TABLE OF CONTENTS—Continued

TABLE OF CONTENTS—Continued

MOTOR AUTO REPAIR MANUAL

51st Edition

First Printing

Robert R. Savasta, SAE
Managing Editor

Dan Irizarry, SAE
Production Manager

Denver Steele
Manager, Electronic Data

Warren Schildknecht, SAE
Senior Editor

Robert J. Ost
Production Assistant

Daniel E. Doku, SAE
Associate Editor

Mark E. Flynn, SAE
Associate Editor

John R. Lypen, SAE
Associate Editor

James M. Garripoli
Assistant Editor

John E. DeGroat
Assistant Editor

Thomas G. Gaeta
Assistant Editor

Published by

MOTOR

**Hearst Books/Business Publishing Group,
A Division of The Hearst Corp.**

555 West 57th St., New York, N.Y. 10019

Printed in the U.S.A.

ISBN 0-87851-650-6

GASOLINE ENGINE TUNE UP SPECIFICATIONS & DIESEL ENGINE PERFORMANCE SPECIFICATIONS

TABLE OF CONTENTS

The following specifications are published from the latest information available. This data should be used only in the absence of a decal affixed in the engine compartment. On some vehicles, it may be necessary to disconnect certain vacuum hoses and/or electrical connectors. Refer to vehicle emission decal.
Before removing wires from distributor cap, determine location of the No. 1 wire in cap, as distributor position may have been altered from that shown at the end of this chart.

Page No.

DIESEL ENGINE PERFORMANCE SPECIFICATIONS

Ford Motor Company

General Motors Corporation

Fuel Pump Pressure—See Last Column of Each Chart

GASOLINE ENGINE TUNE UP SPECIFICATIONS

Chrysler Corporation

Ford Motor Company

General Motors Corporation

GASOLINE ENGINE TUNE UP
AMERICAN MOTORS

Year & Engine/V.I.N.	Spark Plug Gap	Ignition Timing BTDC ① Firing Order Fig.	Ignition Timing Man. Trans.	Ignition Timing Auto. Trans.	Mark Fig.	Curb Idle Speed ② Man. Trans.	Curb Idle Speed Auto. Trans.	Fast Idle Speed Man. Trans.	Fast Idle Speed Auto. Trans.	Fuel Pump Pressure
1982										
4-151/B Concord & Spirit Exc. Calif. & High Alt.	.060	E	10°	10°	D	900⑪	700D⑨	2400	2400⑤	6 1/2-8
4-151/B Eagle Exc. Calif. & High Alt.	.060	E	12°	12°	D	900⑪	700D⑨	2400	2500	6 1/2-8
4-151/B Concord & Spirit Calif.	.060	E	8°	8°	D	900⑪	700D⑨	2400	2400⑤	6 1/2-8
4-151/B Eagle Calif.	.060	E	8°	8°	D	900⑪	700D⑨	2500	2500	6 1/2-8
4-151/B Concord & Spirit High Alt.	.060	E	15°	15°	D	900⑪	700D⑨	2400	2400⑤	6 1/2-8
4-151/B Eagle High Alt.	.060	E	15°	15°	D	900⑪	700D⑨	2500	2500	6 1/2-8
6-258/C Exc. High Alt.	.035	F	15°⑫④	15°⑫④	A	600③	500D⑧	1850	1850	4-5
6-258/C Concord & Spirit High Alt.	.035	F	19°⑫④	19°⑫④	A	600③	500D⑧	1850	1850	4-5
6-258/C Eagle High Alt.	.035	F	21°⑫④	21°⑫④	A	600③	500D⑧	1850	1850	4-5
1983										
4-150/U Exc. High Alt.	.035	B	12°⑩	12°⑩	C	500⑥	500D⑬	2000⑲	2300⑲	4-5
4-150/U High Alt.	.035	B	19°⑩	19°⑩	C	500⑥	500D⑬	2000⑲	2300⑲	4-5
4-151/B Exc. Calif.	.060	E	10°	10°	D	600/900	550/700D	2500㉔	2700㉔	6 1/2-8
4-151/B Calif.	.060	E	12°	12°	D	600/900	500/700D	2500㉔	2700㉔	6 1/2-8
6-258/C Concord & Spirit Exc. High Alt.	.035	F	6°	6°	A	650°⑥	550D⑯	1700⑲	1850⑲	5-6 1/2
6-258/C Eagle Exc. Calif. & High Alt.	.035	F	6°	6°	A	600°⑥	500D⑯	1700⑲	1850⑲	5-6 1/2
6-258/C Eagle Calif.	.035	F	6°	6°	A	650°⑥	550D⑯	1700⑲	1850⑲	5-6 1/2
6-258/C High Alt.	.035	F	13°	13°	A	700°⑰	650D⑱	1700⑲	1850⑲	5-6 1/2
1984										
4-150/U Exc. High Alt.	.035	B	12°⑩	12°⑩	C	⑥	⑬	2000⑲	2300⑲	4-5
4-150/U High Alt.	.035	F	19°⑩	19°⑩	A	⑥	⑬	2000⑲	2300⑲	4-5
1984-86										
6-258/C Exc. High Alt.	.035	F	9°⑩	9°⑩	A	680⑭	600D⑮	1700⑲	1850⑲	5-6 1/2
6-258/C High Alt.	.035	F	16°⑩	16°⑩	A	700⑭	650D⑮	1700⑲	1850⑲	5-6 1/2
1987										
6-258/C Exc. High Alt.	.035	F	9°⑩	9°⑩	A	680⑭	600D⑮	1700⑲	1850⑲	5-6 1/2
6-258/C High Alt.	.035	F	16°⑩	16°⑩	A	700⑭	650D⑮	1700⑲	1850⑲	5-6 1/2

①—BTDC-Before top dead center.

②—Idle speed on man. trans. vehicles is adjusted in Neutral & on auto. trans. equipped vehicles is adjusted in Drive unless otherwise specificed. When two idle speeds are listed, the higher speed is with the A/C or idle solenoid energized.

③—With holding solenoid energized, 750 RPM; with vacuum actuator energized, 900 RPM.

④—With ignition module electronic retard (two wire) connector disconnected and a jumper wire connected between the two module wire connector terminals.

⑤—Models with A/C, 2600 RPM.

⑥—With holding solenoid energized, 750 RPM; with vacuum actuator energized, 750 RPM.

⑦—With fast idle screw on highest step of fast idle cam.

⑧—With holding solenoid energized, 650D RPM; with vacuum actuator energized, 800D RPM.

⑨—On models equipped with A/C, with A/C off & solenoid disconnected, 500D RPM; with A/C on & solenoid connected, 1250D RPM.

⑩—At 1600 RPM with 3 wire electrical connector to vacuum input switches disconnected.

⑪—On models equipped with A/C, with A/C off & solenoid disconnected, 500 RPM; with A/C on & solenoid connected, 950 RPM.

⑫—At 1600 RPM.

⑬—With holding solenoid energized, 700D RPM; with vacuum actuator energized, 850D RPM.

⑭—With holding solenoid energized, 900 RPM; with vacuum actuator energized, 1100 RPM.

⑮—With holding solenoid energized, 800 RPM; with vacuum actuator energized, 900 RPM.

⑯—With holding solenoid energized, 650D RPM; with vacuum actuator energized, 850D RPM.

⑰—With holding solenoid energized, 750 RPM; with vacuum actuator energized, 1000 RPM.

⑱—With holding solenoid energized, 750D RPM; with vacuum actuator energized, 850D RPM.

⑲—With stop screw on 2nd step of fast idle cam and EGR disconnected.

⑳—On models with 2.37 rear axle ratio, set at 12° BTDC.

Continued

AMERICAN MOTORS—Continued

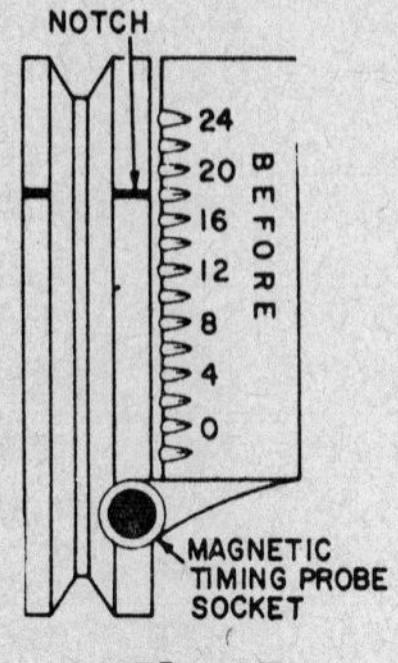

Fig. A

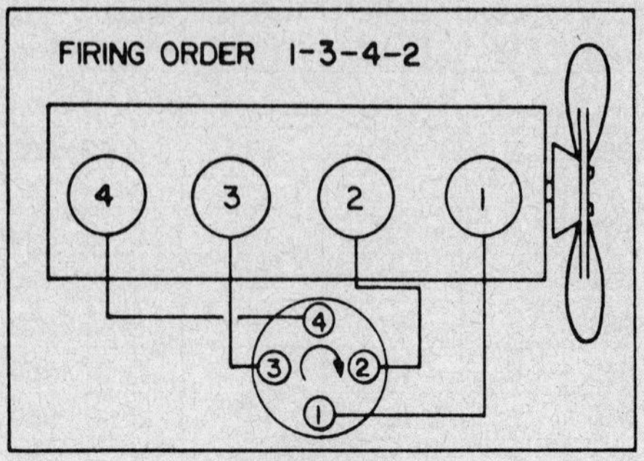

Fig. B

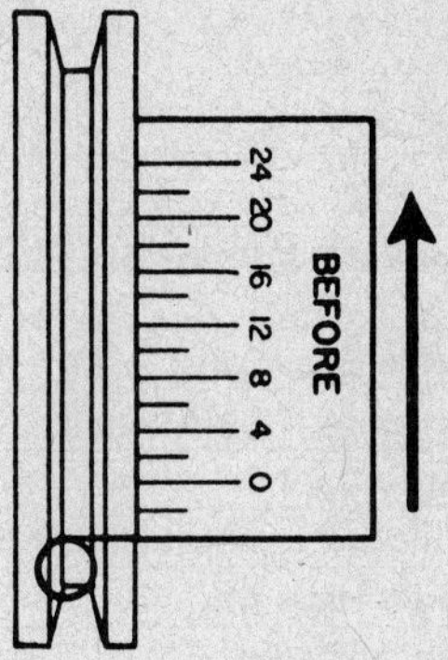

Fig. C

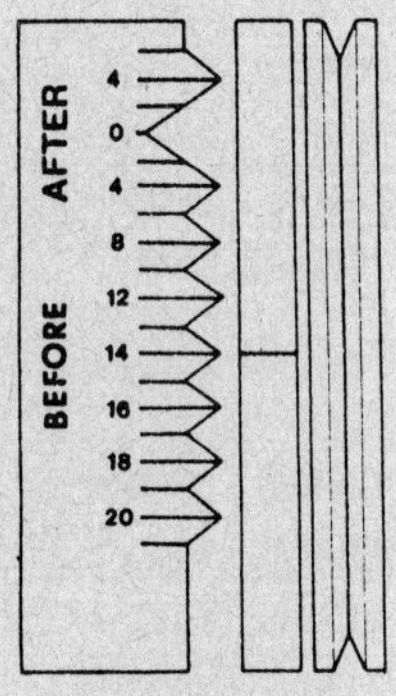

Fig. D

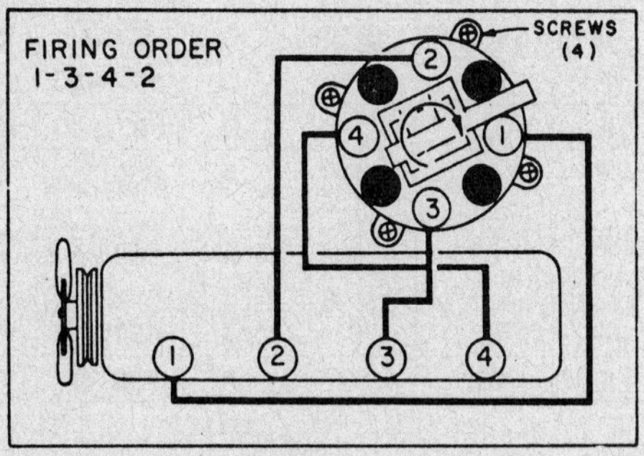

Fig. E

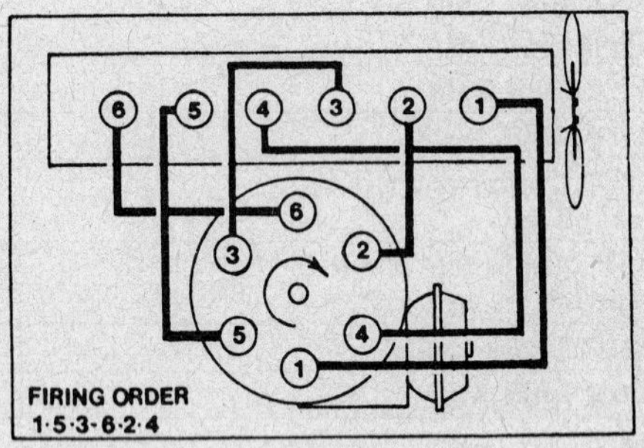

Fig. F

CHRYSLER FRONT WHEEL DRIVE

Year & Engine/VIN Code	Spark Plug Gap	Ignition Timing BTDC ①				Curb Idle Speed		Fast Idle Speed		Fuel Pump Pressure
		Firing Order Fig.	Man. Trans.	Auto. Trans.	Mark Fig.	Man. Trans.	Auto. Trans. ②	Man. Trans.	Auto Trans.	
1982										
4-105/A Man. Trans.	.035	A	20° ④	—	B	850	—	1400	—	4½–6
4-105/A Auto. Trans.	.035	A	—	12°	C	—	900N	—	1400	4½–6
4-135/B Man. Trans.	.035	D	12°	—	C	850	—	1300	—	4½–6
4-135/B Auto. Trans.	.035	D	—	12°	C	—	900N	—	1600	4½–6
4-156/D	.041	F	—	7°	G	—	800N ⑪	—	—	4½–6
1983										
4-97/A	.035	E	12°	—	H	⑦	—	1400	—	4½–6
4-105/B	.035	A	12° ④	12°	③	850	900N	1400	1350	4½–6
4-135/C ⑧	.035	D	10°	10°	C	775	900N	1400	1500	4½–6
4-135/C ⑤	.035	D	6°	6°	C	900	850N	1350	1375	4½–6
4-135/F	.035	D	15°	—	C	850	—	1500	—	4½–6
4-135/D	.035	D	—	—	③	—	⑥	—	—	—
4-156/G	.040	F	—	7°	G	—	800N	—	—	4½–6
1984										
4-97/A	.035	E	12° ⑩	12° ⑩	H	850	1000N	1200 ⑨	1500 ⑨	4½–6
4-135/C	.035	D	10° ⑩	10° ⑩	③	800	900N	1500 ⑨	1600 ⑨	4½–6
4-135/F	.035	D	15° ⑩	—	C	850	—	1500 ⑨	—	4½–6
4-135/D	.035	D	6° ⑩	6° ⑩	③	850 ⑥	750N ⑥	⑥	⑥	34-38 ⑪
4-135 Turbo/E	.035	D	12° ⑩	12° ⑩	C	950 ⑥	800N ⑥	⑥	⑥	51-55 ⑫
4-156/G	.035-.040	F	—	7°	G	—	800N	—	950	4½–6
1985										
4-97/A	.035	E	12° ⑩	12° ⑩	H	850	1000N	1400 ⑨	1400 ⑨	4½–6
4-135/C	.035	D	10° ⑩	10° ⑩	C	800	900N	1700 ⑨	1850 ⑨	4½–6
4-135 H.P./C	.035	D	15° ⑩	—	C	850	—	1700 ⑨	—	4½–6
4-135 EFI/D	.035	D	12° ⑩	12° ⑩	C	850 ⑥	750N ⑥	⑥	⑥	34-38 ⑪
4-135 Turbo/E	.035	D	12° ⑩	12° ⑩	C	950 ⑥	800N ⑥	⑥	⑥	51-55 ⑫
4-156/G	.035-.040	F	—	7° ⑩	G	—	800N	—	950	4½–6
1986										
4-97/A	.035	E	12° ⑩	—	H	800	—	1400 ⑨	—	4½–6
4-135 2 Bbl./C	.035	D	10° ⑩	10° ⑩	C	800	900N	1700 ⑨	1850 ⑨	4½–6
4-135 2 Bbl. H.O./C	.035	D	15° ⑩	—	C	850	—	1700 ⑨	—	4½–6
4-135 EFI/D	.035	D	12° ⑩	12° ⑩	C	900 ⑥	700N ⑥	⑥	⑥	34-38 ⑪
4-135 Turbo/E	.035	D	12° ⑩	12° ⑩	C	950 ⑥	950N ⑥	⑥	⑥	51-55 ⑫
4-153 EFI/K	.035	D	12° ⑩	12° ⑩	C	900 ⑥	700N ⑥	⑥	⑥	34-38 ⑪
1987										
4-135 2 Bbl./C	.035	D	10° ⑩	10° ⑩	C	800	900N	—	—	4½–6
4-135 EFI/D	.035	D	12° ⑬	12° ⑬	C	900 ⑥	700N ⑥	⑥	⑥	—
4-135 Turbo/E	.035	D	12° ⑬	12° ⑬	C	900 ⑥	800N ⑥	⑥	⑥	—
4-153/K	.035	D	12° ⑬	12° ⑬	C	900 ⑥	900N ⑥	⑥	⑥	—
1988										
4-135 EFI/	.035	D	—	—	C	—	700	⑥	⑥	15 ⑭
4-135 Turbo ⑮ /	.035	D	—	—	C	—	800	⑥	⑥	55 ⑭
4-135 Turbo II ⑯ /	.035	D	—	—	C	—	700	⑥	⑥	55 ⑭
4-153/	.035	D	—	—	C	—	700	⑥	⑥	15 ⑭
V6-181.4/	.042	—	—	—	—	—	—	—	—	48 ⑭

Continued

CHRYSLER FRONT WHEEL DRIVE—Continued

①—BTDC-Before top dead center.
②—N: Neutral.
③—Exc. A-412 manual transaxle, Fig. C; A-412 manual transaxle, Fig. B.
④—If an adjustable timing light is unavailable, use following procedure to mark flywheel for standard timing light:

a. On models with A-412 manual transaxle, align 12° BTDC mark on flywheel with pointer on housing, cover flywheel timing marks with tape, then mark tape at 12° and 16° BTDC positions. Remove tape and reposition so that 12° BTDC mark on tape is aligned with 16° BTDC mark on flywheel. Permanently mark flywheel at 16°BTDC mark on tape; a position which should correspond to 20° BTDC.

b. On models with A-460 manual transaxle, align flywheel timing mark with 16° BTDC mark on housing, then scribe a line on flywheel aligned with 12° BTDC mark on housing. When checking or adjusting ignition timing, 20° BTDC will be indicated when scribed line is aligned with 16° BTDC mark on housing.

⑤—High altitude.
⑥—Idle speed controlled by Automatic Idle Speed (AIS) motor.
⑦—Exc. high altitude, 900 RPM; high altitude, 850 RPM.
⑧—Exc. high altitude.
⑨—On low step of fast idle cam.
⑩—With vacuum line to Spark Control Computer disconnected & plugged.
⑪—Loosen gas cap to release pressure in tank. Ground one injector terminal with a jumper wire. Connect the remaining injector terminal to the battery positive post using a jumper wire for no longer than 10 seconds, this will release system pressure. Remove fuel intake hose from throttle body & connect a suitable pressure tester between fuel filter hose & throttle body. Check fuel pressure with engine running.
⑫—Loosen gas cap to release pressure in tank. Ground one terminal of any injector with a jumper wire. Connect remaining terminal of injector to the battery positive post using a jumper for no longer than 10 seconds, this will release fuel system pressure. Remove cover from service valve on fuel rail. Connect a suitable fuel pressure tester to service valve. Check fuel pressure with engine running.
⑬—Check ignition timing with coolant sensor wire disconnected.
⑭—Nominal regulated pressure.
⑮—Less intercooler.
⑯—W/intercooler.

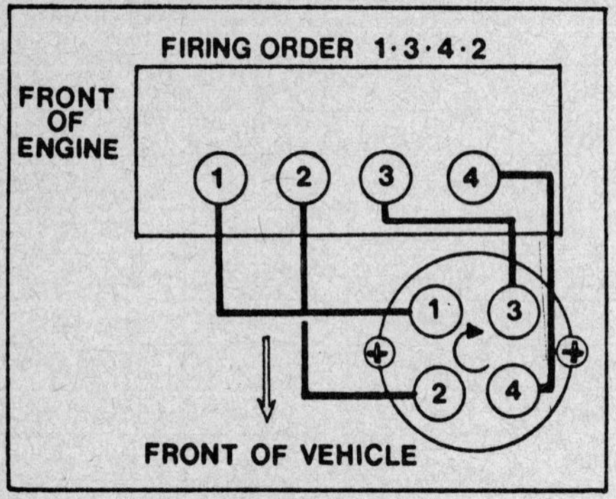

Fig. A

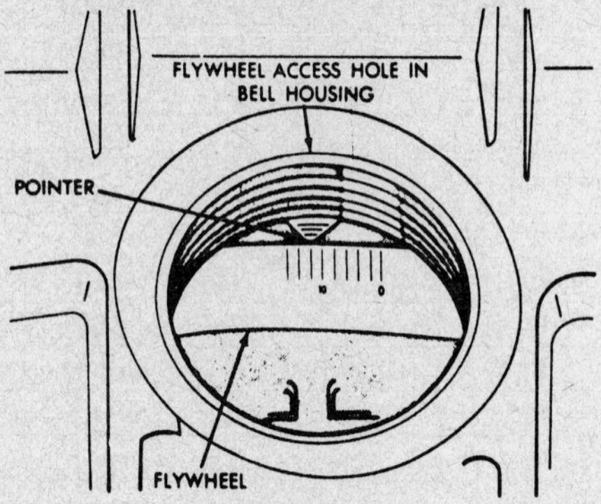

Fig. B

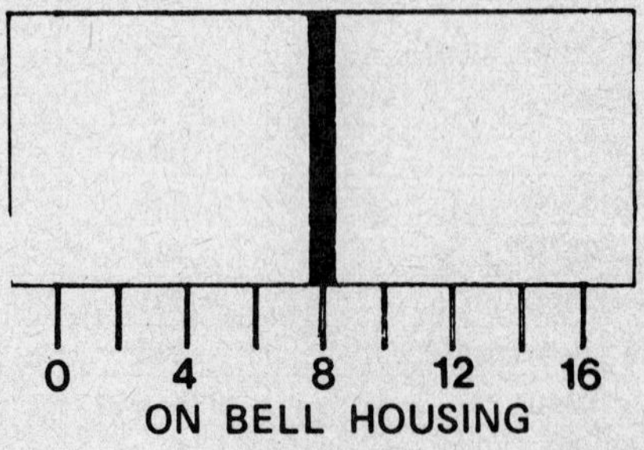

Fig. C

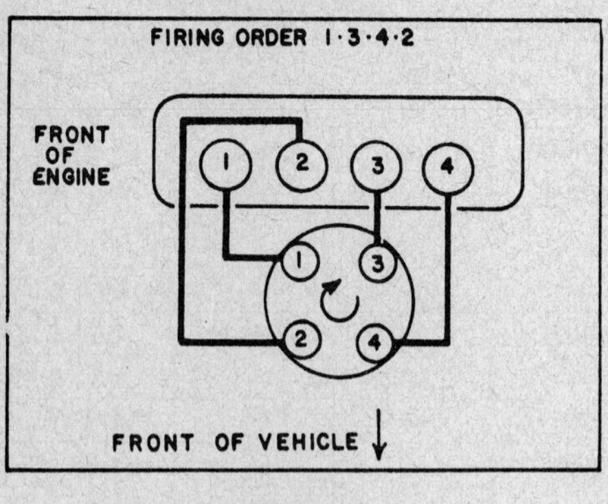

Fig. D

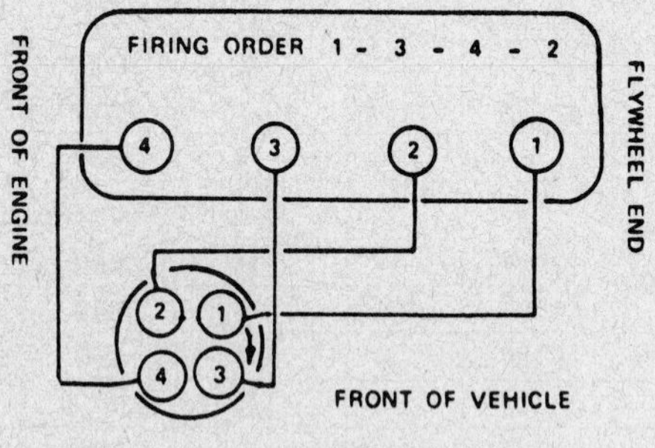

Fig. E

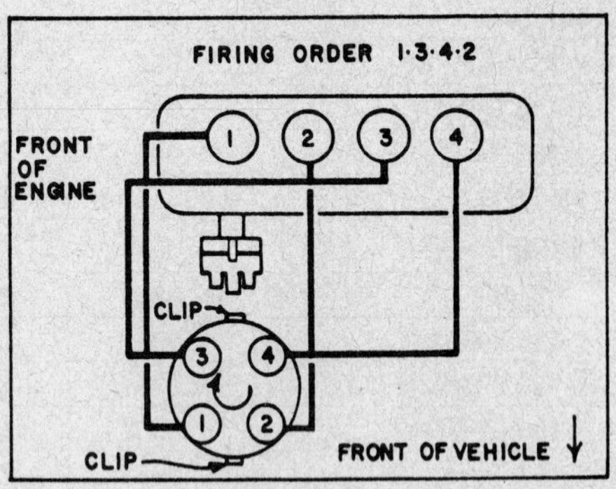

Fig. F

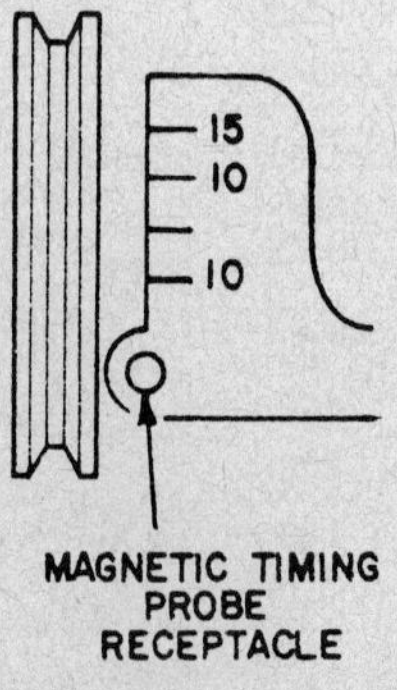

Fig. G

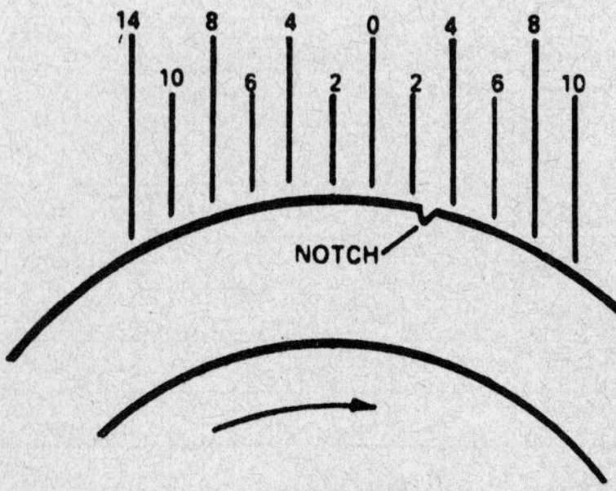

Fig. H

CHRYSLER REAR WHEEL DRIVE

Year & Engine/VIN Code	Spark Plug Gap	Ignition Timing BTDC ①				Curb Idle Speed		Fast Idle Speed		Fuel Pump Pressure
		Firing Order Fig.	Man. Trans.	Auto. Trans.	Mark Fig.	Man. Trans.	Auto. Trans. ②	Man. Trans.	Auto. Trans.	
1982										
6-225/E Exc. Calif.	.035	B	—	12°	D	—	625N	—	1600④	4-5½
6-225/E Calif.	.035	B	—	12°	D	—	725N	—	1950④	4-5½
V8-318/K 2 Barrel	.035	C	—	16°	A	—	600N	—	1400④	5¾-7¼
V8-318/M 4 Barrel	.035	C	—	16°	A	—	650N	—	1400④	5¾-7¼
V8-318/J E.F.I.	.035	C	—	12°	A	—	580N	—	—	7½-11½③
1983										
6-225/H	.035	B	—	16°	D	—	750N	—	2000④	4-5½
V8-318/P 2 Barrel	.035	C	—	16°	A	—	700N	—	1400④	5¾-7½
V8-318/N E.F.I.	.035	C	—	12°	A	—	580N	—	—	7½-11½③
1984										
V8-318/P 2 Barrel Exc. Calif.	.035	C	—	16°	A	—	700N	—	1400④	5¾-7¼
V8-318/P 2 Barrel Calif.	.035	C	—	16°	A	—	730N	—	1400④	5¾-7¼
V8-318/R 4 Bbl.	.035	C	—	16°	A	—	700N	—	1400④	5¾-7¼
1985-87										
V8-318/P 2 Barrel	.035	C	—	7°	A	—	680N	—	1700④	5¾-7¼
V8-318/R,S 4 Bbl.	.035	C	—	16°	A	—	750N	—	1720④	5¾-7¼
1988										
V8-318/	.035	C	—	—	A	—	680N	—	—	5¾-7 ¼

①—BTDC-Before top dead center.
②—N: Neutral. D: Drive.
③—In-tank electric fuel pump.
④—With stop screw on second highest step of fast idle cam.

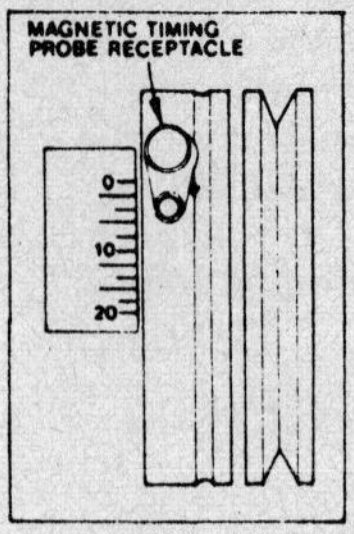

Fig. A

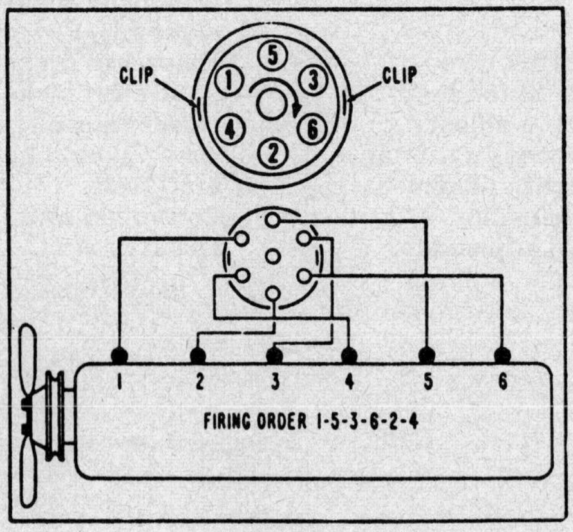

Fig. B

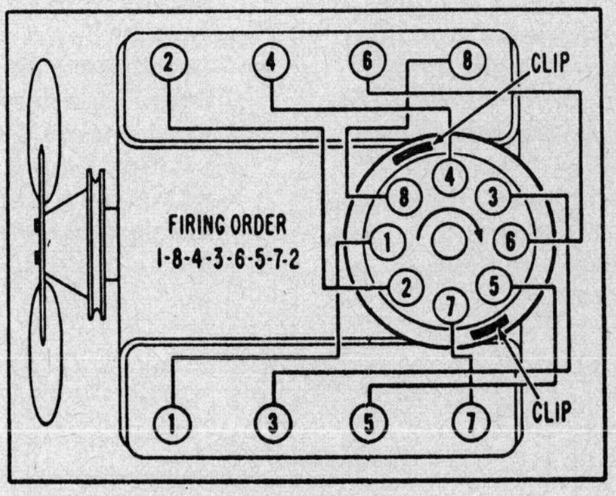

Fig. C

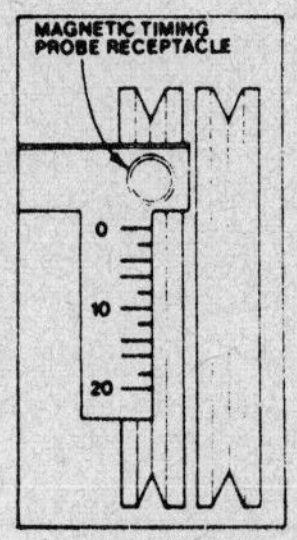

Fig. D

FORD & MERCURY FULL SIZE MODELS

Year & Engine/VIN Code	Spark Plug Gap	Ignition Timing			Curb Idle Speed ②	Fast Idle Speed	Fuel Pump Pressure
		Firing Order Fig.	Degrees BTDC ①	Mark Fig.			
1982							
V8-255/D	.050	A	7°	B	500/650D	1800③	6-8
V8-302/F Exc. High Alt.	.050	A	8°	B	500D	1800③	6-8
V8-302/F High Alt.	.050	A	14°	B	500D	1800③	6-8
1983							
V8-302/F Exc. Calif.	.050	A	⑤	B	500D	2200③	—
V8-302/F Calif.	.050	A	⑤	B	550D	2400③	—
1984							
V8-302/F	.050	A	10°④	B	550D	2300	35-45⑥
1985							
V8-302/F Exc. Calif.	.050	A	10°④	B	550D	⑧	35-45⑥
V8-302/F Calif.	.050	A	10°④	B	550D	2300	35-45⑥
1986							
V8-302/F	.050	A	10°④	B	⑦	⑧	35-45⑥
1987							
V8-302/F	.050	A	10°④	B	⑦	⑧	35-45⑥
1988							
V8-302/	.050	A	—	B	⑦	⑧	35-45⑥

①—BTDC-Before top dead center.

②—Idle speed on manual trans. vehicles is adjusted in Neutral & on auto. trans. equipped vehicles is adjusted in Drive unless otherwise specified. Where two idle speeds are listed, the higher speed is with the A/C or throttle solenoid energized. On models equipped with vacuum release brake, whenever adjusting ignition timing or idle speed, vacuum line to brake release mechanism must be disconnected & plugged to prevent parking brake from releasing when selector lever is moved to Drive.

③—On kickdown step of cam.

④—Disconnect single black wire connector near distributor, then start engine & check & adjust ignition timing as necessary. After completing adjustment, reconnect single black wire connector.

⑤—Ignition timing is not adjustable.

⑥—Wrap shop towel around fitting to prevent fuel spillage, then connect a suitable fuel pressure gauge to fuel diagnostic valve on fuel charging assembly. Energize fuel pump & check fuel pressure gauge reading.

⑦—Controlled by an automatic idle speed control, no adjustment. Idle speed should be between 490 to 615D RPM.

⑧—Controlled by an automatic idle speed control.

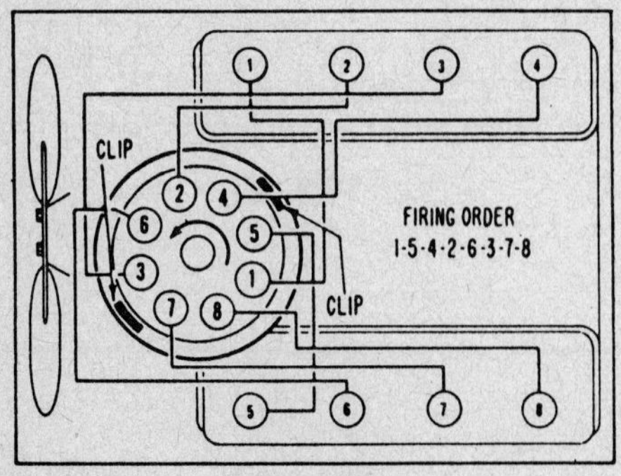

Fig. A

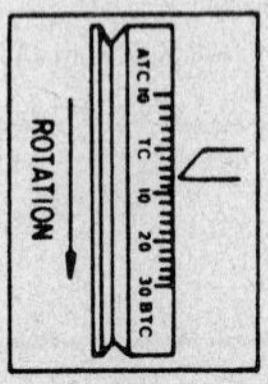

Fig. B

FORD & MERCURY COMPACT & INTERMEDIATE MODELS

Year & Engine/VIN Code	Spark Plug Gap	Ignition Timing BTDC (1) Firing Order Fig.	Man. Trans.	Auto. Trans.	Mark Fig.	Curb Idle Speed (2) Man. Trans.	Auto. Trans.	Fast Idle Speed Man. Trans.	Auto. Trans.	Fuel Pump Pressure
1982										
4-140/A Exc. Calif.	.034	D	6°	12°	E	850	800D	1800 (3)	2000 (3)	5-7 (16)
4-140/A Calif.	.034	D	4°	12°	E	850	800D	1600 (3)	1800 (3)	5-7 (16)
6-200/B Exc. High Alt.	.050	F	—	10°	C	—	450/600D	—	2000 (3)	5-7 (16)
6-200/B High Alt.	.050	F	—	12°	C	—	450/600D	—	2000 (3)	5-7 (16)
V6-232/3 Exc. Calif. & High Alt.	.044	I	—	(10)	A	—	550/650D	—	2200 (4)	6-8
V6-232/3 Calif.	.044	I	—	12°	A	—	550/650D	—	1200 (3)	6-8
V6-232/3 High Alt.	.044	I	—	12°	A	—	550/650D	—	2100 (3)	6-8
V8-255/D Exc. High Alt.	.050	G	—	8°	B	—	500/650D	—	1500 (3)	6-8
V8-255/D High Alt.	.050	G	—	14°	B	—	500/650D	—	1700 (3)	6-8
1983										
4-140/A (13)	.044	D	9°	9°	E	850	800	1800 (3)	2000 (3)	5-7 (16)
4-140/W (14)	.034	D	—	—	E	—	—	—	—	—
6-200/X Exc. High Alt. (11)	.050	F	—	10°	C	—	450/600	—	2000 (3)	6-8
6-200/X High Alt. (11)	.050	F	—	12°	C	—	450/600	—	2000 (3)	6-8
6-200/X Exc. Calif. (9)	.050	F	—	10°	C	—	450/600	—	2200 (3)	6-8
6-200/X Calif. (9)	.050	F	—	10°	C	—	450/600	—	2100 (3)	6-8
V6-232/3 Exc. Calif. & High Alt.	.044	I	—	12°	A	—	550/650	—	2200 (4)	6-8 (16)
V6-232/3 Calif.	.044	I	—	10°	A	—	550/700	—	2200 (4)	6-8 (16)
V6-232/3 High Alt.	.044	I	—	12°	A	—	550/700	—	2100 (4)	6-8 (16)
V8-302/F	.050	G	—	—	B	—	550	—	—	—
1984										
4-140/A (13)	.044	D	10° (20)	10° (20)	E	850	750D	2000 (3)	2200 (3)	5-7 (16)
4-140/W (14)	.034	D	10° (21)	10° (21)	E	900 (5)	1000N (5)	(5)	(5)	35-45 (6)
V6-232/3	.044	I	—	10° (21)	A	—	550D (5)	—	(5)	35-45 (6)
V8-302/F	.050	G	—	10° (21)	B	—	550D (5)	—	(5)	35-45 (6)
[illegible]302 H.O./M	.044	H	—	10° (21)	B	—	550D	—	2400 (4)	7-9
[illegible]										
[illegible]	.044	D	10° (20)	10° (20)	E	850	750	2200 (3)	2200 (3)	5-7 (16)
[illegible]	.034	D	10° (21)	10° (21)	E	900	1000N (5)	(5)	(5)	35-45 (6)
[illegible]	.044	I	—	10° (21)	A	—	550D (5)	—	(5)	35-45 (6)
[illegible]	.054	I	—	10° (21)	A	—	550D (5)	—	(5)	35-45 (6)
[illegible]	.054	I	—	7° (21)	A	—	550D (5)	—	(5)	35-45 (6)
[illegible]	.050	G	—	7° (21)	B	—	550D (5)	—	(5)	35-45 (6)
[illegible]	.050	G	—	10° (21)	B	—	550D (5)	—	(5)	35-45 (6)
[illegible]										
[illegible]	.044	D	10° (20)	10° (20)	E	800	750D	2000 (3)	2200 (3)	5-7 (16)
[illegible]	[illegible]34	D	10° (21)	10° (21)	E	900 (5)	1000N (5)	(5)	(5)	35-45 (6)
[illegible]	[illegible]	I	—	10° (21)	A	—	550D (5)	—	(5)	35-45 (6)
[illegible]	[illegible]	G	—	10° (21)	B	—	550D (5)	—	(5)	35-45 (6)
[illegible]										
[illegible]	[illegible]	[illegible]	10° (20)	10° (20)	E	(5)	(5)	(5)	(5)	35-45 (6)
[illegible]	[illegible]	[illegible]	—	10° (21)	A	—	(5)	—	(5)	35-45 (6)
[illegible]	[illegible]	[illegible]	—	10° (21)	B	—	(5)	—	(5)	35-45 (6)

4-[illegible]
4-14[illegible]
V6-23[illegible]
V6-232[illegible]
V6-232/3[illegible]
V8-302/F [illegible]
V8-302/F (12)
1986
4-140/A (13)
4-140/W (14)
V6-232/3
V8-302/F
1987-88
4-140/W (14)
V6-232/3
V8-302/F

Continued

FORD & MERCURY COMPACT & INTERMEDIATE—Continued

①—BTDC-Before top dead center.
②—Idle speed on manual trans. vehicles is adjusted in Neutral & on auto. trans. equipped vehicles is adjusted in Drive unless otherwise specified. Where two idle speeds are listed, the higher speed is with the A/C or throttle solenold energized. On models equipped with vacuum release brake, whenever adjusting ignition timing or idle speed, vacuum line to brake release mechanism must be disconnected & plugged to prevent parking brake from releasing when selector lever is moved to Drive.
③—On kickdown step of cam.
④—On high step of fast idle cam.
⑤—Controlled by idle speed control motor.
⑥—Wrap shop towel around fuel diagnostic valve to prevent fuel spillage. Attach a suitable fuel pressure gauge to diagnostic valve. Energize fuel pump & check pressure gauge reading.
⑦—With A/C on and clutch de-energized.
⑧—Calibration codes 4-16B-R0, 4-16N-R10, 5-16F-R0, 5-16S-R0 & 5-16S-R10.
⑨—LTD & Marquis.
⑩—Cougar & Granada. 10°BTDC; Cougar XR-7 & Thunderbird, 12°BTDC.
⑪—Fairmont & Zephyr.
⑫—Refer to engine calibration code on engine identification label, located at rear of left valve cover on V6 & V8 engines, on front of valve cover on in line 4 & 6 cyl. engines. The calibration code is located on the label after the engine code number is preceded by the letter C and the revision code is located below the calibration code and is preceded by the letter R.
⑬—Except turbocharged engine.
⑭—Turbocharged engine.
⑮—Calibration codes 5-16B-R5, 5-16B-R11, 5-16N-R5 & 5-16N-R11.
⑯—With pump to fuel tank return line pinched off & a new fuel filter installed.
⑰—Calibration codes 5-16B-R6, 5-16F-R6, 5-16F-R7 & 5-16N-R6.
⑱—Calibration code 4-22F-R10.
⑲—Calibration codes 5-22T-R0 & 5-22T-R10.
⑳—With distributor vacuum line disconnected & plugged.
㉑—With single wire connector near distributor disconnected.

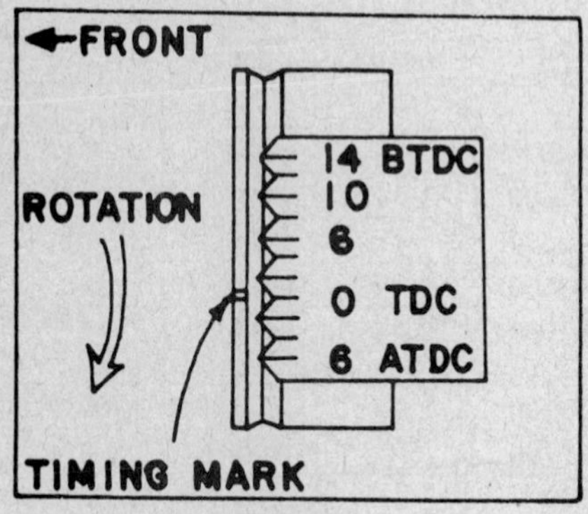

Fig. A

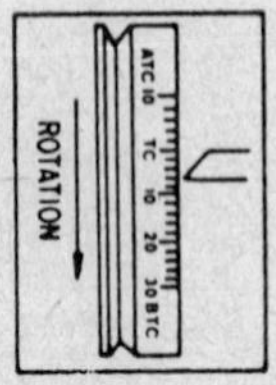

Fig. B

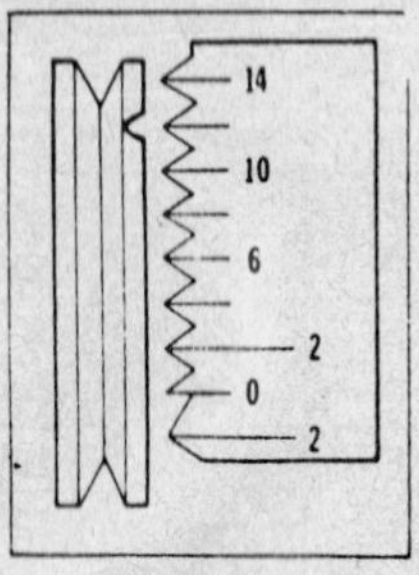

Fig. C

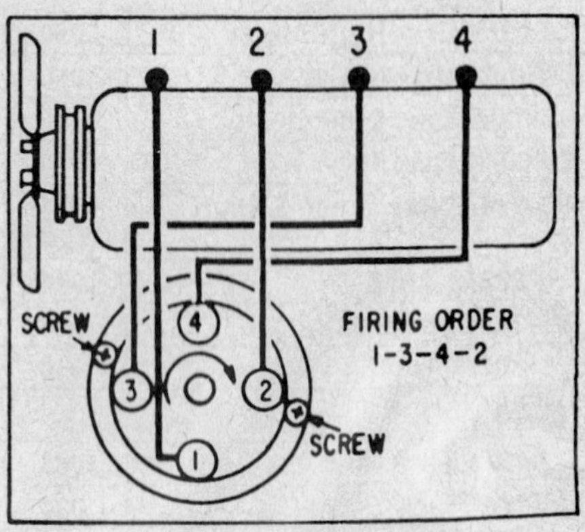

Fig. D

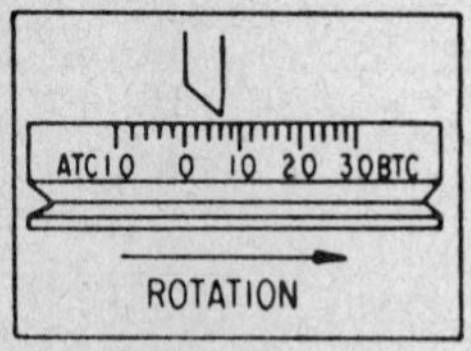

Fig. E

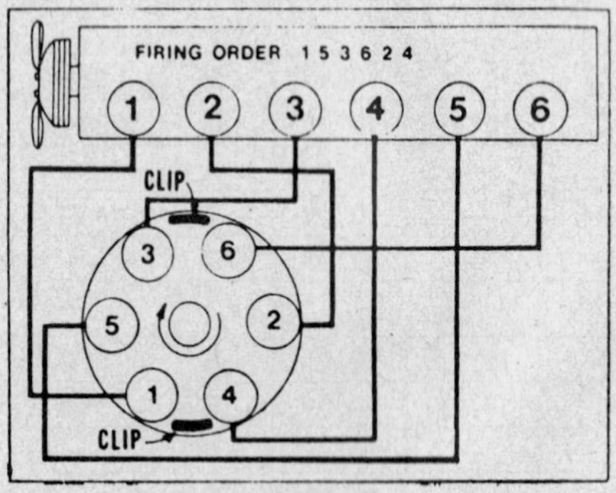

Fig. F

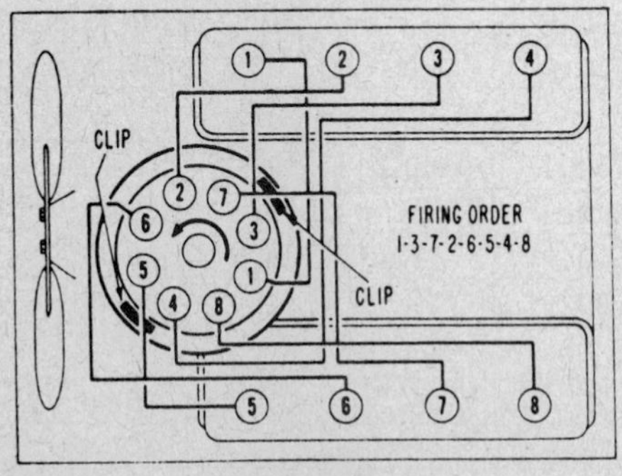

Fig. H

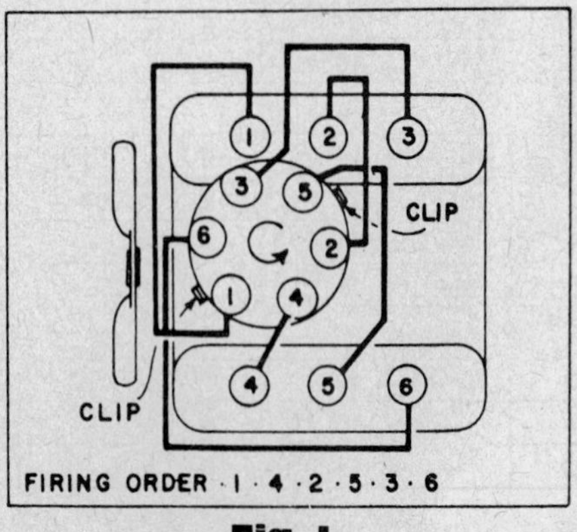

Fig. I

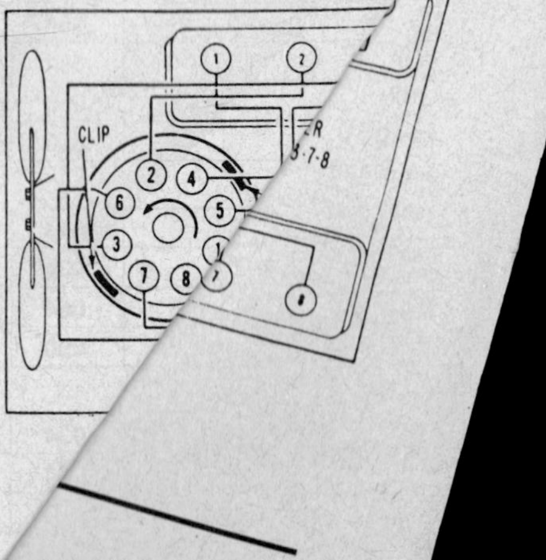

FORD MUSTANG & MERCURY CAPRI

Year & Engine/VIN	Spark Plug Gap	Ignition Timing BTDC (1)				Curb Idle Speed (2)		Fast Idle Speed		Fuel Pump Pressure
		Firing Order Fig.	Man. Trans.	Auto. Trans.	Mark Fig.	Man. Trans.	Auto Trans.	Man. Trans.	Auto Trans.	
1982										
4-140/A Exc. Calif. & High Alt.	.034	G	(6) (26)	12°	E	850	800D	(3) (6) (16)	2000 (3)	5-7 (4)
4-140/A Calif.	.034	G	4°	12°	E	850	800D	1600 (3)	1800 (3)	5-7 (4)
4-140/A High Alt.	.034	G	6°	12°	E	850	800D	1800 (3)	2000 (3)	5-7 (4)
6-200/B	.050	A	—	(24)	B	—	450/600D	—	2000 (3)	5-7
V8-255/D Exc. High Alt.	.050	D	—	8°	C	—	500/700D	—	1500 (3)	6-8
V8-255/D High Alt.	.050	D	—	14°	C	—	500/700D	—	1600 (3)	6-8
V8-302/F	.044	I	12°	—	C	700/900	—	1500 (3)	—	6-8
1983										
4-140/A (8)	.044	G	9°	9°	E	850	800D	1800 (3)	2000 (3)	5-7
4-140/W (9)	.034	G	10°	—	E	825-975 (13)	—	(13)	—	—
V6-232/3 Exc. Calif. & High Alt.	.044	F	—	10°	H	—	(23)	—	2200 (5)	6-8 (10)
V6-232/3 Calif.	.044	F	—	8°	H	—	(23)	—	2200 (5)	6-8 (10)
V6-232/3 High Alt.	.044	F	—	18°	H	—	(23)	—	2100 (5)	6-8 (10)
V8-302/F	.044	I	10°	—	C	700	—	—	2400 (5)	6-8
1984										
4-140/A (8)	.044	G	10° (27)	10° (27)	E	850	750D	2000 (3)	2000 (3)	5-7 (4)
4-140/W (9)	.034	G	10° (28)	—	E	750 (13)	—	(13)	35-45 (11)	
V6-232/3	.044	F	—	10° (28)	H	—	525 (13)	—	(13)	35-45 (11)
V8-302/M	.044	I	10° (27)	—	C	700	—	2400 (5)	—	6-8
1985										
4-140/A (8)	.044	G	10° (27)	10° (27)	E	800	750D	2000 (3)	2200 (3)	5-7 (4)
4-140/T (9) (14)	.034	G	10° (28)	—	E	750 (13)	—	(13)	—	35-45 (11)
V6-232/C (6) (7)	.044	F	—	10° (28)	H	—	525D (13)	—	(13)	35-45 (11)
V6-232/C (6) (15)	.054	F	—	10° (28)	H	—	525D (13)	—	(13)	35-45 (11)
V8-302 H.O. CFI/M Exc. Calif. (6) (18)	.044	I	—	8° (28)	C	—	550D (13)	—	(13)	35-45 (11)
V8-302 H.O. CFI/M Exc. Calif. (6) (19)	.044	I	—	10° (28)	C	—	550D (13)	—	(13)	35-45 (11)
V8-302 H.O. CFI/M Calif. (6) (20)	.044	I	—	8° (28)	C	—	550D (13)	—	—	35-45 (11)
V8-302 H.O. CFI/M Calif. (6) (21)	.044	I	—	4° (28)	C	—	550D (13)	—	—	35-45 (11)
V8-302 H.O. CFI/M Calif. (6) (22)	.044	I	—	6° (28)	C	—	550D (13)	—	(13)	35-45 (11)
V8-302 H.O. 4Bbl./M Exc. Calif.	.044	I	12° (27)	—	C	700	—	2400 (5)	—	6-8
V8-302 H.O. 4 Bbl./M Calif.	.044	I	10° (27)	—	C	700	—	2400 (5)	—	6-8
1986										
4-140/A (8)	.044	G	10° (27)	10° (27)	E	800	750D	2000 (3)	2200 (3)	5-7 (4)
4-140/T (9) (14)	.034	G	10° (28)	—	—	900 (13)	—	(13)	35-45 (11)	—
V6-232/3	.054	F	—	10° (28)	H	—	550D (13)	—	(13)	35-45 (11)
V8-302 H.O./M	.050	I	10° (28)	10° (28)	C	700 (13)	625D (13)	(13)	(13)	35-45 (11)
1987										
4-140/A	.044	G	10° (27)	10° (27)	E	800 (13)	750D (13)	(13)	(13)	35-45 (11)
V8-302 H.O./M	.054	I	10° (28)	10° (28)	C	(13)	(13)	(13)	(13)	35-45 (11)
1988										
4-140/	.044	G	10° (27)	10° (27)	E	—	(13)	—	(13)	35-45 (11)
V8-302/	.054	I	10° (28)	10° (28)	C	—	(13)	—	(13)	35-45 (11)

Continued

FORD MUSTANG & MERCURY CAPRI—Continued

① —BTDC-Before top dead center.
② —Idle speed on manual trans. vehicles is adjusted in Neutral & on auto. trans. equipped vehicles is adjusted in Drive unless otherwise specified. Where two idle speeds are listed, the higher speed is with the A/C or throttle solenoid energized.
③ —On kickdown step of cam.
④ —With pump to fuel tank line pinched off & a new fuel filter installed.
⑤ —On high step of fast idle cam.
⑥ —Refer to engine calibration code on engine identification label located at rear of left valve cover on V6 & V8 engines, on front of valve cover on inline 4 & 6 cyl. engines. The calibration code is located on the label after the engine codes number & is preceded by the letter C & the revision code is located below the calibration code is preceded by the letter R.
⑦ —Calibration codes 4-16A-R10 & 4-16P-R10.
⑧ —Except turbocharged engine.
⑨ —Turbocharged engine
⑩ —If vehicle is equipped with Tripminder, return line should be pinched off when checking pressure.
⑪ —Wrap shop towel around fuel diagnostic valve to prevent fuel spillage. Connect suitable fuel pressure gauge to fuel diagnostic valve. Energize fuel pump & check pressure gauge reading.
⑫ —Fuel tank mounted pump, 6; frame mounted pump, 39.
⑬ —Equipped w/idle speed control.
⑭ —Mustang SVO.
⑮ —Exc. calibration codes 4-16A-R10 & 4-16P-R10.
⑯ —Calibration codes 2-5A-R0 & 2-5B-R0, 1800 RPM; calibration codes 2-5C-R0 & 2-5C-R11, 1600 RPM.
⑰ —Calibration codes 5-22A-R0 & 5-221-R0.
⑱ —Calibration code 4-22A-R13.
⑲ —Calibration codes 5-22A-R0 & 5-22I-R0.
⑳ —Calibration code 4-22P-R12.
㉑ —Calibration code 4-22P-R13.
㉒ —Calibration code 5-22P-R0.
㉓ —With A/C, 550/650D; less A/C, 450/550D.
㉔ —Exc. high altitude, 10°; high altitude, 12°
㉕ —Calibration code 4-22A-R13
㉖ —Calibration codes 2-5A-R0 & 2-2B-R0, 6°; calibration codes 2-5C-R0 & 2-5C-R11, 4°.
㉗ —With distributor vacuum hose disconnected & plugged.
㉘ —With single wire connector near distributor disconnected.

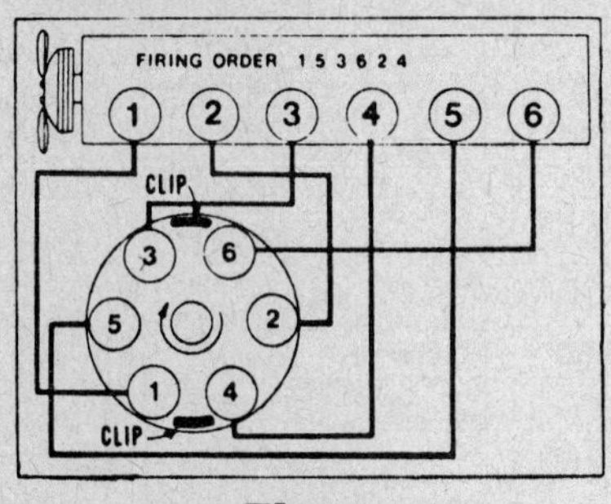

Fig. A

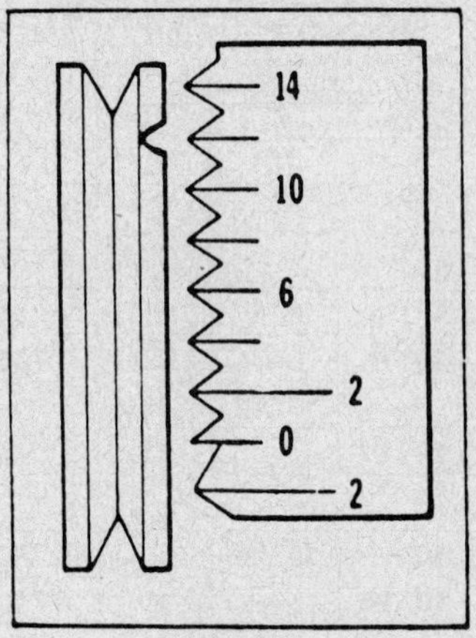

Fig. B

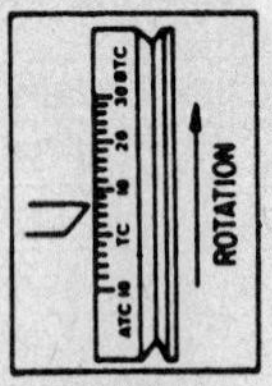

Fig. C

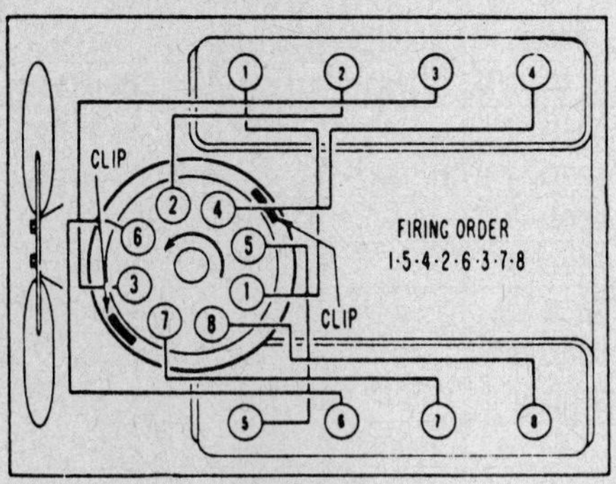

Fig. D

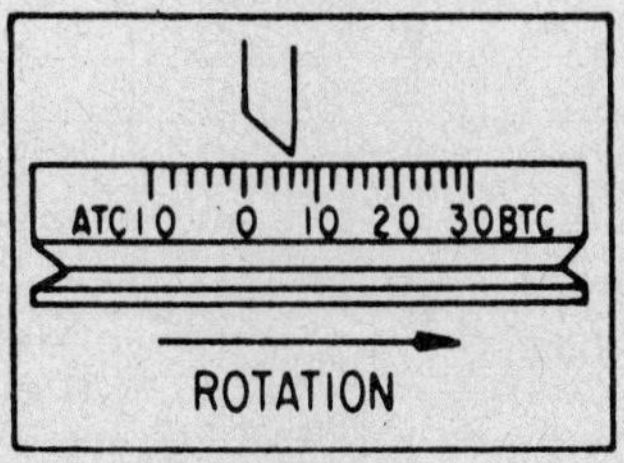

Fig. E

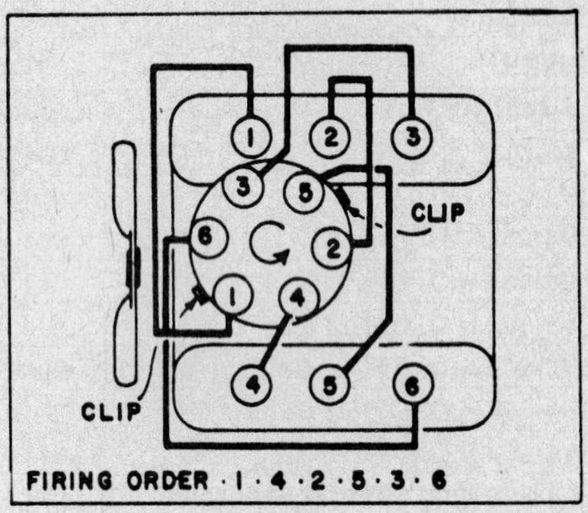

Fig. F

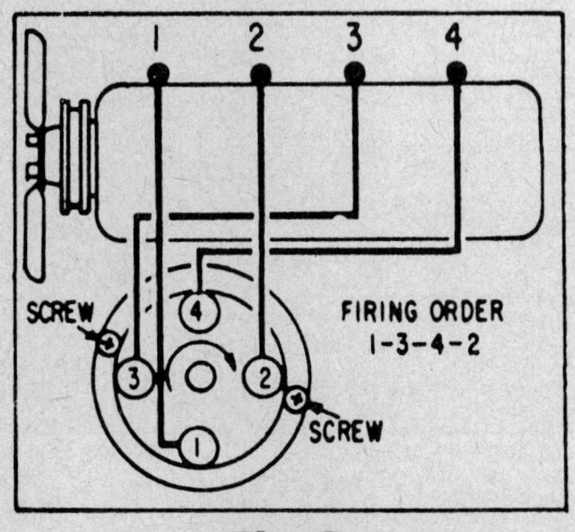

Fig. G

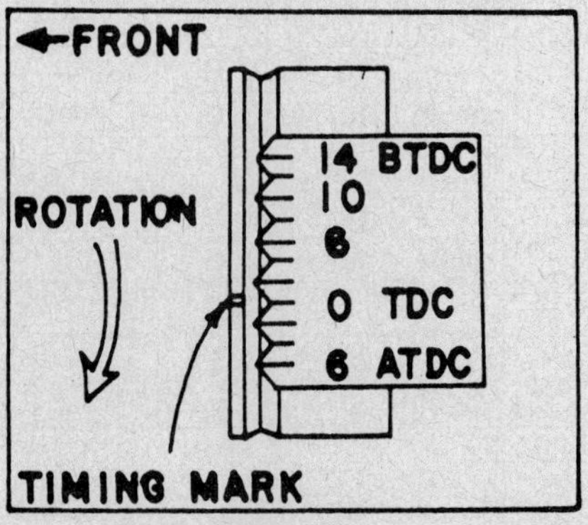

Fig. H

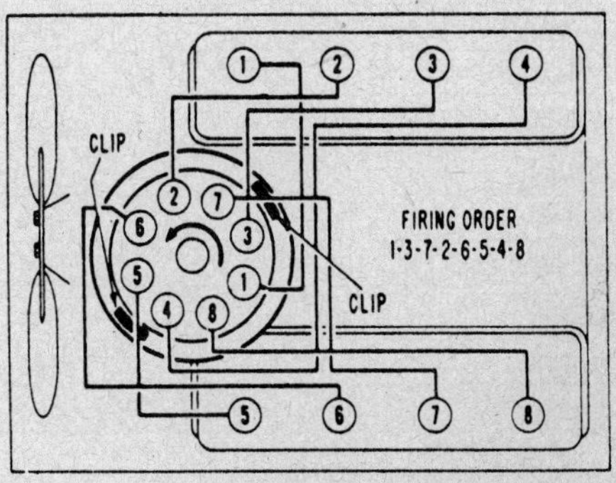

Fig. I

FORD ESCORT, EXP & TEMPO MERCURY LN7, LYNX & TOPAZ

Year & Engine/VIN	Spark Plug Gap	Ignition Timing BTDC (1)				Curb Idle Speed		Fast Idle Speed		Fuel Pump Pressure
		Firing Order Fig.	Man. Trans.	Auto. Trans.	Mark Fig.	Man. Trans.	Auto Trans. (2)	Man. Trans.	Auto Trans.	
1982										
4-97.6/2 Exc. Calif. (10) (11) (12)	.044	A	—	12° (7)	B	—	800D (3)	—	2400 (5)	4½-6½ (6)
4-96.6/2 Exc. Calif. & High Alt. (11) (13) (14)	.044	A	—	10° (7)	B	—	750D (15)	—	2400 (5)	4½-6½ (6)
4-97.6/2 Exc. High Alt. (10) (11) (16)	.044	A	6° (7)	—	B	800 (15)	—	2400 (5)	—	4½-6½ (6)
4-97.6/2 Exc. High Alt. (11) (13) (18)	.044	A	14° (7)	—	B	800 (15)	—	2400 (5)	—	4½-6½ (6)
4-97.6/2 Exc. High Alt. (11) (13) (19) (20)	.044	A	14° (7)	—	B	650/1300	—	2200 (5)	—	4½-6½ (6)
4-97.6/2 Exc. High Alt. (11) (13) (21)	.044	A	12° (7)	—	B	800 (15)	—	2400 (5)	—	4½-6½ (6)
4-97.6/2 Exc. High Alt. (11) (13) (22)	.044	A	10° (7)	—	B	800 (15)	—	2400 (5)	—	4½-6½ (6)
4-97.6/2 Calif. (10) (11) (23)	.044	A	—	12° (7)	B	—	800D (3)	—	2400 (5)	4½-6½ (6)
4-97.6/2 Calif. (10) (11) (24)	.044	A	—	8° (7)	B	—	800D (3)	—	2400 (5)	4½-6½ (6)
4-97.6/2 Calif. (11) (13) (25)	.044	A	—	8° (7)	B	—	750D (15)	—	2400 (5)	4½-6½ (6)
4-97.6/2 Calif. (11) (13) (26)	.044	A	—	10° (7)	B	—	750D (15)	—	2400 (5)	4½-6½ (6)
4-97.6/2 High Alt. (10) (11) (27)	.044	A	8° (7)	—	B	800 (16)	—	2400 (5)	—	4½-6½ (6)
4-97.6/2 High Alt. (11) (13) (28)	.044	A	10° (7)	10° (7)	B	800 (16)	750D (15)	2400 (5)	2400 (5)	4½-6½
4-97.6/2 H.O./2 (29)	.044	A	10° (7)	10° (7)	B	—	750D (15)	—	2200 (5)	4½-6½ (6)
1983										
4-97.6/2 Exc. High Alt. (11) (30)	.044	A	8° (7)	—	B	650	—	2100 (5)	—	4½-6½ (6)
4-97.6/2 Exc. High Alt. (11) (29) (31)	.044	A	10° (7)	—	B	800 (32) / 1200 (33)	—	2400 (5) (9)	—	4½-6½ (6)
4-97.6/2 Exc. High Alt. (11) (34)	.044	A	—	10° (7)	B	—	750D	—	2400 (5)	4½-6½ (6)
4-97.6/2 Calif. (11) (36)	.044	A	8° (7)	10° (7)	B	800 (32) /1200 (33)	750D	2200 (35)	2400 (5)	4½-6½ (6)
4-97.6/2 Calif. (11) (29) (37)	.044	A	—	14° (7)	B	—	750D	—	2400 (5)	4½-6½ (6)
4-97.6/2 High Alt. (11) (29) (38)	.044	A	10° (7)	—	B	900 (32) /1500 (33)	—	2400 (5) (9)	—	4½-6½ (6)
4-97.6/2 High Alt. (11) (29) (41)	.044	A	—	16° (7)	B	—	850D	—	2400 (5)	4½-6½ (6)
4-97.6 EFI/2 (11) (42)	.044	A	13°	—	B	(45)	—	—	—	39 (40)
4-97.6 EFI/2 (11) (43)	.044	A	15°	—	B	(45)	—	—	—	39 (40)
4-97.6 EFI/2 Exc. High Alt. (11) (44)	.044	A	—	15°	B	(45)	—	—	—	39 (40)
1984										
4-97.6/2 (11) (47)	.044	A	8° (4)	—	B	700-1000 (33)	—	2200 (39)	—	5-7
4-97.6/2 (11) (48)	.044	A	8° (4)	—	B	720	—	2200 (39)	—	5-7
4-97.6 H.O./4	.044	A	12° (4)	14° (4)	B	800/1200 (33)	700D	2200 (39)	2400 (39)	5-7
4-97.6 EFI/5	.044	A	10° (8)	10° (8)	B	(45)	(45)	(45)	(45)	39 (40)
4-140/R	.044	C	15° (4)	15° (4)	(46)	800	700D	1900 (5)	2200 (5)	4½-6½
1985										
4-97.6/2	.044	A	8° (4)	—	B	(17)	—	2200 (39)	—	5-7
4-97.6 H.O./4	.044	A	12° (4)	14° (4)	B	800/1200	700D	2200 (39)	2400 (39)	5-7
4-97.6 EFI/5	.044	A	10° (8)	10° (8)	B	800 (45)	750D (45)	(45)	(45)	35-45 (40)
4-97.6 Turbo/8	.044	A	8° (8)	—	B	800 (45)	—	(45)	—	35-45 (40)
4-116/9	.044	A	10° (4)	10° (4)	B	750	750D	2200 (39)	2400 (39)	5-7
4-140/X Exc. Calif.	.044	C	10° (8)	10° (8)	(46)	750 (45)	600D (45)	(45)	(45)	13-16 (40)
4-140/X Calif.	.044	C	10° (8)	10° (8)	(46)	800 (45) °600D (45)	(45)	(45)	13-16 (40)	
4-140 HSO/S	.044	C	10° (8)	10° (8)	(46)	800 (45)	600D (45)	(45)	(45)	13-16 (40)

Continued

FORD ESCORT, EXP & TEMPO, MERCURY LN7, LYNX & TOPAZ—Continued

Year & Engine/VIN	Spark Plug Gap	Ignition Timing BTDC ① Firing Order Fig.	Ignition Timing BTDC ① Man. Trans.	Ignition Timing BTDC ① Auto. Trans.	Ignition Timing BTDC ① Mark Fig.	Curb Idle Speed Man. Trans.	Curb Idle Speed Auto Trans. ②	Fast Idle Speed Man. Trans.	Fast Idle Speed Auto Trans.	Fuel Pump Pressure
1986										
4-116/9	.044	A	10° ④	10° ④	B	750	750D	2200 ㊴	2400 ㊴	5-7
4-116 EFI/J	.044	A	10° ⑧	10° ⑧	B	900 ㊺	800D ㊺	㊺	㊺	35-45 ㊵
4-140 HSC/X	.044	C	10° ⑧	10° ⑧	㊻	750 ㊺	650D ㊺	㊺	㊺	13-16 ㊵
4-140 HSO/S	.044	C	10° ⑧	—	㊻	800 ㊺	—	㊺	—	13-16 ㊵
1987										
4-116 CFI/	.044	A	10° ④	10° ④	B	800 ㊺	800D ㊺	㊺	㊺	14.5-17.5 ㊵
4-116 EFI/J	.044	A	10° ⑧	10° ⑧	B	1000 ㊺	㊺	㊺	㊺	35-45 ㊵
4-140 HSC/X	.044	C	10° ⑧	10° ⑧	㊻	800 ㊺	㊺	㊺	㊺	13.5-17.5 ㊵
4-140 HSO/S	.044	C	10° ⑧	10° ⑧	㊻	800 ㊺	㊺	㊺	㊺	13.5-17.5 ㊵
1988										
4-116 CFI/	.044	A	10° ④	10° ④	B	㊺	㊺	㊺	㊺	14.5-17.5 ㊵
4-116 EFI/	.044	A	10° ⑧	—	B	1000N ㊺	㊺	㊺	㊺	35-45 ㊵
4-140 HSC/	.044	C	10° ⑧	10° ⑧	㊻	㊺	㊺	㊺	㊺	13.5-17.5 ㊵
4-140 HSO/	.044	C	10° ⑧	10° ⑧	㊻	㊺	㊺	㊺	㊺	13.5-17.5 ㊵

①—BTDC-Before top dead center.
②—D: Drive.
③—With A/C on, 1700 RPM, if equipped.
④—With distributor vacuum hose disconnected & plugged.
⑤—On kick down step of cam.
⑥—With pump to tank return pinched off.
⑦—At 800 RPM.
⑧—With single wire connector located near distributor disconnected.
⑨—If mileage on vehicle is less than 100 mi., set at 2200 RPM.
⑩—Early production EXP & LN7.
⑪—Refer to engine calibration code on engine identification label, located at front of engine timing belt cover. The calibration code is located on the label below the engine sequence number (ESN) & is preceded by the letter C. The revision code is located next to the calibration code & is preceded by the letter R.
⑫—Calibration code 1-4E-R0.
⑬—Escort, Lynx & late production EXP & LN7.
⑭—Calibration code 2-4C-R0.
⑮—With A/C on, 1500N RPM, if equipped.
⑯—Calibration codes 1-3S-R0 & 1-3S-R11.
⑰—Less A/C, 720 RPM; with A/C, 700/1200 RPM.
⑱—Calibration codes 2-3A-R10 & 2-3C-R0.
⑲—Calibration codes 2-3D-R0, R1, R14 & R15.
⑳—Models less A/C & power steering.
㉑—Calibration code 2-3E-R0.
㉒—Calibration code 2-3G-R0.
㉓—Calibration code 1-4S-R0.
㉔—Calibration code 1-4S-R10.
㉕—Calibration code 2-4Q-R0.
㉖—Calibration code 2-4Q-R10.
㉗—Calibration code 1-3Y-R10.
㉘—Calibration code, man. trans. 2-3X-R0; auto. trans., 2-4X-R0.
㉙—High output engine.
㉚—Calibration code 3-3D-R01.
㉛—Calibration code 2-3B-R11.
㉜—With VOTM off.
㉝—With VOTM on.
㉞—Calibration code 3-4C-R00.
㉟—If mileage on vehicle is less than 100 miles, set at 2000 RPM.
㊱—Calibration code, man. trans., 3-3C-R00; auto. trans., 3-4Q-R01.
㊲—Calibration code 3-4T-R00.
㊳—Calibration code 2-3Y-R11.
㊴—On second step of fast idle cam.
㊵—On EFI models equipped with fuel diagnostic valve, wrap shop towel around fitting to prevent fuel spillage. Connect a suitable fuel pressure gauge to fuel diagnostic valve. On CFI models & EFI models less fuel diagnostic valve, disconnect electrical connector at inertia switch, then crank engine for approximately 15 seconds to deplete fuel system pressure. Wrap shop towel around connection to be disconnected to avoid fuel spillage. Connect a suitable fuel pressure gauge between throttle body & fuel filter. On all models, energize fuel pump & check fuel pressure gauge reading.
㊶—Calibration code 3-4Y-R00.
㊷—Calibration code 3-03A-R12.
㊸—Calibration code 3-03A-R13.
㊹—Calibration code 3-04A-R10.
㊺—Idle speed not adjustable. Idle speed maintained by computer.
㊻—Refer to Fig. D for manual transaxle models of Fig. E for automatic transaxle models. On manual transaxle models, a cover plate retained by two screws must be removed to view timing marks. On automatic transaxle models, symbols are indented on outer face of flywheel.
㊼—Calibration code 4-03F-R00.
㊽—Exc. calibration code 4-03F-R00.

Continued

FORD ESCORT, EXP & TEMPO, MERCURY LN7, LYNX & TOPAZ—Continued

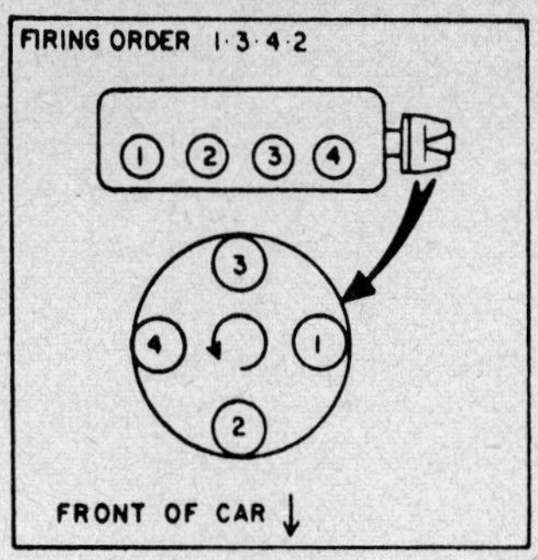

Fig. A

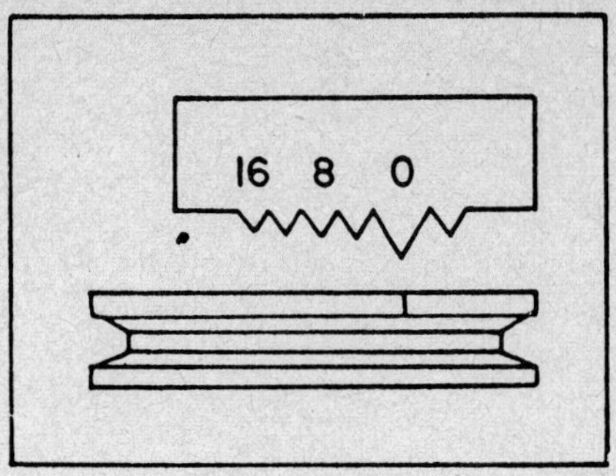

Fig. B

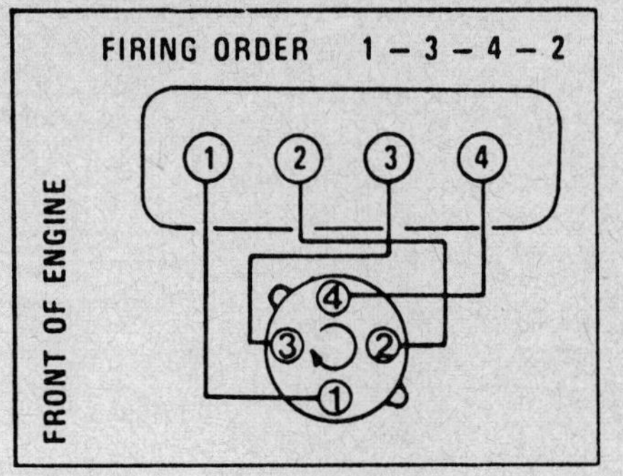

Fig. C

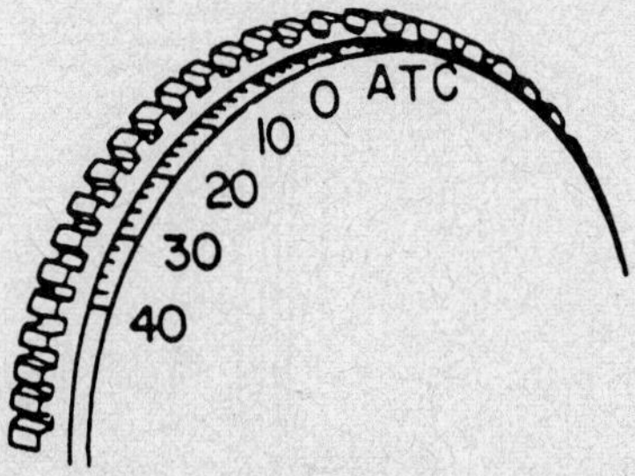

Fig. D

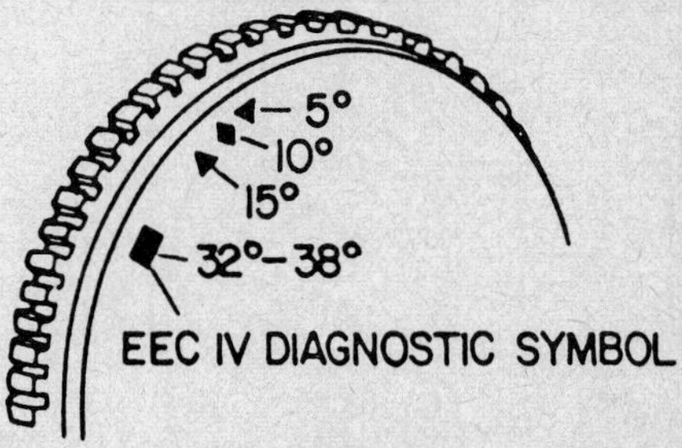

Fig. E

FORD TAURUS & MERCURY SABLE

Year & Engine	Spark Plug Gap	Ignition Timing BTDC ①				Curb Idle Speed ②		Fast Idle Speed		Fuel Pump Pressure
		Firing Order Fig.	Man. Trans.	Auto. Trans.	Mark Location	Man. Trans.	Auto Trans.	Man. Trans.	Auto Trans.	
1986										
4-153/D	.044	A	10° ④	10° ④	B	800 ⑤	700 ⑤	⑤	⑤	13-16 ③
V6-182/U	.044	C	10° ④	10° ④	B	⑤	⑤	⑤	⑤	—
1987										
4-153/D	.044	A	10° ④	10° ④	B	⑤	⑤	⑤	⑤	—
V6-182/U	.044	C	—	10° ④	D	—	⑤	—	⑤	—
1988										
4-153/	.044	A	10° ④	10° ④	B	⑤	⑤	⑤	⑤	13-16 ③
V6-182/	.044	C	—	10° ④	D	—	⑤	—	⑤	35-45 ③
V6-232/	.054	—	—	—	—	—	—	—	—	35-45 ③

①—BTDC-Before top dead center.

②—Idle speed on manual trans. vehicles is adjusted in Neutral & on auto. trans. equipped vehicles is adjusted in Drive unless otherwise specified. Where two idle speeds are listed, the higher speed is with the A/C or throttle solenoid energized. On models equipped with vacuum release brake, whenever adjusting ignition timing or idle speed, vacuum line to brake release mechanism must be disconnected & plugged to prevent parking brake from releasing when selector is moved to Drive.

③—Disconnect electrical connector at inertia switch, then crank engine for approximately 15 seconds to deplete fuel system pressure. Wrap shop towel around connection to be disconnected to prevent fuel spillage. Connect a suitable fuel pressure gauge between throttle body & fuel filter. Energize fuel pump & check pressure gauge reading.

④—With single wire connector located near distributor disconnected.

⑤—Idle speed is controlled by an automatic idle control system.

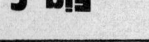

Continued

FORD TAURUS & MERCURY SABLE—Continued

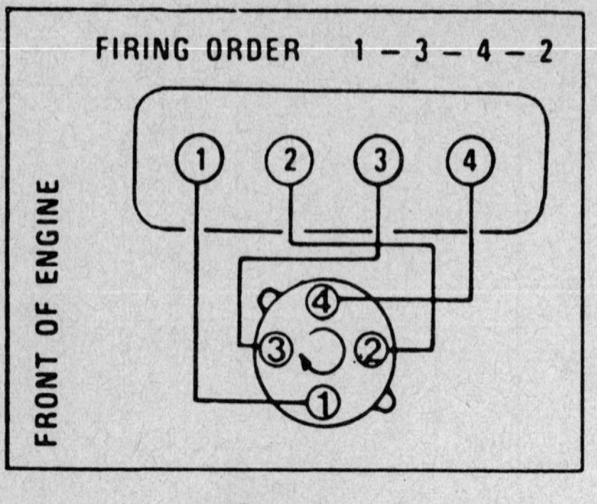

Fig. A

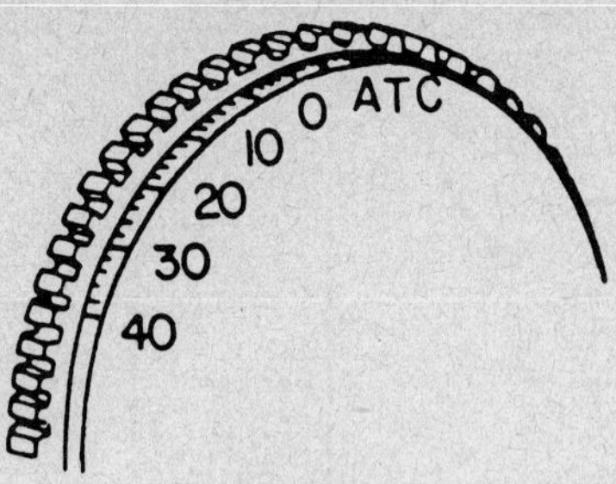

Fig. B

FIRING ORDER 1-4-2-6-3-5

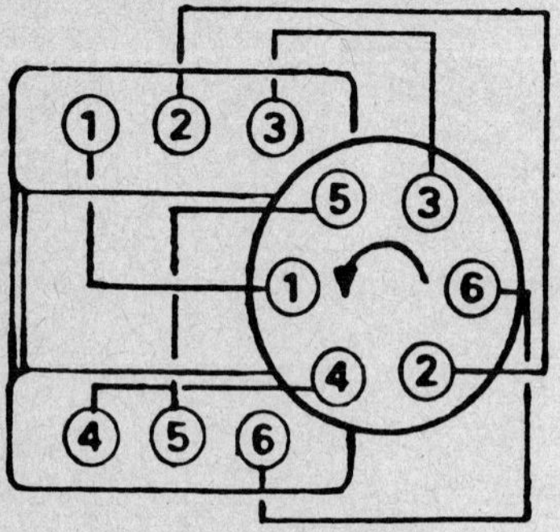

Fig. C

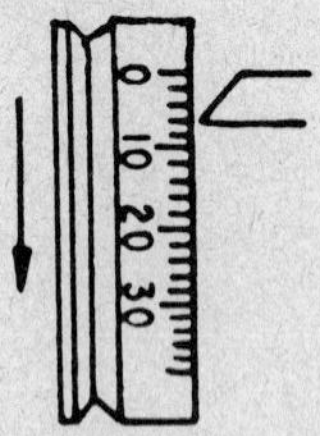

Fig. D

LINCOLN

Year & Engine/VIN	Spark Plug Gap	Ignition Timing			Curb idle speed ②	Fast idle speed	Fuel Pump Pressure
		Firing Order Fig.	Degrees BTDC ①	Mark Fig.			
1982							
V6-232/3 Exc. Calif.	.044	A	12°	D	550/650D	2200④	6-8
V6-232/3 Calif.	.044	A	12°	D	550/650D	2200③	6-8
V8-302/F Exc. Calif.	.050	E	12°	B	550D	1700③	6-8
V8-302/F High Alt.	.050	E	12°	B	550D	1700③	6-8
V8-302/F Calif.	.050	E	—	B	550D	—	6-8
V8-302/F E.F.I. Exc. Calif.	.050	E	⑦	B	550D	2200⑩	—
V8-302/F E.F.I. Calif.	.050	E	⑦	B	550D	2150⑩	—
1983							
V8-302/F E.F.I. Exc. Calif.	.050	E	⑦	B	550D	2200④	39
V8-302/F E.F.I. Calif.	.050	E	⑦	B	550D	2200④	39
1984							
V8-302/F E.F.I. Exc. Calif.	.050	E	10°⑤	B	550D⑪	⑥⑧	35-45
V8-302/F E.F.I. Calif.	.050	E	10°⑤	B	550D⑪	⑥⑨	35-45
1985							
V8-302/F E.F.I.	.050	E	10°⑤	B	550D⑪	2300	35-45
V8-302 H.O./M E.F.I.	.050	C	10°⑤	B	550D⑪	2400	35-45

Continued

LINCOLN—Continued

(11)

Year & Engine/VIN	Spark Plug Gap	Ignition Timing: Firing Order Fig.	Ignition Timing: Degrees BTDC (1)	Ignition Timing: Mark Fig.	Curb idle speed (2)	Fast idle speed	Fuel Pump Pressure
1986							
V8-302/F E.F.I.	.050	E	10° (5)	B	600D	—	35-45 (12)
V8-302 H.O./F E.F.I.	.050	C	10° (5)	B	625D	—	35-45 (12)
1987							
V8-302/F	.050	E	10° (5)	B	—	—	35-45 (12)
V8-302 H.O./F	.050	C	10° (5)	B	—	—	35-45 (12)
1988							
V6-232/	.054	—	—	—	—	—	35-45 (12)
V8-302/	.050	E	10° (5)	B	—	—	35-45 (12)
V8-302 H.O./	.054	F	10° (5)	B	—	—	35-45 (12)

(1)—BTDC-Before top dead center.

(2)—Idle speed on manual trans. vehicles is adjusted in Neutral & on auto. trans. equipped vehicles is adjusted in Drive unless otherwise specified. Where two idle speeds are listed, the higher speed is with the A/C or throttle solenoid energized. On models equipped with vacuum release brake, whenever adjusting ignition timing or idle speed, vacuum line to brake release mechanism must be disconnected & plugged to prevent parking brake from releasing when selector is moved to Drive.

(3)—On kickdown step of cam.

(4)—On high step of fast idle cam.

(5)—Firing order for V8-302, 1-5-4-2-6-3-7-8. Firing order for V8-302 H.O., 1-3-7-2-6-5-4-8. Cylinder numbering (front to rear): Right bank 1-2-3-4, left bank 5-6-7-8. Refer to Fig. C for spark plug wire connections at distributor.

(6)—Refer to engine calibration code on engine identification label, located at rear of left valve cover. The calibration code is located on the label after the engine code number and is preceded by the letter C and the revision code is located below the calibration code and is preceded by the letter R.

(7)—Ignition timing is not adjustable.

(8)—Calibration code 4-22B-R0, 2100 RPM; Exc. calibration code 4-22B-R0, 2300 RPM.

(9)—Calibration code 3-22D-R0, 2200 RPM; Calibration code 4-22Q-R0, 2300 RPM.

(10)—On 1st step of idle cam.

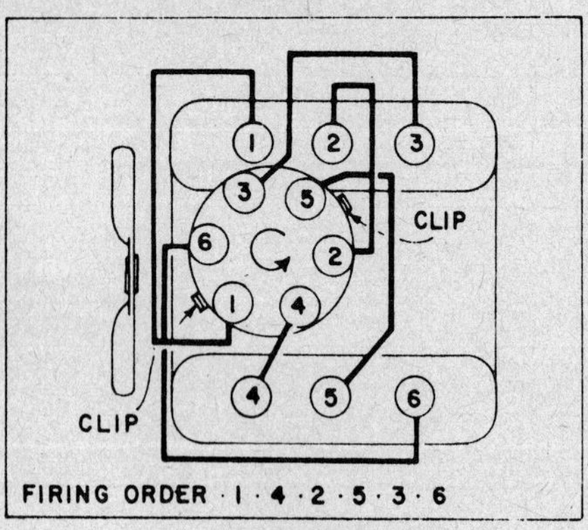

Fig. A

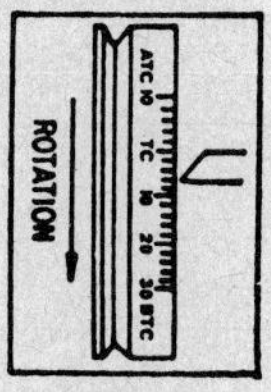

Fig. B

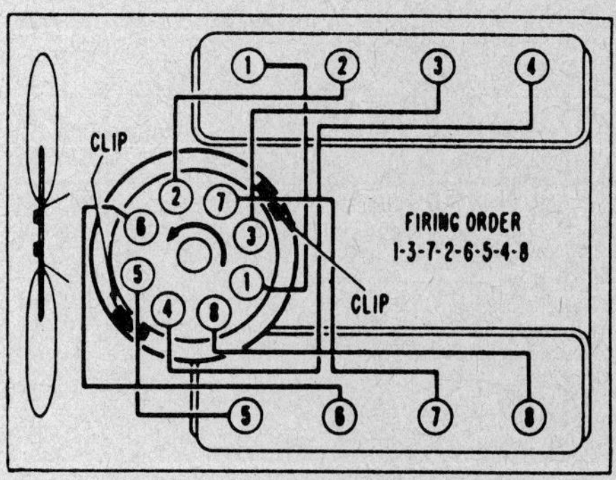

Fig. C

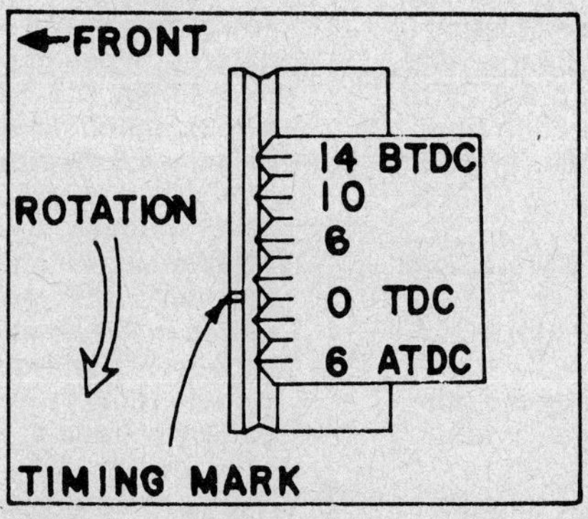

Fig. D

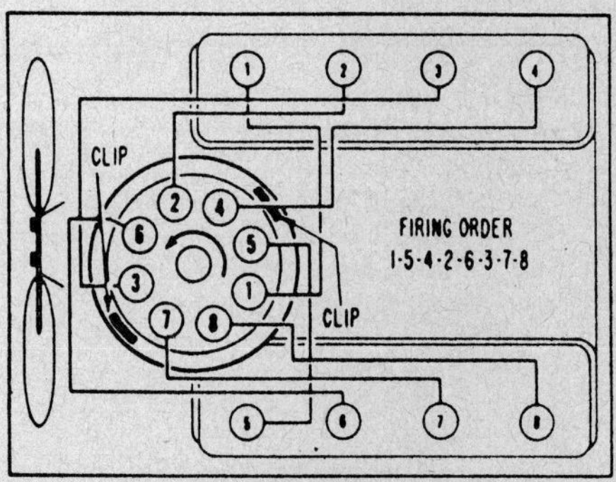

Fig. E

BUICK REAR WHEEL DRIVE & 1982-85 RIVIERA

Year & Engine/ VIN	Spark Plug Gap	Ignition Timing Firing Order Fig.	Degrees BTDC ①	Mark Fig.	Curb Idle Speed	Fast Idle Speed	Fuel Pump Pressure
1982							
V6-231/A⑤	.080	A	15°	B④	500D⑩	2000	5½-6½
V6-231/C⑥	.060	A	15°	B④	500D	2000	5½-6½
V6-252/4	.080	A	15°	B④	500D⑩	2000	5½-6½
V8-307/Y	.080	D	20°⑦	E	⑩	650D	5½-6½
1983							
V6-231/A⑤	.080	A	15°	B④	⑩	2200	5½-6½
V6-231/8⑥	.060	A	15°	B④	⑩	2200	5½-6½
V6-252/4	.080	A	15°	B④	⑩	⑧	5½-6½
V8-307/Y	.080	D	20°⑦	E	⑩	900D	5½-6½
1984							
V6-231/A⑤	.060	A	15°⑬	B④	⑩	2200⑮	4¼-5¾
V6-231/9⑥	.045	⑪	③	⑭	⑨	⑨	34-40②
V6-252/4	.060	A	15°⑬	B④	⑩	⑧	4¼-5¾
V8-307/Y	.080	D	20°⑦	E	⑩	700D⑯	5½-6½
1985							
V6-231/A⑤	.060	A	15°⑬	B④	⑩	2200⑮	4¼-5¾
V6-231/9⑥	.045	⑪	③	⑭	⑨	⑨	37-43②
V8-307/Y	.060	D	20°⑦	E	⑩	550D⑯	6-7½
1986							
V6-231/A⑤	.060	A	15°⑬	B④	⑩	2200⑮	4½-5¾
V6-231/7⑥	.045	⑪	③	⑭	⑨	⑨	37-43②
V6-307/Y	.060	D	20°⑦	E	⑩	550D⑯	6-7½
1987							
V6-231/A	.060	A	15°⑬	B④	⑩	22°⑮	4¼-5¾
V6-231 Turbo/7	.045	⑫	③	⑭	⑨	⑨	37-43②
V8-307/Y	.060	E	20°⑦	E	⑩	550D⑯	6-7½
1988							
V8-307/	.060	E	20°⑦	E	450D⑩	—	6-7½

①—BTDC-Before top dead center.

②—With shop towel wrapped around fuel pressure valve to prevent fuel spillage, connect a suitable fuel pressure gauge to fuel pressure valve. Check fuel pressure with ignition switch in On position, engine not running.

③—Computer controlled, no adjustment.

④—The harmonic balancer on these engines has two timing marks. The timing mark measuring 1/16 in. is used when setting timing with a hand held timing light. The mark measuring 1/8 in. is used when setting timing with magnetic timing equipment.

⑤—Except turbo charged engine.

⑥—Turbo charged engine.

⑦—At 1100 RPM with jumper wire connected between ALCL connector terminals A & B. The ALCL connector is located under the instrument panel to the right of the steering column. After completing adjustment, disconnect jumper wire from between terminals A & B. With engine off, clear trouble code from Electronic Control Module (ECM) by removing battery voltage to ECM for 30 seconds.

⑧—Exc. Riviera, 2200 RPM; Riviera, 2100 RPM.

⑨—Idle speed controlled by idle Air Control (IAC) valve.

⑩—Idle speed is controlled by the idle speed control (ISC) motor or idle load compensator (ILC).

⑪—Cylinder numbering front to rear, left bank 1, 3, 5; right bank 2, 4, 6. Firing order 1-6-5-4-3-2. Refer to Fig. C for spark plug wire connections at coil unit.

⑫—Cylinder numbering front to rear, left bank 1, 3, 5; right bank 2, 4, 6. Firing order 1-6-5-4-3-2. Two different types of coil untis are used, refer to Fig. C & F for spark plug wire connections at coil unit.

⑬—Disconnect distributor four wire electrical connector when checking ignition timing. After completing adjustment, reconnect distributor four wire connector. With ignition switch in Off position, clear trouble code from Electronic Control Module (ECM) memory by removing battery voltage to the ECM for 30 seconds.

⑭—Equipped with crankshaft position sensor.

⑮—On high step of fast idle cam.

⑯—On low step of fast idle cam.

Continued

BUICK REAR WHEEL DRIVE & 1982-85 RIVIERA—Continued

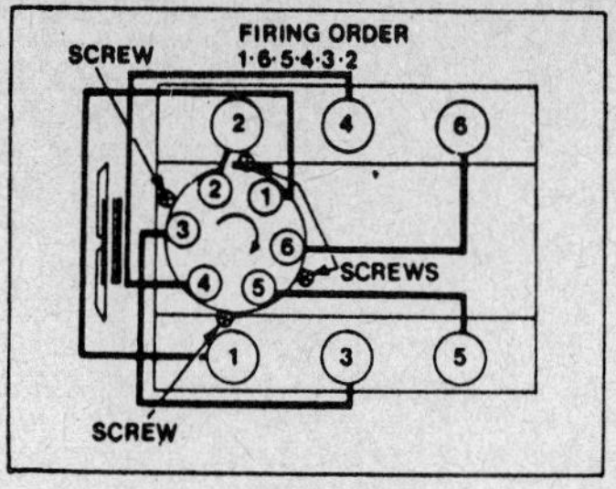

Fig. A

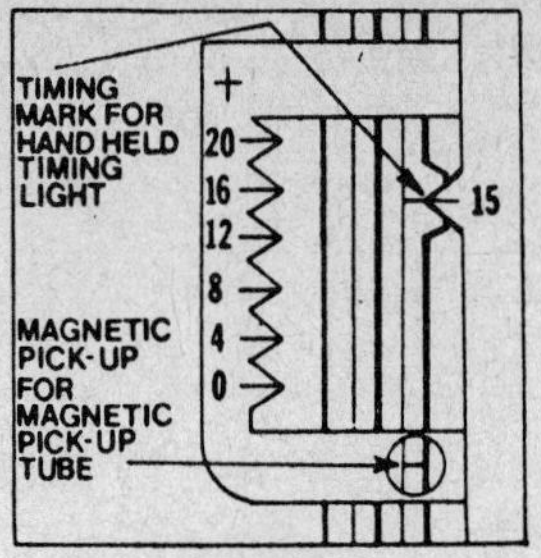

Fig. B

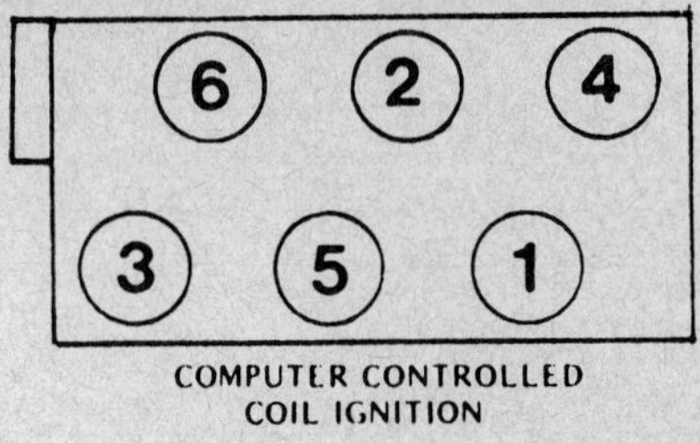

Fig. C

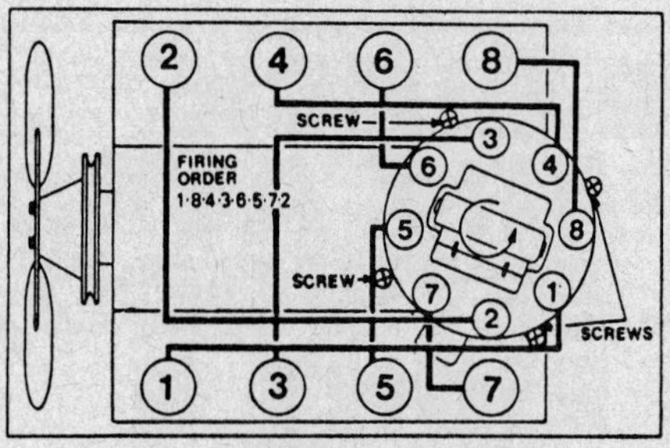

Fig. D

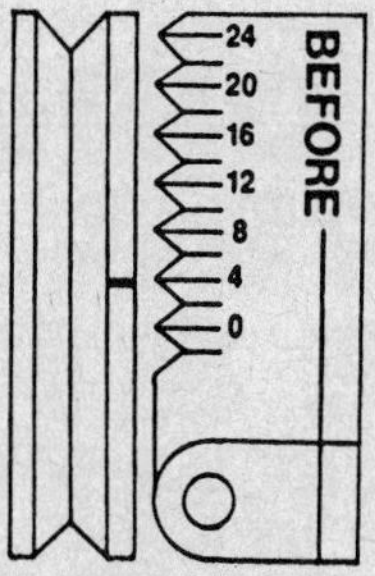

Fig. E

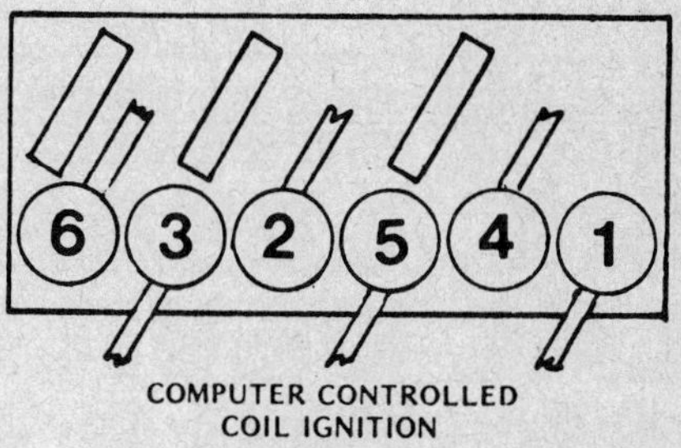

Fig. F

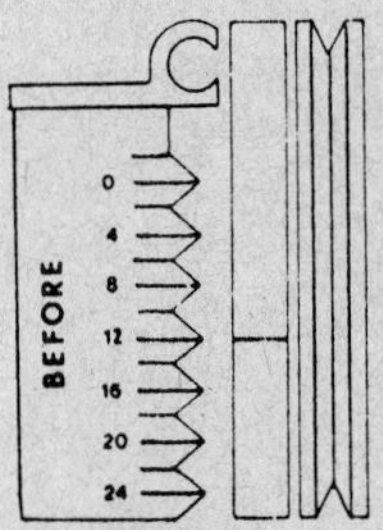

Fig. G

1986-88 BUICK RIVIERA, CADILLAC ELDORADO & SEVILLE & OLDSMOBILE TORONADO

Year & Engine/VIN Code ①	Spark Plug Gap	Ignition Timing			Curb Idle Speed ③	Fast Idle Speed	Fuel Pump Pressure
		Firing Order Fig.	Degrees BTDC	Mark Fig.			
1986							
V6-231/B,3	.045	④	⑤	—	⑥	⑥	37-43 ⑦
V8-250/8	.060	B	10° ⑧	C	⑥	⑥	9-12 ②
1987							
V6-231/B	.045	④	⑤	—	⑥	⑥	37-43 ⑦
V8-250/8	.060	B	10° ⑧	C	⑥	⑥	9-12 ⑦
1988							
V6-231/	—	④	⑤	—	⑥	⑥	—
V8-273/	—	—	—	—	—	—	—

①—The eighth digit of the Vehicle Identification Number (VIN) denotes engine code.

②—Wrap shop towel around fuel hose to steel line connection in engine compartment to prevent fuel spillage. Disconnect fuel hose from steel line & connect a suitable fuel pressure gauge between hose and line. Ensure gauge connections are tight, then start engine & check fuel pressure readings.

③—Idle speed is adjusted in Drive. When adjusting idle speed, set parking brake & block drive wheels.

④—Cylinder numbering from left to right as viewed from front of vehicle, front bank, 1, 3, 5; rear bank, 2, 4, 6. Firing order 1-6-5-4-3-2. Refer to Fig. A for spark plug wire connections at coil unit.

⑤—Computer controlled, no adjustment.

⑥—Idle speed is controlled by an idle speed control (ISC) motor or an idle air control (IAC) valve.

⑦—With shop towel wrapped around fuel pressure valve to prevent fuel spillage, connect a suitable fuel pressure gauge to fuel pressure valve. Check fuel pressure with ignition switch in the On position, engine not running.

⑧—Connect jumper wire between ALCL connector terminals A & B. The ALCL connector is located under the instrument panel to the right of the steering column. After completing adjustment, disconnect jumper wire from between terminals A & B. With engine off, clear trouble code from Electronic Control Module (ECM) by removing battery voltage to ECM for 30 seconds.

Continued

1986-88 BUICK RIVIERA, CAD. ELDORADO & SEVILLE & OLDS. TORONADO—Continued

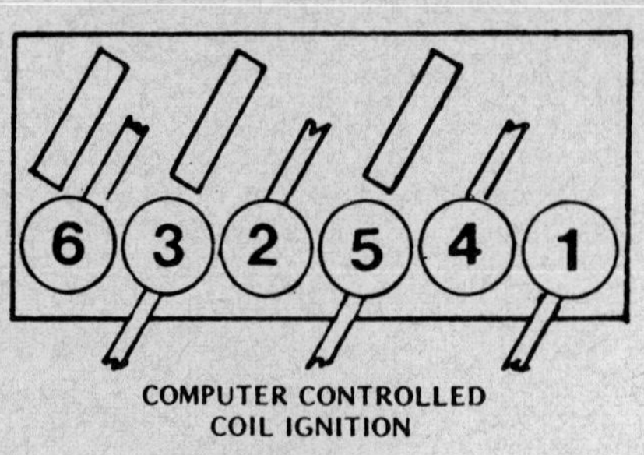

Fig. A

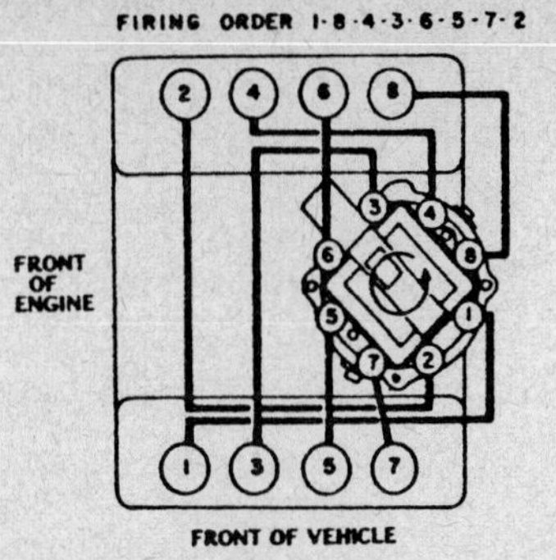

Fig. B

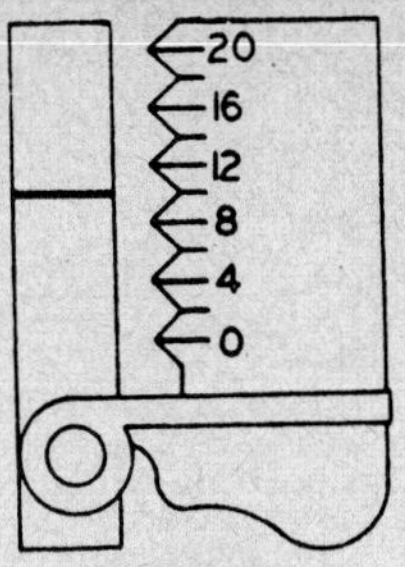

Fig. C

FRONT WHEEL DRIVE BUICK ELECTRA, LESABRE & PARK AVE., CADILLAC DEVILLE & FLEETWOOD, OLDSMOBILE EIGHTY EIGHT & NINETY EIGHT, PONTIAC BONNEVILLE

Year & Engine/VIN Code	Spark Plug Gap	Ignition Timing: Firing Order Fig.	Ignition Timing: Degrees BTDC ①	Ignition Timing: Mark Fig.	Curb Idle Speed ②	Fast Idle Speed	Fuel Pump Pressure
1985							
V6-181/E	.060	A	15° ⑦	B	③	2400 ⑩	3.9-6.5
V6-231 MFI/3	.080	—	15° ⑧	—	③	③	34-40 ⑪
V8-250 DFI/8	.060	E	10° ⑧	F	450 ④	—	9-12 ⑫
1986							
V6-181/L	.045	⑥	⑤	⑨	③	③	37-43 ⑪
V6-231 SFI/B,3	.045	⑥	⑤	⑨	③	③	37-43 ⑪
V8-250 DFI/8	.060	E	10° ⑧	F	③	③	9-12 ⑫
1987							
V6-231 SFI/3	.045	⑥	⑤	⑨	③	③	37-43 ⑪
V8-250 DFI/8	.060	E	—	F	③	③	9-12 ⑫
1988							
V6-231/	—	—	—	—	—	—	—
V8-273/	—	—	—	—	—	—	—

①—BTDC-Before top dead center.
②—D; Drive.
③—Idle speed is controlled by an idle speed control motor or idle air control motor.
④—Minimum RPM.
⑤—Not adjustable.
⑥—Cylinder numbering from left to right as viewed from front of vehicle, front bank 1, 3, 5; rear bank 2, 4, 6. Firing order 1-6-5-4-3-2. Two different types of computer controlled coil ignition system are used. Refer to Figs. C & D for spark plug wire connections at coil unit.
⑦—Disconnect distributor four wire electrical connector when adjusting ignition timing. After completing adjustment, reconnect distributor four wire electrical connector. With engine off, clear trouble code from Electronic Control Module Memory (ECM) by removing battery voltage to ECM for 30 seconds.
⑧—Connect jumper wire between ALCL connector terminals A & B. The ALCL connector is located under the instrument panel to the right of the steering column. After completing adjustment, disconnect jumper wire from between terminals A & B. With engine off, clear trouble code from Electronic Control Module (ECM) memory by removing battery voltage from ECM for 30 seconds.
⑨—Equipped with crankshaft position sensor.
⑩—On high step of fast idle cam.
⑪—With shop towel wrapped around fuel pressure valve to prevent fuel spillage, connect a suitable fuel pressure gauge to fuel pressure valve. Check fuel pressure with ignition switch in the On position, engine not running.
⑫—With shop towel wrapped around fitting to prevent spillage, connect a suitable fuel pressure gauge to fuel line service fitting. Check fuel pressure while cranking engine.

Continued

FRONT WHEEL DRIVE BUICK ELECTRA, LESABRE & PARK AVE., CADILLAC DEVILLE & FLEETWOOD, OLDSMOBILE EIGHTY EIGHT & NINETY EIGHT, PONTIAC BONNEVILLE—Continued

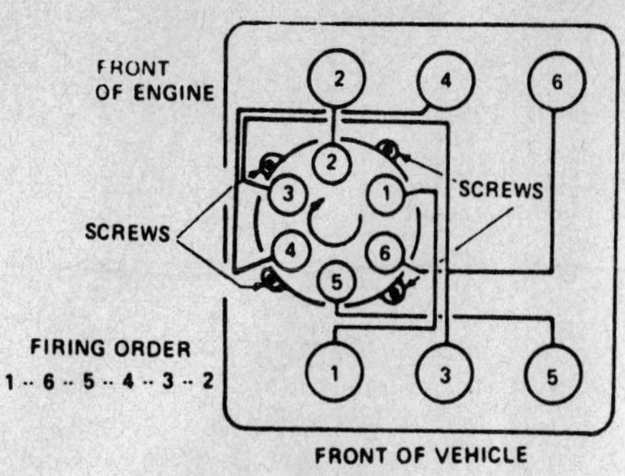

Fig. A

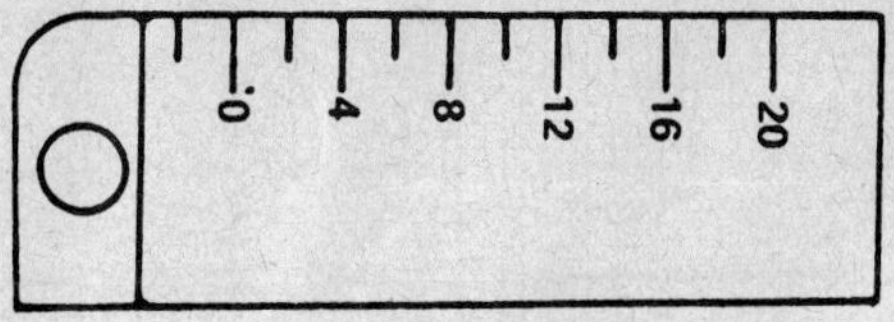

Fig. B

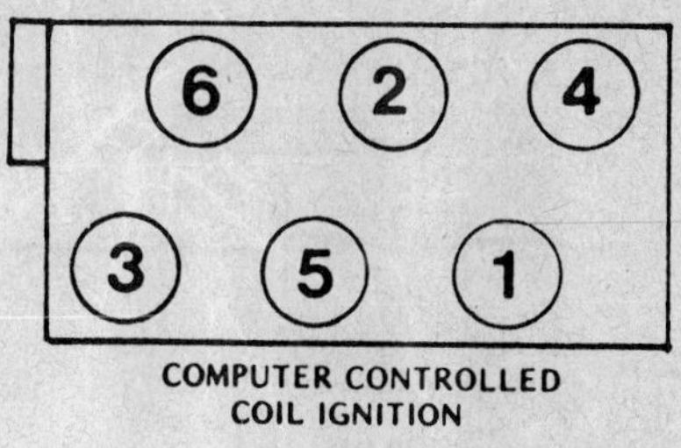

Fig. C

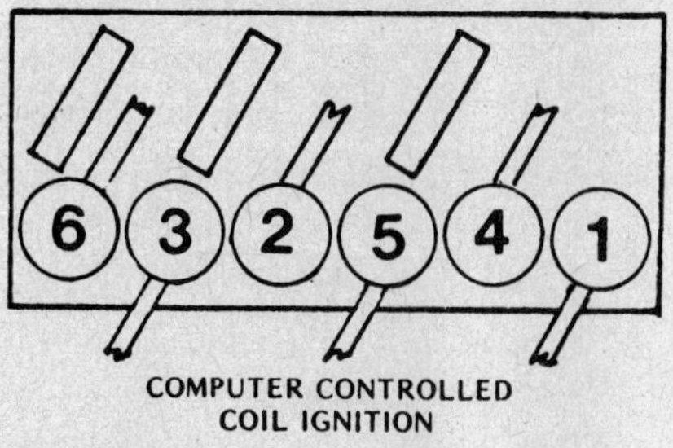

Fig. D

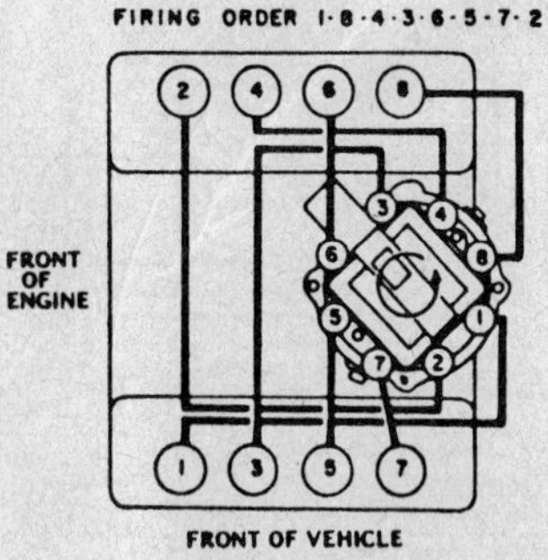

Fig. E

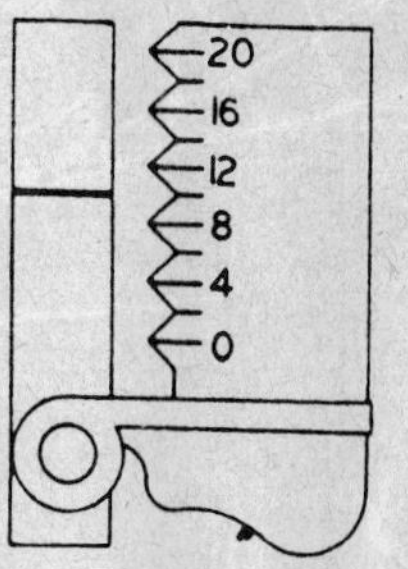

Fig. F

CADILLAC REAR WHEEL DRIVE & 1982-85 ELDORADO & SEVILLE

Year & Engine/VIN	Spark Plug Gap	Ignition Timing			Curb Idle Speed	Fast Idle Speed ③	Fuel Pump Pressure
		Firing Order Fig.	Degrees BTDC ①	Mark Fig.			
1982							
V6-252/4	.080	E	15°②	F④	⑥	⑥	4¼-5¾
V8-250 D.E.F.I./8	.060	C	10°②	D	⑥	⑥	—
1983-85							
V8-250 D.E.F.I./8	.060	C	10°②	D	450D⑦	⑥	9-12⑧
1986-88							
V8-307/Y	.060	A	20°⑤	B	⑥	550D⑨	6-7.5

①—BTDC-Before top dead center.
②—With green reference signal electrical connector located at rear of engine near distributor disconnected.
③—With transmission in Park position & parking brake fully applied.
④—The harmonic balancer on these engines has two timing marks. The timing mark measuring 1/16 in. is used when setting timing with a hand held timing light. The mark measuring 1/8 inch is used when setting timing with magnetic timing equipment.
⑤—At 1100 RPM.
⑥—Idle speed is controlled by an idle speed control motor or idle load compensator.
⑦—Minimum.
⑧—With shop towel wrapped around fitting to prevent fuel spillage, connect a suitable fuel pressure gauge to fuel line service fitting. Check pressure while cranking engine.
⑨—On low step of fast idle cam.

Continued

CADILLAC REAR WHEEL DRIVE & 1982-85 ELDORADO & SEVILLE—Continued

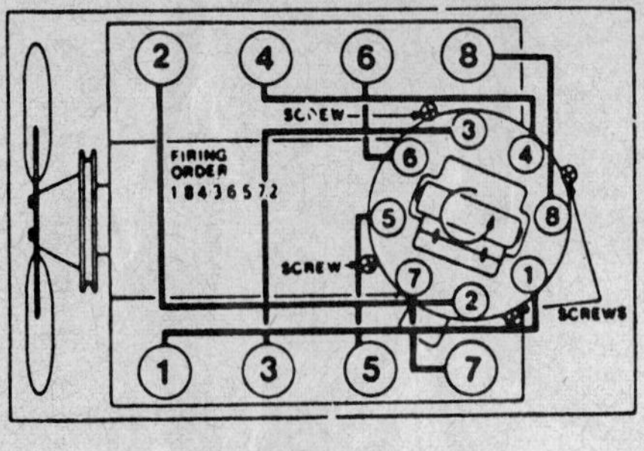

Fig. A

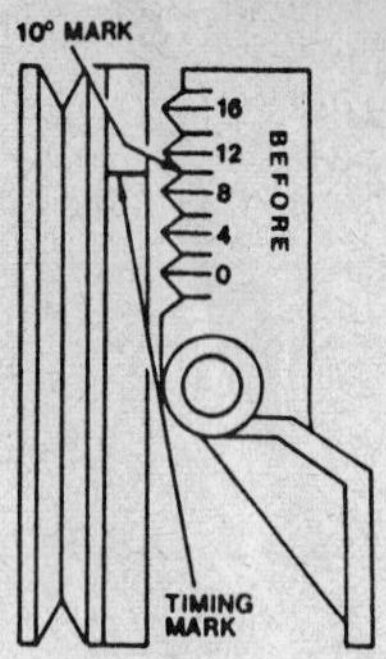

Fig. B

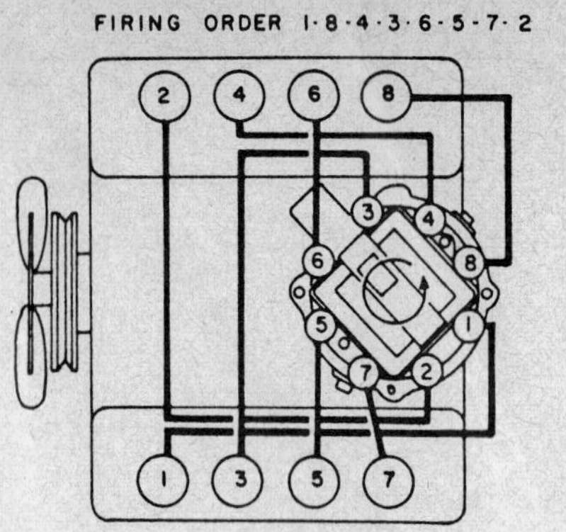

Fig. C

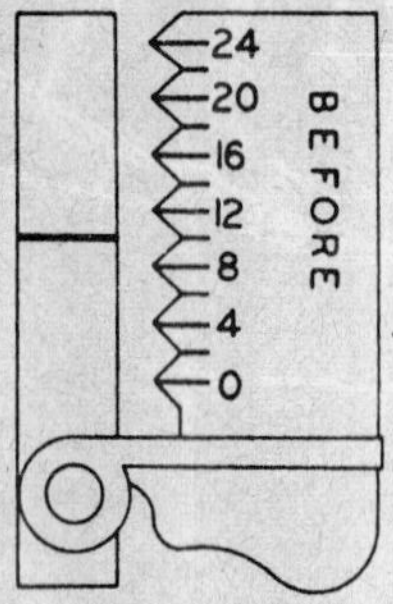

Fig. D

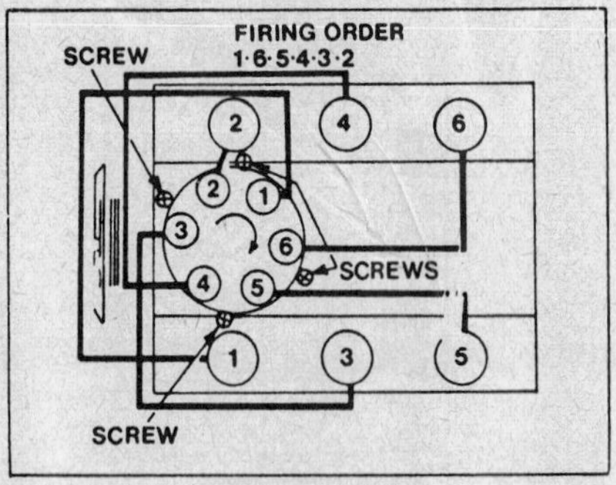

Fig. E

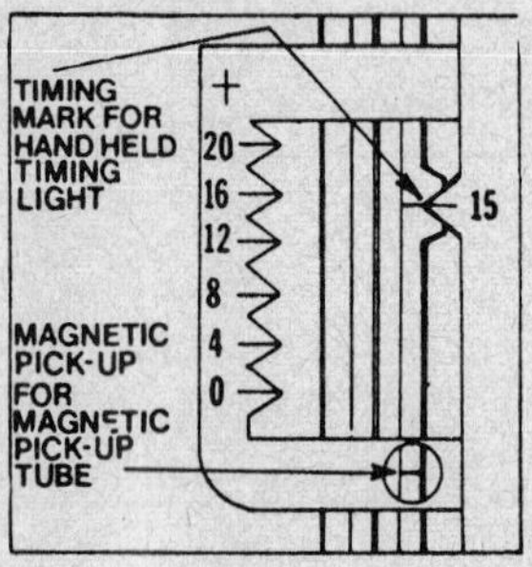

Fig. F

1985-87 BUICK SOMERSET REGAL & OLDS CALAIS; 1985-88 PONT. GRAND AM; 1986-88 BUICK SKYLARK; 1988 CUTLASS CALAIS

Year & Engine/ VIN	Spark Plug Gap	Ignition Timing BTDC ①				Curb Idle Speed ②		Fast Idle Speed		Fuel Pump Pressure
		Firing Order Fig.	Man. Trans.	Auto. Trans.	Mark Fig.	Man. Trans.	Auto. Trans.	Man. Trans.	Auto. Trans.	
1985										
4-151/U	.060	A	8°③⑦	8°④⑦	B	⑤	⑤	⑤	⑤	9-13⑩
V6-181/L	.040	⑨	—	⑥	⑧	—	⑤	⑤	⑤	37-43
1986										
4-151/U	.060	A	8°⑦	8°⑦	B	⑤	⑤	⑤	⑤	9-13⑩
V6-181/L	.040	⑨	—	⑥	⑧	—	⑤	—	⑤	37-43⑪
1987										
4-121 Turbo/M	.060	D	—	—	E	⑤	⑤	⑤	⑤	30-39⑪
4-151/U	.060	A	—	—	B	⑤	⑤	⑤	⑤	9-13⑩
V6-181/L	.045	⑨	—	⑥	⑧	—	⑤	—	⑤	37-43⑪
1988										
4-138/	—	—	—	—	—	—	—	—	—	—
4-151/U	—	—	—	—	—	—	—	—	—	—
4-181/L	—	—	—	—	—	—	—	—	—	—

Continued

1985-87 BUICK SOMERSET REGAL & OLDS. CALAIS • 1985-88 PONT. GRAND AM • 1986-88 BUICK SKYLARK & 1988 CUTLASS CALAIS—Continued

①—BTDC-Before top dead center.
②—D: Drive.
③—At 800 RPM
④—At 750 RPM
⑤—Idle speed is controlled by by an idle air control (IAC) valve or an idle speed control (ISC) motor.
⑥—Not adjustable.
⑦—Connect jumper wire between ALCL terminal A & B. The ALCL connector is located under the instrument panel. Check average timing of cylinder numbers 1 & 4 & reset as necessary. After completing adjustment, remove jumper wire from ALCL connector.
⑧—Equipped with crankshaft oposition sensor.
⑨—Cylinder numbering left to right as viewed from front of vehicle. Front bank; 1, 3, 5; rear bank 2, 4, 6. Firing Order 1-6-5-4-3-2. Two different types of coil units are used, refer to Figs. C & F for spark plug wire connections at coil unit.
⑩—Wrap shop towel around fuel hose to steel line connection in engine compartment to prevent fuel spillage. Disconnect fuel hose from steel line & install a suitable fuel pressure gauge between hose & line. Ensure gauge connections are tight, then start engine & check fuel pressure readings.
⑪—With shop towel wrapped around fuel pressure valve to prevent fuel spillage, connect a suitable fuel pressure gauge to fuel pressure valve. Check fuel pressure with ignition switch in the On position, engine not running.

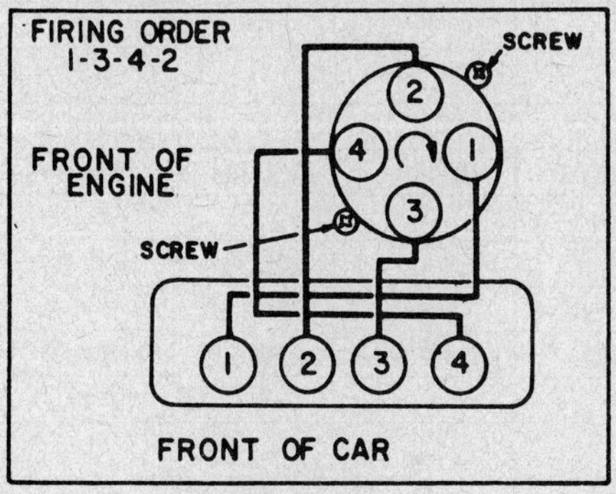

Fig. A

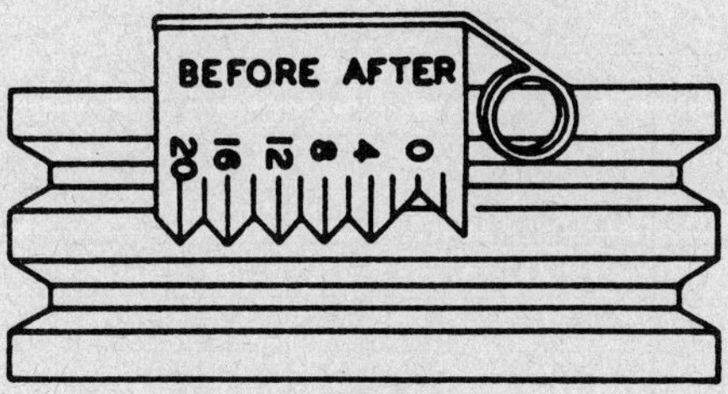

Fig. B

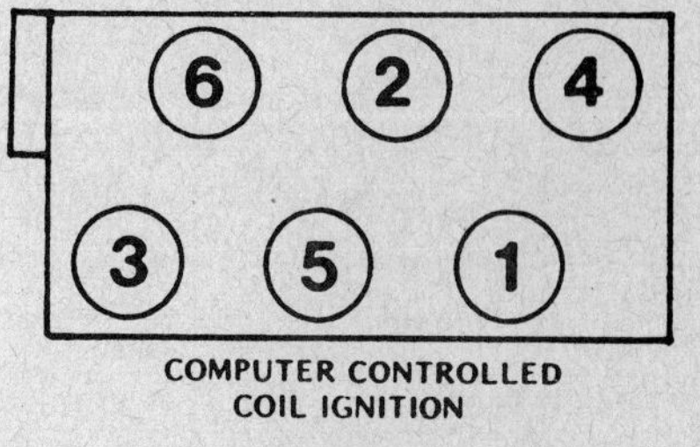

Fig. C

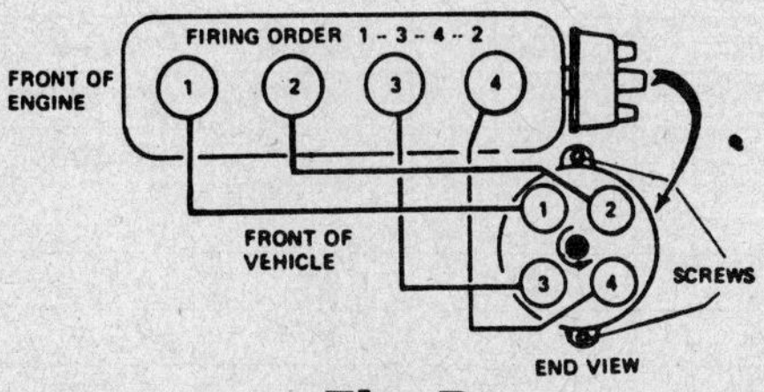

Fig. D

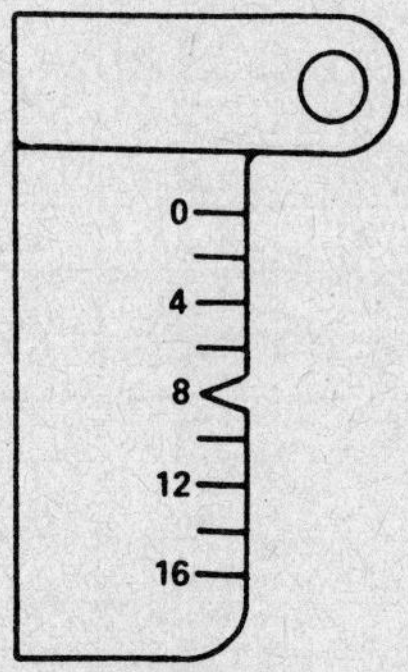

Fig. E

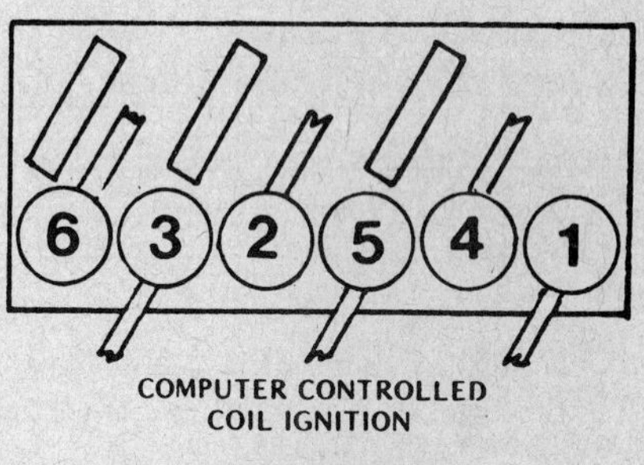

Fig. F

CHEVROLET—CAMARO, CAPRICE, CORVETTE, IMPALA, MALIBU & MONTE CARLO

Year & Engine/V.I.N.	Spark Plug Gap	Ignition Timing BTDC①* Firing Order Fig.♦	Ignition Timing BTDC①* Man. Trans.	Ignition Timing BTDC①* Auto. Trans.	Ignition Timing BTDC①* Mark Fig.	Curb Idle Speed② Man. Trans.	Curb Idle Speed② Auto. Trans.	Fast Idle Speed Man. Trans.	Fast Idle Speed Auto. Trans.	Fuel Pump Pressure
1982										
4-151 E.F.I./2	.060	I	8°⑧	8°⑧	J	⑩	⑩	⑩	⑩	—
V6-173/1	.045	K	10°⑨	10°⑨	L	850④	600D⑥	2600	2500	6-7½
V6-229/K	.045	F	—	TDC	G	—	③	—	2200	4½-6
V6-231/A	.080	D	—	15°⑨	E⑤	—	③	—	1800	3 Min.
V8-267/J	.045	C	—	2°	A	—	500/600D	—	2200	7½-9
V8-305/H	.045	C	6°	6°⑨	A	700/800	500/600D	1800	2200	7½-9
V8-305 E.F.I./7	.045	C	—	6°⑦	A	—	⑩	—	⑩	—
V8-350/6	.045	C	—	6°⑦	A	—	⑩	—	⑩	—

Continued

GASOLINE ENGINE PERFORMANCE SPECIFICATIONS

CHEVROLET CAMARO, CAPRICE, CORVETTE, IMPALA, MALIBU & MONTE CARLO—Continued

Year & Engine/VIN.	Spark Plug Gap	Ignition Timing BTDC ①				Curb Idle Speed ②		Fast Idle Speed		Fuel Pump Pressure
		Firing Order Fig.	Man. Trans.	Auto. Trans.	Mark Fig.	Man. Trans.	Auto. Trans.	Man. Trans.	Auto. Trans.	
1983										
4-151 E.F.I./2	.060	I	—	8° ⑧	J	775N ⑩	550D ⑩	⑩	⑩	—
V6-173/1	.045	K	10° ⑨	10° ⑨	L	775/1100	600/750D	2500	2500	5½-6½
V6-229/9	.045	F	—	TDC	G	—	—	—	—	4½-6
V6-231/A	.080	D	—	15° ⑨	E ⑤	—	③	—	2200	4¼-4¾
V8-305/H	.045	C	6° ⑨	6° ⑨	A	700/800	500/650D	1800	2200	7½-9
V8-305 H.O./G	.045	C	6° ⑨	6° ⑨	A	700	500D	—	—	7½-9
V8-305 E.F.I./S	.045	C	6°	6°	A	⑩	⑩	⑩	⑩	—
1984										
4-151 E.F.I./2	.060	I	8° ⑪	8° ⑧	J	775 ⑩	500D ⑩	⑩	⑩	9-13 ⑯
V6-173/1	.045	K	10° ⑨	10° ⑨	L	775/1100	600/750D	2500 ⑭	2500 ⑭	5½-6½
V6-229/9	.045	F	—	TDC ⑪ ⑫	G	—	⑩	—	⑩	4½-6
V6-231/A	.060	D	—	15° ⑨	E ⑤	—	⑩	—	2200 ⑭	4¼-5¾
V8-305/H	.045	C	6° ⑨	6° ⑨	A	700/800	500/650D	1800 ⑭	2200 ⑭	7½-9
V8-305 H.O./G	.045	C	6° ⑨	6° ⑨	A	700	500D	1800 ⑭	2200 ⑭	7½-9
V8-350/8	.045	C	—	6° ⑦	H	—	⑩	—	⑩	9-13 ⑥
1985										
4-151/E.F.I./2	.060	I	8° ⑪	8° ⑪	J	⑩	⑩	⑩	⑩	9-13 ⑯
V6-173 M.F.I./S	.045	K	10° ⑨	10° ⑨	L	⑩	⑩	⑩	⑩	40.5-47 ⑰
V6-262 E.F.I./Z	.035	M	—	TDC ⑦	Q	—	⑩	—	⑩	9-13 ⑯
V8-305/H	.045	C	TDC ⑨	TDC ⑨	A	700	500D	1800 ⑭	2200 ⑭	7½-9
V8-305 H.O./G	.045	C	6° ⑨	6° ⑨	A	700	500D	1800 ⑭	2200 ⑭	7½-9
V8-305 T.P.I./F	.045	C	—	6° ⑦	A	—	⑩	—	⑩	40.4-47 ⑰
V8-350/8	.045	C	6° ⑦	6° ⑦	H	⑩	⑩	⑩	⑩	30-40 ⑰
1986										
4-151 E.F.I./2	.060	I	8° ⑪	8° ⑪	J	⑩	⑩	⑩	⑩	9-13 ⑯
V6-173 M.F.I./S	.045	K	10° ⑨	10° ⑨	L	⑩	⑩	⑩	⑩	40.5-47 ⑰
V6-262 E.F.I./Z	.035	M	—	TDC ⑨	Q	—	⑩	—	⑩	9-13 ⑯
V8-305/H	.035	C	TDC ⑨	TDC ⑨	A	700	500D	1800 ⑭	2200 ⑭	4-6.5
V8-305 H.O./G	.035	C	6° ⑨	6° ⑨	A	700	500D	1800 ⑭	2200 ⑭	4-6.5 ⑱
V8-305 T.P.I./F	.035	C	—	6° ⑦	A	—	⑩	—	⑩	40.5-47 ⑰
V8-350 T.P.I./8	.045	C	6° ⑦	6° ⑦	H	⑩	⑩	⑩	⑩	34-39 ⑰
1987										
V6-173/S	.045	K	10° ⑲	10° ⑲	L	⑩	⑩	⑩	⑩	34-47 ⑰
V6-262/Z	.035	M	—	TDC ⑲	Q	—	⑩	—	⑩	9-13 ⑯
V8-305/H	.035	C	TDC ⑨	TDC ⑨	A	700	500D	1800N ⑭	2200 ⑭	4-6.5 ⑱
V8-305 H.O. 4 Bbl. /G	.035	C	—	6° ⑲	A	—	600D	—	2200 ⑭	7 4/6.5
V8-305 H.O. TPI/F	.035	C	—	6°	A	⑩	⑩	⑩	⑩	34-47 ⑰
V8-307/Y	.060	N	—	20° ⑪ ⑬	O	—	⑩	—	550D ⑮	6-7½
V8-350/8	.035	C	6° ⑲	6° ⑲	H	⑩	⑩	⑩	⑩	34-47 ⑰
1988										
V6-173/	.045	—	—	—	—	—	—	—	—	—
V6-262/	.035	—	—	—	—	—	—	—	—	—
V8-305 EFI/	.035	—	—	—	—	—	—	—	—	—
V8-305 4 Bbl./	.035	—	—	—	—	—	—	—	—	—
V8-305 TPI/	.035	—	—	—	—	—	—	—	—	—
V8-307/	.060	—	—	—	—	—	—	—	—	—
V8-350/	.035	—	—	—	—	—	—	—	—	—

Continued

CHEVROLET CAMARO, CAPRICE, CORVETTE, IMPALA, MALIBU & MONTE CARLO—Continued

①—BTDC-Before top dead center.

②—Idle speed on man. trans. vehicles is adjusted in Neutral and on auto. trans. equipped vehicles is adjusted in Drive unless otherwise specified. Where two idle speeds are listed, the higher speed is with A/C or idle solenoid energized.

③—Equipped with idle speed control motor.

④—1100N with A/C.

⑤—The harmonic balancer on these engines has two timing marks. The timing mark measuring 1/16 in. is used when setting timing with a hand held timing light. The mark measuring 1/8 in. is used when setting timing with magnetic timing equipment.

⑥—700D with A/C.

⑦—When checking ignition timing, disconnect Electronic Spark Timing bypass connector (tan wire w/black stripe) to place EST in bypass mode.

⑧—Ground diagnostic connector located under dash. The check engine light should flash on & off when in diagnostic mode. Check average ignition timing of cylinder Nos. 1 & 4, & reset as necessary. After completing timing check, remove ground from diagnostic connector & ensure check engine light is off.

⑨—With distributor 4 wire connector disconnected.

⑩—Automatically controlled by Electronic Fuel Injection.

⑪—Connect jumper wire between ALCL connector terminals A & B. The ALCL connector is located under the instrument panel to the right of the steering column. On 4-151 engines, check average timing of cylinders No. 1 & 4 & reset as necessary. On all other engines, check ignition timing at No. 1 cylinder. After completing adjustment, disconnect jumper wire from ALCL terminals A & B. With engine off, clear trouble code from Electronic Control Module (ECM) memory by removing battery voltage to ECM for 30 seconds.

⑫—At 1200 RPM.

⑬—At 1100 RPM.

⑭—On high step of fast idle cam.

⑮—On low step of fast idle cam.

⑯—Wrap shop towel around fuel hose to steel line connection in engine compartment to prevent fuel spillage. Disconnect hose from steel line & install a suitable fuel pressure gauge between hose and line. Ensure gauge connections are tight, then start engine & check fuel pressure readings.

⑰—With shop towel wrapped around fuel pressure valve to prevent fuel spillage, connect a suitable fuel pressure gauge to fuel pressure valve. Check fuel pressure with ignition switch On, engine not running.

⑱—In-tank electric fuel pump, 3 psi.

⑲—With timing connector disconnected.

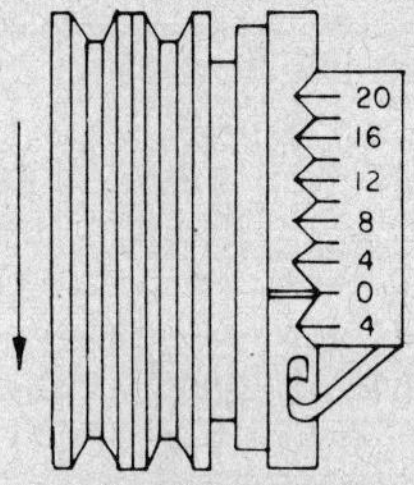

Fig. A

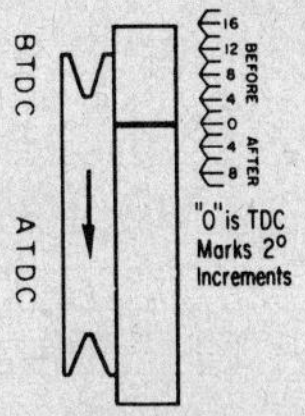

Fig. B

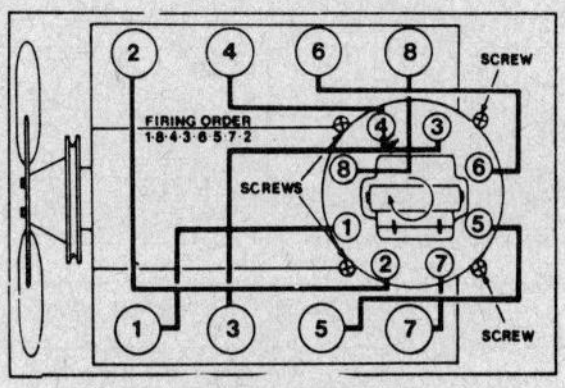

Fig. C

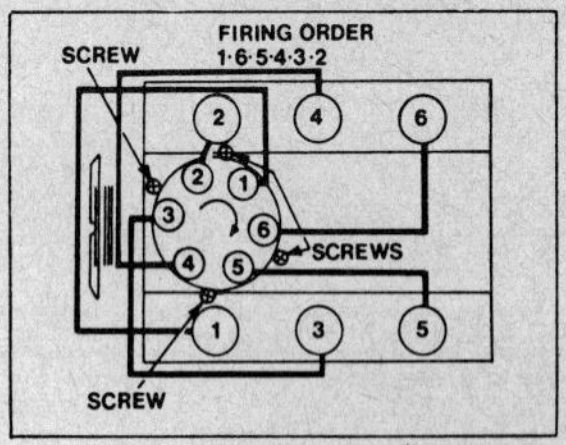

Fig. D

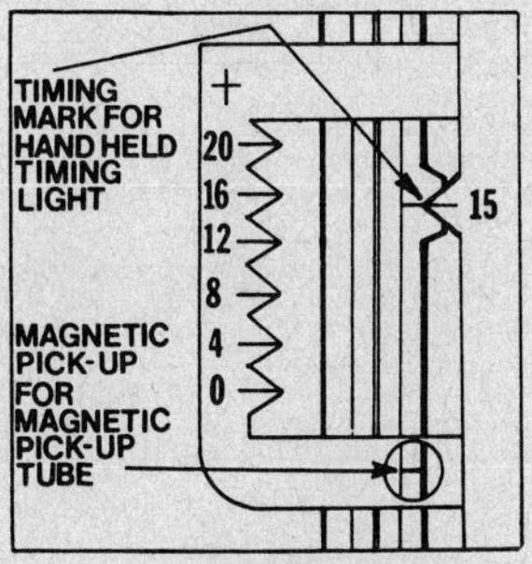

Fig. E

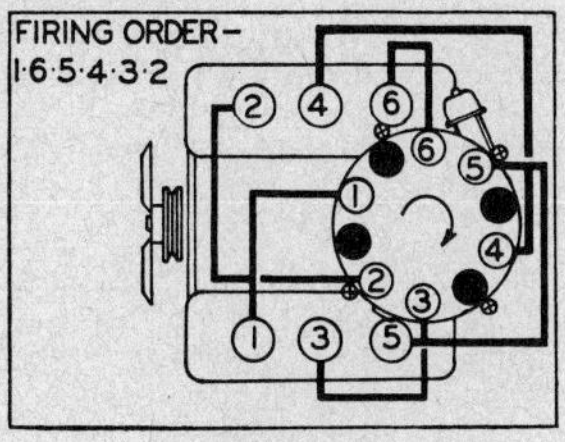

Fig. F

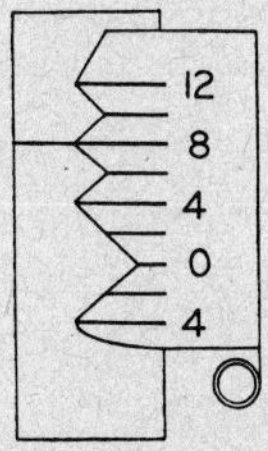

Fig. G

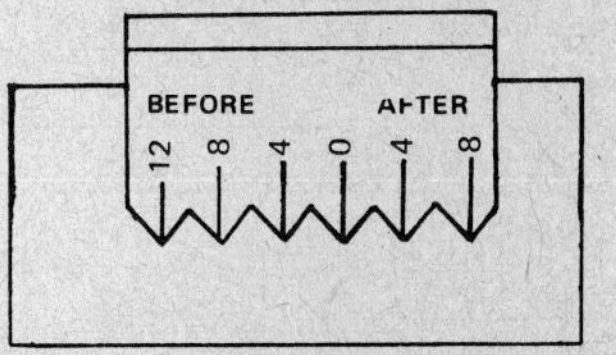

Fig. H

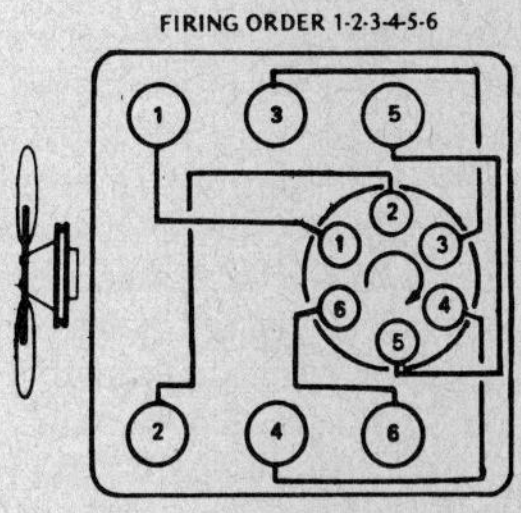

Fig. K

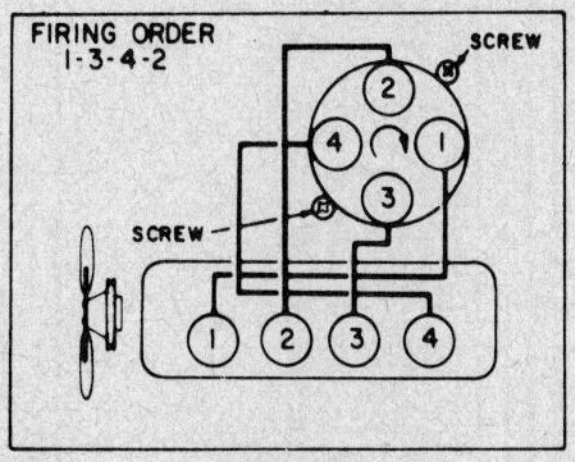

Fig. I

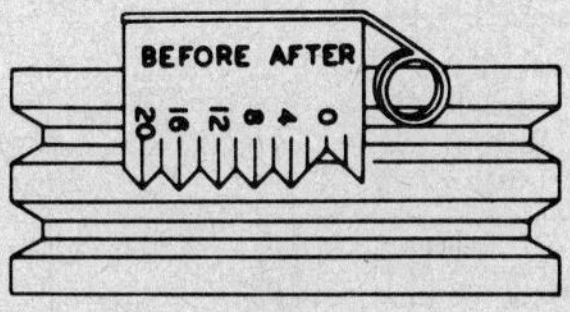

Fig. J

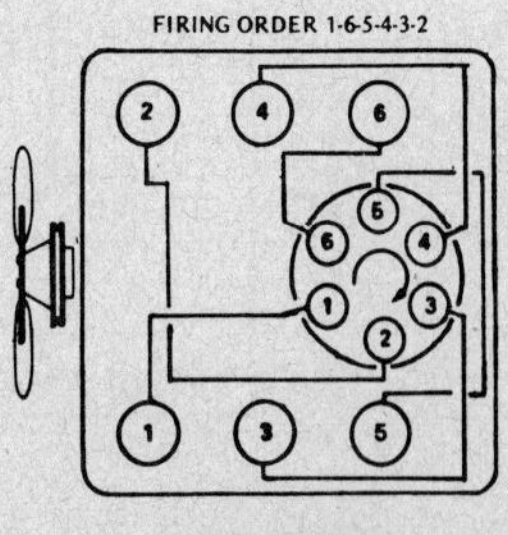

Fig. M

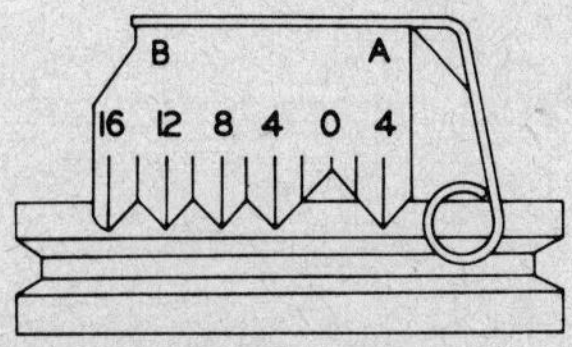

Fig. L

Continued

CHEVROLET CAMARO, CAPRICE, CORVETTE, IMPALA, MALIBU & MONTE CARLO—Continued

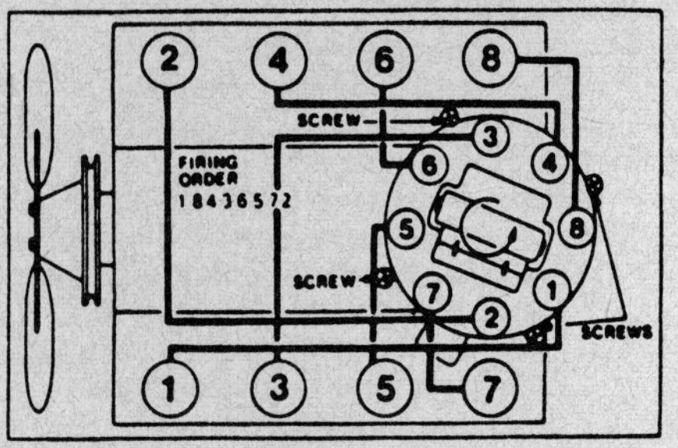

Fig. N

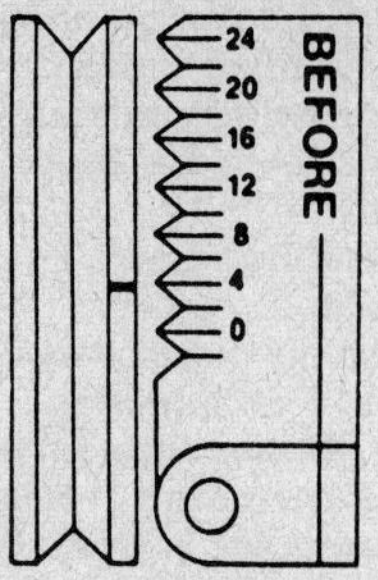

Fig. O

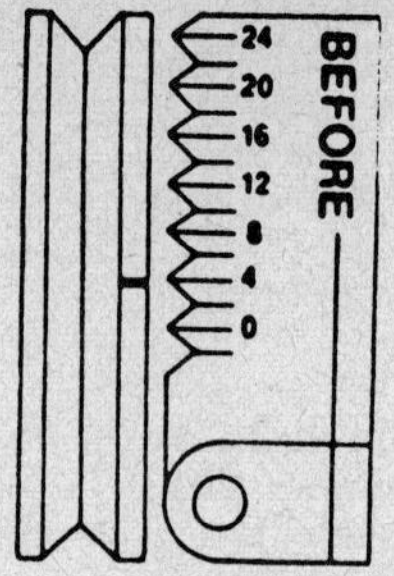

Fig. P

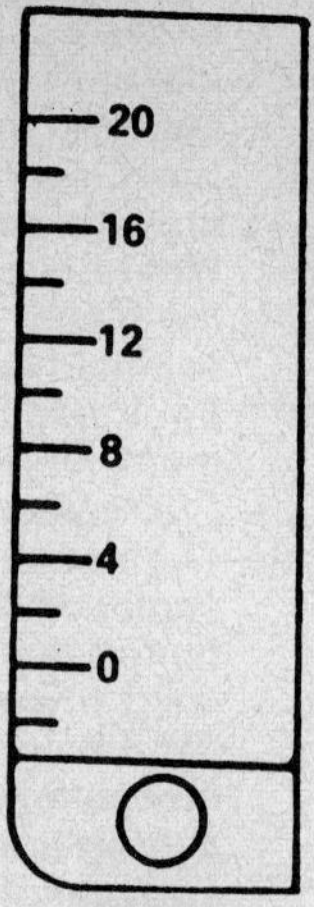

Fig. Q

CHEVROLET CHEVETTE & PONTIAC 1000

Year & Engine/V.I.N.	Spark Plug Gap	Ignition Timing BTDC①*				Curb Idle Speed②		Fast Idle Speed		Fuel Pump Pressure
		Firing Order Fig.♦	Man. Trans.	Auto. Trans.	Mark Fig.	Man. Trans.	Auto. Trans.	Man. Trans.	Auto. Trans.	
1982										
4-97.6/C	.035	A	4°	4°	B	700	700D	2500	2500	2½-6½
1983										
4-97.6/C	.035	A	6°	6°	B	800/1150	700/875D	2500	2500	2½-6½
1984										
4-97.6/C	.035	A	8°⑤	8°⑤	B	800③	700D	2500⑥	2500⑥	5-6½
1985										
4-97.6/C	.035	A	8°⑤	8°⑤	B	④	700D	2500⑥	2500⑥	5-6½
1986										
4-97.6/C	.035	A	8°⑤	8°⑤	B	④	—	2500⑥	2500⑥	5-6½
1987										
4-97.6/C	.035	A	8°⑤	8°⑤	B	800	700D	—	—	5-6½

①—BTDC-Before top dead center.
②—Idle speed on man. trans. vehicles is adjusted in Neutral & on auto, trans. equipped vehicles is adjusted in Drive unless otherwise specified. Where two idle speeds are listed, the higher speed is with the A/C or idle solenoid energized.
③—700 RPM with 3.36:1 axle.
④—4 Speed trans., 800/1250 RPM. 5 speed trans., 1000/1250 RPM.
⑤—With distributor vacuum advance hose disconnected & plugged.
⑥—On high step of fast idle cam.

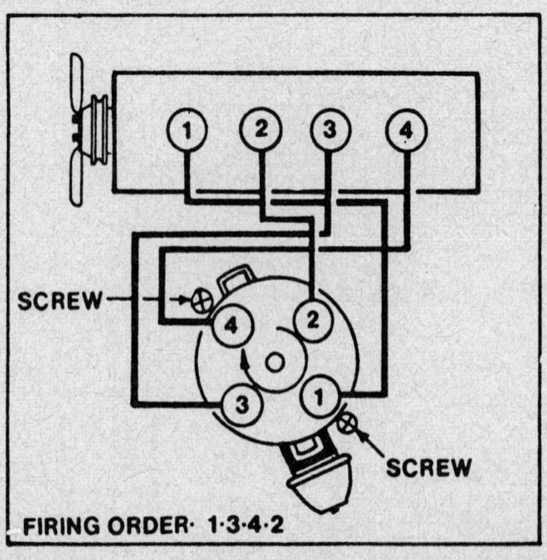

Fig. A

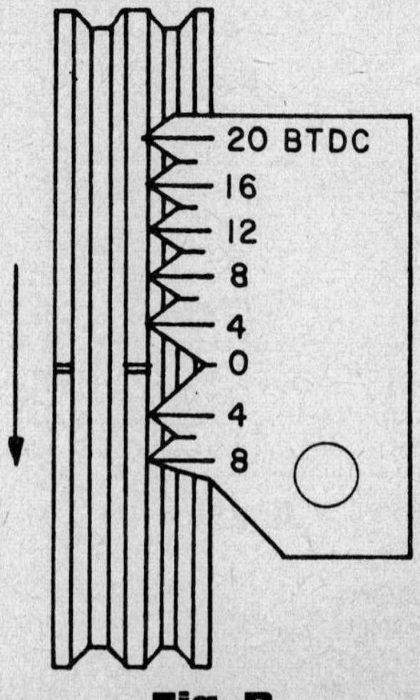

Fig. B

1982-88 CHEV. CAVALIER, BUICK SKYHAWK, CAD. CIMARRON, OLDS. FIRENZA & PONT. 2000 & SUNBIRD

Year & Engine/ VIN	Spark Plug Gap	Ignition Timing BTDC①				Curb Idle Speed②		Fast Idle Speed		Fuel Pump Pressure
		Firing Order Fig.	Man. Trans.	Auto. Trans.	Mark Fig.	Man. Trans.	Auto. Trans.	Man. Trans.	Auto. Trans.	
1982										
4-112/G 2 Barrel③	.035	A	12°⑤	12°⑤	B⑥	⑦	⑦	2400	2300	4½⑧
4-112 E.F.I./O⑨	.060	C	8°⑩	8°⑩	D	④	④	④	④	—
4-121/B③	.035	A	—	12°⑤	B⑥	—	⑦	—	2300	4½⑧
1983										
4-112 E.F.I./O⑨	.035	C	8°⑩	8°⑩	D	④	④	④	④	—
4-121 E.F.I./P③	.035	A	TDC②	TDC②	B⑥	④	④	④	④	—
1984										
4-112 E.F.I./O⑨	.035	C	8°⑩	8°⑩	D	④	④	④	④	9-13⑪
4-112 Turbo/J⑨	.035	C	8°⑩	8°⑩	D	④	④	④	④	34-40⑫
4-121 E.F.I./P③	.035	A	6°②	6°②	B⑥	④	④	④	④	9-13⑬
1985										
4-112 E.F.I./O⑨	.035	C	8°⑩	8°⑩	D	④	④	④	④	9-13⑪
4-112 Turbo/J⑨	.035	C	8°⑩	8°⑩	D	④	④	④	④	30-40⑫
4-121 E.F.I./P③	.035	A	6°⑤	6°⑤	B⑥	④	④	④	④	9-13⑬
V6-173 M.F.I./W	.045	E	10°⑭	10°⑭	F	④	④	④	④	40.5-47⑫
1986										
4-112 E.F.I./O⑨	.035	C	8°⑩	8°⑩	D	④	④	④	④	9-13⑪
4-112 Turbo/J⑨	.035	C	8°⑩	8°⑩	D	④	④	④	④	30-40⑫
4-121 E.F.I./P③	.035	A	6°⑤	6°⑥	B⑥	④	④	④	④	9-13⑬
V6-173 M.F.I./W	.045	E	10°⑭	10°⑭	F	④	④	④	④	40.5-47⑫
1987										
4-121/1	.035	⑮	⑯	⑯	⑰	④	④	④	④	9-13⑬
4-121/K	.060	C	—	—	D	④	④	④	④	9-13⑪
4-121/M Turbo	.035	C	—	—	D	④	④	④	④	35-38⑫
4-173/W	.045	⑱	⑯	⑯	⑰	④	④	④	④	40.5-47⑪
1988										
4-121/K	—	—	—	—	—	—	—	—	—	—
4-121/M Turbo	—	—	—	—	—	—	—	—	—	—
4-121/1	—	—	—	—	—	—	—	—	—	—
V6-173/W	—	—	—	—	—	—	—	—	—	—

①—BTDC-Before top dead center.

②—Disconnect single wire from Electronic Spark Timing (EST) bypass connector to place system in ignition timing bypass mode. Do not disconnect three wire connector to distributor. Connect a suitable inductive pickup timing light to ignition coil high tension lead. When checking ignition timing, the pulley notch will appear to move slightly as each cylinder is fired during timing check. This slight pulley notch movement should be centered at the proper timing degree mark on the timing tab, see note 6. After timing check is complete, reconnect wire to EST bypass connector.

③—Overhead valve engine.

④—Idle speed is controlled by the idle air control assembly.

⑤—Disconnect 4 terminal Electronic Spark Timing (EST) wire connector to place system in ignition timng bypass mode. Connect a suitable inductive pickup timing light to ignition coil high tension lead near distributor. The pulley notch will appear to move slightly as each cylinder is fired during the ignition timing check. This slight pulley notch movement should be centered at the proper timing degree mark on the timing tab, see note 6. After completing adjustment, reconnect EST wire connector.

⑥—The crankshaft pulley has two ignition timing notches located 180°apart. The notch for No. 1 cylinder is scribed across the three pulley sheave surfaces, while the second notch is scribed across the center sheave only.

⑦—Idle speeds are controlled by the idle speed control motor.

⑧—Minimum.

⑨—Overhead cam engine.

⑩—Ground diagnostic connector

Continued

1982-88 CHEV. CAVALIER, BUICK SKYHAWK, CAD. CIMARRON, OLDS. FIRENZA & PONT. 2000 & SUNBIRD—Continued

located under dash panel. The check engine light should be flashing. Check average timing of cylinder Nos. 1 & 4. After completing adjustment, remove ground from diagnostic connector.

(11)—To relieve fuel pressure, remove fuel pump fuse from fuse panel, then start engine & allow to run until fuel supply is deleted. When engine has stopped, engage starter for 3 seconds to dissipate remaining fuel system pressure. Remove air cleaner & plug Thermac port on throttle body unit. Install a suitable fuel pressure gauge on throttle body side of fuel filter at rear of vehicle near fuel tank. Start engine & note fuel pressure reading. Before removing fuel gauge, relieve fuel system pressure.

(12)—With shop towel wrapped around fuel pressure valve to prevent fuel spillage, connect a suitable fuel pressure gauge to fuel pressure valve. Check fuel pressure with ignition switch in the On position, engine not running.

(13)—Wrap shop towel around fuel hose to steel line connection in engine compartment to prevent fuel spillage. Disconnect fuel hose from steel line and connect a suitable fuel pressure gauge between hose & line. Ensure gauge connections are tight, then start engine & check fuel pressure.

(14)—Disconnect set timing connector, which is located in the engine compartment near the blower motor housing along the cowl. This connector branches out of the engine wiring harness near the bulk head connector. After completing timuing adjustment, reconnect set timing connector. With engine off, clear trouble code from Electronic Control Module memory by removing battery voltage to ECM for 30 seconds.

(15)—Cylinder numbering from front of engine to rear of engine, 1, 2, 3, 4. Refer to Fig. G for spark plug wire connections at coil unit.

(16)—No adjustment.

(17)—Equipped with crankshaft sensor.

(18)—Cylinder numbering left to right as viewed from front of vehicle, front bank, 2, 4, 6; rear bank, 1, 3, 5. Firing order 1-2-3-4-5-6. Refer to Fig. H for spark plug wire connections at coil unit.

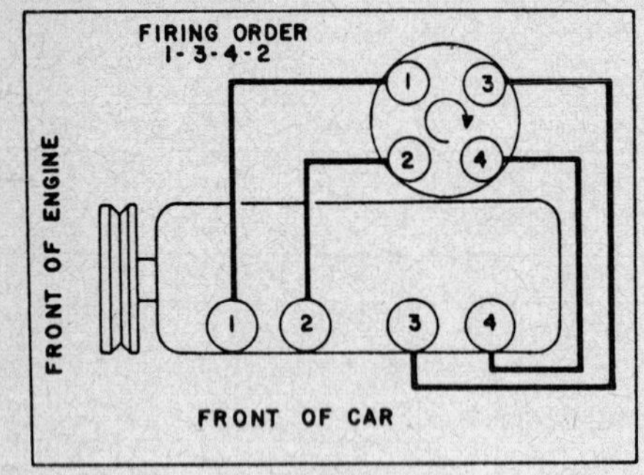

Fig. A

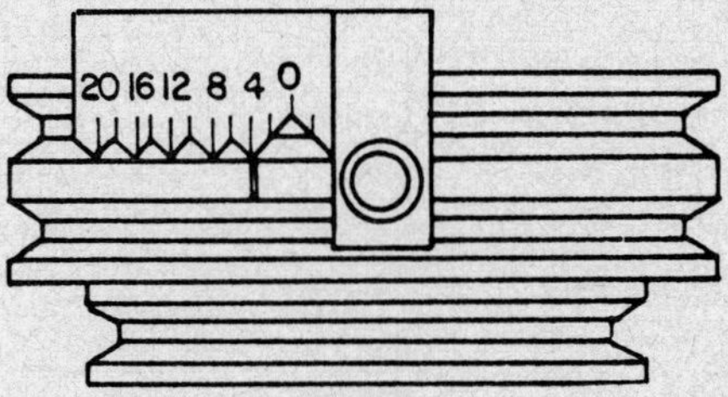

Fig. B

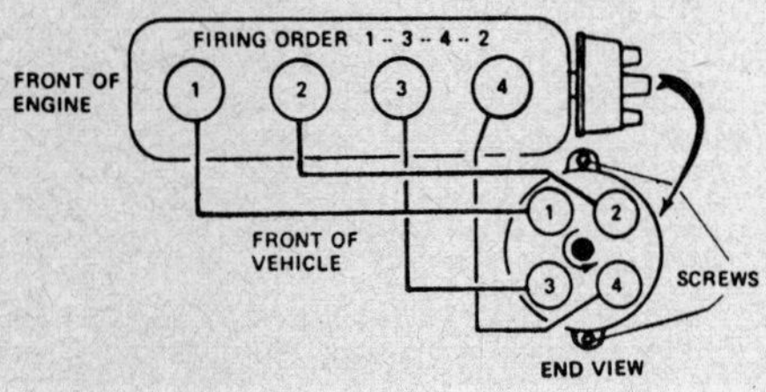

Fig. C

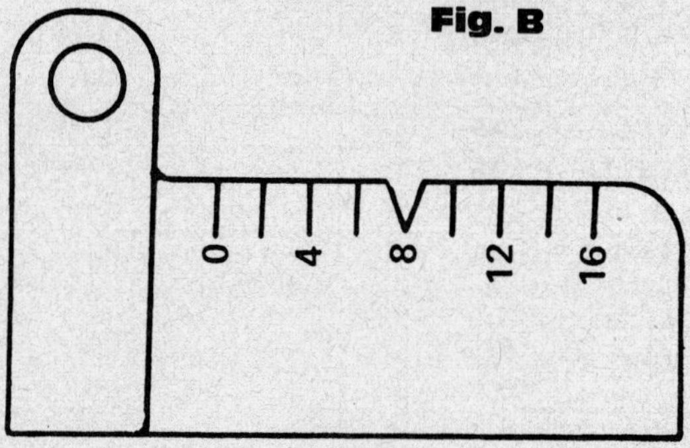

Fig. D

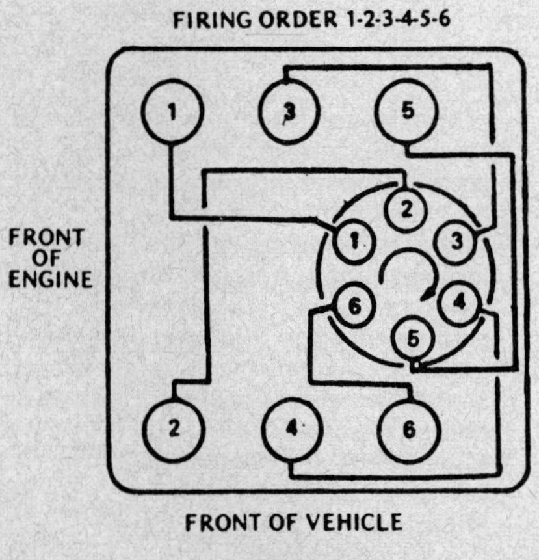

Fig. E

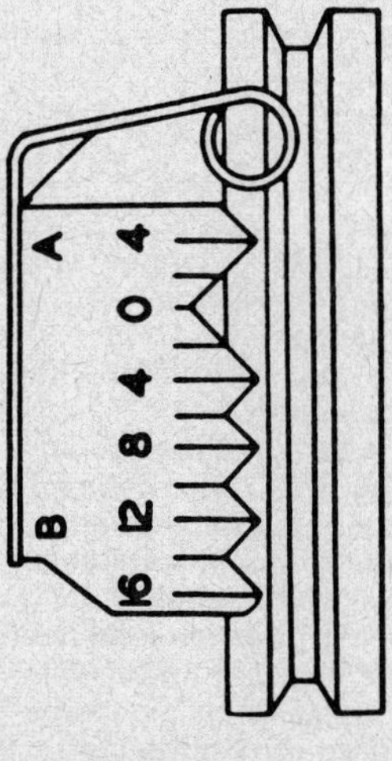

Fig. F

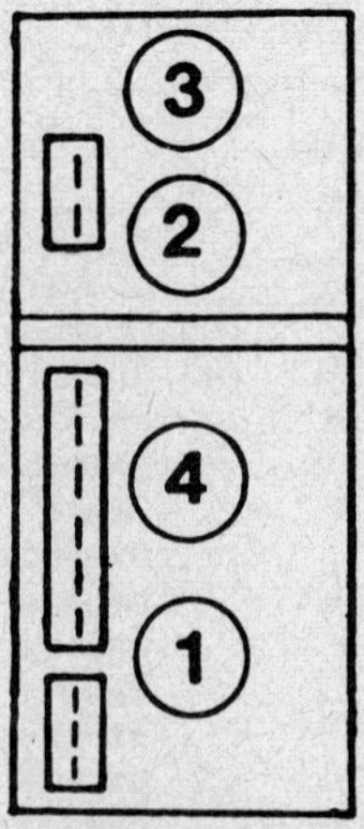

Fig. G

Fig. H

1982-85 CHEV. CITATION, BUICK SKYLARK, OLDS. OMEGA & PONT. PHOENIX

Year & Engine/VIN	Spark Plug Gap	Firing Order Fig.	Ignition Timing BTDC ①			Curb Idle Speed ②		Fast Idle Speed		Fuel Pump Pressure
			Man. Trans.	Auto. Trans.	Mark Fig.	Man. Trans.	Auto. Trans.	Man. Trans.	Auto. Trans.	
1982										
4-151/R	.060	E	8° ⑨ ⑩	8° ⑨ ⑩	B	⑪	⑪	⑪	⑪	—
V6-173/X Exc. H.O.	.045	C	10° ⑤	10° ⑤	D	800/1050	600/800D	⑦	2600	6-7½
V6-173/Z H.O. ⑧	.045	C	6° ⑤	10° ⑤	D	850/1100	750/900D	2600	2800	6-7½
1983										
4-151/R	.060	E	8° ⑨ ⑩	8° ⑨ ⑩	B	⑪	⑪	⑪	⑪	—
V6-173/X Exc. H.O.	.045	A	10° ⑤	10° ⑤	D	775	600D	2500N	2500N	6-7½
V6-173/Z H.O. ⑧	.045	A	10° ⑤	10° ⑤	D	800	725D	2600N	2700N	6-7½
1984										
4-151/R	.060	E	8 ⑩	8 ⑩	B	⑪	⑪	⑪	⑪	9-13 ⑫
V6-173/X Exc. H.O.	.045	A	10° ⑤	10° ⑤	D	800/1100	600/750D	2500N	2500N	6-7½
V6-173/Z H.O. ⑧	.045	A	10° ⑤	10° ⑤	D	800/1100	600/750D	2600N	2700N	6-7½
1985										
4-151/R	.060	E	8° ⑩	8° ⑩	B	⑪	⑪	⑪	⑪	9-13 ⑫
V6-173/W	.045	A	10° ⑤	10° ⑤	D	⑪	⑪	⑪	⑪	40.5-47 ⑬
V6-173/X	.045	A	10° ④	10° ④	D	800	600D	2500	2500	6-7½

①—BTDC-Before top dead center.

②—Idle speed on man. trans. vehicles is adjusted in Neutral & on auto. trans. equipped vehicles is adjusted in Drive unless otherwise specified. Where two idle speeds are listed, the higher speed is with the A/C or idle solenoid energized.

③—At 750 RPM.

④—Disconnect set timing connector, which is located in engine compartment near the blower housing along the cowl. This connector branches out if engine wiring harness near the bulkhead connector. After completing adjustment, reconnect set timing connector.

⑤—Disconnect 4 wire EST connector at distributor, then check & adjust basic ignition timing as needed. After checking timing, reconnect EST connector.

⑥—At 900 RPM.

⑦—Models less A/C, 2400 RPM; models with A/C 2600 RPM.

⑧—High output engine.

⑨—At 1050 RPM.

⑩—Ground diagnostic connector located under dash. The check engine light should flash on and off when in diagnostic mode. Check average ignition timing of cylinder Nos. 1 and 4, and reset as necessary. After completing ignition timing check, remove ground from diagnostic connector and ensure that check engine light is off.

⑪—Idle speed controlled by Idle Air Control (IAC) valve.

⑫—Wrap shop towel around fuel hose to steel line connection to prevent fuel spillage. Disconnect fuel hose from steel line & connect a suitable fuel pressure gauge. Ensure fuel pressure gauge connections are tight, then start engine & check fuel pressure reading.

⑬—With shop towel wrapped around fuel pressure valve to prevent fuel spillage, connect a suitable fuel pressure gauge to fuel pressure valve. Check fuel pressure with ignition switch On, engine not running

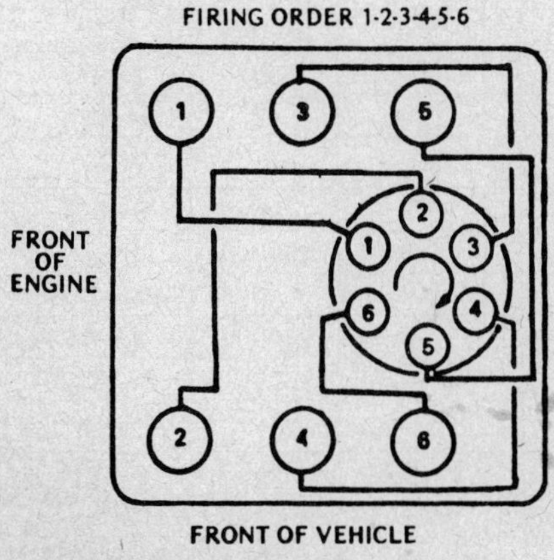

Fig. A

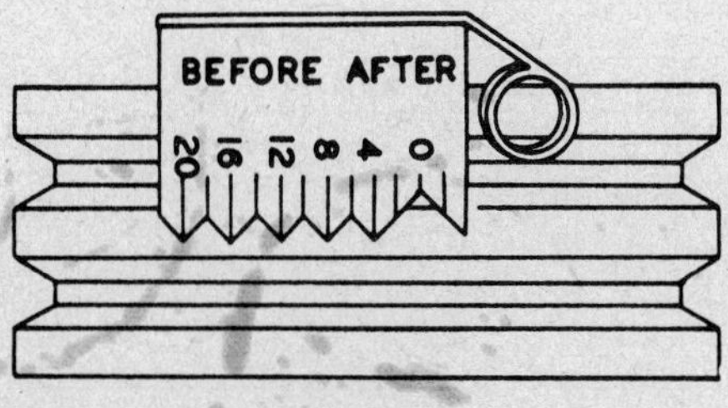

Fig. B

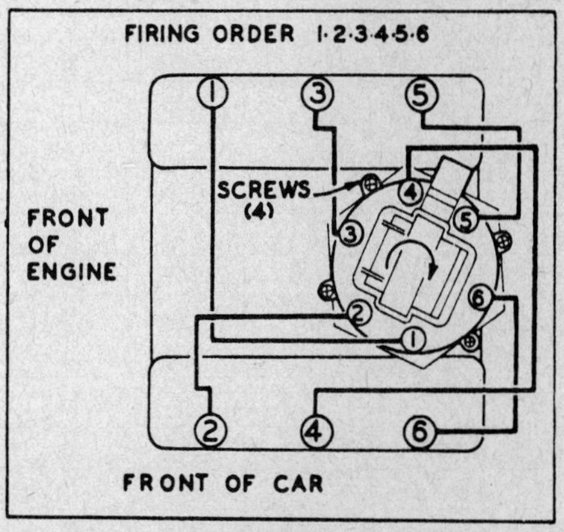

Fig. C

Continued

1982-85 CHEV. CITATION, BUICK SKYLARK, OLDS. OMEGA & PONT PHOENIX—Continued

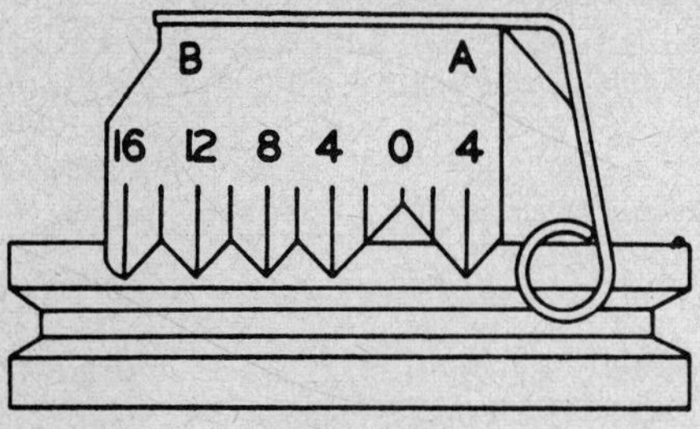

Fig. D

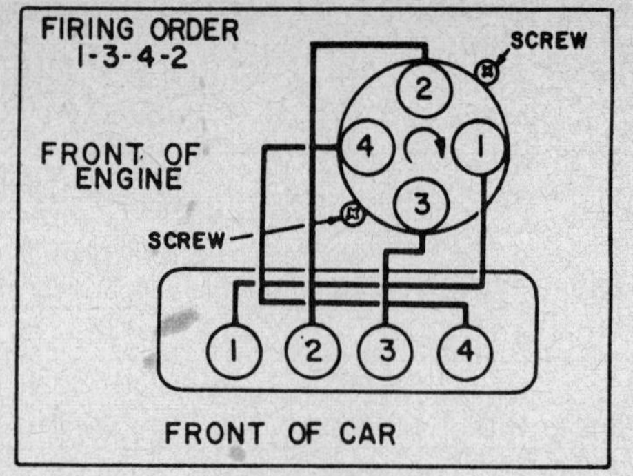

Fig. E

1982-88 CHEV. CELEBRITY, BUICK CENTURY, OLDS. CUTLASS CIERA, PONT. 6000 & 1984-88 CUTLASS CRUISER

Year & Engine/VIN Code	Spark Plug Gap	Ignition Timing BTDC ① Firing Order Fig.	Ignition Timing BTDC ① Man. Trans.	Ignition Timing BTDC ① Auto. Trans.	Ignition Timing BTDC ① Mark Fig.	Curb Idle Speed Man. Trans.	Curb Idle Speed Auto. Trans.	Fast Idle Speed Man. Trans.	Fast Idle Speed Auto. Trans.	Fuel Pump Pressure
1982										
4-151/R	.060	A	—	8° ③ ⑦	B	—	⑩	—	⑩	9-13
V6-173/X	.045	C	—	10° ⑤	D	—	600D	—	2600N	6-7½
V6-181/E	.080	E	—	15°	F	—	⑩	—	2300P	6-7½
1983										
4-151/R	.060	A	—	8° ⑦ ⑪	B	—	⑩	—	⑩	—
V6-173/X	.045	G	—	10°	D	—	600/750D	—	2500	5½-6½
V6-173 H.O./Z ④	.045	G	—	10°	D	—	725/850D	—	2700	5½-6½
V6-181/E Exc. Calif.	.060	E	—	15°	F	—	⑩	—	2400	4-6½
V6-181/E Calif.	.060	E	—	5°	F	—	⑩	—	2300	4-6½
1984										
4-151/R	.060	A	—	8° ⑨	B	—	⑩	—	⑩	9-13 ⑱
V6-173/X	.045	G	—	10° ⑧	D	—	600D	—	2500 ⑰	6-7½
V6-173 H.O./Z ④	.045	G	—	10° ⑧	D	—	725D	—	2700 ⑰	6-7½
V6-181/E	.060	E	—	15° ⑧	F	—	⑩	—	2400 ⑰	3.9-6.5
V6-231 MFI/3	.080	—	—	15° ⑨	—	—	⑩	—	⑩	34-40 ⑲
1985										
4-151/R	.060	A	8° ⑨	8° ⑨	B	⑩	⑩	⑩	⑩	9-13 ⑱
V6-173/X	.045	G	10° ⑧	10° ⑧	D	800/1100	600/750D	2500 ⑰	2500 ⑰	6½-7
V6-173 H.O. MFI/W ④	.045	G	10° ⑥	10° ⑥	D	⑩	⑩	⑩	⑩	40.5-47 ⑲
V6-181/E	.060	E	—	15° ⑧	F	—	⑩	—	2400 ⑰	3.9-6.5
V6-231 MFI/3	.080	—	—	15° ⑦	—	—	⑩	—	⑩	34-40 ⑲
1986										
4-151 EFI/R	.060	A	8° ⑨	8° ⑨	B	⑩	⑩	⑩	⑩	9-13 ⑱
V6-173 2 Barrel/X	.045	G	10° ⑧	10° ⑧	D	800	600/750D	2500 ⑰	2500 ⑰	6-7½
V6-173 MFI/W	.045	G	10° ⑥	10° ⑥	D	⑩	⑩	⑩	⑩	40.5-47 ⑲
V6-231 SFI/B,3	.045	⑬	—	⑮	—	—	⑩	—	⑩	37-43 ⑲

Continued

1982—88 CHEV. CELEBRITY, BUICK CENTURY, OLDS. CUTLASS CIERA, PONT. 6000 & 1984—86 CUTLASS CRUISER—Continued

Year & Engine/VIN Code	Spark Plug Gap	Ignition Timing BTDC ①				Curb Idle Speed		Fast Idle Speed		Fuel Pump Pressure
		Firing Order Fig.	Man. Trans.	Auto. Trans.	Mark Fig.	Man. Trans.	Auto. Trans.	Man. Trans.	Auto. Trans.	
1987										
4-151/R	.060	⑫	⑮	⑮	⑯	⑩	⑩	⑩	⑩	9-13 ⑱
V6-173/W	.045	⑭	⑮	⑮	⑯	⑩	⑩	⑩	⑩	40.5-47 ⑲
V6-231/3	.045	⑬	—	⑮	⑯	—	⑩	—	⑩	37-43 ⑲
1988										
4-151/R	.060	—	⑮	⑮	—	—	—	—	—	—
V6-173 MFI/W	.045	—	⑮	⑮	—	—	—	—	—	—
V6-189 MFI/	—	—	—	—	—	—	—	—	—	—
V6-231 SFI/3	.045	—	—	⑮	—	—	—	—	—	—

①—BTDC-Before top dead center.

②—Idle speed on auto. trans. equipped vehicles is adjusted in Drive unless otherwise specified. Where two idle speeds are listed, the higher speed is with the A/C or idle solenoid energized.

③—At 1050N RPM.

④—High output engine.

⑤—At 600D RPM.

⑥—Disconnect set timing connector, which is located in engine compartment near blower housing along the cowl. This connector branches out of engine wiring harness near bulkhead connector. After completing adjustment, reconnect set timing connector.

⑦—Ground diagnostic connector located under dash. The check engine light should flash on & off when in diagnostic mode. Check average ignition timing of cylinder Nos. 1 & 4, reset as necessary. After completing ignition timing check, remove ground from diagnostic connector & ensure that check engine light is off.

⑧—With distributor 4 wire electrical connector disconnected. After completing adjustment, reconnect distributor wire connector.

⑨—With jumper wire connected between ALCL terminals A & B. The ALCL connector is located on the lower edge of the instrument panel to right of steering column. Remove jumper wire after completing adjustment.

⑩—Idle speeds are controlled by an idle speed control (ISC) motor or idle air control (IAC) valve.

⑪—At 750 RPM.

⑫—Cylinder numbering from front of engine 1, 2, 3, 4. Firing order 1-3-4-2.

⑬—Cylinder numbering left to right as viewed from front of vehicle, front bank 1, 3, 5; rear bank 2, 4, 6. Firing order 1-6-5-4-3-2. Refer to Figs. H & I for spark plug wire connections at coil unit.

⑭—Cylinder numbering left to right as viewed from front of vehicle, front bank 2, 4, 6; rear bank 1, 3, 5. Firing order 1-2-3-4-5-6.

⑮—No adjustment.

⑯—Equiped with crankshaft position sensor.

⑰—On high step of fast idle cam.

⑱—Wrap shop towel around fuel hose to steel line connection to prevent fuel spillage. Disconnect fuel hose from steel line & connect suitable fuel pressure gauge. Ensure pressure gauge connections are tight, then start engine & note fuel pressure reading.

⑲—With shop towel wrapped around fuel pressure valve to prevent fuel spillage, connect a suitable fuel pressure gauge to fuel pressure valve. Check fuel pressure with ignition switch On, engine not running.

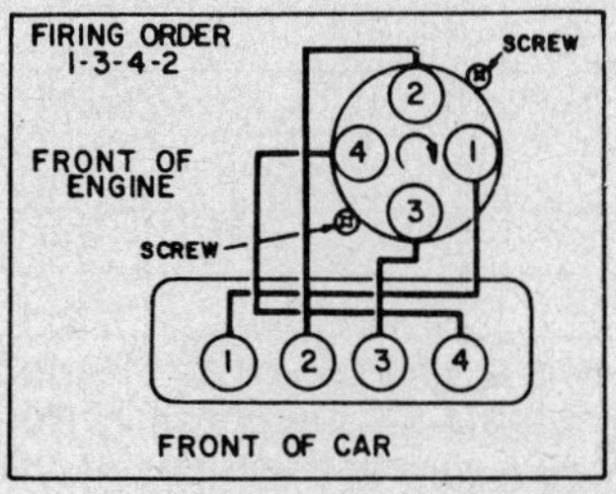

Fig. A

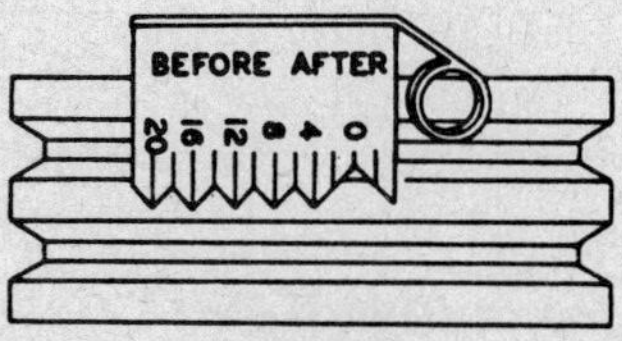

Fig. B

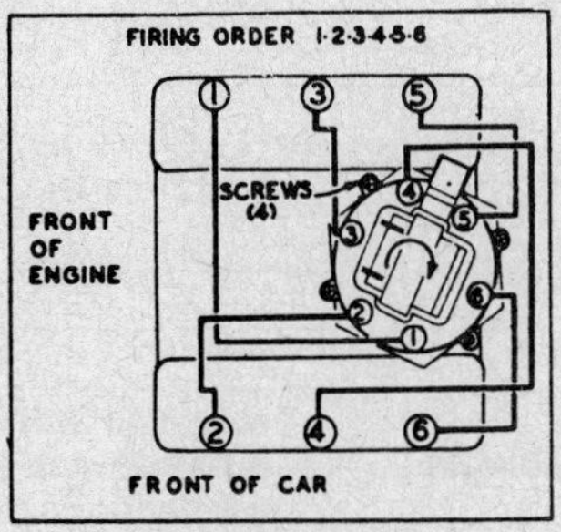

Fig. C

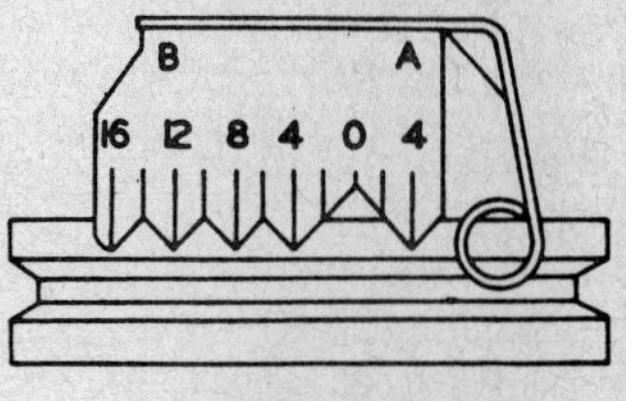

Fig. D

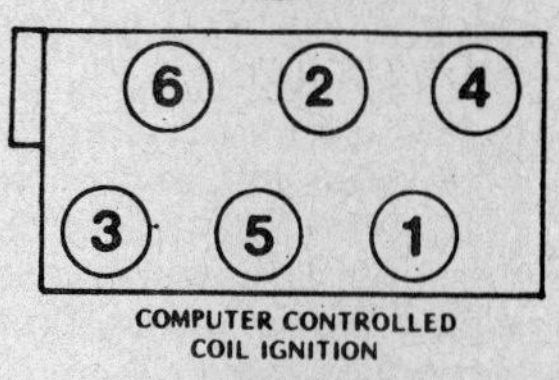

Fig. H

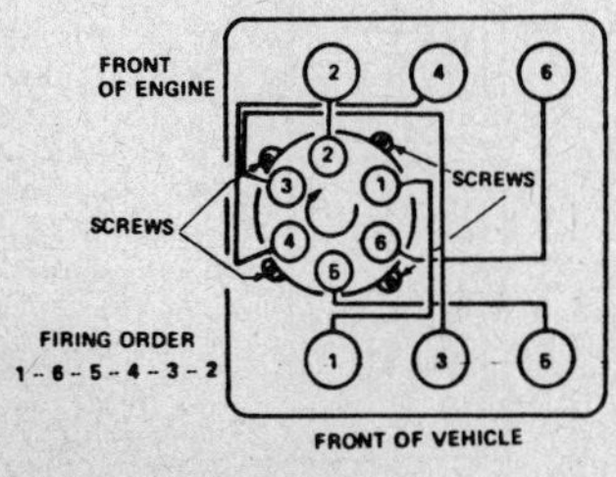

Fig. E

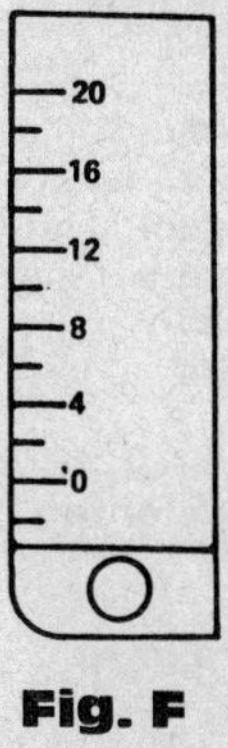

Fig. F

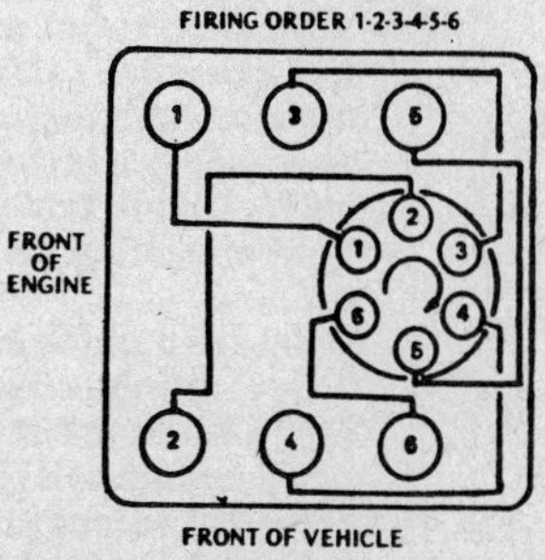

Fig. G

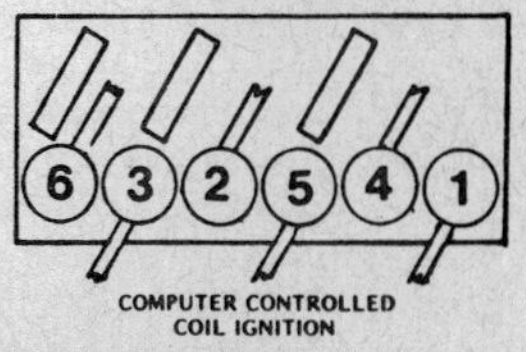

Fig. I

CHEVROLET NOVA

Year & Engine/VIN	Spark Plug Gap	Ignition Timing BTDC ① Firing Order Fig.	Ignition Timing BTDC ① Man. Trans.	Ignition Timing BTDC ① Auto. Trans.	Ignition Timing BTDC ① Mark Fig.	Curb Idle Speed ② Man. Trans.	Curb Idle Speed ② Auto. Trans.	Fast Idle Speed Man. Trans.	Fast Idle Speed Auto. Trans.	Fuel Pump Pressure
1985										
4-97/4 Exc. Calif.	.043	A	8° ③	8° ③	B	650	800N	3000 ④	3000 ④	3.5
4-97/4 Calif.	.043	A	5° ③	5° ③	B	650	800N	3000 ④	3000 ④	3.5
1986										
4-97/4 Exc. Calif.	.043	A	8° ③	8° ③	B	650	750N	3000 ④	3000 ④	3.5
4-97/4 Calif.	.043	A	5° ③	5° ③	B	650	750N	3000 ④	3000 ④	3.5
1987										
4-97/4	.043	A	—	—	B	650	750N	3000 ④	3000 ④	3.5
1988										
4-97 SOHC/	.043	A	—	—	B	650	750N	—	—	—
4-97 DOHC/	.043	—	—	—	—	800	800N	—	—	—

①—BTDC-Before top dead center.
②—Idle speed on auto. trans. equipped vehicles is adjusted in Drive unless otherwise specified. Where two idle speeds are listed, the higher speed is with A/C or idle solenoid energized.
③—Disconnect & plug distributor vacuum line.
④—On high step of fast idle cam.

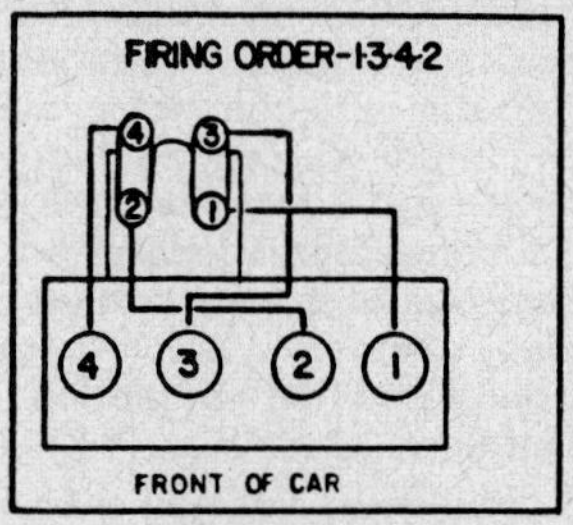

Fig. A

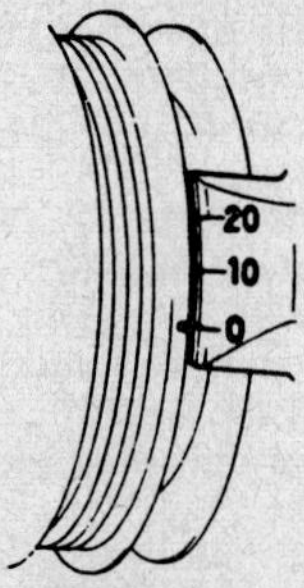

Fig. B

CHEVROLET CORSICA & BERETTA

Year & Engine/ VIN Code ①	Spark Plug Gap	Ignition Timing BTDC Firing Order Fig. ②	Ignition Timing BTDC Man. Trans.	Ignition Timing BTDC Auto. Trans.	Ignition Timing BTDC Mark Fig.	Curb Idle Speed ③ Man. Trans.	Curb Idle Speed ③ Auto. Trans.	Fast Idle Speed Man. Trans.	Fast Idle Speed Auto. Trans.	Fuel Pump Pressure
1987										
4-121/1	.035	⑨	④	④	⑤	⑥	⑥	⑥	⑥	9-13 ⑦
V6-173/W	.045	⑩	④	④	⑤	⑥	⑥	⑥	⑥	40.5-47 ⑧
1988										
4-121/	.035	—	—	—	—	—	—	—	—	—
V6-173/	.045	—	—	—	—	—	—	—	—	—

①—The eighth digit of Vehicle Identification Number (VIN) denotes engine code.
②—Before removing wires from distributor cap, determine location of No. 1 wire in cap, as distributor posiion may have been altered from that shown at the end of this chart.
③—Not adjustable.
④—Computer controlled, no adjustment.
⑤—Equipped with a crankshaft position sensor.
⑥—Idle speeds are controlled by the idle air control assembly.
⑦—Wrap shop towel around fuel hose to steel line connection in engine compartment to prevent fuel spillage. Disconnect fuel hose from steel line and connect suitable fuel pressure gauge. Ensure gauge connections are tight, then st art engine & check fuel pressure readings.
⑧—With shop towel wrapped around fuel pressure valve to prevent fuel spillage, connect a suitable fuel pressure gauge to fuel pressure valve. Check fuel pressure with ignition switch On, engine not running.
⑨—Cylinder numbering front to rear, 1, 2, 3, 4. Firing order 1-3-4-2. Refer to Fig. A for spark plug wire connections at coil unit.
⑩—Cylinder numbering left to right as viewed from front of vehicle, front bank 2, 4, 6; rear bank 1, 3, 5. Firing order, 1-2-3-4-5-6. Refer to Fig. B for spark plug wire connections at coil unit.

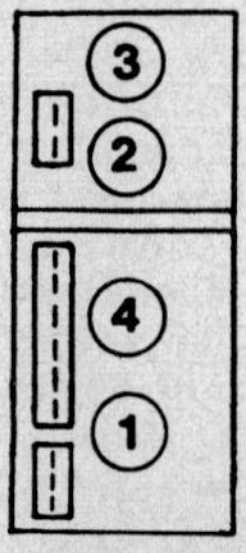

Fig. A

Continued

CHEVROLET CORSICA & BERETTA–Continued

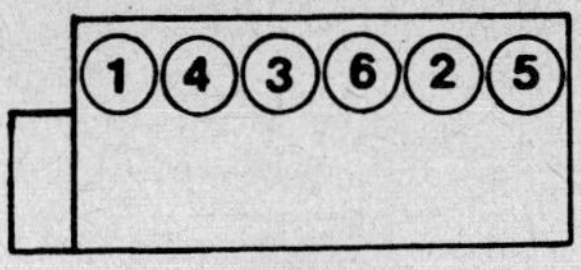

Fig. B

OLDSMOBILE REAR WHEEL DRIVE & 1982-85 TORONADO

Year & Engine/VIN	Spark Plug Gap	Ignition Timing: Firing Order Fig.	Ignition Timing: Degrees BTDC ①	Ignition Timing: Mark Fig.	Curb Idle Speed ②	Fast Idle Speed	Fuel Pump Pressure
1982							
V6-231/A	.080	A	15°	C ⑩	⑤	2200	3 Min.
V6-252/4	.080	A	15°	C ⑩	⑤	⑨	3 Min.
V8-260/8	.080	B	20° ④	D	⑤	700D	5½-6½
V8-307/Y	.080	B	20° ④	D	⑤	650D	5½-6½
1983							
V6-231/A	.080	A	15°	C ⑩	⑤	2200	4¼-5¾
V6-252/4	.080	A	15°	C ⑩	⑤	⑧	4¼-5¾
V8-307/Y ③	.080	B	20° ④	D	⑤	900D	6-7½
V8-307/9 ⑦	.080	B	20° ④	D	500D	900D	6-7½
1984							
V6-231/A	.060	A	15° ⑪	C ⑩	⑤	2200 ⑫	4¼-5¾
V6-252/4	.060	A	15° ⑪	C ⑩	⑤	⑧ ⑫	4¼-5¾
V8-307/Y ③	.080	B	20° ⑤	D	⑤	700D ⑬	6-7½
V8-307/9 ⑦	.080	B	20° ⑤	D	500D	900D ⑬	6-7½
1985							
V6-231/A	.060	A	15° ⑪	C ⑩	⑤	2200 ⑫	4¼-5¾
V8-307/Y ③	.060	B	20° ④	D	⑤	550D ⑬	6-7½
V8-307/9 ⑦	.080	B	20° ④	D	550/650D	750D ⑬	6-7½
1986							
V6-231/A	.060	A	15° ⑪	C ⑩	⑤	2200 ⑫	4½-5¾
V8-307/Y ③	.060	B	20° ④	D	⑤	550D ⑬	6-7½
V8-307/9 ⑦	.060	B	20° ④	D	600/650	750D ⑬	6-7½
1987							
V6-231/A	.060	A	15° ⑪	C ⑩	⑤	⑤ ⑫	4¼-5¾
V8-307/Y	.060	B	20° ④	D	⑤	550D ⑬	6-7½
V8-307/9	.060	B	20° ④	D	600/650D	750D ⑬	6-7½
1988							
V8-305/	.060	—	—	—	500	—	7½-9
V8-307/	.060	B	—	D	450	—	6-7½

①—BTDC-Before top dead center.

②—Idle speed on auto. trans. equipped vehicles is adjusted in in Neutral & on atuo. trans. equipped vehicles is adjusted in Drive unless otherwise specified. Where two idle speeds are listed, the higher the speed is with the A/C or idle solenoid energized.

③—Exc. Hurst option.

④—At 1100 RPM ALDL test lead grounded.

⑤—Idle speed is controlled by the idle speed control (ICS) motor or the idel load compensator (ILC).

⑥—Except Calif. & models w/Computer Controlled Catalytic Converter (C4) System.

⑦—Hurst option.

⑧—Except Toronado, 2200 RPM; Toronado, 2100 RPM.

⑨—Except Toronado Calif. models, 2200 RPM; Toronado California models 2100 RPM.

⑩—The harmonic balancer on these engines has two timing marks. The timing mark measuring 1/16 in. is used when setting timing with magnetic timing equipment.

⑪—Disconnect distributor four wire electrical connector when checking ignition timing. After completing adjustment, reconnect distributor four wire electrical connector. With ignition switch in the off position, clear trouble code from Electronic Control Module (ECM) memory by removing battery voltage to ECM for 30 seconds.

⑫—On high step of fast idle cam.

⑬—On low step of fast idle cam.

Continued

OLDSMOBILE Rear Wheel Drive & 1982-85 Toronado—Continued

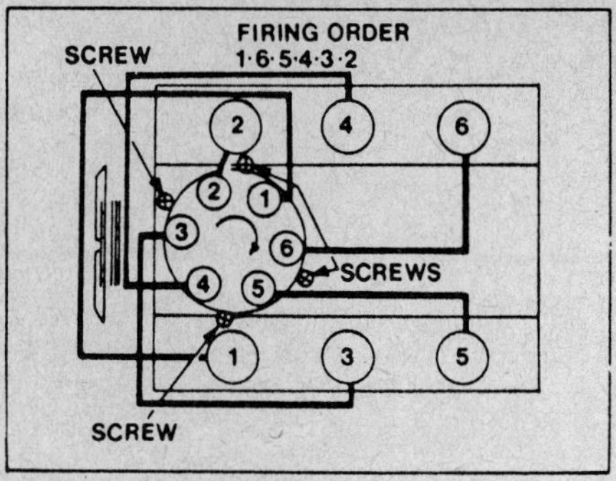

Fig. A

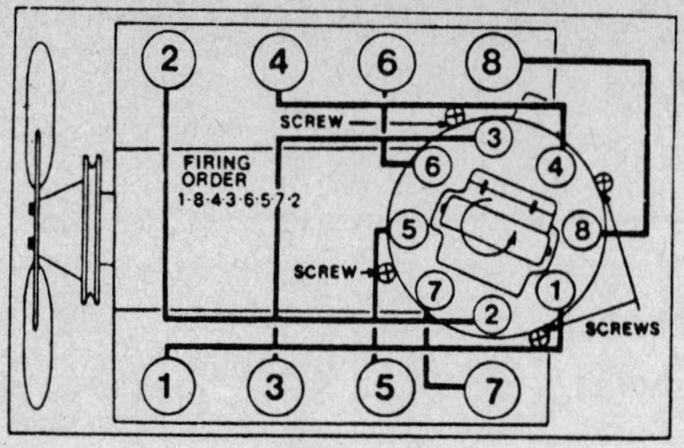

Fig. B

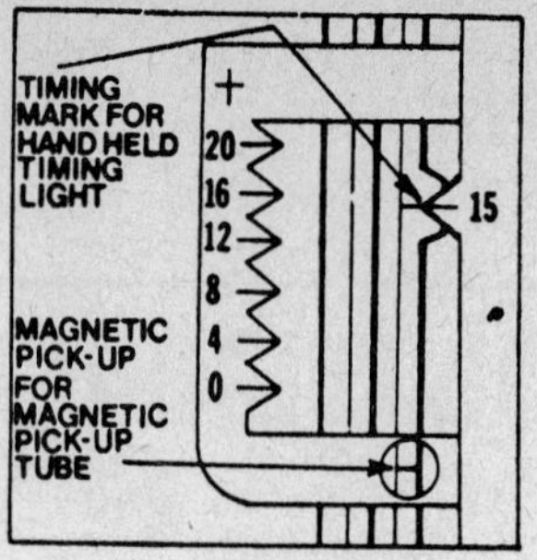

Fig. C

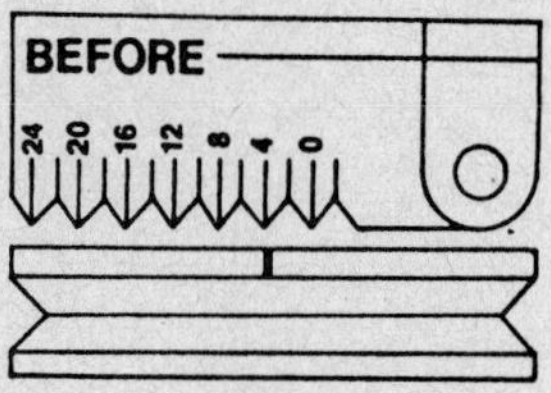

Fig. D

PONTIAC—REAR WHEEL DRIVE MODELS EXC. FIERO & 1000

Year & Engine/VIN	Spark Plug Gap	Ignition Timing BTDC ① Firing Order Fig.	Ignition Timing BTDC ① Man. Trans.	Ignition Timing BTDC ① Auto. Trans.	Ignition Timing BTDC ① Mark Fig.	Curb Idle Speed ② Man. Trans.	Curb Idle Speed ② Auto. Trans.	Fast Idle Speed Man. Trans.	Fast Idle Speed Auto. Trans.	Fuel Pump Pressure
1982										
4-151 T.B.I./2	.060	F	8° ⑨	8° ⑨	N	⑦ ⑧	650D ⑧	⑧	⑧	—
V6-173/1	.045	J	10° ③	10° ③	D	850/1100N	600/700D	2600	2500	6-7½
V6-231/A	.080	B	—	15° ③	E ⑩	—	500D	—	2000	4¼-5¾
V6-252/4	.080	B	—	15° ③	E ⑩	—	500D	—	—	4¼-5¾
V8-305/H	.045	K	6° ③	6° ③	G	700/800N	500/600D	1800 ⑫	2200 ⑫	7½-9
V8-305 T.B.I./7	.045	K	—	6° ⑪	G	—	500D ④	—	1000 ④	—
1983										
4-151 T.B.I./2	.060	F	—	8° ⑨	N	—	⑧	—	⑧	—
V6-173/1	.045	J	10° ③	10° ③	D	775/1100N	600/750D	2500	2500	6-7½
V6-173 H.O./L	.045	J	10° ③	10° ③	D	800/1100N	725/850D	2600	2700	6-7½
V6-229/9	.045	L	—	TDC	M	—	⑧	—	⑧	4½-6
V6-231/A	.080	B	—	15°	C ⑩	—	⑧	—	2200	4¼-5¾
V8-305/H	.045	K	6° ③	6° ③	G	700/800N	500/600D	1800 ⑫	2200 ⑫	7½-9
V8-305 T.B.I./S	.045	K	—	6° ⑪	G	—	④	—	④	—
V8-305 H.O./G	.045	K	—	—	G	700	500D	—	—	7½-9
1984										
4-151/2	.060	F	8° ⑨	8° ⑨	N	775 ⑧	⑧	⑧	⑧	9-13 ⑯
V-173/1	.045	J	10° ③	10° ③	D	775/1100	600/750D	2600 ⑭	2500 ⑭	5½-6½
V-173/L	.045	J	10° ③	10° ③	D	800/1100	725/850D	2600 ⑭	2700 ⑭	6-7½
V6-231/A	.060	B	—	15° ③	C ⑩	—	⑧	—	2200 ⑭	4¼-5¾
V8-305/H	.045	K	6° ③	6° ③	G	700/800	500/650D	1800 ⑭	2200 ⑭	7½-9
V8-305/H.O./G	.045	K	6° ③	6° ③	G	700	600/650D	1800 ⑭	2200 ⑭	7½-9

Continued

PONTIAC–REAR WHEEL DRIVE MODELS EXC. FIERO & 1000—Continued

Year & Engine/VIN	Spark Plug Gap	Firing Order Fig.	Ignition Timing BTDC ① Man. Trans.	Ignition Timing BTDC ① Auto. Trans.	Ignition Timing BTDC ① Mark Fig.	Curb Idle Speed ② Man. Trans.	Curb Idle Speed ② Auto. Trans.	Fast Idle Speed Man. Trans.	Fast Idle Speed Auto. Trans.	Fuel Pump Pressure
1985										
4-151/2	.060	F	8° ⑨	8° ⑨	N	⑧	⑧	⑧	⑧	9-13 ⑯
V6-173 MFI/S	.045	J	10° ③	10° ③	D	⑧	⑧	⑧	⑧	40.5-47 ⑰
V6-231/A	.060	B	—	15° ⑬	C ⑩	—	⑧	—	2200 ⑭	4¼-5¾
V6-262/Z	.035	I	—	TDC ③	O	—	⑧	⑧	⑧	9-13 ⑯
V8-305 4 Bbl./H	.045	K	TDC ③	TDC ③	G	700	500/650D	1800 ⑭	2200 ⑭	7½-9
V8-305 4 Bbl. H.O./G	.045	K	6° ⑬	6° ⑬	G	700	600D	1800 ⑭	2200 ⑭	7½-9
V8-305 TPI/F	.045	K	—	6° ③	G	—	⑧	—	⑧	40.5-47 ⑰
1986										
4-151 EFI/2	.060	F	8° ⑨	8° ⑨	N	⑧	⑧	⑧	⑧	9-13 ⑯
V6-173 MFI/S	.045	J	10° ③	10° ③	D	⑧	⑧	⑧	⑧	40.5-47 ⑰
V6-231/A	.060	B	—	15° ③	C ⑩	—	⑧	—	2200 ⑭	4¼-5¾
V6-262 EFI/Z	.035	I	—	TDC ⑬	O	—	⑧	—	⑧	9-13 ⑯
V8-305 4 Bbl./H	.045	K	TDC ③	TDC ③	G	700	500D	1800 ⑭	2200 ⑭	7½-9
V8-305 H.O. 4 Bbl./G	.035	K	6° ③	6° ③	G	700	600D	1800 ⑭	2200 ⑭	7½-9
V8-305 TPI/F	.035	K	—	6° ⑬	G	—	⑧	—	⑧	40.5-47 ⑰
V8-307/Y	.060	H	—	20° ⑤	E	—	⑧	—	550D ⑮	6-7½
1987										
V6-173/S	.045	J	—	—	D	⑧	⑧	⑧	⑧	34-37
V6-231/A	.060	B	10° ③	15° ③	C ⑩	⑧	⑧	⑧	2200 ⑭	4¼-5¾
V6-262/Z	.035	I	—	—	O	—	⑧	—	⑧	9-13 ⑯
V8-305/H	.035	K	—	TDC ③	G	700	500D	—	2200 ⑭	7½-9
V8-305 H.O./F	.035	K	—	—	G	⑧	⑧	⑧	⑧	34-47 ⑰
V8-307/Y	.060	H	—	20° ⑥ ⑨	E	—	⑧	—	550D ⑮	6-7½
V8-350/8	.035	K	—	6° ⑪	A	⑧	⑧	⑧	⑧	34-47 ⑰
1988										
V6-173/S	—	—	—	—	—	—	—	—	—	—
V8-305/ TBI	—	—	—	—	—	—	—	—	—	—
V8-305/F TPI	—	—	—	—	—	—	—	—	—	—
V8-307/Y	—	H	—	—	E	—	⑧	—	—	—
V8-350/	.035	K	—	—	A	—	⑧	—	⑧	—

①—BTDC-Before top dead center.

②—Idle speed on man. trans. vehicles is adjusted in Neutral & on auto. trans. equipped vehicles is adjusted in Drive unless otherwise specified. Where two idle speeds are listed, the higher speed is with the A/C or idle solenoid energized.

③—With distributor 4-wire connector disconnected.

④—Idle speed controlled by Idle Air Control (IAC) assembly.

⑤—At 1100 RPM with ALDL test lead grounded.

⑥—At 1100 RPM.

⑦—Less A/C, 850 RPM; with A/C, 900 RPM.

⑧—Idle speed is controlled by the idle speed control (ICS) motor or the idle load compensator (ILC).

⑨—Ground diagnostic connector located under dash. The check engine light should flash on & off when in diagnostic mode. Check average ignition timing of cylinder Nos. 1 & 4, and reset as necessary. After completing timing check, remove ground from diagnostic connector & ensure check engine light is off.

⑩—The harmonic balancer on these engines has two timing marks. The mark measuring 1/16 in. is used when setting timing with a hand held timing light. The mark measuring 1/8 in. is used when setting timing with magnetic timing equipment.

⑪—When checking ignition timing, disconnect Electric Spark Timing bypass connector (tan wire w/black stripe) to place EST in bypass mode.

⑫—With EGR vacuum hose disconnected and plugged. Check adjustments within 15 seconds after placing throttle on high step of fast idle cam.

⑬—Disconnect set timing bypass connector (tan/black wire) near the brake booster when adjusting ignition timing. After completing adjustment, reconnect set timing connector. With engine off, clear trouble code from Electronic Control Module (ECM) by removing battery voltage to ECM for 30 seconds.

⑭—On high step of fast idle cam.

⑮—On low step of fast idle cam.

⑯—Wrap shop towel around fuel hose to steel line connection to prevent fuel spillage. Disconnect hose from steel line & install a suitable fuel pressure gauge between hose & steel line. Ensure gauge connections are tight, then start engine & check fuel pressure.

⑰—With shop towel wrapped around fuel pressure valve to prevent fuel spillage, connect a suitable fuel pressure gauge to fuel pressure valve. Check fuel pressure with ignition switch On, engine not running.

Continued

PONTIAC–REAR WHEEL DRIVE MODELS EXC. FIERO & 1000—Continued

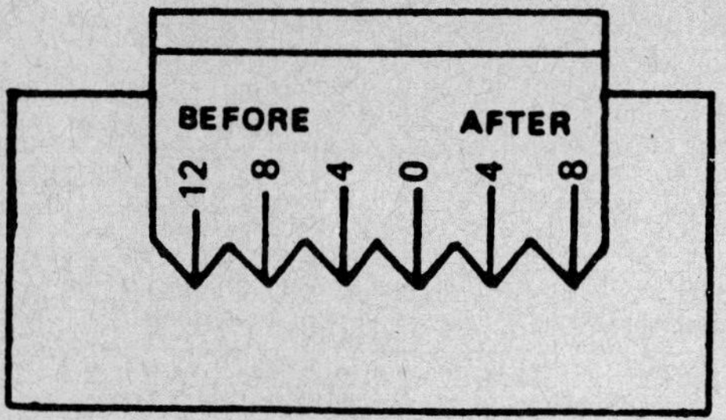

Fig. A

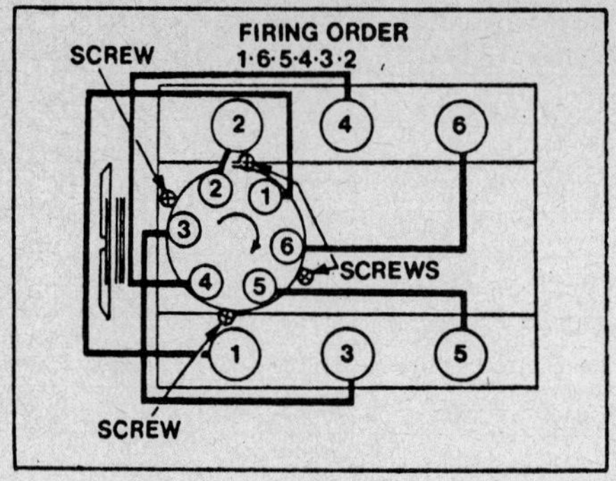

Fig. B

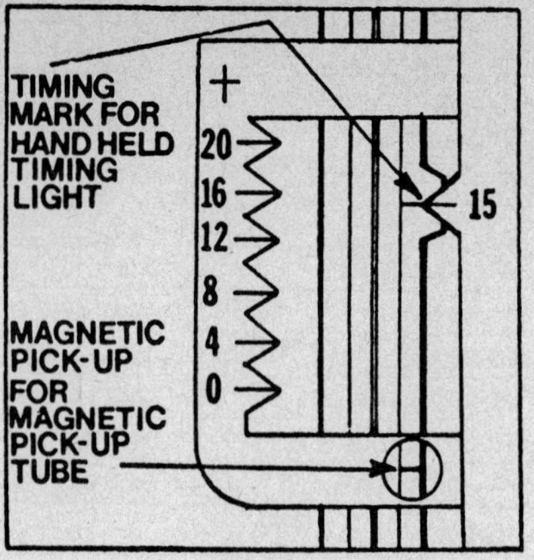

Fig. C

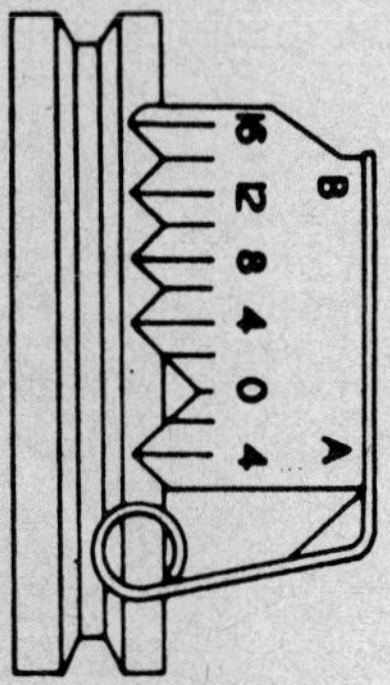

Fig. D

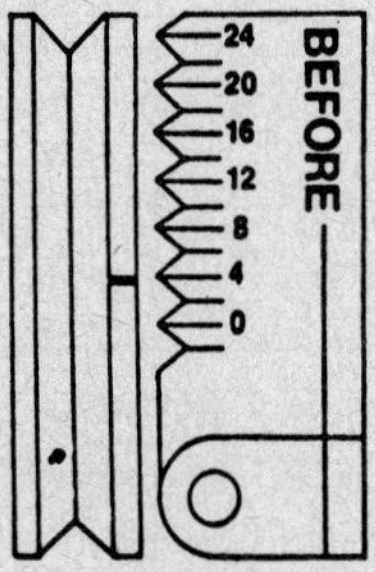

Fig. E

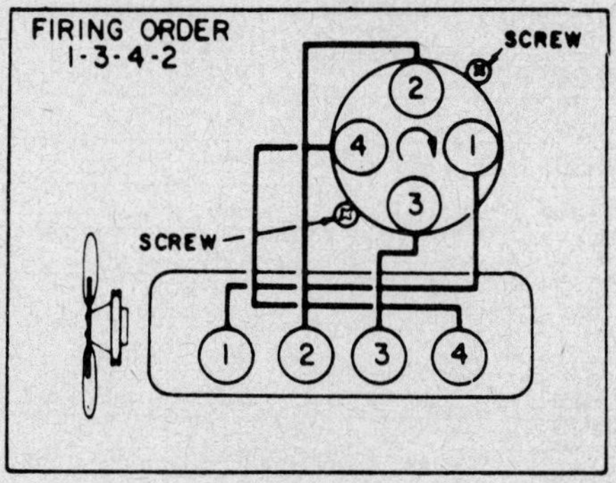

Fig. F

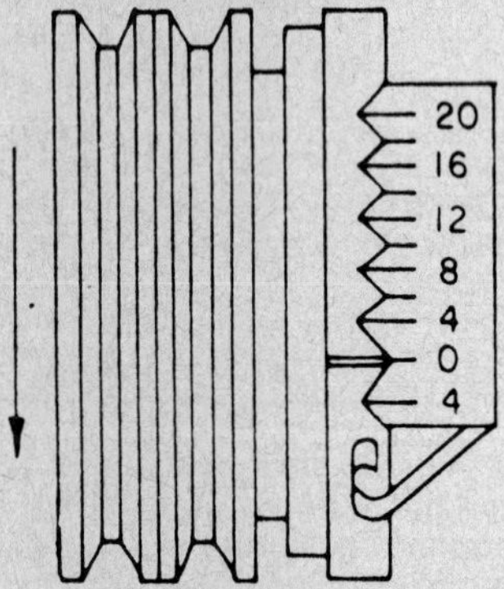

Fig. G

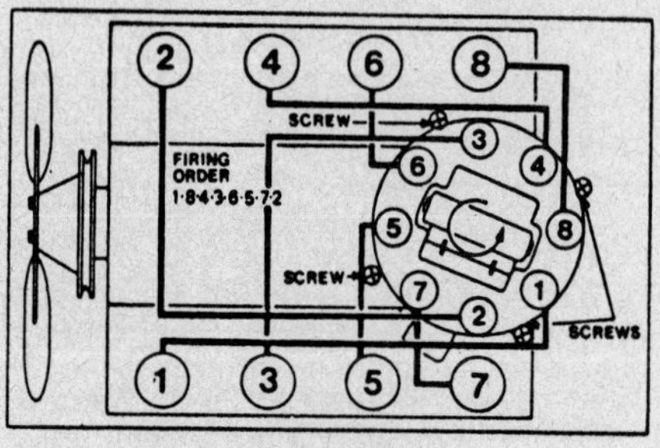

Fig. H

FIRING ORDER 1-6-5-4-3-2

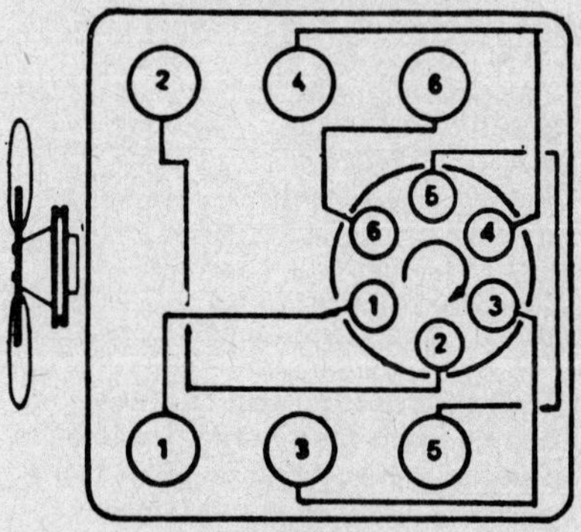

Fig. I

FIRING ORDER 1-2-3-4-5-6

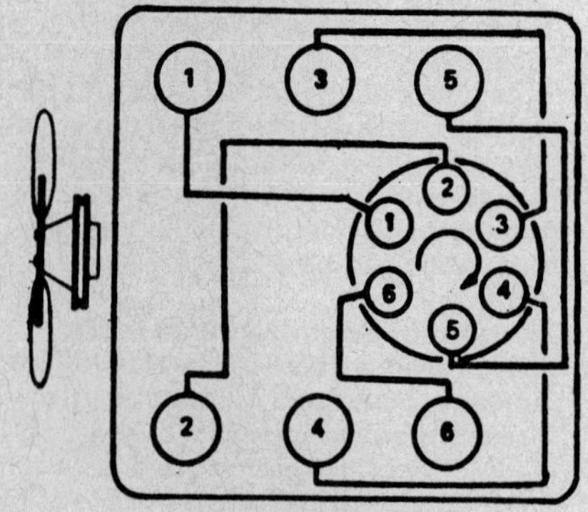

Fig. J

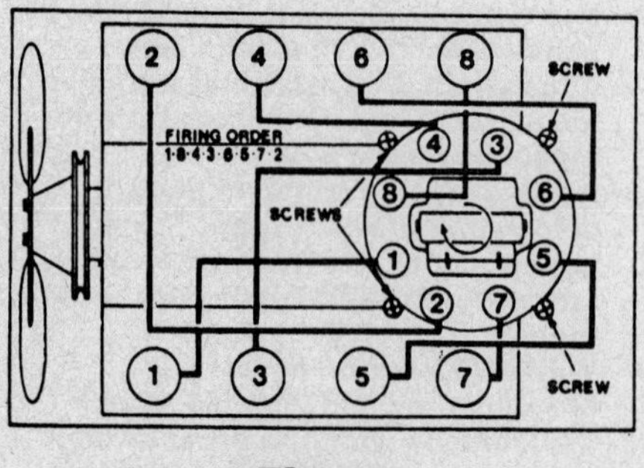

Fig. K

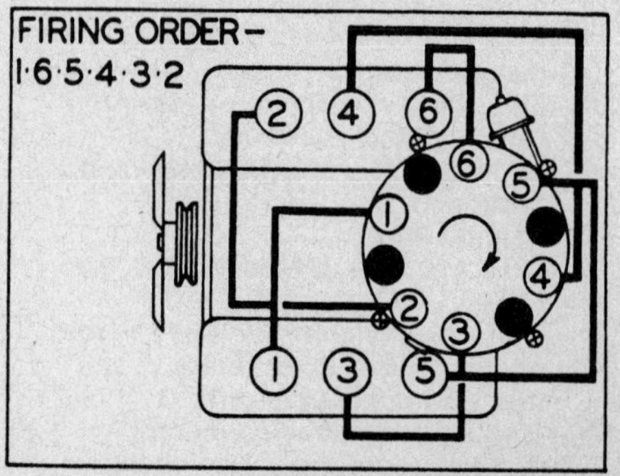

Fig. L

Continued

PONTIAC–REAR WHEEL DRIVE MODELS EXC. FIERO & 1000—Continued

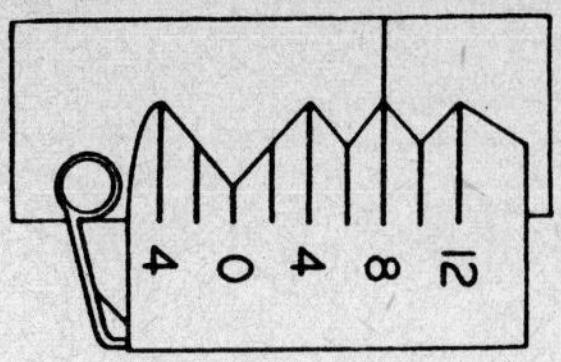

Fig. M

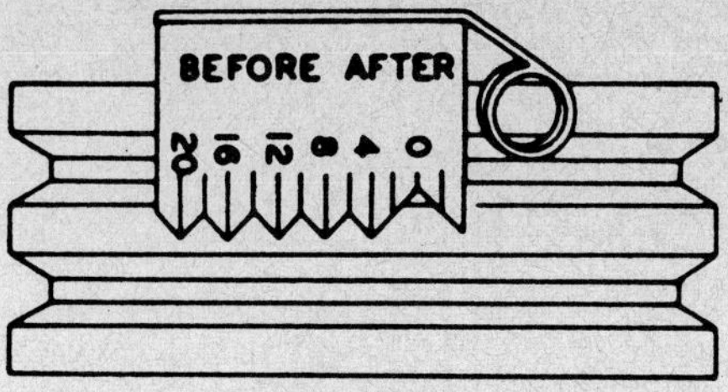

Fig. N

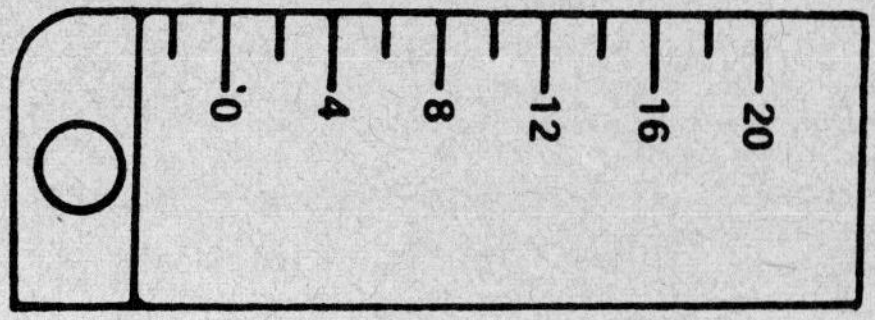

Fig. O

PONTIAC FIERO

Year & Engine/ VIN	Spark Plug Gap	Ignition Timing BTDC ①				Curb Idle Speed ②		Fast Idle Speed		Fuel Pump Pressure
		Firing Order Fig.	Man. Trans.	Auto. Trans.	Mark Fig.	Man. Trans.	Auto. Trans.	Man. Trans.	Auto. Trans.	
1984										
4-151/R	.060	A	8° ③	8° ③	B	④	④	④	④	9-13 ⑤
1985-86										
4-151/R	.060	A	8° ③	8° ③	B	④	④	④	④	9-13 ⑤
V6-173/9	.045	C	10° ③	10° ③	—	④	④	④	④	40.5-47 ⑥
1987										
4-151/R	.060	⑦	⑧	⑧	⑨	④	④	④	④	9-13 ⑤
V6-173/9	.045	⑩	⑧	⑧	⑨	④	④	④	④	40.5-47 ⑥
1988										
4-151/	.060	—	—	—	—	—	—	—	—	—
V6-173/	.045	—	—	—	—	—	—	—	—	—

①—BTDC-Before top dead center.

②—Idle speed on man. trans. vehicles is adjusted in Neutral, & on auto. trans. equipped vehicles is adjusted in Drive unless otherwise specified. Where two idle speeds are listed, the highest speed is with the A/C or idle solenoid energized.

③—Connect jumper wire between ALCL connector terminals A & B. The ALCL connector is located in the console. On 4-151 engines, check average timing of cylinders No. 1 & 4 & reset as necessary. On V6-173 engines, check ignition timing at No. 1 cylinder. After completing ignition timing adjustment, disconnect jumper wire from between ALCL connector terminals A & B. With engine off, clear trouble code from Electronic Control Module (ECM) memory by removing battery voltage to ECM for 30 seconds.

④—Idle speed controlled by Idle Air Control (IAC) valve.

⑤—Wrap shop towel around fuel hose to steel line connection to prevent fuel spillage. Disconnect fuel hose from steel line & connect a suitable fuel pressure gauge between hose & steel line. Ensure gauge connections are tight, then start engine & note fuel pressure readings.

⑥—With shop towel wrapped around fuel pressure valve to prevent fuel spillage, connect a suitable fuel pressure gauge to fuel pressure valve. Check fuel pressure with ignition switch On, engine not running.

⑦—Cylinder numbering from front of engine to rear 1, 2, 3, 4. Firing order 1-3-4-2. Refer to Fig. E for spark plug wire connections at coil unit.

⑧—Electronically controlled, no adjustment.

⑨—Equipped with crankshaft position sensor.

⑩—Cylinder numbering left to right as viewed from front of vehicle, front bank 2, 4, 6; rear bank 1, 3, 5. Firing order 1-2-3-4-5-6. Refer to Fig. F for spark plug wire connections at coil unit.

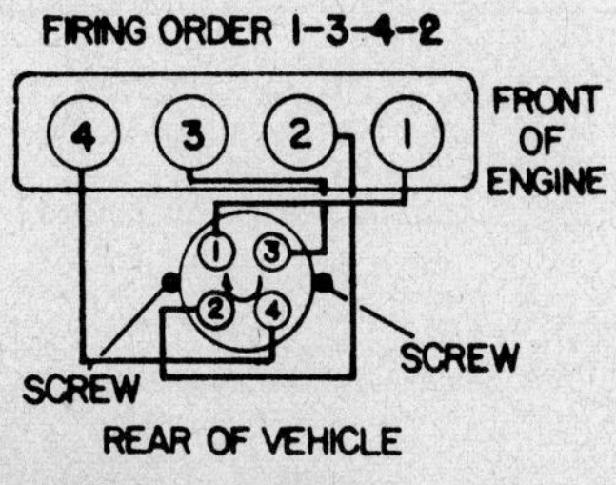

Fig. A

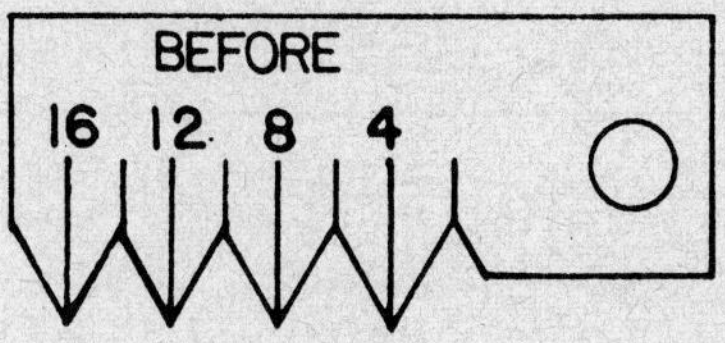

Fig. B

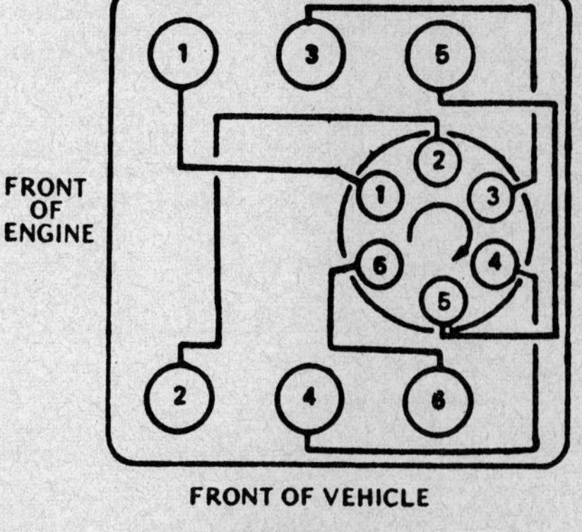

Fig. C

Continued

PONTIAC FIERO—Continued

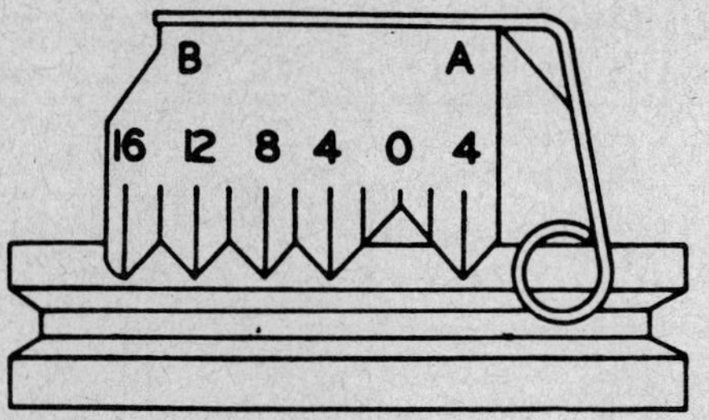

Fig. D

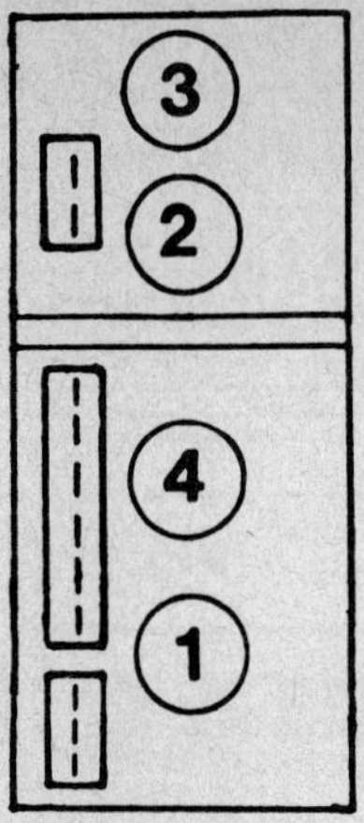

Fig. E

Fig. F

DIESEL ENGINE PERFORMANCE FORD MOTOR COMPANY

FORD ESCORT & TEMPO; MERCURY LYNX & TOPAZ

Year & Engine/VIN	Firing Order	Injection Timing	Injection Nozzle Pressure		Curb Idle Speed RPM	Fast Idle Speed RPM
			New	Used		
1984						
4-120/H	1-3-4-2	TDC①	1990-2105	1849-1990	750②	1500②
1985						
4-120/H	1-3-4-2	TDC①	1990-2105	1849-1990	—	—
1986						
4-120/H	1-3-4-2	TDC①	1990-2105	1849-1990	—	—
1987						
4-120/H	1-3-4-2	—	1914	—	—	—

①—With engine at operating temperature.
②—With manual transmission.

LINCOLN CONTINENTAL & MARK VII

Year & Engine/VIN	Firing Order	Injection Timing BTDC①	Injection Nozzle Opening Pressure②	Curb Idle Speed RPM	Fast Idle Speed RPM
1984-85					
6-149/L	1-5-3-6-2-4	5°③	2133	750-800	900-1050

①—BTDC-Before top dead center.
②—PSI.
③—At 1500 RPM.

GENERAL MOTORS

BUICK, CADILLAC & OLDSMOBILE—REAR WHEEL DRIVE MODELS & 1982-85 Eldorado, Riviera, Seville & Toronado

Year & Engine/V.I.N.	Firing Order	Injection Timing ATDC①	Curb Idle Speed RPM②	Fast Idle Speed RPM②
1982-83				
V6-262/V Exc. High Alt.	1-6-5-4-3-2	7°③⑤	650D	725D
V6-262/V High Alt.	1-6-5-4-3-2	7°③⑥	650D	725D
V8-350/N Exc. High Alt.	1-8-4-3-6-5-7-2	4°③⑦	600D	725D
V8-350/N High Alt.	1-8-4-3-6-5-7-2	4°③⑧	600D	725D
1984				
V6-262/V	1-6-5-4-3-2	7°③⑨	675D	775D
V8-350/N	1-8-4-3-6-5-7-2	4°③⑩	600D	750D
1985				
V8-350/N	1-8-4-3-6-5-7-2	③⑩④	600D	750D

①—ATDC-After top dead center.
②—D: Drive.
③—Using diesel timing meter J-33075.
④—Exc. LeSabre, 6°; LeSabre, 5°.
⑤—At 1300 RPM. At altitudes above 4000 ft., set at 8° ATDC.
⑥—At 1300 RPM. At altitudes below 4000 ft., set at 6° ATDC.
⑦—At 1250 RPM. At altitudes above 4000 ft., set at 5° ATDC.
⑧—At 1250 RPM. At altitudes below 4000 ft., set at 3° ATDC.
⑨—At 1300 RPM.
⑩—At 1250 RPM.

1985 BUICK ELECTRA & PARK AVENUE, CADILLAC DEVILLE & FLEETWOOD & OLDSMOBILE 98

Year & Engine/VIN	Firing Order	Injection Timing ATDC①	Curb Idle Speed RPM②	Fast Idle Speed RPM②
1985				
V6-262/T Exc. Calif.③	1-6-5-4-3-2	5½°④⑤	675D	750D
V6-262/T Calif.③	1-6-5-4-3-2	6½°④⑤	675D	750D
V6-262/T Exc. Calif.⑥	1-6-5-4-3-2	6°④⑤	675D	750D
V6-262/T Calif.⑥	1-6-5-4-3-2	7°④⑤	675D	750D

①—ATDC-After top dead center.
②—D: Drive.
③—Engines with external EGR.
④—Using diesel timing meter J-33075.
⑤—At 1300 RPM.
⑥—Engines with internal EGR.

CHEVROLET & PONTIAC—REAR WHEEL DRIVE MODELS EXC. CHEVETTE & 1000

Year & Engine/VIN	Firing Order	Injection Timing ATDC①	Curb Idle Speed RPM②	Fast Idle Speed RPM②
1982-83				
V6-262/V Exc. High Alt.	1-6-5-4-3-2	7°③⑤	650D	725D
V6-262/V High Alt.	1-6-5-4-3-2	7°③⑥	650D	725D
V8-350/N Exc. High Alt.	1-8-4-3-6-5-7-2	4°③⑦	600D	725D
V8-350/N High Alt.	1-8-4-3-6-5-7-2	4°③⑧	600D	725D
1984				
V8-350/N	1-8-4-3-6-5-7-2	4°③④	600D	750D
1985				
V8-350/N	1-8-4-3-6-5-7-2	5°③④	600D	750D

①—ATDC-After top dead center.
②—D: Drive.
③—Using diesel timing meter J-33075.
④—At 1250 RPM.
⑤—At 1300 RPM. At altitudes above 4000 ft., set at 8° ATDC.
⑥—At 1300 RPM. At altitudes below 4000 ft., set at 6° ATDC.
⑦—At 1250 RPM. At altitudes above 4000 ft., set at 5° ATDC.
⑧—At 1250 RPM. At altitudes below 4000 ft., set at 3° ATDC.

CHEVROLET CHEVETTE & PONTIAC 1000

Year & Engine/VIN	Injection Timing BTDC ①	Curb Idle Speed RPM		Fast Idle Speed RPM	
		Man. Trans.	Auto. Trans. ②	Man. Trans.	Auto. Trans.
1982-83					
4-110/D	18° ③	625	725N	950	950
1984					
4-110/D	18° ③	625	725N	—	—
1985					
4-110/D	18° ③	625	—	—	—
1986					
4-110/D Exc. Calif.	18° ③	700	725N	—	—
4-110/D Calif.	18° ③	625	725N	—	—

①—BTDC-Before top dead center. ②—D: Drive. N: Neutral. ③—Static timing.

1982-85 CHEV. CELEBRITY BUICK CENTURY, OLDS. CUTLASS CIERA, PONT. 6000 & 1984-85 CUTLASS CRUISER

Year & Engine/VIN	Firing Order	Injection Timing ATDC ①	Curb Idle Speed RPM ②	Curb Fast Speed RPM ②
1982				
V6-262/T	1-6-5-4-3-2	5° ③ ④	650D	725D
1983-84				
V6-262/T	1-6-5-4-3-2	6° ③ ④	675D	775D
1985				
V6-262/T Exc. Calif.	1-6-5-4-3-2	5½° ③ ④	650D	750D
V6-262/T Calif.	1-6-5-4-3-2	6½° ③ ④	650D	750D

①—ATDC-After top dead center.
②—D: Drive.
③—Using diesel timing meter J-33075.
④—At 1300 RPM.

TROUBLESHOOTING

INDEX

Condition	Possible Cause	Correction
EXTERNAL OIL LEAKS	(1) Fuel pump gasket broken or improperly seated.	(1) Replace gasket.
	(2) Cylinder head cover RTV sealant broken or improperly seated.	(2) Replace sealant; inspect cylinder head cover sealant flange and cylinder head sealant surface for distortion and cracks.
	(3) Oil filler cap leaking or missing.	(3) Replace cap.
	(4) Oil filter gasket broken or improperly seated.	(4) Replace oil filter.
	(5) Oil pan side gasket broken, improperly seated or opening in RTV sealant.	(5) Replace gasket or repair opening in sealant; inspect oil pan gasket flange for distortion.
	(6) Oil pan front oil seal broken or improperly seated.	(6) Replace seal; inspect timing case cover and oil pan seal flange for distortion.
	(7) Oil pan rear oil seal broken or improperly seated.	(7) Replace seal; inspect oil pan rear oil seal flange; inspect rear main bearing cap for cracks, plugged oil return channels, or distortion in seal groove.
	(8) Timing case cover oil seal broken or improperly seated.	(8) Replace seal.
	(9) Excess oil pressure because of restricted PCV valve.	(9) Replace PCV valve.
	(10) Oil pan drain plug loose or has stripped threads.	(10) Repair as necessary and tighten.
	(11) Rear oil gallery plug loose.	(11) Use appropriate sealant on gallery plug and tighten.

Engine mechanical troubleshooting (part 1 of 6)

Condition	Possible Cause	Correction
	(12) Rear camshaft plug loose or improperly seated.	(12) Seat camshaft plug or replace and seal, as necessary.
	(13) Distributor Base Gasket damaged.	(13) Replace Gasket.
EXCESSIVE OIL CONSUMPTION	(1) Oil level too high.	(1) Drain oil to specified level.
	(2) Oil with wrong viscosity being used.	(2) Replace with specified oil.
	(3) PCV valve stuck closed.	(3) Replace PCV valve.
	(4) Valve stem oil deflectors (or seals) are damaged, missing, or incorrect type.	(4) Replace valve stem oil deflectors.
	(5) Valve stems or valve guides worn.	(5) Measure stem-to-guide clearance and repair as necessary.
	(6) Poorly fitted or missing valve cover baffles.	(6) Replace valve cover.
	(7) Piston rings broken or missing.	(7) Replace broken or missing rings.
	(8) Scuffed piston.	(8) Replace piston.
	(9) Incorrect piston ring gap.	(9) Measure ring gap, repair as necessary.
	(10) Piston rings sticking or excessively loose in grooves.	(10) Measure ring side clearance, repair as necessary.
	(11) Compression rings installed upside down.	(11) Repair as necessary.
	(12) Cylinder walls worn, scored, or glazed.	(12) Repair as necessary.
	(13) Piston ring gaps not properly staggered.	(13) Repair as necessary.
	(14) Excessive main or connecting rod bearing clearance.	(14) Measure bearing clearance, repair as necessary.
NO OIL PRESSURE	(1) Low oil level.	(1) Add oil to correct level.

Engine mechanical troubleshooting (part 2 of 6)

Condition	Possible Cause	Correction
NO OIL PRESSURE (Continued)	(2) Oil pressure gauge, warning lamp or sending unit inaccurate.	(2) Inspect and replace as necessary.
	(3) Oil pump malfunction.	(3) Repair or replace oil pump.
	(4) Oil pressure relief valve sticking.	(4) Remove and inspect oil pressure relief valve assembly.
	(5) Oil passages on pressure side of pump obstructed.	(5) Inspect oil passages for obstructions.
	(6) Oil pickup screen or tube obstructed.	(6) Inspect oil pickup for obstructions.
	(7) Loose oil inlet tube.	(7) Tighten or seal inlet tube.
LOW OIL PRESSURE	(1) Low oil level.	(1) Add oil to correct level.
	(2) Inaccurate gauge, warning lamp or sending unit.	(2) Inspect and replace as necessary.
	(3) Oil excessively thin because of dilution, poor quality, or improper grade.	(3) Drain and refill crankcase with recommended oil.
	(4) Excessive oil temperature.	(4) Correct cause of overheating engine.
	(5) Oil pressure relief spring weak or sticking.	(5) Remove and inspect oil pressure relief valve assembly.
	(6) Oil inlet tube and screen assembly has restriction or air leak.	(6) Remove and inspect oil inlet tube and screen assembly. (Fill inlet tube with lacquer thinner to locate leaks.)
	(7) Excessive oil pump clearance.	(7) Inspect and replace as necessary.
	(8) Excessive main, rod, or camshaft bearing clearance.	(8) Measure bearing clearances, repair as necessary.
HIGH OIL PRESSURE	(1) Improper oil viscosity.	(1) Drain and refill crankcase with correct viscosity oil.
	(2) Oil pressure gauge or sending unit inaccurate.	(2) Inspect and replace as necessary.

Engine mechanical troubleshooting (part 3 of 6)

Condition	Possible Cause	Correction
HIGH OIL PRESSURE (Continued)	(3) Oil pressure relief valve sticking closed.	(3) Remove and inspect oil pressure relief valve assembly.
MAIN BEARING NOISE	(1) Insufficient oil supply.	(1) Inspect for low oil level and low oil pressure.
	(2) Main bearing clearance excessive.	(2) Measure main bearing clearance, repair as necessary.
	(3) Bearing insert missing.	(3) Replace missing insert.
	(4) Crankshaft end play excessive.	(4) Measure end play, repair as necessary.
	(5) Improperly tightened main bearing cap bolts.	(5) Tighten bolts with specified torque.
	(6) Loose flywheel or drive plate.	(6) Tighten flywheel or drive plate attaching bolts.
	(7) Loose or damaged vibration damper.	(7) Repair as necessary.
CONNECTING ROD BEARING NOISE	(1) Insufficient oil supply.	(1) Inspect for low oil level and low oil pressure.
	(2) Carbon build-up on piston.	(2) Remove carbon from piston crown.
	(3) Bearing clearance excessive or bearing missing.	(3) Measure clearance, repair as necessary.
	(4) Crankshaft connecting rod journal out-of-round.	(4) Measure journal dimensions, repair or replace as necessary.
	(5) Misaligned connecting rod or cap.	(5) Repair as necessary.
	(6) Connecting rod bolts tightened improperly.	(6) Tighten bolts with specified torque.
PISTON NOISE	(1) Piston-to-cylinder wall clearance excessive (scuffed piston).	(1) Measure clearance and examine piston.
	(2) Cylinder walls excessively tapered or out-of-round.	(2) Measure cylinder wall dimensions, rebore cylinder.

Engine mechanical troubleshooting (part 4 of 6)

Condition	Possible Cause	Correction
PISTON NOISE (Continued)	(3) Piston ring broken.	(3) Replace all rings on piston.
	(4) Loose or seized piston pin.	(4) Measure piston-to-pin clearance, repair as necessary.
	(5) Connecting rods misaligned.	(5) Measure rod alignment, straighten or replace.
	(6) Piston ring side clearance excessively loose or tight.	(6) Measure ring side clearance, repair as necessary.
	(7) Carbon build-up on piston is excessive.	(7) Remove carbon from piston.
VALVE ACTUATING COMPONENT NOISE	(1) Insufficient oil supply.	(1) Check for: (a) Low oil level. (b) Low oil pressure. (c) Plugged pushrods. (d) Wrong hydraulic tappets. (e) Restricted oil gallery. (f) Excessive tappet to bore clearance.
	(2) Push rods worn or bent.	(2) Replace worn or bent push rods.
	(3) Rocker arms or pivots worn.	(3) Replace worn rocker arms or pivots.
	(4) Foreign objects or chips in hydraulic tappets.	(4) Clean tappets.
	(5) Excessive tappet leak-down.	(5) Replace valve tappet.
	(6) Tappet face worn.	(6) Replace tappet; inspect corresponding cam lobe for wear.
	(7) Broken or cocked valve springs.	(7) Properly seat cocked springs; replace broken springs.
	(8) Stem-to-guide clearance excessive.	(8) Measure stem-to-guide clearance, repair as required.
	(9) Valve bent.	(9) Replace valve.
	(10) Loose rocker arms.	(10) Tighten bolts with specified torque.
	(11) Valve seat runout excessive.	(11) Regrind valve seat/valves.

Engine mechanical troubleshooting (part 5 of 6)

Condition	Possible Cause	Correction
VALVE ACTUATING COMPONENT NOISE (Continued)	(12) Missing valve lock.	(12) Install valve lock.
	(13) Push rod rubbing or contacting cylinder head.	(13) Remove cylinder head and remove obstruction in head.
	(14) Excessive engine oil	(14) Correct oil level.

Engine mechanical troubleshooting (part 6 of 6)

Condition	Possible Cause	Correction
HARD STARTING (ENGINE CRANKS NORMALLY)	(1) Binding linkage, choke valve or choke piston.	(1) Repair as necessary.
	(2) Restricted choke vacuum diaphragm.	(2) Clean passages.
	(3) Improper fuel level.	(3) Adjust float level.
	(4) Dirty, worn or faulty needle valve and seat.	(4) Repair as necessary.
	(5) Float sticking.	(5) Reapir as necessary.
	(6) Faulty fuel pump.	(6) Replace fuel pump.
	(7) Incorrect choke cover adjustment.	(7) Adjust choke cover.
	(8) Inadequate choke unloader adjustment.	(8) Adjust choke unloader.
	(9) Faulty ignition coil.	(9) Test and replace as necessary.
	(10) Improper spark plug gap.	(10) Adjust gap.
	(11) Incorrect ignition timing.	(11) Adjust timing.
	(12) Incorrect valve timing.	(12) Check valve timing; repair as necessary.
ROUGH IDLE OR STALLING	(1) Incorrect curb or fast idle speed.	(1) Adjust curb or fast idle speed.
	(2) Incorrect ignition timing.	(2) Adjust timing to specification.
	(3) Improper feedback system operation	(3) Check operation and repair as necessary.
	(4) Improper fast idle cam adjustment.	(4) Adjust fast idle cam.
	(5) Faulty EGR valve operation.	(5) Test EGR system and replace as necessary.
	(6) Faulty PCV valve air flow.	(6) Test PCV valve and replace as necessary.

Engine performance troubleshooting (part 1 of 6)

Condition	Possible Cause	Correction
ROUGH IDLE OR STALLING (Continued)	(7) Choke binding.	(7) Locate and eliminate binding condition.
	(8) Faulty vacuum motors or valves.	(8) Repair as necessary.
	(9) Air leak into manifold vacuum.	(9) Inspect manifold vacuum connections and repair as necessary.
	(10) Improper fuel level.	(10) Adjust fuel level.
	(11) Faulty distributor rotor or cap.	(11) Replace rotor or cap.
	(12) Improperly seated valves.	(12) Test cylinder compression, repair as necessary.
	(13) Incorrect ignition wiring.	(13) Inspect wiring and correct as necessary.
	(14) Faulty ignition coil.	(14) Test coil and replace as necessary.
	(15) Restricted air vent or idle passages.	(15) Clean passages.
	(16) Restricted air cleaner.	(16) Clean or replace air cleaner filler element.
	(17) Faulty choke vacuum diaphragm.	(17) Repair as necessary.
FAULTY LOW-SPEED OPERATION	(1) Restricted idle transfer slots.	(1) Clean transfer slots.
	(2) Restricted idle air vents and passages.	(2) Clean air vents and passages.
	(3) Restricted air cleaner.	(3) Clean or replace air cleaner filter element.
	(4) Improper fuel level.	(4) Adjust fuel level.
	(5) Faulty spark plugs.	(5) Clean or replace spark plugs.
	(6) Dirty, corroded, or loose ignition secondary circuit wire connections.	(6) Clean or tighten secondary circuit wire connections.
	(7) Improper feedback system operation.	(7) Check operation and repair as necessary.
	(8) Faulty ignition coil high voltage wire.	(8) Replace ignition coil high voltage wire.
	(9) Faulty distributor cap.	(9) Replace cap.
FAULTY ACCELERATION	(1) Improper accelerator pump stroke.	(1) Adjust accelerator pump stroke.
	(2) Incorrect ignition timing.	(2) Adjust timing.
	(3) Inoperative pump discharge check ball or needle.	(3) Clean or replace as necessary.

Engine performance troubleshooting (part 2 of 6)

Condition	Possible Cause	Correction
FAULTY ACCELERATION (Continued)	(4) Worn or damaged pump diaphragm or piston.	(4) Replace diaphragm or piston.
	(5) Leaking carburetor main body cover gasket.	(5) Replace gasket.
	(6) Engine cold and choke set too lean.	(6) Adjust choke cover.
	(7) Improper metering rod adjustment.	(7) Adjust metering rod.
	(8) Faulty spark plug(s).	(8) Clean or replace spark plug(s).
	(9) Improperly seated valves.	(9) Test cylinder compression, repair as necessary.
	(10) Faulty ignition coil.	(10) Test coil and replace as necessary.
	(11) Improper feedback system operation.	(11) Check operation and repair as necessary.
FAULTY HIGH SPEED OPERATION	(1) Incorrect ignition timing.	(1) Adjust timing.
	(2) Faulty distributor centrifugal advance mechanism.	(2) Check centrifugal advance mechanism and repair as necessary.
	(3) Faulty distributor vacuum advance mechanism.	(3) Check vacuum advance mechanism and repair as necessary.
	(4) Low fuel pump volume.	(4) Replace fuel pump.
	(5) Wrong spark plug air gap or wrong plug.	(5) Adjust air gap or install correct plug.
	(6) Faulty choke operation.	(6) Adjust choke cover.
	(7) Partially restricted exhaust manifold, exhaust pipe, catalytic converter, muffler or tailpipe.	(7) Eliminate restriction.
	(8) Restricted vacuum passages.	(8) Clean passages.
	(9) Improper size or restricted main jet.	(9) Clean or replace as necessary.
	(10) Restricted air cleaner.	(10) Clean or replace filter element as necessary.
	(11) Faulty distributor rotor or cap.	(11) Replace rotor or cap.
	(12) Faulty ignition coil.	(12) Test coil and replace as necessary.
	(13) Improperly seated valve(s).	(13) Test cylinder compression, repair as necessary.
	(14) Faulty valve spring(s).	(14) Inspect and test valve spring tension, replace as necessary.
	(15) Incorrect valve timing.	(15) Check valve timing and repair as necessary.

Engine performance troubleshooting (part 3 of 6)

Condition	Possible Cause	Correction
FAULTY HIGH SPEED OPERATION (Continued)	(16) Intake manifold restricted.	(16) Remove restriction or replace manifold.
	(17) Worn distributor shaft.	(17) Replace shaft.
	(18) Improper feedback system operation.	(18) Check operation and repair as necessary.
MISFIRE AT ALL SPEEDS	(1) Faulty spark plug(s).	(1) Clean or replace spark plug(s).
	(2) Faulty spark plug wire(s).	(2) Replace as necessary.
	(3) Faulty distributor cap or rotor.	(3) Replace cap or rotor.
	(4) Faulty ignition coil.	(4) Test coil and replace as necessary.
	(5) Primary ignition circuit shorted or open intermittently.	(5) Troubleshoot primary circuit and repair as necessary.
	(6) Improperly seated valve(s).	(6) Test cylinder compression, repair as necessary.
	(7) Faulty hydraulic tappet(s).	(7) Clean or replace tappet(s).
	(8) Improper feedback system operation.	(8) Check operation and repair as necessary.
	(9) Faulty valve spring(s).	(9) Inspect and test valve spring tension, repair as necessary.
	(10) Worn camshaft lobes.	(10) Replace camshaft.
	(11) Air leak into manifold.	(11) Check manifold vacuum and repair as necessary.
	(12) Improper carburetor adjustment.	(12) Adjust carburetor.
	(13) Fuel pump volume or pressure low.	(13) Replace fuel pump.
	(14) Blown cylinder head gasket.	(14) Replace gasket.
	(15) Intake or exhaust manifold passage(s) restricted.	(15) Pass chain through passage(s) and repair as necessary.
	(16) Incorrect trigger wheel installed in distributor.	(16) Install correct trigger wheel.
POWER NOT UP TO NORMAL	(1) Incorrect ignition timing.	(1) Adjust timing.
	(2) Faulty distributor rotor.	(2) Replace rotor.
	(3) Trigger wheel loose on shaft.	(3) Reposition or replace trigger wheel.
	(4) Incorrect spark plug gap.	(4) Adjust gap.
	(5) Faulty fuel pump.	(5) Replace fuel pump.

Engine performance troubleshooting (part 4 of 6)

Condition	Possible Cause	Correction
POWER NOT UP TO NORMAL (Continued)	(6) Incorrect valve timing.	(6) Check valve timing and repair as necessary.
	(7) Faulty ignition coil.	(7) Test coil and replace as necessary.
	(8) Faulty ignition wires.	(8) Test wires and replace as necessary.
	(9) Improperly seated valves.	(9) Test cylinder compression and repair as necessary.
	(10) Blown cylinder head gasket.	(10) Replace gasket.
	(11) Leaking piston rings.	(11) Test compression and repair as as necessary.
	(12) Worn distributor shaft.	(12) Replace shaft.
	(13) Improper feedback system operation.	(13) Check operation and repair as necessary.
INTAKE BACKFIRE	(1) Improper ignition timing.	(1) Adjust timing.
	(2) Faulty accelerator pump discharge.	(2) Repair as necessary.
	(3) Defective EGR valve.	(3) Replace EGR valve.
	(4) Faulty vacuum motors or valves.	(4) Repair as necessary.
	(5) Lean air/fuel mixture.	(5) Check float level or manifold vacuum for air leak. Remove sediment from bowl.
EXHAUST BACKFIRE	(1) Air leak into manifold vacuum.	(1) Check manifold vacuum and repair as necessary.
	(2) Faulty air injection diverter valve.	(2) Test diverter valve and replace as necessary.
	(3) Exhaust leak.	(3) Locate and eliminate leak.
PING OR SPARK KNOCK	(1) Incorrect ignition timing.	(1) Adjust timing.
	(2) Distributor centrifugal or vacuum advance malfunction.	(2) Inspect advance mechanism and repair as necessary.
	(3) Excessive combustion chamber deposits.	(3) Remove with combustion chamber cleaner.
	(4) Air leak into manifold vacuum.	(4) Check manifold vacuum and repair as necessary.
	(5) Excessively high compression.	(5) Test compression and repair as necessary.
	(6) Fuel octane rating excessively low.	(6) Try alternate fuel source.

Engine performance troubleshooting (part 5 of 6)

Condition	Possible Cause	Correction
PING OR SPARK KNOCK (Continued)	(7) Sharp edges in combustion chamber.	(7) Grind smooth.
	(8) EGR Valve not functioning properly.	(8) Test EGR System and replace as necessary.
SURGING (AT CRUISING TO TOP SPEEDS)	(1) Low carburetor fuel level.	(1) Adjust fuel level.
	(2) Low fuel pump pressure or volume.	(2) Replace fuel pump.
	(3) Metering rod(s) not adjusted properly (BBD Model Carburetor).	(3) Adjust metering rod.
	(4) Improper PCV valve air flow.	(4) Test PCV valve and replace as necessary.
	(5) Air leak into manifold vacuum.	(5) Check manifold vacuum and repair as necessary.
	(6) Incorrect spark advance.	(6) Test and replace as necessary.
	(7) Restricted main jet(s).	(7) Clean main jet(s).
	(8) Undersize main jet(s).	(8) Replace main jet(s).
	(9) Restricted air vents.	(9) Clean air vents.
	(10) Restricted fuel filter.	(10) Replace fuel filter.
	(11) Restricted air cleaner.	(11) Clean or replace air cleaner filter element.
	(12) EGR valve not functioning properly.	(12) Test EGR System and replace as necessary.
	(13) Improper feedback system operation.	(13) Check operation and repair as necessary.

Engine performance troubleshooting (part 6 of 6)

Condition	Possible Cause	Correction
LOW BRAKE PEDAL (Excessive pedal travel required to apply brake)	(1) Excessive clearance between rear linings and drums caused by inoperative automatic adjusters.	(1) Make 10 to 15 alternate forward and reverse brake stops to adjust brakes. If brake pedal does not come up, repair or replace adjuster parts as necessary.
	(2) Worn rear brake lining.	(2) Inspect and replace lining if worn beyond minimum thickness specification.
	(3) Bent, distorted brakeshoes.	(3) Replace brakeshoes in axle sets.
	(4) Caliper pistons corroded.	(4) Repair or replace calipers.
LOW BRAKE PEDAL (pedal may go to floor under steady pressure)	(1) Leak in hydraulic system.	(1) Fill master cylinder to within 1/4-inch of rim; have helper apply brakes and check calipers, wheel cylinders, differential valve, tubes, hoses and fittings for leaks. Repair or replace parts as necessary.
	(2) Air in hydraulic system.	(2) Bleed air from system.
	(3) Incorrect or non-recommended brake fluid (fluid boils away at below normal temp.).	(3) Flush hydraulic system with clean brake fluid. Refill with correct-type fluid.
LOW BRAKE PEDAL (pedal goes to floor on first application — o.k. on subsequent applications)	(1) Disc brakeshoe (pad) knock back; shoes push caliper piston back into bore. Caused by loose wheel bearings or excessive lateral runout of rotor (rotor wobble).	(1) Adjust wheel bearings and check lateral runout of rotor(s). Refinish rotors if runout is over limits. Replace rotor if refinishing would cause rotor to fall below minimum thickness limit.
	(2) Calipers sticking on abutment surfaces of caliper and anchor plate. Caused by buildup of dirt, rust, or corrosion on abutment surfaces.	(2) Clean abutment surfaces and lubricate surfaces with molydisulphide grease.
FADING BRAKE PEDAL (pedal falls away under steady pressure)	(1) Leak in hydraulic system.	(1) Fill master cylinder reservoirs to within 1/4-inch of rim; have helper apply brakes, check calipers, wheel cylinders, differential valve, tubes, hoses, and fittings for leaks. Repair or replace parts as necessary.
	(2) Master cylinder piston seals worn, or master cylinder bore is scored, worn or corroded.	(2) Repair or replace master cylinder.

Brake system troubleshooting (part 1 of 6)

Condition	Possible Cause	Correction
DECREASING BRAKE PEDAL TRAVEL (pedal travel required to apply brakes decreases and may be accompanied by hard pedal)	(1) Caliper or wheel cylinder pistons sticking or seized.	(1) Repair or replace calipers, or wheel cylinders.
	(2) Master cylinder compensator ports blocked (preventing fluid return to reservoirs) or pistons sticking or seized in master cylinder bore.	(2) Repair or replace master cylinder.
	(3) Power brake unit binding internally.	(3) Test unit as follows: (a) Shift transmission into neutral and start engine. (b) Increase engine speed to 1500 RPM, close throttle and fully depress brake pedal. (c) Slowly release brake pedal and stop engine. (d) Have helper remove vacuum check valve and hose from power unit. Observe for backward movement of brake pedal. (e) If pedal moves backward, power unit has internal bind — replace power unit.
SPONGY BRAKE PEDAL (pedal has abnormally soft, springy, spongy feel when depressed)	(1) Air in hydraulic system.	(1) Bleed brakes.
	(2) Brakeshoes bent or distorted.	(2) Replace brakeshoes.
	(3) Brake lining not yet seated to drums and rotors.	(3) Burnish brakes.
HARD BRAKE PEDAL (excessive pedal pressure required to stop car. May be accompanied by brake fade)	(1) Loose or leaking power brake unit vacuum hose.	(1) Tighten connections or replace leaking hose.
	(2) Brake lining contaminated by grease or brake fluid.	(2) Determine cause of contamination and correct. Replace contaminated brake lining in axle sets.
	(3) Incorrect or poor quality brake lining.	(3) Replace lining in axle sets.
	(4) Bent, broken, distorted brakeshoes.	(4) Replace brakeshoes and lining.

Brake system troubleshooting (part 2 of 6)

Condition	Possible Cause	Correction
HARD BRAKE PEDAL (continued)	(5) Calipers binding or dragging on anchor plate. Rear brakeshoes dragging on support plate.	(5) Sand or wire brush anchor plate and caliper abutement surfaces and lubricate surfaces lightly. Clean rust or burrs from rear brake support plate ledges and lubricate ledges. NOTE: If ledges are deeply grooved or scored, do not attempt to sand or grind them smooth — replace support plate.
	(6) Rear brake-drum(s) bell mouthed, flared, or barrel shaped (distorted).	(6) Replace rear drum(s).
	(7) Caliper, wheel cylinder, or master cylinder pistons sticking or seized.	(7) Repair or replace parts as necessary.
	(8) Power brake unit vacuum check valve malfunction.	(8) Test valve as follows: (a) Start engine, increase engine speed to 1500 RPM, close throttle and immediately stop engine. (b) Wait at least 90 seconds then try brake action. (c) If brakes are not vacuum assisted for 2 or more applications, check valve is faulty.
	(9) Power brake unit has internal bind.	(9) Test unit as follows: (a) With engine stopped, apply brakes several times to exhaust all vacuum in system. (b) Shift transmission into neutral, depress brake pedal and start engine. (c) If pedal falls away under foot pressure and less pressure is required to hold pedal in applied position, power unit vacuum system is working. Test power unit as outlined in item (3) under Decreasing Brake Pedal Travel. If power unit exhibits bind condition, replace power unit.
	(10) Master cylinder compensator ports (at bottom of reservoirs) blocked by dirt, scale, rust, or have small burrs (blocked ports prevent fluid return to reservoirs).	(10) Repair or replace master cylinder. CAUTION: Do not attempt to clean blocked ports with wire, pencils, or similar implements. Use compressed air only.

Brake system troubleshooting (part 3 of 6)

Condition	Possible Cause	Correction
HARD BRAKE PEDAL (continued)	(11) Brake hoses, tubes, fittings clogged or restricted.	(11) Use compressed air to check or unclog parts. Replace any damaged parts.
	(12) Brake fluid contaminated with improper fluids (motor oil, transmission fluid, or poor quality brake fluid) causing rubber components to swell and stick in bores.	(12) Replace all rubber components and hoses. Flush entire brake system. Refill system.
GRABBING BRAKES (severe reaction to brake pedal pressure)	(1) Brake lining(s) contaminated by grease or brake fluid.	(1) Determine and correct cause of contamination and replace brakeshoes and lining in axle sets.
	(2) Parking brake cables incorrectly adjusted or seized.	(2) Adjust cables. Replace seized cables.
	(3) Power brake unit binding internally.	(3) Test unit.
	(4) Incorrect brake lining or lining loose on brakeshoes.	(4) Replace brakeshoes in axle sets.
	(5) Brakeshoes bent, cracked, distorted.	(5) Replace brakeshoes in axle sets.
	(6) Caliper anchor plate bolts loose.	(6) Tighten bolts.
	(7) Rear brakeshoes binding on support plate ledges.	(7) Clean and lubricate ledges. Replace support plate(s) if ledges are deeply grooved. Do not attempt to smooth ledges by grinding.
	(8) Rear brake support plates loose.	(8) Tighten mounting bolts.
	(9) Caliper or wheel cylinder piston sticking or seized.	(9) Repair or replace parts as necessary.
	(10) Master cylinder pistons sticking or siezed in bore.	(10) Repair or replace master cylinder.
	(11) Master cylinder compensator ports (at bottom of reservoirs) blocked by dirt, scale, rust, or have small burrs (blocked ports prevent fluid return to reservoirs).	(11) Repair or replace master cylinder. CAUTION: Do not attempt to clean blocked ports with wire, pencils, or similar implements. Use compressed air only.
BRAKES GRAB, PULL, OR WON'T HOLD IN WET WEATHER	(1) Brake lining water soaked.	(1) Drive car with brakes lightly applied to dry out lining. If problem persists after lining has dried, replace brakeshoe lining in axle sets.
	(2) Rear brake support plate bent allowing excessive amount of water to enter drum.	(2) Replace support plate.

Brake system troubleshooting (part 4 of 6)

Condition	Possible Cause	Correction
DRAGGING BRAKES (slow or incomplete release of brakes)	(1) Brake pedal binding at pivot.	(1) Free up and lubricate.
	(2) Power brake unit has internal bind.	(2) Inspect for internal bind.
	(3) Parking brake cables incorrectly adjusted or seized.	(3) Adjust cables. Replace seized cables.
	(4) Rear brakeshoe return springs weak or broken.	(4) Replace return springs. Replace brakeshoe if necessary in axle sets.
	(5) Automatic adjusters malfunctioning.	(5) Repair or replace adjuster parts as required.
	(6) Caliper, wheel cylinder or master cylinder pistons sticking or seized.	(6) Repair or replace parts as necessary.
	(7) Master cylinder compensating ports blocked (fluid does not return to reservoirs).	(7) Use compressed air to clear ports. Do not use wire, pencils, or similar objects to open blocked ports.
CAR PULLS TO ONE SIDE WHEN BRAKES ARE APPLIED	(1) Incorrect front tire pressure.	(1) Inflate to recommended cold (reduced load) inflation pressures.
	(2) Incorrect front wheel bearing adjustment or worn — damaged wheel bearings.	(2) Adjust wheel bearings. Replace worn, damaged bearings.
	(3) Brakeshoe lining on one side contaminated.	(3) Determine and correct cause of contamination and replace brakeshoe lining in axle sets.
	(4) Brakeshoes on one side bent, distorted, or lining loose on shoe.	(4) Replace brakeshoes in axle sets.
	(5) Support plate bent or loose on one side.	(5) Tighten or replace support plate.
	(6) Brake lining not yet seated to drums and rotors.	(6) Burnish brakes.
	(7) Caliper anchor plate loose on one side.	(7) Tighten anchor plate bolts.
	(8) Caliper piston sticking or seized.	(8) Repair or replace caliper.
	(9) Brakeshoe linings watersoaked.	(9) Drive car with brakes lightly applied to dry linings.
	(10) Loose suspension component attaching or mounting bolts, incorrect front end alignment. Worn suspension parts.	(10) Tighten suspension bolts. Replace worn suspension components. Check and correct alignment as necessary.
	(11) Corrosion or dirt buildup on abutment (sliding) surfaces or caliper and anchor plate.	(11) Remove caliper and clean abutment (sliding) surfaces using wire brush and crocus cloth and apply light film of molydisulphide grease to abutment surfaces.

Brake system troubleshooting (part 5 of 6)

Condition	Possible Cause	Correction
CHATTER OR SHUDDER WHEN BRAKES ARE APPLIED (pedal pulsation and roughness may also occur)	(1) Front wheel bearings loose.	(1) Adjust wheel bearings.
	(2) Brakeshoes distorted, bent contaminated, or worn.	(2) Replace brakeshoes in axle sets.
	(3) Caliper anchor plate or support plate loose.	(3) Tighten mounting bolts.
	(4) Excessive thickness variation or lateral run out of rotor(s).	(4) Refinish or replace rotors in axle sets.
	(5) Rear drums(s) out of round, or have hard spots.	(5) Refinish or replace drums if out of round. Replace drums with hard spots.
	(6) Strut rods loose or bushings worn.	(6) Tighten jam nuts or replace bushings.
NOISY BRAKES (squealing, clicking, scraping sound when brakes are applied)	(1) Bent, broken, distorted brake-shoes.	(1) Replace brakeshoes in axle sets.
	(2) Brake lining worn out — shoes contacting drum or rotor.	(2) Replace brakeshoes and lining in axle sets. Refinish or replace drums or rotors.
	(3) Broken or loose holdown or return springs.	(3) Replace parts as necessary.
	(4) Rough or dry drum brake support plate ledges.	(4) Lubricate support plate ledges.
	(5) Cracked, grooved, or scored rotor(s) or drum(s).	(5) Replace rotor(s) or drum(s). Replace brakeshoes and lining in axle sets if necessary.
PULSATING BRAKE PEDAL	(1) Out of round drums or excessive thickness variation or lateral runout in disc brake rotor(s).	(1) Refinish or replace drums or rotors.
	(2) Bent rear axle shaft	(2) Replace axle shaft.

Brake system troubleshooting (part 6 of 6)

Condition	Possible Cause	Correction
NOISE IN COLUMN	(1) One click in OFF-Unlock and when steering wheel is moved.	(1) Normal seating of Lock Bolt.
	(2) Column not correctly aligned.	(2) Align column.
	(3) Flexible coupling pulled apart.	(3) Align column and replace flexible coupling.
	(4) Horn contact ring not lubricated.	(4) Lubricate with Lubriplate or equivalent.
	(5) Lack of grease on bearings or bearing surface.	(5) Lubricate with Lubriplate or equivalent.
	(6) Lower shaft bearing tight or frozen.	(6) Replace bearing. Check shaft and replace if scored.
	(7) Upper shaft bearing tight or frozen.	(7) Replace housing assembly.
	(8) Lock plate retaining ring not seated.	(8) Replace retaining ring. Check for proper seating in groove.
	(9) Steering shaft snap ring not seated.	(9) Replace snap ring. Check for proper seating in groove.
	(10) Shroud or housing loose.	(10) Tighten mounting screws.
ONE CLICK WHEN IN OFF-LOCK POSITION AND STEERING WHEEL IS MOVED	(1) Seating of lock bolt.	(1) None — normal — lock bolt seating; click is characteristic.
HIGH STEERING SHAFT EFFORT	(1) Column assembly misaligned in car.	(1) Align correctly.
	(2) Tight or frozen upper or lower bearings.	(2) Replace.
	(3) Binding intermediate shaft U-joint.	(3) Repair or replace intermediate shaft.
HIGH SHIFT EFFORT	(1) Column not aligned correctly in car.	(1) Realign.
	(2) Lower bowl bearing not aligned correctly.	(2) Assemble correctly.
	(3) Lack of grease on seal or bearing areas.	(3) Lubricate
	(4) Improper ignition switch mounting screws.	(4) Install correct screws.
	(5) Shift tube bent or broken.	(5) Replace shift tube.

Steering column troubleshooting

Condition	Possible Cause	Correction
CHIRP NOISE IN STEERING PUMP	(1) Loose belt	(1) Adjust belt tension to specification
BELT SQUEAL (PARTICULARLY NOTICEABLE AT FULL WHEEL TRAVEL AND STAND STILL PARKING)	(1) Loose belt	(1) Adjust belt tension to specification
GROWL NOISE IN STEERING PUMP	(1) Excessive back pressure in hoses or steering gear caused by restriction	(1) Locate restriction and correct. Replace part if necessary
GROWL NOISE IN STEERING PUMP (PARTICULARLY NOTICEABLE AT STAND STILL PARKING)	(1) Scored pressure plates, thrust plate or rotor (2) Extreme wear of cam ring	(1) Replace parts and flush system (2) Replace parts
GROAN NOISE IN STEERING PUMP	(1) Low oil level (2) Air in the oil. Poor pressure hose connection	(1) Fill reservoir to proper level (2) Tighten connector to specified torque. Bleed system by operating steering from right to left - full turn
RATTLE NOISE IN STEERING PUMP	(1) Vanes not installed properly (2) Vanes sticking in rotor slots	(1) Install properly (2) Free up by removing burrs, varnish, or dirt
SWISH NOISE IN STEERING PUMP	(1) Defective flow control valve.	(1) Replace part
WHINE NOISE IN STEERING PUMP	(1) Pump shaft bearing scored	(1) Replace housing and shaft. Flush system
HARD STEERING OR LACK OF ASSIST	(1) Loose pump belt (2) Low oil level in reservoir NOTE: Low oil level will also result in excessive pump noise (3) Steering gear to column misalignment (4) Lower coupling flange rubbing against steering gear adjuster plug (5) Tires not properly inflated	(1) Adjust belt tension to specification (2) Fill to proper level. If excessively low, check all lines and joints for evidence of external leakage. Tighten loose connectors. (3) Align steering column (4) Loosen pinch bolt and assemble properly (5) Inflate to recommended pressure

Power steering pump troubleshooting (part 1 of 2)

Condition	Possible Cause	Correction
	Further possible causes could be:	
	(6) Sticking flow control valve (7) Insufficient pump pressure output (8) Excessive internal pump leakage (9) Excessive internal gear leakage	In order to diagnose conditions such as listed in (6), (7), (8), (9) a pressure test of the entire power steering system is required.
FOAMING MILKY POWER STEERING FLUID, LOW FLUID LEVEL AND POSSIBLE LOW PRESSURE	(1) Air in the fluid, and loss of fluid due to internal pump leakage causing overflow	(1) Check for leaks and correct. Bleed system. Extremely cold temperatures will cause system aeration should the oil level be low. If oil level is correct and pump still foams, remove pump from vehicle and separate reservoir from body. Check welsh plug and body for cracks. If plug is loose or body is cracked, replace body.
LOW PUMP PRESSURE	(1) Flow control valve stuck or inoperative.	(1) Remove burrs or dirt or replace. Flush system.
	(2) Pressure plate not flat against cam ring	(2) Correct.
MOMENTARY INCREASE IN EFFORT WHEN TURNING WHEEL FAST TO RIGHT OR LEFT	(1) Low oil level in pump.	(1) Add power steering fluid as required.
	(2) Pump belt slipping	(2) Tighten or replace belt.
	(3) High internal leakage	(3) Check pump pressure.
STEERING WHEEL SURGES OR JERKS WHEN TURNING WITH ENGINE RUNNING ESPECIALLY DURING PARKING	(1) Low oil level	(1) Fill as required.
	(2) Loose pump belt	(2) Adjust tension to specification.
	(3) Steering linkage hitting engine oil pan at full turn	(3) Correct clearance.
	(4) Insufficient pump pressure	(4) Check pump pressure.
	(5) Sticking flow control valve	(5) Inspect for varnish or damage, replace if necessary.
EXCESSIVE WHEEL KICKBACK OR LOOSE STEERING	(1) Air in system	(1) Add oil to pump reservoir and bleed by operating steering. Check hose connectors.

Power steering pump troubleshooting (part 2 of 2)

Condition	Possible Source	Action
WANDER — vehicle wander is a condition where the car wanders back and forth on the roadway when it is driven straight ahead while the steering wheel is held in a firm position. Evaluation should be conducted on a level road (little road crown).	• Loose tie rod ends. • Inner ball housing loose or worn. • Gear Assembly loose on body bracket. • Excessive yoke clearance. • Loose suspension struts or ball joints. • Loose front hub. • Column intermediate shaft connecting bolts loose. • Column intermediate shaft universal joints loose or worn. • Improper toe setting.	Replace tie rod end assemblies. Replace tie rod end assemblies. Tighten mounting bolts. Adjust yoke clearance. Adjust or replace as required. Check and replace nut if loose or improperly staked — do not reuse nut. Tighten bolts. Replace intermediate shaft. Set toe to specification.
FEEDBACK — (rattle, chuckle, knocking noises in the steering gear). Feedback is a condition where roughness is felt in the steering wheel by the driver when the car is driven over rough pavement.	• Column U-joints loose. • Loose tie rod ends. • Loose/worn tie rod ball. • Gear assembly loose on body bracket. • Loose pinion bearing cap. • Loose yoke plug/locknut. • Loose pinion bearing locknut. • Piston disengaged or loose on rack. • Oversized pinion shaft bushing. • Steering gear yoke worn. • Column support bracket loose. • Column intermediate shaft connecting bolts loose. • Loose suspension struts on ball joints. • Loose front hub.	Replace if bad. Replace tie rod end assemblies. Replace tie rod assemblies. Tighten mounting bolts. Tighten. Adjust yoke preload to specification. Tighten locknut. Replace rack assembly. Replace gear housing. Replace yoke assembly. Tighten bolts. Tighten bolts. Adjust or replace as necessary. Check and replace nut if loose or improperly staked—do not reuse nut.

Power rack & pinion steering gear troubleshooting (part 1 of 2)

Condition	Possible Source	Action
POOR RETURNABILITY — Sticky Feel — Poor returnability is noticed when the steering fails to return to center following a turn without manual effort from the driver. In addition, when the driver returns the steering to center it may have a sticky or catchy feel.	• Misaligned steering column or column flange rubbing steering wheel and/or flange.	Align column.
	• Check rotational torque of U-joints.	If binding, replace intermediate shaft.
	• Yoke plug too tight.	Adjust yoke preload to specification.
	• Tight ball joints.	Replace as required.
	• Tight tie rod end ball joints.	Replace tie rod end assemblies.
	• Undersized pinion shaft bushing in the housing.	Replace gear housing assemblies.
	• Binding in valve assembly.	Replace input shaft of valve assembly.
	• Bent or damaged rack.	Replace rack assembly.
	• Column bearing binding.	Replace bearing.
	• Tight suspension struts or ball joints.	Adjust or replace as required.
	• Front end lube required.	Lube front end.
	• Improper toe setting.	Set toe to specification.
	• Contamination in system.	Flush Power Steering system.
HEAVY STEERING EFFORTS (Poor or loss of assist) — A heavy effort and poor assist condition is recognized by the driver while turning corners and especially while parking. A road test will verify this condition.	• Leakage/loss of fluid.	
	• Valve plastic ring cut or twisted.	Replace ring.
	• Damaged/worn plastic piston ring.	Replace ring.
	• Loose/missing rubber backup piston O-ring.	Replace/install O-ring.
	• Loose rack piston.	Replace rack assembly.
	• Gear assembly oil passages restricted.	Clear/service as required.
	• Bent/damaged rack assembly.	Replace rack assembly.
	• Valve assembly internal leakage.	Replace valve assembly.
	• Low pump fluid.	Fill as necessary.
	• Pump external leakage.	
	• Improper drive belt tension.	Readjust belt tension.
	• Improper engine idle speed.	Readjust idle.
	• Pully loose or warped.	Replace pulley.
	• Pump/flow pressure not to specification.	
	• Hose/cooler line restrictions or leakage.	Clear or replace as required.

Power rack & pinion steering gear troubleshooting (part 2 of 2)

Condition	Possible Cause	Correction
HISSING NOISE IN STEERING GEAR	(1) There is some noise in all power steering systems. One of the most common is a hissing sound most evident at standstill parking. There is no relationship between this noise and performance of the steering. Hiss may be expected when steering wheel is at end of travel or when slowly turning at standstill.	(1) Slight hiss is normal and in no way affects steering. Do not replace valve unless hiss is extremely objectionable. A replacement valve will also exhibit slight noise and is not always a cure. Investigate clearance around flexible coupling rivets. Be sure steering shaft and gear are aligned so flexible coupling rotates in a flat plane and is not distorted as shaft rotates. Any metal-to-metal contacts through flexible coupling will transmit valve hiss into passenger compartment through the steering column.
RATTLE OR CHUCKLE NOISE IN STEERING GEAR	(1) Gear loose on frame.	(1) Check gear-to-frame mounting screws.
	(2) Steering linkage looseness.	(2) Check linkage pivot points for wear. Replace if necessary.
	(3) Pressure hose touching other parts of car.	(3) Adjust hose position. Do not bend tubing by hand.
	(4) Loose pitman shaft over center adjustment. **NOTE:** A slight rattle may occur on turns because of increased clearance off the "high point." This is normal and clearance must not be reduced below specified limits to eliminate this slight rattle.	(4) Adjust to specifications.
	(5) Loose pitman arm.	(5) Tighten pitman arm nut to specifications.
SQUAWK NOISE IN STEERING GEAR WHEN TURNING OR RECOVERING FROM A TURN	(1) Damper O-ring on valve spool cut.	(1) Replace damper O-ring.
POOR RETURN OF STEERING WHEEL TO CENTER	(1) Tires not properly inflated.	(1) Inflate to specified pressure.
	(2) Lack of lubrication in linkage and ball joints.	(2) Lube linkage and ball joints.
	(3) Lower coupling flange rubbing against steering gear adjuster plug.	(3) Loosen pinch bolt and assemble properly.
	(4) Steering gear to column misalignment.	(4) Align steering column.

Power steering gear troubleshooting exc. rack & pinion (part 1 of 3)

Condition	Possible Cause	Correction
POOR RETURN OF STEERING WHEEL TO CENTER (Continued)	(5) Improper front wheel alignment.	(5) Check and adjust as necessary. With front wheels still on alignment pads of front-end machine, disconnect pitman arm of linkage from pitman shaft of gear. Turn front wheels by hand. If wheels will not turn or turn with considerable effort, determine if linkage or ball joints are binding.
	(6) Steering linkage binding.	(6) Replace pivots.
	(7) Ball joints binding.	(7) Replace ball joints.
	(8) Steering wheel rubbing against housing.	(8) Align housing.
	(9) Tight or frozen steering shaft bearings.	(9) Replace bearings.
	(10) Sticking or plugged valve spool.	(10) Remove and clean or replace valve.
	(11) Steering gear adjustments over specifications.	(11) Check adjustment with gear out of car. Adjust as required.
CAR LEADS TO ONE SIDE OR THE OTHER (KEEP IN MIND ROAD CONDITION AND WIND. TEST CAR IN BOTH DIRECTIONS ON FLAT ROAD)	(1) Front end misaligned.	(1) Adjust to specifications.
	(2) Unbalanced steering gear valve. **NOTE:** If this is cause, steering effort will be very light in direction of lead and normal or heavier in opposite direction.	(2) Replace valve.
MOMENTARY INCREASE IN EFFORT WHEN TURNING WHEEL FAST TO RIGHT OR LEFT	(1) Low oil level.	(1) Add power steering fluid as required.
	(2) Pump belt slipping.	(2) Tighten or replace belt.
	(3) High internal leakage.	(3) Check pump pressure.
STEERING WHEEL SURGES OR JERKS WHEN TURNING WITH ENGINE RUNNING ESPECIALLY DURING PARKING	(1) Low oil level.	(1) Fill as required.
	(2) Loose pump belt.	(2) Adjust tension to specification.
	(3) Steering linkage hitting engine oil pan at full turn.	(3) Correct clearance.
	(4) Insufficient pump pressure.	(4) Check pump pressure.

Power steering gear troubleshooting exc. rack & pinion (part 2 of 3)

Condition	Possible Cause	Correction
	(5) Pump flow control valve sticking	(5) Inspect for varnish or damage, replace if necessary.
EXCESSIVE WHEEL KICKBACK OR LOOSE STEERING	(1) Air in system.	(1) Add oil to pump reservoir and bleed by operating steering. Check hose connectors for proper torque and adjust as required.
	(2) Steering gear loose on frame.	(2) Tighten attaching screws to specified torque.
	(3) Steering gear flexible coupling loose on shaft or rubber disc mounting screws loose.	(3) Tighten flange pinch bolts.
	(4) Steering linkage joints worn enough to be loose.	(4) Replace loose pivots.
	(5) Front wheel bearings incorrectly adjusted or worn.	(5) Adjust bearings or replace with new parts as necessary.
	(6) Worn poppet valve.	(6) Replace poppet valve.
	(7) Loose thrust bearing preload adjustment.	(7) Adjust to specification with gear out of vehicle.
	(8) Excessive overcenter lash.	(8) Adjust to specification with gear out of car.
HARD STEERING OR LACK OF ASSIST	(1) Loose pump belt.	(1) Adjust belt tension to specification.
	(2) Low oil level. **NOTE:** Low oil level will also result in excessive pump noise.	(2) Fill to proper level. If excessively low, check all lines and joints for evidence of external leakage. Tighten loose connectors.
	(3) Steering gear to column misalignment.	(3) Align steering column.
NOTE: IF CHECKS (1) THROUGH (5) DO NOT REVEAL CAUSE OF HARD STEERING, REFER TO PRESSURE TEST	(4) Lower coupling flange rubbing against steering gear adjuster plug.	(4) Loosen pinch bolt and assemble properly.
	(5) Tires not properly inflated.	(5) Inflate to recommended pressure.
	Further possible causes could be:	
	(6) Sticky flow control valve.	In order to diagnose conditions such as listed in (6), (7), (8), (9) a test of the entire power steering system is required.
	(7) Insufficient pump pressure output.	
	(8) Excessive internal pump leakage.	
	(9) Excessive internal gear leakage.	

Power steering gear troubleshooting exc. rack & pinion (part 3 of 3)

Condition	Possible Cause	Correction
TURN SIGNAL WILL NOT CANCEL	(1) Loose switch mounting screws.	(1) Tighten
	(2) Switch or anchor bosses broken.	(2) Replace switch.
	(3) Broken, missing or out of position detent, return or canceling spring.	(3) Reposition or replace springs as required.
TURN SIGNAL DIFFICULT TO OPERATE	(1) Turn signal lever is loose.	(1) Tighten mounting screw
	(2) Cancelling cam or switch broken or distorted.	(2) Replace cam or switch.
	(3) Loose or misplaced switch springs.	(3) Reposition or replace springs.
	(4) Foreign material in switch.	(4) Remove foreign material and clean switch.
	(5) Switch mounted loosely.	(5) Tighten mounting screws
TURN SIGNAL WILL NOT INDICATE LANE CHANGE	(1) Broken lane change pressure pad or spring hanger.	(1) Replace switch.
	(2) Broken, missing, or misplaced lane change spring.	(2) Replace or reposition as required.
	(3) Jammed wires.	(3) Loosen mounting screws, reposition base or wires and retighten screws
TURN SIGNAL WILL NOT STAY IN TURN POSITION	(1) Foreign material or loose parts impeding movement of yoke.	(1) Remove foreign material. Tighten loose parts.
	(2) Worn or cracked switch.	(2) Replace switch.
HAZARD SWITCH CANNOT BE PULLED OUT	(1) Foreign material between support and canceling leg and yoke.	(1) Remove foreign material. If no foreign material is impeding function of hazard switch, replace turn signal switch.
NO TURN SIGNAL LIGHTS	(1) Inoperative turn signal flasher.	(1) Replace turn signal flasher.
	(2) Defective or blown fuse.	(2) Replace fuse.
	(3) Inoperative signal switch.	(3) Replace signal switch. Disconnect column-to-chassis connector. Connect new switch to chassis and operate switch by hand. If lights now operate normally, signal switch is inoperative.

Turn signal switch troubleshooting (part 1 of 3)

Condition	Possible Cause	Correction
NO TURN SIGNAL LIGHTS (Continued)	(4) Loose chassis-to-column connector.	(4) Connect securely.
	(5) If lights do not operate, check chassis wiring for opens, grounds, etc.	(5) Repair chassis wiring as required.
TURN INDICATOR LIGHTS ON, BUT NOT FLASHING	(1) Front or rear bulb burned out.	(1) Replace bulb.
	(2) If vehicle lights do not operate, check light sockets for high resistance connections, the chassis wiring for opens, grounds, etc.	(2) Repair chassis wiring as required.
	(3) Inoperative flasher.	(3) Replace flasher.
	(4) Loose chassis-to-column connection.	(4) Connect securely.
	(5) Inoperative turn signal switch.	(5) Replace turn signal switch. To determine if turn signal switch is defective, substitute new switch into circuit and operate switch by hand. If the vehicle lights operate normally, signal switch is inoperative.
STOP LIGHT NOT ON WHEN TURN INDICATED	(1) Loose column-to-chassis connection.	(1) Connect securely.
	(2) Inoperative signal switch or brake light switch.	(2) Replace signal switch. Disconnect column-to-chassis connector. Connect new switch into system without removing old. Operate switch by hand. If brake lights work with switch in the turn position, signal switch is defective.
	(3) If brake lights do not work check connector to stop light sockets for grounds, opens, etc.	(3) Repair connector to stoplight circuits.

Turn signal switch troubleshooting (part 2 of 3)

Condition	Possible Cause	Correction
TURN INDICATOR PANEL LIGHTS NOT FLASHING	(1) Burned out bulbs. (2) High resistance to ground at bulb socket. (3) Opens, grounds in wiring harness.	(1) Replace bulbs. (2) Replace socket. (3) Locate and repair as required.
TURN SIGNAL LIGHTS FLASH VERY SLOWLY	(1) High resistance ground at light sockets. (2) Incorrect capacity turn signal flasher. (3) Ground in chassis wiring. (4) Loose chassis-to-column connection. (5) Inoperative signal switch.	(1) Repair high resistance grounds at light sockets. (2) Replace turn signal flasher. (3) Locate and repair as required. If the flashing rate is still extremely slow, check chassis wiring harness from the connector to light sockets for grounds, high resistance points, etc. (4) Connect securely. (5) Replace signal switch. Disconnect column-to-chassis connector. Connect new switch into system without removing old. Operate switch by hand. If flashing occurs at normal rate, the signal switch is defective.
HAZARD SIGNAL LIGHTS WILL NOT FLASH — TURN SIGNAL FUNCTIONS NORMALLY	(1) Blown fuse. (2) Inoperative hazard warning flasher. (3) Loose chassis-to-column connection. (4) Inoperative turn signal switch. (5) Harness connector open.	(1) Replace fuse. (2) Replace hazard warning flasher. (3) Connect securely. (4) Replace the turn signal switch. Disconnect column-to-chassis connector. Connect new switch into system without removing old. Depress the hazard warning button and observe the hazard warning lights. If they now work normally, the turn signal switch is defective. (5) Replace harness connector.

Turn signal switch troubleshooting (part 3 of 3)

CONDITION	POSSIBLE CAUSE	ACTION
Headlamps		
• All exterior lamps do not light	• Loose wiring connections.	• Check and secure connection at headlamps switch and dash panel connector.
	• Open wiring.	• Check power to and from headlamp switch. Check ground at bulbs. Service as necessary.
	• Bad ground.	
	• Damaged headlamp switch.	• Replace headlamp switch.
• One headlamp does not work	• Loose connection.	• Secure connection at headlamp.
	• Bad ground.	• Check ground at headlamp.
	• Bulb burnt out.	• Replace sealed beam.
	• Corroded or damaged connector.	• Replace as required.
• Both low beam or both high beam headlamps do not work	• Loose connections.	• Check and secure connections at dimmer switch and headlamp switch.
	• Damaged dimmer switch.	• Check dimmer switch operation. Replace if necessary.
	• Open wiring.	• Service as necessary.
• All headlamps out. Park and tail lamps OK	• Loose connections.	• Check and secure connections at dimmer switch and headlamp switch.
	• Damaged dimmer switch.	• Check dimmer switch operation. Replace if necessary.
	• Damaged headlamp switch.	• Replace if necessary.
	• Open wiring or poor ground.	• Service as necessary.
Taillamps		
• One taillamp out	• Bulb burnt out.	• Replace bulb.
	• Open wiring or poor ground.	• Service as necessary.
	• Corroded bulb socket.	• Service or replace socket.
• All taillamps, park lamps, and instrument panel lamps out — headlamps OK	• Blown fuse in fuse panel.	• Service as necessary.
	• Loose connections.	• Secure wiring connections where accessible.
	• Open wiring or poor ground.	• Service as necessary.
	• Damaged headlamp switch.	• Service headlamps switch.
Back-Up Lamps		
• Back-Up lamps — one does not function	• Check fuse in fuse panel.	• Replace fuse.
	• Bulb burnt out.	• Replace bulb.
	• Loose connection.	• Tighten connectors.
	• Open wiring.	• Service as necessary.

Exterior light troubleshooting (part 1 of 2)

CONDITION	POSSIBLE SOURCE	ACTION
Stoplamps		
• Stoplamps do not light.	• Fuse burnt out.	• Replace fuse. If fuse blows again, check for short circuit.
	• Problem in turn signal circuit.	• Service turn signal circuit or replace turn signal.
	• Loose connections.	• Secure connections at stoplamp switch.
	• Damaged stoplamp switch.	• Replace stoplamp switch.
	• Open wiring.	• Service as required.
Turn Signal Lamps		
• Turn signal lamps — one or more inoperative.	• Bulb burnt out.	• Replace bulb.
	• Loose connections.	• Secure connections.
	• Open wiring or poor ground:	• Service as required.
	• Damaged turn signal switch.	• Replace turn signal switch.
• Turn signal lamps — all lights inoperative.	• Fuse burnt out.	• Replace fuse. If fuse blows again, check for short circuit.
	• Damaged turn signal flasher.	• Substitute a known good flasher.
	• Loose connections.	• Tighten connections.
	• Open wiring or poor grounds.	• Service as required.
	• Damaged turn signal switch.	• Replace turn signal switch.
Hazard Flasher Lamps		
• Hazard flasher lamps — do not flash.	• Damaged turn signal operation.	• Service turn signal system.
	• Fuse burnt out.	• Replace fuse. If fuse blows again, check for short circuit.
	• Damaged hazard flasher.	• Substitute a known good flasher.
	• Open wiring.	• Service as required.
	• Damaged hazard flasher switch.	• Service or replace the turn signal switch assembly which includes the hazard flasher switch.
Cornering Lamps		
• Cornering lamps — both lamps will not operate. Turn signals OK.	• Switch inoperative.	• Replace T/S switch.
	• Fuse burnt out.	• Replace fuse. If fuse blows again, check for short circuit.
	• Loose connections.	• Tighten connectors.
	• Open wiring or poor ground.	• Service as necessary.
• Cornering lamps — one lamp will not operate. Turn signals OK.	• Bulb burnt out.	• Replace bulb.
	• Loose connection.	• Tighten connectors.
	• Open wiring or poor ground.	• Service as necessary.
	• Switch inoperative.	• Replace T/S switch.
	• Cornering lamp relay damaged or worn.	• Replace relay.

Exterior light troubleshooting (part 2 of 2)

Note: Replace burned out bulbs or fuses before proceeding.

CONDITION	POSSIBLE SOURCE	ACTION
Headlamps do not work. Park and tail lamps OK.	• Open or shorted wiring. • Poor ground connections. • Damaged dimmer switch. • Damaged headlamp switch.	• Check wiring and connections between headlamp switch and lamps. Service as necessary. • Check and service as necessary. • Check dimmer switch, replace if necessary. • Check headlamp switch, replace if necessary.
All exterior lamps do not work.	• Open or shorted wiring. • Damaged headlamp switch.	• Check wiring and connections between power source and headlamp switch and between headlamp switch and dash panel connector. • Check headlamp switch, replace if necessary.
Headlamps flash On and Off.	• Shorted circuit. • Damaged headlamp switch.	• Check wiring and connections between headlamp switch and headlamps. • Replace headlamp switch.
All exterior lamps do not work. Headlamps OK.	• Blown fuse. • Open wiring or poor ground. • Damaged headlamp switch.	• Replace fuse. • Check wiring and connections between headlamp switch and lamps. Service as necessary. • Check headlamp switch, replace if necessary.
Instrument panel lamps do not work, or will not dim.	• Blown fuse. • Open or shorted wiring. • Damaged headlamp switch.	• Replace fuse. • Check wiring between headlamp switch and lamps. • Check headlamp switch, replace as necessary.
Dome lamps will not work.	• Blown fuse. • Open or shorted wiring. • Damaged headlamp switch.	• Replace fuse. • Check wiring and connections between headlamp switch and dome lamp and between headlamp switch and fuse panel. • Check headlamp switch, replace if necessary.

Headlight switch troubleshooting

NOTES

GENERAL MAINTENANCE

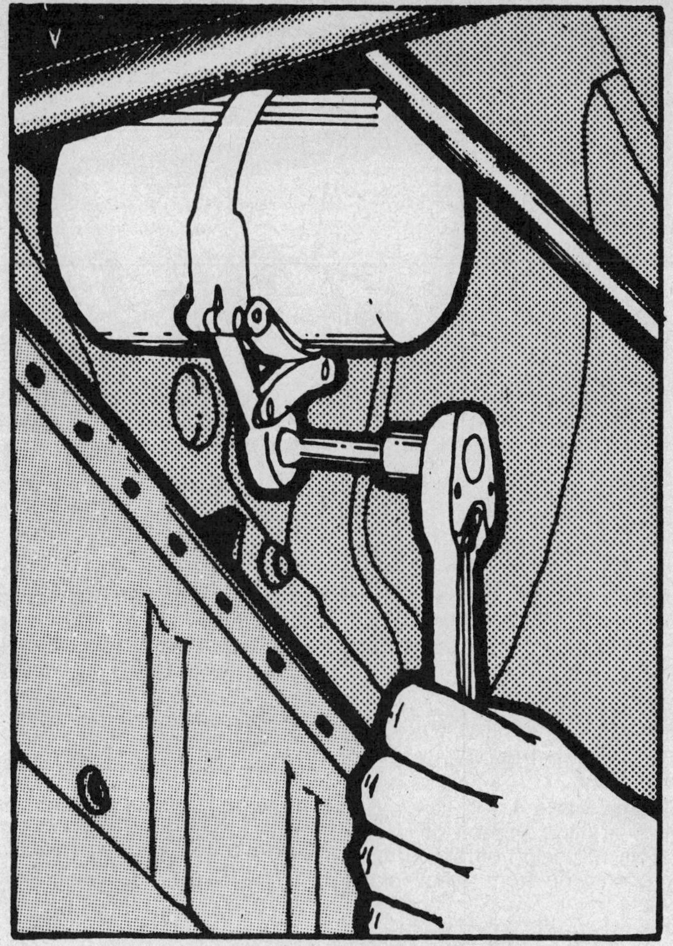

Fig. 1 Oil filter removal (typical)

LUBRICATION & OIL CHANGE

ENGINE OIL & FILTER CHANGE

NOTE: Engine oil and filter should be changed at intervals recommended by the vehicle manufacturer.

1. Operate engine and allow to reach operating temperature, then turn ignition off.
2. Place drain pan under engine oil pan, then using a suitable wrench remove drain plug.
3. Allow engine oil to thoroughly drain into pan, then replace drain plug.

NOTE: Do not overtighten drain plug, as this can strip the threads in oil pan.

4. If oil filter is to be replaced, position drain pan under filter, then install oil filter wrench and remove filter by turning counterclockwise, **Fig. 1.**

NOTE: Ensure old oil filter gasket is not on the filter adapter on the engine. Clean adapter before installing new filter.

5. Coat new oil filter gasket with engine oil, then position filter on adapter, **Fig. 2.** Hand tighten filter until gasket contacts adapter face, then tighten filter one additional turn. Wipe filter and adapter with a clean cloth.

NOTE: Ensure gasket is in position on filter before tightening. Do not use oil filter wrench to tighten filter. Hand tighten only.

Fig. 2 Oil filter installation (typical)

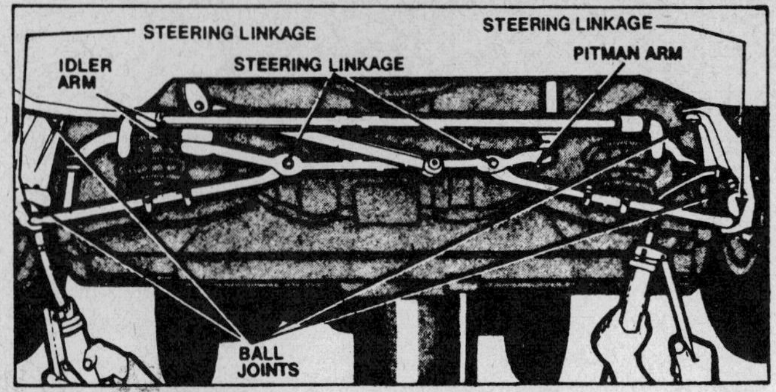

Fig. 3 Typical fitting locations

6. Remove oil filter cap and add quantity of oil specified by manufacturer, then install filler cap.

NOTE: Only add oil which meets the vehicle manufacturer's specifications.

7. Start engine and check to ensure oil filter and drain plug are not leaking, then turn ignition off.
8. Check oil level to ensure crankcase is full but not overfilled. Add oil as necessary.

NOTE: Do not bring oil level above "Full" mark on dipstick. Overfilling could result in damage to engine gaskets or seals causing leaks.

EGR VALVE, CHECK

1. Start engine and allow to warm up.
2. With engine at curb idle speed, disconnect vacuum hose from EGR valve and plug hose to prevent vacuum leak.
3. Attach hand vacuum pump to EGR valve fitting.
4. Operate pump to apply at least 4 inches of vacuum to valve.
5. Observe that engine begins to misfire and run roughly. If there is no change in engine performance, EGR valve is defective or gas passages are clogged with exhaust deposits.
6. Disconnect vacuum hose from valve.
7. Remove the two bolts holding valve to manifold or spacer, and remove valve.
8. Clean old gasket off mating surface with scraper and wire brush.
9. Inspect and clean out gas passages in manifold or spacer with wire gun-bore brush or small round wire brush.
10. Exhaust deposits can be removed from EGR valve with wire brush or by tapping side of valve with soft mallet.
11. Ensure valve stem and diaphragm can move freely by pushing on diaphragm.
12. Check diaphragm for leakage by applying vacuum with hand vacuum pump.
13. Install new valve or reinstall old valve with new gasket and tighten bolts.
14. Reconnect vacuum hose and check operation. With engine warmed up, valve should be seen or felt to operate when throttle opening is increased beyond idle.

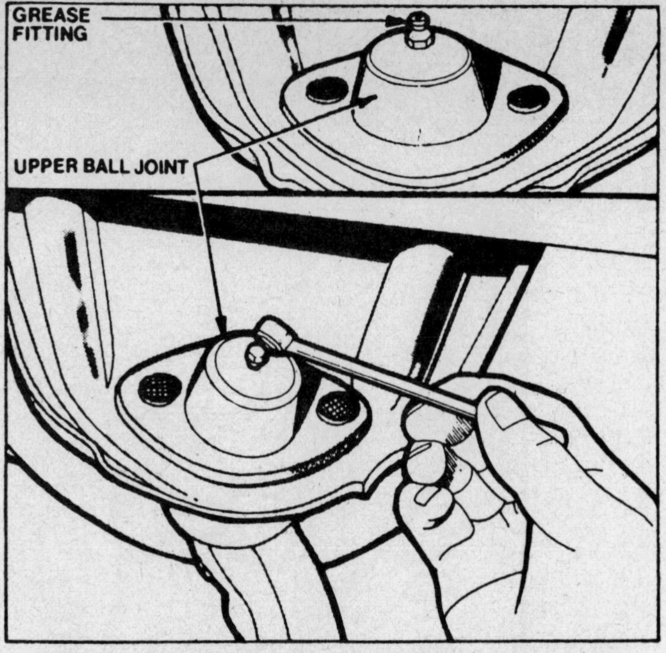

Fig. 4 Identifying grease fittings (typical). If vehicle is equipped with plugs, the plugs must be removed and a grease fitting installed prior to lubricating

CHASSIS LUBRICATING

The first time you perform a grease job, you will spend much of the time looking for the fittings, **Figs. 3 and 4.**

As you find a fitting, wipe it off with a clean rag. This will help you spot it later and also prevent you from injecting dirt with the grease.

The injection tip of the grease gun should be a catch fit on the fitting nipple. That is, once in place it will not slip off. Slight, straight-on pressure is all that is necessary for the gun tip to engage the fitting. Once that is done, pump the handle. To ensure proper lubrication and to prevent damage to the seals, pump slowly until rubber boot or seal can be felt or seen to swell slightly.

NOTE: If the fitting fails to take grease, the lubricant will ooze out between fitting and top of the gun. Do not just keep pumping, hoping some grease is getting in, or you will have a mess. It is normal for a bit of grease to seep out. However, if the fitting is obviously not taking grease, it should be replaced.

REPACKING FRONT WHEEL BEARINGS

1. Remove inner and outer bearings as outlined in car chapters.
2. Clean old lubricant from hub and spindle.
3. Clean inner and outer bearings and bearing races with kerosene.

NOTE: Ensure all old lubricant is removed before repacking. Allow bearings and races to dry thoroughly. Do not use compressed air to clean bearings.

4. Inspect cones, rollers and races for cracks, nicks and wear, and replace as necessary

NOTE: Bearings and race must be replaced as a unit.

5. Place a small amount of wheel bearing grease in palm of hand, then force grease into large end of roller cage until grease protrudes from small end.

NOTE: Use only wheel bearing grease which meets the vehicle manufacturer's specifications.

6. Lubricate remaining bearings in the same manner, then install and adjust bearings as outlined in truck chapter.

NOTE: Apply a light film of grease to lips of grease retainer before installing.

CHECKING & MAINTAINING FLUID LEVELS

NOTE: When checking fluid levels, ensure vehicle is on a level surface. If vehicle is not level, an accurate fluid level reading cannot be obtained.

ENGINE OIL LEVEL

1. Warm up engine, then turn ignition off and allow a few minutes for oil to return to crankcase.
2. Remove dipstick and wipe off.
3. Replace dipstick and ensure it is seated in tube.
4. Remove dipstick and inspect to see if oil level is between "Add" and "Full" marks.

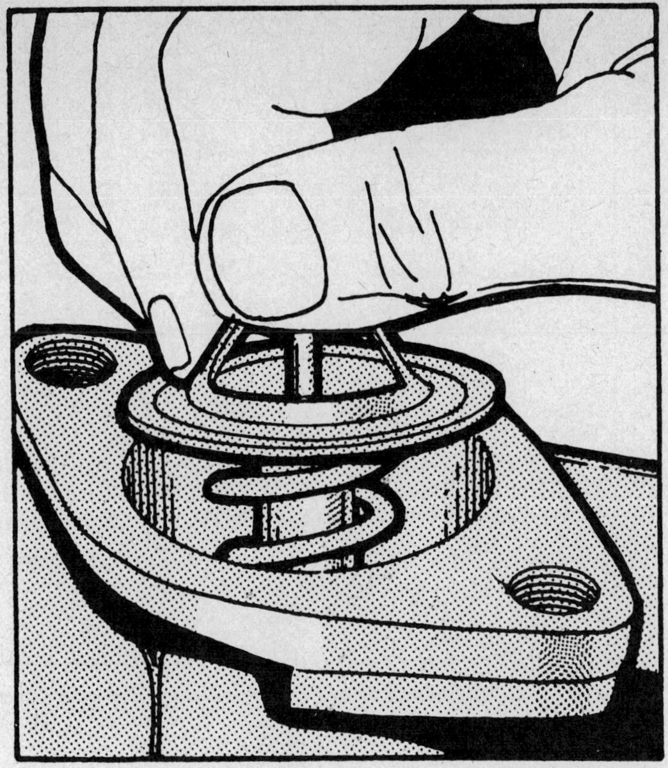

Fig. 5 Replacing thermostat (typical)

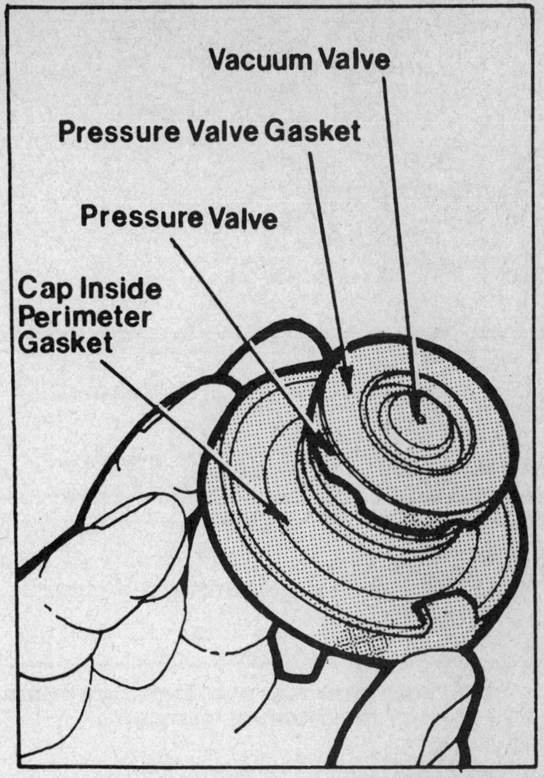

Fig. 6 Radiator cap (typical)

NOTE: Add oil only if level is at or below "Add" mark.

5. If oil level is at "Add" mark, one quart of oil will bring level to "Full" mark. If oil level is below "Add" mark, add sufficent amount of oil to bring level between "Add" & "Full" marks.

NOTE: Do not bring oil level above "Full" mark, as overfilling of crankcase could result in damage to engine gaskets and seals and cause leaks. Only add oil meeting the vehicle manufacturer's specifications.

6. Replace dipstick.

BATTERY

1. Remove filler cap and check fluid level in each cell.

NOTE: Keep flame and sparks away from top of battery as combustible gases present may explode. Do not allow battery electrolyte to contact skin, eyes, fabric or painted surfaces. Flush contacted area with water immediately and thoroughly and seek medical attention if necessary. Wear eye protection when working on or near battery. Do not wear rings or other metal jewelry when working on or near battery.

2. Add water as required to bring fluid level of each cell up to split ring located at bottom of filler well.

NOTE: In areas where water is known to be hard or have a high mineral or alkali content, distilled water must be used. If water is added during freezing temperatures, the vehicle should be driven several miles afterwards to mix the water and battery electrolyte.

3. Install filler caps.

COOLING SYSTEM

NOTE: Add only permanent type antifreeze which meets the vehicle manufacturer's specifications.

CAUTION: Never add large quantities of water into radiator if vehicle has overheated before engine has cooled off. If necessary to service at this time, start engine and add water to coolant slowly. this will avoid damage to the engine.

Less Coolant Recovery System

NOTE: Avoid checking coolant level if engine is hot. If coolant level must be checked when engine is hot, muffle radiator cap with a thick cloth, then turn cap counterclockwise until pressure starts to escape. After pressure has been completely relieved, finish removing cap.

1. With engine cold, remove radiator cap and inspect coolant level.
2. Coolant level should be approximately 1 inch below bottom of filler neck.
3. Add solution of 50% water–50% antifreeze as required.
4. Install radiator cap.

With Coolant Recovery System

NOTE: On these type systems, do not remove radiator cap to check coolant level.

1. Start engine and allow to reach operating temperature.
2. Visually inspect coolant level in plastic reservoir.
3. On all models except Chrysler Corp. vehicles, coolant level should be between "Full" and "Add" marks or at "Full Hot" mark, depending on reservoir. On Chrysler Corp. vehicles, coolant level should be between the one and two quart marks with engine operating at idle speed.
4. Remove reservoir filler cap and add solution of 50% water–50% antifreeze as required.
5. Install reservoir filler cap.

BRAKE MASTER CYLINDER RESERVOIR

1. Clean master cylinder reservoir cover, then using a screwdriver, unsnap retainer(s) and remove cover.

NOTE: Do not hold cover over vehicle, as brake fluid may damage finish.

2. Brake fluid level should be ¼ inch from top of master cylinder reservoir.

NOTE: If brake fluid level is excessively low, the brake linings should be inspected for wear and brake system checked for leaks. Fluid level in reservoirs servicing

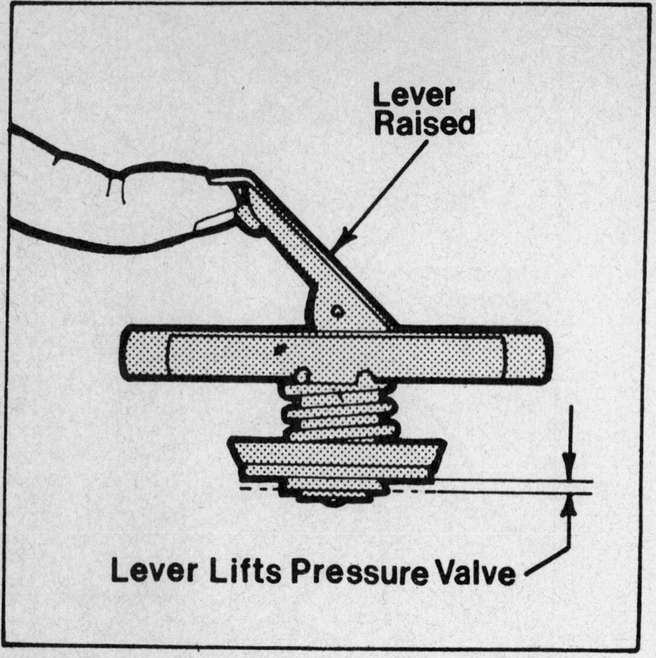

Fig. 7 Radiator cap with pressure release mechanism (typical)

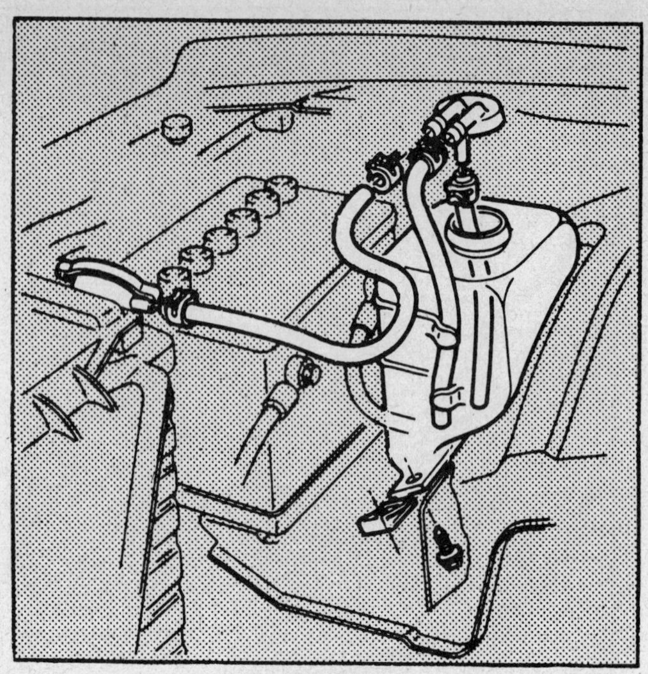

Fig. 8 Factory installed coolant recovery system (typical)

disc brakes will decrease as disc brake pads wear.

3. Add brake fluid as required.

NOTE: Only add brake fluid which meets the vehicle manufacturer's specifications. Use only brake fluid which has been in a tightly closed container to prevent contamination from dirt and moisture. Do not allow petroleum base fluids to contaminate brake fluid, as seal damage may result.

4. Install cover and snap retainer into place.

NOTE: Ensure retainer is locked into cover grooves.

POWER STEERING PUMP RESERVOIR

1. Start engine and allow to reach operating temperature, then turn ignition off.
2. Clean area around filler cap or dipstick, then remove filler cap or dipstick and inspect fluid level.
3. Fluid level should be between "Full" mark and end of dipstick.

NOTE: On models without dipstick, fluid level should be half way up filler neck.

4. Add fluid as necessary, then install filler cap or dipstick.

NOTE: Only add fluid recommended by the vehicle manufacturer.

AUTOMATIC TRANSMISSION

1. Firmly apply parking brake, then start and run engine for approximately 10 minutes to bring transmission fluid to operating temperature.

NOTE: Do not run engine in unventilated area. Exhaust gases contain carbon monoxide which could be deadly in unventilated areas.

2. With engine running at idle speed, shift selector through all positions, then place lever in Neutral or Park as recommended by owner's manual.
3. Clean dipstick cap, then remove dipstick and wipe off.
4. Replace dipstick and ensure it is seated in tube.
5. Remove dipstick and inspect to see if fluid level is between "Add" and "Full" marks.

NOTE: Add fluid only if level is at or below "Add" mark.

6. If fluid level is at "Add" mark, one pint of transmission fluid will bring level to "Full" mark. If fluid level is below "Add" mark, add sufficient amount of fluid to bring level between "Add" and "Full" marks. Transmission fluid is added through the dipstick tube.

NOTE: Do not bring level above "Full" mark, as overfilling could result in damage to transmission. Only add automatic transmission fluid of type and specification recommended by the vehicle manufacturer.

7. Replace dipstick and ensure it is seated in tube.

MANUAL TRANSMISSION

1. Set parking brake and block wheels.
2. Clean area around filler plug, then using a suitable wrench or ratchet, remove filler plug.
3. Fluid should be level with bottom of filler plug hole.
4. Add fluid as required, then install filler plug.

NOTE: Only add lubricant recommended by the vehicle manufacturer.

REAR AXLE

1. Set parking brake and block wheels.
2. Clean area around filler plug, then using a suitable ratchet, remove filler plug.
3. Fluid level should be approximately ½ inch below bottom of filler plug hole.
4. Add fluid as required, then install filler plug.

NOTE: Only add lubricant recommended by vehicle manufacturer.

COOLING SYSTEM SERVICE

CAUTION: Do not attempt to perform any system servicing when the engine is hot or the cooling system is pressurized. Even a simple operation such as removing the radiator cap should be avoided since personal injury and loss of coolant may result.

DRAINING THE SYSTEM

Most cooling systems incorporate a radiator petcock usually located on the engine side of the radiator at either of the lower corners. Some radiator petcocks are locat-

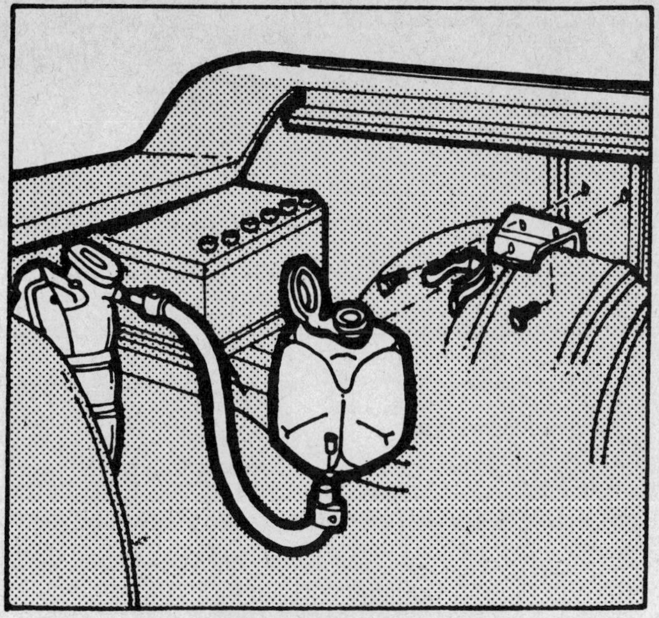

Fig. 9 Aftermarket coolant recovery system installation (typical)

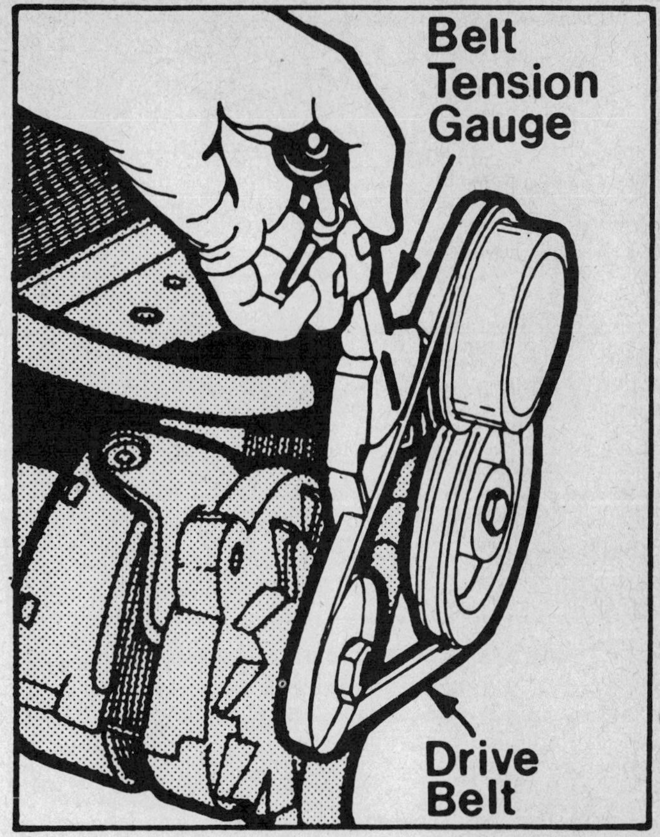

Fig. 10 Checking belt tension with a tension gauge

ed on the side of the radiator. Not all cooling systems are equipped with a radiator petcock.

1. Place a suitable container under radiator to catch coolant.
2. On systems equipped with a radiator petcock, turn the tangs (ears) to open the petcock. However, do not apply excessive pressure in either direction as damage to the petcock may result because some petcocks turn clockwise and others counterclockwise to open.
3. On systems not equipped with a radiator petcock, it will be necessary to remove the lower hose from the radiator.
4. Dispose of coolant.

FLUSHING THE SYSTEM

There are two flushing methods which can be performed without the use of special equipment. One method outlined below requires the use of a garden hose only. The second method requires the use of the garden hose and a "Tee" fitting spliced into one of the heater hoses. The "Tee" fitting and other items and instructions needed to perform this type of flushing are available through aftermarket manufacturers.

1. With coolant system drained, remove thermostat as outlined below:
   a. To located the thermostat housing on most engines follow the upper radiator hose from the radiator to the engine block. On some engines, follow the lower radiator hose from the radiator to the engine block. The point at which these hoses connect is the thermostat housing.
   b. The thermostat housing is usually retained by two bolts or nuts. Remove these bolts or nuts and remove the housing.
   c. Lift the thermostat from the mounting flange, **Fig. 5,** noting the position in which it was installed. This is important to avoid reinstalling the thermostat upside down.
   d. Reinstall thermostat housing, however do not reinstall thermostat. Tighten retaining bolt.
2. Insert garden hose into radiator filler opening, open radiator petcock and turn on water.
3. Start engine and run engine for a few minutes. This should flush out any loose particles in the system.
4. Turn off engine and remove the garden hose.
5. Remove thermostat housing. Thoroughly clean the thermostat housing and engine-surfaces of old gasket and sealer. This is necessary to prevent leakage between the housing and engine surfaces.
6. Install new thermostat housing gasket and the thermostat. Make certain the thermostat is installed exactly in the same position as it was removed.
7. Install thermostat housing and tighten retaining bolts and nuts.
8. Allow radiator to drain.
9. Close radiator petcock, if equipped.
10. Remove coolant overflow tank, if equipped. Thoroughly clean the inside of the tank and reinstall.

REFILLING THE SYSTEM

1. Determine the amount of anti-freeze required to achive a 50/50 solution in the cooling system. Refer to the "Cooling System & Capacity Data" tables in the individual car chapters. Take the total number of quarts listed in the tables and divide by two. This number is the amount of anti-freeze, in quarts, required to achieve the 50/50 solution. This solution will generally provide protection to −35 degrees F.
2. Add the amount of anti-freeze to the radiator determined in the preceding step. If radiator fills before required amount of anti-freeze is installed, start engine and turn on heater. Add the anti-freeze as the coolant level sinks in the radiator.
3. Continue to run engine with the radiator cap removed until the upper radiator hose becomes hot to the touch.
4. Top up the coolant level in the radiator to the bottom of the filler neck with a 50/50 mixture of anti-freeze and water.
5. If equipped with an overflow tank, add a 50/50 mixture of anti-freeze and water to the cold level as marked on the side of the tank.

RADIATOR CAP

The radiator filler cap contains a pressure relief valve and a vacuum relief valve, **Fig. 6.** The pressure relief valve is held against its seat by a spring, which when compressed relieves excessive pressure out the radiator outflow. The vacumm valve is held against its seat by a spring which when compressed opens the valve to

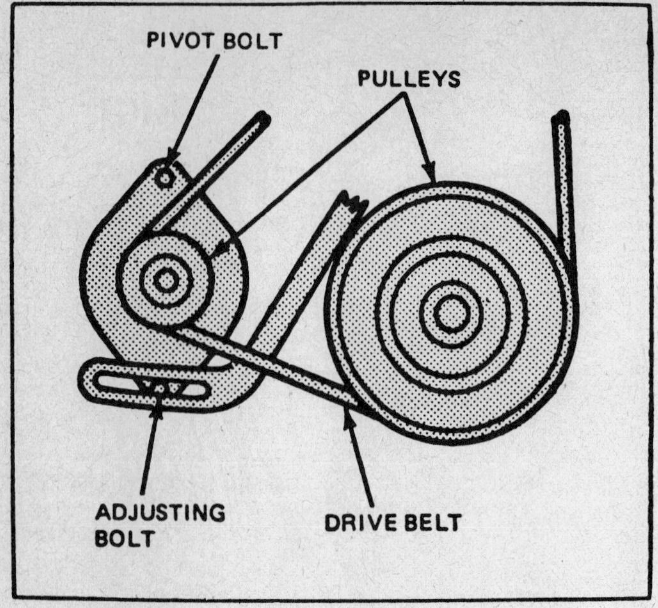

Fig. 11 Pivot bolt and adjusting bolt arrangement

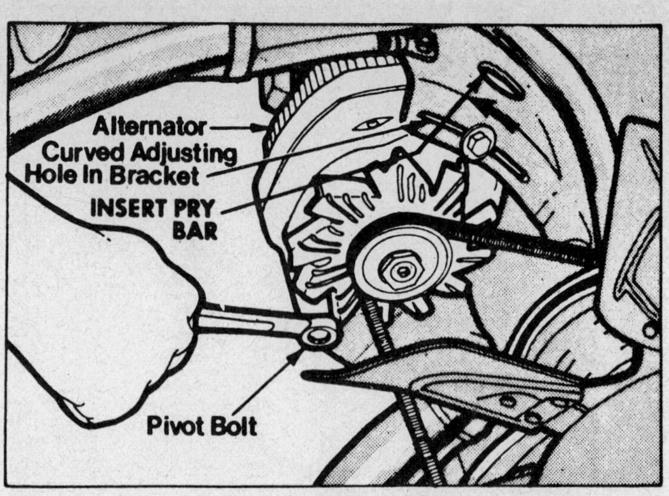

Fig. 12 Loosening adjusting bolt and pivot bolt

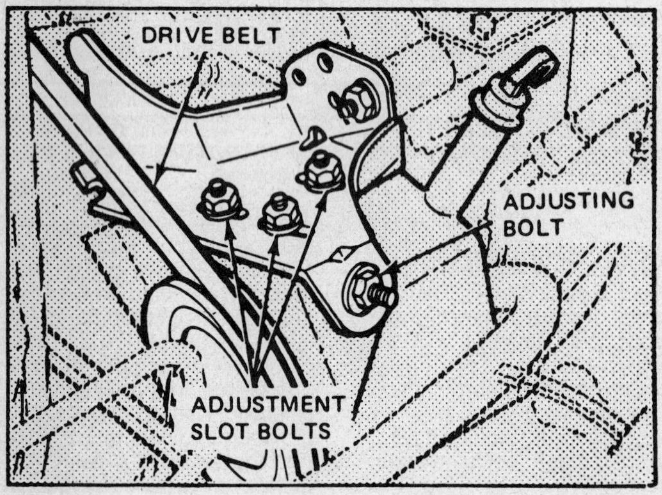

Fig. 13 Adjustment bolt and adjustment slot arrangement

relieve the vacuum created when the system cools.

NOTE: Some aftermarket radiator caps incorporate a pressure release mechanism to relieve cooling system pressure before rotating cap, **Fig. 7**.

The radiator cap should be washed with clean water and pressure checked at regular tune-up intervals. Inspect rubber seal on cap for tears or cracks. If the pressure cap will not hold pressure or does not release at the proper pressure, replace the cap.

COOLANT RECOVERY SYSTEM

The coolant recovery system supplements the standard cooling system in that additional coolant is available from a plastic reservoir, **Fig. 8**.

As the coolant is heated it expands within the cooling system and overflows into the plastic reservoir. As the engine cools, the coolant contacts and is drawn back into the radiator by vacuum. In this way, the radiator is filled to capacity at all times, resulting in increased cooling efficiency.

Air or vapor entering the system will be forced to the reservoir under the coolant and will exit through the reservoir cap.

A special radiator cap is designed to discourage inadvertent removal. The finger grips have been eliminated, replaced by a round configuration.

Overflow Kit

If your vehicle does not have an overflow reservoir, it is easy to fit it with one, **Fig. 9**. A kit should include the following:

1. A clear plastic reservoir with quart markings to indicate fluid level.
2. A replacement radiator cap, with an air sealing gasket in the cap's inside perimeter.
3. Necessary hoses and fittings.

HOSE REPLACEMENT

The radiator, heater and the coolant bypass hoses are held at each end by a clamp. All clamps but the spring design can be loosened with a screwdriver. To save yourself time after you have removed the hose from your radiator or heater, buy the replacement hose and any necessary clamps before starting the job.

Removal

1. Drain the radiator as outlined previously. Use a clean container, large enough to hold the coolant from your cooling system after replacing the hose. If you are removing the radiator upper hose or heater hoses, you need only drain the radiator. If you are removing the lower hose, also drain the block as follows: disconnect the lower hose at the radiator, bend it down and use it as a drain spout.
2. Loosen the clamps with a screwdriver at each end of the hose to be removed. If the clamps are old and corroded, they may be stuck to the hose. Loosening the screw may not be enough on some designs, in which case you'll have to pry the clamp.

CAUTION: Be very careful when prying under the clamp. The fittings are extremely fragile and might bend or break if too much force is exerted.

If the hose is held by spring clamps, you may be in for a struggle unless you have spring clamp pliers. There are many types of pliers designed for these clamps, including ordinary slip-joint pliers with recesses cut into the jaws to grip each end of the clamp. To release the clamp you must squeeze the ends together, and if you try to use ordinary pliers, the ends may split off. The best procedure is to discard the spring type and install a wormdrive band clamp, but if you insist in reusing the one you have, at least invest in a pair of special pliers.

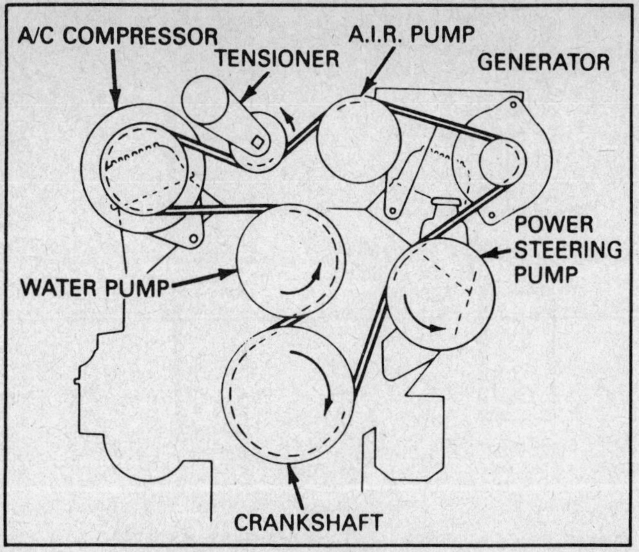

Fig. 14 Serpentine drive belt with spring loaded tensioner

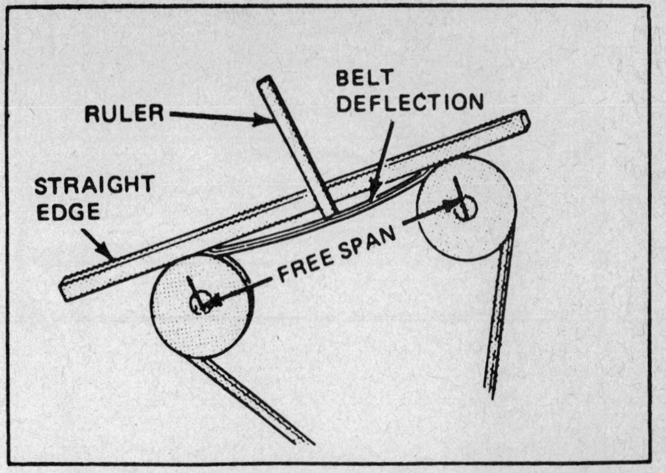

Fig. 15 Checking belt tension without belt tension gauge

3. Twist the hose back and forth to loosen it from the connector. Slide the hose off the connections. If the hose is stuck, shove in a screwdriver and try to pry loose. If the working angle is poor for the screwdriver, or if the hose is really stuck, cut the hose off the neck with a single-edge razor blade. If the hose being removed is dried and cracked and remnants of it remain on either connection, clean the connection thoroughly with a scraper or putty knife.

Installation

1. With the old hose removed, wire brush the hose connections to remove foreign material.
2. To ease installation, coat hose neck with a soap solution.
3. Slide the hose in position so it is completely on the neck at each end, to avoid possibility of kinking and to provide room for proper positiong of the clamp. Except for the wormdrive clamp, which can be opened completely, the clamp must be loosely placed over the hose prior to fitting its end on the neck.
4. Make sure the clamps are beyond the head and placed in the center of the clamping surface of the connections.
5. Tighten the clamps.
6. Refill the cooling system as outlined previously.

COOLING SYSTEM LEAKS

If the coolant level must be adjusted frequently, the cooling system may be leaking either internally or externally. To determine if the system is leaking internally, special equipment must be used such as a pressure tester. To determine if the system is leaking externally, check for leakage in the following locations: radiator and its seams, hoses and their connections, heater core, water pump, coolant temperature sending unit, thermostat housing, hot water choke housing, heater water valve, coolant recovery tank and core plugs.

DRIVE BELTS

Proper belt tension is important not only to minimize noise and prolong belt life, but also to protect the accessories being driven.

Belts which are adjusted too tight may cause failure to the bearing of the accessory which it drives. Premature wear and breakage of the belt may also result. Belts which are too loose will slip on their pulleys and cause a screeching sound. Loose belts can also cause the battery to go dead, the engine to overheat, steering to become hard (if equipped with power steering) and air conditioner to malfunction.

DRIVE BELT TENSION GAUGE

The use of a belt tension gauge will quickly indicate whether a belt is properly adjusted or not. Low cost tension gauges give spot readings while the more expensive ones give continuous readings as the belt tension is adjusted, **Fig. 10.**

DRIVE BELT INSPECTION

All belts should be inspected at regular intervals for uneven wear, fraying and glazing.

CAUTION: Do not inspect belts while engine is running.

Small cracks on the underside of the belt can be enlarged for inspection by flexing the belt. Cracks expose the interior to damage, leading to breakage without warning.

Grease rots ordinary rubber belts. It also causes the belts to slip.

Glazed belts, indicated with a shiny friction surface cause the belts to slip. This can cause overheating, a low charging rate, and hard steering in the case of vehicles with power steering.

Always make sure to inspect the underside of belts. Belts that appear sound from the top, may be severely split on the sides and bottom, ready to fail.

DRIVE BELT TENSION ADJUSTMENT

1. Run engine until it reaches normal operating temperature, then turn engine off.

CAUTION: Do not attempt to check or adjust any drive belt while engine is running. Turn engine off.

2. Using belt tension gauge following manufacturer's instructions, check tension of each belt, individually. Refer to individual vehicle chapter for belt tension specifications.
3. If adjustment is necessary, proceed as follows:
   a. Pivot Bolt and Adjusting Bolt, **Figs. 11 and 12:** using a suitable wrench, loosen adjusting bolt and pivot bolt, then using a pry bar, move accessory toward or away from engine until tension gauge reaches specified reading. Make sure to tighten bolts before relieving force applied to pry bar.

CAUTION: Do not pry against power steering housing or air pump housing.

   b. Adjusting Bolt and Adjusting Bolt Slots, **Fig. 13,** loosen adjusting slot bolts, then loosen or tighten adjusting bolt until tension gauge reaches specified reading. Make sure to tighten adjusting slot bolts.
   c. Idler Pulley Pivot Bolt and Adjusting Bolt: loosen idler pulley pivot bolt and adjusting bolt, then insert a ½ inch flex handle into pulley arm slot and apply force on handle until

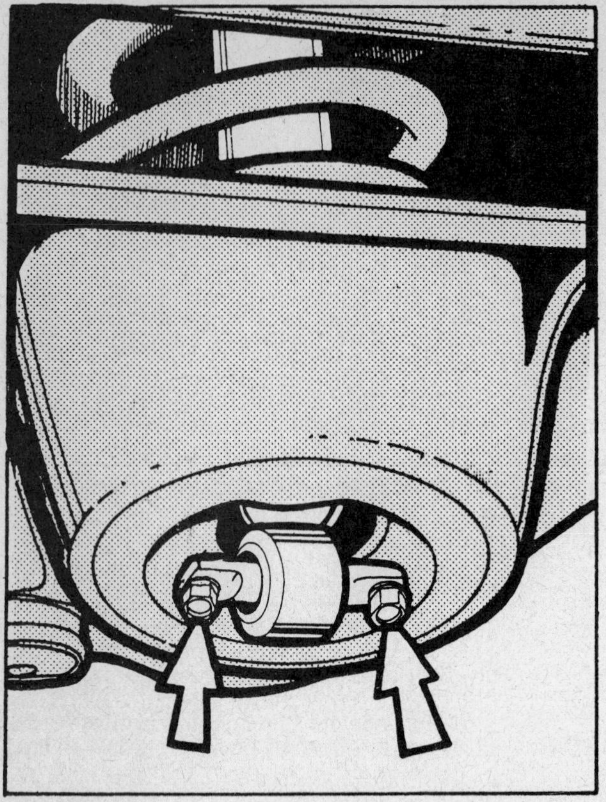

Fig. 16 **Disconnecting lower shock absorber mount (typical)**

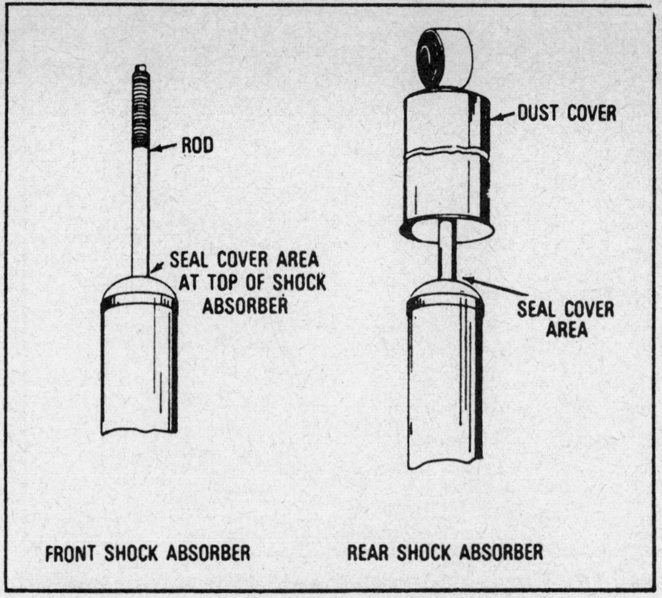

Fig. 17 **Possible source of shock absorber leakage**

tension gauge reaches specified reading. Make sure to tighten pivot and adjusting bolt before relieving force on handle.

NOTE: Some later models use a serpentine drive belt which incorporates a spring loaded tensioner, eliminating the need for adjustment, **Fig. 14.**

4. To check tension on a belt without a belt tension gauge, proceed as follows:
   a. Place a straight edge along the belt from pulley to pulley, **Fig. 15.**
   b. Using a ruler, depress belt at midpoint between pulleys. Measure amount of deflection. For belt with a free span of less than 12 inches between pulleys, amount of deflection should be ¼ inch. For belts with a free span of more than 12 inches between pulleys, amount of deflection should be ½ inch.
   c. Adjust belt tension, if necessary, as described previously.
5. Recheck belt tension, and readjust if necessary.

DRIVE BELT REPLACEMENT

To replace a belt on models not equipped with a serpentine belt with spring loaded tensioner, loosen the adjusting bolt and pivot bolt. Move accessory as required to obtain maximum slack on belt. Remove belt by lifting off the pulleys and working it around the fan or other accessories, as necessary. Occasionally on multiple belt arrangements, it will be necessary to remove one or more additional belts in order to remove the defective belt. To install belt, reverse removal procedure and adjust belt tension as described previously.

NOTE: On accessories which are driven by dual belts, it is adviseable to replace both belts even if only one needs replacement.

To replace a belt on models equipped with a serpentine belt with spring loaded tensioner, lift the tensioner, using a half inch breaker bar.

SHOCK ABSORBERS

ON VEHICLE CHECKS

Bounce Test

Check each shock absorber by bouncing each corner of vehicle. This is best accomplished by alternately lifting up and pushing down at corner of vehicle until maximum up and down movement is reached. Let go of vehicle and ensure movement stops very quickly. Relative damping of shocks should be compared side to side but not front to rear.

Shock Mounts

If noise appears to come from shock mounts, raise vehicle on hoist that supports wheels and check mountings for the following:

1. Worn or defective grommets.
2. Loose mounting nuts or bolts.
3. Possible interference condition.
4. Missing bump stops.

If no apparent faults can be found but noise condition exists when vehicle is bounced, proceed to next check.

Leak Inspection & Manual Operation Check

1. Disconnect each shock lower mount, **Fig. 16,** and pull down on shock absorber until fully extended.
2. Check for leaks in seal cover area, **Fig. 17.** Shock absorber oil is a very thin hydraulic fluid that has a characteristic odor and dark brown color.

NOTE: Shock absorber seals are intended to allow slight seepage to lubricate rod. A trace of oil around seal cover area is not cause for shock absorber replacement since the unit has sufficient reserve fluid to compensate for this seepage.

Ensure oil spray is not from some other source. To check, wipe wet area clean and manually operate shock absorber as described in following step. Fluid will reappear if shock absorber is leaking.

NOTE: Air line must be disconnected from air adjustable shocks before they are manually operated.

3. If necessary, fabricate bracket or handle to enable a secure grip on shock absorber end, **Fig. 18.**
4. Check for internal binding, leakage, and improper or defective valving by pulling down and pushing up shock absorber. Compare rebound resistance (downward) of both shock absorbers, then compression resistance. If any noticeable difference is detected during either stroke, the weaker unit is usually at fault.
5. If shock absorber operates noisily, it

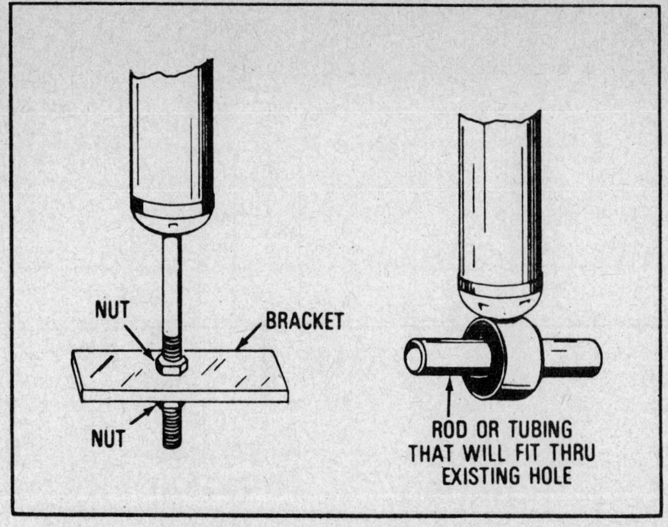

Fig. 18 Methods of gripping shock absorbers

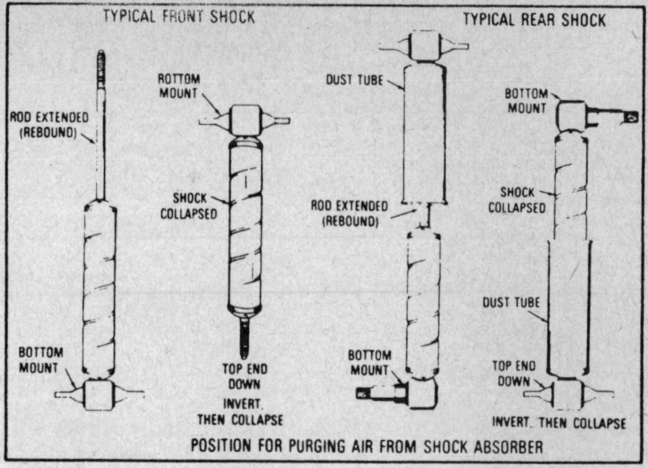

Fig. 19 Purging air from shock absorbers

should be replaced. Noise conditions that require shock asorber replacement are as follows:

a. Grunt or squeal after full stroke in both directions.
b. Clicking noise during fast direction reversal.
c. Skip or lag when reversing direction in mid-stroke.

BENCH CHECKS

If a suitable hoist is not available to perform on-vehicle shock absorber checks, or there is still doubt as to whether the units are defective, the following bench test can be performed.

Spiral Groove Reservoir Shock Absorbers

NOTE: If this style shock absorber is stored or left to lie in a horizontal position for any length of time, an air pocket will form in pressure chamber. If air pocket is not purged, shock absorber may be misdiagnosed as faulty. Purge air from pressure chamber as follows:

a. Extend shock absorber while holding it vertically and right side up, **Fig. 19.**
b. Inverst shock absorber and fully compress unit.
c. Repeat steps a and b at least 5 times to ensure air is completely purged.

1. Obtain known good shock absorber with same part number.
2. Hold both shock absorbers in vertical position and clamp bottom mounts in vise. Do not clamp on mounting threads or on reservoir tube.
3. Operate shock absorbers by hand at different speeds and compare resistance of known good shock to the other. Rebound resistance (extension) is usually greater than compression resistance (about 2:1). Resistance should be smooth and consistent for each stroke rate.
4. Check for the following conditions which indicate a defective shock absorber:

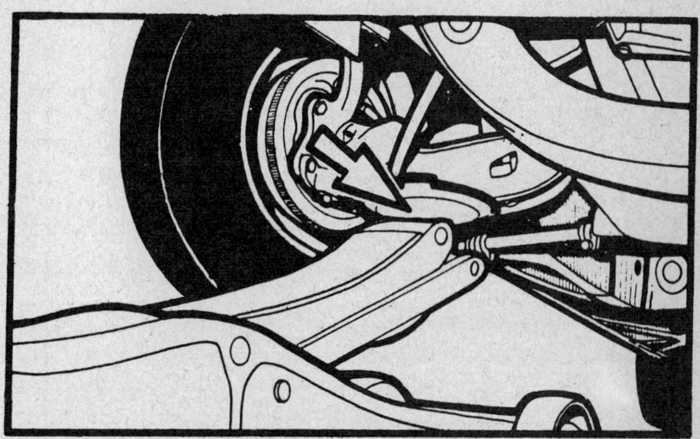

Fig. 20 Supporting control arm on vehicles with spring on lower control arm

a. Skip or lag when reversing direction in mid-stroke.
b. Seizing or binding except at extreme end of stroke.
c. Noises such as grunt or squeal after completing full stroke in either direction.
d. Clicking noise at fast reversal.
e. Fluid leakage.

5. Check for loose piston by extending shock absorber to full rebound position, then give an extra hard pull. If any give is present, piston is loose and unit must be replaced.

Gas Cell Shock Absorbers

These shock absorbers are equipped with a gas-filled cell which takes the place of air in the reservoir. Foaming of the fluid is eliminated since air and fluid cannot mix. Because of this feature, these style shock absorbers must be tested in an upside down position. If a lag is noticed when unit is stroked, gas cell has ruptured and unit must be replaced.

Air Adjustable Shock Absorbers

These shock absorbers have an air chamber similar to the spiral groove reservoir type which must be purged. Refer to note under "Spiral Groove Reservoir Shock Absorbers" to purge air from shock absorbers.

1. Place shock absorber in vise in vertical position with larger diameter tube at top, and clamp at lower mounting ring.
2. Operate unit manually at different speeds. A consistent degree of resistance should be felt through length of stroke A gurgling noise is normal since unit is normally pressurized.
3. Refer to "Spiral Groove Reservoir Shock Absorbers" test procedure for remainder of bench checks.

FRONT SUSPENSION & STEERING CHECKS

To perform the following wear checks, tension must be removed from the suspension parts. Raise the vehicle and support with jack stands. Relieve load from suspension as follows: on vehicles with the spring or torsion bar on the lower control arm, place a floor jack or single piston hydraulic jack under lower arm control as close to ball joint as possible, **Fig. 20,** and raise control arm until vehicle chassis is about to lift off jack stand, then stop; on vehicles with spring on upper control arm, jack up lower control arm as described previously, place block of wood between upper control arm and frame, **Fig. 21,** and

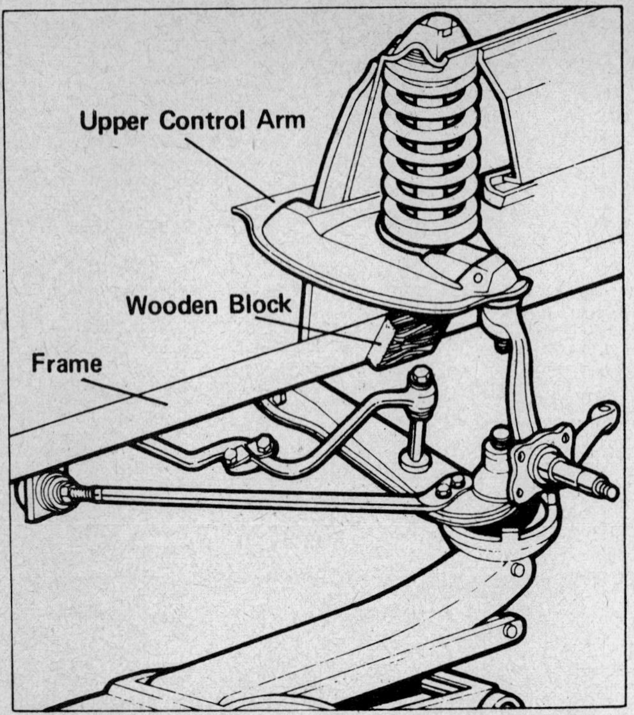

Fig. 21 Blocking control arm of vehicles with spring on upper control arm

slowly lower jack from lower control arm, making sure that neither upper control nor wooden block move. Wooden block must be removed after inspection is completed.

UPPER & LOWER CONTROL ARM BUSHINGS CHECK

1. Have assistant sit in vehicle and apply brake to lock front wheels.
2. Grasp front wheel with both hands and vigorously attempt to rotate it forward

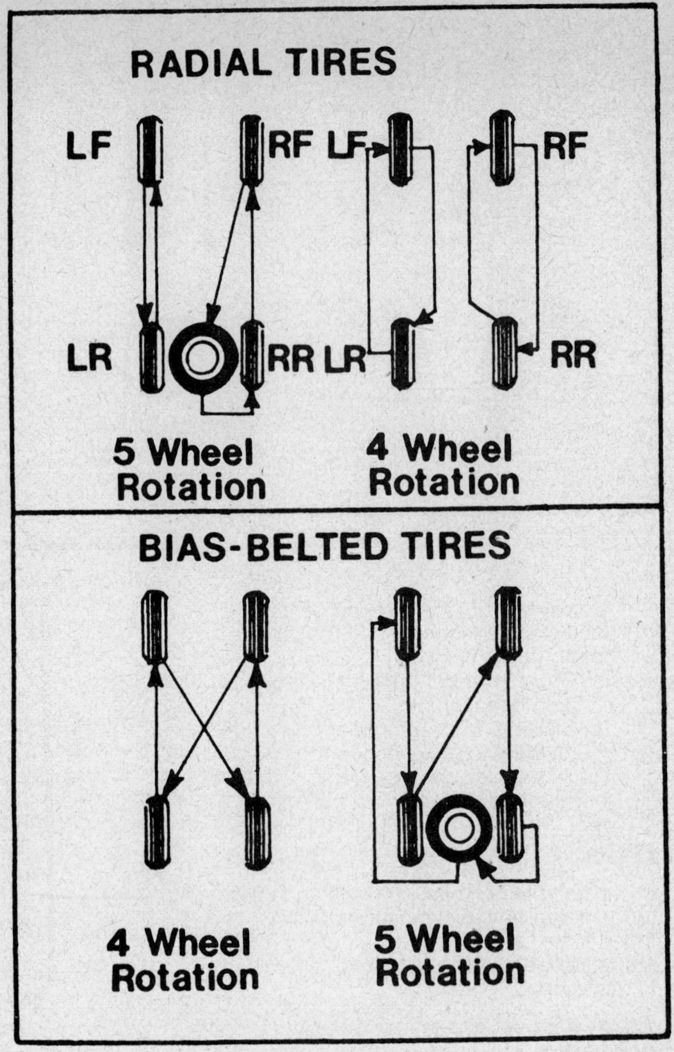

Fig. 22 Tire rotation chart

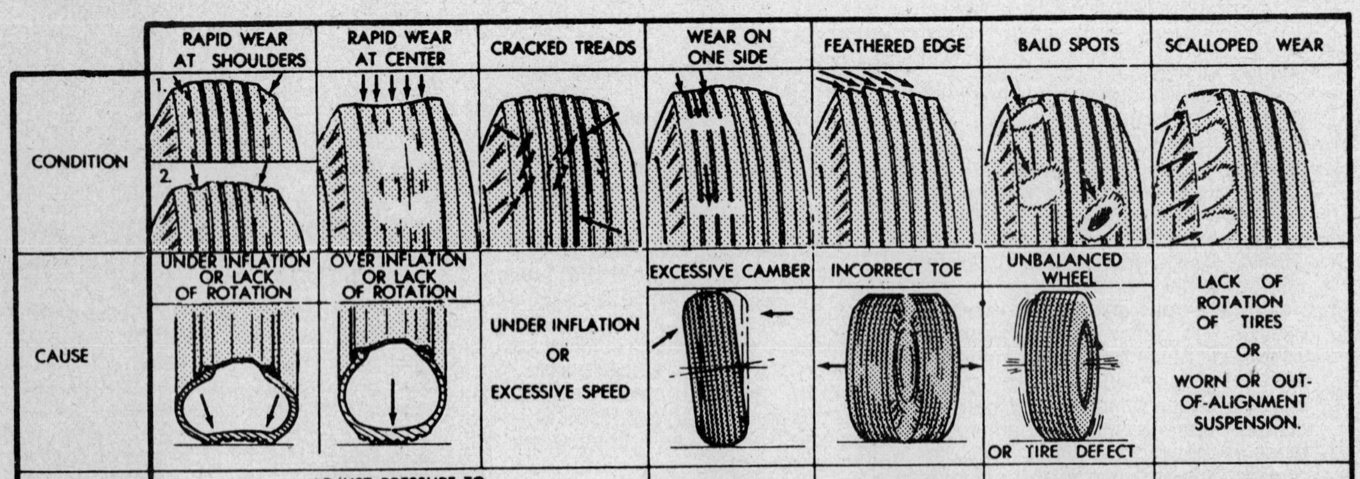

	RAPID WEAR AT SHOULDERS	RAPID WEAR AT CENTER	CRACKED TREADS	WEAR ON ONE SIDE	FEATHERED EDGE	BALD SPOTS	SCALLOPED WEAR
CONDITION	1. 2.						
CAUSE	UNDER INFLATION OR LACK OF ROTATION	OVER INFLATION OR LACK OF ROTATION	UNDER INFLATION OR EXCESSIVE SPEED	EXCESSIVE CAMBER	INCORRECT TOE	UNBALANCED WHEEL OR TIRE DEFECT	LACK OF ROTATION OF TIRES OR WORN OR OUT-OF-ALIGNMENT SUSPENSION.
CORRECTION	ADJUST PRESSURE TO SPECIFICATIONS WHEN TIRES ARE COOL ROTATE TIRES			ADJUST CAMBER TO SPECIFICATIONS	ADJUST TOE-IN TO SPECIFICATIONS	DYNAMIC OR STATIC BALANCE WHEELS	ROTATE TIRES AND INSPECT SUSPENSION

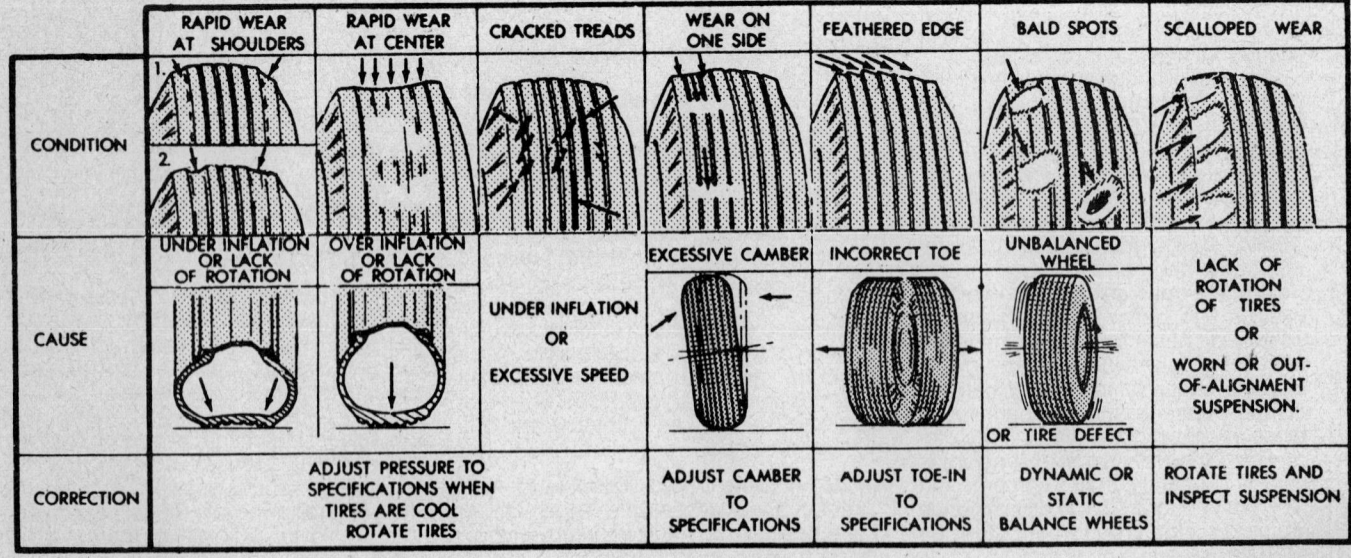

Fig. 23 Tire tread wear patterns

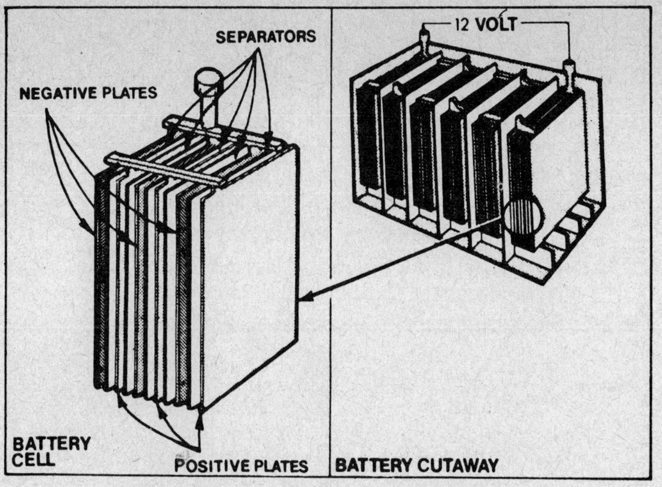

Fig. 24 Battery construction

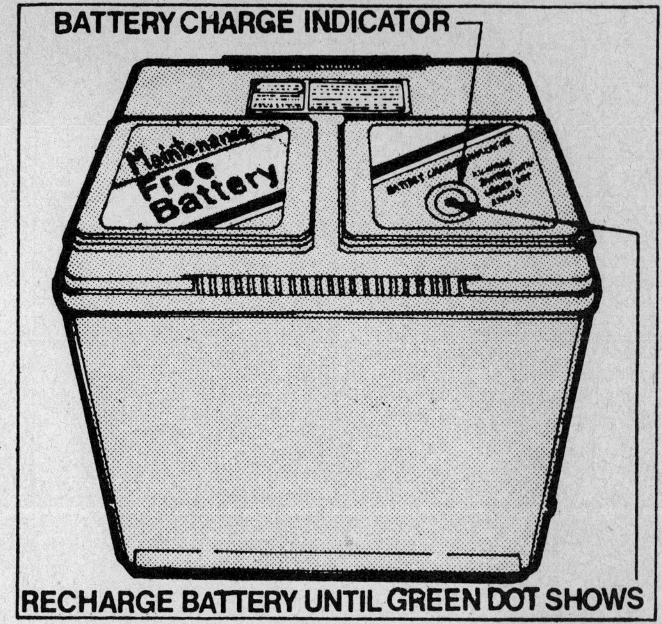

Fig. 25 Typical maintenance free battery

and backward. Observe control arms for excessive front-to-rear movement.

3. Repeat procedure on other front wheel.

UPPER BALL JOINT CHECK

1. Grasp front wheel at top with one hand and at bottom with other.
2. Pull wheel out at bottom while simultaneously pushing in at top. Have assistant watch for play in upper ball joint.
3. Repeat on other front wheel.

LOWER BALL JOINT CHECK

1. Place suitable bar or pipe directly under center of tire.
2. Wedge pipe against ground and lift. Several tries may be necessary to get a good check.
3. Repeat procedure on other wheel.

STEERING LINKAGE CHECK

1. Grasp wheel with both hands and vigorously shake tire from right to left. Have assistant check for wear in tie-rod ends, center link, and idler arm. Idler arm should not move up and down.
2. Repeat procedure on other wheel.

TIRE CARE

TIRE ROTATION

The purpose of tire rotation is to equalize normal wear. By equalizing this wear evenly over the entire tread surface, you extend tire life. Recommended rotation patterns are shown in **Fig. 22.**

It is wise to provide snow tires with rims of their own. They can be kept on rims of their own during both storage and use. In this way, you will protect tires from the bead damage which becomes a possibility when you break a tire away from a rim.

A studded snow tire should always be mounted on the same wheel of the car year after year. When storing studded snow tires, mark tire in chalk for either Right or Left, depending upon which side of the car the tire was mounted.

When storing tires, lay them flat, off the tread to prevent flat spots from developing. Keep tires away from electricity-producing machinery which creates ozone and can damage rubber.

TIRE MAINTENANCE

Tires should be inspected regularly for excessive or abnormal tread wear, fabric breaks, cuts or other damage, **Fig. 23.** A bulge or bump in the sidewall or tread is reason for discarding a tire. A bulge indicates that the tread or sidewall has separated from the tire body. The tire is a candidate for a blowout. Look also for small stones or other foreign bodies wedged in the tread. These can be removed by prying them out carefully with a screwdriver.

BATTERY SERVICE

NOTE: All vehicles are available with a standard two terminal battery. Some later model General Motors vehicles have an optional Power Reserve Battery System. If the battery in your vehicle appears to have three battery terminals, refer to "Power Reserve Battery System" for further information.

CONSTRUCTION & OPERATION

To understand why batteries malfunction, some knowledge of batteries is important. Simply stated, the battery is constructed of two unlike materials, a positive plate and a negative plate with a porous separator between the two plates, **Fig. 24.** This assembly placed in a suitable battery case and filled slightly above the top of the plates with electrolyte (sulphuric acid and distilled water) forms a cell. The 12 volt battery is composed of 6 cells interconnected by plate straps. Note that batteries have varying number of plates per cell, but each cell in any given battery has the same number of plates.

The battery performs the following four basic functions in a vehicle:

1. Supplies electrical energy to the starter motor to crank and start the engine and also to the ignition system while the engine is being started.
2. Supplies electrical energy for accessories such as radio, tape deck, heater, and lights when engine is not running and the ignition switch is in the "OFF" or the "Accessory" position.
3. Supplies additional electrical energy for accessories while the engine is running when the output alternator is exceeded by the various accessories.
4. Stabilizes voltage in the electrical system. Satisfactory operation of the ignition system and any other electrical device is impossible with a damaged, weak or even underpowered (low rating) battery.

Sealed Batteries

Sealed batteries, called "Maintenance Free" or "Freedom" batteries, **Fig. 25,** are available on some vehicles, and can also be purchased from other sources.

The sealed batteries have unique chemistry and construction methods which provide advantages.

Water never needs to be added to the battery.

The battery is completely sealed except for two small vent holes on the side. The vent holes allow what small amount of gases are produced in the battery to escape. The special chemical composition inside the battery reduces the production of gas to an extremely small amount at normal charging voltages.

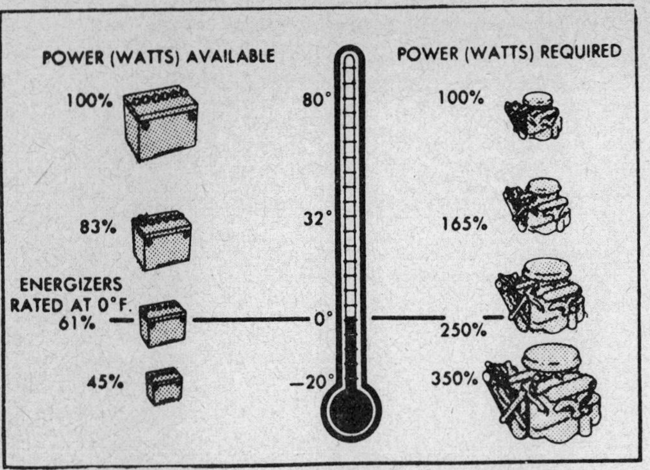

Fig. 26 Battery energy versus falling temperature comparison chart

Watt Rating	5 Amperes	10 Amperes	20 Amperes	30 Amperes	40 Amperes	50 Amperes
Below 2450	10 Hours	5 Hours	2 1/2 Hours	2 Hours		
2450–2950	12 Hours	6 Hours	3 Hours	2 Hours	1 1/2 Hours	
Above 2950	15 Hours	7 1/2 Hours	3 1/4 Hours	2 Hours	1 3/4 Hours	1 1/2 Hours

Fig. 27 Battery charging guide

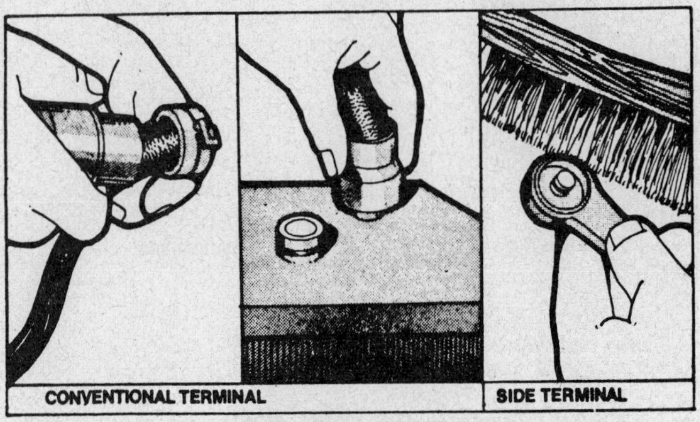

Fig. 28 Cleaning battery terminals

The battery has a very strong ability to withstand damaging effects of overcharge, and the terminals are tightly sealed to minimize leakage. A charge indicator in the cover indicates state of charge.

Compared to a conventional battery in which performance decreases steadily with age, the sealed battery delivers more available power at any time during its life. The battery has a reduced tendency to self-discharge as compared to a conventional battery.

SAFETY PRECAUTIONS

CAUTION: Electrolyte solution in the battery is a strong and dangerous acid. it is extremely harmful to eyes, skin and clothing. If acid contacts any part of the body, flush immediately with water for a period not less than 15 minutes. If acid is accidentally swallowed, drink large quantities of milk or water, followed by milk of magnesia, a beaten raw egg or vegetable oil. Call physician immediately.

When batteries are being charged, highly explosive hydrogen and oxygen gases form in each battery cell. Some of this gas escapes through the vent holes in the plugs on top of battery case and forms an explosive atmosphere surrounding the battery. This explosive gas will remain in and/or around the battery for several hours after the battery has been charged. Sparks or flames can ignite this gas and cause a dangerous battery explosion.

The following precautions must be observed to avoid battery explosion, personal harm and damage to the vehicle's electrical system.

1. Do not smoke near batteries being charged or those which have been recently charged. It is a good practice never to smoke near a battery even though the battery is in the vehicle.
2. Always shield your eyes when working with batteries.
3. Do not disconnect live (working) circuits (lights or accessories operating) at the terminals of batteries since sparking usually occurs at a point where such a circuit is disconnected.
4. Use extreme caution when connecting or disconnecting booster leads or cable clamps from battery chargers. Make sure live (working) circuits are disconnected before connecting or disconnecting the booster leads or cable clamps. Poor booster lead connections are a common cause of electrical arcing causing battery explosions.

CAUSES OF DISCHARGED BATTERIES

There are numerous reasons that could cause a battery to discharge and appear to be defective, therefore the battery should not be targeted as the primary source of electrical and/or starting problems before it has been tested.

The following are some common conditions that could discharge a good battery:

1. Lights left "ON" or doors not closed properly, leaving dome light "ON."
2. Excessive use of accessories with the engine not running.
3. Improper installation of after market accessories.
4. Alternator belt loose or damaged.
5. Dirty battery case causing a self-discharge condition.
6. Loose battery cable terminals.
7. Low alternator output.
8. High resistance in charging circuits caused by other loose electrical connections.

BATTERY RATING & CAPACITY

The two most commonly used ratings are the 20 hour rating of 80° F and the cold cranking load capacity of the battery at 0° F, specified in amps. Batteries are also rated by watts in the Peak Watt Rating (PWR) which is actually the cold cranking ability of the battery at 0° F.

Another battery rating method is the reserve capacity rating in minutes. The purpose of this rating is to determine the length of time a vehicle can be operated with a faulty charging system (malfunctioning alternator or regulator). Batteries are normally marketed by the Ampere-Hour rating which is based on the 20 hour rating. The Ampere-Hour rating is also normally stamped on the battery case or on a label attached to the battery. A battery capable of furnishing 4 amps for a period of 20 hours is classified as an 80 ampere hour battery (4 amps × 20 hour = 80).

The Ampere-Hour rating should not be confused with the cranking performance of a battery at 0° F. Batteries with the same Ampere-Hour ratings can have various 0° F cranking capacities. The higher quality battery will have a higher Ampere-Hour rating and a higher cranking capacity will increase with larger number of plates per cell, larger size of plates, and larger battery case size allowing for more electrolyte solution.

SELECTING A REPLACEMENT BATTERY

Long and troublefree service can be better assured when the capacity or wattage rating of the replacement battery is at least equal to the wattage rating of the battery originally engineered for the application by the manufacturer.

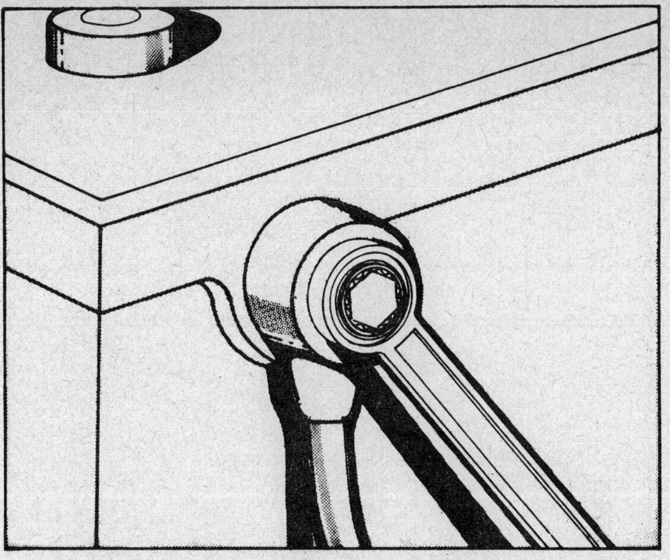

Fig. 29 Removing side type battery terminal

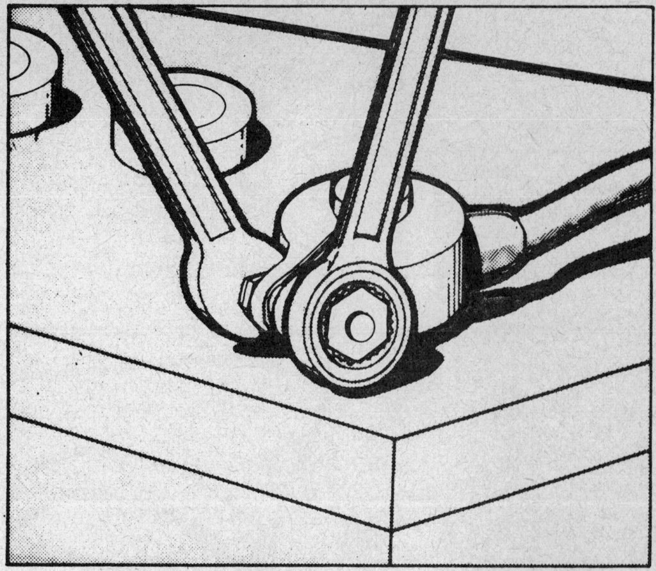

Fig. 30 Removing bolt type terminal

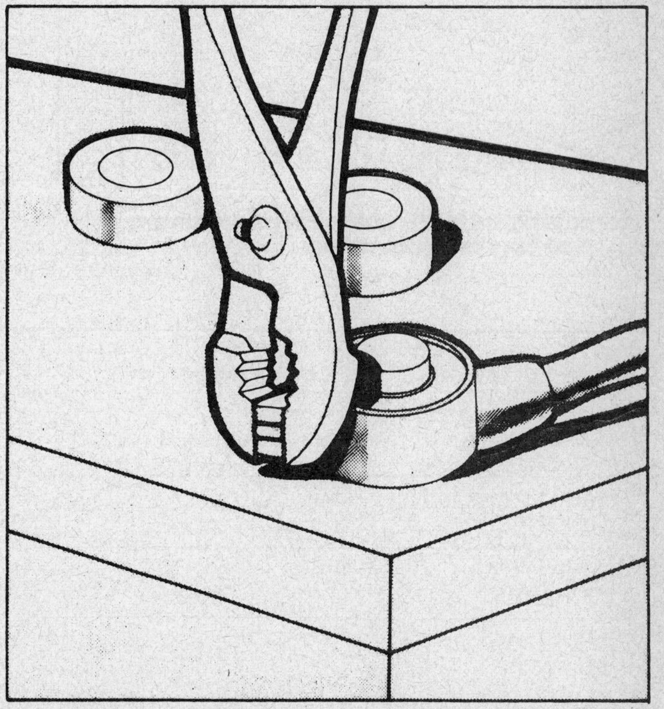

Fig. 31 Removing spread type terminal

The use of an undersized battery may result in poor performance and early failure. **Fig. 26** shows how battery power shrinks while the need for engine cranking power increases with falling temperatures. Sub-zero temperatures reduce capacity of a fully charged battery to 45% of its normal power and at the same time increase cranking load to 3½ times the normal warm weather load.

Hot weather can also place excessive electrical loads on the battery. Difficulty in starting may occur when cranking is attempted shortly after a hot engine has been turned off or stalls. High compression engines can be as difficult to start under such conditions as on the coldest day. Consequently, good performance can be obtained only if the battery has ample capacity to cope with these conditions.

A battery of greater capacity should be considered if the electrical load has been increased through the addition of accessories, or if driving conditions are such that the generator cannot keep the battery charged.

On applications where heavy electrical loads are encountered, a higher output generator that will supply a charge during low speed operation may be required to increase battery life and improve battery performance.

TESTING BATTERY (SPECIFIC GRAVITY)

NOTE: The specific gravity of a sealed battery cannot be checked.

A hydrometer can be used to measure the specific gravity of the electrolyte in each cell. There are several types of hydrometers available, the least expensive consisting of a glass tube, a rubber bulb at the end of the tube and several balls within the tube. To use this type, the specific gravity of the battery must be interpreted by the number of balls which float to the surface of the electrolyte, according to the manufacturer's instructions.

The hydrometer indicates the concentration of the electrolyte.

BOOST STARTING A VEHICLE WITH A DISCHARGED BATTERY

1. Be sure the ignition key is in the off position and all accessories and lights are off.
2. Shield eyes. Use goggles or similar eye protection.
3. Connect the booster cables from the positive (+) battery terminal of the discharged battery (vehicle to be started) to the positive (+) battery terminal of the vehicle used as the booster.
4. Connect one end of the other cable to negative (−) terminal of the good battery.
5. Connect one end of the other cable to engine bolthead or similar good contact spot on the vehicle being started.

CAUTION: Never connect to negative terminal of dead battery.

NOTE: To prevent damage to other electrical components on the vehicle being

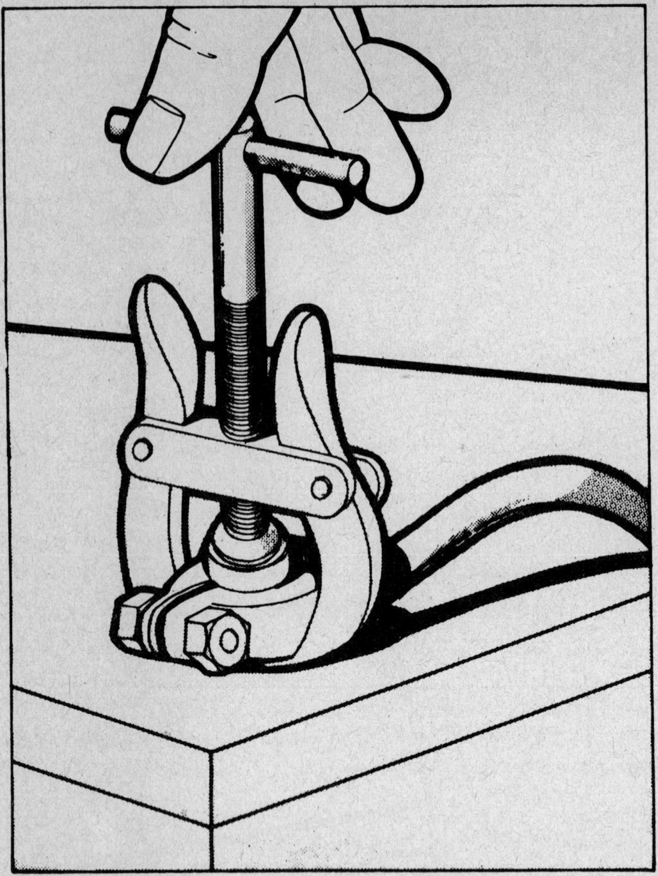

Fig. 32 Removing battery cable terminal using cable terminal puller

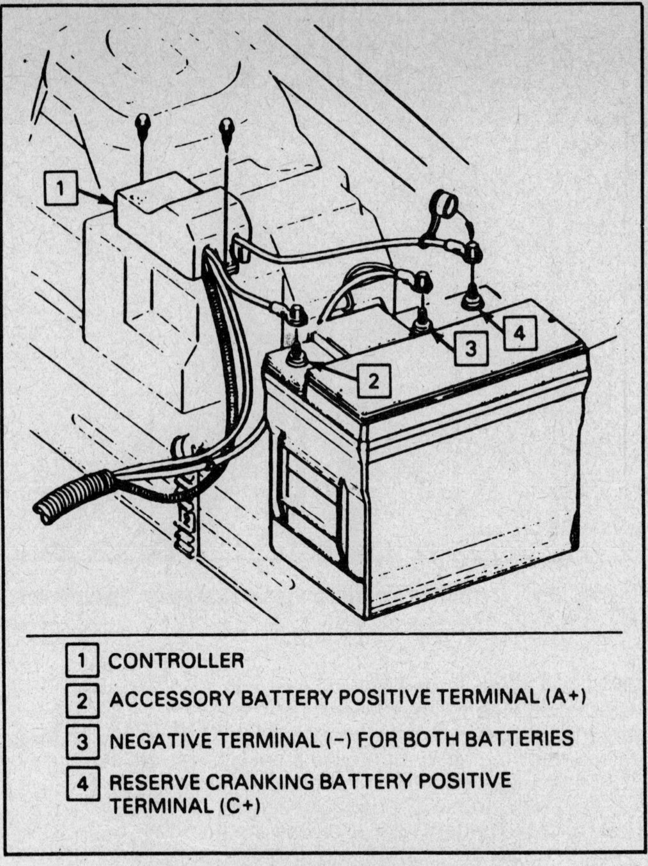

Fig. 33 Posipower battery and controller

VOLTAGE AND ELECTROLYTE TEMPERATURE	
ESTIMATED ELECTROLYTE TEMPERATURE	MINIMUM REQUIRED VOLTAGE UNDER 15 SECOND LOAD
70°F (21°C) & ABOVE	9.6
50°F (10°C)	9.4
30°F (1-1°C)	9.1
15°F (-10°C)	8.8
0°F (-18°C)	8.5
BELOW 0°F	8.0

Fig. 34 Power reserve voltage chart

started, make certain engine is at idle speed before connecting jumper cables.

CHARGING THE BATTERY

There are two separate methods of recharging batteries which differ basically in the rate of charge.

Slow Charging Method

Slow charging is the best and only method of completely recharging a battery. This method, when properly applied, may be used safely under all possible conditions providing the electrolyte is at proper level and the battery is capable of being fully charged. The normal charging rate is 5 amperes.

A fully charged battery is indicated when all cell specific gravities do not increase when checked at three one-hour intervals and all cells are gassing freely.

Charge periods of 24 hours or more may be required because of the low charging rate. See charging guide, **Fig. 27.**

Quick Charging Method

In order to get a car back on the road in the least amount of time, it is sometimes necessary to quick charge a battery. The battery cannot be brought up to full charged condition by the quick charge method. It can, however, be substantially recharged or boosted but, in order to bring it to a fully charged condition, the charging cycle must be finished by charging at a low or normal rate. Some quick chargers have a provision for finishing the charging cycle at a low rate to bring the battery up to a fully charged condition.

CAUTION: Too high a current during quick charging will damage battery plates.

BATTERY CABLE SERVICE

NOTE: At regular intervals, perform a visual inspection of the battery.

This inspection should be performed when any of the underhood maintenance items such as engine oil, transmission fluid or radiator coolant level are checked.

1. Clean any heavy accumulation of dirt or corrosion on the battery terminals and battery tray with a wire brush, **Fig. 28.** Finish cleaning with a solution of baking soda and water. Diluted ammonia can also be used as a washing agent. Thoroughly flush battery with clean water.

NOTE: Baking soda and ammonia neutralize battery acid. Therefore make sure

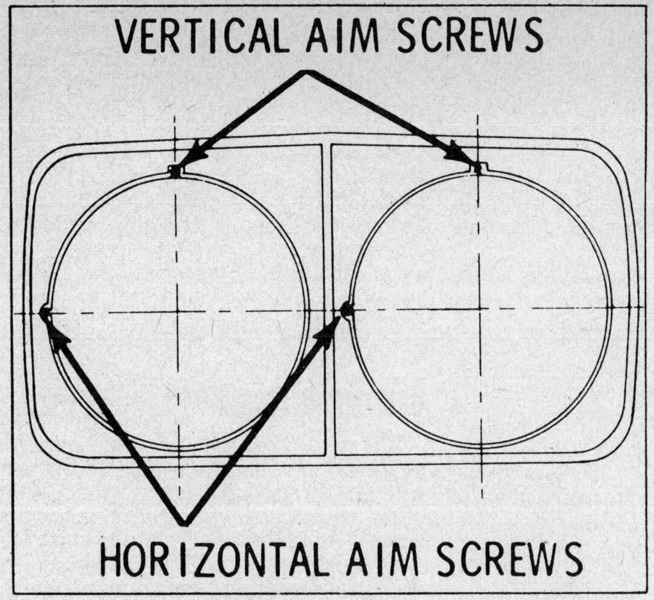

Fig. 35 Headlamp adjusting screws (typical)

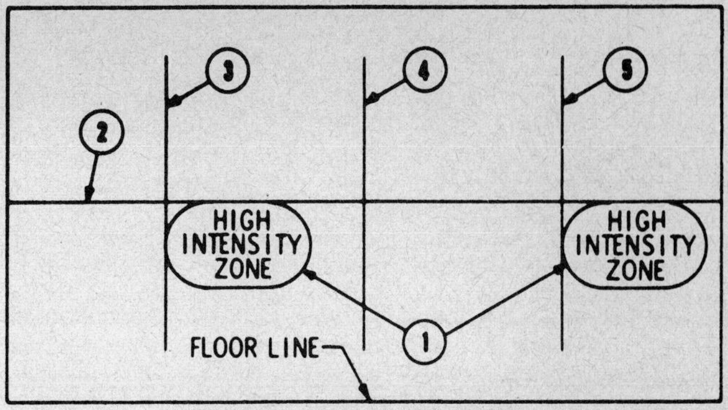

LOW BEAM ADJUSTMENT PATTERN
(VISUAL AIM AT 25 FEET)
5-3/4" TYPE 2 LAMPS (OUTBOARD ONLY) AND 7" TYPE 2 LAMPS

LINE 1	HIGH INTENSITY ZONES.
LINE 2	HORIZONTAL AND VERTICAL AT CENTER OF HEADLAMPS.
LINES 3 & 5	VERTICAL AT CENTER OF HEADLAMPS.
LINE 4	VERTICAL AT CENTER OF CAR.

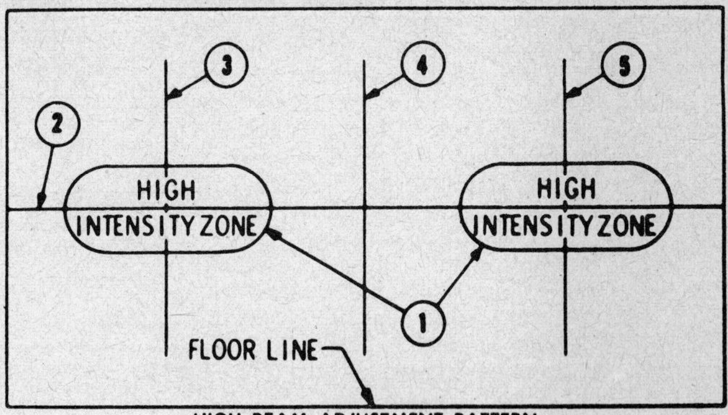

HIGH BEAM ADJUSTMENT PATTERN
(VISUAL AIM AT 25 FEET)
5-3/4" TYPE 1 LAMPS (INBOARD ONLY)

Fig. 36 Headlamp aiming

these agents are kept out of the battery by keeping the battery caps tightly in place.

2. Check for damaged cable insulation. Damaged insulation can cause the cable to short out against the body of the vehicle or other accessories. Cables in this condition should be replaced immediately.
3. Check level of electrolyte. If required, add water as described further on.
4. Make sure battery is securely held in place. A loose or broken bracket can result in battery damage (both internally and externally) from excessive vibration.

Battery Cable, Replace

NOTE: When disconnecting battery cables, first make sure all accessories are off, disconnect the negative battery cable and then the positive cable. Make sure to reconnect cables in the reverse order of removal.

1. On side terminal batteries, loosen the retaining bolts using a ⅝-inch wrench, and disconnect the cable from the battery, **Fig. 29.**
2. On all other type batteries, loosen the cable retaining bolt using a ½ inch or ⁹⁄₁₆ inch box wrench, **Fig. 30,** and lift the cable off the battery posts. Some cables can be removed by squeezing the tabs on the cable terminal using a pair of pliers, **Fig. 31,** and lifting the cable off the battery posts.
3. If the battery terminals are difficult to remove, use a terminal puller, **Fig. 32.** Place the legs of the puller underneath the terminal and tighten the puller screw until the terminal is removed.
4. Clean the cable terminals and battery posts using a terminal and post wire brush, **Fig. 28.**
5. Clean the battery top using a solution of soda and water. Ensure the battery is thoroughly cleaned and dried. Make sure you cover the battery caps to avoid entry of the soda and water solution into the battery.
6. To install the cables on a side terminal battery, place the cables onto the battery and tighten the retaining screws using a ⁵⁄₁₆ inch wrench.
7. To install the cables on all other types of batteries, place the cables on the battery post and force them all the way down. if the cable is not completely bottomed, spread the cable terminal slightly with a screwdriver, until the terminal is properly positioned.
8. Tighten the terminal bolts using a ½ inch or ⁹⁄₁₆ inch box wrench.
9. Coat the outside of the terminals with petroleum jelly to prevent corrosion.

REPLACING BATTERY

Careless installation of a new battery can ruin the battery. In removing the old battery, note the location of the positive battery post so the new battery can be installed in the same position. Always remove the negative (ground) cable first.

Use an open-end wrench to loosen the clamp. If the nut is very tight, use one wrench on the head of the bolt and the other on the nut to avoid straining and possibly cracking the battery cover. A pair of tire pliers can be used to loosen the nut, but a wrench should always be used on the head of the bolt.

If a cable terminal is corroded to the post, do not try to loosen it by hammering, or by resting a tool on the battery and prying—either method can break the battery container. Use a screw type terminal puller, **Fig. 32,** or spread the cable terminals slightly with a screwdriver.

Clean any corrosion from the cables, battery case, or hold-downs, and inspect them. Paint any corroded steel parts with acid-proof paint. Make sure the cable is of the correct size and that its insulation and clamp terminal are in good condition.

Put the new battery in position, making sure it sits level, and tighten the hold-down a little at a time, alternately, to avoid distorting and breaking the battery case. The hold-downs should be snug enough to prevent bouncing, but should not be too tight.

NOTE: Before connecting the cables, check the battery terminals to be sure the battery is not reversed.

Clean the battery post bright with sandpaper or a wire brush.

Don't hammer the terminals down on the posts, as the battery case may crack. Spread the terminals slightly if necessary. Connect the starter cable first and the negative (ground) cable last, tightening the terminal bolts after making sure the cables don't interfere with the vent plugs or rub against the hold-downs.

POWER RESERVE BATTERY SYSTEM

This system, available as an option on some later model General Motors vehicles, is made up of a control box, three battery cables and a Posipower battery case that contains two separate batteries, **Fig. 33.** The terminal marked "A+" is the positive terminal of the "Accessory Battery." It operates as the normal battery in a car, handling all voltage requirements of the vehicle. The terminal marked "C+" is the positive terminal of the "Reserve Cranking Battery". This portion of the battery is used to assist the Accessory Battery for normal starting and to start the engine if the Accessory Battery is run down, due to lights or other accessories being left on, or a malfunction in the electrical section.

The center terminal is the common ground for both batteries. The controller couples the two batteries together when the ignition switch is turned to "START". When the ignition switch is returned to "RUN", the controller removes the Reserve Cranking Battery from the circuit and the Accessory Battery handles all voltage requirements for the vehicle.

If the Accessory Battery is low due to one or more accessories being left on or an electrical malfunction, the Accessory Battery will not be able to start the vehicle. If this is the case, turn the ignition switch to "RUN" or "ON", then "PRESS" and "RELEASE" the Battery Reserve push button switch on the lower instrument panel. The controller will now engage the Reserve Cranking Battery into the system to start the engine. Now turn ignition switch to "START" position and start the engine in the usual manner. After starting, the two batteries will stay coupled together and be charged by the alternator. The two batteries will remain coupled together until the ignition is turned "OFF".

Testing & Charging Posipower Battery

NOTE: The following procedures apply to both batteries contained in the Posipower battery case. Test and charge each battery separately.

1. Check for visible damage, such as cracked or broken case, replacing battery as necessary.
2. Disconnect all load from battery, then, using accurate digital voltmeter, read Open Circuit Voltage (OCV).
3. If OCV is at least 12.4 volts, proceed to "Load Test". If OCV is less than 12.4 volts, proceed to "Charging", then to "Load Test".

Load Test

1. With all other load disconnected from battery, connect a carbon pile load and voltmeter across battery.
2. Adjust carbon pile to obtain load current of 110 amps for Accessory Battery (A+ terminal) or 200 amps for Reserve Cranking Battery (C+ terminal).
3. Observe voltage after 15 seconds with load applied.
4. If voltage is below listed value, **Fig. 34,** replace battery.

Charging

NOTE: Each battery may be charged at any rate in amperes as long as battery temperature does not exceed 125°F. and gassing or spewing of electrolyte does not occur. If either of these conditions occur, reduce charging rate.

1. Using suitable charger, set initial rate at highest rate and charge for one hour.
2. Disconnect charger.
3. Connect carbon pile load and adjust to obtained ampere values of 110 amps (A+ terminal) or 200 amps (C+ terminal) for 15 seconds to remove surface charge.
4. After 15 seconds, disconnect carbon pile load, then wait 45 seconds.
5. Using digital voltmeter, read OCV. If OCV is below 12.4 volts, repeat charging procedure. If OCV is at least 12.4 volts, proceed to "Load Test".

NOTE: The recharge time required to bring OCV to 12.4 volts or above varies according to state of charge at beginning of charge period, battery temperature (the lower the temperature of the battery, the longer the charging time required) or the capacity of the charger.

HEADLAMP AIMING

It is recommended that headlamps be checked for proper aim every 12 months or whenever front body work is repaired. On most vehicles, aiming can be performed without removing headlamp bezels. Vertical adjustment is usually accomplished with a screw at the top of the sealed beam retaining ring (12 o'clock position). Horizontal adjustment is provided by a screw at the right or left (3 or 9 o'clock position) of the sealed beam unit, **Fig. 35.** Headlamp aiming can be performed visually with a screen as follows:

1. Vehicle should be on level floor so headlamps are 25 ft. from screen or light colored wall. Fuel tank should be ½ full. Any heavy loads that are normally in vehicle should remain there. Driver and passengers should not be in vehicle during aiming. Tires should be inflated to specified pressures and headlamps lenses should be cleaned.
2. Mark screen or wall with four lines as shown in **Fig. 36.**
3. Adjust low beam pattern only as shown in top diagram in **Fig. 36.**
4. On vehicles with four headlamp systems, cover low beam (outboard or upper lamps) and adjust high beam lamp pattern as shown in bottom diagram of **Fig. 36.**

AMERICAN MOTORS

VEHICLE INFORMATION

GENERAL SERVICE

AMERICAN MOTORS

INDEX OF SERVICE OPERATIONS

NOTE: Refer to the rear of this manual for vehicle manufacturer's special tool suppliers.

Specifications

GENERAL ENGINE SPECIFICATIONS

Year	Engine CID①/Liter	Engine VIN Code ②	Fuel System	Bore & Stroke	Compression Ratio	Net H.P. @ RPM ③	Maximum Torque Ft. Lbs @ RPM	Normal Oil Pressure Pounds
1982	4-151, 2.5L	B	2SE, 2 Bbl.⑤	4.0 x 3.0	8.24	—	—	36-41
	4-151, 2.5L	B	E2SE, 2 Bbl.⑤⑦	4.0 x 3.0	8.24	—	—	36-41
	6-258, 423L	C	BBD, 2 Bbl.④	3.75 x 3.90	8.6	—	—	37-75
1983	4-151, 2.5L	B	2SE, 2 Bbl.⑤⑥	4.0 x 3.0	8.2	—	—	36-41
1983-84	4-150, 2.46L	U	YFA, 1 Bbl.④⑧	3.88 x 3.19	9.2	—	132 @ 3200	37-75
1983-88	6-258, 4.23L	C	BBD, 2 Bbl.④	3.75 x 3.90	9.2	112 @ 3000	210 @ 2000	37-75

①—CID-cubic inch displacement.
②—The fourth digit denotes engine code.
③—Ratings are net-as installed on vehicle.
④—Carter.
⑤—Rochester.
⑥—Calif. vehicles equipped with E2SE.
⑦—Calif. & auto trans. only.
⑧—Electronic Feedback Carburetor.

ALTERNATOR SPECIFICATIONS

Year	Alternator Make	Alternator Model	Ground Polarity	Rated Output Amperes	Rated Output Volts	Field Current Amperes ①	Field Current Volts	Regulator Model	Regulator Test @ 120°F Ampere Load	Regulator Test @ 120°F Altern. RPM	Regulator Test @ 120°F Volts
1982	Delco	—	Negative	42	—	4.0-5.0	—	1116387②	—	—	13.4-14.4
	Delco	—	Negative	55	—	4.0-5.0	—	1116387②	—	—	13.4-14.4
	Delco	—	Negative	63	—	4.0-5.0	—	1116387②	—	—	13.4-14.4
	Delco	—	Negative	70	—	4.0-5.0	—	1116387②	—	—	13.4-14.4
1983-88	Delco	—	Negative	42	—	4.0-5.0	—	1116387②	—	—	13.4-14.4
	Delco	—	Negative	56	—	4.0-5.0	—	1116387②	—	—	13.4-14.4
	Delco	—	Negative	66	—	4.0-5.0	—	1116387②	—	—	13.4-14.4
	Delco	—	Negative	78	—	4.0-5.0	—	1116387②	—	—	13.4-14.4

①—Excessive current drawn indicates shorted field winding. No current draw indicates an open winding.
②—Integral regulator.

STARTING MOTOR APPLICATIONS

Year	Engine/V.I.N.	Starter Ident. No.
1982-83	4-151/B	1109526②
	4-151/B	3236659②
1982-88	6-258/C	EIFF-BA①
1983-84	4-150/U	EIFF-BA①

①—Motorcraft.
②—Delco-Remy.

WHEEL ALIGNMENT SPECIFICATIONS

Year	Model	Caster Angle, Degrees Limits	Caster Angle, Degrees Desired	Camber Angle, Degrees Limits Left	Camber Angle, Degrees Limits Right	Camber Angle, Degrees Desired Left	Camber Angle, Degrees Desired Right	Toe In. Inch	Toe-Out on Turns, Deg.① Outer Wheel	Toe-Out on Turns, Deg.① Inner Wheel
1982-83	Concord & Spirit	+3½ to +5	+4½	+⅛ to +¾	−⅛ to +½	+⅜	+⅛	1/16 to 3/16	—	—
1983-88	Eagle	+3 to +5	+4	+1/8 to +5/8	−1/8 to +5/8	+3/8	+3/8	1/16 to 3/16	②	38

①—Incorrect toe-out when other adjustments are correct, indicates bent steering arms.
②—Wheels at full turn.

ENGINE TIGHTENING SPECIFICATIONS*

*Torque specifications are for clean and lightly lubricated threads only. Dry or dirty threads produce increased friction which prevents accurate measurement of tightness.

Year	Engine Model/VIN	Spark Plugs Ft. Lbs.	Cylinder Head Bolts Ft. Lbs.	Intake Manifold Ft. Lbs.	Exhaust Manifold Ft. Lbs.	Rocker Arm Shaft Bracket Ft. Lbs.	Rocker Arm Cover Ft. Lbs.	Connecting Rod Cap Bolts Ft. Lbs.	Main Bearing Cap Bolts Ft. Lbs.	Flywheel to Crankshaft Ft. Lbs.	Vibration Damper or Pulley Ft. Lbs.
1983-84	4-150/U	27	85②	23	23	19③	28①	33	80	⑤	80④
1982	4-151/B	11	92	37	37	20③	7	30	65	68	160
1983	4-151/B	11	92	26	37	20③	7	30	65	68	162
1982-88	6-258/C	11	85②	23	23	19③	28①	33	80	105	80④

①—Inch pounds.
②—Coat underside of cylinder head bolt heads & threads with a suitable sealing compound.
③—Rocker arm capscrew.
④—Lubricate bolt threads lightly before assembly.
⑤—Torque bolts to 50 ft. lbs., then tighten bolts an additional 60 degrees.

DRIVE AXLE SPECIFICATIONS

Year	Model	Carrier Type ②	Ring Gear & Pinion Backlash		Pinion Bearing Preload			Differential Bearing Preload		
			Method	Adjustment	Method	New Bearings Inch Lbs.	Used Bearings Inch Lbs.	Method	New Bearings Inch Lbs.	Used Bearings Inch-Lbs.
1982-88	7 9/16" Dr. Gr.③	Integral	Shims	.005-.009	Sleeve	15-25①	15-25①	Shims	.008	.008
	MODEL 30④	Integral	Shims	.005-.010	Shims	20-40①	15-25①	Shims	.015	.015

①—Adjust at drive pinion flange nut with inch pound torque wrench.
②—Rear axle shaft endplay, .006 inch. Eagle front axle shaft endplay, .003 inch.
③—Rear Axle.
④—Eagle front axle.

COOLING SYSTEM & CAPACITY DATA

Year	Model or Engine/VIN	Cooling Capacity, Qts.		Radiator Cap Relief Pressure, Lbs.	Thermo. Opening Temp.	Fuel Tank Gals.	Engine Oil Refill Qts. ①	Transmission Oil		Rear Axle Oils Pint
		Less A/C	With A/C					4 & 5 Speed Pints	Auto Trans. Qts. ②	
1982	4-151/B Spirit & Concord	6.5	6.5	15	195	21⑦	3⑨	④	7.1	3
	4-151/B Eagle	6.5	6.5	15	195	22⑫	3⑨	④⑥	7.1⑥	3③
	6-258/C Spirit & Concord	11⑪	14	15	195	21⑦	4	④	8.5	3
	6-258/C Eagle	11⑪	14	15	195	22⑫	4	④⑥	8.5⑥	3③
1983	4-150/U Eagle	6.5	6.5	15	195	21	3.5⑤	④⑥	7.1⑥	3③
	4-151/B Eagle	6.5	6.5	15	195	⑩	3⑨	④⑥	7.1⑥	3③
	6-258/C Spirit & Concord	11⑪	14	15	195	21⑦	4	⑧	8.5	3
	6-258/C Eagle	14	14	15	195	⑩	4	④⑥	8.5⑥	3③
1984	4-150/U Eagle	9	9	15	195	22	3.5⑤	④⑥	7⑥	3③
	6-258/C Eagle	14	14	15	195	22	4	④⑥	7⑥	3③
1985-88	6-258/C Eagle	14	14	15	195	22	4	4	8.5⑥	3③

①—Add one quart with filter change.
②—Approximate. Make final check with dipstick.
③—Front axle, 2.5 pts.
④—Four speed man. trans., 3.5 pts.; five speed man. trans., 4.0 pts.
⑤—Add .5 qt. with filter change.
⑥—Transfer case, 3.0 qts.
⑦—Concord, 22 gal.
⑧—Four speed man. trans., 4 pts.; five speed man. trans., 4.5 pts.
⑨—With or without filter change.
⑩—Except SX-4, 22 gals.; SX-4, 21 gals.
⑪—With heavy duty cooling system, 14 qts.
⑫—Kammback & SX-4, 21 gals.

Electrical Section

INDEX

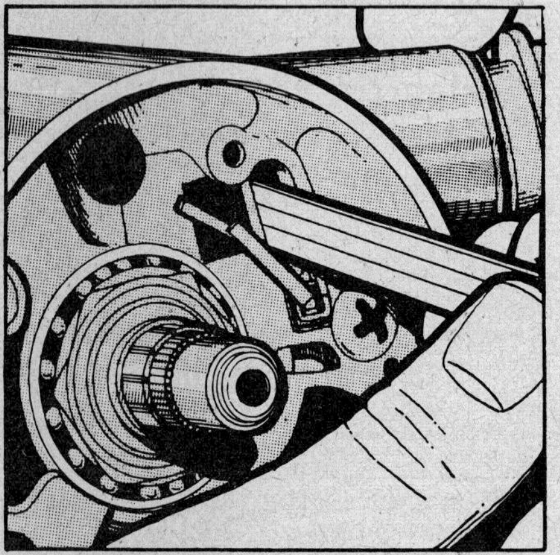

Fig. 1 Lock cylinder removal

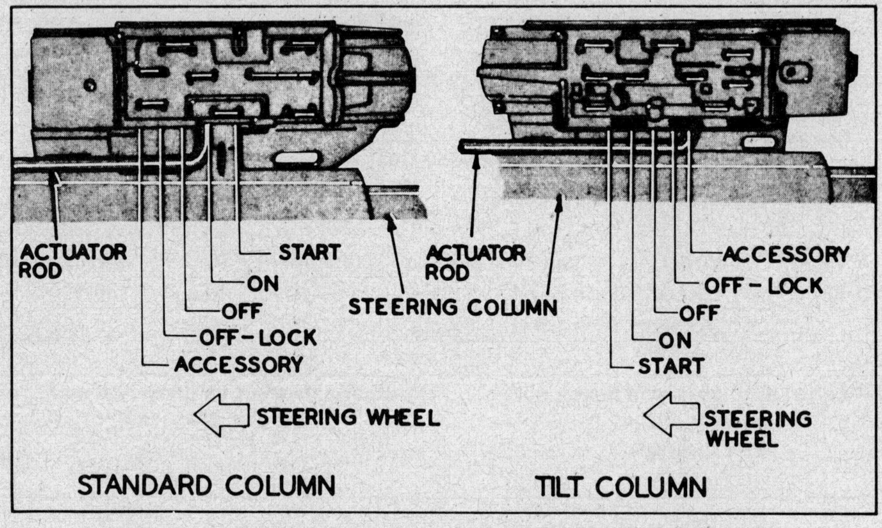

Fig. 2 Ignition switch installation (typical)

STARTER REPLACE

If shims are used to position starter motor, note location of shims, as shims must be reinstalled in the same locations during starter installation.

EXCEPT EAGLE 6-258 & 1982–83 4-151

1. Disconnect battery ground cable.
2. Disconnect cable from starter motor terminal.
3. Remove attaching bolts and remove starter.
4. Reverse procedure to install.

EAGLE 6-258

Man. Trans.

1. Disconnect battery ground cable.
2. Disconnect cable from starter motor terminal.
3. Detach vibration bracket at front axle tube.
4. Remove bolts attaching bracket to flywheel housing, then loosen bolt at starter motor.
5. Swing bracket downward, away from starter motor, then remove remaining attaching bolt and starter motor.
6. Reverse procedure to install.

Auto. Trans.

1. Disconnect battery ground cable.
2. Disconnect cable from starter motor terminal.
3. Detach front section of bracket from front axle tube, then detach rear section of bracket from converter housing.
4. Remove attaching bolts and starter motor.
5. Reverse procedure to install.

1982–83 4-151

1. Disconnect battery ground cable, then remove starter motor to engine brace. On Eagle models it may be necessary to remove an additional brace to remove starter motor.
2. Remove two starter motor to engine attaching bolts, then lower starter motor and disconnect wiring from solenoid.
3. Remove starter motor from vehicle.
4. Reverse procedure to install. Reinstall any shims that were removed.

IGNITION LOCK REPLACE

1. Remove turn signal switch as described further on.
2. Place key lock in "Lock" position and using a small flat blade screwdriver to depress the lock cylinder retaining tab, remove the lock cylinder, **Fig. 1.**
3. Reverse procedure to install.

IGNITION SWITCH REPLACE

On Concord, Eagle and Spirit models, remove package tray, if equipped.

The ignition switch, **Fig. 2,** is mounted on the lower section of the steering column of all models and is connected to the steering lock by a remote control rod.

REMOVAL

1. Disconnect battery ground cable.
2. Place ignition lock in "Off-Lock" position and remove switch attaching screws.
3. Disconnect switch from control rod and wiring connectors from switch, then remove switch from steering column.

INSTALLATION

1. On standard steering columns, move slider to extreme left and on tilt steering columns, move slider to extreme right. This places the switch in the "Accessory" position.

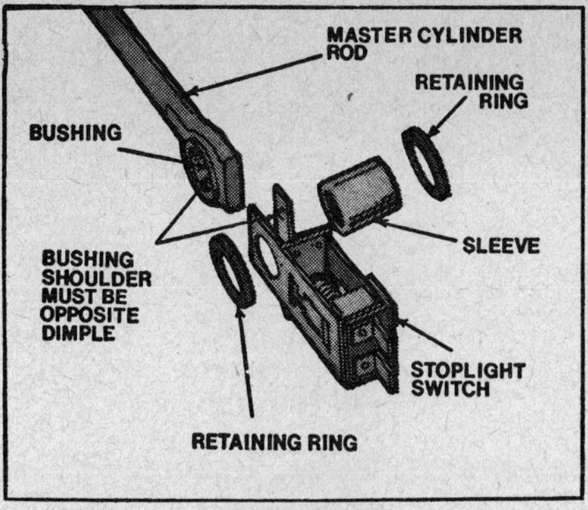

Fig. 3 Stoplight switch (typical)

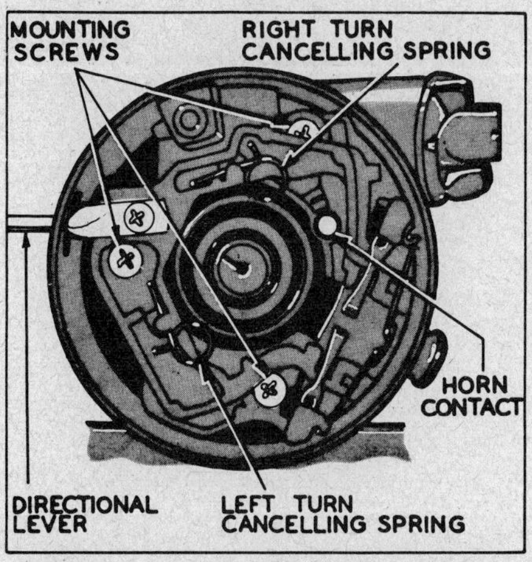

Fig. 5 Turn signal switch

2. Place actuator rod in slider hole and install switch on steering column without moving slider out of detent. Hold key in "Accessory" position and push switch downward to remove slack in linkage and tighten screws.
3. Connect battery ground cable and check for proper operation.

LIGHT SWITCH
REPLACE

1. Disconnect battery ground cable.
2. Remove package tray, if equipped, and disconnect speedometer cable.
3. Remove instrument cluster bezel attaching screws and tilt bezel away from instrument panel.
4. With switch in full "On" position, press release button on switch and remove shaft and knob assembly.
5. Remove switch mounting sleeve nut.
6. Disconnect electrical connectors from switch and remove switch from vehicle.
7. Reverse procedure to install.

STOP LIGHT SWITCH
REPLACE

1. Disconnect battery ground cable.
2. Remove package tray, if equipped.
3. Disconnect wire connector from switch.
4. Remove brake pedal pivot bolt, nylon retaining rings, sleeve, and remove switch.
5. When installing switch, be sure dimple on switch is opposite the bushing collar, Fig. 3. **There are two bolt holes on the brake pedal. On models equipped with power brakes, install bolt in lower hole. On models less power brakes, install bolt in upper hole.**
6. Reverse procedure to install.

NEUTRAL SAFETY SWITCH
REPLACE
EXC. 1982–83 4-151

1. Raise and support vehicle.
2. Disconnect wiring from switch and unscrew from transmission. Allow fluid to drain into a container.
3. Move shift linkage to park and neutral positions and check switch operating fingers for proper positioning.
4. Reverse procedure to install. Correct transmission fluid level as required.

TURN SIGNAL SWITCH
REPLACE

1. Disconnect battery ground cable, then remove steering wheel.
2. Using lock plate compressor tool No. J-23653, depress lock plate and remove and pry round wire snap ring from steering shaft groove, **Fig. 4. On some models, the steering shaft has metric threads and is identified by a blue colored steering wheel nut and/or a groove cut into the steering shaft splines. If shaft has metric threads, replace compressor forcing screw with metric forcing screw J-23653-4 to depress lock plate.**
3. Remove lock plate compressor tool, snap ring, lock plate and directional signal canceling cam from steering shaft.
4. Place directional signal lever in the right turn position, then remove lever and directional signal switch mounting screws, **Fig. 5.**
5. Depress hazard warning switch and remove button by turning in counterclockwise direction.
6. Remove directional signal switch wiring harness connector from mounting bracket on right side of lower column.
7. Remove steering tube cover.
8. Remove steering column lower bracket bolts, then loosen steering column bracket nuts.
9. Fold connector over harness and wrap with tape to avoid snagging, **Fig. 6.** Raise column and pull harness out of column. **On models with tilt column, raise column and remove plastic wiring harness protector.**
10. On Concord models, with column shift, automatic transmission, use stiff wire, such as a paper clip, to depress lock tab which retains shift quadrant light wire to wiring harness connector.

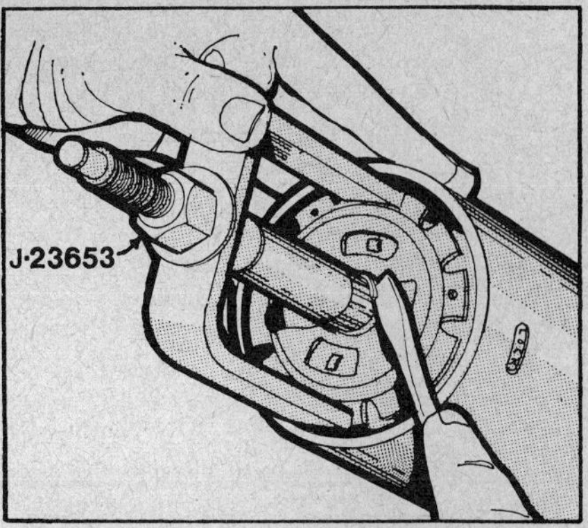

Fig. 4 Compressing lock plate & removing retaining ring

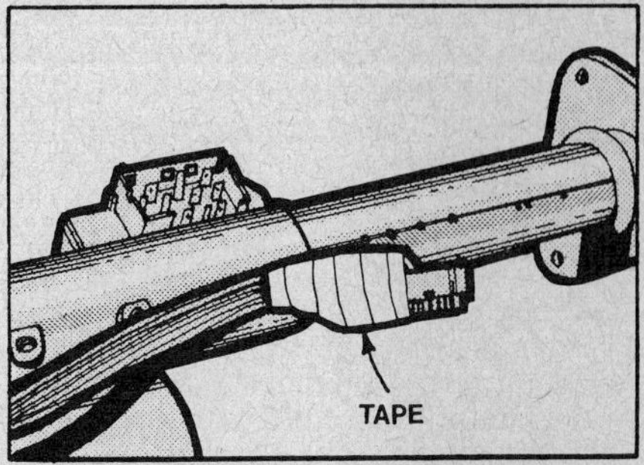

Fig. 6 Taping turn signal connector & wires

The shift quadrant light wire is the gray wire connected to terminal D on wiring harness connector.

11. Reverse procedure to install.

HORN SOUNDER & STEERING WHEEL
REPLACE

1. Disconnect battery ground cable.
2. On steering wheels with horn buttons, remove button by first lifting button upward, and then pulling button out. On steering wheels equipped with horn ring or bar, remove screws from back of steering wheel, then pull wire plastic retainer out of directional signal canceling cam and remove horn ring or bar.
3. Remove steering wheel nut and washer. Note alignment marks on steering wheel and shaft for use during installation. If marks are not present, paint alignment marks on shaft and steering wheel. **Some steering shafts have metric steering wheel nut threads. Metric steering wheel nuts are color coded blue for identification and steering shafts will have an identifying groove on shaft steering wheel splines.**
4. Using a suitable puller, remove steering wheel.
5. Reverse procedure to install.

INSTRUMENT CLUSTER
REPLACE

1. Disconnect battery ground cable.

2. Remove lower steering column cover. On models equipped with column shift automatic transmission, remove gear selector dial actuator cable from steering column shift shroud.
3. Remove instrument cluster bezel attaching screws across top of bezel, above radio and behind glove box door.
4. Tip top of bezel outward and disengage tabs along bottom edge of bezel.
5. If equipped, disconnect glove box lamp wire connector.
6. Depress speedometer cable locking tab and disconnect speedometer cable.
7. Push downward on three illumination lamp housings above bezel, until lamp housings are clear of instrument panel.
8. Disconnect headlamp switch and wiper control connectors and switch lamp. **To disconnect headlamp switch connector, lift two locking tabs.**
9. Twist and remove cluster illumination lamp sockets, then disconnect instrument cluster wire connectors.
10. Remove clock or tachometer attaching screws, if equipped. It is not necessary to remove clock adjusting knob.
11. Disconnect clock or tachometer feed wires from circuit board, if equipped.
12. Remove cluster housing and circuit board to bezel attaching screws.
13. Remove cluster housing and circuit board assembly from bezel, **Fig. 7.** If equipped with clock or tachometer, position aside as necessary.

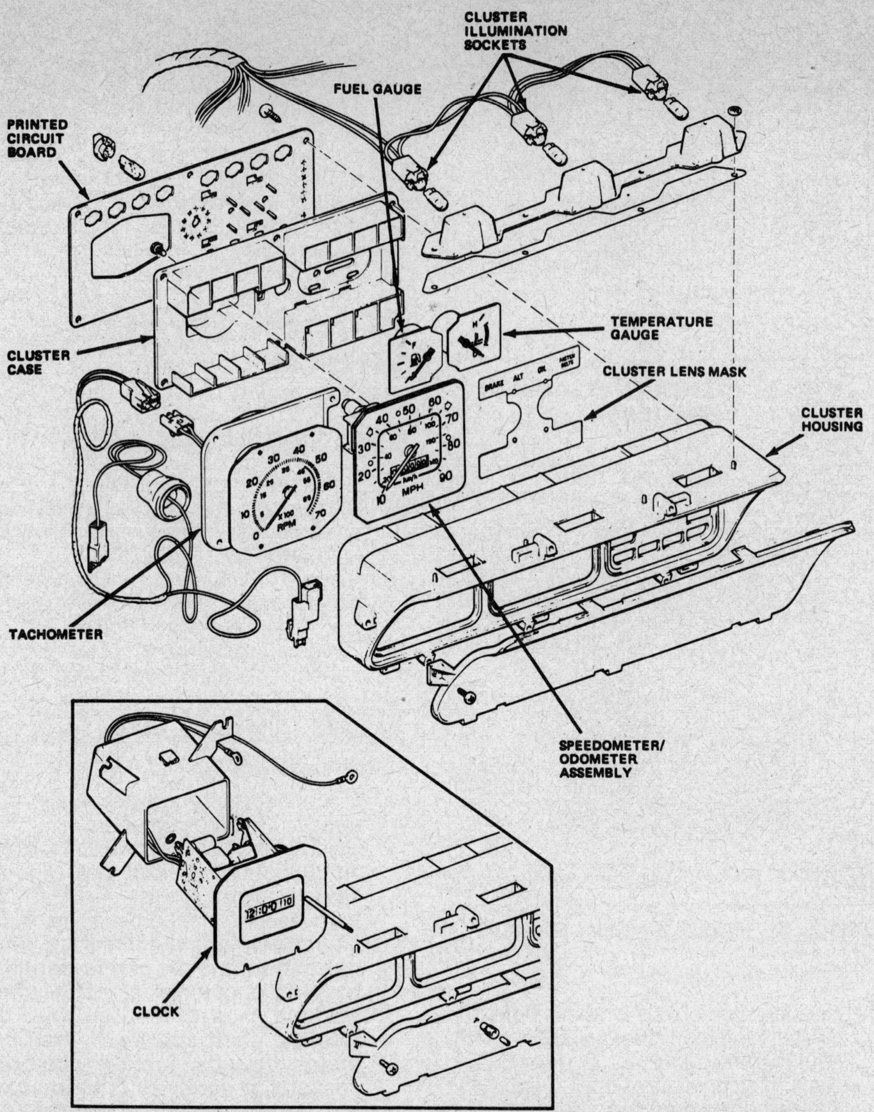

Fig. 7 Instrument cluster (typical). Concord, Eagle & Spirit

WINDSHIELD WIPER MOTOR
REPLACE

1. Disconnect battery ground cable. Remove wiper arms and blades.
2. Remove four screws holding motor to dash.
3. Separate harness connector at the motor.
4. Pull motor and linkage out of opening to expose the drive link to crank stud retaining clip. Raise up the lock tab of the clip with a flat bladed screwdriver and slide clip off stud.
5. Reverse procedure to install.

LIFTGATE WIPER MOTOR
REPLACE

1. Disconnect battery ground cable. Remove wiper arm and blade.
2. Remove liftgate trim pad.
3. Disconnect wiring harness and ground wire.
4. Remove nut and pad securing wiper motor shaft to liftgate.
5. Remove screws securing wiper motor bracket, then separate bracket from motor.
6. Reverse procedure to install.

WINDSHIELD WIPER TRANSMISSION
REPLACE

1. Disconnect battery ground cable. Remove wiper arms and blades.
2. Remove pivot shaft-to-cowl top nuts.
3. Remove wiper motor.
4. Slide pivot shaft body and link assembly to the left to clear right pivot shaft opening and move assembly to the right side of car to remove as a unit.
5. Reverse procedure to install. **When installing pivot shafts to cowl top, flat side of pivot shaft indexes flat side of hole in cowl top when pivot shaft is in up position.**

WINDSHIELD WIPER SWITCH
REPLACE

1. Disconnect battery ground cable.
2. Locate small notch at base of knob and insert a small screwdriver and apply pressure to release spring and pull knob from shaft.
3. Remove slotted trim nut from front of switch.
4. Push switch through instrument panel, then disconnect wiring harness and remove switch.
5. Reverse procedure to install.

RADIO
REPLACE

When installing radio, be sure to adjust antenna trimmer for peak performance.

1. Disconnect battery ground cable.
2. Remove radio knobs and retaining nuts. On models equipped with C.B. radio, remove radio bezel.
3. Remove instrument cluster center housing retaining screws, then remove center housing.
4. Disconnect power and speaker wiring and antenna lead, then remove radio.
5. Reverse procedure to install.

HEATER CORE
REPLACE

1. Disconnect battery ground cable, then drain about 2 qts. from cooling system.
2. Disconnect heater hoses and plug heater core tubes.
3. Remove blower motor and fan.
4. Remove housing attaching nut(s) from inside engine compartment.
5. Remove package tray if so equipped.
6. Disconnect wire connector at resistor.
7. On models with A/C, remove instrument panel bezel, outlet and duct.
8. Disconnect control cables from damper levers.
9. Remove right side windshield pillar molding and the instrument panel upper attaching screws and right side cap screw at the door hinge post.
10. Remove right side kick panel and heater housing attaching screws.
11. Pull the right side of the instrument panel slightly rearward and remove the housing.
12. Remove cover and screws attaching heater core to housing, then remove heater core from housing.
13. Reverse procedure to install.

BLOWER MOTOR
REPLACE

1. Disconnect battery ground cable.
2. Working in engine compartment, disconnect blower motor wire.
3. Remove three retaining nuts for blower scroll cover to which blower assembly is attached and remove blower motor and fan.
4. Reverse procedure to install.

SPEED CONTROL
ADJUST
CENTERING ADJUSTMENT

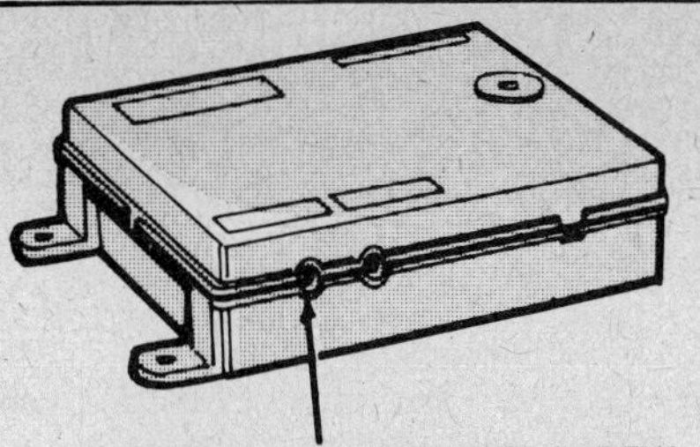

Fig. 8 Centering adjusting screw location.

This adjustment is made by turning the centering adjusting screw on the regulator, **Fig. 8.** If speed control engages at two or more mph higher than selected speed, turn centering adjusting screw counterclockwise a small amount. If engagement speed is two or more mph below selected speed, turn centering adjusting screw clockwise a small amount. Check for proper centering adjustment on a level road after making each adjustment.

VACUUM DUMP VALVE

While holding brake pedal in the depressed position, move vacuum dump valve toward pedal bracket as far as possible, then release brake pedal.

4-150 (2.46L) Engine Section

INDEX

ENGINE MOUNTS
REPLACE

Removal or replacement of any cushion can be accomplished by supporting the weight of the engine or transmission at the area of the cushion to be replaced.

ENGINE
REPLACE

The engine is removed without the transmission as follows:

1. Drain cooling system.
2. Mark hood hinge locations, disconnect underhood lamp, if equipped, and remove hood.
3. Disconnect battery cables, and remove battery.
4. Disconnect alternator wiring and the ignition coil, distributor and oil pressure sender leads.
5. Remove TCS switch bracket from cylinder block, if equipped.
6. Disconnect flexible fuel line from fuel pump and plug line and pump port.
7. Disconnect engine ground strap.
8. Remove the right front engine support cushion to bracket screw.
9. If equipped with air conditioning:
   a. Remove service valve covers and front seat valves.
   b. Loosen service valve to compressor attaching nuts.
   c. Bleed compressor refrigerant charge.
   d. Remove service valves and cap compressor ports and service valves.
   e. Disconnect clutch feed wire.
10. Remove starter.
11. Remove air cleaner and disconnect purge hose from canister and TAC vacuum hose from manifold, if equipped.
12. Disconnect throttle stop solenoid lead, if equipped.
13. Disconnect fuel return hose from fuel filter and the carburetor bowl vent hose from canister.
14. Disconnect throttle cable and remove from bracket. Disconnect throttle valve rod at carburetor and the bellcrank.
15. Disconnect heater and air conditioning system vacuum hose from intake manifold.
16. Disconnect temperature sender wire and TCS vacuum solenoid wiring harness.
17. Disconnect radiator hoses from radiator and the heater hoses from engine.
18. Disconnect transmission oil cooler lines from radiator, if equipped.
19. Remove fan shroud attaching screws, then the radiator and shroud.
20. Remove fan and spacer. Install a 5/16 x 1/2 inch capscrew through fan pulley, into water pump flange.
21. Remove power brake vacuum check valve from power brake unit, if equipped.
22. If equipped with power steering, disconnect hoses from gear and drain reservoir. Cap gear ports and hoses.
23. Remove transmission filler tube bracket screw, if equipped.
24. Raise and support vehicle on jack stands.

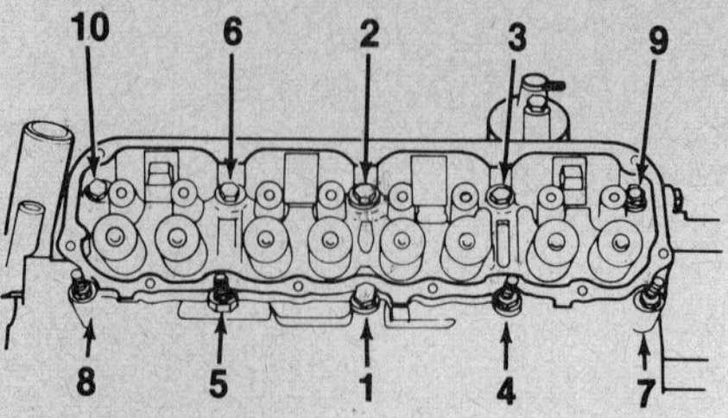

Fig. 1 Cylinder head tightening sequence. 4-150

25. If equipped with automatic transmission:
    a. Remove converter housing spacer cover.
    b. Remove converter attaching screws.
    c. Remove exhaust pipe support from converter housing. This also supports the inner end of the transmission linkage.
26. If equipped with manual transmission:
    a. Remove clutch housing cover and clutch bellcrank inner support screws.
    b. Disconnect springs and remove bellcrank.
    c. Remove outer bellcrank to strut rod bracket retainer.
    d. Disconnect back-up lamp switch wiring harness under hood at dash panel to gain access to clutch housing screw.
27. On all models, remove engine mount cushion to bracket screws.
28. To remove front axle assembly, proceed as follows:
    a. Support axle assembly, then remove half shaft to axle flange attaching bolts.
    b. Compress half shafts inward, toward wheels, and secure to frame side sills with wire.
    c. Remove axle bracket attaching bolts at axle tube and right hand engine mount, then remove axle bracket.
    d. Remove axle bracket attaching bolts at pinion end of axle.
    e. Remove left engine mount support to front axle bracket attaching bolts.
    f. Disconnect axle vent hose, then lower axle assembly and remove from vehicle.
29. Disconnect exhaust pipe from manifold.
30. Remove upper converter or clutch housing screws and loosen the bottom screws.
31. Raise vehicle and support on jackstands.
32. Remove air conditioning compressor drive belt idler pulley and the compressor mounting bracket, if equipped.
33. Install suitable engine lifting equipment and slightly raise engine. Support transmission with a suitable jack.
34. Remove remaining converter or clutch housing screws.
35. Remove engine from vehicle.
36. Reverse procedure to install.

CYLINDER HEAD

REPLACE

1. Disconnect battery ground cable, then drain cooling system.
2. Remove intake and exhaust manifold bolts. Remove manifolds and intake manifold gasket.
3. Remove valve cover bolts and valve cover.
4. Alternately loosen rocker arm capscrews, then remove bridges, pivots and rocker arms.
5. Remove pushrods and spark plugs.
6. Remove cylinder head bolts and cylinder head.
7. Reverse procedure to install. Coat cylinder head gasket with a suitable sealer and install gasket with the word TOP facing upward. Install cylinder head bolts and torque to specifications in sequence, **Fig. 1.** Coat threads of stud No. 8 with a suitable sealer and torque nut to 75 ft. lbs. Torque intake and exhaust manifold bolts to 23 ft. lbs. in sequence, **Fig. 2.**

VALVES

ADJUST

Hydraulic valve lifters are used. No adjustment is required.

VALVE ARRANGEMENT

FRONT TO REAR

4-150.................... E-I-I-E-E-I-I-E

VALVE LIFT SPECIFICATIONS

Engine	Year	Int.	Exh.
4-150	1983-84	.424	.424

VALVE TIMING SPECIFICATIONS

INTAKE OPENS BEFORE TDC

Engine	Year	Degrees
4-150	1983-84	12

ROCKER ARMS

REPLACE

1. Remove rocker arm cover attaching screws, then remove rocker arm cover. **RTV sealant is used between rocker arm cover and cylinder head mating surfaces. To avoid damaging rocker arm cover, do not pry cover upward until seal has been completely broken. When prying cover upward, pry only in areas marked "Pry Here," which are located near rocker arm cover bolt holes.**

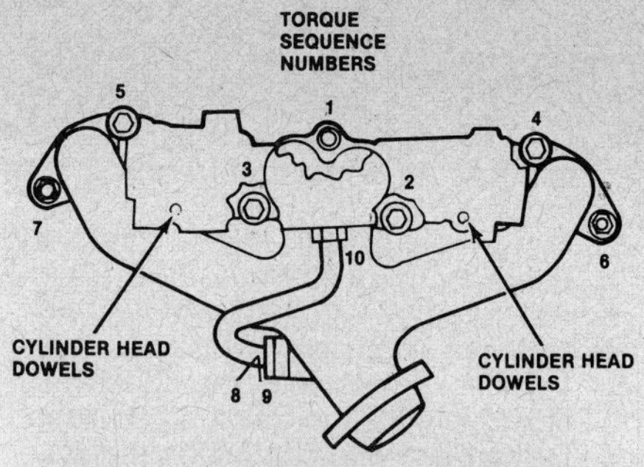

Fig. 2 Intake & exhaust manifold tightening sequence. 4-150

2. Alternately loosen the rocker arm cap screws one turn at a time to prevent damage to bridge, **Fig. 3.**
3. After removing rocker arm cap screws, remove bridge, pivots, rocker arms and pushrods. **Tag all components so they can be reinstalled in the same position as removed.**
4. Reverse procedure to install. When installing rocker arm capscrews, tighten each screw alternately and evenly approximately one turn at a time to prevent damage to bridge.

VALVE GUIDES

The valve guides are an integral part of the cylinder head. If valve stem to guide clearance is excessive, the guide should be reamed to the next oversize and the appropriate oversize valve installed. Valves are available in standard size and oversizes of .003 inch and .015 inch.

VALVE LIFTERS

REPLACE

1. Remove cylinder head cover.
2. Alternately loosen each capscrew one turn at a time, then remove bridge and pivot assemblies, rocker arms and pushrods. **Tag all components so they can be reinstalled in the same positions.**
3. Using tool No. J-21884 or equivalent, remove valve lifters through pushrod openings in cylinder head, **Fig. 4. If lifters are to be reused, retain in same order as removed.**
4. Reverse procedure to install. Before installing, dip each lifter in American Motors Engine Oil Supplement or equivalent. Tighten bridge and pivot assembly capscrews one turn at a time to prevent damage to bridge.

TIMING CASE COVER & TIMING CHAIN

REPLACE

REMOVAL

1. Disconnect battery ground cable, then drain cooling system.
2. Remove bolts securing water and fuel pumps to engine, then remove water and fuel pumps.

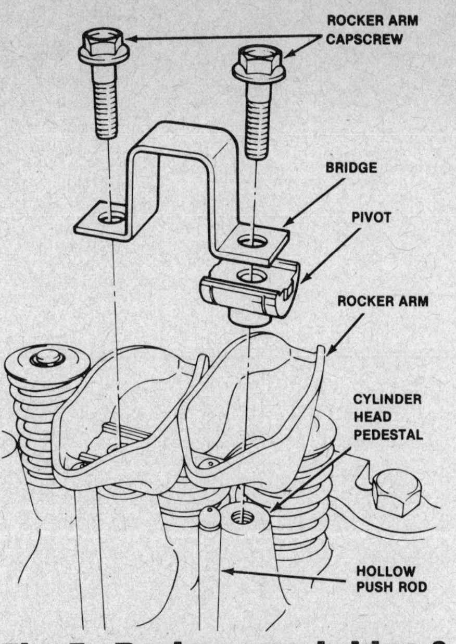

Fig. 3 Rocker arm, bridge & pivot assembly. 4-150

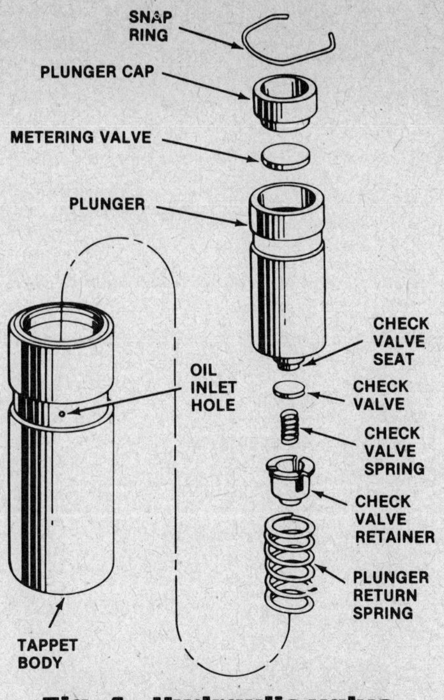

Fig. 4 Hydraulic valve lifter 4-150 assembly

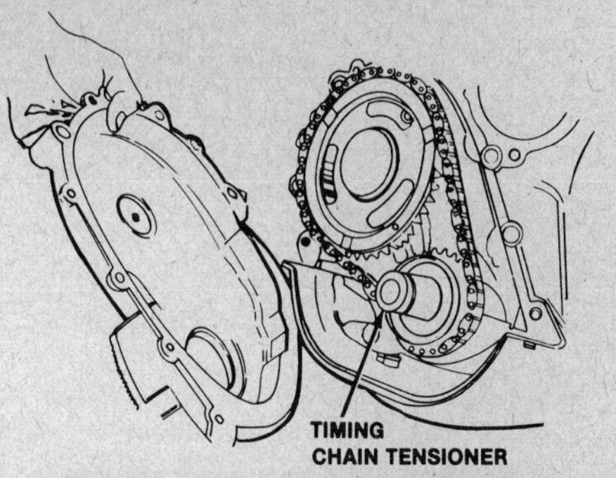

Fig. 5 Removing timing chain cover. 4-150

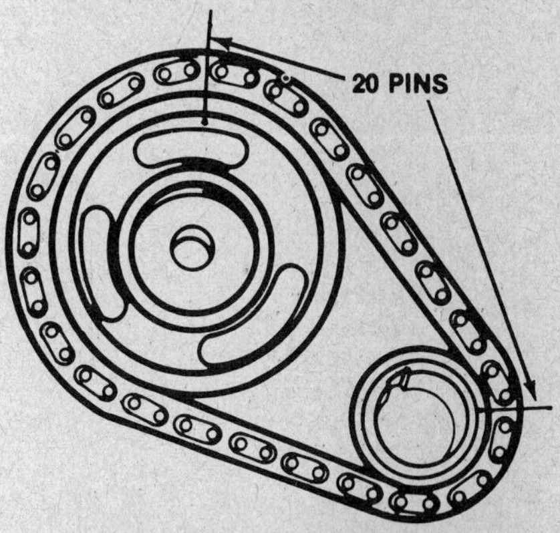

Fig. 8 Timing chain installation check. 4-150

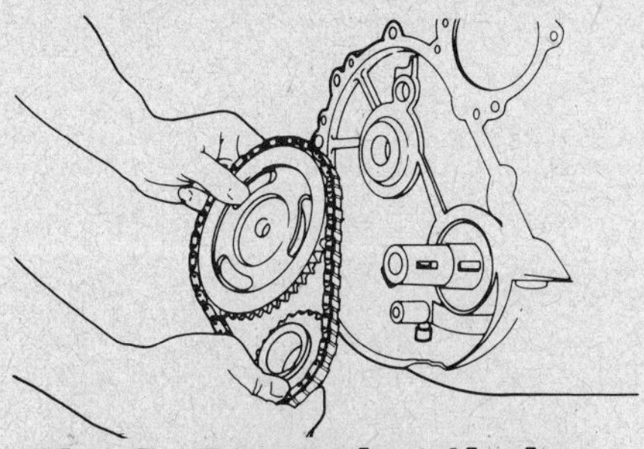

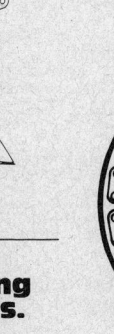

Fig. 6 Removing timing chain & gear sprockets. 4-150

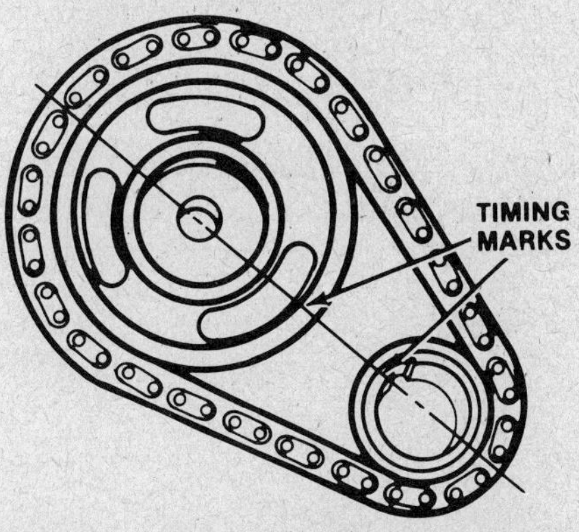

Fig. 7 Valve timing marks. 4-150

3. Remove crankshaft pulley bolts and pulley.
4. Using tool No. J-9256 or equivalent, remove timing chain cover seal.
5. Remove timing chain cover bolts and cover.
6. Remove timing chain tensioner, **Fig. 5.**
7. Remove crankshaft oil slinger.
8. Remove camshaft sprocket retaining bolt and washer, then lift off camshaft sprocket, crankshaft sprocket and timing chain as an assembly, **Fig. 6.**

INSTALLATION

1. Install crankshaft sprocket, camshaft sprocket and timing chain as an assembly. Ensure crankshaft and camshaft sprocket timing marks are aligned, **Fig. 7.**
2. Install camshaft sprocket retaining bolt and washer. Torque camshaft sprocket retaining bolt to 50 ft. lbs. **To verify correct installation of timing chain, rotate crankshaft to position camshaft sprocket timing mark at one o'clock, Fig. 8. The crankshaft sprocket timing mark should now be at the three o'clock position. There should be 20 timing chain pins between the timing marks of both sprockets.**
3. Install timing chain tensioner as follows:
   a. Turn tensioner lever to unlock (down) position, **Fig. 9.**
   b. Pull tensioner block toward tensioner lever. Hold tensioner block and turn tensioner lever to lock (up) position.
   c. Install timing chain tensioner on cylinder block and torque bolts to 14 ft. lbs.
   d. Turn timing chain lever to unlock (down) position. Ensure tensioner is released before installing timing chain cover.
4. Install oil slinger.
5. Using tool No. J-22248 or equivalent for timing chain cover alignment, install timing chain cover, **Fig. 10.** Torque cover bolts to 5 ft. lbs.
6. Coat outside diameter of the timing chain cover seal with suitable sealer and install cover seal. With cover seal in position, coat inside diameter of seal lip with clean engine oil.
7. Insert draw screw of tool No. J-91632 or equivalent into tool No. J-22248, **Fig. 11.** Tighten draw screw nut until tool comes in contact with timing chain cover.
8. Reverse steps 1 through 3 to complete installation procedure.

CAMSHAFT REPLACE

1. Drain cooling system, then remove radiator.
2. Remove A/C condenser and receiver assembly with refrigerant hoses attached and position aside. Do not discharge system.
3. Remove valve lifters as described under "Valve Lifters, Replace."
4. Remove timing case cover and timing chain as described under "Timing Case Cover and Timing Chain, Replace."
5. Remove camshaft.
6. Reverse procedure to install.

PISTON & ROD ASSEMBLE

Pistons are marked with an arrow on the top perimeter, **Fig. 12.** When installing piston in engine, the arrow must face toward front of engine. Always assemble rods and caps with oil squirt holes facing camshaft. Check side clearance between connecting rod and crankshaft journal. Clearance should be .010 to .019 inch.

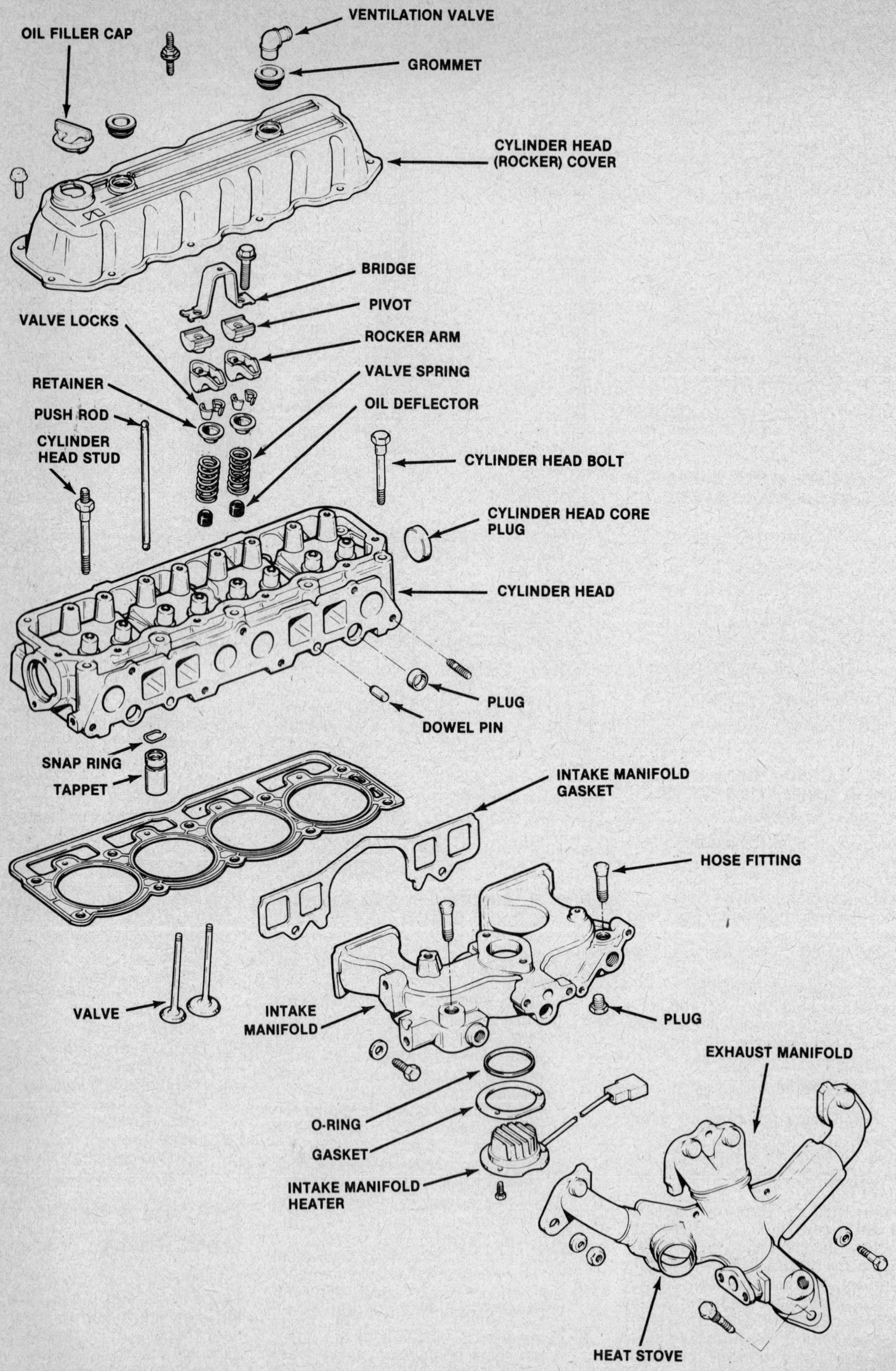

Exploded view of cylinder block & components. 4-150

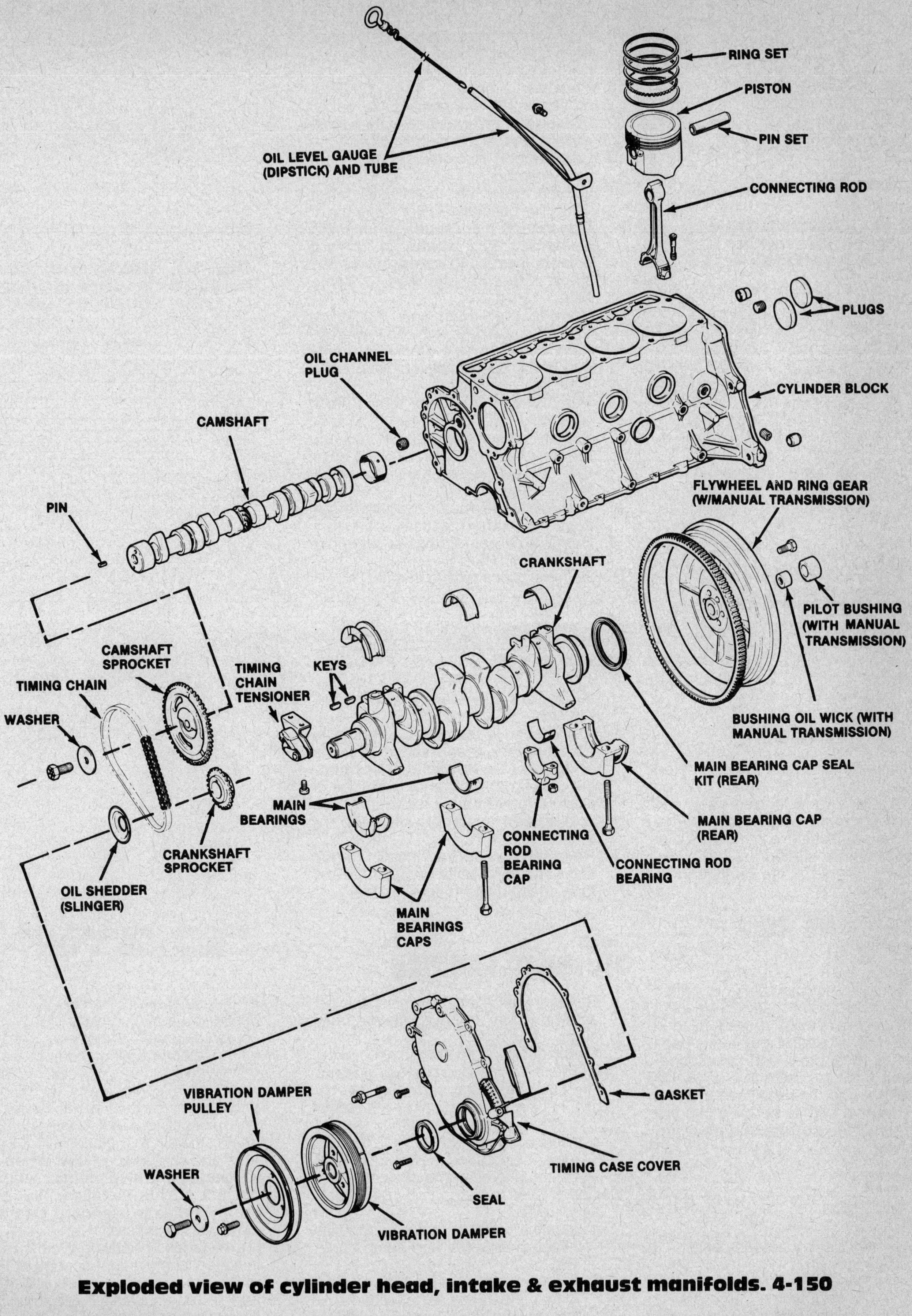
RING SET
PISTON
PIN SET
CONNECTING ROD
OIL LEVEL GAUGE (DIPSTICK) AND TUBE
PLUGS
OIL CHANNEL PLUG
CYLINDER BLOCK
CAMSHAFT
FLYWHEEL AND RING GEAR (W/MANUAL TRANSMISSION)
PIN
CRANKSHAFT
PILOT BUSHING (WITH MANUAL TRANSMISSION)
CAMSHAFT SPROCKET
TIMING CHAIN
TIMING CHAIN TENSIONER
KEYS
WASHER
BUSHING OIL WICK (WITH MANUAL TRANSMISSION)
MAIN BEARING CAP SEAL KIT (REAR)
MAIN BEARINGS
MAIN BEARING CAP (REAR)
CONNECTING ROD BEARING CAP
CRANKSHAFT SPROCKET
CONNECTING ROD BEARING
OIL SHEDDER (SLINGER)
MAIN BEARINGS CAPS
VIBRATION DAMPER PULLEY
GASKET
TIMING CASE COVER
WASHER
SEAL
VIBRATION DAMPER

Exploded view of cylinder head, intake & exhaust manifolds. 4-150

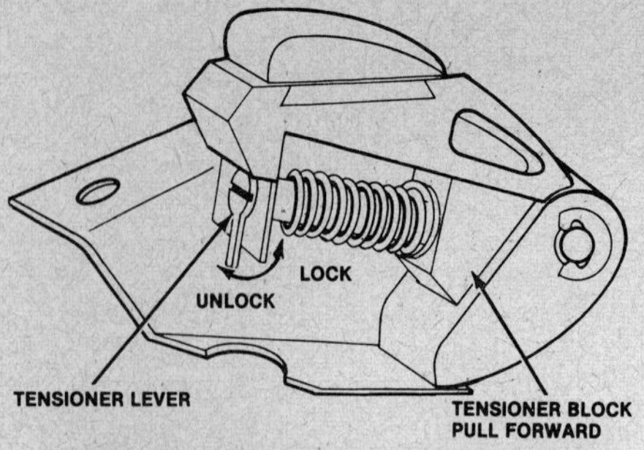

Fig. 9 Position timing chain tensioner in the unlock position. 4-150

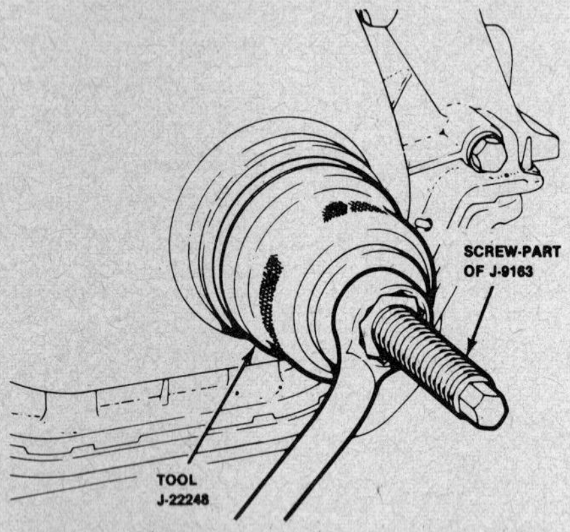

Fig. 11 Installing timing case cover front seal. 4-150

MAIN BEARINGS

The main bearing journal size (diameter) is identified by a color coded paint mark on adjacent cheek toward flanged (rear) end of crankshaft, except for rear main journal which is on crankshaft rear flange. Color codes used to indicate journal and corresponding bearing sizes are listed in **Figs. 13 and 14.**

CONNECTING ROD BEARINGS

The connecting rod journal is identified by a color coded paint mark on adjacent cheek or counterweight toward flanged (rear) end of crankshaft. Color codes used to indicate journal sizes and corresponding bearing sizes are listed in **Fig. 15. Do not intermix the bearing caps. Each connecting rod and its bearing cap are stamped with the corresponding cylinder number.**

OIL PAN
REPLACE

1. Disconnect battery ground cable.
2. Drain engine oil.
3. Lock steering wheel and remove air cleaner.
4. Support engine using a suitable holding fixture.
5. Raise vehicle and support on side sills.
6. Mark for assembly reference and disconnect front driveshaft.
7. Remove engine cushion bolts.
8. Remove bolts from sill-to-crossmember and position bar aside.
9. Loosen pitman arm at gear, then loosen idler arm at steering linkage.
10. Remove bolt from steering damper at crossmember.
11. Loosen sway bar bolts and lower sway bar bolts and lower sway bar.
12. Disconnect half shafts from axle. **Compress half shafts in toward wheels, secure in compressed position with wire attached to frame sills.**
13. Remove bolts from right bracket at axle tube bolt bars, then remove bolts from left upper axle bracket at upper end, and bolts from pinion end bracket at pinion.
14. Remove vent hose and remove axle assembly.
15. Support crossmembers with jack and remove crossmember nuts and bolts, then lower crossmember assembly for clearance.
16. Remove starter motor, then the torque converter housing access cover.
17. Remove oil pan screws and remove oil pan, **Fig. 16.**
18. Reverse procedure to install.

OIL PUMP
REPLACE

1. Drain crankcase, then remove oil pan, **Fig. 16.**
2. Remove bolts attaching oil pump to cylinder block, then remove oil pump and gasket. **Do not disturb positioning of oil pump strainer and tube. If tube is moved a replacement tube and screen assembly must be installed.**
3. Reverse procedure to install. Torque short attaching bolts to 10 ft. lbs. and long attaching bolts to 17 ft. lbs.

OIL PUMP SERVICE

1. Remove oil pump cover retaining screws, then remove cover from pump body.
2. Check gear end clearance as follows:
   a. Place straightedge across ends of gears and pump body, **Fig. 17.**
   b. Check clearance using a suitable feeler gauge.
   c. Clearance should be .002 to .006 inch. If clearance is not within limits, replace oil pump assembly.
3. Check gear to pump body clearance as follows:
   a. Insert a suitable feeler gauge between gear tooth and pump body, **Fig. 18.**
   b. Clearance should be .002 to .004 inch. If clearance is not within limits, replace idler gear, idler shaft and drive gear assembly.

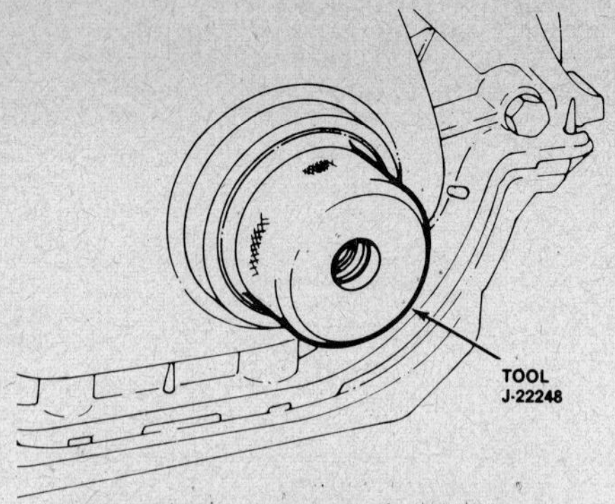

Fig. 10 Using tool No. J-22248 to align timing case cover. 4-150

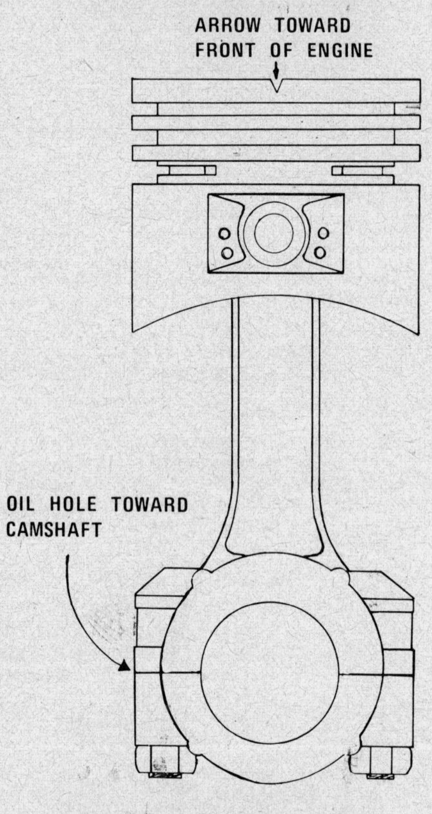

Fig. 12 Piston & rod assemble. 4-150

4. If pressure relief valve is to be checked, move pickup tube and screen assembly out of way. Remove spring retainer, spring and oil pressure relief valve plunger. Check pressure relief valve components for binding and clean or replace as necessary. After reinstalling relief valve components, install a replacement pickup tube and screen assembly. **When replacing relief valve plunger, ensure correct size is installed. Plungers are available in standard size and .010 inch oversize.**
5. If a replacement pickup tube is to be installed, apply a light coating of Permatex No. 2 sealant or equivalent to end of tube. Install pickup tube and screen using tool No. J-21882, **Fig. 19.**

Crankshaft No. 1 Main Bearing Journal Color Codes and Diameter in Inches (mm)	Cylinder Block No. 1 Main Bearing Bore Color Code and Size in Inches (mm)		Bearing Insert Color Code	
			Upper Insert Size	Lower Insert Size
Yellow — 2.5001 to 2.4996 (Standard) (63.5025 to 63.4898 mm)	Yellow —	2.6910 to 2.6915 (68.3514 to 68.3641 mm)	Yellow — Standard	Yellow — Standard
	Black —	2.6915 to 2.6920 (68.3641 to 68.3768 mm)	Yellow — Standard	Black — 0.001-inch Undersize (0.025 mm)
Orange — 2.4996 to 2.4991 (0.0005 Undersize) (63.4898 to 63.4771 mm)	Yellow —	2.6910 to 2.6915 (68.3514 to 68.3641 mm)	Yellow — Standard	Black — 0.001-inch Undersize — (0.001 mm)
	Black —	2.6915 to 2.6920 (68.3461 to 68.3768 mm)	Black — 0.001-inch Undersize (0.025 mm)	Black — 0.001-inch Undersize (0.025 mm)
Black — 2.4991 to 2.4986 (0.001 Undersize) (63.4771 to 63.4644 mm)	Yellow —	2.6910 to 2.6915 (68.3514 to 68.3641 mm)	Black — 0.001-inch Undersize — (0.025 mm)	Black — 0.001-inch Undersize — (0.025 mm)
	Black —	2.6915 to 2.6920 (68.3461 to 68.3768 mm)	Black — 0.001-inch Undersize (0.025 mm)	Green — 0.002-inch Undersize (0.051 mm)
Green — 2.4986 to 2.4981 (0.0015 Undersize) (63.4644 to63.4517 mm)	Yellow —	2.6910 to 2.6915 (68.3514 to 68.3641 mm)	Black — 0.001-inch Undersize — (0.025 mm)	Green — 0.002-inch Undersize — (0.051 mm)
Red — 2.4901 to 2.4896 (0.010 Undersize) (63.2485 to 63.2358 mm)	Yellow —	2.6910 to 2.6915 (68.3514 to 68.3641 mm)	Red — 0.010-inch Undersize (0.254 mm)	Red — 0.010-inch Undersize — (0.254 mm)

Fig. 13 Main bearing selection chart. 4-150 No. 1 main bearing

Crankshaft Main Bearing Journal 2-3-4-5 Color Code and Diameter in Inches (Journal Size)	Bearing Insert Color Code	
	Upper Insert Size	Lower Insert Size
Yellow — 2.5001 to 2.4996 (Standard) (63.5025 to 63.4898 mm)	Yellow — Standard	Yellow — Standard
Orange — 2.4996 to 2.4991 (0.0005 Undersize) (63.4898 to 63.4771 mm)	Yellow — Standard	Black — 0.001-inch Undersize (0.025mm)
Black — 2.4991 to 2.4986 (0.001 Undersize) (63.4771 to 63.4644 mm)	Black — 0.001-inch Undersize (0.025 mm)	Black — 0.001-inch Undersize (0.025 mm)
Green — 2.4986 to 2.4981 (0.0015 Undersize) (63.4644 to 63.4517 mm)	Black — 0.001-inch Undersize (0.025 mm)	Green — 0.002-inch Undersize (0.051 mm)
Red — 2.4901 to 2.4896 (0.010 Undersize) (63.2485 to 63.2358 mm)	Red — 0.010-inch Undersize (0.054 mm)	Red — 0.010-inch Undersize (0.254 mm)

Fig. 14 Main bearing selection chart. 4-150 Nos. 2, 3, 4, 5 main bearings

Connecting Rod Bearing Journal 2-3-4-5 Color Code and Diameter in Inches (Journal Size)	Bearing Insert Color Code	
	Upper Insert Size	Lower Insert Size
Yellow — 2.0955 to 2.0948 (53.2257 - 53.2079 mm) (Standard)	Yellow — Standard	Yellow — Standard
Orange —2.0948 to 2.0941 (53.2079 - 53.1901 mm) (0.0007 Undersize)	Yellow — Standard	Black — 0.001-inch (0.025 mm) Undersize
Black — 2.0941 to 2.0943 (53.1901 to 53.1723 mm) (0.0014 Undersize)	Black — 0.001-inch (0.025 mm) Undersize	Black — 0.001-inch (0.025 mm) Undersize
Red — 2.0855 to 2.0848 (53.9717 to 53.9539 mm) (0.010 Undersize)	Red — 0.010-inch (0.254 mm) Undersize	Red — 0.010-inch (0.245 mm) Undersize

Fig. 15 Connecting rod bearing selection chart. 4-150

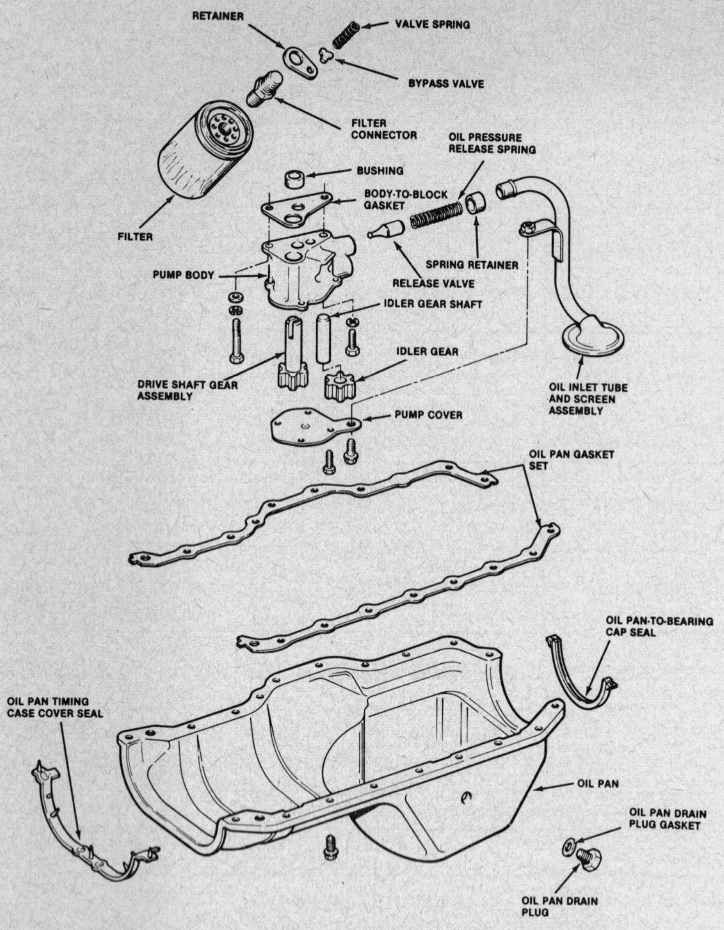

Fig. 16 Oil pan & oil pump. 4-150

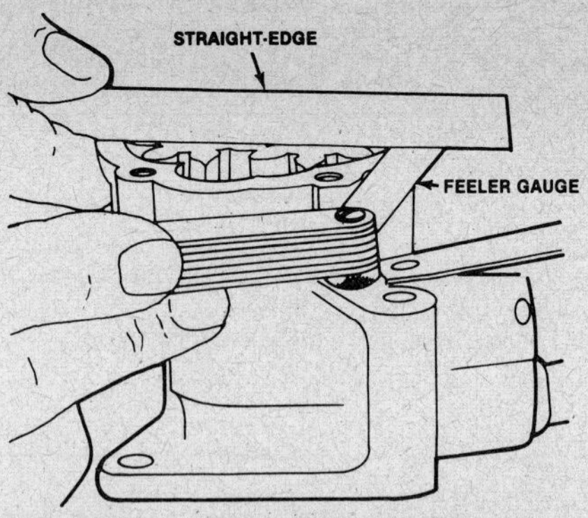

Fig. 17 Checking oil pump gear end clearance. 4-150

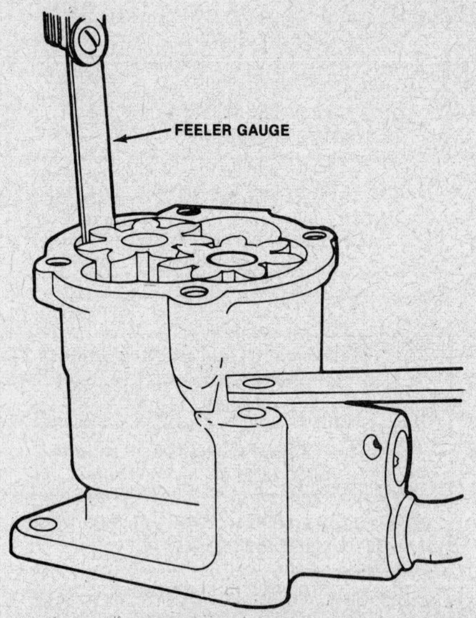

Fig. 18 Checking oil pump gear to body clearance. 4-150

6. Before installing pump cover, fill pump with petroleum jelly.
7. When installing pump cover, torque attaching screws to 70 inch lbs.

BELT TENSION DATA

Belt	New Lbs.	Used Lbs.
V Type Belts		
A/C Comp.	125-155	90-115
Air Pump Less Power Steer.	125-155	90-115°
Air Pump W/Power Steer.	65-75	60-70°
Alternator	125-155	90-115°
Power Steer.	125-155	90-115
Serpentine Type Belt		
All	180-200	140-160

WATER PUMP

REPLACE

1. Drain cooling system.

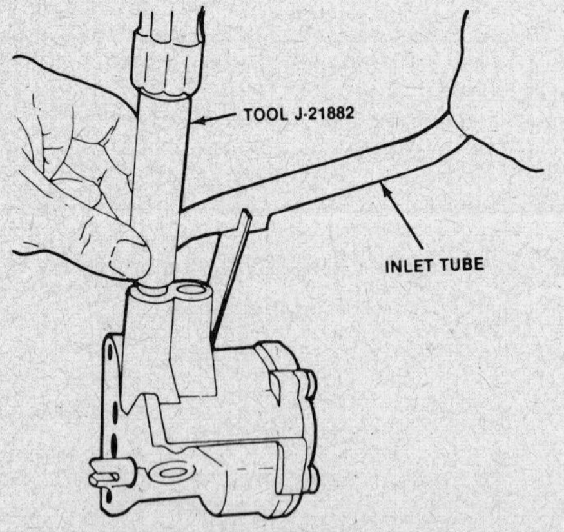

Fig. 19 Installing oil pump pickup screen & tube assembly. 4-150

2. Disconnect radiator and heater hoses from water pump.
3. Remove drive belts.
4. If equipped, remove fan shroud attaching screws, then remove fan and fan shroud.
5. Remove water pump attaching bolts, then remove water pump and gasket.
6. Reverse procedure to install. Torque water pump attaching bolts to 13 ft. lbs.

FUEL PUMP

REPLACE

1. Disconnect fuel lines from pump.
2. Remove retaining screws and fuel pump.
3. Remove all gasket material from the pump and block gasket surfaces. Apply sealer to both sides of new gasket.
4. Position gasket on pump flange and hold pump in position against its mounting surface. Make sure rocker arm is riding on camshaft eccentric.
5. Press pump tight against its mounting. Install retaining screws and tighten them alternately.
6. Connect fuel lines. Then operate engine and check for leaks. **When installing pump, crank engine to place camshaft eccentric in a position as to place the least amount of tension on fuel pump rocker arm. This will ease pump installation.**

4-151 (2.5L) Engine Section

NOTE: The 4-151 (2.5L) engine is a General Motors built engine. Refer to the 4-151 (2.5L) engine section in General Motors chapter 7, for service procedures not covered in this section.

INDEX

ENGINE MOUNTS
REPLACE

Remove fan shroud to radiator attaching screws to prevent damage to shroud.

1982 CONCORD & SPIRIT

Removal or replacement of any cushion can be accomplished by supporting the weight of the engine at the area of the cushion to be replaced.

1982–83 EAGLE

Left Side

1. Disconnect heated air tube from air cleaner and exhaust manifold.
2. Remove bolts attaching engine cushion bracket to axle housing.
3. Remove engine mount through bolt, then support engine using a suitable jack.
4. Remove engine cushion support bracket, then remove engine mount attaching bolts and engine mount.
5. Reverse procedure to install. Torque engine mount to engine bolts to 33 ft. lbs., cushion support bracket to engine bolts to 40 ft. lbs. and engine mount through bolt to 45 ft. lbs.

Right Side

1. Disconnect battery ground cable, then loosen lefthand side engine mount through bolt.
2. Loosen bolts attaching engine cushion bracket to axle housing.
3. Remove rightside engine mount through bolt, then remove engine cushion to bracket attaching bolts.
4. Disconnect axle tube at righthand side, then disconnect axle at pinion support.
5. Position a suitable jack under engine and raise engine slightly, then remove engine mount.
6. Reverse procedure to install. Torque engine mount to engine bolts to 33 ft. lbs., cushion bracket bolts to 40 ft. lbs. and engine mount through bolts to 45 ft. lbs.

ENGINE
REPLACE

1982 CONCORD & SPIRIT

On these models, the engine and transmission are removed as an assembly.

1. Disconnect battery ground cable, then drain cooling system. **Do not loosen cylinder block drain plug with system hot and under pressure because serious burns from coolant can occur.**
2. Disconnect upper and lower radiator hoses at radiator.
3. Mark location of hinges on hood, then remove hood.
4. Remove air cleaner, fan and fan shroud.
5. On models equipped with automatic transmission, disconnect fluid cooler lines from radiator.
6. Remove radiator to support attaching bolts, then remove radiator.
7. Remove power steering pump drive belt, if equipped.
8. On models less A/C, disconnect wire connector from alternator.
9. On models with A/C, remove compressor and condenser attaching bolts, then position compressor and condenser out of way with refrigerant lines connected. Remove evaporator to dryer line from sill clips.
10. Disconnect heater hose from intake manifold, then remove throttle cable clip and remove cable from bracket.
11. On models with A/C, disconnect wire connector from alternator and pull wiring through tube.
12. Disconnect pressure and return hoses from power steering gear, if equipped.
13. Disconnect module control solenoid, choke heater, idle speed solenoid and temperature sending unit wire connectors.
14. Detach dipstick tube from exhaust manifold, then remove tube and dipstick from block.
15. Remove engine mount nuts at crossmember and ground cable from lefthand engine cushion bracket at engine.
16. Disconnect fuel hose from steel tube on righthand frame side rail.
17. Disconnect wiring from starter solenoid, distributor and oil pressure sending unit.
18. Loosen crossmember attaching bolts and lower crossmember slightly, then remove transmission oil cooler lines, if equipped, speedometer cable from transmission, transmission linkage, back-up light switch wire connector, transmission rear mount and crossmember.
19. Disconnect exhaust pipe from exhaust manifold, then suspend exhaust pipe from strut rod bushing with wire.
20. On models equipped with manual transmission, disconnect clutch linkage.
21. Mark propeller shaft and pinion flange so they can be installed in the same position, then remove propeller shaft.
22. Using a suitable engine lifting device, remove engine and transmission from vehicle.
23. Reverse procedure to install.

1982–83 EAGLE

On these models, the engine is removed separately from the transmission.

1. Refer to the 1982 Concord and Spirit Engine, Replace procedure and perform steps 1 through 14.
2. Remove left front engine mount bracket to axle housing attaching bolts.
3. Raise and support vehicle, then remove splash shield and disconnect both half shafts from front axle. Compress half shafts inward, toward wheels and secure to frame side sills with wire.
4. Mark front drive shaft so it can be installed in the same position, then remove front driveshaft.
5. Using a suitable jack, support front axle, then disconnect axle at righthand tube support and at pinion end of axle.
6. Disconnect axle vent tube, then remove front axle.
7. Remove axle support bracket from cylinder block, then remove starter motor and shims.
8. Disconnect wiring from distributor, oil pressure sending unit and back-up light switch.
9. Disconnect fuel hose from steel line.

10. On models with manual transmission, disconnect clutch release cylinder from clutch housing. Position a wooden block between transfer case and skid plate, then remove clutch housing to engine attaching bolts.
11. On models with automatic transmission, disconnect manual linkage, then remove converter housing inspection cover and remove converter to flywheel attaching nuts. Remove converter housing to engine attaching bolts.
12. Disconnect exhaust pipe from exhaust manifold, then lower vehicle.
13. Remove engine mount attaching bolts, then attach a suitable engine lifting device and raise engine slightly.
14. Remove left engine mount bracket, then remove engine from vehicle.
15. Reverse procedure to install.

OIL PAN
REPLACE

1. Disconnect battery ground cable, then remove fan shroud attaching screws and slide shroud toward engine.
2. Raise vehicle and support at frame side sills, then drain crankcase.
3. On Eagle models proceed as follows:
   a. Using a suitable jack, support front axle.
   b. Mark front drive shaft so it can be installed in the same position, then remove drive shaft.
   c. Disconnect both half shafts from axle. Compress shafts inward, toward wheels, and secure to frame side sills with wire.
   d. Disconnect axle assembly at righthand axle tube, at lefthand engine mount and at pinion mount.
   e. Lower axle assembly slightly and disconnect vent tube, then remove axle assembly.
4. Remove starter motor, then remove flywheel housing inspection cover.
5. Remove engine mount to crossmember attaching nuts.
6. Position a suitable jack under vibration damper and raise engine approximately 1 to 2 inches.
7. Remove crossmember righthand nut and screws and loosen lefthand nut, then lower right side of front crossmember.
8. Remove oil pan attaching bolts, then pry crossmember downward on right side and remove oil pan.
9. Reverse procedure to install.

FUEL PUMP
REPLACE
1982–83 EAGLE

1. Disconnect battery ground cable.
2. Remove alternator and harness as an assembly and position aside, then disconnect mounting bracket from cylinder block and intake manifold.
3. Loosen bottom bolt of intake manifold-to-right side engine cushion bracket and move bracket toward fender panel.
4. Disconnect carburetor vent hose and position aside.
5. Temporarily move coolant hoses to heater core to gain clearance, then disconnect vacuum hoses after tagging them.
6. Disconnect fuel inlet pipe at fuel pump, then disconnect fuel pump-to-carburetor pipe at pump.
7. Install engine holding fixture and remove right engine cushion through bolt and raise engine slightly.
8. Raise and support vehicle.
9. Disconnect right side engine cushion bracket from block and axle bracket, then lower vehicle.
10. Raise engine and position bracket to gain access clearance to fuel pump bolts, then remove fuel pump bolts and fuel pump.
11. Clean all gasket material from fuel pump-to-block mating surface, then install new gasket and fuel pump and torque to 15 ft. lbs.
12. Connect fuel pipes to fuel pump.
13. Connect engine cushion bracket to cylinder block and axle bracket, then lower engine onto cushion and remove holding fixture.
14. Install engine cushion through bolt and nut, then connect vacuum hoses and route heater hoses to original locations.
15. Install intake manifold-to-cushion bracket.
16. Install alternator mounting bracket and alternator, then install and adjust belts and reconnect battery ground cable.

6-258 (4.23L) Engine Section

INDEX

ENGINE MARKINGS

A letter code is used to denote size of the bore, main bearings and rod bearings. This code is located on a boss above the oil filter. This letter code is as follows:

Letter "B"-Cyl. bore .010 inch oversize.

Letter "M"-Main bearings .010 inch undersize.

Letter "P"-Rod bearings .010 inch undersize.

Letter "C"-Camshaft block bore .010 inch oversize.

Letters "PM"-Main and rod bearings .010 inch undersize.

ENGINE MOUNTS
REPLACE

Removal or replacement of any cushion can be accomplished by supporting the weight of the engine or transmission at the area of the cushion to be replaced, **Figs. 1 and 2.**

ENGINE
REPLACE

The engine is removed without the transmission as follows:

1. Drain cooling system.
2. Mark hood hinge locations, disconnect underhood lamp, if equipped, and remove hood.
3. Disconnect battery cables and remove battery.
4. Disconnect alternator wiring and the ignition coil, distributor and oil pressure sender leads.
5. Remove TCS switch bracket from cylinder block, if equipped.
6. Disconnect flexible fuel line from fuel pump and plug line and pump port.
7. Disconnect engine ground strap.

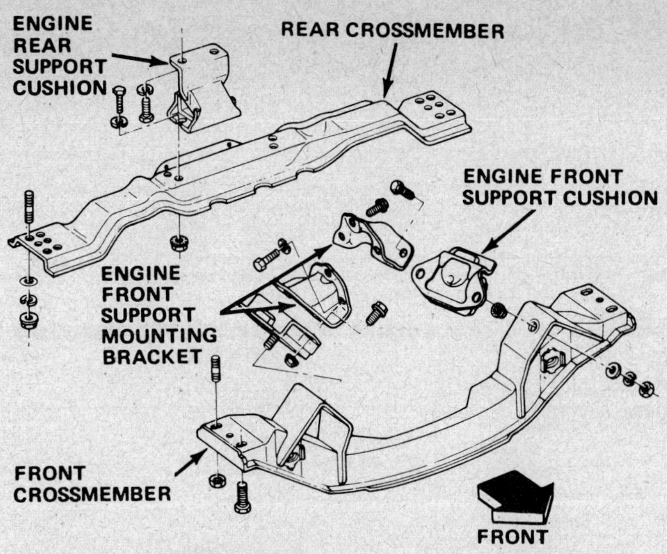

Fig. 1 Engine mounts. Eagle (typical)

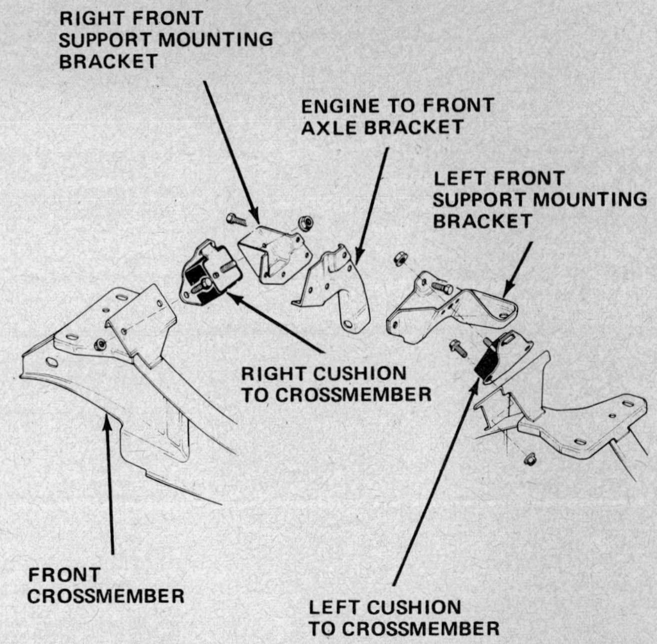

Fig. 2 Engine mounts. Eagle W/6 cylinder engine

8. Remove the right front engine support cushion to bracket screw.
9. If equipped with air conditioning:
   a. Remove service valve covers and front seat valves.
   b. Loosen service valve to compressor attaching nuts.
   c. Bleed compressor refrigerant charge.
   d. Remove service valves and cap compressor ports and service valves.
   e. Disconnect clutch feed wire.
10. Remove starter.
11. Remove air cleaner and disconnect purge hose from canister and TAC vacuum hose from manifold, if equipped.
12. Disconnect throttle stop solenoid lead, if equipped.
13. Disconnect fuel return hose from fuel filter and the carburetor bowl vent hose from canister.
14. Disconnect throttle cable and remove from bracket. Disconnect throttle valve rod at carburetor and the bellcrank.
15. Disconnect carburetor stepper motor and oxygen sensor electrical connectors, if equipped.
16. Disconnect heater and air conditioning system vacuum hose from intake manifold.
17. Disconnect temperature sender wire and TCS vacuum solenoid wiring harness.
18. Disconnect radiator hoses from radiator and the heater hoses from engine.
19. Disconnect transmission oil cooler lines from radiator, if equipped.
20. Remove fan shroud attaching screws, then the radiator and shroud.
21. Remove fan and spacer. Install a 5/16 x 1/2 inch capscrew through fan pulley, into water pump flange.
22. Remove power brake vacuum check valve from power brake unit, if equipped.
23. If equipped with power steering, disconnect hoses from gear and drain reservoir. Cap gear ports and hoses.
24. Remove transmission filler tube bracket screw, if equipped.
25. Raise and support vehicle on jack stands.
26. If equipped with automatic transmission:
   a. Remove converter housing spacer cover.
   b. Remove converter attaching screws.
   c. Remove exhaust pipe support from converter housing. This also supports the inner end of the transmission linkage.
27. If equipped with manual transmission:
   a. Remove clutch housing cover and clutch bellcrank inner support screws.
   b. Disconnect springs and remove bellcrank.
   c. Remove outer bellcrank to strut rod bracket retainer.
   d. Disconnect back-up lamp switch wiring harness under hood at dash panel to gain access to clutch housing screw.
28. On all models, remove engine mount cushion to bracket screws.
29. On Eagle models proceed as follows:
   a. Support axle assembly, then remove half shaft to axle flange attaching bolts.
   b. Compress half shafts inward, toward wheels, and secure to frame side sills with wire.
   c. Remove axle bracket attaching bolts at axle tube and righthand engine mount, then remove axle bracket.
   d. Remove axle bracket attaching bolts at pinion end of axle.
   e. Remove left engine mount support to front axle bracket attaching bolts.
   f. Disconnect axle vent hose, then lower axle assembly and remove from vehicle.
30. Disconnect exhaust pipe from manifold.
31. Remove upper converter or clutch housing screws and loosen the bottom screws.
32. Raise vehicle and support on jack stands.
33. Remove air conditioning compressor drive belt idler pulley and the compressor mounting bracket, if equipped.
34. Install suitable engine lifting equipment and slightly raise engine. Support transmission with a suitable jack.
35. Remove remaining converter or clutch housing screws.
36. Remove engine from vehicle.
37. Reverse procedure to install.

CYLINDER HEAD REPLACE

An excessive oil consumption problem on 1987 Eagle models equipped with the 6-258 engine may be due to defective aluminum valve cover baffle seal. The baffle seal may allow oil to leak past the seal when the engine is operating. Valve covers with potentional baffle seal leaks were used on 1987 engine built prior to engine build code 702C23. If excessive oil consumption was experienced and the engine was built prior to the above date code, replace valve cover.

Tighten cylinder head bolts a little at a time in three steps in the sequence shown in the illustrations. Final tightening should be to the torque specifications listed in the Engine Tightening table.

1. Drain cooling system and disconnect hoses at thermostat housing.
2. Remove air cleaner and disconnect fuel line and vacuum advance line.
3. Remove valve cover and gasket. **During removal of valve cover, use a suitable putty knife or razor blade and break silicone seal between**

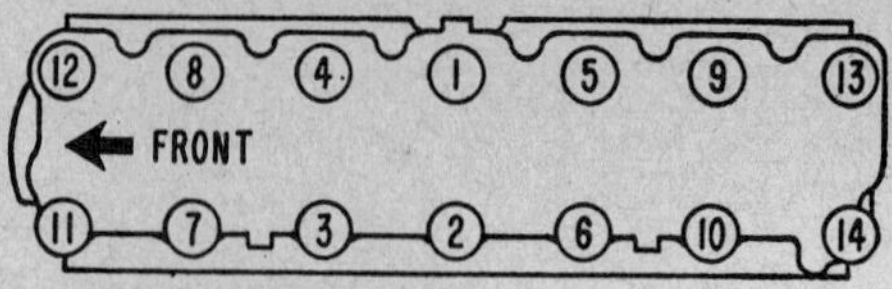

Fig. 3 Cylinder head tightening sequence. The No. 11 bolt must be sealed to prevent coolant leakage.

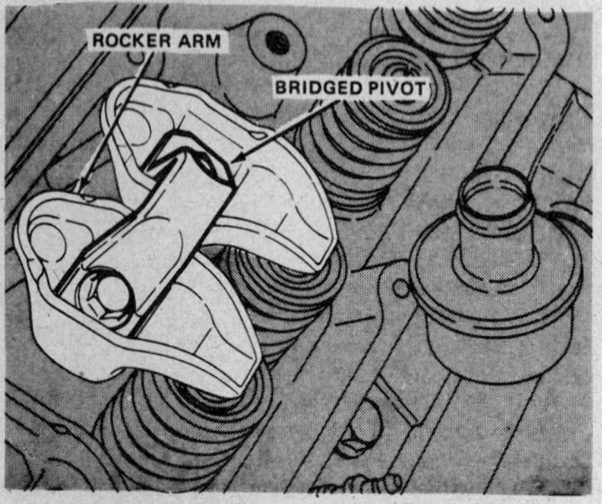

Fig. 5 Rocker arms, pushrod and pivot assembly

valve cover and cylinder head. Do not pry valve cover upward until seal has been completely broken.

4. Remove rocker arms and bridged pivot assemblies. Alternately loosen each cap screw one turn at a time to prevent damage to bridge. **Label pushrods, rocker arms and bridge pivots so they can be installed in the same position.**
5. Disconnect power steering pump and air pump and position pumps and brackets aside. Do not disconnect hoses from pumps.
6. Remove intake and exhaust manifold assembly from cylinder head.
7. On models equipped with A/C, remove A/C drive belt idler bracket from cylinder head. Loosen alternator drive belt, then remove alternator bracket to cylinder head mounting bolt. Remove bolts from compressor mounting bracket and position compressor aside.
8. Disconnect ignition wires and remove spark plugs.
9. Disconnect temperature sending unit wire and battery ground cable.
10. Remove ignition coil and bracket assembly.
11. Remove cylinder head bolts, cylinder head and gasket.
12. Reverse procedure to install. Torque cylinder head bolts in sequence shown in **Fig. 3** and torque manifold bolts in sequence shown in **Fig. 4.**

VALVES

ADJUST

Hydraulic valve lifters are used. No adjustment is required.

VALVE ARRANGEMENT

FRONT TO REAR

6-258 . . . . E-I-I-E-I-E-E-I-E-I-I-E

VALVE LIFT SPECIFICATIONS

Year	Engine	Int.	Exh.
1982-87	6-258	.405	.405

VALVE TIMING

INTAKE OPENS BEFORE TDC

Year	Engine	Degrees
1982-87	6-258 ①	9

①—2 barrel carb.

ROCKER ARMS

All engines have the intake and exhaust rocker arms pivoting on a bridged pivot assembly which is secured to the cylinder head by two capscrews, **Fig. 5.** When installing capscrews, turn each screw one turn at a time to avoid breaking the bridge. Torque capscrews to 19 ft. lbs.

The pushrods are hollow, serving as oil galleries for lubricating each individual rocker arm assembly. Prior to installing, the pushrods should be cleaned thoroughly, inspected for wear and deposits which may restrict the flow of oil to the rocker arm.

The pushrods also serve as guides to maintain correct rocker arm to valve stem relationship; therefore, a contact pattern on the pushrods where they contact the cylinder head is normal.

Lubrication to each rocker arm is supplied by the corresponding hydraulic valve lifter. A metering system located in each valve lifter consists of a stepped lower surface on the pushrod cap that contacts a flat plate, causing a restriction, **Fig. 6.** The restriction meters the amount of oil flow through the pushrod cap, hollow pushrod, and upper valve train components. A loss of lubrication to the rocker arm could be caused by a restricted or plugged pushrod or a defective hydraulic valve lifter.

Correct installation of pushrods in these engines is critical and more than normal care must be taken upon installation. When placing the pushrods through the guide hole in the cylinder head, it is important that the pushrod end is inserted in the plunger cap socket. It is possible that the pushrod may seat itself on the edge of the plunger cap which will restrict valve lifter rotation and lubrication to rocker arms.

It is recommended that, just prior to installation of the cylinder head covers, the engine be operated and the supply of lubrication to each rocker arm be visually inspected. If inspection reveals that an individual rocker arm is not being supplied with lubrication, the pushrod and/or valve lifter must be inspected to determine the cause.

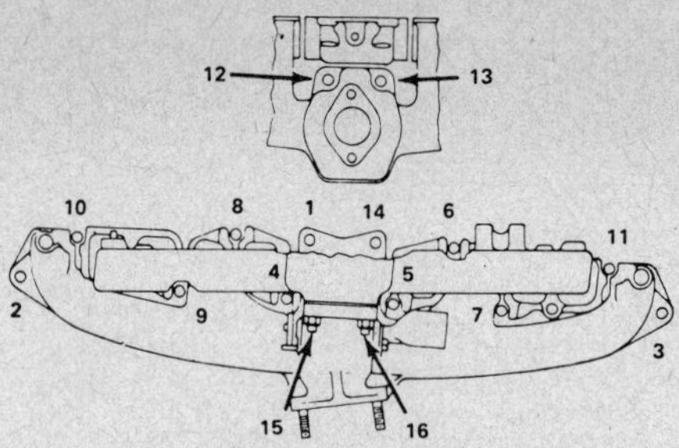

Fig. 4 Manifold tightening sequence

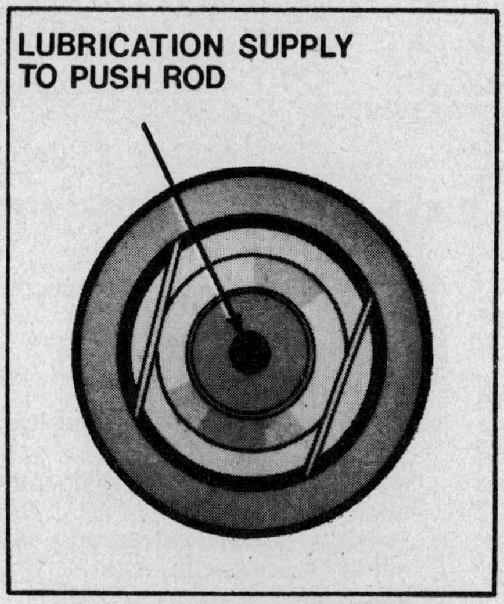

Fig. 6 Hydraulic lifter identification

VALVE GUIDES

Excessive valve stem-to-guide clearance will cause lack of power, rough idling and noisy valves, and may cause valve breakage. Insufficient clearance will result in noisy and sticky functioning of valves and disturb engine smoothness of operation.

Valve stem-to-guide clearances are listed in the Engine Valve Specifications table. By using a micrometer and a suitable telescope hole gauge, check the diameter of the valve stem in three places (top, center and bottom). Insert telescope hole gauge in valve guide bore, measuring at the center. Subtract the highest reading of valve stem diameter from valve guide bore center diameter to obtain valve-to-guide clearance. If clearance is not within specified limits, use the next oversize valve and ream bore to fit. Valves with oversize stems are available in .003 inch, .015 inch and .030 inch.

HYDRAULIC LIFTERS

Valve lifters may be removed from their bores after removing the cylinder head cover. Using Valve Tappet Removal and Installation Tool J-21884 remove the tappets through the pushrod openings in the cylinder head. The type of lifter used on these engines is illustrated in **Fig. 7.**

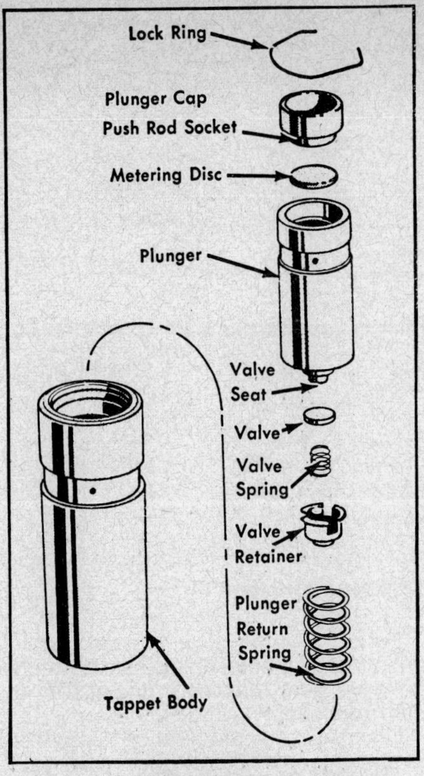

Fig. 7 Hydraulic valve lifter

TIMING CASE COVER
REPLACE

1. Remove drive belts, fan and pulley.
2. Remove vibration damper.
3. Remove oil pan-to-timing chain cover screws and cover-to-block screws.
4. Raise the cover and pull the oil pan front seal up enough to pull the retaining nibs from the holes in the cover.
5. Remove timing chain cover gasket from block. Cut off seal tab flush with front face of cylinder block. Clean gasket surfaces.
6. Remove oil seal.
7. Place gasket in position on cylinder block. Install new oil pan front seal, cut off protruding tab of seal to match portion of the original seal.
8. Insert suitable aligning tool in cover seal bore and on crankshaft. Install cover-to-oil pan screws and tighten lightly. Install cover screws and tighten.
9. Retighten all screws and install new cover seal.

TIMING CHAIN

When installing a timing chain, see that the timing marks on the sprockets are in line as shown in **Fig. 8.**

CAMSHAFT
REPLACE

1. Remove distributor and ignition wires and the fuel pump.
2. Remove radiator from vehicle. If equipped with A/C, remove condenser and receiver with refrigerant lines attached and position out of way.
3. Remove cylinder head and valve lifters.
4. Remove timing chain cover.
5. Rotate crankshaft until timing marks on sprockets are aligned, **Fig. 8.**
6. Remove sprockets and chain.
7. Remove front bumper or grille as required to remove camshaft.
8. Remove camshaft.
9. Reverse procedure to install.

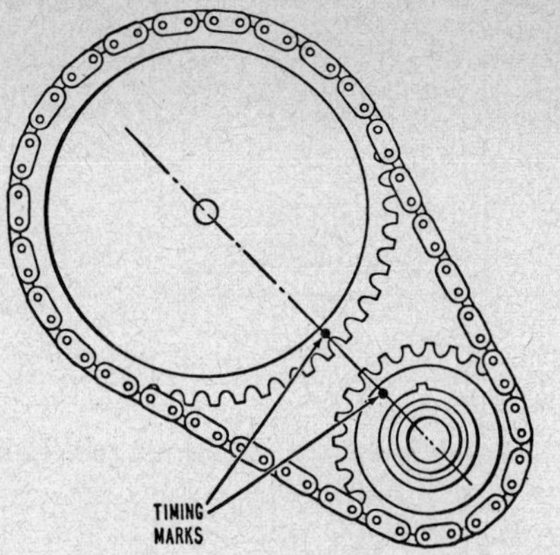

Fig. 8 Valve timing

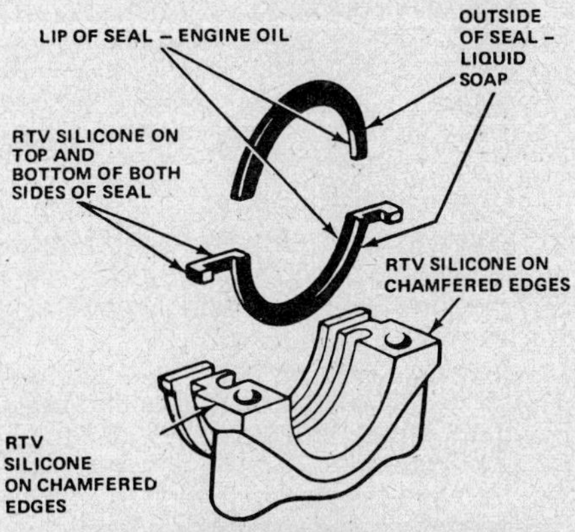

Fig. 10 Rear main bearing sealing

PISTONS & RODS ASSEMBLE

Pistons are marked with a depression notch or arrow on the top perimeter, **Fig. 9.** When installed in the engine, this notch or arrow must be toward the front of the engine. Always assemble rods and caps with the cylinder numbers facing the camshaft side of engine. Check side clearance between connecting rod and crankshaft journals. Clearance should be .010-.019 inch.

PISTONS, PINS & RINGS

Pistons are furnished in standard sizes and oversizes of .002, .005, .010 and .020 inch.

Piston pins are furnished in oversizes of .003 and .005 inch.

Piston rings are available in .020 inch oversizes.

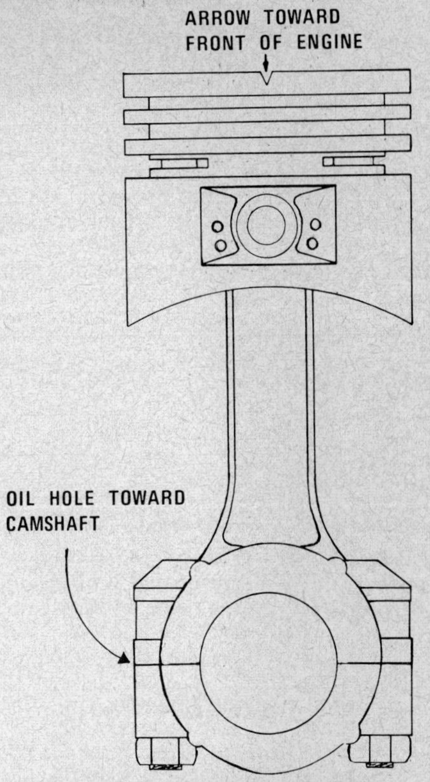

Fig. 9 Piston & rod assembly

MAIN & ROD BEARINGS

Both main and rod bearings are supplied in undersizes of .001, .002, .010 and .012 inch.

CRANKSHAFT REAR OIL SEAL
REPLACE

1. To replace the seal, **Fig. 10,** remove oil pan and scrape oil pan surfaces clean.
2. Remove rear main bearing cap.
3. Remove and discard old seals.
4. Clean cap thoroughly.
5. Loosen all remaining main bearing capscrews.
6. With a brass drift and hammer, tap upper seal until sufficient seal is protruding to permit pulling seal out completely with pliers.
7. Wipe seal surface of crankshaft clean, then oil lightly.
8. Coat back surface of upper seal with soap, and lip of seal with engine oil.
9. Install upper seal into cylinder block. Lip of seal must face to front of engine.
10. Coat cap and cylinder block mating surface portion of seal with RTV Silicone or equivalent, being careful not to apply sealer on lip of seal.
11. Coat back surface of lower seal with soap, and lip of seal with No. 40 engine oil. Place into cap, seating seal firmly into seal recess in cap.
12. Place RTV Silicone or equivalent on both chamfered edges of rear main bearing cap.

13. Install main bearings and install cap. Tighten all caps to correct torque as listed in the Engine Tightening Specifications table.
14. Cement oil pan gasket to cylinder block with tongue of gasket at each end coated with RTV Silicone or equivalent before installing into rear main bearing cap at joint of tongue and oil pan front neoprene seal.
15. Coat oil pan rear seal with soap. Place into recess of rear main bearing cap, making certain seal is firmly and evenly seated.
16. Install oil pan and tighten drain plug securely.

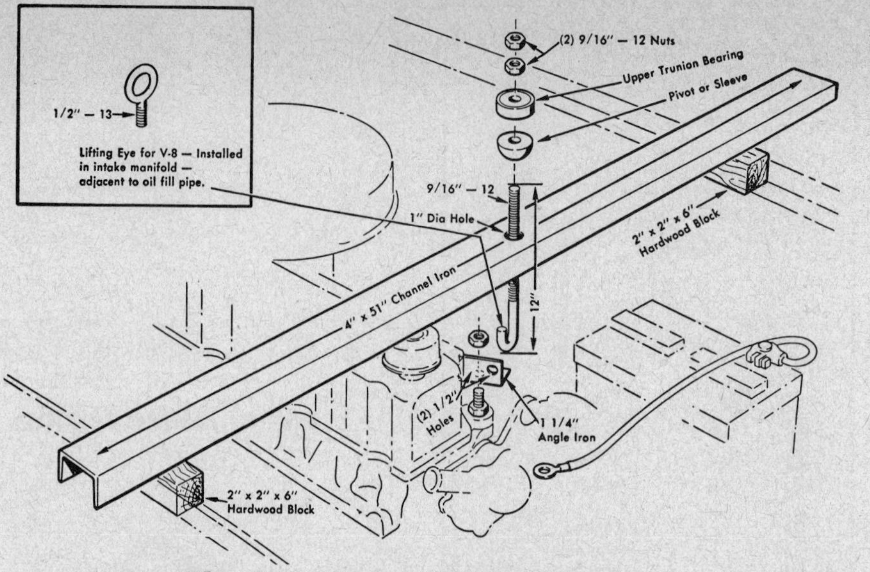

Fig. 11 Engine lifting fixture

OIL PAN

REPLACE

1982–83 ALL EXC. EAGLE

1. Disconnect battery ground cable.
2. Turn steering wheel to full left lock.
3. Support engine using a suitable holding fixture, **Fig. 11.**
4. Raise vehicle and support on side sills.
5. Disconnect steering idler arm at side sill.
6. Disconnect engine front support cushions at engine brackets.
7. Loosen sway bar link nuts to end of threads, if equipped.
8. Remove front crossmember to side sill attaching bolts, then pull crossmember down.
9. Remove engine right support bracket from engine.
10. Loosen strut rods at lower control arms; do not remove screws.
11. Remove starter motor.
12. Drain crankcase, then remove oil pan attaching bolts and oil pan.
13. Clean gasket surfaces of oil pan and engine block. Remove all sludge and dirt from oil pan sump.
14. Reverse procedure to install.

1982–83 EAGLE

1. Disconnect battery ground cable.
2. Drain engine oil.
3. Lock steering wheel and remove air cleaner.
4. Support engine using a suitable holding fixture.
5. Raise vehicle and support on side sills.
6. Mark for assembly reference and disconnect front driveshaft.
7. Remove engine cushion bolts.
8. Remove bolts from sill-to-crossmember and position bar aside.
9. Loosen pitman arm at gear, then loosen idler arm at steering linkage.
10. Remove bolt from steering damper at crossmember.
11. Loosen sway bar bolts and lower sway bar bolts and lower sway bar.
12. Disconnect half shafts from axle. **Compress half shafts in toward wheels, secure in compressed position with wire attached to frame sills.**
13. Remove bolts from right bracket at axle tube bolt bars, then remove bolts from left upper axle bracket at upper end, and bolts from pinion end bracket at pinion.
14. Remove vent hose and remove axle assembly.
15. Support crossmembers with jack and remove crossmember nuts and bolts, then lower crossmember assembly for clearance.
16. Remove starter motor, then the torque converter housing access cover.
17. Remove oil pan screws and remove oil pan.
18. Reverse procedure to install.

1984–87 EAGLE

1. Disconnect battery ground cable.
2. Lock steering wheel, then raise and support vehicle at side sills.
3. Drain engine oil, then mark front driveshaft to ensure correct alignment during assembly.
4. Disconnect driveshaft, then support axle assembly with a suitable jack.
5. Disconnect half shafts from axle. **Compress half shafts in toward wheels, secure in compressed position with wire attached to frame sills.**
6. Remove bolt from right bracket at axle tube bolt bars, then the bolts from left upper axle bracket at the upper end.
7. Remove pinion end bracket to pinion attaching bolts.
8. Remove vent hose and axle assembly.
9. Remove starter motor, then the torque converter housing access cover.
10. Remove oil pan attaching screws, then the oil pan.
11. Reverse procedure to install.

OIL PUMP

When servicing oil pump, if inlet tube is moved out of position a new inlet tube and screen assembly must be installed.

The oil pump is located in the oil pan thus necessitating removal of the pan to gain access to the pump.

Oil pump removal or replacement will not affect distributor timing as the distributor drive gear remains in mesh with the camshaft gear.

Upon disassembly of the oil pump, place a straightedge across gears and pump body and check clearance between straightedge and pump body which should be .006-.004 inch. Clearance between gears and pump housing should be .0005-.0025 inch.

The pump cover should be installed with the pump out of the engine and pump checked for freedom of operation before installation.

The oil pressure relief valve, which is built into the pump, is not adjustable, the correct pressure being built into the relief valve spring.

BELT TENSION DATA

Belt	New Lbs.	Used Lbs.
Air Conditioning	125-155	90-115
Air Pump	65-75	60-70
Fan & Power Steering	125-155	90-115
Serpentine Type Belt	180-200	140-160

WATER PUMP

REPLACE

On engines equipped with a serpentine drive belt, the water pump and fan drive assembly will operate in the reverse rotation of an engine not equipped with a serpentine drive belt. Water pumps for use on these engines can be identified by the letters REV cast into the pump body, while fan components can be identified by the word REVERSE stamped on the fan drive and on the inner side of the fan.

1. Disconnect battery ground cable.
2. Drain cooling system and disconnect radiator and heater hoses from pump.

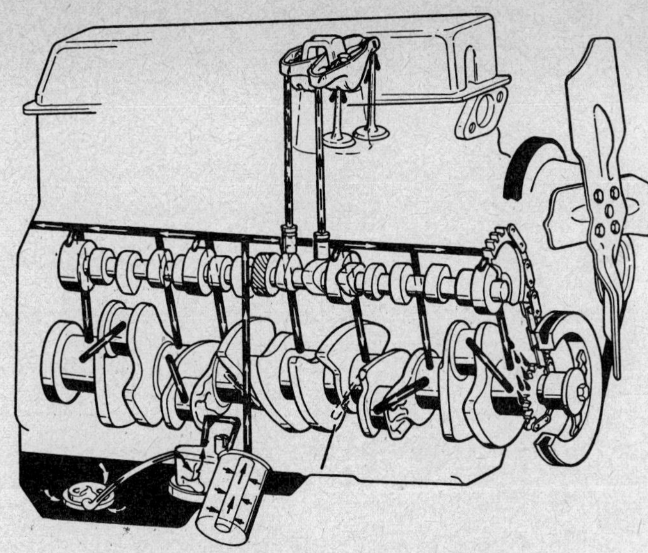

Engine oiling system

3. Remove drive belts. **On some models it will be necessary to remove alternator front bracket and place alternator aside, without disconnecting wires.**
4. Remove fan shroud attaching bolts, then remove fan, hub and shroud.
5. Remove water pump and gasket.
6. Reverse procedure to install.

FUEL PUMP
REPLACE

1. Disconnect fuel lines from pump.
2. Remove retaining screws and fuel pump.
3. Remove all gasket material from the pump and block gasket surfaces. Apply sealer to both sides of new gasket.
4. Position gasket on pump flange and hold pump in position against its mounting surface. Make sure rocker arm is riding on camshaft eccentric.
5. Press pump tight against its mounting. Install retaining screws and tighten them alternately.
6. Connect fuel lines. Then operate engine and check for leaks. **When installing pump, crank engine to place camshaft eccentric in a position as to place the least amount of tension on fuel pump rocker arm. This will ease pump installation.**

Clutch, Manual Transmission & Transfer Case Section

INDEX

CLUTCH PEDAL
ADJUST
PEDAL FREEPLAY

1982–83 4-151, EAGLE W/6-258 & 1983–84 4-150

These models are equipped with a hydraulic actuated clutch and no adjustment is required.

EXC. 4-150, 151 & 6-258

In order to provide sufficient free movement of the clutch release bearing when the clutch is engaged and pedal fully released, pedal free play should be 7/8 inch to 1 1/8 inch with desired freeplay of 1 1/8 inch.

Adjustment for pedal free play is made by varying the length of the beam or link to the release lever rod. Lengthening this rod reduces pedal travel; shortening it increases pedal play, **Fig. 1.**

CLUTCH
REPLACE
EXC. EAGLE

1. Remove transmission as described under Transmission, Replace.
2. Remove clutch housing to engine attaching bolts, then the clutch housing.
3. Remove throwout bearing, then mark pressure plate and flywheel for reassembly.
4. Remove pressure plate to flywheel attaching bolts, then remove pressure plate and clutch disc. **Loosen pressure plate to flywheel bolts alternately and evenly to prevent distorting pressure plate.**
5. Reverse procedure to install. Position clutch and pressure plate on flywheel and install attaching bolts finger tight. Align clutch disc using a suitable alignment tool, then tighten pressure plate attaching bolts alternately and evenly to 23 ft. lbs. Torque clutch housing to engine and transmission to clutch housing attaching bolts to 54 ft. lbs.

EAGLE

1. Remove transmission as described under Transmission, Replace.
2. Remove righthand brace rod and starter motor, then disconnect clutch release cylinder spring from clutch fork.
3. Remove clutch release cylinder, with hydraulic line attached, and clutch housing inspection cover.
4. Disconnect exhaust pipe at exhaust manifold, then remove clutch housing to engine attaching bolts and remove clutch housing.
5. Mark pressure plate and flywheel for reassembly, then remove pressure plate attaching bolts and remove pressure plate and clutch disc. **Loosen pressure plate attaching bolts alternately and evenly to prevent distorting pressure plate.**
6. Reverse procedure to install. Position clutch disc and pressure plate on flywheel and install attaching bolts finger tight. Align clutch disc using a suitable alignment tool, then tighten pressure plate attaching bolts alternately and evenly to 28 ft. lbs. Torque clutch housing to engine upper attaching bolts to 27 ft. lbs. Torque clutch housing lower attaching bolts and dowel bolts to 43 ft. lbs. Torque transmission to engine attaching bolts to 55 ft. lbs.

MANUAL TRANSMISSION

REPLACE

EXC. EAGLE

4-151 & 1982–84 6-258

1. Remove console, if equipped, then remove gearshift lever, bezel and boot.
2. Mark propeller shaft and rear axle pinion flange so they can be installed in the same position, then remove propeller shaft.
3. Disconnect speedometer cable and back-up lamp switch wire connector.
4. Disconnect exhaust pipe, if necessary.
5. Remove starter motor, then disconnect clutch release cylinder spring at clutch fork.
6. Remove inspection cover from clutch housing, then remove bolts attaching catalytic converter support bracket to transmission rear support bracket, if equipped.
7. Place support under front of engine, then remove bolts attaching transmission mount to rear crossmember.
8. Remove nuts attaching rear crossmember to frame side sills, then remove crossmember.
9. Remove transmission to clutch housing attaching bolts, then remove transmission.
10. Reverse procedure to install. Torque transmission to clutch housing attaching bolts to 54 ft. lbs.

EAGLE

4-151 & 6-258

1. Place transmission shift lever in the neutral position, then remove console, if equipped.
2. Remove gearshift lever bezel and boot, then remove gearshift lever from mounting cover on transmission.
3. Remove skid plate, then mark position of speedometer adapter for reassembly, then disconnect speedometer cable. Plug adapter opening in transfer case to prevent lubricant spillage.
4. Mark propeller shafts and axle yokes for reassembly, then disconnect propeller shafts at transfer case.
5. Disconnect back-up lamp switch wire connector, then support engine using a suitable jack.
6. Support transmission and transfer case using a suitable transmission jack, then remove rear crossmember.
7. Remove catalytic converter support bracket from transfer case.
8. Remove transmission to clutch housing attaching bolts, then remove transmission and transfer case as an assembly.
9. Remove nuts from transfer case mounting studs, then separate transfer case from transmission.
10. Reverse procedure to install. Torque transfer case to transmission adapter housing stud nuts to 33 ft. lbs. Torque transmission to clutch housing bolts to 55 ft. lbs.

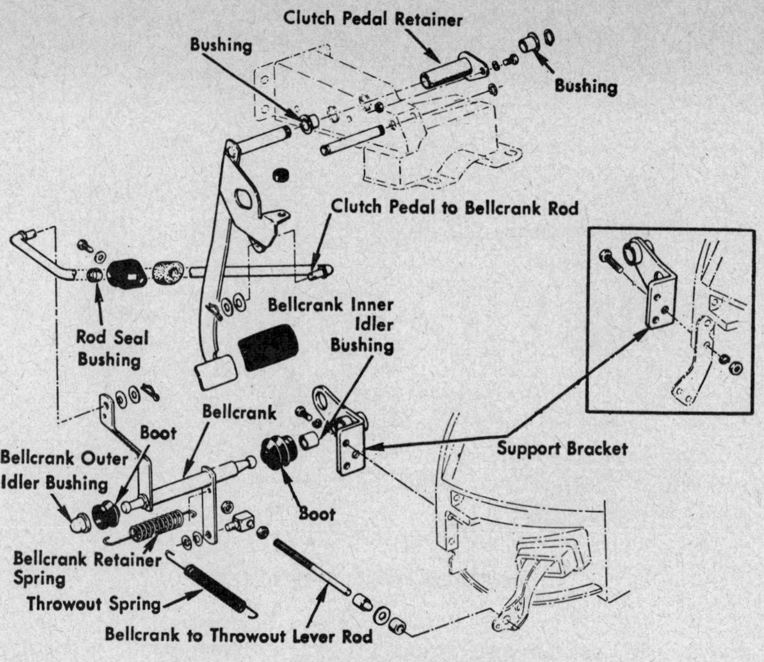

Fig. 1 Typical clutch linkage

TRANSFER CASE

REPLACE

WITH AUTOMATIC TRANSMISSION

1. Raise and support vehicle.
2. Support engine and transmission with a suitable jack or jack stand.
3. Disconnect catalytic converter support bracket from adapter housing.
4. Remove skid plate.
5. Disconnect speedometer cable and adapter from transfer case. Discard adapter O-ring.
6. Mark propeller shafts and transfer case yoke for assembly reference. Then, disconnect propeller shafts from yokes. Secure shafts aside.
7. Disconnect gearshift and throttle linkage from transmission.
8. Remove rear crossmember.
9. Remove transfer case to adapter housing nuts.
10. Remove transfer case from vehicle.
11. Install transfer case on adapter housing.
12. Install and torque transfer case to adapter housing nuts to 33 ft. lbs.
13. Install rear crossmember.
14. Install rear brace rod.
15. Remove jack or jack stand, supporting engine and transmission.
16. Connect gearshift and throttle linkage to transmission.
17. Connect propeller shafts to transfer case yokes.
18. Install new O-ring on speedometer adapter, then the adapter and speedometer cable to transfer case.
19. Install skid plate.
20. Connect catalytic converter support bracket to adapter housing.
21. Check transfer case lubricant level and adjust, if necessary. Also, check transmission linkage adjustments.

WITH MANUAL TRANSMISSION

1. Shift transmission into neutral.
2. Remove screws attaching gear shift lever bezel to floorpan or console (if equipped).
3. Slide bezel and boot up on gear shift lever to gain access to lever attaching bolts, then remove bolts and remove lever.
4. Remove bolts attaching gear shift lever mounting cover to transmission adapter housing and remove cover.
5. Remove nut from transfer case mounting stud from inside transmission adapter housing.
6. Raise and support vehicle.
7. Remove skid plate and stiffening brace, or rear brace rod.
8. Remove speedometer adapter retainer attaching bolt and remove retainer, adapter and cable, then plug adapter opening in transfer case to avoid excessive oil leakage. **Before removing speedometer adapter, mark position for reference during assembly.**
9. Mark propeller shafts and axle yokes for assembly reference and disconnect propeller shafts at transfer case.
10. Remove transfer case shift motor vacuum harness.
11. Support transfer case with transmission jack, then remove nuts from transfer case mounting studs and remove transfer case.
12. Align transmission output and transfer case input shafts and install transfer case on transmission adapter housing, then install and torque transfer case mounting stud nuts to 33 ft. lbs.
13. Remove jack supporting transfer case.
14. Connect propeller shafts to axle

yokes and torque clamp strap bolts to 15 ft. lbs.
15. Install new O-ring on speedometer adapter, then install adapter and cable and retainer, torque retainer bolt to 100 inch lbs.
16. Install skid plate and stiffening brace, or rear brace rod and torque retaining bolts to 30 ft. lbs.
17. Install transfer case shift motor vacuum harness.
18. Check and correct fluid levels in transmission and transfer case, then lower vehicle.
19. Install nut on transfer case mounting stud inside transmission adapter housing, torque nut to 33 ft. lbs.
20. Install gear shift lever mounting cover on transmission adapter housing, then install gear shift lever on mounting cover.
21. Position gear shift lever boot and bezel on floorpan of console (if equipped), and install bezel attaching screws. **Steps 1 through 5 and 19 through 21 apply to SR-4 transmission only.**

Rear Axle, Propeller Shaft & Brakes

INDEX

REAR AXLES

Figs. 1 and 2 illustrate the rear axle assembly used on these cars. When necessary to overhaul the unit, refer to the Rear Axle Specifications table in this chapter.

DESCRIPTION

In these rear axles, **Figs. 1 and 2,** the drive pinion is mounted in two tapered roller bearings. These bearings are preloaded by a washer behind the front bearing. The pinion is positioned by shims located in front of the rear bearing. The differential is supported in the carrier by two tapered roller side bearings. These bearings are preloaded by shims located between the bearings and carrier housing. The differential assembly is positioned for proper ring gear and pinion backlash by varying the position of these shims. The differential case houses two side gears in mesh with two pinions mounted on a pinion shaft which is held in place by a lock pin. The side gears and pinions are backed by thrust washers.

It is not necessary to remove the rear axle assembly. However, the underbody should be washed to prevent particles of road dirt from contaminating the parts.

REAR AXLE & DRIVE SHAFT

REPLACE

1. Remove cotter pins and remove axle shaft nuts.
2. Raise vehicle and position support stands under rear frame side sills.
3. Remove wheels and brake drum retaining screws.
4. Remove brake drums, then disconnect brake lines at wheel cylinders.
5. Using a suitable puller, remove support plates, oil seal, retainer and endplay shims. **Axle shaft endplay shims are installed at left side of axle only.**
6. Using a suitable puller, remove axle shafts.
7. Remove axle housing cover and drain lubricant, then reinstall cover.
8. Disconnect parking brake cables at equalizer.
9. Mark universal joint and rear axle yokes for reassembly, then disconnect propeller at rear yoke.
10. Remove stabilizer bar, if equipped.
11. Disconnect brake hose at body floor pan bracket.
12. Disconnect vent tube from axle tube.
13. Support axle assembly using a suitable jack.
14. Disconnect shock absorbers at spring plates.
15. Remove spring U-bolts, spring plates and spring clip plate, if equipped with a stabilizer bar.
16. Rotate axle until it clears springs, then lower axle assembly and remove from vehicle.
17. Reverse procedure to install.

AXLE SHAFTS

REPLACE

DISASSEMBLY

The hub and drum are separate units, and the hub and axle shaft are serrated to mate and fit together on the taper. Both are punched marked toinsure correct assembly, **Fig. 3.** The axle shaft and bearing may be removed as follows:

1. Remove rear wheel, drum and hub, then disconnect pa rking brake cable at equalizer.
2. Disconnect brake tube from wheel cylinder and remove brake support plate assembly, oil seal and axle shims from axle shaft. **Axle shaft endplay shims are located on the left side only.**
3. Using suitable puller, pull axle shaft and bearing from axle tube, then remove and discard inner oil seal. **The bearing cone must be pressed off the shaft, using an arbor press. On models equipped with Twin Grip differential, do not rotate differential unless both axle shafts are in place.**

ASSEMBLY

When installing hub onto axle, install two well lubricated thrust washers and axle shaft nut. Tighten axle shaft nut until hub is installed to the dimensions shown in **Fig. 3.** Remove axle shaft nut and one thrust washer. Reinstall axle shaft nut and tighten to 250 ft. lbs. If cotter pin hole is not aligned, tighten the nut to the next castellation and install cotter pin.

Do not use an original hub on a replacement axle shaft; use a new hub. A new hub may be installed on an original axle shaft providing the serrations on the shaft are not worn or damaged. Be certain that the hub and axle shaft are punch marked to insure proper alignment on installation. A replacement hub, which is not serrated, can be installed and serrations will be cut in the hub when installed on the shaft due to the difference in hardness of the shaft and the hub.

Replace the parts in the reverse order of their removal. If the old parts are replaced and the shims have not been disturbed, the axle shaft endplay should be correct when the parts are assembled. However, if a new shaft, bearing, differential carrier or housing has been installed, it will be necessary to check the endplay.

The endplay can be checked when all parts have been replaced except the wheel and hub. To make this check, rap each axle shaft after the nuts are tight to be sure the bearing cups are seated. Then place a dial indicator so that its stem contacts the end of the shaft and work the shaft in and out to determine the amount of existing endplay. Axle shaft endplay should be .004-.008 inch. If an adjustment is necessary, remove the outer oil seal and brake support and add or remove shims as

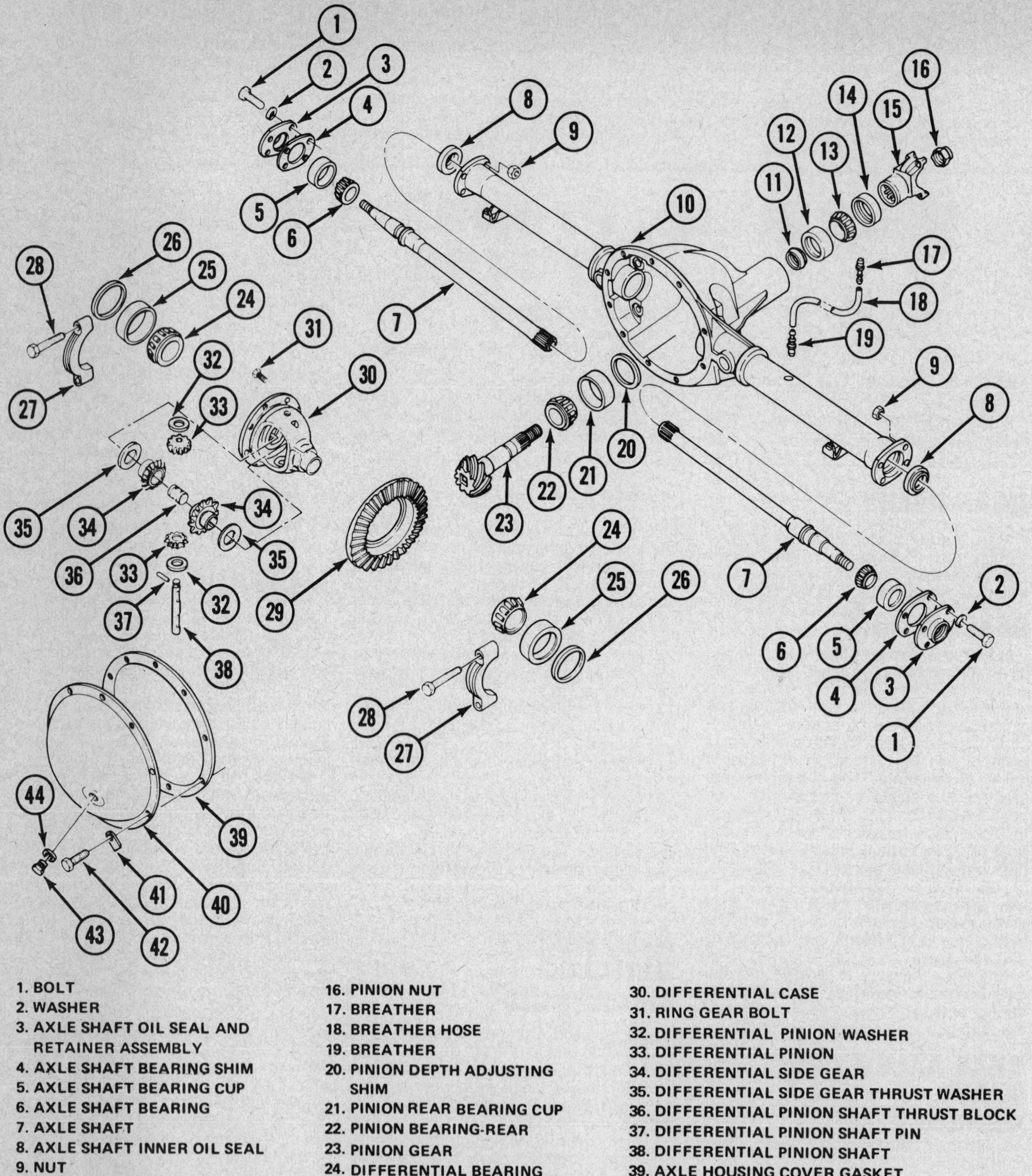

1. BOLT
2. WASHER
3. AXLE SHAFT OIL SEAL AND RETAINER ASSEMBLY
4. AXLE SHAFT BEARING SHIM
5. AXLE SHAFT BEARING CUP
6. AXLE SHAFT BEARING
7. AXLE SHAFT
8. AXLE SHAFT INNER OIL SEAL
9. NUT
10. AXLE HOUSING
11. COLLAPSIBLE SPACER
12. PINION BEARING CUP-FRONT
13. PINION BEARING-FRONT
14. PINION OIL SEAL
15. UNIVERSAL JOINT YOKE
16. PINION NUT
17. BREATHER
18. BREATHER HOSE
19. BREATHER
20. PINION DEPTH ADJUSTING SHIM
21. PINION REAR BEARING CUP
22. PINION BEARING-REAR
23. PINION GEAR
24. DIFFERENTIAL BEARING
25. DIFFERENTIAL BEARING CUP
26. DIFFERENTIAL BEARING SHIM
27. DIFFERENTIAL BEARING CAP
28. DIFFERENTIAL BEARING CAP BOLT
29. RING GEAR
30. DIFFERENTIAL CASE
31. RING GEAR BOLT
32. DIFFERENTIAL PINION WASHER
33. DIFFERENTIAL PINION
34. DIFFERENTIAL SIDE GEAR
35. DIFFERENTIAL SIDE GEAR THRUST WASHER
36. DIFFERENTIAL PINION SHAFT THRUST BLOCK
37. DIFFERENTIAL PINION SHAFT PIN
38. DIFFERENTIAL PINION SHAFT
39. AXLE HOUSING COVER GASKET
40. AXLE HOUSING COVER
41. AXLE IDENTIFICATION TAG
42. BOLT
43. AXLE HOUSING COVER FILL PLUG
44. WASHER

50217

Fig. 1 Rear axle assembly (typical). 7⁹⁄₁₆ in. axle

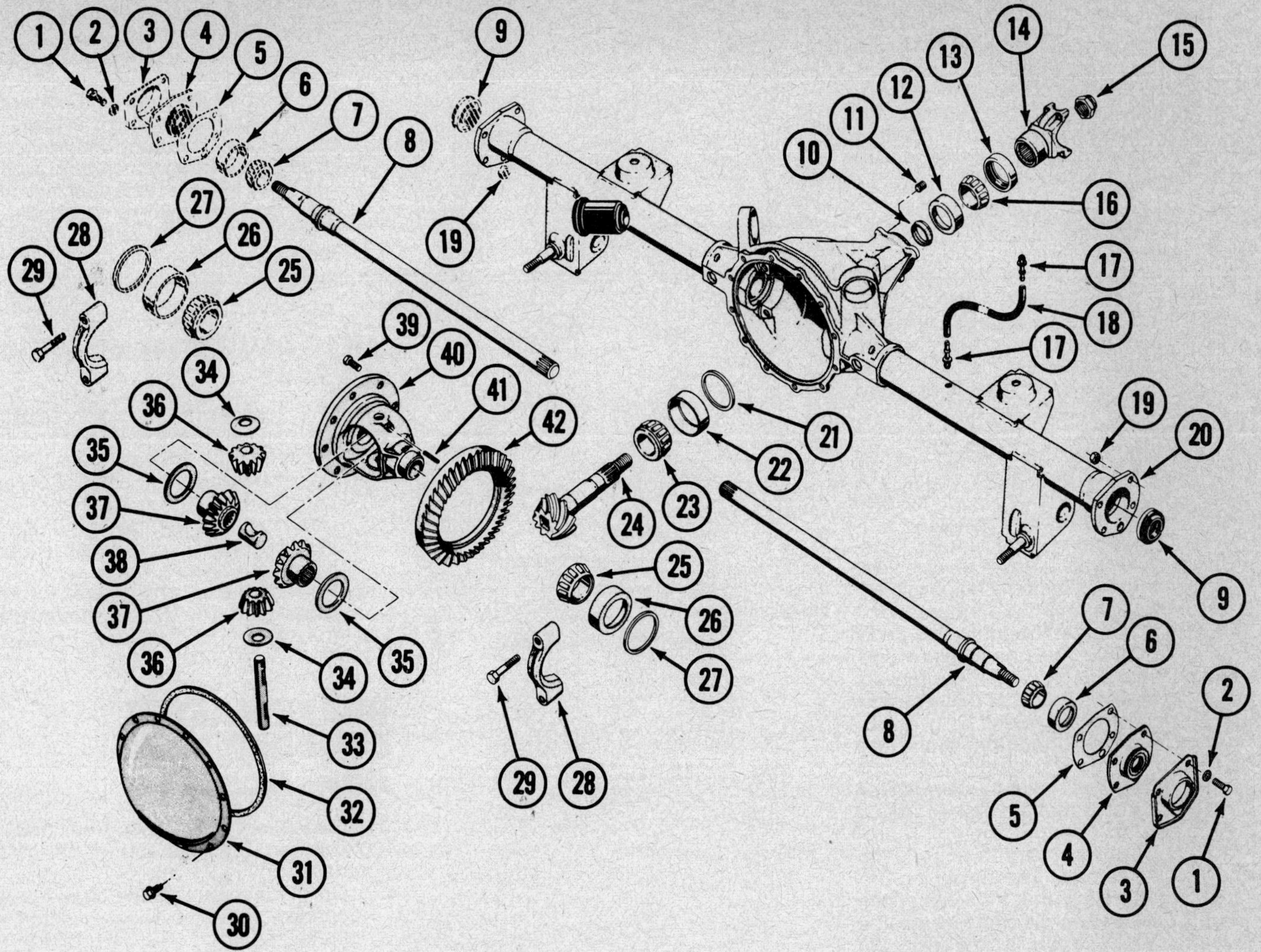

1. BOLT
2. WASHER
3. AXLE SHAFT OIL SEAL RETAINER
4. AXLE SHAFT OIL SEAL
5. AXLE SHAFT BEARING SHIM
6. AXLE SHAFT BEARING CUP
7. AXLE BEARING
8. AXLE SHAFT
9. AXLE SHAFT INNER OIL SEAL
10. PINION COLLAPSIBLE SPACER
11. FILLER PLUG
12. FRONT PINION BEARING CUP
13. PINION OIL SEAL
14. UNIVERSAL JOINT YOKE
15. PINION NUT
16. FRONT PINION BEARING
17. BREATHER
18. BREATHER HOSE
19. NUT
20. REAR AXLE HOUSING
21. DRIVE PINION DEPTH ADJUSTING SHIM
22. REAR PINION BEARING CUP
23. REAR PINION BEARING
24. PINION GEAR
25. DIFFERENTIAL BEARING
26. DIFFERENTIAL BEARING CUP
27. DIFFERENTIAL BEARING SHIM
28. DIFFERENTIAL BEARING CUP
29. BOLT
30. BOLT
31. HOUSING COVER
32. HOUSING COVER GASKET
33. DIFFERENTIAL PINION SHAFT
34. DIFFERENTIAL PINION GEAR THRUST WASHER
35. DIFFERENTIAL SIDE GEAR THRUST WASHER
36. DIFFERENTIAL PINION GEAR
37. DIFFERENTIAL SIDE GEAR
38. DIFFERENTIAL PINION SHAFT THRUST BLOCK
39. BOLT
40. DIFFERENTIAL CASE
41. DIFFERENTIAL PINION SHAFT PIN
42. RING GEAR

Fig. 2 Rear axle assembly (typical). 8⅞ in. axle

required. When making this adjustment, add or subtract shims on left side of axle only.

The application of a bead of sealing material such as "Pliobond" or "Permatex" to the outer diameter of axle tube flange and the brake support contact area is recommended. The sealing material will be used in addition to the gasket for improved sealing.

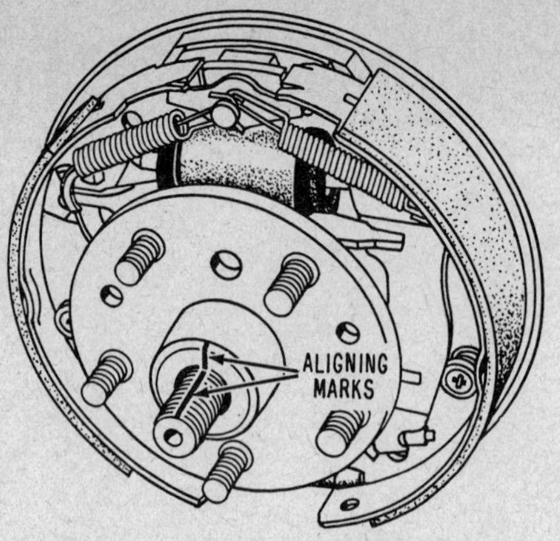

SERVICE BRAKES

ADJUST

These brakes, have self-adjusting mechanisms that assure correct lining-to-drum clearances at all times. The automatic adjusters operate only when the brakes are applied as the car is moving rearward.

Although the brakes are self-adjusting, an initial adjustment is necessary after the brake shoes have been relined or replaced, or when the length of the star wheel adjusting screw has been changed during some other service operation.

Frequent usage of an automatic transmission forward range to halt reverse vehicle motion may prevent the automatic adjusters from functioning, thereby inducing low pedal heights. Should low pedal heights be encountered on these models, it is recommended that numerous forward and reverse stops be made until satisfactory pedal height is obtained.

If a low pedal condition cannot be corrected by making numerous stops (provided the hydraulic system is free of air) it indicates that the self-adjusting mechanism is not functioning. Therefore, it will be necessary to remove the brake drum, clean, free up and lubricate the adjusting mechanisms. Then adjust the brakes as follows, being sure the parking brake is fully released.

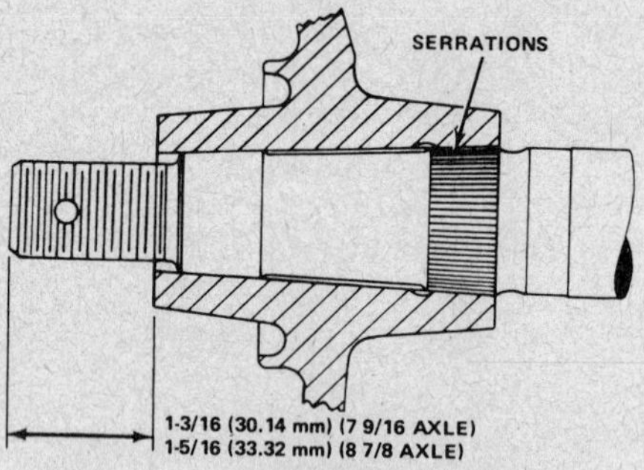

Fig. 3 Installing hub on axle

ADJUSTMENT

1. Remove access slot cover from brake support plate.
2. Using brake adjusting tool or screwdriver, rotate adjuster screw until wheel is locked.
3. Back off adjuster screw one complete turn. **To back off adjuster screw, insert a piece of 1/8 inch rod past adjuster screw and force adjusting lever off adjuster screw.**
4. Install rubber access slot cover.
5. Following the initial adjustment and final assembly, check the brake pedal height to insure brake operation. Then drive the car forward and reverse, making 10 to 15 brake applications prior to road testing. This action balances the adjustment of the four brake units and raises the brake pedal.

PARKING BRAKE

ADJUST

W/ADJUSTMENT GAUGE J-23462

1. Make sure service brakes are properly adjusted.
2. Apply and release parking brake several times.
3. Raise and support vehicle at rear axle using jack stands.
4. Place parking brake in first notch from fully released position.
5. Place an inch lb. torque wrench on Parking Brake Cable Adjustment Gauge J-23462 and place gauge on from parking brake cable, centered between cable housing ferrule and cable equalizer.
6. Apply 50 inch lbs. of torque and note indicator reading. If reading is not within the green band, adjust parking brake at equalizer until satisfactory reading is obtained.
7. Release parking brake and check for brake drag. If brake drag is evident, inspect actuating cables and equalizer for freedom of movement and proper operation. Inspect cable condition, especially at areas where cable passes near exhaust components. Correct as necessary and readjust parking brake cable.

LESS ADJUSTMENT GAUGE J-23462

1. With service brakes properly adjusted, set parking brake pedal on the first notch from fully released position.
2. Adjust front cable at equalizer to obtain .0001-.005 inch (.003-.127 mm) clearance between parking brake lever strut and primary brake shoe at both rear brakes.
3. Release pedal and check for rear wheel drag. The wheels should rotate freely.

BRAKE MASTER CYLINDER

REPLACE

1. Disconnect brake lines from master cylinder. Cap lines and master cylinder ports.
2. On models with manual brakes, disconnect master cylinder pushrod at brake pedal.
3. On all models, remove nuts or bolts attaching master cylinder to dash panel or brake booster and remove master cylinder.
4. Install in the reverse order of removal and bleed the brake system.

POWER BRAKE UNIT

REPLACE

1. Disconnect booster pushrod from brake pedal.
2. Remove vacuum hose from check valve.
3. Remove nuts and washers securing master cylinder to booster unit, then separate master cylinder from booster unit. **Do not disconnect brake lines from master cylinder.**
4. Remove booster unit to firewall attaching nuts and remove booster unit.
5. Reverse procedure to install.

Rear Suspension Section

INDEX

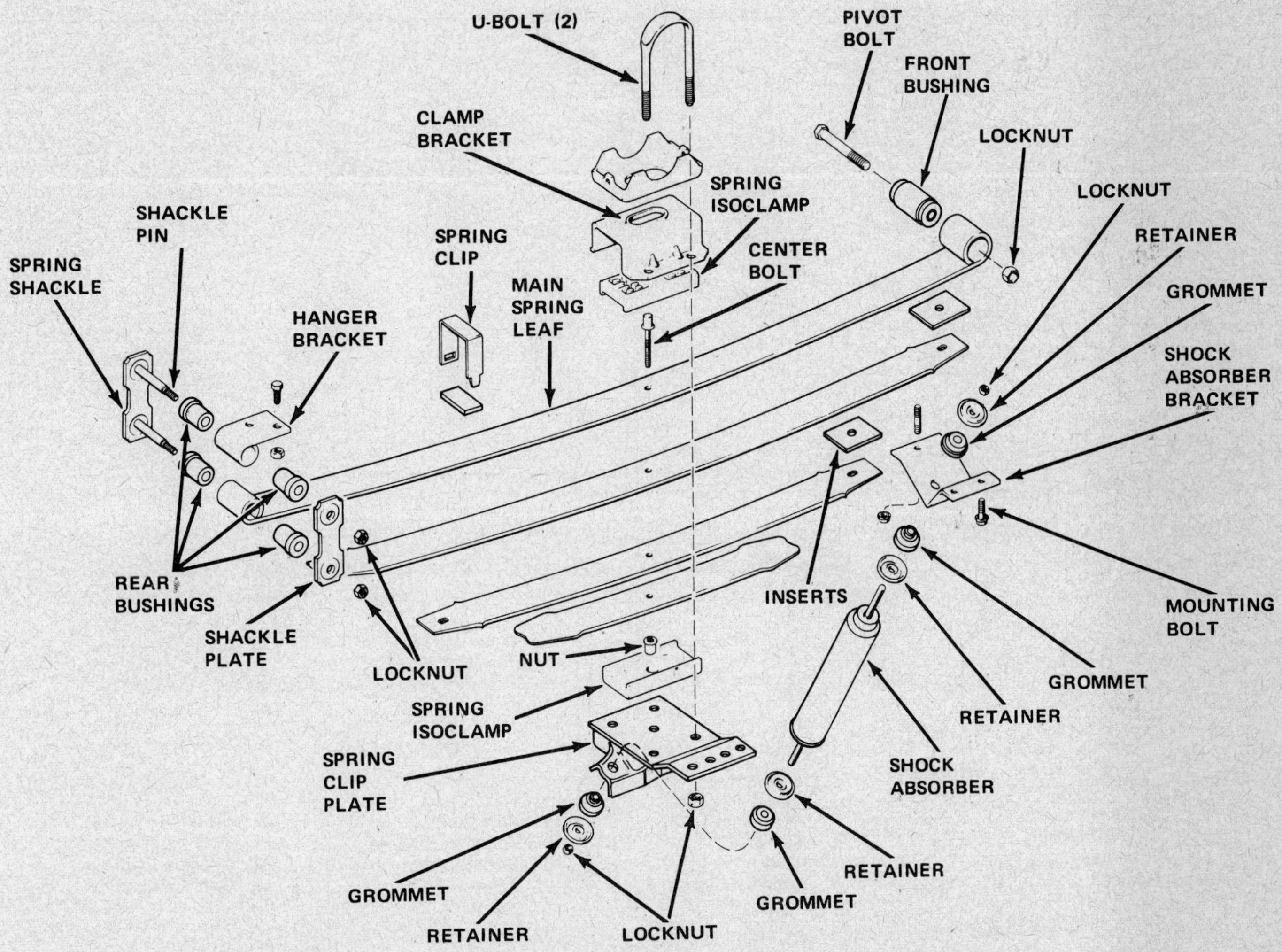

Fig. 1 Rear suspension assembly. Concord & Spirit

SHOCK ABSORBER
REPLACE

1. With the rear axle supported properly, disconnect lower end of shock absorber from stud on mounting bracket.
2. Remove upper mounting bracket from underbody.
3. Reverse procedure to install.

LEAF SPRINGS
REPLACE

1. Support rear axle, removing tension from springs.
2. Disconnect lower end of shock absorber from stud on mounting bracket, **Figs. 1 and 2.**
3. Remove U-bolts securing spring plate and spring to axle tube.
4. Disassemble rear shackle and remove eye bolt from spring forward mounting bracket.
5. Reverse procedure to install. Replace bushings as necessary.

CONTROL ARMS & BUSHINGS
REPLACE

Replace control arms one at a time to prevent axle assembly misalignment, making installation difficult.

UPPER CONTROL ARMS

1. Support vehicle at frame.
2. Remove control arm bolts from frame crossmember and axle tube bracket.
3. To replace axle tube bracket bushings, refer to **Figs. 3 and 4.**
4. Reverse procedure to install.

LOWER CONTROL ARMS

1. Support vehicle at rear axle.
2. Remove stabilizer bar, if equipped.
3. Remove control arm mount bolts from frame and axle tube brackets.

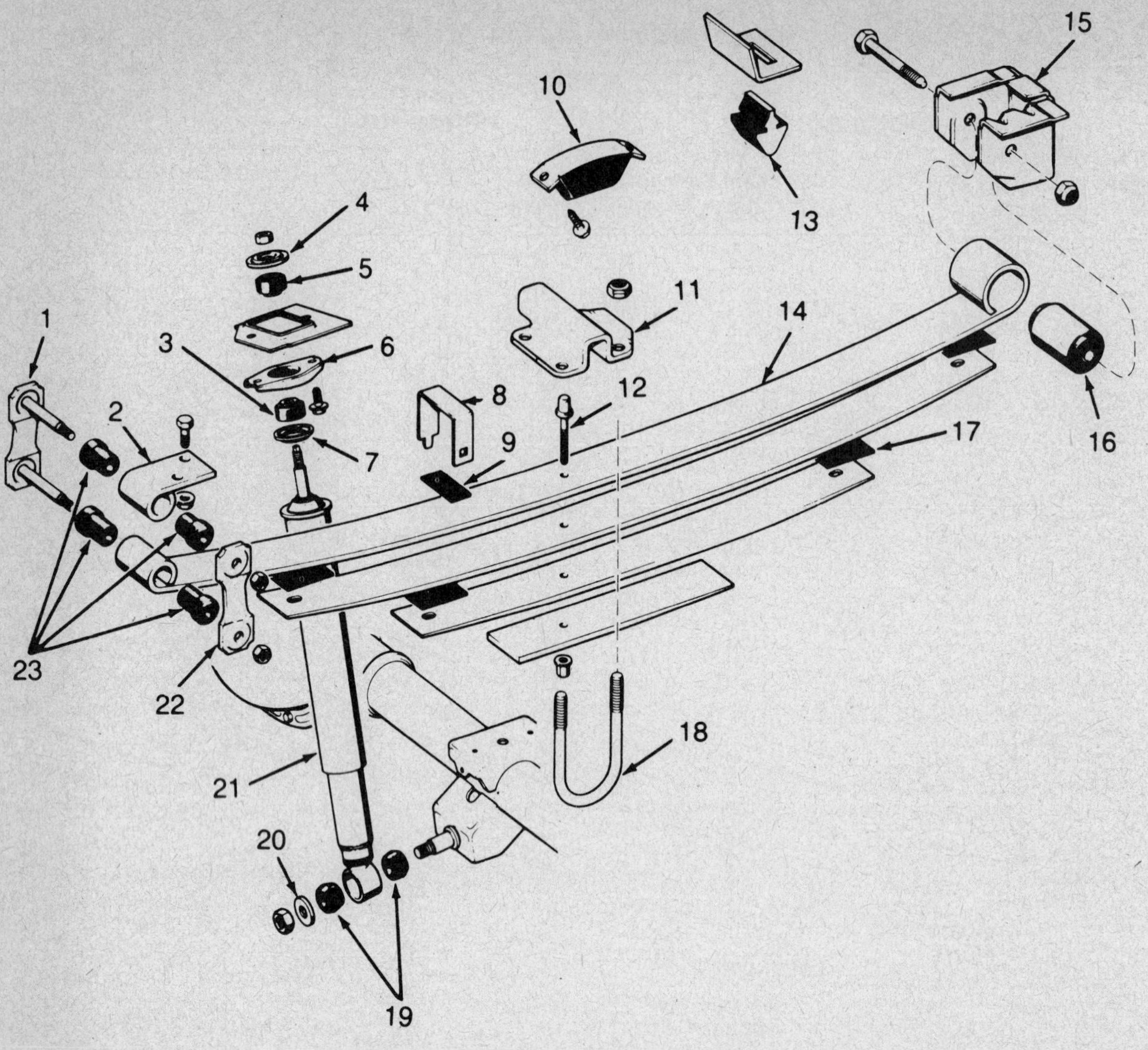

1 - Spring Shackle
2 - Hanger Bracket
3 - Grommet
4 - Retainer
5 - Grommet
6 - Shock Absorber Bracket
7 - Retainer
8 - Spring Clip
9 - Insert
10 - Bumper Cushion
11 - Plate
13 - Cushion
14 - Main Leaf Spring
15 - Mounting Bracket
16 - Front Bushing
17 - Insert
18 - U-Bolt
19 - Grommets
20 - Retainer
21 - Shock Absorber
22 - Shackle Plate
23 - Rear Bushing

Fig. 2 Rear suspension assembly. Eagle

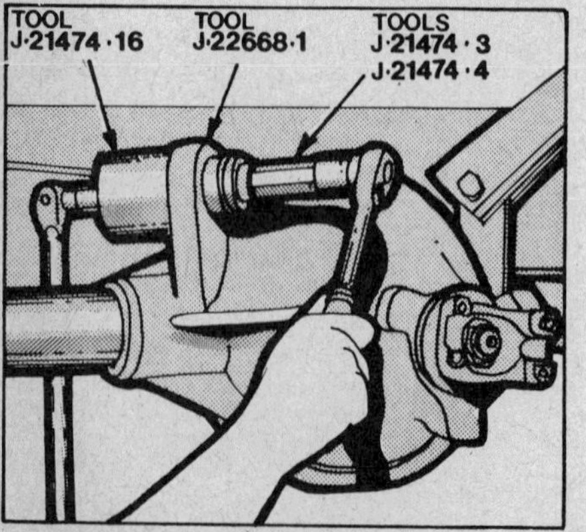

Fig. 3 Upper control arm rear bushing removal

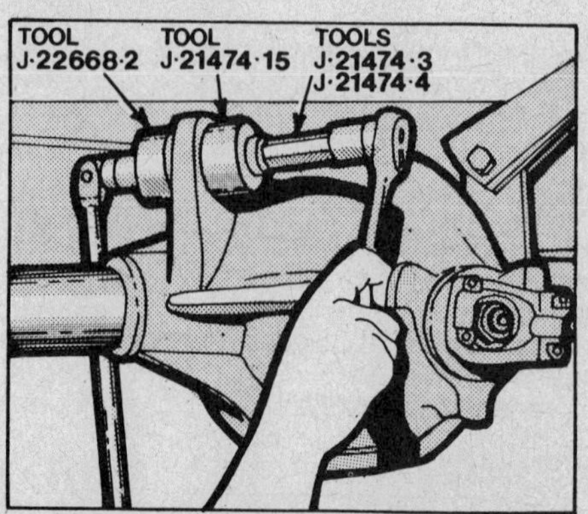

Fig. 4 Upper control arm rear bushing installation

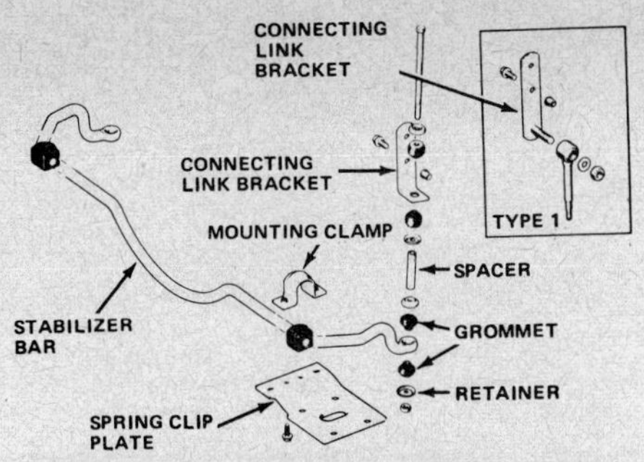

Fig. 5 Rear stabilizer bar. Concord & Spirit

4. Reverse procedure to install. **The lower control arm bushings are not serviceable.**

STABILIZER BAR REPLACE

CONCORD, EAGLE & SPIRIT

1. Raise and support rear of vehicle, then remove nuts and grommets attaching stabilizer to connecting links, **Figs. 5 and 6.**
2. Remove bolts attaching stabilizer bar mounting clamps to spring clip plates and remove stabilizer bar.
3. Reverse procedure to install. Torque link locknuts to 7 ft. lbs. and mounting clamp bolts to 25 ft. lbs.

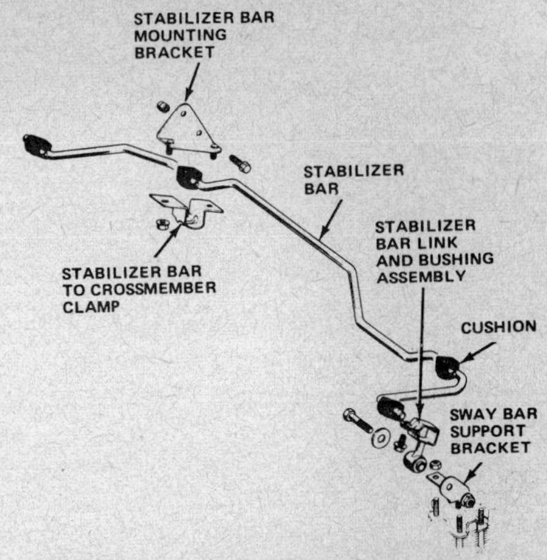

Fig. 6 Rear stabilizer bar. Eagle

Front Suspension & Steering Section

INDEX

DESCRIPTION

EAGLE

These models use an independent front coil spring suspension system, **Fig. 1.** The wheels are suspended on upper and lower control arms with a coil spring located between the upper control arm and a spring seat beneath the wheel housing panels.

Direct acting telescoping shock absorbers are located inside the coil springs. A stabilizer bar attached to each control arm with stabilizer links provides stability, and a dampener dampens steering oscillations.

EXC. EAGLE

The front suspension, **Figs. 2 and 3**, is an independent linked type, with the coil springs located between seats in the wheel house panels and seats attached to the upper control arms.

Directing acting telescoping shock absorbers are located inside the coil springs.

Each upper control arm assembly has two rubber bushings attached to the wheel house panel and a ball joint attached to the steering knuckle.

Each lower control arm has a rubber bushing attached to the front crossmember and a ball joint attached to the steering knuckle.

The lower control arm strut rods are attached to the lower control arms and body side sill brackets.

WHEEL BEARINGS ADJUST

1982–83 EXC. EAGLE

1. To adjust bearings tighten spindle nut to 25 ft. lbs. while rotating the wheel to seat bearings.
2. Then loosen spindle nut 1/3 turn and with wheel rotating, retorque spindle nut to 6 inch pounds.
3. Place the nut retainer on spindle nut with the slots of the retainer aligned with the cotter pin hole on the spindle.
4. Install cotter pin and dust cap.

WHEEL BEARINGS REPLACE

DISC BRAKES

Exc. Eagle

1. Remove two thirds of the total fluid capacity of the master cylinder reservoir to prevent fluid overflow when the caliper pistons are pushed back in their bores.
2. Raise car and remove front wheels.
3. Disconnect hydraulic tube from mounting bracket. Do not disconnect any hydraulic fitting.
4. Holding the lower edge of the caliper, remove the lower bolt. Any shims that fall out at this point should be labeled to insure that they be replaced in their original position.
5. Holding the upper edge of the caliper, remove the upper bolt, tag these shims.
6. Hang caliper from upper suspension to prevent strain being placed on brake hose.
7. Remove spindle nut and hub and disc assembly. Grease retainer and inner bearing can now be removed.
8. Reverse procedure to install.

CHECKING BALL JOINTS FOR WEAR

Before checking ball joints for wear, make sure the front wheel bearings are properly adjusted and that the control arms are tight.

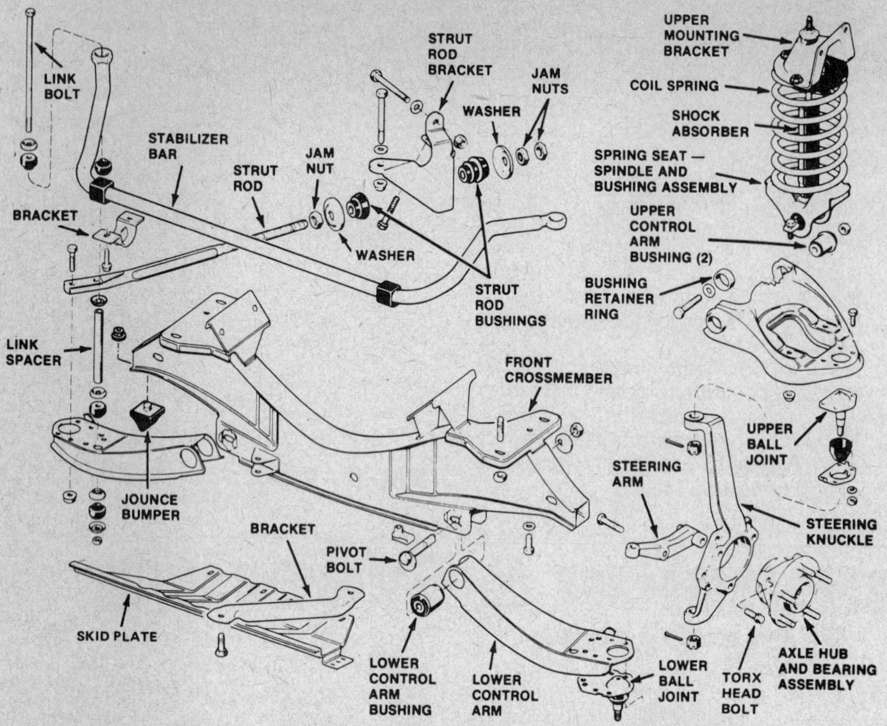

Fig. 1 Front suspension view. Eagle

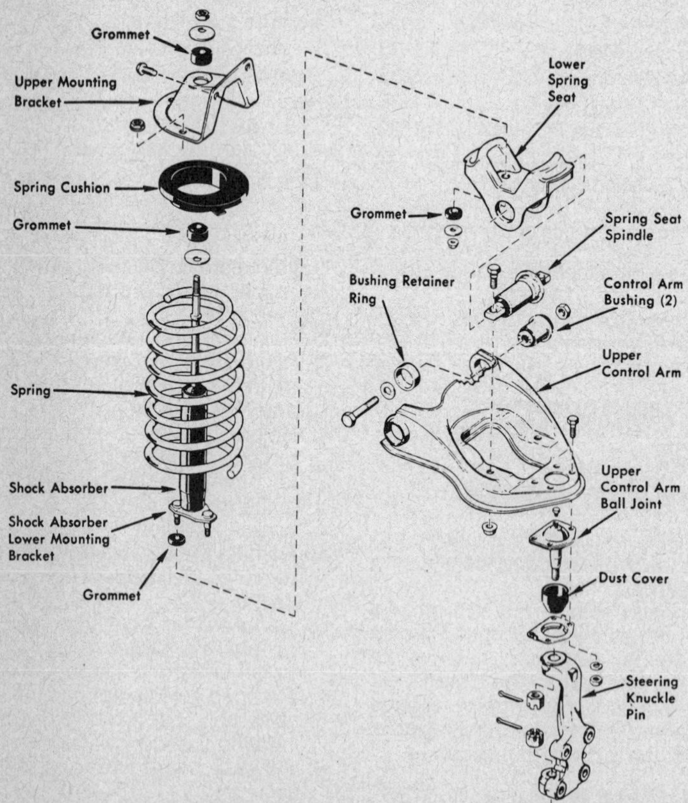

Fig. 2 Front suspension upper control arm components. Exc. Eagle

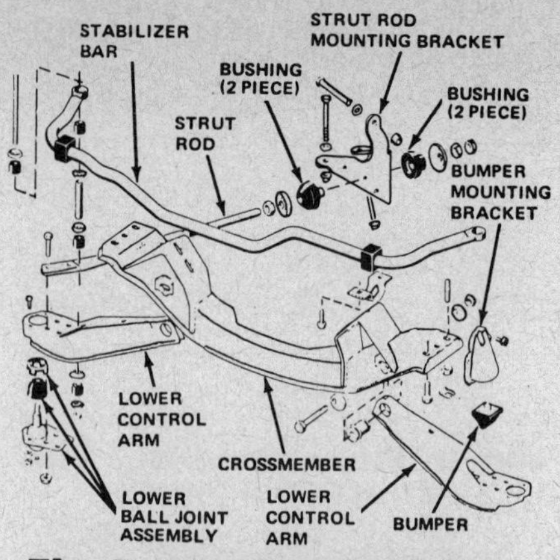

Fig. 3 Front suspension lower control arm components. Exc. Eagle

Raise wheel with a jack placed under the frame as shown. Then test by moving the wheel up and down to check axial play, and rocking it at the top and bottom to measure radial play.

The upper ball joint should be replaced if total travel when rocking and tire exceeds .160 inch.

The lower ball joint is spring loaded and should be replaced if there is any noticeable lateral shake.

On Eagle models, if lower ball joint is worn excessively, the lower control arm and ball joint must be replaced as an assembly.

BALL JOINTS

REPLACE

UPPER BALL JOINT

1. Position a 2x4x5 inch block of wood on side sill under upper control arm.
2. Raise vehicle and support at frame side sills.
3. Remove wheel, brake drum, caliper and rotor assembly. **When removing caliper do not damage brake tubing or hose. Secure caliper to frame with wire.**
4. Remove cotter pin and retaining nut from upper ball joint stud.
5. Install tool No. J-9656 on ball stud, then using a hammer strike tool to loosen ball stud in steering knuckle.
6. Support lower control arm with a suitable jack.
7. Chisel heads from rivets attaching ball joint to upper control arm, then drive rivets out using a punch.
8. Remove tool from ball stud and ball joint from steering knuckle.
9. Position ball joint on control arm and install nuts and bolts. Torque bolts to 25 ft. lbs.
10. Reverse procedure to assemble. Torque ball joint stud nut to 75 ft. lbs.

LOWER BALL JOINT

Exc. Eagle

1. Position a 2x4x5 inch block of wood on side sill under upper control arm.
2. Raise vehicle and support at frame side sills.

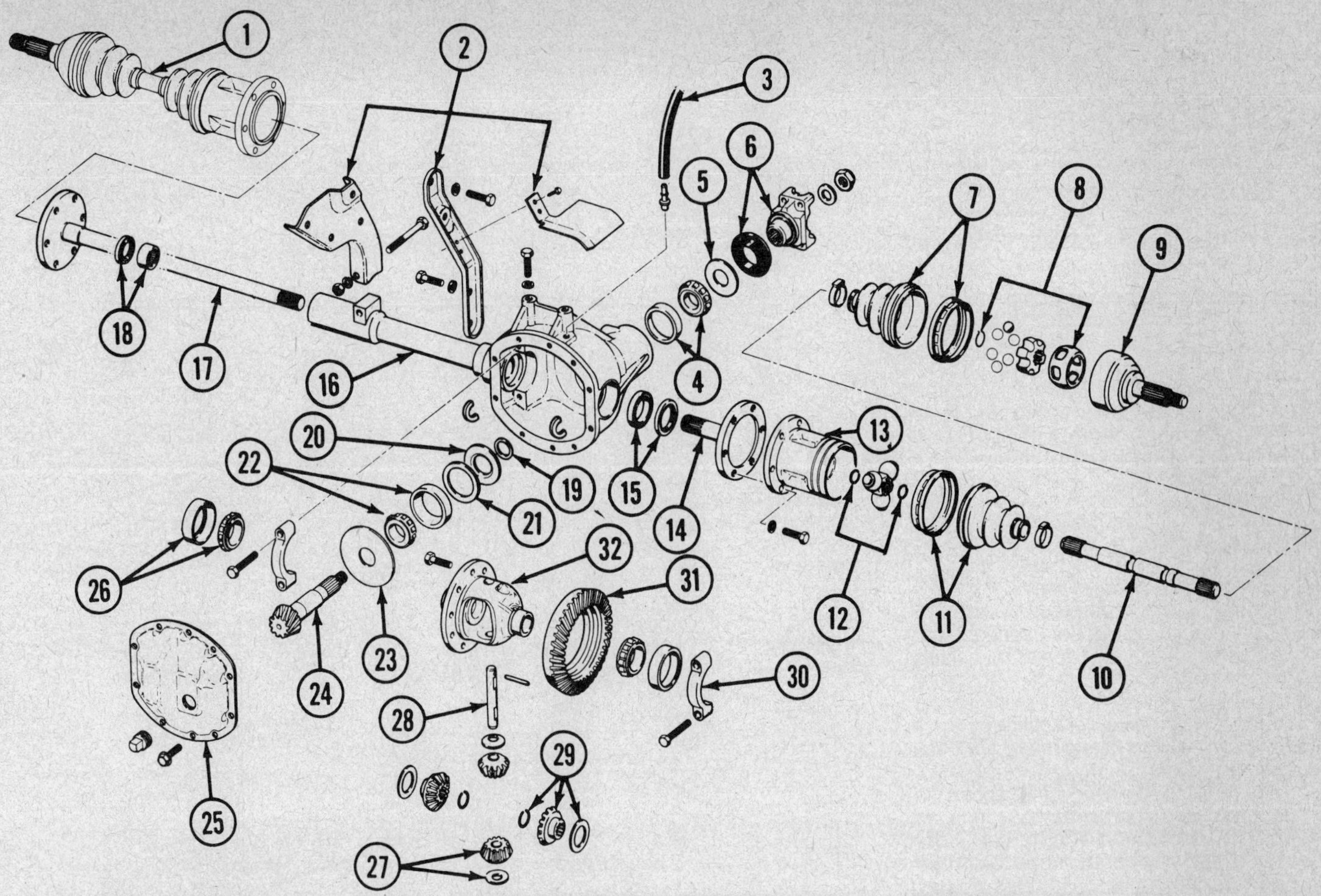

1. HALF-SHAFT ASSEMBLY
2. AXLE MOUNTING BRACKETS
3. VENT HOSE
4. PINION AND FRONT BEARING CUP
5. WASHER
6. YOKE AND SEAL
7. OUTER BOOT AND RETAINER
8. RZEPPA JOINT ASSEMBLY
9. SPINDLE
10. HALF-SHAFT
11. INNER BOOT AND RETAINER
12. TRI-POT JOINT ASSEMBLY
13. TRI-POT HOUSING
14. AXLE SHAFT (SHORT)
15. BALL BEARING AND SEAL
16. AXLE HOUSING
17. AXLE SHAFT (LONG)
18. NEEDLE BEARING AND SEAL
19. PRELOAD SHIM
20. WASHER
21. DEPTH SHIM
22. PINION REAR BEARING AND CUP
23. SLINGER
24. PINION GEAR
25. COVER
26. DIFFERENTIAL BEARING AND CUP
27. DIFFERENTIAL PINION AND THRUST WASHER
28. PINION MATE SHAFT
29. SIDE GEAR, THRUST WASHER AND LOCKRING
30. BEARING CAP
31. RING GEAR
32. DIFFERENTIAL CASE

Fig. 4 Front axle assembly. 1982–84 Eagle less Select Drive System

3. Remove wheel and brake drum or caliper and rotor assembly. **When removing caliper do not damage brake tubing or hose. Secure caliper to frame with wire.**
4. Disconnect strut rod from lower control arm and steering arm from steering knuckle.
5. Remove lower ball joint stud cotter pin and retaining nut.
6. Install tool No. 9656 on ball stud, then strike tool with hammer to loosen ball stud in steering knuckle.
7. Support lower control arm with a suitable jack.
8. Chisel heads from rivets attaching ball joint to upper control arm, then drive rivets out using a punch.
9. Remove tool from ball stud and ball joint from steering knuckle and lower control arm.
10. Position ball joint on lower control arm and install attaching bolts loosely.
11. Connect strut to lower control arm and torque bolts to 75 ft. lbs.
12. Torque ball joint to lower control arm attaching bolts to 25 ft. lbs.
13. Lubricate steering stop, then install ball stud on steering knuckle. Torque stud nut to 75 ft. lbs. Install cotter pin.
14. Install wheel and brake drum or caliper and rotor and lower vehicle.

Eagle

On these models, the lower control arm and lower ball joint must be replaced as an assembly.

1. Remove cotter pin, nut lock and hub nut, then raise and support front of vehicle.
2. Remove wheel, caliper and rotor.
3. Remove lower ball joint cotter pin and retaining nut.
4. Using tool No. J-9656, disconnect lower ball joint from steering knuckle.
5. Remove half shaft flange bolts, then remove half shaft.
6. Remove bolts attaching strut rod to lower control arm, then disconnect stabilizer bar from lower control arm.
7. Remove inner pivot bolt, then remove lower control arm from crossmember.
8. Position control arm on crossmember, then install inner pivot bolt. Do not tighten inner pivot bolt at this time.
9. Position lower ball joint on steering knuckle, then install ball joint stud nut. Torque ball joint stud nut to 75 ft. lbs., then install cotter pin.
10. Connect stabilizer bar to lower control arm and torque locknut to 7 ft. lbs.
11. Connect strut rod to lower control arm and torque attaching bolts to 75 ft. lbs.

12. Install half shaft to axle flange and torque bolts to 45 ft. lbs.
13. Position a suitable jack under control arm and raise control arm slightly to compress coil spring, then tighten inner pivot bolt to 110 ft. lbs.
14. Install rotor, caliper and hub nut. Torque hub nut to 180 ft. lbs., then install nut lock and cotter pin.
15. Install wheel and tire assembly, then lower vehicle and check wheel alignment.

SHOCK ABSORBER
REPLACE

After disconnecting shock absorber from wheelhouse panel at top and lower spring seat at the bottom, withdraw shock absorber out of top of wheelhouse.

SPRING
REPLACE

1. Remove shock absorber.
2. Install spring compressor tool J-23474 through upper spring seat opening, place tool lower attaching screws through shock absorber mounting holes in the lower spring seat. Install tool lower retainer.
3. Remove lower spring seat pivot retaining nuts.
4. Tighten compressor until spring is compressed approximately 1 inch.
5. Raise and support front of car under frame allowing control arms to fall free of lower spring seat. Remove wheel.
6. Pull lower spring seat away from car. Loosen compressor and allow lower spring seat to come out.
7. When all spring tension is released, remove tool lower retainer spring seat and spring.
8. Reverse procedure to install.

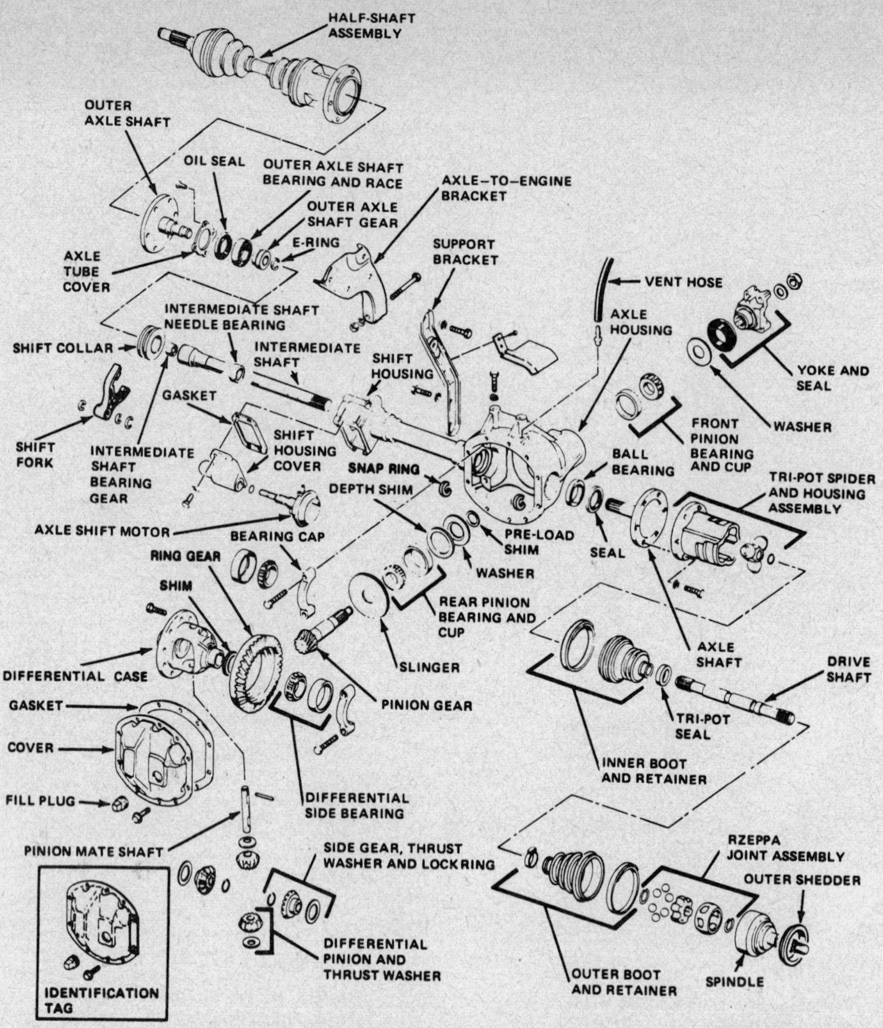

Fig. 5 Front axle assembly. 1982–84 Eagle w/Select Drive System

STABILIZER BAR
REPLACE

1. Raise and support front of vehicle, then remove right side wheel.
2. Disconnect idler arm at frame side sill.
3. Remove stabilizer bar mounting clamps at the frame side sills.
4. Disconnect stabilizer bar link at lower control arms, then remove link bolts, rubber grommets, spacer and retainers.
5. Remove stabilizer bar from right side of vehicle. Move steering linkage and left side wheel, as necessary, to obtain clearance.
6. Reverse procedure to install.

STEERING GEAR
REPLACE
MANUAL STEERING

1. Remove flexible coupling bolts.
2. Remove pitman arm, using a suitable puller.
3. Remove mounting screws and lower steering gear from vehicle.
4. Reverse procedure to install.

POWER STEERING

1. Disconnect pressure and return hoses from gear. Raise hoses above pump level to keep oil from draining out of pump.
2. Remove flexible coupling bolt nuts, noting the different nut sizes to insure correct assembly.
3. On Eagle models, remove skid plate, if equipped, then remove lefthand crossmember to sill support brace and stabilizer bar bracket from frame.
4. Remove pitman arm with a suitable puller.
5. Remove gear attaching bolts.
6. Slide lower shaft free of coupling flange, then remove gear.
7. Reverse procedure to install.

POWER STEERING PUMP
REPLACE
MODELS w/4 CYL. ENGINE

1. Remove air induction hose, then remove power steering pump adjusting bracket mounting bolts.
2. Move power steering pump toward engine and remove drive belt.
3. Loosen return hose clamp and slide back along hose, then pull power steering pump forward and disconnect both pressure and return lines.
4. Remove bolts attaching power steering pump front mounting bracket to rear mounting bracket and engine.
5. Remove power steering pump, pivot bracket and front mounting bracket as an assembly.
6. Reverse procedure to install.

MODELS w/6 CYL. ENGINE
Less A/C

1. On 1982-83 models, remove air pump drive belt, then remove air pump pivot stud nut.
2. On all models, remove power steering pump adjusting stud nuts and pivot bolt, then remove pump drive belt.
3. Disconnect pressure and return lines, then remove bolts attaching power steering pump bracket to engine and remove pump.
4. Reverse procedure to install.

With A/C

1. Remove air induction hoses.
2. On 1982-83 models, remove air

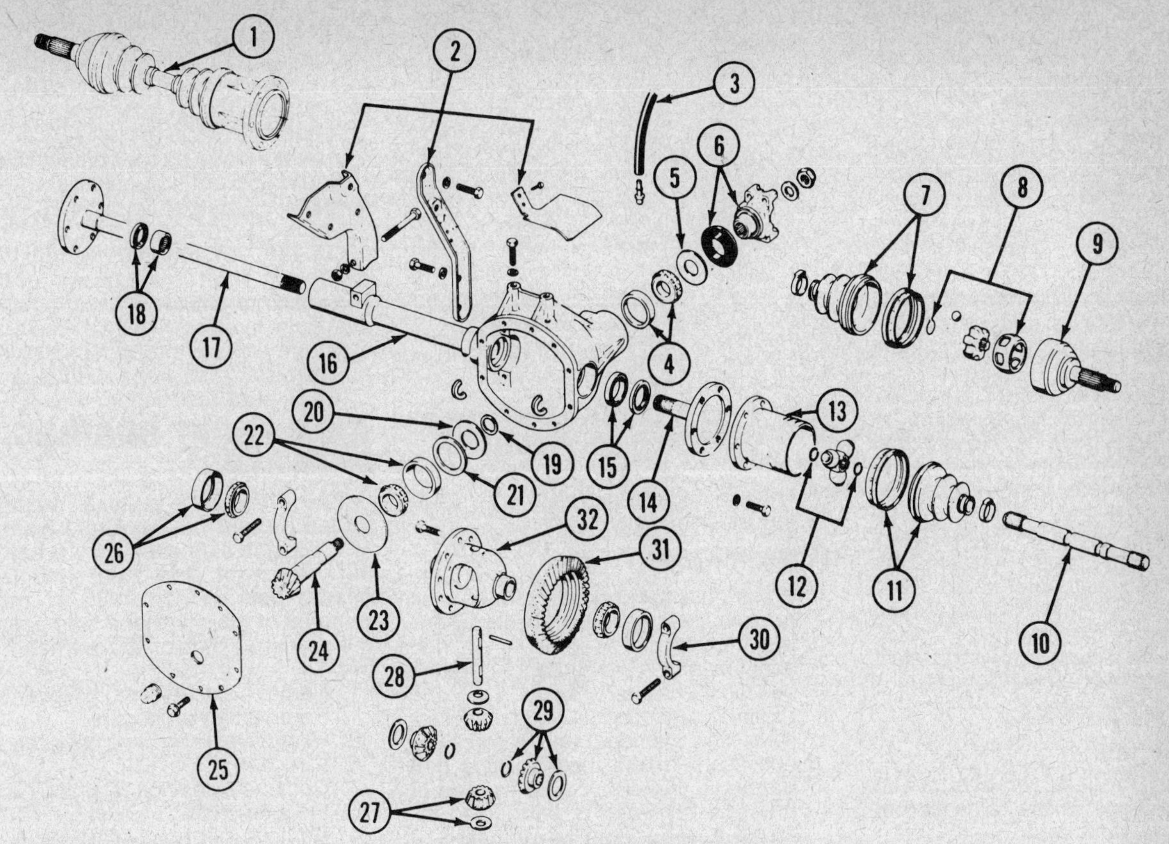

1. HALF-SHAFT ASSEMBLY
2. AXLE MOUNTING BRACKETS
3. VENT HOSE
4. PINION AND FRONT BEARING CUP
5. WASHER
6. YOKE AND SEAL
7. OUTER BOOT AND RETAINER
8. RZEPPA JOINT ASSEMBLY
9. SPINDLE
10. HALF-SHAFT
11. INNER BOOT AND RETAINER
12. TRI-POT JOINT ASSEMBLY
13. TRI-POT HOUSING
14. AXLE SHAFT (SHORT)
15. BALL BEARING AND SEAL
16. AXLE HOUSING
17. AXLE SHAFT (LONG)
18. NEEDLE BEARING AND SEAL
19. PRELOAD SHIM
20. WASHER
21. DEPTH SHIM
22. PINION REAR BEARING AND CUP
23. SLINGER
24. PINION GEAR
25. COVER
26. DIFFERENTIAL BEARING AND CUP
27. DIFFERENTIAL PINION AND THRUST WASHER
28. PINION MATE SHAFT
29. SIDE GEAR, THRUST WASHER AND LOCKRING
30. BEARING CAP
31. RING GEAR
32. DIFFERENTIAL CASE

Fig. 6 Front axle assembly. 1985–87 Eagle

pump adjusting bolt and pivot stud, then remove air pump drive belt.

3. Remove A/C compressor drive belt, then remove compressor pulley and pulley bracket as an assembly.
4. Remove power steering pump pivot bolt attaching lower edge of pump to engine.
5. Remove power steering pump adjusting bracket stud nuts and bolt attaching pump to rear bracket, then slide drive belt from pulley.
6. Pull power steering pump and front mounting bracket forward until bracket clears air pump pivot stud.
7. On 1982-83 models, remove air pump pivot stud and position air pump aside.
8. On all models, disconnect power steering pump pressure and return lines, then remove pump.
9. Reverse procedure to install.

EAGLE FRONT AXLE SERVICE

Refer to **Figs. 4, 5 and 6** during front axle service pro cedures.

AXLE, REPLACE

Removal

1. Raise and support vehicle.
2. Install half shaft boot protectors J-28712 onto boots.
3. Remove half shaft to axle flange bolts and secure half shaft to vehicle underbody.
4. Insert wire through half shaft flange bolt holes, then compress half shaft and wrap wire between boots to prevent half shaft from separating.
5. Mark propeller shaft and axle yoke for reference during reassembly and remove propeller shaft.
6. Support axle assembly using suitable jack.
7. On models equipped with Select Drive System, remove brace rod and shift motor shield.
8. On all models, remove axle mounting bolts. On models less Select Drive System, the axle is secured to the engine block with five bolts. On models with Select Drive System, the axle is secured to the engine block by five bolts on the left hand side and one bolt on the righthand side.
9. On models equipped with Select Drive System, disconnect vacuum hose from axle shift motor, then partially lower axle assembly and disconnect vent hose.
10. On all models, lower axle assembly to allow access to vent hose and remove hose.

11. Remove axle assembly from vehicle. **Do not apply any load or weight on the hub assembly whenever the half shafts are not securely attached to the axle shaft flanges.**

Installation

1. Support axle assembly on suitable jack and position assembly under vehicle.
2. Raise axle assembly slightly and install vent hose.
3. Continue raising axle assembly until properly positioned and install axle mounting bolts. Torque bolts to 50 ft. lbs.
4. Connect propeller shaft to axle yoke. Ensure shaft and yoke are aligned.
5. Remove wire used to prevent half shafts from separating, then install half shaft to axle flange bolts and torque to 45 ft. lbs.
6. On models equipped with Select Drive System, connect vacuum harness on axle shift motor shield.
7. On all models, remove half shaft boot protectors.
8. On models equipped with Select Drive, connect brace rod to axle.

AXLE SHAFT SEAL, REPLACE

On 1985-87 models, removal of the righthand shaft seal is the same as that of the lefthand shaft seal.

1. Remove axle assembly.
2. Remove axle housing cover and drain lubricant.
3. Remove axle shaft retaining clip, then the axle shaft.
4. Remove axle shaft seal using suitable screwdriver.
5. Install replacement axle shaft seal using Installer J-29152 for righthand side axle shaft and Installer J-29154 for lefthand side axle shaft.
6. Install axle shaft, then the axle shaft retaining clip.
7. Apply suitable sealant to axle housing cover and install cover. Torque cover bolts to 20 ft. lbs.
8. Fill axle with 2 1/2 pints of SAE 85W-90 lubricant, then install assembly onto vehicle. Refer to Axle, Installation for procedures.

AXLE HUB & BEARING

Removal

1. Raise and support vehicle, then remove wheel, caliper and rotor.
2. Remove bolts attaching axle shaft flange to half shaft. **Insert wire through half shaft flange bolt holes, then compress half shaft and wrap wire between boots to prevent half shaft from separating.**
3. Remove cotter pin, locknut and axle shaft nut, then the half shaft.
4. Remove steering arm from steering knuckle.
5. Remove caliper anchor plate from steering knuckle, then the three torx head bolts retaining hub assembly using tool J-26359.
6. Remove hub assembly from steering knuckle and clean grease from steering knuckle cavity.

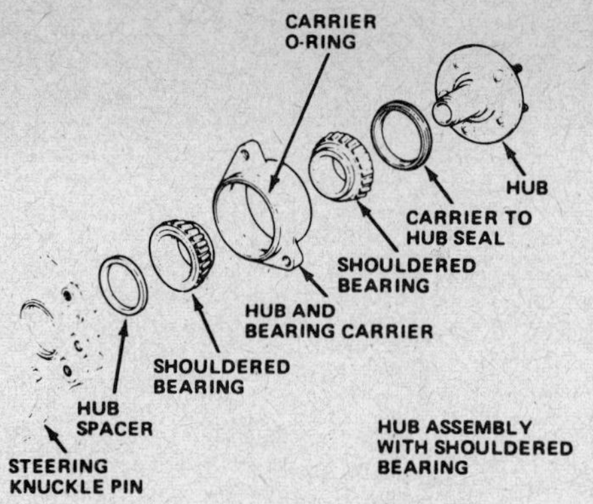

Fig. 7 Disassembled view of axle hub. Eagle

Disassemble

1. Press hub from bearing carrier, then remove bearings, hub spacer, steering knuckle pin seal, carrier to hub seal, carrier O-ring and bearing spacer, if equipped, **Fig. 7.**
2. Clean all components and inspect for wear and damage and replace as necessary. **If hub incorporates ball bearings, the entire hub assembly must be replaced if damage to internal components is indicated. If hub incorporates tapered bearings, internal hub components may be replaced as necessary. Bearings and races must be replaced in matched sets.**
3. Press bearing races from hub carrier, if necessary. Install replacement bearing races using a brass drift or suitable press.

Assemble

1. Fill steering knuckle pin, hub, bearing carrier and lip type seal cavities with lithium base wheel bearing lubricant.
2. Pack bearings with lithium base wheel bearing lubricant, then install bearings into hub carrier, **Fig. 7.**
3. Install seal onto hub side of bearing carrier, then press hub into carrier and install hub spacer on end of hub shaft. **Do not install bearing carrier O-ring at this time.**
4. Install inner seal into steering knuckle pin.
5. Install splash shield onto hub and bearing carrier, then install bearing carrier O-ring.
6. Install splash shield and bearing carrier into steering knuckle pin, then install carrier attaching bolts and torque to 75 ft. lbs.

Installation

1. Partially fill hub cavity of steering knuckle with chassis lubricant and install hub assembly onto steering knuckle. Torque hub torx head bolts to 75 ft. lbs.
2. Install caliper anchor plate and torque plate retaining bolts to 100 ft. lbs.
3. Install steering arm onto steering knuckle and torque retaining bolts to 100 ft. lbs.
4. Install half shaft, then the axle flange to shaft bolts and hub nut. Torque half shaft to flange bolts to 45 ft. lbs. and hub nut 175 ft. lbs.
5. Install locknut, replacement cotter pin, rotor, caliper and wheel.

AXLE SHAFT, REPLACE

On 1985-87 models, removal of the righthand shaft is the same as that of the lefthand shaft.

1. Refer to Axle Shaft Seal, Replace. Perform steps 1 through 3 for axle shaft removal and steps 6 through 8 for axle shaft installation.

AXLE SHAFT BEARING, REPLACE

Two different style axle shaft bearings are used on the Eagle front axle. The left side axle shaft uses a ball bearing. The right side axle shaft uses a needle bearing. On 1985-87 models, removal of the righthand side bearing is the same as that of the lefthand bearing.

1. Remove axle assembly. Refer to Axle, Removal for procedure.
2. Remove axle housing cover and drain lubricant.
3. Remove axle shaft retaining clip, then the axle shaft.
4. Remove axle shaft seal using suitable screwdriver.
5. Remove needle bearing using Tools J-29173 and J-2619-1. Remove ball bearing using suitable brass punch and hammer. **If needle bearing tools are not available, remove the differential, then the bearing using a 15/16 in. socket and three foot extension bar.**
6. Install axle shaft bearings. Use tool J-29153 to install needle bearing and tool J-29154 to install ball bearing.
7. Install axle shaft seals using Installer J-29152 for the righthand side axle shaft and Installer J-29154 for lefthand side axle shaft.
8. Install axle shafts, then the retaining clips.
9. Apply suitable sealant to axle housing cover and install cover. Torque cover bolts to 20 ft. lbs.
10. Fill axle with 2 1/2 pints of SAE 85W-90 lubricant, then install assembly onto vehicle. Refer to Axle, Installation for procedure.

1984-87 HALF SHAFT SERVICE

Care should be taken when removing or replacing drive shaft rubber boots. These boots are relatively fragile and precautions should be taken to avoid damage. Do not drop the drive shafts on the boots. Although no apparent damage is observed, internal damage could result in eventual rupture. Use care when working around the front axle drive shafts to avoid any contact with the boots. Cover the boots with shop towels.

Disassemble

1. Using a suitable tool cut and remove both outer boot clamps, then roll outer boot from constant velocity joint.
2. Position a wooden block against constant velocity joint inner race and drive joint from shaft. If half shaft is to be positioned in a vise, use protective vise jaws.
3. Using a brass drift, tap constant velocity joint cage until cage is tilted outward far enough to remove first ball, then remove remaining balls in the same manner.
4. Align two outer constant velocity joint oblong holes with slots located on interior wall of spindle housing and remove cage and inner race.
5. Align shoulder between race grooves with inside of oblong cage holes, then rotate inner race out of cage using the larger of the two openings.
6. Remove two snap rings from shaft, then remove outer boot.
7. Remove rubber retaining ring from small end of inner boot.
8. Cut inner boot retaining strap, then remove strap from tripod housing. Slide boot away from housing.
9. Remove tripod joint and shaft from housing.
10. Remove snap ring that retains tripod joint on shaft using suitable pliers, then remove tripod joint.
11. Remove inner boot from shaft if replacement is required.
12. Remove any remaining snap rings from shaft, if not removed previously.

Inspection

Clean all components in a suitable solvent and dry with compressed air. Check all components for wear and damage and joints for rough operation, replace components as necessary. **Outer constant velocity joint and inner tripod joint are replaced as an assembly.**

Assemble

1. Pack spindle hub with chassis grease.
2. Install outer constant velocity joint inner into cage, then install cage and race assembly into spindle hub. The smaller diameter of the cage and stopping groove of race must face outward.
3. Using a brass drift, tilt cage outward until first ball can be installed into cage, then install remaining balls in the same manner.
4. Pack constant velocity joint with chassis grease, then install outer boot on half shaft.
5. Install inner and outer snap rings, then constant velocity joint onto shaft until inner race contacts inner snap ring.
6. Position boot over constant velocity joint, then install both boot clamps using tool No. J-22716 or equivalent. **Check and adjust installed length of boot. Total installed length should be 4.134 inch (105 mm). Move small end of boot in or out on shaft to obtain specified length.**
7. Pack tripod joint housing with chassis grease, then install inner small retainer ring, boot and large retainer ring onto half shaft.
8. Install tripod joint and snap ring onto shaft, then install tripod joint and shaft into housing.
9. Position boot and install rubber retainer ring over small end of boot.
10. Install large end boot clamp using a suitable tool.

INTERMEDIATE SHAFT, OUTER AXLE SHAFT & SHIFT HOUSING, REPLACE

Models w/Select Drive System

1. Raise and support front of vehicle.
2. Remove front axle assembly, then drain lubricant.
3. Remove bolts securing shift housing and remove shift fork, shifting housing and shift motor as an assembly.
4. Working through access hole in the outer axle shaft flange, remove screws securing axle tube cover.
5. Remove outer axle shaft assembly by tapping shaft flange with a rubber or plastic mallet.
6. Remove intermediate shaft snap ring, then remove intermediate shaft and shift collar.
7. Using a suitable puller and slide hammer, remove outer axle shaft bearing race.
8. Using adapter tool No. J-26225 and slide hammer J-6471-2, remove intermediate shaft needle bearing from axle tube end.
9. Using spreader tool No. J-29369-1 and slide hammer No. J-2619-01, remove intermediate shaft gear bearing. **The intermediate shaft gear is retained on the axle shaft by an internal type expandable snap ring. When removing the bearing from the gear be sure to support the gear face on vise jaws to avoid pulling the gear off the shaft. The gear and shaft are serviced only as an assembly.**
10. Remove outer axle shaft retaining E-ring.
11. Make a reference mark on outer axle shaft gear (for assembly purposes) and remove gear from shaft.
12. Remove outer axle shaft bearing using an arbor press.
13. Remove axle oil seal and tube cover.
14. Clean and carefully inspect all components for wear or damage. Replace all necessary components.
15. Install axle oil seal and tube cover on axle shaft.
16. Using an arbor press, install axle shaft bearing and race on shaft.
17. Install axle shaft gear on shaft using an arbor press. Be sure to align reference mark. Also ensure gear splines are facing outward.
18. Install axle shaft E-ring.
19. Using tool No. J-29153, install intermediate shaft needle bearing.
20. Install intermediate shaft gear needle bearing in gear bore using an arbor press.
21. Install intermediate shaft, then install shift collar, and seat shaft in differential.
22. Install intermediate shaft lock ring.
23. Install outer axle shaft assembly, torque axle tube cover bolts evenly and in a cross sequence. Torque bolts 144 inch pounds.
24. Install gasket on shift housing cover and install. **Check to ensure the shift fork and tabs are aligned in the shift collar.**
25. Torque shift housing cover bolts to 108 inch pounds.
26. Install axle cover using a new gasket. Torque bolts to 20 ft. lbs.
27. Fill shift housing with five ozs. of specified lubricant, then fill axle housing.

SELECT DRIVE SYSTEM

The Select Drive is a system which permits the full time four wheel drive power train to be operated in a two wheel drive mode. When the vehicle is stopped, the system can be changed from two wheel drive to four wheel or four wheel drive to two wheel drive, by pulling the instrument panel control switch pull release pin downward and moving the control switch lever to the desired position. The two major components of this system are a shifting device in the transfer case and a disconnecting mechanism in the front axle, which are controlled by the instrument panel switch through a series of vacuum actuators.

The vacuum actuated shifter mechanism located on the transfer case slides a splined clutch, located on the transfer case main shaft, rearward to engage or forward to disengage power to the front drive chain sprocket. In the two wheel drive position, the shifter mechanism also locks the transfer case differential. Also the main shaft and differential assembly will turn as a unit, transferring power to the rear driveshaft, while front output shaft, chain and sprocket remain stationary.

A vacuum actuated disconnect device is used to engage or disengage a splined clutch that connects the righthand driveshaft to the righthand half shaft. When four wheel drive is selected, the spline clutch is engaged and the front drive axle operates in a normal manner. When two wheel is selected, the vacuum actuator releases the spline clutch, which releases drive to the righthand half shaft and allows the right hand driveshaft to rotate freely. Due to the design of the differential, to equalize torque between left and right axle shafts, disconnecting the right axle shaft will allow the left axle shaft to rotate freely. The axle disconnect will not release all front drive components in the two wheel drive mode. Half shafts and different side gears will continue to rotate with the front wheels as the vehicle is driven.

AXLE SHIFT MOTOR, REPLACE

Models w/Select Drive System

1. Make a reference mark on fork and housing for assembly purposes.
2. Rotate shift motor and remove retaining snap rings using a suitable screwdriver.
3. Remove shift motor from housing and remove O-ring from motor.
4. Reverse procedure to install.

Wheel Alignment Section

INDEX

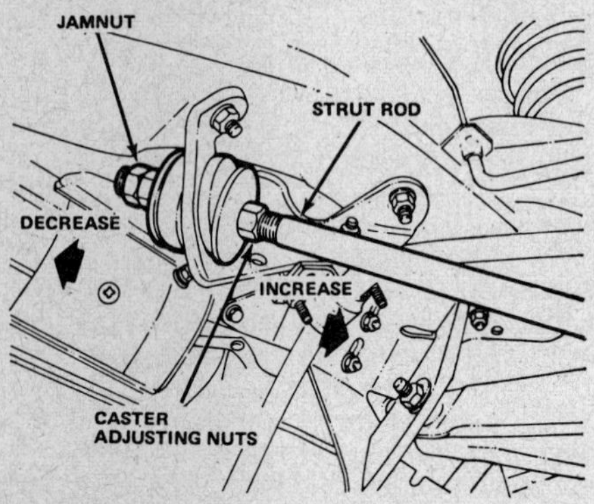

Fig. 1 Caster adjustment

WHEEL ALIGNMENT

CASTER

Caster is obtained by moving the two adjusting nuts on the threaded strut rod, **Fig. 1.** One nut is on each side of the mounting bracket. Therefore, moving the nuts on the rod will move the lower control arm to front or rear for desired caster angle. After adjustment, torque adjusting nuts to 65 ft. lbs. Torque locknuts to 75 ft. lbs.

CAMBER

Camber is obtained by turning on the eccentric lower control arm bolt, **Fig. 2.** After adjustment, torque locknut to 110 ft. lbs.

TOE-IN

ADJUST

To adjust toe-in, loosen the clamps at both ends of the adjustable tubes on each tie rod. Turn the tubes an equal amount until the toe-in is correct. Turning the right tube in the direction the wheels revolve when the car is going forward increases the toe-in and turning the left tube in the opposite direction increases toe-in. To decrease toe-in turn the right tube backward and the left tube forward. It is important that both tubes be turned an equal amount in order to maintain the correct position of the steering wheel. When adjustment is complete, tighten all clamp bolts.

In performing service operations on the steering linkage or when adjusting toe-in, be sure to square the tie rod ball sockets on the studs and align the tie rod stud in the center, or slightly above center, of the cross tube opening, before tightening the steering linkage adjusting tube. This will prevent the stud from contacting the side of the cross tube opening, which would otherwise result in noise problems or damage.

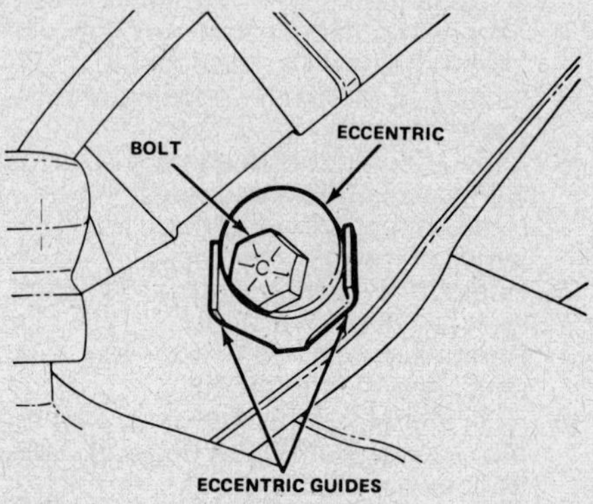

Fig. 2 Camber adjustment

AIR CONDITIONING

TABLE OF CONTENTS

System Testing

INDEX

GENERAL PRECAUTIONS

The Freon refrigerant used is also known as R-12 or F-12. It is colorless and odorless both as a gas and a liquid. Since it boils (vaporizes) at −21.7°F, it will usually be in a vapor state when being handled in a repair shop. But if a portion of the liquid coolant should come in contact with the hands or face, note that its temperature momentarily will be at least 22° below zero.

Protective goggles should be worn when opening any refrigerant lines. If liquid coolant does touch the eyes, bathe the eyes quickly in cold water, then apply a bland disinfectant oil to the eyes. See an eye doctor.

When checking a system for leaks with a torch type leak detector, do not breathe the vapors coming from the flame. Do not discharge refrigerant in the area of a live flame. A poisonous phosgene gas is produced when R-12 or F-12 is burned. While the small amount of this gas produced by a leak detector is not harmful unless inhaled directly at the flame, the quantity of refrigerant released into the air when a system is purged can be extremely dangerous if allowed to come in contact with an open flame. Thus, when purging a system, be sure that the discharge hose is routed to a well ventilated place where no flame is present. Under these conditions the refrigerant will be quickly dissipated into the surrounding air.

Never allow the temperature of refrigerant drums to exceed 125°F. The resultant increase in temperature will cause a corresponding increase in pressure which may cause the safety plug to release or the drum to burst.

If it is necessary to heat a drum of refrigerant when charging a system, the drum should be placed in water that is no hotter than 125°F. Never use a blow torch or other open flame. If possible, a pressure release mechanism should be attached before the drum is heated.

When connecting and disconnecting service gauges on A/C system, ensure that gauge hand valves are fully closed and that compressor service valves, if equipped, are in the back-seated (fully counterclockwise) position. Do not disconnect gauge hoses from service port adapters, if used, while gauges are connected to A/C system. To disconnect hoses, always remove adapter from service port. Do not disconnect hoses from gauge manifold while connected to A/C system, as refrigerant will be rapidly discharged.

After disconnecting gauge lines, check the valve areas to be sure service valves are correctly seated and Schraeder valves, if used, are not leaking.

EXERCISE SYSTEM

An important fact most owners ignore is that A/C units must be used periodically. Manufacturers caution that when the air conditioner is not used regularly, particularly during cold months, it should be turned on for a few minutes once every two or three weeks while the engine is running. This keeps the system in good operating condition.

Checking out the system for the effects of disuse before the onset of summer is one of the most important aspects of A/C servicing.

First clean out the condenser core, mounted in all cases at the front of the radiator. All obstructions, such as leaves, bugs and dirt, must be removed, as they will reduce heat transfer and impair the efficiency of the system. Make sure the space between the condenser and the radiator also is free of foreign matter.

Make certain the evaporator water drain is open. The evaporator cools and dehumidifies the air before it enters the passenger compartment: there, the refrigerant is changed from a liquid to a vapor. As the core cools the air, moisture condenses on it but is prevented from collecting in the evaporator by the water vane.

PERFORMANCE TEST

The system should be operated for at least 15 minutes to allow sufficient time for all parts to become completely stabilized. Determine if the system is fully charged by the use of test gauges and sight glass if one is installed on system. Head pressure will read from 180 psi to 220 psi or higher, depending upon ambient temperature and the type unit being tested. The sight glass should be free of bubbles if a glass is used in the system. Low side pressures should read approximately 15 psi to 30 psi, again depending on the ambient temperature and the unit being tested. It is not feasible to give a definite reading for all types of systems used, as the type control and component installation used on a particular system will directly influence the pressure readings on the high and low sides, **Fig. 1.**

The high side pressure will definitely be affected by the ambient or outside air temperature. A system that is operating normally will indicate a high side gauge reading between 150-170 psi with an 80°F ambient temperature. The same system will register 210-230 psi with an ambient temperature of 100°F. No two systems will register exactly the same, which requires that allowance for variations in head pressures must be considered. Following are the most important normal readings likely to be encountered during the season.

Ambient Temp.	High Side Pressure
80	150-170
90	175-195
95	185-205
100	210-230
105	230-250
110	250-270

RELATIVE TEMPERATURE OF HIGH AND LOW SIDES

The high side of the system should be

Evaporator Pressure Gauge Reading	Evaporator Temperature F°	High Pressure Gauge Reading	Ambient Temperature
0	-21°	45	20°
0.6	-20°	55	30°
2.4	-15°	72	40°
4.5	-10°	86	50°
6.8	- 5°	105	60°
9.2	0°	126	70°
11.8	5°	140	75°
14.7	10°	160	80°
17.1	15°	185	90°
21.1	20°	195	95°
22.5	22°	220	100°
23.9	24°	240	105°
25.4	26°	260	110°
26.9	28°	275	115°
28.5	30°	290	120°
37.0	40°	305	125°
46.7	50°	325	130°
57.7	60°		
70.1	70°		
84.1	80°		
99.6	90°		
116.9	100°		
136.0	110°		
157.1	120°		
179.0	130°		

Fig. 1 Pressure-temperature relationship (Typical). Conditions equivalent to 30 mph or 1750 engine RPM

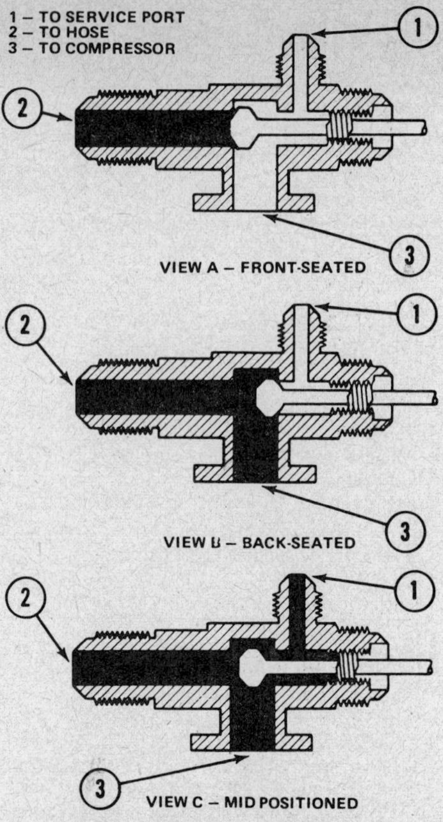

Fig. 2 Service valve positions (Typical)

uniformly hot to the touch throughout. A difference in temperature will indicate a partial blockage of liquid or gas at this point.

The low side of the system should be uniformly cool to the touch with no excessive sweating of the suction line or low side service valve. Excessive sweating or frosting of the low side service valve usually indicates an expansion valve is allowing an excessive amount of refrigerant into the evaporator.

EVAPORATOR OUTPUT

At this point, provided all other inspection tests have been performed, and components have been found to operate as they should, a rapid cooling down of the interior of the vehicle should result. The use of a thermometer is not necessary to determine evaporator output. Bringing all units to the correct operating specifications will insure that the evaporator performs as intended.

DISCHARGING & EVACUATING SYSTEM

On all 1982-87 models, it is not necessary to discharge refrigerant system for compressor removal. The compressor can be isolated from the system, eliminating need for recharging when performing compressor service or oil level check. Proceed as follows:

ISOLATING COMPRESSOR FROM SYSTEM

1. Connect pressure gauge and manifold set, then close both gauge hand valves and crack (mid-position) both service valves, **Fig. 2.**
2. Start engine and operate air conditioning.
3. Slowly turn suction service valve clockwise toward the front seated position, **Fig. 2.** When pressure reading drops to zero or less stop engine and finish front-seating suction service valve, then front-seat discharge service valve, **Fig. 2.**
4. Slowly loosen oil sump filler plug to relieve any internal pressures in the compressor. **A face shield should be worn when loosening the oil filler plug.**
5. Compressor is now isolated from system, service valve can be removed from compressor. Plug all openings to prevent entry of dirt and moisture.

PURGING COMPRESSOR OF AIR

The compressor must be purged of air whenever it has been isolated from the system for oil level check or compressor service.

1. Connect service valve and lines to compressor, then cap service gauge ports on both service valves.
2. Back seat suction valve to allow refrigerant to enter compressor.
3. Place discharge service valve in mid-position, then loosen discharge service valve gauge port cap to allow refrigerant to force air from compressor.
4. Back seat discharge service valve and tighten gauge port cap.
5. Remove manifold and gauge set.

DISCHARGING SYSTEM

1. Connect gauges into system, **Fig. 3,** and adjust controls for maximum cooling. This is necessary when the system has not been operating to return excess oil to the compressor.
2. Operate engine for 10 to 15 minutes to stabilize the system at 1500-1750 RPM.
3. Adjust engine speed to slow idle, then shut off engine and controls.
4. Open low side hand manifold valve slightly, using a container to catch oil and refrigerant. Do not discharge the refrigerant near an open flame as a toxic gas (phosgene) can result.
5. Open high side manifold valve slightly. **Open hand valve(s) only enough to bleed refrigerant from system. Too rapid purging will draw excessive oil from compressor and system.**
6. Close gauge manifold hand valves when refrigerant ceases to bleed from discharge hose and manifold gauges read zero.

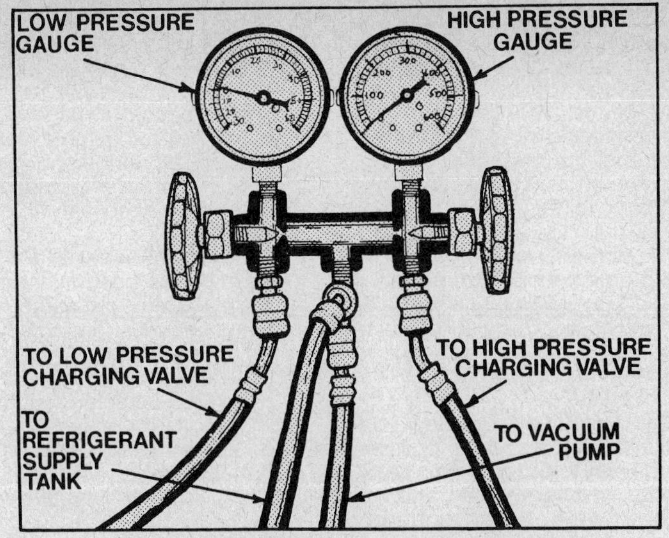

Fig. 3 Manifold gauge set hose connections (Typical)

EVACUATE SYSTEM USING VACUUM PUMP

Vacuum pumps suitable for removing air and moisture from A/C systems are commercially available. A specification for system pump-down used here is 28 to 29½ inches vacuum. This reading can be attained at or near sea level only. For each 1000 feet of altitude this operation is being performed, the reading will be 1 inch vacuum lower. As an example, at 5000 feet elevation, only 23-24½ inches of vacuum can be obtained. **The system must be completely discharged before it can be evacuated. Damage to vacuum pump may result if pressurized refrigerant is allowed to enter.**

1. With gauges connected into system, remove cap from vacuum hose connector. Install center hose from gauge manifold to vacuum pump connector. Mid-position high and low side compressor service valves (if used). Open high and low side gauge manifold hand valves.
2. Operate vacuum pump a minimum of 30 minutes for air and moisture removal. Watch compound gauge that system pumps down into a vacuum. System will reach 28-29½ inches vacuum in not over 5 minutes. If system does not pump down, check all connections and leak-test if necessary.
3. Close gauge manifold hand valves and shut off vacuum pump.
4. Check ability of system to hold vacuum. Watch compound gauge to see that gauge does not rise at a faster rate than 1 inch vacuum every 4 or 5 minutes. If compound gauge rises at too rapid a rate, install partial charge and leak-test. Then evacuate system as outlined above.
5. If system holds vacuum, charge system with refrigerant.

EVACUATE SYSTEM USING CHARGING STATION

A vacuum pump is built into the charging station and is constructed to withstand repeated and prolonged use without damage. Complete moisture removal from the system is possible only with a vacuum pump constructed for the purpose. **The system must be completely discharged before it can be evacuated. Damage to the vacuum pump may result if pressurized refrigerant is allowed to enter.**

1. Connect hose to vacuum pump if system was discharged through charging station.
2. Open high and low side gauge valves of charging station.
3. Connect station into 110-volt current.
4. Engage "Off-On" switch to vacuum pump according to directions of specific station being used.
5. System should pump down into a 28-29½ inch vacuum in not more than 5 minutes. If system fails to meet this specification, repair as necessary.
6. Operate pump a minimum of 30 minutes to remove all air and moisture.
7. Close high and low side gauge valves. Open switch to turn off pump.
8. Check ability of system to hold vacuum by watching compound gauge to see that it does not rise at a rate higher than 1 inch of vacuum every 4 or 5 minutes: If rise rate is not within specifications, repair system as necessary. If rise rate is within specifications, charge system with refrigerant.

CHARGING THE SYSTEM

CHARGING PROCEDURE

USING MULTI-REFRIGERANT CAN OPENER

1. Connect pressure gauge and manifold assembly J-23575 or equivalent. Keep both service valves in mid-position.
2. Close both gauge hand valves and disconnect service hose from vacuum pump.
3. Connect service hose to center of refrigerant can opener. Close valves on dispenser.
4. Attach refrigerant cans to opener. Refer to A/C Data Table for proper weight of refrigerant for vehicle being serviced.
5. Open one petcock valve and loosen center service hose at gauge to allow refrigerant to purge air from hose. Tighten hose and close petcock valve.
6. Open suction gauge hand valve and one petcock valve. Do not open high pressure gauge hand valve.
7. Start engine and set A/C system controls to maximum cooling position. Compressor will help pull refrigerant gas into suction side of system. **Refrigerant cans can be placed in pan of water no hotter than 125°F to aid charging process.**
8. When first can is empty, open next valve to continue charging until specified amount of refrigerant is in system. Frost line on can may be used as a guide when specifications call for using part of full can. If a scale is available, weigh cans before and during charging procedure to ensure accurate filling.
9. When system is fully charged, close suction gauge hand valve and all petcock valves.
10. Operate system for 5-10 minutes to allow it to stabilize and to determine if system cycles properly.
11. After checking operation of system, back-seat suction and discharge service valves to normal operating position by turning valves fully counterclockwise.
12. Loosen pressure gauge and manifold assembly service hoses to release refrigerant trapped in hoses. Remove pressure gauge and manifold assembly and install dust caps on fittings.

USING CHARGING STATION J-23500-01

1. After discharging and evacuating system, close low pressure valve on charging station. Fully open lefthand refrigerant control valve at base of cylinder and high pressure valve on charging station and allow required charge of refrigerant to enter high side of system. When full charge has entered system, close refrigerant control valve and high pressure valve on charging station. **If bubbles appear in the sight glass, tilt the charging station back momentarily. Do not permit level of liquid to drop below zero mark on cylinder sight glass.**
2. After charging is completed, close manifold gauges and check high and low pressures and system operation. **Read gauges with high and low pressure valves closed on charging station. Low pressure gauge can be damaged if both high and low pressure valves are opened.**
3. Close all valves on charging station and close refrigerant drum valve when all operations are finished.
4. After completing operational check, back-seat suction and discharge service valves to their normal operating position by turning them fully counterclockwise.

5. Disconnect high and low pressure charging hoses from compressor.
6. Open valve on top of cylinder to remove remaining refrigerant as charging cylinder is not designed to store refrigerant.
7. Replace quick seal caps on compressor service valves.

LEAK TEST SYSTEM

The propane torch Halide Leak Detector is the most widely used of the detection devices. Therefore, only the procedure for this device will be given. The procedure is the same for any electronic detector, except that the pickup device registers the presence of refrigerant by a flashing light or high pitched squeal instead of changing the color of the flame. All other steps in preparing the system and leak testing are the same and can be followed as outlined below:

1. Stabilize system at 1500-1750 RPM. If system is empty of refrigerant, it will be necessary to install a partial charge before continuing. With gauges connected into system, adjust A/C controls for maximum cooling. Operate for 10 to 15 minutes, then shut off car engine.
2. Light leak detector. Open valve to a low flame that will not blow itself out. Warm up until copper element turns cherry red. Lower flame until flame tip is even with or slightly below center of element. For electronic tester, follow preparation procedure as given in operating instructions.
3. Move leak detector pickup under hoses, joints, seals, and any possible place for a leak to occur. **Freon 12 refrigerant is heavier than air and will move downward. If concentration of refrigerant is located, move pickup upward to locate leak. Do not inhale fumes produced by burning refrigerant.**
4. Watch for color change of flame: Pale blue, no refrigerant; yellow, small amount of refrigerant; purplish-blue, large amount of refrigerant. Repair system as necessary if leaks are located.
5. Check sensitivity of reaction plate: Pass pickup hose over empty can or crack open refrigerant container; flame should show violent reaction. If no color change, replace reaction plate, following instructions accompanying leak detector. Too high a flame will result in short life to reaction plate and poor reaction and will soon burn out element.
6. Charge system if repairs were necessary.

System Servicing

INDEX

OIL CHARGE

DELCO AIR 4 CYLINDER RADIAL COMPRESSOR

OIL CHARGE-COMPONENT REPLACEMENT

If there are no signs of excessive leakage, add the following amount of oil depending on component to be replaced.

Evaporator	3 ounces
Condenser	1 ounce

If accumulator or compressor are to be replaced, drain oil from component to be replaced and measure, then add same amount of new oil to replacement component plus one additional ounce. **The radial 4 cylinder compressor does not have an oil sump.**

OIL CHARGE-LEAK CONDITION

On models with radial 4 cylinder compressor, it will only be necessary to remove and drain and measure oil from accumulator assembly in cases of excessive oil leakage. The radial 4 cylinder compressor does not have an oil sump, therefore it is not necessary to remove compressor in cases of oil leakage. If amount of oil recovered is 2 ounces or more, add same amount of new refrigerant oil to system. If amount of oil recovered is less than 2 ounces, add two ounces of new refrigerant oil to system. **If accumulator is replaced one additional ounce of oil must be added to replace amount captured by desiccant in old accumulator.**

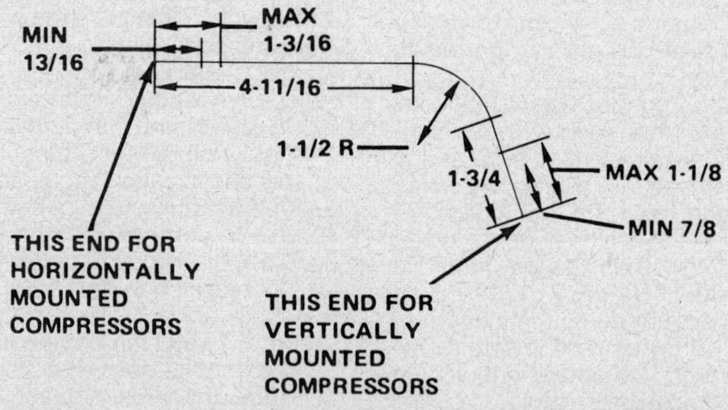

Fig. 1 York compressor oil level dipstick fabrication

OIL LEVEL CHECK

The oil level of these compressors should be checked whenever refrigerant has been lost due to leakage or through normal system servicing.

SANKYO 5 CYL. ROTARY COMPRESSOR

When installing a replacement compressor, proceed as follows:

1. Isolate compressor from system, then remove compressor.
2. Remove oil plug from compressor, then drain refrigerant oil into a calibrated container.
3. Drain refrigerant oil from compressor to be installed.
4. Add the same amount of refrigerant oil removed from compressor to be replaced plus 1 ounce to the compressor to be installed.
5. Install drain plug, then install and purge air from compressor.

YORK

1. Connect manifold gauge set, then operate system for approximately 10 minutes or until system pressures sta-

A/C Data Table

Year	Model	Refrigerant Capacity, Lbs.	Refrigeration Oil			Compressor Clutch Air Gap Inch
			Viscosity	Total System Capacity, Ounces	Compressor Oil Level Check, Inches	
AMERICAN MOTORS						
1982-83	All	2	500	7-8	①	.016-.031
1984-87	All	2	500	4-6	①	.016-.031

①—Note that "Oil Level Inches" cannot be checked. Refer to total capacity in ounces. See text for procedure.

bilize. This will allow oil in the system to return to compressor sump.

2. Isolate compressor as outlined earlier.
3. Slowly loosen compressor oil filler plug to relieve any internal pressures in compressor. **A face shield should be worn when loosening or removing oil filler plug.**
4. Insert clean dipstick into filler plug hole until it bottoms in sump, **Fig. 1. Ensure keyway in shaft faces head of compressor before checking oil level.**
5. Remove dipstick and measure oil level. Refer to "A/C Data Table" and add refrigerant oil as necessary. Install filler plug and O-ring.
6. Purge air from compressor.

CHARGING VALVE LOCATION

On models with 6 cylinder engine, the high and low pressure service ports are located on the compressor; on models with 4 cylinder engine, the high and low pressure service ports are located on service valve adapter.

ENGINE COOLING FANS
Variable Speed Fans

INDEX

Page No.

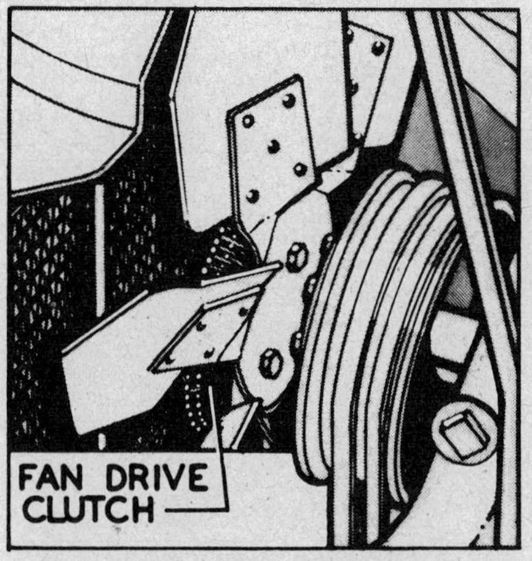

Fig. 1 Typical variable-speed fan installed

DESCRIPTION

The fan drive clutch, **Fig. 1,** is a fluid coupling containing silicone oil. Fan speed is regulated by the torque-carrying capacity of the silicone oil. The more silicone oil in the coupling the greater the fan speed, and the less silicone oil the slower the fan speed.

Two types of fan drive clutches are in use. On one, **Fig. 2,** a bi-metallic strip and control piston on the front of the fluid coupling regulates the amount of silicone oil entering the coupling. The bi-metallic strip bows outward with an increase in surrounding temperature and allows a piston to move outward. The piston opens a valve regulating the flow of silicone oil into the coupling from a reserve chamber. The silicone oil is returned to the reserve chamber through a bleed hole when the valve is closed.

On the other type of fan drive clutch, **Fig. 3,** a heat-sensitive, bi-metal spring connected to an opening plate brings about a similar result. Both units cause the fan speed to increase with a rise in temperature and to decrease as the temperature goes down.

In some cases a flex-fan is used instead of a fan drive clutch. Flexible blades vary the volume of air being drawn through the

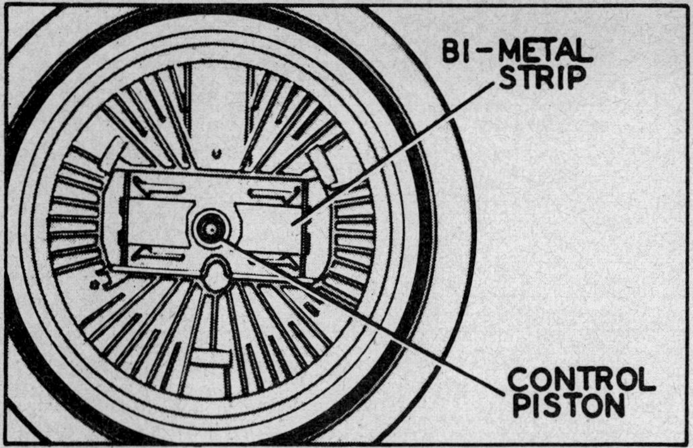

Fig. 2 Variable-speed fan with flat bi-metal thermostatic spring

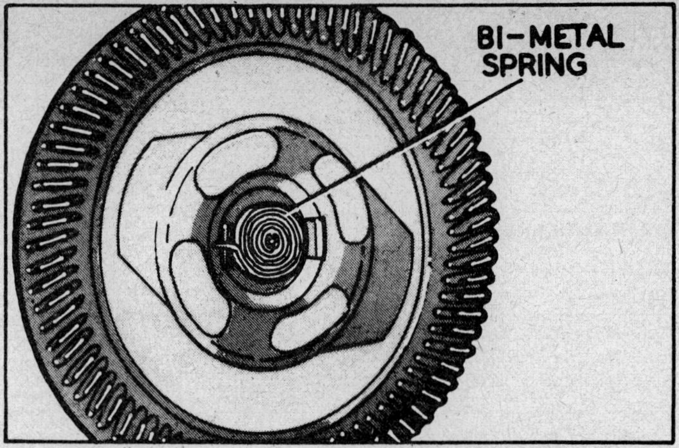

Fig. 3 Variable-speed fan with coiled bi-metal thermostatic spring

radiator, automatically increasing the pitch at low engine speeds.

FAN DRIVE CLUTCH TEST

Do not operate the engine until the fan has been first checked for possible cracks and separations.

Run the engine at a fast idle speed (1000 RPM) until normal operating temperature is reached. This process can be speeded up by blocking off the front of the radiator with cardboard. Regardless of temperatures, the unit must be operated for at least five minutes immediately before being tested.

Stop the engine and, using a glove or a cloth to protect the hand, immediately check the effort required to turn the fan. If considerable effort is required, it can be assumed that the coupling is operating satisfactorily. If very little effort is required to turn the fan, it is an indication that the coupling is not operating properly and should be replaced.

If the clutch fan is the coiled bi-metal spring type, it may be tested while the vehicle is being driven. To check, disconnect the bi-metal spring, **Fig. 4**, and rotate 90° counterclockwise. This disables the temperature-controlled free-wheeling feature and the clutch performs like a conventional fan. If this cures the overheating condition, replace the clutch fan.

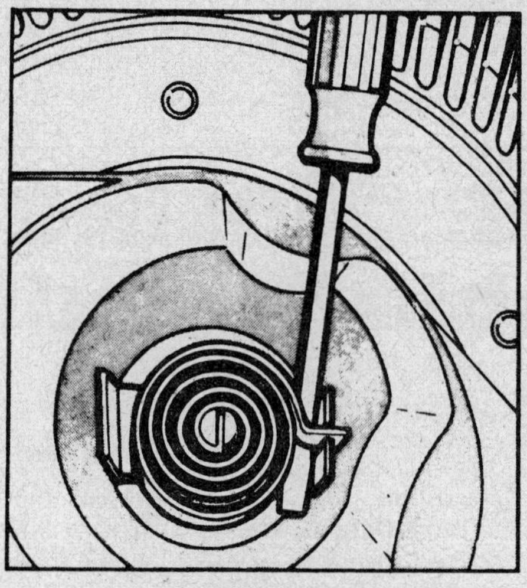

Fig. 4 Disconnecting bi-metal spring

SERVICE PROCEDURE

To prevent silicone fluid from draining into fan drive bearing, do not store or place drive unit on bench with rear of shaft pointing downward.

The removal procedure for either type of fan clutch assembly is generally the same for all cars. Merely unfasten the unit from the water pump and remove the assembly from the car.

The type of unit shown in **Fig. 2** may be partially disassembled for inspection and cleaning. Take off the capscrews that hold the assembly together and separate the fan from the drive clutch. Next remove the metal strip on the front by pushing one end of it toward the fan clutch body so it clears the retaining bracket. Then push the strip to the side so that its opposite end will spring out of place. Now remove the small control piston underneath it.

Check the piston for free movement of the coupling device. If the piston sticks, clean it with emery cloth. If the bi-metal strip is damaged, replace the entire unit. These strips are not interchangeable.

When reassembling, install the control piston so that the projection on the end of it will contact the metal strip. Then install the metal strip. After reassembly, clean the clutch drive with a cloth soaked in solvent. Avoid dipping the clutch assembly in any type of liquid. Install the assembly in the reverse order of removal.

The coil spring type of fan clutch cannot be disassembled, serviced or repaired. If it does not function properly it must be replaced with a new unit.

DASH GAUGES

INDEX

TESTING

Gauge failures are often caused by defective wiring or grounds. The first step in locating trouble should be a thorough inspection of all wiring, terminals and printed circuits. If wiring is secured by clamps, check to see whether the insulation has been severed thereby grounding the wire. In the case of a fuel gauge installation, rust may cause failure by corrosion at the ground connection of the tank unit.

CONSTANT VOLTAGE REGULATOR TYPE (CVR)

The Constant Voltage Regulator (CVR) type indicator is a bi-metal resistance type system consisting of an Instrument Voltage Regulator (IVR), an indicator gauge, and a variable resistance sending unit. Current to the system is applied to the gauge terminals by the IVR, which maintains an average-pulsating value of 5 volts.

The indicator gauge consists of a pointer which is attached to a wire-wound bimetal strip. Current passing through the coil heats the bi-metal strip, causing the pointer to move. As more current passes through the coil, heat increases, moving the pointer farther.

The circuit is completed through a sending unit which contains a variable resistor. When resistance is high, less current is allowed to pass through the gauge, and the pointer moves very little. As resistance decreases due to changing conditions in system being monitored, more current passes through gauge coil, causing pointer to move farther.

OPERATIONAL TEST

1. Disconnect wiring harness connector at sending unit. Connect a test lamp or voltmeter between terminal in wiring harness connector and ground.
2. With ignition switch in ON position, light should pulse or meter reading should fluctuate.
3. If lamp lights but does not pulse, or if meter reading remains steady, check ground to IVR. If ground is satisfactory, IVR is defective.
4. If lamp fails to light, or if meter reads 0 volts, check for open circuit across IVR terminals, indicator gauge terminals, or open circuit in wiring harness and printed circuit between components.
5. Connect test lamp or voltmeter ground lead to ground terminal in sending unit wiring harness connector. Light should pulse or meter reading should fluctuate as in step 2. If not, locate open in ground circuit. **Do not apply battery voltage to system or ground output terminals of IVR, as damage to system components or wiring circuits may result.**

SENDING UNIT TEST

FUEL TANK GAUGE

1. Disconnect wiring harness connector at sending unit and connect ohmmeter between ground terminal and resistor terminal on sending unit.
2. Meter should read 11-61 ohms on Pacer or 31-248 ohms on others. If reading shows no continuity (infinite reading), check ground connection to tank gauge.
3. If ground is satisfactory, but reading is not within specification, tank unit is defective.
4. If reading is within specification, remove fuel tank gauge from vehicle and connect ohmmeter between resistor terminal and ground terminal (metal housing on single terminal units).
5. Observe meter while slowly moving float rod between empty and full stops. Meter should read 61 ohms on Pacer or 248 ohms on others at empty stop and 11 ohms on Pacer or 31 ohms on others at full stop. Change in readings should be smooth, without hesitation or jumping.
6. If tank unit fails to operate as outlined, unit is defective. **Before installing fuel tank gauge, connect wiring harness connector to gauge and move float rod from empty to full position with ignition key in ON position. If dash gauge reading is incorrect, check IVR and dash gauge. If system tests prove satisfactory, but system still does not operate correctly, check that tank gauge rod is not bent or binding and that float is not damaged, loose or filled with fuel.**

OIL & TEMPERATURE SENDING UNITS

1. Test dash gauge and IVR as outlined above.
2. If system is satisfactory, start engine and allow it to reach operating temperature.
3. If no reading is indicated on the gauge, check the sending unit-to-gauge wire by removing the wire from the sending unit and momentarily ground this wire to a clean, unpainted portion of the engine.
4. If the gauge still does not indicate, the wire is defective. Repair or replace the wire.
5. If grounding the new or repaired wire causes the dash gauge to indicate, the sending unit is faulty.

VARIABLE VOLTAGE TYPE

The variable voltage type dash gauge consists of two magnetic coils to which battery voltage is applied. The coils act on the gauge pointer and pull in opposite directions. One coil is grounded directly to the chassis, while the other coil is grounded through a variable resistor within the sending unit. Resistance through the sending unit determines current flow through its coil, and therefore pointer position.

When resistance is high in the sending unit, less current is allowed to flow through its coil, causing the gauge pointer to move toward the directly grounded coil. When resistance in the sending unit decreases, more current is allowed to pass through its coil, increasing the magnetic field. The gauge pointer is then attracted toward the coil which is grounded through the sending unit.

A special tester is required to diagnose this type gauge. Follow instructions included with the tester.

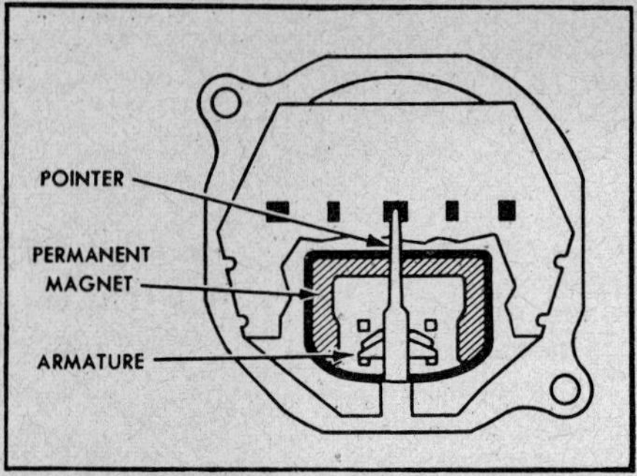

Fig. 1 Conventional type ammeter (typical)

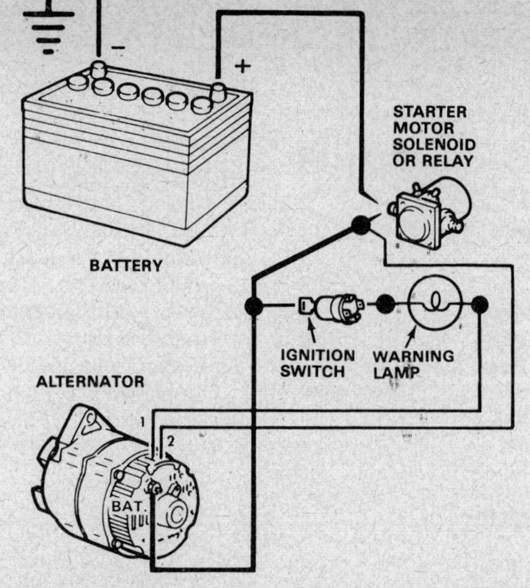

Fig. 2 Charge indicator lamp wiring. Delco SI type charging system

AMMETERS

The ammeter is an instrument used to indicate current flow into and out of the battery. When electrical accessories in the vehicle draw more current than the alternator can supply, current flows from the battery and the ammeter indicates a discharge (−) condition. When electrical loads of the vehicle are less than alternator output, current is available to charge the battery, and the ammeter indicates a charge (+) condition. If battery is fully charged, the voltage regulator reduces alternator output to meet only immediate vehicle electrical loads. When this happens, ammeter reads zero.

CONVENTIONAL AMMETER

A conventional ammeter must be connected between the battery and alternator in order to indicate current flow. This type ammeter, **Fig. 1**, consists of a frame to which a permanent magnet is attached. The frame also supports an armature and pointer assembly. Current in this system flows from the alternator through the ammeter, then to the battery or from the battery through the ammeter into the vehicle electrical system, depending on vehicle operating conditions.

When no current flows through the ammeter, the magnet holds the pointer armature so that the pointer stands at the center of the dial. When current passes in either direction through the ammeter, the resulting magnetic field attracts the armature away from the effect of the permanent magnet, thus giving a reading proportional to the strength of the current flowing.

TROUBLESHOOTING

When the ammeter apparently fails to register correctly, there may be trouble in the wiring which connects the ammeter to the alternator and battery or in the alternator or battery itself.

To check the connections, first tighten the two terminal posts on the back of the ammeter. Then, following each wire from the ammeter, tighten all connections on the ignition switch, battery and alternator. Chafed, burned or broken insulation can be found by following each ammeter wire from end to end.

All wires with chafed, burned or broken insulation should be repaired or replaced. After this is done, and all connections are tightened, connect the battery cable and turn on the ignition switch. The needle should point slightly to the discharge (−) side.

Start the engine and speed it up a little above idling speed. The needle should then move to the charge side (+), and its movement should be smooth.

If the pointer does not behave correctly, the ammeter itself is out of order and a new one should be installed.

SHUNT TYPE AMMETER

The shunt type ammeter is actually a specially calibrated voltmeter. It is connected to read voltage drop across a resistance wire (shunt) between the battery and alternator. The shunt is located either in the vehicle wiring or within the ammeter itself.

When voltage is higher at the alternator end of the shunt, the meter indicates a charge (+) condition. When voltage is higher at the battery end of the shunt, the meter indicates a discharge (−) condition. When voltage is equal at both ends of the shunt, the meter reads zero.

TROUBLESHOOTING

Ammeter accuracy can be determined by comparing reading with an ammeter of known accuracy.

1. With engine stopped and ignition switch in RUN position, switch on headlamps and heater fan. Meter should indicate a discharge (−) condition.
2. If ammeter pointer does not move, check ammeter terminals for proper connection and check for open circuit in wiring harness. If connections and wiring harness are satisfactory, ammeter is defective.
3. If ammeter indicates a charge (+) condition, wiring harness connections are reversed at ammeter.

ALTERNATOR INDICATOR LIGHT

DELCOTRON SI INTEGRAL CHARGING SYSTEM

This system features an integral solid state regulator mounted inside the alternator slip ring end frame. The alternator indicator lamp is installed in the field wire circuit connected between the ignition "Ign." terminal and alternator No. 1 terminal, **Fig. 2.** The resistance provided by the alternator warning light circuit is needed to protect the diode trio. The alternator indicator lamp should light when the ignition switch is turned on before engine is started. If lamp does not light, either lamp is burned out or indicator lamp wiring has an open circuit. After engine is started, the indicator lamp should be out at all times. If indicator lamp comes on, alternator belt may be loose, alternator or regulator may be defective, charging circuit may be defective or fuse may be blown.

TROUBLESHOOTING

1. Switch Off, Lamp On:
   a. Disconnect electrical connector from alternator terminals 1 and 2.
   b. If indicator light remains lit, repair short circuit between leads.
   c. If indicator light goes out, replace alternator rectifier bridge.
2. Switch On, lamp Off, engine not running:
   a. Perform tests described in step 1.
   b. If problem still exists, there may be an open circuit.
   c. To locate open circuit, check for blown fuse or fusible link, burned out bulb, defective bulb socket or an open in No. 1 lead circuit between alternator and ignition switch.
   d. If no faults are found, check charg-

ing system for proper operation.

3. Switch On, lamp On, engine running:
   a. On models so equipped, check condition of fuse between indicator light and ignition switch and fuse in A/C circuit.
   b. Check charging system for proper operation.

VOLTMETER

The voltmeter is a gauge which measures the electrical flow from the battery to indicate whether the battery output is within tolerances. The voltmeter reading can range from 13.5-14.0 volts under normal operating conditions. If an undercharge or overcharge condition is indicated for an extended period, the battery and charging system should be checked.

TROUBLESHOOTING

To check voltmeter, turn key and headlights on with engine off. Pointer should move to 12.5 volts. If no needle movement is observed, check connections from battery to circuit breaker. If connections are tight and meter shows no movement, check wire continuity. If wire continuity is satisfactory, the meter is inoperative and must be replaced.

ELECTRICAL TEMPERATURE GAUGES

This temperature indicating system consists of a sending unit, located on the cylinder head, electrical temperature gauge and an instrument voltage regulator. As engine temperature increases or decreases, the resistance of the sending unit changes, in turn controlling current flow to the gauge. When engine temperature is low, the resistance of the sending unit is high, restricting current flow to the gauge, in turn indicating low engine temperature. As engine temperature increases, the resistance of the sending unit decreases, permitting an increased current flow to the gauge, resulting in an increased temperature reading.

TROUBLESHOOTING

Troubleshooting for the electrical temperature indicating system is the same as for the electrical oil pressure indicating system.

ELECTRICAL OIL PRESSURE GAUGES

This oil pressure indicating system incorporates an instrument voltage regulator, electrical oil pressure gauge and a sending unit which are connected in series. The sending unit consists of a diaphragm, contact and a variable resistor. As oil pressure increases or decreases, the diaphragm actuated the contact on the variable resistor, in turn controlling current flow to the gauge. When oil pressure is low, the resistance of the variable resistor is high, restricting current flow to the gauge, in turn indicating low oil pressure. As oil pressure increases, the resistance of the variable resistor is lowered, permitting an increased current flow to the gauge, resulting in an increased gauge reading.

TROUBLESHOOTING

Disconnect the oil pressure gauge lead from the sending unit, connect a 12 volt test lamp between the gauge lead and the ground and turn ignition ON. If test lamp flashes, the instrument voltage regulator is functioning properly and the gauge circuit is not broken. If the test lamp remains lit, the instrument voltage regulator is defective and must be replaced. If the test lamp does not light, check the instrument voltage regulator for proper ground or an open circuit. Also, check for an open in the instrument voltage regulator to oil pressure gauge wire or in the gauge itself. **If test lamp flashes and gauge is not accurate, the gauge may be out of calibration, requiring replacement.**

OIL PRESSURE INDICATOR LIGHT

Many cars utilize a warning light on the instrument panel in place of the conventional dash indicating gauge to warn the driver when the oil pressure is dangerously low. The warning light is wired in series with the ignition switch and the engine unit—which is an oil pressure switch.

The oil pressure switch contains a diaphragm and a set of contacts. When the ignition switch is turned on, the warning light circuit is energized and the circuit is completed through the closed contacts in the pressure switch. When the engine is started, build-up of oil pressure compresses the diaphragm, opening the contacts, thereby breaking the circuit and putting out the light.

TROUBLESHOOTING

The oil pressure warning light should go on when the ignition is turned on. If it does not light, disconnect the wire from the engine unit and ground the wire to the frame or cylinder block. Then if the warning light still does not go on with the ignition switch on, replace the bulb.

If the warning light goes on when the wire is grounded to the frame or cylinder block, the engine unit should be checked for being loose or poorly grounded. If the unit is found to be tight and properly grounded, it should be removed and a new one installed. (The presence of sealing compound on the threads of the engine unit will cause a poor ground).

If the warning light remains lit when it normally should be out, replace the engine unit before proceeding further to determine the cause for a low pressure indication.

The warning light sometimes will light up or will flicker when the engine is idling, even though the oil pressure is adequate. However the light should go out when the engine speed is increased.

TEMPERATURE INDICATOR LIGHT

The temperature indicator light illuminates whenever engine coolant temperature exceeds a predetermined value. The sending unit is an On-Off switch, and is normally in the "Off" position. Whenever coolant temperature is above the predetermined value of the switch, the switch closes and provides a ground circuit for the indicator light.

TROUBLESHOOTING

If the red light is not lit when the engine is being cranked, check for a burned out bulb, an open in the light circuit, or a defective ignition switch.

If the red light is lit when the engine is running, check the wiring between light and switch for a ground, temperature switch defective, or overheated cooling system. **As a test circuit to check whether the red bulb is functioning properly, a wire which is connected to the ground terminal of the ignition switch is tapped into its circuit. When the ignition is in the "Start" (engine cranking) position, the ground terminal is grounded inside the switch and the red bulb will be lit. When the engine is started and the ignition switch is in the "On" position, the test circuit is opened and the bulb is then controlled by the temperature switch.**

SPEEDOMETERS

The following material covers only that service on speedometers which can be performed by the average service man. Repairs on the units themselves are not included as they require special tools and extreme care when making repairs and adjustments and only an experienced speedometer mechanic should attempt such servicing.

The speedometer has two main parts—the indicator head and the speedometer drive cable. When the speedometer fails to indicate speed or mileage, the cable or housing is probably broken.

SPEEDOMETER CABLE

Most cables are broken due to lack of lubrication or a sharp bend or kink in the housing.

A cable might break because the speedometer head mechanism binds. If such is the case, the speedometer head should be repaired or replaced before a new cable or housing is installed.

A "jumpy" pointer condition, together with a sort of scraping noise, is due, in most instances, to a dry or kinked speedometer cable. The kinked cable rubs on the housing and winds up, slowing down the pointer. The cable then unwinds and the pointer "jumps."

To check for kinks, remove the cable, lay it on a flat surface and twist one end with the fingers. If it turns over smoothly the cable is not kinked. But if part of the cable flops over as it is twisted, the cable is kinked and should be replaced.

LUBRICATION

The speedometer cable should be lubricated with special cable lubricant every 10,000 miles.

Fill the ferrule on the upper end of the

housing with the cable lubricant. Insert the cable in the housing, starting at the upper end. Turn the cable around carefully while feeding it into the housing. Repeat filling the ferrule except for the last six inches of cable. Too much lubricant at this point may cause the lubricant to work into the indicating hand.

INSTALLING CABLE

During installation, if the cable sticks when inserted in the housing and will not go through, the housing is damaged inside or kinked. Be sure to check the housing from one end to the other. Straighten any sharp bends by relocating clamps or elbows. Replace housing if it is badly kinked or broken. Position the cable and housing so that they lead into the head as straight as possible.

Check the new cable for kinks before installing it. Use wide, sweeping, gradual curves when the cable comes out of the transmission and connects to the head so the cable will not be damaged during its installation.

If inspection indicates that the cable and housing are in good condition, yet pointer action is erratic, check the speedometer head for possible binding.

The speedometer drive pinion should also be checked. If the pinion is dry or its teeth are stripped, the speedometer may not register properly.

The transmission mainshaft nut must be tight or the speedometer drive gear may slip on the mainshaft and cause slow speed readings.

ELECTRIC CLOCKS

Regulation of electric clocks used on automobiles is accomplished automatically by merely resetting the time. If the clock is running fast, the action of turning the hands back to correct the time will automatically cause the clock to run slightly slower. If the clock is running slow, the action of turning the hands forward to correct the time will automatically cause the clock to run slightly faster (10 to 15 seconds day).

A lock-out feature prevents the clock regulator mechanism from being reset more than once per wind cycle, regardless of the number of times the time is reset. After the clock rewinds, if the time is then reset, automatic regulation will take place. If a clock varies over 10 minutes per day, it will never adjust sufficiently, and must be repaired or replaced.

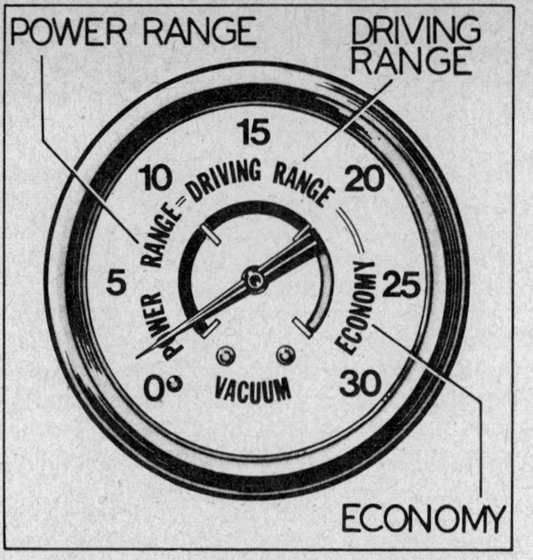

Fig. 3 Typical vacuum gauge

WINDING CLOCK WHEN CONNECTING BATTERY OR CLOCK WIRING

The clock requires special attention when reconnecting a battery that has been disconnected for any reason, a clock that has been disconnected, or when replacing a blown clock fuse. It is very important that the initial wind be fully made. The procedure is as follows:

1. Make sure that all other instruments and lights are turned off.
2. Connect positive cable to battery.
3. Before connecting the negative cable, press the terminal to its post on the battery. Immediately afterward strike the terminal against the battery post to see if there is a spark. If there is a spark, allow the clock to run down until it stops ticking, and repeat as above until there is no spark. Then immediately make the permanent connection before the clock can again run down. The clock will run down in approximately two minutes.
4. Reset clock after all connections have been made. This procedure should also be followed when reconnecting the clock after it has been disconnected, or if it has stopped because of a blown fuse. Be sure to disconnect battery before installing a new fuse.

TROUBLESHOOTING

If clock does not run, check for blown "clock" fuse. If fuse is blown check for short in wiring. If fuse is not blown check for open circuit.

With an electric clock, the most frequent cause of clock fuse blowing is voltage at the clock which will prevent a complete wind and allow clock contacts to remain closed. This may be caused by any of the following: discharged battery, corrosion on contact surface of battery terminals, loose connections at battery terminals, at junction block, at fuse clips, or at terminal connection of clock. Therefore, if in reconnecting battery or clock it is noted that the clock is not ticking, always check for blown fuse, or examine the circuits at the points indicated above to determine and correct the cause.

VACUUM GAUGE

This gauge, **Fig. 3** measures intake manifold vacuum. The intake manifold vacuum varies with engine operating conditions, carburetor adjustments, valve timing, ignition timing and general engine condition.

Since the optimum fuel economy is directly proportional to a properly functioning engine, a high vacuum reading on the gauge relates to fuel economy. For this reason some manufacturers call the vacuum gauge a "Fuel Economy Indicator." Most gauges have colored sectors the green sector being the "Economy" range and red the "Power" range. Therefore, the vehicle should be operated with gauge registering in the green sector or a high numerical number, **Fig. 3**, for maximum economy.

TROUBLESHOOTING

The vacuum gauge is a nonadjustable mechanical gauge. Accuracy may be tested by connecting a test vacuum gauge of known accuracy with the existing gauge using a T-fitting. Compare the vacuum readings of the gauges and replace defective gauge as required.

STARTER MOTORS & SWITCHES

TABLE OF CONTENTS

General Information

INDEX

STARTER TROUBLE CHECKS

When trouble develops in the starting motor circuit, and the starter cranks the engine slowly or not at all, several preliminary checks can be made to determine whether the trouble lies in the battery, in the starter, in the wiring between them, or elsewhere. Many conditions besides defects in the starter itself can result in poor cranking performance.

To make a quick check of the starter system, turn on the headlights. They should burn with normal brilliance. If they do not, the battery may be run down.

If the battery is in a charged condition so that lights burn brightly, operate the starting motor. Any one of three things will happen to the lights: (1) They will go out, (2) dim considerably or (3) stay bright without any cranking action taking place.

IF LIGHTS GO OUT

If the lights go out as the starter switch is closed, it indicates that there is a poor connection between the battery and starting motor. This poor connection will most often be found at the battery terminals. Correction is made by removing the cable clamps from the terminals, cleaning the terminals and clamps, replacing the clamps and tightening them securely. A coating of corrosion inhibitor (petroleum jelly will do) may be applied to the clamps and terminals to retard the formation of corrosion.

IF LIGHTS DIM

If the lights dim considerably as the starter switch is closed and the starter operates slowly or not at all, the battery may be run down, or there may be some mechanical condition in the engine or starting motor that is throwing a heavy burden on the starting motor. This imposes a high discharge rate on the battery which causes noticeable dimming of the lights.

Check the battery state of charge. If it is charged, the trouble probably lies in either the engine or starting motor itself. In the engine, tight bearings or pistons or heavy oil place an added burden on the starting motor. Low temperatures also hamper starting motor performance since it thickens engine oil and makes the engine considerably harder to crank and start. Also, a battery is less efficient at low temperatures.

In the starting motor, a bent armature, loose pole shoe screws or worn bearings, any of which may allow the armature to drag, will reduce cranking performance and increase current draw.

In addition, more serious internal damage is sometimes found. Thrown armature windings or commutator bars, which sometimes occur on over-running clutch drive starting motors, are usually caused by excessive overrunning after starting. This is the result of such conditions as the driver keeping the starting switch closed too long after the engine has started, the driver opening the throttle too wide in starting, or improper carburetor fast idle adjustment. Any of these subject the overrunning clutch to extra strain so it tends to seize, spinning the armature at high speed with resulting armature damage.

Another cause may be engine backfire during cranking which may result, among other things, from ignition timing being too far advanced.

To avoid such failures, the driver should pause a few seconds after a false start to make sure the engine has come completely to rest before another start is attempted. In addition, the ignition timing should be checked if engine backfiring has caused the trouble.

LIGHTS STAY BRIGHT, NO CRANKING ACTION

This condition indicates an open circuit at some point, either in the starter itself, the starter switch or control circuit. The solenoid control circuit can be eliminated momentarily by placing a heavy jumper lead across the solenoid main terminals to see if the starter will operate. This connects the starter directly to the battery and, if it operates, it indicates that the control circuit is not functioning normally. The wiring and control units must be checked to locate the trouble.

If the starter does not operate with the jumper attached, it will probably have to be removed from the engine so it can be examined in detail.

CHECKING CIRCUIT WITH VOLTMETER

Excessive resistance in the circuit between the battery and starter will reduce cranking performance. The resistance can be checked by using a voltmeter to measure voltage drop in the circuits while the starter is operated. There are three checks to be made:

1. Voltage drop between car frame and grounded battery terminal post (not cable clamp).
2. Voltage drop between car frame and starting motor field frame.
3. Voltage drop between insulated battery terminal post and starting motor terminal stud (or the battery terminal stud of the solenoid).

Each of these should show no more than one-tenth (0.1) volt drop when the starting motor is cranking the engine. Do not use the starter for more than 30 seconds at a time to avoid overheating it.

If excessive voltage drop is found in any of these circuits, make correction by disconnecting the cables, cleaning the connections carefully, and then reconnecting the cables firmly in place. A coating of petroleum jelly on the battery cables and terminal clamps will retard corrosion. **On some cars, extra long battery cables may be required due to the location of the battery and starter. This may result in somewhat higher voltage drop than the above recommended 0.1 volt. The only means of determining the normal voltage drop in such cases is to check several of these vehicles. Then when the voltage drop is well above the normal figure for all cars checked, abnormal resistance will be indicated and correction can be made as already explained.**

SOLENOID SWITCHES

The solenoid switch on a cranking motor not only closes the circuit between the battery and the cranking motor but also shifts the drive pinion into mesh with the engine flywheel ring gear. This is done by means of a linkage between the solenoid switch plunger and the shift lever on the cranking motor.

There are two windings in the solenoid; a pull-in winding and a hold-in winding. Both windings are energized when the external control switch is closed. They produce a magnetic field which pulls the plunger in so that the drive pinion is shifted into mesh, and the main contacts in the solenoid switch are closed to connect the battery directly to the cranking motor. Closing the main switch contacts shorts out the pull-in winding since this winding is connected across the main contacts. The magnetism produced by the hold-in winding is sufficient to hold the plunger in, and shorting out the pull-in winding reduces drain on the battery. When the control switch is opened, it disconnects the hold-in winding from the battery. When the hold-in winding is disconnected from the battery, the shift lever spring withdraws the plunger from the solenoid, opening the solenoid switch contacts and at the same time withdrawing the drive pinion from mesh. Proper operation of the switch depends on maintaining a definite balance between the magnetic strength of the pull-in and hold-in windings.

This balance is established in the design by the size of the wire and the number of turns specified. An open circuit in the hold-in winding or attempts to crank with a discharged battery will cause the switch to chatter.

To disassemble the solenoid, remove nuts, washers and insulators from the switch terminal and battery terminal. Remove cover and take out the contact disk assembly.

STARTING MOTOR SERVICE

To obtain full performance data on a starting motor or to determine the cause of abnormal operation, the starting motor should be submitted to a no-load and torque test. These tests are best performed on a starter bench tester with the starter mounted on it.

From a practical standpoint, however, a simple torque test may be made quickly with the starter in the car. Make sure the battery is fully charged and that the starter circuit wires and terminals are in good condition. Then operate the starter to see if the engine turns over normally. If it does not, the torque developed is below standard and the starter should be removed for further checking.

STARTER DRIVE TROUBLES

Starter drive troubles are easy to diagnose and they usually cannot be confused with ordinary starter difficulties. If the starter does not turn over at all or if it drags, look for trouble in the starter or electrical supply system. Concentrate on the starter drive or ring gear if the starter is noisy, if it turns but does not engage the engine, or if the starter won't disengage after the engine is started. After the starter is removed, the trouble can usually be located quickly.

Worn or chipped ring gear or starter pinion are the usual causes of noisy operation. Before replacing either or both of these parts try to find out what caused the damage. With the Bendix type drive, incomplete engagement of the pinion with the ring gear is a common cause of tooth damage. The wrong pinion clearance on starter drives of the over-running clutch type leads to poor meshing of the pinion and ring gear and too rapid tooth wear.

A less common cause of noise with either type of drive is a bent starter armature shaft. When this shaft is bent, the pinion gear alternately binds and then only partly meshes with the ring gear. Most manufacturers specify a maximum of .003 inch radial run-out on the armature shaft.

WHEN CLUTCH DRIVE FAILS

The over-running clutch type drive seldom becomes so worn that it fails to engage since it is directly activated by a fork and lever. The only thing that is likely to happen is that, once engaged, it will not turn the engine because the clutch itself is worn out. A much more frequent difficulty and one that rapidly wears ring gear and teeth is partial engagement. Proper meshing of the pinion is controlled by the end clearance between the pinion gear and the starter housing or pinion stop, if used.

On some starters, the solenoids are completely enclosed in the starter housing and the pinion clearance is not adjustable. If the clearance is not correct, the starter must be disassembled and checked for excessive wear of solenoid linkage, shift lever mechanism, or improper assembly of parts.

Failure of the over-running clutch drive to disengage is usually caused by binding between the armature shaft and the drive. If the drive, particularly the clutch, shows signs of overheating it indicates that it is not disengaging immediately after the engine starts. If the clutch is forced to over-run too long, it overheats and turns a bluish color. For the cause of the binding, look for rust or gum between the armature shaft and the drive, or for burred splines. Excess oil on the drive will lead to gumming, and inadequate air circulation in the flywheel housing will cause rust.

Over-running clutch drives cannot be overhauled in the field so they must be replaced. In cleaning, never soak them in a solvent because the solvent may enter the clutch and dissolve the sealed-in lubricant. Wipe them off lightly with kerosene and lubricate them sparingly with SAE 10 or 10W oil.

WHEN BENDIX DRIVE FAILS

When a Bendix type drive doesn't engage the cause usually is one of three things: either the drive spring is broken, one of the drive spring bolts has sheared off, or the screwshaft threads won't allow the pinion to travel toward the flywheel. In the first two cases, remove the drive by unscrewing the setscrew under the last coil of the drive spring and replace the broken parts. Gummed or rusty screwshaft threads are fairly common causes of Bendix drive failure and are easily cleaned with a little kerosene or steel wool, depending on the trouble. Here again, as in the case of over-running clutch drives, use light oil sparingly, and be sure the flywheel housing has adequate ventilation. There is usually a breather hole in the bottom of the flywheel housing which should be open.

The failure of a Bendix drive to disengage or to mesh properly is most often caused by gummed or rusty screwshaft threads. When this is not true, look for mechanical failure within the drive itself.

Delco-Remy Starters

NOTE: For service procedures and specifications on this starter, refer to "Starter Motors & Switches" chapter in the General Motors section.

Ford Motorcraft Starters

NOTE: For specifications, description and diagnosis procedures on these starters, refer to "Starter Motors & Switches" chapter in the Ford section. For testing, refer to this section.

INDEX

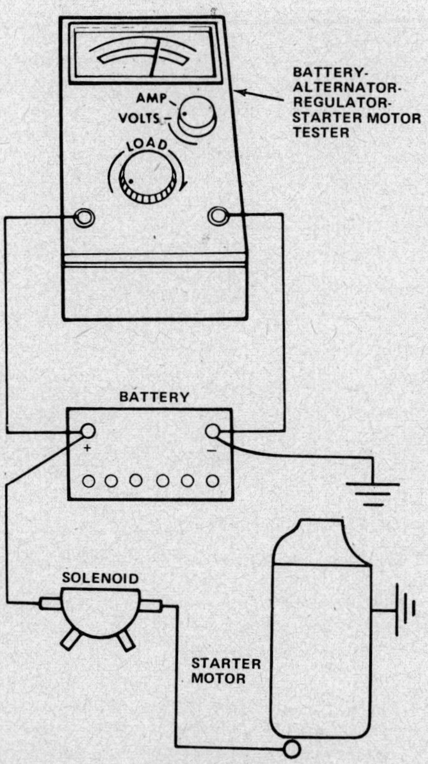

Fig. 1 Full-load current test connections.

IN-VEHICLE TESTING

SOLENOID GROUND TEST

1. Connect one ohmmeter test probe to battery negative post and other probe to sheet metal adjacent to solenoid on manual transmission, or ground terminal on automatic transmission, and note resistance.
2. Move test probe to solenoid S terminal. If resistance increases by more than 5 ohms, check solenoid ground.

SOLENOID PULL-IN COIL WINDING TEST

1. Disconnect S terminal wire from solenoid.
2. Connect ohmmeter leads to S terminal and the mounting bracket on manual transmission, or ground terminal on automatic transmission.
3. If there is no continuity, replace solenoid.

STARTER MOTOR FULL LOAD CURRENT TEST

1. Ensure that battery is fully charged, then disconnect and ground ignition coil secondary wire.
2. Connect remote control starter switch between positive battery terminal and S terminal on starter.
3. Connect circuit tester, **Fig. 1,** then actuate remote starter switch and note voltmeter reading. **Note voltage after starter has reached maximum RPM.**
4. Turn off remote starter switch, then turn load control knob clockwise until indicated voltage is exactly the same as when starter was running.
5. If ammeter does not read 180-220 amps, bench test starter.

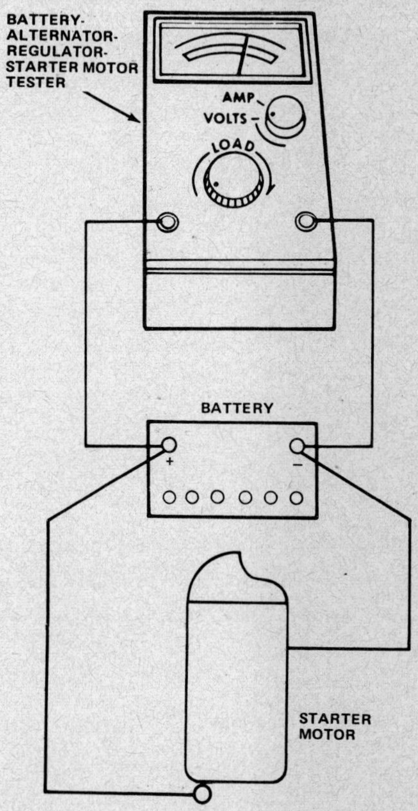

Fig. 2 No-load current test connections

OFF-VEHICLE TESTING

ARMATURE BALANCE TEST

1. Place armature in growler and turn power switch to GROWLER position.
2. Place contact fingers of meter test probe across adjacent commutator bars, then adjust voltage control until pointer indicates highest voltage on scale.
3. Test each commutator bar with adjacent bar. If any reading of zero volts is obtained, replace armature.

ARMATURE GROUND TEST

1. Place armature in growler and turn power switch to TEST position.
2. Place one lead of test lamp on armature core and other lead to each commutator bar.
3. If test lamp lights at any time, replace armature.

ARMATURE SHORT TEST

1. Place armature in growler and turn power switch to GROWLER position.
2. Hold steel blade parallel to and touching armature core, then slowly rotate armature at least one full turn.
3. If steel blade vibrates, replace armature.

FIELD WINDING TERMINAL-TO-BRUSH CONTINUITY TEST

1. Insert a piece of paper between contact points.
2. Touch ohmmeter leads to field winding terminal and insulated brush.
3. If resistance is greater than zero ohms, determine which solder joints have excessive resistance and repair with 600 watt soldering iron.

HOLD-IN COIL WINDING RESISTANCE TEST

1. Insert a piece of paper between contact points.
2. Using ohmmeter, measure resistance between S terminal and starter motor frame.
3. If resistance is not 2.0-3.5 ohms, replace field winding assembly.

INSULATED BRUSH CONNECTION TEST

1. Using ohmmeter, test resistance through solder joint by touching leads to brush and the copper bus bar.
2. If resistance is more than zero ohms, solder joint with 600 watt soldering iron.

NO-LOAD CURRENT TEST

1. Connect test equipment as shown, **Fig. 2**, and turn tester load control knob fully counterclockwise, then operate starter and note voltage.
2. Using mechanical tachometer, determine exact motor RPM. Connect tachometer by removing seal from end of drive end housing and clean grease from end of armature shaft.
3. Disconnect battery cable from starter.
4. Turn load control knob clockwise until voltage reading is exactly that obtained in step 1.
5. If ammeter does not read 67 amps with a starter motor RPM of 7380-9356, repair or replace starter as necessary.

SOLENOID CONTACT POINT TEST

1. Using ohmmeter, test resistance through solder joint.
2. If resistance is more than zero ohms, solder joint using 600 watt soldering iron.

TERMINAL BRACKET INSULATION TEST

1. Using ohmmeter, test resistance between terminal bracket and end cap.
2. If resistance is less than infinite, replace end cap.

ALTERNATOR SYSTEMS

TABLE OF CONTENTS

General Information

INDEX

INTRODUCTION

Alternators are composed of the same functional parts as the conventional D.C. generator but they operate differently. The field is called a rotor and is the turning portion of the unit. A generating part, called a stator, is the stationary member, comparable to the armature in a D.C. generator. The regulator, similar to those used in a D.C. system, regulates the output of the alternator-rectifier system.

The power source of the system is the alternator. Current is transmitted from the field terminal of the regulator through a slip ring to the field coil and back to ground through another slip ring. The strength of the field regulates the output of the alternating current. This alternating current is then transmitted from the alternator to the rectifier where it is converted to direct current.

These alternators employ a three-phase stator winding in which the phase windings are electrically 120 degrees apart. The rotor consists of a field coil encased between interleaved sections producing a magnetic field with alternate north and south poles. By rotating the rotor inside the stator the alternating current is induced in the stator windings. This alternating current is rectified (changed to D.C.) by silicon diodes and brought out to the output terminal of the alternator.

DIODE RECTIFIERS

Six silicon diode rectifiers are used and act as electrical one-way valves. Three of the diodes have ground polarity and are pressed or screwed into a heat sink which is grounded. The other three diodes (ungrounded) are pressed or screwed into and insulated from the end head; these diodes are connected to the alternator output terminal.

Since the diodes have a high resistance to the flow of current in one direction and a low resistance in the opposite direction, they may be connected in a manner which allows current to flow from the alternator to the battery in the low resistance direction. The high resistance in the opposite direction prevents the flow of current from the battery to the alternator. Because of this feature no circuit breaker is required between the alternator and battery.

SERVICE PRECAUTIONS

1. Be certain that battery polarity is correct when servicing units. Reversed battery polarity will damage rectifiers and regulators.
2. If booster battery is used for starting, be sure to use correct polarity in hook up.
3. When a fast charger is used to charge a vehicle battery, the vehicle battery cables should be disconnected unless the fast charger is equipped with a special Alternator Protector, in which case the vehicle battery cables need not be disconnected. Also the fast charger should never be used to start a vehicle as damage to rectifiers will result.
4. Lead connections to the grounded rectifiers (negative) should never be soldered as the excessive heat may damage the rectifiers.
5. Unless the system includes a load relay or field relay, grounding the alternator output terminal will damage the alternator and/or circuits. This is true even when the system is not in operation since no circuit breaker is used and the battery is applied to the alternator output terminal at all times. The field or load relay acts as a circuit breaker in that it is controlled by the ignition switch.
6. When adjusting the voltage regulator, do not short the adjusting tool to the regulator base as the regulator may be damaged. The tool should be insulated by taping or by installing a plastic sleeve.
7. Before making any "on vehicle" tests of the alternator or regulator, the battery should be checked and the circuit inspected for faulty wiring or insulation, loose or corroded connections and poor ground circuits.
8. Check alternator belt tension to be sure the belt is tight enough to prevent slipping under load.
9. The ignition switch should be off and the battery ground cable disconnected before making any test connections to prevent damage to the system.
10. The vehicle battery must be fully charged or a fully charged battery may be installed for test purposes.

Delcotron Type SI Integral Charging System

NOTE: For service procedures on these alternators, refer to the General Motors "Alternators Systems" chapter.

DISC BRAKES

TABLE OF CONTENTS

General Information

INDEX

Fig. 1 Checking rotor for lateral runout

BRAKE SHOES, LININGS & CALIPERS

Remove wheels and inspect brake disc, caliper and linings. The wheel bearings should be inspected at this time and repacked if necessary. Do not get any grease on the linings.

The brake shoe and lining assemblies should be replaced if the lining is worn to within 1/32 inch of rivet heads (riveted linings) or brake shoe (bonded linings). It is recommended that both front and/or rear wheel sets be replaced whenever a respective shoe and lining assembly is replaced.

If a visual inspection does not adequately determine the condition of the linings, the brake shoe and lining assemblies should be removed and inspected. If shoes do not require replacement, reinstall them in their original positions. Brake shoes and linings should also be replaced if cracked or damaged.

If the caliper is cracked or fluid leakage through the casting is evident, it must be replaced as a unit.

BRAKE ROUGHNESS

The most common cause of brake chatter on disc brakes is a variation in thickness of the disc. If roughness or vibration is encountered during highway operation or if pedal pumping is experienced at low speeds, the disc may have excessive thickness variation. To check for this condition, measure the disc at 12 points with a micrometer at a radius approximately one inch from edge of disc. If thickness measurements vary by more than .0005 inch, the disc should be replaced with a new one.

Excessive lateral runout of braking disc may cause a "knocking back" of the pistons, possibly creating increased pedal travel and vibration when brakes are applied.

Before checking the runout, wheel bearings should be adjusted. The readjustment is very important and will be required at the completion of the test to prevent bearing failure. Be sure to make the adjustment according to the recommendations given under Front Wheel Bearings, Adjust, in the car chapter.

DISC BRAKE SERVICE

Servicing of disc brakes is extremely critical due to the close tolerances required in machining the brake disc to insure proper brake operation.

The maintenance of these close controls of the shape of the rubbing surfaces is necessary to prevent brake roughness. In addition, the surface finish must be non-directional and maintained at a micro inch finish. This close control of the rubbing surface finish is necessary to avoid pulls and erratic performance and promote long lining life and equal lining wear of both left and right brakes.

In light of the foregoing remarks, refinishing of the rubbing surfaces should not be attempted unless precision equipment, capable of measuring in micro inches (millionths of an inch) is available.

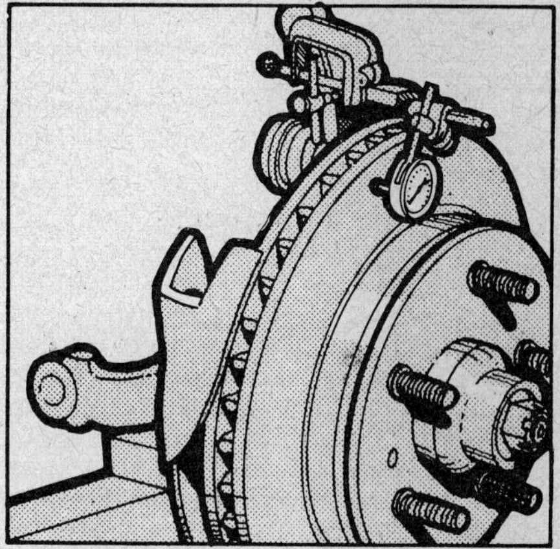

Fig. 2 Checking rotor parallelism (Thickness variation)

To check lateral runout of a disc, mount a dial indicator on a convenient part (steering knuckle, tie rod, disc brake caliper housing) so that the plunger of the dial indicator contacts the disc at a point one inch from the outer edge, **Fig. 1.** If the total indicated runout exceeds specifications, install a new disc.

To check parallelism (thickness variation), mount dial indicators, **Fig. 2,** so the plunger contacts rotor approximately 1 inch from outer edge. If parallelism exceeds specifications, replace rotor.

GENERAL PRECAUTIONS

1. Grease or any other foreign material must be kept off the caliper, surfaces of the disc and external surfaces of the hub, during service procedures. Handling the brake disc and caliper should be done in a way to avoid deformation of the disc and nicking or scratching brake linings.
2. If inspection reveals rubber piston seals are worn or damaged, they should be replaced immediately.

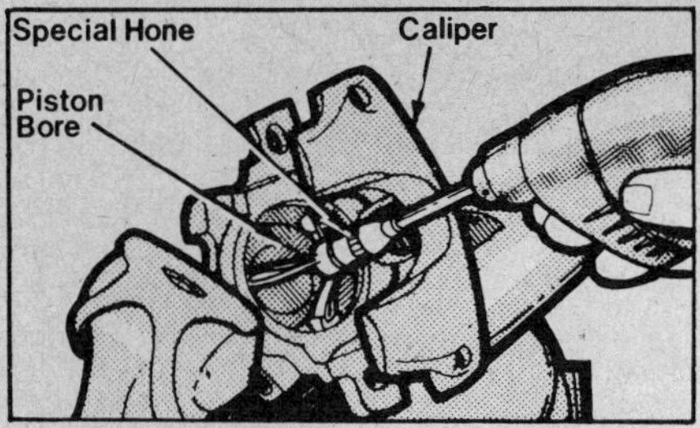

Fig. 3 Honing caliper piston bore

3. During removal and installation of a wheel assembly, exercise care so as not to interfere with or damage the caliper splash shield, or bleeder screw.
4. Front wheel bearings should be adjusted to specifications.
5. Be sure vehicle is centered on hoist before servicing any of the front end components to avoid bending or damaging the disc splash shield on full right or left wheel turns.
6. Before the vehicle is moved after any brake service work, be sure to obtain a firm brake pedal.
7. The assembly bolts of the two caliper housings should not be disturbed unless the caliper requires service.

INSPECTION OF CALIPER

Should it become necessary to remove the caliper for installation of new parts, clean all parts in alcohol, wipe dry using lint-free cloths. Using an air hose, blow out drilled passages and bores. Check dust boots for punctures or tears. If punctures or tears are evident, new boots should be installed upon reassembly.

Inspect piston bores in both housings for scoring or pitting. Bores that show light scratches or corrosion can usually be cleaned with crocus cloth. However, bores that have deep scratches or scoring may be honed, provided the diameter of the bore is not increased more than .002 inch. If the bore does not clean up within this specification, a new caliper housing should be installed (black stains on the bore walls are caused by piston seals and will do no harm).

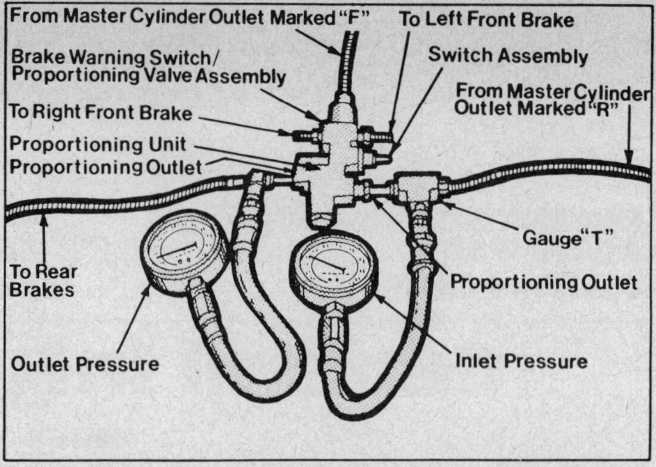

Fig. 4 Gauge hook-up for testing proportioning valve (typical)

When using a hone, **Fig. 3,** be sure to install the hone baffle before honing bore. The baffle is used to protect the hone stones from damage. Use extreme care in cleaning the caliper after honing. Remove all dust and grit by flushing the caliper with alcohol. Wipe dry with clean lint-free cloth and then clean a second time in the same manner.

BLEEDING DISC BRAKES

Pressure bleeding is recommended for all hydraulic disc brake systems.

The disc brake hydraulic system can be bled manually or with pressure bleeding equipment. On vehicles with disc brakes the brake pedal will require more pumping and frequent checking of fluid level in master cylinder during bleeding operation.

Never use brake fluid that has been drained from hydraulic system when bleeding the brakes. Be sure the disc brake pistons are returned to their normal positions and that the shoe and lining assemblies are properly seated. Before driving the vehicle, check brake operation to be sure that a firm pedal has been obtained.

PROPORTIONING VALVE

The proportioning valve (when used), **Fig. 4,** provides balanced braking action between front and rear brakes under a wide range of braking conditions. The valve regulates the hydraulic pressure applied to the rear wheel cylinders, thus limiting rear braking action when high pressures are required at the front brakes. In this manner, premature rear wheel skid is prevented.

TESTING PROPORTIONING VALVE

When a premature rear wheel slide is obtained on a brake application, it usually is an indication that the fluid pressure to the rear wheels is above the 50% reduction ratio for the rear line pressure and that malfunction has occurred within the proportioning valve.

To test the valve, install gauge set shown in **Fig. 4** in brake line between master cylinder and proportioning valve, and at output end of proportioning valve and brake line as shown. Be sure all joints are fluid tight.

Have a helper exert pressure on brake pedal (holding pressure). Obtain a reading on master cylinder output of approximately 700 psi. While pressure is being held as above, reading on valve outlet should be 550-610 psi. If the pressure readings do not meet these specifications, the valve should be removed and a new valve installed.

Bendix Sliding Caliper

INDEX

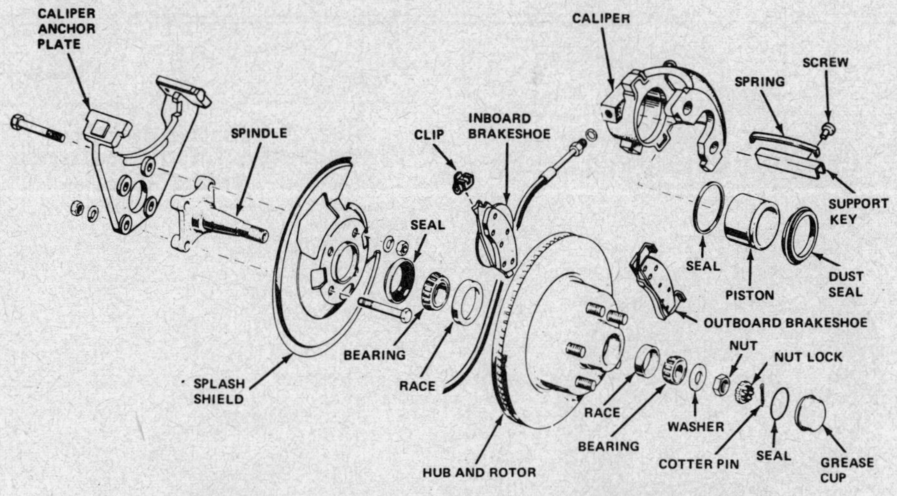

Fig. 1 Bendix sliding caliper disc brake (Typical)

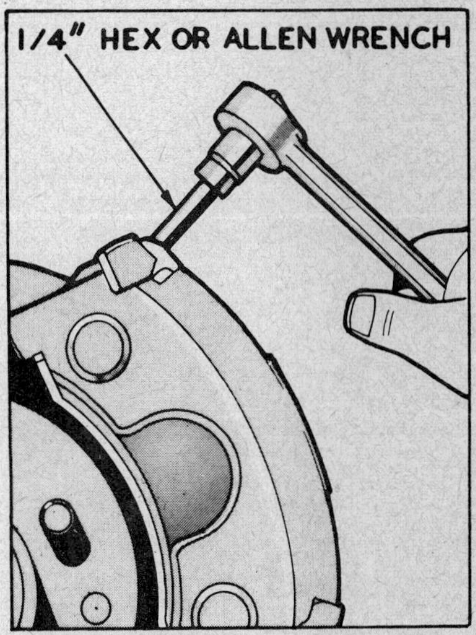

Fig. 3 Removing support key retaining screw

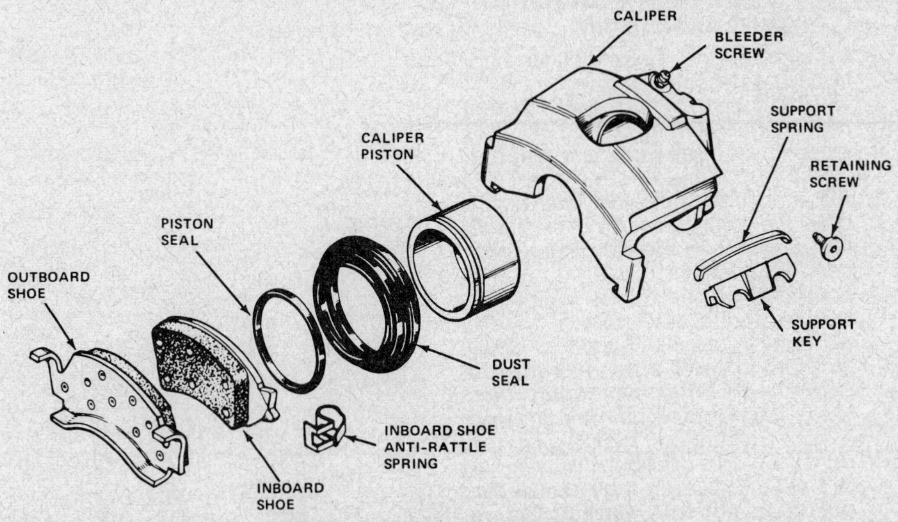

Fig. 2 Caliper assembly

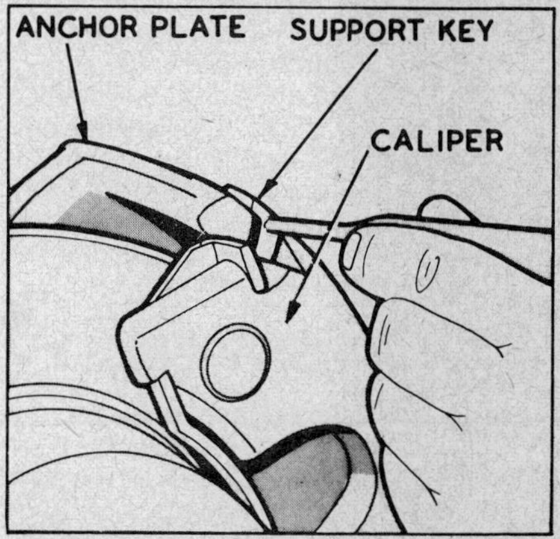

Fig. 4 Removing support key

This sliding caliper disc brake assembly incorporates a hub and rotor assembly, caliper, brake shoes and linings, caliper anchor plate and a splash shield, **Fig. 1.**

Cooling fins are cast into the rotor between the two braking surfaces to ventilate and cool the rotor. The sliding caliper is positioned in, and slides on, the abutment surfaces on the leading and trailing edges of the caliper anchor plate. A caliper support key, located between the forward edge of the caliper and abutment surface, is secured with a retaining screw. A support spring is installed between the support key and caliper to maintain tension on the support key.

The caliper is a one-piece casting containing the piston, piston seal and dust seal, **Fig. 2.** The hydraulic seal between the caliper piston and piston bore is achieved by a square cut piston seal, located in a machined groove in the piston bore. The dust seal seats in a recess machined on the edge of the piston bore and into a groove in the caliper piston.

CALIPER REMOVAL

1. Siphon two-thirds of brake fluid from master cylinder reservoir serving front disc brakes.
2. Raise vehicle, support on jack stands and remove front wheels.
3. Bottom the caliper piston in bore. Insert a screwdriver between inboard shoe and piston, then pry piston back into bore. The piston can also be bottomed in the bore with a large C-clamp.
4. Using a 1/4 inch Allen wrench, remove support key retaining screw, **Fig. 3.**
5. Drive caliper support key and spring from anchor plate with a suitable drift and hammer, **Fig. 4.**

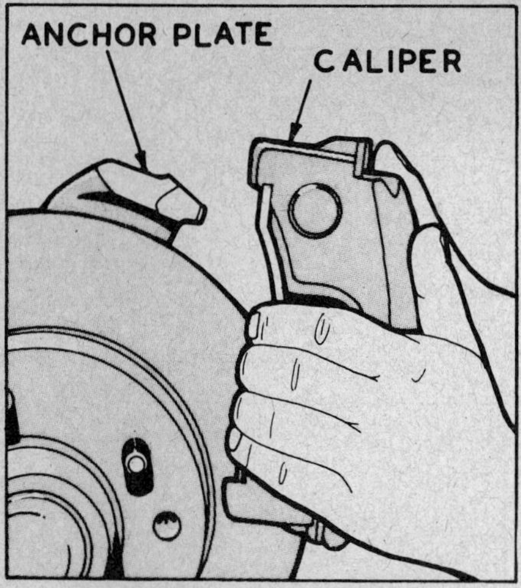

Fig. 5 Removing or installing caliper

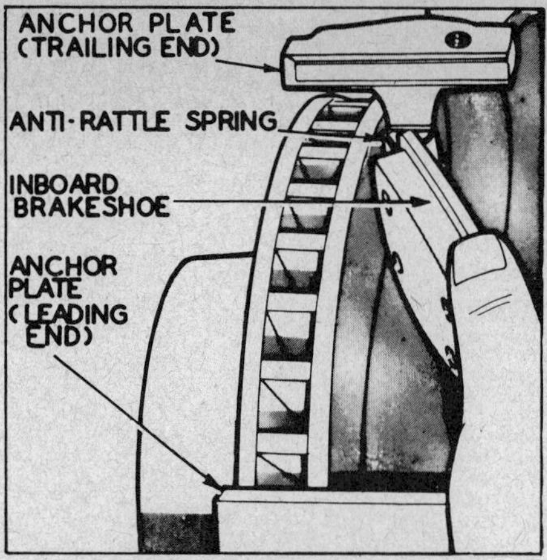

Fig. 6 Removing or installing inboard brake shoe

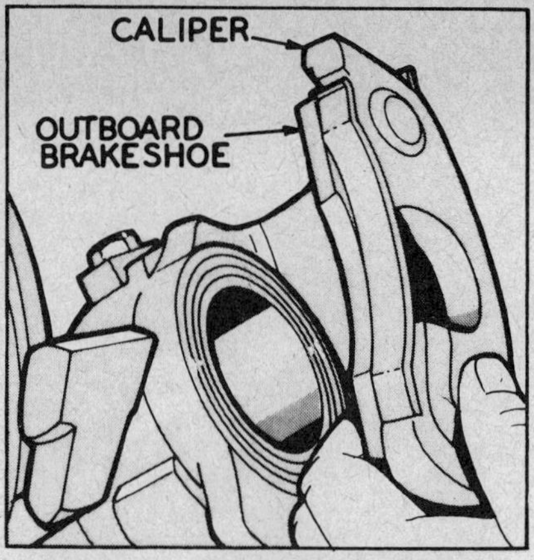

Fig. 7 Removing or installing outboard brake shoe

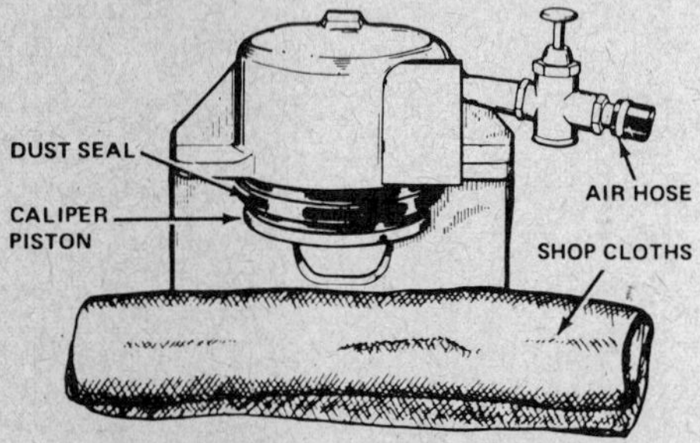

Fig. 8 Removing piston from caliper

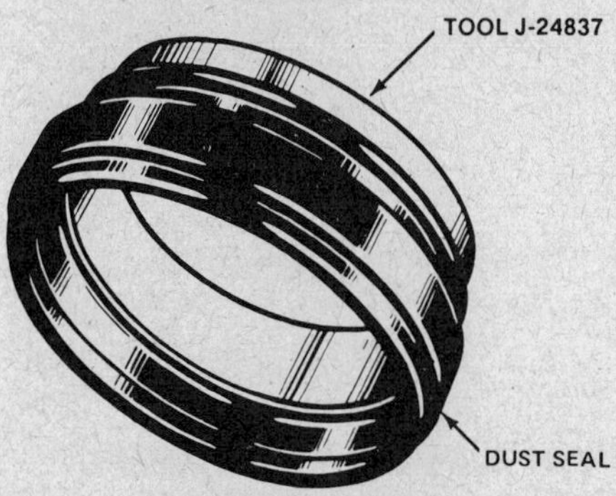

Fig. 9. Dust seal & installer tool assembly

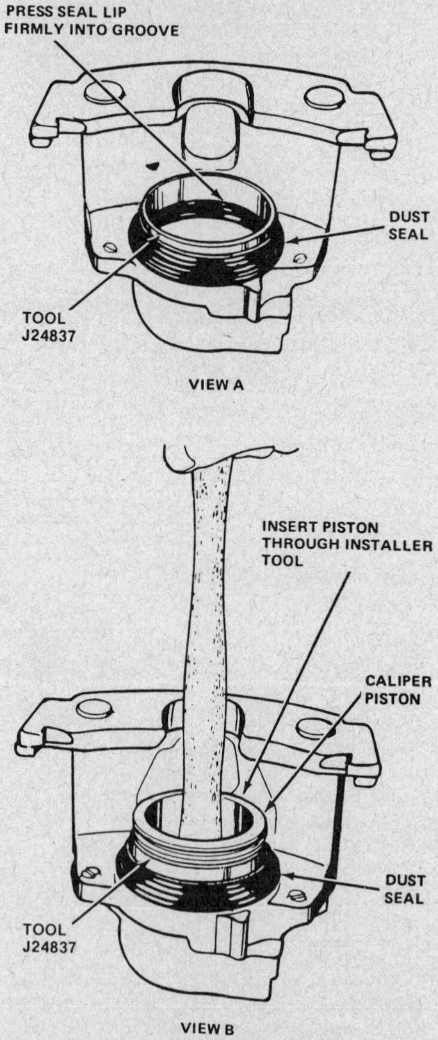

Fig. 10 Installing dust seal & caliper piston

6. Lift caliper from anchor plate and off rotor, **Fig. 5.** Hang caliper from coil spring with wire. Do not allow caliper to hang from brake hose.
7. Remove inboard brake shoe from anchor plate, then the anti-rattle spring from the brake shoe, **Fig. 6.** Remove teflon slipper plate from leading anchor abutment surface, if equipped.
8. Remove outboard brake shoe from caliper, **Fig. 7.** It may be necessary to loosen the brake shoe with a hammer to permit shoe removal.

CALIPER DISASSEMBLY

1. Drain brake fluid from caliper.
2. Position caliper with shop cloths, **Fig. 8,** and apply compressed air to fluid inlet port to ease piston from bore. **Do not attempt to catch piston or to protect it when applying compressed air since personal injury is possible.**
3. Remove dust seal from piston, then the piston seal from bore, **Fig. 2.** Use wooden or plastic tool to remove piston seal since metal tools may damage piston.
4. Remove bleeder screw.

CALIPER ASSEMBLY

1. Coat square cut piston seal with clean brake fluid, then install seal into piston bore. Work seal into groove with clean fingers.
2. Install bleeder screw and plastic cap.
3. Lubricate dust seal and tool J-24387 with clean brake fluid, then place dust seal on tool, allowing 1/4 inch of tool to extend past small lip of dust seal, **Fig. 9.**
4. Place dust seal and tool over piston bore, then work large lip of dust seal into seal groove, **Fig. 10.** Ensure dust seal is fully seated.
5. Lubricate caliper piston and insert through tool. Center piston in bore and use a hammer handle to apply pressure to install piston halfway into bore, **Fig. 10. On some models, disc brake caliper pistons may develop a light coating of rust under the dust seal and outboard of the piston seal. This rust may cause the piston to not fully retract. Before installing piston, apply a light coating of dielectric compound 8126688, or equivalent, to caliper piston bore, Fig. 11.**
6. Remove tool J-24387 and seat small lip of dust seal in caliper piston groove, then bottom piston in bore.

BRAKE SHOE & LINING, REPLACE

The procedures to remove & install the brake shoe and lining assemblies are outlined under "Caliper Removal" and "Caliper Installation." It is not necessary to disconnect the brake hose, however, use caution not to twist or kink hose.

CALIPER INSTALLATION

1. Clean and lubricate abutment surfaces of caliper and the anchor plate with a suitable molydisulfide grease, **Fig. 12.**
2. Install inboard brake shoe anti-rattle

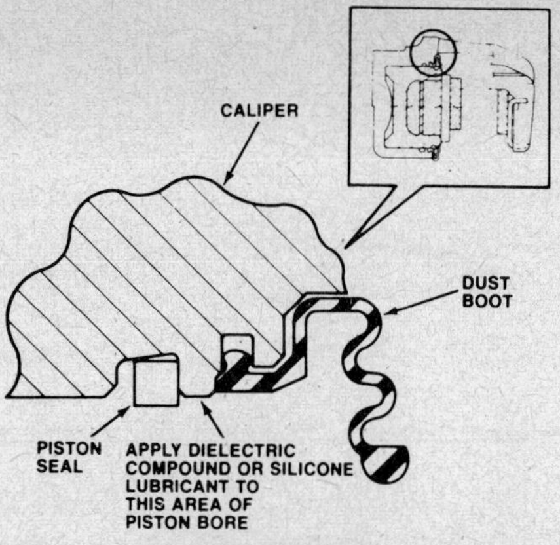

Fig. 11 Lubricating caliper piston bore

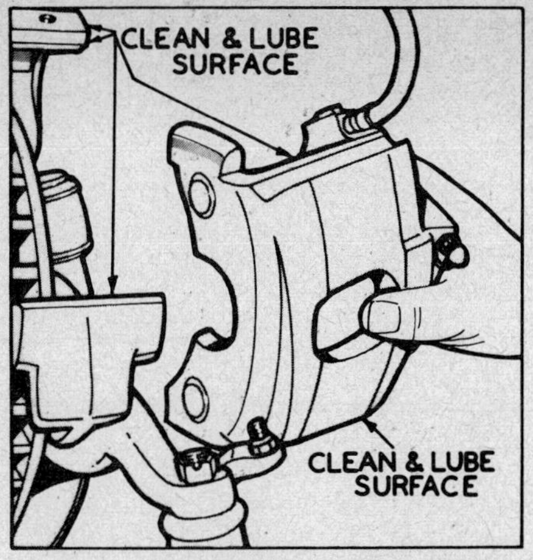

Fig. 12 Caliper & anchor plate abutment surfaces

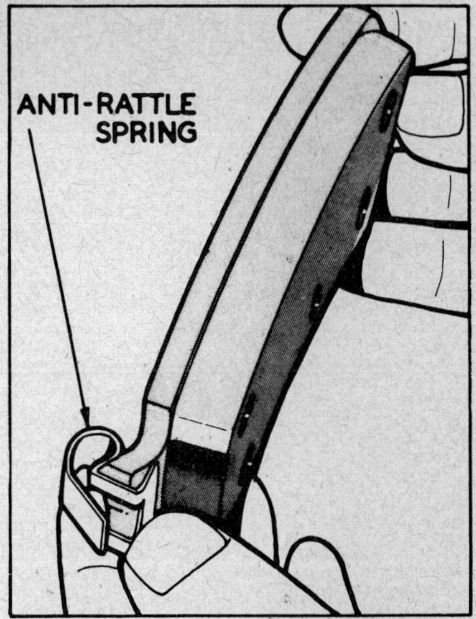

Fig. 13 Installing inboard brake shoe anti-rattle spring

spring on brake shoe rear flange, ensure looped section of clip is facing away from rotor, **Fig. 13.** Install Teflon slipper plate on leading anchor abutment surface, if equipped.

3. Install inboard brake shoe on caliper anchor plate, **Fig. 6.**
4. Install outboard brake shoe in caliper, **Fig. 7.** Ensure the shoe flange is seated fully into outboard arms or caliper. It may be necessary to use a hammer to seat the shoe.
5. Place caliper assembly over rotor and position in caliper anchor plate. Ensure dust boot is not torn or incorrectly positioned by inboard brake shoe during caliper installation.
6. Align caliper with anchor plate abutment surfaces, then insert support key and spring between abutment surfaces, then insert support key and spring between abutment surfaces at the trailing end of caliper and anchor plate. With a hammer and brass drift, drive caliper support key and spring into position, then install and torque support key retaining screw to 15 ft. lbs.
7. Refill master cylinder to within 1/4 inch of rim. Press brake pedal several times to seat shoes.
8. Install front wheels and lower vehicle.

American Motors Dual Pin Sliding Caliper

INDEX

OPERATION

This dual pin sliding caliper assembly incorporates a hub and rotor assembly, a caliper, brake shoes and linings, caliper anchor plate, adapter bracket and splash shield on Spirit and Concord models, **Fig. 1.** On Eagle models, the caliper assembly incorporates a rotor which mounts to the hub assembly, a caliper, brake shoes and linings, caliper anchor plate and splash shield, **Fig. 2.**

The caliper used on all models has a 2.6 inch diameter piston. The caliper is positioned over the rotor and slides on two mounting pins which maintain caliper position relative to the rotor and caliper anchor plate. The caliper is a one-piece casting with a groove machined in the bore to hold the square cut piston seal to maintain a hydraulic seal between the piston and bore wall. The dust boot is seated in a machined recess in the top of the piston bore and a groove in the piston exterior surface.

The inner and outer brake shoes are positioned by the caliper anchor plate. The brake shoe anti-rattle clip is positioned between the brake shoe and caliper anchor plate. The brake linings are riveted to the shoes and the inner and outer brake shoes are not interchangeable.

BRAKE SHOE & LININGS, REPLACE

REMOVAL

1. Drain and discard approximately 2/3 of the brake fluid from the larger brake fluid reservoir.
2. Raise and support vehicle, then remove tire and wheel assembly.
3. Using a suitable screwdriver, pry piston fully into caliper bore. **If piston cannot be bottomed in cylinder bore using a screwdriver, use a C-clamp.**
4. Using a 7 mm Allen wrench, remove caliper mounting pins.
5. Lift caliper from anchor plate and off rotor.
6. Suspend caliper from coil spring with suitable wire to prevent damaging brake hose.
7. Hold anti-rattle clip against caliper anchor plate and remove outer brake shoe. **Note position of anti-rattle clip for assembly reference.**
8. Remove inner brake shoe from caliper anchor plate, then anti-rattle clip.
9. Wipe inside of caliper with dry, clean cloth and inspect piston bore for leakage. If leakage is present, refer to "Caliper Overhaul." **Do not clean caliper with compressed air as damage to the dust boot may result.**

INSTALLATION

1. Inspect caliper and anchor plate abutment surfaces for rust and corrosion. If rust and corrosion are evident, clean surfaces with wire brush.
2. Lightly lubricate caliper and anchor plate abutment surfaces with Molydisulfide grease.
3. Install anti-rattle clip on trailing end of anchor plate. Ensure split end of clip faces away from rotor.
4. While holding anti-rattle clip in position, install inner and outer brake shoes.

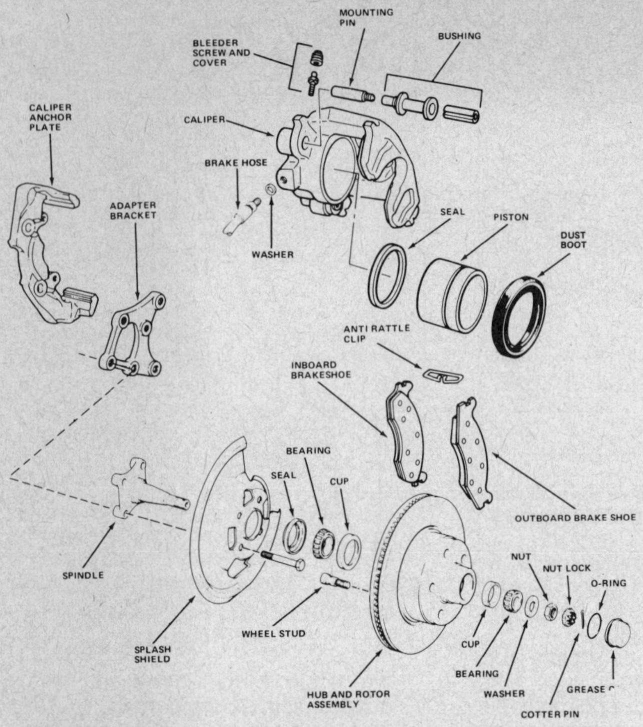

Fig. 1 American Motors dual pin slider disc brake assembly. 1982–83 Spirit & Concord

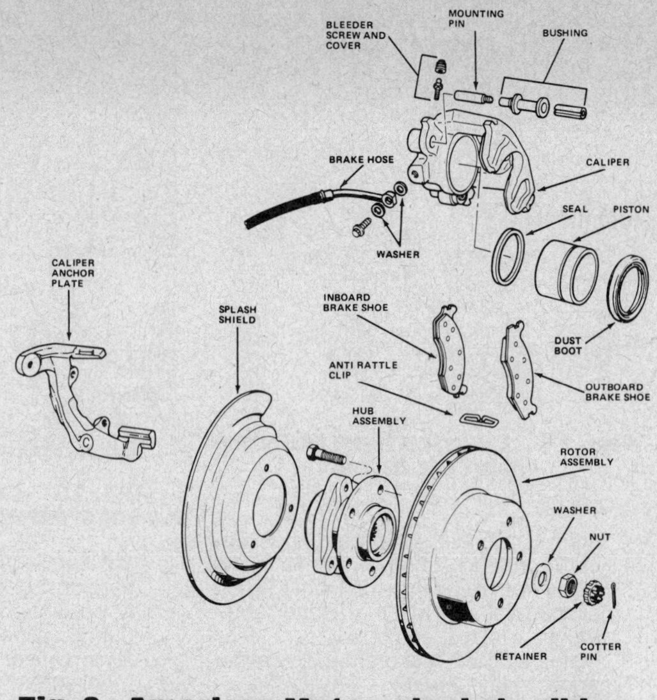

Fig. 2 American Motors dual pin slider disc brake assembly. 1982–87 Eagle

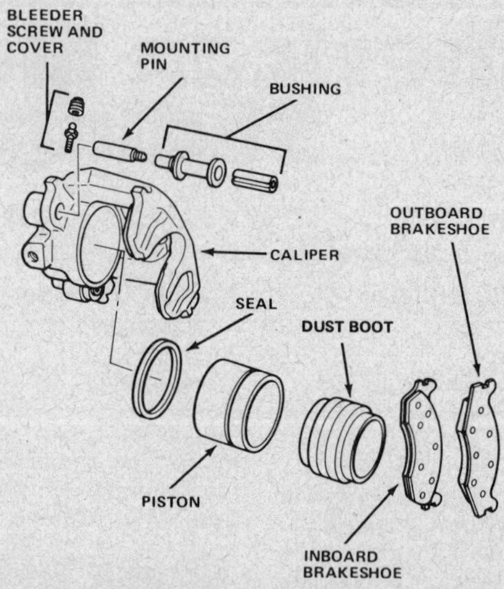

Fig. 3 Disassembled view of disc brake caliper. 1982–87 American Motors (typical)

5. Install caliper over rotor and into position on adapter.
6. Install caliper mounting pins. Torque to 26 ft. lbs. on 1982-84 models, or 30 ft. lbs. on 1985-87 models.
7. Fill master cylinder with clean brake fluid, then pump brake pedal several times to position caliper piston and brake shoes.
8. Install tire and wheel assembly, then lower vehicle.
9. Check brake fluid and refill as necessary. **Before moving vehicle, ensure a firm brake pedal is obtained.**

CALIPER OVERHAUL

REMOVAL

1. Follow steps 1 through 3 of Removal procedure under "Brake Shoe and Linings, Replace."
2. Clean dirt from brake hose fittings.
3. Disconnect brake hose from caliper, then cap open lines to prevent entry of dirt.
4. Discard hose fitting washer.
5. Remove caliper following steps 4 through 8 of Removal procedure under "Brake Shoe and Linings, Replace."

DISASSEMBLY

1. Clean caliper exterior with suitable brake cleaning solvent.
2. Drain caliper, then place on clean work surface.
3. Pad caliper interior with clean shop cloths, then using compressed air, gently apply just enough air pressure into caliper fluid inlet hole to ease piston out of bore. **Do not place fingers in front of piston in an attempt to catch or protect it when applying compressed air. This could result in serious injury.**
4. Using a suitable screwdriver, pry dust boot from bore using care not to damage piston bore, **Fig. 3.**
5. Using a pencil or other suitable wooden object, remove piston seal.
6. Remove bushings from caliper ear and discard.

INSPECTION

1. Clean all parts in brake cleaning solvent or brake fluid, then blow out caliper fluid passages with filtered compressed air.
2. Inspect caliper mounting pins for corrosion, replace as necessary. **Do not attempt to clean or polish caliper mounting pins with abrasives as protective plating will be removed.**
3. Inspect caliper piston. If nicked, scratched, corroded or protective plating is worn off, replace. **Do not attempt to refinish piston in any way as protective plating will be removed, leading to corrosion and eventual failure.**

4. Inspect caliper bore. If nicked, scratched, worn, cracked, or badly corroded, replace caliper. **Minor corrosion and stains can be removed from caliper bore with crocus cloth. Do not attempt to clean caliper bore with any other abrasives.**

ASSEMBLY

1. Lubricate piston bore and seal with brake fluid, then work seal into piston groove using fingers only.
2. Lubricate piston with brake fluid, then slide metal portion of dust seal over open end of piston and pull rearward until seal boot seats in piston groove, then push metal portion of seal forward until retainer is flush with rim and seal fold snaps into position.
3. Insert piston and seal assembly into bore. Do not unseat piston seal.
4. Using a hammer handle, press piston in bore.
5. Using tool No. J-33028, install dust seal in caliper housing.
6. Install bleeder screw and tighten securely.
7. Install replacement plastic sleeves and rubber bushings in caliper ears.

INSTALLATION

1. Follow steps 1 through 6 of Installation procedures under "Brake Shoe and Linings, Replace."
2. Install replacement hose fitting washer on brake hose, then install hose in caliper and torque to 25 ft. lbs.
3. Fill master cylinder with clean brake fluid and bleed brakes.
4. Install tire and wheel assembly, then lower vehicle.
5. Check brake fluid and refill as necessary. **Before moving vehicle, ensure a firm brake pedal is obtained.**

Rotor Specifications

Car	Year	Nominal Thickness	Minimum Refinish Thickness	Thickness Variation (Parallelism)	Lateral Runout (T.I.R.)	Finish (Micro- In.)
Exc. Eagle	1982-83	—	.815	.0005	.003	15-80
Eagle	1982-87	—	.815	.0005	.004	15-80

Caliper Specifications

Year	Model	Caliper Bore Dia. In.
1982-87	All	2.6

DRUM BRAKES

NOTE: Refer to "Application" to determine which type brakes are used on vehicle being serviced.

TABLE OF CONTENTS

Application

	Type No.
1982-83 Concord Exc. Station Wagon W/6 Cylinder Engine	1
1982-83 Concord Station Wagon W/6 Cylinder Engine	2
1982-87 Eagle	2
1982-83 Spirit Exc. GT Models W/Rally Tuned Suspension	1
1982-83 Spirit W/V8 Engine Or Rally Tuned Suspension	2

General Information

INDEX

SERVICE PRECAUTIONS

When working on or around brake assemblies, care must be taken to prevent breathing asbestos dust, as many manufacturers incorporate asbestos fibers in the production of brake linings. During routine service operations the amount of asbestos dust from brake lining wear is at a low level, due to a chemical breakdown during use and a few precautions will minimize exposure.

Do not sand or grind brake linings unless suitable local exhaust ventilation equipment is used to prevent excessive asbestos exposure.

1. Wear a suitable respirator approved for asbestos dust use during all repair procedures.
2. When cleaning brake dust from brake parts, use a vacuum cleaner with a highly efficient filter system. If a suitable vacuum cleaner is not available, use a water soaked rag. Do not use compressed air or dry brush to clean brake parts.
3. Keep work area clean using same equipment as for cleaning brake parts.
4. Properly dispose of rags and vacuum cleaner bags by placing them in plastic bags.
5. Do not smoke or eat while working on brake systems. **Never use gasoline, kerosene, alcohol, motor oil, transmission fluid, or any fluid containing mineral oil to clean brake system components. These fluids will damage the rubber caps and seals. If system contamination is suspected, check brake fluid in the reservoir for dirt, discoloration, or separation (breakdown) of the brake fluid into distinct layers. Drain and flush the hydraulic system with clean brake fluid if contamination is suspected.**

GENERAL INSPECTION

BRAKE DRUMS

Any time the brake drums are removed for brake service, the braking surface diameter should be checked with a suitable brake drum micrometer at several points to determine if they are within the safe oversize limit stamped on the brake drum outer surface. If the braking surface diameter exceeds specifications, the drum must be replaced. If the braking surface diameter is within specifications, drums should be cleaned and inspected for cracks, scores, deep grooves, taper, out of round and heat spotting. If drums are cracked or heat spotted, they must be replaced. Minor scores should be removed with sandpaper. Grooves and large scores can only be removed by machining with special equipment, as long as the braking surface is within specifications stamped on brake drum outer surface. Any brake drum sufficiently out of round to cause vehicle vibration or noise while braking or showing taper should also be machined, removing only enough stock to true up the brake drum.

After a brake drum is machined, wipe the braking surface diameter with a denatured alcohol soaked cloth. If one brake drum is machined, the other should also be machined to the same diameter to maintain equal braking forces.

BRAKE LININGS & SPRINGS

Inspect brake linings for excessive wear, damage, oil, grease or brake fluid contamination. If any of the above conditions exists, brake linings should be replaced. Do not attempt to replace only one set of brake shoes; they should be replaced as an axle set only to maintain equal braking forces. Examine brake shoe webbing, hold-down and return springs for signs of overheating indicated by a slight blue color. If any component exhibits overheating signs, replace hold-down and return springs with new ones. Overheated springs lose their pull and could cause brake linings to wear out prematurely. Inspect all springs for sags, bends and external damage and replace as necessary.

Inspect hold-down retainers and pins for bends, rust and corrosion. If any of the above is found, replace as required.

BACKING PLATE

Inspect backing plate shoe contact surface for grooves that may restrict shoe movement and cannot be removed by lightly sanding with emery cloth or other suitable abrasive. If backing plate exhibits above condition, it should be replaced. Also inspect for signs of cracks, warpage and excessive rust, indicating need for replacement.

ADJUSTER MECHANISM

Inspect all components for rust, corrosion, bends and fatigue. Replace as necessary. On adjuster mechanism equipped with adjuster cable, inspect cable for kinks, fraying or elongation of eyelet and replace as necessary.

PARKING BRAKE CABLE

Inspect parking brake cable end for kinks, fraying and elongation and replace as necessary. Use a small hose clamp to compress clamp where it enters backing plate to remove.

Types 1 & 2

INDEX

Page No.

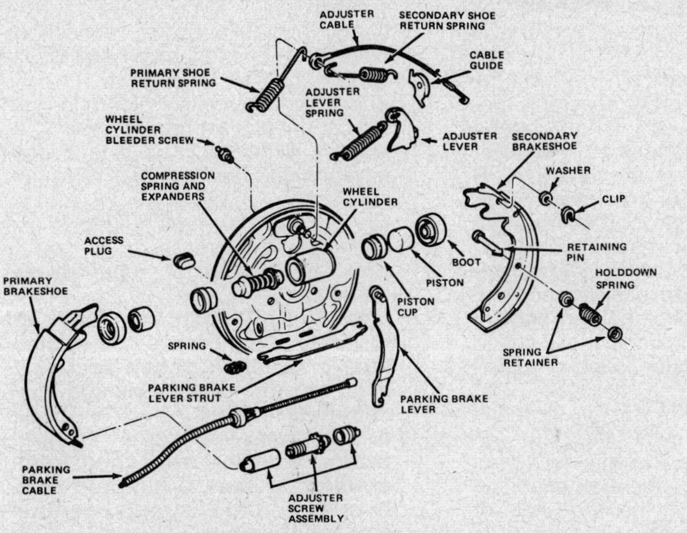

Fig. 1 Drum brake assembly. Type 1

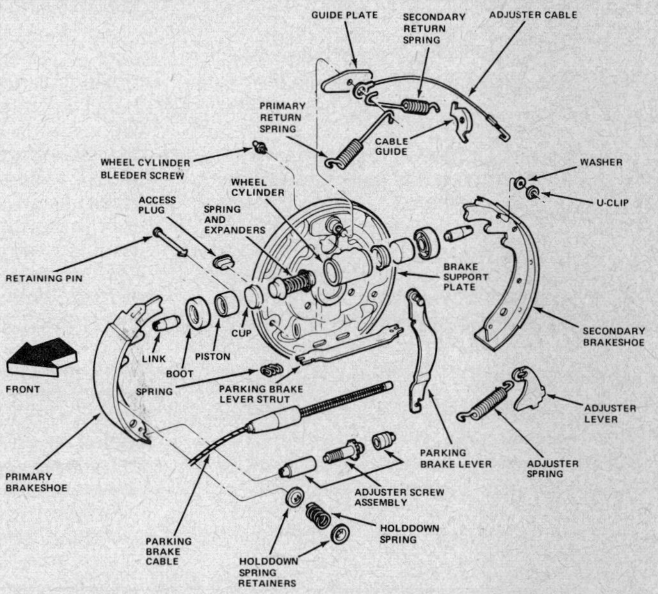

Fig. 2 Drum brake assembly. Type 2

REMOVAL

1. Raise and support rear of vehicle, then remove tire and wheel assembly.
2. Remove brake drum. If brake lining is dragging on brake drum, back off brake adjustment by rotating adjustment screw. Refer to individual car chapter for procedure. **If brake drum is rusted or corroded to axle flange and cannot be removed, lightly tap axle flange to drum mounting surface with a suitable hammer.**
3. Install suitable wheel cylinder clamp over ends of wheel cylinder to retain pistons in bore.
4. Remove parking brake lever retaining clip, **Figs. 1 and 2.**
5. On type 2, **Fig. 2,** remove adjuster lever spring, primary and secondary shoe return springs using a suitable pair of brake spring pliers. On type 1, **Fig. 1,** remove adjuster lever spring, secondary shoe return spring, adjuster cable eyelet and primary shoe return spring.
6. On all types, remove shoe guide plate (if equipped), and adjuster cable and guide plate.
7. Using suitable tool, compress holddown springs, then remove spring retainers, hold down springs and pins.
8. Separate springs and remove from backing plate.
9. Remove parking brake lever from cable.
10. Separate all components from brake shoes.
11. Clean dirt from brake drum, backing plate and all other components. **Do not use compressed air or dry brush to clean brake parts. Many brake parts contain asbestos fibers which, if inhaled, can cause serious injury. Clean brake parts with a water soaked rag or a suitable vacuum cleaner to minimize airborne dust.**

INSPECTION

1. Inspect components for damage and unusual wear. Replace as necessary.
2. Inspect wheel cylinders. Boots which are torn, cut, or heat damaged indicate need for wheel cylinder replacement. Fluid spilling from boot center hole, or wetness around wheel cylinder ends indicates cup leakage and need for wheel cylinder replacement. **A small amount of fluid is always present and is considered normal, acting as a lubricant for the cylinder pistons.**
3. Inspect backing plate for evidence of seal leakage. If leakage exists, refer to individual car chapters for axle seal replacement procedure.
4. Inspect backing plate attaching bolts and ensure they are tight.
5. Check adjuster screw operation. If satisfactory, lightly lubricate adjusting screw and washer with suitable brake lube. If operation is unsatisfactory, replace.
6. Using fine emery cloth or other suitable abrasive, clean rust and dirt from shoe contact surfaces on backing plate.

INSTALLATION

1. Lightly lubricate backing plate shoe

contact surfaces with suitable brake lube.
2. Assemble parking brake lever to secondary shoe and secure with spring washer and retaining clip. Crimp ends of clip with suitable pliers.
3. Position brake shoes on backing plate, primary (short lining) shoe facing front of vehicle and secondary (long lining) facing rear. Secure brake shoes with hold down springs, pins and retainers.
4. Install parking brake link and spring between shoes.
5. Loosen parking brake adjustment nut, then install parking brake cable on parking brake lever.
6. On type 1, proceed as follows:
   a. Using suitable brake spring pliers, install primary return spring from brake shoe to anchor.
   b. Install adjuster cable eyelet on anchor pin with crimp facing out.
   c. Position adjuster cable guide on secondary shoe, then using suitable brake spring pliers, install secondary return spring from brake shoe to anchor.
7. On types 2, proceed as follows:
   a. Install shoe guide plate and adjuster cable eyelet on anchor. Ensure adjuster cable crimp faces out.
   b. Ensure parking brake link is properly positioned between brake shoes and wheel cylinder links are engaged in shoe web.
   c. Using suitable brake spring pliers, install primary return spring from brake shoe to anchor, then secondary return spring from brake shoe to anchor.
8. On all types, remove wheel cylinder clamp installed during removal of brake shoes.
9. Tighten adjuster screw assembly to thread limit and back off one-half turn.

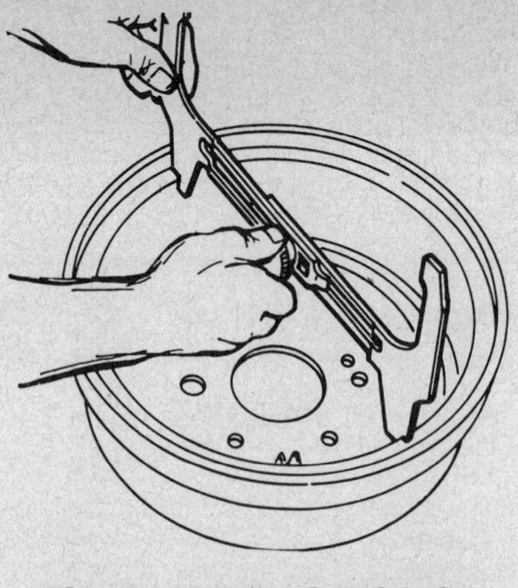

Fig. 3 Measuring brake drum inside diameter

10. Install adjuster screw assembly between shoes. Ensure toothed wheel is on secondary shoe side. **Adjuster screw assemblies are stamped R (right) and L (left). To ensure proper adjuster operation, they must be installed on their respective sides.**
11. Hook adjuster cable hook into adjuster lever hole, then position adjuster spring hook in large hole in primary shoe web. Using suitable brake spring pliers, install adjuster spring in adjuster lever hole.
12. Ensure adjuster cable is properly seated in cable guide, then pull adjuster lever, cable and adjuster spring down and towards the rear, engaging lever pivot hook in the large hole of secondary shoe web.
13. After installation, check adjuster operation by pulling adjuster cable between cable guide and adjuster lever towards secondary shoe sufficiently to lift adjuster lever past one tooth on adjuster screw assembly. The adjuster lever should snap into position behind the next tooth, then upon release of adjuster cable, rotate toothed wheel one notch. If operation is not satisfactory, recheck installation.
14. Ensure brake shoe upper ends are seated against anchor pin and shoe assemblies are centered on backing plate. If not, back off parking brake adjustment.
15. Using suitable brake drum to shoe gauge, **Fig. 3,** measure brake drum inside diameter. Adjust brake shoes to dimension obtained on outside portion of gauge using adjuster screw.
16. Install brake drum, wheel and tire assembly.
17. If any hydraulic brake connections have been opened, bleed brake system.
18. Adjust parking brake. Refer to individual car chapter for procedures.
19. Inspect all hydraulic lines and connections for leakage and repair as necessary.
20. Check master cylinder fluid level and replenish as necessary.
21. Check brake pedal for proper feel and return.
22. Lower vehicle and road test. **Do not severely apply brakes immediately after installation of new brake linings or permanent damage may occur to linings, and/or brake drums may become scored. Brakes must be used moderately during first several hundred miles of operation to ensure proper burnishing of linings.**

Specifications

Year	Model	Brake Drum Inside Dia. In.
1982-83	Exc. Concord & Spirit	10
	Concord	9①
	Spirit	9②
1984-87	Eagle	10

①—Concord Sta. Wag. w/6 cyl. engine, 10".
②—Spirit GT models w/rally tuned suspension, 10".

AUTOMATIC TRANSMISSIONS
Torque-Command Transmission

INDEX

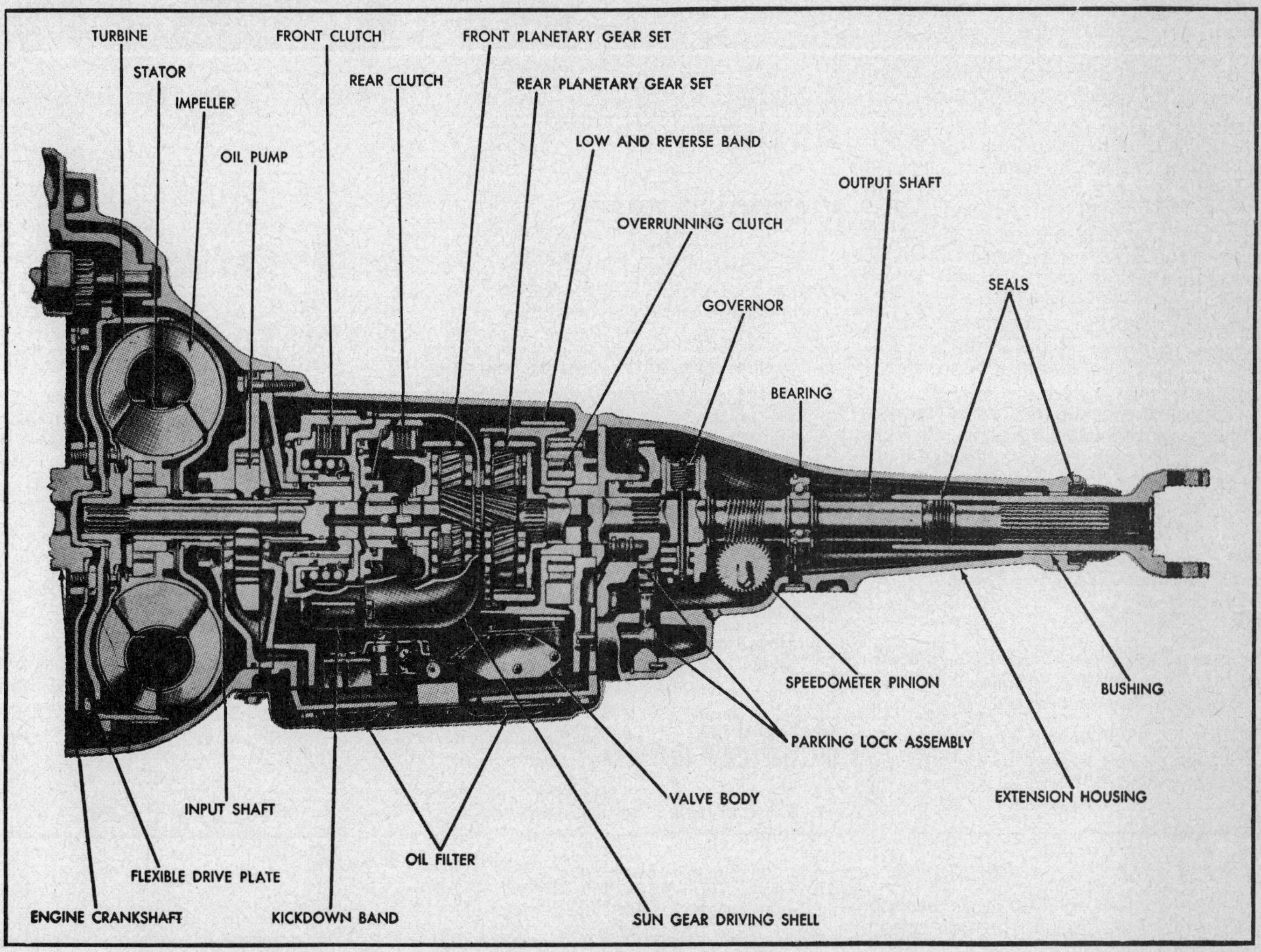

Fig. 1 Series 904 Torqueflite transmission (typical). 998 models similar

IDENTIFICATION

The transmission identification markings, 904 on 4-151 engines or 904 or 998 on 6-258 engines, are cast in raised letters and numerals on the lower left side of the bell housing.

There are sufficient variations to make it necessary to service transmission by serial number, a stamped 7 digit number appearing on the oil pan side rail.

DESCRIPTION

These transmissions, **Fig. 1**, combine a torque converter with a fully automatic three speed gear system. The converter housing and transmission case are an integral aluminum casting. The transmission consists of two multiple disc clutches, an overrunning (one-way) clutch, two servos and bands and two planetary gear sets to provide three forward speeds and reverse.

The common sun gear of the planetary gear sets is connected to the front clutch by a driving shell that is splined to the sun gear and to the front clutch retainer.

The hydraulic system consists of a single oil pump and a valve body that contains all the valves except the governor valve.

Venting of the transmission is accomplished by a drilled passage through the upper part of the front pump housing.

The torque converter is attached to the engine crankshaft through a flexible driving plate. The converter is cooled by circulating the transmission fluid through an oil-to-water type cooler located in the radiator lower tank. The converter is a sealed assembly that cannot be disassembled. On 1982-87 models with 6 cyl. engine, a lockup torque converter is used which eliminates slippage and results in improved fuel economy and reduced fluid temperatures.

The lockup converter system consists of a lockup mechanism within the converter, and a lockup module and switch valve attached to the valve body. The internal lockup mechanism consists of a sliding clutch piston, torsion springs and clutch friction material. The friction material is attached to the front cover, the clutch piston is mounted in the turbine, and the torsion springs are located on the forward side of the turbine. The torsion springs are used to dampen out engine firing impulses, while absorbing the shock loads that occur during lockup.

When the transmission reaches a predetermined speed, transmission fluid is channeled through the input shaft and into the area between the clutch piston and turbine. The fluid pressure forces the piston against the front cover friction material, locking the turbine to the impeller. When vehicle speed decreases, or the transmission shifts out of direct drive, fluid pressure is released, the clutch piston retracts, and the converter operates in a conventional manner.

Because the lockup mechanism is completely enclosed within the converter, lockup converters have a circular decal attached to the front cover stating the converter type and stall ratio.

TROUBLESHOOTING GUIDE

When troubleshooting this transmission, refer to "Torqueflite Automatic Transmission" in the Chrysler section.

MAINTENANCE

CHECKING OIL LEVEL

To check the oil level, apply the parking brake and operate the engine at idle speed with the transmission in Neutral position.

CHANGING OIL

Fluid and filter changes or band adjustments are not required for average passenger car use. Severe usage such as trailer towing or prolonged operation in city traffic, requires that fluid and filter be changed and bands adjusted every 15,000 miles.

Whenever the factory fill fluid is changed, only fluids of the type labeled DEXRON II should be used.

1. Remove drain plug (if equipped) from transmission oil pan and drain oil. **If the oil pan does not have a drain plug, loosen pan bolts and tap pan with a soft mallet to break it loose, permitting fluid to drain.**
2. Remove transmission oil pan, replace filter or clean intake screen and pan, adjust bands and reinstall.
3. Add approximately 4 quarts of automatic transmission fluid through filler tube.
4. Start engine.
5. Allow engine to idle for about two minutes. With parking brake applied, move selector lever momentarily to each position and place in neutral, then check and adjust fluid level as required.

BANDS

ADJUST

KICKDOWN BAND

The kickdown band adjusting screw is located on the left side of the transmission case near the throttle lever shaft.

1. Loosen locknut and back off approximately five turns. Check adjusting screw for free turning in transmission case.
2. Using an inch-pound torque wrench, tighten the band adjusting screw to a reading of 72 inch lbs.
3. Back off adjusting screw as follows: 1982-83 904 with 6 cylinder engines, 2 turns; 1982-83 904 with 4 cylinder engine, 2 1/2 turns and all 1982-87 998 transmissions, 3 turns.
4. Hold adjusting screw in backed off position and tighten locknut.

LOW AND REVERSE BAND

1. Raise vehicle, drain transmission and remove oil pan.
2. Inspect fluid for friction material or metal particles which indicate damaged or worn parts.
3. Loosen adjusting screw locknut and back off nut approximately five turns. Check adjusting screw for free turning in lever.
4. Using an inch pound torque wrench, tighten band adjusting screw to 72 in. lbs. on all except 904 transmissions. On 904 transmissions, tighten adjusting screw to 41 in. lbs.
5. Back off adjusting screw 4 turns on 998 transmission or 7 turns on 904 transmission.
6. Hold adjusting screw and tighten locknut to 35 ft. lbs., then install oil pan and refill transmission.

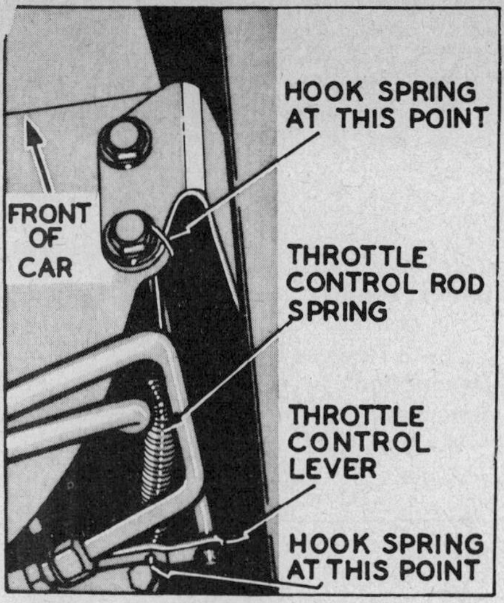

Fig. 2 Install spring on lever.

GEARSHIFT CONTROL LINKAGE

ADJUST

1. Raise and support vehicle.
2. Loosen shift rod trunnion retaining screw, then place gearshift lever in Park position.
3. Move manual lever fully rearward into Park detent, then check that parking pawl is fully engaged in governor support by attempting to rotate propeller shaft. Shaft will not rotate if pawl is properly engaged.
4. Tighten trunnion retaining screw.
5. Move gearshift lever through detents and attempt to start engine. When linkage is properly adjusted, engine should start in Neutral or Park only.

THROTTLE LINKAGE

ADJUST

1. Disconnect throttle control spring, then use spring to hold transmission throttle control lever forward against stop, **Fig. 2.**
2. Block choke open and set throttle off fast idle. **On carburetors equipped with a throttle solenoid, energize solenoid and open throttle part way to allow solenoid to lock and return carburetor to idle.**
3. Loosen retaining bolt on throttle control adjusting link. Do not remove spring clip and nylon washer.
4. Pull on end of link to eliminate lash and tighten retaining bolt, **Fig. 3.**
5. Reconnect throttle control rod spring.

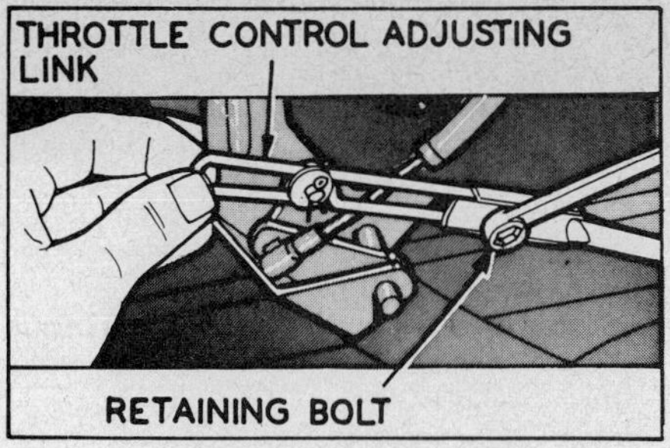

Fig. 3 Six cylinder throttle linkage (Typical)

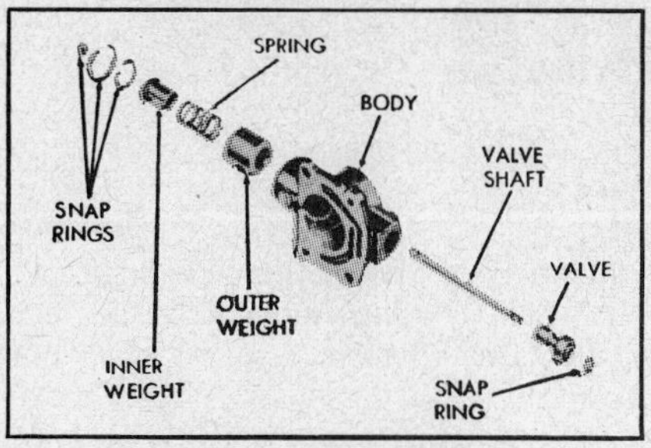

Fig. 4 Governor disassembled

EXTENSION HOUSING/ADAPTER HOUSING SEAL

SPIRIT & CONCORD

1. Raise and support vehicle.
2. Scribe alignment marks on propeller shaft and rear axle yokes, then disconnect and remove propeller shaft.
3. Remove seal from housing using suitable screwdriver.
4. Reverse procedure to install.

EAGLE

1. Scribe alignment marks on propeller shafts and transfer case yokes, then disconnect and remove propeller shafts.
2. Remove transfer case.
3. Remove seal from adapter housing, using care to avoid damaging seal bore.
4. Apply suitable sealant to outside edge of new seal retainer, then coat seal lip with petroleum jelly.
5. Using tool J-29162 or equivalent, install seal flush with edge of seal bore, ensuring seal lip faces toward inside of housing.
6. Reinstall transfer case and propeller shafts.

GOVERNOR

REMOVAL

1. Raise and support vehicle.
2. On Concord and Spirit models, proceed as follows:
   a. Scribe alignment marks on propeller shaft and rear axle yokes, then disconnect and remove propeller shaft.

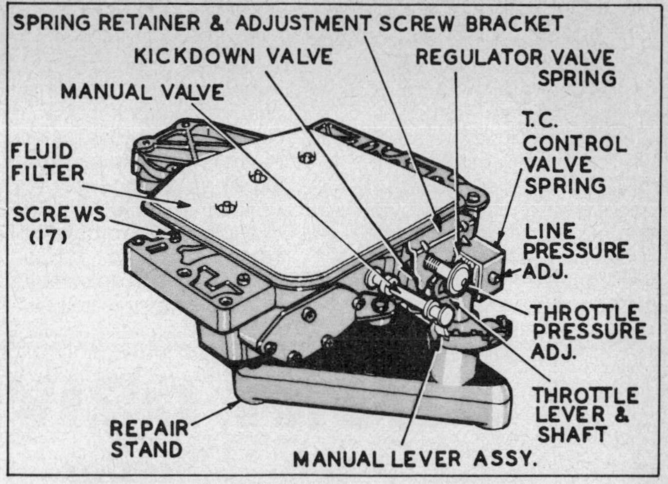

Fig. 5 Valve body external parts

   b. Support transmission with suitable jack, then remove speedometer cable and adapter from extension housing.
   c. Remove rear support crossmember from side sills, then the catalytic converter support bracket from extension housing.
   d. Remove rear support cushion, adapter and rear bearing cover plate from extension housing.
   e. Remove extension housing to case attaching bolts, then install pilot studs into case.
   f. Expand rear bearing snap ring, then tap extension housing off bearing and output shaft.
   g. Remove rear bearing snap ring and bearing.
3. On Eagle models:
   a. Scribe alignment marks on propeller shafts and transfer case yokes, then disconnect and remove propeller shafts.
   b. Remove transfer case and adapter housing.
4. On all models, remove E-clip from weight end of governor valve shaft, then remove valve and shaft from governor body.
5. Rotate output shaft until governor weight faces downward, then remove snap ring, governor body and park gear assembly.

DISASSEMBLY

1. Remove large snap ring from weight end of governor housing, **Fig. 4**, and lift out weight assembly.
2. Remove snap ring from inside governor weight and remove inner weight and spring from outer weight.
3. If park gear or governor body requires replacement, straighten lock tabs, then remove body to support attaching bolts and governor filter. **The primary cause of governor operating failure is due to a sticking governor valve or weights. Rough surfaces may be removed with crocus cloth. Thoroughly clean all parts and check for free movement before assembly.**

ASSEMBLY & INSTALLATION

Reverse above operations to assemble and install governor.

VALVE BODY

1. Drain transmission and remove oil pan.
2. Loosen clamp bolts and remove throttle and gear selector levers from manual lever, **Fig. 5.**
3. Remove neutral safety switch and oil filter.
4. Place a drain pan under transmission and remove the ten valve body to transmission bolts. Hold valve body in place while removing bolts.
5. Carefully lower valve body while pulling it forward to disengage parking control rod. **It may be necessary to rotate output shaft to permit parking control rod to clear sprag.**
6. Remove accumulator piston and spring from transmission case. Inspect piston for nicks, scores and wear. Inspect spring for distortion. Inspect rings for freedom in piston grooves and wear or breakage. Replace parts as necessary.

TRANSMISSION

REPLACE

The hood must be open to prevent damage to hood and air cleaner when removing rear crossmember.

1. Disconnect fan shroud and remove bolt securing fill tube to engine.
2. Place gearshift lever in Neutral, then raise and support vehicle.
3. Scribe alignment marks on propeller shaft(s) and yokes, then remove propeller shaft(s).
4. On Eagle models, remove skid plate, then disconnect exhaust pipe from manifold.

5. On all models, remove starter motor and stiffening braces, if applicable.
6. Remove speedometer adapter, cable assembly and cover adapter bore.
7. Disconnect gearshift and throttle linkages. On vehicles equipped with column shift, remove bolt securing linkage bellcrank to converter housing.
8. Remove converter housing cover, scribe alignment marks on drive plate and converter, then rotate crankshaft and remove converter to drive plate attaching bolts.
9. Support transmission and transfer case, if applicable, using suitable jack.
10. Disconnect cooler lines from transmission, then remove rear support cushion to bracket attaching bolt.
11. Remove rear crossmember attaching nuts, crossmember and support cushion as an assembly.
12. Position suitable support under front of engine, then remove bolts securing catalytic converter support bracket to transmission, if applicable.
13. Remove transmission fill tube.
14. Remove transmission to engine attaching bolts, then move transmission, transfer case (if applicable) and converter rearward until assembly clears crankshaft.
15. Secure converter in position, then lower transmission and remove from vehicle.
16. Reverse procedure to install. Torque transmission to engine attaching bolts to 28 ft. lbs.

FRONT DRIVE AXLE

INDEX

EAGLE FRONT AXLE SERVICE

Refer to Figs. 1, 2 and 3 during front axle service procedures.

AXLE, REPLACE

Removal

1. Raise and support vehicle.
2. Install half shaft boot protectors J-28712 onto boots.
3. Remove half shaft to axle flange bolts and secure half shaft to vehicle underbody.
4. Insert wire through half shaft flange bolt holes, then compress half shaft and wrap wire between boots to prevent half shaft from separating.
5. Mark propeller shaft and axle yoke for reference during reassembly and remove propeller shaft.
6. Support axle assembly using suitable jack.
7. On models equipped with Select Drive System, remove brace rod and shift motor shield.
8. On all models, remove axle mounting bolts. On models less Select Drive System, the axle is secured to the engine block with five bolts. On models with Select Drive System, the axle is secured to the engine block by five bolts on the lefthand side and one bolt on the righthand side.
9. On models equipped with Select Drive System, disconnect vacuum hose from axle shift motor, then partially lower axle assembly and disconnect vent hose.
10. On all models, lower axle assembly to allow access to vent hose and remove hose.
11. Remove axle assembly from vehicle. **Do not apply any load or weight on the hub assembly whenever the half shafts are not securely attached to the axle shaft flanges.**

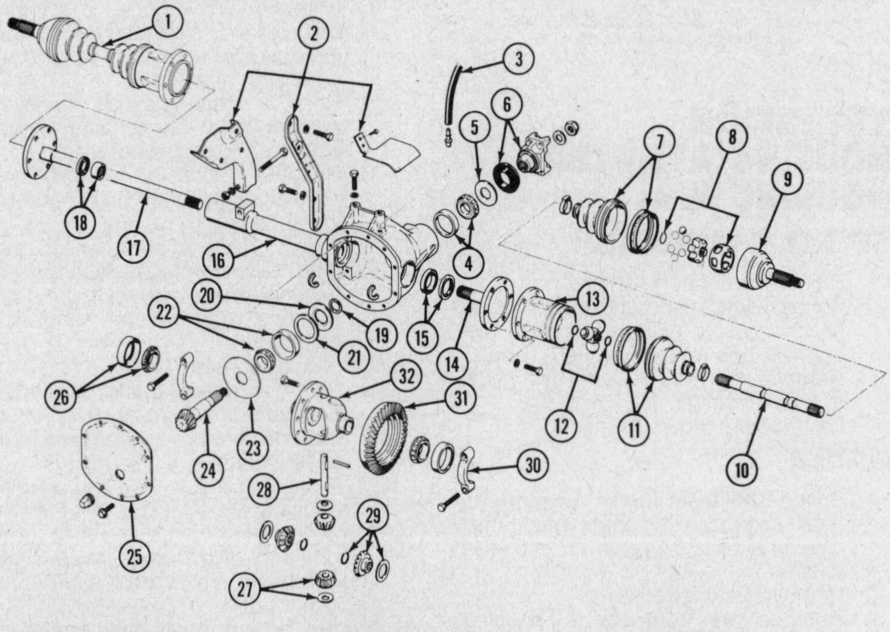

1. HALF-SHAFT ASSEMBLY
2. AXLE MOUNTING BRACKETS
3. VENT HOSE
4. PINION AND FRONT BEARING CUP
5. WASHER
6. YOKE AND SEAL
7. OUTER BOOT AND RETAINER
8. RZEPPA JOINT ASSEMBLY
9. SPINDLE
10. HALF-SHAFT
11. INNER BOOT AND RETAINER
12. TRI-POT JOINT ASSEMBLY
13. TRI-POT HOUSING
14. AXLE SHAFT (SHORT)
15. BALL BEARING AND SEAL
16. AXLE HOUSING
17. AXLE SHAFT (LONG)
18. NEEDLE BEARING AND SEAL
19. PRELOAD SHIM
20. WASHER
21. DEPTH SHIM
22. PINION REAR BEARING AND CUP
23. SLINGER
24. PINION GEAR
25. COVER
26. DIFFERENTIAL BEARING AND CUP
27. DIFFERENTIAL PINION AND THRUST WASHER
28. PINION MATE SHAFT
29. SIDE GEAR, THRUST WASHER AND LOCKRING
30. BEARING CAP
31. RING GEAR
32. DIFFERENTIAL CASE

Fig. 1 Front axle assembly. 1982–84 Eagle less Select Drive System

Installation

1. Support axle assembly on suitable jack and position assembly under vehicle.
2. Raise axle assembly slightly and install vent hose.
3. Continue raising axle assembly until properly positioned and install axle mounting bolts. Torque bolts to 50 ft. lbs.
4. Connect propeller shaft to axle yoke. Ensure shaft and yoke are aligned.
5. Remove wire used to prevent half shafts from separating, then install half shaft to axle flange bolts and torque to 45 ft. lbs.
6. On models equipped with Select Drive System, connect vacuum harness on axle shift motor shield.
7. On all models, remove half shaft boot protectors.

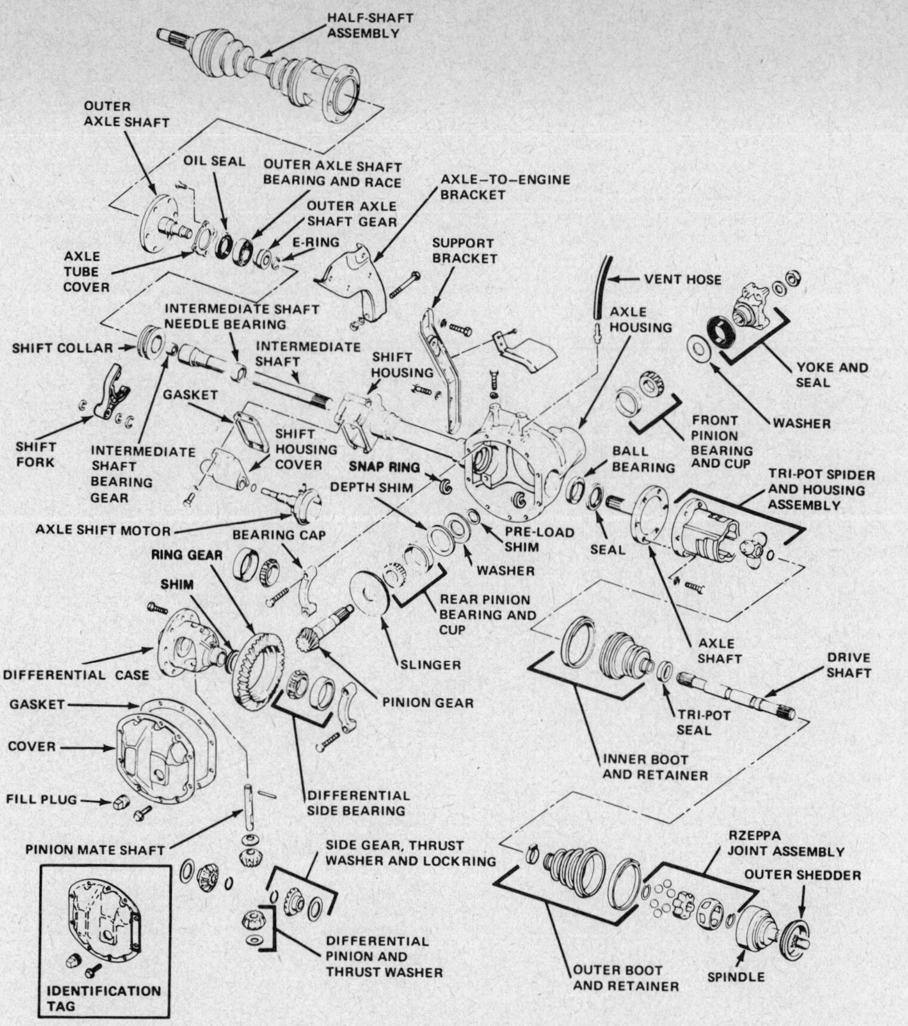

Fig. 2 Front axle assembly. 1982–84 Eagle w/Select Drive System

8. On models equipped with Select Drive, connect brace rod to axle.

AXLE SHAFT SEAL, REPLACE

On 1985-87 models, removal of the righthand shaft seal is the same as that of the lefthand shaft seal.

1. Remove axle assembly.
2. Remove axle housing cover and drain lubricant.
3. Remove axle shaft retaining clip, then the axle shaft.
4. Remove axle shaft seal using suitable screwdriver.
5. Install replacement axle shaft seal using Installer J-29152 for righthand side axle shaft and Installer J-29154 for lefthand side axle shaft.
6. Install axle shaft, then the axle shaft retaining clip.
7. Apply suitable sealant to axle housing cover and install cover. Torque cover bolts to 20 ft. lbs.
8. Fill axle with $2^1/_2$ pints of SAE 85W-90 lubricant, then install assembly onto vehicle. Refer to Axle, Installation for procedures.

AXLE HUB & BEARING

Removal

1. Raise and support vehicle, then remove wheel, caliper and rotor.
2. Remove bolts attaching axle shaft flange to half shaft. **Insert wire through half shaft flange bolt holes, then compress half shaft and wrap wire between boots to prevent half shaft from separating.**
3. Remove cotter pin, locknut and axle shaft nut, then the half shaft.
4. Remove steering arm from steering knuckle.
5. Remove caliper anchor plate from steering knuckle, then the three torx head bolts retaining hub assembly using tool J-26359.
6. Remove hub assembly from steering knuckle and clean grease from steering knuckle cavity.

Disassemble

1. Press hub from bearing carrier, then remove bearings, hub spacer, steering knuckle pin seal, carrier to hub seal, carrier O-ring and bearing spacer, if equipped, **Fig. 11.**
2. Clean all components and inspect for wear and damage and replace as necessary. **If hub incorporates ball bearings, the entire hub assembly must be replaced if damage to internal components is indicated. If hub incorporates tapered bearings, internal hub components may be replaced as necessary. Bearings and races must be replaced in matched sets.**
3. Press bearing races from hub carrier, if necessary. Install replacement bearing races using a brass drift or suitable press.

Assemble

1. Fill steering knuckle pin, hub, bearing carrier and lip type seal cavities with lithium base wheel bearing lubricant.
2. Pack bearings with lithium base wheel bearing lubricant, then install bearings into hub carrier, **Fig. 4.**
3. Install seal onto hub side of bearing carrier, then press hub into carrier and install hub spacer on end of hub shaft. **Do not install bearing carrier O-ring at this time.**
4. Install inner seal into steering knuckle pin.
5. Install splash shield onto hub and bearing carrier, then install bearing carrier O-ring.
6. Install splash shield and bearing carrier into steering knuckle pin, then install carrier attaching bolts and torque to 75 ft. lbs.

Installation

1. Partially fill hub cavity of steering knuckle with chassis lubricant and install hub assembly onto steering knuckle. Torque hub torx head bolts to 75 ft. lbs.
2. Install caliper anchor plate and torque plate retaining bolts to 100 ft. lbs.
3. Install steering arm onto steering knuckle and torque retaining bolts to 100 ft. lbs.
4. Install half shaft, then the axle flange to shaft bolts and hub nut. Torque half shaft to flange bolts to 45 ft. lbs and hub nut 175 ft. lbs.
5. Install locknut, replacement cotter pin, rotor, caliper and wheel.

AXLE SHAFT, REPLACE

On 1985-87 models, removal of the righthand shaft is the same as that of the lefthand shaft.

1. Refer to Axle Shaft Seal, Replace. Perform steps 1 through 3 for axle shaft removal andsteps 6 through 8 for axle shaft installation.

AXLE SHAFT BEARING, REPLACE

Two different style axle shaft bearings are used on the Eagle front axle. The left side axle shaft uses a ball bearing. The right side axle shaft uses a needle bearing. On 1985-87 models, removal of the righthand side bearing is the same as that of the lefthand bearing.

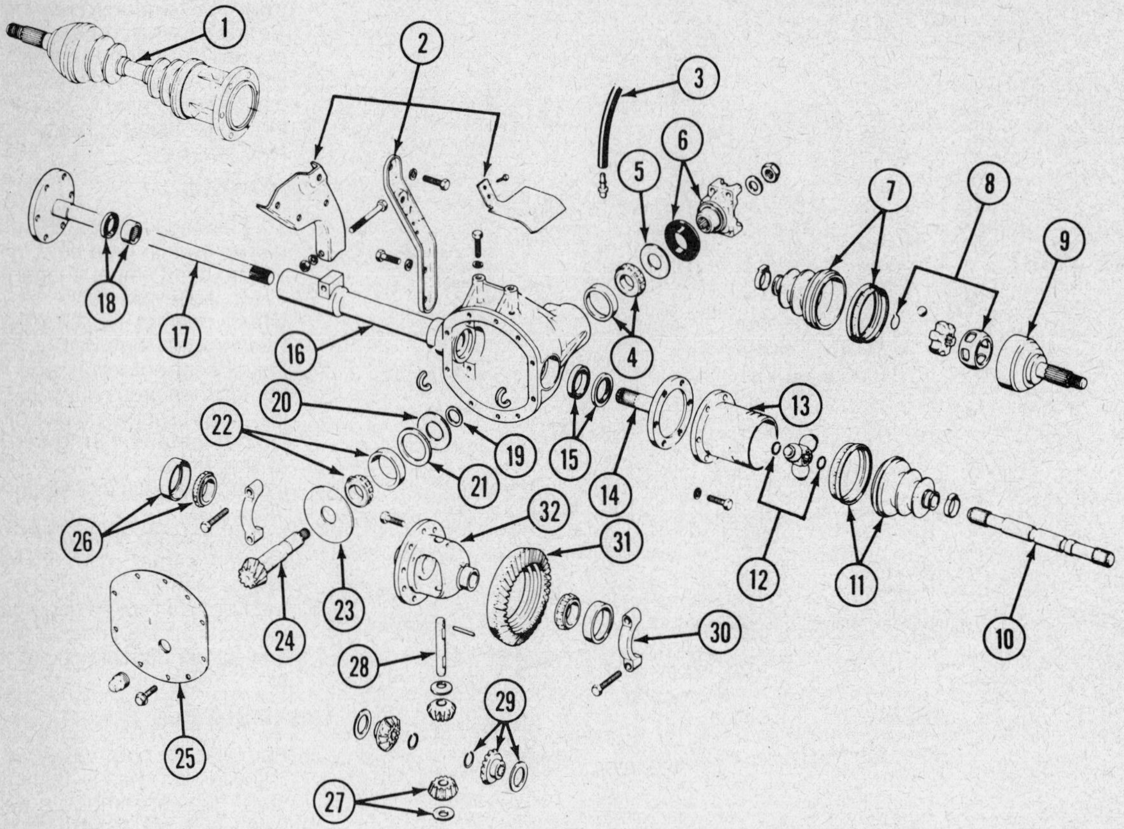

1. HALF-SHAFT ASSEMBLY
2. AXLE MOUNTING BRACKETS
3. VENT HOSE
4. PINION AND FRONT BEARING CUP
5. WASHER
6. YOKE AND SEAL
7. OUTER BOOT AND RETAINER
8. RZEPPA JOINT ASSEMBLY
9. SPINDLE
10. HALF-SHAFT
11. INNER BOOT AND RETAINER
12. TRI-POT JOINT ASSEMBLY
13. TRI-POT HOUSING
14. AXLE SHAFT (SHORT)
15. BALL BEARING AND SEAL
16. AXLE HOUSING
17. AXLE SHAFT (LONG)
18. NEEDLE BEARING AND SEAL
19. PRELOAD SHIM
20. WASHER
21. DEPTH SHIM
22. PINION REAR BEARING AND CUP
23. SLINGER
24. PINION GEAR
25. COVER
26. DIFFERENTIAL BEARING AND CUP
27. DIFFERENTIAL PINION AND THRUST WASHER
28. PINION MATE SHAFT
29. SIDE GEAR, THRUST WASHER AND LOCKRING
30. BEARING CAP
31. RING GEAR
32. DIFFERENTIAL CASE

Fig. 3 Front axle assembly. 1985–87 Eagle

1. Remove axle assembly. Refer to Axle, Removal for procedure.
2. Remove axle housing cover and drain lubricant.
3. Remove axle shaft retaining clip, then the axle shaft.
4. Remove axle shaft seal using suitable screwdriver.
5. Remove needle bearing using Tools J-29173 and J-2619-1. Remove ball bearing using suitable brass punch and hammer. **If needle bearing tools are not available, remove the differential, then the bearing using a 15/16 in. socket and three foot extension bar.**
6. Install axle shaft bearings. Use tool J-29153 to install needle bearing and tool J-29154 to install ball bearing.
7. Install axle shaft seals using Installer J-29152 for the righthand side axle shaft and Installer J-29154 for lefthand side axle shaft.
8. Install axle shafts, then the retaining clips.
9. Apply suitable sealant to axle housing cover and install cover. Torque cover bolts to 20 ft. lbs.
10. Fill axle with 2 1/2 pints of SAE 85W-90 lubricant, then install assembly onto vehicle. Refer to Axle, Installation for procedure.

HALF SHAFT SERVICE, 1984-87

Disassemble

1. Using a suitable tool cut and remove both outer boot clamps, then roll outer boot from constant velocity joint.
2. Position a wooden block against constant velocity joint inner race and drive joint from shaft. If half shaft is to be positioned in a vise, use protective vise jaws.
3. Using a brass drift, tap constant velocity joint cage until cage is tilted outward far enough to remove first ball, then remove remaining balls in the same manner.
4. Align two outer constant velocity joint oblong holes with slots located on interior wall of spindle housing and remove cage and inner race.
5. Align shoulder between race grooves with inside of oblong cage holes, then rotate inner race out of cage using the larger of the two openings.
6. Remove two snap rings from shaft, then remove outer boot.
7. Remove rubber retaining ring from small end of inner boot.
8. Cut inner boot retaining strap, then remove strap from tripod housing. Slide boot away from housing.
9. Remove tripod joint and shaft from housing.
10. Remove snap ring that retains tripod joint on shaft using suitable pliers, then remove tripod joint.
11. Remove inner boot from shaft if replacement is required.
12. Remove any remaining snap rings from shaft, if not removed previously.

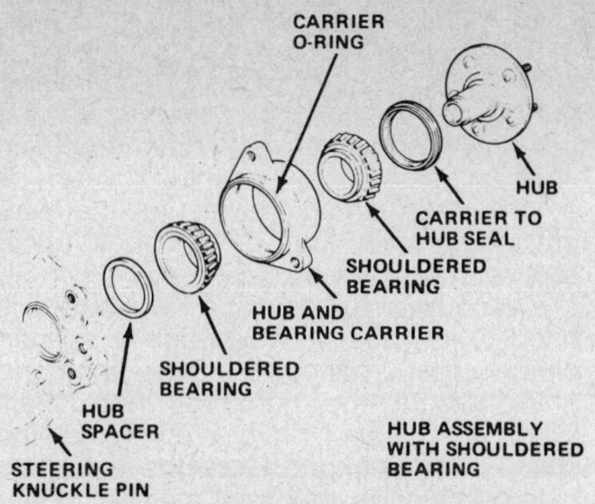

Fig. 4 Disassembled view of axle hub. Eagle

Inspection

Clean all components in a suitable solvent and dry with compressed air. Check all components for wear and damage and joints for rough operation, replace components as necessary. **Outer constant velocity joint and inner tripod joint are replaced as an assembly.**

Assemble

1. Pack spindle hub with chassis grease.
2. Install outer constant velocity joint inner into cage, then install cage and race assembly into spindle hub. The smaller diameter of the cage and stopping groove of race must face outward.
3. Using a brass drift, tilt cage outward until first ball can be installed into cage, then install remaining balls in the same manner.
4. Pack constant velocity joint with chassis grease, then install outer boot on half shaft.
5. Install inner and outer snap rings, then constant velocity joint onto shaft until inner race contacts inner snap ring.
6. Position boot over constant velocity joint, then install both boot clamps using tool No. J-22716 or equivalent. **Check and adjust installed length of boot. Total installed length should be 4.134 inch (105 mm). Move small end of boot in or out on shaft to obtain specified length.**
7. Pack tripod joint housing with chassis grease, then install inner small retainer ring, boot and large retainer ring onto half shaft.
8. Install tripod joint and snap ring onto shaft, then install tripod joint and shaft into housing.
9. Position boot and install rubber retainer ring over small end of boot.
10. Install large end boot clamp using a suitable tool.

INTERMEDIATE SHAFT, OUTER AXLE SHAFT & SHIFT HOUSING, REPLACE

Models w/Select Drive System

1. Raise and support front of vehicle.
2. Remove front axle assembly, then drain lubricant.
3. Remove bolts securing shift housing and remove shift fork, shifting housing and shift motor as an assembly.
4. Working through access hole in the outer axle shaft flange, remove screws securing axle tube cover.
5. Remove outer axle shaft assembly by tapping shaft flange with a rubber or plastic mallet.
6. Remove intermediate shaft snap ring, then remove intermediate shaft and shift collar.
7. Using a suitable puller and slide hammer, remove outer axle shaft bearing race.
8. Using adapter tool No. J-26225 and slide hammer J-6471-2, remove intermediate shaft needle bearing from axle tube end.
9. Using spreader tool No. J-29369-1 and slide hammer No. J-2619-01, remove intermediate shaft gear bearing.

   The intermediate shaft gear is retained on the axle shaft by an internal type expandable snap ring. When removing the bearing from the gear be sure to support the gear face on vise jaws to avoid pulling the gear off the shaft. The gear and shaft are serviced only as an assembly.
10. Remove outer axle shaft retaining E-ring.
11. Make a reference mark on outer axle shaft gear (for assembly purposes) and remove gear from shaft.
12. Remove outer axle shaft bearing using an arbor press.
13. Remove axle oil seal and tube cover.
14. Clean and carefully inspect all components for wear or damage. Replace all necessary components.
15. Install axle oil seal and tube cover on axle shaft.
16. Using an arbor press, install axle shaft bearing and race on shaft.
17. Install axle shaft gear on shaft using an arbor press. Be sure to align reference mark. Also ensure gear splines are facing outward.
18. Install axle shaft E-ring.
19. Using tool No. J-29153, install intermediate shaft needle bearing.
20. Install intermediate shaft gear needle bearing in gear bore using an arbor press.
21. Install intermediate shaft, then install shift collar, and seat shaft in differential.
22. Install intermediate shaft lock ring.
23. Install outer axle shaft assembly, torque axle tube cover bolts evenly and in a cross sequence. Torque bolts 144 inch pounds.
24. Install gasket on shift housing cover and install. **Check to ensure the shift fork and tabs are aligned in the shift collar.**
25. Torque shift housing cover bolts to 108 inch pounds.
26. Install axle cover using a new gasket. Torque bolts to 20 ft. lbs.
27. Fill shift housing with five ozs. of specified lubricant, then fill axle housing.

SELECT DRIVE SYSTEM

The Select Drive is a system which permits the full time four wheel drive power train to be operated in a two wheel drive mode. When the vehicle is stopped, the system can be changed from two wheel drive to four wheel or four wheel drive to two wheel drive, by pulling the instrument panel control switch pull release pin downward and moving the control switch lever to the desired position. The two major components of this system are a shifting device in the transfer case and a disconnecting mechanism in the front axle, which are controlled by the instrument panel switch through a series of vacuum actuators.

The vacuum actuated shifter mechanism located on the transfer case slides a splined clutch, located on the transfer case main shaft, rearward to engage or forward to disengage power to the front drive chain sprocket. In the two wheel drive position, the shifter mechanism also locks the transfer case differential. Also the main shaft and differential assembly will turn as a unit, transferring power to the rear driveshaft, while front output shaft, chain and sprocket remain stationary.

A vacuum actuated disconnect device is used to engage or disengage a splined clutch that connects the righthand driveshaft to the righthand half shaft. When four wheel drive is selected, the spline clutch is engaged and the front drive axle operates in a normal manner. When two wheel is selected, the vacuum actuator releases the spline clutch, which releases drive to the righthand half shaft and allows the righthand driveshaft to rotate freely. Due to the design of the differential, to equalize torque between left and right axle shafts, disconnecting the right axle shaft will allow the left axle shaft to rotate freely. The axle disconnect will not release all front drive components in the two wheel drive mode. Half shafts and different side gears will continue to rotate with the front wheels as the vehicle is driven.

AXLE SHIFT MOTOR, REPLACE

Models w/Select Drive System

1. Make a reference mark on fork and housing for assembly purposes.
2. Rotate shift motor and remove retaining snap rings using a suitable screwdriver.
3. Remove shift motor from housing and remove O-ring from motor.
4. Reverse procedure to install.

UNIVERSAL JOINTS

INDEX

Page No.

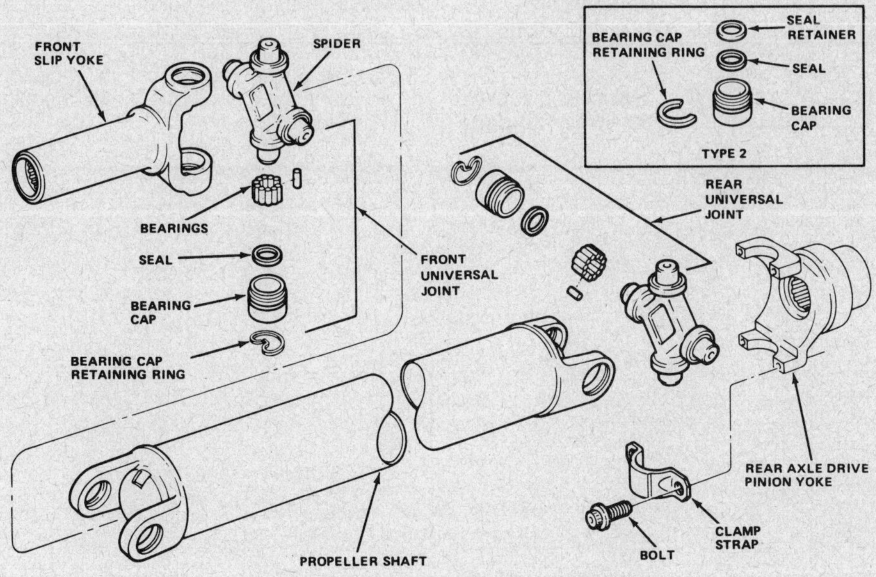

Fig. 1 Cross & roller universal joints (single Cardan type) & propeller shaft (Typical)

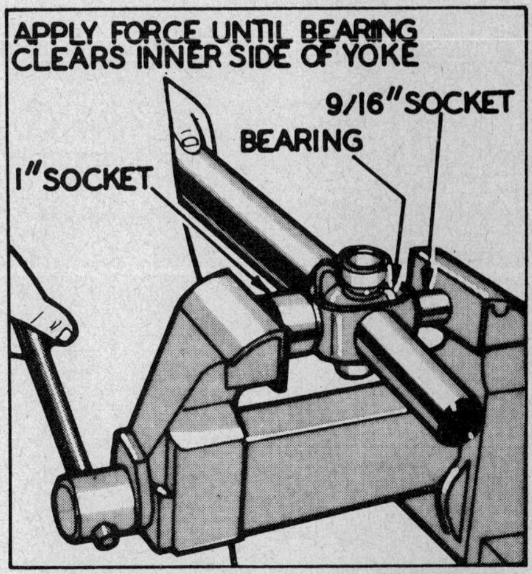

Fig. 2 Removing bearings from yoke using small & large wrench sockets as pusher & receiver tools, respectively

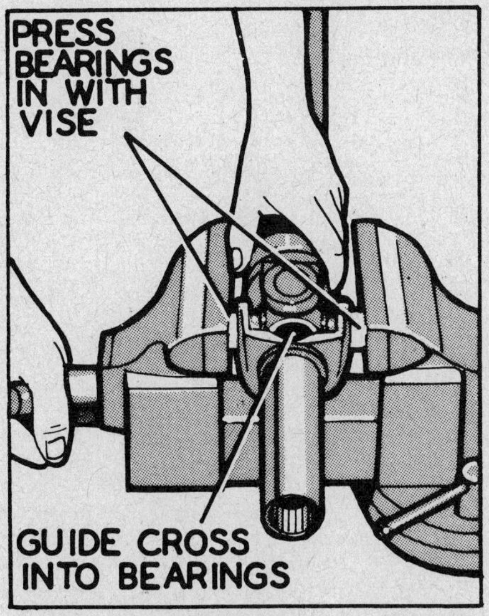

Fig. 3 Installing bearings into drive shaft yoke

SERVICE NOTES

Before disassembling any universal joint, examine the assembly vehicle fully and note the position of the grease fitting (if used). Also, be sure to mark the yokes with relation to the propeller shaft so they may be reassembled in the same relative position. Failure to observe these precautions may produce rough vehicle operation which results in rapid wear and failure of parts, and place an unbalanced load on transmission, engine and rear axle.

When universal joints are disassembled for lubrication or inspection, and the old parts are to be reinstalled, special vehicle must be exercised to avoid damage to universal joint spider or cross and bearing cups.

Some late model vehicles use an injected nylon retainer on the universal joint bearings. When service is necessary, pressing the bearings out will sheer the nylon retainer. Replacement with the conventional steel snap ring type is then necessary.

CROSS & ROLLER TYPE

Fig. 1 illustrates a typical example of a universal joint of this type. They all operate on the same principle and similar service and replacement procedures may be applied to all.

DISASSEMBLY

1. Remove snap rings (or retainer plates) that retain bearings in yoke and drive shaft.
2. Place U-joint in a vise.
3. Select a wrench socket with an outside diameter slightly smaller than the U-joint bearings. Select another wrench socket with an inside diameter slightly larger than the U-joint bearings.
4. Place the sockets at opposite bearings in the yoke so that the smaller socket becomes a bearing pusher and the larger socket becomes a bearing receiver when the vise jaws come together, **Fig. 2.** Close vise jaws until both bearings are free of yoke and remove bearings from the cross or spider.
5. If bearings will not come all the way out, close vise until bearing in receiver socket protrudes from yoke as much as possible without using excessive

Fig. 4 Some units have locating lugs which must face propeller shaft when installed

force. Then remove from vise and place that portion of bearing which protrudes from yoke between vise jaws. Tighten vise to hold bearing and drive yoke off with a soft hammer.

6. To remove opposite bearing from yoke, replace in vise with pusher socket on exposed cross journal with receiver socket over bearing cup. Then tighten vise jaws to press bearing back through yoke into receiving socket.
7. Remove yoke from drive shaft and again place protruding portion of bearing between vise jaws. Then tighten vise to hold bearing while driving yoke off bearing with soft hammer.
8. Turn spider or cross 1/4 turn and use the same procedure to press bearings out of drive shaft.

ASSEMBLY

1. If old parts are to be reassembled, pack bearing cups with universal joint grease. Do not fill cups completely or use excessive amounts as over-lubrication may damage seals during reassembly. Use new seals.
2. If new parts are being installed, check new bearings for adequate grease before assembling.
3. With the pusher (smaller) socket, press one bearing part way into drive shaft. Position spider into the partially installed bearing. Place second bearing into drive shaft. Fasten drive shaft in vise so that bearings are in contact with faces of vise jaws, **Fig. 3.** Some spiders are provided with locating lugs which must face toward drive shaft when installed, **Fig. 4.**
4. Press bearings all the way into position and install snap rings or retainer plates.
5. Install bearings in yoke in same manner. When installation is completed, check U-joint for binding or roughness. If free movement is impeded, correct the condition before installation in vehicle.

ELECTRONIC IGNITION SYSTEMS

TABLE OF CONTENTS

Distributor Specifications

*If unit is checked on vehicle, double the RPM and degrees to get crankshaft figures.

Distributor Part No. ①	Centrifugal Advance Degrees @ RPM of Distributor					Vacuum Advance	
	Advance Starts	Intermediate Advance			Full Advance	Inches of Vacuum to Start Plunger	Max. Adv. Dist. Deg. @ Vacuum
1982							
1103491	−½ to 0 @ 400	¼ to 2½ @ 800	2½ to 4¾ @ 1200	4¼ to 6¼ @ 1600	8 @ 2200	3½ to 5	9¾ @ 8¾
1103492	−½ to 0 @ 400	1 to 2½ @ 800	2½ to 5½ @ 1200	4¼ to 6¼ @ 1600	8 @ 2200	3 to 4½	10½ @ 7
1110598	−½ to 0 @ 400	⅛ to 2⅛ @ 800	2½ to 4½ @ 1200	4⅛ to 6⅛ @ 1600	8⅛ @ 2200	2¼ to 3¾	10½ @ 7
3241333	−1 to ¾ @ 600	—	—	—	7¼ @ 1050	2½ to 4¾	12½ @ 18
1983							
1103527	−½ to 0 @ 400	1 to 2½ @ 800	3 to 5 @ 1200	4½ to 6½ @ 1600	8 @ 2200	3 to 4½	10½ @ 7
1110598	−½ to 0 @ 400	⅛ to 2⅛ @ 800	2½ to 4½ @ 1200	4⅛ to 6⅛ @ 1600	8 @ 2050	2½ to 5	9¾ @ 8¾
3242409	−½ to ½ @ 400	2 to 4 @ 800	—	—	7 @ 2050	3 to 5	12½ @ 18
1984–87							
3242700	−½ to ½ @ 400	1 to 3 @ 1000	3¼ to 5⅛ @ 1300	7 to 9 @ 1600	12 @ 2400	2 to 4	10½ @ 14.5
3242409	−½ to ½ @ 400	0 to 2 @ 700	1½ to 4 @ 800	4½ to 7 @ 1000	7½ @ 2200	2½ to 6	12½ @ 18

①—Stamped on distributor housing plate.

GM High Energy Ignition (H.E.I.)

NOTE: 1982-83 models equipped with 4-151/2.5L engines use the GM HEI system. Refer to the "General Motors Section."

American Motors Solid State Ignition Systems

INDEX

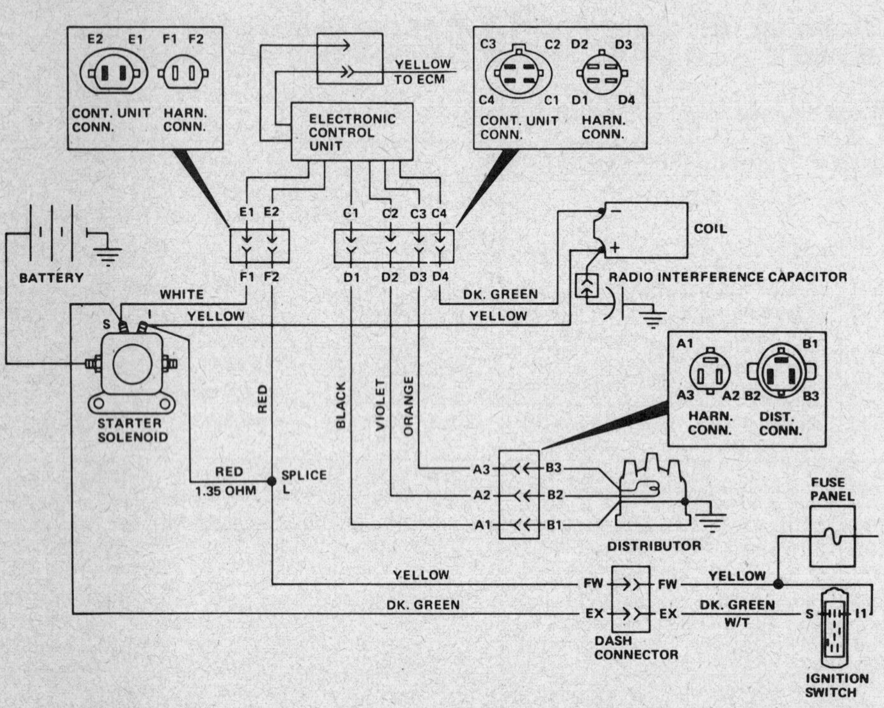

Fig. 1 Schematic view of American Motors solid state ignition system less electronic feedback system

DESCRIPTION

The solid state ignition system, **Figs. 1 and 2,** consists of the ignition switch, electronic ignition control unit, ignition coil, primary resistance wire and bypass, distributor, spark plugs and on some models with electronic feedback system, an electronic spark retard.

The electronic ignition control unit is a solid state, moisture resistant module. The component parts are sealed in a potting material to resist vibration and environmental conditions. The control unit is incorporated with reverse polarity protection and transient voltage protection.

The distributor incorporates a sensor and trigger wheel. Current flowing through the ignition coil creates a magnetic field in the primary windings. When the circuit is opened, the magnetic field collapses and induces a high voltage in the coil secondary windings. This circuit is electronically controlled by the electronic ignition control unit. The distributor sensor and trigger wheel provide the signal to operate the control unit. The trigger wheel is mounted on the distributor shaft and has one tooth for each cylinder. The sensor, a coil of fine wire mounted to a permanent magnet, develops an electromagnetic force that is sensitive to the presence of ferrous metal. The sensor detects the trigger wheel teeth as the teeth pass the sensor. When a trigger wheel tooth approaches the pole piece of the sensor, it reduces the reluctance of the magnetic field, increasing field strength. Field strength decreases as the tooth moves away from the pole piece. This increase and decrease of field strength generates an alternating current which is interpreted by the electronic ignition control unit. The control unit then opens and closes the ignition coil primary circuit.

Since there are no contacting surfaces and no wear occurs, dwell angle requires no adjustment. The dwell angle is electronically controlled by the electronic ignition control unit. When the coil circuit is switched open, an electronic timer in the control unit keeps the circuit open only long enough for the spark to discharge. Then, it automatically closes the ignition coil primary circuit.

TROUBLESHOOTING

SECONDARY CIRCUIT TEST

1. Disconnect coil wire from distributor cap and, using insulated pliers, hold wire approximately 1/2 inch from a good engine ground.
2. Crank engine and observe wire for spark. If no spark occurs, proceed to Step 5. If spark occurs, proceed to Step 3.
3. Reconnect coil wire to distributor cap. Remove wire from one spark plug. **Do not remove wires from spark plugs on cylinder No. 3 on 1984 four cylinder models or cylinders 1 and 5 on 1982-84 6 cylinder models. On eight cylinder models, do not remove spark plug wires from cylinders 3 and 4. Removing these wires during testing could result in sensor damage.**
4. Using insulated pliers, hold wire approximately 1/2 inch from a good engine ground. Crank engine and observe wire for spark. If spark occurs, check for fuel system problems or incorrect ignition timing. If no spark occurs, check for defective distributor cap, rotor or spark plug wires.
5. If no spark occurs at coil wire, measure coil wire resistance. If resistance is greater than 10,000 ohms, replace wire.
6. If malfunction still exists, proceed to the following tests or diagnosis procedures.

INTERMITTENT FAILURE DIAGNOSIS

Since intermittent failure may be caused by loose or corroded terminals, defective components, poor ground connections or defective wiring, it is necessary to check all wiring connections in the ignition system. Also, refer to **Fig. 3** for further diagnosis.

IGNITION COIL PRIMARY CIRCUIT TEST

1. Turn ignition switch "On" and connect a voltmeter between ignition coil positive terminal and the ground. If voltage is 5.5-6.5 volts, proceed to Step 2. If battery voltage is noted, proceed to

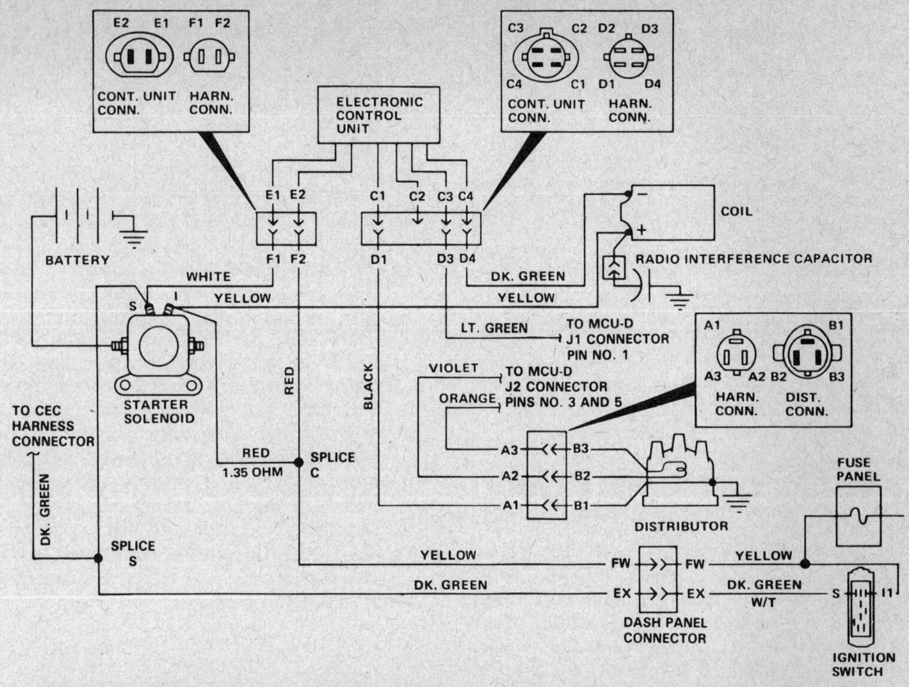

Fig. 2 Schematic view of American Motors solid state ignition system with electronic feedback system

Condition	Possible Cause	Correction
ENGINE FAILS TO START (NO SPARK AT PLUGS)	1. No voltage to ignition system.	1. Check battery, ignition switch and wiring. Repair as required.
	2. Electronic Control Unit ground lead inside distributor open, loose or corroded.	2. Clean, tighten or repair as required.
	3. Primary wiring connectors and fully engaged.	3. Clean and fully engage connectors.
	4. Coil open or shorted.	4. Test coil. Replace if faulty.
	5. Electronic Control Unit defective.	5. Replace Electronic Control Unit.
	6. Cracked distributor cap.	6. Replace cap.
	7. Defective rotor.	7. Replace rotor.
ENGINE BACKFIRES BUT FAILS TO START	1. Incorrect ignition timing.	1. Check timing. Adjust as required.
	2. Moisture in distributor.	2. Dry cap and rotor.
	3. Distributor cap faulty.	3. Check cap for loose terminals, cracks and dirt. Clean or replace as required.
	4. Ignition wire not in correct firing order.	4. Install in correct order.
ENGINE RUNS ONLY WITH KEY IN START POSITION	1. Open in resistance wire or excessive resistance.	1. Repair resistance wire.
ENGINE CONTINUES TO RUN WITH KEY OFF	1. Defective starter solenoid.	1. Replace solenoid.
	2. Defective ignition switch.	2. Replace switch.
ENGINE DOES NOT OPERATE SMOOTHLY AND/OR ENGINE MISFIRES AT HIGH SPEED	1. Spark plugs fouled or faulty.	1. Clean and gap plugs. Replace as required.
	2. Ignition cables faulty.	2. Check cables. Replace as required.
	3. Spark advance system(s) faulty.	3. Check operation. Repair as required.
	4. "I" terminal shorted to starter terminal in solenoid.	4. Replace solenoid.
	5. Trigger wheel pin missing.	5. Install pin.
	6. Distributor wires installed in wrong firing order.	6. Install wires correctly.
EXCESSIVE FUEL CONSUMPTION	1. Incorrect ignition timing.	1. Check timing. Adjust as required.
	2. Spark advance system(s) faulty.	2. Check operation. Repair as required.
ERRATIC TIMING ADVANCE	1. Faulty vacuum advance assembly.	1. Check operation. Replace if required.
	2. Centrifugal weights sticking.	2. Remove dirt, corrosion.
TIMING NOT AFFECTED BY VACUUM	1. Defective vacuum advance unit.	1. Replace vacuum advance unit.
	2. Advance unit adjusting screw too far counterclockwise.	2. Turn screw clockwise to bring advance curve within specifications.
	3. Sensor pivot corroded.	3. Clean pivot.
INTERMITTENT OPERATION	1. Loose or corroded terminals.	1. Clean and tighten terminals. Apply electrical grease.
	2. Defective sensor.	2. Perform sensor tests.
	3. Defective control unit.	3. Perform control unit tests.
	4. Loose ground connector in distributor.	4. Clean and tighten connection.
	5. Wires to distributor shorted together or to ground.	5. Check for frayed, pinched or burned wires.

Fig. 3 American Motors solid state ignition system service diagnosis chart

Step 4. If voltage is below 5.5 volts, disconnect condenser lead. If voltage is not 5.5-6.5 volts, replace condenser. If voltage is still not within specifications, proceed to Step 6.

2. Turn ignition switch to "Start" and measure voltage at coil positive terminal while cranking engine. If battery voltage is present while cranking engine, the ignition coil primary circuit is satisfactory. If voltage present is less than battery voltage, proceed to Step 3.
3. Check for shorted or open circuit in wire attached to starter "I" terminal. Check for defective starter solenoid. Repair as necessary.
4. Place ignition switch in "On" position, disconnect wire from starter solenoid "I" terminal and measure voltage at ignition coil positive terminal. If voltage drops to 5.5-6.5 volts, replace starter solenoid. If voltage remains constant at battery voltage, connect a jumper wire between ignition coil negative terminal and the ground. If voltage drops to 5.5-6.5 volts, proceed to Step 5. If not, repair defective resistance wire and repeat Step 2.
5. Check continuity between ignition coil negative terminal and terminal "D4", **Figs. 1 and 2.** Also, check continuity between terminal "D1" and the ground. If continuity is present, replace electronic ignition control unit. If continuity is not present, locate and repair open circuit.
6. Turn ignition switch "Off" and measure resistance between ignition coil positive terminal and the dash connector "13", **Figs. 1 and 2.** If resistance is greater than 1.40 ohms, repair or replace resistance wire. If resistance is 1.30-1.40 ohms, proceed to Step 7.
7. With ignition "Off", measure resistance between dash connector "13" and ignition switch terminal "I1", **Figs. 1 and 2.** If resistance is greater than .1 ohm, check and repair terminal connections at dash connector or defective wiring.

COIL TEST

1. Inspect ignition coil for oil leaks, exterior damage and carbon tracks. If satisfactory, proceed to Step 2. If not, replace ignition coil.
2. Disconnect ignition coil connector and connect ohmmeter between coil terminals. If resistance is 1.13-1.23 ohms at 75° F or 1.5 ohms at 200° F, proceed to Step 3. If not, replace ignition coil.
3. Connect ohmmeter between ignition coil center tower and the plus or minus terminal. Resistance should be 7700-9300 ohms. If not replace ignition coil.

SENSOR & CONTROL UNIT TEST

1. Disconnect the four wire connector at the control unit, **Figs. 1 and 2.** Disconnect coil wire from center tower of distributor and hold wire approximately 1/2 inch from a good engine ground with insulated pliers, then turn ignition "On." If spark is observed at coil wire, proceed to next step. If not, proceed to Step 5.
2. Measure resistance between terminals "D2" and "D3" of the harness connector, **Figs. 1 and 2.** If resistance is 400-800 ohms, proceed to Step 6. If not, proceed to next step.
3. Disconnect and connect the three wire connector at distributor and measure resistance between terminals "D2" and "D3" of the harness connector, **Figs. 1 and 2.** If resistance is now between 400-800 ohms, proceed to Step 6. If not, disconnect three wire connector at distributor and proceed to next step.
4. Measure resistance between terminals "B2" and "B3" of the distributor connector, **Figs. 1 and 2.** If resistance is not 400-800 ohms, repair or replace harness between three wire and

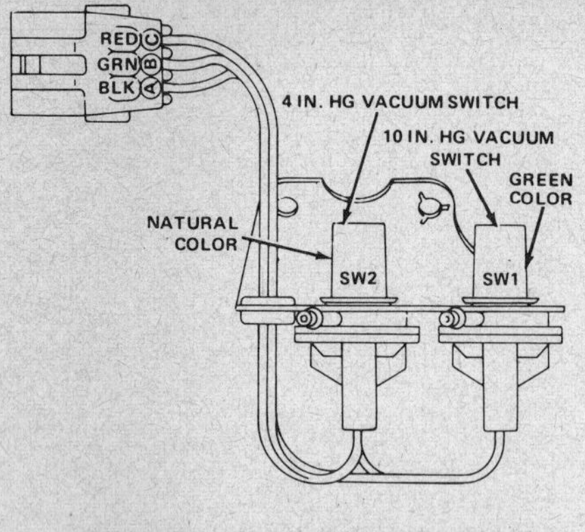

Fig. 4 Vacuum switch assembly

four wire connector.

5. Connect an ohmmeter between terminal "D1" of the harness connector, **Figs. 1 and 2,** and the battery negative terminal. If reading is below .002 ohm, repeat Step 2. If not, check for an improper ground. Check ground cable resistance, distributor to engine block resistance and distributor ground screw to terminal "D1" resistance, **Figs. 1 and 2.**
6. Using a voltmeter connected between terminals "D2" and "D3" of the harness connector, **Figs. 1 and 2,** observed reading while cranking engine. If voltmeter reading fluctuates, it indicates proper sensor and trigger wheel operation. If not, the trigger wheel is defective or the distributor is not rotating.

IGNITION FEED TO CONTROL UNIT TEST

Perform the "Ignition Coil Primary Circuit Test" before performing this test.

1. Disconnect two wire connector from control unit and connect a voltmeter between terminal "F2" and the ground, **Figs. 1 and 2.** Turn ignition "On." If voltmeter reading is within .2 volts of battery voltage, replace control unit and proceed to Step 3. If voltmeter reading is not within .2 volt of battery voltage, proceed to next step.
2. Locate and repair cause of voltage reduction as noted in Step 1. Check for a corroded dash connector or defective ignition switch. Then, check for spark at coil wire. If not, replace control unit.
3. Connect the two wire connector at control unit and disconnect the four wire connector from control unit. Connect an ammeter between terminal "C1" and the ground, **Figs. 1 and 2.** If ammeter reading is 1 ± .1 amp., the system is satisfactory. If ammeter reading is higher or lower, replace module.

CURRENT FLOW TEST

1. Remove connector from coil.
2. Depress plastic barb and remove positive wire from connector. Remove negative wire in same manner.
3. Connect an ammeter between coil positive terminal and the disconnected positive wire.
4. Connect a jumper wire between coil negative terminal and the engine ground.
5. Turn ignition "On" and note ammeter reading. Reading should be approximately 7 amps. and not exceeding 7.6 amps. If reading exceeds 7.6 amps., replace ignition coil.
6. Remove jumper wire from coil negative terminal and connect the coil green wire to negative terminal. Ammeter reading should be approximately 4 amps. If reading is less than 3.5 amps., check for poor connections at the three wire and four wire connectors or a poor ground at distributor ground screw. If reading is greater than 5 amps., the control unit is defective, requiring replacement.
7. Start and run engine. Ammeter reading should be 2-2.4 amps. If not, replace control unit.

ELECTRONIC SPARK RETARD TEST

This test only applies to models with electronic feedback system.

1. Allow engine to reach normal operating temperature.
2. Disconnect vacuum switch assembly wire connector, **Fig. 4.** Disconnect and plug distributor vacuum advance hose.
3. Disconnect knock sensor connector (located on intake manifold), then, using a suitable jumper, wire ground wire to engine block.
4. Increase engine speed to 1600 RPM, then, using a suitable timing light, check timing and compare to specifications. Adjust as necessary.
5. Allow engine to return to idle speed, then connect vacuum switch connector wire connector and increase engine speed to 1600 RPM while observing timing marks. Timing should advance 6° over results found in step 4. If timing did not advance, check for vacuum switch failure. If vacuum switch is satisfactory, check continuity of wiring with a suitable ohmmeter from knock sensor to Micro Computer Unit (MCU). If wiring is satisfactory, replace MCU unit and retest. If timing did advance, proceed to step 6.
6. Allow engine to return to idle speed, then connect knock sensor connector to knock sensor. Increase engine speed to 1600 RPM, then, while observing timing marks with a suitable timing light, knock on intake manifold near the knock sensor. Timing should retard. If timing did not retard, check for continuity of knock sensor harness connector to J2 pin 16 of MCU connector. If satisfactory, replace knock sensor and retest. If timing did retard, the electronic spark retard is operating satisfactory. Allow engine to return to idle speed and connect vacuum hose to distributor.

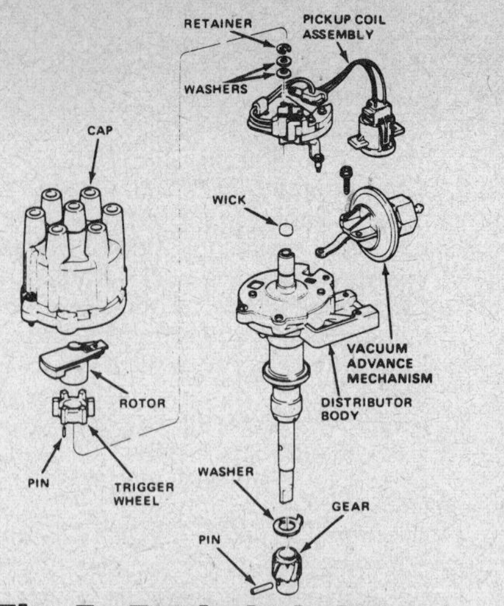

Fig. 5 Exploded view of American Motors distributor used with solid state ignition system

DISTRIBUTOR REPLACE

REMOVAL

1. Remove No. 1 spark plug and crank engine until compression pressure is felt. Slowly rotate engine in direction of normal rotation until timing mark on crankshaft pulley aligns with proper timing mark on timing plate. Remove distributor cap and ensure alignment of rotor and armature with index mark on top of magnetic pickup and mark on distributor housing.
2. Disconnect vacuum advance hose and distributor primary wiring.
3. Remove distributor hold-down bolt and clamp, then remove distributor.

INSTALLATION

1. Clean distributor mounting pad on engine and install a new distributor mounting gasket.
2. Ensure engine is still aligned with the proper timing marks. Align the rotor with the marks on the distributor housing and the armature with the mark on top of the magnetic pickup. It may be necessary to move the rotor slightly or rotate the oil pump shaft with a long, flat bladed screwdriver to mesh distributor gear with camshaft gear. The rotor should align with the housing mark when distributor is installed properly.
3. Install distributor hold-down clamp, bolt and lockwasher, but do not tighten bolt until ignition timing has been set. Connect vacuum line, primary wiring and install distributor cap. Adjust ignition timing to specifications. **If the engine was cranked after the distributor was removed from the engine, refer to step 1 of removal procedure to properly position crankshaft before installing distributor.**

DISTRIBUTOR SERVICE

TRIGGER WHEEL & SENSOR, REPLACE

1. Remove distributor cap and rotor, **Fig. 5.**
2. Remove trigger wheel with a suitable gear puller. Use a flat washer to prevent gear puller from contacting inner shaft. The trigger wheel may also be removed by using two screwdrivers to pry trigger wheel upward. Remove pin.
3. Remove sensor retainer and washers from pivot pin on base plate, then the retaining screws.
4. On all distributors, remove ground screw from harness tab.
5. Remove sensor assembly from distributor housing.
6. Reverse procedure to assemble.

VACUUM UNIT, REPLACE

1. Disconnect vacuum hose.
2. Remove vacuum unit attaching screws and the vacuum unit, **Fig. 5.** It is necessary to tilt the vacuum unit to disengage the link from the sensor pin and also loosen the base plate screws for clearance.
3. Reverse procedure to install. If a new vacuum unit is installed, it must be calibrated as follows:
   a. Insert an appropriate size Allen wrench into vacuum hose tube of original vacuum unit. Rotate Allen wrench clockwise and note the number of turns required to bottom the adjusting screw.
   b. Insert Allen wrench into vacuum hose tube of replacement vacuum unit. Turn the Allen wrench clockwise until the adjusting screw is bottomed, then rotate Allen wrench counterclockwise the number of turns noted in the previous step.

CARBURETOR SECTION

TABLE OF CONTENTS

Carter YFA Series Carburetor

INDEX

ADJUSTMENT SPECIFICATIONS

Year	Carburetor Model	Float Level	Initial Choke Valve Clearance	Choke Unloader Setting	Fast Idle Cam Setting	Choke Setting
1983	7452	.600	.200	.280	.175	①
	7453	.600	.280	.280	.175	①
	7454	.600	.200	.280	.175	①
	7455	.600	.280	.280	.175	①
1984	7700	.600	.240	.370	.175	①
	7701	.600	.240	.370	.175	①
	7702	.600	.240	.370	.175	①
	7703	.600	.240	.370	.175	①

①—Tamper resistant.

IDENTIFICATION LOCATION

This carburetor is identified by a code number and build date which is stamped on the identification tag. The identification tag is attached to the carburetor by one of the cover hold-down bolts.

DESCRIPTION

The YFA carburetor, **Fig. 1,** is a single barrel downdraft unit with feedback control. A Mixture Control (MC) solenoid is an integral part of the carburetor, and provides proper air/fuel ratios by controlling the amount of air mixed with the fuel during given operating conditions. The MC solenoid is controlled by a Micro Computer Unit (MCU), which monitors various engine operating conditions and generates signals to the solenoid to obtain fuel economy and performance.

ADJUSTMENTS

CURB IDLE ADJUSTMENT

1. Connect a calibrated, expanded scale tachometer to coil negative terminal.
2. Start engine and allow to reach normal operating temperature.
3. Turn hex head adjustment screw located at back of solenoid to adjust idle speed to specification.

FAST IDLE ADJUSTMENT

1. Start engine and allow to reach normal operating temperature.
2. Disconnect and plug EGR vacuum hose.
3. Connect calibrated, expanded scale tachometer to coil negative terminal.
4. Turn fast idle adjustment screw in contact with fast idle cam until engine speed is 1500 RPM.

FLOAT LEVEL ADJUSTMENT

Remove air horn and gasket, then invert air horn assembly. Check clearance from top of float to bottom edge of air horn with a float level gauge, **Fig. 2.** Position air horn

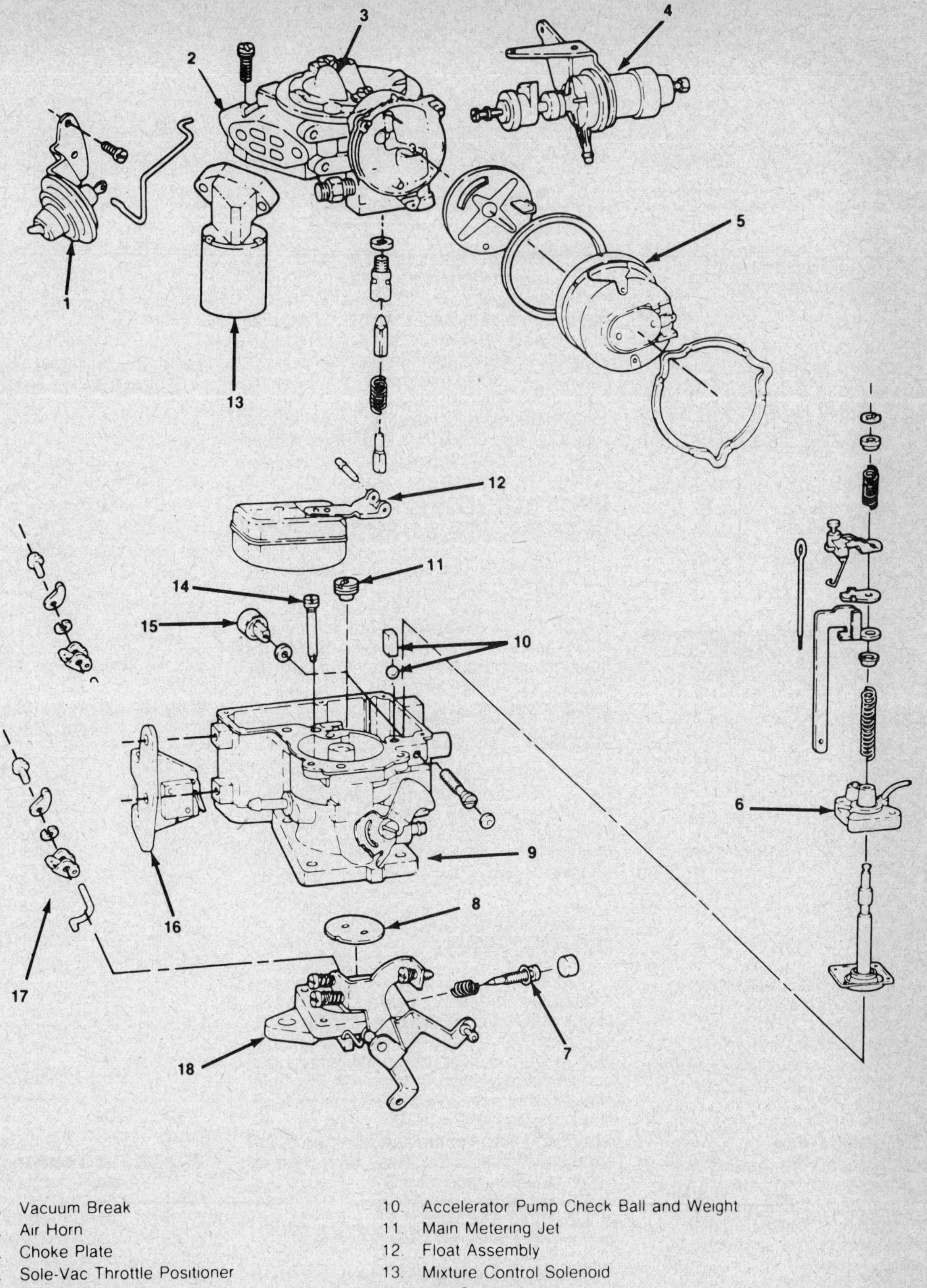

1. Vacuum Break
2. Air Horn
3. Choke Plate
4. Sole-Vac Throttle Positioner
5. Choke Assembly
6. Accelerator Pump Assembly
7. Idle Mixture Screw with O-ring
8. Throttle Plate
9. Main Body
10. Accelerator Pump Check Ball and Weight
11. Main Metering Jet
12. Float Assembly
13. Mixture Control Solenoid
14. Low Speed Jet
15. Accelerator Pump Vent Valve
16. Wide Open Throttle (WOT) Switch
17. Throttle Shaft and Lever
18. Throttle Body

Fig. 1 Carter YFA series carburetor

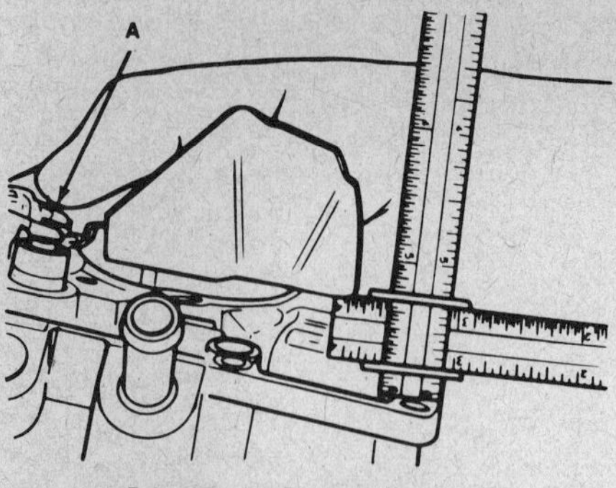

Fig. 2 Float level adjustment

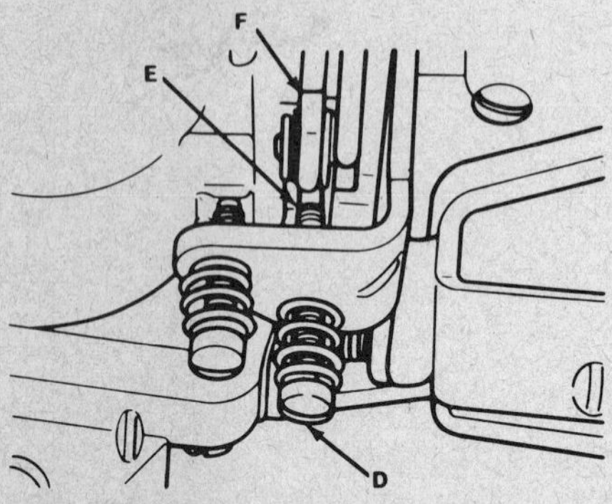

Fig. 5 Positioning fast idle adjusting screw

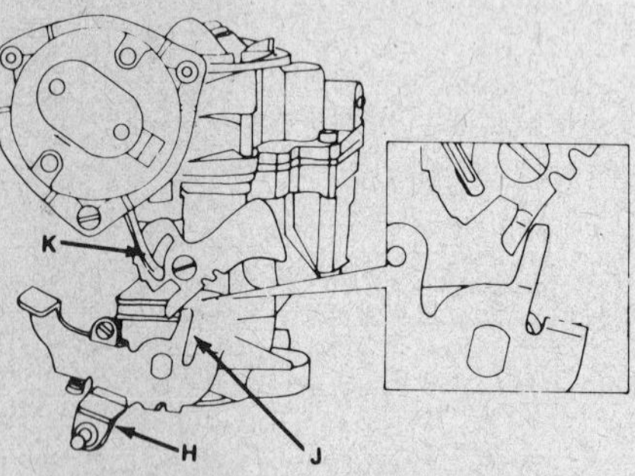

Fig. 7 Choke unloader adjustment

at eye level when measuring float level. The float arm (lever) should be resting on the needle pin when adjusting float level. Bend float arm, (A) **Fig. 2**, to adjust float level to specifications. Hold air horn upright, allowing float to hang freely, then measure maximum clearance from toe end of float to casting surface with air horn at eye level. Bend tab at end of float arm to obtain proper float drop specifications. Attach air horn and new gasket to main body.

METERING ROD ADJUSTMENT

Remove air horn and gasket from main body and ensure idle speed adjustmentscrew allows throttle plate to close tightly in throttle bore. Apply pressure to

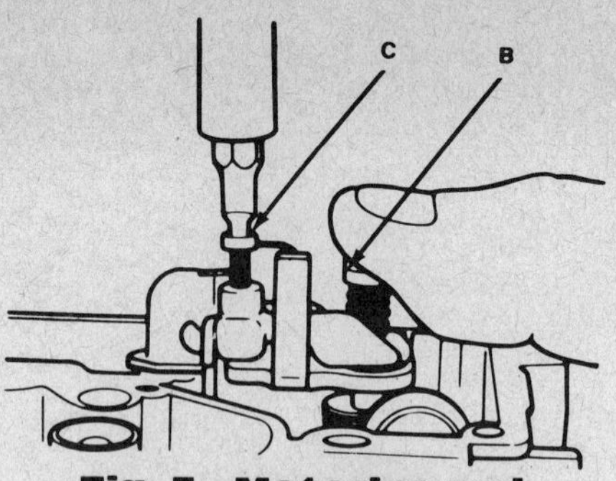

Fig. 3 Metering rod adjustment

top of pump diaphragm shaft until assembly bottoms, (B) **Fig. 3**, then adjust metering rod by turning adjusting screw counterclockwise until metering rod lightly bottoms in main metering jet, (C) **Fig. 3**. Turn metering rod adjusting screw clockwise one turn for final adjustment. Attach air horn and new gasket to main body, then adjust curb idle speed.

INITIAL CHOKE VALVE CLEARANCE ADJUSTMENT

Position fast idle adjustment screw on top step of fast idle cam, then seat the vacuum brake using an external vacuum source, **Fig. 4**. Measure distance between choke plate and air horn, then adjust by bending vacuum brake connector link, (6) **Fig. 4**, to specifications.

FAST IDLE CAM ADJUSTMENT

Position fast idle adjustment screw, (D) **Fig. 5**, on second step (E) of fast idle cam (F) and against the shoulder of high step. Bend fast idle cam link, (G) **Fig. 6**, to obtain specified clearance between lower edge of choke plate and carburetor air horn.

CHOKE UNLOADER ADJUSTMENT

Hold throttle, (H) **Fig. 7**, in wide open position, then measure clearance between choke valve and air horn wall while holding choke valve in position with a suitable plug gauge. Adjust to specifications by bending choke unloader tang (G), **Fig. 7**, in contact with fast idle cam (K). Ensure tang does not interfere with any other component. Bend tang toward fast idle cam to increase clearance, and away from cam to decrease clearance, **Fig. 8**.

SOL-VAC VACUUM ACTUATOR ADJUSTMENTS

Connect a tachometer to engine, then place automatic transmissions in Park, or manual transmissions in Neutral. Start engine and allow to reach normal operating temperature. Connect a suitable external vacuum source to the solenoid vacuum actuator, then apply 10-15 inches of vacu-

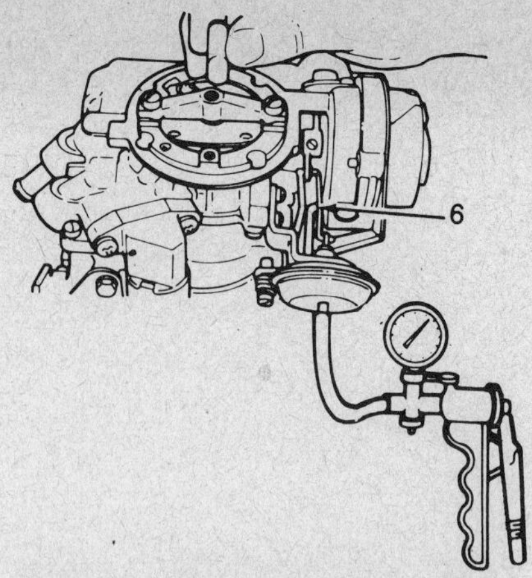

Fig. 4 Initial choke valve clearance adjustment

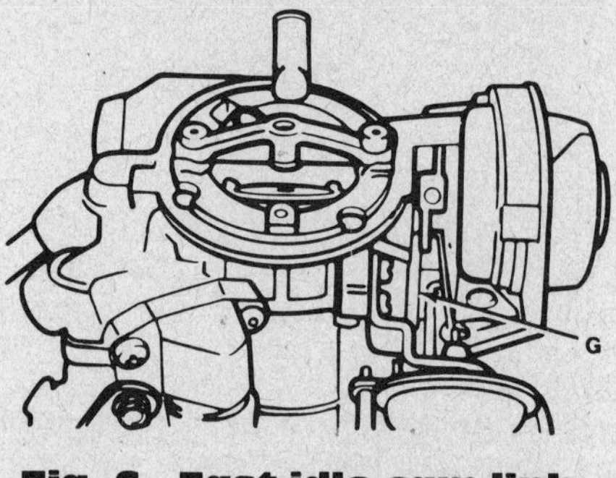

Fig. 6 Fast idle cam link location

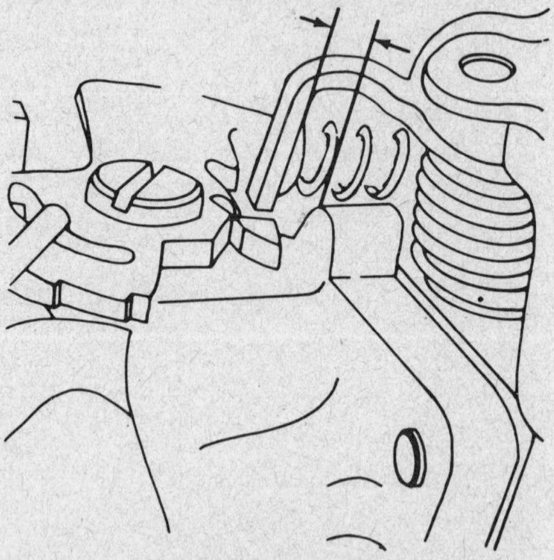

Fig. 8 Automatic choke adjustment

um. Adjust vacuum actuator until an engine speed of approximately 1,000 RPM is obtained. Stop engine and disconnect vacuum source from engine. Disconnect and plug vacuum actuator hose. Turn hexhead idle speed adjustment screw until an engine speed of approximately 500 RPM is obtained, then stop engine and disconnect tachometer. Connect vacuum actuator hose.

Carter BBD Series Carburetor

INDEX

ADJUSTMENT SPECIFICATIONS

Year	Carb. Model	Float Level	Pump Travel Inch	Bowl Vent Clearance	Choke Unloader Clearance	Initial Choke Valve Clearance	Vacuum Piston Gap	Fast Idle Cam Position Clearance	Automatic Choke Setting
1982	8338	1/4	.520	①	.280	.140	.035	.095	②
	8339	1/4	.520	①	.280	.140	.035	.095	②
1983	8360	1/4	.520	①	.280	.140	.035	.095	②
	8362	1/4	.520	①	.280	.140	.035	.095	②
	8364	1/4	.520	①	.280	.140	.035	.095	②
	8367	1/4	.520	①	.280	.140	.035	.095	②
1984-87	8383	1/4	.520	①	.280	.140	.035	.095	1 Rich
	8384	1/4	.520	①	.280	.140	.035	.095	1 Rich

①—Bowl vent should begin to open with fast idle cam on second step of cam.
②—Gold index key, 0; red index key, 1NR; green index key, 2NR.

IDENTIFICATION LOCATION

This carburetor is identified by a code number and build date which is stamped on the identification tag. The identification tag is attached to the carburetor by one of the cover hold-down bolts.

DESCRIPTION

The Carter model BBD 2 barrel carburetor incorporates three lightweight aluminum assemblies, the air horn, main body and throttle body, **Fig. 1.**

The air horn contains the choke valve assembly, mechanical linkage for accelerator pump and the metering rods and bowl vent mechanism.

The main body contains the fuel bowl, accelerator pump, vacuum piston and metering rod assembly, venturi assembly and solenoid, if equipped.

The throttle body contains throttle valves and levers, choke housing, choke vacuum diaphragm and idle mixture screws.

The carburetor used is a feedback type whose stepper motor has two tapered metering pins. Each metering pin is moved in and out of the carburetor to achieve the proper air/fuel ratio.

ADJUSTMENTS

CURB IDLE ADJUSTMENT

1. Disconnect and plug vacuum line at Sol-Vac actuator and disconnect wiring harness connector to holding solenoid.
2. Adjust slow idle speed to specifications by turning throttle stop screw.
3. Apply direct vacuum to Sol-Vac actuator, using a suitable vacuum pump. Adjust idle speed to 850 to 950 RPM on models with manual transmission and 750 to 850 RPM on models with automatic transmission, by turning screw on throttle lever when plunger is fully extended.
4. Disconnect vacuum source from actuator and place A/C control in on position, if so equipped.
5. Apply battery voltage to terminal on holding solenoid, using a jumper wire. **Throttle must be opened momentarily, by hand, to allow plunger to fully extend.**
6. Idle speed should be 750 to 850 RPM on models with manual transmission and 600 to 700 on models with automatic transmission. If not, adjust by turning hex screw on Sol-Vac actuator.
7. Disconnect jumper wire and reconnect wiring harness connector to holding solenoid. Reconnect original vacuum hose to Sol-Vac actuator.

FAST IDLE ADJUSTMENT

Adjust fast idle speed with engine at normal operating temperature and EGR valve hose (if equipped) disconnected. Position fast idle adjusting screw in contact with second step and against shoulder of top step of fast idle cam. Adjust to specifications by turning fast idle adjustment screw.

FLOAT LEVEL ADJUSTMENT

With carburetor body inverted so that weight of floats is forcing needle against its seat, use a T-scale or other suitable tool, and check the float level from surface of fuel bowl to crown of each float at center, **Fig. 2.** If an adjustment is necessary, hold floats on bottom of bowl and bend float lip as required to give the specified dimension. **When bending the float lip, do not allow the lip to push against the needle as the synthetic rubber tip (if used) can be compressed sufficiently to cause a false setting which will affect correct level of fuel in bowl. After being compressed, the tip is very slow to recover its original shape.**

ACCELERATOR PUMP

1. Back off curb idle adjusting screw, completely closing throttle valve, then open choke valve, allowing throttle valves to seat in bores. Ensure accel-

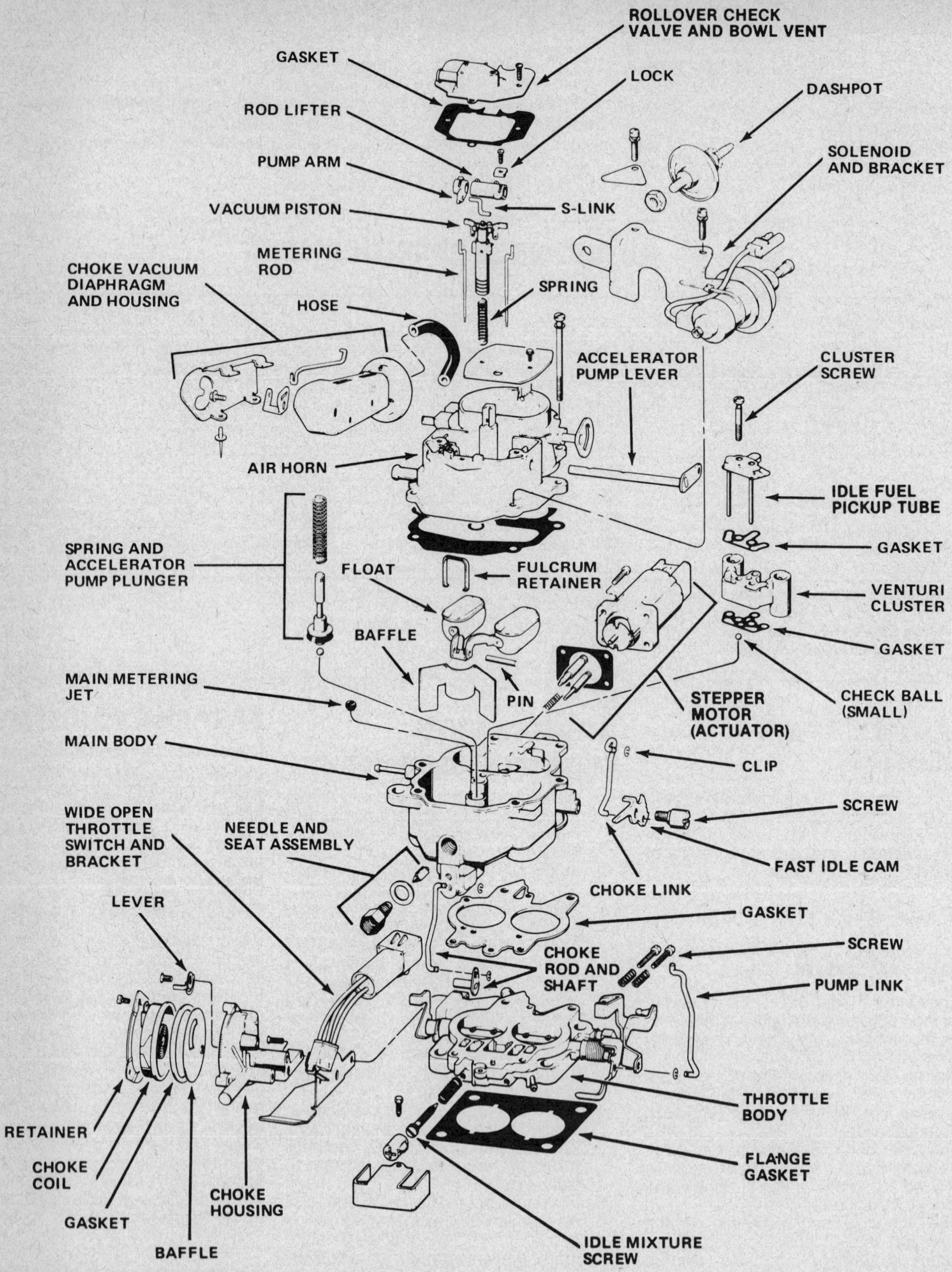

Fig. 1 Carter BBD carburetor

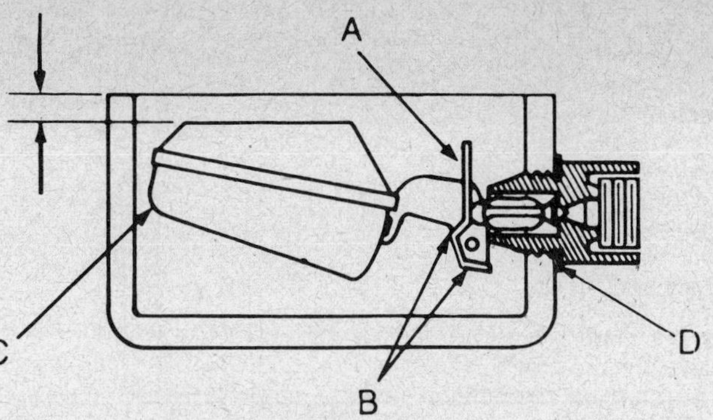

Fig. 2 Float level adjustment

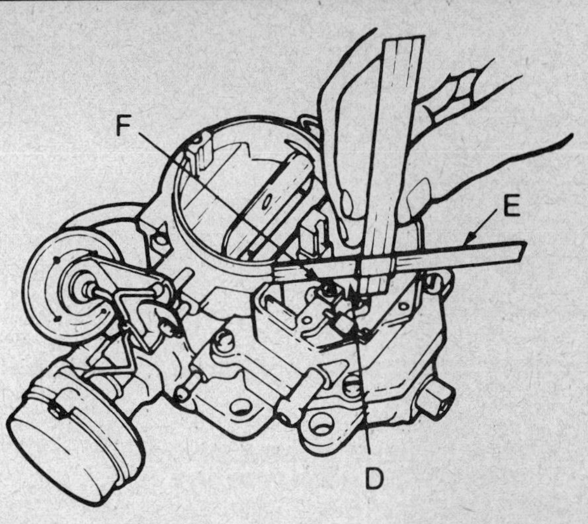

Fig. 3 Accelerator pump adjustment

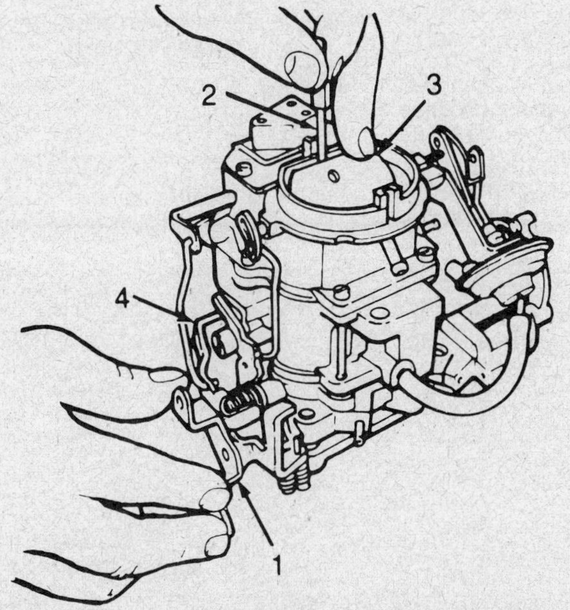

Fig. 4 Choke unloader adjustment

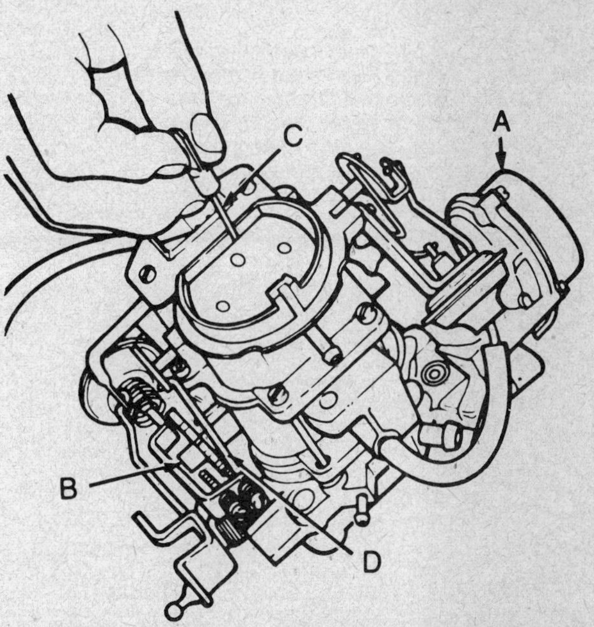

Fig. 5 Fast idle cam position adjustment

erator pump "S" link is located in outer hole or pump arm.

2. Turn curb idle adjusting screw until screw contacts stop, then rotate screw two additional turns.
3. Measure distance between air horn surface and top of accelerator pump shaft, (D) **Fig. 3.** Refer to BBD Specifications Chart.
4. Adjust by loosening pump arm adjusting screw, (F) **Fig. 3,** and rotating sleeve until proper dimension is obtained. Tighten adjusting screw.

CHOKE UNLOADER ADJUSTMENT

The choke unloader is a mechanical device to partially open the choke valve at wide open throttle. It is used to eliminate choke enrichment during engine cranking. Engines that have been flooded or stalled by excessive choke enrichment can be cleared by the use of the unloader. Adjust as follows:

1. Hold throttle valve in wide open position, (1) **Fig. 4.** Insert the specified drill (2) size between upper edge of choke valve and inner wall of air horn (3).
2. With a finger lightly pressing against choke valve, a slight drag should be felt as the drill is being withdrawn.
3. If an adjustment is necessary, bend unloader tang, (4) **Fig. 4,** on throttle lever until specified opening has been obtained, **Fig. 2.**

FAST IDLE CAM POSITION

1. With fast idle adjusting screw contacting second highest step on fast idle cam, move choke valve toward closed position with light pressure on choke shaft lever, **Fig. 3.**
2. Insert the specified size drill between choke valve and air horn wall, (C) **Fig. 5.** An adjustment will be necessary if a slight drag is not obtained as drill is being removed.
3. Adjust by bending fast idle connector rod, (D) **Fig. 5,** at lower angle.

INITIAL CHOKE VALVE CLEARANCE

1. Fully seat choke diaphragm by applying a minimum of 19 inches of mercury from an external vacuum source, (2) **Fig. 6.**
2. Open throttle valve slightly to place fast idle screw on high step of cam.
3. Apply light closing pressure to choke lever or rotate choke coil housing to apply closing pressure to choke, (1) **Fig. 6.**
4. Measure clearance between upper edge of choke plate and air horn wall, (3) **Fig. 6.** To adjust, bend diaphragm connector link, (4) **Fig. 4.**

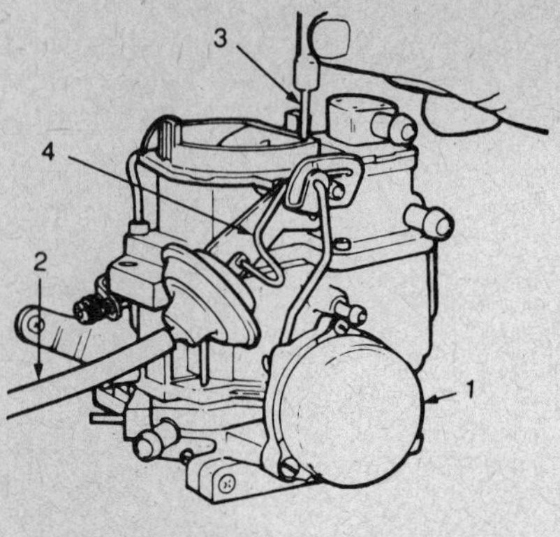

Fig. 6 Initial choke valve clearance adjustment

VACUUM PISTON GAP ADJUSTMENT

1. Adjust vacuum piston gap to specifications. Rotate Allen head screws on top of piston to adjust gap, **Fig. 7.**
2. Install vacuum piston assembly into air horn bore, ensuring metering rods are positioned in the metering jets.
3. Back off curb idle screw until throttle valves are completely closed. Count number of turns so that screw can be returned to its original setting.
4. Fully depress piston and, while applying moderate pressure on rod lifter, tighten rod lifter screw, **Fig. 8.**
5. Release piston and rod lifter and reset curb idle screw.

BOWL VENT VALVE

This adjustment is not precise and is only necessary to ensure that the mechanical fuel bowl vent is open at idle and closed at greater throttle openings.

1. Remove rollover check valve from air horn to provide access to metering rod area.
2. Open throttle and place fast idle speed screw on high step of cam.
3. Move cam manually until fast idle speed screw drops into second step of fast idle cam. Observe the bowl vent which should just begin to open at this time.
4. If valve is not closed on high, fourth or third steps of cam, bend valve tab, (A) **Fig. 9,** until it is closed.
5. If valve does not begin to open with fast idle speed screw on second step of cam, bend tab until it is just off its seat.

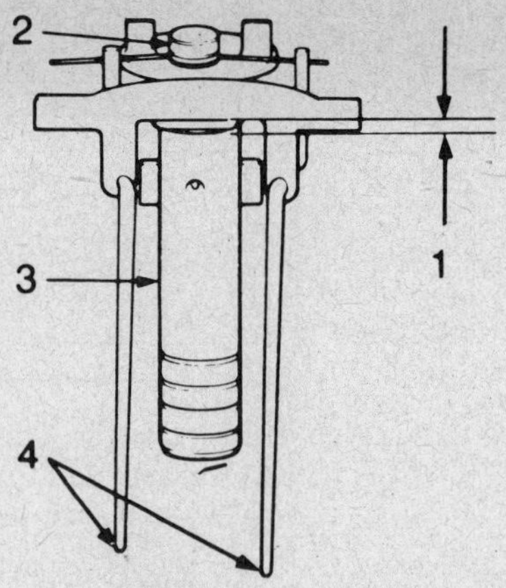

1 - Gap
2 - Adjustment Screw
3 - Vacuum Piston
4 - Metering Rods

Fig. 7 Vacuum piston gap adjustment

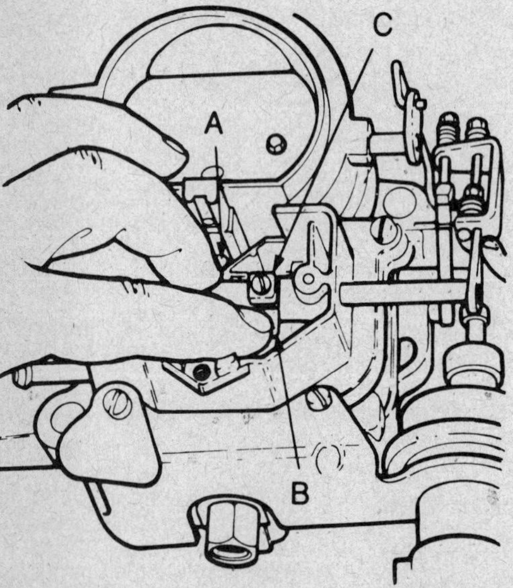

Fig. 8 Vacuum piston adjustment

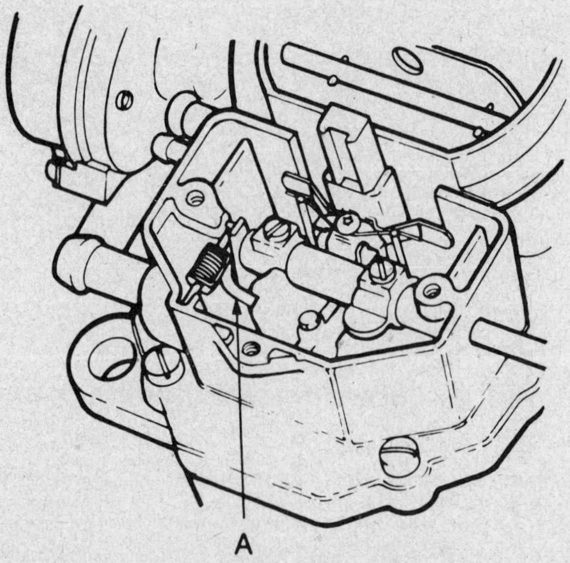

Fig. 9 Fuel bowl vent adjustment

GM Delco/Rochester Model 2SE & E2SE Varajet

INDEX

ADJUSTMENT SPECIFICATIONS

Year	Carb. Production No.	Float Level	Accel. Pump	Choke Coil Lever	Primary Vacuum Break	Air Valve Rod	Choke Setting	Unloader	Secondary Lockout
1982	17082380	.125	.128	.085	21°	2°	②	34°	.050-.080
	17082383	.256	.128	.085	21°	2°	②	34°	.050-.080
	17082385	.256	.128	.085	21°	2°	②	34°	.050-.080
	17082386	.125	.128	.050-.080	19°	2°	②	34°	.050-.080
	17082387	.125	.128	.085	19°	2°	②	34°	.050-.080
	17082388	.125	.128	.085	19°	2°	②	34°	.050-.080
	17082389	.125	.128	.085	19°	2°	②	34°	.050-.080
1983	17082380	①	.128	.085	21°	2°	②	34°	.050-.080
	17083384	.138	.128	.085	19°	2°	②	34°	.050-.080
	17083385	.138	.128	.085	19°	2°	②	34°	.050-.080

①—Man. trans., .216; auto. trans., .138.
②—Tamper resistant.

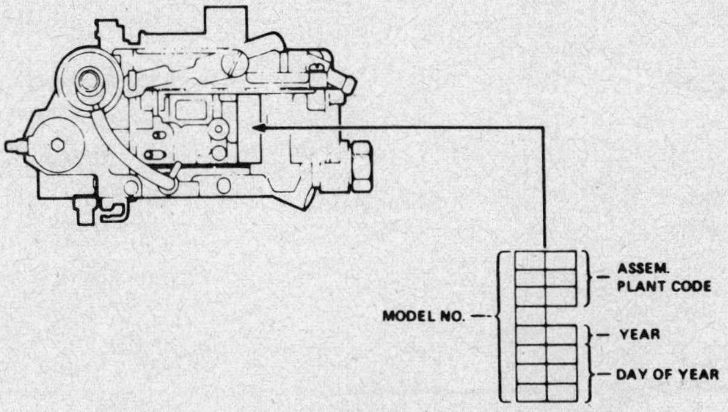

Fig. 1 Identification location

IDENTIFICATION LOCATION

The carburetor model identification is stamped vertically on the float bowl in a flat area adjacent to the vacuum tube, **Fig. 1.** When replacing float bowl, follow manufacturer's instructions included in service kit and ensure that identification number is transferred to new float bowl.

DESCRIPTION

The Varajet models 2SE and E2SE, **Fig. 2,** are two barrel, two stage, downdraft design carburetors. Aluminum die castings are used for the air horn, float bowl and throttle body. A heat insulator gasket is used between the throttle body and float bowl to reduce heat transfer to the float bowl.

The primary stage has a triple venturi, with a small 35 mm bore, resulting in good fuel metering control during idle and part throttle operation. The secondary stage has a 46 mm bore, providing sufficient air capacity for engine power requirements. An air valve is used in the secondary stage with a single tapered metering rod.

The float chamber is internally vented through a vertical vent cavity in the air horn. The float chamber is also externally vented through a tube in the air horn. A hose connects this tube directly to a vacuum operated vapor vent valve located in the vapor canister. When the engine is not running, the canister vapor vent valve is open, allowing fuel vapor from the float chamber to pass into the canister where the vapor is stored until normally purged.

An adjustable part throttle screw is used in the float bowl to aid emission control. This screw is factory pre-set and a plug is installed to prevent further adjustment or fuel leakage. The plug should not be removed or the screw setting disturbed. If float bowl replacement is required, the service float bowl will include a factory pre-set and plugged adjustable part throttle screw.

A hot idle compensator is used on some models and is located in the air horn. The opening and closing of the hot idle compensator valve is controlled by a bi-metal strip that is calibrated to a specific temperature. When the valve opens, additional air is allowed to bypass the throttle valves and enter the intake manifold to prevent rough idle during periods of hot engine operation.

The idle mixture screw is recessed in the throttle body and is sealed with a hardened steel plug to prevent alteration of the factory pre-set mixture setting. The plug should not be removed and the mixture screw readjusted unless required by

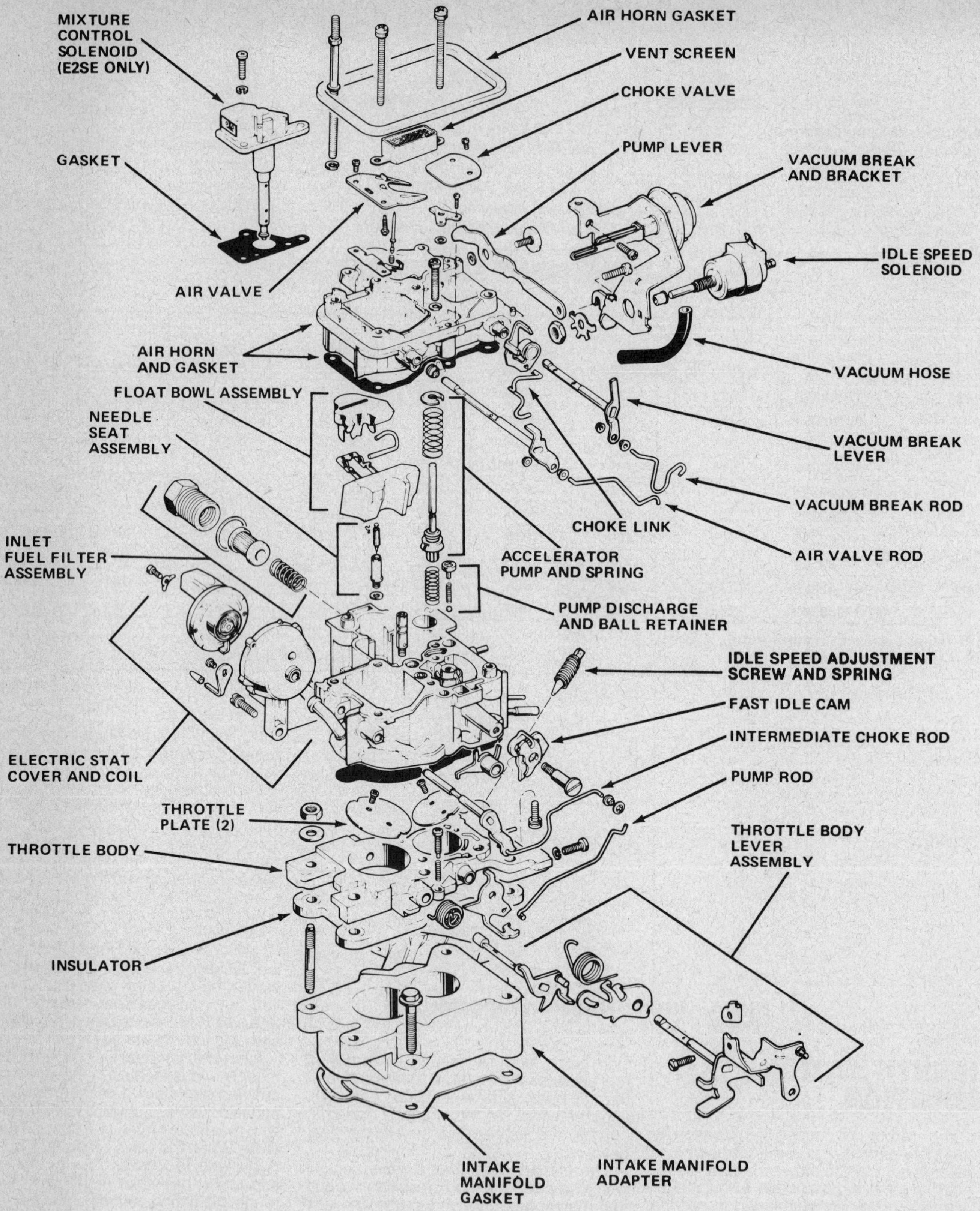
MIXTURE CONTROL SOLENOID (E2SE ONLY)
AIR HORN GASKET
VENT SCREEN
CHOKE VALVE
PUMP LEVER
VACUUM BREAK AND BRACKET
GASKET
IDLE SPEED SOLENOID
AIR VALVE
AIR HORN AND GASKET
VACUUM HOSE
FLOAT BOWL ASSEMBLY
NEEDLE SEAT ASSEMBLY
VACUUM BREAK LEVER
VACUUM BREAK ROD
CHOKE LINK
INLET FUEL FILTER ASSEMBLY
ACCELERATOR PUMP AND SPRING
AIR VALVE ROD
PUMP DISCHARGE AND BALL RETAINER
IDLE SPEED ADJUSTMENT SCREW AND SPRING
FAST IDLE CAM
INTERMEDIATE CHOKE ROD
ELECTRIC STAT COVER AND COIL
PUMP ROD
THROTTLE PLATE (2)
THROTTLE BODY
THROTTLE BODY LEVER ASSEMBLY
INSULATOR
INTAKE MANIFOLD GASKET
INTAKE MANIFOLD ADAPTER

Fig. 2 Carburetor exploded view

major carburetor overhaul or throttle body replacement.

The E2SE carburetor, includes special design features. An electrically operated mixture control solenoid mounted in the air horn, controls air and fuel metered to the idle and main metering systems of the carburetor. The plunger located at the end of the solenoid is submerged in fuel in the fuel chamber of the float bowl. This plunger is controlled by an electrical signal from the Electronic Control Module (ECM). The Electronic Control Module responding to signals from the oxygen sensor in the exhaust and other engine operating condition signals, energizes the solenoid to move the plunger down to the lean position or de-energizes the solenoid to move the plunger up to the rich position to control fuel delivery to the idle and main metering systems. When the plunger is in the lean position, fuel metering is controlled by a lean mixture screw located in the float bowl. When the plunger is in the rich position, the additional fuel is metered to the main fuel well through a rich mixture screw located at the end of the fuel supply channel in the float bowl. Air metered to the idle system is controlled by the up and down movement of the mixture control solenoid plunger. The plunger increases or decreases air supplied to the idle system which is further metered by the idle air bleed screw. The plunger cycles up and down approximately 10 times per second, controlling air and fuel mixtures.

Use care not to remove the special friction reducing coating applied to the primary and secondary throttle shafts, the secondary actuating lever and lockout lever.

ON-VEHICLE ADJUSTMENTS

CURB IDLE SPEED ADJUSTMENT

ROCHESTER 2SE

Apply parking brake and block drive wheels. Place manual transmission in neutral; automatic in drive. Do not accelerate engine.

1. Remove air cleaner and plug associated vacuum hoses. Disconnect and plug purge hose at canister and deceleration valve supply hose.
2. If equipped with A/C, adjust "solenoid off" idle speed to specifications by turning throttle stop screw on carburetor.
   a. Place A/C control in On position and momentarily open throttle to allow solenoid to fully extend.
   b. Adjust "solenoid on" idle speed to specifications by turning solenoid adjusting screw, then place A/C control in Off position.
3. If not equipped with A/C, adjust curb idle to specifications by turning solenoid adjusting screw.
   a. Disconnect wiring harness connector to solenoid and adjust low idle speed by turning throttle stop screw on carburetor.
   b. Reconnect solenoid wire.

Fig. 3 Diagnostic connector. 4-151

4. Place automatic transmission selector in park (manual transmission in neutral) and disconnect vacuum line at EGR valve.
5. With fast idle adjusting screw in highest step of fast idle cam, adjust fast idle to specifications.
6. Reconnect vacuum lines and install air cleaner.

FAST IDLE SPEED ADJUSTMENT

ROCHESTER 2SE

1. Position fast idle adjusting screw on highest step of fast idle cam.
2. Disconnect and plug EGR valve and vacuum hose, then start engine.
3. Turn adjusting screw in or out as required to obtain specified fast idle speed.

ROCHESTER E2SE

1982–83

1. Remove air cleaner and plug associated vacuum hoses. Disconnect and plug purge hose at canister and deceleration valve supply hose.
2. Connect positive lead of dwell meter to terminal 6 on diagnostic connector and connect negative lead of meter to terminal 13 on connector, **Fig. 3.**
3. With meter on 6 cylinder scale, meter pointer should oscillate covering a maximum spread of 15° within the 10°-50° range. If not, engine is not warmed up sufficiently or a problem exists in Mixture Feedback System.
4. On models equipped with A/C:
   a. Adjust "solenoid off" idle speed to specifications by turning throttle stop screw.
   b. Place A/C control in on position and open throttle momentarily to allow solenoid to fully extend.
   c. Adjust "solenoid on" idle speed to specifications by turning solenoid adjusting screw, then place A/C in off position.
5. On models without A/C:
   a. Adjust curb idle speed to specifications by turning solenoid adjusting screw.
   b. Disconnect wiring harness connector to solenoid and adjust low idle speed to specifications by turning throttle stop screw.
   c. Reconnect solenoid wire.
6. Place automatic transmission selector in park (manual transmission in neutral) and disconnect vacuum hose at EGR valve.
7. With fast idle adjusting screw on highest step of fast idle cam, adjust fast idle to specifications.
8. Reconnect all vacuum hoses and replace air cleaner.

FLOAT LEVEL ADJUSTMENT

1. Hold float retainer firmly in place and push float lightly against needle, **Fig. 4.**
2. With an adjustable T-scale, measure distance between float bowl gasket surface (gasket removed) and float toe.
3. To adjust, remove float and bend float arm. **On some 1983 units, a float stabilizing spring is used. Use care when removing this spring.**
4. Check float alignment after adjustment.

PUMP ADJUSTMENT

The pump adjustment should not be altered from the specified setting.

1. With throttle valves in wide open position and fast idle screw off fast idle cam step, measure distance from air horn casting to top of pump stem. Refer to Specifications Chart.
2. To make adjustment, remove pump lever retaining screw and lever by rotating from pump rod. Do not twist or bend lever sideways.
3. Secure lever in a soft-jawed vise and bend end of lever as necessary, then install pump lever and retaining screw.
4. Measure distance between air horn casting and top of pump stem and tighten retaining screw if correct.
5. Open and close throttle valves several times to ensure free movement of linkage and proper alignment of pump lever.

CHOKE COIL LEVER ADJUSTMENT

1. Loosen choke cover retaining screws, then the cover and coil assembly from choke housing, **Fig. 5.** If a riveted choke cover is used, remove choke cover and coil assembly as outlined in the choke cover retainer kit. **On 1982-83 units with riveted choke cover, the cover should not be removed unless a major overhaul is being performed on the carburetor or the choke coil is damaged.**
2. Place fast idle screw on high step of cam.
3. Push the intermediate choke lever until the choke valve closes.
4. Insert specified gauge into hole provided in choke housing. The edge of the lever should just contact gauge.
5. To adjust, bend intermediate choke rod.

CHOKE ROD ADJUSTMENT

The choke coil lever and fast idle adjustments must be made before performing this adjustment.

1. Rotate degree scale until zero is opposite pointer, then with choke valve completely closed, place magnet on top of choke valve and rotate bubble until centered, **Fig. 6.**
2. Rotate scale so specified degree for adjustment is opposite pointer.
3. Place fast idle screw on second step of cam against shoulder of high step.
4. Close choke by pushing intermediate choke lever. **On 1983 units, attach rubber band to intermediate choke lever to hold choke valve closed.**
5. Push vacuum break lever toward open choke position until lever contacts rear tang on choke lever.
6. To adjust, bend fast idle cam rod until bubble is centered.

AIR VALVE ROD ADJUSTMENT

1982–83 Units (Angle Gauge Method)

1. Rotate gauge scale until pointer is opposite zero, **Fig. 7.**
2. With air valve completely closed, place magnet on top of air valve and rotate bubble until centered.
3. Rotate scale so that specified degree for adjustment is opposite pointer.
4. Seat vacuum diaphragm using an external vacuum source.
5. Rotate air valve toward the open position by applying light pressure to the air valve shaft.
6. To adjust, bend air valve rod until bubble is centered.

PRIMARY VACUUM BREAK ADJUSTMENT

1982 E2SE Units

Before performing adjustment procedure, remove primary vacuum break from carburetor and position bracket in vise, then grind off adjusting screw cap and reinstall vacuum break.

1. Rotate degree scale until zero is opposite pointer, then with choke valve completely closed and fast idle screw on high step of fast idle cam, place magnet squarely on top of choke valve and rotate bubble until it is centered, **Fig. 8.**
2. Rotate scale so that specified degree for adjustment is opposite pointer.
3. Seat choke vacuum diaphragm using a vacuum source with over 5 inches Hg of vacuum. Check to ensure that air valve rod is not restricting the vacuum diaphragm from being seated. It may be necessary to bend air valve rod to obtain a slight clearance between rod and end of slot in air valve lever. If the air valve rod adjustment is disturbed, refer to the Air Valve Rod Adjustment procedure after completing the primary vacuum break adjustment.
4. Hold choke valve toward the closed position by lightly pushing on intermediate lever and note angle gauge reading.
5. If adjustment is necessary, use a 1/8 inch hex wrench to rotate adjusting

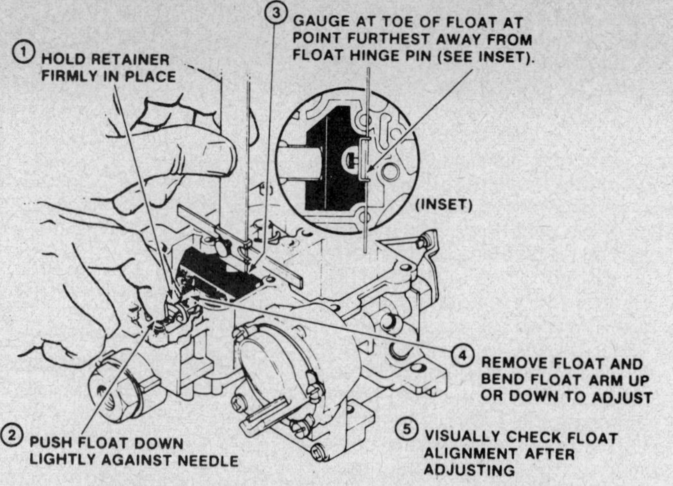

Fig. 4 Float level adjustment

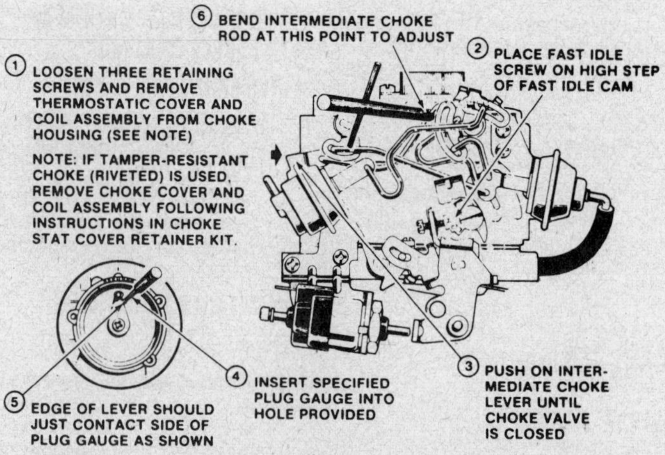

Fig. 5 Choke coil lever adjustment (Typical)

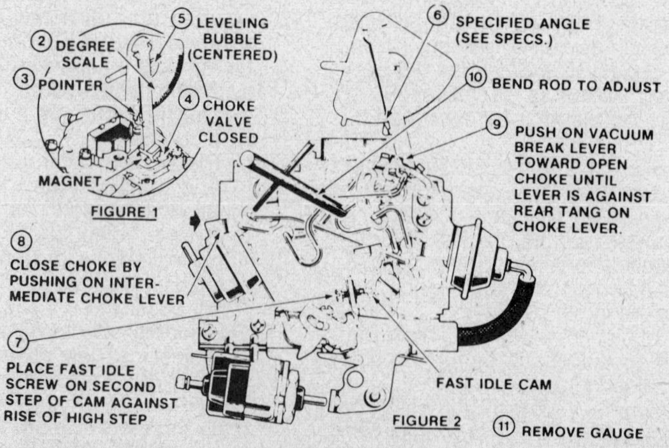

Fig. 6 Choke rod adjustment 1982 units. (Typical)

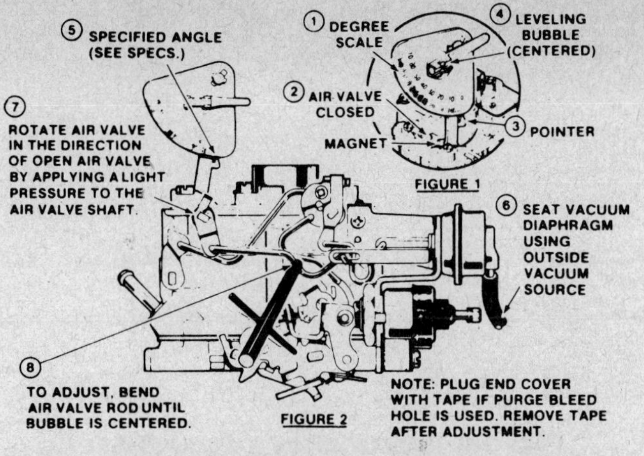

Fig. 7 Air valve rod adjustment (Angle Gauge Method). 1982 units

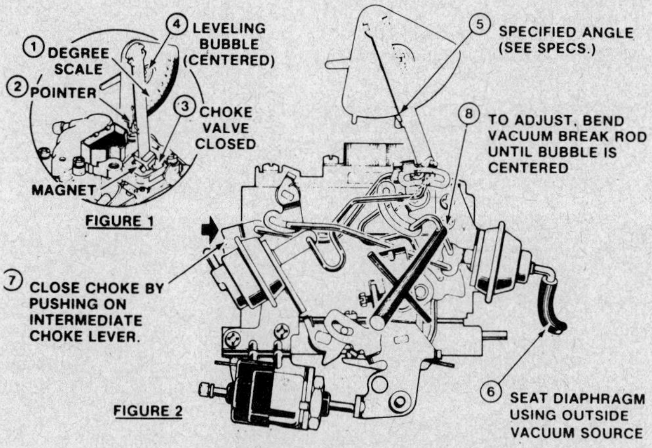

Fig. 8 Primary vacuum break adjustment (Typical). 1982 E2SE units

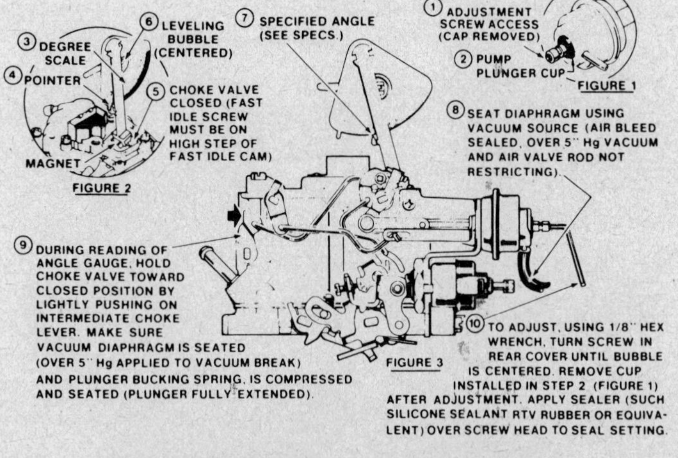

Fig. 9 Primary vacuum break adjustment. 1983 units

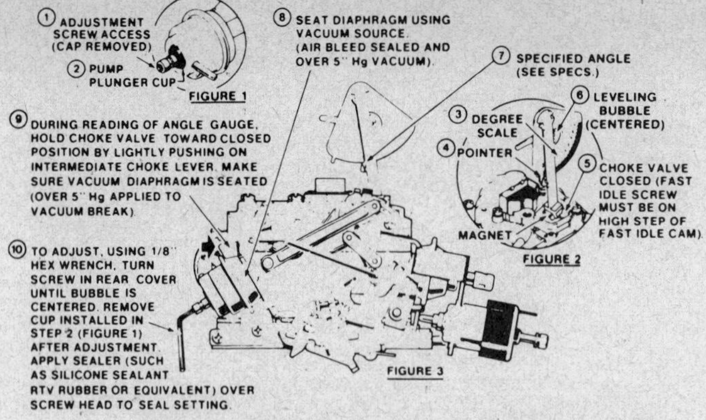

Fig. 10 Secondary vacuum break adjustment (Typical). 1982 units

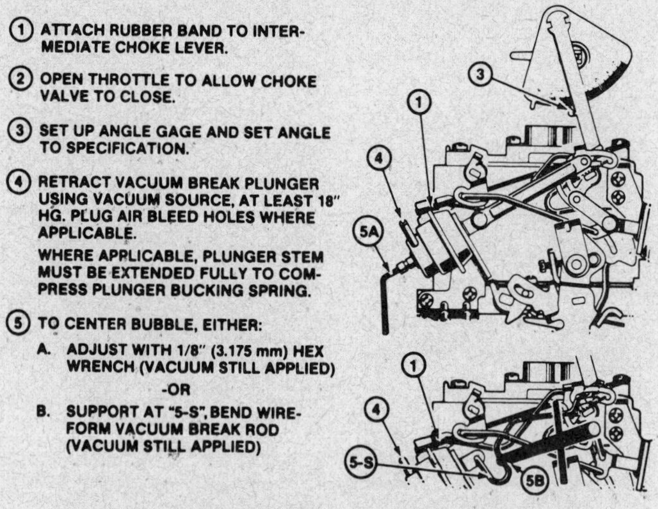

① ATTACH RUBBER BAND TO INTERMEDIATE CHOKE LEVER.
② OPEN THROTTLE TO ALLOW CHOKE VALVE TO CLOSE.
③ SET UP ANGLE GAGE AND SET ANGLE TO SPECIFICATION.
④ RETRACT VACUUM BREAK PLUNGER USING VACUUM SOURCE, AT LEAST 18" HG. PLUG AIR BLEED HOLES WHERE APPLICABLE.
WHERE APPLICABLE, PLUNGER STEM MUST BE EXTENDED FULLY TO COMPRESS PLUNGER BUCKING SPRING.
⑤ TO CENTER BUBBLE, EITHER:
A. ADJUST WITH 1/8" (3.175 mm) HEX WRENCH (VACUUM STILL APPLIED)
-OR
B. SUPPORT AT "5-S", BEND WIRE-FORM VACUUM BREAK ROD (VACUUM STILL APPLIED)
5A
5-S
5B

Fig. 11 Secondary vacuum break adjustment. 1983 units

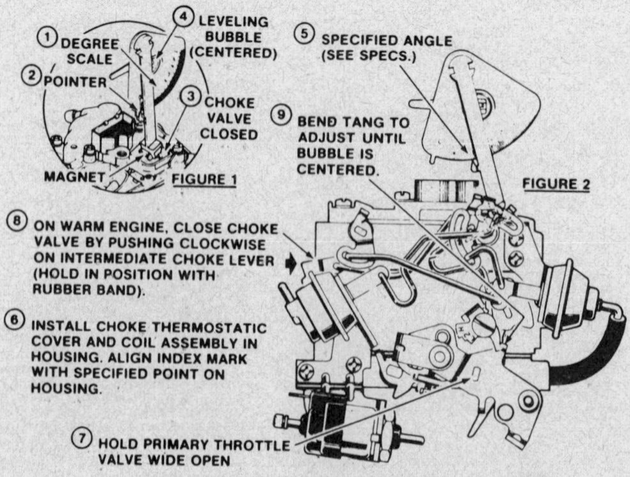

Fig. 12 Unloader adjustment (Typical)

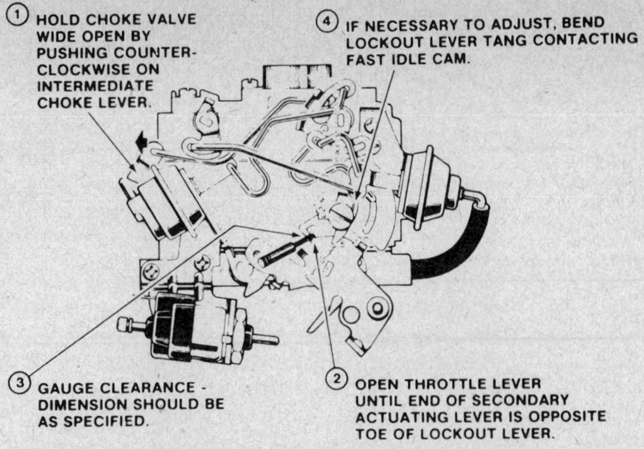
① HOLD CHOKE VALVE WIDE OPEN BY PUSHING COUNTER-CLOCKWISE ON INTERMEDIATE CHOKE LEVER.
④ IF NECESSARY TO ADJUST, BEND LOCKOUT LEVER TANG CONTACTING FAST IDLE CAM.
③ GAUGE CLEARANCE - DIMENSION SHOULD BE AS SPECIFIED.
② OPEN THROTTLE LEVER UNTIL END OF SECONDARY ACTUATING LEVER IS OPPOSITE TOE OF LOCKOUT LEVER.

Fig. 13 Secondary lockout adjustment

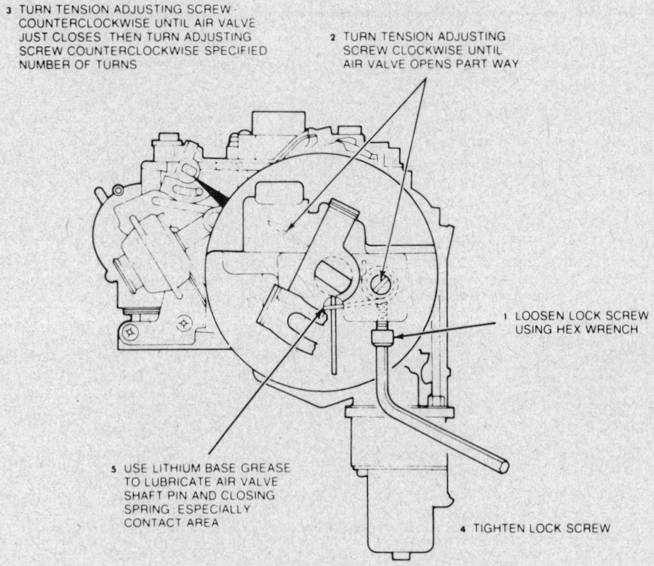
3 TURN TENSION ADJUSTING SCREW COUNTERCLOCKWISE UNTIL AIR VALVE JUST CLOSES THEN TURN ADJUSTING SCREW COUNTERCLOCKWISE SPECIFIED NUMBER OF TURNS
2 TURN TENSION ADJUSTING SCREW CLOCKWISE UNTIL AIR VALVE OPENS PART WAY
1 LOOSEN LOCK SCREW USING HEX WRENCH
5 USE LITHIUM BASE GREASE TO LUBRICATE AIR VALVE SHAFT PIN AND CLOSING SPRING ESPECIALLY CONTACT AREA
4 TIGHTEN LOCK SCREW

Fig. 14 Air valve spring adjustment. 1982–83 E2SE models

screw in rear cover until bubble is centered.
6. After completing adjustment, apply a suitable sealer over adjusting screw head.

1983 Units

1. Attach rubber band to intermediate choke shaft to hold choke valve closed, **Fig. 9.**
2. Install angle gauge and set angle to specifications. Refer to Specifications Chart.
3. Using outside vacuum source, retract vacuum break plunger with a minimum of 15 inches Hg of vacuum.
4. Ensure that air valve rod does not restrict plunger from full retraction. If necessary, bend rod as shown to permit full plunger travel.
5. Make adjustment with vacuum still applied, by rotating adjusting screw with a 1/8 inch Allen wrench, or bending rod as shown until bubble is centered.

SECONDARY VACUUM BREAK ADJUSTMENT

1982 Units

Before performing adjustment procedure, remove secondary vacuum break from carburetor and position bracket in a vise, then grind off adjusting screw cap and reinstall vacuum break. Plug vacuum break end cover using an accelerator pump plunger cup or equivalent. After completing adjustment remove pump plunger cup.

1. Rotate degree scale so that zero is opposite pointer, then with choke valve completely closed and fast idle screw on high step of fast idle cam, place magnet on top of choke valve and rotate until bubble is centered, **Fig. 10.**
2. Rotate scale so that specified degree for adjustment is opposite pointer.
3. Seat choke diaphragm using a vacuum source with over 5 inches Hg of vacuum.
4. Hold choke valve toward the closed position by lightly pushing on intermediate choke lever and note angle gauge reading. When noting reading check to ensure that vacuum diaphragm is seated.
5. Rotate adjusting screw in rear cover until bubble is centered. After completing adjustment, apply a suitable sealer over adjusting screw head. **Remove pump plunger cup from end cover before applying sealer over adjusting screw head.**

1983 Units

1. Attach rubber band to intermediate choke lever to hold choke valve closed. **Fig. 11.**
2. Install angle gauge and set angle to specifications. Refer to Specifications Chart.
3. Using outside vacuum source, retract vacuum break plunger with a mini-

mum of 15 inches Hg of vacuum, then plug air bleed holes if applicable.
4. Make final adjustment with vacuum still applied, by rotating adjusting screw with a 1/8 inch Allen wrench, or bending rod as shown until bubble is centered.

UNLOADER ADJUSTMENT

1. Rotate degree scale until zero is opposite pointer, then with choke valve completely closed, place magnet on top of choke valve and rotate bubble until centered, **Fig. 12.**
2. Rotate degree scale so specified degree for adjustment is opposite pointer.
3. With choke setting properly adjusted, hold primary throttle valve wide open.
4. On warm engines and 1983 units, close choke valve by pushing on intermediate choke lever and hold in position with a rubber band.
5. To adjust, bend tang on throttle lever until bubble is centered.

SECONDARY LOCKOUT ADJUSTMENT

1. Hold choke valve wide open by pulling on intermediate choke lever, **Fig. 13.**
2. Position throttle lever until end of secondary actuating lever is opposite toe of lockout lever. **On 1983 units, it may be necessary to remove the intermediate choke rod to gain access to the lock screw.**
3. Turn adjusting screw counterclockwise.
4. Insert specified gauge between throttle lever and secondary lockout lever toe.
5. To adjust, bend lockout lever tang contacting fast idle cam.

AIR VALVE SPRING ADJUSTMENT

1982–83 E2SE Units

1. Loosen lock screw, then turn adjusting screw clockwise until air valve is partially open, **Fig. 14.**
2. Turn adjusting screw counterclockwise until air valve just closes, then turn screw an additional turn counterclockwise and tighten lock screw. **On 1983 units with part No. 17083650, rotate the screw 1/2 turn only.**
3. Lubricate air valve shaft pin and closing spring with lithium base grease.

EMISSION CONTROL SYSTEMS

INDEX

AIR GUARD SYSTEM

This system, **Figs. 1 and 2** reduces the level of unburned hydrocarbons (HC) and carbon monoxide (CO) emissions by injecting secondary air from an air pump into the exhaust manifolds.

This system consists of a belt driven air pump which injects compressed air through the connecting hoses to a steel distribution manifold and into the stainless steel injection tubes in the exhaust port next to each exhaust valve. This air mixes with the hot and incompletely burned exhaust gases to permit further combustion in the exhaust ports and exhaust manifolds.

The air pump is a positive displacement unit that requires no maintenance, **Figs. 3 and 4.** The early units incorporated a replaceable element type air filter and pressure relief valve. Later units incorporate only a replaceable centrifugal type air filter. The pressure relief valve on early units is located in the exhaust cavity and encloses a preloaded spring, a seat and pressure setting plug.

The air delivery manifold distributes the air from the pump to each of the air delivery tubes in a uniform manner. A check valve which is an integral part of the air delivery manifold prevents the reverse flow of exhaust gases into the pump should the pump fail or the exhaust gas pressures exceed pump output.

The stainless steel air injection tubes are inserted into the machined bosses of the exhaust manifold. These tubes project into the exhaust port and direct the air into the vicinity of the exhaust valve seat.

The bypass valve, used on some engines, is in the normally closed position to allow pump air to flow freely through the valve fittings and into the exhaust manifold. When the throttle is closed quickly and engine manifold vacuum rises, the sudden increase in vacuum (sensed through a vacuum connection at the carburetor base) overcomes the diaphragm spring tension and momentarily moves the valve to the open position. When the valve is in the open position, pump air flow is bypassed to atmosphere or "dumped"

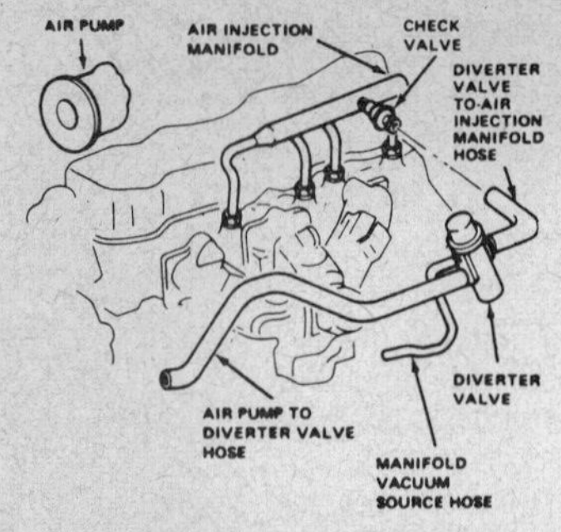

Fig. 1 Air Guard system. 4-151 engine

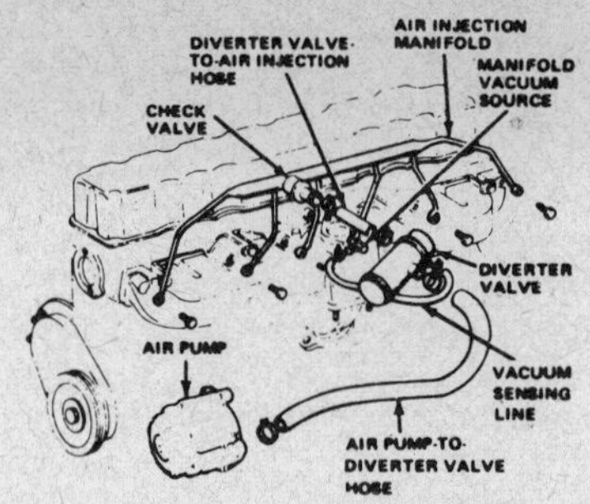

Fig. 2 Air Guard system. 6-258 engine

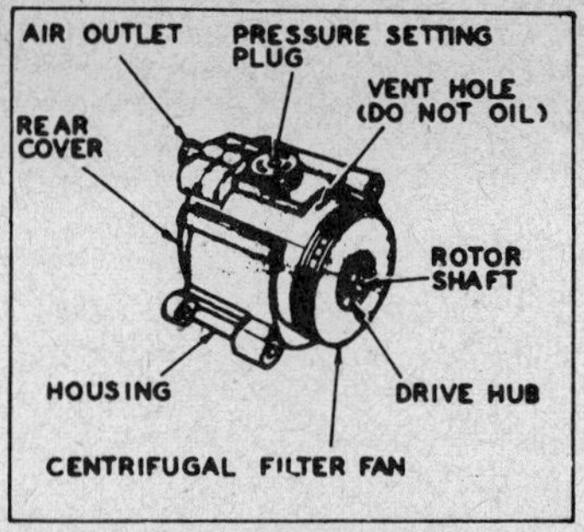

Fig. 3 Air injection pump with integral centrifugal air filter and pressure relief valve

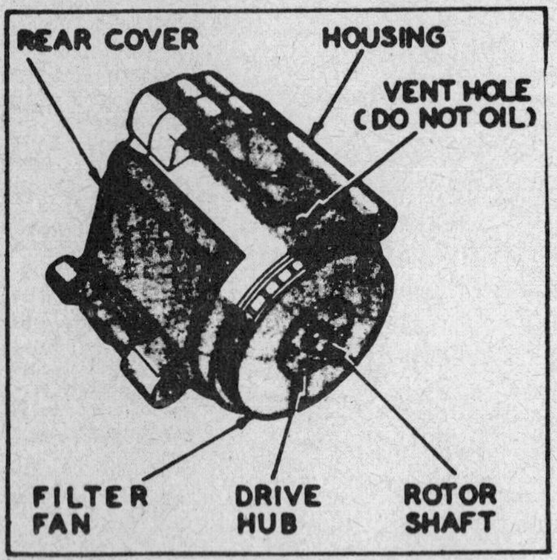

Fig. 4 Air injection pump with integral centrifugal air filter without pressure relief valve

through a bronze silencer pressed into the outlet opening. This action is required to prevent a backfire in the exhaust system which could occur when the throttle is closed suddenly. This valve is operating normally when no exhaust system backfire occurs during rapid throttle closure.

The diverter valve, **Fig. 5**, when triggered by a sharp increase in manifold vacuum, supplies the intake manifold with fresh air to lean out the fuel/air mixture and prevent backfire.

In addition to the above mentioned components, carburetors and distributors specifically calibrated for the Air Guard system must be used.

Service

BELT TENSION, ADJUST

Air pump belt tension should be checked with a belt tension gauge on the longest accessible span of the belt between two pulleys. When adjusting serpentine belt tension, adjust to 180 to 200 pounds for a new belt and 140 to 160 pounds for a used belt. When adjusting V-type belt tension, refer to the following specifications:

Belt	New Belt Pounds	Used Belt Pounds
4-150 & 151	40-60	40-60
6-258 Less Power Steering	125-155	90-115
6-258 With Power Steering	65-75	60-70

AIR FILTER, REPLACE

Pleated Paper Type

This filter is located on the air pump and should be replaced every 12,000 miles or sooner under more adverse conditions.

Centrifugal Filter Fan Type

This filter should be replaced only if damaged. To remove, first pry off the outer disc, **Fig. 6**, and then the remaining portion. Install replacement filter by drawing it into place using the pulley and bolts as tools. Alternately tighten the bolts making sure that outer edge of fan slips into housing. A slight amount of interference with housing bore is normal. After a new fan is installed, it may squeal upon initial operation until its outer diameter lip has worn in. This may take up to 30 miles of operation.

Do not attempt to install fan by hammering or pressing it on as damage to pump may result.

RELIEF VALVE, REPLACE

The relief valve may be removed by using a puller and a bridge over the valve, **Fig. 7**. If the new relief valve has a pressure plug, remove it before installing valve. To install valve, insert it into housing, then place a block of wood over and tap lightly with a hammer until valve is seated, **Fig. 8**. After valve has been installed, the pressure plug must be installed into valve by pressing against its center.

DIVERTER VALVE, REPLACE

This valve is not serviceable and must be replaced if defective. The valve is suspended by the hoses between the air pump and air injection manifolds. To remove valve, disconnect hoses and vacuum sensing line. Reverse this procedure to install. Make sure all connections are tight and not leaking.

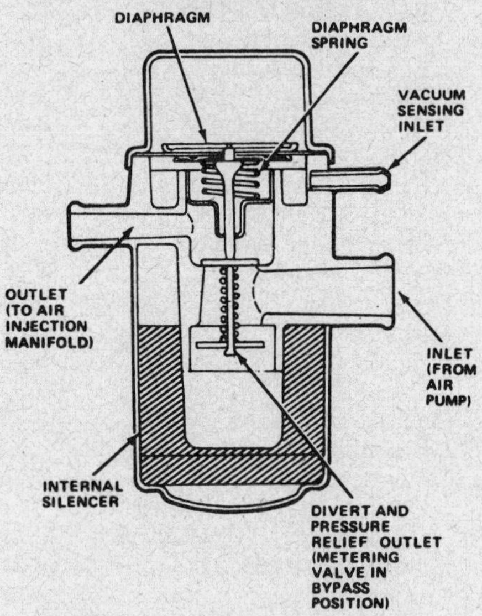

Fig. 5 Diverter valve

AIR PUMP, REPLACE

4-151 Engine

1. Remove drive belt.
2. If equipped with air conditioning, remove A/C compressor-to-mounting bracket attaching bolts and set compressor aside.
3. Remove air pump drive pulley bolts and pulley.
4. Remove fuel vapor canister and mounting bracket.
5. Disconnect output hose from rear of pump.
6. Remove air pump to bracket bolt and remove air pump.
7. Reverse procedure to install. Adjust belt tension to specifications.

6-258 Engine

1. Disconnect output hose from rear of pump.
2. Remove adjusting bolt and drive belt. If a serpentine (single belt) drive belt is used, loosen alternator adjustment and pivot bolts.
3. Remove front mount bracket.
4. Remove adjustment bracket from cylinder head.
5. Remove pump from pivot stud.

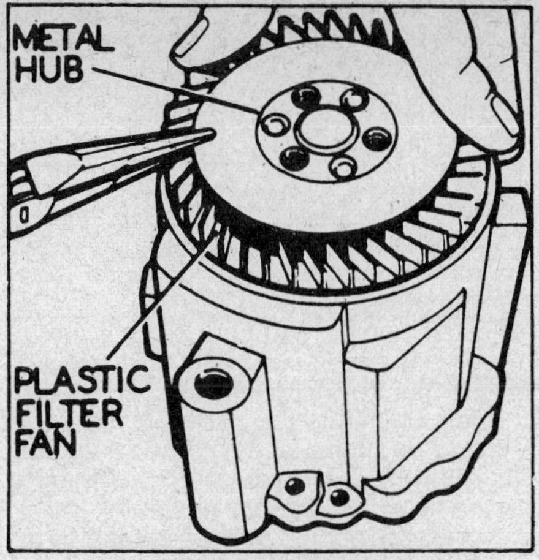

Fig. 6 Removing centrifugal type pump air filter

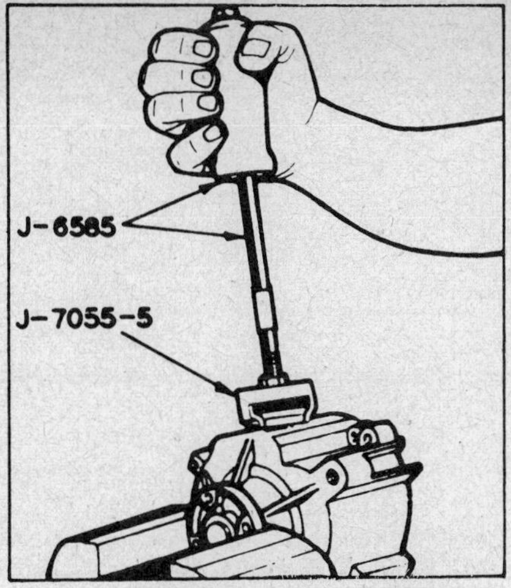

Fig. 7 Removing pressure relief valve with slide hammer and tool

Fig. 8 Installing pressure relief valve

6. Reverse procedure to install. Adjust drive belt to specifications.

AIR MANIFOLDS, REPLACE

1. Disconnect air delivery hose at check valve.
2. Remove injection screws from each cylinder exhaust port. **Some resistance to removal may be encountered due to carbon build-up on the screws.**
3. Remove air injection manifold.
4. Reverse procedure to install.

Diagnosis

CARBURETOR & DISTRIBUTOR

Other than making sure that the carburetor and distributor are functioning properly, make sure that the correct carburetor and distributor are used for the specific engine-transmission combination.

BYPASS VALVE

With transmission in neutral, accelerate engine and allow throttle to close rapidly. The valve is operating properly if no exhaust backfire occurs. Another check is to listen for air momentarily rushing through the bronze silencer immediately after throttle closure.

CHECK VALVE

To check valve for proper operation, disconnect air supply hose from pump at distribution manifold. With engine running, there should be no exhaust gas leakage at check valve.

DIVERTER VALVE

1. Start engine and allow to idle.
2. Check diverter vents. Little or no air should be felt flowing from vents.
3. Accelerate engine to 2000-3000 RPM and quickly close throttle. A strong flow of air should pass from diverter vents. If air does not flow or if backfire occurred, make sure that vacuum sensing line has vacuum and is not leaking. **This valve diverts air pump output when 20 inches Hg or more is applied to vacuum sensing line or pump output exceeds 5 psi.**
4. Slowly accelerate engine. Between 2500 and 3500 RPM, air should begin to flow from diverter valve vents.

AIR PUMP FUNCTIONAL TEST

To check for proper operation, disconnect air outlet hose at pump. With engine running, air discharge should be felt at the pump outlet opening. On early units, the pump output pressure is determined by the relief valve setting which is pre-set and not adjustable.

Pump Noisy Or Seized

The air pump is not completely noiseless. Under normal conditions, noise rises in pitch as engine speed increases. Also, allow a reasonable amount of time for a new pump to wear in before replacing it. Do not confuse air pump noise with other engine components.

1. Check belt tension, adjust as necessary.
2. If pump noise is still heard, remove belt to determine if pump is at fault. Check that pump is operative by turning pulley. A seized pump will not rotate and the noise can be caused by the belt slipping.
3. If pump is not seized, but it is determined that excessive pump noise is present, reinstall belt and proceed as follows:
   a. Check to make sure all hoses are in good condition and properly connected.
   b. With pump operating, check entire system for leaks in the hoses and around clamps. With engine idling, breaks in hoses can be located by feeling for air blowing through any holes.
   c. Check for air leaks around clamps in the same manner or by using a soap and water solution.
   d. Check that pump mounting brackets are not broken and that mounting bolts are tight.
   e. Check relief valve (if used). Valve has failed if air escapes from the valve at engine idle speed.
   f. A chirping or squeaking noise is most likely caused by the vane rubbing in the housing bore. This noise is most noticeable at low speed and is heard intermittently. Frequently vane chirp may be eliminated by allowing the vanes more break in time.
   g. Bearing noise is noticeable at all speeds and makes a rolling sound. This noise does not necessarily indicate bearing failure. However, if bearing noise increases to an objectionable level at certain speeds, the pump may have to be replaced. Rear bearing failure can be distinguished as a continuous knocking sound. Such a sound requires pump replacement.

PUMP INOPERATIVE

If it has been determined that the air pump is not delivering air (check for lack of air flow by disconnecting an air hose and idling engine), proceed as follows:

1. Check belt tension. Note that excessive belt tension can damage the pump. When setting belt tension to specifications, do not pry on pump housing.
2. Check entire system for leaks in the hoses and around the clamps. As the pump is operating with the engine idling, breaks in hoses can be located by feeling for air blowing through any holes. Inspect the entire length of hose.
3. Check for air leaks around clamps in the same manner as above or by using a soap and water solution.
4. If the above steps do not solve the cause of no air delivery, the pump should be replaced.

Troubleshooting

EXHAUST SYSTEM BACKFIRE

1. Check for vacuum leaks, correct as necessary.
2. Check bypass valve. Replace if defective.
3. Check choke operation and setting.

INTAKE SYSTEM BACKFIRE

1. Check ignition timing and point dwell.
2. Check accelerator pump discharge.
3. Check choke operation and setting.

AIR MANAGEMENT SYSTEM & DUAL AIR INJECTION SYSTEM

The Dual Air Injection system, **Fig. 9**, is used on all 1982 models.

This system consists of a belt driven air pump, diverter valve, air switch valve, air injection manifold, "downstream" air injection tube and connecting hoses. This system has two locations for air injection; one is at the exhaust ports, and the other is at the catalytic converter.

This system also uses a reverse delay valve, two-way delay valves and divert solenoid, and upstream solenoid that controls the air switch valve operation which is open by the open Loop 2 (OL2) mode of the CEC system.

Additional components used with the dual air injection system are, 1) divert and upstream solenoids, 2) air switch valve, 3) reverse and two-way delay valves, and 4) downstream air injection tube. This tube injects air to the dual bed catalytic converter.

The air switch valve is located between the diverter valve and air injection manifold and is controlled by vacuum from the upstream solenoid. It directs air pressure either upstream (into the exhaust manifold) or downstream (into the dual bed catalytic converter), depending on whether or not vacuum is applied to the valve. The air mixes with the hot exhaust gases when it enters upstream input and causes a further burning of the particles to reduce hydrocarbon (HC) and carbon monoxide (CO) emissions to the atmosphere. During "downstream" operation, the additional air reacts with HC and CO in the dual bed catalytic converter to create carbon dioxide (CO_2) and water vapor. The air switch valve directs air pressure downstream when vacuum is applied, or upstream when vacuum is not applied.

The upstream solenoid controls the air switch valve and is grounded through the feedback system. When current flows through the circuit, the upstream solenoid opens the air switch valve vacuum to the atmosphere and the air switch valve directs system air pressure "upstream." When the vacuum is allowed to pass through the "upstream" solenoid (de-energized condition) to the air switch valve, air system pressure is directed "downstream."

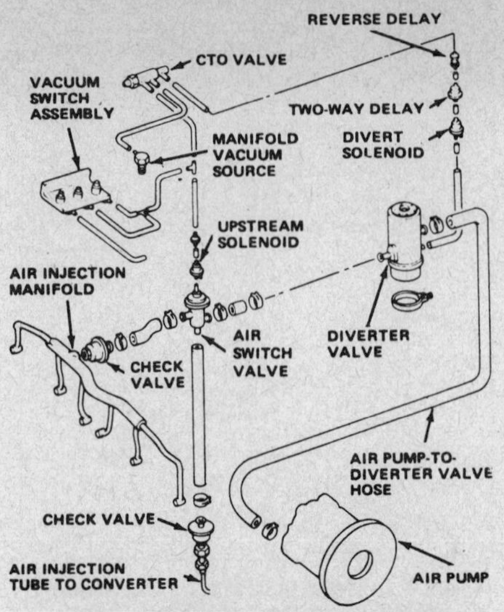

Fig. 9 Dual Air Injection system. 1982 all models

The air bypass circuit operating vacuum is regulated by the divert solenoid, Open Loop 3 vacuum switch (feedback system) and two-way reverse delay valves. The divert solenoid is grounded through the feedback system. When current flows through the circuit, the energized solenoid allows atmospheric pressure to displace the vacuum, allowing the diverter valve to release system air pressure to the atmosphere. The two-way and reverse delay valves are used to prevent a sudden loss of vacuum during a rapid vacuum decrease engine operating condition (acceleration).

Service

DOWNSTREAM AIR INJECTION TUBE, REPLACE

1. Disconnect air delivery hose at check valve. **Remove check valve if it is to be removed.**
2. Remove clamp connecting downstream air injection tube to two-way catalytic converter nipple. Apply heat if necessary.
3. Reverse procedure to install.

AIR PUMP, CHECK VALVES & INJECTION MANIFOLDS

Refer to the appropriate procedure under "Service" in the Air Guard section for service on these components.

Diagnosis

AIR MANAGEMENT SYSTEM

TVS Test

Air cleaner inlet air temperature must be below 40° F. If engine is warm, cool the TVS in the air cleaner to below 40° F.

1. Start engine, then check for manifold vacuum at vacuum hose at reverse delay valve. If there is no vacuum, replace TVS.
2. Disconnect each delay valve and check for vacuum. Replace each valve as necessary.

Air Bypass Valve Test

Engine must be at normal operating temperature.

1. Disconnect hose between air bypass valve and air control valve at air bypass connection, then remove vacuum hose.
2. Start engine and check for air pump pressure output at vent port (directly across from vacuum nipple). System output should be present at vent port and no output at disconnected port.
3. Apply a minimum of 10 inches Hg vacuum to vacuum nipple. Air pump pressure should be present at disconnected port and not at vent port. **If valve does not operate as described above and air pump and diverter valve are functioning properly, replace air bypass valve.**

Divert Solenoid Test

Engine must be at normal operating temperature.

1. Connect one lead of a voltmeter to light green wire at rear of divert solenoid plug and other voltmeter lead to ground.
2. Start engine and idle at 700 RPM.
3. During the first 75 seconds of engine operation, voltmeter should indicate battery voltage. After 75 seconds of engine operation, the voltmeter should indicate 1 volt.
4. Accelerate engine. Voltmeter should indicate battery voltage and the 75 second time period should begin.
5. If a low voltage reading is indicated on the voltmeter before the 75 second time period elapses, check for pinched wire in harness relay. If wire is OK, replace extended idle relay.
6. If voltmeter does not indicate low voltage after the 75 second time delay period elapses, disconnect open loop switch electrical connections and connect a test lamp to Open Loop 3 (red with tracer wire). With engine operating at 700 RPM, test lamp should go on. Disconnect vacuum from Open Loop 3 switch, light should go off. If vacuum switch does not operate as described, replace open loop switch assembly.
7. Reconnect vacuum and electrical connections.
8. Disconnect diverter solenoid electrical connection and connect test lamp to one terminal of solenoid battery positive terminal. Connect other terminal to ground. Test lamp should go on and vacuum should be present through solenoid. If not, replace solenoid and/or locate air leak. If solenoid is operating normally, replace extended idle relay.

Air Control Valve Test

1. Disconnect the two output hoses and vacuum hose.
2. Connect a hand operated vacuum pump to vacuum nipple.

3. Start engine and note output from air control valve. Air pressure should be present at upstream port only. No air pressure should be present at downstream port. If pressure is present at downstream port, replace air control valve.
4. Apply a minimum of 10 inches Hg vacuum to air control valve. Air pump pressure should be present at downstream port and not at upstream port. Replace valve if air is present at upstream port.
5. Reconnect output and vacuum hoses.

Upstream Solenoid Test

1. Connect one lead of voltmeter to light blue wire at rear of upstream solenoid and the other lead to ground.
2. Turn ignition switch on, do not start engine. Voltmeter should indicate battery voltage. If not, check for battery voltage at dark blue wire. If battery voltage is indicated at dark blue wire, replace solenoid. If battery voltage is not indicated at dark blue wire, check for short or open in solenoid voltage circuit.
3. Start engine and idle at 700 RPM. Voltmeter should indicate about 1 volt.
4. Accelerate engine from idle to about 3000 RPM for two seconds. Voltmeter should indicate battery voltage during acceleration and return to about 1 volt when engine returns to idle.
5. If system operation is not as described in step 4:
   a. Disconnect open loop switch electrical connector. Connect one lead of test lamp to battery positive terminal and other lead to Open Loop 2 pin (blue wire).
   b. When manifold vacuum is present at Open Loop 2 switch nipple, lamp should not go on.
   c. Disconnect vacuum hose. Lamp should go on. If not, replace Open Loop 2 switch assembly.
   d. If vacuum switches are operating normally, replace upstream solenoid and reconnect all connections, hoses, etc.
6. Accelerate engine as described in step 4 and observe voltmeter for proper operation. If voltmeter indication does not change, locate short circuit in harness between upstream solenoid and Open Loop 2 switch.

Diverter Valve Test

If engine is at operating temperature, temporarily connect manifold vacuum to the valve during test, since the AGE/CTO switch directs manifold vacuum to the air control valve circuit.

1. Start engine and run at idle.
2. Check diverter valve vents. Little or no air should flow from vents.
3. Accelerate engine to 2000-3000 RPM and rapidly close throttle. A strong flow of air should flow from the diverter valve vents for about 5 seconds. The high air flow diverter valve used on some engines should vent for about 3 seconds. If air does not vent, or if backfire occurs, make sure that vacuum hose is not leaking. **The diverter valve diverts air pump output when a vacuum of 20 inches Hg or more is applied to diaphragm. The diverter valve diverts air when the pump output exceeds 5 psi.**
4. Slowly accelerate engine to 3500 RPM. Between 2500-3500 RPM, air should begin to flow from the diverter vents.

Air Control Valve

Engine must be at normal operating temperature.

1. Disconnect hoses from air control valve, noting which hose was connected to downstream port and which hose to upstream port.
2. Start engine and disconnect vacuum hose from small valve nipple. **There should be vacuum at vacuum hose when engine coolant temperature is below about 160°F, and no vacuum when temperature is above 160°F. If coolant is below 160°F and there is no vacuum present at hose, check hose for air leaks. If there are no leaks, replace AGE/CTO switch.**
3. Air pressure should be present at air control valve port which connects to downstream hose. A small amount of air pressure should be present at upstream port of air control valve.
4. Apply at least 10 inches Hg of vacuum to small nipple on air control valve. Air pressure should be present at upstream port and very little air pressure at downstream port.

DUAL AIR INJECTION SYSTEM

Air Bypass Circuit Functional Test

1. Disconnect hoses from ports A and B of air switch valve. Hose A is connected to air injection manifold and hose B is connected to catalytic converter.
2. Start engine and allow to reach normal operating temperature, then turn engine off.
3. Restart engine and increase speed to 1500 RPM. Air should flow from port A of air switch valve for about 30 seconds, then flow from port B.
4. If there is no air flow as described previously, check base of diverter valve for air exhaust.
5. If air does not flow according to step 4, increase engine speed to 1500 RPM and check that vacuum is being applied to diverter valve. If there is vacuum, replace diverter valve and recheck. If there is no vacuum, check diverter solenoid.
6. If air does not flow, inspect air pump for proper operation.
7. If air flow from air switch valve is normal, depress accelerator pedal to floor, then return engine to idle and check base of diverter valve for air flow. If there is air flow, circuit is operating normally. If there is no air flow, check diverter vacuum hose for vacuum. If there is no vacuum, replace diverter valve. If there is vacuum, check diverter solenoid.

Air Switch Circuit Functional Test

1. Perform steps 1 thru 6 under "Air Bypass Circuit Functional Test."
2. If air flows only from port B, remove vacuum hose and check for vacuum during the first 30 seconds of operation. If there is no vacuum, replace air switch valve and recheck. If there is vacuum, check upstream solenoid.
3. If air flow is normal, depress accelerator to floor, then return engine to idle and check base of diverter valve for air flow.
4. If air flows, system is operating normally. If there is no air flow, check diverter valve vacuum hose for vacuum. If there is no vacuum, replace diverter valve. If there is vacuum, check diverter solenoid.

CATALYTIC CONVERTERS

Catalytic converters are used to convert carbon monoxide (CO), hydrocarbon (HC) and oxides of nitrogen (NOx) into water vapor (H_2O), carbon dioxide (CO_2) and nitrogen (N_2). The catalyst used to create these conversions are platinum, palladium and rhodium (depending on type of converter).

During engine operation, all of the exhaust gases flow through the converter where a chemical change takes place. This change causes the temperature inside the converter to be higher than the temperature of the exhaust gases when they leave the engine. Due to this increase in heat, the converter is insulated so that its outside temperature is about the same temperature as the muffler. However, due to its solid mass, the converter remains hot much longer than the muffler.

The body of the catalytic converter is made of stainless steel designed to last the life of the vehicle. Excessive heat can bulge or distort the converter. Since excessive heat built up is not the fault of the converter, the carburetion or ignition system should be checked whenever a converter is damaged by overheating.

Although all vehicles with catalytic converter must use unleaded fuel, small amounts of leaded fuel can be used in case of an emergency. To prevent adding leaded fuel, the fuel tank filler nozzle has a built-in restrictor, **Fig. 10.**

CONVENTIONAL OXIDIZING CATALYTIC (COC) PELLET TYPE

This type of converter, **Fig. 11,** changes carbon monoxide (CO) and hydrocarbon (HC) into water vapor (H_2O) and carbon dioxide (Co_2). The catalyst in the converter which produce the chemical change are platinum, and palladium included as a fine coating on the substrate (beads of alumina).

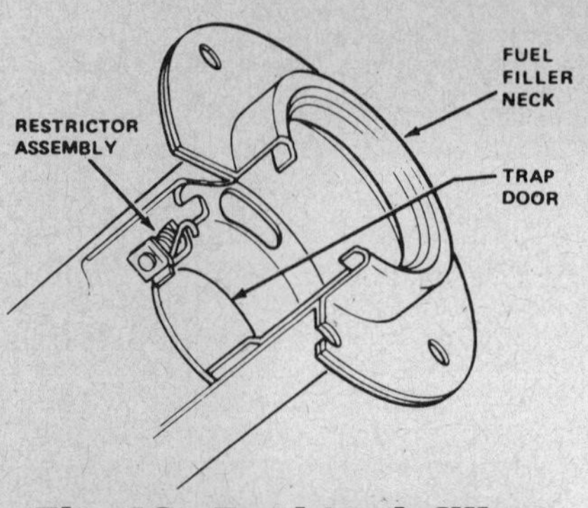

Fig. 10 Fuel tank filler neck with restrictor used on vehicles with catalytic converters

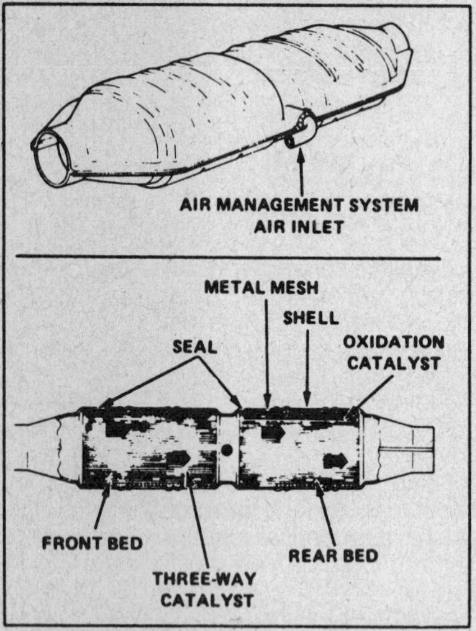

Fig. 13 Dual bed catalytic converter

THREE-WAY CATALYTIC (TWC) PELLET TYPE

This type of converter, **Fig. 12,** contains platinum and palladium as conventional oxidizing agents in addition to rhodium. The addition of rhodium allows the converter to convert carbon monoxide (CO) and oxides of nitrogen (NOx) to carbon dioxide (CO_2) and nitrogen (N_2).

During operation, as the air fuel mixture is leaned, the converter's efficiency for converting HC and CO increases but decreases NOx. If the air fuel mixture were increased, NOx formation would be reduced, but HC and CO would be increased. In order to optimize the simultaneous reduction of all these pollutants, the carburetor must be able to provide an air fuel mixture of approximately 14.7:1. In order to provide this air fuel mixture, a feedback carburetor system is used along with this type of converter.

DUAL BED (TWC & COC) MONOLITHIC TYPE CONVERTER

This type of converter, **Fig. 13,** is two converters in one container. The front half is a three-way catalytic (TWC) converter

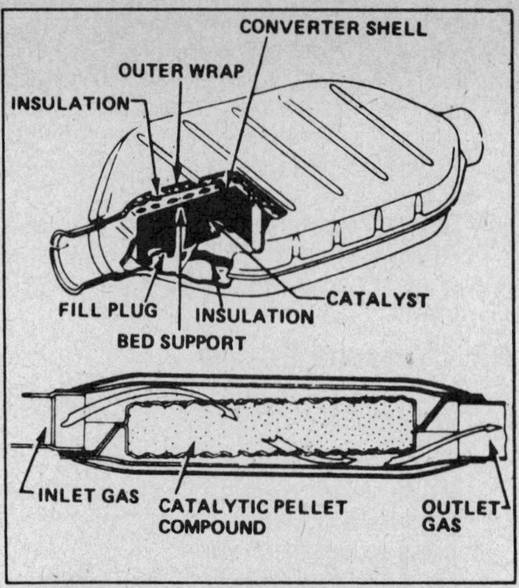

Fig. 11 Conventional catalytic converter

while the rear half is a conventional oxidizing catalytic (COC) converter. The rear half of the converter has a provision for "downstream" air injection.

As with the three-way catalytic (TWC) converter, this converter must be used in conjunction with a feedback carburetor system in order to maintain high efficiency.

WARM-UP MONOLYTHIC TYPE

This converter, **Fig. 14,** is installed in the exhaust system ahead of the pellet type converter. This converter operates on the same principle as the pellet type converter but it reacts more rapidly to incoming gases. It is especially effective in converting gases immediately after start up.

Service

CATALYST, REPLACE

The catalyst in the monolithic type converter is not replaceable. If it is determined that the converter has lost its effectiveness, it must be replaced.

1. Raise and support vehicle.
2. Connect hose of vacuum pump J-25077 on tailpipe and tighten clamp, **Fig. 15.**
3. Connect shop air to fitting on vacuum pump. **Shop air must provide a minimum of 80 psi.**
4. On early model converters, remove fill plug using a 3/4 inch Allen wrench or tool J-25077-3. On later model converters, remove fill plug as follows:
   a. Drive a small chisel between plug and converter housing. Use care to avoid damaging converter housing.
   b. Continue to drive chisel into plug to deform it.
   c. Repeat steps a and b at several locations around plug until it is deformed sufficiently to be removed with pliers. Do not pry on converter housing.
5. Position vibrator (part of tool J-25077) on converter and lock it in place, **Fig. 16.**

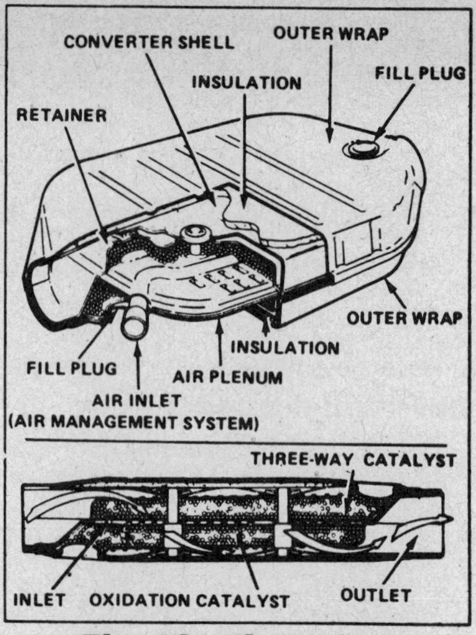

Fig. 12 Three-way catalytic converter

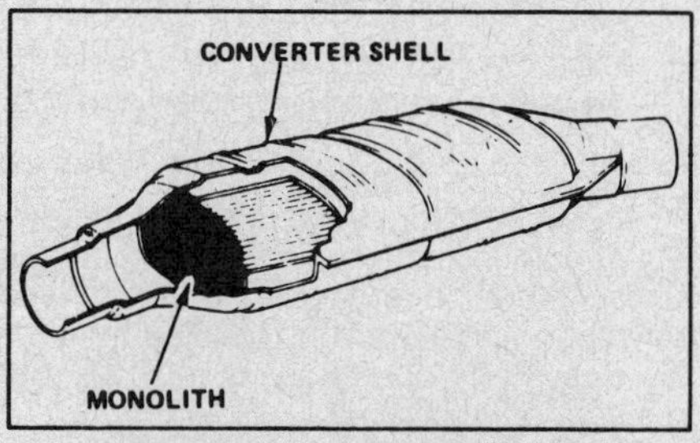

Fig. 14 Warm-up monolythic converter

6. Disconnect air hose from vacuum pump and connect it to vibrator. Catalyst pellets will fall into can for about 10 minutes.
7. When converter is empty, disconnect air hose, remove can and discard pellets.
8. Install refill can on vibrator and connect air hose to vacuum pump attached to tailpipe. Pellets will be drawn into converter. **If any pellets exit from the tailpipe, the converter housing is defective and must be replaced.**
9. When converter is full, remove vibrator from converter.
10. On early model converters with threaded plug, coat plug threads with an anti-seize compound, then install plug and torque to 40 ft. lbs. On later models with non-threaded plug, **Fig. 17,** proceed as follows:
    a. Insert screw into bridge and position bridge inside filler plug opening.
    b. Remove screw from bridge, being careful not to disturb position of bridge.
    c. Insert screw through washer and plug, then thread screw into bridge and tighten.
11. Disconnect air hose from vacuum pump and remove vacuum pump.

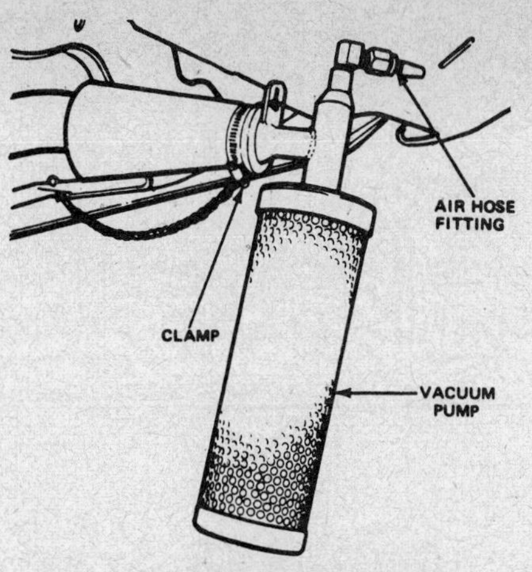

Fig. 15 Vacuum pump installation

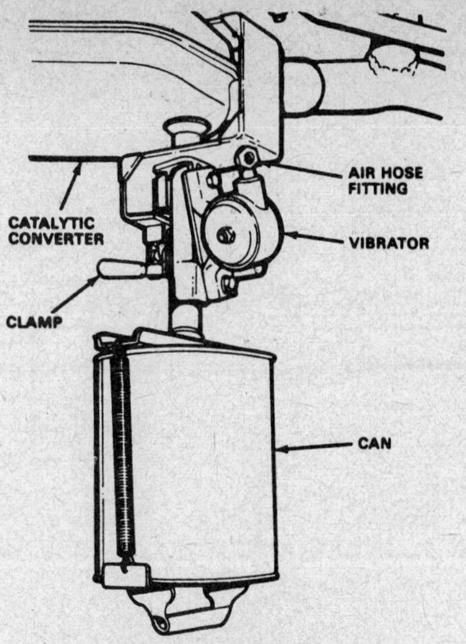

Fig. 16 Vibrator tool installation

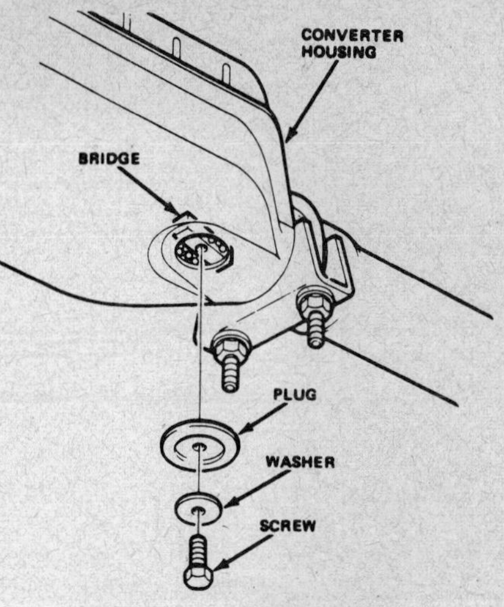

Fig. 17 Filler plug replacement kit

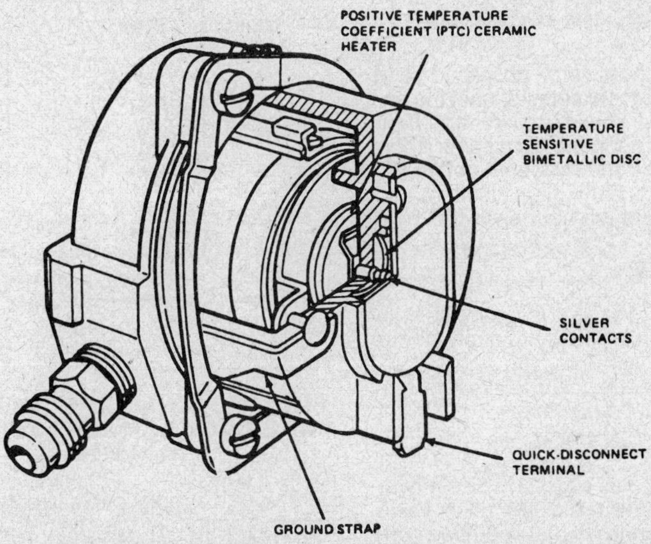

Fig. 18 Electric choke assembly. 4-150 & 6-258 engines

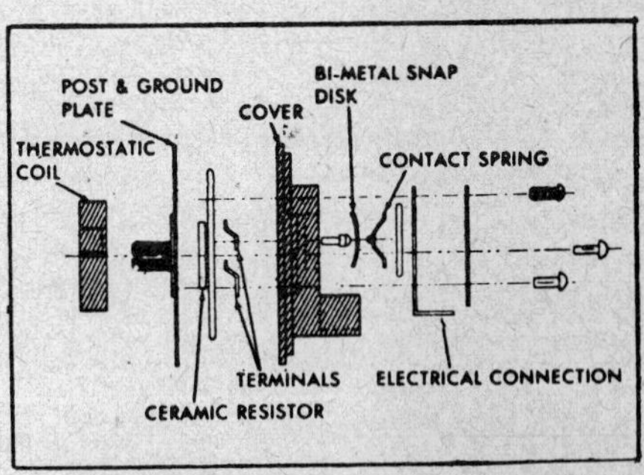

Fig. 19 Electric choke assembly. 4-151 engines

ELECTRIC ASSIST CHOKE

The electric assist choke reduces carbon monoxide (CO) and hydrocarbon (HC) emissions during warm up. It provides supplemental heat to the choke bimetal to speed up choke valve opening after the choke cover interior reaches a predetermined temperature.

4-150 & 6-258 ENGINES

On this system, **Fig. 18,** a special tap is provided on the alternator to supply power to the electric assist choke. A thermostatic switch within the choke cover closes when the interior of the choke cover reaches the modulating temperature. This allows current to flow to the heating element when the circuit is completed through the choke cover ground strap and choke housing to the engine. As the heating element becomes hot, heat is absorbed by an attached metal plate which heats the choke bi-metal coil. When the engine is turned off, the thermostatic switch remains closed until the choke cover interior modulating temperature is reached. If the engine is started immediately after shut-down and before the modulating temperature is reached, current will immediately begin warming up the heating element to open the choke. Once the choke cover interior temperature falls below the modulating temperature, the thermostatic switch opens and current flow to the heating element is shut off. If the engine is restarted at this time, the electric assist function will not operate until choke cover interior reaches its modulating temperature.

4-151 ENGINES

The main components of this electric assist choke system, **Fig. 19,** consist of the thermostatic coil, ceramic resistor, cover, bi-metal snap disc and contact spring. The ceramic resistor is divided into a small center section for gradual heating and a large outer section for rapid heating of the thermostatic coil. The electric actuated ceramic resistor heats the thermostatic coil, gradually relaxing coil tension and allowing the choke valve to open.

When air temperature is below 50°F, electric current applied to the small section of the ceramic resistor allows slow opening of the choke valve for good engine warm-up. As the small section of the ceramic resistor continues to heat, a bi-metal disc causes the spring loaded contact to close and apply electric current to the large section of the ceramic resistor which increases the heat flow to the thermostatic coil for more rapid opening of the choke valve.

When air temperature is between 50-70°F, electric current applied to the small section or both to the large and small sections, produce the required amount of heat to control the choke valve for good engine operation within this temperature range.

When air temperature is above 70°F, current is applied to the small section of the ceramic resistor and through the spring contact to the large section of the ceramic to provide rapid heating of the thermostatic coil for quicker choke valve opening when leaner air/fuel mixtures are required at warmer temperatures.

Service

The only service required is to make

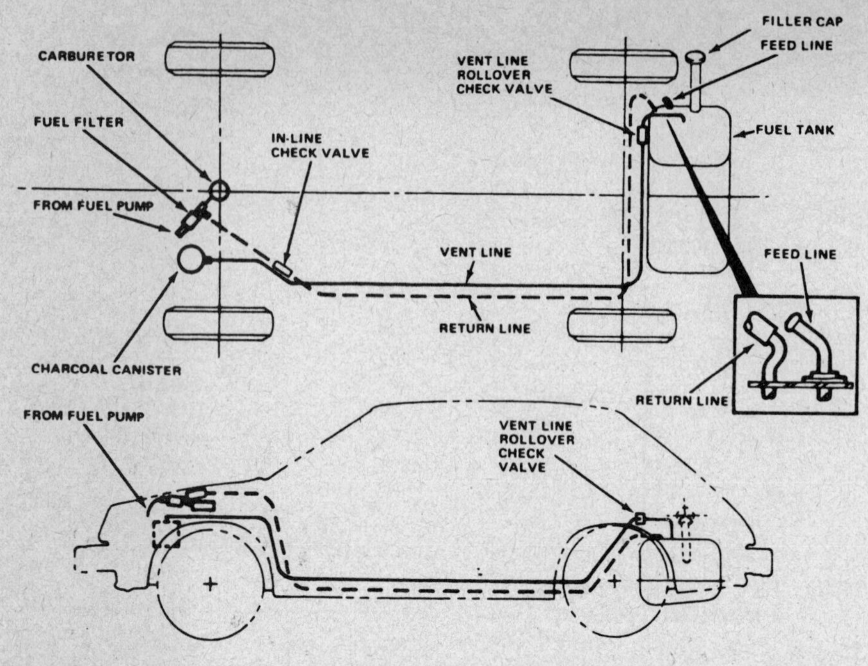

Fig. 20 Evaporative Emission Control system (typical)

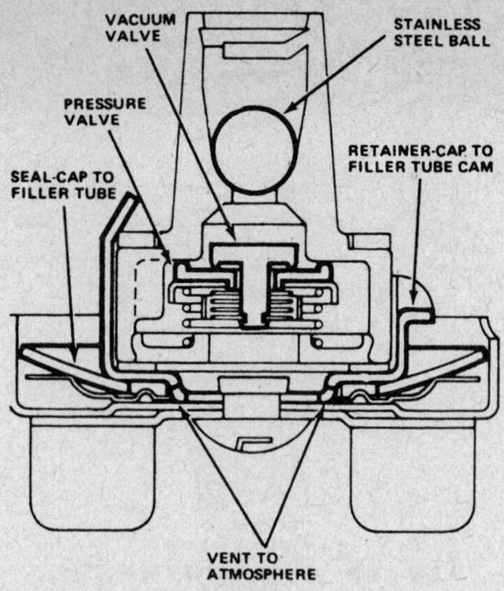

Fig. 21 Fuel filler cap

sure that the electrical connection to the electric choke is clean and tight and that the choke linkage is clean and operates freely.

Diagnosis

EXCEPT 151 ENGINES

1. Disconnect electric assist choke wire from choke housing.
2. Connect one lead of a test light to spade connector at choke housing and other lead of test light to choke wire.
3. Disconnect choke heat tube at choke housing and start engine.
4. Using a small thermometer, position bulb end of thermometer inside heat tube passage of choke housing.
5. Note thermometer reading and observe test light. Lamp should be out when 60-80°F is noted on thermometer. Lamp should be off when temperature readings are below or above those specified previously. **If test light does not go on at all, check 7 volt supply from alternator.**
6. If test light does not go on within the 60-80°F range, replace choke cover.

EVAPORATIVE EMISSION CONTROL/FUEL VAPOR CONTROL

This system, **Fig. 20,** is used to prevent fuel vapors emitted from the fuel tank and carburetor from escaping into the atmosphere. This is accomplished through the use of a non-vented fuel tank, a special fuel filler cap, charcoal canister, vapor separators, check valves, non-vented carburetor, and hoses necessary to connect these components together.

The fuel vapors are absorbed and stored in the charcoal canister until the engine is started. These vapors are then drawn either through the air cleaner snorkel or through a ported vacuum port in the carburetor (depending on application) and burned along with the normal air fuel mixture.

FUEL TANK

The fuel tank, **Fig. 20,** is designed with an expansion area directly above the fuel. Some vehicles with this type of fuel tank have a liquid check valve to prevent fuel from entering the vapor lines.

FUEL FILLER CAP

The fuel filler cap, **Fig. 21,** uses a two-way (vacuum and pressure) relief valve that is closed during normal operating conditions. The relief valve is calibrated to open only when pressure in excess of .8 psi or vacuum in excess of .1 inch Hg develops in the fuel tank. When vacuum or pressure is relieved, the valve returns to its normally closed position.

Some filler caps have a rollover check valve. This valve consists of a stainless steel ball in a plastic housing mounted on the fuel tank side of the cap. Should the vehicle be overturned or tipped sufficiently, the steel ball drops into an orifice closing the vent to prevent fuel leakage. **It is normal to occasionally encounter an air pressure release when removing the fuel filler cap.**

FUEL VAPOR STORAGE CANISTER (CHARCOAL CANISTER)

The fuel resistant nylon body of the canister contains activated charcoal granules which absorb and store fuel vapors until they are drawn into the induction system to be burned along with the normal air fuel mixture. Outside air is drawn into the canister through a replaceable filter pad located at the bottom of the canister.

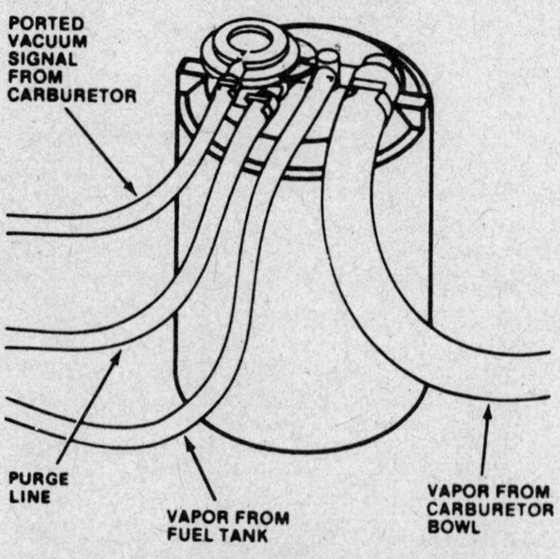

Fig. 22 Charcoal canister hose connections. 1982 all models

On 1982 models, the canister, **Fig. 22,** has a staged dual feature and four nipples. Two of the nipples are inlets, one for fuel tank vapor and the other for carburetor float bowl vapor. The other two nipples are outlets, one is connected to intake manifold vacuum while the other is for carburetor ported vacuum. When the engine is running, manifold vacuum causes fresh air to enter through the inlet filter in the canister and purge the stored vapor. When ported vacuum increases due to increased throttle opening, the secondary purge circuit is opened and the canister is purged at a much higher rate.

LIQUID CHECK VALVE

This valve, **Figs. 23 and 24,** contains a float and viton needle assembly. Should liquid fuel enter the check valve, the float will rise and force the needle upward closing the vent passage and preventing fuel from flowing through the valve. Two different design valves are used, one picks up vapors from the lines while the other picks up vapors from the fuel tank. Both operate the same.

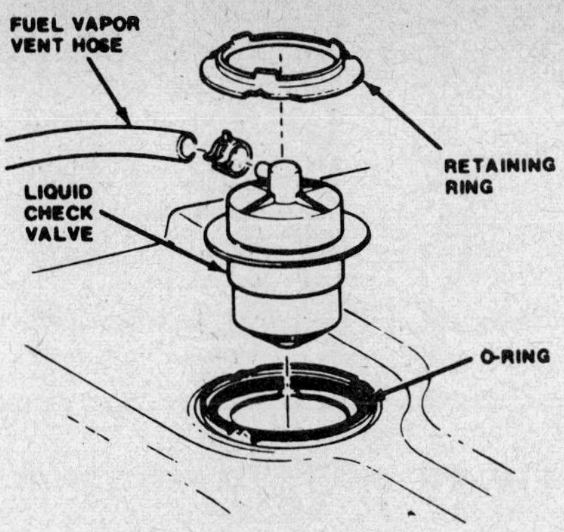

Fig. 23 Liquid check valve. Tank mounted type

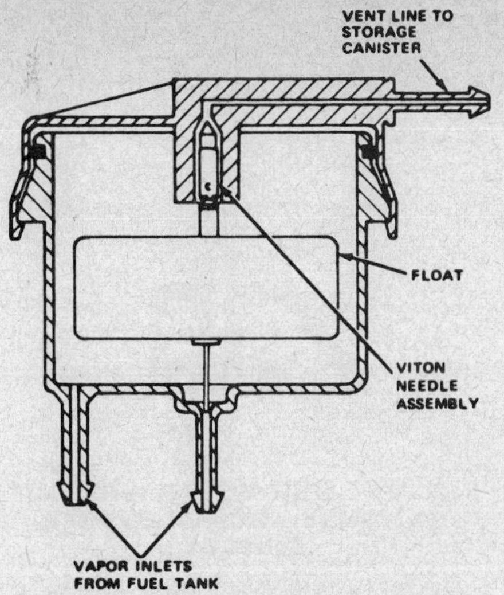

Fig. 24 Liquid check valve. Externally mounted type

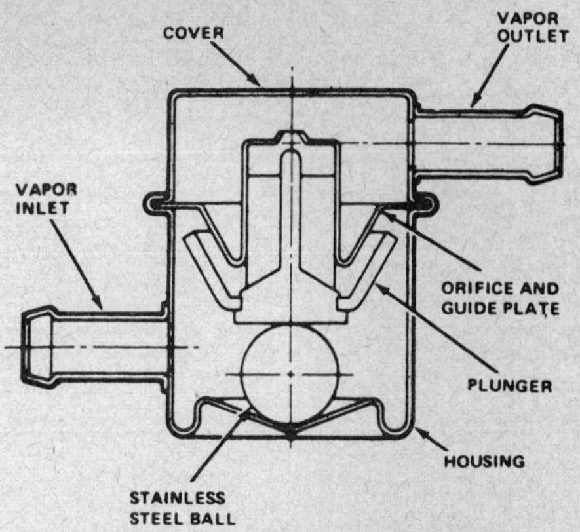

Fig. 25 Rollover check valve

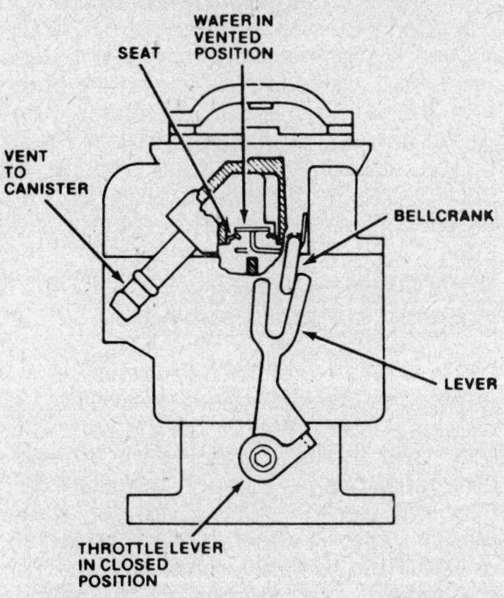

Fig. 26 Bowl vapor vent

After passing through the check valve, the fuel vapor is routed forward through a vent line to the vapor storage canister in the engine compartment.

ROLLOVER CHECK VALVE

This valve, **Fig. 25,** prevents the flow of fuel through the fuel line should the vehicle be rolled over. The check valve consists of a plunger and a stainless steel ball. When inverted, the stainless steel ball pushes the plunger against its seat.

CARBURETOR EXTERNAL BOWL VENT

This vent, **Fig. 26,** used on some carburetors provides an outlet from fuel vapors when the engine is not running. If this vent were not provided, raw fuel vapors would enter the atmosphere. Some vapors would also enter the intake manifold making hot restarts difficult. When the engine is running, the fuel bowl must be vented to the inside of the air cleaner for proper fuel flow.This is accomplished by automatically closing the bowl vent. Some carburetors use manifold vacuum to accomplish this while others use a mechanical link to the throttle.

FUEL RETURN

Most vehicles use a fuel return system to reduce the possibility of high temperature fuel problems. This system consists of a line connecting an extra nipple on the fuel filter to an extra nipple on the fuel tank sending unit. During normal engine operation, a small amount of fuel returns to the fuel tank. During periods of high underhood temperatures, vaporized fuel is returned to the fuel tank instead of entering the carburetor.

Some vehicles have an inline check valve, **Fig. 27,** in the fuel return system at the fuel filter to eliminate the possibility of fuel feeding back to the carburetor through the fuel return line. This valve uses a stainless steel spring loaded check ball to close the orifice. It is located on the fuel return line and secured by a clamp.

Service

FUEL VAPOR STORAGE CANISTER FILTER, REPLACE

This filter is located on the bottom of the canister and should be replaced every 30,000 miles. To replace filter, remove canister from its mounting bracket, then invert canister and remove filter screen and filter. Reverse procedure to install.

Maintenance

The fuel tank, filler cap, fuel lines and vent lines must be maintained in good condition to prevent raw fuel vapors (hydrocarbon) from entering the atmosphere.

1. Inspect filler cap for fuel leakage as indicated by stains at the filler neck opening. Remove cap and check condition of sealing gasket. Replace cap if gasket is damaged or deteriorated.
2. Inspect fuel tank for evidence of leakage as indicated by stains. Trace any stain back to its source and repair or replace the tank as necessary.

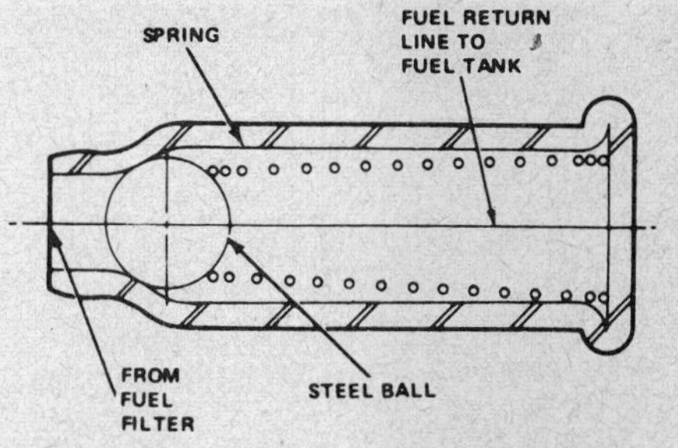

Fig. 27 Inline check valve

3. Inspect all lines and hoses for leakage or damage and repair or replace as necessary. Make sure all connections are tight.
4. If liquid fuel is present at fuel vapor storage canister, inspect liquid check valve and replace if necessary.
5. Replace charcoal canister filter at the recommended intervals.

Diagnosis

Fuel vapors are extremely flammable. Do not smoke or use an open flame in area during test.

1. Inspect carburetor for proper external bowl vent operation and possible flooding.
2. Inspect air cleaner and if equipped, trap door mechanism for proper operation.
3. If equipped, inspect fuel return pipe.
4. Inspect engine compartment for any obvious fuel leakage onto or near power train components and exhaust system.
5. Weigh fuel vapor canister. If it weighs more than 2.5 pounds, replace it.
6. Start engine and check for the following conditions:
   a. Erratic engine operation due to air leakage into vacuum hoses especially at the canister. Repair as necessary.
   b. Fuel leakage from any high pressure pipe fitting located between fuel pump and filter, and between fuel filter and carburetor. Repair as necessary.
7. Turn engine off and test integrity of fuel vapor control system as follows:

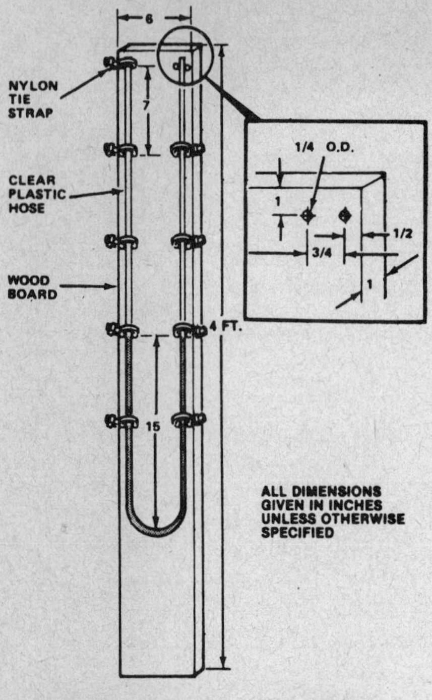

Fig. 28 Manometer fabrication dimensions

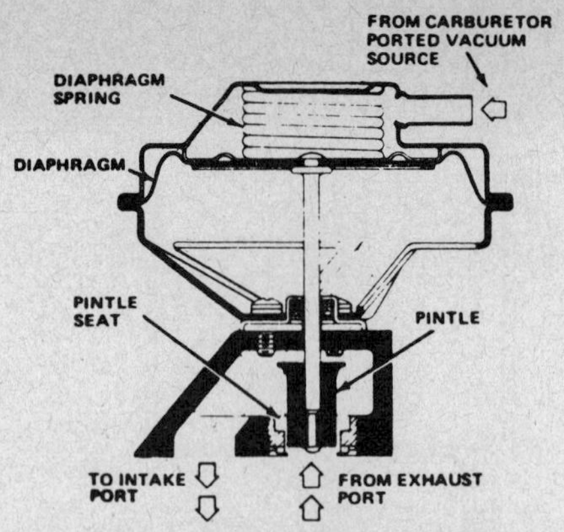

Fig. 29 EGR valve without exhaust back pressure sensor

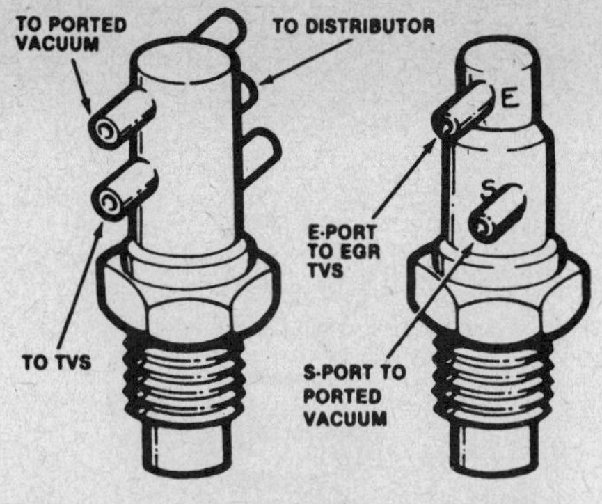

Fig. 30 EGR CTO switches. 1982

a. If a manometer is not available, fabricate one according to **Fig. 28.** Attach a 6 foot length of 3/8 inch clear plastic tubing to a 4 foot x 6 inch x 1 inch board.
b. Fill tube with water to a height of 15 inches.
c. Visually inspect fuel vapor control system for loose or damaged hoses, clamps etc. Repair as necessary.
d. Inspect fuel filler neck sealing surface for scratches and dents. Small dents and scratches may be removed by sanding entire surface with sand paper. If dents or scratches are severe, replace fuel filler neck.
e. Disconnect fuel tank vapor hose from canister at engine compartment and apply pressure to make sure hose is not obstructed.
f. Using a T-fitting, connect plastic tube or rubber hose between manometer and fuel tank vapor hose. Make sure that fuel tank is no more than 3/4 full. **Do not pressurize system more than 1.5 psi (41.5 inches of water) in the following step.**
g. Connect a hand pump to open tee fitting and pressurize system until column of water in manometer rises 15 inches from no pressure level. **Fuel vapor is highly combustible, do not smoke or use an open flame in area during test.**
h. Inspect all fuel lines, hoses and connections for leaks indicated by stains, liquid fuel and bubbles. Repair as necessary.
i. Using a soap and water solution, test all system connections for vapor leaks as indicated by bubbles. Repair as necessary.
j. Check for fuel odor at fuel filler cap. Replace cap if odors are detected.

8. Relieve pressure in system by slowly removing fuel filler cap and reconnect fuel tank vapor hose to canister.

EXHAUST GAS RECIRCULATION (EGR)

The purpose of this system is to reduce the formation of oxides of nitrogen (NOx) by diluting the fresh intake air fuel charge with a metered amount of exhaust gas. This reduces the peak combustion temperatures of the burning gases in the combustion chambers.

EGR VALVE

The EGR valve is mounted on the side of the intake manifold on 6-258 engines. On 4-151 engines the EGR valve is located on a spacer plate located beneath the carburetor.

The EGR valve without an exhaust back pressure sensor, **Fig. 29,** is normally held closed by a spring located above the diaphragm. The valve opens when enough vacuum is applied through the hoses connecting the coolant temperature override (CTO) switch, **Fig. 30,** to the EGR vacuum port at the carburetor. When vacuum overcomes the spring tension, a pintle within the valve is lifted off its seat and exhaust gas is metered into the intake manifold.

The EGR valve with an integral exhaust back pressure sensor, **Fig. 31,** combines the functions of the EGR valve and separate back pressure sensor into a single unit. This unit is calibrated by the use of selective diaphragm spring loads and flow control orifices. The exhaust gas flow is controlled by a moveable pintle. When no vacuum is applied to the diaphragm, the pintle is held against its seat by spring tension, confining exhaust gases to the exhaust manifold. When vacuum is applied to the diaphragm, the pintle is forced from its seat, however, this cannot occur if the vacuum bleed valve in the power diaphragm is opened. Exhaust gas back pressure from inside the exhaust manifold flows through the hollow pintle stem into the control diaphragm chamber. If this pressure is enough to overcome the control spring tension, the control diaphragm moves against its bleed valve. Full vacuum is now applied to the power diaphragm and the pintle moves, allowing exhaust gas to flow to the intake manifold. If the exhaust back pressure drops enough, the control diaphragm moves away from the bleed valve and the pintle returns to its seat.

EXTERNAL BACK-PRESSURE SENSOR

The EGR system, when equipped with an external back-pressure sensor, **Fig. 32,** obtains a vacuum signal at the carburetor spark port and not the EGR port. The vacuum signal passes through the EGR CTO (Coolant Temperature Override) switch (when coolant temperature exceeds 115° or 160°F) to the valve portion of the sensor where it is modulated by exhaust back-pressure.

When exhaust back-pressure is relatively high, as during acceleration and some cruising conditions, exhaust back-pressure traveling through the metal tube overcomes spring tension on the diaphragm within the back-pressure sensor valve, and closes the valve atmospheric vent.

With the back-pressure sensor valve no longer vented to atmosphere, the vacuum signal now passes through the back-pressure sensor valve, and the EGR valve. When vacuum signals the EGR valve, exhaust gas recirculation commences.

When exhaust back-pressure is too low to overcome diaphragm spring tension, the vacuum signal is vented to atmosphere and does not pass through to the EGR valve. With no vacuum signal applied to the EGR valve, exhaust gas does not recirculate.

All 6-258 engines incorporate a steel restrictor plate, **Fig. 33,** under the exhaust back-pressure sensor. The restrictor plate limits the rate of EGR flow, thereby improving driveability.

The back-pressure sensor is not serviceable and must be replaced if defective.

COOLANT TEMPERATURE OVERRIDE SWITCH

This switch, **Fig. 30,** is located on the

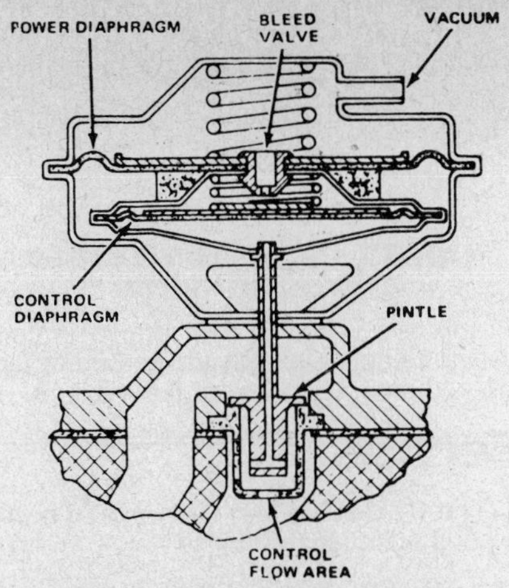

Fig. 31 EGR valve with integral exhaust back pressure sensor

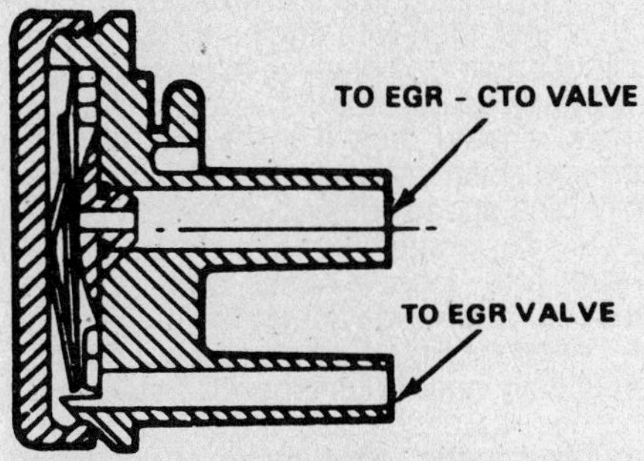

Fig. 34 Thermal vacuum switch

left side of the engine block on 6-258 engines.

On 4-151 engines, the switch is located in the coolant passage at the right rear of the cylinder head.

When coolant temperature is below the specified rating of the CTO switch, there is no vacuum signal to the EGR system. The switch for the 4-151 engine, opens at 100°F. On all other engines, opening temperature is 85°F for switch with white body, 115°F for switch with black body or paint dab and 160°F for switch with yellow body or paint dab.

THERMAL VACUUM SWITCH (TVS)

This switch, **Fig. 34,** is used on 1982 6-258 engines with 2 barrel carburetors. The switch is located in the air cleaner and functions as an on/off switch controlled by the air temperature of the air cleaner. The thermal vacuum switch controls vacuum between the EGR CTO and EGR valve. At temperatures below 40° to 55°F, the thermal vacuum switch limits vacuum to the EGR valve, thus improving cold engine driveability.

LOW TEMPERATURE VACUUM SIGNAL MODULATOR

This unit is located at the left side of the front upper crossmember, just ahead of

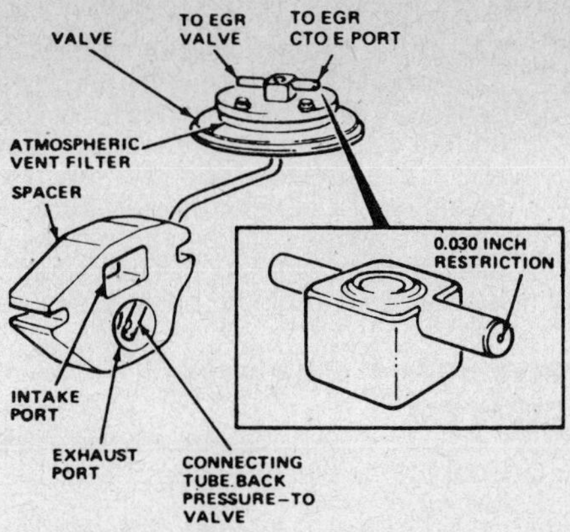

Fig. 32 External exhaust back-pressure sensor

the radiator, on the same mounting bracket as the TCS ambient temperature override switch and is connected to the EGR vacuum signal hose. The modulator is open when ambient temperatures are below 60°F. This causes a weakened vacuum signal to the EGR valve and a resultant decrease in the amount of exhaust gas being recirculated.

HIGH TEMPERATURE VACUUM SIGNAL MODULATOR

This unit is located at the rear of the engine compartment and is connected to the EGR vacuum signal hose. The modulator opens when the underhood air temperature reaches 115°F and causes a weakened vacuum signal to the EGR valve. As a result, the amount of exhaust gas being recirculated is decreased.

VACUUM DUMP VALVE

This valve, **Fig. 35,** is connected in parallel with the EGR vacuum signal source and the EGR valve. It stops EGR operation when manifold vacuum drops to a level of 3 to 5 inches Hg, by dumping the vacuum signal to the EGR valve.

Maintenance

The EGR valve on the intake manifold must be removed, cleaned and inspected at the mileage intervals as specified. The exhaust gas passages in the intake manifold also should be inspected and cleaned as required.

After cleaning, open the EGR valve manually by pressing down on the pintle, then release.

If the valve does not return to the fully closed position, it must be replaced.

Inspect the exhaust gas inlet and discharge passages of the intake manifold for any restriction caused by carbon or lead deposits.

On six cylinder engines, lead or carbon deposits build up rapidly in the exhaust gas discharge passage upper hole. If the deposits cannot be removed a 9/16 inch drill bit may be used.

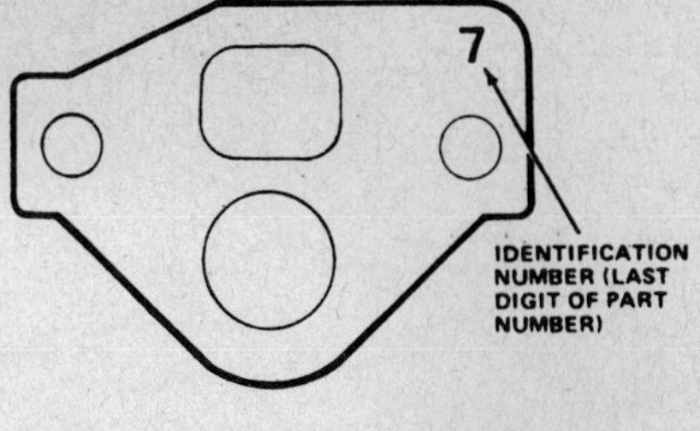

Fig. 33 Restrictor plate

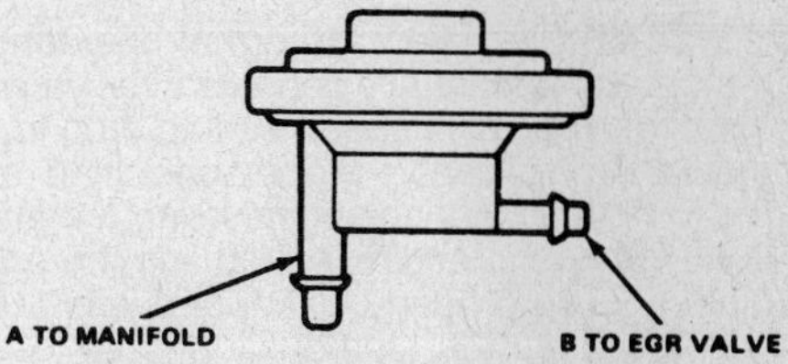

Fig. 35 Vacuum dump valve

Service

EGR VALVE, REPLACE

1. Disconnect vacuum hoses.
2. Remove retaining nuts, then remove EGR valve and gasket.
3. Discard gasket and clean mating surfaces.
4. Reverse procedure to install using a new gasket.

EGR CTO SWITCH, REPLACE

1. Drain coolant from radiator.
2. Disconnect vacuum hoses from switch.
3. Using a 7/8 inch wrench, remove switch.
4. Reverse procedure to install. Add coolant to cooling system. On 6 cylinder engines, removing the temperature switch will allow air to be purged from cooling system.

RESTRICTOR PLATE, REPLACE

The restrictor plate located between the spacer and the intake manifold can be removed after removing the EGR valve. The stainless steel restrictor plate is calibrated for a particular engine-exhaust system combination and should never be altered or replaced with one of a different calibration.

Diagnosis

EGR VALVE

1982

With engine idling at normal operating temperature, accelerate engine to 1500 RPM and release throttle. A definite movement should be noticed in the EGR diaphragm. If diaphragm does not move, check for leaking vacuum lines, faulty vacuum signal to EGR valve, defective EGR valve or back pressure sensor.

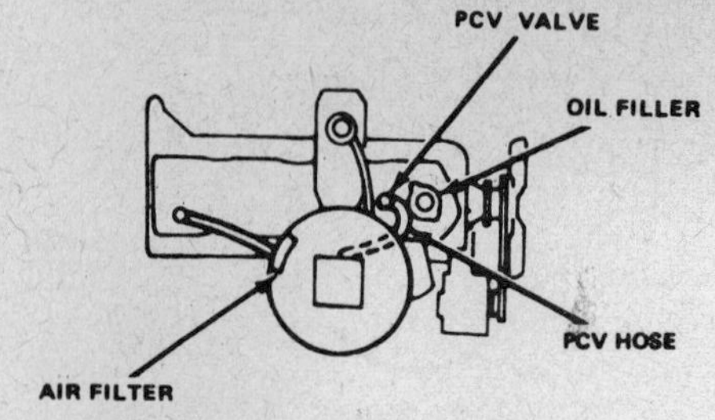

Fig. 36 PCV system (typical)

With engine idling at normal operating temperature, manually depress EGR valve diaphragm. Engine speed should drop immediately, indicating proper operation of the EGR valve during engine idling. If there is no change in engine speed and the engine is idling properly, exhaust gases are not reaching the combustion chamber, and the probable cause is a plugged passage between the EGR valve and the intake manifold. If the engine idles poorly and the speed is not greatly affected when the EGR valve diaphragm is closed, the EGR valve is not stopping the flow of exhaust gases to the combustion chambers. Check for defective hoses, incorrectly routed hoses or defective EGR valve.

EGR CTO SWITCH

Engine coolant temperature should be below 100°F.

1. Check vacuum lines for leaks and correct routing.
2. Disconnect vacuum line at EGR valve and connect a vacuum gauge.
3. Operate engine at approximately 1500 RPM, no vacuum should be indicated on gauge. **If vacuum is indicated, replace EGR CTO switch.**
4. Idle engine until coolant temperature exceeds 115°F (black color coded), 160°F (yellow color coded) or 100°F on 4-151 engines.
5. Operate engine at 1500 RPM, ported carburetor vacuum should be indicated on gauge. **If vacuum is not indicated, replace EGR CTO switch.**

BACKPRESSURE SENSOR

1. Inspect all EGR vacuum lines for leaks and correct routing. **Make certain vacuum line from EGR CTO is connected to nipple with .030 inch restriction.**
2. Using a T-fitting, connect a vacuum gauge in line between EGR valve and exhaust back pressure sensor.
3. With engine idling there should be no vacuum indicated on gauge. **If vacuum is indicated at idle speed, check for correct vacuum line connections. Make certain manifold vacuum is not being used as a vacuum source. If carburetor is providing vacuum, check for partially open throttle plate which could be providing premature ported vacuum to back pressure sensor.**
4. Accelerate engine to 2000 RPM and observe vacuum gauge for no reading when coolant temperature is below 115°F and vacuum reading when coolant temperature is above 115°F.
5. If no vacuum was indicated during test, make certain vacuum is being applied to inlet side of back pressure sensor. If vacuum connections are correct, remove back pressure sensor and inspect spacer port and tube for restrictions. Deposits caused by carbon or lead deposits can be removed using a spiral wire brush. If no vacuum is obtained, replace back pressure sensor.

THERMAL VACUUM SWITCH

1. Cool the air cleaner assembly to below 40°F.
2. Disconnect vacuum hoses from TVS and connect an external vacuum source to large fitting, **Fig. 34.**
3. Apply vacuum to TVS. If TVS does not hold vacuum, replace it.
4. Start engine and allow air cleaner temperature to rise above 55°F. If vacuum is held by TVS, replace it.

VACUUM SIGNAL DUMP VALVE

1. Start engine and allow to reach normal operating temperature.
2. Disconnect vacuum signal dump valve vacuum hose from connection at manifold and plug the manifold connection, **Fig. 35.**
3. Accelerate engine to 2000 RPM. Vacuum should be present at exhaust ports at bottom of valve. If not, replace valve.
4. Connect vacuum signal dump valve vacuum hose to manifold and accelerate engine to 2000 RPM. There should be no vacuum at exhaust ports at bottom of valve. If there is vacuum replace valve.

POSITIVE CRANKCASE VENTILATION (PCV) SYSTEM

This system, **Fig. 36,** prevents crankcase vapors from entering the atmosphere by scavenging the blow-by gases in the crankcase and routing them into the intake manifold where they are burned along with the normal air fuel mixture. In addition to controlling the emission of crankcase vapors into the atmosphere, this system continuously ventilates the crankcase with fresh air which aids in the prevention of sludge formation.

Manifold vacuum controls the airflow through the PCV system. When manifold vacuum is relatively high, such as at idle or at cruising speed, fresh air is drawn through the air inlet filter into the crankcase. After circulating through the crankcase, the vapor-laden air is drawn through the PCV valve, **Fig. 37,** and into the intake manifold. The vapor mixes with the air fuel mixture and is burned in the combustion chambers. The PCV valve is calibrated to control airflow at a rate acceptable to the intake system.

If crankcase vapor pressure (blow-by) exceeds the flow capacity of the PCV valve, airflow in the system reverses.

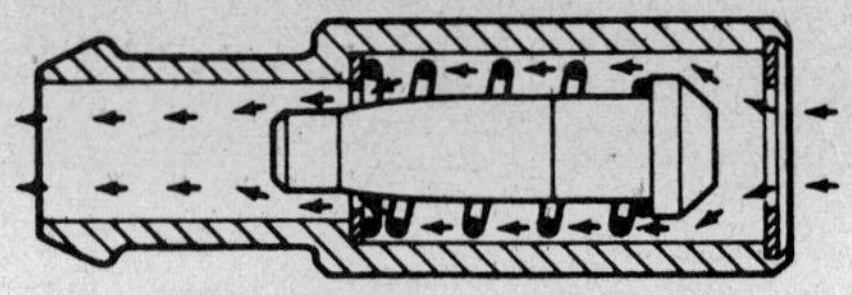

Fig. 37 PCV valve cross sectional view

Crankcase vapor is then drawn through the air cleaner element and carburetor and burned along with the air fuel mixture.

Service

The PCV valve and filter should be replaced every 30,000 miles.

Diagnosis

SYSTEM QUICK CHECK

A quick check of the system can be made by pulling end of valve out of valve cover and, then with engine idling, placing a finger over end of valve to block air flow. A strong vacuum should be felt and engine speed should drop if the system is performing satisfactorily. If there is no change in engine speed, a clogged system is indicated. To isolate problem, remove PCV valve from hose. If hoses and passages are clear, a strong vacuum will be felt with the engine idling. Engine idle will change drastically and the engine may stall when the hose is uncovered. If this occurs, the trouble is in the valve. If the engine continues to idle approximately as it did before the hose was uncovered, the hoses or passages are blocked.

PCV VALVE QUICK CHECK

1. Replace existing PCV valve with a known good one.
2. Start engine and compare existing engine idle quality with prior idle quality.
3. If loping or rough idle condition remains when the PCV valve is replaced, the PCV system is not at fault. Further engine component diagnosis must be made to determine cause of malfunction.
4. If idle quality improves, replace PCV valve and clean hoses and fittings.

PCV VALVE TEST

PCV valve tester J-23111, **Fig. 38,** can be used to test valve and system for proper operation. To use tester, proceed as follows:

1. Remove PCV valve from its mounting grommet.
2. Connect vacuum gauge to read intake manifold vacuum. **The PCV valve must be in a horizontal position and lightly tapped during testing.**
3. Start engine and allow to idle. Compare vacuum and tester readings to flow chart, **Fig. 39,** and record readings.
4. Stop engine, then disconnect coil secondary wire from distributor cap and ground it to engine.
5. Crank engine while comparing vacuum and tester readings with chart, **Fig. 39. Throttle must be at curb idle**

position during cranking speed test.
6. If valve flow is above or below the chart specifications, clean or replace valve.

PULSE AIR INJECTION REACTOR (PAIR)

This system, **Fig. 40,** utilizes exhaust pressure pulsations to draw fresh air from the air into the exhaust system.

This system uses a series of pipes and check valves in the pulse air valve to route fresh air into the exhaust manifold, **Fig. 40.**

Engine operation causes a pulsating flow of exhaust gases which are of positive or negative pressure depending on whether the exhaust valve is seated or not. If pressure is positive, the disc is forced to the closed position, allowing no air flow into the exhaust system. If pressure is negative, the disc will open allowing fresh air flow into the exhaust system. Due to the inertia at high engine RPM, the disc fails to follow pressure pulsations. Therefore, the disc will remain closed preventing air flow into the exhaust system.

Throttle closure during deceleration, momentarily causes air fuel mixtures too rich to burn. These mixtures, when combined with air, will become combustible, causing after fire.

Service

PULSE AIR VALVE, INSPECTION

Inspect valve and vacuum hose for air leaks and cracks. Replace valve and/or hose as required.

PULSE AIR VALVE, REPLACE

1. Remove air cleaner assembly and disconnect vacuum hose from Pulsair valve.
2. Disconnect support bracket, then loosen retaining nuts and remove Pulsair valve.
3. Lightly lubricate Pulsair valve tubes with oil.
4. Install Pulsair valve. Torque nuts to 10-13 ft. lbs.
5. Connect support bracket.
6. Connect vacuum hose to valve and install air cleaner assembly.

Diagnosis

FUNCTIONAL CHECK

1. Connect hand operated vacuum pump to rubber hose of Pulse Air valve.
2. Apply 15 inches Hg or greater to valve. If vacuum drops in less than two seconds, replace valve.

PULSE AIR SYSTEM

The system which is used on 1983-84 6-258 engines, uses the alternating exhaust pressure pulsations instead of an air pump to inject air into the exhaust system, **Fig. 41.** Air is routed from the air cleaner through a hose to the air control valve which is controlled by an air switch solenoid. The air switch solenoid is in turn controlled by the CEC system Micro Computer Unit (MCU). At the appropriate signal from the CEC system the air control valve is opened and air is allowed to flow through the air injection check valve. From there the air enters the exhaust stream either at the front exhaust pipe (upstream) or at the catalytic converter (downstream) depending on which of the air injection circuits has been opened.

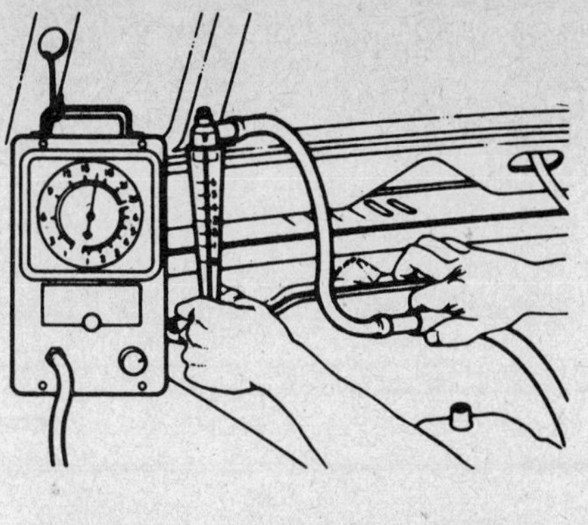

Fig. 38 PCV valve test

SPARK CONTROL SWITCHES & VALVES

SPARK COOLANT TEMPERATURE OVERRIDE (CTO) SYSTEM

On some models, vacuum spark advance operates on carburetor ported vacuum after engine has reached operating temperature. While engine is warming up, driveability can be improved by operating the distributor vacuum spark advance with manifold vacuum while engine is cold. On 4-151 engines, the CTO switch is threaded into the bottom of the thermostat housing. On 6 cyl. models except Eagle, the CTO switch is located in the heater hose CTO fitting on models less A/C and in the heater valve on models with A/C. On Eagle models, the CTO switch is located at the left rear of the cylinder block. A thermal sensor switch is in contact with the engine coolant. Depending on engine coolant temperature, the CTO switch, **Fig. 30,** will permit either manifold vacuum or carburetor ported vacuum to be applied to the distributor vacuum advance unit. On 4-151 engines, when coolant temperature is below 120°F, manifold vacuum is routed through switch port 1 into port D allowing manifold vacuum to be applied to the distributor vacuum advance unit. On 6 cyl. engines, when coolant temperature is below 160°F on models except California or 165°F on California models, vacuum is routed through switch port 1 to port D allowing manifold vacuum to be applied to the distributor vacuum unit. On 4-151 and 6 cyl. engines, when coolant reaches the specified temperature, port 1 closes and port 2 is connected to port D applying carburetor ported vacuum to the distributor vacuum advance unit.

NON-LINEAR VACUUM REGULATION VALVE

The non-linear vacuum regulator (NLVR) **Fig. 42,** combines regulated vacuum at idle speed and carburetor ported vacuum to provide a regulated output signal to control the ignition spark advance mechanism. It is mounted in series between the vacuum source port and distributor vacuum advance unit. The NLVR has two input ports, intake manifold vacuum and carburetor ported vacuum, and one outlet port at the distributor advance unit. At curb idle, the NLVR provides regulated vacuum. Under these conditions, manifold vacuum is high and ported vacuum is either very low or non-existent. The NLVR, as determined by the calibration of the valve, provides a signal between the two vacuum levels. As engine load increases and the signal increases above the regulation point (7.5 in Hg @ 75°F ± 5), the regulator valve switches to ported vacuum output.

FORWARD DELAY VALVE

On some models, a vacuum spark advance forward delay valve is added to the vacuum advance circuit to improve driveability and lower emission of hydrocarbons. This valve gradually applies vacuum to the vacuum advance unit diaphragm.

REVERSE DELAY VALVE

On some models, the vacuum spark control reverse delay valve is added to the vacuum advance circuit to provide improved driveability when engine is cold and to lower emission of hydrocarbons. When a cold engine is started, manifold vacuum is applied to the distributor vacuum advance unit. As engine speed is increased, manifold vacuum drops and distributor vacuum advance is lost. To prevent the retarding of the spark advance, a one-way check valve is installed in the vacuum line. With this check valve, the distributor will remain in a full advance mode until the spark CTO is switched to ported vacuum after the engine has reached operating temperature. The vacuum trapped by the check valve will slowly bleed down when the engine is not operating.

THERMAL VACUUM SPARK CONTROL DELAY VALVE

On some models, this valve is added to the air cleaner to control vacuum between the intake manifold source and the spark CTO switch. The purpose of the valve is to allow the flow of controlled manifold vacuum when air passing through the air cleaner is below 63°F for 4-151 engine or 55°F for 6 cyl. engines. At temperatures above this level, manifold vacuum is prevented from reaching the spark CTO until coolant temperature reaches the spark CTO switch point.

VACUUM SPARK CONTROL DELAY VALVE

On models equipped with 4-151 engine, a spark control delay valve, **Fig. 43,** is added to the vacuum advance circuit. The pur-

Year	Color of Valve	Cubic Feet Per Minute (CFM) @ Engine Manifold Vacuum													
		2	3	4	5	6	7	8	10	12	13	14	16	18	20
1980–84	Black	—	1.22–2.21	—	—	.77–1.66	—	—	—	—	—	—	.69–1.13	—	—
	Blue	—	1.50–2.50	—	—	1.05–1.85	—	—	—	—	—	—	.50–1.00	—	—

Fig. 39 PCV flow rate chart

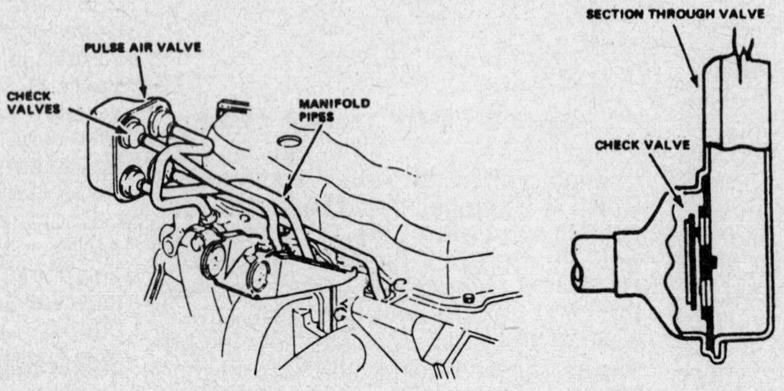

Fig. 40 Pulse Air Injection Reactor (PAIR) system

pose of this valve is to provide improved driveability when the engine is cold. The valve uses a separate external thermal vacuum switch that connects ports 2 and 3 when the vacuum spark control delay valve is open. Ports 1 and 2 and 3 and 4 are connected internally.

VACUUM SOLENOID VALVE-SPARK

This electrically-operated solenoid valve, **Fig. 44** is used on models with 4-151 engine, automatic transmission and air conditioning. The solenoid is energized when the A/C compressor clutch engages and switches the vacuum signal to the advance unit from manifold vacuum to carburetor ported vacuum. Ports 1 and 2 of the valve are connected when the solenoid is energized. Ports 3 and 4 of the valve are connected when the solenoid is de-energized and switches from carburetor ported vacuum to manifold vacuum.

Testing

VACUUM SPARK CONTROL CHECK VALVE TEST

1. Disconnect hose from vacuum advance unit, and connect gauge to disconnected hose.
2. Start engine. Gauge should indicate manifold vacuum.
3. Stop engine and observe gauge. If vacuum drops off rapidly, the check valve is defective. **A very gradual loss of vacuum is normal because of slight leakage in the CTO switch.**

THERMAL VACUUM SWITCH (TVS)

1. Cool air cleaner to below the TVS calibration point of 40 to 50°F.
2. Disconnect vacuum lines from TVS and connect a vacuum gauge to one port and a vacuum pump to the other port.
3. Apply vacuum to TVS. There should be no vacuum reading indicated on the gauge when TVS temperature is below its calibration point. If there is, replace the TVS.
4. Start engine and allow temperature of TVS to reach 40 to 50°F. Vacuum should be indicated through TVS. If not, replace TVS.

NON-LINEAR VACUUM REGULATOR (NLVR)

1. Connect a vacuum gauge to distributor port (Dist.) of NLVR.
2. With engine idling, a vacuum reading of 7 in. Hg should be indicated.
3. Gradually, open throttle. As engine speed increases, ported vacuum from the carburetor should be indicated on the vacuum gauge.

REVERSE DELAY, FORWARD DELAY & 2-WAY DELAY VALVE

1. Apply a constant vacuum of 10 inches Hg to colored side of delay valve.
2. Connect one end of a 24 inch piece of vacuum hose to a vacuum gauge and other end to white side of valve to check reverse delay or colored side to check forward delay.
3. Observe time in seconds for gauge to move from 0 to 8 inches Hg with a constant 10 inches Hg vacuum applied. Refer to chart in **Figs. 45 through 48** for minimum and maximum time for each valve to reach 8 inches Hg.
4. Replace valve if time limits are not within specifications listed.

VACUUM SPARK CONTROL DELAY VALVE

1. Connect vacuum gauge to fitting at port 1, **Fig. 43.**
2. Connect a second vacuum gauge to fitting at port 4, **Fig. 43.**
3. Vacuum should be equal on both gauges when TVS is open (cold).
4. When TVS is closed (warm) and vacuum at port 1 is greater than vacuum at port 4, air from port 4 moves through unseated check valve to port 1.
5. When the TVS is closed and vacuum at port 1 decreases to less than vacuum at port 4, check valve seals and air from port 1 moves through orifice to port 4. When the vacuum is greater at port 1 than at port 4, air can move freely through the unseated check valve. When vacuum at port 4 is greater than at port 1, air moves through the orifice creating a delay in the flow of air through the valve.

VACUUM SOLENOID VALVE

1. Connect vacuum to port 2 of valve, **Fig. 44.**
2. Start engine and turn off A/C.
3. Manifold vacuum should be indicated on gauge.
4. Turn on A/C and accelerate engine. Ported vacuum should be indicated on gauge.
5. If operation is not as described above, replace valve.

THERMOSTATICALLY CONTROLLED AIR CLEANER (TAC)

This system provides heated air for the carburetor during engine warm-up. Heated intake air allows the carburetor air fuel mixture to be calibrated leaner to reduce hydrocarbon (HC) emissions. It also improves engine performance during warm-up and minimizes carburetor icing.

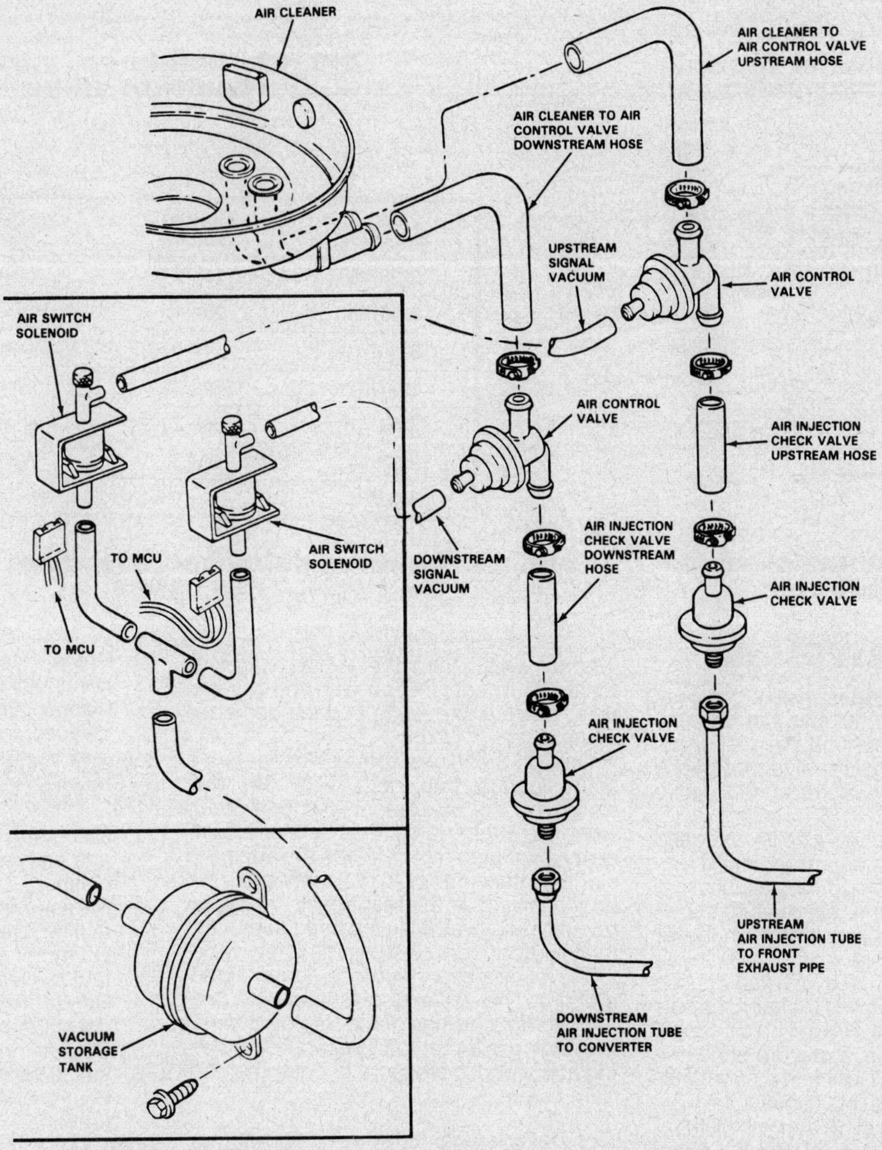
AIR CLEANER
AIR CLEANER TO AIR CONTROL VALVE UPSTREAM HOSE
AIR CLEANER TO AIR CONTROL VALVE DOWNSTREAM HOSE
UPSTREAM SIGNAL VACUUM
AIR CONTROL VALVE
AIR SWITCH SOLENOID
AIR CONTROL VALVE
AIR INJECTION CHECK VALVE UPSTREAM HOSE
AIR INJECTION CHECK VALVE DOWNSTREAM HOSE
AIR SWITCH SOLENOID
TO MCU
DOWNSTREAM SIGNAL VACUUM
AIR INJECTION CHECK VALVE
TO MCU
AIR INJECTION CHECK VALVE
UPSTREAM AIR INJECTION TUBE TO FRONT EXHAUST PIPE
DOWNSTREAM AIR INJECTION TUBE TO CONVERTER
VACUUM STORAGE TANK

Fig. 41 Pulse air system. 1983–84 6-258

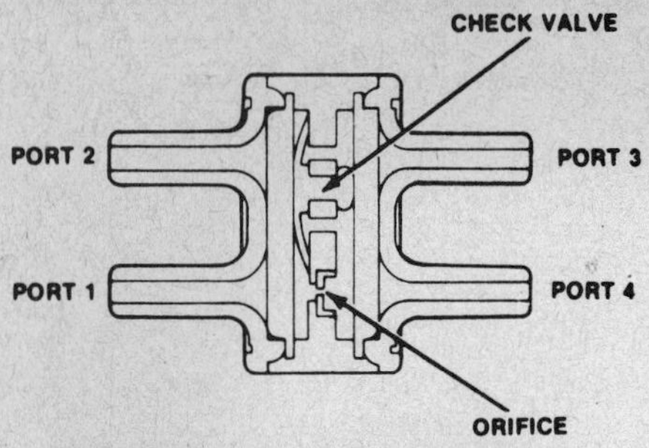

Fig. 43 Vacuum spark control delay valve

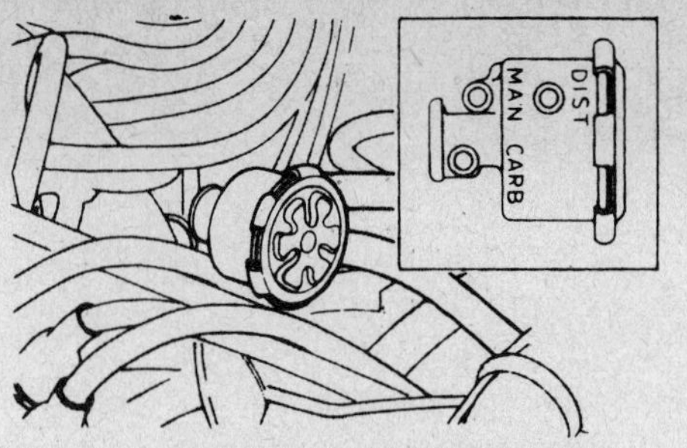

Fig. 42 Non-linear vacuum regulator valve

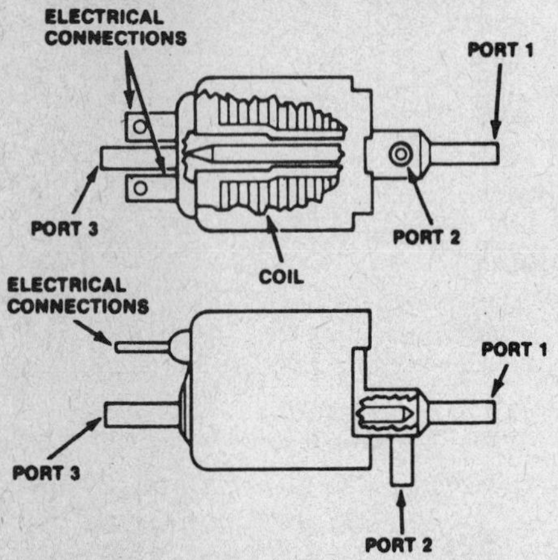

Fig. 44 Vacuum solenoid valve

Part Numbers	Time in Seconds	Color and Identification
3235738	10 ± 2	White and Gray
3235739	20 ± 4	White and Brown
3236285	4 ± 0.8	White and Purple
3237131	375 ± 75	White and Red
3237141	100 ± 20	White and Yellow
3237184	15 ± 3	White and Gold
3237383	2 ± 0.5	White and Orange

Fig. 45 Reverse delay valve (except 4 port) test chart. 1982

VACUUM CONTROLLED

This system, **Fig. 49,** consists of a heat stove that partially encloses the exhaust manifold, a heated air tube, thermal vacuum switch, reverse delay valve(s), a check valve and a vacuum motor and air valve assembly.

The position of the air valve is controlled by manifold vacuum opposing spring tension. Manifold vacuum to the vacuum motor is controlled by the temperature sensitive thermal switch that is located in the air cleaner housing. This switch has an air vent valve that regulates vacuum applied to the vacuum motor and thereby controls the position of the air valve. The air supply is either all heated air, a mixture of heated and ambient air or all ambient air from outside of the vehicle. This regulation of air maintains the intake air to the carburetor at a near optimum temperature for the existing engine operating conditions.

During high underhood air temperature or high ambient air temperature conditions, the air valve is maintained at the full heat off position to prevent excessively high temperature intake air from entering the carburetor.

To improve cold weather driveability, this system uses a reverse delay valve in the hose between the thermal switch and vacuum motor. Upon sudden acceleration (decrease in manifold vacuum) during cold weather operation, the delay valve momentarily maintains manifold vacuum at the vacuum motor and prevents an abrupt intake of cold ambient air, that may cause the engine to stall or hesitate. A one-way check valve, located between the thermal switch and the vacuum source, functions in conjunction with the reverse delay valve to prevent a sudden decrease in vacuum.

On 6-258 engines, the air cleaner has a spring-loaded trap door, **Fig. 50,** that closes off the air cleaner and carburetor when the engine is off. This door is actuated by a vacuum motor. When the engine is started, intake manifold vacuum opens the door allowing air to enter the air cleaner. A reverse delay valve is also used to prevent the trap door from closing during low vacuum level operation (such as during acceleration). The valve also functions to prevent abrupt closings of the trap door when the engine is turned off by gradually allowing atmospheric pressure to enter the vacuum motor.

Service

THERMAL SWITCH, REPLACE

The heated air duct is attached to the snorkel either by a screw or a clamp depending on engine. If the duct is not detached before air cleaner removal, the heated air duct and stove may be damaged.

1. Remove air cleaner and disconnect hoses from switch.
2. Pry up tabs on switch retaining clip, then remove clip and switch from air cleaner.
3. Install replacement switch and gasket assembly in original position.
4. Press retainer clip on hose nipple connectors, **Fig. 51.**
5. Connect vacuum hoses and install air cleaner.

TRAP DOOR VACUUM MOTOR, REPLACE

1. Disconnect vacuum hoses, heated and ambient air ducts and remove air cleaner.
2. Remove trap door vacuum motor retaining rivet from bracket.
3. Lift motor away from bracket, then rotate to clear door arm and remove.
4. Rotate replacement motor to clear door arm and lower into bracket.
5. Secure motor to bracket with rivet.
6. Install air cleaner, ducts and vacuum hoses. Check trap door for proper operation.

AIR VALVE VACUUM MOTOR, REPLACE

1. Disconnect heated air duct. Make sure to remove clamp or screw before removal, as damage to the duct may result.
2. Remove air cleaner assembly.
3. Disconnect vacuum hoses from air valve motor, thermal switch and trap door (if used).
4. Remove rivet attaching air valve vacuum motor to snorkel.
5. Lift motor, tilt to one side to disconnect linkage from air valve assembly and remove.
6. Insert replacement vacuum motor assembly linkage into air valve assembly and position in snorkel.

Part Numbers	Time in Seconds	Color and Identification
527011	8.0 ± 1.6	Black and Blue
547833	3.0 ± 0.6	Black and Brown

Fig. 46 Reverse delay valve (4 port) test chart. 1982

Part Numbers	Time in Seconds	Color and Identification
3230422	200 ± 40	Black and Green
3231118	100 ± 20	Black and Yellow
3231379	63.5 ± 13.5	Black and White
3235261	10 ± 2	Black and Gray
3236284	4 ± 0.8	Black and Purple
3237293	20 ± 4	Black and Brown
3239134	2 ± 0.5	Black and Orange

Fig. 47 Forward delay valve test chart. 1982

Part Numbers	Time in Seconds	Color and Identification
3237255	2.0 ± 0.5	Orange and Orange

Fig. 48 2-way delay valve test chart. 1982

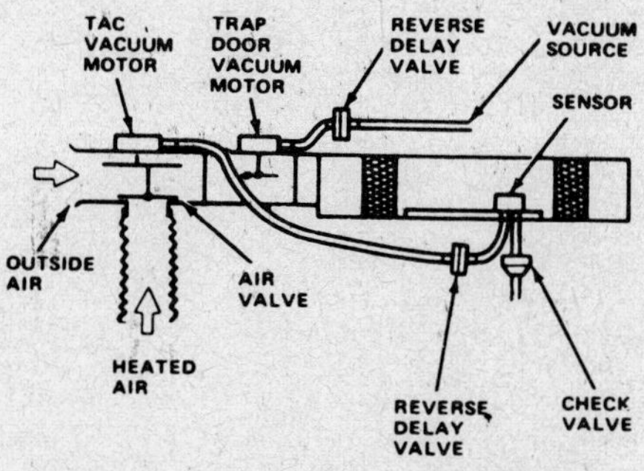

Fig. 49 Vacuum controlled thermostatic air cleaner.

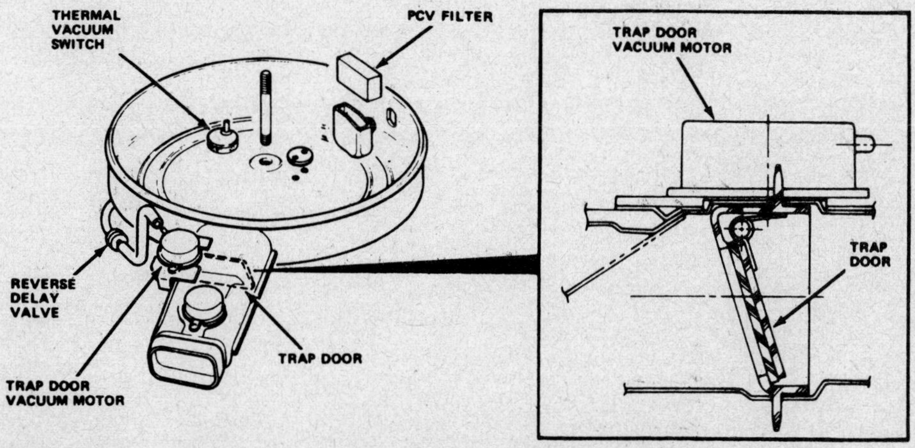

Fig. 50 Trap door. 1982–84 6-258

7. Attach motor to snorkel with rivet. **Make sure rivet does not interfere with movement of air valve.**
8. Reconnect vacuum hoses, install air cleaner assembly, reconnect heated air ducts and check system for proper operation.

Diagnosis

1. Disconnect ambient air duct and observe position of air diverter valve. It should be fully open to incoming ambient air (heat off position).
2. Start engine and observe position of air diverter valve. It should be fully closed to incoming ambient air (heat on position).
3. Quickly open throttle 1/2-3/4 open and release. Air diverter valve should momentarily remain stationary and then move toward heat off position and back to heat on position.
4. Loosely attach flexible ambient air duct and allow engine to reach normal operating temperature. Remove ambient air duct and observe air diverter valve. It should be either fully open to ambient air or an in-between position that allows correct inlet air temperature. Stop engine and reconnect air duct.
5. If operation of diverter door is not as outlined, inspect for a mechanical bind in the snorkel, disconnected vacuum hoses or leaking vacuum motor, thermal switch, reverse delay valve and check valve.

TRAP DOOR TEST

1. With engine off, remove air cleaner cover and observe position of trap door. It should be closed.
2. Disconnect vacuum hose from intake manifold vacuum source and apply an external vacuum of 2-4 inches Hg. Trap door should open.
3. If door does not open, apply vacuum directly to vacuum motor on air cleaner intake duct. If door does not open, check for binding or distortion and adjust as necessary. Replace vacuum motor if door swings freely.
4. If door opens when vacuum is applied in step 3, inspect vacuum hose for obstructions, cracks and kinks. Correct as necessary and retest.

5. If vacuum hose is satisfactory, remove reverse delay valve, then join vacuum hoses and perform step 2. If door opens, replace reverse delay valve.

REVERSE DELAY VALVE TEST

This valve provides delay before allowing the trap door to completely close.

1. Disconnect yellow hose from yellow end of valve and apply an external vacuum source of 2 to 4 inches Hg.
2. Note amount of time required for atmospheric pressure to pass through valve and eliminate vacuum.
3. Replace valve if amount of time noted in step 2 is less than 4.5 seconds or more than 13.2 seconds.

THERMAL SWITCH TEST

1. Disconnect hoses from thermal switch.
2. Connect vacuum pump and vacuum gauge to switch.

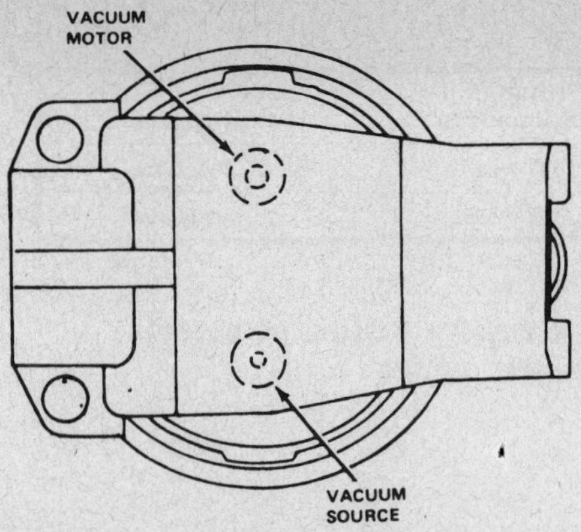

Fig. 51 Thermal switch installation

3. Apply 14 inches Hg to switch.
4. Valve should hold vacuum when its temperature is below 40°F and should release vacuum when switch temperature is above 55°F. Replace switch if defective.

CHRYSLER MOTORS

CHRYSLER

DODGE

IMPERIAL

PLYMOUTH

GENERAL SERVICE

CHRYSLER REAR WHEEL DRIVE

NOTE: The following models are covered in this chapter: CHRYSLER–Cordoba (1982-83), Fifth Avenue (1984-88), Imperial (1982-83), New Yorker (1982), New Yorker Fifth Avenue (1983); DODGE–Diplomat (1982-88), Mirada (1982-83); PLYMOUTH–Gran Fury (1982-88).

INDEX OF SERVICE OPERATIONS

NOTE: Refer to rear of this manual for manufacturer's special service tool suppliers.

Specifications

GENERAL ENGINE SPECIFICATIONS

Year	Engine		Fuel System	Bore & Stroke	Com-pression Ratio	Net H.P. @ RPM③	Maximum Torque Ft. Lbs. @ RPM	Normal Oil Pressure Pounds
	CID①/Liter	VIN Code②						
CHRYSLER & IMPERIAL								
1982	6-225, 3.7L⑥	E	1945, 1 Bbl.⑦	3.40 x 4.12	8.4	90@ 3600	160 @ 1600	30-70
	6-225, 3.7L④	E	6145, 1 Bbl.⑦	3.40 x 4.12	8.4	90 @ 3600	160 @ 1600	30-70
	V8-318, 5.2L⑥	K	BBD, 2 Bbl.⑤	3.91 x 3.31	8.5	130 @ 4000	230 @ 2000	30-80
	V8-318, 5.2L④	M	TQ, 4 Bbl.⑤	3.91 x 3.31	8.5	165 @ 4000	240 @ 2000	30-80
	V8-318, 5.2L	J	E.F.I.⑧	3.91 x 3.31	8.5	140 @ 4000	245 @ 2000	30-80
1983	6-225, 3.7L	H	6145, 1 Bbl.⑦	3.40 x 4.12	8.4	90 @ 3600	165 @ 1600	30-70
	V8-318, 5.2L	P	BBD, 2 Bbl.⑤	3.91 x 3.31	8.5	130 @ 4000	230 @ 1600	30-80
	V8-318, 5.2L	N	E.F.I.⑧	3.91 x 3.31	8.5	140 @ 4000	245 @ 2000	30-80
1984	V8-318, 5.2L	P	BBD, 2 Bbl.⑤	3.91 x 3.31	8.6	130 @ 4000	235 @ 1600	30-80
1985-88	V8-318, 5.2L	P	6280, 2 Bbl.⑦	3.91 x 3.31	9.0	140 @ 3600	265 @ 1600	30-80
DODGE								
1982	6-225, 3.7L⑥	E	1945, 1 Bbl.⑦	3.40 x 4.12	8.4	90 @ 3600	160 @ 1600	30-70
	6-225, 3.7L④	E	6145, 1 Bbl.⑦	3.40 x 4.12	8.4	90 @ 3600	160 @ 1600	30-70
	V8-318, 5.2L⑥	K	BBD, 2 Bbl.⑤	3.91 x 3.31	8.5	130 @ 4000	230 @ 2000	30-80
	V8-318, 5.2L④	M	TQ, 4 Bbl.⑤	3.91 x 3.31	8.5	165 @ 4000	240 @ 2000	30-80
1983	6-225, 3.7L	H	6145, 1 Bbl.⑦	3.40 x 4.12	8.4	90 @ 3600	165 @ 1600	30-70
	V8-318, 5.2L	P	BBD, 2 Bbl.⑤	3.91 x 3.31	8.5	130 @ 4000	230 @ 1600	30-70
1984	V8-318, 5.2L	P	BBD, 2 Bbl.⑤	3.91 x 3.31	8.6	135 @ 4000	230 @ 1600	30-80
1985-88	V8-318, 5.2L	P	6280, 2 Bbl.⑦	3.91 x 3.31	9.0	140 @ 3600	265 @ 1600	30-80
PLYMOUTH								
1982	6-225, 3.7L⑥	E	1945, 1 Bbl.⑦	3.40 x 4.12	8.4	90 @ 3600	160 @ 1600	30-70
	6-225, 3.7L④	E	6145, 1 Bbl.⑦	3.40 x 4.12	8.4	90 @ 3600	160 @ 1600	30-70
	V8-318, 5.2L⑥	K	BBD, 2 Bbl.⑤	3.91 x 3.31	8.5	130 @ 4000	230 @ 2000	30-80
	V8-318, 5.2L④	M	TQ, 4 Bbl.⑤	3.91 x 3.31	8.5	165 @ 4000	240 @ 2000	30-80
1983	6-225, 3.7L	H	6145, 1 Bbl.⑦	3.40 x 4.12	8.4	90 @ 3600	165 @ 1600	30-70
	V8-318, 5.2L	P	BBD, 2 Bbl.⑤	3.91 x 3.31	8.5	130 @ 4000	230 @ 1600	30-70
1984	V8-318, 5.2L	P	BBD, 2 Bbl.⑤	3.91 x 3.31	8.6	130 @ 4000	235 @ 1600	30-80
1985-88	V8-318, 5.2L	P	6280, 2 Bbl.⑤	3.91 x 3.31	9.0	140 @ 3600	265 @ 1600	30-80

①—CID-Cubic Inch Displacement.
②—On 1980 vehicles, the fifth digit in the VIN denotes engine code. On 1981-86 vehicles, the eighth digit in the VIN denotes engine code.
③—Ratings are net-as installed in vehicle.
④—California.
⑤—Carter.
⑥—Exc. California.
⑦—Holley.
⑦—Electronic Fuel Injection.

ALTERNATOR & REGULATOR SPECIFICATIONS

Year	Unit Number	Ground Polarity	Field Coil Draw Amperes	Current Output			Operating Voltage		
				Engine R.P.M.	Amperes	Volts	Engine R.P.M.	Volts	Voltage @ 80°F ①
1982-83	Yellow Tag ③	Negative	4.5-6.5②	1250	47⑤	15	1250	15	13.9-14.6
	Brown Tag	Negative	4.5-6.5②	1250	58⑤	15	1250	15	13.9-14.6
	Yellow Tag ④	Negative	4.75-6.0②	900	97⑤	13	900	13	13.9-14.6
1984-88	Yellow Tag ③	Negative	2.5-5.0②	1250	47⑤	15	1250	15	13.9-14.6
	Brown Tag	Negative	2.5-5.0②	1250	58⑤	15	1250	15	13.9-14.6
	Yellow Tag ④	Negative	2.5-5.0②	900	97⑤	13	900	13	13.9-14.6

①—For each 10 degree rise in temperature subtract .04 volt. Temperature is checked with thermometer two inches from installed voltage regulator cover.
②—Current draw at 12 volts while turning rotor shaft by hand.
③—60 amp rating.
④—114 amp rating.
⑤—Minimum output.

STARTING MOTOR APPLICATIONS

Year	Engine	Starter Ident. No.
1982-83	6-225, V8-318	4111860
1984-88	V8-318	4111860

ENGINE TIGHTENING SPECIFICATIONS*

*Torque specifications are for clean and lightly lubricated threads only. Dry or dirty threads produce increased friction which prevents accurate measurement of tightness.

Year	Engine/VIN	Spark Plugs Ft. Lbs.	Cylinder Head Bolts Ft. Lbs.	Intake Manifold Ft. Lbs.	Exhaust Manifold Ft. Lbs.	Rocker Arm Shaft Bracket Ft. Lbs.	Rocker Arm Cover In. Lbs.	Connecting Rod Cap Bolts Ft. Lbs.	Main Bearing Cap Bolts Ft. Lbs.	Flywheel to Crankshaft Ft. Lbs.	Vibration Damper to Crankshaft Ft. Lbs.
1982-83	6-225/E,H	10	70	④	120①	24	80	45	85	55	②
	V8-318⑤	30	95	45	③	200①	80	45	85	55	100
1984-88	V8-318/P	30	95	45	③	200①	95	45	85	55	100

①—Inch pounds.
②—Press fit.
③—Screw, 20 ft. lbs.; Nut, 15 ft. lbs.
④—Intake to exhaust manifold stud nut 240 in. lbs., Intake to exhaust manifold bolts 200 in. lbs.
⑤—Refer to General Engine Specifications for VIN code.

REAR AXLE SPECIFICATIONS

Year	Model	Carrier Type	Ring Gear & Pinion Backlash		Pinion Bearing Preload			Differential Bearing Preload		
			Method	Adjustment	Method	New Bearings Inch Lbs.	Used Bearings Inch Lbs.	Method	New Bearings Inch Lbs.	Used Bearings Inch Lbs.
1982-83	8¼"⑤	Integral	②	.006-.008	①	20-35④	10-25④	②	③	③
	9¼"⑤	Integral	②	.006-.008	①	20-35④	10-25④	②	③	③
	7¼"⑤	Integral	②	.004-.006	①	15-25	—	②	③	③
1984-88	7¼"	Integral	②	.006-.008	①	20-35④	10-25④	②	③	③
	8¼"	Integral	②	.006-.008	①	20-35④	10-25④	②	③	③

①—Collapsible spacer.
②—Threaded adjusters.
③—Preload is correct when ring gear & pinion backlash is properly adjusted.
④—Adjust by turning pinion shaft nut with an inch-pound torque wrench with seal removed.
⑤—"C" lock type.

WHEEL ALIGNMENT SPECIFICATIONS

NOTE: See that riding height is correct before checking wheel alignment.

Year	Model	Caster Angle, Degrees		Camber Angle, Degrees				Toe-In. Inch	Toe-Out on Turns, Deg.	
				Limits		Desired				
		Limits	Desired	Left	Right	Left	Right		Outer Wheel	Inner Wheel
CHRYSLER & IMPERIAL										
1982-88	All	+1¼ to +3¾	+2½	−¼ to +1¼	−¼ to +1¼	+½	+½	1/16 to 3/16	18	20
DODGE										
1982-88	All	+1¼ to +3¾	+2½	−¼ to +1¼	−¼ to +1¼	+½	+½	1/16 to 3/16	18	20
PLYMOUTH										
1982-88	All	+1¼ to +3¾	+2½	−¼ to +1¼	−¼ to +1¼	+½	+½	1/16 to 3/16	18	20

COOLING SYSTEM & CAPACITY DATA

Year	Model or Engine/VIN	Cooling Capacity, Qts.		Radiator Cap Relief Pressure, Lbs.	Thermo. Opening Temp.	Fuel Tank Gals.	Engine Oil Refill Qts. ①	Auto. Trans. Qts. ②	Rear Axle Oil Pints
		Less A/C	With A/C						
CHRYSLER									
1982-83	Cordoba 6-225/E, H	11½	15	16	195	18	4	8½	④
	Cordoba V8-318③	15	15½	16	195	18	4	8½	④
	New Yorker 6-225/E, H	11½	12½	16	195	18	4	8½	④
	New Yorker V8-318③	15	15½	16	195	18	4	8½	④
1984-88	Fifth Avenue V8-318/P	15½⑦	15½⑦	16	195	18	4	⑧⑨	⑤
IMPERIAL									
1982-83	All	15½	16½	16	195	18	4	8½	4.4
DODGE									
1982-83	Diplomat 6-225/E, H	11½	⑥	16	195	18	4	8½	④
	Diplomat V8-318③	15	15½	16	195	18	4	8½	④
	Mirada 6-225/E, H	11½	12½	16	195	18	4	8½	④
	Mirada V8-318③	15	15½	16	195	18	4	8½	④
1984-88	Diplomat V8-318/P	15½⑦	15½⑦	16	195	18	4	⑧⑨	⑤
PLYMOUTH									
1981	Gran Fury 6-225/E	11½	14½	16	195	21	4	8.15	④
	Gran Fury V8-318/K, M	15	17½	16	195	21	4	8.15	④
1982-83	Gran Fury 6-225/E, H	11½	12½	16	195	18	4	8½	④
	Gran Fury V8-318③	15	15½	16	195	18	4	8½	④
1984-88	Gran Fury V8-318/P	15½⑦	15½⑦	16	195	18	4	⑧⑨	⑤

①—Add 1 qt. with filter change.
②—Approximate. Make final check with dipstick.
③—Refer to General Engine Specifications for V.I.N. code.
④—With 7¼" ring gear, 2½ pts.; with 8¼" ring gear, 4.4 pts.; with 9¼" ring gear, 4½ pts.
⑤—7¼ inch axle, 2.5 pts.; 8¼ inch axle, 4.4 pts.
⑥—1982, 15 qts.; 1983, 12½ qts.
⑦—Heavy duty cooling system, 16½ qts.
⑧—A904 trans., 8.15 qts., A727 trans., 8 qts.
⑨—Add an additional ¼ qt. with auxiliary cooler.

Electrical Section

INDEX

STARTER

REPLACE

1. Disconnect ground cable at battery.
2. Remove cable at starter.
3. Disconnect wires at solenoid.
4. Remove one stud nut and one bolt attaching starter motor to flywheel housing.
5. Slide transmission oil cooler bracket off stud (if so equipped).
6. Remove starter motor and removable seal.
7. Reverse above procedure to install. **When tightening attaching bolt and nut be sure to hold starter away from engine to insure proper alignment.**

IGNITION SWITCH & LOCK

REPLACE

1. Disconnect battery ground cable and remove turn signal switch as outlined elsewhere in this chapter.
2. Remove ignition key lamp assembly retaining screw and the assembly.
3. Remove snap ring from upper end of steering shaft.
4. Remove bearing housing to lock housing retaining screws, then the bearing housing from shaft.
5. Remove bearing lower snap ring from shaft.
6. Pry sleeve from steering shaft lock plate hub, then, using a suitable punch, drive lock plate groove pin from lock plate. **Drive pin from end without grooves.**
7. Remove lock plate from shaft, then the shaft through lower end of column.
8. Remove shift indicator pointer screw, if equipped.
9. Remove buzzer switch retaining screw and the switch.
10. Remove lock lever guide plate retaining screws and the guide plate.
11. Place lock cylinder in the "Lock" position and remove key. With a suitable tool, depress spring loaded lock retainer and pull lock cylinder from housing bore, **Figs. 1 and 2.**
12. Remove ignition switch retaining screws and the ignition switch.
13. Reverse procedure to install.

IGNITION SWITCH

ADJUST

EXCEPT CORDOBA & MIRADA

1. Disconnect battery ground cable.
2. Place transmission in Park and ignition lock in the lock position.
3. If switch was not removed from column, loosen two mounting bolts and insert a lock pin into hole on switch marked lock. If switch was removed from column, pin switch in the lock position, then place switch into rod and rotate 90 degrees over mounting holes. Loosely install mounting bolts. Replacement switches are supplied with locking pins.
4. Apply light upward pressure to align rod and switch and hold switch in this position while tightening retaining bolts. Remove locking pin.
5. Remove lock pin from switch.
6. Reverse procedure to install.

COLUMN MOUNTED DIMMER SWITCH

ADJUST

1982–83 CORDOBA, IMPERIAL & MIRADA

1. Loosen two switch mounting screws, then depress switch plunger slightly and insert locking pin.
2. Apply light upward pressure to remove freeplay between switch and rod.
3. While holding switch with slight upward pressure tighten the two mounting screws.
4. Remove locking pin and check switch for proper operation.

LIGHT SWITCH

REPLACE

1982–83 CORDOBA, IMPERIAL & MIRADA

1. If equipped, remove intermittent wipe and power antenna module assembly.
2. Disconnect battery ground cable.
3. Depress switch stem release button and pull knob and stem from switch.
4. Using a small screwdriver, snap out switch trim bezel, then remove mounting nut.
5. Pull switch from cluster and disconnect wire connector.
6. Reverse procedure to install.

DIPLOMAT, 1982 NEW YORKER, GRAN FURY & FIFTH AVENUE

1. Disconnect battery ground cable.
2. Remove cluster bezel.
3. Remove switch mounting plate attaching screws and pull switch and plate assembly outward.
4. Depress headlight switch stem, then depress release button and pull knob and stem from switch.
5. Remove switch mounting nut, then disconnect electrical connector and remove switch.
6. Reverse procedure to install.

STOP LIGHT SWITCH

REPLACE

1. Disconnect battery ground cable.
2. Disconnect wiring from switch and remove switch from brake pedal bracket.
3. Reverse procedure to install.

NEUTRAL SAFETY & BACK-UP SWITCH

REPLACE

1. Unscrew switch from transmission case, allowing fluid to drain into a container, **Fig. 3.**

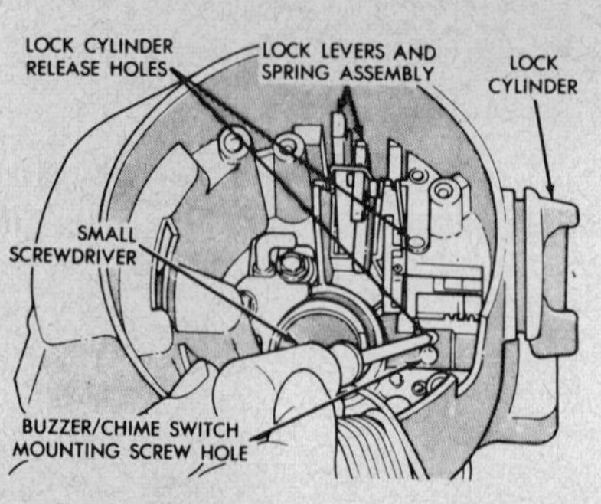

Fig. 1 Ignition lock removal. Model less tilt column

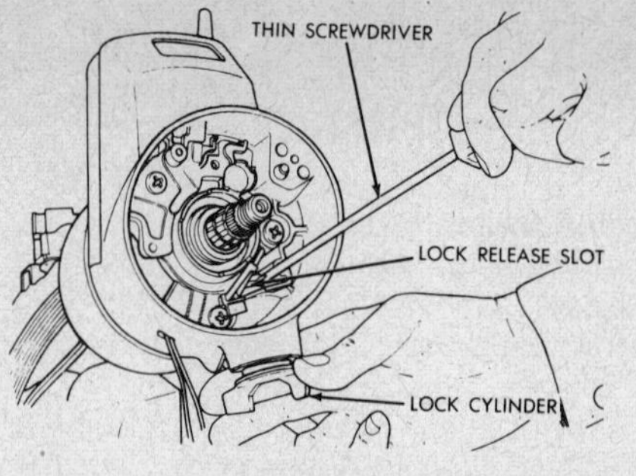

Fig. 2 Ignition lock removal. Models w/tilt column

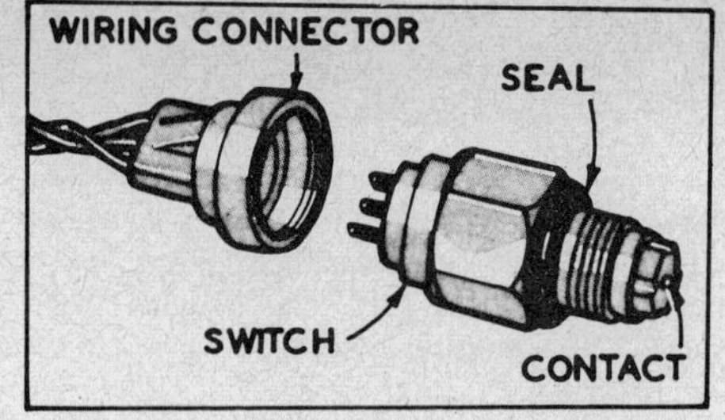

Fig. 3 Neutral safety switch

2. Move shift lever to Park and then to Neutral positions and inspect to see that switch operating lever is centered in switch opening in case.
3. Screw switch into transmission case and torque to 24 ft. lbs.
4. Add fluid to proper level.
5. Check to see that switch operates only in Park and Neutral.

HORN SOUNDER & STEERING WHEEL

REPLACE

1. Disconnect ground cable at battery.
2. On steering wheels with center horn button, remove button by pulling outward. On steering wheels with pressure sensitive switch pad, remove mounting screws from underside of wheel, then disconnect horn wire when removing pad.
3. On models with center horn button, disconnect horn switch wire and remove switch and ring.
4. On all models, remove steering wheel nut and use a suitable puller to remove steering wheel. **Do not bump or hammer on steering shaft to remove wheel as damage to shaft may result.**
5. Reverse procedure to install.

TURN SIGNAL SWITCH

REPLACE

1. Disconnect battery ground cable.
2. Remove steering wheel as described under "Steering Wheel, Replace."
3. On models equipped with tilt column, remove lock plate cover and lock plate.
4. On all models, remove lower instrument panel bezel.
5. On Diplomat, 1982 New Yorker, Gran Fury, and 1983 New Yorker Fifth Avenue and 1984-88 Fifth Avenue models equipped with tilt column, remove gear shift indicator, then the two steering column to lower instrument panel reinforcement retaining screws. Remove mounting bracket from steering column.
6. On all models, unsnap four plastic retainers and remove wiring through steering column.
7. Disconnect light blue wire connector, then remove turn signal lever attaching screw and allow lever assembly to hang loosely from column.
8. Remove turn signal/hazard warning switch attaching screws, then pull switch from steering column, while carefully guiding wires up through column opening.
9. Reverse procedure to install.

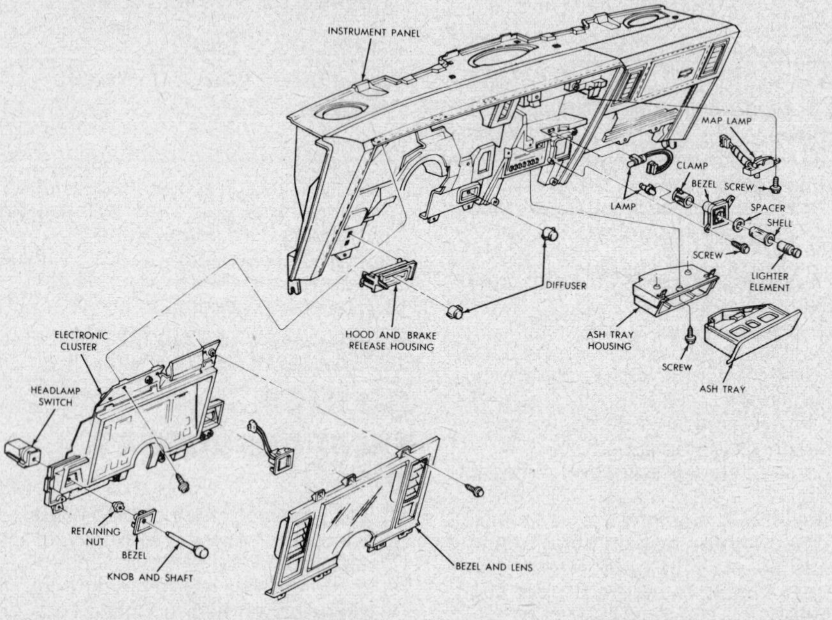

Fig. 4 Electronic instrument cluster. 1982–83 Imperial

INSTRUMENT CLUSTER

REPLACE

1982–83 IMPERIAL

1. Disconnect battery ground cable.
2. Remove cigar lighter and ashtray from instrument panel, **Fig. 4.**
3. Remove instrument panel cluster overlay attaching screws, then the overlay.
4. Remove lower instrument panel cluster bezel attaching screws, then the bezel.
5. Remove instrument cluster bezel attaching screws and bezel. Remove plastic pins retaining cluster mask to cluster and the mask.
6. Remove instrument cluster to panel attaching screws, then pull cluster forward and disconnect wire connectors from cluster.
7. Remove cluster assembly.
8. Reverse procedure to install.

1982–83 CORDOBA & MIRADA

1. Disconnect battery ground cable.
2. Remove five hood and brake release bezel screws, then the bezel.
3. Remove four accessory switch bezel screws, then the bezel.
4. Pull gearshift pointer cable from steering column.
5. Remove lower left and righthand bezels and gearshift pointer cable.
6. Remove three steering column toe plate bolts at firewall, then the nuts and washers attaching steering column bracket to instrument panel steering column support bracket. Lower the steering column, allowing steering wheel to rest on seat.
7. Disconnect speedometer cable and right hand mirror control cable.
8. Remove five screws securing instrument cluster to panel, **Fig. 5.**
9. Roll cluster downward and disconnect headlamp switch electrical connector and instrument cluster wiring.
10. Remove instrument cluster from vehicle.
11. Reverse procedure to install.

DIPLOMAT, 1982 NEW YORKER, GRAN FURY & FIFTH AVENUE

1. Disconnect battery ground cable.
2. Remove lower panel assembly.
3. Remove left lower reinforcement by removing two screws located at left end.
4. Remove gear shift indicator.
5. Remove steering column toe plate mounting bolts and upper steering column mounting nuts, then lower the steering column.
6. Disconnect speedometer cable.
7. Remove two mounting screws and detach fuse block from mid-reinforcement.
8. Remove one screw attaching radio to mid-reinforcement.
9. Remove four upper and four lower cluster mounting screws, **Fig. 6.**
10. Pull cluster out from instrument panel and disconnect wire connectors, control cables and vacuum harness, then remove cluster assembly.
11. Reverse procedure to install.

WINDSHIELD WIPER MOTOR
REPLACE

1. Disconnect battery ground cable.
2. Remove wiper arm and blades.
3. Remove cowl screen.
4. Remove drive crank arm retaining nut and drive crank. Disconnect wiring to motor.
5. Unfasten and remove wiper motor.
6. Reverse procedure to install.

WINDSHIELD WIPER TRANSMISSION
REPLACE

1. Disconnect battery ground cable.
2. Remove top plastic screen.
3. Remove arm and blade assemblies.
4. Remove drive crank from motor by removing the attaching nut.
5. On all models except Diplomat, LeBaron, 1982 New Yorker, Gran Fury and Fifth Avenue, remove six pivot mounting screws.
6. On Diplomat, LeBaron, 1982 New Yorker, Gran Fury and Fifth Avenue, remove pivot mounting nut and washer.
7. Reverse procedure to install.

WINDSHIELD WIPER SWITCH
REPLACE

Refer to "Turn Signal Switch, Replace" procedure.

1. Disconnect battery ground cable.
2. Remove instrument cluster bezel.
3. Remove switch module assembly attaching screws, then pull assembly out and let hang in order to gain access to switch.

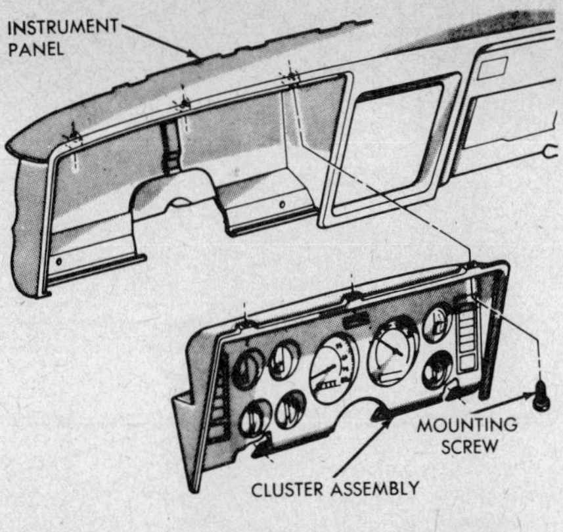

Fig. 5 Instrument cluster removal. 1982–83 Cordoba & Mirada

4. Remove switch knob from stem, then remove switch mounting screws.
5. Disconnect switch wire connector and remove switch.
6. Reverse procedure to install.

RADIO
REPLACE

When installing radio, be sure to adjust antenna trimmer for peak performance.

1982–83 CORDOBA, IMPERIAL & MIRADA

1. Disconnect battery ground cable.
2. Remove center bezel, then the radio to panel attaching screws.
3. Pull radio from instrument panel, then disconnect antenna and electrical leads.
4. Reverse procedure to install.

EXC. 1982–83 CORDOBA, IMPERIAL & MIRADA

1. Disconnect battery ground cable.
2. Remove instrument cluster bezel, then the radio mounting screws.
3. Pull radio from panel and disconnect all wiring, then remove radio from vehicle.
4. Reverse procedure to install.

HEATER CORE
REPLACE

Before attempting to remove a heater core, disconnect the battery ground cable, drain the radiator and remove inlet and outlet hoses from heater assembly in engine compartment.

1982–83 CORDOBA, IMPERIAL & MIRADA

Less Air Conditioning

1. Disconnect battery ground cable and drain cooling system.
2. Disconnect heater hoses from heater core.
3. Disconnect vacuum hoses from water valve and manifold tee, then push hoses and grommet through dash panel.
4. Remove four nuts securing heater assembly to dash panel.
5. Move front seat rearward and remove console, if equipped.
6. Remove heater control and disconnect vacuum harness from extension harness, if equipped.
7. Remove glove box, ashtray and housing, righthand lap cooler duct, lower right hand trim panel or bezel, and the righthand cowl trim pad.
8. Disconnect blower motor electrical connections.
9. Disconnect temperature control cable from heater housing, then remove heater distribution housing, **Figs. 7 and 8.**
10. Support heater housing and remove the heater housing to plenum mounting brace. Pull housing rearward and move toward right side to remove.
11. Remove heater housing top cover, then the heater core retaining screw.
12. Lift heater core from housing.
13. Reverse procedure to install.

With Air Conditioning

1. Disconnect battery ground cable and drain cooling system.
2. Discharge air conditioning refrigerant system.
3. Disconnect heater hoses from heater core.
4. Remove "H" valve and cap refrigerant lines. Remove condensate drain tube.
5. Disconnect vacuum lines from engine compartment and push grommet and vacuum lines through dash panel. **On manual air conditioning systems, the vacuum lines are connected to the manifold vacuum tee and water valve. On semi-automatic air conditioning systems, the vacuum lines are connected to the vacuum reservoir and water valve.**
6. Remove four nuts attaching evaporator heater assembly to dash panel.
7. Move front seat rearward and remove console, if equipped.
8. Remove air conditioning switch control from dash panel and disconnect vacuum harness from harness extension, if equipped.
9. Remove ashtray and housing and glove box assembly.
10. Disconnect righthand lap cooler tube from lap cooler and remove the righthand trim panel or bezel.
11. Remove righthand cowl trim pad and disconnect blower motor electrical connections.
12. Disconnect vacuum harness from harness extension, then remove heater distribution duct.
13. Disconnect temperature control cable from evaporator heater housing.
14. Remove heater distribution housing and the center distribution duct, if equipped.
15. Remove the hi/lo door actuator, **Figs. 9 and 10.**
16. On models with semi-automatic air conditioning system, remove vacuum servo actuator from housing and the in-car air hose from compensator.
17. Support housing and remove brace between housing and plenum. Then,

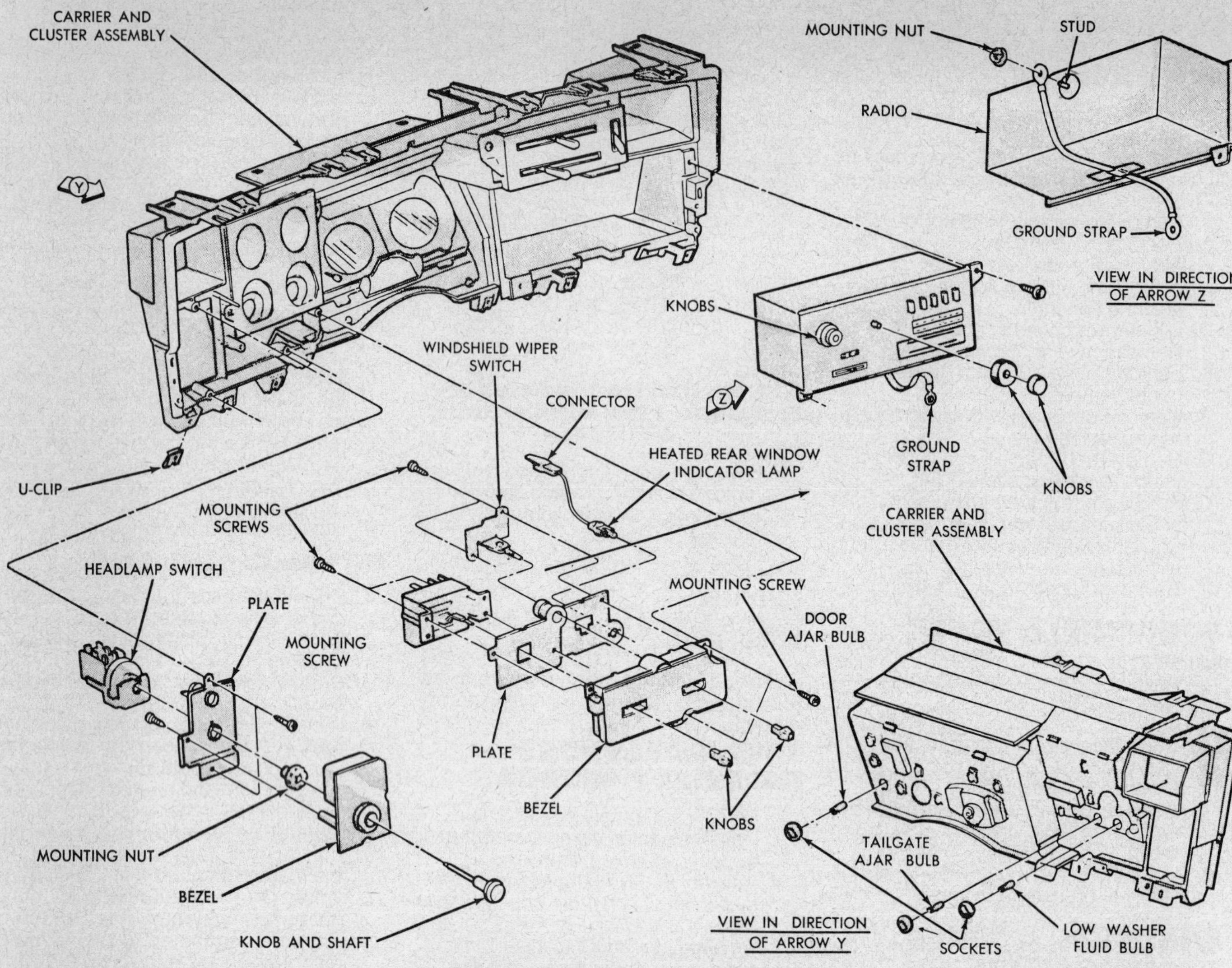

Fig. 6 Instrument cluster (Typical). Diplomat, 1982 New Yorker, Gran Fury, 1983 New Yorker & Fifth Avenue

pull housing rearward and move toward right side to remove.

18. Remove housing top cover and the heater core retaining screw.
19. Lift heater core from housing.
20. Reverse procedure to install.

EXC. 1982–83 CORDOBA, IMPERIAL & MIRADA

Less Air Conditioning

1. Disconnect battery ground cable and drain cooling system.
2. Disconnect and plug heater hoses from dash panel.
3. Remove heater core tube dash panel seals and retainer.
4. Remove instrument cluster bezel assembly, upper cover, steering column cover, right intermediate side cowl trim panel and the lower instrument panel.
5. Remove instrument panel center to lower reinforcement.
6. Remove right vent control cable from unit.
7. Disconnect temperature and mode door control cables from unit, then the blower motor resistor block wiring.
8. Remove heater assembly mounting nuts in engine compartment.
9. Remove heater support to plenum bracket and pull heater unit from dash panel.
10. Separate heater housing by removing retainer clips.
11. Remove heater core tube support clamp and slide heater core from housing.
12. Reverse procedure to install.

With Air Conditioning

1. Disconnect battery ground cable and drain cooling system.
2. Discharge refrigerant system.
3. Remove air cleaner, then disconnect heater hoses from heater core. Install plugs in heater core tubes to prevent coolant from spilling when removing unit.
4. Remove "H" valve, then cap refrigerant lines to prevent dirt and moisture from entering.
5. Remove instrument cluster bezel assembly.
6. Remove instrument panel upper cover, steering column cover and right intermediate side cowl trim panel.
7. Remove lower instrument panel.
8. Remove instrument center to lower reinforcement.
9. Remove floor console, if equipped.
10. Remove right center air distribution duct.
11. Disconnect locking tab on defroster distribution duct.
12. Disconnect temperature control cable from evaporator housing.
13. Disconnect blower motor resistor block wire connector.
14. Disconnect vacuum lines from water valve and vacuum source tee.
15. Remove wiring from evaporator housing and vacuum lines from inlet air housing, then disconnect vacuum harness coupling.
16. Remove drain tube from engine compartment.
17. Remove nuts from evaporator housing mounting studs on engine side of dash panel.
18. Remove hanger strap from plenum stud above evaporator housing, then tilt evaporator housing back to clear dash panel and remove housing from vehicle.

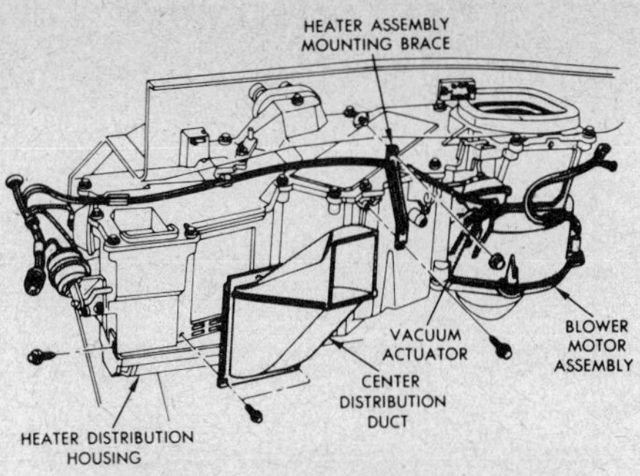

Fig. 7 Heater core & blower motor assembly (less A/C). 1982–83 Cordoba & Mirada

19. Remove blend air door lever from shaft.
20. Remove top cover screws and the cover.
21. Remove heater core from housing.
22. Reverse procedure to install.

BLOWER MOTOR REPLACE

EXC. 1982–83 CORDOBA, IMPERIAL & MIRADA

The blower motor is accessible from under right side of instrument panel.

Less A/C

1. Disconnect battery ground cable.
2. Disconnect blower motor ground and feed wires.
3. Remove blower motor to heater housing attaching screws, then remove blower motor.
4. Reverse procedure to install.

With A/C

1. Disconnect battery ground cable.
2. Disconnect blower motor feed wire, then remove blower motor housing to recirculation housing attaching nuts and separate blower motor housing from upper housing.
3. Remove blower motor plate attaching screws, then remove wire grommet, mounting plate and blower motor and wheel as an assembly.
4. Reverse procedure to install.

1982–83 CORDOBA, IMPERIAL & MIRADA

The blower motor is accessible from under right side of instrument panel.

1. Disconnect battery ground cable.
2. Remove glove box assembly.
3. Disconnect blower motor electrical connections.
4. Remove heater housing or evaporator-heater housing to plenum brace.
5. Remove blower motor mounting screws and the blower motor, **Figs. 7 and 8.**
6. Reverse procedure to install.

SPEED CONTROLS ADJUST

LOCK-IN SCREW ADJUSTMENT

Lock-in accuracy, **Fig. 9,** will be affected by poor engine performance (need for tuneup), loaded gross weight of car (trailering), improper slack in control cable. After the foregoing items have been considered and the speed sags or drops more than 2 to 3 mph when the speed control is activated, the lock-in adjusting screw should be turned counterclockwise approximately 1/4 turn per one mph correction required.

If a speed increase of more than 2 to 3 mph occurs, the lock-in adjusting screw should be turned clockwise 1/4 turn per one mph correction required. **This adjustment must not exceed two turns in either direction or damage to the unit may occur.**

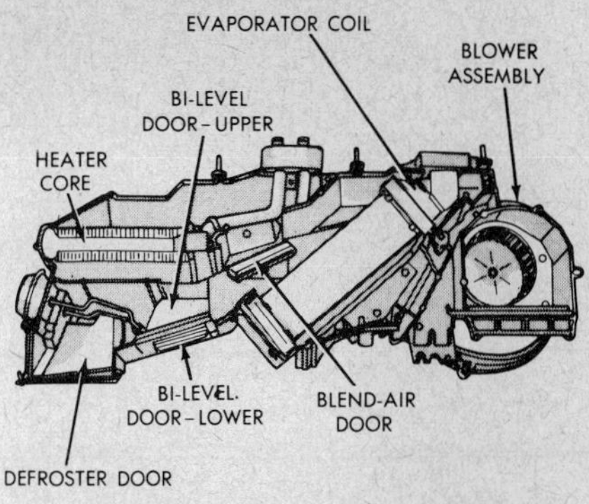

Fig. 8 Heater core & blower motor assembly (with A/C). 1982–83 Cordoba, Imperial & Mirada

Throttle Cable Adjustment

Optimum servo performance is obtained with a given amount of freeplay in the throttle control cable, **Fig. 10.** To obtain proper freeplay, insert a 1/16 inch diameter pin between forward end of slot in cable end of carburetor linkage pin (hair pin clip removed from linkage pin). With choke in full open position and carburetor at curb idle, pull cable back toward dash panel without moving carburetor linkage until all freeplay is removed. Tighten cable clamp bolt to 45 inch pounds, remove 1/16 inch pin and install hair pin clip.

Brake Switch Adjustment

1. Loosen switch bracket.
2. Insert a .130 inch spacer gauge between brake pushrod and switch with pedal in free position.
3. Push switch bracket assembly toward brake pushrod until plunger is fully depressed and switch contacts spacer.
4. Tighten bracket bolt to 75 inch lbs. and remove spacer.

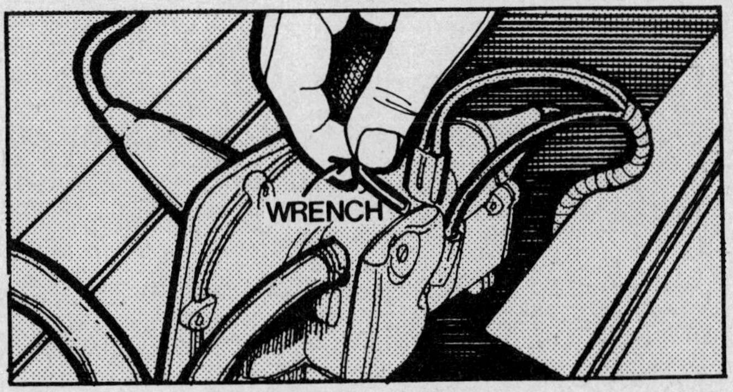

Fig. 9 Speed Control lock-in screw adjustment

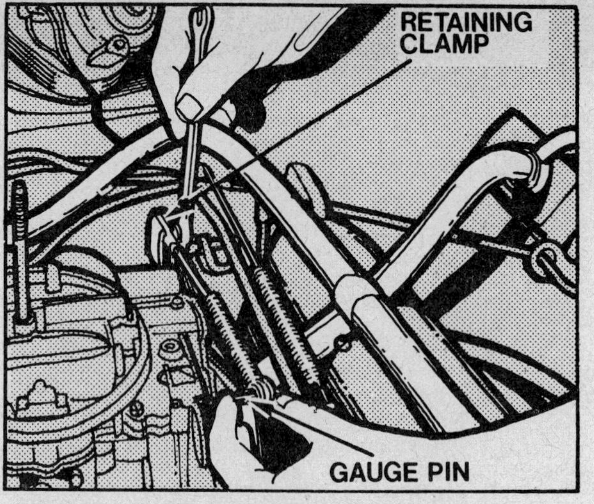

Fig. 10 Speed Control servo cable throttle adjustment

6-225 (3.7L) & V8-318 (5.2L) Engine Section

INDEX

ENGINE MOUNTS
REPLACE

1. Disconnect throttle linkage at transmission and at carburetor.
2. Raise hood and position fan to clear radiator hose and radiator top tank.
3. Remove torque nuts from insulator studs.
4. Raise engine just enough to remove front engine mount.
5. Reverse above to install.

ENGINE
REPLACE
V8-318

1. Scribe a line on hinge brackets on hood to assure proper adjustments when installing. Then remove hood.
2. Remove battery, drain cooling system, remove all hoses, fan shroud, disconnect oil cooler lines and remove radiator.
3. On models with A/C, remove compressor from mounting bracket and position on right fender. **Do not tilt compressor when removed from mounting bracket. Before installing compressor turn pulley several revolutions by hand to ensure all oil is back in compressor oil sump.**
4. On all models, remove distributor cap, vacuum lines and wiring.
5. Remove carburetor, linkage, starter wires and oil pressure wire.
6. Disconnect power steering hoses, if equipped.

7. Remove starter, alternator, charcoal canister and horns.
8. Disconnect exhaust pipe at manifold.
9. On vehicles with automatic transmission:
   a. Mark converter and drive plate to aid in installation.
   b. Remove torque converter drive plate bolts.
   c. Install a C-clamp on bottom front of torque converter, to assure that converter remains properly positioned in transmission housing.
   d. Remove converter housing to engine bolts.
   e. Support transmission in its normal position to assure ease of installation.
10. On vehicles with manual transmission, remove transmission.
11. Attach engine lifting fixture.
12. Remove engine front mounting bolts, then raise and work engine out of chassis.
13. Reverse procedure to install.

6-225

1. Scribe hood hinge outlines on hood and remove hood.
2. Drain cooling system and remove battery and carburetor air cleaner.
3. Disconnect transmission cooler lines at radiator (if equipped).
4. Remove radiator and hoses.
5. On models with A/C, remove compressor from mounting bracket and position on right fender. **Do not tilt compressor when removed from mounting bracket. Before installing compressor turn pulley several revolutions by hand to ensure all oil is back in compressor sump.**
6. On all models, remove closed ventilation system and evaporative control system from cylinder head cover.
7. Disconnect fuel lines, vacuum lines, carburetor linkage and wiring to engine.
8. Disconnect power steering hoses, if equipped.
9. Remove starter, alternator and horns.
10. Disconnect exhaust pipe at manifold.
11. Remove converter cover plate.
12. On manual transmission equipped vehicles disconnect propeller shaft, tie out of the way and disconnect wires and linkage at transmission.
13. On manual transmission equipped vehicles attach engine support fixture, remove engine rear crossmember and remove transmission.
14. On automatic transmission equipped vehicles disconnect torque converter drive plate from engine. Mark converter and drive plate to aid in installation. Support transmission in its normal position in relation to the vehicle, to insure ease of installation.
15. Attach lifting fixture to cylinder head and attach chain hoist.
16. Remove engine support and front engine mounting bolts and lift engine from chassis.
17. Reverse procedure to install.

CYLINDER HEAD & INTAKE MANIFOLD

REPLACE

6-225

1. Drain cooling system.
2. Remove carburetor air cleaner and fuel line.
3. Disconnect accelerator linkage.
4. Remove vacuum control tube at carburetor and distributor.
5. Disconnect spark plug wires, heater hose and clamp holding bypass hose.
6. Disconnect heat indicator sending unit wire. **On models equipped with air pump, disconnect diverter valve vacuum line from intake manifold and remove air tubes from cylinder head.**
7. Disconnect exhaust pipe at manifold.
8. On all models, remove closed vent system and rocker arm cover.
9. Remove rocker shaft assembly and pushrods. **During disassembly note location of pushrods so they can be installed in the same position.**
10. Remove cylinder head bolts, then remove cylinder head and intake and exhaust manifold as an assembly.
11. Install the head in the reverse order of removal, and tighten the bolts in the sequence shown in **Fig. 1.**
12. When installing the manifolds, loosen the three bolts holding the intake and exhaust manifolds together. This is required to maintain proper alignment. Install intake and exhaust manifolds with cup side of the conical washers against the manifolds.

V8-318

The intake manifold attaching bolts on some engines are tilted upward about 30 degrees at an angle to the manifold-to-cylinder head gasket face. The purpose of this design is to provide more effective sealing at the cylinder block end gaskets. If the intake manifold is removed the installation should be such that the bolt tightening is done evenly and in the sequence shown in Fig. 2.

With gaskets in place start all bolts, leaving them loose. Run bolts 1 through 4 down so the heads just touch manifold. Then tighten these four bolts to 25 ft. lbs. torque. After checking to see that gaskets are properly seated at all surfaces, tighten remaining bolts to 25 ft. lbs. Finally tighten all bolts in the sequence shown to specifications.

1. Drain cooling system and disconnect battery ground cable.
2. Remove alternator, carburetor air cleaner and fuel line. Disconnect accelerator linkage.
3. Remove vacuum advance hose and distributor cap and wires.
4. Disconnect coil wires, heat indicator wire, heater and bypass hoses.
5. Remove closed ventilation system and rocker arm covers.
6. Remove intake manifold, coil and carburetor as an assembly.
7. Remove exhaust manifolds.
8. Remove rocker arm and shaft assemblies. Remove pushrods. **During disassembly note location of pushrods so they can be installed in the same position.**
9. Remove head bolts and cylinder heads.
10. Reverse procedure to install heads and tighten bolts in sequence, **Fig. 3. V8-318 engines have cylinder head bolt holes drilled through the block into the water jacket in certain locations, Fig. 4. Cylinder head bolts in these locations must have sealer 4057989 or equivalent applied to the threads to prevent engine coolant leakage. Ensure old sealer is cleaned from the threads before applying new sealer.**

VALVES

ADJUST

6-225

Hydraulic valve lifters are used. No adjustment is required.

V8-318

1982-84 models are equipped with standard hydraulic valve lifters. 1985-88 models are equipped with roller type hydraulic tappets. No adjustment is required.

VALVE ARRANGEMENT

FRONT TO REAR

V8-318. . . . . E-I-I-E-E-I-I-E
6-225. . . . . E-I-E-I-E-I-I-E-I-E-I-E

VALVE LIFT SPECIFICATIONS

Engine	Year	Int.	Exh.
6-225	1982-83	.378	.378
V8-318	1982-86	.373	.400

VALVE TIMING SPECIFICATIONS

INTAKE OPENS BEFORE TDC

Engine	Year	Degrees
6-225	1982-83	6
V8-318	1982-86	10

ROCKER ARMS

REPLACE

6-225

Removal

1. Remove closed ventilation and evaporation control systems.
2. Remove rocker arm cover.
3. Remove rocker shaft bolts and retainers.
4. Lift off rocker arms and shaft.

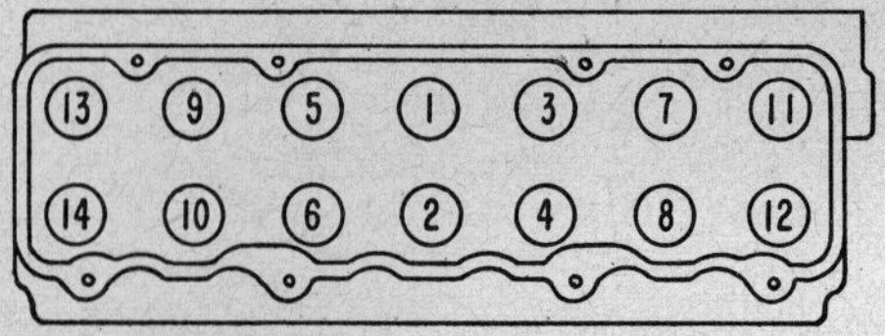

Fig. 1 Cylinder head tightening sequence. 6-225

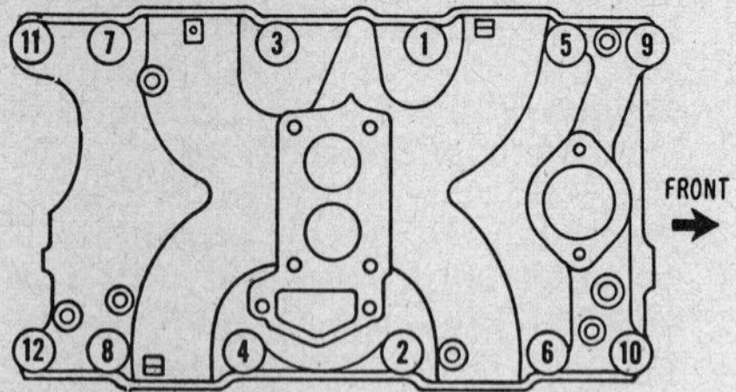

Fig. 2 Intake manifold tightening sequence. V8-318

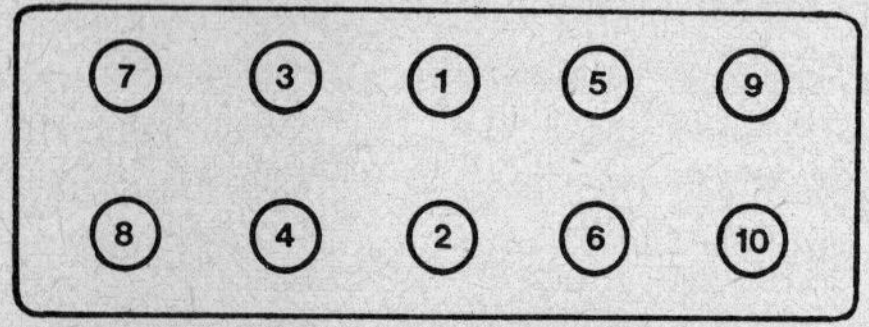

Fig. 3 Cylinder head tightening sequence. V8-318

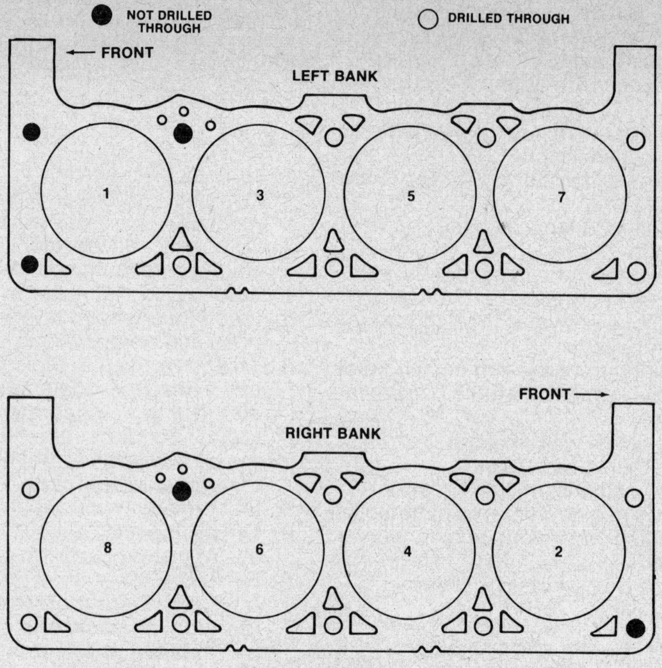

Fig. 4 Cylinder head bolt hole identification. V8-318 engines.

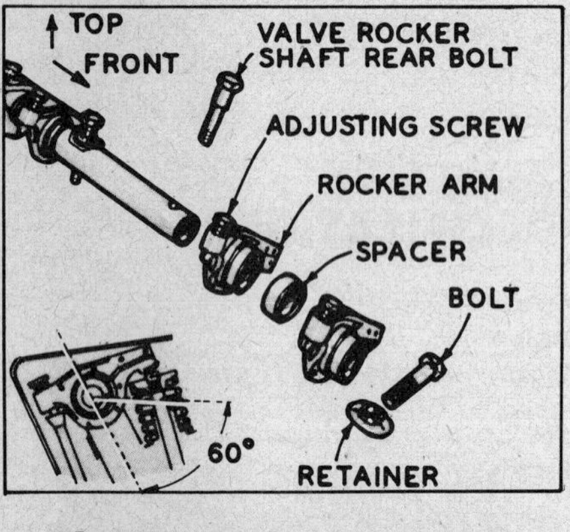

Fig. 5 Rocker arm and shaft assembly. 6-225

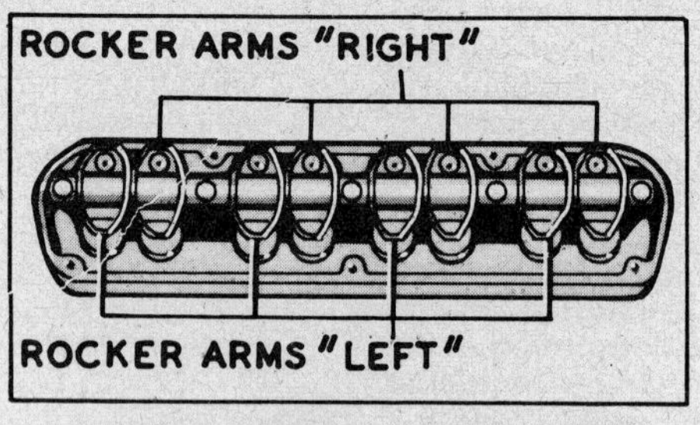

Fig. 6 Rocker arm and shaft assembly installed. V8-318

Inspection

Clean all parts with a suitable solvent. Be sure the inside of the shaft is clean and the oil holes are open. The drilled oil hole in the bore of the rocker arm must be open to the trough and valve end of the arms. The trough also feeds oil to the adjusting screw and pushrod.

The shaft should be free from excessive wear in arm contact areas. The shaft should be smooth in retainer contact areas. The adjusting screws in the rocker arms should have a uniform round end. The drag torque should be smooth and uniform. The retainers should be smooth and undamaged in the shaft contact area.

Assembly & Installation

1. Referring to **Fig. 5**, note position of oil hole on forward end of shaft which denotes the upper side of shaft. Rocker arms must be put on the shaft with the adjusting screw to the right side of the engine. Place one of the small retainers on the one long bolt and install the bolt in the rear hole in the shaft from the top side.
2. Install one rocker arm and one spacer; then two rocker arms and a spacer. Continue in same sequence until all rocker arms and spacers are on the shaft.
3. Place a bolt and small retainer in front hole in shaft.
4. Place a bolt and the one wide retainer through the center hole in the shaft with six rocker arms on each side of center.
5. Install remaining bolts and retainers.
6. Locate the assembly on the cylinder head and position rocker arm adjusting screws in pushrods.
7. Tighten bolts finger tight, bringing retainers in contact with the shaft between rocker arms.
8. Tighten bolts to specified torque.
9. Reverse remaining procedure to complete installation.

V8-318

To provide correct lubrication for the rocker arms on these engines, the rocker shafts have a small notch machined at one end and these notches must always face inward toward the center of the engine when installed. In other words, the notched end must be toward the rear of the engine on the right bank, and to the front of the engine on the left bank.

Rocker arms must be correctly positioned on the shaft prior to installation on cylinder head, **Fig. 6.**

It is also important when installing the rocker shaft assembly on the cylinder head to position the short retainers at each end and in the center, and to place long retainers in the two remaining positions.

VALVE GUIDES

Valves operate in guide holes bored directly in the cylinder head. When valve stem-to-guide clearance becomes excessive, valves with oversize stems of .005, .015 and .030 inch are available for service

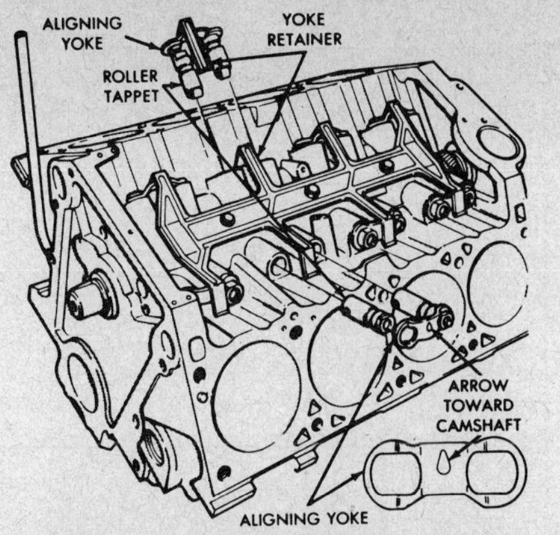

Fig. 7 Hydraulic roller lifter installation. 1985–88 V8-318

Fig. 10 Removing valve lifter

replacement. When necessary to install valves with oversize stems the valve bores should be reamed to provide the proper operating clearance.

VALVE LIFTERS

REPLACE

1985–88 V8-318

1985-88 V8-318 engines are equipped with roller type hydraulic lifters.

Removal

1. Remove valve covers, rocker shaft assembly and pushrods, noting installation position so that components can be installed in original position.
2. Remove intake manifold as outlined in "Cylinder Head, Replace."
3. Remove yoke retainer and aligning yokes, **Fig. 7.**
4. Insert puller C-4129 or equivalent through opening in cylinder head, seat tool securely in head of lifter, then pull lifter from bore. **If more than one lifter is to be removed, identify lifters to ensure reinstallation in original position.**

Inspection

1. Inspect bore in cylinder block, and if bore is scored or shows signs of wear or sticking, ream bore and install oversized lifter assembly.
2. Pry out plunger retaining, then disassemble lifter as shown in **Fig. 8. Plunger and body assemblies are not interchangeable, and plunger valve must always be installed in original body. Disassemble only one lifter at a time to avoid mixing components.**

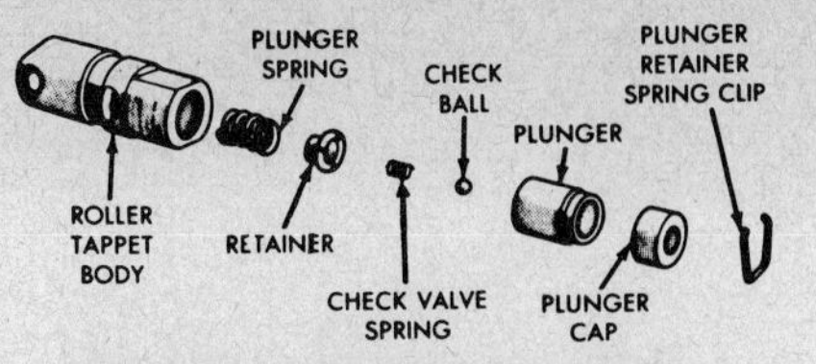

Fig. 8 Hydraulic roller lifter exploded view. 1985–88 V8-318

3. Clean components with solvent suitable for removing all varnish and blow dry with compressed air.
4. Inspect plunger for scoring, wear and pitting, and inspect valve seat for any condition that may prevent seating. If any defect is found, replace lifter assembly.
5. Coat components with clean engine oil or suitable assembly lubricant, then reassemble lifter as shown in **Fig. 8.**

Installation

1. Lubricate lifters, then install in original bores.
2. Install aligning yokes ensuring that arrow points toward camshaft, **Fig. 7.**
3. Install yoke retainers and torque screws to 200 inch lbs.
4. Reverse remaining procedure to complete installation, start engine and run at approximately 15000 RPM until it reaches normal operating temperature. **To prevent engine damage, do not run engine above fast idle until all lifters have filled with oil and become quiet.**

EXC. 1985–88 V8-318

After taking off rocker arm and shaft assembly, lift out push rods. The valve lifters, **Fig. 9,** may then be removed with a suitably long magnet rod. If the lifters cannot be removed with the magnet rod, a special tool (C-4129) may be used, **Fig. 10.** Insert the tool through the pushrod opening in the cylinder head and into lifter. Turn the handle to expand the tool in the lifter, then with a twisting motion remove the lifter from its bore.

TIMING CHAIN COVER

REPLACE

6-225

1. To remove cover, drain cooling system and remove radiator and fan.
2. Remove vibration damper with a puller.
3. Loosen oil pan bolts to allow clearance and remove chain case cover.
4. Reverse above procedure to install cover.

V8-318

1. Remove radiator, fan and belt.
2. Remove water pump and housing as a unit.
3. Remove power steering pump, if necessary.
4. Remove crankshaft pulley.
5. Remove key from crankshaft.
6. Remove fuel pump.
7. Loosen oil pan bolts and remove front bolt at each side.

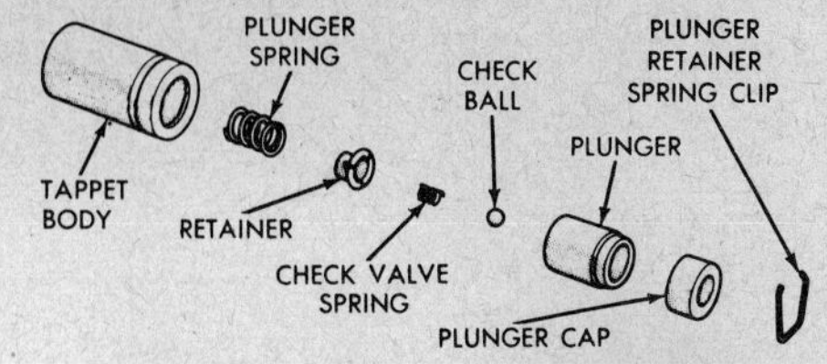

Fig. 9 Hydraulic valve lifter. 1982–84

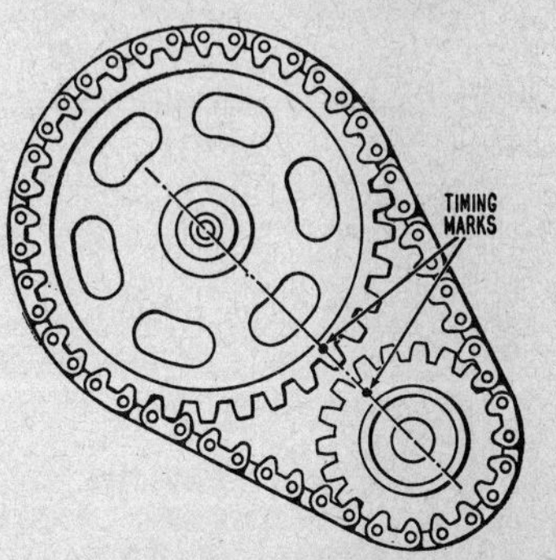

Fig. 11 Valve timing marks aligned for correct valve timing. 6-225

8. Remove chain case cover and gasket, using extreme caution to avoid damaging oil pan gasket otherwise oil pan will have to be removed. It is normal to find particles of neoprene collected between crankshaft seal retainer and oil slinger.
9. Reverse procedure to install.

TIMING CHAIN

REPLACE

6-225

Removal

1. After removing chain case cover as outlined above, take off camshaft sprocket attaching bolt.
2. Remove chain with camshaft sprocket.
3. Clean all parts and dry with compressed air.
4. Inspect timing chain for broken or damaged links. Inspect sprockets for cracks and chipped, worn or damaged teeth.

Installation

1. Turn crankshaft so sprocket timing mark is toward and directly in line with center line of camshaft.
2. Temporarily install camshaft sprocket. Rotate camshaft to position sprocket timing mark toward and directly in line with center line of crankshaft; then remove camshaft sprocket.
3. Place chain on crankshaft sprocket and position camshaft sprocket in chain so sprocket can be installed with timing marks aligned without moving camshaft, **Fig. 11.**
4. Install parts removed in reverse order of removal.

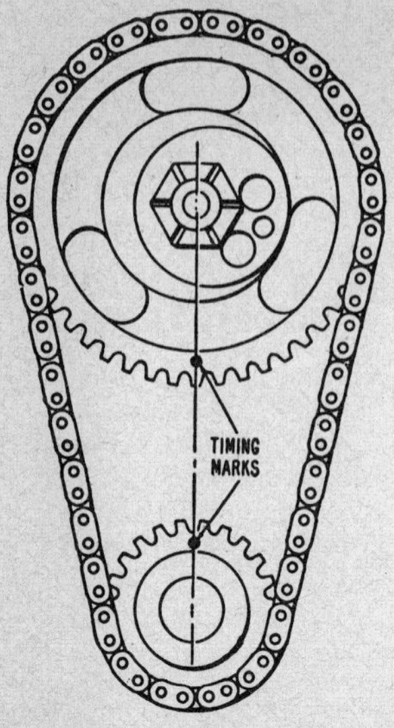

Fig. 12 Valve timing marks aligned for correct valve timing. V8-318

V8-318

To install chain and sprockets, lay both the camshaft and crankshaft sprockets on the bench. Position the sprockets so that the timing marks are next to each other. Place the chain on both sprockets, then push the gears apart as far as the chain will permit. Use a straightedge to form a line through the exact centers of both gears. The timing marks must be on this line, **Fig. 12.**

Slide the chain with both sprockets on the camshaft and crankshaft at the same time; then recheck the alignment. **On V8 engines, use tool No. C-3509 to prevent camshaft from contacting welch plug in rear of engine block. Remove distributor and oil pump-distributor drive gear. Position tool against rear side of cam gear and attach tool with distributor retainer plate bolt.**

CAMSHAFT & BEARINGS REPLACE

6-225

The camshaft is supported by four precision type, steel backed, babbitt-lined bearings. Rearward thrust is taken by the rear face of the sprocket hub contacting the front of the engine block.

The camshaft, **Fig. 13,** can be removed after removing the grille, radiator and timing chain. To remove the camshaft bearings, the engine must be removed from the vehicle.

1. Remove valve lifters, oil pump, fuel pump and distributor.
2. Install a long bolt into front of camshaft to aid removal. Remove camshaft using care not to damage bearings.
3. Remove welch plug back of rear camshaft bearing.
4. Remove bearings with suitable puller equipment.
5. Install new bearings, being sure the oil holes in bearings line up with the corresponding oil holes in the crankcase. **Install No. 1 camshaft bearing 3/32 inch inward from front face of cylinder block.**
6. Apply sealer to welch plug and plug bore, then install plug at rear of camshaft.

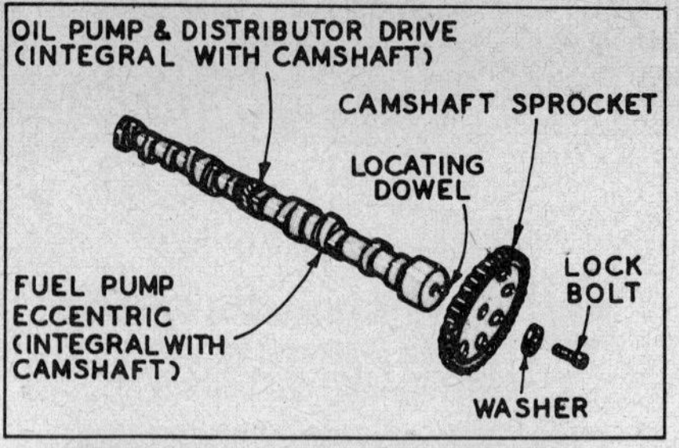

Fig. 13 Camshaft and related parts. 6-225

V8-318

To remove the camshaft, remove all valve lifters, timing chain and sprockets. Remove distributor and oil pump-distributor drive gear. Remove fuel pump and see that pushrod has moved away from eccentric drive cam. Remove thrust plate, noting installation position of timing chain oil tab so it can be installed in the same manner. Withdraw camshaft from engine, using care to see that camshaft lobes do not damage the camshaft bearings.

If camshaft bearings are to be replaced, it is recommended that the engine be removed from the chassis and the crankshaft taken out in order that any chips or foreign material may be removed from the oil passages.

PISTON & ROD ASSEMBLE

6-225

Piston and rod assemblies must be installed as shown in **Fig. 14.**

V8-318

When installing piston and rod assemblies in the cylinders, the compression ring gaps should be diametrically opposite one another and not in line with the oil ring gap. The oil ring expander gap should be toward the outside of the "V" of the engine. The oil ring gap should be turned toward the inside of the engine "V."

Immerse the piston head and rings in clean engine oil and, with a suitable piston ring compressor, insert the piston and rod assembly into the bore. Tap the piston down into the bore, using the handle of a hammer.

Assemble the pistons to the rods as shown in **Fig. 15.**

PISTONS, PINS & RINGS

Pistons are available in standard sizes and the following oversize: .020 inch.

Pins are available in the following oversizes: V8-318, .003, .008 inch. Not furnished on all other engines.

Rings are available in the following oversizes: std. to .009, .020-.029, .040-.049 inch.

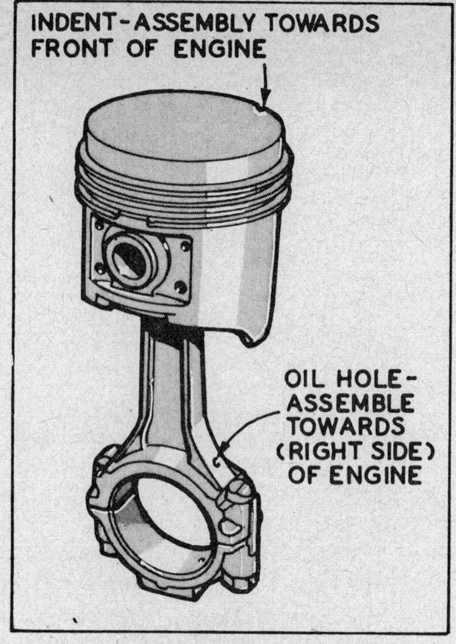

Fig. 14 Piston and rod assembly. 6-225

MAIN & ROD BEARINGS

Main bearings are furnished in standard sizes and the following undersizes: .001, .002, .003, .010, .012 inch.

Rod bearings are furnished in standard sizes and the following undersizes: .001, .002, .003, .010, .012 inch.

6-225 engines may be equipped with either a cast or forged crankshaft. The following parts are not interchangeable between cast and forged crankshaft engines: crankshaft, crankshaft bearings, connecting rods and bearings and cylinder block. On models equipped with manual transmission, cast crankshaft engine vibration damper is not interchangeable with forged crankshaft engine and requires that a crankshaft screw and washer be used and torque to 135 ft. lbs. On models equipped with automatic transmission, vibration damper and torque converter are interchangeable between cast and forged crankshaft engines.

CRANKSHAFT REAR OIL SEAL REPLACE

6-225

Crankshaft oil seal leaks on 1981-83 6-225 engines can sometimes be difficult to locate and repair without proper diagnosis. When a seal leak is suspected, always perform an air test to verify the condition and location before you begin disassembly. Test for oil leaks as follows, using regulated air adjusted to 4 psi to air test engine.

1. Remove crankcase vent valve and cap and plug valve cover holes.
2. Remove dipstick, then install rubber hose connected to air source into dipstick tube.

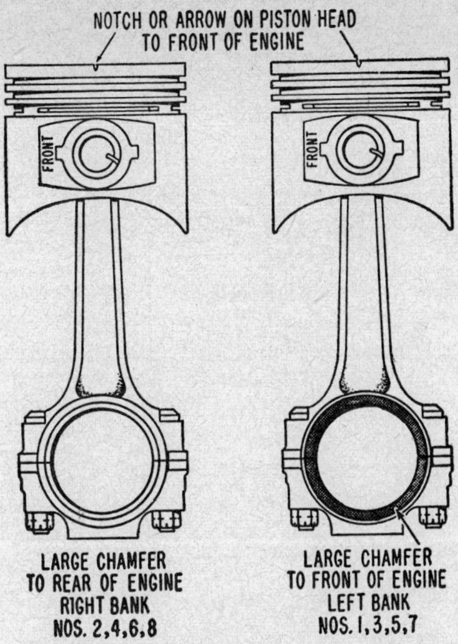

Fig. 15 Piston and rod assembly. V8-318

3. Raise and support vehicle, then remove torque convertor or clutch housing cover.
4. Visually inspect rear of engine block for leakage. Leakage between rear seal and crankshaft will cause oil spray in a circular pattern. Leakage from retainer side seals, retainer joint face or back side of rear seal will tend to run straight down. Other possible leak paths are a porous block and rear cam and gallery plugs.
5. Apply air pressure to crankcase and check seal area for leaks. If leakage is evident, check seal or seal retainer. If no leakage is detected, rotate crankshaft and watch for leakage. If a leak is detected while crankshaft is being rotated, check crankcase seal surface for damage or scratches. If no leakage is detected, pressurize lubrication system and check for leaking oil passage.
6. Remove rear seal retainer. Inspect retainer and seal sides for proper sealing and half round seal for correct positioning. If leak is evident only when crankshaft is rotated, inspect crankshaft for nicks, scratches or cuts in seal area. Polish nicks or scratches with emery cloth.
7. Clean old sealer from seal retainer and block, and remove upper seal half. Ensure seal was not installed backwards, since this can cause leakage. Check outside diameter of seal for cuts or peeled rubber.

Replacement seals are of two piece rubber type composition which make possible the replacement of upper rear seal without removing crankshaft. Both halves must be used. After removing oil pan, rear main bearing cap and seal retainer, pry lower rope seal from retainer with small screwdriver. Screw a special tool into upper rope seal and carefully pull to remove seal while rotating crankshaft.

Install upper half of new seal into block, making sure stripe on seal faces rear of engine. Shim stock or equivalent may be

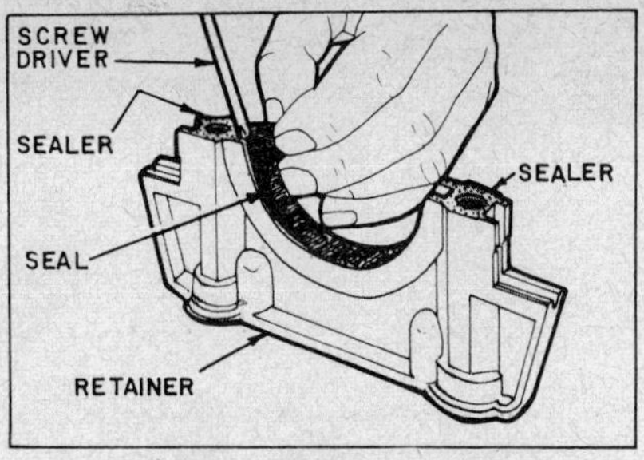

Fig. 16 Lower oil seal & retainer. 6-225

used to protect back side of seal against sharp side of block. Rotate crankshaft to ease installation. Apply a 1/8 inch bead of RTV sealant into groove in retainer, starting and ending 1/2 inch from ends of groove. Install other half of seal into retainer, ensuring stripe on seal faces rearward, then install rear main bearing cap and torque to specifications. Install side seals onto retainer using bonder part 4057988 or equivalent. Apply a small amount of RTV sealer to retainer in areas shown in **Fig. 16.** Install retainer and torque to 30 ft. lbs. **Do not apply sealer to seal lip surface, as leakage may result.**

V8-318

Replacement of rear main bearing oil seals is similar to procedure given above for 6 cylinder engines. A seal retainer is not found on these engines; lower half of seal is installed into groove in rear main bearing cap.

The 318 engine has cap seals in addition to lower seal secured by rear main bearing cap. Cap seal with yellow paint is installed, narrow sealing edge up, into right side with bearing cap in engine position. Cap seals must be flush with shoulder of bearing cap to prevent oil leakage.

The 360 engine requires sealer to be applied adjacent to rear main bearing oil seal as cap seals are not used, **Fig. 17.** After applying sealer, quickly assemble rear main bearing cap to block and torque to specifications.

Some 1984-86 V8-318 engines are equipped with a rope-type rear crankshaft oil seal, and on these engines the upper portion of the seal cannot be replaced with the crankshaft installed. When diagnosis and inspection reveal oil leakage caused by a rotated upper seal, evident by a gap between the seal end and the right side bearing cap/engine block parting line, do not remove the upper seal half. Leave the upper seal in the block, then modify and install a replacement lower seal as follows:

1. Remove lower rope seal half from bearing cap.
2. Install new lower seal half in cap, seating seal in cap groove with suitable driver.
3. Cut right bank end of seal flush with cap surface.
4. Remove seal from cap.
5. Reseat seal in cap with cut end protruding sufficiently to tightly fill the gap left by the compressed upper seal, **Fig. 18.**
6. Hold seal in position with installation

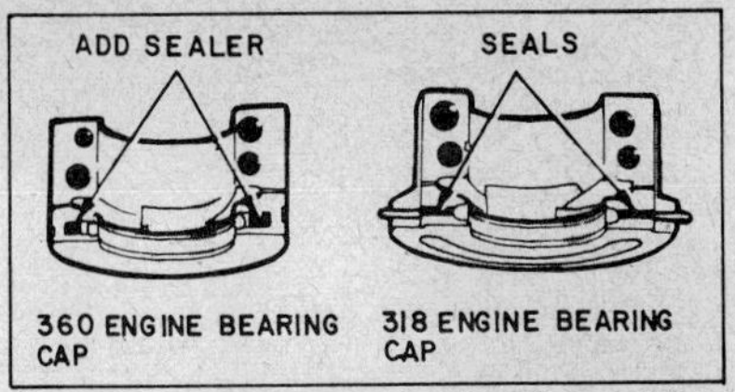

Fig. 17 Rear main bearing caps. V8-318

tool and cut left bank side flush with block surface.
7. Lightly lubricate lower seal surface with engine oil.
8. Install cap side seals, **Fig. 17,** ensuring that seal identified with yellow paint is on the right side.
9. Install bearing cap, taking care not to crimp extended side of lower seal between block and cap, then torque bolts to specifications.
10. Reinstall oil pump and pan, fill engine and check for leaks.

OIL PAN

REPLACE

6-225

1. Drain radiator, disconnect battery ground cable and radiator hoses and remove oil dipstick.
2. Remove shroud attaching screws, separate shroud from radiator and position rearward on engine.
3. Raise vehicle and drain oil pan.
4. Remove engine to transmission support bracket.
5. Disconnect exhaust pipe, then torque converter inspection shield.
6. Remove center link from steering arm and idler arm ball joints.
7. Support front of engine with a jack stand placed under the right front corner of oil pan.
8. Remove engine front mount bolts. Raise engine approx. 1 1/2 to 2 inch.
9. Remove oil pan attaching screws, rotate engine crankshaft to clear counterweights and remove oil pan.
10. Reverse procedure to install.

V8-318

1. Disconnect battery ground cable and remove engine oil level dipstick.
2. Raise vehicle and drain crankcase.
3. Remove exhaust crossover pipe, then disconnect and lower center link.
4. Remove starter and starter mounting stud.
5. Remove torque converter inspection cover.
6. Remove oil pan attaching bolts and oil pan.
7. Reverse procedure to install.

OIL PUMP

REPLACE

6-225

1. Drain radiator and disconnect upper and lower hoses.
2. Remove fan shroud (if equipped).
3. Raise vehicle on a hoist, support front of engine with a jack stand place under right front corner of engine oil pan. Do not support engine at crankshaft

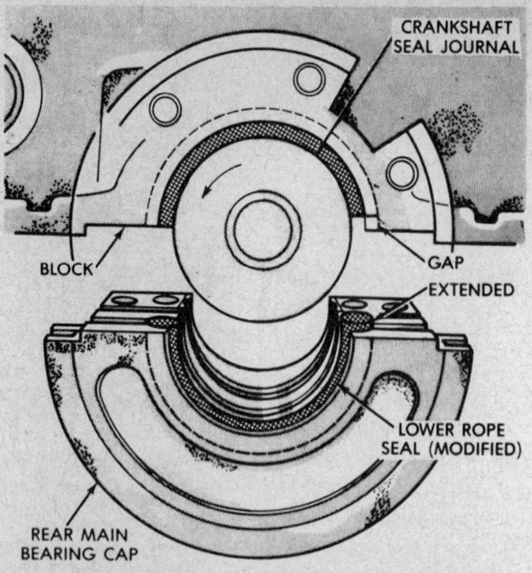

Fig. 18 Installing modified rear crankshaft oil seal. V8-318 w/rope type seal

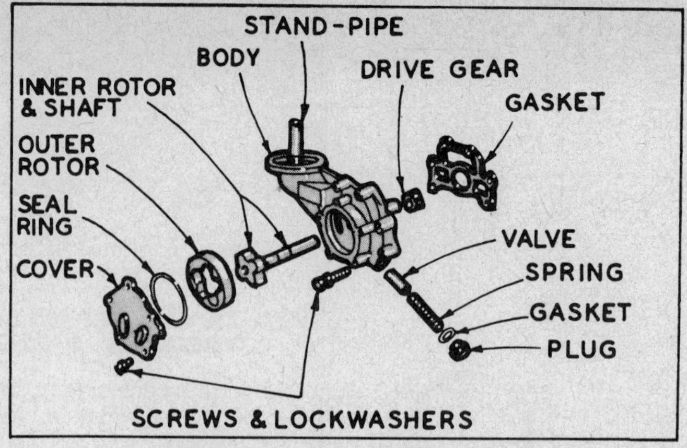

Fig. 19 Oil pump. 6-225

pulley or vibration damper.
4. Remove front engine mounts.
5. Raise engine $1\frac{1}{2}$ to 2 inches.
6. Remove oil filter, pump attaching bolts and remove pump assembly.
7. Reverse procedure to install.

V8-318

Remove oil pan as outlined, then remove pump from rear main bearing cap. Reverse procedure to install, torquing retaining bolts to 30 ft. lbs.

OIL PUMP SERVICE

6-225

To disassemble, remove the pump cover seal ring, **Fig. 19.** Press off the drive gear, supporting the gear to keep load off aluminum body. Remove rotor and shaft and lift out outer pump rotor. Remove oil pressure relief valve plug and lift out spring and plunger. Remove oil pressure sending unit.

Inspection

1. The rotor contact area and the bores for the shaft and valve in the pump body should be smooth, free from scratches, scoring or excessive wear.
2. The pump cover should be smooth, flat and free from scoring or ridges. Lay a straightedge across the cover. If a .0015 inch feeler gauge can be inserted under the straightedge, the cover should be replaced.
3. All surfaces of the outer rotor should be smooth and uniform, free from ridges, scratches or uneven wear. Discard a rotor less than .825 inch thick and/or less than 2.469 inch in diameter.
4. The inner rotor and shaft assembly should be smooth, free from scoring and uneven wear. Discard rotors less than .825 inch thick.
5. Place outer rotor in pump body and measure clearance between rotor and body. Discard pump body if clearance is more than .014 inch.
6. Install inner rotor and shaft in pump body. Shaft should turn freely but without side play. If clearance between rotor teeth is more than .010 inch, replace both rotors.
7. Measure rotor end clearance. If feeler gauge of more than .004 inch can be inserted between straightedge and rotors, install a new pump body.
8. The oil pressure relief valve should be smooth, free from scratches or scoring, and should be a free fit in its bore.
9. The relief valve spring has a free length of $2\frac{1}{4}$ inches and should test between 22.3 and 23.3. pounds when compressed to $1\frac{19}{32}$ inch. If not, replace the spring.

Assembly & Installation

1. With pump rotors in body, press drive gear on shaft, flush with end of shaft.
2. Install seal ring in groove in body and install cover. Tighten bolts to 95 inch lbs. Test pump for free turning.
3. Install oil pressure relief valve spring. Use new washer (gasket) and tighten plug securely.
4. If pump shaft turns freely, remove pump cover and outer rotor before installation of pump on engine.
5. Install oil pressure sending unit and tighten to 60 inch lbs. (5 ft. lbs.).
6. Using a new gasket, install pump on engine and tighten bolts to 200 inch lbs. (16 ft. lbs.).
7. Install oil filter reservoir on pump. Install filter element and tighten cover nuts to 25 ft. lbs.
8. Connect oil pressure sending unit wire.
9. Complete the installation by reversing steps as given under Oil Pump, Replace.

V8-318

After removing the pump from the engine, it should be disassembled, cleaned and inspected for wear, **Fig. 20.**

1. To remove the relief valve, remove the cotter pin and drill a $\frac{1}{8}$ inch hole into the relief valve retainer cap and install a self-threading sheet metal screw.
2. Clamp screw into vise and tap on housing lightly with a soft hammer to remove the retaining cap, then remove the relief valve spring and valve.
3. Remove the oil pump cover and discard the oil seal ring.

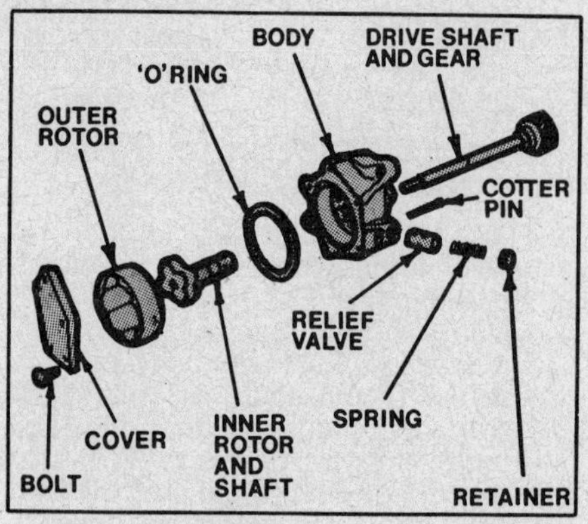

Fig. 20 Oil pump. V8-318

4. Remove pump rotor, shaft and lift out outer rotor.
5. Mating surface of the pump cover should be smooth. If scratched or grooved, replace the pump.
6. Lay a straightedge across the cover. If a .0015 inch feeler gauge can be inserted between the cover and the straightedge, replace the pump.
7. Measure thickness and diameter of outer rotor. If rotor thickness is .825 inch or less, or if the diameter of rotor is 2.429 inches or less, replace outer rotor.
8. If the inner rotor is .825 inch or less, replace the inner rotor and shaft assembly.
9. Install the outer rotor into the housing. Press rotor to one side with the fingers and measure the clearance between the rotor and body with a feeler gauge. If the measurement is .014 inch or greater, replace the pump.
10. Place the inner rotor and shaft into the pump. If clearance between the rotors is .010 inch or greater, replace the shaft and both rotors.
11. Place a straightedge across the face of the pump between bolt holes. If a feeler gauge of .004 inch or greater can be inserted, replace the pump.
12. Check the oil pump relief valve plunger for scoring and free operation in the bore. Small marks may be removed with 400-grit sand paper.
13. The relief valve spring should have a free length of $2\frac{1}{32}$ to $2\frac{3}{64}$ inch and

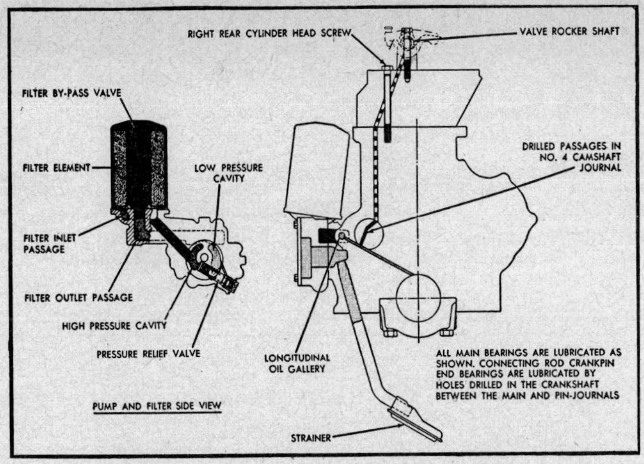

Engine oiling system. 6-225

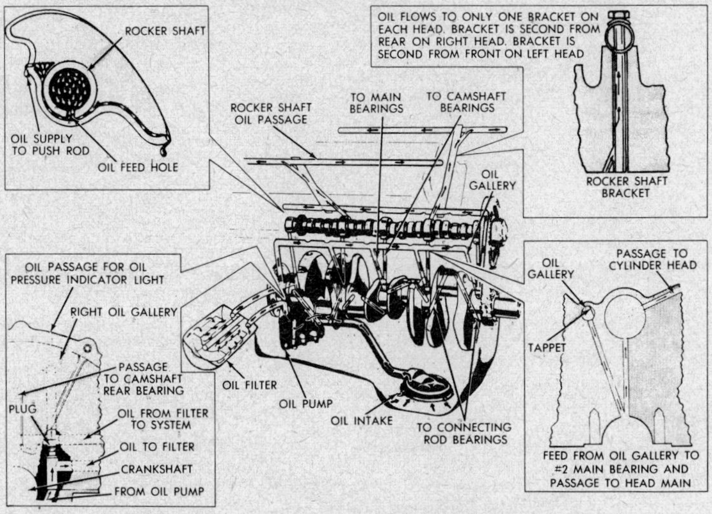

Engine Oiling System. V8-318

should test between 16.2 and 17.2 pounds when compressed to $1^{11}/_{32}$ inch. If not, replace the spring.

BELT TENSION DATA

Belt	New Lbs.	Used Lbs.
1982-88 All	120	70

WATER PUMP

REPLACE

When it becomes necessary to remove a fan clutch of the silicone type, the assembly must be supported in the vertical position to prevent leaks of silicone fluid from the clutch mechanism. This loss of fluid will render the fan clutch inoperative.

6-225

1. Drain cooling system, then remove battery, upper and lower radiator hoses and fan shroud.
2. Remove all drive belts, then remove fan attaching bolts, fan, spacer and pulley.
3. Remove A/C compressor and air pump bracket to water pump attaching bolts, then position compressor and air pump aside. Keep compressor in upright position.
4. Disconnect bypass and heater hoses from water pump.
5. Remove water pump attaching bolts and remove pump assembly.
6. Reverse procedure to install.

V8-318

1. Drain cooling system and disconnect battery ground cable.
2. Remove all drive belts, then remove radiator shroud and position over fan.
3. Remove fan assembly, pulley and fan shroud.
4. Remove alternator adjusting strap and mounting bolts and position alternator aside.
5. Remove A/C compressor with mounting brackets and position aside, if equipped. Keep compressor in upright position.
6. Remove power steering pump mounting bolts and position pump aside, if equipped.
7. Remove air pump and mounting brackets, if equipped. Disconnect air hose at pump fittings.
8. Disconnect bypass and heater hoses at water pump.
9. Disconnect lower radiator hose from pump.
10. Remove remaining water pump attaching bolts and remove pump assembly.
11. Reverse procedure to install.

When replacing a cup-type core hole plug in an engine, the size of the hole in the cylinder head, water jacket or rear bearing bore for the camshaft should be checked. At these locations a $^1/_{16}$ inch oversize hole is sometimes bored in production and an oversize core plug installed. Core plugs $^1/_{16}$ inch oversize are available for replacement should they be required at these locations.

FUEL PUMP

REPLACE

Before installing the pump, it is good practice to crank the engine so that the nose of the camshaft eccentric is out of the way of the fuel pump rocker arm when the pump is installed. In this way there will be the least amount of tension on the rocker arm, thereby easing the installation of the pump.

1. Disconnect fuel lines from fuel pump.
2. Remove fuel pump attaching bolts and fuel pump.
3. Remove all gasket material from the pump and block gasket surfaces. Apply sealer to both sides of new gasket.
4. Position gasket on pump flange and hold pump in position against its mounting surface. Make sure rocker arm is riding on camshaft eccentric.
5. Press pump tight against its mounting. Install retaining screws and tighten them alternately.
6. Connect fuel lines. Then operate engine and check for leaks.

Rear Axle, Propeller Shaft & Brakes

INDEX

Figs. 1 through 3 shows the $7^1/_4$ and $8^1/_4$ inch rear axle assemblies. When necessary to overhaul any of these units, refer to the Rear Axle Specifications table in this chapter.

INTEGRAL TYPE REAR AXLE

The following changes have been made in the design of the $7^1/_4$ inch rear axle during the 1982 model year for all models except Imperial.

1. The inboard ends of the $8^1/_4$ inch axle shaft tubes are tapered down in size and pressed into the $7^1/_4$ inch carrier, **Fig. 2.**
2. The $7^1/_4$ inch axle shafts ball bearings are replaced with the $8^1/_4$ inch axle shaft roller bearings.
3. The axle shafts are retained with the standard $8^1/_4$ inch axle "C" lock washer, **Fig. 4.**
4. The $7^1/_4$ inch differential side gears now have a counterbore to incorporate the "C" lock washers. These side gears can be used on the early design $7^1/_4$ inch axles, but the early design side gears cannot be used on the later design $7^1/_4$ inch axle.
5. The late design carrier has two cast holes to allow lube to flow into the tubes to lubricate the axle shaft roller bearings, **Fig. 3.**

Servicing the late design $7^1/_4$ inch rear axle is the same as the early design $7^1/_4$ differential, except for the axle shaft and axle shaft bearing. When replacing axle shaft or axle shaft bearing refer to "Axle Shaft, Replace **(Fig. 2)**" for service procedures.

Two types of integral carrier axles are used. In both types, the drive pinion is mounted in two opposing tapered roller bearings which are preloaded by a spacer positioned between them.

In the unit shown in **Fig. 1**, the differential is supported by two tapered roller side bearings. These bearings are preloaded by spacers located between the bearings and carrier housing. The differential assembly is positioned for ring and pinion backlash by varying these spacers.

Axle shafts in this unit are held in place by retainers at the outer ends of the shafts. These retainers are bolted through the brake backing plates to the rear axle tubes.

In the unit shown in **Fig. 2**, the differential is also supported by two tapered roller bearings. A threaded differential bearing

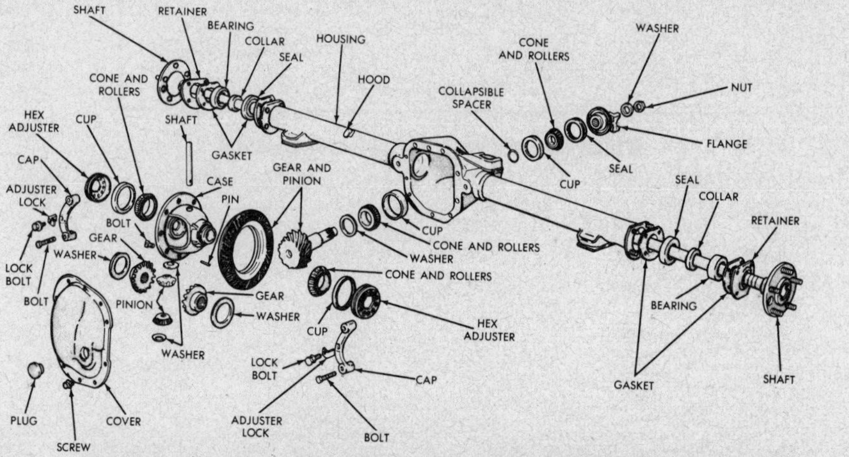

Fig. 1 Integral carrier rear axle exploded view (type 1). Early production 1982 w/$7^1/_4$ inch ring gear

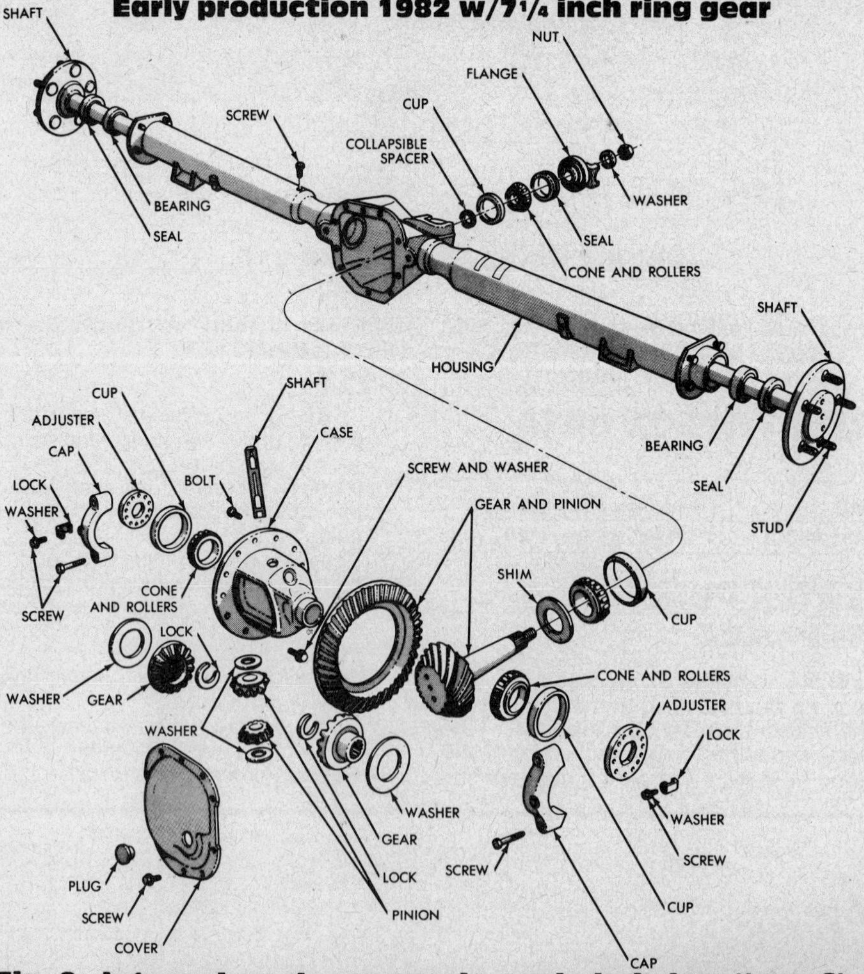

Fig. 2 Integral carrier rear axle exploded view (type 2). Late 1982 & 1983–88 w/$7^1/_4$ inch ring gear

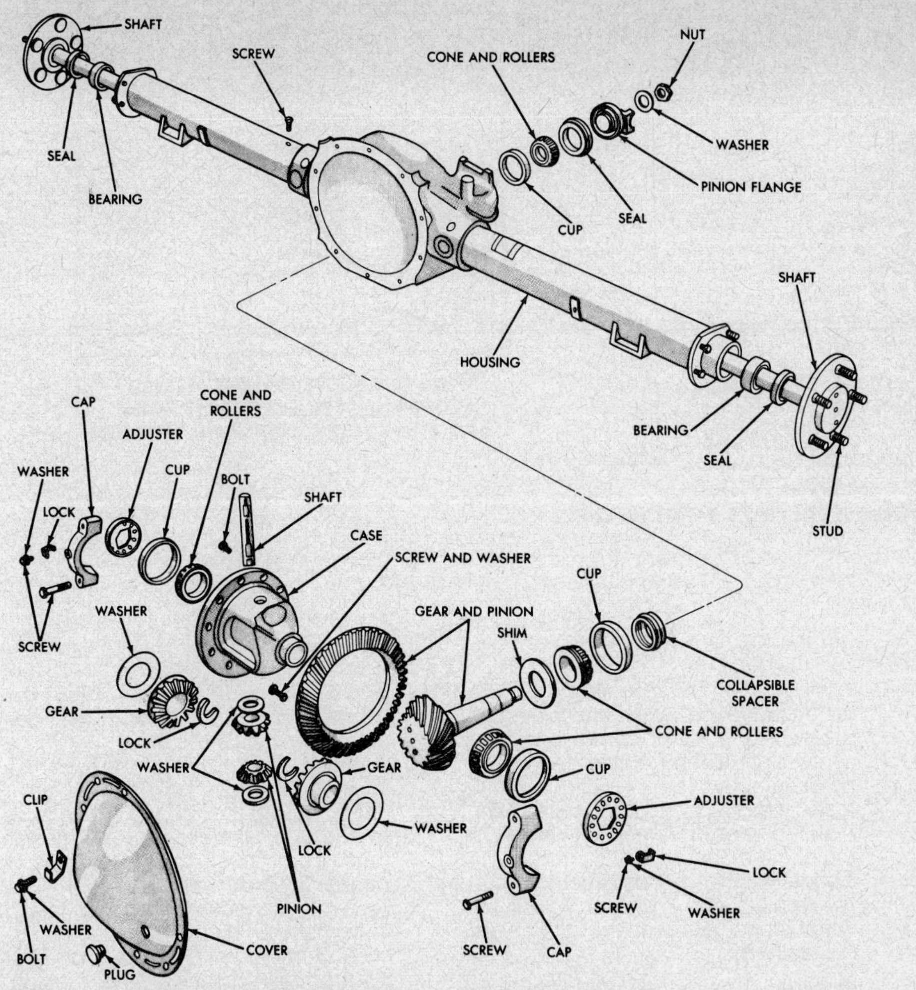

Fig. 3 Integral carrier rear axle exploded view (type 3). Models w/8¹/₄ inch ring gear

adjuster is located in each bearing pedestal cap to eliminate differential side play, adjust and maintain ring and pinion backlash and provide a means of obtaining differential bearing preload.

Axles are retained by means of a "C" washer which is installed into a groove in the inner end of the axle shaft inside the differential unit.

On both these units, a removable stamped steel cover, bolted to the rear of the carrier, permits inspection and service of the differential without removal of the complete axle assembly from the vehicle.

7¹/₄ and 8¹/₄ in. axle differentials have balanced side and pinion gears. Any attempt to mix these side or pinion gears with previously manufactured ones will result in lock up or excessive differential backlash. Side and pinion gears must be replaced as a set.

REAR AXLE
REPLACE

1. Raise rear of vehicle and position safety stands at front of rear springs.
2. Remove rear wheels, then disconnect brake lines at wheel cylinders. Cap brake line fittings to prevent loss of fluid.
3. Disconnect parking brake cables.
4. Mark drive shaft and pinion flanges for reassembly, then remove drive shaft.
5. Disconnect shock absorbers from spring plate studs, then loosen rear spring U-bolt nuts and remove U-bolts.
6. Remove axle assembly from vehicle.

AXLE SHAFT
REPLACE
TYPE 1

1. With wheel removed, remove clips holding brake drum on wheel studs and remove drum, **Fig. 1.**
2. Disconnect brake lines at wheel cylinders.
3. Using access hole in axle flange, remove retainer nuts from end of housing.
4. Remove axle shaft and brake assembly, using a slide hammer-type puller.
5. Remove brake assembly from axle shaft with care to avoid damaging shaft in seal contact area.
6. Remove oil seal from axle housing.
7. Remove axle shaft bearings only when necessary. Discard bearings, if removed.

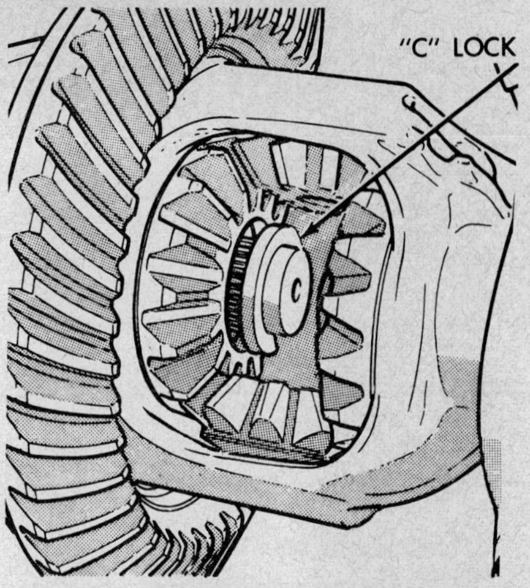

Fig. 4 Axle shaft 'C' lock installation

8. Axle shaft endplay is pre-set and not adjustable. Endplay is accomplished by the amount of endplay built into the bearings. The two axle housing brake support plate gaskets on each side are used for sealing purposes only. Replace gaskets.
9. Press bearing and collar on shaft firmly against shoulders on shaft.
10. Install new oil seal in housing.
11. Install brake assembly on axle housing and carefully slide axle shaft through oil seal and into side gear splines.
12. Tap end of axle shaft lightly to position axle shaft bearing into bearing bore and attach retainer plate to housing.
13. Install brake drums and wheels.

TYPES 2 & 3

1. With wheel and brake drum removed, or caliper and rotor assembly removed, loosen differential housing cover and drain lubricant. Remove cover, **Figs. 2 and 3.**
2. Turn differential case to make pinion shaft lock screw accessible and remove lock screw and shaft.
3. Push axle shaft inward toward center of car and remove "C" washer from groove in axle shaft, **Fig. 4.**
4. Remove axle shaft from housing, being careful not to damage the axle bearing, which will remain in the housing.
5. The axle bearing and/or seal can now be removed if necessary.
6. Reverse procedure to install.

PROPELLER SHAFT
REPLACE

1. Remove both rear universal joint roller and bushing assembly clamps from pinion yoke. Do not disturb retaining strap holding roller assemblies on cross.
2. Lower front of vehicle slightly to prevent loss of transmission oil and pull drive shaft out as an assembly.
3. To install, carefully slide yoke into splines on transmission output shaft.

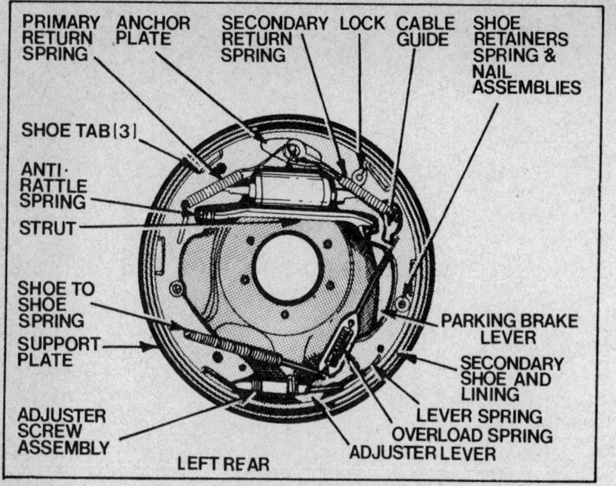

Fig. 5 Brake & related components, left rear brake shown

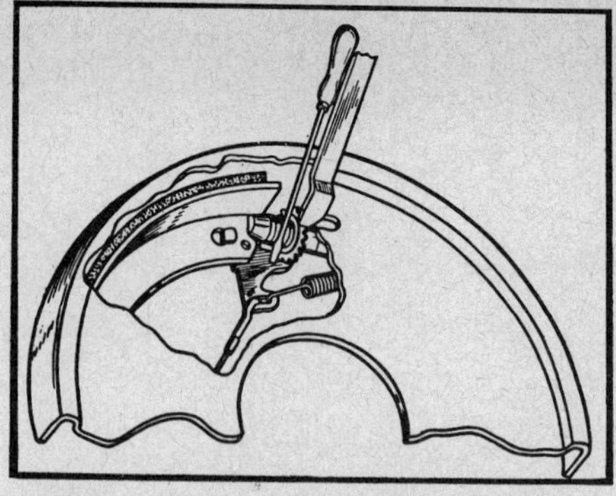

Fig. 6 Releasing brake lever with screwdriver while adjusting star wheel

4. Align rear of propeller shaft with pinion yoke and position roller and bushing assemblies into seats of pinion yoke.
5. Install bushing clamps and tighten clamp bolts to 170 inch lbs.

BRAKE ADJUSTMENTS

These brakes, **Fig. 5,** have self-adjusting shoe mechanisms that assure correct lining-to-drum clearances at all times. The automatic adjusters operate only when the brakes are applied as the car is moving rearward.

Although the brakes are self-adjusting, an initial adjustment is necessary when the brake shoes have been relined or replaced, or when the length of the star wheel adjuster has been changed during some other service operation.

Frequent usage of an automatic transmission forward range to halt reverse vehicle motion may prevent the automatic adjusters from functioning, thereby inducing low pedal heights. Should low pedal heights be encountered, it is recommended that numerous forward and reverse stops be made until satisfactory pedal height is obtained.

If a low pedal height condition cannot be corrected by making numerous reverse stops (provided the hydraulic system is free of air) it indicates that the self-adjusting mechanism is not functioning. Therefore, it will be necessary to remove the drum, clean, free up and lubricate the adjusting mechanism. Then adjust the brakes, being sure the parking brake is fully released.

SERVICE BRAKE ADJUSTMENT

1. Each backing plate has two adjusting hole covers; remove the rear cover and turn the adjusting screw upward with a screwdriver or other suitable tool to expand the shoes until a slight drag is felt when the drum is rotated.
2. While holding the adjusting lever out of engagement with the adjusting screw, **Fig. 6,** back off the adjusting screw until wheel rotates freely with no drag.
3. Install wheel and adjusting hole cover. Adjust brakes on remaining wheels in the same manner.
4. If pedal height is not satisfactory, drive the vehicle and make sufficient reverse stops until proper pedal height is obtained.

PARKING BRAKE ADJUST

1. Release parking brake lever and loosen cable adjusting nut to be sure cable is slack.
2. With rear wheel brakes properly adjusted tighten cable adjusting nut until a slight drag is felt when the rear wheels are rotated. Then loosen the cable adjusting nut until both rear wheels can be rotated freely.
3. To complete the operation, back off an additional two turns of the cable adjusting nut.
4. Apply and release parking brake several times to be sure rear wheels are not dragging when cable is in released position.

MASTER CYLINDER REPLACE

MANUAL BRAKES

1. Disconnect brake lines from master cylinder. Install plugs in outlets to prevent fluid leakage.
2. From under instrument panel, disconnect stop lamp switch mounting bracket and position aside.
3. Grasp brake pedal and pull backward to disengage pushrod from master cylinder piston. **This will require a pull of about 50 pounds. Also, the retention grommet will be destroyed.**
4. Remove master cylinder to cowl retaining nuts and remove master cylinder by pulling straight out. **Make sure to remove all traces of old grommet from pushrod groove and master cylinder piston.**
5. Reverse procedure to install. Install new grommet on pushrod, then lubricate grommet with water and align pushrod with master cylinder piston. Using brake pedal, apply pressure to fully seat pushrod into piston.

POWER BRAKES

1. Disconnect primary and secondary brake tubes from master cylinder, then cap lines and master cylinder fitting.
2. Remove nuts attaching master cylinder to power brake unit, then slide master cylinder from power brake unit.
3. Reverse procedure to install.

POWER BRAKE UNIT REPLACE

1. Remove master cylinder retaining nuts, then carefully slide out master cylinder from power brake and allow it to rest on fender shield.
2. Disconnect vacuum hose from power brake.
3. From under instrument panel, disconnect push rod from brake pedal. On linkage type power brake unit, also remove lower pivot retaining bolt.
4. Remove power brake retaining nuts and remove power brake unit.
5. Reverse procedure to install.

Rear Suspension

INDEX

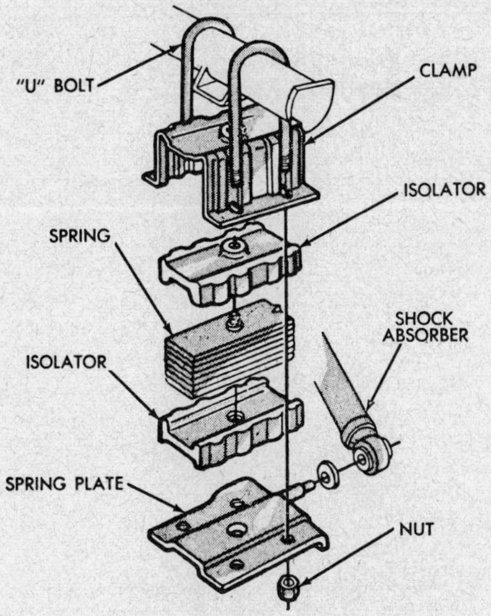

Fig. 1 Rear spring isolator

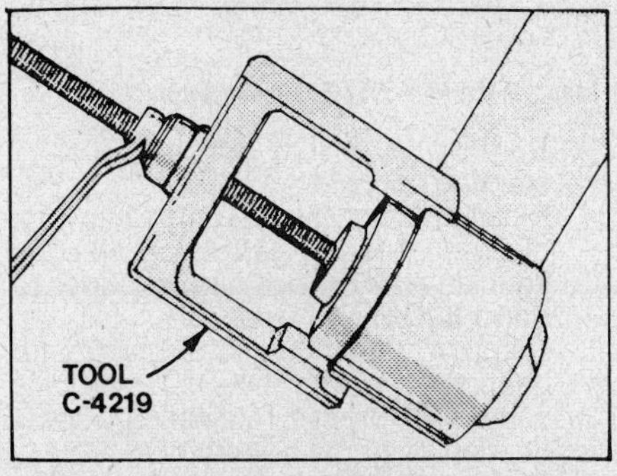

Fig. 3 Spring pivot bushing replacement

LEAF SPRINGS & BUSHINGS REPLACE

1. Support rear axle, relieving tension from spring.
2. Disconnect shock absorber from lower mounting.
3. Remove U-bolts and spring plate, or lower spring seat isolator retainer and isolator, **Fig. 1.**
4. Remove spring front hanger to body mount bracket nuts, **Fig. 2.**
5. Remove rear shackle bolts, lower spring, thus pulling spring front hanger bolts out of holes.
6. Remove front hanger and rear shackle from spring. To replace pivot bushings, refer to **Fig. 3.** Bushing replacement is accomplished in one operation.
7. Reverse procedure to install.

LEAF SPRING SERVICE

To replace interliners, remove spring alignment clips and on all models except Imperial, discard alignment clips. Separate spring leaves with a screwdriver or other suitable tool and remove interliners. Thoroughly clean spring surfaces before installation of new interliners.

To replace zinc interleaves, clamp spring in a vise and remove center bolt. Open vise carefully, allowing spring to expand. Interleaves can now be serviced. Install a drift through spring center bolt holes and clamp spring in a vise. Remove drift and install center bolt.

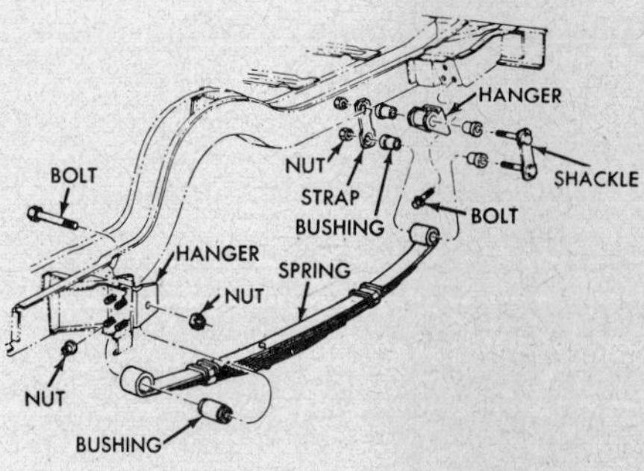

Fig. 2 Rear spring (typical)

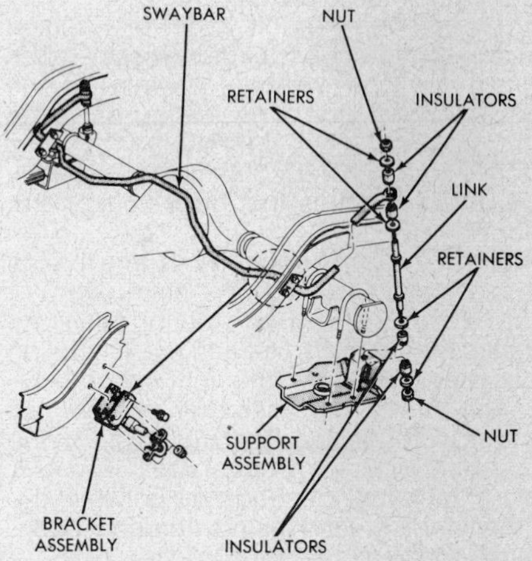

Fig. 4 Sway bar installation

SHOCK ABSORBER REPLACE

To replace shock absorber, support rear axle properly and disconnect shock absorber at upper and lower mountings.

SWAY BAR REPLACE

1. Remove nuts, retainers and rubber insulators from sway bar upper links, **Fig. 4.**
2. Disconnect sway bar brackets from frame.
3. Remove link from support assembly and replace insulators. Reverse procedure to install.

Front Suspension & Steering Section

INDEX

FRONT SUSPENSION

TRANSVERSE TORSION BAR FRONT SUSPENSION

This front suspension, **Figs. 1 and 2**, incorporates two transverse torsion bars which react on the outboard end of the lower control arms. The torsion bars are anchored in the front crossmember opposite the affected wheel. The torsion bars are mounted parallel to the front crossmember through a "Pivot Cushion Bushing," attached to the crossmember, and turns and extends rearward to the lower control arm. The torsion bar ends are provided with an isolated bushing, bolted to the lower control arm and sway bar, which acts as the lower control arm strut.

Riding height is controlled by the torsion bar adjusting bolts on the anchor end of the torsion bar. The right torsion bar is adjusted from the left side and the left torsion bar is adjusted from the right side.

The torsion bar assembly incorporates the "Pivot Cushion Bushing," **Fig. 3**, and "Bushing to Lower Control Arm." The lower control arm inner ends are bolted to the crossmember and pivots through bushings.

Caster and camber settings are made by loosening the upper control arm pivot bar bolt nuts and adjusting as necessary.

LONGITUDINAL TORSION BAR FRONT SUSPENSION

This suspension, **Fig. 4**, consists of two torsion bar springs (right and left), two sets of upper and lower control arms, four ball joints and two struts.

The front ends of the torsion bar springs engage the lower control arms at the inner pivot points. The rear end of the torsion bars engage adjustable anchor and cam assemblies that are supported by brackets welded to the frame side rails and a removable crossmember.

The upper control arms are mounted on removable brackets that are bolted to the frame side rails. The lower control arms are attached to the frame front crossmember by a pivot shaft and bushing assembly.

The pivot shafts are mounted in replaceable rubber bushings.

The steering knuckles are connected to the upper and lower control arms by means of ball joints. To prevent the possibility of fore and aft movement of the lower control arms, a strut is attached to the front crossmember and to the lower control arm.

This suspension has a rubber mounted crossmember, a torsion bar crossmember, more serviceable struts and a lower control arm with pressed in ball joints. Caster and camber settings are made by loosening the upper control arm pivot bar bolt nuts and adjusting as necessary.

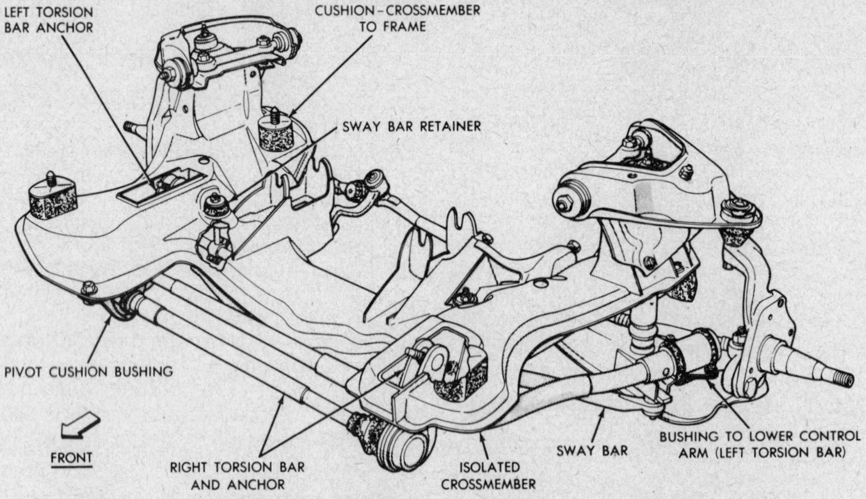

Fig. 1 Transverse torsion bar front suspension

WHEEL BEARINGS ADJUST

1. Tighten adjusting nut to 20-25 ft. lbs. while rotating wheel.
2. Back off adjusting nut 1/4 turn.
3. Finger tighten adjusting nut while rotating wheel, then align nut lock with cotter pin slot and install cotter pin.
4. The resulting adjustment should be .0001-.003 end play.

WHEEL BEARINGS REPLACE

1. Raise car and remove front wheels.
2. Remove grease cap, cotter pin, locknut and bearing adjusting nut.
3. Remove bolts that attach caliper to steering knuckle.
4. Slowly slide caliper up and away from disc and support caliper on steering knuckle arm. **Do not allow caliper to hang by brake hose.**
5. Remove thrust washer and outer bearing cone. Remove hub and disc assembly. Grease retainer and inner bearing can now be removed.
6. Reverse procedure to install.

CHECKING BALL JOINTS FOR WEAR

UPPER BALL JOINT

1. Position a suitable jack under lower control arm and raise wheel and tire assembly clear of floor, then remove wheel cover and wheel bearing dust cover and cotter pin.
2. Tighten wheel bearing adjusting nut just enough to remove all play between hub, bearings and spindle.
3. Lower jack positioned under lower control arm to allow tire to lightly contact floor.
4. Grasp top of tire and move wheel and tire assembly inward and outward. While moving tire inward and outward, check for movement at ball joints between steering knuckle and upper control arm.

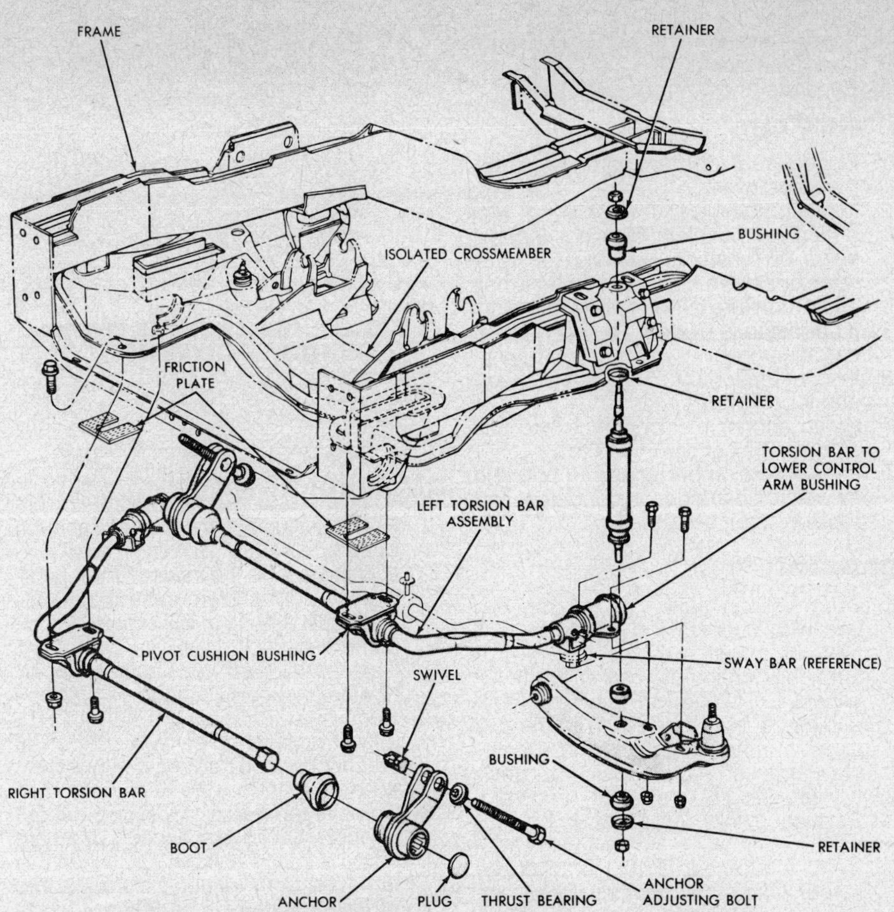

Fig. 2 Transverse torsion bar installation

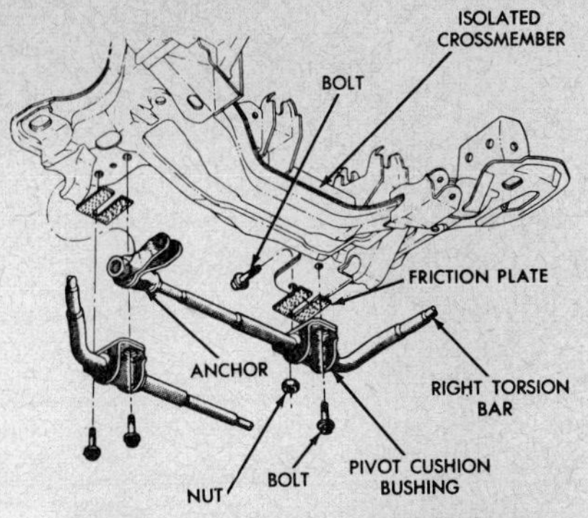

Fig. 3 Pivot cushion bushing & torsion bars

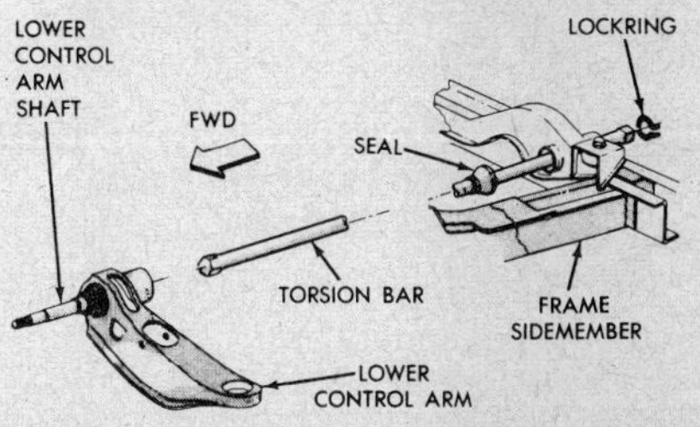

Fig. 4 Longitudinal torsion bar & lower control arm

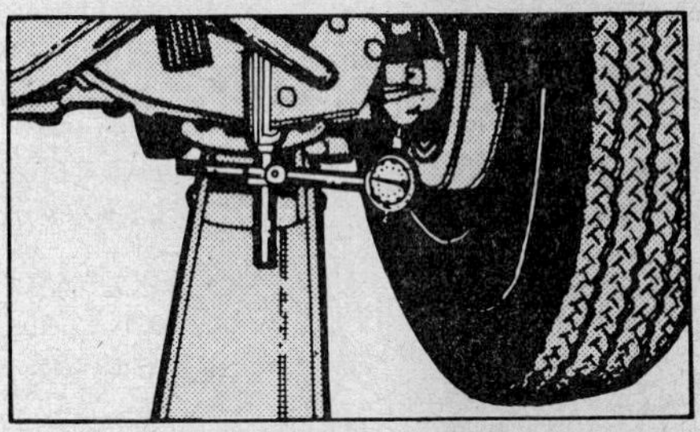

Fig. 5 Checking lower ball joint for wear

5. If any lateral movement is present, the upper ball joint should be replaced.
6. After completing upper ball joint check, readjust wheel bearing as described under "Wheel Bearings, Adjust."

LOWER BALL JOINT

If loose ball joints are suspected, first make sure the front wheel bearings are properly adjusted and that the control arms are tight.

1. Raise front of vehicle and place jack stands underneath each lower control arm as far out as possible. **The upper control arms must not contact the rubber rebound bumpers.**
2. With weight of vehicle on lower control arms, attach dial indicator onto lower control arm, **Fig. 5.**
3. Place dial indicator plunger tip against ball joint housing and zero dial indicator.
4. Using a pry bar under the center of the tire, raise and lower the tire and measure the axial travel of the ball joint housing with respect to the ball joint. If the axial travel is .030 inch or more than specified, the ball joint should be replaced.

BALL JOINTS

REPLACE

UPPER BALL JOINT

1. Place ignition switch in the "Off" position.
2. Using a suitable jack raise front of vehicle and position a jack stand under lower control arm as close to wheel and tire assembly as possible. Check to ensure that jack stand is not in contact with brake splash shield. Also check to ensure that rubber rebound bumper is not in contact with frame. **The torsion bar will remain in the loaded position.**
3. Remove wheel and tire assembly.
4. Remove cotter pin and nut from lower ball joint stud. Position tool No. C3564-A over lower ball joint stud, **Fig. 6,** allowing tool to rest on knuckle arm, then set tool securely against upper ball joint stud.
5. Tighten tool to apply pressure against upper ball joint stud, then strike knuckle with hammer to loosen stud.
6. Remove tool, then detach upper ball joint from knuckle. **Support knuckle and brake assembly to prevent damage to lower ball joint and brake hoses.**
7. Remove upper ball joint from upper control arm, using tool No. C3560.
8. Reverse procedure to install. Thread upper ball joint into control arm as far as possible by hand. Torque upper ball joint into control arm to 100 ft. lbs. After tightening lower ball joint stud nut, install cotter pin. **Ball joint seals should be replaced whenever they have been removed.**

LOWER BALL JOINT

1. Place ignition switch in the "Off" position.
2. Raise vehicle and support so front suspension is in the full rebound position. Position jack stands under front frame for additional support.
3. Remove wheel and tire assembly, then remove disc brake caliper and support with wire hook to prevent brake hose from becoming damaged.
4. Remove disc brake hub and rotor assembly and splash shield, then disconnect shock absorber at lower mounting.
5. Release load on torsion bar by rotating adjusting bolt counterclockwise.
6. Remove upper and lower ball joint stud nuts and cotter pin, then position tool No. C3564-A over upper ball joint stud so that tool is resting on steering knuckle, **Fig. 6.**
7. Rotate threaded portion of tool to lock it against lower ball joint stud. Tighten tool to place pressure on lower ball joint stud, then strike steering knuckle with a hammer to loosen stud. Remove tool and disconnect lower ball joint.

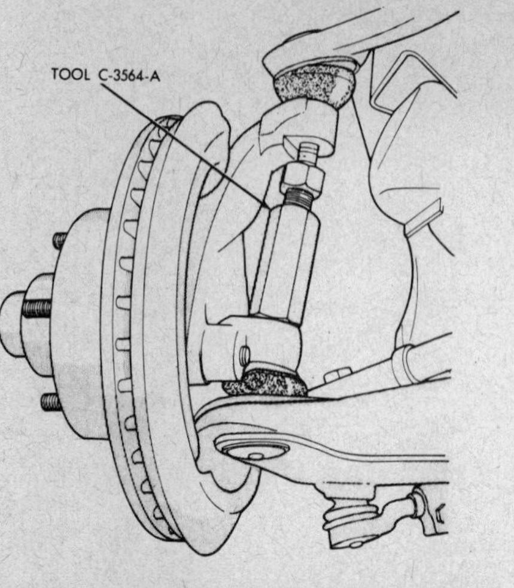

Fig. 6 Removing upper ball joint stud using tool C-3564-A

8. Use tool No. C4212 to press ball joint from lower control arm.
9. Position replacement ball joint on lower control arm, then press into control arm using tool No. C4212.
10. Install seal over lower ball joint. Use tool No. C4039 to press retainer portion of seal until it is locked in position.
11. Position lower ball joint to steering knuckle, then install upper and lower stud nuts and torque to 100 ft. lbs. After tightening stud nuts, install cotter pin.
12. Place tension on torsion bar by rotating adjusting bolt clockwise.
13. Install disc brake assembly and wheel and tire assembly, then adjust front wheel bearing as described under "Wheel Bearings, Adjust."
14. Lubricate ball joint, then lower vehicle and adjust vehicle riding height.

TORSION BAR REPLACE

MODELS W/TRANSVERSE TORSION BARS

Removal

1. Raise vehicle and support so front suspension is in full rebound position.
2. Rotate anchor adjusting bolts located in frame crossmember, counterclockwise to release load on both torsion bars. Then, remove anchor adjusting bolt from torsion bar to be removed.
3. Raise lower control arms until 2 7/8 inch clearance is obtained between crossmember ledge at jounce bumper and the torsion bar end bushing and support lower arms at this height. **This procedure will align the sway bar and the lower control arm attaching points for disassembly and component realignment and attachment during assembly.**
4. Remove sway bar to control arm attaching bolt and retainers, then the two bolts securing torsion bar end bushing to lower control arm.
5. Remove two bolts securing torsion bar pivot cushion bushing to crossmember, then the torsion bar and anchor assembly from crossmember.
6. Separate anchor from torsion bar.

Inspection

1. Inspect seal for damage and replace, if necessary.
2. Inspect bushing to lower control arm and pivot cushion bushing. Inspect seals on cushion bushing for cuts, tears or severe deterioration that may allow moisture to enter under cushion. If corrosion is evident, replace torsion bar assembly.
3. Inspect torsion bars for paint damage and touch up, if necessary.
4. Clean anchor hex openings and torsion bar hex ends.
5. Inspect torsion bar adjusting bolt and swivel for damage or corrosion and replace, if necessary.

Installation

1. Slide balloon seal over torsion bar end with cupped end facing toward hex.
2. Lubricate torsion bar hex end with lubricant, P/N 2525035, and install hex end into anchor bracket. With the torsion bar in horizontal position, the anchor bracket ears should be positioned nearly straight upward. Position swivel into anchor bracket ears.
3. Install torsion bar anchor bracket assembly into crossmember anchor retainer, then the anchor adjusting bolt and bearing.
4. Install two bolt and washer assemblies securing pivot cushion bushing to crossmember. Leave assemblies loose enough to install friction plates.
5. With lower control arms supported as outlined in step 3 under "Removal," install the two bolt and nut assemblies securing torsion bar bushing to lower control arm and torque nuts to 70 ft. lbs.
6. Ensure that torsion bar anchor bracket is fully seated in crossmember. Then install friction plates between crossmember and pivot cushion bushing with open end of slot to rear and bottomed out on mounting bolt. Tighten cushion bushing bolts to 85 ft. lbs. Place balloon seal over anchor bracket.
7. Install new bolt through sway bar, retainer cushions and sleeve and attach to lower control arm end bushing, then torque bolt to 50 ft. lbs.
8. Rotate anchor adjusting bolt clockwise to load torsion bar.
9. Lower vehicle and adjust riding height.

MODELS W/LONGITUDINAL TORSION BARS

The torsion bars are not interchangeable side for side. The bars are marked either right or left by an "R" or an "L" stamped on one end of the bar. The general procedure for replacing a torsion bar is as follows.

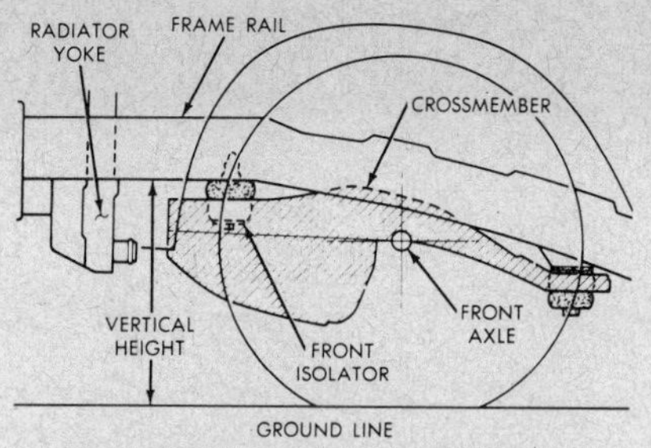

Fig. 7 Measuring front suspension height

Removal

1. Remove upper control arm rebound bumper.
2. If vehicle is to be raised on a hoist, make sure it is lifted on the body only so suspension is in full rebound position (no load).
3. Release all load from torsion bar by turning anchor adjusting bolt counterclockwise.
4. Slide rear anchor balloon seal off of rear anchor and remove lock ring from anchor.
5. Remove torsion bar, by sliding bar out through rear of rear anchor. Use care not to damage balloon seal when it is removed from torsion bar. **On some models, it may be necessary to remove transmission torque shaft to provide clearance.**

Inspection

1. Inspect balloon seal for damage and replace if necessary.
2. Inspect torsion bar for scores or nicks. Dress down all scratches and nicks to remove sharp edges, then paint repaired areas with a rust preventive.
3. Remove all foreign material from hex openings in anchors and from hex ends of torsion bars.
4. Inspect adjusting bolt and swivel and replace if there is any sign of corrosion or other damage. Lubricate for easy operation.

Installation

1. Insert torsion bar through rear anchor.
2. Slide balloon seal over torsion bar with cupped end toward rear of bar.
3. Coat both ends of torsion bar with a long mileage lubricant.
4. Slide torsion bar in hex opening of lower control arm.
5. Install lock ring, making sure it is seated in groove.
6. Pack annular opening in rear anchor completely full of a long mileage lubricant.
7. Position lip of balloon seal in groove of anchor.
8. Turn adjusting bolt clockwise to place a load on torsion bar.
9. Lower vehicle to floor and adjust front suspension height.
10. Install upper control arm rebound bumper.

SWAY BAR
REPLACE

1. Raise and support front of vehicle. **Sway bar to lower control arm attaching points are aligned only when lower control arms are at design height. If frame contact or twin post hoist is used, release load on torsion bar by turning adjuster bolts counterclockwise, then raise lower control arms until clearance between crossmember ledge and torsion bar to lower control arm bushing is 2$^{7}/_{8}$ inches. Support lower control arms with jack stand during sway bar removal and installation.**
2. With lower control arms properly supported, remove sway bar to torsion bar bushing attaching bolts, retainers, cushions and sleeves.
3. Remove retainer assembly strap bolts and retainer straps, then remove sway bar.
4. Reverse procedure to install. Inspect cushions and bushings for excessive wear or deterioration and replace as necessary.

RIDING HEIGHT
ADJUST

Before taking measurements, grasp the bumpers at the center (rear bumper first) and jounce the car up and down several times. Jounce the car at the front bumper the same number of times and release the bumper at the same point in the cycle each time.

1. Ride height is measured from the head of the front suspension front crossmember insulator bolt to ground, **Fig. 7.**
2. If necessary, turn torsion bar adjusting bolt clockwise to increase height and counterclockwise to decrease height.
3. After completing adjustment, jounce vehicle and recheck riding height. Both sides must be measured even though only one side may have been adjusted. Front vehicle height should not vary more than $^{1}/_{4}$ inch from the specified riding height. Riding height should also be within $^{1}/_{4}$ inch side to side.

Year	Model	Height
CHRYSLER & IMPERIAL		
1982-83	Cordoba, LeBaron	12½ inch
1982-83	Imperial	12½ inch
1982	New Yorker	12½ inch
1983	New Yorker Fifth Ave.	12½ inch
1984–88	Fifth Avenue	12½ inch
DODGE		
1982-83	Diplomat, Mirada	12½ inch
1984-88	Diplomat	12½ inch
PLYMOUTH		
1982–88	Gran Fury	12½ inch

MANUAL STEERING GEAR
REPLACE

To avoid damage to the energy absorbing steering column, it is recommended that the steering column be completely detached from floor and instrument panel before steering gear is removed.

1. Use a suitable puller to remove steering arm from under vehicle.
2. Remove gear to frame retaining bolts and remove gear.
3. Reverse procedure to install.

POWER STEERING GEAR
REPLACE

1. Disconnect battery ground cable.
2. Remove steering column.
3. Disconnect fluid hoses from steering gear and support free ends above pump to avoid loss of fluid. Plug fittings on gear.
4. Disconnect steering arm from gear with suitable puller.
5. Remove gear to frame retaining bolts or nuts and remove gear.
6. Reverse procedure to install.

POWER STEERING PUMP
REPLACE

1. Loosen power steering pump mounting and locking bolts, then remove drive belt.
2. Disconnect pressure and return lines at power steering pump.
3. Remove pump mounting bolts, then remove pump and mounting bracket.
4. Reverse procedure to install.

There may be cases when the vehicle may not have sufficient positive camber adjustment. Upper control arm plate spacers are available that will allow more positive camber adjustment, if required. If this condition is encountered, use spacer 1-4014352 for front suspension upper control arm front pivot support and spacer 1-4014353 for the rear pivot support. To install spacers, proceed as follows:

1. Loosen but do not remove caster/camber adjustment nut.
2. Raise vehicle and remove wheel and tire assembly.
3. Loosen but do not remove shock absorber upper mounting nut.
4. Remove two support plate bolts at front end of plate, then loosen two rear bolts enough to slide front spacer between support plate and frame.
5. Align holes in spacer with holes in support plate and frame.
6. Insert two front bolts and start threads. Do not tighten.
7. Repeat steps 4 through 6 for rear spacer.
8. Torque the four support plate bolts to 65 ft. lbs. and the shock absorber upper nut to 25 ft. lbs.
9. Lower vehicle and adjust alignment on side that spacers were installed.

Wheel Alignment Section

INDEX

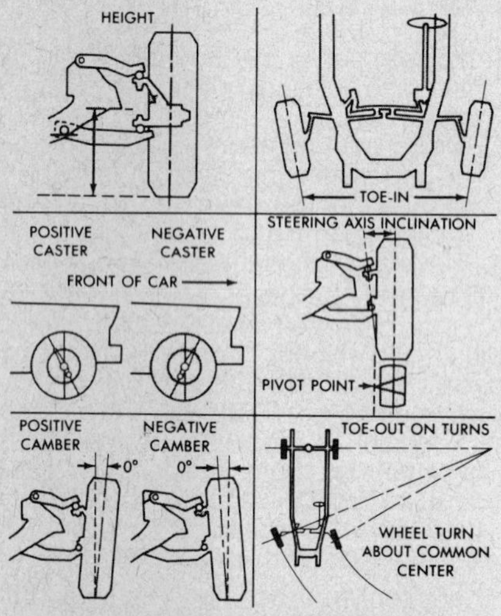

Fig. 1 Alignment factors

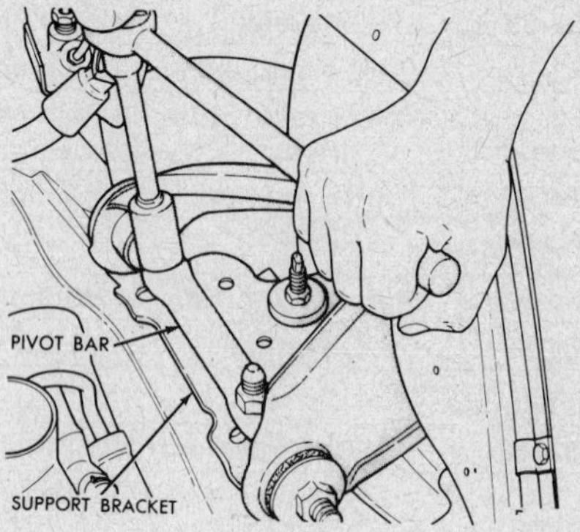

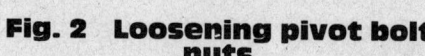

Fig. 2 Loosening pivot bolt nuts

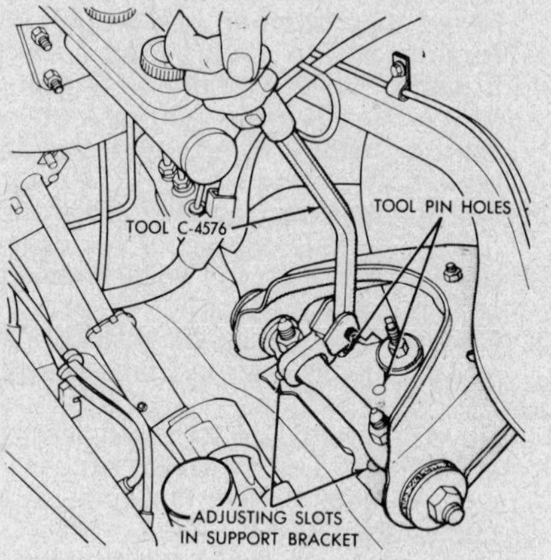

Fig. 3 Adjusting camber & caster using tool C-4576

WHEEL ALIGNMENT

CASTER & CAMBER, ADJUST

Front suspension height must be checked and corrected as necessary before performing wheel alignment.

1. Remove all foreign material from exposed threads of cam adjusting bolt nuts or pivot bar adjusting bolt nuts.
2. Record initial camber and caster readings before loosening cam bolt nuts or pivot bar bolt nuts, **Fig. 1.**
3. On vehicles using cam bolts, the camber and caster is adjusted by loosening the cam bolt nuts and turning the cam bolts as necessary until the desired setting is obtained. On vehicles using pivot bars, tool C-4576 is required to adjust caster and camber. When performing adjustments, the camber settings should be held as close as possible to the "desired" setting, and the caster setting should be held as nearly equal as possible on both wheels, **Figs. 2 and 3.**

TOE-IN, ADJUST

With the front wheels in straight ahead position, loosen the clamps at each end of both adjusting tubes. Adjust toe-in by turning the tie rod sleeve which will "center" the steering wheel spokes. If the steering wheel was centered, make the toe-in adjustment by turning both sleeves an equal amount. Position the clamps so they are on the bottom and tighten bolts to 15 ft. lbs.

CHRYSLER MOTORS FRONT WHEEL DRIVE

NOTE: The following models are covered in this chapter: CHRYSLER—E-Class (1983-84), Executive (1983-85), Laser (1984-87), LeBaron (1982-88), LeBaron GTS (1986-88), LeBaron Coupe/Convertible (1987-88), New Yorker (1983-87) & New Yorker Turbo (1988), New Yorker & New Yorker Landau (1988), Town & Country (1982-88); DODGE—Aries (1982-88), Charger (1983-87), Daytona (1984-88), Dynasty (1988), 400 (1982-83), Lancer (1985-88), Omni (1982-88), 024 (1982), Shelby Charger (1983-86) 600 (1983-88), Shadow (1987-88); PLYMOUTH—Caravelle (1985-88), Horizon (1982-88), Reliant (1982-88), TC-3 (1982), Sundance (1987-88), Turismo (1983-86).

INDEX OF SERVICE OPERATIONS

NOTE: Refer to rear of this manual for vehicle manufacturer's special service tool suppliers.

Specifications

GENERAL ENGINE SPECIFICATIONS

Year	Engine CID①/Liter	Engine VIN Code②	Fuel System	Bore & Stroke Inch (Millimeters)	Compression Ratio	Net H.P. @ RPM ③	Maximum Torque Ft. Lbs. @ RPM	Normal Oil Pressure Pounds @ 2000 RPM
1982	4-105, 1.7L ⑥	A	6520, 2 Bbl. ⑦	3.13 x 3.40 (79.5 x 86.4)	8.2	63 @ 4800	83 @ 2400	60-90
	4-135, 2.2L ⑧	B	6520, 2 Bbl. ⑦	3.44 x 3.62 (87.5 x 92)	8.5	84 @ 4800	111 @ 2400	50
	4-156, 2.6L ⑨	D	Mikuni, 2 Bbl.	3.59 x 3.86 (91.1 x 98)	8.2	92 @ 4500	131 @ 2500	57
1983	4-97, 1.6L ⑩	A	6520, 2 Bbl. ⑦	3.17 x 3.07 (80.6 x 78)	8.8	62 @ 4800	86 @ 3200	58-87 ⑪
	4-105, 1.7L ⑥	B	6520, 2 Bbl. ⑦	3.13 x 3.40 (79.5 x 86.4)	8.2	63 @ 4800	83 @ 2400	60-90
	4-135, 2.2L ⑧	C	6520, 2 Bbl. ⑦	3.44 x 3.62 (87.5 x 92.0)	9.0	94 @ 5200	117 @ 3200	50
	4-135, 2.2L ⑧ ⑫	F	6520, 2 Bbl. ⑦	3.44 x 3.62 (87.5 x 92)	9.6	107 @ 5600	126 @ 3600	50
	4-135, 2.2L ⑧	D	E.F.I. ⑬	3.44 x 3.62 (87.5 x 92)	9.0	94 @ 5200	120 @ 3200	50
	4-156, 2.6L ⑨	G	Mikuni, 2 Bbl.	3.59 x 3.86 (91.1 x 98.0)	8.2	93 @ 4500	131 @ 2500	57
1984	4-97, 1.6L ⑩	A	6520, 2 Bbl. ⑦	3.17 x 3.07 (80.6 x 78)	8.8	64 @ 4800	87 @ 2800	58-87 ⑪
	4-135, 2.2L ⑧	C	6520, 2 Bbl. ⑦	3.44 x 3.62 (87.5 x 92)	9.0	96 @ 5200	119 @ 3200	50
	4-135, 2.2L ⑧ ⑫	F	6520, 2 Bbl. ⑦	3.44 x 3.62 (87.5 x 92)	10.0	100 @ 5600	129 @ 3600	50
	4-135, 2.2L ⑧	D	E.F.I. ⑬	3.44 x 3.62 (87.5 x 92)	9.0	99 @ 5600	121 @ 3200	50
	4-135, 2.2L ⑧ ④	E	E.F.I. ⑬	3.44 x 3.62 (87.5 x 92)	8.5	142 @ 5600	160 @ 3600	50
	4-156, 2.6L ⑨	G	Mikuni, 2 Bbl.	3.59 x 3.86 (91.1 x 98)	8.7	101 @ 4800	140 @ 2800	85 ⑤
1985	4-97, 1.6L ⑩	A	6520, 2 Bbl ⑦	3.17 x 3.07 (80.6 x 78)	8.8	64 @ 4800	87 @ 2800	40-90 ⑪
	4-135, 2.2L ⑧	C	6520, 2 Bbl. ⑦	3.44 x 3.62 (87.5 x 92)	9.5	96 @ 5200	119 @ 3200	25-90 ⑪
	4-135, 2.2L ⑧ ⑫	F	6520, 2 Bbl. ⑦	3.44 x 3.62 (87.5 x 92)	10	110 @ 5600	129 @ 3600	25-90 ⑪
	4-135, 2.2L ⑧	D	E.F.I. ⑬	3.44 x 3.62 (87.5 x 92)	9.0	99 @ 5600	121 @ 3200	25-90 ⑪
	4-135, 2.2L ⑧ ④	E	E.F.I. ⑬	3.44 x 3.62 (87.5 x 92)	8.5	146 @ 5200	168 @ 3600	25-90 ⑪
	4-156, 2.6L ⑨	G	Mikuni, 2 Bbl.	3.59 x 3.86 (91.1 x 98)	8.7	101 @ 4800	140 @ 2800	45-90 ⑪
1986-88	4-97, 1.6L ⑩	A	6520, 2 Bbl. ⑦	3.17 x 3.07 (80.6 x 78)	8.8	64 @ 4800	87 @ 2400	72.5
	4-135, 2.2L ⑧	C	6520, 2 Bbl. ⑦	3.44 x 3.62 (87.5 x 92)	9.5	96 @ 5200	119 @ 3200	50
	4-135, 2.2L ⑧ ⑫	F	6520, 2 Bbl. ⑦	3.44 x 3.62 (87.5 x 92)	9.6	110 @ 5600	129 @ 3600	50
	4-135, 2.2L ⑧	D	E.F.I. ⑬	3.44 x 3.62 (87.5 x 92)	9.0	97 @ 5200	122 @ 3200	50
	4-135, 2.2L ⑧ ④	E	E.F.I. ⑬	3.44 x 3.62 (87.5 x 92)	8.1	146 @ 5200	170 @ 3600	50
	4-153, 2.5L	K	E.F.I. ⑬	3.44 x 4.09 (87.5 x 104)	9.0	100 @ 4800	136 @ 2800	50

①—CID-cubic inch displacement.
②—On 1982-86 models, the 8th digit of the VIN denotes engine code.
③—Ratings are net-as installed in vehicle.
④—Turbocharged engine.
⑤—At 2500 RPM.
⑥—1700 cc.
⑦—Holley.
⑧—2200 cc.
⑨—2600 cc.
⑩—1600 cc.
⑪—At 3000 RPM.
⑫—High output engine.
⑬—Electronic fuel injection.

ENGINE TIGHTENING SPECIFICATIONS*

*Torque specifications are for clean and lightly lubricated threads only. Dry or dirty threads produce increased friction which prevents accurate measurement of tightness.

Year	Engine Model/VIN	Spark Plugs Ft. Lbs.	Cylinder Head Bolts Ft. Lbs.	Intake Manifold Inch Lbs.	Exhaust Manifold Inch Lbs.	Camshaft Cover Inch Lbs.	Connecting Rod Cap Bolts Ft. Lbs.	Main Bearing Cap Bolts Ft. Lbs.	Flywheel to Crankshaft Ft. Lbs.	Crankshaft Pulley Ft. Lbs.
1982-83	4-105/④1700 cc	20	60①	200②	200	48	35	47	⑤	58
1982-85	4-135/④2200 cc	26	①	200	200	105	40①	30①	65	20.8
	4-156/④2600 cc	18.3	③	150	150	53	34	58	100	87
1983-86	4-97/A 1600 cc	⑦	52	133	180	44⑥	28	48	—	110
1986-88	4-135/④	26	①	200	200	105	40①	30①	70	20.8
	4-153/K	26	①	200	200	105	40①	30①	70	20.8

①—Refer to text for procedure.
②—Intake to exhaust mainfold inboard nut, 150 inch lbs. Intake to exhaust manifold outboard nut, 200 inch lbs.
③—Cold engine, 69 ft. lbs.; warm engine, 76 ft. lbs.
④—For VIN code, refer to the General Engine Specifications at the front of the chapter.
⑤—Man. trans., 60 ft. lbs.; auto trans., 40 ft. lbs.
⑥—Rocker arm covers.
⑦—1983 models, 20 ft. lbs.; 1984-88 models, 22 ft. lbs.

ALTERNATOR & REGULATOR SPECIFICATIONS

	Alternator				Regulator	
Year	Part Number	Rated Hot Output Amps.	Field Current 12 Volts @ 80° F	Output @ 15 Volts 1250 RPM	Part Number	Voltage @ 80°F
1982-83	Yellow①	60	4.5-6.5	45	4111990	13.9-14.6
	Brown①	78	4.5-6.5	56	4111990	13.9-14.6
1982-85	A4T25191②	75	—	63-70③	Integral	14.1-14.7④
1983-86	K1⑤	65	2.5-5.0	50	—	—
1984-85	Yellow	60	2.5-5.0	45	—	13.9-14.6
	Brown	78	2.5-5.0	56	—	13.9-14.6
	B120 427 850MP⑤	90	—	78-85③	Integral	13.8-14.2⑥
1985	①⑦	40/90	2.5-5.0	96	—	—
	⑤⑦	40/90	2.5-5.0	87	—	—
1986-88	Yellow	60	2.5-5.0	45	—	13.9-14.6
	Brown	78	2.5-5.0	56	—	13.9-14.6
	①⑦	40/90	2.5-5.0	87	—	—
	⑤⑦	40/90	2.5-5.0	80	—	—
	⑤⑧	40/100	2.5-5.0	87	—	—

①—Chrysler alternator.
②—Mitsubishi alternator.
③—At 13.5 volts & 1000 RPM.
④—At 68° F.
⑤—Bosch alternator.
⑥—At 77° F.
⑦—40/90 AMP alternator w/voltage regulator in engine electronics.
⑨—40/90 AMP alternator w/voltage regulator in engine electronics.

STARTING MOTOR APPLICATIONS

Year	Engine/VIN	Model	Ident. Number
1982-83	4-105 (1700 cc)②③	Bosch	5206255
	4-105 (1700 cc)②③	Nippondenso	5206265
	4-105 (1700 cc) ①③	Bosch	5213395
	4-105 (1700 cc) ①③	Nippondenso	5213295
	4-135 (2200 cc) ①③	Bosch	5213045
	4-135 (2200 cc)②③	Bosch	5213395
	4-135 (2200 cc)③	Nippondenso	5213645
1982-85	4-156/③(2600 cc)	Nippondenso	5213235
1983-86	4-97/A (1600 cc)	Mitsubishi	5213301
1984-85	4-135 (2200 cc)④	Bosch	5213045
	4-135 (2200 cc)④	Nippondenso	5213645
	4-135/E (2200 cc)	Bosch	5213450
1986-88	4-135④	Bosch	5226442
	4-135④	Nippondenso	5226742
	4-135④	Bosch	5226441
	4-153/K	Bosch	5226444

①—Automatic Transmission.
②—Manual Transmission.
③—For VIN code, refer to the General Engine Specifications at the front of the chapter.
④—VIN codes C, D, & F.

WHEEL ALIGNMENT SPECIFICATIONS

Year	Model	Camber Angle, Degrees				Toe In Inch
		Limits		Desired		
		Left	Right	Left	Right	
1982-83	Aries & Reliant①	−1/4 to +3/4	−1/4 to +3/4	+5/16	+5/16	⑤
	Aries & Reliant③	−1 to 0	−1 to 0	−1/2	−1/2	⑥
	Horizon & Omni①	−1/4 to +3/4	−1/4 to +3/4	+5/16	+5/16	②
	Horizon & Omni③	⑦	⑦	⑦	⑦	④
	LeBaron & 400①	−1/4 to +3/4	−1/4 to +3/4	+5/16	+5/16	⑤
	LeBaron & 400③	−1 to 0	−1 to 0	−1/2	−1/2	⑥
1983	Charger & Turismo①	−1/4 to +3/4	−1/4 to +3/4	+5/16	+5/16	⑤
	Charger & Turismo③	−1/4 to −1 1/4	−1/4 to −1 1/4	−3/4	−3/4	④
	New Yorker, E Class & 600①	−1/4 to +3/4	−1/4 to +3/4	+5/16	+5/16	⑤
	New Yorker, E Class & 600③	−1 to 0	−1 to 0	−1/2	−1/2	⑥
1984-85	All①	−1/4 to +3/4	−1/4 to +3/4	+5/16	+5/16	⑤
	Charger, Horizon, Omni & Turismo③	−1 1/4 to −1/4	−1 1/4 to −1/4	−3/4	−3/4	④
	Exc. Charger, Horizon, Omni & Turismo③	−1 to 0	−1 to 0	−1/2	−1/2	⑥
1986-88	All①	−1/4 to +3/4	−1/4 to +3/4	+5/16	+5/16	⑤
	Charger, Horizon, Omni & Turismo③	−1 1/4 to −1/4	−1 1/4 to −1/4	−1/2	−5/16	⑧
	Exc. Charger, Horizon, Omni & Turismo③	−1 1/4 to +1/4	−1 1/4 to +1/4	+1/2	1/2	⑨

①—Front wheel alignment.
②—7/32" out to 1/8" in. (.4° out to .2° in).
③—Rear wheel alignment
④—5/32" out to 11/32" in. (.3° out to .7° in).
⑤—7/32" out to 1/8" in (.4° out to .2° in).
⑥—3/16" out to 3/16" in. (.38° out to .38° in).
⑦—1981 Limits, −1 1/4° to −1/2°; Desired, −1°. 1982-83 Limits, −1 1/4 to −1/4°, Desired, −3/4°
⑧—3/16" out to 13/32" in. (.40 out to .8° in).
⑨—5/16" out to 5/16" in. (.60 out to .60° in).

COOLING SYSTEM & CAPACITY DATA

Year	Model or Engine/VIN	Cooling Capacity		Radiator Cap Relief Pressure, Lbs.	Thermo. Opening Temp. Degrees F. (Centigrade)	Fuel Tank Gals. (Litres)	Engine Oil Refill Qts. (Litres)	Transmission Oil		Final Drive Pints (Litres)②
		Less A/C Qts. (Litres)	With A/C Qts. (Litres)					4 & 5 Speed Pints (Litres)	Auto. Trans. Qts. (Litres)①	
1982	4-105/A (1.7L)	6 (5.7)	6 (5.7)	16	195 (90.6)	13 (49)	4④ (3.8)	3 (1.4)	7.3⑤ (6.9)	2.4 (1.1)
	4-135/B (2.2L)	7 (6.6)	7 (6.6)	16	195 (90.6)	13 (49)	4④ (3.8)	4 (1.8)	7.5⑤ (7.1)	2.4 (1.1)
	4-156/D (2.6L)	8.5 (8.1)	8.5 (8.1)	16	190 (88)	13 (49)	5⑥ (5)	4 (1.8)	8.5⑤ (8.1)	2.4 (1.1)
1983	4-97 (1.6L)/A	7 (6.6)	7 (6.6)	16	195 (90.6)	13 (49)	3.5⑥ (3.3)	⑪	—	—
	4-105 (1.7L)/B	6 (5.7)	6 (5.7)	16	195 (90.6)	13 (49)	4④ (3.8)	⑪	8.4⑦ (7.9)	2.4 (1.1)
	4-135 (2.2L)/⑧	9 (8.5)	9 (8.5)	16	195 (90.6)	13⑩ (49)	4④ (3.8)	⑪	8.9⑦⑫ (8.4)	2.4 (1.1)
	4-156 (2.6L)/G	9 (8.5)	9 (8.5)	16	190 (88)	13 (49)	4④ (3.8)	⑪	8.9⑦⑫ (8.4)	2.4 (1.1)
1984–85	4-97 (1.6L)/A	6.8 (6.4)	6.8 (6.4)	16	195 (90.6)	13 (49)	3.5⑥ (3.3)	3.8⑬ (1.7)	8.9⑦ (8.4)	2.4 (1.1)
	4-135 (2.2L)/⑧	9 (8.5)	9 (8.5)	16	195 (90.6)	⑨	4.0④ (3.8)	4.0⑬ (1.8)	8.9⑦⑫ (8.4)	2.4 (1.1)
	4-156 (2.6L)/G	9 (8.5)	9 (8.5)	16	190 (88)	14 (53)	5.0⑥ (4.8)	—	8.9⑦⑫ (8.4)	2.4 (1.1)
1988	4-97 (1.6L)/A	6.8 (6.4)	6.8 (6.4)	16	195 (90.6)	13 (49)	3.5⑥ (3.3)	3.8③ (1.7)	8.9⑦ (8.4)	2.4 (1.1)
	4-135 (2.2L)/⑧	9 (8.5)	9 (8.5)	16	195 (90.6)	⑨	4.0④ (3.8)	4.0③ (1.8)	8.9⑦⑫ (8.4)	2.4 (1.1)
	4-153 (2.5L)/K	9 (8.5)	9 (8.5)	16	195 (90.6)	14 (53)	4.0 (3.8)	4.0③ (1.8)	8.9⑫ (8.4)	2.4 (1.1)

①—Approximate. Make final check with dipstick.
②—Automatic trans. only.
③—5 spd. transaxle, 4.6 pts.
④—With or without filter change.
⑤—Drain & refill, 3 qts.
⑥—Includes ½ qt. for filter change.
⑦—Drain & refill, 4 qts.
⑧—For V.I.N. code, refer to "General Engine Specifications" at the front of the chapter.
⑨—Exc. Charger, Horizon, Omni & Turismo—14.0 gals.; Charger, Horizon, Omni & Turismo—13.0 gals.
⑩—EFI models, 14.0 gals.
⑪—A-412, 3.0 pts.; A-460, 4.0 pts.; A-465 (5 spd.), 4.6 pts.
⑫—Vehicles with fleet option package, 9.2 qts.

Electrical Section

INDEX

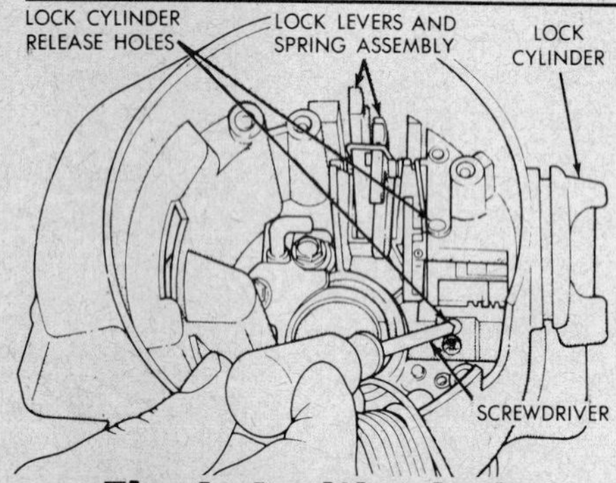

Fig. 1 Ignition lock cylinder removal. Models with standard column exc. Horizon, Omni, Charger & Turismo

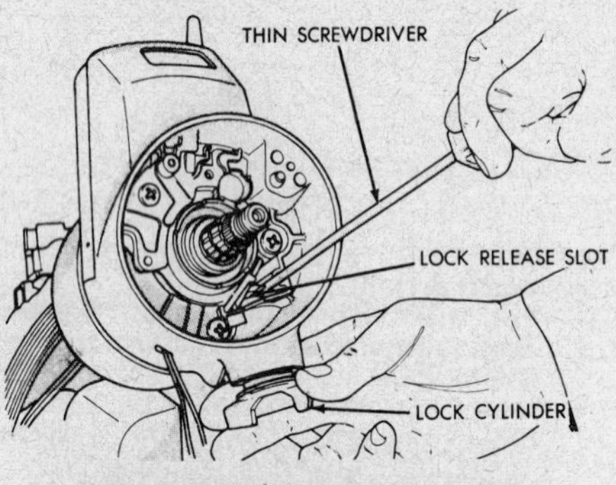

Fig. 2 Ignition lock cylinder removal. Models with tilt column exc. Horizon, Omni, Charger & Turismo

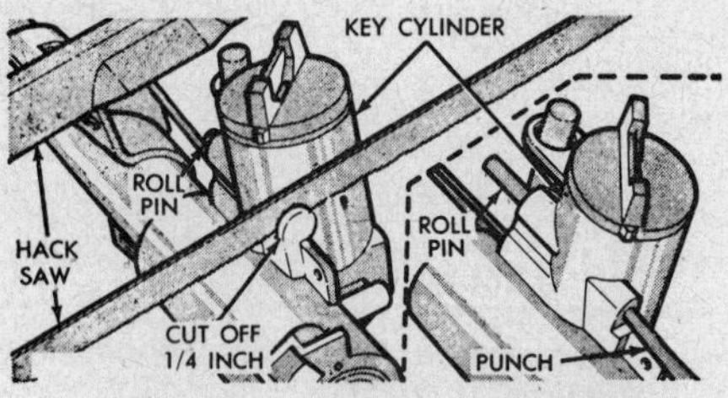

Fig. 3 Ignition lock cylinder retaining pin removal. Horizon, Omni, Charger & Turismo

STARTER REPLACE

EXC. 4-156 ENGINE

1. Disconnect battery ground cable.
2. Remove starter to flywheel housing and rear bracket to engine or transaxle attaching bolts.
3. On models equipped with 4-135 engine, loosen air pump tube at exhaust manifold, then position tube bracket away from starter motor.
4. If equipped, remove heat shield clamp and heat shield.
5. Disconnect starter cable at starter motor and solenoid leads at solenoid, then remove starter motor.
6. Reverse procedure to install.

4-156 ENGINE

1. Disconnect battery ground cable.
2. Disconnect starter cable at starter.
3. Disconnect solenoid lead wire from solenoid.
4. Remove starter attaching bolts and starter.
5. Reverse procedure to install.

IGNITION LOCK REPLACE

EXC. HORIZON, OMNI, CHARGER & TURISMO

Models Less Tilt Column

1. Disconnect battery ground cable.
2. Remove turn signal switch as described under "Turn Signal Switch, Replace."
3. Disconnect horn and ignition key lamp ground wires, then remove ignition key lamp attaching screw and lamp.
4. Remove four screws attaching upper bearing housing to lock housing and the snap ring from upper end of steering shaft, then the upper bearing housing.
5. Remove lock plate spring and lock plate from steering shaft.
6. Position lock cylinder in Lock position and remove ignition key.
7. Remove key warning buzzer attaching screws and buzzer.
8. Remove two screws attaching ignition switch to steering column, then rotate switch 90° and slide from rod.
9. Remove two screws attaching dimmer switch, then disengage dimmer switch from actuator rod.
10. Remove two bellcrank attaching screws, then slide bellcrank up into lock housing until it can be disconnected from ignition switch actuator rod.
11. With lock cylinder in Lock position, insert a small diameter screwdriver into lock cylinder release holes and push inward until spring loaded lock cylinder retainers release, **Fig. 1.**
12. Grasp lock cylinder and pull from lock housing bore.
13. Reverse procedure to install. The lock cylinder and ignition switch must be in the Lock position.

Models W/Tilt Column

1. Disconnect battery ground cable.
2. Remove turn signal switch as described under "Turn Signal Switch, Replace."
3. Remove ignition key lamp.
4. Position ignition lock cylinder in Lock position, then remove ignition key.

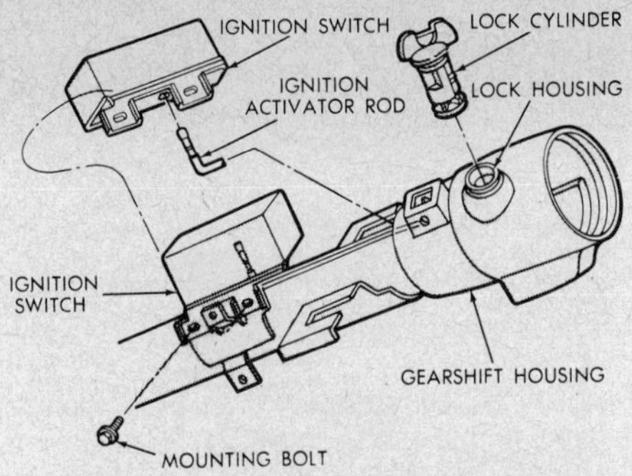

Fig. 4 Ignition switch replacement. Exc. Horizon, Omni, Charger & Turismo

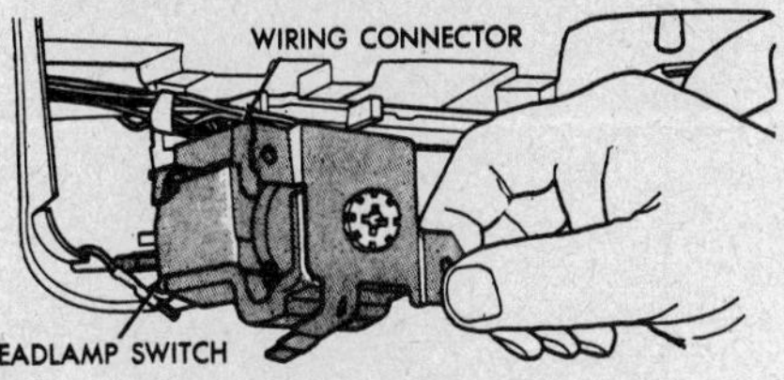

Fig. 6 Light switch replacement (Typical)

5. Insert a thin screwdriver into lock cylinder release slot and depress spring latch which releases lock cylinder, then grasp lock cylinder and remove from column, **Fig. 2.**
6. Reverse procedure to install.

HORIZON, OMNI, CHARGER & TURISMO

1. Remove steering wheel, column covers and turn signal switch.
2. With a hacksaw blade, cut upper 1/4 inch from retainer pin boss, **Fig. 3.**
3. Using a suitable drift, drive roll pin from housing and remove lock cylinder.
4. Insert new cylinder into housing, ensuring that it engages lug or ignition switch driver.
5. Install roll pin.
6. Check for proper operation.

IGNITION SWITCH REPLACE

EXC. HORIZON, OMNI, CHARGER & TURISMO

1. Disconnect battery ground cable.
2. Remove under panel sound deadener.
3. Disconnect speed control switch.
4. Remove two switch attaching screws, then rotate switch 90° and pull-up to disengage switch from rod, **Fig. 4.**
5. Reverse procedure to install. When installing new switch push up gently on switch relieve slack in rod system.

HORIZON, OMNI, CHARGER & TURISMO

1. Disconnect battery ground cable.
2. Remove connector from ignition switch.
3. Place ignition lock in "Lock" position and remove key.
4. Remove two ignition switch mounting screws and permit switch and pushrod to drop below column jacket, **Fig. 5.**
5. Rotate switch 90° for removal of switch from pushrod.
6. Position ignition switch in "Lock" position, second detent from top of the switch.
7. Place switch at right angle to column and insert pushrod.
8. Align switch on bracket and loosely install screws.
9. With a light rearward load on switch, tighten attaching screws.
10. Connect ignition switch wiring connector and battery ground cable.
11. Check for proper operation.

LIGHT SWITCH REPLACE

EXC. HORIZON, OMNI, CHARGER, TURISMO, LANCER & LEBARON

1. Disconnect battery ground cable, then place gearshift lever in "1" position.
2. Remove left upper and lower instrument cluster bezel attaching screws, then detach bezel from five retaining clips. Remove bezel.
3. Remove three screws attaching headlamp switch retainer plate to instrument panel.
4. Pull headlamp switch and retainer plate rearward and disconnect wire connector, then depress button on switch and remove switch knob and stem.
5. Remove switch retainer plate escutcheon, then the nut attaching switch to plate.
6. Reverse procedure to install.

HORIZON, OMNI, CHARGER & TURISMO

1. Disconnect battery ground cable.
2. Reach under instrument panel and depress light switch knob release button, then pull light switch knob and shaft from switch.
3. Remove four bezel attaching screws and bezel.
4. Remove switch attaching screws and disconnect electrical connector from switch, **Fig. 6.**
5. Remove switch from panel.
6. Reverse procedure to install.

LANCER & LEBARON

1. Disconnect battery ground cable.
2. Remove cluster bezel attaching screws, then the cluster bezel.
3. Remove headlight and accessory switch module attaching screws, then pull module assembly away from dash panel and disconnect all electrical connectors.
4. Depress button on bottom of headlight switch, then remove switch knob and stem.
5. Remove switch assembly to switch module attaching screws.

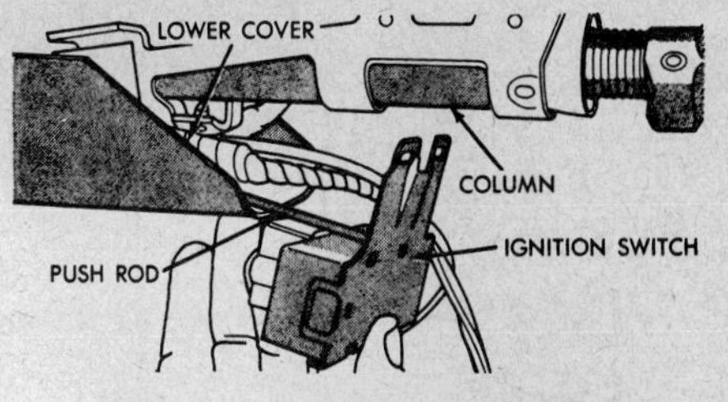

Fig. 5 Ignition switch replacement. Horizon, Omni, Charger & Turismo

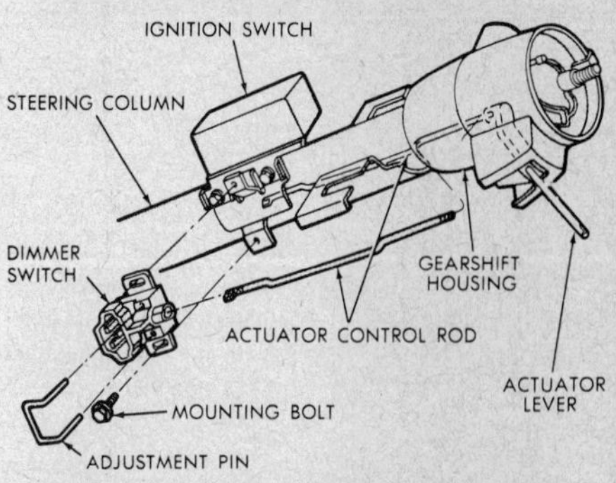

Fig. 7 Dimmer switch replacement. Exc. Horizon, Omni, Charger & Turismo; models less tilt column

6. Remove switch assembly from module, then switch assembly retaining plate from switch.
7. Reverse procedure to install.

DIMMER SWITCH REPLACE

EXC. HORIZON, OMNI, CHARGER & TURISMO

Models Less Tilt Column

1. Disconnect battery ground cable, then disconnect electrical connector from switch.
2. Remove two screws attaching switch to column, **Fig. 7.**
3. Reverse procedure to install. During installation, gently push up on switch to take up slack on rod.

Models W/Tilt Column

Refer to "Horizon, Omni, Charger & Turismo" for Dimmer Switch, Replace procedure.

HORIZON, OMNI, CHARGER & TURISMO

1. Disconnect battery ground cable, then disconnect connector from switch.
2. Remove two switch mounting screws and disengage switch from pushrod, **Fig. 8.**
3. To install switch, firmly seat pushrod into switch, then compress switch until two .093 inch drill shanks can be inserted into alignment holes. Position upper end of pushrod in pocket of washer/wiper switch. **This can be done by feel, or if necessary, by removing lower column cover.**

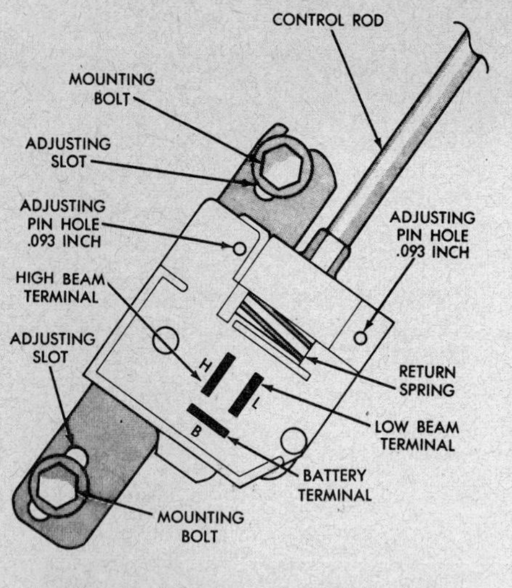

Fig. 8 Dimmer switch installation. Horizon, Omni, Charger & Turismo; Models w/Tilt Column

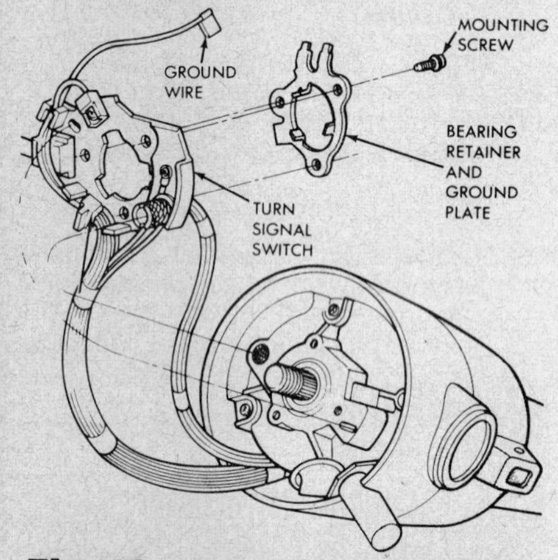

Fig. 10 Turn signal switch replacement. Exc. Horizon, Omni, Charger & Turismo

4. Apply a light rearward pressure on switch, then install screws and remove drills. **The switch should click when lever is lifted, and again as lever returns, just before it reaches its stop in the down position.**
5. Reconnect wiring connector to switch and connect battery ground cable.

TURN SIGNAL SWITCH REPLACE

EXC. HORIZON, OMNI, CHARGER & TURISMO

1. Disconnect battery ground cable.
2. Remove horn button and switch and steering wheel nut, then the steering wheel using a suitable puller.
3. Remove instrument panel lower bezel and steering column cover.
4. On models with tilt steering column, remove transmission gearshift indicator, then two nuts attaching steering column to lower panel. Remove four attaching bolts, then the bracket from column.
5. On models less tilt column, position gearshift lever into its full clockwise position. On models with tilt column, place gearshift lever to its midway position.
6. On models with tilt column, carefully remove plastic cover from lock plate, then depress lock plate with tool No. C-4156 and remove snap ring, **Fig. 9.** Remove lock plate, canceling cam and upper bearing spring from steering shaft.
7. Remove turn signal lever attaching screws and lever. On models with speed control allow lever to hang from column.
8. Remove turn signal switch and upper bearing attaching screws. Carefully remove turn signal switch, while guiding wire up through column opening, **Fig. 10.**
9. Reverse procedure to install.

HORIZON, OMNI, CHARGER & TURISMO

Removal

1. Disconnect battery ground cable.
2. Remove horn button or horn pad, then the horn switch.
3. Remove steering wheel nut and steering wheel with a suitable puller.
4. Remove four screws from lower steering column cover and cover.
5. Remove screw securing washer-wiper switch and position switch aside.
6. Disconnect turn signal and hazard warning wiring connector, disengage wiring harness from support bracket and remove vinyl tape securing key in buzzer wires to turn signal harness.
7. Remove three turn signal switch retainer screws, **Fig. 11.**
8. Remove turn signal and hazard warning switch while guiding wiring harness out from column.

Installation

1. Guide wiring harness downward through column until switch is properly seated.
2. Install switch retainer and three screws.
3. Snap plastic harness retainer into support bracket, connect harness connector and tape key in buzzer wires to harness.
4. Install washer-wiper switch and retaining screw.
5. Install lower steering column cover.
6. Install steering wheel, horn switch and horn button.
7. Connect battery ground cable.

INSTRUMENT CLUSTER REPLACE

1982–84 ARIES & RELIANT; 1982–83 LEBARON & 400; 1983 E CLASS, EXECUTIVE, NEW YORKER & 600

1. Disconnect battery ground cable.
2. Remove screws securing instrument cluster bezel and pull bezel from retaining clips, **Fig. 12.**
3. Remove screws securing upper right bezel and bezel.
4. Remove screws securing instrument panel pad, as needed, and raise pad slightly to allow cluster removal.
5. Remove 4 screws securing instrument cluster and pull cluster away from dash.
6. Disconnect electrical connectors and speedometer cable, then remove cluster.
7. Reverse procedure to install.

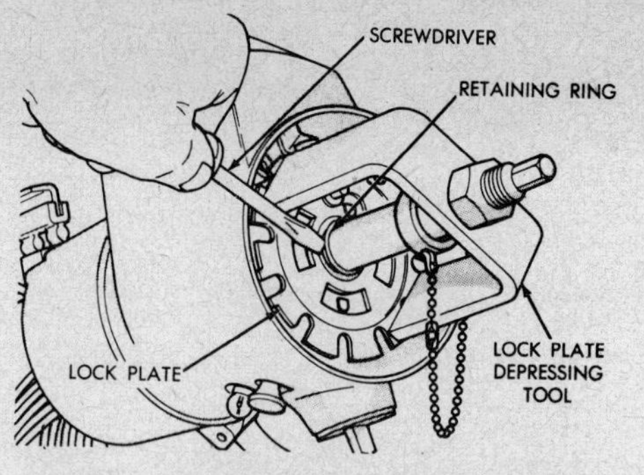

Fig. 9 Lock plate removal. Models with tilt column exc. Horizon, Omni, Charger & Turismo

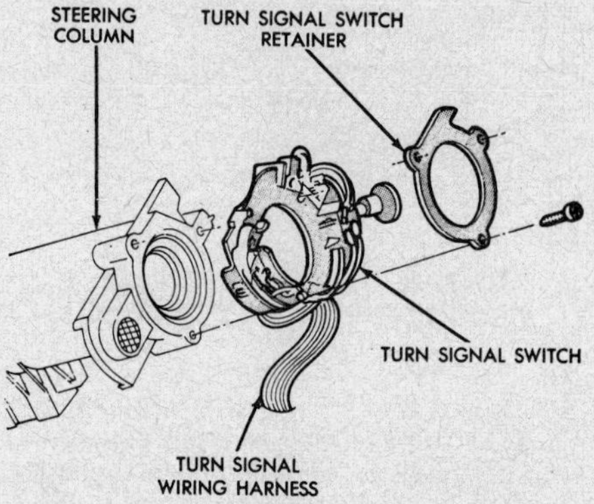

Fig. 11 Turn signal switch replacement. Horizon, Omni, Charger & Turismo

1984 E CLASS & LEBARON; 1984–85 EXECUTIVE; 1984–87 NEW YORKER & 600; 1985–88 ARIES, CARAVELLE, LEBARON EXC. GTS, TOWN & COUNTRY & RELIANT

1. Disconnect battery ground cable.
2. Remove screws securing instrument cluster bezel, **Fig. 13,** and bezel.
3. Remove screws securing instrument panel pad, **Fig. 14,** and raise pad slightly to allow cluster removal.
4. Remove 4 screws securing cluster and pull cluster from dash.
5. Disconnect electrical connectors and speedometer cable, if equipped, then remove cluster.
6. Reverse procedure to install.

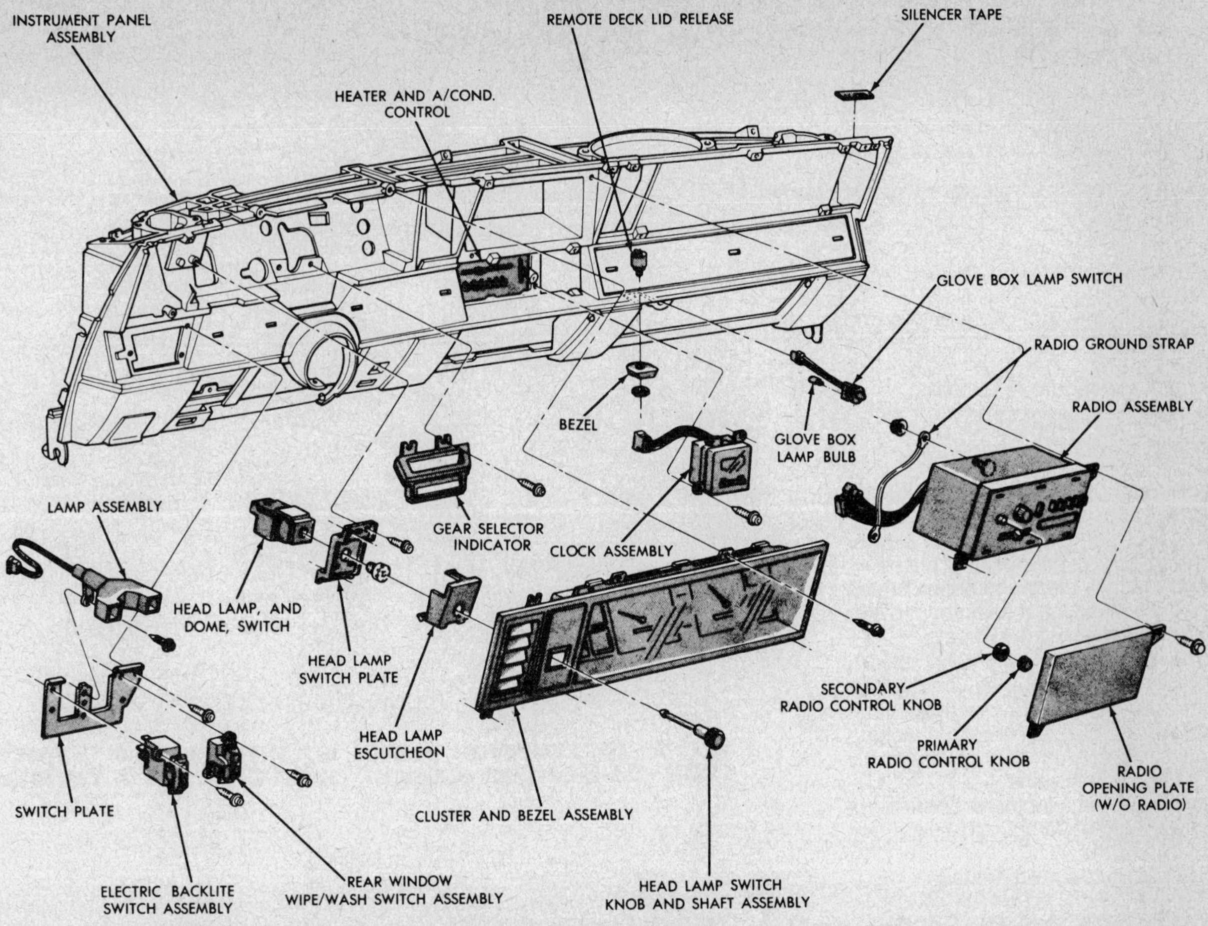

Fig. 12 Instrument panel, exploded view (Typical). 1982–84 Aries & Reliant; 1982–83 LeBaron & 400; 1983 E Class, Executive, New Yorker & 600

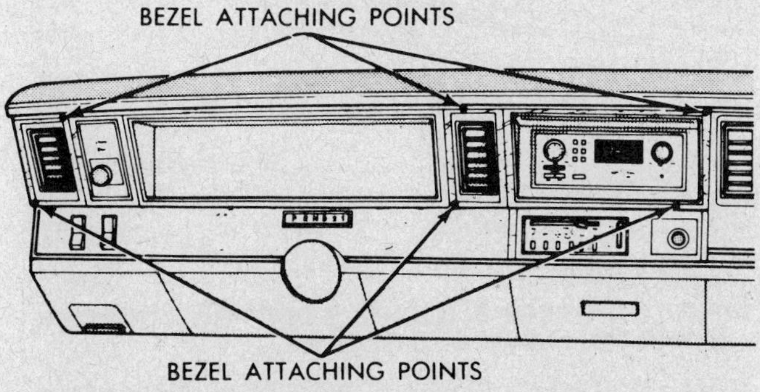

Fig. 13 Instrument cluster removal. 1984 E Class & LeBaron; 1984–85 Executive; 1984–87 New Yorker & 600; 1985–88 Aries, Caravelle, LeBaron Exc. GTS, Town & Country & Reliant

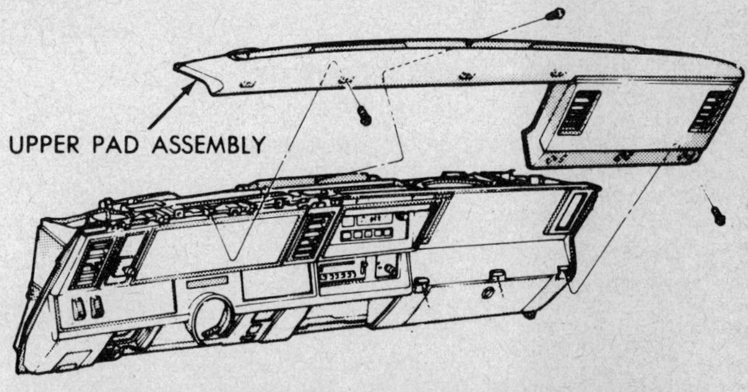

Fig. 14 Instrument panel pad removal. 1984 E Class & LeBaron; 1984–85 Executive; 1984–-86 New Yorker & 600; 1985–88 Aries, Caravelle, LeBaron Exc. GTS, Town & Country & Reliant

1984–88 DAYTONA & LASER

1. Disconnect battery ground cable.
2. Remove screws securing cluster bezel and bezel.
3. Remove 4 screws securing cluster and pull cluster away from dash.
4. Disconnect electrical connectors and speedometer cable, if equipped, then remove cluster.
5. Reverse procedure to install.

1982–83 HORIZON, OMNI & 1983 CHARGER & TURISMO

1. Disconnect battery ground cable.
2. Remove two mask-lens assembly lower attaching spring pins by pulling rearward with suitable pliers.
3. Pull mask-lens rearward, lower slightly and remove from cluster.
4. Disconnect speedometer cable.
5. Remove two speedometer attaching screws and speedometer.
6. Disengage two wiring harness connectors. On Rallye cluster disconnect three harness connectors.
7. Remove two cluster attaching screws, **Fig. 15.** On Rallye cluster remove four screws.
8. Remove cluster upper attaching spring pins and pull cluster from panel.
9. Disconnect clock wiring, if equipped.
10. Remove cluster from vehicle.
11. Reverse procedure to install.

1984–88 CHARGER, HORIZON, OMNI & TURISMO

1. Disconnect battery ground cable.
2. Remove 2 lower cluster bezel retaining screws, **Fig. 16.**
3. Allow bezel to drop slightly, then remove bezel.
4. Remove 4 screws securing instrument cluster and pull cluster away from dash.
5. Disconnect electrical connectors and speedometer cable, then remove cluster.
6. Reverse procedure to install.

1985–88 LANCER & LEBARON GTS

1. Disconnect battery ground cable.
2. Place gear selector lever in lowest position, then remove instrument cluster bezel attaching screws and bezel.
3. Remove lower steering column cover, then disconnect gear selector cable at steering column shift housing.
4. Remove mask and lens assembly.
5. Remove speedometer assembly, then disconnect speedometer cable.
6. Remove cluster assembly attaching screws, then pull cluster assembly away from dash panel.
7. Disconnect all electrical connectors from cluster assembly, then remove cluster, **Fig. 17.**
8. Reverse procedure to install.

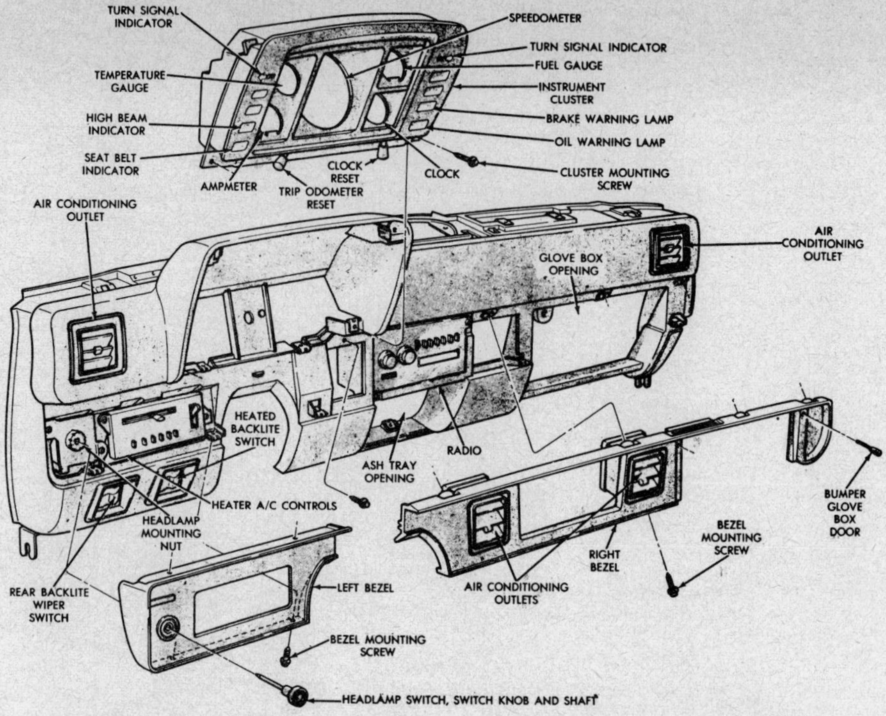

Fig. 15 Instrument panel, exploded view (Typical). 1982–83 Horizon & Omni; 1983 Charger & Turismo

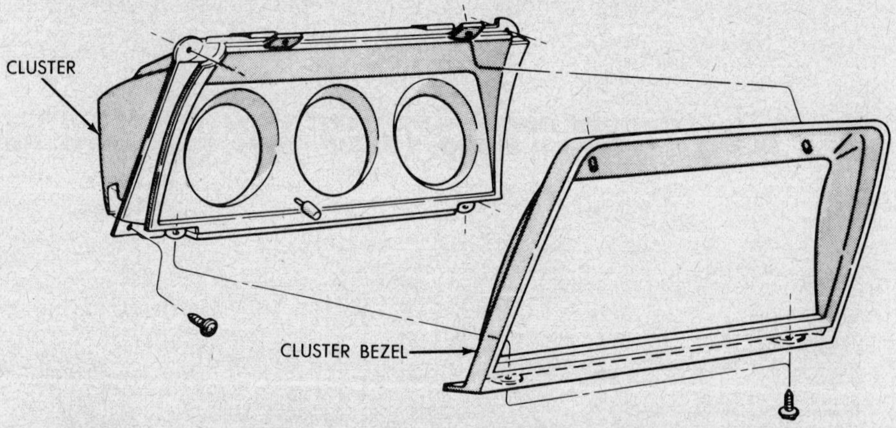

Fig. 16 Instrument cluster & bezel. 1984–88 Charger, Horizon, Omni & Turismo

WIPER SWITCH REPLACE

FRONT

Exc. Horizon, Omni, Charger & Turismo

1. Disconnect battery ground cable and remove steering wheel, using a suitable puller.
2. On models equipped with intermittent wiper system, remove two screws attaching turn signal lever cover to lock housing and the turn signal lever cover.
3. Remove screw attaching windshield wiper switch and switch, **Fig. 18.**
4. Reverse procedure to install.

Horizon, Omni, Charger & Turismo

1. Disconnect battery ground cable.
2. Disconnect wiper switch and turn signal switch wiring harness connectors.
3. Remove lower column cover.
4. Remove horn button.
5. Place ignition lock in "Off" position and turn steering wheel so access hole in hub area is at 9 o'clock position on except 1982 models, and in the 3 o'clock position on 1982 models.
6. With a suitable screwdriver, loosen turn signal lever screw through access hole.
7. Disengage dimmer pushrod from wiper switch.
8. Unsnap wiring clip and remove wiper switch.
9. Reverse procedure to install.

REAR

Exc. Charger, Horizon, Omni, Turismo, Lancer & LeBaron GTS

1. Disconnect battery ground cable.
2. Remove cluster bezel, then seven lower trim bezel attaching screws.
3. Remove trim bezel by unsnapping two retaining clips.
4. Disconnect switch assembly electrical connector.
5. Remove two switch attaching screws and the switch.
6. Reverse procedure to install.

Charger, Horizon, Omni & Turismo

1. Disconnect battery ground cable.
2. Depress two spring clips on top of bezel, using a thin blade screwdriver.
3. Tip bezel rearward and pull out switch assembly.
4. Remove switch and lamp electrical connector, then the switch assembly.
5. Reverse procedure to install.

Lancer & LeBaron GTS

1. Disconnect battery ground cable.
2. Remove headlight and accessory switch module from instrument panel.
3. Remove two rear wiper and washer switch attaching screws from module, then the switch.
4. Reverse procedure to install.

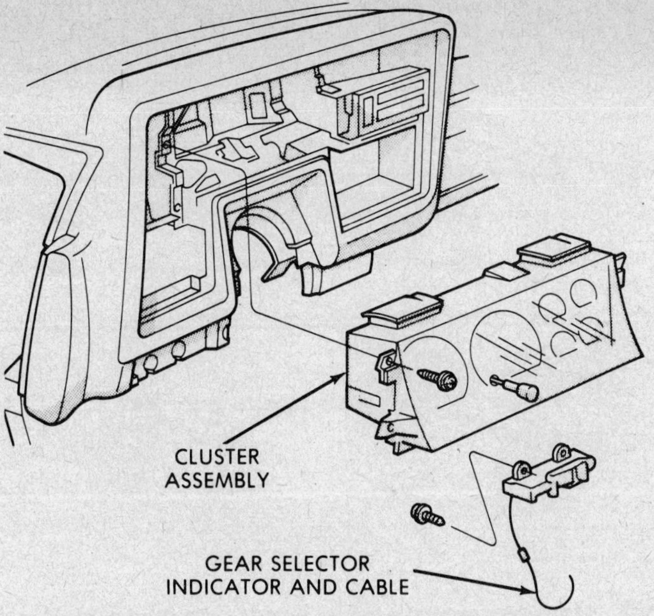

Fig. 17 Instrument cluster assembly. Lancer & LeBaron GTS

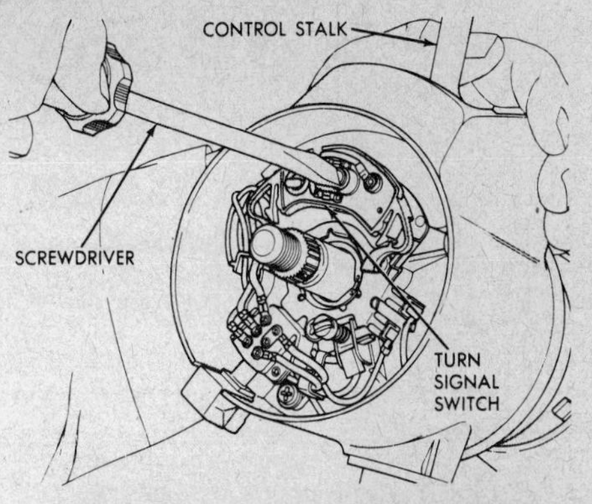

Fig. 18 Windshield wiper switch removal. Exc. Horizon, Omni, Charger & Turismo

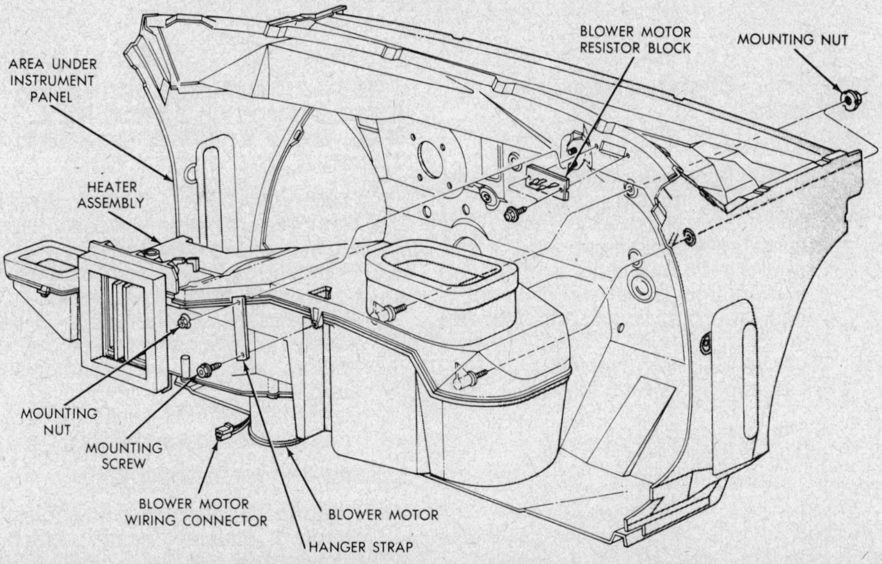

Fig. 19 Heater assembly. Models less A/C exc. Horizon & Omni; 1983–87 Charger & Turismo; 1985–88 Daytona, Lancer, Laser & LeBaron GTS

WINDSHIELD WIPER MOTOR

REPLACE

FRONT

Exc. Horizon, Omni, Charger & Turismo

1. Disconnect battery ground cable, then remove wiper arms and pivot attaching nuts.
2. Remove plastic screen covering cowl, if equipped, and disconnect reservoir hose from "T" connector on Daytona and Laser.
3. Remove wiper motor cover and disconnect electrical connectors to motor.
4. Push pivots downward into plenum chamber, then pull motor outward to clear mounting stud. Move wiper motor toward driver's side of vehicle as far as possible and pull righthand pivot and link assembly through opening, then move motor toward passenger side of vehicle and remove wiper motor, and lefthand pivot and link assembly.
5. Remove nut from end of motor shaft, then the motor crank.
6. Reverse procedure to install.

Horizon, Omni, Charger & Turismo

1. Remove wiper arm assemblies.
2. Remove nuts from left and right pivots.
3. Remove wiper motor plastic cover.
4. Disconnect wiper motor wiring harness.
5. Remove three bolts from wiper motor mounting bracket.
6. Disengage pivots from cowl top mounting positions.
7. Remove wiper motor, cranks, pivots and drive link assembly from cowl plenum chamber.
8. Remove wiper motor from drive crank linkage.
9. Reverse procedure to install.

REAR

Aries, Reliant, Lebaron, Executive, Lancer & Town & Country

1. Disconnect battery ground cable.
2. Remove wiper arm and blade assembly.
3. Remove wiper motor cover, then disconnect wire connector from motor.
4. Remove four screws attaching wiper motor bracket to liftgate, then the wiper motor.
5. Reverse procedure to install.

Daytona & Laser

1. Disconnect battery ground cable.
2. Raise wiper arm, release latch and remove arm assembly.
3. Remove inner trim panel and disconnect electrical connector to motor.
4. Remove grommet from liftgate glass.
5. Remove 2 screws securing motor and the motor.
6. Reverse procedure to install.

Horizon, Omni, Charger & Turismo

1. Disconnect battery ground cable and remove wiper arm assembly.
2. Remove pivot shaft nut, bezel and seal.
3. Remove wiper motor cover and disconnect electrical connector to motor.
4. Remove screws securing wiper motor and motor.
5. Reverse procedure to install.

RADIO

REPLACE

EXCEPT MODELS W/COMPACT DISC PLAYER

1982–84 Aries & Reliant; 1982–83 LeBaron & 400; 1983 E Class, Executive, New Yorker & 600

1. Disconnect battery ground cable, then remove center bezel.
2. On vehicles equipped with mono-speaker, remove speaker and disconnect from radio.
3. Remove two screws attaching radio to base panel, then pull radio through front face of base panel.
4. Disconnect wiring harness, antenna lead and ground strap.
5. Reverse procedure to install.

1984 E Class, Executive Sedan, LeBaron, New Yorker & 600

1. Disconnect battery ground cable.
2. Remove screws securing instrument cluster bezel, **Fig. 13,** and bezel.
3. Remove screws securing radio and pull radio away from dash panel.
4. Disconnect electrical connectors and antenna lead, then remove radio.
5. Reverse procedure to install.

Daytona & Laser

1. Disconnect battery ground cable.
2. Remove 2 screws securing bottom of console bezel, then lift bezel from console.
3. Remove 2 screws securing radio and pull radio away from console.
4. Disconnect electrical connectors and antenna lead, then remove radio.
5. Reverse procedure to install.

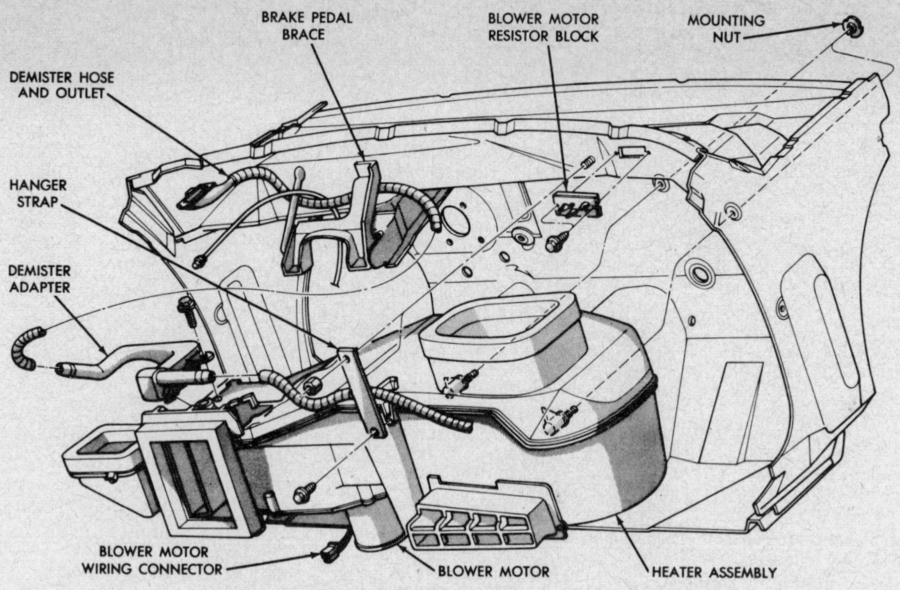

Fig. 20 Heater assembly. 1985–88 Daytona, Lancer, Laser & LeBaron GTS less A/C

Horizon, Omni, Charger & Turismo

1. Disconnect battery ground cable.
2. Remove right bezel attaching screws and open glove box.
3. Remove bezel, guiding right end around glove box as needed.
4. Remove radio mounting screws.
5. Pull radio from panel and disconnect wiring, ground strap and antenna lead from radio.
6. Remove radio from vehicle.
7. Reverse procedure to install.

1985–88 Aries, Caravelle, Executive, LeBaron Exc. GTS, New Yorker, Reliant, Town & Country & 600

1. Disconnect battery ground cable.
2. Remove left instrument bezel attaching screws, then the bezel.
3. Remove two radio and radio bezel to base panel attaching screws.
4. Pull radio through front face of base panel, then disconnect electrical connectors, antenna lead and ground strap.
5. Remove radio from vehicle.
6. Reverse procedure to install.

Lancer & LeBaron GTS

1. Disconnect battery ground cable.
2. Remove cluster bezel attaching screws, then the cluster bezel.
3. Remove radio attaching screws, then pull radio away from dash panel.
4. Disconnect electrical connectors, antenna lead and ground strap.
5. Remove radio from vehicle.
6. Reverse procedure to install.

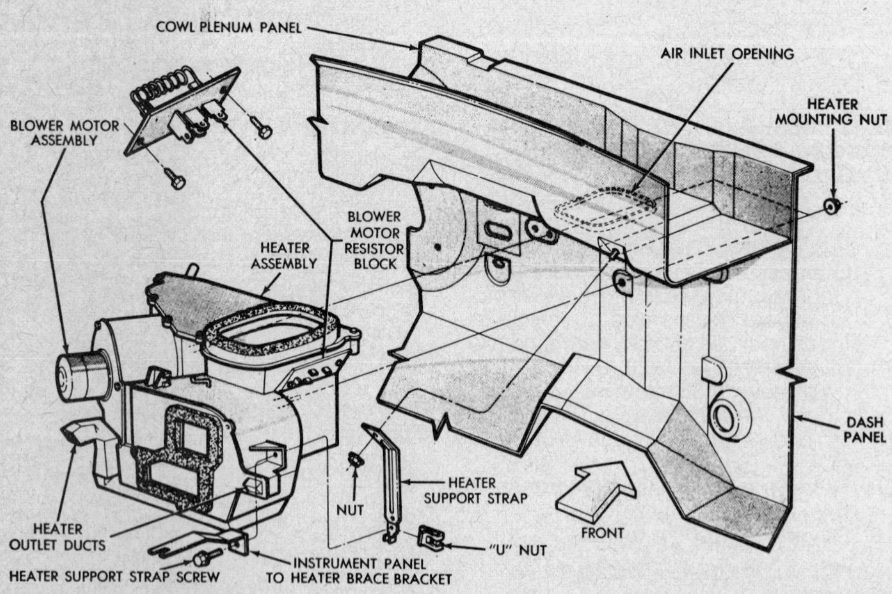

Fig. 21 Heater assembly. Horizon, Omni, Charger & Turismo less A/C

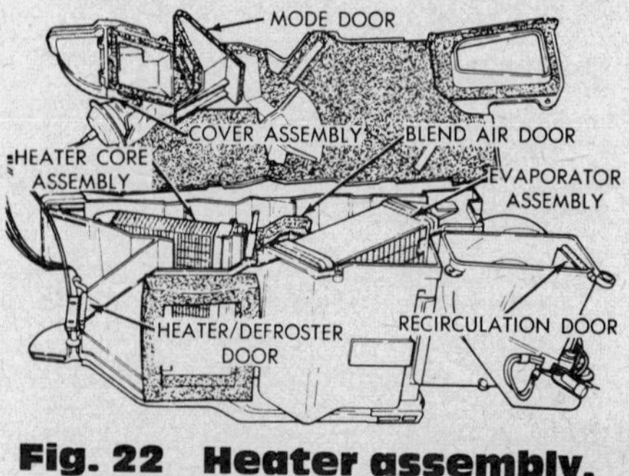

Fig. 22 Heater assembly. Models with A/C exc. Horizon, Omni, Charger & Turismo

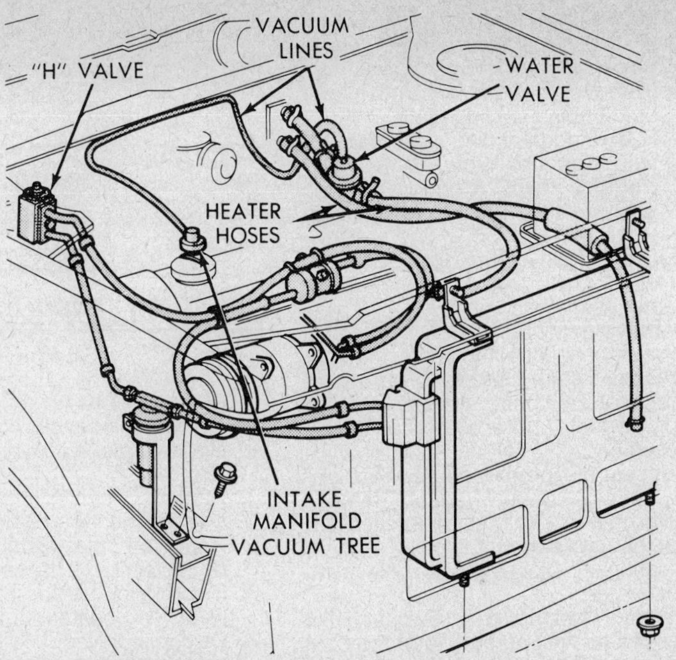

Fig. 23 Air conditioning & heater hose routing. Horizon, Omni, Charger & Turismo

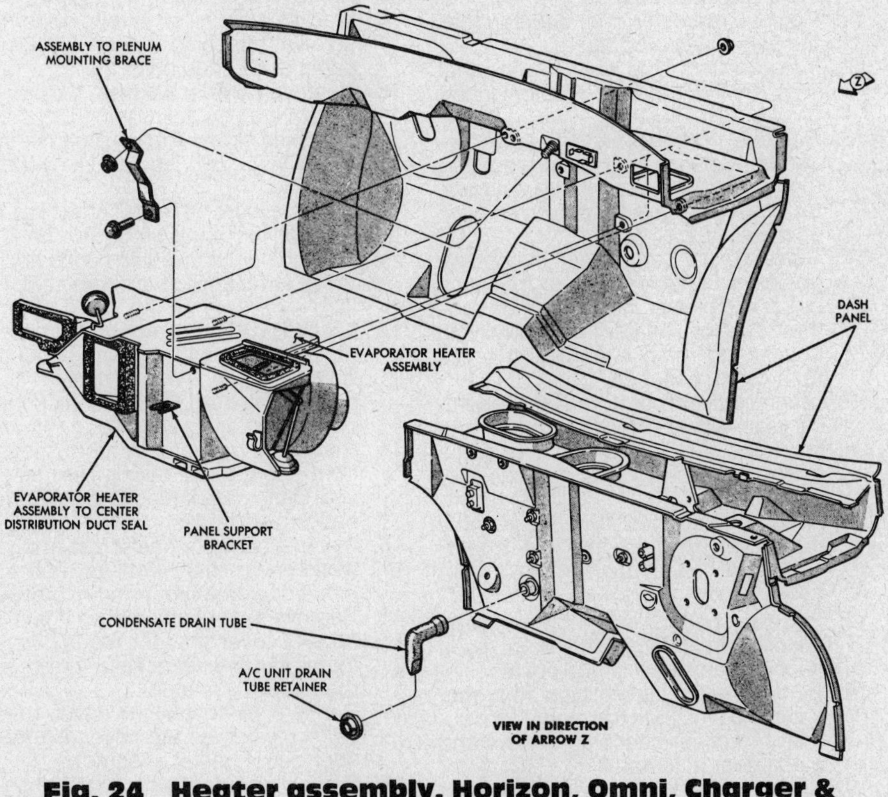

Fig. 24 Heater assembly. Horizon, Omni, Charger & Turismo with A/C

HEATER CORE REPLACE

LESS A/C

Exc. Horizon, Omni, Charger & Turismo

1. Disconnect battery ground cable, then drain cooling system.
2. Disconnect wire connector from blower motor, then disconnect control cable from mode door.
3. Disconnect heater hoses from heater core, then cap heater core tube openings to prevent coolant spillage.
4. Remove glove box, then the nut attaching hanger bracket to heater assembly through glove box opening. **On Daytona, Lancer, Laser & Le-Baron GTS, remove 2 screws and disconnect demister adapter from top of heater case.**
5. From engine compartment of dash panel, remove two nuts attaching heater assembly.
6. Carefully slide heater assembly out from under instrument panel, **Figs. 19 and 20.**
7. Remove insulation from around heater core tubes, then the upper core mounting screw.
8. Using a screwdriver, pry retainer tabs from outer edges of heater housing cover, then remove cover.
9. Remove lower heater core to housing attaching screws, then slide heater core from housing.
10. Reverse procedure to install.

Horizon, Omni, Charger & Turismo

1. Disconnect battery ground cable, then drain cooling system.
2. Disconnect blower motor electrical connector, then remove ashtray.
3. Depress red color coded tab on end of temperature control cable, and pull control cable out of receiver on heater assembly.
4. Remove glove box and door assembly.
5. Disconnect heater hoses and plug heater core tube openings.
6. Remove two heater assembly to dash panel attaching nuts, **Fig. 21.**
7. Disconnect blower resistor electrical connector, then remove heater support brace to instrument panel attaching screws.
8. Remove heater support bracket nut, then disconnect strap from plenum stud and lower heater assembly from under instrument panel.
9. Depress yellow color coded tab on end of mode door control cable out of receiver on heater assembly.
10. Move heater unit toward right side of vehicle, then out from under instrument panel.
11. Remove left heater outlet duct attaching screws, then the heater outlet duct.
12. Remove four blower motor mounting plate attaching screws, then the blower motor assembly.
13. Remove four outside air and defroster door cover attaching screws, then the door cover.
14. Remove defroster door assembly, then lift defroster door control rod out of heater assembly.
15. Remove 8 heater core cover attaching screws, then the core cover.
16. Slide heater core up and out of heater assembly.
17. Reverse procedure to install.

WITH A/C

Exc. Horizon, Omni, Charger & Turismo

1. Disconnect battery ground cable, drain cooling system and discharge A/C system.
2. Disconnect heater hoses from heater core, then cap heater core tube openings to prevent coolant spillage.

Fig. 25 Blower motor replacement. Horizon, Omni, Charger & Turismo less A/C

3. Disconnect vacuum lines at engine intake manifold and water valve.
4. Remove right scuff plate and cowl side trim panel.
5. Remove A/C control panel, then the center console, if equipped.
6. Remove forward console mounting bracket, if equipped.
7. Remove center distribution duct, then the demister adapter on Daytona, Lancer, Laser & LeBaron Hatchback.
8. Remove defroster duct from under panel, then disconnect condensation drain tube from engine side of dash panel.
9. Disconnect electrical connectors and control cables from A/C and heater housing.
10. Remove right side cowl to plenum brace, then pull carpet rearward from under unit.
11. Remove A/C and heater housing hanger bracket attaching screw, then the four nuts attaching unit to dash panel from engine compartment.
12. Pull unit rearward so that mounting studs clear dash panel, then carefully remove unit from under instrument panel.
13. Place evaporator heater assembly on workbench, then on 1982 models, remove 1/4-20 nut from mode door actuator arm on top cover. On 1983-88 models, remove actuator arm by squeezing it off its mounting clips.
14. Remove two retaining clips from front edge of cover.
15. Remove two mode door actuator to cover attaching screws, then the actuator.
16. Remove 15 screws securing cover to evaporator heater assembly, then lift off cover, **Fig. 22.**
17. Lift mode door out of unit.
18. Remove screw from heater core tube retaining bracket, then the heater core from evaporator heater assembly.
19. Reverse procedure to install.

1982–83 Horizon, Omni, 1983 Charger & Turismo

1. Disconnect battery ground cable, then drain cooling system and discharge A/C system.
2. Disconnect heater hose at heater core. Plug heater core tube opening.
3. Disconnect vacuum lines at engine intake manifold and water valve, **Fig. 23.**
4. Remove expansion valve ("H" valve), **Fig. 23,** as follows:
   a. Disconnect low pressure cut-off switch electrical connector, located on side of "H" valve.
   b. Remove hex head bolt from center of plumbing sealing plate.
   c. Pull refrigerant line assembly toward front of vehicle.
   d. Remove two Allen head cap screws, then the disassembled valve.
5. Remove hose clamp, then the condensate drain tube from evaporator heater assembly.
6. Remove evaporator heater assembly to dash panel attaching nuts, then depress red color coded tab on end of temperature control cable and pull control cable out of receiver on heater assembly.
7. Remove glove box and door assembly, then disconnect vacuum harness from heater A/C control, located under instrument panel.
8. Disconnect blower motor electrical connector.
9. Remove right trim bezel to instrument panel attaching screws, then the right trim bezel.
10. Remove center distribution duct to instrument panel attaching screws, then the distribution duct.
11. Remove defroster duct adapter, then the panel support bracket.
12. Remove right side cowl lower panel, then the right side instrument panel pivot bracket screw.
13. Remove screws attaching lower instrument panel to steering column, then pull carpet from under evaporator heater assembly as far rearward as possible.
14. Remove nut attaching evaporator heater assembly to plenum mounting brace and blower motor ground cable, then support heater assembly with hands and remove mounting brace from its stud, **Fig. 24.**
15. Lift and pull evaporator heater assembly rearward to clear dash panel and liner. The panel will also have to be pulled rearward to allow assembly clearance.
16. Remove evaporator heater assembly from dash panel, taking care to prevent dash panel attaching studs from hanging up in dash liner.
17. Place evaporator assembly on workbench, then remove nut from mode door actuator arm on top cover.
18. Remove two retaining clips from front edge of cover, then the mode door actuator to cover attaching screws and mode door actuator.
19. Remove 15 heater assembly cover attaching screws, then lift cover door out of heater assembly.
20. Remove heater core tube retaining bracket attaching screw, then lift core from heater assembly.
21. Reverse procedure to install.

1984–88 Charger, Horizon, Omni & Turismo

1. Disconnect battery ground cable, then drain cooling system and discharge A/C system.

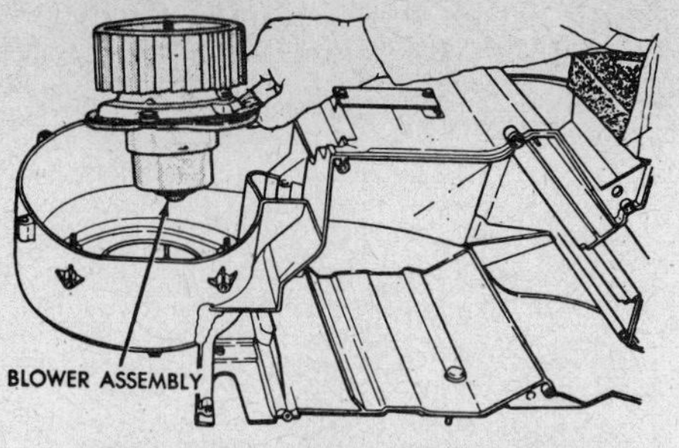

Fig. 26 Blower motor replacement. Models with A/C

2. Disconnect blend air door cable and disengage from clip on heater air duct.
3. Remove glove box and door assembly.
4. Remove center bezel attaching screws, then the center bezel.
5. Remove center distribution duct and defroster duct adapter.
6. Disconnect heater hoses and A/C lines. Plug heater core tube openings.
7. Disconnect vacuum lines at engine and water valve, **Fig. 23.**
8. Remove four dash retaining nuts, then the right side cowl trim panel.
9. Remove right instrument panel pivot bracket attaching screw, then two screws attaching lower instrument panel at steering column.
10. Remove panel top cover.
11. Remove all but left panel to fenceline attaching screw, then pull carpet from under A/C unit as far rearward as possible.
12. Remove support strap attaching nut and blower motor ground cable, then support heater unit with hands and remove strap from its plenum stud, **Fig. 24.**
13. Lift and pull evaporator heater assembly rearward to clear dash panel and liner. The panel will also have to be pulled rearward to allow assembly clearance.
14. Remove evaporator heater assembly from dash panel, taking care to prevent dash panel attaching studs from hanging up in dash liner.
15. Place evaporator heater assembly on workbench, then remove nut from mode door actuator arm on top cover.
16. Remove two retaining clips from front edge of cover, then the mode door actuator to cover attaching screws and mode door actuator.
17. Remove 15 heater unit cover attaching screws, then the cover. Lift mode door out of heater assembly.
18. Remove heater core tube retaining bracket attaching screw, then lift core from heater assembly.
19. Reverse procedure to install.

BLOWER MOTOR REPLACE

LESS A/C

Exc. Horizon, Omni, Charger & Turismo

1. Perform steps 1 through 14 as described under "Heater Core, Replace."

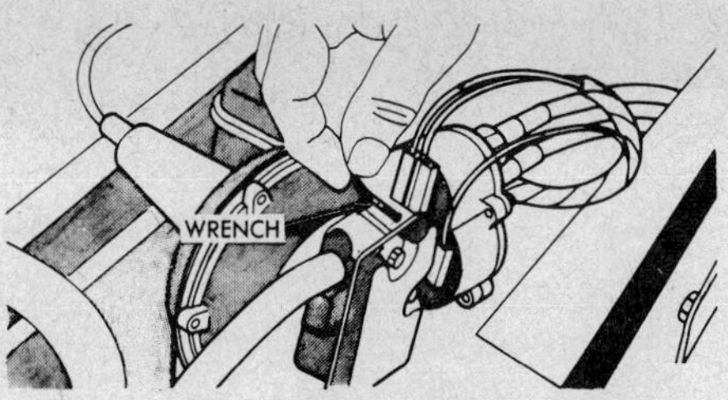

Fig. 27 Speed control lock-in screw adjustment

2. Remove blower motor to heater housing attaching screws and the blower motor.
3. Remove clamp retaining blower motor wheel to shaft, the two nuts attaching retainer plate to blower motor and the plate.
4. Reverse procedure to install.

Horizon, Omni, Charger & Turismo

1. Disconnect battery ground cable.
2. Disconnect blower motor wiring connector.
3. Remove left heater outlet duct.
4. Remove screws retaining blower motor mounting plate to heater unit.
5. Remove blower motor assembly, **Fig. 25.**
6. Reverse procedure to install.

WITH A/C

1. Disconnect battery ground cable.
2. Remove three screws securing glove box to instrument panel and glove box.
3. Disconnect blower motor feed and ground wires. Remove wires from retaining clip on recirculating housing.
4. Disconnect blower motor vent tube from A/C unit.
5. Loosen recirculation door actuator from bracket and remove actuator from housing. Do not disconnect vacuum lines.
6. Remove seven screws securing recirculating housing to A/C unit, then the housing.
7. Remove three blower motor mounting flange nuts and blower motor, **Fig. 26.**
8. Reverse procedure to install.

SPEED CONTROL

LOCK-IN SCREW ADJUSTMENT

Lock-in accuracy will be affected by poor engine performance (need for tuneup), loaded gross weight of car (trailering), improper slack in control cable. After the foregoing items have been considered and the speed sags or drops more than 2 to 3 mph when the speed control is activated, the lock-in adjusting screw should be turned counterclockwise approximately 1/4 turn per one mph correction required, **Fig. 27.**

If a speed increase of more than 2 to 3 mph occurs, the lock-in adjusting screw should be turned clockwise 1/4 turn per one mph correction required. **This adjustment must not exceed two turns in either direction or damage to the unit may occur.**

THROTTLE CABLE ADJUSTMENT

Optimum servo performance is obtained with a given amount of freeplay in the throttle control cable. To obtain proper freeplay, insert a 1/16 inch diameter pin, **Fig. 28,** between forward end of slot in cable end of carburetor linkage pin (hair pin clip removed from linkage pin). With choke in full open position and carburetor at curb idle, pull cable back toward dash panel without moving carburetor linkage until all freeplay is removed. Tighten cable clamp bolt to 45 inch pounds, remove 1/16 inch pin and install hair pin clip.

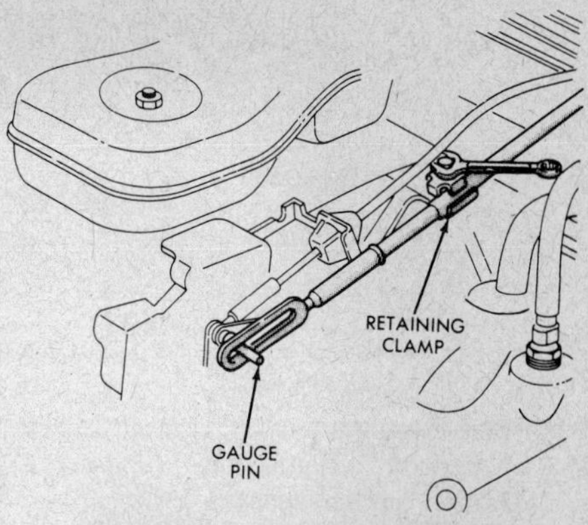

Fig. 28 Speed control servo throttle cable adjustment (Typical)

BRAKE SWITCH ADJUSTMENT

Exc. Horizon, Omni, Charger & Turismo

Position stop light switch to retaining bracket, then with brake pedal depressed, push switch forward into retaining bracket until it is fully seated. Slowly release brake pedal and allow pedal striker to rachet switch rearward in bracket to the correct position. No further adjustment is necessary.

Horizon, Omni, Charger & Turismo

1. Loosen switch bracket.
2. Insert .130 spacer gauge between brake pushrod and switch with pedal in free position.
3. Pushswitch brackek assembly toward brake push rod until plunger is fully depressed and switch contacts spacer.
4. Tighten bracket bolt to 75 inch lbs. and remove spacer.

4-97 (1.6L) Engine Section

INDEX

ENGINE MOUNTS REPLACE

When positioning the engine, check driveshaft length as outlined in the "Front Suspension & Steering Section" under "Driveshaft Length, Adjust." The engine mounts incorporate slotted bolt holes to permit side-to-side positioning of the engine thereby affecting length of the driveshaft. Failure to properly position engine may result in extensive damage to the engine.

Refer to **Figs. 1 and 2** when replacing engine mounts.

ENGINE REPLACE

MANUAL TRANSMISSION

The engine and transmission are removed as an assembly.

1. Disconnect battery cables and drain cooling system.
2. Scribe hood hinge locations and remove hood.
3. Remove radiator hoses, radiator and fan shroud assembly.
4. Remove air cleaner.
5. Remove A/C compressor mounting bolts and position compressor aside, if equipped.
6. Disconnect all wiring, hoses, lines and cables from engine.
7. Remove air diverter valve and lines from air pump.
8. Remove alternator belt and alternator.
9. Disconnect clutch and speedometer cables.
10. Raise and support vehicle.
11. Disconnect drive shafts from transmission and secure aside with wire.
12. Disconnect exhaust pipe from manifold.
13. Remove air pump hoses and lines, air pump belt and air pump.
14. Disconnect transmission linkage.
15. Lower vehicle.
16. Attach suitable engine lifting equipment to engine.
17. Raise engine slightly and remove front engine mount bolt.
18. Remove right and left engine mount bolts.
19. Remove engine and transmission assembly from vehicle.
20. Reverse procedure to install.

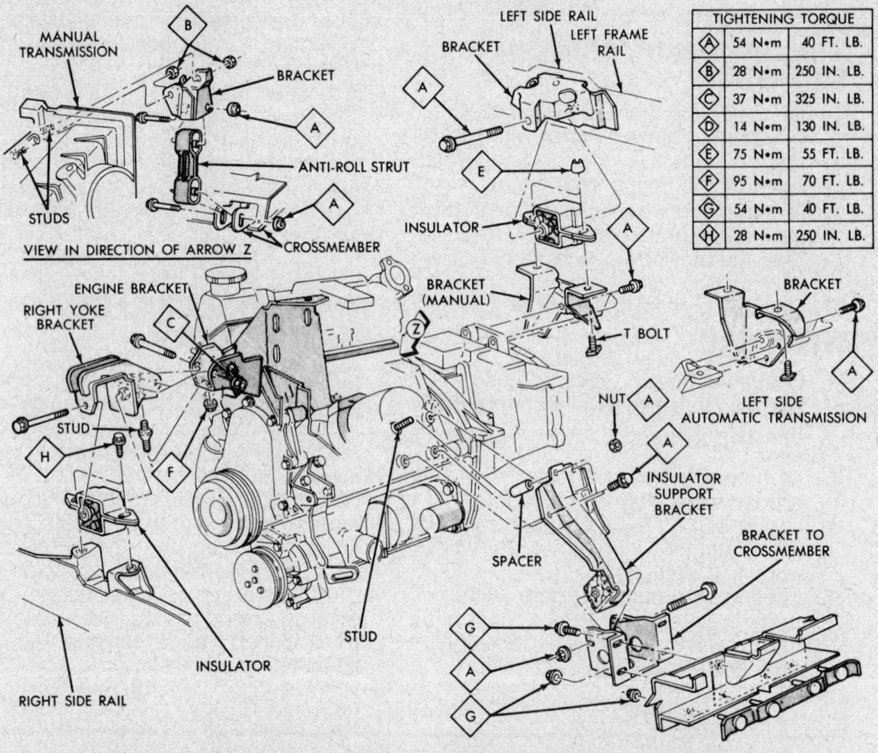

TIGHTENING TORQUE		
A	54 N•m	40 FT. LB.
B	28 N•m	250 IN. LB.
C	37 N•m	325 IN. LB.
D	14 N•m	130 IN. LB.
E	75 N•m	55 FT. LB.
F	95 N•m	70 FT. LB.
G	54 N•m	40 FT. LB.
H	28 N•m	250 IN. LB.

Fig. 1 Engine mount replacement. 1983

AUTOMATIC TRANSMISSION

The engine is removed without the transmission.

1. Disconnect battery cables and drain cooling system.
2. Scribe hood hinge locations and remove hood.
3. Remove radiator hoses and air cleaner.
4. Remove A/C compressor mounting bolts and position compressor aside, if equipped.
5. Disconnect all wiring, hoses, lines and cables from engine.
6. Remove air diverter valve and lines from air pump, if equipped.
7. Remove alternator belt and alternator.
8. Remove upper bellhousing bolts.
9. Raise and support vehicle and remove front wheels.
10. Remove left and right splash shields.
11. Remove power steering pump belt and pump mounting bolts. Position pump aside.
12. Remove water pump and crankshaft pulleys.
13. Remove front engine mounting bolt.
14. Remove transmission inspection cover, then the flex plate bolts.
15. Remove starter motor.
16. Remove lower bellhousing bolts.
17. Lower vehicle and support transmission with a suitable jack.
18. Attach suitable engine lifting equipment to engine.
19. Remove engine oil filter and right engine mount.
20. Lift and remove engine from vehicle.
21. Reverse procedure to install.

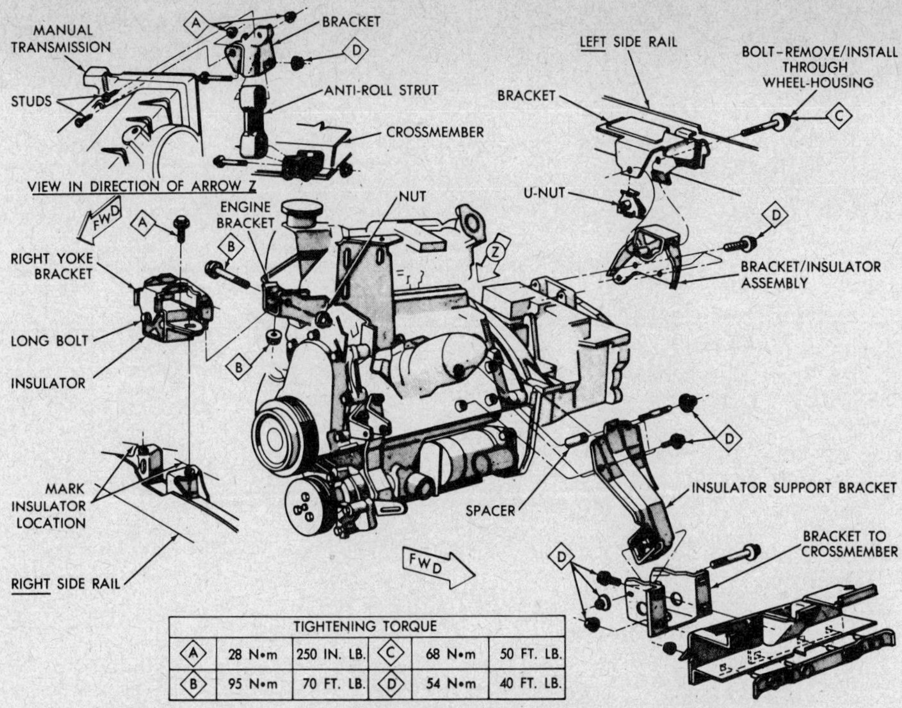

TIGHTENING TORQUE					
A	28 N•m	250 IN. LB.	C	68 N•m	50 FT. LB.
B	95 N•m	70 FT. LB.	D	54 N•m	40 FT. LB.

Fig. 2 Engine mount replacement. 1984–86

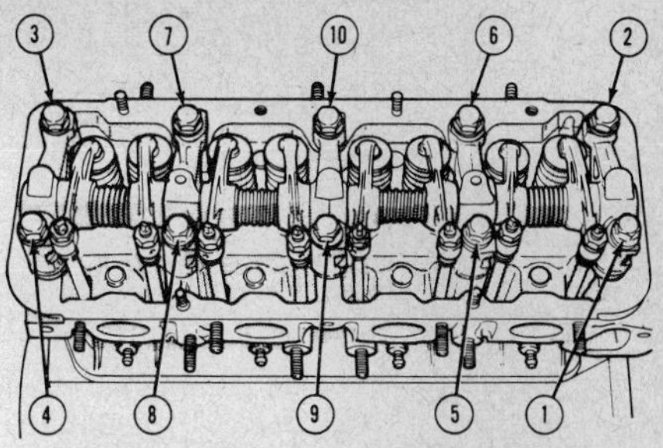

Fig. 3 Cylinder head bolt removal sequence

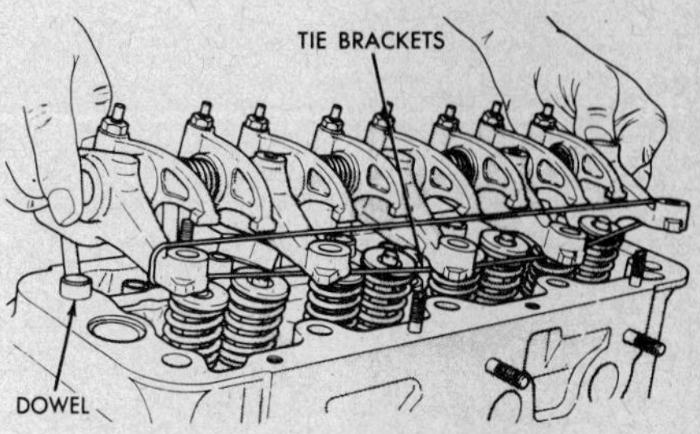

Fig. 4 Rocker arm assembly removal

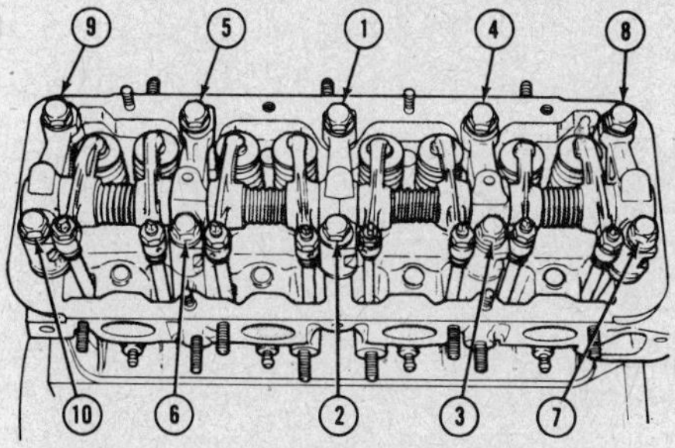

Fig. 5 Cylinder head bolt tightening sequence

CYLINDER HEAD & INTAKE MANIFOLD

REPLACE

Cylinder head must be cool prior to removal to avoid cylinder head distortion.

1. Drain cooling system.
2. Remove intake and exhaust manifolds from cylinder head.
3. Remove rocker arm cover.
4. Loosen and remove cylinder head bolts evenly in sequence, **Fig. 3. Rocker arm supporting brackets are located on dowels and are retained by head bolts. Only brackets 2 and 4 are pinned to rocker arm shaft.**
5. Tie rocker arm assembly together with suitable wire, then remove, **Fig. 4.**
6. Remove pushrods, noting location of each to facilitate installation, and the cylinder head.
7. Reverse procedure to install. **Refer to Fig. 5 for cylinder head bolt tightening sequence. Bolts are to be torqued progressively to 52 ft. lbs.**

VALVE ARRANGEMENT

FRONT TO REAR

4-97 .... I-E-I-E-I-E-I-E

VALVE TIMING

INTAKE OPENS BEFORE TDC

Engine	Year	Degrees
4-97	1983	13
4-97	1984-86	16½

VALVE CLEARANCE SPECIFICATIONS

Year	Engine	Int.	Exh.
1983-84	4-97	.010C	.012C
1985-86	4-97	.010C	.010C

VALVES

ADJUST

For proper clearance, valve adjustment must be set with piston at TDC on compression stroke with engine cold.

1. Rotate crankshaft noting exhaust valve movement. When one valve begins to close continue turning slowly until intake valve on same cylinder just starts to open. This is the "Valve Rocking" position. In this position, clearance in the opposite cylinder can be adjusted.
2. After checking both clearances, **Fig. 6,** rotate crankshaft one half turn to bring next cylinder in firing order to the "Valve Rocking" position and the paired cylinder can be adjusted. Valve rocking cylinders are paired to valve adjust cylinders as follows: 4-1, 2-3, 1-4, 3-2.
3. Adjust valve clearance by loosening locknut and turning screw until a sliding fit is obtained between valve stem and rocker, **Fig. 6.**

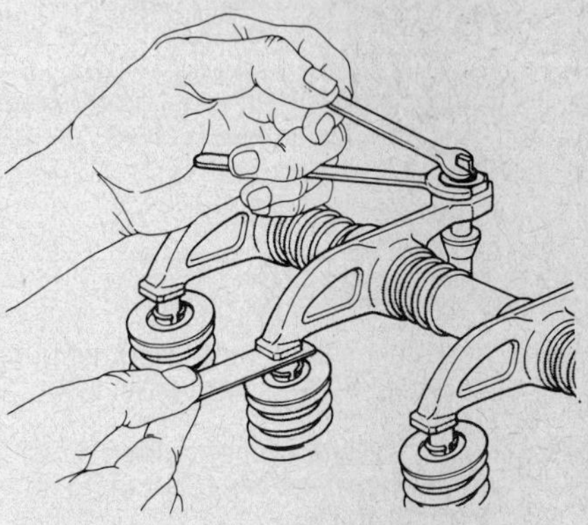

Fig. 6 Checking valve clearance

VALVE GUIDE SERVICE

Remove varnish and carbon deposits from valve guide interior with a suitable guide cleaner.

VALVE GUIDE WEAR

1. Insert valve into guide leaving .400 inch above cylinder gasket surface.
2. Firmly attach a dial indicator to cylinder head so indicator needle is in contact with valve margin.
3. Move valve to and from indicator and note total indicator reading, **Fig. 7.**

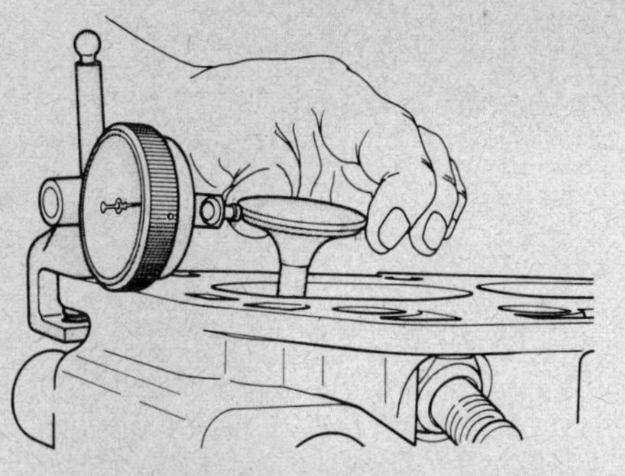

Fig. 7 Checking valve guide wear

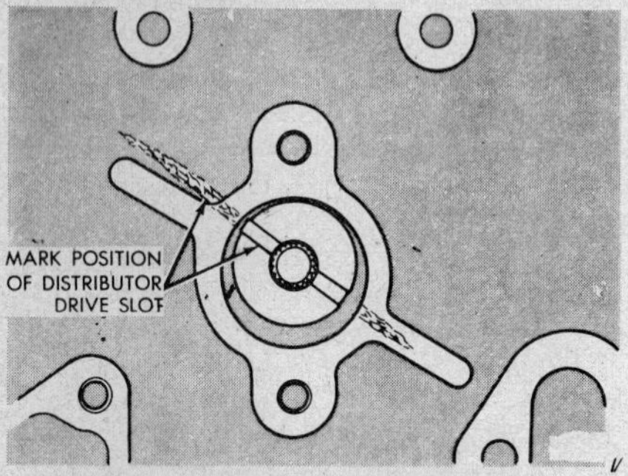

Fig. 8 Distributor drive slot marking

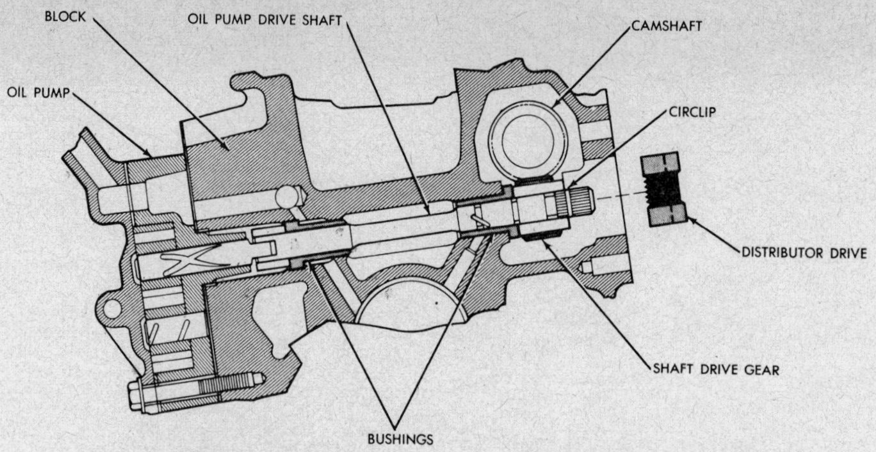

Fig. 9 Oil pump driveshaft assembly

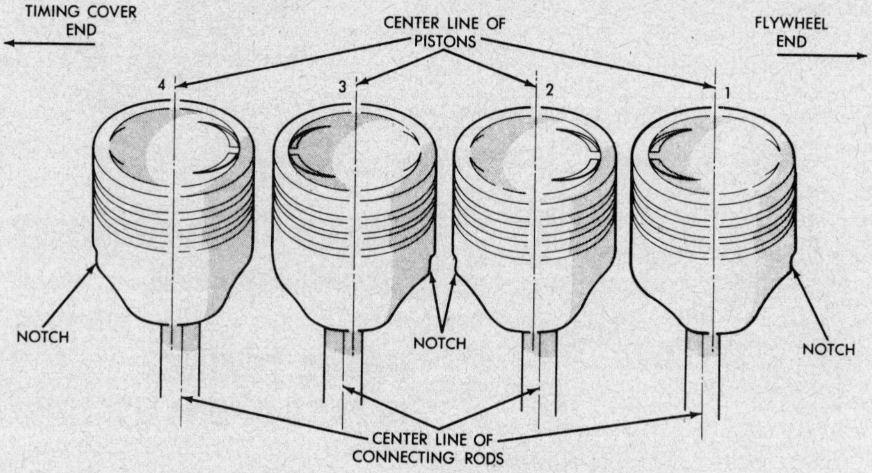

Fig. 10 Piston installation

4. Total indicator reading shows valve guide wear. Wear must not exceed .020 inch for intake valves, or .027 inch for exhaust valves.

CAMSHAFT REPLACE

1. Remove oil filter, then the 7 oil pump attaching screws and pull assembly from block.
2. Remove distributor and drive housing. Mark crankcase in relation to drive slot, **Fig. 8.**
3. Remove distributor drive from drive shaft spindle using a suitable magnet, **Fig. 9.**
4. Remove shaft drive gear circlip. **Insert a shop towel into cavity around gear to prevent circlip from falling into crankcase during removal or installation.**
5. Move driveshaft toward pump side of crankcase with a tapping motion until gear is free of spline, and remove gear.
6. Remove fuel pump and tappets, noting location of tappets to facilitate proper installation.
7. Remove camshaft thrust plate and camshaft.
8. Reverse procedure to install.

PISTON & ROD ASSEMBLY

When installing piston and connecting rod assembly, notches on pistons 1 and 3 must face toward flywheel end of engine and notches on pistons 2 and 4 must be facing timing chain, **Fig. 10.**

TIMING CHAIN COVER REPLACE

1. Disconnect battery ground cable.
2. Loosen AIR pump adjusting screw and bracket and remove belt.
3. Raise vehicle and remove right inner splash shield.
4. Loosen alternator adjusting screw, then move alternator inward and remove alternator/water pump drive belt.
5. Remove crankshaft pulley belt, washer and pulley.
6. Drain cooling system and remove water pump to timing cover hose.
7. Slightly raise and support engine at the timing cover end and remove engine mount bracket to timing cover and block attaching bolts.
8. Remove crankcase extension to cover screws and the cover to block attaching screws. **Two cover to block screws extend through tubular locating dowels, Fig. 11. During removal, ensure dowels do not fall into crankcase extension.**
9. Remove timing cover.
10. Reverse procedures to install.

TIMING COVER SEAL REPLACE

1. Perform steps 1 through 5 under "Timing Chain Cover, Replace."
2. Using tool No. C-4762-1 on 1983 models, or C-748 on 1984-86 models, and a suitable wrench, insert tool over crankshaft nose and turn tool firmly into seal.
3. Tighten thrust screw to remove seal, then tap side of thrust screw to remove seal.
4. Using tool No. C-4761 and a new seal drive seal into timing cover with lips of seal toward engine until tool stops against cover.
5. Examine pulley hub for dirt and defects and polish with 400 grit sandpaper as necessary.
6. Lubricate pulley hub and seal lip using a suitable lubricant, then align keyway and install crankshaft pulley, washer and bolt.
7. Torque retaining bolt to 110 ft. lbs.
8. Reverse steps 1 through 4 to assemble.

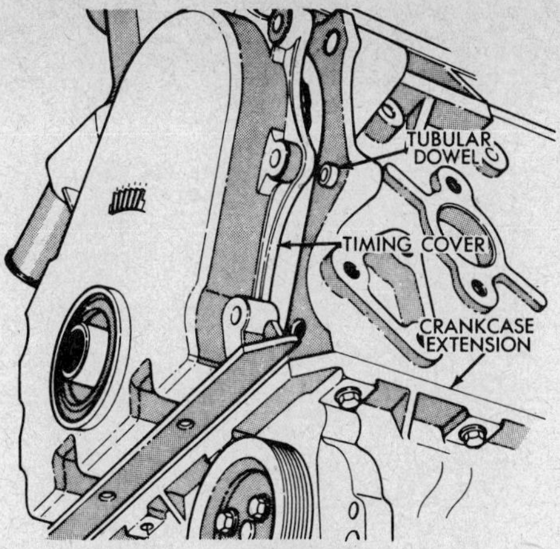

Fig. 11 Tubular dowel location

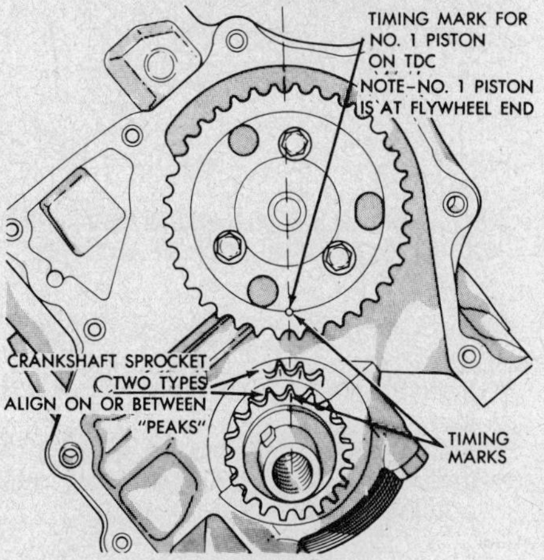

Fig. 14 Timing mark alignment

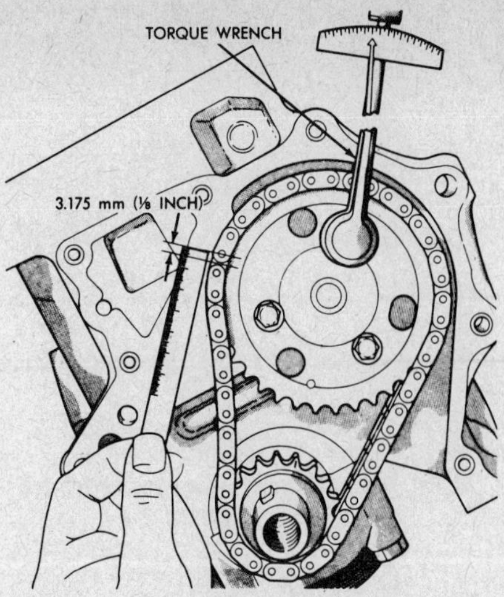

Fig. 12 Measuring timing chain stretch

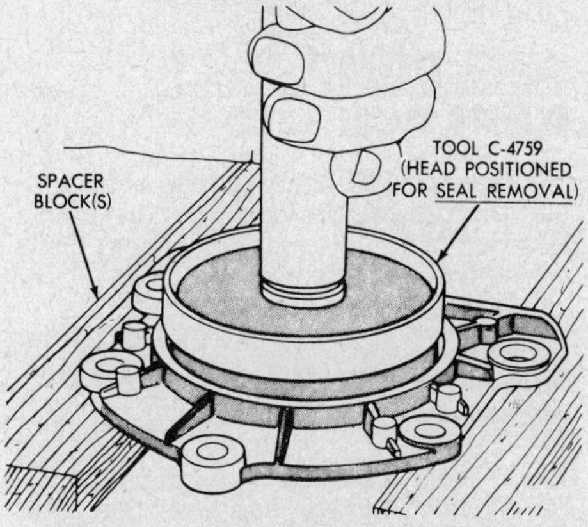

Fig. 15 Crankshaft rear oil seal removal

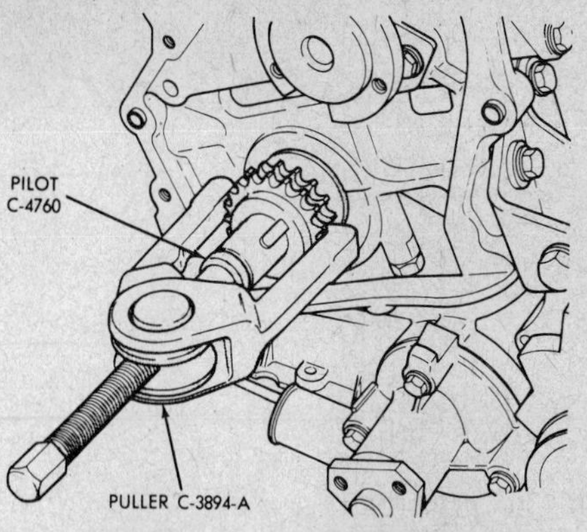

Fig. 13 Crankshaft sprocket removal

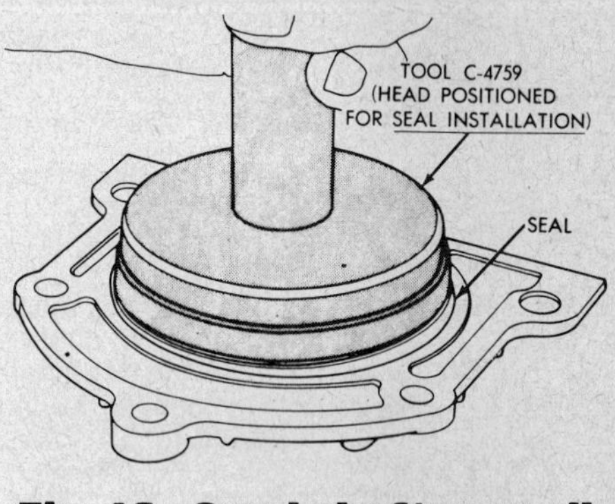

Fig. 16 Crankshaft rear oil seal installation

TIMING CHAIN

REPLACE

1. Remove timing chain cover as described under "Timing Chain Cover, Replace."
2. Before removing timing chain, check timing chain stretch as follows:
   a. Rotate crankshaft until one of the three camshaft sprocket bolts is located at top of crankshaft and camshaft center lines.
   b. Using a suitable size socket and torque wrench, apply torque in direction of crankshaft rotation to the camshaft sprocket bolt, **Fig. 12.** Apply 30 ft. lbs. of torque if cylinder head is installed on engine and 15 ft. lbs. of torque if cylinder head is removed from engine. **Do not allow engine to turn while applying torque.**
   c. Hold a ruler alongside a link in the chain and apply same torque as described previously in opposite direction and note amount of chain movement, **Fig. 12.** If movement exceeds 1/8 inch, timing chain must be replaced.
3. Remove camshaft sprocket attaching bolts, sprocket and chain.
4. Remove crankshaft sprocket using tools C-4760 (adapter) and C-3894-A (puller) or equivalent, **Fig. 13.**
5. Align crankshaft sprocket with key and drive firmly onto crankshaft.
6. Loosely install camshaft sprocket onto camshaft.
7. Rotate crankshaft and camshaft until timing marks on both sprockets are on a line passing through crankshaft and camshaft center lines, **Fig. 14.**
8. Remove camshaft sprocket without disturbing timing marks, then reinstall sprocket and timing chain making sure marks are aligned as described previously.
9. Install camshaft sprocket bolts and torque to 113 inch lbs.
10. Reverse remainder of procedure to assemble.

REAR CRANKSHAFT OIL SEAL SERVICE

1. Place inner surface of seal housing on spacers to allow clearance for seal removal.
2. Install tool No. C-4759 or equivalent and drive seal from housing, **Fig. 15. Tool No. C-4759 with universal driver C-4171 is used as both a seal remover and, when reversed, a seal installer, Figs. 15 and 16.**
3. Place outer seal housing on a flat surface, **Fig. 16.**
4. Using tool No. C-4759 with tool No. C-4171 (driver) tap seal into housing to full depth.

OIL PAN

REPLACE

1. Drain engine oil.
2. Remove 16 oil pan attaching screws, oil pan and gasket.
3. Clean pan and gasket surfaces.
4. Install new gasket and reinstall pan.
5. Torque oil pan attaching screws to 9.4 ft. lbs. (111 inch lbs.) for 1983-84 models or 7.4 ft. lbs. (89 inch lbs.) for 1985-86 models.
6. Refill engine oil.

OIL PUMP

REPLACE

REMOVAL

1. Remove oil filter.
2. Remove seven oil pump mounting bolts while holding pump together as an assembly, **Fig. 17.**
3. Pull assembly from block.

REPLACE

Seal all oil pump attaching bolt threads with suitable sealer before installation.

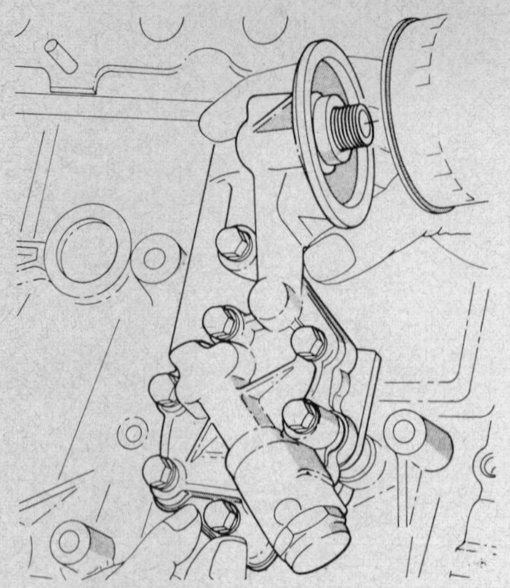

Fig. 17 Oil pump replacement

1. Install new housing to block and housing to cover gaskets.
2. Place cover on housing and insert two bolts to maintain alignment.
3. Install housing into block, then rotate assembly as necessary to engage drive gear shaft with slot in driveshaft.
4. Align bolt pattern, install remaining bolts and torque bolts to 9.4 ft. lbs. (111 inch lbs.).

OIL PUMP SERVICE

DISASSEMBLY

1. For oil pump disassembly, refer to **Fig. 18.**
2. Disassemble oil pressure relief valve by unscrewing dome nut and removing sealing washer, **Fig. 19.**
3. Remove relief valve sleeve using a suitable Allen wrench.
4. Remove spring and ball. **Examine ball for defects such as grooves or scuffing. Check ball for roundness using a micrometer and replace if defective.**

ASSEMBLY

1. Place ball on its seat in relief valve cover, then using a soft rod, tap ball into place with a small hammer.
2. Insert spring into sleeve and screw sleeve into cover and torque to 62 inch lbs., **Fig. 19.**

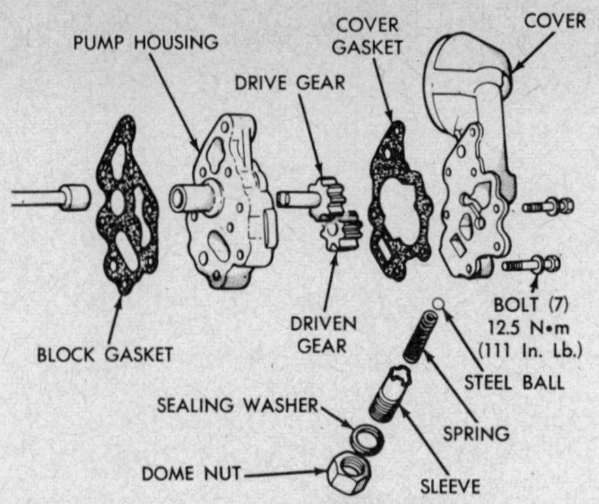

Fig. 18 Exploded view of oil pump

3. Install sealing washer and dome nut and torque to 30 ft. lbs., **Fig. 19.**
4. Refer to **Fig. 18** to reassemble oil pump.

FUEL PUMP

REPLACE

1. Disconnect battery ground cable.
2. Disconnect fuel lines from fuel pump.
3. Remove fuel pump mounting bolts and fuel pump.
4. Reverse procedure to install.

WATER PUMP

REMOVAL

1. Disconnect battery ground cable.
2. Remove radiator cap and drain cooling system from water pump drain plug.
3. Remove pump to block coolant hose at water pump.
4. Loosen alternator/water pump drive belt, then remove pump pulley.
5. Remove 4 pump to crankcase extension screws and pull assembly from crankcase.

INSTALLATION

1. Position water pump on crankcase extension with new gasket.
2. Install 4 pump to crankcase extension screws and torque to 9 ft. lbs.
3. Install pump to block hose and torque clamp to 35 inch lbs.

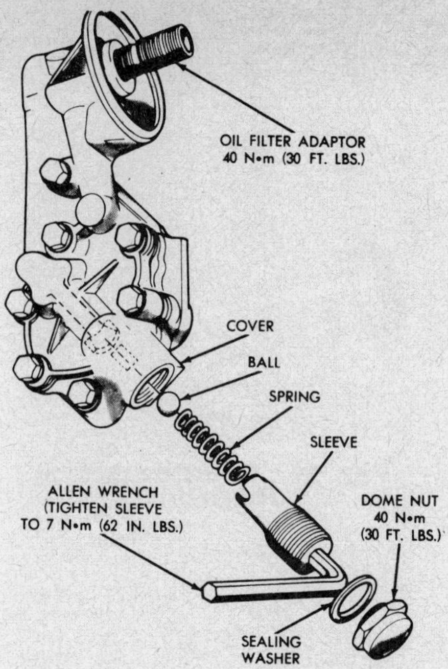

Fig. 19 Exploded view of oil pressure relief valve

4. Install drain plug and torque to 13 ft. lbs.
5. Install pump pulley and adjust belt tension to specifications, then refill cooling system.

BELT TENSION DATA

Belt	New Lbs.	Used Lbs.
1983		
Air Pump	**95**	**70**
Alternator/Water Pump	**115**	**95**
Power Steering	**95**	**70**
1984–86		
Air Pump	**95**	**70**
Alternator/Water Pump	**115**	**80**
Power Steering	**95**	**70**

4-105 (1.7L) Engine Section

INDEX

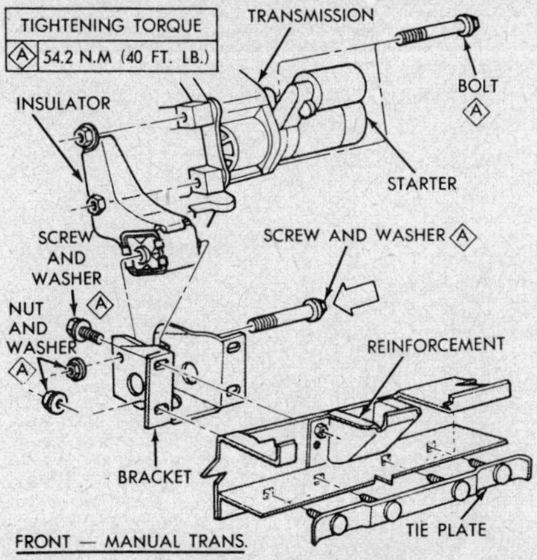

Fig. 1 Front engine mount

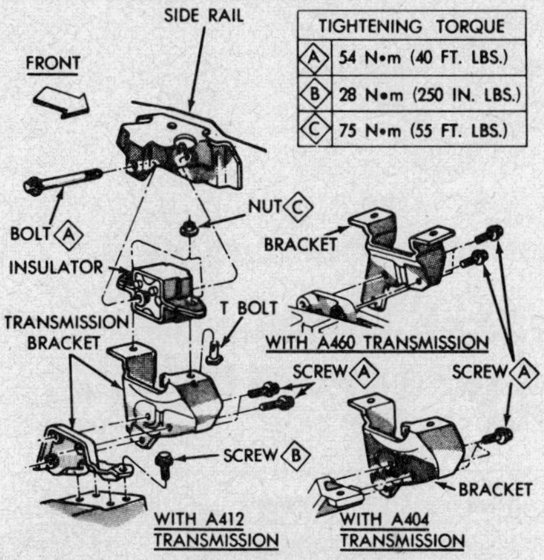

Fig. 4 Left engine mount. 1983

ENGINE MOUNTS

When positioning the engine, check driveshaft length as outlined in the "Front Suspension & Steering Section" under "Driveshaft Length, Adjust." The engine mounts incorporate slotted bolt holes to permit side-to-side positioning of the engine thereby affecting the length of the driveshaft. Failure to properly position engine may result in extensive damage to the engine.

Refer to **Figs. 1 through 5** when replacing the engine mounts.

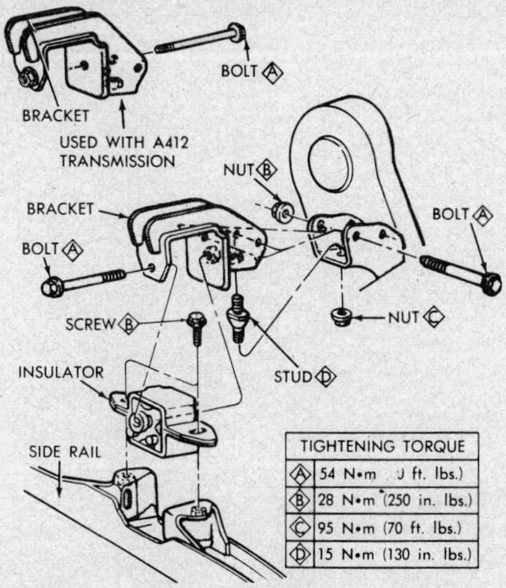

Fig. 2 Right engine mount

The left engine mount is attached with two types of mounting screws. Two of the three are of the pilot type with extended tips. Extended tip screws must be installed in the proper position, Fig. 5. Damage to the shift cover or difficult shifting may occur if the screws are incorrectly installed.

ENGINE REPLACE

MANUAL TRANSMISSION

The engine and transmission are removed as an assembly.

1. Disconnect battery cables and drain cooling system.
2. Scribe hood hinge locations and remove hood.
3. Remove radiator hoses, radiator and shroud assembly.
4. Remove air cleaner.
5. Remove A/C compressor mounting bolts and position compressor aside, if equipped.
6. Disconnect all wiring, hoses, lines and cables from engine.
7. Remove air diverter valve and lines from air pump.
8. Remove alternator belt and alternator.
9. Disconnect clutch and speedometer cables.
10. Raise and support vehicle.

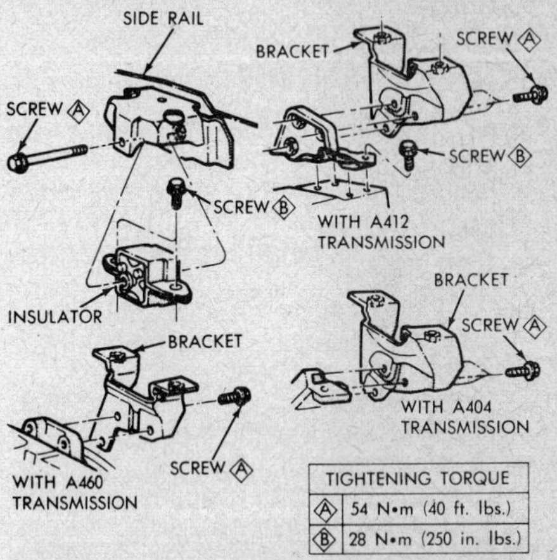

Fig. 3 Left engine mount. 1982

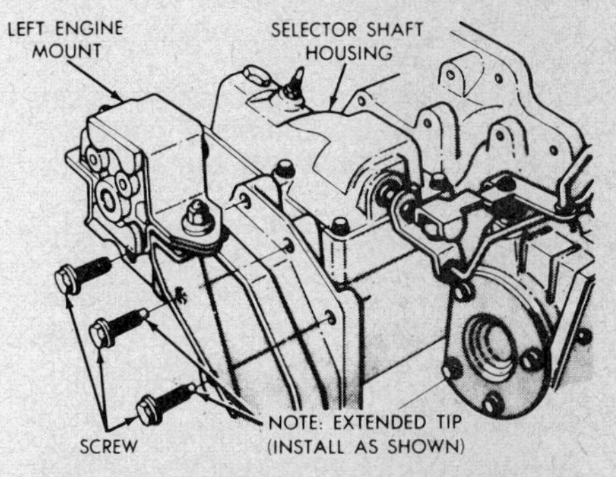

Fig. 5 Correct positioning of extended tip mount bolts

11. On models with A-412 transaxle, disconnect drive shaft from transaxle and secure aside. On models with A-460 transaxle, remove driveshafts as outlined in "Front Suspension and Steering."
12. Disconnect exhaust pipe from manifold.
13. Remove air pump hoses and lines, air pump belt and air pump.
14. Disconnect transmission linkage.
15. Lower vehicle.
16. Attach suitable engine lifting equipment to engine.
17. Raise engine slightly and remove front engine mount bolt.
18. Remove right and left engine mount bolts.

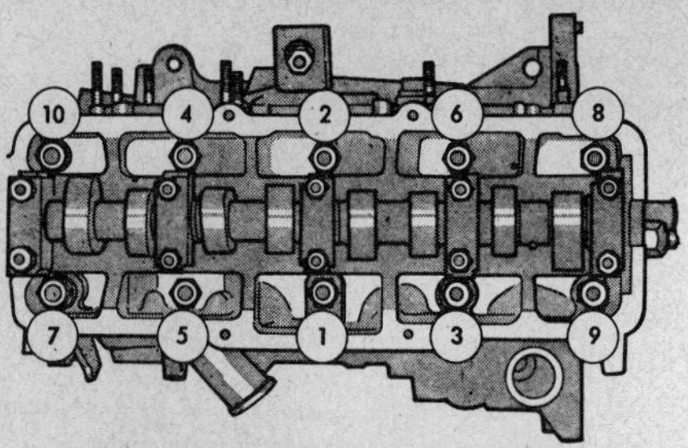

Fig. 6 Cylinder head tightening sequence

19. Remove engine and transmission assembly from vehicle.
20. Reverse procedure to install. Align engine as outlined in "Front Suspension and Steering," to ensure proper driveshaft length.

AUTOMATIC TRANSMISSION

The engine is removed without the transmission.

1. Disconnect battery cables and drain cooling system.
2. Scribe hood hinge locations and remove hood.
3. Disconnect transmission cooler lines and radiator hoses, then remove radiator, hoses and cooling fan.
4. Remove air cleaner assembly, then the A/C compressor, if equipped, and position aside.
5. Disconnect all wiring, hoses, lines and cables from engine.
6. Remove air diverter valve and lines from air pump, if equipped.
7. Remove alternator belt and alternator.
8. Remove upper bellhousing bolts.
9. Raise and support vehicle and remove front wheels.
10. Remove left and right splash shields.
11. Remove power steering pump belt and pump mounting bolts. Position pump aside.
12. Remove water pump and crankshaft pulleys.
13. Remove front engine mounting bolt.
14. Remove transmission inspection cover, then the flex plate bolts.
15. Remove starter motor.
16. Remove lower bellhousing bolts.
17. Lower vehicle and support transmission with a suitable jack.
18. Attach suitable engine lifting equipment to engine.
19. Remove engine oil filter and right engine mount.
20. Lift and remove engine from vehicle.
21. Reverse procedure to install. Align engine as outlined in "Front Suspension And Steering," to ensure proper driveshaft length.

CYLINDER HEAD & INTAKE MANIFOLD

REPLACE

1. Drain cooling system and perform Steps 1 through 15 as outlined under "Timing Belt, Replace" procedure.
2. Remove intake and exhaust manifolds from cylinder head.
3. Disconnect all wiring, hoses and cables attached to cylinder head.
4. Remove cam cover bolts and cam cover.
5. Loosen cylinder head attaching bolts in reverse sequence found in **Fig. 6.**
6. Remove cylinder head, **Fig. 7.**
7. Reverse procedure to install. Insert bolts No. 8 and 10 first, to center cylinder head on engine block. Torque bolts to specifications in sequence, **Fig. 6.** To properly tension timing belt, perform Steps 16 through 22 as outlined under "Timing Belt, Replace" procedure.

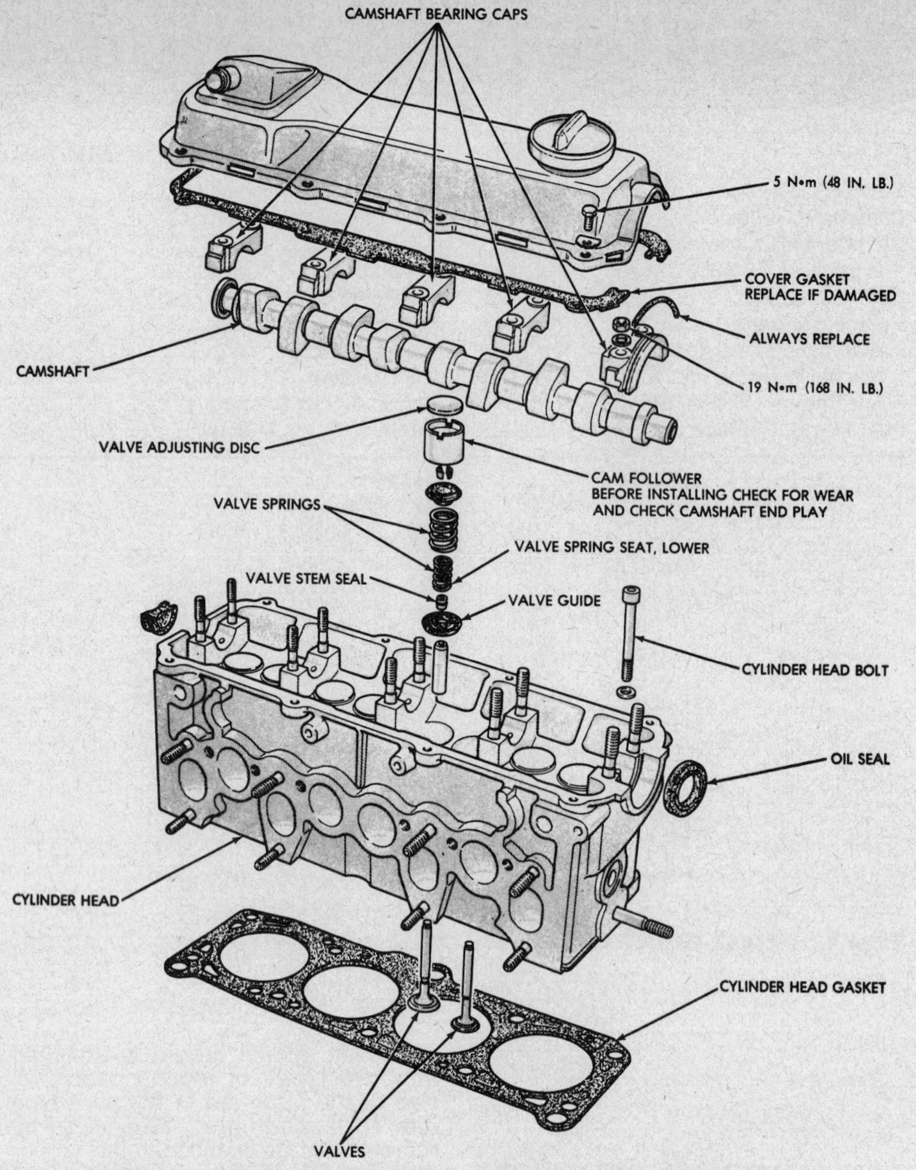

Fig. 7 Cylinder head assembly, exploded view

VALVE ARRANGEMENT

FRONT TO REAR

4-105 .... E-I-E-I-I-E-I-E

VALVE LIFT SPECIFICATIONS

Engine	Year	Int.	Exh.
4-105	1982-83	.406	.406

VALVE TIMING

INTAKE OPENS BEFORE TDC

Engine	Year	Degrees
4-105	1982-83	14

VALVE CLEARANCE SPECIFICATIONS

Year	Engine	Int.	Exh.
1982-83	4-105	.010H	.018H

VALVES

ADJUST

1. Using feeler gauges, check valve clearance with cam lobe in position shown in **Fig. 8. Engine should be at normal operating temperature, with thermostat open and coolant temperature approximately 195°F.**

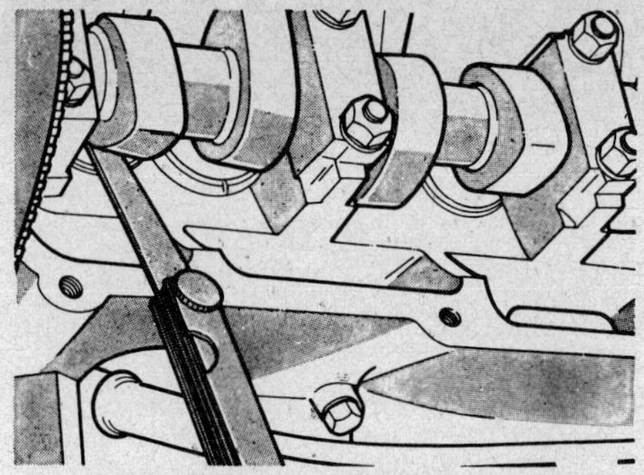

Fig. 8 Checking valve clearance

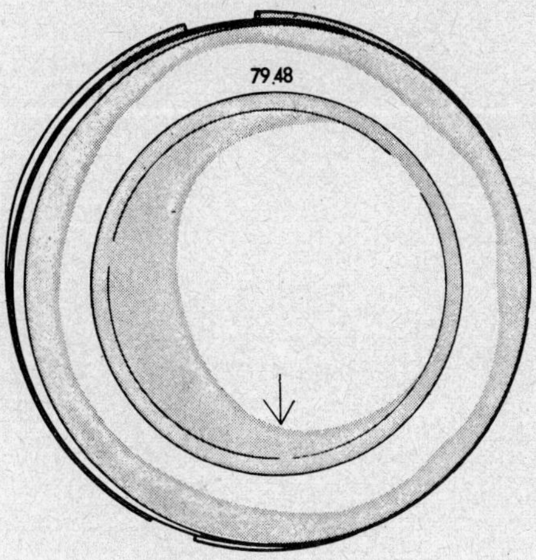

Fig. 11 Piston identification markings

If necessary to check valve clearance with cylinder head cold, use following specifications: Intake, .006-.010 inch; Exhaust, .014-.018 inch, then recheck after engine has reached normal operating temperature.

2. If valve clearance is greater than specified, remove valve adjusting disc and insert a thicker disc to obtain proper clearance.
3. If valve clearance is less than specified, remove valve adjusting disc and insert a thinner disc to obtain proper clearance.
4. To replace valve adjusting disc, depress cam follower with tool L-4417 or equivalent and remove with a narrow screwdriver, **Fig. 9,** and a magnet. Install new disc and recheck clearance.
5. Valve adjusting discs are available in thicknesses of 3.00 mm to 4.25 mm in increments of .05 mm.

VALVE GUIDES

The valve guides may be removed by pressing out from combustion chamber side. Coat new valve guide with oil and press into cold cylinder head until the shoulder is seated. The replacement valve guides have a shoulder. Do not exert a pressure greater than one ton after valve guide shoulder is seated since shoulder may break. Ream valve guide to .315-.316 inch.

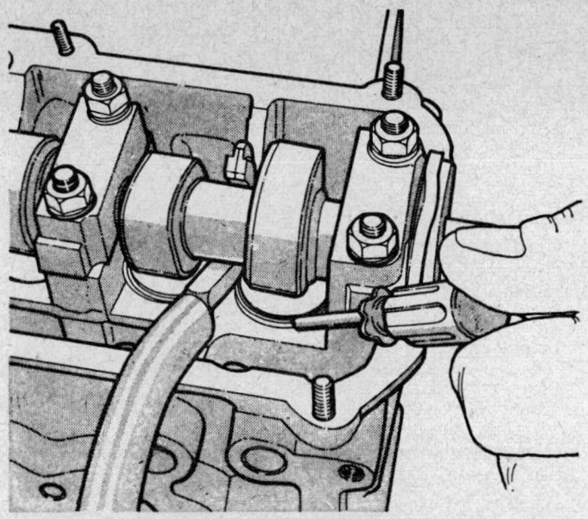

Fig. 9 Valve adjusting disc replacement

CAMSHAFT REPLACE

1. Remove timing belt as outlined under "Timing Belt, Replace."
2. Remove camshaft sprocket.
3. Remove bearing caps 5, 1 and 3, **Fig. 10.**
4. Diagonally loosen and remove bearing caps 2 and 4, **Fig. 10.**
5. Remove camshaft from cylinder head.
6. Lubricate bearing shells, journals and contact faces of bearing caps.
7. Install caps in proper order, observing off center bearing position.
8. Reverse Steps 1 through 5 to complete installation.

PISTON & ROD ASSEMBLY

When installing piston and connecting rod assembly the arrow on top of piston must face toward front of engine, **Fig. 11,** and forged mark on connecting rod must face toward intermediate shaft, **Fig. 12.**

Connecting rod side clearance should be .015 inch maximum.

There are two types of connecting rod assemblies. One uses a stud and nut to retain bearing cap and the other uses a bolt to retain bearing cap, Fig. 12.

PISTONS, RINGS & PINS

Pistons are available in standard sizes and oversizes of 0.25, 0.50 and 1.0 mm.

Rings are available in standard sizes and oversizes of 0.25, 0.50 and 1.0 mm.

MAIN & ROD BEARINGS

Main bearings are available in standard sizes and undersizes of 0.25, 0.50 and 0.75 mm. Refer to **Fig. 13** for bearing installation.

Rod bearings are available in standard sizes and undersizes of 0.25, 0.50 and 0.75 mm.

TIMING BELT REPLACE

1. Disconnect battery ground cable.

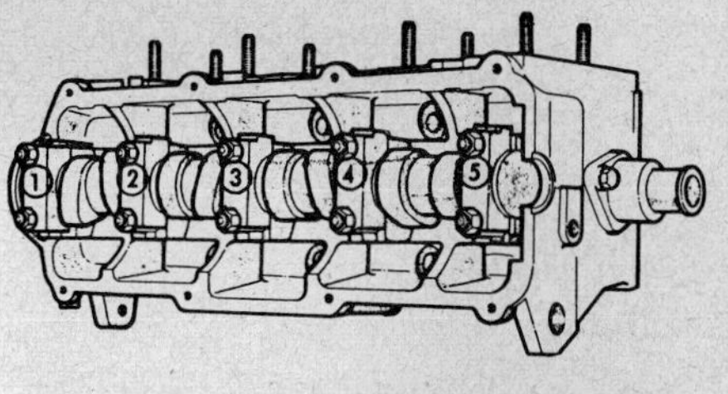

Fig. 10 Camshaft bearing cap identification

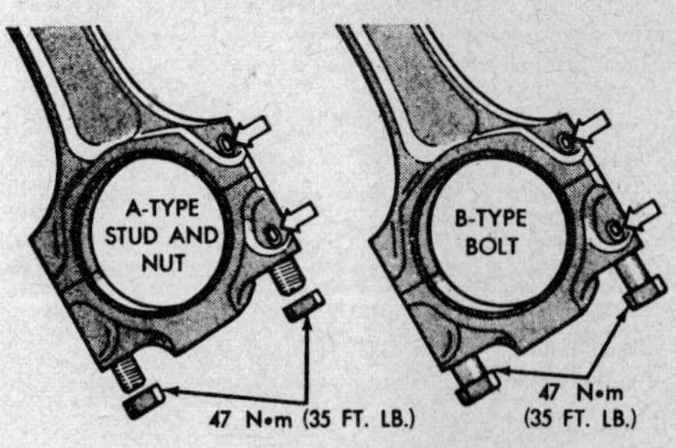

Fig. 12 Connecting rod assemblies

2. Remove A/C compressor adjusting strap screws and drive belt, if equipped. Remove screws from compressor mount and stabilizer brackets, then position compressor aside. Remove compressor bracket from alternator and compressor mount bracket.
3. Loosen alternator adjusting strap and remove drive belt.
4. Remove alternator mount bolts and position alternator aside.
5. Remove alternator and compressor mounting bracket from retainer bracket.
6. Loosen power steering pump drive belt, if equipped.
7. Raise and support vehicle.
8. Remove inner fender shield.
9. Remove air compressor, water pump and air pump drive belts, if equipped.
10. Remove idler pulley assembly.
11. Remove crankshaft pulley, **Fig. 14,** and power steering belt, if equipped.
12. Remove lower plastic timing belt cover.
13. Lower vehicle and support engine with a suitable jack.
14. Remove right engine mounting bolt and raise engine slightly.
15. Loosen timing belt tensioner and remove timing belt.
16. Rotate crankshaft and intermediate sprockets until markings are aligned on sprockets, **Fig. 15.**
17. Rotate camshaft sprocket until marking on sprocket is aligned with cylinder head cover, **Fig. 16.**
18. Install timing belt.
19. Install belt tensioning tool L-4502 on large belt tensioner nut in horizontal position, **Fig. 17.**
20. Reset tool index, as needed, to maintain axis within 15° of horizontal with tensioner bearing against belt.
21. Rotate engine clockwise, 2 full revolutions, then tighten tensioner locknut. **Ensure that timing marks are properly aligned with No. 1 cylinder at TDC of compression stroke.**

22. Remove tensioning tool, then reverse remaining procedure to complete installation.

FRONT ENGINE OIL SEAL SERVICE

Refer to **Figs. 18 and 19** to replace crankshaft, intermediate shaft or camshaft seal.

REAR CRANKSHAFT OIL SEAL SERVICE

1. Using a suitable screwdriver, pry oil seal out. Use caution not to nick or damage crankshaft flange seal surface.
2. Place tool L-4455-1 over crankshaft, **Fig. 20.**
3. Place replacement oil seal over tool and tap seal into position with a mallet.

OIL PUMP

REPLACE

REMOVAL

1. Remove oil pan and gasket.
2. Remove oil pump mounting screws, then the oil pump from engine block, **Fig. 21.**

INSTALLATION

1. Install oil pump with shaft in bore until pump mounting face contacts engine block. It may be necessary to rotate pump body to engage pump shaft tongue in distributor shaft groove.
2. Install oil pump mounting screws.
3. Install oil pan gasket and oil pan.

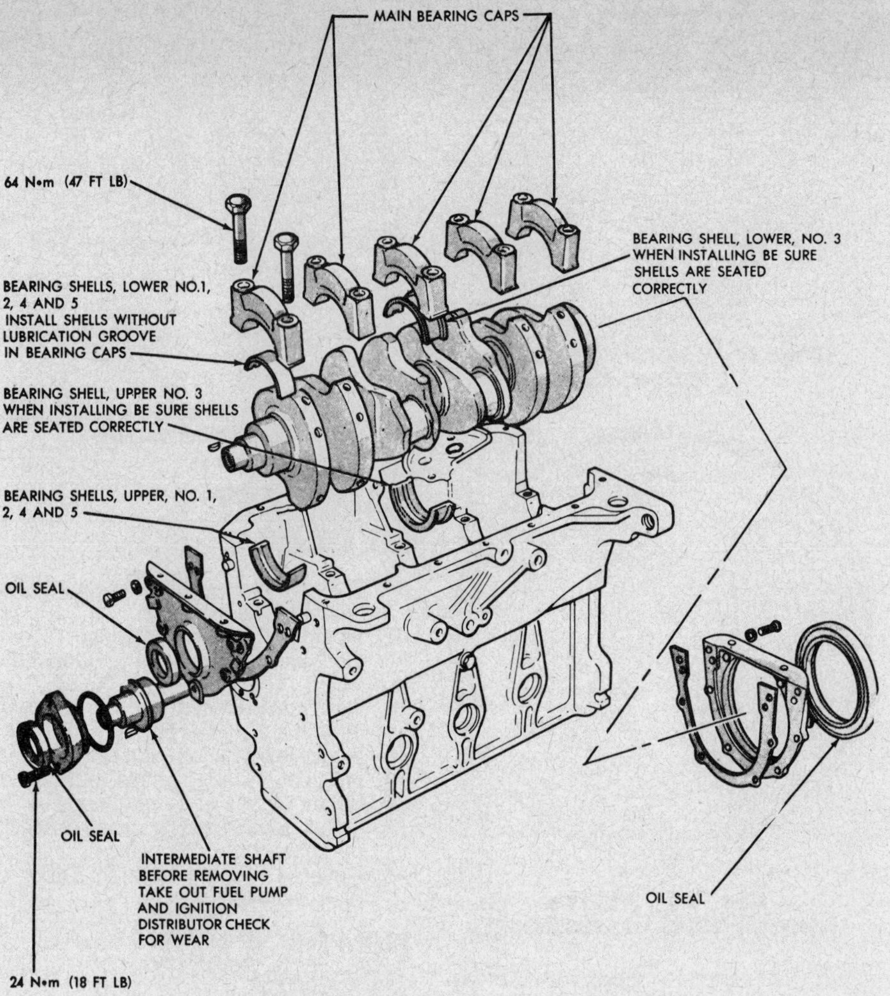

Fig. 13 Crankshaft & bearing assembly, exploded view

OIL PUMP SERVICE

DISASSEMBLY

1. Lightly clamp oil pump in a vise with shaft facing downward.
2. Remove two screws from cover.
3. Push shaft upward and remove shaft and drive gear assembly.
4. Pry deflector plate from assembly and remove strainer. **The relief valve is staked into place and is not serviceable.**

INSPECTION

1. Check endplay, **Fig. 22.** Endplay should be .001-.006 inch.
2. Check gear backlash, **Fig. 23.** Backlash should be .002-.008 inch. If not, replace pump gears.
3. Check cover for flatness with a .002 inch feeler gauge, **Fig. 24.**
4. Use compressed air to check relief valve for proper movement, **Fig. 25.**

ASSEMBLY

1. Lightly lubricate all parts.
2. Install driven gear and drive gear/shaft assembly.
3. Place cover on pump body and install cover screws.
4. Rotate shaft in each direction. If any binding is detected, disassemble pump and inspect for nicks on gears and/or foreign material.

FUEL PUMP

REPLACE

1. Disconnect fuel lines from fuel pump.
2. Remove fuel pump mounting bolts and fuel pump.
3. Reverse procedure to install.

WATER PUMP

REPLACE

1. Disconnect battery ground cable.
2. Drain cooling system.
3. Disconnect radiator hoses and bypass hose from water pump.
4. Remove A/C compressor from mounting brackets and position aside with refrigerant lines attached, if equipped.
5. Remove alternator.
6. Disconnect diverter valve hose at valve, then remove rear air pump bracket and front air pump bracket, if equipped.
7. Remove alternator bracket from water pump.
8. Remove timing belt cover bolt and two top water pump attaching bolts.
9. Remove water pump.
10. Reverse procedure to install.

BELT TENSION DATA

Belt	New Lbs.	Used Lbs.
1982-83		
Air Cond.	90	45
Air Pump	70	40
Alternator	65	40
Power Steer.	80	50

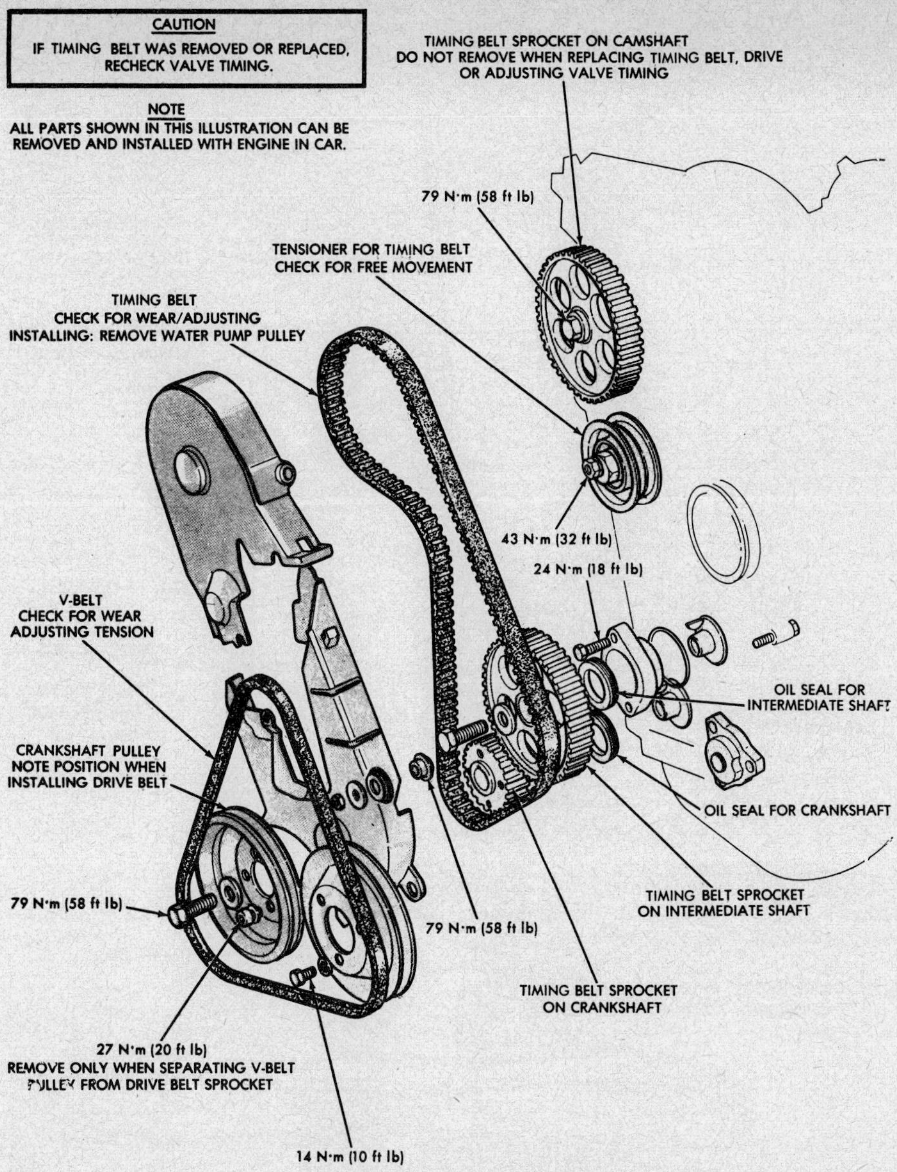

Fig. 14 Timing belt & sprocket assembly, exploded view

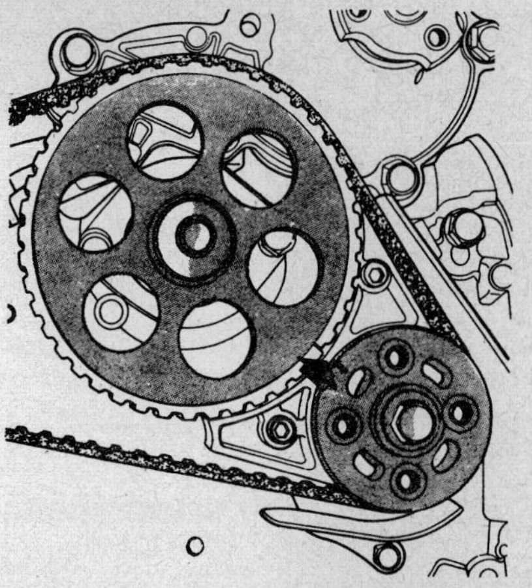

Fig. 15 Aligning timing marks on crankshaft & intermediate shaft sprockets

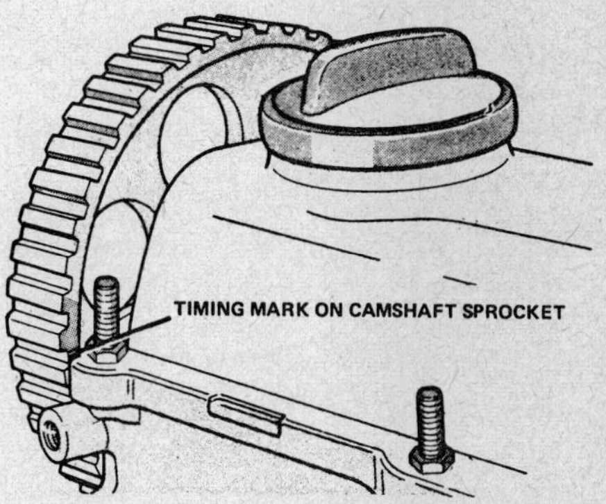

Fig. 16 Aligning timing mark on camshaft sprocket

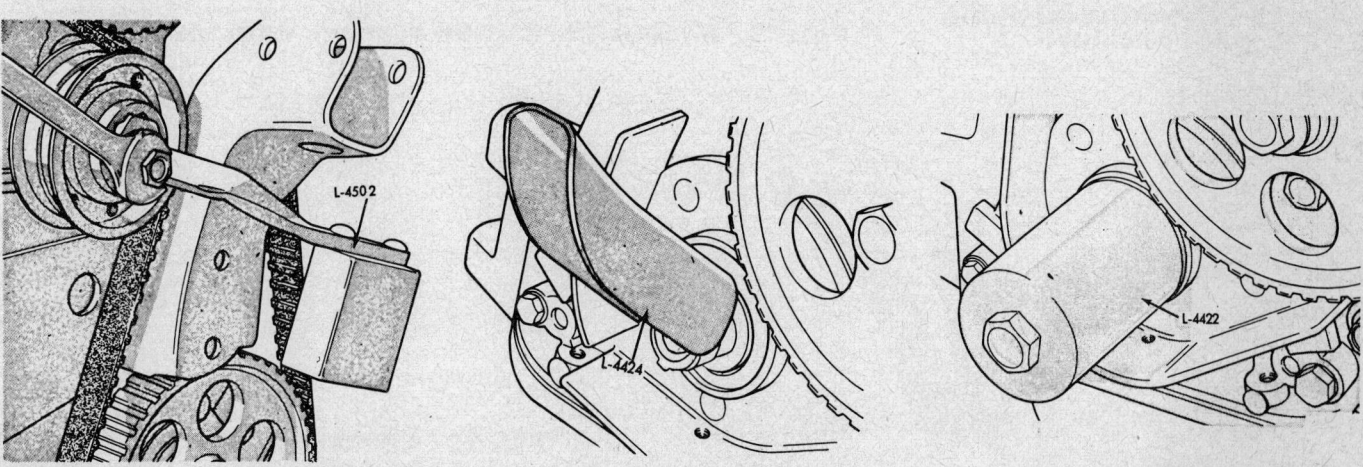

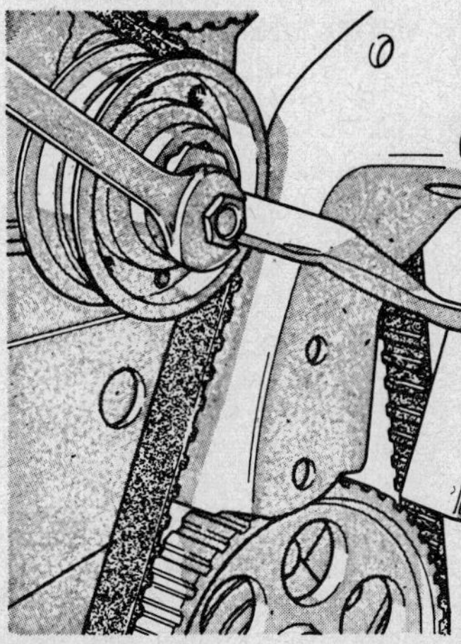

Fig. 17 Timing belt tensioner tool installation

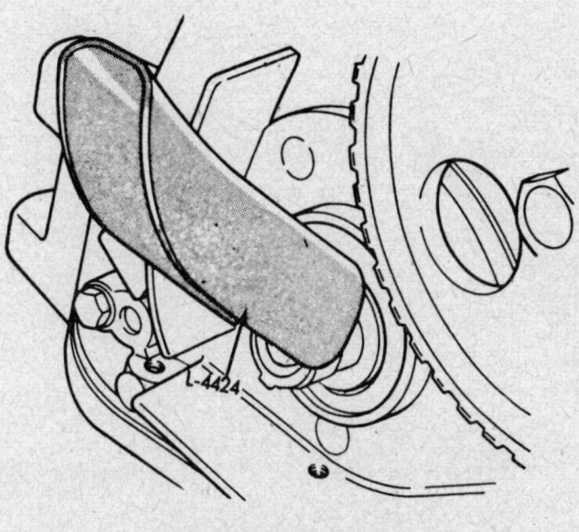

Fig. 18 Front engine oil seal removal

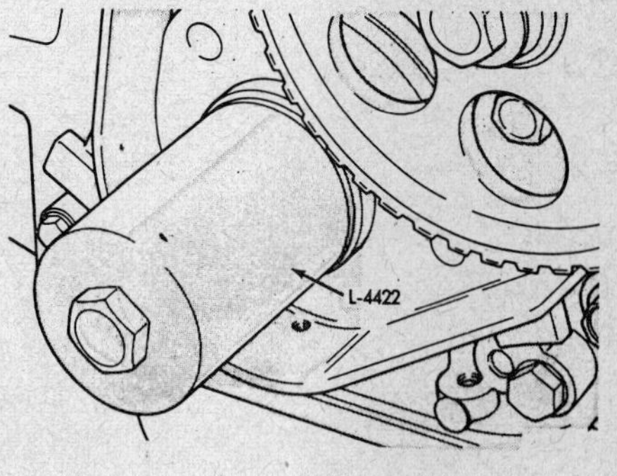

Fig. 19 Front engine oil seal installation

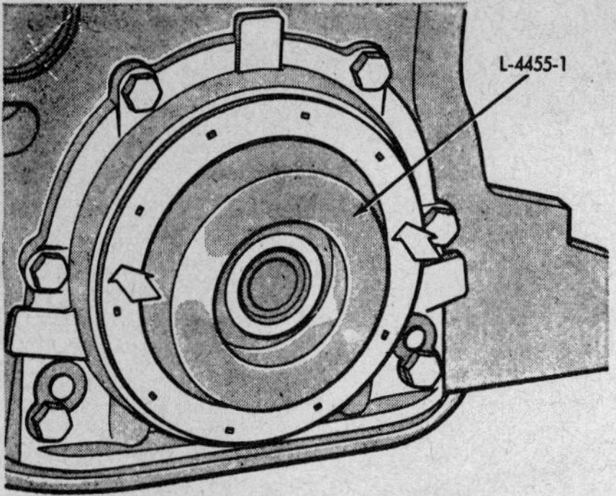

Fig. 20 Rear crankshaft seal installation

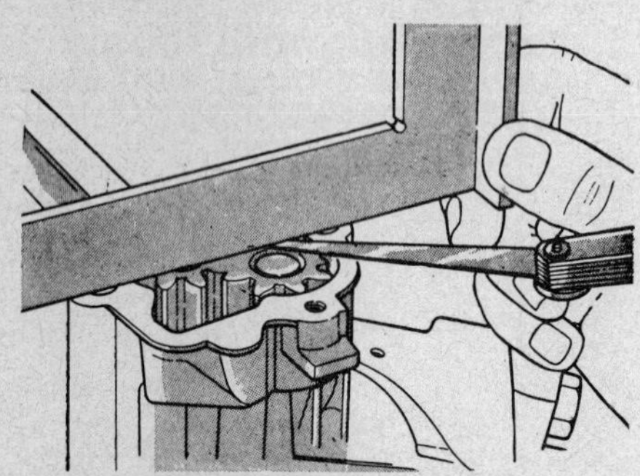

Fig. 22 Checking oil pump gear end play

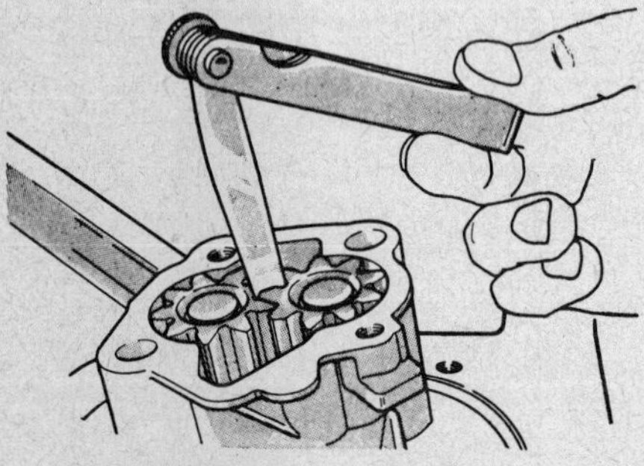

Fig. 23 Checking oil pump gear backlash

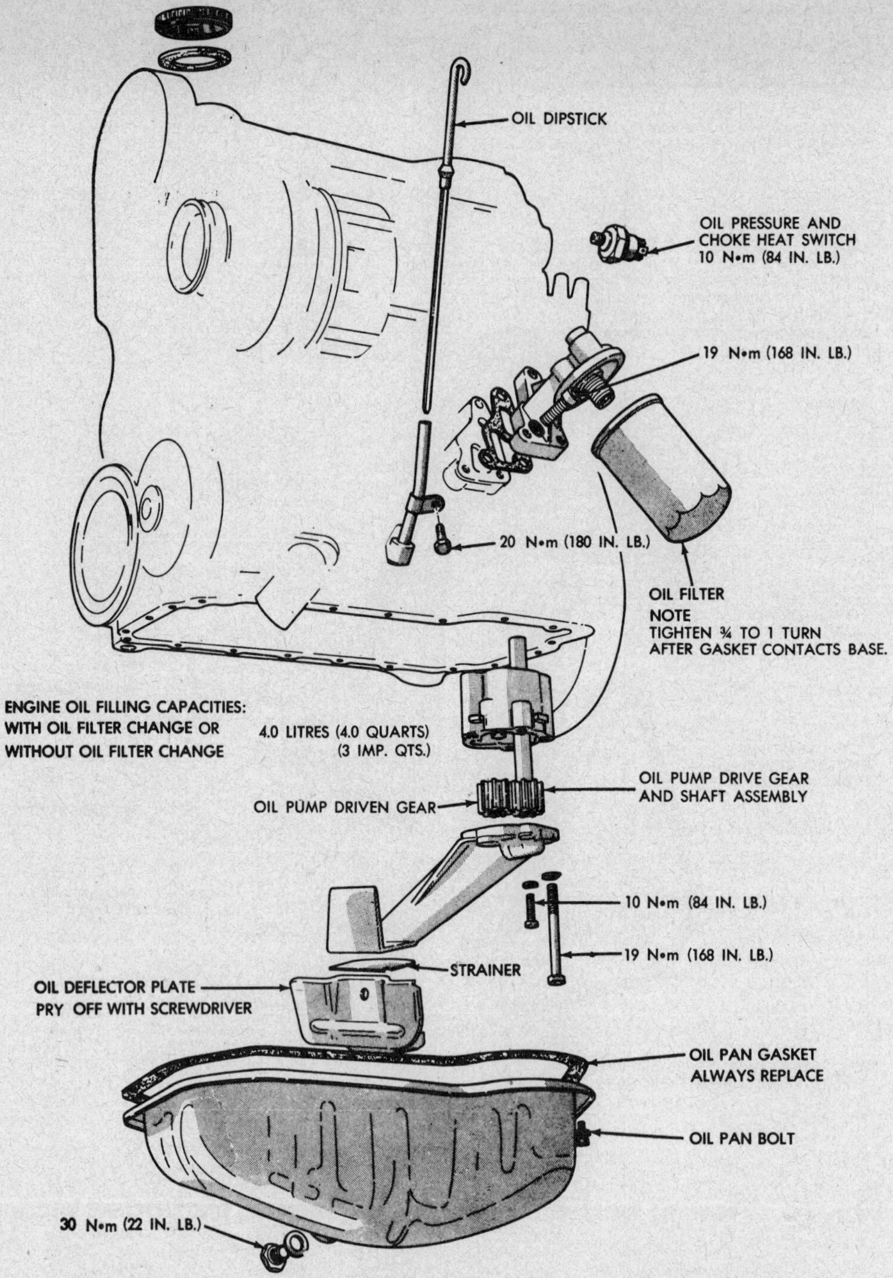

Fig. 21 Engine lubrication system, exploded view

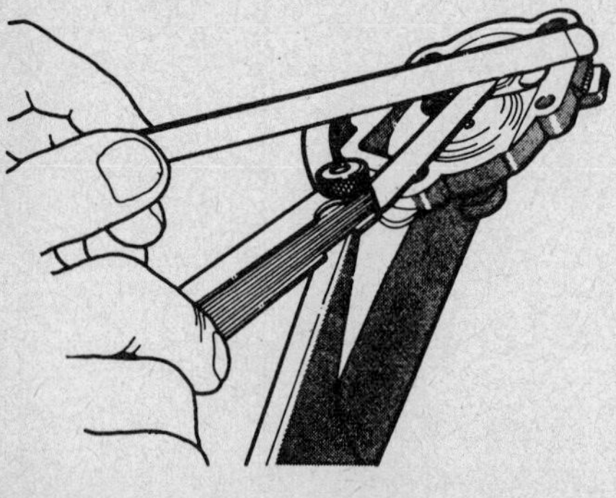

Fig. 24 Checking oil pump gear cover flatness

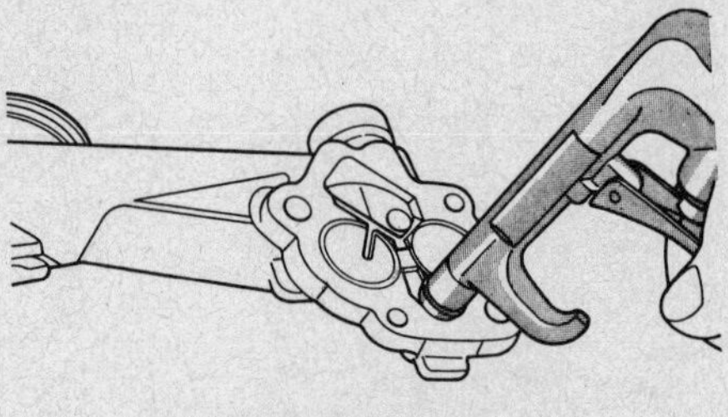

Fig. 25 Checking oil pump relief valve with compressed air

4-135 (2.2L) & 4-153 (2.5L) Engine Section

INDEX

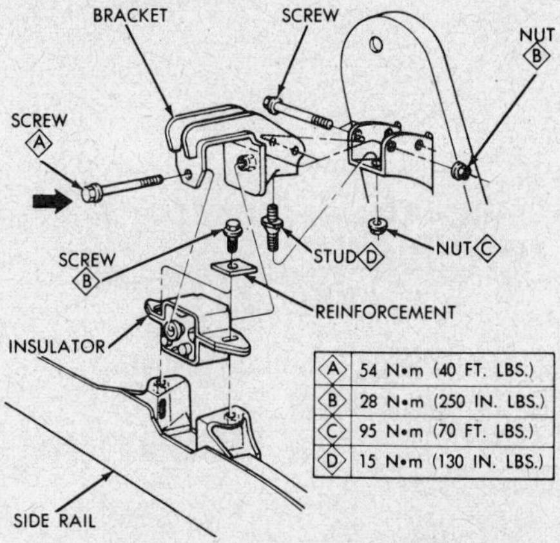

Fig. 1 Engine mount. 1982–83 right side

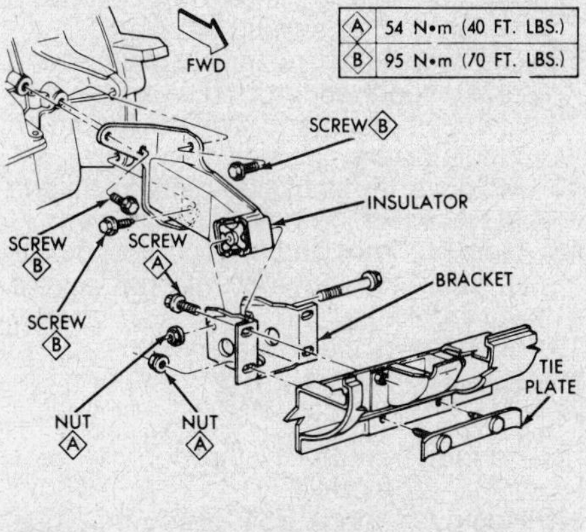

Fig. 2 Front engine mount. 1982–83

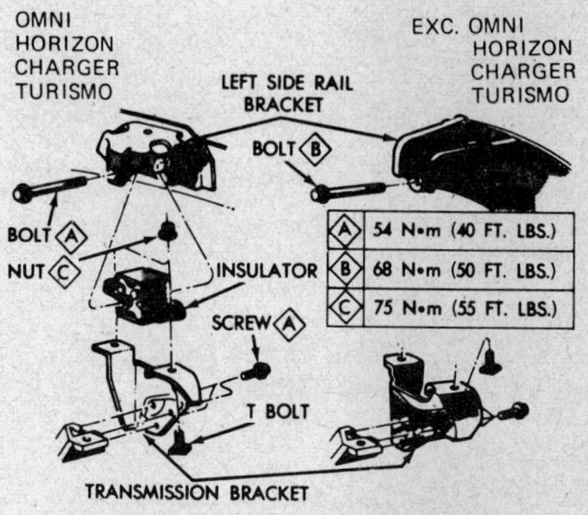

Fig. 3 Engine mount. 1982–83 left side Automatic transaxle

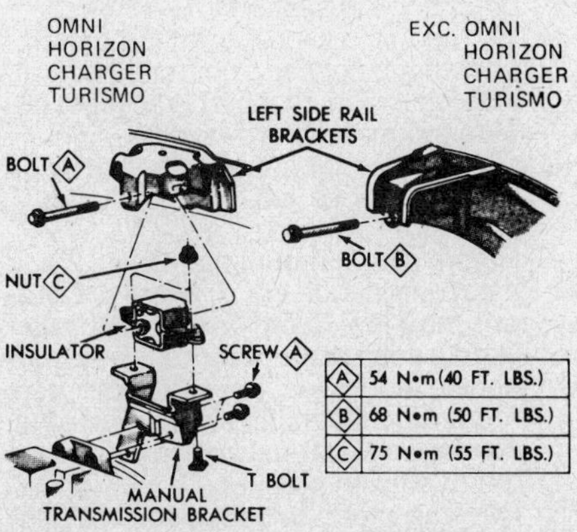

Fig. 4 Engine mount. 1982–83 left side Manual transaxle

ENGINE MOUNTS

When positioning the engine, check driveshaft length as outlined in the "Front Suspension & Steering Section" under "Driveshaft Length, Adjust." The engine mounts incorporate slotted bolt holes to permit side-to-side positioning of the engine thereby affecting the length of the driveshaft. Failure to properly position engine may result in extensive damage to the engine.

Refer to **Figs. 1 through 8** when replacing the engine mounts.

On 1982-83 vehicles, the left engine mount is attached with two types of mounting screws. Two of the three are of the pilot type with extended tips. Extended tip screws must be installed in the proper position, Fig. 8. Damage to the shift cover or difficult shifting may occur if screws are incorrectly installed.

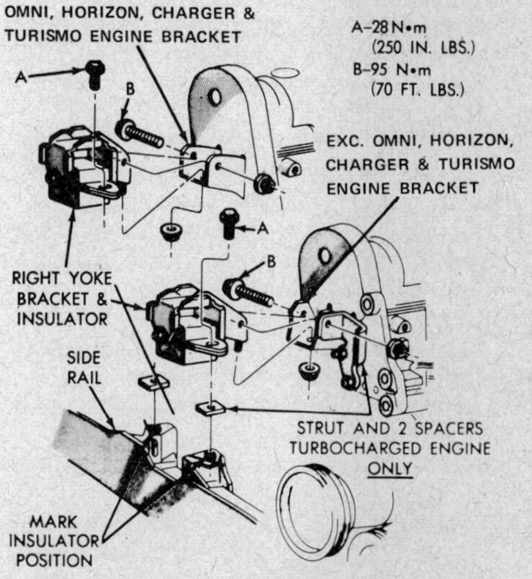

Fig. 5 Engine mount. 1984–85 right side shown, 1986–88 similar

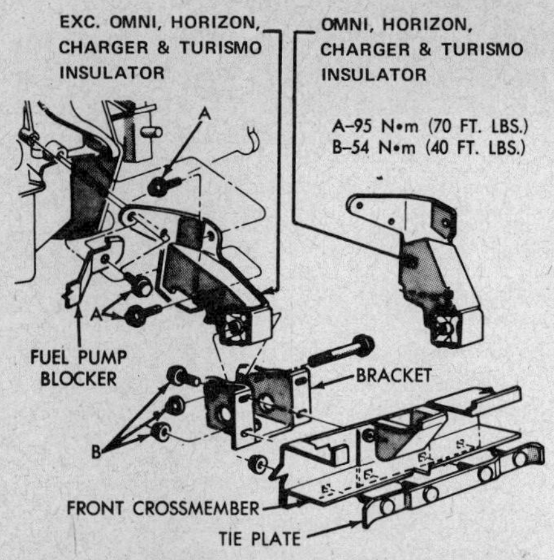

Fig. 6 Front engine mount. 1984–85 shown, 1986–88 similar

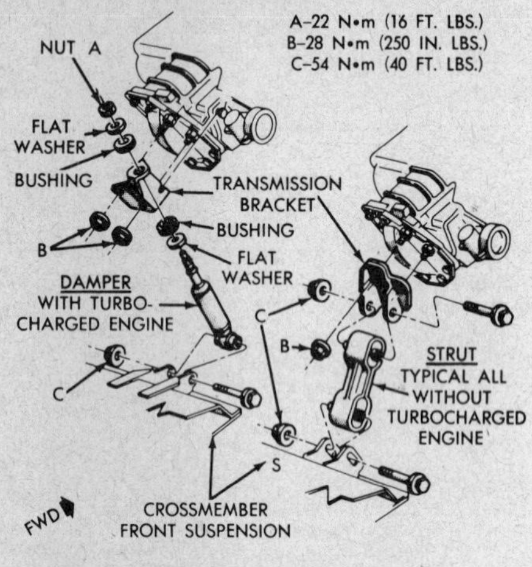

Fig. 9 Anti roll strut & damper

ENGINE REPLACE

1982–83

1. Disconnect battery ground cable.
2. Scribe alignment marks on hood and hood hinge, then remove hood.
3. Drain cooling system, then disconnect radiator hoses at radiator and engine.
4. Remove air cleaner, radiator and fan shroud.
5. Remove A/C compressor from mounting bracket and position aside with hoses attached, if equipped.
6. Remove power steering pump from mounting bracket and position aside with hoses attached, if equipped.
7. Drain crankcase and remove oil filter.
8. Disconnect wire connectors at alternator, carburetor and engine.
9. Disconnect fuel line, heater hose and accelerator cable.
10. Remove alternator from mounting bracket and position aside.
11. On models equipped with manual transmission, disconnect clutch cable, then remove transmission lower cover.
12. On all models, disconnect exhaust pipe from exhaust manifold, then remove starter motor.

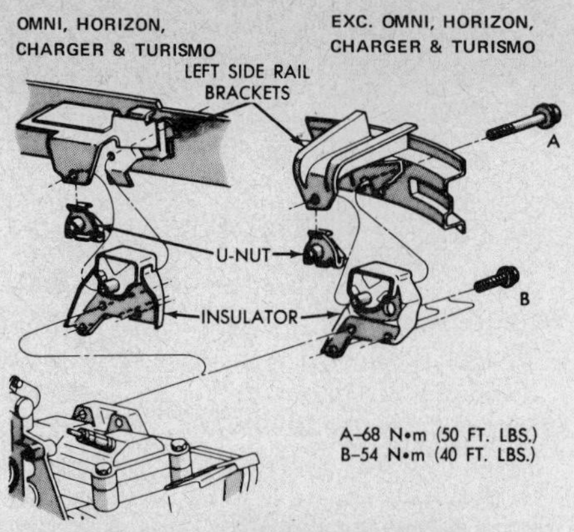

Fig. 7 Engine mount. 1984–85 left side shown, 1986–88 similar

13. On models equipped with automatic transmission, remove transmission case lower cover and place alignment marks on flex plate and torque converter. Remove converter to flex plate attaching screws. Attach a C-clamp to front lower portion of converter housing to retain torque converter in housing when engine is being removed.
14. On all models, install a suitable transmission holding fixture and attach a suitable engine lifting device.
15. Remove righthand inner splash shield and disconnect ground strap.
16. Remove righthand engine mount to insulator through bolt.
17. Remove transmission case to engine block attaching bolts.
18. Remove front engine mount to bracket bolt, then carefully lift engine from vehicle.
19. Reverse procedure to install.

EXCEPT 1982–83

1. Perform steps 1 through 15 for 1982-83 models.
2. Remove long bolt through yoke bracket and insulator. **If insulator screws are to be removed, mark position on side rail for exact reinstallation.**
3. Remove transmission case to cylinder block mounting screws.
4. Remove front engine mount screw and nut.
5. On vehicles with manual transmission, remove anti-roll strut or damper, **Fig. 9.**
6. On vehicles with manual transmission, remove insulator through bolt from inside wheel house, or insulator bracket to transmission screws.
7. On all vehicles, carefully lift engine from vehicle.
8. Reverse procedure to install.

TIMING BELT, SPROCKETS & OIL SEALS

ALTERNATOR BELT REMOVAL

1. Disconnect battery ground cable.
2. Loosen alternator locking screw, then loosen adjusting screw and remove belt.

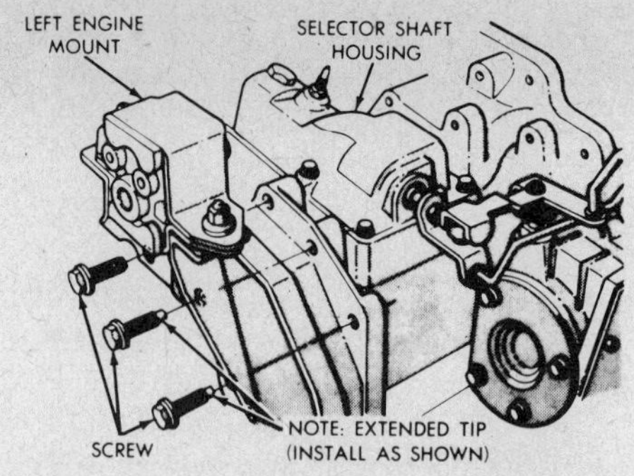

Fig. 8 Correct positioning of extended tip screws

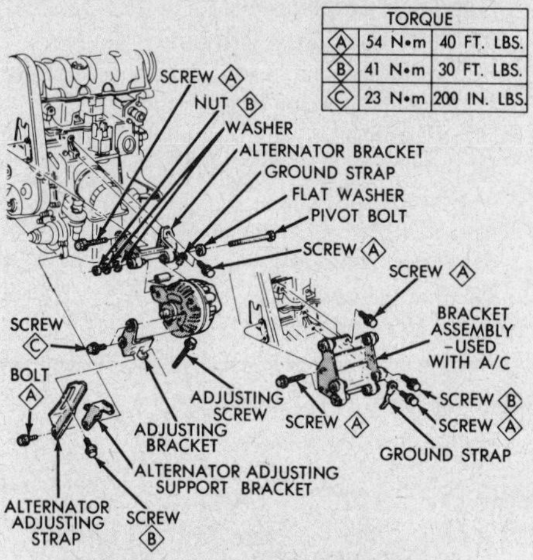

Fig. 10 Alternator & compressor mounting bracket, replacement. 1982–84

3. Reverse procedure to install.

ALTERNATOR & COMPRESSOR MOUNTING BRACKET

1982–84

For replacement of alternator and compressor mounting bracket refer to **Fig. 10.**

Exc. 1982–84

1. Disconnect battery ground cable and drain cooling system.
2. On models equipped with turbocharger, remove right engine mount bolt attaching isolator support bracket to engine mount bracket.
3. On all models, remove five side mounting bolts No. 1, 4, 5, 6 and 7, **Fig. 11.**
4. Remove front mounting nut No. 2 and loosen front bolt No. 3, **Fig. 11. Coolant may leak from No. 3 bolt hole.**
5. Rotate solid mount bracket away from engine and slide on stud until free. Front mounting bolt, spacer and strut, if equipped with turbocharger, will be removed with bracket.
6. Reverse procedure to install. Attaching bolts should be tightened in sequence and to specified torque as follows:
   a. Bolt No. 1 to 30 inch lbs.
   b. Nut No. 2 and Bolt No. 3 to 40 ft. lbs.

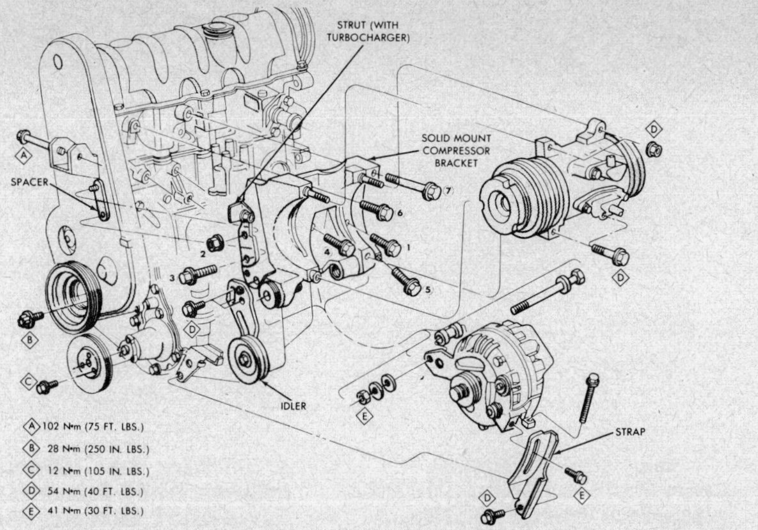

Fig. 11 Accessory & solid mount compressor bracket, replacement. 1985–88

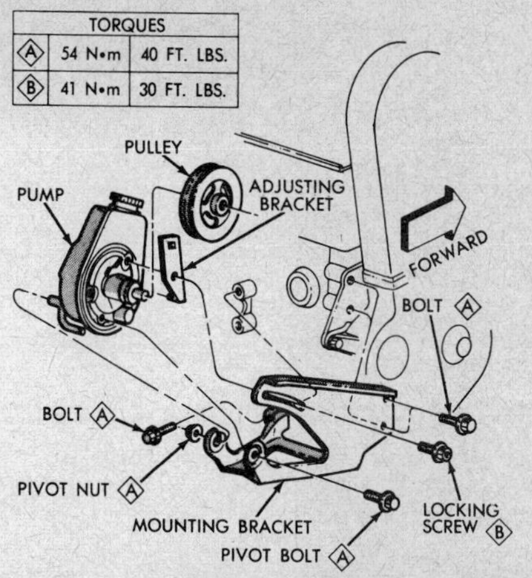

Fig. 12 Power steering pump & mounting bracket, replacement

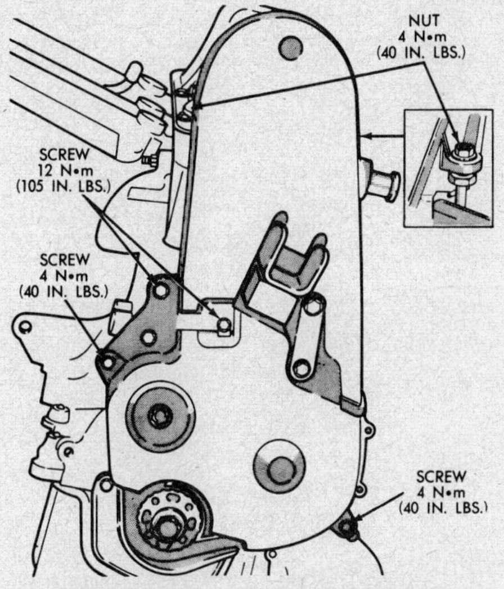

Fig. 13 Timing belt cover removal. 1982–85

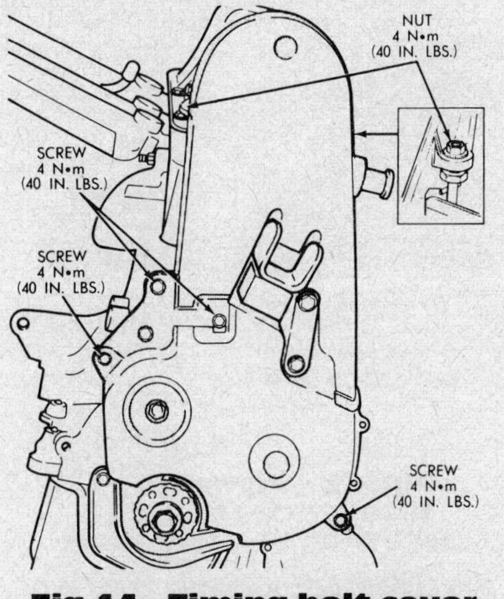

Fig.14 Timing belt cover removal. 1986–88

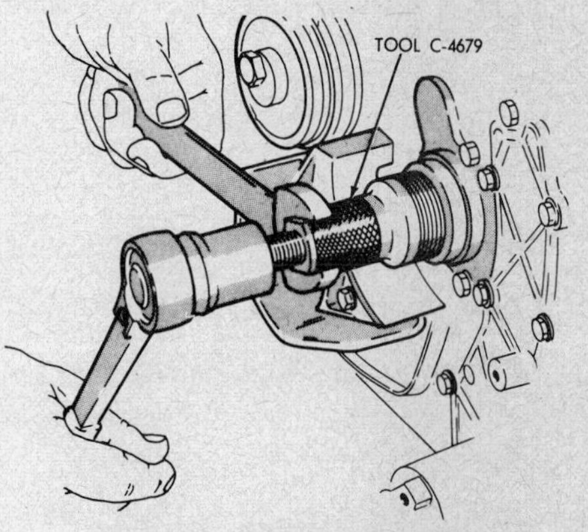

Fig. 15 Crankshaft, intermediate shaft & camshaft oil seal removal

c. Bolts No. 1 (second tightening), 4 and 5 to 40 ft. lbs.
d. Bolts No. 6 and 7 to 40 ft. lbs.

POWER STEERING PUMP MOUNTING BRACKET

1. Remove pump locking screw, **Fig. 12.**
2. Remove pivot bolt and nut, and the drive belt.
3. Remove power steering pump and position aside.
4. Remove mounting bracket bolts and bracket.
5. Reverse procedure to install.

CRANKSHAFT PULLEY & WATER PUMP PULLEY

1. Remove screws retaining water pump pulley to pump shaft.
2. Remove bolts retaining crankshaft pulley.
3. Raise and support front of vehicle, then remove right inner splash shield and crankshaft pulley.
4. Reverse procedure to install.

TIMING BELT & COVER

Timing belt tooth skipping on 1982-83 models less A/C may be caused by snow and/or ice accumulation in the timing belt area. This condition may happen when operating in very deep snow or during blizzard conditions. A timing cover sealing package, part No. 4293186, should be used to correct this problem.

1. Remove nuts securing cover to cylinder head, **Figs. 13 and 14.**
6. Rotate crankshaft to align timing marks as outlined in "Crankshaft and Intermediate Shaft Timing," and ensure camshaft is aligned as outlined in "Camshaft Timing."
3. Position a suitable jack under engine, then remove righthand engine mount bolt and raise engine slightly.
4. Loosen timing belt tensioner, then remove timing belt.
5. Ensure crankshaft and intermediate shaft timing marks are aligned, install timing belt as outlined in "Camshaft Timing," then reverse remaining procedure to complete installation.

CRANKSHAFT SPROCKET

1. With timing belt removed from engine, remove crankshaft sprocket bolt.
2. Remove crankshaft sprocket using a suitable puller.

CRANKSHAFT, INTERMEDIATE SHAFT & CAMSHAFT OIL SEAL SERVICE

Refer to **Figs. 15 and 16** for removal and installation of crankshaft, intermediate shaft or camshaft seals.

On late model 1981 2.2L engines, the camshaft oil seals were changed from steel backed to uni-directional rubber backed type seals. This change made necessary an increase in the cylinder rear seal bore to prevent accidental mixing of the uni-directional front and rear seals.

The replacement seal for early built 2.2L engines will also be rubber backed with arrows indicating direction of rotation and location in the head marked on seal. The seals must be installed as indicated.

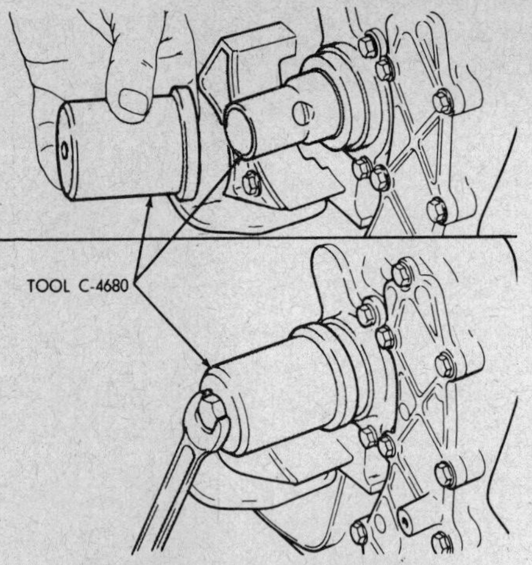

Fig. 16 Crankshaft, intermediate shaft & camshaft oil seal installation

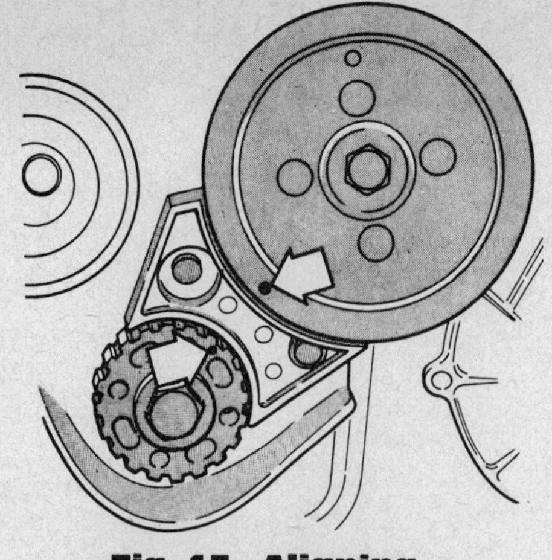

Fig. 17 Aligning crankshaft & intermediate shaft timing marks. 1982–84

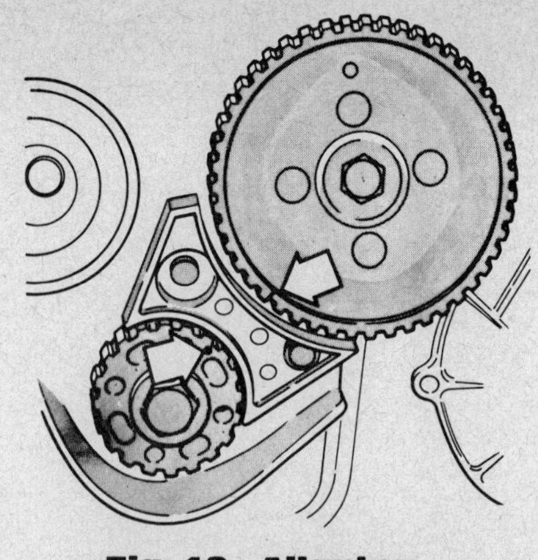

Fig. 18 Aligning crankshaft & intermediate shaft timing marks. 1985–88

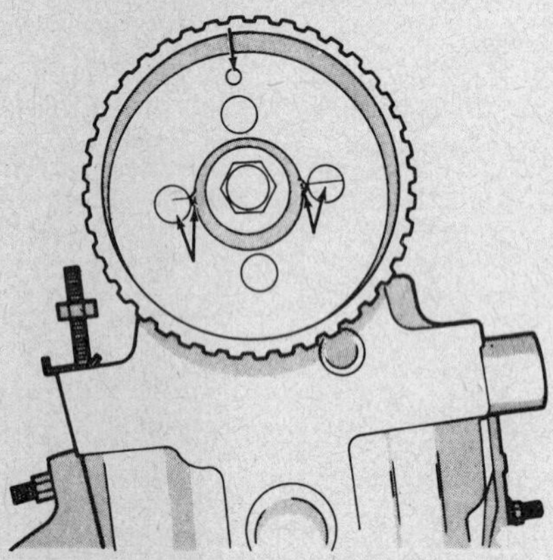

Fig. 19 Aligning camshaft timing marks

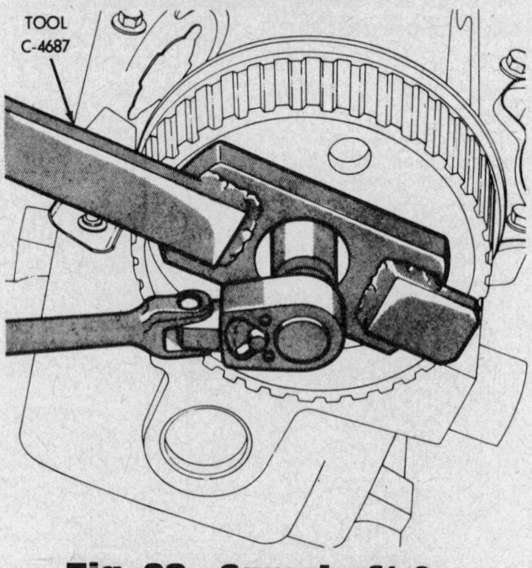

Fig. 20 Camshaft & intermediate shaft sprocket replacement

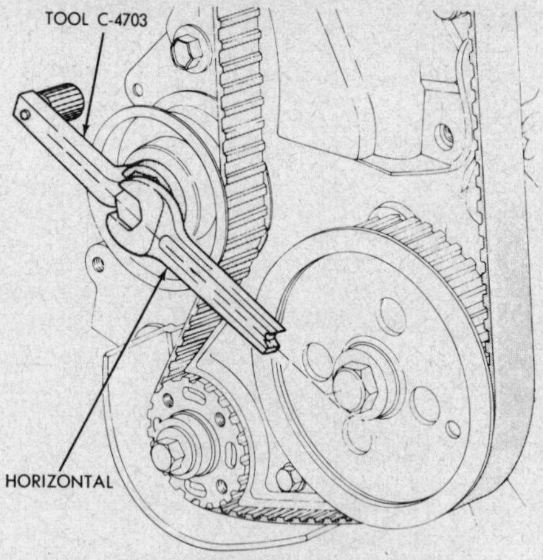

Fig. 21 Adjusting drive belt tension

CRANKSHAFT & INTERMEDIATE SHAFT TIMING

1. Rotate crankshaft and intermediate shaft until markings on sprockets are aligned, **Figs. 17 and 18.**

CAMSHAFT TIMING

1. Rotate camshaft until arrows on hub are aligned with No. 1 camshaft cap to cylinder head line, **Fig. 19.** Small hole must be located along vertical center line.
2. Install timing belt. Refer to "Adjusting Drive Belt Tension" described elsewhere for proper drive belt adjustment.
3. Rotate crankshaft two full revolutions and recheck timing. **Do not allow oil or solvents to contact timing belt since they will deteriorate the rubber and cause tooth skippage.**

CAMSHAFT & INTERMEDIATE SHAFT REMOVAL & INSTALLATION

Refer to **Fig. 20** for removal and installation of camshaft and intermediate shaft sprocket.

ADJUSTING DRIVE BELT TENSION

1. Remove spark plugs then rotate crankshaft to TDC position.
2. Using a suitable tool, loosen tensioner locknut, **Fig. 21.**
3. Reset belt tension so that belt tensioning tool axis is within 15° of horizontal.
4. Rotate crankshaft two revolutions in clockwise direction and position at TDC, then tighten tensioner locknut.

BALANCE SHAFTS

The 4-153 engine is equipped with two balance shafts installed in a carrier attached to the lower crankcase.

The shafts are interconnected through gears to rotate in opposite directions. These gears are driven by a short chain from the crankshaft, to rotate at two times crankshaft speed. This counterbalances certain engine reciprocating masses.

SHAFT, REPLACE

1. Remove oil pan, oil pickup, timing belt cover, belt, crankshaft belt sprocket and front crankshaft oil seal retainer.
2. Remove chain cover, guide and tensioner, **Fig. 22.**
3. Remove balance shaft gear and chain sprocket retaining screws and crankshaft chain sprocket torx screws, then the chain and sprocket assembly, **Fig. 23.**
4. Remove double-ended gear cover retaining stud, then the cover and balance shaft gears.
5. Remove carrier rear cover and balance shafts.
6. Remove six carrier to crankshaft attaching bolts to separate carrier.
7. Reverse procedure to install, then adjust crankshaft to balance shaft timing.

CARRIER ASSEMBLY, REPLACE

The gear cover, gears, balance shafts and rear cover will remain intact during carrier removal.

1. Remove chain cover and driven balance shaft chain sprocket screw.
2. Loosen tensioner pivot and adjusting screws, then move driven balance shaft inboard (through) driven chain sprocket. Sprocket will hang in lower chain loop.

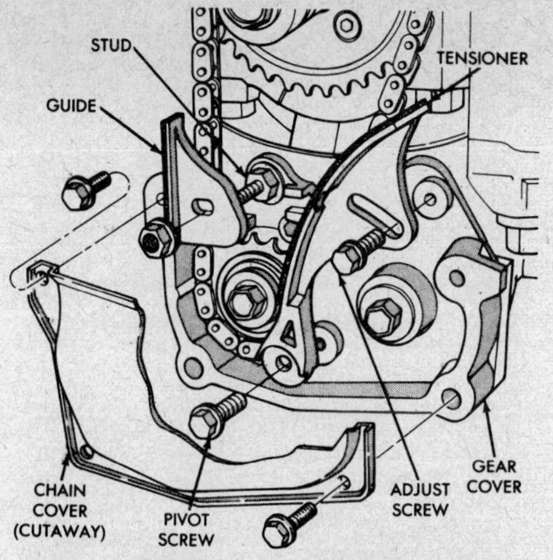

Fig. 22 Removing chain cover, guide & tensioner

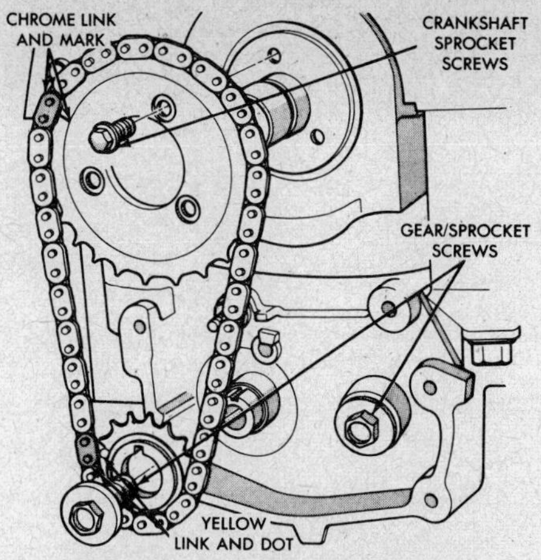

Fig. 23 Removing drive chain & sprockets

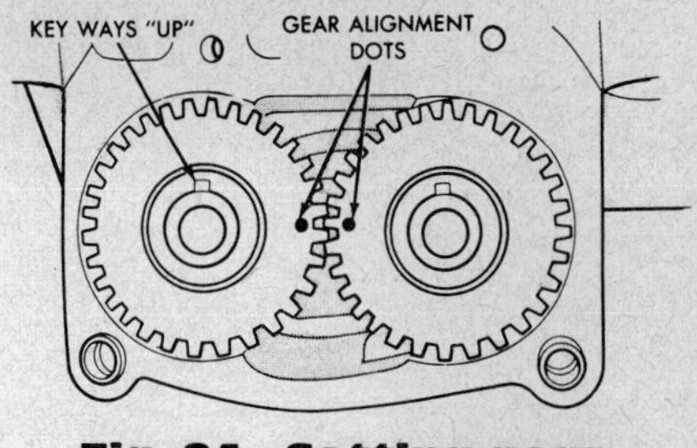

Fig. 24 Setting gear timing

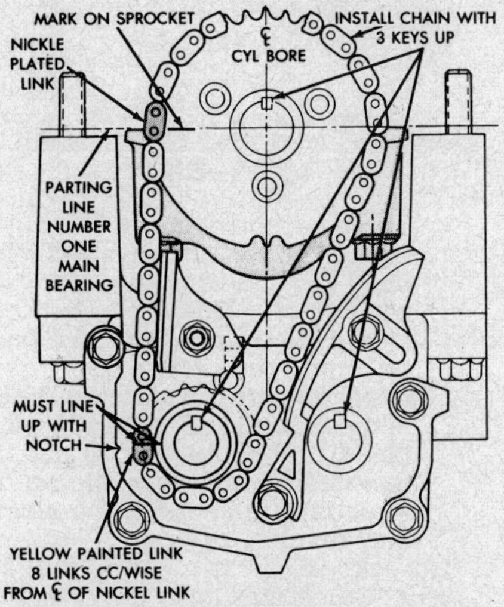

Fig. 25 Setting balance shaft timing

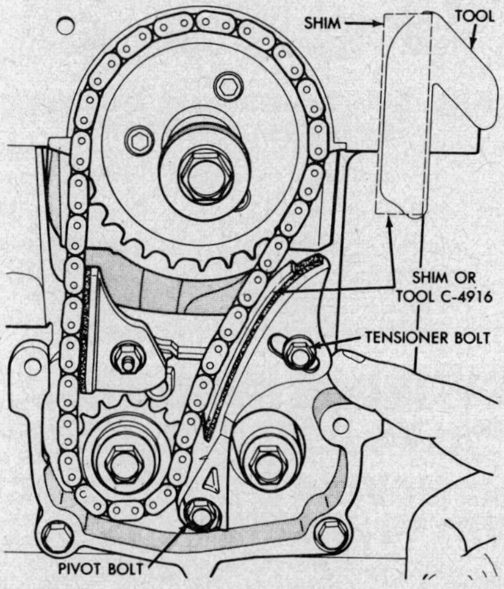

Fig. 26 Adjusting chain tension

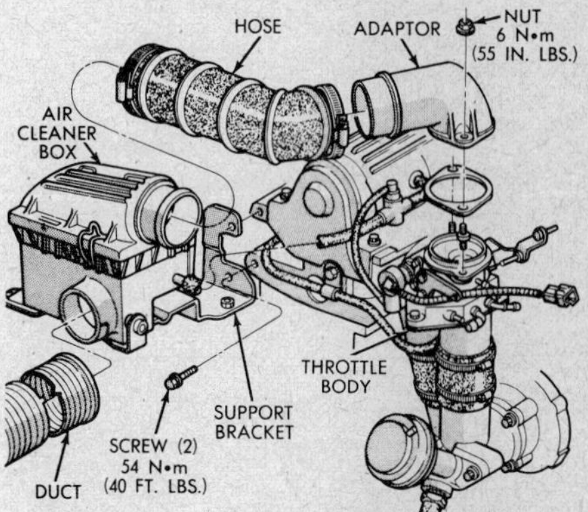

Fig. 27 Air cleaner box & support, hoses, & throttle body adapter

3. Remove carrier to crankshaft attaching bolts and carrier.
4. Reverse procedure to install, then adjust crankshaft to balance shaft timing.

TIMING, ADJUST

1. With balance shafts installed in carrier, position carrier on crankshaft and install six attaching bolts, torquing to 40 ft. lbs.
2. Rotate balance shafts until both shaft keyways are parallel to vertical centerline of engine, then install short hub drive gear on sprocket driven shaft. After installation, gear and balance shaft keyways must face up with gear timing marks meshed as shown, **Fig. 24.**
3. Install gear cover and torque double ended stud/washer fastener to 105 inch lbs.
4. Install crankshaft sprocket and torque socket head torx screws to 130 inch lbs.
5. Rotate crankshaft until number one cylinder is at top dead center (TDC). The timing marks on chain sprocket should line up with parting line on left side of number one main bearing cap, **Fig. 25.**
6. Place chain over crankshaft sprocket so that nickel plated link of chain is over timing mark on crankshaft sprocket, **Fig. 25.**
7. Place balance shaft sprocket into timing chain so that timing mark on sprocket (yellow dot) mates with yellow painted link on chain.
8. With balance shaft keyways at 12 o'clock, slide balance shaft sprocket onto nose of balance shaft. Balance shaft may have to be pushed in slightly to allow for clearance. **Balance shaft timing is correct if the timing mark on sprocket, painted link and arrow on side of gear cover are aligned.**
9. If sprockets are timed correctly, install balance shaft bolts, torquing to 250 inch lbs. A wood block placed between crankcase and crankshaft counterbalance will prevent gear rotation.

TENSIONING CHAIN

1. Install chain tensioner loosely assembled.
2. Place a .039 inch thick by 2.75 inch long shim between tensioner and chain, push tensioner and shim up against chain and apply firm pressure directly behind adjustment slot to take up all slack. Chain must have shoe radius contact as shown, **Fig. 26.**
3. With load applied, tighten top tensioner bolt first, then bottom pivot bolt, torquing both to 105 inch lbs., then remove shim.
4. Position guide on double ended stud, ensuring tab on guide fits into slot on gear cover, then install nut/washer assembly, torquing to 105 inch lbs.
5. Install carrier covers, torquing screws to 105 inch lbs.

INTAKE & EXHAUST MANIFOLD

EXCEPT TURBO

1. Disconnect battery ground cable and drain coolant system.
2. Remove air cleaner and disconnect all vacuum and fuel lines and electrical connectors from carburetor.
3. Disconnect throttle linkage, then remove power steering pump drive belt.
4. Disconnect power brake vacuum hose from manifold, if equipped.
5. Disconnect hoses from water crossover, then raise and support vehicle and disconnect exhaust pipe from exhaust manifold.
6. Remove power steering pump and position aside. Remove intake manifold support bracket.
7. Remove EGR tube and the intake manifold retaining screws.

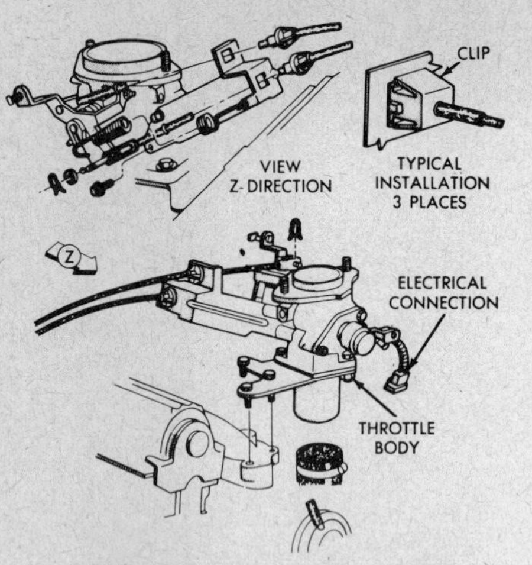

Fig. 28 Accelerator linkage & throttle body

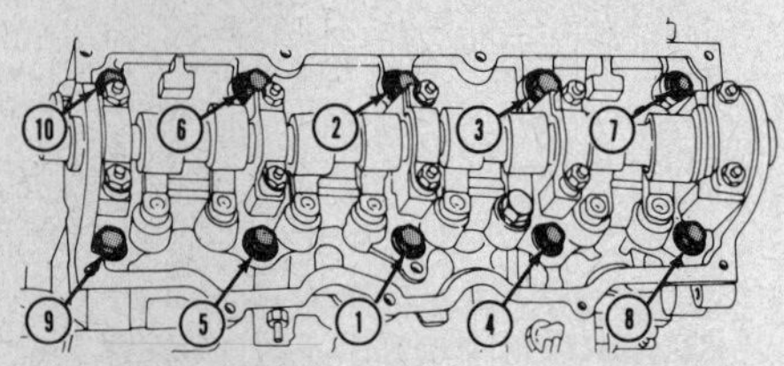

Fig. 31 Cylinder head bolt tightening sequence

8. Lower vehicle and remove intake manifold.
9. Remove exhaust manifold retaining nuts and exhaust manifold.
10. Reverse procedure to install.

TURBO

1. Disconnect battery ground cable and drain cooling system.
2. Raise and support vehicle.
3. Disconnect exhaust pipe at articulated joint and disconnect oxygen sensor at electrical connectors.
4. Remove turbocharger to block support bracket.
5. Loosen oil drain back tube connector hose clamps and move tube down on block fitting.
6. Disconnect turbocharger coolant inlet tube at cylinder block and disconnect tube support bracket.
7. Lower vehicle.
8. Remove air cleaner assembly including throttle body adapter, hose, and air cleaner box with support bracket, **Fig. 27.**
9. Disconnect accelerator linkage, throttle body electrical connector, and vacuum hoses, **Fig. 28.**
10. Remove four bracket to intake manifold screws and two bracket to heat shield retaining clips, then lift and secure fuel rail, with injectors, wiring harness, and fuel lines intact, up out of way.
11. Disconnect turbocharger oil feed line at oil sending unit tee.
12. Disconnect upper radiator hose at thermostat housing.

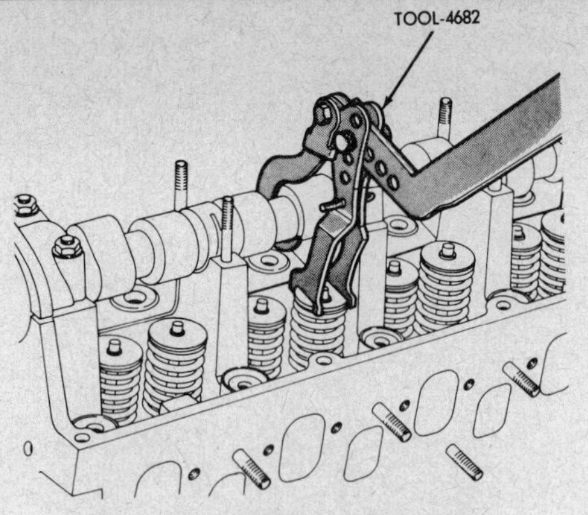

Fig. 29 Valve spring, replace

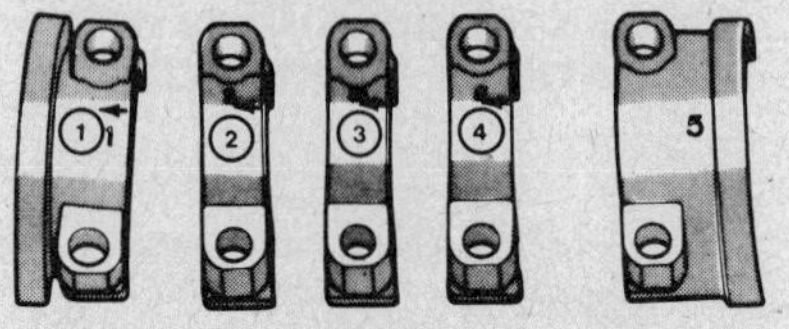

Fig. 32 Camshaft bearing cap installation

13. Remove cylinder head with manifolds and turbocharger as an assembly as described under "Cylinder Head & Valve Assembly."
14. Reverse procedure to install.

CYLINDER HEAD & VALVE ASSEMBLY

REMOVING & INSTALLING VALVE SPRINGS

Cylinder Head Off Engine

1. Using suitable tool to hold valves in head, compress valve spring enough to remove and install valve bead locks, **Fig. 29.**

Cylinder Head On Engine

1. Rotate crankshaft until piston is at TDC on compression stroke.
2. Apply 90-100 psi of compressed air into spark plug hole of valve being removed.
3. Using suitable tool, compress valve spring enough to remove valve stem locks.
4. Remove valve spring and spring seat.
5. Remove valve seal.

CYLINDER HEAD BOLT REMOVAL SEQUENCE

When removing cylinder head, remove cylinder head bolts in proper sequence, **Fig. 30.**

CYLINDER HEAD BOLT TIGHTENING SEQUENCE

1. On 1982-84 and early production 1985 engines, refer to tightening sequence, **Fig. 31,** and tighten cylinder head bolts in 3 steps as follows:
   a. Torque all bolts to 30 ft. lbs.
   b. Torque all bolts to 45 ft. lbs.

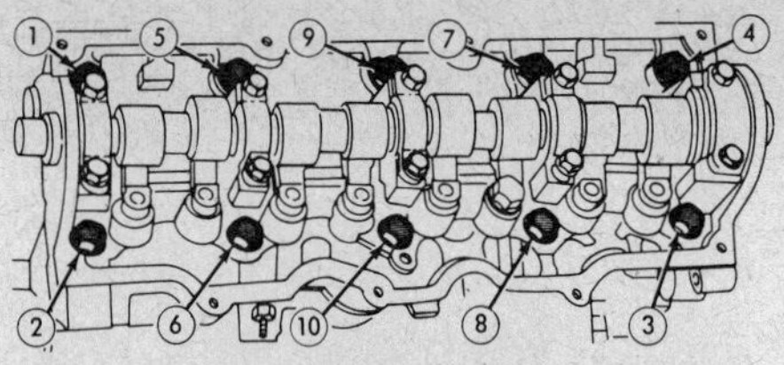

Fig. 30 Cylinder head bolt removal sequence

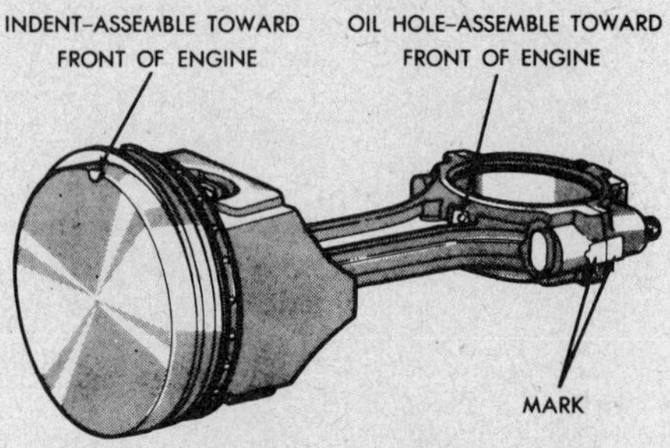

Fig. 33 Piston & connecting rod assembly. 1982–85

   c. Tighten each bolt an additional 1/4 turn (90°). **During 1985 an 11 mm head bolt was introduced in production. This bolt can be identified by an "11" stamped on bolt head. These bolts are used on late production 1985 engines and all 1986-88 engines. Do not intermix 10 and 11 mm head bolts, as stripping of threads or cracking of the block may result.**
2. On late production 1985 and all 1986-88 engines, refer to tightening sequence, **Fig. 31,** and tighten cylinder head bolts in 4 steps as follows:
   a. Torque all bolts 45 ft. lbs.
   b. Torque all bolts to 65 ft. lbs.
   c. Torque all bolts again to 65 ft. lbs.
   d. Tighten each bolt an additional 1/4 turn (90°), noting bolt torque. **If bolt torque is not over 90 ft. lbs. after tightening an additional 1/4 turn, bolt should be replaced.**

CAMSHAFT, REPLACE

1. Mark rocker arms to ensure installation in original position.
2. Evenly loosen camshaft bearing bolts until all bolts have been loosened 3-4 turns.
3. Tap rear of camshaft with suitable mallet to break caps free.
4. Continue loosening bearing cap bolts, ensuring camshaft does not cock, then remove bearing caps and camshaft. **Loosen bearing cap bolts evenly. If camshaft cocks in bearing bores, bearing surfaces may be damaged.**
5. With caps removed from engine, check oil holes for obstructions. **Some engines may be equipped with oversize camshaft bearings. Engines with oversize camshaft bearings can be identified by green markings on cylinder head and**

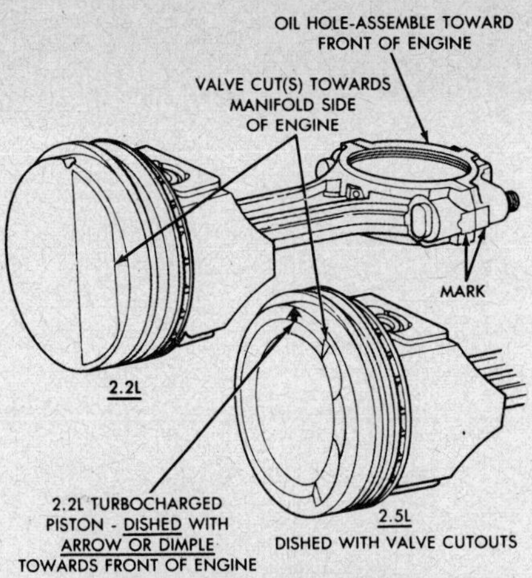

Fig. 34 Piston & connecting rod assembly. 1986–88

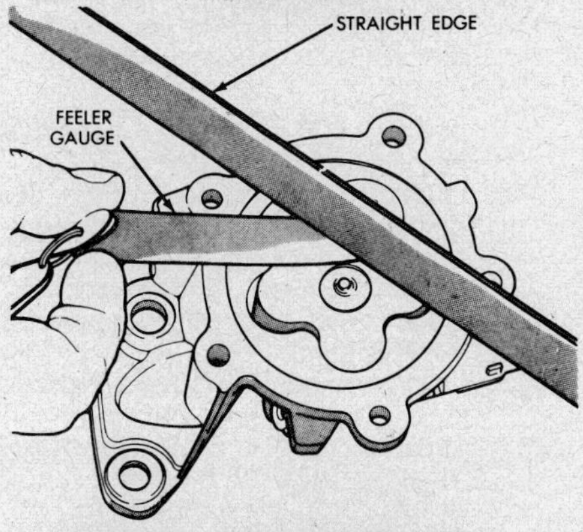

Fig. 37 Measuring oil pump endplay

camshaft at AIR pump side of engine.

6. Check camshaft lobe height in center (contact area) and on shoulders of lobe. If difference in reading exceeds .101 inch, camshaft should be replaced.
7. Install rocker arms in original positions, then position camshaft in bearing saddles of cylinder head.
8. Apply suitable sealant to No. 1 and No. 5 bearing cap.
9. Align caps in proper sequence, with No. 1 cap at timing belt end and No. 5 cap at flywheel end of engine, and ensure arrow on caps 1, 2, 3 and 4 point toward timing belt, **Fig. 32. Install caps before installing camshaft seals.**
10. Torque cap bolts to 165 inch lbs. on 1981-83 engines or 215 inch lbs. on 1984-88 engines. Torque cap bolts evenly in crossing pattern to ensure camshaft remains properly aligned.
11. Install camshaft seals as outlined.

VALVE LIFT SPECIFICATIONS

Engine	Year	Int.	Exh.
4-135	1982-88	.430	.430

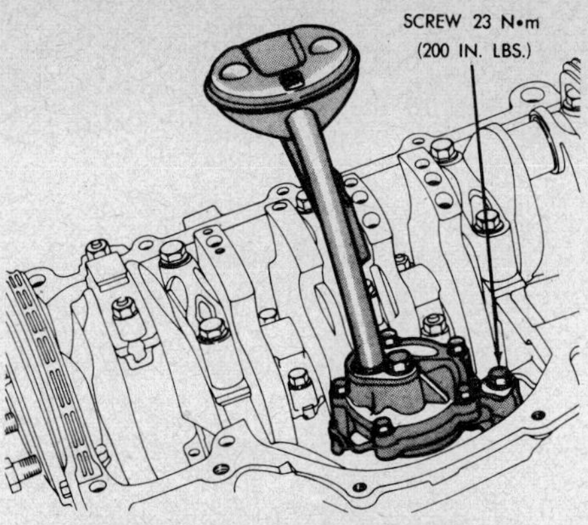

Fig. 35 Oil pump replacement. 1982–84

VALVE TIMING

INTAKE OPENS BEFORE TDC

Engine	Year	Degrees
4-135	1982	12
	1983	16
	1984-85 exc. Shelby Opt. & Turbocharged	16
	1984-85 Shelby	10.5
	1984-85 Turbocharged	10
	1986–88 exc. Turbocharged	16
	1986–88 Turbocharged	10
4-153	1986–88	12

VALVES

ADJUST

Hydraulic valve lifters are used; no adjustment is necessary.

PISTON & ROD ASSEMBLY

1982–85

When installing piston and rod assembly, indentation on top of piston must face towards timing belt side of engine, **Fig. 33.** The oil hole on connecting rod must face timing belt side of engine and be on same side as indented mark on piston.

Connecting rod clearance should be .005-.013 inch.

1986–88

When installing piston and rod assembly, valve cut must face toward manifold side of engine, **Fig. 34.** Turbocharged engine pistons will have an arrow or dimple toward front of engine. Oil hole on connecting rod must face timing belt side of engine.

Connecting rod clearance should be .005-.013 inch.

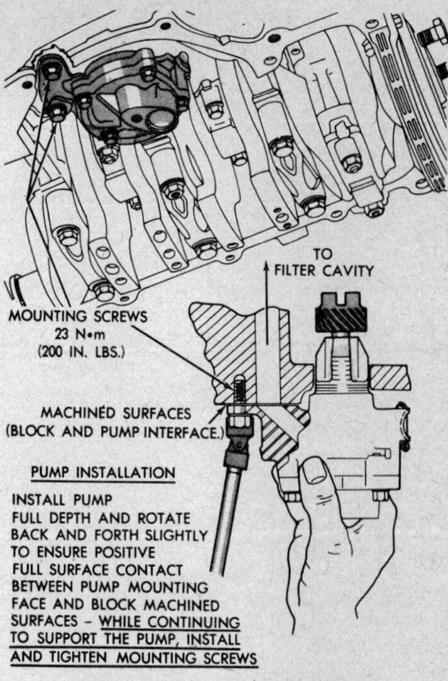

Fig. 36 Oil pump replacement. 1985–88

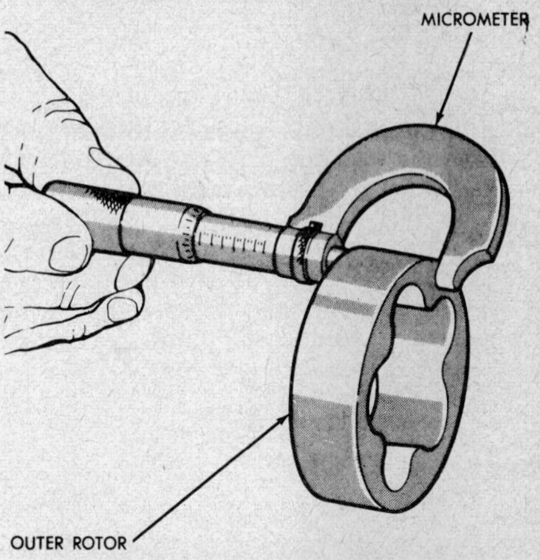

Fig. 38 Measuring oil pump outer rotor thickness

ENGINE LUBRICATION SYSTEM

OIL PUMP ASSEMBLY

1982–84

1. With oil pan removed, remove screw securing oil pump to cylinder block, **Fig. 35.**
2. Reverse procedure to install. Torque oil pump attaching screws to 200 inch lbs. **The oil pump must fully seat on the cylinder block before the mounting bolts are tightened. Check for proper seating by rotating pump body on block. The pump body should move a few degrees in both directions with no further movement into the block. If not, mating surfaces should be cleaned of any foreign material preventing proper seating, otherwise damage to oil pump, pump**

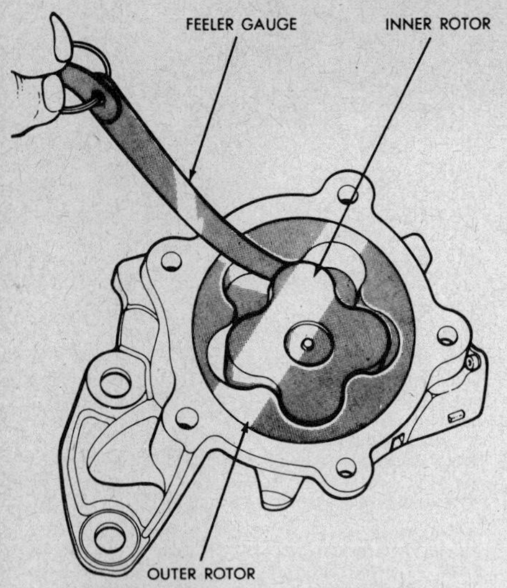

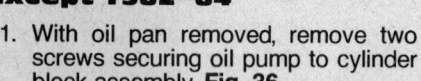

Fig. 39 Measuring clearance between oil pump rotors

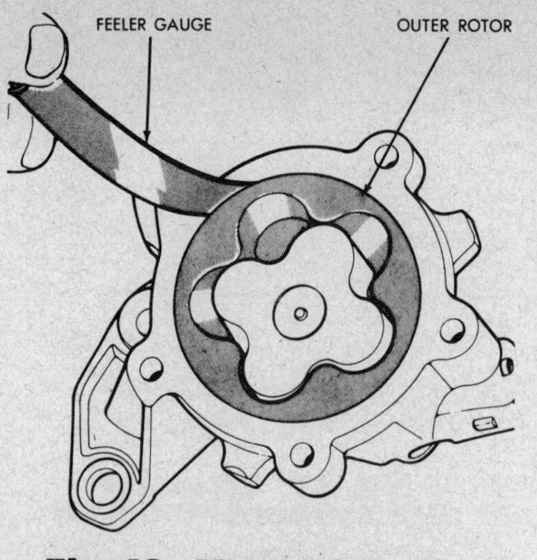

Fig. 40 Measuring oil pump outer rotor clearance

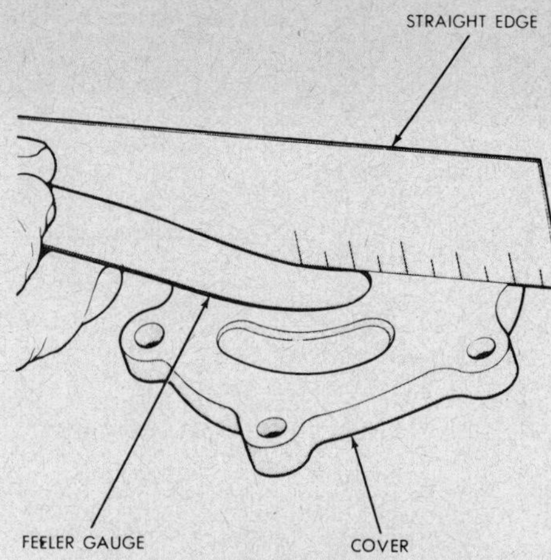

Fig. 41 Measuring oil pump cover clearance

driveshaft and gear, or distributor drive may result.

Except 1982–84

1. With oil pan removed, remove two screws securing oil pump to cylinder block assembly, **Fig. 36.**
2. Apply suitable sealant to pump to block interface.
3. Lubricate oil pump rotor and shaft and the drive gear.
4. Install pump full depth and rotate back and forth slightly to ensure proper positioning and alignment through full surface contact of pump and block machined interface surfaces. **Pump must be held in fully seated position while installing screws.**
5. Torque attaching screws to 200 inch lbs.

OIL PUMP SERVICE

1. Measure the following oil pump clearances:
   a. Endplay, **Fig. 37.** Endplay should be .001-.006 in on 1982 models, .001-.004 in. on 1983-85 models or .001-.004 in. on 1986-88 models.
   b. Outer rotor thickness, **Fig. 38.** Thickness should be .825 in. minimum on 1982-85 models or .944 in. minimum on 1986-88 models. Install outer rotor with chamfered edge in pump body.
   c. Clearance between rotors, **Fig. 39,** should be .010 in. maximum on 1982-85 models or .008 in. maximum on 1986-88 models.
   d. Outer rotor clearance, **Fig. 40.** Clearance should be .014 in. maximum.

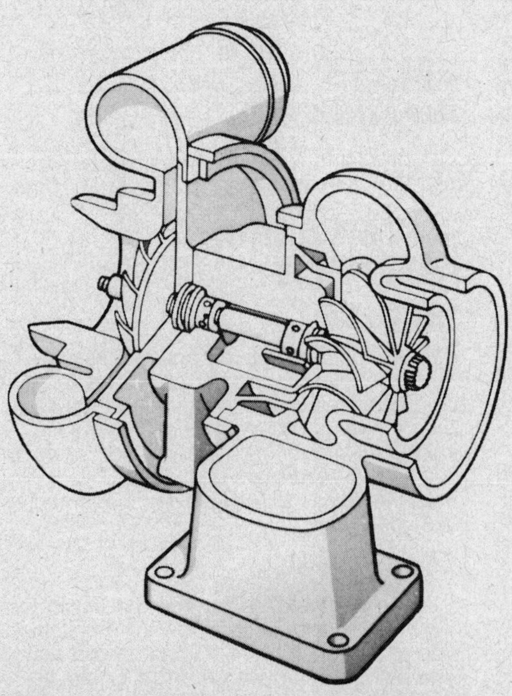

Fig. 42 Section view of Garret-AiResearch T3 type turbocharger

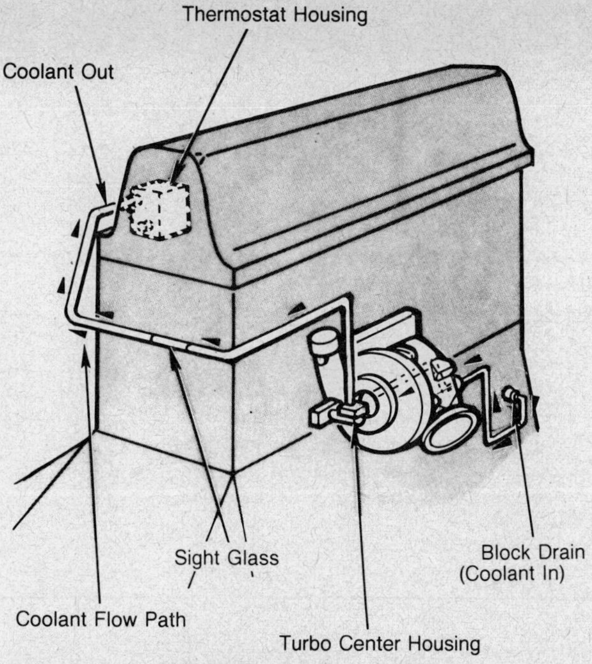

Fig. 43 Turbocharger water cooling system

e. Oil pump cover, **Fig. 41.** Clearance should be .015 in. maximum on 1982 models or .003 in. maximum on 1983-88 models.
f. Oil pressure relief valve spring length should be 1.95 inch.

WATER PUMP REPLACE

1. Disconnect battery ground cable.
2. Drain cooling system, and remove upper radiator hose.
3. Remove A/C compressor from mounting brackets and position aside with refrigerant lines attached, if equipped.
4. Remove alternator.
5. Disconnect lower radiator hose, bypass hose. Remove four water pump to engine attaching screws and water pump.
6. Reverse procedure to install.

TURBOCHARGER

The turbocharged engine is similar to the standard 4-135 engine. However, many components have been upgraded in order to withstand more than fifty percent higher power output generated by the turbocharger. This upgrading includes more durable intake and exhaust valve materials, better sealing piston rings, a larger capacity oil pump, select-fit bearings, and a revised camshaft. Dished piston tops are incorporated to lower the compression ratio.

The turbocharged engine integrates a Garrett-AiResearch T-3 center housing and wastegate assembly with a Chrysler built compressor and turbine housing, and exhaust outlet elbow, **Fig. 42.** The wastegate is calibrated to regulate maximum boost pressure at 7.5 psi. Turbo boost begins at 1200 RPM, rises to 7.2 psi at 2050 RPM, and peaks at 7.5 psi at 6000 RPM.

This turbocharger also incorporates a water cooled turbine end shaft bearing which lowers bearing temperatures, especially after a hot shut-off, to increase durability of the turbocharger, **Fig. 43.**

BELT TENSION DATA

Belt	New Lbs.	Used Lbs.
1982–84		
Air Cond.	95	80
Air Pump	—	—
Alternator	115	80
Power Steer.	95	80
1985–88		
Air Cond.	105	80
Air Pump	—	—
Alternator	115	80
Power Steer.	105	80

4-156 (2.6L) Engine Section

INDEX

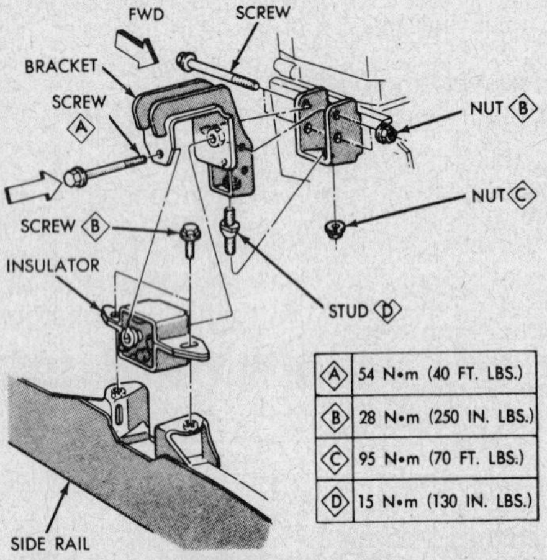

Fig. 1 Engine mount, right side. 1982–83

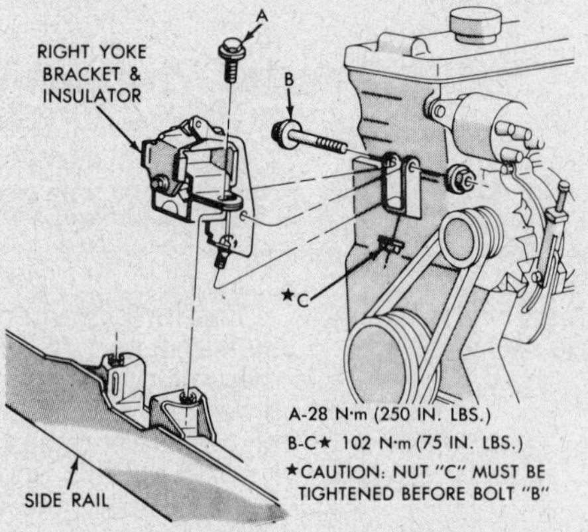

Fig. 2 Engine mount, right side. 1984–85

ENGINE MOUNTS

When positioning the engine, check driveshaft length as outlined in the "Front Suspension & Steering Section" under "Driveshaft Length, Adjust." The engine mounts incorporate slotted bolt holes to permit side-to-side positioning of the engine thereby affecting the length of the driveshaft. Failure to properly position engine may result in extensive damage to the engine.

Refer to **Figs. 1 through 5** when replacing the engine mounts.

The left engine mount is attached with two types of mounting screws. Two of the three are of the pilot type with extended tips. Extended tip screws must be installed in the proper position, Fig. 6. Damage to the shift cover or difficult shifting may occur if the screws are incorrectly installed.

ENGINE REPLACE

1. Disconnect battery ground cable.
2. Scribe alignment marks on hood and hood hinge, then remove hood.
3. Drain cooling system, then disconnect radiator hoses at radiator and engine.
4. Remove air cleaner, radiator and fan shroud.
5. Remove A/C compressor from mounting bracket and position aside with hoses attached, if equipped.
6. Remove power steering pump from mounting bracket and position aside with hoses attached, if equipped.
7. Drain crankcase and remove oil filter.
8. Disconnect wire connectors at alternator, carburetor and engine.
9. Disconnect fuel line, heater hose and accelerator cable.
10. Remove alternator from mounting bracket and position aside.
11. Disconnect exhaust pipe from exhaust manifold, then remove starter motor.
12. Remove transmission case lower cover and place alignment marks on flex plate and torque converter. Remove converter to flex plate attaching screws. Attach a C-clamp to front lower portion of converter housing to retain torque converter in housing when engine is being removed.
13. Install a suitable transmission holding fixture and attach a suitable engine lifting device.
14. Remove righthand inner splash shield, then disconnect ground strap.
15. Remove righthand engine mount to insulator through bolt.
16. Remove transmission case to engine block attaching bolts.
17. Remove front engine mount to bracket bolt, then carefully lift engine from vehicle.
18. Reverse procedure to install.

TIMING GEARS & OIL SEALS

TIMING CHAIN CASE COVER, REMOVAL

1. Disconnect battery ground cable.
2. Remove alternator locking screw, then loosen jam nut and adjusting screw. Remove drive belt.

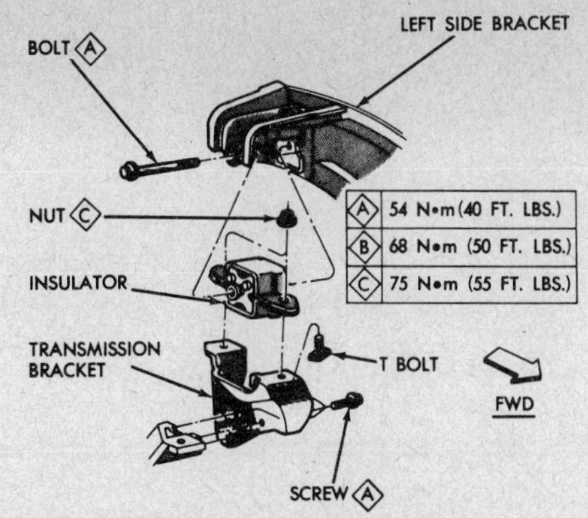

Fig. 3 Engine mount, left side. 1982–83

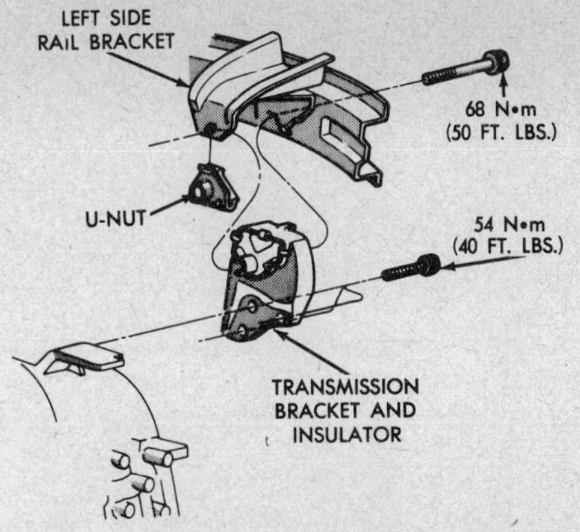

Fig. 4 Engine mount, left side. 1984–85

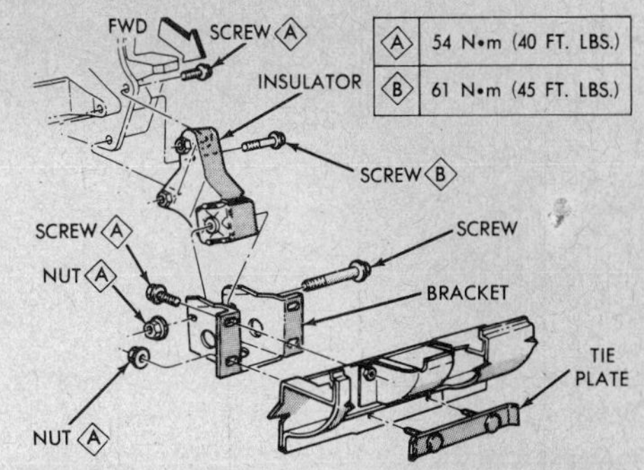

Fig. 5 Front engine mount

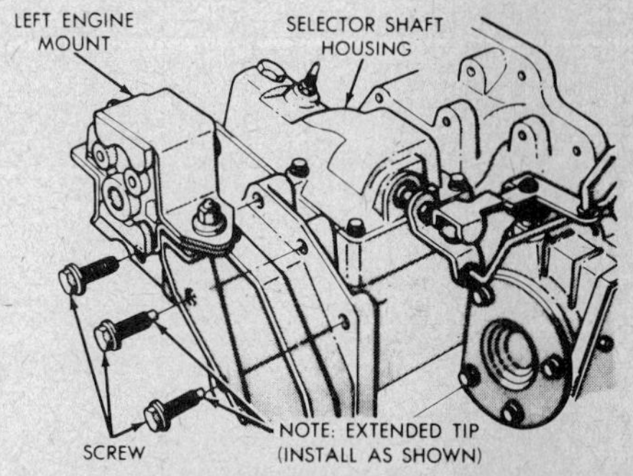

Fig. 6 Correct positioning of extended tip screws

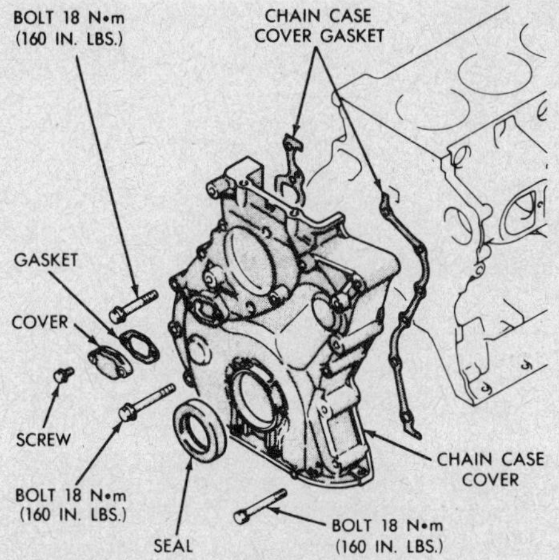

Fig. 7 Chain case cover removal

3. Remove distributor retaining nut, then the distributor from cylinder head and position aside.
4. Remove front and rear A/C compressor to bracket attaching screws and A/C compressor and position aside.
5. Remove power steering pump pivot and lock screws, then the drive belt.
6. Remove power steering pump mounting screw and nut, then position power steering pump aside.
7. Remove power steering pump bracket to engine attaching screws and bracket.
8. Raise vehicle and remove right inner splash shield.
9. Drain crankcase, then remove crankshaft drive pulley.
10. Lower vehicle and position a suitable jack under engine.
11. Remove engine mount to frame side rail through bolt, then the engine oil dipstick.
12. Remove air cleaner assembly.
13. Disconnect battery ground cable, then the spark plug wires.
14. Disconnect vacuum hoses from cylinder head cover.
15. Remove cylinder head cover screws and cylinder head cover.
16. Remove oil pan attaching screws and oil pan.
17. Remove timing indicator plate from timing chain case cover.
18. Remove engine mounting plate from timing chain case cover.
19. Remove cylinder head cover as previously described.
20. Remove two front cylinder head screws. Do not disturb any other cylinder head bolts.
21. Refer to **Fig. 7** and remove remaining screws securing chain case cover to engine.

SILENT SHAFT DRIVE CHAIN, REMOVAL

1. Remove chain case cover as previously described.
2. Remove sprocket screws, then the drive chain, crankshaft sprocket and silent shaft sprocket, **Fig. 8.**

CAMSHAFT DRIVE CHAIN, REMOVAL

1. Remove chain case cover as previously described.
2. Remove camshaft sprocket holder, then the left and right timing chain guides, **Fig. 9.**
3. Depress tensioner to remove drive chain.
4. Remove crankshaft and camshaft sprockets.

CAMSHAFT INSTALLATION

1. With camshaft bearing caps installed, rotate camshaft until timing marks are aligned as shown in **Fig. 10.**

TIMING CHAIN INSTALLATION

1. Install sprocket holder, then left and right chain guides, **Fig. 8.**
2. Rotate crankshaft until No. 1 piston is at TDC on compression stroke.
3. Install tensioner spring assembly onto oil pump body, **Fig. 9.**
4. Install timing chain on camshaft sprocket and crankshaft sprocket. Ensure timing marks are aligned, **Fig. 11.** Timing marks on sprockets are punch marks on teeth while timing marks on chain are plated links.
5. Align crankshaft sprocket to crankshaft keyway and slide into place. Align camshaft sprocket dowel hole to camshaft dowel hole.
6. Install dowel pin, then the distributor drive gear. Install sprocket screw onto camshaft and torque to 40 ft. lbs.

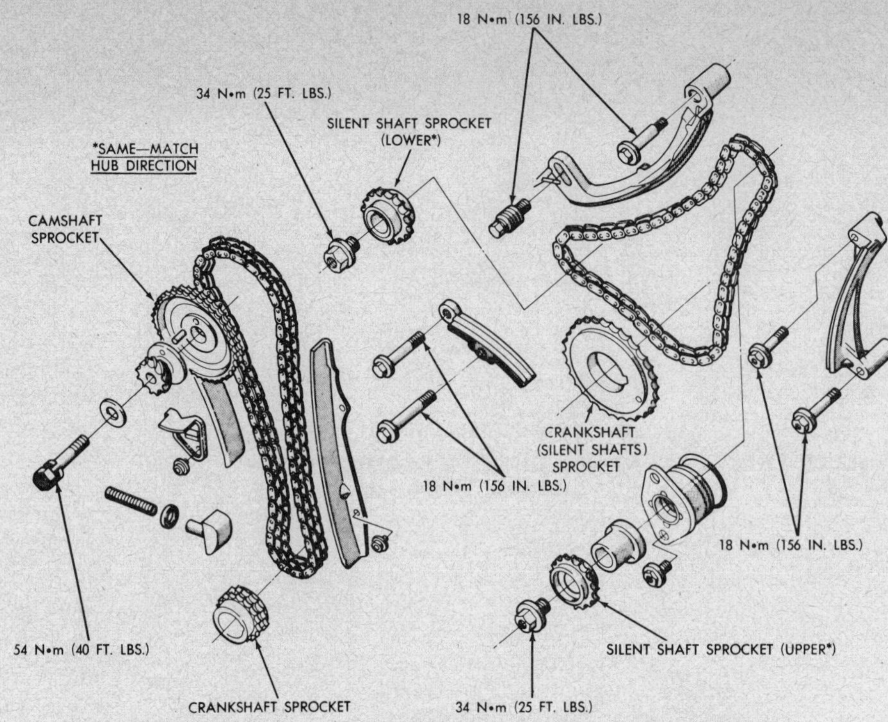

Timing gears & chain assembly. 1982–84

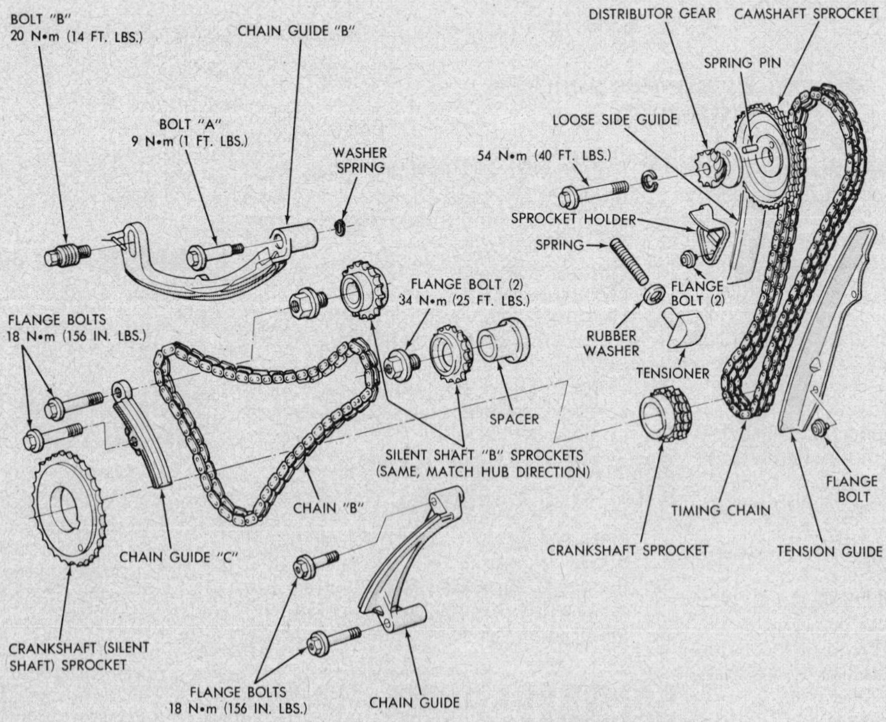

Timing gears & chain assembly. 1985

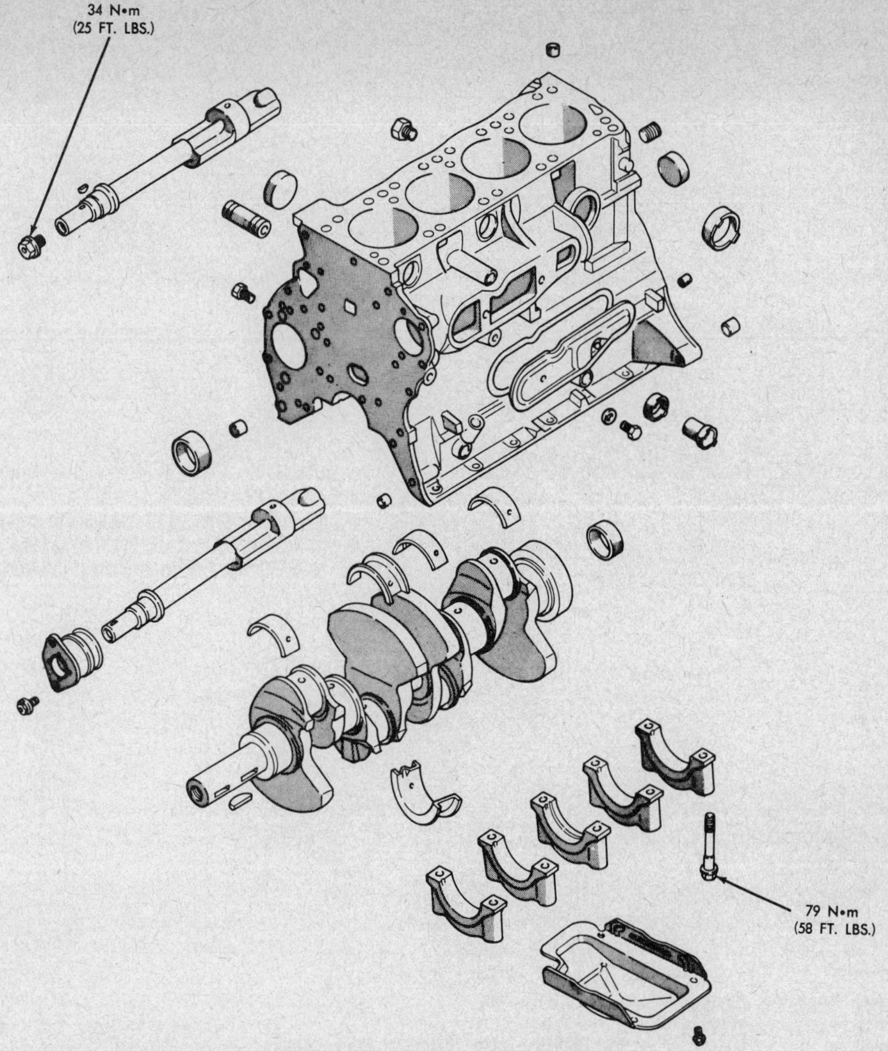

Crankshaft, bearings & silent shaft assembly

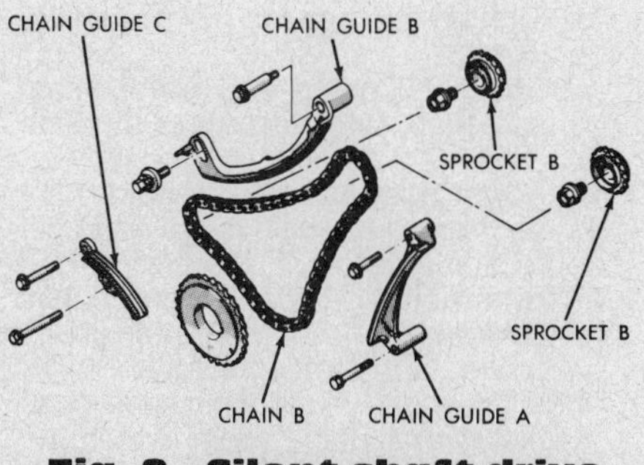

Fig. 8 Silent shaft drive chain, replace

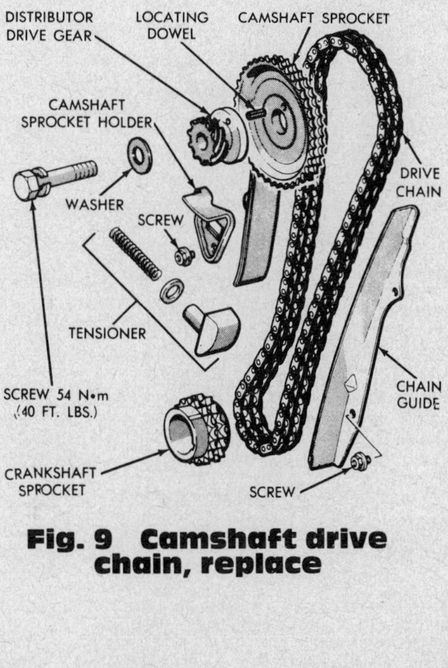

Fig. 9 Camshaft drive chain, replace

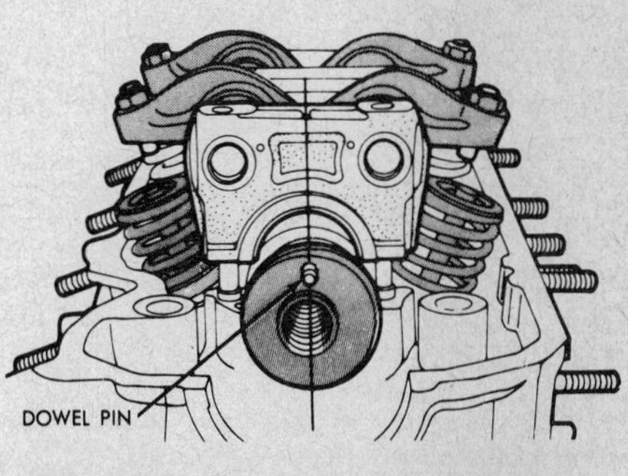

Fig. 10 Camshaft timing mark alignment

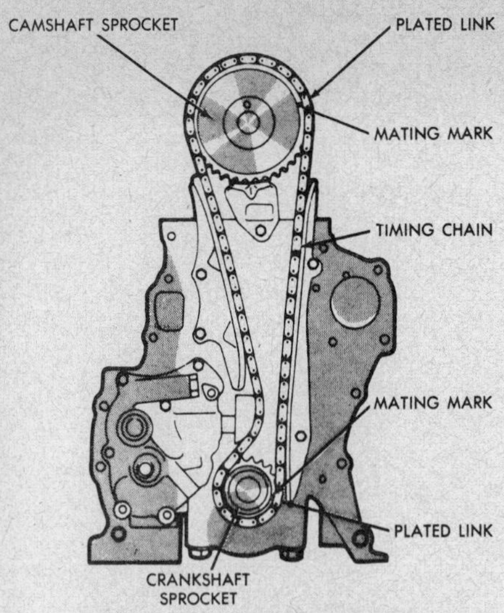

Fig. 11 Timing chain installation

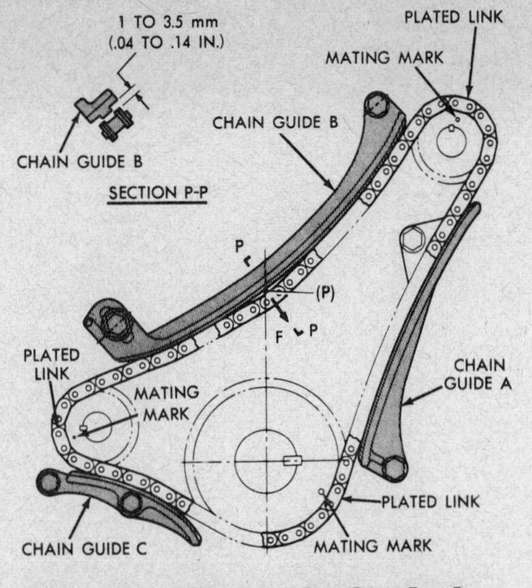

Fig. 12 Silent shaft chain adjustment & installation with engine removed

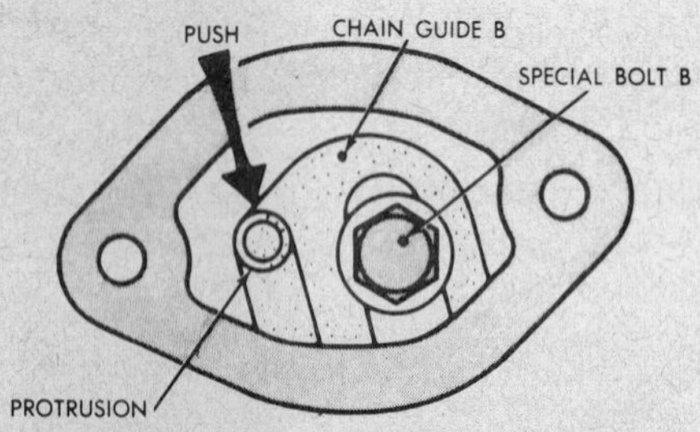

Fig. 13 Silent Shaft chain adjustment with engine installed

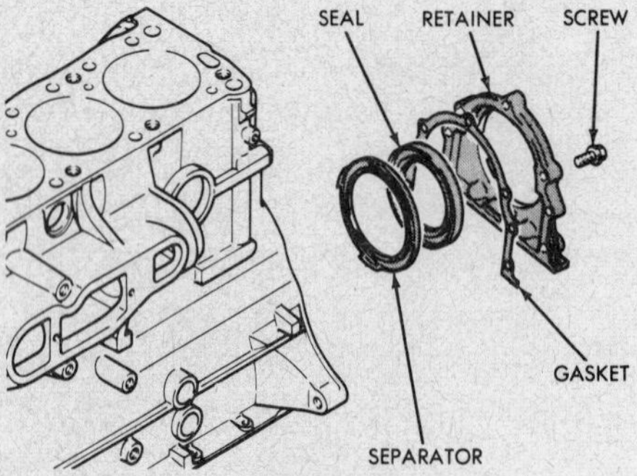

Fig. 14 Rear oil seal, replace

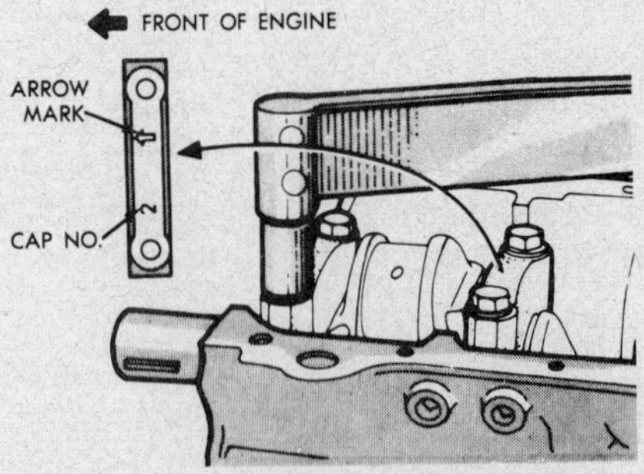

Fig. 15 Main bearing cap installation

SILENT SHAFT CHAIN INSTALLATION & ADJUSTMENT

1. Install silent shaft chain drive pulley onto crankshaft.
2. Install silent shaft chain onto oil pump sprocket and silent shaft sprocket, **Fig. 12.**
3. Ensure timing marks are aligned. Timing marks on sprockets are punch marks on teeth, while timing marks on chain are plated links.
4. Align crankshaft sprocket plated link with punch mark on sprocket.
5. Position chain on crankshaft sprocket, then install oil pump sprocket and silent shaft sprockets on their respective shafts.
6. Install oil pump and silent shaft sprocket screws and torque to 25 ft. lbs.
7. Install three chain guides. Snug tighten retaining bolts.
8. Refer to **Fig. 12** and adjust silent shaft chain tension as follows:

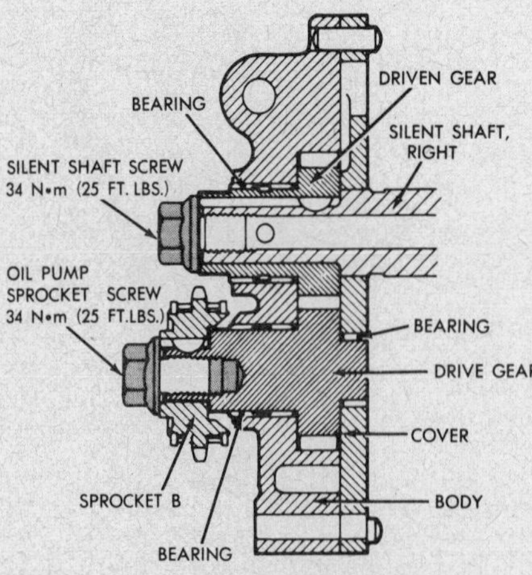

Fig. 16 Oil pump & silent shaft, removal

a. Tighten chain guide "A" mounting screws.
b. Tighten chain guide "C" mounting screws.
c. Shake oil pump and silent shaft sprockets to collect slack at point "P."
d. Adjust position of chain guide "B" so that when chain is pulled in direction of arrow "F," clearance between chain guide "B" and chain links will be .4-.14 in. Tighten chain guide "B" mounting screws.

9. Install new gasket on chain case, coat gasket with suitable sealant, then install chain case to block and torque attaching screws to 156 in. lbs.

TENSION ADJUSTMENT WITH ENGINE INSTALLED

1. Remove cover over access hole in chain case cover, **Fig. 13.**
2. Loosen bolt "B," **Fig. 13.**
3. Apply pressure by hand on boss indicated in **Fig. 13,** then torque bolt "B" to 160 inch lbs.

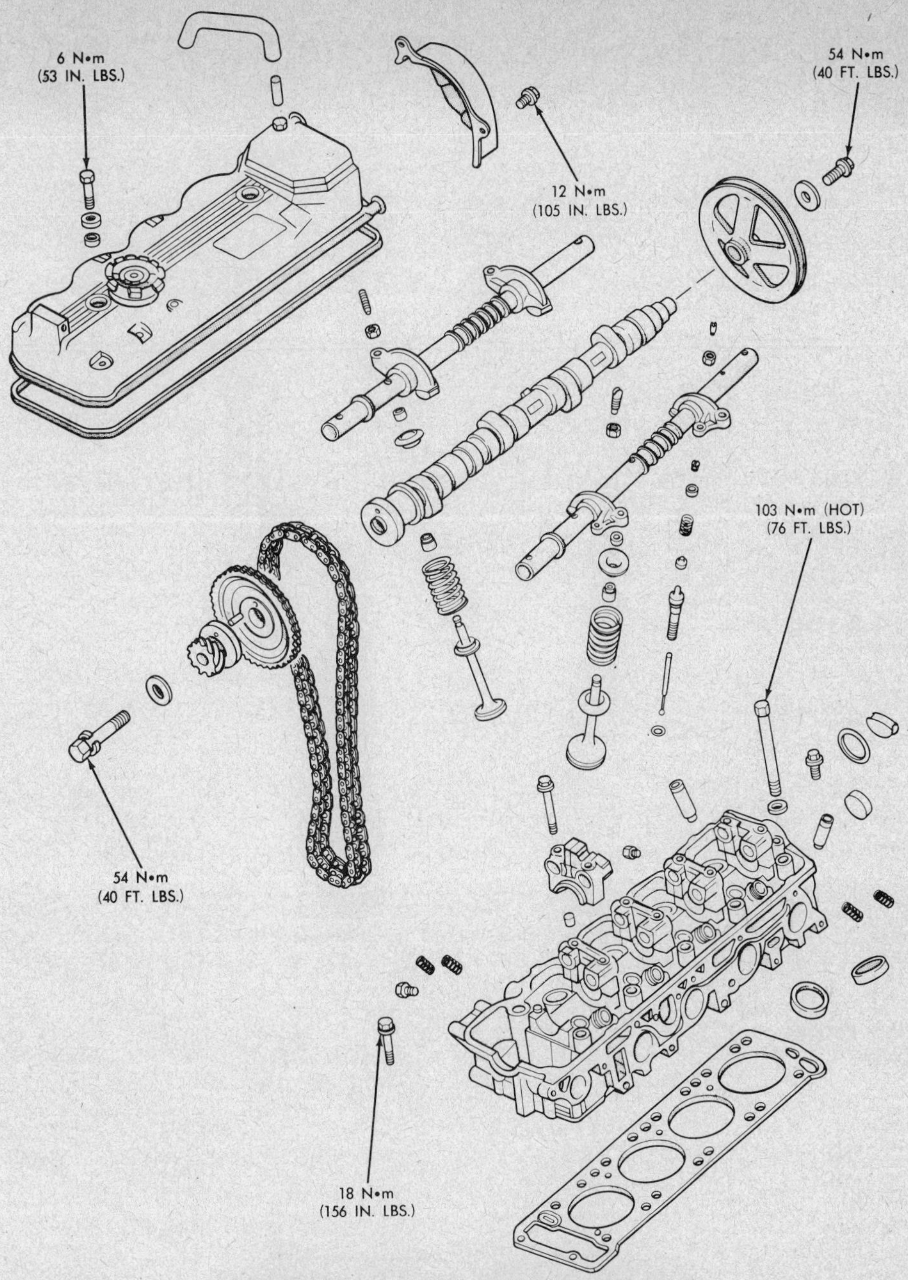

Cylinder head & valve assembly

CRANKSHAFT, BEARINGS & SILENT SHAFT

REAR OIL SEAL, REPLACE

1. Remove screws attaching crankshaft rear oil seal retainer and the retainer, **Fig. 14.**
2. Remove separator from retainer, then the oil seal.
3. Install new seal into retainer, then the separator. Ensure oil hole is positioned at separator bottom.

MAIN BEARING CAPS

1. Install main bearing caps in sequence and ensure arrows on caps are pointed in direction of timing chain, **Fig. 15.**

OIL PUMP & SILENT SHAFT

1. Refer to **Fig. 16** and remove silent shaft screw and the silent shaft.
2. Remove oil pump to cylinder block screw and oil pump.

SILENT SHAFT CLEARANCES

Before installing silent shaft, measure outer diameter to outer bearing clearance. Clearance should be .0008-.0024 in. (.02-.06 mm). Measure inner diameter to inner bearing clearance. Clearance should be .0020-.0035 in. (.05-.09 mm).

PISTON & ROD ASSEMBLY

During installation of piston and rod assembly, arrow at top of piston must face toward front of engine (timing chain), **Fig. 17.** Refer to **Fig. 18** for correct piston ring installation and note following groove clearances:

1. No. 1 upper: .0024-.0039 in. (.06-.10 mm). Wear limit: .004 in. (.1 mm).
2. No. 2 intermediate: .0008-.0024 in. (.02-.06 mm). Wear limit: .004 in. (.1 mm).
3. Oil ring upper: .010-.018 in. (.25-.45 mm). Wear limit: .039 in. (.1 mm).
4. Oil ring intermediate: .010-.018 in. (.25-.45 mm). Wear limit: .039 in. (.1 mm).
5. Oil ring side rail: .008-.035 in. (.2-.4 mm) Wear limit: .059 in. (.15 mm). Connecting rod side clearance should be .004-.010 inch.

INSTALLING PISTON RING SIDE RAIL

1. Place one end of side rail between

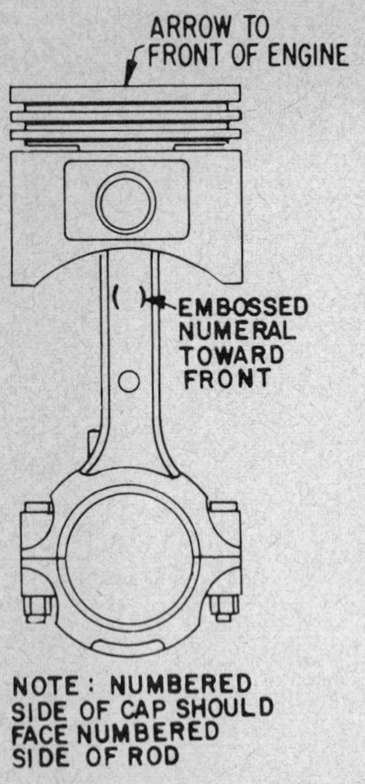

Fig. 17 Piston & rod assembly

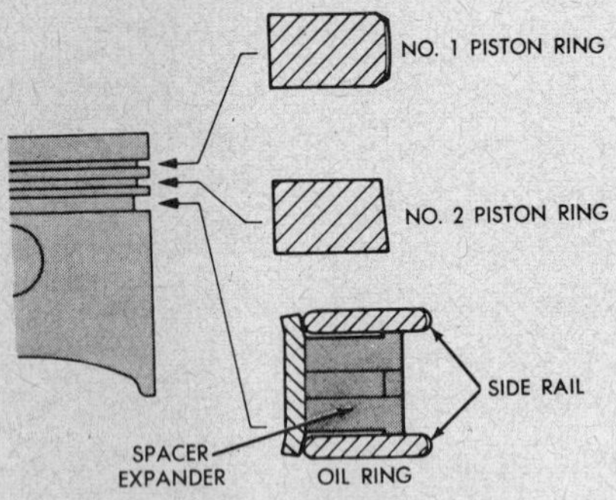

Fig. 18 Piston ring installation

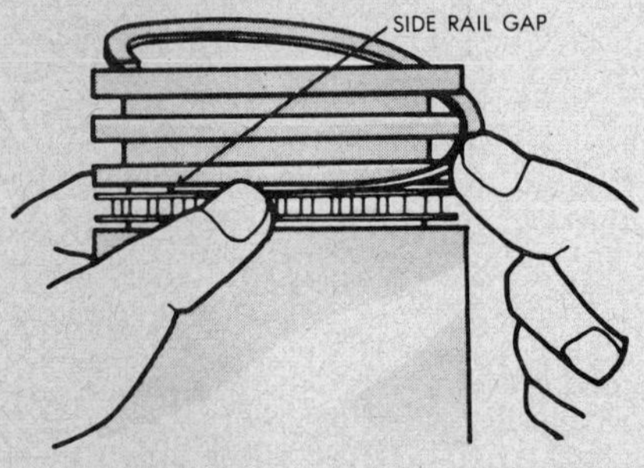

Fig. 19 Installing oil ring side rail

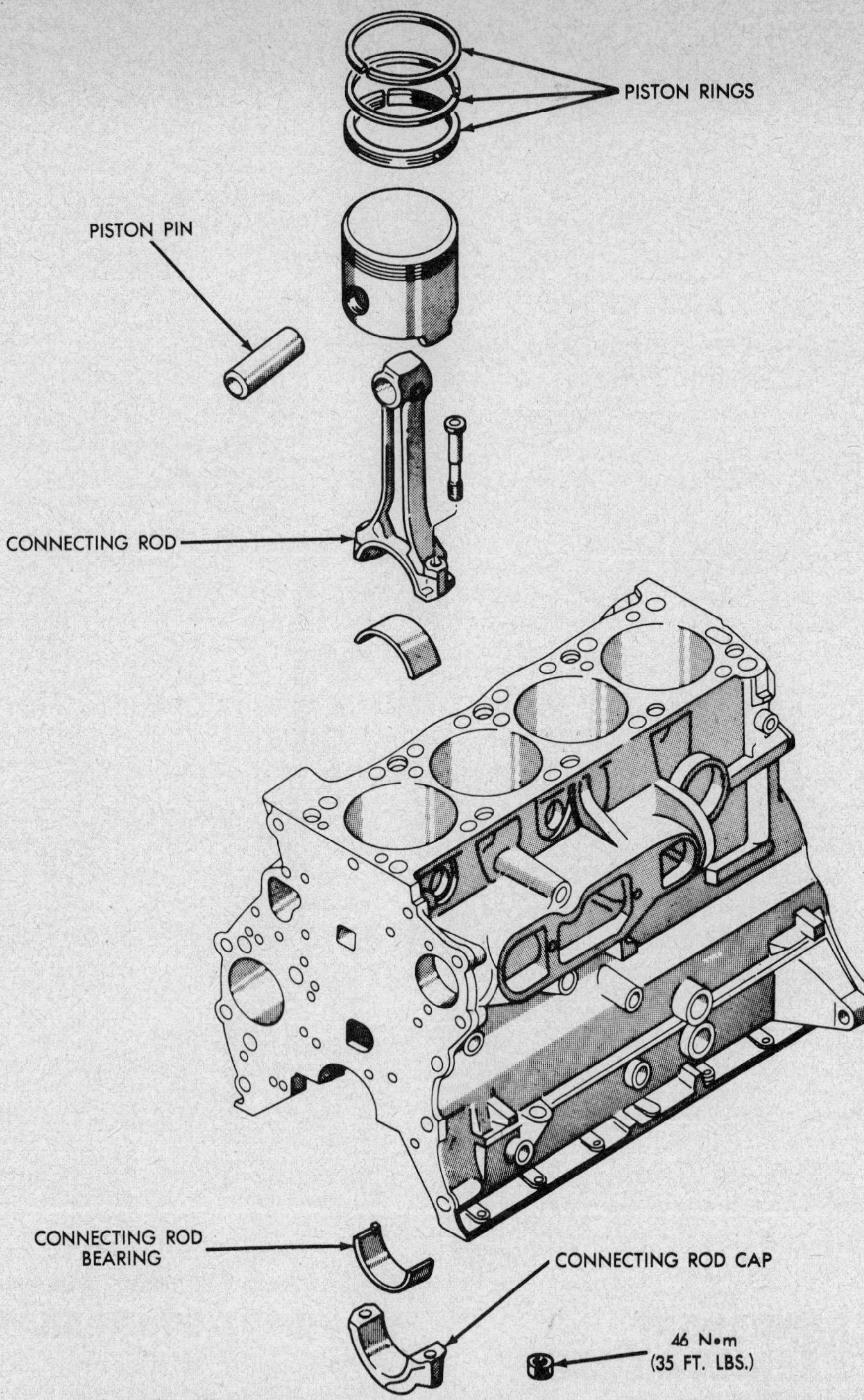

Cylinder block, piston & connecting rod assembly

piston ring groove and spacer expander, **Fig. 19.**

2. Hold end of ring firmly and press downward on portion to be installed until side rail is in position. Do not use a piston ring expander.
3. Install upper side rail first, then the lower side rail.

PISTON RING END GAP LOCATION

1. Position piston ring end gaps as shown in **Fig. 20.**
2. Position oil ring expander gap at least 45° from side rail gaps but not on piston pin center line or in thrust direction.

CYLINDER HEAD & VALVE ASSEMBLY

CYLINDER HEAD, REPLACE

1. Disconnect battery ground cable, then drain cooling system. Disconnect upper radiator hose and heater hoses.
2. Disconnect spark plug wires from spark plugs, then remove distributor.
3. Remove carburetor to valve cover bracket.
4. Disconnect fuel lines from fuel pump, then remove fuel pump.
5. Remove cylinder head cover bolts and cylinder head cover.
6. Disconnect all electrical connectors and vacuum lines from cylinder head.
7. Disconnect throttle linkage from carburetor.

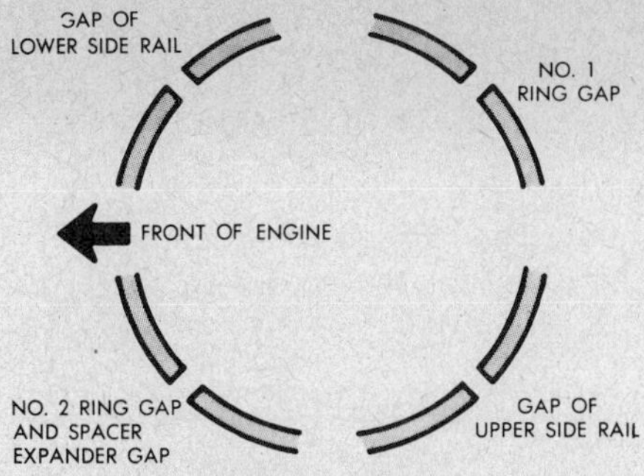

Fig. 20 Piston ring end gap location

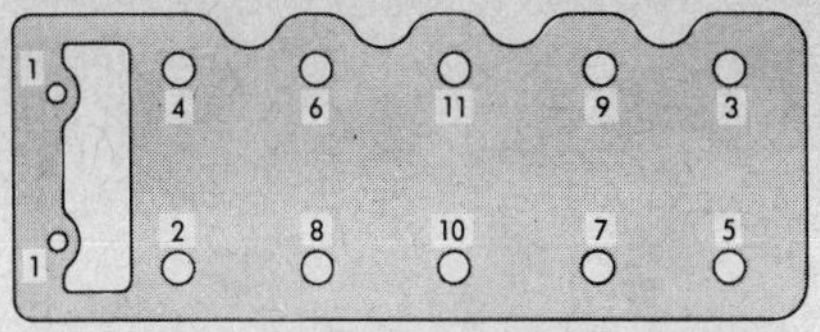

Fig. 21 Cylinder head bolt removal sequence

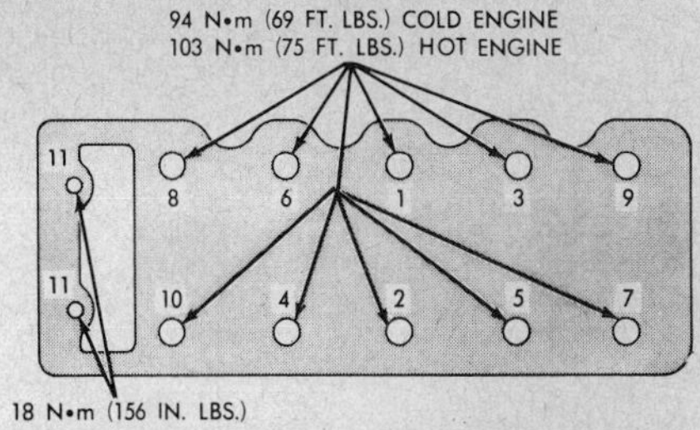

Fig. 22 Cylinder head bolt tightening sequence

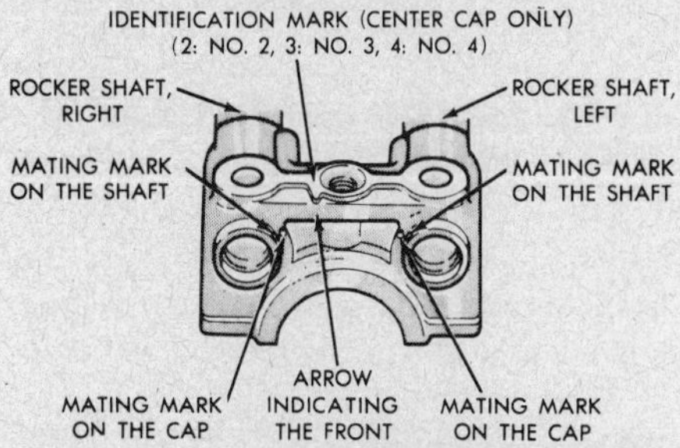

Fig. 23 Camshaft bearing cap installation

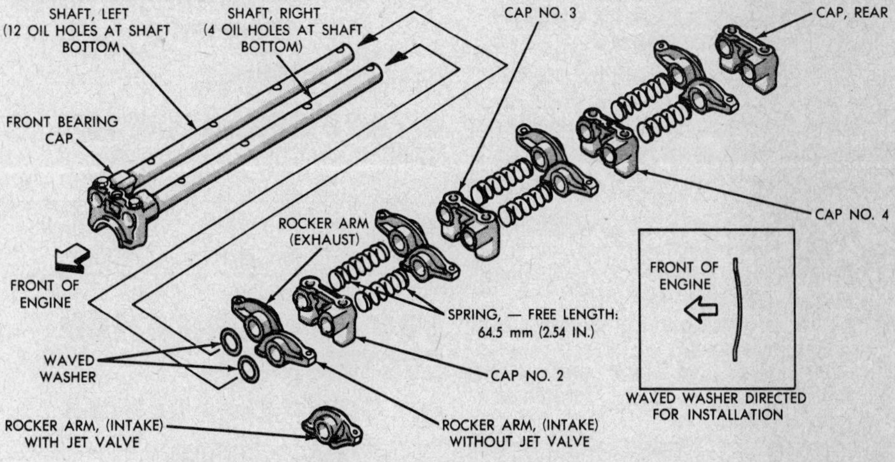

Fig. 24 Rocker arm shaft assembly

8. Remove water pump belt and pulley.
9. Rotate crankshaft until No. 1 piston is at TDC.
10. Paint a white reference mark on timing chain in line with timing mark on camshaft sprocket.
11. Remove camshaft sprocket bolt, sprocket and distributor drive gear.
12. Raise and support vehicle.
13. Disconnect air feed lines.
14. Remove power steering pump and position aside.
15. Disconnect ground strap and remove dipstick tube.
16. Remove exhaust manifold heat shield, then disconnect exhaust pipe from catalytic converter. Lower vehicle.
17. Remove cylinder head bolts in sequence shown in **Fig. 21.**
18. Reverse procedure to install. Refer to cylinder head bolt tightening sequence, **Fig. 22,** tighten cylinder head bolts in three steps as follows:
    a. Torque all bolts except No. 11 to 35 ft. lbs.
    b. Torque all bolts except No. 11 to 69 ft. lbs. on a cold engine or 75 ft. lbs. on a hot engine.
    c. Torque cylinder head to chain case cover bolts (No. 11) to 156 inch lbs.

CAMSHAFT BEARING CAP

1. Align camshaft bearing caps with arrows pointing toward timing chain, **Fig. 23.** Install caps in numerical order.

ROCKER ARM SHAFT ASSEMBLY

1. Refer to **Fig. 24** and install bolts into front bearing caps.

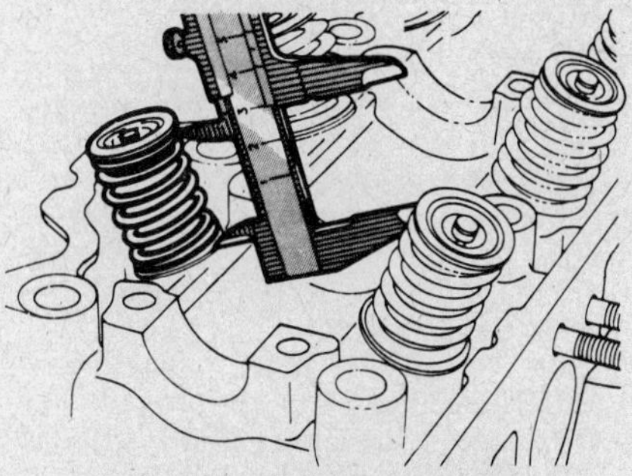

Fig. 25 Measuring installed valve spring height

2. Install wave washers, rocker arms, bearing caps and springs in order shown, **Fig. 24.**
3. Place rocker shaft assembly into position, then rotate camshaft until dowel pin hole is at vertical center line, **Fig. 10.**
4. Tighten camshaft bearing cap bolts in the following order:
    a. No. 3 cap bolts to 85 inch. lbs.
    b. No. 2 cap bolts to 85 inch. lbs.
    c. No. 4 cap bolts to 85 inch. lbs.
    d. Front cap bolts to 85 inch. lbs.
    e. Rear cap bolts to 85 inch. lbs.
5. Repeat step 4, increasing torque to 175 inch lbs.

INSTALLED VALVE SPRING HEIGHT

1. Measure installed height of valve spring between spring seat and spring retainer, **Fig. 25.** Installed height should be 1.590 in. If height is greater than 1.629 in., replace spring.

VALVE CLEARANCE ADJUSTMENT

Check hot torque on cylinder head bolts before performing valve adjustments.

1. With engine at operating temperature, position piston at TDC on compression stroke.
2. Loosen valve adjuster locknut, then adjust valve clearance by rotating adjusting screw while measuring with a feeler gauge, **Fig. 26.**
3. Valve clearance should be as follows: Intake–.006 in.; Exhaust–.010 in.
4. Tighten locknut securely while holding adjusting screw with screwdriver.

JET VALVE SERVICE

1. Install jet valve assembly into cylinder head.
2. Using suitable socket, torque jet valve to 168 inch lbs. (14 ft. lbs.). **Ensure that socket wrench is not tilted with respect to center line of jet valve as damage to valve stem may result. Check hot torque on cylinder head bolts before performing jet valve adjustments.**
3. With engine at operating temperature, position piston at TDC of compression stroke.
4. Loosen jet valve adjuster locknut, **Fig. 27.**
5. Proper valve clearance is obtained by rotating adjusting screw while measuring clearance with feeler gauge.

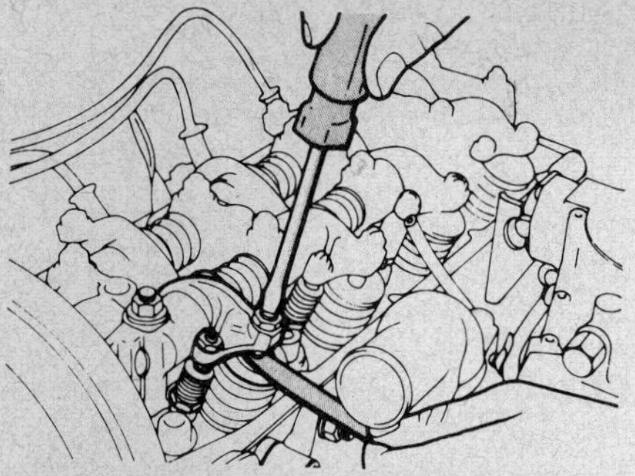

Fig. 26 Adjusting valve clearance

6. Valve clearance should be .006 in.
7. Tighten locknut securely while holding adjusting screw with screwdriver.

INTAKE MANIFOLD, REPLACE

1. Disconnect battery ground cable and drain coolant system.
2. Disconnect hose between water pump and intake manifold.
3. Disconnect carburetor air horn and position aside.
4. Disconnect carburetor and intake manifold vacuum hoses, throttle linkage, and fuel line.
5. Remove fuel filter and fuel pump and position aside.
6. Remove mounting nuts and washers securing intake manifold and the intake manifold.

VALVE CLEARANCE SPECIFICATIONS

Year	Engine	Int.	Exh.
1982-85	4-156	.006H	.010H

VALVE LIFT SPECIFICATIONS

Engine	Year	Int.	Exh.
4-156	1982-85	.410	.410

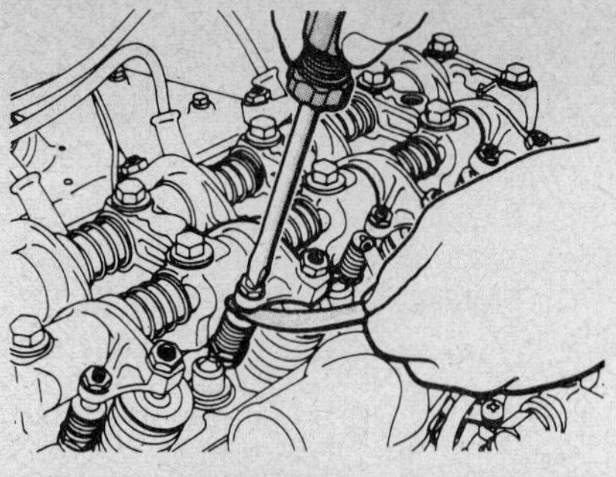

Fig. 27 Adjusting jet valve clearance

VALVE TIMING

INTAKE OPENS BEFORE TDC

Engine	Year	Degrees
4-156	1982-85	25

ENGINE LUBRICATION SYSTEM

OIL PUMP CLEARANCES

Refer to **Fig. 16** and measure the following clearances:

1. Drive gear to body—.0043-.0059 in. (.11-.15 mm).
2. Driven gear endplay—.0024-.0047 in. (.06-.10 mm) for 1984-85 models.
3. Driven gear endplay—.0024-.0047 in. (.06-.12 mm) for 1982-83 models; .0016-.0039 in. (.04-.10 mm) for 1984-85 models.
4. Drive gear endplay—.0016-.0028 in. (.04-.07 mm) for 1982-83 models; .0020-.0043 in. (.05-.11 mm) for 1984-85 models.
5. Drive gear to body clearance—.0043-.0059 in. (.11-.15 mm).
6. Drive gear to bearing—.0008-.0020 in (.02-.05 mm).
7. Relief valve spring length—1.850 in. (47 mm).
8. Relief valve spring load—9.5 lbs. at 1.575 in. (40 mm).

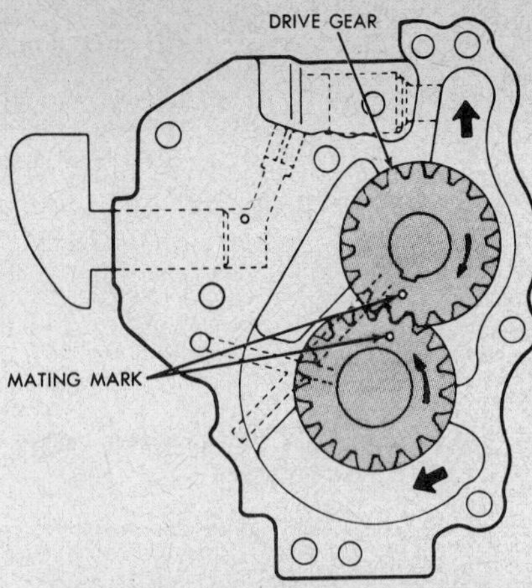

Fig. 28 Oil pump gear alignment

Refer to **Fig. 28** and align mating marks of drive and driven gears, then prime pump with clean oil and install onto engine.

WATER PUMP REPLACE

1. Disconnect battery ground cable.
2. Drain cooling system.
3. Disconnect radiator hose, bypass hose, and heater hose from water pump.
4. Remove drive pulley shield.
5. Remove locking screw and pivot screws.
6. Remove drive belt and the water pump from engine.
7. Reverse procedure to install.

BELT TENSION DATA

Belt	New Lbs.	Used Lbs.
1982–85		
Power Steer.	95	80
Alternator	115	80
Air Cond.	115	80

Clutch & Manual Transaxle Section

INDEX

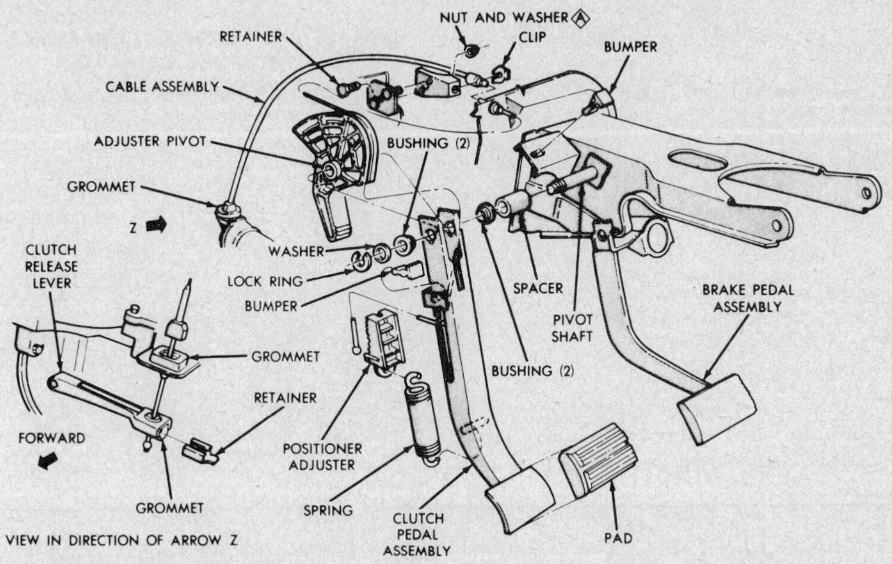

Fig. 1 Clutch cable routing. Except models w/4-105 engine

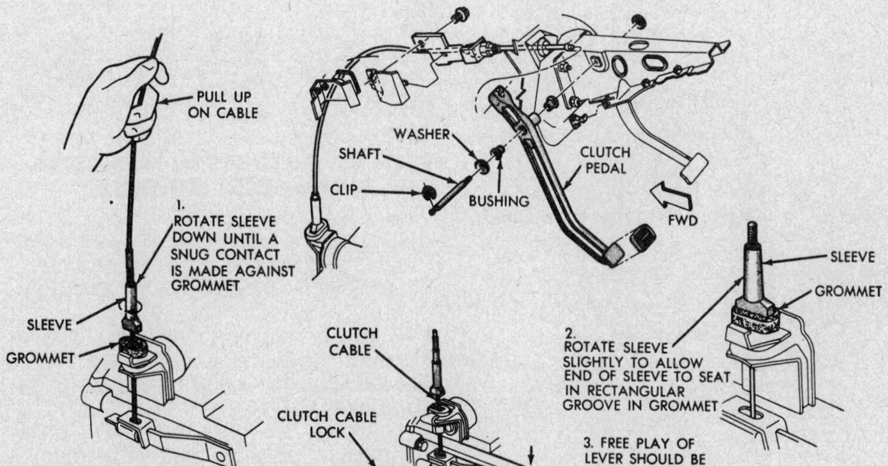

Fig. 2 Clutch pedal freeplay adjustment. Models w/4-105 engine

CLUTCH

ADJUST

EXCEPT MODELS W/4-105 ENGINE

The clutch release cable, **Fig. 1,** on these models cannot be adjusted. When the cable is properly routed, the spring between clutch pedal and positioner adjuster will hold clutch cable in proper position. An adjuster pivot is used to hold release cable in place to ensure complete clutch release when clutch pedal is depressed.

MODELS W/4-105 ENGINE

1. Pull upward on clutch cable at housing attachment, **Fig. 2.**
2. Rotate sleeve downward until sleeve snugly contacts grommet.
3. Rotate sleeve so end of sleeve seats into rectangular groove in grommet.
4. Check for proper operation.

CLUTCH

REPLACE

EXCEPT MODELS W/4-105 ENGINE

1. Remove transaxle as outlined under "Manual Transaxle, Replace" procedure.
2. Mark relationship between clutch cover and flywheel for reference during reassembly, then insert suitable clutch disc aligning tool through clutch disc hub.
3. Gradually loosen clutch cover attaching bolts, then remove pressure plate and cover assembly and disc from flywheel.
4. Remove clutch release shaft and slide release bearing assembly off input shaft seal retainer. Remove fork from release bearing thrust plate.
5. Reverse procedure to install. Align reference marks made during disassembly, then using a clutch disc alignment tool, install disc, plate and cover to flywheel. Refer to **Figs. 3 and 4** for torque specifications.

MODELS W/4-105 ENGINE

Removal

1. Remove transaxle as outlined under "Manual Transaxle, Replace" procedure.

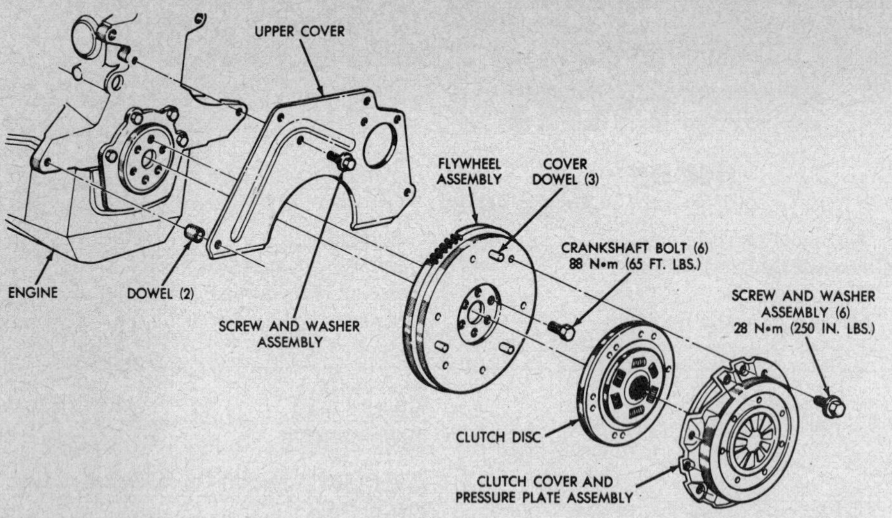

Fig. 3 Clutch assembly. Models w/4-135 & 4-153 engines

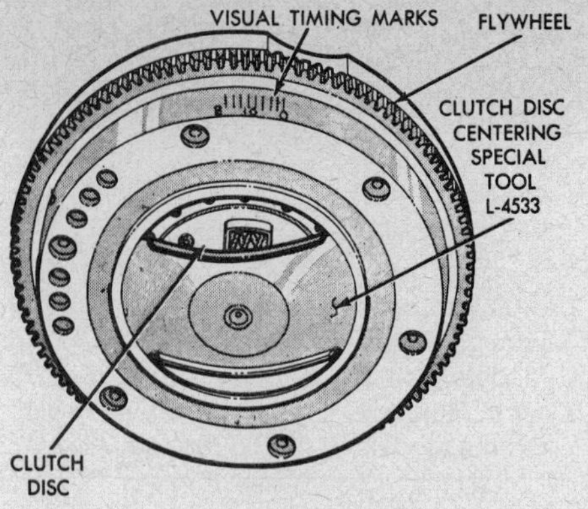

Fig. 6 Centering clutch disc. Models w/4-105 engine

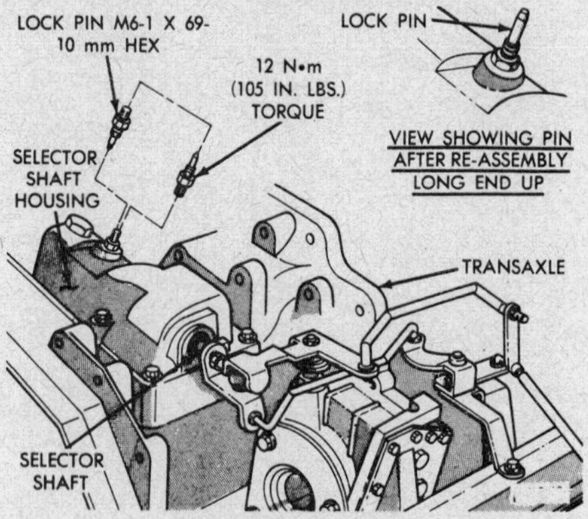

Fig. 7 Lock pin removal & installation

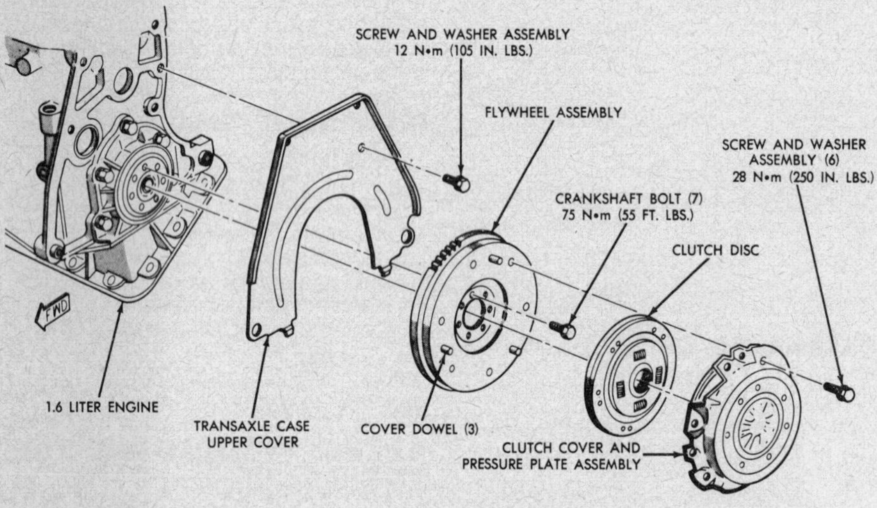

Fig. 4 Clutch assembly. Models w/4-97 engine

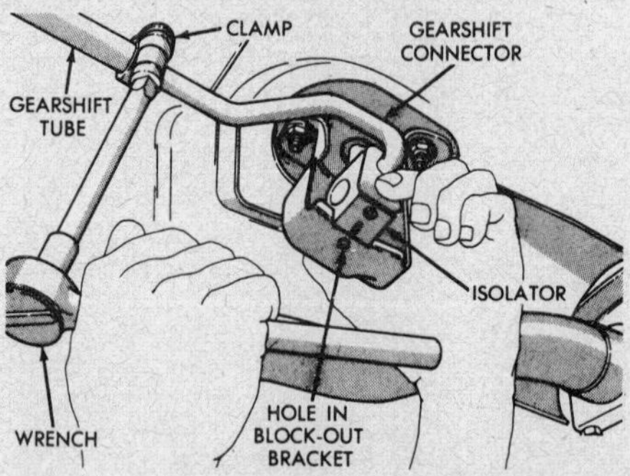

Fig. 8 Adjusting rod-type gear shift linkage

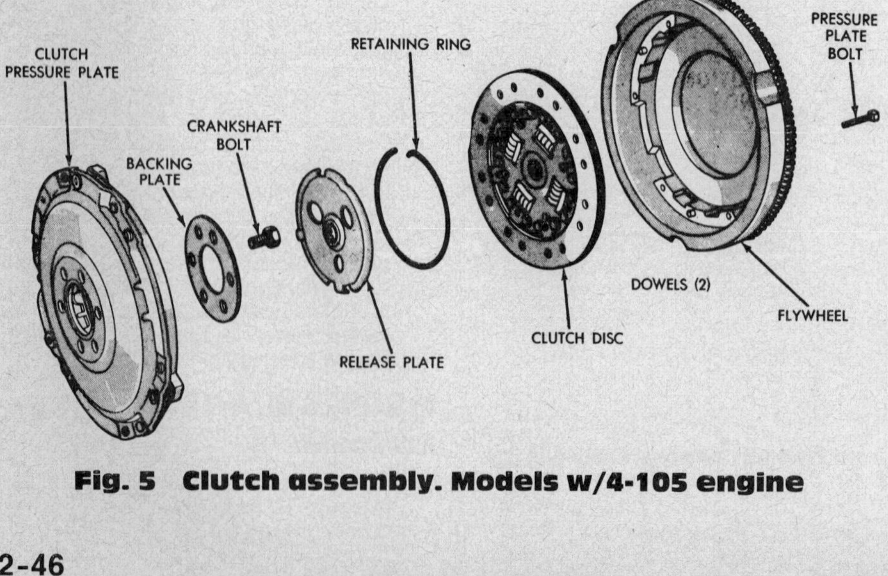

Fig. 5 Clutch assembly. Models w/4-105 engine

2. Gradually loosen and remove bolts attaching flywheel to pressure plate.
3. Remove flywheel and clutch disc, **Fig. 5.**
4. Remove retaining ring and release plate.
5. Mark position of pressure plate on crankshaft.
6. Gradually loosen and remove bolts attaching pressure plate to flywheel.
7. Remove spacer and pressure plate.

Installation

1. Thoroughly clean surfaces of flywheel and pressure plate with fine sandpaper or crocus cloth. Also, ensure that all oil or grease has been removed.

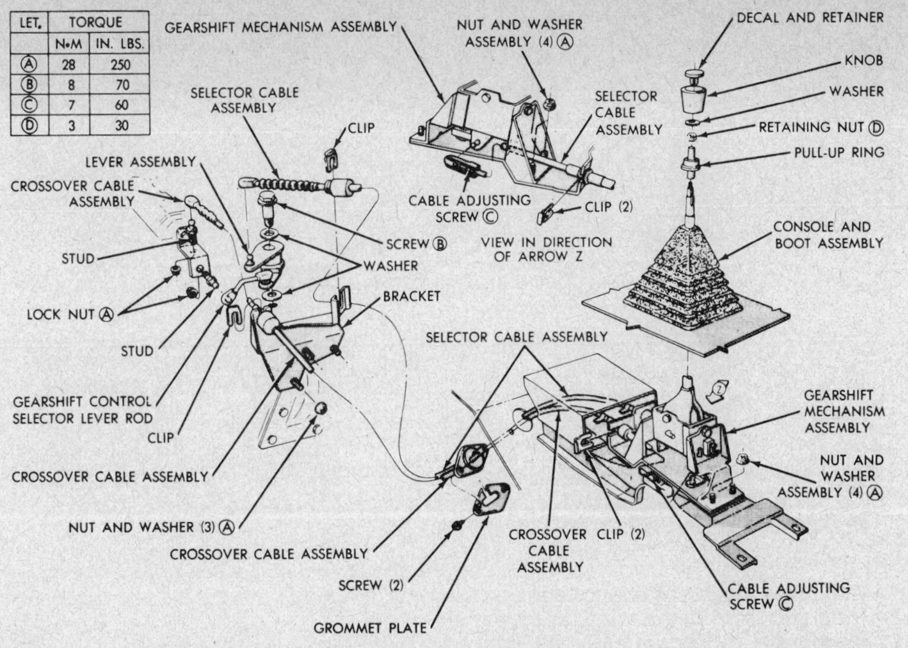

LET.	TORQUE	
	N•M	IN. LBS.
Ⓐ	28	250
Ⓑ	8	70
Ⓒ	7	60
Ⓓ	3	30

Fig. 9 Cable operated gearshift linkage. 1982–83 models w/4-135 engine

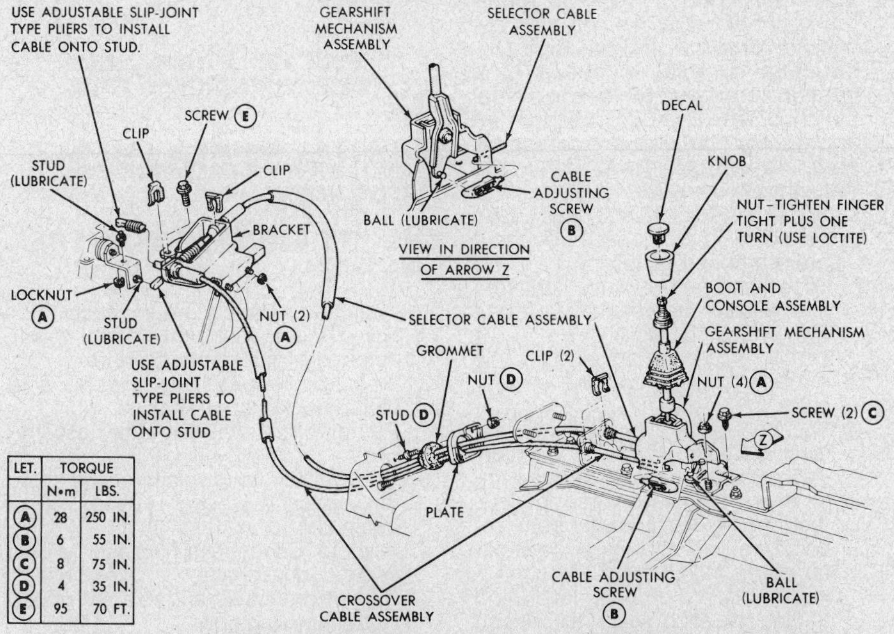

LET.	TORQUE	
	N•m	LBS.
Ⓐ	28	250 IN.
Ⓑ	6	55 IN.
Ⓒ	8	75 IN.
Ⓓ	4	35 IN.
Ⓔ	95	70 FT.

Fig. 10 Cable operated gearshift linkage. Except 1982–83 models w/4-135 engine

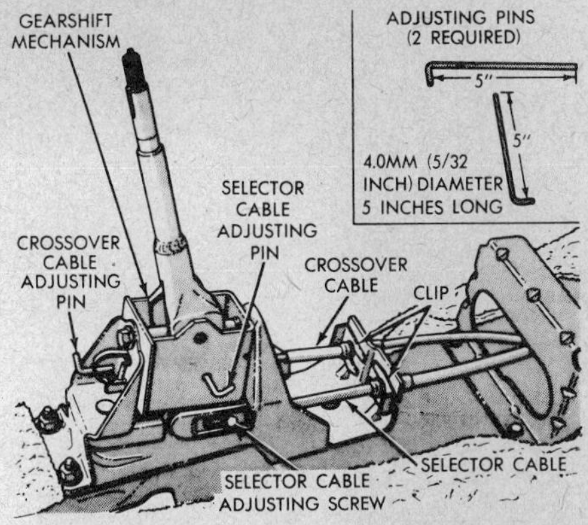

Fig. 11 Cable adjusting pins

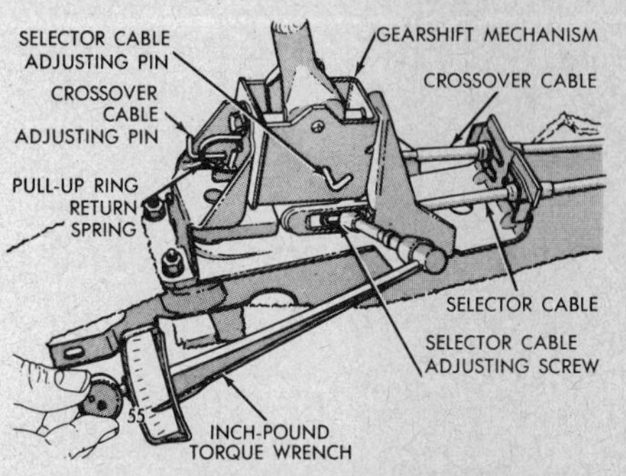

Fig. 12 Adjusting selector cable

2. Align marks on pressure plate and crankshaft and install pressure plate and spacer on crankshaft. Install and torque attaching bolts to 55 ft. lbs. (75 Nm).
3. Install release plate and retaining ring.
4. Using tool L-4533 to center clutch disc, **Fig. 6,** install disc and flywheel onto pressure plate. Ensure the drilled mark on flywheel is at the top so the two dowels in flywheel align proper holes in pressure plate.
5. Install and torque flywheel to pressure plate attaching bolts to 15 ft. lbs. (20 Nm).
6. Remove centering tool.
7. Install transaxle and adjust clutch.
8. Check for proper operation.

GEARSHIFT LINKAGE

ADJUST

ROD LINKAGE

1. Remove lock pin from transaxle selector shaft housing, **Fig. 7.**
2. Reverse lock pin so long end is facing downward, and insert pin into same threaded hole while pushing selector shaft into selector housing.
3. Raise and support vehicle then loosen clamp bolt that secures gearshift tube to gearshift rod.
4. Check that gearshift connector slides and rotates freely in gearshift tube.
5. Position shifter mechanism connector assembly so that isolator is spaced .050 inch away from upstanding flange, while rib on isolator is aligned fore and aft with hole in blocker bracket. Hold connector isolator in this position and torque clamp bolt on gearshift tube to 170 inch lbs. No significant force should be placed on linkage during this procedure, **Fig. 8.**
6. Lower vehicle, remove lock pin from selector shaft housing and reinstall lock pin in reversed position. Torque pin to 105 in. lbs.
7. Check for proper operation.

CABLE LINKAGE

1. Remove lock pin from transaxle selector shaft housing, **Figs. 7 through 10.**
2. Reverse lock pin so long end is down, and insert lock pin into same threaded hole while pushing selector shaft in 1-2 neutral position.
3. Remove gearshift knob, retaining nut and pull-up ring.
4. On all models except Daytona and Laser, remove console attaching screws and console.
5. On Daytona and Laser models, remove console as follows:
   a. Remove front seat assemblies.
   b. Remove 2 forward console bezel attaching screws and bezel.
   c. Remove carpet retaining clips from console.

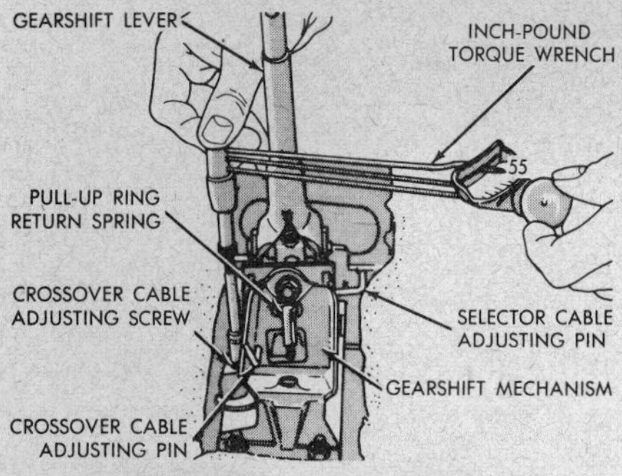

Fig. 13 Adjusting crossover cable

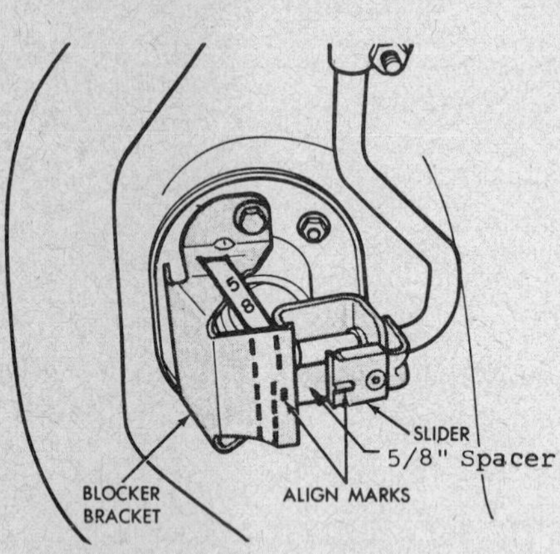

Fig. 16 Revised gearshift blocker bracket. Models w/4-105 engine

d. Remove console attaching bolts and screws.
e. Disconnect electrical connectors from console, then remove console from vehicle.

6. On all models, fabricate 2 cable adjusting pins as shown in **Fig. 11.**
7. Adjust selector cable and torque adjusting screw to 60 inch lbs. (7 Nm) on 1982-83 models, or 55 inch lbs. (6 Nm) on except 1982-83 models, **Fig. 12. The selector cable adjusting screw must be properly torqued.**
8. Adjust crossover cable and torque adjusting screw to 60 inch lbs. (7 Nm) on 1982-83 models, or 55 inch lbs. (6 Nm) on except 1982-83 models, **Fig. 13. The crossover cable adjusting screw must be properly torqued.**
9. Remove lock pin from selector shaft housing and reinstall lock pin so long end is up in selector shaft housing, **Fig. 7.**
10. Check for proper operation and reinstall console, pull-up ring, retaining nut and gearshift knob. **High shift effort or gear blockage on Daytona and Laser models, and 1985-88 Lancer and LeBaron GTS models with 5 speed manual transaxle, may be caused by improper shifter crossover adjustment. To check crossover adjustment place selector in third gear and, with engine**

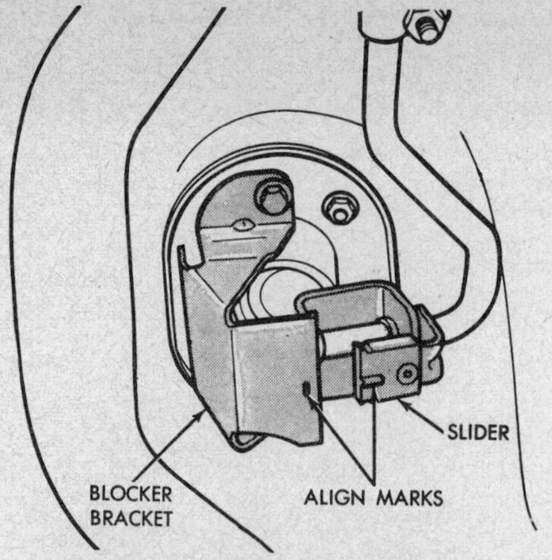

Fig. 14 Aligning slider & block bracket marks. Models w/4-105 engine

off, make rapid shifts between second and third gears while applying moderate (approximately 20 lbs.) preload toward reverse/neutral position. Place selector in second gear and make slow shifts between first and second gears while applying minimal crossover preload toward reverse/neutral position. Obstruction or total blockage of a gear during above tests, after initial synchronizer line-up, indicates an improperly adjusted crossover gate. Adjust crossover using the following procedure:

a. Shift transaxle into first gear. Leave transaxle in first gear throughout adjustment procedure.
b. Slide driver's seat fully rearward and remove carpet pad from left side of floor console.
c. Locate crossover adjusting screw through left side opening of console.
d. Loosen adjusting screw until shift lever is free in crossover direction.
e. Push shift lever toward reverse until lever contacts reverse lockout, then move lever away from reverse toward fifth gear approximately 1/8 inch.
f. Hold position of shift lever and torque adjusting screw to 55 inch lbs.
g. Replace carpet, then recheck operation of shifter.

MODELS W/4-105 ENGINE

1. Place shift lever in neutral at 3-4 position.
2. Loosen shift tube clamp.
3. Align tab on slider with hole in blocker bracket, **Fig. 14.**
4. Install a 1/2 inch spacer, **Fig. 15**, to set gearshift unit lock-out. **If blocker bracket has a 5/8 stamp imprint at forward vertical face of the reinforcement strap, Fig. 16, it indicates that a 5/8 inch spacer must be used in place of the 1/2 inch spacer.**
5. Tighten shift tube clamp and remove spacer.
6. Check for proper operation.

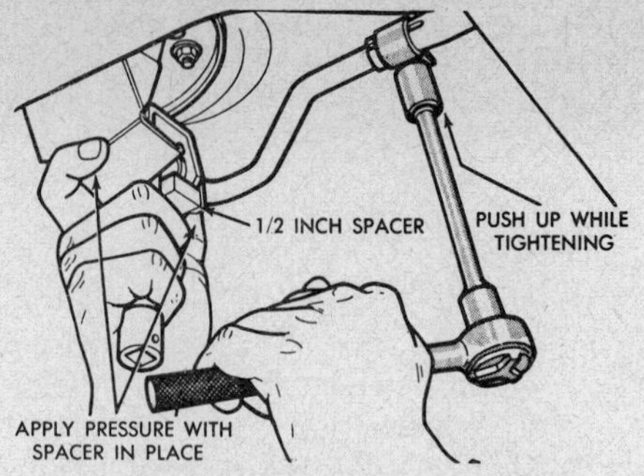

Fig. 15 Installing spacer. Models w/4-105 engine

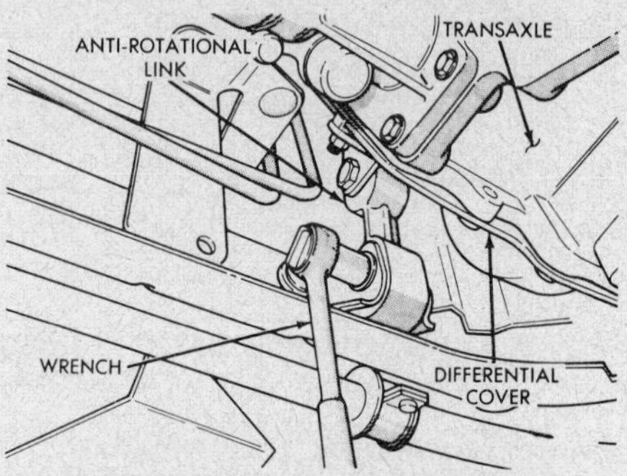

Fig. 17 Removing anti-rotational link

MANUAL TRANSAXLE REPLACE

EXCEPT MODELS W/4-105 ENGINE

1. Disconnect battery ground cable.
2. Raise and support vehicle and install suitable engine support fixture.
3. Disconnect gearshift linkage and clutch cable from transaxle.
4. Remove front wheel and tire assemblies.
5. Remove left front splash shield, then the impact bracket from transaxle if so equipped.
6. Refer to "Driveshafts, Replace" to disconnect driveshafts.
7. Support transaxle and remove upper clutch housing bolts.
8. Remove left engine mount from transaxle noting location of bolts.
9. Remove anti-rotational link, **Fig. 17.**
10. Move engine and transaxle toward left side of vehicle until mainshaft clears clutch and lower and remove transaxle.
11. Reverse procedure to install. When installing left engine mount, refer to "Engine mounts" section.

MODELS W/4-105 ENGINE

1. Disconnect battery ground cable.
2. Disconnect shift linkage rods, starter wiring and back-up lamp switch wiring.
3. Remove starter and disconnect clutch cable.
4. Remove bolt attaching speedometer adapter to transaxle.

5. With speedometer cable housing connected, pull adapter and pinion from transaxle.
6. Raise and support vehicle. Also, support engine with suitable equipment.
7. Disconnect righthand drive shaft and position aside.
8. Remove lefthand drive shaft.
9. Remove left splash shield.
10. Drain transaxle fluid.
11. Remove bolts from left engine mount.
12. Remove transaxle to engine attaching nuts and bolts.
13. Slide transaxle toward left side of vehicle until mainshaft clears clutch.
14. Lower and remove transaxle from vehicle.
15. Reverse procedure to install.

Rear Axle, Rear Suspension & Brakes Section

INDEX

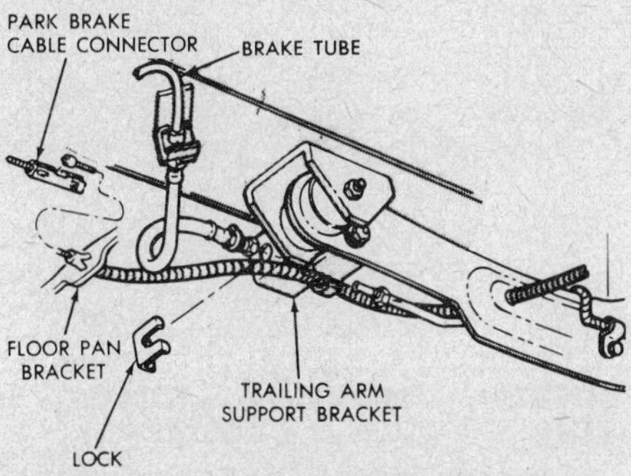

Fig. 1 Parking brake cable & brake tube assemblies. Exc. Horizon, Omni, Charger & Turismo

REAR AXLE
REPLACE
EXC. HORIZON, OMNI, CHARGER & TURISMO

1. Raise and support vehicle, support rear axle, and remove rear wheels.
2. Disconnect parking brake cable at connector and cable housing at floor pan bracket, **Fig. 1.**
3. Disconnect brake tube assembly from brake line on trailing arm support bracket, and remove lock.
4. On 1986-88 models equipped with automatic load leveling, disconnect link from sensor to track bar.
5. Disconnect shock absorbers and track bar at rear axle. Support track bar end.
6. Lower axle until spring and isolator assemblies, **Figs. 2, 3 and 4,** come free and can be removed.
7. Support pivot ends of trailing arms and remove pivot bracket bolts. Lower and remove axle from vehicle.
8. Reverse procedure to install. Torque brake tube assembly to hose fitting to 140 inch lbs. Torque other components as shown in **Figs. 2, 3 and 4.**

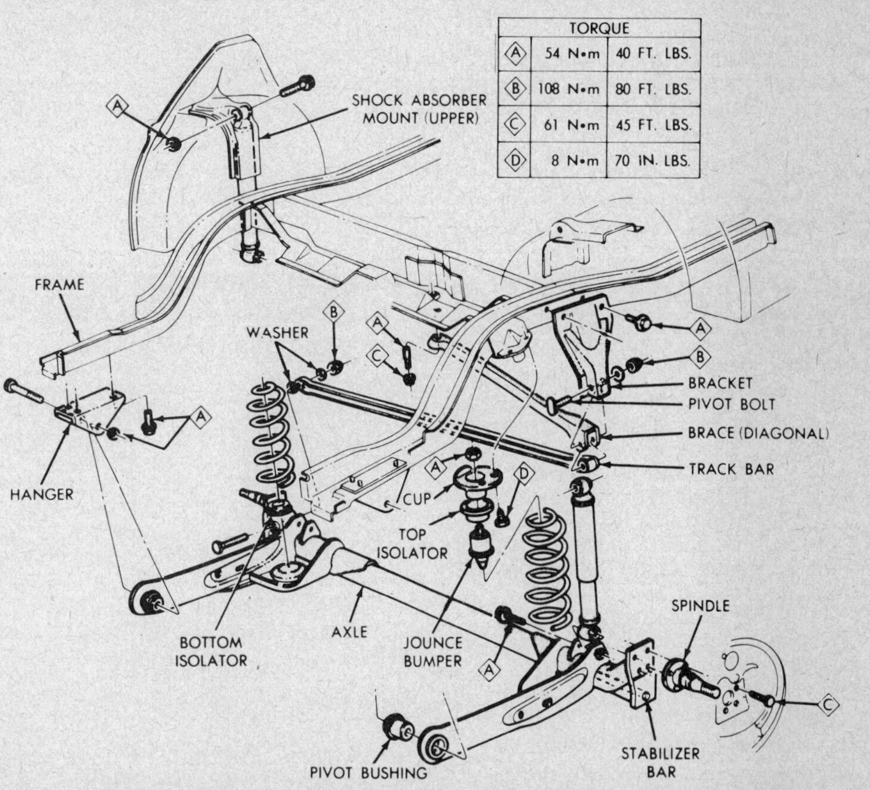

TORQUE		
A	54 N•m	40 FT. LBS.
B	108 N•m	80 FT. LBS.
C	61 N•m	45 FT. LBS.
D	8 N•m	70 IN. LBS.

Fig. 2 Rear axle & suspension assembly. 1982–83 Aries & Reliant; 1982–83 LeBaron & 400; 1983 New Yorker, E Class, Executive & 600

HORIZON, OMNI, CHARGER & TURISMO

1. Raise and support vehicle.
2. Remove wheels.
3. Remove brake fitting and retaining clips securing flexible brake line.
4. Remove parking brake cable adjusting connection nut.
5. Release parking brake cables from bracket by slipping ball-end of cables through brake connectors.
6. Pull parking brake cable through bracket.
7. Remove brake drums.
8. Remove brake assembly and spindle retaining bolts, **Fig. 5.**
9. Position spindle aside using a piece of wire.
10. Support axle and suspension with a suitable jack.
11. Remove shock absorber mounting bolts.
12. Remove trailing arm to hanger bracket mounting bolt.
13. Lower rear axle from vehicle.
14. Reverse procedure to install.

SHOCK ABSORBER & COIL SPRING

REPLACE

EXC. HORIZON, OMNI, CHARGER, TURISMO

Removal

1. Raise and support vehicle.
2. Support axle assembly and remove both upper and lower shock absorber attaching bolts and the shock absorbers. On 1986-88 models equipped with automatic load leveling, remove link from track bar to sensor.
3. Lower axle assembly until spring and spring upper isolater can be removed, **Figs. 2, 3 and 4.**

Installation

1. Position jounce bumper to rail, install and torque attaching screws to 70 in. lbs. (7 Nm).
2. Install isolator over jounce bumper and install spring.
3. Raise axle and install shock absorber. Loosely assemble lower shock absorber attaching bolts and torque upper attaching bolts to 40 ft. lbs. On 1986-88 models with load leveling, attach link to track bar
4. With suspension supporting vehicle, torque shock absorber attaching screws to 40 ft. lbs. (54 Nm).

HORIZON, OMNI, CHARGER & TURISMO

Replacement

1. Remove upper shock absorber mounting protective cap, located inside vehicle at upper rear wheelwell area. **On two door models, it is necessary to remove the lower rear quarter trim panel for access.**
2. Remove upper shock absorber mounting nut, isolator retainer and upper isolator, **Fig. 5.**
3. Raise and support vehicle.
4. Remove shock absorber lower mounting bolt.
5. Remove shock absorber and coil spring assembly from vehicle.
6. Reverse procedure to install.

Service

1. Install coil spring retractors, tool L-4514, or equivalent, on coil spring and support in a vise, **Fig. 6.** Grip 4 or 5 coils of the spring in the retractors. Also, do not extend retractors more than 9¹/₄ inches.
2. Tighten retractors evenly until spring pressure is released from upper spring seat.
3. Hold flat end of pushrod and loosen retaining nut. **Ensure that spring is properly compressed before loosening retaining nut since personal injury may result.**
4. Remove lower isolator, pushrod sleeve and upper spring seat.
5. Remove shock absorber from coil spring.

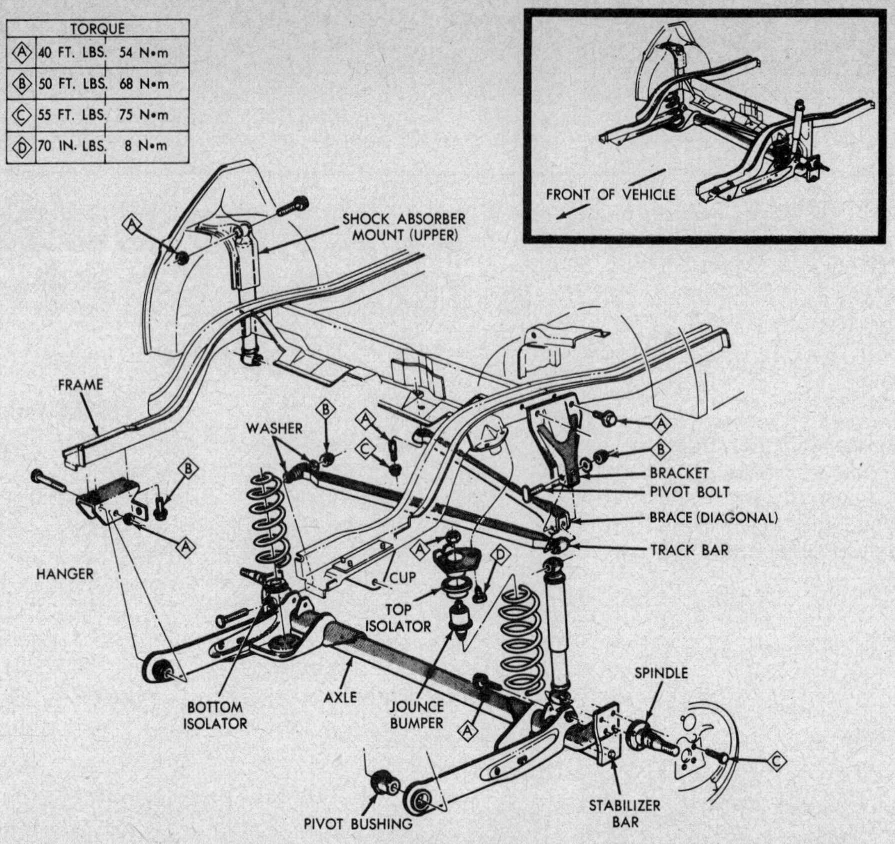

Fig. 3 Rear axle & suspension assembly. 1984–85 Aries, Reliant, Daytona, Laser, New Yorker, Caravelle, Lancer, LeBaron & 600; 1985 Executive & Town & Country

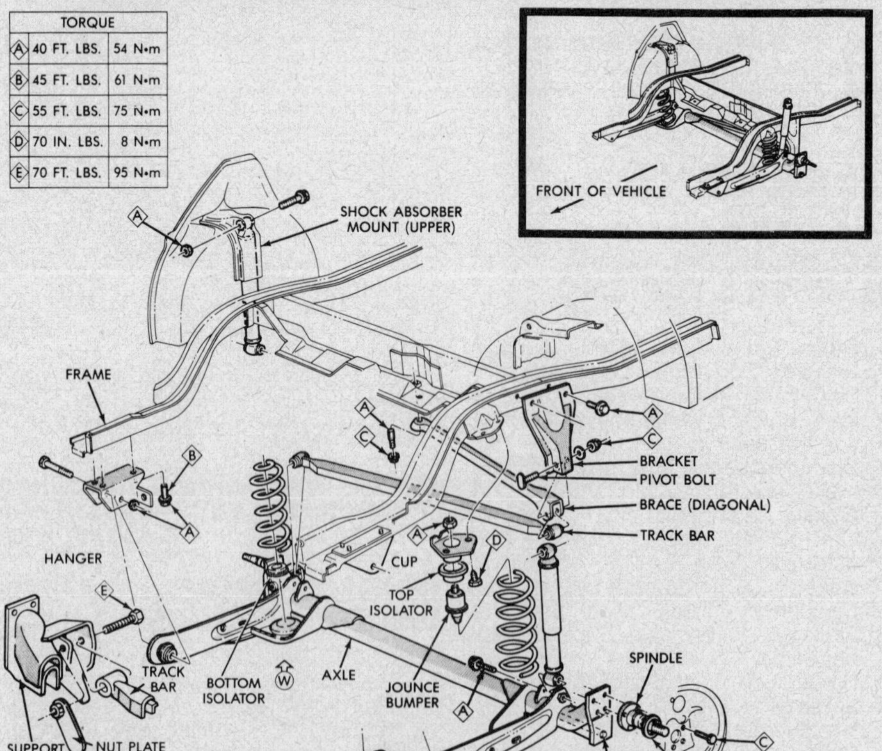

Fig. 4 Rear axle & suspension assembly. 1986–88 Aries, Reliant, Daytona, Laser, New Yorker, Caravelle, Lancer, Lebaron, 600 & Town & Country

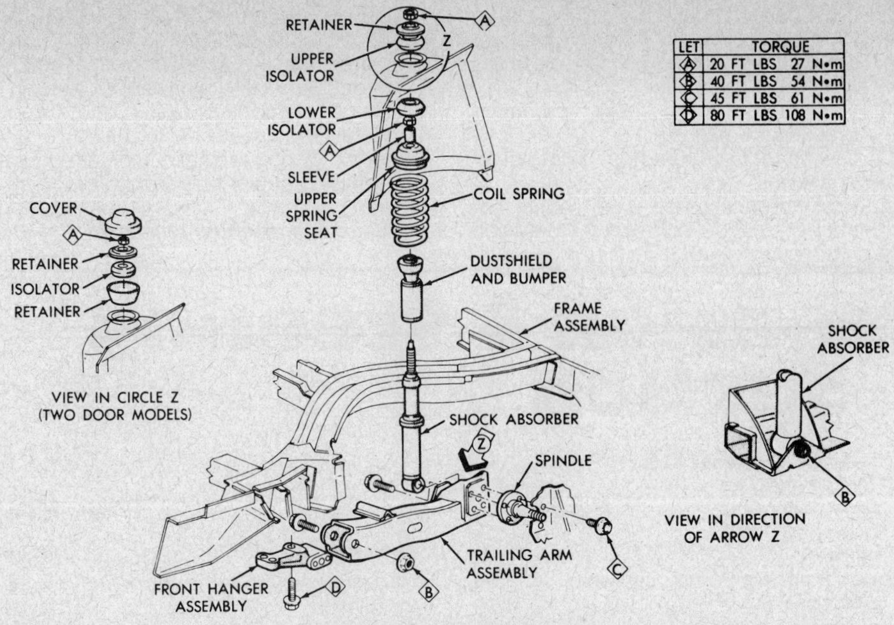

LET	TORQUE
A	20 FT LBS 27 N•m
B	40 FT LBS 54 N•m
C	45 FT LBS 61 N•m
D	80 FT LBS 108 N•m

Fig. 5 Rear axle & suspension assembly. Horizon, Omni, Charger & Turismo

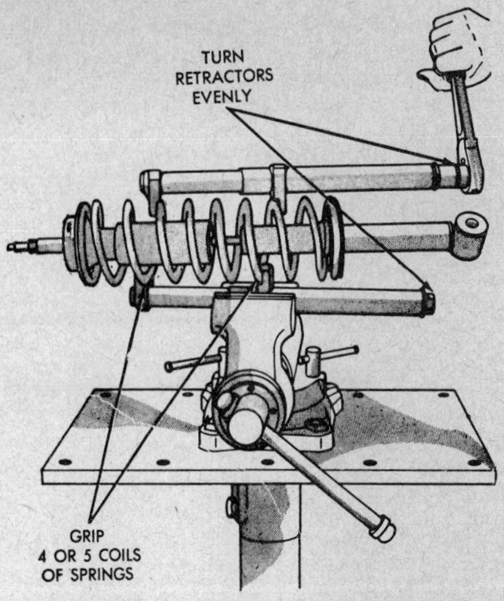

Fig. 6 Retracting coil spring

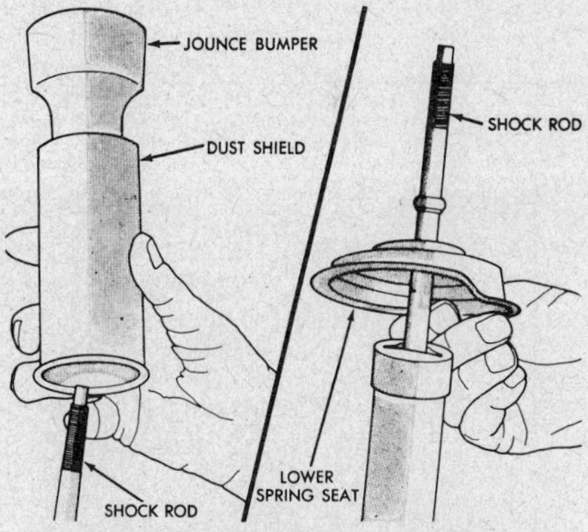

Fig. 7 Jounce bumper, dust shield & lower spring seat replacement

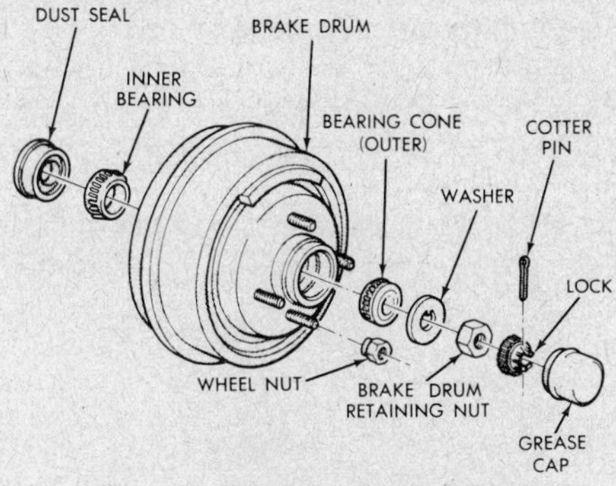

Fig. 8 Wheel bearing assembly

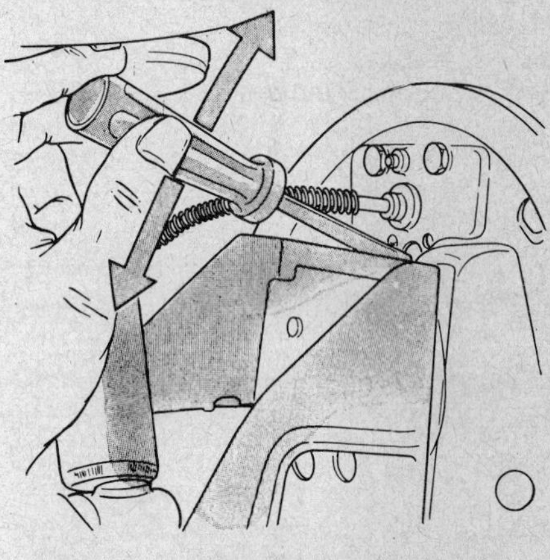

Fig. 9 Adjusting service brakes

6. Remove jounce bumper and dust shield from pushrod, **Fig. 7.**
7. Remove lower spring seat. **Fig. 7.**
8. Reverse procedure to assemble.

REAR WHEEL BEARING

ADJUST

1. Torque adjusting nut to 270 inch lbs. (30 Nm) while rotating wheel.
2. Stop wheel and loosen adjusting nut, **Fig. 8.**
3. Tighten adjusting nut finger tight. End-play should be .001-.003 inch.
4. Install castle lock with slots aligned with cotter pin hole.
5. Install cotter pin and grease cap.

SERVICE BRAKES

ADJUST

The rear brakes on 1983-88 models are self-adjusting and no adjustment is necessary. On 1982 models, the rear brakes are not self-adjusting and periodic adjustment is required as follows:

1. Raise and support vehicle.
2. Remove adjusting hole covers from brake supports.
3. Release parking brake and back off cable adjustment to slacken cable.
4. Insert a narrow screwdriver into adjusting nut hole. Move screwdriver handle downward on left side or upward on right side until wheels are locked, **Fig. 9.**
5. Back off nut 10 clicks.
6. Adjust parking brake.

PARKING BRAKE

ADJUST

1. Raise and support vehicle.
2. Release parking brake and back off adjustment to slacken cable.
3. Tighten cable adjusting nut until a slight drag is obtained while rotating wheels.
4. Loosen cable adjusting nut until wheels rotate freely, then an additional two turns.
5. Apply and release parking brake to check for proper operation. The rear wheels should rotate without dragging.

MASTER CYLINDER

REPLACE

MANUAL BRAKES

1. Disconnect and plug brake tubes from master cylinder. Cap master cylinder ports.
2. Disconnect stop lamp switch mounting bracket from beneath instrument panel.
3. Pull brake pedal rearward to disengage pushrod from master cylinder. **Pulling brake pedal rearward will destroy grommet. Install a new grommet when installing push rod.**
4. Remove master cylinder attaching nuts.
5. Remove master cylinder from vehicle.
6. Reverse procedure to install.

POWER BRAKES

1. Disconnect and plug brake tubes from master cylinder. Cap master cylinder ports.
2. Remove master cylinder attaching

nuts and master cylinder from power brake unit.
3. Reverse procedure to install.

POWER BRAKE UNIT REPLACE

1. Remove master cylinder attaching nuts, slide master cylinder from mounting studs and support on fender shield. Do not disconnect brake tubes from master cylinder.
2. Remove clutch cable mounting bracket, if equipped.
3. Disconnect vacuum hose from power brake unit.
4. From beneath instrument panel, install a suitable screwdriver between center tang on retainer clip and brake pedal pin. Rotate screwdriver so retainer center tang will pass over brake pedal pin. Pull retainer clip from pin.
5. Remove stop light switch and striker plate, if equipped.
6. Remove power brake unit attaching nuts and power brake unit from vehicle.
7. Reverse procedure to install.

Front Suspension & Steering Section

INDEX

DESCRIPTION

These vehicles use a MacPherson type front suspension with vertical shock absorber struts attached to the upper fender reinforcement and steering knuckle, **Fig. 1.** The lower control arms are attached inboard to a crossmember and outboard to the steering knuckle through a ball joint to provide lower steering knuckle position. During steering maneuvers, the strut and steering knuckle rotate as an assembly.

The driveshafts are attached inboard to the transaxle output drive flanges and outboard to the driven wheel hub.

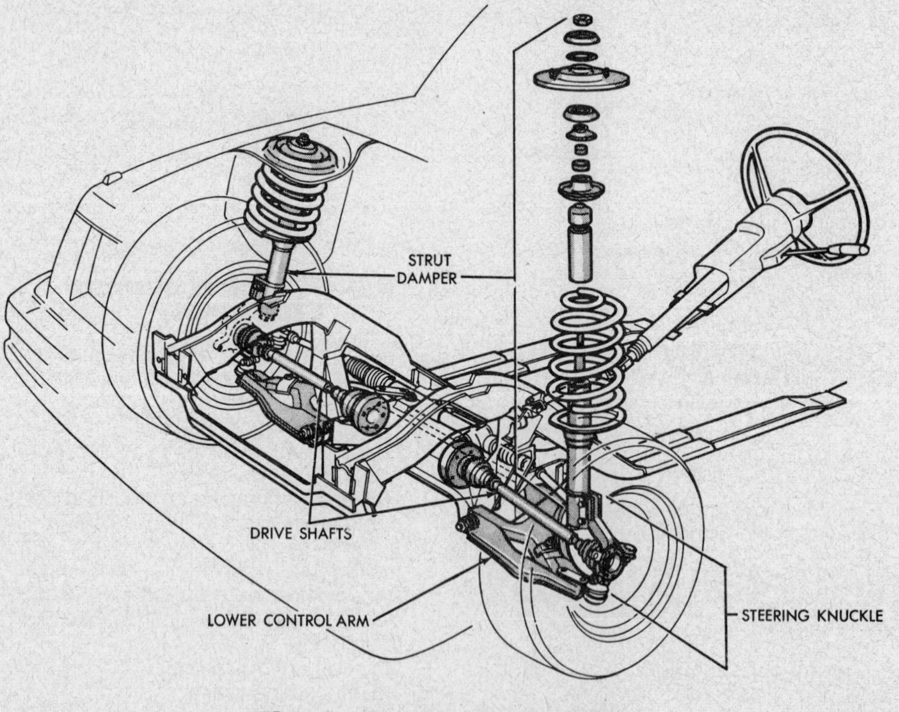

Fig. 1 Front suspension

STRUT DAMPER ASSEMBLY REPLACE

REMOVAL

1. Raise and support vehicle, then remove front wheels.
2. On all models exc. 1985-88 Lancer and LeBaron GTS, mark position of camber adjusting cam for proper alignment during installation.
3. On 1985-88 Lancer and LaBaron GTS, mark outline of strut on knuckle for proper alignment during installation.
4. On all models, remove cam bolt, knuckle bolt or bolts, washer plate and brake hose to damper bracket attaching screw, **Figs. 2 through 5. On 1985 Lancer and LeBaron GTS, discard one knuckle bolt and washer plate.**
5. Remove strut damper to fender shield attaching nut and washer assemblies.
6. Remove strut damper from vehicle.

INSTALLATION

1. Position strut assembly into fender reinforcement, then install retaining nuts and washers and torque to 20 ft. lbs.
2. Position steering knuckle and washer plate to strut, then install upper cam and lower through bolts. **On 1985 Lancer and LeBaron GTS, replace one knuckle bolt with a new cam bolt.**
3. Install brake hose retainer on damper, then index alignment marks made during removal.
4. Position a 4 inch or larger C-clamp on steering knuckle and strut, then tighten clamp just enough to eliminate any looseness between strut and knuckle. Check alignment of marks made during removal. On all 1982-83 models and 1984-87 Charger, Horizon, Omni and Turismo, torque cam bolt nuts to

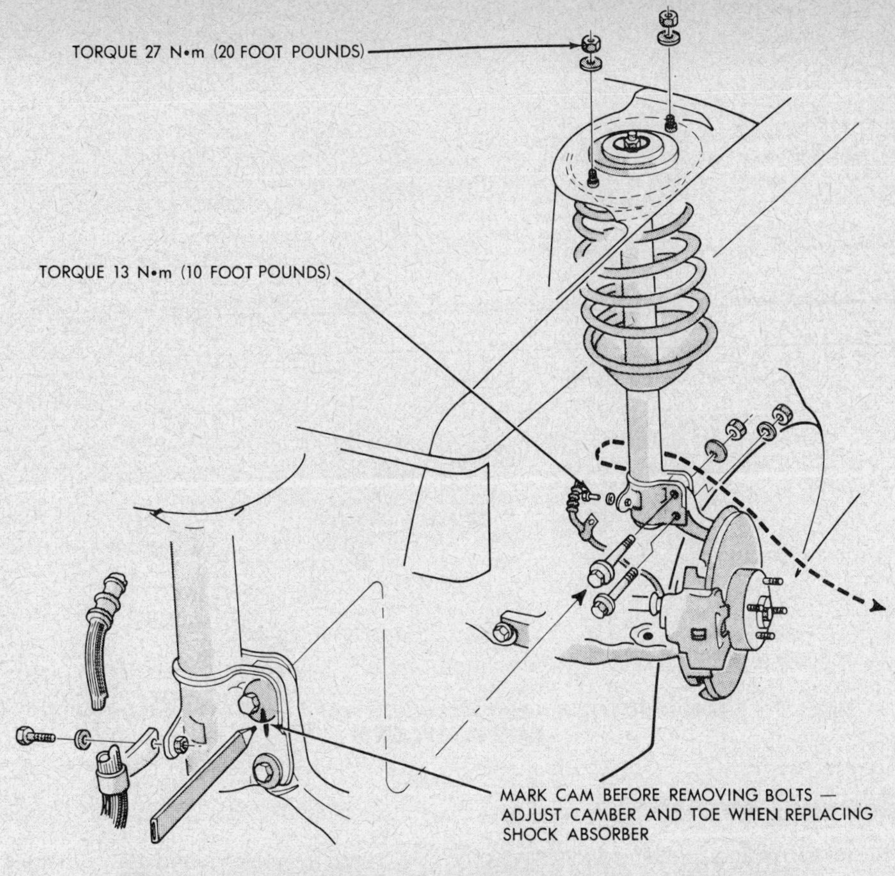

Fig. 2 Strut damper replacement. 1982–83

45 ft. lbs., then advance nuts an additional 1/4 turn. On 1984-88 models except Charger, Horizon, Omni and Turismo, torque nuts to 75 ft. lbs., then advance an additional 1/4 turn.

5. Remove C-clamp, then install wheel and tire assembly.

COIL SPRING REPLACE

1. Remove strut damper assembly as outlined previously.
2. Using a suitable tool, compress coil spring.
3. Remove strut rod nut while holding strut rod to prevent rotation.
4. Remove mount assembly, **Figs. 6 through 8.**
5. Remove coil spring from strut damper.
6. Inspect mount assembly for deterioration of rubber isolator, retainers for cracks and distortion and bearings for binding.
7. Install bumper dust shield assembly.
8. Install spring and seat, upper spring retainer, bearing and spacer, mount assembly and rebound bumper, retainer and rod nut upper. **On all 1982-83 models and 1984-88 exc. Charger, Horizon, Omni and Turismo, position spring upper retainer tab or notch parallel to damper lower attaching bracket, Fig. 9. On 1984-87 Charger, Horizon, Omni and Turismo, position spring upper retainer tab 180° to damper lower attaching bracket, Fig. 10.**

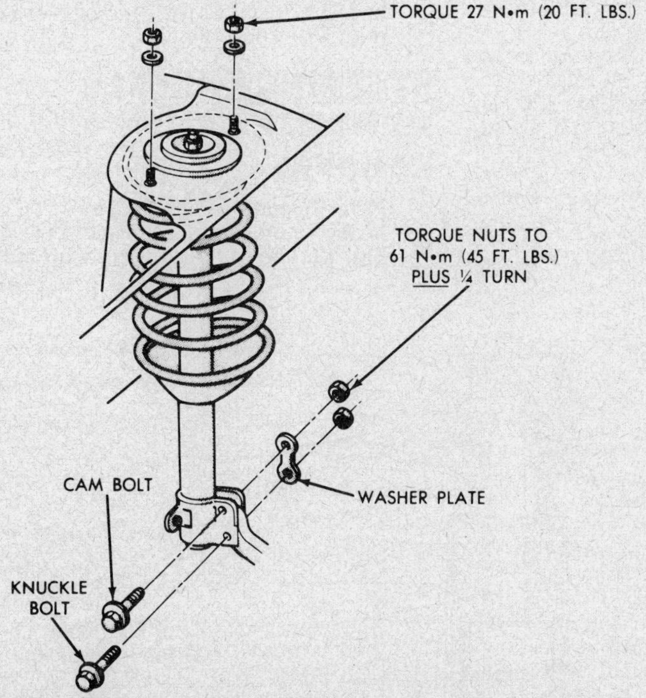

Fig. 3 Strut damper replacement. 1984–87 Charger, Horizon, Omni & Turismo

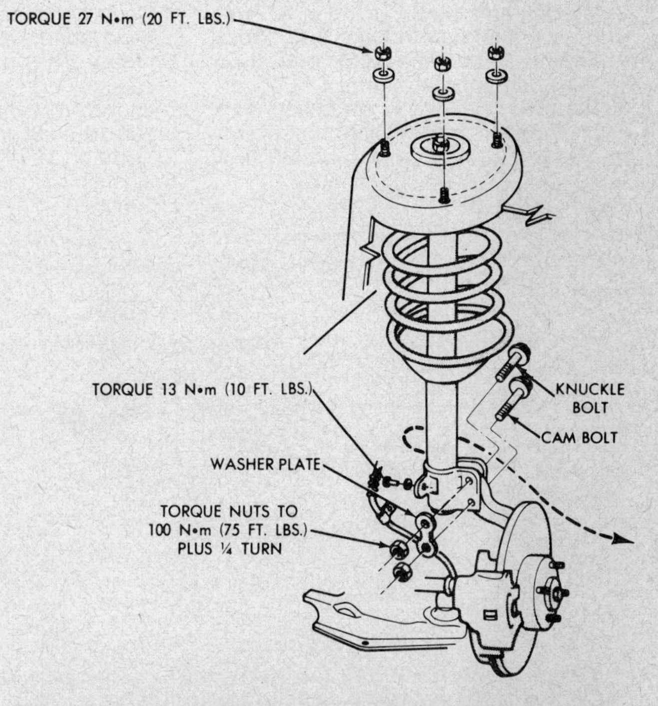

Fig. 4 Strut damper replacement. 1984 E-Class; 1984–85 Executive; 1984–86 Aries, Daytona, Laser, LeBaron Exc. GTS, New Yorker, Reliant, Town & Country & 600 & Caravelle

9. Torque strut rod nut to 60 ft. lbs. (81 Nm). **Do not release spring compressor before torquing nut.**
10. Remove spring compressor.

BALL JOINTS

The lower control arm ball joints operate with no freeplay. The ball joint is pressed into the lower control arm. Ball joints can be pressed from lower control arm using a 1 1/16 inch deep socket and tool No. C-4699-2. When pressing ball joint into lower control arm, use tool Nos. C-4699-1 and C-4699-2. Install ball joint seal using a 1 1/2 socket and tool No. C-4699-2. **On some models the ball joint is welded to the lower control arm. On these models the ball joint and lower control arm must be replaced as an assembly.**

CHECKING BALL JOINTS

With weight of vehicle resting on wheel and tire assembly, attempt to move grease fitting with fingers, **Fig. 11.** Do not use a tool or added force to attempt to move grease fitting. If grease fitting moves freely, then ball joint is worn and should be replaced.

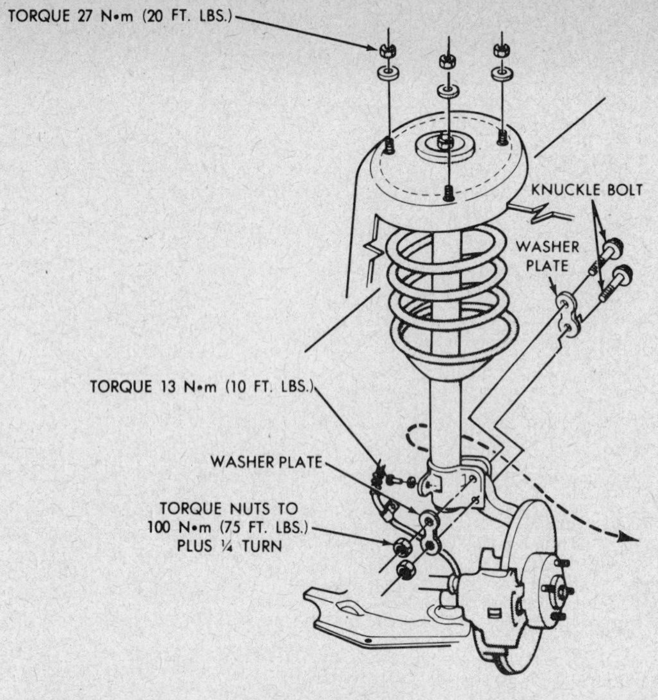

Fig. 5 Strut damper replacement. 1985–88 Lancer & LeBaron GTS

LOWER CONTROL ARM REPLACE

REMOVAL

1. Raise and support vehicle.
2. Remove front inner pivot through bolt, rear stub strut nut, retainer and bushing and the ball joint to steering knuckle clamp bolt, **Fig. 12.**
3. Separate the ball joint from steering knuckle by prying between ball stud retainer and lower control arm. **Pulling steering knuckle "Out" from vehicle after releasing from ball joint can separate inner C/V joint.**
4. Remove sway bar to control arm nut and reinforcement. Rotate control arm over sway bar. Remove rear stub strut bushing, sleeve and retainer.

INSTALLATION

1. Install retainer, bushing and sleeve on stub strut.
2. Position control arm over sway bar and install rear stub strut and front pivot into crossmember.
3. Install front pivot bolt and loosely assemble nut, **Fig. 12.**
4. Install stub strut bushing and retainer and loosely assemble nut.
5. Place sway bar bracket stud through control arm and install retainer and nut. Torque nut to 22 ft. lbs. (30 Nm) on 1982-83 vehicles or 25 ft. lbs. (34 Nm) on 1984-88 vehicles.
6. Install ball joint stud into steering knuckle, then the clamp bolt. Torque bolt to 50 ft. lbs. (68 Nm) on all 1982-83 vehicles and 1984 Charger, Horizon, Omni and Turismo, or 70 ft. lbs. (94 Nm) on all 1984 models except Charger, Horizon, Omni and Turismo and all 1985-88 models.
7. Lower vehicle and with suspension support vehicle torque front pivot bolt to 105 ft. lbs. (142 Nm) and stub strut nut to 70 ft. lbs. (94 Nm).

STEERING KNUCKLE REPLACE

REMOVAL

1. Remove cotter pin and nut lock.
2. Loosen hub nut with brakes applied, **Fig. 13. The hub and driveshaft are**

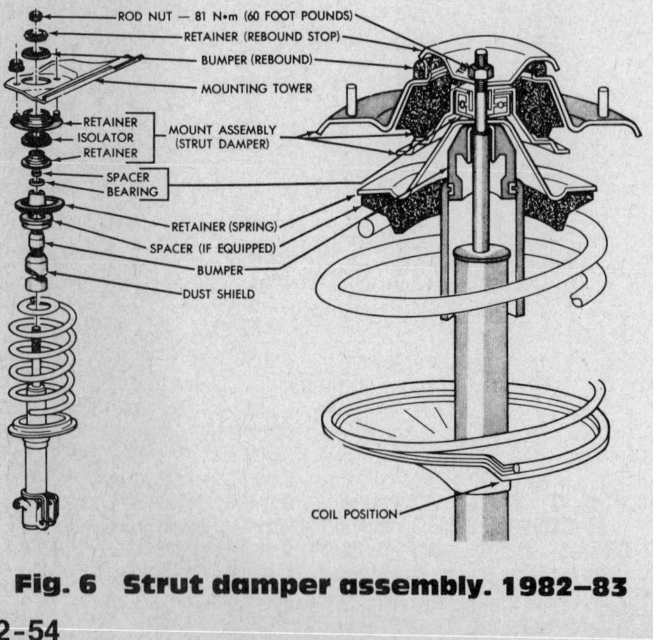

Fig. 6 Strut damper assembly. 1982–83

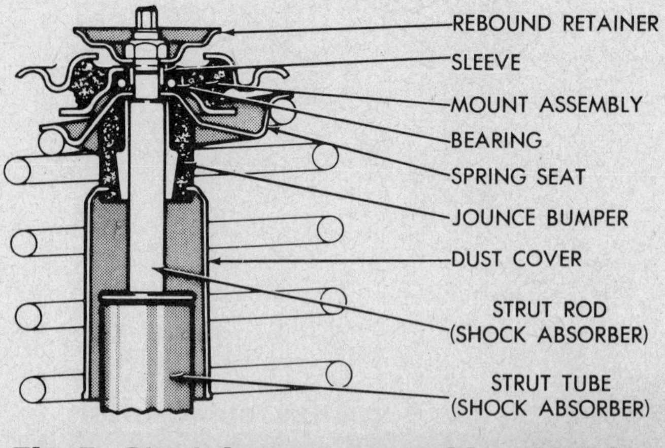

Fig. 7 Strut damper assembly. 1984–87 Charger, Horizon, Omni & Turismo

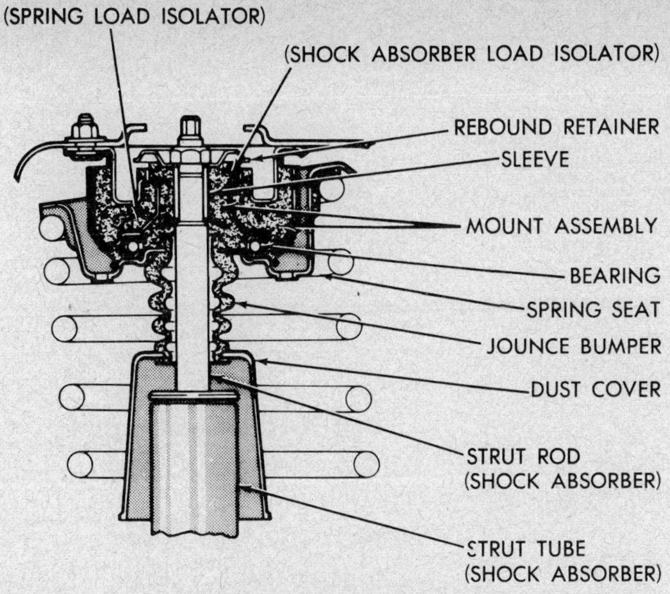

Fig. 8 Dual path strut damper assembly. Exc. 1984–87 Charger, Horizon, Omni & Turismo

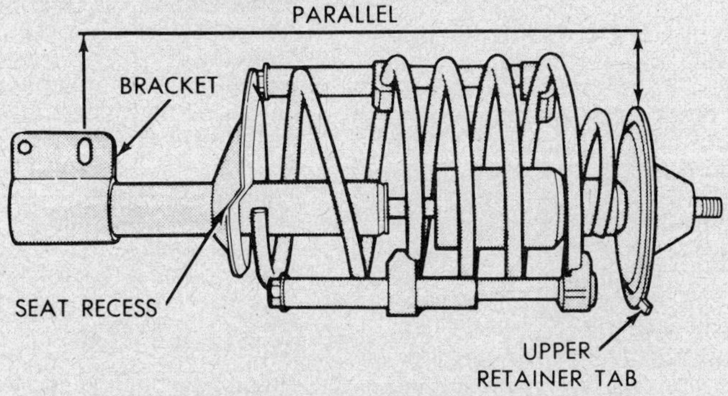

Fig. 10 Spring seat & retainer position. 1984–87 Charger, Horizon, Omni & Turismo

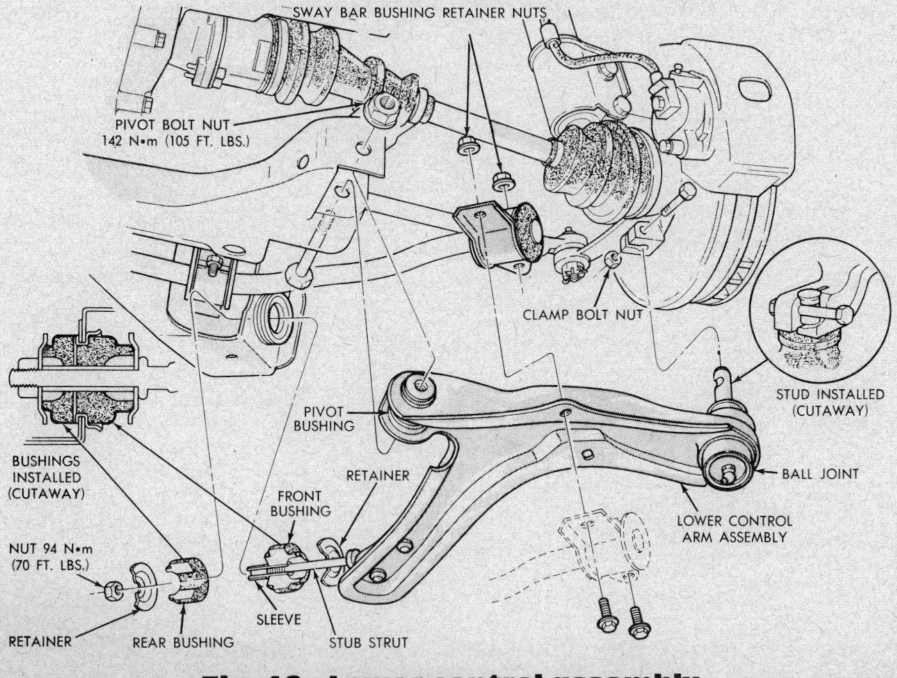

Fig. 12 Lower control assembly

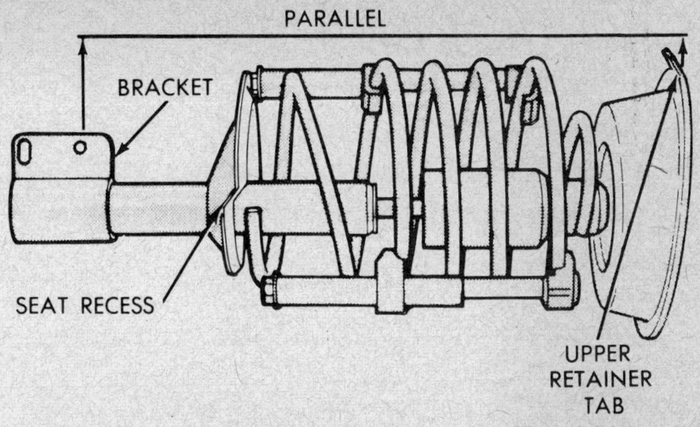

Fig. 9 Spring seat & retainer position. 1982–83 models & 1984–88 Exc. Charger, Horizon, Omni & Turismo

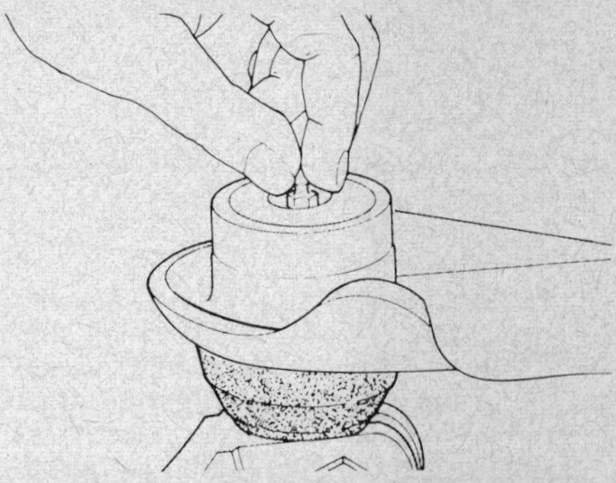

Fig. 11 Checking ball joint for wear

splined together through the knuckle (Bearing) and retained by hub nut.

3. Raise and support vehicle, then remove front wheel.
4. Remove hub nut. Ensure that splined driveshaft is free to separate from spline in hub during knuckle removal. A pulling force on the shaft can separate the inner C/V joint. Tap lightly with a brass drift, if required.
5. Disconnect tie rod end from steering arm with a suitable puller.
6. Disconnect brake hose retainer from strut damper.
7. Remove clamp bolt securing ball joint stud into steering knuckle and brake caliper adapter screw and washer assemblies.
8. Support caliper with a piece of wire. Do not hang by brake hose.
9. Remove rotor.
10. Mark position of camber cam upper adjusting bolt and loosen both bolts.
11. Support steering knuckle and remove cam adjusting and through bolts. Move upper knuckle "Leg" from strut damper bracket and lift knuckle from ball joint stud. **Support driveshaft during knuckle removal. Do not permit driveshaft to hang after separating steering knuckle from vehicle.**

INSTALLATION

1. Place steering knuckle on lower ball joint stud and driveshaft through hub.

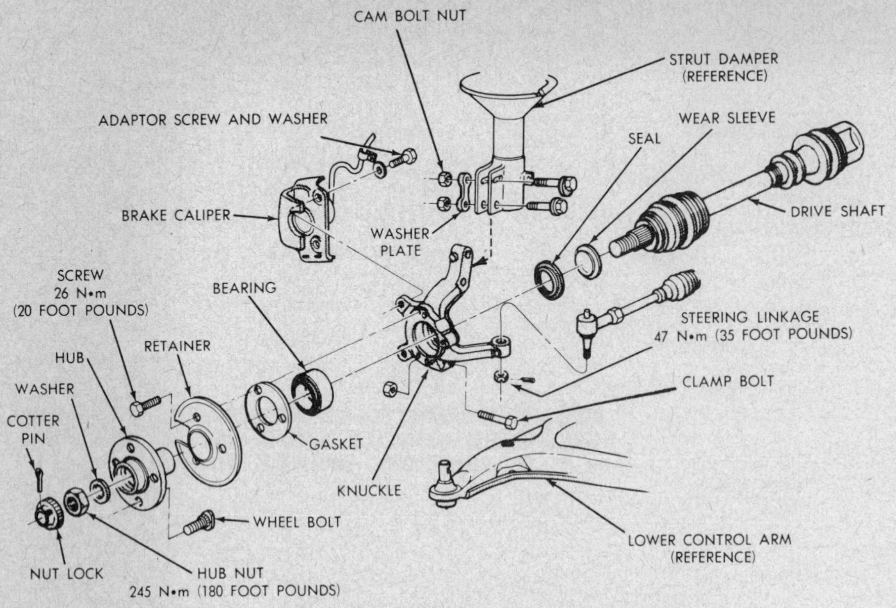

Fig. 13 Steering knuckle assembly

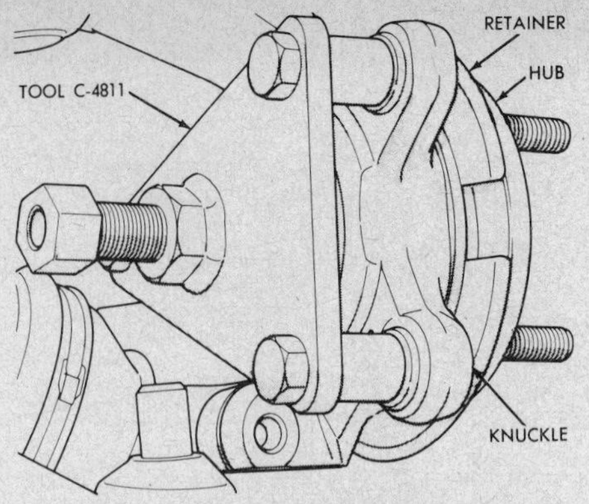

Fig. 14 Hub removal

2. Position upper "Leg" of knuckle into strut damper bracket and install cam and through bolts. Place cam in original position. Place a 4 inch or larger C-clamp on strut and steering knuckle, then tighten clamp just enough to eliminate looseness between knuckle and strut. Ensure cam alignment marks are aligned. On all 1982-83 models and 1984-87 Charger, Horizon, Omni and Turismo, torque cam bolt nuts to 45 ft. lbs. (61 Nm), then advance nuts an additional 1/4 turn. On 1984-88 models except Charger, Horizon, Omni and Turismo, torque nuts to 75 ft. lbs. (100 Nm), then advance an additional 1/4 turn.
3. Install and torque ball joint to steering knuckle clamp bolt to 50 ft. lbs. (68 Nm) on all 1983 models and 1984 Charger, Horizon, Omni and Turismo, or 70 ft. lbs. (95 Nm) on 1984 models except Charger, Horizon, Omni and Turismo and all 1985-88 models.
4. Install tie rod end into steering arm and torque nut to 35 ft. lbs. (47 Nm). Install cotter pin.
5. Install rotor.
6. Install caliper over rotor and position adapter to steering knuckle. Install adapter to knuckle bolts and torque to 85 ft. lbs. (115 Nm) on 1982 models, or 160 ft. lbs. (216 Nm) on 1983-85 models.
7. Attach brake hose retainer to strut damper and torque screw to 10 ft. lbs. (13 Nm).
8. Install washer and hub nut.
9. Torque hub nut to 180 ft. lbs. (245 Nm) with brakes applied.
10. Install nut lock and new cotter pin.

HUB & BEARING REPLACE

On 1984 Models except Charger, Horizon, Omni and Turismo there are two designs or types of front knuckle/hub bearings used, tapered roller or ball bearing design. It is possible to have either or both types of bearings on same vehicle. No functional problems result from a mixed bearing condition, however, a service problem may arise as a result of different characteristics of these bearings.

If there is movement noted on one or both wheels but no bearing noise, measure move ment at wheel outer rim diameter with a dial gauge. The maximum allowable movement on a 13 inch wheel at the rim lip is .020 inch, on a 14 inch wheel .023 inch and .025 inch on a 15 inch wheel. Do not replace bearings for looseness if movement is as specified. Also do not over torque the axle retaining nut beyond 180 ft. lbs. to minimize bearing freeplay.

REMOVAL

1. Remove steering knuckle as described under "Steering Knuckle, Replace."
2. Remove hub from bearing using tool No. C-4811 or equivalent, **Fig. 14. Back out three bearing attaching screws from knuckle until hub is unseated. Also install adapter screw into rear attaching screw threads and place thrust button inside hub bore.**
3. Remove three screws and bearing retainer from knuckle.
4. Pry bearing seal from machined recess in knuckle.
5. Press bearing out of knuckle using tool No. C-4811 or equivalent.

INSTALLATION

1. Press new bearing into knuckle using tool No. C-4811 or equivalent.
2. On 1982-83 models, install brake dust shield.
3. On all models, install new seal and bearing retainer. Torque retainer screws to 20 ft. lbs. (27 Nm).

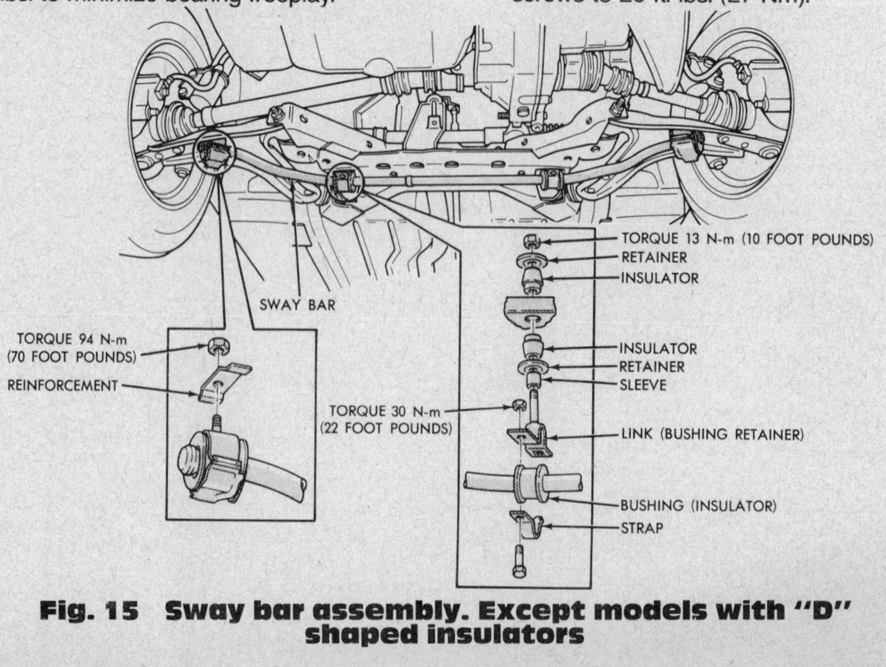

Fig. 15 Sway bar assembly. Except models with "D" shaped insulators

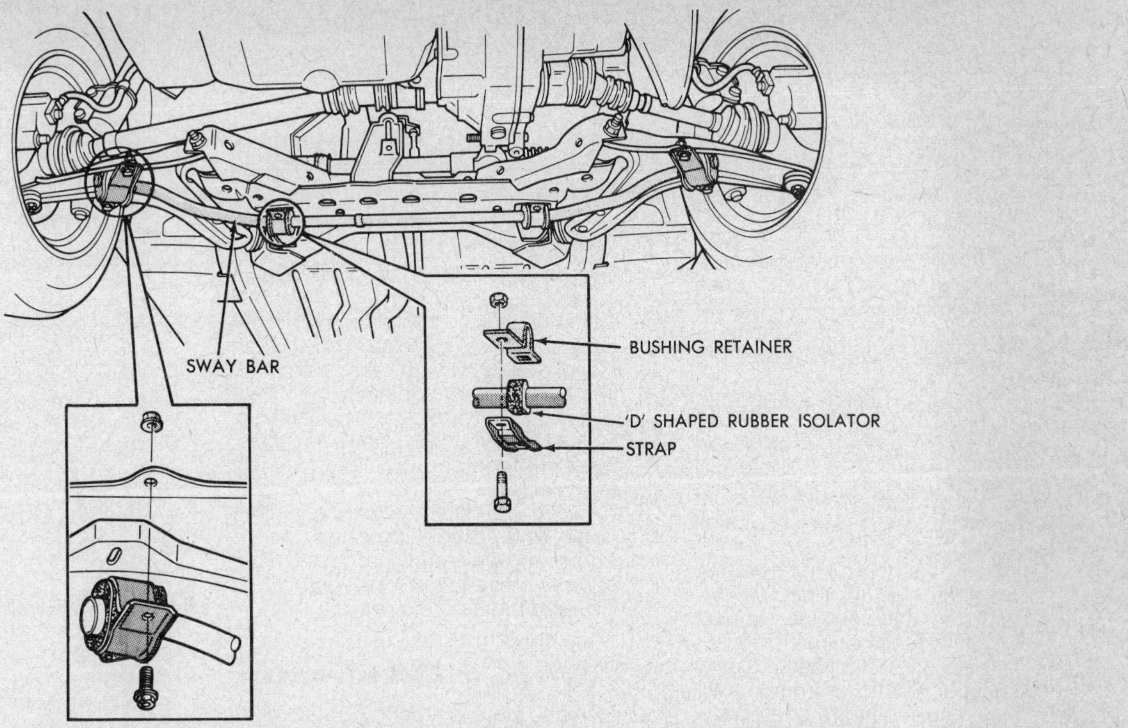

Fig. 16 Sway bar assembly. 1982–83. (1984–88 similar)

4. Press hub into bearing using tool No. C-4811 or equivalent.
5. Install new bearing seal using tool No. C-4698 or equivalent.

SWAY BAR REPLACE

REMOVAL

1. Raise and support front of vehicle.
2. On except models with "D" shaped insulators, remove end bushing to control arm nut and reinforcement plate, **Fig. 15.** On models with "D" shaped insulators, remove nuts, bolts and retainer at control arm, **Fig. 16.**
3. On except models with "D" shaped insulators, remove sway bar to crossmember linkage (nut, retainer and insulators at top of crossmember). Bushing are permanently installed on sway bars. On models with "D" shaped insulators, remove bolts at crossmember clamps, then remove clamps.
4. Remove sway bar.

INSTALLATION

Some vehicles have a linkless sway bar in the front suspension. The new sway bar is nearly symmetric looking and it is possible to install the sway bar improperly in the vehicle when it is removed for service. Always mark the sway bar prior to removal to assure proper installation. Sway bars used for production and service replacement are marked on the left (driver side) by a dab or stripe of paint.

1. Position crossmember bushings on bar with curved surface up and split to front of vehicle. Set upper clamps onto crossmember bushings, lirt bar assembly into crossmember and install lower clamps and bolts.
2. Position retainers at control arms, then insert bolts and install nuts.
3. With lower control arms raised to design height, tighten bolts, **Figs. 15 and 16.** Refer to **Fig. 15** for bolt torques on except models with "D" shaped insulators. Torque bolts to 22 ft. lbs. (30 Nm) on 1982-83 models, or 25 ft. lbs. (34 Nm) on 1984-88 models with "D" shaped insulators. **A bushing retainer is not used on 1984-88 models.**

RACK & PINION STEERING GEAR REPLACE

1. Raise and support vehicle, then remove front wheels.
2. Remove tie rod ends with a suitable puller.
3. On all models except Omni, Horizon, Charger and Turismo, remove steering column as follows:
   a. Disconnect battery ground cable.
   b. On column shift vehicles, disconnect cable rod by prying rod out of grommet in shift lever.
   c. Disconnect all wiring connectors at steering column jacket and remove steering wheel center pad.
   d. Disconnect horn wires and horn switch, then pull steering wheel from column.
   e. Expose steering column bracket, remove instrument panel steering column cover and lower reinforcement. Remove bezel.
   f. Remove indicator setscrew and shaft indicator pointer from shift housing.
   g. Remove nuts attaching steering column bracket to instrument panel support, then lower the bracket support to floor. **Do not remove roll pin to remove steering column assembly.**
   h. Pull steering column rearward, and disconnect lower shaft from coupling.
   i. Reinstall anti-rattle clips into lower coupling tube slot.
   j. Remove column assembly out through passenger compartment, being careful not to damage paint or trim.
   k. Cut plastic grommets from shift levers and install new grommets from rod side of lever using pliers and a backup washer. Apply grease to grommets.
4. On Omni, Horizon, Charger and Turismo, drive out lower roll pin attaching pinion shaft to lower universal joint.
5. On all models except Omni, Horizon, Charger and Turismo, support the front suspension crossmember with a suitable jack, then remove bolts attaching steering gear to front crossmember. Lower crossmember from vehicle frame.
6. On Omni, Horizon, Charger and Turismo, remove 2 rear crossmember nuts and loosen 2 front bolts, then lower crossmember slightly to gain access to boot seal shields.
7. Remove splash shields and boot seal shields.
8. On power steering units, disconnect hoses from steering gear.
9. Disconnect tie rod ends from steering knuckles.
10. Remove gear to front suspension crossmember attaching bolts, then the gear from left side of engine.

11. Reverse procedure to install. On all models except Omni, Horizon, Charger and Turismo, reinstall steering column as follows:
   a. Align and insert lower stub shaft into coupling, raise column into position and loosely install bracket nuts. Pull column assembly rearward and torque nuts to 105 inch lbs.
   b. With needle nose pliers, pull coupling spring upward until it touches the universal flange.
   c. Snap gearshift rods into grommets.
   d. Readjust gearshift linkage as necessary.
   e. Install steering wheel and torque nut to 45 ft. lbs.
   f. Install horn switch and horn switch wire.
   g. Connect all wiring connectors at steering column jacket and install steering wheel pad.
   h. Connect battery ground cable and test operation of lights and horn.
   i. On column shift vehicles, connect gearshift indicator pointer to its approximate original location. Slowly move gear shift lever from 1 (low) to park, pausing briefly at each position. The indicator pointer must align with each selector position. If necessary, loosen and readjust pointer correctly.
   j. Install instrument panel steering column cover.

POWER STEERING PUMP REPLACE

4-97 ENGINE

1. Loosen pressure hose connector at pump.
2. Remove drive belt adjustment nut from top rubber isolator stud, then loosen 3 locknuts on rear studs.
3. Place a suitable container on top of radiator yoke to catch any spilled fluid.
4. Remove drive belt and 3 locknuts, then lift pump and bracket assembly from vehicle.
5. Remove pump reservoir cap and drain fluid, then disconnect hoses from pump. Plug pump ports and hose ends to prevent contamination.
6. Reverse procedure to install.

4-105, 135 & 153 ENGINES

1. Remove power steering pump drive belt adjusting bolt and nut, then the nut attaching pump end hose bracket, if equipped.
2. Raise and support vehicle, then remove nut attaching pump pressure hose bracket to crossmember.
3. Disconnect pressure hose from steering gear and allow fluid to drain into a suitable container.
4. Remove drive belt splash shield, then disconnect both pressure and return hoses at power steering pump. Cap hoses and fittings to prevent entry of dirt.
5. Remove lower stud nut and pivot bolt from power steering pump, then lower the vehicle.
6. Remove pulley from pump, then move pump rearward to clear mounting bracket and remove adjusting bracket.
7. Rotate pump so pulley faces rear of vehicle, then lift pump assembly from vehicle.
8. Reverse procedure to install.

4-156 ENGINE

1. Disconnect pressure and return lines from pump. Cap all lines and fittings.
2. Remove belt adjustment and pivot bolts, and drive belt from pulley.
3. Remove power steering pump and mounting bracket as an assembly.
4. Reverse procedure to install.

Wheel Alignment Section

INDEX

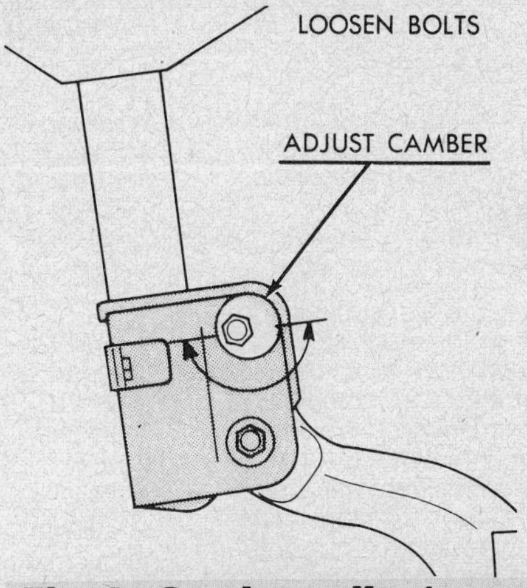

Fig. 1 Camber adjustment. 1982–83 All & 1984–87 Charger, Horizon, Omni & Turismo

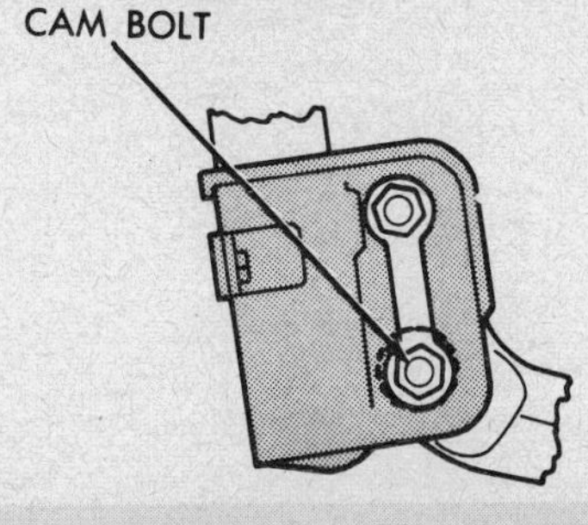

Fig. 2 Camber adjustment. 1984–88 exc. Charger, Horizon, Omni & Turismo

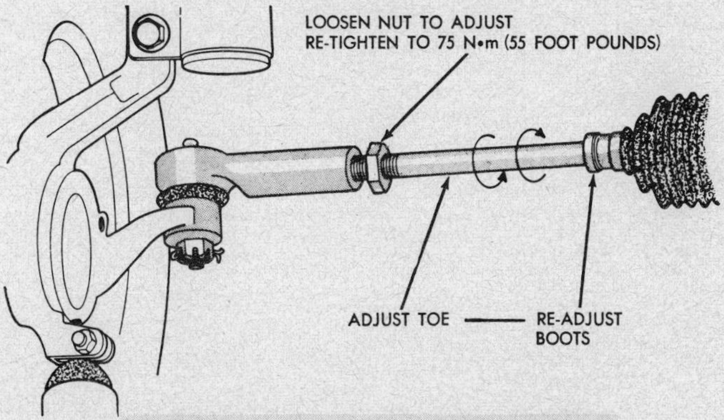

Fig. 3 Toe-in adjustment

FRONT WHEEL ALIGNMENT

Prior to wheel alignment ensure tires are at recommended pressure, are of equal size and have approximately the same wear pattern. Check front wheel and tire assembly for radial runout and inspect lower ball joints and steering linkage for looseness. Check front and rear springs for sagging or damage. Front suspension inspections should be performed on a level floor or alignment rack with fuel tank at capacity and vehicle free of luggage and passenger compartment load. The vehicle should be bounced an equal number of times from the center of the bumper alternately, first from the rear, then the front, releasing at bottom of down cycle.

CASTER

The caster angle on these vehicles cannot be adjusted.

CAMBER

To adjust camber, loosen the cam and through bolts, **Figs. 1 and 2.** On 1985-88 Lancer and LeBaron GTS, remove rear washer plate and one of the knuckle bolts and replace with a new cam bolt. On all models, rotate cam bolt to move top of wheel in or out to obtain specified camber angle. On all 1982-83 models and 1984-87 Charger, Horizon, Omni and Turismo, torque cam bolt nuts to 45 ft. lbs., then advance nuts an additional 1/4 turn. On 1984-88 models except Charger, Horizon, Omni and Turismo, torque nuts to 75 ft. lbs., then advance an additional 1/4 turn.

TOE-IN

To adjust toe-in, center steering wheel and hold in position with a suitable tool. Loosen tie rod locknuts and rotate the rod, **Fig. 3,** to adjust toe-in to specifications. Use care not to twist steering gear rubber boots. Torque tie rod locknuts to 55 ft. lbs. (75 Nm). Adjust position of steering gear rubber boots. Remove steering wheel holding tool.

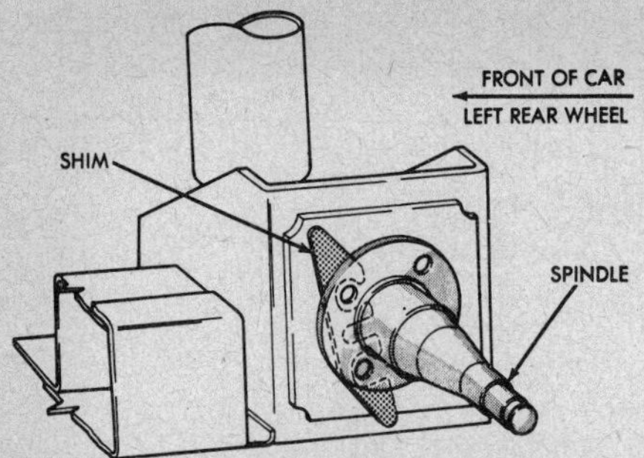

Fig. 4 Shim installation for toe-out

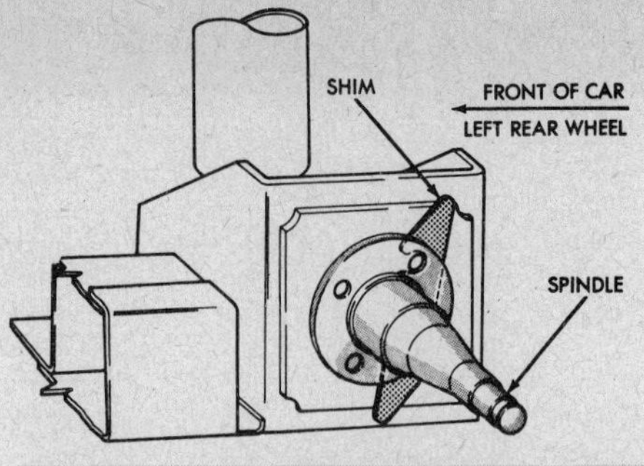

Fig. 5 Shim installation for toe-in

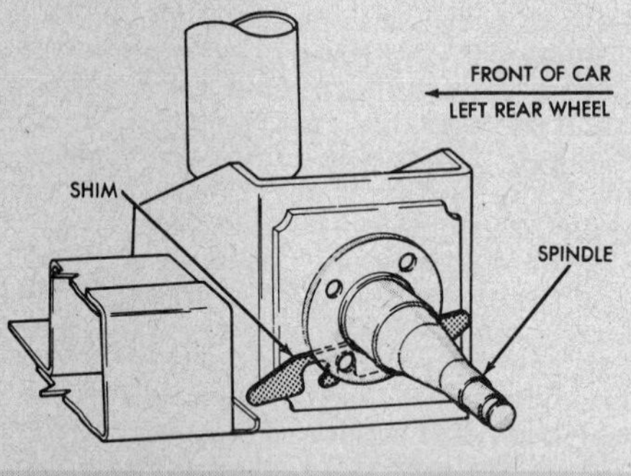

Fig. 6 Shim installation for positive camber

REAR WHEEL ALIGNMENT

Due to the design of the rear suspension and the incorporation of stub axles or wheel spindles, it is possible to adjust the camber and toe of the rear wheels on these vehicles. Adjustment is controlled by adding shims approximately .010 inch thick between the spindle mounting surface and spindle mounting plate. The amount of adjustment is approximately 0° 18' per shim. Refer to **Figs. 4 through 7** for proper placement of shims.

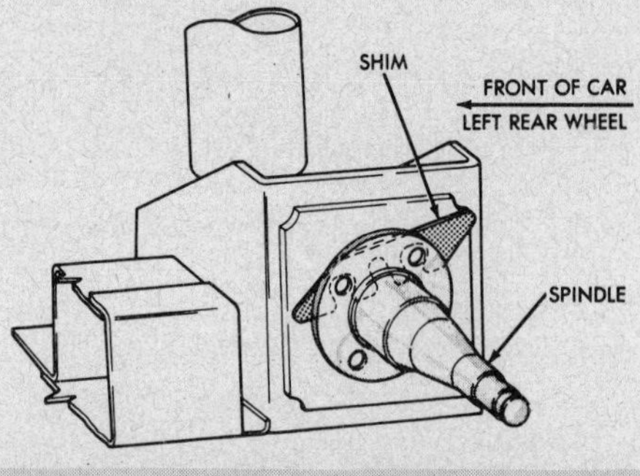

Fig. 7 Shim installation for negative camber

AIR CONDITIONING

TABLE OF CONTENTS

System Testing

INDEX

GENERAL PRECAUTIONS

The Freon refrigerant used is also known as R-12 or F-12. It is odorless and colorless both as a gas and a liquid. Since it boils (vaporizes) at −21.7°F, it will usually be in a vapor state when being handled in a repair shop. But if a portion of the liquid coolant should come in contact with the hands or face, note that its temperature momentarily will be at least 22° below zero.

Protective goggles should be worn when opening any refrigerant lines. If liquid coolant does touch the eyes, bathe the eyes quickly in cold water, then apply a bland disinfectant oil to the eyes. See an eye doctor.

When checking a system for leaks with a torch type leak detector, do not breathe the vapors coming from the flame. Do not discharge refrigerant in the area of a live flame. A poisonous phosgene gas is produced when R-12 or F-12 is burned. While the small amount of gas produced by a leak detector is not harmful unless inhaled directly at the flame, the quantity of refrigerant released into the air when a system is purged can be extremely dangerous if allowed to come in contact with an open flame. Thus, when purging a system, be sure that the discharge hose is routed to a well ventilated place where no flame is present. Under these conditions the refrigerant will be quickly dissipated into the surrounding air.

Never allow the temperature of refrigerant drums to exceed 125°F. The resultant increase in temperature will cause a corresponding increase in pressure which may cause the safety plug to release or the drum to burst.

If it is necessary to heat a drum of refrigerant when charging a system, the drum should be placed in water that is no hotter than 125°F. Never use a blow torch or other open flame. If possible, a pressure release mechanism should be attached before the drum is heated.

When connecting and disconnecting service gauges on A/C system, ensure that gauge hand valves are fully closed and that compressor service valves, if equipped, are in the back-seated (fully counterclockwise) position. Do not disconnect gauge hoses from service port adapters, if used, while gauges are connected to A/C system. To disconnect hoses, always remove adapter from service port. Do not disconnect hoses from gauge manifold while connected to A/C system, as refrigerant will be rapidly discharged.

After disconnecting gauge lines, check the valve areas to be sure service valves are correctly seated and Schraeder valves, if used, are not leaking.

EXERCISE SYSTEM

An important fact most owners ignore is that A/C units must be used periodically. Manufacturers caution that when the air conditioner is not used regularly, particularly during cold months, it should be turned on for a few minutes once every two or three weeks while the engine is running. This keeps the system in good operating condition.

Checking out the system for effects of disuse before the onset of summer is one of the most important aspects of A/C servicing.

First clean out the condenser core, mounted in all cases in front of the radiator. All obstructions, such as leaves, bugs and dirt, must be removed, as they will reduce heat transfer and impair the efficiency of the system. Make sure the space between the condenser and the radiator is also free of foreign matter.

Make certain the evaporator water drain is open. The evaporator cools and dehumidifies the air before it enters the passenger compartment; there, the refrigerant is changed from a liquid to a vapor. As the core cools the air, moisture condenses on it but is prevented from collecting in the evaporator by the water drain.

PERFORMANCE TEST

The system should be operated for at least 15 minutes to allow sufficient time for all parts to become completely stabilized. Determine if the system is fully charged by the use of test gauges and sight glass if one is installed on system. Head pressure will read from 180 psi to 220 psi or higher, depending upon ambient temperature and the type unit being tested. The sight glass should be free of bubbles if a glass is used in the system. Low side pressures should read approximately 15 psi to 30 psi, again depending on the ambient temperature and the unit being tested. It is not feasible to give a definite reading for all types of systems used, as the type control and component installation used on a particular system will directly influence the pressure readings on the high and low sides, **Fig. 1.**

The high side pressure will definitely be affected by the ambient or outside air temperature. A system that is operating normally will indicate a high side gauge reading between 150-170 psi with an 80°F ambient temperature. The same system will register 210-230 psi with an ambient temperature of 100°F. No two systems will register exactly the same, which requires that allowance for variations in head pressures must be considered. Following are the most important normal readings likely to be encountered during the season.

Ambient Temp.	High Side Pressure
80	150-170
90	175-195
95	185-205
100	210-230
105	230-250
11	250-270

RELATIVE TEMPERATURE OF HIGH & LOW SIDES

The high side of the system should be uniformly hot to the touch throughout. A difference in temperature will indicate a partial blockage of liquid or gas at this point.

Evaporator Pressure Gauge Reading	Evaporator Temperature F°	High Pressure Gauge Reading	Ambient Temperature
0	-21°	45	20°
0.6	-20°	55	30°
2.4	-15°	72	40°
4.5	-10°	86	50°
6.8	- 5°	105	60°
9.2	0°	126	70°
11.8	5°	140	75°
14.7	10°	160	80°
17.1	15°	185	90°
21.1	20°	195	95°
22.5	22°	220	100°
23.9	24°	240	105°
25.4	26°	260	110°
26.9	28°	275	115°
28.5	30°	290	120°
37.0	40°	305	125°
46.7	50°	325	130°
57.7	60°		
70.1	70°		
84.1	80°		
99.6	90°		
116.9	100°		
136.0	110°		
157.1	120°		
179.0	130°		

Fig. 1 Pressure-temperature relationship (Typical). Conditions equivalent to 30 mph or 1750 engine RPM.

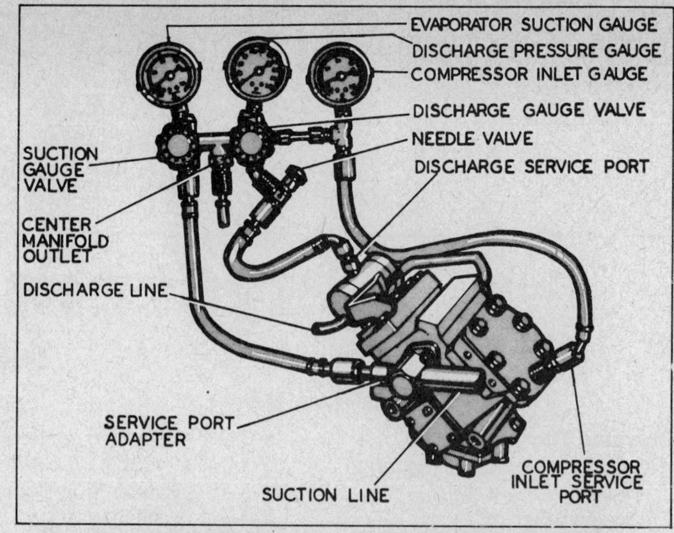

Fig. 2 Manifold gauge set connections. Chrysler Airtemp RV2 compressor

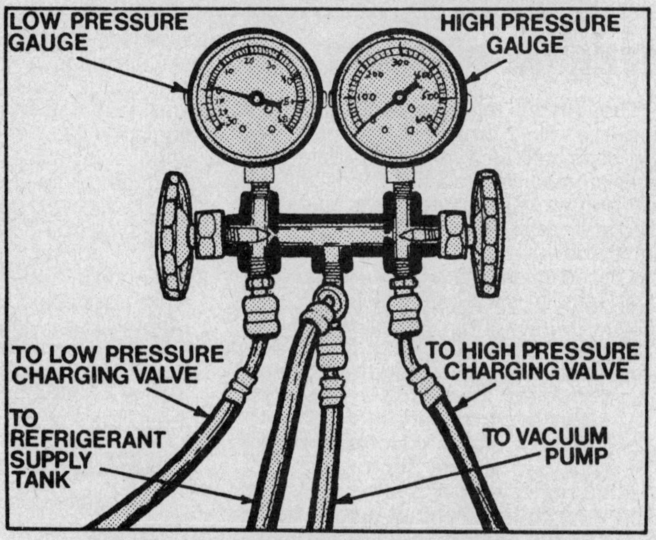

Fig. 3 Manifold gauge set hose connections (Typical). Exc. Chrysler Airtemp RV2 compressor

The low side of the system should be uniformly cool to the touch with no excessive sweating of the suction line or low side service valve. Excessive sweating or frosting of the low side service valve usually indicates an expansion valve is allowing an excessive amount of refrigerant into the evaporator.

EVAPORATOR OUTPUT

At this point, provided all other inspection tests have been performed, and components have been found to operate as they should, a rapid cooling down of the interior of the vehicle should result. The use of a thermometer is not necessary to determine evaporator output. Bringing all units to the correct operating specifications will insure that the evaporator performs as intended.

DISCHARGING & EVACUATING SYSTEM

DISCHARGING SYSTEM

1. Connect gauges into system, **Figs. 2 and 3,** and adjust controls for maximum cooling. This is necessary when the system has not been operating to return excess oil to the compressor.
2. Operate engine for 10 to 15 minutes to stabilize the system at 1500-1750 rpm.
3. Adjust engine speed to slow idle, then shut off engine and controls.
4. Open low side hand manifold valve slightly, using a container to catch oil and refrigerant. **Do not discharge the refrigerant near an open flame as a toxic gas (phosgene) can result.**
5. Open high side manifold valve slightly. **Open hand valve(s) only enough to bleed refrigerant from system. Too rapid purging will draw excessive oil from compressor and system.**
6. Close gauge manifold hand valves when refrigerant ceases to bleed from discharge hose and manifold gauges read zero.

EVACUATE SYSTEM WITH VACUUM PUMP

Vacuum pumps suitable for removing air and moisture from A/C systems are commercially available. A specification for system pump-down used here is 28 to 29½ inches vacuum. This reading can be attained at or near sea level only. For each 1000 feet of altitude this operation is being performed, the reading will be 1 inch vacuum lower. As an example, at 5000 feet elevation, only 23-24½ inches of vacuum can be obtained.

The system must be completely discharged before it can be evacuated. Damage to vacuum pump may result if pressurized refrigerant is allowed to enter.

1. With gauges connected into system, remove cap from vacuum hose connector. Install center hose from gauge manifold to vacuum pump connector. Mid-position high and low side compressor service valves (if used). Open high and low side gauge manifold hand valves.
2. Operate vacuum pump a minimum of 30 minutes for air and moisture removal. Watch compound gauge that system pumps down into a vacuum. System will reach 28-29½ inches vacuum in not over 5 minutes. If system does not pump down, check all connections and leak-test if neces-

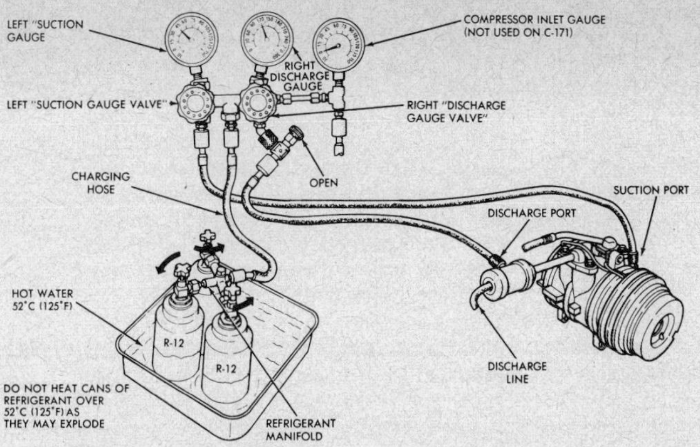

Fig. 4 Complete charging of system

sary.

3. Close gauge manifold hand valves and shut off vacuum pump.
4. Check ability of system to hold vacuum. Watch compound gauge to see that gauge does not rise at a faster rate than 1 inch vacuum every 4 or 5 minutes. If compound gauge rises at too rapid a rate, install partial charge and leak-test. Then evacuate system as outlined above.
5. If system holds vacuum, charge system with refrigerant.

EVACUATE SYSTEM USING CHARGING STATION

A vacuum pump is built into the charging station and is constructed to withstand repeated and prolonged use without damage. Complete moisture removal from the system is possible only with a vacuum pump constructed for the purpose.

The system must be completely discharged before it can be evacuated. Damage to the vacuum pump may result if pressurized refrigerant is allowed to enter.

1. Connect hose to vacuum pump if system was discharged through charging station.
2. Open high and low side gauge valves of charging station.
3. Connect station into 110-volt current.
4. Engage "Off-On" switch to vacuum pump according to directions of specific station being used.
5. System should pump down into a 28-29$^{1}/_{2}$ inches vacuum in not more than 5 minutes. If system fails to meet this specification, repair as necessary.
6. Operate pump a minimum of 30 minutes to remove all air and moisture.
7. Close high and low side gauge valves. Open switch to turn off pump.
8. Check ability of system to hold vacuum by watching compound gauge to see that it does not rise at a rate higher than 1 inch of vacuum every 4 or 5 minutes. If rise rate is not within specifications, repair system as necessary. If rise rate is within specifications, charge system with refrigerant.

CHARGING THE SYSTEM

CHARGING WITH 14 OUNCE CANS

Never use cans to charge into high pressure side of system (compressor discharge port) or into system at high temperature, as high system pressure transferred into charging can may cause it to explode.

1. Attach center hose from manifold gauge set to refrigerant dispensing manifold. Turn refrigerant manifold valves completely counterclockwise to open fully, and remove protective caps from refrigerant manifold.
2. Screw refrigerant cans into manifold, ensuring gasket is in place and in good condition. Torque can and manifold nuts to 6-8 ft. lbs.
3. Turn refrigerant manifold valves clockwise to puncture cans, and close manifold valves, **Fig. 4.**
4. Loosen charging hose at gauge set manifold and turn a refrigerant valve counterclockwise to release refrigerant and purge air from charging hose. When refrigerant gas escapes from loose connection, retighten hose.
5. Fully open all refrigerant manifold valves being used and place refrigerant cans into pan of hot water at 125°F to aid transfer of refrigerant gas. **Do not heat refrigerant cans over 125°F as they may explode. Place water pan and refrigerant cans on scale and note weight.**
6. Connect a jumper wire across cycling clutch switch terminals located on suction line near H valve so clutch will remain engaged.
7. Start engine and set controls to A/C low blower position. Low pressure cut-out switch will prevent clutch from engaging until refrigerant is added to system. If clutch does engage, replace switch before continuing.
8. Charge through suction side of system by slowly opening suction manifold valve. Adjust valve so charging pressure does not exceed 50 psig.
9. Adjust engine speed to fast idle of 1400 RPM.
10. After specified refrigerant charge has entered system, close gauge set manifold valves, refrigerant manifold valves, and reconnect wiring.

CHARGING WITH BULK REFRIGERANT SUPPLY

Only a charging bottle may be used to charge liquid refrigerant through the compressor discharge muffler. Never charge with liquid through compressor inlet or suction line ports, as damage to compressor is likely to occur. Do not run compressor while adding liquid refrigerant.

Beginning with 1984 models, charging system with liquid on compressor discharge side is no longer recommended due to safety reasons.

1. Warm charging bottle in pan of 125°F water. **Do not heat R-12 with a torch, as it may explode.**
2. Loosen charging hose at gauge set manifold and slowly open refrigerant supply valve until refrigerant has purged air from hose. Retighten the hose.
3. Place refrigerant container upside down on scale and note weight.
4. Open refrigerant supply valve and compressor discharge gauge valve to charge system. When scale indicates proper amount of charge has entered system, close valves.

If required amount of refrigerant does not enter system, close compressor discharge valve on manifold gauge set. Turn charging bottle right side up so gas, not liquid, will enter system. Start engine and set A/C control in A/C position. Slowly open suction line valve on manifold gauge set. The compressor will draw refrigerant into system. Charging line valve should be set so suction pressure does not exceed 50 psig.

LEAK TEST SYSTEM

The propane torch Halide Leak Detector is the most widely used of the detection devices. Therefore, only the procedure for this device will be given. The procedure is the same for any electronic detector, except that the pickup device registers the presence of refrigerant by a flashing light or high pitched squeal instead of changing the color of the flame. All other steps in preparing the system and leak testing are the same and can be followed as outlined below:

1. Stabilize system at 1500-1750 RPM. If system is empty of refrigerant, it will be necessary to install a partial charge before continuing. With gauges connected into system, adjust A/C controls for maximum cooling. Operate for 10 to 15 minutes, then shut off car engine.
2. Light leak detector. Open valve to a low flame that will not blow itself out. Warm up until copper element turns cherry red. Lower flame until flame tip is even with or slightly below center of element. For electronic tester, follow preparation procedure as given in operating instructions.
3. Move leak detector pickup under hoses, joints, seals, and any possible place for a leak to occur. **Freon 12 refrigerant is heavier than air and will move downward. If concentration of refrigerant is located, move pickup upward to locate leak. Do not inhale fumes produced by burning refrigerant.**
4. Watch for color change of flame: Pale blue, no refrigerant; yellow, small amount of refrigerant; purplish-blue, large amount of refrigerant. Repair system as necessary if leaks are located.
5. Check sensitivity of reaction plate: Pass pickup hose over empty can or crack open refrigerant container; flame should show violent reaction. If no color change, replace reaction plate, following instructions accompanying leak detector. Too high a flame will result in short life to reaction plate and poor reaction and will soon burn out element.
6. Charge system if repairs were necessary.

System Servicing

INDEX

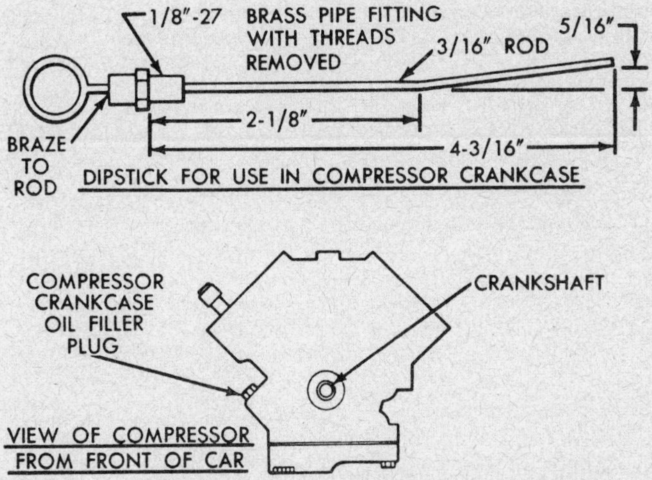

Fig. 1 Air Temp compressor oil level dipstick fabrication & MDBO—MDNM filler plug location

OIL CHARGE

C-171

1. Discharge system and remove suction and discharge lines from compressor.
2. Remove compressor assembly from vehicle, then drain compressor oil from suction and discharge ports.
3. Add 5 fl. oz. of refrigerant oil to compressor through suction port.
4. Install compressor assembly and, using new gaskets, attach suction and discharge lines.
5. Evacuate and charge system. If any of the following components are to be replaced, oil must be added to the system:
   Evaporator................ 2 ounces
   Condenser..................1 ounce
   Filter-Drier..................1 ounce

OIL LEVEL CHECK

The oil level of these compressors should be checked whenever refrigerant has been lost due to leakage or through normal system servicing.

CHRYSLER AIR TEMP COMPRESSORS

RV2 COMPRESSOR

1. Connect gauge and manifold assembly and slowly discharge refrigerant system. Near completion of discharge, flush dipstick with existing freon. This will ensure dipstick is clean and at approximately the same temperature as refrigerant oil in compressor sump.
2. Carefully remove compressor oil sump filler plug, then insert dipstick into hole until it bottoms in sump, **Fig. 1. When removing compressor oil sump filler plug a face shield should be worn. Refrigerant dissolved in compressor oil could cause oil to percolate out through filler plug opening.**
3. Remove dipstick and measure oil level, refer to A/C Specification Tables. Add refrigerant oil as necessary to bring oil level within limits. **Oil level should be checked only after refrigerant has boiled off and oil surface has stabilized.**
4. If any of the following components are to be replaced, it will be necessary to add additional oil to system. Evaporator, 2 ounces; Condenser, 1 ounce; Filter Drier, 1 ounce.
5. On all models, install filler plug, then evacuate and recharge system.

C-171 COMPRESSOR

1. Discharge refrigerant from system.
2. Remove compressor from vehicle, then invert compressor and allow oil to drain from suction and discharge ports.
3. Add 5 fluid ounces of clean refrigerant oil through suction port, then install compressor and connect suction and discharge lines using new gaskets.
4. Evacuate and recharge system. **The C-171 compressor contains 9 to 10 ounces of refrigerant oil on 1982-84 models, or 7 to 7 1/4 ounces of refrigerant oil on 1985-86 models. While the A/C system is in operation, the oil is carried through the entire system by the refrigerant. Some of the oil will be retained in the various components of the system. If a replacement evaporator coil is installed, add 2 ounces of refrigerant oil to system. If a replacement condenser coil or filter-drier is installed, add one additional ounce of refrigerant oil to system. This additional oil must be added to compensate for oil removed with the component. Before installing a replacement compressor, drain and measure oil from old compressor and adjust level in new compressor to equal this amount.**

CHARGING VALVE LOCATION

All charging valves are located on the compressor except the high pressure valve for the C-171 compressor, which is located on the muffler.

A/C Data Table

Year	Model	Refrigerant Capacity, Lbs.	Refrigerant Oil: Viscosity	Refrigerant Oil: Total System Capacity, Ounces	Refrigerant Oil: Compressor Oil Level Check, Inches	Compressor Clutch Air Gap, Inch
1982-85	Front Wheel Drive ①	2.125	500	③	④	.020-.025
	Front Wheel Drive ②	2.375	500	③	④	.020-.035
1986-87	Front Wheel Drive	2.625	500	7-7.25	⑤	.020-.035
1982-87	Rear Wheel Drive	2.625	500	③	④	.020-.035

①—Horizon, Omni, Charger, Turismo, 024 & TC3
②—Except Horizon, Omni, Charger, Turismo, 024 & TC3
③—RV2 compressor, 10-12 ounces. Refer to text procedure for C-171 compressor.
④—RV2 compressor, 10-12 ounces. Refer to text procedure for C-171 compressor.
⑤—Refer to text for procedure.

ENGINE COOLING FANS

TABLE OF CONTENTS

Variable Speed Fans

INDEX

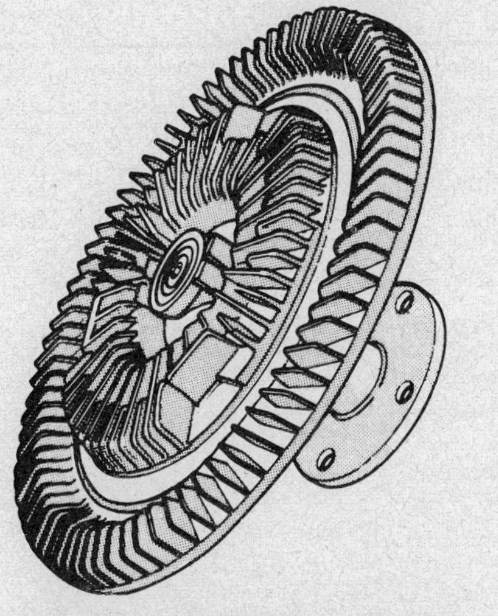

Fig. 1 Fan drive clutch (typical of Chrysler rear wheel drive vehicles)

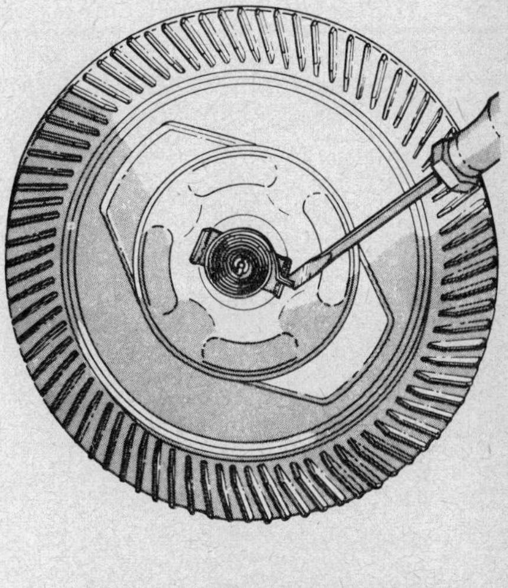

Fig. 2 Disconnecting thermostatic spring

DESCRIPTION

The fan drive clutch, **Fig. 1,** is a fluid coupling containing silicone oil. Fan speed is regulated by the torque-carrying capacity of the silicone oil. The more silicone oil in the coupling the greater the fan speed, and the less silicone oil the slower the fan speed.

Chrysler rear wheel drive vehicles use a bi-metal coil spring type of fan drive clutch, **Fig. 1.** The bi-metal coil on the face of the fan clutch senses the temperature of the air after it passes through the radiator. Until the thermostat is open, the fan will "Idle" at a reduced speed. Once the thermostat is open and the incoming air is heated (to a specified temperature), thereby causing a reaction in the bi-metal coil, will the fan clutch engage and drive the fan for required engine cooling. When the fan clutch is engaged, the fan speed will increase with the engine speed until a specified fan speed is reached. At this point the fan will rotate at the maximum speed despite any increase in engine RPM.

FAN DRIVE CLUTCH TEST

Do not operate the engine until the fan has been first checked for possible cracks and separations.

Run the engine at a fast idle speed (1000 RPM) until normal operating temperature is reached. This process can be speeded up by blocking off the front of the radiator with cardboard. Regardless of temperatures, the unit must be operated for at least five minutes immediately before being tested.

Stop the engine and, using a glove or a cloth to protect the hand, immediately check the effort required to turn the fan. If considerable effort is required, it can be assumed that the coupling is operating satisfactorily. If very little effort is required to turn the fan, it is an indication that the coupling is not operating properly and should be replaced.

Another test is to disconnect the bi-metal spring, **Fig. 2,** and rotate counterclockwise until a stop is felt. Measure the gap between end of coil and housing clip, **Fig. 3.** The gap should be 1/2 inch. If not, replace fan clutch.

SERVICE

To prevent silicone fluid from draining into fan drive bearing, store with flange facing upward, Fig. 4.

Also, the coil spring type of fan clutch cannot be disassembled, serviced or repaired. If defective, replace with a new unit.

1. Disconnect battery ground cable.
2. Remove fan shroud attaching screws and position shroud rearward on engine.
3. Remove fan attaching bolts. **The fan and fan drive clutch are removed as an assembly.**
4. On some models it is necessary to partially drain coolant and remove upper radiator hose to provide clearance for fan and clutch removal.
5. Separate fan drive clutch from fan.
6. Reverse procedure to install. Torque fan attaching bolts to 200 inch pounds.

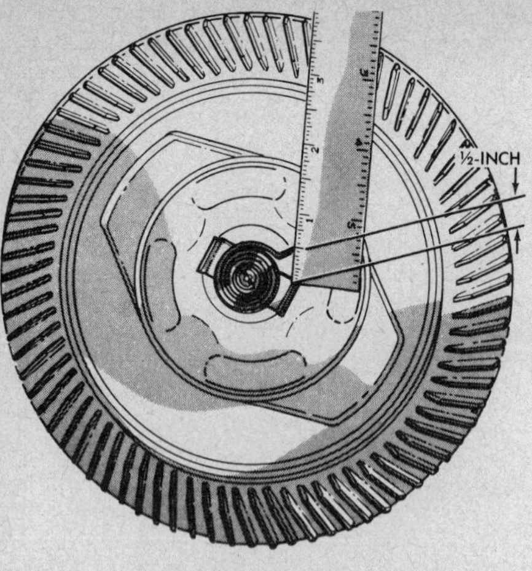

Fig. 3 Checking spring & shaft rotation

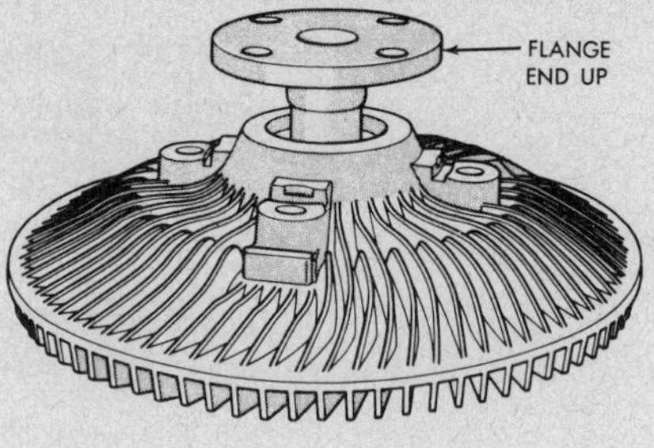

Fig. 4 Proper position for storage of fan drive clutch

Electric Cooling Fans

INDEX

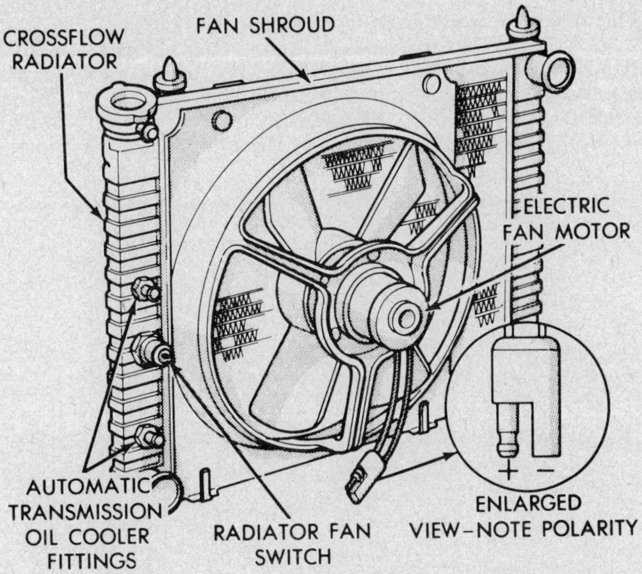

Fig. 1 Electric engine cooling fan (typical)

On models equipped with electric engine cooling fans, the battery ground cable should be disconnected whenever underhood service is performed.

DESCRIPTION

On all models except 1985-87 equipped with 2.2L/4-135 and 1986-87 2.5L/4-153 engines, the fan is controlled by a fan switch which is located on the radiator, **Fig. 1.** The switch will automatically turn on when coolant temperature reaches approximately 193 to 207 degrees F. On all models with A/C, when the A/C system is in operation, the fan motor will operate continually regardless of engine coolant temperature. When the ignition switch is turned off the fan motor will stop operating, except on models equipped with 2.6 L engine and air conditioning. On models equipped with 2.6L/4-156 engines and air conditioning, and others, the fan will remain operating with ignition off for approximately 5 to 10 minutes if ambient temperature at radiator is above a predetermined level (after-run fan).

On 1985-87 models equipped with 2.2L/4-135 engines and 1986-87 models equipped with 2.5L/4-153 engines, the fan is controlled by the on-board computer. The computer shuts off the fan motor automatically when it is not needed on vehicles less air conditioning, or when the A/C is shut off on vehicles with air conditioning. The fan motor is always on when the air conditioning compressor is running. With A/C off or on models less A/C, the fan runs with vehicle speed above 40 mph only if coolant temperature reaches 230°F and will turn off when temperature drops to 220°F. At speeds below 40 mph, the fan switches on at 210°F and off at 200°F. The fan motor does not operate when the ignition is turned off.

RADIATOR FAN SWITCH

The radiator fan switch is located on left-hand radiator tank. The switch is normally open and incorporates a bi-metal disc which pushes the plunger when coolant temperature reaches approximately 200 degrees F. If the fan motor turns on and off at the appropriate temperature, the switch is operating properly.

To check switch continuity, drain coolant until level is below switch. The switch can be viewed by looking downward through the radiator filler neck. Disconnect electrical connector from switch and remove switch from radiator. Dip switch into an oil bath which has achieved a temperature of 208 degrees F or higher and check switch for continuity using a test lamp or ohmmeter. If continuity is not indicated, replace switch.

AMBIENT TEMPERATURE SWITCH

AFTER-RUN FAN

Some models use an ambient temperature switch. The switch is located on the radiator cooling fan mounting bracket and is used in conjunction with the time delay relay to activate the radiator cooling fan for approximately 5 to 10 minutes with engine off during periods of radiator ambient temperature of 105° F or above.

The switch is tested using a suitable ohmmeter. When the switch is cold, continuity should not exist. When the switch is warmed to 105° F or above, continuity should be present. Replace if defective.

ELECTRIC FAN MOTOR DIAGNOSIS

Disconnect wire connector from fan motor terminal, then connect a 14 gauge jumper wire from battery to fan motor terminal. If fan motor does not operate properly, replace fan motor.

FAN MOTOR, REPLACE

1982 MODELS

1. Disconnect wire connectors from fan motor and fan switch, then drain cooling system.
2. Disconnect upper and lower radiator hoses from radiator. On models equipped with automatic transmission, disconnect fluid cooling hoses from radiator, if necessary.
3. Remove upper fan shroud attaching screws, then lift shroud upward and out of bottom shroud retaining clips, separating shroud from radiator. **When removing shroud from radiator, use care not to damage fan or radiator cooling fans.**
4. Remove fan motor to shroud attaching screws, then while supporting fan motor and shaft, remove fan motor retaining clip and fan motor.
5. Reverse procedure to install.

1983–87 MODELS

1. Disconnect fan motor electrical connector.
2. Remove fan motor, fan and fan shroud or support as an assembly from radiator support.
3. To remove fan blade from motor, support motor and shaft assembly on workbench, then remove fan blade retaining clip. Use caution to prevent bending motor shaft. **Do not allow fan blades to become bent or damaged in any way.**
4. Reverse procedure to install.

ELECTRIC FAN MOTOR RELAY

The fan motor relay is used on models equipped with A/C, except for 1985-87 models with 2.2L/4-135 engines and 1986-87 models equipped with 2.5L/4-153 engines. The relay is located on the lefthand shock absorber housing. If radiator fan switch and fan motor test results are satisfactory, but fan motor will not operate the fan motor relay is then suspected. After replacing relay, disconnect wire connector from radiator fan switch and connect a 14 gauge jumper wire between wire connector terminals. Place ignition switch in the Accessory position. Fan motor should operate.

On models equipped with 2.6L/4-156 engines and others, the electric engine cooling fan relay also contains the time delay, which operates the cooling fan when ignition is off and the radiator ambient temperature is 105° F or above.

DASH GAUGES

INDEX

GAUGES

Gauge failures are often caused by defective wiring or grounds. The first step in locating trouble should be a thorough inspection of all wiring, terminals and printed circuits. If wiring is secured by clamps, check to see whether the insulation has been severed thereby grounding the wire. In the case of a fuel gauge installation, rust may cause failure by corrosion at the ground connection of the tank unit.

VOLTAGE LIMITER TYPE

The voltage limiter type indicator is a bi-metal resistance type system consisting of a voltage limiter, an indicator gauge, and a variable resistance sending unit. Current to the system is applied to the gauge terminals by the voltage limiter, which maintains an average-pulsating value of 5 volts.

The indicator gauge consists of a pointer which is attached to a wire-wound bi-metal strip. Current passing through the coil heats the bi-metal strip, causing the pointer to move. As more current passes through the coil, heat increases, moving the pointer farther.

The circuit is completed through a sending unit which contains a variable resistor. When resistance is high, less current is allowed to pass through the gauge, and the pointer moves very little. As resistance decreases due to changing conditions in system being monitored, more current passes through gauge coil, causing pointer to move farther.

VOLTAGE LIMITER TEST

1. Connect one lead of a suitable voltmeter to temperature sending unit and other lead to a good ground. Do not disconnect sending unit lead from sending unit.
2. Turn ignition switch to the "On" position and observe voltmeter.
3. A fluctuating voltmeter indicates that voltage limiter is operating.

AMMETERS

The ammeter is an instrument used to indicate current flow into and out of the battery. When electrical accessories in the vehicle draw more current than the alternator can supply, current flows from the battery and the ammeter indicates a discharge (−) condition. When electrical loads of the vehicle are less than alternator output, current is available to charge the battery, and the ammeter indicates a charge (+) condition. If battery is fully charged, the voltage regulator reduces alternator output to meet only immediate vehicle electrical loads. When this happens, ammeter reads zero.

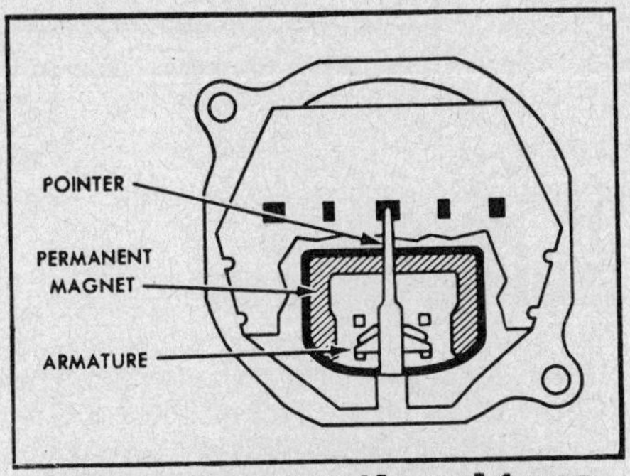

Fig. 1 Conventional type ammeter (typical)

CONVENTIONAL AMMETER

A conventional ammeter must be connected between the battery and alternator in order to indicate current flow. This type ammeter, **Fig. 1,** consists of a frame to which a permanent magnet is attached. The frame also supports an armature and pointer assembly. Current in this system flows from the alternator through the ammeter, then to the battery or from the battery through the ammeter into the vehicle electrical system, depending on vehicle operating conditions.

When no current flows through the ammeter, the magnet holds the pointer armature so that the pointer stands at the center of the dial. When current passes in either direction through the ammeter, the resulting magnetic field attracts the armature away from the effect of the permanent magnet, thus giving a reading proportional to the strength of the current flowing.

TROUBLESHOOTING

When the ammeter apparently fails to register correctly, there may be trouble in the wiring which connects the ammeter to the alternator and battery or in the alternator or battery itself.

To check the connections, first tighten the two terminal posts on the back of the ammeter. Then, following each wire from the ammeter, tighten all connections on the ignition switch, battery and alternator. Chafed, burned or broken insulation can be found by following each ammeter wire from end to end.

All wires with chafed, burned or broken insulation should be repaired or replaced. After this is done, and all connections are tightened, connect the battery cable and turn on the ignition switch. The needle should point slightly to the discharge (−) side.

Start the engine and speed it up a little above idling speed. The needle should then move to the charge side (+), and its movement should be smooth.

If the pointer does not behave correctly, the ammeter itself is out of order and a new one should be installed.

SHUNT TYPE AMMETER

The shunt type ammeter is actually a specially calibrated voltmeter. It is connected to read voltage drop across a resistance wire (shunt) between the battery and alternator. The shunt is located either in the vehicle wiring or within the ammeter itself.

When voltage is higher at the alternator end of the shunt, the meter indicates a charge (+) condition. When voltage is higher at the battery end of the shunt, the meter indicates a discharge (−) condition. When voltage is equal at both ends of the shunt, the meter reads zero.

TROUBLESHOOTING

Ammeter accuracy can be determined by comparing reading with an ammeter of known accuracy.

1. With engine stopped and ignition switch in RUN position, switch on headlamps and heater fan. Meter should indicate a discharge (−) condition.
2. If ammeter pointer does not move, check ammeter terminals for proper connection and check for open circuit in wiring harness. If connections and wiring harness are satisfactory, ammeter is defective.
3. If ammeter indicates a charge (+) condition, wiring harness connections are reversed at ammeter.

VOLTMETER

The voltmeter is a gauge which measures the electrical flow from the battery to indicate whether the battery output is within tolerances. The voltmeter reading can range from 13.5-14.0 volts under normal operating conditions. If an undercharge or overcharge condition is indicated for an extended period, the battery and charging system should be checked.

TROUBLESHOOTING

To check voltmeter, turn key and headlights on with engine off. Pointer should move to 12.5 volts. If no needle movement is observed, check connections from battery to circuit breaker. If connections are tight and meter shows no movement, check wire continuity. If wire continuity is satisfactory, the meter is inoperative and must be replaced.

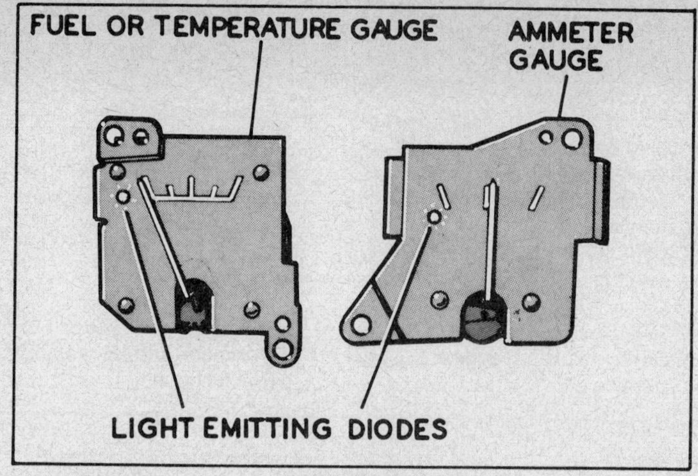

Fig. 2 Gauges incorporating the LED system

ELECTRICAL TEMPERATURE GAUGES

This temperature indicating system consists of a sending unit, located on the cylinder head, electrical temperature gauge and an instrument voltage regulator. As engine temperature increases or decreases, the resistance of the sending unit changes, in turn controlling current flow to the gauge. When engine temperature is low, the resistance of the sending unit is high, restricting current flow to the gauge, in turn indicating low engine temperature. As engine temperature increases, the resistance of the sending unit decreases, permitting an increased current flow to the gauge, resulting in an increased temperature reading.

TROUBLESHOOTING

A special tester is required to diagnosis this type of gauge. Follow instructions included with the tester.

ELECTRICAL OIL PRESSURE GAUGES

This oil pressure indicating system incorporates an instrument voltage regulator, electrical oil pressure gauge and a sending unit which are connected in series. The sending unit consists of a diaphragm, contact and a variable resistor. As oil pressure increases or decreases, the diaphragm actuated the contact on the variable resistor, in turn controlling current flow to the gauge. When oil pressure is low, the resistance of the variable resistor is high, restricting current flow to the gauge, in turn indicating low oil pressure. As oil pressure increases, the resistance of the variable resistor is lowered, permitting an increased current flow to the gauge, resulting in an increased gauge reading.

TROUBLESHOOTING

A special tester is required to diagnosis this type of gauge. Follow instructions included with the tester.

OIL PRESSURE INDICATOR LAMP

Many cars utilize a warning lamp on the instrument panel in place of the conventional dash indicating gauge to warn the driver when the oil pressure is dangerously low. The warning lamp is wired in series with the ignition switch and the engine unit which is an oil pressure switch.

The oil pressure switch contains a diaphragm and a set of contacts. When the ignition switch is turned on, the warning lamp circuit is energized and the circuit is completed through the closed contacts in the pressure switch. When the engine is started, build-up of oil pressure compresses the diaphragm, opening the contacts, thereby breaking the circuit and putting out the lamp.

TROUBLESHOOTING

The oil pressure warning lamp should light when the ignition is turned on. If it does not light, disconnect the wire from the engine unit and ground the wire to the frame or cylinder block. If the warning lamp still does not light with the ignition switch on, replace the bulb.

If the warning lamp lights when the wire is grounded to the frame or cylinder block, the engine unit should be checked for being loose or poorly grounded. If the unit is found to be tight and properly grounded, it should be removed and a new one installed. (The presence of sealing compound on the threads of the engine unit will cause a poor ground).

If the warning lamp remains lit when it normally should be out, replace the engine unit before proceeding further to determine the cause for a low pressure indication.

The warning lamp will sometimes light or flicker when the engine is idling, even though the oil pressure is adequate. However, the lamp should go out when the engine is speeded up. There is no cause for alarm in such cases; it simply means that the pressure switch is not calibrated precisely correct.

TEMPERATURE INDICATOR LAMP

A bimetal temperature switch located in the cylinder head control the operation of a temperature indicator lamp with a red lens. If the engine cooling system is not functioning properly and coolant temperature exceeds a predetermined value, the warning lamp will illuminate.

TROUBLESHOOTING

If the red lamp is not lit when the engine is being cranked, check for a burned out bulb, an open in the light circuit, or a defective ignition switch.

If the red lamp is lit when the engine is running, check the wiring between lamp and switch for a ground, temperature switch defective, or overheated cooling system.

As a test circuit to check whether the red bulb is functioning properly, a wire which is connected to the ground terminal of the ignition switch is tapped into its circuit. When the ignition is in the "Start" (engine cranking) position, the ground terminal is grounded inside the switch and the red bulb will be lit. When the engine is started and the ignition switch is in the "On" position, the test circuit is opened and the bulb is then controlled by the temperature switch.

GAUGE ALERT SYSTEM

LED (LIGHT EMITTING DIODE)

The fuel, temperature and ammeter gauges are equipped with a LED (Light Emitting Diode) mounted in each of the gauge dials, **Fig. 2.** This diode will illuminate and alert the driver that the system the gauge is monitoring is malfunctioning. The electronic sensor circuit is mounted on the gauge housing. The printed circuit board is permanently attached and is not serviceable. If the LED is malfunctioning, the gauge and the printed circuit board must be replaced as an assembly.

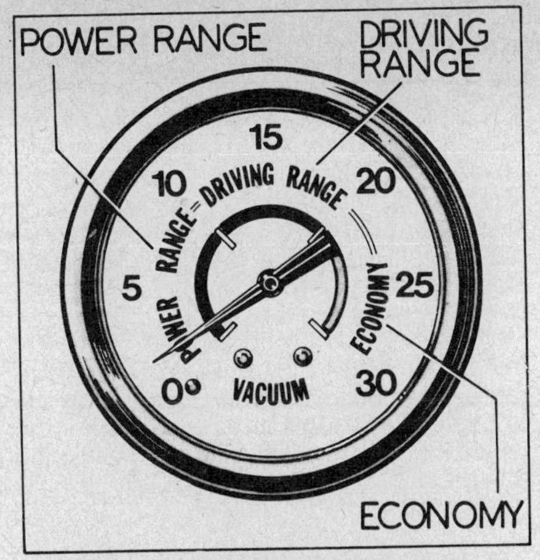

Fig. 3 Typical vacuum gauge

OPERATION

FUEL GAUGE

When gauge indicator shows approximately 1/8 of a tank of fuel remaining, the LED will light alerting the driver of a low fuel situation.

TEMPERATURE GAUGE

When gauge indicator shows engine temperature approximately 240 to 260 degrees F the LED will light alerting the driver of an overheat condition.

AMMETER GAUGE

This LED operates independently of the gauge indicator and monitors system voltage. The LED will alert the driver of three charging system potential malfunctions.

1. A discharging condition, caused by excessive electrical demand on charging system (engine at idle RPM).
2. A weak or defective battery with ignition switch in the "On" position, (before the ignition switch is moved to the "Start" position).
3. A weak or defective battery with minimum demand on charging system, while vehicle is being used in stop and go driving (intermittent LED illumination occurring).

TESTING

FUEL & TEMPERATURE LED

Use tester C-3826 for diagnosing systems.

AMMETER LED

Only if battery and charging system are functioning properly can the following test be performed.

Turn ignition switch to the "On" position and turn on headlights, windshield wipers and stoplights. This will cause excessive demand on charging system activating the LED immediately or within approximately one minute. If the LED does not light there is a malfunction in the system. If LED lights, run engine at approximately 2000 RPM, LED should stop emitting light, if the LED continues to emit light there is a malfunction in the system. **In all cases of system malfunctions the complete gauge must be replaced.**

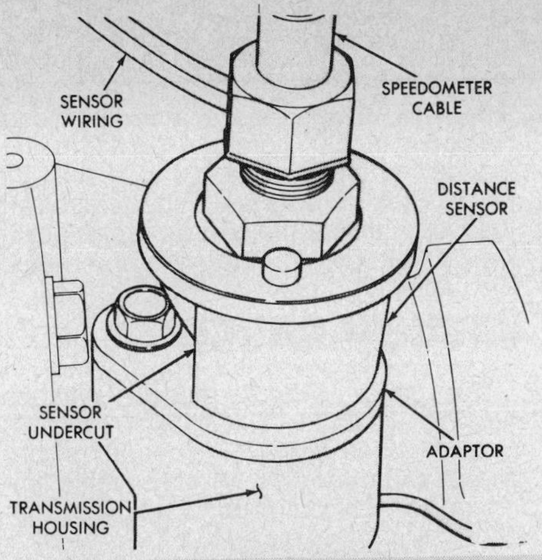

Fig. 4 Distance sensor installation

SPEEDOMETERS

The following material covers only that service on speedometers which can be performed by the average service man. Repairs on the units themselves are not included as they require special tools and extreme care when making repairs and adjustments and only an experienced speedometer mechanic should attempt such servicing.

The speedometer has two main parts: the indicator head and the speedometer drive cable. When the speedometer fails to indicate speed or mileage, the cable or housing is probably broken.

SPEEDOMETER CABLE

Most cables are broken due to lack of lubrication or a sharp bend or kink in the housing.

A cable might break because the speedometer head mechanism binds. If such is the case, the speedometer head should be repaired or replaced before a new cable or housing is installed.

A "jumpy" pointer condition, together with a sort of scraping noise, is due, in most instances, to a dry or kinked speedometer cable. The kinked cable rubs on the housing and winds up, slowing down the pointer. The cable then unwinds and the pointer "jumps."

To check for kinks, remove the cable, lay it on a flat surface and twist one end with the fingers. If it turns over smoothly the cable is not kinked. But if part of the cable flops over as it is twisted, the cable is kinked and should be replaced.

LUBRICATION

The speedometer cable should be lubricated with special cable lubricant every 10,000 miles.

Fill the ferrule on the upper end of the housing with the cable lubricant. Insert the cable in the housing, starting at the upper end. Turn the cable around carefully while feeding it into the housing. Repeat filling the ferrule except for the last six inches of cable. Too much lubricant at this point may cause the lubricant to work into the indicating hand.

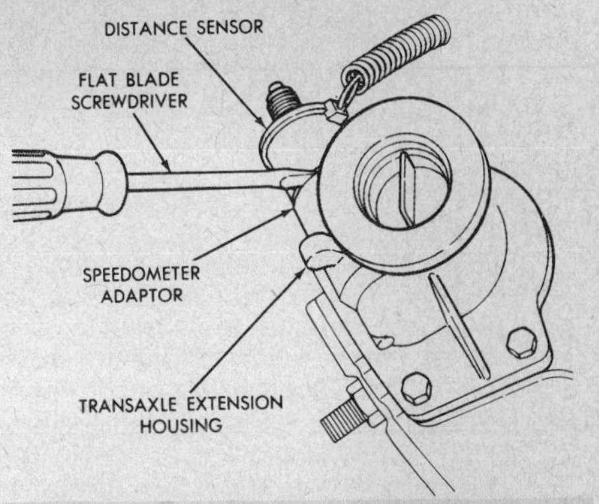

Fig. 5 Distance sensor removal

INSTALLING CABLE

During installation, if the cable sticks when inserted in the housing and will not go through, the housing is damaged inside or kinked. Be sure to check the housing from one end to the other. Straighten any sharp bends by relocating clamps or elbows. Replace housing if it is badly kinked or broken. Position the cable and housing so that they lead into the head as straight as possible.

Check the new cable for kinks before installing it. Use wide, sweeping, gradual curves when the cable comes out of the transmission and connects to the head so the cable will not be damaged during its installation.

If inspection indicates that the cable and housing are in good condition, yet pointer action is erratic, check the speedometer head for possible binding.

The speedometer drive pinion should also be checked. If the pinion is dry or its teeth are stripped, the speedometer may not register properly.

The transmission mainshaft nut must be tight or the speedometer drive gear may slip on the mainshaft and cause slow speed readings.

ELECTRIC CLOCKS

Regulation of electric clocks used on automobiles is accomplished automatically by merely resetting the time. If the clock is running fast, the action of turning the hands back to correct the time will automatically cause the clock to run slightly slower. If the clock is running slow, the action of turning the hands forward to correct the time will automatically cause the clock to run slightly faster (10 to 15 seconds day).

A lock-out feature prevents the clock regulator mechanism from being reset more than once per wind cycle, regardless of the number of times the time is reset. After the clock rewinds, if the time is then reset, automatic regulation will take place. If a clock varies over 10 minutes per day, it will never adjust sufficiently, and must be repaired or replaced.

WINDING CLOCK WHEN CONNECTING BATTERY OR CLOCK WIRING

The clock requires special attention

when reconnecting a battery that has been disconnected for any reason, a clock that has been disconnected, or when replacing a blown clock fuse. It is very important that the initial wind be fully made. The procedure is as follows:

1. Make sure that all other instruments and lights are turned off.
2. Connect positive cable to battery.
3. Before connecting the negative cable, press the terminal to its post on the battery. Immediately afterward strike the terminal against the battery post to see if there is a spark. If there is a spark, allow the clock to run down until it stops ticking, and repeat as above until there is no spark. Then immediately make the permanent connection before the clock can again run down. The clock will run down in approximately two minutes.
4. Reset clock after all connections have been made. The foregoing procedure should also be followed when reconnecting the clock after it has been disconnected, or if it has stopped because of a blown fuse. Be sure to disconnect battery before installing a new fuse.

TROUBLESHOOTING

If clock does not run, check for blown clock fuse. If fuse is blown check for short in wiring. If fuse is not blown check for open circuit.

With an electric clock, the most frequent cause of clock fuse blowing is voltage at the clock which will prevent a complete wind and allow clock contacts to remain closed. This may be caused by any of the following: discharged battery, corrosion on contact surface of battery terminals, loose connections at battery terminals, at junction block, at fuse clips, or at terminal connection of clock. Therefore, if in reconnecting battery or clock it is noted that the clock is not ticking, always check for blown fuse, or examine the circuits at the points indicated above to determine and correct the cause.

VACUUM GAUGE

This gauge, **Fig. 3,** measures intake manifold vacuum. The intake manifold vacuum varies with engine operating conditions, carburetor adjustments, valve timing, ignition timing and general engine condition.

Since the optimum fuel economy is directly proportional to a properly functioning engine, a high vacuum reading on the gauge relates to fuel economy. For this reason some manufacturers call the vacuum gauge a "Fuel Economy Indicator." Most gauges have colored sectors the green sector being the "Economy" range and red the "Power" range. Therefore, the vehicle should be operated with gauge registering in the green sector or a high numerical number, **Fig. 3,** for maximum economy.

ELECTRONIC VOICE ALERT

On some Chrysler models, an 11 function voice alert system is available as an option. All messages are preceded by a group of beeps and, on some models, followed with a tone. Warning messages are repeated with each "key on" until the condition is corrected.

Some messages will not be heard unless the vehicle is in forward motion. These are controlled by a distance sensor, **Fig. 4,** and the back-up lamp switch. The distance sensor delays selected messages until the vehicle is in motion and the back-up lamp switch locks out others when in reverse gear.

A volume control is located under the electronic control module and is adjustable. An on-off switch is provided on the module (depending on model year). If the voice alert system is turned off, all warning lamps and tones will function normally.

DISTANCE SENSOR TEST

Do not use a test lamp for this test.

1. Disconnect speedometer cable from distance sensor, **Fig. 4.**
2. Insert a flat bladed screwdriver between the sensor and adapter. Rotate screwdriver 90 degrees to release sensor from adapter spring clip, **Fig. 5.**
3. Disconnect sensor wiring connector and remove from vehicle.
4. Using an ohmmeter that will read in tenths of an ohm, connect ohmmeter leads to sensor terminals.
5. Rotate the sensor shaft and observe ohmmeter. Eight pulses should be observed for each complete revolution of the sensor shaft. Also, each reading should have a value of .5 ohm. Any reading higher would indicate a defective sensor.

STARTER MOTORS & SWITCHES

TABLE OF CONTENTS

General Information

INDEX

STARTER TROUBLE CHECK OUT

When trouble develops in the starting motor circuit, and the starter cranks the engine slowly or not at all, several preliminary checks can be made to determine whether the trouble lies in the battery, in the starter, in the wiring between them, or elsewhere. Many conditions besides defects in the starter itself can result in poor cranking performance.

To make a quick check of the starter system, turn on the headlights. They should burn with normal brilliance. If they do not, the battery may be run down.

If the battery is in a charged condition so that lights burn brightly, operate the starting motor. Any one of three things will happen to the lights: (1) They will go out, (2) dim considerably or (3) stay bright without any cranking action taking place.

IF LAMP GOES OUT

If the lamps go out as the starter switch is closed, it indicates that there is a poor connection between the battery and starting motor. This poor connection will most often be found at the battery terminals. Correction is made by removing the cable clamps from the terminals, cleaning the terminals and clamps, replacing the clamps and tightening them securely. A coating of corrosion inhibitor (petroleum jelly will do) may be applied to the clamps and terminals to retard the formation of corrosion.

IF LAMP DIMS

If the lamps dim considerably as the starter switch is closed and the starter operates slowly or not at all, the battery may be run down, or there may be some mechanical condition in the engine or starting motor that is throwing a heavy burden on the starting motor. This imposes a high discharge rate on the battery which causes noticeable dimming of the lamps.

Check the battery state of charge. If it is charged, the trouble probably lies in either the engine or starting motor itself. In the engine, tight bearings or pistons or heavy oil place an added burden on the starting motor. Low temperatures also hamper starting motor performance since it thickens engine oil and makes the engine considerably harder to crank and start. Also, a battery is less efficient at low temperatures.

In the starting motor, a bent armature, loose pole shoe screws or worn bearings, any of which may allow the armature to drag, will reduce cranking performance and increase current draw.

In addition, more serious internal damage is sometimes found. Thrown armature windings or commutator bars, which sometimes occur on overrunning clutch drive starting motors, are usually caused by excessive overrunning after starting. This is the result of such conditions as the driver keeping the starting switch closed too long after the engine has started, the driver opening the throttle too wide in starting, or improper carburetor fast idle adjustment. Any of these subject the overrunning clutch to extra strain so it tends to seize, spinning the armature at high speed with resulting armature damage.

Another cause may be engine backfire during cranking which may result, among other things, from ignition timing being too far advanced.

To avoid such failures, the driver should pause a few seconds after a false start to make sure the engine has come completely to rest before another start is attempted. In addition, the ignition timing should be checked if engine backfiring has caused the trouble.

LAMP STAYS BRIGHT, NO CRANKING ACTION

This condition indicates an open circuit at some point, either in the starter itself, the starter switch or control circuit. The solenoid control circuit can be eliminated momentarily by placing a heavy jumper lead across the solenoid main terminals to see if the starter will operate. This connects the starter directly to the battery and, if it operates, it indicates that the control circuit is not functioning normally. The wiring and control units must be checked to locate the trouble.

If the starter does not operate with the jumper attached, it will probably have to be removed from the engine so it can be examined in detail.

CHECKING CIRCUIT WITH VOLTMETER

Excessive resistance in the circuit between the battery and starter will reduce cranking performance. The resistance can be checked by using a voltmeter to measure voltage drop in the circuits while the starter is operated. There are three checks to be made:

1. Voltage drop between car frame and grounded battery terminal post (not cable clamp).
2. Voltage drop between car frame and starting motor field frame.
3. Voltage drop between insulated battery terminal post and starting motor terminal stud (or the battery terminal stud of the solenoid).

Each of these should show no more than one-tenth (0.1) volt drop when the starting motor is cranking the engine. Do not use the starter for more than 30 seconds at a time to avoid overheating it.

If excessive voltage drop is found in any of these circuits, make correction by disconnecting the cables, cleaning the connections carefully, and then reconnecting the cables firmly in place. A coating of petroleum jelly on the battery cables and terminal clamps will retard corrosion. **On some cars, extra long battery cables may be required due to the location of the battery and starter. This may result in somewhat higher voltage drop than the above recommended 0.1 volt. The only means of determining the normal voltage drop in such cases is to check several of these vehicles. Then when the voltage drop is well above the nor-**

mal figure for all cars checked, abnormal resistance will be indicated and correction can be made as already explained.

SOLENOID SWITCHES

The solenoid switch on a cranking motor not only closes the circuit between the battery and the cranking motor but also shifts the drive pinion into mesh with the engine flywheel ring gear. This is done by means of a linkage between the solenoid switch plunger and the shift lever on the cranking motor.

There are two windings in the solenoid; a pull-in winding and a hold-in winding. Both windings are energized when the external control switch is closed. They produce a magnetic field which pulls the plunger in so that the drive pinion is shifted into mesh, and the main contacts in the solenoid switch are closed to connect the battery directly to the cranking motor. Closing the main switch contacts shorts out the pull-in winding since this winding is connected across the main contacts. The magnetism produced by the hold-in winding is sufficient to hold the plunger in, and shorting out the pull-in winding reduces drain on the battery. When the control switch is opened, it disconnects the hold-in winding from the battery. When the hold-in winding is disconnected from the battery, the shift lever spring withdraws the plunger from the solenoid, opening the solenoid switch contacts and at the same time withdrawing the drive pinion from mesh. Proper operation of the switch depends on maintaining a definite balance between the magnetic strength of the pull-in and hold-in windings.

This balance is established in the design by the size of the wire and the number of turns specified. An open circuit in the hold-in winding or attempts to crank with a discharged battery will cause the switch to chatter.

To disassemble the solenoid, remove nuts, washers and insulators from the switch terminal and battery terminal. Remove cover and take out the contact disk assembly.

STARTING MOTOR SERVICE

To obtain full performance data on a starting motor or to determine the cause of abnormal operation, the starting motor should be submitted to a no-load and torque test. These tests are best performed on a starter bench tester with the starter mounted on it.

From a practical standpoint, however, a simple torque test may be made quickly with the starter in the car. Make sure the battery is fully charged and that the starter circuit wires and terminals are in good condition. Then operate the starter to see if the engine turns over normally. If it does not, the torque developed is below standard and the starter should be removed for further checking.

STARTER DRIVE TROUBLES

Starter drive troubles are easy to diagnose and they usually cannot be confused with ordinary starter difficulties. If the starter does not turn over at all or if it drags, look for trouble in the starter or electrical supply system. Concentrate on the starter drive or ring gear if the starter is noisy, if it turns but does not engage the engine, or if the starter won't disengage after the engine is started. After the starter is removed, the trouble can usually be located quickly.

Worn or chipped ring gear or starter pinion are the usual causes of noisy operation. Before replacing either or both of these parts try to find out what caused the damage. With the Bendix type drive, incomplete engagement of the pinion with the ring gear is a common cause of tooth damage. The wrong pinion clearance on starter drives of the overrunning clutch type leads to poor meshing of the pinion and ring gear and too rapid tooth wear.

A less common cause of noise with either type of drive is a bent starter armature shaft. When this shaft is bent, the pinion gear alternately binds and then only partly meshes with the ring gear. Most manufacturers specify a maximum of .003 inch radial run-out on the armature shaft.

WHEN CLUTCH DRIVE FAILS

The overrunning clutch type drive seldom becomes so worn that it fails to engage since it is directly activated by a fork and lever. The only thing that is likely to happen is that, once engaged, it will not turn the engine because the clutch itself is worn out. A much more frequent difficulty and one that rapidly wears ring gear and teeth is partial engagement. Proper meshing of the pinion is controlled by the end clearance between the pinion gear and the starter housing or pinion stop, if used.

On some starters, the solenoids are completely enclosed in the starter housing and the pinion clearance is not adjustable. If the clearance is not correct, the starter must be disassembled and checked for excessive wear of solenoid linkage, shift lever mechanism, or improper assembly of parts.

Failure of the overrunning clutch drive to disengage is usually caused by binding between the armature shaft and the drive. If the drive, particularly the clutch, shows signs of overheating it indicates that it is not disengaging immediately after the engine starts. If the clutch is forced to overrun too long, it overheats and turns a bluish color. For the cause of the binding, look for rust or gum between the armature shaft and the drive, or for burred splines. Excess oil on the drive will lead to gumming, and inadequate air circulation in the flywheel housing will cause rust.

Overrunning clutch drives cannot be overhauled in the field so they must be replaced. In cleaning, never soak them in a solvent because the solvent may enter the clutch and dissolve the sealed-in lubricant. Wipe them off lightly with kerosene and lubricate them sparingly with SAE 10 or 10W oil.

WHEN BENDIX DRIVE FAILS

When a Bendix type drive doesn't engage the cause usually is one of three things: either the drive spring is broken, one of the drive spring bolts has sheared off, or the screwshaft threads won't allow the pinion to travel toward the flywheel. In the first two cases, remove the drive by unscrewing the setscrew under the last coil of the drive spring and replace the broken parts. Gummed or rusty screwshaft threads are fairly common causes of Bendix drive failure and are easily cleaned with a little kerosene or steel wool, depending on the trouble. Here again, as in the case of overrunning clutch drives, use light oil sparingly, and be sure the flywheel housing has adequate ventilation. There is usually a breather hole in the bottom of the flywheel housing which should be open.

The failure of a Bendix drive to disengage or to mesh properly is most often caused by gummed or rusty screwshaft threads. When this is not true, look for mechanical failure within the drive itself.

Starter Motor Specifications

Starter Make	Starter Model Number	Brush Spring Tension, Ounces	Free Speed Test			Solenoid	
			Amps	Volts	RPM	Hold-In Windings	Pull-In Windings
Bosch	5206255	—	47	11	6600	—	—
	5206260	—	47	11	6600	—	—
	5213045	—	47	11	6600	—	—
	5213080	—	47	11	6600	—	—
	5213395	—	47	11	6600	—	—
	5213450	—	47	11	6600	—	—
	5226441	47	47	11	6600	—	—
	5226442	47	47	11	6600	—	—
	5226444	85	85	11	3700	—	—
	5227282	—	—	—	—	—	—
Chrysler	3755250	32-36	90	11	5700	8-11	13-15
	3755900	32-36	90	11	3700	8-11	13-15
	4111855	32-36	90	11	5700	8-11	13-15
	4111860	32-36	91	11	5700	8-11	13-15
Mitsubishi	5213301	—	120-160	11	6600	—	—
Nippondenso	5206265	—	47	11	6600	—	—
	5206270	—	47	11	6600	—	—
	5213085	—	47	11	6600	—	—
	5213190	—	85	11	3700	—	—
	5213235	—	47①	11	6600②	—	—
	5213295	—	47	11	6600	—	—
	5213301	—	47	11	6600	—	—
	5213645	—	47	11	6600	—	—
	5226742	—	47	11	6600	—	—
	5226842	—	85	11	3700	—	—
	5226844	—	85	11	3700	—	—

①—1984-85, 85 amps.
②—1984-85, 3700 RPM.

Bosch Starter Motors

INDEX

DESCRIPTION

The Bosch starter used on 1.7 and 2.2 L engines is a direct drive starter motor with an overrunning clutch type starter drive. A solenoid switch is mounted on the starter motor.

The Bosch starter used on 2.5 L engines is a gear reduction starter. The starter uses six permanent magnets in place of conventional wound field magnets to save weight. The gear reduction system uses a planetary gear train to transmit armature rotation to the pinion shaft. A solenoid switch is mounted on the starter motor drive end shield.

DIAGNOSIS

Refer to **Fig. 1** when diagnosing starter.

IN-VEHICLE TESTING

Before starting any tests, ensure that battery is fully charged and that all connections are good.

AMPERAGE DRAW TEST

1. Run engine until it reaches operating temperature, then turn engine off.
2. Connect a suitable battery-starter tester according to manufacturer's instructions.
3. Turn battery-starter tester control knob to "Off" position.
4. Turn voltmeter selector knob to "16 Volt" position.
5. Turn battery-starter function selector to "Starter System Test" (0-500 amp scale).
6. Connect red positive ammeter lead to positive battery terminal and the black negative ammeter lead to negative battery terminal.
7. Connect red positive voltmeter lead to positive battery terminal and the black negative voltmeter lead to the negative battery terminal.
8. Connect a remote starter jumper ac-

cording to manufacturer's instructions. **Do not crank engine excessively during testing.**

9. Disconnect coil wire from distributor cap center tower and secure to good ground.
10. Crank engine with remote starter switch and observe exact voltmeter reading, then stop cranking engine.
11. Turn tester control knob clockwise until voltmeter reads exactly the same as when engine was being cranked. On direct drive starters, ammeter should read 120-160 amps. On reduction gear starters, ammeter should read 150-210 amps.

STARTER RESISTANCE TEST

1. Disconnect positive battery cable and connect 0-300 scale ammeter between disconnected lead and battery terminal post.
2. Connect a voltmeter, graduated in tenths, between positive post on battery and starter relay terminal on starter solenoid.
3. Crank engine while observing reading on voltmeter and ammeter. A voltage reading exceeding .3 volts indicates high resistance caused by loose circuit connections, a faulty cable, burned starter relay or solenoid switch contacts. A high current combined with slow cranking speed indicates need for starter repair.
4. Reconnect positive battery lead to battery.

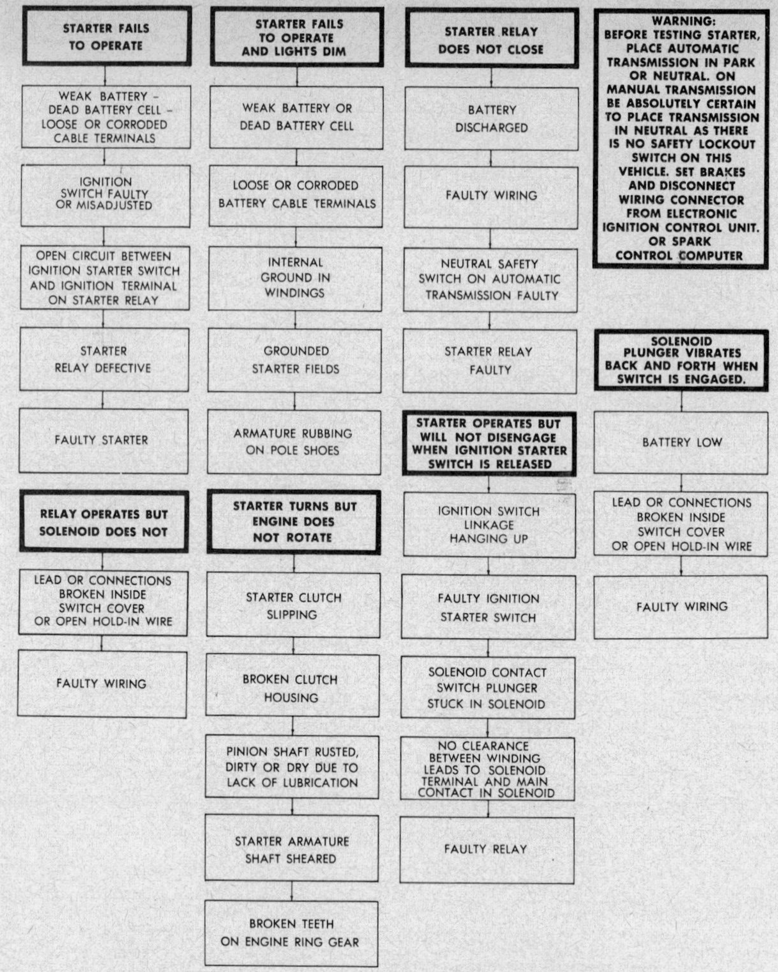

Fig. 1 Starter motor diagnosis

INSULATED CIRCUIT TEST

1. Turn voltmeter selector knob to 4 volt position.
2. Disconnect ignition coil secondary cable.
3. Connect voltmeter positive lead to battery positive post and voltmeter negative lead to solenoid connector that connects to starter field coils. **It may be necessary to peel back rubber boot on solenoid to reach solenoid connection.**
4. Connect remote control starter switch to battery solenoid terminal of starter relay.
5. Crank engine with remote control starter switch while observing voltmeter reading. If voltmeter reading exceeds .3 volt, there is high resistance in starter insulated coil, proceed as follows:
   a. Remove voltmeter lead from solenoid connector and connect to following points, repeating test at each connection. Starter terminal of solenoid, battery terminal of solenoid, battery cable terminal at solenoid, starter relay and cable clamp at battery.
   b. A small change will occur each time a normal portion of the circuit is removed from test. A definite change in voltmeter reading indicates that last part eliminated in test is at fault.

STARTER GROUND TEST

1. Connect voltmeter positive lead to starter through bolt and negative voltmeter lead to battery negative post.
2. Crank engine with remote control starter switch and observe voltmeter reading.
3. If voltmeter reading exceeds .2 volt, make following tests to isolate points of excessive voltage loss, repeating test at each connection; starter drive housing, cable terminal at engine, cable clamp at battery.
4. A small change will occur each time a normal portion of circuit is removed from test. A definite change in voltmeter reading indicates last part eliminated in test is at fault.

STARTER SOLENOID TEST

1. Connect heavy jumper wire on starter relay between battery and solenoid terminals. If engine cranks, perform starter relay test.
2. If engine does not crank or solenoid chatters, check wiring and connectors from relay to starter for loose or corroded connections.
3. Repeat test and, if engine still does not crank properly, repair or replace starter as necessary.

STARTER SOLENOID BENCH TEST

1. Disconnect field coil wire from field coil terminal.
2. Check for continuity between solenoid terminal and field coil terminal. There should be continuity.
3. Check for continuity between solenoid terminal and solenoid housing. There should be continuity.
4. If there is no continuity in either test, replace solenoid assembly.
5. Connect field coil wire to field coil terminal.

STARTER RELAY TEST

1. Place transmission in Neutral and apply parking brake.
2. Check for battery voltage between starter relay battery terminal and ground.
3. Connect jumper wire on starter relay between battery and ignition terminals.
4. If engine does not crank, connect a second jumper wire to starter relay between ground terminal and good ground and repeat test.
5. If engine cranks in step 4, transmission linkage is improperly adjusted or neutral safety switch is defective.
6. If engine does not crank in step 4, starter relay is defective.

Chrysler Reduction Gear Starter

INDEX

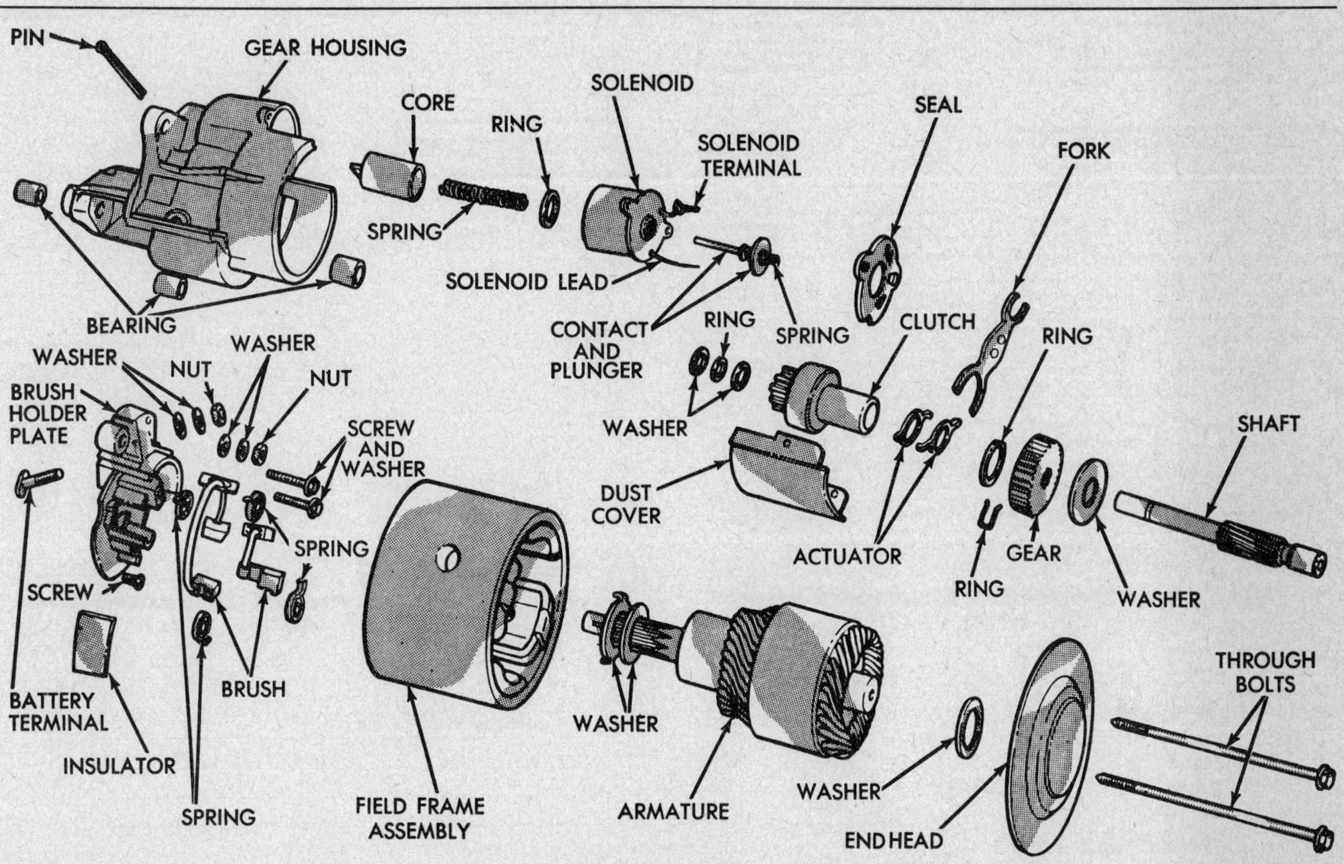

Fig. 1 Chrysler built reduction gear starting motor

DESCRIPTION

This reduction gear starting motor, **Fig. 1**, has an armature-to-engine crankshaft ratio of 2 to 1 or a $3^1/_2$ to 1 reduction gear set is built into the motor assembly. The starter utilizes a solenoid shift. The housing of the solenoid is integral with the starter drive end housing.

DIAGNOSIS

Refer to **Fig. 2** when diagnosing starter.

IN-VEHICLE TESTING

AMPERAGE DRAW TEST

1982 MODELS

1. Run engine until it reaches operating temperature, then turn engine off.
2. Connect battery-starter tester following manufacturer's instructions.
3. Turn variable resistor control knob on tester to zero or off position.
4. Connect remote starter switch following manufacturer's instructions.
5. Crank engine just long enough to read cranking voltage on voltmeter.
6. Turn variable resistor control knob on tester until voltmeter reads cranking voltage previously noted. Amperage should be 165-180 amps on 225 and 318 cubic inch engines, or 180-200 amps on 225 (equipped with 1.8 horsepower starter).

1983–87 MODELS

When performing this test on these vehicles refer to amperage draw test for Bosch starters.

CIRCUIT RESISTANCE TEST

1. Connect voltmeter leads across each connection shown in circuit resistance chart, **Fig. 3**.
2. If readings are higher than specified, clean or repair connection, then repeat test.

STARTER SOLENOID TEST

1. Connect heavy jumper wire on starter relay between battery and solenoid terminals.
2. If starter does not crank, or solenoid chatters, check wiring and connectors from relay to starter for loose or corroded connections, then repeat test.
3. If engine still will not crank, repair or replace starter as necessary.

STARTER SOLENOID BENCH TEST

1. Remove solenoid assembly.
2. Connect solenoid to 6 volt DC power supply with an ammeter in series. Connect positive lead of power supply to solenoid terminal, positive lead of ammeter to solenoid sleeve and negative lead of power supply to other ammeter terminal.
3. Turn on circuit and check current draw for hold-in coil.
4. Transfer positive ammeter lead to solenoid lead terminal and check current

STARTER MOTOR DIAGNOSIS

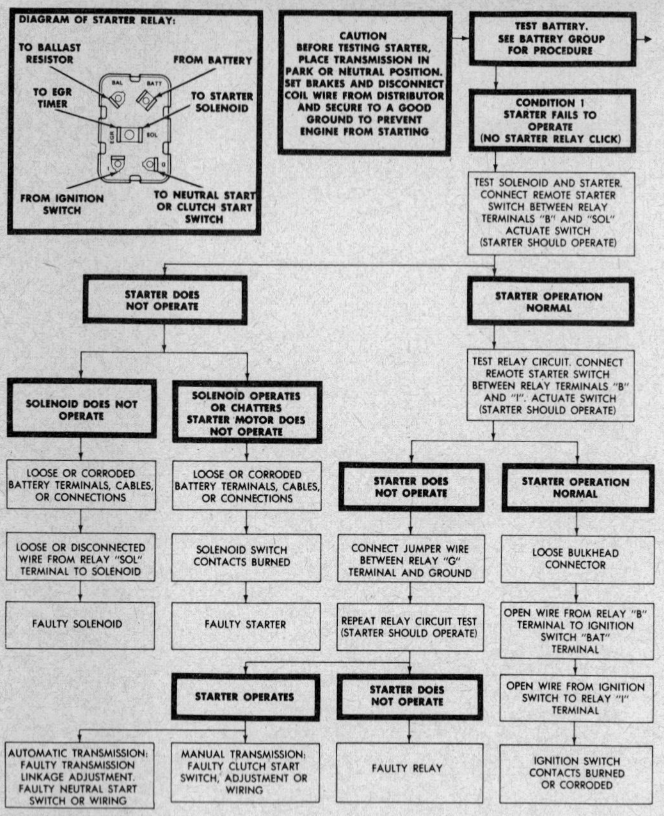

Fig. 2 Starter motor diagnosis (Part 1 of 2)

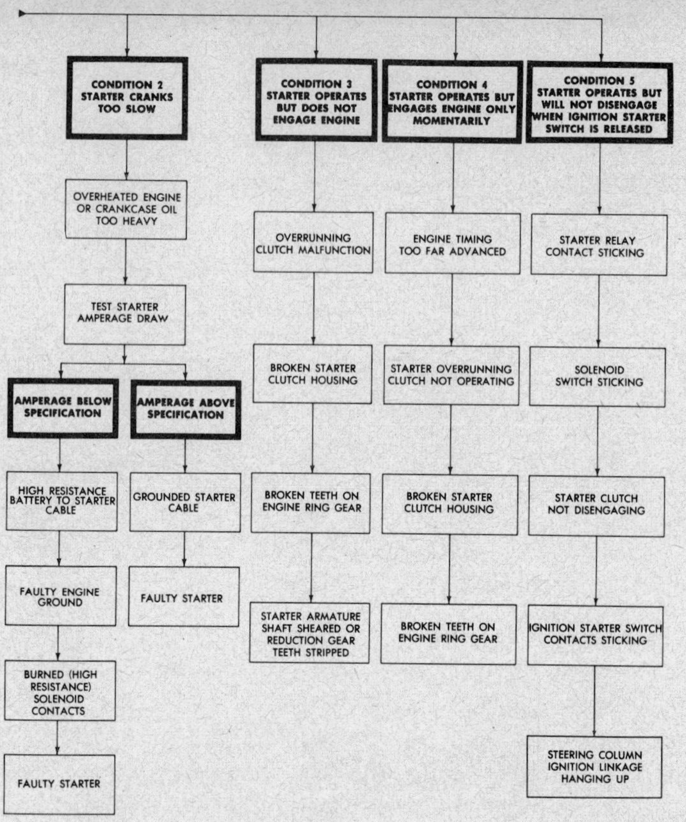

Fig. 2 Starter motor diagnosis (Part 2 of 2)

draw for pull-in coil.

5. If current draw for hold-in coil is not 8-9 amps @ 77°F, current draw for pull-in coil is not 13-15 amps @ 77°F or winding appears burnt or damaged, replace solenoid assembly.

STARTER RELAY TEST

VEHICLES W/AUTOMATIC TRANSMISSION

1. Place shift lever in Neutral, then connect jumper wire on starter relay between battery and ignition terminals.
2. If engine does not crank, connect a second jumper wire on starter relay between ground terminal and good ground.
3. If engine now cranks, transmission linkage is improperly adjusted or neutral safety switch is defective.
4. If engine still does not crank, replace starter relay.

CIRCUIT RESISTANCE CHART

Connection	Voltmeter Lead Connection Positive	Negative	Voltmeter Reading
Positive post on battery to cable clamp	To post	To clamp	0
Negative post on battery to cable clamp	To post	To clamp	0
Battery ground cable to engine block	To bolt	To cable connector	Not to exceed 0.2 volts
Battery Cable to Starter	To Battery Postive Post	To Battery Terminal on Starter	Not to exceed 0.2 volts
Starter housing to ground	To starter housing	To negative post on battery	Not to exceed 0.2 volts

Fig. 3 Circuit resistance chart

VEHICLES W/MANUAL TRANSMISSION

1. Have assistant depress clutch pedal.
2. Connect jumper wire on starter relay between battery and ignition terminals.
3. If engine does not crank, connect second jumper wire on starter relay between ground terminal and good ground.
4. If engine cranks, clutch neutral start switch is improperly adjusted or defective. If engine does not crank, replace starter relay.

Mitsubishi Starters

INDEX

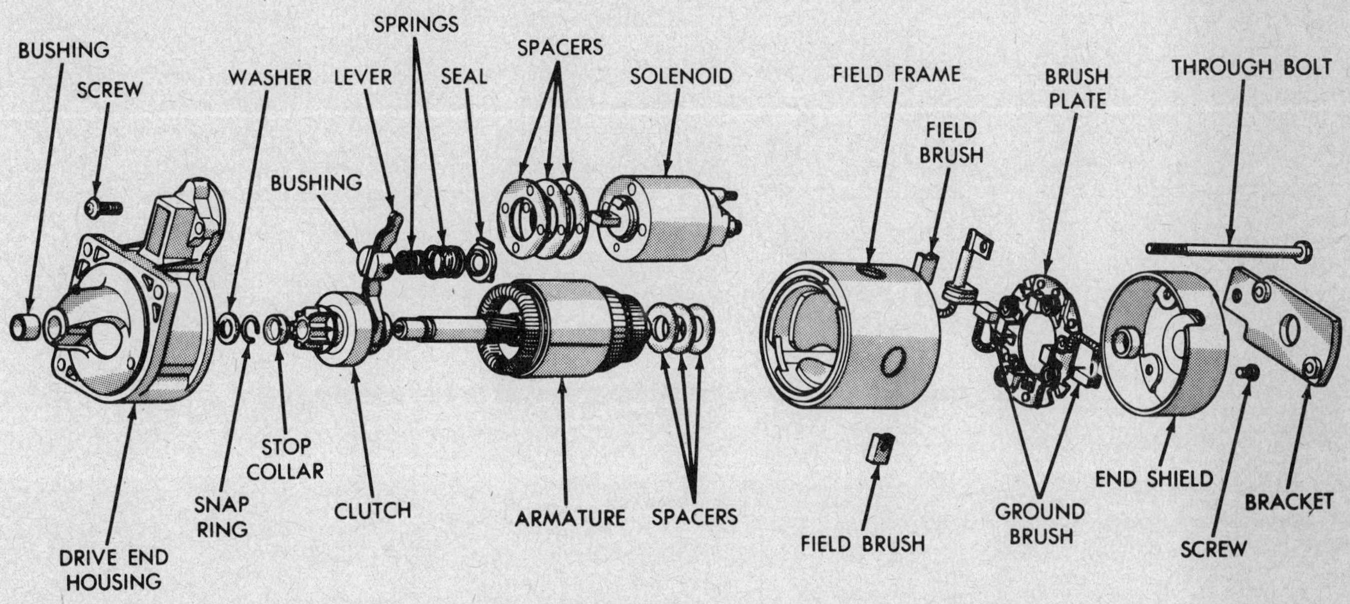

Fig. 1 Nippondenso direct drive starter exploded view

DESCRIPTION

The Mitsubishi starter, **Fig. 1,** is a direct drive starter motor with an overrunning clutch type starter drive. A solenoid switch is mounted on the starter motor.

DIAGNOSIS

For diagnosis of this starter, refer to "Bosch Starters."

IN-VEHICLE TESTING

When testing this starter, refer to "Bosch Starters."

Nippondenso Starters

INDEX

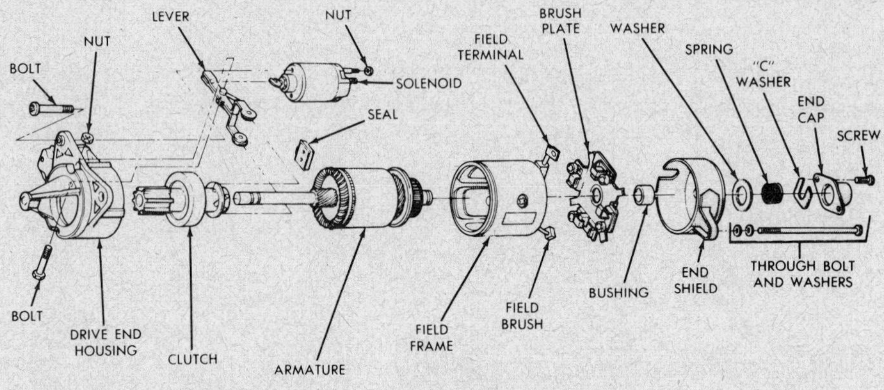

Fig. 2 Nippondenso reduction gear starter exploded view

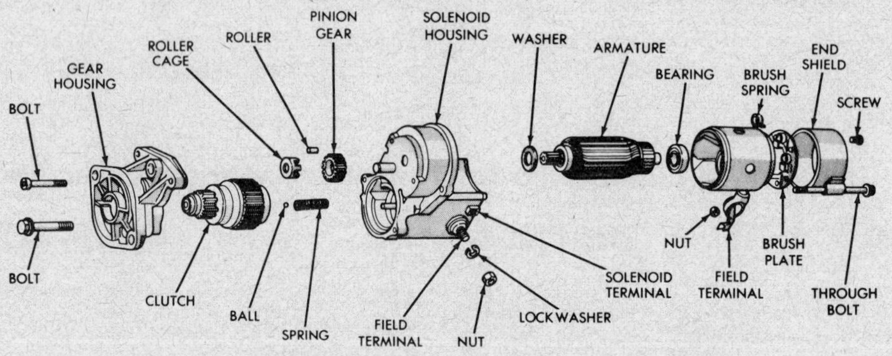

Fig. 1 Mitsubishi starter exploded view

DESCRIPTION

Nippondenso starters, **Figs. 1 and 2,** are either direct drive or reduction gear types. The direct drive starter has an overrunning clutch type starter drive and a solenoid switch is mounted on the starter motor. The structure of the reduction gear type starter differs from that of the direct drive type, but the electrical wiring is the same for both types.

DIAGNOSIS & TESTING

When diagnosing or testing Nippondenso starters, refer to "Bosch Starters."

ALTERNATOR SYSTEMS

TABLE OF CONTENTS

General Information

INDEX

INTRODUCTION

Alternators are composed of the same functional parts as the conventional D.C. generator but they operate differently: The field is called a rotor and is the turning portion of the unit. A generating part, called a stator, is the stationary member, comparable to the armature in a D.C. generator. The regulator, similar to those used in a D.C. system, regulates the output of the alternator-rectifier system.

The power source of the system is the alternator. Current is transmitted from the field terminal of the regulator through a slip ring to the field coil and back to ground through another slip ring. The strength of the field regulates the output of the alternating current. This alternating current is then transmitted from the alternator to the rectifier where it is converted to direct current.

These alternators employ a three-phase stator winding in which the phase windings are electrically 120 degrees apart. The rotor consists of a field coil encased between interleaved sections producing a magnetic field with alternate north and south poles. By rotating the rotor inside the stator the alternating current is induced in the stator windings. This alternating current is rectified (changed to D.C.) by silicon diodes and brought out to the output terminal of the alternator.

DIODE RECTIFIERS

Six or more silicon diode rectifiers are used and act as electrical one-way valves. One half of the diodes have ground polarity and are pressed or screwed into a heat sink which is grounded. The other diodes (ungrounded) are pressed or screwed into and insulated from the end head; these diodes are connected to the alternator output terminal.

Since the diodes have a high resistance to the flow of current in one direction and a low resistance in the opposite direction, they may be connected in a manner which allows current to flow from the alternator to the battery in the low resistance direction. The high resistance in the opposite direction prevents the flow of current from the battery to the alternator. Because of this feature no circuit breaker is required between the alternator and battery.

SERVICE PRECAUTIONS

1. Be certain that battery polarity is correct when servicing units. Reversed battery polarity will damage rectifiers and regulators.
2. If booster battery is used for starting, be sure to use correct polarity in hook up.
3. When a fast charger is used to charge a vehicle battery, the vehicle battery cables should be disconnected unless the fast charger is equipped with a special Alternator Protector, in which case the vehicle battery cables need not be disconnected. Also the fast charger should never be used to start a vehicle as damage to rectifiers will result.
4. Lead connections to the grounded rectifiers (negative) should never be soldered as the excessive heat may damage the rectifiers.
5. Unless the system includes a load relay or field relay, grounding the alternator output terminal will damage the alternator and/or circuits. This is true even when the system is not in operation since no circuit breaker is used and the battery is applied to the alternator output terminal at all times. The field or load relay acts as a circuit breaker in that it is controlled by the ignition switch.
6. Before making any "on vehicle" tests of the alternator or regulator, the battery should be checked and the circuit inspected for faulty wiring or insulation, loose or corroded connections and poor ground circuits.
7. Check alternator belt tension to be sure the belt is tight enough to prevent slipping under load.
8. The ignition switch should be off and the battery ground cable disconnected before making any test connections to prevent damage to the system.
9. The vehicle battery must be fully charged or a fully charged battery may be installed for test purposes.

Bosch Alternators

INDEX

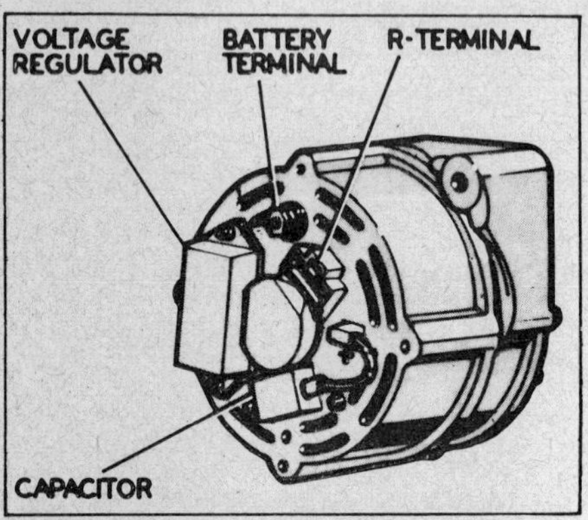

Fig. 1 Bosch alternator w/integral regulator

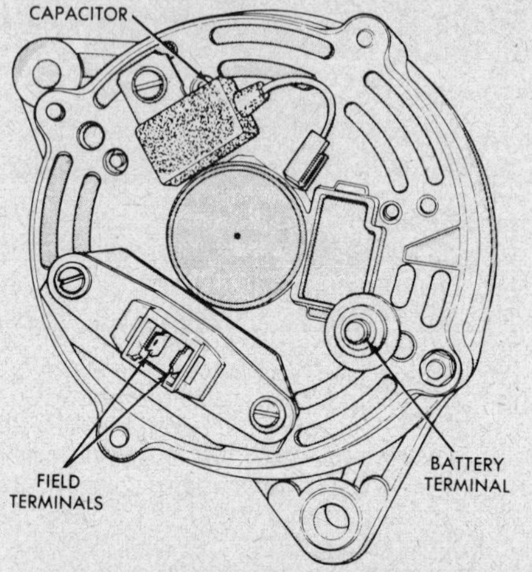

Fig. 2 Rear view of Bosch alternator w/external regulator

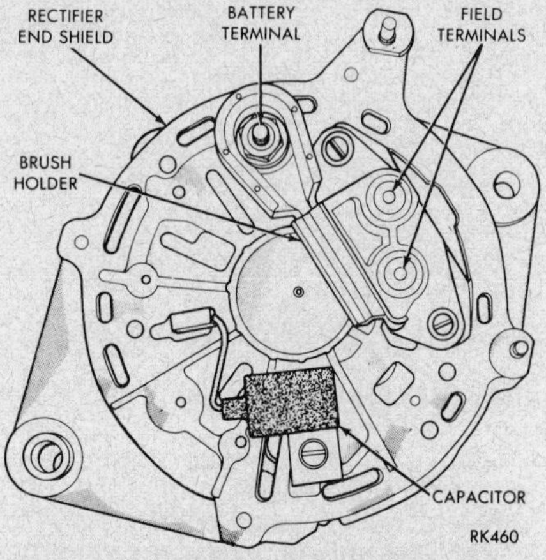

Fig. 3 Rear view of Bosch alternator w/regulator in-engine electronics

DESCRIPTION

The main components of the Bosch alternator, **Figs. 1 through 3,** are the front and rear housings, stator windings, rotor and rectifying diodes. Current is supplied to the rotor through slip rings and two brushes which, on integral regulator units, are built into the voltage regulator positioned on the rear housing. The rotor is supported in the front and rear housings by ball bearings. The stator windings are assembled inside a laminated core which forms part of the alternator frame. A diode plate containing positive and negative diodes is soldered to the stator winding leads.

Alternator field current is supplied through a diode trio which is also connected to the stator windings. A capacitor which is mounted to the rear housing, protects the diode plate assembly from high voltages and suppresses radio noises. On all units, the voltage regulator is solid state, which is not serviceable or adjustable. On integral regulator units, the voltage regulator can be replaced without disassembling the alternator. On units with voltage regulator in-engine electronics, the electronic voltage regulator is contained within engine electronics Power Module and Logic Module.

IN-VEHICLE TESTING

INTEGRAL REGULATOR UNITS

CHARGING CIRCUIT RESISTANCE TEST

1. Disconnect ground cable from battery and the "Bat" lead from alternator output terminal.
2. Complete test connections as shown in **Fig. 4.**

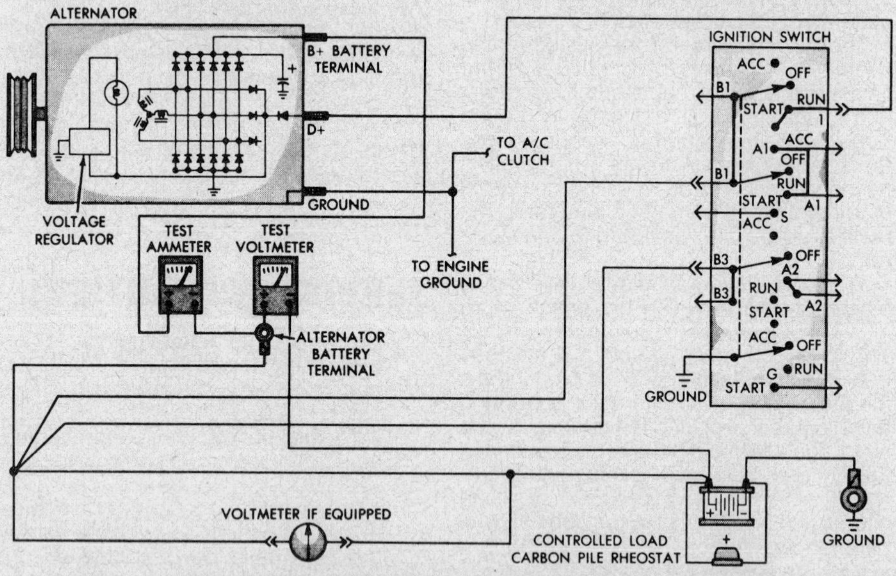

Fig. 4 Charging circuit resistance test. Models w/integral regulator

3. Connect battery ground cable, then start engine and operate at idle.
4. Adjust engine speed and carbon pile rheostat to obtain 20 amps in the circuit and check voltmeter reading. Reading should not exceed .5 volts. If a higher voltage drop is indicated, inspect, clean and tighten all connections in the circuit. A voltage drop test at each connection can be performed to isolate the problem.

CURRENT OUTPUT TEST

1. Disconnect ground cable from battery and the "Bat" lead from alternator output terminal.
2. Complete test connections as shown in **Fig. 5.**
3. Connect battery ground cable, then start engine and operate at idle.
4. Adjust carbon pile rheostat and engine speed to obtain 28-35 amps at 13.5 volts and 500 RPM, 75-85 amps at 13.5 volts and 1000 RPM and 89 amps at 13.5 volts and 2000 RPM. **While increasing engine speed, do not allow voltage to exceed 16 volts.**
5. If amperage does not meet specifications, remove alternator from vehicle

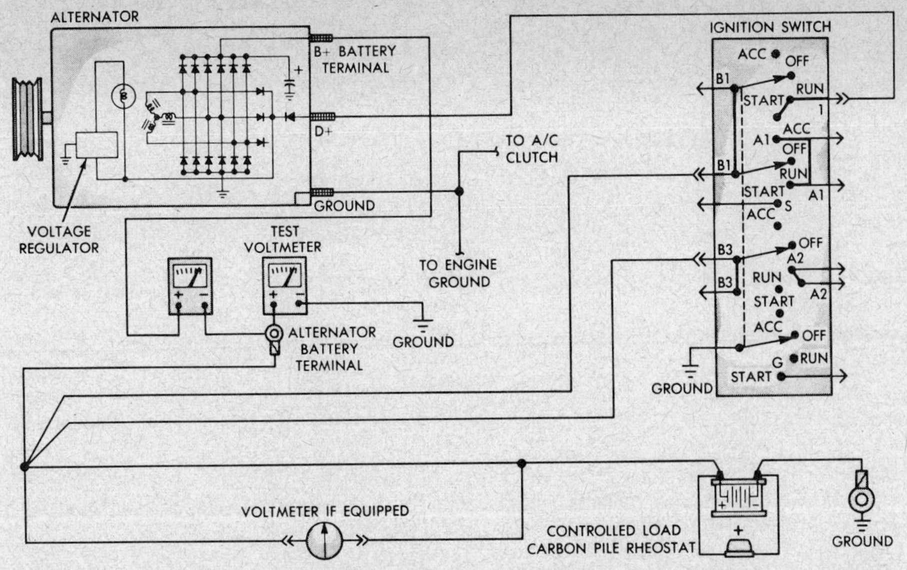

Fig. 5 Current output test. Models w/integral regulator

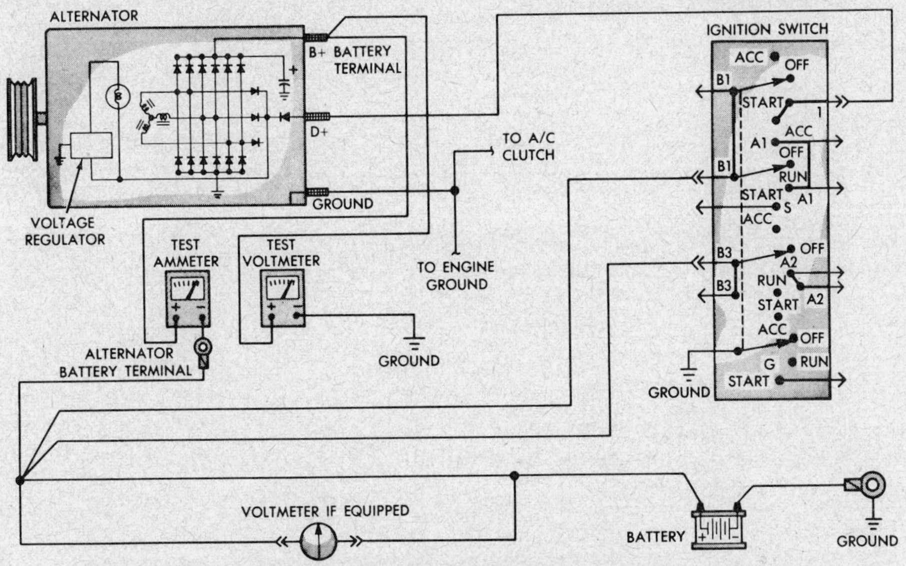

Fig. 6 Voltage regulator test. Models w/integral regulator

and perform bench tests.

VOLTAGE REGULATOR TEST

1. Disconnect ground cable from battery and the "Bat" lead from alternator output terminal.
2. Complete test connections as shown in **Fig. 6.**
3. Ensure voltmeter reads zero. Any other voltage reading indicates a defective alternator.
4. Turn ignition switch to On position and ensure voltmeter reads within one-half volt of battery voltage.
5. Connect a suitable tachometer to engine, then start engine with a jumper wire connected between test ammeter terminals.
6. Remove jumper wire from ammeter terminals and immediately increase engine speed to 2000-3000 RPM while noting ammeter reading.
7. If ammeter reading is 10 amps or less, recheck voltmeter reading without changing engine speed to obtain a correct charging voltage reading. Charging voltage should be 13.9-14.2 volts at 77°F, with an allowance of .05-.09 volt for each 18°F variation of temperature.
8. If ammeter reading is more than 10 amps, continue charging battery until amperage falls below 10 amps, or replace battery with a fully charged one.

EXC. INTEGRAL REGULATOR UNITS

CHARGING CIRCUIT RESISTANCE TEST

1. Disconnect battery ground cable and the "Bat" lead from alternator output terminal.
2. Complete test connections as shown in **Figs. 7 and 8.**
3. On units with external regulator, disconnect wiring harness electrical connector from the electronic voltage regulator.
4. On units with regulator in-engine electronics, remove air hose between power module and air cleaner, then the wiring harness electrical connector.
5. On all models, connect a suitable jumper wire from wiring harness connector green wire terminal to ground. **Do not connect blue J2 lead of wiring electrical connector to ground.**
6. Connect battery ground cable, then start engine and operate at idle.
7. Adjust engine speed and carbon pile rheostat to obtain 20 amps in the circuit and check voltmeter reading. Reading should not exceed .5 volts. If a higher voltage drop is indicated, inspect, clean and tighten all connections in the circuit. A voltage drop test at each connection can be performed to isolate the problem.

CURRENT OUTPUT TEST

1. Disconnect battery ground cable and "Bat" lead from alternator output terminal.
2. Complete test connections as shown in **Figs. 9 and 10.**
3. On units with external regulator, disconnect wiring harness electrical connector from the electronic voltage regulator.
4. On units with regulator in-engine electronics, remove air hose between power module and air cleaner, then the wiring harness electrical connector.
5. On all models, connect a suitable jumper wire from wiring harness connector green wire terminal to ground. **Do not connect blue J2 lead of wiring electrical connector to ground.**
6. Connect battery ground cable, then start engine and operate at idle.
7. Adjust carbon pile rheostat and engine speed to obtain 15 volts at 1250 RPM. **While increasing engine speed, do not allow voltage to exceed 16 volts.**
8. If ammeter reading is not approximately 87 amps, proceed to "Bench Tests."

VOLTAGE REGULATOR TEST

Units W/External Regulator

1. Disconnect battery ground cable and connect suitable tachometer.
2. Complete test connections as shown in **Fig. 11.**
3. Connect battery ground cable, then start engine and operate at 1250 RPM with all lights and accessories turned off.
4. Check voltmeter. If voltage readings are as specified in **Fig. 12**, regulator is satisfactory. If voltage readings are below limits or fluctuate, perform steps 5 through 7. If voltage readings are above limits, proceed to steps 8 through 10.

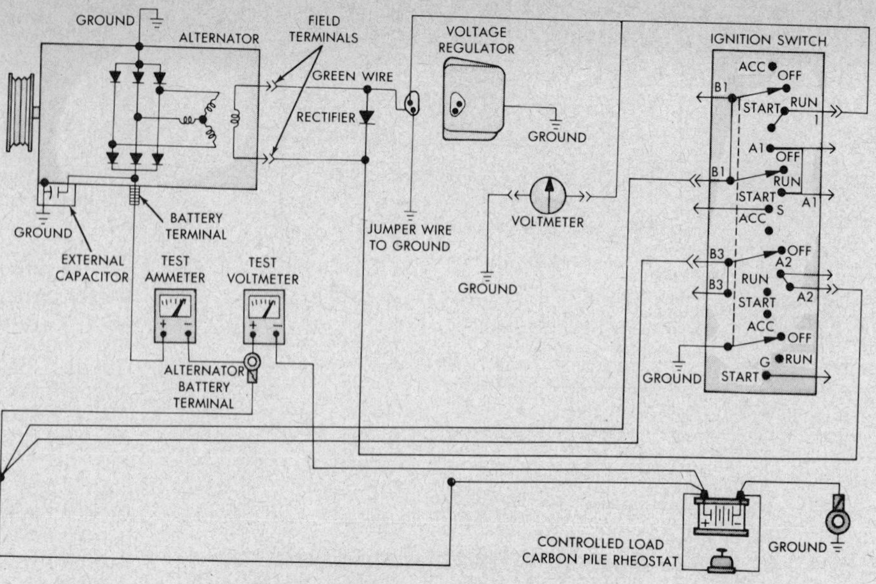

Fig. 7 Charging circuit resistance test. Models w/external regulator

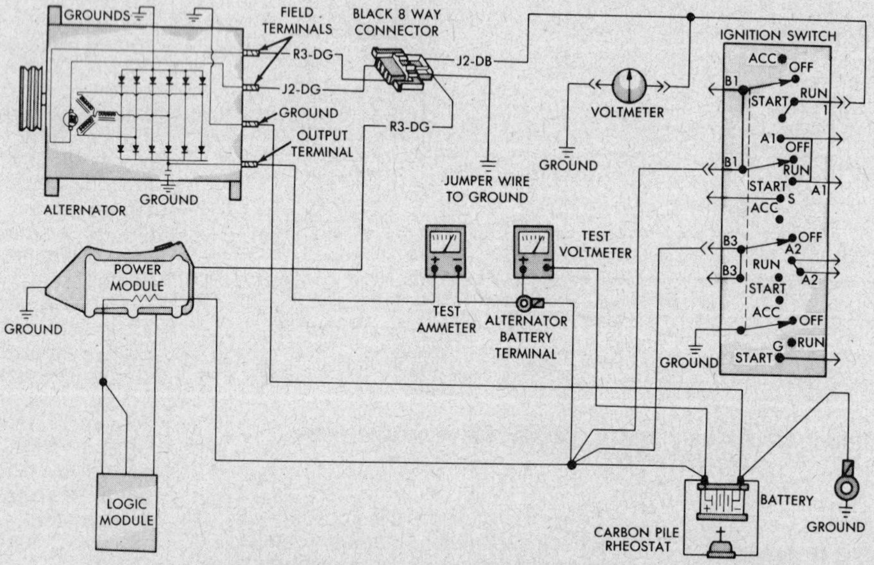

Fig. 8 Charging circuit resistance test. Models w/regulator in-engine electronics

5. Ensure voltage regulator is properly grounded through the regulator case, then turn ignition switch to the "Off" position and disconnect voltage regulator wiring harness connector. **Ensure terminals of connector have not spread open to cause open or intermittent connection.**
6. Turn ignition switch to the "On" position, then check battery voltage at voltage regulator wiring harness connector terminals. Both blue and green terminals should read battery voltage.
7. If steps 5 and 6 are satisfactory, replace regulator and repeat test.
8. Turn ignition switch to the "Off" position and disconnect voltage regulator wiring harness connector. **Ensure terminals of connector have not spread open to cause open or intermittent connection.**
9. Turn ignition switch to the "On" position, then check battery voltage at voltage regulator wiring harness connector terminals. Both blue and green terminals should read battery voltage.
10. If steps 8 and 9 are satisfactory, replace regulator and repeat test.

Units w/Regulator In-Engine Electronics

Voltage regulator is controlled by Electronic Control Unit.

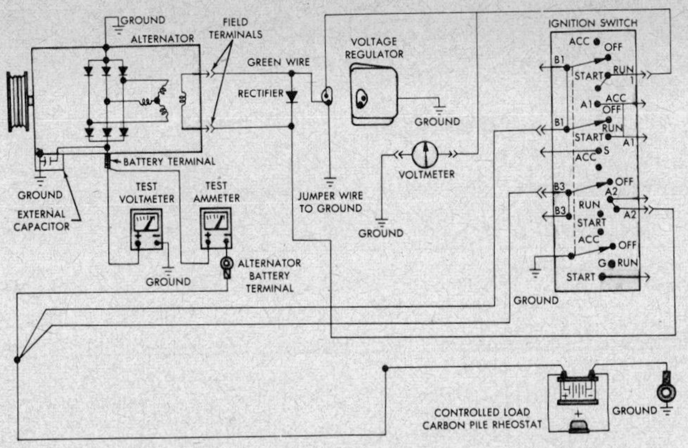

Fig. 9 Current output test. Models w/external regulator

VOLTAGE CHART	
AMBIENT TEMPERATURE NEAR VOLTAGE REGULATOR	VOLTAGE RANGE
−30°C −20°F	14.9 to 15.8
27°C 80°F	13.9 to 14.4
60°C 140°F	13.0 to 13.7
Above 60°C Above 140°F	Less than 13.60

Fig. 12 Voltage regulator test chart. Models w/external regulator

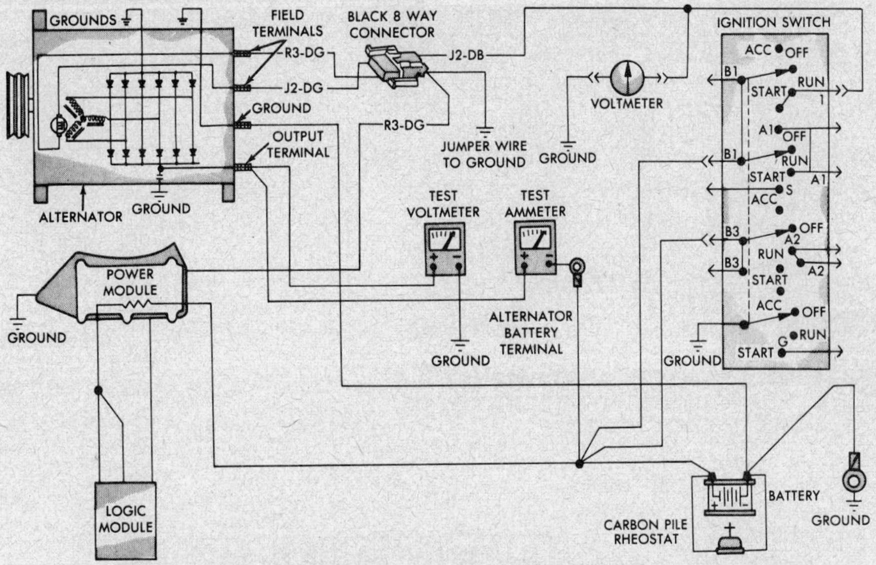

Fig. 10 Current output test. Models w/regulator in-engine electronics

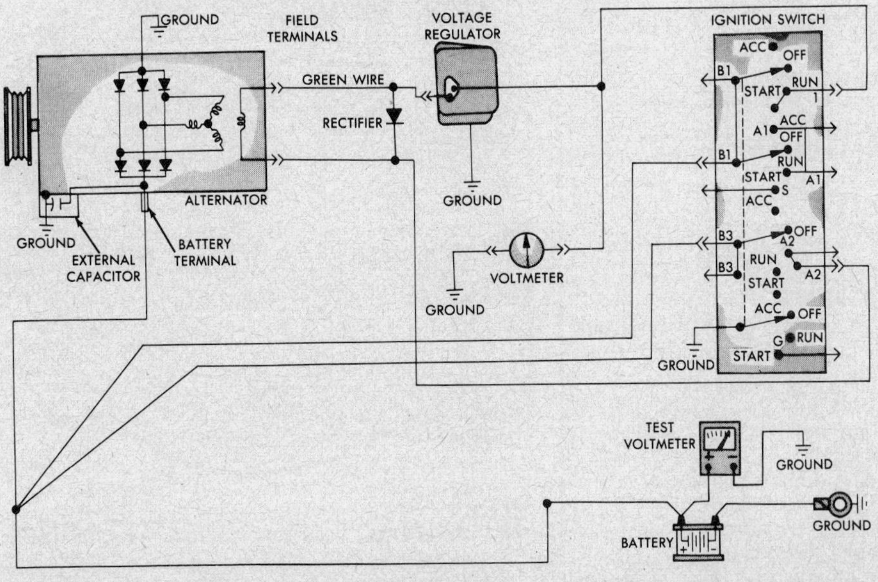

Fig. 11 Voltage regulator test. Models w/external regulator

Chrysler Alternators

INDEX

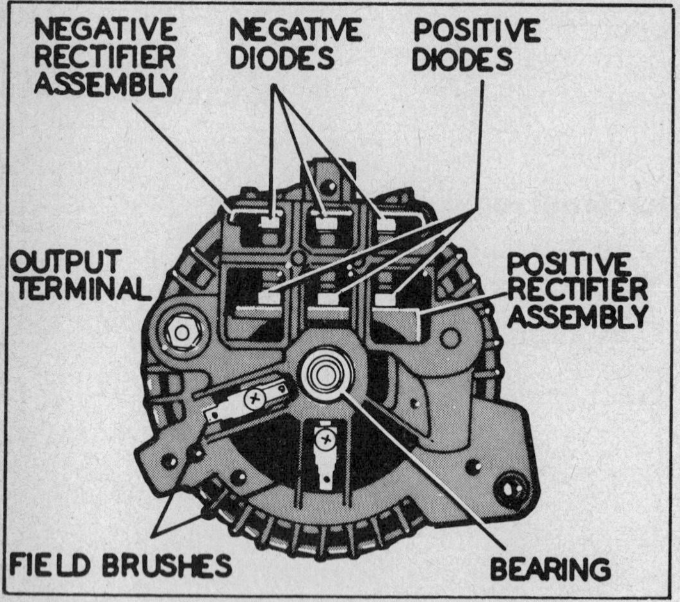

Fig. 1 Alternator assembly exc. 100 & 114 amp units & units w/regulator in engine electronics

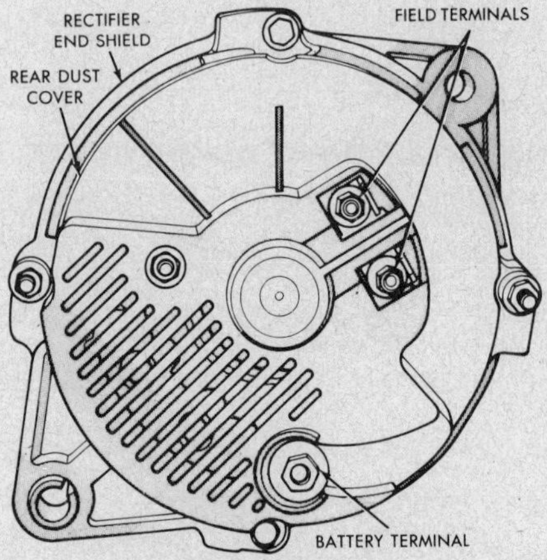

Fig. 2 Alternator assembly. Units w/regulator in engine electronics

DESCRIPTION

All Chrysler alternators except the 100 and 114 amp units are equipped with six silicon rectifiers, **Figs. 1. and 2.** The 100 and 114 amp alternators are equipped with twelve silicon rectifiers, **Fig. 3.**

IN-VEHICLE TESTING

When testing alternators except 100 and 114 amp units, use a 0-100 amp ammeter. When testing 100 and 114 amp alternators, use a 0-150 amp ammeter.

CHARGING CIRCUIT RESISTANCE TEST

EXC. UNITS W/REGULATORS IN-ENGINE ELECTRONICS

1. Disconnect battery ground cable. Disconnect "Batt" lead at the alternator.
2. Complete test connections as shown in **Figs. 4 and 5.**
3. Connect battery ground cable, start engine and operate at idle.
4. Adjust engine speed and carbon pile to obtain 20 amps in the circuit and check voltmeter reading. Reading should not exceed .7 volts. (.5 volts on 1984-87 models). If a voltage drop is indicated, inspect, clean and tighten all connections in the circuit. A voltage drop test at each connection can be performed to isolate the trouble.

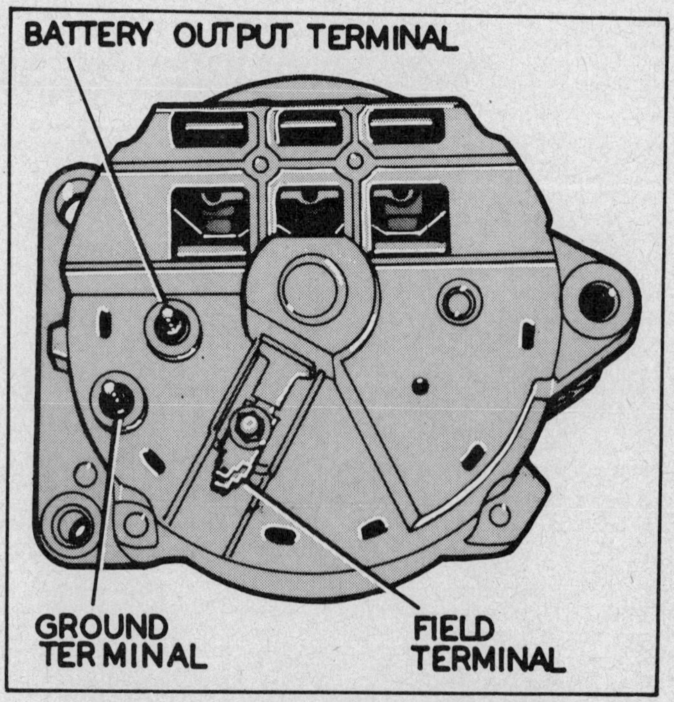

Fig. 3 100 & 114 amp alternator assembly

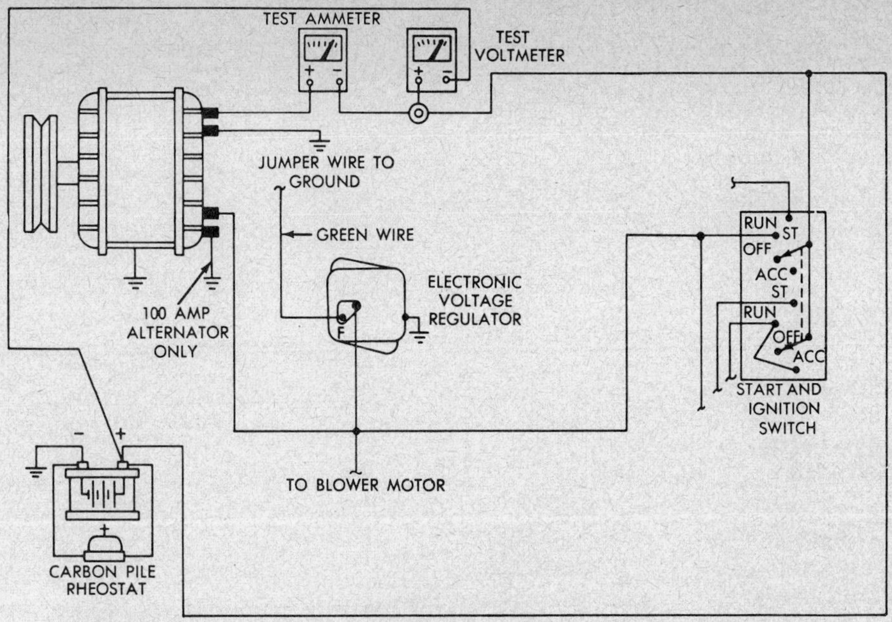

Fig. 4 Charging circuit resistance test. 1982–83 alternators

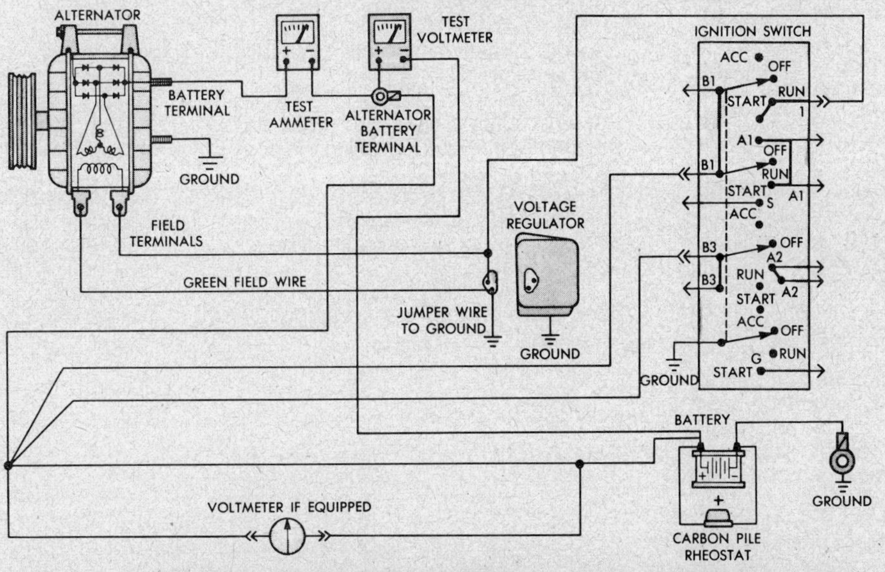

Fig. 5 Charging circuit resistance test. 1984–87 exc. units w/regulator in engine electronics

UNITS W/REGULATOR IN-ENGINE ELECTRONICS

1. Disconnect battery ground cable and the "Bat" lead from alternator output terminal.
2. Complete test connections as shown in **Fig. 6.**
3. Remove air hose between power module and air cleaner, then the wiring harness electrical connector.
4. Connect a suitable jumper wire from wiring harness connector green wire terminal to ground. **Do not connect blue J2 lead of wiring electrical connector to ground.**
5. Connect battery ground cable, then start engine and operate at idle.
6. Adjust engine speed and carbon pile rheostat to obtain 20 amps in the circuit and check voltmeter reading. Reading should not exceed .5 volts. If a higher voltage drop is indicated, inspect, clean and tighten all connections in the circuit. A voltage drop test at each connection can be performed to isolate the problem.

CURRENT OUTPUT TEST

EXC. UNITS W/REGULATOR IN-ENGINE ELECTRONICS

1. Disconnect battery ground cable, complete test connections as per **Figs. 7 and 8** and start engine and operate at idle. Immediately after starting, reduce engine speed to idle.
2. Adjust the carbon pile and engine speed in increments until a speed of 1250 RPM and 15 volts are obtained on all units except 100 and 114 amp alternators. On 100 and 114 amp alternators, obtain engine speed of 900 RPM and 13 volts. **While increasing speed, do not allow voltage to exceed 16 volts.**
3. Check ammeter reading. Output current should be within specifications.

UNITS W/REGULATOR IN ENGINE ELECTRONICS

1. Disconnect battery ground cable and "Bat" lead from alternator output terminal.
2. Complete test connections as shown in **Fig. 9.**
3. Remove air hose between power module and air cleaner, then the wiring harness electrical connector.
4. Connect a suitable jumper wire from wiring harness connector green wire terminal to ground. **Do not connect blue J2 lead of wiring electrical**

connector to ground.

5. Connect battery ground cable, then start engine and operate at idle.
6. Adjust carbon pile rheostat and engine speed to obtain 15 volts at 1250 RPM. **While increasing engine speed, do not allow voltage to exceed 16 volts.**
7. If ammeter reading is not approximately 96 amps (1986-87, 87 amps) repair or replace alternator.

VOLTAGE REGULATOR TEST

Battery must be fully charged for test to be accurate.

EXC. UNITS W/REGULATOR CONTROLLED BY ENGINE ELECTRONICS

1. Connect test equipment, **Figs. 10 and 11.**
2. Start and run engine at 1250 RPM with all lights and accessories turned "Off." Voltage should be as specified in **Fig. 12.**
3. It is normal for the vehicle ammeter to indicate an immediate charge, then gradually return to the normal position.
4. If voltage is below limits or is fluctuating, proceed with the following:
   a. Check voltage regulator for proper ground. The ground is obtained through the regulator case to mounting screws, then to the vehicle sheet metal.
   b. With ignition switch "Off," disconnect voltage regulator connector. Turn ignition "On" and check for battery voltage at the wiring harness terminal. Both green and blue leads should have battery voltage.
   c. If voltage regulator was grounded properly and battery voltage was present at the green and blue leads, replace voltage regulator except on systems incorporating a field-loads relay. On systems with a field-loads relay, test the relay as outlined under "Field-Loads Relay Test." If relay tests satisfactory, replace voltage regulator. On all systems, repeat test.
5. If voltage is above limits, refer to Steps 4b and 4c.

UNITS W/REGULATOR IN-ENGINE ELECTRONICS

Voltage regulator is controlled by Electronic Control Unit.

BENCH TESTS

To remove the alternator, disconnect the battery ground cable and the leads at the alternator. Then unfasten and remove the alternator from the vehicle.

FIELD COIL DRAW

1. Place alternator on an insulated surface.
2. On all units, connect a jumper wire between one alternator field terminal and the negative terminal of a fully charged battery.
3. Connect test ammeter positive lead to the other alternator field terminal and the ammeter negative lead to the positive battery terminal.
4. On 1982-83 units except 100 and 114 amp, connect a jumper wire between alternator end shield and negative terminal of battery.
5. On all units, slowly rotate rotor by hand and note ammeter reading. On units except 100 and 114 amp, field current at 12 volts should be 4.5 to 6.5 amps (1984-87, 2.5-5.0 amps). On 100 and 114 amp units, field current should be 4.75 to 6.0 amps.
6. A low rotor coil draw is an indication of high resistance in the field coil circuit (brushes, slip rings or rotor coil). A high rotor coil draw indicates shorted rotor coil or grounded rotor. No reading indicates an open rotor or defective brushes.

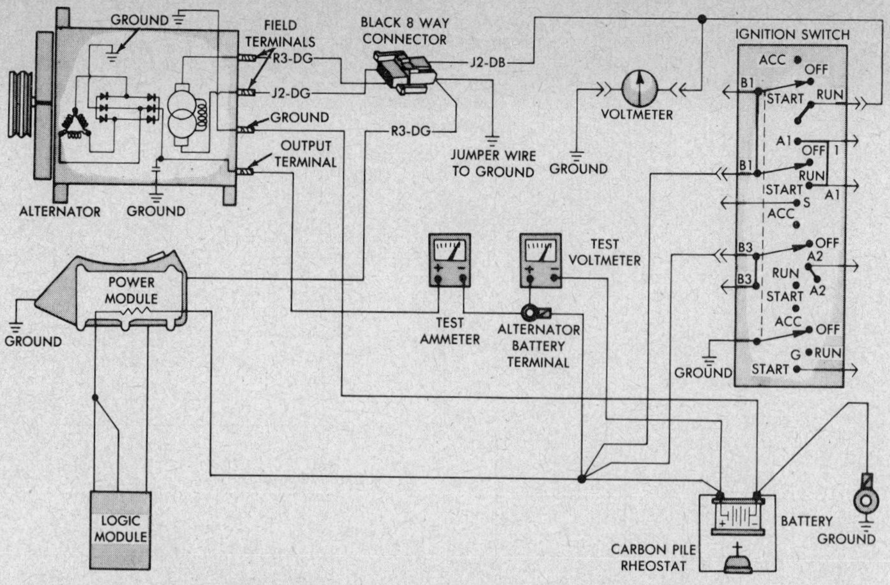

Fig. 6 Charging circuit resistance test. 1985–87 units w/regulator in engine electronics

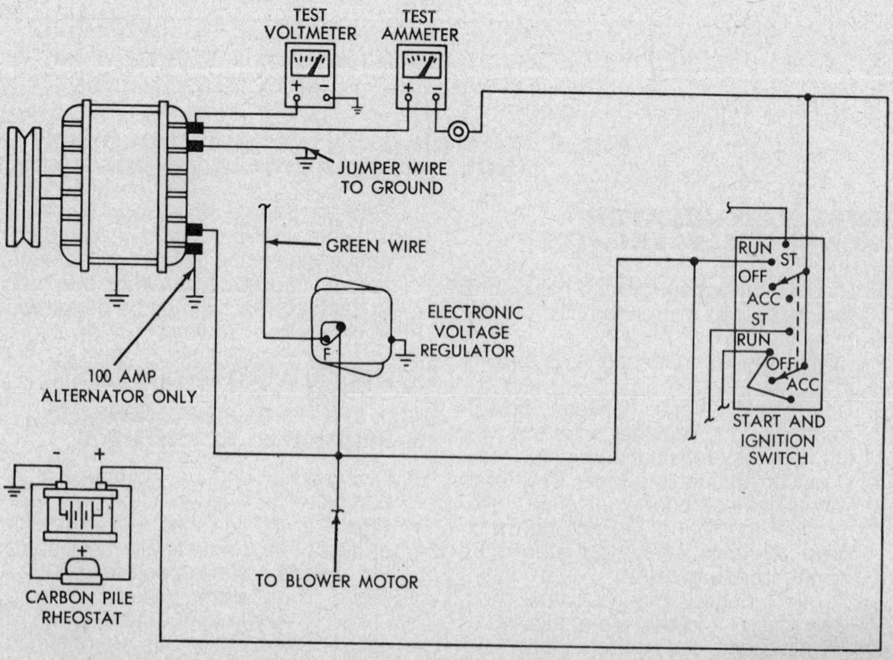

Fig. 7 Current output test. 1982–83 alternators

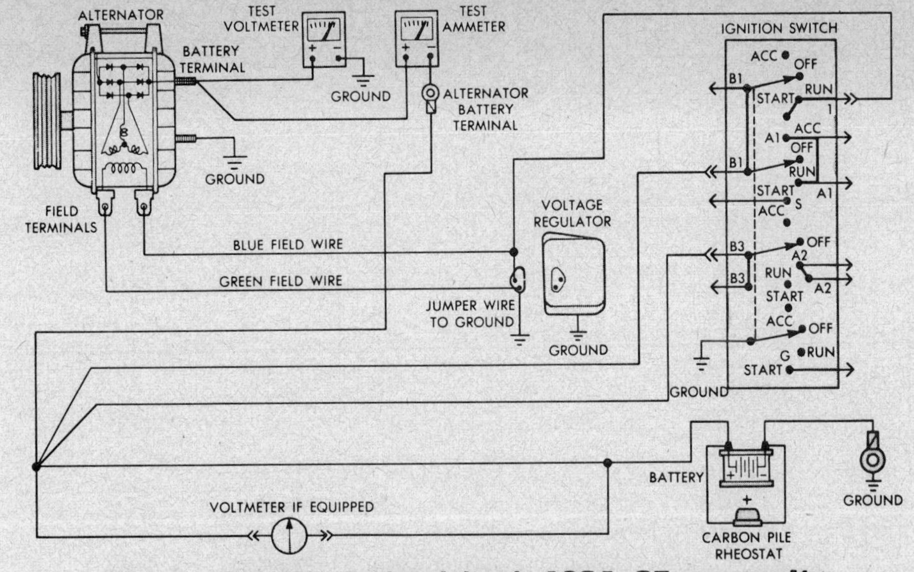

Fig. 8 Current output test. 1984–87 exc. units w/regulator in engine electronics

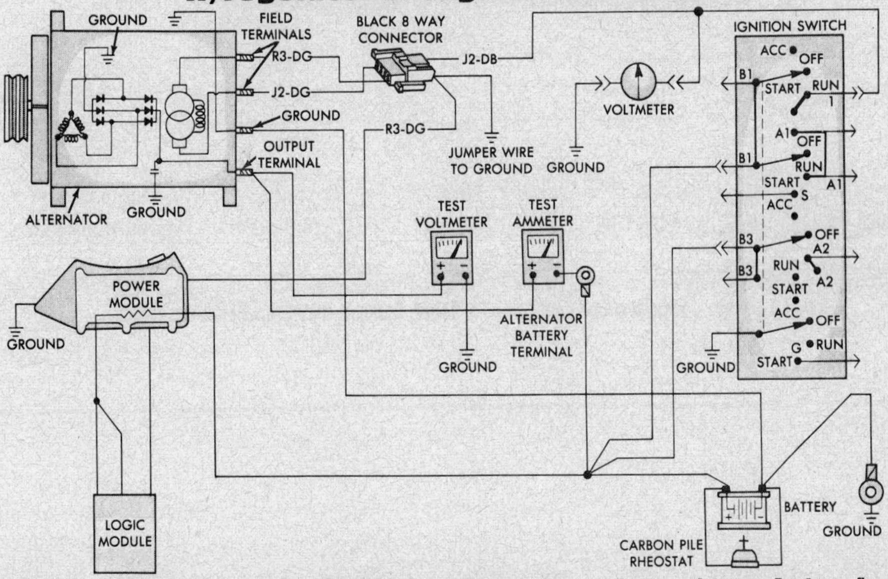

Fig. 9 Current output test. 1985–87 units w/regulator in engine electronics

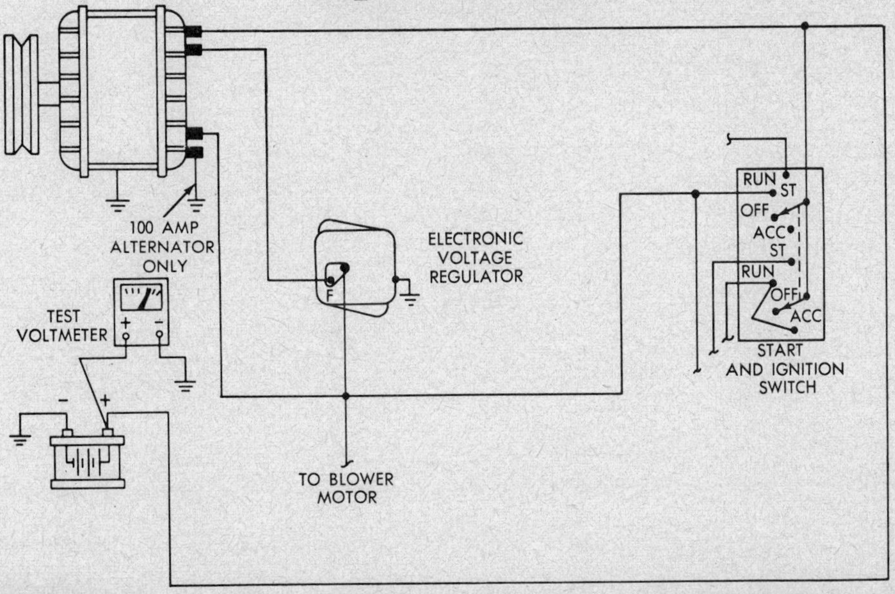

Fig. 10 Voltage regulator test. 1982–83 alternators

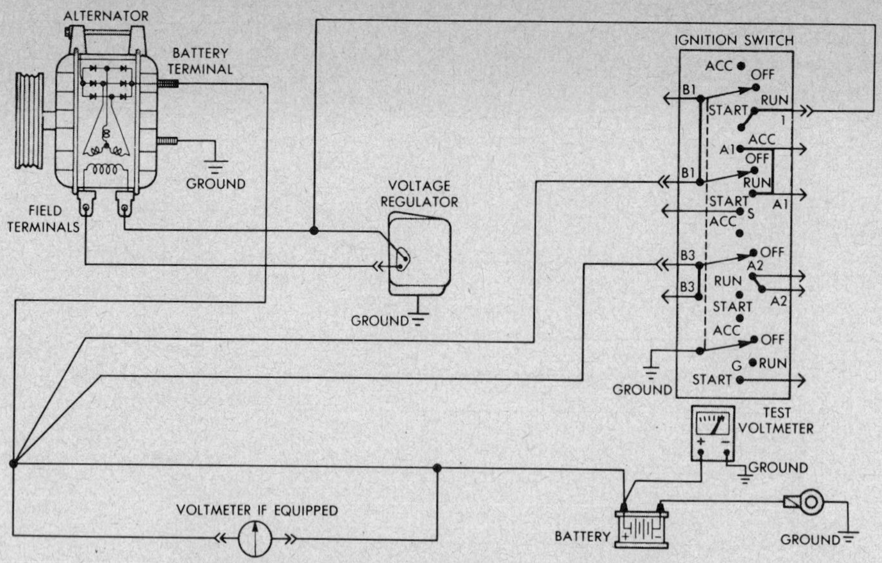

Fig. 11 Voltage regulator test. 1984–87 exc. units w/regulator in engine electronics

Ambient Temperature Near Regulator	−20°F	80°F	140°F	Above 140°F
1982-83	14.9-15.9	13.9-14.6	13.3-13.9	Less than 13.6
1984-87	14.6-15.8	13.9-14.4	13.0-13.7	Less than 13.6

Fig. 12 Voltage regulator test specifications

Mitsubishi Alternator

INDEX

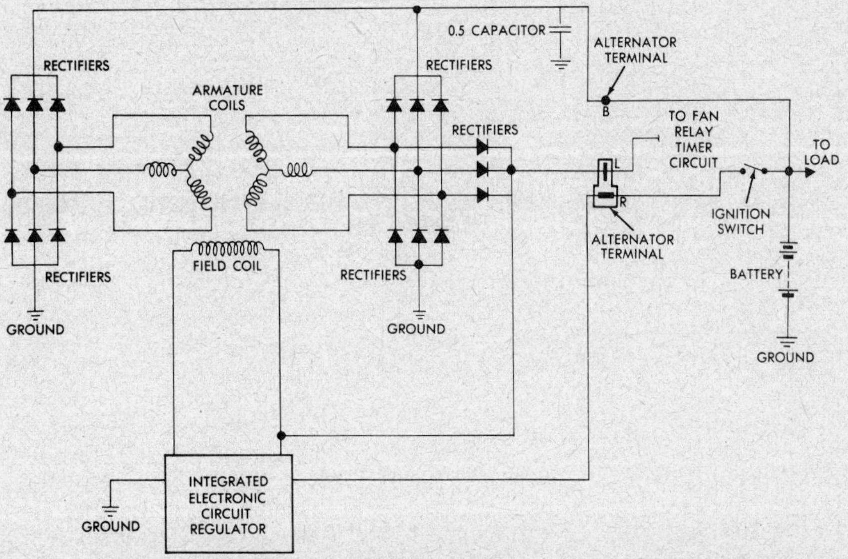

Fig. 1 Wiring diagram of Mitsubishi charging system. 1982–83

DESCRIPTION

On these units the regulator is incorporated into the alternator rear housing, **Figs. 1 and 2.** The electronic voltage regulator has the ability to vary regulated system voltage upward or downward as temperature changes. No voltage regulated adjustments are required on these units.

IN-VEHICLE TESTING

VOLTAGE REGULATOR TEST

1. With ignition switch in the Off position, disconnect battery positive cable and connect an ammeter between battery positive post and battery cable, **Figs. 3 and 4.**
2. Connect a voltmeter between alternator L terminal and ground, **Figs. 3 and 4.** Voltmeter should indicate zero voltage. If voltage is present, the alternator or charging system wiring is defective.
3. Place ignition switch in the On position and note voltmeter reading. Voltmeter reading should be 1 volt or less, if a higher reading is indicated, the alternator should be removed for bench tests.
4. Connect a tachometer to engine, then start and operate engine at approximately 2000 to 3000 RPM and note ammeter reading. **When starting engine, ensure that no starting current is applied to ammeter.**
5. If ammeter reading is 5 amps or less on 1982-83 models, or 10 amps or less on 1984-85 models, check voltmeter reading with engine operating at 2000-3000 RPM. The charging voltage should be 14.4 volts at 68°F.
6. If ammeter reading is above 5 amps on 1982-83 models, or above 10 amps on 1984-85 models, continue to charge battery until reading drops below this value and check voltmeter reading at 2000-3000 RPM. If voltage is not within limits, remove alternator for bench tests.

CURRENT OUTPUT TEST

1. With ignition switch in the Off position, disconnect battery ground cable, then disconnect battery lead from alternator output terminal.
2. Connect an ammeter set at the 0 to 100 amp scale between alternator output terminal and the disconnected battery lead, **Figs. 5 and 6.**
3. Connect positive lead of voltmeter to alternator output terminal and negative lead to ground, **Figs. 5 and 6.**
4. Connect suitable tachometer to engine and reconnect battery ground cable.
5. Connect a variable carbon pile regulator between battery terminals. When installing carbon pile regulator, ensure that regulator is in the Open or Off position.
6. Adjust carbon pile regulator and accelerate engine to the specified RPM, noting ammeter and voltmeter readings, **Fig. 7.**
7. If ammeter reading is less than specified, the alternator should be removed for bench tests.

CHARGING CIRCUIT RESISTANCE TEST

1984–85

1. Disconnect ground cable from battery and the "Bat" lead from alternator output terminal.
2. Complete test connections as shown in **Fig. 8.**
3. Connect battery ground cable, then start engine and operate at idle.
4. Adjust engine speed and carbon pile rheostat to obtain 20 amps in the circuit and observe voltmeter reading, which should not exceed .5 volt.
5. If a higher voltage drop is indicated, inspect, clean and tighten all connections in the circuit. A voltage drop test at each connection can be performed to isolate the problem.

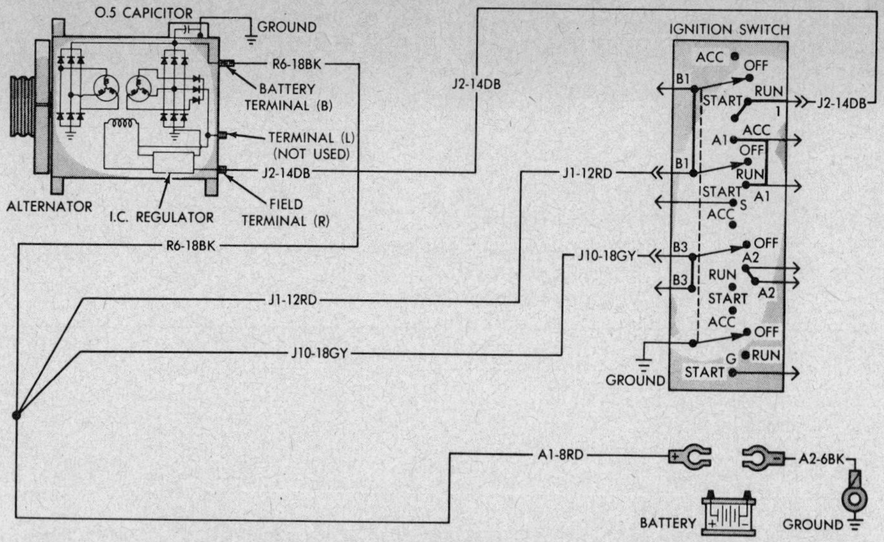

Fig. 2 Wiring diagram of Mitsubishi charging system. 1984–85

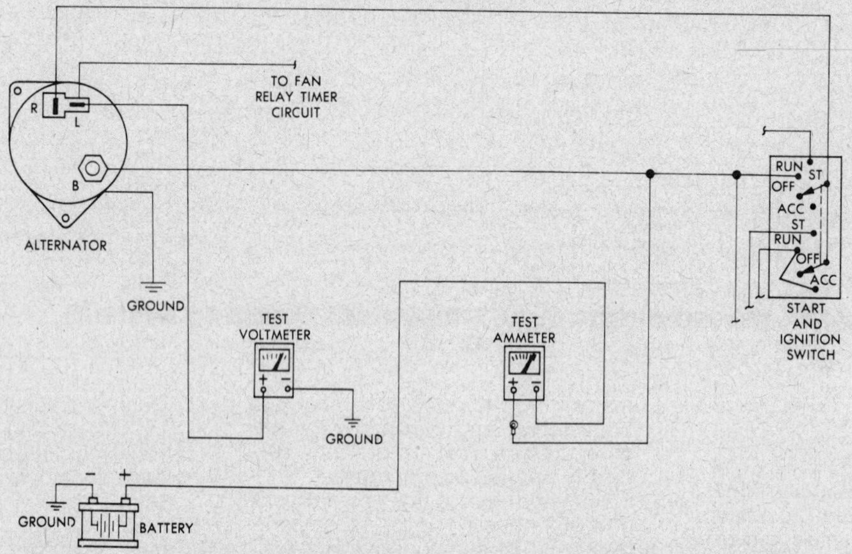

Fig. 3 Voltage regulator test connections. 1982–83

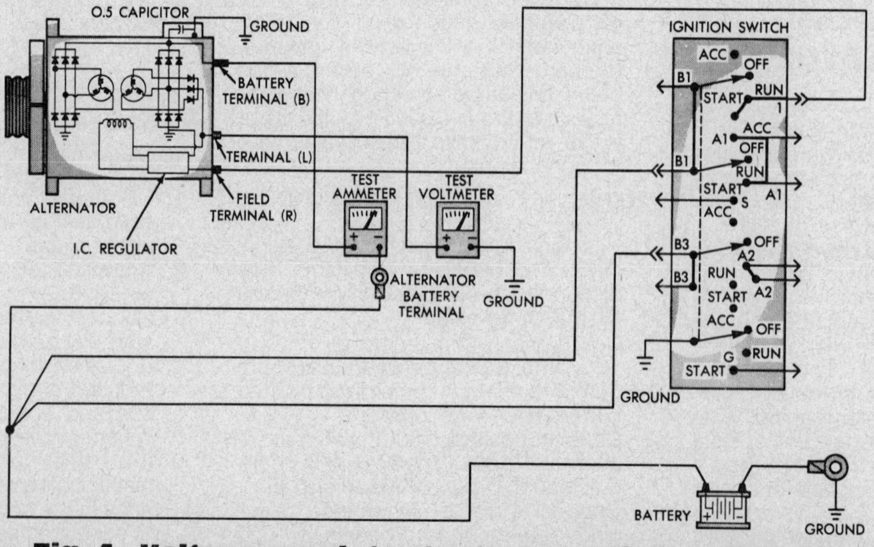

Fig. 4 Voltage regulator test connections. 1984–85

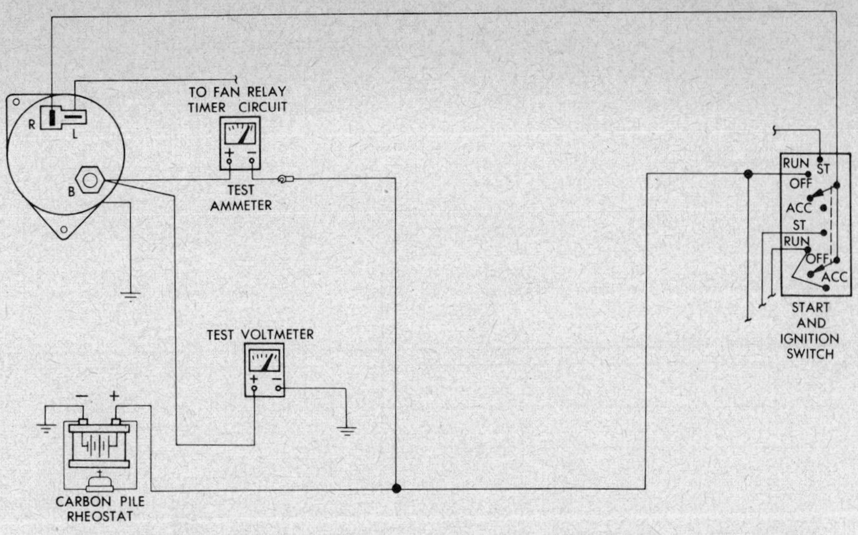

Fig. 5 Current output test connections. 1982–83

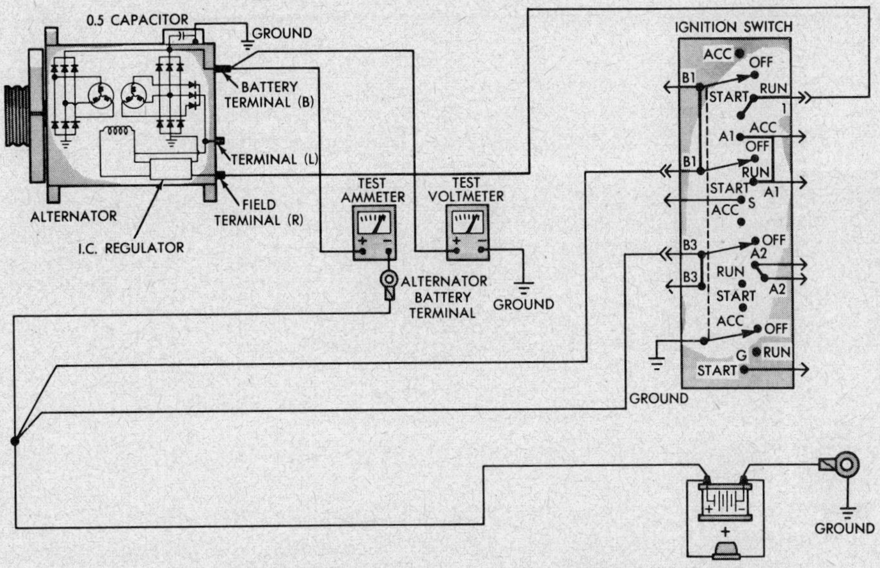

Fig. 6 Current output test connections. 1984–85

Engine RPM	Alternator Current Output Hot or Cold At 13.5 Volts
500	17-25 Amps
1000	63-70 Amps
2000	74 Amps

Fig. 7 Alternator output test specifications

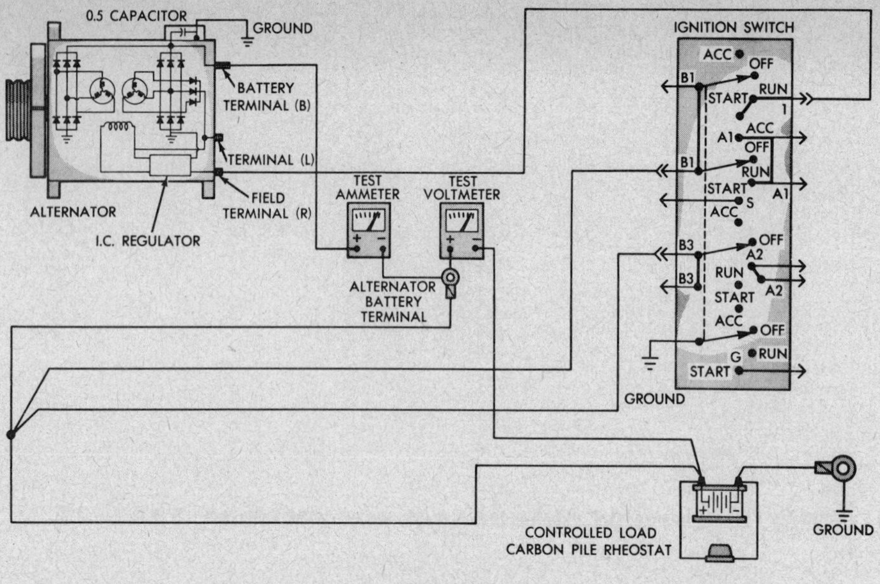

Fig. 8 Charging circuit resistance test connections. 1984–85

DISC BRAKES

TABLE OF CONTENTS

Application

General Information

INDEX

BRAKE SHOES, LININGS & CALIPERS

Remove wheels and inspect brake rotor, caliper and linings. The wheel bearings should be inspected at this time and repacked if necessary. Do not get any grease on the linings.

On rear wheel drive models, the brake shoe and lining assemblies should be replaced if the lining is worn to within 1/32 inch of rivet heads (riveted linings) or brake shoe (bonded linings). On front wheel drive models, the brake shoe and lining assemblies should be replaced when the combined thickness of the shoe and lining is 5/16 inch or less. It is recommended that both front and/or rear wheel sets be replaced whenever a respective shoe and lining assembly is replaced.

If a visual inspection does not adequately determine the condition of the linings, the brake shoe and lining assemblies should be removed and inspected. If shoes do not require replacement, reinstall in original positions. Brake shoes and linings should also be replaced if cracked or damaged.

If the caliper is cracked or fluid leakage through the casting (porosity) is evident, the caliper must be replaced.

BRAKE ROUGHNESS

The most common cause of brake chatter on disc brakes is a variation in thickness of the disc. If roughness or vibration is encountered at high speed or if pedal pumping is experienced at low speeds, the disc may have excessive thickness variation. To check for this condition, measure the disc at 12 points with a micrometer at a radius approximately one inch from edge of disc. If thickness measurements vary by more than .0005 inch, the disc should be replaced.

Excessive lateral runout of braking disc may cause a "knocking back" of the pistons, possibly creating increased pedal travel and vibration when brakes are applied.

Before checking the runout, wheel bearings should be adjusted. The readjustment is very important and will be required at the completion of the test to prevent bearing failure. Be sure to make the adjustment according to the recommendations given under Front Wheel Bearings, Adjust in the Chrysler Front Wheel Drive or Rear Wheel Drive car chapters.

DISC BRAKE SERVICE

Servicing of disc brakes is extremely critical due to the close tolerances required in machining the brake disc to insure proper brake operation.

The maintenance of these close tolerances controls of the shape of the rubbing surfaces is necessary to prevent brake roughness. In addition, the surface finish must be non-directional and maintained at a micro inch finish. This controls the rubbing surface finish to avoid pulls and erratic performance and promotes long lining life and equal lining wear of both left and

Fig. 1 Checking rotor for lateral runout

Fig. 2 Checking rotor parallelism (Thickness variation)

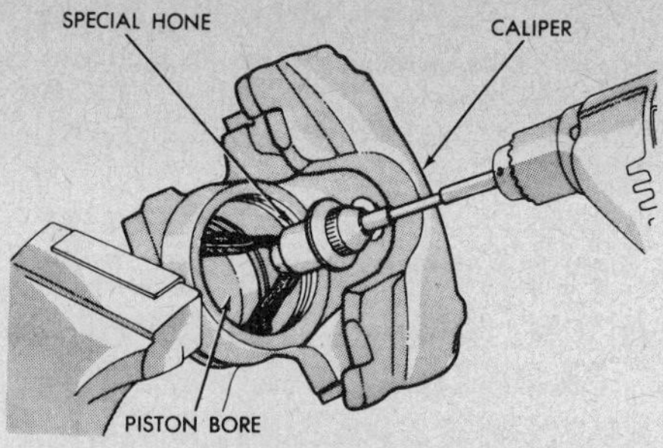

Fig. 3 Honing caliper piston bore

right brakes.

Refinishing of the rubbing surfaces should not be attempted unless precision equipment, capable of measuring in micro inches (millionths of an inch) is available.

To check lateral runout of a disc, mount a dial indicator on a convenient part (steering knuckle, tie rod, disc brake caliper housing) so that the plunger of the dial indicator contacts the disc at a point one inch from the outer edge, **Fig. 1.** If the total indicated runout exceeds specifications, install a new disc.

To check parallelism (thickness variation), mount dial indicators, **Fig. 2,** so the plunger contacts rotor approximately 1 inch from outer edge. If parallelism exceeds specifications, replace the rotor.

GENERAL PRECAUTIONS

1. Grease or any other foreign material must be kept off the caliper, surfaces of the disc and external surfaces of the hub, during service procedures. Handling the brake disc and caliper should be done in a way to avoid deformation of the disc and nicking or scratching brake linings.
2. If inspection reveals that the rubber piston seals are worn or damaged, they should be replaced.
3. During removal and installation of a wheel assembly, exercise care so as not to interfere with or damage the caliper splash shield or bleeder screw.
4. Front wheel bearings should be adjusted to specifications.
5. Be sure vehicle is centered on hoist before servicing any of the front end components to avoid bending or damaging the disc splash shield on full right or left wheel turns.
6. Before the vehicle is moved after any brake service work, be sure to obtain a firm brake pedal.
7. The assembly bolts of the two caliper housings (if a two piece caliper) should not be disturbed unless the caliper requires service.

INSPECTION OF CALIPER

Should it become necessary to remove the caliper for installation of new parts, clean all parts in alcohol, wipe dry using lint-free cloths. Using an air hose, blow out drilled passages and bores. Check dust boots for punctures or tears. Generally, new boots should be installed upon reassembly.

Inspect piston bores for scoring or pitting. Bores that show light scratches or corrosion can usually be cleaned with crocus cloth. However, bores that have deep scratches or scoring may be honed, provided the diameter of the bore is not increased more than .002 inch. If the bore does not clean up within this specification, a new caliper housing should be installed (black stains on the bore walls are caused by piston seals and will do no harm).

When using a hone, **Fig. 3,** be sure to install the hone baffle before honing bore. The baffle is used to protect the hone stones from damage. Use extreme care in cleaning the caliper after honing. Remove all dust and grit by flushing the caliper with alcohol. Wipe dry with clean lint-free cloth and then clean a second time in the same manner.

Kelsey-Hayes Sliding Caliper

INDEX

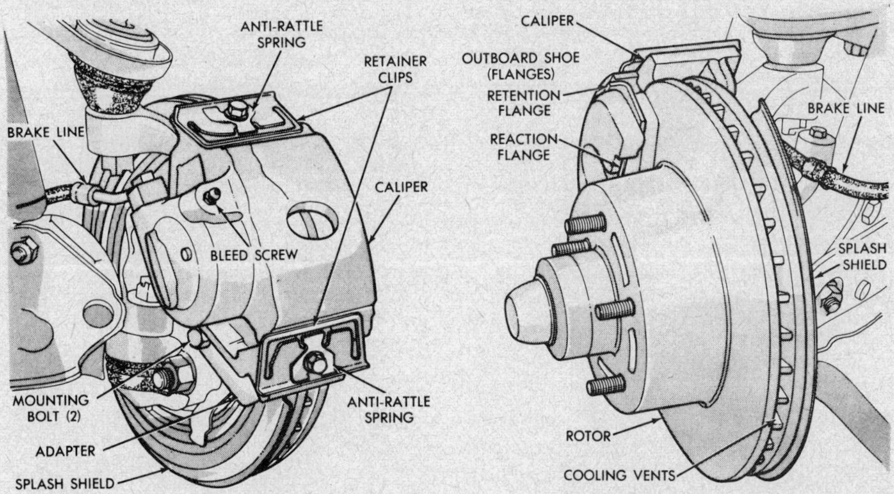

Fig. 1 Kelsey-Hayes sliding caliper front disc brake

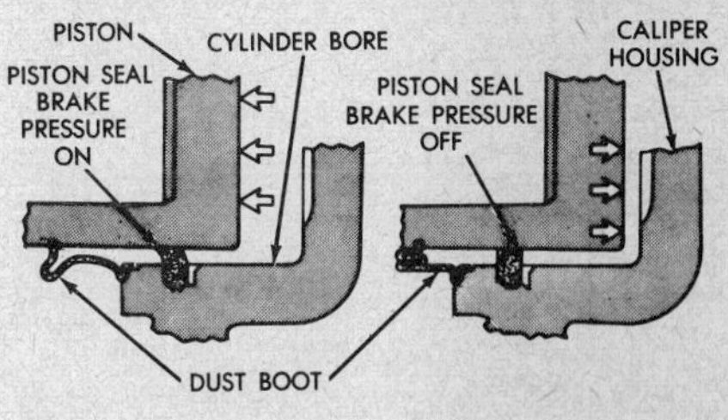

Fig. 2 Piston seal function

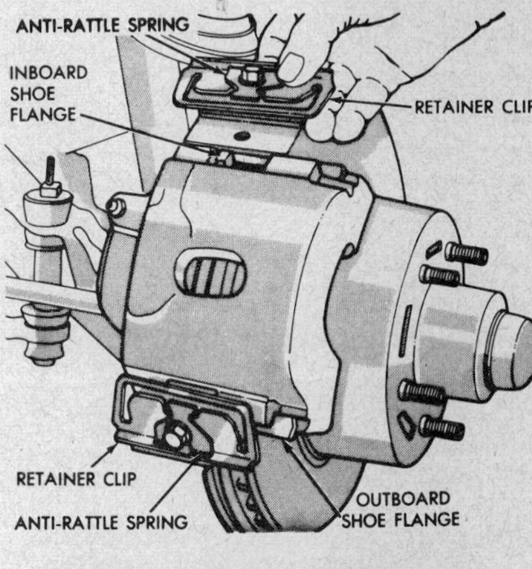

Fig. 3 Retainer clips & anti-rattle spring replacement

OPERATION

This sliding caliper single piston system uses a one piece hub and is actuated by the hydraulic system and disc assembly, Fig. 1. Alignment and positioning of the caliper is achieved by two machined guides or "ways" on the adapter, while caliper retaining clips allow lateral movement of the caliper. Outboard shoe flanges are used to position and locate the shoe on the caliper fingers, while the inboard shoe is retained by the adapter. Braking force applied onto the outboard shoe is transferred to the caliper, while braking force applied onto the inboard shoe is transferred directly to the adapter.

A square cut piston seal provides a hydraulic seal between the piston and the cylinder bore, Fig. 2. A dust boot with a wiping lip installed in a groove in the cylinder bore and piston, prevents contamination in the piston and cylinder bore area. Adjustment between the disc and the shoe is obtained automatically by the outward relocation of the piston as the inboard lining wears and inward movement of the caliper as the outboard lining wears.

CALIPER REMOVAL

1. Raise the vehicle and remove front wheel.
2. Remove caliper retaining clips and anti-rattle springs, **Fig. 3.**
3. Remove caliper from disc by slowly sliding caliper assembly out and away from disc. **Use some means to support caliper. Do not let caliper hang from hydraulic line.**

BRAKE SHOE REMOVAL

1. Remove caliper assembly as outlined above.
2. Remove outboard shoe by prying between the shoe and the caliper fingers, **Fig. 4,** since flanges on outboard shoe retain caliper firmly. **Caliper should be supported to avoid damage to the flexible brake hose.**
3. Remove inboard brake shoe from the adapter, **Fig. 5.**

BRAKE SHOE INSTALLATION

Remove approximately 1/3 of the brake fluid out of the reservoir to prevent overflow when pistons are pushed back into the bore.

1. With care, push piston back into bore until bottomed.
2. Install new outboard shoe in recess of caliper. **No freeplay should exist between brake shoe flanges and caliper fingers, Fig. 6. If up and down (vertical) movement of the shoe shows freeplay, shoe must be removed and flanges bent to provide a slight interference fit, Fig. 7. Reinstall shoe after modification, if shoe cannot be finger snapped into place, use light C-clamp pressure, Fig. 8.**
3. Position inboard shoe with flanges inserted in adapter "ways," **Fig. 5.**
4. Carefully slide caliper assembly into adapter and over the disc while aligning caliper on machined "ways" of adapter. **Make sure dust boot is not pulled out from groove when piston and boot slide over the inboard shoe.**
5. Install anti-rattle springs and retaining clips and torque retaining screws to 180 inch pounds. **The inboard shoe anti-rattle spring is to be installed on top of the retainer spring plate, Fig. 3.**

CALIPER DISASSEMBLY

1. With caliper and shoes removed as described previously, place caliper onto the upper control arm and slowly depress brake pedal to hydraulically push piston from bore. **The pedal will fall when piston passes bore opening.**
2. Support pedal below first inch of pedal travel to prevent excessive fluid loss.
3. To remove piston from the opposite caliper, disconnect flexible brake line at frame bracket at vehicle side where piston has been removed previously and plug tube to prevent pressure loss. By depressing brake pedal this

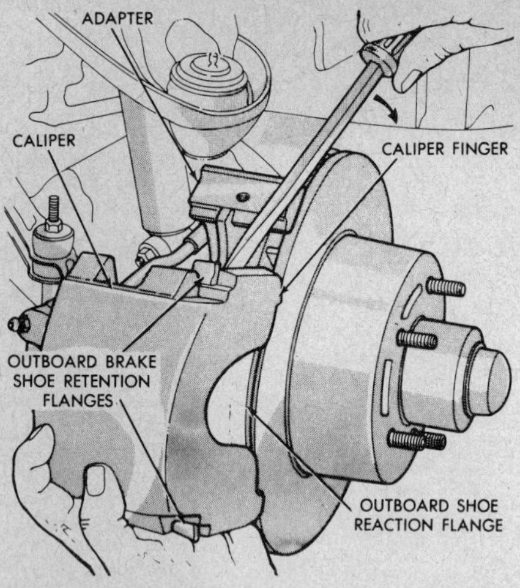

Fig. 4 Removing outboard shoe

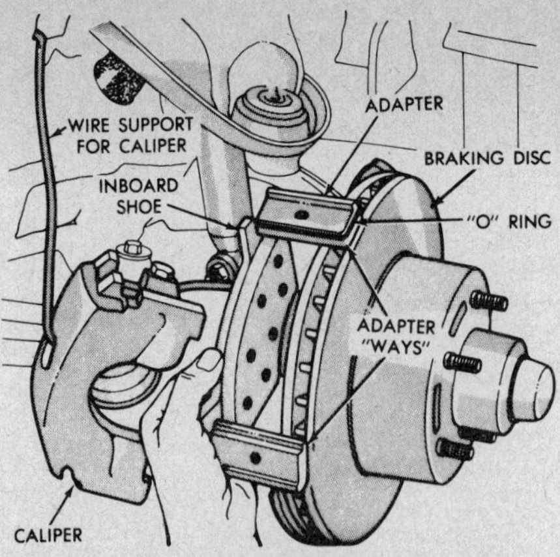

Fig. 5 Replacing inboard shoe

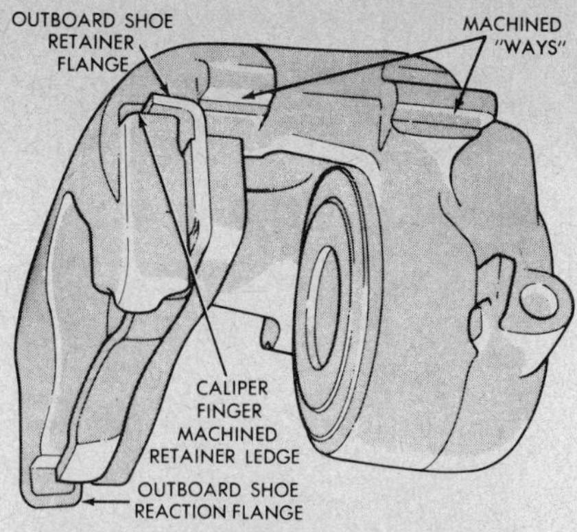

Fig. 6 Caliper finger & outboard shoe retainer flange

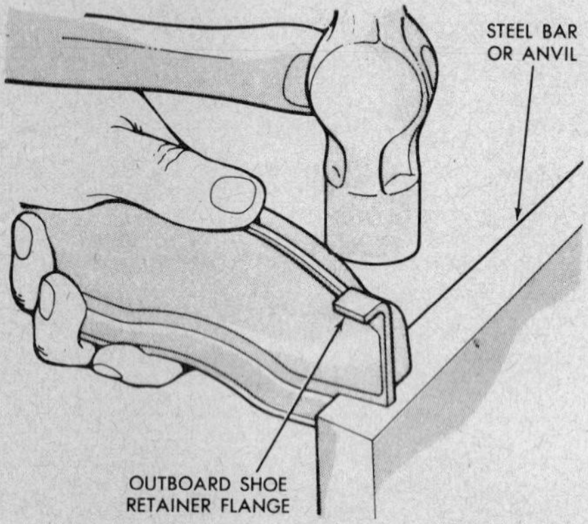

Fig. 7 Bending outboard shoe retaining flange

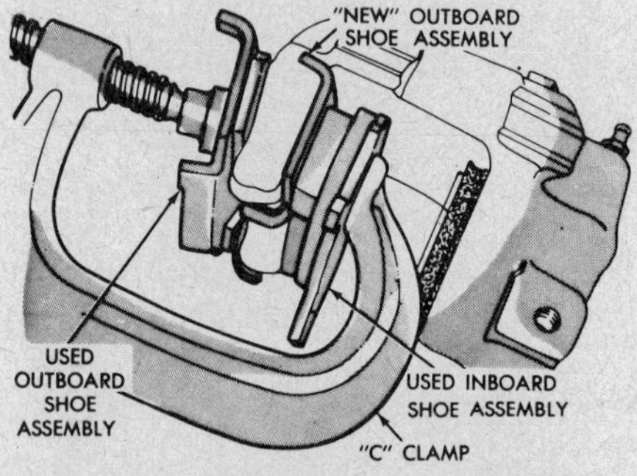

Fig. 8 Installing outboard shoe using C-clamp

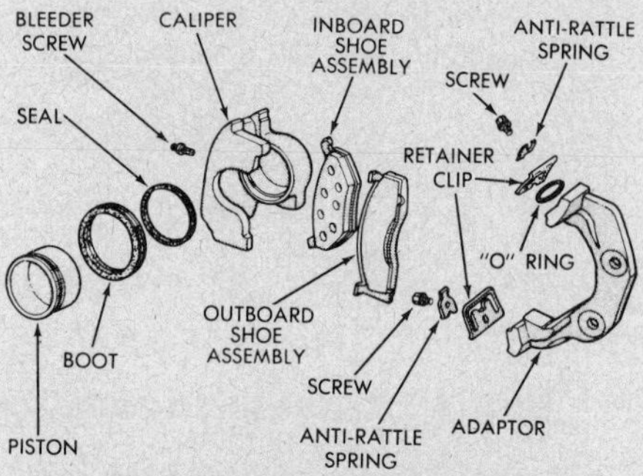

Fig. 9 Exploded view of Kelsey-Hayes sliding caliper disc brake

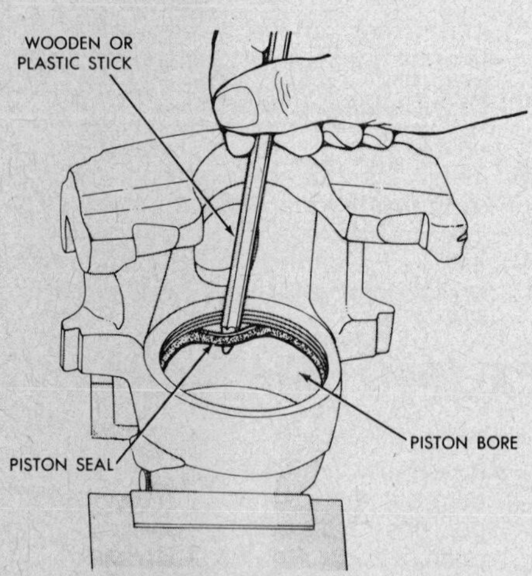

Fig. 10 Piston seal removal

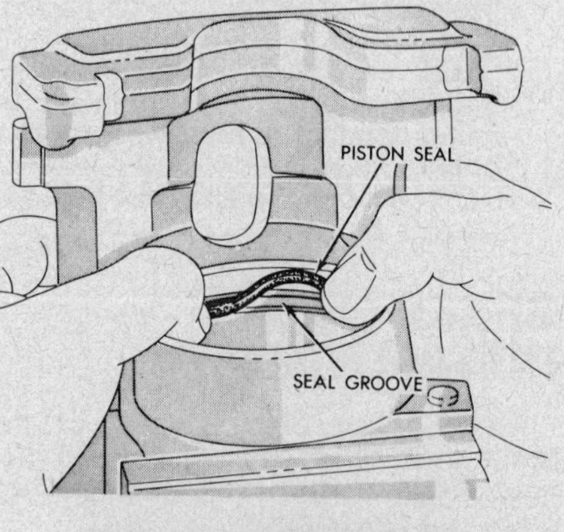

Fig. 11 Piston seal installation

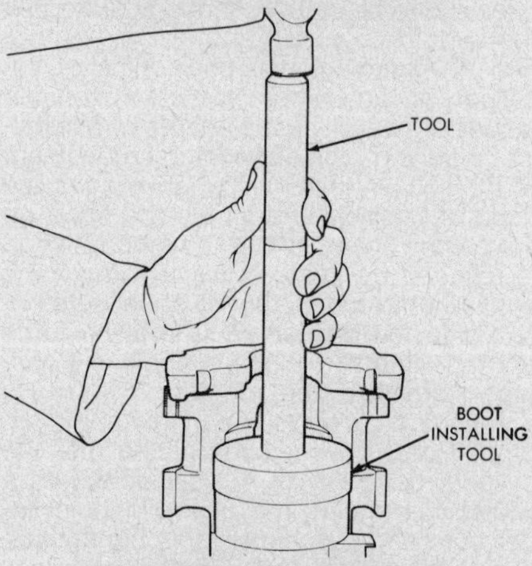

Fig. 12 Dust boot installation

piston can also be hydraulically pushed out.

4. Mount caliper in a soft-jawed vise. **Excessive vise pressure will distort caliper bore.**
5. Remove the dust boot, **Fig. 9.**
6. Insert a suitable tool such as a small, pointed wooden or plastic object between the cylinder bore and the seal and work seal out of the groove in the piston bore, **Fig. 10. A metal tool such as a screwdriver should not be used since it can cause damage to the piston bore or burr the edges of the seal groove.**

CALIPER ASSEMBLY

1. Dip new piston seals in clean brake fluid. Work seal gently into the groove (using clean fingers) until seal is properly seated, make sure that seal is not twisted or rolled, **Fig. 11. Do not reuse old seals.**
2. Install piston into bore and push past seal until piston bottoms in bore.
3. Lubricate piston boot generously with clean brake fluid. Position dust boot in counterbore and install piston boot with tool C-4689 and handle C-4171, **Fig. 12.**
4. Install brake hose to caliper using new seal washers.
5. Install caliper and shoes as described under "Brake Shoe Installation."

A.T.E. (Front) Dual Pin Floating Caliper Disc Brake

INDEX

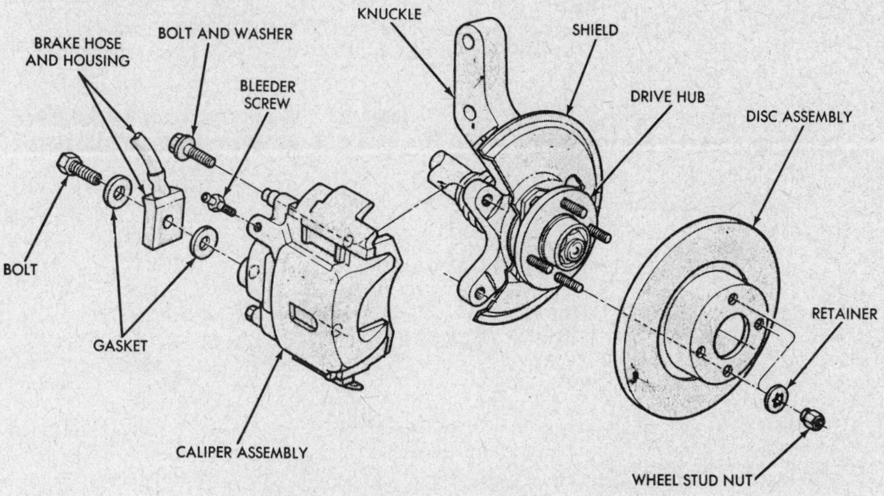

Fig. 1 A.T.E. (front) dual pin floating caliper disc brake. Front wheel drive models

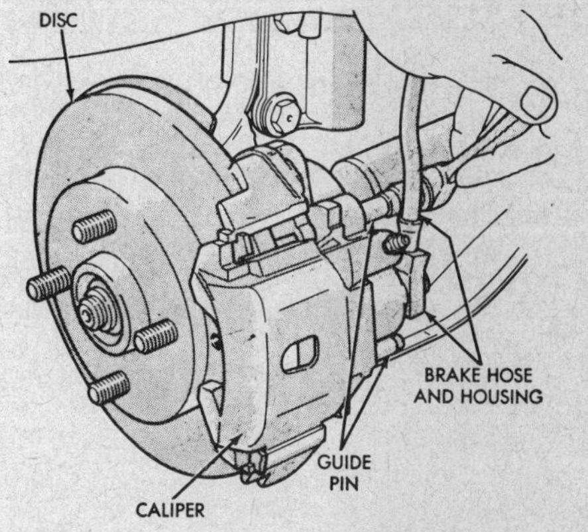

Fig. 2 Removing caliper guide pins

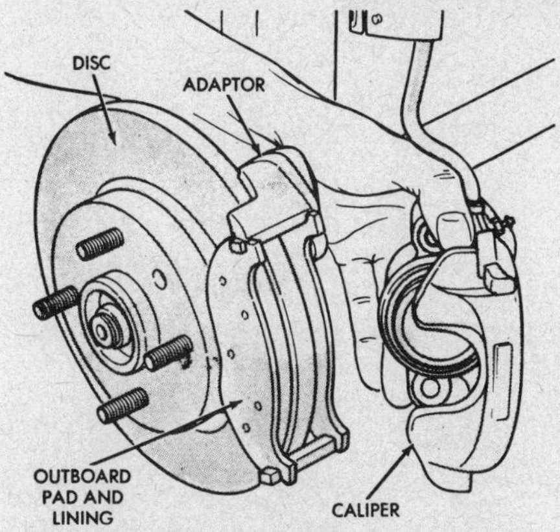

Fig. 3 Removing caliper

OPERATION

The single piston floating caliper disc brake assembly consists of the hub and disc brake rotor assembly, caliper, shoes and linings, splash shield and adapter, **Fig. 1.**

The caliper assembly floats on two rubber bushings riding on two steel guide pins threaded into the adapter. The bushings are inserted on the inboard portion of the caliper. Two machined abutments on the adapter position and align the caliper fore and aft. Guide pins and bushings control caliper and piston seal movement to assist in maintaining proper shoe clearance. All braking force is taken directly by the adapter.

BRAKE SHOE & LINING REPLACE

1982–84 OMNI & HORIZON & 1983–84 CHARGER & TURISMO

1. Raise and support front of vehicle, then remove wheel and tire assembly.
2. Remove caliper guide pins and anti-rattle spring, **Fig. 2.**
3. Carefully slide caliper assembly away from disc, **Fig. 3.** Support caliper assembly to prevent damage to brake hose.
4. Remove outboard shoe and lining assembly from adapter, **Fig. 4.**
5. Remove rotor from drive axle flange and studs, **Fig. 5.**
6. Remove inboard shoe and lining assembly from adapter, **Fig. 6.**
7. Carefully push piston into caliper bore. **Remove some brake fluid from reservoir to prevent overflowing when pushing piston into caliper bore.**
8. Position inboard shoe and lining on adapter. Ensure metal portion of shoe is properly positioned in recess of adapter.
9. Install rotor over studs and drive flange.
10. While holding outboard shoe in position on adapter, carefully position adapter over disc brake rotor.
11. Carefully lower caliper over disc brake rotor and adapter.

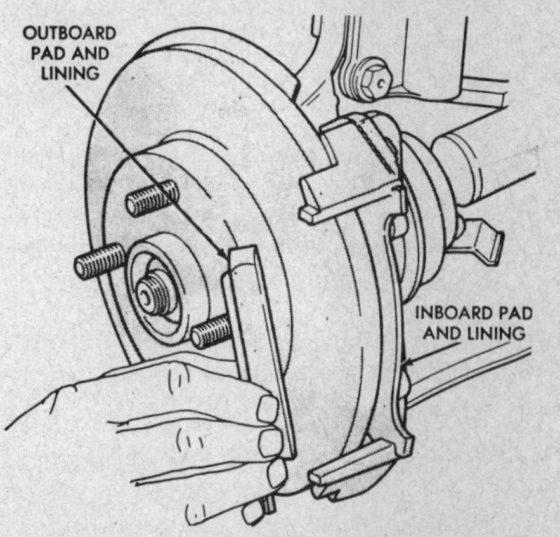

Fig. 4 Removing outboard pad & lining assembly

12. Install guide pins through bushings, caliper and adapter.
13. Press in on guide pins and thread pin into adapter. Torque pins to 25 to 40 ft. lbs.
14. Install wheel and tire assembly, then lower vehicle.

ALL FRONT WHEEL DRIVE EXC. 1982–84 OMNI & HORIZON & 1983–84 CHARGER & TURISMO

1. Raise and support vehicle, then remove wheel and tire assemblies.
2. Remove hold-down spring from caliper assembly by pressing spring outward.

3. Loosen, but do not remove, caliper guide pins, then remove caliper from disc. Inboard shoe will remain inside caliper. Support caliper assembly to prevent damage to hydraulic brake hose. **Remove caliper guide pins only if bushings or sleeves are to be replaced.**
4. Remove inboard shoe from caliper and outboard shoe from adapter.
5. Push caliper piston into bore. **Remove some brake fluid from master cylinder reservoir to prevent overflowing when piston is pushed into bore.**
6. Install new inboard shoe into caliper with retainer positioned in piston bore.
7. Install outboard shoe onto adapter.
8. Position caliper over brake disc and adapter, then torque guide pins to 18-22 ft. lbs.
9. Install hold-down spring, then install tire and wheel assemblies and lower vehicle to ground.
10. Check master cylinder reservoir for proper level of brake fluid and add as necessary.

CALIPER OVERHAUL

DISASSEMBLE

1. Remove caliper assembly as described under Brake Shoe & Lining, Replace.
2. With brake hose attached to caliper, **Figs. 7 and 8,** carefully depress brake pedal to push piston out of caliper bore. Prop brake pedal to any position below first inch of brake pedal travel to prevent brake fluid loss.
3. If pistons are to be removed from both calipers, disconnect brake hose at frame bracket after removing piston, then cap brake line and repeat procedure to remove piston from other caliper.
4. Disconnect brake hose from caliper.
5. Mount caliper in a soft jawed vise.
6. Support caliper and remove dust boot and discard.
7. Using a small wooden or plastic stick, remove seal from groove in piston bore and discard.
8. Using a suitable tool, remove bushings from caliper.

ASSEMBLE

1. Mount caliper in a soft jawed vise.
2. Lubricate piston seal with clean brake fluid and install seal in caliper bore groove, **Fig. 9.** Ensure seal is properly seated, **Figs. 7 and 8.**
3. Lubricate piston boot with clean brake fluid and install boot in caliper bore groove, **Fig. 10.**
4. Using a hammer and small steel plate or a suitable C-clamp, drive into caliper until seated, **Fig. 11.** Ensure boot is properly seated in caliper bore.
5. Plug brake hose inlet boss and bleeder screw hole, then lubricate piston with clean brake fluid.
6. Spread boot with finger and work piston into boot, then press down on piston.

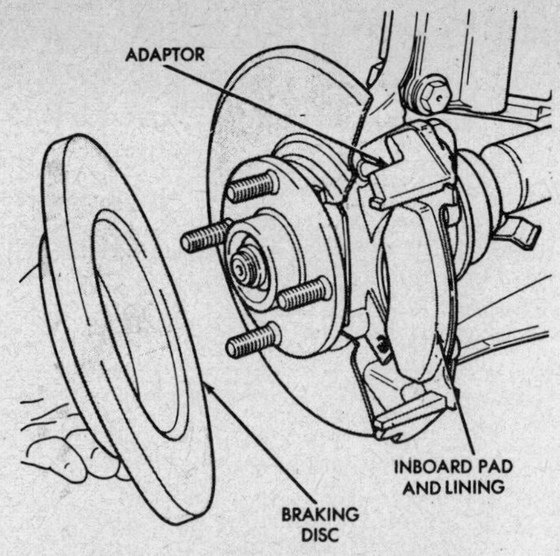

Fig. 5 Removing disc brake rotor from hub

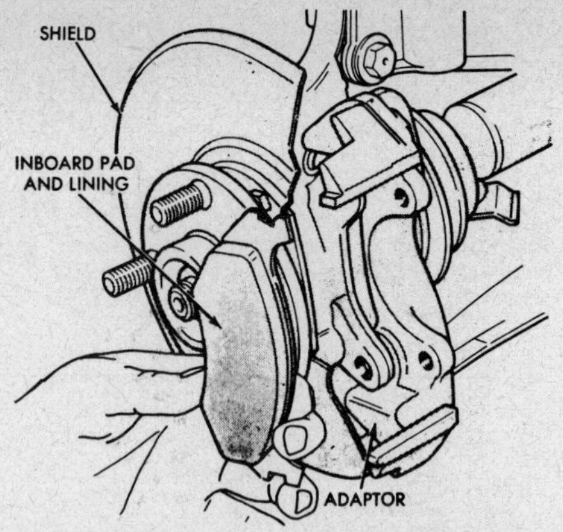

Fig. 6 Removing inboard pad & lining assemblies

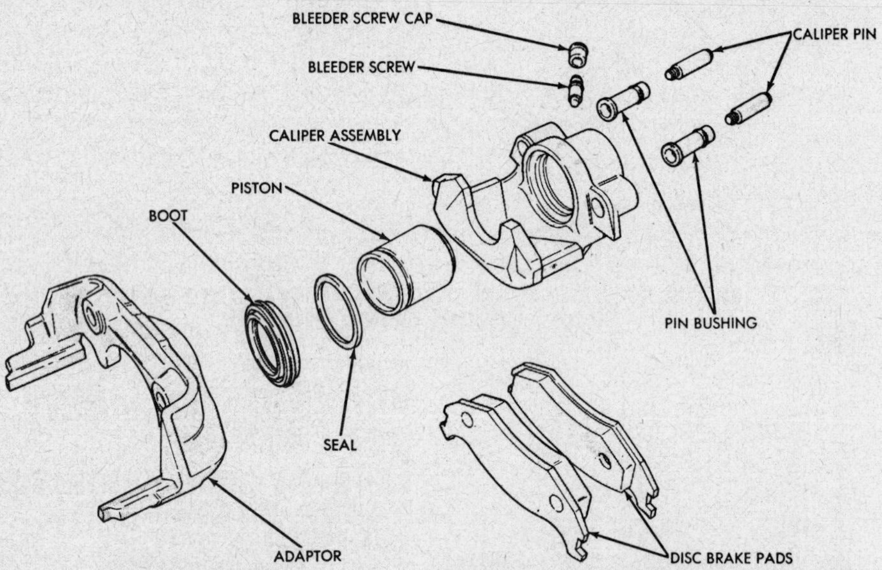

Fig. 7 Disassembled view of disc brake caliper. 1982–84 Omni & Horizon; 1983–84 Charger & Turismo

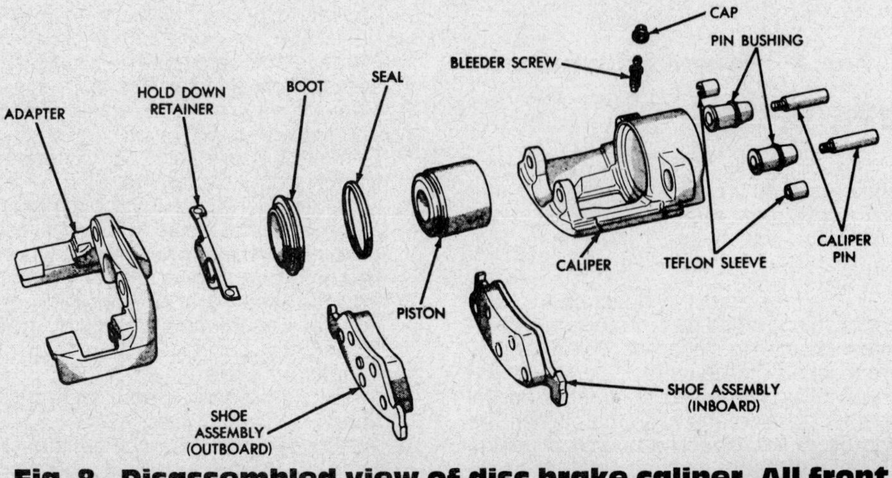

Fig. 8 Disassembled view of disc brake caliper. All front wheel drive exc. 1982–84 Omni & Horizon; 1983–84 Charger & Turismo

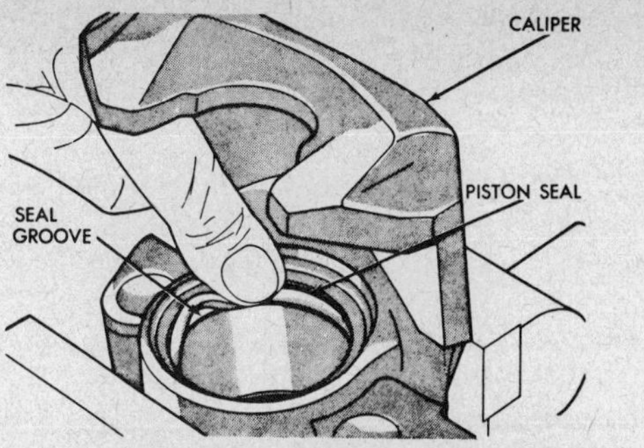

Fig. 9 Installing piston seal

7. Remove plug and carefully push piston down in bore until bottomed.
8. Compress flanges of guide pin bushings and install bushings on caliper housing. Ensure that bushing flanges extend evenly over caliper housing on both sides. **On all front wheel drive except 1982-84 Omni and Horizon and 1983-84 Charger and Turismo, remove Teflon sleeves from guide pin bushings prior to installing bushings into caliper. After bushings are installed into caliper, reinstall Teflon sleeves into bushings.**

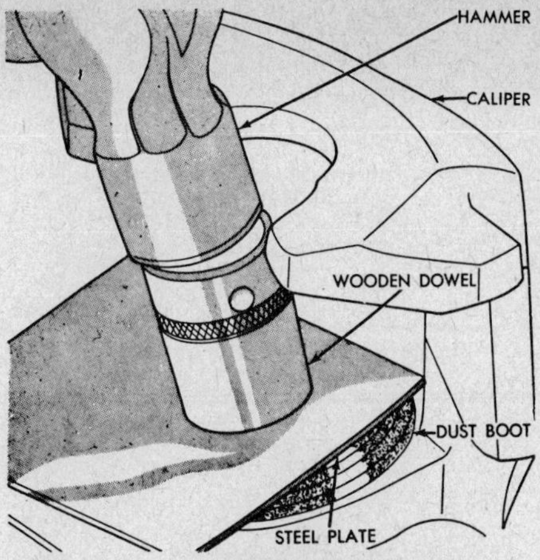

Fig. 10 Installing piston dust boot

9. Connect brake hose to brake line at frame bracket.

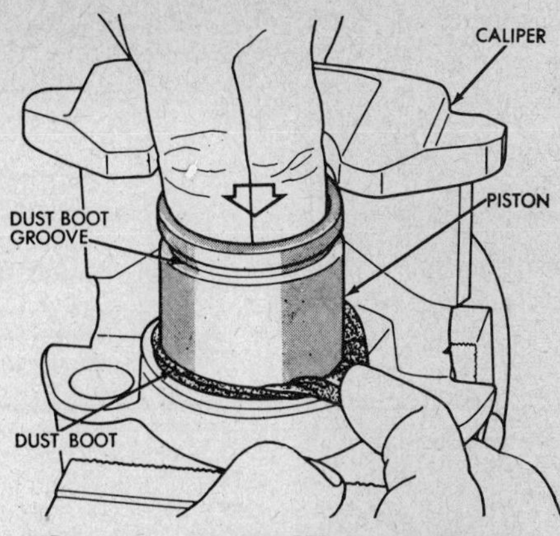

Fig. 11 Installing caliper piston

10. Install caliper on vehicle as described under Brake Shoe & Lining, Replace.
11. Check brake fluid level of master cylinder reservoir, then open caliper bleed screw and bleed brake system. Continue bleeding procedure until firm pedal is obtained.

A.T.E. (Rear) Dual Pin Floating Caliper Disc Brake

INDEX

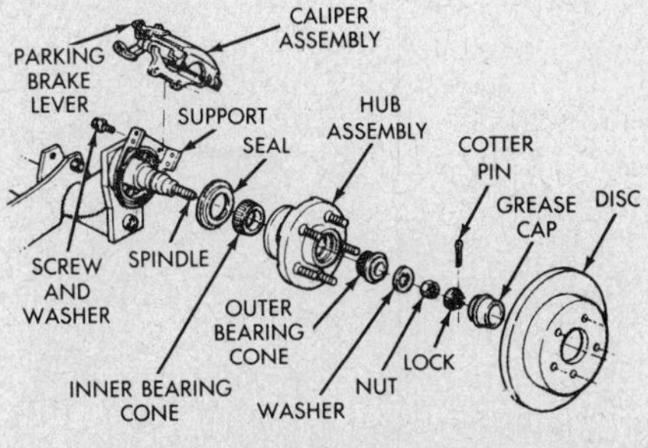

Fig. 1 A.T.E. (Rear) floating caliper disc brake

DESCRIPTION

This disc brake, **Fig. 1,** is a single piston, floating caliper type that incorporates a mechanically actuated parking brake mechanism. The caliper is a one piece casting with the single piston located on the inboard side. An automatic adjuster within the piston maintains a constant running clearance between the brakes and disc. The parking brake mechanism is self-adjusting.

The caliper floats on rubber bushings, with teflon inner sleeves, on the two guide pins threaded into the adapter. Two machined abutments on the adapter position and align the caliper and brake shoes for fore and aft movement.

BRAKE SHOES REPLACE

1. Raise and properly support vehicle.
2. Remove rear wheels, then clean caliper in area of access plug, **Fig. 2.**
3. Remove access plug and insert a 4 mm Allen wrench through access hole, and engage retraction shaft, **Fig. 3.** Rotate retraction shaft with Allen wrench counterclockwise to increase clearance between brake shoes and disc.
4. Remove outboard anti-rattle spring, **Fig. 4. Use care not to deform spring.**
5. Back out the caliper guide pins to free caliper from adapter. **Remove guide pins only if bushings or sleeve require replacement.**
6. Lift caliper upward and away from disc, **Fig. 5.** The inboard shoe will remain in caliper, attached to piston. Suspend caliper from a suspension member with suitable wire. **Do not allow caliper to hang by brake hose.**
7. Remove inboard shoe from piston (caliper), **Fig. 6,** and outboard shoe from adapter.
8. When installing shoes and the caliper, note the following:
   a. It will be necessary to retract the piston further with the Allen

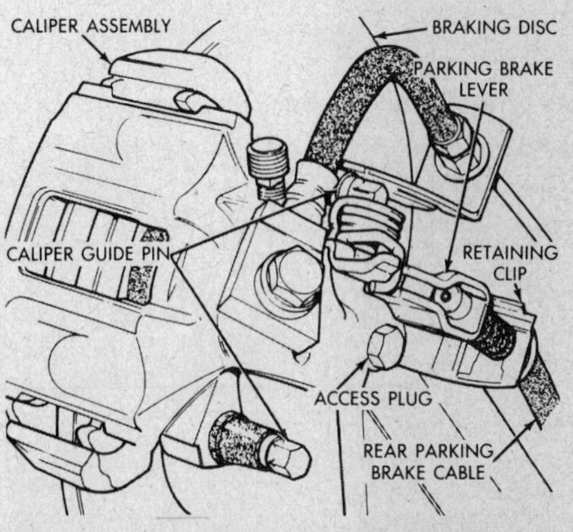

Fig. 2 Access plug location (parking brake retractor)

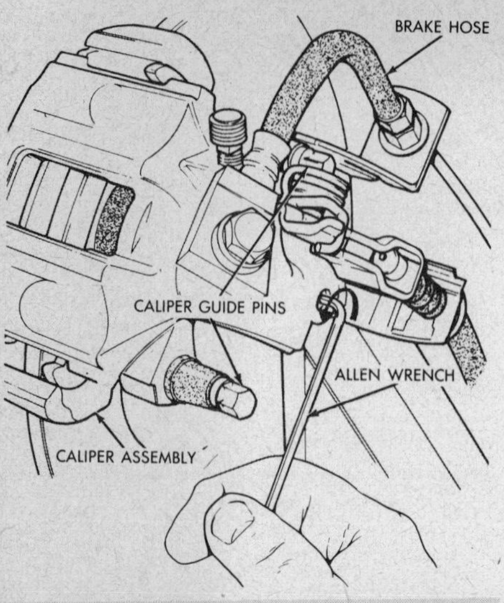

Fig. 3 Retracting brake shoes from disc

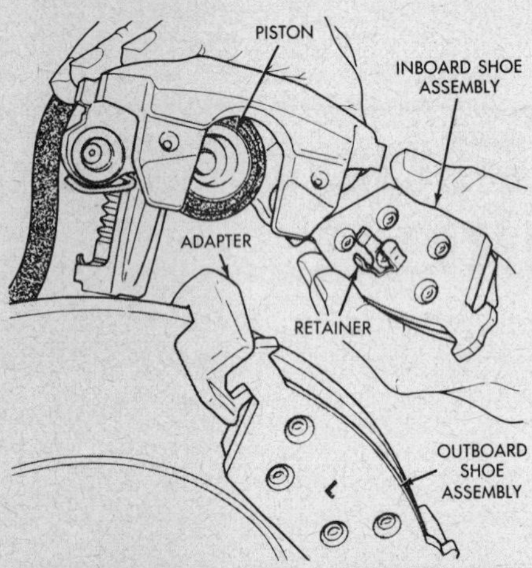

Fig. 6 Brake shoe replacement

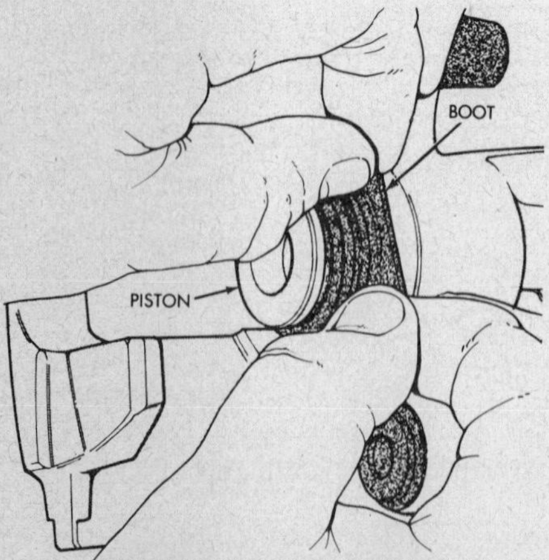

Fig. 9 Dust boot installation

wrench due to the thickness of the new shoes. When retracting the piston, stop rotation of Allen wrench when slight resistance is encountered. This indicates that the piston has bottomed. **Do not use excessive force since damage to retraction and actuation shafts may occur.**

b. The inboard shoes are interchangeable and may be used on either side of the vehicle. **The outboard shoes are not interchangeable and are marked "L" for left side or "R" for right side of vehicle, Fig. 7.**
c. Fit the retainer on inboard shoe into piston. Install proper outboard shoe on adapter. Lower caliper over disc and outboard shoe. Install and torque guide pins to 18-26 ft. lbs. **Be sure not to crossthread the pins.** Install anti-rattle spring.
d. To set the initial clearance between the brake shoes and disc, rotate the retraction shaft with the Allen wrench clockwise until snug, then back off 1/3 turn.

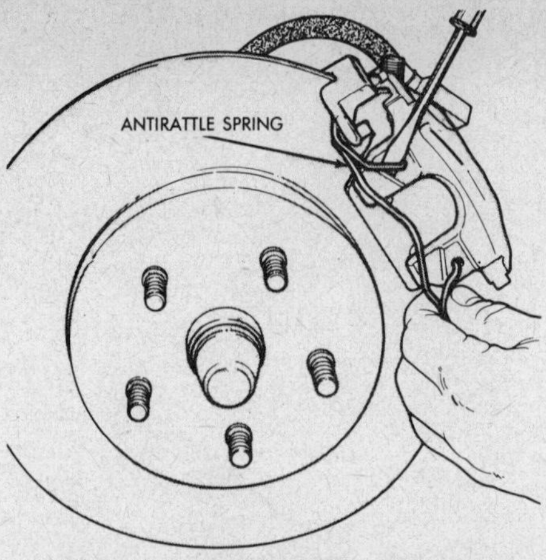

Fig. 4 Anti-rattle spring removal

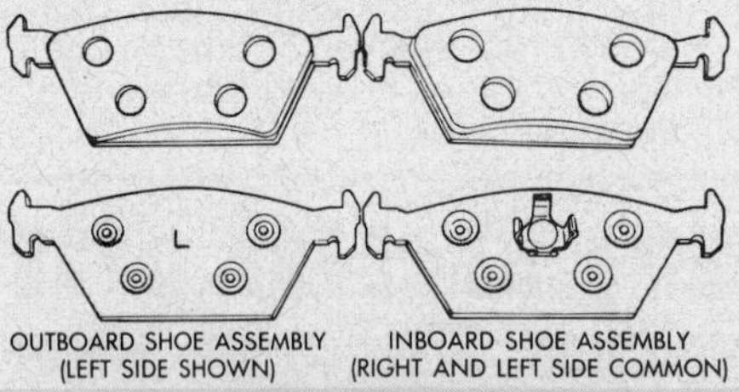

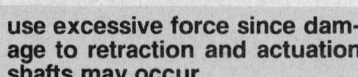

Fig. 7 Brake shoe identification

CALIPER SERVICE

DUST BOOT, REPLACE

1. Remove dust boot retainer with a suitable screwdriver, **Fig. 8.**
2. Remove dust boot from caliper and piston grooves.
3. Clean piston and caliper grooves, then coat new boot with clean brake fluid.
4. Place boot over piston and into the piston and caliper grooves, **Fig. 9.**
5. Install dust boot retainer into caliper groove.

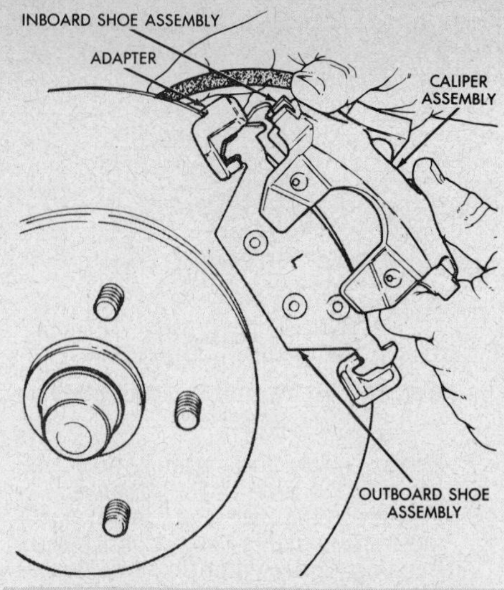

Fig. 5 Caliper removal

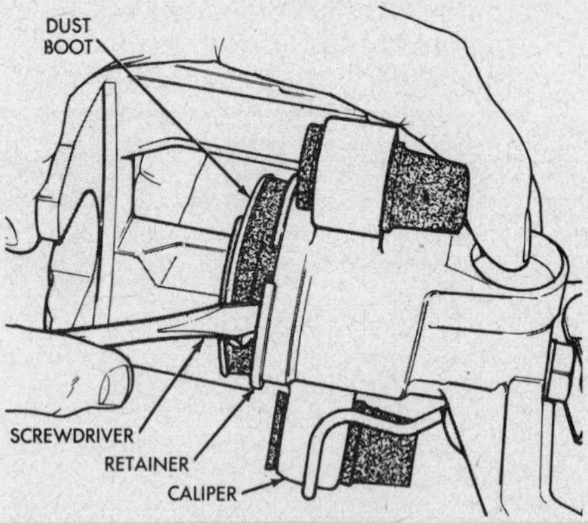

Fig. 8 Removing dust boot retainer

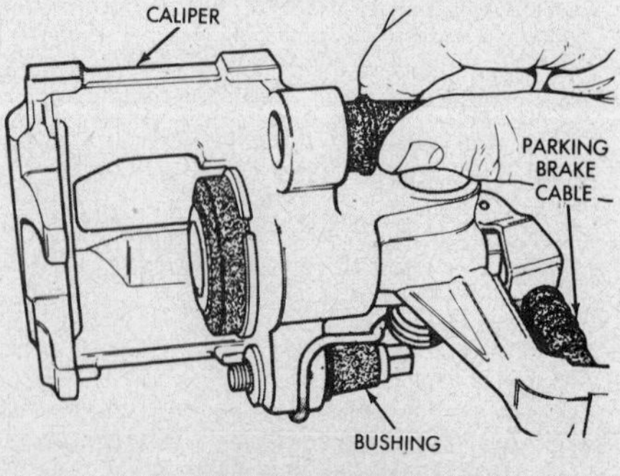

Fig. 10 Guide pin bushing installation

GUIDE PIN BUSHING, REPLACE

1. Remove bushings from caliper with a suitable tool. Discard bushings and Teflon sleeves.
2. Remove Teflon sleeves from new bushings prior to bushing installation.
3. Compress bushing flange with fingers and push bushing into seated position, **Fig. 10.**
4. Install Teflon sleeves into bushings.

Kelsey-Hayes Single Pin Floating Caliper Disc Brake

INDEX

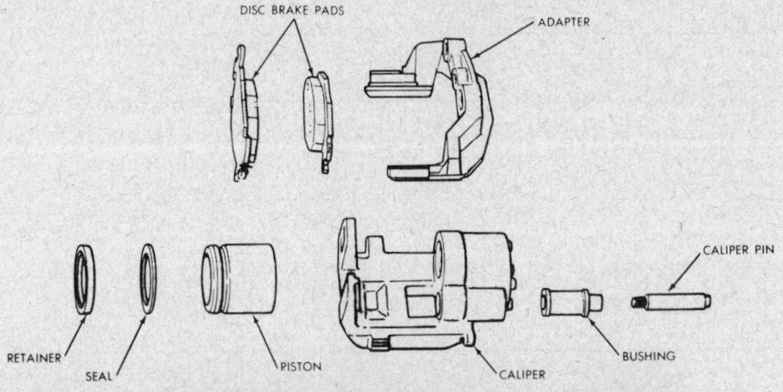

Fig. 1 Disassembled view of Kelsey-Hayes single pin floating caliper

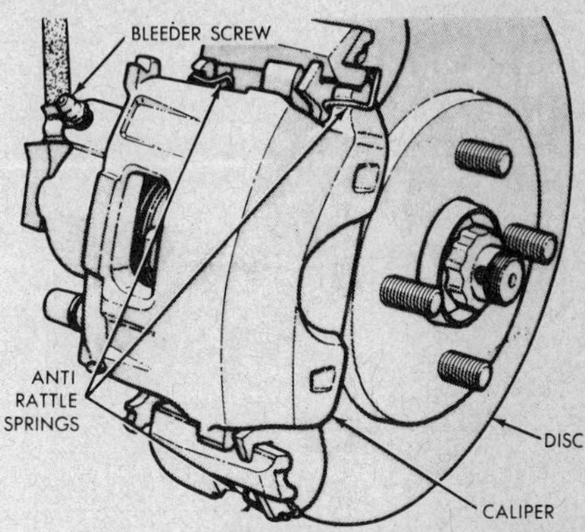

Fig. 2 Anti-rattle spring location

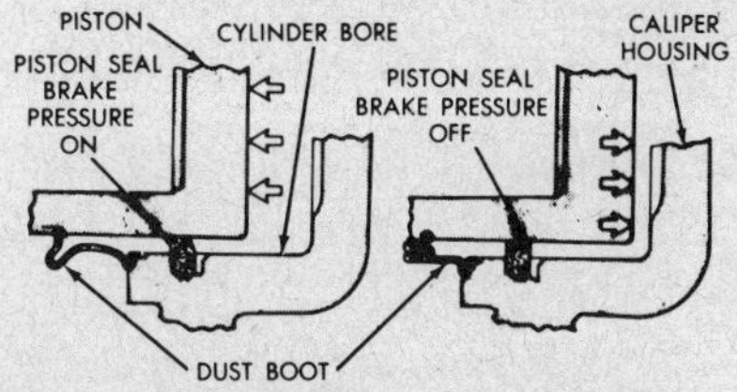

Fig. 3 Sectional view of piston seal & dust boot

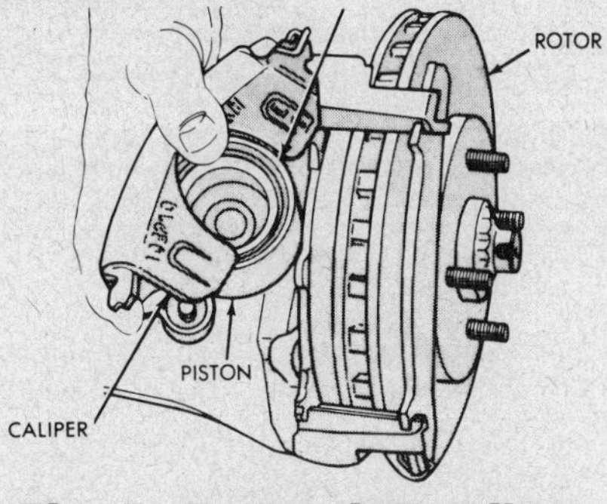

Fig. 4 Removing caliper

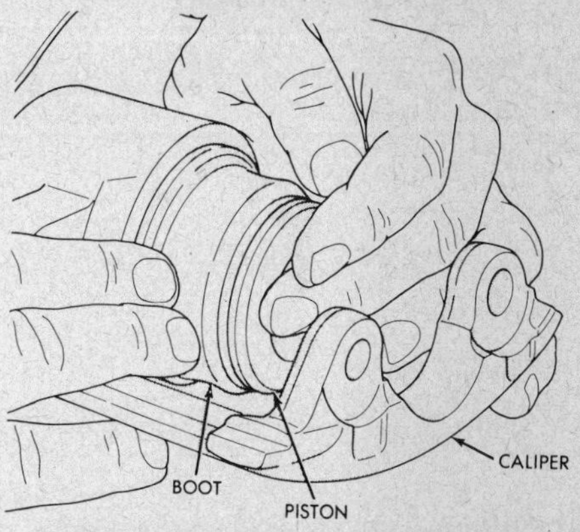

Fig. 5 Piston installation

OPERATION

The caliper assembly consists of a rotor, caliper, shoes and linings, and adapter, **Fig. 1.** The single piston caliper assembly floats through a rubber bushing on a single pin, threaded into the adapter. The bushing is inserted into the inboard portion of the caliper. Two machined abutments on the adapter, position and align the caliper fore and aft. The guide pin and bushing controls the movement of the caliper and the piston seal, to assist in maintaining proper shoe clearance.

This assembly has three anti-rattle clips. One is on top of the inboard shoe, one clip is on the bottom of the outboard shoe, and one clip is on top of the caliper, **Fig. 2.**

All of the braking force is taken directly by the adapter. The caliper is a one piece casting with the inboard side containing a single piston cylinder bore.

A square cut rubber piston seal is located in a machined groove in the caliper bore and provides a seal between piston and caliper bore, **Fig. 3.**

A molded rubber dust boot installed in a groove in the cylinder bore and piston keeps contamination from the caliper bore and piston. The boot mounts in the caliper bore and in a groove in the piston, **Fig. 3.**

BRAKE SHOE & LINING REPLACE

REMOVAL

1. Remove brake fluid until reservoir is half full.
2. Raise and support front of vehicle, then remove wheel and tire assembly.
3. Remove caliper guide pin and anti-rattle clips.
4. Remove caliper from disc by sliding caliper assembly out and away from braking disc, **Fig. 4.** Suspend caliper with wire so as not to damage flexible brake hose.
5. Remove outboard brake lining, then lift off rotor and remove inboard brake lining.

INSTALLATION

1. Push piston back into cylinder bore with uniform pressure until it is bottomed, **Fig. 5.**
2. Position inboard shoe and lining on adapter, then install rotor.
3. While holding outboard shoe in position on adapter, carefully position caliper over disc brake rotor.
4. Lower caliper over rotor and adapter.
5. Install guide pin through bushing, caliper and adapter.
6. Press in on guide pin and thread pin into adapter. Torque pin to 25 to 40 ft. lbs. on 1982-83 models and 25 to 35 ft. lbs. on 1984-87 models.
7. Install wheel and tire assembly, then lower vehicle.

CALIPER OVERHAUL

Refer to Caliper Overhaul under "A.T.E. (Front) Dual Pin Floating Caliper Disc Brake" for procedure.

Rotor Specifications

Car	Year	Nominal Thick-ness	Minimum Refinish Thick-ness	Thickness Variation Parallelism	Lateral Runout (T.I.R.)	Finish (Micro-In.)
Rear Wheel Drive	1982–87	1.010	.940	.0005	.004	15–80
Horizon & Omni	1982–87	.498	.431	.0005	.005	15–80
Charger & Turismo	1983–84	.498	.431	.0005	.005	15–80
All Other Front Wheel Drive ①	1982–87	.935	.882	.0005	.005	15–80
All Other Front Wheel Drive ②	1987	.344	.291	.0005	.005	15–80

①—Front wheel disc brake.
②—Rear wheel disc brake.

Caliper Specifications

Year	Model	Caliper Bore Dia. In.
FRONT WHEEL DRIVE		
1982	Horizon & Omni	1.894
1982–87	All Others ①	2.130
1987	All Others ②	1.30

①—Front wheel disc brake.
②—Rear wheel disc brake.

DRUM BRAKES

TABLE OF CONTENTS

Application

	Type No.
1982 Front Wheel Drive	2
1983-87 Front Wheel Drive	3
Rear Wheel Drive	1

General Information

INDEX

SERVICE PRECAUTIONS

When working on or around brake assemblies, care must be taken to prevent breathing asbestos dust, as many manufacturers incorporate asbestos fibers in the production of brake linings. During routine service operations the amount of asbestos dust from brake lining wear is at a low level, due to a chemical breakdown during use and a few precautions will minimize exposure.

Do not sand or grind brake linings unless suitable local exhaust ventilation equipment is used to prevent excessive asbestos exposure.

1. Wear a suitable respirator approved for asbestos dust use during all repair procedures.
2. When cleaning brake dust from brake parts, use a vacuum cleaner with a highly efficient filter system. If a suitable vacuum cleaner is not available, use a water soaked rag. **Do not use compressed air or dry brush to clean brake parts.**
3. Keep work area clean using same equipment as for cleaning brake parts.
4. Properly dispose of rags and vacuum cleaner bags by placing them in plastic bags.
5. Do not smoke or eat while working on brake systems. **Never use gasoline, kerosene, alcohol, motor oil, transmission fluid, or any fluid containing mineral oil to clean brake system components. These fluids will damage the rubber caps and seals. If system contamination is suspected, check brake fluid in the reservoir for dirt, discoloration, or separation (breakdown) of the brake fluid into distinct layers. Drain and flush the hydraulic system with clean brake fluid if contamination is suspected.**

GENERAL INSPECTION

BRAKE DRUMS

Any time the brake drums are removed for brake service, the braking surface diameter should be checked with a suitable brake drum micrometer at several points to determine if they are within the safe oversize limit stamped on the brake drum outer surface. If the braking surface diameter exceeds specifications, the drum must be replaced. If the braking surface diameter is within specifications, drums should be cleaned and inspected for cracks, scores, deep grooves, taper, out of round and heat spotting. If drums are cracked or heat spotted, they must be replaced. Minor scores should be removed with sandpaper. Grooves and large scores can only be removed by machining with special equipment, as long as the braking surface is within specifications stamped on brake drum outer surface. Any brake drum sufficiently out of round to cause vehicle vibration or noise while braking or showing taper should also be machined, removing only enough stock to true up the brake drum.

After a brake drum is machined, wipe the braking surface diameter with a denatured alcohol soaked cloth. If one brake drum is machined, the other should also be machined to the same diameter to maintain equal braking forces.

BRAKE LININGS & SPRINGS

Inspect brake linings for excessive wear, damage, oil, grease or brake fluid contamination. If any of the above conditions exists, brake linings should be replaced. Do not attempt to replace only one set of brake shoes; they should be replaced as an axle set only to maintain equal braking forces. Examine brake shoe webbing, hold-down and return springs for signs of overheating indicated by a slight blue color. If any component exhibits overheating signs, replace hold-down and return springs with new ones. Overheated springs lose their pull and could cause brake linings to wear out prematurely. Inspect all springs for sags, bends and external damage and replace as necessary.

Inspect hold-down retainers and pins for bends, rust and corrosion. If any of the above is found, replace as required.

BACKING PLATE

Inspect backing plate shoe contact surface for grooves that may restrict shoe movement and cannot be removed by lightly sanding with emery cloth or other suitable abrasive. If backing plate exhibits above condition, it should be replaced. Also inspect for signs of cracks, warpage and excessive rust, indicating need for replacement.

ADJUSTER MECHANISM

Inspect all components for rust, corrosion, bends and fatigue. Replace as necessary. On adjuster mechanism equipped with adjuster cable, inspect cable for kinks, fraying or elongation of eyelet and replace as necessary.

PARKING BRAKE CABLE

Inspect parking brake cable end for kinks, fraying and elongation and replace as necessary. Use a small hose clamp to compress clamp where it enters backing plate to remove.

Type 1

INDEX

Page No.

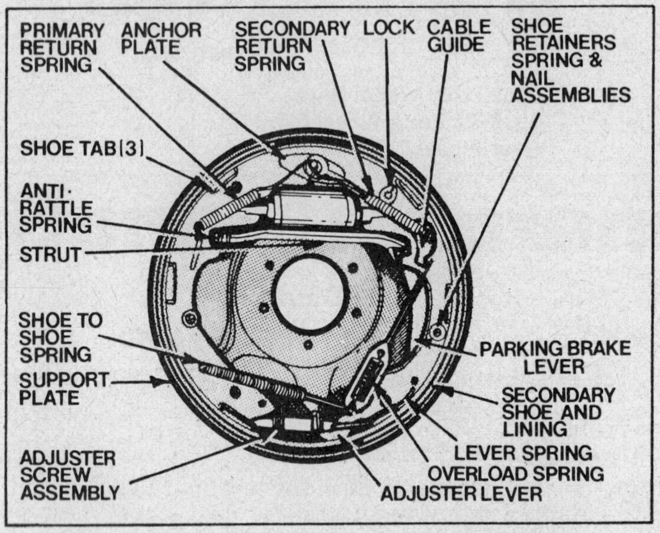

Fig. 1 Drum brake assembly. Type 1

REMOVAL

1. Raise and support rear of vehicle and remove tire and wheel assembly.
2. Remove brake drum. If brake lining is dragging on brake drum, back off brake adjustment by rotating adjustment screw. **If brake drum is rusted or corroded to axle flange and cannot be removed readily, lightly tap axle flange to drum mounting surface with a suitable hammer.**
3. Using brake spring pliers or equivalent, remove primary and secondary shoe return springs, **Fig. 1.**
4. Remove automatic adjuster cable from anchor plate and unhook from adjuster lever.
5. Remove adjuster cable, overload spring, cable guide and anchor plate.
6. Unhook adjuster lever spring from lever and remove spring and lever.
7. Remove shoe to shoe spring from secondary shoe web, then the primary shoe.
8. Spread shoes apart and remove parking brake strut and spring.
9. Using suitable tool, remove shoe retainers, then the springs and nails.
10. Disconnect parking brake cable from lever and remove brake shoes.
11. Remove parking brake lever from secondary shoe.
12. Clean dirt from brake drum, backing plate and all other components. **Do not use compressed air or dry brush to clean brake parts. Many brake parts contain asbestos fibers which, if inhaled, can cause serious injury. To clean brake parts, use a water soaked rag or a suitable vacuum cleaner to minimize airborne dust.**

INSPECTION

Refer to the General Information section at the front of this chapter.

INSTALLATION

1. Lubricate parking brake lever fulcrum with suitable brake lube, then attach lever to secondary brake shoe. Ensure that the lever operates smoothly.
2. Lightly lubricate backing plate shoe contact surfaces with suitable brake lube.
3. Connect parking brake lever to cable and slide secondary brake shoe into position.
4. Connect wheel cylinder link to brake shoe (if equipped).
5. Slide parking brake lever strut behind axle flange and into parking brake lever slot, then place parking brake anti-rattle spring over strut.
6. Position primary brake shoe on backing plate and connect wheel cylinder link (if equipped) and parking brake strut.
7. Install anchor plate and position adjuster cable eye over anchor pin.
8. Install primary shoe return spring using brake spring pliers or equivalent.
9. Place protruding hole rim of cable guide in secondary shoe web hole, then holding guide in position, install secondary shoe return spring through cable guide and secondary shoe. Install spring on anchor pin using brake spring pliers or equivalent. **Ensure cable guide remains flat against secondary shoe web during and after return spring installation. Also ensure secondary spring end overlaps primary spring end on anchor pin.**
10. Using suitable pliers, squeeze spring ends around anchor pin until parallel.
11. Install adjuster screw assembly between primary and secondary brake shoes with star wheel on secondary shoe side. **The left side adjuster assembly stud is stamped "L" and is cadmium-plated. The right side adjuster assembly is not stamped and is colored black.**
12. Install shoe to shoe spring, then position adjusting lever spring over pivot pin on shoe web.
13. Install adjusting lever under spring and over pivot pin, then slide lever slightly rearward.
14. Install nails, springs and retainers.
15. Thread adjuster cable over guide and hook end of overload spring in lever. Ensure eye of cable is pulled tight

against anchor and in a straight line with guide.
16. Install brake drum, tire and wheel assembly.
17. Adjust brakes. Refer to the Chrysler Rear Wheel Drive car chapter for procedure.
18. If any hydraulic connections have been opened, bleed brake system.
19. Check master cylinder fluid level, and replenish as necessary.
20. Check brake pedal for proper feel and return.
21. Lower vehicle and road test. **Do not severely apply brakes immediately after installation of new brake linings or permanent damage may occur to linings, and/or brake drums may become scored. Brakes must be used moderately during first few hundred miles of operation to ensure proper burnishing of linings.**

Type 2

INDEX

Page No.

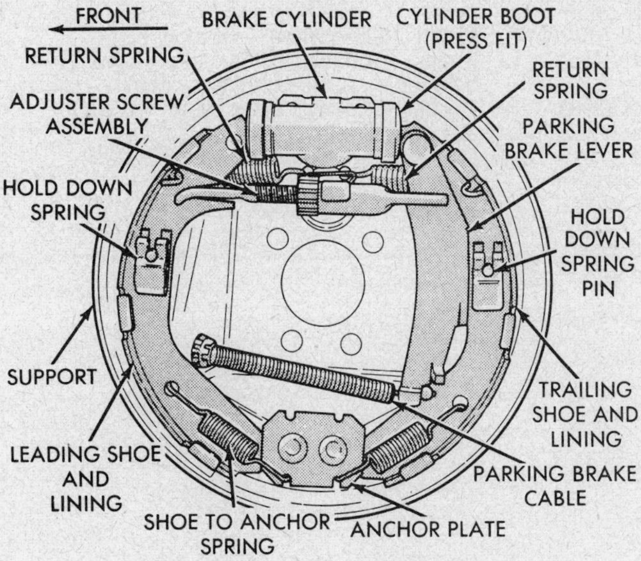

Fig. 1 Drum brake assembly. Type 2

REMOVAL

1. Raise and support rear of vehicle, then remove tire and wheel assembly.
2. Remove brake drum. If brake lining is dragging on brake drum, back off brake adjustment by rotating adjustment screw.
3. Disconnect parking brake cable from parking brake lever, **Fig. 1.**
4. Using suitable pliers, remove brake shoe to anchor springs and hold-down springs.
5. Fully seat adjuster nut, then spread shoes apart and remove adjuster screw assembly.
6. Raise parking brake lever, then pull trailing shoe away from support to ease return spring tension and disengage spring end from support. Remove trailing shoe.
7. Pull leading shoe away from support to ease return spring tension and disengage spring end from support. Remove leading shoe.
8. Remove parking brake lever from trailing shoe.
9. Clean dirt from brake drum, support plate and all other components. **Do not use compressed air or dry brush to clean brake parts. Many brake parts contain asbestos fibers which, if inhaled, can cause serious injury. To clean brake parts, use a water soaked rag or a suitable vacuum cleaner to minimize airborne dust.**

INSPECTION

Refer to the General Information section at the front of this chapter.

INSTALLATION

1. Lightly lubricate support plate shoe contact surfaces with suitable brake lube.
2. Remove brake drum hub grease seal and bearings, then clean and repack bearings and reinstall. Install new grease seal.
3. Position leading shoe return spring on shoe, then while holding shoe away from support, engage return spring in support plate, **Fig. 2,** and swing shoe end into position under anchor.
4. Install parking brake lever on trailing shoe.
5. Install trailing shoe return spring on shoe, then while holding shoe away from support, engage return spring in support plate, **Fig. 3,** and swing shoe end into position under anchor.
6. Spread shoes apart and install adjuster screw assembly. Ensure forked end enters the leading shoe with curved tines facing down, **Fig. 1.**
7. Using a suitable pair of pliers, install hold-down springs and shoe to anchor springs.

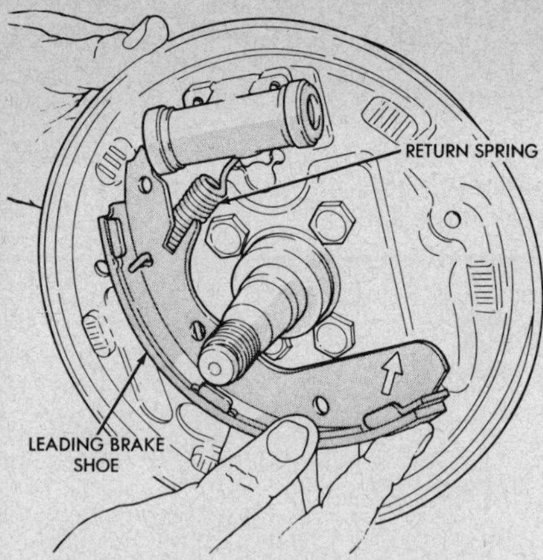

Fig. 2 Installing leading brake shoe. Type 2

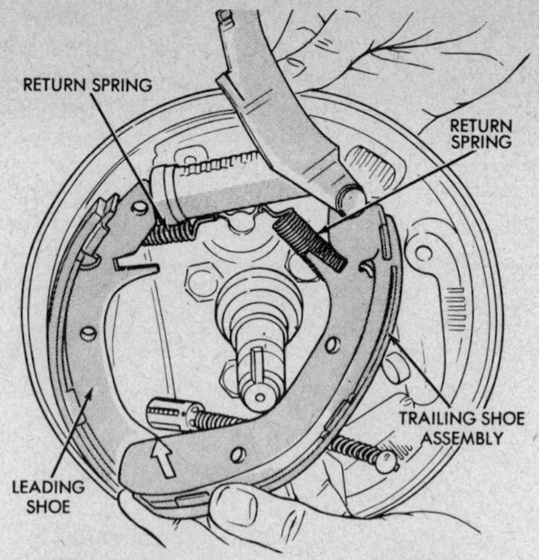

Fig. 3 Installing trailing brake shoe. Type 2

8. Pull back parking brake cable return spring slightly to expose cable, then slide parking brake cable into parking brake lever and release spring.
9. Install brake drum and bearings. Refer to individual car chapter for wheel bearing adjustment procedure.
10. Adjust brakes. Refer to Chrysler Front Wheel Drive car chapter for procedure.
11. Install tire and wheel assembly.
12. If any hydraulic connections have been opened, bleed brake system.
13. Check master cylinder level, replenish as necessary.
14. Check brake pedal for proper feel and return.
15. Lower vehicle and road test. **Do not severely apply brakes immediately after installation of new brake linings or permanent damage may occur to linings and/or brake drums may become scored. Brakes must be used moderately during first several hundred miles of operation to ensure proper burnishing of linings.**

Type 3

INDEX

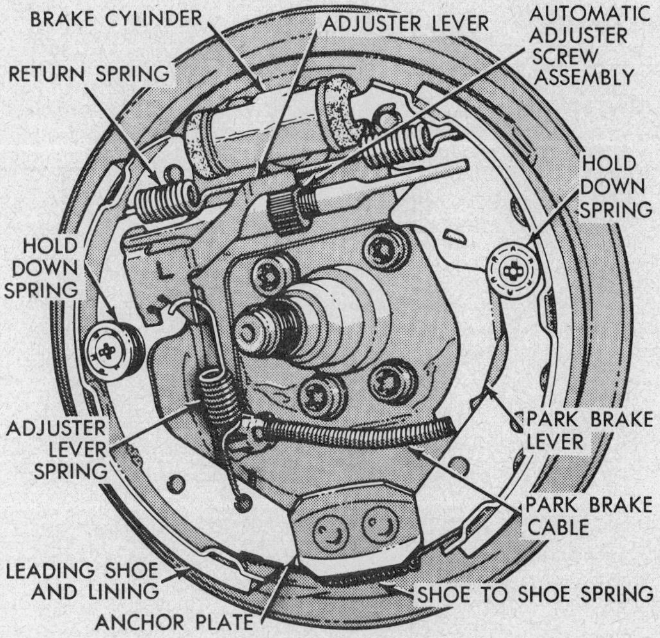

Fig. 1 Drum brake assembly. Type 3

REMOVAL

1. Raise and support rear of vehicle, then remove tire and wheel assembly.
2. Remove brake drum. If brake lining is dragging on brake drum, back off brake adjustment by rotating adjustment screw.
3. Using suitable pliers, remove adjuster lever spring, **Fig. 1.**
4. Remove adjuster lever.
5. Turn automatic adjuster screw out to expand shoes past wheel cylinder boot.
6. Using suitable tool, remove hold-down springs.
7. Pull brake shoe assembly down and away from anchor plate.
8. Remove C-clip retaining parking brake lever to trailing brake shoe webbing.
9. Disassemble shoe assembly.
10. Clean dirt from brake drum, anchor plate and all other components. **Do not use compressed air or dry brush to clean brake parts. Many brake parts contain asbestos fibers, which, if inhaled, can cause serious injury. To clean brake parts, use a water soaked rag or a suitable vacuum cleaner to minimize airborne dust.**

INSPECTION

Refer to the General Information section at the front of this chapter.

INSTALLATION

1. Lightly lubricate anchor plate shoe contact surfaces with suitable brake lube.
2. Remove brake drum hub grease seal and bearings, then clean and repack bearings and reinstall. Install new grease seal.
3. Assemble automatic adjuster screw assembly, return spring and shoe-to-shoe spring to brake shoe assembly.
4. Position lining assembly near anchor plate, then assemble parking brake lever to trailing shoe webbing. Secure with C-clip.
5. Install lining assembly onto anchor plate. When positioned, back off adjuster nut to seat brake shoe ends in wheel cylinder.
6. Install hold-down springs.
7. Position adjuster lever, then using suitable pliers, install adjuster lever spring.
8. Install brake drum and bearings. Refer to individual car chapter for wheel bearing adjustment procedure.
9. Adjust brakes. Refer to individual car chapter for procedure.
10. Install tire and wheel assembly.
11. If any hydraulic connections have been opened, bleed brake system.
12. Check master cylinder level, and replenish as necessary.
13. Check brake pedal for proper feel and return.
14. Lower vehicle and road test. **Do not severely apply brakes immediately after installation of new brake linings or permanent damage may occur to linings and/or brake drums may become scored. Brakes must be used moderately during first several hundred miles of operation to ensure proper burnishing.**

Specifications

Year	Model	Brake Drum Inside Dia. In.	Rear Wheel Cylinder Bore Dia. In.
FRONT WHEEL DRIVE			
1982–87	Exc. Caravelle, E-Class, Executive, New Yorker & 600	7.87	5/8 ①
1982–87	All Others	8.66	5/8 ①
REAR WHEEL DRIVE			
1982–87	All	10 ②	15/16

①—Heavy duty, 9/16 inch.
②—Heavy duty, 11 inches.

AUTOMATIC TRANSMISSIONS/TRANSAXLES

TABLE OF CONTENTS

Torqueflite Automatic Transmission

INDEX

IDENTIFICATION

Transmission identification markings are cast in raised letters and numerals on the lower left side of the bellhousing. **There are sufficient variations within each of the main categories to make it necessary to service them by serial number, a stamped 7-digit number appearing on the oil pan side rail.**

DESCRIPTION

These transmissions, **Fig. 1**, combine a torque converter with a fully automatic three speed gear system. The converter housing and transmission case are an integral aluminum casting. The transmission consists of two multiple disc clutches, an overrunning (one-way) clutch, two servos and bands and two planetary gear sets to provide three forward speeds and reverse.

The common sun gear of the planetary gear sets is connected to the front clutch by a driving shell that is splined to the sun gear and to the front clutch retainer.

The hydraulic system consists of a single oil pump and a valve body that contains all the valves except the governor valve.

Venting of the transmission is accomplished by a drilled passage through the upper part of the front pump housing.

The torque converter is attached to the engine crankshaft through a flexible driving plate, and is cooled by circulating the transmission fluid through an oil-to-water type cooler located in the radiator lower tank. A lockup feature is used on most applications.

The lockup converter system consists of a lockup mechanism within the converter, and a lockup module and switch valve attached to the valve body. The internal lockup mechanism consists of a sliding clutch piston, torsion springs and clutch friction material. The friction material is attached to the front cover, the clutch piston is mounted in the turbine, and the torsion springs are located on the forward side of the turbine. The torsion springs are used to dampen out engine firing impulses, while absorbing the shock loads that occur during lockup.

When the transmission reaches a predetermined speed, transmission fluid is channeled through the input shaft and into the area between the clutch piston and turbine. The fluid pressure forces the piston against the front cover friction material, locking the turbine to the impeller. When vehicle speed decreases, or the transmission shifts out of direct drive, fluid pressure is released, the clutch piston retracts, and the converter operates in a conventional manner.

Because the lockup mechanism is completely enclosed within the converter, lockup converters have a circular decal attached to the front cover stating the converter type and stall ratio.

TROUBLESHOOTING GUIDE

HARSH ENGAGEMENT IN D-1-2-R

1. Engine idle speed too high.
2. Hydraulic pressures too high or too low.
3. Low-reverse band out of adjustment.
4. Accumulator sticking, broken rings or spring.
5. Low-reverse servo, band or linkage malfunction.
6. Worn or faulty front and/or rear clutch.
7. Valve body malfunction or leakage.
8. Throttle linkage sticking or incorrect adjustment.
9. Accumulator broken seal rings, scratched bore, broken or collapsed spring, cracked piston.

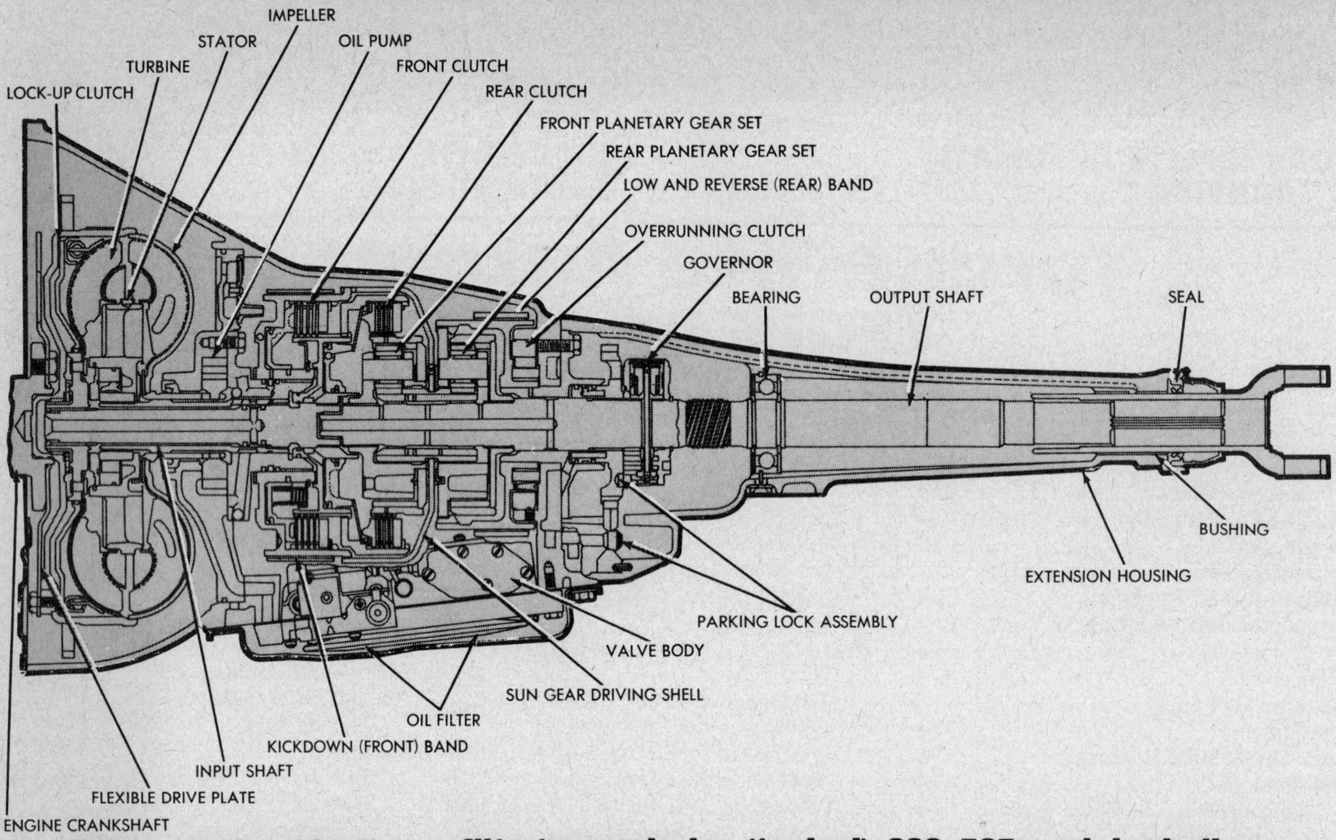

Fig. 1 Series 904 Torqueflite transmission (typical). 999, 727 models similar

DELAYED ENGAGEMENT IN D-1-2-R

1. Low fluid level.
2. Incorrect manual linkage adjustment.
3. Oil filter clogged.
4. Hydraulic pressures too high or low.
5. Valve body malfunction or leakage.
6. Accumulator sticking, broken rings or spring.
7. Clutches or servos sticking or not operating.
8. Faulty front oil pump.
9. Worn or faulty front and/or rear clutch.
10. Worn or broken input shaft and/or reaction shaft support seal rings.
11. Aerated fluid.
12. Incorrect idle adjustment.
13. Incorrect low and reverse band adjustment.

RUNAWAY OR HARSH UPSHIFT & 3-2 KICKDOWN

1. Low fluid level.
2. Incorrect throttle linkage adjustment.
3. Hydraulic pressures too high or low.
4. Kickdown band out of adjustment.
5. Valve body malfunction or leakage.
6. Governor malfunction.
7. Accumulator sticking, broken rings or spring.
8. Clutches or servos sticking or not operating.
9. Kickdown servo, band or linkage malfunction.
10. Worn or faulty front clutch.
11. Worn or broken input shaft and/or reaction shaft support seal rings.
12. Aerated oil.
13. Clogged oil filter.

NO UPSHIFT

1. Low fluid level.
2. Incorrect throttle linkage adjustment.
3. Kickdown band out of adjustment.
4. Hydraulic pressures too high or low.
5. Governor sticking.
6. Valve body malfunction or leakage.
7. Accumulator sticking, broken rings or spring.
8. Clutches or servos sticking or not operating.
9. Faulty oil pump.
10. Kickdown servo, band or linkage malfunction.
11. Worn or faulty front clutch.
12. Worn or broken input shaft and/or reaction shaft support seal rings.
13. Incorrect gearshift linkage adjustment.
14. Governor support seal rings broken or worn.

DELAYED UPSHIFT

1. Incorrect throttle linkage adjustment.
2. Kickdown band out of adjustment.
3. Governor support seal rings broken or worn.
4. Worn or broken reaction shaft support seal rings.
5. Governor malfunction.
6. Kickdown servo band or linkage malfunction.
7. Worn or faulty front clutch.

NO KICKDOWN OR NORMAL DOWNSHIFT

1. Incorrect throttle linkage adjustment.
2. Incorrect gearshift linkage adjustment.
3. Kickdown band out of adjustment.
4. Hydraulic pressure too high or low.
5. Governor sticking.
6. Valve body malfunction or leakage.
7. Accumulator sticking, broken rings or spring.
8. Clutches or servos sticking or not operating.
9. Kickdown servo, band or linkage malfunction.
10. Overrunning clutch not holding.
11. Low fluid level.

ERRATIC SHIFTS

1. Low fluid level.
2. Aerated fluid.
3. Incorrect throttle linkage adjustment.
4. Incorrect gearshift control linkage adjustment.
5. Hydraulic pressures too high or low.
6. Governor sticking.
7. Oil filter clogged.
8. Valve body malfunction or leakage.
9. Clutches or servos sticking or not operating.
10. Faulty oil pump.
11. Worn or broken input shaft and/or reaction shaft support rings.
12. Governor support seal rings broken or worn.
13. Kickdown servo band or linkage malfunction.
14. Worn or faulty front clutch.

SLIPS IN FORWARD DRIVE POSITIONS

1. Low oil level.
2. Aerated fluid.
3. Incorrect throttle linkage adjustment.
4. Incorrect gearshift control linkage adjustment.
5. Hydraulic pressures too low.
6. Valve body malfunction or leakage.

7. Accumulator sticking, broken rings or springs.
8. Clutches or servos sticking or not operating.
9. Worn or faulty front and/or rear clutch.
10. Overrunning clutch not holding.
11. Worn or broken input shaft and/or reaction shaft support seal rings.
12. Clogged oil filter.
13. Faulty oil pump.
14. Overrunning clutch worn, broken or seized.
15. Incorrect kickdown band adjustment.

SLIPS IN REVERSE ONLY

1. Low fluid level.
2. Aerated fluid.
3. Incorrect gearshift control linkage adjustment.
4. Hydraulic pressures too high or low.
5. Low-reverse band out of adjustment.
6. Valve body malfunction or leakage.
7. Front clutch or rear servo sticking or not operating.
8. Low-reverse servo, band or linkage malfunction.
9. Faulty oil pump.
10. Worn or broken reaction shaft support seal rings.
11. Worn or faulty front clutch.

SLIPS IN ALL POSITIONS

1. Low fluid level.
2. Hydraulic pressures too low.
3. Valve body malfunction or leakage.
4. Faulty oil pump.
5. Clutches or servos sticking or not operating.
6. Worn or broken input shaft and/or reaction shaft support seal rings.
7. Oil filter clogged.
8. Aerated oil.

NO DRIVE IN ANY POSITION

1. Low fluid level.
2. Hydraulic pressures too low.
3. Oil filter clogged.
4. Valve body malfunction or leakage.
5. Faulty oil pump.
6. Clutches or servos sticking or not operating.
7. Planetary gear sets broken or seized.
8. Torque converter failure.
9. Incorrect gearshift linkage adjustment.

NO DRIVE IN FORWARD POSITIONS

1. Hydraulic pressures too low.
2. Valve body malfunction or leakage.
3. Accumulator sticking, broken rings or spring.
4. Clutches or servos sticking or not operating.
5. Worn or faulty rear clutch.
6. Overrunning clutch not holding.
7. Worn or broken input shaft and/or reaction shaft support seal rings.
8. Low fluid level.
9. Planetary gear sets broken or seized.
10. Overrunning clutch worn, broken or seized.
11. Incorrect gearshift linkage adjustment.

NO DRIVE IN REVERSE

1. Incorrect gearshift control linkage adjustment.
2. Hydraulic pressures too low.
3. Low-reverse band out of adjustment.
4. Valve body malfunction or leakage.
5. Front clutch or rear servo sticking or not operating.
6. Low-reverse servo, band or linkage malfunction.
7. Worn or faulty front and/or rear clutch.
8. Worn or broken reaction shaft support seal rings.
9. Planetary gear sets broken or seized.

NO LOW GEAR IN D2

1. Governor valve:
   a. Burrs, nicks, scores or binding on weights, shaft and valve.
   b. Collapsed or distorted springs or snap rings.
   c. Cracked or warped body.
   d. Dirty filter.
2. Valve body:
   a. Nicks, scratches or burrs on valves and plugs.
   b. Damaged valve lands or bores.
   c. Collapsed springs.
   d. Damaged or warped mating surfaces.

DRIVES IN NEUTRAL

1. Incorrect gearshift control linkage adjustment.
2. Valve body malfunction or leakage.
3. Rear clutch worn, faulty, dragging or inoperative.
4. Insufficient clutch plate clearance.

DRAGS OR LOCKS

1. Kickdown band out of adjustment.
2. Low-reverse band out of adjustment.
3. Kickdown and/or low-reverse servo, band or linkage malfunction.
4. Front and/or rear clutch faulty.
5. Planetary gear sets broken or seized.
6. Overrunning clutch worn, broken or seized.
7. Hydraulic pressure too low.
8. Valve body: nicks, scratches and burrs on valve and plugs. Rounded edges on valve lands. Scratches on bores, collapsed springs. Nicked or warped mating surfaces.
9. Accumulator, broken seal rings, scratched bore, broken or collapsed spring, cracked piston.

GRATING, SCRAPING OR GROWLING NOISE

1. Kickdown band out of adjustment.
2. Low-reverse band out of adjustment.
3. Output shaft bearing and/or bushing damaged.
4. Governor support binding or broken seal rings.
5. Oil pump scored or binding.
6. Front and/or rear clutch faulty.
7. Planetary gear sets broken or seized.
8. Overrunning clutch worn, broken or seized.
9. Low fluid level.
10. Clogged oil filter.

BUZZING NOISE

1. Low fluid level.
2. Pump sucking air.
3. Valve body malfunction.
4. Overrunning clutch inner race damaged.
5. Aerated oil.
6. Governor valve: burrs, nicks, scores or binding on weights, shaft and valve.
7. Collapsed or distorted springs or distorted snap ring. Cracked or warped body. Dirty filter.

HARD TO FILL, OIL FLOWS OUT FILLER TUBE

1. High fluid level.
2. Breather clogged.
3. Oil filter clogged.
4. Aerated fluid.
5. Clogged lines to cooler.

TRANSMISSION OVERHEATS

1. Low fluid level.
2. Kickdown band adjustment too tight.
3. Low-reverse band adjustment too tight.
4. Faulty cooling system.
5. Cracked or restricted oil cooler line or fitting.
6. Faulty oil pump.
7. Insufficient clutch plate clearance in front and/or rear clutches.
8. Engine idle too low.
9. Hydraulic pressures too low.
10. Incorrect gearshift linkage adjustment.
11. Kickdown band adjustment too tight.
12. Clogged oil filter.
13. Valve body: Nicks, scratches and burrs on valve and plugs. Rounded edges on valve lands. Scratches on bores, collapsed springs. Nicked or warped mating surfaces.

STARTER WILL NOT ENERGIZE IN NEUTRAL OR PARK

1. Incorrect gearshift control linkage adjustment.
2. Faulty or incorrectly adjusted neutral starting switch.
3. Broken lead to neutral switch.

SLUGGISH ACCELERATION, EXCESSIVE THROTTLE NEEDED TO MAINTAIN SPEED

1. Low fluid level.
2. Sticking or incorrect throttle linkage adjustment.
3. Faulty torque converter or clutches.
4. Incorrect hydraulic pressures.

NO LOCK-UP

1. Faulty input shaft, seal ring, locking clutch or torque converter.
2. Sticking failsafe switch, lock-up valve or switch valve.
3. Faulty oil pump.

WILL NOT UNLOCK

1. Sticking failsafe valve, lock-up valve, switch valve or governor valve.
2. Valve body malfunctioning.

REMAINS LOCKED-UP AT TOO LOW A SPEED IN DRIVE

1. Sticking failsafe valve, lock-up valve or governor valve.

LOCKS UP OR DRAGS IN LOW OR SECOND

1. Sticking failsafe valve.
2. Faulty oil pump.

ENGINE STALLS OR IS SLUGGISH IN REVERSE

1. Plugged cooler lines or fittings.
2. Valve body malfunctioning or, faulty oil pump.

LOUD CHATTER WHILE LOCKING-UP WHEN COLD

1. Leaking turbine hub seal.
2. Faulty torque converter.

VIBRATIONS AFTER LOCK-UP

1. Throttle linkage improperly adjusted, or sticking governor valve.
2. Engine requires tune up, or otherwise not performing properly.
3. Exhaust system contacting vehicle.

VIBRATION WHEN VEHICLE IS ACCELERATED IN NEUTRAL

1. Unbalanced torque converter.

OVERHEATING (OIL BLOWING OUT OF DIPSTICK OR PUMP SEAL)

1. Sticking switch valve.
2. Plugged cooler lines or fittings.

MAINTENANCE

CHECKING OIL LEVEL

To check the oil level, apply the parking brake and operate the engine at idle speed with the transmission in Neutral position.

CHANGING OIL

Fluid and filter changes or band adjustments are not required for average passenger car use. Severe usage such as police, taxi, trailer towing or prolonged operation in city traffic, requires that fluid and filter be changed and bands adjusted every 15,000 miles.

Whenever the factory fill fluid is changed, only fluids of the type labeled Dexron II should be used.

1. Remove drain plug (if equipped) from transmission oil pan and drain oil. **If the oil pan does not have a drain plug, loosen pan bolts and tap pan with a soft mallet to break it loose, permitting fluid to drain.**
2. Remove transmission oil pan, replace filter or clean intake screen and pan, adjust bands and reinstall.
3. Add 4 quarts of automatic transmission fluid through filler tube.
4. Start engine.
5. Allow engine to idle for about two minutes. With parking brake applied, move selector lever momentarily to each position and place in neutral.

BANDS

ADJUST

KICKDOWN BAND

The kickdown band adjusting screw is located on the left side of the transmission case near the throttle lever shaft.

1. Loosen locknut and back off approximately five turns. Check adjusting screw for free turning in transmission case.
2. Using an inch-pound torque wrench, tighten the band adjusting screw to a reading of 72 inch lbs.
3. Back off adjusting screw 2½ turns.
4. Hold adjusting screw in this position and tighten locknut.

LOW & REVERSE BAND

1. Raise vehicle, drain transmission and remove oil pan.
2. Inspect fluid for friction material or metal particles which indicate damaged or worn parts.
3. Loosen adjusting screw locknut and back off nut approximately five turns. Check adjusting screw for free turning in lever.
4. Using an inch pound torque wrench, tighten band adjusting screw to 72 inch lbs. on all except 1982 904 series transmissions equipped with Allen-type adjustment screw. On 1982 904 series transmissions equipped with Allen-type adjusting screw, tighten screw to 41 inch lbs.
5. Back off adjusting screw the number of turns indicated:

A-904 w/6-225	7 turns
A-904 w/V8-318	4 turns
A-904-LA, A-904T, A-999	4 turns
A-727	2 turns

6. Hold adjusting screw and tighten locknut to 35 ft. lbs., then install oil pan and refill transmission.

GEARSHIFT CONTROL LINKAGE

ADJUST

EXC. IMPERIAL

1. Loosen adjustable lock swivel lock bolt, **Fig. 2.**
2. Place selector lever in Park and move transmission control lever all the way to rear (in Park detent).
3. With both levers still in Park position, torque swivel clamp screw to 90 inch lbs.

IMPERIAL

Shift lever should be in Park detent before proceeding with adjustment.

1. Loosen the 2 screws that secure PRND21 switch to steering column.
2. Hold PRND21 switch in position on column jacket, apply downward force to switch, then tighten switch screws.
3. Check each gear position to ensure proper gear position is illuminated on the PRND21 switch and that no double characters (double gear positions) are illuminated. **It is normal for more than one gear position to be illuminated during transition from one gear position to another.**

THROTTLE LINKAGE

ADJUST

Before proceeding with the adjustment, disconnect the choke rod at the carburetor or block the choke valve wide open. Open the throttle slightly to release the fast idle cam, then return carburetor to the hot idle position.

Hold or fasten the transmission lever firmly forward against the stop while performing the adjustment to insure a proper adjustment.

1. Support vehicle on hoist and loosen swivel lock screw, **Fig. 3. To insure correct adjustment, swivel must be free to slide along flat end of throttle rod so that preload spring action is not restricted. If necessary, disassemble and clean or repair parts to assure free action.**
2. Hold transmission lever firmly forward against its internal stop and tighten swivel lock screw to 100 inch lbs. **Adjustment is now finished. Linkage backlash was automatically removed by the preload spring.**
3. Lower vehicle and test linkage operation by moving throttle rod rearward and slowly releasing it making certain that it returns fully.

EXTENSION HOUSING & PARKING LOCK CONTROL ROD, REPLACE

On some models, it is necessary to unload both torsion bars, remove the left torsion bar, then lower one side of the torsion bar crossmember to provide clearance for extension housing removal.

1. Mark parts for reassembly and remove propeller shaft.
2. Remove speedometer pinion and adapter assembly, then drain about two quarts of fluid from transmission.
3. Remove extension housing to crossmember bolts, then raise transmission with jack and remove crossmember.
4. Remove extension housing to transmission bolts. On console shift models, remove torque shaft lower bracket to extension housing bolts. **In the following step, the gearshift must be in "low" therefore positioning the parking lock control rod rearward so it can be disengaged or engaged with the parking lock sprag.**
5. Remove two screws, plate and gasket from bottom of extension housing mounting pad, then spread snap ring from output shaft bearing, **Fig. 4,** and carefully tap extension housing off output shaft bearing.
6. Slide extension housing off shaft to remove parking sprag and spring, then remove snap ring and slide reaction plug and pin assembly out of

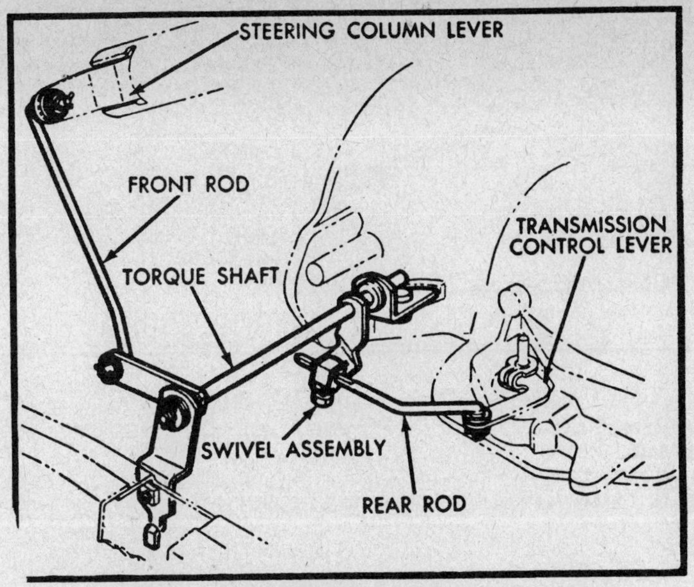

Fig. 2 Gearshift linkage (typical)

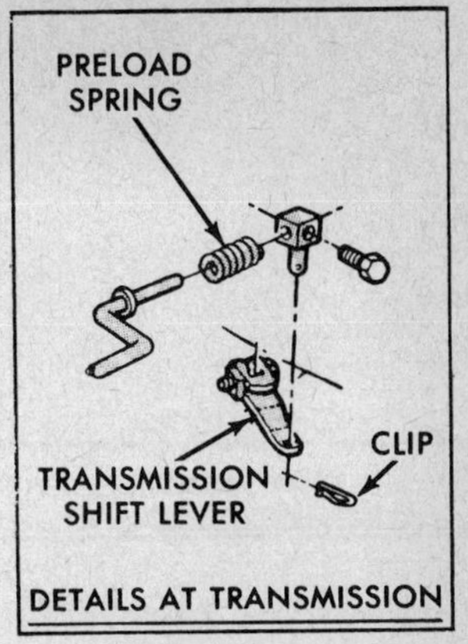

Fig. 3 Throttle linkage adjustment

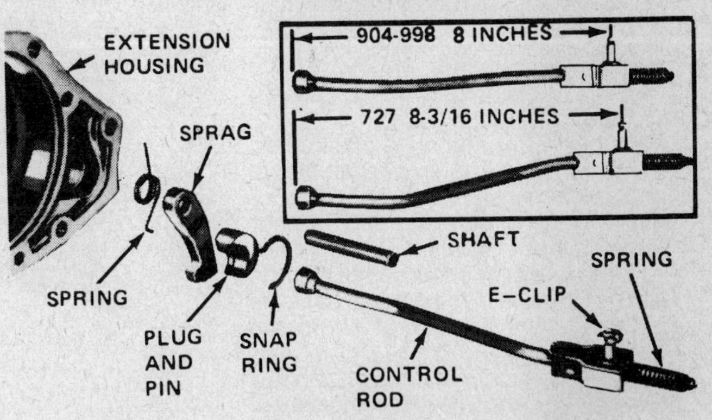

Fig. 5 Parking lock components

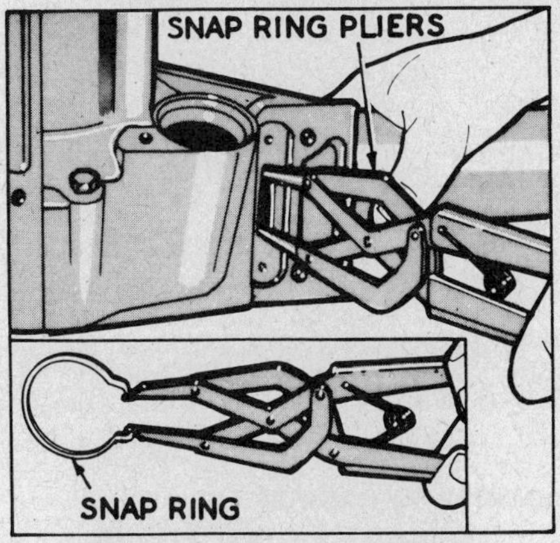

Fig. 4 Removing or installing extension housing snap ring

housing, **Fig. 5.**

7. To replace parking lock control rod, refer to "Valve Body."

OUTPUT SHAFT OIL SEAL, REPLACE

1. Mark propeller shaft to aid in reassembly and remove propeller shaft being careful not to scratch or nick surface on sliding spline yoke.
2. Using a screwdriver and hammer, drive between extension housing and seal and remove seal.
3. Position new seal and drive it into extension housing using tool C-3995 or C-3972.
4. Carefully install yoke into housing, then align marks made at removal and install propeller shaft.

GOVERNOR SERVICE

1. Remove extension housing, then remove output shaft bearing rear snap ring and remove bearing. On 727 Series, remove remaining snap ring from shaft.
2. Remove snap ring, **Fig. 6,** from weight end of governor valve shaft and remove valve and shaft from governor body.
3. Remove large snap ring from weight end of governor housing, and lift out weight assembly.
4. Remove snap ring from inside governor weight and remove inner weight and spring from outer weight.
5. Remove snap ring from behind governor housing, then slide governor housing and parking brake sprag assembly off output shaft. If necessary, separate governor housing from sprag (4 screws). **The primary cause of governor operating failure is due to a sticking governor valve or weights. Rough surfaces may be removed with crocus cloth. Thoroughly clean all parts and check for free movement before assembly.**
6. Reverse above operations to assemble and install governor.

VALVE BODY SERVICE

1. Drain transmission and remove oil pan.
2. Loosen clamp bolts and remove throttle and gear selector levers from manual lever, **Fig. 7.**
3. Remove neutral safety switch and oil filter.
4. Place a drain pan under transmission and remove the ten valve body to transmission bolts. Hold valve body in place while removing bolts.
5. Carefully lower valve body while pulling it forward to disengage parking control rod. **It may be necessary to rotate output shaft to permit parking control rod to clear sprag.**
6. Remove accumulator piston and spring from transmission case. Inspect piston for nicks, scores and wear. Inspect spring for distortion. Inspect rings for freedom in piston grooves and wear or breakage. Replace parts as necessary.

LOCK-UP MODULE, REPLACE

1. Remove end plate retaining screws and end plate from module, **Fig. 8.**
2. Remove lock-up spring and valve and failsafe valve and spring. Tag springs to aid reassembly.
3. Remove lock-up module from valve body.
4. Reverse procedure to install.

TRANSMISSION REPLACE

The transmission and converter must be removed as an assembly, otherwise, the converter drive plate, front pump bushing and oil seal will be damaged. The drive plate will not support the load; therefore, none of the weight of the transmission should be allowed to rest on the plate during removal.

1. Disconnect battery ground cable. **Some models will require that the**

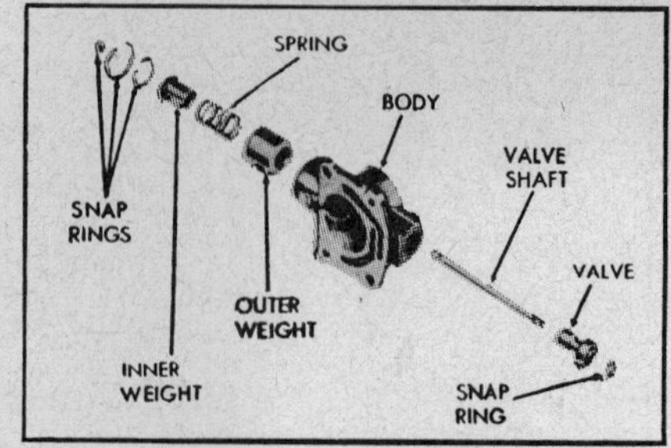

Fig. 6 Governor disassembled

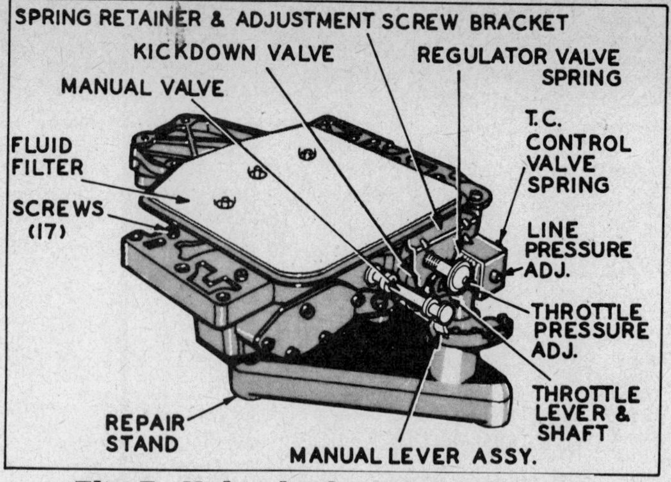

Fig. 7 Valve body external parts

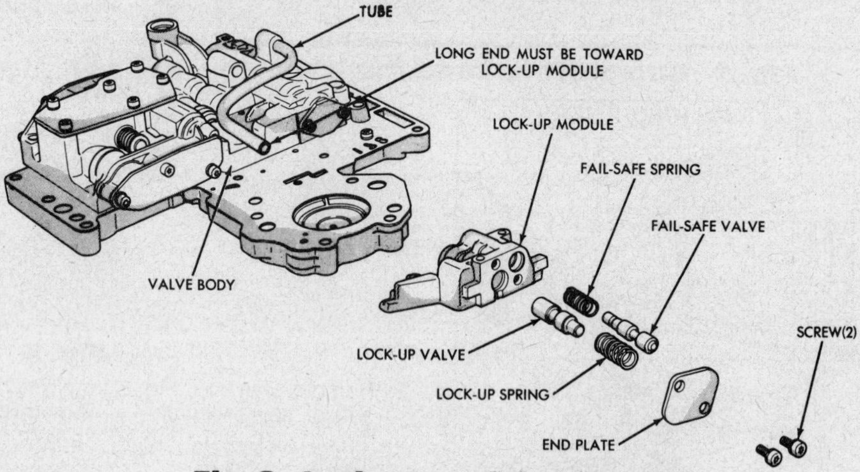

Fig. 8 Lock-up module removal

exhaust system be lowered for clearance.

2. Remove engine to transmission struts (if equipped), then disconnect transmission cooler lines and remove starter motor, cooler line bracket and converter access cover.
3. Drain fluid from transmission as described in "Changing Oil."
4. Mark converter and drive plate to aid in reassembly. The crankshaft flange bolt circle, inner and outer circle of holes in the drive plate, and the four tapped holes in front face of converter all have one hole offset so these parts will be installed in the original position. This maintains balance of the engine and converter.
5. Remove converter to drive plate bolts. Rotate engine clockwise using socket wrench to gain access to all bolts. **Do not rotate converter or drive plate by prying with a screwdriver or similar tool, as the drive plate might become distorted.**
6. Mark driveshaft to aid in reassembly and remove driveshaft.
7. Disconnect neutral and back-up light switch connector and gearshift and torque shaft assembly from transmission. **When disassembling linkage rods from levers which use plastic grommets as retainers, the grommets should be replaced with new ones.**
8. Disconnect throttle rod from lever at left side of transmission, then remove linkage bellcrank from transmission, if so equipped.
9. Remove oil filler tube and disconnect speedometer cable.
10. Install a suitable fixture or jack that will support engine, then raise transmission slightly with a jack to relieve the load on the supports, and remove the crossmember. **Some models have a torsion bar anchor crossmember that remains in place and requires a careful downward tilt on front of transmission as it is being lowered. If these models have a vibration dampening weight bolted to rear of extension housing, it must be removed.**
11. Remove transmission to engine bolts and carefully work transmission and converter assembly rearward off engine block dowels and disengage converter hub from end of crankshaft. Using a small C-clamp on edge of bellhousing, hold converter in place during transmission removal.
12. Remove transmission assembly from under vehicle.
13. Reverse procedure to install.

Torqueflite Automatic Transaxle

INDEX

IDENTIFICATION

A seven digit part number is stamped on a pad located at the rear of the transaxle on the transaxle oil pan flange. This number must be referred to when servicing the transaxle due to differences in some internal components.

DESCRIPTION

These transaxles combine a torque converter, automatic 3 speed transaxle, final drive gearing and differential combined into one unit. The torque converter, transaxle and differential assemblies are housed in an integral aluminum die cast housing, Fig. 1. **The differential oil sump is separate from the transaxle pump. Ensure differential oil lever is 1/8 to 3/8 inch below the oil filler hole on the differential cover.**

The torque converter is connected to the crankshaft through a flexible drive plate. Converter cooling is accomplished by an oil to water type cooler, located in the radiator side tank. The torque converter cannot be disassembled.

The transaxle consists of two multiple disc clutches, an overrunning clutch, two servos, a hydraulic accumulator, two bands and two planetary gear assemblies to provide three forward and one reverse gear. The sun gear is connected to the front clutch retainer. The hydraulic system consists of an oil pump, and a single valve body which contains all of the valves except the governor valves. Output torque from the main drive gears is transferred through helical gears to the transfer shaft. An integral ring gear on the transfer shaft drives the differential ring gear.

TROUBLESHOOTING GUIDE

HARSH ENGAGEMENT FROM NEUTRAL TO DRIVE OR REVERSE

1. High idle speed.
2. Defective or leaking valve body.
3. High hydraulic pressure.
4. Worn or damaged rear clutch.
5. Low-reverse band worn out.

DELAYED ENGAGEMENT FROM NEUTRAL TO DRIVE OR REVERSE

1. Low hydraulic pressure.
2. Defective or leaking valve body.
3. Low-reverse servo, band or linkage malfunction.
4. Low fluid level.
5. Incorrect gearshift linkage adjustment.
6. Clogged transaxle oil filter.
7. Faulty oil pump.
8. Worn or damaged input shaft seal rings.
9. Aerated fluid.
10. Low idle speed.
11. Worn or damaged reaction shaft support seal rings.
12. Worn or defective front clutch.
13. Worn or defective rear clutch.

RUNAWAY UPSHIFTS

1. Low hydraulic pressure.
2. Defective or leaking valve body.
3. Low fluid level.
4. Clogged transaxle oil filter.
5. Aerated fluid.
6. Incorrect throttle linkage adjustment.
7. Worn or damaged reaction shaft support seal rings.
8. Kickdown servo, band or linkage malfunction.
9. Worn or faulty front clutch.

NO UPSHIFT

1. Low hydraulic pressure.
2. Defective or leaking valve body.
3. Low fluid level.
4. Incorrect gearshift linkage adjustment.
5. Incorrect throttle linkage adjustment.
6. Worn or damaged governor support seal rings.
7. Worn or damaged reaction shaft support seal rings.
8. Faulty governor.
9. Kickdown servo, band or linkage malfunction.
10. Worn or faulty front clutch.

3-2 KICKDOWN RUNAWAY

1. Low hydraulic pressure.
2. Defective or leaking valve body.
3. Low fluid level.
4. Aerated fluid.
5. Incorrect throttle linkage adjustment.
6. Kickdown band adjustment.
7. Worn or damaged governor support seal rings.
8. Kickdown servo, band or linkage malfunction.
9. Worn or faulty front clutch.

NO KICKDOWN OR NORMAL DOWNSHIFT

1. Defective or leaking valve body.
2. Incorrect throttle linkage adjustment.
3. Faulty governor.
4. Kickdown servo, band or linkage malfunction.

ERRATIC SHIFTS

1. Low hydraulic pressure.
2. Defective or leaking valve body.
3. Low fluid level.
4. Incorrect gearshift linkage adjustment.
5. Clogged transaxle oil filter.
6. Faulty oil pump.
7. Aerated fluid.
8. Incorrect throttle linkage adjustment.
9. Worn or damaged governor support seal rings.
10. Worn or damaged reaction shaft support seal rings.
11. Faulty governor.
12. Kickdown servo, band or linkage malfunction.
13. Worn or faulty front clutch.

SLIPS IN 1, 2 OR DRIVE

1. Low hydraulic pressure.
2. Defective or leaking valve body.
3. Low fluid level.
4. Incorrect gearshift linkage adjustment.
5. Clogged transaxle oil filter.
6. Faulty oil pump.
7. Worn or damaged input shaft seal rings.
8. Aerated fluid.
9. Incorrect throttle linkage adjustment.
10. Overrunning clutch not holding.
11. Worn or faulty rear clutch.
12. Overrunning clutch worn damaged or seized.

SLIPS IN REVERSE ONLY

1. Low hydraulic pressure.
2. Low-reverse band adjustment.
3. Defective or leaking valve body.

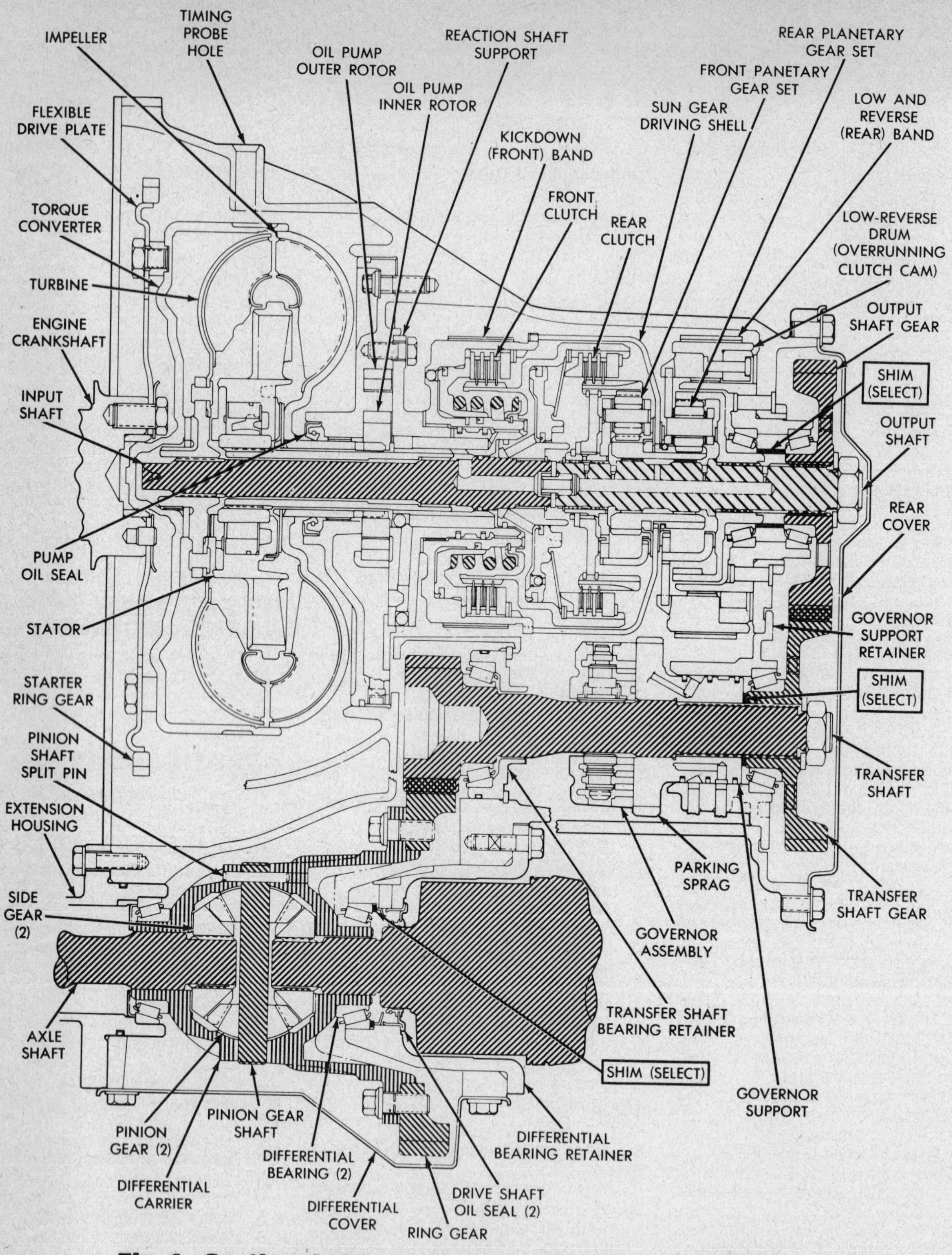

Fig. 1 Sectional view of automatic transaxle. Typical

4. Low-reverse servo, band or linkage malfunction.
5. Low fluid level.
6. Incorrect gearshift linkage adjustment.
7. Faulty oil pump.
8. Aerated fluid.
9. Worn or damaged reaction shaft seal rings.
10. Worn or faulty front clutch.

SLIPS IN ALL RANGES

1. Low hydraulic pressure.
2. Defective or leaking valve body.
3. Low fluid level.
4. Clogged transaxle oil filter.
5. Faulty oil pump.
6. Worn or damaged input shaft seal rings.
7. Aerated fluid.

NO DRIVE IN ANY RANGE

1. Low hydraulic pressure.
2. Defective or leaking valve body.
3. Low fluid level.
4. Clogged transaxle oil filter.
5. Faulty oil pump.
6. Planetary gear sets damaged or seized.

NO DRIVE IN 1, 2 OR DRIVE

1. Low hydraulic pressure.
2. Defective or leaking valve body.
3. Low fluid level.
4. Worn or damaged input shaft seal rings.
5. Overrunning clutch not holding.
6. Worn or faulty rear clutch.
7. Planetary gear sets damaged or seized.
8. Overrunning clutch worn, damaged or seized.

NO DRIVE IN REVERSE

1. Low hydraulic pressure.
2. Low-reverse band adjustment.
3. Defective or leaking valve body.
4. Low-reverse servo, band or linkage malfunction.
5. Incorrect gearshift linkage adjustment.
6. Worn or damaged reaction shaft support seal rings.
7. Worn or faulty front clutch.
8. Worn or faulty rear clutch.
9. Planetary gear sets damaged or seized.

DRIVE IN NEUTRAL

1. Defective or leaking valve body.
2. Incorrect gearshift linkage adjustment.
3. Insufficient clutch plate clearance.
4. Worn or faulty rear clutch.
5. Rear clutch dragging.

DRAGS OR LOCKS

1. Low-reverse band adjustment.
2. Kickdown band adjustment.
3. Planetary gear sets damaged or seized.
4. Overrunning clutch worn, damaged or seized.

HARD TO FILL (OIL BLOWS OUT FILLER TUBE)

1. Clogged transaxle oil filter.
2. Aerated fluid.
3. High fluid level.
4. Breather clogged.

TRANSAXLE OVERHEATS

1. Stuck switch valve.
2. High idle speed.
3. Low hydraulic pressure.
4. Low fluid level.
5. Incorrect gearshift adjustment.
6. Faulty oil pump.
7. Kickdown band adjustment too tight.
8. Faulty cooling system.
9. Insufficient clutch plate clearance.

HARSH UPSHIFTS

1. Low hydraulic pressure.
2. Incorrect throttle linkage adjustment.
3. Kickdown band adjustment.
4. High hydraulic pressure.

DELAYED UPSHIFT

1. Incorrect throttle linkage adjustment.
2. Kickdown band adjustment.
3. Worn or damaged governor support seal rings.
4. Worn or damaged reaction shaft support seal rings.
5. Faulty governor.
6. Kickdown servo, band or linkage malfunction.

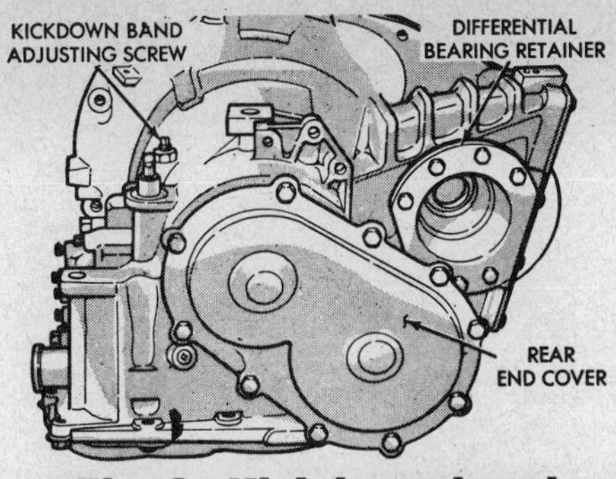

Fig. 2 Kickdown band adjusting screw location

7. Worn or faulty front clutch.

GRATING, SCRAPING OR GROWLING NOISE

1. Low-reverse band out of adjustment.
2. Kickdown band adjustment.
3. Output shaft bearing or bushing damaged.
4. Planetary gear sets damaged or seized.
5. Overrunning clutch worn, damaged or seized.

BUZZING NOISE

1. Defective or leaking valve body.
2. Low fluid level.
3. Aerated fluid.
4. Overrunning clutch inner race damaged.

MAINTENANCE

ADDING OIL

To check fluid level, apply the parking brake and operate engine at idle speed with transaxle in Neutral or Park position. Add fluid as necessary.

CHANGING OIL

Fluid and filter changes are not required for average passenger car use. Severe usage such as commercial type usage or prolonged operation in city traffic, requires that fluid be changed and bands adjusted every 15,000 miles.

Whenever factory fill fluid is changed, only fluid of the type labeled Dexron should be used.

1. Raise vehicle and place a suitable drain pan under transaxle oil pan.
2. Loosen transaxle oil pan attaching bolts and allow fluid to drain, then remove oil pan.
3. Replace oil filter and adjust bands if necessary, then install oil pan and gasket.
4. Add four quarts of approved automatic transaxle fluid through the filler tube.
5. Start engine and allow to idle for at least two minutes, then with parking brake applied move selector lever momentarily to each position. Place selector lever in Neutral or Park and check fluid level. Add fluid to bring level to Add mark.
6. Recheck fluid level after transaxle has reached operating temperature. The level should be between Add and Full marks.

BANDS

ADJUST

KICKDOWN BAND

1. Loosen locknut and back off nut approximately five turns, **Fig. 2.**
2. Using tool No. C-3380-A and adapter C-3705, tighten band adjusting screw to 47 to 50 inch lbs. If adapter C-3705 is not used, tighten adjusting screw to 72 inch lbs.
3. Back off adjusting screw 2¾ turns 1982-83 A-413 and A-470 models, 2½ turns on 1984-87 A-413 and A-470 models, and 3 turns on A-415 and 1982-83 A-404 models. Torque locknut to 35 ft. lbs. while preventing adjusting screw from turning.

LOW-REVERSE BAND

A-404 & A-415

The low-reverse band is not adjustable on these transaxles. If excessive band wear is suspected, checking may be done as follows:

1. Remove oil pan and pressurize low-reverse servo with 30 psi air pressure.
2. Measure gap between band ends. If gap is less than .080 inch, the band is excessively worn and should be replaced.

A-413 & A-470

Before adjustment is attempted, the low-reverse band should be checked for correct end gap as indicated above. To adjust band, proceed as follows:

1. Loosen locknut and back off nut approximately five turns.
2. Torque adjusting nut to 41 inch lbs.
3. Back off adjusting nut 3½ turns.
4. Torque locknut to 20 ft. lbs. on 1982 models, or 10 ft. lbs. on 1983-87 models.

GEARSHIFT LINKAGE

ADJUST

1. Place selector lever in Park position.
2. Raise vehicle, then loosen swivel lock bolt.
3. Move transaxle lever to front detent (Park) position.
4. Torque swivel lock bolt to 90 inch lbs., then check adjustment. **On 1982-84 models with column shift, apply a 10 pound forward load on the cable housing insulator while torquing swivel lock bolt. On models with console shift, apply a minimum forward load of 10 pounds on the console shift lever knob while torquing swivel lock bolt. On some models, it may be necessary to apply the forward load to the transaxle lever while tightening lock bolt.**

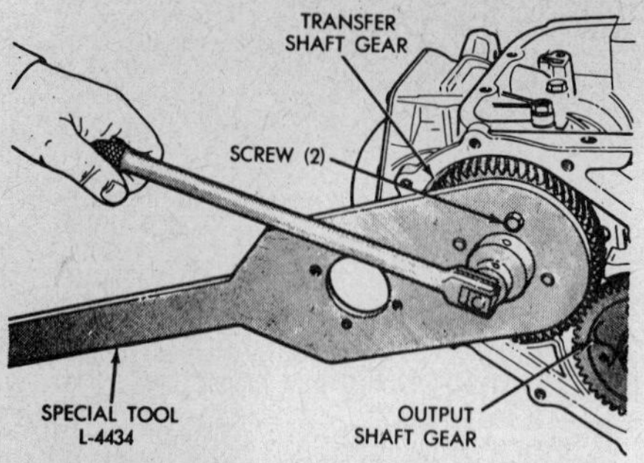

Fig. 3 Loosening transfer shaft gear retaining nut

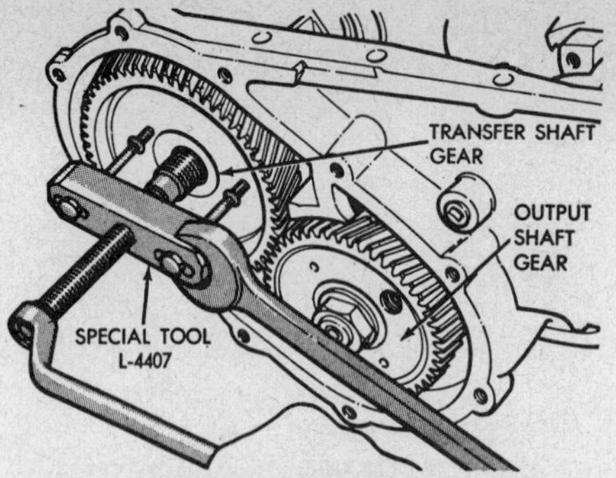

Fig. 4 Removing transfer shaft gear

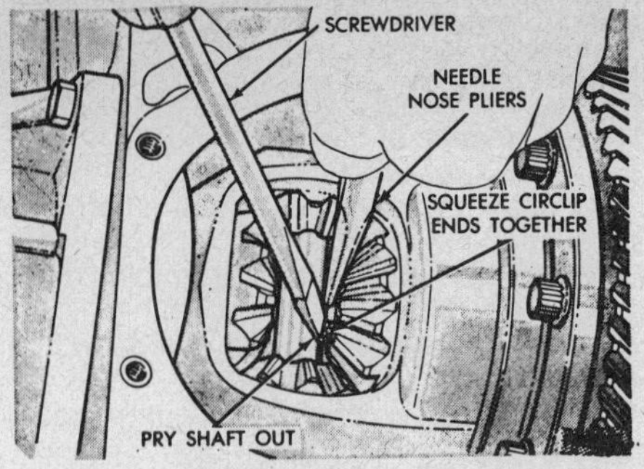

Fig. 5 Prying driveshaft out of side gear

THROTTLE CABLE
ADJUST

1. Perform adjustment with engine at operating temperature, otherwise ensure carburetor is not on fast idle cam by disconnecting choke.
2. Loosen cable mounting bracket lock screw.
3. On 1982-84 and early 1985 models, hold transaxle lever rearward against internal stop and tighten adjusting bracket lock screw to 105 inch lbs.
4. On late 1985 and all 1986-87 models, proceed as follows:
   a. Position mounting bracket with both alignment tabs touching transaxle cast surface.
   b. Release cross-lock on cable assembly by pulling the cross-lock upward. **To ensure proper adjustment, the cable must be free to slide all the way toward engine, against its stop, after the cross-lock is released.**
   c. Move transaxle throttle control lever fully clockwise against its internal stop, and press cross-lock downward into locked position.
5. On all models, reconnect choke, if disconnected, then check cable for freedom of movement by moving throttle control lever.

VALVE BODY
REPLACE

1. Loosen transaxle oil pan attaching bolts and allow transaxle to drain, then remove oil pan.
2. Remove oil filter attaching screws and oil filter.
3. Using a screwdriver, remove E-clip, then remove parking rod.
4. Remove seven valve body attaching bolts, then remove valve body and governor oil tubes.

GOVERNOR & TRANSFER SHAFT OIL SEAL
REPLACE

1. Remove rear cover attaching bolts and rear cover.
2. Using tool No. L-4434, remove transfer shaft gear retaining nut, **Fig. 3.**
3. Using tool No. L-4407, remove transfer shaft gear and shim, **Fig. 4.**
4. Remove governor support retainer, then remove low-reverse band anchor pin.
5. Remove governor assembly.
6. Remove transfer shaft retainer snap ring, then using tool No. L-4512 and a suitable puller, remove transfer shaft and retainer assembly.
7. Remove transfer shaft retainer from shaft.
8. Using a screwdriver, remove oil seal from transfer shaft retainer.
9. Using suitable tool, tap oil seal into shaft retainer.
10. Reverse procedure to install. Torque transfer shaft gear retaining nut to 200 ft. lbs.

TRANSAXLE
REPLACE

The transaxle and converter are removed as an assembly.

1. Disconnect battery cables.
2. Disconnect transaxle shift control and throttle cables from transaxle and position aside.
3. On 1982 vehicles, remove upper oil cooler tube.
4. On 1983-87 vehicles, remove upper and lower oil cooler hoses.
5. On all vehicles, support engine with suitable engine lifting equipment.
6. Remove three upper bellhousing bolts.
7. Remove hub castle locks, nuts and cotter pins.
8. Raise and support vehicle, then remove front wheels.
9. Remove left splash shield.
10. On 1982 vehicles, drain fluid from differential, then remove cover.
11. On all vehicles, remove speedometer adapter, cable and pinion as an assembly.
12. Remove sway bar and both lower ball joint to steering knuckle bolts.
13. Pry lower ball joint from steering knuckle, then remove driveshaft from hub.
14. On 1982 vehicles, rotate both driveshafts until circlip ends are visible in the opening, then while squeezing circlip ends together, remove driveshaft from side gear, **Fig. 5.**
15. On all vehicles, remove both driveshafts, supporting both joints at housing.
16. Remove dust cover if equipped, then mark position of torque converter to drive plate and remove torque converter retaining bolts.
17. Remove access plug in right splash shield to rotate engine.
18. On 1982 vehicles, remove lower cooler tube.
19. On all vehicles, disconnect neutral/park safety switch wire, then remove engine mount bracket from front crossmember.
20. Remove front engine mount insulator through bolt and bellhousing bolts.
21. Support transaxle with a suitable jack.
22. Remove left engine mount and long through bolt.
23. On 1983-87 vehicles, remove starter.
24. On all vehicles, remove lower bellhousing bolts.
25. Move transaxle away from engine and lower from vehicle. **It may be necessary to pry transaxle away from vehicle between the extension housing and engine block for clearance.**
26. Reverse procedure to install. Use RTV sealant when installing differential cover.

FRONT DRIVE AXLE

INDEX

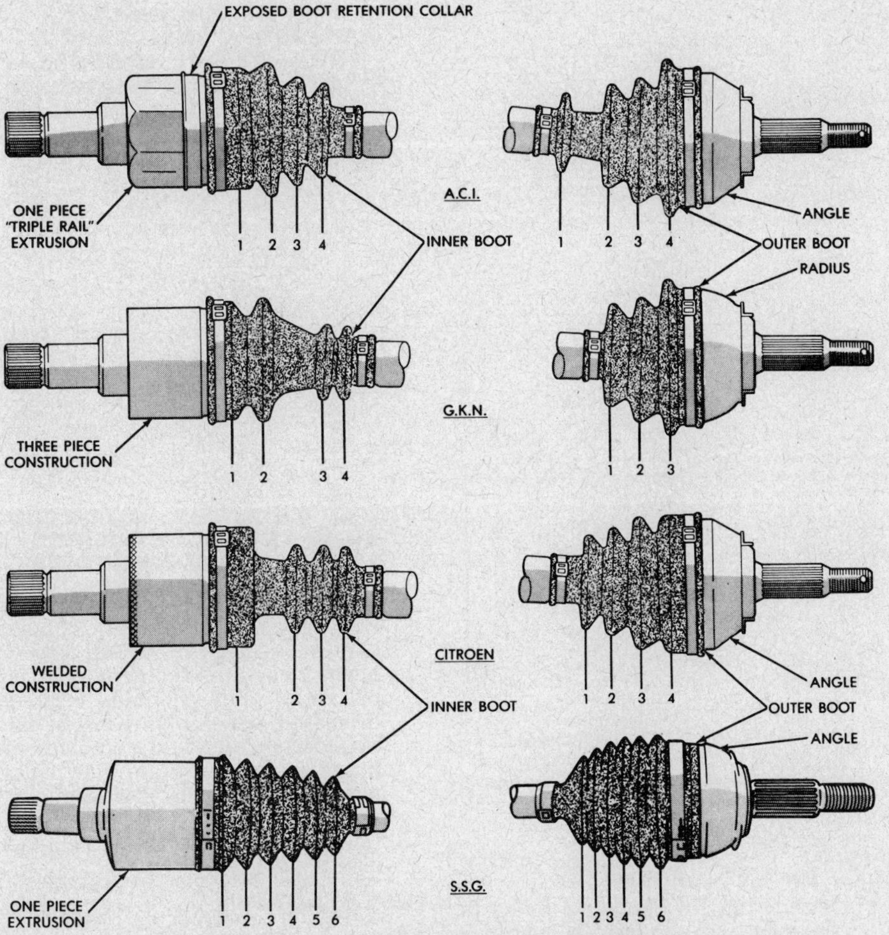

Fig. 1 Driveshaft identification

DRIVESHAFT IDENTIFICATION

Driveshafts are identified as "A.C.I.," "CITROEN," "G.K.N." or "S.S.G." assemblies, **Fig. 1.** Vehicles can be equipped with any of these assemblies, however they should not be intermixed.

Two different driveshaft systems are used. All 1984-87 turbocharged models use an "equal length" system while all others use an "unequal length" system. The "equal length" system has short solid interconnecting shafts of equal length on the left and right sides. The "unequal length" system has a short solid interconnecting shaft on left side with a longer tubular interconnecting shaft on right.

Procedures for installation and removal of driveshafts are essentially the same for all types of assemblies used.

DRIVESHAFTS REPLACE

1982–83 MODELS W/A412 MANUAL TRANSAXLE

REMOVAL

1. Remove hub nut as outlined under "Steering Knuckle, Replace" procedure.
2. Remove clamp bolt securing ball joint stud into steering knuckle.
3. Separate ball joint stud from steering knuckle.
4. Separate outer C/V joint splined shaft from hub while moving knuckle/hub assembly away from C/V joint, **Fig. 2. The separated outer joint and shaft must be supported during inner joint separation from transaxle drive flange. Secure assembly to control arm during next step. Also, the grease slinger must not be bent or damaged during service procedures. Do not attempt to remove, repair or replace.**
5. Using a suitable tool or tool L-4550, remove six 8 mm Allen head screws attaching inner C/V joint to transaxle drive flange. Clean foreign material from C/V joint and drive flange. **Remove plastic caps installed over Allen head screws.**
6. Release outer assembly from control arm.
7. To remove driveshaft assembly, hold both inner and outer housings parallel and rotate outer assembly downward and inner assembly upward at drive flange.
8. Remove driveshaft from vehicle.

INSTALLATION

1. If lubricant was lost during handling, fill C/V joint housing with lubricant, P/N 4131389 or equivalent.
2. Clean grease from joint housing, face, screw holes and transaxle drive flange prior to installation.
3. Support assembly vertically with inner housing upward. **Do not move inner joint in or out during reassembly to drive flange since this movement can force lubricant from the joint.**
4. Position inner housing to drive flange and rotate assembly upward. Locate inner housing in drive flange. Support the outer end of driveshaft. Do not permit assembly to hang.
5. Secure inner C/V joint to drive flange with new Allen head screws. Then, using tool L-4550 or equivalent, torque the six screws to 440 inch lbs. (50 Nm). Install plastic caps over Allen head screws. **Failure to properly torque screws may result in failure during vehicle operation.**
6. Push knuckle/hub assembly out and install splined outer C/V joint shaft into hub.
7. Install knuckle assembly on ball joint stud. Install and torque clamp bolt to 50 ft. lbs. (68 Nm).
8. Install washer and hub nut. Torque nut to 180 ft. lbs. (245 Nm). Install nut lock and cotter pin.

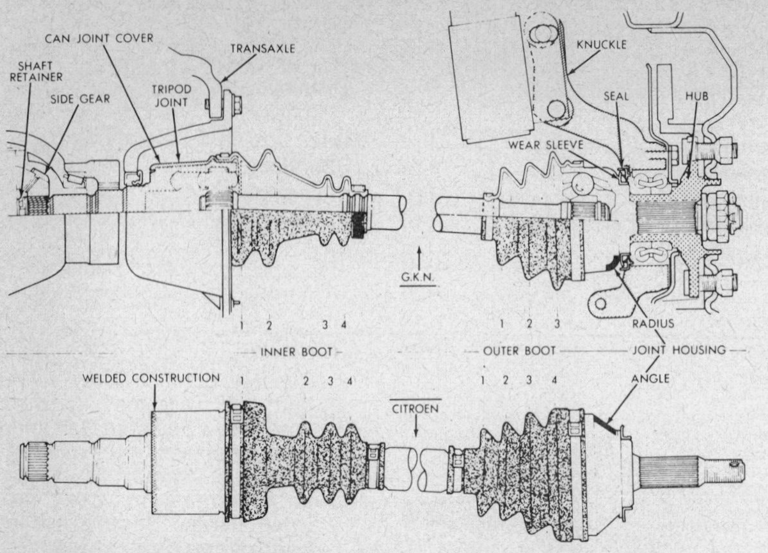

Fig. 2 Driveshaft assemblies. Early 1982

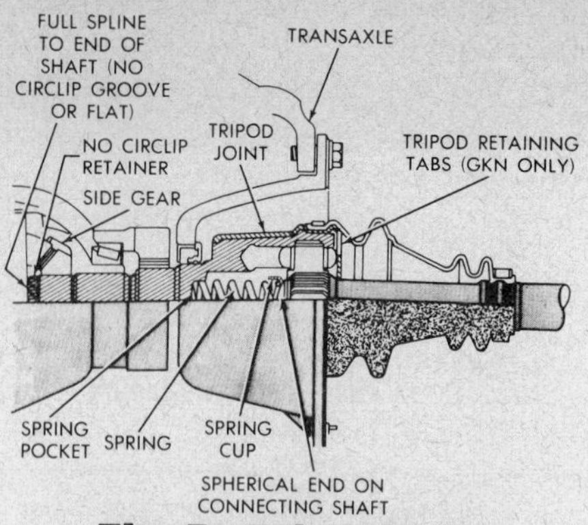

Fig. 3 Driveshaft assembly. Late 1982 & 1983–87 exc. models w/A412 manual transaxle

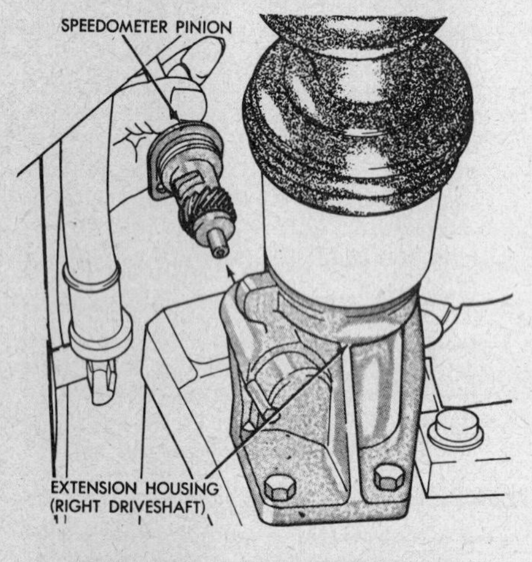

Fig. 4 Speed pinion replacement. Exc. 1982–83 models w/A412 manual transaxle

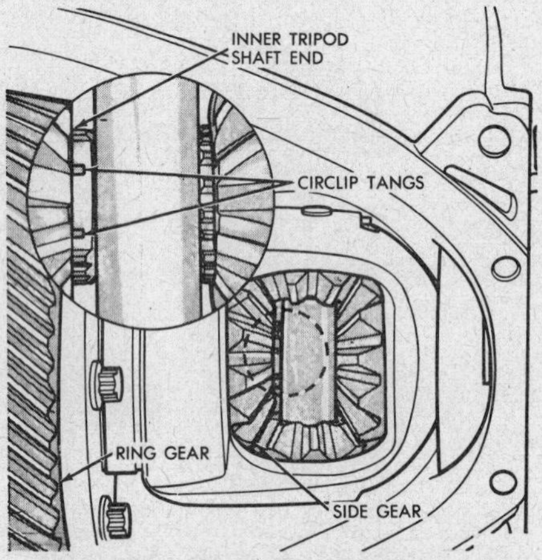

Fig. 5 Circlips exposed. Early 1982 models less A412 manual transaxle

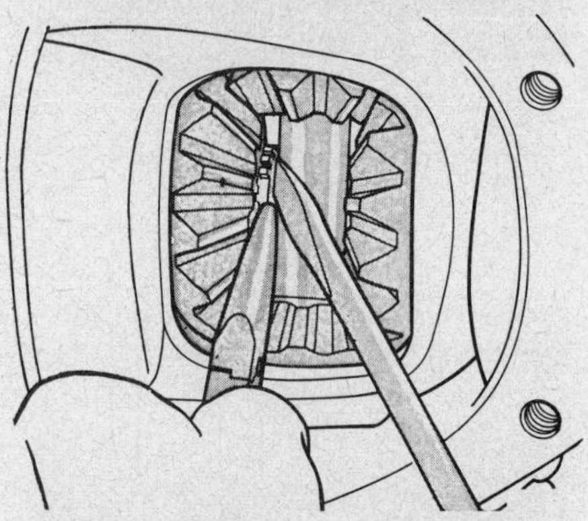

Fig. 6 Compressing circlip. Early 1982 models less A412 manual transaxle

9. If, after attaching driveshaft assembly in vehicle the inboard boot appears collapsed or deformed, vent the inner boot by inserting a round tipped, small diameter rod between the boot and shaft. As venting occurs, the boot will return to normal shape. **After installation of driveshaft, check driveshaft length as outlined in "Driveshaft Length, Adjust."**

EXC. 1982–83 MODELS W/A412 MANUAL TRANSAXLE

REMOVAL

On early 1982 models, inboard C/V joints have stub shafts splined into differential side gears and are retained with circlips, Fig. 2. The circlip "Tangs" are located on a machined surface on inner end of stub shafts and are removed and installed with shaft. On late 1982 and 1983-87 models, driveshafts are spring loaded and are retained to side gears by constant spring pressure provided by spring contained in C/V joints, Fig. 3.

1. On early 1982 models, drain transaxle differential unit and remove cover.
2. On all models, if removing the right hand driveshaft, speedometer pinion must be removed prior to driveshaft removal, **Fig. 4.**
3. On early 1982 models, rotate driveshaft to expose circlip tangs, **Fig. 5.** Using needle nose pliers, compress circlip tangs while prying shaft into side gear splined cavity, **Fig. 6.** The circlip will be compressed in the cavity with shaft.
4. On all models, remove clamp bolt securing ball joint clamp bolt to steering knuckle, then separate ball joint stud from steering knuckle. Do not damage ball joint or C/V joint boots.
5. Separate outer C/V joint splined shaft from hub by holding C/V housing while moving knuckle/hub assembly away from C/V joint. **Do not damage slinger on outer C/V joint. Do not attempt to remove, repair or replace.**
6. Support assembly at C/V joint housings and remove by pulling outward on the inner C/V joint housing. Do not pull on shaft. **If removing lefthand driveshaft assembly, removal may be aided by inserting a screwdriver blade between differential pinion shaft and carefully prying against end face of stub.**
7. Remove driveshaft assembly from vehicle.

INSTALLATION

On early 1982 units, install new circlips on inner joint shaft before installation, Fig. 7.

1. On early 1982 units, ensure tang on circlips are aligned with flattened end of shaft before inserting shaft into transaxle. If not, this can cause jamming or component damage.
2. On all models, hold inner joint assembly at housing while aligning and guiding inner joint spline into transaxle.
3. On early 1982 units, while holding inner joint housing, quickly thrust shaft into differential. This will complete lock-up of driveshaft to axle side gear. **Inspect circlip positioning in side gears to verify lock-up.**
4. On all models, push knuckle/hub assembly out and install splined outer C/V joint shaft into hub.
5. Install knuckle assembly on ball joint stud.

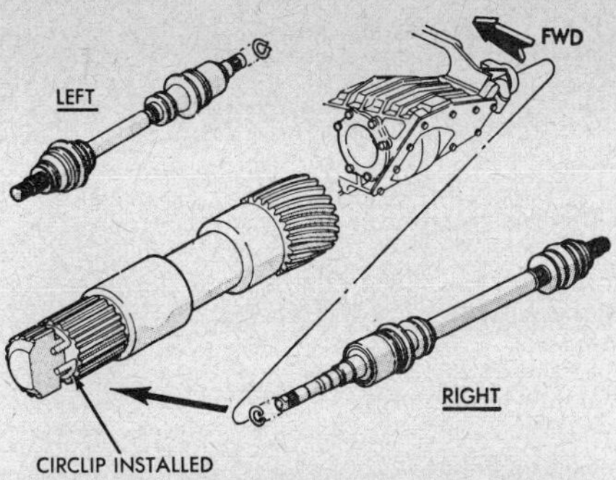

Fig. 7 Circlip installation. Early 1982 models less A412 manual transaxle

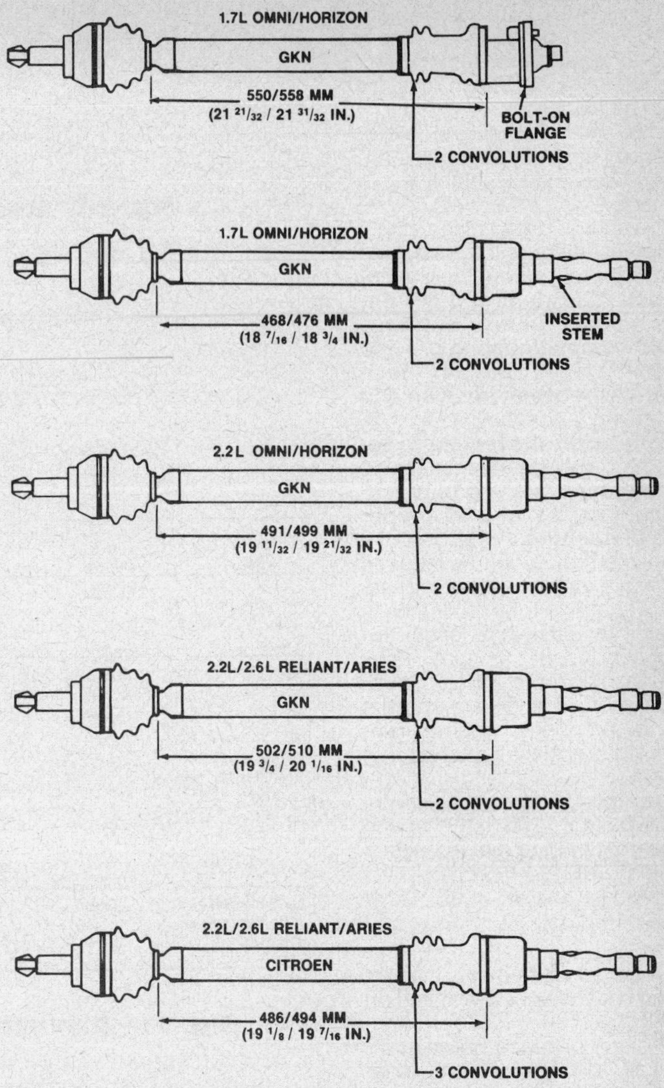

Fig. 8 Right side driveshaft length. 1982

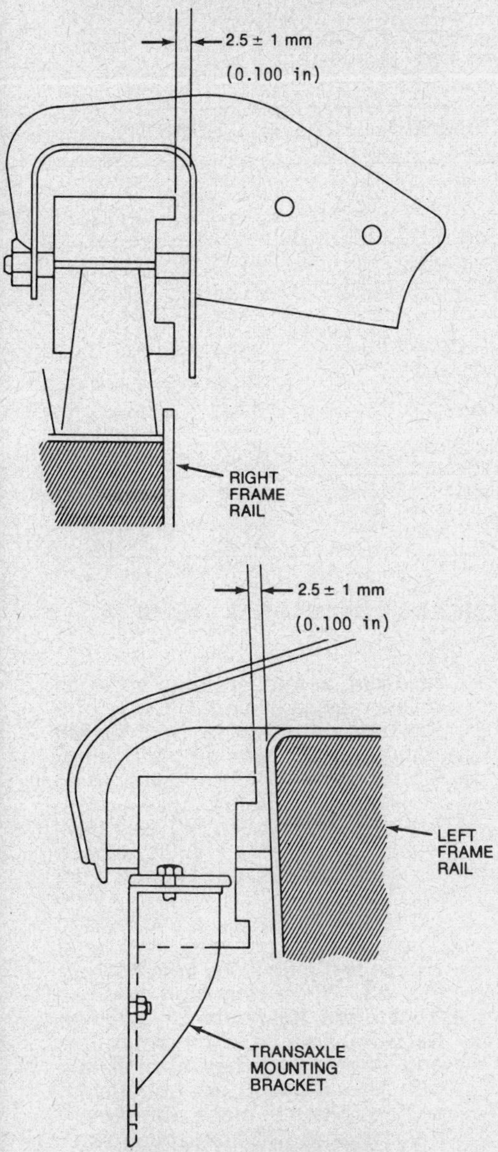

Fig. 9 Measuring clearance between bushing and support bracket. 1982

6. Install clamp bolt. Torque to 50 ft. lbs. (68 Nm) on all 1982-83 models and 1984 Charger, Horizon, Omni and Turismo, or 70 ft. lbs. (95 Nm) on all 1984 models except Charger, Horizon, Omni and Turismo and 1985-87 models.
7. Install speedometer pinion, **Fig. 4.**
8. On early 1982 models, apply a 1/16 inch bead of silicone sealant, part number 4026070, to differential cover sealing surface and mating surface of transaxle case after both have been properly cleaned and inspected.
9. On early 1982 models, install differential cover and torque retaining screws to 250 inch lbs. (28 Nm).
10. On all models, fill differential to bottom of filler plug hole with Dexron automatic transaxle fluid.
11. Install washer and hub nut. Torque hub nut to 180 ft. lbs. (245 Nm). Install nut lock and cotter pin.
12. If, after attaching driveshaft assembly in vehicle, the inboard boot appears collapsed or deformed, vent the inner boot by inserting a round tipped, small diameter rod between boot and shaft. As venting occurs, the boot will return to normal shape. **After installation of driveshaft, check driveshaft length as outlined in "Driveshaft Length, Adjust."**

DRIVESHAFT LENGTH ADJUST

If the vertical bolts on both engine mounts have been loosened, or vehicle has experienced front structural damage, driveshaft length must be checked.

The engine mounts incorporate slotted bolt holes to permit side-to-side positioning of the engine, thereby affecting length of driveshaft. To check driveshaft length proceed as follows.

1982

Measuring of the right driveshaft (passenger side) will indicate proper positioning of both sides.

1. Position vehicle so that weight of the body is on all four wheels.
2. Using a tape measure or other suitable measuring device, measure direct distance from inner edge of outboard boot to inner edge of inboard boot, **Fig. 8.**

3. If measurement matches length shown in **Fig. 8**, no further action is required. If measurement is not within given range, engine position must be corrected as follows:
   a. Remove load on engine motor mounts by carefully supporting engine and transaxle assembly with a floor jack.
   b. Loosen right and left engine mount vertical fasteners and front engine mount bracket to front crossmember bolts. **The right and left engine mount rubber bushings should be positioned to provide approximately .06-.14 inch clearance between bushing and supporting bracket, Fig. 9. When bracket movement is required, it will be necessary to obtain proper bushing to bracket clearance as well as proper driveshaft length.**
   c. Pry engine right or left as required to achieve proper driveshaft assembly length. A total of .47 inch is available for driveshaft length adjustment. Insert 3 mm thick spacers adjacent to isolator snubber on each side. These spacers must be in place when engine mount fasteners are tightened, **Fig. 9.**
   d. Torque right and left engine mount vertical bolts to 250 inch lbs. and torque front engine mount bolts to 40 ft. lbs.

1983–87

1. Position vehicle with wheels straight ahead and body weight distributed on all 4 tires.
2. Measure direct distance between inner edge of outboard boot to inner edge of inboard boot on both driveshafts, **Fig. 10. On 1983 models equipped with 4-105 engine and manual transaxle, measure from outer edge of inboard flange.**
3. Driveshaft length must be within specifications in chart, **Figs. 11 through 15.** If measurement is not within specifications, engine position must be corrected as follows:
   a. Remove load from engine mounts by carefully supporting engine and transaxle assembly with a suitable jack.
   b. Loosen right and left engine mount vertical bolts (1984-87 models, right only) and front engine mount bracket-to-crossmember attaching bolts.
   c. Pry engine to right or left as necessary to bring driveshaft length within specifications. **On 1984-87 models, left engine mount is sleeved over long support bolt and shaft, Fig. 16,** to provide lateral adjustment whether or not engine weight is removed.
   d. Torque engine mount vertical bolts to 250 inch lbs. and front engine mount bolts to 40 ft. lbs.
   e. On 1984-87 models, center left engine mount.

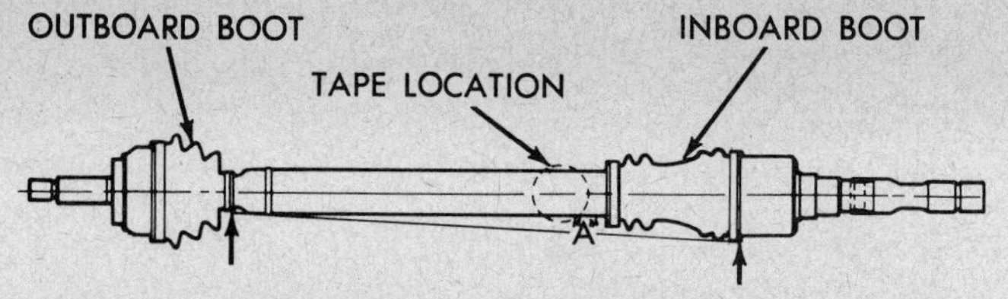

Fig. 10 Measuring driveshaft. 1983–85

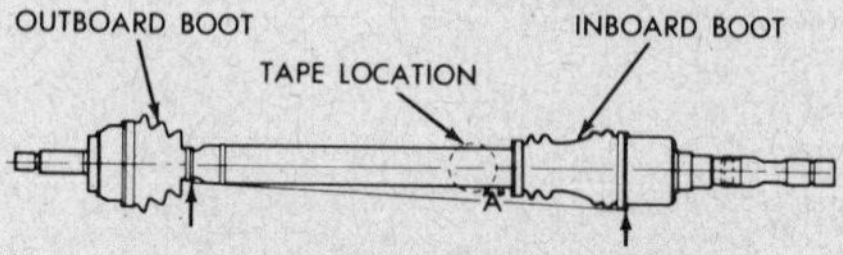

		Driveshaft Identification			"A" Dimension	
Body	Engine	Type	Side	Tape Color	mm	Inch
CHARGER, HORIZON, OMNI & TURISMO	1.6L/2.2L	G.K.N.	Right	Yellow	498-509	19.6-20.0
			Left	Yellow	240-253	9.5-10.0
		A.C.I.	Right	Red	469-478	18.5-19.0
			Left	Red	208-218	8.2- 8.6
EXC. CHARGER, DAYTONA, HORIZON, LASER, OMNI & TURISMO	2.2L	G.K.N.	Right	Blue	505-515	19.9-20.3
			Left	Blue	259-277	10.2-10.9
		A.C.I.	Right	Green	477-485	18.8-19.1
			Left	Green	229-244	9.0- 9.6
		G.K.N./A.C.I.	Right	Orange	492-500	19.4-19.7
			Left	Orange	243-258	9.6-10.2
		Citroen	Right	White	480-492	18.9-19.4
			Left	White	238-255	9.4-10.0
	2.6L	G.K.N.	Right	Silver	501-510	19.7-20.1
			Left	Silver	254-269	10.0-10.6
		Citroen	Right	Yellow	480-492	18.9-19.4
			Left	Yellow	238-255	9.4-10.0
EXC. CHARGER, HORIZON, OMNI & TURISMO	2.2L Turbo	G.K.N.	Right	Tan	257-265	10.1-10.4
			Left	Silver	254-269	10.0-10.6
		Citroen	Right	Red	241-251	9.5- 9.9
			Left	Yellow	238-255	9.4-10.0

Fig. 11 Driveshaft length specifications. 1984

INNER CONSTANT VELOCITY JOINT SERVICE

DISASSEMBLY

1. Remove clamp and boot from joint and discard, **Fig. 17.**
2. On Citroen units, separate tripod from housing by slightly deforming retaining ring at three locations, **Fig. 18.** If necessary, cut retaining ring from housing and install replacement retaining ring with inner flange rolled, then stake into machined groove with a suitable punch. **When removing tripod from housing, secure rollers. After tripod has been removed, secure assembly with tape.**
3. On early 1982 G.K.N. non-spring loaded units, slide tripod from housing, **Fig. 19.** On late 1982-87 G.K.N. spring loaded units, bend tabs on joint cover using needle nose pliers, then remove tripod from housing, **Fig. 20.**
4. On 1984 A.C.I. units, position housing so all 3 rollers are flush with retaining tabs. Pull housing out by hand at a slight angle to pop one roller at a time out of retaining tabs, **Fig. 21.** Do not hold joint at too severe an angle, as rollers may be damaged. **The retaining tabs must not be bent during removal or installation of housing.**
5. On 1985-87 A.C.I. units, hold housing and lightly compress C/V joint retention spring while bending tabs back with a pair of pliers, **Fig. 22.** Support housing, then separate tripod from housing.
6. On 1986-87 S.S.G. units, use flathead screwdriver to pry wire ring out of groove and slide tripod from housing, **Fig. 23. When removing housing from tripod, hold rollers in place on the trunion studs to prevent rollers and needle bearings from falling out. After tripod is out of housing, secure rollers in place with tape.**
7. Remove snap ring from end of shaft then the tripod using a brass drift.

INSPECTION

Remove grease from assembly and inspect bearing race and tripod components for wear and damage and replace as necessary. On late 1982-87 spring loaded joints inspect spring, spring cup and spherical end of connecting shaft for wear and damage and replace as necessary. **Components of spring loaded and non-**

Body	Engine	Driveshaft Identification Type	Side	Tape Color	"A" Dimension mm	Inch
CHARGER, HORIZON, OMNI & TURISMO	1.6L/2.2L	G.K.N.	Right	Yellow	498-509	19.6-20.0
			Left	Yellow	240-253	9.5-10.0
		A.C.I.	Right	Red	469-478	18.5-19.0
			Left	Red	208-218	8.2- 8.6
	2.2L Turbo	Citroen	Right	Orange	211-220	8.3-8.7
			Left	Orange	211-220	8.3-8.7
CHARGER, DAYTONA, HORIZON, LANCER, LASER, LEBARON GTS, OMNI & TURISMO	2.2L	Citroen	Right	Green	465-477	18.3-18.8
			Left	Green	211-220	8.3-8.7
		A.C.I.	Right	Blue	463-472	18.2-18.6
			Left	Blue	204-213	8.0-8.4
EXC. CHARGER, HORIZON, OMNI & TURISMO	2.2L	G.K.N.	Right	Blue	505-515	19.9-20.3
			Left	Blue	259-277	10.2-10.9
		A.C.I.	Right	Green	477-485	18.8-19.1
			Left	Green	229-244	9.0- 9.6
		G.K.N./A.C.I.	Right	Orange	492-500	19.4-19.7
			Left	Orange	243-258	9.6-10.2
		Citroen	Right	White	480-492	18.9-19.4
			Left	White	238-255	9.4-10.0
	2.6L	G.K.N.	Right	Silver	501-510	19.7-20.1
			Left	Silver	254-269	10.0-10.6
		Citroen	Right	Yellow	480-492	18.9-19.4
			Left	Yellow	238-255	9.4-10.0
EXC. CHARGER, HORIZON, OMNI & TURISMO	2.2L Turbo	G.K.N.	Right	Tan	257-265	10.1-10.4
			Left	Silver	254-269	10.0-10.6
		Citroen	Right	Red	241-251	9.5- 9.9
			Left	Yellow	238-255	9.4-10.0

Fig. 12 Driveshaft length specifications. 1985

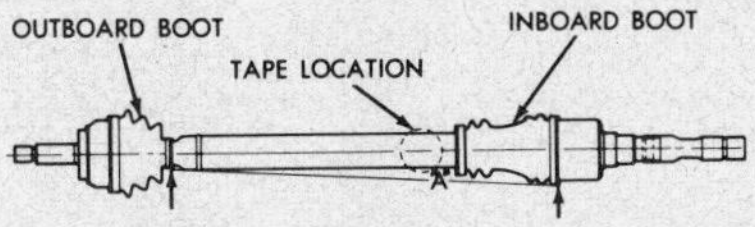

Body	Engine	Driveshaft Identification Type	Side	Tape Color	"A" Dimension mm	Inch
CHARGER, HORIZON OMNI & TURISMO	1.6L/2.2L	G.K.N.	Right	Yellow	498-509	19.6-20.0
			Left	Yellow	240-253	9.5-10.0
		A.C.I.	Right	Red	469-478	18.5-19.0
			Left	Red	208-218	8.2- 8.6
	2.2L Turbo	Citroen	Right	Orange	211-220	8.3-8.7
			Left	Orange	211-220	8.3-8.7
CHARGER, DAYTONA, HORIZON, LANCER, LASER, LEBARON GTS, OMNI & TURISMO	2.2L	Citroen	Right	Green	465-477	18.3-18.8
			Left	Green	211-220	8.3-8.7
		A.C.I.	Right	Blue	463-472	18.2-18.6
			Left	Blue	204-213	8.0-8.4
EXC. CHARGER, HORIZON, OMNI, & TURISMO	2.2L/2.5L	G.K.N.	Right	Blue	505-515	19.9-20.3
			Left	Blue	259-277	10.2-10.9
		A.C.I.	Right	Green	477-485	18.8-19.1
			Left	Green	229-244	9.0- 9.6
		G.K.N./A.C.I.	Right	Orange	492-500	19.4-19.7
			Left	Orange	243-258	9.6-10.2
		Citroen	Right	White	480-492	18.9-19.4
			Left	White	238-255	9.4-10.0
		S.S.G	Right	Gold	457-469	17.9-18.5
			Left	Gold	216-232	8.5- 9.1
	2.6L	G.K.N.	Right	Silver	501-510	19.7-20.1
			Left	Silver	254-269	10.0-10.6
		Citroen	Right	Yellow	480-492	18.9-19.4
			Left	Yellow	238-255	9.4-10.0
EXC. CHARGER, HORIZON, OMNI, & TURISMO	2.2L Turbo	G.K.N.	Right	Tan	257-265	10.1-10.4
			Left	Silver	254-269	10.0-10.6
		Citroen	Right	Red	241-251	9.5- 9.9
			Left	Yellow	238-255	9.4-10.0

Fig. 13 Driveshaft length specifications. 1986

spring loaded inner C/V joints cannot be interchanged.

ASSEMBLY

1. On 1984 models equipped with turbocharged engine, install a new slinger, **Fig. 24.** Tap slinger down until collar is flush with journal, then on 1984-87 models, slide rubber seal over stub shaft and into groove.
2. On all models, slide small end of boot over shaft. On Tubular type shafts, align boot lip with mark on shaft outer diameter. On solid type shafts, position small end of boot in groove on shaft.
3. Place rubber clamp over groove on boot.
4. Install tripod on shaft with non-chamfered face of tripod body facing shaft retainer groove.
5. Lock tripod assembly on shaft by installing retaining ring in shaft groove.
6. Distribute two packets of grease provided with boot and clamp kit into boot assembly on G.K.N. units, one packet on A.C.I. units, 2/3 packet on Citroen units or 1/2 packet on S.S.G. units.
7. On 1982-83 models with 4-105 engine and manual transaxle, install joint housing over tripod, then position large end of boot in groove in housing. Add two additional packets of grease after boot has been secured to housing.
8. On early 1982 models less 4-105 engine with manual transaxle, distribute one packet of grease in housing before positioning housing over tripod. On Citroen units, reform retainer ring. On all units, secure boot to housing with boot clamp.
9. On late 1982 and 1983-87 models less 4-105 engine and manual transaxle, distribute remaining grease supplied into housing. Position spring, with spring cup attached to exposed end, into spring pocket. Place a small amount of grease on spring cup, then position housing over tripod. On Citroen units, reform or replace retainer ring. On G.K.N. units, bend retaining tabs. On 1984 A.C.I. units, align rollers with retaining tabs and housing tracks and pop one roller at a time through retaining tabs. On 1985-87 A.C.I. units, slide tripod onto housing. On 1986-87 S.S.G. units, slip tripod into housing and install tripod wire retaining ring into position, ensuring retaining ring retains tripod in housing. Care must be taken to ensure proper spring positioning. The spring must remain centered in housing spring pocket when tripod is installed and seated in spring cup. Do not bend retaining tabs back to original position at this time, tripod must be engaged in housing when driveshaft is installed. On all units, position boot over boot groove in housing, then install clamp. **When installing housing, check to ensure that spring remains in pocket and centered in housing. Also ensure that spring cup contacts spherical end of connecting shaft.**

OUTER CONSTANT VELOCITY JOINT SERVICE

DISASSEMBLY

1. Cut boot clamps from boot and discard boot and clamps, **Fig. 25.**
2. Clean grease from joint.
3. Exc. on S.S.G. units support shaft in a soft jawed vise, support outer joint and tap with a mallet to dislodge joint from internal circlip installed in a groove at outer end of shaft, **Fig. 26.** Do not remove slinger from housing.
4. On S.S.G. units, loosen damper weight bolts and slide weight and boot toward inner joint, then expand circlip with suitable pliers, slide joint from shaft and reinstall damper weight.
5. Remove circlip from shaft groove and discard, **Fig. 27.**
6. Unless shaft requires replacement, do not remove heavy lock ring from shaft, **Fig. 27.**
7. If constant velocity joint was operating satisfactorily and grease does not appear contaminated, proceed to "Assembly" procedure, Step 8.
8. If constant velocity joint is noisy or badly worn, replace entire unit. The repair kit will include boot, clamps, cir-

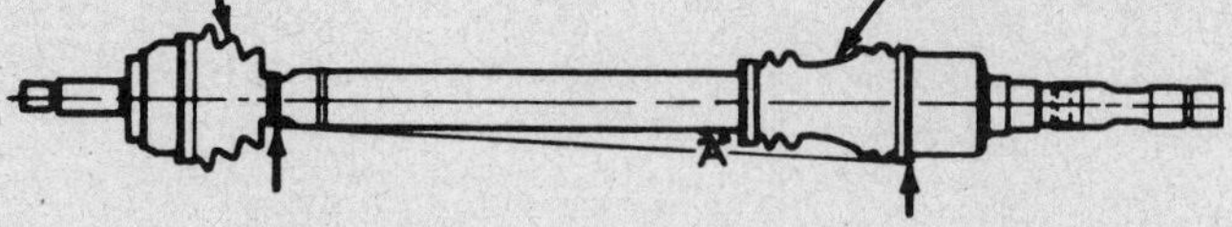

Body	Engine	Driveshaft Identification			"A" Dimension	
		Type	Side	Transaxle	mm	Inch
Charger, Horizon, Omni & Turismo	2.2L	G.K.N.	Right	Auto.	498-504	19.6-20.0
			Left	Auto.	208-221	8.2- 8.7
		G.K.N.	Right	Manual	498-504	19.6-20.0
			Left	Manual	240-253	9.4-10.0
	2.2L Turbo I	G.K.N.	Right	All	211-220	8.3-8.7
			Left	All	211-220	8.3-8.7
		Citroen	Right	All	227-232	8.9- 9.1
			Left	All	227-232	8.9- 9.1
Exc. Charger, Horizon, Omni & Turismo	2.2L/2.5L	G.K.N.	Right	All	505-515	19.9-20.3
			Left	All	227-245	8.9- 9.6
		A.C.I.	Right	All	477-485	18.8-19.1
			Left	All	197-212	7.8- 8.3
		G.K.N./A.C.I.	Right	All	492-500	19.4-19.7
			Left	All	211-226	8.3- 8.9
		Citroen	Right	All	480-492	18.9-19.4
			Left	All	206-223	8.1- 8.8
		S.S.G	Right	All	457-469	17.9-18.5
			Left	All	184-200	7.2- 7.9
	2.6L	G.K.N.	Right	All	501-510	19.7-20.1
			Left	All	222-237	8.7- 9.3
		Citroen	Right	All	480-492	18.9-19.4
			Left	All	206-223	8.1- 8.8
Exc. Charger, Horizon, Omni & Turismo	2.2L Turbo I	G.K.N.	Right	All	257-265	10.1-10.4
			Left	All	257-265	10.1-10.4
		Citroen	Right	All	241-251	9.5- 9.9
			Left	All	241-251	9.5- 9.9
		S.S.G.	Right	All	219-228	8.6- 9.0
			Left	All	219-228	8.6- 9.0
Daytona	2.2L Turbo II	G.K.N.	Right	Manual	227-234	8.9- 9.2
			Left	Manual	227-234	8.9- 9.2

Fig. 14 Driveshaft length specifications. 1987 exc. Shadow & Sundance

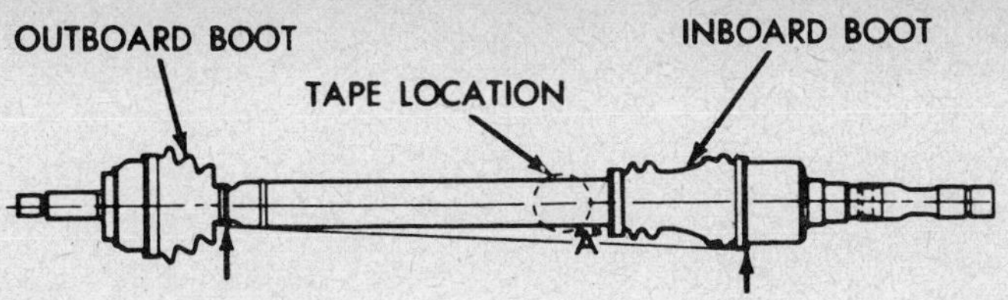

	Driveshaft Identification			"A" Dimension	
Engine	Type	Side	Tape Color	mm	Inch
2.2L	G.K.N.	Right	Blue	505-515	19.9-20.3
		Left	Blue	259-277	10.2-10.9
	A.C.I.	Right	Green	477-485	18.8-19.1
		Left	Green	229-244	9.0-9.6
	G.K.N./A.C.I.	Right	Orange	492-500	19.4-19.7
		Left	Orange	243-258	9.6-10.2
	Citroen	Right	White	480-492	18.9-19.4
		Left	White	238-255	9.4-10.0
	S.S.G.	Right	Gold	457-469	17.9-18.5
		Left	Gold	216-232	8.5-9.1
2.2L Turbo	G.K.N.	Right	Tan	257-265	10.1-10.4
		Left	Silver	254-269	10.1-10.6
	Citroen	Right	Red	241-251	9.5-9.9
		Left	Yellow	238-255	9.4-10.0
	S.S.G.	Right	Turquoise	219-228	8.6-9.0
		Left	Gold	216-232	8.5-9.1

Fig. 15 Driveshaft length specifications. 1987 Shadow & Sundance

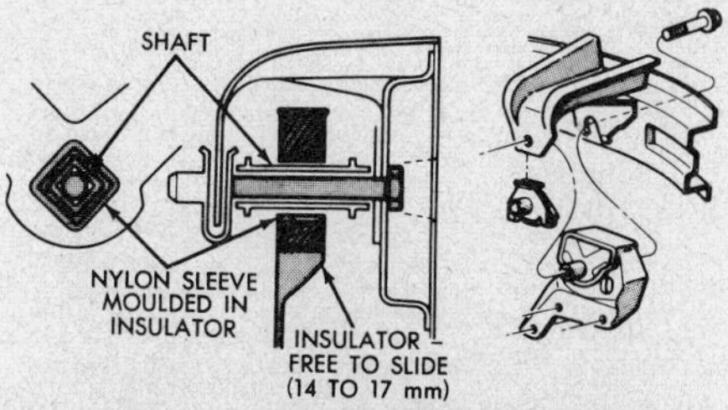

Fig. 16 Left engine mount adjustment. 1984–87

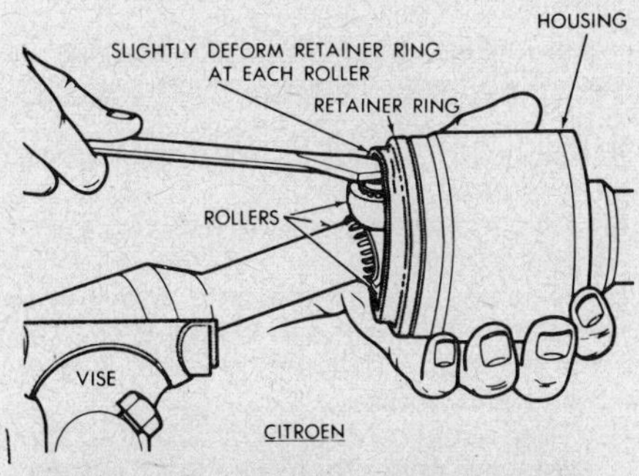

Fig. 18 Removing 3 ball tripod housing. Citroen inner C/V joint

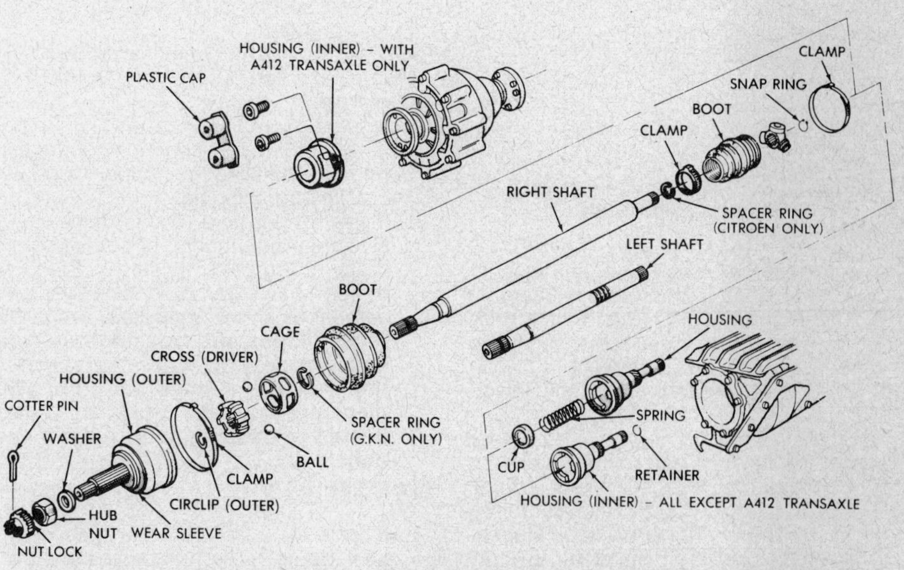

Fig. 17 Driveshaft components. 1982–83 (1984–87 similar)

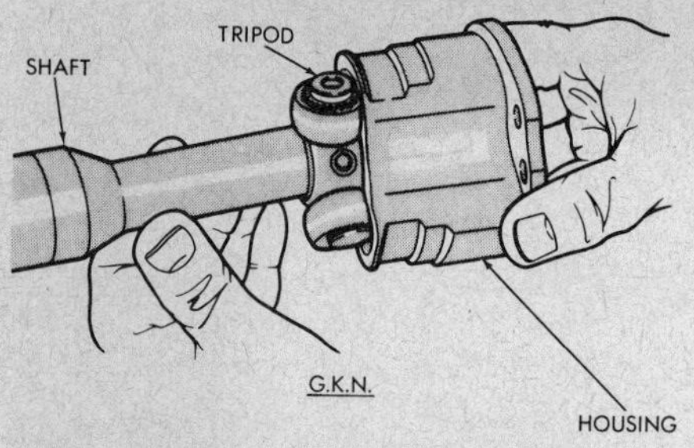

Fig. 19 Removing 3 ball tripod housing. 1982 & early 1982 G.K.N. inner C/V joint

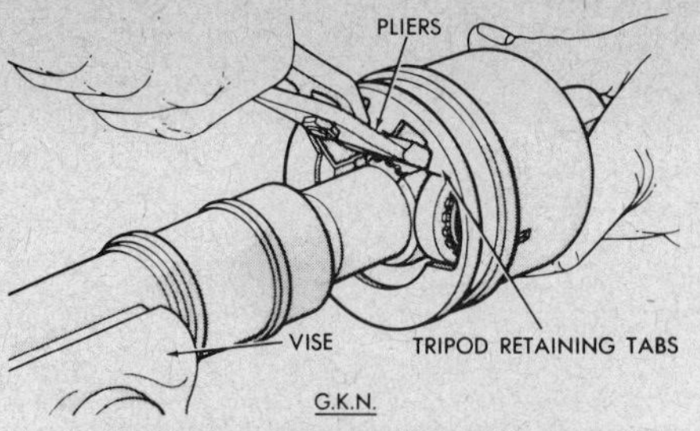

Fig. 20 Removing 3 ball tripod housing. Late 1982–87 G.K.N. inner C/V joint

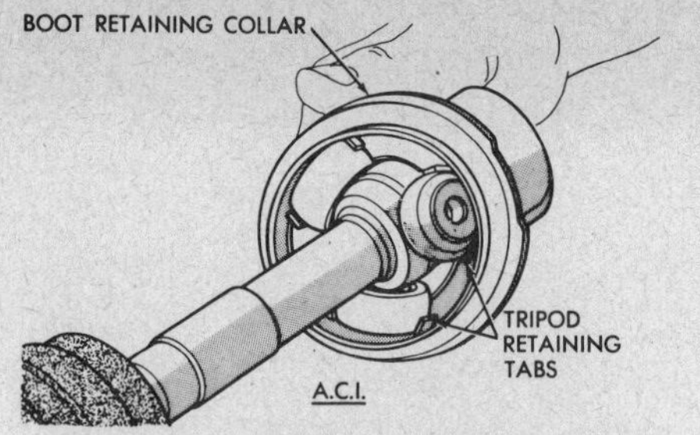

Fig. 21 Removing 3 ball tripod housing. 1984 A.C.I. inner C/V joint

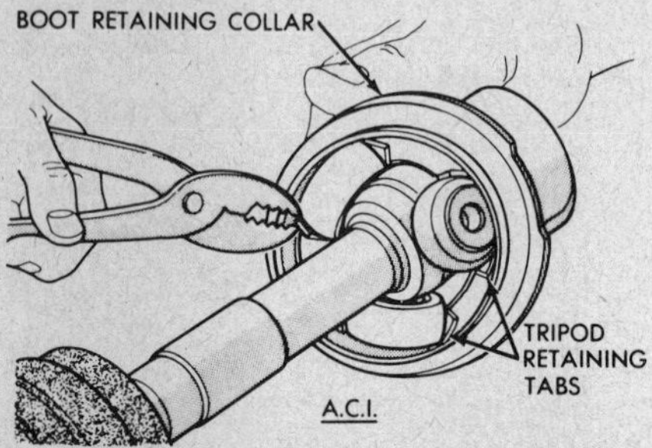

Fig. 22 Removing 3 ball tripod housing. 1985–87 A.C.I. inner C/V joint

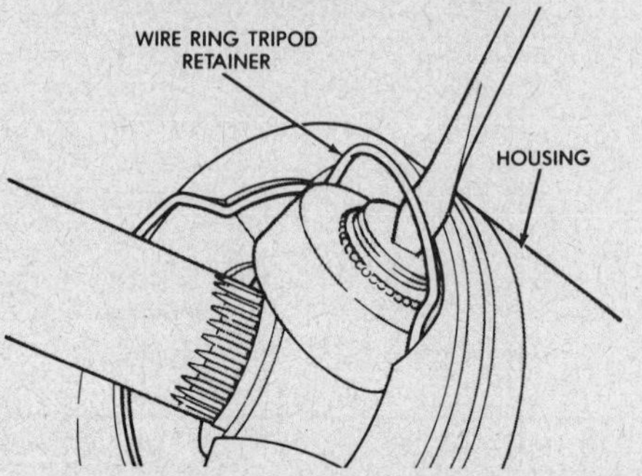

Fig. 23 Separating tripod from housing. 1986–87 S.S.G. inner C/V joint

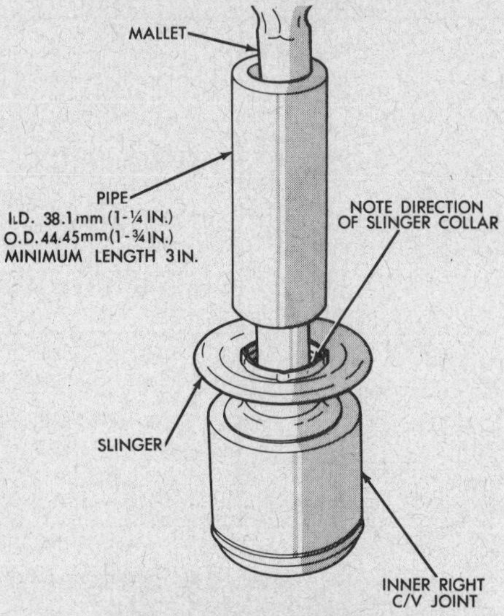

Fig. 24 Slinger installation. 1984 w/turbocharged engine

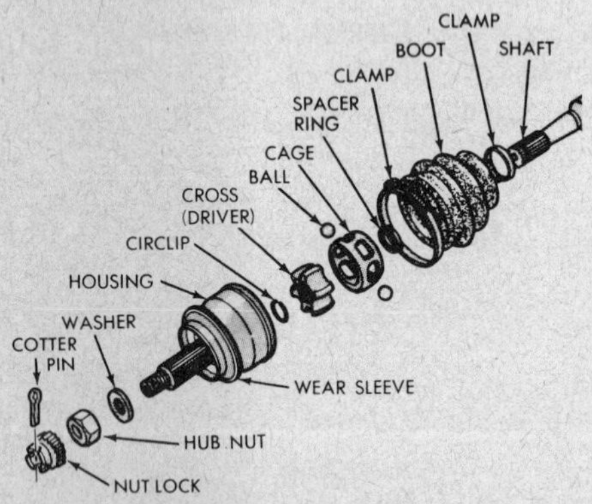

Fig. 25 Outer C/V joint disassembled

clip and lubricant. Clean and inspect joint outlined in the following steps.

9. Clean surplus grease and mark relative position of inner cross, cage and housing with a dab of paint.
10. Hold joint vertically in a soft jawed vise.
11. Press downward on one side of inner race to tilt cage and remove ball from opposite side, **Fig. 28.** If joint is tight, use a hammer and a brass drift to tap inner race. Do not strike cage. Repeat this step until all six balls are removed. A screwdriver may be used to pry balls loose.
12. Tilt cage assembly vertically and position two opposing, elongated cage windows in area between ball grooves. Remove cage and inner race assembly by pulling upward from housing, **Fig. 29.**
13. Rotate inner cross 90 degrees to cage and align one of race spherical lands with an elongated cage window. Raise land into cage window and remove inner race by swinging outward, **Fig. 30.**

INSPECTION

1. Check housing ball races for excessive wear.
2. Check splined shaft and nut threads for damage.
3. Inspect balls for pitting, cracks, scouring and wear. Dulling of the surface is normal.
4. Inspect cage for excessive wear on inner and outer spherical surfaces, heavy brinelling of cage, window cracks and chipping.
5. Inspect inner race (Cross) for excessive wear or scouring of ball races.
6. If any of the defects listed in Steps 1 through 5, are found, replace C/V assembly as a unit. **Polished areas in races (Cross and housing) and on cage spheres are normal and does not indicate a need for joint replacement unless they are suspected of causing noise and vibration.**

ASSEMBLY

1. If removed, position wear sleeve on joint housing, then tap sleeve onto housing using tool No. C-4698.
2. Lightly oil components, then align marks made during disassembly.
3. Align one of the inner race lands with elongated window of cage, then insert race into cage and pivot 90°.
4. Align elongated cage windows with housing land, then pivot cage 90°.

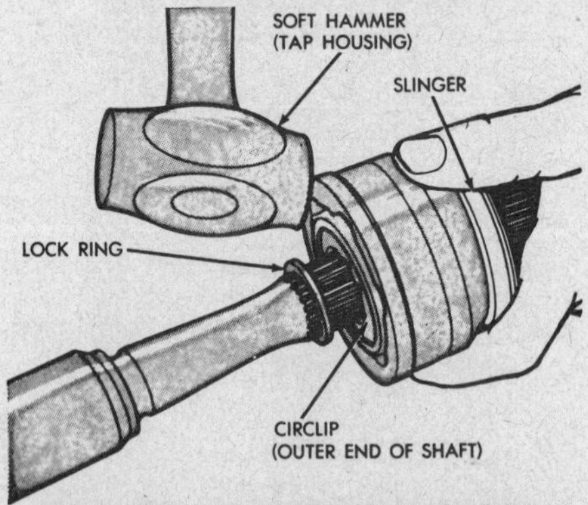

Fig. 26 Removing joint from shaft. Outer C/V joints

5. Lubricate ball races with one packet of grease from kit.
6. Tilt cage and inner race assembly and insert balls.
7. With shaft supported in a soft jawed vise, install boot. On G.K.N. and A.C.I. units, slip small clamp over spacer ring and shaft.
8. Slide small end of boot over spacer ring and shaft, then position boot end in machined groove. **On Citroen units, position vent sleeve under boot at clamp area.**
9. Install snap ring on shaft. When installing use care not to overexpand snap ring.

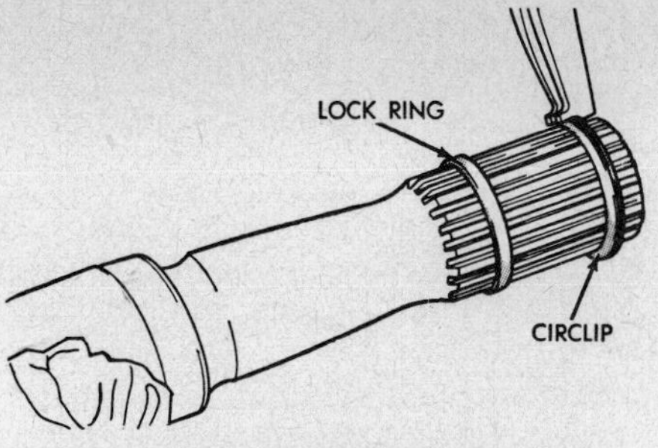

Fig. 27 Circlip removal. Outer C/V joints

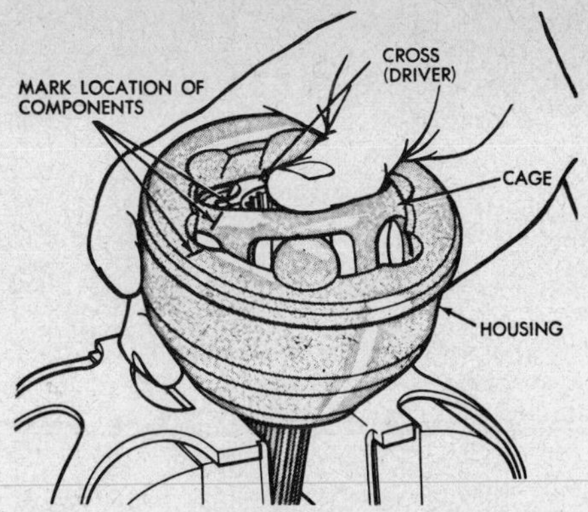

Fig. 28 Ball removal. Outer C/V joints

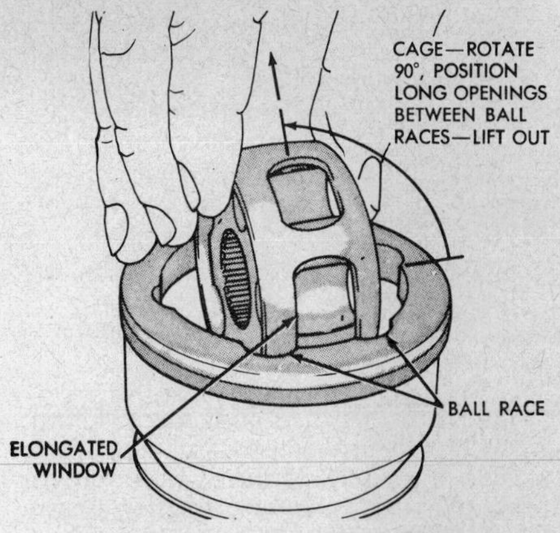

Fig. 29 Cage & cross assembly removal. Outer C/V joints

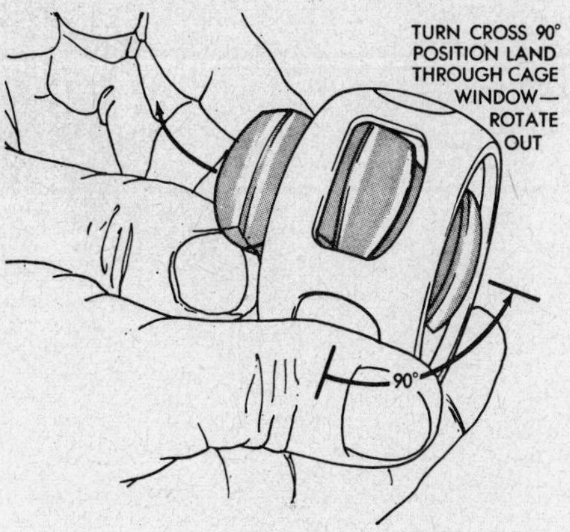

Fig. 30 Removing cross from cage. Outer C/V joints

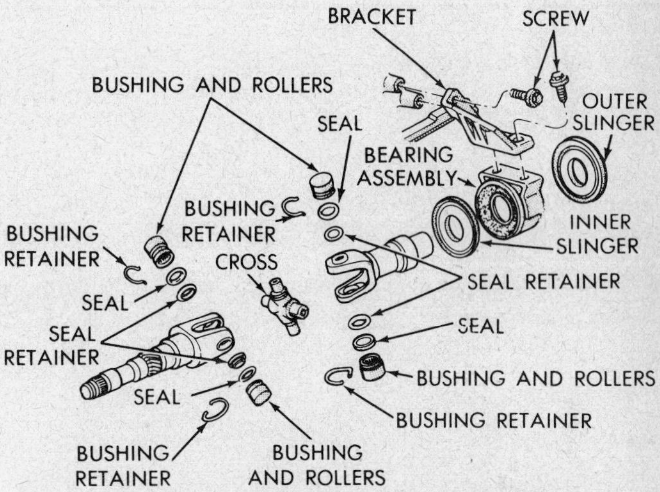

Fig. 31 Intermediate shaft assembly. 1984–87 turbocharged models

10. Position joint housing on shaft, then engage by tapping sharply with a soft faced mallet.
11. Check to ensure that snap ring is properly seated, by attempting to pull joint from shaft.
12. Locate large end of boot over housing.
13. On G.K.N. and A.C.I. units, secure boot clamps using tool No. C-4124. On Citroen units, secure boot clamps using tool C-4653. **G.K.N. and A.C.I. units use steel clamps, while Citroen units use a strap type clamp.**

INTERMEDIATE SHAFT ASSEMBLY

The intermediate shaft assembly, Fig. 31, is used on all 1984-87 turbocharged models.

REMOVAL

1. Remove right driveshaft, refer to "Driveshaft, Replace" procedure.
2. Remove speedometer pinion from extension housing, **Fig. 32.**
3. Remove two screws from bearing assembly bracket to engine block, **Fig. 31.**
4. Remove intermediate shaft assembly from transaxle extension by pulling yoke outward.

SUBASSEMBLY SERVICE

UNIVERSAL JOINT & ROLLER

Disassemble

1. Mark relationship of shafts to insure proper alignment during assembly. Apply penetrating oil to bushing, then remove snap rings.
2. Support yoke in vise, then position 1 1/8 inch socket over bushing on top of yoke.
3. Strike socket with a suitable hammer until bushing moves up out of yoke into socket.
4. Turn assembly in vise and remove remaining bushings in same manner.

Assemble

1. Hold cross in position between yoke ears with one hand and start one bushing assembly into yoke with other hand.
2. Hammer bushing assembly into yoke, then install snap ring.
3. Install remaining bushing assemblies in same manner.

BRACKET, BEARING & SLINGER ASSEMBLY

Disassemble

1. Remove two bearing assembly to support bracket attaching screws, then separate bearing from bracket.
2. Press intermediate shaft out of bearing assembly and outer slinger. **Do not dent or damage inner slinger or end of stub shaft.**
3. If either slinger is damaged, it should be replaced by carefully pressing shaft through slinger. **The bearing assembly is not serviceable and must be replaced as an assembly.**

Assemble

1. Place new slinger on stub shaft, then using a suitable tool, drive slinger down until it bottoms out on shoulder of shaft. Ensure slinger is properly seated.
2. Press bearing assembly onto shaft, leaving a minimum of 1/32 inch (1 mm) clearance between slinger and bear-

ing assembly. **Apply pressure only to inner race of bearing assembly during installation.**

3. Press outer slinger into position using a suitable tool. The slinger must bottom out on shoulder of shaft.

INSTALLATION

1. Attach bracket loosely to bearing assembly.
2. Hold stub yoke and install spline into transaxle.
3. Attach bracket to engine. Torque attaching screws to 40 ft. lbs. (54 Nm).
4. Push intermediate shaft assembly into transaxle as far as it can travel, then torque bracket to bearing attaching screws to 21 ft. lbs. (28 Nm).
5. Apply suitable grease inside spline and pilot bore on bearing end of intermediate shaft.
6. Install speedometer pinion, then the right driveshaft, refer to "Driveshaft, Replace" procedure.

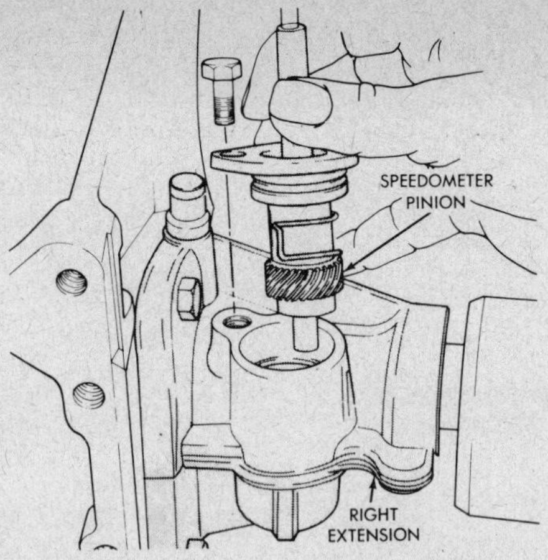

Fig. 32 Removing speedometer pinion from extension housing

UNIVERSAL JOINTS

INDEX

Page No.

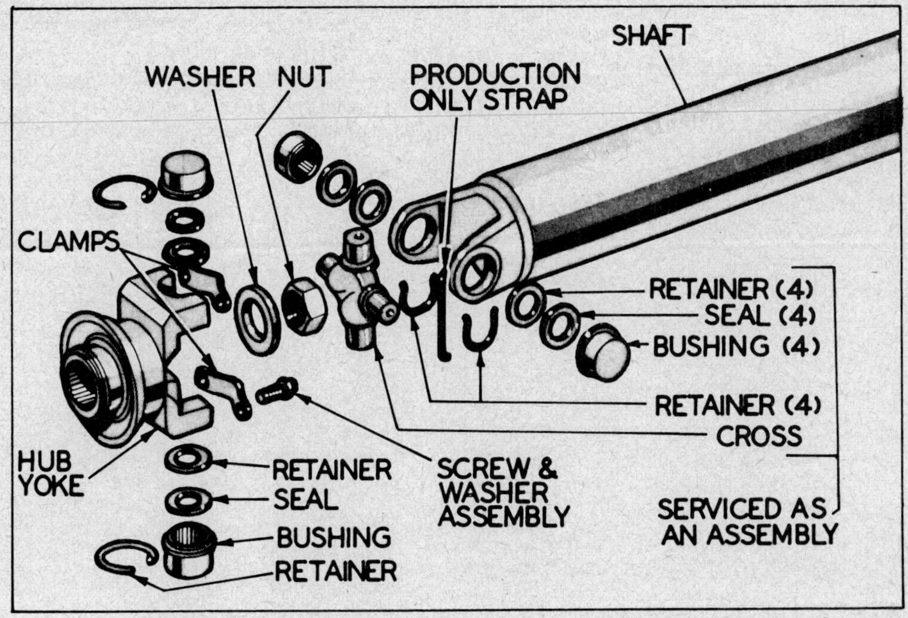

Fig. 1 Rear cross & roller type universal joint

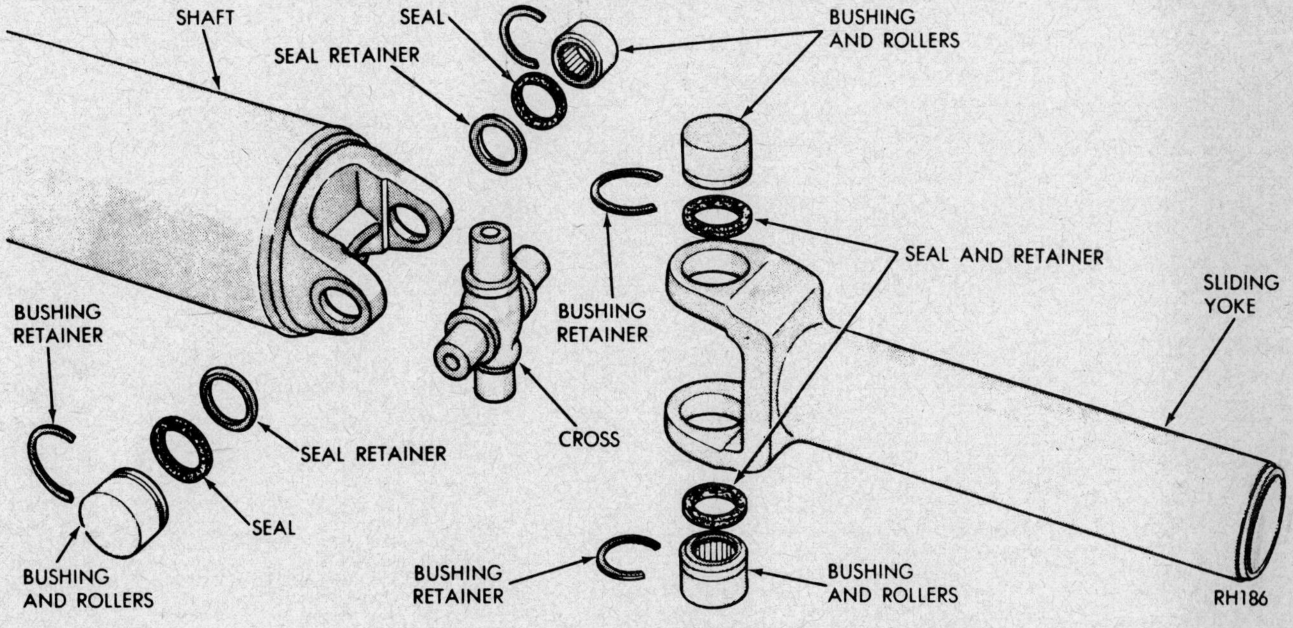

Fig. 2 Front cross & roller type universal joint

SERVICE NOTES

Before disassembling any universal joint, examine the assembly carefully and note the position of the grease fitting (if used). Also, be sure to mark the yokes with relation to the propeller shaft so they may be reassembled in the same relative position. Failure to observe these precautions may produce rough car operation which results in rapid wear and failure of parts, and place an unbalanced load on transmission, engine and rear axle.

When universal joints are disassembled for lubrication or inspection, and the old parts are to be reinstalled, special care must be exercised to avoid damage to universal joint spider or cross and bearing cups.

CROSS & ROLLER TYPE

DISASSEMBLY

1. Mark relationship of yoke to shaft to ensure proper alignment during assembly, then apply penetrating oil to bushing and remove snap rings, **Figs. 1 and 2.**
2. Support one yoke in vise and place socket, large enough to receive bushing, on top of other yoke.
3. Strike socket with hammer, causing yoke to move down and bushing to move up out of yoke and into socket.
4. Rotate driveshaft in vise and remove remaining bushing as previously described.

ASSEMBLY

1. Align marks made during disassembly, then hold cross in position between yoke ears with one hand and start one bushing assembly into yoke with other hand.
2. Continuing to hold cross in position, hammer bushing into yoke ear and install snap ring.
3. Install opposite bushing and snap ring as previously described.
4. Repeat procedure for sliding yoke or, in case of axle end of driveshaft, install snap rings on two remaining bushings and use tape or wire to hold bushings on cross.

ELECTRONIC IGNITION SYSTEMS

TABLE OF CONTENTS

Distributor Specifications

FRONT WHEEL DRIVE MODELS

***Note: If unit is checked on vehicle, double the RPM and degrees to get crankshaft figures.**

Distributor Part No. ①	Centrifugal Advance Degrees @ RPM of Distributor			Vacuum Advance	
	Advance Starts	Intermediate Advance	Full Advance	Start Dist. Degrees @ Inches of Vacuum	Maximum Dist. Degrees
1982					
4243694③	0 @ 600	6 @ 1400	10 @ 3000	0 @ 5.1	7.5
4243705②	0 @ 600	6 @ 1400	10 @ 3000	0 @ 3.1	10
5206945	—	—	—	—	—
5206975	—	—	—	—	—
1983					
4243694③	0 @ 600	6 @ 1400	10 @ 3000	0 @ 5.1	7.5
4243705②	0 @ 600	6 @ 1400	10 @ 3000	0 @ 3.1	10

①—Stamped on distributor housing.
②—Exc. Calif.
③—Calif.

DISTRIBUTOR SPECIFICATIONS—Continued

REAR WHEEL DRIVE MODELS

***Note: If unit is checked on vehicle, double the RPM and degrees to get crankshaft figures.**

Distributor Part No. ①	Centrifugal Advance Degrees @ RPM of Distributor			Vacuum Advance	
	Advance Starts	Intermediate Advance	Full Advance	Inches of Vacuum to Start Plunger	Max. Adv. Dist. Deg. @ Vacuum
1982					
4145954	0-1.6 @ 600	0-2 @ 900	4.5 @ 2500	4	12 @ 11
1982–83					
4145751②	—	—	—	—	—
4145753②	—	—	—	—	—
1984					
4145752②	—	—	—	—	—
1985					
4091140②	—	—	—	—	—
1986–87					
4091140②	—	—	—	—	—
4145753②	—	—	—	—	—

①—Stamped on distributor.
②—Electronic Spark Control system distributor, cannot be checked on vehicle.

Electronic Spark Control Specifications

1982 FRONT WHEEL DRIVE

Spark Control Computer	5213437	5213438	5213480	5213481	5213482	5213483
Basic Timing	12°	20°	12°	12°	12°	12°
Vacuum Advance (Range)	0–10″	0–12″	0–12″	0–12″	0–12″	0–12″
Accumulator Time (In Minutes)	0	0	0	0	0	0
Spark Advance Test @ 2000 RPM②	55° ± 4°	50° ± 4°	45° ± 4°	47° ± 4°	45° ± 4°	45° ± 4°

Spark Control Computer	5213542	5213544	5213546	5213546①	5213594	
Basic Timing	12°	12°	12°	12°	12°	
Vacuum Advance (Range)	0–10″	0–10″	0–10″	0–12″	0–10″	
Accumulator Time (In Minutes)	0	0	0	0	0	
Spark Advance Test @ 2000 RPM②	55° ± 4°	50° ± 4°	43° ± 4°	31° ± 4°	37° ± 4°	

①—High Altitude.
②—Plus basic timing.

ELECTRONIC SPARK CONTROL SPECIFICATIONS—Continued

1983 FRONT WHEEL DRIVE

Spark Control Computer	5213438	5213641	5213691	5213832	5213834	5213836
Basic Timing	20°	12°	10°	10°	10°	10°
Vacuum Advance (Range)	0–12″	0–12″	2–12″	2–12″	2–12″	2–12″
Accumulator Time (In Minutes)	0	0	0	0	0	0
Spark Advance Test @ 2000 RPM②	30° ± 4°	23° ± 4°	28° ± 4°	28° ± 4°	28° ± 4°	34° ± 4°

Spark Control Computer	5213838	5213840①	5213974③	5213976③	5213978③	
Basic Timing	10°	6°	15°	15°	15°	
Vacuum Advance (Range)	2–12″	2–21″	—	—	—	
Accumulator Time (In Minutes)	0	0	—	—	—	
Spark Advance Test @ 2000 RPM②	31° ± 4°	34° ± 4°	30° ± 4°	25° ± 4°	18° ± 4°	

①—High Altitude. ②—Plus basic timing. ③—Shelby option.

1984 FRONT WHEEL DRIVE

Spark Control Computer	5226106	5226118	5226122	5226158①	5226160①
Basic Timing	12°	10°	10°	15°	15°
Vacuum Advance (Range)	—	—	—	—	—
Accumulator Time (In Minutes)	—	—	—	—	—
Spark Advance Test @ 2000 RPM②	33° ± 4°	42° ± 4°	40° ± 4°	43° ± 4°	43° ± 4°

Spark Control Computer	5226162	5226166③	5226188	5226174	
Basic Timing	10°	10°	10°	10°	
Vacuum Advance (Range)	—	—	—	—	
Accumulator Time (In Minutes)	—	—	—	—	
Spark Advance Test @ 2000 RPM②	40° ± 4°	38° ± 4°	40° ± 4°	40° ± 4°	

①—Shelby option. ②—Basic timing included. ③—High altitude.

1985-87 FRONT WHEEL DRIVE

Spark Control Computer	5226411	5226433	5226439	5226449②
Basic Timing	12°	10°	10°	15°
Vacuum Advance (Range)	—	—	—	—
Accumulator Time (In Minutes)	—	—	—	—
Spark Advance Test @ 2000 RPM①	33° ± 4°	41° ± 4°	42° ± 4°	38° ± 4°

Spark Control Computer	5226451	5226455	5226645	5227097③
Basic Timing	10°	10°	15°	15°
Vacuum Advance (Range)	—	—	—	—
Accumulator Time (In Minutes)	—	—	—	—
Spark Advance Test @ 2000 RPM①	37° ± 4°	42° ± 4°	36° ± 4°	43° ± 4°

①—Basic timing included. ②—1985 models only. ③—1986 models only.

ELECTRONIC SPARK CONTROL SPECIFICATIONS—Continued

1982 REAR WHEEL DRIVE

Spark Control Computer	4145452	4145701	4145726	4145907
Basic Timing	16°	12°	12°	12°
Vacuum Advance (Range)	4–14	2–12	2–12	1–14
Accumulator Time In Minutes	0	0	0	0
Spark Advance Test @ 2000 RPM	29 ± 4	23 ± 4	23 ± 4	34 ± 4
Electronic EGR Time Delay	35 sec.	—	—	20 sec.
Electronic Throttle Control Time Delay	—	AIS①	AIS①	20 sec.
Oxygen Feedback Electronic Air Switching Time	—	70 sec.	70 sec.	90 sec.

Spark Control Computer	4145980	4145996	4145998	4289034
Basic Timing	16°	16°	16°	12°
Vacuum Advance (Range)	1–14	4–14	4–14	3–10
Accumulator Time In Minutes	0	0	0	0.5
Spark Advance Test @ 2000 RPM	34 ± 4	34 ± 4	34 ± 4	20 ± 4
Electronic EGR Time Delay	20 sec.	60 sec.	60 sec.	60 sec.
Electronic Throttle Control Time Delay	—	60 sec.	60 sec.	60 sec.
Oxygen Feedback Electronic Air Switching Time	90 sec.	20 sec.	20 sec.	65 sec.

①—Automatic idle speed motor.

1983 REAR WHEEL DRIVE

Spark Control Computer	4145726	4145996	4289058	4289061
Basic Timing	12°	16°	16°	16°
Vacuum Advance (Range)	2–12	4–14	3–10	3–10
Accumulator Time In Minutes	0	0	60 sec.	60 sec.
Spark Advance Test @ 1500 RPM	23 ± 4	18 ± 4	14 ± 4	8 ± 4②
Electronic EGR Time Delay	—	60 sec.	65 sec.	65 sec.
Electronic Throttle Control Time Delay	①	—	—	—
Oxygen Feedback Electronic Air Switching Time	70 sec.	—	—	—

Spark Control Computer	4289063	4289065	4289104
Basic Timing	16°	16°	12°
Vacuum Advance (Range)	2–14	2–14	2–12
Accumulator Time In Minutes	0	0	0
Spark Advance Test @ 1500 RPM	30 ± 4	30 ± 4	20 ± 4
Electronic EGR Time Delay	60 sec.	60 sec.	—
Electronic Throttle Control Time Delay	—	—	①
Oxygen Feedback Electronic Air Switching Time	—	—	70 sec.

①—Automatic idle speed motor.
②—At 2000 RPM.

ELECTRONIC SPARK CONTROL SPECIFICATIONS—Continued

1984 REAR WHEEL DRIVE

Spark Control Computer	4289340	4289344	4289348	4289354
Basic Timing	16°	16°	16°	16°
Vacuum Advance (Range)	—	—	—	—
Accumulator Time In Minutes	—	—	—	—
Spark Advance Test @ 2000 RPM	51 ± 4	51 ± 4	41 ± 4	41 ± 4
Electronic EGR Time Delay	20 sec.	20 sec.	30 sec.	30 sec.
Oxygen Feedback Electronic Air Switching (Electronic)	Equipped	Equipped	Equipped	Equipped

1985 REAR WHEEL DRIVE

Spark Control Computer	4289673	4289811	4289819	4289821
Basic Timing	7°	7°	16°	16°
Vacuum Advance (Range)	—	—	—	—
Accumulator Time In Minutes	—	—	—	—
Spark Advance Test @ 2000 RPM①	46° ± 4	46° ± 4	38° ± 4	38° ± 4
Electronic EGR Time Delay	20 sec.	20 sec.	50 sec.	30 sec.
Oxygen Feedback Electronic Air Switching	Equipped	Equipped	Equipped	Equipped

①—Includes basic timing.

1986 REAR WHEEL DRIVE

Spark Control Computer	4289813	4289913	4289919	4289921
Basic Timing	7°	7°	16°	16°
Vacuum Advance (Range)	—	—	—	—
Accumulator Time In Minutes	—	—	—	—
Spark Advance Test @ 2000 RPM①	46° ± 4	46° ± 4	38° ± 4	38° ± 4
Electronic EGR Time Delay	40 sec.	40 sec.	40 sec.	40 sec.
Oxygen Feedback Electronic Air Switching	Equipped	Equipped	Equipped	Equipped

①—Includes basic timing.

1987 REAR WHEEL DRIVE

Spark Control Computer	4289813	4289913	4379228
Basic Timing	7°	7°	16°
Vacuum Advance Range	—	—	—
Accumulator Time In Minutes	—	—	—
Spark Advance Test @ 2000 RPM①	46±4	46±4	38±4
Electronic EGR Time Delay	40 sec.	40 sec.	40 sec.
Oxygen Feedback Electronic Air Switching	Equipped	Equipped	Equipped

①—Includes basic timing.

Front Wheel Drive w/4-156 (2.6L) Engine, Less Electronic Spark Control

INDEX

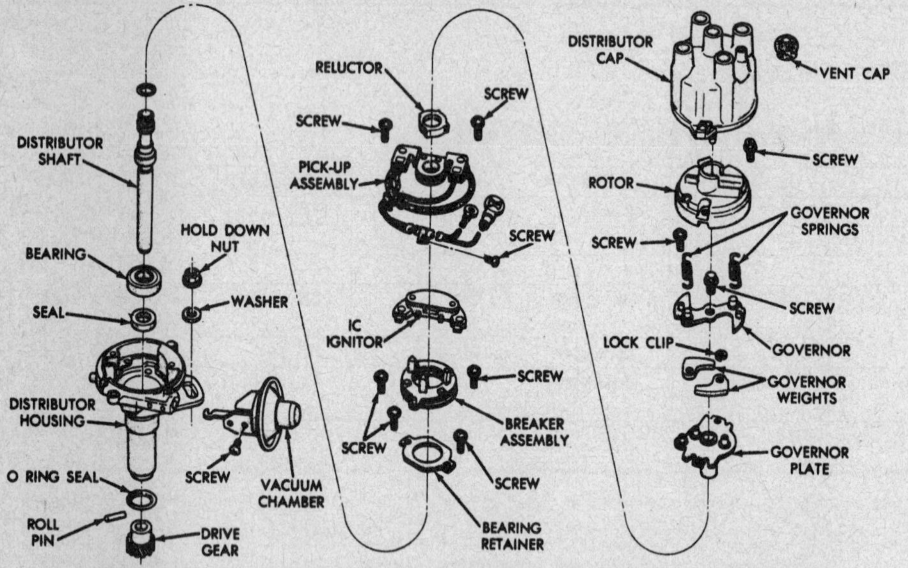

Fig. 1 Disassembled view of electronic ignition distributor. Front wheel drive models w/4-156 (2.6L) engine

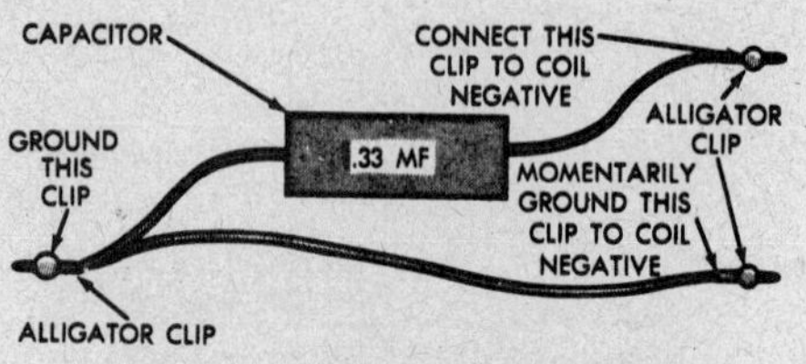

Fig. 2 Coil negative terminal jumper wire

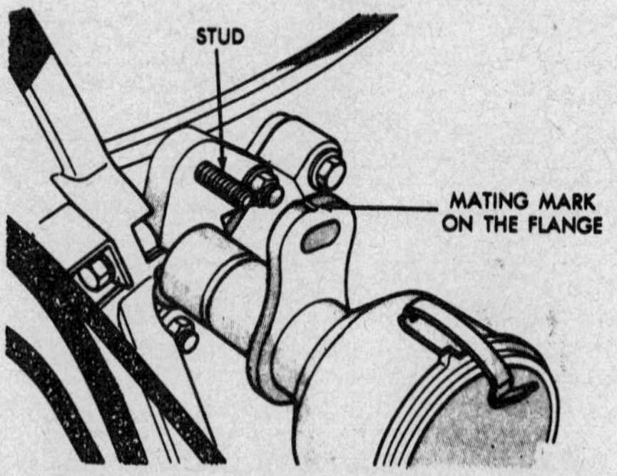

Fig. 3 Aligning distributor and engine mating marks

DESCRIPTION

This system consists of the distributor, **Fig. 1,** ignition switch, ignition coil, ECU igniter and spark plugs. Primary circuit current is controlled by the ECU igniter in response to timing signals produced by the distributor pickup. The distributor consists of the power distribution section, signal generator, ECU igniter, advance mechanism and drive gear section. The signal generator is a small magneto which produces a signal that is processed by the ECU to determine the exact time to open the coil primary circuit and produce a high voltage.

SYSTEM TESTING

1. Disconnect high tension lead from distributor and hold end of cable 3/16–3/8 inch from good engine ground. Crank engine and check for spark at end of high tension lead.
2. If spark is present, continue cranking engine while slowly moving coil high tension lead away from engine ground. If arcing occurs at coil tower, replace coil. If no spark is present at coil high tension lead or spark is weak, turn ignition On and check voltage at coil negative terminal using suitable voltmeter.
3. If voltage reading obtained is the same as battery voltage, system is operating satisfactorily. If reading is three volts or less, the distributor is defective and must be checked further. If zero reading is obtained, check for open circuit in ignition wiring and repair as necessary.
4. Connect special jumper wire, **Fig. 2,** to coil negative terminal. Turn ignition On, position coil high tension lead as described in step 1, then momentarily touch other end of jumper wire to a good ground.
5. If no spark is observed at coil high tension lead, check for presence of voltage at coil positive terminal. If battery voltage reading is obtained at coil positive terminal, replace coil. If proper voltage cannot be obtained, check for loose connections or damaged wiring and repair as necessary.

DISTRIBUTOR SERVICE

DISTRIBUTOR, REPLACE

Removal

1. Rotate engine until No. 1 cylinder is at TDC on compression stroke.
2. Disconnect battery ground cable.
3. Remove distributor cap and mark relationship of rotor to distributor housing.
4. Remove distributor wiring harness.
5. Disconnect vacuum hose from distributor.
6. Remove distributor retaining nut, then the distributor.

Installation

1. Align mating mark on distributor housing with rotor.
2. Install distributor into engine aligning mating mark on distributor mounting flange with center of distributor retaining stud, **Fig. 3.** Also ensure rotor aligns with reference marks on distributor housing made during removal.
3. Install retaining nut, vacuum hose, secondary ignition cables and distributor wiring harness.
4. Connect battery ground cable, start engine and adjust ignition timing.

DISASSEMBLY

1. Remove distributor rotor.
2. Remove governor assembly retaining screw, **Fig. 1,** and governor assembly. **Governor springs are not interchangeable and must be installed**

in their original positions. Note position of each spring during disassembly for reference during assembly.

3. Remove wire retaining clamp from side of distributor.
4. Remove pickup coil and ECU igniter retaining screws, then remove pickup coil and ECU igniter as an assembly.
5. Remove vacuum chamber retaining screws, then the vacuum chamber assembly.
6. Remove breaker assembly retaining screws, then the breaker assembly.
7. Remove bearing retainer plate screws, then the bearing retainer plate.
8. Mark relationship of distributor drive gear to distributor shaft, then punch out distributor drive gear retaining pin and remove gear from shaft.
9. Remove distributor shaft and bearing assembly from housing.
10. Remove distributor housing seal.

ASSEMBLY

1. Lubricate distributor housing seal with suitable grease and install into distributor housing.
2. Install distributor shaft and bearing assembly into distributor housing.
3. Install distributor drive gear onto shaft and align marks made during disassembly.
4. Install drive gear roll pin, then install bearing retainer and retaining screws.
5. Install breaker assembly and retaining screws.
6. Install vacuum chamber onto distributor housing and secure with retaining screws.
7. Install pickup coil and ECU igniter as an assembly into housing, then install retaining screws.
8. Install wire retaining clamp and governor assembly. If governor assembly was disassembled, check to ensure that governor springs are installed in original positions.
9. Install governor assembly retaining screw and rotor.

PICKUP ASSEMBLY, REPLACE

1. Remove distributor as outlined under "Distributor, Replace."
2. Perform steps 1 through 4 as outlined under "Disassembly."
3. Reverse procedure to install.

Front Wheel Drive w/Electronic Spark Control

INDEX

SYSTEM TESTING

IGNITION SYSTEM STARTING TEST

1. Remove coil wire from distributor cap and hold end of wire approximately 1/4 inch from a good engine ground. Crank engine and observe spark at coil wire.
2. The spark at the coil wire must be constant and bright blue in color. If so, continue to crank engine and slowly move coil wire away from the ground. If arcing occurs at the coil tower, replace coil. If spark is weak, not constant or there is no spark, proceed to the "Failure To Start Test."
3. If spark is satisfactory and no arcing occurs at the coil tower, the ignition system is producing the necessary high secondary voltage. However, this voltage is transmitted to the spark plugs by the distributor rotor, cap, spark plug wires and spark plugs and must also be checked. If satisfactory, the ignition system is not at fault. It will be necessary to check the fuel system and engine mechanical components.

FAILURE TO START TEST

Before performing this test, perform the "Ignition System Starting Test." Failure to do so may lead to unnecessary diagnostic time and incorrect test results.

1. With a voltmeter, measure and note battery voltage. Battery specific gravity must be at least 1.220, temperature corrected, to deliver the necessary voltage to operate the cranking and ignition systems properly.
2. Disconnect wire from ignition coil negative terminal.
3. Remove coil wire from distributor cap.
4. With ignition switch in "On" position, and using jumper wire, **Fig. 1**, momentarily ground ignition coil negative terminal while holding coil wire 1/4 inch from a good engine ground. A spark should be observed.
5. If spark was obtained, proceed to step 8. If not, turn ignition Off, then disconnect 10-wire electrical connector at Spark Control Computer. **Do not remove grease from harness connector or connector cavity since grease is used to prevent moisture from corroding the terminals. There must be at least 1/8 inch of grease on bottom of computer connector cavity. If not, apply a liberal amount of Mopar multi-purpose grease, part number 2932524 or equivalent over end of connector plug before installation.**
6. Turn ignition On, hold coil wire 1/4 inch from ground and momentarily ground coil negative terminal using jumper wire, **Fig. 1.** If spark is present, replace Spark Control Computer. If spark is not present, measure voltage at coil positive terminal using suitable voltmeter. Voltage reading should be within one volt of battery voltage.
7. If no voltage was obtained at coil positive terminal, check for open circuit between battery and coil and repair as necessary. If voltage was obtained, measure voltage at coil negative terminal. Reading should be within one volt of battery voltage. If no voltage is present or voltage is present but spark is not, replace coil.
8. If spark was obtained in step 5, but engine will not start, hold open carburetor switch with thin piece of paper and measure voltage at carburetor switch. Reading should be within 1 volt of battery voltage. If voltage reading is satisfactory, proceed to step 12. If no voltage is present, turn ignition Off, then disconnect 10-wire connector from Spark Control Computer.
9. Turn ignition On and measure voltage between connector cavity 2 and ground, **Fig. 2.** Reading should be within one volt of battery voltage. If not, check for continuity between battery and cavity 2 using ohmmeter. If continuity is not present, check for open circuit between battery and cavity 2 and repair as necessary.
10. If battery voltage is present in step 6, turn ignition Off and check continuity between carburetor switch and cavity 7 of 10 way connector. If continuity is not present, check for open circuit between cavity 7 and carburetor switch and repair as necessary.
11. If continuity is present in step 10, check continuity between cavity 10 and ground. If continuity is present, replace Spark Control Computer. If continuity is not present between cavity 10 and ground, check for damaged wiring or an open circuit and repair as necessary. If wiring is satisfactory, but engine will not start, proceed to step 12.

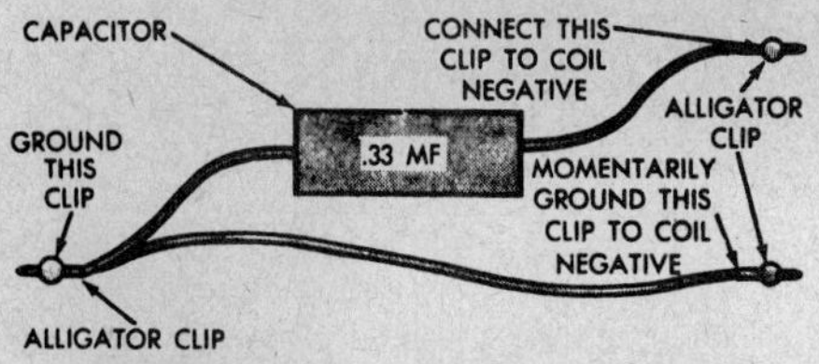

Fig. 1 Coil negative terminal jumper wire

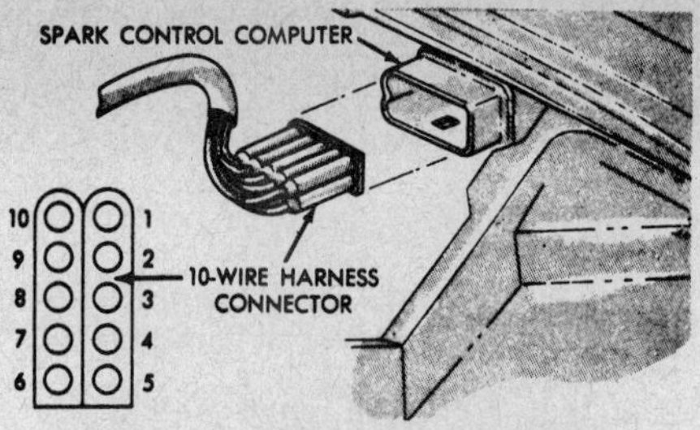

Fig. 2 Spark control computer 10-wire connector

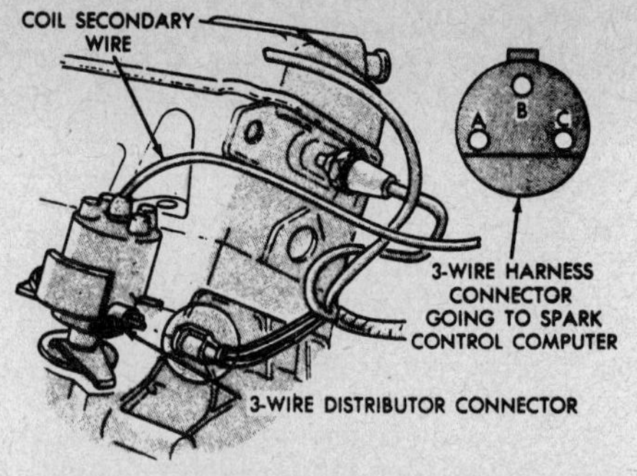

Fig. 3 Distributor 3-wire harness connector (Typical)

12. Reconnect 10-wire connector into Spark Control Computer, turn ignition On and hold coil wire 1/4 inch from ground. Disconnect distributor electrical connector and connect jumper wire between terminals A and C of connector, **Fig. 3.** Spark should be observed at coil wire.
13. If spark is present at coil wire, but engine will not start, replace pickup assembly and perform rotor test as described in step 19. **When replacing Hall effect pickup assembly, check to ensure rotor shutter blades are grounded, Fig. 4. Connect one lead of suitable ohmmeter to shutter blade and other lead to ground. If continuity is not present, press downward on rotor shaft and recheck continuity. If continuity is still not present, replace rotor. Check to ensure that new rotor is marked ESA on top. Do not start engine until continuity has been obtained.**
14. If no spark is present at coil wire check voltage between cavity B of distributor connector and ground, **Fig. 3.** Reading obtained should be within one volt of battery voltage. If battery voltage is not present, proceed to step 16. If battery voltage is present, turn ignition off and disconnect 10-way connector from Spark Advance Computer. Check for continuity between cavity C of distributor connector, **Fig. 3,** and cavity 9 of 10-way connector. Repeat procedure between cavity A of distributor connector and cavity 5 of 10-way connector.
15. If continuity is not present, open circuit exists in harness wiring. Repair as necessary. If continuity is present, replace Spark Advance Computer.
16. If no battery voltage is present at cavity B of distributor connector, turn ignition Off, then disconnect 10-wire connector from Spark Control Computer.
17. Check for continuity between cavity B of distributor connector and cavity 3 of 10-wire connector. If continuity is not present, repair open circuit in wire between cavities as necessary.
18. If continuity is present, turn ignition On and check for voltage between cavity 2 and 10 of 10-wire connector. If battery voltage is present, replace Spark Control Computer. If battery voltage is not present, check for proper computer ground circuit connection and repair as necessary.
19. To perform rotor test, check to ensure that rotor is stamped ESA on top. Turn ignition Off, then, using suitable ohmmeter, check for good rotor ground contact at distributor shaft. If continuity is indicated, rotor is satisfactory. If continuity is not indicated, check to ensure that rotor is properly seated on shaft.

POOR PERFORMANCE TESTS

CARBURETOR SWITCH TEST

Grounding the carburetor switch eliminates spark advance on most models. On models with feedback carburetor it also provides a fixed fuel/air ratio.

1. With ignition switch in "Off" position, disconnect 10-wire harness connector from "Spark Control Computer."
2. With throttle completely closed, check continuity between terminal 7 and the engine ground, **Fig. 2.** Continuity should exist. If not, check wiring and carburetor switch.
3. With throttle opened, check continuity between terminal 7 and the engine ground, **Fig. 2.** Continuity should not exist.

COOLANT SWITCH TEST

1982–83

1. With ignition switch in "Off" position, disconnect wire from coolant switch.
2. Check continuity between coolant switch terminal and the engine ground. The ohmmeter readings should be as follows: Engine cold, below 150°—Continuity should exist. If not, replace coolant switch. Engine hot, above 150°—No continuity should exist. If continuity exists, replace coolant switch.

COOLANT SENSOR TEST

1984–86

1. With ignition Off, disconnect coolant sensor electrical connector.
2. Connect ohmmeter leads to terminals of sensor.
3. With coolant sensor at room temperature (70°), the ohmmeter should read 5000-6000 ohms.
4. Replace coolant sensor if specifications cannot be obtained.

1987

1. With ignition Off, disconnect coolant sensor electrical connector.
2. Measure resistance between sensor terminals 1 and 2, **Fig. 5.**
3. The ohmmeter should indicate 10500-13000 ohms at approximately 70°F and 650-750 ohms at approximately 200°F.
4. Replace coolant sensor if resistance readings are not within specifications.

SPARK ADVANCE TEST

1. Run engine until normal operating temperature is reached, then disconnect carburetor switch electrical connector. Check to ensure that coolant sensor is operating as described in "Poor Performance Tests" under "Coolant Sensor Test," or "Coolant Switch Test."
2. Disconnect and plug vacuum transducer vacuum hose.
3. Apply 16 inches Hg vacuum from outside vacuum source to vacuum transducer.
4. Increase engine speed to 2000 RPM, wait one minute, then check amount of advance timing. Refer to "Front Wheel Drive Electronic Spark Control Specification Chart" for specification. **On certain models equipped with an accumulator, the accumulator must be allowed to time out with the carburetor switch disconnected before checking spark advance.**
5. If spark advance specifications cannot be obtained, replace Spark Control Computer.

BASIC ADVANCE TIMING TEST

1. Connect a suitable tachometer and adjustable timing light to engine.
2. Connect a jumper wire from carburetor switch to ground.
3. Set parking brake and start vehicle, then using the timing light adjustment feature, adjust timing light so specified timing mark is lined up with pointer.
4. The adjustable timing light meter should show amount of advance as shown in "Front Wheel Drive Electronic Spark Control Specification Chart."

DISTRIBUTOR SERVICE

REMOVAL

1.6 Liter Engines

1. Disconnect primary wiring connector at distributor, then remove splash shield from distributor.
2. Loosen distributor cap retaining screws, then remove distributor cap.
3. Rotate crankshaft until rotor is pointing in direction of engine block, then

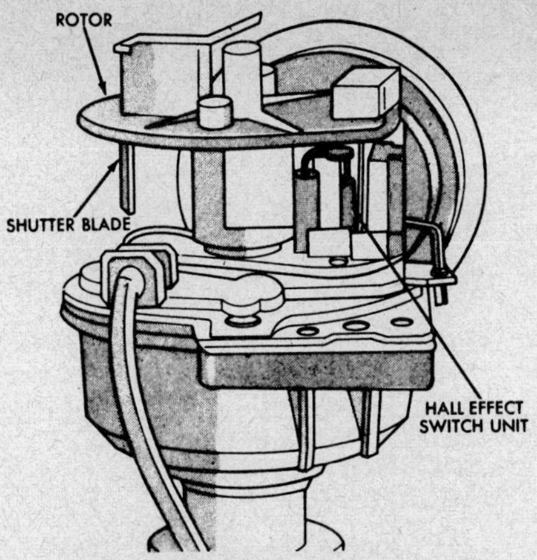

Fig. 4 Rotor shutter blades. Exc. 1986 2.2 & 2.5 liter engine

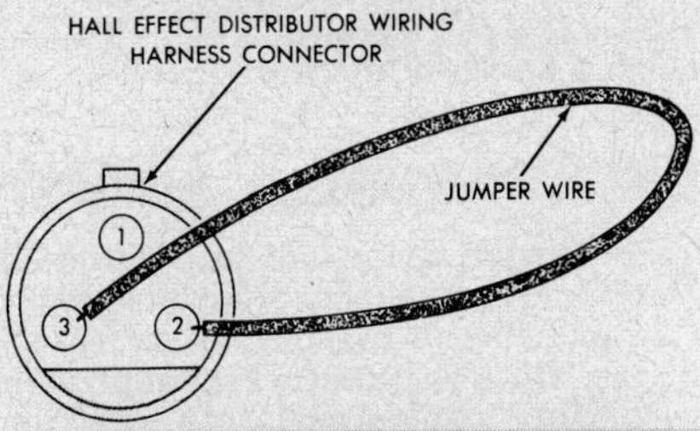

Fig. 5 Coolant sensor terminal identification. 1987

scribe a line on block to indicate rotor position during installation.

4. Remove distributor hold-down bolt, then carefully lift distributor from engine.

1.7, 2.2 & 2.5 Liter Engines

1. Disconnect primary wiring connector at distributor, then remove pickup coil lead retaining screw.
2. Remove splash shield from retaining screws, then remove shield.
3. On all models, loosen distributor cap retaining screws, then remove distributor cap.
4. Rotate crankshaft until rotor is pointing in direction of engine block, then scribe a line on block to indicate rotor position during installation.
5. Remove distributor hold-down bolt, then carefully lift distributor from engine.

INSTALLATION

1.6 Liter Engine

1. With gasket or O-ring installed on base of distributor, position distributor in engine.
2. Engage distributor drive with camshaft offset drive tang so distributor rotor will align with scribe mark made during removal.
3. If engine was cranked while distributor was removed, proceed as follows:
   a. Rotate crankshaft until No. 1 piston is at top dead center of compression stroke. The mark on crankshaft pulley should be aligned with "0" mark on timing cover.
   b. Rotate distributor rotor to a position ahead of No. 1 distributor cap terminal.
   c. Install distributor into engine, engaging distributor drive with camshaft offset drive tang. The rotor should be properly positioned under distributor cap No. 1 terminal.
4. Install distributor cap.
5. Install distributor hold-down screw finger tight.
6. Install splash shield, then connect primary wiring connector at distributor.
7. Adjust ignition timing. Refer to "Tune Up Specifications."

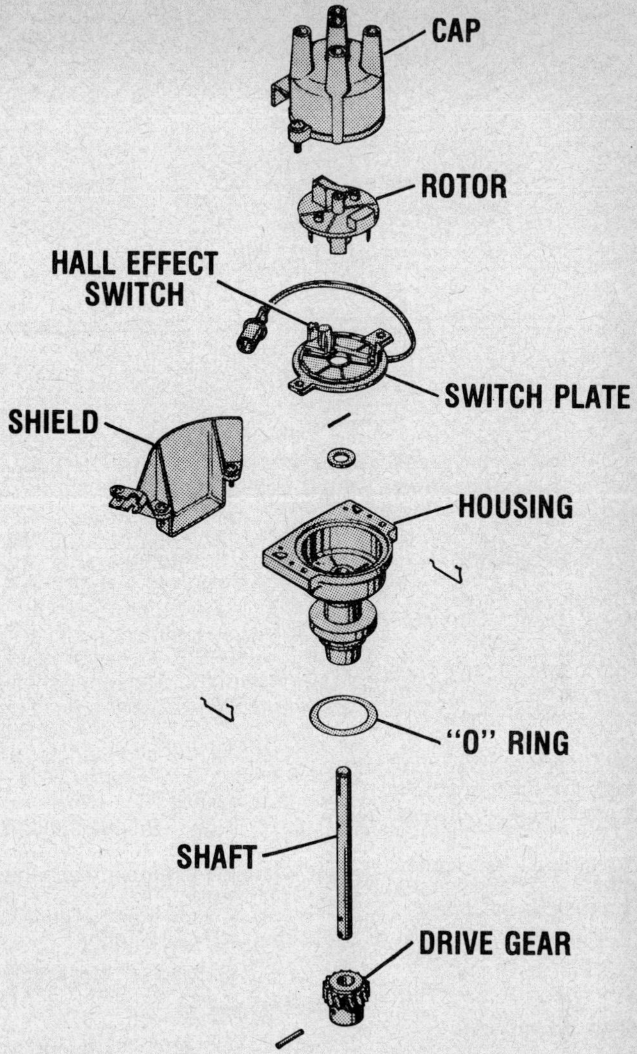

Fig. 6 Typical Hall Effect electronic ignition distributor

1.7, 2.2 & 2.5 Liter Engines

1. With gasket installed on base of distributor, position distributor into engine.
2. Engage distributor drive gear with camshaft drive gear so distributor rotor will align with scribe mark made during removal.
3. If engine was cranked while distributor was removed, proceed as follows:
   a. Rotate crankshaft until No. 1 piston is at top dead center of compression stroke. The pointer on clutch housing or bellhousing should align with "0" mark on flywheel.
   b. Rotate distributor rotor to a position ahead of No. 1 distributor cap terminal.
   c. Install distributor into engine, engaging distributor drive with camshaft drive gear. The rotor should be properly positioned under distributor cap No. 1 terminal.
4. Install distributor cap, then the distributor hold-down screw finger tight.
5. Install splash shield.
6. Connect primary wiring connector to distributor.
7. Install pickup coil lead retaining screw.
8. Adjust ignition timing. Refer to "Tune Up Specifications."

DISASSEMBLY

1.6 & 1.7 Liter Engines

1. Remove rotor from shaft, **Fig. 6.**
2. Remove Hall Effect Pickup Assembly lock springs and the pickup assembly.
3. Mark position of drive gear on distributor shaft.
4. Remove roll pin with a suitable punch.
5. Remove drive gear, then the distributor shaft from housing.
6. Remove nylon spacer from shaft.

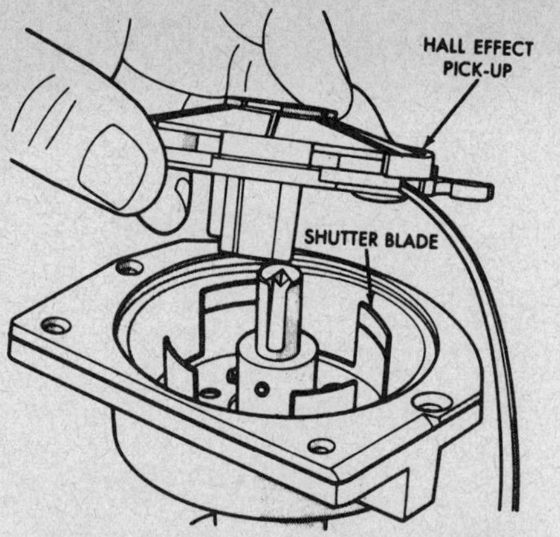

Fig. 7 Hall Effect pickup installation. 1986 2.2 & 2.5 engines

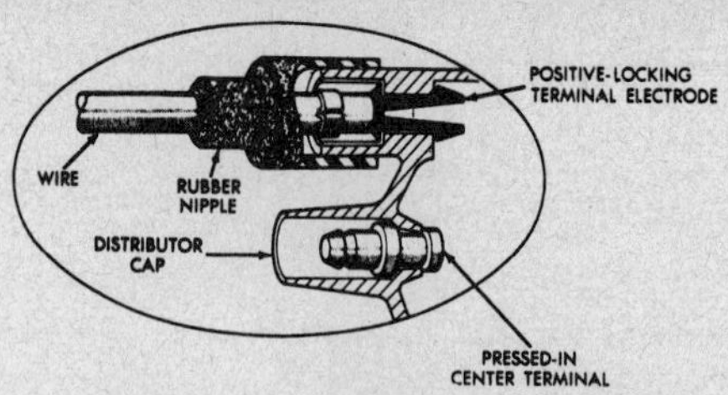

Fig. 8 Spark plug wire positive locking terminal electrode

2.2 & 2.5 Liter Engines

1. Remove rotor from shaft and disconnect pickup electrical connector on 1982-85 models.
2. On 1982-85 models, remove Hall effect pickup retaining clips. On 1986 models, pickup is held in place by cap retaining screws.
3. Remove Hall Effect Pickup Assembly.
4. Remove distributor drive gear roll pin using punch, then remove drive gear, **Fig. 6.**
5. Remove drive gear thrust washer and distributor shaft.
6. Remove distributor to block seal.

ASSEMBLY

1.6 & 1.7 Liter Engines

1. Lightly lubricate housing bushings with engine oil.
2. Install shaft into housing, ensuring nylon spacer is resting on housing bushing.
3. Install drive gear onto distributor shaft in original position, aligning mating marks.
4. Drive in roll pin.
5. Place Hall Effect Pick-Up Assembly into housing and secure with lock springs.
6. Install rotor onto shaft.

2.2 & 2.5 Liter Engines

1. Lubricate distributor housing bushings with engine oil, then install engine seal onto distributor housing.
2. Install distributor shaft thrust washer onto distributor shaft, then install shaft into distributor housing.
3. Install distributor drive gear thrust washer, then install distributor drive gear onto distributor shaft.
4. Install drive gear roll pin using punch.
5. On 1982-85 models, position Hall effect pickup in distributor and connect electrical connector, then install retaining clips.
6. On 1986-87 models, install Hall effect pickup, **Fig. 7,** ensuring that lead wire retainer is properly engaged in retaining slot.
7. Press rotor onto shaft, ensuring that rotor is fully seated.

SPARK PLUG WIRES, REPLACE

The coil wire and spark plug end of spark plug wires are replaced in a conventional manner. To replace distributor end of spark plug wires, use the following procedure.

1. Remove distributor cap.
2. Using a pair of suitable long nosed piers, remove spark plug wires from distributor cap by squeezing wire clips and pushing out, **Fig. 8. Do not remove spark plug wires from distributor cap unless nipples are damaged or cable testing indicates high resistance or broken insulation.**
3. Refer to **Fig. 8** for proper installation of spark plug wires. Ensure positive locking terminal electrode is fully seated in cap.

SERVICE NOTE

IGNITION TIMING, ADJUST

1. Connect a suitable tachometer to engine and a suitable adjustable timing light to No. 1 cylinder secondary cable. **Do not puncture ignition secondary cables or boots with test probes.**
2. Set parking brake, start engine and place gear selector in neutral. Run engine until warm.
3. On vehicles equipped with carburetor switch, connect a jumper wire between carburetor switch and a known good ground. Disconnect and plug vacuum line from transducer.
4. Ensure curb idle speed is set at or below specifications. Adjust as necessary.
5. Check ignition timing. If within $\pm 2^\circ$ of specifications, shut engine "Off" and remove timing light, tachometer and carburetor ground wire. If outside of tolerance, proceed to step 6.
6. Loosen distributor hold-down arm screw, rotate distributor housing until correct timing marks are lined up, ensuring idle speed is still at or below specified curb idle speed.
7. Tighten distributor hold-down screw, then recheck idle speed and ignition timing.
8. Turn engine "Off" and remove timing light, tachometer and carburetor ground wire.
9. Reconnect vacuum hose.

Rear Wheel Drive Less Electronic Spark Control

INDEX

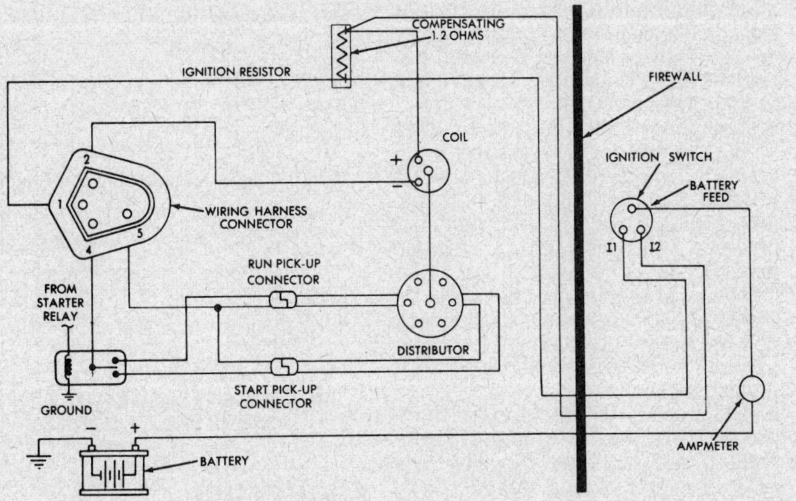

Fig. 1 Chrysler electronic ignition wiring

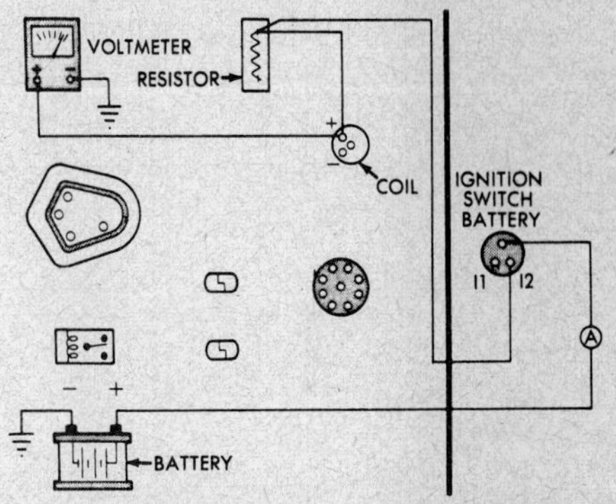

Fig. 2 Checking battery voltage at coil positive terminal

DESCRIPTION

This system, **Fig. 1,** is composed of a magnetic distributor, an electronic control unit, a wiring harness, a production coil and a single or dual ballast resistor.

The distributor is essentially the same as the conventional type except the contacts have been replaced by a pickup coil or coils and the cam by a reluctor. With a conventional contact type system, the voltage necessary to fire the spark plugs is developed by interrupting the current flowing through the primary circuit of the ignition coil by opening a set of contacts. With the Electronic System, the voltage is produced the same way except that the current is interrupted by a transistor in the electronic control unit. This happens each time the control unit receives a "timing" pulse from the distributor magnetic pickup(s).

Since the magnetic pickup(s), reluctor and the control unit, which replace the contact points and cam, do not normally change or wear out with service, engine timing and dwell do not require periodic adjusting. This minimizes regular ignition maintenance of cleaning and replacing the spark plugs.

TROUBLESHOOTING

ENGINE WILL NOT START—FUEL SYSTEM OK

1. Wiring harness electrical terminals covered with grease.
2. Faulty ballast resistor.
3. Faulty ignition coil.
4. Faulty pickup(s) or improper pickup air gap(s).
5. Faulty wiring.
6. Faulty control unit.

ENGINE SURGES SEVERELY—NOT LEAN CARBURETOR

1. Wiring.
2. Faulty pickup leads.
3. Ignition coil.

ENGINE MISSES—CARBURETION GOOD

1. Spark plugs.
2. Secondary cables.
3. Ignition coil.
4. Wiring.
5. Control unit.

SYSTEM TESTING

1982–84

To completely test components and circuits of the electronic ignition system, special testers should be used. However, in event the testers are not available, the following procedures may be utilized. A voltmeter with a 20,000 ohm/volt rating, and an ohmmeter with a 9 volt battery should be used for testing. Before performing any electrical tests, ensure all wiring is properly connected.

1. Visually check all spark plug cables and spark plugs for proper installation or damage.
2. Check for proper installation of primary ignition coil wire at coil terminals and at ballast resistor.
3. If above checks are satisfactory, check and record battery voltage.
4. Disconnect coil secondary lead from distributor cap. Turn ignition On, then momentarily ground negative terminal of coil using suitable jumper wire while holding coil secondary lead 1/4 inch from good ground. If no spark is observed, turn ignition Off, then disconnect four-wire electrical connector at electronic control unit. If spark is observed, proceed to step 10. **Before connecting or disconnecting the harness connector from the control unit, check to ensure that the ignition switch is in the Off position.**

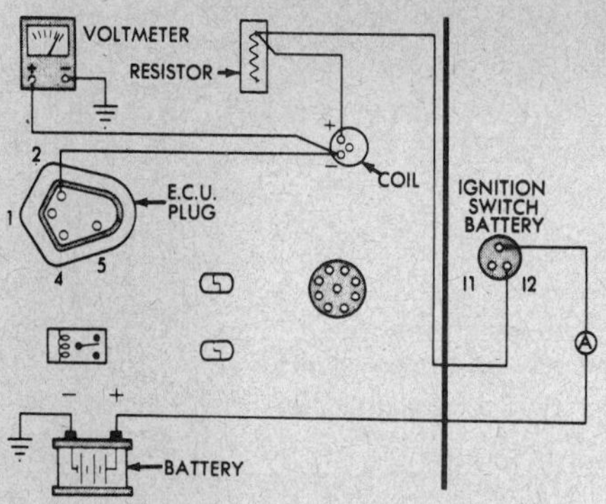

Fig. 3 Checking battery voltage at coil negative terminal

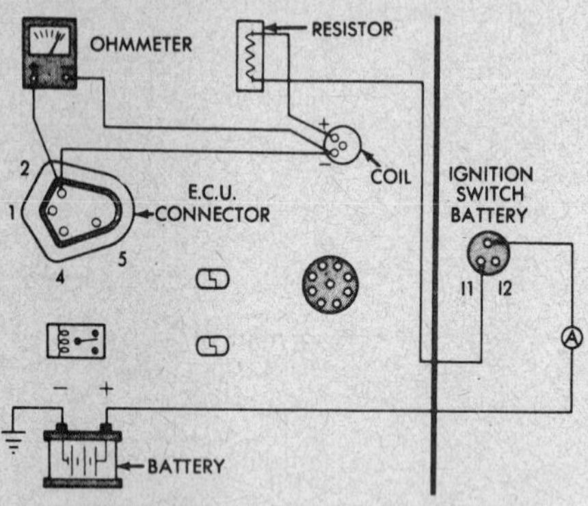

Fig. 5 Checking continuity between coil negative terminal and No. 2 cavity

5. Repeat step 4. If spark is observed, replace electronic control unit.
6. If no spark is observed, measure voltage at coil positive terminal. Reading obtained should be within one volt of previously recorded battery voltage.
7. If voltage reading is zero, replace starter relay and check wiring between battery positive terminal and coil, **Fig. 2.**
8. If voltage reading obtained in step 6 is not continuous, replace ignition resistor and repeat step 6.
9. Check battery voltage at coil negative terminal, **Fig. 3.** Reading obtained should be within one volt of battery voltage. If voltage reading is satisfactory, but no spark is observed when coil negative terminal is grounded, replace coil.
10. If spark was obtained in step 4 or step 9, but engine will not start, disconnect four-wire connector from electronic control unit (if not previously removed), then with ignition On, check for battery voltage at cavity 2 of ECU harness connector. Reading obtained should be within one volt of battery voltage, **Fig. 4.**
11. If voltage reading is not satisfactory, turn ignition Off, and check for continuity between cavity 2 and coil negative terminal using suitable ohmmeter, **Fig. 5.** If continuity is not present, check for damaged wiring or loose connections and repair as necessary.
12. If voltage reading in step 10 is satisfactory, check for battery voltage at cavity 2 of ECU connector. If battery voltage is not obtained, turn ignition Off and check for continuity between cavity 1 and ignition switch using suitable ohmmeter, **Fig. 6.** If continuity is not present, check for damaged wiring or loose connections and repair as necessary.
13. If battery voltage is obtained at cavity 2 of ECU connector, turn ignition Off and check resistance between cavities 4 and 5 of ECU harness connector using suitable ohmmeter, **Fig. 7.** Reading of 150-900 ohms should be obtained.
14. If reading is satisfactory, check wiring between cavities 4 and 5 for open or short circuit and repair as necessary. If wiring is satisfactory, check for proper operation of dual pickup start-run relay as described under "Dual Pickup Start-Run Relay Test."
15. If ohmmeter reading obtained in step 13 is not between 150-900 ohms, disconnect pickup leads and measure resistance at distributor side of pickup lead, **Fig. 8.** If reading obtained is not between 150-900 ohms, replace pickup coils as necessary.
16. Check for short circuit at each distributor side of pickup lead by connecting ohmmeter as indicated in **Fig. 9.** If ohmmeter indicates pickup is shorted, replace pickup coil.
17. If pickup coil is satisfactory, check for proper ECU ground contact by connecting ohmmeter between pin 5 of ECU and ground. If ohmmeter indicates poor ECU ground contact, check for proper ECU installation or poor ECU electrical connections.
18. If ECU is properly grounded, reconnect all electrical connections and check again for spark. If no spark is available, replace ECU.

Dual Pick-Up Start-Run Relay Test, 1982–84 Models

1. Disconnect two-way connector from pins 5 and 4 of dual pickup start-run relay, **Fig. 10.**
2. Connect suitable ohmmeter between pins 4 and 5 of relay.
3. If ohmmeter reading of 20-30 ohms cannot be obtained, replace relay.

DISTRIBUTOR SERVICE

DISTRIBUTOR, REPLACE

Removal

1. Disconnect vacuum line at distributor (if equipped).
2. Disconnect distributor pickup lead(s) at wiring harness connector, then remove distributor cap.
3. Mark position of rotor on distributor body and engine block surface so that distributor can be installed in the same position.
4. Remove hold-down and/or bolt and lift distributor from engine.

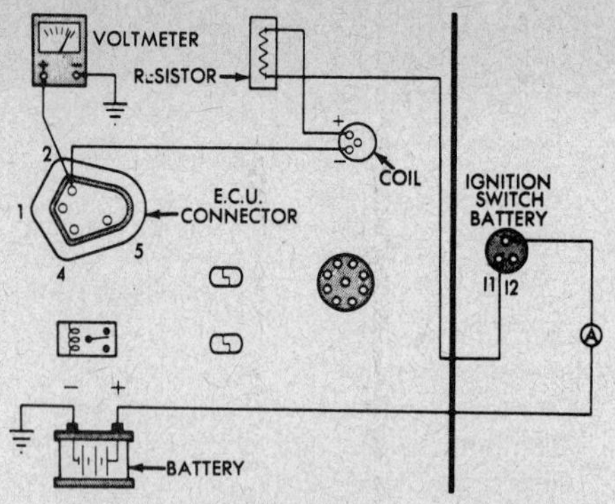

Fig. 4 Checking battery voltage at No. 2 cavity

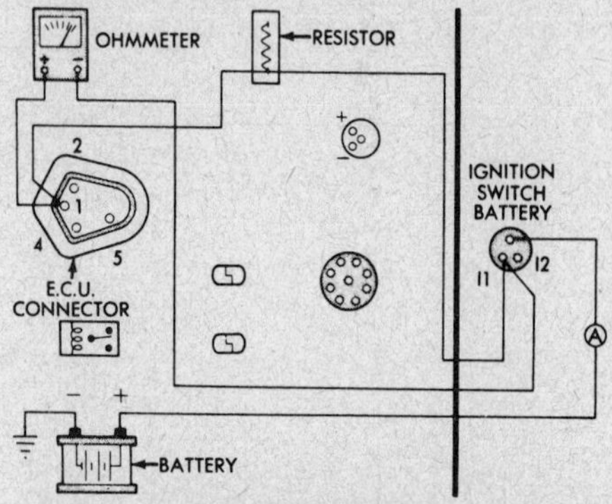

Fig. 6 Checking continuity between ignition switch and No. 1 cavity

Installation

1. If engine was cranked after distributor was removed from engine, rotate crankshaft to bring No. 1 piston up on its compression stroke and align timing mark on crankshaft pulley with "O" (TDC) mark on timing cover.
2. With distributor gasket or O-ring in place, hold distributor over mounting pad.
3. Turn rotor to a position just ahead of the No. 1 distributor cap terminal.
4. Install distributor, engaging distributor gear with camshaft drive gear on 6 cylinder engines. On V-8 engines, engage tang of distributor shaft with slot in oil pump drive gear. With distributor fully seated on engine, rotor should be under No. 1 cap terminal.
5. Install distributor hold-down and/or bolt, distributor cap, pickup lead(s) and vacuum line (if equipped).
6. Adjust ignition timing to specifications found in the individual car chapters.

DISTRIBUTOR SHAFT & BUSHING WEAR TEST

1. Remove distributor from vehicle and clamp distributor in a vise. Use extreme caution not to damage distributor.
2. Attach a dial indicator to housing so plunger rests against reluctor sleeve.
3. Place a wire loop around reluctor sleeve and hook a spring scale on the other end of the loop. Apply a one pound pull in line with indicator plung-

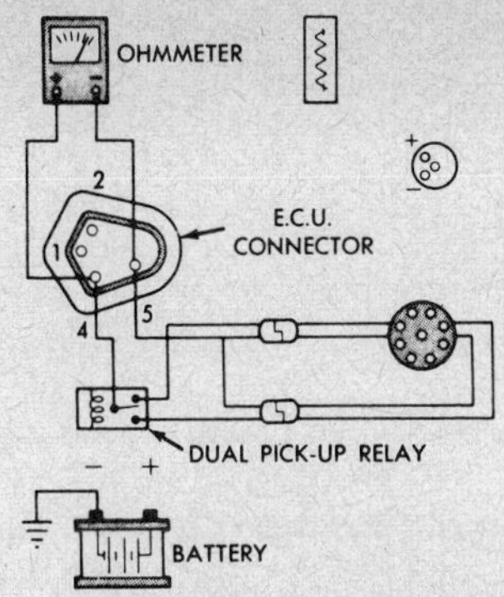

Fig. 7 Checking resistance between cavities No. 4 & 5

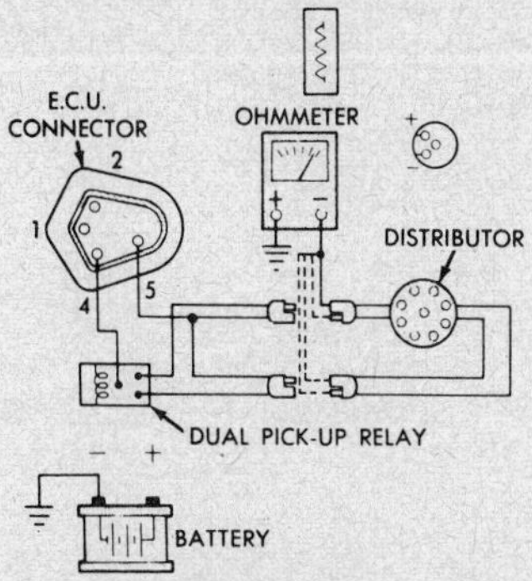

Fig. 9 Checking for short circuit at pickup coil terminal

er and read movement on indicator. Movement must not exceed .006 inch. If movement exceeds limit, replace either housing or shaft to bring movement back within tolerance.

DISTRIBUTOR DISASSEMBLE

1. Remove rotor and vacuum advance unit (if equipped), **Figs. 11 through 13.**
2. Remove reluctor by prying up from bottom of reluctor using two screwdrivers with a maximum blade width of 7/16 in. Use care not to damage or distort reluctor teeth.
3. Remove two screws and lockwashers attaching lower plate to distributor housing, then lift out lower plate, upper plate and pickup coil as an assembly. Do not remove distributor cap clamp springs.
4. On six cylinder units, if distributor housing, or shaft and governor assembly are to be replaced, proceed as follows:
   a. If gear is worn or damaged, scribe a line on end of shaft from center to edge, so that line is centered between two gear teeth, **Fig. 14.** Do not scribe line completely across shaft. Remove distributor drive gear retaining pin and slide gear off end of shaft. **Support hub of gear so that pin can be driven out without damaging shaft.**
   b. If necessary use a file to clean burrs from around pin hole area on shaft, then remove lower thrust washer.
   c. Push shaft upward and remove from distributor body.
5. On eight cylinder units, if distributor housing, shaft, reluctor sleeve or governor weights are to be replaced, proceed as follows:
   a. Remove distributor shaft retaining pin and slide retainer off end of shaft.
   b. If necessary, use a file to clean burrs from around pin hole area on shaft, then remove lower thrust washer.
   c. Push shaft upward and remove from distributor housing.

DISTRIBUTOR ASSEMBLE

1. Lubricate and test operation of governor weights. Inspect weight springs for distortion and bearing surfaces and pins for damage.
2. Lubricate upper thrust washer and install onto shaft. Install shaft into housing, **Figs. 11 through 13.**
3. On 6 cylinder units, install lower thrust washer and distributor gear and roll pin. If a replacement distributor gear is to be installed, proceed as follows:
   a. Install thrust washer and replacement gear on rotor shaft. Position pin hole in replacement gear approximately 90 degrees from hole in distributor shaft, with scribed line made during disassembly between gear teeth, **Fig. 14. On replacement distributor gears, the roll pin hole is located higher than the original gear roll pin hole, so that distributor shaft will not be weakened when the shaft is rotated 90 degrees and drilled to accommodate the replacement gear.**
   b. Before drilling through shaft and gear, place a .007 in. feeler gauge between gear and thrust washer and observe that center line between two gear teeth is in line with center line of rotor electrode, **Fig. 15.** Drill a .124 to .129 in. hole and install roll pin. **Support gear hub when installing roll pin so gear teeth will not be damaged.**
4. On eight cylinder units, install distributor shaft retainer and pin, **Fig. 15.**
5. On all units, install lower plate, upper plate and pickup coil assembly, **Figs. 11 through 13.**
6. Attach vacuum advance unit to pickup plate, then install vacuum advance unit attaching screws and washers (if equipped).
7. Position reluctor keeper pin into place on reluctor sleeve, then slide reluctor down reluctor sleeve and press firmly into position. Install keeper pin.
8. Lubricate felt pad located in top of reluctor sleeve with one drop of light engine oil, then install rotor.

PICKUP REPLACEMENT & AIR GAP ADJUSTMENT

1. With distributor removed from vehicle, perform Steps 1 to 3 as outlined in Distributor Disassemble.

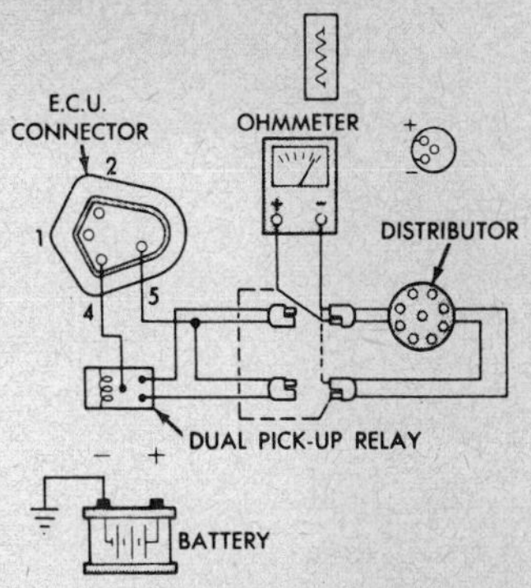

Fig. 8 Testing pickup coil resistance

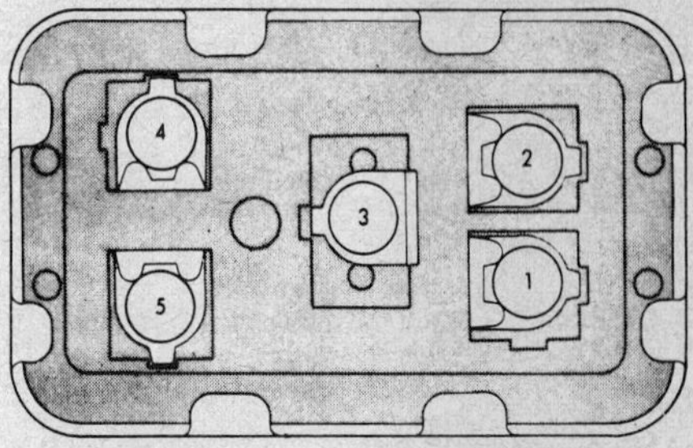

Fig. 10 Dual pickup start-run relay

2. Remove pickup coil and upper plate by depressing retainer clip and moving it away from mounting stud. Pickup coil cannot be removed from upper plate.
3. Lightly lubricate upper plate pivot pin and lower plate support pins with distributor lubricant. Install upper plate pivot pin through smallest hole in lower plate and install retainer clip. **The upper plate must ride on the support pins on the lower plate.**
4. Install lower and upper plates and pickup coil as an assembly and install distributor into vehicle. **On dual pickup distributors, the start pickup may be identified by a two prong male connector and the run pickup may be identified by a male-female plug, Fig. 16.**
5. To set air gap on all single pickup distributors and on start pickup of dual pickup distributors, align one reluctor tooth with pickup pole and install a .006 inch non-magnetic feeler gauge between reluctor tooth and pickup pole, **Figs. 16 and 17.** Rotate pickup coil until contact is made between reluctor tooth, feeler gauge and pickup pole. Tighten pickup coil hold-down screw and remove feeler gauge. The feeler gauge should be removed without force. If it cannot, readjust gap.
6. To set air gap on run pickup of dual pickup distributors, first adjust start pickup as described in step 5, then adjust run pickup as described in step 5. Use a .012 inch non-magnetic feeler gauge to adjust run pickup air gap.
7. Perform a second gap check using a .008 inch non-magnetic feeler gauge on all single pickup distributors and

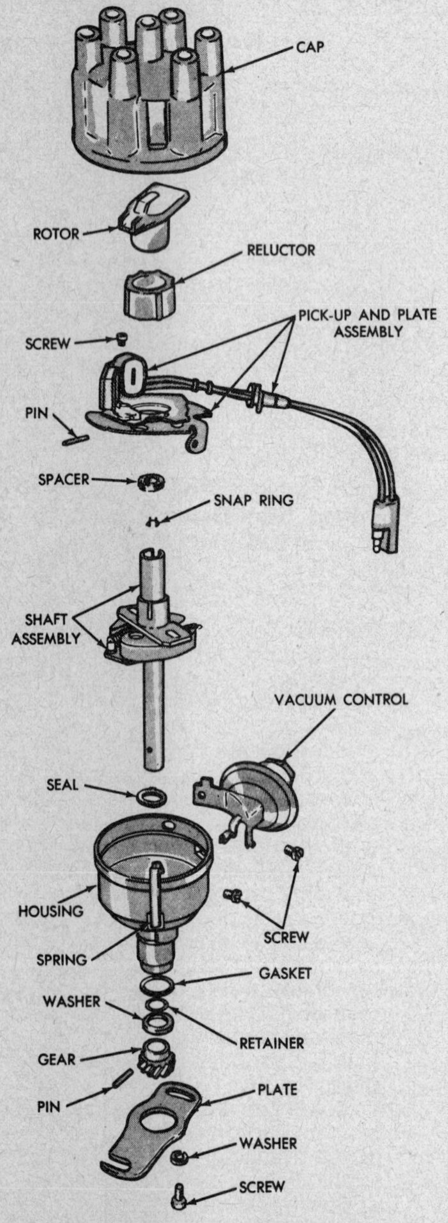

Fig. 11 Disassembled view of Chrysler 6 cylinder engine electronic distributor with single pickup (typical)

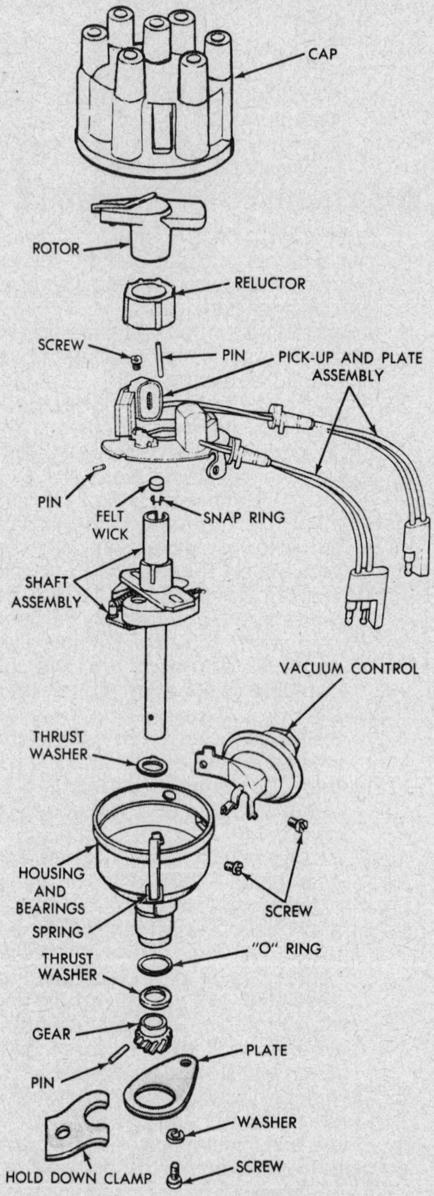

Fig. 12 Disassembled view of Chrysler 6 cylinder engine electronic distributor with dual pickup (typical)

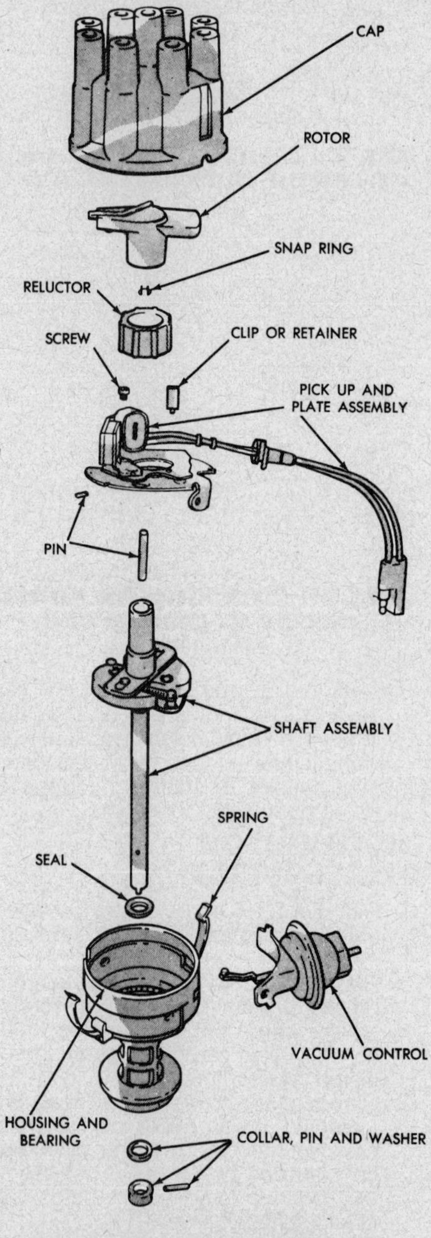

Fig. 13 Disassembled view of Chrysler 8 cylinder engine electronic distributor (typical)

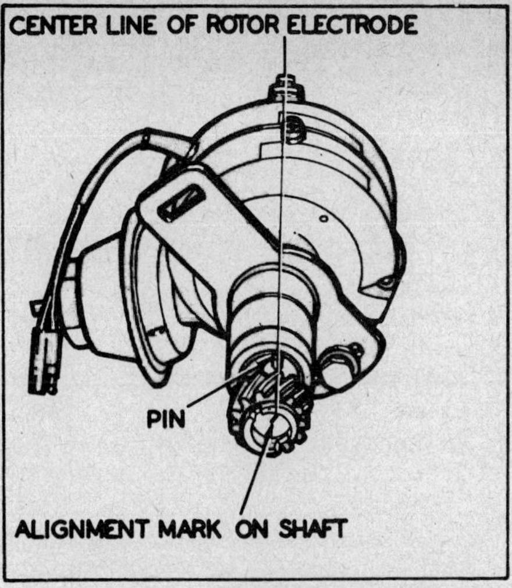

Fig. 14 Scribe line on distributor shaft. 6 cylinder units

on start pickup of dual pickup distributor or a .014 inch non-magnetic feeler gauge on run pickup of dual pickup distributors. Do not force feeler gauge between reluctor tooth and pickup pole as it is possible to do so. The feeler gauge should not be able to fit between the reluctor tooth and pickup pole if air gap is correctly set. Apply vacuum to vacuum control unit (if equipped). Pickup should not contact reluctor tooth. Readjust air gap if contact occurs. **If pickup contacts reluctor teeth on one side of shaft only, the distributor shaft is most likely bent and shaft replacement required.**

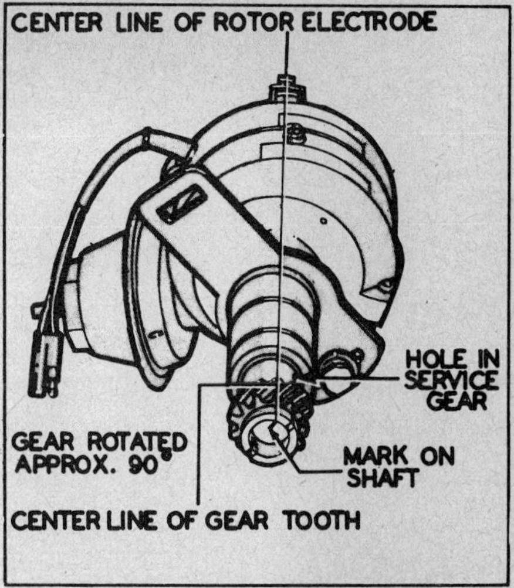

Fig. 15 Aligning gear teeth with center line of rotor electrode. 6 cylinder units

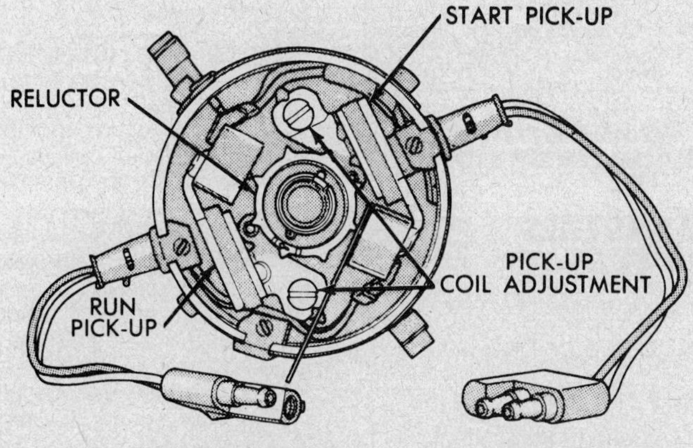

Fig. 16 Air gap adjustment. Distributors equipped with dual pickup

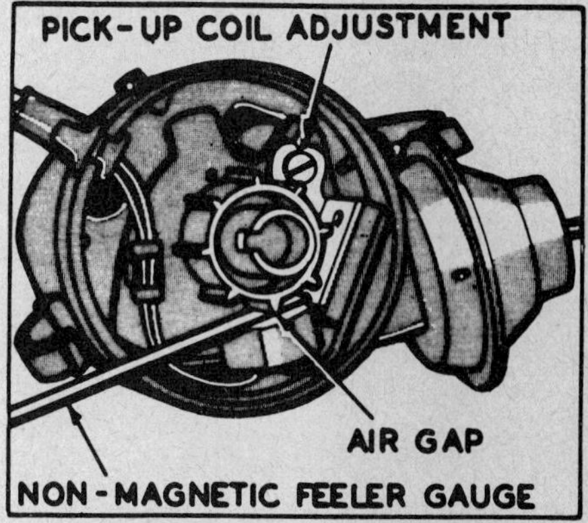

Fig. 17 Air gap adjustment. Distributors equipped with single pickup

Rear Wheel Drive w/Electronic Spark Control

INDEX

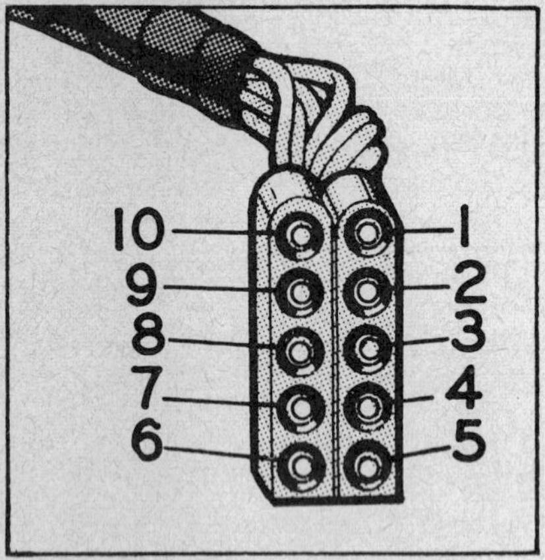

Fig. 1 Dual connector

SYSTEM TESTING

BASIC IGNITION TIMING, ADJUST

1. Connect a suitable tachometer to engine and a suitable adjustable timing light to No. 1 cylinder secondary cable. **Do not puncture ignition secondary cables or boots with test probes.**
2. Set parking brake, start engine and place gear selector in neutral. Run engine until warm.
3. On vehicles equipped with carburetor switch, connect a jumper wire between carburetor switch and a known good ground.
4. Ensure curb idle speed is set at or below specifications. Adjust as necessary.
5. Check ignition timing. If within ± 2° of specifications, shut engine "Off" and remove timing light, tachometer and carburetor ground wire. If outside of tolerance, proceed to step 6.
6. Loosen distributor hold-down arm screw, rotate distributor housing until correct timing marks are lined up, ensuring idle speed is still at or below specified curb idle speed.
7. Tighten distributor hold-down screw, then recheck idle speed and ignition timing.
8. Turn engine "Off" and remove timing light, tachometer and carburetor ground wire.

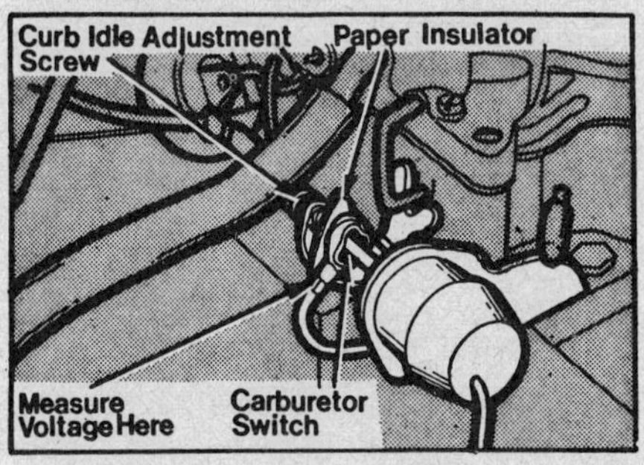

Fig. 2 Power & vacuum transducer tests

IGNITION SYSTEM STARTING TEST

Prior to testing the ignition system, ensure battery is fully charged. Make a note of battery voltage to be used during testing procedures.

1. Remove the coil wire from distributor cap and hold end of wire about 1/4 in. from a good engine ground. Turn ignition "On," then intermittently jump coil negative terminal to a good ground while observing coil wire.
2. The spark at the coil wire must be constant and bright blue. If spark is satisfactory, intermittently jump coil negative terminal while slowly moving coil wire end away from ground. If arcing occurs at the coil tower, replace coil. If spark is weak or not constant or there is no spark, proceed to the "Failure To Start Test."
3. If spark is satisfactory and no arcing occurs at coil tower, the ignition system is producing the necessary high secondary voltage. However, ensure this voltage is transmitted to the spark plugs by checking the distributor rotor, cap, spark plug wires, and spark plugs. If satisfactory, the ignition system is not faulty. It will be necessary to check the fuel system and engine mechanical components.

FAILURE TO START TEST

Before proceeding with this test, perform "Ignition System Starting Test." Failure to do so may lead to unnecessary diagnostic time and incorrect test results.

1. Turn ignition "Off." Remove 10-way connector from base of Spark Control

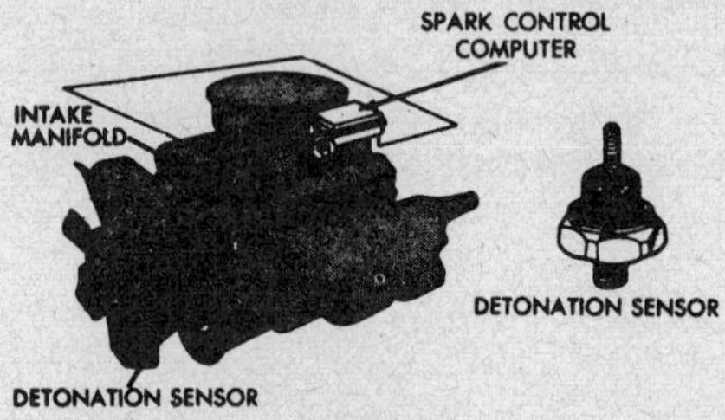

Fig. 3 Detonation sensor location

Computer. Turn ignition "On," then holding end of coil wire about 1/4 inch away from a ground, momentarily short coil negative wire to ground. If a spark is obtained, replace Spark Control Computer. If no spark is obtained, proceed to step 2.
2. Using a voltmeter, check for battery voltage at coil positive terminal with the ignition "On." If voltage is within 1 volt of battery voltage, proceed to step 4. If not, proceed to step 3.
3. Check continuity of wiring between battery and coil positive, repair as necessary and repeat step 2.
4. Using a voltmeter, check for battery voltage at coil negative. If within 1 volt of battery voltage, proceed to step 5. If not, replace coil.
5. If voltage is correct, but no spark is obtained when grounding coil negative, replace coil.
6. If spark is obtained, but engine will not start, place ignition switch in "On" position. Using a suitable voltmeter, measure voltage of disconnected 10-way connector cavity 1, **Fig. 1**, to ground. Voltage should be within 1 volt of battery voltage. If voltage is within 1 volt of battery voltage, proceed to step 8. If not, proceed to step 7.
7. Check wire for opens and repair as necessary (no power between coil negative and 10 way connector). Repeat step 6.
8. Place a piece of paper between curb idle adjusting screw and carburetor switch, **Fig. 2**, or ensure curb idle adjusting screw is not contacting carburetor switch.
9. Connect negative lead of voltmeter to a good engine ground.
10. Rotate ignition switch to "On" position and measure voltage at carburetor

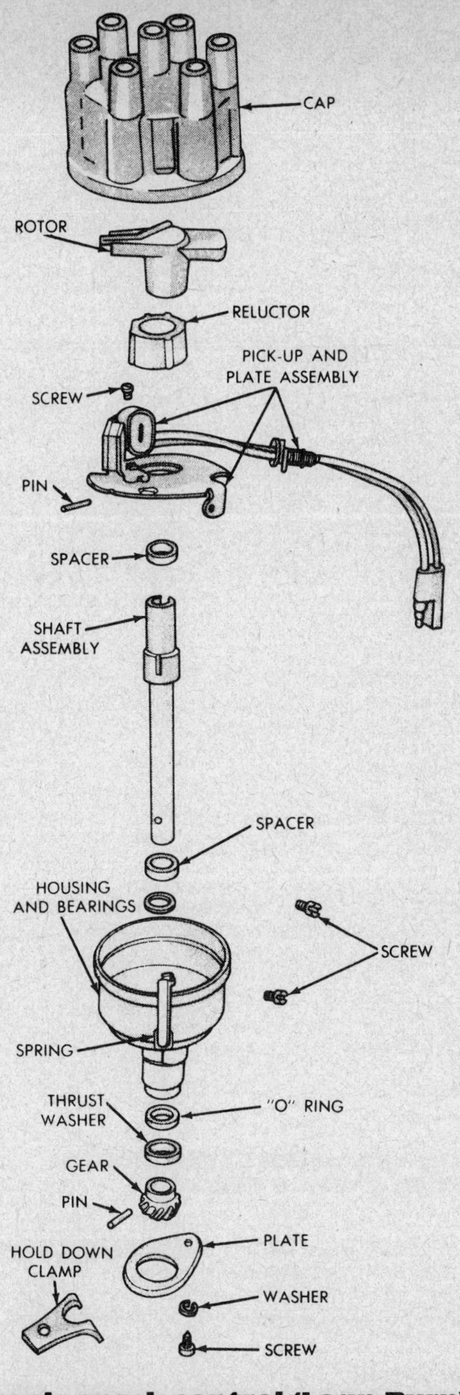

Fig. 4 Electronic spark control (Lean Burn) distributor with single pickup exploded view. 6 cylinder

switch terminal. If voltage is approximately 5 volts, proceed to step 12. If voltage is not at least 5 volts, place ignition switch in "Off" position and disconnect wire connector from bottom of Spark Control Computer, **Fig. 1.** Rotate ignition switch back to the "On" position and measure voltage at wire connector terminal 2, **Fig. 1.** Voltage should be within one volt of battery voltage noted previously. If voltage is correct proceed to step 11. If voltage is incorrect check wiring between wire terminal 2 and ignition switch for open or short circuits or improper connections.

11. With ignition switch in the "Off" position, disconnect wire connector from Spark Control Computer. Using an ohmmeter, check for continuity between connector terminal 7, **Fig. 1**, and carburetor switch terminal. Continuity should exist between these two points. If not, check wiring for open or short circuit or improper connections. If continuity is noted, check for continuity between connector terminal 10 and engine ground. If continuity exists, replace Spark Control Computer. If not, check wiring for open circuit or improper connections and proceed to step 12 only if engine still fails to start.
12. Place ignition switch in the "Off" position, then, using an ohmmeter, measure resistance between terminals No. 5 and 9 for run pickup coil and terminals 3 and 9 for start pickup coil **Fig. 1.** Resistance should be between 150 and 900 ohms. If not, disconnect pickup coil leads from distributor and measure resistance at lead going into distributor. If resistance is now between 150 and 900 ohms, this would indicate an open or short circuit or improper connection between distributor connector and terminals 5 and 9 or terminals 3 and 9 of dual connector. If resistance is not within specifications, pickup coil is defective.
13. Connect one ohmmeter lead to engine ground and with the other lead check for continuity at each terminal going to the distributor. There should be no continuity. Reconnect distributor lead and proceed to step 14. If there is continuity, replace pickup coil.
14. Remove distributor cap and check air gap of pickup coil. Refer to Pick-up Coil Replacement and Air Gap Adjustment and adjust gap as necessary.
15. Install distributor cap and reconnect all wiring, then start engine. If engine fails to start, replace spark control computer.
16. After installing new computer and engine still fails to start, reinstall original computer and repeat test procedure since one of the test procedures may have been performed incorrectly.

COMPONENT TESTING

CHARGE TEMPERATURE & COOLANT SWITCH TEST

Turn ignition Off, then connect suitable ohmmeter between center terminal of temperature switch and ground for coolant temperature switch and ground for coolant temperature switch or between center terminal and ground terminal of charge temperature switch.

With engine cold, continuity should be present with resistance less than 100 ohms. If not, replace switch. Charge temperature switch must be cooler than 60°F in order to perform test properly.

With engine hot, terminal reading should show no continuity. If continuity is present, replace coolant switch.

DETONATION SENSOR TEST

1. Connect a suitable timing light to engine.
2. Set parking brake. Start engine and position throttle on second step of fast idle cam (at least 1200 RPM).
3. Using a suitable hand operated vacuum pump, apply 16 inch of vacuum to Spark Control Computer transducer.
4. Using a small metal object, tap lightly on the intake manifold near the detonation sensor, **Fig. 3.** At the same time, using the timing light, look for a decrease in spark advance at the timing marks. The decrease is proportional to the strength and frequency of

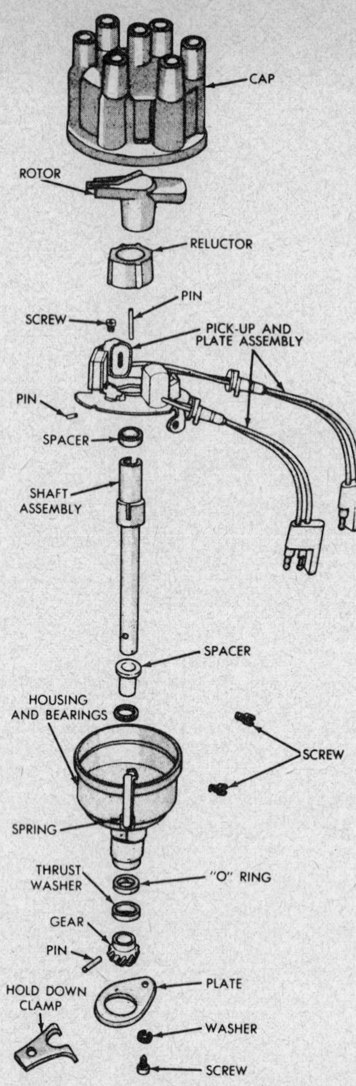

Fig. 5 Electronic spark control (Lean Burn) distributor with dual pickup exploded view. 6 cylinder

the tapping. 11° is the maximum timing decrease.

5. Kick engine down to normal idle speed and turn ignition "Off." Remove timing light and vacuum pump.

COOLANT SENSOR TEST

1. Connect ohmmeter to terminals of coolant sensor.
2. With engine cold and ambient temperature less than 90°F, resistance should be 500-1000 ohms.
3. With engine at normal operating temperature, resistance should be greater than 1300 ohms.
4. If resistance is not as specified, replace sensor.

SPARK ADVANCE COMPUTER ADVANCE TEST

1. Ensure engine is fully warmed up and the temperature sensor is connected and operating properly.
2. Set ignition timing to specifications.
3. Place a piece of paper between curb idle adjusting screw and carburetor switch, **Fig. 2**, or ensure curb idle adjusting screw is not contacting carburetor switch.
4. Remove and plug vacuum transducer line.
5. Using a suitable hand operated vacuum pump, apply 16 inch of vacuum to Spark Control Computer transducer on all 8 cylinder models. On all 6 cylinder models, apply 10 inch of vacuum to Spark Control Computer transducer.
6. Increase engine speed to specifications, wait 1 minute (or specified clock up time, see specifications). Advance specifications are in addition to basic timing advance. On systems equipped with an accumulator the specified time must be reached with the carburetor switch ungrounded before checking the specified spark advance schedule (see Specifications).
7. If the computer fails to obtain specified settings, replace computer.

CARBURETOR SWITCH TEST

On most systems, grounding the carburetor switch eliminates all spark advance.

1. Turn ignition Off, then disconnect 10-way connector from computer.
2. Check to ensure throttle is fully closed, then check continuity between pin 7 of harness connector and ground using suitable ohmmeter, **Fig. 1.**
3. If continuity is not present, check for open circuit in carburetor switch wiring circuit and repair as necessary.
4. Open throttle and check continuity between pin 7 of harness connector and ground. Continuity should not be present.

EGR SYSTEM TEST

The electronic EGR control is incorporated into the Spark Control Computer on all models. On 1982 6 cylinder non-California models, the EGR time delay is located in a cowl mounted timer. On

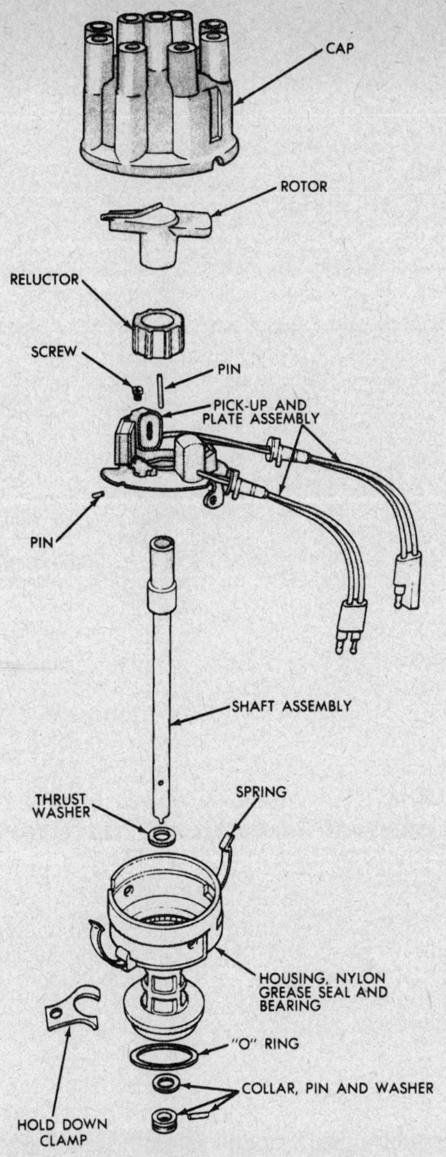

Fig. 6 Electronic spark control (Lean Burn) distributor with dual pickup exploded view. 8 cylinder

1982-84 8 cylinder models, 1982 6 cylinder California models and all 1983 6 cylinder models, the time delay is integral with the Spark Control Computer. Before proceeding with test, ensure engine temperature sensors are operating properly.

1. With engine cold and ignition Off, connect one lead of suitable voltmeter to gray wire terminal on EGR solenoid. Connect second voltmeter lead to ground.
2. Start engine and check voltmeter reading. Reading should be less than one volt. Reading will remain at this value until engine reaches normal operating temperature and electronic EGR schedule has timed out. EGR Solenoid will then de-energize and voltmeter will indicate charging system voltage.
3. If system does not de-energize in specified amount of time, replace solenoid.
4. If voltmeter indicates charging system voltage before EGR schedule is complete, replace Spark Control Computer or cowl mounted timer as necessary. **All 1982-84 V8-318 non-California models equipped with 2 barrel carburetors have no thermal delay at ambient temperatures below 60°F. This engine will operate according to EGR time delay schedule only. Refer to Chrysler Electronic Spark Control Specification Chart for delay schedules.**
5. If an engine is started warm, the EGR solenoid will be energized for the duration of time delay schedule only. It will then de-energize.

ELECTRONIC THROTTLE CONTROL TEST

1982–84

The electronic throttle control system is incorporated in the Spark Control Computer on 8 cylinder models and all 6 cylinder California models. On 1982 6 cylinder models except California and all 1983 6 cylinder models, the electronic throttle control utilizes two cowl mounted timers. A carburetor mounted solenoid is energized whenever the air conditioner, electronic heated backlite or electronic timers are activated. The timers operate with a two second delay after the throttle is closed or with an EGR time delay after an engine start condition.

1. Connect tachometer to engine, then start engine and run until operating temperature is reached.
2. Depress accelerator, then release. Curb idle speed should increase for length of time of EGR schedule.
3. Curb idle speed should increase when air conditioner, and/or electronic heated backlite are operated and return to normal when components are turned Off. **Air conditioner clutch will cycle on and off as air conditioner operates and should not be mistaken as part of electronic control system operation.**
4. If curb idle speed does not increase and decrease as described above, disconnect three-way electrical connector from carburetor.
5. Connect ohmmeter between carburetor solenoid black wire terminal and ground. Resistance should be 15-35 ohms. If not, replace solenoid.
6. Start engine and measure voltage between black wire of three-way connector and ground before time delay has timed out. Voltmeter reading should indicate charging system voltage. If not, replace Spark Control Computer or cowl mounted gray start timer as necessary.
7. With engine operating and voltmeter connected as described in step 6, turn on air conditioner and/or electronic heated backlite. Voltmeter should read charging system voltage after time delay has timed out. If not, check wiring between three-way harness connector and instrument panel for damage and repair as necessary.

DISTRIBUTOR REPLACE

Refer to "Rear Wheel Drive Models Less Electronic Spark Control" for distributor replacement procedure.

DISTRIBUTOR SERVICE

DISASSEMBLY

1. Remove rotor. If necessary, use two screwdrivers under upper part of rotor to pry off, **Figs. 4 through 7.**
2. Remove reluctor by prying up from bottom of reluctor with two screwdrivers (7/16 inch maximum width of screwdrivers). Use care not to distort or damage reluctor teeth.
3. Remove the two screws retaining plate to housing and lift out the plate and pickup coil as an assembly. **The distributor clamp springs are held in place by peened metal around**

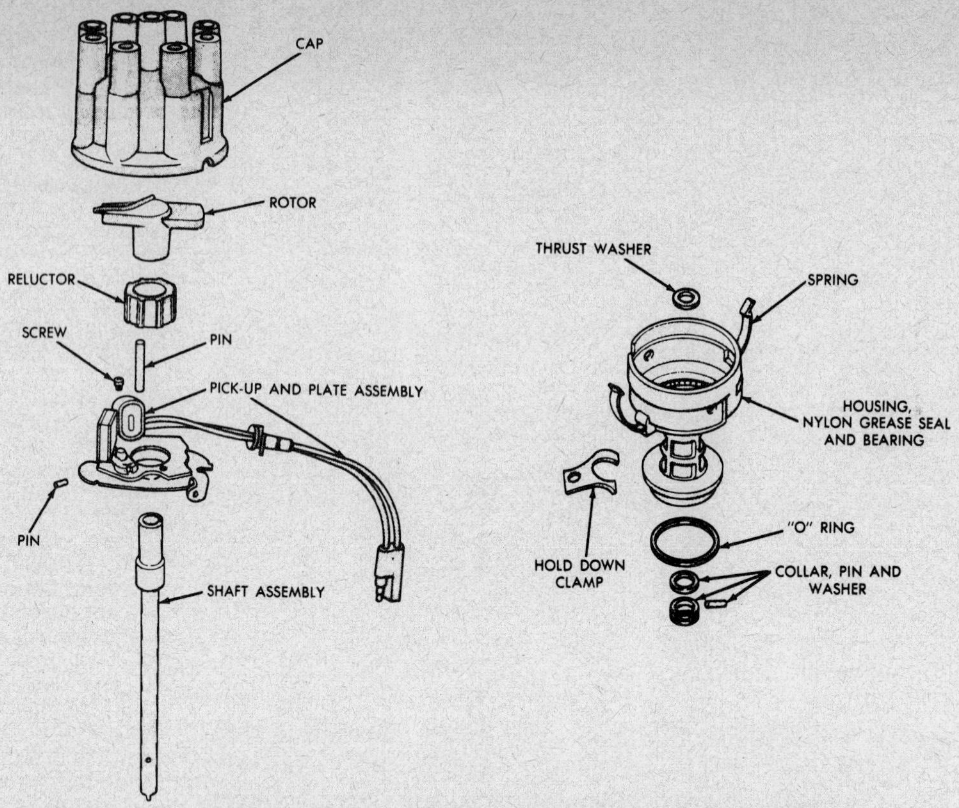

Fig. 7 Electronic spark control (Lean Burn) distributor exploded view. Electronic Fuel Injection

the openings and should not be removed.

4. On 6 cylinder distributors, refer to "Rear Wheel Drive Models W/Electronic Ignition System" for procedures.
5. On V8 distributors, refer to "Rear Wheel Drive Models Less Electronic Spark Control System" and perform the "Distributor Shaft & Bushing Wear Test." If side play exceeds .006 inch, replace housing shaft and reluctor sleeve as follows:
   a. Remove distributor shaft retaining pin and slide retainer off end of shaft.
   b. Using a file, clean burrs from around pin hole in shaft and remove lower thrust washer.
   c. Push shaft up and remove through top of distributor body.

ASSEMBLY

1. Lubricate and install upper thrust washer(s) on shaft and slide shaft into distributor body.
2. Install distributor shaft retainer and pin, **Figs. 4 through 7.**
3. Install plate and pickup coil assembly and retaining screws.
4. Position reluctor keeper pin into position on reluctor sleeve.
5. Slide reluctor down reluctor sleeve and press firmly into place, then install keeper pin.

PICKUP REPLACEMENT & AIR GAP ADJUSTMENT

For pickup replacement and/or pickup air gap adjustment, refer to "Rear Wheel Drive Less Electronic Spark Control" for procedures.

CARBURETORS

TABLE OF CONTENTS

Carter Model BBD 2 Barrel Carburetor

INDEX

ADJUSTMENT SPECIFICATIONS

Year	Carb. Model	Float Level	Pump Travel Inch	Choke Unloader Clearance	Choke Vacuum Kick Clearance	Fast Idle Cam Position Clearance
1982	8291S	1/4	1/2 ①	.280	.130	.070
1983	8291S	1/4	15/32 ①	.280	.130	.070
1984	8385S	1/4	15/32 ①	.280	.130	.070

①—At idle.

IDENTIFICATION LOCATION

The location of the carburetor identification depends on the year and type of carburetor. On all 1982-83 models less Electronic Feedback Carburetor System, the carburetor identification is located on an identification tag that is attached to the carburetor by one of the cover hold-down bolts. On 1984 models less Electronic Feedback Carburetor System, the identification number is stamped on the carburetor near the bowl vent nipple. On all models with Electronic Feedback Carburetor System, the identification number is stamped on the step-up piston cover plate.

DESCRIPTION

The Carter model BBD dual venturi carburetor, **Figs. 1 thru 4,** uses three basic fuel metering systems. An idle system provides the mixture for idle and low speed performance, the accelerator pump system provides additional fuel during acceleration and the main metering system provides an economical mixture for normal cruising conditions.

In addition to the three basic metering systems, there is a fuel inlet system that constantly supplies fuel to the basic metering systems and a choke system with electric assist that temporarily enriches the mixture to aid in starting or running a cold engine.

All BBD model carburetors have an EGR vacuum port because the EGR system is controlled by the venturi vacuum control system. Carburetors used with an Electronic Feedback Carburetor System have various components to enable a computer to help control the air/fuel ratio.

ON-VEHICLE ADJUSTMENTS

CURB IDLE SPEED

1. Disconnect and plug vacuum hose at EGR valve, distributor or carburetor, if equipped.
2. On models equipped with carburetor ground switch, connect jumper wire between switch and ground.
3. On models not equipped with spark control computer (SCC), disconnect and plug vacuum hose from carburetor at heated air temperature sensor and orifice spark advance control valve (OSAC), if equipped.
4. On all, models, disconnect and plug control hose at canister.
5. Remove PCV valve from cylinder head cover and allow to draw underhood air.
6. Connect tachometer, then start engine and allow to reach normal operating temperature.
7. Adjust Solenoid Idle Stop, if equipped, as follows:
   a. On models with A/C, turn on A/C and set blower on low, then disconnect A/C clutch wire.
   b. On models less A/C, connect jumper wire between battery positive terminal and the SIS lead wire. **Ensure correct jumper wire installation. Applying battery voltage to other than correct wire will damage the wiring harness.**
   c. On all models, open throttle slightly to allow solenoid plunger to extend.

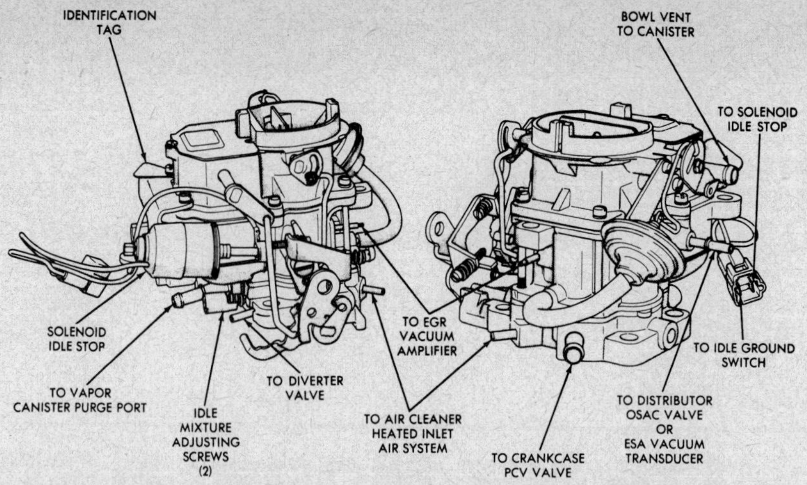

Fig. 1 BBD carburetor assembly. 1982–83 units less Electronic Feedback Carburetor System (Typical)

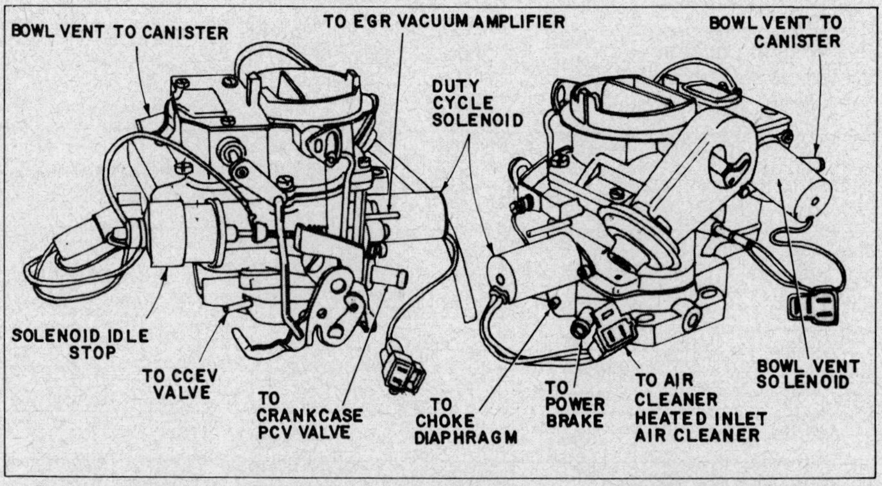

Fig. 2 BBD carburetor assembly. 1982–83 units with Electronic Feedback Carburetor System (Typical)

d. Turn adjusting screw on throttle lever to obtain 850 RPM.
e. Turn off A/C and reconnect clutch wire or remove jumper, if equipped.

8. On models equipped with oxygen sensor feedback, disconnect electrical connector from oxygen sensor and ground connector.
9. Remove and plug vacuum hose at vacuum transducer on SCC, then install suitable vacuum pump to vacuum transducer and apply 16 inches of vacuum.
10. Allow engine to run for two minutes. If idle is not as specified, turn adjusting screw on solenoid to obtain correct RPM.
11. On models not equipped with oxygen sensor feedback, allow engine to run for one minute.
12. If idle RPM is not as specified, turn idle speed screw to obtain correct RPM.
13. On all models, turn off engine, connect vacuum lines and remove tachometer. Remove jumper wire and connect oxygen sensor electrical connector, if equipped. **After step 13 has been completed, idle speed may change slightly. This condition is normal and engine speed should not be readjusted.**

FAST IDLE SPEED

1982–84

1. Disconnect and plug vacuum hose at EGR valve and distributor, if equipped.
2. On models equipped with carburetor ground switch, connect jumper wire between switch and ground.
3. On models not equipped with spark control computer (SCC), disconnect and plug vacuum hose from carburetor at heated air temperature sensor.
4. On all models, disconnect and plug control hose at canister.
5. Remove PCV valve from cylinder head cover and allow to draw underhood air.
6. Connect tachometer, then start engine and allow to reach normal operating temperature.
7. On models equipped with oxygen sensor feedback, disconnect electrical connector from oxygen sensor and ground connector, then allow engine to run for two minutes.
8. On models not equipped with oxygen sensor feedback, allow engine to run for one minute.
9. On all models, open throttle slightly and position fast idle adjusting screw on second highest step of fast idle cam.
10. Open choke fully, then adjust fast idle speed screw to obtain specified RPM.
11. Return to idle, then reposition adjusting screw on second highest step of fast idle cam to ensure correct RPM. Repeat adjustment if necessary.
12. Turn off engine, then connect vacuum hoses and remove tachometer. Remove jumper wire and connect oxygen sensor electrical connector, if equipped. **After step 12 has been completed, idle speed may change slightly. This condition is normal and engine speed should not be readjusted.**

FLOAT LEVEL

With carburetor body inverted so that weight of floats ONLY is forcing needle against its seat, use a T-scale or the tool shown, **Fig. 5,** and check the float level from surface of fuel bowl to crown of each float at center.

If an adjustment is necessary, hold floats on bottom of bowl and bend float lip as required to give the specified dimension. **When bending the float lip, do not allow the lip to push against the needle as the synthetic rubber tip (if used) can be compressed sufficiently to cause a false setting which will affect correct level of fuel in bowl. After being compressed, the tip is very slow to recover its original shape.**

QUALIFYING STEP-UP PISTON

If step-up piston assembly is removed or the mechanical rod lifter adjustment is disturbed, the step-up piston must be readjusted or "Qualified." Qualifying places the piston in a central position.

1. Remove step-up piston cover plate and gasket.
2. Remove rod lifter lock screw, then the step-up piston assembly.
3. Adjust gap in step-up piston, **Fig. 6,** by turning Allen head calibration screw on top of piston. Adjust gap to .035 inch. Record number of turns and direction required to obtain this gap as screw must be reset to original position after vacuum step-up piston adjustment has been made.
4. Install step-up piston assembly and rod lifter lock screw.
5. Adjust vacuum step-up piston.

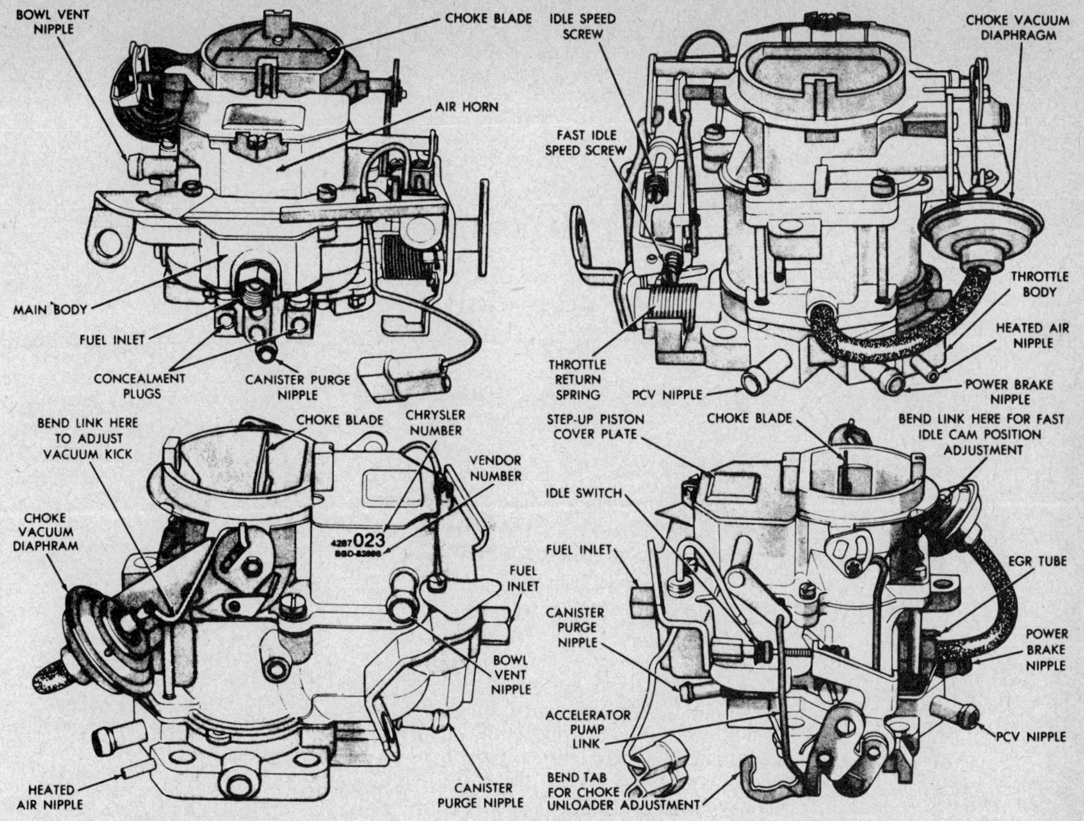

Fig. 3 BBD carburetor assembly. 1984 units less Electronic Feedback Carburetor System

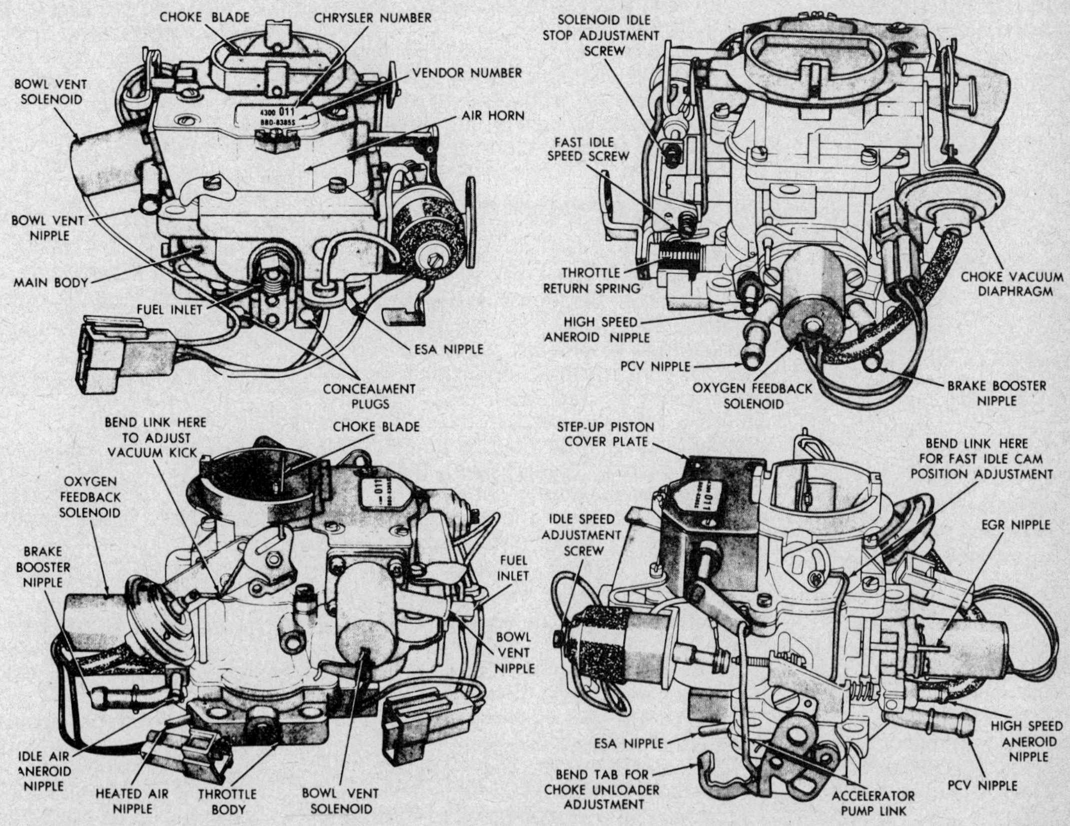

Fig. 4 BBD carburetor assembly. 1984 units with Electronic Feedback Carburetor System

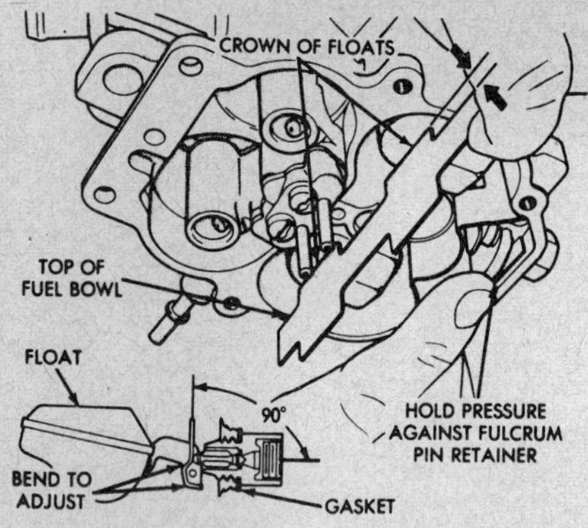

Fig. 5 Qualifying step-up piston adjustment

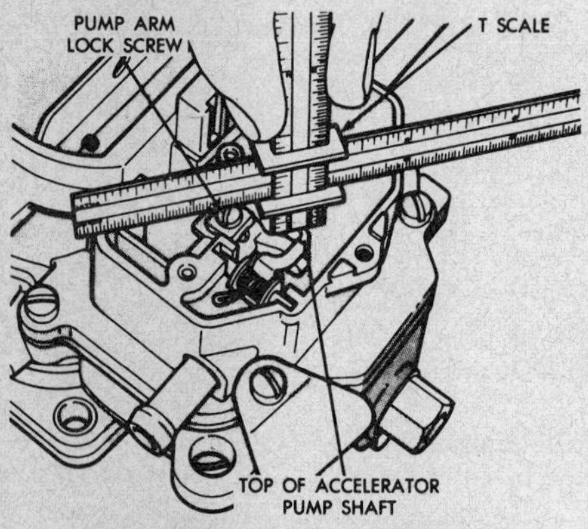

Fig. 8 Adjusting accelerator pump stroke. BBD carburetors

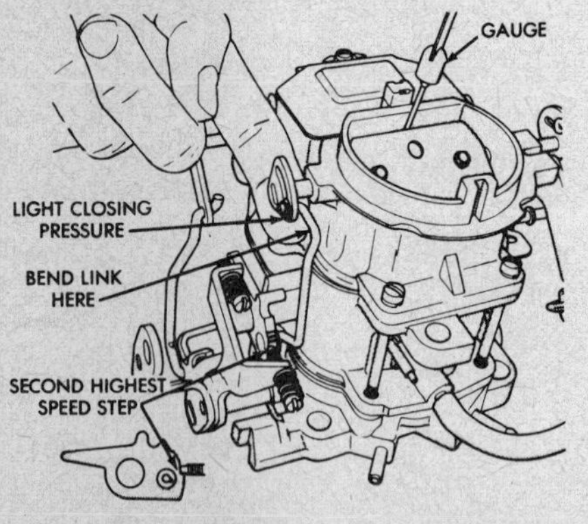

Fig. 10 Adjusting fast idle cam position. BBD carburetors

VACUUM STEP-UP PISTON

1. Back off idle speed screw until throttle valves are completely closed. Count number of turns so that screw can be returned to its original position.
2. Fully depress step-up piston while holding moderate pressure on rod lifter tab and tighten rod lifter lock screw, **Fig. 7.**
3. Release piston and rod lifter, then return idle speed screw to its original position.

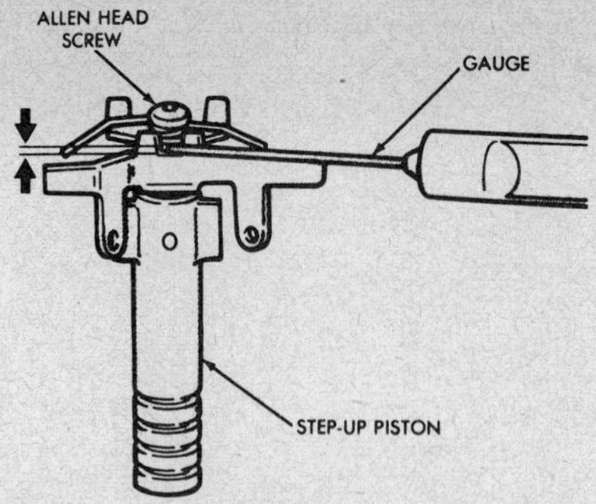

Fig. 6 Adjusting float. BBD carburetor

4. Reset Allen head calibration screw on top of step-up piston to its original position as measured when qualifying step-up piston.

ACCELERATOR PUMP STROKE

To establish an approximate idle RPM on newly assembled carburetors, back off idle speed screw to completely close throttle valve (fast idle cam must be in open choke position). Turn idle speed screw clockwise until it just contacts stop, then two complete turns further.

1. Ensure that accelerator pump "S" link is in outer hole of pump arm if arm has two holes.
2. Measure distance between surface of air horn and top of accelerator pump shaft, **Fig. 8.**
3. If accelerator pump stroke is not within specifications, adjust by loosening pump arm adjusting lock screw and rotating sleeve until proper measurement is obtained, then tighten lock screw.

CHOKE VACUUM KICK

Open throttle and close choke, then close throttle to trap fast idle cam at closed choke position, **Fig. 9.** Using an external vacuum source, apply 15 or more inches of vacuum to diaphragm. Apply a closing force on choke lever to completely compress spring in diaphragm stem without distorting linkage. Note that the solid rod stem of diaphragm extends to an internal stop as spring compresses. Measure clearance between top of choke valve and air horn wall at throttle lever side. Adjust clearance by bending diaphragm link at "U" bend. Remove external vacuum source and linkage for free movement.

FAST IDLE CAM POSITION

1. With fast idle speed adjusting screw contacting second highest speed step on fast idle cam, move choke valve toward closed position with light pressure on choke shaft lever, **Fig. 10.**
2. Measure by inserting specified gauge between top of choke valve and air horn wall at throttle lever side.
3. Adjust to specifications as necessary by bending fast idle connector rod at angle until correct valve opening is obtained.

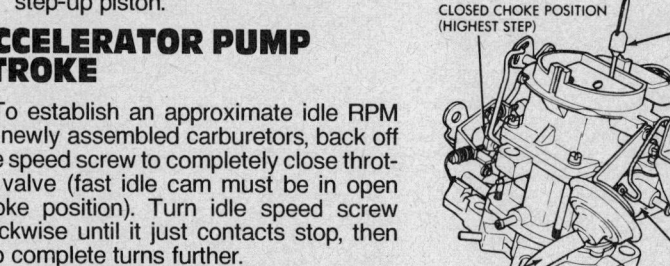

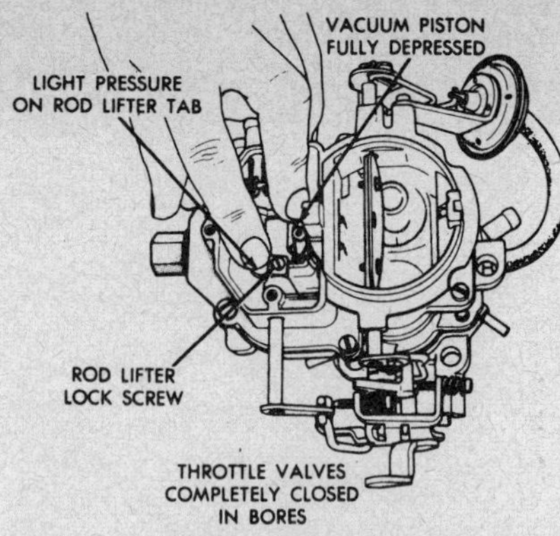

Fig. 7 Adjusting vacuum step-up piston. BBD carburetors

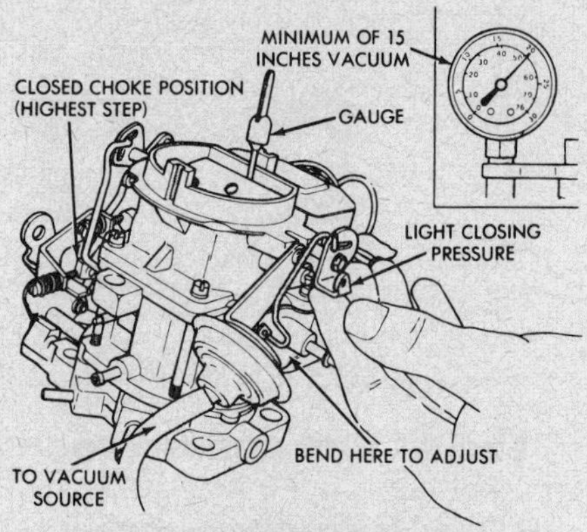

Fig. 9 Adjusting choke vacuum kick. BBD carburetors

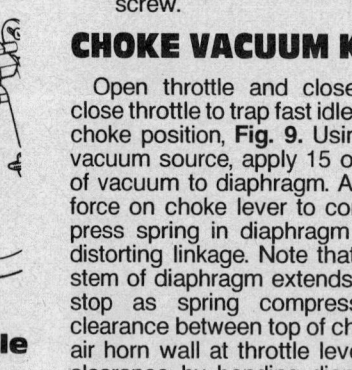

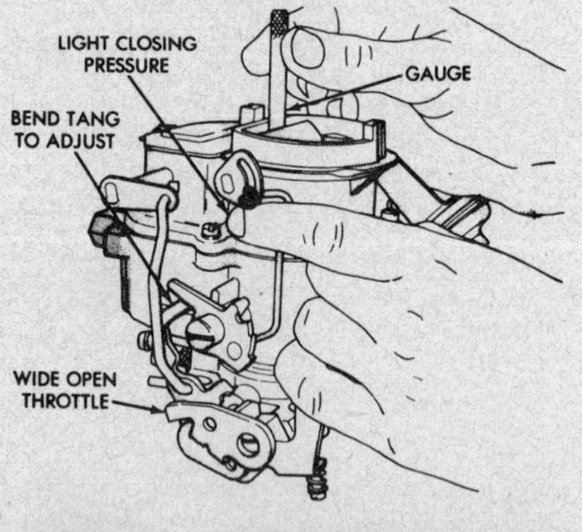

Fig. 11 Adjusting choke unloader. BBD carburetors

CHOKE UNLOADER

1. Hold throttle valve in wide open position.
2. Lightly press finger against control lever to move choke valve toward closed position, **Fig. 11.**
3. Measure by inserting specified gauge between top of choke valve and air horn wall at throttle lever side.
4. Adjust as necessary by bending tang on throttle lever.

Carter Thermo-Quad 4 Barrel Carburetor

INDEX

ADJUSTMENT SPECIFICATIONS

Year	Carb. Model	Float Setting	Secondary Throttle Linkage	Secondary Air Valve Opening	Secondary Air Valve Spring	Pump Travel	Choke Control Lever (Off Car)	Choke Vacuum Kick	Choke Unloader	Choke Setting
1982	9337S	29/32	①	13/32	1 3/4 Turns	33/64 ② ③	3 3/8	.130	.312	④
	9372S	29/32	①	13/32	1 3/4 Turns	33/64 ② ③	3 3/8	.130	.312	④
	9385S	29/32	①	13/32	1 3/4 Turns	33/64 ② ③	3 3/8	.130	.312	④
1983	9374S	29/32	①	13/32	1 3/4 Turns	33/64 ② ③	3 3/8	.130	.310	④
	9385S	29/32	①	13/32	1 3/4 Turns	33/64 ② ③	3 3/8	.130	.310	④
1984	9389S	29/32	①	13/32	1 3/4 Turns	33/64 ② ③	3 3/8	.130	.310	④

①—Adjust link so primary and secondary stops both contact at same time.
②—Slot No. 2.
③—Secondary stage pickup adjustment, 25/64 inch.
④—Tamper-resistant.

IDENTIFICATION LOCATION

The identification is stamped on driver side face of carburetor, **Fig. 1.**

DESCRIPTION

The TQ (Thermo-Quad) carburetor, **Fig. 1,** is unique in design in that it has a black main body or fuel bowl of molded phenolic resin. This acts as an effective heat insulator. Fuel is kept cooler by about 20 degrees Fahrenheit than in carburetors of all metal design. Another reason for the lower operating temperatures is its suspended design metering system. All calibration points, with the exception of the idle adjusting screws, are in the upper aluminum casting or air horn and are in effect suspended on cavities in the plastic main body.

ON-VEHICLE ADJUSTMENTS

The metering rods are preset to specifications by the manufacturer. No additional adjustment should be attempted since an accurate adjustment cannot be made in the field. An improper adjustment may result in the exhaust emissions exceeding specifications. Also, inproper adjustment of the metering rods may prevent the carburetor from returning to the idle position from wide open throttle (WOT) due to throttle shaft binding, resulting in poor fuel economy.

CURB IDLE SPEED

1. Disconnect and plug vacuum hose at EGR valve, distributor or carburetor, if equipped.
2. On models equipped with carburetor ground switch, connect jumper wire between switch and ground.
3. On models not equipped with spark control computer (SCC), disconnect and plug vacuum hose from carburetor or at heated air temperature sensor and orifice spark advance control valve (OSAC), if equipped.
4. On all, models, disconnect and plug control hose at canister.
5. Remove PCV valve from cylinder head cover and allow to draw underhood air.
6. Connect tachometer, then start engine and allow to reach normal operating temperature.
7. Adjust Solenoid Idle Stop, if equipped, as follows:
   a. On models with A/C, turn on A/C and set blower on low, then disconnect A/C clutch wire.
   b. On models less A/C, connect jumper wire between battery positive terminal and the SIS lead wire. **Ensure correct jumper wire installation. Applying battery voltage to other than correct wire will damage the wiring harness.**
   c. On all models, open throttle slightly to allow solenoid plunger to extend.
   d. Turn adjusting screw on throttle lever to obtain 850 RPM.
   e. Turn off A/C and reconnect clutch wire or remove jumper, if equipped.
8. On models equipped with oxygen sensor feedback, disconnect electrical connector from oxygen sensor and ground connector.
9. Remove and plug vacuum hose at vacuum transducer on SCC, then install suitable vacuum pump to vacuum transducer and apply 16 inches of vacuum.
10. Allow engine to run for two minutes. If idle is not as specified, turn adjusting screw on solenoid to obtain correct RPM.
11. On models not equipped with oxygen sensor feedback, allow engine to run for one minute.
12. If idle RPM is not as specified, turn idle speed screw to obtain correct RPM.
13. On all models, turn off engine, connect vacuum lines and remove tachometer. Remove jumper wire and connect oxygen sensor electrical connector, if equipped. **After step 13 has been completed, idle speed may change slightly. This condition is normal and engine speed should not be readjusted.**

FAST IDLE SPEED

1. Disconnect and plug vacuum hose at EGR valve and distributor, if equipped.
2. On models equipped with carburetor

ground switch, connect jumper wire between switch and ground.
3. On models not equipped with spark control computer (SCC), disconnect and plug vacuum hose from carburetor or at heated air temperature sensor.
4. On all models, disconnect and plug control hose at canister.
5. Remove PCV valve from cylinder head cover and allow to draw underhood air.
6. Connect tachometer, then start engine and allow to reach normal operating temperature.
7. On models equipped with oxygen sensor feedback, disconnect electrical connector from oxygen sensor and ground connector, then allow engine to run for two minutes.
8. On models not equipped with oxygen sensor feedback, allow engine to run for one minute.
9. On all models, open throttle slightly and position fast idle adjusting screw on second highest step of fast idle cam.
10. Open choke fully, then adjust fast idle speed screw to obtain specified RPM.
11. Return to idle, then reposition adjusting screw on second highest step of fast idle cam to ensure correct RPM. Repeat adjustment if necessary.
12. Turn off engine, then connect vacuum hoses and remove tachometer. Remove jumper wire and connect oxygen sensor electrical connector, if equipped. **After step 12 has been completed, idle speed may change slightly. This condition is normal and engine speed should not be readjusted.**

FLOAT SETTING

With a bowl cover inverted, gasket installed and floats resting on seated needle, the dimension of each float from bowl cover gasket to bottom side of float should be within specifications, **Fig. 2.** To adjust, bend float lever.

When adjusting, do not allow lip of float lever to be pressed against needle.

SECONDARY THROTTLE LINKAGE

Hold fast idle lever in curb idle position and invert carburetor, **Fig. 3.** Open primary throttle valve until the primary and secondary stops contact simultaneously. To adjust, bend secondary throttle operating rod at angle until correct adjustment is obtained.

SECONDARY AIR VALVE OPENING

1. With air valve in closed position, the opening along air valve at its long side must be at its maximum and parallel with air horn gasket surface, **Fig. 4.**
2. With air valve wide open, the opening of the air valve at the short side and airhorn must be within specifications. The corner of air valve is notched for adjustment. Bend the corner with a pair of pliers to give proper opening.

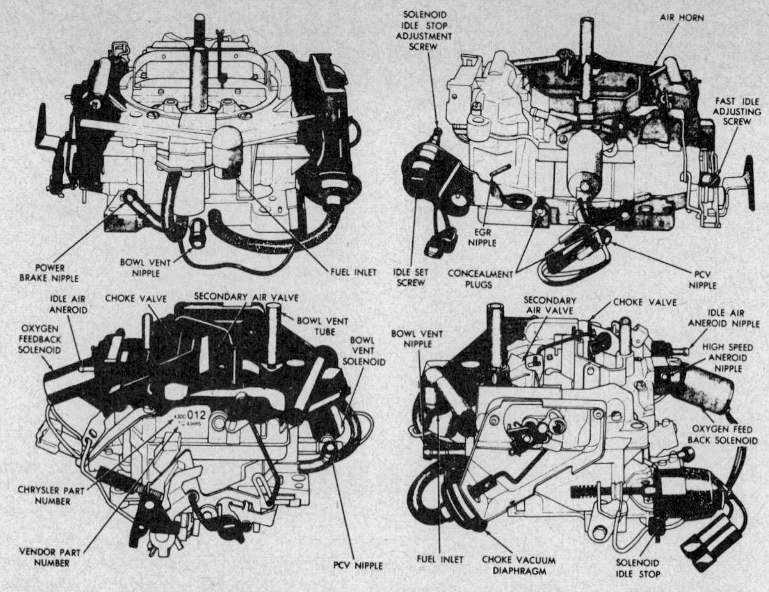

Fig. 1 TQ carburetor assembly 1982–84 (Typical)

SECONDARY AIR VALVE SPRING TENSION

1. Loosen air valve lock plug and turn air valve adjustment plug clockwise to allow air valve to position itself to wide open position. **Hold air valve adjustment plug with screwdriver when loosening lock plug or spring may snap out of position, requiring disassembly of carburetor to retrieve spring.**
2. With a long screwdriver that will enter center of tool C-4152-B or equivalent positioned on air valve adjustment plug, turn plug counterclockwise until air valve contacts stop lightly, then an additional turn, **Fig. 5.**
3. Hold adjustment plug with screwdriver and tighten lock plug securely, ensuring that adjustment does not move.
4. Check air valve for freedom of movement.

ACCELERATOR PUMP STROKE

1983–84 Units

First Stage. Ensure throttle connector rod is in center hole on three hole pump arm or inner hole on two hole pump arm, **Fig. 6.** With idle adjusting screw adjusted to the specified curb idle speed, measure distance from air horn surface to top of accelerator pump plunger. If equipped with an idle stop solenoid the ignition switch must be in the on position. Dimensions should be within specifications. Bend throttle connector rod at lower angle to adjust.

Second Stage. With choke in the open position, open throttle until secondary lockout latch is just applied. Plunger downward travel stops at this point. Measure distance from air horn surface to top of accelerator pump plunger. Dimension should be within specifications. Bend tang on throttle to adjust.

1982 Units

Ensure that throttle connector rod is in the specified hole of the pump arm, **Fig. 7.** With idle adjusting screw adjusted to the specified curb idle speed, measure distance from air horn surface to top of accelerator pump plunger. Dimensions should be within specifications. Adjust plunger height by bending throttle connector rod in area indicated in **Fig. 5.**

CHOKE CONTROL LEVER

Place carburetor on a flat surface, **Fig. 8.** Close choke by pushing on choke lever with throttle partly open. Measure vertical distance between top of rod hole in control lever and base of carburetor (flat surface). Dimension should be within specifications. Adjust by bending link connecting the two choke shafts.

CHOKE DIAPHRAGM CONNECTOR ROD

Apply a vacuum of 15 inches Hg or more to fully depress diaphragm, **Fig. 9.** An auxiliary source like a distributor test machine can be used for this purpose. With air valve closed, adjust connector rod to give .040 inch clearance between air valve and stop.

CHOKE VACUUM KICK

Measure at the lowest edge of the choke valve (throttle lever side).

1. Open throttle and close choke, then close throttle to trap fast idle cam at closed choke position.
2. Disconnect vacuum hose from carburetor and connect to hose of auxiliary vacuum source with small length of tube.
3. Apply a vacuum of at least 15 inches Hg.
4. Apply sufficient closing pressure on choke control lever to move kick ad-

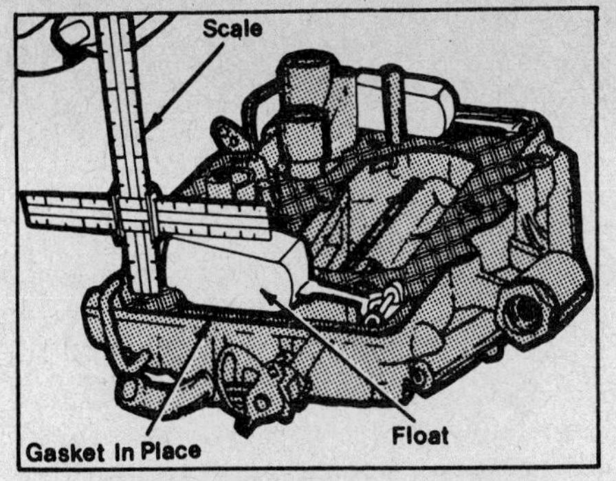

Fig. 2 TQ float setting

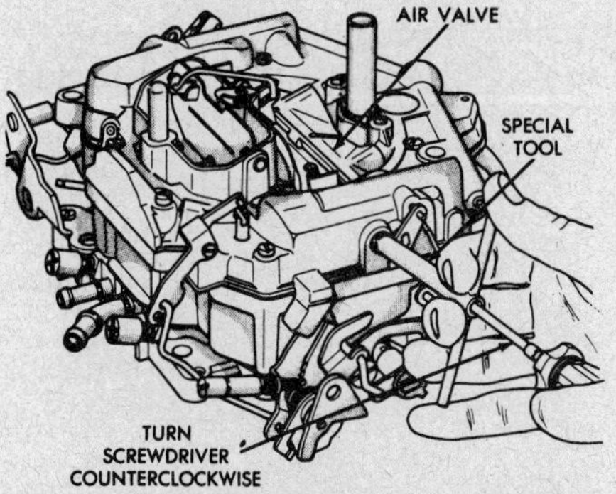

Fig. 5 Adjusting secondary air valve spring tension

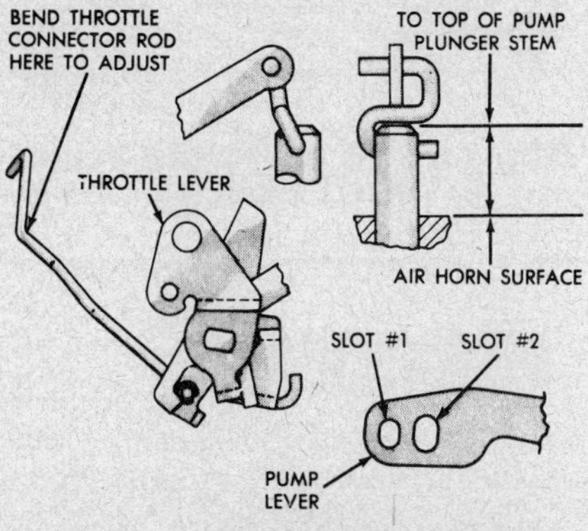

Fig. 7 TQ accelerator pump stroke adjustment. 1982 units

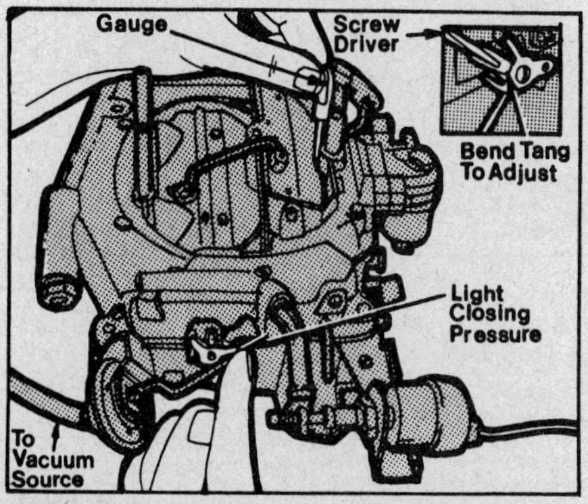

Fig. 10 TQ vacuum kick adjustment

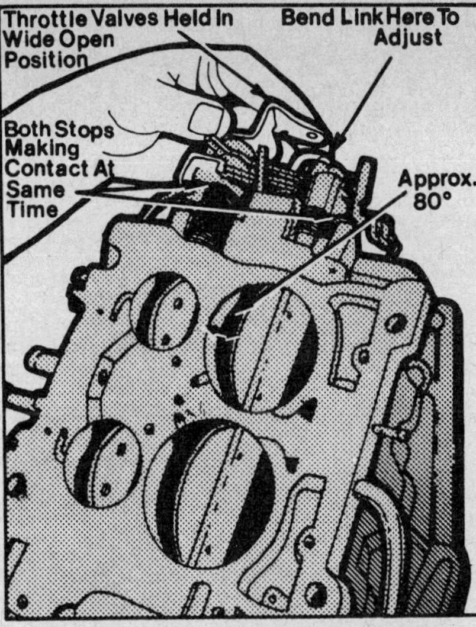

Fig. 3 TQ secondary throttle adjustment

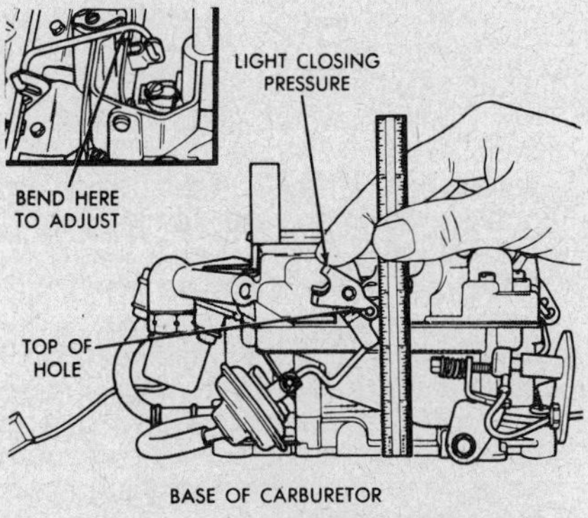

Fig. 8 TQ choke control lever adjustment

justment tang against its stop without distorting linkage, **Fig. 10.**

5. Measure by inserting specified gauge between bottom of choke valve and air horn wall at throttle lever side. **Do not change position of choke with gauge during measurement.**
6. Adjust by twisting screwdriver in tang slot. Do not adjust diaphragm rod.
7. Check for free movement between open and adjusted positions, correct any improper alignment or interference and repeat adjustment as necessary.
8. Reconnect vacuum hose on correct carburetor fitting.

FAST IDLE CAM POSITION

Measure at lowest edge of choke valve (throttle lever side).

1. With fast idle speed adjusting screw contacting second highest speed step on fast idle cam, move choke valve toward closed position with light pressure on fast idle control lever, **Fig. 11.**
2. Measure by inserting specified gauge between bottom of choke valve and air horn wall at throttle lever side. **Do not change position of choke with gauge during measurement.**

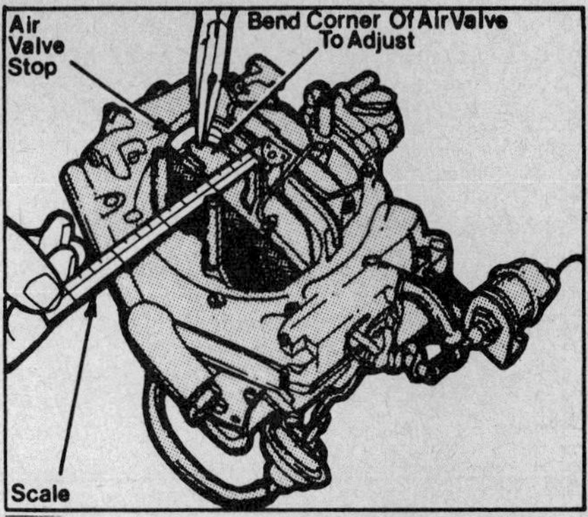

Fig. 4 TQ secondary air valve opening

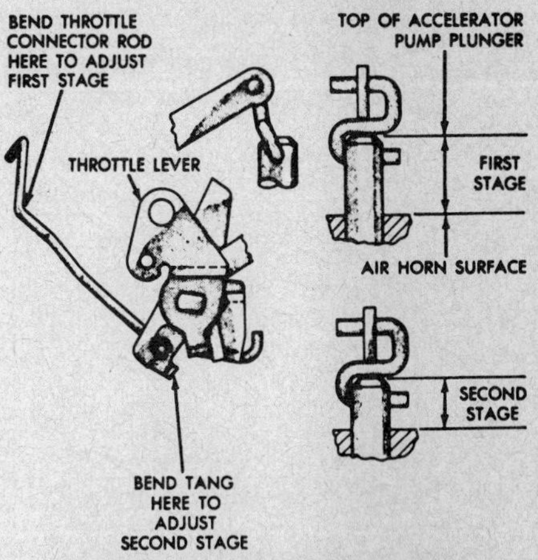

Fig. 6 TQ accelerator pump stroke adjustment, with staged pump system. 1983–84 units

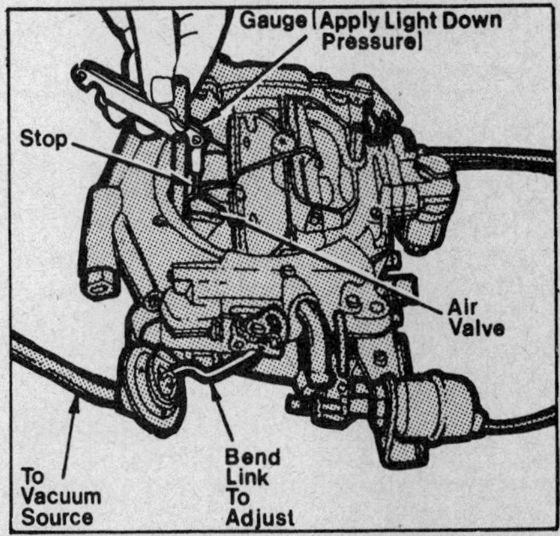

Fig. 9 TQ choke diaphragm connector rod

3. Adjust by bending fast idle connector rod at angle until correct valve opening has been obtained. **If fast idle cam position adjustment is changed, the choke unloader and secondary throttle lockout adjustments must be reset.**

CHOKE UNLOADER ADJUSTMENT

Hold the throttle valves in wide open position and insert specified drill between long side (lower edge) of choke valve and

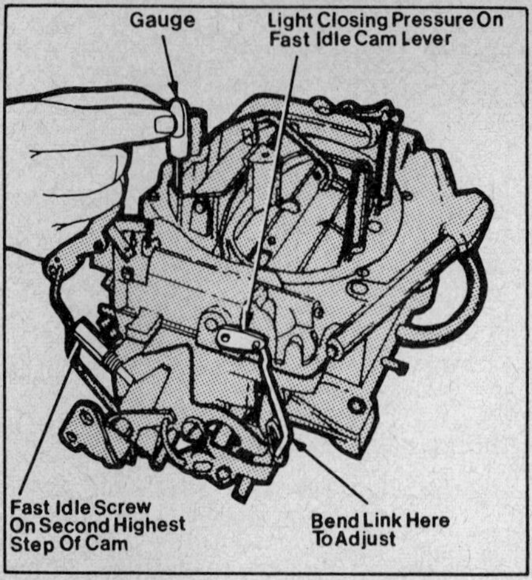

Fig. 11 TQ fast idle cam & linkage adjustment

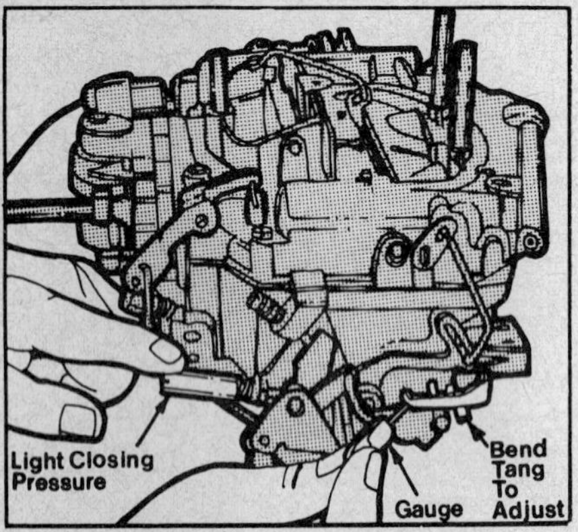

Fig. 13 TQ secondary throttle lockout

inner wall of air horn, **Fig. 12.** With finger lightly pressing against choke valve control lever, a slight drag should be felt as drill is withdrawn. Refer to Specifications for proper drill size or dimension. Adjust by bending tang on fast idle control lever.

SECONDARY THROTTLE LOCKOUT

Move choke control lever to open choke position, **Fig. 13.** Measure clearance between lockout lever and stop. Clearance should be .060-.090 inch. Adjust by bending tang on fast idle control lever.

SOLENOID BOWL VENT VALVE CHECK

Fig. 14

1. Remove air cleaner.
2. Disconnect vacuum hose from solenoid bowl vent diaphragm.
3. Connect an external vacuum source and apply 15 inches of vacuum to the diaphragm.
4. Observe valve movement through air horn vent tube. Valve should move when vacuum is applied.
5. Turn ignition switch "On" and disconnect external vacuum source. The valve should remain in the downward position until the ignition switch is turned "Off."
6. If the valve does not move when vacuum is applied, the diaphragm is defective and requires replacement. If the valve does not remain in the downward position when the ignition switch is turned "On" and the vacuum source removed, the solenoid or wiring is defective.
7. Install air cleaner.

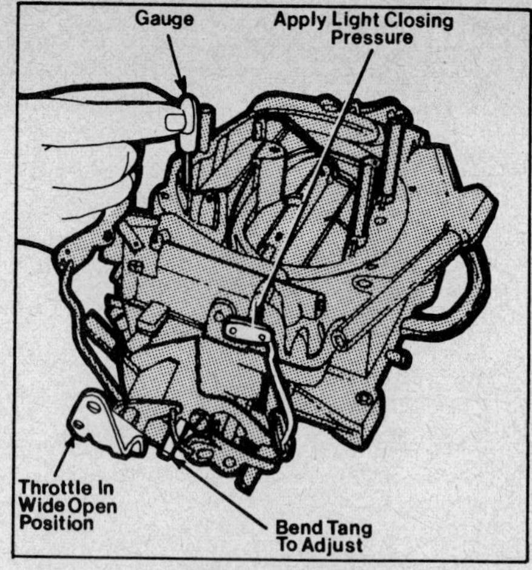

Fig. 12 TQ choke unloader adjustment

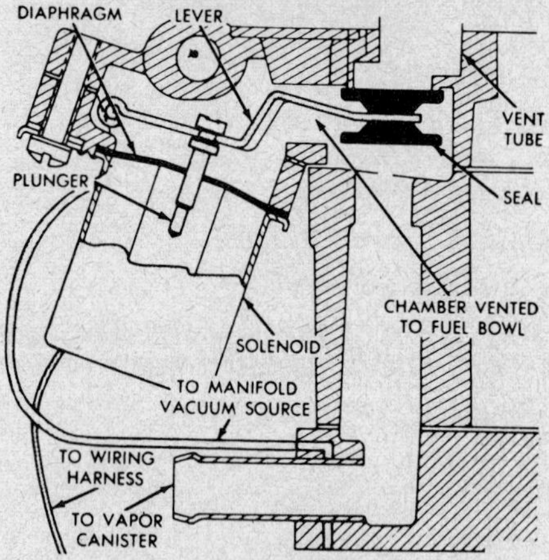

Fig. 14 TQ solenoid bowl vent check

Holley Model 1945 1 Barrel Carburetor

INDEX

ADJUSTMENT SPECIFICATIONS

Year	Carb. Part No.①	Float Level (Dry)	Pump Setting	Fast Idle Bench	Choke Unloader Clearance	Vacuum Kick Drill Size	Cam Position Drill Size	Choke Setting
1982	R-6928A	③	1.615④	.090	.250	.150	.090	②
	R-9687A	③	1.615④	.090	.250	.150	.090	②

①—Located on tag attached to carburetor or on casting.
②—Tamper-resistant.
③—Flush with top of bowl casting to .050 inch above the bowl inverted.
④—Hole position No. 2.

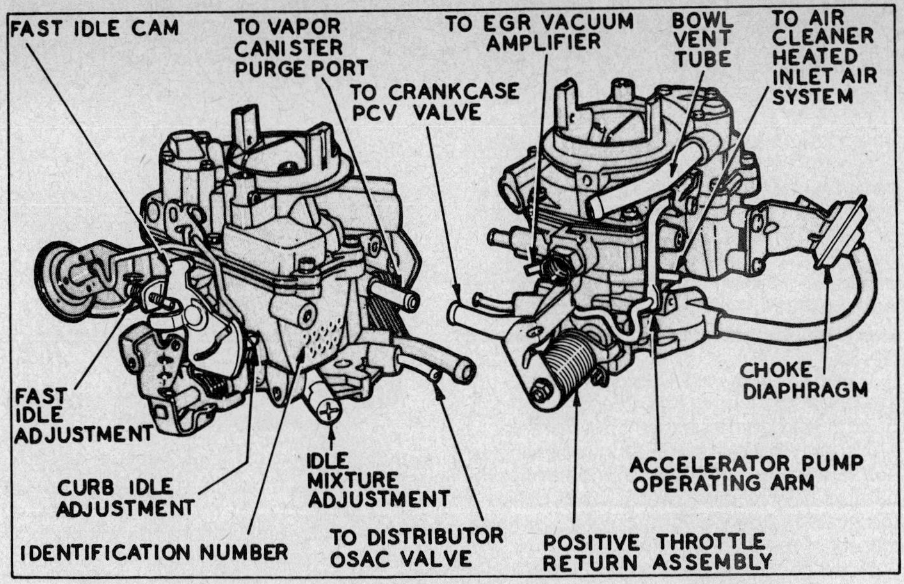

Fig. 1 Holley model 1945 single barrel carburetor (Typical)

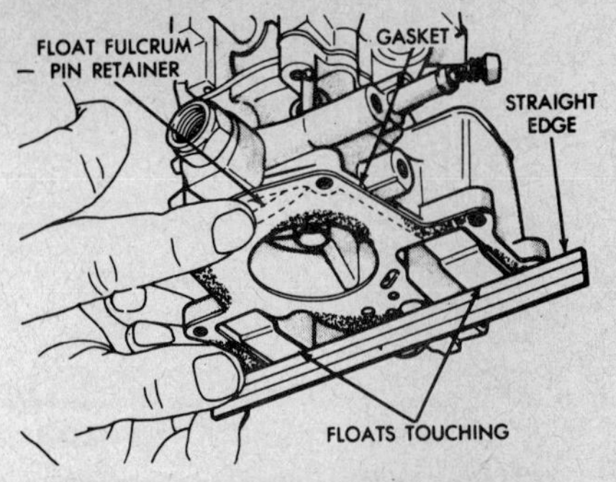

Fig. 2 Adjusting float setting

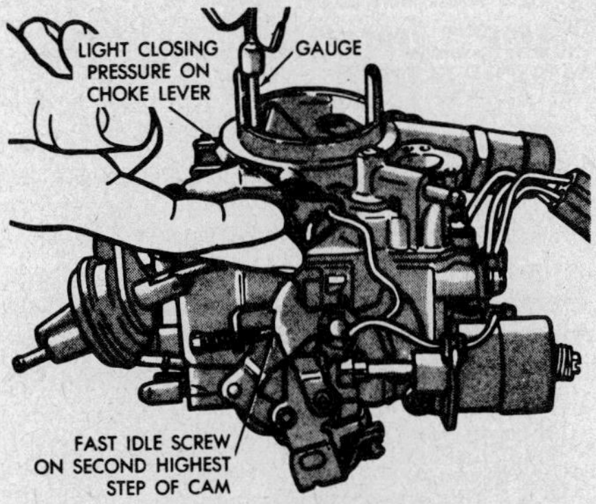

Fig. 3 Adjusting fast idle cam position

IDENTIFICATION LOCATION

The carburetor identification number is located on either a tag attached to the carburetor by one of the cover hold-down bolts or is stamped on the front face of the carburetor body.

DESCRIPTION

This single barrel carburetor, **Fig. 1**, utilizes dual nitrophyl floats to control the fuel level, thus permitting high angularity operation during the most severe operating conditions. Also, the float construction eliminates the possibility of a malfunction due to a punctured float. An electric choke system is incorporated to open the choke at approximately 60 degrees F.

The accelerator pump is of the piston type and is operated by a rod and a link connected to the throttle lever.

The power enrichment system on all units, consists of a power valve installed near the center of the carburetor body and a vacuum piston located in the bowl cover.

A spring-loaded modulated power valve is used. A vacuum passage in the throttle body transmits manifold vacuum to the vacuum piston chamber in the bowl cover. Under light throttle and load conditions, vacuum acting on the vacuum piston is sufficient to overcome the spring tension. When the throttle valve is opened to 55 degrees, vacuum acting on the vacuum piston is bled to the atmosphere and manifold vacuum is closed off. The throttle shaft is provided with a small hole which aligns with a port in the base of the carburetor when the throttle valve is opened to 55 degrees. This vents the vacuum piston chamber to the atmosphere, allowing the spring tension to open the power valve.

ON-VEHICLE ADJUSTMENTS

CURB IDLE SPEED

1. Disconnect and plug vacuum hose at EGR valve, then the 3/16 inch diameter control hose at canister.
2. Remove PCV valve from cylinder head cover and allow to draw underhood air.
3. Ground carburetor switch with jumper wire, if equipped.
4. Install tachometer, then start engine and allow to reach normal operating temperature.
5. Adjust Solenoid Idle Stop, if equipped, as follows:
   a. On models with A/C, turn on A/C and set blower on low, then disconnect A/C clutch wire.
   b. On models less A/C, connect jumper wire between battery positive terminal and the SIS lead wire. **Ensure correct jumper wire installation. Applying battery voltage to other than correct wire will damage wiring harness.**
   c. On all models, open throttle slightly to allow solenoid plunger to extend.
   d. Remove adjusting screw and spring from solenoid.

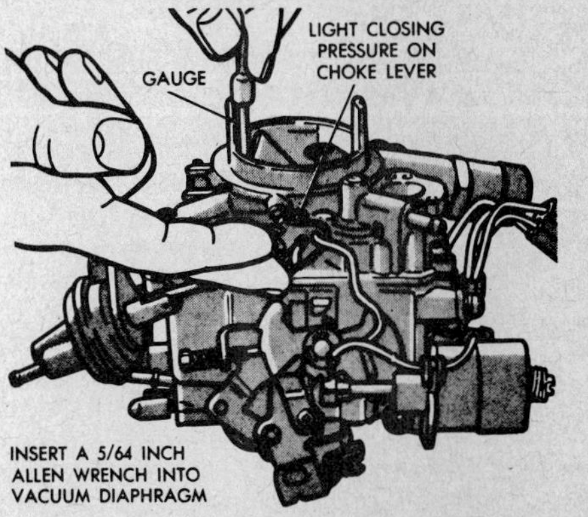

Fig. 4 Adjusting choke vacuum kick

   e. Insert 1/8 inch Allen wrench into the solenoid and adjust to 875 RPM.
   f. Turn off A/C and replace clutch wire or remove jumper wire.
   g. Install solenoid screw and spring.
6. Allow engine to run at idle for one minute. If idle is not as specified, turn adjusting screw to obtain correct RPM.
7. Turn off engine, connect vacuum lines and remove tachometer. Install PCV valve, then remove jumper wire if equipped. **After step 7 has been completed, idle speed may change slightly. This condition is normal and engine speed should not be readjusted.**

FAST IDLE SPEED

1. Disconnect and plug vacuum hose at EGR valve, then the control hose at canister.
2. Remove PCV valve from cylinder head cover and allow to draw underhood air.
3. Ground carburetor switch with jumper wire, if equipped.
4. Install tachometer, then start engine and allow to reach normal operating temperature.
5. Open throttle and place fast idle screw on second highest step of fast idle cam.
6. Open choke fully, then adjust fast idle speed screw to obtain specified RPM.
7. Return to idle, then reposition adjusting screw on second highest step of fast idle cam to ensure correct RPM. Readjust as necessary.
8. Turn off engine, connect vacuum lines and remove tachometer. Install PCV

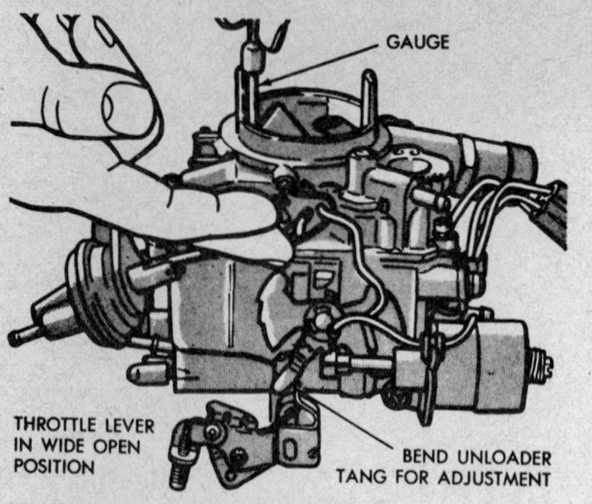

Fig. 5 Choke unloader adjustment

valve, then remove jumper wire, if equipped. **After step 8 has been completed, idle speed may change slightly. This condition is normal and engine speed should not be readjusted.**

DRY FLOAT SETTING

Hold float fulcrum retaining pin in position and invert carburetor bowl, **Fig. 13.** Place a straightedge across surface of bowl, contracting float toes. Remove straightedge and measure distance float dropped from surface of fuel bowl. Refer to Adjustment Specifications. Adjust by bending float tang to obtain proper dimension.

FAST IDLE CAM POSITION

With fast idle speed adjusting screw contacting second highest step on fast idle cam, move choke valve toward closed position with light pressure on choke shaft lever, **Fig. 3.** Insert specified gauge between top of choke valve and wall of air horn. Refer to adjustment specifications. An adjustment will be necessary if a slight drag is not obtained as drill shank is being removed. Adjust by bending fast idle link at lower angle, until correct valve opening has been obtained.

CHOKE VACUUM KICK

Test can be made on or off vehicle.

Fig. 4—If adjustment is to be made with engine running, back off fast idle speed screw until choke can be closed to the kick position with engine at curb idle. (Note number of screw turns required so that fast idle can be returned to original adjustment.) If an auxiliary vacuum source is to be used, open throttle valve (engine not running) and move choke to closed position. Release throttle first, then release choke.

When using an auxiliary vacuum source, disconnect vacuum hose from carburetor and connect it to hose from vacuum supply with a small length of tube to act as a fitting. Removal of hose from diaphragm may require forces which damage the system. Apply a vacuum of 15 or more inches of mercury.

Insert gauge between top of choke valve and wall of air horn. Refer to adjustment specifications. Apply sufficient closing pressure on lever to which choke rod attaches to provide a minimum choke valve opening without distortion of diaphragm link.

The cylindrical stem of diaphragm extends as the internal spring is compressed. This spring must be fully compressed for proper measurement of vacuum kick adjustment.

Adjustment is necessary if slight drag is not obtained when removing the gauge. Shorten or lengthen diaphragm link to obtain correct choke valve opening. Length changes should be made by carefully opening or closing the U-bend provided in the link. Improper bending causes contact between the U-section and the diaphragm assembly.

Do not apply twisting or bending force to diaphragm.

After completion of adjustment, reinstall vacuum hose on correct carburetor fitting. Return fast idle screw to its original location if disturbed. Make following check. With no vacuum applied to diaphragm, the choke valve should move freely between open and closed positions. If movement is not free, examine linkage for improper alignment or interferences caused by bending operation.

On 1982 models, adjustment is made by means of a 5/64 inch Allen wrench inserted into vacuum diaphragm.

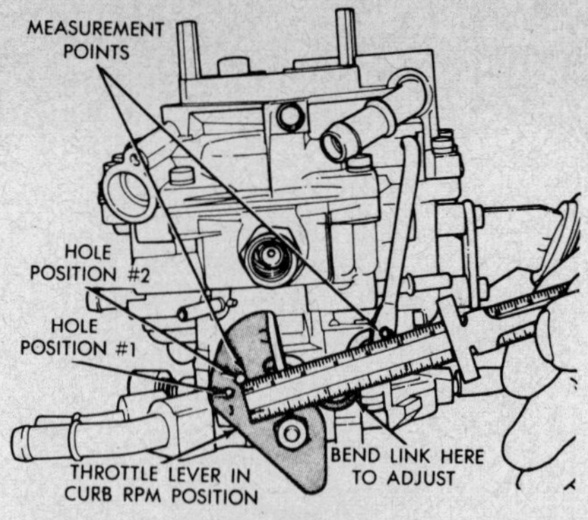

Fig. 6 Accelerator pump adjustment

CHOKE UNLOADER (WIDE OPEN KICK)

With throttle valves in wide open position, **Fig. 5,** insert drill gauge between upper edge of choke valve and inner wall of air horn. Refer to adjustment specifications. With a finger lightly pressing against shaft lever, a slight drag should be felt as drill is being withdrawn. Adjust by bending unloader tang on throttle lever until correct opening has been obtained.

ACCELERATOR PUMP SETTING

With throttle at curb idle position, **Fig. 6,** measure length of pump operating link. Refer to adjustment specification. Adjust by bending link between throttle lever and pump operating rod.

Holley Model 5220 2 Barrel Carburetor

INDEX

ADJUSTMENT SPECIFICATIONS

Year	Model No.	Float Level	Float Drop	Acc. Pump Hole No.	Choke Vacuum Kick	Choke Setting
1982	R-9582A	.480	1 7/8"	3	.060	①
	R-9583A	.480	1 7/8"	3	.060	①
	R-9584A	.480	1 7/8"	3	.060	①
	R-9585A	.480	1 7/8"	3	.060	①

①—Tamper-resistant.

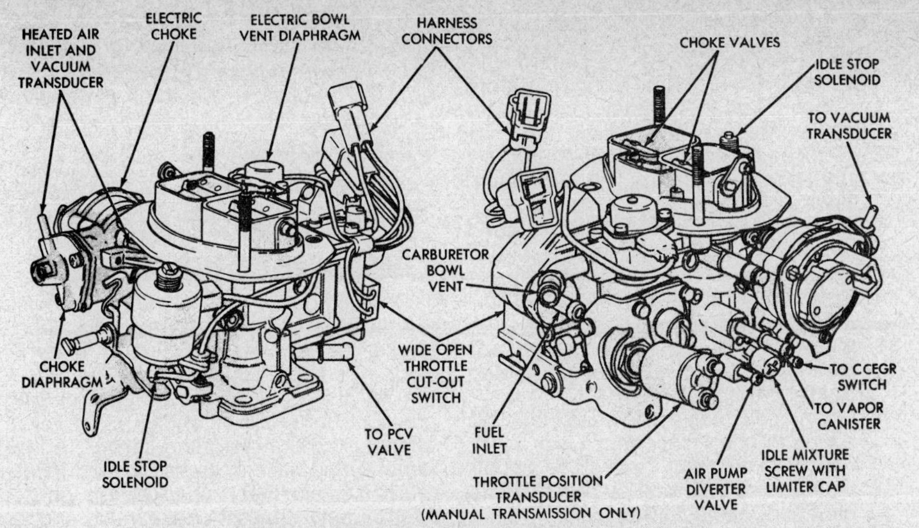

Fig. 1 Holley model 5220 carburetor. Vehicles equipped with air conditioning (Typical)

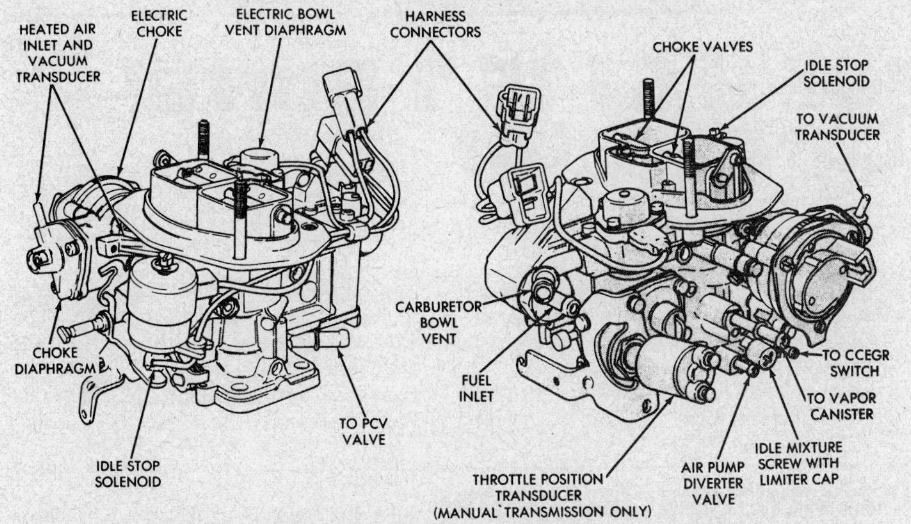

Fig. 2 Holley model 5220 carburetor. Vehicles less air conditioning (Typical)

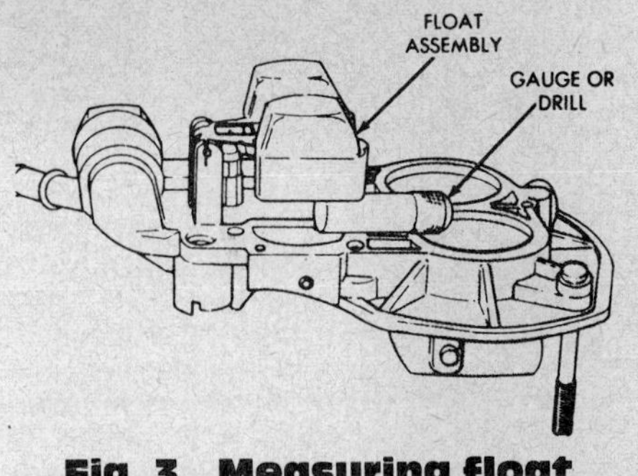

Fig. 3 Measuring float level

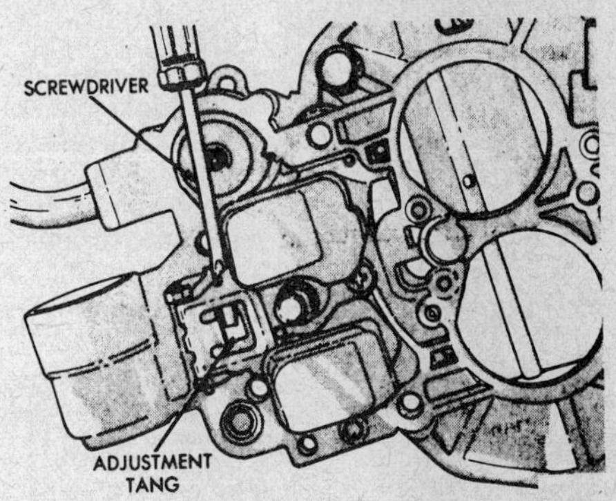

Fig. 4 Adjusting float level

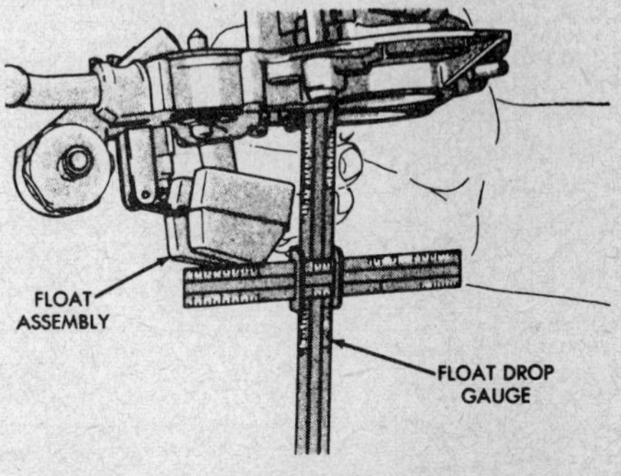

Fig. 5 Measuring float drop

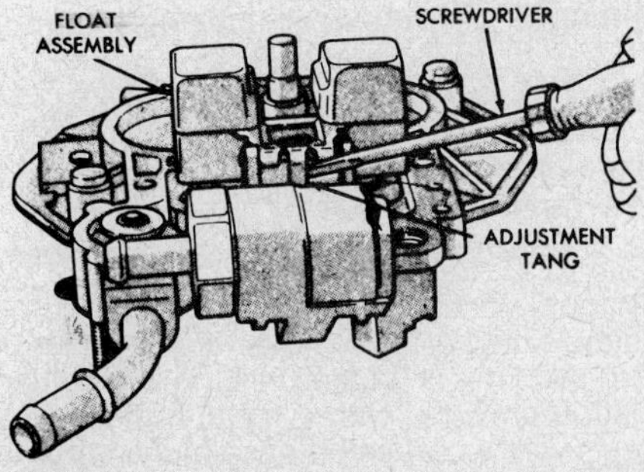

Fig. 6 Adjusting float drop

IDENTIFICATION LOCATION

The carburetor identification number is stamped on side of float bowl.

DESCRIPTION

The Holley model 5220, **Figs. 1 and 2**, is a staged dual venturi carburetor. The primary bore or venturi is smaller than the secondary bore. The secondary stage is mechanically operated by linkage connecting the primary and secondary throttle levers. The primary stage includes a curb idle and transfer system, diaphragm type accelerator pump system, main metering system and power enrichment system. The secondary stage includes a main metering system and power system. Both the primary and secondary venturi draw fuel from a common fuel bowl. The electric automatic choke has a bi-metal two stage heating element. The carburetor also has an electronic solenoid and a vacuum operated bowl vent.

ON-VEHICLE ADJUSTMENTS

CURB IDLE SPEED

1. Disconnect and plug vacuum hose at EGR valve and distributor, if equipped.
2. Disconnect electrical connector at radiator fan, then install jumper wire so fan will run continuously.

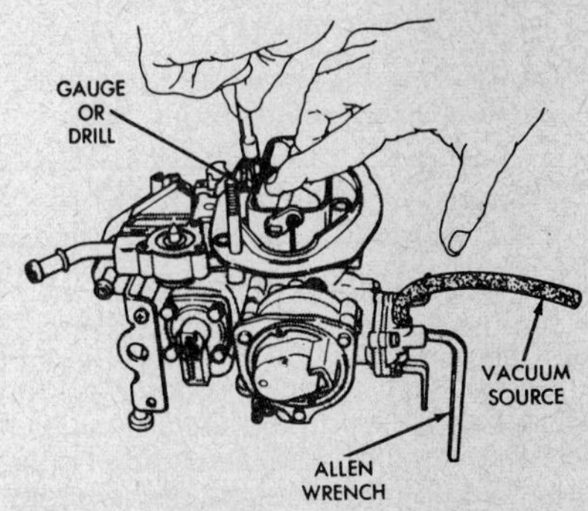

Fig. 7 Choke vacuum kick adjustment

3. Remove PCV valve from connector and allow to draw underhood air, then plug the 3/16 inch diameter vacuum hose from canister.
4. On models equipped with fuel control computer, connect jumper wire between carburetor switch and ground.

5. On all models, connect tachometer, then start engine and allow to reach normal operating temperature.
6. Turn off all lights and accessories.
7. On models equipped with A/C, proceed as follows:
   a. Turn on A/C, then open throttle slightly to energize solenoid.
   b. Remove adjusting screw and spring from top of A/C solenoid.
   c. Adjust solenoid to specified idle speed using a 1/8 inch Allen wrench. **Ensure A/C clutch is operating during idle speed adjustment.**
   d. Install adjusting screw and spring on solenoid.
8. On all models, note tachometer reading. If not within specifications, turn idle speed screw on top of solenoid to obtain correct idle speed. **On all models equipped with A/C, allow engine speed to stabilize one minute after performing A/C idle speed adjustment.**

FAST IDLE SPEED

1. Disconnect electrical connector from radiator fan, then install jumper wire so fan will run continuously.
2. Remove PCV valve and allow to draw underhood air, then plug vacuum hose at canister.
3. Connect tachometer, then ground carburetor switch with jumper wire, if equipped.
4. Start engine and allow to reach normal operating temperature.
5. Open throttle slightly and place adjustment screw on slowest speed step of fast idle cam.
6. Open choke valve and adjust fast idle speed to specifications.
7. Return to curb idle, then place adjusting screw on slowest step of fast idle cam and readjust if necessary.
8. Connect PCV valve and vacuum connectors, then remove radiator fan jumper wire.

FLOAT LEVEL

Invert air horn and insert specified gauge between float and air horn, **Figs. 3 and 4.** To adjust, use a small screwdriver to bend tang.

FLOAT DROP

Using a suitable depth gauge, measure float drop, **Figs. 5 and 6.** To adjust, use a small screwdriver to bend tang.

CHOKE VACUUM KICK

Open throttle, close choke, then close throttle to trap fast idle system in closed choke position, **Fig. 7.** Using an external vacuum source, apply 15 inches of vacuum to choke diaphragm. Apply closing pressure to position choke at smallest opening without distorting linkage. An internal spring will compress to a stop inside choke system. Insert specified gauge between upper edge of choke valve and air horn wall at primary throttle end of carburetor. To adjust, rotate Allen head screw in center of diaphragm housing.

Holley Model 6145 1 Barrel Carburetor

INDEX

ADJUSTMENT SPECIFICATIONS

Year	Carb. Part No. ①	Float Level (Dry)	Pump Setting Fast Idle Bench		Choke Unloader Clearance	Vacuum Kick Drill Size	Cam Position Drill Size	Choke Setting
1982	R-9695A	②	1.615③	.090	.250	.150	.090	④
1983	R-4042A	②	1.615③	.090	.250	.150	.090	④

①—Located on tag attached to carburetor or on casting.
②—Flush with top of bowl casting to .050 inch above with bowl inverted.
③—Hole position No. 2.
④—Tamper resistant.

IDENTIFICATION LOCATION

The carburetor identification number can be found on a sticker located on the float bowl on the throttle linkage side of carburetor where the throttle cable hooks, or stamped on opposite side of carburetor by solenoid kicker.

DESCRIPTION

This single barrel carburetor, **Fig. 1**, utilizes dual nitrophyl floats to control the fuel level, thus permitting high angularity operation during the most severe operating conditions. Also, the float construction eliminates the possibility of a malfunction due to a punctured float. An electric choke system is incorporated to open the choke at approximately 60 degrees F.

The accelerator pump is of the piston type and is operated by a rod and a link connected to the throttle lever.

The power enrichment system on all units, consists of a power valve installed near the center of the carburetor body and a vacuum piston located in the bowl cover.

A spring-loaded modulated power valve is used. A vacuum passage in the throttle body transmits manifold vacuum to the vacuum piston chamber in the bowl cover. Under light throttle and load conditions, vacuum acting on the vacuum piston is sufficient to overcome the spring tension. When the throttle valve is opened to 55 degrees, vacuum acting on the vacuum piston is bled to the atmosphere and manifold vacuum is closed off. The throttle shaft is provided with a small hole which aligns with a port in the base of the carburetor when the throttle valve is opened to 55 degrees. This vents the vacuum piston chamber to the atmosphere, allowing the spring tension to open the power valve.

The 6145 electronic feedback carburetor also incorporates a duty cycle solenoid which provides a limited topulation of air-fuel ratio in response to electrical signals from the spark control computer. The solenoid meters the main fuel system and operates in parallel with a conventional fixed main metering jet. When there is no electrical signal applied to the solenoid, the valve spring pushes upward through the main

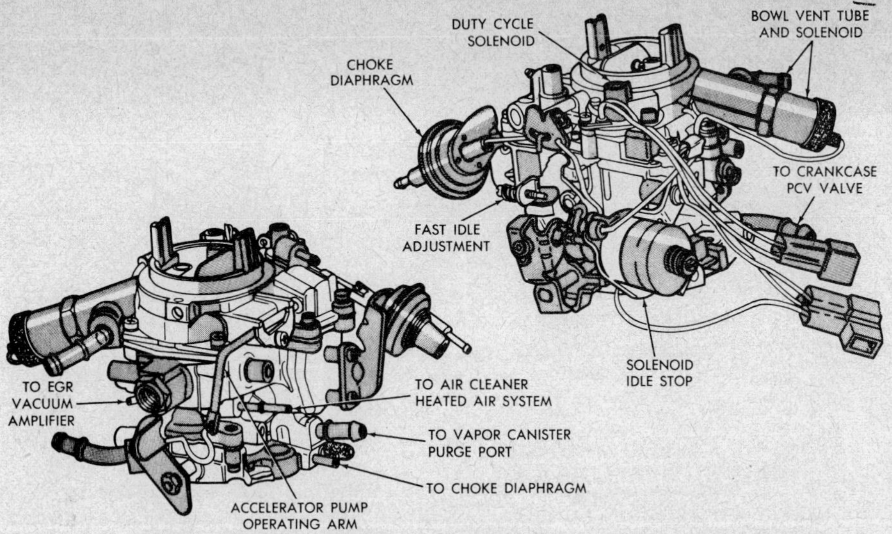

Fig. 1 Holley model 6145 electronic feedback single barrel carburetor

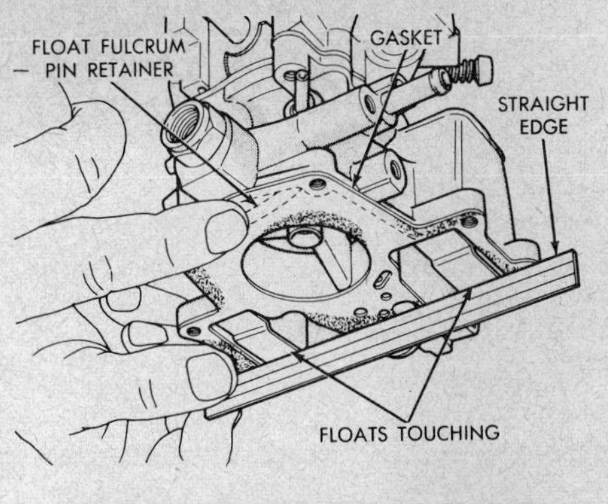

Fig. 2 Measuring float level. 6145 carburetor

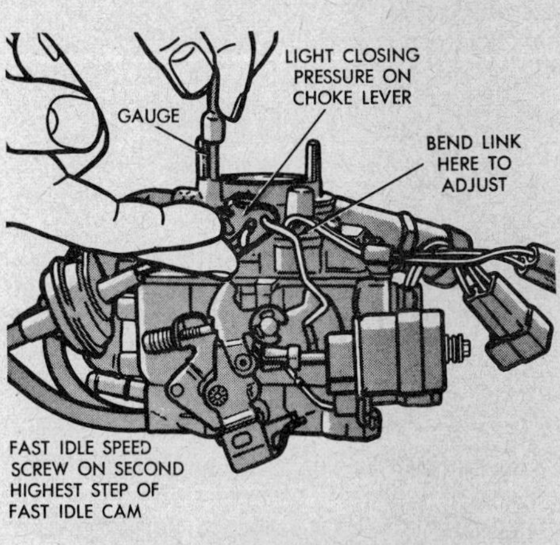

Fig 3 Fast idle cam position adjustment. 6145 carburetor

system fuel valve, fully uncovering the solenoid controlled main metering orifice so that the richest condition exists within the carburetor for any given airflow. When the electrical signal is applied to the solenoid, the field windings are energized, thus causing the armature to move the pushrod and main system valve downward against the valve spring. This movement will continue until the main system valve bottoms against the main system valve seat. In this position the solenoid controlled main metering orifice is fully sealed so that the leanest condition exists within the carburetor for any given airflow. This condition will remain unchanged until the signal from the spark control computer to the solenoid is switched off. The main system fuel may be regulated between richest and leanest limits by controlling the amount of time that the solenoid is in the power on position. Under normal operating conditions, 12 volts at a frequency of 10 Hz is applied to the field windings. By controlling the duration of the voltage signal, the power on time to total time, referred to as the duty cycle, is established.

ON-VEHICLE ADJUSTMENTS

CURB IDLE SPEED

1. Disconnect and plug vacuum hose at EGR valve, distributor or carburetor, if equipped.
2. On models equipped with carburetor ground switch, connect jumper wire between switch and ground.
3. On models not equipped with spark control computer (SCC), disconnect and plug vacuum hose from carburetor at heated air temperature sensor and orifice spark advance control valve (OSAC), if equipped.
4. On all models, disconnect and plug control hose at canister.
5. Remove PCV valve from cylinder head cover and allow to draw underhood air.
6. Connect tachometer, then start engine and allow to reach normal operating temperature.
7. Adjust Solenoid Idle Stop, if equipped, as follows:
   a. On models with A/C, turn on A/C and set blower on low, then disconnect A/C clutch wire.
   b. On models less A/C, connect jumper wire between battery positive terminal and the SIS lead wire. **Ensure correct jumper wire installation. Applying battery voltage to other than correct wire will damage wiring harness.**
   c. On all models, open throttle slightly to allow solenoid plunger to extend.
   d. Remove adjusting screw and spring from solenoid, then insert 1/8 inch Allen wrench into the solenoid and adjust to 900 RPM.
   e. Turn off A/C and reconnect clutch wire or remove jumper, if equipped.
   f. Install solenoid screw and spring.
8. On models equipped with oxygen sensor feedback, remove exhaust manifold heat shield, then disconnect electrical connector from oxygen sensor and ground connector.
9. Remove and plug vacuum hose at vacuum transducer on SCC, then install suitable vacuum pump to vacuum transducer and apply 16 inches of vacuum.
10. Allow engine to run for 2 minutes. If idle is not as specified, turn adjusting screw to obtain correct RPM.
11. On models not equipped with oxygen sensor feedback, allow engine to run for one minute.
12. If idle RPM is not as specified, turn idle speed screw to obtain correct RPM.
13. On all models, turn off engine, connect vacuum lines and remove tachometer. Remove jumper wire and connect oxygen sensor electrical connector, if equipped. **After step 13 has been completed, idle speed may change slightly. This condition is normal and engine speed should not be readjusted.**

FAST IDLE SPEED

1. Disconnect and plug vacuum hose at EGR valve and distributor, if equipped.
2. On models equipped with carburetor ground switch, connect jumper wire between switch and ground.
3. On models not equipped with spark control computer (SCC), disconnect and plug vacuum hose from carburetor at heated air temperature sensor.
4. On all models, disconnect and plug control hose at canister.
5. Remove PCV valve from cylinder head cover and allow to draw underhood air.
6. Connect tachometer, then start engine and allow to reach normal operating temperature.
7. On models equipped with oxygen sensor feedback, disconnect electrical connector from oxygen sensor and ground connector, then allow engine to run for two minutes.
8. On models not equipped with oxygen sensor feedback, allow engine to run for one minute.
9. On all models, open throttle slightly and position fast idle adjusting screw on second highest step of fast idle cam.
10. Open choke fully, then adjust fast idle speed screw to obtain specified RPM.
11. Return to idle, then reposition adjusting screw on second highest step of fast idle came to ensure correct RPM. Readjust if necessary.

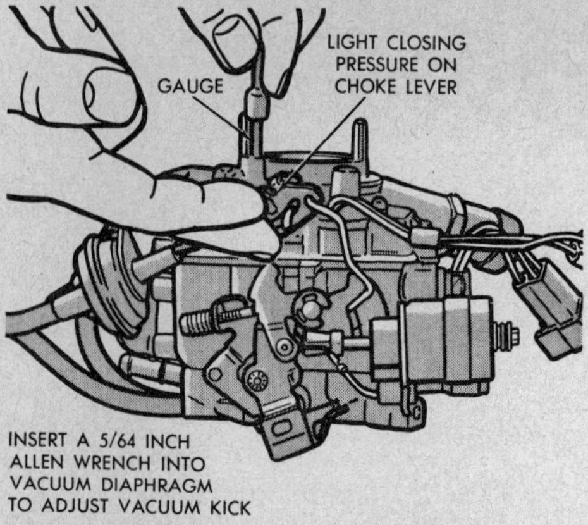

Fig. 4 Choke vacuum kick adjustment 6145 carburetor (Typical)

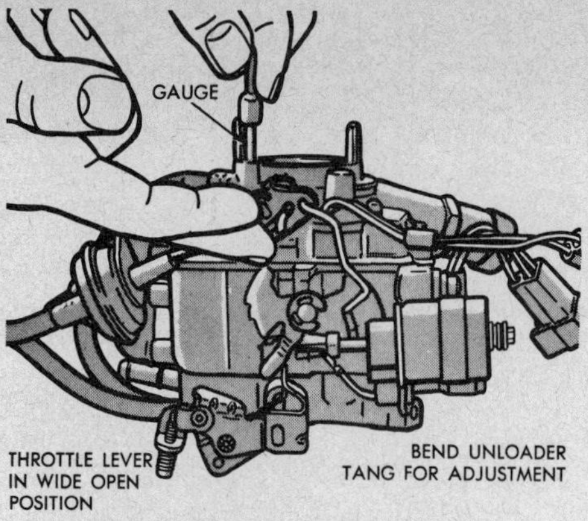

Fig. 5 Choke unloader adjustment. 6145 carburetor

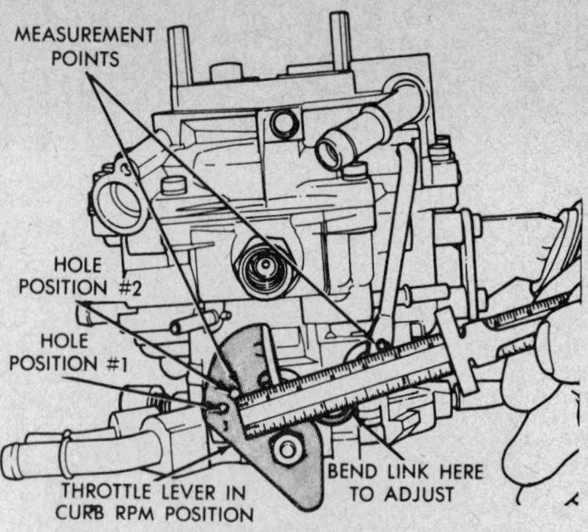

Fig. 6 Accelerator pump adjustment. 6145 carburetor

DRY FLOAT SETTING

Hold float fulcrum retaining pin in position and invert carburetor bowl, **Fig. 2.** Place a straightedge across surface of bowl, contracting float toes. Remove straightedge and measure distance float dropped from surface of fuel bowl. Refer to adjustment specifications. Adjust by bending float tang to obtain proper dimension.

FAST IDLE CAM POSITION

With fast idle speed adjusting screw contacting second highest step on fast idle cam, **Fig. 3,** move choke valve toward closed position with light pressure on choke shaft lever. Insert specified gauge between top of choke valve and wall of air horn. Refer to adjustment specifications. An adjustment will be necessary if a slight drag is not obtained as drill shank is being removed. Adjust by bending fast idle link at lower angle, until correct valve opening has been obtained.

CHOKE VACUUM KICK

Test can be made on or off vehicle.

If adjustment is to be made with engine running, back off fast idle speed screw until choke can be closed to the kick position with engine at curb idle, **Fig. 4.** (Note number of screw turns required so that fast idle can be returned to original adjustment). If an auxiliary vacuum source is to be used, open throttle valve (engine not running) and move choke to closed position. Release throttle first, then release choke.

When using an auxiliary vacuum source, disconnect vacuum hose from carburetor and connect it to hose from vacuum supply with a small length of tube to act as a fitting. Removal of hose from diaphragm may require forces which damage the system. Apply a vacuum of 15 or more inches of mercury.

Insert gauge between top of choke valve and wall of air horn. Refer to adjustment specifications. Apply sufficient closing pressure on lever to which choke rod attaches to provide a minimum choke valve opening without distortion of diaphragm link.

The cylindrical stem of diaphragm extends as the internal spring is compressed. This spring must be fully compressed for proper measurement of vacuum kick adjustment.

Adjustment is necessary if slight drag is not obtained when removing the gauge. Shorten or lengthen diaphragm link to obtain correct choke valve opening. Length changes should be made by carefully opening or closing the U-bend provided in the link. Improper bending causes contact between the U-section and the diaphragm assembly.

Do not apply twisting or bending force to diaphragm.

After completion of adjustment, reinstall vacuum hose on correct carburetor fitting. Return fast idle screw to its original location if disturbed. Make following check. With no vacuum applied to diaphragm, the choke valve should move freely between open and closed positions. If movement is not free, examine linkage for improper alignment or interferences caused by bending operation.

On 1982-83 models, adjustment is made by means of a 5/64 inch Allen wrench inserted into vacuum diaphragm.

CHOKE UNLOADER (WIDE OPEN KICK)

With throttle valves in wide open position, insert drill gauge between upper edge of choke valve and inner wall of air horn, **Fig. 5.** Refer to adjustment specifications. With a finger lightly pressing against shaft lever, a slight drag should be felt as drill is being withdrawn. Adjust by bending unloader tang on throttle lever until correct opening has been obtained.

ACCELERATOR PUMP SETTING

With throttle at curb idle position, measure length of pump operating link, **Fig. 6.** Refer to adjustment specification. Adjust by bending link between throttle lever and pump operating rod.

Holley Model 6280 2 Barrel Carburetor

INDEX

ADJUSTMENT SPECIFICATIONS

Year	Carb. Part No.	Float Level (Dry) ①	Pump Setting	Vacuum Kick	Fast Idle Cam	Choke Unloader	Choke Setting
1985	R-40121A	9/32	②	.130	.060	.280	③
1986-87	R-40276A	9/32	②	.130	.060	.280	③

①—Measured at end of floats furthest from pivot.

②—Flush with top of bowl vent casting.

③—Tamper-resistant.

IDENTIFICATION LOCATION

The identification number is generally located on the left side on the front of the carburetor base.

DESCRIPTION

These dual venturi carburetors, **Fig. 1**, use four basic metering systems. The basic idling system provides a mixture for idle and low speed. The accelerator pump system provides fuel needed for acceleration. The main metering system provides an economical mixture for normal cruising conditions. The power enrichment system combines a mechanical and vacuum operated power valve to provide a richer mixture when high power output is necessary.

These carburetors also have a fuel inlet system to constantly supply fuel to the basic metering systems and a choke system to temporarily enrich the mixture for efficient starting and running of a cold engine.

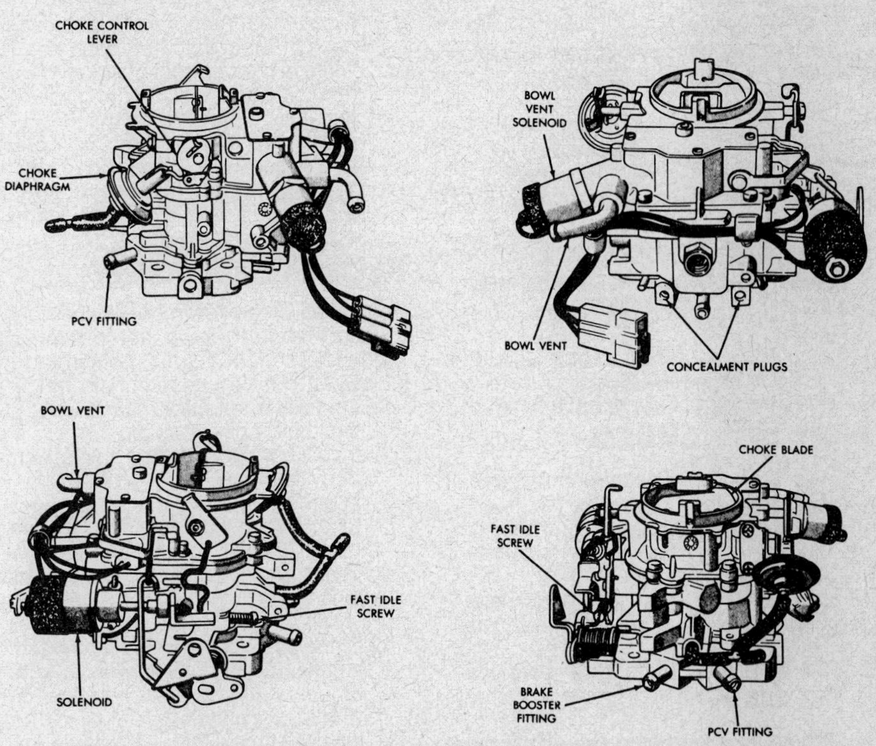

Fig. 1 Holley model 6280 carburetor assembly

ON-VEHICLE ADJUSTMENTS

CURB IDLE SPEED

1. Disconnect and plug vacuum hose at EGR valve.
2. Disconnect and plug hose from carburetor at the heated air temperature sensor.
3. Remove air cleaner, then disconnect and plug canister purge hose at canister.
4. Remove PCV valve from valve cover and allow valve to draw underhood air.
5. Disconnect and plug vacuum advance at ESA unit.
6. Connect suitable tachometer to engine.
7. Disconnect carburetor electrical connector, then remove green duty cycle wire and blue idle solenoid wire from connector. Reconnect carburetor electrical connector less the two removed wires.
8. Ground carburetor switch using a suitable jumper wire.
9. Attach a suitable jumper wire between solenoid idle stop terminal blue wire and positive battery terminal. **Use caution in jumping proper wire on solenoid. If battery voltage is applied to incorrect wire, damage to wiring harness may occur.**
10. Start engine and allow to reach normal operating temperature, then open throttle slightly to allow solenoid plunger to extend.
11. Remove solenoid outer spring and screw, then insert a suitable Allen wrench into the solenoid and adjust idle speed to 775 RPM.
12. Install screw and spring until outer screw lightly bottoms out.
13. Remove jumper wire, then turn out solenoid screw until specified curb idle RPM is obtained.
14. Remove tachometer, connect vacuum hoses and install PCV valve and air cleaner.
15. Disconnect carburetor electrical con-

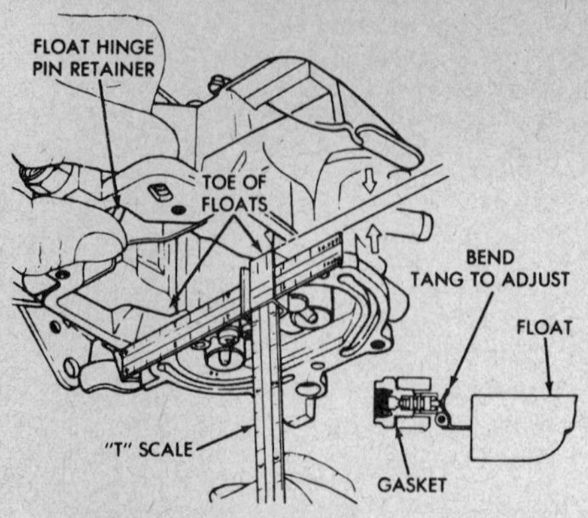

Fig. 2 Adjusting float setting

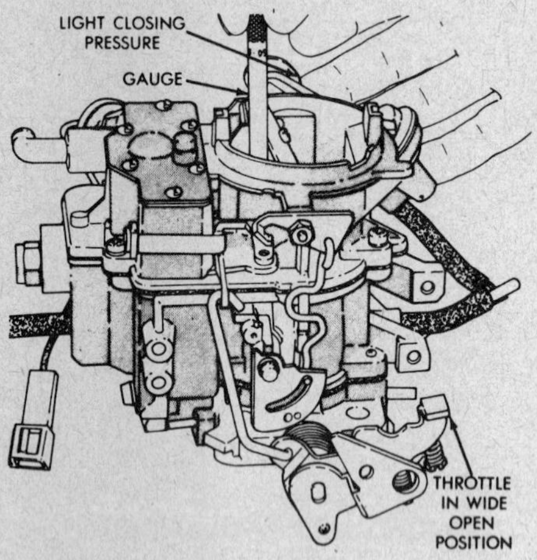

Fig. 5 Adjusting choke unloader

nector, then install green and blue wires in their correct positions. Reconnect carburetor electrical connector.

FAST IDLE SPEED

1. Disconnect and plug vacuum hose at EGR valve.
2. Disconnect and plug hose from carburetor at the heated air temperature sensor.
3. Remove air cleaner, then disconnect and plug canister purge hose at canister.
4. Remove PCV valve from valve cover and allow valve to draw underhood air.
5. Disconnect and plug vacuum hose at distributor.
6. Connect suitable tachometer, then start engine and allow to reach normal operating temperature.
7. Disconnect carburetor electrical connector, then remove green duty cycle wire and blue idle solenoid wire from the connector. Reconnect carburetor electrical connector less the two removed wires.
8. Ground carburetor switch using a suitable jumper wire.
9. Open throttle and place fast idle adjusting screw on the second highest step of fast idle cam.
10. With choke fully open, turn fast idle adjusting screw until specified fast idle speed is obtained.

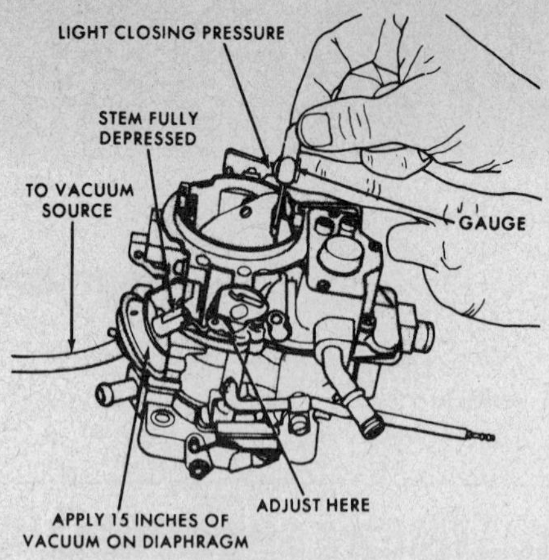

Fig. 3 Adjusting choke valve kick

11. Return to idle, then reposition adjusting screw on the second highest step of fast idle cam to ensure speed is correct. Readjust as necessary.
12. Connect vacuum hoses, then remove jumper wires.
13. Disconnect carburetor electrical connector, then install green and blue wires in their correct positions. Reconnect carburetor electrical connector.
14. Install air cleaner, then the PCV valve. **After step 14 has been completed, idle speed may change slightly. This condition is normal and engine speed should not be readjusted.**

FLOAT LEVEL (DRY)

1. Install hinge pin in float assembly, insert hinge through slot in float baffle with tabs on baffle pointing downward, position assembly in hinge pin cradle in carburetor main body and install hinge pin retainer.
2. Install needle, seat and gasket in main body and tighten securely.
3. Invert main body, catching pump intake check ball, so that weight of floats only is forcing needle against seats and hold finger against hinge pin retainer to fully seat in float pin cradle.
4. Using straightedge, **Fig. 2,** check float setting. If measurement from surface of fuel bowl to toe of each float is not within specifications, adjust by bending float tang. Bend either float arm to equalize individual float positions.

CHOKE VALVE KICK

1. Open throttle and close choke, then close throttle to trap fast idle cam at closed choke position.
2. Disconnect vacuum hose at carburetor and connect to hose of auxiliary vacuum source with small length of tube, then apply a vacuum of at least 15 inches Hg, **Fig. 3.**
3. Apply enough force on choke lever to completely compress spring in diaphragm stem without distorting linkage.
4. Measure by inserting .13 inch gauge in center of area between top of choke valve and air horn wall.

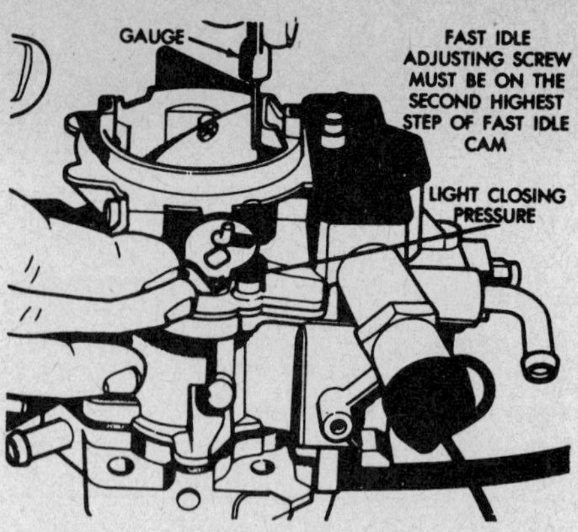

Fig. 4 Adjusting fast idle cam position

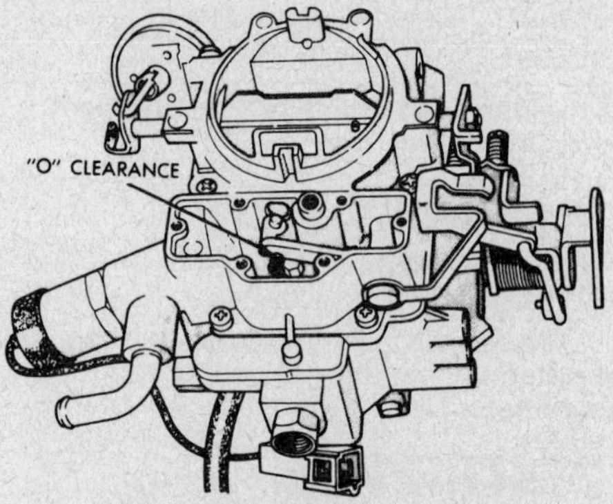

Fig. 6 Measuring accelerator pump stroke

5. Adjust as necessary by changing diaphragm link length by opening or closing U-bend.
6. Check for free movement between open and adjusted positions, correcting any improper alignment or interference.
7. Install vacuum hose on correct carburetor fitting.

FAST IDLE CAM POSITION

1. With fast idle speed adjusting screw contacting second highest speed step on fast idle cam, move choke valve toward closed position with light pressure on choke shaft lever.
2. Measure by inserting .06 inch gauge in center of area between choke valve and air horn wall, **Fig. 4.**
3. Adjust by opening or closing U-bend in fast idle connector link until correct valve opening has been obtained.

CHOKE UNLOADER (WIDE OPEN KICK)

1. Hold throttle valves in wide open position.
2. Lightly press finger against control lever to move choke valve toward closed position.
3. Measure by inserting .28 inch gauge in center of area between top of choke valve and air horn wall, **Fig. 5.**
4. Adjust by bending tang on accelerator pump lever.

ACCELERATOR PUMP STROKE

1. Remove bowl vent cover plate and gasket.
2. With all pump links and levers installed, adjust accelerator pump cap nut for zero clearance between pump lever and cap nut, **Fig. 6.**
3. Ensure wide open throttle can be reached without binding.
4. Install gasket and bowl vent cover plate.

Holley Model 6520 2 Barrel Carburetor

INDEX

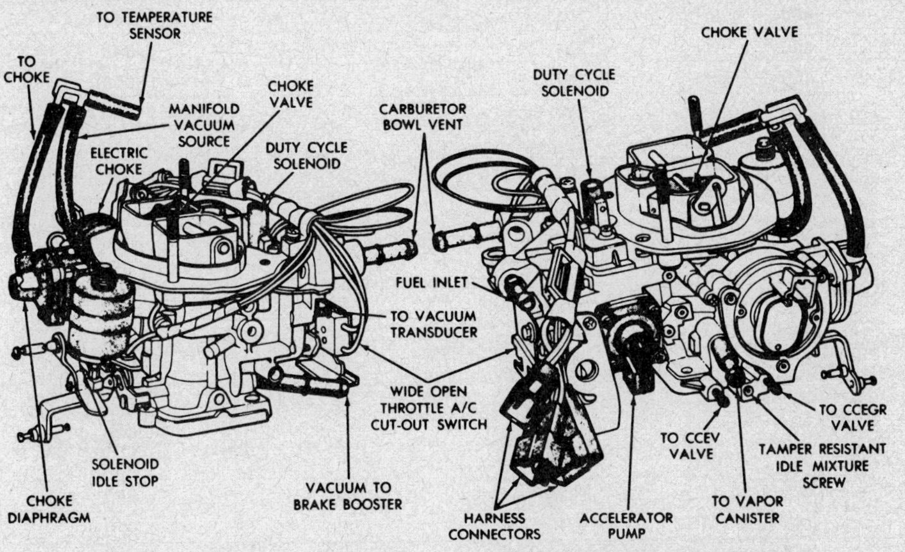

Fig. 1 Holley Model 6520 Carburetor (Typical)

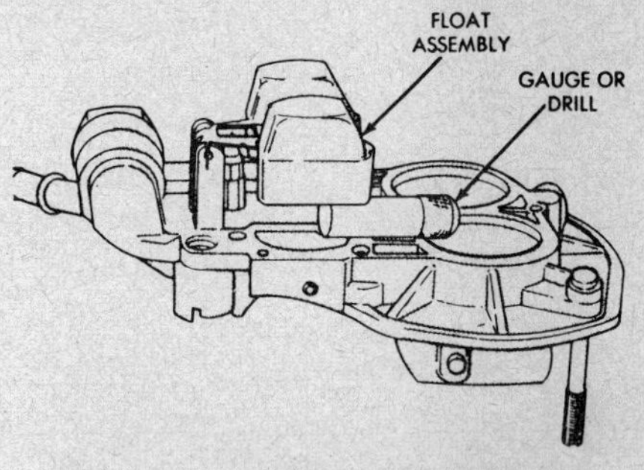

Fig. 2 Measuring float level. 6520 carburetor

IDENTIFICATION LOCATION

The carburetor identification number is stamped on the carburetor body on either the driver or passenger side.

DESCRIPTION

1982–84 UNITS

The Holley model 6520, **Fig. 1,** is a staged dual venturi electronic feedback carburetor. The primary bore is smaller than the secondary bore. The secondary stage is mechanically operated by linkage connecting the primary and secondary throttle levers. The primary stage includes a curb idle and transfer system, diaphragm type accelerator pump system, main metering system and a fuel regulator solenoid responsive to oxygen sensor. The secondary stage includes a main metering system and power system. Both the primary and secondary venturi draw fuel from a common fuel bowl. The electronic automatic choke incorporates a two stage heating element. On manual transmission carburetors, only one choke valve is used, while on automatic transmission carburetors, two choke valves are used.

The 6520 electronic feedback carburetor also incorporates a duty cycle solenoid which provides a limited regulation of air-fuel ratio in response to electrical signals from the spark control computer. The solenoid meters the main fuel system and operates in parallel with a conventional fixed main metering jet. When there is no electrical signal applied to the solenoid, the valve spring pushes upward through the main system fuel valve, fully uncovering the solenoid controlled main metering orifice so that the richest condition exists within the carburetor for any given airflow. When the electrical signal is applied to the solenoid, the field windings are energized, thus causing the armature to move the pushrod and main system valve downward against the valve spring. This movement will continue until the main system valve bottoms against the main system valve seat. In this position the solenoid controlled main metering orifice is fully sealed so that the leanest condition exists within the carburetor for any given airflow. This condition will remain unchanged until the signal from the spark control computer to the solenoid is switched off. The main system fuel may be regulated between richest and leanest limits by controlling the amount of time that the solenoid is in the power on position. Under normal operating conditions, 12 volts at a frequency of 10 Hz is applied to the field windings. By controlling the duration of the voltage signal, the power on time to total time, referred to as the duty cycle, is established.

1983 units incorporate a deceleration fuel shut off system which provides a very lean air-fuel mixture during deceleration. This is accomplished by opening a solenoid controlled idle air bleed. This system also prevents engine dieseling by making the air-fuel mixture too lean to support combustion when the engine is turned off. The fuel shut off solenoid opens the additional idle air bleed when the throttle is closed and engine RPM is above a preset speed.

1985–87 UNITS

These are staged venturi carburetors. The primary bore or venturi is smaller than the secondary bore. The secondary stage is operated by a vacuum controlled diaphragm.

The primary stage includes a curb idle and transfer system, diaphragm type accelerator pump system, main metering system, power enrichment system and oxygen feedback solenoid that is responsive to the oxygen sensor.

The secondary stage includes a main metering system and power system. Both

ADJUSTMENT SPECIFICATIONS

Year	Model No.	Float Level	Float Drop	Acc. Pump Hole No.	Choke Vacuum Kick
1982	R-9503A	.480	1⁷/₈	3	.060
	R-9504A	.480	1⁷/₈	3	.070
	R-9505A	.480	1⁷/₈	3	.070
	R-9506A	.480	1⁷/₈	3	.070
	R-9507A	.480	1⁷/₈	3	.085
	R-9508A	.480	1⁷/₈	3	.085
	R-9509A	.480	1⁷/₈	3	.085
	R-9510A	.480	1⁷/₈	3	.085
	R-9750A	.480	1⁷/₈	3	.060
	R-9751A	.480	1⁷/₈	3	.060
	R-9752A	.480	1⁷/₈	3	.070
	R-9753A	.480	1⁷/₈	3	.070
	R-9822A	.480	1⁷/₈	2	.047
	R-9823A	.480	1⁷/₈	2	.047
	R-9824A	.480	1⁷/₈	2	.040
	R-9940A	.480	1⁷/₈	3	.050
	R-9941A	.480	1⁷/₈	3	.050
	R-9942A	.480	1⁷/₈	3	.050
	R-9943A	.480	1⁷/₈	3	.050
1983	R-40003A	.480	1⁷/₈	3	.070
	R-40004A	.480	1⁷/₈	3	.065
	R-40006A	.480	1⁷/₈	3	.080
	R-40007A	.480	1⁷/₈	3	.070
	R-40008A	.480	1⁷/₈	3	.070
	R-40010A	.480	1⁷/₈	3	.065
	R-40012A	.480	1⁷/₈	3	.070
	R-40014A	.480	1⁷/₈	3	.080
	R-40080A	.480	1⁷/₈	2	.045
	R-40081A	.480	1⁷/₈	2	.045
1984	R-400581A	.480	1⁷/₈	2	.070
	R-400641A	.480	1⁷/₈	3	.080
	R-400651A	.480	1⁷/₈	3	.080
	R-40071A	.480	1⁷/₈	3	.080
	R-40081-1A	.480	1⁷/₈	2	.080
	R-400821A	.480	1⁷/₈	2	.080
	R-401071A	.480	1⁷/₈	2	.055
	R-40122A	.480	1⁷/₈	2	.080
1985	R-40058-A	.480	1⁷/₈	2	.070
	R-40134-A	.480	1⁷/₈	3	.075
	R-40135-A	.480	1⁷/₈	3	.075
	R-40138-A	.480	1⁷/₈	3	.075
	R-40139-A	.480	1⁷/₈	3	.075
1986	R-40058-1A	.480	1⁷/₈	—	.070
	R-40134-A	.480	1⁷/₈	—	.075
	R-40135-1A	.480	1⁷/₈	—	.075
	R-40138-A	.480	1⁷/₈	—	.075
	R-40138-1A	.480	1⁷/₈	—	.075
	R-40139-1A	.480	1⁷/₈	—	.075
1987	R-40295-A	.480	1⁷/₈	—	.075
	R-40296-A	.480	1⁷/₈	—	.075

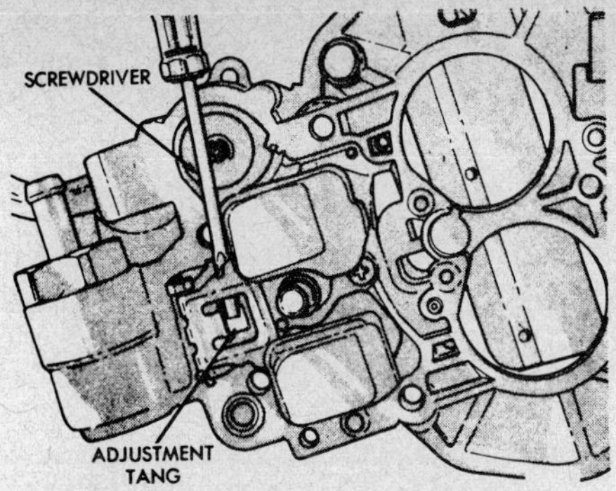

Fig. 3 Adjusting float level. 6520 carburetor

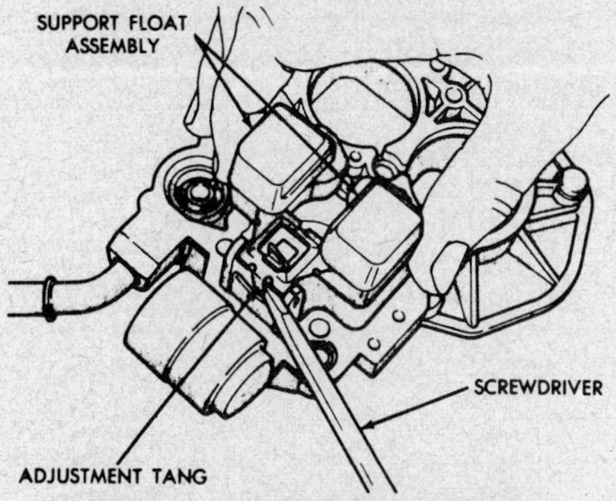

Fig. 5 Adjusting float drop. 6520 carburetor

the primary and secondary venturi draw fuel from a common fuel bowl.

The electric automatic choke has a bi-metal two stage heating element.

ON-VEHICLE ADJUSTMENTS

CURB IDLE SPEED

1982

1. Disconnect and plug vacuum hose at EGR valve and distributor, if equipped.
2. Disconnect electrical connector at radiator fan, then install jumper wire so fan will run continuously.
3. Remove PCV valve from connector and allow to draw underhood air, then plug the 3/16 inch diameter vacuum hose from canister.
4. On models equipped with fuel control computer, connect jumper wire between carburetor switch and ground.
5. On all models, connect tachometer, then start engine and allow to reach normal operating temperature.
6. Turn off all lights and accessories.
7. On models equipped with A/C, proceed as follows:
   a. Turn on A/C, then open throttle slightly to energize solenoid.
   b. Remove adjusting screw and spring from top of A/C solenoid.
   c. Adjust solenoid to specified idle speed using a 1/8 inch Allen wrench. **Ensure A/C clutch is operating during idle speed adjustment.**
   d. Install adjusting screw and spring on solenoid.
8. On all models, note tachometer reading. If not within specifications, turn idle speed screw on top of solenoid to obtain correct idle speed. **On all models equipped with A/C, allow engine speed to stabilize one minute after performing A/C idle speed adjustment.**

1983–87

1. Disconnect and plug vacuum connectors from Coolant Controlled EGR valve (CCEGR) or Coolant Vacuum Switch Cold Closed Valve (CVSCC), if equipped.
2. Disconnect electrical connector at radiator fan, then install jumper wire so fan will run continuously.
3. Remove PCV valve and allow valve to draw underhood air.
4. Connect tachometer, then ground carburetor switch with suitable jumper wire.
5. On 4-105 engines equipped with A/C, proceed as follows:
   a. Turn on A/C, then open throttle slightly to energize solenoid.
   b. Remove adjusting screw and spring from top of A/C solenoid.
   c. Adjust solenoid to specified idle speed using a 1/8 inch Allen wrench. **Ensure A/C clutch is operating during idle speed adjustment.**
   d. Install adjusting screw and spring on solenoid.
6. On 1984-87 models, disconnect oxygen sensor system test connector located on left fender shield.
7. On all models, start engine and allow to reach normal operating temperature, then note engine RPM.
8. If RPM is not within specifications, turn idle speed adjusting screw until specified speed is obtained.
9. Connect PCV valve, oxygen sensor connector and vacuum connectors, then remove jumper wire and connect fan electrical connector. **After step 9 has been completed, idle speed may change slightly. This condition is normal and engine speed should not be readjusted.**

FAST IDLE SPEED

1. Disconnect and plug vacuum hose from EGR valve on 1982 models or CCEGR/CVSCC valve on 1983-87 models.
2. Disconnect electrical connector from radiator fan, then install jumper wire so fan will run continuously.
3. Remove PCV valve and allow to draw underhood air, then, on 1982 models, plug vacuum hose at canister.
4. Connect tachometer, then ground carburetor switch with suitable jumper wire, if equipped.
5. On 1983-87 models, disconnect oxygen sensor system test connector located on left fender shield, if equipped.
6. On all models, start engine and allow to reach normal operating temperature.
7. Open throttle slightly and place adjustment screw on slowest speed step of fast idle cam.

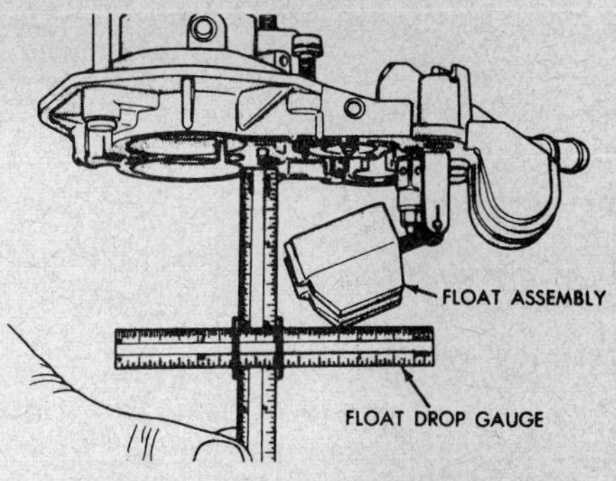

Fig. 4 Measuring float drop. 6520 carburetor

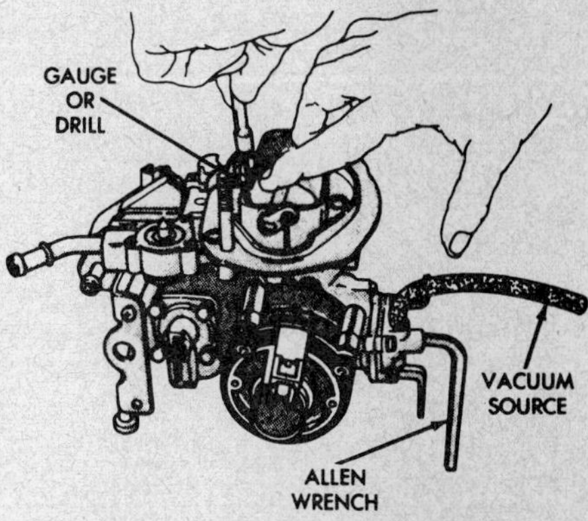

Fig. 6 Adjusting choke vacuum kick. 6520 carburetor

8. Open choke valve and adjust fast idle speed to specifications.
9. Return to curb idle, then place adjusting screw on slowest step of fast idle cam and readjust if necessary.
10. Connect PCV valve, oxygen sensor connector and vacuum connectors, then remove radiator fan jumper wire.

FLOAT LEVEL (DRY)

Invert air horn and insert specified gauge between float and air horn, **Figs. 2 abd 3.** To adjust, use a small screwdriver to bend tang.

FLOAT DROP

Using a suitable depth gauge measure float drop, **Figs. 4 and 5.** To adjust, use a small screwdriver to bend tang.

CHOKE VACUUM KICK

Open throttle and close choke valve, **Fig. 6,** then close throttle to retain choke valve in the closed position. Disconnect vacuum hose from carburetor and connect an external vacuum source. Apply 15 inches Hg of vacuum or more. Apply sufficient closing pressure to choke valve, using care not to distort linkage. Note that an internal spring will compress to a stop within the choke system. Insert the specified gauge in center area between top of choke valve and air horn wall at primary throttle end of carburetor. Adjust clearance by rotating the Allen head screw in center of diaphragm housing.

Mikuni 2 Barrel Carburetor

INDEX

ADJUSTMENT SPECIFICATIONS

Year	Model No.	Float Level	Fast Idle Opening at 68°F	Choke Breaker Opening at 14°F	Unloader Opening at 32°F
1982	MD025430	.779	15.5°	.067	.051
	MD025432	.779	15.5°	.067	.051
1983	MD017066	.779	15.5°	.067	.051
	MD017306	.779	15.5°	.067	.051
	MD017307	.779	15.5°	.067	.051
1984	4243740	.779	—	.067	.051
	4243743	.779	—	.067	.051
1985	MD082758	.779	—	.067	.051
	MD088137	.779	—	.067	.051

IDENTIFICATION LOCATION

The carburetor identification number is stamped on carburetor air horn surface near bowl vent valve.

DESCRIPTION

1982–83 ALL & 1984 CALIFORNIA MODELS

The Mikuni non-feedback carburetor, **Fig. 1**, is a conventional downdraft two barrel compound type carburetor. The automatic choke on these units is of the thermo-wax type which is controlled by engine coolant temperature. The main body on these units consists of a black resin compound. Other features of these units include a diaphragm type accelerator pump, bowl vent, fuel cut-off solenoid, air switching valve, sub-EGR valve, coasting air valve and jet air control valve. California units also incorporate a high altitude compensation system.

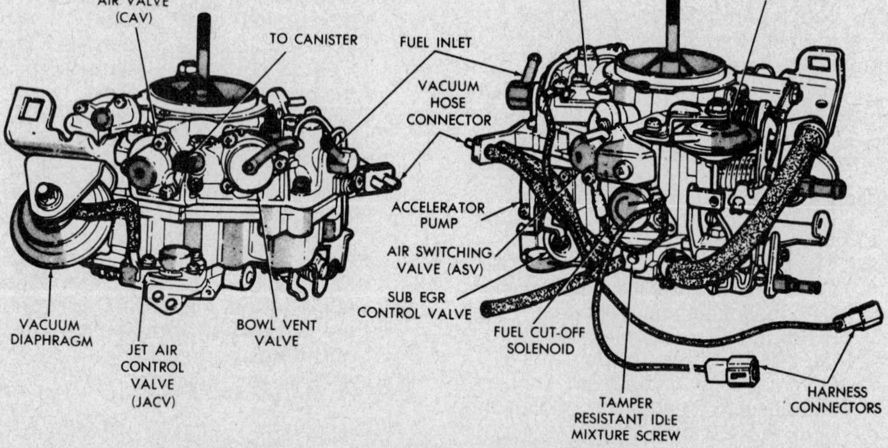

Fig. 1 Mikuni non-feedback carburetor assembly

1984 EXC. CALIFORNIA MODELS & 1985 ALL

The Mikuni feedback carburetor, **Fig. 2**, is a two barrel down draft carburetor designed for electronic fuel control and closed loop operation.

With a closed loop system of mixture control, this carburetor provides optimum air/fuel control during all ranges of engine operation. Fuel metering is accomplished through the use of three solenoid valves that reduce or add fuel to the engine.

The fuel flow through the valves is controlled by the length of time electrical current is supplied to the solenoids. The solenoids operate at a fixed frequency generated by the electronic control unit. By varying the amount of time that the solenoid is energized during each duty cycle, the air/fuel mixture delivered to the engine can be precisely controlled. The duty cycle applied to the solenoid is controlled by the electronic control unit in response to signals received from various sensors.

There are eight basic systems in the feedback carburetor: fuel inlet, primary metering, secondary metering accelerator pump, choke, jet mixture, enrichment and fuel cut-off. The first five systems are basically the same as those on the non-feedback carburetor while the last three are unique to the feedback carburetor.

ON-VEHICLE ADJUSTMENTS

CURB IDLE SPEED

1. Apply parking brake and place transaxle in Neutral position.
2. Turn off all lights and accessories, then disconnect radiator fan electrical connector.
3. Connect tachometer, then start engine and allow to reach normal operating temperature.
4. On models equipped with oxygen sensor, proceed as follows:
   a. Turn off engine.
   b. Disconnect battery ground cable

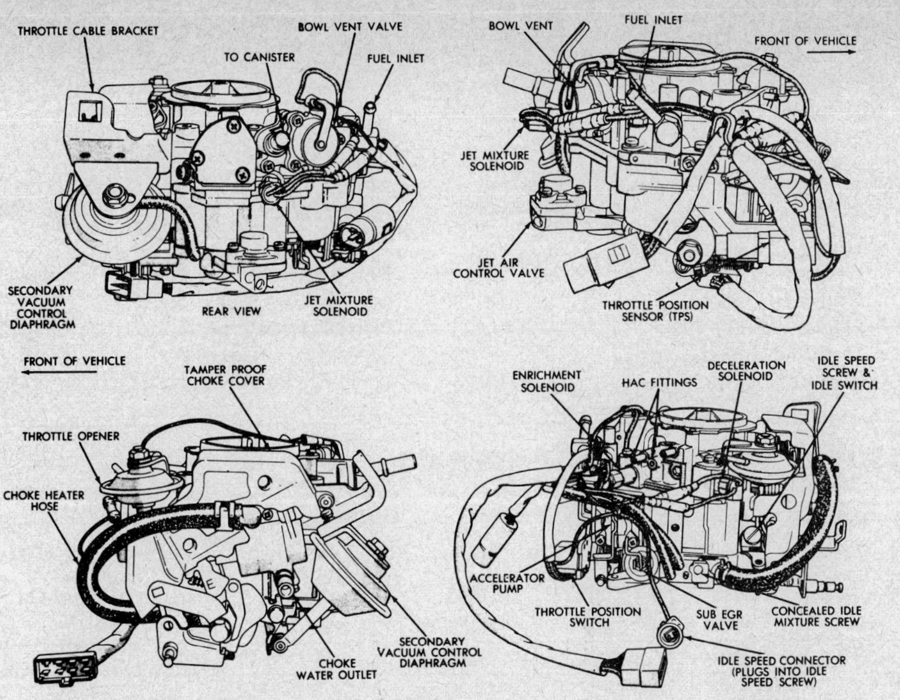

Fig. 2 Mikuni feedback carburetor assembly

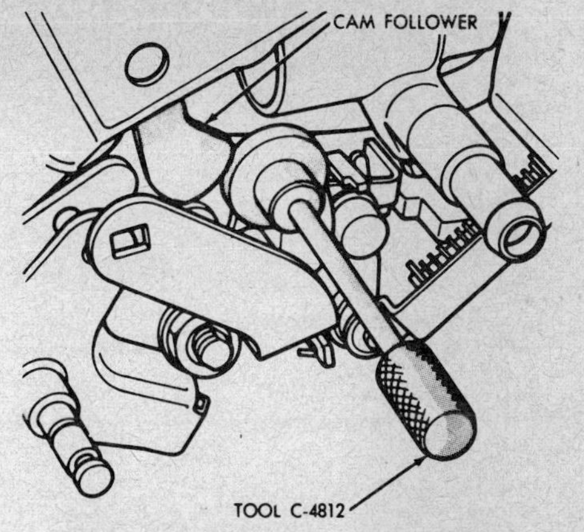

Fig. 3 Typical fast idle speed adjustment tool installation. Mikuni carburetor

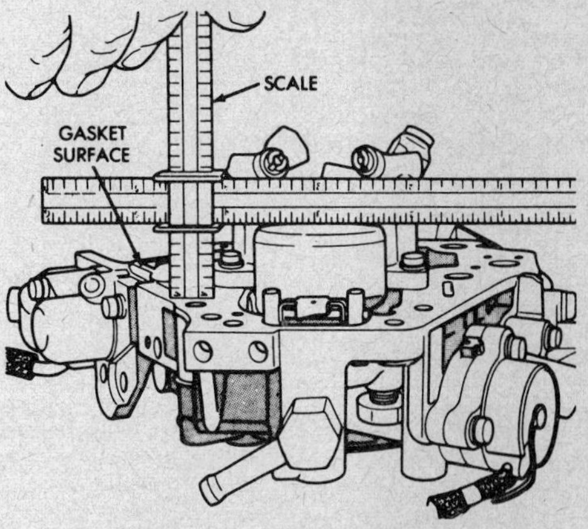

Fig. 4 Float level adjustment. Mikuni carburetor

for three seconds, then reconnect cable.

c. Disconnect oxygen sensor electrical connector. **Use caution when working around sensor as exhaust manifold may be extremely hot.**

d. Start engine and allow to run at 2500 RPM for 10 seconds, then return to idle.

5. On all models, allow engine speed to stabilize, then note engine RPM. If not within specifications, turn adjusting screw to obtain correct idle speed.
6. On models equipped with oxygen sensor, remove idle switch connector, then turn off engine and connect oxygen sensor electrical connector.
7. On models equipped with A/C, allow engine idle speed to stabilize, then set temperature control lever to coldest position and turn on A/C. Set engine speed to 900 RPM by turning idle up screw. **Ensure A/C compressor is operating during idle speed adjustment.**
8. On all models, turn off engine, reconnect fan, disconnect tachometer and connect idle speed connector, if equipped.

FAST IDLE SPEED

1984–85

1. Set parking brake and place transaxle in Neutral position.
2. Turn off lights and accessories, then disconnect radiator fan electrical connector.
3. Connect tachometer, then start engine and allow to reach normal operating temperature.
4. Disconnect and plug vacuum hose from distributor.
5. Open throttle and install tool No. C-4812 or equivalent on choke cam follower pin, **Fig. 3.**
6. Release throttle lever and adjust fast idle speed to specifications.
7. Remove tool, then turn off engine, connect fan and vacuum hose and remove tachometer.

FLOAT LEVEL

Invert air horn, with gasket removed, and measure distance from bottom of float to surface of air horn, using a suitable depth gauge, **Fig. 4.** If reading is not within limits, the shim located under needle seat must be changed. Use shim kit MD606952 or equivalent, which has three shims with thicknesses of .012 inch, .016 inch and .02 inch. Adding or removing a shim will change float level by three times the thickness of the shims.

Rochester Quadrajet 4 Barrel Carburetor

INDEX

ADJUSTMENT SPECIFICATIONS

Year	Model No.	Float Level	Choke Rod	Choke Coil Lever	Choke Vacuum Kick	Air Valve Rod	Secondary Lockout	Choke Unloader	Air-Valve Spring Wind-Up
1985	17085407	7/16	.143	.120	.193	.025	.015	.250	7/8
1986-87	17085433	7/16	.120	.120	.140	.025	.015	.180	7/8

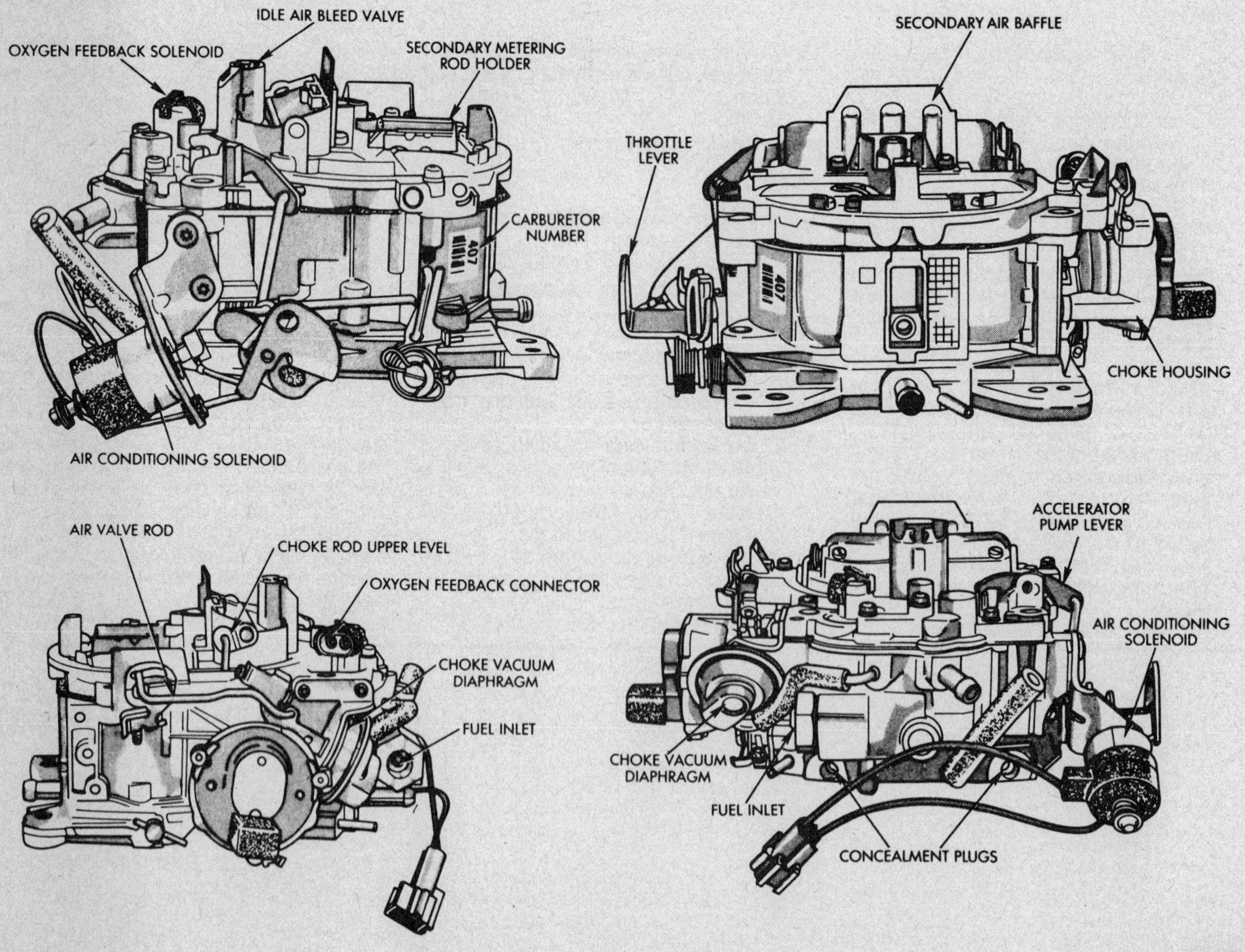

Fig. 1 Rochester Quadrajet carburetor assembly

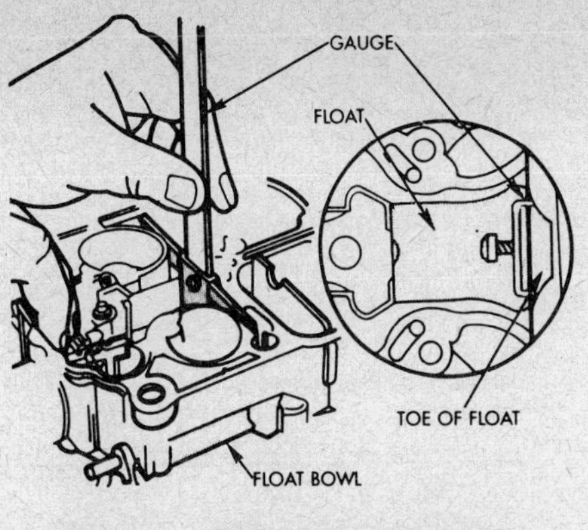

Fig. 2 Adjusting float

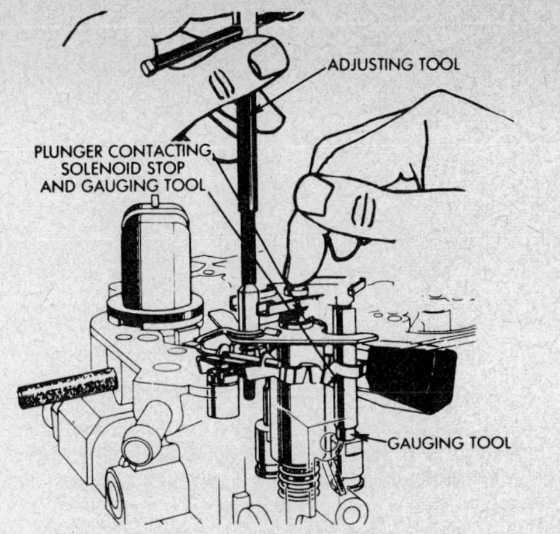

Fig. 3 Adjusting lean mixture screw

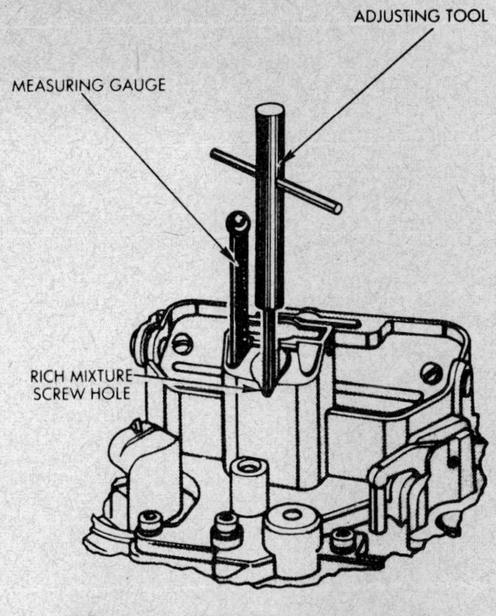

Fig. 4 Adjusting rich mixture stop screw

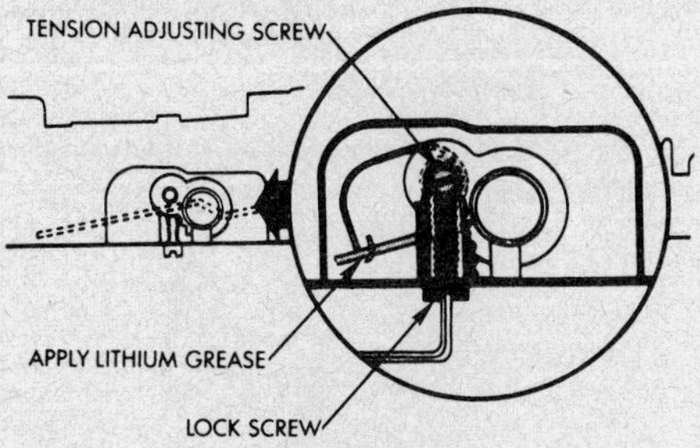

Fig. 5 Adjusting air valve spring

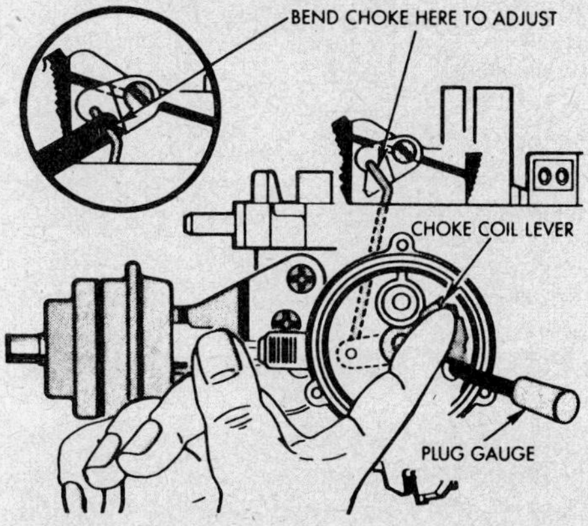

Fig. 6 Adjusting choke coil lever

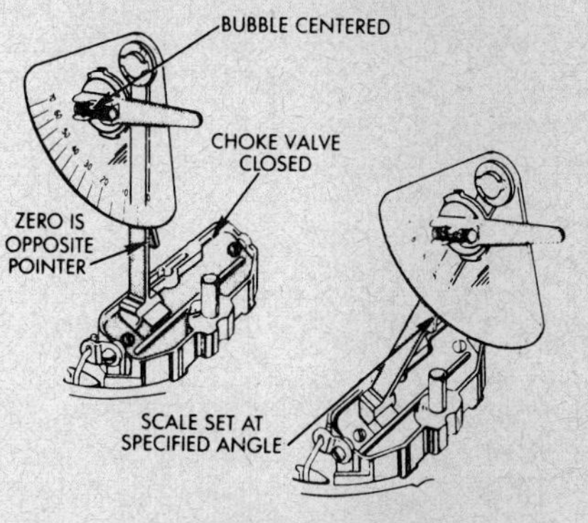

Fig. 7 Using choke valve angle gauge

IDENTIFICATION LOCATION

The carburetor identification number is a vertically stamped eight digit number. The number can be found on the left rear corner of the float bowl casting, adjacent to the secondary pickup lever.

DESCRIPTION

The Rochester Quadrajet carburetor, **Fig. 1**, is a four barrel two stage carburetor with three main carburetor assemblies; the air horn, float bowl and throttle body. There are six basic operating systems; the float system, idle system, main metering system, power system, pump system and choke system.

The float system maintains an adequate supply of fuel in the fuel bowl for use by various fuel delivery systems. A single float chamber supplies fuel to all carburetor bores. A closed cell rubber float, brass needle seat and plastic tipped float needle with pull clip are used to control fuel level in the float chamber.

Each carburetor bore has a separate and independent idle system to provide the correct air/fuel mixture to the engine during idle and off-speed operations. The idle system is necessary because air flow through the carburetor venturi is not sufficient to obtain efficient metering from the main discharge nozzles.

The main metering system supplies fuel to the engine from off-idle to wide open throttle. The system supplies air and fuel during this range through plain tube nozzles and the venturi principal. The multiple venturi in each bore produces excellent fuel metering control because of its sensitivity to air flow.

The power system provides additional mixture enrichment to meet power requirements under heavy engine loads and high speed operation. The richer mixtures are supplied by the main metering systems in the primary and secondary sides of the carburetor.

Air flow through the carburetor bores and intake manifold changes almost instantly during quick accelerations when the throttle is opened rapidly. The fuel, which is heavier, tends to lag behind, causing a momentary leanness. The accelerator pump system prevents this by providing the additional fuel necessary for smooth acceleration.

The offset choke valve is mounted in the air horn above the primary carburetor venturi. The closed choke valve provides the correct air/fuel mixture enrichment for cold engine starting. The choke valve also aids engine performance during warm up.

An electric choke coil is mounted in the choke housing. This system uses electric current supplied to the choke coil, which, combined with the offset choke valve and throttle position, control choke operation.

Fuel metering is controlled by two special shaped metering rods, operating in the main metering jets, and positioned by a plunger in the oxygen feedback solenoid. The solenoid plunger is controlled by an electrical output signal generated by a computer. The computer, responding to an electrical signal from the oxygen sensor in the exhaust manifold, alternately energizes the solenoid, moving the metering rods to the lean position, and de-energizes the solenoid, moving the metering rods to the rich position.

ON-VEHICLE ADJUSTMENTS

CURB IDLE SPEED

1. Disconnect and plug vacuum hose at EGR valve.
2. Disconnect and plug hose from carburetor at the heated air temperature sensor.
3. Remove air cleaner, then disconnect and plug canister purge hose at canister.
4. Remove PCV valve from valve cover and allow valve to draw underhood air.
5. Disconnect and plug vacuum advance at ESA unit.
6. Connect suitable tachometer to engine.
7. Disconnect carburetor electrical connector, then remove the green duty

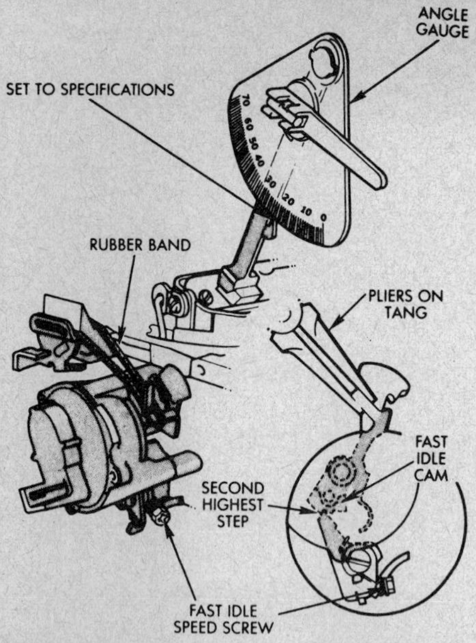

Fig. 8 Adjusting choke rod fast idle cam using angle gauge

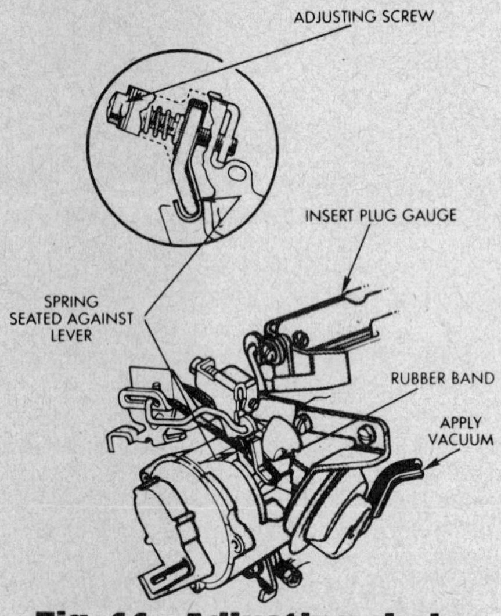

Fig. 11 Adjusting choke vacuum kick using plug gauge

cycle wire and blue idle solenoid wire from the connector. Reconnect carburetor electrical connector less the two removed wires.

8. Ground carburetor switch using a suitable jumper wire.
9. Attach suitable jumper wire between solenoid idle stop terminal blue wire and battery positive terminal. **Use caution in jumping proper wire on solenoid. If battery voltage is applied to incorrect wire, damage to wiring harness may occur.**
10. Start engine and allow to reach normal operating temperature, then open throttle slightly to allow solenoid plunger to extend.
11. Remove solenoid outer spring and screw, then insert a suitable Allen wrench into the solenoid and adjust idle speed to 775 RPM.
12. Install screw and spring until outer screw lightly bottoms out.

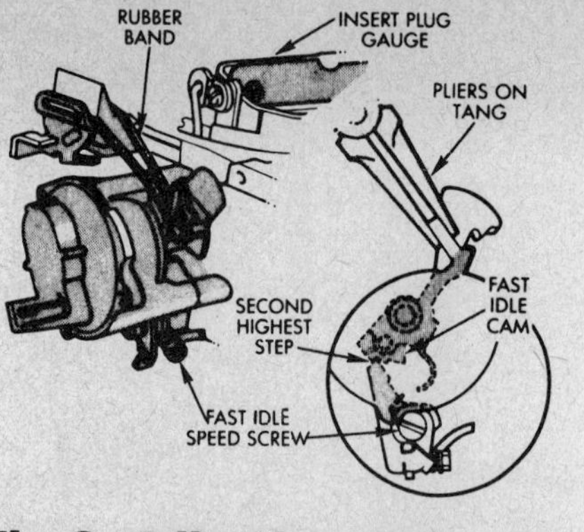

Fig. 9 Adjusting choke rod fast idle cam using plug gauge

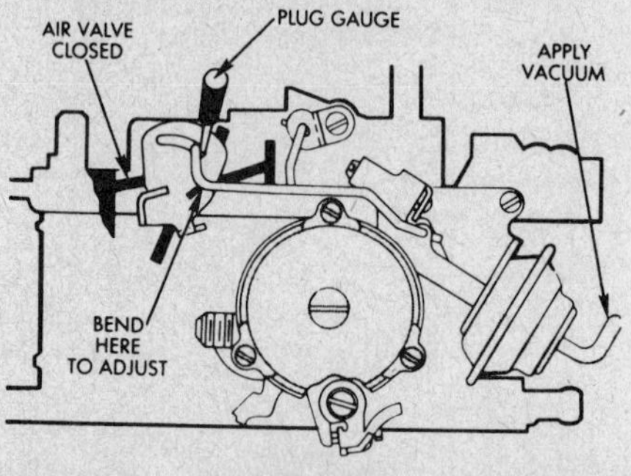

Fig. 12 Adjusting air valve rod

13. Remove jumper wire, then turn out solenoid screw until specified curb idle RPM is obtained.
14. Remove tachometer, connect vacuum hoses and install PCV valve and air cleaner.
15. Disconnect carburetor electrical connector, then install green and blue wires in their correct positions. Reconnect carburetor electrical connector.

FAST IDLE SPEED

1. Disconnect and plug vacuum hose at EGR valve.
2. Connect suitable jumper wire between carburetor switch and ground.
3. Disconnect and plug vacuum hose at canister.
4. Disconnect PCV valve from cylinder head cover and allow to draw underhood air.
5. Connect suitable tachometer, then start engine and allow to reach normal operating temperature.
6. Disconnect and ground oxygen sensor electrical connector.
7. Allow engine to run for 4 minutes, then open throttle slightly and place fast idle adjusting screw on the second highest step of fast idle cam.
8. With choke fully open, turn fast idle adjusting screw until specified fast idle speed is obtained.
9. Return to idle, then reposition adjusting screw on the second highest step of fast idle cam to ensure speed is correct. Readjust as necessary.
10. Connect vacuum hoses, then remove jumper wires.

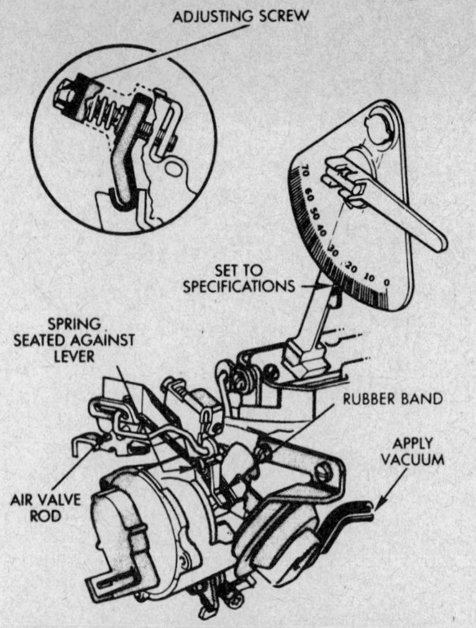

Fig. 10 Adjusting choke vacuum kick using angle gauge

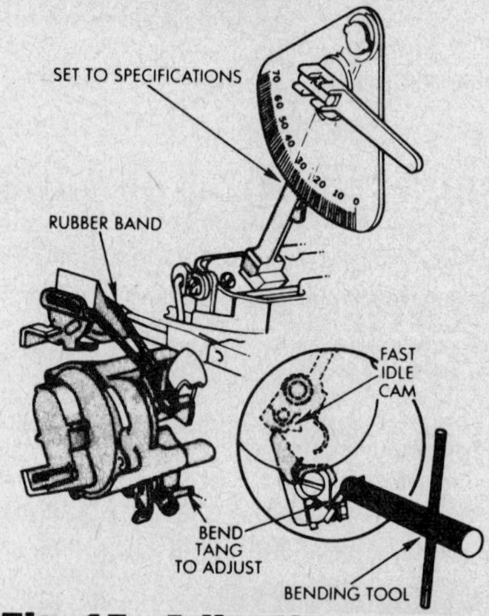

Fig. 13 Adjusting choke unloader using angle gauge

11. Connect oxygen sensor electrical connector. **After step 11 has been completed, idle speed may change slightly. This condition is normal and engine speed should not be readjusted.**

FLOAT

1. Remove air horn, feedback solenoid plunger and air horn gasket.
2. Remove plastic float bowl insert.
3. Hold float bowl retainer firmly in place.
4. Push float down lightly against needle.
5. Measure float height from top of casting to top of float at a point 3/16 inch from end of float, **Fig. 2.**
6. If float level is too high, hold retainer in place and push down on center of float pontoon to obtain correct setting.
7. If float level is too low, proceed as follows:
   a. Remove metering rods and feedback solenoid connector screw.
   b. Count and record number of turns necessary to lightly bottom lean mixture screw.

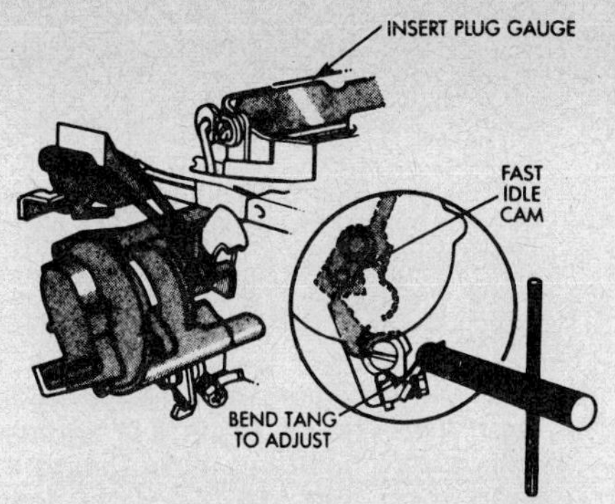

Fig. 14 Adjusting choke unloader using plug gauge

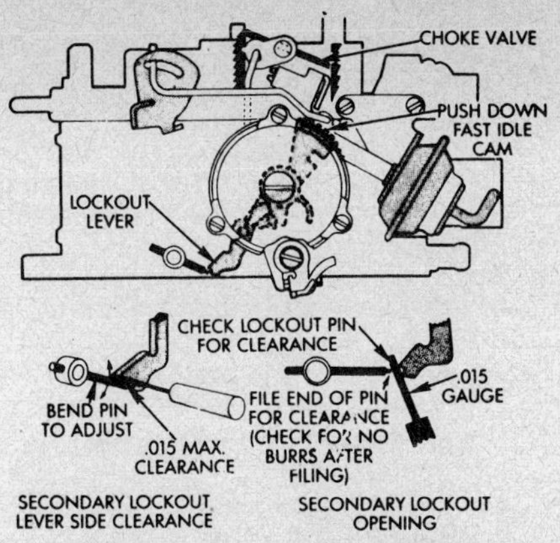

Fig. 15 Adjusting secondary lockout

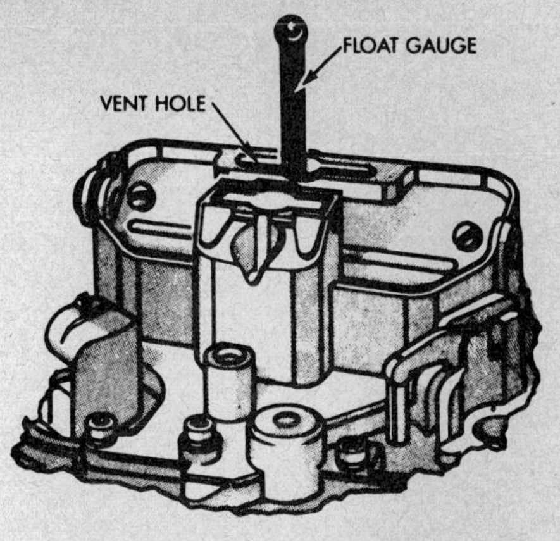

Fig. 16 Performing float level external check

c. Remove feedback solenoid assembly.
d. Bend float upward to adjust, then recheck float level.
e. Reassemble float bowl components, lightly bottom lean mixture screw and back out number of turns previously recorded, then install air horn.

LEAN MIXTURE SCREW

Lean mixture screw must have at least its first six threads engaged in float bowl to ensure proper installation.

1. Install gauging tool C-4899 or equivalent over left metering rod guide and install solenoid plunger, **Fig. 3.**
2. Hold plunger against solenoid and, using tool C-4898 or equivalent, turn lean mixture screw until solenoid plunger contacts gauging tool.
3. Remove gauging tool.

RICH MIXTURE SCREW

1. Install external float gauging tool C-4900 or equivalent in vertical "D" shaped vent hole in air horn and allow it to float freely, **Fig. 4.**
2. Read at eye level the mark on the gauge in inches that lines up with top of air horn casting and record reading.
3. Lightly press on gauge and again read and record the mark on the gauge that lines up with the top of the air horn casting.
4. Subtract dimension recorded in step 2 from dimension recorded in step 3 to determine total solenoid plunger travel.
5. Insert tool C-4898 or equivalent into access hole in air horn and adjust rich mixture screw to obtain 1/8 inch total solenoid plunger travel.
6. Remove tool.

AIR VALVE SPRING

1. Loosen lock screw, **Fig. 5.**
2. Turn tension adjusting screw counterclockwise until air valve is partially open.
3. Turn tension adjusting screw clockwise until air valve just closes, then turn adjusting screw clockwise proper number of turns.
4. Tighten lock screw.
5. Apply lithium base grease to lubricate contact area.

CHOKE COIL LEVER

1. Remove choke cover.
2. Place fast idle cam follower on highest step of fast idle cam.
3. Push up on choke coil lever to close choke valve.
4. Insert .12 inch plug gauge, **Fig. 6.**
5. Bend choke rod as necessary so lower edge of lever just contacts gauge.

USING CHOKE VALVE ANGLE GAUGE

1. Close choke valve.
2. Rotate degree scale until zero is opposite pointer, **Fig. 7.**
3. Center leveling bubble.
4. Rotate scale to specified angle.
5. Adjust linkage to center bubble.

CHOKE ROD FAST IDLE CAM

Angle Gauge Method

1. Attach rubber band to green tang of intermediate choke shaft, **Fig. 8.**
2. Open throttle to allow choke valve to close.
3. Set up angle gauge and set angle to specification.
4. Place cam follower on second highest step of cam against rise of high step. If cam follower does not contact cam, turn in fast idle screw until it does.
5. Adjust by bending tang of fast idle cam until bubble is centered.

Plug Gauge Method

1. Attach rubber band to green tang of intermediate choke shaft, **Fig. 9.**
2. Open throttle to allow choke valve to close.
3. Place cam follower on second step of fast idle cam against rise of high step. If cam follower does not contact cam, turn in fast idle speed screw until it does.
4. Apply a slight opening pressure on choke blade and insert specified plug gauge between top of choke blade and air horn casting.
5. Adjust as necessary by bending tang of fast idle cam until a slight drag is felt when gauge is withdrawn.

CHOKE VACUUM KICK

Angle Gauge Method

1. Attach rubber band to green tang of intermediate choke shaft, **Fig. 10.**
2. Open throttle to allow choke valve to close.
3. Set up angle gauge and set to specifications.
4. Using tool C-4207A or equivalent, apply at least 18 inches Hg vacuum to nipple on choke diaphragm. The air valve rod must not restrict plunger from retracting fully. If necessary, bend rod to permit full plunger travel. Final rod clearance must be set after vacuum kick setting has been made.
5. With vacuum applied, adjust screw to center bubble.

Plug Gauge Method

1. Attach rubber band to green tang of intermediate choke shaft, **Fig. 11.**
2. Open throttle to allow choke valve to close.
3. Using tool C-4207A or equivalent, apply at least 18 inches Hg vacuum to nipple on choke diaphragm. The air valve rod must not restrict plunger from retracting fully. If necessary, bend rod to permit full plunger travel. Final rod clearance must be set after vacuum kick setting has been made.
4. With vacuum still applied, apply slight opening pressure on choke blade and insert specified plug gauge between top of choke blade and air horn casting.
5. Adjust as necessary by adjusting screw until a slight drag is felt when gauge is withdrawn.

AIR VALVE ROD

1. Using tool C-4207A or equivalent, apply at least 18 inches Hg vacuum to vacuum nipple on choke vacuum diaphragm, **Fig. 12.**
2. Close air valve.
3. Insert specified gauge plug between rod and end of slot.
4. Bend rod to adjust clearance to specifications.

CHOKE UNLOADER

Angle Gauge Method

1. Attach rubber band to green tang of intermediate choke shaft, **Fig. 13.**
2. Open throttle to allow choke valve to close.
3. Set up angle gauge and set angle to specification.
4. Hold secondary lockout lever away from pin.
5. Hold throttle lever in wide open position.
6. Adjust as necessary by bending tang of fast idle lever until bubble is centered.

Plug Gauge Method

1. Attach rubber band to green tang of intermediate choke shaft, **Fig. 14.**
2. Open throttle to allow choke valve to close.
3. Hold secondary lockout lever away from pin.
4. Hold throttle lever in wide open position.
5. Apply slight opening pressure on choke blade and insert specified plug gauge between top of choke blade and air horn casting.
6. Adjust as necessary by bending tang of fast idle lever until a slight drag is felt when gauge is withdrawn.

SECONDARY LOCKOUT

1. Check secondary lockout lever adjustment as follows:
   a. Close choke valve.
   b. Close throttle valve.
   c. Insert .015 inch plug gauge, **Fig. 15.**
   d. Bend pin to obtain .015 inch clearance.
2. Check secondary lockout opening clearance as follows:
   a. Hold choke valve wide open by pushing down on tail of fast idle cam.
   b. Insert .015 inch plug gauge, **Fig. 15.**
   c. File pin as necessary to achieve .015 inch clearance, being sure to remove all burrs after filing.

FLOAT LEVEL EXTERNAL CHECK

1. With engine idling and choke wide open, insert gauge C-4900 or equivalent in vent hole and allow gauge to float freely, **Fig. 16.** Do not press down on gauge.
2. Observe mark on gauge that lines up with top of casting. Setting should be within $1/16$ inch of specified float level setting. **Incorrect fuel pressure will cause false readings.**
3. If float level is not within specifications, remove air horn and adjust float.

FUEL INJECTION

TABLE OF CONTENTS

Rear Wheel Drive Models

INDEX

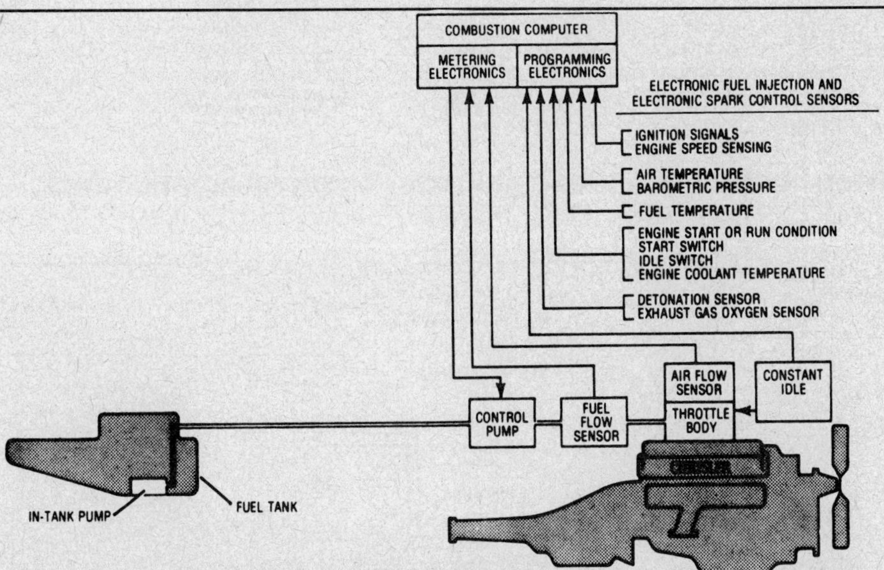

Fig. 1 Chrysler EFI combustion computer & electronic spark control operation

DESCRIPTION

The Chrysler EFI system is a continuous flow, single point, fully electronically controlled system. The combustion computer continuously monitors critical engine functions and adjusts air/fuel ratio to provide a balanced driving condition, **Figs. 1 and 2.** Air and fuel entering the engine are electronically measured. The EFI system maintains air/fuel ratio by arranging the throttle blades and bore in geometrical relationships that make air shear, entrain and distribute the fuel evenly into each cylinder. This system also electronically establishes the base air to fuel ratio for each individual vehicle, thus there is no need for a manifold absolute pressure sensor. The combustion computer also controls spark advance electronically.

The EFI system consists of three major systems. The first major system is the fuel supply system which is located in the fuel tank. In addition to conventional fuel delivery components, this system incorporates an electric turbine pump and several check valves, **Fig. 3.** The second major system isthe air cleaner, which contains the airflow sensor and the metering and ignition modules, **Fig. 4.** The third major system is the throttle body and fuel controller assembly, which includes the control pump and control pump electronics, fuel flow sensor, pressure regulating valves, spray bars and automatic idle speed motor, **Fig. 4.**

The computer basically senses the flow of air into the engine, the flow of fuel and the oxygen content in the exhaust gas. These signals are compared to an ideal calibration programmed into the computer. When any of these signals vary from the programmed calibration, the computer signals the control pump to deliver more or less fuel, depending on whether fuel ratio is too lean or rich.

The fuel pump in the fuel tank delivers fuel to the control pump. The control pump then delivers a small portion of the fuel, at 21 psi at idle, through the fuel flow sensor and low pressure regulator valve, into the spray bars, through the nozzles and into the engine, **Figs. 5, 6 and 7.** Since fuel openings are fixed, the pressure has to vary with engine speed. At high vehicle speeds, the control pump will deliver fuel at pressures up to 60 psi. The spray bar is designed to deliver fuel evenly at low speed. At higher speeds, a second spray bar will open and deliver the full amount of fuel at the correct pressure. Fuel that is not required for engine operation is returned to the fuel tank through the low pressure regulator valve and return line.

As air enters the air flow sensor, the blades set the air into a swirling motion in through the air vortex. The swirling air creates a low pressure at the center of the vortex. As the swirling air expands, the low pressure center begins to rotate around the wall. The air then passes over a silicon chip which converts the low pressure differential into an electrical signal. As the volume of air increases, the pulsation of the electrical signal increases, thus informing the computer as to the quantity of air entering the air cleaner. The fuel flow sensor basically consists of a paddle wheel, a light emitting diode and a phototransistor. As the paddle wheel spins, the flow of light from the diode to the phototransistor is interrupted, which in turn creates a pulsating electrical signal. As fuel flow increases, the paddle wheel rotates faster, thus increasing pulsation of the electrical signal. The information obtained from the air and fuel flowmeters triggers one shot pulses of opposite polarities, positive and negative, which create electrical signals that are fed into multiplier, which are combined with reading obtained from additional sensors to create a mass signal, **Fig. 8.** The mass signal is then directed to an integrator which controls the pump motor.

An automatic calibration system establishes the fuel to air ratio and also compensates for changes in barometric pressure. A temperature sensor, located on the air cleaner, signals the computer of changes in air temperature that will affect

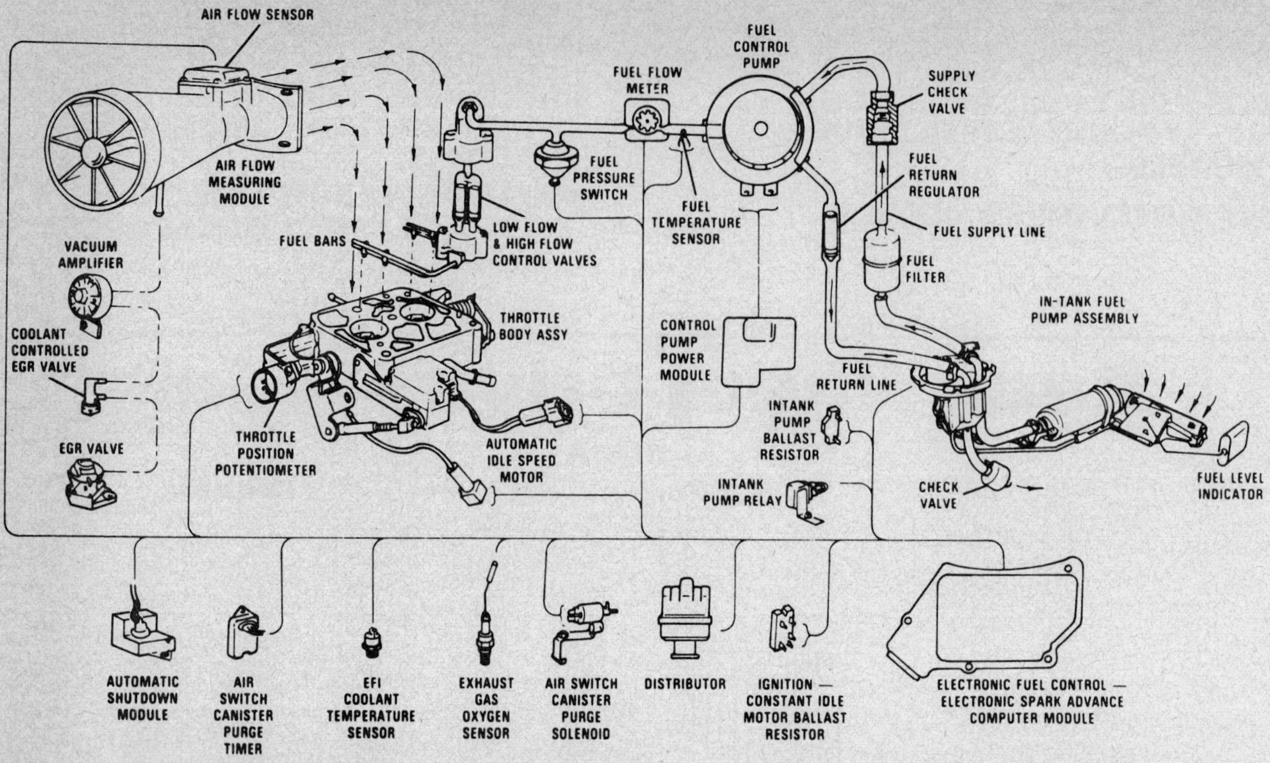

Fig. 2 Chrysler EFI combustion computer & electronic spark control components

the density of the air. The oxygen sensor in the exhaust system signals the computer when air/fuel mixture is too rich or lean. The system is designed to operate on an air/fuel ratio as lean as 21:1.

The air control device is a conventional two part, single throttle shaft design, similar to the air horn on a carburetor, with several important differences, **Fig. 9**. All fuel is introduced above the throttle blades on the air control device. Two fuel distribution bars are located over each port, a primary fuel bar for low fuel flow and a power bar for high fuel flow. The throttle blade has a fuel film spreader mounted above the blade and a mixture deflector mounted below. When the engine is cranking, idling or under light load, only the primary bar nozzles are delivering fuel. As engine speed increases and fuel flow reaches approximately 35 pounds per hour, the power regulator valve opens and allows fuel to flow from the power orifices. The fuel flow from the spray bar nozzles contacts the film spreader, which distributes the fuel into a thin film. The lower velocity air at the larger throttle blade openings, draws the fuel film to the sharp edges of the blade, resulting in a highly atomized fuel and air mixture. The lower mixture deflector is used to improve cylinder to cylinder air/fuel mixture.

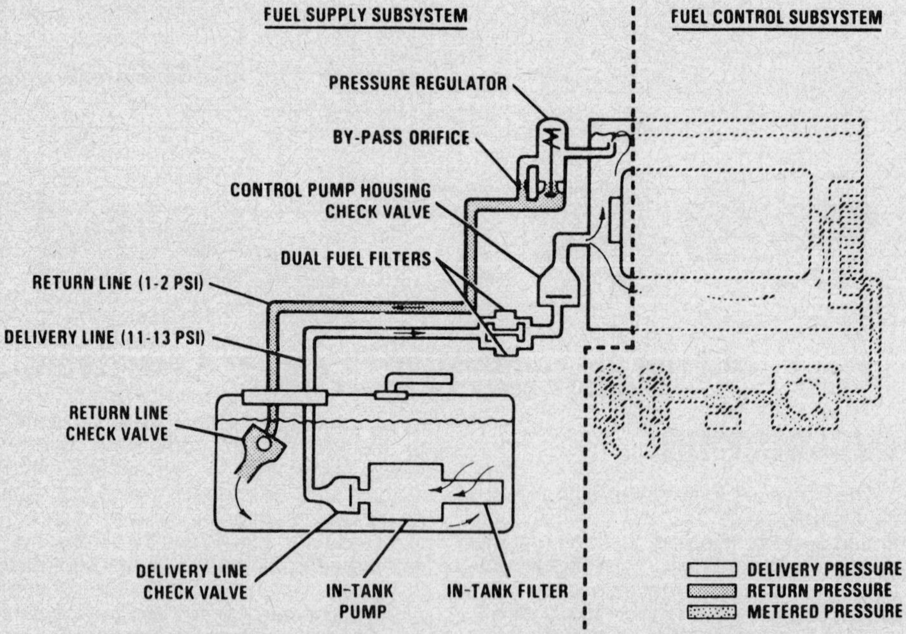

Fig. 3 Fuel flow supply & return circuits

SYSTEM SERVICE

PRELIMINARY INSPECTION

Before attempting to service the EFI system, observe the following:

1. Use caution when performing electrical tests or disconnecting electrical connectors to prevent accidental grounding, shorting or energizing terminals which are electrically connected to the Combustion Control Computer (CCC).
2. If it is necessary to crank the engine with high tension lead from ignition coil disconnected from distributor cap, the high tension lead must be grounded, or the CCC will be damaged.
3. Perform fuel flow test as quickly as possible to prevent flooding or hydrostatic damage to the engine.
4. When servicing the fuel supply system, ensure all fittings are secured properly to prevent leaks while system is under pressure.

VISUAL INSPECTION

Most problems with the EFI system can usually be traced to poor hose or wiring connections. Before proceeding with system diagnosis, perform the following visual inspections.

Inside Air Cleaner

1. Ensure pump control is connected to power module control pump connec-

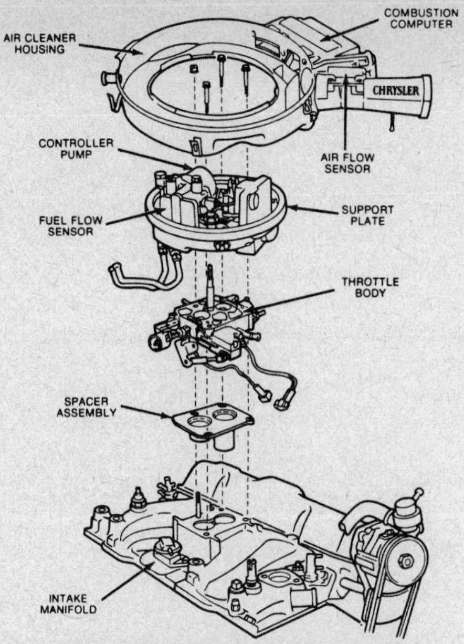

Fig. 4 Chrysler EFI throttle body & fuel controller assembly & air cleaner mounted components

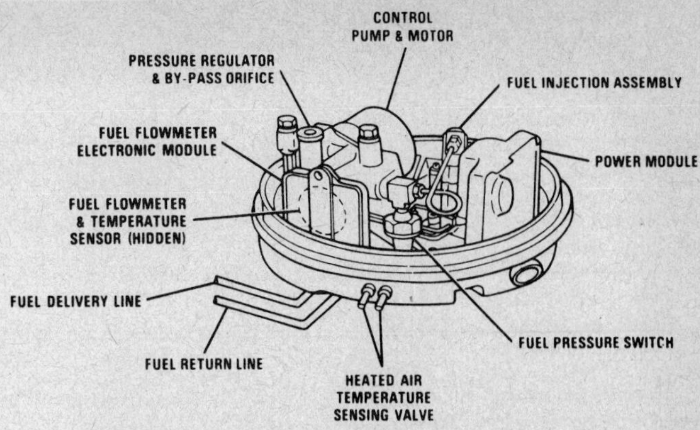

Fig. 5 Fuel control subassembly

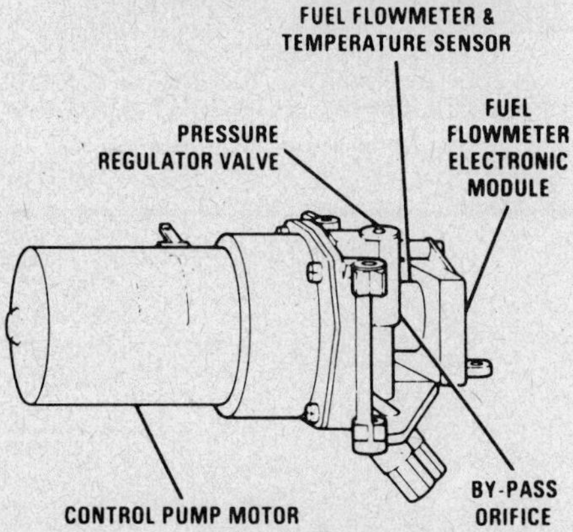

Fig. 6 Fuel control pump assembly

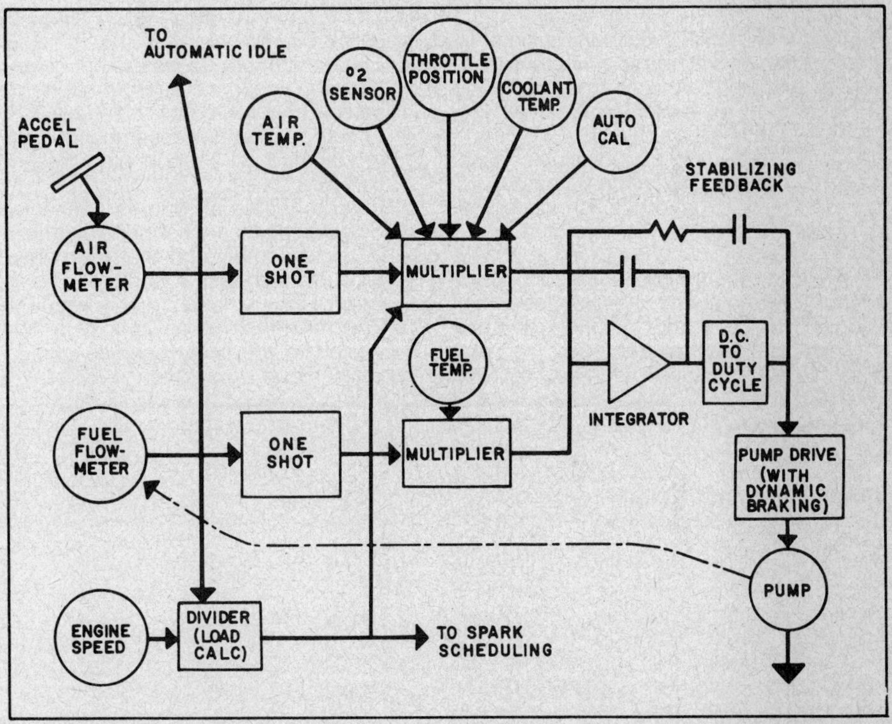

Fig. 8 Chrysler EFI flowmeter & sensor operation

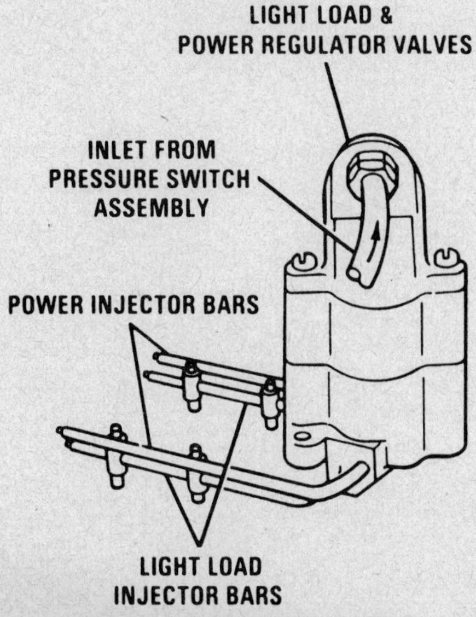

Fig. 7 Fuel injection assembly

tor.

2. Ensure pressure switch wire is connected to power module pressure switch connector.
3. Ensure power module wire is grounded to the support plate assembly attaching screws.
4. Ensure fuel flowmeter is connected to the power module fuel flowmeter connector.
5. Ensure fuel line from control pump is properly secured to the fuel bar regulator valve assembly and control pump.
6. Ensure pressure switch is tightly seated to fuel line.
7. Ensure wires from power module are not cut where they route over top of module and retaining clips.
8. Ensure all wires and their retaining clips are properly attached to the side of support plate.

Outside Air Cleaner

1. Ensure ESA harness plug is fully seated into rearmost socket connector.
2. Ensure automatic calibration connector is connected to wiring harness.
3. Ensure EFI harness plug is fully seated into front socket connector.
4. Ensure throttle body ground relay is connected to harness.
5. Ensure oxygen sensor is connected to the EFI electronics.
6. Ensure vacuum delay valve in heated air door vacuum line is installed for the proper flow direction.
7. Ensure vacuum hoses are connected between intake manifold, vacuum solenoid, and air switching valve.
8. Ensure power module connector on the lower front side of support plate is connected to wire harness and secured in place.

9. Ensure wire harness is properly secured into air flowmeter.
10. Ensure water temperature sensor is properly connected to wiring harness.
11. Ensure vacuum hose is properly connected between vacuum solenoid and vacuum signal.
12. Ensure auto-shutdown module is properly connected.
13. Ensure ignition ballast resistor on the firewall is connected to wiring harness.
14. Ensure in-tank pump ballast resistor on the firewall is connected to wiring harness.
15. Ensure in-tank relay on the right inner fender is connected to wiring harness.
16. Ensure throttle body potentiometer is properly connected to wiring harness.
17. Ensure throttle idle ground switch is properly connected to engine harness.
18. Ensure automatic idle control motor is properly connected to wiring harness.
19. Ensure dash wiring harness is connected to air switching timer on the firewall.
20. Ensure two radio suppression chokes are connected to wiring harness.
21. Ensure vacuum hose is connected between charcoal canister and throttle body.
22. Ensure vacuum hoses are connected between vacuum amplifier, reservoir, EGR valve, intake manifold and air horn and vacuum tree.

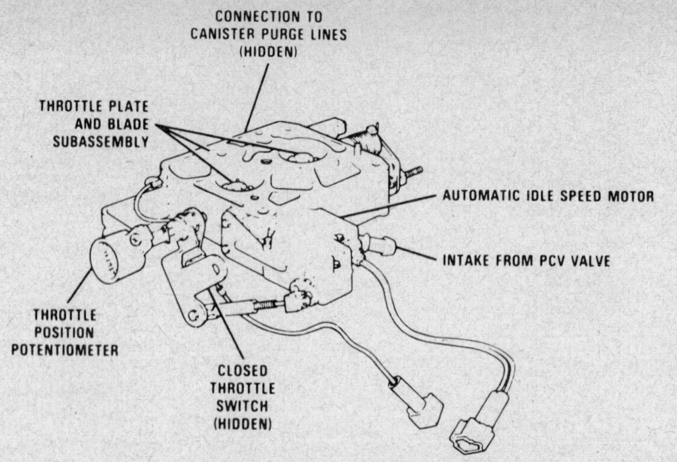

Fig. 9 Throttle body assembly

23. Ensure vacuum hoses are connected between vacuum source, temperature sensor and heated air assembly.
24. Ensure air cleaner assembly is properly seated on support plate sealing gasket.
25. Ensure heated air duct is connected between air cleaner snorkel and heated air assembly and that the heated air door operates properly.
26. Ensure in-tank fuse is not burned out.
27. Ensure in-tank pump jumper is connected to the body harness and in-tank pump at fuel tank. Check inline gas filter for leaks.
28. Ensure six way and eight way connectors at right valve cover are properly connected.
29. Ensure there is no gasoline in crankcase oil.

DIAGNOSIS

A special electronic fuel injection tester must be used to diagnose this system. Follow instructions included with tester.

Single Point Fuel Injection, 1983–85 Front Wheel Drive Models

INDEX

DESCRIPTION

This system, used on 1983-85 front wheel drive models with a 2.2L engine, is a computer-controlled, single-point fuel injection system which provides a precise air/fuel ratio under all driving conditions. The system utilizes a logic module, a digital pre-programmed computer, to regulate ignition timing, idle speed, emission devices and air/fuel ratio.

Various sensors and switches located throughout the vehicle provide information to the logic module, **Fig. 1.** All inputs to the logic module are converted to signals sent to the power module. According to these signals, the power module changes fuel flow at the injector and/or ignition timing.

The logic module tests many of its own input and output circuits. If a problem is detected in a major system, the information is stored in the logic module. This information can be displayed by a flashing light emitting diode (LED) located on the module, or by connecting a diagnostic readout and reading a numbered display which corresponds to a specific problem.

COMPONENTS

Power Module

The power module houses the circuits needed to power the ignition coil and fuel injector, and energizes the automatic shutdown (ASD) relay which activates the fuel pump, ignition coil and power module itself. The module also receives a signal from the distributor and relays this signal to the logic module. If no distributor signal is received, the ASD relay is not activated and power is shut off from the fuel pump and ignition coil. A voltage converter in the power module reduces battery voltage to a regulated 8 volt output which powers the distributor as well as the module.

Logic Module

The logic module is a digital computer which contains a microprocessor. Input signals from various switches, sensors and components are sent to the module, which then computes the fuel injector pulse width, spark advance, ignition coil dwell, idle speed and purge and EGR control solenoid cycles.

Automatic Shutdown (ASD) Relay (1983–84)

The ASD relay is powered and controlled through the power module. During engine cranking, the power module senses a distributor signal and grounds the relay. This completes the circuit for the electric fuel pump, ignition coil and power module. If for any reason the distributor signal is lost, the ASD relay interrupts this circuit in less than one second, preventing fuel, spark and engine operations. This rapid shutdown provides added safety in the event of an accident.

Manifold Absolute Pressure (MAP) Sensor

The MAP sensor, located in the right side passenger compartment, monitors manifold vacuum. The sensor is connected to a vacuum nipple on the throttle body and electrically to the logic module. This device relays information on manifold vacuum and barometric pressure to the logic module which is used in determining the proper air/fuel mixture.

Oxygen Sensor

The oxygen sensor, located in the exhaust manifold, produces voltage when exposed to oxygen present in exhaust gasses. The sensor produces a low voltage when the air/fuel mixture is lean and a high voltage when the mixture is rich. The voltage signal is transmitted to the logic module which signals the power module to trigger the fuel injector. The injector adjusts the mixture accordingly.

Coolant Temperature Sensor

The coolant temperature sensor, located in the thermostat housing, provides the logic module with information on engine operating temperature. This data, in conjunction with data provided by the charge temperature switch, permits the logic module to provide slightly richer air/fuel mixtures and higher idle speeds until normal operating temperatures are reached.

Charge Temperature Sensor

The charge temperature sensor on 1983 models, located in the intake manifold, measures the temperature of the air/fuel mixture. The logic module uses this information to determine engine operating temperature and engine warm-up cycles should the coolant temperature sensor fail.

Switch Input

Several switches located throughout the vehicle provide information to the logic module. These switches include the idle, neutral safety, electric backlight, air conditioning, air conditioning clutch and brake light switches. When one or more of these switches is in the on position, the logic module signals the automatic idle speed (AIS) motor to increase idle speed to a specific RPM.

When air conditioning is on and the throttle valve is above a preset angle, the wide open throttle cut out relay prevents the air conditioning clutch from engaging until the throttle valve is below this angle.

Power Loss Lamp

The power loss lamp on the instrument panel will illuminate if the logic module receives an incorrect signal or no signal from the coolant temperature sensor, MAP sensor or throttle position sensor. This lamp indicates that the logic module has gone into the "limp in mode" to keep the system operational, and indicates an immediate need for service.

The power loss lamp will also light for several seconds each time the ignition key is turned on as a bulb check.

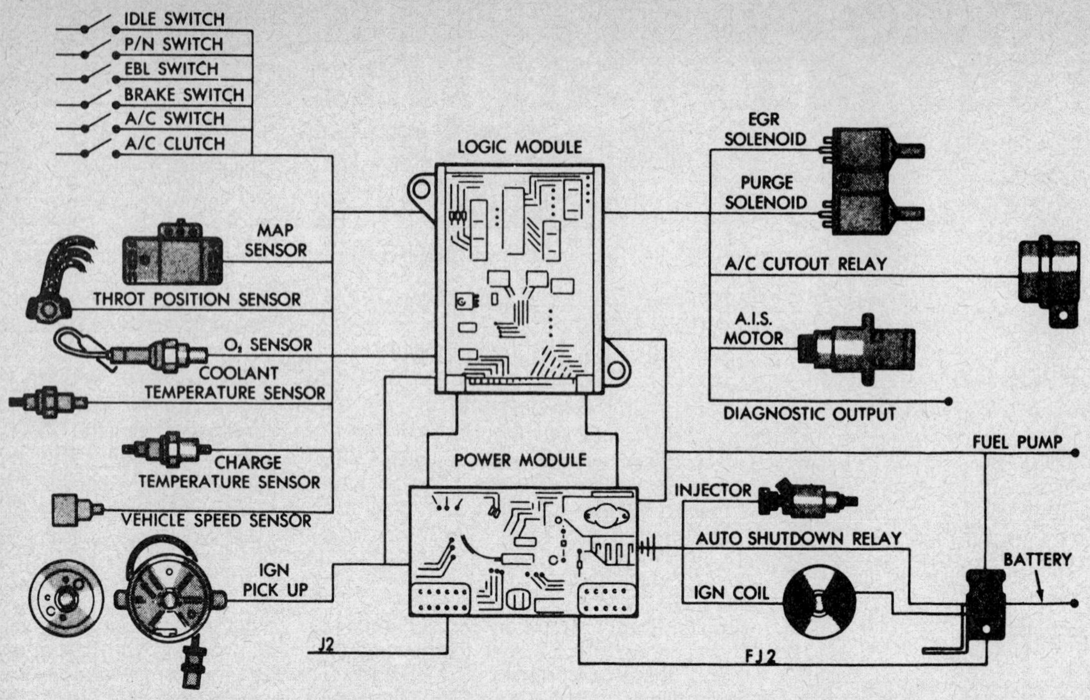

Fig. 1 Single point electronic fuel injection (EFI) system components. 1983 front wheel drive w/2.2L engine (1984–85 similar)

Exhaust Gas Recirculation (EGR) Solenoid

The EGR solenoid is energized by the logic module when engine temperature is below 70°F. This closes the solenoid and prevents ported vacuum from reaching the EGR valve. When engine temperature exceeds 70°F, the solenoid is de-energized and ported vacuum from the throttle body will pass through to the EGR valve. At idle and wide open throttle the solenoid is energized, preventing EGR operation.

Purge Solenoid

The purge solenoid is energized by the logic module when engine temperature is below 160°F for 1983 models or 145°F for 1984-85 models. This prevents vacuum from reaching the charcoal canister valve. When engine temperature exceeds 160°F for 1983 models or 145°F for 1984-85 models, the solenoid is de-energized and vacuum will flow to the canister purge valve and purge vapors through the throttle body.

Air Conditioning Cut Out Relay

The air-conditioning cut out relay is wired in series with the cycling clutch switch and low pressure cut out switch. When the throttle position sensor sends a wide open throttle signal to the logic module, the relay is energized and air conditioning clutch engagement is prevented.

Throttle Body

The throttle body assembly, located on top of the intake manifold, contains the fuel injector, pressure regulator, throttle position sensor and AIS motor. A cable-operated throttle valve in the base of the throttle body controls air flow through the assembly. The throttle body provides the chamber for metering, atomizing and distributing fuel throughout the air entering the engine.

Fuel Injector

The fuel injector, **Fig. 2**, is an electric solenoid powered by the power module and controlled by the logic module. According to ambient, mechanical and sensor input, the logic module determines when and how long the power module will operate the fuel injector.

Fuel Pressure Regulator

The fuel pressure regulator, **Fig. 3**, located downstream of the fuel injector on the throttle body, maintains a constant fuel pressure of 36 psi across the injector tip. The spring-loaded diaphragm in the regulator is assisted by vacuum in the throttle body above the throttle valve. As venturi vacuum increases, less pressure is needed to supply the same amount of fuel into the air flow. In order to fine tune the fuel pressure under all operating conditions, the vacuum assists in opening the fuel port during high vacuum conditions.

Throttle Position Sensor (TPS)

The TPS, located on the throttle body, is an electric resistor which is activated by the movement of the throttle shaft. The sensor produces a voltage which increases or decreases according to the throttle valve opening. The voltage signal is transmitted to the logic module where it is used with data from other sensors to adjust the air/fuel mixture accordingly.

Automatic Idle Speed (AIS) Motor

The AIS motor, operated by the logic module, adjusts the air portion of the air/fuel mixture through an air bypass on the back of the throttle body. Base idle is determined by the minimum air flow through the throttle body. The AIS motor opens or closes off the air bypass as needed according to engine loads or ambient conditions. The logic module senses the change in air/fuel mixture and increases or decreases fuel accordingly to change engine idle. The AIS motor also prevents stalling during deceleration by increasing engine idle when the throttle is closed quickly.

Fuel Pump

The fuel pump used in the EFI system is a positive displacement, roller vane, immersible pump with a permanent magnet electric motor. The pump uses two check valves: one valve relieves internal pump pressure and regulates maximum pump output, and the other valve, located near the pump outlet, restricts fuel flow in either direction when the pump is not operational. Operating voltage is supplied to the pump through the ASD relay.

Fuel Reservoir

The fuel reservoir is located in the fuel tank and houses the fuel pump. The reservoir provides fuel at the pump intake under all driving conditions. The fuel return line directs fuel to a container on the side of the reservoir. The flow of fuel into this container creates a low pressure area and causes additional fuel from the main tank to flow into the reservoir. This combination of re-

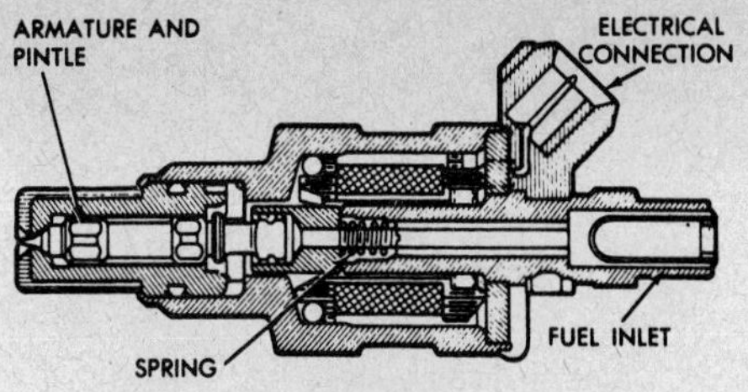

Fig. 2 Fuel injector

turn fuel and fuel from the main tank maintains a full fuel condition in the reservoir even if fuel level is below the reservoir walls.

Exhaust Gas Recirculation (EGR) System

The EGR system is a back pressure type and is controlled by a back pressure transducer and the logic module. The logic module controls vacuum through the EGR solenoid, turning the circuit on or off according to operating conditions. The back pressure transducer measures the amount of exhaust back pressure on the exhaust side of the EGR valve. The logic module prevents EGR operation by turning the EGR solenoid off at idle, at wide open throttle or when engine temperature is below 70°F. The back pressure transducer vents the vacuum circuit of the EGR valve to the atmosphere whenever less than 0 psi is sensed at the exhaust side of the EGR valve.

DIAGNOSIS

VISUAL INSPECTION

Most problems with the EFI system can usually be traced to poor hose or wiring connections. Before proceeding with system tests or diagnosis, inspect the following:

1. Ensure that vacuum connections on front and rear of throttie body are secure and not leaking.
2. Check that vacuum connections at EGR and purge solenoids are secure and not leaking.
3. Ensure hoses are securely attached to vapor canister and back pressure transducer.
4. Check PCV valve for proper installation.
5. Make sure proper connections exist between air heater and throttle body.
6. Inspect the MAP sensor for proper vacuum connections.
7. Check electrical connectors for proper installation at the following components: logic module, MAP sensor, ASD relay, power module, EGR and purge solenoids, speed sensor, charge temperature sensor on 1983 models, AIS motor, throttle position sensor, fuel injector, oxygen sensor, coolant temperature sensor, distributor and radiator fan relay on 1984-85 models.
8. Ensure ground eyelet is attached securely to the intake manifold under bracket.

ON BOARD DIAGNOSTICS

The logic module is programmed to monitor various circuits in the EFI system. If a problem is sensed often enough to indicate an actual fault, its fault code is stored in the logic module for display. If the problem ceases to exist or is repaired, the fault code will be cancelled by the logic module after 30 ignition key on/off cycles.

FAULT CODES

Fault codes can be displayed either by a light emitting diode (LED) on the module or by connecting diagnostic readout tool No. C-4805 to the system. To obtain fault codes using diagnostic readout tool No. C-4805, connect the unit to the diagnostic connector located in the passenger compartment near the right side strut tower. Start the engine if possible, then cycle the transmission selector and air conditioning switch and shut off the engine. Cycle the ignition switch on and off twice, then turn ignition on and record all diagnostic codes displayed within five seconds. Note that the power loss lamp should light for two seconds as a bulb check.

After all codes have been displayed and Code 55 has been received, actuate the following component switches and make sure that the display changes when the switch is activated and released; brake pedal, gearshift selector, A/C switch and electric backlight switch.

Fault codes indicate the results of a failure but do not always identify the component at fault. Fault code indications are as follows:

CODE 11

Indicates a fault in the distributor circuit. This code will appear when the logic module has not received a distributor signal since the battery was reconnected.

CODE 12

Indicates a fault in the stand by memory circuit on 1984-85 models. This code appears if direct battery feed to the logic module is interrupted.

CODE 13

Indicates a fault in the MAP sensor pneumatic system. This code will appear if the MAP sensor vacuum level does not change between start and start/run transfer speed (500-600 RPM).

CODE 14

Indicates a fault in the MAP sensor electrical sensor. This code will appear if the MAP sensor signal is too low (below .02 volts) or too high (above 4.9 volts).

CODE 15

Indicates a fault in the speed sensor circuit. This code will appear if engine speed is above 1468 RPM and the speed sensor indicates less than 2 mph. Note that this code is only valid if it is sensed while vehicle is moving.

CODE 16

Indicates a loss of battery voltage.

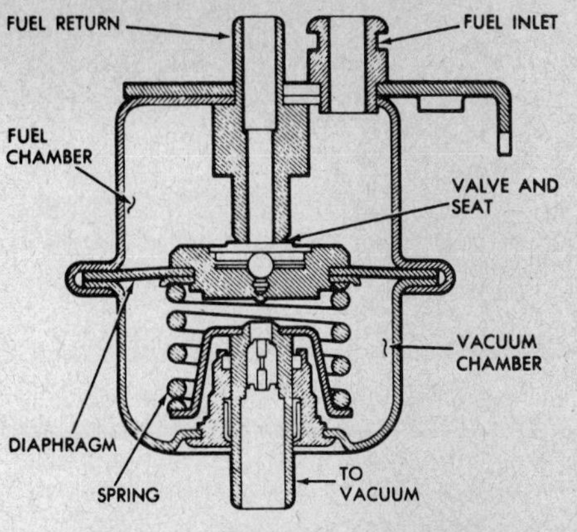

Fig. 3 Fuel pressure regulator

CODE 21

Indicates a problem in the oxygen feedback circuit. On 1983 models, this code will appear if engine temperature is above 170°F, engine speed is above 1500 RPM, and the oxygen sensor stays rich or lean for more than one minute. On 1984 models, this code appears if there has been no oxygen sensor signal for more than 5 seconds.

CODE 22

Indicates a fault in the coolant temperature sensor circuit. This code will appear if the circuit indicates an incorrect temperature or a temperature that changes unusually fast.

CODE 23

Indicates a fault in the charge temperature sensor circuit. This code will appear if the circuit indicates an incorrect temperature or a temperature that changes unusually fast.

CODE 24

Indicates a fault in the throttle position sensor circuit. This code will appear if the sensor signal is too low (below .16 volts) or too high (above 4.7 volts).

CODE 25

Indicates a fault in the AIS control circuit. This code will appear if proper voltage from the AIS system is not present. Note than an open harness or wire will not activate this code.

CODE 26

Indicates that peak injector current has not been reached.

CODE 27

Indicates internal problem in logic module fuel circuit.

CODE 31

Indicates an open or short in the canister purge solenoid circuit.

CODE 32

Indicates an open or short in the power loss lamp circuit.

CODE 33

Indicates an open or short in the air conditioning wide open throttle cutout relay circuit.

CODE 34

On 1983-84 models, indicates an open or short in EGR solenoid circuit. On 1985 models, indicates problem in spare driver circuit.

CODE 35

Indicates a problem in the fan relay circuit on 1984-85 models. This code appears if the radiator fan is either not operating or operating at the incorrect time.

CODE 36

On 1985 models, indicates problem in spare driver circuit.

CODE 37

On 1985 models, indicates problem in shift indicator lamp circuit.

CODE 41

Indicates a fault in the charging system. This code will appear if battery voltage from the ASD relay is less than 11.75 volts.

CODE 42

Indicates a fault in the ASD relay circuit. This code will appear if, during cranking, battery voltage from the ASD relay is not present for at least 1/3 second after first distributor pulse. This code will also appear if, after engine stall, battery voltage is not off within 3 seconds after last distributor pulse.

CODE 43

Indicates a fault in the interface circuit. This code will appear if there is no anti-dwell or injector control signal between the logic module and power module.

CODE 44

On 1983-84 models, indicates internal failure in Logic Module. On 1985 models, indicates battery temperature is out of range.

CODE 51

On 1983 models, indicates a fault in standby memory. This code will appear if direct battery feed to the logic module is interrupted. When the module receives a distributor signal, the code will disappear after approximately 30 ignition key on/off cycles. On 1984 models, indicates a problem in the closed loop fuel system. This code appears if during closed loop conditions, the oxygen sensor signal is either low or high for more than 2 minutes. On 1985 models, indicates oxygen sensor feedback system is latched lean.

CODE 52

On 1983-84 models, indicates internal failure in Logic Module. On 1985 models, indicates oxygen sensor feedback system is latched rich.

CODE 53

Indicates internal failure in Logic Module.

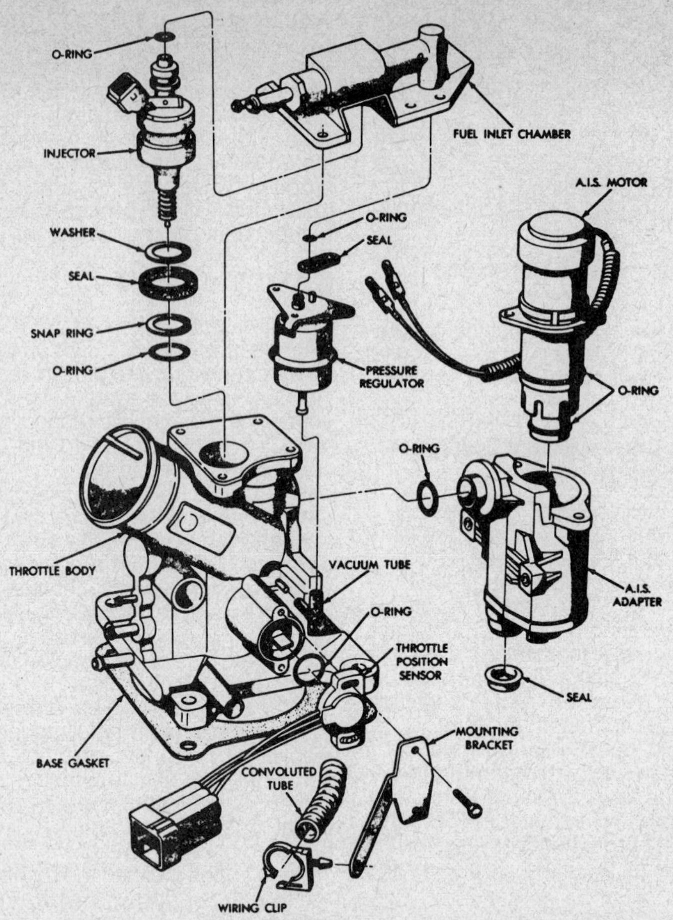

Fig. 4 Exploded view of throttle body assembly

CODE 54

On 1983-84 models, indicates internal failure in Logic Module.

CODE 55

Indicates end of message. This code will appear after all other codes have been displayed.

CODE 88

Indicates start of message. This code will appear only on diagnostic readout tool No. C-4805 before any other codes are displayed.

ACTUATOR TEST MODE (ATM)

1983–84

1. Remove coil wire from distributor cap and place 1/4 inch from ground. **If the coil wire is more than 1/4 inch from ground, the power module may be damaged.**
2. Disconnect air cleaner hose from throttle body, then connect diagnostic readout tool No. C-4805 to diagnostic connector.
3. Depress ATM button on readout tool and observe the following:
   a. Three sparks from coil wire to ground.
   b. Two AIS motor movements, one open and one closed. Listen closely for AIS operation.
   c. One fuel pulse from injector into throttle body. **ATM capability duration is 5 minutes from the time the ignition is turned on. This capability can be reinstated by cycling the ignition switch on and off three times, ending in the on position.**
4. When ATM button is depressed, Code 42 is activated as the ASD relay is bypassed. After ATM operation, this code must not be used for diagnostics.
5. The ATM test verifies three categories of operation:
   a. The coil firing three times indicates that the coil, logic module and power module are operational and that the interface between modules is working.
   b. The AIS motor movement indicates that the AIS motor is operational.
   c. The injector fuel pulse into the throttle body indicates that the fuel pump and injector are operational and the fuel lines are intact.

1985

1. Place system in diagnostic test mode and wait for code 55 to appear on display screen.
2. Press ATM button on tool to activate display. To obtain specific ATM test, hold ATM button down until desired

test code appears. Computer will continue to turn selected circuit on and off for as long as 5 minutes or until either ATM button is pressed again or ignition switch is turned off.
3. Actuator test codes are as follows: Code 01, spark activation; Code 02, injector activation; Code 03, AIS activation; Code 04, radiator fan activation Code 05, A/C cutout relay activation.

FUEL SYSTEM PRESSURE TEST

Fuel system pressure must be released any time a fuel line is to be disconnected.

1. Disconnect fuel inlet hose from throttle body and connect pressure testers C- 3293 and C-4749 between fuel filter hose and throttle body.
2. Start engine and observe pressure gauge. Gauge should indicate 34-38 psi pressure. If indicated, reinstall fuel hose using a new clamp and torque to 10 inch lbs.
3. If fuel pressure is below 34 psi, install tester between fuel filter hose and fuel line and start engine. If pressure is now within specifications, replace fuel filter. If pressure does not increase, gently squeeze fuel hose. If pressure now increases, replace pressure regulator. If fuel pressure still does not increase, either the fuel pump is defective or the filter sock is obstructed.
4. If fuel pressure exceeds 38 psi, remove fuel return hose from throttle body. Install a suitable length of hose to throttle body and place open end of hose into a clean container. Start engine and recheck fuel pressure. If pressure is now within specifications, check fuel return line for restrictions. If fuel pressure does not decrease to within specifications, replace pressure regulator.

SYSTEM SERVICING

IGNITION TIMING

1. Connect a suitable timing light to No. 1 cylinder, or a magnetic timing unit to engine.
2. Connect tachometer to engine, then start engine and run until operating temperature is reached.
3. Disconnect, then reconnect the water temperature sensor connector on thermostat housing. The loss of power lamp must illuminate and engine RPM should be within specifications given on vehicle emission label.
4. Direct timing light at timing hole in bellhousing, or read magnetic timing unit, and adjust timing as necessary by loosening distributor and turning until specifications are met.
5. Shut engine off, then disconnect and reconnect positive battery quick disconnect.
6. Start engine and observe loss of power lamp, which should be off.
7. Shut engine off, then cycle ignition switch on and off twice.
8. Turn ignition on and observe fault code display. Fault codes should be clear with Codes 88, 51, and 55 displayed.

SPARK ADVANCE

1. Check basic timing and adjust if necessary as previously described.
2. With engines running at 2000 RPM, check timing, which should now be approximately 40°.
3. If timing advance does not meet specifications, replace logic module.

FUEL SYSTEM PRESSURE RELEASE

The EFI system is under a constant fuel pressure of approximately 36 psi. Fuel system pressure must be released prior to servicing fuel tank, fuel pump, fuel lines, fuel filter or fuel components of the throttle body.

1. Loosen gas cap to release any residual pressure in the fuel tank.
2. Disconnect electrical connector from fuel injector.
3. Using a suitable jumper wire, ground one injector terminal, then connect another jumper wire to other injector terminal and touch battery positive post for no more than 10 seconds.
4. Remove jumper wires from injector terminals.

THROTTLE BODY, REPLACE

1. Release pressure from fuel system as previously described.
2. Disconnect battery ground cable.
3. Disconnect electrical connector at injector and the 6-way connector at throttle body.
4. Remove air cleaner hose, then the throttle cable.
5. If equipped, disconnect speed control and transmission kickdown cables.
6. Remove return spring and disconnect vacuum hoses from throttle body.
7. Loosen fuel inlet and return hose clamps. Wrap a clean towel around each hose, then disconnect the hoses.
8. Remove throttle body attaching screws, then the throttle body.
9. Reverse procedure to install, noting the following:
   a. Use a new gasket on throttle body mounting flange. Install gasket with tabs facing forward.
   b. Torque throttle body attaching screws to 200 inch lbs.
   c. Use new hose clamps on fuel lines and torque clamps to 10 inch lbs.

INJECTOR, REPLACE

1. Release pressure from fuel system as previously described.
2. Disconnect battery ground cable.
3. Remove inlet chamber-to-throttle attaching screws.
4. Remove vacuum hose between pressure regulator and throttle body. **Place a clean towel around fuel inlet chamber to avoid fuel leakage.**
5. Remove fuel inlet chamber and injector from throttle body, **Fig. 4.**
6. Remove injector from fuel inlet chamber.
7. Remove O-rings, snap ring, seal and washer from injector.
8. Reverse procedure to install, using new O-rings, washer and seal. Torque fuel inlet chamber attaching screws to 35 inch lbs.

PRESSURE REGULATOR, REPLACE

1. Release pressure from fuel system as previously described.
2. Disconnect battery ground cable.
3. Remove pressure regulator-to-fuel inlet chamber attaching screws. **Place a clean towel around fuel inlet chamber to avoid fuel leakage.**
4. Remove vacuum hose between pressure regulator and throttle body.
5. Remove pressure regulator from throttle body, **Fig. 4.**
6. Remove O-ring and seal from regulator.
7. Reverse procedure to install, using new O-ring and seal. Torque pressure regulator attaching screws to 40 inch lbs.

THROTTLE POSITION SENSOR (TPS), REPLACE

1. Disconnect battery ground cable.
2. Disconnect 6-way connector at throttle body.
3. Remove TPS-to-throttle body attaching screws.
4. Unfasten wiring clip from convoluted tube, then remove mounting bracket, **Fig. 4.**
5. Lift TPS off throttle shaft and remove O-ring.
6. Disconnect three TPS wires from convoluted tubing.
7. Lift each locking tab inside 6-way connector with a small screwdriver and remove TPS wire blade terminals. Note position of wires for assembly reference.
8. Reverse procedure to install, using new O-ring. Torque TPS attaching screws to 20 inch lbs.

AUTOMATIC IDLE SPEED (AIS) MOTOR, REPLACE

1. Disconnect battery ground cable.
2. Disconnect 6-way connector at throttle body.
3. Remove AIS motor-to-adapter attaching screws. **Do not remove clamp on motor, as damage may result.**
4. Remove two AIS wires from 6-way connector. Lift each locking tab inside connector with a small screwdriver and remove blade terminals. Note position of wires for assembly reference.
5. Remove AIS motor from adapter and remove O-rings from motor, **Fig. 4.**
6. Reverse procedure to install, using new O-rings. Torque motor attaching screws to 20 inch lbs.

AUTOMATIC IDLE SPEED (AIS) MOTOR ADAPTER, REPLACE

1. Disconnect battery ground cable.
2. Disconnect 6-way connector at throttle body.
3. Remove throttle body-to-adapter at-

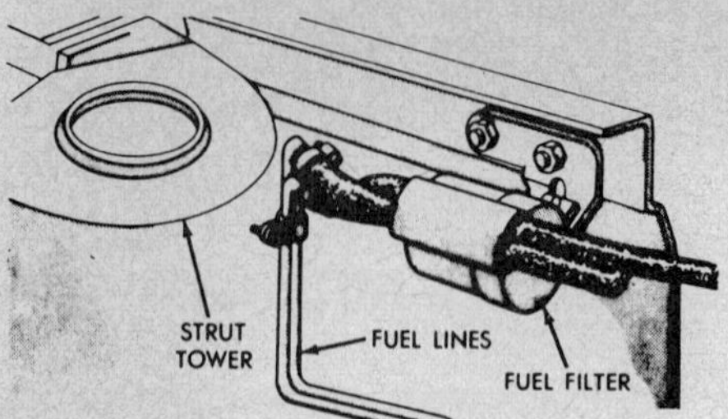

Fig. 5 1983 Fuel filter replacement. 1984–85 Similar

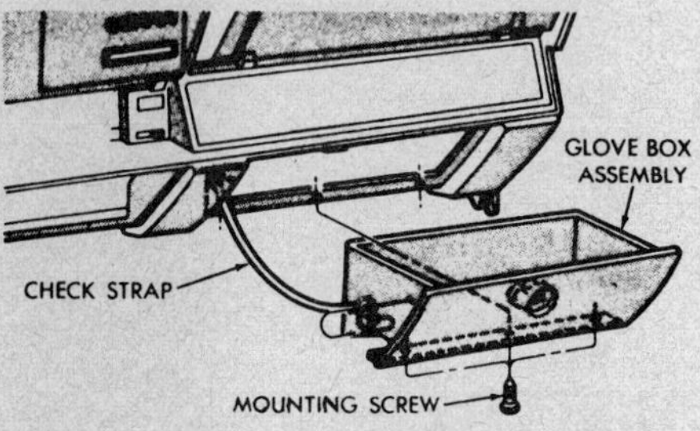

Fig. 8 Glove compartment removal

taching screws.

4. Remove wiring clips and the two AIS wires from 6-way connector. Lift each locking tab inside connector with a small screwdriver and remove blade terminals. Note position of wires for assembly reference.
5. Remove AIS adapter with motor from rear of throttle body, **Fig. 4.**
6. Remove O-ring and seal from adapter.
7. Reverse procedure to install, using new O-ring and seal. Torque adapter attaching screws to 65 inch lbs.

FUEL FILTER, REPLACE

1. Release pressure from fuel system as previously described.
2. Remove filter bracket attaching nuts, **Fig. 5.**
3. Loosen fuel line clamps, then disconnect fuel lines at filter. **Wrap a clean towel around fuel lines to prevent leakage of residual fuel.**
4. Remove filter assembly from vehicle.
5. Reverse procedure to install, using new clamps. Torque clamps to 10 inch lbs.

LOGIC MODULE, REPLACE

1. Remove right side kick panel, then the module attaching screws, **Fig. 6.**
2. Disconnect electrical connectors from module, then remove module from vehicle.
3. Reverse procedure to install.

POWER MODULE, REPLACE

1. Remove air cleaner duct from module.
2. Remove battery from vehicle.

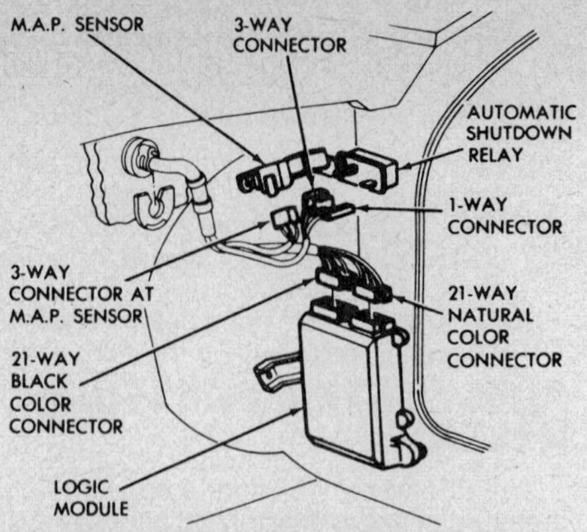

Fig. 6 Logic module & automatic shutdown (ASD) relay replacement

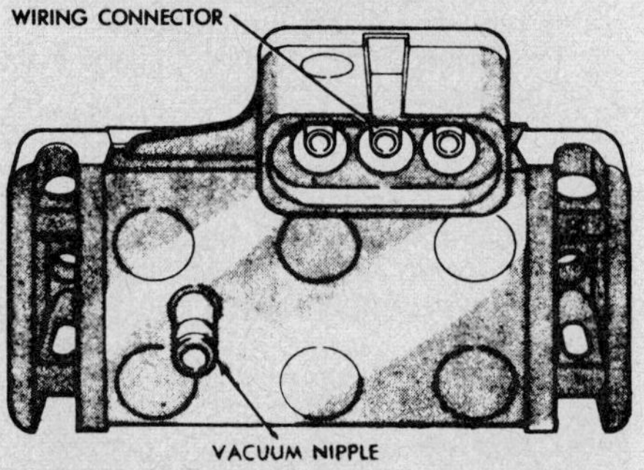

Fig. 9 Manifold absolute pressure (MAP) sensor replacement. 1983–84

3. Remove module attaching screws, **Fig. 7.**
4. Disconnect electrical connectors from module, then remove module from vehicle.
5. Reverse procedure to install.

AUTOMATIC SHUTDOWN (ASD) RELAY, REPLACE

1. Remove glove compartment, **Fig. 8.**
2. Disconnect wiring harness from relay, **Fig. 6.**
3. Remove relay attaching screw, then the relay.
4. Reverse procedure to install.

MANIFOLD ABSOLUTE PRESSURE (MAP) SENSOR, REPLACE

1983–84

1. Remove glove compartment, **Fig. 8.**
2. Disconnect vacuum hose and wiring harness from sensor, **Fig. 9.**
3. Remove sensor attaching screws, then the sensor.
4. Reverse procedure to install.

1985

1. Remove right side kick panel.
2. Disconnect vacuum hose from sensor.

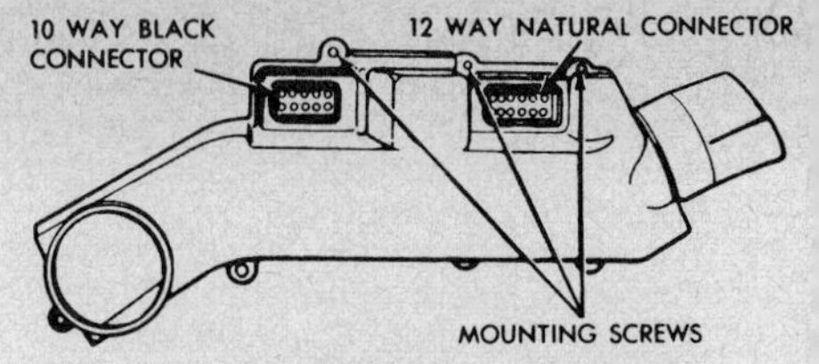

Fig. 7 Power module replacement

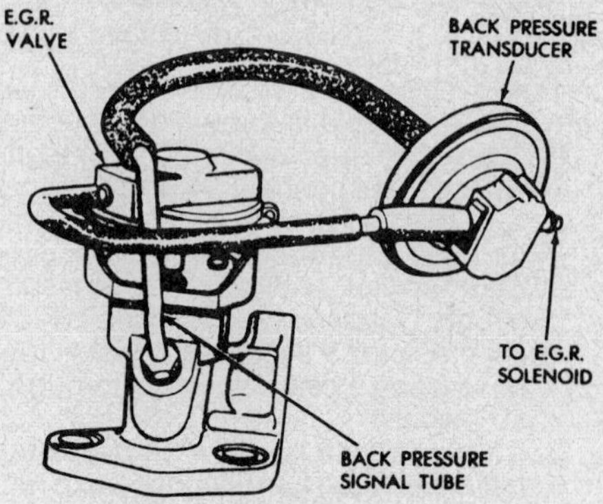

Fig. 10 EGR valve & backpressure transducer assembly replacement

3. Remove sensor mounting screws and remove sensor from logic module.
4. Reverse procedure to install taking care that vacuum hose is attached and sensor is mounted correctly.

OXYGEN SENSOR, REPLACE

1. Remove sensor from exhaust manifold using tool No. C-4589, or equivalent.
2. Clean threads in manifold using an 18 mm x 1.5 x 6E tap.
3. Install new sensor and torque to 20 ft. lbs. **If original sensor is to be reinstalled, coat threads with a suitable anti-seize compound. New sensors are pre-coated and need no additional compound.**

EGR VALVE & BACKPRESSURE TRANSDUCER ASSEMBLY, REPLACE

1. Disconnect vacuum hose from backpressure transducer, **Fig. 10.**
2. Pull transducer straight out from mounting clip.
3. Remove EGR valve attaching screws, then the EGR valve and backpressure transducer assembly.
4. Reverse procedure to install.

Single Point Fuel Injection, 1986–87 Front Wheel Drive Models

INDEX

DESCRIPTION

The electronic, single point fuel injection system used in 1986-87 models uses a pre-programmed "Logic Module" to control air/fuel mixtures delivered to the engine, ignition timing, idle speed, various emission control devices, the engine cooling fan and the charging system. The logic module monitors inputs from various engine and vehicle sensors, computes ideal operating parameters for the controlled subsystems based on these inputs, and controls operation of the subsystems. Sensors used to control system operations include: an exhaust gas oxygen sensor, Manifold Absolute Pressure (MAP) sensor, throttle position sensor, coolant and throttle body temperature sensors, distributor reference signal, vehicle distance sensor, and the neutral safety and A/C compressor clutch switches, **Fig. 1.**

All inputs to the logic module are converted to signals which are transmitted to the power module. These signals cause the power module to alter fuel injector delivery and/or ignition timing to maintain ideal air fuel mixtures and ignition timing for all vehicle operating conditions.

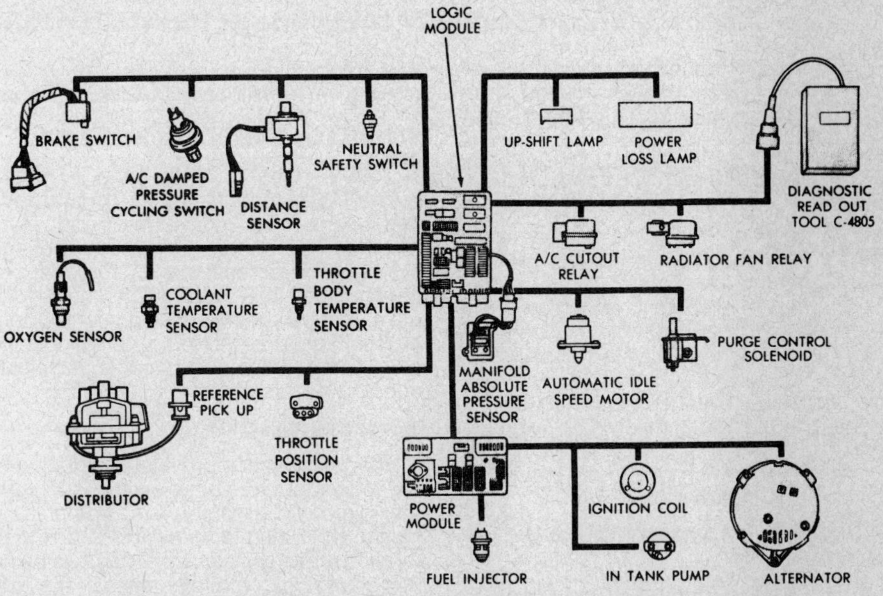

Fig. 1 Fuel injection system schematic

In addition, the logic module tests many of its input and output circuits, and, if a fault is found in one of the monitored circuits, information relating to the malfunction is stored in the module's memory. Information relating to monitored circuit malfunctions can be accessed by the technician through the instrument panel mounted power loss lamp, or by connecting a diagnostic read-out instrument to the system. Both access methods provide numerical type codes which relate to specific circuit malfunctions.

POWER MODULE & AUTOMATIC SHUT DOWN (ASD) RELAY

The power module is mounted on the air cleaner along with the spark control computer and contains circuits necessary to energize the ignition coil, fuel injectors and alternator field in order to minimize electrical noise in the passenger compartment. The module contains a power converter which converts battery voltage into a regulated 8 volt output to energize the logic module and ignition pickup coil. The power module also houses and energizes the Automatic Shut Down (ASD) relay which activates the fuel pump, ignition coil injector and portions of the power module.

The ASD relay is turned on and off by the logic module in response to distributor reference pulses. When distributor reference pulses are transmitted to the logic module, the module activates the ASD relay. However, when no reference pulse is transmitted to the logic module the ASD relay is deactivated and power is shut off to the fuel control system and ignition coil.

SENSORS & SWITCHES

Manifold Absolute Pressure (MAP) Sensor

The MAP sensor is mounted on the logic module and monitors intake manifold vacuum through a line connected to the throttle body. The sensor converts manifold vacuum (negative pressure) and barometric pressure into electrical signals and transmits these signals to the logic module. The module uses these signals to monitor engine load and atmospheric conditions in order to determine the correct air fuel mixture for vehicle operating conditions.

Oxygen Sensor

The oxygen sensor produces voltage

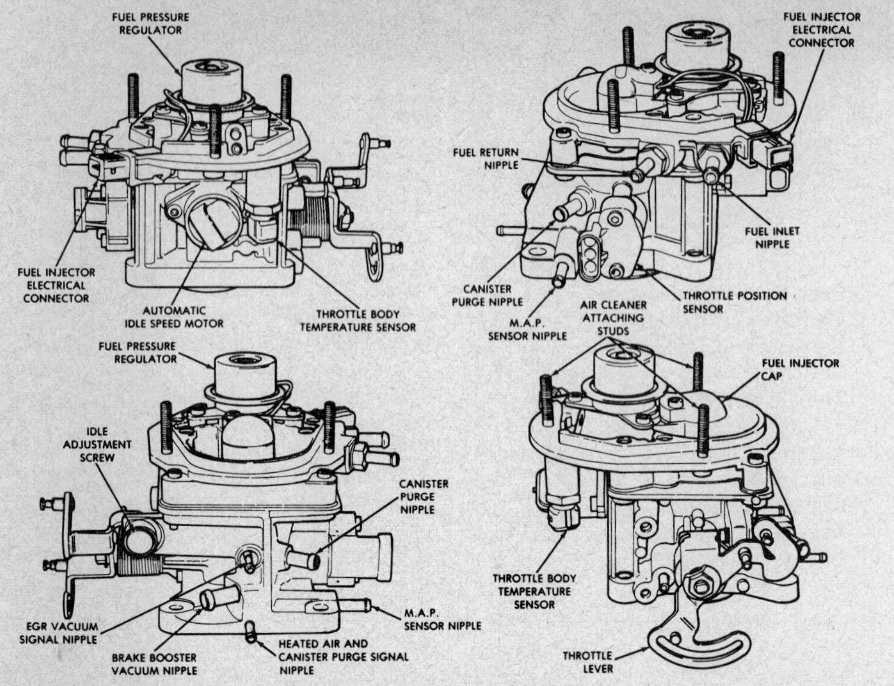

Fig. 2 Throttle body assembly component identification

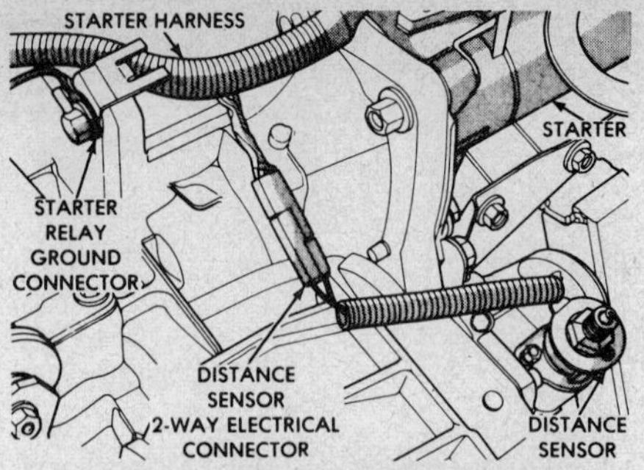

Fig. 3 Speed/distance sensor installation

signals when exposed to oxygen in the exhaust gasses. The oxygen content in the exhaust gasses is directly proportional to the air fuel mixture entering the engine, and the voltage signal produced by the sensor is inversely proportional to the amount of oxygen remaining in the exhaust gasses. The logic module uses these signals to determine air fuel mixtures entering the engine.

The oxygen sensor is mounted in the exhaust manifold, and the sensing element must be heated by exhaust gasses before the sensor begins to produce voltage signals. When exhaust gas oxygen content is high (lean mixtures), the sensor produces a low voltage. When oxygen content is low (rich mixtures), the sensor produces a higher voltage.

Coolant Temperature Sensor

The coolant temperature sensor is mounted in the thermostat housing and allows the logic module to monitor engine operating temperature in order to provide proper air/fuel mixtures. The sensor provides a variable resistance which is proportional to coolant temperature. When the engine is cold and sensor resistance is low, the logic module provides richer air/fuel mixtures and increases engine idle speed to provide acceptable cold engine performance and allow quick warm up. When coolant temperature and sensor resistance increase, the logic module provides leaner air/fuel mixtures and lowers engine idle speed to provide proper exhaust emission control and increased fuel economy.

Throttle Body Temperature Sensor

The throttle body mounted temperature sensor allows the logic module to monitor fuel temperature. The logic module uses this information to provide the proper air/fuel mixtures for a hot restart condition.

Throttle Position Sensor (TPS)

The TPS is mounted on the throttle body and is senses the angle of the throttle plate opening. The sensor produces a voltage signal which increases and decreases according to throttle position. The logic module uses these voltage signals to tailor air/fuel mixtures for varying conditions such as idle, wide open throttle, acceleration and deceleration.

Switch Inputs

Various switches provide information to the logic module. These switches include the idle, neutral safety, A/C compressor clutch and brake lamp switches. If one or more of these switches is sensed as being "on", the logic module signals the idle speed motor to change idle speed to a preset RPM. In addition, when the A/C is on and the throttle plate is above a specified angle, the wide open throttle cut-out relay prevents the A/C clutch from being energized until throttle angle is reduced.

AUTOMATIC IDLE SPEED (AIS) MOTOR

The AIS motor is operated by the logic module and controls engine idle speed by controlling air flow through the throttle body bypass channel. The logic module computes proper idle speed based in signals from vehicle and engine sensors and the switch inputs, and transmits voltage signals to the AIS motor to open or close the bypass channel in order to maintain the proper engine speed.

Basic, no-load idle speed is determined by the amount of air flowing through the throttle body past the closed throttle plate. The AIS motor alters idle speed by allowing increased air flow through the bypass channel; increasing idle speed when the channel is opened and decreasing idle speed when the channel is closed. In addition, the AIS motor is signaled to open the bypass channel during deceleration to prevent stalling and mixture enrichment caused by sudden closing of the throttle plate.

FUEL SYSTEM CONTROLS

Throttle Body & Fuel Injector

The throttle body assembly is mounted on the intake manifold and houses the throttle plate, fuel injector, fuel pressure regulator, temperature and position sensors, and the AIS motor, **Fig. 2.** Intake air flow is controlled by the cable operated throttle plate and by a separate bypass channel which is controlled by the AIS motor. The throttle body provides the chamber for fuel metering, atomization, and mixing atomized fuel with incoming air.

The fuel injector is a solenoid operated valve which is energized by the power module but controlled by the logic module. Fuel is supplied to the injector at a constant pressure of 14.5 psi, and excess fuel is returned to the tank. When voltage is applied to the injector solenoid, a spring loaded ball is lifted off its seat and fuel is sprayed into the throttle body through 6 spray orifices. The spray orifices and injector tip design cause the fuel to be sprayed in an even conical pattern prior to entering the intake air stream.

The amount of fuel delivered by the injector is determined by the amount of time that the injector solenoid is energized. The logic module determines the amount of fuel necessary to maintain ideal air/fuel mixtures based upon various sensor inputs. The logic module then directs the power module to energize the fuel injector for a sufficient amount of time to deliver the necessary amount of fuel.

Fuel Pressure Regulator

The mechanical fuel pressure regulator is used to maintain fuel pressure at the injector tip at a constant 14.5 psi. The pressure regulator uses a spring loaded diaphragm to control the fuel return port in order to maintain constant pressure. Pressurized fuel is delivered first to the fuel injector and then flows to the pressure regulator. When fuel pressure acting on the regulator diaphragm exceeds 14.5 psi, the regulator spring is compressed and the

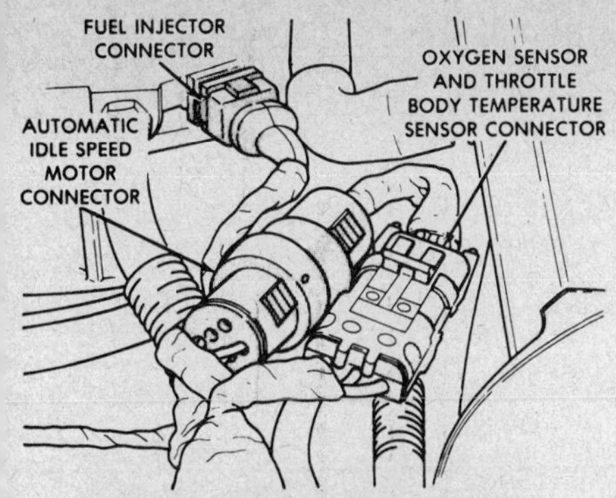

Fig. 4 Throttle body electrical connector identification

fuel return port is opened. When fuel pressure drops below 14.5 psi spring tension causes the diaphragm to block the fuel return port. The diaphragm and spring move constantly between the open and closed positions in order to maintain constant fuel pressure at the injector tip.

Fuel Pump & Reservoir

An electric fuel pump is located in a specially designed reservoir within the fuel tank. The reservoir ensures that fuel is available at the pump inlet during all operating conditions, particularly when little fuel remains in the tank. The fuel pump is energized by the ASD relay and operates whenever the relay is activated. Fuel is drawn into the pump through a "sock type" filter screen, and the pump contains an integral fuel inlet check valve to prevent drain back.

EMISSION CONTROLS

The charcoal canister purge control solenoid is operated by the logic module. When engine temperature is below 145 degrees F, the logic module completes the purge solenoid ground circuit, the solenoid is energized and purge vacuum is prevented from being applied to the canister. When engine temperature is above 145 degrees F, the solenoid is de-energized and purge vacuum is applied from the port on the throttle body.

DIAGNOSIS & TESTING

The logic module has been programmed to monitor several different circuits of the fuel injection system in order to provide a self-diagnosis function. In conjunction with the self-diagnosis function, a power loss lamp is wired into the system to indicate a failure in the monitored circuits. The power loss lamp is illuminated for 3 seconds whenever the engine is started as a "bulb test." However, if the logic module detects a malfunction in one of the monitored circuits the power loss lamp will be illuminated and will remain on as long as the ignition key remains in the on position. Illumination of the power loss lamp indicates that the system has entered the "limp-in" mode and signals an immediate need for system service.

If vehicle performance or the power loss lamp indicate fuel injection system malfunctions, certain procedures should be followed. Prior to suspecting the fuel injection service as the cause for complaints, ensure that the engine and all related systems are in proper operating condition. After checking related systems, inspect fuel injection components and connecting harnesses as outlined in "Visual Inspection," repair system as indicated, the road test vehicle to check system operation. If service performed during visual inspection does not correct observed malfunctions, or if power loss lamp remains illuminated, refer to "System Testing" to call up fault codes stored in the logic module memory and correct as needed.

Pin	Circuit	Color	Function
1	—	—	5 Volt Supply
2	K16	18 VT/YL	Injector Control
3	—	—	Not Used
4	—	—	Not Used
5	R31	20 DG/OR	Alternator Field Control
6	K15	18 YL	Dwell Control
7	K14	18 DB	Fused J2
8	K14	18 DB	Fused J2
9	—	—	Not Used
10	N 7	18 GY	Distributor Reference
11	DK21	20 PK	SCI Interface Transmit
12	T21	20 GY/LB	Tachometer Signal
13	DK20	20 LG	SCI Interface Receive
14	Z 6	20 LB	Fuel Monitor
15	U 3	20 OR/LG	Shift Indicator Light
16	N 4	18 VT/BK	AIS Motor
17	K19	20 DB/YL	ASD Relay Control
18	N 1	18 GY/RD	AIS Motor Open
19	—	—	Not Used
20	N3	18 VT	AIS Motor
21	C27	20 DB/PK	Radiator Fan Relay
22	N 2	18 BR	AIS Motor Close
23	N 6	18 OR	7.5 Volts Input
24	K 5	18 BK	Signal Ground
25	N 5	18 BK/LB	Sensor Return

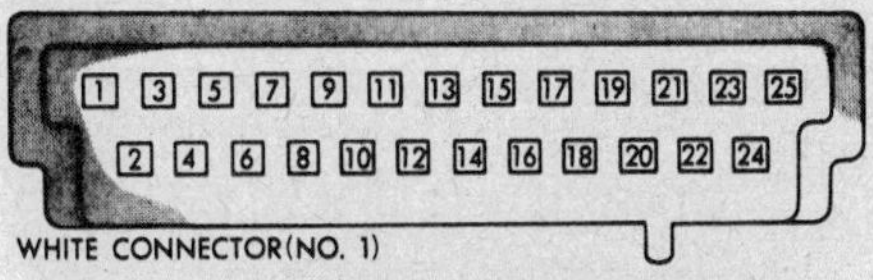

Fig. 5 Logic module white connector terminal identification. 1986 all & 1987 Shadow & Sundance

Visual Inspection

A visual inspection for loose, disconnected or improperly routed wiring and hoses should be made prior to attempting to diagnose fuel injection system malfunctions. The visual inspection should include the following checks:

1. Ensure that vacuum connections on rear of throttle body, **Fig. 2**, are secure.
2. Ensure that vacuum connection and purge control solenoid and charcoal canister are secure and not leaking.
3. Inspect PCV valve and ensure that valve and hose are in satisfactory condition.
4. Inspect alternator and ensure that electrical connectors are secure and that belt is properly adjusted.
5. Ensure that MAP sensor hose is securely connected at firewall connection and at sensor.
6. Ensure that air intake heated air door vacuum hose is securely connected.
7. Inspect fuel pump and fuel lines, ensuring that pump electrical connectors and fuelhoses are securely connected.
8. Inspect back pressure transducer and EGR valve, ensuring that components are securely mounted and free from leaks.

Pin	Circuit	Color	Function
1	K8	20 VT/WT	5 Volt Supply
2	K16	22 VT/YL	Injector Control
3	—	—	Not Used
4	K3	22 BK/PK	Power Loss Light
5	R31	22DG/OR	Alternator Field Control
6	K15	22 YL	Dwell Control
7	K14	18 DB	Fused J2
8	K14	18 DB	Fused J2
9	G7	22 WT/OR	Vehicle Distance Sensor
10	N 7	18 GY	Distributor Reference
11	DK21	20 PK	SCI Interface Transmit
12	T21	22 GY/LB	Tachometer Signal
13	DK20	20 LG	SCI Interface Receive
14	Z 6	22 LB	Fuel Monitor
15	U 3	22 OR/LG	Shift Indicator Light (Manual)/Part Throttle Unlock (Automatic)
16	N 4	18 BK/YL	AIS Motor
17	K19	20 DB/YL	ASD Relay Control
18	N 1	18 GY/RD	AIS Motor
19	—	—	Not Used
20	N3	18 VT/BK	AIS Motor
21	C27	20 DB/PK	Radiator Fan Relay
22	N 2	18 BR	AIS Motor
23	N 6	18 OR	9.0 Volts Input
24	K 5	18 BK	Signal Ground
25	N 5	18 BK/LB	Sensor Return

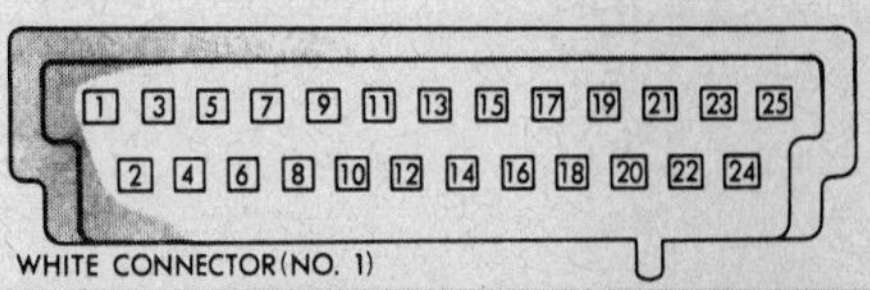

Fig. 6 Logic module white connector terminal identification. 1987 exc. Shadow & Sundance

9. Ensure that black and white 25 pin connectors are securely seated in proper sockets in logic module.
10. Ensure that 10 pin and 12 pin connectors are securely seated in proper sockets in power module. **When inspecting system electrical connectors, ensure that connector terminals are not bent or damaged, preventing proper current transfer. Do not clean conductive grease from connector cavities, where applicable, as this could adversely affect system performance.**
11. Ensure that starter relay ground connector (man. trans.) and distance sensor connectors, **Fig. 3**, are secure.
12. Ensure that Fuel injector, AIS motor, and throttle body oxygen sensor and temperature sensor electrical connectors are secure, **Fig 4.**
13. Ensure that coolant sensor is properly mounted in thermostat housing and that electrical connector is secure.
14. Ensure that 3 wire distributor connector and oxygen sensor lead connector are secure and free from corrosion.
15. Inspect engine harness connectors, ensuring that terminals are not bent or damaged and that connectors are properly locked.
16. Ensure that all relay electrical connectors are fully seated and that battery cable connections are clean and free from corrosion.
17. Ensure that radiator fan relay and radiator temperature sensor connectors are properly seated.
18. Inspect ignition system primary and secondary wiring, ensuring that all connections are secure and free from corrosion.
19. Ensure that neutral safety switch is operating properly and that electrical connector is secure.

Pin	Circuit	Color	Function
1	K 6	18 OR/WT	TPS 5 Volts
2	J11	20 RD/WT	Battery Standby
3	N13	20 DB/OR	A/C Cut-out Relay
4	K 3	20 BK/PK	Power Loss Lamp
5	K 1	18 PK	Purge Solenoid
6	—	—	Not Used
7	K 9	18 LB/RD	Power Ground
8	K 9	18 LB/RD	Power Ground
9	—	—	Not Used
10	—	—	Not Used
11	C 2B	18 BR	A/C Clutch
12	S 4	20 BR/YL	P/N Switch
13	D 4	18 WT/TN	Brake Switch
14	G 7	20 WT/OR	Distance Sensor
15	—	—	Not Used
16	—	—	Not Used
17	—	—	Not Used
18	N11	18 BK	Oxygen Sensor
19	—	—	MAP Sensor Signal
20	K22	20 RD/BK	Battery Temperature Signal
21	K 7	18 OR/DB	TPS
22	J11	20 RD/WT	Battery Sense
23	K10	18 TN	Coolant Sensor
24	—	—	Not Used
25	K13	18 BK/RD	Throttle Body Temperature Sensor

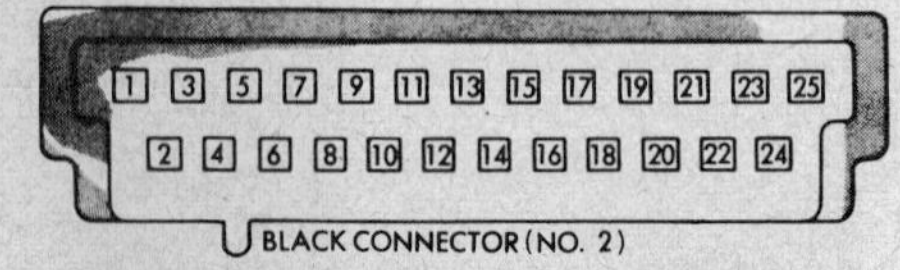

Fig. 7 Logic module black connector terminal identification. 1986 all & 1987 Shadow & Sundance

20. Ensure that engine ground strap is secure at dash panel and intake manifold.

System Testing

OBTAINING FAULT CODES

If a problem is sensed by the logic module, often enough to be considered a malfunction, a fault code is stored in the module memory. If the problem is repaired, or ceases to occur, the module will cancel the fault code after 20-40 engine cycles. Fault codes that remain in the module memory can be called up and displayed either by using diagnostic tool C-4805 or by observing flashes of the power loss lamp. Fault codes can be obtained using the following procedures:

Using Tester C-4805

1. Connect tester to diagnostic connector located in engine compartment near passenger side strut tower.
2. Start engine, if possible, move transmission selector through range and cycle A/C compressor on and off, then stop engine.
3. Turn ignition switch on, off, on, off and on within 5 seconds.
4. Power loss lamp should light for 3 seconds, then go out and stored fault codes will be displayed on tool. **After obtaining fault codes using tester C-4805, test circuits as outlined in "Switch Tests" and "Actuation Test Mode (ATM) Tests."**

Using Power Loss Lamp

If suitable tester is not available, stored fault codes and be accessed directly through the power loss lamp. To call up codes, cycle ignition switch on, off, on, off and on within 5 seconds. Stored codes will be indicated by flashes of the power loss lamp.

Pin	Circuit	Color	Function
1	K 6	18 OR/WT	TPS 5 Volts
2	J11	20 RD/WT	Battery Standby
3	N13	20 DB/OR	A/C Cut-out Relay
4	X36	20 TN/RD	Speed Control Vacuum
5	K 1	18 PK	Purge Solenoid
6	X35	20 LG/RD	Speed Control Vent Solenoid
7	K 9	18 LB/RD	Power Ground
8	K 9	18 LB/RD	Power Ground
9	X31	22 BR/RD	Speed Control Set
10	X33	22 WT	Speed Control Resume
11	C 2B	18 BR	A/C Clutch
12	S 4	20 BR/YL	P/N Switch
13	D 4	18 WT/TN	Brake Switch
14	—	—	Not Used
15	X32	22 YL/RD	Speed Control On/Off
16	—	—	Not Used
17	—	—	Not Used
18	N11	18 BK	Oxygen Sensor
19	K4	20 DG/RD	MAP Sensor Signal
20	K22	22 RD/BK	Battery Temperature Signal
21	K 7	18 OR/DB	TPS
22	J11	20 RD/WT	Battery Sense
23	K10	20 TN	Coolant Sensor
24	—	—	Not Used
25	K13	18 BK/RD	Throttle Body Temperature Sensor

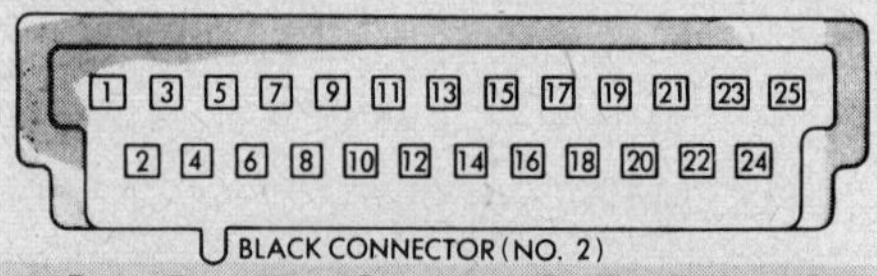

Fig. 8 Logic module black connector terminal identification. 1987 exc. Shadow & Sundance

FAULT CODE DIAGNOSIS

These fault codes indicate the result of a failure, but do not identify the failed component in the following areas:
Code 88—Start of test.
Code 11—Engine not cranked since battery was disconnected.
Code 12—Memory Standby power lost.
Code 13—MAP sensor pneumatic circuit.
Code 14—MAP sensor electrical circuit.
Code 15—Vehicle speed/distance sensor.
Code 16—Loss of battery voltage sense.
Code 17—Engine running too cool.
Code 21—Oxygen sensor circuit.
Code 22—Coolant temperature sensor circuit.
Code 23—Throttle body temperature sensor circuit.
Code 24—Throttle position sensor.
Code 25—AIS motor driven circuit.
Code 26—Peak injector current not reached.
Code 27—Internal problem in logic module fuel circuit.
Code 31—Purge solenoid circuit.
Code 33—A/C cutout relay circuit.
Code 35—Fan control relay circuit.
Code 37—Shift indicator lamp circuit.
Code 41—Charging system excess or no field circuit.
Code 42—ASD relay driver.
Code 43—Spark interface circuit.
Code 44—Battery temperature out of range.
Code 46—Battery voltage too high.
Code 47—Battery voltage too low.
Code 51—Oxygen feedback system stuck at lean position.
Code 52—Oxygen feedback system stuck at rich position.
Code 53—Internal logic module problem.
Code 55—End of message.

Codes indicated by an asterisk will cause the power loss lamp to remain illuminated when set in the logic module memory.

Pin	Circuit	Color	Function
1	J 5	18 BK/YL	Coil (–) Terminal
2	J 2	14 DB	Ignition Switch Input
3	K14	18 DB	Fused J2 Output
4	J 1	12 PK	Direct Battery
5	K18	18 TN	Injector
6	Z 1	14 DG/BK	Switched Battery
7	K17	18 WT	Injector
8	R 3	18 DG	Alternator Field
9	J 9	14 BK	Power Ground
10	J 9	14 BK	Power Ground

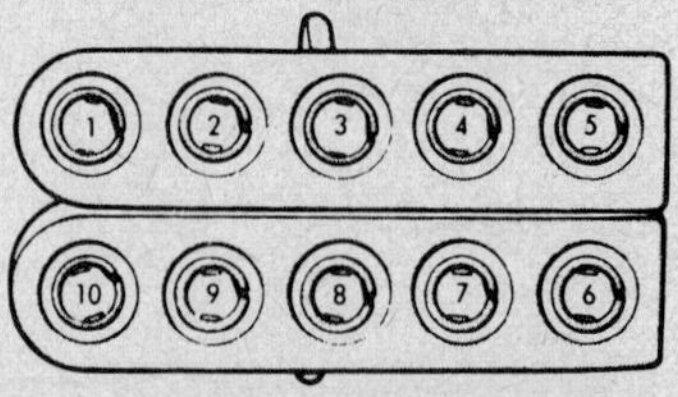

Fig. 9 Power module 10 pin connector terminal identification. 1986 all & 1987 Shadow & Sundance

Test continuity of wiring in each circuit indicated by fault codes or in other circuit tests, referring to **Figs. 5 through 12,** for logic and power module terminal identification. Repair wiring as needed and check operation of components as outlined in "Description." Replace any components that fail to perform properly, then recheck system operation.

SWITCH TESTS

1. Connect tester C-4805 or equivalent and access fault codes as outlined.
2. After Code 55 has been displayed, indicating end of fault code display, observe tester display and operate switches as follows:
   a. Operate brake lamp switch by depressing and releasing brake pedal.
   b. Operate neutral safety and indicator lamp switches by moving shift selector through range.
   c. Ensure that A/C dampened pressure switch is closed, then cycle A/C compressor clutch on and off with blower switch in on position.
   d. Raise and support vehicle and rotate drive wheels to operate speed sensor.
3. As each switch is opened and closed, numerical read-out on tester should change.
4. If read-out does not change as switch is operated, check continuity of wiring between switch and logic module and repair as needed.
5. If wiring is satisfactory, test each switch individually.

ACTUATION TEST MODE (ATM) TEST

1. Connect tester C-4895 or equivalent and access fault codes as outlined.
2. Wait until Code 55 has been displayed indicating end of fault code display.
3. Depress ATM button on tool to activate display, holding button down until desired display code appears.
4. Each display code will activate a specific current as follows:
   a. 01—Spark activation once every 2 seconds.

Pin	Circuit	Color	Function
1	J 5	18 BK/YL	Coil (–) Terminal
2	J 2	14 DB	Ignition Switch Input
3	K14	18 DB	Fused J2 Output
4	J 1	12 PK	Direct Battery
5	K18	18 TN	Injector
6	Z 1	14 DG/BK	Switched Battery
7	K17	18 WT	Injector
8	R 3	18 DG	Alternator Field
9	J 9	16 BK	Power Ground
10	J 9	16 BK	Power Ground

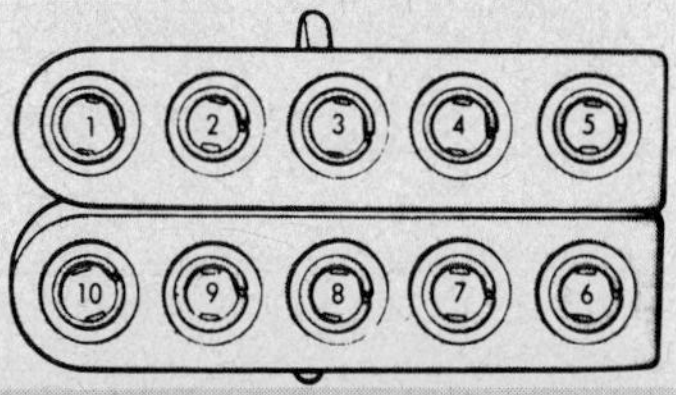

Fig. 10 Power module 10 pin connector terminal identification. 1987 exc. Shadow & Sundance

b. 02—Injector activation once every 2 seconds.
c. 03—AIS activation; one step open/one step closed every 4 seconds.
d. 04—Radiator fan relay activation once every 2 seconds.
e. 05—A/C WOT relay activation once every 2 seconds.
f. 06—ASD relay activation once every 2 seconds.
g. 07—Purge solenoid activation; one toggle every 2 seconds.
h. 08—Shift indicator lamp activation; one toggle every 2 seconds.
i. 09—Alternator field control activation; one toggle every 2 seconds.

5. The computer will continue to turn the selected circuit on and off for as long as 5 minutes to allow operation to be observed.
6. If selected circuit fails to operate, check continuity of wiring and operation of individual components and repair or replace as needed.
7. To stop test cycle, either depress ATM button to move to the next circuit or turn off ignition.
8. If ATM button is not depressed and the ignition switch is left on, the computer will continue cycling the selected circuit for 5 minutes and then shut the system off.

SENSOR READ TEST MODE

1987

1. Connect tester C-4805 or equivalent and access fault codes as outlined.
2. After Code 55 has been displayed, indicating end of fault code display, press ATM button on tool to activate display. If a specific sensor read test is desired, hold ATM button down until desired test code appears.
3. Slide Read/Hold switch to the "Hold" position to display the corresponding sensor output level.
4. Sensor read test display code descriptions are as follows:
   a. 01—Battery temperature sensor-display number 10 equals sensor temperature.
   b. 02—Oxygen sensor voltage-display number 10 equals sensor voltage.

Pin	Circuit	Color	Function
1	K16	22 VT/YL	Injector Control
2	Y 5	18 BK/LB	Signal Ground
3	K22	22 RD/BK	Battery Temperature Sensor
4	—	—	Not Used
5	K19	20 DB/YL	ASD Relay Control
6	J11	20 RD/WT	Battery Sense and Standby
7	—	—	Not Used
8	—	—	Not Used
9	—	—	Not Used
10	K15	22 YL	Dwell Control
11	R31	22 DG/OR	Alternator Field Control
12	N 6	18 OR	8 Volts Output

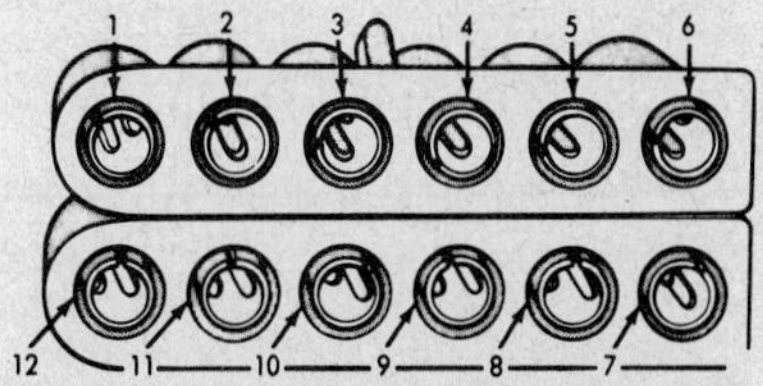

Fig. 11 Power module 12 pin connector terminal identification. 1986 all & 1987 Shadow & Sundance

c. 03—Throttle body temperature sensor voltage-display number 10 equals sensor voltage.
d. 04—Engine coolant temperature sensor-display number 10 equals degrees of engine coolant sensor.
e. 05—Throttle position sensor voltage-display number 10 equals sensor voltage.
f. 07—Battery voltage-display number equals battery voltage.
g. 08—Map sensor voltage-display number 10 equals sensor voltage.
h. 09—Cruise control switches. Cruise Off-display is blank; Cruise On-display shows 00; Cruise Set-display shows 10; Cruise Resume-display shows 01.

5. If sensor tested corresponds to previously noted fault code, check sensor wiring. If wiring is satisfactory, replace sensor.

ENGINE RUNNING TEST MODE

1987

This system monitors sensors on vehicle which check operating conditions while engine is running. Using number displayed on tester C-4805 or equivalent, follow instructions given in code description for values of each test. The engine running test mode can be performed with engine idling in neutral with parking brake applied or while driving down the road. With diagnostic tester read/hold switch in read position, engine running test mode is initiated after engine is started.

To select test code, place read/hold switch in the read position and depress actuator button until desired code appears. Release actuator button and switch read/hold switch to hold position. The logic module will monitor that system test and results will be displayed. Using the code description, the display number must be adjusted as required.

Engine running test display code descriptions are as follows:

1. 61—Battery temperature sensor-display number 10 equals volts.
2. 62—Oxygen sensor-display number 10 equals volts.

Pin	Circuit	Color	Function
1	K16	18 VT/YL	Injector Control
2	Y 5	18 BK/LB	Signal Ground
3	K22	20 RD/BK	Battery Temperature Sensor
4	—	—	Not Used
5	K19	20 DB/YL	ASD Relay Control
6	J11	20 RD/WT	Battery Sense and Standby
7	—	—	Not Used
8	—	—	Not Used
9	—	—	Not Used
10	K15	18 YL	Dwell Control
11	R31	20 DG/OR	Alternator Field Control
12	N 6	18 OR	8 Volts Output

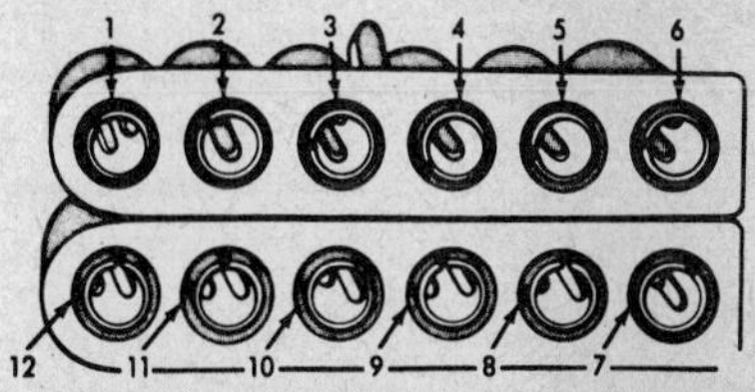

Fig. 12 Power module 12 pin connector terminal identification. 1987 exc. Shadow & Sundance

3. 63—Fuel injector temperature sensor-display number 10 equals volts.
4. 64—Engine coolant temperature sensor-display number x 10 equals degrees F.
5. 65—Throttle position sensor-display number 10 equals volts.
6. 67—Battery voltage sensor-display equals volts.
7. 68—Manifold vacuum sensor-display is inches Hg.
8. 69—Minimum throttle position sensor-display number 10 equals volts.
9. 70—Minimum air flow idle speed sensor-display number 10 equals RPM.
10. 71—Vehicle speed sensor-display is mph.
11. 72—Engine speed sensor-display number 10 equals RPM.

THROTTLE BODY MINIMUM AIR FLOW TEST

1987

1. Remove air cleaner assembly, then plug heated air door vacuum hose.
2. Start engine and allow cooling fan to cycle on and off at least once.
3. Connect suitable timing light, then disconnect coolant thermistor and set basic timing to 12° BTDC.
4. Stop engine and reconnect coolant thermistor wire.
5. Disconnect PCV valve hose from intake manifold nipple.
6. Attach tool No. C-5004 or equivalent (.125 inch orifice in attached hose) to intake manifold PCV nipple.
7. Connect diagnostic readout box C-4805, then start engine and allow to idle for at least one minute.
8. Using readout box, place read/hold switch in read position and depress ATM button until code 70 appears.
9. Place read/hold switch to hold position, then the following should occur:
   a. AIS motor will fully close.
   b. Idle spark advance will become fixed.
   c. Idle fuel will become enriched.
   d. Engine RPM will be displayed on diagnostic readout box in units of

RPM x 10. For example, display 95 equals 95 x 10 which indicates 950 RPM.

10. Check idle RPM. If idle RPM is within 1100-1300 RPM for 4-135 engines or 1050-1250 RPM for 4-153 engines, then throttle body minimum air flow is satisfactory. If idle RPM is not as specified, replace throttle body.
11. Shut off engine, then remove tool No. C-5004 from intake manifold PCV nipple. Install PVC valve hose.
12. Remove readout box, then install air cleaner assembly and heated air door vacuum hose.

SYSTEM SERVICE

The electronic fuel injection system is under a constant pressure of approximately 14.5 psi. Before servicing the fuel pump, fuel lines, fuel filter, throttle body or fuel injector, the fuel system pressure must be released.

IGNITION TIMING

1. Connect a suitable timing light to No. 1 cylinder, or a magnetic timing unit to engine.
2. Connect tachometer to engine, then start engine and run until operating temperature is reached.
3. Disconnect, then reconnect the water temperature sensor connector on thermostat housing. The loss of power lamp must illuminate and engine RPM should be within specifications given on vehicle emission label.
4. Direct timing light at timing hole in bellhousing, or read magnetic timing unit, and adjust timing as necessary by loosening distributor and turning until specifications are met.
5. Shut engine off, then disconnect and reconnect positive battery quick disconnect.
6. Start engine and observe loss of power lamp, which should be off.
7. Shut engine off, then cycle ignition switch on and off twice.
8. Turn ignition on and observe fault code display. Fault codes should be clear with Codes 88, 51, and 55 displayed.

FUEL SYSTEM PRESSURE RELEASE

1. Loosen gas cap and allow tank pressure to release.
2. Remove wiring harness connector from injector, then ground one injector terminal.
3. Connect a suitable jumper wire to a second terminal, then touch the positive post of the battery for approximately 10 seconds and release system pressure.
4. Remove jumper wires and service fuel system as required.

THROTTLE BODY, REPLACE

1. Remove air cleaner.
2. Perform fuel system pressure release procedures as previously described.
3. Disconnect battery ground cable.
4. Disconnect vacuum hoses, then the electrical connector.
5. Remove throttle cable, then if equipped, the speed control and transaxle kickdown cables.
6. Remove return spring, then the fuel system intake and return hoses.
7. Remove throttle body attaching bolts, then lift throttle body from vehicle.
8. Reverse procedure to install. Torque attaching bolts to 200 inch lbs.

PRESSURE REGULATOR, REPLACE

1. Remove air cleaner assembly.
2. Perform fuel system pressure release procedures as previously described.
3. Disconnect battery ground cable.
4. Place a suitable shop towel around fuel inlet chamber as to contain any remaining fuel in system, then remove three pressure regulator to throttle body attaching screws.
5. Pull pressure regulator from throttle body.
6. Remove O-ring from pressure regulator, then the gasket.
7. Reverse procedure to install, noting the following:
   a. Install new pressure regulator gasket and new O-ring.
   b. Torque pressure regulator to throttle body attaching screws to 40 inch lbs.
   c. Pressurize system and check for leaks after assembly.

FUEL INJECTOR, REPLACE

1. Remove air cleaner.
2. Perform fuel system pressure release procedures as previously described.
3. Disconnect battery ground cable.
4. Remove torx screw retaining injector cap, then lift cap from injector using two suitable screwdrivers.
5. Pry injector from pod by placing a suitable screwdriver into hole at side of electrical connector.
6. Remove lower O-ring from pod.
7. Place new lower O-ring on injector and new O-ring on injector cap.
8. Place injector in pod, positioning injector as to allow cap to be installed without interference.
9. Rotate cap and injector to align attachment hold, then press down on cap to ensure proper seal.
10. Install torx screw, then torque to 35-45 inch lbs.
11. Connect battery ground cable, then pressurize system and check for leaks.
12. Reinstall air cleaner.

THROTTLE POSITION SENSOR, REPLACE

1. Disconnect battery ground cable, then remove air cleaner.
2. Disconnect three-way connector at throttle position sensor (TPS), then remove TPS to throttle body mounting screws.
3. Lift TPS from throttle shaft, then remove O-ring.
4. Reverse procedure to install. Install new O-ring and torque TPS to throttle body mounting screw to 20 inch lbs.

THROTTLE BODY TEMPERATURE SENSOR, REPLACE

1. Remove air cleaner, then disconnect throttle cables from throttle body linkage.
2. Remove two throttle cable bracket attaching screws, then position bracket aside.
3. Disconnect electrical connector, then unscrew sensor.
4. Apply heat transfer compound to tip of new sensor.
5. Install new sensor, then torque to 80-120 inch lbs.
6. Reconnect electrical connector, then install throttle cable bracket with attaching screws.
7. Connect throttle cables to throttle body linkage, then install retaining clips.
8. Install air cleaner.

AUTOMATIC IDLE SPEED (AIS) MOTOR ASSEMBLY, REPLACE

1. Disconnect battery ground cable, then remove air cleaner assembly.
2. Disconnect four pin connector from AIS, then remove temperature sending unit from throttle body housing.
3. Remove two AIS to throttle body torx head retaining screws.
4. Remove AIS from throttle body housing with O-ring.
5. Reverse procedure to install. Install new O-ring and torque retaining screws to 20 inch lbs.

MANIFOLD ABSOLUTE PRESSURE SENSOR, REPLACE

1. Remove kick panel at passenger side of vehicle.
2. Remove vacuum hose from sensor.
3. Remove sensor attaching screws, then the sensor.
4. Reverse procedure to install. Ensure proper installation of vacuum hose to sensor and sensor to logic module.

POWER MODULE, REPLACE

1. Remove air cleaner duct from power module.
2. Remove battery.
3. Remove three module mount screws.
4. Remove module electrical connectors.
5. Remove module.
6. Reverse procedure to install.

OXYGEN SENSOR, REPLACE

The oxygen sensor is to be removed using tool No. C-4589 or equivalent. After removal, clean threads in exhaust manifold using an 18 mm x 1.5 x 6E tap. If reinstalling the same sensor, apply a suitable sealant to threads of sensor. New sensors are packaged with an anti-seize compound already applied to the threads and no further application is required. When installing sensor, torque to 20 ft. lbs.

Multi-Point Fuel Injection, 1984–87 Front Wheel Drive Models

INDEX

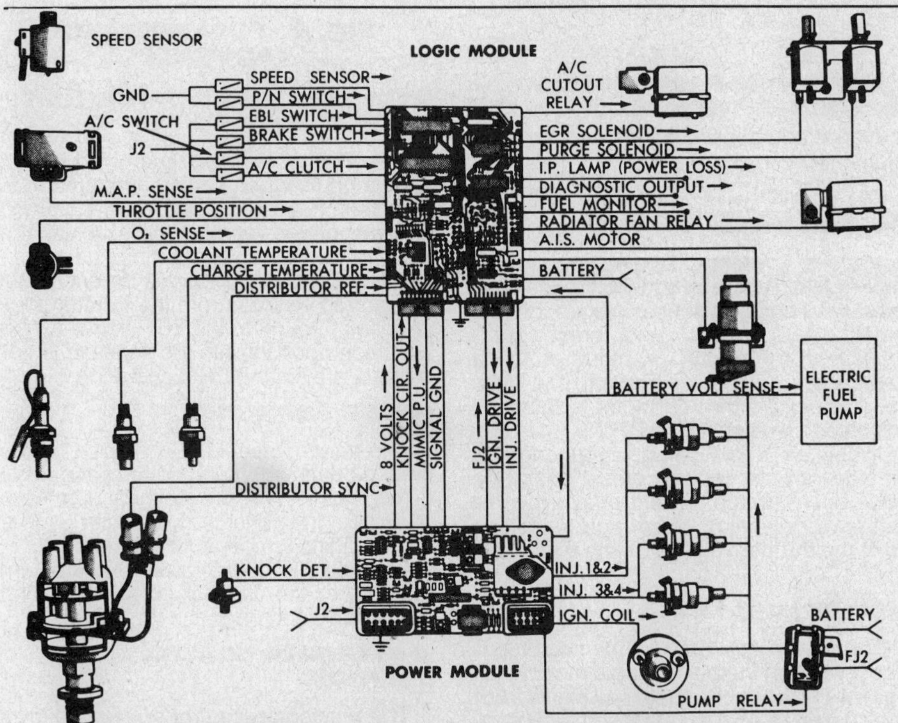

Fig. 1 Multi-point electronic fuel injection system components. 1984 front wheel drive w/2.2L turbocharged engine

DESCRIPTION

This system combines an electronic fuel and spark advance control system with a turbocharged intake system to provide a precise air/fuel ratio under all driving conditions. This system utilizes a logic module, a digital pre-programmed computer, to regulate ignition timing, air/fuel ratio, emission control devices and idle speed.

Various sensors provide the input necessary for the logic module to correctly regulate fuel flow at the fuel injectors, **Figs. 1 and 2.** These include manifold absolute pressure, throttle position, oxygen feedback, coolant temperature, charge temperature, and vehicle speed sensors. In addition to the sensors, various switches also provide important information. These include transmission neutral safety, heated backlite, A/C, & A/C clutch switches.

Inputs to the logic module are converted into signals sent to the power module. These signals cause the power module to change either the fuel flow at the injector, ignition timing or both.

The logic module tests many of its own input and output circuits. If a problem is detected in a major system, the information is stored in the logic module. This information can be displayed by a flashing light emitting diode (LED) located on the instrument panel, or by connecting a diagnostic readout and reading a numbered display which corresponds to a specific problem.

COMPONENTS

Power Module

The power module houses the circuits needed to power the ignition coil and fuel injector, and energizes the automatic shutdown (ASD) relay which activates the fuel pump, ignition coil and power module itself. The module also receives a signal from the distributor and relays this signal to the logic module. If no distributor signal is received, the ASD relay is not activated and power is shut off from the fuel pump and ignition coil. A voltage converter in the power module reduces battery voltage to a regulated 8 volt output which powers the distributor as well as the module.

Logic Module

The logic module is a digital computer which contains a microprocessor. Input signals from various switches, sensors and components are sent to the module, which then computes the fuel injector pulse width, spark advance, ignition coil dwell, idle speed and purge and EGR control solenoid cycles.

Automatic Shutdown (ASD) Relay

The ASD relay is powered and controlled through the power module. During engine cranking, the power module senses a distributor signal and grounds the relay. This completes the circuit for the electric fuel pump, ignition coil and power module. If for any reason the distributor signal is lost, the ASD relay interrupts this circuit in less than one second, preventing fuel, spark and engine operations. This rapid shutdown provides added safety in the event of an accident.

Manifold Absolute Pressure (MAP) Sensor

The MAP sensor, located in the right side passenger compartment, monitors manifold vacuum. The sensor is connected to a vacuum nipple on the throttle body and electrically to the logic module. This device relays information on manifold vac-

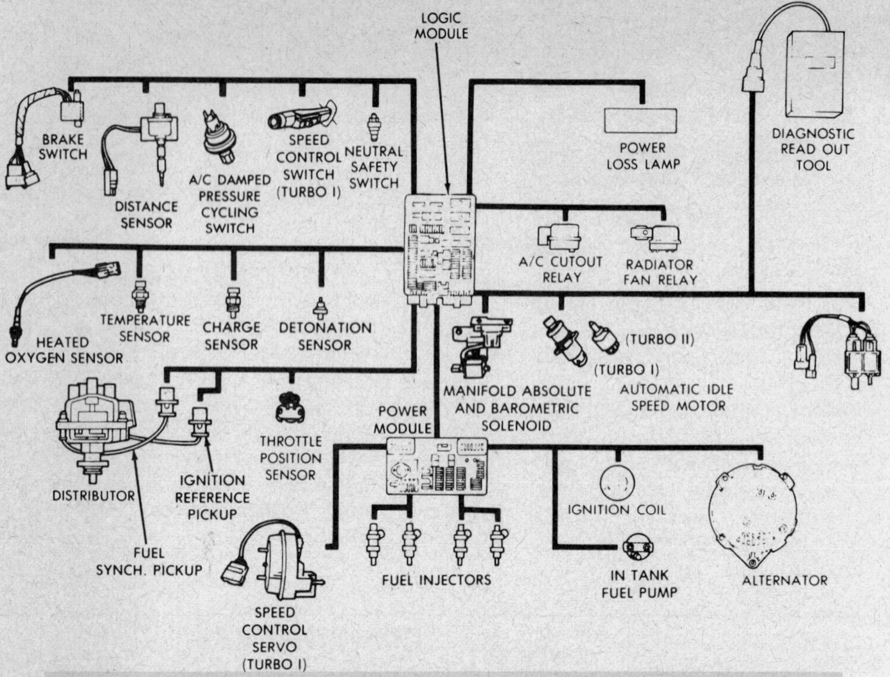

Fig. 2 Typical multi-point electronic fuel injection system components. 1985–87 models

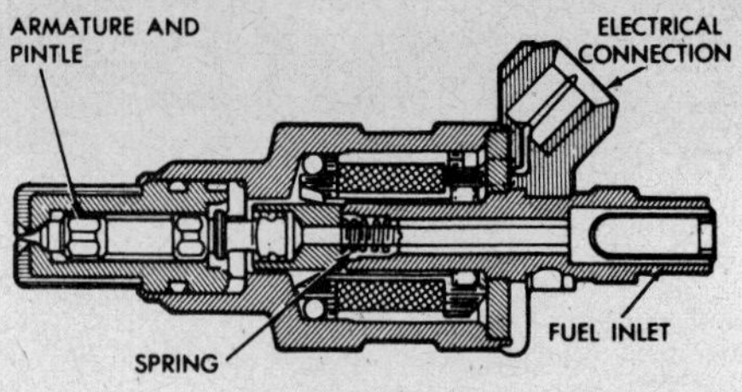

Fig. 3 Typical fuel injector

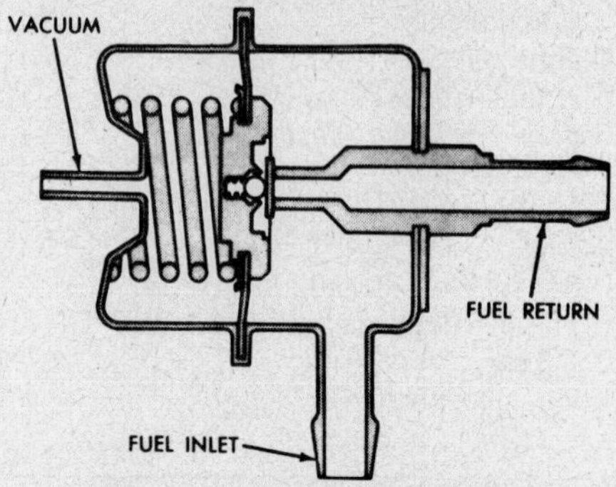

Fig. 4 Fuel pressure regulator

uum and barometric pressure to the logic module which is used in determining the proper air/fuel mixture.

Oxygen Sensor

The oxygen sensor, located in the exhaust manifold, produces voltage when exposed to oxygen present in exhaust gasses. The sensor produces a low voltage when the air/fuel mixture is lean and a high voltage when the mixture is rich. The voltage signal is transmitted to the logic module which signals the power module to trigger the fuel injector. The injector adjusts the mixture accordingly.

Coolant Temperature Sensor

The coolant temperature sensor, located in the thermostat housing, provides the logic module with information on engine operating temperature. This data, in conjunction with data provided by the charge temperature switch, permits the logic module to provide slightly richer air/fuel mixtures and higher idle speeds until normal operating temperatures are reached.

Charge Temperature Sensor

The charge temperature sensor, located in the intake manifold, measures the temperature of the air/fuel mixture. The logic module uses this information to determine engine operating temperature and engine warm-up cycles should the coolant temperature sensor fail.

Detonation Sensor (Knock Sensor)

The detonation sensor generates a signal when spark knock occurs. It is mounted on the intake manifold in a position where detonation is each cylinder can be detected. The logic module uses information from the knock sensor to modify spark advance and boost schedules to eliminate detonation.

Switch Input

Various switches located throughout the vehicle provide information to the logic module. These switches include neutral safety, A/C clutch, and brake lightswitches. When one or more of these switches is in the on position, the logic module signals the AIS motor to increase idle speed to a specified RPM.

When air conditioning is on and the throttle valve is above a preset angle, the wide open throttle cut out relay prevents the air conditioning clutch from engaging until the throttle valve is below this angle.

Power Loss Lamp

The power loss lamp on the instrument panel will illuminate if the logic module receives an incorrect signal or no signal from the coolant temperature sensor, MAP sensor or throttle position sensor. This lamp indicates that the logic module has gone into the "limp in mode" to keep the system operational, and indicates an immediate need for service.

The power loss lamp will also light for several seconds each time the ignition key is turned on as a bulb check.

Limp In Mode

In this mode, the Logic Module compensates for the failure of certain components by substituting information from other sources. If the Logic Module senses incorrect data at all from the MAP Sensor, Throttle Position Sensor, Charge Temperature Sensor, or Coolant Temperature Sensor, the system is placed into Limp In Mode and the Power Loss Lamp on instrument panel is activated.

Exhaust Gas Recirculation (EGR) Solenoid

The EGR solenoid is energized by the logic module when engine temperature is below 70°F. This closes the solenoid and prevents ported vacuum from reaching the EGR valve. When engine temperature exceeds 70°F, the solenoid is de-energized and ported vacuum from the throttle body will pass through to the EGR valve. At idle and wide open throttle the solenoid is energized, preventing EGR operation.

Purge Solenoid

The purge solenoid is energized by the logic module when engine temperature is below 145°F. This prevents vacuum from reaching the charcoal canister valve. When engine temperature exceeds 145°F, the solenoid is de-energized and vacuum will flow to the canister purge valve and purge vapors through the throttle body.

Wastegate Control Solenoid

The wastegate control solenoid allows the Logic Module to adjust maximum boost by varying the duty cycle of the solenoid.

Barometric Read Solenoid

This solenoid, which is controlled by Logic Module, is located in the MAP sensor line. The solenoid measures barometric pressure at closed throttle, once per throttle closure, but no more than once every 30 seconds and below a specified RPM. The barometric information is used primarily for boost control.

Air Conditioning Cut Out Relay

The air conditioning cut out relay is wired in series with the cycling clutch switch and low pressure cut out switch. When the throttle position sensor sends a wide open throttle signal to the logic module, the relay is energized and air conditioning clutch engagement is prevented.

Throttle Body

The throttle body is connected to both the turbocharger and intake manifold and houses the TPS and AIS motor. Air flow through the throttle body is controlled by a cable operated throttle blade located in the base of the throttle body.

Fuel Injector

The fuel injector, **Fig. 3,** is an electric solenoid powered by the power module and controlled by the logic module. According to ambient, mechanical and sensor input, the logic module determines when and how long the power module will operate the fuel injector.

Fuel Pressure Regulator

The fuel pressure regulator, **Fig. 4,** located downstream of the fuel injector on the throttle body, maintains a constant fuel pressure of 55 psi across the injector tip. The spring-loaded diaphragm in the regulator is assisted by vacuum in the throttle body above the throttle valve. As venturi vacuum increases, less pressure is needed to supply the same amount of fuel into the air flow. In order to fine tune the fuel pressure under all operating conditions, the vacuum assists in opening the fuel port during high vacuum conditions.

Throttle Position Sensor (TPS)

The TPS, located on the throttle body, is an electric resistor which is activated by the movement of the throttle shaft. The sensor produces a voltage which increases or decreases according to the throttle valve opening. The voltage signal is transmitted to the logic module where it is used with data from other sensors to adjust the air/fuel mixture accordingly.

Automatic Idle Speed (AIS) Motor

The AIS motor, operated by the logic module, adjusts the air portion of the air/fuel mixture through an air bypass on the back of the throttle body. Base idle is determined by the minimum air flow through the throttle body. The AIS motor opens or closes off the air bypass as needed according to engine loads or ambient conditions. The logic module senses the change in air/fuel mixture and increases or decreases fuel accordingly to change engine idle. The AIS motor also prevents stalling during deceleration by increasing engine idle when the throttle is closed quickly.

Fuel Pump

The fuel pump used in the EFI system is a positive displacement, roller vane, immersible pump with a permanent magnet electric motor. The pump uses two check valves: one valve relieves internal pump pressure and regulates maximum pump output, and the other valve, located near the pump outlet, restricts fuel flow in either direction when the pump is not operational. Operating voltage is supplied to the pump through the ASD relay.

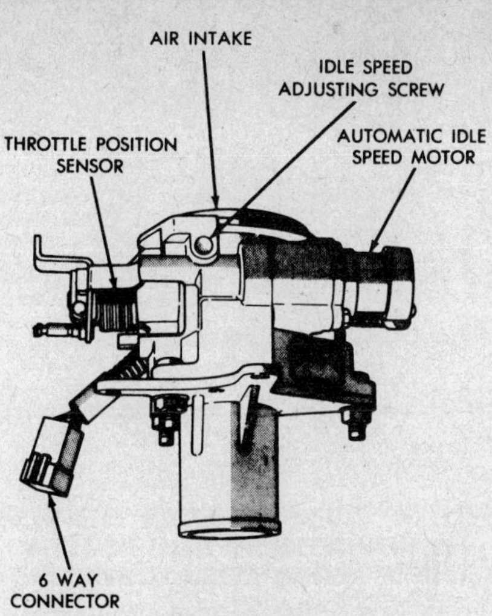

Fig. 5 Typical throttle body assembly

Fuel Reservoir

The fuel reservoir is located in the fuel tank and houses the fuel pump. The reservoir provides fuel at the pump intake under all driving conditions. The fuel return line directs fuel to a container on the side of the reservoir. The flow of fuel into this container creates a low pressure area and causes additional fuel from the main tank to flow into the reservoir. This combination of return fuel and fuel from the main tank maintains a full fuel condition in the reservoir even if fuel level is below the reservoir walls.

Exhaust Gas Recirculation (EGR) System

The EGR system is a back pressure type and is controlled by a back pressure transducer and the logic module. The logic module controls vacuum through the EGR solenoid, turning the circuit on or off according to operating conditions. The back pressure transducer measures the amount of exhaust back pressure on the exhaust side of the EGR valve. The logic module prevents EGR operation by turning the EGR solenoid off at idle, at wide open throttle or when engine temperature is below 70°F. The back pressure transducer vents the vacuum circuit of the EGR valve to the atmosphere whenever less than 0 psi is sensed at the exhaust side of the EGR valve.

DIAGNOSIS

VISUAL INSPECTION

Most problems with the EFI system can usually be traced to poor hose or wiring connections. Before proceeding with system tests or diagnosis, inspect the following:

1. Check harness ground eyelet mounting to intake manifold.
2. Check electrical connectors for proper installation at the following components: charge temperature sensor, throttle body, MAP sensor, detonation sensor, fuel injector, distributor, oxygen sensor, speed sensor, power module, purge solenoid, EGR solenoid, water temperature sensor, logic module and automatic shut down relay.
3. Check vacuum hose connectors for proper routing and installation at the following components: throttle body, PVC valve and turbocharger, fuel pressure regulator, EGR solenoid, purge solenoid, charcoal canister, EGR system, and MAP sensor.
4. Check fuel pump electrical and hydraulic connections.
5. Check fuse No. 16 for continuity.

ON BOARD DIAGNOSTICS

The logic module is programmed to monitor various circuits in the EFI system. If a problem is sensed often enough to indicate an actual fault, its fault code is stored in the logic module for display. If the problem ceases to exist or is repaired, the fault code will be cancelled by the logic module after 30 ignition key on/off cycles.

FAULT CODES

Fault codes can be displayed either by a light emitting diode (LED) on the module or by connecting diagnostic readout tool No. C-4805 to the system. Fault codes indicate the results of a failure but do not always identify the component at fault. Fault codes and their indications are as follows:

CODE 11–Indicates a fault in the distributor circuit. This code will appear when the logic module has not received a distributor signal since the battery was reconnected.

CODE 12–Indicates a fault in the stand by memory circuit. This code appears if direct battery feed to the logic module is interrupted.

CODE 13–Indicates a fault in the MAP sensor pneumatic system. This code will appear if the MAP sensor vacuum level does not change between start and start/run transfer speed (500-600 RPM).

CODE 14–Indicates a fault in the MAP sensor electrical sensor. This code will appear if the MAP sensor signal is too low (below .02 volts) or too high (above 4.9 volts).

CODE 15–Indicates a fault in the speed sensor circuit. This code will appear if engine speed is above 1468 RPM and the speed sensor indicates less than 2 mph. Note that this code is only valid if it is sensed while vehicle is moving.

CODE 16–Indicates loss of battery voltage sense.

CODE 17–On 1985 models, indicates problem in knock sensor circuit. On 1986-87 models, indicates engine running too cool.

CODE 21–Indicates a problem in the oxygen feedback circuit. This code appears if engine temperature is above 170°F, engine speed above 1500 RPM, and there has been no oxygen sensor signal for more than 5 seconds.

CODE 22–Indicates a fault in the coolant temperature sensor circuit. This code will appear if the circuit indicates an incorrect temperature or a temperature that changes unusually fast.

CODE 23–Indicates a fault in the charge temperature sensor circuit. This code will appear if the circuit indicates an incorrect

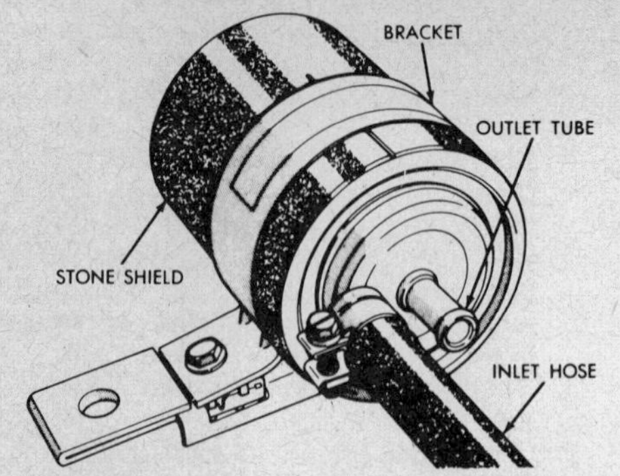

Fig. 6 Fuel filter assembly

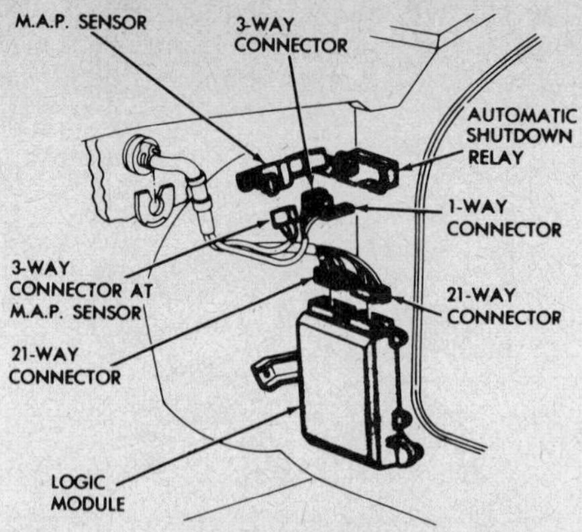

Fig. 7 Typical logic module & automatic shutdown (ASD) relay replacement

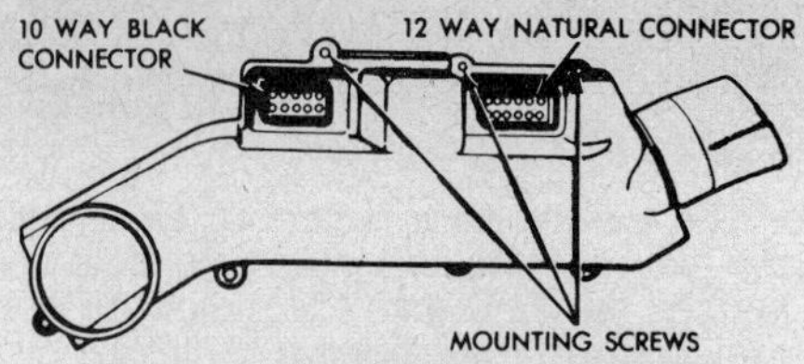

Fig. 8 Power module replacement

temperature or a temperature that changes unusually fast.

CODE 24—Indicates a fault in the throttle position sensor circuit. This code will appear if the sensor signal is too low (below .16 volts) or too high (above 4.7 volts).

CODE 25—Indicates a fault in the AIS control circuit. This code will appear if proper voltage from the AIS system is not present. Note than an open harness or wire will not activate this code.

CODE 26—Indicates problem in No. 1 injector circuit.

CODE 27—Indicates problem in No. 2 injector circuit.

CODE 31—Indicates an open or short in the canister purge solenoid circuit.

CODE 32—Indicates an open or short in the power loss lamp circuit.

CODE 33—Indicates an open or short in the air conditioning wide open throttle cut out relay circuit.

CODE 34—On 1984-86 models, indicates an open or short in the EGR solenoid circuit. On 1987 models, indicates a speed control problem.

CODE 35—Indicates a problem in the fan relay circuit. This code appears if the radiator fan is either not operating or operating at the incorrect time.

CODE 37—On 1987 models, barometric read solenoid circuit.

CODE 41—Indicates a fault in the charging system. This code will appear if battery voltage from the ASD relay is less than 11.75 volts.

CODE 42—Indicates a fault in the ASD relay circuit. This code will appear if, during cranking, battery voltage from the ASD relay is not present for at least 1/3 second after first distributor pulse. This code will also appear if, after engine stall, battery voltage is not off within 3 seconds after last distributor pulse.

CODE 43—Indicates a fault in the interface circuit. This code will appear if there is no anti-dwell or injector control signal between the logic module and power module.

CODE 44—Indicates a fault in the logic module. This code will appear if an incorrect PROM has been installed in the logic module.

CODE 44—On 1984 models, indicates problem in Logic Module, caused by installation of incorrect PROM. On 1986-87 models, indicates battery temperature is out of range.

CODE 45—Indicates a fault in the overboost shut off circuit. This code will appear if MAP sensor electrical signal rises above 10 psi boost.

CODE 46—On 1985-87 models, indicates battery voltage is too high.

CODE 47—On 1985-87 models, indicates battery voltage is too low.

CODE 51—On 1984 models, indicates problem in closed loop fuel system, caused when oxygen signal is low or high for more than 2 minutes. On 1985 models, indicates oxygen feedback system is latched up; on 1986-87 models, indicates oxygen feedback system is latched lean.

CODE 52—On 1984 models, indicates problem in Logic Module caused by internal failure. On 1985 models, indicates problem in battery temperature circuit. On 1986-87 models, oxygen feedback system is latched rich.

CODE 53—Indicates internal problem in Logic Module.

CODE 54—Indicates a fault in the synchronization pickup circuit. This code appears, if at start/run transfer speed, the reference pickup signal is present but the synchronization pickup is missing at the logic module.

CODE 55—Indicates end of message. This code will appear after all other codes have been displayed.

CODE 88—Indicates start of message. This code will appear only on diagnostic readout tool No. C-4805 before any other codes are displayed.

After all codes have been displayed and Code 55 has been received, actuate the following component switches and make sure that the display changes when the switch is activated and released: brake pedal, gearshift selector, A/C switch and electric back light switch.

To obtain fault codes using diagnostic readout tool No. C-4805, connect the unit to the diagnostic connector located in the engine compartment near the passenger side strut tower. Start the engine if possible, then cycle the transmission selector and air conditioning switch and shut off the engine. Cycle the ignition switch on and off twice, then turn ignition on and record all diagnostic codes displayed within 5 seconds. Note that the power loss lamp should light for 2 seconds as a bulb check.

ACTUATOR TEST MODE (ATM)

1984

1. Remove coil wire from distributor cap and place 1/4 inch from ground. **If the coil wire is more than 1/4 inch from ground, the power module may be damaged.**
2. Disconnect air cleaner hose from throttle body, then connect diagnostic readout tool No. C-4805 to diagnostic connector.
3. Depress ATM button on readout tool and observe the following:
   a. Three sparks from coil wire to ground.
   b. Two AIS motor movements, one open and one closed. Listen closely for AIS operation.
   c. With the ATM button still depressed, install a jumper wire between pins 2 and 3 or the gray distributor synchronizer connector. Listen for the click which indicates one set of injectors has been activated. Remove jumper wire and second set of injectors will be activated. Reconnect distributor connector.
   d. One fuel pulse from injector into throttle body. **ATM capability duration is 5 minutes from the time the ignition is turned on. This capability can be reinstated by cycling the ignition switch on and off three times, ending in the on position.**
4. When ATM button is depressed, Code 42 is activated as the ASD relay is bypassed. After ATM operation, this code must not be used for diagnostics.
5. The ATM test verifies three categories of operation:
   a. The coil firing three times indicates that the coil, logic module and power module are operational and that the interface between modules is working.
   b. The AIS motor movement indicates that the AIS motor is operational.
   c. The injector fuel pulse into the throttle body indicates that the fuel pump and injector are operational and the fuel lines are intact.

1985–87

1. Place system in diagnostic test mode and wait for code 55 to appear on display screen.
2. Press ATM button on tool to activate display. A specific ATM test can be

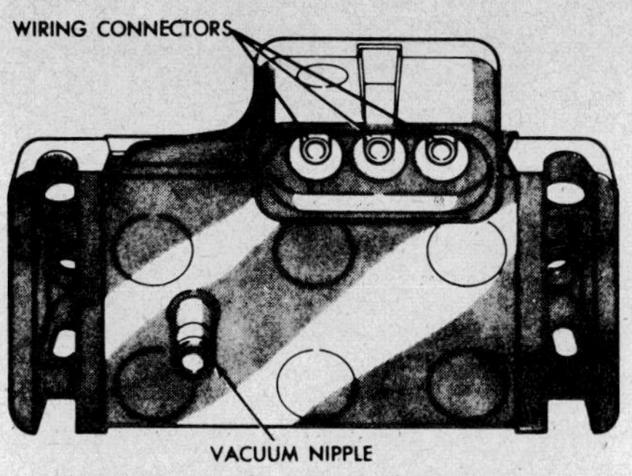

Fig. 9 Manifold absolute pressure (MAP) sensor replacement

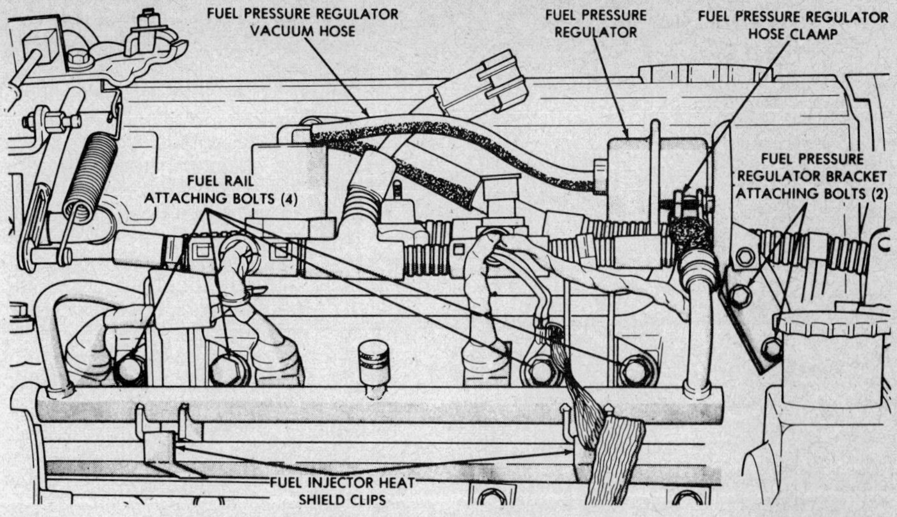

Fig. 10 Fuel injection components. All 1984–86 models & 1987 models w/Turbo I

called by holding down ATM button until desired code appears.

The computer will continue to turn selected circuit on and off for up to 5 minutes or until ATM is pressed again or if ignition switch is turned off.

Actuator Test Display Codes

CODE 01

Spark Activation—Once every 2 seconds.

CODE 02

Injector Activation—Once every 2 seconds.

CODE 03

AIS Activation—One pulse open/one pulse closed every 4 seconds.

CODE 04

Radiator Fan Activation—One pulse every 2 seconds.

CODE 05

A/C Cutout Relay Activation—One pulse every 2 seconds.

CODE 06

ASD Relay Activation—One toggle every 2 seconds.

CODE 07

Purge Solenoid Activation—One toggle every 2 seconds.

CODE 08

EGR Solenoid Activation (1985-86)—One toggle every 2 seconds. Control Vacuum And Vent Solenoid Activation (1987)—Once every 2 seconds.

CODE 09

Wastegate Solenoid Activation—One toggle every 2 seconds.

CODE 10

Barometric Read Solenoid Activation—One toggle every 2 seconds.

CODE 11

Alternator Full Field Activation (1986-87)—One toggle every 2 seconds.

SENSOR READ TEST MODE

1986–87

1. Place system in diagnostic test mode and wait for code 55 to appear on display screen.
2. Press ATM button on tool to activate display. A specific sensor read test can be called by holding ATM button down until desired test code appears.
3. Slide read/hold switch to Hold position to display corresponding sensor output level.

SENSOR READ REST DISPLAY CODES

CODE 01

Battery Temperature Sensor—Units are Volts x 10

CODE 02

Oxygen Sensor Voltage—Units are for Volts x 10

CODE 03

Charge Temperature Sensor Voltage—Units are Volts x 10

CODE 04

Engine Coolant Temperature Sensor—Units are degrees F/10

CODE 05

Throttle Position Sensor—Units are Volts x 10

CODE 06

Peak Knock Sensor Voltage—Units are Volts

CODE 07

Battery Voltage—Units are Volts

CODE 08

MAP Sensor Voltage—Units are Volts x 10

CODE 09

Control switches (1987)—cruise Off, display is blank; cruise On, display shows 00; cruise set, display shows 10; cruise Resume, display shows 01.

ENGINE RUNNING TEST MODE

1987

This system monitors sensors on vehicle which check operating conditions while engine is running. Using number displayed on tester C-4805 or equivalent, follow instructions given in code description for values of each test. The engine running test mode can be performed with engine idling in neutral with parking brake applied or while driving down the road. With diagnostic tester read/hold switch in read position, engine running test mode is initiated after engine is started.

To select test code, place read/hold switch in the read position and depress actuator button until desired code appears. Release actuator button and switch read/hold switch to hold position. The logic module will monitor that system test and results will be displayed. Using the code description, the display number must be adjusted as required.

Engine running test display code descriptions are as follows:

1. 61 Battery temperature sensor—display number 10 equals volts.
2. 62 Oxygen sensor—display number 10 equals volts.
3. 63 Intake charge temperature sensor—display number 10 equals volts.
4. 64 Engine coolant temperature sensor—display number x 10 equals degrees F.
5. 65 Throttle position sensor—display number 10 equals volts.
6. 66 Spark retard due to spark—display is cylinder number (upper digit)/degrees (lower digit).
7. 67 Battery voltage sensor—display equals volts.
8. 68 Manifold vacuum/pressure sensor—display is inches Hg.
9. 69 Minimum throttle position sensor—display number 10 equals volts.
10. 70 Minimum air flow idle speed

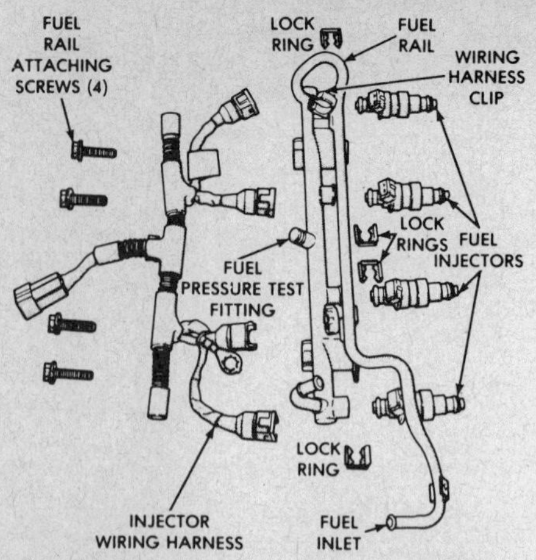

Fig. 11 Fuel rail & injector assembly. All 1984–86 models & 1987 models w/Turbo I

sensor—display number x 10 equals RPM.

11. 71 Vehicle speed sensor—display is mph.
12. 72 Engine speed sensor—display number 10 equals RPM.

THROTTLE BODY MINIMUM AIR FLOW TEST

1987

1. Start engine and allow cooling fan to cycle on and off at least once.
2. Connect suitable timing light, then disconnect and connect coolant thermistor and set basic timing.
3. Stop engine, then connect diagnostic readout box C-4805. Start engine and allow to idle for at least one minute.
4. Using readout box, place read/hold switch in read position and depress ATM button until code 70 appears.
5. Place read/hold switch to hold position, then the following should occur:
   a. AIS motor will fully close.
   b. Spark stabilization will be inhibited.
   c. Idle fuel will become enriched.
   d. Engine RPM will be displayed on diagnostic readout box in units of RPM x 10. For example, display 95 equals 95 x 10 which indicates 950 RPM.
6. Check idle RPM. If idle RPM is within 700-900 RPM, then throttle body minimum air flow is satisfactory. If idle RPM is not as specified, replace throttle body.
7. Shut off engine and remove readout box.

FUEL SYSTEM PRESSURE TEST

Fuel system pressure must be released any time a fuel line is to be disconnected.

1. Connect fuel pressure gauge C-3292 and hose adapter C-4749 or equivalent to fuel rail service valve.
2. On 1984-85 models, start engine and observe pressure gauge. On 1986-87 models, using ATM tester C-4805, place ignition switch in Run position and depress ATM button to activate fuel pump. Gauge should indicate 51-55 psi pressure. If pressure is as specified, remove gauge and adapter from fuel rail.
3. If fuel pressure is below 51 psi, install tester between fuel filter hose and fuel line and start engine. If pressure is now within specifications, replace fuel filter. If pressure does not increase, gently squeeze fuel hose. If pressure now increases, replace pressure regulator. If fuel pressure still does not increase, either the fuel pump is defective or the filter sock is obstructed.
4. If fuel pressure exceeds 55 psi, remove fuel return hose from pressure regulator end. Install suitable length of hose to pressure regulator and place open end of hose into a clean container. Start engine and recheck fuel pressure. If pressure is now within specifications, check fuel return line for restrictions. If fuel pressure is not as specified, replace fuel regulator.

SYSTEM SERVICING

IGNITION TIMING

1. Connect a suitable timing light to No. 1 cylinder, or a magnetic timing unit to engine.
2. Connect tachometer to engine, then start engine and run until operating temperature is reached.
3. Disconnect, then reconnect the water temperature sensor connector on thermostat housing. The loss of power lamp must illuminate and engine RPM should be within specifications given on vehicle emission label.
4. Direct timing light at timing hole in bellhousing, or read magnetic timing unit, and adjust timing as necessary by loosening distributor and turning until specifications are met.
5. Shut engine off, then disconnect and reconnect positive battery quick disconnect.
6. Start engine and observe loss of power lamp, which should be off.
7. Shut engine off, then cycle ignition switch on and off twice.
8. Turn ignition on and observe fault code display. Fault codes should be clear with Codes 88, 51, and 55 displayed.

FUEL SYSTEM PRESSURE RELEASE

The EFI system is under a constant fuel pressure of approximately 53 psi. Fuel system pressure must be released prior to servicing fuel tank, fuel pump, fuel lines, fuel filter or fuel components of the throttle body.

1. Loosen gas cap to release any residual pressure in the fuel tank.
2. Disconnect electrical connector from fuel injector.
3. Using a suitable jumper wire, ground one injector terminal, then connect another jumper wire to other injector terminal and touch battery positive post for no more than 10 seconds.
4. Remove jumper wires from injector terminals.

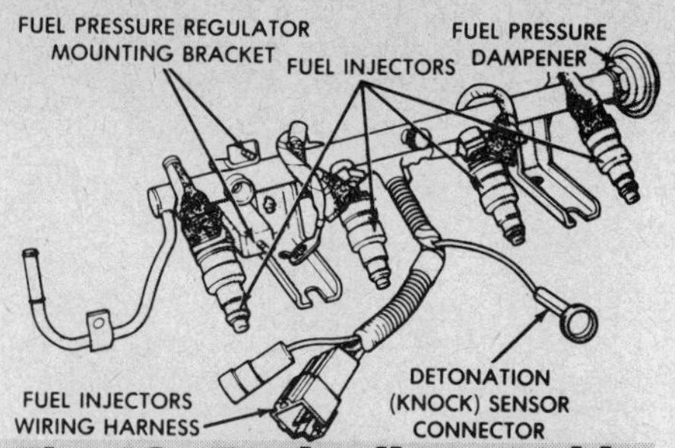

Fig. 12 Fuel rail assembly. 1987 models w/Turbo II

THROTTLE POSITION SENSOR (TPS), REPLACE

All 1984–86 Models & 1987 Models w/Turbo I

1. Disconnect battery ground cable.
2. Disconnect throttle body 6-way connector on all 1984-86 models and 1987 Shelby Charger or TPS electrical connector on 1987 models except Shelby Charger, **Fig. 5.**
3. Remove TPS-to-throttle body attaching screws.
4. Unfasten wiring clip from convoluted tube, then remove mounting bracket.
5. Lift TPS off throttle shaft and remove O-ring.
6. Disconnect three TPS wires from convoluted tubing on all 1984-86 models and 1987 Shelby Charger.
7. Lift each locking tab inside 6-way connector with a small screwdriver and remove TPS wireblade terminals. Note position of wires for assembly reference.
8. Reverse procedure to install, using new O-ring. Torque TPS attaching screws to 20 inch lbs.

1987 Models w/Turbo II

1. Disconnect battery ground cable.
2. Disconnect throttle position sensor electrical connector.
3. Remove throttle position sensor-to-throttle body attaching screws, then lift throttle position sensor off throttle shaft.
4. Reverse procedure to install. Torque sensor attaching screws to 17 inch lbs.

AUTOMATIC IDLE SPEED (AIS) MOTOR, REPLACE

All 1984–86 Models & 1987 Models w/Turbo I

1. Disconnect battery ground cable.
2. Disconnect throttle body 6-way connector on all 1984-86 models and 1987 Shelby Charger or AIS motor electrical connector on 1987 models except Shelby Charger.
3. Remove wiring clip from convoluted tube if necessary, then the AIS motor attaching screws and motor. **Do not remove clamp on motor, as damage may result.**
4. Remove two AIS wires from 6-way connector or from convoluted tubing on all 1984-86 models and 1987

Shelby Charger models. On all models, lift each locking tab inside connector with a small screwdriver and remove blade terminals. Note position of wires for assemble reference.
5. Remove AIS motor from adapter and remove O-rings from motor.
6. Reverse procedure to install, using new O-rings. Torque motor attaching screws to 17-20 inch lbs.

1987 Models w/Turbo II

1. Disconnect battery ground cable.
2. Disconnect AIS motor electrical connector.
3. Disconnect AIS motor-to-throttle body attaching screws, then the AIS motor from throttle body. Ensure O-ring is on AIS motor during removal.
4. Reverse procedure to install. If pintle measures more than 1¼ inch, it must be retracted by using ATM Code 03.

AUTOMATIC IDLE SPEED (AIS) MOTOR ADAPTER, REPLACE

1. Disconnect battery ground cable.
2. Disconnect 6-way connector at throttle body, **Fig. 5.**
3. Remove throttle body-to-adapter attaching screws.
4. Remove wiring clips and the two AIS wires from 6-way connector. Lift each locking tab inside connector with a small screwdriver and remove blade terminals. Note position of wires for assembly reference.
5. Remove AIS adapter with motor from rear of throttle body.
6. Remove O-ring and seal from adapter.
7. Reverse procedure to install, using new O-ring and seal. Torque adapter attaching screws to 65 inch lbs.

FUEL FILTER, REPLACE

1. Release pressure from fuel system as previously described.
2. Remove filter bracket attaching nuts, **Fig. 6.**
3. Loosen fuel line clamps, then disconnect fuel lines at filter. **Wrap a clean towel around fuel lines to prevent leakage of residual fuel.**
4. Remove filter assembly from vehicle.
5. Reverse procedure to install, using new clamps. Torque clamps to 10 inch lbs.

LOGIC MODULE, REPLACE

1. Remove right side kick panel, then the module attaching screws, **Fig. 7.**
2. Disconnect electrical connectors from module, then remove module from vehicle.
3. Reverse procedure to install.

POWER MODULE, REPLACE

1. Remove air cleaner duct from module.
2. Remove battery from vehicle.
3. Remove module attaching screws, **Fig. 8.**
4. Disconnect electrical connectors from module, then remove module from vehicle.
5. Reverse procedure to install.

AUTOMATIC SHUTDOWN (ASD) RELAY, REPLACE

1. Remove glove compartment.
2. Disconnect wiring harness from relay, **Fig. 7.**
3. Remove relay attaching screw, then the relay.
4. Reverse procedure to install.

MANIFOLD ABSOLUTE PRESSURE (MAP) SENSOR, REPLACE

1. Disconnect vacuum hose and wiring harness from sensor, **Fig. 9.**
2. Remove sensor attaching screws, then the sensor.
3. Reverse procedure to install.

OXYGEN SENSOR, REPLACE

1. Remove sensor from exhaust manifold using tool No. C-4589, or equivalent.
2. Clean threads in manifold using an 18 mm x 1.5 x 6E tap.
3. Install new sensor and torque to 20 ft. lbs. **If original sensor is to be reinstalled, coat threads with a suitable anti-seize compound. New sensors are pre-coated and need no additional compound.**

THROTTLE BODY, REPLACE

All 1984–86 Models & 1987 Models w/Turbo I

1. Disconnect battery ground cable.
2. Remove air cleaner to throttle body attaching screws, then loosen hose clamp and remove air cleaner adapter.
3. Remove accelerator, speed control and transmission kickdown cables and return spring.
4. Remove throttle cable bracket from throttle body, then disconnect six way connector.
5. Disconnect vacuum hoses from throttle body, then loosen throttle body to turbocharger hose clamp.
6. Remove throttle body to intake manifold screws, then the throttle body.
7. Reverse procedure to install.

1987 Models w/Turbo II

1. Disconnect battery ground cable.
2. Remove air cleaner hose clamp to throttle body, then the hose.
3. Remove accelerator cable, then disconnect AIS motor and TPS electrical connectors.
4. Disconnect vacuum hoses from throttle body.
5. Remove throttle body-to-intake manifold attaching nuts, then the throttle body and gasket.
6. Reverse procedure to install.

FUEL INJECTOR RAIL ASSEMBLY, REPLACE

All 1984–86 Models & 1987 Models w/Turbo I

1. Release fuel system pressure.
2. Loosen supply hose clamps at fuel rail inlet and remove hose.
3. Disconnect fuel pressure regulator vacuum hose from intake manifold vacuum tree.
4. Remove fuel pressure regulator bolts from intake manifold bracket, **Fig. 10.**
5. Loosen fuel rail to pressure regulator hose clamp at rail end and remove hose and regulator.
6. Remove screw from fuel rail to valve cover bracket.
7. Disconnect fuel injector wiring harness.
8. Remove clips from fuel injector heat shield, **Fig. 10.**
9. Remove fuel rail to intake manifold bolts, then fuel rail and injector assembly by pulling rail so that injectors come straight out of their ports. Take care not to damage rubber injector O-rings.
10. Remove fuel rail assembly from vehicle, **Fig. 11.** Do not remove fuel injectors until fuel rail assembly has been completely removed from vehicle.
11. Be sure injectors are seated in receiver cup with lock ring in place.
12. Make sure injector openings are clean and that any plugs have been removed.
13. Apply drop of oil to injector O-rings.
14. Draw injector assembly into intake manifold taking care to seat each injector in its hole. Once all injectors are seated properly, torque bolts to 250 inch lbs.
15. Connect injector wiring harness to injectors.
16. Install heat shield clips.
17. Connect injector wiring harness to main harness.
18. Install fuel rail to valve cover bracket.
19. Reconnect fuel pressure regulator vacuum hose to vacuum tree.
20. Install fuel pressure regulator hose clamp and hose to fuel rail.
21. Install fuel pressure regulator on intake manifold bracket and tighten screws.
22. Connect fuel supply hose and clamp to fuel rail inlet. Torque clamp to 10 inch lbs. Check that all ground straps, hoses, and wiring harnesses are located properly.
23. Connect battery ground cable.
24. Check system for leaks.

1987 Models w/Turbo II

1. Release fuel system pressure, then disconnect battery ground cable.
2. Remove air cleaner assembly, then disconnect detonation (knock) sensor and fuel injector electrical connectors.
3. Disconnect AIS motor and TPS electrical connectors from throttle body.
4. Remove throttle body and PCV system vacuum hoses.
5. Loosen fuel supply hose clamp at fuel rail inlet, then remove hose.
6. Loosen fuel return hose clamp at fuel pressure regulator, then remove hose.
7. Remove EGR tube attaching nut from EGR valve.
8. Remove accelerator cable, then disconnect upper plenum support at battery ground cable on cylinder head.

9. Remove intake manifold upper plenum attaching bolts, then the upper plenum and gasket from lower manifold.
10. Remove fuel pressure regulator attaching nuts, then the fuel pressure regulator from rail.
11. Remove fuel rail-to-valve cover bracket attaching screws, then disconnect detonation (knock) sensor electrical connector.
12. Remove fuel rail-to-intake manifold attaching screws, then the fuel rail and injector assembly by pulling rail so that injectors come straight out of their ports. **Use caution not to damage rubber injector O-rings during removal.**
13. Remove fuel rail assembly from vehicle, **Fig. 12.**
14. Reverse procedure to install, noting the following:
    a. Lubricate injector and fuel pressure regulator O-ring with clean oil to facilitate installation.
    b. Torque fuel rail attaching bolts to 250 inch lbs.
    c. Torque fuel rail pressure regulator attaching bolts to 65 inch lbs.
    d. Torque upper plenum-to-intake manifold attaching bolts to 200 inch lbs. and upper plenum support bracket to 40 ft. lbs.

FUEL PRESSURE REGULATOR, REPLACE

1987 Models w/Turbo II

1. Release fuel system pressure, then disconnect battery ground cable.
2. Remove vacuum hose harness and wire harness from valve cover bracket.
3. Loosen fuel supply hose clamp at fuel rail inlet, then remove hose.
4. Loosen fuel return hose clamp at fuel pressure regulator, then remove hose.
5. Remove pressure regulator attaching nuts, then the fuel pressure regulator.
6. Reverse procedure to install. Torque fuel pressure regulator attaching nuts to 65 inch lbs.

FUEL PRESSURE DAMPENER, REPLACE

1987 Models w/Turbo II

1. Release fuel system pressure.
2. Remove PCV system hose assembly from intake manifold and valve cover.
3. Remove fuel pressure dampener and copper washer using two wrenches, one on the flats or the fuel rail and the other on fuel pressure dampener.
4. Reverse procedure to install.

FUEL INJECTOR, REPLACE

1. Disconnect wiring connector from injector.
2. Position fuel rail assembly so that fuel injectors are easily accessible.
3. Remove injector clip from injector and fuel rail, **Fig. 10.**
4. Pull injector straight out of fuel rail receiver cup.
5. Check injector O-ring for damage. Replace O-ring if damaged. If injector will be reused, install protective cap on injector tip to prevent damage.
6. Reverse procedure to install. Install injector clip by sliding open end into top slot of injector and onto receiver cup ridge into side slots of clip.

EMISSION CONTROL SYSTEMS

INDEX

AIR INJECTION SYSTEM

Description

This system, **Fig. 1,** is used to reduce carbon monoxide (CO) and hydrocarbon (HC) emissions by adding a controlled amount of air to the exhaust gases in the exhaust system. This addition of air causes further oxidation of the exhaust gases with an appreciable reduction of carbon monoxide and hydrocarbon emissions.

This system consists of an air pump, an air switching valve, a check valve, an air manifold and the necessary tubes and hoses to connect the various components. Cylinder heads used on engines with this system have drilled passages to conduct the air to the exhaust ports.

The air injection system is designed so that air injection will not interfere with the ability of the EGR system to control NOx emissions and on vehicles equipped with an oxygen sensor, to ensure air/fuel distribution for maximum fuel economy. Air is injected at the exhaust ports for a short period during engine warm-up, which assists in the oxidation process in the upstream catalyst. On 6 and V8 engines, the air flow is then switched to a point downstream where it will assist the oxidation process in the main catalyst. On 6 cylinder engines, the downstream location is in the exhaust pipe, behind the upstream catalyst. On V8 engines the downstream location is in the main catalyst between the reduction and oxidation catalyst. On 4-97, 4-105 and 4-135 engines, after engine warm-up, the air flow is switched to a point in the 3-way catalyst between the reduction and oxidation catalysts reducing CO and HC emissions. On all 1982 and 1983-84 4-97, 4-105 and 4-135 engines, air flow switching is controlled by the CCEVS or by a vacuum solenoid. On 1983-86 6 and V8 engines and 1985-87 4 cylinder engines, air flow switching is controlled by the CVSCO or by a vacuum solenoid.

AIR PUMP

The belt driven air pump, **Fig. 2,** is mounted on the front of the engine. Intake

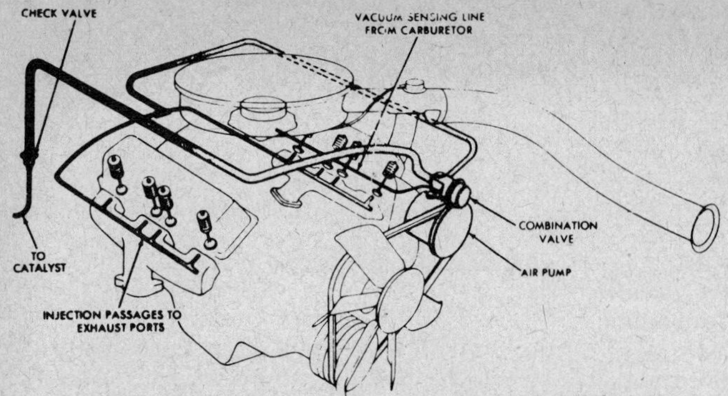

Fig. 1 Air injection system (Typical)

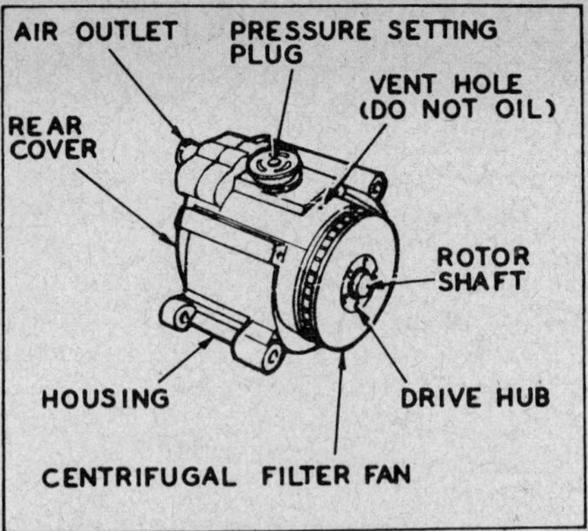

Fig. 2 Air injection pump w/integral centrifugal air filter & pressure relief valve

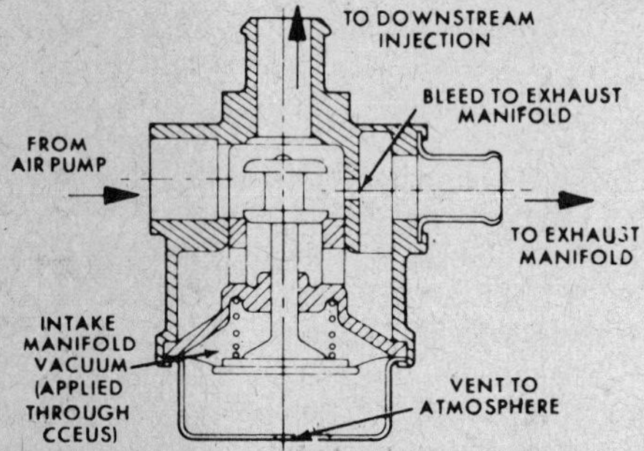

Fig. 3 Air switching valve. 1982

air passes through a centrifugal fan at the front of the pump, where foreign materials are separated from the air by a centrifugal force. Air is delivered to the air injection manifold and tube assembly by a rubber hose through the air switching valve mounted on the rear of the pump.

AIR SWITCHING VALVE

1982 Exc. Rear Wheel Drive w/EFI

This valve, **Fig. 3**, is used to switch air injection from the exhaust ports to an injection point further downstream in the exhaust system after engine warm-up so that air injection will not offset the effect on NOx emissions by the EGR.

When the engine is warming up and NOx emissions are low, air injection to the exhaust ports is acceptable, however, as the gases become hotter they tend to oxidize more rapidly by the addition of secondary air causing an increase of NOx emissions. At this time, the air switching valve switches the air injection.

A vacuum signal from the CCEVS causes the switching valve to open, allowing all air injection into the exhaust ports. When CCEVS shuts off vacuum to the switching valve, the valve closes and bypasses most of the air injection to the injection point downstream in the exhaust system. A bleed hole in the switching valve permits a small amount of air pump air to be injected into the exhaust ports at all times to assist in CO and HC reduction.

AIR SWITCHING VALVE (COMBINATION SWITCH/RELIEF VALVE)

Exc. Rear Wheel Drive Models w/EFI

This valve, **Fig. 4**, directs air injection flow to the exhaust ports or to the downstream injection point. The valve also regulates air pump output during high speed operation. When air pressure reaches a predetermined level, some of the air pump air is vented to the atmosphere through the silencer. Initially, air is injected at the upstream location as close to the exhaust valves as possible. As engine temperature increases, EGR and oxygen sensor systems will begin functioning. When this occurs, the air injection point will be switched to the downstream location. On 1982-87 engines, except 1983 4-105 and 1983-87 4-135 engines, the valve is controlled by manifold vacuum with a CCEVS valve and/or a vacuum solenoid. On 1983 4-105 and 1983-87 4-135 engines, the valve is controlled by manifold vacuum with a CCEVS/CVSCO valve and/or a vacuum solenoid. When the engine is cold, a manifold vacuum signal is sent to the valve, which directs air injection to the exhaust ports. As engine temperature increases, the CCEVS valve or CCEVS/CVSCO valve shuts off the manifold vacuum signal to the valve. Without the vacuum signal, the air switching valve (combination switch/relief valve) directs air to the downstream location.

1982–83 Rear Wheel Drive Models With EFI

The air switching system, **Fig. 5**, is basically the same as that for other vehicles with an air switching valve. However, the controls and operation are slightly different.

The vacuum-actuated air switching valve used in this system, directs air from the air pump to either the "upstream" or "downstream" air injection nozzles. A vacuum signal causes air to be directed upstream from the air switch valve. When there is no vacuum, the air is directed downstream. The shuttle-type vacuum solenoid valve, when energized, allows engine vacuum to reach the air switching valve, causing upstream air injection. When de-energized, the solenoid valve blocks the vacuum signal to the air switching valve, causing it to switch to downstream air injection.

The vacuum solenoid valve is controlled by the ignition key, a 70 second-delay time and the presence or absence of a cold enrichment signal from the EFI electronics. When the engine is started, the vacuum solenoid valve is energized, causing upstream air injection. After starting, the solenoid remains energized until the circuit is interrupted by the conclusion of the 70-second delay from the timer. At this point, downstream air injection starts. If the engine is cold when started, the cold enrichment signal from the EFI must first end before the 70 second time delay can begin. If the engine is hot, there will be no cold enrichment signal and downstream air injection occurs after 70 seconds.

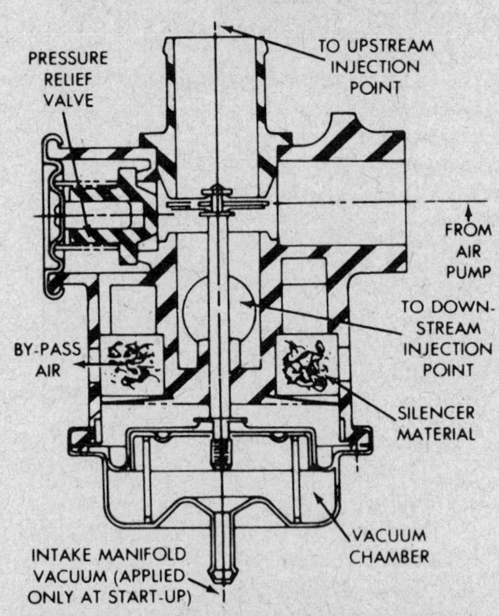

Fig. 4 Air switching valve (combination switch/relief valve)

CHECK VALVE

On 4 cylinder and V8 engines, the check valve is located in the injection tube assembly that leads to the exhaust manifold and catalyst. On 6 cylinder engines, the check valve is located on the cylinder head and exhaust pipe. The check valve will protect the system in the event of pump belt failure, excessively high exhaust system pressure or air hose ruptures.

COOLANT CONTROLLED ENGINE VACUUM SWITCH (CCEVS)

The CCEVS is used to improve hot driveability by preventing the operation of

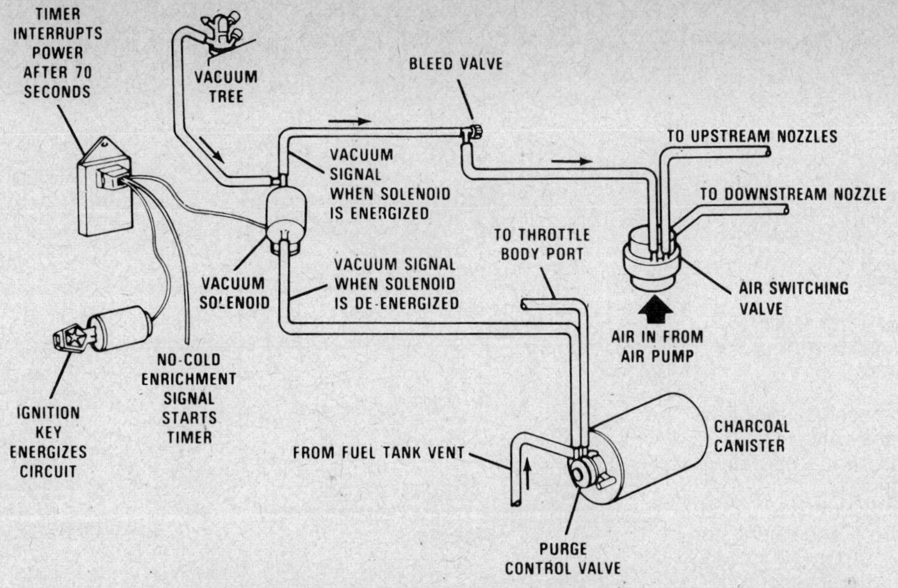

Fig. 5 Air switching & canister purging control circuits. 1982 rear wheel drive models w/EFI

the Power Heat Valve, if equipped, and air injection switching system after coolant temperature reaches a predetermined level. The CCEVS valve is mounted in the cylinder head on 6 cylinder engines and in the intake manifold on V8 engines.

COOLANT CONTROLLED ENGINE VACUUM/VACUUM SWITCH COLD OPEN (CCEVS/CVSCO)

1983–84 4-97, 4-105, 4-135 & 4-151 Engines

This switch, **Fig. 6,** provides manifold vacuum to the air switching system after a cold engine start until coolant temperature reaches a predetermined level. After the coolant temperature reaches this level, the switch closes and vacuum is cut off from the air switching system. The CCEVS/CVSCO is mounted in the thermostat housing.

COOLANT VACUUM SWITCH COLD OPEN (CVSCO)

1983–86 6 & V8, 1985–87 4 Cylinder Engines

The CVSCO serves the same purpose as the CCEVS.

Diagnosis

SYSTEM DIAGNOSIS

1. Excessive belt noise:
   a. Loose belt.
   b. Seized pump.
2. Excessive pump noise:
   a. Insufficient air pump break-in time.
   b. Hose leakage.
   c. Loose hose connection.
   d. Hose contacting other engine components.
   e. Air switching valve (combination switch/relief valve) inoperative.
   f. Check valve inoperative.
   g. Air pump mounting bolts loose.
   h. Air pump inoperative.
3. No air supply:
   a. Loose drive belt.
   b. Leak in air supply hose.
   c. Air hose fittings are leaking.
   d. Air switching valve (combination switch/relief valve) leaking.

AIR PUMP TEST

1. Accelerate engine to about 1500 RPM and observe air flow from hose(s). If air flow increases as engine is accelerated, the pump is operating satisfactorily. If not, proceed as follows:
2. Check for proper drive belt tension.
3. Check for leaky pressure relief valve. Air may be heard leaking with the pump running. **The air pump is not completely noiseless. Under normal conditions noise rises in pitch as engine speed increases. To determine if excessive noise is the fault of the system, operate the engine with the pump drive belt removed. If excessive noise does not exist with the belt removed, proceed as follows:**
4. Check for proper installation of the relief valve silencer if so equipped.
5. Check for seized air pump.
6. Check hoses, tubes, air manifolds and all connections for leaks and proper routing.
7. Check carburetor air cleaner for proper installation.
8. Check air pump for proper mounting.
9. If none of the above conditions exists and the air pump has excessive noise, replace the pump.

Air Switching Valve (Combination Switch/Relief Valve) Test

Apply vacuum to the valve. Ensure air injection is applied upstream. If there is no vacuum upstream, replace valve.

CHECK VALVE TEST

1. Check valve should be inspected whenever the hose is disconnected from the valve or check valve failure is suspected. **Any indication of exhaust gases in the air pump indicates check valve failure.**
2. Orally blow through the check valve (toward air manifold) then attempt to suck back. Flow should be toward air manifold only.
3. When replacing a check valve, be careful not to bend or twist the air manifold.

COOLANT CONTROLLED ENGINE VACUUM SWITCH (CCEVS) TEST

1. Check for disconnected vacuum hoses and proper valve installation. Check engine coolant level, add coolant as necessary.
2. With the CCEVS valve properly installed, disconnect molded connector from valve.
3. Connect a 1/8 inch I.D. hose to bottom port on valve.
4. With valve no warmer than 75°F, blow through hose. If it is not possible to blow through the valve, the valve is faulty and must be replaced.
5. Operate engine until normal operating temperature is obtained and connect a suitable vacuum gauge to bottom port on valve.
6. Apply 10 inches of vacuum to the valve. If vacuum level drops more than one inch in 15 seconds, replace valve.

COOLANT VACUUM SWITCH COLD OPEN (CVSCO) TEST

1. Check vacuum hoses for correct routing and installation.
2. With valve installed, disconnect molded connector from valve. Connect a 1/8 inch inside diameter hose to bottom port of valve.
3. With radiator top tank warm (no warmer than 75°F), blow through

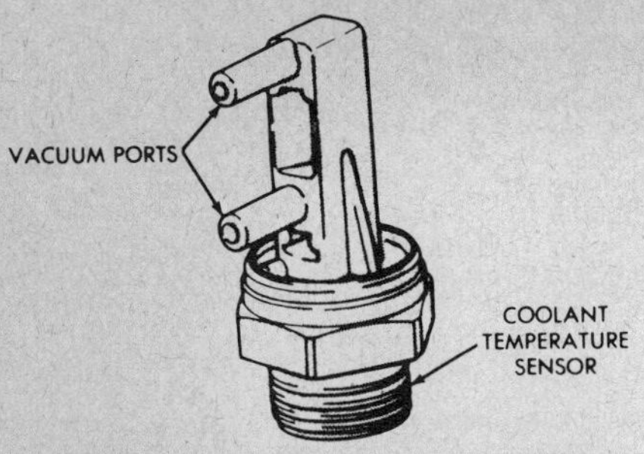

Fig. 6 CCEVS/CVSCO valve. 1983–86 4-97, 4-105 & 4-135 engines

hose. If it is not possible to blow through hose, replace valve.
4. Operate engine until normal operating temperature is obtained.
5. Connect a suitable vacuum pump and gauge No. C-4207 or equivalent, to bottom port of valve. Apply 10 inches Hg vacuum to the valve. If vacuum level drops more than one inch in 15 seconds, replace valve.

System Service

AIR PUMP, REPLACE

Servicing of the air pump is limited to replacement of the centrifugal fan filter or the entire air pump assembly. Do not disassemble the air pump assembly.

1. Disconnect battery ground cable.
2. Disconnect air and vacuum hoses from diverter or air switching valves.
3. Remove air switching valve (combination switch/relief valve) from air pump.
4. Loosen air pump pivot and adjusting bolts. Remove drive belt.
5. On vehicles equipped with air conditioning, remove bracket retaining bolts and bracket from air pump.
6. Remove air pump bolts, pulley and air pump from vehicle.
7. Reverse procedure to install. On 4 cylinder engines, torque air pump mounting bolts to 29 ft. lbs. Torque air pump bracket bolts to 40 ft. lbs. Torque air pump pulley bolts to 105 inch lbs. On 4-135 engines, torque air pump pulley shield nuts and bolts and air switching valve (combination switch/relief valve) mounting bolts to 125 inch lbs. On 4-97 and 4-105 engines, torque air pump pivot and adjusting bolts to 250 inch lbs. On 6 and V8 engines, torque air pump mounting bolts to 220 inch lbs. Torque air pump pulley bolts to 105 inch lbs. Torque air pump bracket bolts to 30 ft. lbs. Torque air switching valve (combination switch/relief valve) bolts to 125 inch lbs.

AIR SWITCHING VALVE (COMBINATION SWITCH/RELIEF VALVE), REPLACE

1. Disconnect air and vacuum hoses from valve.
2. Remove bolts securing valve to air pump mounting flange.
3. Reverse procedure to install. Torque mounting bolts to 125 inch lbs.

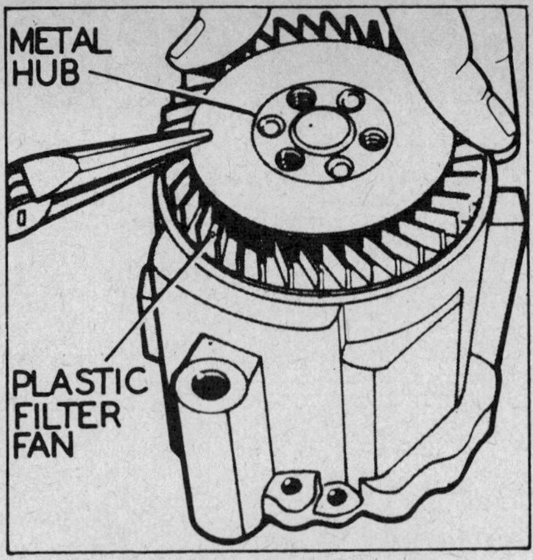

Fig. 7 Removing centrifugal type pump air filter

CHECK VALVE, REPLACE

4 Cylinder Engines

1. Release clamp and disconnect air hose from check valve inlet.
2. Remove tube nut securing injection tube to exhaust manifold or catalyst.
3. On 4-97 and 4-105 engines, remove top nut from water valve outlet and bolts from bracket, then injection tube from engine. On 4-135 engines, loosen starter motor mounting bolt and remove injection tube from engine.
4. Remove catalyst injection tube bolt from catalyst flange and injection tube from exhaust system.
5. Reverse procedure to install. Torque injection tube to catalyst flange bolt to 125 inch lbs. Torque injection tube nut to 25-35 ft. lbs. On 4-97 and 4-105 engines, torque injection tube nut to 25-35 ft. lbs. and bracket assembly bolts to 125 inch lbs. On 4-135 engines, torque starter motor mounting bolt to 40 ft. lbs., and injection tube nut to 25-35 ft. lbs.

6 & V8 Engines

1. To replace the check valve, release clamp and disconnect air hose from check valve inlet.
2. Remove screws or tube nut securing injection tube to exhaust manifold or exhaust pipe.
3. Remove injection tube from engine.
4. Remove any gasket material remaining on exhaust manifold and injection tube flange.
5. Reverse procedure to install. Torque flange mounting and injection tube bracket bolts to 200 inch lbs. On tube nut joint assemblies, torque tube nut to 25-35 ft. lbs.

COOLANT CONTROLLED ENGINE VACUUM SWITCH (CCEVS), REPLACE

1. Disconnect air and vacuum hoses from valve.
2. Remove valve from engine.
3. Reverse procedure to install.

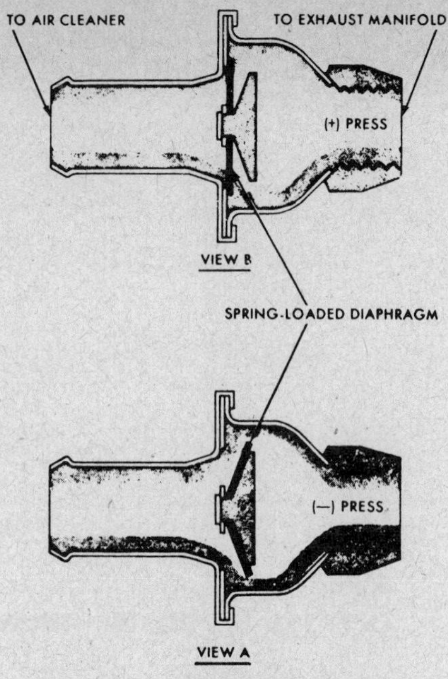

Fig. 8 Aspirator valve

COOLANT CONTROLLED ENGINE VACUUM/COOLANT VACUUM SWITCH COLD OPEN (CCEVS/CVSCO), REPLACE

1. Disconnect hoses from valve.
2. Remove CCEVS/CVSCO from thermostat housing.
3. Reverse procedure to install.

COOLANT VACUUM SWITCH COLD OPEN (CVSCO), REPLACE

1. Disconnect vacuum hoses from valve.
2. On 6 cylinder engines, remove CVSCO from cylinder head. On V8 engines, remove CVSCO from intake manifold.
3. Reverse procedure to install.

CENTRIFUGAL PUMP FILTER, REPLACE

1. To replace filter, **Fig. 7,** remove drive belt and pump pulley. Pry loose outer disc of filter fan, being careful to prevent fragments from entering the air intake hole.
2. Install the new filter by drawing it on the pulley and pulley bolts, by alternately tightening the bolts. Ensure outer edge of the filter slips into the pump housing. The slight amount of interference with the pump housing bore is normal. Do not attempt to install a filter by hammering or pressing it on.

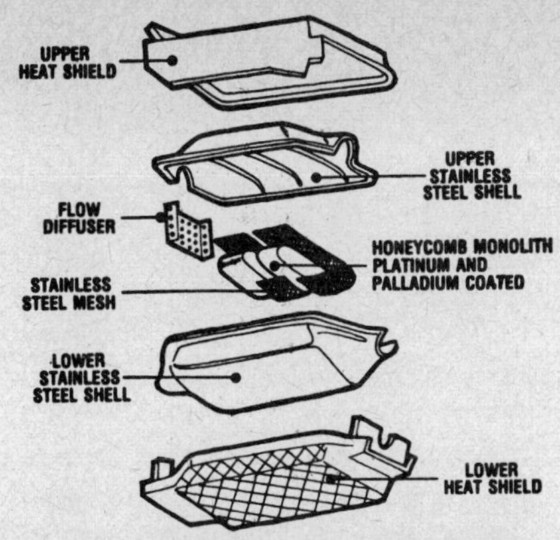

Fig. 9 Catalytic converter

AIR SWITCHING VALVE, COASTING AIR VALVE & DECELERATION SPARK ADVANCE SYSTEMS

Description

4-156 ENGINE

1982–85

These deceleration devices are incorporated to decrease HC emissions during vehicle deceleration. The system comprises of an air switching valve (ASV), coasting air valve (CAV) and a deceleration spark advance system (DSAS).

In order to decrease HC emissions emitted during vehicle deceleration, the ASV, which is activated by carburetor ported vacuum, cuts off fuel flow to the bypass holes and pilot outlet by supplying additional air into the low speed passage. The CAV, which is activated by carburetor ported vacuum also, supplies additional air into the intake manifold. The DSAS advances ignition timing, while the ignition timing is usually controlled by carburetor ported vacuum as well as engine speed.

Activation of the ASV & CAV is interrupted by opening the solenoid valve, when the engine speed sensor detects engine speed below 1300 RPM, in order to maintain smooth vehicle operation and to eliminate engine stall.

Diagnosis

ASV & CAV TEST

1. Start and operate engine at idle.
2. Disconnect solenoid valve connector. If the idle speed falls excessively or the engine stalls, the ASV, CAV and solenoid valve are operating properly.
3. If idle speed does not change, check condition of the vacuum passage for clogging and condition of ASV, CAV and solenoid valve.
4. With engine idling, use a voltmeter and check for battery voltage at the solenoid connector. If voltage is present, electrical wiring or engine speed sensor is defective. Replace wiring or engine speed sensor.
5. Increase engine speed to 2500 RPM. Check to ensure voltage is present at solenoid connector. If no voltage, engine speed sensor is defective. Replace engine speed sensor.

DSAS TEST

1. Connect a timing light to the vehicle.
2. Start and operate engine at idle.
3. Disconnect solenoid valve connector while watching the timing marks.
4. If ignition timing advances, the solenoid valve and advance mechanism are operating properly. If not, replace solenoid valve.

ASPIRATOR AIR SYSTEM

Description

The valve, **Fig. 8**, in this system uses exhaust pressure pulsations to draw air into the exhaust system to reduce CO and HC emissions. It draws fresh air from the "clean" side of the air cleaner and past a one-way spring loaded diaphragm. The diaphragm opens to permit fresh air to mix with the exhaust gases during negative pressure (vacuum) pulses. When the pressure is positive, the diaphragm closes and no exhaust gases are allowed to flow past the valve. The aspirator valve works most efficiently at idle and slightly above idle when the negative pulses are maximum. At higher engine speeds, the aspirator valve remains closed.

Diagnosis

The aspirator valve is not repairable and, if necessary, should be replaced with a new valve. Aspirator valve failure results in excessive exhaust system noise under the hood at idle and hardening of the rubber hose from the valve to the air cleaner. If there is excessive exhaust noise from under the hood, first check the aspirator tube exhaust manifold assembly joint and hose connections at the aspirator valve and air cleaner for leakage. If the aspirator tube exhaust manifold assembly joint is leaking, remove aspirator tube assembly and replace the gasket. If either hose connection is leaking and the rubber hose has not hardened, install suitable hose clamps. To determine if the aspirator valve is inoperative, disconnect hose from aspirator valve inlet. With the engine idling and the transmission in neutral, the vacuum exhaust pulses can be felt at the aspirator valve inlet. If hot exhaust gas is escaping from the aspirator inlet, the aspirator valve is inoperative and must be replaced.

System Service

ASPIRATOR VALVE, REPLACE

1. Disconnect air hose from aspirator valve inlet.
2. Remove aspirator valve from aspirator tube assembly.
3. Reverse procedure to install. Torque valve to 25 ft. lbs.

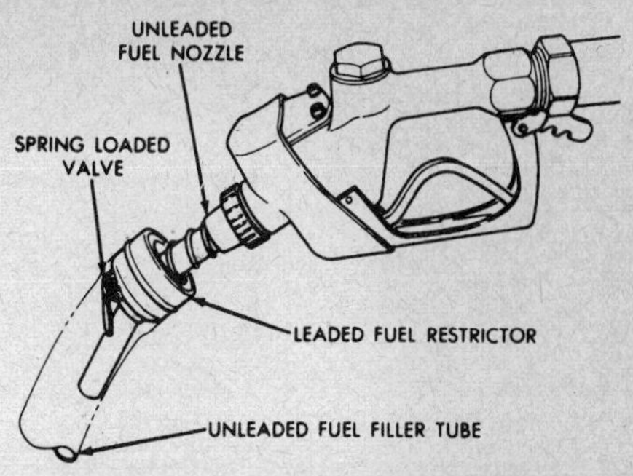

Fig. 10 Fuel tank filler safety neck for all vehicles equipped w/catalytic converters (Typical)

ASPIRATOR TUBE ASSEMBLY, REPLACE

1. Disconnect air hose from aspirator valve inlet.
2. Remove bolts securing aspirator tube assembly to exhaust manifold and engine.
3. Remove aspirator tube assembly from engine.
4. Remove any remaining gasket material from exhaust manifold and aspirator tube flange.
5. Reverse procedure to install. On 4 cylinder engines, torque aspirator tube nut to 40 ft. lbs., and aspirator tube bracket bolt to 95 ft. lbs. On 6 cylinder and V8 engines, torque flange mounting bolt to 200 inch lbs. On 6 cylinder engines, torque aspirator tube assembly bolts to 40 ft. lbs., on V8 engines, torque tube assembly bolts to 115 inch lbs.

CATALYTIC CONVERTERS

Description

The catalytic converter serves two purposes: it permits a faster chemical reaction to take place and, although it enters into the chemical reaction, it remains the same, ready to repeat the process. The catalytic converter combines hydrocarbons (HC) and carbon monoxide (CO) with oxygen to form water (H_2O) and carbon dioxide (CO_2).

The catalyst is structured in the form of a honeycomb monolith, **Fig. 9.** The catalyst consists of a porous substrate of an inert material, coated with platinum and other metals, the catalytically active materials.

This device, located in the exhaust system between the exhaust manifold and muffler, requires the use of heat shields, in some cases, due to its high operating temperatures.

The heat shields are necessary to protect chassis components, passenger compartment and other areas from heat related damage.

A smaller diameter fuel tank filler tube neck, **Fig. 10,** is incorporated to prevent the larger service station pump nozzle, used for leaded fuels, being inserted into the filler tube, thereby preventing system contamination.

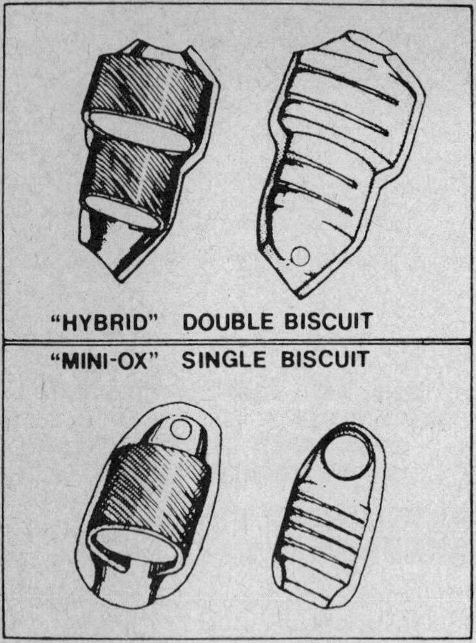

Fig. 11 Mini catalytic converters

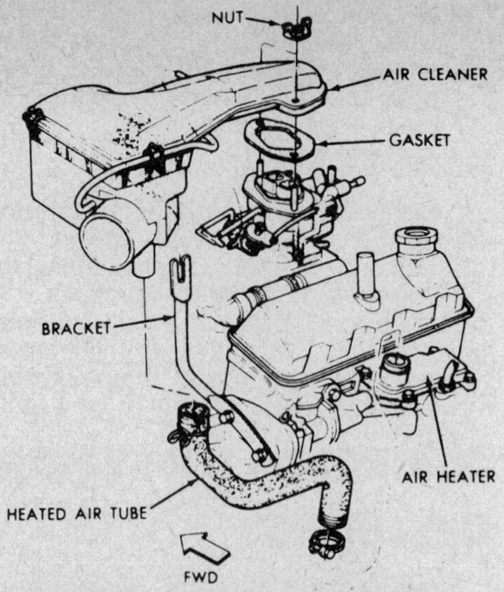

Fig. 12 Heated inlet air system. 4-97 engine

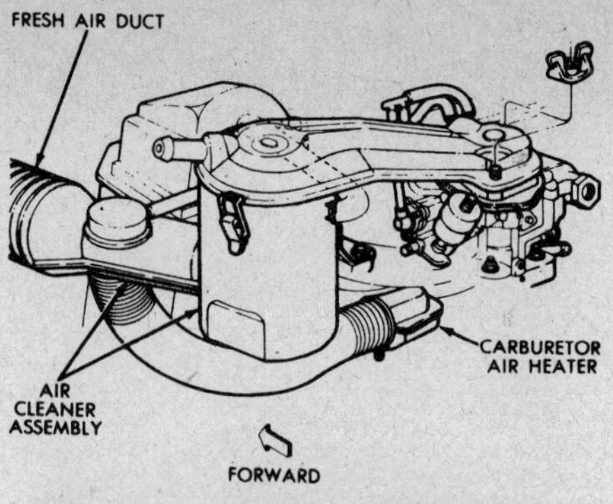

Fig. 13 Heated inlet air system. 4-105 engine

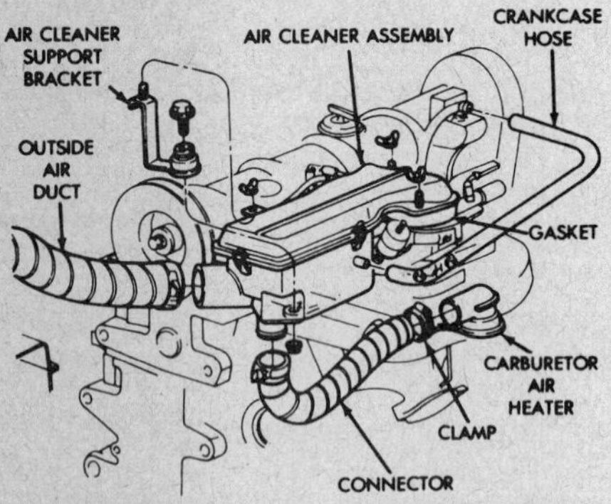

Fig. 14 Heated inlet air system. 4-135 engine less EFI

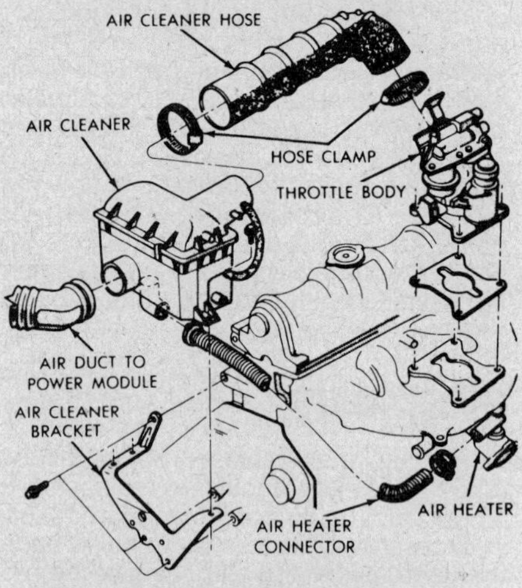

Fig. 15 Heated inlet air system. 1983–85 4-135 engine w/EFI

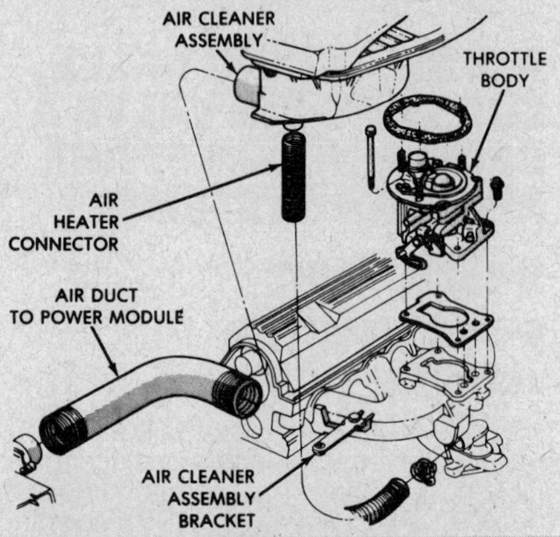

Fig. 16 Heated inlet air system. 1986–87 4-135 & 4-153 w/EFI

Since the use of leaded fuels contaminates the catalysts, deteriorating its effectiveness, the use of unleaded fuels is mandatory in vehicles equipped with catalytic converters. The catalytic converter can tolerate very small amounts of leaded fuels without permanently reducing the catalyst effectiveness.

Some vehicles incorporate two mini-oxidation catalytic converters in conjunction with the main underfloor converter. Their main purpose is to initiate exhaust gas oxidation before the gases reach the underfloor converter. The mini-ox, **Fig. 11**, is a single biscuit catalytic converter and is shaped so that only one small biscuit can fit inside the can.

The "hybrid" converter, **Fig. 11**, utilizes a larger biscuit and a smaller biscuit. A Power Heat Control Valve is incorporated to increase the flow of exhaust gases through the lefthand exhaust manifold to rapidly bring the mini-catalyst up to operating temperature.

System Service

The catalytic converters are not serviceable. After determining that the catalyst has lost its effectiveness, the catalytic converter assembly must be replaced.

HEATED INLET AIR SYSTEM

Description

These systems, **Figs. 12 thru 19**, use a thermostatically controlled air cleaner to maintain a predetermined air temperature entering the carburetor when underhood temperatures are less than 100°F. By maintaining this temperature, the carburetor can be calibrated leaner, improve engine warm-up and minimize carburetor icing. Temperature is controlled by intake manifold vacuum, a temperature sensor and a vacuum diaphragm which operates the heat control door in the air cleaner snorkel.

During engine warm-up, air is heated by a shroud surrounding the exhaust manifold, then the air is piped to the air cleaner snorkel and into the carburetor. The vacuum diaphragm controls the air control valve which is closed to outside air. Therefore all air entering the carburetor is heated.

During normal operation, as the air entering the air cleaner increases, the air control valve opens to allow heated air to mix with cold air to keep the air entering the carburetor at about 100°F.

During wide-open throttle operation or at any time engine vacuum is below 4-6 inches Hg, the hot air duct is closed off allowing only cold air to enter the carburetor.

DUAL SNORKEL

The dual snorkel air cleaner performs basically like a single snorkel air cleaner except that on deep throttle acceleration, both snorkels are open (when manifold vacuum drops between 5 inch Hg).

The "non-heat" air snorkel is connected to manifold vacuum through a tee in the vacuum hose between the carburetor and the sensor.

Check the second snorkel vacuum diaphragm as one with the heat connector.

LOWER COMPRESSION RATIOS

Compression ratios have been lowered by various modifications in the piston head design and in the quench height. This reduction in the compression ratio permits the engine to operate satisfactorily on lower octane fuel, thereby achieving a slight reduction in HC and NOx emission levels.

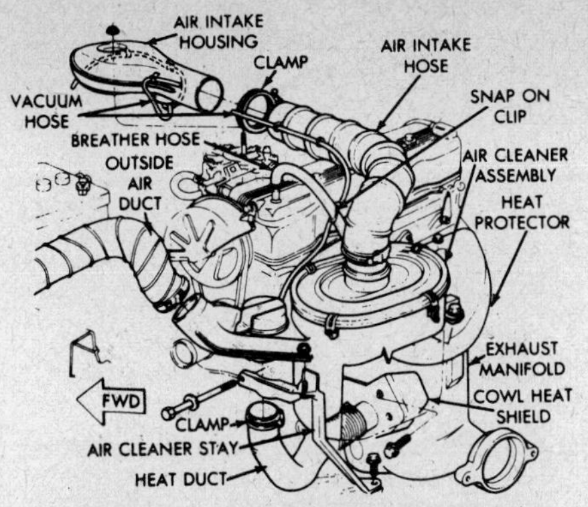

Fig. 17 Heated inlet air system. 4-156 engine

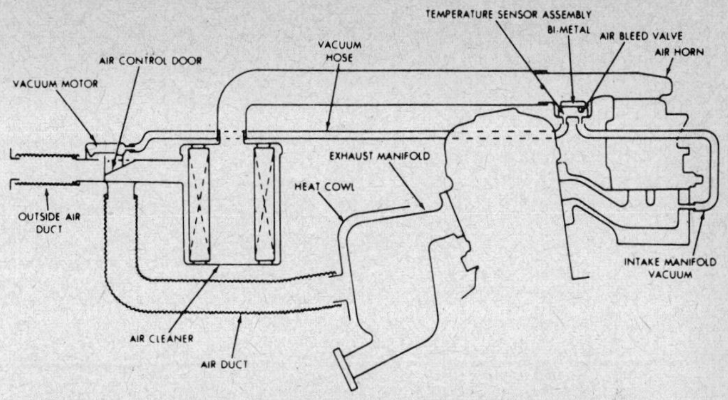

Fig. 18 Heated inlet air system hose & duct routing. 4-156 engine

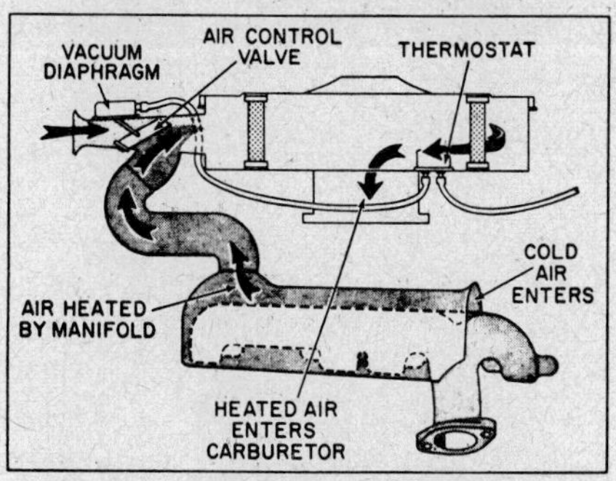

Fig. 19 Heated inlet air system. 6 cylinder & V8 engines

COMBUSTION CHAMBER DESIGN

The combustion chamber is designed to eliminate pockets and close clearance spaces which have a tendency to quench the flame before all the air/fuel mixture is burned. By increasing the quench heights, more complete burning of air/fuel ratio is achieved, thereby substantially reducing the HC emission levels.

INCREASED OVERLAP CAMSHAFT

The increased valve overlap produced by the camshaft causes some dilution of the incoming air/fuel mixture. This dilution lowers the peak combustion temperature which results in lowered NOx emission levels.

INTAKE MANIFOLD DESIGN

Intake manifolds are designed to promote rapid fuel vaporization during engine warm-up. The exhaust crossover floor of the intake manifold between the inlet gases and exhaust gases has been thinned out with improved thickness control, thereby reducing the time required to get the heat from the exhaust manifold gases into the inlet gases. By adding this additional heat, fuel vaporizes quicker, and leaner air/fuel mixtures can be used, resulting in lower CO emissions.

DISTRIBUTOR SOLENOID

Some engines have a solenoid incorporated in the distributor vacuum advance mechanism to retard ignition timing when the throttle is closed. At a closed throttle, and with the idle adjusting screw in the closed position, electrical contacts on the carburetor throttle stop cause the distributor solenoid to energize. This reduces the ignition timing to reduce emissions during hot idle conditions. Cold or part throttle starting is not penalized because the distributor solenoid is not energized unless hot idle adjusting screw is against the throttle stop contact.

Ignition timing must be set at closed throttle to give accurate setting.

Diagnosis

1. Ensure all vacuum hoses and the stove to the air cleaner flexible connector are properly installed and in good condition.
2. With engine cold and ambient temperature in the engine compartment below 65°F on 1982-85 4-97, 4-105 and 4-135 and 1986-87 4 cylinder carbureted engines, 84°F on 4-156 engine, 50°F on 6 and V8 engines or 115°F on 1986-87 4 cylinder engines with fuel injection, the heat control door in the snorkel should be in the up (heat on) position.
3. With the engine warmed to operating temperature and running, check the air temperature entering the snorkel or at the sensor. When temperature is 85°F or higher on 1982-85 4-97, 4-105 and 4-135 engines, 113°F or higher on 4-156 engine, 100°F or higher on 6 and V8 engines, 90°F or higher on 1986-87 carbureted 4 cylinder engines, or 140°F or higher on 1986-87 4 cylinder fuel injected engines, then door should be in the down (heat off) position.
4. Remove air cleaner from engine and allow engine to cool down to temperature specified in step 2. Using a suitable vacuum pump, apply 20 inches Hg vacuum on all engines except 4-156 to the sensor. On 4-156 engine, apply 15 inches Hg vacuum to sensor. The door should be in the up (heat on) position. If not, check vacuum diaphragm.
5. To check the vacuum diaphragm, apply vacuum directly to diaphragm with a vacuum gauge in the line and bleed valve to control the vacuum inserted in the line between the gauge and the vacuum source. Apply 20 inches Hg vacuum to the diaphragm on all 4 cylinder engines, except 4-156 and 1982-83 6 and V8 engines. On 4-156 engines, apply 10 inches Hg vacuum to the diaphragm. On 1984-87 6 and V8 engines, apply 25 inches Hg vacuum to the diaphragm. On all engines except 4-156, the diaphragm should not bleed off more than 10 inches of vacuum in 5 minutes. On 4-97, 4-105, 4-135 and 4-153 engines, the door should not lift off the bottom of the snorkel at less than 2 inches Hg vacuum and should be in full up (heat on) position with no more than 4 inches Hg vacuum. On 1982-83 6 and V8 engines, the door should not lift off the bottom of the snorkel at less than 5 inches Hg vacuum and should be in full up (heat on) position with no more than 9 inches Hg vacuum. On 1984-87 6 and V8 engines, the door should not lift off the bottom of the snorkel at less than 5.5 inches Hg vacuum and should be in full up (heat on) position with no more than 8.5 inches Hg vacuum. On 4-156 engine, with 10 inches Hg vacuum applied to the diaphragm, the door should be in the full up (heat on) position. If diaphragm does not operate as described, it must be replaced.
6. If the diaphragm performs properly but proper temperature is not maintained, replace the sensor and repeat procedure.

System Service

VACUUM DIAPHRAGM, REPLACE

1. Remove air cleaner housing from vehicle.
2. Disconnect vacuum hose from diaphragm, drill through rivets, then tilt diaphragm slightly forward and rotate unit counterclockwise to disengage lock.
3. When diaphragm is free from snorkel, slide assembly to one side to disengage operating rod from heat control door and remove from air cleaner snorkel.
4. Reverse procedure to install.

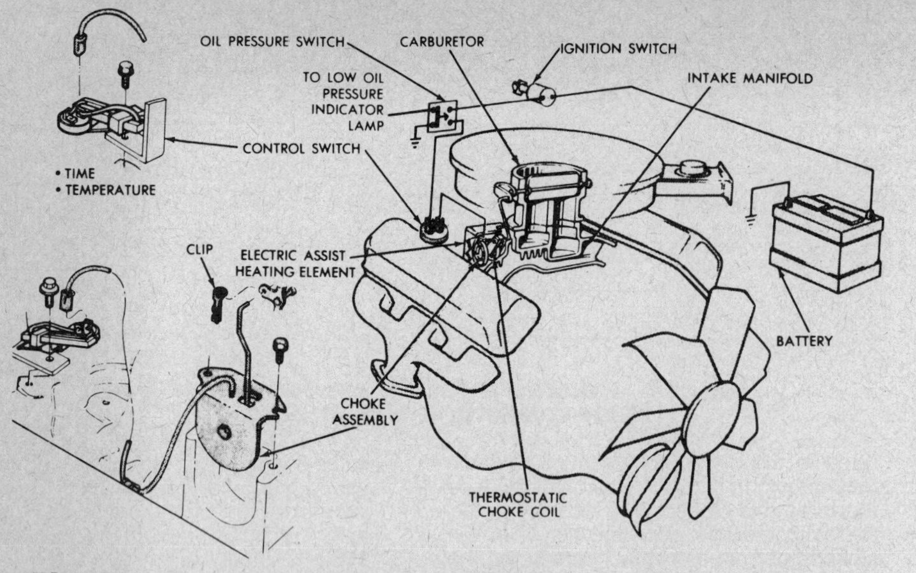

Fig. 20 Electric assist choke system. 1984–87 shown, 1982–83 similar

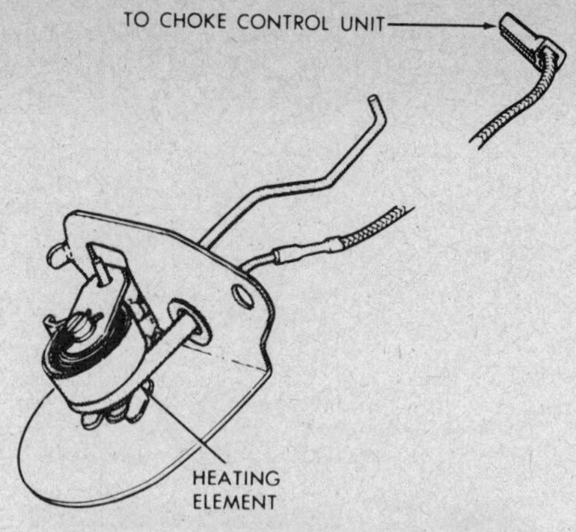

Fig. 21 Electric assist choke heating element. 1984–87 shown, 1982–83 similar

SENSOR, REPLACE

1. Remove air cleaner housing from vehicle.
2. Disconnect vacuum hose from sensor and remove sensor retaining clips.
3. Remove sensor and gasket assembly from air cleaner.
4. Reverse procedure to install.

ELECTRIC ASSIST CHOKE

Description

The electric assist choke system, **Fig. 20**, is used to reduce HC and CO emissions during engine start and warm up. The choke thermostatic coil spring reacts to engine temperature.

An electric heating element located next to a bi-metallic spring inside the choke well assists engine heat to shorten choke duration.

A wire from the choke heater is connected to an electrical control switch. The control switch, **Fig. 21**, is connected to the ignition switch from which electrical power is obtained and transferred through an electrical connection to the control switch.

The single stage control switch, **Fig. 22**, operates as follows:

The single stage control switch shortens choke duration only above 80°F. Below 55°F, electric heat is not available until the engine is at normal operating temperature. Normal engine heat will then warm the control and energize the choke heater, but only after the choke has opened by engine heat.

The dual stage control switch operates as follows:

The dual stage control switch shortens choke duration above 80°F and stabilizes choke duration during cold weather operation. During hot weather operation, electric assist heater is hotter then during cold weather operation assist level.

Cold weather heat levels are regulated by an electrical resistor connected to both terminals of the control. Below 55°F, electrical power is reduced by the resistor. Above 80°F, the resistor is bypassed by a switch inside the control to supply full power.

Engines started during cold weather conditions will experience two levels of choke heat, low during engine warm-up and high after engine warm-up. High heat levels occur after the choke is open to insure an open choke condition under all driving conditions and minimize choking action which can occur after short stops during cold weather operation.

Engines started in hot weather conditions will not experience low choke heat levels. Engines started hot will only experience high heat because the switch is normally warmer than 80°F.

The heating element should not be exposed to or immersed in any fluid for any purpose. An electric short in the wiring to the heater or within the heater will be a short in the ignition system.

Diagnosis

CHOKE CONTROL SWITCH TEST

1. On dual stage control switch, connect a test light to battery terminals. Note intensity of test light.
2. Before starting the engine, disconnect ignition harness electrical connector from control switch.
3. Connect a test light to load (choke) terminal of control switch and ground.
4. Start engine and allow it to reach normal operating temperature.
5. Apply 12 volts to ignition harness terminal of control switch. If test light does not light or does not have the same intensity as when checked in step 1, replace control switch.

CHOKE HEATING ELEMENT TEST

1. Disconnect electric heating element at the control switch.

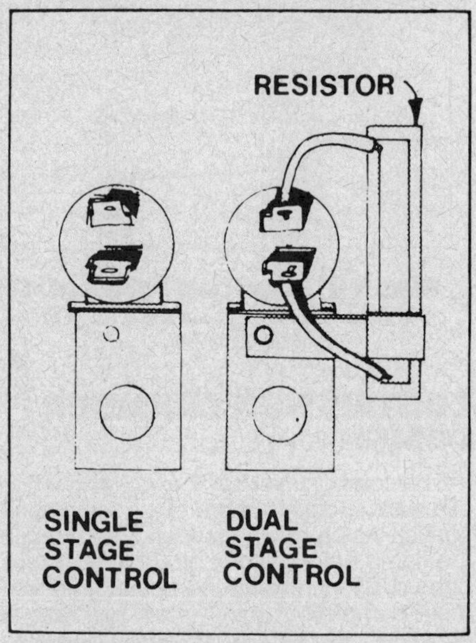

Fig. 22 Choke control unit

2. Connect an ohmmeter to crimped junction of this wire at choke end. **Do not connect to steel heater casing.**
3. Hold the other ohmmeter lead against the choke housing or engine manifold.
4. Electrical resistance of 4-12 ohms is normal. If reading is not 4-12 ohms, replace choke assembly. **The electric assist choke system does not change any carburetor service procedures and cannot be adjusted. However, the choke linkage and shaft must move freely hot or cold.**

If the system is found out of calibration, a new heater control switch or choke unit must be installed.

System Service

The electric assist choke does not require adjustment. However, the choke linkage and shaft must move freely hot or cold. Check choke rods for damage and bending. A bent choke rod will prevent proper operation of the electric assist choke.

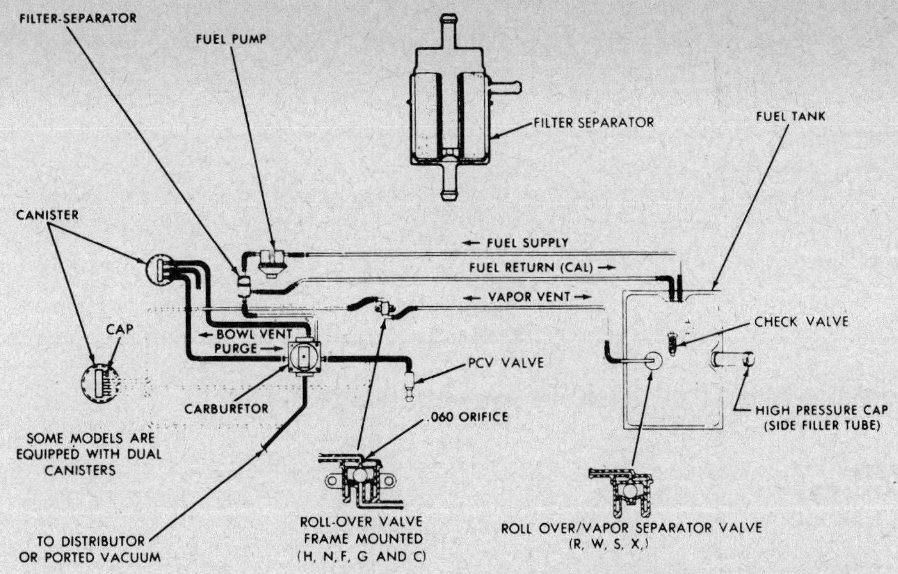

Fig. 23 Evaporative emission control system. 6 cylinder & V8 engine

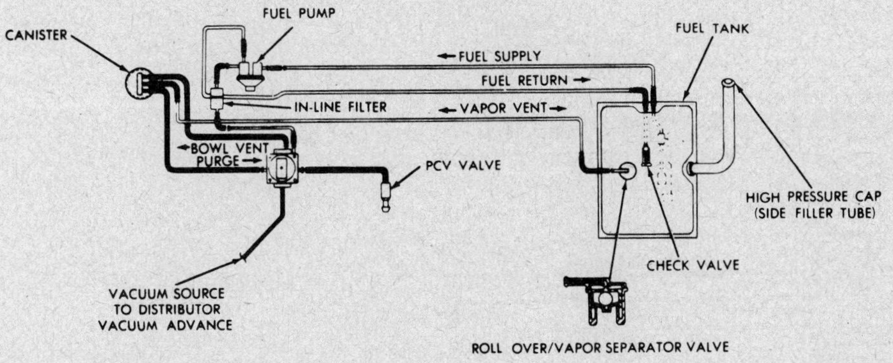

Fig. 24 Evaporative emission control system. 1982 4-105 engine

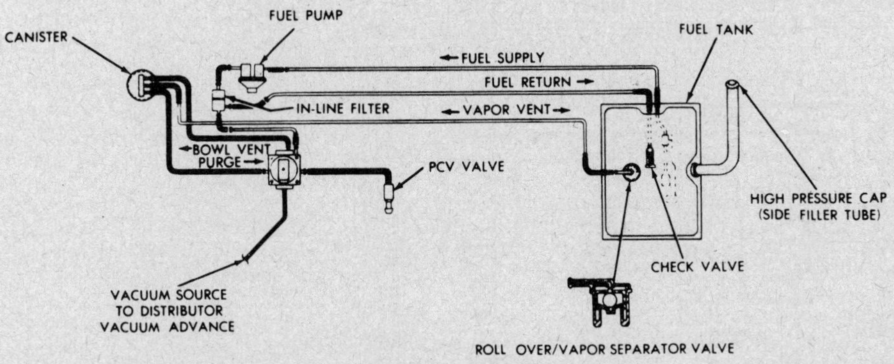

Fig. 25 Evaporative emission control system. 1982 4-135 engine

EVAPORATIVE EMISSION CONTROL SYSTEM

Description

4 CYLINDER ENGINES

In this system, **Figs. 23 through 29,** when fuel evaporates in the carburetor float chamber or fuel tank, the vapors pass through the vent hoses to the charcoal canister where they are temporarily held until they can be drawn into the intake manifold during engine operation.

On fuel injected and turbocharged engines, the vapors are drawn into the engine at idle as well as off idle. This system is called bi-level purge system where there is a dual source of vacuum to remove fuel vapor from canister.

On fuel injected and turbocharged engines, then source of vacuum at idle is a tee in the PCV system. On carbureted engines, it may have a vacuum source at the carburetor.

6 CYLINDER & V8 ENGINES

In this system, **Fig. 23,** when the fuel tank is filled to the base of the filler tube, vapors can no longer escape, they become trapped above the fuel. Vapor flow through the vent line is blocked by the limiting valve, and the filler tube is blocked by fuel preventing more fuel from entering the tank. At any time pressures in the tank rise above operating pressures of the limiting valve, the valve opens and allows vapors to flow forward to the charcoal canister. Due to the configuration of the fuel tank on some models and all station wagons, vapor separator tanks are not required. The charcoal canister is a feature on all models for the storage of fuel vapors from the fuel tank and carburetor bowl. A vacuum port located in the base of the carburetor governs vapor flow to the engine. On some models, each corner of the fuel tank is vented and each of the hoses from these vents is connected to a vapor separator. A tube from the separator leads to the charcoal canister. Evaporated fuel vapor from the fuel tank, flows through the separator to the canister. The canister used has three hoses and no purge valve. The purge valve previously located on top of the canister has been eliminated by using an additional ported vacuum connection on the carburetor for purging the canister. This utilizes the throttle plates of the carburetor as purge valve. This system will improve hot idle quality by eliminating canister purging during idle. Some limited production, high performance vehicles will continue to use the earlier type two stage canister which utilizes an integral purge valve. This canister can be identified by four hose connections while the new type canister uses only three.

SYSTEM COMPONENTS

Overfill Limiting Valve

The overfill limiting valve, located in the engine compartment on some models, is not serviceable. In the event that replace-

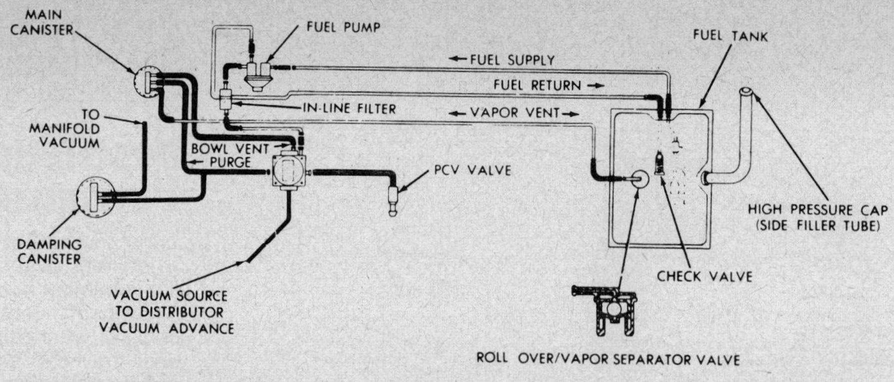

Fig. 26 Evaporative emission control system. 1982 4-156 engine

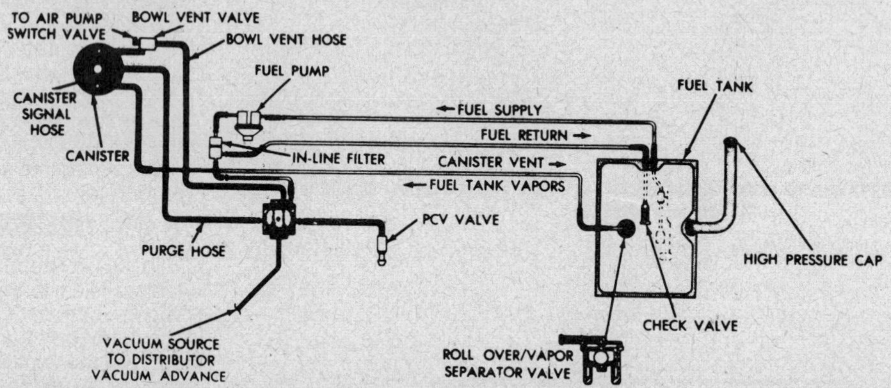

Fig. 27 Evaporative emission control system (Typical). 1983 4-97 & 4-105 engines

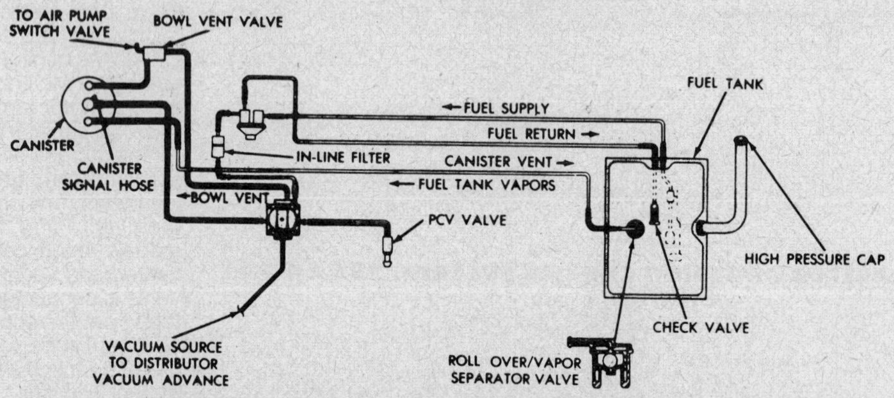

Fig. 28 Evaporative emission control system. 1983–85 4-135 & 1985 4-97 engines (1986–87 similar)

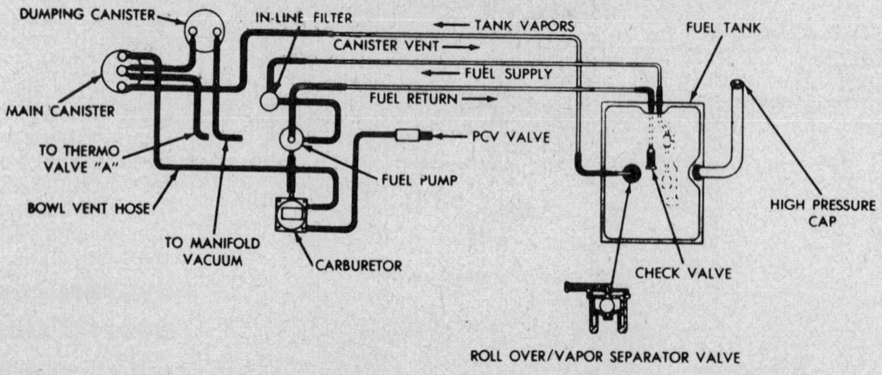

Fig. 29 Evaporative emission control system. 1983–85 4-156 engine

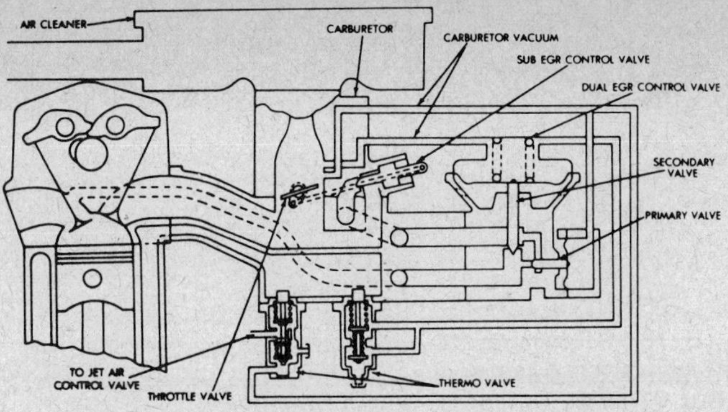

Fig. 30 EGR system. 4-156 engine

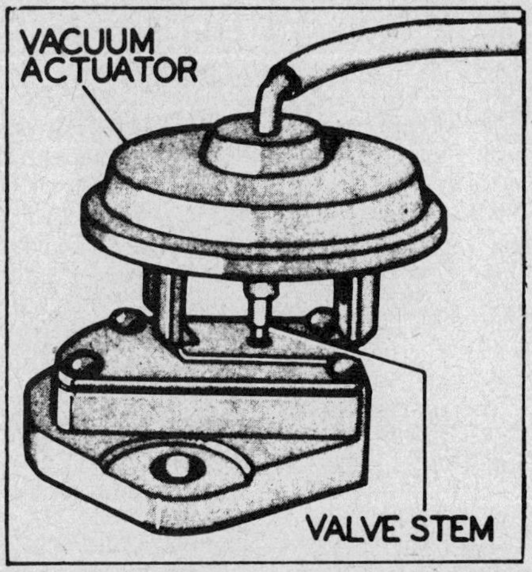

Fig. 31 EGR control valve

ment is required, cut the old valve out using a tubing cutter. Flare the end of the existing tube to insure a good vapor seal and install the replacement valve in the same position as the old valve. If overfill limiting valve is part of the vapor separator, the entire vapor separator must be replaced if the overfill limiting valve requires replacement.

It is important that all overfill limiting valves be installed as vertical as possible, in order to function properly.

Rollover Check Valve

A rollover check valve is used in the fuel tank vent line and the charcoal canister to prevent fuel leakage if the vehicle is accidentally rolled over.

Pressure-Vacuum Filler Cap

The fuel tank is sealed with a specially engineered pressure vacuum relief filler cap. The relief valves in the filler cap are a safety feature, and operate only to prevent excessive pressure or vacuum in the tank caused by malfunction in the system or damage to the vent lines.

Charcoal Canister

The service free canister is constructed of polypropylene and is located in the wheelwell area of the engine compartment. The canister is purged into the air cleaner using air pump pressure or intake manifold vacuum.

Damping Canister

The damping canister is a purge control device and does not store carburetor bowl or fuel tank vapor. The damping canister is isolated from these vapors by the purge control valve. The damping canister is connected to the purge line in series with the primary canister and the intake manifold port. The damping canister cushions the effect of a sudden release of fuel rich vapors when the purge control valve is opened. These vapors are temporarily held, then gradually released into the intake manifold.

Bowl Vent Valve

The bowl vent valve is connected to the carburetor fuel bowl, charcoal canister and air pump outlet. When the engine is not operating, there is a direct connection between the fuel bowl and canister. When the engine is operating, air pump pressure closes the connection between the fuel bowl and canister. When the engine is switched off, air pressure in the valve bleeds off and the fuel bowl is allowed to vent into the canister.

Purge Control Valve

This valve is installed on the carbon canister and controls the flow of fuel vapors during various engine operating modes. The control is provided by a vacuum signal from either the spark port, EGR port or intake manifold and opens or closes the valve accordingly. When the engine is off, the vapors from the fuel tank and carburetor fuel bowl are routed through the purge control valve and into the carbon canister for storage.

During normal cruise conditions, spark port or EGR vacuum is strong enough to open the orifice in the purge control valve to allow fuel vapors to flow from the carburetor canister through the purge line to a connection in the PCV tube or into the carburetor spacer. At the same time, the vapors from the fuel tank are also directed into the purge line. At idle and low speed cruise conditions, spark port or EGR port vacuum is not enough to open the orifice in the purge control valve so that the fuel vapors are then routed to the carbon canister.

Vacuum Controlled Orifice Tank Vapor Valve

1986-87 vehicles use this valve (VCOTVV) in the fuel tank vent line, between the fuel tank and vapor canister, to retain the fuel vapor within the tank until tank pressure reaches a predetermined level. With the engine off, when the tank vapor level reached that predetermined level, the valve opens, allowing the vapor to flow to the vapor canister. With the engine running and manifold vacuum connected to the valve's signal port, the valve is open, allowing vapor to flow to the canister.

Rollover & Pressure Relief Valve

1986-87 fuel injected 4 cylinder engines, except some turbocharged models, are equipped with a combination pressure relief and rollover valve. This valve provides a path for fuel vapors to travel from the fuel tank to the canister and provides fuel leakage protection when a vehicle rollover occurs. This valve also incorporates a pressure relief mechanism designed to release pressure to the atmosphere when fuel tank pressure exceeds that of the calibrated sealing valve.

Canister Purge Solenoid

The canister purge solenoid, used on 1987 vehicles with 4 cylinder, fuel injected

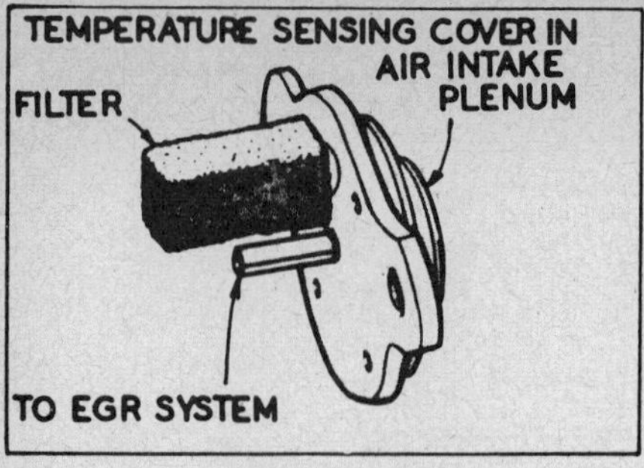

Fig. 32 EGR temperature control valve

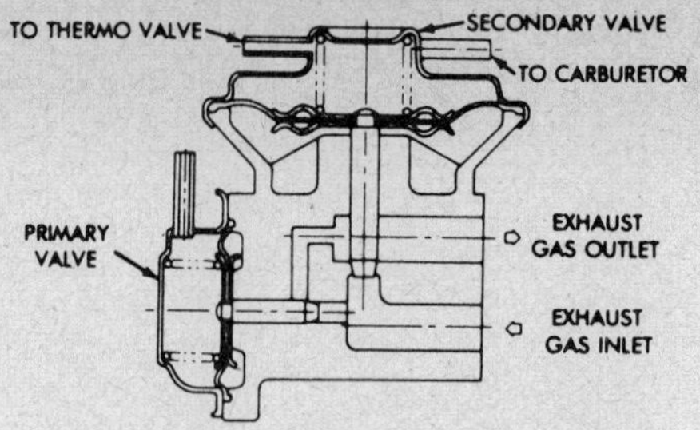

Fig. 33 Dual EGR control valve. 4-156 engine

engines, is controlled by the logic module. When engine temperature is below 145°F, the logic module grounds the purge solenoid valve to energize it. This prevents vacuum from reaching the charcoal canister valve. When engine temperature reaches 145°F, the logic module de-energizes the solenoid by turning the ground off. Once this occurs, vacuum will flow to the canister purge valve and purge fuel vapors through the throttle body.

System Service

Ensure all vacuum hoses and electrical wires are routed clear of the exhaust manifold to prevent deterioration due to the high temperature. Vacuum hoses should always be a minimum of three inches from the exhaust manifold. When servicing the charcoal canister, mark, then disconnect vacuum hoses from charcoal canister to ensure proper installation.

EXHAUST GAS RECIRCULATION (EGR)

Description

CARBURETED MODELS

This system is used to reduce oxides of nitrogen emissions at the engine's exhaust. This is accomplished by introducing exhaust gases into the intake manifold at throttle positions other than idle. The system uses an EGR valve. The exhaust gas intake port of the EGR valve is connected to the intake manifold exhaust crossover channels where it can pick up exhaust gases. As the throttle valves are opened and the engine accelerates, vacuum is applied to a vacuum diaphragm in the EGR valve through a connecting tube. As the diaphragm moves up, it opens the valve in the exhaust port which allows exhaust gas to be pulled into the intake manifold and enter the cylinders.

On 4-156 engines, exhaust gas is partially recirculated from an exhaust port of the cylinder head into a port located at the intake manifold below the carburetor, while EGR flow is controlled by the EGR control valve and thermo valve, **Fig. 30.**

Two different type systems are used to control EGR operation. A Ported Vacuum Control System and Venturi Vacuum Control System. Both systems use the same

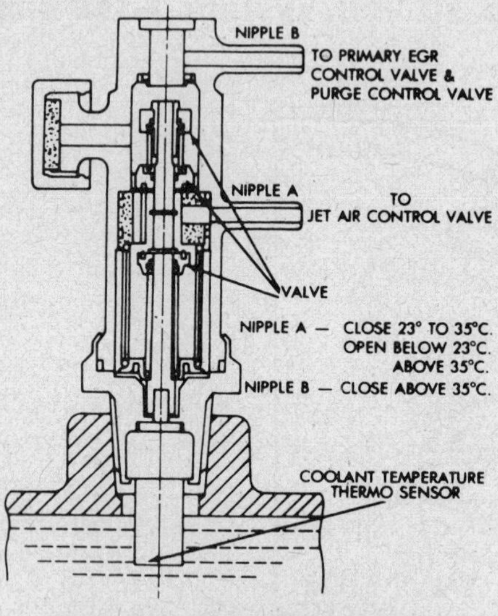

Fig. 34 Thermo valve. 4-156 engine

type exhaust gas recirculation (EGR) control valve, **Fig. 31,** only the method of controlling the valve is different. The valve is a vacuum actuated, poppet type unit used to modulate exhaust gas flow from the exhaust gas crossover into the incoming air fuel mixture.

FUEL INJECTED MODELS

1982–85

This system is a back pressure type and is controlled in two ways. The vacuum through the EGR solenoid is controlled by a logic module which cycles the vacuum circuit "On" or "Off." The amount of exhaust back pressure is measured by the back pressure transducer, located on the exhaust side of the EGR valve. EGR operation is discontinued by the logic module by turning the EGR solenoid "Off" at idle, wide open throttle or when engine temperature is below 70°F. The EGR signal is adjusted by the back pressure transducer to provide programmed amounts of exhaust gas recirculation under all other conditions.

The EGR solenoid is also operated by the logic module and, when engine temperature falls below 70°F, the solenoid is energized by the logic module by grounding it. This closes the solenoid and prevents ported vacuum from reaching the EGR valve. When engine temperature exceeds 70°F, the logic module bypasses the ground signal, thereby de-energizing the solenoid and allowing ported vacuum from the throttle body to pass through the EGR valve. At idle and wide open throttle, the solenoid is energized, which prevents EGR operation.

1986

This system uses either a ported or manifold vacuum controlled backpressure EGR valve to modulate exhaust gas flow from the exhaust manifold to the intake manifold. EGR flow is further controlled by a backpressure transducer in the EGR signal line. The transducer uses exhaust system backpressure to control EGR valve signal vacuum, bleeding the signal vacuum off to atmosphere when exhaust backpressure at the EGR valve drops below a calibrated value.

1987 Models Exc. Turbo

This system is a backpressure type. A backpressure transducer measures the amount of exhaust backpressure on the exhaust side of the EGR valve and varies the strength of the vacuum signal applied to the EGR valve. The backpressure transducer adjusts the EGR signal to provide programmed amounts of exhaust gas recirculation under all other conditions.

1987 Turbo Models

This system is a backpressure type that is controlled in two ways. The logic module controls vacuum through the EGR solenoid, turning the vacuum circuit on or off. A backpressure transducer measures the amount of exhaust backpressure on the exhaust side of the EGR valve and varies the strength of the vacuum signal applied to the EGR valve. The logic module will prevent EGR operation by turning the EGR solenoid off when engine temperature is below 80°F or is above 80°F for less than 7 seconds. The backpressure transducer adjusts the EGR signal to provide programmed amounts of exhaust recirculation under all other conditions.

PORTED VACUUM CONTROL SYSTEM

4 Cylinder Engines

The ported vacuum control system utilizes a slow type port in the carburetor throttle body which is exposed to an increasing ratio of manifold vacuum as the throttle blade opens. This throttle bore port is connected through an external nipple directly to the EGR valve. The flow rate is dependent on three variables, 1) manifold

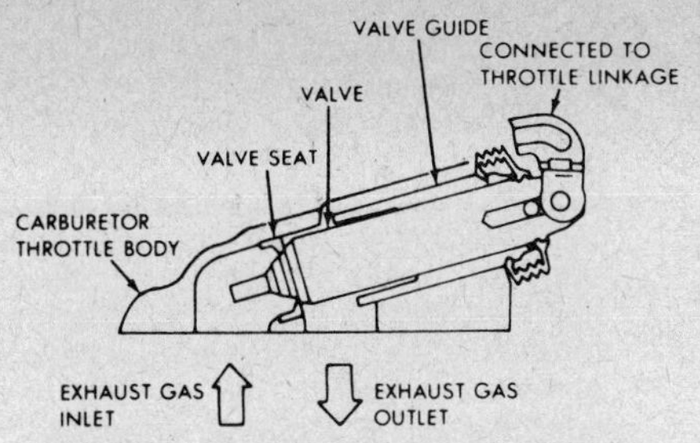

Fig. 35 Sub-EGR control valve

vacuum, 2) throttle position, and 3) exhaust gas back pressure. Recycle at wide open throttle is eliminated by calibrating the valve opening point above manifold vacuums available at wide open throttle as port vacuum cannot exceed manifold vacuum. Elimination of wide open throttle recycle provides maximum performance.

VENTURI VACUUM CONTROL SYSTEM

6 Cylinder & V8 Engines

The venturi vacuum control system utilizes a vacuum tap at the throat of the carburetor venturi to provide a control signal. This vacuum signal is amplified to the level required to operate the EGR control valve. Elimination of recycle at wide open throttle is accomplished by a dump diaphragm which compares venturi and manifold vacuum to determine when wide open throttle is achieved. At wide open throttle, the internal reservoir is "dumped," limiting output to the EGR valve to manifold vacuum. The valve opening point is set above the manifold vacuums available at wide open throttle.

This system is dependent primarily on engine intake airflow as indicated by the venturi signal, and is also affected by intake vacuum and exhaust gas back pressure.

TEMPERATURE CONTROL VALVE

The plenum mounted temperature control valve, **Fig. 32**, is utilized on the ported vacuum control system. The valve reduces the recycle rate at low ambient temperature for improved driveability. The unit contains a temperature sensitive bi-metal disc which senses plenum air temperature. The snap action of the disc unplugs a calibrated orifice to provide the bleed air. Calibration is protected by an air filter unit.

COOLANT CONTROL EXHAUST GAS RECIRCULATION (CCEGR)

On engines equipped with EGR use a CCEGR valve mounted in the radiator top tank, engine block or water pump housing. The purpose of this valve is to allow exhaust gas recirculation only after the engine has reached a predetermined temperature.

COOLANT CONTROLLED EXHAUST GAS RECIRCULATION/COOLANT VACUUM SWITCH COLD CLOSED (CCEGR/CVSCO)

1983–87 4 Cylinder Engines

The CCEGR/CVSCO is mounted in the thermostat housing. This switch prevents vacuum from being supplied to the EGR system or other systems after a cold start, until coolant temperature reaches a predetermined level. After coolant temperature reaches this level, the valve opens and vacuum is supplied to the EGR valve, allowing exhaust gas to recirculate.

COOLANT CONTROLLED ENGINE VACUUM SWITCH (CCEVS)

Refer to "Air Injection System" described under "Coolant Controlled Engine Vacuum Switch (CCEVS)" for description and service procedures.

CHARGE TEMPERATURE SWITCH (CTS)

This switch is used on 6 and V8 engines, and is installed in the intake manifold where it is exposed to the incoming air/fuel mixture charge. When the charge temperature is below 60°F, the CTS will be closed permitting no EGR valve operation. When the charge temperature is above 60°F, the CTS will open, permitting the EGR time delay device to count down and resume normal EGR operation.

The EGR time delay device used with this system is unique and not interchangeable with those of previous years.

DUAL EGR CONTROL VALVE

1982–85 4-156 Engine

The dual EGR control valve, **Fig. 33**, consists of primary and secondary valves, which are controlled by different carburetor vacuums in response to throttle valve openings, while the EGR flow is suspended at idle and wide open throttle operation. The primary valve controls EGR flow during part throttle operation, while the secondary control valve allows recirculation of exhaust gas into the intake manifold when the throttle valve is further opened. Vacuum applied to the dual EGR control valve is controlled by a thermo valve, **Fig. 34.**

SUB-EGR CONTROL VALVE

On vehicles equipped with the 4-156 engine, a Sub-EGR Control Valve is incorporated in conjunction with the EGR system. The Sub-EGR closely modulates EGR flow in response to throttle valve opening. The Sub-EGR Control Valve is an integral part of the carburetor, and is directly opened and closed through linkage that is connected to the throttle valve, **Fig. 35.**

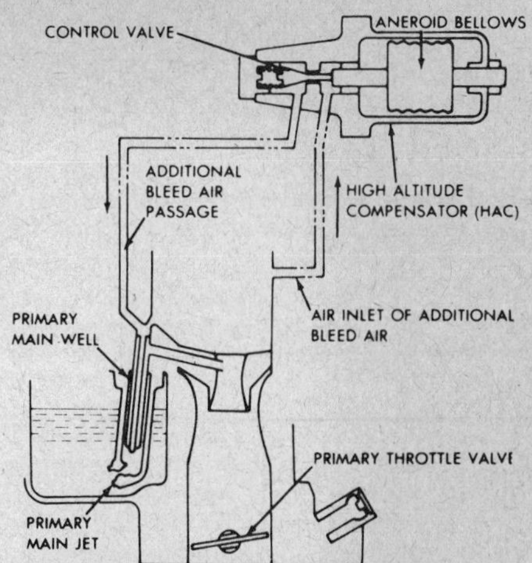

Fig. 36 High altitude compensation system. 1982–85 4-156 engine

EGR TIME-DELAY & IDLE ENRICHMENT SYSTEM

On most engine models, a time-delay device is incorporated into the EGR system which works in conjunction with the idle enrichment system to improve engine starting and performance. This system consists of an electronic timer and either one or two vacuum solenoids. The electronic timer energizes the solenoid(s) during starting and for 35 seconds thereafter. When the solenoid(s) energize(s), vacuum to the EGR amplifier is cut off, thereby stopping exhaust gas recirculation.

CHARGE TEMPERATURE SENSOR

This sensor, used on 1987 V8 engines, located in the intake manifold runner, monitors engine temperature. The sensor signals the computer when to operate the air switching, EGR and spark advance systems.

COOLANT VACUUM SWITCH COLD CLOSED (CVSCC)

Some vehicles are equipped with a CVSCC mounted in the thermostat housing. When engine coolant temperature reaches 108-125°F, the switch opens and vacuum is applied to open the EGR control valve, allowing exhaust gas to recirculate.

EGR DELAY SYSTEM

Some vehicles are equipped with an EGR delay system that has an electric timer mounted on the dash panel in the engine compartment which controls an engine mounted solenoid. The solenoid is connected by vacuum hoses between the carburetor venturi signal nipple and the vacuum amplifier. The purpose of this system is to prevent exhaust gas recirculation for approximately 60 seconds after the ignition is turned on.

Diagnosis

EGR SYSTEM TEST

The complete EGR system should be

inspected and tested at the time intervals recommended by the manufacturer. To assure proper operation of this system all passages and moving parts must operate properly free of deposits, also hoses and connections must be free from leaks.

Ambient temperature in the area of the vehicle must be above 68°F for this test.

Exc. 4-156 (2.6 Liter) & Turbocharged 4-135 (2.2 Liter) Engines

Warm up engine and allow the engine to idle, in neutral, with the carburetor throttle closed; then abruptly accelerate the engine to approximately 2000 RPM, but not over 3000 RPM. Visible movement of the EGR valve stem should occur during this operation. This can be determined by change in the relative position of the groove on the EGR valve stem. This operation should be repeated several times to confirm movement. Movement of the stem indicates that the control system is functioning correctly.

If control system is functioning properly, the valve and passages may be checked for exhaust gas flow by applying a vacuum of at least 10 inches Hg directly to the EGR control valve with the engine warm and idling in neutral. Idle speed should drop 150 RPM or more when vacuum is applied. This reduction in idle speed confirms that exhaust gas recirculation is taking place. If the speed change does not occur, or is less than that specified, exhaust deposits in the EGR valve or intake manifold EGR passages are indicated.

4-156 (2.6 Liter) Engines

1. Make sure that vacuum hoses are not leaking and that they are properly routed.
2. With engine cold and idling, increase engine speed to 2500 RPM and make sure that increased engine speed does not cause secondary EGR valve to operate. If it does, replace thermo valve.
3. Allow engine temperature to exceed 149°F, then increase engine speed to 2500 RPM and check that secondary valve operates. If it does not operate, inspect EGR control valve or thermo valve.
4. Disconnect green striped hose from carburetor and connect a vacuum pump to hose.
5. While opening the sub-EGR valve by pulling it by hand, apply 6 inches Hg vacuum with pump.
6. If idle speed becomes unstable, the secondary valve is operating properly. If idle speed does not change, the secondary EGR valve or thermo valve is not operating. Replace defective component.
7. Disconnect vacuum pump and reconnect hose to carburetor.
8. Disconnect yellow striped hose from carburetor and connect a vacuum pump to hose.
9. While opening the sub-EGR valve by pulling it by hand, apply 6 inches Hg vacuum with pump.

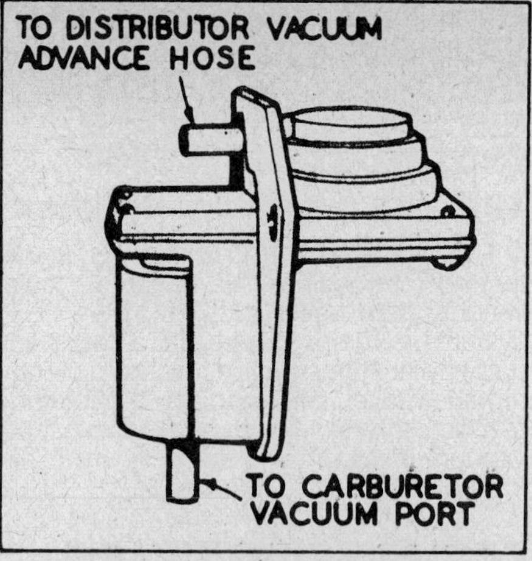

Fig. 37 OSAC valve. 1982–83 rear wheel drive models

10. If idle speed becomes unstable, the primary valve is operating properly. If idle speed does not change, the primary EGR valve or thermo valve is not operating. Replace defective component.

Turbocharged 4-135 (2.2 Liter) Engine

To ensure proper operation of backpressure EGR system, all passages and moving parts must be free of clogging or sticking as a result of deposits. The entire system should be free of leaks. Any vacuum lines or components found to be leaking should be replaced.

Inspect all vacuum line connections between the throttle body, EGR control valve and backpressure transducer. Replace any split or otherwise damaged vacuum lines or connectors.

The EGR valve stem is not visible on 4-135 turbo EGR valves. Therefore, it is necessary to proceed as follows to verify system operation.

1. Disconnect vacuum hose from EGR valve and connect suitable vacuum gauge, then start engine and accelerate to 2000 RPM. With engine temperature below 90°F, vacuum gauge should show a steady reading of zero. If so, proceed to step 2. If gauge shows an unsteady reading above zero, replace EGR solenoid.
2. Disconnect vacuum line to EGR backpressure transducer from EGR solenoid. Connect a vacuum gauge to this line, then start engine and wait until sufficiently warm for solenoid to operate, then raise engine speed to 2000 RPM. If gauge reads at least 5 inches Hg of vacuum, repair vacuum supply from throttle body and solenoid, then disconnect vacuum gauge from vacuum line and reconnect vacuum line to EGR backpressure transducer.
3. Disconnect vacuum line to EGR valve vacuum motor from EGR backpressure transducer and connect a suitable vacuum gauge to this line, then start engine and raise engine speed to 2000 RPM. If vacuum gauge reads approximately 5 inches Hg vacuum, proceed to step 4. If vacuum gauge does not read approximately 5 inches Hg vacuum, replace EGR valve/backpressure transducer assembly.
4. Connect an auxiliary vacuum supply to EGR valve vacuum motor and, with engine running at idle speed, slowly apply vacuum. If engine speed begins to drop when applied vacuum reaches 2.0-3.5 inches Hg vacuum, proceed to step 5. If engine speed does not drop, replace EGR valve/backpressure transducer assembly, then repeat step 4. **Before replacing assembly, check for clogged EGR supply tube or passages.**
5. With engine set up as in step 4, apply 10 inches Hg vacuum. If vacuum holds without bleeding for 10 seconds, system is satisfactory. If vacuum does not hold, replace EGR valve/backpressure transducer assembly.

COOLANT CONTROL EXHAUST GAS RECIRCULATION (CCEGR) VALVE TEST

The CCEGR valve can be tested for proper operation by placing it in ice and cooling it to below 40°F. Using vacuum pump and gauge tool C-4207 or equivalent, apply a vacuum of at least 10 inches or mercury to the valve nipple corresponding to the blue striped hose. If vacuum reading drops off more than 1 inch in one minute, the valve should be replaced.

COOLANT CONTROLLED EXHAUST GAS RECIRCULATION/COOLANT VACUUM SWITCH COLD CLOSED (CCEGR/CVSCO) TEST

1. Remove valve from housing, and submerge threaded portion of valve into a container of cold water. Water temperature should be approximately 40°F.
2. Disconnect yellow striped hose from valve and connect a suitable vacuum pump and gauge to valve nipple.
3. Apply 10 inches Hg vacuum to the valve. There should be no more than 1 inch drop in vacuum in 1 minute. If there is excessive vacuum drop, replace the valve.

CHARGE TEMPERATURE SWITCH (CTS) TEST

1. No EGR operation with engine warm:
    a. Check hose routing and EGR solenoid operation.
    b. Remove center connector from CTS and wait 90 seconds.
    c. If EGR operation now resumes, replace CTS.
2. EGR operation with engine cold:
    a. Check hose routing and EGR solenoid operation.
    b. Remove center connector from CTS and check for 10 ohms resistance between center terminal of CTS and ground.

c. If ohmmeter indicates an open circuit, replace CTS.
d. If ohmmeter does not indicate an open circuited CTS, check for open circuit in the CTS to engine ground wire. **When replacing CTS switch, do not torque more than 60 inch lbs. Over-torquing will break off the nylon threads in the intake manifold.**

COOLANT CONTROLLED ENGINE VACUUM SWITCH (CCEVS) TEST

1. Check vacuum hoses for proper routing and make sure that valve is properly installed. Also make sure that engine coolant is at proper level.
2. Disconnect molded connector from valve and connect a 1/8 inch inside diameter hose to bottom port of valve.
3. With engine coolant at 75°F or less, blow air through hose. If air does not flow freely, replace valve.
4. Start engine and warm to normal operating temperature, then, using an external vacuum source, apply 10 inches Hg to valve. If vacuum level drops more than one inch in 15 seconds, replace valve.

TIME DELAY SYSTEM TEST

Timer

1. Check wiring for proper connections and correct as necessary.
2. With ignition switch off, remove wiring connector from solenoid valve.
3. Connect a test light across terminals of connector disconnected in step 2.
4. Start engine. Test light should go on and remain on for 35 seconds for black color coded valves, 60 seconds for orange color coded valves, and 90 seconds for red color coded valves after engine starts.
5. If test light does not go on, remains on indefinitely, or does not remain on the amount of time specified in step 4, replace timer. **In order to avoid overloading of timer, current draw of test light should not exceed .5 amps.**

Solenoid

1. Make sure that vacuum hose routing is correct and that hoses are not leaking.
2. Disconnect electrical plug from solenoid valve.
3. Connect either solenoid terminal to ground and the other to battery positive terminal to activate the solenoid valve. This will interrupt the vacuum flow to the EGR system. **A click should be heard from the solenoid as it is connected to the battery.**
4. To check solenoid operation, allow engine to idle, then increase engine speed to 2000 RPM while observing EGR control valve stem. If stem does not move, replace solenoid.

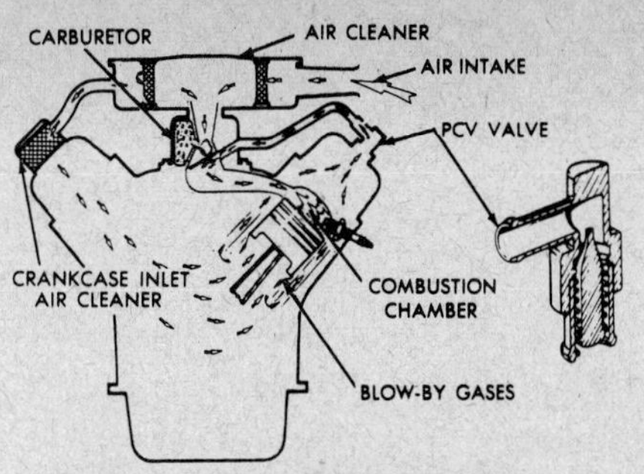

Fig. 38 PCV system (Typical)

IDLE ENRICHMENT SYSTEM TEST

Idle Enrichment System

1. Warm engine to normal operating temperature, then remove air cleaner. **Do not cap any fittings opened by hose removal as leakage is needed for testing.**
2. Disconnect hose from idle enrichment diaphragm at plastic connector and remove connector from hose.
3. Connect 3-4 feet of hose to enrichment diaphragm, then start engine and run at slow idle.
4. Apply vacuum to other end of hose and observe engine speed change. If engine speed changes when vacuum is applied, the idle enrichment system is operating properly. If engine speed does not change when vacuum is applied, replace valve assembly on Holley carburetors, or proceed to steps 5 and 6 if equipped with Carter carburetor.
5. Cover air inlet passage and observe engine speed change. If speed changes, the diaphragm is leaking or the air valve is stuck open. If speed does not change, the air valve is stuck closed.
6. Clean valve and repeat step 4. If not operating properly, replace diaphragm.

COOLANT VACUUM SWITCH COLD CLOSED TEST

6 Cylinder & V8 Engines

1. Ensure vacuum hoses are in good condition and properly routed and check engine coolant level.
2. With switch installed in its proper location, disconnect molded connector from valve and attach a 1/8 inch hose to bottom port of valve.
3. With radiator top tank warm to touch, but no warmer than 75°F, blow through hose. If it is not possible to blow through hose, valve is defective and must be replaced.

4 Cylinder Engines

1. Remove valve from engine and place it in an ice bath below 40°F so that the threaded portion is covered.
2. Attach a suitable vacuum pump and gauge tool No. C-4207 or equivalent to bottom nipple.
3. Apply a vacuum signal of at least 10 inches.
4. If vacuum drops more than 1 inch in 1 minute, replace switch.

EGR SOLENOID TEST

1. Ensure all vacuum hose connections are correct and not leaking.
2. Disconnect electrical connector from solenoid valve.
3. Apply 12 volts to solenoid and ensure clicking noise is heard as voltage is applied.
4. Start engine and run at idle. Increase engine speed to 2000 RPM and ensure EGR control valve stem moves. If valve stem does not move, replace delay solenoid.

System Service

EGR CONTROL VALVE

The EGR control valve should be checked for deposits with particular attention to the poppet and seat area, **Fig. 31.** If deposits exceed a thin film condition, the EGR valve should be cleaned. If wear of the stem or other moving components is noted, the EGR valve should be replaced. **Extreme care should be exercised during the cleaning operation to prevent spilling of solvent on the valve diaphragm, as this will cause diaphragm failure. Do not push on diaphragm to operate valve, use the vacuum source only.**

HIGH ALTITUDE COMPENSATION SYSTEM

Description

This system is used on 1982-85 California models with 4-156 engine to maintain the correct air fuel ratio at high altitudes.

An aneroid bellows, **Fig. 36,** is mounted on the body panel in the engine compartment and connected to the carburetor with hoses and is vented to the atmosphere through the top of the carburetor. As atmospheric pressure expands or contracts the bellows, the brass tapered seat control valve regulates the air flow to the main air bleeds.

During high altitude engine operation, the fuel mixture tends to become richer due to low atmospheric pressure. When the atmospheric pressure reaches a predetermined value, the aneroid begins to open, allowing air to enter the main air bleeds. This auxiliary air, in addition to the present air source, provides the system with the proper amount of air necessary to maintain the correct air fuel ratio.

This system supplies varying amounts of additional air depending upon the altitude. When sufficient atmospheric pressure is restored, the valve closes and system returns to its normal operation.

ORIFICE SPARK ADVANCE CONTROL VALVE (OSAC)

Description

The OSAC valve, **Fig. 37,** is incorporated to aid in the control of NOx (Oxides of Nitrogen). The valve controls the vacuum to the vacuum advance actuator of the distributor. A tiny orifice is incorporated in the OSAC valve which delays the change in ported vacuum to the distributor by about 17 seconds (10 or 27 seconds on some applications) when going from idle to part throttle. When going from part throttle to idle, the change in ported vacuum is instantaneous.

Vacuum is obtained by a vacuum tap just above the throttle plates of the carburetor. This type of tap provides no vacuum at idle, but provides manifold vacuum as soon as the throttle plates are opened slightly. Proper operation of this valve depends on air tight fittings and hoses and freedom from sticking or plugging due to deposits.

Diagnosis

Ambient temperature in area of vehicle must be above 68°F for this test.

1. Inspect hose connections and replace any hoses which may allow vacuum leakage.
2. With engine at operating temperature and running at 2000 RPM, "tee" a vacuum gauge into hose leading to distributor.
3. On all vehicles, if a gradual increase in vacuum is observed, about 15-20 seconds, the valve is operating properly. If vacuum immediately goes up to manifold vacuum or there is no vacuum, the OSAC valve is not operating properly and should be replaced.

System Service

To remove the OSAC valve, mark and disconnect vacuum line from valve. Remove OSAC valve screws and valve from firewall.

POSITIVE CRANKCASE VENTILATION (PCV) SYSTEM

Description

This system, **Fig. 38,** is used on all engines to prevent the emission of blow-by gases from the engine's crankcase. These blow-by gases are the result of high pressures developed within the combustion chamber during the combustion process and contain undesirable pollutants.

When the engine is running, air is drawn by manifold vacuum from the air cleaner through a hose, to the crankcase inlet air cleaner. From the crankcase inlet air cleaner, the air mixes with the vapors in the rocker arm chamber and crankcase and are then drawn up through the PCV valve in the cylinder head cover to a hose connected to either the intake manifold or carburetor base. These gases become part of the calibrated air/fuel mixture and are then drawn into the combustion chamber, burned and expelled with the exhaust gases.

Diagnosis

1. With engine idling, remove PCV valve from rocker cover. If valve is not plugged, a hissing sound will be heard as air passes through the valve, and a strong vacuum should be felt when a finger is placed over the inlet of the valve.
2. Reinstall the PCV valve, then remove crankcase inlet air cleaner. With engine idling, loosely hold a piece of stiff paper (such as a parts tag) over the opening in the rocker arm cover. After allowing about a minute for the crankcase pressure to reduce, the paper should be drawn against the opening in the rocker arm cover.
3. With engine off, remove PCV valve from rocker cover and shake the valve. A clicking noise should be heard, indicating that the valve is free.
4. If the system passes the above tests, no further service is required. If not, replace the PCV valve and recheck the system. **Do not attempt to clean the PCV valve.**
5. With a new PCV valve installed, if the paper is not drawn against the crankcase inlet air cleaner opening with considerable force, it will be necessary to clean the passage in the lower part of the carburetor. Also, the PCV hose will have to be cleaned or replaced.

Service

Every 30,000 miles, replace PCV valve and clean crankcase inlet air cleaner. If vehicle is used extensively for short trips with frequent idling, this service may have to be performed sooner.

To clean the passage in the carburetor, remove carburetor from engine. Turn a 1/4 inch drill bit by hand through the passage to dislodge the solid particles, then blow clean using compressed air. If necessary, use a smaller drill bit so that no metal will be removed.

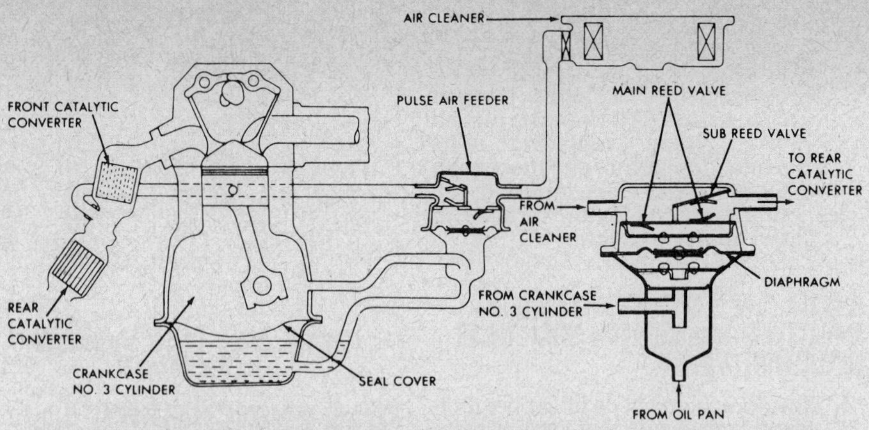

Fig. 39 Pulse air feeder (PAF) system. 4-156 engine

PULSE AIR FEEDER (PAF) SYSTEM

Description

This system, **Fig. 39,** is used on 4-156 (2.6 liter) engines. It supplies secondary air into the exhaust system between the front and rear catalytic converters in order to promote the oxidation of exhaust emissions in the rear catalytic converter.

The PAF consists of a main reed valve and sub-reed valve.

The main reed valve is actuated in response to movement of a diaphragm which is activated by pressure pulsation generated by the reciprocating motion of the number 3 piston. The number 3 cylinder crankcase is sealed by a seal cover which has a small hole for discharging engine oil and blow by gases.

The sub-reed valve is actuated by exhaust vacuum generated from pulsation in the exhaust system between the front and rear catalytic converters.

System Service

PULSE AIR FEEDER, REPLACE

1. Remove screw and air deflector duct from right side of radiator.
2. Remove carburetor protection shield.
3. Remove oil dipstick and oil dipstick tube.
4. Remove three pulse air feeder mounting bolts, raise and support front of vehicle.
5. Disconnect hoses from pulse air feeder and remove pulse air feeder from vehicle.
6. Reverse procedure to install.

FORD MOTOR COMPANY

FORD

LINCOLN

MERCURY

GENERAL SERVICE

FORD & MERCURY Full Size Models

NOTE: This chapter includes service procedures for the 1982 LTD, Marquis & 1983-88 LTD Crown Victoria & Grand Marquis. For service procedures on 1983-86 LTD & Marquis models, refer to "Ford & Mercury—Compact & Intermediate Models Chapter." Refer to rear of this manual for vehicle manufacturer's special service tool suppliers.

INDEX OF SERVICE OPERATION

GENERAL ENGINE SPECIFICATIONS

Year	Engine CID①/Liter	Engine VIN Code ②	Carburetor	Bore and Stroke	Compression Ratio	Net H.P. @ RPM③	Maximum Torque Ft. Lbs. @ RPM	Normal Oil Pressure Pounds
FORD								
1982	V8-255, 4.2L	D	7200VV, 2 Bbl.④	3.68 x 3.00	8.2	122 @ 3400	209 @ 2400	40-60
	V8-302, 5.0L	F	7200VV, 2 Bbl.④	4.00 x 3.00	8.4	132 @ 3400	236 @ 1800	40-60
1983-85	V8-302, 5.0L	F	E.F.I.⑤	4.00 x 3.00	8.4	140 @ 3200	250 @ 1600	40-60
1986-88	V8-302, 5.0L	F	S.E.F.I.⑥	4.00 x 3.00	8.9	150 @ 3200	270 @ 2000	40-60
MERCURY								
1982	V8-255, 4.2L	D	7200VV, 2 Bbl④	3.68 x 3.00	8.2	122 @ 3400	209 @ 2400	40-60
	V8-302, 5.0L	F	7200VV, 2 Bbl.④	4.00 x 3.00	8.4	132 @ 3400	236 @ 1800	40-60
1983-85	V8-302, 5.0L	F	E.F.I.⑤	4.00 x 3.00	8.4	140 @ 3200	250 @ 1600	40-60
1986-88	V8-302, 5.0L	F	S.E.F.I.⑥	4.00 x 3.00	8.9	150 @ 3200	270 @ 2000	40-60

①—C.I.D.-cubic inch displacement.
②—On 1982-88 models, the eighth digit of VIN denotes engine code.
③—Rating are net-as installed in vehicle.
④—Motorcraft.
⑤—E.F.I.-electronic fuel injection
⑥—S.E.F.I.-sequential electronic fuel injection.

ENGINE TIGHTENING SPECIFICATIONS*

*Torque specifications are for clean and lightly lubricated threads only. Dry or dirty threads produce increased friction which prevents accurate measurement of tightness.

Year	Engine Model/VIN	Spark Plugs Ft. Lbs.	Cylinder Head Bolts Ft. Lbs.	Intake Manifold Ft. Lbs.	Exhaust Manifold Ft. Lbs.	Rocker Arm Stud Nut or Bolt Ft. Lbs.	Rocker Arm Cover Ft. Lbs.	Connecting Rod Cap Bolts Ft. Lbs.	Main Bearing Cap Bolts Ft. Lbs.	Flywheel to Crankshaft Ft. Lbs.	Vibration Damper or Pulley Ft. Lbs.
1982	V8-255/D	10-15	65-72	18-20	18-24	18-25	3-5	19-24	60-70	75-85	70-90
1982-85	V8-302/F	10-15	65-72	23-25	18-24	18-25	3-5	19-24	60-70	75-85	70-90
1986-88	V8-302	10-15	65-72	23-25	18-24	18-25	3-5	19-24	60-70	75-85	70-90

STARTING MOTOR APPLICATIONS

Year	Engine/VIN	Ident. No.
1982	V8-255/D, 302/F	E1AF-BA
1983	V8-302/F	E3AF-AA
1984	V8-302/F	①
1985-88	V8-302/F	E4AF-AA

①—E3AF-AA, models built prior to December, 1983; E4AF-AA, models built from December, 1983.

ALTERNATOR & REGULATOR SPECIFICATIONS

Year	Stamp Color Code	Current Rating		Field Current @ 75°F		Voltage Regulator	
		Amperes	Volts	Amperes	Volts	Part No. (10316)	Voltage @ 75°F
1982	Orange ② ④	40	15	4.0	12	E1AF-BA ①	13.8-14.6
	Black ② ④	65	15	4.0	12	E1AF-BA ①	13.8-14.6
	Green ② ④	60	15	4.0	12	E1AF-BA ①	13.8-14.6
	Black ③ ④	70	15	4.0	12	E1AF-BA ①	13.8-14.6
	Red ③ ④	100	15	4.0	12	E1AF-BA ①	13.8-14.6
1983	Orange ② ④	40	15	4.25	12	E2AF-AA ①	—
	Black ② ④	65	15	4.25	12	E2AF-AA ①	—
	Green ② ④	60	15	4.25	12	E2AF-AA ①	—
	Black ③ ④	70	15	4.25	12	E2AF-AA ①	—
	Red ③ ④	100	15	4.25	12	E2AF-AA ①	—
1984-85	Orange ② ④	40	15	4.25	12	E4AF-AA ①	—
	Green ② ④	60	15	4.25	12	E4AF-AA ①	—
	Black ③ ④	70	15	4.25	12	E4AF-AA ①	—
	Red ③ ④	100	15	4.25	12	E4AF-AA ①	—
1986	Green ④	60	15	4.25	12	E6TZ-AA ⑤	—
	Black ④	65	15	4.25	12	E6TZ-AA ⑤	—
	③	70	15	4.25	12	—	—
	③	100	15	4.25	12	—	—
1987-88	Orange	40	15	4.25	12	E6TZ-AA	—
	Red	40	15	4.25	12	E6TZ-AA	—
	Green	60	15	4.25	12	E6TZ-AA	—
	Black	65	15	4.25	12	E6TZ-AA	—
	③	70	15	4.25	12	—	—
	③	100	15	4.25	12	—	—

①—Electronic voltage regulator. These units are color coded black for systems w/warning indicator lamp & blue for systems w/ammeter.
②—Rear terminal alternator.
③—Side terminal alternator.
④—Solid state alternator.
⑤—Integral regulator.

REAR AXLE SPECIFICATIONS

Year	Carrier Type	Ring Gear & Pinion Backlash Inch	Nominal Pinion Locating Shim, Inch	Pinion Bearing Preload		Differential Bearing Preload	Pinion Nut Torque Ft. Lbs. ①
				New Bearings With Seal Inch Lbs.	Used Bearings With Seal Inch Lbs.		
1982-83	Integral	.008-.015	.030	16-29	8-14	.016 ②	③
1984-88	Integral	.008-.015	.030	16-19	8-14	.006 ② ④	③

①—If torque cannot be obtained, install new spacer.
②—Differential case spread.
③—With 7.5 inch ring gear, 170 ft. lbs.; with 8.5 & 8.8 inch ring gear, 140 ft. lbs.
④—On each side of differential case.

WHEEL ALIGNMENT SPECIFICATIONS

Year	Model	Caster Angle, Degrees		Camber Angle, Degrees				Toe-In. Inch	Toe-Out on Turns, Deg.	
		Limits	Desired	Limits Left	Limits Right	Desired Left	Desired Right		Outer Wheel	Inner Wheel
1982	All	+2¼ to +3¾	+3	−¼ to +1¼	−¼ to +1¼	+½	+½	1/16	18.51	20
1983-87	All	+2¼ to +4	+3	−¼ to +1¼	−¼ to +1¼	+½	+½	1/16	18.51	20
1988	All	+3¼ to +5	+4	−¼ to +1¼	−¼ to +1¼	+½	+½	1/16	—	—

COOLING SYSTEM & CAPACITY DATA

Year	Model or Engine/VIN	Cooling Capacity, Qts. Less A/C	Cooling Capacity, Qts. With A/C	Radiator Cap Relief Pressure, Lbs.	Thermo. Opening Temp.	Fuel Tank Gals.	Engine Oil Refill Qts.①	Auto. Trans. Qts.②	Rear Axle Oil Pints
FORD									
1982	V8-255/D	14.7	15	16	191	20	4⑤	12	3¾
1982-83	V8-302/F	13	13.4	16	196	20	4⑤	12	3¾
1984-85	V8-302/F	13	13.4③	16	196	18④	4⑤	12.3	4
1986	V8-302	13	13.4③	16	196	18	4⑤	12.3	3.75
1987-88	V8-302	14.1⑥	14.1⑥	16	196	18	4⑤	12.3	3.75
MERCURY									
1982	V8-255/D	14.7	15	16	191	20	4⑤	12	3¾
1982-83	V8-302/F	13	13.4	16	196	20	4⑤	12	3¾
1984-85	V8-302/F	13	13.4③	16	196	18④	4⑤	12.3	4
1986	V8-302	13	13.4③	16	196	18	4⑤	12.3	3.75
1987-88	V8-302	14.1⑥	14.1⑥	16	196	18	4⑤	12.3	3.75

①—Add one quart with filter change.
②—Approximate. Make final check with dipstick.
③—Trailer tow, 14.6 qts.
④—Sta. Wag., 18.5 gals.
⑤—When changing engine oil on these models, both drain plugs must be removed to fully drain crankcase. One drain plug is located at the front of the oil pan, while the other drain plug is located at rear left side of the oil pan.
⑥—Trailer tow, 16.2 qts.

Electrical Section

INDEX

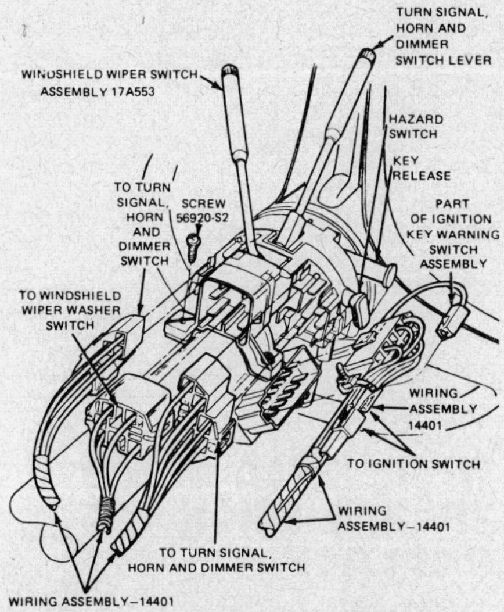

Fig. 1 Typical ignition switch. 1982–88

STARTER
REPLACE

STARTER PROBLEMS: If the starter is noisy or if it locks up, before condemning the starter, loosen the three mounting bolts enough to hand fit the starter properly into the pilot plate. Then tighten the mounting bolts, starting with the top bolt.

1. Disconnect battery ground cable.
2. Raise and support vehicle.
3. Disconnect starter cable from motor.
4. Remove mounting bolts and starter. **On some models it may be necessary to turn the wheels right or left to remove starter.**
5. Reverse procedure to install. Torque bolts to 15-20 ft. lbs.

IGNITION LOCK
REPLACE
1982–88

1. Disconnect battery ground cable.
2. Remove steering column trim shroud.
3. Disconnect key warning switch electrical connector.
4. Turn ignition lock to "On" or "Run" position.
5. Using a 1/8 inch pin or punch located in the 4 o'clock hole and 1 1/4 inch from outer edge of lock cylinder housing, depress retaining pin while pulling the lock cylinder from housing.
6. Turn lock cylinder to "On" or "Run" position and insert cylinder into housing. Ensure that the lock cylinder is fully seated and aligned into the interlocking washer before turning key to "Off" position. This will permit the retaining pin to extend into the lock cylinder housing hole.
7. Rotate key to check for proper mechanical operation.
8. Connect key warning switch electrical connector.
9. Connect battery ground cable.
10. Check for proper operation.

IGNITION SWITCH
REPLACE
1982–88

1. Disconnect battery ground cable.
2. Remove upper column shroud.
3. Disconnect ignition switch electrical connector.
4. With a 1/8 inch twist drill, drill out the switch retaining bolt heads, then remove the bolts with a "Easy Out" or equivalent.
5. Disengage ignition switch from actuator and remove from vehicle, **Fig. 1.**
6. Adjust ignition switch to "Run" position. Insert a .050 inch drill or equivalent through the switch housing and into the carrier to prevent movement. **A replacement ignition switch includes an installed adjusting pin.**
7. Place lock cylinder in the "Run" position, which is approximately 90° from the "Lock" position.
8. Install ignition switch on actuator pin.
9. Install switch break-off head mounting bolts and tighten until the bolt heads shear.
10. Remove adjusting pin or drill.
11. Connect ignition switch electrical connector.
12. Connect battery ground cable and check for proper operation.
13. Install column shroud.

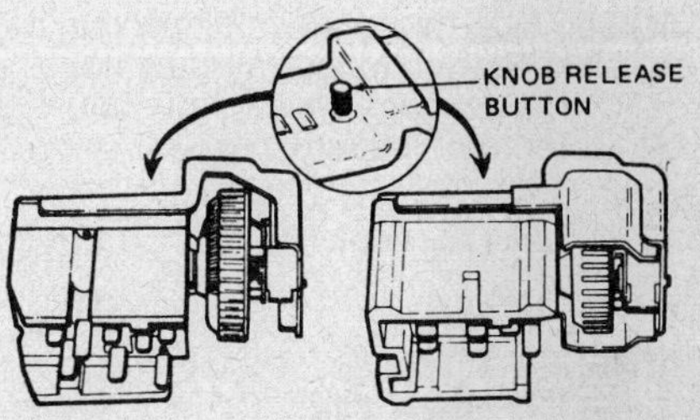

Fig. 2 Typical light switch

LIGHT SWITCH
REPLACE
1982–88

1. Disconnect battery ground cable.
2. Under instrument panel, depress light switch knob and shaft retainer button on side of switch and, while holding button in, pull knob and shaft assembly from switch, **Fig. 2.**
3. Unscrew trim bezel and remove locknut.
4. From under instrument panel, pull switch from panel while tilting downward, disconnect electrical connector and remove switch.
5. Reverse procedure to install.

STOP LIGHT SWITCH
REPLACE

1. Referring to **Fig. 3,** disconnect wires at connector.
2. Remove hairpin retainer and slide switch, pushrod and nylon washers and bushing away from pedal, and remove switch.
3. Position the new switch, pushrod, bushing and washers on brake pedal pin and secure with hairpin retainer.
4. Connect wires at connector and install wires in retaining clip.

TURN SIGNAL SWITCH

REPLACE

1982–88

1. Disconnect battery ground cable.
2. On models with tilt column, unsnap extension shroud, located below steering wheel, from retaining clip. On all models, remove attaching screws, then remove steering column trim shroud.
3. Remove turn signal switch lever by grasping lever and using a pulling twisting motion of the hand, while pulling lever straight out of switch.
4. Peel foam sight shield from switch, then disconnect two turn signal switch wire connectors.
5. Remove two screws attaching turn signal switch to lock cylinder housing, then disengage switch from housing.
6. Reverse procedure to install.

NEUTRAL SAFETY SWITCH

EXC. MODELS W/AUTOMATIC OVERDRIVE TRANSMISSION

The neutral safety switch has been eliminated and is replaced by a series of steps incorporated into the steering column selector lever hub casting.

MODELS W/AUTOMATIC OVERDRIVE TRANSMISSION

1. Disconnect battery ground cable.
2. Remove air cleaner assembly.
3. Place transmission selector lever in manual low position, then disconnect neutral safety switch electrical connector from switch. Lift connector straight off without any side-to-side motion.
4. Remove switch and O-ring using a 24 inch extension, universal adapter and socket No. T74P-77247-A. **Use of any tools other than those specified may result in damage to the vehicle.**
5. Reverse procedure to install. Torque switch to 7-10 ft. lbs.

HORN SOUNDER

REPLACE

1982–88

Refer to "Turn Signal Switch, Replace" for horn switch replacement.

INSTRUMENT CLUSTER

REPLACE

1982–88

1. Disconnect battery ground cable.
2. Disconnect speedometer cable.
3. Remove instrument cluster trim cover attaching screws and the trim cover.

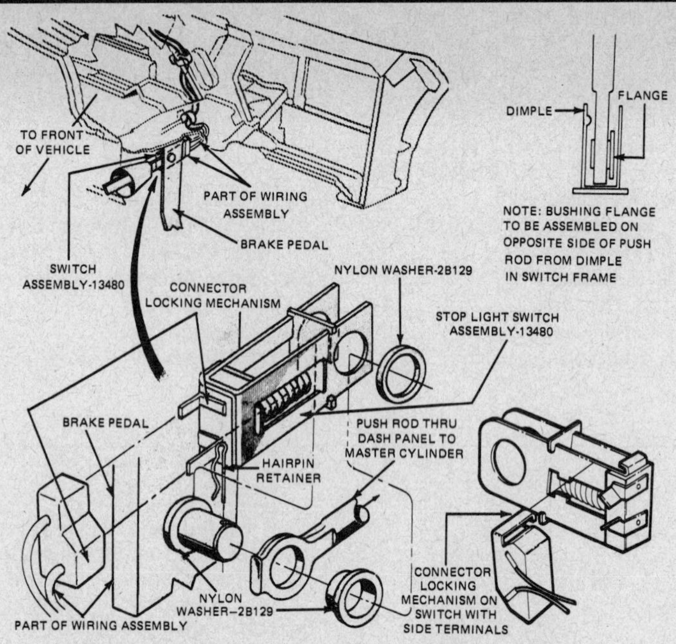

Fig. 3 Mechanical stop light switch

4. Remove the two lower steering column cover attaching screws and the cover.
5. Remove steering column shroud lower half.
6. Remove screws securing transmission indicator column bracket to steering column. Detach cable loop from pin on shift lever and remove bracket from column.
7. Remove four instrument cluster attaching screws.
8. Disconnect cluster feed plug and remove cluster assembly from vehicle.
9. Reverse procedure to install.

WINDSHIELD WIPER MOTOR

REPLACE

1982–88

1. Disconnect battery ground cable.
2. Disconnect right side washer nozzle hose and remove right side wiper arm and blade assembly from pivot shaft.
3. Remove wiper motor and linkage cover.
4. Disconnect linkage drive arm from the motor output arm crankpin by removing retaining clip.
5. Disconnect the wiring connectors from the motor.
6. Remove three bolts retaining the motor to the dash panel extension and the motor.
7. Reverse procedure to install.

WINDSHIELD WIPER SWITCH

REPLACE

1982–88

1. Disconnect battery ground cable.
2. Remove the steering column cover screws and separate the two halves.
3. Remove wiper switch retaining screws, disconnect wiring connector and remove switch.
4. Reverse procedure to install.

WINDSHIELD WIPER TRANSMISSION

REPLACE

1982–88

1. Disconnect battery ground cable.
2. Remove wiper arm and blade assemblies from the pivot shafts. Remove rear hood seal.
3. Remove wiper motor and linkage cover for access to linkage.
4. Disconnect the linkage drive arm from the motor crank pin by removing the retaining clip.
5. Remove the six bolts retaining the left and right pivot shafts to the cowl, and remove the complete linkage assembly.
6. Reverse procedure to install.

RADIO

REPLACE

When installing radio, be sure to adjust antenna trimmer for peak performance.

1982–88

For an all-electronic radio, perform step 6 first.

1. Disconnect battery ground cable.
2. Remove radio knobs and screws attaching the bezel to instrument panel.
3. Remove the radio mounting plate attaching screws.
4. Pull radio to disengage it from the lower rear support bracket.
5. Disconnect radio wiring and remove radio.

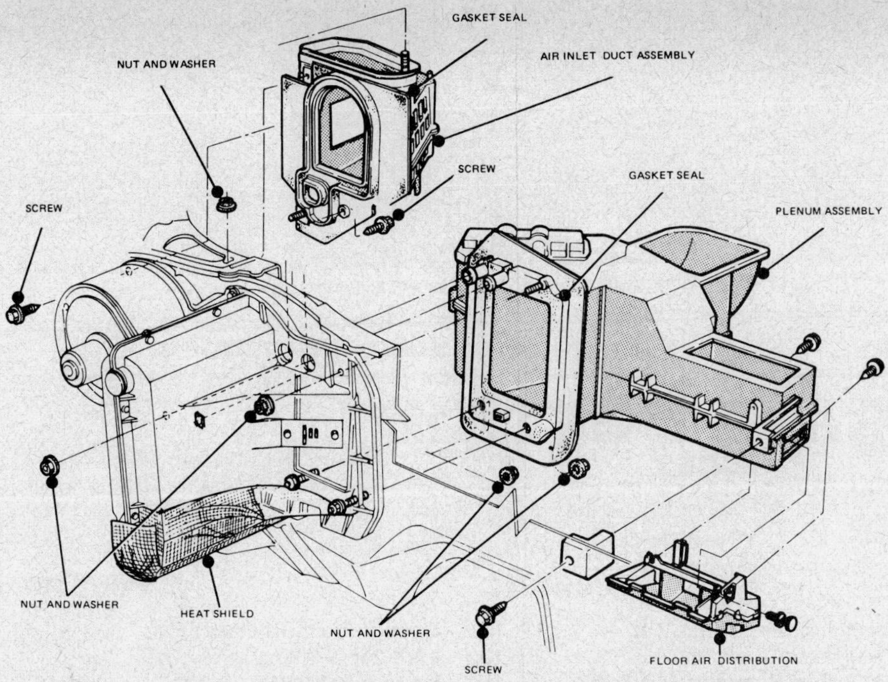

Fig. 4 Typical plenum assembly removal. 1982–88

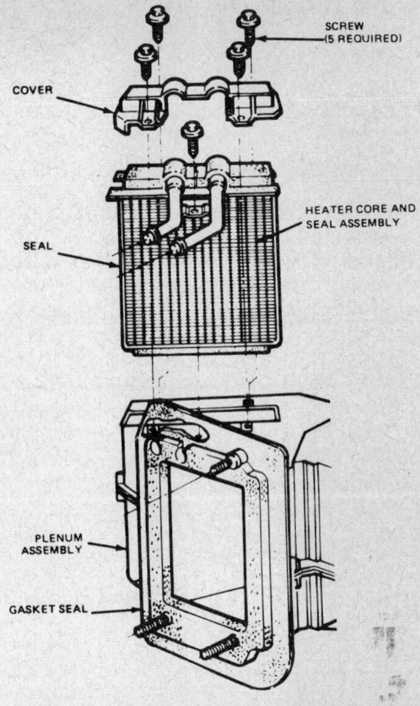

Fig. 5 Typical heater core removal. 1982–88

6. Remove the radio to mounting plate retaining nuts and washers and remove the mounting plate.
7. Remove the rear upper support retaining nut and remove the support.
8. Reverse procedure to install. Perform step 6 first if equipped with all-electronic radio.

HEATER CORE REPLACE

1982–88

1. Disconnect battery ground cable, then drain cooling system.
2. Disconnect heater hoses from heater core. Plug heater hoses and core fittings to prevent coolant spillage.
3. Remove bolt located below windshield wiper motor, attaching left end of plenum to dash panel.
4. Remove nut attaching upper lefthand corner of evaporator or heater case to dash panel.
5. Disconnect vacuum control system supply hose from vacuum source, then push grommet and hose into passenger compartment.
6. Remove glove box, then loosen righthand door sill plate and remove side cowl trim panel.
7. Remove bolt attaching righthand side of instrument panel to side cowl.
8. Remove instrument panel pad as follows:
   a. Remove two screws from each defroster nozzle opening in pad.
   b. From front lower edge of panel pad, remove five attaching screws.
   c. From each end of pad, remove one attaching screw.
   d. Lift pad assembly from instrument panel.
9. On models less ATC, disconnect temperature control cable from plenum bracket and blend air door crank.
10. On models equipped with ATC, disconnect temperature control cable and vacuum harness connector from ATC sensor. Disconnect ATC sensor tube from sensor and evaporator case connector, then disconnect wire connector from EV relay.
11. On all models, remove push clip attaching center duct bracket to plenum, then rotate bracket upward and to the right.
12. Disconnect vacuum harness at vacuum connector near floor air distribution duct.
13. Disconnect the white vacuum hose from the outside recirculating air door vacuum motor.
14. Remove two screws from rear side of floor air distribution duct to plenum, **Fig. 4.** To remove the righthand screw, it may be necessary to remove the two screws attaching the lower panel door vacuum motor to the mounting bracket.
15. Remove push fastener attaching floor air distribution duct to left end of plenum, then remove floor air distribution duct.
16. Remove two nuts located along lower flange of plenum.
17. Carefully move plenum rearward, so that heater core tubes and plenum case upper stud clear openings in dash panel, then remove plenum from vehicle by rotating upper portion of the plenum forward, down and out from under instrument panel. It may be necessary to carefully pull the lower edge of the instrument panel rearward while the plenum is being removed from behind the instrument panel.
18. Remove retaining screws from heater core cover, then the cover from the plenum assembly, **Fig. 5.**
19. Remove retaining screw from heater core inlet and outlet tube bracket.
20. Pull heater core and seal assembly from plenum assembly.
21. Reverse procedure to install.

BLOWER MOTOR REPLACE

1982–88

1. Disconnect battery ground cable.
2. Disconnect blower motor ground wire and the engine ground wire and position wiring aside.
3. Disconnect blower motor lead connector from wiring harness hard shell connector.
4. Remove blower motor cooling tube from blower motor.
5. Remove blower motor retaining screws.
6. Rotate blower motor slightly to the right so the bottom edge of the mounting plate follows the contour of the wheelwell splash panel. Then, lift blower motor up and out of housing assembly.
7. Reverse procedure to install.

SPEED CONTROLS

1982–88

Actuator Cable Adjustment

1. Remove cable retaining clip.
2. Deactivate the throttle positioner, as required.

3. Set throttle plate in closed position.
4. Pull the actuator cable to remove slack.
5. While maintaining light tension on the actuator cable, insert the cable retaining clip.

Vacuum Dump Valve

The vacuum dump valve is mounted on a moveable mounting bracket, **Fig. 6.** The valve should be adjusted so that it is closed when the brake pedal is not depressed and opens when the brake pedal is depressed.

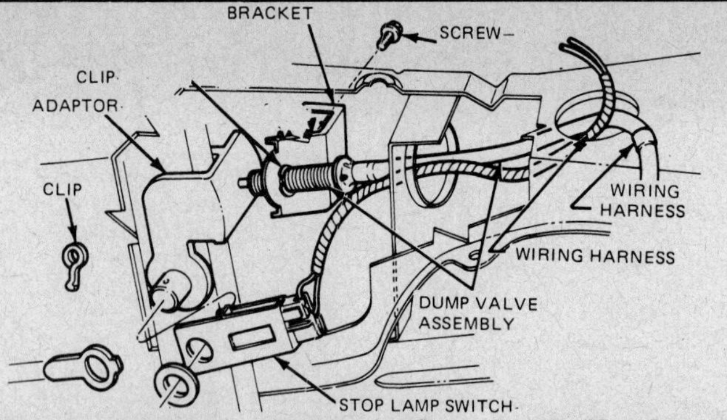

Fig. 6 Vacuum pump valve installation

Engine Section

INDEX

ENGINE MOUNTS

REPLACE

Whenever self-locking mounting bolts and nuts are removed, they must be replaced with new self-locking bolts and nuts.

1982–88 V8-255 & 302

1. Remove fan shroud attaching screw.
2. On all models, remove nut and through bolt attaching insulator to support bracket, **Fig. 1.**
3. Raise the engine slightly with a jack and a wood block placed under the oil pan.
4. Remove the engine insulator assembly to cylinder block attaching bolts. Remove the engine insulator assembly and the heat shield, if so equipped.
5. Reverse procedure to install.

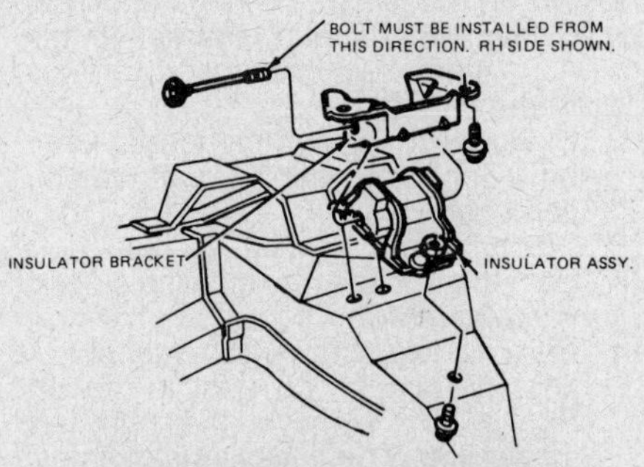

Fig. 1 Engine mount. 1982–88 V8-255 & 302

ENGINE

REPLACE

Because of engine compartment tolerances, the engine should not be removed and installed with the transmission attached.

1982–88 V8-255 & 302

1. Disconnect battery and alternator ground cables.
2. Drain cooling system and oil pan.
3. Remove hood.
4. Remove air cleaner and intake duct assembly.
5. Disconnect radiator hoses from engine.
6. Disconnect transmission oil cooler lines from radiator.
7. Remove fan shroud attaching bolts, then the radiator, fan, spacer, pulley and shroud.
8. Remove alternator mounting bolts and position alternator aside.
9. Disconnect oil pressure sending unit electrical connector.
10. Relieve fuel pressure, then disconnect fuel tank line at fuel pump and plug line.
11. Disconnect accelerator cable and speed control cable, if equipped, from carburetor or throttle body.
12. Disconnect throttle valve vacuum line from intake manifold, if equipped.
13. Disconnect manual shift rod and retracting spring at shift rod stud.
14. Disconnect transmission filler tube bracket from engine block.
15. Isolate and remove A/C compressor from vehicle, if equipped.
16. Disconnect power steering pump bracket from cylinder head and water pump and position aside, if equipped.
17. Disconnect power brake vacuum line from intake manifold, if equipped.
18. Disconnect heater hoses from engine.
19. Disconnect coolant temperature sending unit electrical connector.
20. Remove upper converter housing to engine attaching bolts.
21. Disconnect ignition coil and distributor wiring. Remove harness from left-hand rocker arm cover and position aside. Disconnect ground strap from engine block.
22. Raise and support front of vehicle.
23. Disconnect starter motor wiring and remove starter motor.

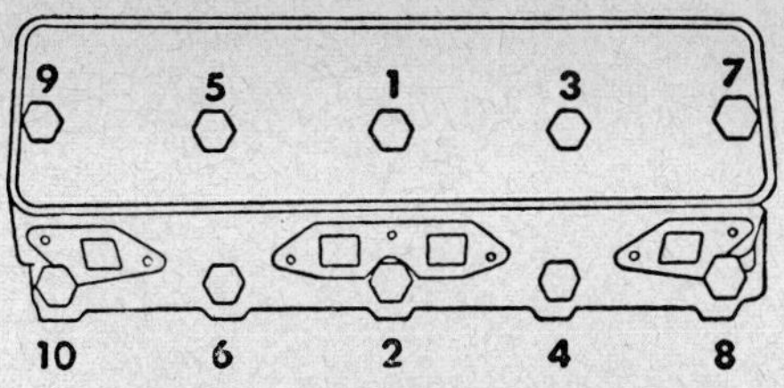

Fig. 2 Cylinder head tightening sequence

24. Disconnect exhaust pipes from manifold.
25. Disconnect engine mounts from frame brackets.
26. Disconnect secondary air line to catalytic converter, if equipped.
27. Disconnect transmission oil cooler lines from retainer.
28. Remove converter housing inspection cover.
29. Disconnect converter from flywheel. Secure converter in housing.
30. Remove remaining converter housing to engine bolts.
31. Lower vehicle and support transmission. Attach suitable engine lifting equipment to engine.
32. Raise engine slightly and pull forward to disengage from transmission.
33. Remove engine from vehicle.
34. Reverse procedure to install.

CYLINDER HEAD
REPLACE

Tighten cylinder head bolts a little at a time in three steps in the sequence shown in **Fig. 2.** Final tightening should be to the torque specifications listed in the "Engine Tightening" table. After bolts have been tightened to specifications, they should not be disturbed.

1982–88 V8-255 & 302

1. Disconnect battery ground cable.
2. Remove intake manifold as an assembly.
3. Remove rocker arm cover.
4. If left cylinder head is being removed, isolate and remove A/C compressor, if equipped.
5. Remove EGR cooler, if equipped.
6. If left cylinder head is being removed, disconnect power steering pump bracket from cylinder head and engine block and position assembly aside.
7. Remove Thermactor crossover tube from rear of cylinder heads.
8. If right cylinder head is being removed, remove alternator bracket bolt and spacer and, if equipped, the A/C compressor mounting bracket.
9. Loosen rocker arm stud nuts or bolts so that rocker arms can be rotated to the side.
10. Remove pushrods, keeping them in sequence so they may be returned to their original locations. Remove exhaust valve stem caps.
11. Disconnect exhaust pipes from exhaust manifold.
12. Unfasten and remove cylinder head.

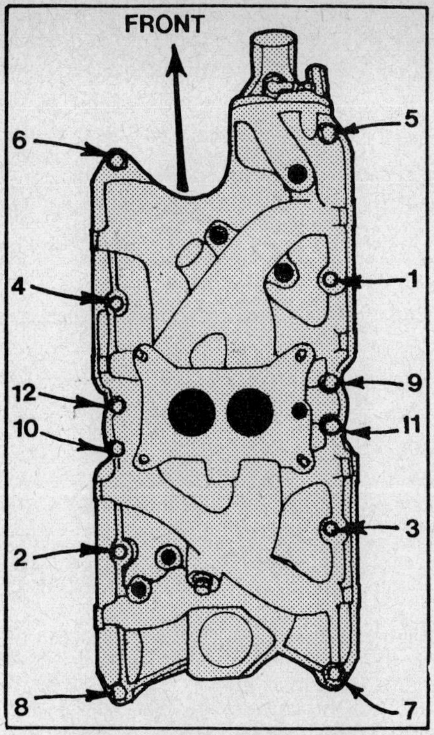

Fig. 3 Typical intake manifold tightening sequence. V8-255 & 302

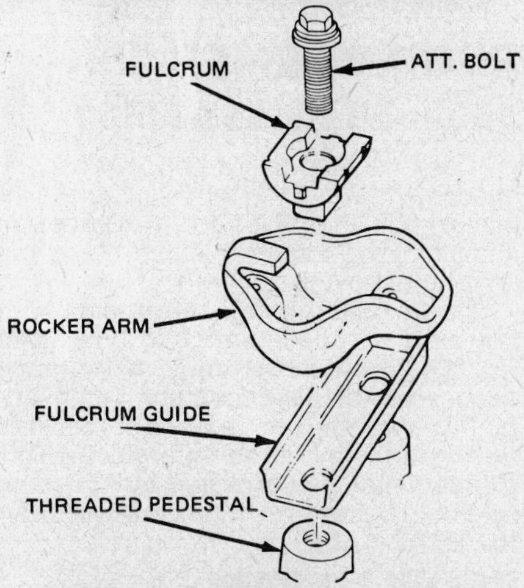

Fig. 5 Rocker arm. 1982–88 V8-255 & 302

13. Reverse removal procedure to install the head. Tighten cylinder head down in the sequence shown in **Fig. 2.** When installing intake manifold refer to **Fig. 3** for bolt tightening sequence.

When installing intake manifold, a 1/8 inch bead of RTV sealer should be applied at mating surfaces of intake manifold, cylinder head and cylinder block, **Fig. 4.** After intake manifold seals and gaskets have been positioned, apply a 1/16 inch bead of RTV sealer to the outer end of each intake manifold seal for the entire width of the seal, **Fig. 4.**

On V8-302 engines equipped with cork intake manifold seals, both the front and rear seals should be replaced with RTV sealer. Apply a 1/4 inch bead of sealer to front and rear sealing surfaces of engine block.

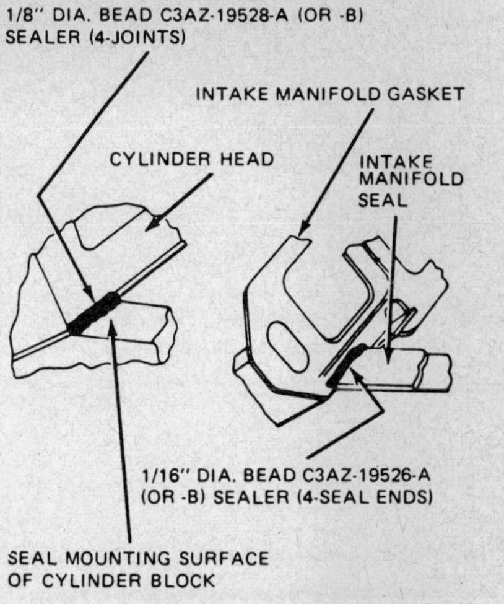

Fig. 4 Applying RTV sealer for intake manifold installation

VALVE ARRANGEMENT
FRONT TO REAR

Right .... I-E-I-E-I-E-I-E
Left...................... E-I-E-I-E-I-E-I

VALVE LIFT SPECIFICATIONS

Engine	Year	Intake	Exhaust
V8-255	1982	.375	.375
V8-302	1982-88	.375	.391

VALVE TIMING
INTAKE OPENS BEFORE TDC

Engine	Year	Degrees
V8-255	1982	16
V8-302	1982-88	16

VALVE CLEARANCE SPECIFICATIONS

Engine	Year	Clearance
V8-255	1982	.096-.146
V8-302	1982-88	.096-.146

Clearance specified is at valve stem tip with lifter collapsed, refer to text for procedure.

VALVES
ADJUST

To eliminate the need of adjusting valve lash, a positive stop fulcrum bolt and seat is used on 1982-88 V8-255 and 302 engines, **Fig. 5.**

It is very important that the correct pushrod be used and all components be in-

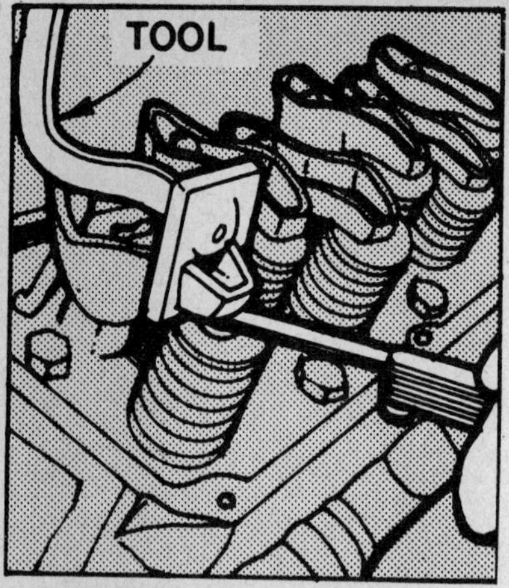

Fig. 6 Checking valve clearance

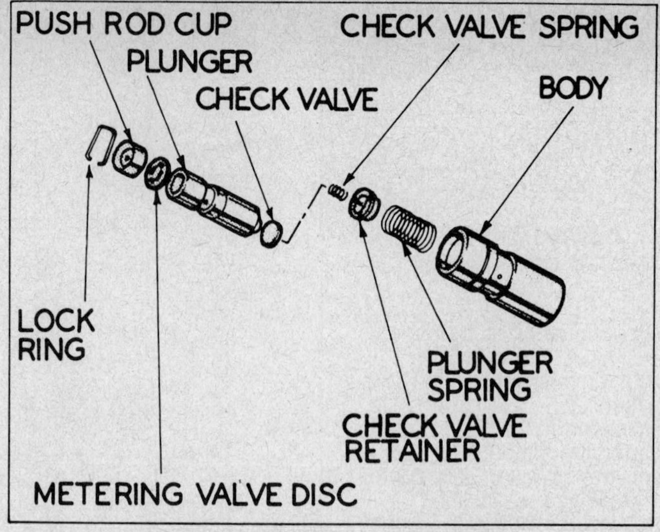

Fig. 7 Typical conventional hydraulic valve lifter disassembled

stalled and torqued as follows:

1. Position the piston of the cylinder being worked on at TDC of its compression stroke.
2. Install rocker arm, fulcrum seat and oil deflector. Install fulcrum bolt and torque to 18-25 ft. lbs.

A .060 inch shorter pushrod or a .060 inch longer rod are available for service to provide a means of compensating for dimensional changes in the valve mechanism. Valve stem-to-rocker arm clearance should be .096-.146 inch, with the hydraulic lifter completely collapsed, **Fig. 6.** Repeated valve grind jobs will decrease this clearance to the point that if not compensated for the lifters will cease to function.

When checking valve clearance, if the clearance is less than the minimum, the .060 inch shorter pushrod should be used. If clearance is more than the maximum, the .060 inch longer pushrod should be used. To check valve clearance, proceed as follows:

1. Mark crankshaft pulley at three locations, with number 1 location at TDC timing mark (end of compression stroke), number 2 location one half turn (180°) clockwise from TDC and number 3 location three quarter turn clockwise (270°) from number 2 location.
2. Turn the crankshaft to the number 1 location and check the clearance on the following valves:
   a. Intake Nos. 1, 7 and 8; exhaust Nos. 1, 4 and 5.
3. Turn the crankshaft to the number 2 location and check the clearance on the following valves:
   a. Intake Nos. 4 and 5; exhaust Nos. 2 and 6.
4. Turn the crankshaft to the number 3 location and check the clearance on the following valves:
   a. Intake Nos. 2, 3 and 6; exhaust Nos. 3, 7 and 8.

VALVE GUIDES

Valve guides in these engines are an integral part of the head and, therefore, cannot be removed. For service, guides can be reamed oversize to accommodate one of three service valves with oversize stems (.003 inch, .015 inch and .030 inch).

Check the valve stem clearance of each valve (after cleaning) in its respective valve guide. If the clearance exceeds the service limits of .0055 inch, ream the valve guides to accommodate the next oversize diameter valve.

ROCKER ARMS

1982–88 V8-255 & 302

These engines use a bolt and fulcrum attachment, **Fig. 5.** To remove, remove attaching bolt, then the fulcrum, rocker arm and fulcrum guide, if the other rocker arm is being removed.

Some 1982 models equipped with low profile rocker arm fulcrums (part No. E1TZ-6A528-A) may experience excessive oil displacement when engine is operated for extended periods during high ambient temperatures. This problem may be corrected by replacing original rocker arm fulcrums with part No. D7AZ-6A528-A.

VALVE LIFTERS REPLACE

The internal parts of each hydraulic valve lifter assembly are a matched set. If these are mixed, improper valve operation may result. Therefore, disassemble, inspect and test each assembly separately to prevent mixing the parts.

Fig. 7 illustrates one type of hydraulic lifter used. On some late model V8-302 engines, a roller type hydraulic lifter is used instead of the conventional lifter.

1. Remove intake manifold and related parts.
2. Remove rocker arm covers.
3. Loosen rocker arm stud nuts or bolts and rotate rocker arms to the side.
4. Lift out pushrods, keeping them in sequence in a rack so they may be installed in their original location. **On some late model V8-302 engines with roller type lifters, pushrods have a collar at upper end and can only be installed one way.**
5. On V8-302 engines with roller type lifters, remove lifter guide retainer attaching bolts, then the guide retainer and guide plates. Ensure guide retainer and plates are marked so they may be installed in their original location.
6. On all models, remove valve lifters, using a magnet rod, and place them in sequence in a rack so they may be installed in their original location.
7. Reverse procedure to install.

TIMING CASE COVER REPLACE

To replace seal in timing gear cover, it is necessary to remove the cover as outlined below.

1982–88 V8-255 & 302

1. Drain cooling system and oil pan.
2. Disconnect lower radiator hose from water pump.
3. Disconnect heater hose from water pump and slide water pump bypass hose clamp toward pump.
4. Unfasten and position alternator and bracket out of way.
5. If equipped with power steering or air conditioning, remove the drive belts.
6. Remove the fan, spacer, pulley and drive belt.
7. Remove crankshaft pulley and vibration damper. **Disconnect crankshaft position sensor electrical connector, if equipped.**
8. Disconnect fuel pump outlet line from pump and remove pump retaining bolts and lay pump to one side with flex line attached.
9. Remove oil dipstick and the oil pan to front cover attaching bolts.
10. Unfasten and remove the front cover and water pump as an assembly.
11. Reverse procedure to install.

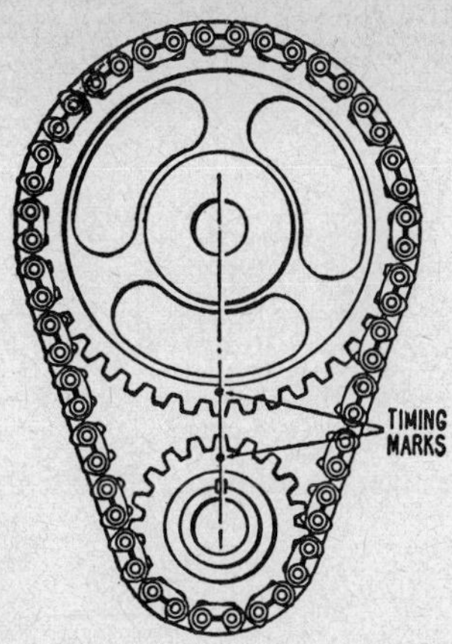

Fig. 8 Timing marks aligned for correct valve timing

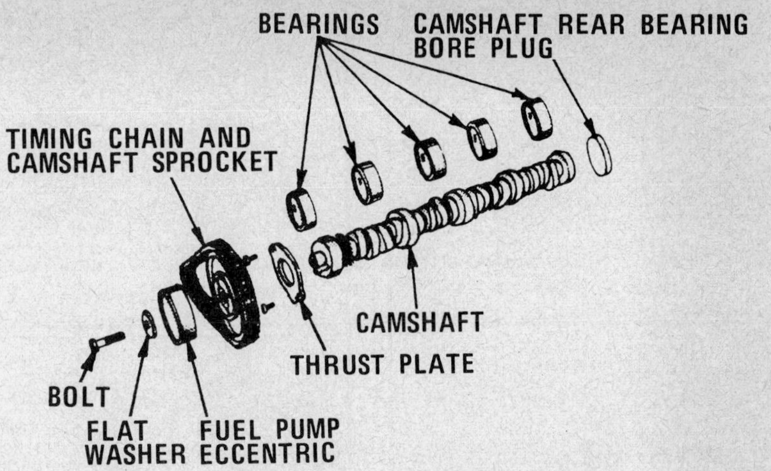

Fig. 9 Camshaft & related parts

TIMING CHAIN
REPLACE
1982–88 V8-255 & 302

After removing the cover as outlined above, crank the engine until the timing marks are aligned as shown in **Fig. 8.** Remove camshaft sprocket retaining bolt, washer, fuel pump eccentric and spacer, if equipped. Slide both sprockets and chain forward and remove them as an assembly.

Reverse procedure to install the chain and sprockets, being sure the timing marks are aligned.

CAMSHAFT
REPLACE

It may be necessary to remove or reposition radiator, A/C compressor and grille components to provide adequate clearance.

1. To remove camshaft, remove cylinder front cover and timing chain.
2. Remove distributor cap and spark plug wires, then remove distributor.
3. Disconnect automatic transmission oil cooler lines from radiator and remove radiator.
4. Remove intake manifold as an assembly.
5. Remove rocker arm covers.
6. Loosen rocker arm stud nuts or bolts and rotate rocker arms to one side.
7. Remove pushrods, keeping them in sequence in a rack so they may be installed in their original location.
8. Using a magnet, remove valve lifters and place them in a rack in sequence so they may be installed in their original location.
9. Remove camshaft thrust plate, **Fig. 9** and carefully pull camshaft from engine, using care to avoid damaging camshaft bearings.
10. Reverse procedure to install.

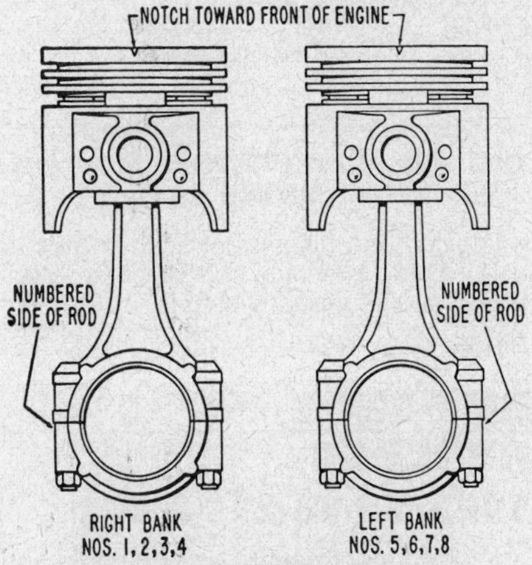

Fig. 10 Piston & rod assembly

CAMSHAFT BEARINGS

When necessary to replace camshaft bearings, the engine will have to be removed from the vehicle and the plug at the rear of the cylinder block will have to be removed in order to utilize the special camshaft bearing removing and installing tools required to do this job. If properly installed, camshaft bearings require no reaming—nor should this type bearing be reamed or altered in any manner in an attempt to fit bearings.

PISTON & ROD
ASSEMBLE

Assemble the pistons to the rods so the notch or arrow faces toward the front of engine and the numbered side of rod faces away from center of engine, **Fig. 10.** After installation, check side clearance between connecting rods at each crankshaft journal. Clearance should be .010-.020 in.

PISTONS, PINS & RINGS

Pistons and rings are available in standard sizes and oversizes of .003, .020, .030 and .040 inch.

Oversize piston pins of .001 and .002 inch are available.

MAIN & ROD BEARINGS

Main and rod bearings are available in standard sizes and the following undersizes: .001, .002, .010, .020, .030, .040 inch.

CRANKSHAFT OIL SEAL
REPLACE
1982–83

A rubber split-lip rear crankshaft oil seal is available for service. This seal can be installed without removal of the crankshaft and also eliminates the necessity of seal installation tools.

1. Remove oil pan and, if necessary, the oil pump.
2. Remove rear main bearing cap.
3. Loosen remaining bearing caps, allowing crankshaft to drop down about $1/32$ inch.
4. Remove old seals from both cylinder block and rear main bearing cap. Use a brass rod to drift upper half of seal from cylinder block groove. Rotate crankshaft while drifting to facilitate removal.
5. Carefully clean seal groove in block with a brush and solvent. Also clean seal groove in bearing cap. Remove the oil seal retaining pin from the bearing cap if so equipped. The pin is not used with the split-lip seal.
6. Dip seal halves in clean engine oil.
7. Carefully install upper seal half in its groove with undercut side of seal toward front of engine, **Fig. 11,** by rotating it on shaft journal of crankshaft until approximately $3/8$ inch protrudes below the parting surface. Be sure no rubber has been shaved from outside diameter of seal by bottom edge of groove.

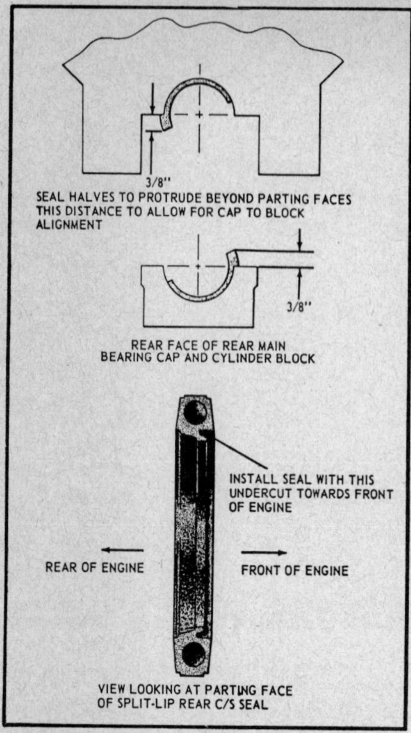

Fig. 11 Split-lip rear crankshaft seal installation. 1982–83

8. Retighten main bearing caps and torque to specifications.
9. Install lower seal in main bearing cap with undercut side of seal toward front of engine, and allow seal to protrude about 3/8 inch above parting surface to mate with upper seal upon cap installation.
10. Apply suitable sealer to parting faces of cap and block. Install cap and torque to specifications. If difficulty is encountered in installing the upper half of the seal in position, lightly lap (sandpaper) the side of the seal opposite the lip side using a medium grit paper. After sanding, the seal must be washed in solvent, then dipped in clean engine oil prior to installation.

A revised crankshaft rear oil seal has been released for service. This new seal may be received when ordering an oil pan gasket kit and is installed in the same manner as described previously, Fig. 12.

1984–88

A one piece crankshaft rear main oil seal must be used when replacement of seal required.

1. Punch one hole into seal metal surface between seal lip and engine block using a suitable tool.
2. Screw threaded end of suitable slide hammer into hole and remove seal. Use caution not to damage oil seal surface.
3. Lubricate new seal with engine oil, then position seal on rear oil seal installer T82L-6701-A or equivalent.
4. Position tool and seal on rear of engine, then install tool attaching bolts. Tighten attaching bolts alternately until seal is properly seated.

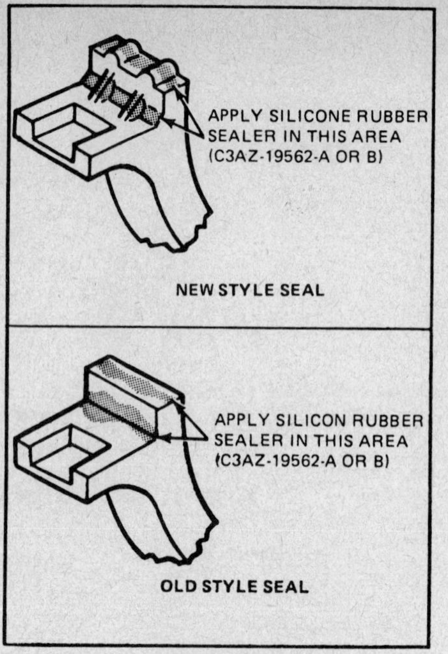

Fig. 12 Crankshaft rear oil seals

OIL PAN

REPLACE

1982–88 V8-255 & 302

1. Disconnect battery ground cable and remove air cleaner assembly.
2. Disconnect accelerator cable and kickdown rod from carburetor or TV cables from throttle body.
3. Remove accelerator mounting bracket bolts and bracket, then the EGR valve, if necessary.
4. Remove fan shroud attaching screws and position shroud over fan.
5. Disconnect wiper motor electrical connector and remove wiper motor.
6. Disconnect windshield washer hose.
7. Remove wiper motor mounting cover.
8. Remove oil level dipstick, then the dipstick tube retaining bolt from exhaust manifold.
9. If equipped with EGR cooler or EEC, remove Thermactor air dump tube retaining clamp, then the Thermactor crossover tube at rear of engine.
10. On all models, raise and support vehicle.
11. Drain oil pan.
12. On vehicles equipped with EGR cooler or EEC, remove filler tube from transmission oil pan and drain transmission, then remove starter motor.
13. Disconnect fuel line at fuel pump and plug line. **Vehicles equipped with electronic fuel injection use a high pressure electric fuel pump. Prior to disconnecting fuel lines from the pump, pressure must be released at the Schrader valve on the fuel charging assembly.**
14. Disconnect exhaust pipes from manifolds.
15. If equipped with EGR cooler or EEC, remove exhaust gas sensor from exhaust manifold, then the Thermactor secondary air tube to converter housing clamps.
16. Loosen rear engine mount attaching nuts.
17. Remove engine mount through bolts.
18. Remove shift crossover bolts at transmission.
19. If equipped with EGR cooler or EEC, disconnect exhaust pipes from catalytic converter outlet, then the catalytic converter secondary air tube and inlet pipes to exhaust manifold.
20. On all models, disconnect transmission kickdown rod.
21. Remove torque converter housing cover.
22. Remove brake line retainer from front crossmember.
23. With a suitable jack, raise engine as far as possible.
24. Place a block of wood between each engine mount and chassis bracket. When engine is secured in this position, remove jack.
25. Remove oil pan attaching bolts and lower the oil pan.
26. Remove oil pickup tube bolts and lower tube in oil pan.
27. Remove oil pan from vehicle.
28. Reverse procedure to install.

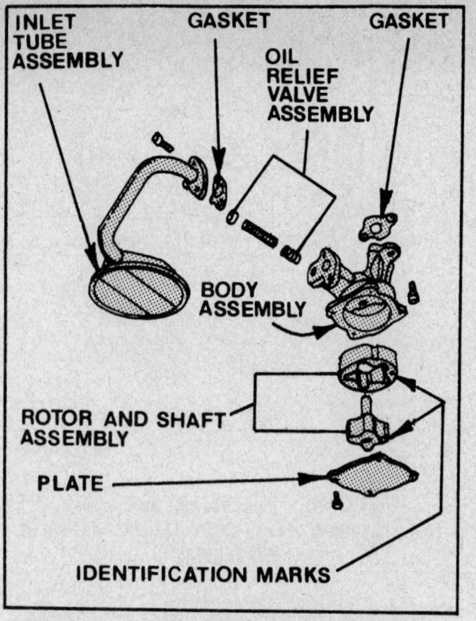

Fig. 13 Typical oil pump. V8-255 & 302

OIL PUMP

REPLACE

1. Remove oil pan as described under "Oil Pan, Replace" procedure.
2. Remove oil inlet pickup tube and screen assembly.
3. Remove oil pump attaching bolts, then the oil pump and intermediate drive shaft.

4. Reverse procedure to install. Prime oil pump with engine oil before installing. Position intermediate drive shaft into distributor sprocket. With intermediate drive shaft firmly seated, the stop on the shaft should contact crankcase surface. Remove shaft and adjust as necessary. Position pump with intermediate drive shaft insert to cylinder block, then install and torque attaching bolts to 22 to 32 ft. lbs.

Do not force oil pump into position on cylinder block. If pump drive shaft is misaligned with distributor shaft, rotate drive shaft to a new position.

OIL PUMP SERVICE

1. With all parts clean and dry, check the inside of the pump housing and the outer race and rotor for damage or excessive wear, **Fig. 13.**
2. Check the mating surface of the pump cover for wear. If this surface is worn, scored or grooved, replace the pump.
3. Measure the clearance between the outer race and housing. This clearance should be .001-.013 inch.
4. With the rotor assembly installed in the housing, place a straightedge over the rotor assembly and housing. Measure the clearance between the straightedge and the rotor and outer race. Maximum recommended limits is .004 inch. The outer race, shaft and rotor are furnished only as an assembly.
5. Check the drive shaft-to-housing bearing clearance by measuring the O.D. of the shaft and the I.D. of the housing bearing. The recommended clearance limits are .0015-.0030 inch.
6. Inspect the relief valve spring for a collapsed or worn condition.
7. Check the relief valve piston for scores and free operation in the bore. The specified piston clearance is .0015-.0030 inch.

BELT TENSION DATA

Belt	New Lbs.	Used Lbs.
1982–88		
1/4 inch V Belt	65	50
All other V Belts	140	105
4K Exc. Air Pump①	130	115
4K Air Pump①	110	105
5K②	150	135
6K③	113	110
6K④	160	145

①—4 grooves.
②—5 grooves fixed.
③—6 grooves with tensioner.
④—6 grooves fixed.

WATER PUMP REPLACE

1. Drain cooling system, then remove carburetor air inlet tube.
2. On models equipped with a fan shroud, remove shroud attaching bolts and place shroud over fan and spacer. Remove fan and spacer from water pump shaft, then remove fan shroud.
3. Remove alternator drive belt, A/C drive belt and idler pulley bracket, if so equipped. Remove power steering drive belt and power steering pump, if so equipped. Remove all brackets from water pump, then remove water pump.
4. Disconnect radiator lower hose and heater hose at water pump.
5. Remove drive belt, fan, spacer or fan drive clutch and pulley.
6. Reverse procedure to install.

FUEL PUMP REPLACE

MECHANICAL TYPE

1. Loosen, then retighten fuel line connection(s) using a suitable wrench. Do not disconnect lines at this time.
2. Loosen fuel pump attaching bolts one or two turns. Apply hand force to pump to loosen gasket.
3. Rotate engine until fuel pump cam lobe is near low position to reduce pressure on pump.
4. Disconnect fuel lines and, if equipped, the vapor return line from pump.
5. Remove fuel pump attaching bolts and pump. Remove and discard gasket.
6. Clean all gasket material from engine and fuel pump.
7. Install attaching bolts into fuel pump, then install new gasket over bolts.
8. Install pump and tighten attaching bolts alternately and evenly.
9. Connect fuel lines and vapor return line, if equipped, then operate engine and check for leaks.

Rear Axle, Propeller Shaft & Brakes

INDEX

REAR AXLE

Fig. 1 illustrates the rear axle assembly used on these vehicles. When necessary to overhaul these units, refer to the "Rear Axle Specifications" table in this chapter.

The gear set consists of a ring gear and an overhung drive pinion which is supported by two opposed tapered roller bearings, **Fig. 1.** The differential case is a one-piece design with openings allowing assembly of the internal parts and lubricant flow. The differential pinion shaft is retained with a threaded bolt (lock) assembled to the case.

The roller type wheel bearings have no inner race, and the rollers directly contact the bearing journals of the axle shafts. The axle shafts do not use an inner and outer bearing retainer. Rather, they are held in the axle by means of C-locks, **Fig. 2.** These C-locks also fit into a machined recess in the differential side gears within the differential case. There is no retainer bolt access hole in the axle shaft flange.

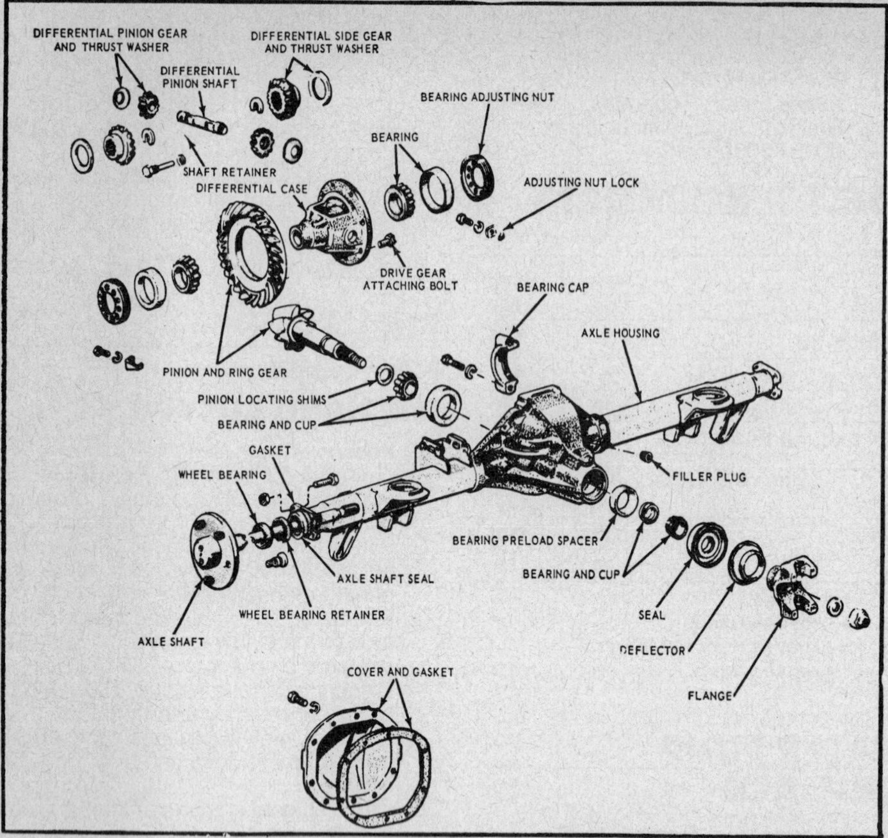

Fig. 1 Integral type rear axle assembly (typical)

Fig. 2 Axle shaft C locks. Integral type axle

Fig. 3 Using hook-type tool to remove oil seal

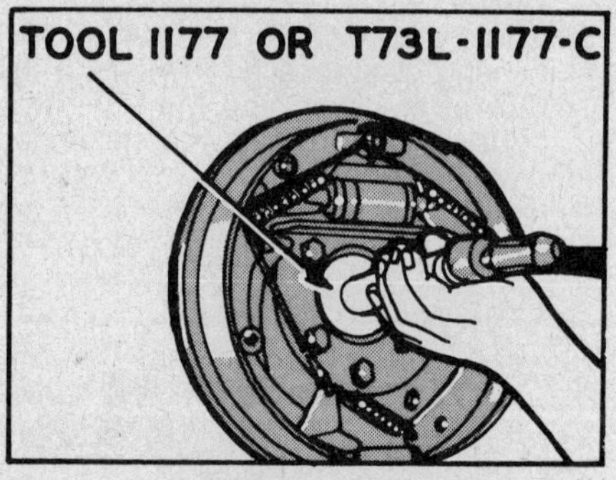

Fig. 4 Using special driver to install oil seal

REAR AXLE, REPLACE

1. Raise vehicle and support using jack stands under both frame side rails.
2. Mark drive shaft and pinion flange for reassembly, then disconnect drive shaft at pinion flange and remove drive shaft from transmission extension housing. Install seal replacer tool in extension housing to prevent leakage.
3. Disconnect parking brake cable and brake lines. Cover brake lines to prevent contamination.
4. Support axle with jack, then lower axle far enough to relieve spring tension.
5. Disconnect shock absorbers at lower mounting brackets.
6. If equipped, disconnect track bar from axle housing stud.
7. Remove nuts, washers and pivot bolts connecting lower suspension arms to axle housing, then disconnect both arms from housing.
8. Remove nuts, bolts, washers and two eccentric washers, then disconnect upper suspension arm from axle housing.
9. Lower rear axle and remove from vehicle.

AXLE SHAFT, BEARING & SEAL, REPLACE

1. Raise car on hoist and remove wheels.
2. Drain differential lubricant.
3. Remove brake drums.
4. Remove differential housing cover.
5. Position safety stands under rear frame member and lower hoist to allow axle to lower as far as possible.
6. Working through differential case opening, remove pinion shaft lock bolt and pinion shaft.
7. Remove wheel speed sensor, if equipped.
8. Push axle shaft(s) inward toward center of axle housing and remove C-lock(s) from housing, **Fig. 2.**
9. Remove axle shaft, using extreme care to avoid contact of shaft seal lip with any portion of axle shaft except seal journal.
10. Use a hook-type puller to remove seal and bearing, **Fig. 3.**
11. Reverse procedure to install, using suitable driving tools, **Fig. 4,** to install seal and bearing. New seals are prepacked with lubricant and do not require oil soaking before installation.

PROPELLER SHAFT REPLACE

1. Mark the relationship of the driveshaft to pinion flange, then disconnect rear U-joint or companion flange from drive pinion flange.
2. Pull drive shaft toward rear of car until front U-joint yoke clears transmission extension housing and output shaft.
3. Install a suitable tool, such as a seal driver, in seal to prevent lube from leaking from transmission.
4. Before installing, check U-joints for freedom of movement. If a bind has resulted from misalignment after overhauling the U-joints, tap the ears of the drive shaft sharply to relieve the bind.
5. If rubber seal installed on end of transmission extension housing is damaged, install a new seal.
6. Lubricate yoke spline with special spline lubricant. This spline is sealed so that transmission fluid does not "wash" away spline lubricant.
7. Install yoke on transmission output shaft.
8. Align marks on driveshaft and pinion flange, then install U-bolts and nuts which attach U-joint to pinion flange. Tighten U-bolts evenly to prevent binding U-joint bearings.

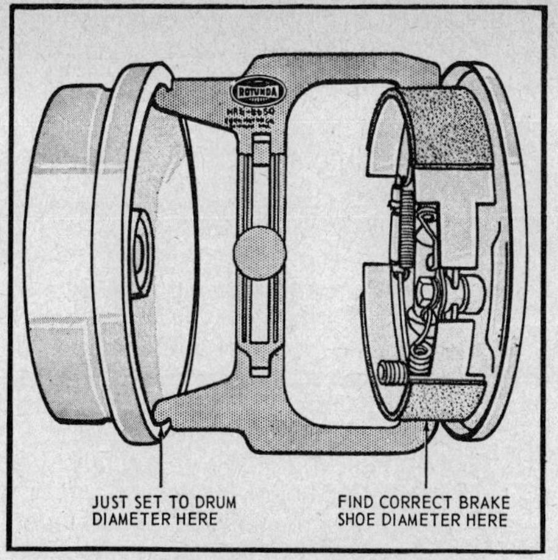

Fig. 5 Brake adjustment gauge

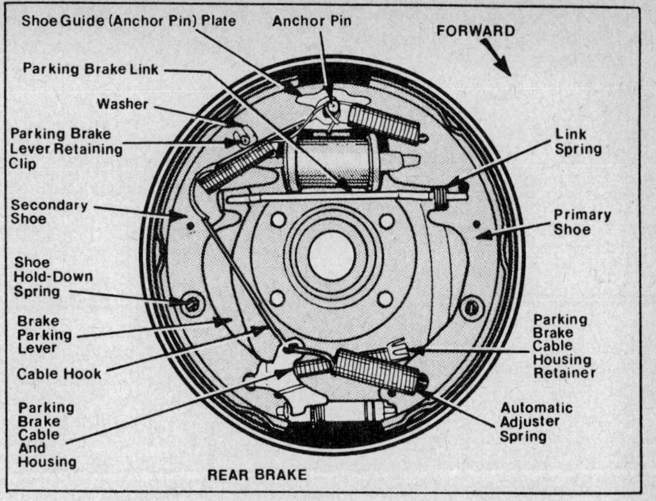

Fig. 6 Rear drum type brakes

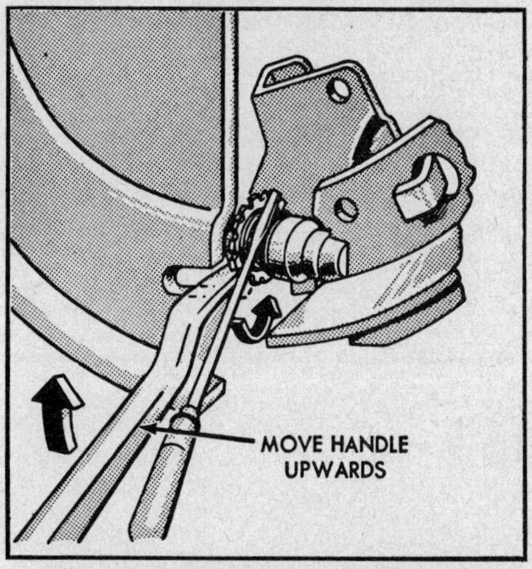

Fig. 7 Backing off brake adjustment by disengaging adjusting lever with screwdriver

BRAKE ADJUSTMENTS

1. Use the brake shoe adjustment gauge shown in **Fig. 5** to obtain the drum inside diameter as shown. Tighten the adjusting knob on the gauge to hold this setting.
2. Place the opposite side of the gauge over the brake shoes and adjust the shoes by turning the adjuster screw until the gauge just slides over the linings. Rotate the gauge around the lining surface to assure proper lining diameter adjustment and clearance.
3. Install brake drum and wheel. Final adjustment is accomplished by making several firm reverse stops, using the brake pedal.

SELF-ADJUSTING BRAKES

These brakes, **Fig. 6,** have self-adjusting shoe mechanisms that assure correct lining-to-drum clearances at all times. The automatic adjusters operate only when the brakes are applied as the car is moving rearward.

Although the brakes are self-adjusting, an initial adjustment is necessary after the brake shoes have been relined or replaced, or when the length of the star wheel adjuster has been changed during some other service operation.

Frequent usage of an automatic transmission forward range to halt reverse vehicle motion may prevent the automatic adjusters from functioning, thereby inducing low pedal heights. Should low pedal heights be encountered, it is recommended that numerous forward and reverse stops be performed with a firm pedal effort until satisfactory pedal height is obtained.

If a low pedal height condition cannot be corrected by making numerous reverse stops (provided the hydraulic system is free of air), it indicates that the self-adjusting mechanism is not functioning. Therefore, it will be necessary to remove the brake drums, clean, free up and lubricate the adjusting mechanism. Then adjust the brakes, being sure the parking brake is fully released.

INITIAL ADJUSTMENT

1. Remove adjusting hole cover from brake backing plate and, from the backing plate side, turn the adjusting screw upward with a screwdriver or other suitable tool to expand the shoes until a slight drag is felt when the drums are rotated.
2. Remove the drum.
3. While holding the adjusting lever out of engagement with the adjusting screw, **Fig. 7,** back off the adjusting screw about one full turn with the fingers. **If finger movement will not turn the screw, free it up. If this is not done, the adjusting lever will not turn the screw during vehicle operation. Lubricate the screw with oil and coat with wheel bearing grease. Any other adjustment procedure may cause damage to the adjusting screw with consequent self-adjuster problems.**
4. Install wheel and drum, and adjusting hole cover. Adjust brakes on remaining wheels in the same manner.
5. If pedal height is not satisfactory, drive the vehicle and make sufficient reverse stops with a firm pedal effort until proper pedal height is obtained.

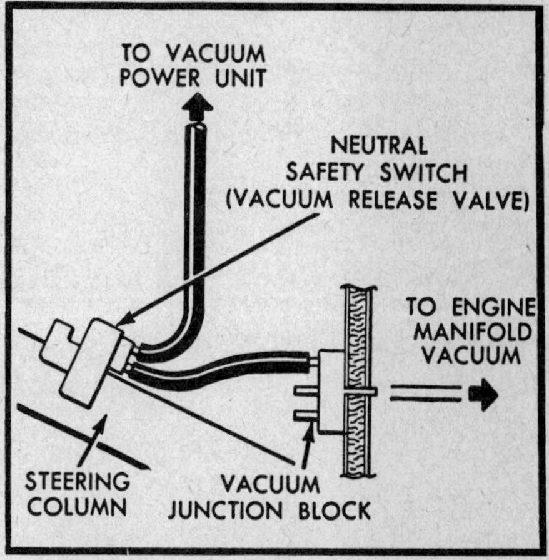

Fig. 8 Connections for automatic parking brake release. Typical

PARKING BRAKE

ADJUST

Check parking brake cables when brakes are fully released. If cables are loose, adjust as follows:

1982–88 REAR DRUM BRAKES

1. Make sure parking brake is released.
2. Place transmission in neutral and raise the vehicle.
3. Tighten the adjusting nut against the cable equalizer to cause rear brakes to drag.
4. Then loosen the adjusting nut until the rear wheels are fully released. There should be no drag.
5. Lower vehicle and check operation.

VACUUM RELEASE PARKING BRAKE

The vacuum power unit will release the parking brakes automatically when the shift lever is moved into any drive position with the engine running. The brakes will not release automatically, however, when the shift lever is in neutral or park position with the engine running, or in any position with the engine off.

The power unit piston rod is attached to the release lever. Since the release lever pivots against the pawl, a slight movement of the release lever will disengage the pawl from the ratchet, allowing the brakes to release. The release lever pivots on a rivet pin in the pedal mount.

As shown in **Fig. 8,** hoses connect the power unit and the engine manifold to a vacuum release valve in the transmission neutral safety switch. Moving the transmission selector lever into any drive position with the engine running will open the release valve to connect engine manifold vacuum to one side of the actuating piston in the power unit. The pressure differential thus created will cause the piston and link to pull the release lever.

MASTER CYLINDER

REPLACE

1. Disconnect brake lines from master cylinder.
2. Remove nuts retaining master cylinder to brake booster.
3. Remove master cylinder.
4. Reverse procedure to install.

HYDRO-BOOST BRAKE BOOSTER

REPLACE

1. Working under instrument panel, disconnect stop light switch wires at connector. Remove hairpin retainer. Slide switch off brake pedal pin just far enough for switch outer hole to clear pin. Then lift switch straight upward from pin. Slide master cylinder pushrod and nylon washers and bushing off brake pedal pin.
2. Open hood and disconnect brake line at master cylinder outlet fitting.
3. Disconnect the pressure, steering gear and return lines, then plug lines and ports.
4. Remove Hydro-Boost to dash panel nuts and remove assembly from panel, sliding pushrod link from engine side of dash panel.
5. Reverse procedure to install. To purge system, disconnect coil wire so that engine will not start. Fill power steering pump reservoir, then while engaging starter, pump brake pedal. Do not cycle steering wheel until all residual air has been purged from the hydro boost unit. Check fluid level, then connect coil wire and start engine. Apply brakes with a pumping action and cycle steering wheel, then check system for leaks.

VACUUM BRAKE BOOSTER

REPLACE

1. Disconnect battery ground cable.
2. Disconnect master cylinder from booster and position aside. **It is not necessary to disconnect brake lines, but care should be taken to avoid twisting or kinking lines.**
3. Disconnect manifold vacuum hose from booster check valve.
4. Working inside vehicle, disconnect stop lamp switch electrical connector under instrument panel.
5. Remove stop lamp switch retaining pin. Slide switch off brake pedal pin enough so outer plate of switch clears the pin, then remove switch from pin.
6. Remove booster-to-dash panel attaching screws.
7. Slide booster pushrod, nylon washers and bushing off brake pedal pin.
8. Slide pushrod out from engine side of dash panel and remove booster from vehicle.
9. Reverse procedure to install.

Rear Suspension

INDEX

SHOCK ABSORBER

REPLACE

1. With the rear axle supported properly disconnect shock absorber at upper mounting and compress it to clear hole in spring seat.
2. Disconnect shock absorber from stud on axle bracket.
3. Reverse procedure to install.

COIL SPRING

REPLACE

1. Raise rear of vehicle and support at frame. Support rear axle with a suitable jack.
2. Disconnect shock absorbers at lower mountings.
3. Disconnect brake line from rear brake hose and remove hose to bracket clip.
4. Lower axle to remove springs. **On some models, it may be necessary to disconnect the righthand parking brake cable from righthand upper arm retainer before lowering axle.**
5. Reverse procedure to install. Install an insulator between upper seat and spring, if necessary.

CONTROL ARMS

REPLACE

Control arms must be replaced in pairs.

1. Raise rear of vehicle and support at frame. Support axle with a suitable jack.
2. Remove stabilizer bar, if necessary.
3. Lower axle and install a second jack under differential pinion nose.
4. Disconnect parking brake cable from upper arm retainer.
5. Disconnect control arm from axle bracket. On upper arms, disconnect arm from crossmember and on lower arms, disconnect arm from frame attachment bracket.
6. Reverse procedure to install.

STABILIZER BAR

REPLACE

1. Raise and support vehicle at frame side rails.
2. Support rear axle with a suitable jack and position axle so the shock absorbers are fully extended.
3. Remove bolts, nuts and spacers attaching stabilizer bar to lower arms, **Fig. 1.**
4. Remove stabilizer bar from vehicle.
5. Reverse procedure to install.

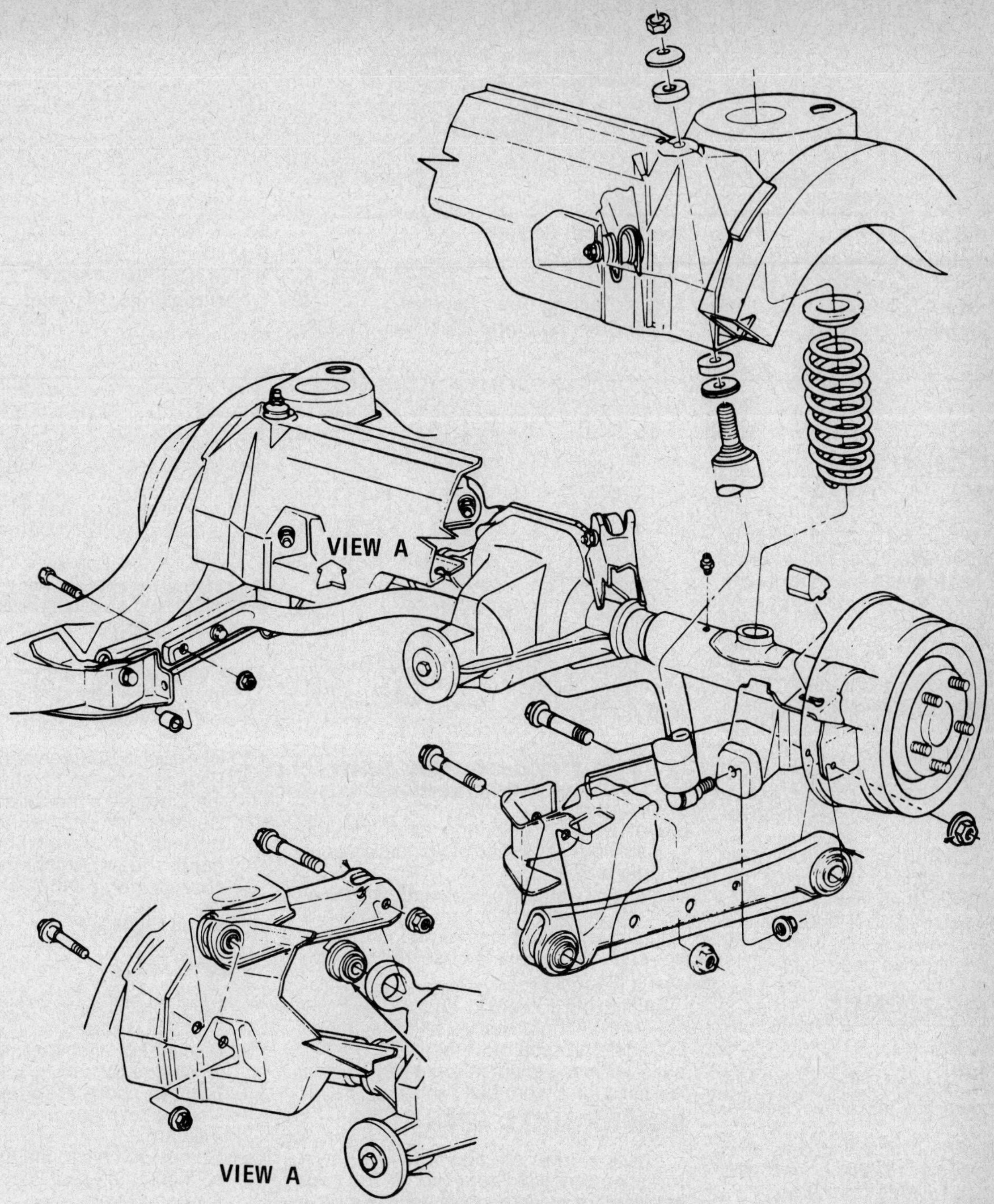

Fig. 1 Rear suspension. 1982–88

Front Suspension & Steering Section

INDEX

WHEEL BEARINGS
ADJUST

1. Raise and support vehicle so front wheels are free to turn.
2. Remove wheel cover, then the grease cap from hub.
3. Clean excess grease from end of spindle, then remove cotter pin and nut lock.
4. Back off adjusting nut three turns, then rock wheel assembly in and out several times to push shoe and linings away from rotor.
5. Torque adjusting nut to 17-25 ft. lbs. while rotating the wheel assembly.
6. Back off adjusting nut 1/2 turn, then retighten nut to 10-12 inch lbs.
7. Install nut lock on nut so castellations on lock are aligned with cotter pin hole in spindle, then install cotter pin.
8. Check wheel rotation. If wheel rotates roughly or makes noise, lubricate or replace bearings as necessary.

WHEEL BEARINGS
REPLACE

1. Raise and support front of vehicle, then remove tire and wheel assemblies.
2. Remove caliper mounting bolts. **It is not necessary to disconnect the brake lines for this operation.**
3. Slide caliper off of disc, inserting a spacer between the shoes to hold them in their bores after the caliper is removed. Position caliper assembly out of the way. **Do not allow caliper to hang by brake hose.**
4. Remove hub and disc assembly. Grease retainer and inner bearing can now be removed.
5. Reverse procedure to install.

CHECKING BALL JOINTS FOR WEAR
UPPER BALL JOINT

1. Raise car on floor jacks placed beneath lower control arms.
2. Grasp lower edge of tire and move wheel in and out.

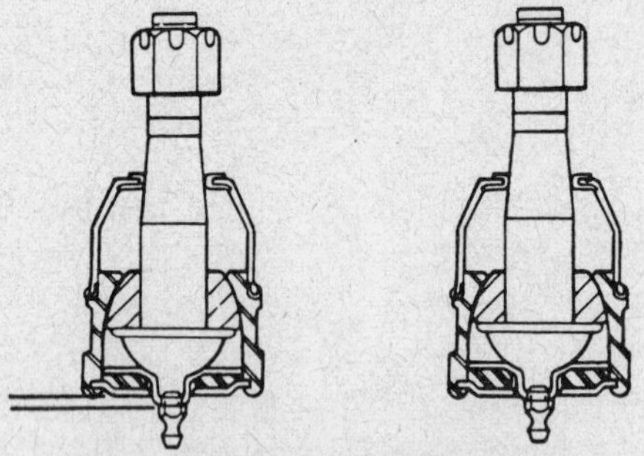

Fig. 1 Lower ball joint wear indicators

3. As wheel is being moved in and out, observe upper end of spindle and upper arm.
4. Any movement between upper end of spindle and upper arm indicates ball joint wear and loss of preload. If any such movement is observed, replace upper ball joint.

During the foregoing check, the lower ball joint will be unloaded and may move. Disregard all such movement of the lower ball joint. Also, do not mistake loose wheel bearings for a worn ball joint.

LOWER BALL JOINT

These models are equipped with lower ball joint wear indicators, **Fig. 1.** To check ball joint for wear, support vehicle in normal driving position with both ball joints loaded. Observe the checking surface of the ball joint. If the checking surface is inside the cover, **Fig. 1**, replace the ball joint.

BALL JOINTS
REPLACE

Ford Motor Company recommends that new ball joints should not be installed on used control arms and that the control arm be replaced if ball joint replacement is required. However, aftermarket ball joint repair kits which do not require control arm replacement, are available and can be installed using the following procedure.

The ball joints are riveted to the upper and lower control arms. The ball joints can be replaced on the car by removing the rivets and retaining the new ball joint to the control arm with the attaching bolts, nuts and washers furnished with the ball joint kit.

When removing a ball joint, use a suitable pressing tool to force the ball joint out of the spindle.

SHOCK ABSORBER
REPLACE

1. Remove nut, washer and bushing from shock absorber upper end.
2. Raise vehicle and install safety stands.
3. Remove two thread-cutting screws from lower end of shock absorber, then remove shock absorber.
4. Reverse procedure to install. **If threads in lower arm become damaged, reuse original thread-cutting screws along with 5/16-18 locknuts.**

COIL SPRING
REPLACE

1. Raise and support vehicle.
2. Remove wheel.
3. Disconnect stabilizer bar link from lower control arm.
4. Remove shock absorber.
5. Remove steering center link from pitman arm.
6. Compress coil spring with a suitable spring compressor, tool D-78P-5310-A or equivalent.
7. Remove two lower control arm pivot bolts and disengage arm from crossmember.
8. Remove spring from vehicle.
9. Reverse procedure to install. Torque stabilizer bar to lower control arm nuts to 9-12 ft. lbs. Torque lower control arm to crossmember bolts to 120-140 ft. lbs.

STABILIZER BAR
REPLACE

1. Raise and support vehicle.
2. Remove stabilizer bar attaching clamps, then the stabilizer bar attaching bolts from each stabilizer link.
3. Remove stabilizer bar assembly.
4. Reverse procedure to install.

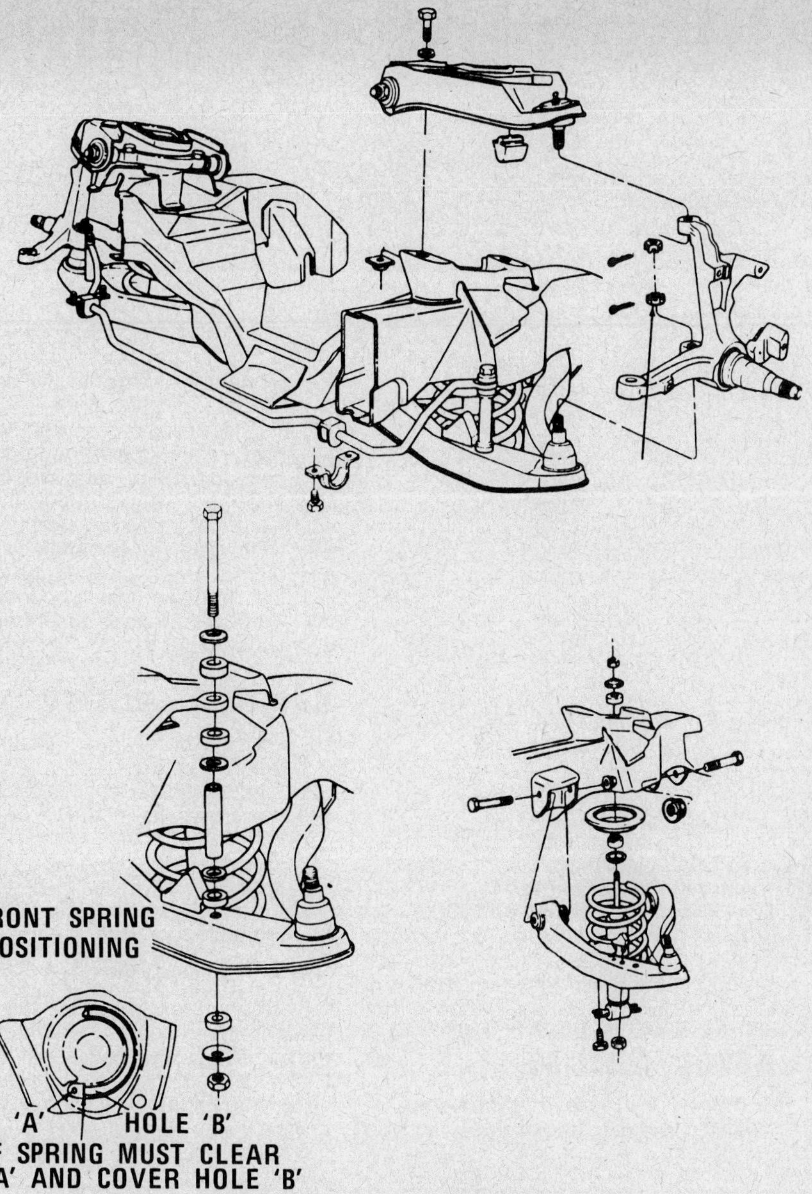

Fig. 2 Typical front suspension

CONTROL ARM REPLACE

LOWER CONTROL ARM

1. Raise and support front of vehicle, then remove front wheels.
2. Remove brake caliper, rotor and dust shield.
3. Remove jounce bumper, if equipped.
4. Remove shock absorber.
5. Disconnect stabilizer bar link from lower control arm.
6. Disconnect steering center link from pitman arm.
7. Remove lower ball joint attaching nut cotter pin, then loosen lower ball joint nut one or two turns. **Do not remove nut from stud at this time.**
8. Install ball joint press tool T57P-3006-B or equivalent between upper and lower ball joint studs.
9. Compress ball joint with tool, then tap spindle, near lower stud, to loosen stud in spindle.
10. Remove ball joint press tool, then position a suitable jack under lower control arm.
11. Install suitable coil spring compression tool, then remove coil spring.
12. Remove ball joint nut, then the lower control arm assembly.
13. Reverse procedure to install, noting the following:
    a. Torque ball joint attaching nut to 100-120 ft. lbs.
    b. Ensure coil spring is properly aligned, **Fig. 2.**
    c. Torque control arm-to-crossmember attaching bolts and nuts to 100-140 ft. lbs.
    d. Check wheel alignment, refer to "Wheel Alignment Section."

UPPER CONTROL ARM

1. Raise and support front of vehicle, then remove front wheels.
2. Remove upper ball joint attaching nut cotter pin, then loosen upper ball joint nut one or two turns. **Do not remove nut from stud at this time.**
3. Install ball joint press tool T57P-3006-B or equivalent between upper and lower ball joint studs.
4. Compress ball joint with tool, then tap spindle, near upper stud, to loosen stud in spindle.
5. Remove ball joint press tool, then position a suitable jack under lower control arm.
6. Remove upper control arm attaching bolts, then the upper control arm assembly.
7. Reverse procedure to install, noting the following:
    a. Torque ball joint attaching nut to 60-90 ft. lbs.
    b. Torque upper control arm attaching bolts to 120-140 ft. lbs.
    c. Check wheel alignment, refer to "Wheel Alignment Section."

POWER STEERING GEAR REPLACE

1. Remove stone shield, if equipped.
2. Disconnect pressure and return lines from steering gear. Plug lines and ports in gear to prevent entry of dirt.
3. Remove two bolts that secure flex coupling to steering gear and to column.
4. Raise car and remove sector shaft nut.
5. Use a puller to remove pitman arm.
6. Support steering gear, then remove attaching bolts.
7. Work steering gear free of flex coupling and remove it from car.
8. Reverse procedure to install.

POWER STEERING PUMP REPLACE

1. Disconnect power steering pump return line and allow power steering pump fluid to drain into a suitable container.
2. Disconnect power steering pump pressure hose from pump fitting.
3. Disconnect drive belt from power steering pump pulley, remove pulley, then remove pump.
4. Reverse procedure to install. Torque pump to mounting bracket bolts to 30-45 ft. lbs. **On Ford model CII power steering pump, torque pressure hose to pump fitting to 10-15 ft. lbs. Endplay on this fitting is normal and does not indicate a loose fitting.**

Wheel Alignment Section

INDEX

WHEEL ALIGNMENT

Wheel balancing differs on vehicles with disc brakes, dynamic balancing of the wheel-and-tire assembly on the vehicle should not be attempted without first pulling back the shoe and lining assemblies from the rotor. If this is not done, brake drag may burn out the motor on the wheel spinner.

The drag can be eliminated by removing the wheel, taking out the two bolts holding the caliper splash shield, and detaching the shield. Then push the pistons into their cylinder bores by applying steady pressure on the shoes on each side of the rotor for at least a minute. If necessary, use water pump pliers to apply the pressure.

After the pistons have been retracted, reinstall the splash shield and wheel. The wheel-and-tire assembly can then be dynamically balanced in the usual way. After the balancing job has been completed, be sure to pump the brake pedal several times until the shoes are seated and a firm brake pedal is obtained.

Caster and camber can be adjusted by loosening the bolts that attach the upper suspension arm to the shaft at the frame side rail, and moving the arm assembly in or out in the elongated bolt holes, **Fig. 1.** Since any movement of the arm affects both caster and camber, both factors should be balanced against one another when making the adjustment.

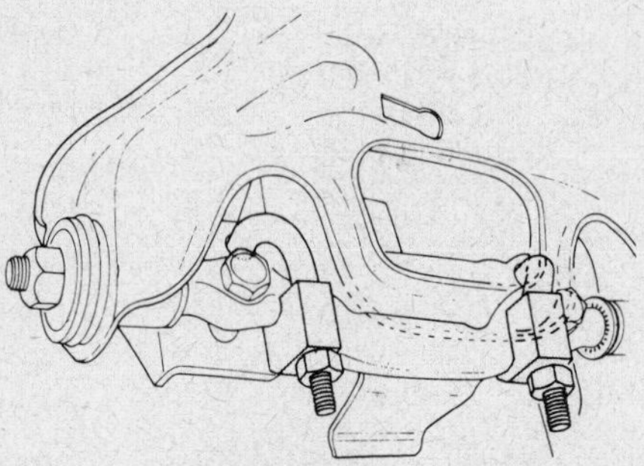

Fig. 1 Adjusting caster & camber

Use alignment tool T79P-3000A or equivalent, **Fig. 1.** Install the tool with the pins in the frame holes and the hooks over the upper arm inner shaft. Tighten the hook nuts snug before loosening the upper arm inner shaft attaching bolts.

CASTER, ADJUST

1. Tighten the tool front hook nut or loosen the rear hook nut as required to increase caster to the desired angle.
2. To decrease caster, tighten the rear hook nut or loosen the front hook nut as required. **The caster angle can be checked without tightening the inner shaft retaining bolts.**
3. Check the camber angle to be sure it did not change during the caster adjustment and adjust if necessary.
4. Torque the upper arm inner shaft retaining bolts to 120-140 ft. lbs. and remove tool.

CAMBER, ADJUST

1. Loosen both inner shaft retaining bolts.
2. Tighten or loosen the hook nuts as necessary to increase or decrease camber.
3. Recheck caster and readjust if necessary.
4. Torque upper arm inner shaft retaining bolts to 120-140 ft. lbs.

TOE-IN, ADJUST

Position the front wheels in their straight-ahead position. Then turn both tie rod adjusting sleeves an equal amount until the desired toe-in setting is obtained. Torque tie rod sleeve clamp bolt to 20-22 ft. lbs.

FORD & MERCURY Compact & Intermediate Models

NOTE: The Capri, Mustang, Sable & Taurus are located elsewhere in this manual. Refer to rear of this manual for vehicle manufacturer's special service tool suppliers.

INDEX OF SERVICE OPERATIONS

Specifications

GENERAL ENGINE SPECIFICATIONS

Year	Engine CID ①/Liter	Engine VIN Code ②	Fuel System	Bore and Stroke	Compression Ratio	Net H.P. @ RPM ③	Maximum Torque Lbs. Ft. @ RPM	Normal Oil Pressure Pounds
1982	4-140, 2.3L	A	6500, 2 Bbl. ⑪	3.781 x 3.126	9.0	86 @ 4600	117 @ 2600	40-60
	6-200, 3.3L	B	1946, 1 Bbl. ⑪	3.68 x 3.13	8.6	87 @ 3800	154 @ 1400	30-50
	V6-232, 3.8L ④	3	2150, 2 Bbl. ⑩	3.81 x 3.39	8.8	112 @ 4000	175 @ 2600	54-59
	V6-232, 3.8L ⑧	3	7200VV, 2 Bbl. ⑩	3.81 x 3.39	8.8	118 @ 4000	186 @ 2600	54-59
	V8-255, 4.2L ④	D	2150, 2 Bbl. ⑩	3.68 x 3.00	8.2	122 @ 3400	209 @ 2400	40-60
	V8-255, 4.2L ⑧	D	7200VV, 2 Bbl. ⑩	3.68 x 3.00	—	—	—	40-60
1983	4-140, 2.3L ⑤	A	YFA, 1 Bbl. ⑥	3.78 x 3.12	9.0	86 @ 4600	117 @ 2600	50
	4-140, 2.3L ⑦	W	E.F.I ⑨	3.78 x 3.12	8.0	—	—	55
	6-200, 3.3L	X	1946, 1 Bbl. ⑪	3.68 x 3.12	8.6	87 @ 3800	154 @ 1400	50
	V6-232, 3.8L	3	2150, 2 Bbl. ⑩	3.8 x 3.4	8.7	112 @ 4000	175 @ 2600	40-60
	V8-302, 5.0L	F	E.F.I ⑨	4.00 x 3.00	—	—	—	40-60
1984-85	4-140, 2.3L ⑤	A	YFA, 1 Bbl. ⑥	3.78 x 3.12	9.0	88 @ 4000	1220 @ 2400	50
	4-140, 2.3L ⑦	W	E.F.I ⑨	3.78 x 3.12	8.0	145 @ 4600	180 @ 3600	55
	V6-232, 3.8L	3	E.F.I ⑨	3.80 x 3.40	8.7	120 @ 3600	205 @ 1600	40-60
	V8-302, 5.0L	F	E.F.I. ⑨	4.00 x 3.00	8.4	140 @ 3200	250 @ 1600	40-60
	V8-302, H.O., 5.0L	M	E.F.I. ⑨	4.00 x 3.00	8.3	165 @ 3800	245 @ 2000	40-60
1986	4-140, 2.3L ⑤	A	YFA, 1 Bbl. ⑥	3.78 x 3.12	9.5	88 @ 4200	122 @ 2600	50
	4-140, 2.3L ⑦ ⑬	T,W	E.F.I. ⑨	3.78 x 3.12	8.0	145 @ 4400	180 @ 3000	55
	4-140, 2.3L ⑦ ⑭	T,W	E.F.I. ⑨	3.78 x 3.12	8.0	155 @ 4600	190 @ 2800	55
	V6-232, 3.8L	3	E.F.I. ⑨	3.80 x 3.40	8.7	120 @ 3600	205 @ 1600	40-60
	V8-302, 5.0L	F	S.E.F.I. ⑫	4.00 x 3.00	8.9	150 @ 3400	270 @ 2000	40-60
1987	4-140, 2.3L ⑦	W	E.F.I. ③	3.78 x 3.12	8.0	190 @ 4600	240 @ 3400	40-60
	V6-232, 3.8L	3	E.F.I. ③	3.80 x 3.40	8.7	120 @ 3600	205 @ 1600	40-60
	V8-302, 5.0L	F	S.E.F.I. ⑫	4.00 x 3.00	8.9	150 @ 3200	270 @ 2000	40-60
1988	4-140, 2.3L ⑦	—	E.F.I. ③	3.78 x 3.12	8.0	190 @ 4600	240 @ 3400	55
	V6-232, 3.8L	—	E.F.I. ③	3.80 x 3.40	9.0	140 @ 3800	215 @ 2400	40-60
	V8-302, 5.0L	—	S.E.F.I. ⑫	4.00 x 3.00	8.9	155 @ 3400	265 @ 2200	40-60

①—CID-cubic inch displacement.
②—The eighth digit of the VIN denotes engine code.
③—Rating are NET-as installed on vehicle.
④—Except California.
⑤—Non-Turbocharged.
⑥—Carter.
⑦—Turbocharged.
⑧—California.
⑨—Electronic fuel injection.
⑩—Motorcraft.
⑪—Holley.
⑫—Sequential electronic fuel injection.
⑬—Auto. trans.
⑭—Man. trans.

ENGINE TIGHTENING SPECIFICATIONS*

*Torque specifications are for clean and lightly lubricated threads only. Dry or dirty threads produce increased friction which prevents accurate measurement of tightness.

Year	Engine/VIN	Spark Plugs Ft. Lbs.	Cylinder Head Bolts Ft. Lbs.	Intake Manifold Ft. Lbs.	Exhaust Manifold Ft. Lbs.	Rocker Arm Shaft Bracket Ft. Lbs.	Rocker Arm Cover Ft. Lbs.	Connecting Rod Cap Bolts Ft. Lbs.	Main Bearing Cap Bolts. Ft. Lbs.	Flywheel to Crankshaft Ft. Lbs.	Vibration Damper or Pulley Ft. Lbs.
1982	4-140/A	5-10	80-90	14-21	16-23	—	5-8	30-36	80-90	56-64	100-120
	6-200/B	10-15	70-75	—	18-24	30-35	3-5	21-26	60-70	75-85	85-100
	V6-232/3	15-22	②	18.4	15-22	18.4-25.8	3-5	31-36	65-81	54-64	93-121
	V8-255/D	10-15	65-72	18-20	18-24	18-25⑥	3-5	19-24	60-70	75-85	70-90
1983	4-140/A,W	5-10	80-90	14-21	16-23	—	5-8	30-36	80-90	56-64	100-120
	6-200/X	10-15	70-75	—	18-24	30-35	3-5	21-26	60-70	75-85	85-100
	V6-232/3	5-11	②	18.4	15-22	18.4-25.8	3-5	31-36	65-81	54-64	93-121
	V8-302/F	10-15	65-72	23-25	18-24	18-25⑥	3-5	19-24	60-70	75-85	70-90
1984	4-140/A,W	5-10	80-90	14-21	16-23	—	5-8	30-36	80-90	56-64	100-120
	V6-232/3	5-11	⑤	⑧	15-22	18.4-25.8⑥	6.6-8.8	31-36	65-81	56-64	93-121
	V8-302/F	10-15	65-72	23-25	18-24	18-25⑥	3-5	19-24	60-70	75-85	70-90
	V8-302H.O./M	10-15	④	23-25	18-24	18-25⑥	3-5	19-24	60-70	75-85	70-90
1985	4-140/A,W	5-10	⑨	14-21	⑩	—	5-8	⑪	⑦	56-64	100-120
	V6-232/3	5-11	⑤	⑧	15-22	①⑥	80-106③	31-36	65-81	54-64	93-121
	V8-302/F	10-15	④	23-25	18-24	18-25⑥	3-5	19-24	60-70	75-85	70-90
	V8-302/M	10-15	④	23-25	18-24	18-25⑥	3-5	19-24	60-70	75-85	70-90
1986	4-140	5-10	⑨	14-21	⑩	—	5-8	⑪	⑦	56-64	100-120
	V6-232	5-11	⑤	⑧	15-22	①⑥	80-106③	31-36	65-81	54-64	93-121
	V8-302	10-15	④	23-25	18-24	18-25⑥	3-5	19-24	60-70	75-85	70-90
1987	4-140/W	5-10	⑨	14-21	20-30	—	5-8	⑪	⑫	56-64	103-133
	V6-232/3	5-11	⑤	⑧	15-22	①⑥	80-106③	31-36	65-81	54-64	93-121
	V8-302/F	10-15	④	23-25	18-24	18-25⑥	3-5	19-24	60-70	75-85	70-90
1988	4-140	5-10	—	—	—	—	5-8	⑪	⑫	56-64	103-133
	V6-232	5-11	—	—	—	—	80-106③	31-36	65-81	54-64	93-121
	V8-302	10-15	—	—	—	—	3-5	19-24	60-70	75-85	70-90

①—Torque in 2 steps: 1, 5-11 ft. lbs.; 2, 18-4-25.8 ft. lbs.

②—Tighten in 4 steps: 1, 47 ft. lbs.: 2, 55 ft. lbs.; 3, 63 ft. lbs.; 4, 74 ft. lbs. Back off all bolts 2-3 turns, retorque in 4 steps.

③—Inch lbs.

④—Torque in 2 steps: 1, 55-65 ft. lbs.; 2, 65-72 ft. lbs.

⑤—Tighten in 4 steps: 1, 37 ft. lbs.; 2, 45 ft. lbs.; 3, 52 ft. lbs.; 4, 59 ft. lbs. Back off all bolts 2-3 turns, retorque in 4 steps.

⑥—Fulcurm bolt to cylinder head.

⑦—Torque in 2 steps: 1, 50-60 ft. lbs.; 2, 80-90 ft. lbs.

⑧—Torque in 3 steps: 1, 7 ft. lbs.; 2, 15 ft. lbs.; 3, 24 ft. lbs.

⑨—Torque in 2 steps: 1, 50-60 ft. lbs.; 2, 80-90 ft. lbs.

⑩—Torque in 2 steps: 1, 5-7 ft. lbs.; 2, 16-23 ft. lbs.

⑪—Torque in 2 steps: 1, 25-30 ft. lbs.; 2, 30-36 ft. lbs.

⑫—Torque in two steps: 1, 50-60 ft. lbs.; 2, 75-85 ft. lbs.

ALTERNATOR & REGULATOR SPECIFICATIONS

Year	Color Code Stamp	Current Rating ①		Field Current @ 75°F		Voltage Regulator				Field Relay Armature Air Gap
		Amperes	Volts	Amperes	Volts	Model No. (10316)	Voltage @ 75°F	Contact Gap	Armature Air Gap	
1982	Orange ③ ⑤ ⑦	40	15	4.0	12	E1AF-AA ⑥	13.8-14.6	④	④	
	Green ③ ⑤ ⑦	60	15	4.0	12	E1AF-AA ⑥	13.8-14.6	④	④	
	Black ③ ⑤ ⑦	65	15	4.0	12	E1AF-AA ⑥	13.8-14.6	④	④	
	Black ③ ⑤ ⑧	70	15	4.0	12	E1AF-AA ⑥	13.8-14.6	④	④	
	Red ③ ⑤ ⑧	100	15	4.0	12	E1AF-AA ⑥	13.8-14.6	④	④	
1983	Orange ③ ⑤ ⑦	40	15	4.25	12	—	—	—	—	—
	Black ③ ⑤ ⑦	65	15	4.25	12	—	—	—	—	—
	Green ③ ⑤ ⑦	60	15	4.25	12	—	—	—	—	—
	Black ③ ⑤ ⑧	70	15	4.25	12	—	—	—	—	—
	Red ③ ⑤ ⑧	100	15	4.25	12	—	—	—	—	—
1984	Orange ③ ⑤ ⑦	40	15	4.25	12	—	—	—	—	—
	Green ③ ⑤ ⑦	60	15	4.25	12	—	—	—	—	—
	Black ③ ⑤ ⑧	70	15	4.25	12	—	—	—	—	—
	Red ③ ⑤ ⑧	100	15	4.25	12	—	—	—	—	—
1985-86	Orange ③ ⑤ ⑦	40	15	4.25	12	E4AF-AA ⑥	—	④	④	④
	Green ③ ⑤ ⑦	60	15	4.25	12	E4TF-AA ⑥	—	④	④	④
	Black ③ ⑤ ⑦	70	15	4.25	12	E4TF-AA ⑥	—	④	④	④
	Red ③ ⑤ ⑦	100	15	4.25	12	E4TF-AA ⑥	—	④	④	④
1987-88	Orange ③ ⑤ ⑨	40	15	4.25	12	E6TZ-AA	—	④	④	④
	Red ③ ⑤ ⑨	40	15	4.25	12	E6TZ-AA	—	④	④	④
	Green ③ ⑤ ⑨	60	15	4.25	12	E6TZ-AA	—	④	④	④
	Black ③ ⑤ ⑨	65	15	4.25	12	E6TZ-AA	—	④	④	④
	⑦	40	15	4.25	12	—	—	—	—	—
	⑦	60	15	4.25	12	—	—	—	—	—
	⑧	70	15	4.25	12	—	—	—	—	—
	⑧	100	15	4.25	12	—	—	—	—	—

①—Current rating stamped on housing.
②—Voltage regulation stamped on cover.
③—Stamp color.
④—Not adjustable.
⑤—Solid state alternator.
⑥—Electronic voltage regulator. These units are color coded black for systems w/warning indicator lamp & blue for systems w/ammeter.
⑦—Rear terminal alternator.
⑧—Side terminal alternator.
⑨—Integral regulator alternator.

REAR AXLE SPECIFICATIONS

Year	Ring Gear Diameter	Carrier Type	Ring Gear & Pinion Backlash Inch	Nominal Pinion Locating Shim, Inch	Pinion Bearing Preload		Differential Bearing Preload	Pinion Nut Torque Ft. Lbs. ①
					New Bearings With Seal Inch-Lbs.	Used Bearings With Seal Inch-Lbs.		
1982-88	7½"	Integral	.008-.015	.030	16-29	8-14	.016 ②	170

①—If torque cannot be obtained, install new spacer.
②—Case spread across differential.

STARTING MOTOR APPLICATIONS

Year	Engine/VIN	Ident. No.
1982	4-140/A	E2BF-AA
	6-200/B ①	E1AF-BA
	6-200/B ②	E1BF-BA
	V6-232/3 ③	E2SF-AA
	V6-232/3 ④	E25F-AA
	V8-255/D ⑩	E1AF-BA
	V8-255/D ⑪	E3AF-AA
1983	4-140/A,W	E2BF-AA
	6-200/X ⑦	E3AF-AA
	6-200/X ⑧	E1AF-BA
	V6-232/3	E25F-AA
	V8-302/F	E3AF-AA
1984	4-140/A ⑨	E2BF-AA
	4-140/A ⑫	E4DF-AA
	4-140/W	E4SF-AA
	V6-232/3	E25F-AA
	V8-302/F ⑨	E3AF-AA
	V8-302/F ⑫	E4AF-AA
	V8-302 H.O./M	—
1985	4-140/A	E4DF-AA
	4-140/W	—
	V6-232/3	E4DF-BA
	V8-302/F	E4AF-AA
	V8-302 H.O./M	—
1986	4-140 ⑤	—
	4-140 ⑥	E4SF-AA
	V6-232	E4DF-BA
	V8-302	E4AF-AA
1987-88	4-140 ⑥	—
	V6-232	—
	V8-302	—

①—Except Thunderbird & XR-7 with C5 automatic trans., serial no. PEB-Z2.
②—Thunderbird & XR-7 with C5 automatic trans., serial no. PEB-Z2.
③—Vehicles manufactured before 1-18-82.
④—Vehicles manufactured after 1-17-82.
⑤—Non-Turbocharged.
⑥—Turbocharged.
⑦—Except Fairmont & Zephyr high alt.
⑧—Fairmont & Zephyr high alt.
⑨—Vehicles manufactured before 12/83.
⑩—Vehicles manufactured before 5-17-82.
⑪—Vehicles manufactured after 5-16-82.
⑫—Vehicles manufactured from 12/83.

WHEEL ALIGNMENT SPECIFICATIONS

Year	Model	Caster Angle, Degrees		Camber Angle, Degrees				Toe-In. Inch	Toe-Out on Turns, Deg.	
				Limits		Desired				
		Limits	Desired	Left	Right	Left	Right		Outer Wheel	Inner Wheel
1982	Cougar Sedan	+1/8 to 1 7/8	+1	−5/16 to +1 3/16	−5/16 to +1 3/16	+7/16	+7/16	3/16	19.84	20
	Cougar Sta. Wag.	+1/8 to 1 5/8	+3/4	−1/4 to +1 1/4	−1/4 to +1 1/4	+1/2	+1/2	3/16	19.84	20
	Cougar XR-7	+1/8 to 1 7/8	+1	−1/2 to +1 1/4	−1/2 to +1 1/4	+3/8	+3/8	3/16	19.73	20
	Fairmont	+1/8 to 1 7/8	+1	−5/16 to +1 3/16	−5/16 to +1 3/16	+7/16	+7/16	3/16	19.84	20
	Granada Sedan	+1/8 to 1 7/8	+1	−5/16 to +1 3/16	−5/16 to +1 3/16	+7/16	+7/16	3/16	19.84	20
	Granada Sta. Wag.	+1/8 to 1 5/8	+3/4	−1/4 to +1 1/4	−1/4 to +1 1/4	+1/2	+1/2	3/16	19.84	20
	Thunderbird	+1/8 to 1 7/8	+1	−1/2 to +1 1/4	−1/2 to +1 1/4	+3/8	+3/8	3/16	19.73	20
	Zephyr	+1/8 to 1 7/8	+1	−5/16 to +1 3/16	−5/16 to +1 3/16	+7/16	+7/16	3/16	19.84	20
1983	Cougar	+1/2 to 2	+1 1/4	−1/2 to +1	−1/2 to +1	+1/4	+1/4	3/16	19.73	20
	Fairmont	+1/8 to 2 1/8	+1 1/8	−5/16 to +1 3/16	−5/16 to +1 3/16	+7/16	+7/16	3/16	19.84	20
	LTD Sedan	+1/8 to 2 1/8	+1 1/8	−5/16 to +1 3/16	−5/16 to +1 3/16	+7/16	+7/16	3/16	19.84	20
	LTD Sta. Wagon	−1/8 to 7/8	+7/8	−1/4 to +1 1/4	−1/4 to +1 1/4	+1/2	+1/2	3/16	19.84	20
	Marquis Sedan	+1/8 to 2 1/8	+1 1/8	−5/16 to +1 3/16	−5/16 to +1 3/16	+7/16	+7/16	3/16	19.84	20
	Marquis Sta. Wagon	−1/8 to 1 7/8	+7/8	−1/4 to +1 1/4	−1/4 to +1 1/4	+1/2	+1/2	3/16	19.84	20
	Thunderbird	+1/2 to 2	+1 1/4	−1/2 to +1	−1/2 to +1	+1/4	+1/4	3/16	19.73	20
	Zephyr	+1/8 to 2 1/8	+1 1/8	−5/16 to +1 3/16	−5/16 to +1 3/16	+7/16	+7/16	3/16	19.84	20
1984	Cougar	+1/4 to 1 3/4	+1	−1/2 to +1	−1/2 to +1	+1/4	+1/4	3/16	19.73	20
	LTD Sedan	+1/4 to 2 1/4	+1	−1/4 to +1 1/4	−1/4 to +1 1/4	+1/2	+1/2	3/16	19.84	20
	LTD Sta. Wagon	+1/4 to 2 1/4	+1	−1/4 to +1 1/4	−1/4 to +1 1/4	+1/2	+1/2	3/16	19.84	20
	Marquis Sedan	+1/4 to 2 1/4	+1	−1/4 to +1 1/4	−1/4 to +1 1/4	+1/2	+1/2	3/16	19.84	20
	Marquis Sta. Wagon	+1/4 to 2 1/4	+1	−1/4 to +1 1/4	−1/4 to +1 1/4	+1/2	+1/2	3/16	19.84	20
	Thunderbird	+1/4 to 1 3/4	+1	−1/2 to +1	−1/2 to +1	+1/4	+1/4	3/16	19.73	20
1985-86	Cougar	0 to 1 1/2	+3-4	−1/2 to +1	−1/2 to +1	+1/4	+1/4	3/16	19.73	20
	LTD Sedan	+1/8 to 2 1/8	+7/8	−3/8 to +1 1/8	−3/8 to +1 1/8	+3/8	+3/8	3/16	19.84	20
	LTD Sta. Wagon	0 to 2	+3/4	−5/16 to +1 3/16	−5/16 to +1 3/16	+7/16	+7/16	3/16	19.84	20
	Marquis Sedan	+1/8 to +2 1/8	+7/8	−3/8 to +1 1/8	−3/8 to +1 1/8	+3/8	+3/8	3/16	19.84	20
	Marquis Sta. Wagon	0 to +2	+3/4	−5/16 to +1 3/16	−5/16 to +1 3/16	+7/16	+7/16	3/16	19.84	20
	Thunderbird	0 to +1 1/2	+3/4	−1/2 to +1	−1/2 to +1	+1/4	+1/4	3/16	19.73	20
1987	Cougar	+15/32 to +1 31/32	+1 7/32	−1 13/32 to +3/32	−1 13/32 to +3/32	−2 1/32	−21/32	3/16	19.73	20
	Thunderbird ①	+15/32 to +1 31/32	+1 7/32	−1 13/32 to +3/32	−1 13/32 to +3/32	−21/32	−21/32	3/16	19.73	20
	Thunderbird ② +19/32 to +2 3/32	+1 11/32	−3/4 to +3/4	−3/4 to +3/4	0	0	3/16	19.73	20	
1988	Cougar	+15/32 to +19/32	+1 7/32	−1 13/32 to +3/32	−1 13/32 to +3/32	−21/32	−21/32	3/16	—	—
	Thunderbird ①	+15/32 to +19/32	+1 7/32	−1 13/32 to +3/32	−1 13/32 to +3/32	−21/32	−21/32	3/16	—	—
	Thunderbird ②	+19/32 to +1 13/32	+1 11/32	−3/4 to +3/4	−3/4 to +3/4	0	0	3/16	—	—

①—Exc. Turbo.
②—Turbo.

COOLING SYSTEM & CAPACITY DATA

Year	Model or Engine/VIN	Cooling Capacity Qts.		Radiator Cap Relief Pressure, Lbs.	Thermo. Opening Temp.	Fuel Tank Gals.	Engine Oil Refill Qts. ①	Transmission Oil		Rear Axle Oil Pints
		Less A/C	With A/C					4 & 5 Speed Pints	Auto Trans. Qts.	
1982	4-140/A ③	8.6	9.4	④	191	⑫	4	2.8	8	3.50
	4-140/A ⑦	8.4	8.5	④	191	⑫	4	2.8	8	3.25
	6-200/B ③ ⑦	8.4	8.5	16	196	⑫	4	2.8	⑬	⑥
	6-200/B ⑨	8.4	8.5	16	196	21	4	—	⑭	3.25
	V6-232/3	10.7	10.8	16	196	⑫	4	—	⑭	3.25
	V8-255/D ③	15.2	15.2	16	191	⑫	4 ⑩	—	11	⑥
	V8-255/D ⑨	14.9	14.0	16	191	21	4 ⑩	—	⑭	3.25
1983	4-140/A ③ ⑮	8.6	9.4	④	191	⑫	4 ⑯	2.8	8	3.25
	4-140 ⑰ ⑱	8.4	8.7	④	191	18	4.5 ⑯ ⑲	4.75	—	3.25
	6-200/X ③	8.4	8.5	16	191	⑫	4	—	⑪	3.25
	6-200/X ③	8.4	8.5	16	191	⑫	4	—	⑧	3.25
	V6-232/3 ⑮	10.7	10.8	16	196	⑫	4	—	⑤	3.25
	V6-232/3 ⑰	10.7	10.8	16	196	21	4	—	⑤	3.25
1984	4-140/A ⑮	8.6	9.4	16	191	⑫	4 ⑯	2.8	8	3.50
	4-140/W ⑰ ⑱	10.5	10.5	16	191	21	4.5 ⑯ ⑲	5.6	8	3.50
	V6-232/3 ⑮	10.7	10.8	16	196	⑫	4	—	11	3.50
	V6-232/3 ⑰	10.7	10.8	16	196	21	4	—	⑤	3.50
	V8-302/F ⑰	14	14.2	16	196	21	4 ⑩	—	12.3	3.50
1985	4-140/A ⑮	9.5	10.2	16	191	⑫	4 ⑯	—	8	3.50
	4-140/W ⑰ ⑱	10.8	10.8	16	191	21	4.5 ⑯ ⑲	5.6	8	3.50
	V6-232/3 ⑮	11.5	11.5	16	196	⑫	4	—	11	3.50
	V6-232/3 ⑰	11.7	11.7	16	196	21	4	—	⑤	3.50
	V8-302/F ⑰	14.2	14.2	16	196	21	4 ⑩	—	12.3	3.50
1986	4-140/A ⑮	9.6	10	16	191	⑫	4 ⑯	—	8	3.5
	4-140/W ⑰ ⑱	10	10	16	191	18	4.5 ⑯ ⑲	5.6	8	3.5
	V6-232/3 ⑮	11.3	11.5	16	196	⑫	4	—	11	3.5
	V6-232/3 ⑰	11.8	11.8	16	196	18.8	4	—	⑤	3.5
	V8-302/F ⑰	14.1	14.1	16	196	18.8	4 ⑩	—	12.3	3.5
1987	4-140/W ⑱	10	10	16	191	18	4 ⑯ ⑲	5.6	9.5	3.75
	V6-232/3	11.8	11.8	16	196	18.8	4	—	⑪	3.75
	V8-302/F	14.1	14.1	16	196	18.8	4 ⑩	—	12.3	3.75
1988	4-140 ⑱	8.9	8.9	16	188	22.1	4 ⑯ ⑲	5.6	9.5	3.75
	V6-232	12.2	12.3	16	197	22.1	4	—	12.3	3.75
	V8-302	13.3	13.4	16	193	22.1	4 ⑩	—	12.3	3.75

①—Add 1 qt. with filter change.
②—Approximate. Make final check with dipstick.
③—Faimont & Zephyr.
④—Less A/C, 13 psi.; with A/C 16 psi.
⑤—C5, 11 qts.; Automatic overdrive transmission. 12 qts.
⑥—With 7.5 inch ring gear, 3.2 pts.; with 6.75 inch ring gear, 2.5 pts.
⑦—Cougar & Granada.
⑧—C3, 8 qts.; C5 except Calif., 10.3 qts.; C5 Calif., 7.5 qts.
⑨—Cougar, XR-7 & Thunderbird.
⑩—Dual sump oil pan. Remove both drain plugs to fully drain oil. One drain plug located at front of oil pan. Second drain plug located at left side of oil pan.
⑪—C3, 8 qts.; C5 except high altitude models, 11 qts.; C5 high altitude models, 7.5 qts.
⑫—Standard, 16 gals.; optional 20 gals.
⑬—C3, 8 qts., C5, 11 qts.
⑭—C5, 11 qts., Automatic overdrive transmission, 12 qts.
⑮—LTD & Marquis.
⑯—Add 1/2 qt. with filter change.
⑰—Cougar & Thunderbird.
⑱—Turbocharged engine.
⑲—Before starting engine after changing oil, disconnect ignition switch connector from distributor & crank engine several times (not longer than 30 seconds for each cranking interval) until oil lamp goes out or a steady oil pressure reading is observed, then reconnect switch connector & start engine.

Electrical Section

INDEX

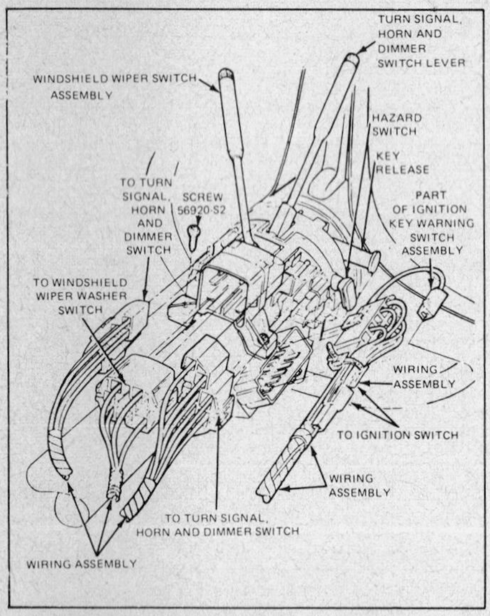

Fig. 1 Ignition switch

STARTER
REPLACE

1. Disconnect battery ground cable.
2. Raise and support vehicle.
3. Remove starter shield, if equipped.
4. Disconnect starter cable from motor.
5. Remove starter attaching bolts and remove starter.
6. Reverse procedure to install noting the following:
   a. Torque starter motor attaching bolts to 15-20 ft. lbs.
   b. Torque starter cable attaching bolt to 70-110 inch lb.

IGNITION LOCK
REPLACE

1. Disconnect battery ground cable.
2. On models equipped with tilt column, remove upper extension shroud by detaching from retaining clip at 9 o'clock position.
3. On all models, remove both trim shroud halves.
4. Disconnect key warning switch electrical connector.
5. Turn ignition key to "Run." Place gear shift lever in "Park" if equipped with column shift.
6. Insert a 1/8 inch diameter wire pin into hole in casting around lock cylinder. Remove lock cylinder while depressing retaining pin with wire.
7. Reverse procedure to install. Lock cylinder must be in "Run" and retaining pin depressed during installation. Following installation, turn the key to check for correct operation in all positions.

IGNITION SWITCH
REPLACE

1. Disconnect battery ground cable.
2. On models equipped with tilt column, remove upper extension shroud by detaching from retaining clip at 9 o'clock position.
3. On all models, remove steering column shroud attaching screws, then the steering column shroud.
4. Disconnect ignition switch electrical connector, **Fig. 1,** then rotate ignition key lock cylinder to "Run" position.
5. On 1982-86 models, drill out bolt heads that attach switch to lock cylinder housing using a 1/8 in. drill, then remove the two bolts using an easy-out or equivalent. On 1987-88 models, remove switch to lock cylinder attaching bolts.
6. Remove ignition switch from actuator pin.

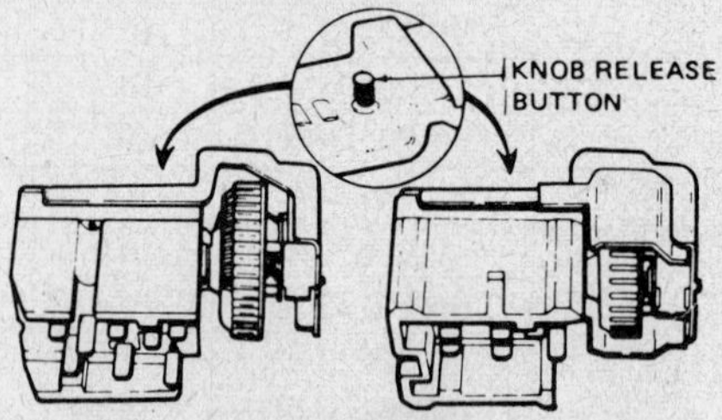

Fig. 2 Light switches. Exc. 1985–87 Thunderbird & Cougar

7. Adjust ignition switch by sliding carrier to "Run" position. **A new replacement switch assembly will be preset in "Run" position.**
8. Place ignition key lock cylinder in "Run" position by rotating cylinder approximately 90° from "Lock" position.
9. Install ignition switch on actuator pin. **Slightly move switch back and forth to align mounting holes with column lock housing threaded holes.**
10. On 1982-86 models, install switch to lock cylinder housing using new break away bolts and torque bolts until heads break away. On 1987-88 models, install switch to lock cylinder attaching bolts and torque bolts to 50-60 inch lbs.
11. Connect switch electrical connector.
12. Install steering column trim shrouds, then check ignition for proper operation.

LIGHT SWITCH
REPLACE
EXC. 1985–88 THUNDERBIRD & COUGAR

1. Disconnect battery ground cable.

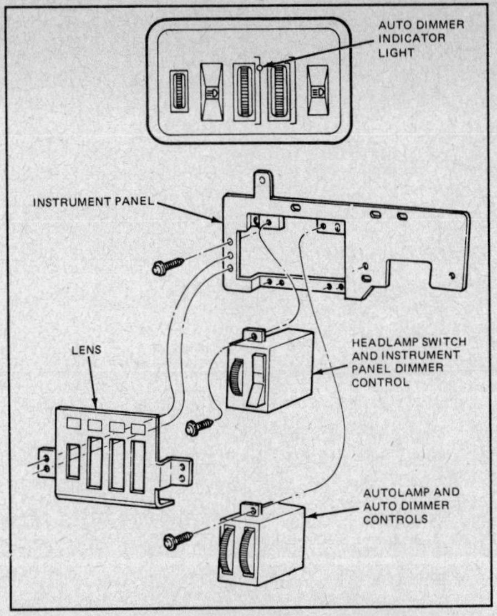

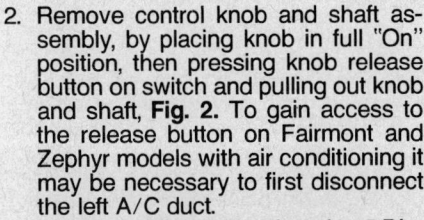

Fig. 3 Removing headlamp switch. 1985–88 Thunderbird & Cougar

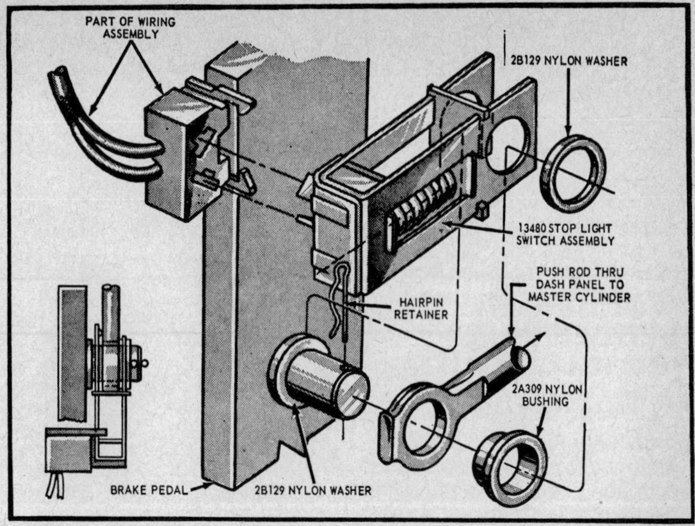

Fig. 4 Mechanical stop light switch (Typical)

2. Remove control knob and shaft assembly, by placing knob in full "On" position, then pressing knob release button on switch and pulling out knob and shaft, **Fig. 2.** To gain access to the release button on Fairmont and Zephyr models with air conditioning it may be necessary to first disconnect the left A/C duct.
3. On all models, remove bezel nut. Disconnect multiple plug connector, vacuum hoses if vehicle is equipped with headlight doors and remove switch.
4. Reverse procedure to install. Install knob and shaft by inserting shaft into the switch until a distinct click is heard. In some instances it may be necessary to rotate the shaft slightly until it engages the switch carrier.

1985–88 THUNDERBIRD & COUGAR

1. Disconnect battery ground cable.
2. Remove lens assembly attaching screws and the lens assembly, **Fig. 3.**
3. Remove switch assembly attaching screws from instrument panel, pull switch from panel, then disconnect electrical connector. **On vehicles equipped with auto lamp/dimmer switch, remove this switch before removing light switch.**
4. Reverse procedure to install.

STOP LIGHT SWITCH

REPLACE

1. Disconnect battery ground cable and disconnect wires at switch connector.
2. Remove hairpin retainer and slide stop light switch, pushrod, nylon washers and bushings away from brake pedal, and remove switch, **Fig. 4.**
3. Reverse procedure to install.

NEUTRAL SAFETY SWITCH

REPLACE

TRANSMISSION MOUNTED SWITCH

Except Automatic Overdrive Transmission

1. Remove downshift linkage rod from transmission downshift lever.
2. Apply penetrating oil to downshift lever shaft and nut; then remove downshift outer lever.
3. Remove switch attaching bolts.
4. Disconnect multiple wire connector and remove switch from transmission.
5. Install new switch.
6. With transmission manual lever in neutral, rotate switch and install gauge pin (43 drill) into gauge pin holes, **Fig. 5. The shank end of the drill must be inserted approximateld 15/32 inch into each of the gauge pin holes.**
7. Tighten switch attaching bolts and remove gauge pin.
8. Complete the installation in reverse order of removal.

Automatic Overdrive Transmission

1. Disconnect battery ground cable.
2. Place transmission gear selector in manual low position.
3. Raise and support vehicle.
4. Disconnect electrical connector from neutral start switch. Lift connector straight up off switch using a long screwdriver under the rubber plug of connector.
5. Remove switch and O-ring using socket No. T74P-77247-A or equivalent. **Use of any tools other than those specified may result in damage to the vehicle.**
6. Reverse procedure to install. Torque switch to 7-10 ft. lbs.

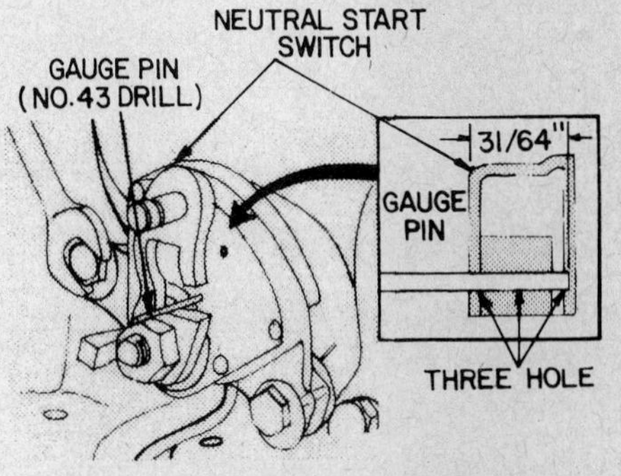

Fig. 5 Neutral safety switch. Transmission mounted

TURN SIGNAL SWITCH

REPLACE

1. Disconnect battery ground cable.
2. On 1982-84 models with tilt column, remove upper extension shroud. Unsnap shroud from retaining clip located at the 9 o'clock position.
3. On all models, remove trim shroud or shroud halves.
4. Remove turn signal switch lever from switch. Grasp lever and use a pulling and twisting motion while pulling lever straight out from switch.
5. Peel back foam shield from turn signal switch, then disconnect two electrical connectors from switch.
6. Remove turn signal switch attaching screws and the switch from vehicle.
7. Reverse procedure to install.

HORN SOUNDER
REPLACE
MODELS EQUIPPED W/TURN SIGNAL MOUNTED SWITCH

On these models, the horn sounder is located on the turn signal, headlight dimmer and horn lever. Refer to "Turn Signal Switch, Replace" when replacing switch.

MODELS EQUIPPED W/STEERING WHEEL MOUNTED HORN SWITCH

Cougar & Thunderbird

1. Disconnect battery ground cable.
2. Pry switch cover off top. Use caution not to damage cover when removing.
3. Remove switch attaching screws, then lift switch from steering wheel. Use caution not to loose contact spring.
4. Reverse procedure to install.

LTD & Marquis

1. Disconnect battery ground cable.
2. With steering wheel in straight ahead position, pry off steering wheel hub cover and horn switch.
3. Remove horn switch electrical connectors.
4. Reverse procedure to install.

STEERING WHEEL
REPLACE

1. Disconnect battery ground cable.
2. Remove steering wheel trim pad, horn button or ring. **On 1982-83 models with 4-spoke steering wheel, alternately push out on the cover retaining posts using a 9/32 inch rod through two access holes in back of steering wheel.**
3. Disconnect horn and speed control wiring, if equipped.
4. Remove steering wheel nut.
5. Mark relationship between steering shaft and steering wheel hub for proper reinstallation.
6. Remove steering wheel with a suitable puller.
7. Reverse procedure to install.

INSTRUMENT CLUSTER
REPLACE
1985–86 LTD & MARQUIS & 1985–88 THUNDERBIRD COUGAR

STANDARD CLUSTER

Thunderbird & Cougar Exc. Turbo Coupe

1. Disconnect battery ground cable.
2. Remove two lower trim covers.
3. Remove steering column cover, then disconnect shift indicator bracket and cable assembly from steering column.
4. Move shift lever, then remove cluster trim cover.

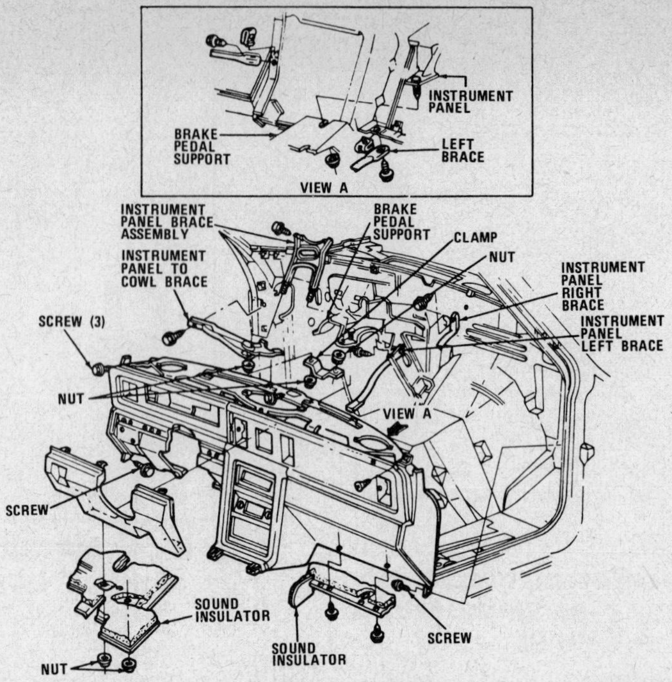

Fig. 6 Typical instrument panel. 1983–88 Cougar & Thunderbird

5. Remove 4 cluster attaching screws, then pull bottom of cluster toward steering wheel.
6. Working from behind and underneath cluster, disconnect the two electrical connectors.
7. Swing bottom of cluster outward to gain adequate clearance, then remove cluster from vehicle.
8. Reverse procedure to install ensuring that shift indicator is properly adjusted.

Turbo Coupe

1. Disconnect battery ground.
2. Remove steering column shroud, if applicable.
3. Remove the ten retaining screws, then the cluster trim cover.
4. Remove the four instrument cluster to instrument panel attaching screws, then pull cluster outward.
5. Disconnect cluster feed plug from receptacle and boost gauge rubber tube from gauge nipple.
6. Remove cluster from vehicle.
7. Reverse procedure to install.

LTD & Marquis

1. Disconnect battery ground cable.
2. Disconnect speedometer cable from cluster.
3. Remove instrument trim cover, then the steering column shroud.
4. Remove shift control cable clamp retaining screw, then disconnect cable loop from shift cane lever pin. Remove plastic clamp from steering column.
5. Remove the four cluster attaching screws, then disconnect feed plug from receptacle.
6. Disconnect engine warning lamp, then remove cluster from vehicle.
7. Reverse procedure to install, noting the following:
   a. When reconnecting shift control cable, place loop of cable over pin on shift cane lever.
   b. Position shift lever in Drive, then rotate cable clamp until indicator pointer is centrally located on D. Torque cable clamp retaining screw to 20-30 inch lbs.
   c. Move shift lever through all shift positions and check indicator pointer for proper position.

ELECTRONIC CLUSTER

Thunderbird & Cougar Exc. Turbo Coupe

Refer to "Standard Cluster" for removal procedures on the above mentioned vehicles.

1982 COUGAR XR-7, 1982–84 THUNDERBIRD & 1983–84 COUGAR, LTD & MARQUIS

STANDARD CLUSTER

1983–84 Cougar & Thunderbird

1. Disconnect battery ground cable.
2. Remove steering column shroud and instrument cluster trim cover.
3. Remove 6 instrument cluster-to-instrument panel attaching screws.
4. Pull cluster away from instrument panel and disconnect speedometer cable and cluster feed plugs.
5. Remove instrument cluster from vehicle.
6. Reverse procedure to install.

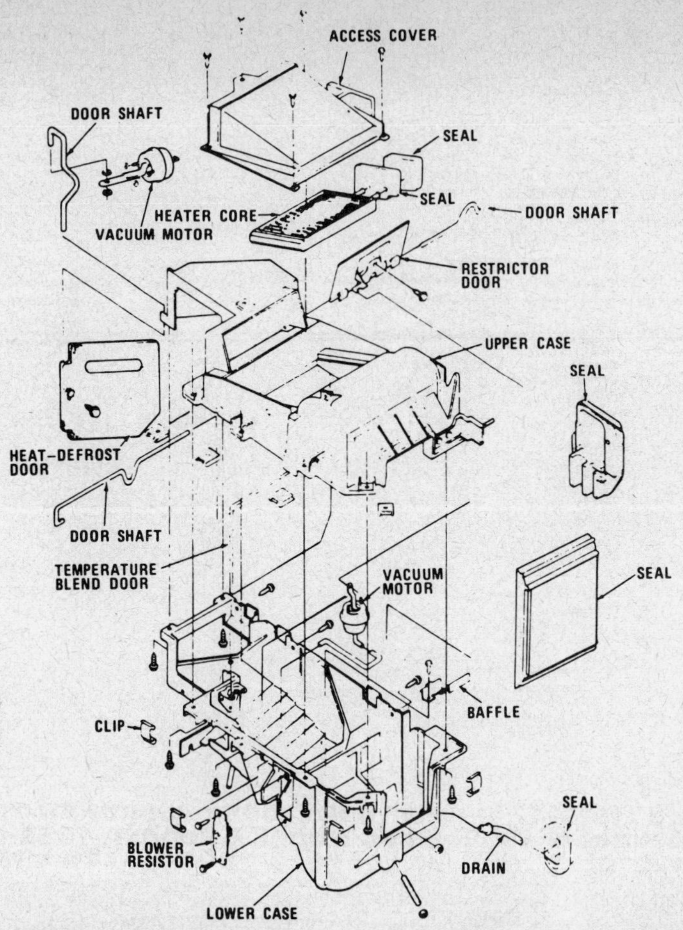

Fig. 7 Heater core less A/C. 1982 Cougar XR-7, 1982–88 Thunderbird, 1983–88 Cougar & 1983–86 LTD & Marquis

1982–84 Exc. 1983–84 Cougar & Thunderbird

1. Disconnect battery ground cable.
2. Disconnect speedometer cable, then remove instrument panel trim cover and steering column shroud.
3. Remove screw attaching transmission shift lever indicator cable bracket to steering column, then detach cable loop from pin on shift cane lever and remove plastic clamp from around steering column.
4. Remove four instrument cluster retaining screws, then disconnect cluster feed plug and remove instrument cluster.
5. Reverse procedure to install.

ELECTRONIC CLUSTER

1. Disconnect battery ground cable.
2. Remove four instrument panel lower trim cover attaching screws, then remove trim cover.
3. Remove steering column shroud.
4. Remove six instrument cluster trim panel attaching screws, then remove trim panel.
5. Remove four instrument cluster to instrument panel attaching screws.
6. Remove screw attaching transmission selector lever indicator cable bracket to steering column, then detach cable loop from pin on steering column.
7. Carefully pull cluster assembly away from instrument panel.
8. Disconnect speedometer cable and cluster feed plug and ground wire from cluster back plate, then remove cluster assembly.
9. Reverse procedure to install.

1982 COUGAR & GRANADA & 1982–83 FAIRMONT, ZEPHYR

1. Disconnect battery ground cable.
2. Remove steering column shroud.
3. Remove instrument cluster trim cover.
4. Remove screw retaining PRND21 control cable clamp to steering column. Then, disconnect the cable from pin on steering column. Remove plastic clamp from steering column.
5. Remove two upper and two lower screws retaining instrument cluster to instrument panel.
6. Pull cluster from instrument panel and disconnect speedometer cable.
7. Disconnect electrical connectors from instrument cluster.
8. Remove instrument cluster from vehicle.
9. Reverse procedure to install.

WINDSHIELD WIPER MOTOR

REPLACE

EXC. STA. WAG. LIFTGATE WIPER MOTOR

1. On 1983-88 Cougar and Thunderbird models, operate wipers and turn ignition key off when blades are straight up on the windshield.
2. On all models, disconnect battery ground cable.
3. On 1982 Cougar XR-7 and Thunderbird, and 1983-86 LTD and Marquis models, remove righthand wiper and blade assembly. On Fairmont, Granada, Zephyr, 1982-88 Cougar and 1983-88 Thunderbird models, remove both wiper arm and blade assemblies.
4. On all models, remove cowl grille or trash screen attaching screws, then remove cowl grille or trash screen.
5. Remove clip, then disconnect linkage drive arm from motor crankpin.
6. Disconnect wire connector from wiper motor, then remove wiper motor attaching bolts and lift motor from cowl opening.

STA. WAG. LIFTGATE WIPER MOTOR

1. Disconnect battery ground cable.
2. Remove wiper arm and blade assembly.
3. Remove pivot shaft attaching nut and spacers.
4. On 1982-85 models, remove liftgate inner trim panel.
5. On all models, remove license plate housing attaching screws, then disconnect lamp electrical connector and remove housing.
6. Disconnect wiper motor wire connector.
7. Remove linkage arm lock clip, then pry off arm and remove linkage.
8. Remove wiper motor and bracket attaching bolts, then remove motor and bracket.

WINDSHIELD WIPER, TRANSMISSION REPLACE

1. On 1983-88 Cougar and Thunderbird models, operate wipers and turn ignition key off when blades are straight up on windshield.
2. On all models, disconnect battery ground cable.
3. On all models except 1983-88 Cougar and Thunderbird, remove both wiper arm and blade assemblies.
4. On 1983-88 Cougar and Thunderbird models, remove right wiper arm and blade assembly.
5. On all models, remove cowl grille or left trash screen attaching screws then the cowl grille or screen.
6. Remove retaining clip, then disconnect linkage drive arm from wiper motor crankpin.

7. On Fairmont, Granada, Zephyr and 1982 Cougar models, remove 4 bolts attaching left and right pivot shafts to cowl, then remove linkage assembly.
8. On Cougar XR-7, Thunderbird and 1983-86 LTD and Marquis models, remove 2 bolts attaching right pivot shaft to cowl, then remove nut, washer and spacer from left pivot shaft and remove linkage assembly.
9. On 1983-88 Cougar and Thunderbird models, remove pivot shaft attaching screws, then remove linkage assembly out through cowl chamber.
10. Reverse procedure to install.

WINDSHIELD WIPER SWITCH

REPLACE

EXC. STA. WAG. LIFTGATE WIPER MOTOR

1. Disconnect battery ground cable.
2. Remove four steering column shroud attaching screws, then grasp top and bottom of shroud and separate.
3. Using a screwdriver, disconnect wire connector from wiper switch.
4. Remove two wiper switch attaching screws, then remove switch.
5. Reverse procedure to install.

STA. WAG. LIFTGATE WIPER MOTOR

1. Disconnect battery ground cable.
2. Remove wiper switch knob, then remove two bezel retaining screws.
3. Pull switch retainer away from instrument panel.
4. Remove wiper switch retaining nut, then separate switch from retainer.
5. Disconnect wire connector from wiper switch, then remove switch.
6. Reverse procedure to install.

RADIO

REPLACE

When installing radio, be sure to adjust antenna trimmer for peak performance.

1982 COUGAR XR-7, 1982–88 THUNDERBIRD, 1983–88 COUGAR & 1983–86 LTD & MARQUIS

1. Disconnect battery ground cable.
2. Remove radio knobs, then remove instrument panel center trim panel.
3. Remove radio mounting plate attaching screws.
4. Pull radio to disengage from lower rear support bracket, then disconnect power antenna, speaker leads and floor switch lead, if equipped and remove radio.
5. Reverse procedure to install.

1982 COUGAR & GRANADA & 1982–83 FAIRMONT, ZEPHYR

1. Disconnect battery ground cable.
2. Disconnect power lead, speaker leads and antenna lead from radio.

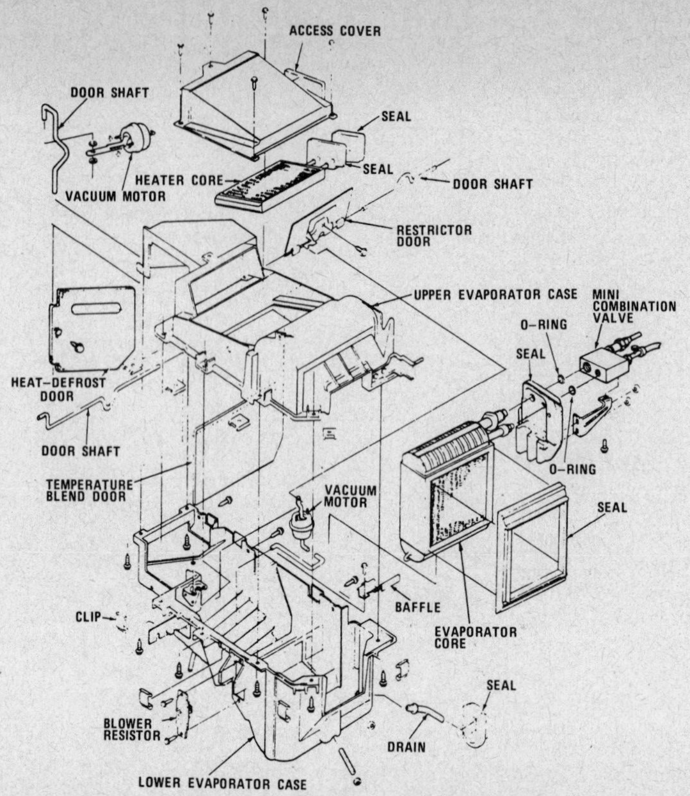

Fig. 8 Heater core with A/C. 1982 Cougar XR-7, 1982 Granada, 1982–83 Fairmont & Zephyr, 1982–88 Thunderbird, 1983–88 Cougar & 1983–86 LTD & Marquis

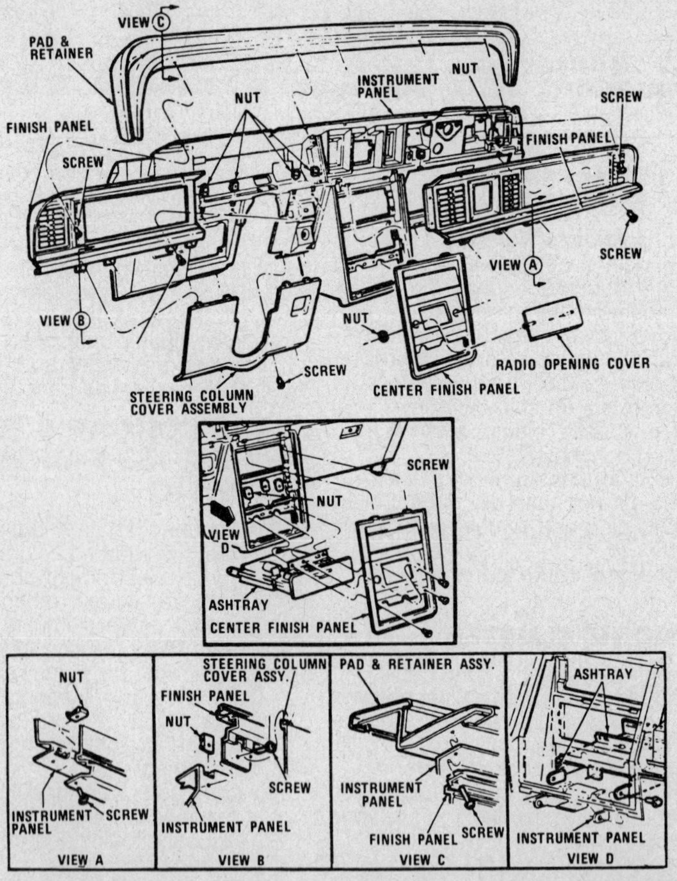

Fig. 9 Instrument panel trim panel (Typical). 1982 Cougar XR-7, Thunderbird & 1983–86 LTD & Marquis

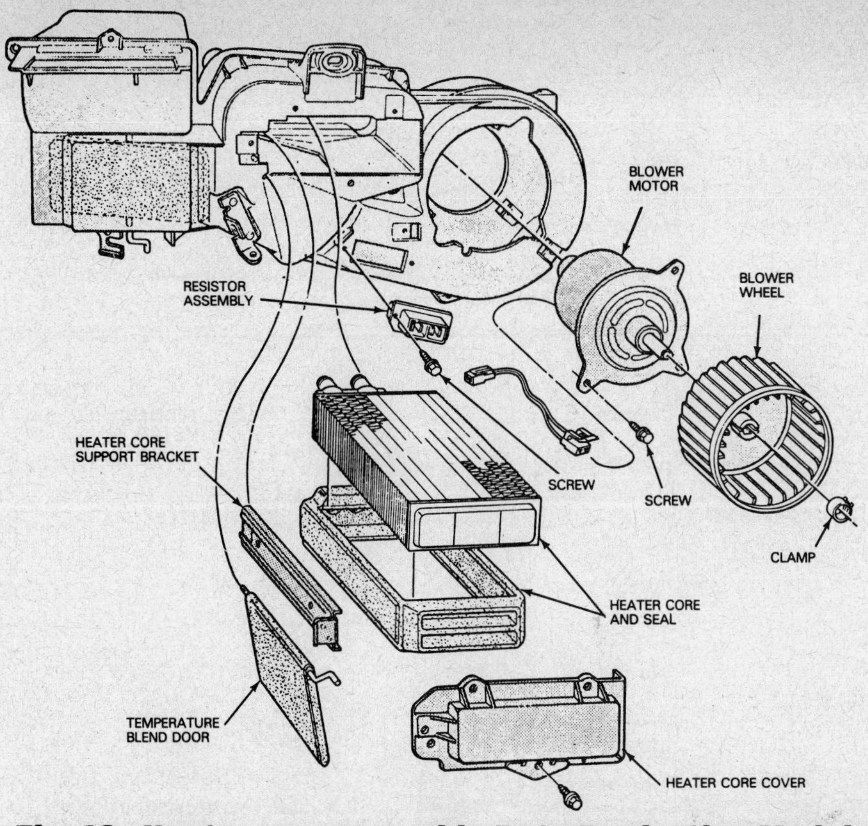

Fig. 10 Heater core assembly (Late Production Models). 1982 Cougar & Granada & 1982–83 Fairmont & Zephyr

3. Remove control knobs, discs, control knob shaft nuts and washers.
4. Remove ashtray and bracket.
5. Remove radio rear support attaching nut.
6. Remove instrument panel lower reinforcement.
7. Remove heater or A/C floor ducts.
8. Remove radio from bezel and rear support, then lower radio from instrument panel.
9. Reverse procedure to install.

HEATER CORE

REPLACE

1983–88 COUGAR & THUNDERBIRD

Less Air Conditioning

1. Disconnect battery ground cable.
2. Remove steering column cover, then the instrument panel reinforcement under steering column opening.
3. Remove 2 nuts securing hood latch release handle mounting bracket to brake pedal support under steering column.
4. Remove sound insulator from lower left side of instrument panel, **Fig. 6.**
5. Remove 2 steering column clamp attaching nuts and lower steering column to rest on front seat.
6. Remove instrument panel pad attaching screws and the pad.
7. Disconnect speedometer cable from speedometer.
8. Remove console cover or tray.
9. Remove 4 console switch panel cover attaching screws, then disconnect electrical connectors and remove switch panel.
10. Remove console attaching screws, then disengage console from instrument panel and position aside.
11. Remove 2 pins attaching glove compartment door straps to glove compartment and allow door to hang down on hinge.
12. Remove instrument panel brace attaching bolt from glove compartment opening.
13. Remove brake pedal support attaching nut from lower edge of instrument panel.
14. Remove instrument panel brace attaching bolt from lower edge of instrument panel on left side of console extension.
15. Remove instrument panel-to-cowl side panel attaching bolt from both sides of instrument panel.
16. Support instrument panel and remove 3 instrument panel-to-cowl top panel attaching screws.
17. Move instrument panel rearward, disconnect necessary electrical connectors and vacuum hoses, and rest panel on front seat.
18. Drain cooling system, then disconnect hoses from heater core. Cover hoses and heater core tubes to prevent leakage.
19. Remove 2 nuts securing heater case to dash panel from engine compartment.
20. Working in passenger compartment, remove screws attaching heater case support bracket and air inlet duct support bracket to cowl top panel.
21. Remove nut retaining bracket at left end of heater case to dash panel and nut securing bracket below case to dash panel.
22. Pull heater case away from dash panel to gain access to heater core access cover attaching screws.
23. Remove heater core access cover attaching screws and the cover.
24. Remove heater core and seals from heater case, **Fig. 7.**
25. Remove the 2 seals from heater core tubes.
26. Reverse procedure to install.

With Air Conditioning

1. Perform steps 1 through 17 as described under "Heater Core, Replace," "1983-88 Cougar & Thunderbird, Less Air Conditioning."
2. Discharge refrigerant from A/C system at the service valve on suction line. When system is fully discharged, disconnect and cap high and low pressure lines.
3. Drain cooling system, then disconnect hoses from heater core. Cover hoses and heater core tubes to prevent leakage.
4. Remove screw securing air inlet duct and blower housing assembly support brace to cowl top panel.
5. Disconnect black vacuum supply hose from inline check valve in engine compartment.
6. Disconnect blower motor electrical connectors from harness.
7. Remove 2 evaporator case-to-dash panel attaching nuts from engine compartment.
8. Working in passenger compartment, remove evaporator case support bracket-to-cowl top panel attaching screw.
9. Remove nut securing bracket below evaporator case to dash panel.
10. Carefully remove evaporator case assembly from vehicle.
11. Remove 5 heater core access cover attaching screws and the cover.
12. Remove heater core and seals from evaporator case, **Fig. 8.**
13. Remove the 2 seals from heater core tubes.
14. Reverse procedure to install.

1982 COUGAR XR-7 & THUNDERBIRD & 1983–86 LTD & MARQUIS

1. Disconnect battery ground cable.
2. Remove steering column cover assembly, then remove left and right finish panels, **Fig. 9.**
3. Remove two screws from sides of instrument panel pad and retainer assembly.
4. Remove pad and retainer assembly and upper finish panel.
5. Remove steering column attaching bolts, then carefully lower steering

column just enough to allow access to transmission gear selector lever cable assembly. Reach between steering column and instrument panel, then carefully lift selector lever cable from lever and remove cable clamp from steering column tube.
6. Lower steering column and allow to rest on front seat.
7. Remove screw attaching instrument panel to brake pedal support through steering column opening.
8. Disconnect temperature door cable from door and heater/evaporator cable bracket.
9. Disconnect vacuum hose connectors at evaporator housing.
10. Disconnect blower motor resistor wire from resistor on heater/evaporator case and blower motor feed wire at inline connector.
11. Support instrument panel, then remove three screws attaching top of instrument panel to cowl.
12. Remove one screw attaching each end of instrument panel to cowl side panels, then remove two screws attaching instrument panel to floor.
13. Move instrument panel rearward and disconnect speedometer cable and any wires that will prevent instrument panel from being placed on front seat. **Use care when removing instrument panel to prevent damage to panel or steering column surfaces.**
14. On 1982-86 models less A/C, perform steps 18 through 26 under "Heater Core, Replace," "1983-88 Cougar & Thunderbird, Less Air Conditioning."
15. On 1983-86 models with A/C, perform steps 2 through 14 under "Heater Core, Replace," "1983-88 Cougar & Thunderbird, With Air Conditioning."

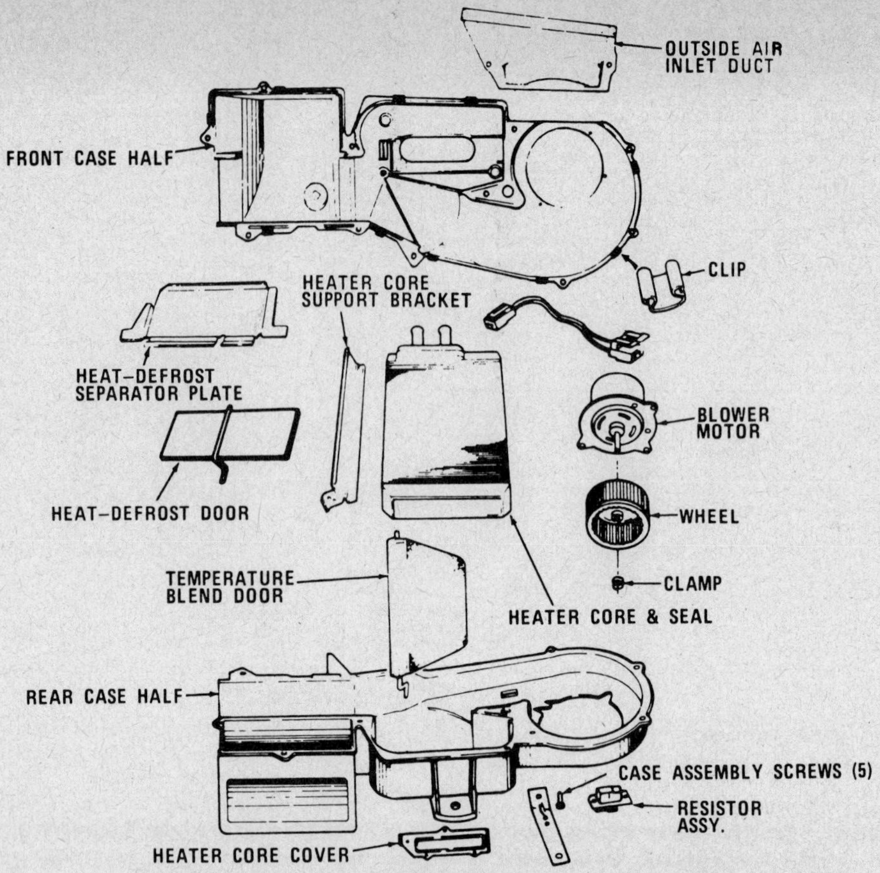

Fig. 11 Heater case assembly (Early Production Models). 1982 Fairmont, Zephyr, Cougar & Granada

1982–83 FAIRMONT, ZEPHYR & 1982 COUGAR & GRANADA

Models with heater cases built after 11-1-81 use a one piece case, Fig. 10. This type case cannot be separated and all interior case components must be removed and installed through openings in case.

Less Air Conditioning

1. Disconnect battery ground cable and drain cooling system.
2. Disconnect heater hoses from heater core and seal the core tubes.
3. Remove glove box liner.
4. Remove instrument panel to cowl brace retaining screws and brace.
5. Place temperature control lever in the warm position.
6. Remove heater core cover retaining screws and the cover, **Figs. 10 and 11.**
7. From engine compartment, remove heater case assembly mounting stud nuts.
8. Push heater core tubes and seal toward passenger compartment to loosen heater core from case assembly.
9. Remove heater core through glove box opening.
10. Reverse procedure to install.

With Air Conditioning

1. Disconnect battery ground cable.
2. Remove screws attaching instrument cluster trim panel to instrument panel pad.
3. Remove instrument panel pad to instrument panel screws at each defroster opening.
4. Remove instrument panel pad edge to instrument panel screws, and pad.
5. Remove steering column lower cover to instrument panel screws then the cover.
6. On 1982-83 models, proceed as follows:
   a. Remove steering column trim shroud attaching screws and the trim shrouds.
   b. Remove steering column attaching nuts, then carefully lower steering column just enough to allow access to transmission gear selector lever cable assembly. Reach between steering column and instrument panel and carefully lift selector lever cable from lever and remove cable clamp from steering column tube.
   c. Lower steering column and allow to rest on front seat.
7. On all models, remove instrument panel to brake pedal support screw at steering column opening.
8. Remove screw attaching lower brace to lower edge of instrument panel below radio.
9. Remove screw attaching the brace to lower edge of instrument panel.
10. Disconnect temperature control cable from blend door and evaporator case bracket.
11. Disconnect vacuum hose connectors from evaporator case.
12. Disconnect blower resistor wire connector from resistor on evaporator housing, then the blower motor feed wire at inline connector.
13. Support instrument panel and, with an angle Phillips screwdriver, remove three screws attaching top of instrument panel to the cowl.
14. Remove screws attaching instrument panel to cowl side panels.
15. Move instrument panel rearward and disconnect speedometer cable and any wiring that will not permit the instrument panel to be positioned on the front seat.
16. On 1982-83 models, proceed as follows:
   a. Discharge refrigerant from A/C system at the service valve on suction line. When system is fully discharged, disconnect and cap high and lower pressure lines.
   b. Drain cooling system, then disconnect hoses from heater core. Cover hoses and heater core tubes to prevent leakage.
   c. Remove screw securing air inlet

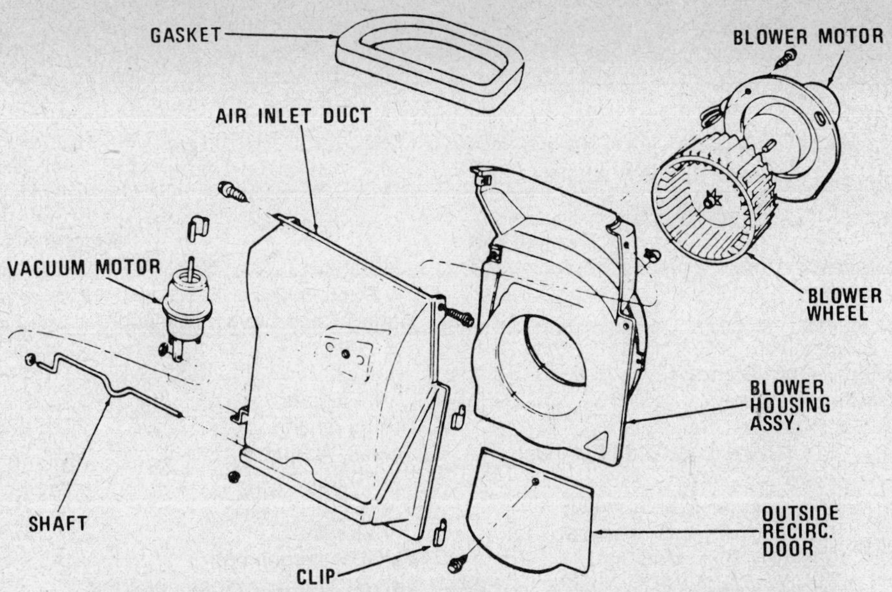

Fig. 12 Blower motor. 1982 Cougar XR-7, 1982–83 Fairmont & Zephyr with A/C, 1982–88 Thunderbird, 1983–88 Cougar & 1983–86 LTD & Marquis

duct and blower housing assembly support brace to cowl top panel.

d. Disconnect black vacuum supply hose from inline check valve in engine compartment.
e. Disconnect blower motor electrical connectors from harness.
f. Disconnect electrical connector from blower motor resistor.
g. Remove two evaporator case-to-dash panel attaching nuts from engine compartment.
h. Working in passenger compartment, remove evaporator case support bracket-to-cowl top panel attaching screws.
i. Remove screw retaining bracket below evaporator case to dash panel.
j. Carefully remove evaporator case assembly from vehicle.

17. On all models, remove five heater core access cover attaching screws and the access cover, **Fig. 8.**
18. Remove heater core and seals from evaporator case.
19. Remove the two seals from heater core tubes.
20. Reverse procedure to install.

BLOWER MOTOR REPLACE

1982–83 FAIRMONT & ZEPHYR & 1982 COUGAR & GRANADA LESS AIR CONDITIONING

1. Disconnect battery ground cable.
2. Remove screw securing right register duct mounting bracket to lower edge of instrument panel.
3. Remove screws securing ventilator control cable lever assembly to lower edge of instrument panel.
4. Remove glove box liner.
5. Remove plastic rivets securing grille to ventilator floor outlet, then the grille from the bottom of the ventilator assembly.
6. Remove right register duct and register assembly.
7. Remove screws securing ventilator assembly to blower housing portion of the heater case assembly.
8. Slide ventilator assembly toward the right, then downward to remove from under instrument panel.
9. Remove push nut from door crank arm.
10. Remove control cable housing retaining screw, then control cable assembly from ventilator assembly.
11. Remove hub clamp spring from blower wheel hub, then slide wheel off shaft.
12. Remove blower motor attaching screws and the blower motor. Disconnect motor electrical connector before removing from vehicle.
13. Reverse procedure to install.

1982 COUGAR XR-7, 1982–83 FAIRMONT & ZEPHYR WITH A/C, 1982–88 THUNDERBIRD, 1983–86 LTD & MARQUIS & 1983–88 COUGAR

1. Disconnect battery ground cable.
2. Remove glove box and disconnect vacuum hose from outside–recirc air door motor.
3. Remove instrument panel lower right to side attaching bolt.
4. Remove screw attaching support brace to top of air inlet duct.
5. Disconnect blower motor lead wire.
6. Remove nut securing blower motor housing lower bracket to evaporator case.
7. Remove side cowl trim panel and the blower ground wire screw.
8. Remove screw securing top of air inlet duct to evaporator case.
9. Move air inlet duct and blower housing assembly downward from evaporator case, **Fig. 12.**
10. Remove blower motor mounting plate screws and the blower motor. **Do not remove mounting plate from motor.**
11. Reverse procedure to install.

SPEED CONTROLS

BEAD CHAIN ADJUSTMENT

This adjustment should be made to remove as much slack as possible from the chain without restricting the carburetor lever from returning to the idle speed position. On vehicles equipped with a solenoid throttle positioner, the adjustment should be performed with the throttle positioner disengaged.

VACUUM DUMP VALVE

The vacuum dump valve is mounted on a movable mounting bracket. The valve should be adjusted so that it is closed when the brake pedal is not depressed and open when the brake pedal is depressed.

ACTUATOR CABLE ADJUSTMENT

1. Remove cable retaining clip.
2. On all carbureted models, deactivate the throttle positioner and set carburetor at hot idle.
3. On all models, pull the actuator cable to remove slack.
4. Insert cable retaining clip while maintaining light tension on the actuator cable.

Engine Section

NOTE: The following engines are covered in this section: 4-140 (2.3L), 6-200 (3.3L), V6-232 (3.8L), V8-255 (4.2L) & V8-302 (5.0L). Refer to "Ford Mustan g • Mercury Capri" Section for service procedures on the 4-140 (2.3L) engine not covered in this section.

INDEX

ENGINE MOUNTS

Whenever self-locking mounting bolts and nuts are removed, they must be replaced with new self-locking bolts and nuts.

On some 1982 Granada, 1982-83 Cougar and Thunderbird and 1983 LTD and Marquis models, a silver colored flange nut which retains the engine mounts to No. 2 crossmember has replaced the black nut previously used. Reduce torque on this type nut to 50-65 ft. lbs.

1985–86 LTD & MARQUIS & 1985–88 COUGAR & THUNDERBIRD 4-140

1. Support engine using a suitable jack and wooden block placed under oil pan.
2. On LTD and Marquis models, remove bolt securing lower end of engine damper to No. 2 crossmember bracket, Fig. 1.
3. On turbocharged engine, remove through bolts attaching both insulators to No. 2 crossmember bracket.
4. On all models, remove nuts and washers attaching both insulators to No. 2 crossmember.

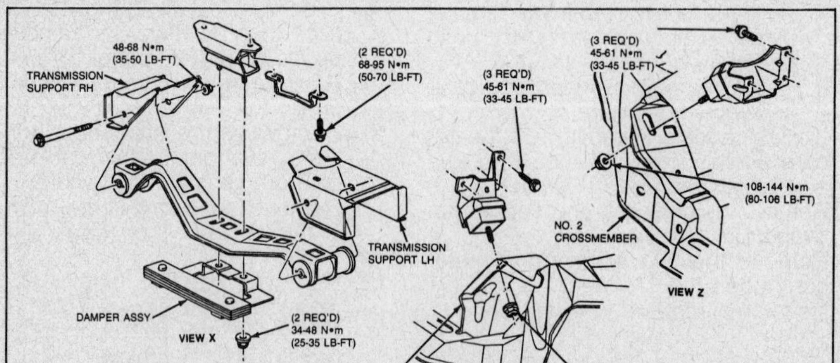

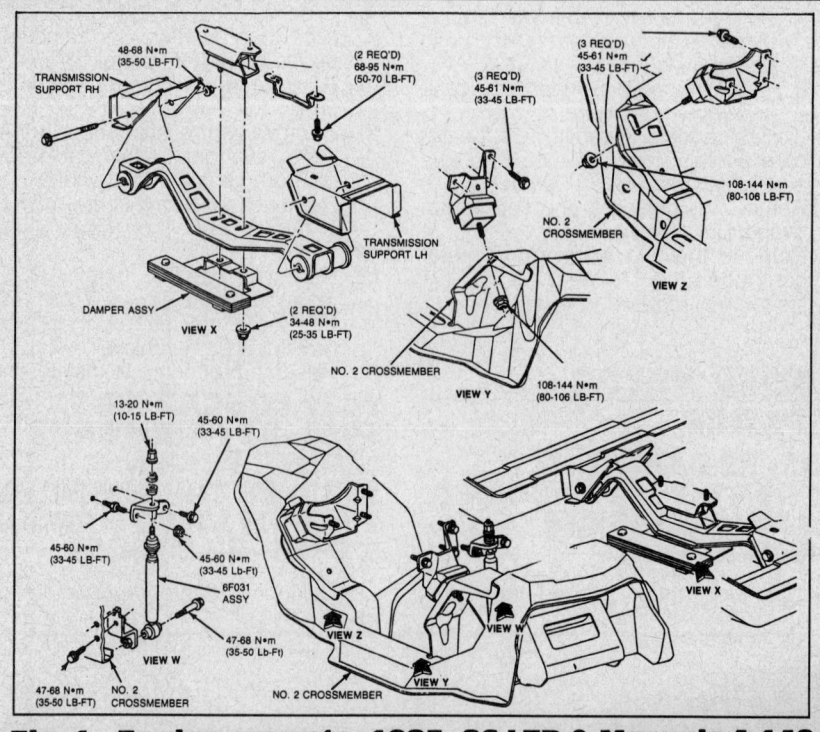

Fig. 1 Engine mounts. 1985–86 LTD & Marquis 4-140

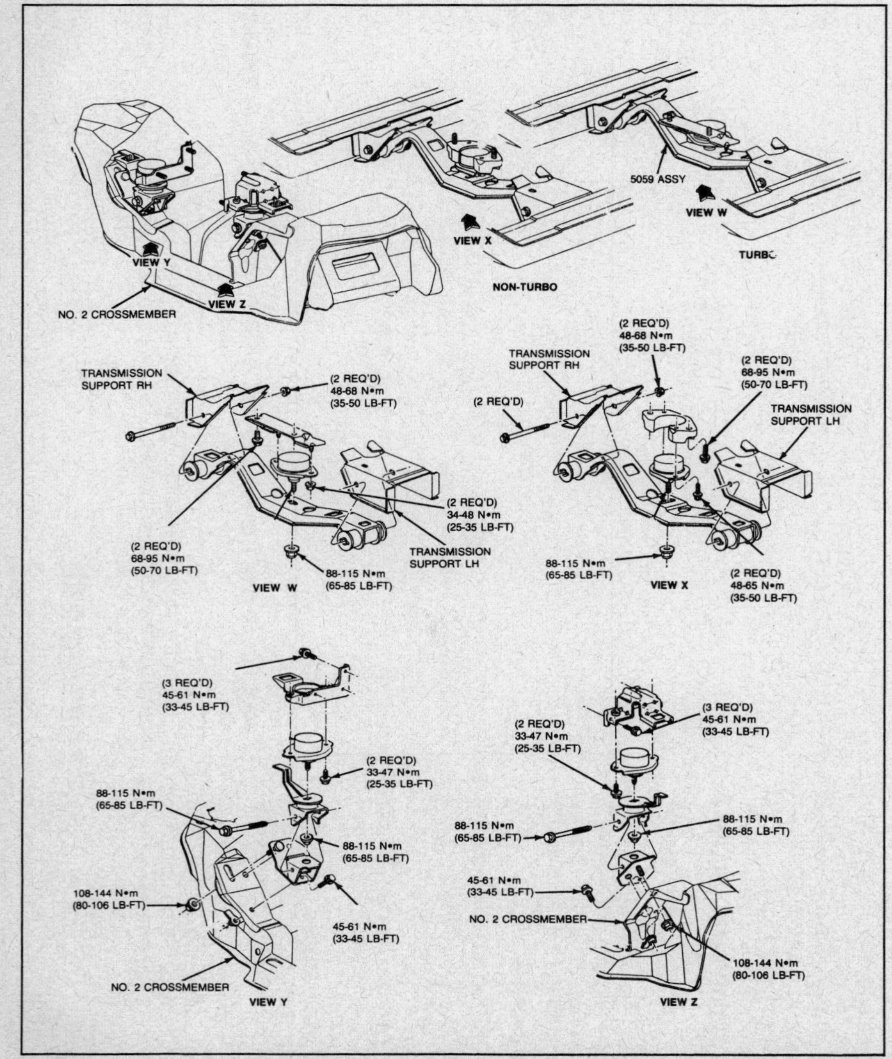

Fig. 2 Engine mounts. 1985 Cougar & Thunderbird 4-140

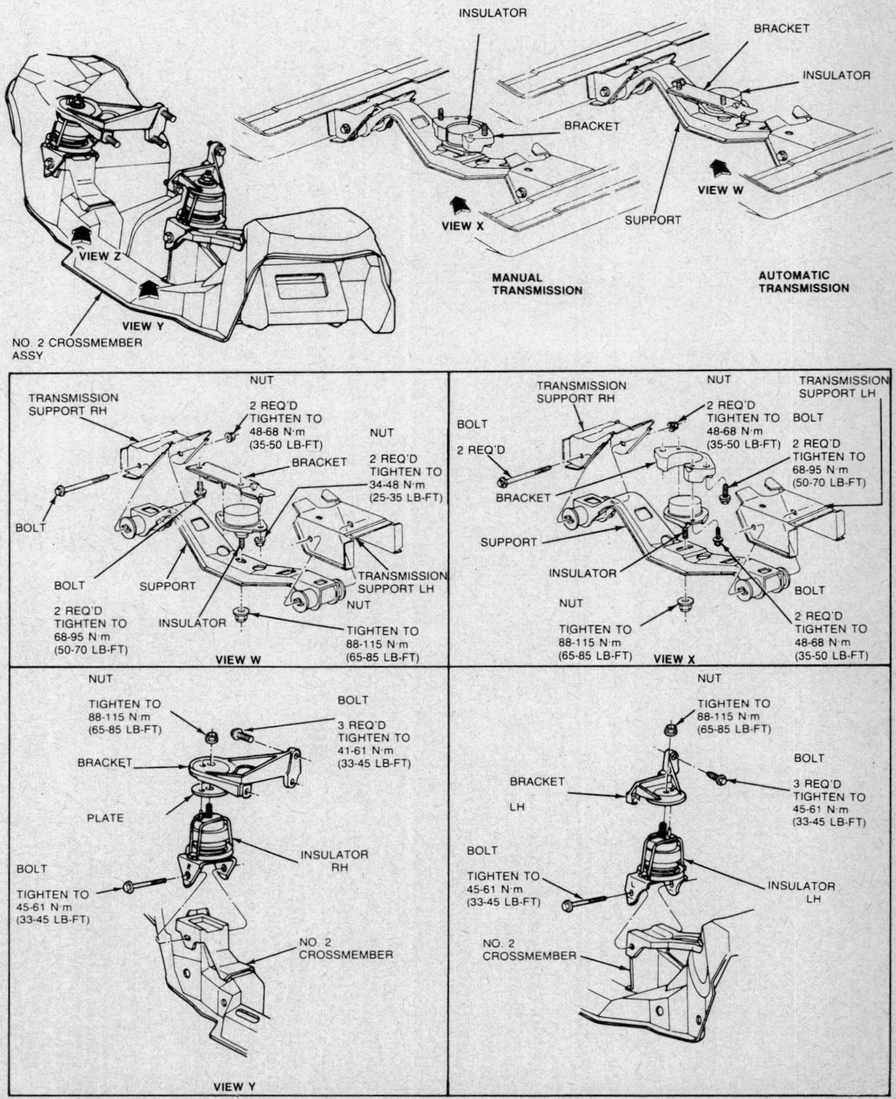

Fig. 3 Engine mounts. 1986–88 Cougar & Thunderbird

5. Disconnect shift linkage, then raise engine just enough to disengage insulator from crossmember bracket.
6. Remove insulator and bracket attaching bolts, then the insulator and bracket assembly, **Figs. 1, 2 and 3.**
7. Reverse procedure to install.

1983–84 COUGAR, LTD, MARQUIS & THUNDERBIRD 4-140

1. Support engine using a suitable jack and wooden block placed under oil pan.
2. Remove fuel pump shield attaching screw, if equipped, from lefthand engine support bracket.
3. On LTD and Marquis models, remove bolt securing lower end of engine damper to No. 2 crossmember bracket, **Fig. 4.**
4. On Cougar and Thunderbird models, remove through bolts from bottom of mounts, **Fig. 5.**
5. Remove nuts and washers attaching both insulators to No. 2 crossmember.
6. Raise engine just enough to clear insulator studs from crossmember.
7. Remove insulator and bracket attaching bolts, then the insulator and bracket assembly from vehicle.
8. Reverse procedure to install.

1982 COUGAR, GRANADA & THUNDERBIRD 1982–83 FAIRMONT, ZEPHYR & 1983 LTD & MARQUIS 6-200

1. Remove fan shroud screws.
2. Support engine with suitable jack and wooden block.
3. On LTD and Marquis models, remove engine damper lower bolt and No. 2 crossmember bracket, **Fig. 6.**
4. On all models, remove nut and washer assemblies from insulators at No. 2 crossmember.
5. Raise engine with jack until insulator studs clear crossmember.
6. Disconnect bracket from engine and remove engine mount.
7. Reverse procedure to install. Torque fasteners according to **Figs. 6 and 7.**

1983–88 V6-232

1. Remove fan shroud attaching screws.
2. Support engine using a suitable jack and wooden block placed under oil pan.
3. Remove nuts or bolts and washers attaching insulators to No. 2 crossmember, **Fig. 8 and 9.**
4. On LTD and Marquis models, remove bolt securing lower end of engine damper to No. 2 crossmember bracket, if necessary.
5. Disconnect shift linkage, if necessary.
6. On all models, raise engine sufficiently to clear insulator studs or clevis brackets from crossmember.
7. Remove fuel pump shield, if equipped, from righthand side of engine.
8. Disconnect oil cooler line attaching clips and starter ground cable from righthand engine support bracket.
9. Remove insulator and bracket attaching bolts, then the insulator and bracket assembly from vehicle.
10. Reverse procedure to install.

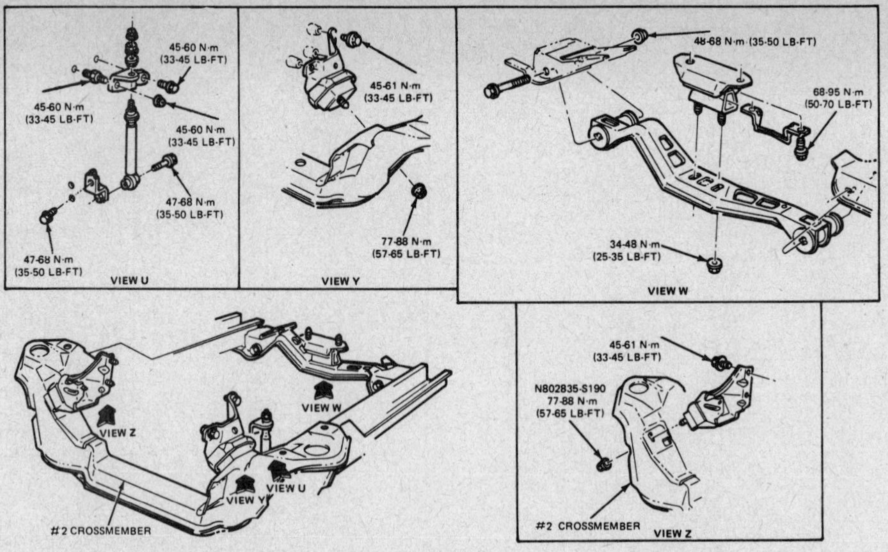

Fig. 4 Engine mounts. 1983–84 LTD & Marquis 4-140

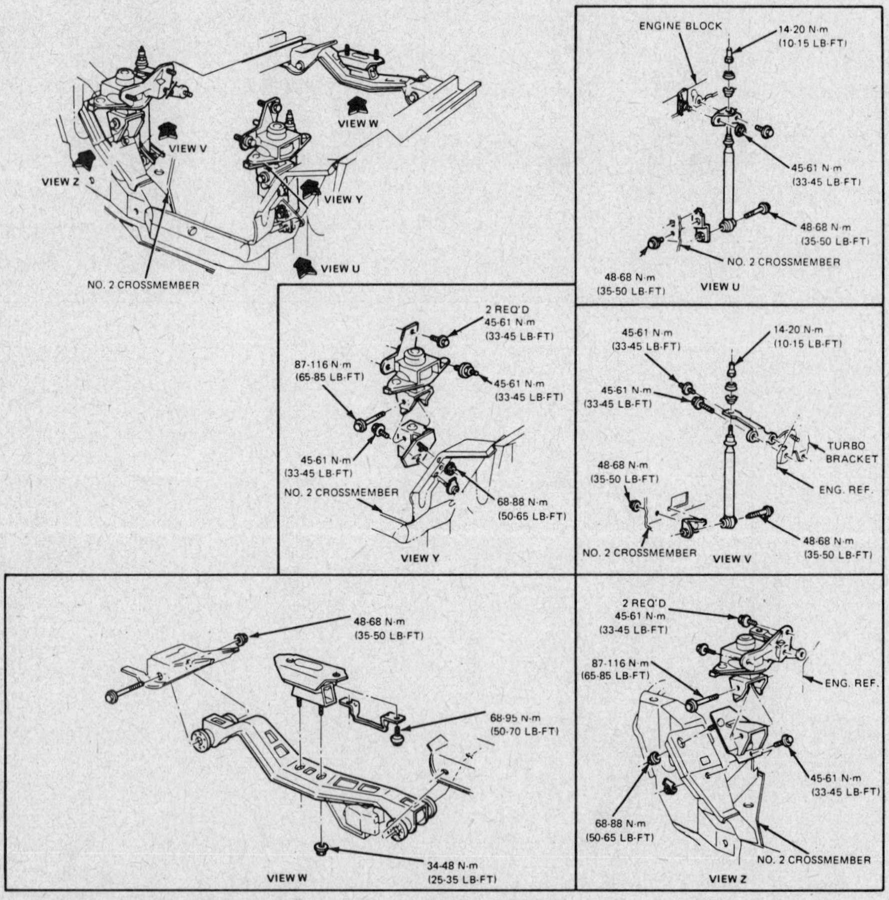

Fig. 5 Engine mounts. 1983–84 Cougar & Thunderbird 4-140

1982 V6-232

1. Support engine using a suitable jack and wooden block placed under oil pan.
2. Remove nut and washer attaching mount to chassis, then raise engine slightly, **Fig. 10.**
3. Remove bolts attaching engine mount and bracket to engine, then remove mount.
4. Reverse procedure to install.

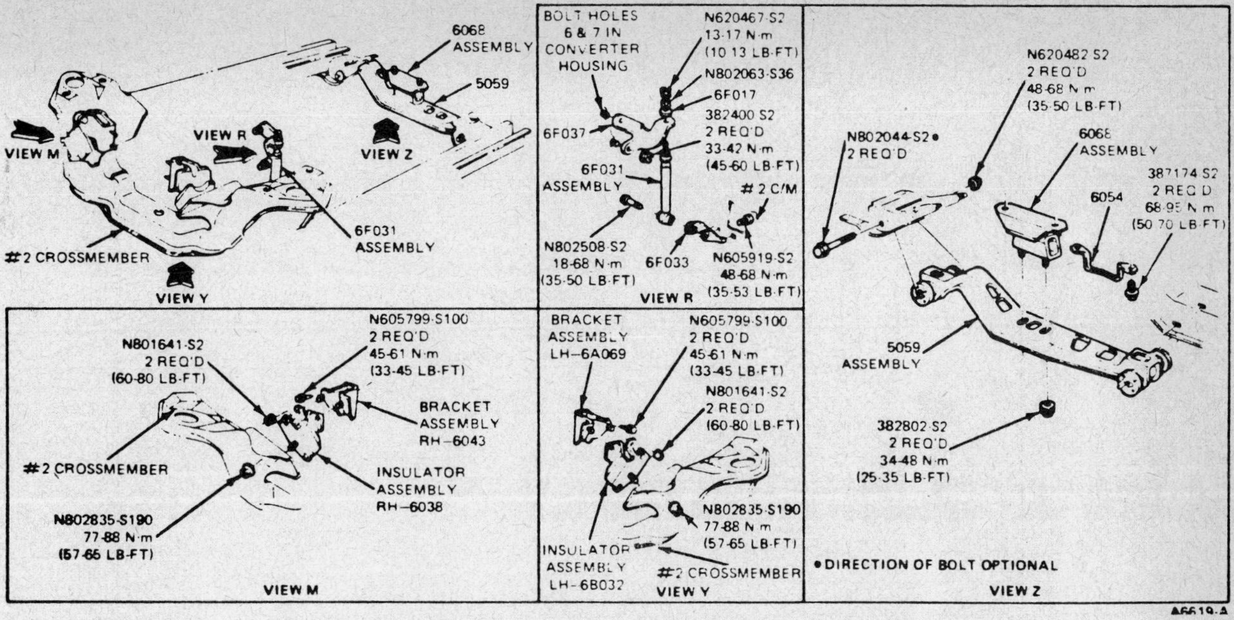

Fig. 6 Engine mounts. 1983 LTD & Marquis 6-200

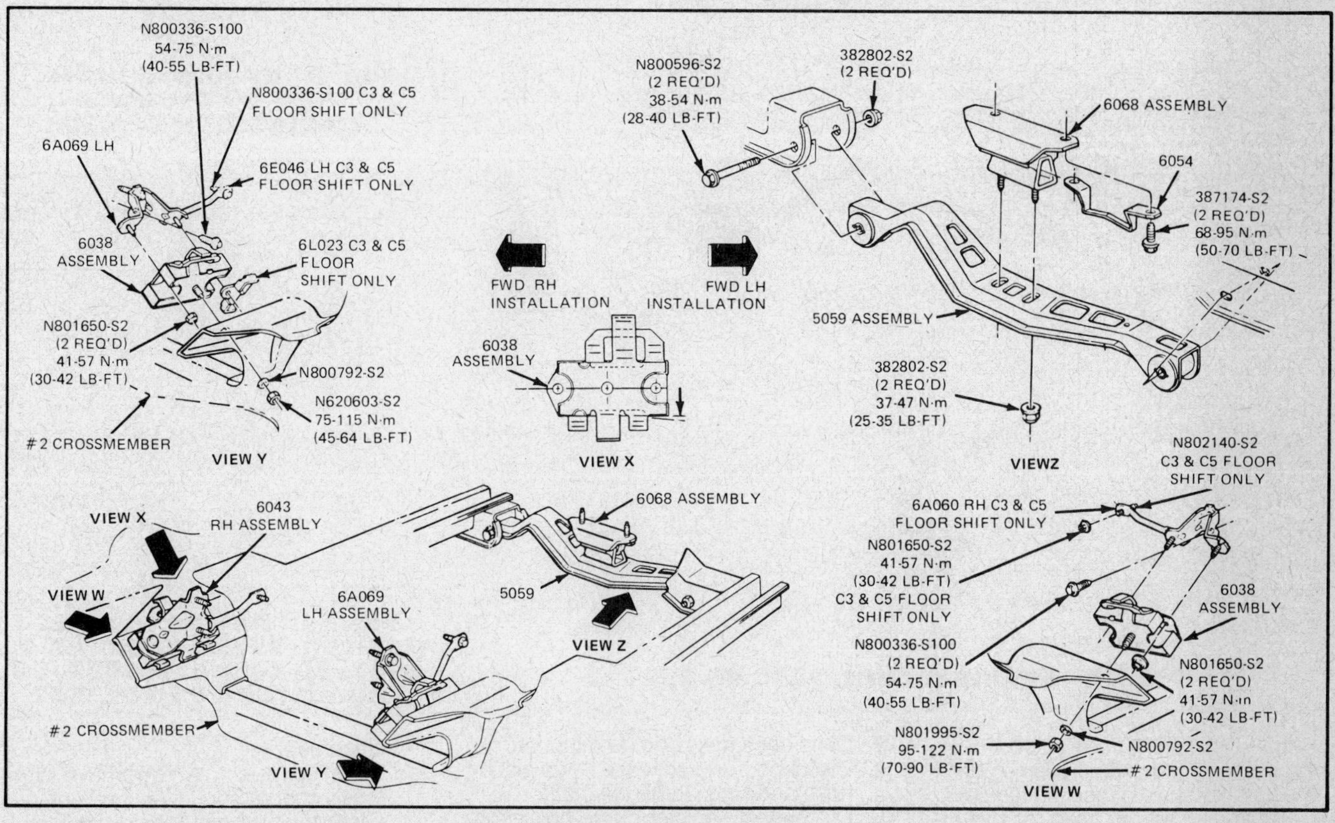

Fig. 7 Engine mounts. 1982–83 Fairmont & Zephyr, 1982 Cougar XR-7, Granada & Thunderbird 6-200

1984–86 LTD & MARQUIS V8-302

1. Remove fan shroud attaching screws.
2. Position block of wood under oil pan, then support engine with suitable jack.
3. Remove insulator to crossmember attaching nuts.
4. Disconnect shift linkage, then raise engine and remove insulator.
5. Reverse procedure to install.

1982 COUGAR XR-7, 1982–88 THUNDERBIRD & 1983–88 COUGAR V8-255 & 302

1. Remove fan shroud attaching screws.
2. Using a suitable jack with a wooden block placed under oil pan, support engine.

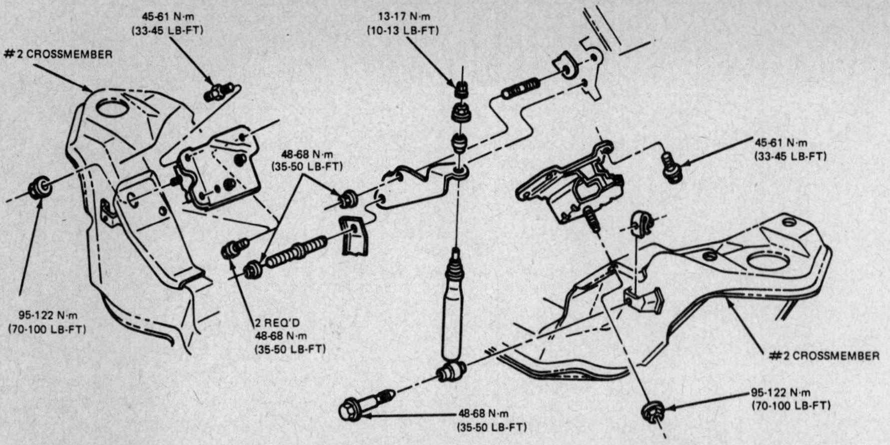

Fig. 8 Engine mounts. 1983–86 LTD & Marquis V6-232 (Typical of 1983–85 Cougar & Thunderbird V6-232)

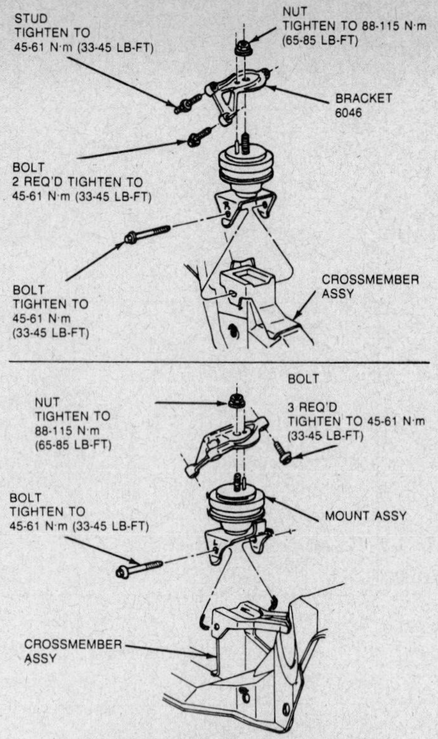

Fig. 9 Engine mounts. 1986–88 Cougar & Thunderbird V6-232

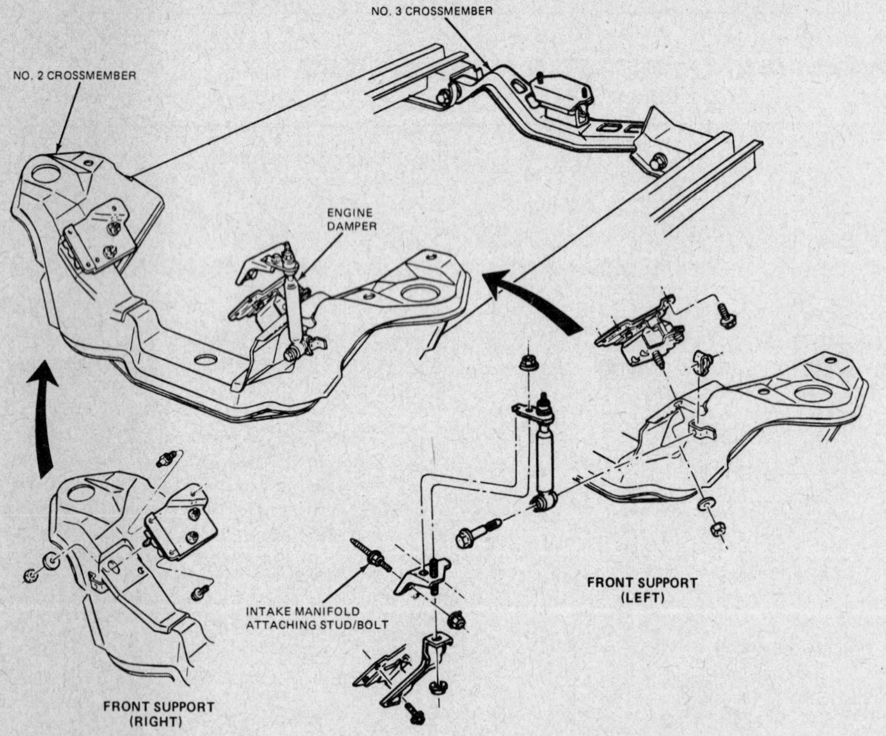

Fig. 10 Engine mount. 1982 V6-232

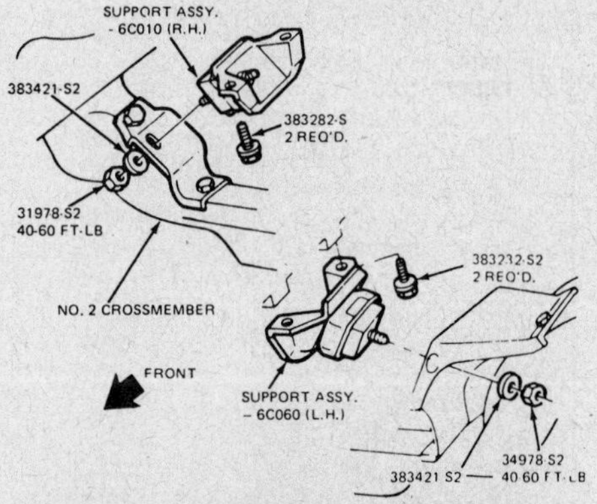

Fig. 11 Engine mounts (typical). 1982 Cougar XR-7, 1983–88 Cougar & 1982–88 Thunderbird V8-255, 302

3. Remove nut and through bolt attaching insulator to frame crossmember.
4. Disconnect shift linkage, as required.
5. Raise engine slightly, then remove insulator and heat shield, if equipped, **Fig. 11.**
6. Reverse procedure to install.

ENGINE REPLACE

6-200

1. Remove battery ground cable.
2. Remove hood assembly.
3. Drain cooling system and oil pan.
4. Disconnect crankcase ventilation hose and remove air cleaner.
5. Disconnect canister purge hose from P.C.V. valve.
6. Disconnect radiator and heater hoses and remove all drive belts.
7. If equipped with automatic transmission, disconnect transmission oil cooler lines from radiator.
8. On all models, remove radiator, then the fan, spacer and pulley.
9. Disconnect alternator and starter wiring, then the accelerator cable.
10. If equipped with Thermactor system, remove or disconnect components that may interfere with engine replacement.
11. If equipped with A/C, remove compressor from mounting bracket and position aside with refrigerant line attached.
12. On all models, disconnect and plug fuel pump inlet line.
13. Disconnect ignition coil wires, then the oil pressure and water temperature wiring from sending units.
14. Remove starter motor.
15. If equipped with manual transmission, disconnect clutch retracting spring, then the clutch equalizer shaft and arm bracket from underbody rail. Remove arm bracket and equalizer shaft.
16. On all models, raise vehicle and re-

move flywheel or converter housing upper attaching bolts.
17. Disconnect exhaust pipe from manifold. Loosen exhaust pipe clamp and slide off support bracket on engine.
18. Disconnect front engine mounts from underbody bracket.
19. Remove flywheel or converter housing cover.
20. If equipped with manual transmission, remove flywheel housing lower attaching bolts.
21. If equipped with automatic transmission, remove converter to flywheel bolts, then the converter housing lower attaching bolts.
22. On all models, lower vehicle and support transmission and flywheel or converter housing with a suitable jack.
23. Attach suitable lifting equipment to engine and remove engine from vehicle.
24. Reverse procedure to install.

V6-232

1. Disconnect battery ground cable, then drain cooling system and crankcase.
2. On models equipped with underhood light, disconnect electrical connector from the light.
3. Mark position of hood hinges, then remove hood.
4. Remove air cleaner, air inlet duct and heat tube.
5. Remove fan shroud and fan assembly, then loosen accessory drive belt idler and remove drive belt and water pump pulley.
6. Disconnect upper and lower radiator hoses at radiator.
7. Disconnect Thermactor hose at air tube check valve, then remove air tube valve bracket attaching bolt at rear of righthand cylinder head.
8. Remove secondary wire from ignition coil.
9. Remove bolts attaching power steering pump mounting bracket, then remove pump and bracket assembly and position aside with hoses attached, if equipped.
10. On models with A/C, remove compressor mounting bracket attaching bolts, then remove compressor and mounting bracket assembly and secure to righthand shock absorber tower with refrigerant lines attached.
11. Remove alternator and position aside.
12. Disconnect heater hoses from water pump and heater tube.
13. On models equipped with speed control, disconnect cable at carburetor or fuel charging assembly.
14. Disconnect all necessary vacuum hoses and wiring connectors.
15. Remove engine ground strap to dash panel attaching screw.
16. Disconnect transmission downshift linkage and throttle cable from carburetor, or fuel charging assembly, then remove throttle cable bracket attaching bolts.
17. Disconnect fuel line and PCV valve hose from carburetor, or flexible fuel lines from steel lines over the rocker arm cover, on models equipped with fuel injection.

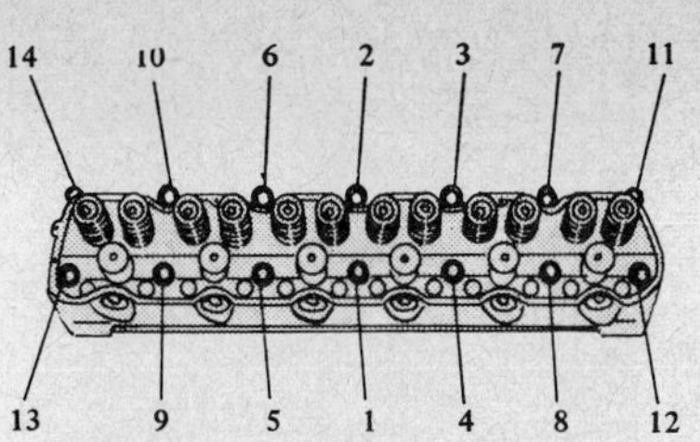

Fig. 12 Cylinder head tightening sequence. 1982–83 6-200

18. Remove carburetor assembly from intake manifold. On models equipped with 7200 VV two barrel carburetor, remove spark knock intensity sensor and adapter assembly which is located between carburetor and thermostat housing.
19. With EGR spacer and phenolic gasket in position, install engine lifting plate T75T-6000-A or equivalent over carburetor mounting studs, then install nuts.
20. Raise vehicle and disconnect fuel inlet hose from fuel pump. Cap fuel hose to prevent entry of dirt.
21. Remove inspection cover from torque converter housing, then remove nuts attaching flex plate to torque converter.
22. Remove starter motor.
23. Remove transmission cooler line retaining clips, then disconnect exhaust pipe from exhaust manifold.
24. Remove four lower engine to transmission attaching bolts.
25. Remove engine mount to crossmember attaching nuts or bolts.
26. Lower vehicle and position a suitable transmission jack under transmission. Raise jack just enough to support weight of transmission.
27. Remove two upper engine to transmission attaching bolts, then place a 1/4 inch piece of plywood or other suitable material between engine and radiator to prevent damage to radiator.
28. Carefully raise engine slightly, then pull away transmission and lift from vehicle.

V8-255, 302

1. Disconnect battery ground cable.
2. Remove hood.
3. Drain cooling system and oil pan.
4. Remove air cleaner and intake duct assembly.
5. Disconnect radiator and heater hoses, then remove all drive belts.
6. If equipped with automatic transmission, disconnect transmission oil cooler lines from radiator.
7. On all models, remove fan shroud attaching bolts, then the radiator, fan, spacer, pulley and shroud.
8. Remove alternator mounting bolts and position alternator aside with wiring attached.
9. Disconnect oil pressure and water temperature wiring from sending units, then the accelerator cable from carburetor or throttle body.
10. Disconnect and plug fuel pump inlet line.
11. If equipped with automatic transmission, disconnect throttle valve vacuum line from intake manifold. Disconnect manual shift rod and the retracting spring at shift rod stud. Disconnect transmission filler tube bracket from engine block.
12. If equipped with Thermactor system, remove or disconnect components that may interfere with engine replacement.
13. If equipped with A/C, isolate and remove compressor.
14. If equipped with power steering, disconnect pump bracket from cylinder head and position assembly aside.
15. If equipped with power brakes, disconnect brake vacuum line from intake manifold.
16. On all models, remove flywheel or converter housing upper attaching bolts.
17. Disconnect ignition coil wiring.
18. On models equipped with EEC IV system, disconnect air charge temperature sensor, engine coolant temperature sensor and exhaust gas oxygen sensor electrical connectors.
19. On all models, disconnect wiring harness from left side rocker arm cover and position aside. Disconnect ground strap from engine block.
20. Raise front of vehicle. Disconnect starter wiring, then remove starter motor.
21. Disconnect exhaust pipes from manifolds.
22. Disconnect engine mounts from brackets on frame.
23. If equipped with manual transmission, remove bolts attaching clutch equalizer bar to frame rail, then the equalizer from engine block. Remove remaining flywheel housing to engine bolts.
24. If equipped with automatic transmission, disconnect transmission oil cooler lines from retainer and remove converter housing inspection cover. Remove converter to flywheel bolts and secure converter in housing. Remove remaining converter housing to engine bolts.
25. On all models, lower vehicle and support transmission with a suitable jack.
26. Attach suitable engine lifting equipment to engine.
27. Lift engine slightly and pull forward to disengage from transmission, then remove engine from vehicle.
28. Reverse procedure to install.

CYLINDER HEAD REPLACE

Tighten cylinder head bolts a little at a time in steps in the sequence shown in the illustrations. Final tightening should be to the torque specifications listed in the Engine Tightening table. After tightening the bolts to specifications, they should not be disturbed.

6-200

1. Drain cooling system and remove air cleaner.

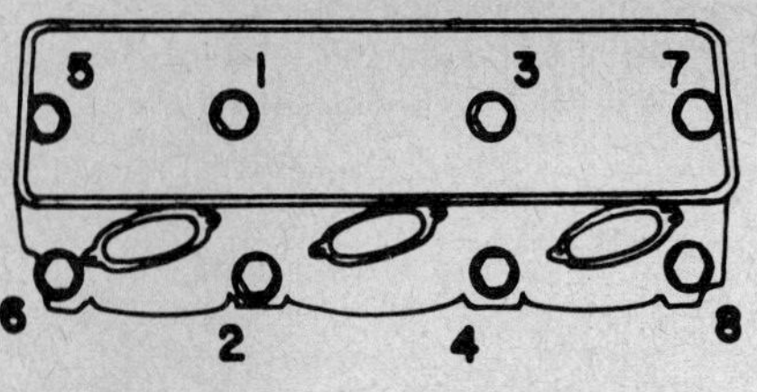

Fig. 13 Cylinder head tightening sequence. 1982–88 V6-232

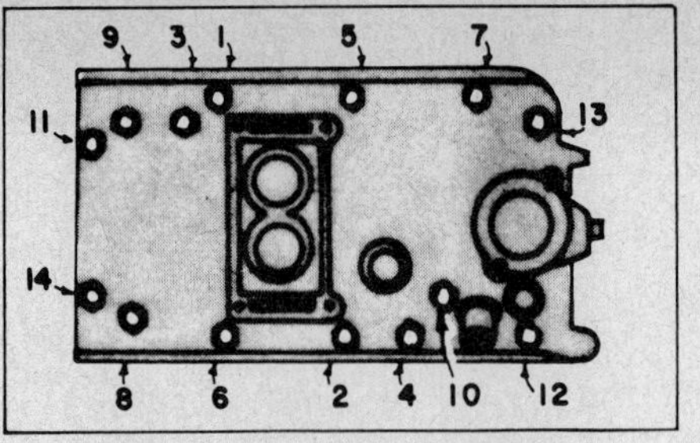

Fig. 14 Intake manifold tightening sequence. 1982–88 V6-232

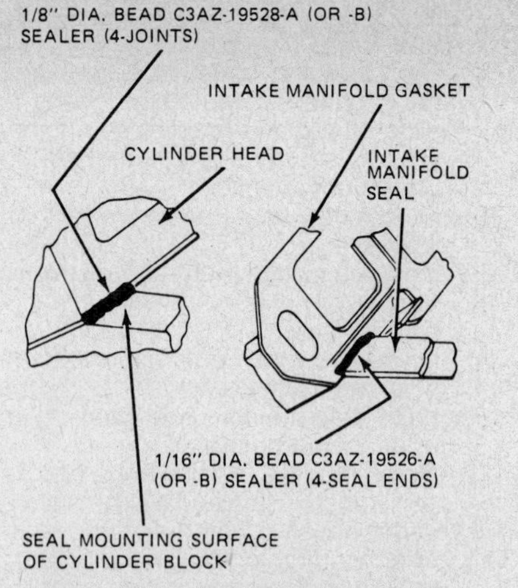

Fig. 15 Applying RTV sealer for intake manifold installation. 1982–88 V8-255, 302 & 1982–88 V6-232

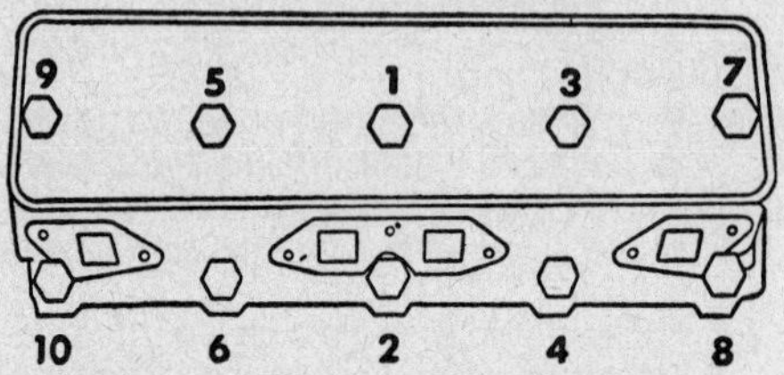

Fig. 16 Cylinder head tightening. V8 engines

2. Disconnect exhaust pipe from manifold and pull it down.
3. Disconnect accelerator cable and transmission downshift rod from carburetor.
4. Disconnect fuel inlet line at fuel filter hose, and distributor vacuum line at carburetor.
5. Disconnect coolant lines at carburetor spacer, if equipped. Remove radiator upper hose at outlet housing.
6. Disconnect distributor vacuum line at distributor. Disconnect carburetor fuel inlet line at fuel pump. Remove lines as an assembly.
7. Disconnect spark plug wires at plugs and temperature sending unit wire at sending unit.
8. Remove crankcase ventilation system. Remove hoses from Thermactor system as necessary for accessibility.
9. Remove valve rocker arm cover.
10. Remove rocker arm shaft assembly.
11. Remove valve pushrods.
12. Remove remaining cylinder head bolts and lift off head.
13. Reverse procedure to install. Torque cylinder head according to sequence shown in **Fig. 12** in three steps: step 1, 50-55 ft. lbs.; step 2, 60-65 ft. lbs.; step 3, 70-75 ft. lbs.

V6-232

1. Disconnect battery ground cable, then drain cooling system.
2. Remove air cleaner, air intake duct and heat tube.
3. Loosen accessory drive belt idler and remove drive belt.
4. If left cylinder head is to be removed, proceed as follows:
   a. Remove oil filler cap.
   b. If equipped with power steering, remove pump bracket attaching bolts, then remove pump and bracket assembly and position pump aside with hoses attached.
   c. If equipped with A/C, remove compressor bracket attaching bolts, then position compressor and bracket assembly aside with refrigerant lines attached.
5. If right cylinder head is to be removed, proceed as follows:
   a. Remove Thermactor diverter valve and hose assembly.
   b. Remove accessory drive belt idler, then remove alternator.
   c. Remove Thermactor pump pulley, then remove Thermactor pump.
   d. Remove alternator mounting bracket. **On models equipped with Tripminder, the fuel supply line from the fuel pump to the fuel sensor will have to be disconnected to gain access to the upper alternator bracket bolt.**
   e. Remove PCV valve.
6. Remove intake manifold and exhaust manifolds.
7. Remove rocker arm cover attaching screws, then loosen cover by using a putty knife under cover flange and remove cover. Do not use excess force when loosening rocker arm cover as cover may become damaged.
8. Loosen rocker arm fulcrum bolt enough to allow rocker arms to be rotated to one side, then remove pushrods. **Tag pushrods so they can be installed in the same position.**
9. Remove cylinder head attaching bolts, then remove cylinder head and gasket.
10. Reverse procedure to install. Apply a thin coating of pipe sealant D8AZ-19558-A or equivalent to the shorter cylinder head bolts which are installed on the exhaust manifold side of the cylinder head. Do not apply pipe sealant to long bolts which are installed on the intake manifold side of the cylinder head. Tighten cylinder head bolts in four steps to torque listed under Engine Tightening Specifications using sequence shown in **Fig. 13.** On 1982-83 models: step 1, 47 ft. lbs.; step 2, 55 ft. lbs.; step 3, 63 ft. lbs.; step 4, 74 ft. lbs. On 1984-87 models: step 1, 37 ft. lbs.; step 2, 45 ft. lbs.; step 3, 52 ft. lbs.; step 4, 59 ft. lbs. Loosen cylinder bolts approximately 2 to 3 turns, then retighten bolts in four steps to specified torque in sequence, **Fig. 13.**

When installing intake manifold, tighten mounting bolts to torque specified under Engine Tightening Specifications in sequence shown in **Fig. 14.** Before installing intake manifold, apply a 1/8 inch bead of silicone rubber sealer D6AZ-19562-B or equivalent at mating surfaces of intake manifold, cylinder heads and cylinder block, **Fig. 15.** Also apply a 1/8 inch bead of sealer to the outer end of each intake manifold seal for the full width of the seal.

V8-255, 302

1. Remove intake manifold and carburetor or throttle body as an assembly.
2. Disconnect battery ground cable at cylinder head.
3. If left head is being removed, remove A/C compressor (if equipped). Also remove and wire power steering pump out of the way. If equipped with Thermactor System, disconnect hose from air manifold on left cylinder head.
4. If right head is to be removed, remove alternator mounting bracket bolt and spacer, ground wire and air cleaner inlet duct.
5. If right head is to be removed on an engine with Thermactor System, remove air pump from bracket. Disconnect hose from air manifold.
6. Disconnect exhaust manifolds at exhaust pipes.
7. Remove rocker arm covers. If equipped with Thermactor System, remove check valve from air manifold.
8. Remove fulcrum bolts, oil deflector (if used), fulcrum and rocker arms. On all engines, remove pushrods. Keep push rods and rocker arm components in order so they may be installed in original position.
9. Remove head bolts and lift head off block.
10. Reverse procedure to install. Torque cylinder head bolts in sequence shown in **Fig. 16,** and on carbureted models, torque intake manifold bolts

in sequence shown in **Fig. 17.** On 1982 V8-255 and 1982-87 V8-302 engines, before installing intake manifold, apply a 1/8 inch bead of silicone rubber sealer D6AZ-19563-A or B or equivalent at mating surfaces of intake manifold, cylinder heads and cylinder block, **Fig. 15.** Also apply a 1/16 inch bead of sealer to the outer end of each intake manifold seal for the full width of the seal.

On V8-302 engines equipped with cork intake manifold seals, both the front and rear seals should be replaced with RTV sealer. Apply a 1/4 inch bead of sealer to the front and rear sealing surfaces of engine block.

INTAKE MANIFOLD REPLACE

6-200 ENGINE

On these engines, the intake manifold is an integral part of the cylinder head and cannot be removed separately.

V6-232 ENGINE

1. Disconnect battery ground cable, then drain cooling system into suitable container.
2. Remove air cleaner, air cleaner air inlet and hot air tube.
3. Disconnect accelerator cable and transmission linkage from carburetor.
4. Remove accelerator cable bracket mounting bolts, then position cable aside.
5. On models equipped with cruise control, disconnect servo chain at carburetor, then remove servo and bracket assembly attaching bolts and position unit aside.
6. Disconnect carburetor bowl vent hose from carburetor and position aside.
7. Disconnect thermactor air supply hose from check valve located at rear of intake manifold.
8. Disconnect fuel line from carburetor.
9. Disconnect upper radiator hose from thermostat housing and water pump bypass hose from intake manifold.
10. Disconnect heater hose from intake manifold, then the heater hose support bracket attaching nut.
11. Label, then disconnect all necessary vacuum hoses and electrical connections that would interfere with intake manifold removal.
12. On models equipped with A/C, remove A/C compressor support bracket from intake manifold.
13. Loosen EGR tube at EGR valve adapter, then disconnect PCV hose from carburetor.
14. Remove carburetor and discard gasket.
15. Remove carburetor attaching studs from intake manifold, then the EGR spacer attaching bolts.
16. Remove EGR valve and adapter from intake manifold. Discard gasket.
17. Remove PCV hose, then the intake manifold attaching bolts and the intake manifold.

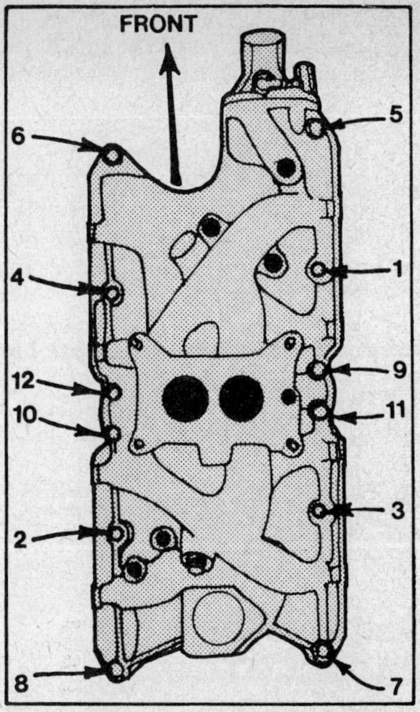

Fig. 17 Intake manifold tightening sequence for carbureted V8-255 & V8-302 engines (fuel injected models similar)

18. Reverse procedure to install, noting the following:
    a. Clean all cylinder head/block to intake manifold contact areas.
    b. Apply a dab of contact cement D7AZ-19B508-A or equivalent in three places on each cylinder head to intake manifold mating surface, then press new gaskets into position over locating dowels.
    c. Apply bead of silicone sealer D6AZ-19562-B or equivalent to each corner where the intake manifold joins the cylinder block.
    d. Apply bead of silicone sealer D6AZ-19562-B or equivalent to each end where the intake manifold joins the cylinder block.
    e. Install intake manifold carefully to avoid smearing gasket compound.
    f. Apply pipe sealant D8AZ-19558-A or equivalent to intake manifold attaching bolts and underside of bolt heads.
    g. Torque bolts in sequence, **Fig. 14,** in the following increments; 5 ft. lbs., 10 ft. lbs., then to the final torque of 18 ft. lbs.

V8-255 & 302 ENGINES

Less E.F.I.

1. Disconnect battery ground cable, then drain cooling system into suitable container.
2. Remove air cleaner, crankcase ventilation hose and air cleaner inlet duct.
3. Disconnect automatic choke heat tube, then the accelerator cable and cruise control linkage (if equipped) from carburetor. Remove accelerator cable bracket.
4. Disconnect vacuum hoses at intake manifold, then the ignition coil primary and secondary wiring.
5. Disconnect spark plug wiring from spark plugs, then remove spark plug wiring and bracket assemblies from rocker arm cover studs. Remove distributor cap adapter and secondary wiring as an assembly.
6. Remove fuel line from carburetor and fuel pump.
7. Disconnect distributor vacuum hose (if equipped), then the distributor wiring connector. Remove distributor hold-down bolt, then the distributor.
8. Disconnect radiator hose from coolant outlet housing, then remove coolant temperature sensor wire.
9. Disconnect heater hose from intake manifold, then the water pump bypass hose.
10. Remove PCV valve from rocker arm cover.
11. Remove the intake manifold attaching bolts, then the intake manifold and carburetor as an assembly. **It may be necessary to pry the intake manifold from the cylinder heads. If prying is necessary, use caution to avoid damaging gasket sealing surfaces.**
12. Reverse procedure to install, noting the following:
    a. Clean all cylinder head/block to intake manifold contact areas.
    b. Apply 1/8 bead of silicone sealer D6AZ-19562-B or equivalent to each corner where the cylinder heads joins the cylinder block.
    c. Position replacement gaskets and seals on cylinder heads and block. Ensure gaskets are interlocked with tab locks on seals.
    d. Apply 1/16 bead of silicone sealer D6AZ-19562-B or equivalent to each end where the intake manifold gaskets join the cylinder block seals. **Do not drip any sealer into engine lifter galley.**
    e. Install intake manifold carefully to avoid smearing gasket compound. **Run a finger around the seal area to ensure seals are properly in place.**
    f. Torque bolts in sequence, **Fig. 17,** to 24 ft. lbs.

W/E.F.I.

1. Disconnect battery ground cable, then drain cooling system into suitable container.
2. Remove air inlet hose, crankcase ventilation hose and evaporative purge hoses.
3. Disconnect accelerator cable, transmission T.V. cable and cruise control linkage (if equipped) from throttle body. Remove accelerator cable bracket.
4. Disconnect vacuum hoses at intake manifold.
5. Disconnect spark plug wiring from spark plugs, then remove spark plug wiring and bracket assemblies from rocker arm cover studs. Remove distributor cap adapter and secondary wiring as an assembly.

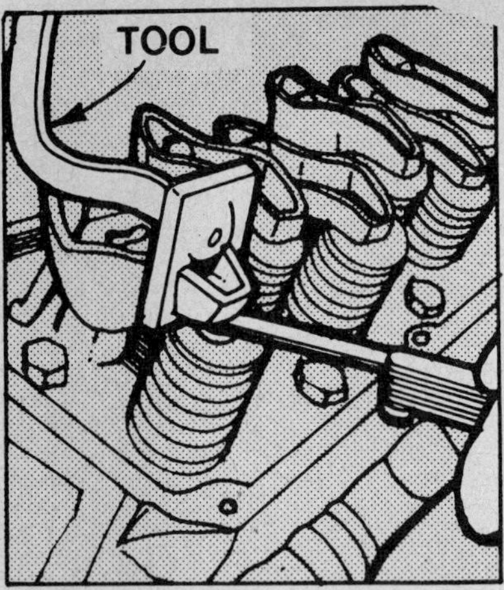

Fig. 18 Compressing lifter to check valve clearance. V8 engines (typical of 6 cylinder engines)

6. Disconnect fuel pressure and return lines. **Prior to removing fuel lines, relieve fuel system pressure by tapping suitable pressure gauge onto fuel rail valve and allowing system to drain through the drain tube.**
7. Disconnect distributor vacuum hose (if equipped), then the distributor wiring connector. Remove distributor hold-down bolt, then the distributor.
8. Disconnect radiator hose from coolant outlet housing, then remove coolant temperature sensor wire.
9. Disconnect heater hose from intake manifold and throttle body cooler, then the water pump bypass hose.
10. Disconnect ECT, ACT, TP, ISC solenoid and EGR sensor wiring.
11. Disconnect injector wiring connectors, then remove fuel charging assembly wiring.
12. Disconnect crankcase vent hose assembly.
13. Remove the upper intake manifold attaching bolts, then the upper intake manifold.
14. Remove lower intake manifold attaching bolts, then the lower intake manifold. **It may be necessary to pry the lower intake manifold from the cylinder heads. If prying is necessary, use caution to avoid damaging gasket sealing surfaces.**
15. Reverse procedure to install, noting the following:
    a. Clean all cylinder head/block to intake manifold contact areas.
    b. Apply 1/8 bead of silicone sealer D6AZ-19562-B or equivalent to each corner where the cylinder heads joins the cylinder block.
    c. Position replacement gaskets and seals on cylinder heads and block. Ensure gaskets are interlocked with tab locks on seals.
    d. Apply 1/16 bead of silicone sealer D6AZ-19562-B or equivalent to each end where the intake manifold gaskets join the cylinder block seals. **Do not drip any sealer into engine lifter galley.**
    e. Install lower intake manifold carefully to avoid smearing gasket compound. **Run a finger around the seal area to ensure seals are properly in place.**
    f. Torque bolts in sequence, **Fig. 17,** to 24 ft. lbs.

VALVE ARRANGEMENT

FRONT TO REAR

4-140	E-I-E-I-E-I-E-I
6-200	E-I-I-E-I-E-E-I-E-I-I-E
V6-232 Right	I-E-I-E-I-E
V6-232 Left	E-I-E-I-E-I
V8-255, 302 Right	I-E-I-E-I-E-I-E
V8-255, 302 Left	E-I-E-I-E-I-E-I

VALVE LIFT SPECIFICATIONS

Engine	Year	Intake	Exhaust
4-140	1982–88	.3997	.3997
6-200	1982–83	.372	.372
V6-232	1982–88	.415	.417
V8-255	1982	.3753	.3753
V8-302	1983–88	.3753	.3909
V8-302 H.O.	1984–85	.4130	.4420

VALVE TIMING

INTAKE OPENS BEFORE TDC

Engine	Year	Degrees
4-140	1982–88	22
6-200	1982	20
V6-232	1982–88	13
V8-255	1982	16
V8-302 (Exc. H.O.)	1983–88	16

VALVE CLEARANCE SPECIFICATIONS

When adjusting valves, note the following valve lash specifications: 4-140, .040-.050 inch; 6-200, .110-.184 inch; V6-232, .088-.189 inch; V8-255, .096-.146 inch; V8-302, .096-.146 inch; V8-302 H.O., .123-.264 inch.

VALVES

ADJUST

6-200

A .060 inch longer or a .060 inch shorter pushrod is available to compensate for dimensional changes in the valve train. If clearance is less than the minimum, the .060 inch shorter pushrod should be used. If clearance is more than the maximum, the .060 inch longer pushrod should be used.

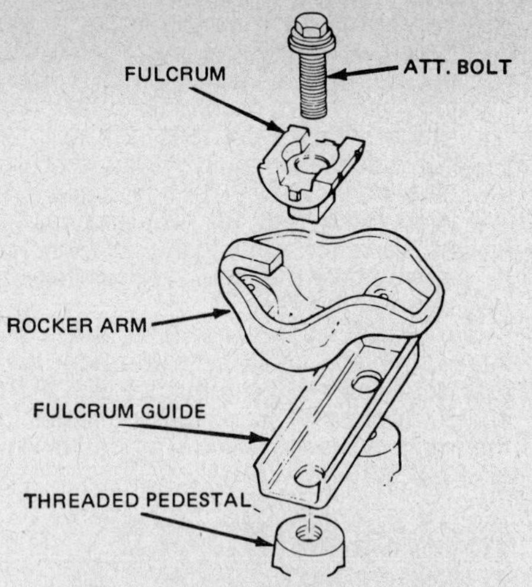

Fig. 19 Rocker arm assembly. V6-232, V8-255, 302

The procedure used to check the valve clearance is to rotate the crankshaft with an auxiliary starter switch until the No. 1 piston is near TDC at the end of the compression stroke, and then compress the valve lifter using tool 6513-K or equivalent, **Fig. 18.** At this point the following valves can be checked: intake Nos. 1, 2 and 4; exhaust Nos. 1, 3 and 5.

After the clearance of these valves have been checked, rotate the crankshaft until the No. 6 piston is on TDC at the end of its compression stroke (1 revolution of the crankshaft), and then compress the valve lifter using tool 6513-K or equivalent, **Fig. 18,** and check the following valves: intake Nos. 3, 5 and 6; exhaust Nos. 2, 4 and 6.

V6-232

A .060 inch longer or a .060 inch shorter pushrod is available to compensate for dimensional changes in the valve train. If clearance is less than specified, the .060 inch shorter pushrod should be used. If clearance is more than the maximum specified, the .060 inch longer pushrod should be used.

Using an auxiliary starter switch crankshaft until No. 1 cylinder is at TDC compression stroke, then compress valve lifter using tool T82C-6500-A or equivalent, **Fig. 18.** At this point, the following valves can be checked: intake Nos. 1, 3 and 6; exhaust Nos. 1, 2 and 4.

After clearance on these valves has been checked, rotate crankshaft until No. 5 cylinder is at TDC compression stroke (1 revolution of crankshaft), and then compress valve lifter using tool No. T82C-6500-A or equivalent, **Fig. 18,** and check the following valves: intake Nos. 2, 4 and 5; exhaust Nos. 3, 5 and 6.

V8 ENGINES

For these engines, a .060 inch longer or a .060 inch shorter pushrod is available to provide a means of compensating for dimensional changes in the valve train and

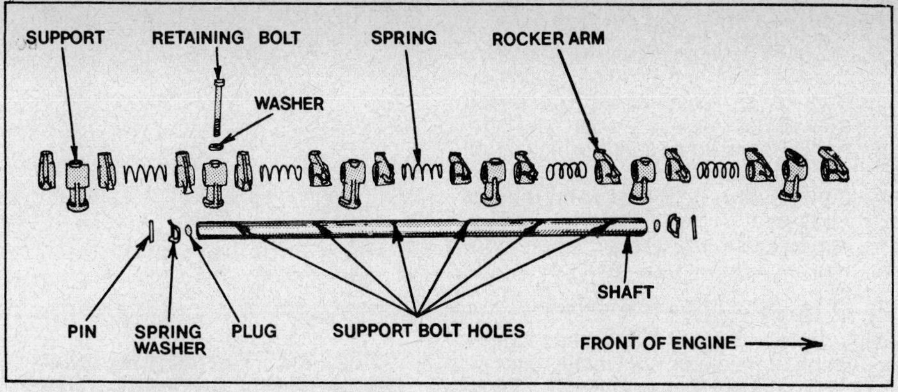

Fig. 20 Rocker arm shaft assembly. 6-200

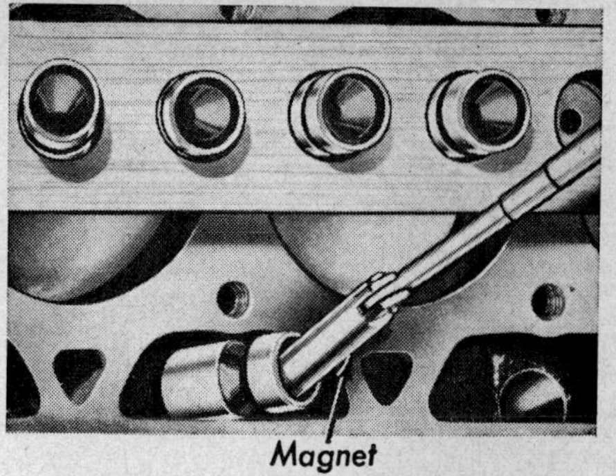

Fig. 21 Removing valve lifter with magnetic rod

rocker arm. If the clearance is less than the minimum, the .060 inch shorter pushrod should be used. If clearance is more than the maximum the .060 inch longer pushrod should be used.

All engines use a bolt and fulcrum attachment, **Fig. 19.**

To check valve clearance, proceed as follows:

1. Mark crankshaft pulley at three locations with number 1 location at TDC timing mark (end of compression stroke), number 2 location one half turn (180°) clockwise from TDC and number 3 location three quarter turn clockwise (270°) from TDC.
2. Turn the crankshaft to the number 1 location, then compress valve lifter using tool T71P-6513-A or equivalent, **Fig. 18,** and check the clearance on the following valves:
   a. V8-255, 302 (Exc. H.O.): intake Nos. 1, 7 and 8; exhaust Nos. 1, 4 and 5.
   b. V8-302 (H.O.): intake Nos. 1, 4 and 8; exhaust Nos. 1, 3 and 7.
3. Turn the crankshaft to the number 2 location, then compress valve lifter using tool T71P-6513-A or equivalent, **Fig. 18,** and check the clearance on the following valves:
   a. V8-255, 302 (Exc. H.O.): intake Nos. 4 and 5; exhaust Nos. 2 and 6.
   b. V8-302 (H.O.): intake Nos. 3 and 7; exhaust Nos. 2 and 6.
4. Turn the crankshaft to the number 3 location, then compress valve lifter using tool T71P-6513-A or equivalent, **Fig. 18,** and check the clearance on the following valves:
   a. V8-255, 302 (Exc. H.O.): intake Nos. 2, 3 and 6; exhaust Nos. 3, 7 and 8.
   b. V8-302 (H.O.): intake Nos. 2, 5 and 6; exhaust Nos. 4, 5 and 8.

VALVE GUIDES

Valve guides consist of holes bored in the cylinder head. For service the guide holes can be reamed oversize to accommodate valves with oversize stems of .015 and .030 inch.

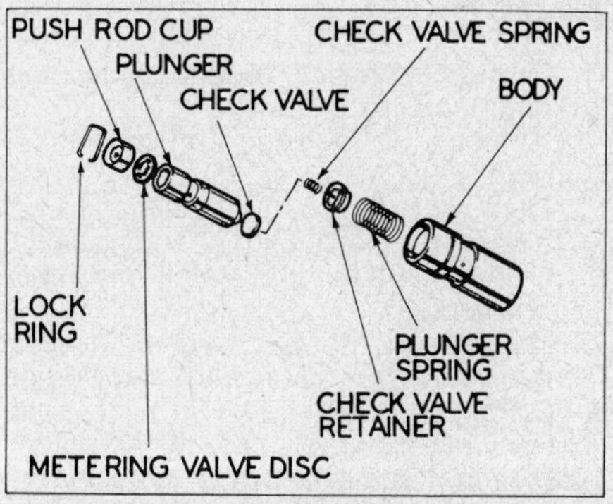

Fig. 22 Typical hydraulic valve lifter

ROCKER ARM SERVICE

6-200

Disassemble

1. To disassemble, remove pin and spring washer from each end of rocker shaft, **Fig. 20.**
2. Slide rocker arms, springs and supports off the shaft, being sure to identify location of parts for reassembly.
3. If it is necessary to remove the plugs from the shaft ends, drill or pierce the plug on one end. Then use a steel rod to knock out the plug on the opposite end. Working from the open end, knock out the remaining plug.

Assemble

1. Lubricate all parts with engine oil. Apply Lubriplate to the rocker arm pads.
2. If plugs were removed from shaft ends, use a blunt tool or large diameter pin punch and install a plug (cup side out) in each end of shaft.
3. Install spring washer and pin on one end of shaft.
4. Install rocker arms, supports and springs in order shown in **Fig. 20.** Be sure oil holes in shaft are facing downward.
5. Complete the assembly by installing remaining spring washer and pin.

V6-232

These engines use stamped steel rocker arms retained by a fulcrum seat which bolts directly to the cylinder head and guides the rocker arm. Torque fulcrum bolts in two steps as follows: For each valve rotate crankshaft until tappet rests on heel (base circle) of camshaft lobe and torque fulcrum bolt to 5-11 ft. lbs. After initial torquing all fulcrum bolts, final torque to 19-25 ft. lbs. Final torque may be done with camshaft in any position.

V8-255 & V8-302

These engines use stamped steel rocker arms retained by a fulcrum seat, **Fig. 19.** The fulcrum seat bolts directly to the cylinder head and guides the rocker arm.

VALVE LIFTERS

REPLACE

6-200

When necessary to replace valve lifters, remove cylinder head and related parts as outlined previously. Then, using a magnet rod, **Fig. 21,** remove and install one lifter at a time to be sure they are placed in their original bores.

When installing, apply Lubriplate to each lifter foot and coat the remainder of lifter with oil before installation.

V6-232, V8-255, 302

1. On V6-232 engine, disconnect secondary ignition wires from spark plugs using wire remover T74P-6666-A or equivalent. Remove ignition wire routing clips from rocker arm cover attaching bolt studs and position wires aside.
2. On all models, remove intake manifold.
3. Remove rocker arm covers. On engines with stud mounted rocker arms, loosen stud nuts and rotate rocker arms to one side. On other engines, remove fulcrum bolt, fulcrum, rocker arm and fulcrum guide (if used).
4. Remove pushrods in sequence so they can be installed in their original bores. **On 1985-88 V8 engines equipped with roller lifters, the**

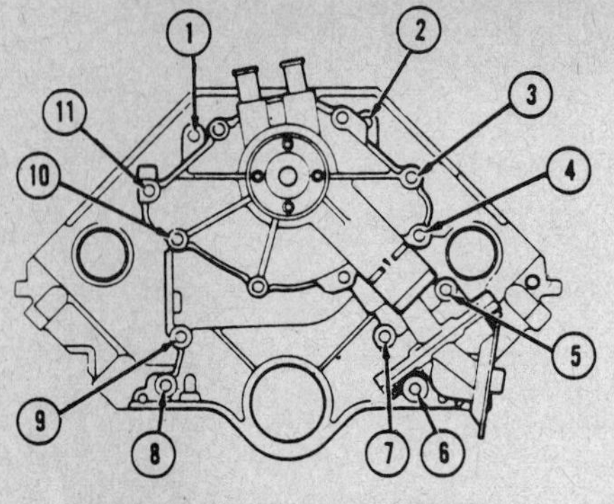

Fig. 23 Front cover attaching bolt locations. V6-232

pushrods have a collar at the upper end and can only be installed one way. When installing lifters, ensure that lifter is correctly oriented so that roller rotates in same direction.

5. Remove lifter guide retainer bolts, retainer and guide plate, if equipped.
6. Using a magnet rod, **Fig. 21,** remove the lifters and place them in a numbered rack so they can be installed in their original bores. If the lifters are stuck in their bores by excessive varnish, etc., it may be necessary to use a plier-type tool to remove them. Rotate the lifter back and forth to loosen it from the gum or varnish.
7. The internal parts of each lifter are matched sets. Do not intermix parts. Keep the assemblies intact until they are to be cleaned, **Fig. 22.**

TIMING CASE COVER REPLACE

To replace the seal in the timing gear cover, it is necessary to remove the cover as outlined below.

6-200

Removal

1. Disconnect battery ground cable.
2. Drain cooling system and oil pan.
3. Disconnect radiator hoses from engine, then the transmission oil cooler lines from radiator, if equipped.
4. Remove radiator, then the drive belt, fan and pulley.
5. If equipped with A/C, remove condenser attaching bolts and position condenser forward with refrigerant lines attached. Remove compressor drive belt.
6. On all models, remove accessory drive pulley and the crankshaft damper with a suitable puller.
7. Remove front cover attaching screws from cover and oil pan. Pry cover from cylinder block slightly and cut oil pan gasket flush with front face of cylinder block.
8. Clean mating surfaces of cylinder block and front cover.

Installation

1. Apply oil resistant sealer to new front cover gasket and position gasket on front cover. Apply sealer to exposed area of gasket.
2. Apply sealer to gasket surface of oil pan. Cut and position the required portions of a new gasket on oil pan. Apply sealer to exposed areas of gasket, including the corners where contact is made with the front cover gasket.
3. Install front cover.
4. Lubricate hub of crankshaft damper with Lubriplate or equivalent, then install damper. Torque attaching bolt to specifications.
5. Install accessory drive pulley.
6. Reverse "Removal" steps 1 through 5 to complete installation.

V6-232

1. Disconnect battery ground cable, then drain cooling system.
2. Remove air cleaner and air intake duct.
3. Remove fan shroud attaching screws and fan and fan clutch attaching bolts, then remove fan and clutch assembly and shroud.
4. Loosen accessory drive belt idler, then remove drive belt and water pump pulley.
5. On models equipped with power steering, remove pump bracket attaching bolts, then position pump aside with hoses attached.
6. On models equipped with A/C, remove compressor front support bracket.
7. Disconnect coolant bypass hose and heater hose at water pump and upper radiator hose at thermostat housing.
8. Disconnect ignition coil secondary wire from distributor cap, then remove distributor cap with ignition wires attached.
9. With No. 1 cylinder at TDC compression stroke, mark position of rotor to distributor housing and position of distributor housing to front cover.
10. Remove distributor hold-down clamp, then lift distributor from front cover.
11. On models equipped with Tripminder, remove fuel flow meter support bracket. Do not remove flow meter or disconnect fuel lines.
12. On 1982-86 models, raise and support front of vehicle, then remove crankshaft pulley using a suitable puller.
13. On 1982-83 models, remove fuel pump shield, if equipped, then disconnect fuel pump to carburetor fuel line at fuel pump.
14. On all models, remove fuel pump attaching bolts and position aside with fuel hose attached, if necessary.
15. Remove oil filter, then disconnect lower radiator hose from water pump.
16. Remove oil pan as described under "Oil Pan, Replace."
17. Lower vehicle and remove front cover attaching bolts, **Fig. 23. One of the front cover attaching bolts is located behind the oil filter adapter. Also tag bolts as they are removed so that they can be installed at the same location.**
18. Remove ignition timing indicator, then remove front cover and water pump as an assembly.
19. Remove camshaft thrust button and spring from camshaft.
20. Reverse procedure to install. Before installing front cover attaching bolts at location 10, **Fig. 23,** coat threads of bolt with pipe sealant D8AZ-19558-A or equivalent. Also lubricate camshaft thrust button with polyethylene grease before installing. Torque front cover attaching bolts to 15 to 22 ft. lbs. **If a replacement front cover is to be installed, the water pump, oil pump, oil filter adapter and intermediate shaft must be removed from the front cover to be replaced and reinstalled on the replacement front cover. Also it may be necessary to rotate crankshaft 180° from the No. 1 cylinder TDC location to position fuel pump eccentric for fuel pump installation. When installing distributor, No. 1 cylinder must be at TDC position and marks made during removal must be aligned.**

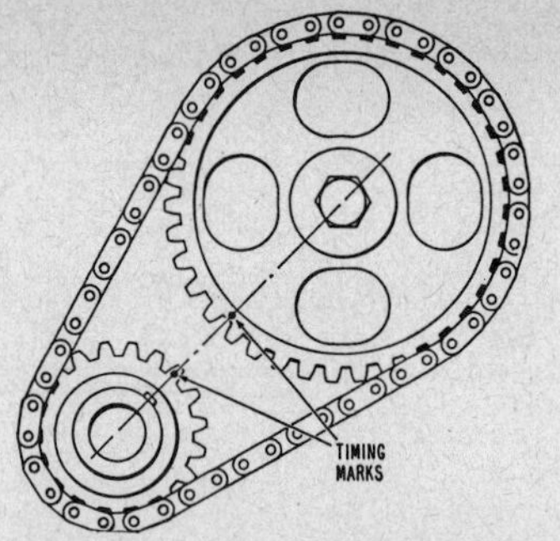

Fig. 24 Timing marks aligned for correct valve timing. 6-200

V8 ENGINES

1. To remove cover, drain cooling system and crankcase. Remove air cleaner and disconnect battery ground cable.
2. Remove water hose as necessary.
3. Remove generator support bolt at water pump, and loosen generator mounting bolts.
4. Remove fan, spacer and pulley.
5. Remove power steering and compressor drive belts, as required.
6. Remove crankshaft pulley and adapter.
7. Remove fuel pump and lay it to one side with flexible fuel line attached.
8. Remove oil level dipstick tube bracket and oil filler tube bracket.
9. Remove oil pan-to-front cover bolts.
10. Remove cover and water pump as an assembly.
11. Drive out cover seal with a pin punch. Clean out recess in cover.

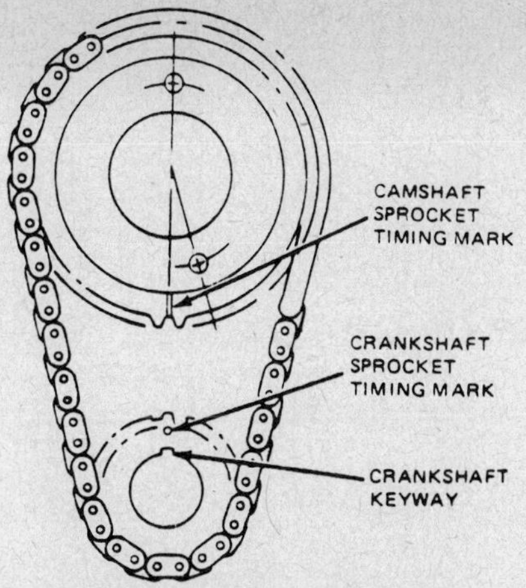

Fig. 25 Timing marks aligned for correct valve timing. V6-232

12. Coat a new seal with grease and drive seal in until it is fully seated in recess. Check seal after installation to be sure spring is properly positioned in seal.
13. Reverse removal procedure to install cover.

TIMING CHAIN

After removing the cover as outlined above, remove the crankshaft front oil slinger. Crank the engine until the timing marks are aligned as shown in **Figs. 24, 25 and 26.** Remove camshaft sprocket retaining bolt(s) and washer. Slide both sprockets and chain forward and remove them as an assembly.

Reverse the order of the foregoing procedure to install the chain and sprockets, being sure the timing marks are aligned.

1988 V6-232 W/BALANCE SHAFT

This engine is basically the same design used on previous models for the exception of a balance shaft assembly. In conjuction with the balance shaft assembly, the cylinder block, camshaft, pistons and oil pump have been revised.

CYLINDER BLOCK & BALANCE SHAFT ASSEMBLY

This cylinder block incorporates a specially designed, cast iron balance shaft. In addition, this counter rotating shaft offsets the Noise Vibration Harshness (NVH) qualities for improved driving and vehicle operation.

CAMSHAFT

The full circumference design camshaft and balance shaft thrust plates are incorporated for balance shaft accommodation. In addition, a steel gear balance drive has been incorporated and the camshaft bearings have also been revised.

PISTONS

Revised dish pistons are incorporated for a 9.0:1 compression ratio. These pistons utilize new, low tension design compression piston rings and a reduced tension oil control ring spacer for improved performance. A shrouded valve design is utilized to enhance fast burn combustion.

OIL PUMP

A special design gear and gear shaft oil pumps have been incorporated to provide improved oil cooling, and also, uses separate, die cast aluminum housing for the oil pump gears. Special oil drain-back passages, gasket cover and an oil pan which uses stiffer ribs to reduce resonance is used.

CAMSHAFT REPLACE

6-200

1. Remove air cleaner, then drain cooling system and crankcase.
2. Remove radiator and grille.
3. On models equipped with A/C, remove condenser attaching bolts and position condenser aside. **Do not disconnect refrigerant lines from condenser.**
4. On 1982-84 models, disconnect accelerator control cable from carburetor and bracket, then the bracket from carburetor.

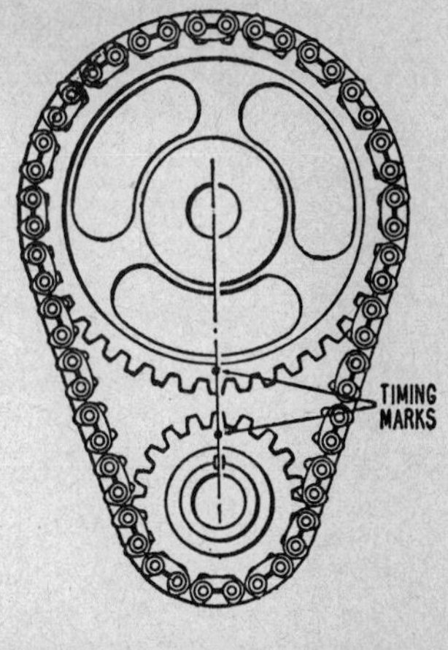

Fig. 26 Timing marks aligned for correct valve timing. Typical of V8 engines

5. On all models, disconnect fuel inlet line from fuel filter.
6. Disconnect connectors and vacuum hoses connected to cylinder head from carburetor.
7. Disconnect exhaust pipe from manifold. Pull pipe down and remove gasket.
8. Disconnect carburetor fuel inlet line from fuel pump.
9. Disconnect ignition wires from spark plugs and the high tension lead from ignition coil.
10. Disconnect engine temperature sending unit electrical connector from sending unit.
11. Remove distributor, fuel pump and oil filter.
12. Remove crankcase vent hose, regulator valve, rocker arm cover, cylinder head and lifters.
13. Remove drive belt, fan and pulley, then the damper using a suitable puller.
14. On all models, remove front cover, gasket, timing chain and sprockets.
15. Remove camshaft thrust plate, then the camshaft by pulling toward front of engine, **Fig. 27. Use care to avoid damaging crankshaft bearings.**
16. Reverse procedure to install.

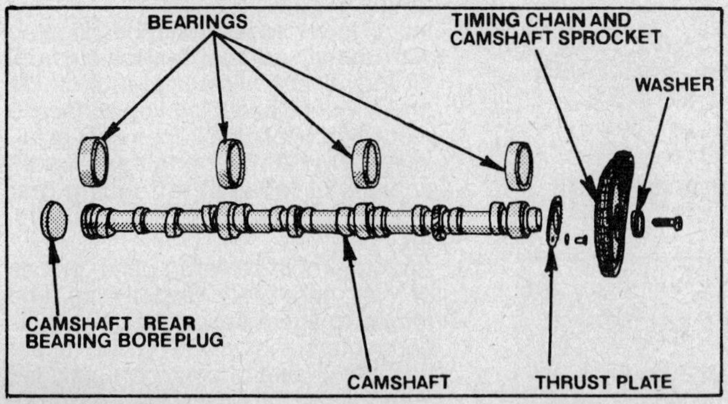

Fig. 27 Camshaft and related parts. 6-200

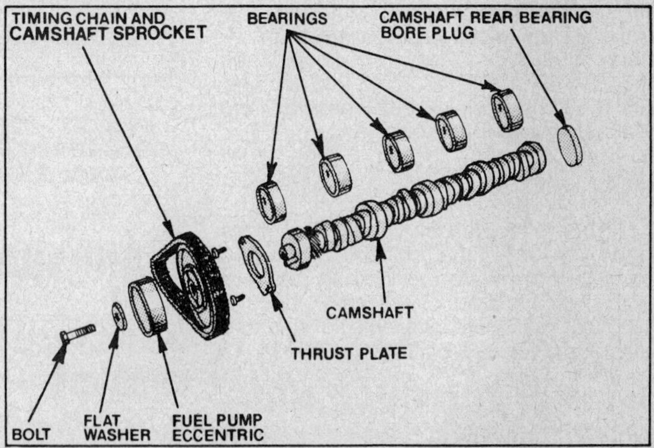

Fig. 28 Camshaft and related parts. V8 engines

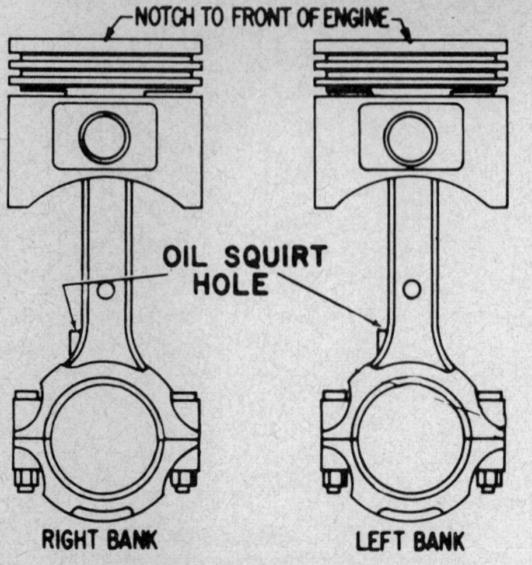

Fig. 29 Piston & rod assembly. 6-200

V6 & V8 ENGINES

1. Drain cooling system and remove radiator and grille.
2. If equipped with air conditioning:
   a. On 255 and 302 engines, remove condenser retaining bolts and position condenser aside without disconnecting refrigerant lines.
   b. On V6-232 engine, purge refrigerant from system and remove condenser.
3. Remove front cover, timing chain and sprockets.
4. Remove intake manifold.
5. Remove pushrods and lifters.
6. On V6-232 engine, remove oil pan.
7. On all models, remove thrust plate, then carefully remove camshaft by pulling toward front of engine, **Fig. 28. Use care to avoid damaging camshaft bearings.**
8. Reverse procedure to install.

PISTON & ROD ASSEMBLY

When installed, piston and rod assembly should have the notch or arrow in piston head toward front of engine with connecting rod numbers positioned as shown in **Figs. 29, 30 and 31.** Check side clearance between connecting rods at each crankshaft journal. Clearance should be .0035-.0105 for 4-140 and 6-200 engines, .0047-.0114 for V6-232 engine, and .010-.020 for V8-302 engine.

PISTONS, PINS & RINGS

Pistons are available in standard sizes and oversizes of .003, .020, .030 and .040 in. Piston rings are available in standard sizes and oversizes of .020, .030 and .040 in. Piston pins are available in standard size and oversizes of .001 and .002 in.

MAIN & ROD BEARINGS

Main and rod bearings are available in standard sizes and undersizes of .001, .002, .010, .020 and .030 in.

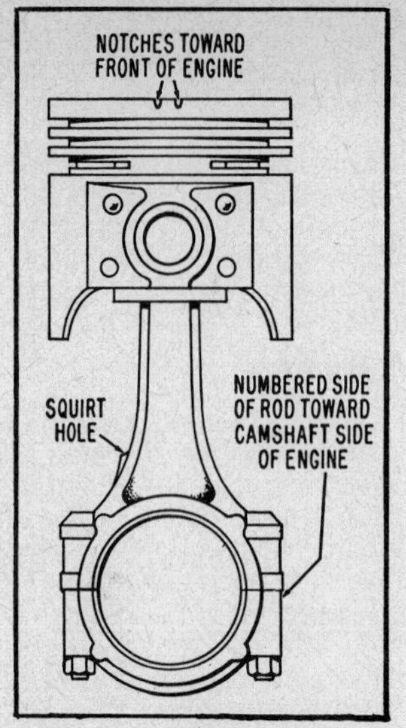

Fig. 30 Piston & rod assembly. V6-232

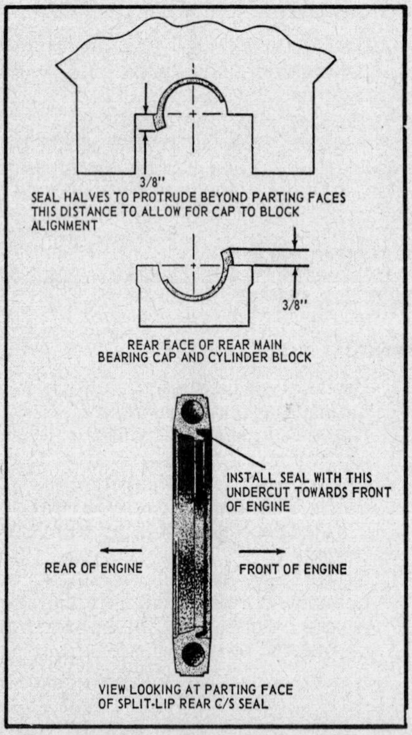

Fig. 32 Crankshaft rear seal installation. 1982–83 exc. 1982–83 V6-232

CRANKSHAFT REAR OIL SEAL

REPLACE

1982–83

1. On all except V6-232 engines, remove oil pan and oil pump as described under "Oil Pan, Replace" and "Oil Pump, Replace."

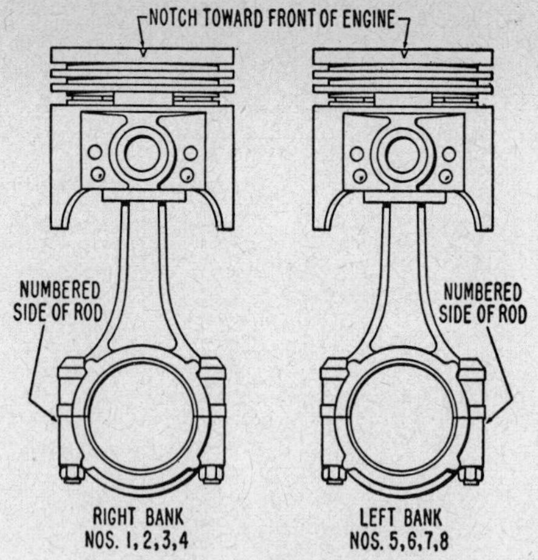

Fig. 31 Piston & rod assembly. V8s

2. Loosen all main bearing cap bolts, allowing crankshaft to drop slightly. Do not let crankshaft drop more than 1/32 inch.
3. Remove rear main bearing cap.
4. Remove old seals from both cylinder block and rear main bearing cap. To remove block half of seal, use a seal removal tool or install a small screw in one end of seal and pull on screw to remove seal. **Use care to prevent damaging the crankshaft seal surfaces.**
5. Carefully clean seal groove in block with a brush and solvent. Also clean seal groove in bearing cap. Remove the oil seal retaining pin from the bearing cap if so equipped. The pin is not used with the split-lip seal.
6. Dip seal halves in clean engine oil.
7. Carefully install upper seal half in its groove with undercut side of seal toward front of engine, **Fig. 32,** by rotating it on shaft journal of crankshaft until approximately 3/8 inch protrudes below the parting surface. Be sure no rubber has been shaved from outside diameter of seal by bottom edge of groove. **On V6-232 engines, seal ends should be flush with the block and cap.**
8. Retighten main bearing caps and torque to specifications.
9. Install lower seal in main bearing cap with undercut side of seal toward front of engine, and allow seal to protrude about 3/8 inch above parting surface to mate with upper seal upon cap installation. **On V6-232 engines, install seals with locating tab facing rear of engine, then remove the tab, Fig. 33.**
10. Apply suitable sealer to parting faces of cap and block. Install cap and torque to specifications. If difficulty is encountered in installing the upper half of the seal in position, lightly lap (sandpaper) the side of the seal opposite the lip side using a medium grit paper. After sanding, the seal must be

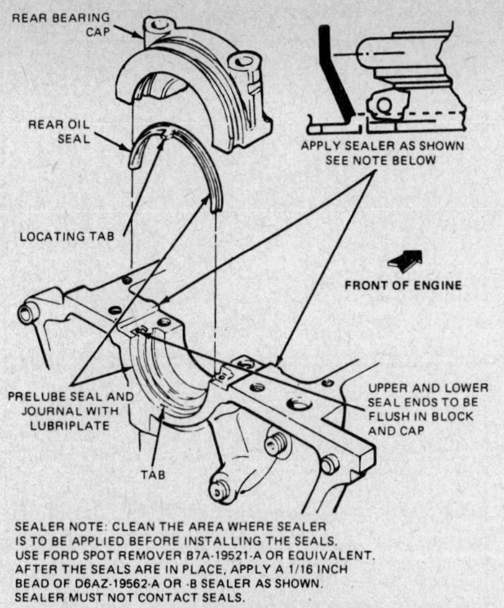
REAR BEARING CAP
REAR OIL SEAL
APPLY SEALER AS SHOWN SEE NOTE BELOW
LOCATING TAB
FRONT OF ENGINE
PRELUBE SEAL AND JOURNAL WITH LUBRIPLATE
UPPER AND LOWER SEAL ENDS TO BE FLUSH IN BLOCK AND CAP
TAB
SEALER NOTE: CLEAN THE AREA WHERE SEALER IS TO BE APPLIED BEFORE INSTALLING THE SEALS. USE FORD SPOT REMOVER B7A-19521-A OR EQUIVALENT. AFTER THE SEALS ARE IN PLACE, APPLY A 1/16 INCH BEAD OF D6AZ-19562-A OR -B SEALER AS SHOWN. SEALER MUST NOT CONTACT SEALS.

Fig. 33 Crankshaft rear seal installation. 1982–83 V6-232

washed in solvent, then dipped in clean engine oil prior to installation.

A new crankshaft rear oil seal has been released for service. This new seal may be received when ordering an oil pan gasket kit and is installed in the same manner as described above, **Fig. 34.**

1984–88

1. Using a sharp tool, punch one hole into seal metal surface between seal lip and engine block.
2. Remove seal using slide hammer No. T82L-9533-B or equivalent. Use care to prevent damaging the sealing surface.
3. Lubricate new seal with clean engine oil and install using tool No. T82L-6701-A or equivalent. Tighten bolts alternately to seat seal properly, **Fig. 35.**

OIL PAN

REPLACE

1982 GRANADA & COUGAR XR-7, 1982–83 FAIRMONT & ZEPHYR, 1983–86 LTD & MARQUIS & 1983–88 COUGAR & THUNDERBIRD 4-140

1. Disconnect battery ground cable.
2. Raise and support vehicle.
3. Drain cooling system and crankcase.
4. Remove right and left engine support nuts and washers or bolts.
5. Raise engine as far as possible using a suitable jack. Place wooden blocks between the mounts and chassis bracket or No. 2 crossmember pedestals, then remove jack.
6. Remove steering gear attaching nuts and bolts and the steering gear-to-flex coupling attaching bolt. Position steering gear forward and down.

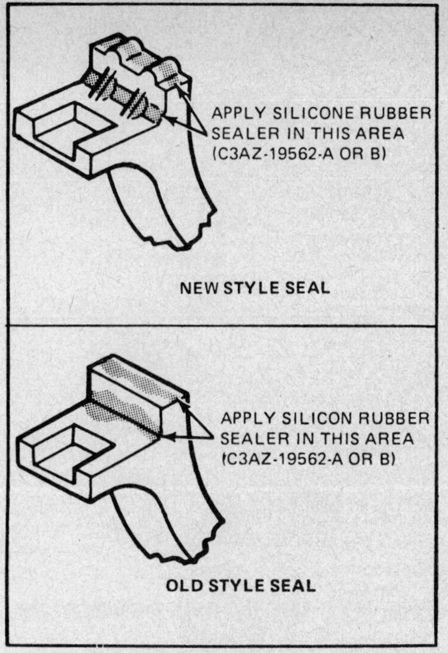
APPLY SILICONE RUBBER SEALER IN THIS AREA (C3AZ-19562-A OR B)
NEW STYLE SEAL
APPLY SILICON RUBBER SEALER IN THIS AREA (C3AZ-19562-A OR B)
OLD STYLE SEAL

Fig. 34 Crankshaft oil seals

7. Remove shake brace, then the starter motor.
8. Remove engine rear support-to-crossmember attaching nuts.
9. Raise and support transmission with a suitable jack.
10. Remove oil pan attaching bolts and the oil pan.
11. Reverse procedure to install.

1982 COUGAR, GRANADA & THUNDERBIRD & 1982–83 FAIRMONT & ZEPHYR 6-200

1. If equipped with automatic transmission, disconnect transmission oil cooler lines at radiator.
2. On all models, remove radiator top support, then the oil level dipstick.
3. Raise and support vehicle, and drain oil pan.
4. Remove nuts and bolts attaching sway bar to chassis and allow sway bar to hang downward.
5. Remove "K" brace.
6. Lower rack and pinion steering gear.
7. Remove starter motor.
8. Remove nuts attaching engine mounts to support brackets.
9. Loosen rear insulator to crossmember attaching bolts.
10. Slightly raise engine and place a 1/4 inch spacer between engine support insulator and chassis bracket. **Loosen fan shroud attaching screws to prevent damage to fan when raising engine.**
11. Support and raise transmission slightly with a suitable jack.
12. Remove oil pan attaching bolts and lower oil pan to crossmember.
13. Remove oil pump intermediate driveshaft, pickup tube and screen assembly and allow components to drop into oil pan.
14. Position transmission oil cooler lines aside, if equipped, and remove oil pan from vehicle. It may be necessary to rotate crankshaft.
15. Reverse procedure to install.

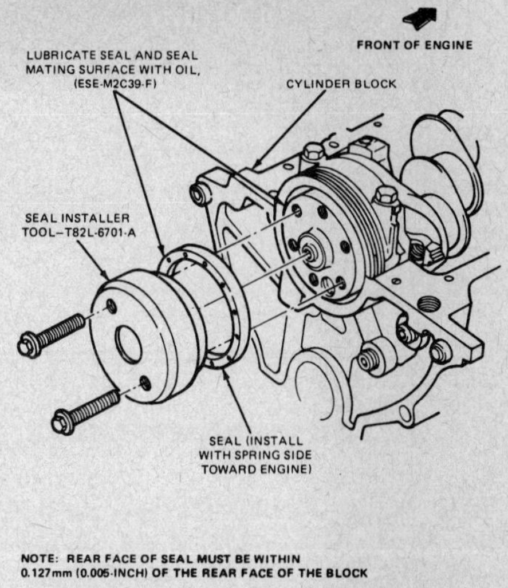
FRONT OF ENGINE
LUBRICATE SEAL AND SEAL MATING SURFACE WITH OIL, (ESE-M2C39-F)
CYLINDER BLOCK
SEAL INSTALLER TOOL—T82L-6701-A
SEAL (INSTALL WITH SPRING SIDE TOWARD ENGINE)
NOTE: REAR FACE OF SEAL MUST BE WITHIN 0.127mm (0.005-INCH) OF THE REAR FACE OF THE BLOCK

Fig. 35 Crankshaft rear seal installation. 1984–88

1982 COUGAR XR-7 & GRANADA, 1982–88 COUGAR & THUNDERBIRD & 1983–86 LTD & MARQUIS V6-232

1. Disconnect battery ground cable, then remove air cleaner and air intake duct.
2. Remove fan shroud attaching screws and position shroud over fan, then remove engine oil dipstick.
3. Remove vacuum solenoid(s) from dash panel and position on engine with vacuum hoses attached.
4. Raise and support front of vehicle, then remove exhaust pipe to exhaust manifold attaching nuts.
5. Drain crankcase, then remove oil filter.
6. Remove shift linkage bracket to converter housing attaching bolts.
7. Disconnect transmission oil cooler lines at radiator. Remove four converter cover attaching bolts, then remove converter cover.
8. Remove bolts attaching engine damper to No. 2 crossmember.
9. Disconnect steering gear at flex coupling, then remove steering gear to main crossmember attaching bolts and allow steering gear to rest on frame.
10. Remove nuts and bolts attaching from engine mounts to chassis, then raise engine approximately 2 to 3 inches and insert wooden block between engine mounts and frame. **On some models, it may be necessary to raise engine as much as 5 inches to provide clearance for oil pan removal. On these models, transmission fluid dipstick tube may contact Thermactor air tube. If contact**

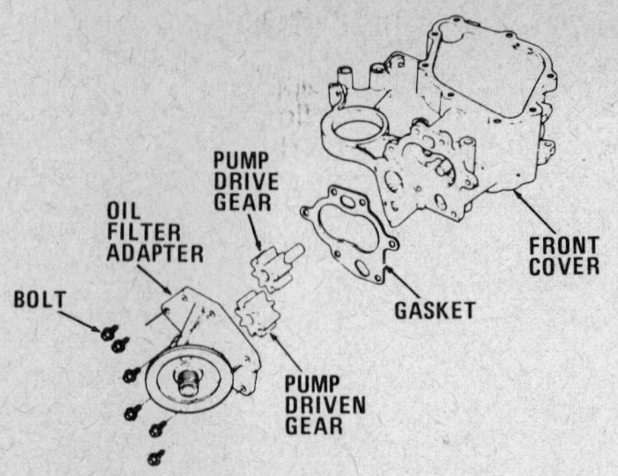

Fig. 36 Oil pump assembly. V6-232

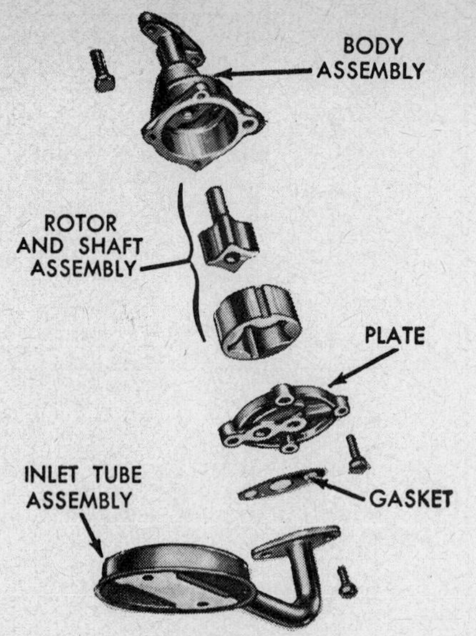

Fig. 37 Oil pump assembly. 6-200

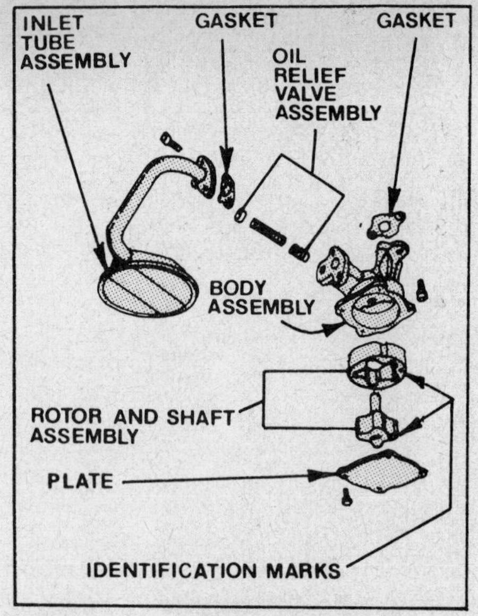

Fig. 38 Oil pump assembly. V8-255, 302

occurs, lower engine and remove dipstick and air tube.

11. Remove oil pan attaching bolts, then lower oil pan to crossmember.
12. Remove oil pump pickup tube attaching bolts and pickup tube bracket attaching nut, then lower pickup tube into oil pan.
13. Remove oil pan through front of vehicle, then remove oil pan gaskets and seals.
14. Reverse procedure to install. Using a small screwdriver, work tabs of oil pan seal into gap between rear main bearing cap and cylinder block, then with tabs positioned, work seal into groove on rear main bearing cap. Apply a 1/8 inch bead of silicone sealer D6AZ-19562-B or equivalent where front cover and cylinder block join and where rear main bearing cap and cylinder block join. Apply a 1/8 inch bead along oil pan rail surface of cylinder block and a 1/4 inch bead along front cover to oil pan surface.

1983–88 COUGAR & THUNDERBIRD & 1984–86 LTD & MARQUIS V8-302

1. Disconnect battery ground cable.
2. Remove oil level indicator from left side of rear oil sump.
3. Remove air cleaner assembly.
4. Remove fan shroud attaching bolts and position shroud over fan.
5. Raise and support vehicle.
6. Drain engine oil and transmission fluid.
7. Disconnect driveshaft, then remove speedometer cable from transmission.
8. Remove transmission shift linkage lever from transmission.
9. Remove flywheel housing cover attaching bolts and the cover.
10. Remove flywheel-to-converter attaching bolts, then the transmission kickdown control shaft.
11. Remove gear selector valve rod, then the starter motor.
12. Remove catalytic converter and muffler inlet pipes.
13. Support transmission with a suitable jack and remove converter housing-to-cylinder block attaching bolts.
14. Remove No. 3 crossmember and rear insulator support assemblies.
15. Disconnect neutral start switch electrical connector from transmission.
16. Disconnect transmission oil cooler lines, then lower transmission and converter assembly from vehicle.
17. Remove flywheel attaching bolts, then the engine rear cover plate.
18. Remove steering gear attaching bolts and position gear aside.
19. Raise engine sufficiently to provide clearance for oil pan removal.
20. Remove oil pan attaching bolts and the oil pan.
21. Reverse procedure to install.

1982 COUGAR XR-7 & THUNDERBIRD V8-255 & 302

1. Disconnect battery ground cable.
2. Remove fan shroud attaching screws and position shroud over fan, then remove dipstick and tube assembly.
3. Raise vehicle and drain crankcase.
4. Disconnect steering flex coupling, then remove two bolts attaching steering gear to main crossmember and let steering gear rest on frame away from oil pan.
5. Unclip and position splash pan away from ends of stabilizer.
6. Remove brackets attaching stabilizer bar to frame, then pull bar downward.
7. Remove transmission shift linkage bracket from frame rail.
8. Remove engine mount attaching bolts, then disconnect and plug transmission oil cooler lines.
9. Disconnect exhaust pipe at exhaust manifolds.
10. Loosen transmission mount nuts, then position a suitable jack under engine and raise engine until engine mount bolts clear frame mounts and pry engine as far forward as it will slide on the transmission mounts.
11. Position two wooden blocks between engine mounts and frame.
12. Remove oil pan attaching bolts, then lower oil pan to frame.
13. Remove oil pump attaching bolts and inlet tube attaching nut, then lower oil pump assembly into oil pan.
14. Remove oil pan. When removing, pull pan forward of stabilizer bar and steering gear flex coupling. **It may be necessary to rotate the crankshaft so that oil pan will clear crankshaft counterweights.**
15. Reverse procedure to install.

OIL PUMP REPLACE

6-200

1. Remove oil pan and related parts as directed above.
2. Unfasten and remove pump, gasket and intermediate drive shaft.
3. Prime pump by filling either the inlet or outlet port with engine oil. Rotate pump shaft to distribute oil within pump body.
4. Position intermediate drive shaft into distributor socket.
5. Position new gasket on pump housing. Insert intermediate drive shaft into oil pump.
6. Install pump and shaft as an assembly.
7. Install oil pan.

V6-232

On these engines, the oil pump is contained within the front cover, **Fig. 36.**

V8-255, 302

1. Remove oil pan as outlined above.
2. Remove pump inlet tube and screen.
3. Remove pump retaining bolts and remove pump, gasket and intermediate shaft.
4. To install, position intermediate drive shaft into distributor socket. With shaft seated in socket, stop on shaft should touch roof of crankcase. Remove shaft and position stop as necessary.
5. With new gasket on pump housing and stop properly positioned, insert intermediate shaft into oil pump. Install pump and shaft as a unit. Do not force pump into position if it will not seat readily. The drive shaft hex may be misaligned with distributor shaft. To align, rotate shaft into new position.
6. Prime pump by filling either inlet or outlet port with engine oil. Rotate pump shaft to distribute oil within pump body.
7. Position new gasket on pump housing.
8. Insert intermediate drive shaft into oil pump.
9. Install pump and shaft as a unit.
10. Complete installation in reverse order of removal.

OIL PUMP, REPAIRS

V6-232 & V8-255, 302

Referring to **Figs. 36 through 38,** disassemble pump. To remove the oil pressure relief valve, insert a self-threading sheet metal screw of the proper diameter into the oil pressure relief valve chamber cap and pull cap out of chamber. Remove spring and plunger.

The inner rotor and shaft and the outer race are serviced as an assembly. One part should not be replaced without replacing the other.

BELT TENSION DATA

Belt	New	Used
Exc. 1/4 Inch Belts	140	105
1/4 Inch Exc. Air Pump	65	50
1/4 Inch Air Pump	110	105
4 Ribs Exc. Air Pump	130	115
4 Ribs Air Pump	110	105
5 Ribs	150	135
6 Ribs, V6	175	145
6 Ribs, V8	113	110

WATER PUMP REPLACE

6-200

1. Drain cooling system, then remove Thermactor pump, power steering and A/C drive belts, if equipped.
2. Disconnect lower radiator hose, then remove fan belt, fan and drive clutch and water pump pulley.
3. Disconnect heater hose at water pump.
4. Remove water pump attaching bolts, then remove water pump.
5. Reverse procedure to install.

V6-232

1. Drain cooling system, then remove air cleaner and air intake duct.
2. Remove fan shroud attaching screws then the fan and fan clutch attaching bolts. Remove fan and fan clutch and shroud.
3. Loosen accessory drive belt idler, then remove drive belt and water pump pulley.
4. On models equipped with power steering, remove pump mounting bracket attaching bolts, position pump aside with hoses attached.
5. On models equipped with A/C, remove compressor front support bracket.
6. Disconnect lower radiator hose, coolant bypass hose and heat hose from water pump.
7. On models equipped with Tripminder, remove fuel flow sensor support bracket. Do not disconnect fuel lines.
8. Remove water pump attaching bolts, then remove water pump.
9. Reverse procedure to install.

V8-255, 302

1. Drain cooling system.
2. Remove air inlet tube.
3. On models equipped with a fan shroud, remove shroud attaching bolts and position shroud over fan.
4. On all models remove fan, spacer and fan shroud.
5. Remove A/C compressor drive belt and idler pulley bracket, if equipped.
6. Remove alternator drive belt, then remove power steering drive belt and pump, if equipped.
7. Remove all accessory brackets attached to water pump, then remove water pump pulley.
8. Disconnect lower radiator hose, heater hose and bypass hose from water pump.
9. Remove water pump to front cover attaching bolts, then remove water pump.
10. Reverse procedure to install.

FUEL PUMP REPLACE

1. Loosen fuel line connections, then retighten hand tight. Do not disconnect lines at this time.
2. Loosen fuel pump attaching bolts one or two turns. Apply hand force to break pump free from gasket.
3. Rotate engine slightly until pump cam lobe is near lowest position.
4. Disconnect inlet and outlet lines and the vapor return line from pump, if equipped.
5. Remove fuel pump attaching bolts and pump. Remove and discard gasket.
6. Reverse procedure to install.

Clutch & Transmission Section

INDEX

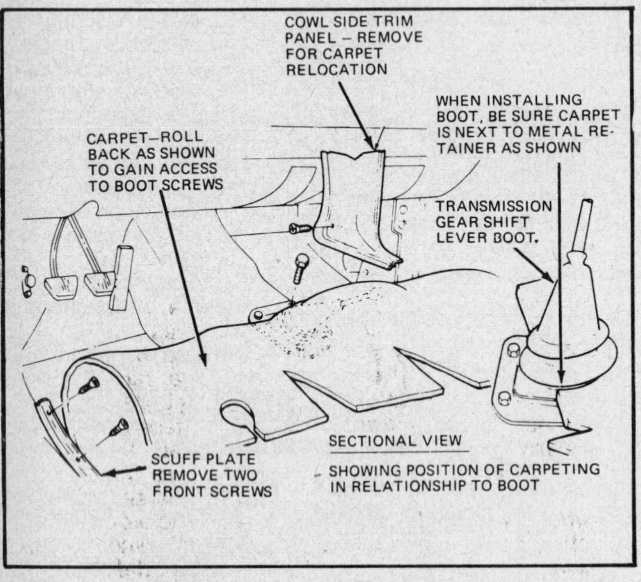

Fig. 1 Shift lever boot removal. Models w/four speed transmission

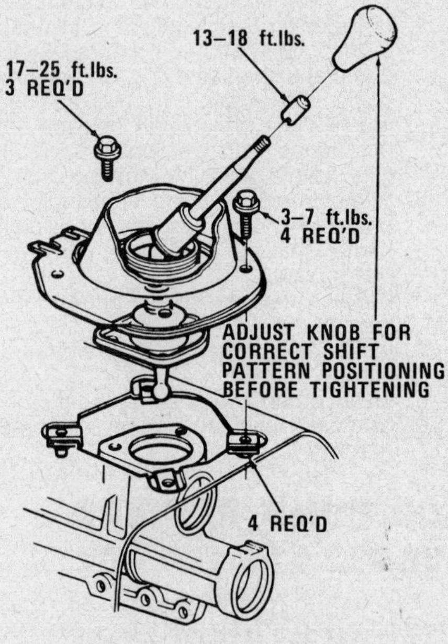

Fig. 2 Shift lever installation. Models w/five speed transmission

CLUTCH PEDAL
ADJUST

These models incorporate a self adjusting clutch mechanism. The adjust mechanism consists of a spring loaded ratchet quadrant attached to the clutch cable. To accomplish this adjustment, grasp clutch pedal and pull upward, then slowly depress clutch pedal. If a click is heard during the procedure, an adjustment was necessary and has been accomplished. This procedure should be performed at least every 5000 miles.

CLUTCH
REPLACE

Lift clutch pedal upward to disengage clutch cable self adjuster pawl and quadrant. Push quadrant forward, then detach cable from quadrant and allow quadrant to swing rearward slowly.

4-140

1. Raise vehicle and remove release lever spring and dust shield.
2. On turbocharged models, remove clutch slave cylinder.
3. On non-turbocharged models, loosen clutch cable locknut and adjusting nut, then disconnect clutch cable from release lever.
4. On non-turbocharged models, remove retaining clip, then remove clutch cable from clutch housing.
5. Remove starter motor.
6. Remove bolts attaching engine rear plate to lower front portion of flywheel housing.
7. Remove transmission and flywheel housing as described under "Transmission, Replace."
8. Remove clutch release lever from housing by pulling lever through opening in housing until retainer spring is disengaged from pivot.
9. Remove release bearing from release lever.
10. Remove pressure plate cover attaching bolts. **Loosen bolts evenly to relieve spring tension without distorting cover. Mark cover and flywheel so that pressure plate can be installed in the same position.**
11. Remove pressure plate and clutch disc from flywheel.
12. Reverse procedure to install. **Prior to installing throw-out bearing, apply a light film of lithium base lubricant No. C1AZ-19590-B or equivalent to transmission front bearing retainer outside diameter, the clutch release fork and anti-rattle spring where they contact the release bearing hub and to the throw-out bearing where the bearing contacts the pressure plate release fingers. In addition, fill the throw-out bearing grease groove with the same lubricant. Clean up all excess lubricant.**

6-200 & V8-302

1. Raise vehicle, then remove transmission as described under "Transmission, Replace."
2. Remove dust shield and loosen clutch cable adjusting nut, then disengage clutch cable from release lever.
3. Disengage clutch cable from flywheel housing.
4. Remove starter.

5. Remove bolts attaching engine rear plate to front lower portion of flywheel housing.
6. Remove bolts attaching housing to cylinder block.
7. Move housing back just far enough to clear pressure plate and remove housing.
8. Remove clutch release lever from housing by pulling lever through housing opening until retainer spring is disengaged from pivot.
9. Remove pressure plate cover attaching bolts. **Loosen bolts evenly to relieve spring tension without distorting cover. Mark cover and flywheel so that pressure plate can be installed in the same position.**
10. Remove pressure plate and clutch disc from flywheel.
11. Reverse procedure to install. **Prior to installing throw-out bearing, apply a light film of lithium base lubricant No. C1AZ-19590-B or equivalent to transmission front bearing retainer outside diameter, the clutch release fork and anti-rattle spring where they contact the release bearing hub and to the throw-out bearing where the bearing contacts the pressure plate release fingers. In addition, fill the throw-out bearing grease groove with the same lubricant. Clean up all excess lubricant.**

FOUR SPEED TRANS. REPLACE

1. Remove coin tray, then remove four screws attaching boot to floor pan and pull boot up on shift lever. Remove three lever attaching screws, then remove shift lever and boot assembly, **Figs. 1 and 2.**
2. From under hood, remove flywheel housing to engine block upper attaching bolts or nuts.
3. Raise and support vehicle.
4. Mark driveshaft so that it can be installed in the same position, then remove driveshaft and install a plug in transmission extension housing to prevent lubricant leakage.
5. Remove clutch release lever dust cover, then disconnect clutch cable from release lever.
6. Remove starter motor.
7. Remove speedometer cable attaching screw, then lift cable from extension housing.
8. Support rear of engine using a suitable jack, then remove bolts attaching crossmember to body.
9. Remove bolts attaching crossmember to extension housing and remove crossmember.
10. Lower engine as required to permit removal of bolts attaching flywheel housing to engine. Slide transmission rearward from engine and lower from vehicle. **It may be necessary to slide mounting bracket forward from catalytic converter heat shield to provide clearance to move transmission rearward for removal.**
11. Remove cover attaching bolts and drain lubricant.
12. Remove flywheel housing to transmission attaching bolts, then remove flywheel housing.
13. Reverse procedure to install.

FIVE SPEED TRANS. REPLACE

1. Raise and support vehicle.
2. Mark driveshaft for assembly reference, then disconnect driveshaft from rear U-joint flange. Slide driveshaft from transmission output shaft, then install an extension housing seal installation tool into extension housing opening to prevent lubricant spillage.
3. Remove 4 catalytic converter attaching bolts and the converter with inlet pipe.
4. Remove rear transmission support attaching bolts.
5. Support engine and transmission using a suitable jack, then remove crossmember attaching bolts. Raise engine slightly and remove crossmember.
6. Lower transmission to gain access to 2 shift handle attaching bolts, then remove the bolts and shift handle.
7. Disconnect back-up light electrical connector, then the top gear and neutral sensing switch electrical connectors, if equipped.
8. Remove speedometer cable retainer bolt, then the speedometer driven gear from transmission.
9. Remove transmission-to-flywheel attaching bolts.
10. Move transmission rearward until input shaft clears flywheel housing, then lower transmission from vehicle. It may be necessary to lower engine slightly to provide clearance for transmission removal. **Do not depress clutch pedal while transmission is removed from vehicle.**
11. Reverse procedure to install.

Rear Axle, Propeller Shaft & Brakes Section

INDEX

REAR AXLES

FORD INTEGRAL CARRIER w/BOLT-ON TYPE AXLE RETENTION

This rear axle, **Fig. 1**, is an integral design hypoid with the center line of the pinion set below the center line of the ring gear. The semi-floating axle shafts are retained in the housing by ball bearings and bearing retainers at axle ends.

The differential is mounted on two opposed tapered roller bearings which are retained in the housing by removable caps. Differential bearing preload and drive gear backlash is adjusted by nuts located behind each differential bearing cup.

The drive pinion assembly is mounted on two opposed tapered roller bearings. Pinion bearing preload is adjusted by a collapsible spacer on the pinion shaft. Pinion and ring gear tooth contact is adjusted by shims between the rear bearing cone and pinion gear.

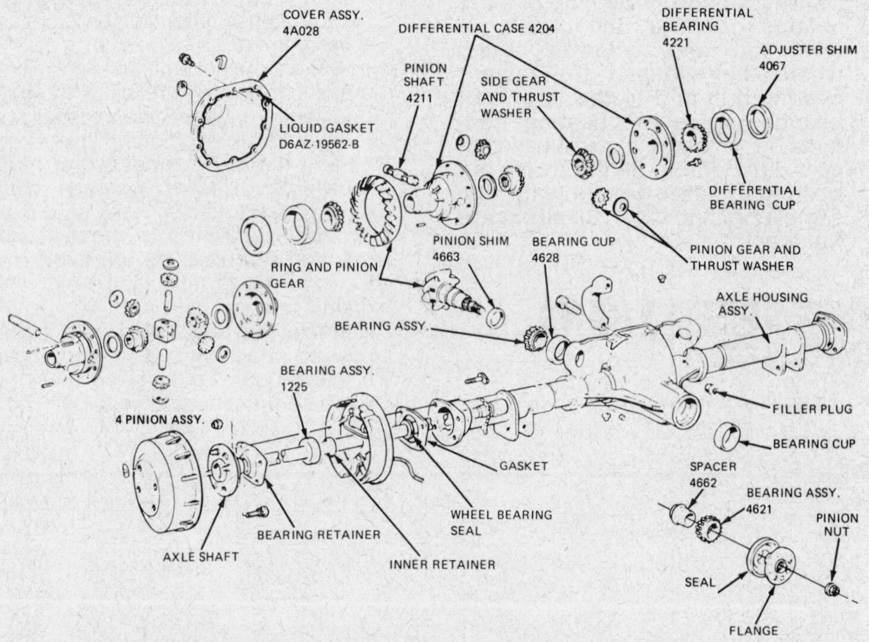

Fig. 1 Disassembled view of Ford integral carrier type rear axle assembly w/bolt on type axle retention

FORD INTEGRAL CARRIER w/C-LOCK TYPE AXLE RETENTION

The gear set, **Fig. 2**, consist of a ring gear and an overhung drive pinion which is supported by two opposed tapered roller bearings. Pinion bearing preload is maintained by a collapsible spacer on the pinion shaft and adjusted by the pinion nut. The differential case is a one piece design with two openings to allow assembly of internal components and lubricant flow. The pinion shaft is retained with a threaded bolt assembled to the case. The differential case is mounted in the carrier between two opposed tapered roller bearings. The bearings are retained in the carrier by removable bearing caps. Differential bearing preload and ring gear backlash are adjusted by the use of shims located between the differential bearing cups and the carrier housing. Axle shafts are held in the housing by C-locks positioned in a slot on the axle shaft splined end, **Fig. 3.**

REAR AXLE REPLACE

1. Raise rear of vehicle support at frame members and rear axle, then remove wheel and tire assembly.
2. Remove brake drums and disconnect brake lines at wheel cylinders.
3. Make marks on drive shaft yoke and pinion flange for reassembly, then disconnect drive shaft at rear U-joint and remove drive shaft from transmission extension housing. Install seal replacer tool in extension housing to prevent leakage.
4. Position a drain pan under differential carrier, then remove carrier attaching bolts and allow differential to drain.
5. Disconnect stabilizer bar, if equipped.
6. Disconnect shock absorbers from lower mountings.
7. Remove brake lines from retaining clips on rear axle housing, then remove brake line junction block retaining screw.
8. Position a suitable jack under axle housing to prevent housing from tilting when removing control arms.
9. Disconnect lower control arms from axle housing and position control arms downward.
10. Disconnect upper control arms from axle housing and position control arms upward.
11. Disconnect air vent line.
12. Lower axle slightly and remove coil springs and insulators.
13. Lower axle housing and remove from vehicle.

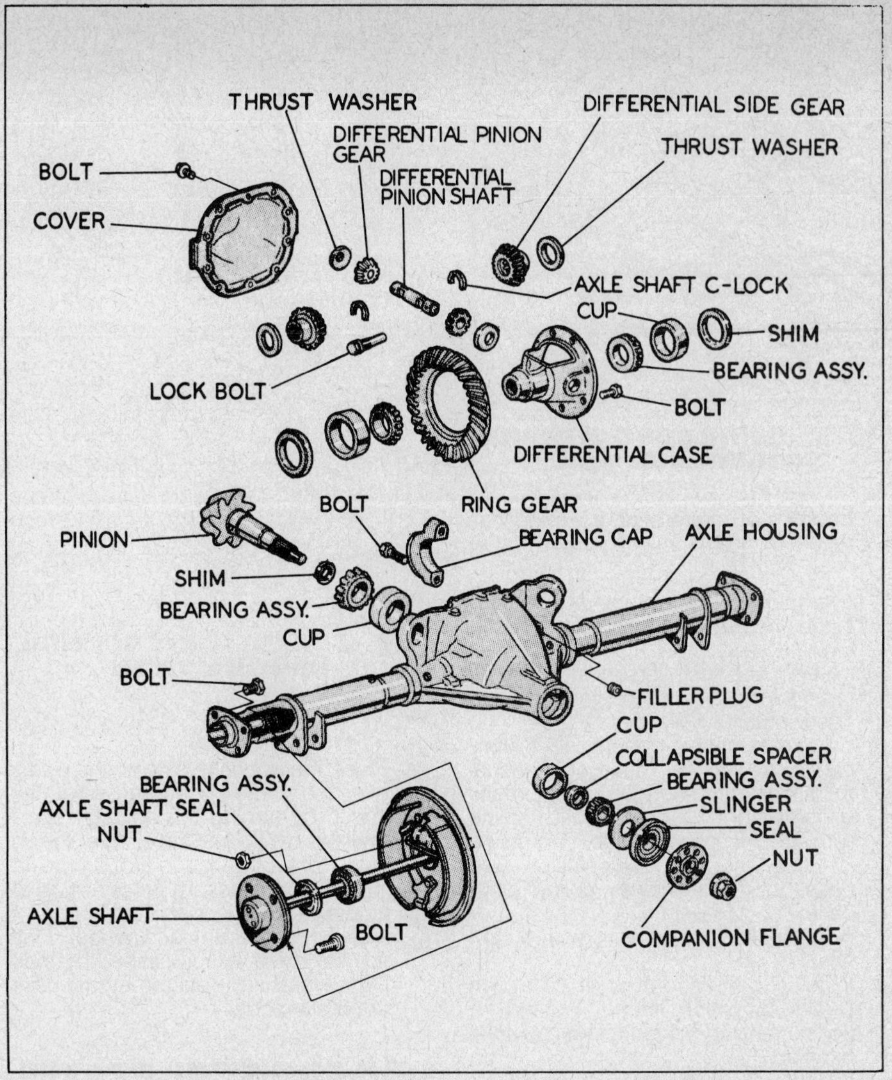

Fig. 2 Disassembled view of Ford integral carrier type rear axle assembly w/C-lock type axle retention

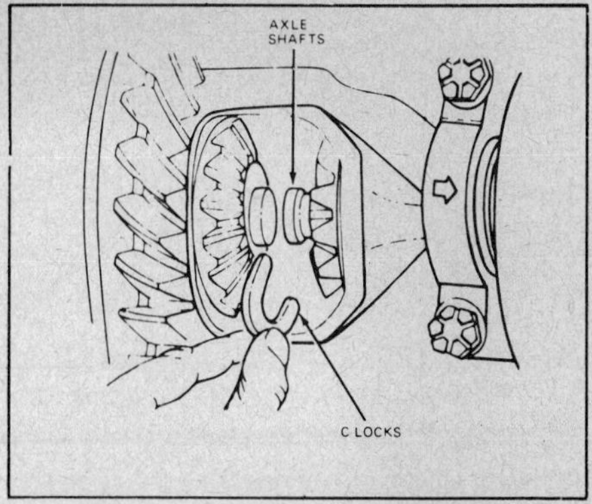

Fig. 3 Axle shaft C-lock

Fig. 4 Removing nuts from wheel bearing retainer

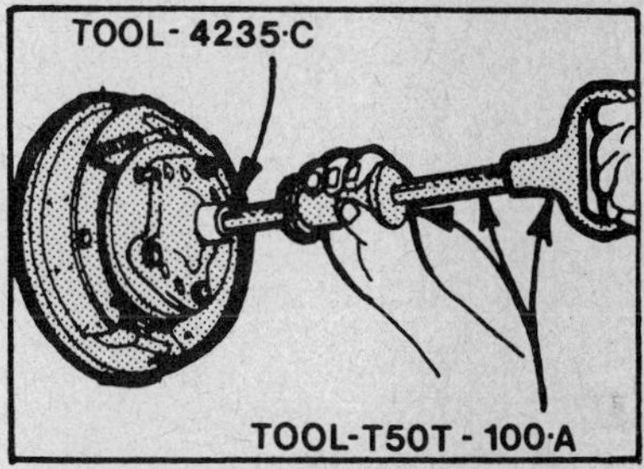

Fig. 5 Removing axle shaft with slide hammer-type puller

AXLE SHAFT REPLACE

FORD INTEGRAL CARRIER W/BOLT ON TYPE AXLE RETENTION

1. Remove wheel and tire assembly, then remove nuts attaching brake drum to axle shaft flange and remove brake drum.
2. Working through opening in axle shaft flange, remove nuts securing axle shaft bearing retainer, **Fig. 4.**
3. Using a suitable puller, pull axle shaft from housing, **Fig. 5.**
4. Remove brake backing plate and attach to frame side rail with a piece of wire.
5. If rear wheel bearing is to be replaced, loosen inner retainer ring by nicking it deeply in several places with a chisel, **Fig. 6,** then slide retainer from axle shaft.
6. Press bearing from axle shaft using tool No. T71P-4621-B.
7. Using a hook type puller, remove oil seal from axle housing, **Fig. 7.**
8. Position bearing retainer and bearing on axle shaft, then using tool No. T62F-4621-A, press bearing onto shaft until firmly seated against shoulder.
9. Using bearing installation tool, press inner retainer onto shaft until retainer is firmly seated against bearing.
10. Wipe all lubricant from oil seal area of axle housing, then install oil seal using tool No. T79P-1177-A, **Fig. 8.**
11. Install gasket on housing flange, then install brake backing plate.
12. Carefully slide axle shaft into housing using care not to damage oil seal, then install bearing retainer attaching nuts and torque to 20 to 40 ft. lbs.
13. Install brake drum and retaining nuts, then install wheel and tire assembly.

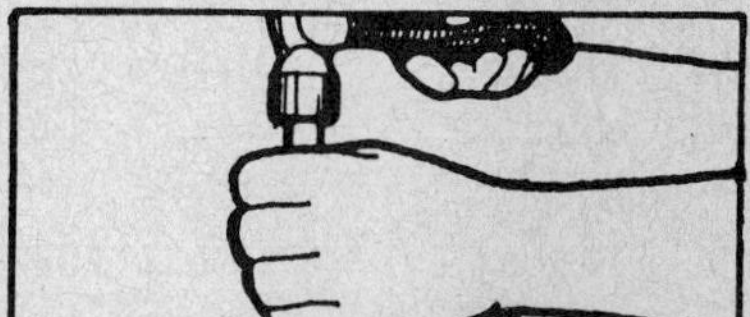

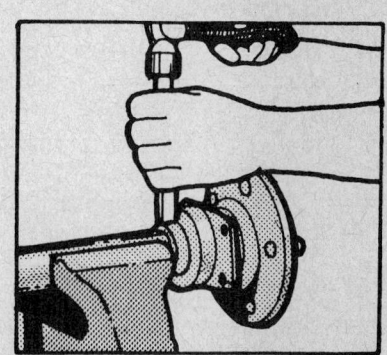

Fig. 6 Splitting bearing inner retainer for bearing removal

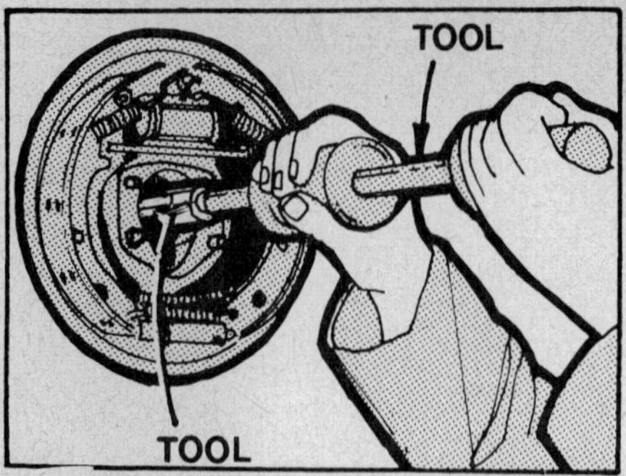

Fig. 7 Using hook-type tool to remove oil seal

FORD INTEGRAL CARRIER W/C-LOCK TYPE AXLE RETENTION

1. Raise and support rear of vehicle.
2. Remove wheel and tire assembly and brake drum.
3. Remove rear axle housing cover and drain lubricant.
4. Remove differential pinion lock screw and differential pinion shaft.
5. Remove wheel speed sensor, if equipped. **Damage to sensor may occur if sensor is not removed before axle shaft.**
6. Push axle shafts inward and remove C-locks, **Fig. 3.**
7. Remove axle shaft from housing using care not to damage oil seal.
8. Remove bearing and seal as an assembly using a suitable slide hammer, **Fig. 7**, if necessary. **Two types of bearing are used, Fig. 9. One requires a light press fit in the housing flange, while on the other a loose fit is acceptable. Therefore, if a loose fitting bearing is encountered, it does not indicate excessive wear or damage.**
9. Lubricate bearing with rear axle lubricant and install bearing into housing bore using tool No. T78P-1225-A.
10. Install axle shaft seal into housing using tool No. T78P-1177-A, **Fig. 8.**
11. Reverse procedure to install axle shaft.

PROPELLER SHAFT REPLACE

1. Mark relationship of driveshaft to pinion flange, then disconnect rear U-joint or companion flange from drive pinion flange.
2. Pull drive shaft toward rear of car until front U-joint yoke clears transmission extension housing and output shaft.
3. Install a suitable tool, such as a seal driver, in seal to prevent lube from leaking from transmission.
4. Before installing, check U-joints for freedom of movement. If a bind has resulted from misalignment after overhauling the U-joints, tap the ears of the drive shaft sharply to relieve the bind.
5. If rubber seal installed on end of transmission extension housing is damaged, install a new seal.
6. On a manual shift transmission, lubricate yoke spline with conventional transmission grease. On an automatic transmission, lubricate yoke spline with special spline grease. This spline is sealed so that transmission fluid does not "wash" away spline lubricant.
7. Install yoke on transmission output shaft.
8. Install U-bolts and nuts which attach U-joint to pinion flange. Tighten U-bolts evenly to prevent binding U-joint bearings.

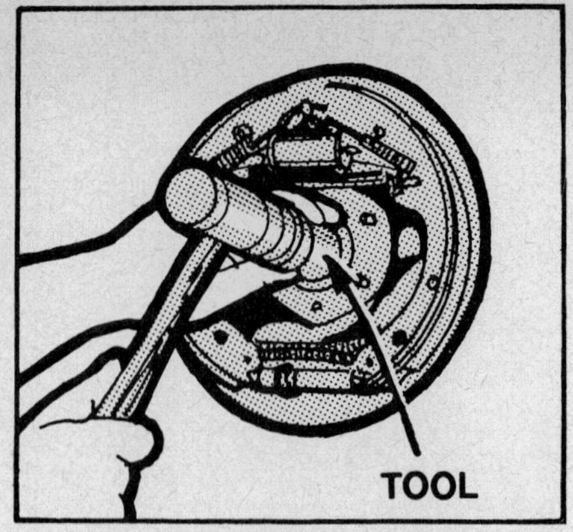

Fig. 8 Using special driver to install oil seal

BRAKE ADJUSTMENTS

Some models use a new front and rear brake backing plate which omits the adjusting slot for manual brake adjustment. The backing plates have a partially stamped knock-out slot for use ONLY when the brake drums cannot be removed in a normal manner. The open slot is then covered with a rubber plug as used in the past to prevent contamination of the brakes.

When servicing a vehicle requiring a brake adjustment, the metal knock-out plugs should NOT be removed. Rather the drums should be removed and brakes inspected for a malfunction.

Although the brakes are self-adjusting, an initial adjustment will be necessary after a brake repair, such as relining or replacement. The initial adjustment can be obtained by the new procedure which follows:

1. Use the brake shoe adjustment gauge shown in **Fig. 10** to obtain the drum inside diameter as shown. Tighten the adjusting knob on the gauge to hold this setting.

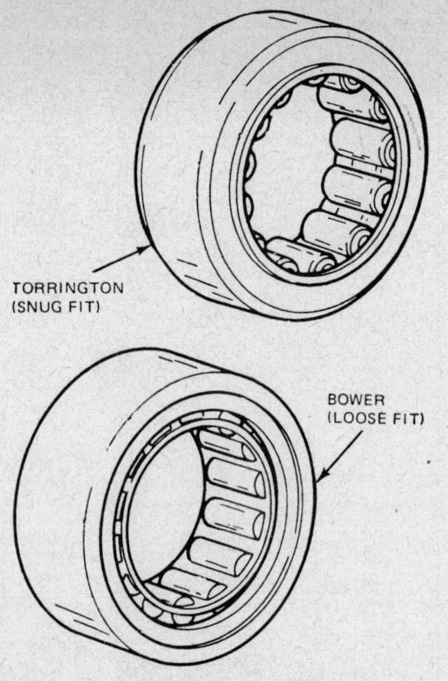

Fig. 9 Axle shaft bearing identification

2. Place the opposite side of the gauge over the brake shoes and adjust the shoes by turning the adjuster screw until the gauge just slides over the linings. Rotate the gauge around the lining surface to assure proper lining diameter adjustment and clearance.
3. Install brake drum and wheel. Final adjustment is accomplished by making several firm reverse stops, using the brake pedal.

SELF-ADJUSTING BRAKES

These brakes, **Fig. 11** have self-adjusting shoe mechanisms that assure correct lining-to-drum clearances at all times. The automatic adjusters operate only when the brakes are applied as the car is moving rearward.

Although the brakes are self-adjusting, an initial adjustment is necessary after the brake shoes have been relined or replaced, or when the length of the star wheel adjuster has been changed during some other service operation.

Frequent usage of an automatic transmission forward range to halt reverse vehicle motion may prevent the automatic adjusters from functioning, thereby inducing low pedal heights. Should low pedal heights be encountered, it is recommended that numerous forward and reverse stops be made until satisfactory pedal height is obtained.

If a low pedal condition cannot be corrected by making numerous reverse stops (provided the hydraulic system is free of air) it indicates that the self-adjusting mechanism is not functioning. Therefore, it will be necessary to remove the brake drum, clean, free up and lubricate the adjusting mechanism. Then adjust the brake, being sure the parking brake is fully released.

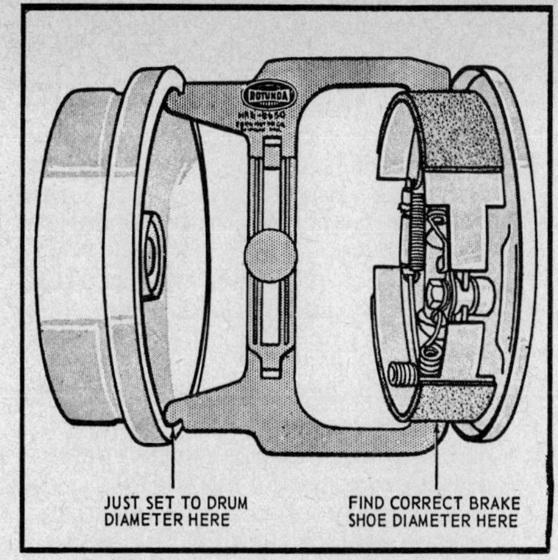

Fig. 10 Revised brake adjustment

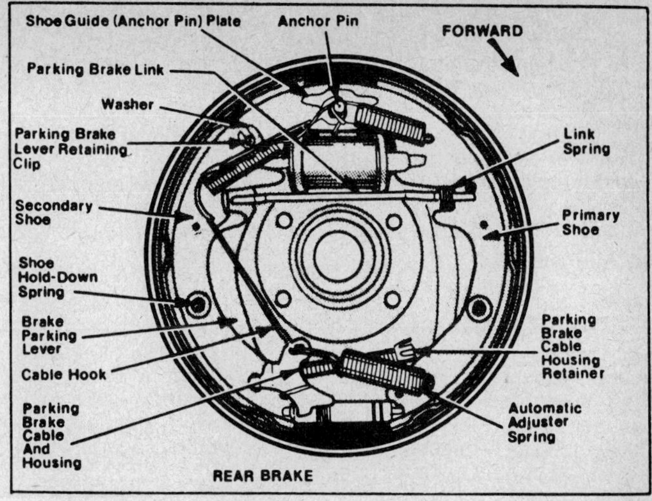

Fig. 11 Rear drum brake mechanism

PARKING BRAKE ADJUST

REAR DRUM BRAKES

1. Make sure parking brake is released.
2. Place transmission in neutral and raise the vehicle.
3. Tighten the adjusting nut against the cable equalizer to cause rear brakes to drag.
4. Then loosen the adjusting nut until the rear wheels are fully released. There should be no drag.
5. Lower vehicle and check operation.

REAR DISC BRAKES

1. Fully release parking brake, then place transmission in neutral and support vehicle at rear axle.
2. Tighten adjuster nut until levers on calipers just start to move, then loosen the nut just enough to obtain full travel to the off position. **If brake cables are replaced in any system having a foot-actuated control assembly, stroke parking brake control with about 100 pounds pedal effort, then repeat adjustment.**
3. The lever is in the off position when a 1/4 inch diameter pin can be freely inserted past the side of the lever into the 1/4 inch diameter holes in the cast iron housing.
4. Apply and release the parking brake, then apply and release the service brake pedal with moderate force. Check parking brake levers on calipers to determine if they are fully returned to the off position. **If the 1/4 inch pin cannot be freely inserted, the adjustment is too tight. Repeat adjustment procedure. Also, if levers do not return to off position, parking and service brake function will be affected as the vehicle is driven.**

VACUUM RELEASE UNIT

The vacuum power unit will release the parking brake automatically when the transmission selector lever is moved into any driving position with the engine running. The brakes will not release automatically, however, when the selector lever is in neutral or park position with the engine running, or in any other position with the engine off.

The lower end of the release handle extends out for alternate manual release in the event of vacuum power failure or for optional manual release at any time.

MASTER CYLINDER REPLACE

LESS POWER BRAKES

1. Disconnect battery ground cable.
2. Disconnect stop light switch wires, remove hairpin retainer and slide stop light switch off brake pedal pin just far enough to clear end of pin. Then lift switch straight upward from pin.
3. Slide master cylinder pushrod with nylon washers and bushings from brake pedal pin.
4. Remove brake tubes from outlet ports of master cylinder.
5. Remove locknuts that secure master cylinder to dash panel and lift cylinder forward and upward from vehicle.
6. Reverse procedure to install.

WITH POWER BRAKES

1. Disconnect brake lines from master cylinder.
2. Disconnect brake warning lamp electrical connector, if equipped.
3. On all models, remove master cylinder to power brake unit attaching nuts, then lift master cylinder from mounting studs.
4. Reverse procedure to install.

POWER BRAKE UNIT REPLACE

EXC. HYDRO-BOOST

Exc. 1985–87 4-140

1. Disconnect battery ground cable and remove air cleaner.
2. On 1982-84 models equipped with 4-140 engine, disconnect accelerator cable from carburetor, then remove screw that secures accelerator cable to to shaft bracket and remove cable bracket. Remove two screws that secure accelerator shaft bracket to manifold and rotate bracket toward engine. Remove RPO horn, if equipped.
3. On all models, disconnect manifold vacuum hose from booster check valve.
4. Disconnect brake lines from primary and secondary outlet ports of master cylinder.
5. Remove master cylinder-to-booster attaching nuts and the master cylinder.
6. Working under instrument panel, disconnect electrical connector from stop lamp switch.
7. Remove hairpin type retainer. Slide stop lamp switch off brake pedal pin just far enough for the switch outer hole to clear the pin, then lower switch away from pin.
8. Remove booster-to-dash panel attaching nuts.
9. On models equipped with speed control, unfasten control amplifier from lower outboard booster stud and position aside.
10. On all models, slide booster pushrod, bushing and inner nylon washer off brake pedal pin.
11. Move booster forward in engine compartment until booster studs clear dash panel, then rotate front of booster toward engine and remove booster.
12. Reverse procedure to install.

1985–87 4-140

1. Disconnect battery ground cable and remove air cleaner.
2. Disconnect accelerator cable from throttle plate.
3. Remove screw that secures accelerator cable to shaft bracket and remove cable from bracket.
4. Remove two screws that secure accelerator shaft bracket to manifold and rotate bracket toward engine.

5. On LTD and Marquis models, remove RPO horn.
6. On Cougar and Thunderbird models, release fuel system pressure, then disconnect the two manifold injector connectors located near oil dipstick retaining bracket. Disconnect two fuel lines to fuel supply manifold assembly.
7. On all models, remove engine oil dipstick tube and bracket.
8. Remove windshield wiper motor.
9. Disconnect vacuum lines located over brake booster at dash panel vacuum tee.
10. Remove bolt securing clutch cable stand, then move bracket to side rail at fender inner panel.
11. On models equipped with speed control, move speed control cable to one side to clear booster.
12. On all models, disconnect manifold booster line from booster check valve.
13. Disconnect brake lines from master cylinder, then remove master cylinder attaching nuts and the master cylinder.
14. Working under instrument panel, disconnect electrical connector from stop lamp switch.
15. Remove hairpin type retainer and outer nylon washer from brake pedal pin, then slide stop lamp switch off brake pedal pin just enough for outer arm to clear pin.
16. On models equipped with speed control, unfasten control amplifier from lower outboard booster stud and position aside.
17. On all models, slide booster pushrod link and nylon washers off brake pedal pin.
18. Move booster forward in engine compartment until booster studs clear dash panel, then rotate front of booster toward engine and remove booster.
19. Reverse procedure to install.

HYDRO-BOOST

1. Disconnect stoplight switch wires at connector and remove hairpin retainer, then slide stoplight switch off brake pedal pin far enough for switch outer hole to clear pin and remove pin from switch.
2. Slide hydro-boost pushrod and nylon washers and bushing off brake pedal pin.
3. Remove master cylinder and position to one side without disturbing hydraulic lines. **It is not necessary to disconnect brake lines, but care should be taken not to deform lines.**
4. Disconnect pressure, steering gear and return lines from booster, then plug lines and ports in hydro-boost to prevent entry of dirt.
5. Remove hydro-boost retaining nuts, and remove assembly sliding pushrod link from engine side of dash panel.
6. Reverse procedure to install. To purge system, disconnect coil wire so that engine will not start. Fill power steering pump reservoir, then while engaging starter, pump brake pedal. Do not cycle steering wheel until all residual air has been purged from the hydro boost unit. Check fluid level, then connect coil wire and start engine. Apply brakes with a pumping action and cycle steering wheel, then check system for leaks.

Rear Suspension Section

INDEX

SHOCK ABSORBER
REPLACE

1. On sedans, open trunk to gain access to upper shock absorber attachment. On station wagons, remove side panel trim covers.
2. Remove rubber cap from shock absorber stud.
3. On all models, remove shock absorber attaching nut, washer and insulator.
4. Raise vehicle and support rear axle.
5. Compress shock absorber to clear hole in upper shock absorber tower.
6. On Fairmont, LTD, Marquis, Zephyr and 1982 Cougar and Granada models, remove nut or bolt and washer from shock absorber lower mounting stud, then the shock absorber. On Thunderbird, 1982 Cougar XR-7 and 1983-87 Cougar models, remove shock absorber protective cover, then the shock absorber attaching bolt and shock absorber.

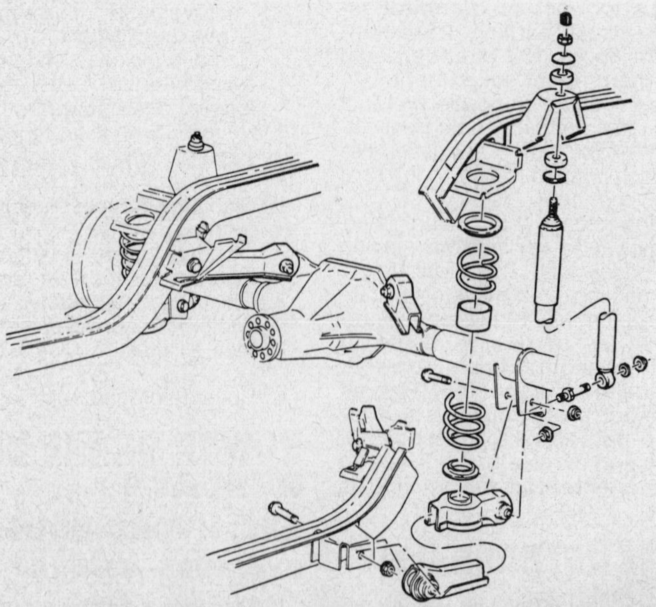

Fig. 1 Rear suspension (typical)

7. Reverse procedure to install. Torque upper shock mount bolts to 26 ft. lbs. Torque lower attaching bolt to 60-65 ft. lbs. on 1982 models, or 55-70 ft. lbs. on 1983-87 models. **On 1984-87 Thunderbird and Cougar models equipped with optional handling package, torque lower attaching bolt to 45-60 ft. lbs.**

AXLE DAMPER REPLACE

COUGAR & THUNDERBIRD W/4-140 TURBOCHARGED ENGINE

1. Raise and support vehicle at rear axle.
2. Remove wheel.
3. Remove axle damper front attaching nut and pivot bolt.
4. Remove rear attaching nut, then the axle damper and spacer.
5. Reverse procedure to install. Torque all attaching nuts and bolts to 55-70 ft. lbs.

STABILIZER BAR REPLACE

1. Raise and support rear of vehicle.
2. Remove four bolts attaching stabilizer bar to lower control arms.
3. Remove stabilizer bar from vehicle.

COIL SPRING REPLACE

1. Remove stabilizer bar as described under "Stabilizer Bar, Replace," if equipped.
2. Position a suitable jack under rear axle, then raise vehicle and support body at rear body crossmember.
3. Lower axle until shock absorbers are fully extended. **Support axle with jack stands or a suitable jack.**
4. Position a suitable jack under lower control arm pivot bolt and remove nut and bolt. Carefully and slowly lower the control arm until all spring tension is relieved.
5. Remove coil spring and insulators from vehicle, **Fig. 1.**

CONTROL ARMS REPLACE

Upper and lower control arms must be replaced in pairs.

UPPER ARM

1. Raise vehicle and support body at rear body crossmember.
2. Remove upper arm pivot bolt and nut, **Fig. 1.**
3. Remove front pivot bolt and nut, then remove upper arm from vehicle.

LOWER ARM

1. Remove stabilizer bar as described under "Stabilizer Bar, Replace," if equipped.
2. Position a suitable jack under rear axle, then raise vehicle and support body at rear body crossmember.
3. Lower axle until shock absorbers are fully extended. **Support axle with jack stands or a suitable jack.**
4. Position a suitable jack under lower control arm rear pivot bolt and remove nut and bolt, **Fig. 1.** Carefully and slowly lower the control arm until all spring tension is relieved, then remove coil spring and insulators.
5. Remove lower control arm front pivot bolt and nut, then remove lower control arm assembly.

Front Suspension & Steering Section

INDEX

FRONT SUSPENSION

This suspension, **Fig. 1,** is a modified MacPherson strut design, which uses shock struts and coil springs. The springs are mounted between the lower control arm and a spring pocket in the crossmember.

WHEEL BEARINGS ADJUST

1. With wheel rotating, tighten adjusting nut to 17-25 ft. lbs.
2. Back off adjusting nut 1/2 turn, then retighten nut to 10-15 inch lbs. on 1982-83 models, or 10-12 inch lbs. on 1984-87 models.
3. Place nut lock on nut so that castellations on lock are aligned with cotter pin hole in spindle and install cotter pin, **Fig. 2.**
4. Check front wheel rotation, if it rotates noisily or rough, clean, inspect or replace wheel bearings as necessary.

WHEEL BEARINGS REPLACE

DISC BRAKES

1. Raise car and remove front wheels.
2. Remove caliper mounting bolts. **It is not necessary to disconnect the brake lines for this operation.**
3. Slide caliper off of disc, inserting a clean spacer between the shoes to hold them in their bores after the caliper is removed. Position caliper out of the way. **Do not allow caliper to hang by brake hose.**
4. Remove hub and disc assembly. Grease retainer and inner bearing can now be removed.

CHECKING BALL JOINTS FOR WEAR

1. Support vehicle in normal driving position with both ball joints loaded.
2. Clean area around grease fitting and checking surface. **The checking surface is the round boss into which the grease fitting is installed.**
3. The checking surface should project outside the cover, **Fig. 3.** If surface is inside cover replace lower arm assembly.

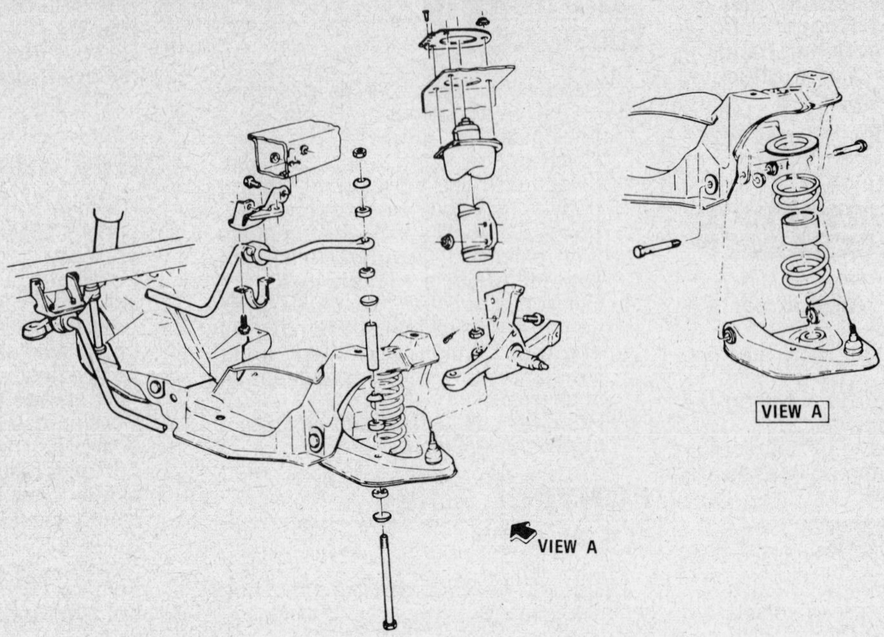

Fig. 1 Typical front suspension

BALL JOINTS
REPLACE

Ford Motor Company recommends that new ball joints should not be installed on used control arms and that the control arm be replaced if ball joint replacement is required. However, aftermarket ball joint repair kits which do not require control arm replacement, are available and can be installed using the following procedure.

These ball joints are not serviceable. If they require replacement, the control arm and ball joint must be replaced as an assembly.

SHOCK STRUT
REPLACE

1. Place ignition switch in the Unlocked position so that front wheels are free to move.
2. From engine compartment, remove one strut to upper mounting nut. Use a screwdriver in rod slot to hold rod stationary when removing nut.
3. Raise front of vehicle by lower control arms, then place safety stands under frame jack pads located rearward of wheels.
4. Remove wheel and tire assembly, then remove brake caliper, rotor assembly and dust shield.
5. Remove two nuts and bolts attaching lower strut to spindle. **Gas pressurized struts (LTD, Marquis and 1983-87 Cougar and Thunderbird) must be held firmly during removal of the last spindle-to-strut bolt since gas pressure will cause strut to extend fully when bolt is removed.**
6. Lift strut upward from spindle to compress rod, then pull downward and remove strut.
7. On 1983-87 models, remove jounce bumper.
8. Reverse procedure to install. Torque upper mount attaching nut to 60-75 ft. lbs. on 1982 models, or 55-92 ft. lbs. on 1983-87 models. Remove suspension load from lower control arm by lowering front of vehicle, then torque lower mounting nuts to 150-180 ft. lbs. on 1982 models, or 120-179 ft. lbs. on 1983-87 models.

COIL SPRING
REPLACE

1. Raise front of vehicle and position safety stands under jack pads located rearward of wheels, then remove wheel and tire assembly.
2. Disconnect caliper and wire it out of the way without disconnecting brake lines.
3. Disconnect stabilizer bar link from lower control arm.
4. Remove steering gear attaching bolts, and position gear aside.
5. Disconnect tie rod from spindle using tool 3290-C, or equivalent.
6. Using spring compressor tool T82P-5310-A, compress spring until it is free from lower seat.
7. Remove two lower control arm pivot bolts and disengage control arm from frame, then remove spring from seat. If a replacement spring is to be installed, measure compressed length of spring being removed to assist in compressing and installing the replacement spring.
8. Reverse procedure to install. When installing spring, locate lower end of coil between two holes in lower control arm spring pocket. On 1982 models, torque lower control arm pivot nuts to 215-260 ft. lbs., stabilizer bar to lower control arm nut 6-12 ft. lbs. and steering gear to crossmember bolts to 90-100 ft. lbs. On 1983-87 models, torque control arm pivot nuts to approximately 150 ft. lbs., stabilizer bar link nut to 6-12 ft. lbs., steering gear to crossmember nuts to 90-100 ft. lbs., and tie rod end to 35 ft. lbs.

STABILIZER BAR AND/OR INSULATOR
REPLACE

1. Raise vehicle and place jack stands under lower control arms.

WITH WHEEL ROTATING, TORQUE ADJUSTING NUT, TO 17-25 FT. LBS.
BACK ADJUSTING NUT OFF 1/2 TURN
TIGHTEN ADJUSTING NUT TO 10-15 IN.-LBS.
INSTALL THE LOCK AND A NEW COTTER PI

Fig. 2 Front wheel bearing adjustment

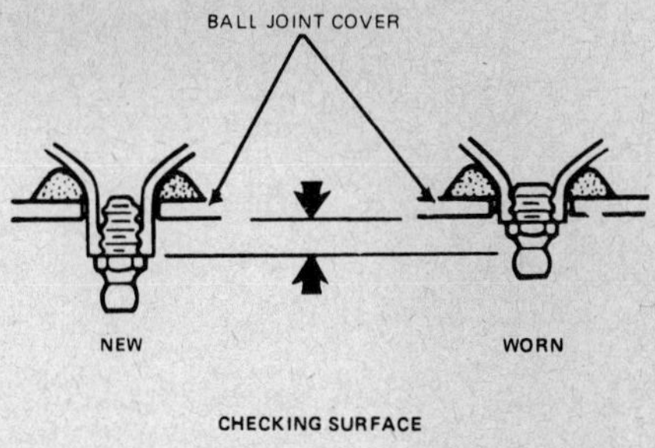
BALL JOINT COVER
NEW
WORN
CHECKING SURFACE

Fig. 3 Checking lower ball joint

2. Disconnect stabilizer bar from links, then remove stabilizer insulator retaining clamps and remove stabilizer.
3. To remove insulator, cut insulators and plastic sleeves from stabilizer bar. Before installing new insulators, coat the necessary parts of the stabilizer with grease, then install the insulators and sleeves.
4. Reverse procedure to install stabilizer bar. Install new stabilizer link bolts with heads facing down and torque to 6-12 ft. lbs. Using new bolts, install stabilizer insulator retaining clamps and torque to 20 to 25 ft. lbs.

POWER STEERING GEAR
REPLACE

INTEGRAL POWER RACK & PINION

1. Disconnect battery ground cable.
2. Remove bolt retaining flexible coupling to input shaft.
3. Turn ignition key "On" and raise vehicle.
4. Remove the two tie rod end retaining nuts, then separate studs from spindle arms, using a suitable tool.
5. Support gear and remove attaching bolts, then lower gear enough to gain access to pressure and return lines, and remove bolt attaching the hose bracket to the gear.
6. Disconnect pressure and return lines and remove steering gear. Plug lines and ports to prevent entry of dirt.
7. Reverse procedure to install. Torque pressure and return line fittings to 10-15 ft. lbs., gear housing to crossmember mounting bolt to 80-100 ft. lbs., steering flex coupling bolt to 20-30 ft. lbs. and tie rod end to spindle arm nut to 35-47 ft. lbs. **On some models, hoses can swivel when torqued properly. Do not over-tighten.**

INTEGRAL POWER STEERING GEAR

1. Disconnect pressure and return lines from gear and plug openings to prevent entry of dirt.
2. Remove two bolts that secure flex coupling to gear and column.
3. Raise vehicle and remove pitman arm with suitable puller.
4. If vehicle is equipped with synchromesh transmission, remove clutch release retracting spring to provide clearance to remove gear.
5. Support gear and remove three gear attaching bolts.

MANUAL STEERING GEAR
REPLACE

RACK & PINION

1. Disconnect battery ground cable, turn ignition "On" and raise vehicle.
2. Remove tie rod end retaining nuts and using ball joint separator, separate tie rod ends from spindle arms.
3. Remove pinion shaft to flexible coupling bolt and the bolts securing steering gear to crossmember.
4. Turn front wheels, then remove steering gear from left side of vehicle.
5. Reverse procedure to install. Torque connecting rod end to spindle arm nut to 41-47 ft. lbs., flex coupling to 20-37 ft. lbs. and torque steering gear to crossmember bolts to 90-100 ft. lbs.

EXC. RACK & PINION

1. Remove flex coupling bolts.
2. Remove pitman arm nut and remove arm from shaft using a puller.
3. With manual transmission it may be necessary to disconnect the clutch linkage and on V8 models it may be necessary to lower the exhaust system.
4. Unfasten and remove steering gear.
5. Reverse procedure to install. Torque steering gear to side rail bolts to 50-60 ft. lbs. and pitman arm to sector shaft nut to 200-225 ft. lbs.

POWER STEERING PUMP
REPLACE

1. Disconnect return hose from power steering pump and allow fluid to drain into a suitable container.
2. Remove pressure hose from power steering pump fitting.
3. On models less fixed pump, remove mounting bracket attaching bolts, then disconnect drive belt from pulley and remove pump.
4. On models with fixed pump, remove drive belt from pulley, then remove pulley and lift pump from engine compartment.
5. Reverse procedure to install.

CONTROL VALVE
REPLACE

NON-INTEGRAL POWER STEERING

1. Disconnect fluid fittings at control valve and drain fluid from lines by turning wheels to left and right.
2. Loosen clamp at righthand end of sleeve. Remove roll pin from steering arm-to-idler arm rod through slot in sleeve.
3. Using tool 3290-C, remove ball stud from sector shaft arm. **The use of any other tool may result in damage to the control valve assembly.**
4. Turn wheels fully to left and unthread control valve from idler arm rod.
5. Reverse procedure to install. Measure distance between center of left spindle connect-rod hole in idler arm to edge of control valve. Distance must be 2.55-2.65 inches. Torque valve sleeve clamp nut to 13-17 ft. lbs., ball stud nut to 35-47 ft. lbs., worm screw hose clamp to 30-60 in. lbs., return line to control valve to 16-25 ft. lbs., pressure line to control valve to 15-19 ft. lbs. and pressure and return lines to power cylinder to 15-19 ft. lbs. Connect short control valve to power cylinder hose to valve port "C" and other hose to valve port "A."

Wheel Alignment Section

INDEX

CASTER

ADJUST

The caster angle of this suspension is factory set and cannot be adjusted.

CAMBER

ADJUST

1982

The camber angles of this suspension are factory set and cannot be adjusted in the field.

1983–87

1. Remove pop rivet from camber plate.
2. Loosen 3 camber plate-to-body apron nuts.
3. Move top of shock strut as needed to bring camber angle within specifications, then tighten nuts. **It is not necessary to replace the pop rivet.**

TOE-IN

ADJUST

1. Check to see that steering shaft and steering wheel marks are in alignment and in the top position.

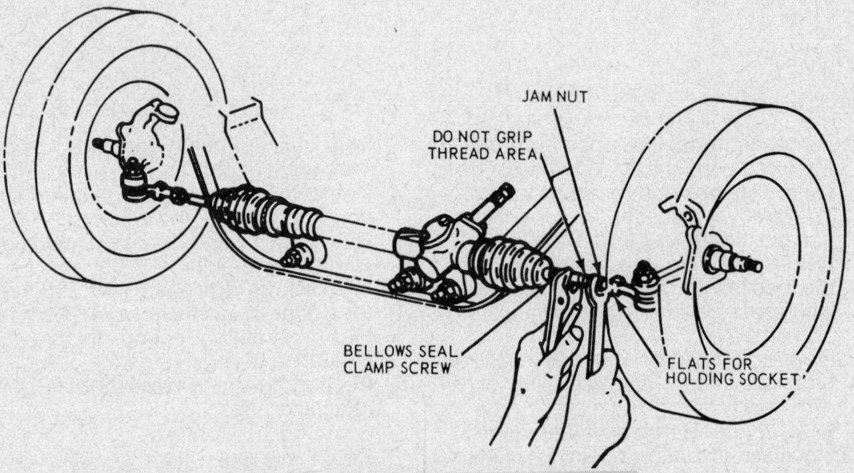

Fig. 1 Toe-in adjustment

2. Loosen clamp screw on the tie rod bellows and free the seal on the rod to prevent twisting of the bellows, **Fig. 1.**
3. Place opened end wrench on flats of tie rod socket to prevent socket from turning, then loosen tie rod jam nuts.
4. Use suitable pliers to turn the tie rod inner end to correct the adjustment to specifications. Do not use pliers on tie rod threads. Turning to reduce number of threads showing will increase toe-in. Turning in the opposite direction will reduce toe-in.
5. Torque tie rod jam nuts to 43-50 ft. lbs.

FORD ESCORT, EXP & TEMPO
MERCURY LN7, LYNX & TOPAZ

INDEX OF SERVICE OPERATIONS

NOTE: Refer to rear of this manual for vehicle manufacturer's special service tool suppliers.

Specifications

GENERAL ENGINE SPECIFICATIONS

Year	Engine CID①/Liter	Engine VIN Code ②	Fuel System	Bore & Stroke	Compression Ratio	Net H.P. @ RPM③	Maximum Torque Ft. Lbs. @ RPM	Normal Oil Pressure Pounds
1982	97.6, 1.6 L	2	740, 2 Bbl.④	3.15 x 3.13	8.8	70 @ 4600	89 @ 3000	30-50
1983	97.6, 1.6 L	2	740, 2 Bbl.④	3.15 x 3.13	8.8	70 @ 4600	89 @ 3000	30-50
	97.6, 1.6 L	2	EFI	3.15 x 3.13	9.5	88 @ 5400	—	30-50
	97.6, 1.6 L H.O.	2	740, 2 Bbl.④	3.15 x 3.13	—	—	—	—
1984	97.6, 1.6 L	2	740, 2 Bbl.④	3.15 x 3.13	8.8	70 @ 4600	88 @ 2600	30-50
	97.6, 1.6 L	5	EFI	3.15 x 3.13	9.5	80 @ 5400	88 @ 3000	30-50
	97.6, 1.6 L H.O.	4	740, 2 Bbl.④	3.15 x 3.13	9.0	80 @ 5400	88 @ 3000	30-50
	120, 2.0 L⑥	H	Fuel Injection	3.39 x 3.39	22.5	52 @ 3600	82 @ 2400	—
	140, 2.3 L⑦	R	6149, 1 Bbl.⑤	3.68 x 3.30	9.0	84 @ 4600	118 @ 2600	55-70
1985	97.6, 1.6L	2	740, 2 Bbl.④	3.15 x 3.13	9.0	70 @ 4600	88 @ 2600	30-50
	97.6, 1.6L H.O.	4	740, 2 Bbl.④	3.15 x 3.13	9.0	80 @ 5400	88 @ 3000	30-50
	97.6, 1.6L⑧	5	EFI	3.15 x 3.13	9.0	84 @ 5200	90 @ 2800	30-50
	97.6, 1.6L⑨	5	EFI	3.15 x 3.13	8.0	120 @ 5200	120 @ 3400	30-50
	116, 1.9L	9	2 Bbl.④	3.23 x 3.46	9.0	86 @ 4800	100 @ 3000	35-65
	120, 2.0L⑥	H	Fuel Injection	3.39 x 3.39	22.5	52 @ 3600	82 @ 2400	—
	140, 2.3L⑦	S,X	EFI	3.68 x 3.30	9.0	100 @ 4600	125 @ 3200	55-70
1986-88	116, 1.9L, Exc. H.O.	9	2 Bbl.⑤	3.23 x 3.46	9.0	86 @ 4800	100 @ 3000	35-65
	116, 1.9L, H.O.	—	EFI	3.23 x 3.46	9.0	108 @ 5200	114 @ 4000	35-65
	120, 2.0L⑥	H	Fuel Injection	3.39 x 3.39	22.7	52 @ 4000	82 @ 2400	—
	140, 2.3L⑦	X	EFI	3.68 x 3.30	9.0	100 @ 4600	125 @ 3200	—

①—CID-Cubic inch displacement.
②—The eighth digit in the VIN denotes engine code.
③—Ratings are net-as installed in vehicle.
④—Motorcraft.
⑤—Holley.
⑥—Diesel.
⑦—Tempo & Topaz.
⑧—Exc. turbocharged engine.
⑨—Turbocharged engine.

STARTING MOTOR APPLICATIONS

Year	Engine Model/VIN	Ident. No.①
1982	4-97.6, 1.6L/2	EIEF-AD
1983	4-97.6, 1.6L/2	E3EF-AA
		E4EF-BA
1984	4-97.6, 1.6L/②	E3EF-AA
		E4EF-BA
	4-120, 2.0L/H	E4EF-AA
	4-140, 2.3L/R	E43F-AA

Year	Engine Model/VIN	Ident. No.①
1985	4-97.6, 1.6L/②	E4EF-BA
	4-116, 1.9L	E6EF-AA
	4-120, 2.0L/H	E4EF-AA
	4-140, 2.3L/S,X	E43F-AA
1986—88	4-116, 1.9L	E6EF-AA
	4-120, 2.0L/H	EFEF-AA
	4-140, 2.3L/S,X	E43F-AA

①—Basic Ident. No., 11001.
②—V.I.N. Codes, 2, 5 and 4.

ALTERNATOR & REGULATOR SPECIFICATIONS

Year	Ident. Stamp Color	Current Rating		Field Current @ 75°F		Regulator	
		Amps	Volts	Amps	Volts	Ident. No. ①	Voltage @ 75°F
1982-83	Orange	40	15	4	12	②	13.8-14.6
	Green	60	15	4	12	②	13.8-14.6
	Black	65	15	4	12	②	13.8-14.6
1984-88	Orange	40	15	4.25	12	—	—
	Green	60	15	4.25	12	—	—
	Black	65	15	4.25	12	—	—

①—Basic Ident. No., 10316.

②—1982 Escort & Lynx, EIAF-AA; 1982 EXP & LN7, EITF-AA; 1983 Escort & Lynx, E2AF-AA; 1983 EXP & LN7, E2TF-AA.

ENGINE TIGHTENING SPECIFICATIONS

Year	Engine/VIN	Spark Plugs Ft. Lbs.	Cylinder Head Bolts Ft. Lbs.	Intake Manifold Ft. Lbs.	Exhaust Manifold Ft. Lbs.	Rocker Arm Shaft Bracket Ft. Lbs.	Rocker Arm Cover Ft. Lbs.	Connecting Rod Cap Bolts Ft. Lbs.	Main Bearing Cap Bolts Ft. Lbs.	Flywheel to Crankshaft Ft. Lbs.	Vibration Damper or Pulley Ft. Lbs.
1982	4-97.6, 1.6L/2	17-23	44①	12-15	15-20	7-11②	6-8	19-25	67-80	59-69	74-90
1983	4-97.6, 1.6L/2	8-15	44①	12-15	15-20	7-11②	6-8	19-25	67-80	54-64	74-90
1984	4-97.6, 1.6L/2, 4 & 5	8-15	③	12-15	15-20	7-11②	6-8	19-25	67-80	54-64	74-90
	4-120, 2.0L/H Diesel	④	—	11-16	15-19	—	⑤	50-54	60-65	130-137	115-123
	4-140, 2.3L/R, S,X⑥	5-10	⑦ ⑫	15-23	⑧	⑨ ⑩	3-5	21-26⑪	60-74	54-64	82-103
1985	4-97.6, 1.6L/2,4,5	8-15	⑮	12-15	15-20	7-11②	6-8	19-25	67-80	54-64	74-90
	4-120, 2.0L/H Diesel	④	—	12-17	16-20	—	⑤	48-51	61-65	130-137	116-123
	4-140, 2.3L/RSX⑥	5-10	⑫	15-23	⑧	⑨ ⑩	21-26⑪	51-66	51-66	54-64	140-170
1985-88	4-116, 1.9L	8-15	⑬ ⑭	12-15	15-20	15-19②	6-8	19-25⑪	67-80	54-64	74-90
1986-88	4-120, 2.0L/H Diesel	④	—	12-17	16-20	—	⑤	48-51	61-65	130-137	116-123
	4-140, 2.3L/X⑥	5-10	⑫	15-23	⑧	⑨ ⑩	21-26⑪	51-66	51-66	54-64	140-170

①—Then tighten bolts an additional 1/2 turn in 1/4 turn increments after specified torque has been obtained.

②—Rocker arm stud to cylinder head.

③—Torque bolts to 30-45 ft. lbs., then turn bolts an additional 180° in 90° increments.

④—Glow plug torque, 10-14 ft. lbs.

⑤—Cylinder Head cover torque, 5-7 ft. lbs.

⑥—Tempo & Topaz.

⑦—Tighten bolts in 2 steps. Final torque of bolts must be 81 ft. lbs.

⑧—Tighten bolts in 2 steps. First to 5-7 ft. lbs., then 20-30 ft. lbs.

⑨—Tighten bolts in 2 steps. First to 4-7 ft. lbs., then 19-26 ft. lbs.

⑩—Rocker arm fulcrum bolt to cylinder head.

⑫—Torque bolts in 2 steps. First to 51-59 ft. lbs., then 70-76 ft. lbs.

⑬—Torque to 44 ft. lbs., then loosen 2 turns and retorque to 44 ft. lbs.

⑭—Turn bolts an additional 90°, then complete torquing by turning bolts an additional 90°.

⑪—Connecting rod cap nut.

WHEEL ALIGNMENT SPECIFICATIONS

Year	Model	Caster Angle, Degrees		Camber Angle, Degrees				Toe-In. Inch	Toe-Out on Turns, Deg.	
				Limits		Desired				
		Limits	Desired	Left	Right	Left	Right		Outer Wheel	Inner Wheel
1982-83	Front	+.55 to +2.05	+1.3	+1.4 to +2.9	+.95 to +2.45	+2.15	+1.7	①	③	20
	Rear	—	—	−1.45 to +.25	−1.45 to +.25	−.6	−.6	.09	—	—
1984	Front④	+5/8 to +2 1/8	+1 2/3	+1 3/8 to +2 7/8	+15/16 to +2 7/16	+2 1/8	+1 11/16	①	—	—
	Rear④	—	—	−2 1/8 to −3/8	−1 1/2 to +1/4	−1 1/4	−5-8	1/16	—	—
	Front⑤	+1/2 to +2	+1 1/4	+1 1/4 to +2 3/4	+3/4 to +2 1/4	+2	+1 1/4	①	—	—
	Rear⑤	—	—	−1 to +1/2	−1 to +1/2	−1/4	−1/4	1/16	—	—
1985	Front④⑥	+5/16 to +2 1/16	+1 5/16	+1 1/2 to +2 5/8	+11/16 to +2 3/16	+1 7/8	+1 1/16	①	—	—
	Front④②	+1/4 to +1 3/4	+1	+7/16 to +1 15/16	0 to +1 1/2	+1 3/16	+3/4	①	—	—
	Rear④	—	—	−1 3/32 to +19/32	−1 3/32 to +19/32	−1/4	−1/4	3/32	—	—
	Front⑤	+1/2 to +2	+1 1/4	+1 1/4 to +2 3/4	+3/4 to 2 1/4	+2	+3/4	①	—	—
	Rear⑤	—	—	−9/16 to +15/16	−9/16 to +15/16	−3/16	−3/16	7/64	—	—
1986-88	Front④	+1 5/8 to 3 1/8	+2 3/8	+5/16 to +1 13/16	0 to +1 1/2	+1 1/16	+3/4	−1/8	—	—
	Rear④	—	—	−1 9/32 to +13/32	−1 9/32 to +13/32	−7/16	−7/16	3/16	—	—
	Front⑤	+1 11/16 to +3 3/16	+2 7/16	+21/32 to +2 5/32	+7/32 to +1 23/32	+1 13/32	+13/32	−1/8	—	—
	Rear⑤	—	—	−29/32 to +19/32	−29/32 to +19/32	−5/32	−5/32	0	—	—

①—Toe out, .10 inch.
②—Turbocharged engine.
③—Left wheel, 20°; right wheel, 17°.
④—All models, Except Tempo & Topaz.
⑤—Tempo & Topaz.
⑥—Except turbocharged engine.

COOLING SYSTEM & CAPACITY DATA

Year	Model or Engine/VIN	Cooling Capacity, Qts.		Radiator Cap Relief Pressure, Lbs.	Thermo. Opening Temp.	Fuel Tank Gals.	Engine Refill Qts. ①	Transaxle Oil	
		Less A/C	With A/C					4 & 5 Speed Pints	Auto Trans. Qts. ①
1982	4-97.6, 1.6L/2	8	8	16	191	11.3	4③	5	9.8
1983	4-97.6, 1.6L/2	6.7	8	16	191	11.3	4③	④	8.3
1984	4-97.6, 1.6L/2	6.7	8.1	16	192	13	3.5	④	7.8
	4-120, 2.0/H	8.1	8.1	16	190	13	5	6.1	7.8
	4-140, 2.3/R	8.1	8.1	16	192	14	4	④	8.3
1985	4-97.6, 1.6L/2,4,5	6.7	8.1	16	192	13	3.5	④	7.8
	4-120, 2.0L/H⑤	9.2	9.2	16	190	13	5.28	6.1	—
	4-120, 2.0L/H②	9.2	9.2	16	190	15.2	5.28	6.1	—
	4-140, 2.3L/S,X②	8.1	8.1	16	192	15.2	4	6.1	7.8
1985-86	4-116, 1.9L	6.5	7.1	16	192	13	3.5	6.1	7.4
1986-88	4-120, 2.0L/H⑤	9.2	9.2	16	190	13	5.28	6.1	—
	4-120, 2.0L/H②	9.2	9.2	16	190	15.2	5.28	6.1	—
	4-140, 2.3L/X②	8.1	8.1	16	192	15.2	4	6.1	7.8

①—Approximate. Make final check with dipstick.
②—Tempo & Topaz.
③—Includes filter.
④—4 speed trans., 5 pints; 5 speed trans., 6.1 pints.

Electrical Section

INDEX

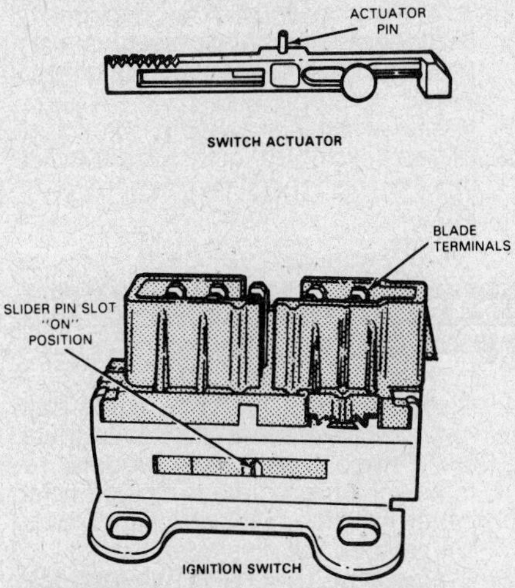

Fig. 1 Ignition switch

STARTER REPLACE

EXCEPT DIESEL ENGINE

1. Disconnect battery ground cable and raise and support vehicle. Disconnect starter cable from starter motor terminal.
2. On vehicles equipped with manual transmission, remove three nuts attaching roll restrictor brace to transmission-side starter studs and remove brace.
3. Remove two bolts attaching starter rear support bracket. Remove retaining nut from rear of starter stud bolt, then remove bracket.
4. Remove three starter mounting nuts or bolts and the starter.
5. Reverse procedure to install.

DIESEL ENGINE

1. Remove battery cover, then disconnect battery ground cable located in luggage compartment.
2. Disconnect cable assembly from fender apron relay and starter solenoid.
3. Remove upper starter mounting stud bolt.
4. Raise and support vehicle.
5. Disconnect vacuum hose from vacuum pump.
6. Remove starter support bracket attaching screws, then the bracket.
7. Remove power steering hose bracket.
8. Remove ground wire assembly and cable support from starter bolt studs.
9. Remove 2 starter mounting studs.
10. Remove vacuum pump bracket.
11. Remove starter.
12. Reverse procedure to install.

IGNITION SWITCH REPLACE

MODELS LESS PASSIVE RESTRAINT SYSTEM

1. Disconnect battery ground cable, then remove five steering column shroud attaching screws.
2. Remove two bolts and two nuts attaching steering column to column bracket, then lower steering column assembly to seat and remove column shrouds.
3. Disconnect ignition switch wire connector, then rotate ignition switch lock cylinder to the Run position.
4. Using a 1/8 inch drill bit, drill out shear bolts retaining ignition switch to lock cylinder housing.
5. Remove the two shear bolts using an easy out.
6. Detach ignition switch from actuator pin, then remove switch.
7. Check to ensure that ignition switch actuator pin slot and ignition switch lock cylinder are in the Run position. **Replacement ignition switches are set in the Run position. The Run position on the ignition switch lock cylinder is located approximately 90° from the lock position.**
8. Position ignition switch on actuator pin. It may be necessary to move switch slightly to align switch to column mounting bolt holes, **Fig. 1.**
9. Install and tighten shear bolts until heads break off.
10. Connect wire connector to ignition switch, then connect battery ground cable and check ignition switch for proper operation.
11. Position upper shroud on column, then raise steering column and install column mounting bracket to instrument panel attaching bolts. Torque bolts to 15 to 25 ft. lbs.
12. Position lower shroud on column and install attaching bolts.

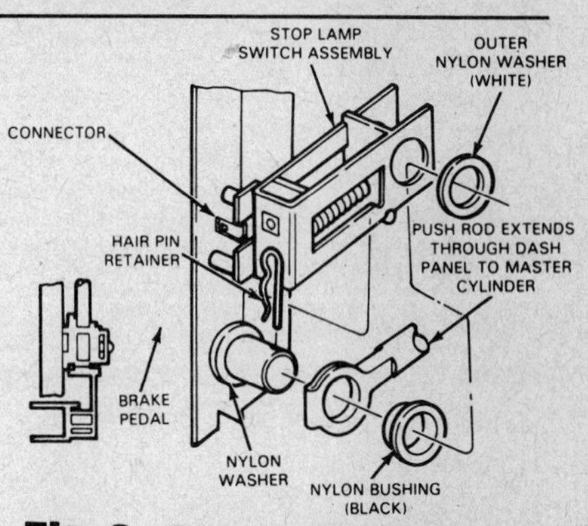

Fig. 2 Stop light switch

MODELS W/PASSIVE RESTRAINT SYSTEM

1. Park vehicle with wheels in the straight ahead position. Turn ignition switch to "Lock" position and rotate steering wheel 16° counterclockwise until locked into position.
2. Disconnect battery ground cable.
3. Remove five steering column shroud attaching screws.
4. Remove two bolts and two nuts holding steering column assembly to steering column bracket assembly. Lower steering column to seat.
5. Remove steering column shrouds.
6. Disconnect ignition switch electrical

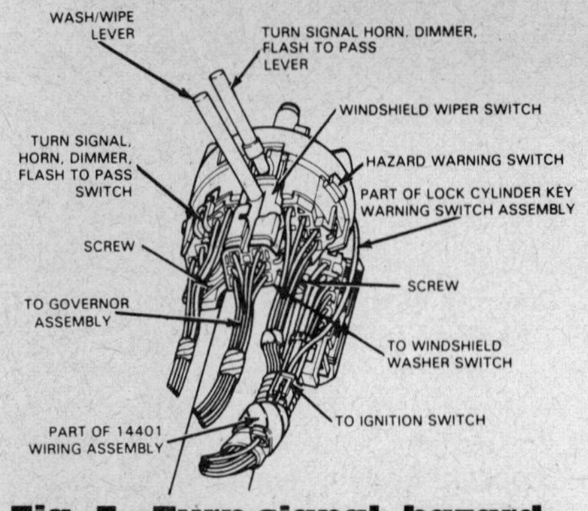

Fig. 3 Turn signal, hazard, horn, flash-to-pass & dimmer switch

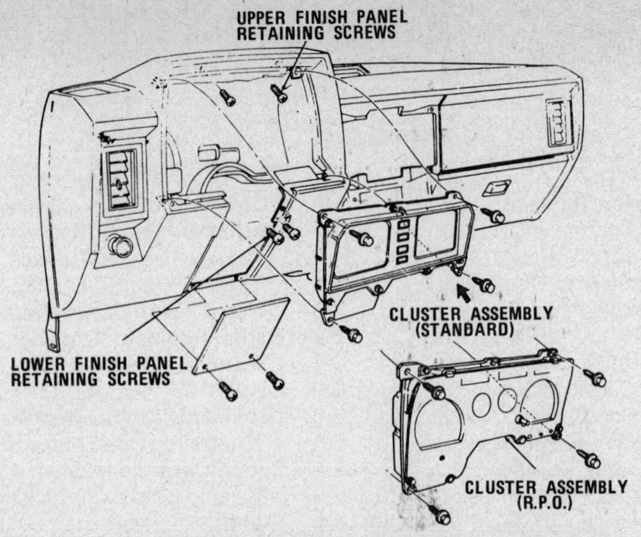

Fig. 4 Instrument cluster removal. Exc. Tempo & Topaz

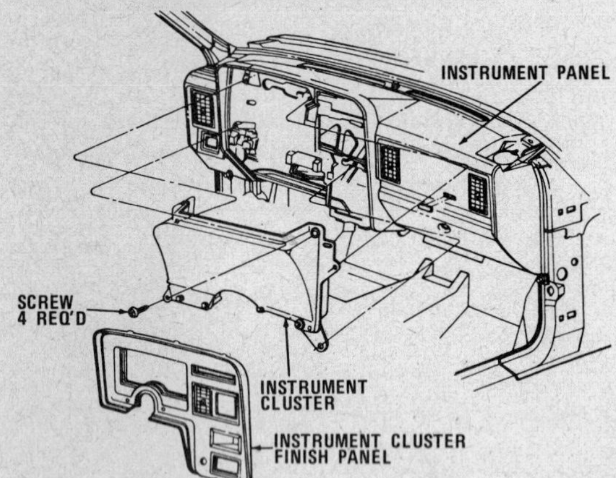

Fig. 5 Instrument cluster removal. Tempo & Topaz

connectors slip ring connector to column harness.

7. Drill out break-off head bolts attaching switch to lock cylinder. Use a 1/8 inch drill bit.
8. Remove two bolts using a ES-3 easy out tool or equivalent.
9. Disengage ignition switch from actuator pin.
10. Reverse procedure to install.

STOPLIGHT SWITCH
REPLACE

1. Disconnect battery ground cable.
2. Disconnect electrical connector from switch. **On vehicles equipped with standard brakes, the locking tab must be lifted before electrical connector can be removed.**
3. On vehicles equipped with standard brakes, remove retainer, then slide the switch, pushrod, white nylon washer and bushing away from pedal. Remove switch from vehicle, **Fig. 2.**
4. On vehicles equipped with power brakes, remove retainer and outer white nylon washer from pedal pin. Slide switch off brake pedal pin far enough so that outer side of plate of switch clears pin. Remove switch, **Fig. 2.**

TURN SIGNAL, HAZARD, HORN, FLASH-TO-PASS & DIMMER SWITCH
REPLACE

MODELS LESS PASSIVE RESTRAINT SYSTEM

1. Disconnect battery ground cable.
2. Remove 5 shroud screws, then the lower shroud.
3. Remove upper shroud assembly.
4. Grasp switch lever and pull lever straight out from switch assembly, **Fig. 3.**
5. Peel back foam switch cover from turn signal switch.
6. Disconnect 2 electrical connectors.
7. Remove 2 self tapping screws attaching switch assembly to lock cylinder housing, then disconnect switch from housing.
8. Reverse procedure to install.

MODELS W/PASSIVE RESTRAINT SYSTEM

1. Disconnect battery ground cable.
2. Remove five shroud attaching screws, then lower shroud.
3. Remove upper shroud.
4. Remove switch lever by grasping lever and pulling lever straight out from switch.
5. Peel back foam switch cover from turn signal switch.
6. Disconnect two switch electrical connectors and air bag slip ring connector from column harness.
7. Remove two self tapping screws attaching switch to lock cylinder housing, then disengage switch from housing.
8. Reverse procedure to install.

INSTRUMENT CLUSTER
REPLACE

1. Disconnect battery ground cable, then remove steering column lower cover.
2. On Tempo and Topaz models, remove eight instrument cluster finish panel retaining screws and radio knobs, then the finish panel.
3. On Escort EXP, LN7 & Lynx models, remove four cluster opening finish panel retainer screws, then the finish panel.
4. From under instrument panel, disconnect speedometer cable, then pull cluster away from instrument panel, **Figs. 4 and 5.**
5. Disconnect cluster electrical connector from printed circuit.
6. Reverse procedure to install.

INSTRUMENT PANEL
REPLACE

1. Disconnect battery ground cable.
2. Remove sound insulator from underside of instrument panel, **Figs. 6 and 7.**
3. Remove steering column opening cover from instrument panel.
4. Remove lower half of shroud from steering column.
5. Remove steering column to support attaching screws, then allow steering wheel to rest on front seat.
6. Remove one nut attaching instrument panel to steering column support bracket at the top of the steering column opening.

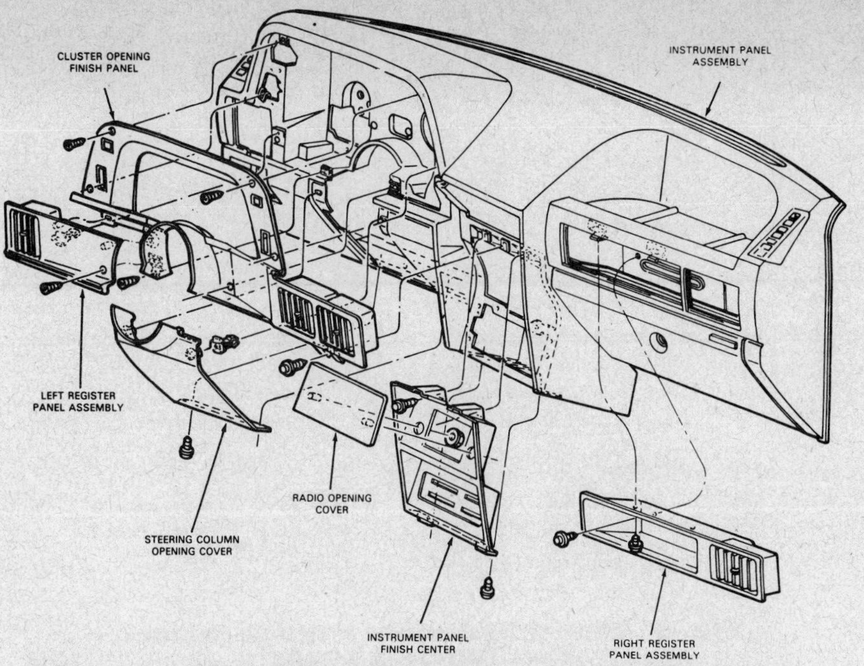

Fig. 6 Instrument panel removal. Escort & Lynx

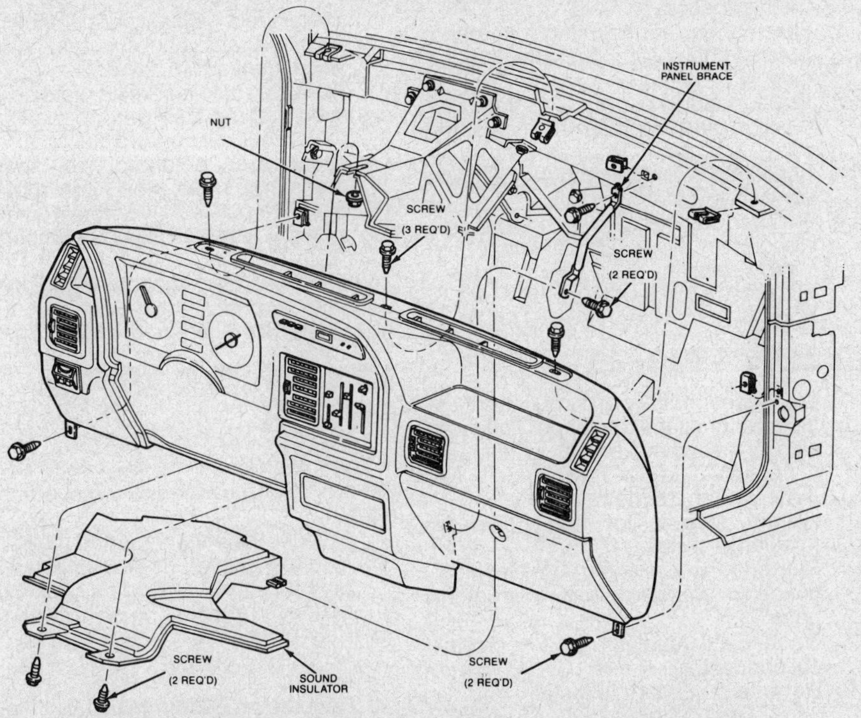

Fig. 7 Instrument panel removal. Tempo & Topaz

7. Disconnect center brace from lower flange on instrument panel.
8. Remove radio speaker opening covers from instrument panel.
9. Remove one screw attaching instrument panel to the top of the dash panel at each radio speaker opening and at the top center of the instrument panel.
10. Disconnect speedometer cable from transmission.
11. Disconnect wire harness connectors from the blower motor and the blower motor resistor.
12. Move temperature control lever to cool and function control cable to OFF. Then disconnect the temperature and function cables from the heater core using tool T83P-18532-AH or equivalent.
13. Disconnect wires from right door dome lamp switch, if equipped, and remove wires from A-pillar.
14. Remove one screw attaching each end of the instrument panel to cowl side panels.
15. Pull instrument panel rearward away from the dash panel and cowl top panel, disconnecting any wires as necessary.
16. Reverse procedure to install.

AUXILIARY CLUSTER, REPLACE

EXP, LN7 & Tempo

1. Disconnect battery ground cable.
2. Pull trim cover at bottom edge and slide out of tabs at top edge.
3. Remove three cluster to console attaching screws. On Tempo models, remove four cluster to console attaching screws, then pull cluster outward and disconnect electrical connector.
4. Remove cluster from console.
5. Reverse procedure to install.

TEMPERATURE GAUGE, REPLACE

Topaz

1. Disconnect battery ground cable.
2. Remove instrument cluster as described under "Instrument Cluster, Replace."
3. Remove retaining screws, mask and lens from cluster backplate.
4. Remove two gauge retaining nuts and gauge.
5. Reverse procedure to install.

GRAPHIC WARNING DISPLAY, REPLACE

Escort, Lynx, Tempo & Topaz

1. Disconnect battery ground cable, then remove console finish panel by prying at bottom edge to disengage retainers.
2. Remove module to console attaching screws, then pull module outward and disconnect electrical connector.
3. Remove module from console.
4. Reverse procedure to install.

STEERING WHEEL REPLACE

MODELS LESS PASSIVE RESTRAINT SYSTEM

1. Disconnect battery ground cable.
2. Remove steering hub cover assembly, then the steering wheel attaching nut. Discard nut.
3. Remove steering wheel from steering shaft using tool T67L3600A. Do not use a knock-off type steering wheel puller or strike end of steering column with a hammer since damage to steering column bearings will result.
4. Reverse procedure to install. Install new wheel retaining nut, then torque to 30-40 ft. lbs. On non-tilt models, install steering wheel cover, then insert attaching bolts and torque to 13-20 inch lbs.

MODELS W/PASSIVE RESTRAINT SYSTEM

Carefully follow the following procedure to avoid serious injury and/or vehicle damage.

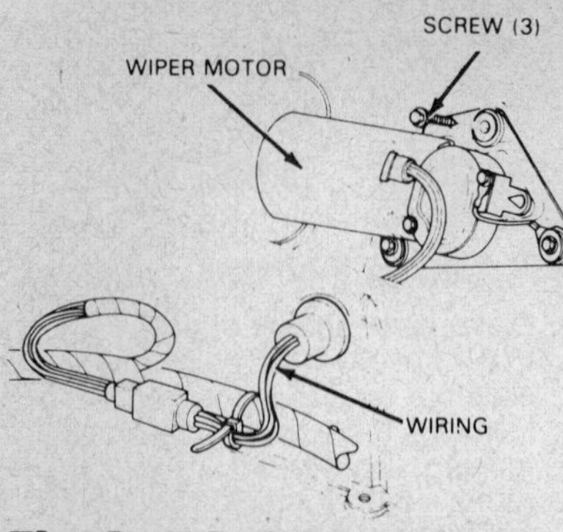

Fig. 8 Windshield wiper motor

Removal

1. Park vehicle with wheels in straight ahead position, then turn ignition switch to "Lock" position and rotate steering wheel approximately 16° counterclockwise until locked into position.
2. Disconnect battery ground cable.
3. Remove steering wheel as follows:
   a. Working from rear of steering wheel, remove four nuts attaching air bag module to steering wheel. Place an alignment mark on the steering wheel and shaft.
   b. Lift air bag module from wheel and disconnect air bag module to slip ring clock spring electrical connector.
   c. Remove and discard steering wheel attaching nut.
   d. Using tool T67L-3600-A or equivalent only, remove steering wheel from upper shaft. **Do not use a knock-off type steering wheel puller or strike end of steering column upper shaft with a hammer.**

Installation

1. Position steering wheel on end of steering wheel shaft, aligning marks made during removal.
2. Install a new steering wheel attaching nut. Torque nut to 30-40 ft. lbs.
3. Connect air bag module wire to slip ring electrical connector and place module onto steering wheel. Install four attaching nuts. Torque nuts to 35-53 inch lbs.
4. Connect battery ground cable.

HORN SOUNDER REPLACE

On these models, the horn sounder is located on the turn signal, headlight dimmer and horn lever. Refer to Turn Signal, Hazard, Horn, Flash-To-Pass & Dimmer Switch, Replace when replacing lever.

HEADLAMP SWITCH REPLACE

1982–83

1. Disconnect battery ground cable, then on vehicles without A/C, the lefthand air vent control cable from the instrument panel.
2. Remove screws securing fuse panel bracket and position fuse panel to the side.
3. Place headlamp switch in the "On" position and depress the headlamp knob and shaft retainer button on headlamp switch. Remove knob and shaft assembly.
4. Remove headlamp switch bezel and disconnect electrical connector, then remove switch.
5. Reverse procedure to install.

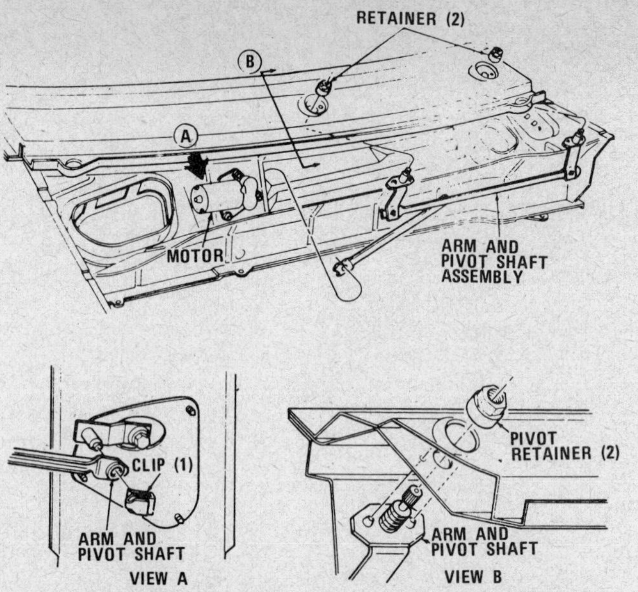

Fig. 9 Windshield wiper linkage replace. Exc. Tempo & Topaz

EXCEPT 1982–83

1. Disconnect battery ground cable.
2. Insert a thin flat blade under flange at side of headlamp switch to depress spring retaining clip. Twist blade to remove switch from one side.
3. Repeat step 2 for other side of headlamp switch.
4. Pull headlamp switch and electrical connector outward from instrument panel.
5. Disconnect headlamp switch electrical connector.
6. Reverse procedure to install.

RADIO REPLACE

1982–83

1. Disconnect battery ground cable.
2. Remove A/C floor duct, if equipped.
3. Disconnect power, speaker and antenna leads from radio.
4. Remove knobs, discs, control shaft, nuts and washers from radio.
5. Remove ashtray and bracket, then the radio.
6. Remove radio rear support attaching nut.
7. Reverse procedure to install.

EXCEPT 1982–83

1. Disconnect battery ground cable.
2. Remove radio knobs and instrument panel center trim panel.
3. Remove radio mounting plate screws, then pull radio outward to disengage lower rear support bracket.
4. Disconnect antenna and speaker leads from radio, then remove radio.
5. Remove nuts and washers from radio control shafts. Remove mounting plate.
6. Remove rear support retaining nut and support.
7. Reverse procedure to install.

WINDSHIELD WIPER SWITCH

The switch handle is an integral part of the switch and cannot be removed separately.

1. Disconnect battery ground cable.
2. Remove upper steering column trim shroud, then disconnect electrical connector.
3. Pull back shield, then remove two screws securing switch. Remove switch.
4. Reverse procedure to install.

WINDSHIELD WIPER MOTOR REPLACE

1. Disconnect battery ground cable.
2. Lift passenger side water shield cover from cowl, then disconnect motor electrical connector.
3. Remove linkage retaining clip from motor arm, then the three bolts attaching motor to mounting bracket, **Fig. 8.**
4. Disconnect operating arm from motor, then separate motor from mounting bracket and remove from vehicle.
5. Reverse procedure to install.

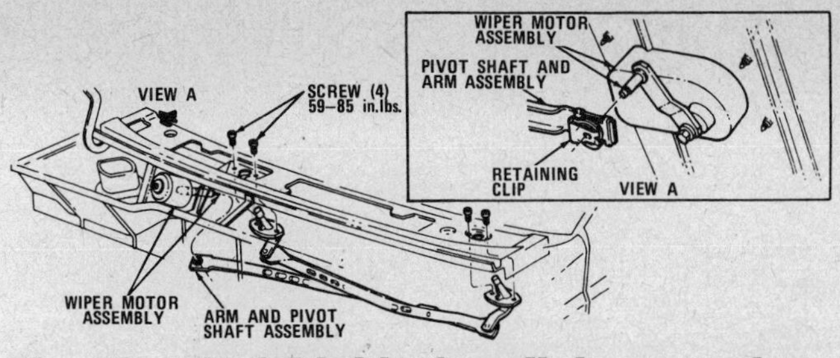

Fig. 10 Windshield wiper linkage replace. Tempo & Topaz

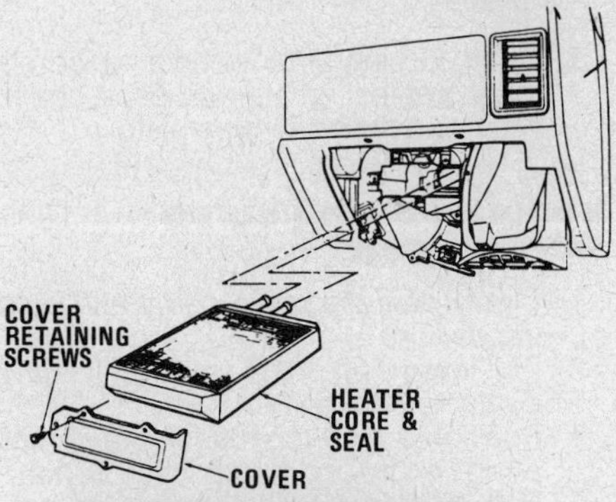

Fig. 11 Heater core removal. Less air conditioning

REAR WIPER MOTOR REPLACE

EXCEPT TEMPO & TOPAZ

1. Disconnect battery ground cable.
2. Remove liftgate inner trim panel.
3. On station wagon models, remove license plate housing attaching screws, disconnect lamp electrical connector, then the housing.
4. Pull wiper motor electrical connector clip out from retaining hole.
5. Disconnect electrical connector halves.
6. Remove motor.
7. Reverse procedure to install.

WINDSHIELD WIPER TRANSMISSION REPLACE

1. Remove wiper arm and blade assemblies from pivot shaft.
2. Disconnect battery ground cable, then remove clip and disconnect linkage drive arm from motor crank pin.
3. On Tempo and Topaz models, remove top grille from left and right cowl, then the pivot to cowl attaching screws.
4. On Escort, EXP, LN7 and Lynx models, remove pivot shaft retaining nuts.
5. On all models, remove linkage and pivots from cowl chamber, **Figs. 9 and 10.**
6. Reverse procedure to install.

HEATER CORE REPLACE

LESS AIR CONDITIONING

1. Disconnect battery ground cable and drain cooling system.
2. Disconnect heater hoses from heater core and plug all open lines and fittings to prevent spillage.
3. Remove glove box and liner and move temperature lever to warm position.
4. Remove heater core cover, then working from engine compartment, loosen two nuts attaching heater case assembly to dash panel.
5. Push heater core toward passenger compartment, then pull heater core through glove box opening and remove from vehicle, **Fig. 11.**
6. Reverse procedure to install.

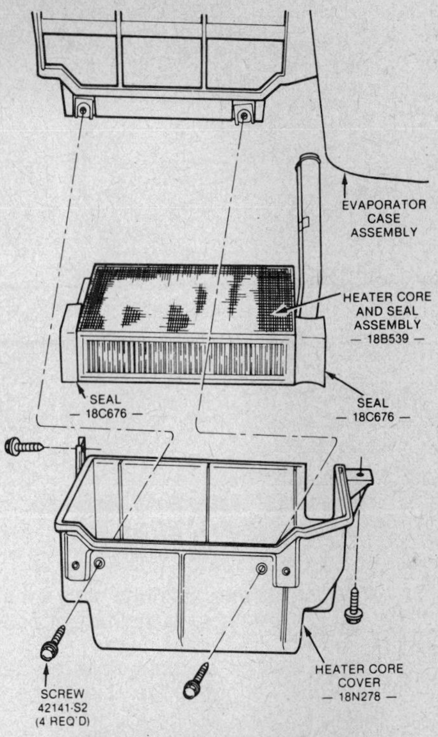

Fig. 12 Heater core removal. With air conditioning

WITH AIR CONDITIONING

1. Disconnect battery ground cable and drain cooling system.
2. Disconnect heater hoses from heater core and plug all lines and fittings.
3. Remove floor duct from plenum.
4. Remove screws attaching heater core cover to plenum, then the cover and heater core, **Fig. 12.**
5. Reverse procedure to install.

BLOWER MOTOR REPLACE

LESS AIR CONDITIONING

1. Disconnect battery ground cable.

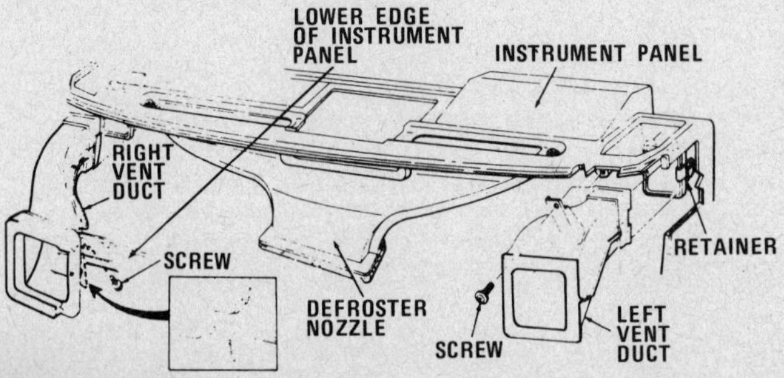

Fig. 13 Vent assembly removal. 1982–83

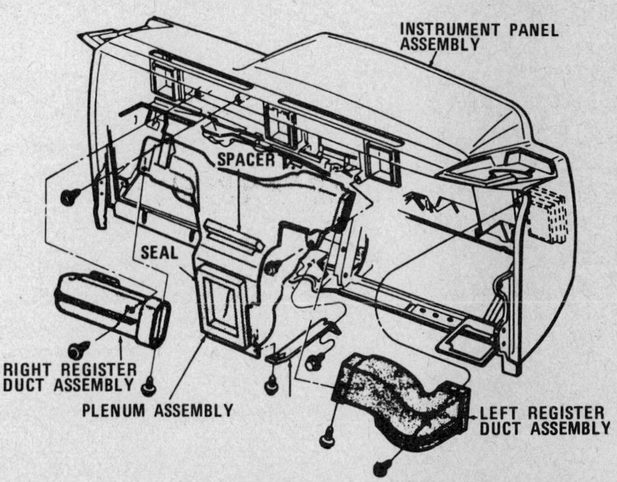

Fig. 14 Vent assembly removal. Except 1982–83

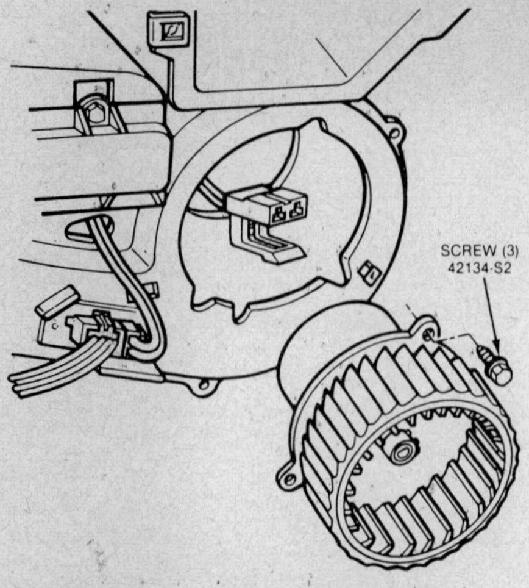

Fig. 15 Blower motor removal. Less air conditioning

2. Remove screws securing right ventilator control cable to instrument panel.
3. Remove screw securing right register duct to lower right edge of instrument panel.
4. Remove glove box and hinge bar from instrument panel.
5. Pull right register duct from installed position between air inlet duct and right register opening, **Figs. 14 and 15.**
6. Remove ventilator grille from bottom of ventilator assembly, then screws securing right ventilator assembly to blower housing.
7. Remove hub clamp spring from blower wheel hub, **Fig. 15.**
8. Pull blower wheel from blower shaft, then remove three blower motor flange attaching screws.
9. Pull blower motor from housing, disconnect electrical connector, then remove motor from vehicle.
10. Reverse procedure to install.

WITH AIR CONDITIONING

1. Disconnect battery ground cable.

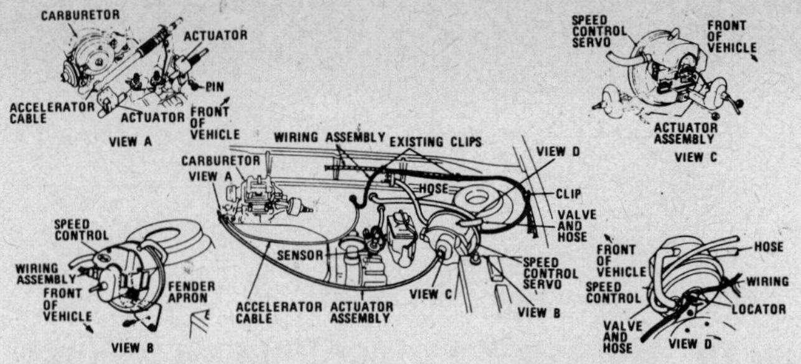

Fig. 16 Speed control actuator cable assembly

2. Remove glove box door and instrument panel lower reinforcement from instrument panel.
3. Disconnect blower motor electrical connector, then remove blower motor and mounting plate from evaporator housing.
4. Rotate motor until mounting plate flats clear edge of glove box opening, then remove motor.
5. Remove hub clamp wheel spring from blower wheel hub and remove blower wheel from motor shaft.
6. Reverse procedure to install.

SPEED CONTROLS

ACTUATOR CABLE ADJUSTMENT

Escort, EXP, LN7 & Lynx

1. Remove cable retaining clip, then disengage throttle positioner.
2. Place carburetor throttle lever at the curb idle speed position.
3. Pull on actuator cable end tube to remove slack from cable, **Fig. 16.**
4. While maintaining light tension on actuator cable, insert cable retaining clip.

Tempo & Topaz

1. With ignition "Off," adjust carburetor so throttle plate is closed and choke linkage is completely off cam.
2. Remove beaded chain locking pin, then pull bead chain through adjuster.
3. Insert locking pin into hole which allows greatest tension on bead chain, without opening throttle plate.

Vacuum Dump Valve Adjustment

1. Firmly depress brake pedal and hold in position.
2. Pull inward on dump valve until collar contacts retaining clip.
3. Position a .050 to .100 inch shim between pedal and dump valve button.
4. Pull brake pedal rearward to its normal position and allow dump valve to ratchet into retaining clip.

Clutch Switch Adjustment

This adjustment should be performed on models with manual transmission, when speed control will not engage.

1. Position and support clutch pedal in the full upward position against pedal stop.
2. Loosen switch attaching screw and slide switch forward toward clutch pedal, until clearance between switch plunger cap and switch housing is .030 inch, then tighten attaching screw.
3. Remove support holding clutch pedal in the full upward position and check speed control for proper operation. Ensure that speed control disengages when clutch pedal is depressed.

4-97.6 (1.6L) Gasoline Engine Section

INDEX

ENGINE MOUNTS

Refer to **Figs. 1 through 6,** when replacing the engine mounts.

ENGINE

REPLACE

EXCEPT TURBOCHARGED ENGINE

1. Disconnect battery ground cable, then mark location of hinges and remove hood.
2. Remove air cleaner, fresh air intake tube and hot air tube.
3. Drain cooling system, then disconnect secondary coil wire from distributor.
4. Remove alternator and thermactor pump.
5. Disconnect A/C compressor clutch wire from compressor.
6. On models with automatic transaxle, disconnect upper and lower oil cooler lines at radiator, then remove transmission oil cooler line clips.
7. Disconnect upper and lower radiator hoses.
8. Disconnect heater hoses from engine.
9. Disconnect wire connector from electric cooling fan and remove fan motor and shroud assembly, then remove radiator.
10. Remove power steering pump filler tube and cap pump opening to prevent fluid spillage, if equipped.
11. Disconnect all necessary vacuum hose and electrical connections.
12. Disconnect fuel supply and return hoses at metal connector to engine.
13. On models with automatic transaxle, disconnect throttle kickdown linkage.
14. Disconnect vacuum hose at power brake booster, if equipped.
15. Disconnect hose to thermactor valve, then disconnect accelerator cable at carburetor and bracket.
16. Disconnect fuel evaporation hose at metal tube located on lefthand fender.
17. Loosen upper power steering pump pivot bolt, then remove upper pump to adjusting bracket attaching bolts, if equipped.
18. Remove upper rear thermactor pump bracket bolt, then install lifting eye.
19. Remove upper A/C compressor to mounting bracket attaching bolts, then remove clip retaining A/C compressor inlet line to exhaust manifold.
20. Raise and support vehicle, then loosen power steering pump lower adjusting bolt and remove drive belt. Remove power steering pump to lower bracket attaching bolts, then remove pump from bracket by passing pulley through adjusting bracket opening. Secure power steering pump against dash panel.
21. Remove heater supply and return tube clamps.
22. Remove starter motor ground cable and engine ground strap, then remove knee brace located at front of starter motor.
23. On models with manual transaxle, remove roll restrictor.
24. Remove starter motor and knee brace rear section, then disconnect exhaust pipe at inlet connector.
25. On models with automatic transaxle, remove converter cover and bracket. On models with manual transaxle, remove lower flywheel cover and brackets.
26. Using tool No. T81P-6312-A, remove crankshaft pulley.
27. On models with automatic transaxle, remove converter to flywheel attaching nuts, then remove lower converter housing to engine attaching bolts.
28. On models with manual transaxle, remove lower clutch housing to engine attaching bolts.
29. Remove coolant by pass hose from intake manifold, then remove lower No. 3-A engine mount bolt and nut from under insulator, **Figs. 1 through 6.**
30. Remove A/C compressor lower bracket bolt, if equipped.
31. Lower vehicle and attach a suitable lifting device to engine. Attach lifting device to engine using a 10 mm bolt to exhaust side of cylinder head at the transaxle end and at lifting eye of thermactor pump bracket. A stabilizer chain may also be attached to alternator bracket bolt.
32. Remove engine mount No. 3-A through bolt, then remove engine mount, **Fig. 1 through 6.**
33. Remove A/C compressor bracket, if equipped.
34. On models with manual transaxle, remove timing belt cover.
35. Position a suitable transmission jack under transaxle.
36. On models with automatic transaxle, remove upper converter housing to engine attaching bolts. On models with manual transaxle, remove upper clutch housing to engine attaching bolts.
37. Remove engine from vehicle. **On models with automatic transaxle, check to ensure that torque converter studs are free from flywheel before removing engine.**

TURBOCHARGED ENGINE

1. Mark position of hood hinges and remove hood.
2. Disconnect battery ground cable.
3. Remove air cleaner and air intake tube assembly.
4. Drain cooling system.
5. Disconnect secondary wire from ignition coil.
6. Remove alternator drive belt, alternator mounting bolts, then position alternator aside.
7. Disconnect upper and lower radiator hoses from engine.
8. Disconnect heater hoses from engine.
9. Remove radiator guard, then the radiator assembly from vehicle.
10. Disconnect heater assembly from metal tube.
11. Mark then disconnect all electrical connectors and vacuum hoses from engine.
12. Disconnect fuel supply and return lines from intake manifold brackets.
13. On models with power brakes, disconnect power booster vacuum hose from engine.
14. Disconnect accelerator cable from air throttle body assembly, then remove

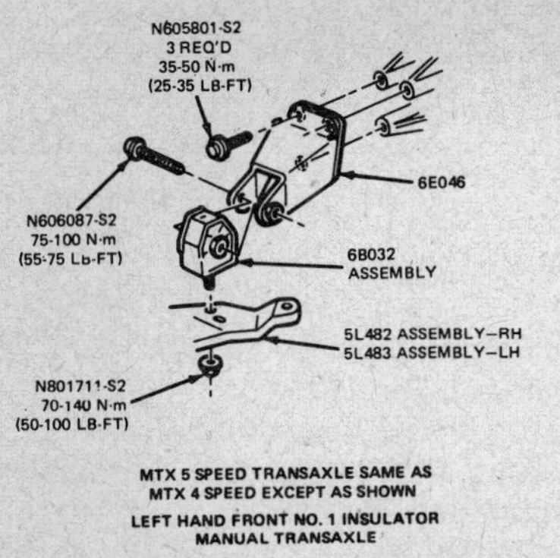

Fig. 1 Lefthand front No. 1 insulator. 5 speed manual transaxle

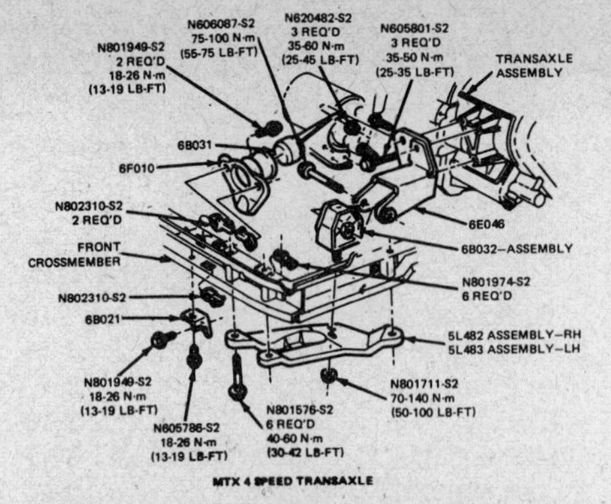

Fig. 2 Lefthand front No. 1 insulator. 4 speed manual transaxle

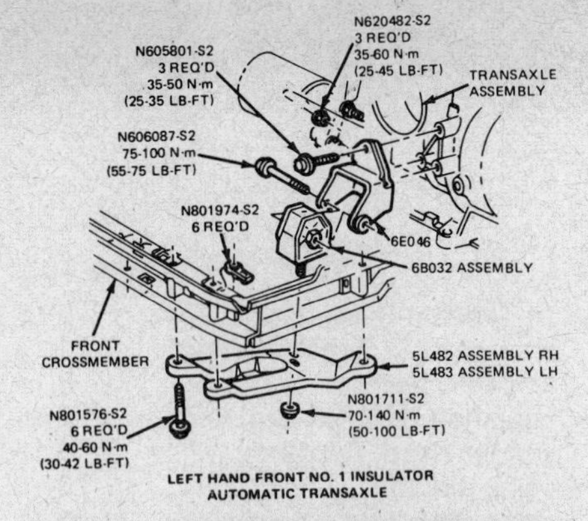

Fig. 3 Lefthand front No. 1 insulator. Automatic transaxle

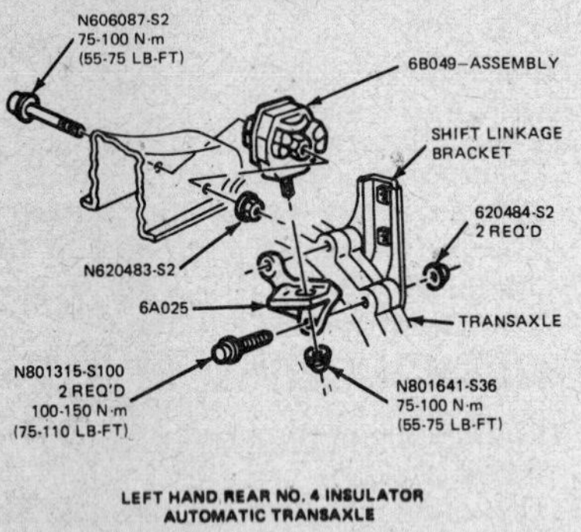

Fig. 4 Lefthand rear No. 4 insulator. Automatic transaxle

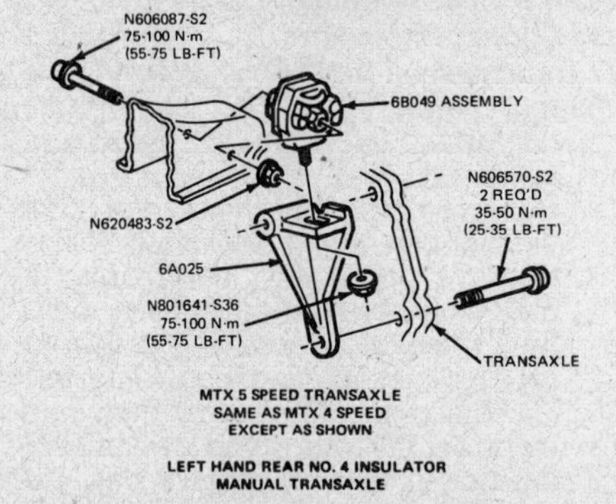

Fig. 5 Lefthand rear No. 4 insulator. Manual transaxle

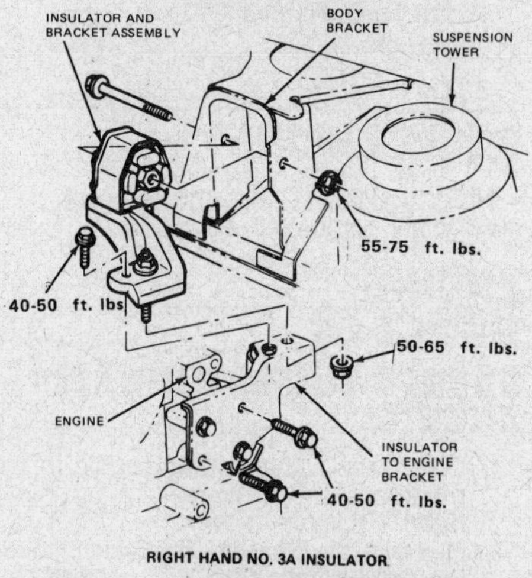

Fig. 6 Righthand No. 3A insulator. All

cable routing bracket attaching screws.
15. Disconnect vapor hose from carbon canister tube.
16. Disconnect purge hose from canister purge solenoid.
17. Raise and support vehicle.
18. Remove oil cooler assembly.
19. Remove clamp from heater supply and return lines.
20. Disconnect battery cable from starter motor.
21. Remove brace from front of starter motor.
22. Remove starter motor assembly from engine.
23. Disconnect exhaust pipe from turbocharger assembly.
24. Remove inspection cover, exhaust pipe support bracket and crankshaft pulley.
25. Remove timing belt cover lower attaching bolts.
26. Remove flywheel housing lower attaching bolts.
27. Remove bolt securing battery ground cable to cylinder block.
28. Remove nut and bolt attaching No. 3A insulator bracket to the engine bracket located at front of engine, **Figs. 1 through 6.**
29. Disconnect EGR tube from intake manifold.
30. Disconnect pulse air hose at check valve and air cleaner assembly.
31. Lower vehicle.
32. Install suitable engine lifting equipment onto engine lifting eyes.
33. Remove nuts attaching casting to No. 3A insulator, then the casting.
34. Remove remaining timing belt cover attaching bolts, then the cover.
35. Position a suitable jack under transaxle assembly. Raise jack enough to support the weight of the transaxle.
36. Remove flywheel housing upper attaching bolts.
37. Remove engine from vehicle.
38. Reverse procedure to install.

CYLINDER HEAD REPLACE

Some engines may have an oversize camshaft. Engines having an oversize camshaft will be identified by a stamping marked ".38/OC" on the outside of the cylinder head above the No. 4 exhaust port. The camshaft will also be stamped ".38/OC" at the distributor drive end. If a cylinder head necessitating replacement incorporates an oversize camshaft, a standard size camshaft must be used with the replacement cylinder head.

1983-85 models incorporate three internal vent tubes located at the oil drain holes on the cylinder head assembly which replace an external hose vent system. The external vent system had a hose routed from the rear of the rocker cover to the lower area of the engine block. The function of the internal tube is to permit venting from the oil pan while simultaneously permitting engine oil to drain from the top of the cylinder head. Removing these tubes will restrict return oil flow to the oil pan. These tubes must be in place whenever removing/installing cylinder head assembly.

1. Disconnect battery ground cable.
2. On non-turbocharged engine models, disconnect heater hose from intake manifold. Remove air cleaner.
3. On turbocharged engine models, disconnect radiator upper hose from cylinder head, then remove air supply hose from air throttle body assembly.
4. On all models, disconnect electrical connector from cooling fan switch.
5. Remove PCV oil separator, if equipped.
6. Disconnect PCV hose from air cleaner assembly.
7. Remove rocker arm cover, drive belts, crankshaft pulley and timing belt cover.
8. Set No. 1 cylinder to TDC of compression stroke by turning crankshaft until pulley keyway is at 12 o'clock and camshaft sprocket keyway is at 6 o'clock. Then, remove distributor cap and spark plug wires as an assembly.
9. Using a suitable tool, loosen both timing belt tensioner attaching bolts.

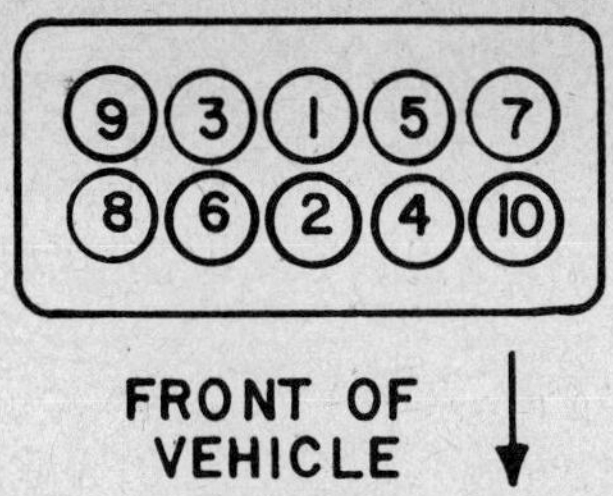

Fig. 7 Cylinder head bolt tightening sequence

10. Position timing belt tensioner as far left as possible and remove timing belt.
11. Disconnect EGR tube from EGR valve.
12. Disconnect choke cap electrical connector, if equipped.
13. Disconnect and cap fuel supply and return lines from engine.
14. Disconnect accelerator cable and speed control cable, if equipped.
15. On turbocharged engine models, disconnect EGO electrical connector and EGR valve vacuum hose.
16. On power steering models, remove thermactor pump, drive belt and bracket.
17. Disconnect altitude compensator from dash panel, if equipped.
18. Disconnect alternator air intake tube, if equipped and electrical connector.
19. Remove alternator and bracket.
20. On turbocharged models, disconnect air intake tube. Disconnect turbocharger oil supply tube from coolant outlet.
21. Disconnect exhaust pipe from exhaust manifold or turbocharger assembly.
22. On turbocharged engine models, disconnect oil drain from turbocharger.
23. Remove cylinder head bolts and washers. Discard bolts and washers.
24. Remove cylinder head, exhaust manifold, intake manifold and turbocharger, if equipped as an assembly. **Before installing cylinder head, rotate crankshaft so pulley keyway is positioned at 9 o'clock (viewed from the front of the engine). Turn camshaft to position its keyway at 6 o'clock and install cylinder head. Then, turn crankshaft so pulley keyway is positioned at 12 o'clock. The camshaft and crankshaft are now properly timed and should not be rotated from this position until after the timing belt and sprockets have been installed.**
25. Reverse procedure to install. **Before FINAL installation of the cylinder head to the engine block, piston "squish height"must be checked. Squish height is the clearance of the piston dome to the cylinder head dome at piston TDC. No rework of the head gasket surfaces (slabbing), or use of replacement compone nts (crankshaft, piston and connecting rod) causing the assembled "squish height" to over or under the tolerance specification is permitted. If no parts other than the cylinder head gasket are replaced, the piston squish height should be within specification. If parts other than the cylinder head gasket are replaced, check the squish height. If the squish height is not within specification, replace the parts again, and check piston squish height as follows:**
    a. Clean all gasket material from the mating surfaces on the cylinder head and engine block.
    b. Place a small amount of soft lead solder on the piston spherical areas.
    c. Rotate the crankshaft to lower the piston in the bore and install the head gasket and cylinder head. A compressed (used) head gasket is preferred.
    d. Install used head bolts and tighten the cylinder head bolts to 30-44 ft. lbs. in sequence.
    e. Rotate crankshaft to move the piston through its TDC position.
    f. Remove the cylinder head and measure the thickness of the compressed solder to determine squish height at TDC. The solder should be .039-.070 inch.
26. Torque cylinder head bolts in sequence shown in **Fig. 7**, to 44 ft. lbs. Loosen all attaching bolts approximately 2 turns, and torque bolts again to 44 ft. lbs. After tightening all bolts, turn bolts an additional 90 degrees again in the same sequence. Complete bolt tightening sequence by turning cylinder head bolts an additional 90 degrees again in the same sequence. Refer to "Timing Belt, Replace" for belt tension data.

VALVE ARRANGEMENT

FRONT TO REAR

1.6 L....................... I-E-I-E-I-E-I-E

CAM LOBE LIFT SPECIFICATIONS

Engine	Year	Int.	Exh.
1.6L	1982-85	.229	.229
1.6L, E.F.I., H.O. & Turbocharged	1983-85	.396	.396

VALVE LIFT SPECIFICATIONS

Engine	Year	Intake	Exhaust
1.6L	1982-85	.377	.377
1.6L, E.F.I.,	983-85		
H. O. & Turbocharged	1983-85	.396	.396

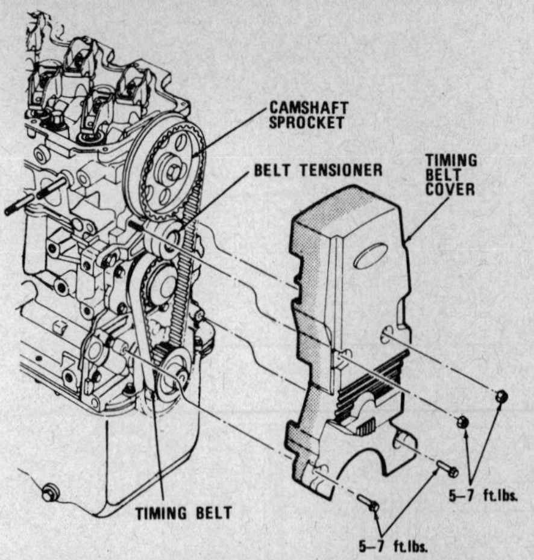

Fig. 8 Timing belt cover removal

VALVE TIMING

INTAKE OPENS BEFORE TDC

Engine	Year	Degrees
1.6L	1982	20

VALVE CLEARANCE SPECIFICATIONS

Year	Engine	Valve Lash
1982-85	4-97.6	.059-.194①

①—With hydraulic valve lash adjuster completely collapsed.

VALVES

ADJUST

The 1.6L engines are equipped with overhead camshafts and hydraulic lash adjusters. Valve stem to rocker arm clearance is measured with the tappet completely collapsed. Perform the following procedure when measuring valve tappet clearance.

Some engines may incorporate oversize valve tappets. The cylinder head assembly will be identified by metal stamping .254 OT on the machined pad below the rocker arm rail and above the No. 1 exhaust port.

1. Rotate engine until No. 1 piston is on TDC of compression stroke.
2. Position suitable hydraulic lifter compressor tool onto rocker arm and slowly apply pressure to bleed tappet. Continue applying pressure until lifter plunger bottoms. Hold tappet in this position and check clearance between rocker arm and valve stem tip with feeler gauge. Collapsed tappet gap should be .059-.194 in. If clearance is less than specified, check for worn or damaged fulcrums, tappets or camshaft lobes.
3. With No. 1 piston on TDC of compression stroke, check the following valves:

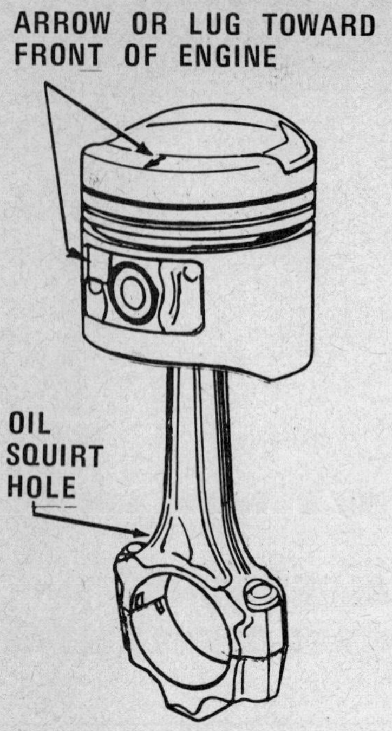
ARROW OR LUG TOWARD FRONT OF ENGINE
OIL SQUIRT HOLE

Fig. 9 Piston & rod assembly

a. Intake Nos. 1 and 2; exhaust No.1.
6. Rotate crankshaft 180° from above position and check the following valves:
   a. No. 3 intake & No. 3 exhaust.
4. Rotate crankshaft another 180° from above position and check the following valves:
   a. Intake No. 4; exhaust Nos. 2 and 4.

VALVE GUIDES

Valve guide reamers are available in oversizes of .003, .015 and .030 in. When reaming a valve guide to an oversize, use the reamer in sequence from the smallest oversize first, to the next largest, etc. Always reface the valve seat after the valve guide has been reamed and use a suitable tool to remove the corner that forms on the inner diameter of the top of the valve guide.

CAMSHAFT
REPLACE

1. Disconnect battery ground cable and remove air cleaner assembly.
2. Disconnect PCV hose and remove accessory drive belts.
3. Remove crankshaft pulley, then the timing belt cover, **Fig. 8.**
4. Remove valve cover, then rotate engine until No. 1 piston is on TDC of compression stroke. **Ensure crankshaft is positioned at TDC and do not turn the crankshaft until the timing belt is installed.**
5. Remove rocker arm hex flange nuts, fulcrums and rocker arms.
6. Remove fulcrum washers, then the tappets.
7. Remove crankshaft sprocket, then the timing belt. Refer to "Timing Belt, Replace" for procedure.
8. Remove camshaft sprocket, key and distributor assembly.
9. Loosen both timing belt tensioner attaching bolts using tool T81P-6254A or equivalent.
10. Remove camshaft thrust plate, then the fuel pump assembly.
11. Remove ignition coil and bracket.
12. Remove camshaft from back of head towards transaxle.
13. Reverse procedure to install. Lubricate camshaft with suitable oil before installing. Check camshaft seal for damage and wear.

PISTON & ROD ASSEMBLE

Assemble the piston to the rod with arrow or lug facing front of engine and numbered side of rod facing exhaust manifold side of engine, **Fig. 9.** Check side clearance between connecting rods at each connecting rod crankshaft journal. Clearance should be .004-.011 in.

PISTONS, RINGS & PINS

Standard size pistons and rings are color coded red or blue and oversize pistons and rings have .004 OS stamped on their dome. Piston to bore clearance should be .0012-.0020 in. on 1982 models and .0018-.0026 in. on except 1982 models. Measure cylinder bore and select a piston to ensure proper clearance. When the piston to bore clearance is in the lower 1/3 of the specified range, a red piston should be used; in the middle 1/3 range a blue piston should be used and in the upper 1/3 range a .004 OS piston should be used. Piston pins are not available in oversize.

MAIN & ROD BEARINGS

Main and rod bearings are available in standard size and undersizes of .001 and .002 in.

TIMING BELT
REPLACE

Replacement of the timing belt when the belt tension is released is not necessary. Replace a damaged timing belt as required.

1. Disconnect battery ground cable.
2. Remove timing belt cover, **Fig. 8.** Turn crankshaft until crankshaft pulley keyway is at 12 o'clock and camshaft sprocket keyway is at 6 o'clock (sprocket pointer at timing mark on cylinder head), **Fig. 10.**
3. Install timing belt cover and ensure that timing mark on crankshaft pulley aligns with TDC mark on front cover. Remove timing belt cover.
4. Loosen both timing belt tensioner attaching bolts using tool T81P-6254A or equivalent.
5. Position belt tensioner away from belt as far as possible, then tighten one of the tensioner attaching bolts, **Fig. 11.**
6. Remove crankshaft pulley, then the timing belt. Discard timing belt, if damaged.

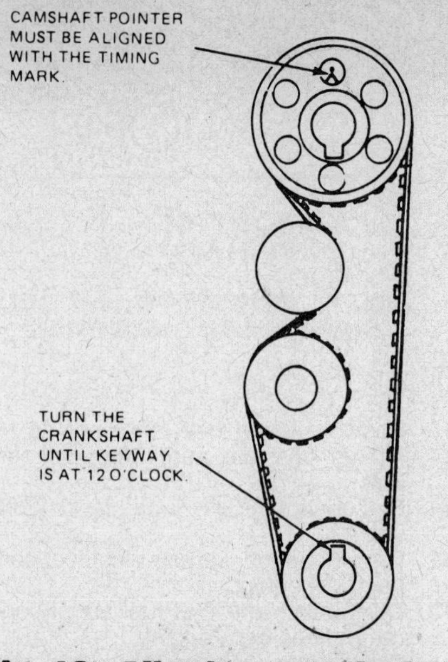
CAMSHAFT POINTER MUST BE ALIGNED WITH THE TIMING MARK.
TURN THE CRANKSHAFT UNTIL KEYWAY IS AT 12 O'CLOCK.

Fig. 10 Aligning camshaft to cylinder head timing marks

7. Install timing belt over sprocket in clockwise direction starting at crankshaft. Ensure belt span between crankshaft and camshaft is kept tight as belt is installed over remaining sprockets, **Fig. 12.** Do not alter relationship between camshaft and crankshaft as shown in **Fig. 10.**
8. Loosen belt tensioner attaching bolts and allow tensioner to locate against belt.
9. Tighten one tensioner attaching bolt using tool T81P-6254A or equivalent.
10. Install crankshaft pulley, drive plate and pulley attaching bolt.
11. Hold crankshaft pulley stationary using tool YA-826 or equivalent and torque pulley attaching bolt to 74-90 ft. lbs.
12. To seat timing belt on sprocket teeth, proceed as follows:
    a. Connect battery ground cable.
    b. Crank engine for approximately 30 seconds.
    c. Disconnect battery ground cable.
    d. Turn crankshaft to align timing pointer on camshaft sprocket with timing mark on cylinder head.
    e. Position timing belt cover on engine and confirm timing mark on crankshaft aligns with TDC pointer on the cover. If timing marks do not align, remove timing belt, align timing marks, **Fig. 10,** and repeat steps 7 through 13.
13. Loosen belt tensioner attaching bolt tightened in step 9.
14. Secure crankshaft so it cannot rotate, then using tool No. D81P-6256 or equivalent and a torque wrench, turn camshaft sprocket counterclockwise. Tighten timing belt tensioner attaching bolt when torque wrench indicates 27-32 ft. lbs., for a new timing belt and 10 ft. lbs., for a used timing belt. **Engine must be cold when torque is applied to camshaft sprocket.**
15. Remove crankshaft pulley and install timing belt cover.

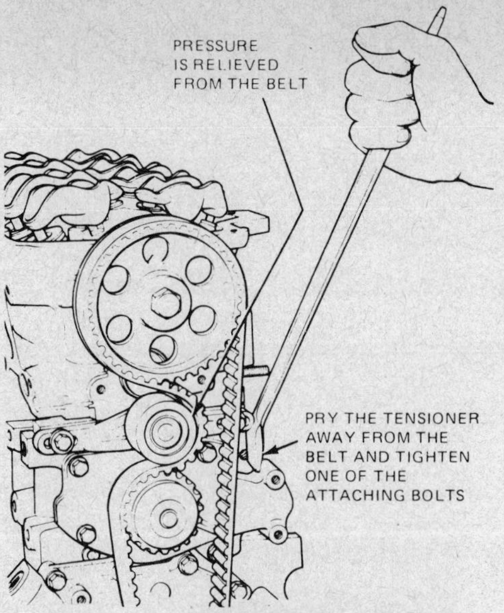

Fig. 11 Relieving timing belt tension

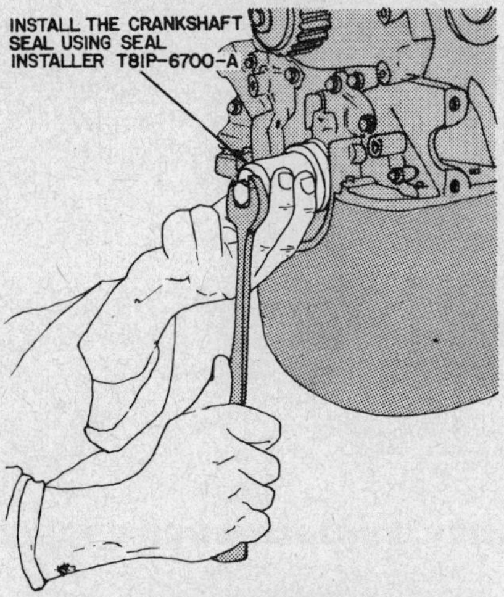

Fig. 14 Crankshaft front oil seal installation

16. Install pulley and drive belts.

FRONT ENGINE OIL SEAL SERVICE

1. Remove timing belt as described under "Timing Belt, Replace."
2. Remove camshaft sprocket or crankshaft pulley as necessary.
3. Remove appropriate seal, **Figs. 13 and 14.**
4. Reverse procedure to install.

CRANKSHAFT REAR OIL SEAL SERVICE

1. Remove engine as described under "Engine, Replace."
2. Remove rear cover plate, **Fig. 15,** then the flywheel.
3. Using suitable tool, pierce seal metal casing.
4. Insert sheet metal screw into hole until screw forces seal out of retainer.

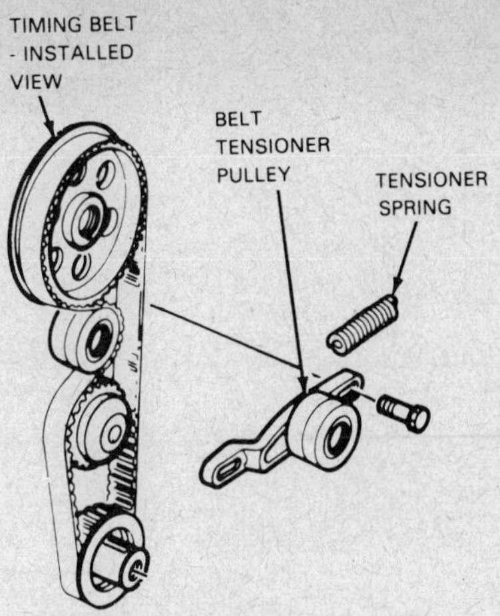

NOTE: WHEN THE CRANKSHAFT KEYWAY IS AT THE 12 O'CLOCK POSITION, NUMBER ONE PISTON IS AT TDC. WHEN THE KEYWAY IS AT THE 9 O'CLOCK POSITION, NUMBER ONE PISTON IS 90° BEFORE TDC.

Fig. 12 Timing belt installed

5. Reverse procedure to install using suitable seal installation tool to install seal.

INTAKE MANIFOLD REPLACE

EXCEPT TURBOCHARGED & EFI ENGINES

1. Disconnect battery ground cable and drain coolant system.
2. Disconnect heater hose from intake manifold and remove air cleaner assembly.
3. Disconnect vacuum hoses as necessary, then the electrical connectors from idle fuel solenoid, bowl vent and choke.
4. Remove EGR supply tube.
5. Raise and support vehicle, then disconnect PVS hose using tool T81P-8564A or equivalent.
6. Remove intake manifold nuts Nos. 2, 3, and 6, **Fig. 16,** then lower vehicle.
7. Disconnect fuel line at fuel filter and return line at carburetor.
8. Disconnect accelerator cable and, if equipped, speed control cable.
9. On vehicles equipped with automatic transmission, disconnect throttle valve linkage at carburetor, then remove cable bracket attaching bolts.
10. On vehicles equipped with power steering, remove thermactor pump drive belt, thermactor pump, mounting bracket and bypass hose.
11. Remove fuel pump, then three remaining manifold attaching nuts. Remove intake manifold. **Do not place manifold on flat surface as damage to gasket surfaces may result.**

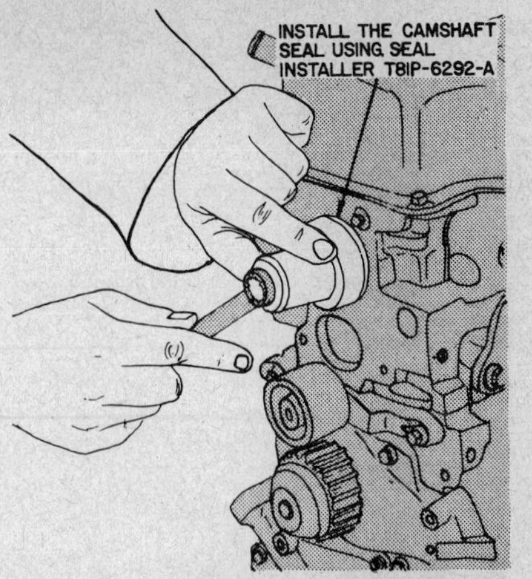

Fig. 13 Camshaft front oil seal installation

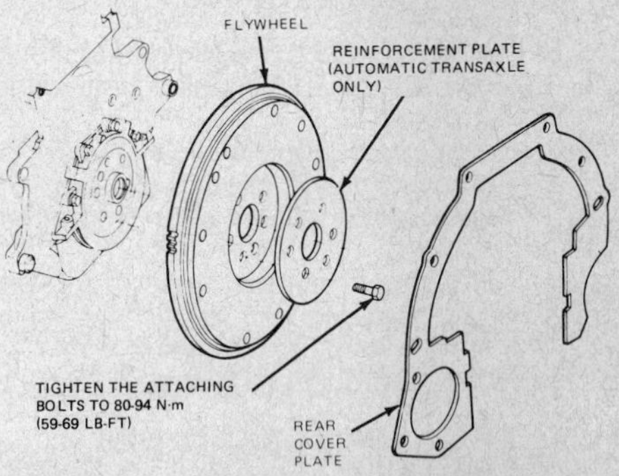

Fig. 15 Rear cover plate, removal

12. Reverse procedure to install. Tighten intake manifold stud nuts in sequence shown in **Fig. 16,** to torque listed in Engine Tightening Specifications.

TURBOCHARGED & EFI ENGINES

Refer to "Fuel Pump, Replace" (electric fuel pump) to relieve system pressure.

1. Disconnect battery ground cable.
2. Remove air supply hose from throttle body assembly.
3. Mark then disconnect all electrical connectors and vacuum hoses from intake manifold.
4. Remove EGR supply tube.
5. Disconnect electrical connector from throttle air bypass solenoid.
6. Raise and support vehicle.
7. Remove the bottom 3 intake manifold attaching nuts, **Fig. 17.**
8. Lower vehicle.
9. Disconnect fuel supply and return lines from intake manifold.
10. Disconnect accelerator cable from throttle body assembly.
11. Disconnect engine wiring harness from shock tower bracket.
12. Disconnect PCV hose from rocker cover and intake manifold.
13. Remove PCV valve.
14. Remove remaining 3 intake manifold attaching nuts, intake manifold and gasket.

15. Reverse procedure to install. Tighten intake manifold stud nuts in sequence shown in **Fig. 17**, to torque listed in Engine Tightening Specifications.

EXHAUST MANIFOLD REPLACE

EXCEPT TURBOCHARGED & EFI ENGINES

1. Disconnect battery ground cable.
2. Remove air cleaner.
3. Disconnect electrical connector from fan switch.
4. Remove radiator shroud bolts, then the shroud.
5. Disconnect EGR tube from exhaust manifold.
6. Disconnect thermactor tube from exhaust manifold.
7. Remove A/C hose bracket, if equipped.
8. Remove exhaust manifold heat stove.
9. Remove exhaust manifold attaching nuts, **Fig. 18.**
10. Raise and support vehicle.
11. Remove anti-roll brace.
12. Disconnect water tube mounting brackets.
13. Disconnect exhaust pipe from exhaust manifold.
14. Remove exhaust manifold.
15. Reverse procedure to install.

TURBOCHARGED & EFI ENGINES

1. Disconnect battery ground cable.
2. Remove cooling fan shield from radiator support.
3. Loosen compressor outlet hose clamp from throttle housing.
4. Disconnect hose from turbocharger compressor inlet.
5. Remove alternator and bracket assembly.
6. Disconnect EGO sensor electrical connector, **Fig. 19.**
7. Raise and support vehicle.
8. Disconnect oil supply line from turbocharger coolant outlet.
9. Disconnect oil return line from cylinder block.
10. Remove exhaust pipe to turbocharger assembly attaching nuts, then position exhaust pipe away from mounting studs.
11. Remove exhaust shield from water outlet connector.
12. Remove nuts attaching exhaust manifold to cylinder head. Slide exhaust manifold and turbocharger assembly away from cylinder head.
13. Remove turbocharger and exhaust manifold as an assembly. **If exhaust manifold is being replaced, replace EGO sensor.**
14. Reverse procedure to install. Torque exhaust manifold nuts to 16-19 ft. lbs.

OIL PAN REPLACE

1. Disconnect battery ground cable, then raise and support vehicle.

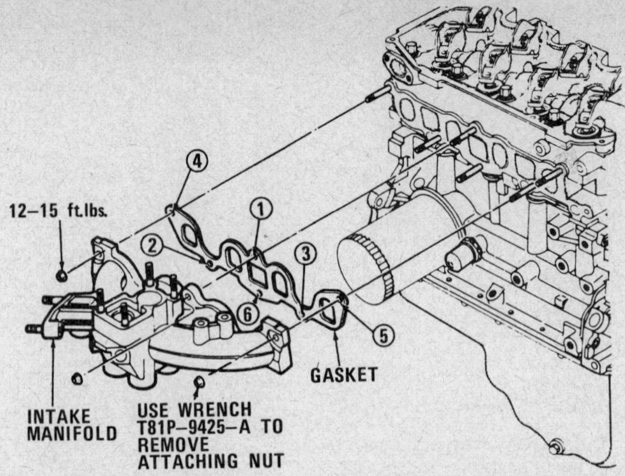

Fig. 16 Intake manifold bolt tightening sequence

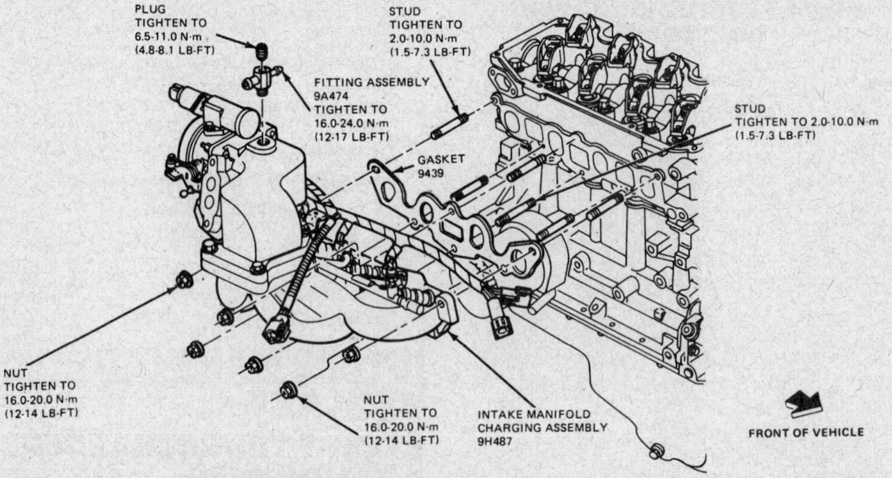

Fig. 17 Intake manifold assembly. Turbocharged engine

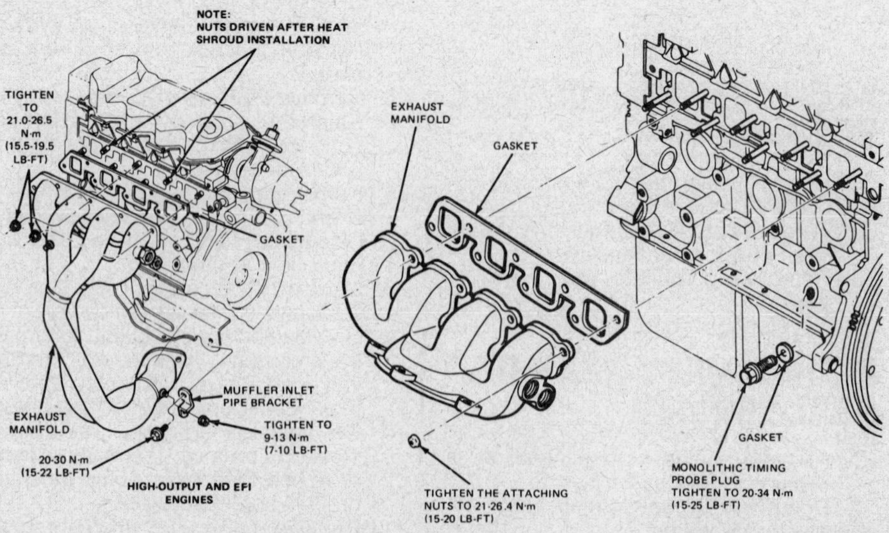

Fig. 18 Exhaust manifold assembly. Except turbocharged engine

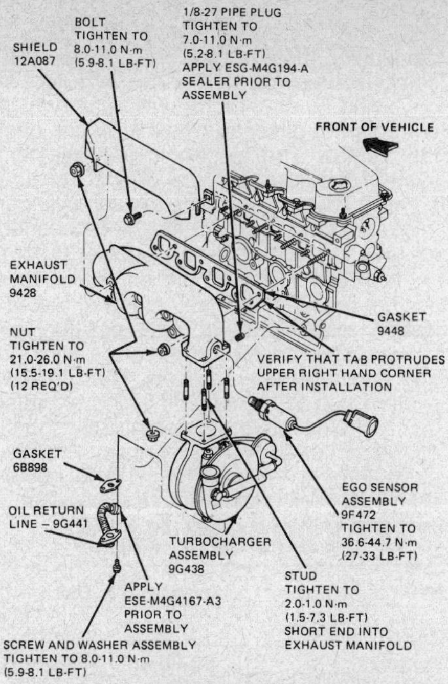

Fig. 19 Exhaust manifold assembly. Turbocharged engine

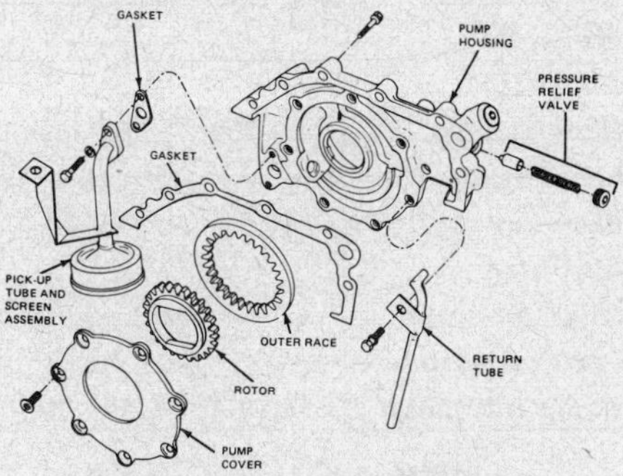

Fig. 22 Oil pump

2. Drain engine oil, then disconnect starter electrical connectors.
3. Remove knee brace, then the starter.
4. Remove transaxle knee braces, then the oil pan retaining bolts. Remove the oil pan and discard gaskets.
5. On turbocharged engines, remove EGR tubes from exhaust inlet pipe. Disconnect exhaust inlet pipe from exhaust manifold. Remove exhaust inlet pipe support bracket and pipe.
6. Reverse procedure to install using suitable sealant on all pan gaskets. Refer to **Fig. 20**, for oil pan bolt tightening sequence.

OIL PUMP REPLACE

1. Perform steps 1 thru 4 as described under "Timing Belt, Replace."
2. Remove timing belt from camshaft and crankshaft pulleys and water pump gear.
3. Raise and support vehicle, then drain engine oil.
4. Remove crankshaft pulley, then the timing belt. Discard timing belt.

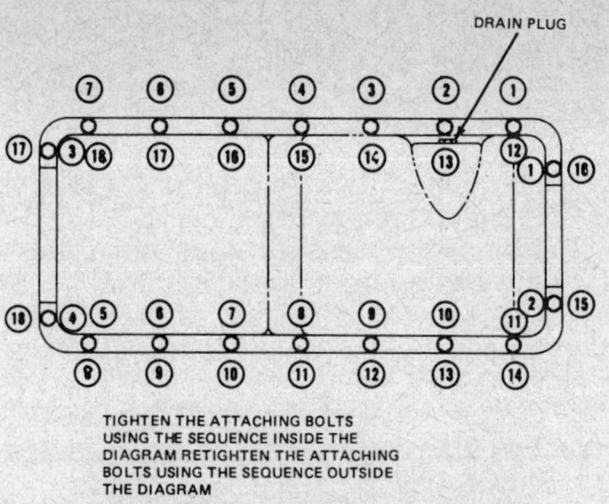

Fig. 20 Oil pan bolt tightening sequence

5. Remove crankshaft drive plate assembly, then the crankshaft pulley and gear.
6. Disconnect starter electrical connectors, then remove knee brace from engine.
7. Remove starter, then the rear section of knee brace. Remove transmission inspection plate.
8. Remove oil pan retaining bolts, then the oil pan.
9. Remove oil pick up tube brace to cylinder block bolt.
10. Remove oil pump attaching bolts, oil pump and gaskets, **Fig. 21.**
11. Reverse procedure to install using suitable sealant on all pan gaskets.

OIL PUMP SERVICE

Refer to **Fig. 22,** and measure the following clearances:

a. Outer race to housing: .0027-.0055 in. (.069-.140 mm).
b. Outer race and rotor to cover: .001-.0025 in. (.040-.66 mm.).
c. Relief valve to bore: .007-.0031 in. (.02-.08 mm). **An engine oil leak at the oil pump hex socket plug on some 1982 vehicles may be serviced by applying sealer to the oil pump hex plug threads above the pressure relief valve plug. Remove hex plug and clean plug threads with a suitable solvent. Apply sealer No. E0AZ-19554A or equivalent to the plug threads. Torque plug to 21-24 ft. lbs. These plugs are not interchangeable and must not be overtorqued. On some engines built after March 31, 1983, a new gerotor gear design oil pump is being used, Fig. 23. The oil pump, oil pan and crankshaft used on models equipped with gerotor gear type oil pumps are not interchangeable with those used with the crescent type oil pump.**

OIL COOLER REPLACE

TURBOCHARGED & EFI ENGINES ONLY

1. Disconnect battery ground cable.

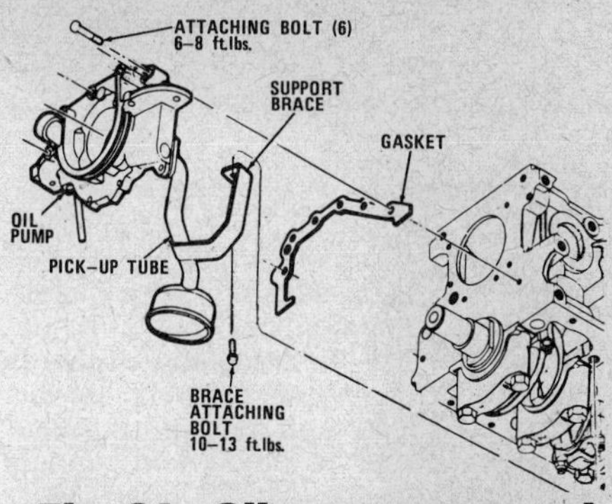

Fig. 21 Oil pump removal

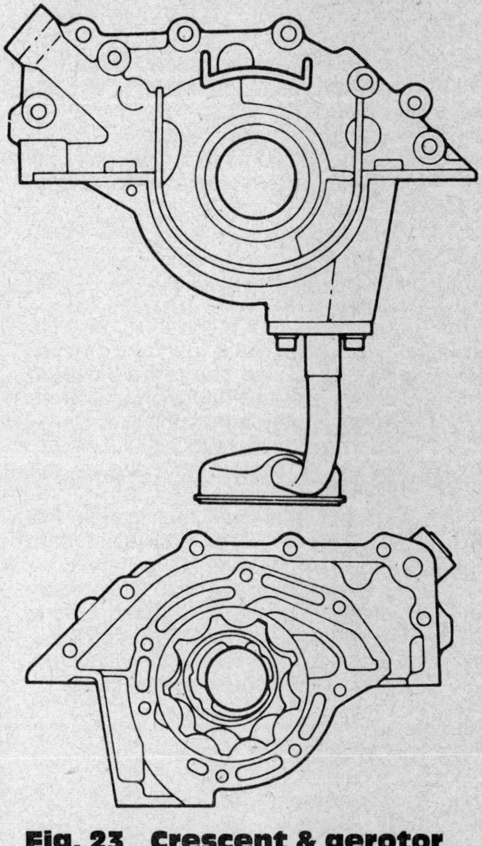

Fig. 23 Crescent & gerotor type oil pumps

2. Drain engine oil and remove oil filter.
3. Drain cooling system.
4. Remove clamps retaining coolant hoses onto oil cooler, then the hoses.
5. Remove oil filter adapter insert, then the oil cooler from engine.
6. Reverse procedure to install.

FUEL PUMP REPLACE

MECHANICAL

1. Loosen fuel supply attaching nut at fuel pump outlet and the fuel pump mounting bolts.
2. Manually rotate engine until pump pushrod is positioned on low side of cam.
3. Disconnect fuel lines from fuel pump.

4. Remove pump mounting bolts, then the pump and gasket.
5. Reverse procedure to install.

ELECTRIC

Fuel supply lines will remain pressurized for long periods of time after engine shutdown. This pressure must be relieved before any service is attempted. A valve is provided on the fuel rail assembly for this purpose. To relieve system pressure, remove air cleaner assembly and connect pressure gauge tool No. T80L-9974-A or equivalent, onto fuel diagnostic valve on the fuel rail assembly. Gradually release fuel system pressure.

1. Disconnect battery ground cable.
2. Depressurize fuel system as described previously.
3. Raise and support vehicle.
4. Loosen fuel pump mounting bolt until fuel pump can be removed from vehicle.
5. Remove parking brake cable from pump clip.
6. Disconnect electrical connector and fuel pump outlet fitting.
7. Disconnect fuel pump inlet line from pump. **Either drain fuel tank or raise end of fuel line above fuel level in tank to prevent fuel siphon action.**
8. Remove pump from vehicle.
9. Reverse procedure to install. To pressurize fuel system, proceed as follows:
   a. Install pressure tool gauge No. T80L-9974-A or equivalent onto fuel rail pressure fitting.
   b. Turn ignition switch to ON position for 2 seconds and repeat turning ignition switch ON and OFF at 2 second intervals until gauge tool indicates approximately 35 psi.

WATER PUMP

REPLACE

1. Disconnect battery ground cable and drain coolant system.
2. Remove accessory drive belts, then the engine front timing cover.
3. Position No. 1 cylinder at TDC, then loosen both belt tensioner attaching bolts.
4. Secure tensioner as far left as possible, then remove timing belt. Discard timing belt.
5. Remove camshaft sprocket, then the rearward front timing cover stud.
6. Disconnect heater return tube hose connection at water pump inlet tube.
7. Remove water pump inlet tube fasteners, then the tube and gasket.
8. Remove water pump to cylinder block bolts, then the water pump.
9. Reverse procedure to install. Refer to "Timing Belt, Replace" for proper belt tension procedures.

TURBOCHARGER

The turbocharger is used to increase engine power on a demand basis. As engine load increases and the throttle opens, more air-fuel mixture flows into the combustion chambers. As the increased flow is burned a larger volume of high energy exhaust gases enters the engine exhaust system and is directed through the turbocharged turbine housing. Some of the exhaust gas energy is used to increase the speed of the turbine wheel which is connected to the compressor wheel. The increased speed of the compressor wheel compresses the air-fuel mixture and delivers the compressed air-fuel mixture to the intake manifold. The high pressure in the intake manifold allows a denser charge to enter the combustion chambers, in turn developing more engine power during the combustion cycle. Turbocharger output is governed by an integral wastegate which controls the passage of exhaust gas past the turbine. The electronic fuel injection system provides precise air-fuel mixture control. The fuel injectors at each cylinder intake port deliver more fuel when needed for high turbocharger boost power output.

The EEC-1V electronic engine control system provides precise control of fuel injection response to throttle position, air temperature, engine temperature, altitude and engine emission levels. The EEC-1V system also controls spark timing, exhaust gas recirculation and automatically shuts-off the air conditioner compressor at wide-open throttle to eliminate engine power drag when full engine output is needed.

BELT TENSION DATA

Belt	New	Used
1982–83		
1/4 inch	50-80	40-60
Air Pump	90-130	90-120
4 Ribs Exc.		
Air Pump	110-150	100-130
5 ribs	130-170	120-150
1984–85		
Air Pump		
(Low Mount)	90-130	80-100
Less Power		
Steering	50-90	40-60
Air Pump		
(High Mount) &		
Power Steering		
Pump Alternator	150-190	140-10

4-116 (1.9L) Gasoline Engine Section

INDEX

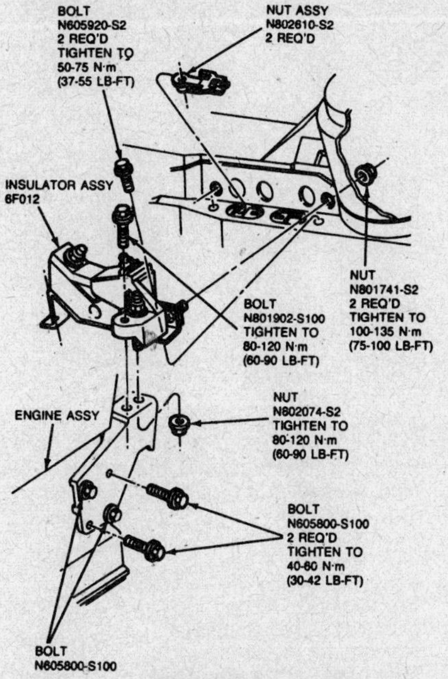

Fig. 1 Righthand No. 3A insulator

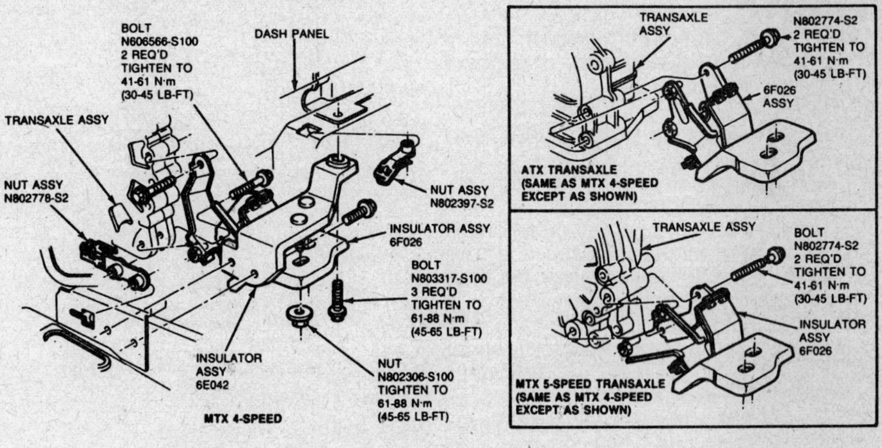

Fig. 2 Lefthand rear No. 4 insulator

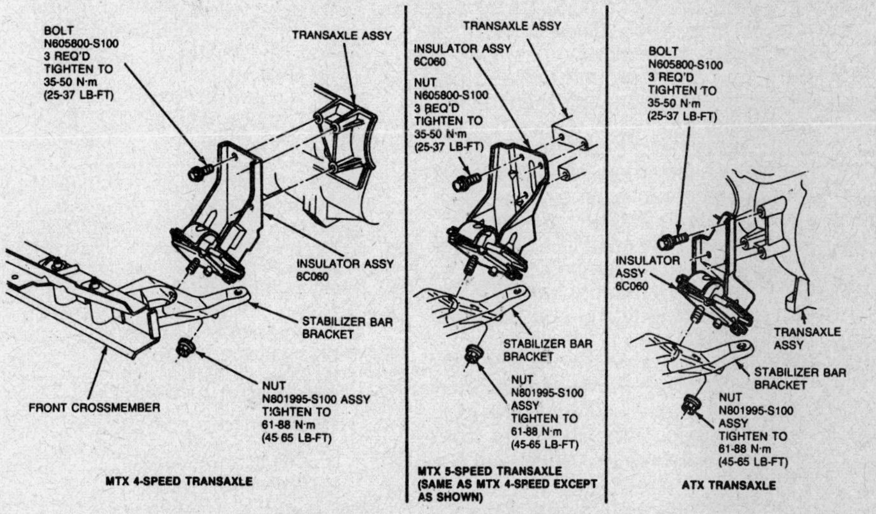

Fig. 3 Lefthand front No. 1 insulator

ENGINE MOUNTS

Refer to **Figs. 1 through 3** when replacing engine mounts.

ENGINE REPLACE

When performing engine removal and installation procedures, check and record the distance between the crankshaft pulley and the frame rail, and the distance between the transmission and frame rail. Models with manual transaxle, check distance at transaxle case. Models with automatic transaxle, check distance at the oil pump housing. This check should be done before the engine is removed and after the engine is installed. If necessary, loosen the motor mount-to-engine bolts to shift the engine to obtain proper engine/transaxle to frame rail clearances. Proper clearances are necessary to ensure half-shaft alignment. Crankshaft pulley-to-frame rail clearance should be .62 inch plus or minus .15 inch. Transaxle to frame rail clearance should be .98 inch plus or minus .19 inch.

1. Mark position of hood hinges, then remove hood.
2. Disconnect battery ground cable, then remove air cleaner, intake duct and heat tube.
3. Remove alternator air intake tube, then drain engine coolant.
4. Remove secondary coil wire, then the alternator drive belt.
5. Remove alternator mount bolts, then position alternator aside.
6. Disconnect thermactor air supply hose at pump, then remove pump.
7. On models with automatic transaxle, disconnect cooler lines at radiator.
8. On all models, disconnect the engine coolant hoses at radiator, then the heater hoses at engine block.
9. Disconnect electric cooling fan, then remove fan and shroud as an assembly.
10. On models with automatic transaxle,

remove transaxle coolant line routing clip at radiator.
11. On all models, remove radiator.
12. Disconnect heater at metal tube, then the necessary engine electrical connectors.
13. Disconnect vacuum hoses, then the fuel pump supply and return lines.
14. On models with power assist brakes, disconnect brake booster vacuum hose at engine.
15. On models with automatic transaxle, disconnect kickdown rod at carburetor.
16. On all models, disconnect vacuum hose at thermactor valve.
17. Disconnect accelerator cable at carburetor, then remove cable routing bracket attaching screws.
18. Disconnect vapor hose at carbon canister, then raise and support vehicle.
19. Remove clamp from heater supply and return tubes, then disconnect starter battery cable.
20. Remove knee brace from front of starter motor, then pull starter from vehicle.
21. Disconnect exhaust pipe, then remove support bracket.
22. Remove converter cover on automatic transaxle models or inspection cover on manual transaxle models, then the crankshaft pulley.
23. On models with automatic transaxle, remove torque converter to flywheel attaching bolts, then the converter housing lower attaching bolts.
24. On models with manual transaxle, remove timing belt cover lower attaching bolts, then the flywheel attaching bolts.
25. On all models, loosen coolant bypass hose clamp, then disconnect hose from intake manifold.
26. Remove battery ground cable to engine block attaching bolt, then the No. 3A casting bracket to engine bracket attaching nut and bolt, **Fig. 1.**
27. Lower vehicle, then attach suitable lifting brackets to engine, then attach lifting device to engine brackets.
28. Remove No. 3A casting to insulator retaining nut, then the casting.
29. On models with manual transaxle, remove remaining timing belt cover attaching bolts, then the cover.
30. On all models, remove insulator attaching bracket from engine, then support transaxle with a suitable jack.
31. Remove upper attaching bolts from converter housing on models with automatic transaxle or flywheel housing on models with manual transaxle.
32. On all models, remove engine from vehicle.
33. Reverse procedure to install.

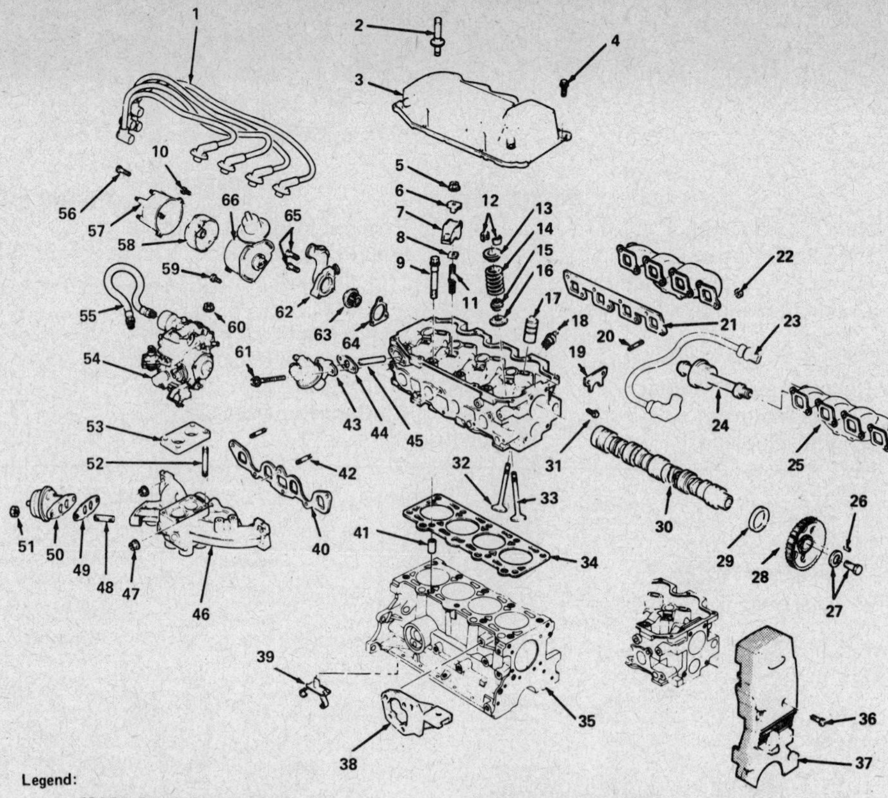

Legend:

1. SPARK PLUG CABLE SET
2. BOLT/STUD, COVER ATTACHING (2)
3. ROCKER ARM COVER
4. SCREW, COVER ATTACHING (7)
5. NUT, FULCRUM ATTACHING (8)
6. FULCRUM, ROCKER ARM
7. ROCKER ARM
8. WASHER, FULCRUM (8)
9. BOLT, CYLINDER HEAD ATTACHING (10)
10. SCREW, ROTOR ATTACHING (2)
11. STUD, FULCRUM ATTACHING (8)
12. KEYS, VALVE SPRING RETAINER
13. RETAINER, VALVE SPRING
14. VALVE SPRING
15. SEAL, VALVE STEM
16. SEAT, VALVE SPRING
17. HYDRAULIC TAPPET
18. SPARK PLUG
19. PLATE, CAMSHAFT THRUST
20. STUD, MANIFOLD ATTACHING (8)
21. GASKET, EXHAUST MANIFOLD
22. NUT, MANIFOLD ATTACHING (8)
23. EGR TUBE
24. CHECK VALVE, AIR INJECTION
25. EXHAUST MANIFOLD
26. SHAFT KEY, CAM SPROCKET
27. BOLT/WASHER SPROCKET ATTACHING (1)
28. SPROCKET, CAMSHAFT
29. SEAL, CAMSHAFT
30. CAMSHAFT
31. BOLT, THRUST PLATE ATTACHING (2)
32. INTAKE VALVE
33. EXHAUST VALVE
34. GASKET, CYLINDER HEAD
35. CYLINDER BLOCK
36. BOLTS (2) & NUTS (2), COVER ATTACHING
37. TIMING BELT COVER
38. ENGINE MOUNT
39. CRANKCASE VENTILATION BAFFLE
40. GASKET, INTAKE MANIFOLD
41. DOWEL, CYLINDER HEAD ALIGNMENT (2)
42. STUD, MANIFOLD ATTACHING (6)
43. FUEL PUMP
44. GASKET, FUEL PUMP
45. PUSH ROD, FUEL PUMP
46. INTAKE MANIFOLD
47. NUT, MANIFOLD ATTACHING (6)
48. STUD, VALVE ATTACHING (2)
49. GASKET, EGR VALVE
50. EGR VALVE
51. NUT, VALVE ATTACHING (2)
52. STUD, CARBURETOR ATTACHING (4)
53. GASKET, CARBURETOR MOUNTING
54. CARBURETOR
55. FUEL LINE
56. SCREW, CAP ATTACHING (2)
57. DISTRIBUTOR CAP
58. ROTOR
59. BOLT, DISTRIBUTOR ATTACHING (3)
60. NUT, CARBURETOR ATTACHING (4)
61. BOLT, PUMP ATTACHING (2)
62. THERMOSTAT HOUSING
63. THERMOSTAT
64. GASKET, HOUSING
65. BOLT, HOUSING ATTACHING (2)
66. DISTRIBUTOR

Cylinder head assembly & related components exploded view

CYLINDER HEAD
REPLACE

Some 1985 Escort, Exp and Lynx models may exhibit an oil leak condition at the intake manifold side of the engine. If this condition occurs, a revised cylinder head gasket part No. E6FZ-6051-B should be installed to service the oil leak condition. The cylinder head gasket is manufactured with a double bead of silicone rubber seal around the oil transfer hole on the cylinder head surface of the gasket and a single bead around the hole on the engine block side of the gasket. This gasket is used in current production engines and replaces the previous (E6FZ-6051-A) service gasket.

1. Raise and secure hood in open position.
2. Disconnect battery ground cable.
3. Drain cooling system and disconnect heater hose at the fitting located under the intake manifold.
4. Disconnect cooling fan switch electrical connector.
5. Remove air cleaner assembly.
6. Remove PCV hose from air cleaner

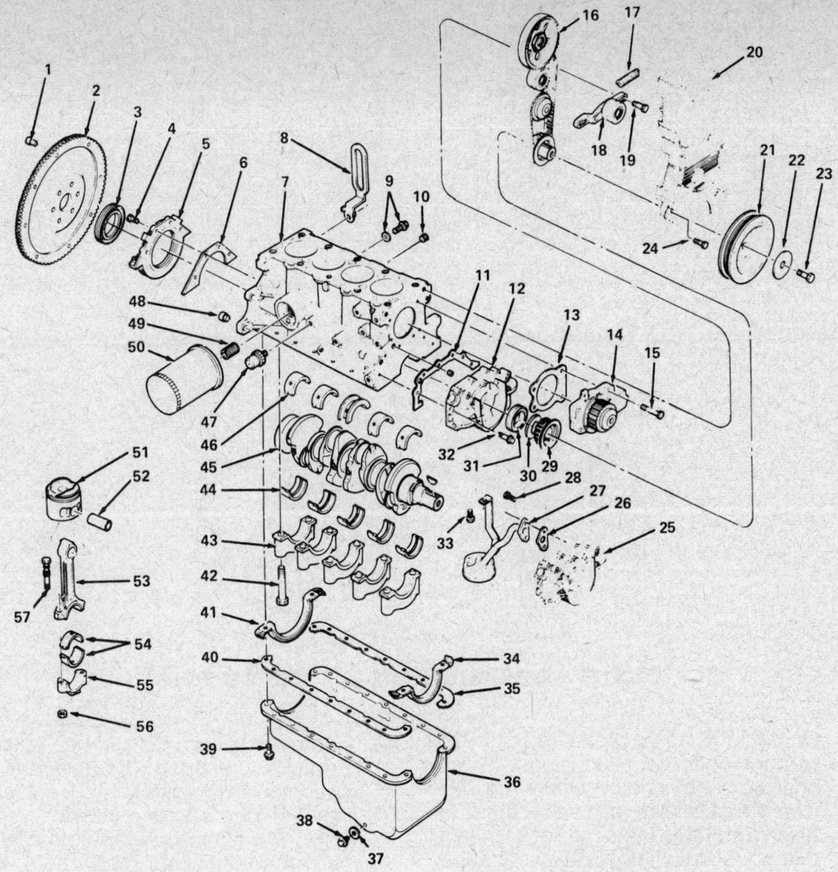

1. DOWEL, PRESSURE PLATE ALIGNMENT
2. FLYWHEEL
3. SEAL, CRANKSHAFT REAR
4. BOLT, RETAINER ATTACHING (6)
5. SEAL RETAINER
6. GASKET, RETAINER
7. CYLINDER BLOCK
8. ENGINE LIFTING EYE
9. PLUG AND GASKET, MONOLITHIC TIMING
10. PLUG, COOLANT DRAIN
11. GASKET, PUMP (OIL)
12. OIL PUMP
13. GASKET, PUMP (WATER)
14. WATER PUMP
15. BOLT, PUMP (WATER) ATTACHING (4)
16. TIMING BELT – INSTALLED VIEW
17. SPRING, TENSIONER
18. BRACKET AND IDLER, TENSIONER
19. BOLT, TENSIONER ATTACHING (2)
20. TIMING BELT COVER
21. CRANKSHAFT PULLEY
22. WASHER, PULLEY BOLT (1)
23. BOLT, PULLEY ATTACHING (1)
24. BOLT, COVER ATTACHING (4)
25. OIL PUMP ASSEMBLY
26. GASKET, PICKUP TUBE
27. SCREEN AND COVER ASSEMBLY
28. BOLT, PICK UP ATTACHING (2)
29. SPROCKET, CRANKSHAFT
30. GUIDE, TIMING BELT
31. SEAL, CRANKSHAFT FRONT
32. BOLT, PUMP (OIL) ATTACHING (6)
33. BOLT, BRACE ATTACHING (1)
34. SEAL, PAN FRONT
35. GASKET, PAN SIDE
36. OIL PAN
37. SEAL, DRAIN PLUG
38. PLUG, OIL PAN DRAIN
39. BOLT, PAN ATTACHING (18)
40. GASKET, PAN SIDE
41. SEAL, PAN REAR
42. BOLT, CAP ATTACHING (10)
43. MAIN BEARING CAPS
44. MAIN BEARING INSERTS, LOWER (NON-GROOVED)
45. CRANKSHAFT
46. MAIN BEARING INSERTS, UPPER
47. OIL PRESSURE SENDING UNIT
48. DOWEL, TRANSMISSION ALIGNMENT
49. ADAPTER, OIL FILTER
50. OIL FILTER
51. PISTON
52. PISTON PIN
53. CONNECTING ROD
54. CONNECTING ROD BEARINGS
55. CONNECTING ROD CAP
56. NUT, CAP ATTACHING
57. BOLT, CAP ATTACHING

Cylinder block, crankshaft & related components exploded view

assembly.

7. Label, then disconnect all electrical connectors and vacuum hoses from cylinder head assembly.
8. Remove rocker arm cover.
9. Remove accessory drive belts.
10. Remove crankshaft pulley.
11. Remove timing belt cover.
12. Turn crankshaft until No. 1 cylinder is at TDC of compression stroke.
13. Remove distributor cap and spark plug wires as an assembly.
14. Using torque wrench adapter T81P-6254-A or equivalent, loosen both belt tensioner attaching bolts.
15. Secure belt tensioner as far left toward front of vehicle as possible.
16. Remove timing belt.
17. Disconnect EGR tube from EGR valve.
18. Disconnect fuel supply and return lines from metal connectors, located on the right side of the engine and set rubber lines aside.
19. Disconnect accelerator cable and speed control cable, if equipped.
20. On models with power steering, remove thermactor pump drive belt, pump and pump mounting bracket.
21. Disconnect altitude compensator, if equipped, from dash panel.
22. Disconnect alternator air intake tube, if equipped and electrical connectors.
23. Remove alternator and mounting bracket.
24. Raise and support vehicle.
25. Disconnect front exhaust pipe from exhaust manifold.
26. Lower vehicle.
27. Remove cylinder head bolts and washers. Discard bolts and washers.
28. Remove cylinder head with exhaust and intake manifolds attached.
29. Remove cylinder head gasket. Do not lay cylinder head flat. Damage to the spark plugs, valves or gasket surfaces may result.
30. Reverse procedure to install. **Before FINAL installation of the cylinder head, check piston squish height. Squish height is the clearance of the piston dome to the cylinder head dome at piston TDC. No rework of the cylinder head gasket surfaces (slabbing) or use of replacement components (crankshaft, piston and connecting rod) causing the assembled squish height to be over or under the tolerance specification is permitted. If no other parts other than the cylinder head gasket are replaced, the piston squish height should be within specification. If parts other than the cylinder head gasket are replaced, check the squish height. Ifthe squish height is out of specification, replace the parts again, and check the piston squish height again. Check squish height as follows:**
    a. Clean all gasket material from the mating surfaces on the cylinder head and engine block.
    b. Place a small amount of soft lead solder of appropriate thickness on the piston spherical areas.
    c. Rotate crankshaft to lower the piston in the bore and install the cylinder head gasket. A compressed (used) gasket is preferred.
    d. Install the used cylinder head bolts and tighten the head bolts to 30-44 ft. lbs. in sequence.
    e. Rotate the crankshaft to move the piston through its TDC position.
    f. Remove the cylinder head and measure the thickness of the compressed solder to determine squish height at TDC. The solder should be .039-.070 inch. **Before installing the cylinder head the crankshaft must be rotated so that the No. 1 piston is 90 degrees before top dead center (BTDC). To position the piston, turn crankshaft until the pulley keyway is at 9 o'clock position. To time the valve train to this piston position, turn the camshaft until keyway is at the 6**

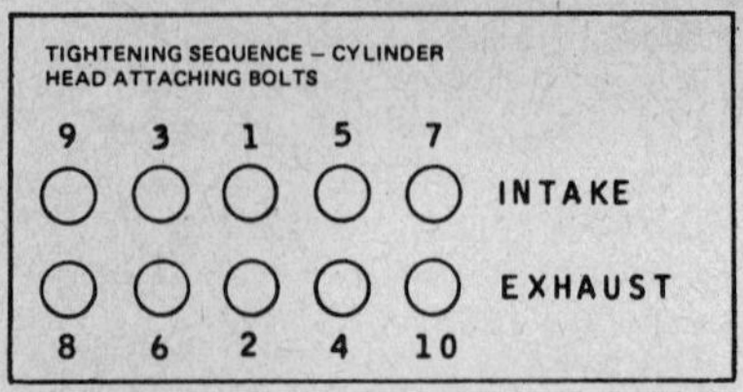

Fig. 4 Cylinder head bolt tightening sequence

o'clock position. The camshaft and the crankshaft must not be turned until after the installation of the timing gears and timing belt.

31. Torque new cylinder head bolts in sequence shown in **Fig. 4,** to 44 ft. lbs. Loosen all attaching bolts approximately two turns, then torque attaching bolts in sequence shown to 44 ft. lbs. After tightening cylinder head bolts, turn all bolts 90 degrees, again in sequence shown. Complete bolt tightening by turning all bolts in sequence an additional 90 degrees.

VALVE ARRANGEMENT
FRONT TO REAR

1.9L . . . . I-E-I-E-I-E-I-E

CAM LOBE LIFT SPECIFICATIONS

Engine	Year	Intake	Exhaust
1.9L	1985–88	.240	.240

VALVE LIFT SPECIFICATIONS

Engine	Year	Intake	Exhaust
1.9L	1985–88	.396	.396

VALVE CLEARANCE SPECIFICATIONS

Year	Engine	Valve Lash
1985-88	4-116	.059-.194①

①—With hydraulic valve lash adjuster completely collapsed.

VALVES
ADJUST

The 1.9L engine is equipped with an overhead camshaft and hydraulic lash adjuster. Valve stem to rocker arm clearance is measured with tappet completely collapsed. Perform the following procedure when measuring valve tappet clearance:

1. Rotate engine until piston of No. 1 cylinder is at TDC of compression stroke.
2. Position suitable hydraulic lifter compressor tool onto rocker arm, then slowly apply pressure to bleed tappet. Continue to apply pressure until lifter plunger bottoms. Hold tappet in this position and check clearance between rocker arm and valve stem tip using a suitable feeler gauge with less than a 3/8 inch width. Collapsed tappet gap clearance should be .059-.194 inch. If clearance is less than specified, check for worn or damaged fulcrums, tappets or camshaft lobes.
3. With No. 1 piston on TDC of compression stroke, check the following valves as outlined: Nos. 1 and 2 intake & No. 1 exhaust.
4. Rotate crankshaft 180° from present position, then check the following valves: No. 3 intake & No. 3 exhaust.
5. Rotate crankshaft 180° from present position, then check the following valves: No. 4 intake & Nos. 2 and 4 exhaust.

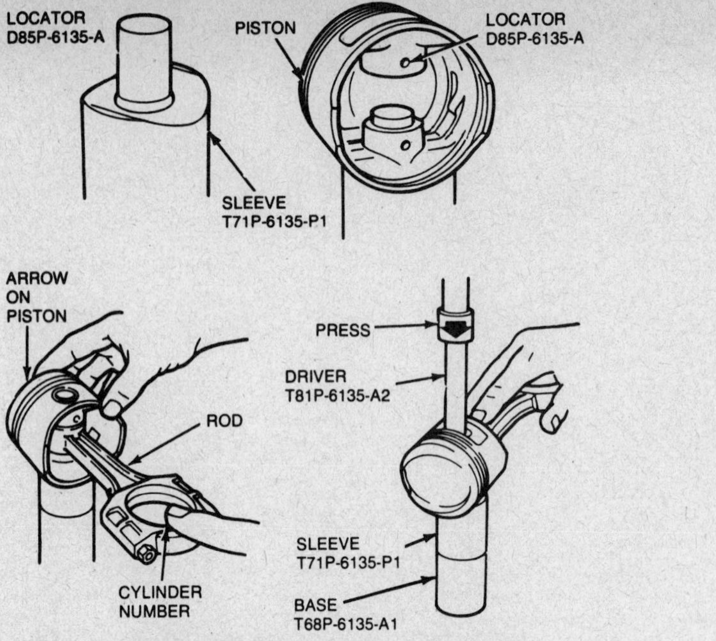

Fig. 5 Assembling piston to rod

CAMSHAFT
REPLACE

1. Disconnect battery ground cable, then remove air cleaner assembly.
2. Remove PCV hose, then the accessory drive belts.
3. Remove crankshaft pulley, then the timing belt cover.
4. Remove valve cover attaching bolts and studs, then the valve cover.
5. Set piston of No. 1 cylinder at TDC of compression stroke, then remove rocker arm hex flange nuts, fulcrums and rocker arms.
6. Remove fulcrum washers, then the tappets.
7. Remove distributor assembly, then loosen timing belt tensioner attaching bolts using torque wrench adapter tool No. T81P-6254-A or equivalent.
8. Remove timing belt, then the camshaft sprocket and key.
9. Remove thrust plate, then the fuel pump.
10. Remove ignition coil and coil bracket.
11. Remove camshaft through rear of head, toward transaxle.
12. Reverse procedure to install.
13. Apply a suitable lubricant to camshaft prior to installation, then check seal for wear and damage and replace as necessary.

PISTON & ROD
ASSEMBLE

Position locator tool D85P-6135-A or equivalent into center hole of sleeve T71P-6135-P1, **Fig. 5,** then place piston onto locator. Locator will align pin bores in piston and rods and will also serve as a pilot for piston pin. Press piston into place using tool No. T81P-6135-A2 or equivalent. Assemble piston to rod with arrow facing front of engine and numbered side of rod facing exhaust manifold side of engine, **Fig. 6.** Check side clearance between connecting rods at each crankshaft journal. Clearance should be .004-.011 inch.

TIMING BELT
REPLACE

1. Disconnect battery ground cable, then remove accessory drive belts.
2. Remove timing cover. **Align timing mark on camshaft sprocket with timing mark on cylinder head.**
3. Install timing belt cover, then ensure timing mark on crankshaft pulley aligns with TDC mark on front cover.
4. Remove timing belt cover.
5. Loosen both timing tensioner attaching bolts using torque wrench adapter T81P-6254-A or equivalent.
6. Pry tensioner away from belt as far as possible, then tighten one attaching bolt.

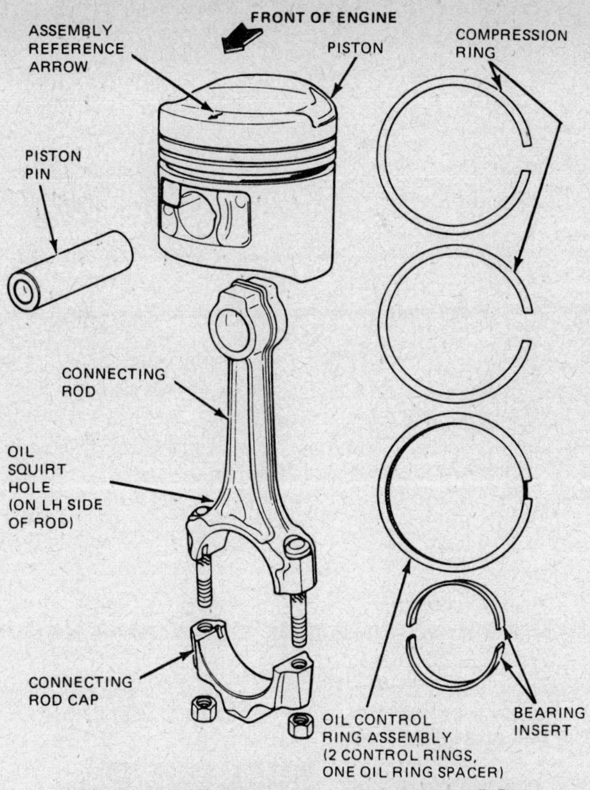

Fig. 6 Piston & rod assembly

7. Remove crankshaft pulley, then the timing belt. Discard timing belt if damaged.
8. Install timing belt over sprockets in a counterclockwise direction starting at crankshaft. Ensure belt span between crankshaft and camshaft is kept tight as belt is installed over remaining sprocket.
9. Loosen belt tensioner attaching bolt and allow to locate against belt.
10. Tighten one tensioner attaching bolt using previously mentioned tool, then install crankshaft pulley, drive plate and pulley attaching bolt.
11. Retain crankshaft pulley using tool No. YA-826, then torque pulley nut to 74-90 ft. lbs.
12. To seat timing belt on sprocket teeth, proceed as follows:
    a. Connect battery ground cable, then crank engine for approximately 30 seconds.
    b. Disconnect battery ground cable, then rotate crankshaft as necessary to align timing pointer on cam sprocket with timing mark on cylinder head.
    c. Position timing belt cover on engine, then ensure timing mark on crankshaft aligns with TDC pointer on cover.
    d. If timing marks do not align, remove belt, align timing marks and repeat steps 8-12.
13. Loosen tensioner attaching bolt, then secure crankshaft and ensure it will not rotate.
14. Using tool No. D81P-6256-A or equivalent and a suitable torque wrench, turn camshaft sprocket counterclockwise. Torque belt tensioner attaching bolt to 27-32 ft. lbs. for new belt or 10 ft. lbs. on new belt. **Ensure engine is cold when applying torque to camshaft sprocket. Do not set torque on hot engine.**
15. Install timing belt cover, accessory drive belts, then connect battery ground cable.

CRANKSHAFT OIL SEAL SERVICE

FRONT

1. Remove timing belt as described under "Timing Belt, Replace."
2. Remove crankshaft pulley, then the front seal.
3. Install new front seal using tool No. T81P-6700-A or equivalent.
4. Install crankshaft pulley, then the timing belt.

REAR

1. Remove transaxle assembly.
2. Remove rear cover plate, then the flywheel.
3. Using a suitable tool, punch a hole into seal metal surface between lip and block. Screw in threaded end of suitable slide hammer, then remove seal. Use care not to damage oil seal surface.
4. Inspect crankshaft seal area for damage that may cause new seal to leak. If damage is present, repair or replace crankshaft as necessary.
5. Apply a suitable lubricant to new seal, then install seal using tool No. T81P-6701-A or equivalent.

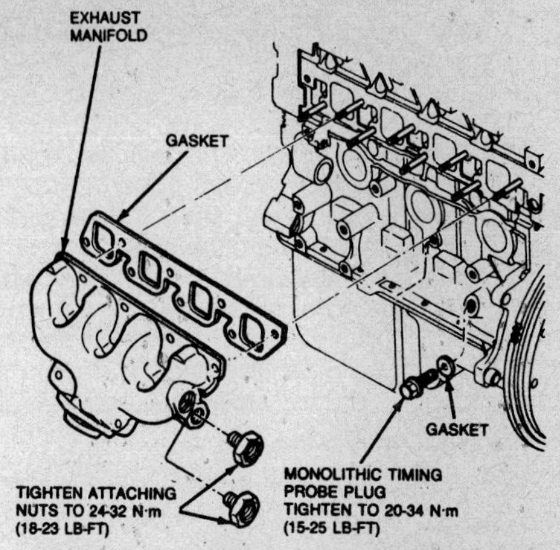

Fig. 7 Exhaust manifold assembly

6. Tighten bolts evenly as to allow seal to seat straight, then install flywheel and torque attaching bolts to 54-64 ft. lbs.
7. Install rear cover plate, then the transaxle.

EXHAUST MANIFOLD REPLACE

1. Disconnect battery ground cable, then remove air cleaner tray.
2. Disconnect electric cooling fan electrical connector, then remove radiator shroud attaching bolts and shroud.
3. Disconnect thermactor tube at exhaust manifold, then remove air conditioning hose bracket.
4. Remove exhaust manifold retaining nuts, then raise and support vehicle.
5. Remove anti-roll brace, then disconnect water tube brackets.
6. Disconnect exhaust pipe at catalytic converter, then remove exhaust manifold.
7. Reverse procedure to install. Refer to **Fig. 7,** during installation procedure.

INTAKE MANIFOLD REPLACE

EXCEPT EFI ENGINES

1. Raise and secure hood in open position, then disconnect battery ground cable.
2. Partially drain cooling system, then disconnect heater hose from intake manifold.
3. Remove air cleaner assembly, then disconnect vacuum hoses.
4. Disconnect electrical connectors from choke cap wire, bowl vent and idle fuel solenoid, then remove EGR supply tube.
5. Raise and support vehicle, then remove PVS hose connectors using tool No. T81P-8564-A or equivalent. Label connectors, then position aside.
6. Remove bottom three intake manifold attaching nuts, then lower vehicle.
7. Disconnect fuel line at fuel filter, then the return line at carburetor.
8. Disconnect accelerator, then the speed control cable, if equipped.
9. On models with automatic transaxle, Disconnect throttle valve linkage at

carburetor, then remove cable bracket attaching bolts.
10. On models with power steering, remove thermactor pump drive belt, pump, pump mounting bracket, then the thermactor bypass hose.
11. Remove fuel pump, then the remaining intake valve attaching bolts.
12. Reverse procedures to install. Tighten retaining nuts in sequence shown, **Fig. 8,** to torque value listed in Engine Tightening Specifications.

EFI ENGINES

Refer to "Fuel Pump, Replace" (electric) to relieve fuel system pressure.

To remove upper intake manifold assembly, proceed as follows:
1. Disconnect engine air cleaner outlet tube from throttle body.
2. Unplug throttle position sensor from wiring harness.
3. Disconnect vacuum lines from upper manifold assembly.
4. Disconnect EGR tube at manifold connection.
5. Unplug air bypass valve connector.
6. Remove manifold upper support bracket top bolt.
7. Remove five upper manifold attaching bolts.
8. Remove upper manifold assembly and gasket.
9. Reverse procedure to install.

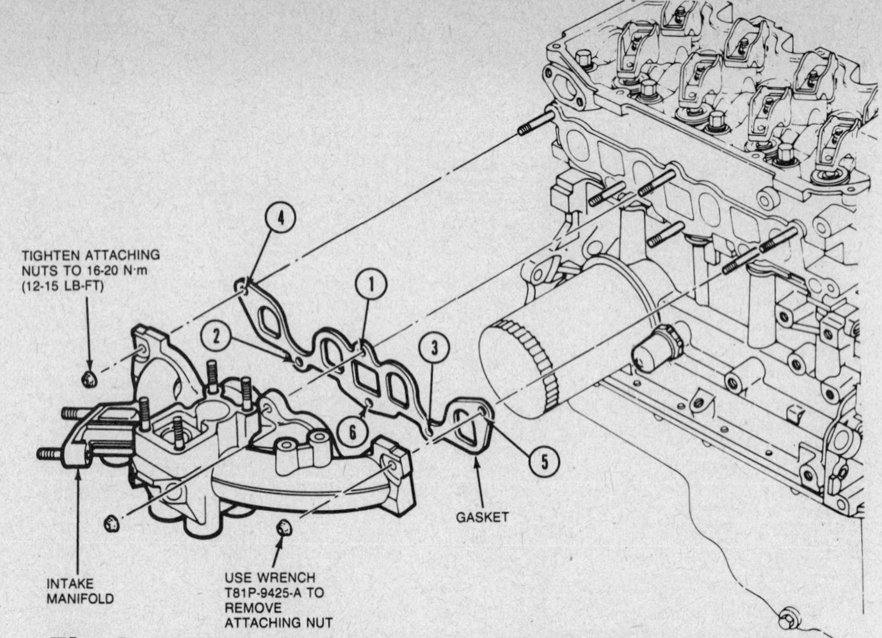

Fig. 8 Intake manifold bolt tightening sequence

OIL PAN REPLACE

1. Disconnect battery ground cable.
2. Raise and support vehicle.
3. Drain oil from engine.
4. Disconnect starter cable.
5. Remove starter motor from engine.
6. Remove two oil pan-to-transaxle attaching bolts.
7. Disconnect exhaust pipe from manifold and converter.
8. Remove oil pan attaching bolts and oil pan.
9. Reverse procedure to install. If the oil pan is installed on engine with engine removed from vehicle, a transaxle case or equivalent fixture must be bolted to the block to align the oil pan up, flush with the rear face of the block. Torque the two M-10 pan-to-transaxle bolts to 30-40 ft. lbs., then loosen bolts one-half turn. Torque oil pan flange-to-cylinder block M-8 bolts to 15-22 ft. lbs. Torque the two M-10 pan-to-transaxle bolts to 29-40 ft. lbs.

OIL PUMP REPLACE

1. Secure hood in open position, then disconnect battery ground cable.
2. Loosen alternator bolt at adjusting arm, then remove accessory drive belt.
3. Remove timing belt cover. Place No. 1 cylinder at T.D.C. of compression stroke by turning crankshaft until pulley keyway is at 12 o'clock and camshaft sprocket keyway is at 6 o'clock. Loosen belt tensioner, then pry tensioner away from belt and tighten one attaching bolt.
4. Disengage timing belt from camshaft sprocket, water pump sprocket and crankshaft sprocket. Raise vehicle on a suitable hoist, then drain crankcase.
5. Remove timing belt, then the crankshaft drive plate assembly.
6. Remove crankshaft pulley, then the crankshaft sprocket.
7. Disconnect starter cable at starter, then remove knee brace from engine.
8. Remove starter, then the rear section of knee brace and inspection plate at transaxle.
9. Remove oil pan retaining bolts, then the oil pan.
10. Remove front and rear oil pan seals and side gaskets, then the oil pump attaching bolts, oil pump and gasket.
11. Remove oil pump seal.
12. Reverse procedure to install. Apply a suitable sealant to oil pan gasket surfaces. Torque oil pump screen and pickup tube attaching bolts to 6-9 ft. lbs. Torque oil pump attaching bolts to 5-7 ft. lbs. Torque oil pan attaching bolts to 15-20 ft. lbs.

BELT TENSION DATA

Belt	New Lbs.	Used Lbs.
1986–88		
Air Pump (Low Mount) Less Power Steering	**90-130**	**80-100**
Air Pump (High Mount) & Power Steering Pump	**50-90**	**40-60**
Alternator	**150-190**	**140-160**

FUEL PUMP REPLACE

MECHANICAL

1. Loosen fuel supply attaching nuts at fuel pump outlet using suitable tool.
2. Loosen fuel pump attaching bolts approximately two turns, then manually rotate engine to position pump pushrod on low side of cam.
3. Remove rubber hose and clamp from fuel pump inlet, then disconnect fuel line from fuel pump inlet.
4. Disconnect fuel line from fuel pump outlet, then remove pump attaching bolts, fuel pump gasket and pushrod.
5. Reverse procedure to install.

ELECTRIC

Fuel supply lines will remain pressurized for long periods of time after engine shutdown. This pressure must be relieved before any service is attempted. A valve is provided on the fuel rail assembly for this purpose. To relieve system pressure, remove air cleaner assembly and connect pressure gauge tool No. T80L-9974-A or equivalent, onto fuel diagnostic valve on the fuel rail assembly. Gradually release fuel system pressure.
1. Disconnect battery ground cable.
2. Depressurize fuel system as described previously.
3. Raise and support vehicle.
4. Loosen fuel pump mounting bolt until fuel pump can be removed from vehicle.
5. Remove parking brake cable from pump clip.
6. Disconnect electrical connector and fuel pump outlet fitting.
7. Disconnect fuel pump inlet line from pump. **Either drain fuel tank or raise**

end of fuel line above fuel level in tank to prevent fuel siphon action.

8. Remove pump from vehicle.
9. Reverse procedure to install. To pressurize fuel system, proceed as follows:
   a. Install pressure tool gauge No. T80L-9974-A or equivalent onto fuel rail pressure fitting.
   b. Turn ignition switch to ON position for 2 seconds and repeat turning ignition switch ON and OFF at 2 second intervals until gauge tool indicates approximately 35 psi.

WATER PUMP
REPLACE

1. Disconnect battery ground cable, then drain cooling system.
2. Remove accessory drive belts, then the engine front timing cover.
3. Place No. 1 cylinder at T.D.C. of compression stroke by turning crankshaft until pulley keyway is at 12 o'clock and camshaft sprocket keyway is at 6 o'clock. Loosen belt tensioner, then pry tensioner away from belt and tighten one attaching bolt.
4. Secure tensioner as far left as possible, then remove timing belt.
5. Remove camshaft sprocket, then the rearward front timing cover stud.
6. Disconnect heater return tube hose connection at water pump inlet tube.
7. Remove water pump inlet tube fasteners, then the tube and gasket.
8. Remove water pump to cylinder block bolts, then the water pump.
9. Reverse procedure to install. Refer to "Timing Belt, Replace" for proper belt tension procedures.

4-140 (2.3L) Gasoline Engine Section

INDEX

ENGINE MOUNTS
REPLACE

Refer to **Figs. 1 through 5** when replacing engine mounts.

ENGINE
REPLACE

Engine and transaxle are removed as an assembly.

1. Mark position of hood hinges, then remove hood.
2. Disconnect battery ground cable, then remove air cleaner assembly.
3. Remove lower radiator hose and drain coolant from engine. Remove upper radiator hose from engine.
4. On models equipped with automatic transaxle, disconnect transaxle cooler lines from rubber hoses below radiator.
5. Remove coil assembly from cylinder head. Disconnect coolant fan electrical connector.
6. Remove radiator shroud, cooling fan and radiator.
7. Carefully discharge refrigerant from air conditioning system, if equipped. Remove inlet and outlet lines from compressor.
8. Mark and disconnect all electrical and vacuum lines from engine.
9. On models equipped with automatic transaxle, disconnect TV linkage from transaxle. On models equipped with manual transaxle, disconnect clutch cable from transaxle shift lever.
10. Disconnect accelerator linkage, fuel supply and return lines from engine.
11. Disconnect thermactor pump discharge hose from pump.
12. Disconnect power steering pressure and return lines from pump, if equipped. Remove power steering line bracket from cylinder head.
13. Install engine support tool No. D79P-6000-A or equivalent, to engine lifting eye.
14. Raise and support vehicle.
15. Remove starter cable from starter.
16. Remove air hose from catalytic converter.
17. Remove bolt securing exhaust pipe bracket to oil pan. Remove two exhaust pipes to exhaust manifold nuts, then pull exhaust pipe out of rubber insulating grommets and position aside.
18. Disconnect speedometer cable from transaxle.
19. Remove water pump inlet hose from engine.
20. Remove bolts securing control arms to body. Remove stabilizer bar bracket bolts and brackets.
21. Remove half shaft assembly from transaxle.
22. On models equipped with manual transaxle, remove roll restrictor nuts from transaxle. Remove shift stabilizer bar to transaxle bolts. Remove shift mechanism to shift shaft nut and bolt from transaxle.
23. On models equipped with automatic transaxle, disconnect manual shift cable clip from transaxle shift lever. Remove manual shift linkage bracket bolts and bracket from transaxle.
24. Remove nuts and lefthand rear No. 4 insulator mount bracket from body bracket.
25. Lower vehicle and install suitable lifting hoist to engine. **Do not allow front wheels to touch floor.**
26. Remove engine support tool No. D79L-6000-A or equivalent from engine.
27. Remove righthand No. 3 insulator intermediate bracket to engine bracket bolts and intermediate bracket to insulator nuts. Remove nut on the bottom of double ended stud which secures intermediate bracket to engine bracket. Remove bracket.
28. Carefully lower engine and transaxle assembly from vehicle.
29. Reverse procedure to install. When installing engine/transaxle assembly, position assembly directly below engine compartment. Slowly lower vehicle over engine and transaxle. Do not allow front wheels to contact floor.

CYLINDER HEAD
REPLACE

1. Disconnect battery ground cable.
2. Remove lower radiator hose and drain coolant from engine.
3. Disconnect heater hose from fitting located under intake manifold.
4. Disconnect upper radiator hose from cylinder head.
5. Disconnect electric cooling fan switch from electrical connector.
6. Remove air cleaner assembly from engine.
7. Mark and disconnect all vacuum hoses from cylinder head.
8. Remove rocker arm cover.
9. Remove all accessory drive belts from engine.

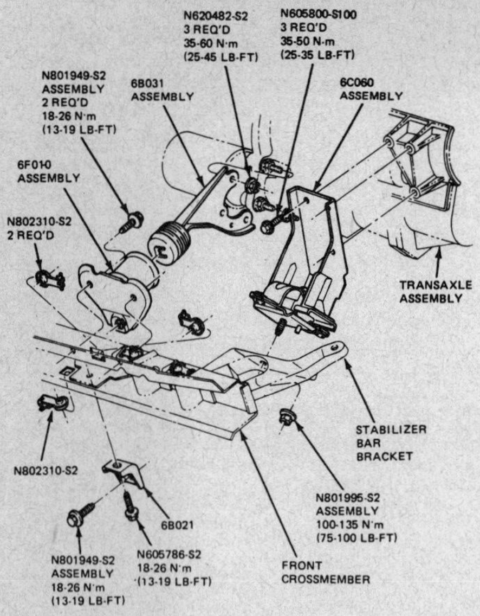

LEFT HAND FRONT NO. 1 INSULATOR
MTX 4 AND 5-SPEED APPLICATIONS

Fig. 1 Lefthand front No. 1 insulator. 4 & 5 speed manual transaxle

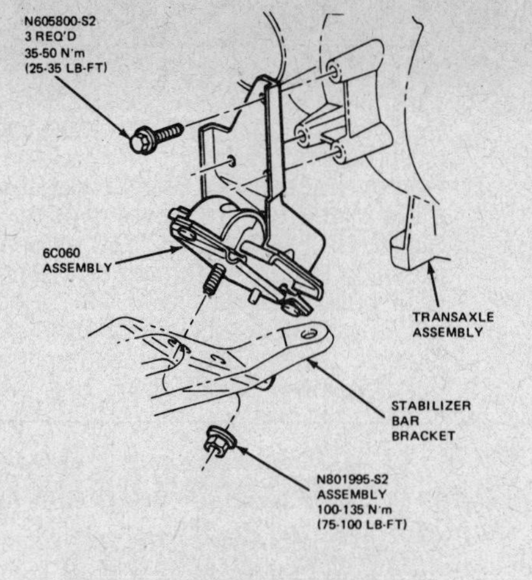

LEFT HAND FRONT NO. 1 INSULATOR
ATX APPLICATIONS

Fig. 2 Lefthand front No. 1 insulator. Automatic transaxle

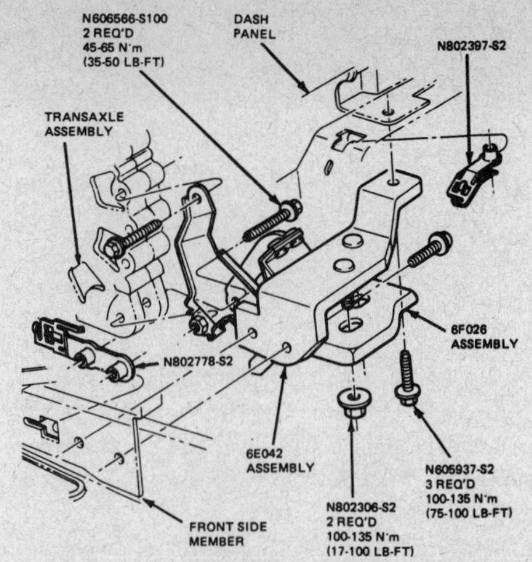

Fig. 3 Lefthand rear No. 4 insulator. 4 speed manual transaxle

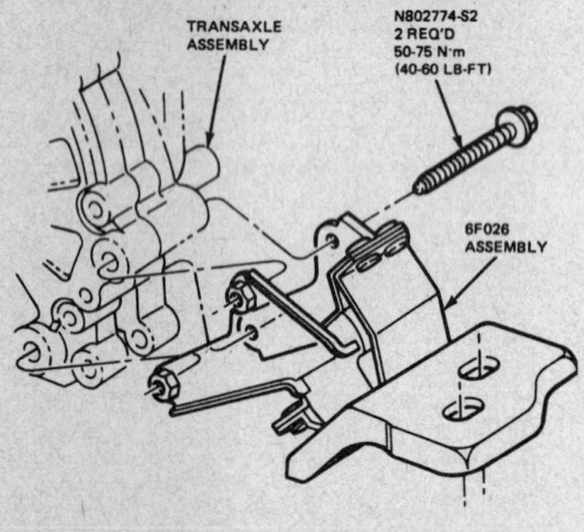

LEFT HAND REAR NO. 4 INSULATOR
MTX 5-SPEED AND ATX APPLIATIONS
(SAME AS MTX 4-SPEED EXCEPT AS SHOWN)

Fig. 4 Lefthand rear No. 4 insulator. 5 speed manual & automatic transaxle

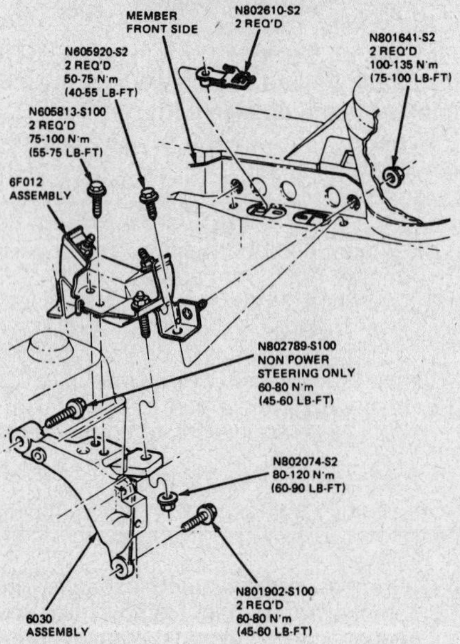

ALL APPLICATIONS

Fig. 5 Righthand No. 3A insulator. All

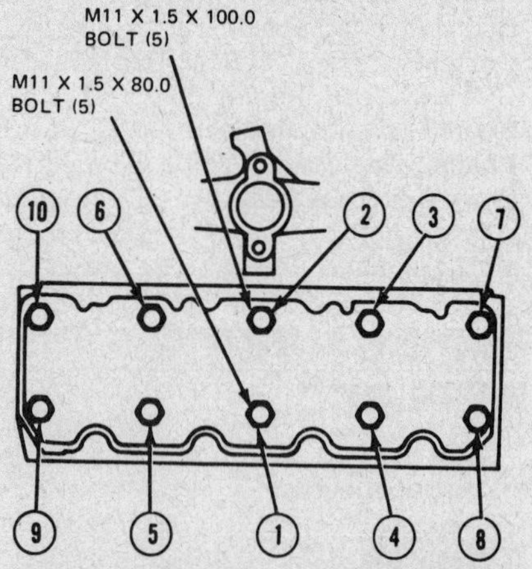

Fig. 6 Cylinder head bolt tightening sequence

10. Remove distributor cap and spark plug wires as an assembly.
11. Disconnect EGR tube from EGR valve. Disconnect choke cap wire.
12. Disconnect fuel supply and return lines from rubber connector.
13. Disconnect accelerator cable and speed control cable, if equipped.
14. Loosen thermactor pump belt pulley.
15. Raise and support vehicle.
16. Disconnect exhaust system from exhaust pipe. Lower vehicle.
17. Remove cylinder head bolts, cylinder head and gasket with thermactor pump, exhaust and intake manifolds attached. **Do not lay cylinder head flat. Damage to spark plugs or gasket surfaces may result.**
18. Reverse procedure to install. Torque cylinder head bolts in sequence shown in **Fig. 6,** to 53-59 ft. lbs. on early 1984 production models, 81 ft. lbs. on later production 1984 models or 70-76 ft. lbs. on 1985-86 models.

VALVE ARRANGEMENT

FRONT TO REAR

4-140 . . . . I-E-I-E-E-I-E-I

VALVE CLEARANCE SPECIFICATIONS

Valve Lash Year	Engine	Int.	Exh.
1984-88	4-140	.070-.170①	

①—With hydraulic valve lash adjuster completely collapsed.

HYDRAULIC VALVE LIFTERS

REPLACE

Before replacing a hydraulic valve lifter for noisy operation, ensure the noise is not caused by improper collapsed tappet gap, worn rocker arms, pushrods or valve tips.

To check collapsed tappet gap, proceed as follows:

1. Rotate camshaft to position A as shown in **Fig. 7.**
2. Check intake and exhaust valves on compression stroke under camshaft position A. With camshaft in position A, tappet gap should be .072-.174 inch with tappet collapsed on base circle. Check No. 1 cylinder intake and exhaust valves. Check No. 2 cylinder intake valve. Check No. 3 cylinder exhaust valve. Tighten fulcrum bolts to specifications.
3. Rotate camshaft 180 degrees to position B as shown in **Fig. 7.** Check No. 2 cylinder exhaust valve. Check No. 3 cylinder intake valve. Check No. 4 cylinder intake and exhaust valve. Tighten fulcrum bolts to specification.

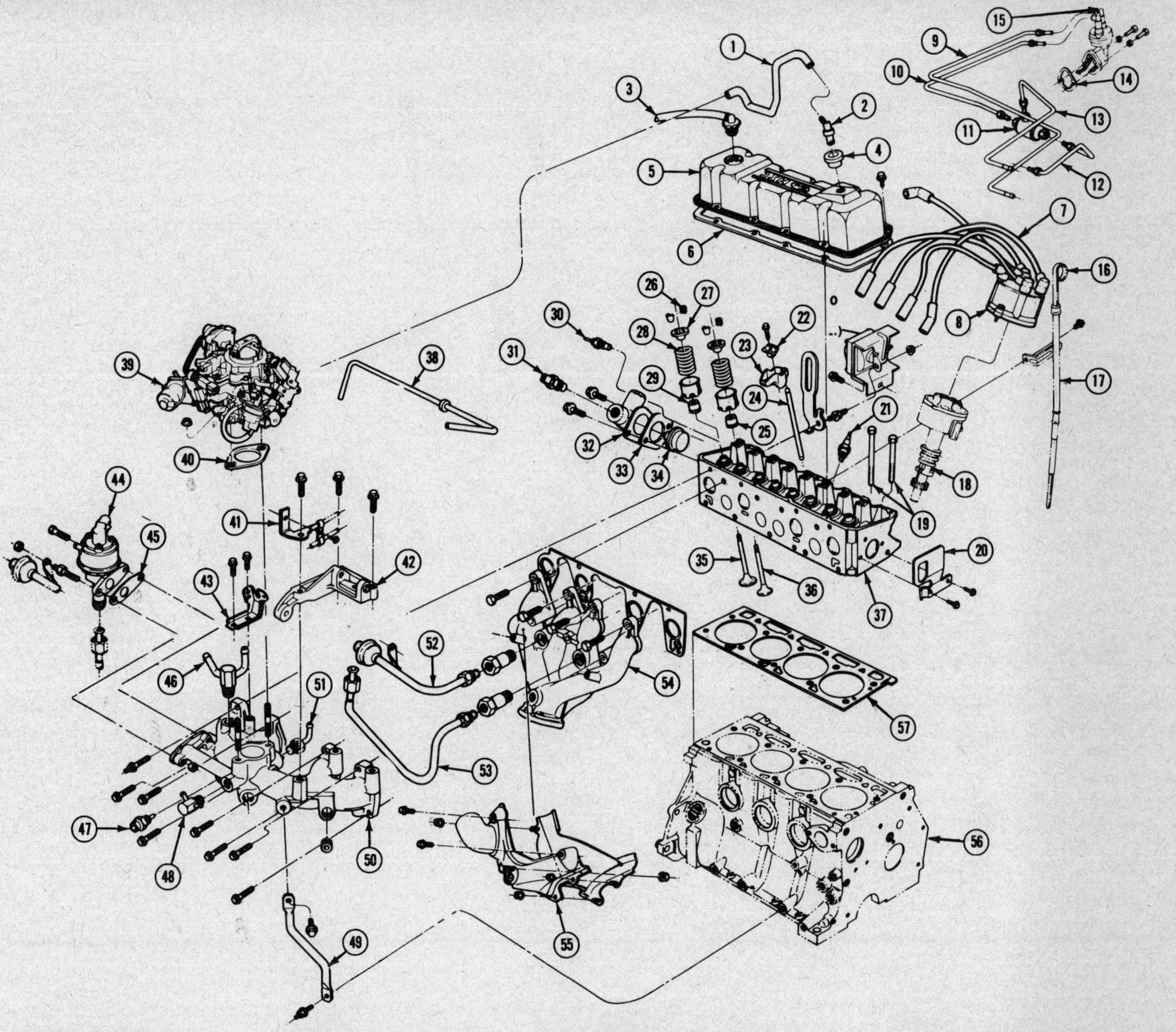

1 VACUUM TUBE
2 VENT VALVE ASSEMBLY
3 TUBE ASSEMBLY
4 GROMMET
5 ROCKER ARM COVER
6 ROCKER ARM COVER GASKET
7 SPARK PLUG WIRES
8 DISTRIBUTOR CAP
9 FUEL LINES
10 FUEL LINES
11 FUEL FILTER
12 FUEL FILTER LINES
13 FUEL FILTER LINES
14 FUEL PUMP GASKET
15 FUEL PUMP ASSEMBLY
16 DIPSTICK
17 DIPSTICK TUBE ASSEMBLY
18 DISTRIBUTOR
19 CYLINDER HEAD BOLTS
20 ENGINE LIFTING EYE
21 SPARK PLUG
22 ROCKER ARM FULCRUM
23 ROCKER ARM
24 PUSHROD
25 EXHAUST VALVE STEM SEAL
26 KEY
27 SPRING RETAINER
28 SPRING
29 INTAKE VALVE STEM SEAL
30 TEMPERATURE SENSOR
31 FAN SWITCH
32 WATER OUTLET CONNECTION
33 WATER OUTLET CONNECTION GASKET
34 THERMOSTAT ASSEMBLY
35 INTAKE VALVE
36 EXHAUST VALVE
37 CYLINDER HEAD
38 CARBURETOR FUEL LINE
39 CARBURETOR ASSEMBLY
40 CARBURETOR GASKET
41 BRACKET
42 BRACKET
43 ACCELERATOR SHAFT BRACKET
44 EGR VALVE ASSEMBLY
45 EGR VALVE GASKET
46 VACUUM FITTING
47 SENSOR
48 VACUUM FITTING
49 BRACE
50 INTAKE MANIFOLD ASSEMBLY
51 VACUUM FITTING
52 TUBE ASSEMBLY
53 TUBE ASSEMBLY
54 EXHAUST MANIFOLD
55 HEAT SHIELD
56 CYLINDER BLOCK
57 CYLINDER HEAD GASKET

Cylinder head assembly & components

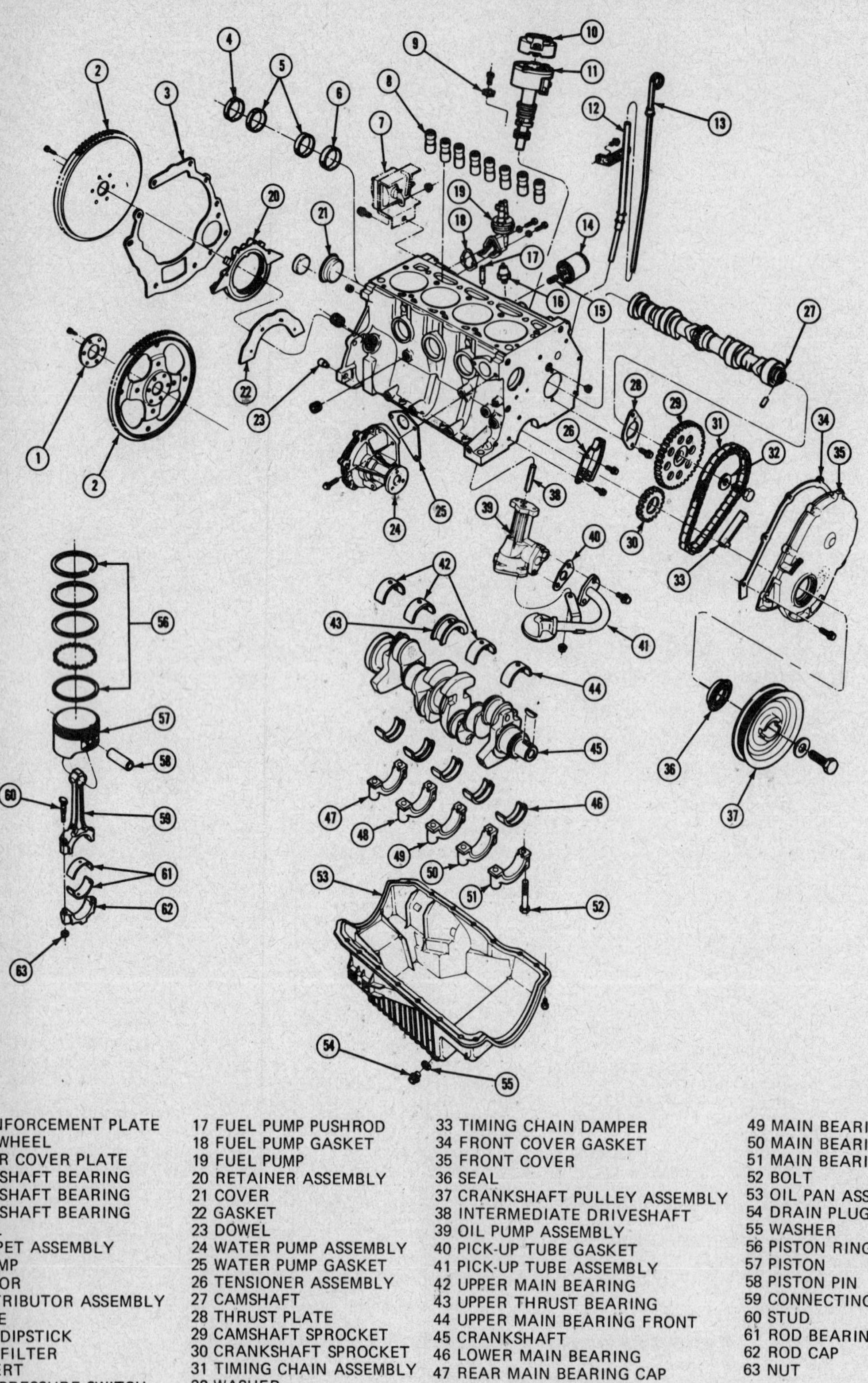

1 REINFORCEMENT PLATE
2 FLYWHEEL
3 REAR COVER PLATE
4 CAMSHAFT BEARING
5 CAMSHAFT BEARING
6 CAMSHAFT BEARING
7 COIL
8 TAPPET ASSEMBLY
9 CLAMP
10 ROTOR
11 DISTRIBUTOR ASSEMBLY
12 TUBE
13 OIL DIPSTICK
14 OIL FILTER
15 INSERT
16 OIL PRESSURE SWITCH
17 FUEL PUMP PUSHROD
18 FUEL PUMP GASKET
19 FUEL PUMP
20 RETAINER ASSEMBLY
21 COVER
22 GASKET
23 DOWEL
24 WATER PUMP ASSEMBLY
25 WATER PUMP GASKET
26 TENSIONER ASSEMBLY
27 CAMSHAFT
28 THRUST PLATE
29 CAMSHAFT SPROCKET
30 CRANKSHAFT SPROCKET
31 TIMING CHAIN ASSEMBLY
32 WASHER
33 TIMING CHAIN DAMPER
34 FRONT COVER GASKET
35 FRONT COVER
36 SEAL
37 CRANKSHAFT PULLEY ASSEMBLY
38 INTERMEDIATE DRIVESHAFT
39 OIL PUMP ASSEMBLY
40 PICK-UP TUBE GASKET
41 PICK-UP TUBE ASSEMBLY
42 UPPER MAIN BEARING
43 UPPER THRUST BEARING
44 UPPER MAIN BEARING FRONT
45 CRANKSHAFT
46 LOWER MAIN BEARING
47 REAR MAIN BEARING CAP
48 MAIN BEARING CAP
49 MAIN BEARING CAP
50 MAIN BEARING CAP
51 MAIN BEARING CAP FRONT
52 BOLT
53 OIL PAN ASSEMBLY
54 DRAIN PLUG
55 WASHER
56 PISTON RINGS
57 PISTON
58 PISTON PIN
59 CONNECTING ROD
60 STUD
61 ROD BEARINGS
62 ROD CAP
63 NUT

Cylinder block assembly & components

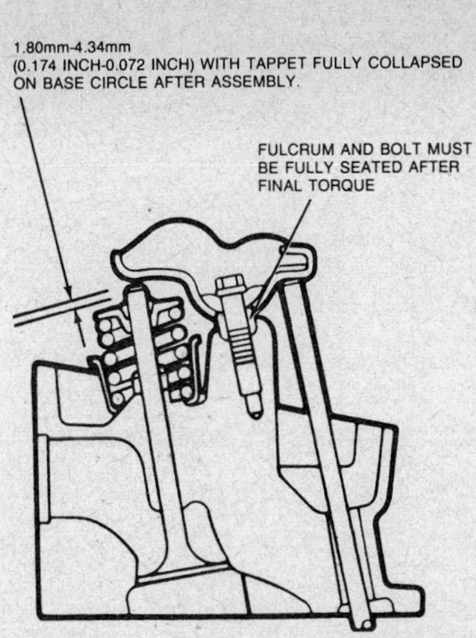

Fig. 7 Checking collapsed tappet gap

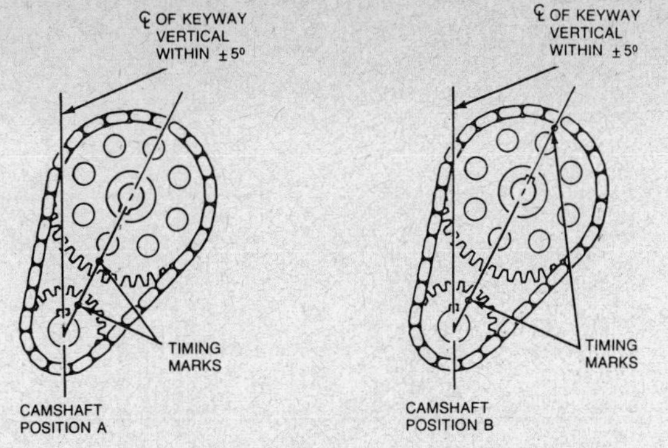

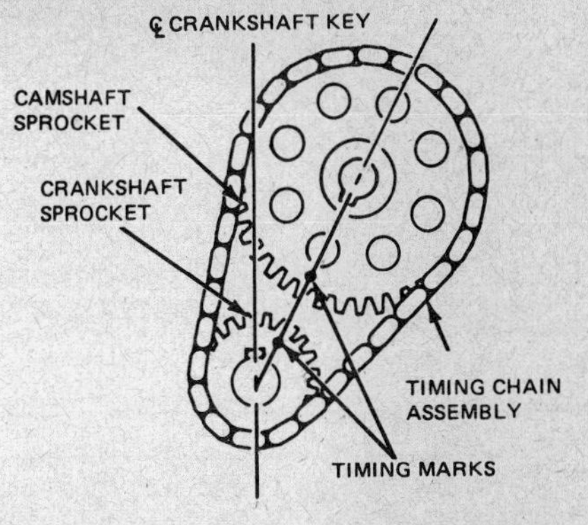

Fig. 9 Valve timing marks

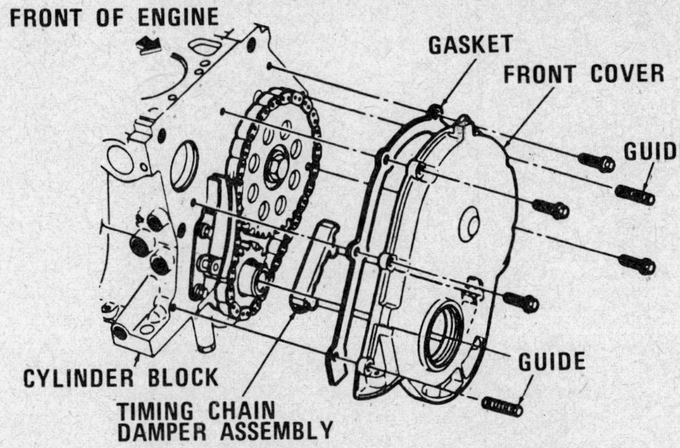

Fig. 8 Front cover removal

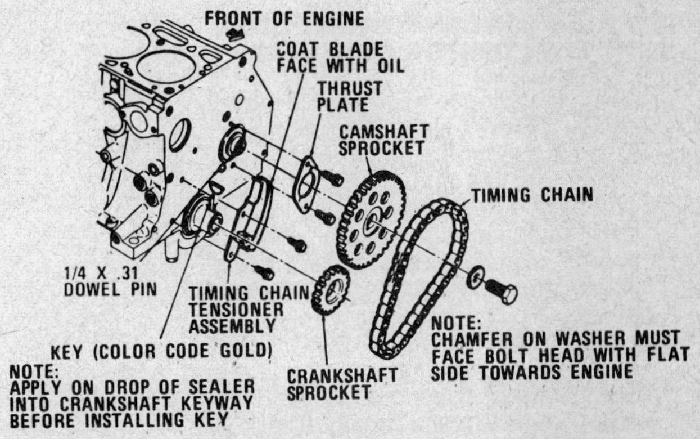

Fig. 10 Timing chain & sprockets removal

Remove lifters as follows:

1. Remove cylinder head as described previously.
2. Using a suitable magnet, remove lifters from lifter bores.
3. Place valve lifters in a rack so they can be installed in their original positions. **If the lifters are stuck in their bores by excessive varnish or gum buildup, use tool No. T70L-6500-A or equivalent to remove valve lifters.**
4. Reverse procedure to install.

ROCKER ARM COVER

REPLACE

1. Disconnect battery ground cable.
2. Remove oil filler cap.
3. Disconnect PCV hose from PCV valve.
4. Disconnect throttle linkage cable from rocker arm cover.
5. Disconnect speed control cable from rocker arm cover, if equipped.
6. Remove rocker arm cover bolts and cover.
7. Reverse procedure to install.

FRONT COVER OIL SEAL

REMOVAL

The following removal and installation procedure can only be performed with the engine removed from the vehicle. Remove engine as described under "Engine, Replace."

1. Remove bolt and washer from crankshaft pulley.
2. Using tool No. T77F-4220-B1 or equivalent, remove crankshaft pulley.
3. Using tool No. T74P-6700-A or equivalent, remove front cover oil seal.

INSTALLATION

1. Coat new front cover oil seal with a suitable lubricant.
2. Using tool No. T83T-4676-A or equivalent, install oil seal into front cover. Drive oil seal in until it is fully seated into front cover recess. Check oil seal after installation to ensure spring is properly positioned in oil seal.
3. Install crankshaft pulley, washer and bolt. Torque crankshaft pulley bolt to specification.

FRONT COVER, TIMING CHAIN & SPROCKETS

REPLACE

The following procedure can only be performed with the engine removed from the vehicle. Remove engine as described under "Engine, Replace."

1. Remove dipstick, crankshaft pulley bolt, washer and pulley.
2. Remove front cover bolts and front cover, **Fig. 8.**
3. Align camshaft and crankshaft sprocket timing marks as shown in **Fig. 9.**
4. Remove camshaft sprocket bolt and washer.
5. Remove sprockets and timing chain from engine as an assembly, **Fig. 10.** Check timing chain vibration damper for wear. Replace if necessary.
6. Remove oil pan.
7. Reverse procedure to install. Ensure to align timing marks as shown in **Fig. 8.**

CAMSHAFT

REPLACE

The following procedure can only be performed with the engine removed from the vehicle. Remove engine as described under "Engine, Replace."

1. Remove dipstick. Drain coolant and oil from engine.
2. Remove accessory drive belts and pulleys.
3. Position No. 1 piston at TDC with distributor rotor at No. 1 firing position, then remove distributor.

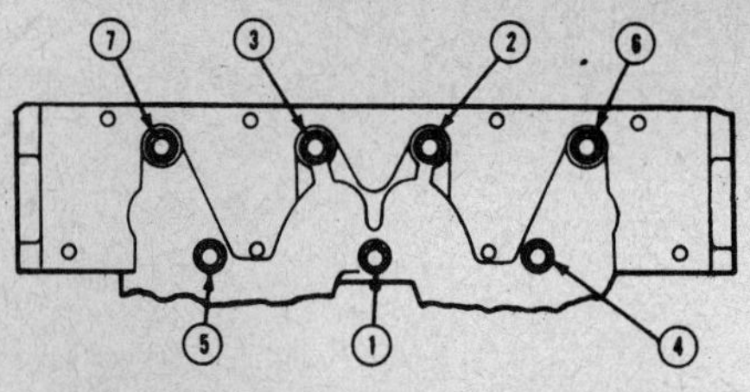

Fig. 11 Exhaust manifold bolt tightening sequence

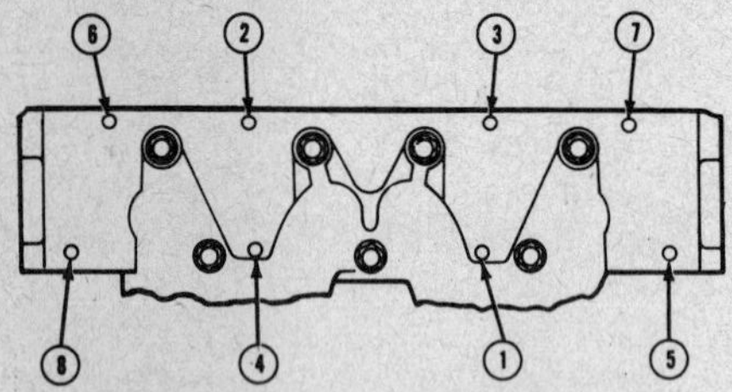

Fig. 12 Intake manifold bolt tightening sequence

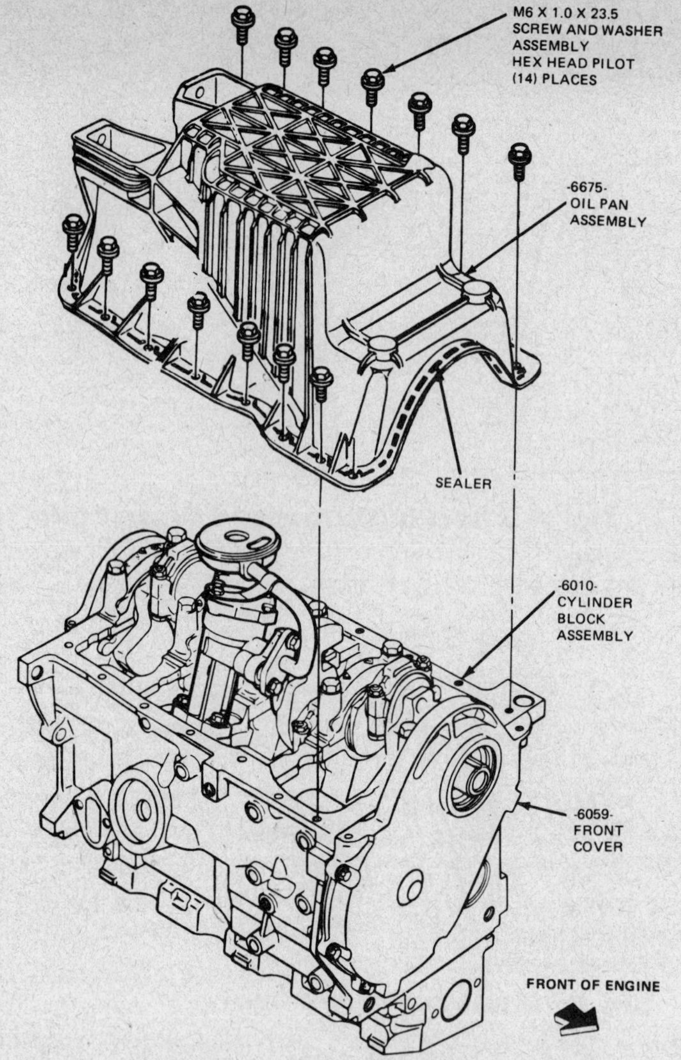

Fig. 13 Oil pan removal

4. Remove cylinder head as described under "Cylinder Head, Replace."
5. Using a suitable magnet, remove hydraulic tappets and position in order so that they can be installed in their original locations. If tappets are stuck in their bores, use tool No. T70L-6500A or equivalent to remove tappets.
6. Loosen then remove fan drive belt, fan and crankshaft pulley.
7. Remove front cover as described under "Front Cover, Timing Chain & Sprockets, Replace."
8. Remove fuel pump, gasket and fuel pump pushrod.
9. Remove timing chain, sprockets and timing chain tensioner as described under "Front Cover, Timing Chain & Sprockets, Replace."
10. Remove camshaft thrust plate. Carefully remove camshaft from engine to avoid damaging camshaft bearings, journals and lobes.
11. Reverse procedure to install. Lubricate camshaft with suitable oil before installing. Ensure No. 1 piston is at TDC with distributor rotor at No. 1 firing position.

MAIN BEARINGS

Main bearings are available in standard sizes and undersizes of .010, .020, .030 and .040 inch.

CRANKSHAFT REAR OIL SEAL

REPLACE

1. Remove engine and transaxle from vehicle as described under "Engine, Replace."
2. Remove transaxle from engine.
3. Remove rear cover plate.
4. Using a suitable tool, punch a hole into the seal metal surface between the lip and block. Using Tool No. T77L-9533-B or equivalent, remove seal.
5. Reverse procedure to install.

INTAKE & EXHAUST MANIFOLD

REPLACE

1. Disconnect battery ground cable and drain coolant from engine.
2. Disconnect accelerator cable.
3. Remove air cleaner assembly and heat stove duct from heat shield.
4. Disconnect all vacuum lines from intake manifold.
5. Remove thermactor belt from pulley, thermactor hose and thermactor pump from engine.
6. Remove exhaust pipe to exhaust manifold nuts and disconnect exhaust pipe from exhaust manifold.
7. Remove exhaust manifold heat shield.
8. Disconnect EGO sensor electrical connector.
9. Disconnect thermactor check valve hose from tube assembly. Remove EGR valve bracket nuts and EGR valve bracket.
10. Disconnect water inlet hose from intake manifold.
11. Disconnect EGR hose from EGR valve.
12. Remove bolts, intake manifold and gasket from engine.
13. Remove bolts and exhaust manifold from engine.
14. Reverse procedure to install. Torque exhaust manifold bolts in two steps. Torque bolts in sequence shown in **Fig. 11** to 7-10 ft. lbs., then 20-30 ft. lbs. Torque intake manifold bolts in sequence shown in **Fig. 12** to 15-23 ft. lbs.

OIL PAN

REPLACE

1. Disconnect battery ground cable.
2. Raise and support vehicle.
3. Drain coolant and oil from engine.
4. On models equipped with manual transaxle, remove roll restrictor.
5. Remove starter from engine.
6. Disconnect exhaust pipe from oil pan.
7. Remove engine coolant tube located at the lower radiator hose, at the water pump and from tabs on oil pan.
8. Remove oil pan bolts and oil pan, **Fig. 13,** from engine.
9. Reverse procedure to install.

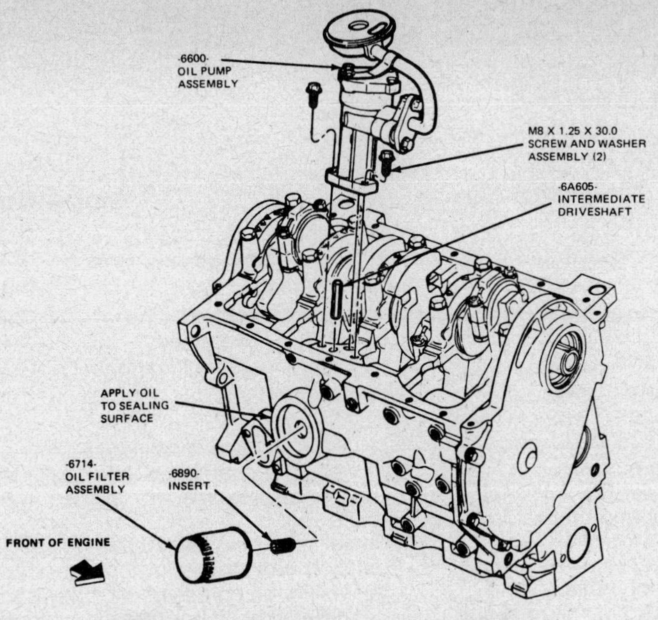

Fig. 14 Oil pump removal

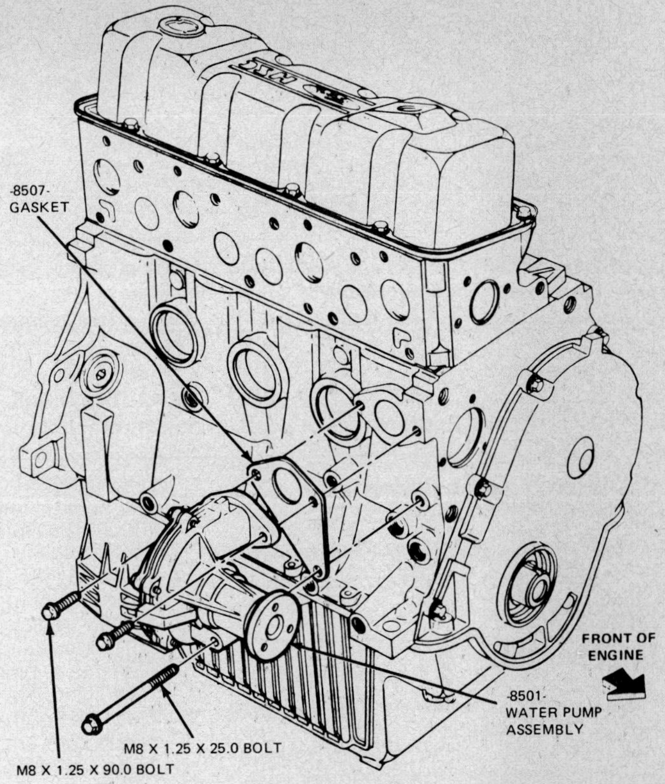

Fig. 15 Water pump removal

OIL PUMP REPLACE

1. Disconnect battery ground cable.
2. Remove oil pan as described under "Oil Pan, Replace."
3. Remove oil pump bolts and oil pump, **Fig. 14**, from engine. Remove intermediate driveshaft from oil pump.
4. Reverse procedure to install.

WATER PUMP REPLACE

1. Disconnect battery ground cable and drain coolant from engine.
2. Loosen thermactor pump adjusting bolt and remove belt.
3. Remove thermactor air pump hose clamp, thermactor pump bracket bolts, pump and bracket assembly from engine.
4. Loosen water pump idler pulley bolt and remove belt from water pump pulley.
5. Remove water pump inlet tube.
6. Remove water pump bolts and water pump, **Fig. 15.**
7. Reverse procedure to install.

FUEL PUMP REPLACE

Fuel supply lines will remain pressurized for long periods of time after engine shutdown. This pressure must be relieved before any service is attempted. A valve is provided on the fuel rail assembly for this purpose. To relieve system pressure, remove air cleaner assembly and connect pressure gauge tool No. T80L-9974-A or equivalent onto fuel valve on fuel rail assembly.

1. Disconnect battery ground cable.
2. Depressurize fuel system as described previously.
3. Remove fuel from fuel tank by pumping fuel out of fuel filler neck.
4. Raise and support vehicle.
5. Disconnect then remove fuel filler neck.
6. Support fuel tank, then remove tank support straps. Lower fuel tank partially and remove fuel lines, electrical connectors and vent lines from tank.
7. Turn fuel pump locking ring counterclockwise and remove locking ring.
8. Remove fuel pump, bracket and gasket assembly.
9. Reverse procedure to install. To pressurize fuel system, proceed as follows:
   a. Install pressure gauge tool No. T80L-9974-A or equivalent onto fuel rail pressure fitting.
   b. Turn ignition switch to ON position for 3 seconds, repeatedly 5 to 10 times until pressure gauge indicates 13 psi.

BELT TENSION DATA

Belt	New Lbs.	Used Lbs.
Alternator, Power Steering & Air Conditioning	150-190	140-160
Water Pump & Air Pump	50-90	40-60

4-120 (2.0L) Diesel Engine Section

INDEX

ENGINE MOUNTS

Refer to **Fig. 1** when replacing the engine mounts.

ENGINE

REPLACE

Engine and transaxle are removed from vehicle as an assembly.

1. Disconnect battery ground cable located in luggage compartment.
2. Remove air cleaner assembly.
3. Remove lower radiator hose, then drain coolant from engine.
4. Disconnect cooling fan electrical connector.
5. Remove radiator shroud, cooling fan and radiator from vehicle.
6. Remove starter cable from starter.
7. Carefully discharge refrigerant from air conditioning system, if equipped. Disconnect pressure and return lines from compressor.
8. Mark then disconnect all electrical and vacuum lines from engine.
9. Disconnect clutch cable from transaxle shift lever.
10. Disconnect injection pump throttle linkage. Disconnect fuel supply and return lines from engine.
11. Disconnect power steering pressure and return lines from power steering pump, if equipped. Remove power steering line bracket from cylinder head.
12. Install suitable engine support tool to engine lifting eye.
13. Raise and support vehicle.
14. Remove bolt securing exhaust pipe bracket to oil pan. Remove exhaust pipe to exhaust manifold nuts, then disconnect exhaust pipe from exhaust manifold.
15. Disconnect speedometer cable from transaxle.
16. Disconnect heater hoses from heater and oil cooler.
17. Remove bolts securing control arms to body. Remove stabilizer bar bracket bolts and bracket.
18. Remove halfshaft assembly from transaxle.
19. On models equipped with manual transaxle, remove shift stabilizer bar to transaxle bolts. Remove shift shaft nut and bolt from transaxle.
20. Remove lefthand rear No. 4 insulator mount bracket nuts and bracket from body bracket.
21. Remove lefthand front No. 1 insulator to transaxle mounting bolts.
22. Lower vehicle. Do not allow front wheels to touch floor.
23. Remove engine support tool from engine lifting eye.
24. Remove righthand No. 3A insulator intermediate bracket to engine bracket bolts, intermediate bracket to insulator nuts and bottom nut of double ended stud securing intermediate bracket to engine bracket. Remove bracket.
25. Lower engine and transaxle from vehicle.
26. Reverse procedure to install.

CYLINDER HEAD & PRE-CHAMBER

REPLACE

1. Disconnect battery ground cable and drain cooling system.
2. Remove camshaft cover, front and rear timing belt covers and belts.
3. Raise and support vehicle.
4. Disconnect exhaust pipe from exhaust manifold.
5. Lower vehicle.
6. Remove air inlet duct from air cleaner and intake manifold. Install cap, **Fig. 2**, onto intake manifold.
7. Disconnect all electrical connectors and vacuum hoses from temperature sensors.
8. Remove upper and lower coolant hoses and upper radiator hose from thermostat housing.
9. Remove injection lines from injection pump and nozzles. Cap all lines and fittings with cap set No. T84P-9395 or equivalent, **Fig. 3**.
10. Disconnect glow plug harness from engine harness.
11. Loosen cylinder head bolts in sequence shown in **Fig. 4**, then remove cylinder head.
12. Remove glow plugs.
13. Using a brass drift and hammer, remove pre-chambers from cylinder head, **Fig. 5**.
14. Clean pre-chamber cups, pre-chambers, cylinder head and crankcase gasket surfaces.
15. Install pre-chambers into cylinder head. Ensure pins are aligned with slots, **Fig. 5**.
16. Install glow plugs and torque to specification. Note the following:
    a. Using compressed air, blow out cylinder head bolt threads in crankcase.
    b. Install new cylinder head gasket. Ensure cylinder head oil feed hole is not restricted, **Fig. 6**.
    c. Measure dimension A, **Fig. 7**, of each cylinder head bolt. If dimension A is more than 4.5 in., replace cylinder head bolt.
    d. Rotate camshaft until both intake and exhaust valves for No. 1 cylinder are closed. Rotate crankshaft clockwise until No. 1 piston is halfway up in the cylinder bore toward TDC.
    e. Install cylinder head.
    f. Before installing cylinder head bolts, paint a white reference mark on each bolt, **Fig. 8**, then apply a light coat of clean engine oil to bolt threads.
    g. Torque cylinder head bolts in sequence shown in **Fig. 9** to 22 ft. lbs. Using the painted reference marks, tighten each cylinder head bolt in sequence an additional 90°, **Fig. 8.** Tighten cylinder head bolts another 90° to complete cylinder head bolt installation.
17. Reverse procedure to install.

INTAKE MANIFOLD

REPLACE

1. Disconnect battery ground cable and drain cooling system.
2. Remove air inlet duct from air cleaner and intake manifold. Install cap, **Fig. 2**, onto intake manifold.
3. Disconnect resistor electrical connectors from glow plugs.
4. Remove breather hose from engine and upper radiator hose from thermostat housing.
5. Disconnect upper and lower coolant hoses from thermostat housing.
6. Disconnect electrical connectors from temperature sensors.
7. Remove intake manifold to cylinder head bolts, then the intake manifold.
8. Reverse procedure to install.

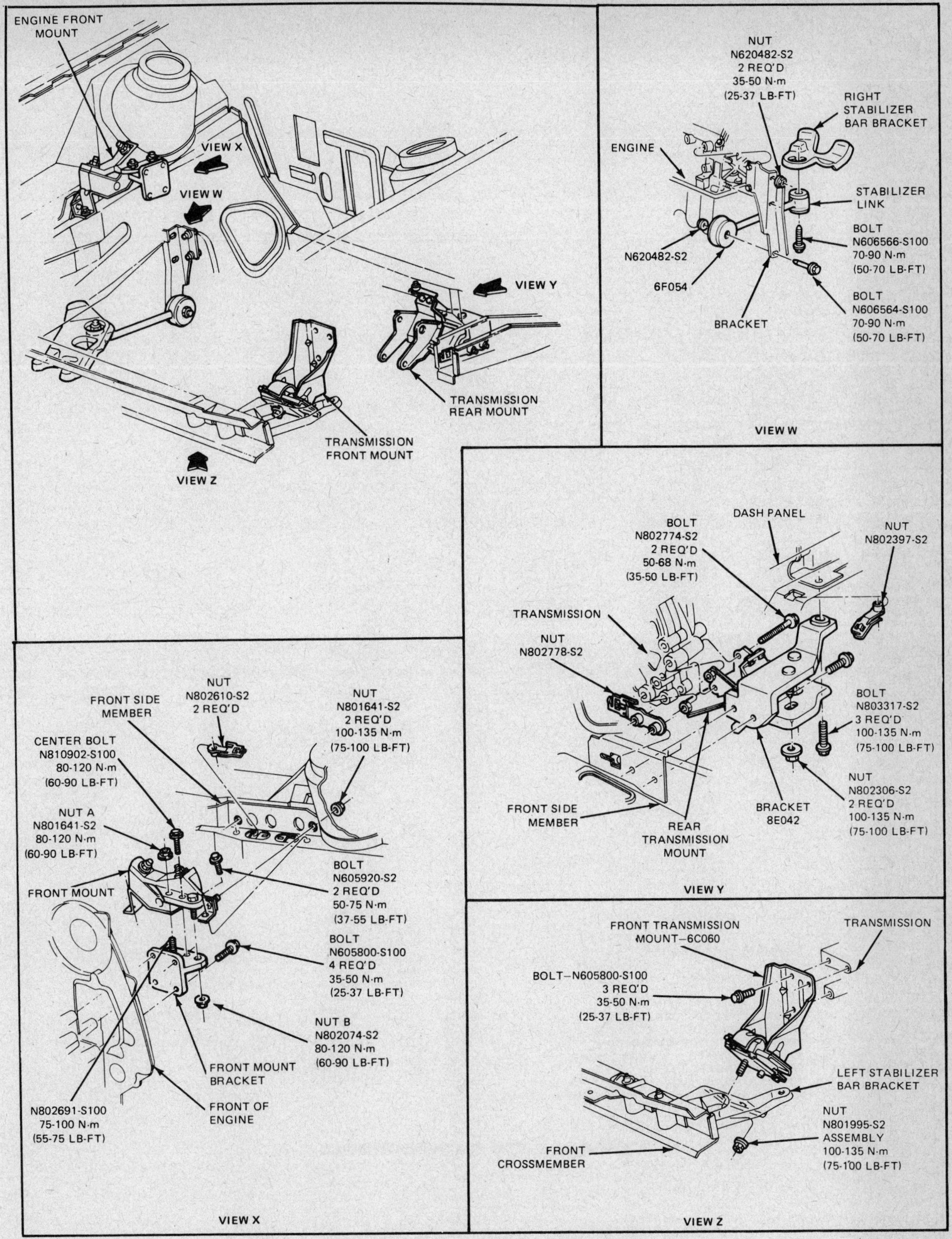

Fig. 1 Engine mount assembly

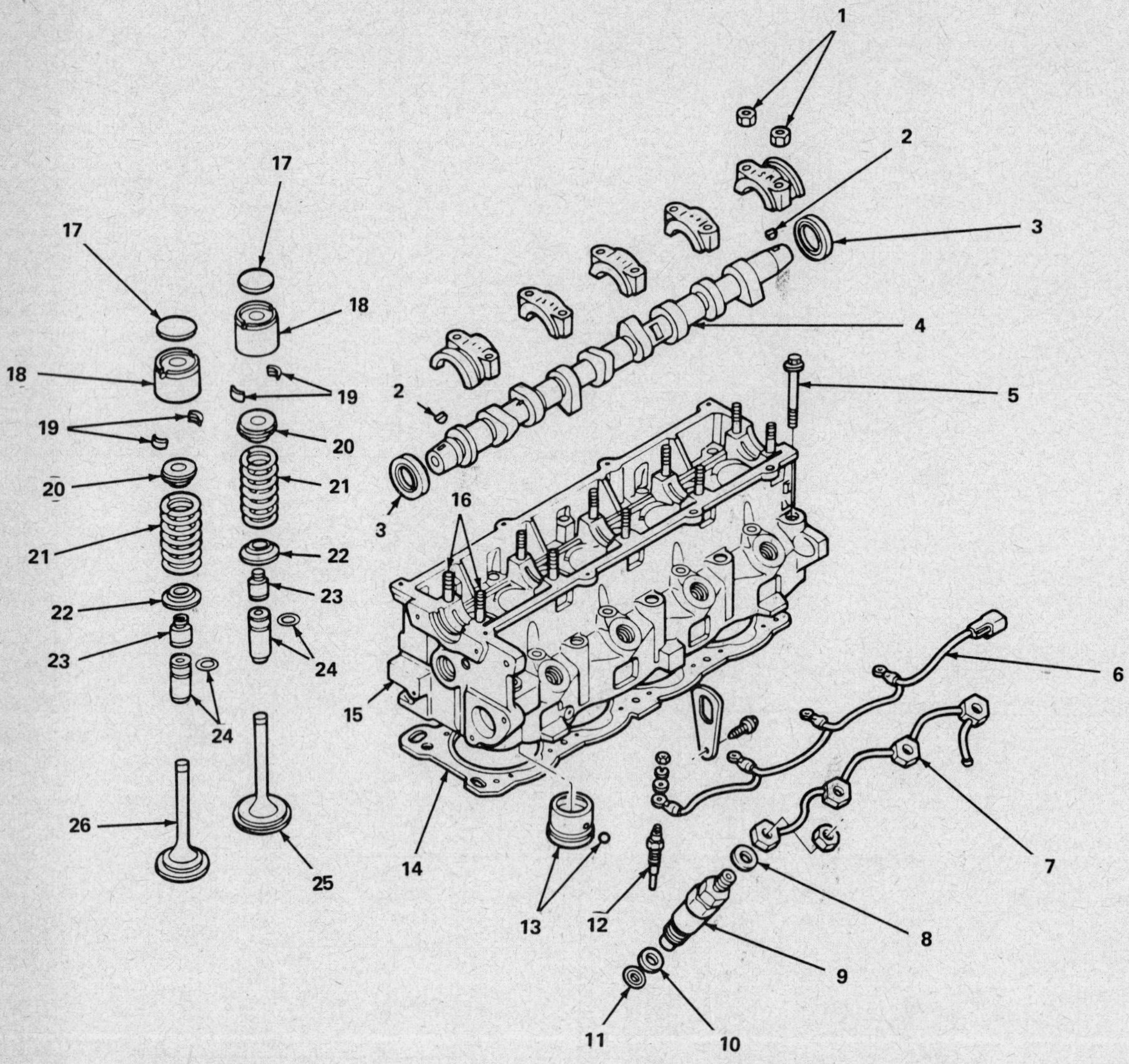

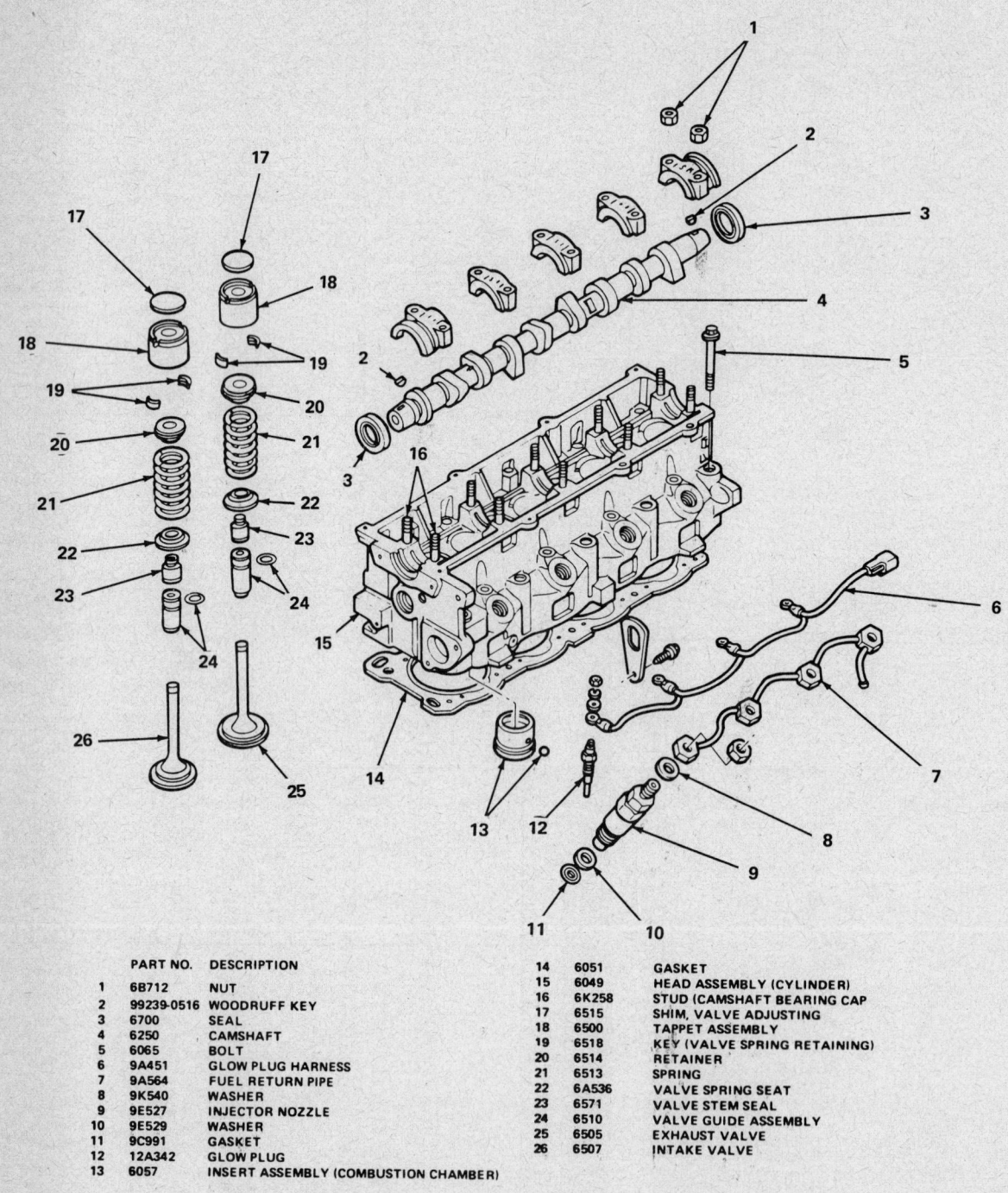

	PART NO.	DESCRIPTION
1	6B712	NUT
2	99239-0516	WOODRUFF KEY
3	6700	SEAL
4	6250	CAMSHAFT
5	6065	BOLT
6	9A451	GLOW PLUG HARNESS
7	9A564	FUEL RETURN PIPE
8	9K540	WASHER
9	9E527	INJECTOR NOZZLE
10	9E529	WASHER
11	9C991	GASKET
12	12A342	GLOW PLUG
13	6057	INSERT ASSEMBLY (COMBUSTION CHAMBER)
14	6051	GASKET
15	6049	HEAD ASSEMBLY (CYLINDER)
16	6K258	STUD (CAMSHAFT BEARING CAP
17	6515	SHIM, VALVE ADJUSTING
18	6500	TAPPET ASSEMBLY
19	6518	KEY (VALVE SPRING RETAINING)
20	6514	RETAINER
21	6513	SPRING
22	6A536	VALVE SPRING SEAT
23	6571	VALVE STEM SEAL
24	6510	VALVE GUIDE ASSEMBLY
25	6505	EXHAUST VALVE
26	6507	INTAKE VALVE

Cylinder head & components

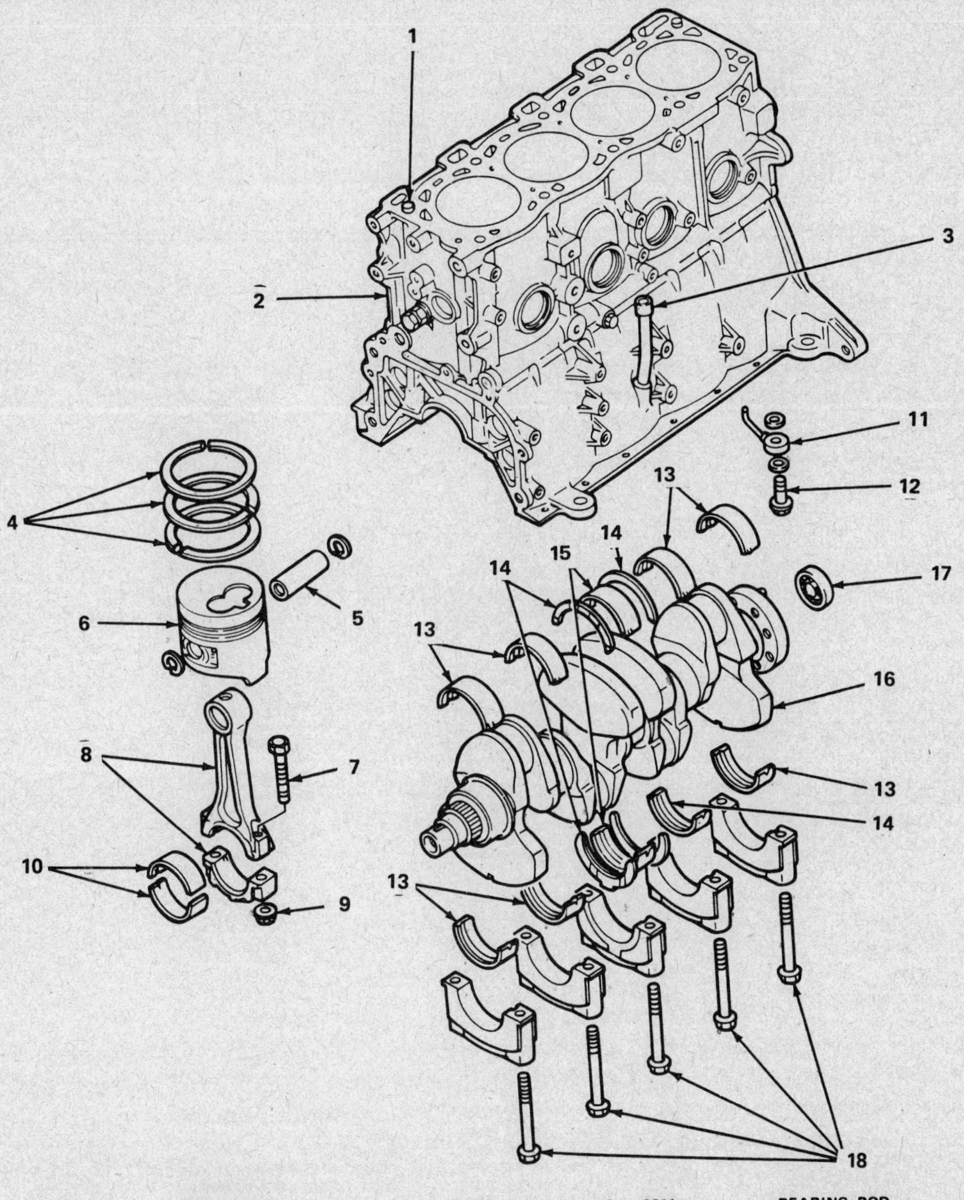

	PART NO.	DESCRIPTION
1	6A008	DOWEL PIN (CYLINDER HEAD TO CYLINDER BLOCK)
2	6010	BLOCK ASSEMBLY (CYLINDER)
3	6754 (LOWER)	TUBE ASSEMBLY (OIL LEVEL INDICATOR)
4	6148	PISTON RINGS
5	6135	PISTON PIN
6	6108	PISTON
7	6214	BOLT
8	6200	ROD ASSEMBLY
9	6212	NUT
10	6211	BEARING, ROD
11	6C327	OIL JET ASSEMBLY (PISTON COOLING)
12	6K757	BOLT
13	6333	BEARING, MAIN
14	6334	BEARING, THRUST
15	6337	BEARING, MAIN
16	6303	CRANKSHAFT
17	6701	SEAL (CRANKSHAFT REAR OIL)
18	6345	BOLT

Cylinder block & components

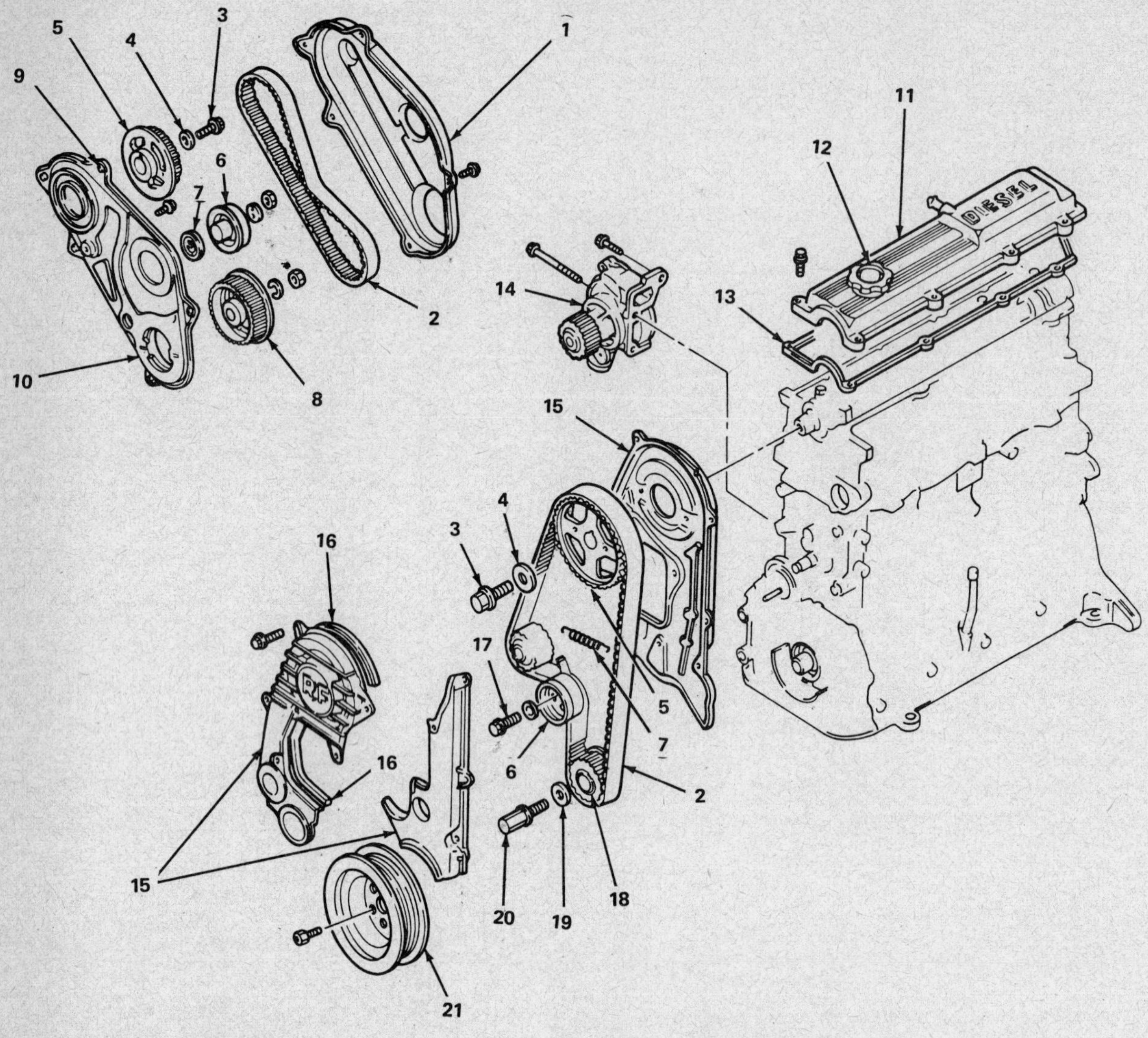

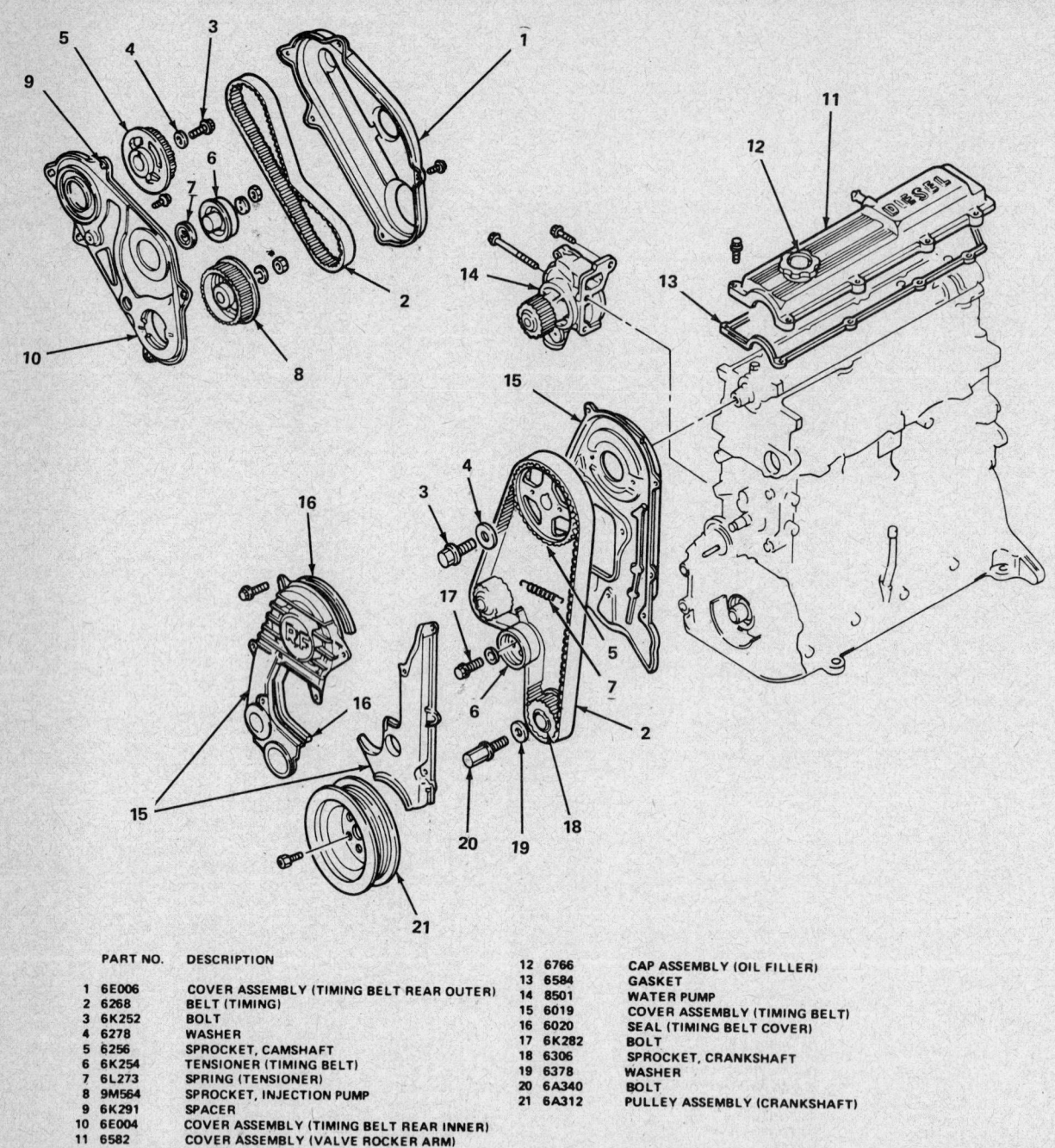

	PART NO.	DESCRIPTION
1	6E006	COVER ASSEMBLY (TIMING BELT REAR OUTER)
2	6268	BELT (TIMING)
3	6K252	BOLT
4	6278	WASHER
5	6256	SPROCKET, CAMSHAFT
6	6K254	TENSIONER (TIMING BELT)
7	6L273	SPRING (TENSIONER)
8	9M564	SPROCKET, INJECTION PUMP
9	6K291	SPACER
10	6E004	COVER ASSEMBLY (TIMING BELT REAR INNER)
11	6582	COVER ASSEMBLY (VALVE ROCKER ARM)
12	6766	CAP ASSEMBLY (OIL FILLER)
13	6584	GASKET
14	8501	WATER PUMP
15	6019	COVER ASSEMBLY (TIMING BELT)
16	6020	SEAL (TIMING BELT COVER)
17	6K282	BOLT
18	6306	SPROCKET, CRANKSHAFT
19	6378	WASHER
20	6A340	BOLT
21	6A312	PULLEY ASSEMBLY (CRANKSHAFT)

Timing belt, sprockets & related components

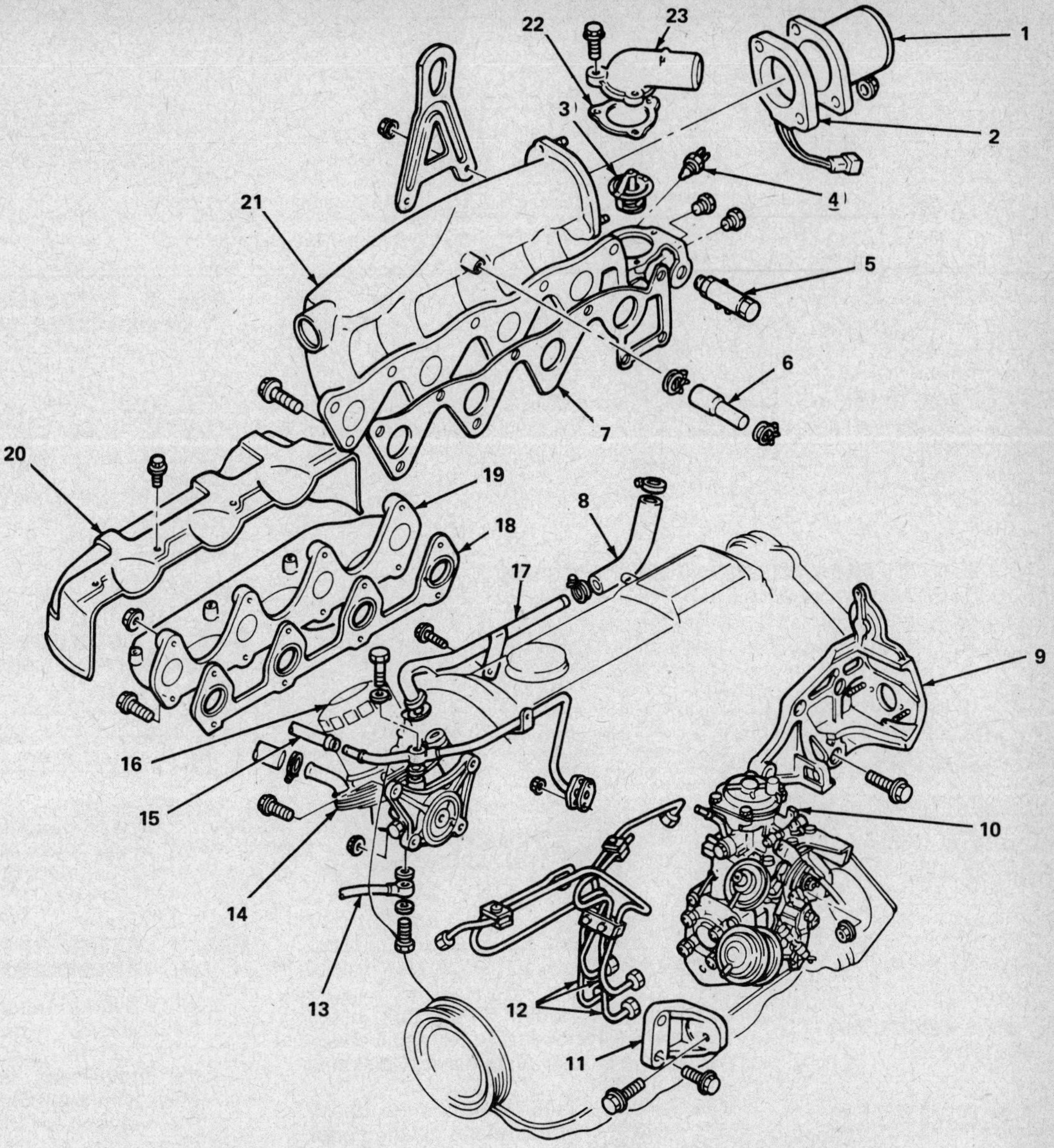

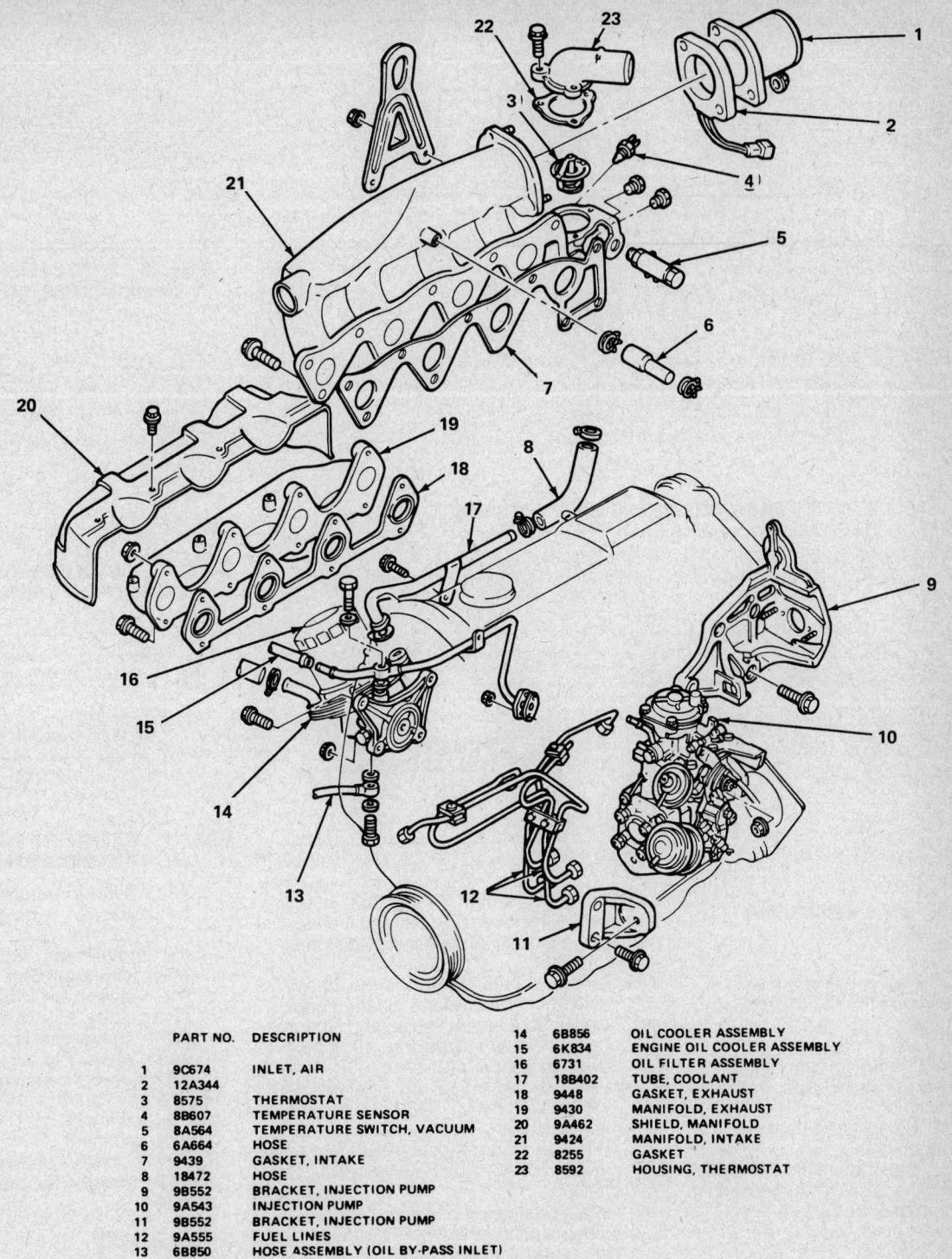

	PART NO.	DESCRIPTION
1	9C674	INLET, AIR
2	12A344	
3	8575	THERMOSTAT
4	8B607	TEMPERATURE SENSOR
5	8A564	TEMPERATURE SWITCH, VACUUM
6	6A664	HOSE
7	9439	GASKET, INTAKE
8	18472	HOSE
9	9B552	BRACKET, INJECTION PUMP
10	9A543	INJECTION PUMP
11	9B552	BRACKET, INJECTION PUMP
12	9A555	FUEL LINES
13	6B850	HOSE ASSEMBLY (OIL BY-PASS INLET)
14	6B856	OIL COOLER ASSEMBLY
15	6K834	ENGINE OIL COOLER ASSEMBLY
16	6731	OIL FILTER ASSEMBLY
17	18B402	TUBE, COOLANT
18	9448	GASKET, EXHAUST
19	9430	MANIFOLD, EXHAUST
20	9A462	SHIELD, MANIFOLD
21	9424	MANIFOLD, INTAKE
22	8255	GASKET
23	8592	HOUSING, THERMOSTAT

Intake manifold, exhaust manifold & injection pump components

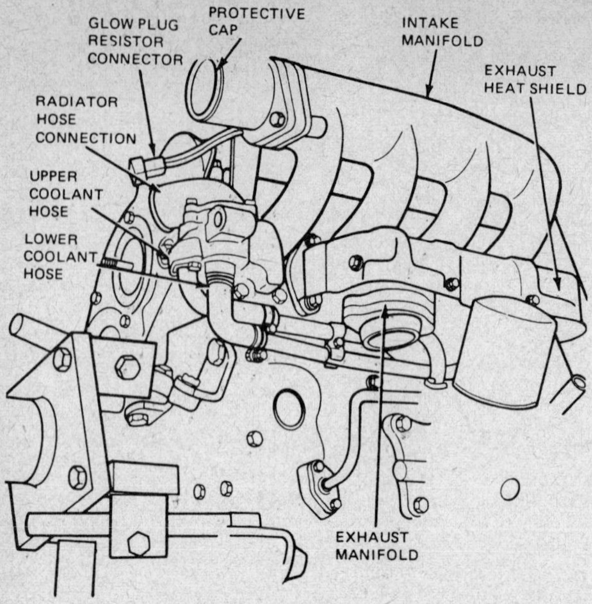

Fig. 2 Intake manifold removal

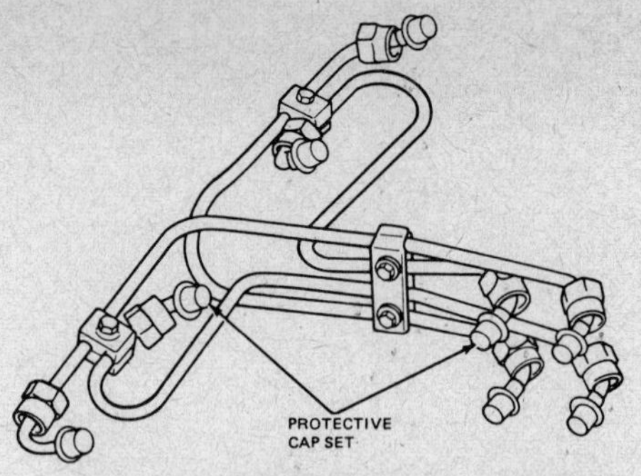

Fig. 3 Injection nozzle protective cap set

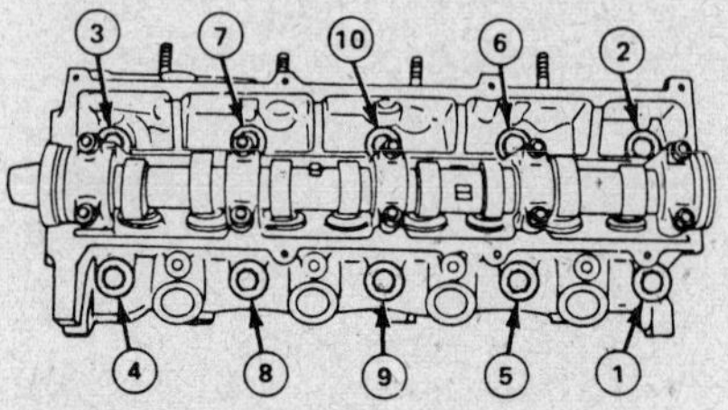

Fig. 4 Cylinder head bolt loosening sequence

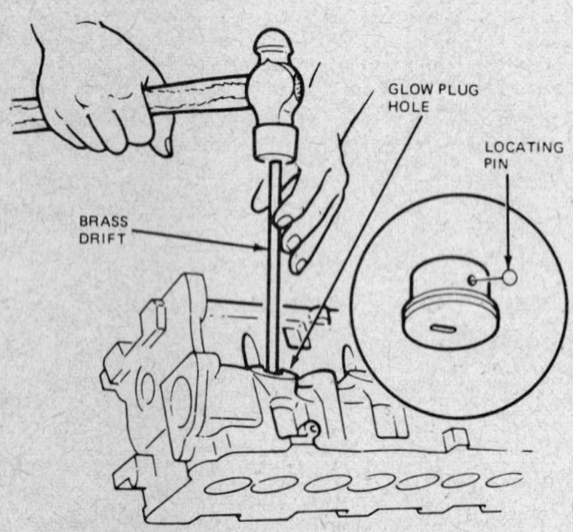

Fig. 5 Pre-chamber removal

EXHAUST MANIFOLD
REPLACE

1. Disconnect battery ground cable.
2. Disconnect exhaust pipe from exhaust manifold.
3. Remove bolts securing heat shield to exhaust manifold.
4. Remove exhaust manifold to cylinder head nuts, then the exhaust manifold.
5. Reverse procedure to install.

VALVE CLEARANCE SPECIFICATIONS

Year	Engine	Valve Lash
1984-86	4-120	①
1987-88	4-120	②

①—Intake .008-.011; exhaust .011-.015.
②—Intake .0098-.0020; exhaust .0138-.0020.

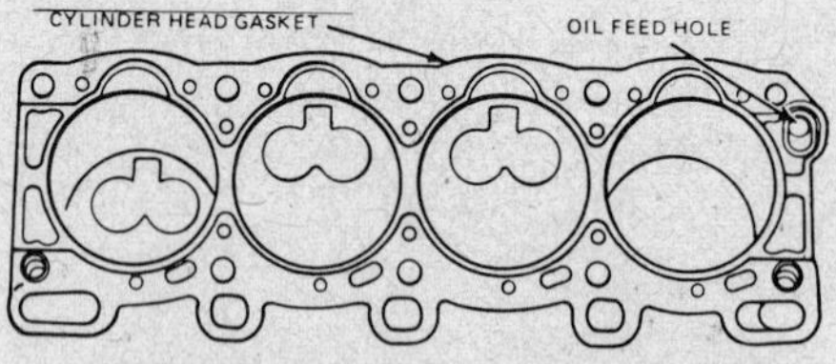

Fig. 6 Cylinder head gasket installation

VALVES
ADJUST

1. Disconnect breather hose from intake manifold and remove camshaft cover.
2. Rotate crankshaft until No. 1 piston is at TDC.
3. Using a suitable feeler gauge, check valve shim to cam lobe clearance for Nos. 1 and 2 intake valves and Nos. 1 and 3 exhaust valves, **Fig. 10.** Intake valve clearance should be .008-.011 in. on except 1987-88 engines or .0098-.0020 in. on 1987-88 engine, exhaust valves clearance should be .011-.015 in. on except 1987-88 engines or .0138-.0020 in. on 1987-88 engines.
4. Rotate crankshaft one complete revolution. Measure valve clearance for Nos. 3 and 4 intake valves and Nos. 2 and 4 exhaust valves. If measured clearance is not to specification, proceed as follows:
   a. Rotate crankshaft until lobe of valve to be adjusted is facing downward.
   b. Install cam follower retainer tool No. T84P-6513B or equivalent as shown in **Fig. 11.**
   c. Rotate crankshaft until cam lobe is on base circle as shown in **Fig. 12.** Using tool No. T71P-19703C or equivalent, pry valve adjusting shim out of the cam follower, **Fig. 12. Valve shims are available in thicknesses ranging from .134-.181 in. (3.40-4.60 mm) If the valve was tight, select a shim with a smaller thickness. If the valve was loose, select a shim with a larger thickness. Shim thickness is stamped on valve shim, Fig. 13. Install shim with numbers facing downward.**
5. Rotate crankshaft until cam lobe is facing downward and remove cam follower retainer.
6. Recheck valve clearance. Repeat steps 2 through 4 for each valve to be adjusted.

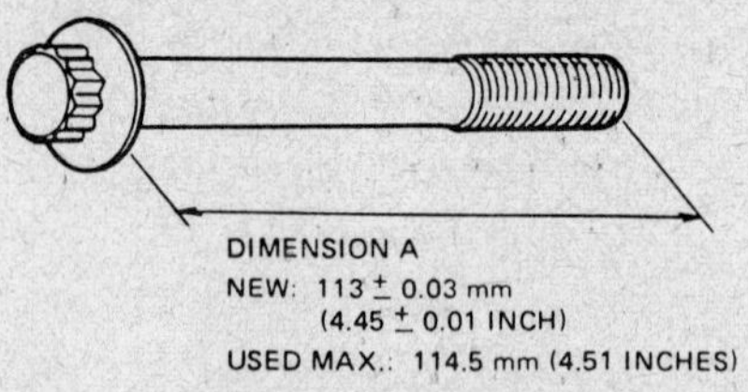

Fig. 7 Cylinder head bolt dimension A

CAMSHAFT
REPLACE

1. Disconnect battery ground cable.
2. Disconnect breather hose from camshaft cover.
3. Remove camshaft cover bolts, then the camshaft cover.
4. Remove flywheel timing mark cover from clutch housing.
5. Rotate crankshaft until No. 1 cylinder is at TDC.
6. Remove front and rear timing belt covers.
7. Loosen front timing belt tensioner,

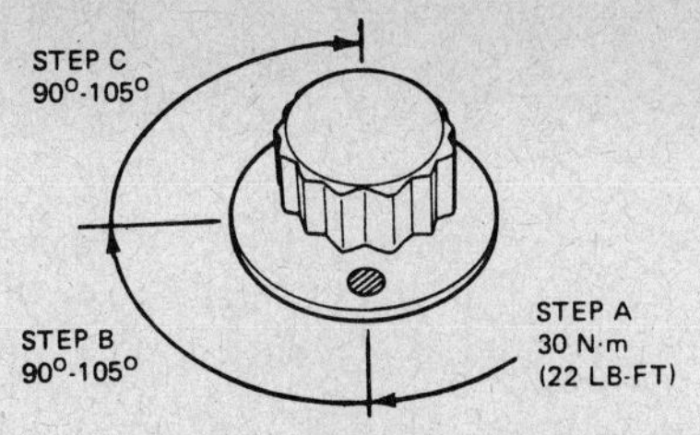

Fig. 8 Cylinder head bolt tightening steps

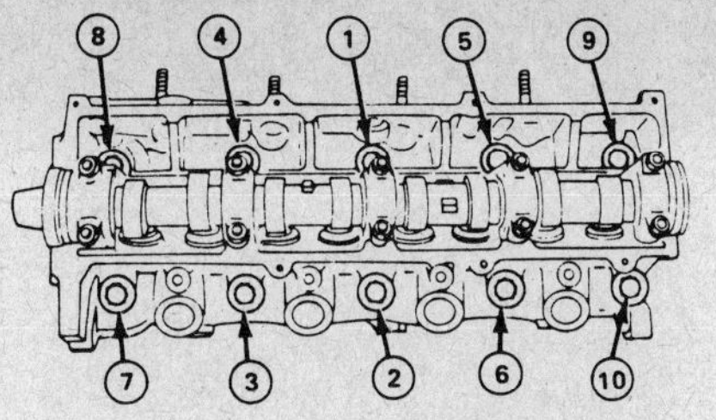

Fig. 9 Cylinder head bolt tightening sequence

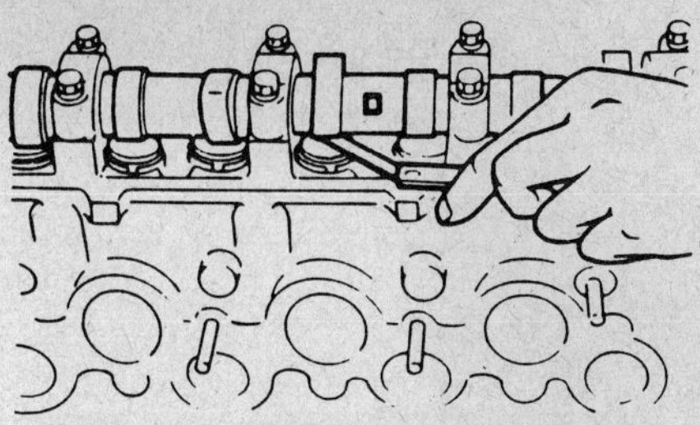

Fig. 10 Checking valve clearance

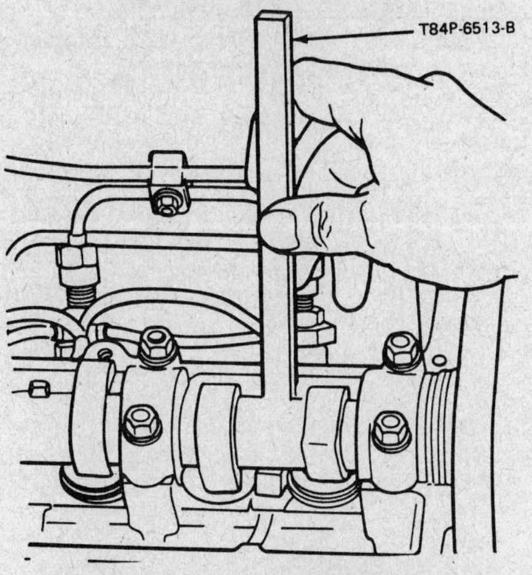

Fig. 11 Installing cam follower retainer

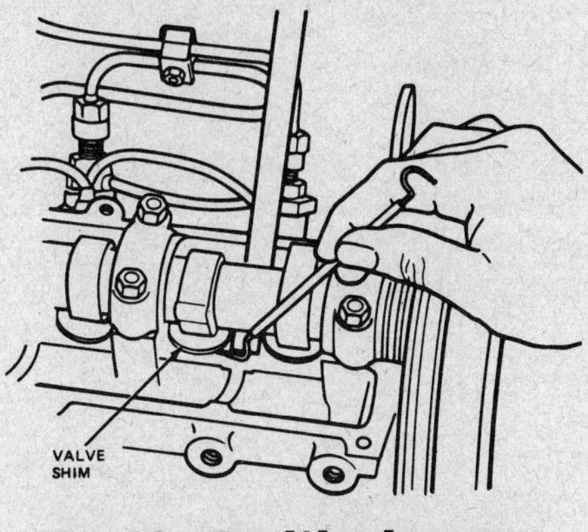

Fig. 12 Positioning cam lobe on base circle for valve shim removal

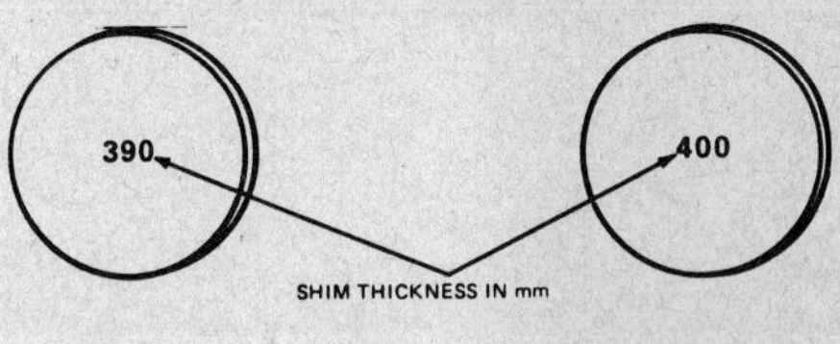

Fig. 13 Valve shim sizes

then remove timing belt from camshaft sprocket.

8. Install an adjustable wrench onto camshaft boss, then loosen front camshaft sprocket bolt.
9. Hold camshaft with wrench then remove rear camshaft sprocket bolt.
10. Using tool Nos. T77F-4220B1 and D80L-625-4 or equivalents, remove camshaft sprockets. Retain camshaft sprocket Woodruff keys.
11. Remove No. 1, 3 and 5 camshaft bearing caps.
12. Remove No. 2 and 4 camshaft bearing caps as follows:
    a. Loosen one of the camshaft bearing nuts two or three turns.
    b. Loosen the remaining camshaft bearing nuts one at a time, two or three turns.
    c. Repeat steps 12a and 12b, turning each nut two or three turns at a time, until all camshaft bearing cap nuts are loose.
13. Remove camshaft and discard camshaft seals.
14. Remove cam followers and note their location for installation in their original positions.
15. Reverse procedure to install. For installation of camshaft bearings, proceed as follows. **Install camshaft bearings with arrows pointing toward front of engine. No. 2, 3 and 4 camshaft bearing caps have their numbers stamped on the top surface of the bearing cap. No. 1 and 5 bearing caps are not marked. No. 1 bearing cap has a slot to fit over camshaft thrust flange.**
    a. Install No. 2 and 4 bearing caps, tightening one of the nuts two or three turns.
    b. Tighten the remaining nuts one at a time, two or three turns.
    c. Repeat steps 15a and 15b, turning each nut two or three turns at a time until No. 2 and 4 bearing caps are seated.
    d. Install No. 1, 3 and 5 bearing caps, and torque nuts to 15-19 ft. lbs.

TIMING BELT REPLACE

FRONT

Removal

1. With engine removed from vehicle, remove front timing belt upper cover bolts, then the upper cover.
2. Install flywheel holding tool T84P-6375 or equivalent onto flywheel.
3. Remove crankshaft pulley to crankshaft sprocket bolts.
4. Using tool Nos. T58P-6316 and T74P-6700B or equivalents, remove crankshaft pulley.
5. Remove front timing belt lower cover bolts, then the lower cover. Loosen tensioner pulley, then remove timing belt.

Installation

1. Align camshaft sprocket with timing marks as shown in **Fig. 14. Ensure crankshaft sprocket timing marks are aligned, Fig. 15.**
2. Remove tensioner spring from front timing belt upper cover, then install spring into tensioner lever slot and over crankcase stud, **Fig. 16.**
3. Push tensioner lever toward water pump and tighten lock bolt.
4. Install timing belt as shown in **Fig. 14.** Adjust timing belt as described in "Front Timing Belt, Adjust".
5. Install front timing belt lower cover. Torque lower cover bolts to 5-7 ft. lbs.
6. Install crankshaft pulley. Torque pulley bolts to 17-24 ft. lbs.
7. Install front timing belt upper cover. Torque upper cover bolts to 5-7 ft. lbs.

REAR

1. With engine removed from vehicle, remove rear timing belt cover bolts, then the rear cover.
2. Remove flywheel timing mark cover from clutch housing.
3. Rotate crankshaft until flywheel timing mark is at TDC on No. 1 cylinder, **Fig. 17. Ensure injection pump and camshaft sprocket timing marks are aligned with their marks, Fig. 18.**
4. Loosen tensioner locknut. Using a suitable tool, insert tool into tensioner slot, **Fig. 19.** Rotate tensioner clockwise, then tighten locknut.
5. Remove rear timing belt.
6. Install rear timing belt as shown in **Fig. 20.**
7. Loosen tensioner locknut and adjust timing belt as described under "Rear Timing Belt, Adjust".
8. Install rear timing belt cover. Torque the 6 mm rear cover bolts to 5-9 ft. lbs., torque the 8 mm rear cover bolts to 12-16 ft. lbs.

TIMING BELT ADJUST

FRONT

1. Remove flywheel timing mark cover.
2. Remove front timing belt upper cover.
3. Remove timing belt tension spring from front cover.

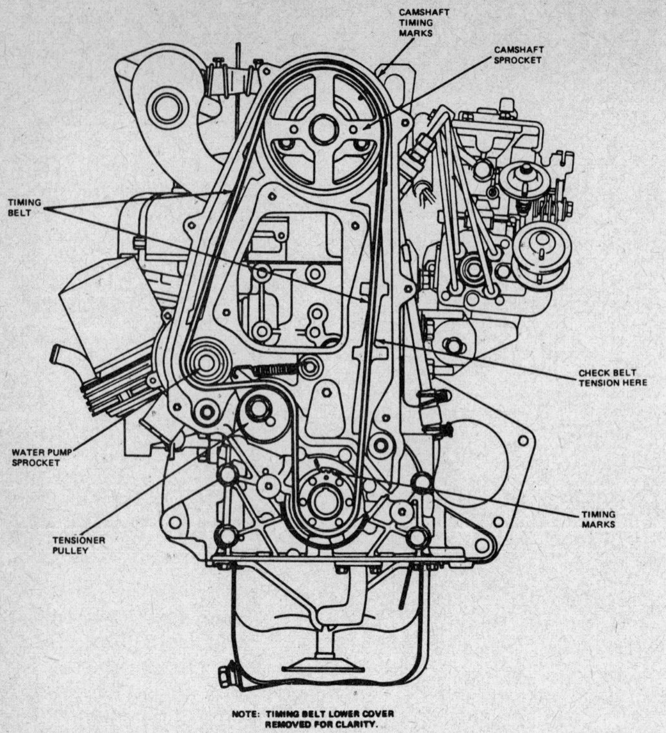

Fig. 14 Front timing belt installation

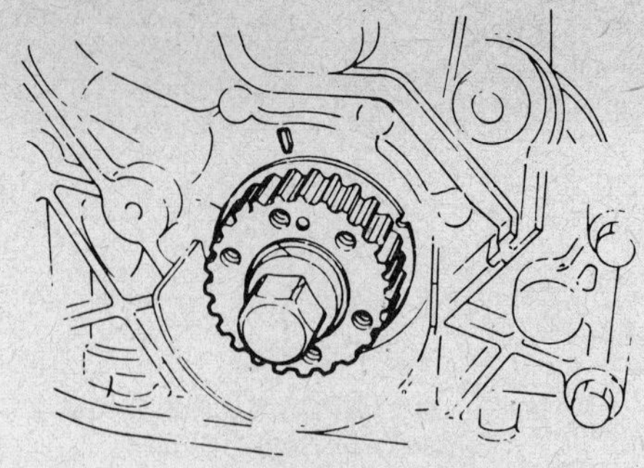

Fig. 15 Crankshaft pulley timing marks

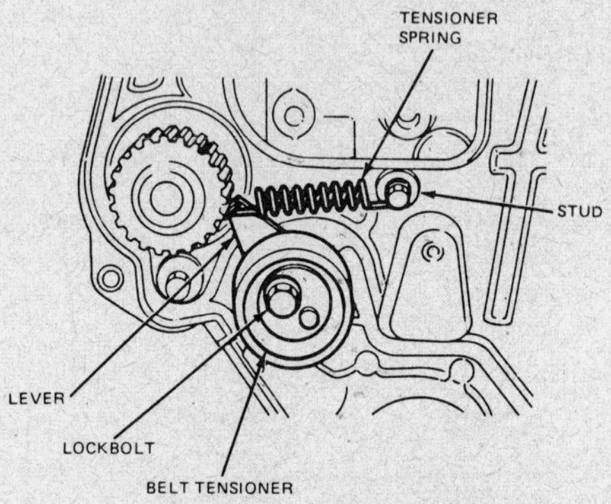

Fig. 16 Front timing belt tensioner spring installation

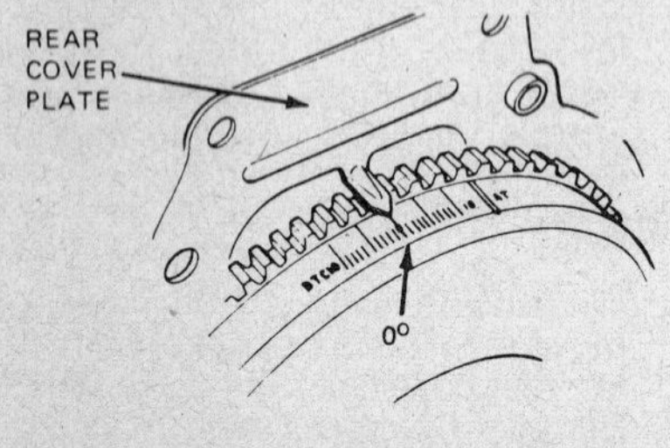

Fig. 17 Flywheel timing marks

4. Install tensioner spring into belt tensioner lever and over crankcase stud, **Fig. 16.**
5. Loosen tensioner pulley lock bolt.
6. Rotate crankshaft pulley two revolutions clockwise until flywheel TDC timing mark aligns with pointer on rear cover plate, **Fig. 17. Ensure front camshaft sprocket is aligned with its timing mark, Fig. 21.**
7. Torque tensioner lock bolt to 23-34 ft. lbs. Using a suitable belt tension gauge, check belt tension, **Fig. 14.** Belt tension should be 33-44 lbs.
8. Remove tensioner spring and install spring into front cover.
9. Install front cover. Torque front cover bolts to 5-7 ft. lbs.
10. Install flywheel timing mark cover.

REAR

1. Remove flywheel timing mark cover.
2. Remove rear timing belt cover.
3. Rotate crankshaft pulley two revolutions clockwise until flywheel TDC timing mark aligns with pointer on rear

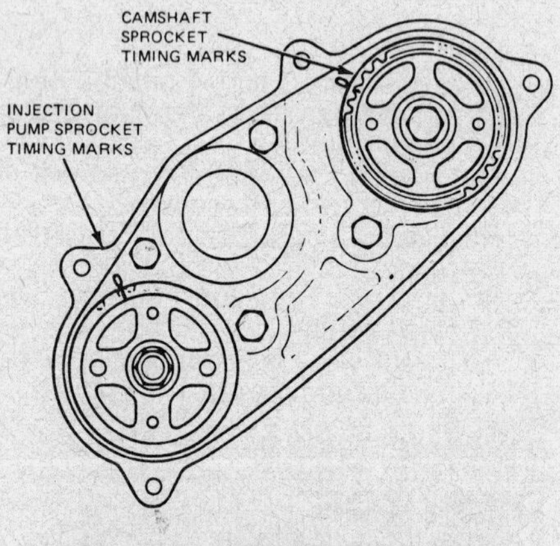

Fig. 18 Camshaft and injection pump timing marks

cover plate, **Fig. 17. Ensure injection pump and camshaft sprocket timing marks are aligned withtheir marks, Fig. 18.**

4. Torque tensioner locknut to 15-20 ft. lbs.
5. Using a suitable belt tension gauge, check belt tension, **Fig. 20.** Belt tension should be 22-33 lbs.
6. Install rear timing belt cover. Torque the 6 mm rear cover bolts to 5-9 ft. lbs., torque the 8 mm rear cover bolts to 12-16 ft. lbs.
7. Install flywheel timing mark cover.

INJECTION PUMP REPLACE

1. Disconnect battery ground cable lo-

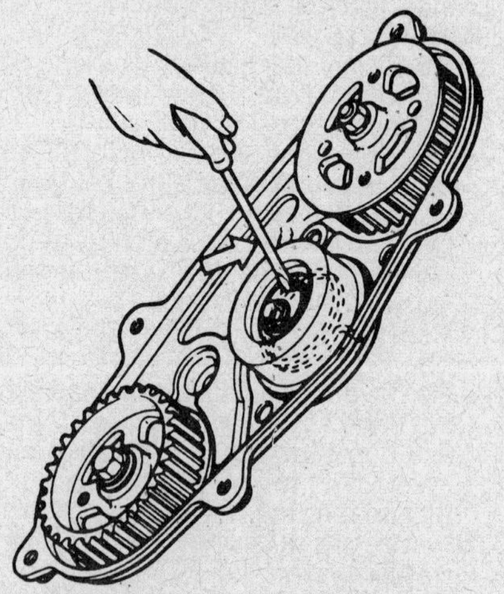

Fig. 19 Loosening tensioner pulley

cated in luggage compartment.
2. Disconnect air inlet duct from air cleaner and intake manifold. Install cap, **Fig. 2,** onto intake manifold.
3. Remove rear timing belt cover and flywheel timing mark cover.
4. Remove rear timing belt as described under "Rear Timing Belt, Replace."
5. Disconnect throttle and speed control cable, if equipped.
6. Disconnect vacuum lines from altitude compensator and cold start diaphragm.
7. Disconnect fuel supply and return lines from injection pump.

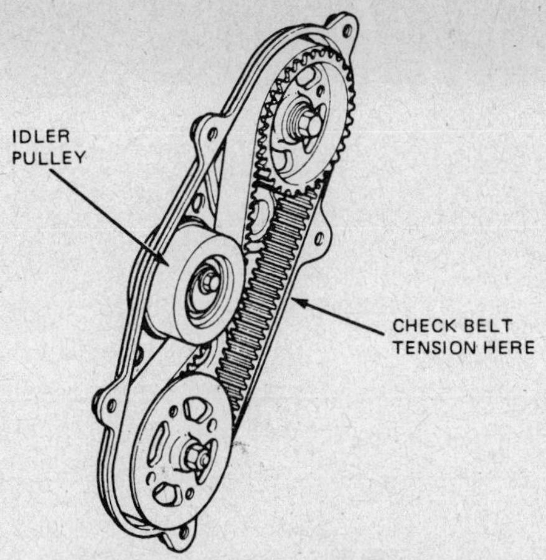

Fig. 20 Rear timing belt tensioner

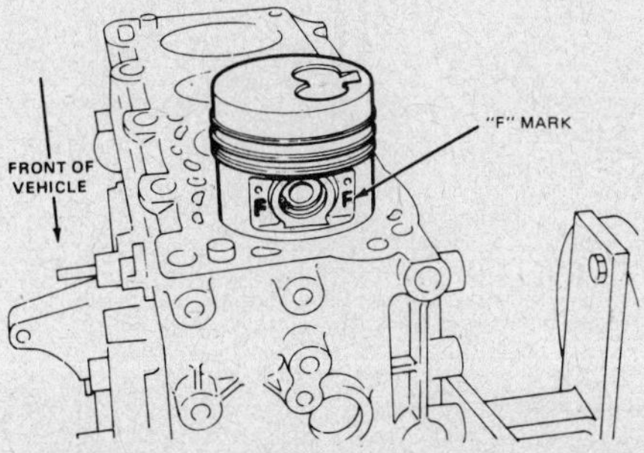

Fig. 23 Piston alignment

8. Disconnect electrical connector from fuel cut-off solenoid.
9. Remove injection lines from injection pump and nozzles. Cap all lines and fittings with cap set No. T84P-9395 or equivalent, **Fig. 3.**
10. Rotate injection pump sprocket until injection pump and camshaft sprocket timing marks align with their marks, **Fig. 18.**
11. Install two M8 x 1.25 bolts into injection pump sprocket holes, **Fig. 22,** to secure injection pump sprocket. Remove injection pump sprocket bolt.
12. Using tool Nos. T77F-4220B1 and D80L-625-4 or equivalents, remove injection pump sprocket.
13. Remove bolt securing injection pump to pump front bracket.
14. Remove injection pump nuts, then the injection pump.
15. Reverse procedure to install.

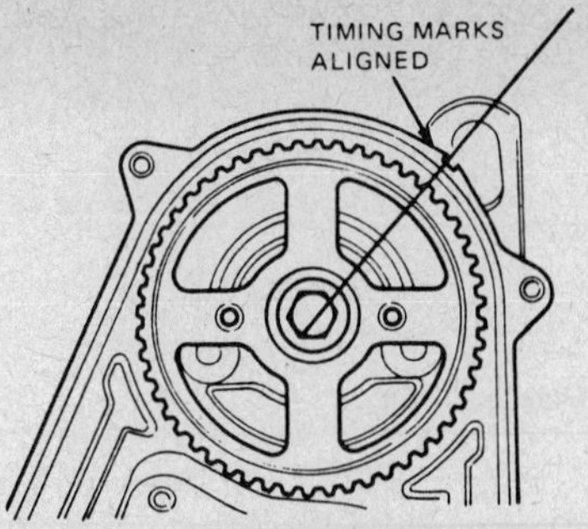

Fig. 21 Camshaft timing mark

PISTON & ROD ASSEMBLE

Pistons are available in standard size and oversize of .020 in. Install piston with an "F" mark, **Fig. 23,** on piston toward front of engine. Connecting rods have alignment marks stamped on one side of main bearing bore boss, **Fig. 24.** After piston and connecting rod assemblies have been installed, check side clearance between connecting rods on each crankshaft journal. Clearance should be .0043-.0103 inch.

MAIN & ROD BEARINGS

Main bearings are available in standard size and undersizes of .010, .020 and .030 inch. Connecting rod bearings are available in standard sizes and undersizes of .003, .010, .020, and .030 inch.

CRANKSHAFT REAR OIL SEAL

REPLACE

1. Disconnect battery ground cable.
2. Remove transaxle and clutch assemblies from engine.
3. Install flywheel holding tool No. T84P-6375A or equivalent, and remove flywheel bolts and flywheel.
4. Remove oil seal from crankshaft.
5. Reverse procedure to install.

OIL PAN

REPLACE

1. Disconnect battery ground cable.
2. Raise and support vehicle.
3. Remove oil pan bolts, then the oil pan.
4. Reverse procedure to install.

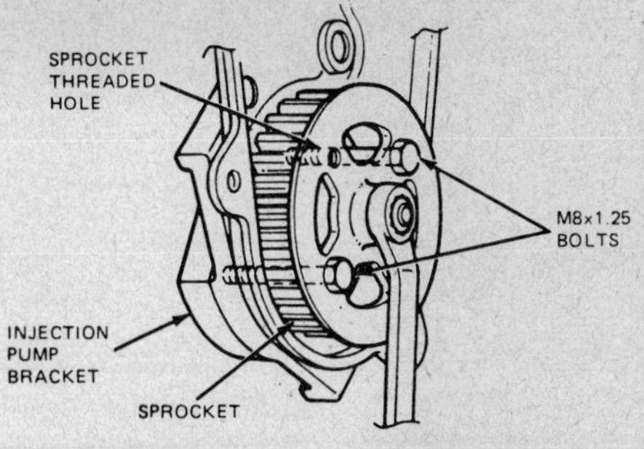

Fig. 22 Injection pump sprocket removal

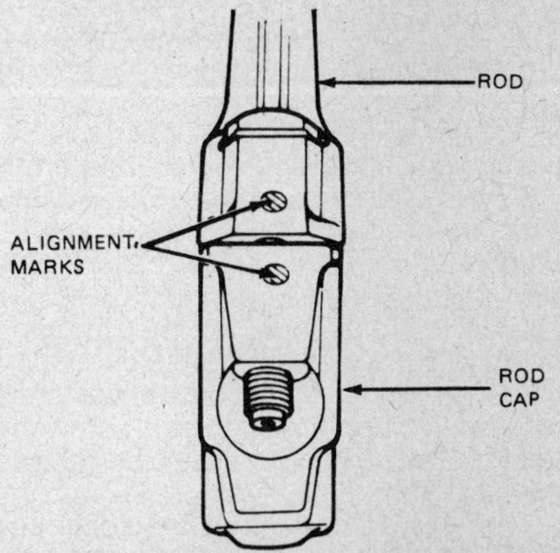

Fig. 24 Connecting rod cap alignment marks

OIL PUMP

REPLACE

1. Disconnect battery ground cable.
2. With engine removed from vehicle, remove accessory drive belts.
3. Drain engine oil and remove oil pan.
4. Remove crankshaft pulley, front timing belt, front timing belt tensioner and crankshaft sprocket.
5. Remove bolts securing oil pump to crankcase, then the oil pump.
6. Reverse procedure to install.

BELT TENSION DATA

Belt	New Lbs.	Used Lbs.
Alternator Exc. V ribbed	120-160	110-130
Power Steering & Air Conditioning	150-190	140-160

Clutch & Manual Transaxle Section

INDEX

CLUTCH
ADJUST

Lift clutch pedal to the uppermost position when connecting or disconnecting the clutch cable. Whenever the clutch cable is disconnected for any reason, such as transmission removal or clutch, clutch pedal components, or clutch cable replacement, it is important that the proper method for installing the clutch cable be followed. Under no circumstances should a prying instrument such as a screwdriver or a pry bar be used to install the cable into the quadrant.

The cable operated clutch control system, **Fig. 1,** is self adjusting and periodic adjustments are not required. If the clutch cable is replaced for any reason, an initial adjustment is performed by pulling the clutch pedal to its full upward position.

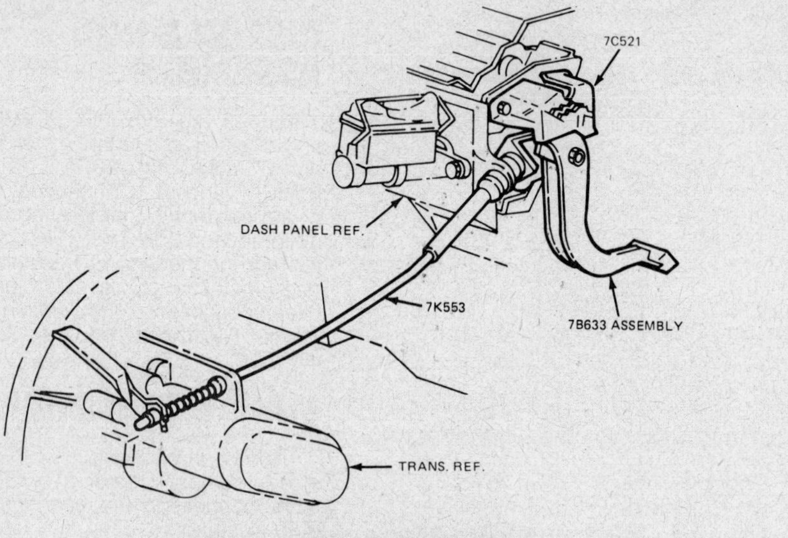

Fig. 1 Clutch linkage

CLUTCH
REPLACE

1. Remove transmission as described under "Manual Transaxle, Replace" procedure.
2. Loosen pressure plate cover attaching bolts evenly to avoid distorting cover. If same pressure plate and cover are to be installed, mark cover and flywheel so pressure plate can be installed in original position.
3. Remove pressure plate and clutch disc from flywheel, **Fig. 2.**
4. Position clutch disc and pressure plate onto flywheel with flatter side of clutch disc facing toward flywheel.
5. Ensure three dowel pins on flywheel are aligned with dowel pins on pressure plate.
6. Snug tighten cover attaching bolts, then align clutch disc using tool T81P-7550A or equivalent. Torque bolts to 12-24 ft. lbs. (17-32 Nm.).
7. Remove alignment tool, then install transaxle and perform initial clutch adjustment.

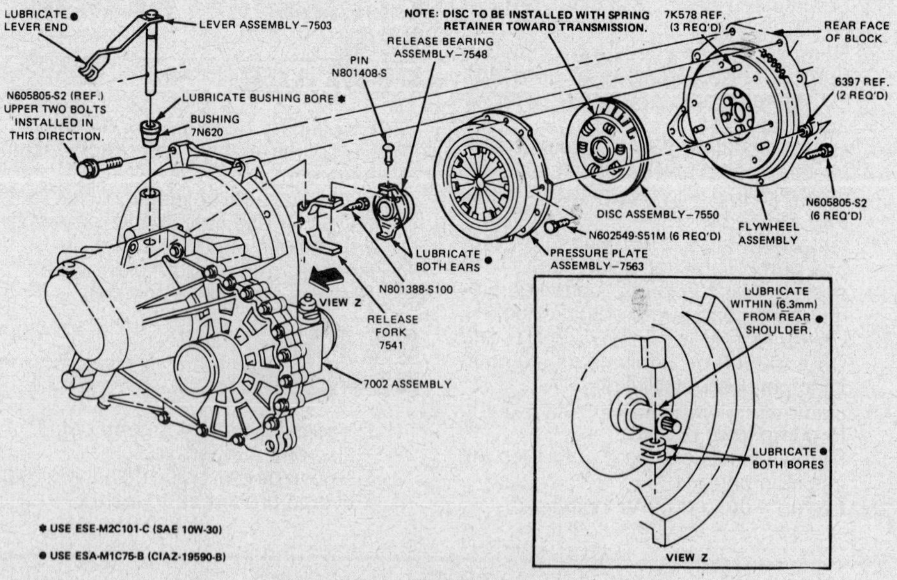

Fig. 2 Clutch assembly

GEARSHIFT LINKAGE
ADJUST

Adjustment of the external gearshift linkage is not necessary and no provision is made for adjustment, **Fig. 3.**

MANUAL TRANSAXLE
REPLACE

On models equipped with all wheel drive system, refer to "Transfer Case Section" to remove transfer case.

4 SPEED
Except Tempo & Topaz

1. Disconnect battery ground cable.
2. Remove 2 top transaxle to engine mounting bolts.

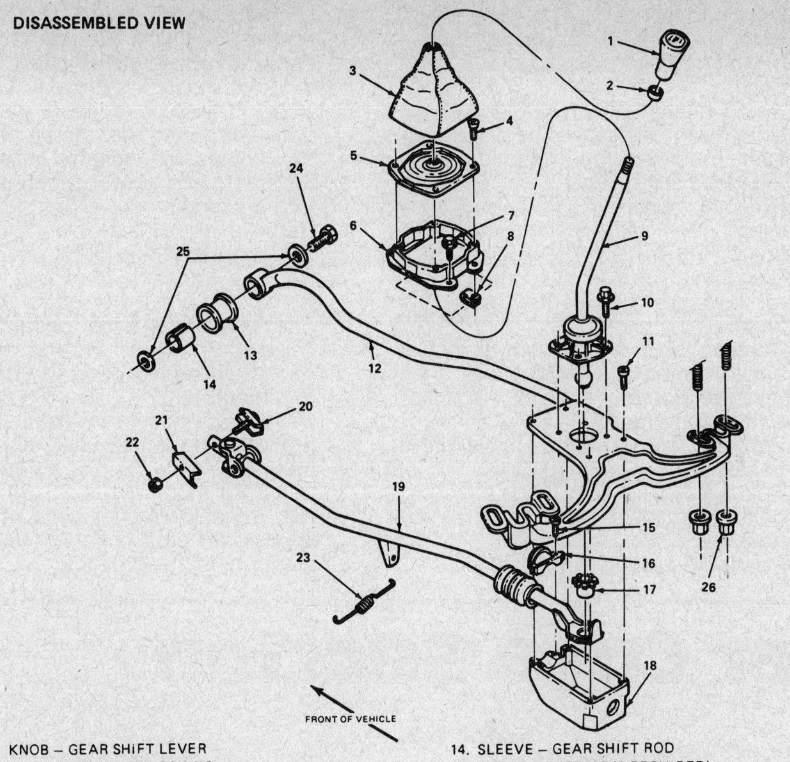

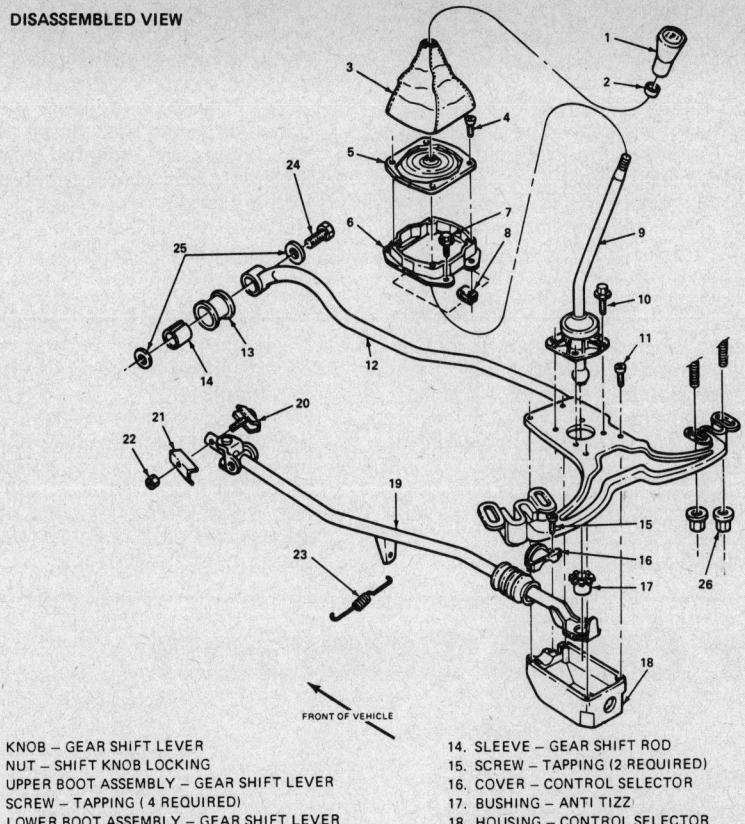

1. KNOB – GEAR SHIFT LEVER
2. NUT – SHIFT KNOB LOCKING
3. UPPER BOOT ASSEMBLY – GEAR SHIFT LEVER
4. SCREW – TAPPING (4 REQUIRED)
5. LOWER BOOT ASSEMBLY – GEAR SHIFT LEVER
6. BOOT RETAINER ASSEMBLY – GEAR SHIFT LEVER
7. BOLT – BOOT RETAINER (4 REQUIRED)
8. NUT – SPRING (4 REQUIRED)
9. LEVER ASSEMBLY – GEARSHIFT
10. BOLT – TAPPING (4 REQUIRED)
11. SCREW – TAPPING (4 REQUIRED)
12. SUPPORT ASSEMBLY (SHIFT STABILIZER BAR)
13. BUSHING – GEAR SHIFT STABILIZER BAR
14. SLEEVE – GEAR SHIFT ROD
15. SCREW – TAPPING (2 REQUIRED)
16. COVER – CONTROL SELECTOR
17. BUSHING – ANTI TIZZ
18. HOUSING – CONTROL SELECTOR
19. ASSEMBLY – SHIFT ROD AND CLEVIS
20. ASSEMBLY – CLAMP
21. CLAMP – GEAR SHIFT LEVER (2 REQUIRED)
22. NUT – CLAMP ASSEMBLY
23. RETAINING SPRING – GEAR SHIFT TUBE
24. BOLT -- STABILIZER BAR ATTACHING
25. WASHER – FLAT (2 REQUIRED)
26. ASSEMBLY – NUT/WASHER (4 REQUIRED)

Fig. 3 Gearshift linkage

3. Grasp and pull clutch cable forward, disconnecting cable from clutch release lever.
4. Remove clutch cable casing from rib on the top surface of transaxle case.
5. Raise and support vehicle.
6. Remove brake hose routing clip to suspension strut bracket mounting bolt.
7. Remove bolt securing lower control arm ball joint onto steering knuckle assembly. Pry lower control arm away from knuckle.
8. Using tool No. D83P-4026-A or equivalent, pry right inboard CV joint assembly from transaxle.
9. Remove inner CV joint from transaxle by grasping righthand steering knuckle and swing knuckle and shaft outward from transaxle.
10. Wire halfshaft assembly in level position to prevent overextending CV joint.
11. Repeat steps 8 through 10 on left inboard CV joint assembly. **If the CV joint cannot be pried from the transaxle, insert tool T81P-4026-A or equivalent through right side of case and tap CV joint out.**
12. Remove both front stabilizer bar to control arm attaching nut and washer.
13. Remove 2 front stabilizer bar mounting brackets, then the stabilizer bar.
14. Disconnect speedometer cable from transaxle.
15. Disconnect back-up light switch electrical connector from transaxle switch.
16. Remove clutch housing stiffener brace attaching bolts.
17. Remove shift mechanism stabilizer bar to transaxle attaching bolt.
18. Disconnect then remove transaxle control selector indicator switch and bracket.
19. Remove shift mechanism to shift shaft attaching bolt, then the shift mechanism.
20. Position a suitable jack under transaxle assembly.
21. Loosen rear mount stud nut, then remove bottom rear mount attaching bolt.
22. Remove 3 bolts securing front mount to transaxle case.
23. Lower transaxle slightly until transaxle clears rear mount.
24. Position a suitable jack under engine oil pan.
25. Remove remaining 4 transaxle to engine attaching bolts.
26. Lower transaxle from vehicle.
27. Reverse procedure to install. **During installation of transaxle assembly, ensure transaxle is flush with rear face of engine before installing and tightening attaching bolts.**

Tempo & Topaz

1. Disconnect battery ground cable.
2. Position a suitable block of wood approximately 7 inches of length under clutch pedal to hold clutch pedal up.
3. Grasp and pull clutch cable forward, disconnecting cable from clutch release shaft lever assembly.
4. Remove clutch casing from top rib of transaxle case.
5. Remove 2 top transaxle to engine attaching bolts.
6. Remove air cleaner assembly.
7. Raise and support vehicle, then remove front stabilizer bar to control arm attaching nut and washer.
8. Remove stabilizer bar mounting brackets.
9. Remove nut and bolt attaching lower control ball joint to steering knuckle assembly.
10. Using a suitable tool, pry lower control arm away from steering knuckle.
11. Using tool D83P-4026-A or equivalent, pry left inboard CV joint assembly from transaxle. Remove inboard CV joint from transaxle by grasping the lefthand steering knuckle and swinging the knuckle and halfshaft outward from transaxle. **If the CV joint cannot be pried from transaxle, insert tool T81P-4026-A or equivalent through right side of case and tap CV joint out.**
12. Wire halfshaft assembly in level position to prevent overextending CV joint.
13. Repeat steps 10 through 12 for other CV joint.
14. Remove back-up light switch electrical connector from transaxle.
15. Remove starter motor and position aside.
16. Remove engine roll restricter.
17. Remove shift mechanism, shift indicator and bracket assembly.
18. Disconnect speedometer cable from transaxle.
19. Remove oil pan to clutch housing stiffener brace attaching bolts.
20. Position a suitable jack under transaxle assembly.
21. Remove 2 nuts securing lefthand rear No. 4 insulator to body bracket.
22. Remove bolts securing lefthand front No. 1 insulator to body bracket.
23. Lower transaxle slightly until transaxle clears rear mount.
24. Position a suitable jack under engine.
25. Remove 4 transaxle to engine attaching bolts.
26. Lower transaxle from vehicle.
27. Reverse procedure to install.

5 SPEED

1. Disconnect battery ground cable and drain transaxle fluid.
2. Wedge a seven inch wood block under clutch pedal.
3. Disconnect clutch cable from clutch release shaft assembly, then remove the clutch cable casing from rib on top surface of transaxle case.
4. Remove two top transaxle to engine mounting bolts.
5. Remove top bolt that secures air

management valve bracket to transaxle.

6. Raise vehicle, then remove lower control arm ball joint to steering knuckle attaching nut and bolt. Discard nut and bolt and repeat procedure on opposite side.
7. Pry lower control arm from knuckle on both sides of vehicle using suitable pry bar. Use care not to damage or cut ball joint.
8. Pry left inboard CV joint assembly from transaxle using suitable pry bar. **Lubricant will drain from the seal at this time. Install two plugs.**
9. Remove inboard CV joint from transaxle. Repeat procedure on other side. **If the CV joint assembly cannot be pried from the transaxle, insert tool T81P-4026-A or other suitable tool through the left side and tap the joint out. Tool can be used from either side of the transaxle.**
10. Wire left and right half shaft assemblies in level position.
11. Remove back-up lamp switch connector from transaxle back-up lamp switch.
12. Remove engine roll restricter bracket.
13. Remove three heater pipe bracket attaching screws, then remove engine roll restricter.
14. Remove starter.
15. Disconnect shift mechanism from shaft.
16. Disconnect and remove control selector indicator switch arm from shift shaft.
17. Remove shift mechanism stabilizer bar to transaxle attaching bolt, then remove control selector indicator switch and bracket.
18. Remove speedometer cable from transaxle.
19. Remove two stiffener brace attaching bolts from lower position of clutch housing.
20. Position a jack under transaxle.
21. Remove two rear mount and air management valve to transaxle securing bolts, then remove three bolts attaching front mount to transaxle.
22. Lower transaxle support jack until transaxle clears rear mount and support engine with suitable jack. Use a suitable piece of wood between the jack and engine.
23. Remove remaining four engine-to-transaxle attaching bolts.
24. Remove transaxle from rear face of the engine and lower it from vehicle. **The transaxle case casting may have sharp edges. Wear protective gloves when handling the transaxle assembly.**
25. Reverse procedure to install. Torque the following as specified, engine-to-transaxle bolts 26-31 ft. lbs., front transaxle mount bolts 25-35 ft. lbs., rear transaxle mount bolts 40-51 ft. lbs., starter stud bolts 30-40 ft. lbs., starter nuts 25-30 ft. lbs.

Transfer Case Section

Page No.

DESCRIPTION

TRANSFER CASE

The transfer case used on 1987-88 Tempo and Topaz models with the All Wheel Drive system, is actuated by an electrically controlled vacuum servo system. When the AWD (all wheel drive) switch is turned on, a relay activates the 4WD solenoid valve. The 4WD solenoid valve allows a vacuum to be created in the lefthand chambers of the vacuum servo. Vacuum in the lefthand chambers moves the servo rod and sliding collar into engagement with the transfer case output gears, driveshaft and rear axle. When the AWD switch is turned OFF, a relay activates the 2WD solenoid valve. The 2WD solenoid valve then allows a vacuum to be created in the righthand chambers of the vacuum servo. Vacuum in the righthand chambers then returns the servo rod and sliding collar, disengaging the transfer case, driveshaft and rear axle output gears.

TRANSFER CASE REPLACE

1. Raise and support vehicle.
2. Drain fluid from transfer case by removing drive housing lower lefthand attaching bolt.
3. Remove vacuum line attaching bracket bolt.
4. Remove drive shaft front attaching bolts and caps. Disconnect front of drive shaft from drive yoke.
5. Remove three bolts attaching vacuum motor shield, then the shield.
6. Remove vacuum lines from servo.
7. Support transfer case assembly, then remove transfer case to transaxle attaching bolts.
8. Remove transfer case.
9. Reverse procedure to install.

Rear Axle, Suspension & Brakes Section

INDEX

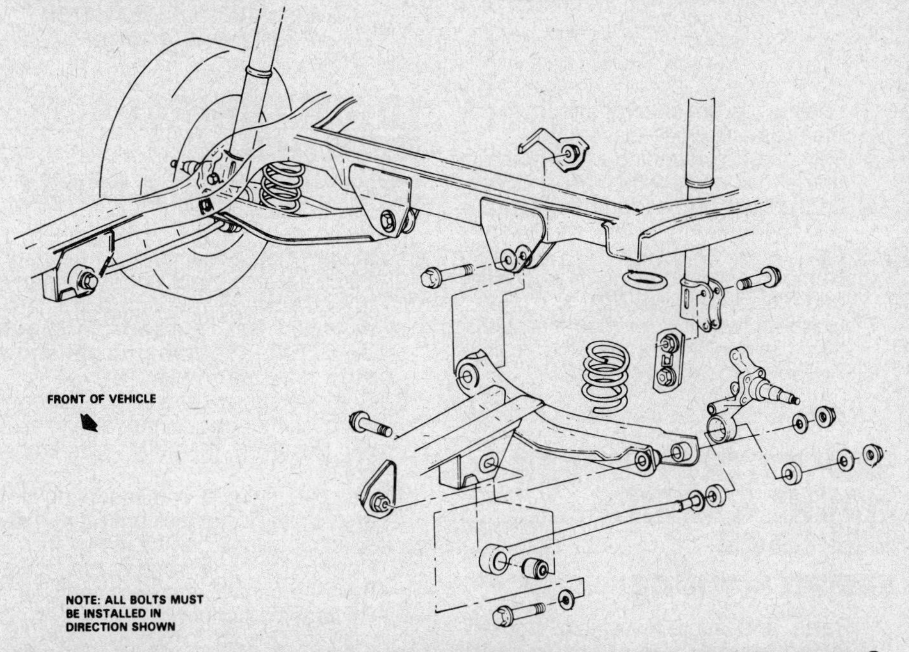

FRONT OF VEHICLE
NOTE: ALL BOLTS MUST BE INSTALLED IN DIRECTION SHOWN

Fig. 1 Rear suspension, exploded view. Except Tempo & Topaz

DESCRIPTION

EXCEPT TEMPO & TOPAZ

These vehicles use a modified MacPherson strut independent rear suspension, **Fig. 1.** Each side consists of a shock strut, lower control arm, tie rod, spindle and a coil spring mounted between the lower control arm and body crossmember side rail.

TEMPO & TOPAZ

These vehicles use a new MacPherson strut independent rear suspension, **Fig. 2.** Each side consists of a shock absorber strut assembly, two parallel control arms per side, tie rod, spindle and a jounce bumper and bracket.

The shock absorber strut assembly includes a rubber isolated top mount, upper spring seat, coil spring insulator, coil spring and a lower spring seat. the strut assembly is attached at the top by two studs, which retain the top mount of the strut to the inner body side panel. The lower end of the assembly is bolted to the spindle. The two control arms are attached to the underbody and spindle with nuts and bolts. The tie rod is attached to the underbody and the spindle. The jounce bumper bracket is bolted to the strut.

1987–88 TEMPO & TOPAZ MODELS W/ALL WHEEL DRIVE SYSTEM

REAR AXLE ASSEMBLY, REPLACE

Remove rear axle assembly to a suitable workbench to conduct all axle repairs.

1. Disconnect battery ground cable.
2. Raise and support vehicle. Position a suitable jack under the rear axle assembly.
3. Disconnect and remove exhaust system components from catalytic converter to rear of vehicle.
4. Remove rear U-joints bolts and caps retaining driveshaft from torque tube yoke flange. Lower driveshaft.
5. Remove four attaching bolts from torque tube support bracket.
6. Remove axle attaching bolt from left-hand differential support bracket.
7. Remove axle attaching bolt from center differential support bracket.
8. Lower axle assembly and remove inboard U-joint attaching bolts and caps from each half shaft. Remove and wire half shaft assemblies aside.
9. Reverse procedure to install. Torque inboard U-joint cap attaching nuts to 15-17 ft. lbs. Torque differential housing to left hand and center differential support bracket attaching bolts to 70-80 ft. lbs. Torque mounting bracket and torque tube to crossmember attaching bolts to 28-35 ft. lbs. Torque driveshaft to torque tube yoke flange attaching bolts to 15-17 ft. lbs.

HALF SHAFT, REPLACE

1. Remove rear suspension control arm attaching bolt.
2. Remove outboard U-joint attaching bolts and caps.
3. Remove inboard U-joint attaching bolts and caps.
4. Carefully slide shafts together. Do not allow splined shafts to contact with excessive force. Remove half shafts. **Do not drop the half shafts as the impact may damage U-joint bearing cups.**
5. Remove and retain bearing cups.
6. Inspect U-joint assemblies for wear and/or damage. Replace U-joints, if necessary.
7. Reverse procedure to install. Note the following:
   a. The inboard shaft has a larger diameter than the outboard shaft.

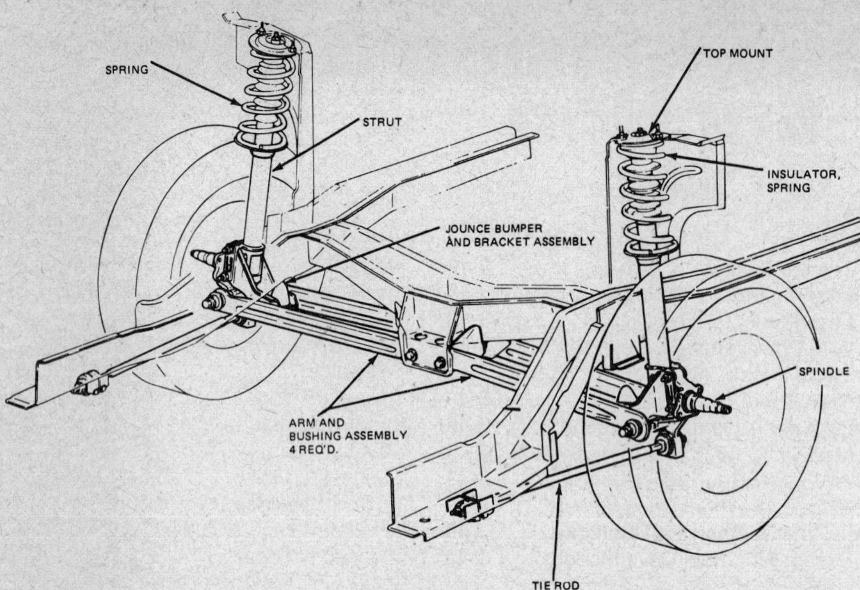

Fig. 2 Rear suspension components. Tempo & Topaz

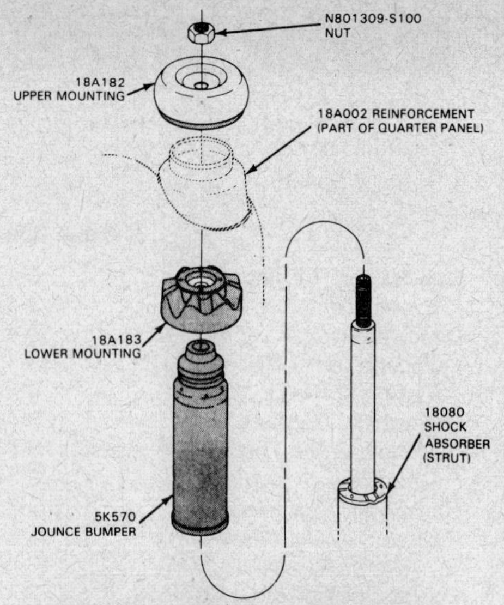

Fig. 3 Shock absorber strut upper mounting components. Except Tempo & Topaz

b. Torque inboard U-joint attaching bolts to 15-17 ft. lbs.
c. Torque outboard U-joint attaching bolts to 15-17 ft. lbs.
d. Torque rear suspension control arm attaching bolt to 60-86 ft. lbs.

DRIVESHAFT, REPLACE

During removal and installation, support driveshaft using a suitable jack or hoist under the center bearing assembly.

1. To maintain driveshaft balance, mark U-joints so they may be installed in their original positions. **Do not use a sharp tool to place alignment marks on any component.**
2. Remove front U-joint attaching bolts and caps.
3. Slide driveshaft toward rear of vehicle and disengage driveshaft.
4. Remove rear U-joint attaching bolts and caps attaching driveshaft, from torque tube yoke flange.
5. Slide driveshaft toward front of vehicle and disengage driveshaft. **Do not allow splined shafts to contact with excessive force.**
6. Remove center bearing attaching bolts.
7. Remove driveshaft and retain bearing cups with tape, if necessary.
8. Inspect U-joint assemblies for wear or damage. Replace, if necessary.
9. Reverse procedure to install. Torque U-joint retaining caps and bolts to 15-17 ft. lbs. Torque center bearing and attaching bolts to 23-30 ft. lbs.

SHOCK STRUT REPLACE

EXCEPT TEMPO & TOPAZ

1. Raise and support vehicle.
2. Remove rear compartment access panels. On four-door models, remove quarter trim panel.
3. Loosen top shock strut attaching nut, then remove wheel assembly.
4. Remove clip retaining brake hose to rear shock and position hose aside.
5. Loosen but do not remove two nuts and bolts securing shock strut to spindle.
6. Remove top mounting nut, washer and rubber insulator, **Fig. 3.**
7. Remove two bottom mounting bolts, then the shock strut from the vehicle.
8. Reverse procedure to install.

SHOCK STRUT, UPPER MOUNT & SPRING REPLACE

TEMPO & TOPAZ

1. Raise and support vehicle. Loosen upper strut mount to body nuts located in luggage compartment.
2. Remove wheel assembly.
3. Place a suitable jack under control arms.
4. Remove brake hose bracket to strut bolt and position brake hose bracket aside.
5. Remove jounce bumper bracket.
6. Remove two upper mount to body nuts, then the strut.
7. Place strut, spring and upper mount assembly into a suitable spring compressor tool. **Do not remove the spring from the strut without first compressing the spring.**
8. With spring compressed, remove strut shaft to mount nuts. Remove spring, strut and mount, **Fig. 4,** from spring compressor tool.
9. Reverse procedure to install. Torque shaft nut to 35-50 ft. lbs., torque jounce bumper bracket to strut mount bolts to 70-96 ft. lbs., torque top mount to body nuts to 25-30 ft. lbs.

LOWER CONTROL ARM REPLACE

EXCEPT TEMPO & TOPAZ

1. Raise and support vehicle, then remove wheel assembly.
2. Place a suitable jack under lower control arm between spring and spindle mounting. **Rear suspension should be at full rebound and the shock strut fully extended.**
3. Remove control arm to body mounting nuts, then the control arm to spindle mounting nuts. Do not remove bolts.
4. Remove spindle end mounting bolt, then slowly lower jack until spring and spring insulator can be removed.
5. Remove bolts from body mountings, then the control arm from vehicle.
6. Reverse procedure to install.

TEMPO & TOPAZ

1. Raise and support vehicle.
2. Remove wheel assembly.
3. Remove control arm to spindle nut and bolt.
4. Remove center mounting nut and bolt.
5. Remove control arm from vehicle.
6. Reverse procedure to install. Torque control arm to body bolt to 40-55 ft. lbs., torque control arm to spindle nut to 60-86 ft. lbs. **When installing new control arms the bushing with the 10 mm hole is installed toward the center of the vehicle and the bushing with the 12 mm hole toward the spindle. The offset on the control arm must face up on the right side of the vehicle and down on the left side of the vehicle, Fig. 5. The flanged edge of the control arm stamping must face the rear of the vehicle.**

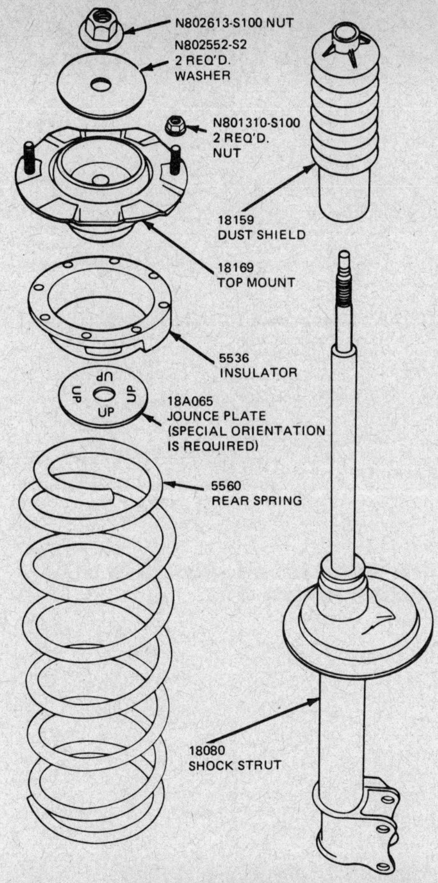

Fig. 4 Strut, spring & upper mount components. Tempo & Topaz

TIE ROD
REPLACE
EXCEPT TEMPO & TOPAZ

1. Raise and support vehicle.
2. Scribe a reference mark on tie rod front bracket at bolt head center line for use during reassembly.
3. Remove nut, washer and insulators attaching tie rod to spindle.
4. Remove nut and bolt attaching tie rod to body bracket, then the tie rod. **It may be necessary to pry front bracket sheet metal apart slightly to remove tie rod from body.**
5. Place a new dished washer over tie rod end with flange toward middle of rod, **Fig. 6.**
6. Install tie rod through spindle bushings and place eye of rod into body bracket. Secure rod to bracket using a new nut and bolt. Do not tighten.
7. Place another dished washer over end of rod with flange toward end of rod, then install a new nut and torque to 65-75 ft. lbs.
8. Using suitable jack, raise lower control arm to curb height.
9. Align center of bolt head with reference mark on body bracket, then torque tie rod front bolt to 90-100 ft. lbs. This bolt must be installed with head inboard on vehicle.
10. Lower vehicle to ground.

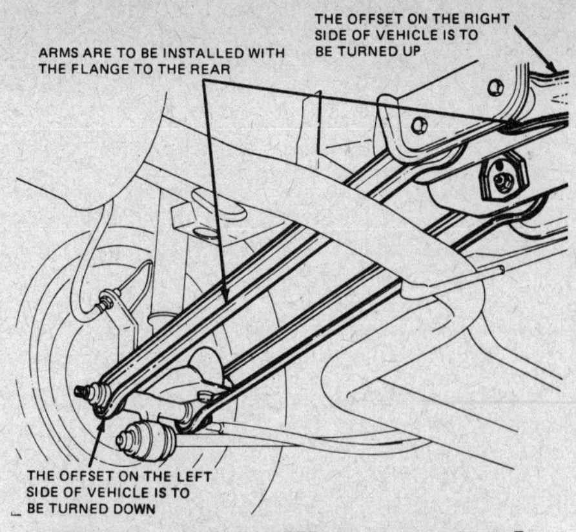

Fig. 5 Installing control arm. Tempo & Topaz

TEMPO & TOPAZ

1. Raise and support vehicle.
2. From inside of luggage compartment, loosen two strut top mount to body nuts.
3. Raise vehicle. Position a suitable jack under lower control arm with a piece of wood between jack and control arm.
4. Remove wheel assembly.
5. Remove two top mount studs, then tie rod to spindle retaining nut.
6. Remove tie rod to body retaining nut.
7. Lower jack until upper strut mount studs clear body mount holes.
8. Move spindle rearward until tie rod can be removed.
9. Place new washers and bushings on both ends of tie rod, **Fig. 6. Front and rear bushings are not interchangeable. The rear bushings have indentations incorporated in them.**
10. Insert tie rod into body bracket, then install new bushing, washer and nut. Do not tighten nut.
11. Pull back on spindle until tie rod can be installed into the spindle. Install new bushing, washer and nut. Do not tighten nut.
12. Raise jack enough to secure the two strut mounting studs in place.
13. Install two strut to body mount nuts. Torque nuts to 20-30 ft. lbs.
14. Using a suitable jack, raise lower control arm to curb height. Install tie rod nuts and torque to 52-74 ft. lbs.
15. Remove jack and install wheel assembly. Lower vehicle.

SPINDLE
REPLACE
EXCEPT TEMPO & TOPAZ

If a frame contact hoist is used, a jack stand must be placed under lower control arm to raise it to curb height.

1. Raise and support vehicle.
2. Remove wheel assembly, then the brake drum and wheel bearings.
3. Remove brake backing plate assembly, then the tie rod retaining nut and dished washer.
4. Remove two nuts and bolts securing strut to spindle.

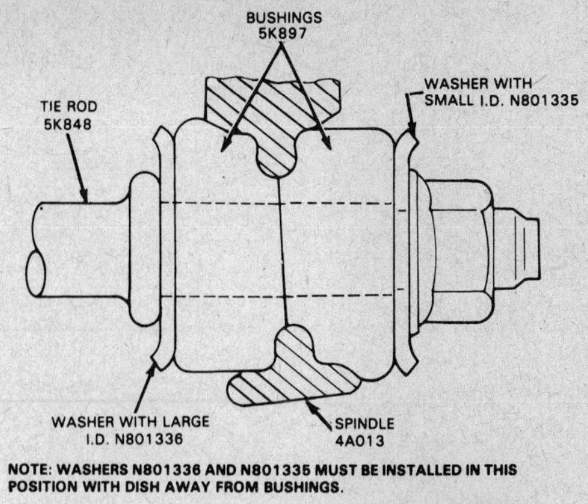

Fig. 6 Tie rod installation

5. Remove nut and bolt securing lower control arm to spindle, then the spindle.
6. Reverse procedure to install.

TEMPO & TOPAZ

1. Raise and support vehicle.
2. Remove wheel assembly.
3. Remove brake drum. Remove brake flex hose bracket to strut bolt.
4. Remove brake backing plate to spindle bolts, then the brake backing plate. **Care should be taken to ensure that brake flex hose is not stretched and brake tube is not bent.**
5. Remove lower control arm to spindle bolt, washer and nut.
6. Remove tie rod nut, bushing and washer.
7. Remove spindle to strut bolts, then the spindle.
8. Reverse procedure to install. Torque spindle to strut bolts to 70-96 ft. lbs. Torque tie rod nut to 52-74 ft. lbs. Torque lower control arm to spindle nut to 60-86 ft. lbs.

COIL SPRING
REPLACE
EXCEPT TEMPO & TOPAZ

1. Raise and support vehicle. Support lower control arm with suitable jack.
2. Remove tire and wheel assembly.
3. Remove nut, bolt and washer securing lower control arm to spindle.
4. Lower control arm until spring can be removed.
5. Reverse procedure to install. A new spring insulator must be used when replacing the spring.

BRAKE ADJUSTMENTS

Although the brakes are self-adjusting, **Figs. 7 and 8,** an initial adjustment will be necessary after a brake repair. The initial adjustment can be obtained as follows:

1. On 7 in. brakes, pivot adjuster quadrant until it meshes with knurled pin and is in third or fourth notch of the outboard end of the quadrant, **Fig. 9.**
2. On 8 in. brakes, determine inside diameter of drum brake surface using brake shoe gauge tool D81L-1103-A

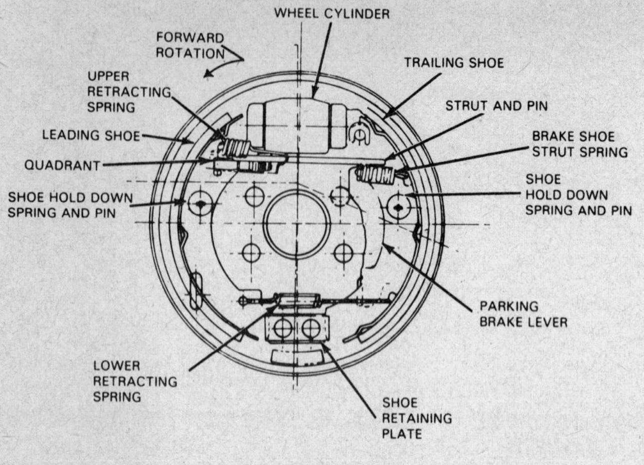

Fig. 7 Rear brake assembly. Models w/7 inch brake drum dia.

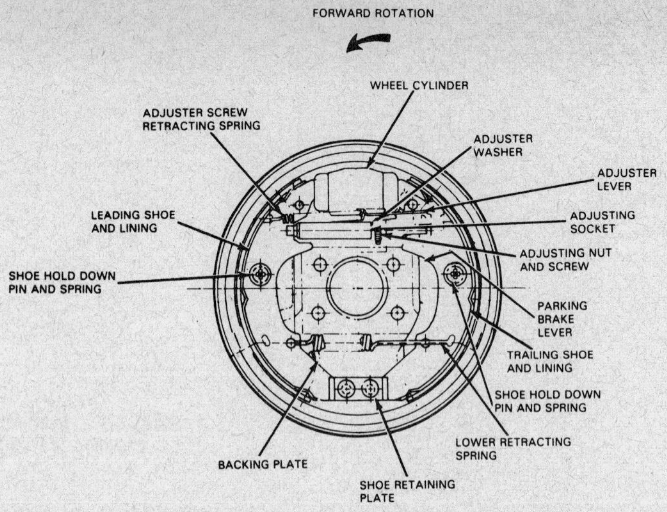

Fig. 8 Rear brake assembly. Models w/8 inch brake drum dia.

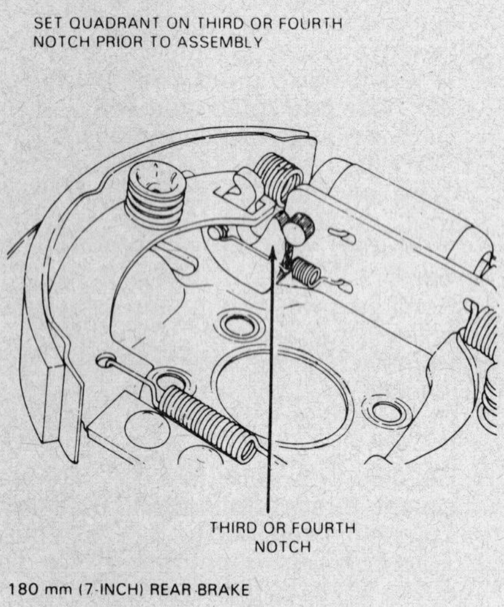

Fig. 9 Initial brake adjustment

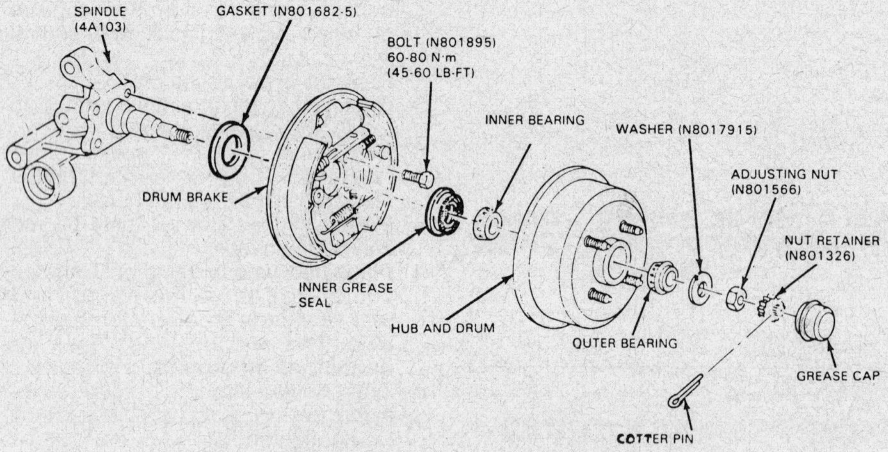

Fig. 10 Rear wheel bearing assembly. Except models with all wheel drive system

or equivalent. Adjust brake shoe diameter to fit gauge. Hold automatic adjusting lever out of engagement while rotating adjusting screw and ensure that screw rotates freely.

3. Install drum and wheel assembly, then adjust wheel bearings as described in **Fig. 10.**
4. Complete adjustment by applying brakes several times, then check brake operation by making several stops from varying speeds. **If brake drum cannot be removed for brake servicing, remove rubber plug from backing plate inspection hole. On 7 in. brakes, insert a suitable tool into the hole until it contacts adjuster assembly pivot. apply pressure sideways on the pivot point allowing adjuster quadrant to ratchet and release the brake adjustment. On 8 in. brakes remove the brake line to axle retention bracket. This will allow sufficient room for insertion of a suitable tool to disengage adjusting lever and back off the adjusting screw.**

PARKING BRAKE

ADJUST

1. Pump brake pedal three times before making adjustment.
2. Place transmission in neutral, then raise and support vehicle.
3. Position parking brake control assembly in 12th notch position (two notches from full application). Tighten adjusting nut until rear wheel brakes drag slightly with control assembly fully released. Repeat procedure as necessary to ensure proper adjustment.
4. Position control assembly in 12th notch, then loosen adjusting nut enough to eliminate rear brake drag with the control assembly fully released.
5. Lower vehicle and check operation of parking brake.

MASTER CYLINDER

REPLACE

LESS POWER BRAKES

1. Disconnect battery ground cable.
2. Disconnect stop lamp switch electrical connector and remove switch retainer.
3. Slide stop lamp switch off pedal pin far enough to clear end of pin, then remove switch from pin.
4. From inside engine compartment loosen two master cylinder attaching nuts, then slide master cylinder pushrod, nylon washers and bushings from brake pedal pin.
5. Disconnect brake lines from master

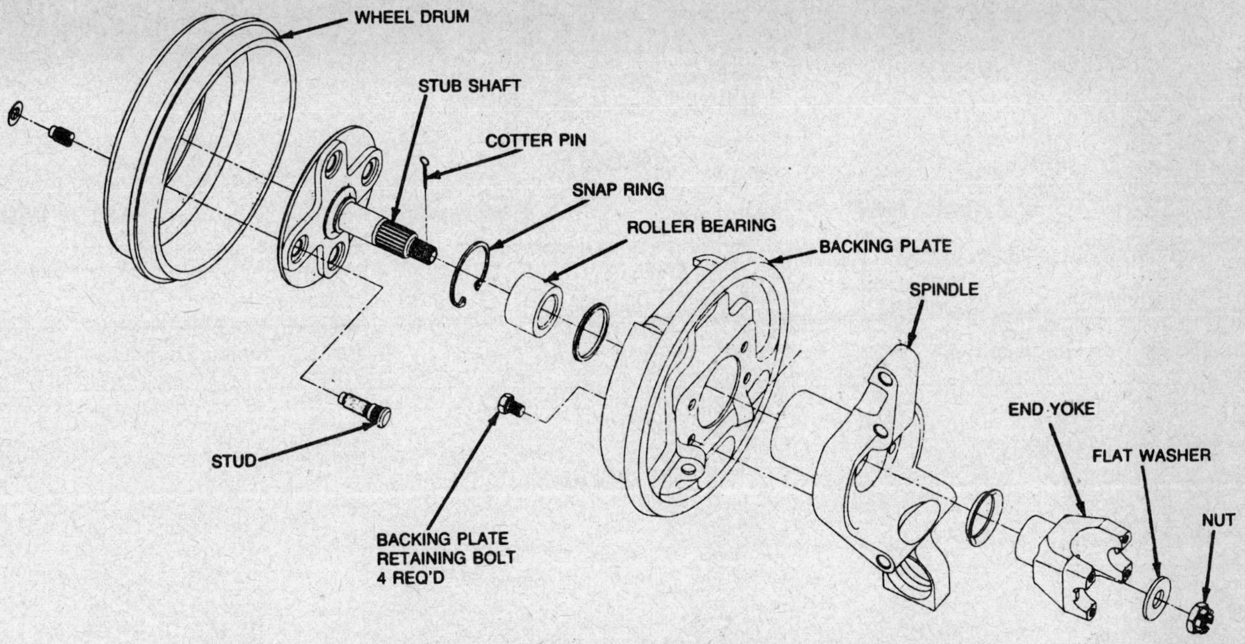

Fig. 11 Rear wheel bearing assembly. Models w/all wheel drive system

cylinder, then remove nuts securing master cylinder to dash panel. List cylinder forward and upward and remove from vehicle.

6. Reverse procedure to install.

WITH POWER BRAKES

1. Disconnect brake lines from master cylinder. Cap all lines and fittings.
2. On late 1983 models and all 1984-86 models, disconnect brake warning lamp switch wire connector.
3. Remove master cylinder to power brake unit attaching nuts, then remove master cylinder.
4. Reverse procedure to install.

POWER BRAKE UNIT REPLACE

1. Remove master cylinder as described under Master Cylinder, Replace, Power Brakes.
2. From inside passenger compartment, disconnect stop lamp switch electrical connector.
3. Remove pushrod retainer and outer nylon washer from pedal pin, then slide switch along brake pedal far enough for outer hole to clear pin. Slide switch upward and remove.
4. Remove booster to dash panel attaching nuts, then slide booster pushrod and pushrod bushing from brake pedal pin.
5. From inside engine compartment, disconnect manifold vacuum hose from booster check valve.
6. Move booster forward until booster studs clear dash panel, then remove booster.
7. Reverse procedure to install.

REAR WHEEL BEARING ADJUST

EXCEPT ALL WHEEL DRIVE MODELS

1. Raise and support vehicle. Remove dust cover from hub. Remove wheel assembly, if necessary.
2. Remove cotter pin and nut retainer.
3. Back off adjusting nut 1 full turn.
4. Torque adjusting nut, **Fig. 10**, to 17-25 ft. lbs., while rotating drum assembly.
5. Back off adjusting nut 1/2 turn, then retighten adjusting nut to 10-15 inch lbs. Position adjusting nut retainer over nut so slots are aligned with cotter pin hole, then install cotter pin.
6. Install dust cover, wheel assembly, if necessary and lower vehicle to ground.

REAR WHEEL BEARING REPLACE

EXCEPT ALL WHEEL DRIVE MODELS

1. Raise and support vehicle.
2. Remove grease cap from hub. Remove cotter pin, nut retainer, adjusting nut and flat washer from spindle, **Fig. 10.** Discard cotter pin.
3. Pull hub and drum assembly off spindle being careful not to drop outer bearing assembly.
4. Remove outer bearing assembly.
5. Using tool 1175-AC or equivalent, remove and discard grease seal. Remove inner bearing assembly from hub.
6. Reverse procedure to install.

MODELS W/ALL WHEEL DRIVE SYSTEM

1. Raise and support vehicle.
2. Remove wheel and tire assembly.
3. Remove brake drum, parking brake cable from brake backing plate.
4. Remove brake line from wheel cylinder.
5. Remove outboard U-joint attaching bolts and caps. Remove outboard end of halfshaft from wheel stub shaft yoke and wire to control arm, **Fig. 11.**
6. Remove and discard control arm to spindle bolt, washers and nut.
7. Remove tie rod nut, bushing and washer. Discard nut.
8. Remove and discard two bolts attaching spindle to strut. Remove spindle from vehicle.
9. Mount spindle and backing plate assembly into a suitable vise.
10. Remove cotter pin and nut attaching stub shaft yoke to stub shaft. Discard cotter pin.
11. Remove spindle and backing plate assembly from vise. Remove stub shaft yoke using a suitable tool.
12. Mount spindle and backing plate assembly in a vise. Remove wheel stub shaft.
13. Remove snap ring retaining bearing.
14. Remove four bolts attaching spindle to backing plate. Remove backing plate.
15. Remove spindle from vise and mount into a suitable press. With spindle side facing upward, carefully press bearing out of spindle. Discard bearing after removal.
16. Reverse procedure to install.

Front Suspension & Steering Section

INDEX

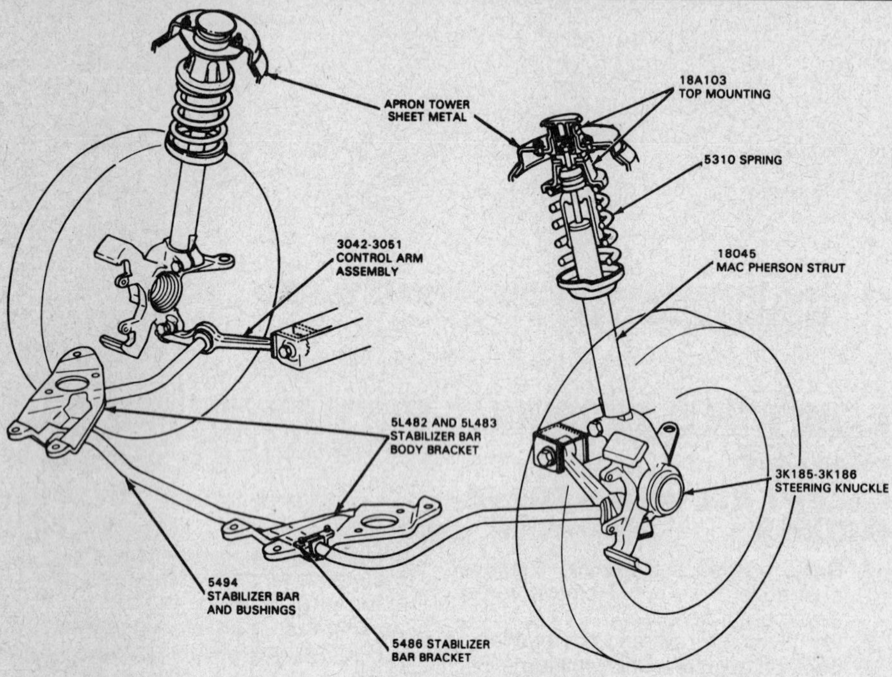

Fig. 1 Front suspension

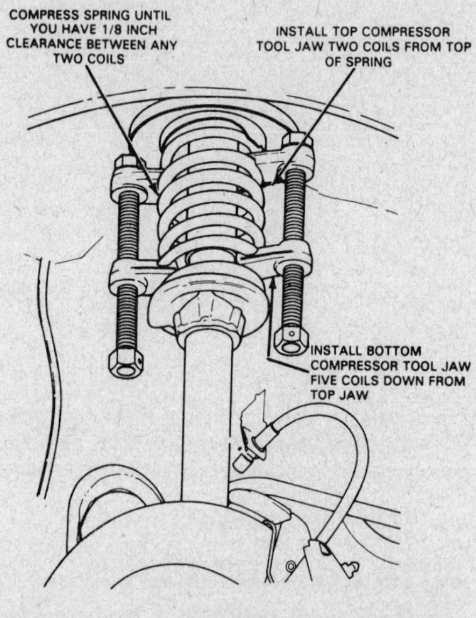

Fig. 2 Installing coil spring compressor. Except Tempo & Topaz

DESCRIPTION

These vehicles use a MacPherson type front suspension with the vertical shock absorber struts attached to the upper fender reinforcements and the steering knuckle, **Fig. 1.** The lower control arms are attached inboard to a crossmember and outboard to the steering knuckle through a ball joint to provide lower steering knuckle position.

STRUT ASSEMBLY REPLACE

1. Raise and support vehicle, then remove tire and wheel assembly.
2. Remove brake hose retaining bracket from strut.
3. On Tempo and Topaz models, remove brake caliper, brake rotor, and tie rod end.
4. Place suitable jack under lower control arm and raise strut as far as possible without raising vehicle.
5. On models except Tempo and Topaz, install spring compressor tool No. T81P-5310A or equivalent by placing top jaw on second coil from top and bottom jaw so as to grip a total of 5 coils, then compress spring until there is about 1/8 inch between any 2 coils, **Fig. 2.**
6. On Tempo and Topaz models, install spring compressor tool No. 14-0259 or 86-0016 by placing top jaw on 5th or 6th coil from bottom, then compress spring a minimum of 3 1/2 inches, **Fig. 3. Spring must be compressed before strut is removed to insure that no excessive force is applied to constant velocity universal joints.**
7. Remove steering knuckle-to-strut pinch bolt, then loosen two top mount to apron nuts and top strut shaft nut. **When loosening or tightening strut-to-mount nut, hold 6 mm Allen wrench, Fig. 4, or hold 8 mm hex with a deep socket 1/4-inch drive wrench, Figs. 5 and 6, and turn only the nut.**
8. Lower jack from control arm, then using a large screwdriver, spread knuckle-to-strut pinch joint.
9. Place block of wood 2 x 4 x 7 1/2 inches against knuckle shoulder. Using suitable pry bar between wood block and lower spring seat, separate strut from knuckle, **Fig. 7.**
10. Remove two top mounting nuts, then the strut, spring, and top mount assembly from vehicle.
11. On 1981-82 vehicles, install 18 mm deep socket onto strut shaft nut. Insert 6 mm Allen wrench into shaft end, then clamp mount into vise, **Fig. 4.**
12. On 1983-86 except Tempo and Topaz, place 18 mm deep socket tool No. D81P-18045-A1 or equivalent on strut shaft nut. Place an 8 mm deep socket, 1/4 inch drive onto shaft end and clamp mount into vise, **Fig. 5.**
13. On Tempo and Topaz, place 18 mm deep socket tool No. D81P-18045-A1 or equivalent on strut shaft nut. Insert an 8 mm hex deep socket with 1/4-inch drive wrench and clamp strut into vise, **Fig. 6.**
14. On all vehicles, remove top shaft mounting nut from shaft while holding Allen wrench or 1/4-inch drive socket. **Do not clamp directly on strut with vise as damage to strut may result.**
15. Remove strut top mount components and, except on Tempo and Topaz,

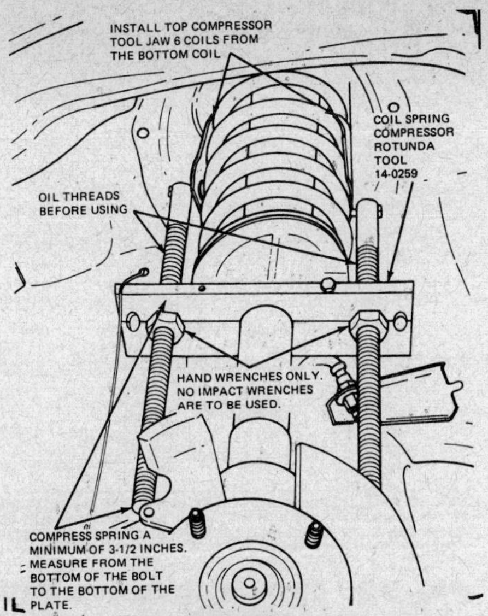

Fig. 3 Installing coil spring compressor. Tempo & Topaz

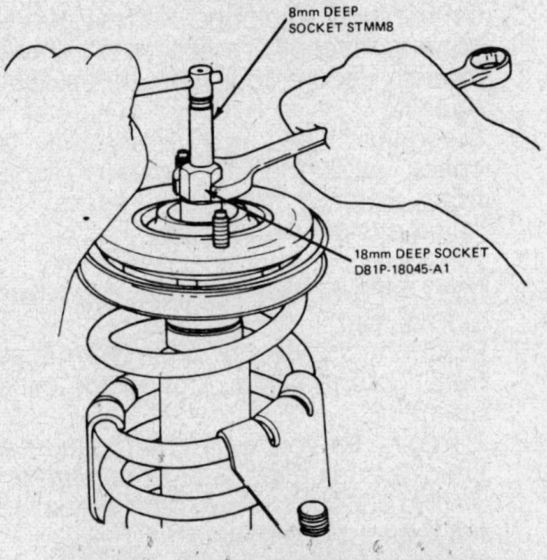

Fig. 6 Removing shock absorber strut top mounting nut. Tempo & Topaz

spring. **On Tempo and Topaz models, check spring insulator for damage to splash shield.**

16. On Tempo and Topaz models, remove spring compressor from strut and remove spring.
17. Reverse procedure to install. Refer to **Figs. 8 and 9** for proper installation sequence of top mount components. On except Tempo and Topaz models, torque strut shaft nut to 48-62 ft. lbs., on Tempo and Topaz models, torque strut shaft nut to 35-50 ft. lbs. Install new steering knuckle pinch nut and torque to 66-81 ft. lbs. On except Tempo and Topaz models, torque two top mount attaching nuts to 22-29 ft. lbs. On Tempo and Topaz models, torque two top mount attaching nuts to 25-30 ft. lbs.

CHECKING BALL JOINTS

1. Raise and support vehicle.
2. With suspension in full rebound position, grasp lower edge of tire and move wheel in and out, **Fig. 10.**

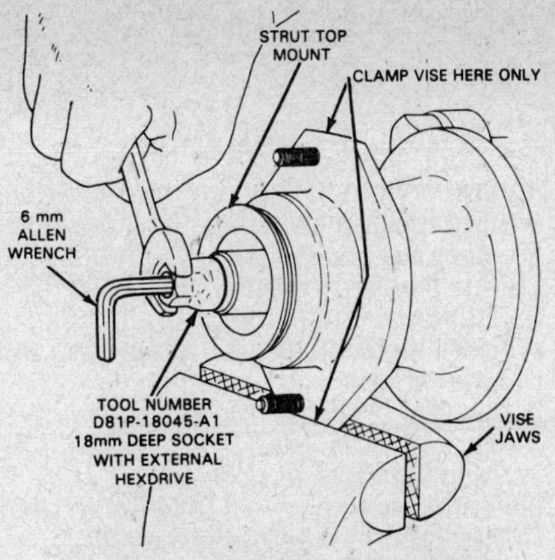

Fig. 4 Removing shock absorber strut top mounting nut. 1981–82

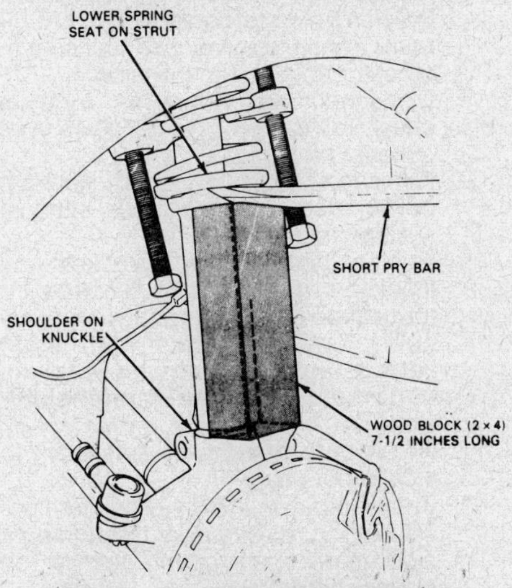

Fig. 7 Separating shock absorber strut from knuckle

3. Observe lower end of knuckle and lower control arm as wheel is being moved in and out. Any movement between lower end of knuckle and lower arm indicates excessive ball joint wear.
4. If any movement is observed, install a new lower control arm assembly. The lower ball joint and control arm are serviced as an assembly only. Refer to Lower Control Arm, Replace in this section.

LOWER CONTROL ARM REPLACE

1. Raise and support vehicle.
2. Remove nut from stabilizer bar, then the large dished washer.
3. Remove lower control arm inner pivot bolt and nut.
4. Remove lower control arm ball joint pinch bolt, then using a screwdriver, separate the control arm from the steering knuckle and remove from vehicle. **Ensure steering column is in unlocked position. Do not use a hammer to separate ball joint from knuckle.**

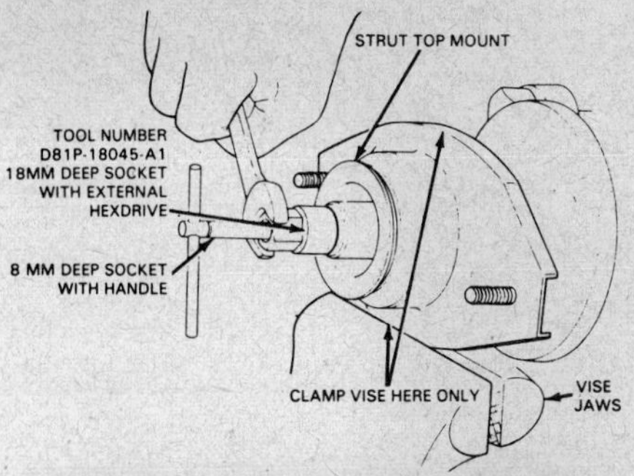

Fig. 5 Removing shock absorber strut top mounting nut. 1983–86 exc. Tempo & Topaz

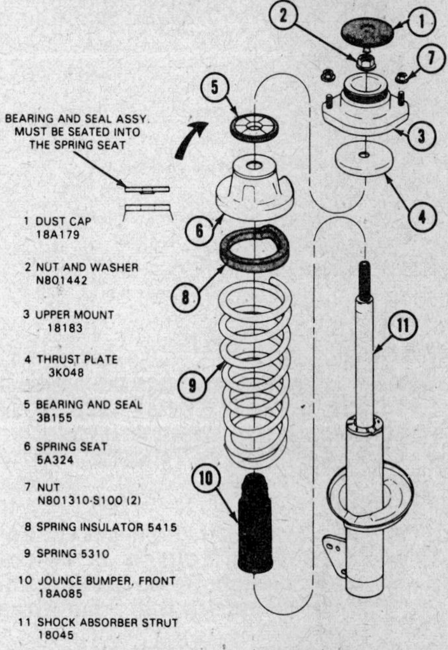

Fig. 8 Installation of shock absorber strut top mounting components. Except Tempo & Topaz

5. Reverse procedure to install. Torque pinch bolt and nut to 37-44 ft. lbs. On 1981-83 vehicles, torque lower control arm inner pivot nut to 44-55 ft. lbs. On 1984-86 vehicles, torque lower control arm inner pivot nut to 50-60 ft. lbs. Torque stabilizer bar nut to 98-115 ft. lbs.

STEERING KNUCKLE REPLACE

1. Raise and support vehicle, then remove wheel assembly.
2. Remove cotter pin from tie rod end stud, then the slotted nut.
3. Using tool 3290C and adapter T81P3504W, remove tie rod end from knuckle.
4. Remove brake caliper, then the hub from the driveshaft.
5. On 1984-86 vehicles, loosen two top mount nuts. Do not remove nuts.
6. On all vehicles, remove pinch bolt and nut securing lower arm to steering knuckle, then using a screwdriver,

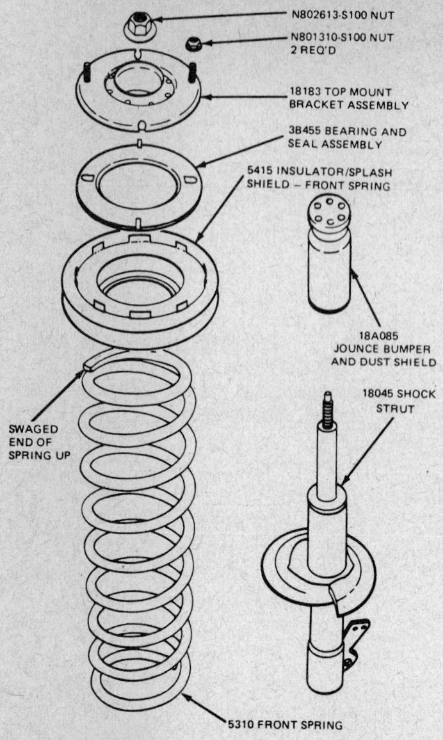

Fig. 9 Installation of shock absorber strut top mounting components. Tempo & Topaz

separate lower arm from knuckle. **Ensure steering column is in unlocked position. Do not use a hammer to separate ball joint from knuckle.**

7. Remove shock absorber strut to steering knuckle pinch bolt, then using a screwdriver, slightly open knuckle to strut pinch joint.
8. Remove steering knuckle from shock absorber strut, **Fig. 7**, then from the vehicle.
9. Reverse procedure to install. Torque steering knuckle to shock strut assembly pinch bolt to 66-81 ft. lbs., torque lower control arm to steering knuckle pinch bolt to 37-44 ft. lbs. On 1984-88 vehicles, torque two top mount nuts to 25-30 ft. lbs. Install new slotted nut then torque to 23-35 ft. lbs.

STABILIZER BAR REPLACE

1. Raise and support vehicle.
2. Remove stabilizer insulator mounting bracket bolts.
3. Remove stabilizer bar to control arm attaching bolts, then the stabilizer bar assembly.
4. Remove worn insulators from stabilizer bar.
5. Reverse procedure to install. Torque stabilizer bar to control arm attaching bolt to 98-115 ft. lbs. Torque stabilizer insulator mounting bracket bolts to 60-70 ft. lbs.

STEERING GEAR REPLACE

MANUAL STEERING

1. Disconnect battery ground cable, then turn ignition switch to "On" position.
2. Remove access panel from dash below steering column.
3. Remove intermediate shaft bolts at gear input shaft and at steering column shaft.
4. Using a wide blade screwdriver, spread slots enough to loosen intermediate shaft at both ends.
5. Turn steering wheel fully left to allow clearance for tie rod removal.
6. Remove tie rod ends from steering knuckles using tool 3290C and adapter T81P3504W. Turn right wheel to full left position.
7. Remove left tie rod end from tie rod, then on vehicles equipped with automatic transmission disconnect speedometer cable at transmission.
8. Disconnect secondary air tube at check valve, then exhaust pipes from exhaust manifold.
9. Remove exhaust hanger bracket from below steering gear. Wire exhaust system aside.
10. Remove gear mounting brackets and insulators, then separate gear from intermediate shaft while simultaneously pulling upward on shaft from inside vehicle. **Right and lefthand brackets and insulators are not interchangeable.**
11. Rotate gear forward and downward to clear input shaft.
12. Ensure input shaft is in full left turn position, then remove gear through right side apron opening until left tie rod clears shift linkage.
13. Lower left side of gear and remove gear from vehicle.
14. Reverse procedure to install. Ensure input shaft is at full left turn stop and right wheel assembly is in full left turn position. Use caution not to damage steering gear bellows.

POWER STEERING

1. Disconnect battery ground cable, then turn ignition switch to On position.
2. Remove access panel from dash below steering column.
3. Remove four screws from dash panel steering column boot, then slide boot along intermediate shaft.
4. Remove intermediate shaft bolts at gear input shaft and from steering column shaft.
5. Using wide blade screwdriver, spread slot wide enough to loosen intermediate shaft at both ends.
6. Turn steering wheel to full left stop to facilitate gear removal.
7. On all 1982 vehicles except 1.6 L. engine and manual transmission without air conditioning, remove pressure switch electrical connector, then the switch.

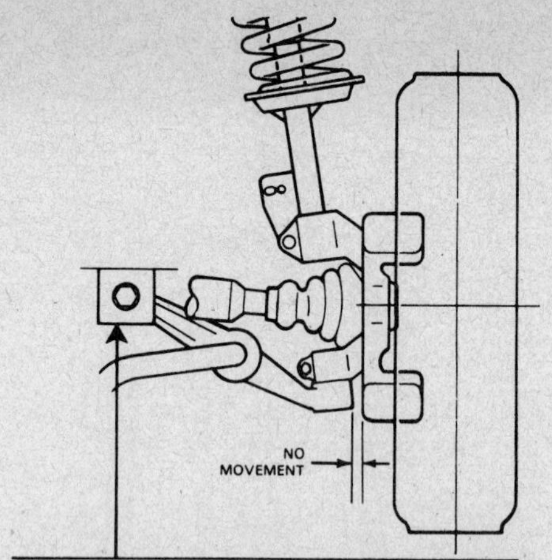

NOTE: AS WHEEL IS BEING MOVED IN AND OUT, OBSERVE THE LOWER END OF THE KNUCKLE AND THE LOWER CONTROL ARM. ANY MOVEMENT BETWEEN LOWER END OF THE KNUCKLE AND THE LOWER ARM INDICATES ABNORMAL BALL JOINT WEAR

Fig. 10 Checking lower ball joint

8. On 1984-88 vehicles, remove air cleaner.
9. On vehicles equipped with air conditioning, except Tempo and Topaz models, secure liquid line above dash opening.
10. Disconnect secondary air tube at check valve, then the exhaust pipes from exhaust manifold. Secure exhaust system to the side.
11. Remove exhaust hanger brackets from below steering gear and from side apron.
12. Disconnect pressure and return lines from intermediate connector and drain fluid.
13. Remove tie rod ends from steering knuckles using tool 3290C and adapter T81P3504W. Turn right wheel to full left turn position.
14. On vehicles equipped with manual transmission, remove left tie rod end from tie rod.
15. On vehicles equipped with automatic transmission, disconnect speedometer cable from transmission.
16. On vehicles equipped with automatic transmission, disconnect shift cable assembly from transmission.
17. Except on Tempo and Topaz models, remove screws securing heater water tube to brace below oil pan.
18. Except on Tempo and Topaz models, remove nut from lower bolt securing engine mounting bracket to transmission housing. Tap bolt out as far as possible.
19. Remove gear mounting brackets and insulators.
20. Remove gear from intermediate shaft by pushing upward on shaft with bar while pulling gear downward.
21. Rotate gear downward and forward to clear input shaft.
22. Ensure input shaft is in full left turn position, then move gear through right side apron opening until left tie rod clears opening. Use caution to avoid damaging bellows.
23. Lower left side of gear and remove gear from vehicle.
24. Reverse procedure to install.

POWER STEERING PUMP REPLACE

WITH DIESEL ENGINE

1. Remove drive belts.
2. On vehicles with air conditioning, remove alternator.
3. On vehicles with air conditioning, remove both braces from support bracket.
4. Disconnect power steering lines and drain fluid from pump.
5. Remove four bracket mounting bolts.
6. Install pulley removal tool No. T69L-10300-B or equivalent on pulley hub. Hold small hex head of tool and turn tool nut counterclockwise to remove pulley.
7. Remove pump from bracket.
8. Reverse procedure to install.

WITH GASOLINE ENGINE

Escort, EXP, LN7 & Lynx

1. Remove air cleaner, thermactor pump drive belt and thermactor pump.
2. Remove power steering reservoir filler extension. Cover opening to prevent entry of dirt.
3. From underneath vehicle, loosen one power steering pump adjusting bolt and remove one pump to mounting bracket bolt, then disconnect return hose.
4. Form engine compartment, loosen one power steering pump adjusting bolt, then loosen pivot and remove drive belts.
5. Remove the remaining two power steering pump to bracket retaining bolts, then remove pump from bracket by passing pulley through adjusting bracket opening.
6. Disconnect pressure hose from power steering pump, then remove pump.
7. Reverse procedure to install.

Tempo & Topaz

1. Remove alternator drive belt.
2. Place alternator in upper most position.
3. Remove radiator overflow bottle.
4. Remove power steering pump drive belt.
5. Disconnect return line from pump.
6. Completely back off power steering pump pressure line nut. The pressure line will separate when the pump bracket is removed.
7. Remove power steering pump mounting bolts and pump.
8. Reverse procedure to install.

FRONT WHEEL BEARINGS

The front wheel bearings are cartridge design and are pregreased, sealed and require no maintenance. The bearings are preset and cannot be adjusted.

WHEEL BEARINGS, REPLACE

1. Raise and support vehicle, then remove tire and wheel assembly.
2. Remove brake caliper and rotor.
3. Disconnect lower control arm and tie rod from knuckle (leave strut attached).
4. Loosen two strut top mount to apron attaching nuts.
5. Using suitable tools, remove hub bearing and knuckle assembly by pushing out constant velocity joint outer shaft until it is free of assembly.
6. Install tool D80L-1002-L and D80L-625-1 or equivalents, onto knuckle bosses and remove hub.
7. Remove snap ring retaining bearing in knuckle assembly. Discard snap ring.
8. Using a suitable press and tools T83P-1104-AH3 and T83P-1104-AH2, press bearing from knuckle assembly. Discard bearing.
9. Remove half shaft assembly. Place shaft into a suitable vise and remove bearing dust shield. Discard dust shield.
10. Reverse procedure to install.

Wheel Alignment Section

INDEX

FRONT WHEEL ALIGNMENT

CASTER & CAMBER

Caster and camber angles are preset at the factory and cannot be adjusted.

TOE-IN

To adjust toe-in, **Fig. 1**, lock steering wheel in the straight ahead position using suitable steering wheel holder. Remove small outer clamp from steering boot to prevent boot from twisting during adjustment procedure. Loosen tie rod adjusting nuts, then adjust left and right tie rods until each wheel has 1/2 the desired total toe specification. Tighten tie rod adjusting nuts, replace steering gear rubber boots and tighten clamp. Remove steering wheel holding tool.

REAR WHEEL ALIGNMENT

CASTER & CAMBER

Caster and camber cannot be adjusted and factory set.

TOE-IN & TOE-OUT

Toe-in and toe-out can be adjusted wheel wheel it is determined that the vehicle is not within alignment specifications. To adjust toe of either wheel, loosen bolt attaching rear control arm to body **Fig. 2**, and rotate alignment cam until therequired alignment setting is obtained. Tight control arm attaching bolt to 40-55 ft. lbs.

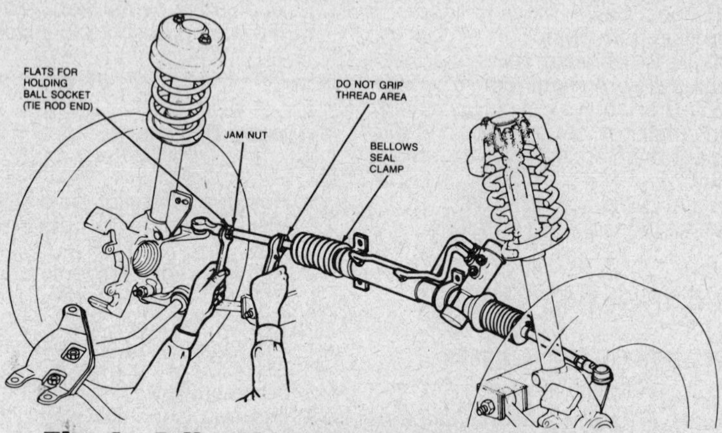

Fig. 1 Adjusting front wheel toe-in and toe-out

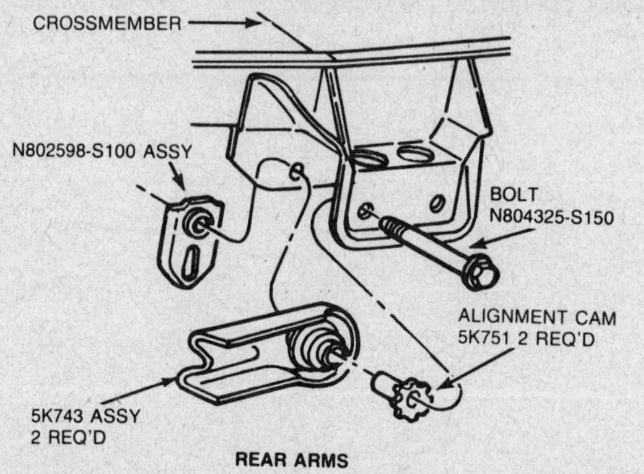

Fig. 2 Rear wheel toe-in and toe-out alignment cam

LINCOLN

INDEX OF SERVICE OPERATIONS

NOTE: Refer to rear of this manual for vehicle manufacturer's special service tool suppliers.

GENERAL ENGINE SPECIFICATIONS

Year	Engine C.I.D./Liter ①	Engine VIN Code ②	Fuel System	Bore & Stroke	Compression Ratio	Net H.P. @ RPM ③	Maximum Torque Ft. Lbs. @ RPM	Normal Oil Pressure Pounds
1982	V6-232/3.8L ⑤	3	2150, 2 Bbl. ④	3.81 x 3.39	8.8	112 @ 4000	175 @ 2600	54-59
	V6-232/3.8L ⑥	3	7200VV, 2 Bbl. ④	3.81 x 3.39	8.8	118 @ 4000	186 @ 2600	54-59
	V8-302/5.0L ⑤	F	2150, 2 Bbl. ④	4.00 x 3.00	8.4	—	—	40-60
	V8-302/5.0L ⑥	F	7200VV, 2 Bbl. ④	4.00 x 3.00	8.4	131 @ 3400	229 @ 1200	40-60
	V8-302/5.0L	F	⑦	4.00 x 3.00	8.4	134 @ 3400	232 @ 3200	40-60
1983	V8-302/5.0L ⑤	F	⑦	4.00 x 3.00	8.4	⑧	⑨	40-60
	V8-302/5.0L ⑥	F	⑦	4.00 x 3.00	8.4	130 @ 3200	240 @ 2000	40-60
	6-149/2.4L ⑩	L	⑬	3.15 x 3.19	22	144 @ 4800	150 @ 2400	58
1984	V8-302/5.0L	F	⑦	4.00 x 3.00	8.4	⑪	⑫	40-60
1985	6-149/2.4L ⑩	L	⑬	3.15 x 3.19	22	114 @ 4800	150 @ 2400	58
	V8-302/5.0L	F	⑦	4.00 x 3.00	8.4	⑪	⑫	40-60
	V8-302 H.O./5.0L	M	⑦	4.00 x 3.00	8.3	180 @ 4200	260 @ 2600	40-60
1986-87	V8-302/5.0L	F	⑦	4.00 x 3.00	8.9	150 @ 3400	270 @ 2000	40-60
	V8-302 H.O./5.0L	M	⑦	4.00 x 3.00	9.2	200 @ 4000	285 @ 3000	40-60
1988	V6-232/3.8L	—	⑦	3.80 x 3.40	9.0	140 @ 3800	215 @ 2200	40-60
	V8-302/5.0L	—	⑦	4.00 x 3.00	8.9	⑭	⑮	40-60
	V8-302 H.O./5.0L	—	⑦	4.00 x 3.00	9.2	225 @ 4000	300 @ 3200	40-60

①—C.I.D.-cubic inch displacement.
②—The eighth digit of the VIN denotes engine code.
③—Ratings are net-as installed in vehicle.
④—Motorcraft.
⑤—Exc. Calif.
⑥—Calif.
⑦—Electronic Fuel Injection.
⑧—Single exhaust, 103 @ 3200; Dual exhaust 145 @ 3600.
⑨—Single exhaust, 240 @ 2000; Dual exhaust 245 @ 2200.
⑩—Turbocharged diesel engine.
⑪—Single exhaust, 140 @ 3200; Dual exhaust, 155 @ 3600.
⑫—Single exhaust, 250 @ 1600; Dual exhaust, 265 @ 2000.
⑬—Fuel injection.
⑭—Single exhaust, 150 @ 3200; dual exhaust, 160 @ 3400.
⑮—Single exhaust, 270 @ 2000; dual exhaust, 280 @ 2200.

Specifications

ENGINE TIGHTENING SPECIFICATIONS*

*Torque specifications are for clean and lightly lubricated threads only. Dry or dirty threads produce increased friction which prevents accurate measurement of tightness.

Year	Engine/ VIN	Spark Plugs Ft. Lbs.	Cylinder Head Bolts Ft. Lbs.	Intake Manifold Ft. Lbs.	Exhaust Manifold Ft. Lbs.	Rocker Arm Stud Nut or Bolt Ft. Lbs.	Rocker Arm Cover Ft. Lbs.	Connecting Rod Cap Bolts Ft. Lbs.	Main Bearing Cap Bolts Ft. Lbs.	Flywheel to Crankshaft Ft. Lbs.	Vibration Damper or Pulley Ft. Lbs.
1982	V6-232/3	17-23	④	⑤	15-22	⑥	⑦	31-36	65-81	54-64	93-121
1982-88	V8-302/F, M	10-15	⑨	23-25	18-24	③	3-5	19-24	60-70	75-85	70-90
1984-85	6-149/L ⑧	—	②	14-17	14-17	—	6-7	①	43-48	77-85	282-311
1988	V6-232	—	—	—	—	—	—	—	—	—	—

①—Torque in two steps: No. 1, 14 ft. lbs.; No. 2, torque bolts an additional 70° from step 1.
②—Torque in four steps: No. 1, 22-29 ft. lbs.; No. 2, 36-43 ft. lbs.; No. 3, torque bolts an additional 70° from step 2; No. 4, start engine and allow to run 25 minutes, then torque bolts an additional 90° from step 3.
③—Rocker arm fulcrum bolt to cylinder head, 18-25 ft. lbs.
④—Tighten bolts in 4 steps; No. 1, 47 ft. lbs.; No. 2, 55 ft. lbs.; No. 3, 63 ft. lbs.; No. 4, 74 ft. lbs.; then back off all bolts 2-3 turns and repeat sequence.
⑤—Tighten bolts in three steps; No. 1, 5.1 ft. lbs.; No. 2, 10.3 ft. lbs.; No. 3, 18.4 ft. lbs.
⑥—Rocker arm fulcrum bolt to cylinder head, tighten bolts in two steps; No. 1, 5.1-11.0 ft. lbs.; No. 2, 18.4-25.8 ft. lbs.
⑦—36-61 inch lbs.
⑧—Diesel engine.
⑨—Tighten bolts in two steps; No. 1, 55-65 ft. lbs.; No. 2, 65-72 ft. lbs.

STARTING MOTOR APPLICATIONS

Year	Application	Ident. No.
1982	Exc. Continental ①	E1AF-BA
	Exc. Continental ②	E3AF-AA
	Continental	E25F-AA
1983	All	E3AF-AA
1984	Diesel Models	E4LF-AB
	Gas Models ③	E3AF-AA
	Gas Models ④ ⑤	E4DF-BA
	Gas Models ④ ⑥	E4AF-AA
1985	Diesel Models ⑦	E4LB-AB
	Diesel Models ⑧	E5LF-AA
	Gas Models	E4AF-AA
1986-88	Exc. 1988 Continental	E4AF-AA
1988	Continental	E4DF-AA

①—To 5/82. ③—To 12/83. ⑤—Exc. Town Car. ⑦—To 1/85.
②—From 5/82. ④—From 12/83. ⑥—Town Car. ⑧—From 1/85.

ALTERNATOR & REGULATOR SPECIFICATIONS

Year	Indent. No. ①	Current Rating ②		Field Current @ 75°F		Voltage Regulator	
		Amperes	Volts	Amperes	Volts	Ident. No. ③ ⑥	Voltage @ 75°F
1982	Orange ④ ⑦	40	15	4.0	12	E2PZ-A ⑧	13.8-14.6
	Black ④ ⑦	65	15	4.0	12	E2PZ-A ⑧	13.8-14.6
	Green ④ ⑦	60	15	4.0	12	E2PZ-A ⑧	13.8-14.6
	Black ⑤ ⑦	70	15	4.0	12	E2PZ-A ⑧	13.8-14.6
	Red ⑤ ⑦	100	15	4.0	12	E2PZ-A ⑧	13.8-14.6
1983	Orange ④ ⑦	40	15	4.25	12	E2PZ-A ⑧	—
	Black ④ ⑦	65	15	4.25	12	E2PZ-A ⑧	—
	Green ④ ⑦	60	15	4.25	12	E2PZ-A ⑧	—
	Black ⑤ ⑦	70	15	4.25	12	E2PZ-A ⑧	—
	Red ⑤ ⑦	100	15	4.25	12	E2PZ-A ⑧	—
1984-86	Orange ④ ⑦	40	15	4.25	12	E2PZ-A	—
	Green ④ ⑦	60	15	4.25	12	E2PZ-A	—
	Black ⑤ ⑦	70	15	4.25	12	E2PZ-A	—
	Red ⑤ ⑦	100	15	4.25	12	E2PZ-A	—
1987-88	Green ④ ⑦	60	15	4.25	12	E2PZ-A	—
	Black ④ ⑦	65	15	4.25	12	E2PZ-A	—
	⑤	70	15	4.25	12	E4AF-AA ⑧	
	⑤	100	15	4.25	12	E4AF-AA ⑧	

①—Basic No. 10300.
②—Stamped on housing.
③—Stamped on cover.
④—Rear terminal alternator.
⑤—Side terminal alternator.
⑥—Basic No. 10316.
⑦—Solid state alternator.
⑧—Electronic voltage regulator. These units are color coded black for system w/warning indicator lamp & blue for systems w/ammeter.

REAR DRIVE AXLE SPECIFICATIONS

Year	Model	Carrier Type	Ring Gear & Pinion Backlash Inch	Nominal Pinion Locating Shim, Inch	Pinion Bearing Preload New Bearings With Seal Inch Lbs.	Pinion Bearing Preload Used Bearings With Seal Inch Lbs.	Differential Bearing Preload	Pinion Nut Torque Ft. Lbs.
1982-88	All	Integral	.008-.015	.030	16-29	8-14	.016①	②

①—Case spread.
②—With 7.5 inch ring gear, 170 ft. lbs., with 8.5 and 8.8 inch ring gear, 140 ft. lbs.

FRONT WHEEL ALIGNMENT SPECIFICATIONS

Year	Model	Caster Angle, Degrees		Camber Angle, Degrees				Toe-In Inch	Toe-Out on Turns, Deg.①	
		Limits	Desired	Limits Left	Limits Right	Desired Left	Desired Right		Outer Wheel	Inner Wheel
1982	Town Car	+2¼ to +3¾	+3	−¼ to + 1¼	−¼ to +1¼	+½	+½	1/16	18.51	20
	Mark VI	+2¼ to +3¾	+3	−¼ to +1 ¼	−¼ to +1¼	+½	+½	1/16	18.51	20
	Continental	+⅛ to +1⅞	+1	−½ to +1 ¼	−½ to +1¼	+⅜	+⅜	3/16	19.13	20
1983	Town Car	+2¼ to +4	+3	−¼ to + 1¼	−¼ to +1¼	+½	+½	1/16	18.51	20
	Mark VI	+2¼ to +4	+3	−¼ to +1¼	−¼ to +1¼	+½	+½	1/16	18.51	20
	Continental	+⅜ to +2⅛	+1¼	−½ to +1¼	−½ to +1¼	+⅜	+⅜	⅛	19.13	20
1984	Town Car	+2½ to +4	+3	−¼ to + 1¼	−¼ to +1¼	+½	+½	1/16	18.51	20
	Mark VII②	+7/10 to +2½	+1¾	−¾ to +¾	−¾ to +¾	0	0	⅛	17.14	20
	Continental②	+7/10 to +2½	+1¾	−¾ to +¾	−¾ to +¾	0	0	⅛	17.14	20
1985-87	Town Car	+2¼ to +4	+3	−¼ to + 1¼	−¼ to +1¼	+½	+½	1/16	18.51	20
	Mark VII②	+⅝ to +2¾	+1½	−¾ to +¾	−¾ to +1¾	0	0	⅛	17.14	20
	Continental②	+⅝ to +2¾	+1½	−¾ to +¾	−¾ to +1¾	0	0	⅛	17.14	20
1988	Continental	+4¼ to +5¾	+5	−1½ to −½	−1½ to −½	−1	−1	0	—	—
	Town Car	+3¼ to +5	+4	−1¼ to +¼	−1¼ to +¼	−½	−½	1/16	—	—
	Mark VII②	+⅝ to +2¾	+1½	−¾ to +¾	−¾ to +¾	0	0	⅛	—	—

①—Incorrect toe-out, when other adjustments are correct, indicates bent steering arms.
②—Set ride height before performing alignment check.

REAR WHEEL ALIGNMENT SPECIFICATIONS

Year	Model	Camber Angle, Degrees Limits Left	Camber Angle, Degrees Limits Right	Camber Angle, Degrees Desired Left	Camber Angle, Degrees Desired Right	Toe-In Inch
1988	Continental	−2½ to −½	−2½ to −½	−1½	−1½	1/20

COOLING SYSTEM & CAPACITY DATA

Year	Model or Engine	Cooling Capacity, Qts.	Radiator Cap Relief Pressure, Lbs.	Thermo. Opening Temp.	Fuel Tank Gals.	Engine Oil Refill Qts.①	Auto. Trans. Qts.②	Rear Axle Oil Pints
1982-83	Town Car	13.4	16	195	18	4	12.0	3.75
	Mark VI	13.4	16	195	18	4	12.0	3.75
	Continental	④	16	195	⑥	4	12.0	3.25
1984-85	Town Car	13.4	16	195	18	4	12.	3.75
	Mark VII	③	⑦	195	22.3	⑤	12	3.5
	Continental	③	⑦	195	22.3	⑤	12	3.5
1986-87	Town Car	13.4	16	195	18	4	12.	3.75
	Mark VII	14.1	16	195	22.3	4	12	3.5
	Continental	14.1	16	195	22.3	4	12	3.5
1988	Town Car	13.4	16	195	18	4	12.3	3.8
	Mark VII	14.1	16	195	22.1	4	12.3	3.8
	Continental	11.5	16	195	18.6	4⑧	13.1⑨	—

①—Add one quart with filter change.
②—Approximate. Make final check with dipstick.
③—Exc. diesel engine, 13.4; diesel engine, 11.8.
④—V8-302, 13.4 qts; V6-232, 11.1 qts.
⑤—Gasoline engines, 4.0 qts.; diesel engine 6.5 qts. less oil filter.
⑥—V8-302, 22.6 gals; V6-232, 20 gals.
⑦—Gasoline engines, 16 lbs.; diesel engines, 15 lbs.
⑧—Add .5 qts. with filter change.
⑨—Includes differential.

Electrical Section

INDEX

STARTER
REPLACE

EXC. DIESEL ENGINE MODELS & 1988 CONTINENTAL

1. Disconnect battery ground cable, then raise and support vehicle.
2. Disconnect starter cable at starter terminal, then remove starter mounting bolts.
3. Remove starter. On some models, it may be necessary to turn wheels to the left or right to gain clearance for removal.
4. Reverse procedure to install. Torque starter cable to starter motor bolt to 70-110 inch lbs.

1988 CONTINENTAL

1. Disconnect battery ground cable, then the starter electrical cable.
2. If applicable, remove cable support and ground cable connection from upper starter stud bolt.
3. If applicable, remove brace at starter motor and cylinder block.
4. Remove starter mounting bolts, then the starter from area between subframe and radiator.
5. Reverse procedure to install.

DIESEL ENGINE MODELS

1. Disconnect battery ground cables.
2. Raise and support vehicle, then remove starter retaining bolts.
3. Lower vehicle, then disconnect starter motor relay to solenoid wire assembly.
4. Remove oil level indicator tube assembly retaining bolts.
5. Disconnect accelerator pedal from throttle cable assembly.
6. Remove starter from vehicle.
7. Reverse procedure to install.

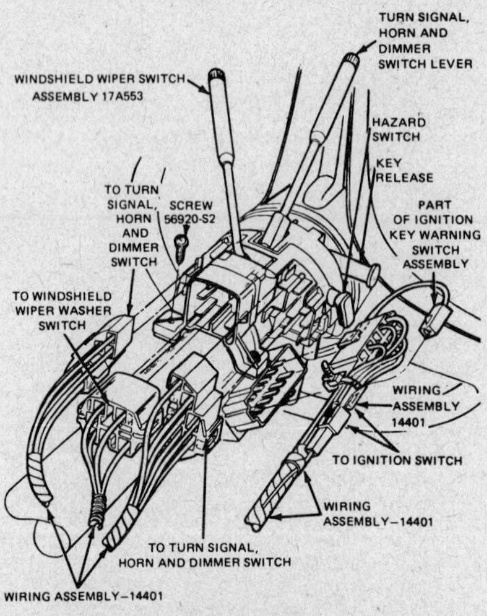

Fig. 1 Ignition switch installation

IGNITION LOCK
REPLACE

1. Disconnect battery ground cable.
2. On models with tilt wheel, remove upper column extension shroud by unsnapping from retaining clip at 9 o'clock position.
3. Remove steering column trim shroud.
4. Disconnect key warning switch electrical connector.
5. Turn ignition lock to "On" position.
6. Using a 1/8 inch pin or punch located in the 4 o'clock hole and 1 1/4 inch from outer edge of lock cylinder housing, depress retaining pin while pulling the lock cylinder from housing.
7. Turn lock cylinder to "On" position and insert cylinder into housing. Ensure that the lock cylinder is fully seated and aligned into the interlocking washer before turning key to "Off" position. This will permit the retaining pin to extend into the lock cylinder housing hole.
8. Rotate key to check for proper mechanical operation.
9. Connect key warning switch electrical connector.
10. Connect battery ground cable.
11. Check for proper operation.

IGNITION SWITCH
REPLACE

1. Disconnect battery ground cable.
2. For tilt wheel only, remove upper column extension shroud by unsnapping from retaining clip at 9 o'clock position.
3. Remove steering column trim shrouds.
4. Disconnect ignition switch electrical connector. Turn the lock cylinder to the "On" position.
5. With a 1/8 inch drill, drill out the switch retaining bolt heads. Then, remove the bolts with an "Easy Out" or equivalent.
6. Disengage ignition switch from actuator and remove from vehicle, **Fig. 1.**
7. Adjust ignition switch by sliding the carrier to the switch "On" position. **A replacement ignition switch will be pre-set in the "On" position.**
8. Ensure the lock cylinder is in approximately the "On" position and install the ignition switch onto the actuator pin.
9. Install switch break-off head mounting bolts and tighten until heads shear.
10. Reconnect switch electrical connector and battery ground cable. Check the ignition switch for proper operation in all switch positions. Be sure the column is locked in the lock position.
11. Reinstall shrouds.

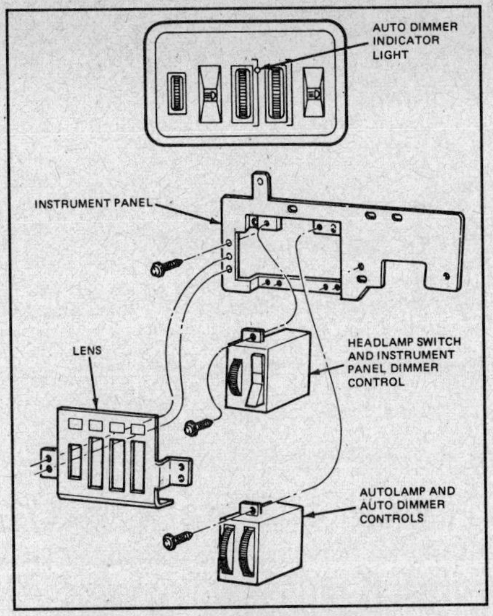

Fig. 2 Light switch replacement. 1984–87 Continental & 1984–88 Mark VII

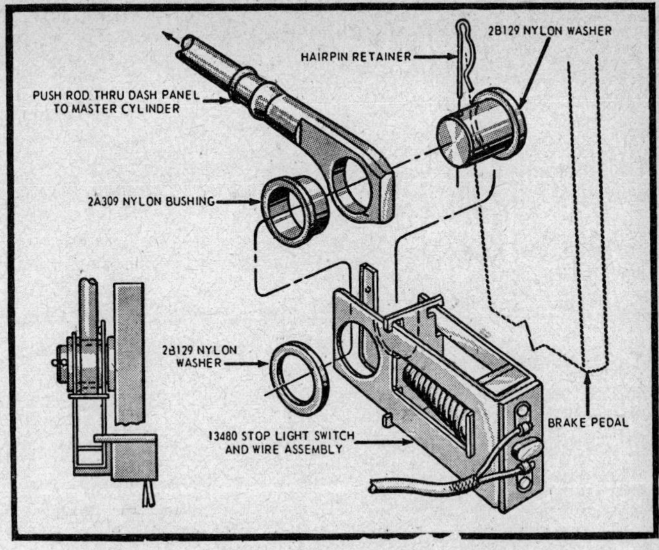

Fig. 3 Stop light switch (typical)

LIGHT SWITCH REPLACE

1984–87 CONTINENTAL & 1984–88 MARK VII

1. Remove lens assembly attaching screws and the lens assembly.
2. Remove switch assembly attaching screws, then pull switch out from instrument panel, **Fig. 2.**
3. Disconnect switch electrical connector and remove switch.
4. Reverse procedure to install.

1982–83 CONTINENTAL

1. Disconnect battery ground cable.
2. Remove steering column trim shrouds.
3. Unsnap the instrument panel cluster lower molding to expose five screws along bottom of cluster lens and remove.
4. Remove the lefthand lower pad retaining screws and carefully tilt the pad out from under the cluster lens.
5. Disconnect the headlamp switch wiring connectors.
6. Insert a hooked tool into headlight switch knob slot and remove spring tension on knob, then pull off.
7. Remove switch retaining nut and lens.
8. Remove second nut and screw retaining the switch to lower pad and remove.
9. Reverse procedure to install.

1982–83 MARK VI & 1982–88 TOWN CAR

1. Disconnect battery ground cable.
2. Insert a hooked tool into headlight switch knob slot and remove spring tension on knob, then pull off.
3. Remove steering column lower shroud and lower lefthand instrument panel trim bezel.
4. Remove five headlight switch mounting bracket retaining screws.
5. Carefully pull switch and bracket from instrument panel and disconnect switch wiring.
6. On Mark VI models, mark and remove vacuum hoses from switch distributor valve.
7. Remove locknut and screw retaining switch to switch bracket.
8. Reverse procedure to install.

STOP LIGHT SWITCH REPLACE

1. Disconnect wires at switch connector.
2. Remove hairpin retainer, slide switch, pushrod and nylon washers and bushing away from brake pedal, and remove switch, **Fig. 3.**
3. Reverse above procedure to install.

NEUTRAL SAFETY SWITCH REPLACE

CONTINENTAL & MARK VII WITH AOD TRANSMISSION

1. Disconnect battery ground cable.
2. Position transmission selector lever in "Lo" position.
3. Raise and support vehicle, then working from underneath vehicle, disconnect electrical harness from switch by lifting harness straight up off switch.
4. Using tool T74P-77247-A or equivalent, remove neutral start switch and O-ring seal by positioning tool over the extension housing area to gain access to switch.
5. Reverse procedure to install. Torque switch to 7-10 ft. lbs. using tool mentioned above.

TOWN CAR & MARK VI WITH AOD TRANSMISSION

1. Disconnect battery ground cable, then remove air cleaner assembly.
2. Position transmission selector lever in "Lo."
3. Disconnect electrical harness from switch by lifting harness straight up off switch.
4. Using tool T74P-77247-A or equivalent, remove neutral start switch and O-ring seal through access path at left side of dash panel.
5. Reverse procedure to install. Torque switch to 7-10 ft. lbs. using tool mentioned above.

1988 CONTINENTAL WITH AXOD TRANSAXLE

1. Disconnect battery ground cable.
2. Place shift lever in Neutral, then disconnect linkage from manual shift lever.
3. Disconnect switch wiring connector, then remove switch attaching bolts and switch.
4. Install switch and attaching bolts, but do not tighten bolts at this time.
5. Insert a No. 43 (.089 inch) drill bit through hole in switch, then torque attaching bolts to 7-9 inch lbs. and remove drill bit.
6. Reconnect switch connector and battery cable, then ensure that starter engages in Neutral or Park positions only.

TURN SIGNAL SWITCH REPLACE

1. Disconnect battery ground cable.
2. On models with tilt wheels, remove upper column extension shroud by unsnapping from retaining clip at 9 o'clock position.

3. Remove steering column cover attaching screws and the cover, then the signal lever.
4. Carefully lift wiring connector plug retainer tabs and disconnect the plugs from switch.
5. Remove switch retaining screws and lift up switch assembly.
6. Reverse procedure to install.

HORN SOUNDER & STEERING WHEEL REPLACE

On 1982-84 models, refer to "Turn Signal Switch, Replace" for horn switch replacement. On 1985-88 models, the horn switch is integral with the steering wheel hub cover.

1. Working from behind steering wheel, remove steering wheel hub cover by pushing retaining posts outward with a suitable drift.
2. Remove steering wheel to shaft retaining nut. Discard nut.
3. If no marks are present, scribe alignment marks on steering wheel and shaft to aid in installation.
4. Using a suitable puller, remove steering wheel from shaft.
5. Reverse procedure to install. Torque new retaining nut to 30-40 ft. lbs. **On vehicles equipped with speed control, check slip ring for damage and slip ring grease for contamination before installing steering wheel.**

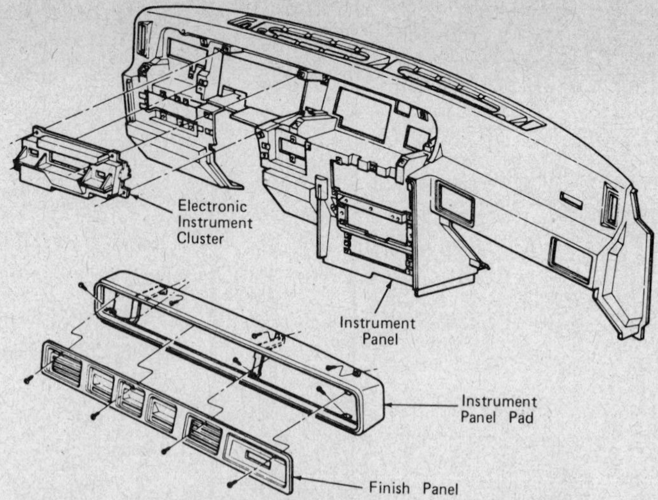

Fig. 4 Electronic instrument cluster. Mark VII

INSTRUMENT CLUSTER REPLACE

MARK VII

1. Remove the four finish panel retaining screws, then rotate top of panel towards steering wheel and remove from vehicle, **Fig. 4.**
2. Remove the six instrument panel pad retaining screws, then rotate pad toward steering wheel and remove from vehicle.
3. Remove the four instrument cluster to instrument panel retaining screws, then pull cluster away from instrument panel.
4. Disconnect cluster electrical connector and remove cluster.
5. Reverse procedure to install.

1982–87 CONTINENTAL

1. Disconnect battery ground cable.
2. Remove steering column shroud.
3. Snap off instrument panel mouldings.
4. Remove seventeen instrument panel assembly to instrument panel and instrument panel pad retaining screws, then remove trim assembly, **Fig. 5.**
5. Disconnect transmission indicator cable from steering column.
6. Remove four cluster retaining screws from instrument panel and move cluster away from instrument panel.
7. Disconnect wiring harness connector and remove cluster.
8. Reverse procedure to install.

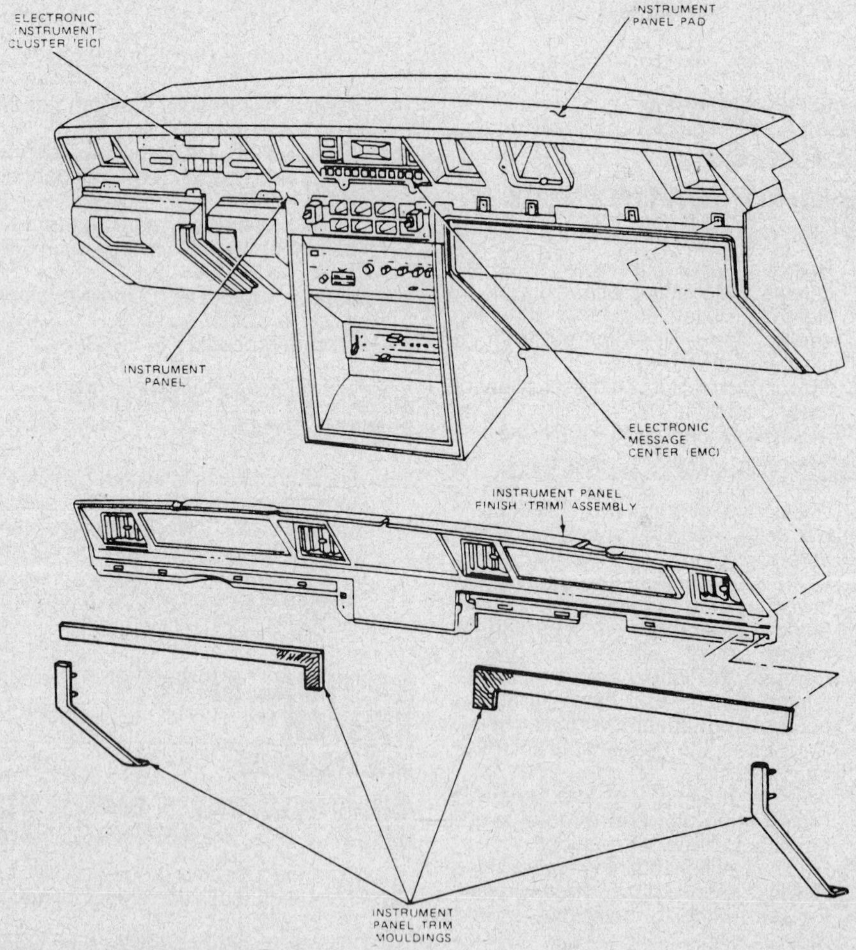

Fig. 5 Electronic instrument panel. 1982–87 Continental

MARK VI & 1982–88 TOWN CAR

Less Electronic Cluster

1. Disconnect battery ground cable.
2. Disconnect speedometer cable, then remove trim cover screws and remove trim cover.
3. Remove lower steering column cover screws and remove cover.
4. Remove transmission indicator bracket retaining screw, then disconnect cable loop and bracket pin from steer-

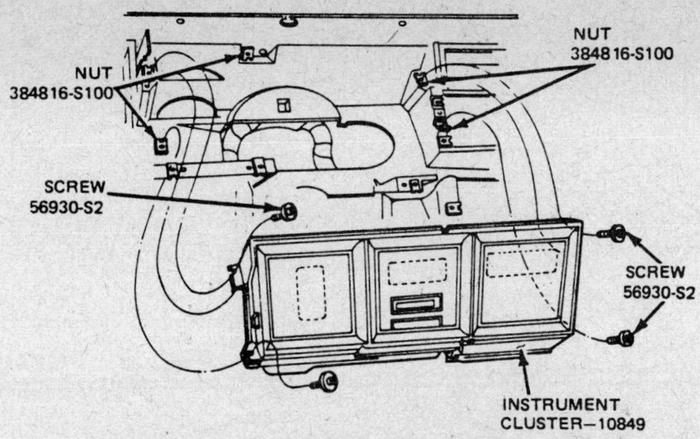

Fig. 6 Electronic instrument cluster. Mark VI & 1982–88 Town Car

ing column. Also remove the column bracket from column.
5. Remove cluster retaining screws, then disconnect electrical feed plug from connector and remove cluster.

With Electronic Cluster

1. Disconnect battery ground cable.
2. Remove steering column cover, lower instrument panel trim cover, keyboard trim panel and panel on left of column.
3. Remove the ten instrument cluster trim cover retaining screws, then remove trim cover.
4. Remove the four screws retaining instrument cluster to instrument panel and pull cluster forward. Disconnect both electrical plugs and ground wire from their receptacles, then disconnect speedometer cable by pressing on flat surface of plastic connector.
5. Remove transmission indicator cable bracket retaining screw, then disconnect cable loop and bracket pin from steering column.
6. Remove plastic clamp from around steering column, then remove cluster, **Fig. 6.**
7. Reverse procedure to install.

WINDSHIELD WIPER MOTOR

REPLACE

MARK VII

1. Turn wipers on, then with wiper blades straight up on windshield, turn ignition key to "Off" position.
2. Disconnect battery ground cable and remove arm and blade assemblies.
3. Remove left side cowl top grille.
4. Remove drive arm to motor crankpin retaining clip, then disconnect drive arm from crankpin.
5. Disconnect wiper motor electrical connector, then remove wiper motor retaining screws and the wiper motor from opening.
6. Reverse procedure to install.

1982–87 CONTINENTAL

1. Disconnect battery ground cable.
2. Remove righthand side wiper and blade assembly.
3. Remove cowl top grille retaining screws and grille.
4. Disconnect linkage drive arm from the motor output arm crankpin by removing retainer clip.
5. Disconnect electrical connector and remove three motor attaching screws.
6. Pull the motor from the opening.
7. Reverse procedure to install.

MARK VI & 1982–88 TOWN CAR

1. Disconnect battery ground cable.
2. Disconnect right side washer nozzle hose clip and remove right side wiper arm and blade assembly from pivot shaft.
3. Remove wiper motor linkage cover.
4. Disconnect linkage drive arm from the motor output arm crankpin by removing retainer clip.
5. Disconnect the wiring connectors from the motor.
6. Remove three bolts retaining the motor to the dash panel extension and the motor.
7. Reverse procedure to install.

WINDSHIELD WIPER TRANSMISSION

REPLACE

MARK VII

The wiper transmission is mounted below the cowl top panel and can be reached by raising the hood. Because the pivot shaft and transmission assemblies are connected with unremovable plastic ball joints, the right and left pivot shafts and transmission are serviced as a unit.

1. Perform steps 1 and 2 as outlined under "Windshield Wiper Motor, Replace" procedure.
2. Raise hood, then remove left and right cowl top grilles.
3. Remove drive arm to wiper motor crankpin retaining clip, then disconnect drive arm from crankpin.
4. Remove pivot shaft attaching screws, then guide transmission and pivots from cowl chamber.
5. Reverse procedure to install, ensuring wiper motor is in "Park" position.

1982–87 CONTINENTAL

1. Disconnect battery ground cable.
2. Remove righthand side wiper arm and blade assembly.
3. Remove cowl top grille retaining screws and remove grille.
4. Disconnect linkage drive arm from the motor output arm crankpin by removing retainer clip.
5. Remove the right side pivot shaft retaining screws then, remove the large nut and spacer from the left side pivot shaft.
6. Remove linkage.
7. Reverse procedure to install.

MARK VI & 1982–88 TOWN CAR

1. Disconnect battery ground cable.
2. Remove wiper arm and blade assemblies from the pivot shafts.
3. Remove wiper motor and linkage cover for access to linkage.
4. Disconnect the linkage drive arm from the motor crank pin by removing the retaining clip.
5. Remove the six bolts retaining the left and right pivot shafts to the cowl, and remove the complete linkage assembly.
6. Reverse procedure to install.

WINDSHIELD WIPER SWITCH

REPLACE

1. Disconnect battery ground cable.
2. Remove the steering column cover screws and separate the two halves.
3. Remove wiper switch retaining screws, disconnect wiring connector and remove switch.
4. Reverse procedure to install.

RADIO

REPLACE

When installing radio, be sure to adjust antenna trimmer for peak performance.

1982–87 CONTINENTAL & 1984–88 MARK VII

1. Disconnect battery ground cable.
2. Remove center instrument panel trim panel.
3. Remove four radio and mounting bracket to instrument panel retaining screws.
4. Push radio towards the front of vehicle and raise back end slightly so rear support bracket clears clip in instrument panel and carefully pull out radio.
5. Disconnect radio wiring and remove radio.
6. Remove rear support bracket.
7. Reverse procedure to install.

MARK VI & 1982–88 TOWN CAR

1. Disconnect battery ground able.
2. Remove radio plate to instrument panel retaining screws.

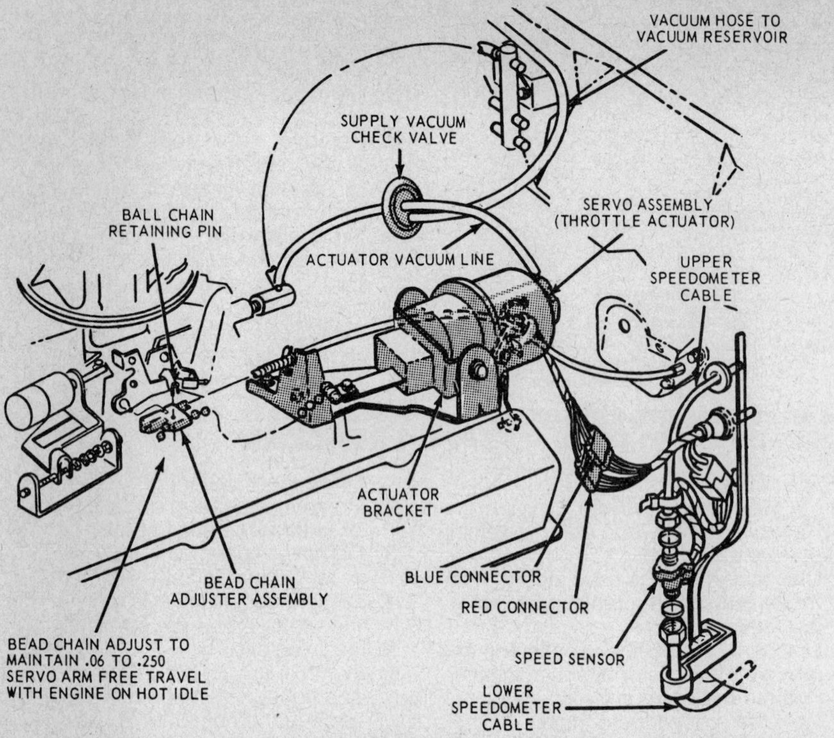

Fig. 7 Servo assembly & throttle linkage installation. (typical)

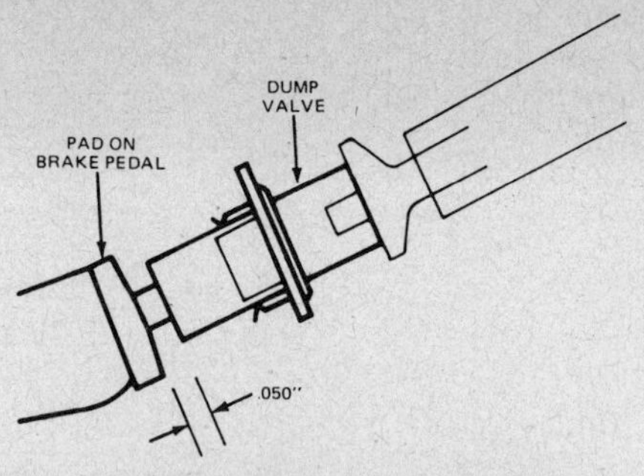

Fig. 8 Vacuum dump valve adjustment (typical)

3. Pull radio rearward until the rear support bracket is clear of instrument panel.
4. Disconnect radio wiring and antenna lead. Remove radio.
5. Remove screws securing front bracket to radio and remove, remove rear support bracket.
6. Reverse procedure to install.

SPEED CONTROLS

ADJUST

BEAD CHAIN

Adjust bead chain cable to obtain desired free travel with engine warm and carburetor at idle position. Desired free travel is 1/8-1/4 inch, **Fig. 7.** The adjustment should be made to take as much slack as possible out of the bead chain without restricting the carburetor lever from returning to idle. On vehicles with solenoid anti-diesel valve, perform the adjustment with the ignition switch in the ON position.

ACTUATOR CABLE

1. Remove actuator cable retaining clip from speed control connection adjuster.
2. Disengage throttle positioner.
3. With carburetor in hot idle position, pull the actuator cable end tube until all slack is removed from cable.
4. While maintaining light tension on cable, install cable retaining clip.

VACUUM DUMP VALVE

The vacuum dump valve is fully adjustable in its mounting bracket. When correctly adjusted, the valve should be closed when the brake pedal is in the released position, enabling the black housing of the valve to clear the adapter or pad on the brake pedal. If adjustment is necessary, hold the brake pedal down and push the dump valve forward through its adjustment collar. Position a .050 inch shim on the adapter or pad, **Fig. 8,** then pull brake pedal fully rearward. Release brake pedal and remove shim. The white plunger on the valve should be in contact with the adapter or pad, while the threaded black housing should have sufficient clearance away from it.

HEATER CORE

REPLACE

1984–88 MARK VII

1. Remove instrument panel.
2. Discharge refrigerant from A/C system, then disconnect high and low pressure hoses. Cap hose ends to prevent entry of dirt and moisture.
3. Drain coolant and disconnect hoses from heater core. Plug hoses and core to prevent spillage.
4. Remove air inlet duct/blower housing assembly support brace to cowl top panel retaining screw.
5. Disconnect A/C wiring, if necessary, then working from engine compartment, remove the two evaporator case to dash panel retaining nuts.
6. Working from passenger compartment, remove evaporator case support bracket to cowl panel attaching screw.
7. Carefully pull evaporator case away from dash panel and remove from vehicle.
8. Remove heater core access cover to evaporator case attaching screws.
9. Remove heater core and seals from case, then remove seals from heater core tubes.
10. Reverse procedure to install.

1982–87 CONTINENTAL

1. Disconnect battery ground cable.
2. Remove steering column cover assembly, then remove left and right finish panels, **Fig. 5.**
3. Remove two screws from sides of instrument panel pad and retainer assembly.
4. Remove pad and retainer assembly and upper finish panel.
5. Remove steering column attaching bolts, then carefully lower steering column just enough to allow access to transmission gear selector lever cable assembly. Reach between steering column and instrument panel, then carefully lift selector lever cable from lever and remove cable clamp from steering column tube.
6. Lower steering column and allow to rest on front seat.
7. Remove screw attaching instrument panel to brake pedal support through steering column opening.
8. Disconnect temperature door cable from door and heater/evaporator cable bracket.
9. Disconnect vacuum hose connectors at evaporator housing.
10. Disconnect blower motor resistor wire from resistor on heater/evaporator case and blower motor feed wire at in-line connector.
11. Support instrument panel, then remove three screws attaching top of instrument panel to cowl.
12. Remove one screw attaching each end of instrument panel to cowl side panels, then remove two screws attaching instrument panel to floor.
13. Move instrument panel rearward and disconnect speedometer cable and any wires that will prevent instrument panel from being placed on front seat. **Use care when removing instrument panel to prevent damage to panel or steering column surfaces.**
14. Drain cooling system, then disconnect heater hoses from heater core. Plug heater core tubes to prevent coolant spillage.

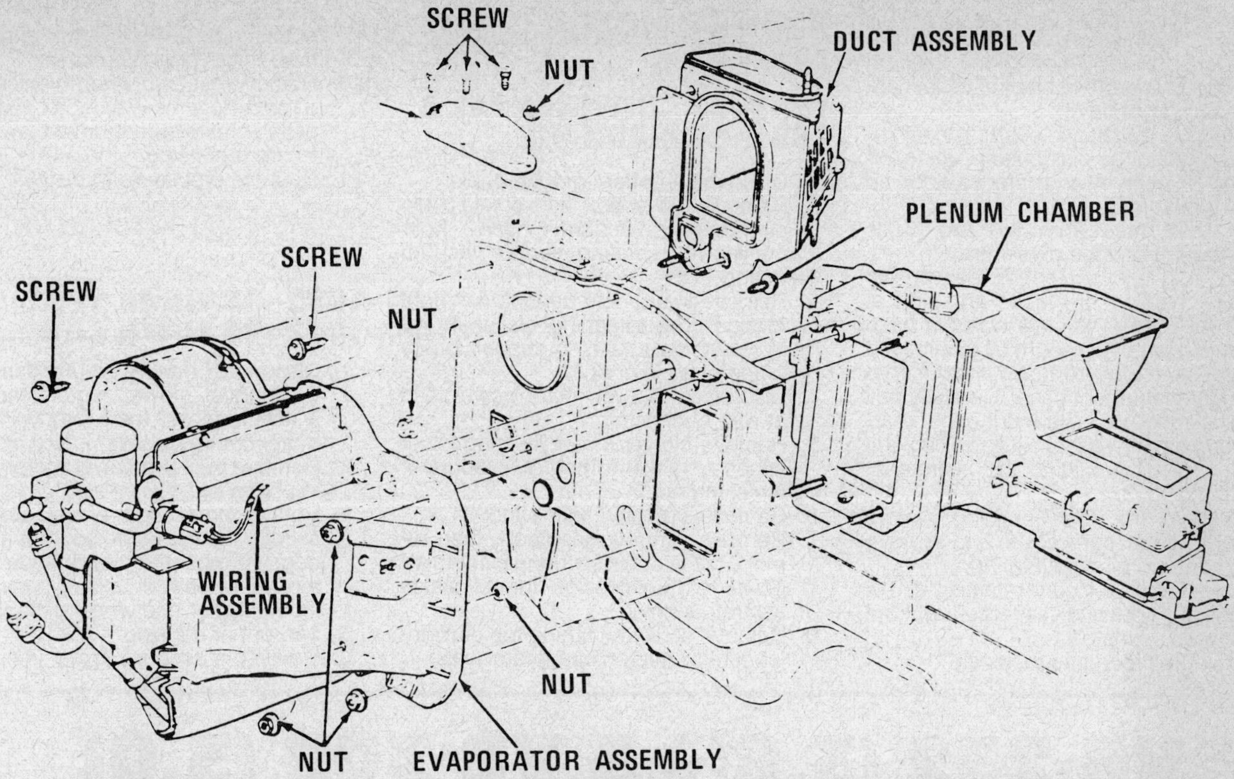

Fig. 9 Plenum & air inlet duct assembly. Mark VI & 1982–88 Town Car

15. Discharge A/C system, then remove high and low side pressure hoses. Cap the hose openings to prevent entry of dirt or moisture.
16. From engine compartment, remove two nuts attaching heater/evaporator case to dash panel.
17. From passenger compartment, remove bolts attaching heater/evaporator case and air inlet duct support brackets to cowl top panel.
18. Remove one nut attaching bracket at left side of heater/evaporator case to dash panel, then remove one nut retaining bracket below case to dash panel.
19. Carefully pull case away from dash panel to gain access to heater core cover attaching bolts.
20. Remove five heater core cover attaching bolts, then remove cover.
21. Remove heater core and seals from case, then remove seals from heater core tubes.
22. Reverse procedure to install.

1982–83 MARK VI & 1982–88 TOWN CAR

1. Disconnect battery ground cable.
2. Disconnect heater hoses from core. Plug hoses and heater core tubes to prevent coolant loss during core removal.
3. Remove one bolt located below the windshield wiper motor retaining left end of plenum to dash panel.
4. Remove one nut retaining the upper left corner of evaporator case to dash panel.
5. Disconnect vacuum supply hose from vacuum source, then push grommet and hose into passenger compartment.
6. Remove glove compartment, then loosen door sill plates and remove side cowl trim panels. **On some models, it may be necessary to lower the steering column to remove the instrument panel. On these models, disconnect harnesses from multiple connectors and transmission shift indicator from column, then remove steering column to instrument panel brace attaching nuts and lower steering column to seat.**
7. Disconnect speedometer cable from speedometer and antenna lead from radio.
8. Remove bolt retaining lower right end of instrument panel to side cowl, then remove instrument panel pad as follows:
   a. Remove screws retaining instrument panel pad to instrument panel at each defroster opening.
   b. Remove the one screw retaining each outboard end of pad to instrument panel.
   c. Remove the five screws retaining lower edge of instrument panel pad, then pull instrument panel pad rearward and remove it.
9. Disconnect temperature control cable housing from bracket at top of plenum, then disconnect cable from temperature blend door crank arm.
10. Remove push clip retaining the center register duct bracket to the plenum and rotate bracket to the right.
11. Disconnect vacuum jumper harness at multiple vacuum connector near the floor air distribution duct, then disconnect white vacuum hose from the outside-recirculating door vacuum motor.
12. Remove screws retaining the passenger side of floor air distribution duct to

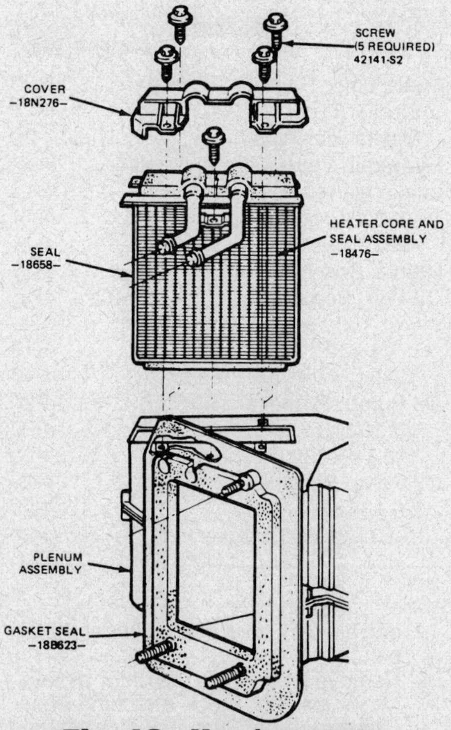

Fig. 10 Heater core removal. Mark VI & 1982–88 Town Car

the plenum. It may be necessary to remove the two screws retaining the partial (lower) panel door vacuum motor to mounting bracket to gain access to right screw.

13. Remove the plastic push fastener retaining floor air distribution duct to left end of plenum and remove floor air distribution duct.
14. Remove nuts from the two studs along lower edge of plenum.
15. Carefully move plenum rearward to allow heater core tubes and stud at top of plenum to clear holes in dash panel. Remove plenum by rotating top of plenum forward, down and out from under instrument panel. Carefully pull lower edge of instrument panel rearward as necessary while rolling the plenum from behind the instrument panel, **Fig. 9.**
16. Remove the four retaining screws from heater core cover and remove cover from plenum, **Fig. 10.**
17. Remove heater core retaining screw then pull core and seal assembly from plenum assembly.
18. Reverse procedure to install.

BLOWER MOTOR REPLACE

1982–87 CONTINENTAL & 1984–88 MARK VII

1. Disconnect battery ground cable.
2. Remove glove box and shield, then disconnect vacuum hose from outside-recirculating air door vacuum motor.
3. Remove instrument panel lower right to side cowl attaching bolt then, remove screw attaching support brace to top of air inlet duct.
4. Disconnect blower motor power lead at wire connector.
5. Remove blower motor housing lower support bracket to heater/evaporator attaching nut.
6. Remove side cowl trim panel.
7. Remove ashtray receptacle, then remove two screws securing instrument panel to transmission tunnel inside ashtray opening.
8. Remove screw attaching top of air inlet duct to heater/evaporator case.
9. Remove air inlet duct and blower housing assembly down and away from the evaporator case.
10. Remove assembly from vehicle, then remove four blower motor mounting plate screws and remove blower motor from housing.
11. Reverse procedure to install.

1982–83 MARK VI & 1982–88 TOWN CAR

1. Disconnect battery ground cable.
2. Disconnect blower motor lead from wiring harness, then remove blower motor cooling tube from blower motor.
3. Remove the four blower motor retaining screws.
4. Rotate motor and wheel assembly slightly to the right so that bottom edge of mounting plate follows contour of wheelwell splash panel, then lift the motor and wheel assembly up and out of housing.
5. Reverse procedure to install.

V6-232 (3.8L) & V8-302 (5.0L) Gasoline Engines

INDEX

ENGINE MOUNTS REPLACE

EXC. 1988 CONTINENTAL

Whenever self-locking mounting bolts and nuts are removed, they must be replaced with new self-locking boits and nuts.

1. Remove fan shroud attaching screws, if necessary.
2. Remove the nut and through bolt attaching the insulator to the support bracket, **Figs. 1, 2 and 3.**
3. Raise the engine slightly with a jack and a wood block placed under the oil pan.
4. Remove the engine insulator assembly to cylinder block attaching bolts. Remove the engine insulator assembly and the heat shield, if so equipped.
5. Reverse procedure to install.

1988 CONTINENTAL

This vehicle is equipped with two RH (front and rear) and one LH internally restrained hydraulic engine mounts. The two RH mounts are equipped with nylon heat shields. All mounts are located and attached to the front sub-frame assembly.

ENGINE REPLACE

1982 CONTINENTAL V6-232

1. Disconnect battery ground cable, then drain cooling system and crankcase.
2. Mark position of hood hinges, then remove hood.
3. Remove air cleaner, air inlet duct and heat tube.
4. Remove fan shroud and fan assembly, then loosen accessory drive belt

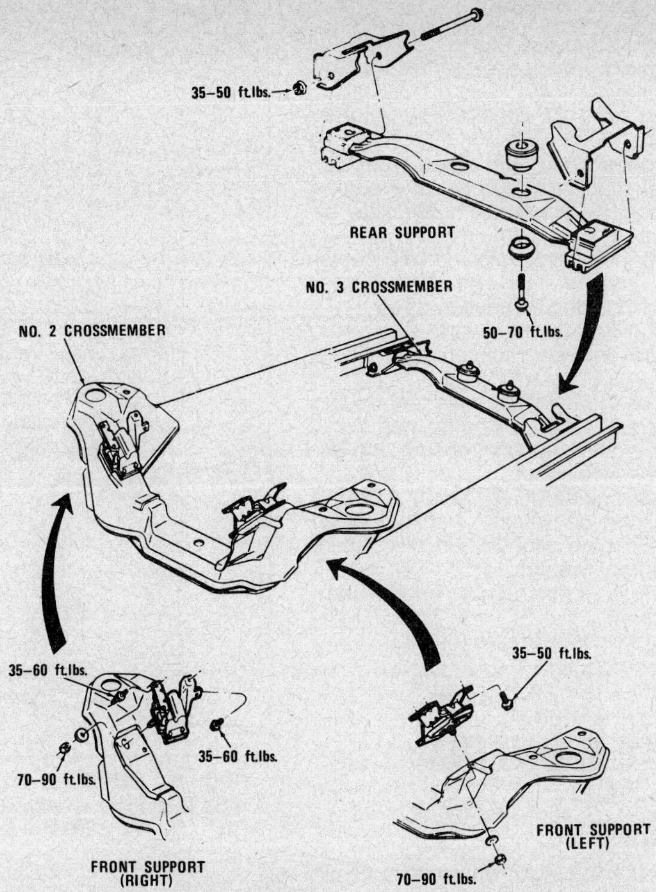

Fig. 1 Engine mounts. 1982 Continental V6-232

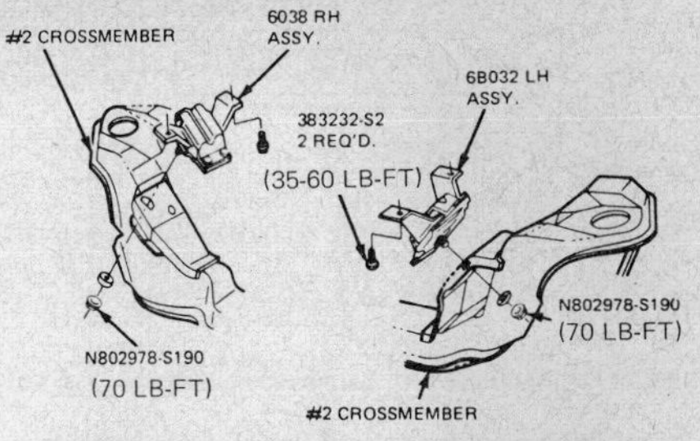

Fig. 2 Engine mounts. 1982–87 Continental & 1984–88 Mark VII V8-302

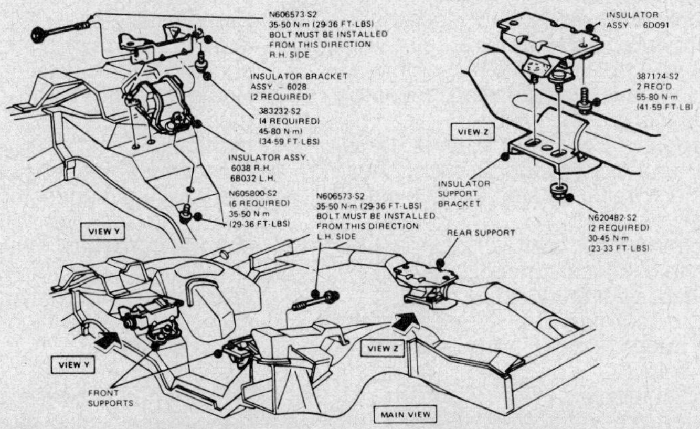

Fig. 3 Engine mounts. 1982–83 Mark VI & 1982–88 Town Car V8-302

idler and remove drive belt and water pump pulley.

5. Disconnect upper and lower radiator hoses at radiator.
6. Disconnect Thermactor hose atair tube check valve, then remove air tube valve bracket attaching bolt at rear of righthand cylinder head.
7. Remove secondary wire from ignition coil.
8. Remove bolts attaching power steering pump mounting bracket, then remove pump and bracket assembly and position aside with hoses attached if equipped.
9. On models with A/C, remove compressor mounting bracket attaching bolts, then remove compressor and mounting bracket assembly and secure to righthand shock absorber tower with refrigerant lines attached.
10. Remove alternator and position aside.
11. Disconnect heater hoses from water pump and heater tube.
12. On models equipped with speed control, disconnect servo chain at carburetor, then remove servo bracket attaching bolts and servo.
13. Disconnect all necessary vacuum hoses and wiring connectors.
14. Remove engine ground strap to dash panel attaching screw.
15. Disconnect transmission downshift linkage, throttle cable from carburetor, then remove throttle cable bracket attaching bolts.
16. Disconnect fuel line and PCV valve hose from carburetor.
17. Remove carburetor assembly from intake manifold. On models equipped with 7200 VV two barrel carburetor, remove spark knock intensity sensor and adapter assembly which is located between carburetor and thermostat housing.
18. With EGR spacer and phenolic gasket in position, install engine lifting plate T75T-6000-A or equivalent over carburetor mounting studs, then install nuts.
19. Raise vehicle and disconnect fuel inlet hose from fuel pump. Cap fuel hose to prevent entry of dirt.
20. Remove inspection cover from torque converter housing, then remove nuts attaching flex plate to torque converter.
21. Remove starter motor.
22. Remove transmission cooler line retaining clips, then disconnect exhaust pipe from exhaust manifold.
23. Remove four lower engine to transmission attaching bolts, then lower vehicle.
24. Remove engine mount to crossmember attaching nuts.
25. Lower vehicle and position a suitable transmission jack under transmission. Raise jack just enough to support weight of transmission.
26. Remove two upper engine to transmission attaching bolts, then place a 1/4 inch piece of plywood or other suitable material between engine and radiator to prevent damage to radiator.
27. Carefully raise engine slightly, then pull away from transmission and lift from vehicle.
28. Reverse procedure to install. Torque

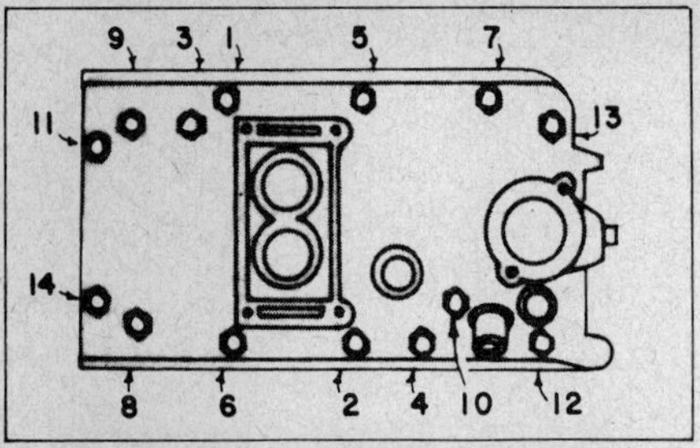

Fig. 4 Intake manifold tightening sequence. 1982 V6-232

fasteners according to numbers in **Fig. 1:** 1, 35-50 ft. lbs.; 2, 50-70 ft. lbs.; 3, 35-60 ft. lbs.; 4, 35-60 ft. lbs.; 5, 70-90 ft. lbs.; 6, 35-50 ft. lbs.; 7, 70-90 ft. lbs.

EXC. 1982 & 1988 CONTINENTAL V6-232

On models equipped with Thermactor system, remove or disconnect components that will interfere with engine removal or installation.

1. Drain cooling system and crankcase.
2. Remove hood, then disconnect battery and alternator ground cables from cylinder block.
3. Remove air cleaner and duct assembly.
4. Disconnect upper and lower radiator hoses from engine block and transmission oil cooler lines from radiator.
5. Remove bolts attaching fan shroud to radiator.
6. Remove radiator, fan, spacer, pulley and fan shroud.
7. Remove alternator mounting bolts and position alternator aside.
8. Disconnect oil pressure sending unit wire connector and fuel line at fuel pump. Plug fuel tank line. **On models equipped with electronic fuel injection, relieve pressure at the Schrader type valve on the fuel charging valve before disconnecting fuel lines.**
9. Disconnect accelerator cable from throttle and throttle valve vacuum line at intake manifold.
10. Disconnect transmission manual shift rod, then disconnect retracting spring at shift rod stud.
11. Disconnect transmission oil filler tube bracket from engine block.
12. On models equipped with A/C, isolate and remove compressor.
13. Remove power steering pump bracket from cylinder head and position pump aside. Position pump so that fluid will not drain from reservoir.
14. Disconnect heater hoses from water pump and intake manifold and temperature sending unit wire connector.
15. Remove converter housing to engine upper attaching bolts.
16. Disconnect primary wire connector from ignition coil, then remove wiring harness from left rocker arm cover and position out of way. Disconnect ground strap from block. On EEC-IV equipped vehicles, disconnect wiring at sensors.
17. Raise front of vehicle and remove starter.
18. Disconnect exhaust pipes from exhaust manifold, then remove engine support insulators from brackets on frame.
19. Disconnect transmission oil cooler lines from retainer and remove converter housing inspection cover.
20. Disconnect flywheel from converter, secure converter to converter housing.
21. Remove remaining converter housing to engine attaching bolts, then lower vehicle and support transmission using a suitable jack.
22. Attach engine lifting device to lifting brackets on intake manifold, then raise engine slightly and disconnect from transmission.
23. Carefully lift engine from engine compartment.
24. Reverse procedure to install.

INTAKE MANIFOLD REPLACE

1982 V6-232

1. Drain cooling system, then remove air cleaner assembly.
2. Disconnect throttle linkage at carburetor, then remove accelerator linkage mounting bracket and position accelerator cable aside.
3. If applicable, disconnect speed control bead chain from carburetor, then remove servo/bracket assembly attaching nuts and position assembly aside.
4. Disconnect bowl vent hose at carburetor and thermactor air supply hose at check valve located at back end of intake manifold.
5. Disconnect and mark all vacuum hoses and electrical connections that will interfere with manifold removal.
6. Disconnect fuel line from carburetor and upper radiator hose from intake manifold.
7. If applicable, remove A/C compressor support bracket from manifold.
8. Loosen EGR tube at adapter, then disconnect PCV hose from carburetor.
9. Remove carburetor and EGR spacer.
10. Remove intake manifold attaching bolts, then the manifold.
11. Reverse procedure to install, and note the following:
    a. Before installing intake manifold, apply a 1/8 inch bead of silicone rubber sealer D6AZ-19562-B or equivalent at mating surfaces of intake manifold, cylinder heads and cylinder block. Also apply a 1/8 inch bead of sealer to the outer end of each intake manifold seal for the full width of the seal.
    b. Torque bolts to specification in sequence shown in **Fig. 4.**

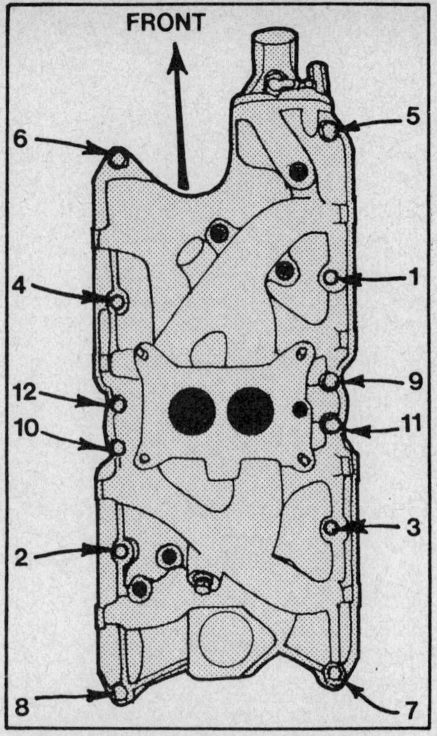

Fig. 5 Intake manifold tightening sequence. V8-302

V8-302

1982–85

1. Disconnect battery ground cable and drain cooling system.
2. Remove air cleaner, PCV hose and air intake duct, then disconnect electric choke heater tube, if applicable.
3. Remove accelerator cable bracket, then disconnect all vacuum lines from manifold.
4. Disconnect high tension lead and primary wiring connector from ignition coil, then remove coil and support bracket from manifold.
5. Disconnect high tension leads from spark plugs, then remove distributor cap, adapter and high tension leads as an assembly.
6. Disconnect fuel line from carburetor or fuel charging assembly on throttle body (fuel injected models). **On fuel injected models, relieve fuel pressure at Schrader type valve on fuel charging assembly before disconnecting fuel line.**
7. Disconnect vacuum hoses, if applicable, and electrical leads from distributor, then remove hold-down bolt and distributor. Mark position of rotor to aid installation.
8. Disconnect upper radiator hose and coolant temperature sending wire from manifold.
9. Disconnect all remaining wiring that will interfere with manifold removal.
10. Remove EGR cooler, if applicable, from rear of manifold.
11. Remove intake manifold attaching bolts, then the intake manifold.

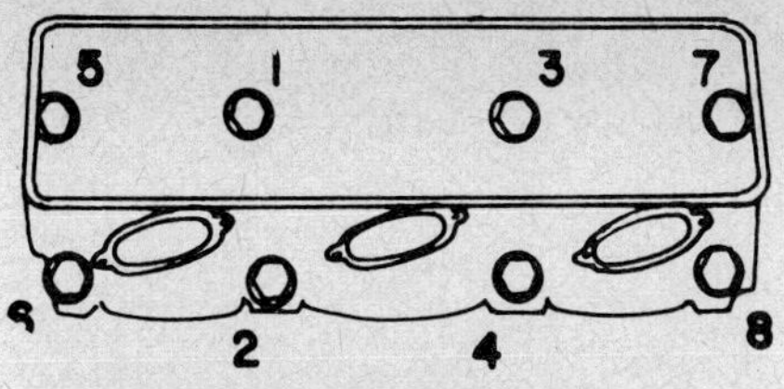

Fig. 6 Cylinder head tightening sequence. 1982 V6-232

12. Reverse procedure to install. Torque intake manifold bolts to specification in sequence shown in **Fig. 5. Some 1982-85 V8-302 engines may exhibit engine oil leakage at the front or rear intake manifold end seals. To correct this condition, RTV sealer should be used instead of the conventional cork seals provided in the gasket set. Remove intake manifold and gaskets, then clean cylinder block and intake manifold sealing surfaces with suitable solvent. Install side runner gaskets onto cylinder block, then apply a 1/4 inch bead of RTV sealer across the front and rear sealing surfaces of the cylinder block. When applying the sealer, ensure sealer does not get inside engine, as damage may result. Install manifold and torque bolts to specifications.**

1986–88

1. Disconnect battery ground cable and drain cooling system.
2. Remove air cleaner, PCV hose and air intake duct, then disconnect electric choke heater tube, if applicable.
3. Remove accelerator cable bracket, then disconnect speed control linkage, TV cable and all vacuum lines from manifold.
4. Disconnect high tension lead and primary wiring connector from ignition coil, then remove coil and support bracket from manifold.
5. Disconnect high tension leads from spark plugs, then remove distributor cap, adapter and high tension leads as an assembly.
6. Disconnect fuel return and supply lines. **Relieve fuel pressure at valve on metal fuel rail located at LH front corner of engine before disconnecting fuel lines.**
7. Disconnect electrical leads from distributor, then remove hold down bolt and distributor. Mark position of rotor to aid installation.
8. Disconnect upper radiator hose, coolant temperature sending wire and throttle body cooler hoses at manifold.
9. Loosen hose clamp, then slide bypass hose off outlet housing.
10. Disconnect all remaining electrical connections that will interfere with manifold removal.
11. Disconnect crankcase vent hose assembly at rear of lower intake manifold, then the fuel evaporative purge tube, if so equipped.
12. Remove attaching bolts, then the upper intake manifold.
13. Remove lower intake manifold, together with fuel rails.
14. Reverse procedure to install.

CYLINDER HEAD REPLACE

Before installing cylinder head, wipe off engine block gasket surface and be certain no foreign material has fallen into cylinder bores, bolt holes or in the valve lifter area. It is good practice to clean out bolt holes with compressed air.

Some cylinder head gaskets are coated with a special lacquer to provide a good seal once the parts have warmed up. Do not use any additional sealer on such gaskets. If the gasket does not have this lacquer coating, apply suitable sealer to both sides.

Tighten cylinder head bolts a little at a time in three steps in the sequence shown in the illustrations. Final tightening should be to the torque specifications listed in the Engine Tightening table. After the bolts have been torqued to specifications, they should not be disturbed.

1982 V6-232

1. Disconnect battery ground cable, then drain cooling system.
2. Remove air cleaner, air intake duct and heat tube.
3. Loosen accessory drive belt idler and remove drive belt.
4. If left cylinder head is to be removed, proceed as follows:
   a. Remove oil filler cap.
   b. If equipped with power steering, remove pump bracket attaching bolts, then remove pump and bracket assembly and position pump aside with hoses attached.
   c. If equipped with A/C, remove compressor bracket attaching bolts, then position compressor and bracket assembly aside with refrigerant lines attached.
5. If right cylinder head is to be removed, proceed as follows:
   a. Remove Thermactor diverter valve and hose assembly.
   b. Remove accessory drive belt idler, then remove alternator.
   c. Remove Thermactor pump pulley, then remove Thermactor pump.
   d. Remove alternator mounting bracket. **On models equipped with Tripminder, the fuel supply line from the fuel pump to the fuel sensor will have to be disconnected to gain access to the upper alternator bracket bolt.**
   e. Remove PCV valve.
6. Remove intake manifold, and exhaust manifolds.
7. Remove rocker arm cover and attaching screws, then loosen cover by using a putty knife under cover flange and remove cover. Do not use excess force when loosening rocker arm cover as cover may become damaged.
8. Loosen rocker fulcrum bolt enough to allow rocker arms to be rotated to one side, then remove pushrods. **Tag pushrods so they can be installed in the same position.**
9. Remove cylinder head attaching bolts, then remove cylinder head and gasket.
10. Reverse procedure to install. Apply a thin coating of pipe sealant D8AZ-19558-A or equivalent to the shorter cylinder head bolts which are installed on the exhaust manifold side of the cylinder head. Do not apply pipe sealant to long bolts which are installed on the intake manifold side of the cylinder head. Tighten cylinder head bolts in four steps to torque listed under Engine Tightening Specifications using sequence shown in **Fig. 6.** Loosen cylinder bolts approximately 2 to 3 turns, then retighten bolts in four steps to specified torque in sequence, **Fig. 6.**

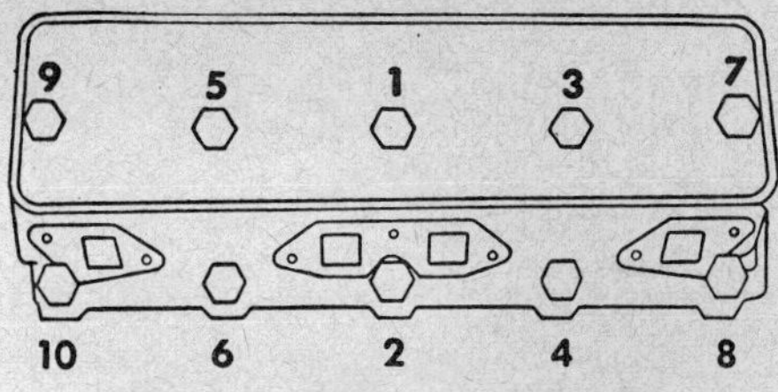

Fig. 7 Cylinder head tightening sequence. V8-302

V8-302

1. Remove intake manifold.
2. Disconnect battery ground cable at cylinder head.
3. If left head is being removed, remove A/C compressor (if equipped). Also remove and wire power steering pump out of the way. If equipped with Thermactor System, disconnect hose from air manifold on left cylinder head.
4. If right head is to be removed, remove alternator mounting bracket bolt and spacer, ground wire and air cleaner inlet duct, and A/C compressor bracket.
5. If right head is to be removed on an engine with Thermactor System, remove air pump from bracket. Disconnect hose from air manifold.
6. Disconnect exhaust manifolds at exhaust pipes.
7. Remove rocker arm covers. If equipped with Thermactor System, remove check valve from air manifold.
8. Remove fulcrum bolts, oil deflectors (if used), fulcrums and rocker arms. On all engines, remove pushrods. Keep rocker arms and pushrods in order so they can be installed in the same position.
9. Remove head bolts and lift head off block.
10. Reverse procedure to install. Torque cylinder head bolts in sequence shown in **Fig. 7. Some 1982 V8-302 engines may exhibit excessive oil consumption caused by low profile rocker arm fulcrums, Part No. E1TZ-6A528-A, allowing excessive**

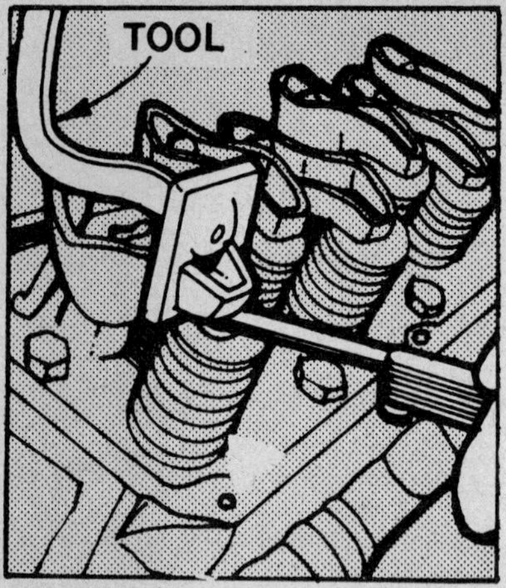

Fig. 8 Compressing lifter to check valve clearance

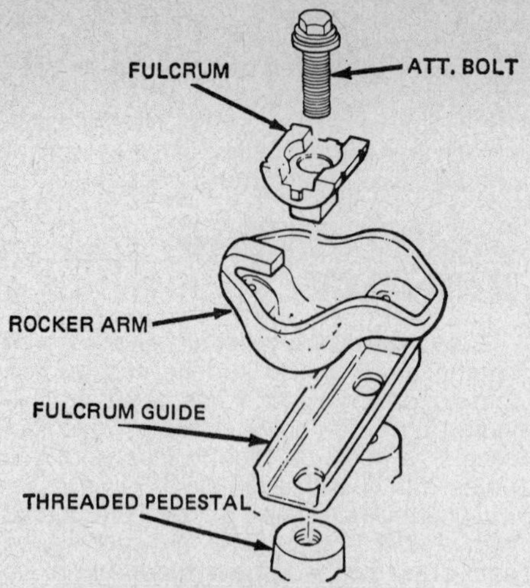

Fig. 9 Rocker arm & related parts

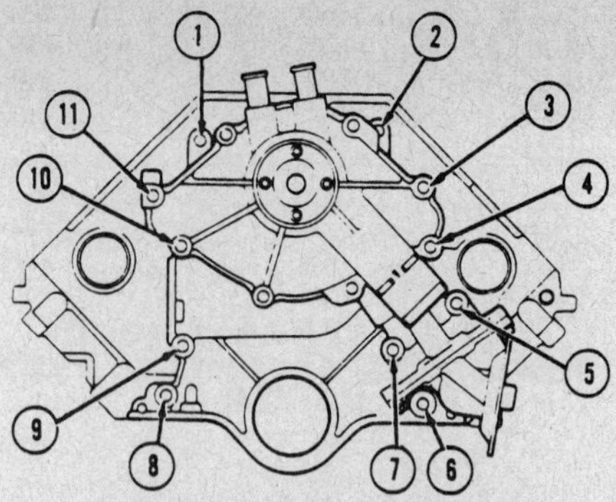

Fig. 10 Front cover attaching bolt location. 1982 V6-232

oil displacement when the engine is operated for an extended period during high ambient temperatures. To service the above problem, replace the fulcrums indicated above with new fulcrums, Part No. D7AZ-6A528-A.

VALVE CLEARANCE SPECIFICATIONS

Engine	Year	Int.	Exh.
V6-232	1982	.088-.189①	.088-.189①
V8-302	1982-88	.096-.146①	.096-.146①
V8-302 H.O.	1985-88	.123-.146①	.123-.146①

①—With hydraulic lifter fully collapsed.

VALVES

ADJUST

1982 V6-232

A .060 inch longer or a .060 inch shorter pushrod is available to compensate for dimensional changes in the valve train. If clearance is less than specified, the .060 inch shorter pushrod should be used. If clearance is more than the maximum specified, the .060 inch longer pushrod should be used.

Using an auxiliary starter switch crank engine until No. 1 cylinder is at TDC compression stroke, then compress valve lifter using tool T82C-6500-A or equivalent, **Fig. 8.** At this point, the following valves can be checked: intake Nos. 1, 3 and 6; exhaust Nos. 1, 2 and 4.

After clearance on these valves has been checked, rotate crankshaft until No. 5 cylinder is at TDC compression stroke (1 revolution of crankshaft), and then compress valve lifter using tool No. T82C-6500-A or equivalent, **Fig. 8,** and check the following valves: intake Nos. 2, 4 and 5; exhaust Nos. 3, 5 and 6.

V8-302

To eliminate the need of adjusting valve lash, a positive stop nut fulcrum bolt and seat is used on these engines, **Fig. 9.**

It is very important that the correct pushrod be used and all components be installed and torqued as follows:

1. Position the piston of the cylinder being worked on at TDC of its compression stroke.
2. Install rocker arm, fulcrum seat and oil deflector. Install fulcrum bolt and torque to 18-25 ft. lbs.

A .060 inch shorter pushrod or a .060 inch longer rod is available for service to provide a means of compensating for dimensional changes in the valve mechanism. Valve stem-to-rocker arm clearance should be as specified, with the hydraulic lifter completely collapsed, **Fig. 8.** Repeated valve grind jobs will decrease this clearance to the point that if not compensated for the lifters will cease to function.

When checking valve clearance, if the clearance is less than the minimum, the .060 inch shorter pushrod should be used. If clearance is more than the maximum, the .060 inch longer pushrod should be used. To check valve clearance, proceed as follows:

1. Mark crankshaft pulley at three locations, with number 1 location at TDC timing mark (end of compression stroke), number 2 location one half turn (180°) clockwise from TDC and number 3 location three quarter turn clockwise (270°) from number 2 location.
2. Turn the crankshaft to the number 1 location and check the clearance on the following valves:
   a. V8-302: intake Nos. 1, 7 and 8; exhaust Nos. 1, 4 and 5.
   b. V8-302 H.O.: intake Nos. 1, 4 and 8; exhaust Nos. 1, 3 and 7.
3. Turn the crankshaft to the number 2 location and check the clearance on the following valves:
   a. V8-302: intake Nos. 4 and 5; exhaust Nos. 2 and 6.
   b. V8-302 H.O.: intake Nos. 3 and 7; exhaust Nos. 2 and 6.
4. Turn the crankshaft to the number 3 location and check the clearance on the following valves:
   a. V8-302: intake Nos. 2, 3 and 6; exhaust Nos. 3, 7 and 8.
   b. V8-302 H.O.: intake Nos. 2, 5 and 6; exhaust Nos. 4, 5 and 8.

VALVE ARRANGEMENT

FRONT TO REAR

V6-232, Right Bank........... I-E-I-E-I-E
V6-232, Left Bank............ E-I-E-I-E-I
V8-302, Right Bank........ I-E-I-E-I-E-I-E
V8-302, Left Bank......... E-I-E-I-E-I-E-I

VALVE LIFT SPECIFICATIONS

Engine	Year	Intake	Exhaust
V6-232	1982	.415	.417
V8-302	1982-88	.375	.390
V8-302H.O.	1985-88	.413	.442

ROCKER ARM

REPLACE

V6-232 & V8-302

The rocker arm is supported by a fulcrum bolt which fits through the fulcrum seat and threads into the cylinder head. To disassemble, remove the bolt, fulcrum seat, fulcrum guide and rocker arm, **Fig. 9.**

VALVE GUIDES

Valve guides in these engines are an integral part of the head and, therefore, cannot be removed. For service, guides can be reamed oversize to accommodate one of three service valves with oversize stems (.003 inch, .015 inch and .030 inch).

Check the valve stem clearance of each valve (after cleaning) in its respective valve guide. If the clearance exceeds the service limits of .0055 inch, ream the valve guides to accommodate the next oversize diameter valve.

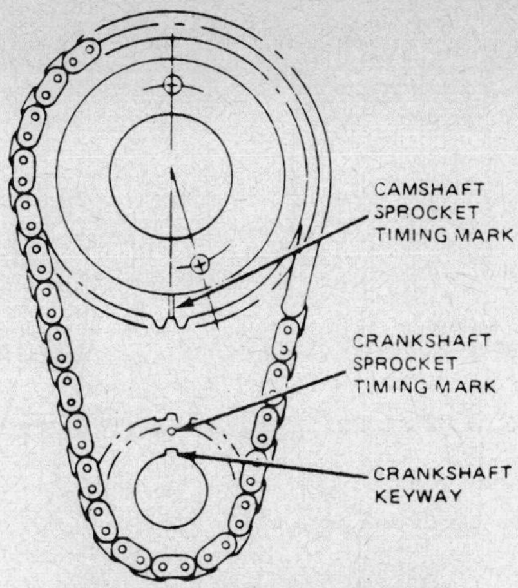

Fig. 11 Valve timing marks. 1982 V6-232

HYDRAULIC VALVE LIFTERS
REPLACE

The internal parts of each hydraulic valve lifter assembly are a matched set. If these are mixed, improper valve operation may result. Therefore, disassemble, inspect and test each assembly separately to prevent mixing the parts.

Conventional type hydraulic lifters are used on all 1982-85 engines, except 1985 V8-302 H.O. 1985 V8-302 H.O. and all 1986-88 V8-302 engines are equipped with roller hydraulic lifters. Pushrods used on these engines have a collar at the upper end and must be installed in this position. To replace valve lifters, proceed as follows:

1. Remove intake manifold and related parts.
2. Remove rocker arm covers.
3. Loosen rocker arm stud nuts or bolts and rotate rocker arms to the side.
4. Lift out pushrods, keeping them in sequence in a rack so they may be installed in their original location.
5. Using a magnet rod, remove valve lifters and place them in sequence in a rack so they may be installed in their original location.
6. Reverse procedure to install.

TIMING CASE COVER
REPLACE

If necessary to replace the cover oil seal the cover must first be removed.

1982 V6-232

1. Disconnect battery ground cable and drain cooling.
2. Remove air cleaner and air duct assembly.
3. Remove fan shroud and clutch assembly
4. Loosen accessory drive belt idler, then remove drive belt and water pump pulley.
5. On models equipped with power steering, remove pump bracket attaching bolts, then position pump and bracket assembly aside with hoses attached.
6. If equipped with A/C, remove compressor front support bracket.
7. Disconnect bypass hose, heater hoses and upper radiator hose from engine.
8. Position No. 1 cylinder at TDC compression stroke, then disconnect coil wire from distributor cap. Remove distributor cap and mark position of rotor to distributor body and distributor body to front cover. Remove distributor hold-down clamp, then remove distributor.
9. On models equipped with Tripminder, remove fuel flow meter support bracket.
10. Raise vehicle and support, then remove crankshaft damper using a suitable puller.
11. Remove fuel pump shield, then remove fuel pump attaching bolts and position pump aside with fuel hose attached.
12. Remove oil filter, then disconnect lower radiator hose at water pump.
13. Remove oil pan as described under Oil Pan, Replace.
14. Lower vehicle, then remove front cover attaching bolts, **Fig. 10. One of the front cover attaching bolts is located behind the oil filter adapter.**
15. Remove ignition timing indicator, then remove front cover and water pump as an assembly.
16. Reverse procedure to install. Coat threads of bolt located at position 10, **Fig. 10,** with a suitable sealer before installing. Torque front cover attaching bolts to 15 to 22 ft. lbs. **Lubricate camshaft thrust button with Polyethylene grease before installing front cover. Also ensure that thrust button and spring are properly seated.**

V8-302

1. Drain cooling system and crankcase.
2. Remove fan shroud attaching bolts and position shroud over engine fan.
3. Remove engine fan, spacer and shroud.
4. Remove drive belts and A/C idler pulley bracket.
5. Remove power steering pump and position aside.
6. Remove all accessory brackets attached to water pump, then remove water pump pulley.
7. Disconnect lower radiator hose, heater hose and bypass hose from water pump.
8. Remove crankshaft pulley from vibration damper.
9. Remove damper attaching screw and washer, then using a suitable puller, remove damper.
10. If applicable, disconnect fuel pump outlet line, then remove fuel pump attaching bolts and position pump aside.
11. Remove oil level dipstick.
12. Remove oil pan to front cover attaching bolts.

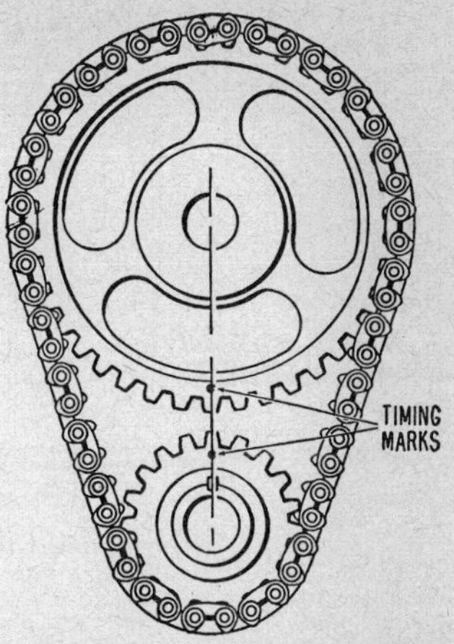

Fig. 12 Valve timing marks. V8-302

13. Remove front cover to engine block attaching bolts, then remove front cover and water pump as an assembly. **Use a thin blade knife to cut oil pan gasket flush with cylinder block face prior to separating front cover from cylinder block.**
14. Reverse procedure to install.

TIMING CHAIN
REPLACE
EXC. 1988 V6-232

1. Remove timing case cover as outlined previously.
2. Crank the engine until the timing mark on the camshaft sprocket is adjacent to the timing mark on the crankshaft sprocket, **Figs. 11 & 12.**
3. Remove capscrews, lock plate and fuel pump eccentric from front of camshaft.
4. Place a screwdriver behind the camshaft sprocket and carefully pry the sprocket and chain off the camshaft.
5. Reverse the foregoing procedure to install the chain, being sure to align the timing marks as shown in **Figs. 11 and 12.**

CAMSHAFT
REPLACE
EXC. 1988 V6-232

If it is necessary to replace the camshaft only, it may be accomplished without removing the engine from the chassis. However, if the camshaft bearings are to be replaced, the engine will have to be removed. To remove the camshaft, refer to the procedure outlined below. **It may be necessary to remove or reposition radiator, A/C compressor and grille components to provide adequate clearance.**

1. To remove camshaft, remove front cover and timing chain.
2. Remove distributor cap and spark plug wires, then remove distributor.
3. Disconnect automatic transmission

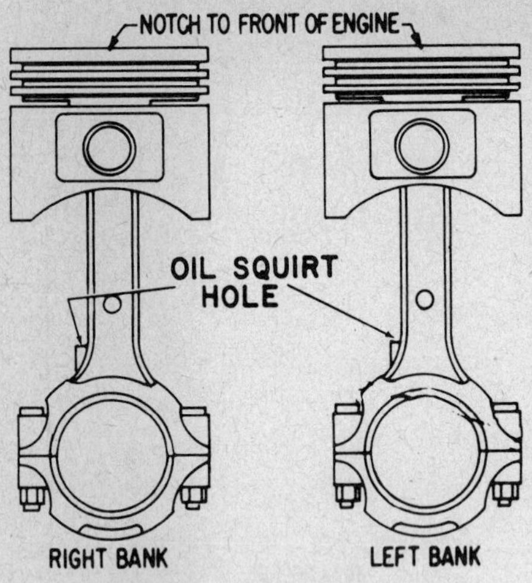

Fig. 13 Piston & rod assembly. V6-232

oil cooler lines from radiator and remove radiator.
4. Remove intake manifold and carburetor (if equipped) as an assembly.
5. Remove rocker arm covers.
6. Loosen rocker arm fulcrum or bolts and rotate rocker arms to one side.
7. Remove pushrods, keeping them in sequence in a rack so they may be installed in their original location.
8. Using a magnet, remove valve lifters and place them in a rack in sequence so they may be installed in their original location.
9. Remove camshaft thrust plate, and carefully pull camshaft from engine, using care to avoid damaging camshaft bearings.
10. Reverse procedure to install. **Prior to installation of the camshaft, lubricate push rods and camshaft lobes with lubricant part No. D9AZ-19579-C or equivalent on V6-232 engines and D0AZ-19584-A or equivalent for V8-302 engines. Using engine oil SF, lubricate valve tappets & bores.**

BALANCE SHAFT SYSTEM

1988 V6-232

A new balance shaft system is used on 1988 V6-232 engines to provide increased engine smoothness. The counter-rotating shaft, driven by a gear mounted on the camshaft snout between the camshaft thrust plate and sprocket, is located above the camshaft in the cylinder block valley area. The balance shaft is retained in the cylinder block by a thrust plate, and rides on bearings very similar to that of the camshaft.

PISTON & ROD ASSEMBLE

If the old pistons are serviceable, make certain that they are installed on the rods from which they were removed. The assembly must be assembled as shown in **Figs. 13 and 14.**

Check side clearance between connecting rods and crankshaft journal. Clearance should be .010-.020 inch for all engines except V6-232. V6-232 clearance should be .0047-.0114 inch.

PISTONS, RINGS & PINS

Pistons are available in oversizes of .003, .020, .030 and .040 inch.

Piston pins are available in oversizes of .001 and .002 inch.

Rings are available in oversizes of .020, .030 and .040 inch.

MAIN & ROD BEARINGS

Main and rod bearings are available in standard size and undersizes of .001, .002, .010, 020, .030 and .040 inch.

CRANKSHAFT REAR OIL SEAL

REPLACE

1982—83

1. Remove oil pan and oil pump, if necessary.
2. Remove rear bearing cap.
3. Loosen remaining bearing caps, allowing crankshaft to drop down about 1/32 inch.
4. Remove old seals from both cylinder block and rear main bearing cap. Use a brass rod to drift upper half of seal from cylinder block groove. Rotate crankshaft while drifting to facilitate removal.
5. Carefully clean seal groove in block with a brush and solvent. Also clean seal groove in bearing cap. Remove the oil seal retaining pin from the bearing cap if so equipped. The pin is not used with the split-lip seal.
6. Dip seal halves in clean engine oil.
7. Carefully install upper seal half in its groove with undercut side of seal toward front of engine, **Fig. 15,** by rotating it on shaft journal of crankshaft until approximately 3/8 inch protrudes below the parting surface. Be sure no rubber has been shaved from outside diameter or seal by bottom edge of groove.
8. Retighten main bearing caps and torque to specifications.
9. Install lower seal in main bearing cap with undercut side of seal toward front of engine, and allow seal to protrude about 3/8 inch above parting surface to mate with upper seal upon cap installation.
10. Apply suitable sealer to parting faces of cap and block. Install cap and torque to specifications. **If difficulty is encountered in installing the upper half of the seal in position, lightly lap (sandpaper) the side of the seal opposite the lip side using a medium grit paper. After sanding, the seal must be washed in solvent, then dipped in clean engine oil prior to installation.**

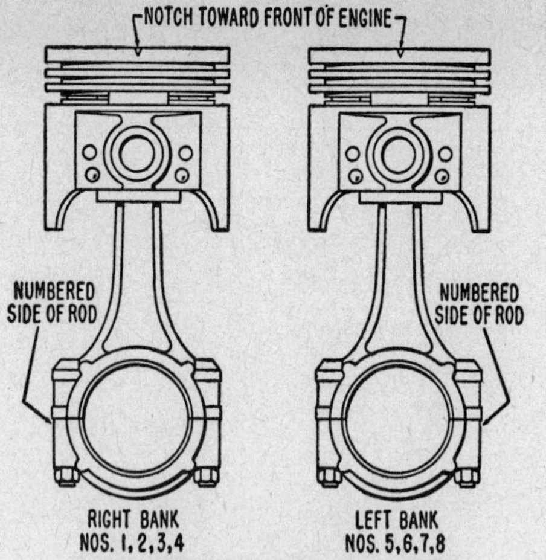

Fig. 14 Piston & rod assembly. V8-302

1984–88 EXC. 1988 V6-232

A one-piece rear oil seal is used on 1984-88 engines. To replace seal, proceed as follows:

1. Using a sharp awl, punch one hole into seal metal surface between seal lip and engine block.
2. Using slide hammer tool T82L-9533-B orequivalent, screw tool into hole in seal and remove seal by gently pulling rear ward. Use caution to avoid damaging sealing surface.
3. Lubricate new seal with engine oil, then position seal on installer tool T82L-6701-A, or equivalent, **Fig. 16.**
4. With spring end of seal facing towards engine, install tool, then alternately tighten bolts until rear face of seal is within .005 inch of the engine block.

OIL PAN

REPLACE

1982 CONTINENTAL V6-232

1. Disconnect battery ground cable, then remove air cleaner and air intake duct.
2. Remove fan shroud attaching screws and position shroud over fan, then remove engine oil dipstick.
3. Remove vacuum solenoid from dash panel and position on engine with vacuum hoses attached.
4. Raise and support front of vehicle, then remove exhaust pipe to exhaust manifold attaching nuts.
5. Drain crankcase, then remove oil filter.
6. Remove shift linkage bracket to converter housing attaching bolts.
7. Disconnect transmission oil cooler lines at radiator. Remove four converter cover attaching bolts, then remove converter cover.
8. Remove bolts attaching engine damper to No. 2 crossmember.
9. Disconnect steering gear at flex coupling, then remove steering gear to main crossmember attaching bolts

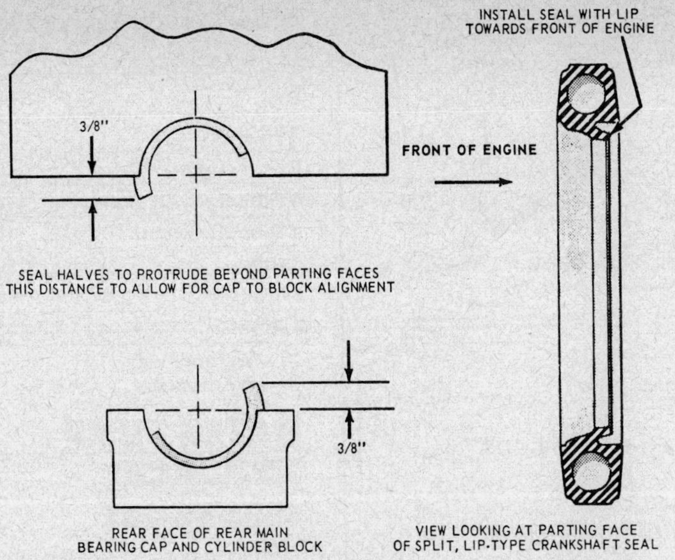

Fig. 15 Rear crankshaft seal installation. 1982–83

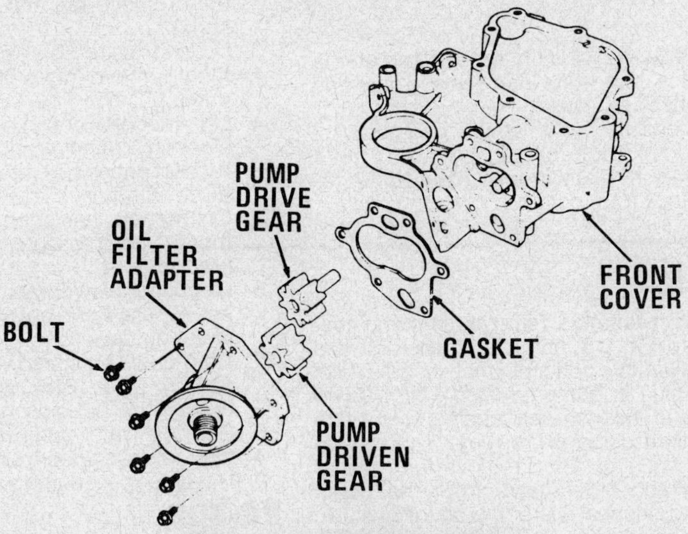

Fig. 16 Rear oil seal installation. 1984–88 Exc. 1988 V6-232

and allow steering gear to rest on frame.

10. Remove nuts and bolts attaching from engine mounts to chassis, then raise engine approximately 2 to 3 inches and insert wooden block between engine mounts and frame. **On some models, itmay be necessary to raise engine as much as 5 inches to provide clearance for o il pan removal. On these models, transmission fluid dipstick tube may contact Thermactor air tube. If contact occurs, lower engine and remove dipstick and air tube.**
11. Remove oil pan attaching bolts, then lower oil pan to crossmember.
12. Remove oil pump pickup tube attaching bolts and pickup tube bracket attaching nut, then lower pickup tube into oil pan.
13. Remove oil pan through front of vehicle, then remove oil pan gaskets and seals.
14. Reverse procedure to install. Using a small screwdriver, work tabs of oil pan seal into gap between rear main bearing cap and cylinder block, then with tabs positioned, work seal into groove on rear main bearing cap. Apply a 1/8 inch bead of silicone sealer D6AZ-19562-B or equivalent where front cover and cylinder block join and where rear main bearing cap and cylinder block join. Apply a 1/8 inch bead along oil pan rail surface of cylinder block and a 1/4 inch bead along front cover to oil pan surface. **When using silicone sealant, assembly must occur within 15 minutes after sealant application. After this time, the sealer may start to set, and its sealing effectiveness may be reduced.**

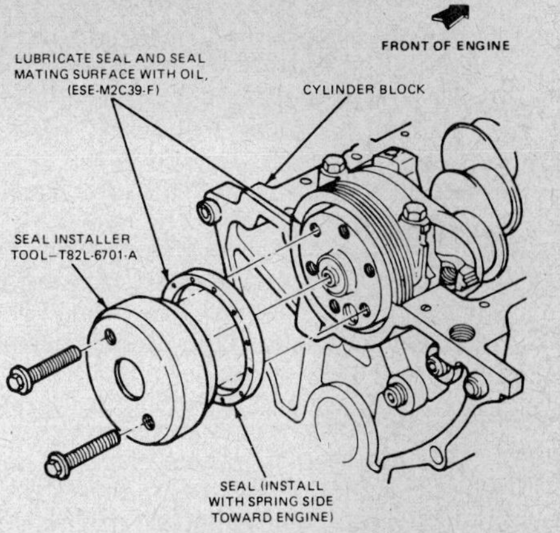

Fig. 17 Oil pump assembly. 1982 V6-232

EXC. 1982 & 1988 CONTINENTAL V6-232

1. Disconnect battery ground cable and remove air cleaner assembly.
2. Disconnect accelerator cable and kickdown rod from throttle.
3. Remove accelerator mounting bracket bolts and bracket, then the EGR valve and cooler, if applicable.
4. Remove fan shroud attaching screws and position shroud over fan.
5. Disconnect wiper motor electrical connector and remove wiper motor.
6. Disconnect windshield washer hose.
7. Remove wiper motor mounting cover.
8. Remove oil level dipstick, then the dipstick tube retaining bolt from exhaust manifold.
9. If equipped with EGR cooler, remove Thermactor air dump tube retaining clamp, then the Thermactor crossover tube at rear of engine.
10. Raise and support vehicle, then drain engine oil.
11. Remove starter motor.
12. Disconnect fuel tank fuel line at fuel pump and plug line. **Vehicles equipped with electronic fuel injection have high pressure at the electric fuel pump. Pressure must be relieved at the schrader type valve on the fuel charging assembly (CFI), or at valve on metal fuel rail located at LH front corner of engine (SFI) before disconnecting fuel lines.**
13. Disconnect exhaust pipes from manifolds.
14. If equipped with EGR cooler, remove thermactor secondary air tube to converter housing clamps.
15. On all models, remove dipstick tube from oil pan.
16. Loosen transmission mount attaching nuts.
17. Remove engine mount through bolts.
18. Remove shift crossover bolts at transmission.
19. On all models, disconnect transmission kickdown rod.
20. Remove brake line retainer from front crossmember.

21. With a suitable jack, raise engine as far as possible.
22. Place a block of wood between each engine mount and chassis bracket. When engine is secured in this position, remove jack, then the low oil level sensor, if equipped.
23. If equipped, remove stabilizer bar attaching bolts and lower stabilizer bar.
24. Remove transmission cooling line clamp retaining bolt, then position cooling lines aside.
25. Remove oil pan attaching bolts and lower pan to crossmember.
26. Remove oil pickup tube and oil pump retaining nuts and bolts, then lower tube and oil pump into oil pan.
27. Remove oil pan, together with pump, through front of vehicle.
28. Reverse procedure to install.

OIL PUMP REPLACE

1982 V6-232

On these engines, the oil pump is contained within the front cover, **Fig. 17.**

V8-302

The oil pan must be removed to gain access to the oil pump. Refer to "Oil Pan, Replace" for procedure.

OIL PUMP SERVICE

1982 V6-232 ENGINE

To disassemble, remove oil filter (if necessary), oil pump, cover bolts and cover. Lift oil pump gears from front cover pocket and remove cover gasket. Remove cotter pin from relief valve plug in pump housing. Drill a small hole and insert a self-tapping screw into the plug, then using pliers, remove plug from pump housing. Remove retainer spring and relief valve from pump housing. Using a suitable solvent, thoroughly clean oil pump components. Inspect oil pump as follows:

1. Check oil pump cover gasket surface. Remove any remaining gasket material, burrs and nicks.
2. Position a straightedge across oil pump gears and gasket surface.
3. Using a feeler gauge, measure clearance between straightedge and gasket surface. Clearance should be .002-.005 inch. If clearance is less than .002 inch, proceed to step 4.
4. Using a micrometer, measure oil pump gear thickness. Gear thickness should be .872-.873 inch. If gear is less than .872 inch, replace gear and check reading.
5. Measure front cover gear pocket depth. Depth should be .868-.870 inch. If depth exceeds .870 inch, replace oil pump front cover.
6. Using a feeler gauge, measure side clearance between gear tooth and gear pocket side wall. Clearance should be .002-.005 inch. If clearance exceeds .005 inch, proceed to step 7.
7. Using a micrometer, measure gear diameter. Gear diameter should be 1.664-1.666 inch. If gear diameter is less than 1.664 inch, replace gear and check reading.
8. Measure front cover gear pocket width. Width should be 1.671-1.674 inch. If width is less than 1.671, replace front cover.

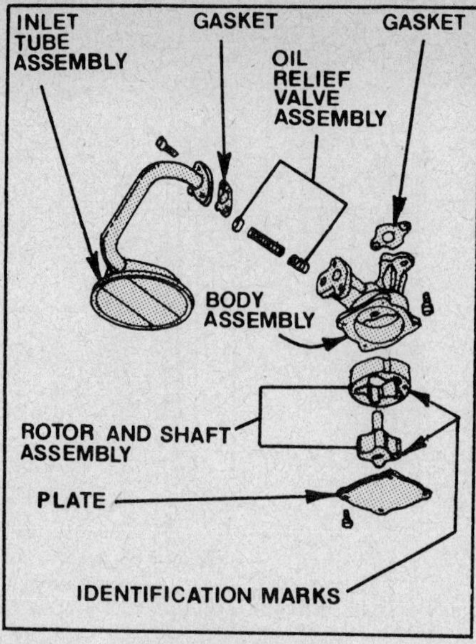

Fig. 18 Oil pump assembly. V8-302

V8-302

To disassemble, remove the pump cover plate, **Fig. 18,** and lift out the rotor and shaft. Remove cotter pin that secures relief valve plug in pump housing. Drill a small hole and insert a self-tapping screw into plug, then using pliers remove plug from pump housing. Then remove the retainer spring and relief valve from the pump housing. Inspect the pump as follows:

1. With all parts clean and dry, check the inside of the pump housing and the outer race and rotor for damage or excessive wear.
2. Check the mating surface of the pump cover for wear. If this surface is worn, scored or grooved, replace the cover.
3. Measure the clearance between the outer race and housing. This clearance should be .001-.013.
4. With the rotor assembly installed in the housing, place a straightedge over the rotor assembly and housing. Measure the clearance between the straightedge and the rotor and outer race. Recommended limits are .0016-.004 inch.
5. Check the drive shaft-to-housing bearing clearance by measuring the O.D. of the shaft and the I.D. of the housing bearing. The recommended clearance limits are .0015-.0030 inch.
6. Inspect the relief valve spring for a collapsed or worn condition.
7. Check the relief valve piston for scores and free operation in the bore. The specified clearance is .0015-.0030 inch.

BELT TENSION DATA

Belt	New	Used
1982–88		
Exc. 1/4 inch	140	105
4 Ribs Exc. Air Pump	130	115
4 Ribs Air Pump	110	105
5 Ribs	150	135
6 Ribs ①	160	145
6 Ribs ②	113	110

①—W/tensioner.
②—W/absorber.

WATER PUMP REPLACE

1982 V6-232

1. Drain cooling system, then remove air cleaner and air intake duct.
2. Remove fan shroud attaching screws and fan and fan clutch attaching bolts, then remove fan and fan clutch and shroud.
3. Loosen accessory drive belt idler, then remove drive belt and water pump pulley.
4. On models equipped with power steering, remove pump mounting bracket attaching bolts, position pump aside with hoses attached.
5. On models equipped with A/C, remove compressor front support bracket.
6. Disconnect lower radiator hose, coolant bypass hose and heat hose from water pump.
7. On models equipped with Tripminder, remove fuel flow sensor support bracket. Do not disconnect fuel lines.
8. Remove water pump attaching bolts, then remove water pump.
9. Reverse procedure to install.

V8-302

1. Drain cooling system, then remove fan shroud attaching bolts and position shroud over fan.
2. Remove fan, spacer and shroud.
3. Remove drive belts, then remove A/C idler pulley bracket.
4. Remove power steering pump and position aside.
5. Remove all accessory brackets which attach to water pump, then remove water pump pulley.
6. Remove lower radiator hose, heater hose and bypass hose from water pump.
7. Remove water pump to front cover attaching bolts, then remove water pump.
8. Reverse procedure to install.

FUEL PUMP REPLACE

MECHANICAL TYPE

1. Disconnect fuel lines from fuel pump.
2. Remove fuel pump attaching bolts and the fuel pump and gasket.

3. Remove all gasket material from the pump and block gasket surfaces. Apply sealer to both sides of new gasket.
4. Position gasket on pump flange and hold pump in position against its mounting surface. Make sure rocker arm is riding on camshaft eccentric.
5. Press pump tight against its mounting. Install retaining screws and tighten them alternately.
6. Connect fuel lines. Then operate engine and check for leaks. **Before installing the pump, it is good practice to crank the engine so that the nose of the camshaft eccentric is out of the way of the fuel pump rocker arm when the pump is installed. In this way there will be the least amount of tension on the rocker arm, thereby easing the installation of the pump.**

ELECTRIC TYPE

When the electric fuel pump is removed from the fuel tank, all the rubber hoses, clamps and mounting gaskets should be replaced, as exposure to the air causes the hoses to become brittle and will lead to premature failure.

Removal

1. Remove air cleaner.
2. Depressurize fuel system as follows:
   a. On CFI engines, attach tool T80L-9974-A or equivalent to fuel diagnostic valve on the fuel charging assembly, then slowly depressurize fuel system.
   b. On EFI engines, depressurize fuel system at valve located in fuel rail on LH front corner of engine.
3. Siphon fuel from fuel tank, then raise and support vehicle.
4. Disconnect fuel supply, return and vent lines at the left and right side rear axle frame kickdowns.
5. Disconnect electrical connector in front of fuel tank.
6. Disconnect and remove fuel filler tube.
7. Remove fuel tank support straps, then the fuel tank.
8. Clean all dirt accumulated around fuel pump attaching flange, then disconnect supply and return line fittings and the electrical connector.
9. Turn fuel pump lock ring counterclockwise and remove lock ring.
10. Remove fuel pump and bracket assembly from fuel tank. Discard seal ring.

Installation

1. Clean fuel tank mounting surface and seal ring groove.
2. Lightly coat new seal ring with heavy grease to hold it in place, then install into fuel ring groove.
3. Carefully install fuel pump and bracket assembly into tank, ensuring filter is not damaged during installation. Ensure locating keys are positioned in keyways and seal ring remains in groove.
4. Holding pump assembly in place, install lock ring finger tight, ensuring all locking tabs are positioned under fuel tank ring tabs. Continue to turn lock ring clockwise until ring contacts stop.
5. Connect fuel pump electrical connector, then lubricate fittings and reconnect fuel lines.
6. Install fuel tank and tighten support straps.
7. Reconnect fuel sender and fuel pump wiring harness, then lower vehicle.
8. Install fuel filler tube and reconnect vent line.
9. Lubricate fittings at right and lefthand side of rear axle frame, reconnect finger tight, then tighten an additional 1/4 turn.
10. Fill fuel tank with at least 10 gallons of fuel and check for leaks.
11. Activate fuel pump until system is fully pressurized, then check all fittings for leakage. Repair leaks as necessary.
12. Start engine and recheck for leaks.

6-149 (2.4L) Diesel Engine

INDEX

ENGINE MOUNTS REPLACE

1. Raise and support vehicle.
2. Remove insulator to crossmember attaching nuts, then raise engine with suitable jack, **Fig 1.**
3. Remove insulator to bracket attaching bolts and the insulator.
4. Reverse procedure to install. Refer to **Fig. 1,** for proper torque specifications.

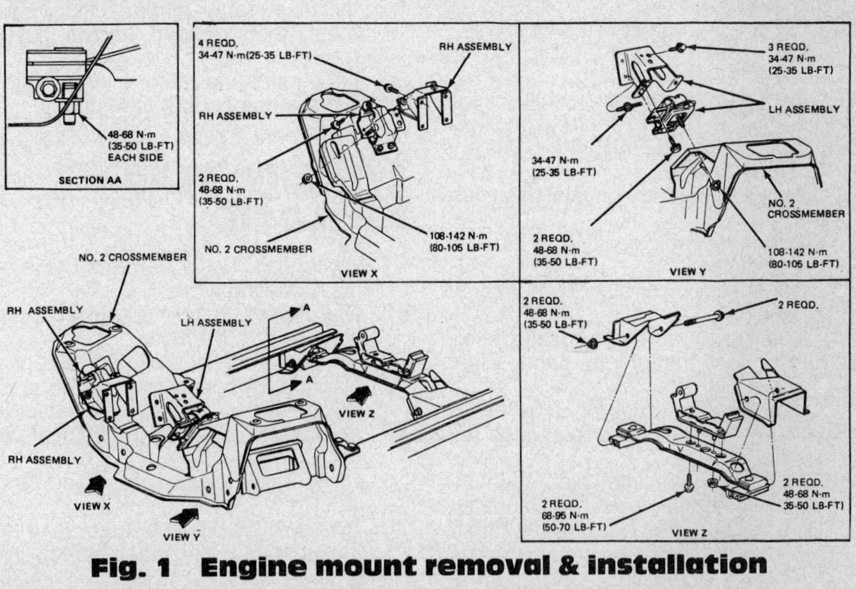

Fig. 1 Engine mount removal & installation

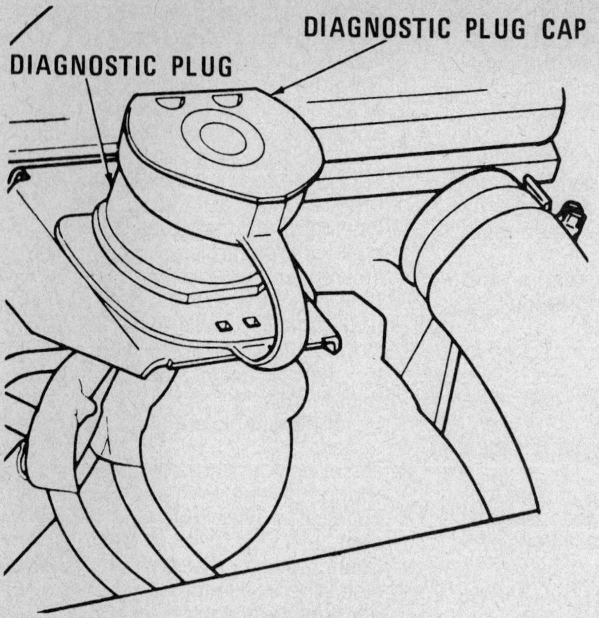

Fig. 2 Diagnostic connector

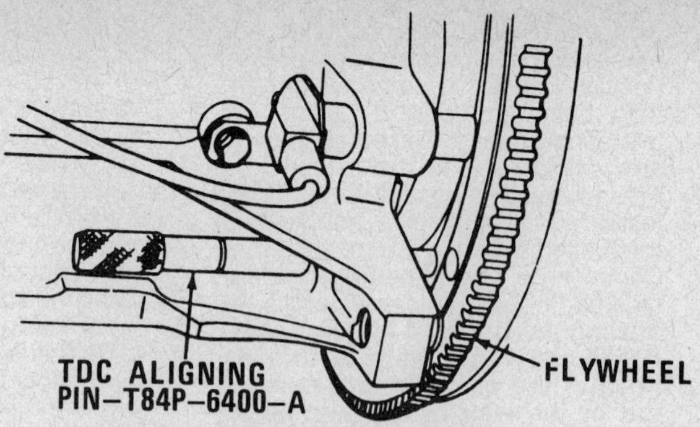

Fig. 3 TDC aligning pin installed

ENGINE
REPLACE

1. Disconnect battery ground cable.
2. Disconnect under hood lamp wiring connector.
3. Scribe hinge mark locations, then remove hood.
4. Drain cooling system and oil pan, then remove air cleaner assembly.
5. Remove fan shroud attaching bolts, then the fan shroud.
6. Remove cooling fan, then disconnect upper and lower radiator hoses.
7. Disconnect transmission oil cooler lines, then remove radiator.
8. Discharge A/C system, then disconnect hoses from compressor. Plug hoses to prevent dirt entry.
9. Disconnect muffler inlet pipe.
10. Disconnect vacuum hoses and wiring harnesses that will interfere with engine removal.
11. Disconnect engine oil cooler lines.
12. Disconnect accelerator cable and fuel line from injection pump.
13. Disconnect transmission shift linkage.
14. Disconnect ground cable at engine.
15. Remove coolant expansion bottle and position aside.
16. Disconnect heater hoses at dash panel.
17. Disconnect electrical lead at A/C compressor.
18. Disconnect power steering pump and position aside.
19. Disconnect fuel lines from injectors.
20. Disconnect instrument panel wiring harness.
21. Install engine support tool D79F-6000-A or equivalent, then raise and support vehicle.
22. Remove muffler inlet pipe, then the engine oil cooler bracket and brace.
23. Remove stabilizer bar bracket attaching bolts and position stabilizer bar forward.
24. Remove left fender splash shield, then disconnect steering column shaft coupling from steering gear.
25. Remove engine mount insulator retaining nuts, then raise engine with suitable jack.
26. Position steering gear, as necessary, then lower engine.
27. Remove converter housing cover, then the converter to drive plate retaining nuts. Position locking pliers in housing to support converter.
28. Remove crossmember retaining nuts, then the transmission shift lever bellcrank.
29. Raise transmission with suitable jack, then remove crossmember retaining bolts.
30. Lower transmission, then remove engine to converter housing retaining bolts.
31. Reinstall crossmember retaining bolts, then lower vehicle.
32. Install suitable engine lifting equipment, then remove engine support tool.
33. Lift engine and remove from vehicle.
34. Reverse procedure to install.

CYLINDER HEAD
REPLACE

1. Disconnect battery ground cable and drain cooling system.
2. Disconnect heater hose, then remove accessory drive belts.
3. Remove valve cover, then disconnect diagnostic connectors, **Fig. 2.**
4. Disconnect coolant temperature switch and glow plug electrical connectors.
5. Disconnect breather hose and bracket.
6. Remove oil dipstick tube to intake manifold attaching clamp and position tube aside.
7. Disconnect boost pressure switch electrical connector.
8. Disconnect radiator hose from cylinder head, then the idle boost coolant hose.
9. Remove vacuum pump from cylinder head.
10. Disconnect No. 1 injector nozzle to injection pump leak hose.
11. Using tool T84P-9395-B or equivalent, disconnect injection lines from nozzles and injection pump. Cap nozzles and lines to prevent dirt entry.
12. Disconnect turbocharger oil lines.
13. Rotate crankshaft pulley until No. 1 cylinder is at TDC, compression stroke, then install TDC aligning pin, tool No. T84P-6400-A or equivalent between cylinder block flange and flywheel, **Fig. 3.**
14. Loosen camshaft drive sprocket retaining bolt, then camshaft drive belt tensioning roller nut and bolt. Remove drive belt.
15. Loosen cylinder head attaching bolts following sequence shown in **Fig. 4,** then remove cylinder head.
16. Clean cylinder head and crankcase sealing surfaces using suitable spray solvent. **Do not score or scratch sealing surfaces, since leakage may occur due to high compression pressures.**
17. Check cylinder head for warpage. If warpage exceeds .006 inch, replace cylinder head.
18. Select cylinder head gasket thickness as follows:
    a. Mount dial indicator D82L-4201-A and height gauge D84P-6100-A so that indicator pointer is on top of No. 1 position.
    b. Rotate crankshaft until piston is at TDC.
    c. Zero indicator on crankcase, then move indicator pointer to front of piston. Record measurement. Move pointer to rear of piston and again record measurement. Average the two measurements.
    d. Repeat steps a through c for remaining pistons.
    e. Using measurement of highest piston, select the correct cylinder head gasket using chart shown, **Fig. 5.**

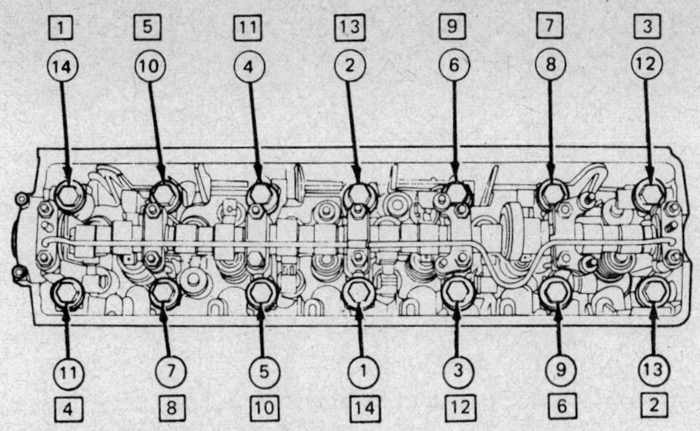

Fig. 4 Cylinder head bolt removal & installation

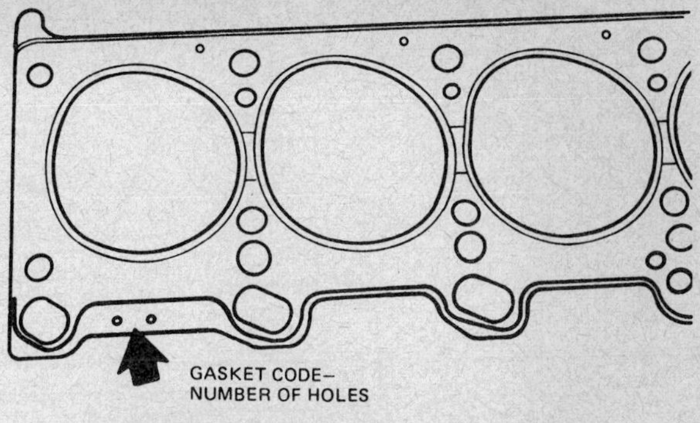

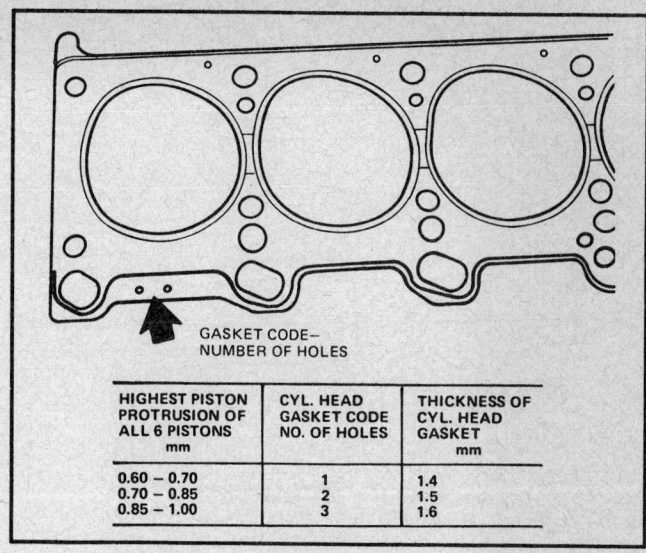

HIGHEST PISTON PROTRUSION OF ALL 6 PISTONS mm	CYL. HEAD GASKET CODE NO. OF HOLES	THICKNESS OF CYL. HEAD GASKET mm
0.60 – 0.70	1	1.4
0.70 – 0.85	2	1.5
0.85 – 1.00	3	1.6

Fig. 5 Cylinder head gasket selection chart

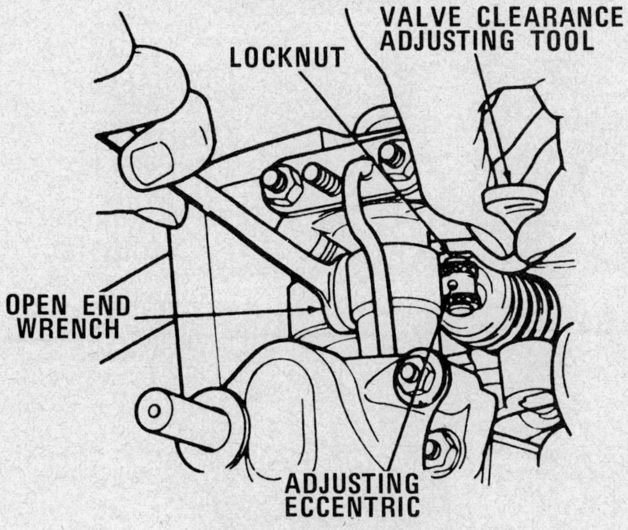

Fig. 6 Loosening adjustment eccentric

19. Clean carbon and oil deposits from head bolts. **Keep oil and/or anti-freeze from entering cylinder head bolt holes, since damage to crank-case may result. If either enters bolt holes, blow out using compressed air.**
20. Position head gasket onto crankcase, then install cylinder head.
21. Install and torque cylinder head bolts in sequence shown, **Fig. 4.**
22. Reverse steps 1 through 13 to complete installation, noting the following:
    a. Torque turbocharger oil lines to 14-17 ft. lbs.
    b. Torque injection line fittings to nozzles and pump to 14-18 ft. lbs.
    c. Torque vacuum pump-to-cylinder head attaching bolts to 6-7 ft. lbs.
    d. After installation is complete, start and run engine for 15 minutes, checking for any fuel, coolant or oil leaks. Repair as necessary.
    e. After running engine for 25 minutes, stop engine and remove valve cover. Using a suitable breaker bar, tighten cylinder head bolts an additional quarter turn (90 degrees). Adjust valves to specifications, then install valve cover.

INTAKE MANIFOLD REPLACE

1. Disconnect battery ground cable.
2. Remove diagnostic plug bracket and position aside, **Fig. 2.**
3. Disconnect turbocharger boost pressure indicator connector.
4. Remove oil dipstick tube to intake manifold attaching clamp and position tube aside.
5. Loosen turbocharger crossover pipe boot clamp.
6. Remove intake manifold to cylinder head attaching bolts, then the intake manifold.
7. Reverse procedure to install.

EXHAUST MANIFOLD REPLACE

1. Disconnect battery ground cable, then remove air cleaner assembly.
2. Disconnect muffler inlet pipe from turbocharger outlet. Plug outlet to prevent dirt entry.
3. Disconnect EGR valve vacuum line.
4. Disconnect inlet duct from turbocharger. Plug inlet to prevent dirt entry.
5. Loosen turbocharger crossover pipe boot clamp, then remove oil feed tube to exhaust manifold retaining clamp.
6. Remove oil feed line to turbocharger attaching bolts. Plug oil feed line and oil inlet port on turbocharger to prevent contamination of turbocharger oiling system.
7. Disconnect oil return line from turbocharger oil drain port. Plug line and port to prevent contamination of turbocharger oiling system.
8. Remove exhaust manifold to cylinder head attaching bolts, then the exhaust manifold and turbocharger assembly. Plug crossover pipe to prevent dirt entry.
9. Reverse procedure to install. Torque manifold attaching bolts and oil feed line to 14-17 ft. lbs., oil return line to 29-36 ft. lbs. and muffler inlet pipe to turbocharger outlet bolts to 31-35 ft. lbs.

VALVE TIMING

INTAKE OPENS BEFORE TOP DEAD CENTER

Engine	Year	Degrees
6-149	1984-85	6

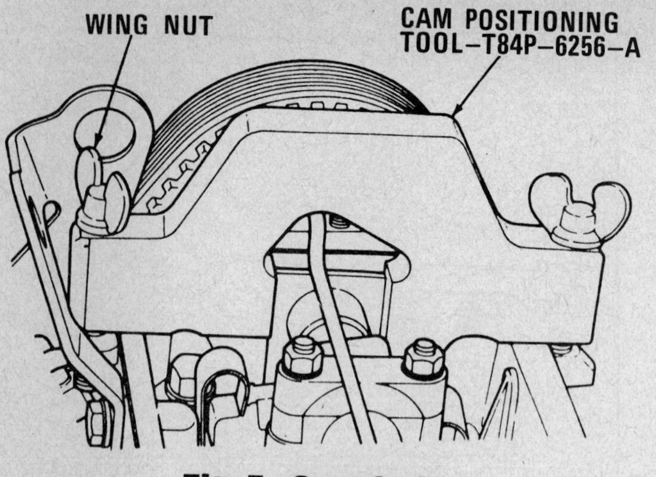

Fig. 7 Camshaft positioning tool installation

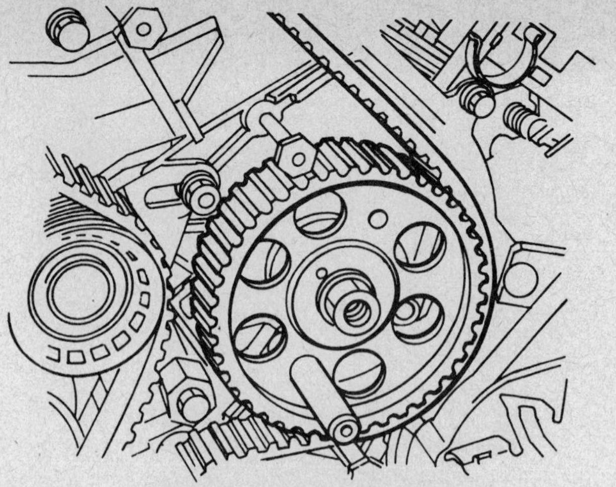

Fig. 8 Injection pump timing aligning pin installation

VALVE LIFT SPECIFICATIONS

Engine	Year	Intake	Exhaust
6-149	1984-85	.374	.376

ROCKER ARM
REPLACE

1. Remove valve cover and vacuum pump.
2. Rotate engine until cam lobe for rocker arm being replaced faces upward.
3. Remove rocker arm retaining clip.
4. Using tool T84P-6513-C or equivalent, compress valve spring.
5. Remove rocker arm assembly. **Ensure valve spring retainer remain locked in valve stem.**
6. Reverse procedure to install. Coat barrel of pivot ball pin with Loctite 270 or equivalent, before installing rocker arm.
7. Adjust valve clearances as outlined in "Valves, Adjust" procedure.

VALVE CLEARANCE SPECIFICATIONS

Engine	Year	Int.	Exh.
6-149	1984-85	.014①	.014①

①—With engine warm.

VALVES
ADJUST

1. Remove valve cover.
2. Rotate engine until camshaft lobe of valve being adjusted faces upward.
3. Using tool T84P-6575-A or equivalent and a 12 mm open end wrench, loosen adjusting eccentric locknut, **Fig. 6.**
4. Position feeler gauge, then rotate eccentric with a suitable punch until clearance is within specifications.
5. Tighten adjusting eccentric locknut.

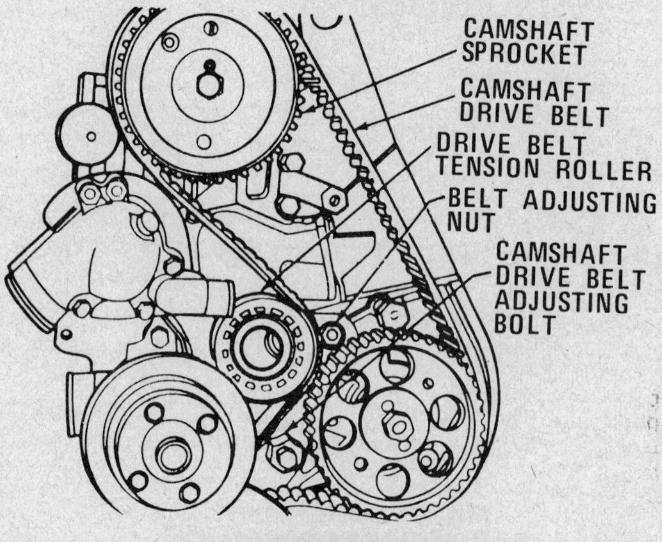

Fig. 9 Timing belt installation

TIMING BELT
REPLACE

1. Disconnect battery ground cable, then drain cooling system.
2. Disconnect upper radiator hose, then remove fan shroud.
3. Remove accessory drive belts, then the fan and clutch assembly.
4. Remove crankshaft pulley and vibration damper retaining bolts, then the pulley and damper.
5. Disconnect heater hose from thermostat housing.
6. Remove timing belt cover-to-crankcase attaching bolts, then the cover.
7. Remove valve cover.
8. Rotate engine until No. 1 cylinder is at TDC compression stroke, then install TDC aligning pin, T84P-6400-A or equivalent, **Fig. 3.**
9. Install camshaft positioning tool T84P-6256-A or equivalent onto cylinder head, **Fig. 7. Flat side of nut or cam position tool should be facing down.**
10. Loosen camshaft sprocket bolt.
11. If old belt will be reinstalled, mark direction of engine rotation on belt.
12. Loosen belt tensioner attaching bolts, then remove timing belt.
13. If using new belt or belt with less than 10,000 miles, insert .098 inch feeler gauge between camshaft positioning tool, **Fig. 7,** and right corner of cylinder head.
14. Install injection pump aligning pin T84P-9000-A or equivalent, through injection pump sprocket, **Fig. 8.**
15. Rotate camshaft sprocket clockwise against aligning pin, then install timing belt. Starting at crankshaft sprocket, route belt around intermediate shaft sprocket, injection pump sprocket, camshaft sprocket and tension roller, **Fig. 9. Ensure V side of belt is correctly positioned in pulley V.**

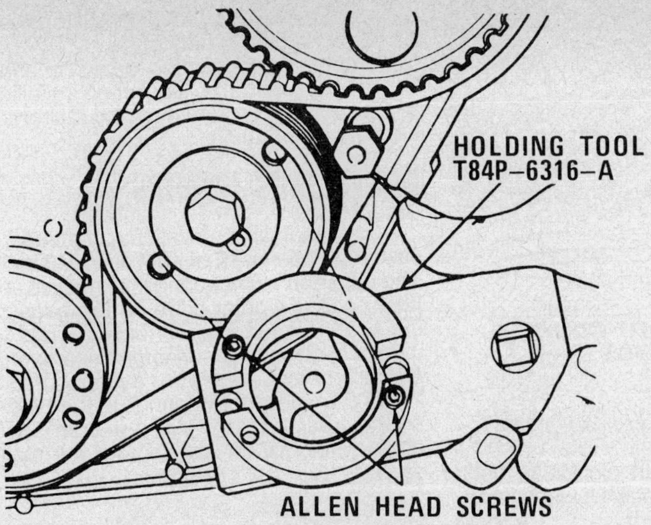

Fig. 10 Aligning Allen head screws

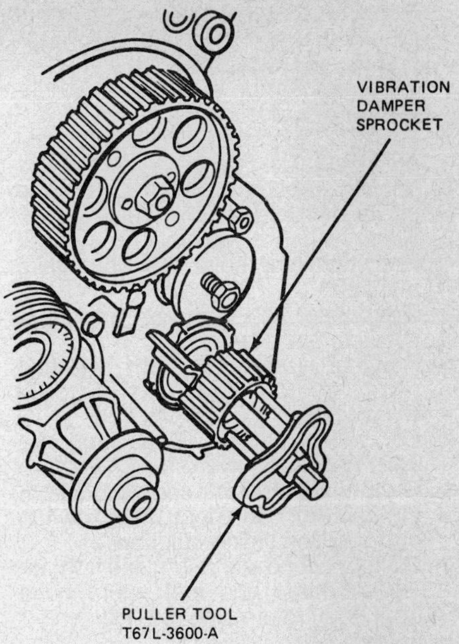

Fig. 11 Vibration damper sprocket removal

16. Hand tighten belt tensioner until all slack is removed from timing belt.
17. Remove injection pump aligning pin.
18. Torque belt tensioner to 35 ft. lbs. for belts with less than 10,000 miles, or 24 ft. lbs. for belts greater than 10,000 miles.
19. Torque belt tensioner attaching bolts to 17 ft. lbs.
20. Torque camshaft sprocket bolt to 44 ft. lbs.
21. Reverse steps 1 through 9 to complete installation. Torque crankshaft pulley and vibration damper retaining bolts to 15-22 ft. lbs.
22. Adjust injection pump timing.

CAMSHAFT
REPLACE

1. Disconnect battery ground cable, then remove valve cover.
2. Remove vacuum pump, cooling fan and fan clutch.
3. Remove accessory drive belts and tensioner, then the camshaft drive belt cover.
4. Remove rocker arms as outlined previously.
5. Rotate engine until cylinder No. 1 is at TDC compression stroke, then install TDC aligning pin, tool No. T84P-6400-A or equivalent, between cylinder block flange and flywheel, **Fig. 3.**
6. Loosen camshaft sprocket bolt, then the timing belt tensioner roller nut and bolt.
7. Remove camshaft sprocket retaining bolt and the sprocket.
8. Scribe alignment marks on camshaft bearing caps and cylinder head so that they can be installed in original position.
9. Remove bearing cap retaining nuts, then the bearing caps.
10. Remove camshaft.
11. Position camshaft onto cylinder head.
12. Install bearing caps and retaining nuts. Torque 6 mm nuts to 7 ft. lbs. and 8 mm nuts to 16 ft. lbs.
13. Loosely install camshaft sprocket, then install timing belt.
14. Torque camshaft sprocket retaining bolt to 44 ft. lbs.
15. Remove TDC alignment pin, then install rocker arms.
16. Install camshaft drive belt cover. Torque bolts to 6-7 ft. lbs.
17. Install accessory drive belt tensioner, drive belts, fan and fan clutch.
18. Install vacuum pump and rocker arm cover.
19. Connect battery ground, then run engine while checking for oil, intake air and coolant leaks.

ENGINE FRONT COVER
REPLACE

1. Perform steps 1 through 6 of "Timing Belt, Replace" procedure.
2. Remove intermediate shaft sprocket retaining bolt using tool T84P-6316-A or equivalent, **Fig. 10. Ensure Allen head screws are aligned with holes in intermediate shaft sprocket, Fig. 10.**
3. Remove vibration damper flange and sprocket retaining bolt. Using tool T67L-3600-A or equivalent, remove flange and sprocket, **Fig. 11.**
4. Remove the three oil pan to front cover attaching bolts, then loosen the remaining oil pan bolts.
5. Remove the six front cover to crankcase attaching bolts, then the front cover.
6. Clean front cover and crankcase mating surfaces.
7. Inspect and, if necessary, replace crankshaft and intermediate shaft oil seals.
8. Install new front cover gasket. Coat areas where front cover gasket meets oil pan gasket with a 1/4 inch bead of RTV sealant.
9. Position front cover onto crankcase and install attaching bolts. Torque 6 mm bolts to 7 ft. lbs. and 8 mm bolts to 16 ft. lbs.
10. Install the three front cover to oil pan attaching bolts. Torque all bolts to 7 ft. lbs.
11. Install vibration damper flange and sprocket onto crankshaft with shoulder facing toward front of vehicle.
12. Position intermediate shaft sprocket onto intermediate shaft, guiding locating pin into bore.
13. Install holding tool T84P-6316-A or equivalent, ensuring that Allen head screws in tool align with holes in intermediate shaft.
14. Install vibration damper flange and sprocket retaining bolt. Torque bolt to 282-311 ft. lbs.
15. Install intermediate shaft sprocket retaining bolt and torque to 44 ft. lbs.
16. Install and adjust timing belt as outlined previously.
17. Perform steps 1 through 6 of "Timing Belt, Replace" procedure in reverse sequence to complete installation.

INJECTION PUMP
REPLACE

1. Remove timing belt as outlined previously.
2. Install injection pump sprocket aligning pin T84P-9000-A or equivalent, then remove sprocket retaining nut and washer.
3. Using suitable puller, remove sprocket from injection pump.
4. Remove Woodruff key from pump shaft.

5. Remove oil dipstick tube to intake manifold attaching clamp, then position dipstick tube aside.
6. Disconnect turbo pressure switch indicator electrical connector.
7. Remove diagnostic plug bracket and position aside, **Fig. 2.**
8. Loosen turbo crossover pipe boot to intake manifold attaching clamp.
9. Remove intake manifold to cylinder head attaching bolts, then the intake manifold.
10. Disconnect and plug fuel lines from injection nozzles.
11. Remove fuel lines from injection pump. Note location of each line to aid reassembly.
12. Disconnect coolant hoses from idle speed boost housing.
13. Disconnect electrical connectors from fuel shut-off solenoid, micro-switch and injection timing solenoid.
14. Disconnect nozzle return line from injection pump and fuel return hose from fuel return line on left fender apron.
15. Disconnect fuel inlet hose from fuel return line on left fender apron.
16. Disconnect vacuum hoses from altitude compensation valve. Note location of hoses to aid reassembly.
17. Disconnect throttle cable and speed control cable, if equipped, from injection pump.
18. Remove injection pump attaching nuts and bolts, then the injection pump.
19. Reverse procedure to install. When installing injection pump, ensure that mark on front cover aligns with mark on injection pump mounting boss. Bleed fuel system as outlined under "Fuel System Bleeding," then adjust pump timing.

INJECTION PUMP TIMING

Refer to "Diesel Engine Performance Specifications" at the front of this manual for specified injection pump timing.

1. With transmission in Park, start engine and allow to reach normal operating temperature.
2. Open cover on diagnostic connector, **Fig. 2,** and install adapter from dynamic timing gauge Rotunda model 078-00116 or equivalent.
3. Check pump timing with engine running. If timing is not as specified, proceed as follows:
   a. Stop engine, then rotate crankshaft until No. 1 cylinder is at TDC of compression stroke.
   b. Remove injection pump distributor head bolt and sealing washer, then install adapter D84P-9000-D and Rotunda tool 014-00420 or equivalent onto injection pump, following tool manufacturer's instructions. **The plunger portion of adapter must project into injection pump sufficiently to contact the pump plunger.**
   c. Install suitable dial indicator into adapter, ensuring that there is at least a .100 inch preload on dial indicator.
   d. Rotate crankshaft clockwise until dial indicator displays lowest value, then zero indicator.
   e. Continue to rotate crankshaft until No. 1 cylinder is again at TDC of compression stroke, then install TDC aligning pin, **Fig. 3,** to secure crankshaft in position.
   f. On timing belts with less than 10,000 miles of use, dial indicator reading should be .0256 inch. On timing belts with more than 10,000 miles of use, the indicator reading should be .0248 inch.
4. If reading obtained is not as specified, rotate injection pump clockwise to increase reading, or counterclockwise to decrease reading on dial indicator.
5. After adjustment is completed, torque rear, then front injection pump mounting bolts to 7 ft. lbs.

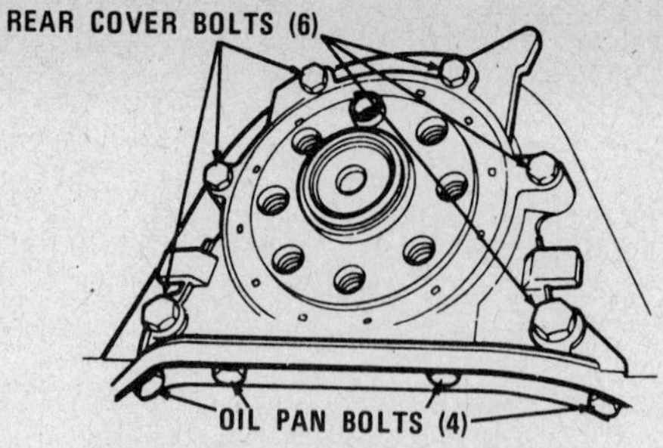

Fig. 12 Rear cover removal

FUEL SYSTEM BLEEDING

1. Ensure that vent screw is closed and that power is available to fuel shut-off solenoid.
2. Turn ignition "On" and allow pump to operate for approximately two minutes, then start engine. If engine runs correctly, system does require bleeding. If engine does not run correctly, proceed to next step.
3. Loosen coupling nuts on injector nozzles, then crank engine until all air is bled from lines. **Use extreme caution not to allow high pressure fuel to contact skin.**
4. Start engine. If engine runs correctly, no further bleeding is required. If engine does not run correctly, proceed to next step.
5. Crank engine and bleed system in the following locations:
   a. Fuel return line banjo bolt (labeled OUT).
   b. Injection pump distributor head plug bolt.
   c. Fuel shut-off solenoid.
   d. Fuel lines at injection pump.

PISTON & ROD ASSEMBLE

Pistons are supplied by three different manufacturers, Alcan-Nural, KS and Mahle. Both standard size and oversize pistons are available, however, pistons can be replaced only in sets of six.

Numbers on connecting rod and bearing cap must be on same side when installing piston. Install piston with arrow facing toward front of engine.

MAIN BEARINGS

Main bearings are available in standard size and undersizes of .010 and .020 inch. The different main bearing thicknesses are identified by a color code on the edge of the bearing shell. The correct bearings to use for each journal are determined during production and are shown by paint marks in the crankcase for bearings in the block; and by paint marks on the crankshaft counterweights, for bearings in the main caps.

CRANKSHAFT REAR OIL SEAL

REPLACE

1. Raise and support vehicle.
2. Remove transmission.
3. Remove drive plate assembly.
4. Remove the four oil pan to rear engine cover attaching bolts.
5. Loosen, but do not remove, the remaining oil pan bolts.
6. Remove rear cover attaching bolts, then the rear cover, **Fig. 12.**
7. Clean crankcase and rear engine cover mating surfaces.
8. Press oil seal from rear cover using an arbor press.
9. Using seal replacer T84P-6701-A or equivalent, press new seal into rear cover.
10. Lubricate sealing lips with engine oil, then install new cover gasket onto crankcase.
11. Apply gasket sealer at points where rear cover gasket meets oil pan gasket.
12. Install rear cover onto crankcase. Torque 6 mm bolts to 7 ft. lbs. and 8 mm bolts to 16 ft. lbs.
13. Install the four oil pan to rear cover attaching bolts, then torque all oil pan bolts to 7 ft. lbs.
14. Install drive plate assembly.
15. Install transmission, then lower vehicle.
16. Start engine and check for oil leaks.

OIL PAN & PUMP

REPLACE

1. Remove engine as outlined in "Engine, Replace" procedure.
2. Remove oil pan attaching bolts, then the oil pan.
3. Remove oil pump to crankcase attaching bolts, then the oil pump and shaft.
4. Install oil pump shaft, ensuring that it is fully engaged with intermediate shaft.
5. Install oil pump and attaching bolts, then torque bolts to 16 ft. lbs.

6. Clean oil pan and crankcase mating surfaces, then apply a 1/4 inch bead of RTV sealant on split lines of engine front and rear covers and crankcase.
7. Position new oil pan gasket onto oil pan, then install oil pan and attaching bolts. Torque bolts to 7 ft. lbs.

WATER PUMP
REPLACE

1. Drain cooling system.
2. Remove drive belts, then the cooling fan and clutch assembly.
3. Remove water pump pulley, then disconnect heater hose from thermostat housing.
4. Remove timing belt cover.
5. Remove water pump attaching bolts, then the water pump.
6. Reverse procedure to install.

Rear Axle, Propeller Shaft & Brakes (Rear Wheel Drive Models)

INDEX

DESCRIPTION

Fig. 1 illustrates the rear axle assembly used on these vehicles. When necessary to overhaul these units, refer to the rear axle specifications table at the beginning of this chapter.

The gear set consists of a ring gear and an overhung drive pinion which is supported by two opposed tapered roller bearings, **Fig. 1.** The differential case is a one-piece design with openings allowing assembly of the internal parts and lubricant flow. The differential pinion shaft is retained with a threaded bolt (lock) assembled to the case.

The roller type wheel bearings have no inner race, and the rollers directly contact the bearing journals of the axle shafts. The axle shafts do not use an inner and outer bearing retainer. Rather, they are held in the axle by means of C-locks. These C-locks also fit into a machined recess in the differential side gears within the differential case. There is no retainer bolt access hole in the axle shaft flange.

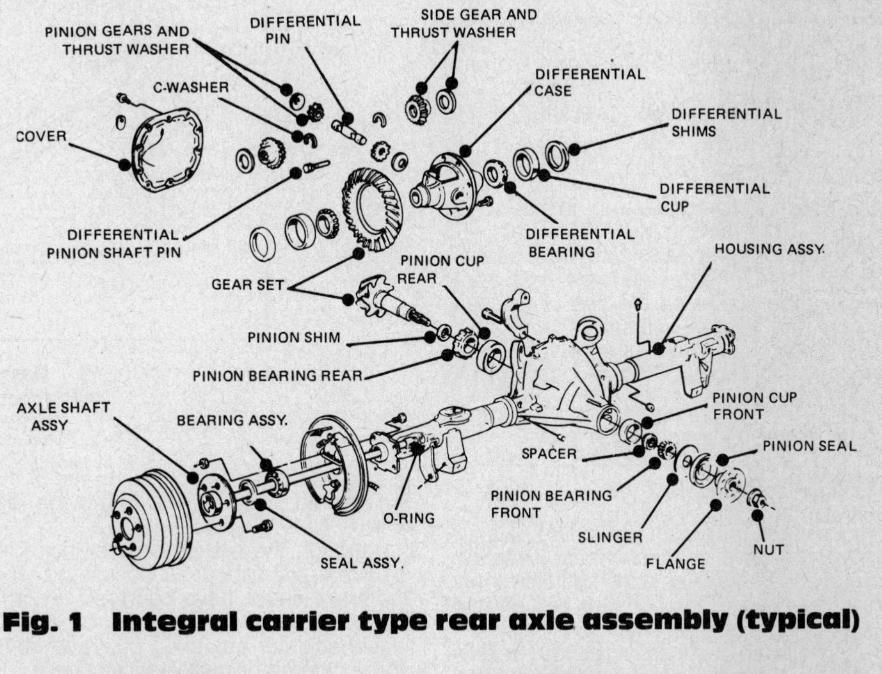

Fig. 1 Integral carrier type rear axle assembly (typical)

REAR AXLE
REPLACE

1. Raise vehicle and position safety stands under the rear frame crossmember.
2. Disconnect drive shaft at companion flange and secure it to vehicle using wire.
3. Remove wheels and brake drums. If equipped with rear disc brakes, remove calipers from anchor plates and rotors from shafts.
4. Support axle housing with floor jack.
5. Disconnect brake line from clips that retain line to axle housing, then disconnect vent from rear axle housing. **Some axle vents may be secured to the housing assembly through the brake junction block. When reinstalling, apply thread locking compound E0AZ-19554-B or equivalent to ensure proper retention.**
6. Disconnect shock absorbers from axle housing.
7. Disconnect upper control arms from mountings on axle housing.
8. Lower axle housing assembly until coils springs are released, then remove springs.
9. Disconnect lower control arms from mountings on axle housing, then lower the axle housing and remove it from vehicle.
10. Reverse procedure to install.

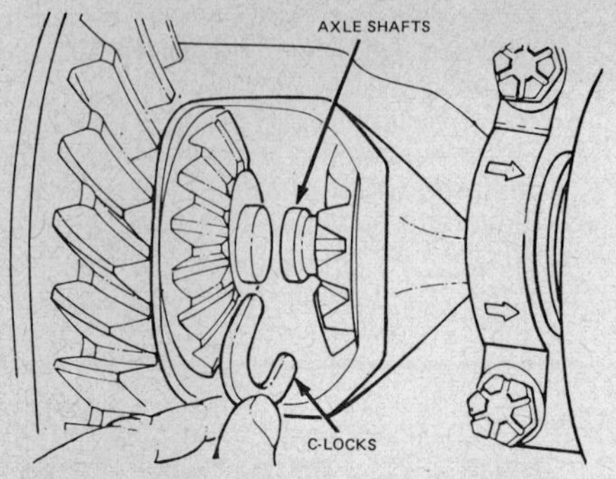

Fig. 2 Axle shaft "C" locks

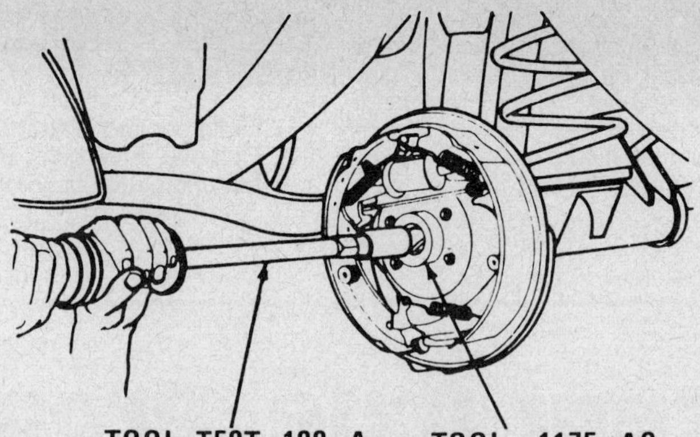

Fig. 3 Removing axle shaft seal and bearing

AXLE SHAFT, BEARING & SEAL

REPLACE

1. Raise car on hoist and remove wheels.
2. Drain differential lubricant.
3. Remove brake drums.
4. Remove differential housing cover.
5. Position safety stands under rear frame member and lower hoist to allow axle to lower as far as possible.
6. Working through differential case opening, remove pinion shaft lock bolt and pinion shaft.
7. Push axle shaft inward toward center of axle housing and remove C-lock(s) from housing, **Fig. 2.**
8. Remove axle shaft, using extreme care to avoid contact of shaft seal lip with any portion of axle shaft except seal journal.
9. Use a hook-type puller to remove seal and bearing, **Fig. 3.**
10. Reverse procedure to install, using suitable driving tools to install seal and bearing. Lubricate new bearing with rear axle lubricant and apply grease between the lips of the seal. Apply silicone sealant to carrier casting face as shown, **Fig. 4,** then install housing cover. Torque cover bolts to 30 ft. lbs.

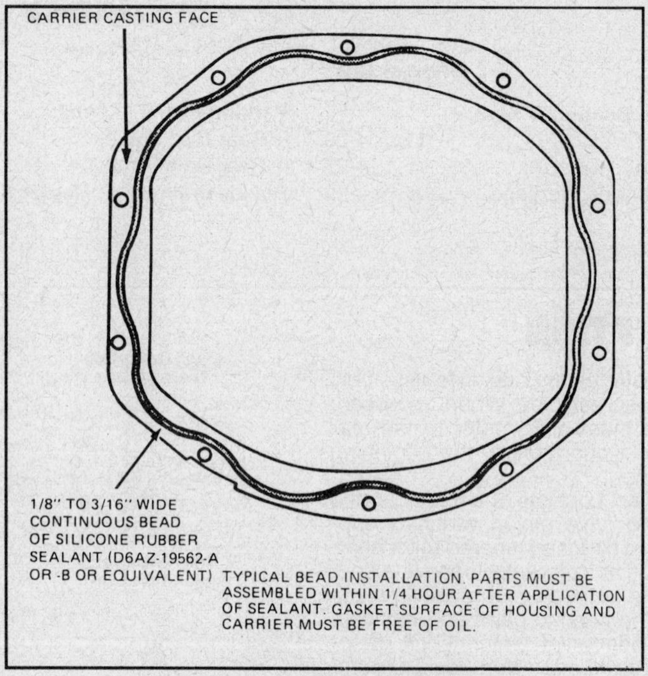

Fig. 4 Applying sealant to carrier casting face

PROPELLER SHAFT

REPLACE

To maintain proper drive line balance, mark the drive shaft, universal joints, slip yoke and companion flange before removing the shaft assembly so it can be reinstalled in its original position.

1. Remove companion flange to drive pinion flange attaching bolts.
2. Pull drive shaft rearward until slip yoke clears transmission extension housing.
3. Reverse procedure to install.

SERVICE BRAKES

ADJUST

These brakes have self-adjusting shoe mechanisms that assure correct lining-to-drum clearances at all times. The automatic adjusters operate only when the brakes are applied when the car is moving rearward.

Although the brakes are self-adjusting, an initial adjustment is necessary when the brake shoes have been relined or replaced, or when the length of the star wheel adjuster has been changed during some other service operation.

Frequent usage of an automatic transmission forward range to halt reverse vehicle motion may prevent the automatic adjusters from functioning, thereby inducing low pedal heights. Should low pedal heights be encountered, it is recommended that numerous forward and reverse stops be made until satisfactory pedal height is obtained.

If a low pedal height condition cannot be corrected by making numerous reverse stops (provided the hydraulic system is free of air) it indicates that the automatic adjusting mechanism is not functioning. Therefore, it will be necessary to remove the brake drum, clean, free up and lubricate the adjusting mechanism. Then adjust the brakes, being sure the parking brake is fully released.

ADJUSTMENT

When servicing a vehicle requiring a brake adjustment, the metal knock-out plugs should NOT be removed. Rather the drums should be removed and brakes inspected for a malfunction.

Although the brakes are self-adjusting, an initial adjustment will be necessary after a brake repair, such as relining or replacement. The initial adjustment can be obtained by the procedure outlined below.

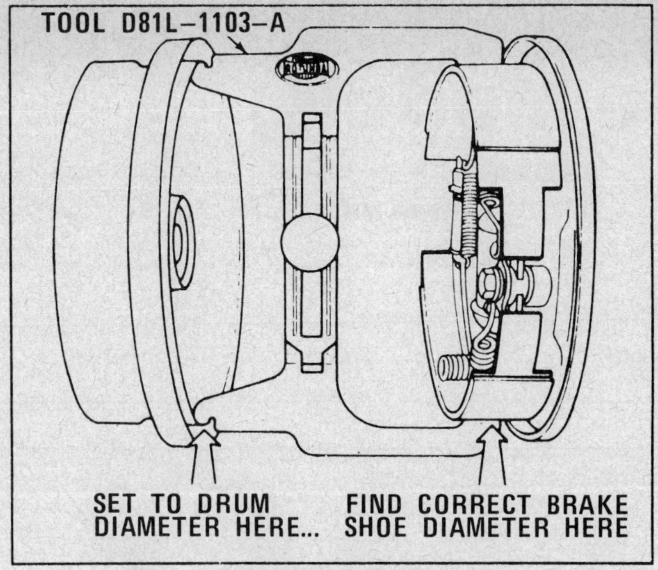

Fig. 5 Brake adjustment with gauge

If after removing brake drum retainers, the brake drum cannot be removed, remove steel knock-out plugs (if equipped) with suitable hammer and chisel. If equipped with rubber plugs, pry plug from backing plate. Insert a narrow screwdriver through hole in backing plate and disengage lever from adjusting screw. While holding lever away from adjusting screw, back off adjusting screw using a suitable tool to retract brake shoes.

1. Use the brake shoe adjustment gauge shown in **Fig. 5** to obtain the drum inside diameter as shown. Tighten the adjusting knob on the gauge to hold this setting.
2. Place the opposite side of the gauge over the brake shoes and adjust the shoes by turning the adjuster screw until the gauge just slides over the linings. Rotate the gauge around the lining surface to assure proper lining diameter adjustment and clearance.
3. Install brake drum and wheel. Final adjustment is accomplished by making several firm reverse stops, using the brake pedal.

PARKING BRAKES

ADJUST

REAR DISC BRAKES

1. Fully release parking brake, then place transmission in neutral and support vehicle at rear axle.
2. Tighten adjuster nut until levers on calipers just begin to move, then loosen adjuster nut until levers just return to stop position.
3. Apply and release parking brake. Check levers on caliper to determine if they are fully returned by attempting to pull lever rearward. If lever moves, the adjustment is too tight and must be readjusted.

REAR DRUM BRAKES

1. Make sure the parking brake is fully released.
2. Place transmission in neutral and raise the vehicle.
3. Tighten the adjusting nut against the cable equalizer to cause rear wheel brake drag. Then loosen the adjusting nut until the rear brakes are fully released. There should be no brake drag.
4. Lower the vehicle and check operation.

VACUUM RELEASE UNIT

The vacuum power unit will release the parking brake automatically when the transmission selector lever is moved into any driving position with the engine running. The brakes will not release automatically, however, when the selector lever is in neutral or park position with the engine running, or in any other position with the engine off.

The lower end of the release handle extends out for alternate manual release in the event of vacuum power failure or for optional manual release at any time.

To detect leaks in the vacuum release parking brake lines or to find disconnected or an improperly connected line, listen for a hissing sound along the line routings.

Do not apply compressed air to the vacuum system when conducting a leak test. The actuator diaphragm in the parking brake vacuum motor may be damaged.

Perform the following to detect leaks in the vacuum release system:

1. Start and operate engine at idle. Position transmission gear shift lever into Neutral and apply parking brake.
2. Position transmission gear shift lever into Drive and check parking brake sector to insure sector returns to its stop (zero travel position), when the parking brake releases. **The parking brake vacuum release does not operate with the transmission in Reverse.**
3. If parking brake does not release, disconnect vacuum line from parking brake release vacuum motor and connect a suitable vacuum gauge to the line. A minimum of 10 inches Hg is required to actuate the parking brake vacuum motor. If a minimum reading is obtained, replace parking brake release vacuum line. If a minimum reading is not obtained, replace parking brake vacuum release motor.

MASTER CYLINDER

REPLACE

1. Disconnect brake lines from master cylinder.
2. Remove two nuts attaching master cylinder to power brake unit.
3. Slide master cylinder off mounting studs and remove from vehicle.
4. Reverse procedure to install.

POWER BRAKE UNIT

REPLACE

1. Disconnect battery ground cable, then remove air cleaner.
2. Disconnect vacuum hose from power brake unit check valve.
3. Disconnect brake lines from master cylinder, then remove two nuts attaching master cylinder to power brake unit and remove master cylinder.
4. Working from under instrument panel, disconnect stop lamp switch wire connector, then remove clip and washer from brake pedal pin. Slide brake lamp switch off brake pedal pin just far enough for outer arm to clear pin, then remove switch. Slide power brake pushrod and washer from brake pedal pin.
5. On models equipped with speed control, remove amplifier unit from lower power brake unit mounting stud.
6. Move power brake unit forward until studs clear dash panel, then remove unit.
7. Reverse procedure to install.

Rear Suspension, (Rear Wheel Drive Models)

INDEX

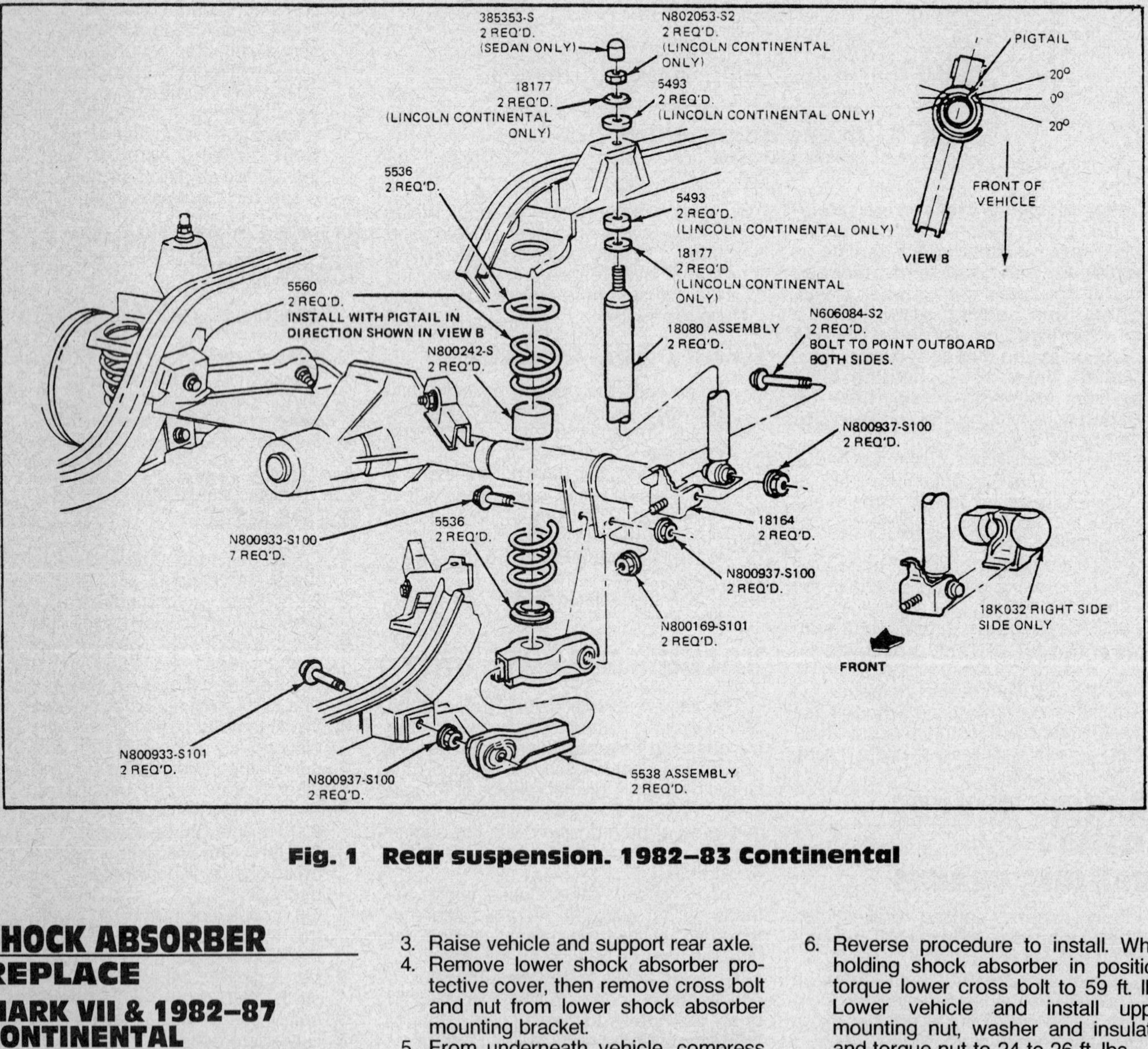

Fig. 1 Rear suspension. 1982–83 Continental

SHOCK ABSORBER REPLACE

MARK VII & 1982–87 CONTINENTAL

On 1984-88 vehicles, turn air suspension switch off before replacing shock absorber.

1. Open trunk to gain access to upper shock absorber attachment.
2. Remove rubber cap if equipped, from shock absorber stud, then remove nut, washer and insulator.
3. Raise vehicle and support rear axle.
4. Remove lower shock absorber protective cover, then remove cross bolt and nut from lower shock absorber mounting bracket.
5. From underneath vehicle, compress shock absorber to clear hole in upper shock tower, then remove shock absorber. **These models are equipped with gas pressurized shock absorbers which extend unassisted during removal. Do not apply heat or flame to the shock absorber tube during removal.**
6. Reverse procedure to install. While holding shock absorber in position, torque lower cross bolt to 59 ft. lbs. Lower vehicle and install upper mounting nut, washer and insulator and torque nut to 24 to 26 ft. lbs.

EXC. MARK VII & 1982–87 CONTINENTAL

1. With the rear axle supported properly disconnect shock absorber at upper mounting and compress it to clear hole.

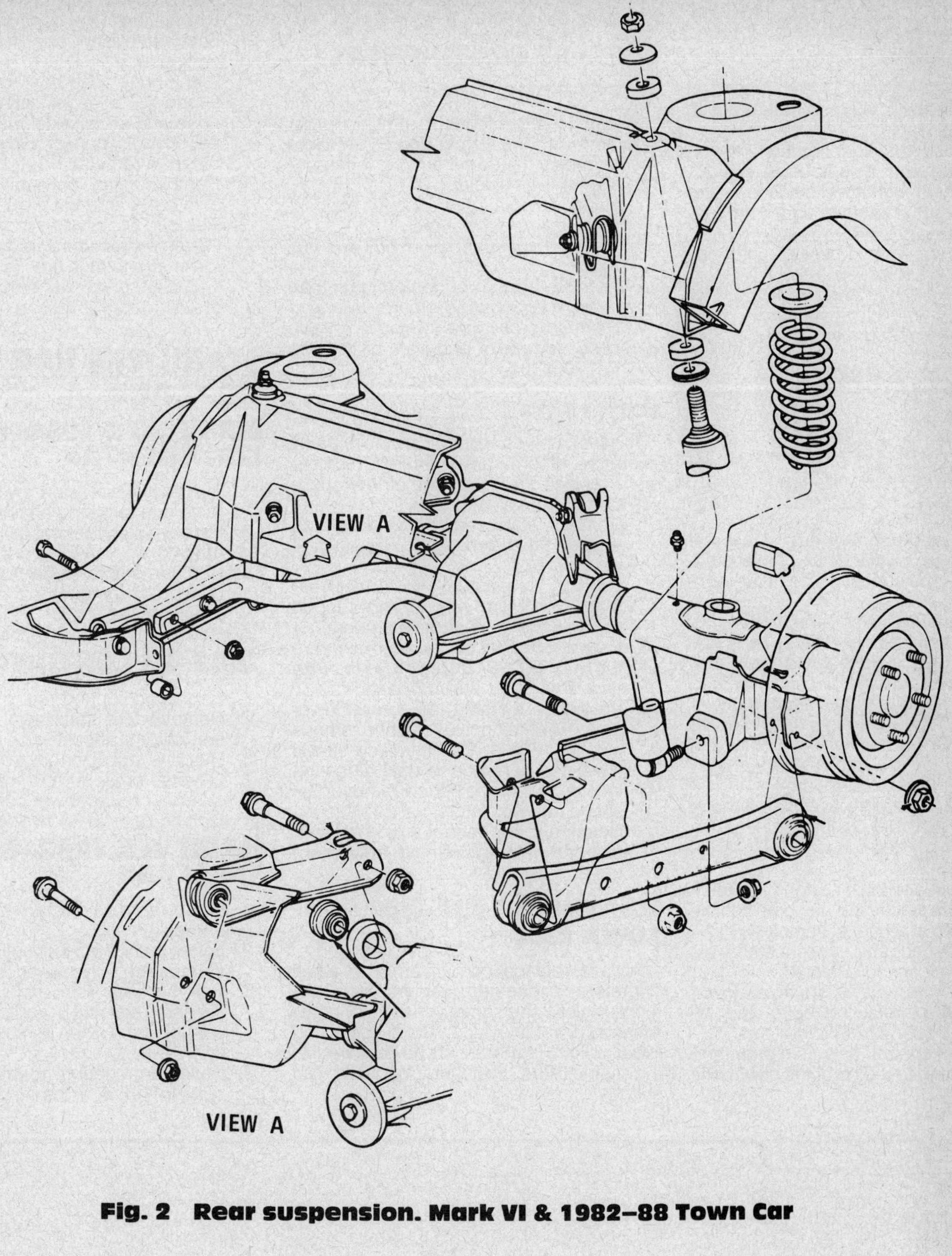

Fig. 2 Rear suspension. Mark VI & 1982–88 Town Car

2. Disconnect shock absorber from lower attachment.
3. Reverse procedure to install. **The 1984-88 Town Car is equipped with gas pressurized shock absorbers which extend unassisted during removal. Do not apply heat or flame to the shock absorber tube during removal.**

COIL SPRINGS REPLACE

1982–83 CONTINENTAL

1. Remove stabilizer bar as described under Stabilizer Bar, Replace, if equipped.
2. Position a suitable jack under rear axle, then raise vehicle and support body at rear body crossmember.
3. Lower axle until shock absorbers are fully extended. **Support axle with jack stands or a suitable jack.**
4. Position a suitable jack under lower control arm pivot bolt and remove nut and bolt. Carefully and slowly lower the control arm until all spring tension is relieved.

5. Remove coil spring and insulators from vehicle, **Fig. 1.**

MARK VI & 1982–88 TOWN CAR

1. Raise rear of vehicle and support at frame side sills. Support rear axle with a suitable jack.
2. Disconnect shock absorbers and stabilizer bar from axle housing, **Fig. 2.**
3. Disconnect righthand parking brake cable from righthand upper arm retainer.
4. Lower the axle housing until coil springs are released.
5. Remove springs and insulators, **Fig. 2.**
6. Reverse procedure to install.

CONTROL ARMS

REPLACE

MARK VII & 1984–87 CONTINENTAL

Upper Arm

Always replace control arm in pairs. If one arm requires replacement, replace the same arm on the opposite side of the vehicle.

1. Turn air suspension switch off.
2. Raise and support vehicle, then disconnect rear height sensor from side arm. Note position of sensor adjustment bracket to aid in reassembly.
3. Remove upper arm to axle and upper arm to frame bracket pivot bolts and nuts.
4. Remove upper control arm.
5. Reverse procedure to install. Torque pivot bolts to 100 ft. lbs.

Lower Arm

1. Turn air suspension switch to off position, then raise and support vehicle and remove wheel assembly.
2. Vent air springs to atmosphere by removing air spring solenoid.
3. Remove the two air spring to lower control arm retaining bolts, and remove air spring from lower arm.
4. Remove control arm to frame and control arm to axle bracket pivot bolts and nuts.
5. Remove lower control arm.
6. Reverse procedure to install. Torque pivot bolts to 100 ft. lbs.

1982–83 CONTINENTAL

Upper Arm

Always replace control arms in pairs. Therefore, if one arm requires replacement, replace the same arm on the opposite side of the vehicle.

1. Raise vehicle and support body at rear body crossmember.
2. Remove upper arm pivot bolt and nut, **Fig. 1.**
3. Remove front pivot bolt and nut, then remove upper arm from vehicle.
4. Reverse procedure to install. Torque upper arm pivot and front pivot bolts to 100 ft. lbs.

Lower Arm

Always replace control arms in pairs. Therefore, if one arm requires replacement, replace the same arm on the opposite side of the vehicle.

1. Remove stabilizer bar as described under Stabilizer Bar, Replace, if equipped.
2. Position a suitable jack under rear axle, then raise vehicle and support body at rear body crossmember.
3. Lower axle until shock absorbers are fully extended. **Support axle with jack stands or a suitable jack.**
4. Position a suitable jack under lower control arm rear pivot bolt and remove nut bolt, **Fig. 1.** Carefully and slowly lower the control arm until all spring tension is relieved, then remove coil spring and insulators.
5. Remove lower control arm front pivot bolt and nut, then remove lower control arm assembly.

MARK VI & 1982–88 TOWN CAR

Always replace control arms in pairs. Therefore, if one arm requires replacement, replace the same arm on the opposite side of vehicle. Also, if both upper and lower control arms are to be removed at the same time, first remove both coil springs.

1. Raise vehicle and support at frame side rails with jack stands.
2. If removing lower control arm, disconnect stabilizer bar from arm (if equipped).
3. With shock absorbers fully extended, support axle under differential pinion nose and under axle. If removing upper arm, disconnect parking brake cable from retainer.
4. Remove pivot bolts and nuts from axle and frame brackets, **Fig. 2.**
5. Remove control arm from vehicle.
6. Reverse procedure to install. Torque lower arm to axle bracket pivot bolt to 118 ft. lbs. and lower arm to frame pivot bolt to 135 ft. lbs.

STABILIZER BAR

REPLACE

MARK VII & 1984–87 CONTINENTAL

1. Turn air suspension switch off, then raise and support vehicle.
2. Remove stabilizer bar to link attaching nuts.
3. Remove stabilizer bar to bushing U-clamp attaching nuts, then the stabilizer bar.
4. Reverse procedure to install.

1982–83 CONTINENTAL

1. Raise and support rear of vehicle.
2. Remove four stabilizer bar to lower control arm attaching bolts.
3. Remove stabilizer bar from vehicle.
4. Reverse procedure to install. Torque stabilizer bar to lower control arm attaching bolts to 45 to 50 ft. lbs.

MARK VI & 1982–88 TOWN CAR

1. Raise rear of vehicle and support at frame side sills.
2. Lower axle housing until shock absorbers are fully extended.
3. Remove the four bolts, nuts and spacers retaining stabilizer bar lower control arms, then remove stabilizer bar.
4. Reverse procedure to install. Torque bolts to 70-92 ft. lbs.

Rear Suspension & Brakes (Front Wheel Drive Models)

INDEX

REAR SUSPENSION

The 1988 Continental utilizes a fully independent rear suspension consisting of MacPherson struts with integral air springs and dual-damping shock absorbers, counterbalancing torsion springs and a height sensor.

The air suspension and dual damping functions are controlled by a microcomputer based module which receives inputs for vehicle speed, door switch position, damping actuator feedback, steering wheel turning rate and angle, engine vacuum, throttle position, brake actuation, ignition switching, and vehicle ride height. The dual-damping function automatically switches from a soft to firm ride when the driving situation (hard cornering, acceleration or braking, etc.) dictates the need for increased damping effect.

The rear struts, **Fig. 1**, use a dual path mount which separates the strut and air spring mounting surfaces, to help provide for maximum isolation. The counterbalancing torsion springs, fitted between the strut and lower control arm, produce an outward force on the strut that tends to offset the binding forces induced by the rear wheels. The rotary design Hall effect type height sensor, **Fig. 2**, permits multiple height positions to be defined, resulting in specialized leveling during all types of driving and load characteristics.

SERVICE PRECAUTION

Always place the air suspension switch in the Off position before performing any work, or whenever raising the rear suspension.

STRUT ASSEMBLY REPLACE

1. Position suitable jack or hoist under vehicle, then raise just enough to contact body.
2. Disconnect air suspension electrical wiring and all related parts that will interfere with strut removal.
3. Loosen, but do not remove, the strut to inner body attaching nuts.
4. Raise and support vehicle, then remove wheel and tire assembly.

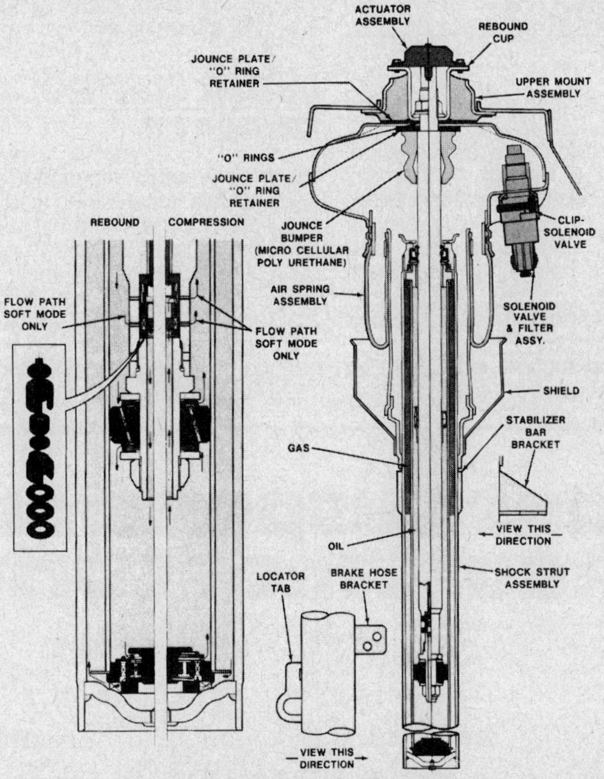

Fig. 1 Crossectional view of rear strut assembly

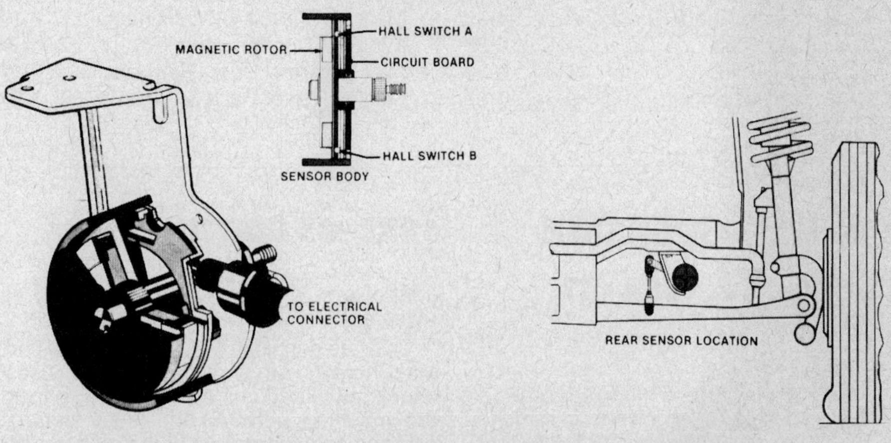

Fig. 2 Rotary height sensor

5. Remove brake hose to strut bracket attaching clip, then position hose aside.
6. If applicable, remove stabilizer bar attaching hardware and insulators, then separate stabilizer bar from link.
7. If applicable, remove tension strut to spindle attaching nut, washer and insulator, then move spindle rearward until it can be separated from tension strut.
8. Remove strut to spindle pinch bolt, then using a pry bar or other suitable tool, separate pinch joint as necessary to allow for strut removal.
9. Disengage strut from pinch joint, then lower vehicle as necessary to allow removal of upper attaching nuts.
10. Remove strut from vehicle.
11. Reverse procedure to install.

TENSION STRUT
REPLACE

1. If necessary, disconnect air suspension electrical wiring and all related parts that will interfere with tension strut removal.
2. Raise vehicle on frame contact hoist using lift pads located rearward of front wheels and forward of rear wheels. Raise hoist only enough to contact body.
3. Loosen, but do not remove, the upper strut to inner body attaching nuts, then raise and support vehicle.
4. Remove wheel and tire assembly.
5. Remove tension strut to spindle and tension strut to body attaching nuts.
6. While moving spindle rearward, remove tension strut from vehicle.
7. Reverse procedure to install, using new washers and bushings.

STABILIZER BAR
REPLACE

1. If necessary, disconnect air suspension electrical wiring and all related parts that will interfere with stabilizer bar removal.
2. Raise and support vehicle.
3. Remove stabilizer bar to link attaching nuts, washers and insulators.
4. Remove U-bracket attaching bolts, then the stabilizer bar.
5. Reverse procedure to install, using new attaching parts.

LOWER CONTROL ARM
REPLACE

1. If necessary, disconnect air suspension electrical wiring and all related parts that will interfere with control arm removal.
2. Raise and support vehicle.
3. Remove control arm to spindle attaching bolt, nut, and washer.
4. Remove control arm to body attaching bolt and nut, then the control arm.
5. Reverse procedure to install, then check rear wheel alignment and adjust as necessary.

BRAKE SYSTEM

A four-wheel disc, computer controlled anti-lock brake system (ABS) is standard equipment on 1988 Continental models.

The system uses four sensors (one at each wheel), which constantly send signals to the central microprocessor. The microprocessor then compares the rotational speed of all four wheels simultaneously. By comparing the rotational speed of all four wheels, the microprocessor can detect if one wheel begins to slow down more quickly than the others, indicating that lockup of that wheel may occur. If this is evident, it will command valves in the three hydraulic circuits (one for each front wheel, one for both rear wheels) to reduce and modulate line pressure, thereby preventing lockup from occurring.

The ABS system is self-monitoring. If a malfunction of the anti-lock system should occur, normal braking operation is retained and the driver is alerted by both an instrument panel warning light and a message center warning. As part of the self-monitoring design, two microprocessors are used within the central unit. Each computer checks itself against the other, and against pre-programmed tests to ensure complete operational reliability.

Power assist for the system is provided by an electric pump which charges a nitrogen filled accumulator upon demand.

Front Suspension & Steering (Rear Wheel Drive Models)

INDEX

FRONT SUSPENSION
MARK VII & 1984–87 CONTINENTAL

This suspension is a modified MacPherson strut design which is very similar to the suspension used in the 1982-83 Continental. The difference is a stamped lower control arm and the use of air bags in place of the coil springs.

1982–83 CONTINENTAL

This suspension, **Fig. 1**, is a modified MacPherson strut design, which uses shock struts and coil springs. The springs are mounted between the lower control arm and a spring pocket in the crossmember.

MARK VI & 1982–88 TOWN CAR

Referring to **Fig. 2**, each wheel rotates on a spindle. The upper and lower ends of the spindle are attached to upper and lower ball joints that are mounted to an upper and lower control arm. The upper control arm pivots on a shaft assembly that is bolted to the frame. The lower control arm pivots on a bolt in the front crossmember.

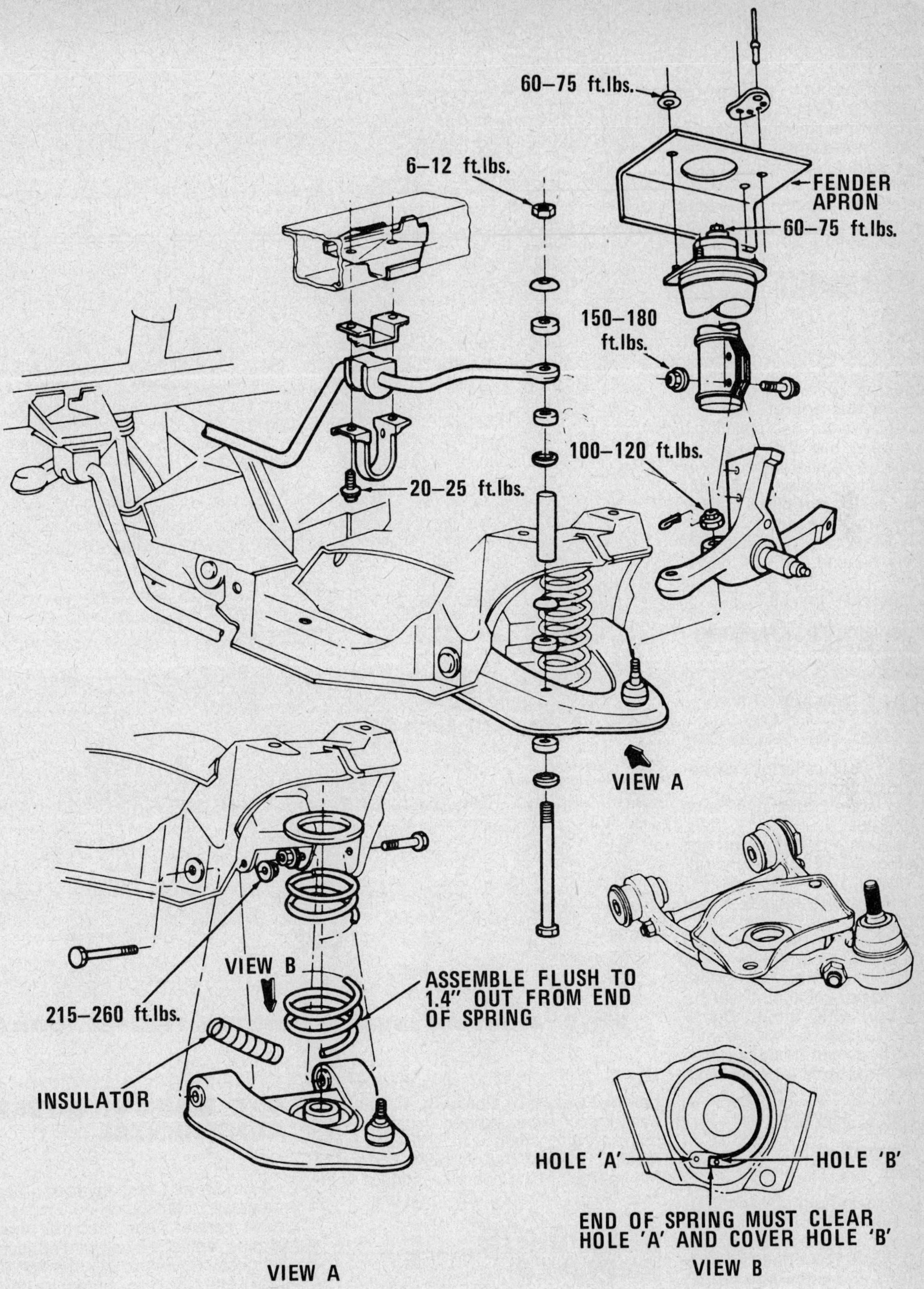

Fig. 1 Front suspension. 1982–83 Continental

WHEEL BEARINGS
ADJUST

1. With wheel rotating, tighten adjusting nut to 17-25 ft. lbs.
2. Back off adjusting nut 1/2 turn and retighten nut to 10-15 inch lbs.
3. Place nut lock on nut so that castellations on lock are aligned with cotter pin hole in spindle and install cotter pin.
4. Check front wheel rotation, if it rotates noisily or rough, clean, inspect or replace wheel bearings as necessary.

WHEEL BEARINGS
REPLACE

1. Raise car and remove front wheels.
2. Remove caliper mounting bolts. **It is not necessary to disconnect the brake line for this operation.**
3. Slide caliper off of the disc, inserting a spacer between the shoes to hold them in their bores after the caliper is removed. Position caliper assembly out of the way. **Do not allow caliper to hang by brake hose.**
4. Remove hub and disc. Grease retainer and inner bearing can now be removed.
5. Reverse procedure to install.

CHECKING BALL JOINTS FOR WEAR
UPPER BALL JOINT
Mark VI & 1982–88 Town Car

1. Raise car on floor jacks placed beneath lower control arms.
2. Grasp lower edge of tire and move wheel in and out.
3. As wheel is being moved in and out, observe upper end of spindle and upper arm.
4. Any movement between upper end of spindle and upper arm indicates ball joint wear and loss of preload. If such movement is observed, replace upper ball joint. **During the foregoing check, the lower ball joint will be unloaded and may move. Disregard all such movement of the lower joint. Also, do not mistake loose wheel bearings for a worn ball joint.**

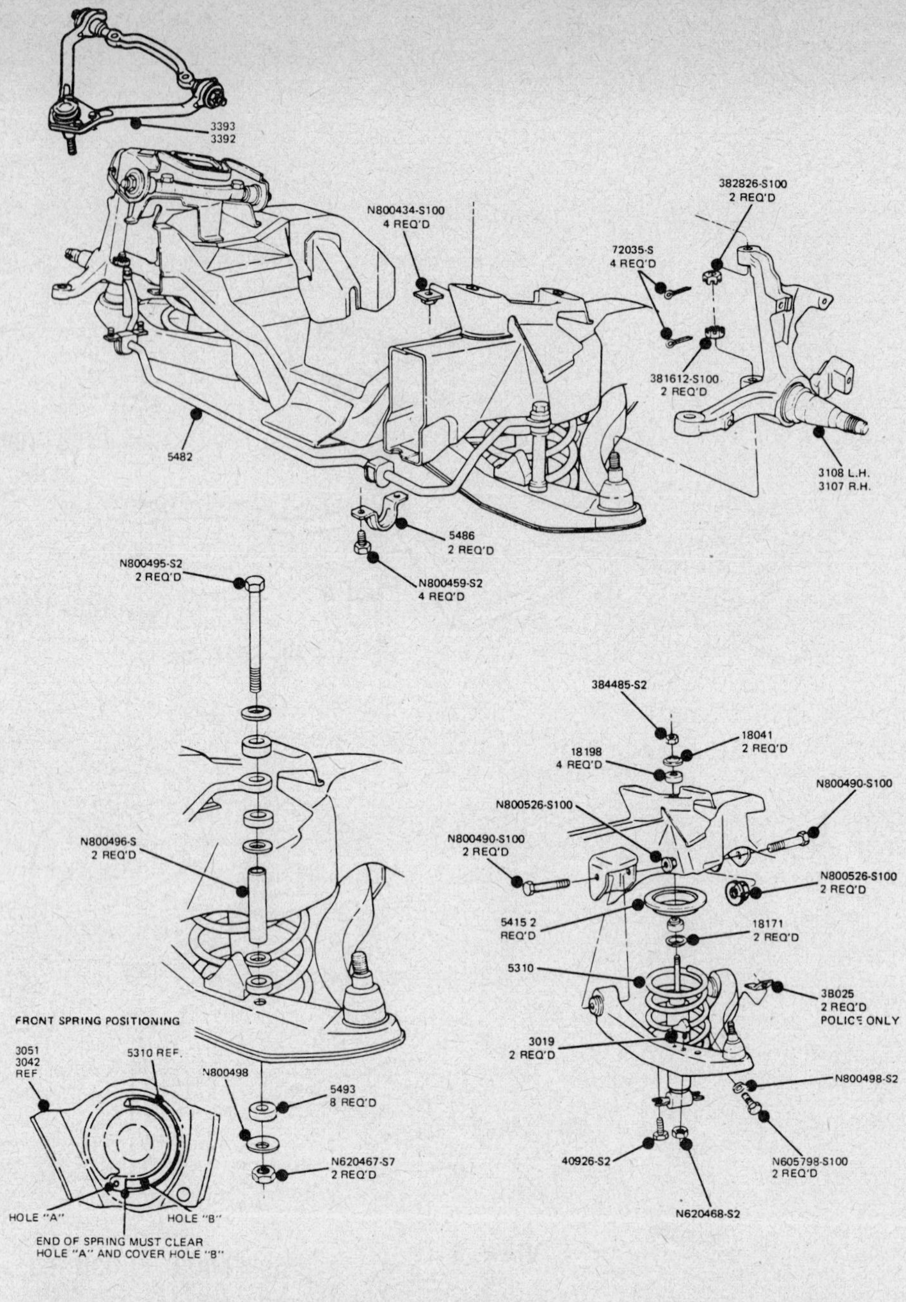

Fig. 2 Front suspension. Mark VI & 1982–88 Town Car

LOWER BALL JOINT
Mark VII & 1982–87 Continental

1. Support vehicle in normal driving position with both ball joints loaded.
2. Clean area around grease fitting and checking surface. **The checking surface is the round boss into which the grease fitting is installed.**
3. The checking surface should project outside the cover, **Fig. 3.** If surface is inside cover replace lower arm assembly.

Mark VI & 1982–88 Town Car

These models are equipped with lower ball joint wear indicators, **Fig. 4.** To check ball joint for wear, support vehicle in normal driving position with both ball joints loaded. Observe the checking surface of the ball joint. If the checking surface is inside the cover, replace the ball joint.

BALL JOINTS
REPLACE
MARK VII & 1982–87 CONTINENTAL

These ball joints are not serviceable. If they require replacement, the control arm and ball joint must be replaced as an assembly. Torque ball joint stud nut to 100-120 ft. lbs.

EXC. MARK VII & 1982–87 CONTINENTAL

Ford Motor Company recommends that new ball joints should not be installed on used control arms, and that the control arm be replaced if ball joint replacement is required. However, aftermarket ball joint repair kits which do not require control arm replacement, are available and can be installed using the following procedure.

When replacing a riveted joint, remove the rivets and retain the new joint in its control arm with the bolts, nuts and washers furnished with the ball joint kit.

Use a suitable pressing tool to force the ball joint from the spindle.

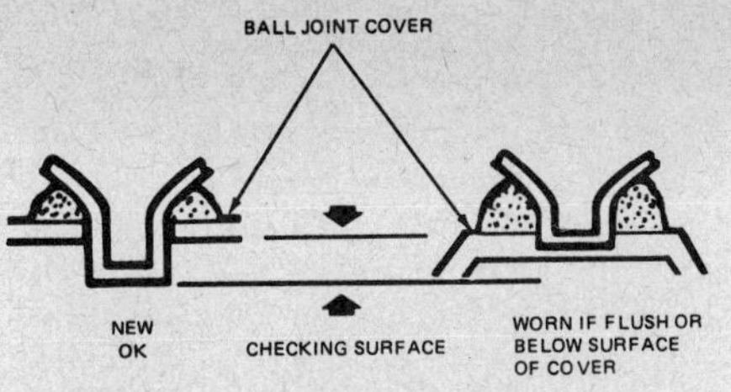

Fig. 3 Lower ball joint wear indicator. Mark VII & 1982–87 Continental

SHOCK STRUT REPLACE

MARK VII & 1982–87 CONTINENTAL

On 1984-88 vehicles, turn air suspension switch off before removing shock strut.

1. Place ignition switch in the Unlocked position so that front wheels are free to move.
2. From engine compartment, remove one strut to upper mounting nut. Use a screwdriver in rod slot to hold rod stationary when removing nut.
3. Raise front of vehicle by lower control arms, then place safety stands under frame jack pads located rearward of wheels.
4. Remove wheel and tire assembly, then remove brake caliper, rotor assembly and dust shield.
5. Remove two nuts and bolts attaching lower strut to spindle. **When removing the second lower strut to spindle nut, hold strut firmly as gas pressure will cause strut to fully extend.**
6. Lift strut upward from spindle to compress rod, then pull downward and remove strut.
7. Reverse procedure to install. Torque upper mount attaching nut to 60 to 75 ft. lbs. Remove suspension load from lower control arm by lowering front of vehicle, then torque lower mounting nuts to 150 to 180 ft. lbs.

SHOCK ABSORBER REPLACE

MARK VI & 1982–88 TOWN CAR

1. Remove nut, washer and bushing from upper end of shock absorber.
2. Raise vehicle and support on stands.
3. Remove screws retaining shock absorber to lower control arm and remove shock absorber.
4. Reverse procedure to install.

COIL SPRING REPLACE

1982–83 CONTINENTAL

1. Raise front of vehicle and position safety stands under jack pads located rearward of wheels, then remove wheel and tire assembly.
2. Disconnect stabilizer bar link from lower control arm.
3. Remove steering gear attaching bolts, then position gear out of way.
4. Using tool 3290-C or equivalent, disconnect tie rod from spindle.
5. Using spring compressor D78P-5310-A or equivalent, compress spring until it is free from lower seat.
6. Remove two lower control arm pivot bolts and disengage control arm from frame, then remove spring from seat. If a replacement spring is to be installed, measure compressed length of spring being removed to assist in compressing and installing the replacement spring.
7. Reverse procedure to install. When installing spring, locate lower end of coil between two holes in lower control arm spring pocket. Torque control arm pivot bolt nuts to 215 to 260 ft. lbs., stabilizer bar link nut to 6 to 12 ft. lbs. and steering gear to crossmember attaching bolts to 90 to 100 ft. lbs.

MARK VI & 1982–88 TOWN CAR

1. Raise and support vehicle.
2. Remove wheel.
3. Disconnect stabilizer bar link from lower control arm.
4. Remove shock absorber.
5. Remove steering center link from pitman arm.
6. Compress coil spring with a suitable spring compressor, tool D-78P-5310-A or equivalent.
7. Remove two lower control arm pivot bolts and disengage arm from crossmember.
8. Remove spring from vehicle.
9. Reverse procedure to install. Torque pivot bolts to 120-140 ft. lbs. **Tail end of spring must be positioned as shown in Fig. 2.**

POWER STEERING GEAR REPLACE

INTEGRAL POWER RACK & PINION

Mark VII & 1982–87 Continental

1. Disconnect battery ground cable.
2. Remove bolt retaining flexible coupling to input shaft.
3. Turn ignition key "On" and raise vehicle.
4. Remove the tie rod end retaining nuts, then separate studs from spindle arms.
5. Support gear and remove attaching bolts, then lower gear enough to gain access to pressure and return lines, and remove bolt attaching the hose bracket to the gear, and bolts from the crossmember.
6. Disconnect and cap pressure and return lines, then remove steering gear.
7. Reverse procedure to install. Torque pressure and return line fittings to 15-20 ft. lbs. Torque steering gear to crossmember bolts to 80-100 ft. lbs. Torque tie rod ends to spindle arm nuts to 35-47 ft. lbs.

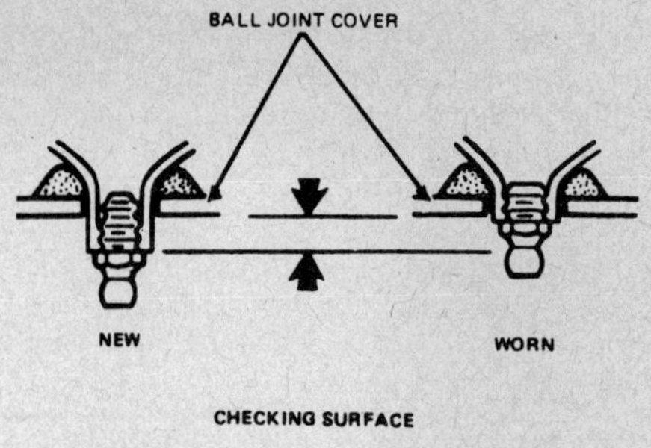

Fig. 4 Lower ball joint wear indicator. Mark VI & 1982–88 Town Car

INTEGRAL POWER STEERING GEAR

Exc. Mark VII & 1982–87 Continental

1. Disconnect lines from steering gear and plug lines and ports.
2. Remove the two bolts securing flex coupling to steering gear and to column.
3. Raise vehicle and remove sector shaft nut and pitman arm. **Do not damage the seals.**
4. Support steering gear and remove three attaching bolts. Remove flex coupling clamp bolt and work steering gear free of coupling, then remove steering gear.
5. Reverse procedure to install.

POWER STEERING PUMP REPLACE

1. Disconnect fluid return hose at reservoir and drain power steering fluid into a container.
2. Remove pressure hose from pump fitting. Do not remove fitting from pump.
3. Disconnect belt from pulley. If necessary, remove pulley from pump installing pulley remover tool T75L-3733-A or equivalent so small diameter threads engage in pump shaft. While holding small hex head, rotate tool nut to remove pulley. Do not apply in and out pressure on pump shaft as this will damage the internal thrust areas.
4. Remove pump.
5. If pulley was removed, install tool and while holding small hex head, turn tool nut clockwise to install pulley. Pulley must be flush within .010 inch of the end of the pump shaft. Do not apply in and out pressure on shaft. Remove tool.

Front Suspension & Steering (Front Wheel Drive Models)

INDEX

FRONT SUSPENSION

The 1988 Continental front suspension consists of MacPherson struts with integral air springs and dual-damping shock absorbers, and two height sensors, one at each control arm.

The air suspension and dual damping functions are controlled by a microcomputer based module which receives inputs for vehicle speed, door switch position, damping actuator feedback, steering wheel turning rate and angle, engine vacuum, throttle position, brake actuation, ignition switching, and vehicle ride height. The dual-damping function automatically switches from a soft to firm ride when the driving situation (hard cornering, acceleration or braking, etc.) dictates the need for increased damping effect.

The front struts, **Fig. 1,** are mounted to the body through a precision ball bearing and rubber mount system. The ball bearing provides a durable pivot for the strut/wheel assembly, while the rubber mount provides for a smooth ride on rough roads with minimal noise. The rotary design Hall effect type height sensor, identical to the rear sensor, permits multiple height positions to be defined, resulting in specialized leveling during all types of driving and load characteristics.

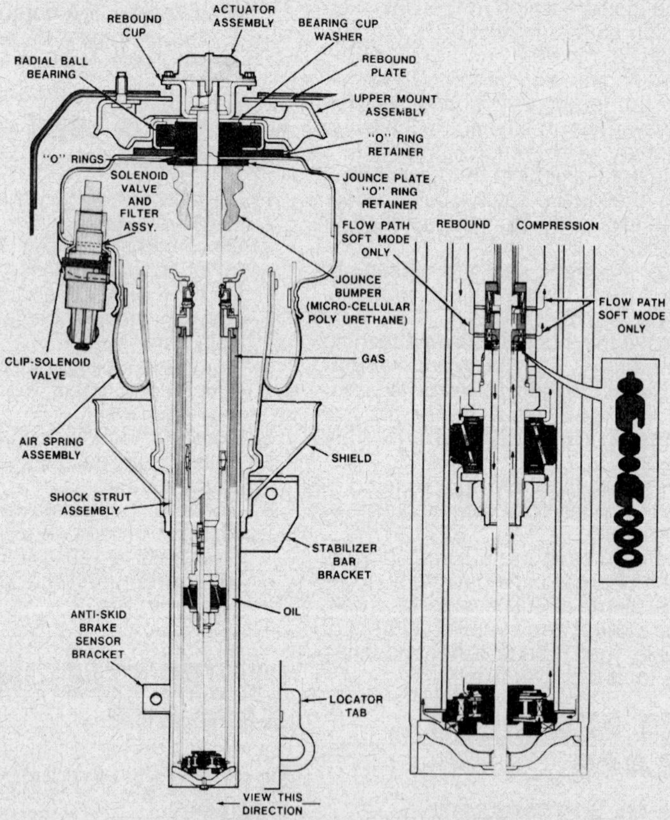

Fig. 1 Cross sectional view of front strut assembly

SERVICE PRECAUTION

Always place the air suspension switch in the Off position before performing any work, or whenever raising the front suspension.

STRUT ASSEMBLY
REPLACE

1. Remove hub nut and loosen the upper strut attaching nuts, then raise and support vehicle. **Do not lift vehicle from lower control arm.**
2. Disconnect air suspension electrical wiring and all related parts that will interfere with strut removal.
3. Remove wheel and tire assembly.
4. Remove brake caliper and support with suitable wire, then disconnect tie rod end.
5. Remove stabilizer bar link nut, then remove link from strut.
6. Remove lower control arm to steering knuckle pinch nut and bolt, then spread joint as necessary and disengage control arm from knuckle.
7. Using a suitable hub installation/removal tool, press axle from hub/rotor assembly. Wire axle shaft as necessary to maintain level position. **Do not permit axle shaft to move outward during disengagement from hub, since damage to CV joints could result.**
8. Remove strut to steering knuckle pinch bolt, then spread joint and remove steering knuckle and hub assembly.
9. Remove strut upper attaching nuts, then remove strut from vehicle.
10. Reverse procedure to install.

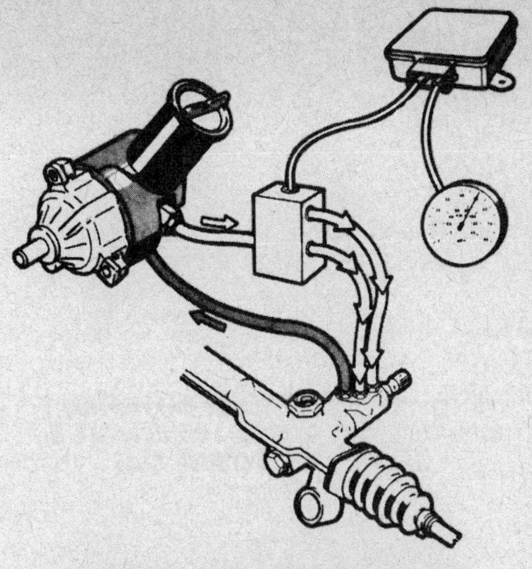

Fig. 2 Variable assist power rack & pinion steering gear system

LOWER CONTROL ARM REPLACE

1. Raise and support vehicle.
2. Disconnect air suspension electrical wiring and all related parts that will interfere with control arm removal.
3. Remove wheel and tire assembly, then the tension strut nut and washer.
4. Remove lower control arm to steering knuckle pinch nut and bolt, then spread joint and separate ball joint from knuckle.
5. Remove lower control arm inner pivot bolt and nut, then the lower control arm.
6. Reverse procedure to install.

STABILIZER BAR REPLACE

1. Raise and support vehicle.
2. Remove stabilizer bar link to strut and link to bar attaching nuts.
3. Remove stabilizer bar mounting brackets, then the stabilizer bar. It may be necessary to move steering gear from sub-frame and lower rear of sub-frame to gain access to mounting brackets.
4. Reverse procedure to install.

POWER RACK & PINION STEERING GEAR SYSTEM

The 1988 Continental uses a new electro-hydraulic, speed sensitive variable assist rack and pinion power steering system. The system is designed to generate higher levels of power assist during low vehicle speeds and while parking, while progressively reducing power assist as vehicle speed increases.

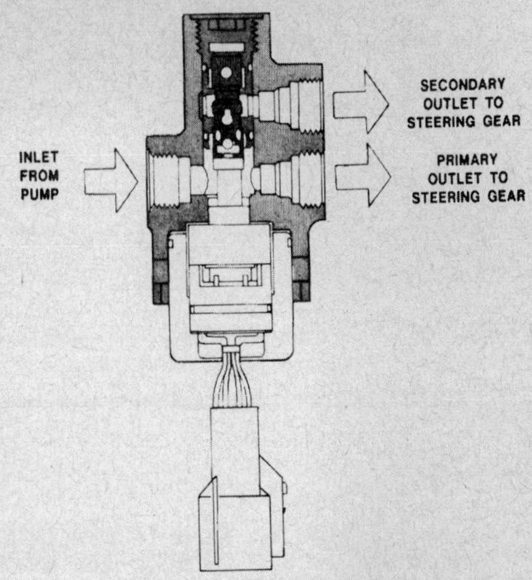

Fig. 3 Cross sectional view of actuator valve

The system is comprised of a new control valve, an electro-hydraulic actuator valve, and an electronic control module that is programmed to provide the right amount of assist during all vehicle speeds, **Figs. 2 and 3.**

The control module also has built-in diagnostic capabilities, which enables quicker troubleshooting in the event of a system malfunction.

Wheel Alignment Section

INDEX

FRONT WHEEL ALIGNMENT

MARK VII & 1984-87 CONTINENTAL

Before performing wheel alignment check on these vehicles, ensure vehicle ride height is correct.

Caster & Camber

Caster is pre-set at the factory and is not adjustable.

To adjust camber, drill out pop rivet located on top of camber plate. Loosen the camber plate to body apron retaining nuts, then move the top of the shock strut to the desired location. Retighten the retaining nuts. It is not necessary to replace the pop rivet after the camber adjustment is completed.

Toe-In

1. Check to see that steering shaft and steering wheel marks are in alignment

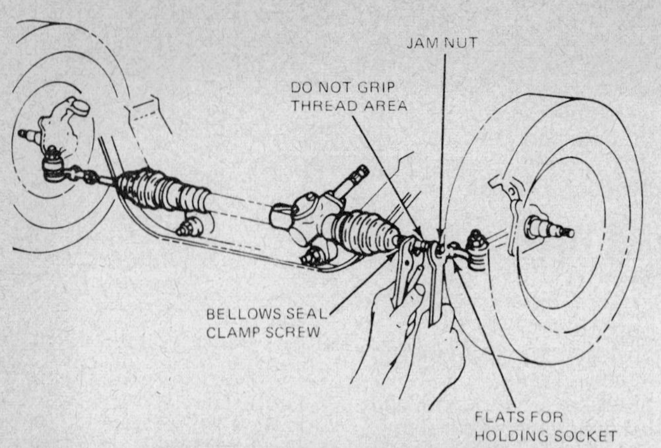

Fig. 1 Toe-in adjustment. Mark VII & 1982–87 Continental

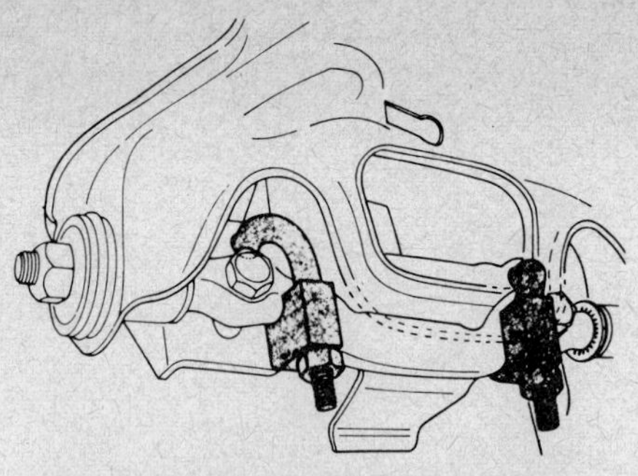

Fig. 2 Caster & camber adjusting tools. Mark VI & 1982–88 Town Car

and in the top position.
2. Loosen clamp screw on the tie rod bellows and free the seal on the rod to prevent twisting of the bellows, **Fig. 1.**
3. Place open end wrench on flats of tie rod socket to prevent socket from turning, then loosen tie rod jam nuts.
4. Use suitable pliers to turn the tie rod inner end to correct the adjustment to specifications. Do not use pliers on tie rod threads. Turning to reduce number of threads showing will increase toe-in. Turning in the opposite direction will reduce toe-in.

1982–83 CONTINENTAL

Caster & Camber

The caster and camber angles of this suspension are factory pre-set and cannot be adjusted in the field.

Toe-In

1. Check to see that steering shaft and steering wheel marks are in alignment and in the top position.
2. Loosen clamp screw on the tie rod bellows and free the seal on the rod to prevent twisting of the bellows, **Fig. 1.**
3. Place open end wrench on flats of tie rod socket to prevent socket from turning, then loosen tie rod jam nuts.
4. Use suitable pliers to turn the tie rod inner end to correct the adjustment to specifications. Do not use pliers on tie rod threads. Turning to reduce number of threads showing will increase toe-in. Turning in the opposite direction will reduce toe-in.

MARK VI & 1982–88 TOWN CAR

Caster and camber can be adjusted by loosening the bolts that attach the upper suspension arm to the shaft at the frame side rail, and moving the arm assembly in or out in the elongated bolt holes. Since any movement of the arm affects both caster and camber, both factors should be balanced against one another when making the adjustment.

Caster, Adjust

1. To adjust caster, install the adjusting tool as shown in **Fig. 2.**
2. Loosen both upper arm inner shaft retaining bolts and move either front or rear of the shaft in or out as necessary to increase or decrease caster angle. Then tighten bolt to retain adjustment.

Camber, Adjust

1. Loosen both upper arm inner retaining bolts and move both front and rear ends of shaft inward or outward as necessary to increase or decrease camber angle.
2. Tighten bolts and recheck caster and readjust if necessary.

Toe-In

Position the front wheels in their straight-ahead position. Then turn both tie rod adjusting sleeves an equal amount until the desired toe-in setting is obtained.

1988 CONTINENTAL

Toe-In

To adjust toe-in, lock steering wheel in straight ahead position using suitable steering wheel holder. Loosen, then slide off small outer clamps from steering boot to prevent boot from twisting during adjustment procedure. Loosen tie rod adjusting and jam nuts, then adjust length of left and right tie rods until each wheel has 1/2 the desired total toe specification. After adjustment is completed, tighten jam nuts, reinstall outer clamps and remove steering wheel holder.

REAR WHEEL ALIGNMENT

1988 CONTINENTAL

Camber

Camber is factory set and cannot be adjusted.

Toe-In

Toe-In is adjusted by rotating the cams located inside the rear inner lower control arm bushings.

FORD MUSTANG & MERCURY CAPRI

INDEX OF SERVICE OPERATIONS

NOTE: Refer to the rear of this manual for vehicle manufacturer's special service tool suppliers.

GENERAL ENGINE SPECIFICATIONS

Year	Engine CID ① Liter	Engine VIN Code ②	Fuel System	Bore & Stroke	Compression Ratio	Net H.P. @ RPM ③	Maximum Torque Ft. Lbs. @ RPM	Normal Oil Pressure Pounds
1982	4-140, 2.3L	A	5200, 2 Bbl. ⑤ ⑩	3.781 x 3.126	9.0	⑬	⑭	40-60
	6-2000, 3.3L	B	1946, 1 Bbl. ④	3.68 x 3.13	8.6	87 @ 3800	154 @ 1400	40-60
	V8-255, 4.2L ⑪	D	2150, 2 Bbl. ⑤	3.68 x 3.00	8.2	83 @ 111	194 @ 1600	30-50
	V8-255, 4.2L ⑫	D	7200VV, 2 Bbl. ⑤	3.68 x 3.00	8.2	83 @ 111	194 @ 1600	40-60
	V8-302, 5.0L H.O.	F	2150A, 2 Bbl. ⑤	4.00 x 3.00	8.4	160 @ 4200	247 @ 2400	40-60
1983	4-140, 2.3L ⑧	A	YFA, 1 Bbl. ⑱	3.781 x 3.126	9.0	90 @ 4600	122 @ 2600	40-60
	4-140, 2.3L ⑨	W	E.F.I ⑰	3.781 x 3.126	8.0	—	—	40-60
	V6-232, 3.8L	3	2150, 2 Bbl. ⑤	3.8 x 3.4	8.7	112 @ 4000	175 @ 2600	54-59
	V8-302 H.O., 5.0L	F	4180, 4 Bbl. ④	4.0 x 3.0	8.3	174 @ 4200	244 @ 2400	40-60
1984	4-140, 2.3L ⑧	A	YFA, 1 Bbl. ⑱	3.781 x 3.126	9.0	88 @ 4000	122 @ 2400	40-60
	4-140, 2.3L ⑨	W	E.F.I. ⑰	3.781 x 3.126	8.0	175 @ 4400	210 @ 3000	40-60
	V6-232, 3.8L	3	E.F.I. ⑰	3.8 x 3.4	8.7	120 @ 3600	205 @ 1600	54-59
	V8-302 H.O., 5.0L ⑮	M	4180-C ④	4.0 x 3.0	8.3	⑲	⑳	40-60
	V8-302 H.O., 5.0L ⑯	M	E.F.I. ⑰	4.0 x 3.0	8.3	165 @ 3800	245 @ 2000	40-60
1985	4-140, 2.3L ⑧	A	YFA, 1 Bbl. ⑱	3.781 x 3.126	9.0	88 @ 4000	122 @ 2400	50
	4-140, 2.3L ⑨	T	E.F.I. ⑰	3.781 x 3.126	8.0	200 @ 5000	240 @ 3000	50
	V6-232, 3.8L	3	C.F.I. ㉑	3.8 x 3.4	8.7	120 @ 3600	205 @ 1600	40-60
	V8-302, 5.0L ⑯	M	C.F.I. ㉑	4.0 x 3.0	8.3	180 @ 4200	260 @ 2600	40-60
	V8-302, 5.0L ⑥	M	4180-C ④	4.0 x 3.0	8.3	210 @ 4400	270 @ 3200	40-60
1986-88	4-140, 2.3L ⑧	A	YFA, 1 Bbl. ⑱	3.781 x 3.126	9.5	88 @ 4200	122 @ 2600	50
	4-140, 2.3L ⑨	T	E.F.I. ⑰	3.781 x 3.126	8.0	200 @ 5000	240 @ 3200	50
	V6-232, 3.8L	3	C.F.I. ㉑	3.8 x 3.4	8.7	120 @ 3600	205 @ 1600	40-60
	V8-302, 5.0L	—	S.E.F.I. ⑦	4.0 x 3.0	9.2	200 @ 4000	285 @ 3000	40-60

①—CID-cubic inch displacement.
②—The eighth digit denotes engine code.
③—Net rating-as installed on vehicle.
④—Holley.
⑤—Motorcraft.
⑥—Vehicles equipped with 5 speed manual overdrive trans.
⑦—S.E.F.I.-Sequential electronic fuel injection.
⑧—Non-Turbocharged.
⑨—Turbocharged.
⑩—Some vehicles equipped with model 6500 Feedback Carburetor.
⑪—Exc. Calif.
⑫—Calif. only.
⑬—Vehicles less A/C, 86 @ 4600; vehicles with A/C, 92 @ 4600.
⑭—Vehicles less A/C, 117 @ 2600; vehicles with A/C, 119 @ 2600.
⑮—Vehicles equipped with 5 speed manual trans.
⑯—Vehicles equipped with automatic overdrive trans.
⑰—Electronic fuel injection.
⑱—Carter.
⑲—Prior to 12/1/83, 175 @ 4000; from 12/1/83, 205 @ 4400.
⑳—Prior to 12/1/83, 245 @ 2200; from 12/1/83, 265 @ 3200.
㉑—C.F.I.-Central fuel injection.

REAR AXLE SPECIFICATIONS

Year	Ring Gear Diameter	Carrier Type	Ring Gear & Pinion Backlash Inch	Nominal Pinion Locating Shim, Inch	Pinion Bearing Preload: New Bearings With Seal Inch-Lbs.	Pinion Bearing Preload: Used Bearings With Seal Inch-Lbs.	Differential Bearing Preload	Pinion Nut Torque Ft. Lbs.
1982	7 1/2" WGX ①	Integral	.008-.015	.030	16-29	8-14	.016 ②	170
	6 3/4" WGG ①	Integral	.008-.015	.030	16-29	8-14	.016 ②	140
1983-88	7 1/2" WGX ①	Integral	.008-.015	.030	16-29	8-14	.016 ②	170
	8.8	Integral	.008-.015	.030	16-29	8-14	—	—

①—Identification tag code.
②—Case spread.

ENGINE TIGHTENING SPECIFICATIONS

Torque specifications are for clean and lightly lubricated threads only. Dry or dirty threads produce increased friction which prevents accurate measurement of tightness.

Year	Engine Model/ VIN	Spark Plugs Ft. Lbs.	Cylinder Head Bolts Ft. Lbs.	Intake Manifold Ft. Lbs.	Exhaust Manifold Ft. Lbs.	Rocker Arm Shaft Bracket Ft. Lbs.	Rocker Arm Cover Ft. Lbs.	Connecting Rod Cap Bolts Ft. Lbs.	Main Bearing Cap Bolts Ft. Lbs.	Flywheel to Crankshaft Ft. Lbs.	Vibration Damper or Pulley Ft. Lbs.
1982	4-140/A	5-10	80-90	14-21	16-23	—	5-8	30-36	80-90	56-64	100-120
	6-200/B	10-15	70-75	—	18-24	30-35	3-5	21-26	60-70	75-85	85-100
	V8-255/D ①	10-15	65-72	18-20	18-24	18-25 ③	3-5	19-24	60-70	75-85	70-90
	V8-302 H.O./F ①	10-15	65-72	23-25	18-24	18-25 ③	3-5	19-24	60-70	75-85	70-90
1983	4-140/A ⑤	5-10	80-90	14-21	16-23	—	5-8	30-36	80-90	56-64	100-120
	4-140/W ⑥	5-10	80-90	14-21	16-23	—	5-8	30-36	80-90	54-64	100-120
	V6-232/3	5-11	④	18.4	15-22	18.4-25.8 ③	3-5	31-36	65-81	56-64	93-121
	V8-302 H.O./F	10-15	65.72	23-25	18-24	18-25 ③	3-5	19-24	60-70	75-85	70-90
1984	4-140/A ⑤	5-10	80-90	14-21	16-23	—	5-8	30-36	80-90	56-64	100-120
	4-140/W ⑥	5-10	80-90	14-21	16-23	—	5-8	30-36	80-90	56-64	100-120
	V6-232/3	5-11	⑦	24	15-22	18.4-25.8 ③	80-106 ⑧	31-36	65-81	54-64	93-121
	V8-302 H.O./M	10-15	65-72	23-25	18-24	18-25 ③	3-5	19-24	60-70	75-85	70-90
1985-88	4-140/A,T	5-10	⑨	14-21	⑫	—	5-8	⑮	②	56-64	100-120
	V6-232/3	5-11	⑦	⑪	15-22	③ ⑬	80-106 ⑭	31-36	65-81	54-64	93-121
	V8-302 H.O./M	10-15	⑩	23-25	18-24	18-25 ③	3-5	19-24	60-70	75-85	70-90

①—Refer to the Ford & Mercury-Compact & Intermediate Chapter for service procedures.
②—Torque in 2 steps: 1, 50-60 ft. lbs.; 2, 80-90 ft. lbs.
③—Rocker fulcrum bolt to cylinder head.
④—Tighten in (4) steps: (1) 47 ft. lbs., (2) 55 ft. lbs., (3) 63 ft. lbs., (4) 74 ft. lbs., then back off all bolts 2-3 revolutions and repeat steps 1 through 4.
⑤—Except turbocharged engine.
⑥—Turbocharged engine.
⑦—Tighten in (4) steps: (1) 37 ft. lbs., (2) 45 ft. lbs., (3) 52 ft. lbs., (4) 59 ft. lbs., then back off all bolts 2-3 revolutions & repeat steps 1 through 4.
⑧—Inch lbs.
⑨—Torque in 2 steps: 1, 50-60 ft. lbs.; 2, 80-90 ft. lbs.
⑩—Torque in 2 steps: 1, 55-65 ft. lbs.; 2, 65-72 ft. lbs.
⑪—Torque in 3 steps: 1, 7 ft. lbs.; 2, 15 ft. lbs.; 3, 24 ft. lbs.
⑫—Torque in 2 steps: 1, 5-7 ft. lbs.; 2, 16-23 ft. lbs.
⑬—Torque in 2 steps: 1, 5-11 ft. lbs.; 2, 18.4-25.8 ft. lbs.
⑭—Inch lbs.
⑮—Torque in 2 steps: 1, 25-30 ft. lbs.; 2, 30-36 ft. lbs.

ALTERNATOR & REGULATOR SPECIFICATIONS

Year	Make or Model	Current Rating		Field Current @ 75°F		Voltage Regulator	
		Amperes	Volts	Amperes	Volts	Make or Model	Voltage @ 75°F
1982	Orange ① ② ④	40	15	4.0	12	E1TF-AA	13.8-14.6
	Green ① ② ④	60	15	4.0	12	E1TF-AA	13.8-14.6
	Black ① ② ④	65	15	4.0	12	E1TF-AA	13.8-14.6
	Black ① ③ ④	70	15	4.0	12	E1TF-AA	13.8-14.6
	Red ① ③ ④	90	15	4.0	12	E1TF-AA	13.8-14.6
1983	Orange ① ② ④	40	15	4.25	12	E2TF-AA	—
	Green ① ② ④	60	15	4.25	12	E2TF-AA	—
	Black ① ② ④	65	15	4.25	12	E2TF-AA	—
	Black ① ③ ④	70	15	4.25	12	E2TF-AA	—
	Red ① ③ ④	100	15	4.25	12	E2TF-AA	—
1984-88	Orange ① ② ④	40	15	4.25	12	E4TF-AA	—
	Green ① ② ④	60	15	4.25	12	E4TF-AA	—
	Black ① ③ ④	70	15	4.25	12	E4TF-AA	—
	Red ① ③ ④	100	15	4.25	12	E4TF-AA	—

①—Color of identification tag.
②—Rear terminal alternator.
③—Side terminal alternator.
④—Solid state alternator.

STARTING MOTOR APPLICATIONS

Year	Engine Model/VIN	Ident. No.
1982	4-140/A	E2BF-AA
	6-200/B	E1AF-BA
	V8-255/D ⑤	E1AF-BA
	V8-255/D ⑬	E3AF-AA
	V8-302/F ⑤	E1AF-BA
	V8-302/F ⑥	E3AF-AA
1983	4-140/A	E2BF-AA
	V6-232/A	E25F-AA
	V8-302/F	E3AF-AA
1984	4-140/A ①	E2BF-AA
	4-140/A ②	E4DF-AA
	4-140/W ②	E4SF-AA
	V6-232/3	E25F-AA
	V8-302/M ①	E3AF-AA
	V8-302/M ②	E4AF-AA
1985	4-140/A ③	E4DF-AA
	4-140/T ④	E4SF-AA
	V6-232/3	E4DF-BA
	V8-302/M	E4AF-AA
1986-88	4-140/A ③	—
	4-140/T ④	—
	V6-232/3	—
	V8-302 H.O./M	—

①—Vehicles manufactured before December 1983.
②—Vehicles manufactured after December 1983.
③—Except turbocharged engine.
④—Turbocharged engine.
⑤—Vehicles manufactured before 5-17-82.
⑥—Vehicles manufactured after 5-16-82.

WHEEL ALIGNMENT SPECIFICATIONS

Year	Model	Caster Angle, Degrees		Camber Angle Degrees				Toe-In Inch	Toe-Out on Turns, Deg.	
				Limits		Desired				
		Limits	Desired	Left	Right	Left	Right		Outer Wheel	Inner Wheel
1982	Capri & Mustang	+3/8 to +1 7/8	+1 1/8	−1/2 to +1	−1/2 to +1	+1/4	+1/4	3/16	19.84	20
1983	Capri & Mustang	+1/2 to +2	+1 1/4	−3/4 to +3/4	−3/4 to +3/4	Zero	Zero	3/16	19.84	20
1984	Capri & Mustang	+1/2 to +2	+1 1/4	−3/4 to +3/4	−3/4 to +3/4	Zero	Zero	3/16	19.84	20
	Mustang SVO	+1/8 to +1 7/8	+1	−3/4 to +3/4	−3/4 to +3/4	Zero	Zero	1/8	19.84	20
1985-88	All	+1/4 to +1 3/4	+1	−3/4 to +3/4	−3/4 to +3/4	Zero	Zero	3/16	19.84	20

COOLING SYSTEM & CAPACITY DATA

Year	Model or Engine/VIN	Cooling Capacity, Qts.		Radiator Cap Relief Pressure, Lbs.	Thermo. Opening Temp.	Fuel Tank Gals.	Engine Oil Refill Qts.①	Transmission Oil			Rear Axle Oil Pints
		Less A/C	With A/C					4 Speed Pints	5 Speed Pints	Auto. Trans. Qts.②	
1982	4-140/A	8.6	9.4	⑦	191	15.4	4	2.8	3.7	8	⑧
	6-200/B	8.4	8.4	16	196	15.4	4	—	—	⑤	⑧
	V8-255/D	14.7	15	16	191	15.4	4⑥	—	—	11	⑧
	V8-302 H.O./F	13.1	13.4	16	196	15.4	4⑥	4.5	—	—	⑧
1983	4-140/A③	8.6	9.4	⑦	191	15.4	4	2.8	—	8	⑩
	4-140/W④	10.5	10.5	⑦	191	15.4	4	—	5.6	—	⑩
	V6-232/3	—	—	16	196	15.4	4	—	—	11	⑩
	V8-302/F	13.1	13.4	16	196	15.4	4⑥	4.5	—	—	3.5
1984	4-140/A③	8.6	9.4	⑦	191	15.4	4	2.8	—	8	⑩
	4-140/W④	10.5	10.5	⑦	191	15.4	4	—	5.6	8	⑩
	V6-232/3	10.7	10.8	16	196	15.4	4	—	—	11	⑩
	V8-302/M	13.1	13.4	16	196	15.4	4⑥	—	—	11	3.5
1985	4-140/A③	8.6	9.2	⑦	191	15.4	4	2.8	—	8	3.25
	4-140/T④	10.8	10.8	16	192	15.4	4	—	5.6	—	3.25
	V6-232/3	10.7	10.8	16	198	15.4	4	—	—	11	3.25
	V8-302/M⑪	14.1	14.1	16	198	15.4	4⑥	—	5.6	—	3.25
	V8-302/M⑫	14.1	14.1	16	198	15.4	4⑥	—	—	12.3	3.25
1986-88	4-140/A③	10	9.7	9	191	15.4	4	2.8	—	8	3.25
	4-140/T④	10.4	10.2	9	191	15.4	4	—	5.6	—	3.25
	V6-232/3	11.5	11.5	16	196	15.4	4	—	—	12.3	3.25
	V8-302 H.O./M	14.1	14.1	16	198	15.4	4	—	5.6	12.3	3.75

①—Add 1 qt. with filter change unless otherwise noted.
②—Approximate. Make final check with dipstick.
③—Non-turbocharged.
④—Turbocharged.
⑤—C3, 8 qts.; C4 trans., 10 qts.
⑥—Dual sump oil. When draining oil, it is necessary to remove both drain plugs. One drain plug is located at front of oil pan. The second plug is located on left side of oil pan.
⑦—Less A/C, 13 psi.; with A/C, 16 psi.
⑧—6 3/4" ring gear axle, 2.5 pts.; 7 1/2" ring gear axle, 3.5 pts.
⑨—Less A/C. 14 psi.; with A/C, 16 psi.
⑩—Standard rear axle, 3.25 pts.; tractionlok rear axle, 3.55 pts.
⑪—Except fuel injected engine.
⑫—Fuel injected engine.

Electrical Section

INDEX

STARTER
REPLACE

1. Disconnect battery ground cable.
2. Raise and support front of vehicle.
3. On all models, disconnect starter cable from starter.
4. Remove starter motor attaching bolts and the starter.
5. Reverse procedure to install.

IGNITION LOCK
REPLACE

1. Disconnect battery ground cable.
2. On models with tilt steering column, remove upper extension shroud. Unsnap shroud from retaining clip located at the 9 o'clock position.
3. On all models, remove trim shroud or shroud halves, then disconnect key warning switch electrical connector.
4. Place gear shift lever in PARK on models with automatic trans. or in any gear on models with manual trans.
5. Insert a 1/8 inch diameter pin in the hole in casting surrounding lock cylinder. Pull lock cylinder out of housing while depressing retaining pin.
6. To install, turn lock cylinder to RUN position and depress retaining pin.
7. Install lock cylinder into housing. Turn key to OFF position after checking that cylinder is fully seated and aligned in the interlocking washer.
8. Turn the key to check for proper operation in all positions.
9. Install trim shroud and extension shroud if applicable.
10. Reconnect battery ground cable.

IGNITION SWITCH
REPLACE
REMOVAL

1. Disconnect battery ground cable.
2. Remove steering column trim shroud. **For tilt column only, remove upper extension shroud.**

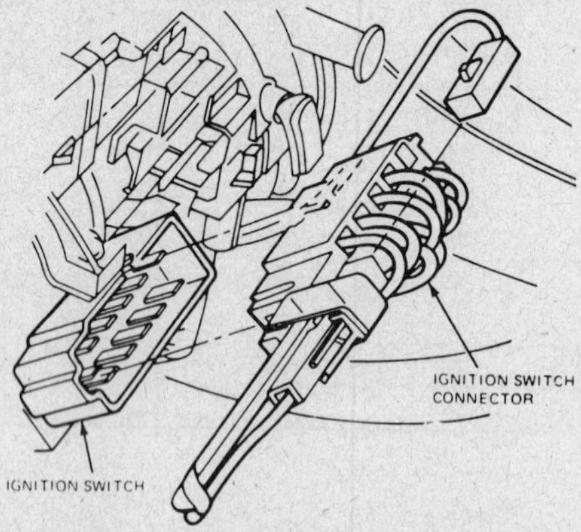

Fig. 1 Ignition switch

3. Disconnect electrical connector from switch, **Fig. 1.**
4. Rotate ignition key to On (Run) position.
5. Drill out bolt heads securing switch to lock cylinder using a 1/8 inch twist drill. Remove bolts using an "Easy Out" or equivalent.
6. Disengage switch from the actuator pin.

INSTALLATION

1. Adjust switch by sliding the carrier to the switch On (Run) position.
2. Check to ensure that the ignition key lock cylinder is in the On (Run) position by rotating the key lock cylinder approximately 90 degrees from the Lock position.
3. Install switch onto the actuator pin.
4. Secure the switch with new break-off head bolts. Tighten bolts until heads shear.
5. Connect electrical connector to switch.
6. Install steering column trim shroud. **For tilt column only, install upper extension shroud.**
7. Connect battery ground cable.
8. Check for proper operation.

STOP LIGHT SWITCH
REPLACE

1. Disconnect wires at connector.
2. Remove hairpin retainer, slide switch, pushrod and nylon washers and bushing away from the pedal and remove the switch, **Fig. 2.**
3. Reverse procedure to install.

NEUTRAL SAFETY, SWITCH
REPLACE
C4 & C5 TRANSMISSIONS
Removal

1. Remove downshift linkage rod from transmission downshift lever.
2. Remove downshift outer lever retaining nut and lever.
3. Remove two switch attaching bolts.
4. Disconnect wire connector and remove switch.

Installation

1. Install switch on transmission and replace attaching bolts.
2. With transmission manual lever in neutral, rotate switch and install gauge pin (No. 43 drill) into gauge pin hole, **Fig. 3.**
3. Tighten switch attaching bolts and remove gauge pin.
4. Install outer downshift lever and attaching nut.
5. Install downshift linkage rod to downshift lever.
6. Install switch wire connector and check operation of switch. The engine should start only with lever in NEUTRAL or PARK.

AOD & C3 TRANSMISSIONS

1. Place selector lever in the manual LOW position.
2. Disconnect battery ground cable.
3. Raise and support vehicle.
4. Disconnect neutral safety switch electrical connector.
5. Using Neutral Start Switch Socket

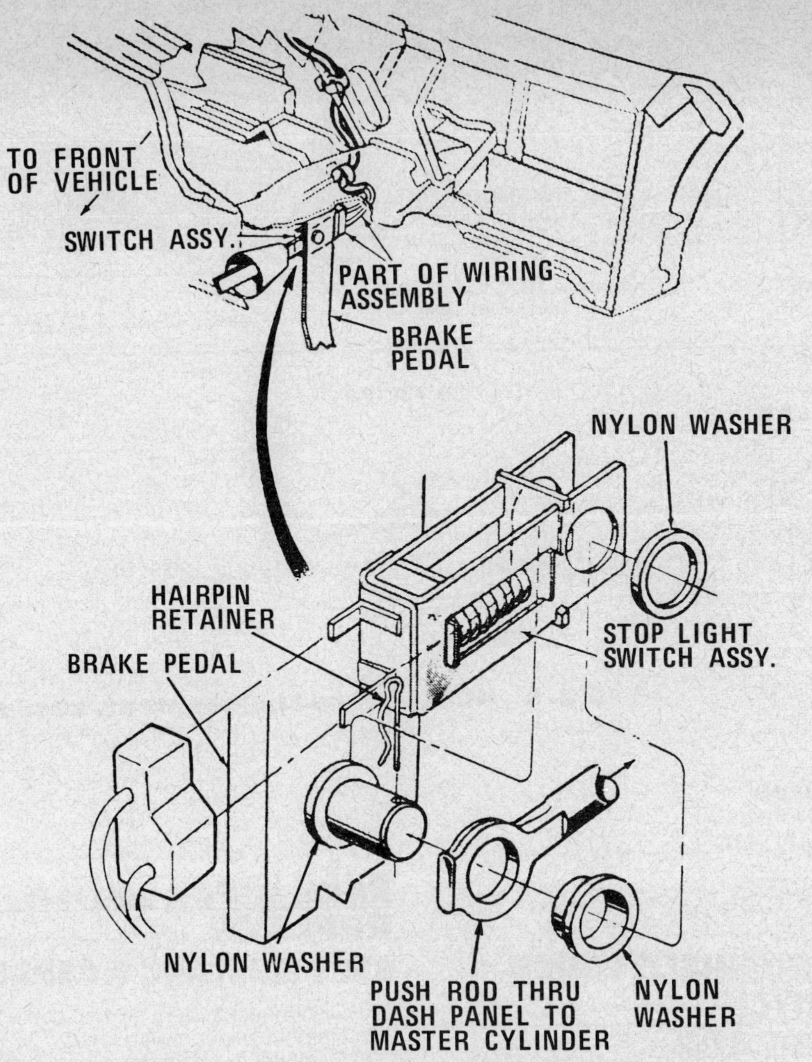

Fig. 2 Stop light switch installation

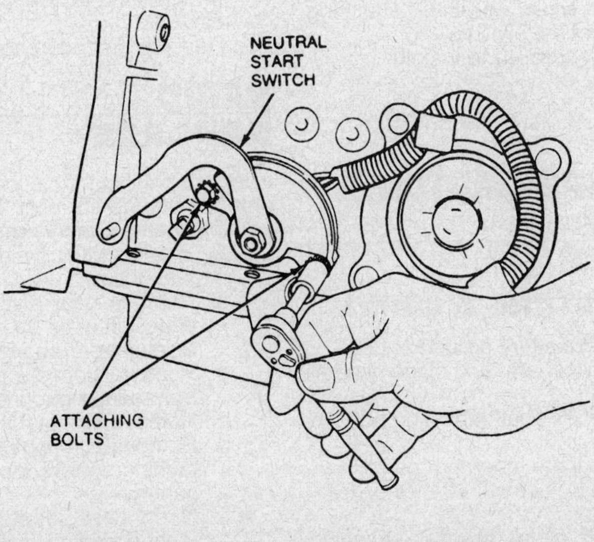

Fig. 3 Neutral safety switch adjustment

T74P-77247-A or equivalent, and a ratchet, remove neutral start switch and O-ring.
6. Reverse procedure to install. Torque switch to 8-11 ft. lbs.

LIGHT SWITCH
REPLACE

1. Disconnect battery ground cable.
2. Depress shaft release button by inserting a screwdriver through hole in underside of instrument panel, then remove knob and shaft.
3. Remove bezel nut, lower switch, disconnect electrical connector and remove switch.

TURN SIGNAL SWITCH
REPLACE

1. Disconnect battery ground cable.
2. On models with tilt column, remove upper extension shroud by unsnapping shroud retaining clips at the 9 o'clock position.
3. Remove five attaching screws, then separate and remove two trim shroud halves.
4. Grasp turn signal switch lever by grasping and using a twisting pulling motion while pulling lever outward.
5. Peel back foam shield from turn signal switch, then disconnect two turn signal switch electrical connectors.
6. Remove two screws attaching turn signal switch to lock housing, then disengage switch from housing and remove.
7. Reverse procedure to install.

HORN SOUNDER
REPLACE

1. Disconnect battery ground cable, then remove steering column cover attaching screws and steering column cover.
2. With wire connectors exposed, carefully lift connector retaining tabs and disconnect connectors.
3. Remove switch attaching screws and the switch.
4. Reverse procedure to install.

INSTRUMENT CLUSTER
REPLACE

1. Disconnect battery ground cable.
2. Remove three upper retaining screws from instrument cluster trim cover, then the trim cover.
3. On Mustang SVO models, remove four screws retaining instrument cluster to instrument panel. Disconnect turbo-boost pressure hose from retaining brace.
4. Remove upper and lower screws retaining instrument cluster to instrument panel.
5. Pull cluster from panel slightly and disconnect speedometer cable and the printed circuit electrical connectors.

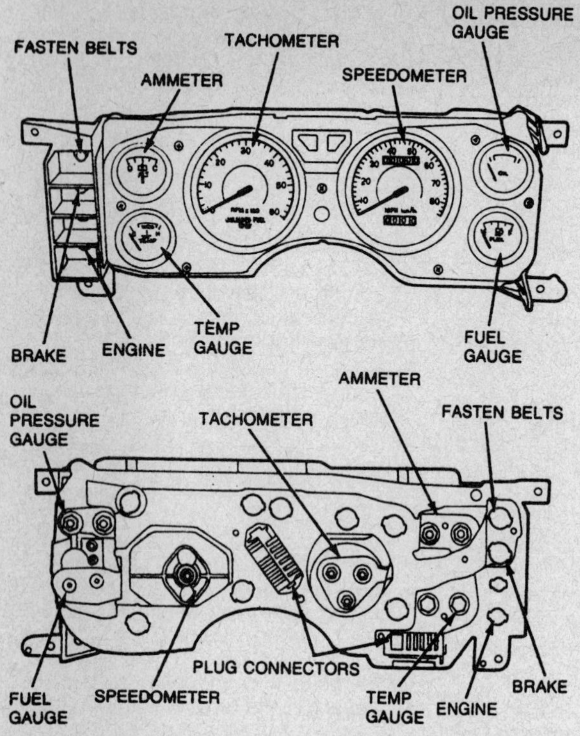

Fig. 4 Instrument cluster (Typical)

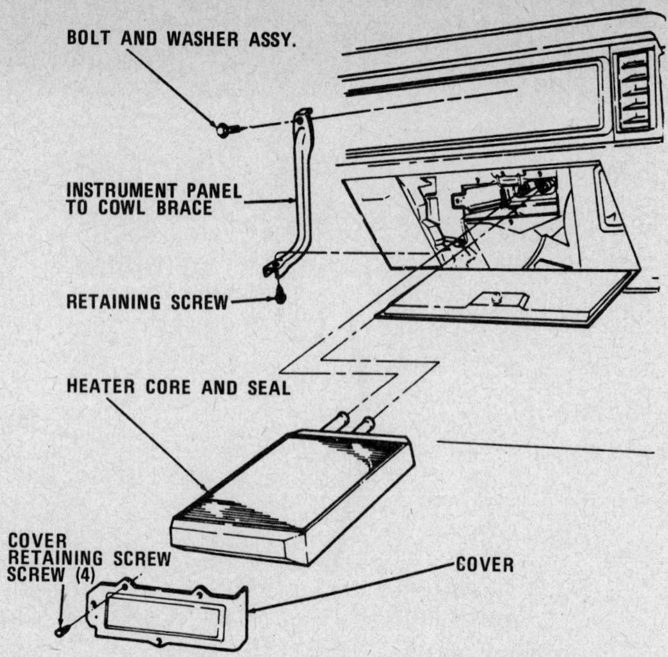

Fig. 5 Heater core replacement. Less A/C

6. Remove instrument clusters from instrument panel, **Fig. 4.**
7. Reverse procedure to install.

WINDSHIELD WIPER MOTOR
REPLACE

1. Disconnect battery ground cable, then remove righthand wiper arm and blade assembly.
2. Remove cowl grille, then remove clip and disconnect linkage drive arm from motor crank pin.
3. Disconnect wiper motor wire connector, then remove three motor attaching screws and pull motor through opening.
4. Reverse procedure to install.

WINDSHIELD WIPER TRANSMISSION
REPLACE

1. Disconnect battery ground cable, then remove right wiper arm and blade assembly from pivot shaft.
2. Remove cowl grille, then remove clip and disconnect linkage drive arm from wiper motor crank pin.
3. Remove two screws retaining righthand pivot shaft to cowl and large nut and spacer from left pivot shaft, then remove linkage assembly.
4. Reverse procedure to install.

WINDSHIELD WIPER SWITCH
REPLACE

1. Disconnect battery ground cable.
2. Remove steering column shroud attaching screws and the shroud.
3. Disconnect electrical connector from wiper switch.
4. Remove wiper switch attaching screws and the switch.
5. Reverse procedure to install.

REAR WIPER MOTOR & LINKAGE
REPLACE
1982 MUSTANG & CAPRI

1. Disconnect battery ground cable.
2. Remove wiper arm and blade assembly.
3. Remove pivot shaft attaching nut and spacers.
4. Remove liftgate inner trim panel.
5. Disconnect electrical connector from wiper motor.
6. Remove 3 motor bracket attaching screws.
7. Remove motor, bracket and linkage assembly from vehicle.
8. Reverse procedure to install.

REAR WIPER SWITCH
REPLACE
1982 MUSTANG & CAPRI

1. Disconnect battery ground cable.
2. Remove wiper switch knob.
3. Remove 2 bezel attaching screws, then pull switch retainer away from instrument panel.
4. Remove switch retaining nut and separate switch from retainer.
5. Disconnect electrical connector from switch and remove switch from vehicle.
6. Reverse procedure to install.

RADIO
REPLACE

When installing radio, be sure to adjust antenna trimmer for peak performance.

1. Disconnect battery ground cable.
2. On models with console, remove console as follows:
   a. Remove gear shift lever opening plate. Lift plate up at front end and disengage from clip.
   b. Remove console panel moulding from center of console.
   c. Remove front ashtray.
   d. Remove 2 console-to-floor pan attaching screws located under the ashtray.
   e. Open console storage compartment door and remove 4 console-to-floor pan attaching screws.
   f. Disconnect all electrical connectors from console, then remove console from vehicle.

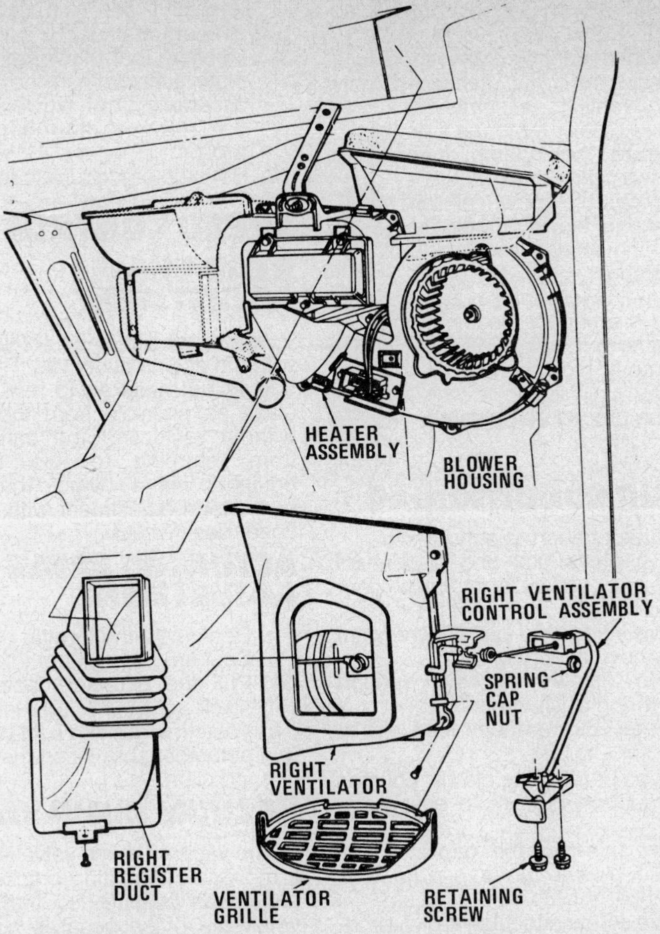

Fig. 6 Right ventilator assembly removal. Less A/C

3. On all models, disconnect all electrical connectors from radio.
4. Remove control knobs, discs, control shaft nuts and washers.
5. Remove ashtray and bracket.
6. Remove radio rear support attaching nut.
7. Remove instrument panel lower reinforcement.
8. Remove A/C or heater floor ducts.
9. Remove radio from bezel and rear support, then lower from instrument panel.
10. Reverse procedure to install.

HEATER CORE REPLACE

LESS AIR CONDITIONING

1. Drain cooling system and disconnect battery ground cable.
2. Disconnect heater hoses from heater core and plug core openings.
3. Remove glove box liner.
4. Remove instrument panel to cowl brace retaining screws and the brace.
5. Move temperature control lever to warm position.
6. Remove the four heater core cover retaining screws, then the cover through the glove box opening.
7. Remove heater core assembly mounting stud nuts from engine compartment.
8. Push core tubes and seal toward passenger compartment to loosen core from case assembly.
9. Remove heater core from case through the glove box opening, **Fig. 5.**
10. Reverse procedure to install.

WITH AIR CONDITIONING

1. Disconnect battery ground cable.
2. Remove screws securing the left side of instrument panel pad retaining tabs to the instrument panel, in the upper right and left corners of the instrument panel cluster area.
3. Remove screws securing the right side of instrument panel pad retaining tabs to instrument panel, located in the two openings at the top edge of the right instrument panel trim applique, above the glove box.
4. Remove screws securing leading edge of instrument panel pad to defroster openings. Use a magnetic or locking tang type phillips screwdriver. Do not let screws drop into defroster openings since plenum door damage may result.
5. Raise the overhanging edge of the instrument panel pad to clear retaining tabs and pull pad rearward to remove from top of instrument panel.
6. Remove screws attaching steering column opening lower cover to instrument panel, then the cover.
7. Remove steering column trim shrouds.
8. Remove nuts securing steering column to brake pedal support and lower steering column for access to gearshift selector lever and cable assembly.
9. Reach between steering column and instrument panel and lift selector lever cable off selector lever. Then, remove cable clamp from steering column tube.
10. Rest steering column on front seat.
11. Remove screw attaching instrument panel to brake pedal support at steering column opening.
12. Remove screw attaching lower brace to lower edge of instrument panel, below the radio.
13. Remove screw attaching brace to lower edge of instrument panel.
14. Disconnect temperature control cable from temperature blend door and evaporator case bracket.
15. Disconnect seven-port vacuum hose connectors at evaporator case.
16. Disconnect blower resistor wire connector from resistor and the blower motor feed wire at inline connector near the blower resistor wire connector.
17. Support instrument panel and remove three screws securing top of instrument panel to the cowl.
18. Remove screw at each side of instrument panel securing instrument panel to cowl side panels.
19. Move instrument panel rearward and disconnect speedometer cable and any wiring that will not permit the panel to lay on the front seat.
20. Drain cooling system.
21. Discharge refrigerant from A/C system at the service valve on suction line. When system is fully discharged, disconnect and cap high and low pressure lines.
22. Disconnect hoses from heater core. Cover hoses and heater core tubes to prevent leakage.
23. Remove screw securing air inlet duct and blower housing assembly support brace to cowl top panel.
24. Disconnect black vacuum supply hose from inline check valve in engine compartment.
25. Disconnect blower motor electrical connectors from harness.
26. Disconnect electrical connector from blower motor resistor.
27. Remove 2 evaporator case-to-dash panel attaching nuts from engine compartment.
28. Working in passenger compartment, remove 2 evaporator case support bracket-to-cowl top panel attaching screws.
29. Remove screw securing bracket below evaporator case to dash panel.
30. Carefully remove evaporator case assembly from vehicle.
31. On all models, remove 5 heater core

access cover attaching screws and the access cover.

32. Remove heater core and seals from evaporator case.
33. Remove the 2 seals from heater core tubes.
34. Reverse procedure to install.

BLOWER MOTOR REPLACE

LESS AIR CONDITIONING

1. Disconnect battery ground cable.
2. Remove right ventilator assembly as follows:
   a. Remove screw securing right register duct to lower edge of instrument panel, **Fig. 6.**
   b. Remove 2 screws securing ventilator control cable lever assembly to lower edge of instrument panel.
   c. Remove glove compartment liner to gain access to upper left ventilator attaching screw.
   d. Remove 2 plastic rivets securing grille to ventilator floor outlet opening. Remove grille from bottom of ventilator assembly to gain access to lower right ventilator assembly attaching screw.
   e. Remove right register duct and register assembly to gain access to upper right ventilator attaching screw.
   f. Remove 4 screws securing ventilator assembly to blower housing section of heater case.
   g. Move ventilator assembly to the right and down and remove from under instrument panel.
   h. Remove push nut from door crank arm.
   i. Remove control cable snap lock tab and the control cable assembly from ventilator assembly.
3. Remove blower motor as follows:
   a. Remove hub clamp spring from blower wheel hub.
   b. Remove blower wheel from shaft.
   c. Remove blower motor flange attaching screws from inside blower housing.
   d. Slide blower motor out of housing and disconnect electrical connectors from motor.
   e. Remove blower motor from vehicle.
5. Reverse procedure to install.

WITH AIR CONDITIONING

1. Disconnect battery ground cable.
2. Remove glove box and disconnect hose from outside-recirculation door vacuum motor.
3. Remove instrument panel lower right to side cowl attaching bolt.
4. Remove screw attaching support brace to top of air inlet duct.
5. Disconnect blower motor feed wire at connector.
6. Remove nut retaining blower housing lower support bracket to evaporator case.
7. Remove side cowl trim panel.
8. Remove blower motor ground wire screw.
9. Remove screw attaching top of air inlet duct to evaporator case.
10. Pull air inlet duct and blower housing assembly downward and away from evaporator case.
11. Remove four blower motor mounting plate screws, then the blower motor assembly from blower housing. **Do not remove mounting plate from motor.**
12. Reverse procedure to install.

SPEED CONTROL

BEAD CHAIN ADJUSTMENT

Adjust bead chain to obtain a taut chain with the engine at hot idle. The adjustment should be made as to remove as much slack as possible from the bead chain without restricting the carburetor lever from returning to idle. On vehicles equipped with a solenoid throttle positioner, perform adjustment with throttle positioner deactivated.

ACTUATOR CABLE ADJUSTMENT

1. Deactivate the throttle positioner.
2. Set carburetor at hot idle.
3. Pull the actuator cable to remove slack.
4. While maintaining light tension on the actuator cable, insert the cable retaining clip.

VACUUM DUMP VALVE

The vacuum dump valve is mounted on a moveable mounting bracket. The valve should be adjusted so that it is closed when the brake pedal is not depressed and opens when the brake pedal is depressed.

4-140 (2.3L) Engine Section

INDEX

ENGINE MOUNTS REPLACE

1. Support engine using a wood block and jack placed under the engine.
2. Remove fan shroud, if necessary.
3. Remove screw attaching fuel pump shield to lefthand support bracket, if so equipped.
4. Remove nut and washer assemblies attaching both insulators to the crossmember, **Figs. 1 and 2.**
5. Disconnect transmission shift linkage.
6. Raise engine sufficiently to clear the insulator studs from the crossmember.
7. Remove bolts attaching insulator and bracket assembly from engine and remove insulator and bracket assembly.
8. Reverse procedure to install. Torque insulator and bracket assembly to 40-45 ft. lbs. on 1982 models, 33-45 ft. lbs. on except 1982 models. Torque crossmember nut assemblies onto insulator studs to 70-90 ft. lbs. on 1982 models, 70-100 ft. lbs. on 1983 models, 65-85 ft. lbs. on 1984-88 turbocharged models, 50-65 ft. lbs. on 1984 models, and 80-106 ft. lbs. on 1985-88 models.

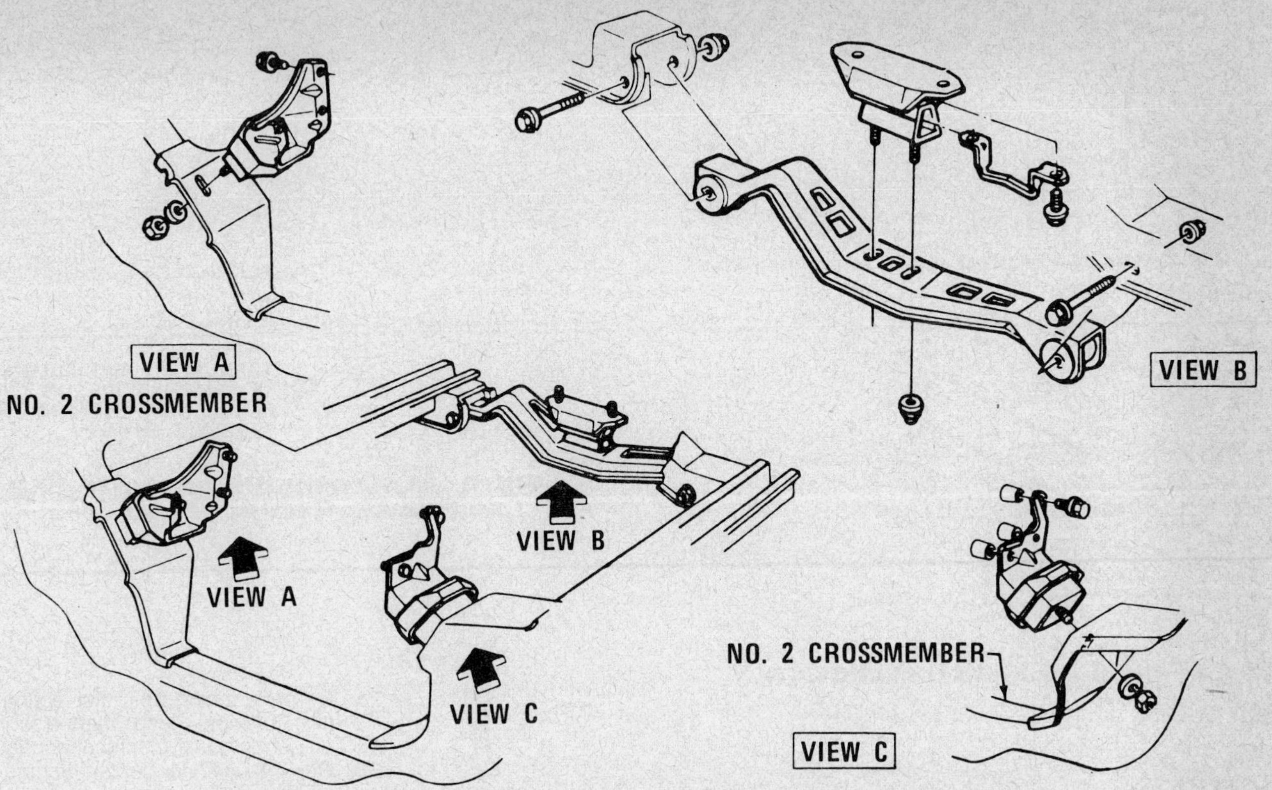

Fig. 1 Engine mounts installation. Capri, Mustang & Mustang SVO

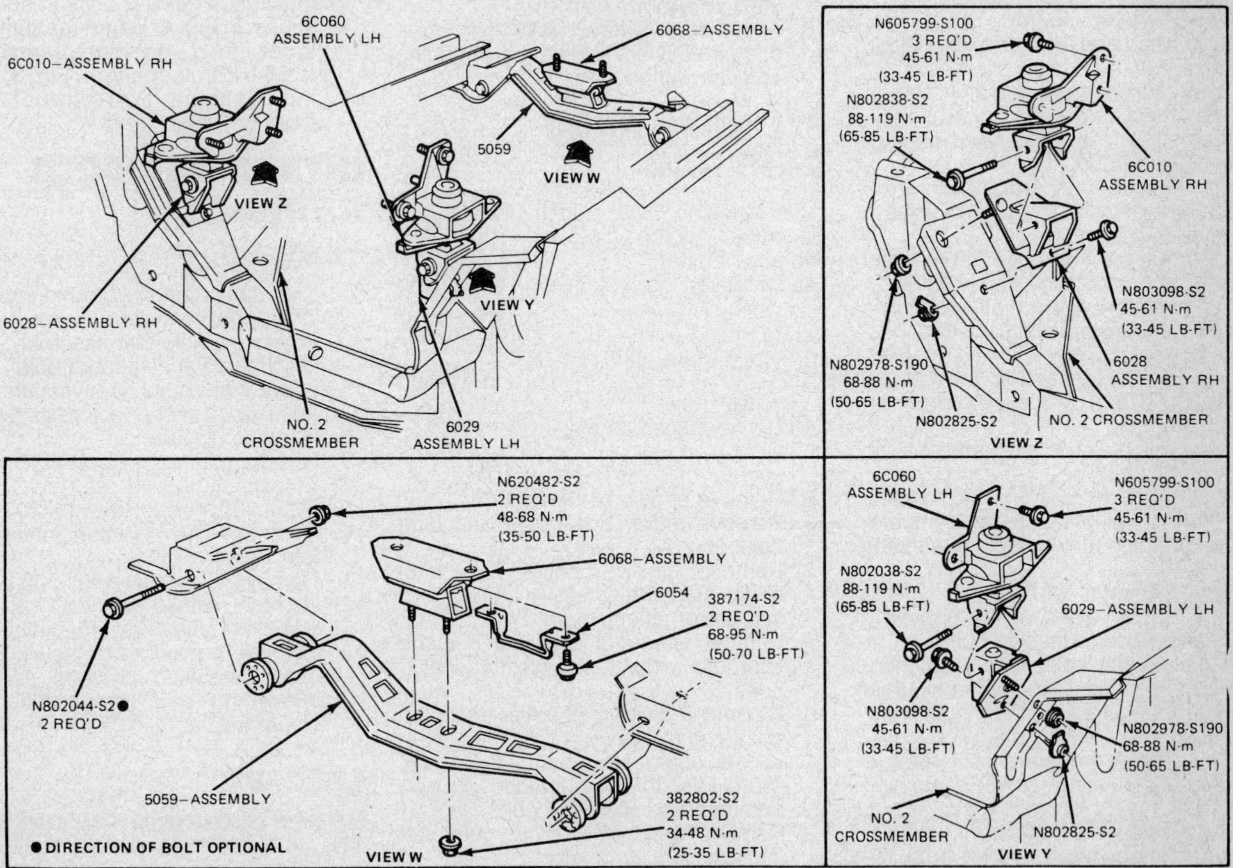

Fig. 2 Engine mount installation. 4-140 turbocharged engine

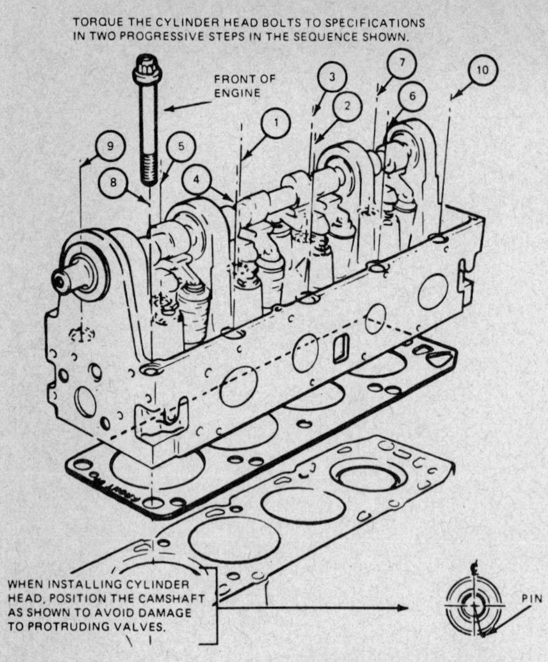

TORQUE THE CYLINDER HEAD BOLTS TO SPECIFICATIONS IN TWO PROGRESSIVE STEPS IN THE SEQUENCE SHOWN.
FRONT OF ENGINE
WHEN INSTALLING CYLINDER HEAD, POSITION THE CAMSHAFT AS SHOWN TO AVOID DAMAGE TO PROTRUDING VALVES.
PIN

Fig. 3 Cylinder head installation

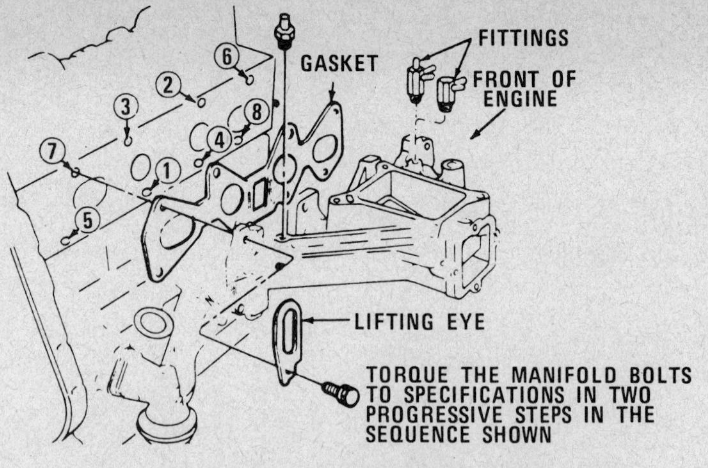

Fig. 4 Intake manifold tightening sequence. Except EFI models

ENGINE
REPLACE

1. Raise hood and secure in vertical position.
2. Drain coolant from radiator and oil from crankcase.
3. Remove air cleaner and exhaust manifold shroud.
4. Disconnect battery ground cable.
5. Remove radiator hoses and remove radiator and fan.
6. Disconnect heater hoses from water pump and carburetor choke fitting.
7. Disconnect wires from alternator and starter and disconnect accelerator cable from carburetor. On A/C vehicles, remove compressor from bracket and position it out of way with lines attached.
8. Disconnect flex fuel line from tank line and plug tank line.
9. Disconnect primary wire at coil and disconnect oil pressure and temperature sending unit wires at sending units.
10. Remove starter and raise vehicle to remove the flywheel or converter housing upper attaching bolts.
11. Disconnect inlet pipe at exhaust manifold. Disconnect engine mounts at underbody bracket and remove flywheel or converter housing cover.
12. On vehicle with manual shift, remove flywheel housing lower attaching bolts.
13. On vehicle with automatic transmission, disconnect converter from flywheel and remove converter housing lower attaching bolts. Disconnect transmission oil cooler lines if attached to engine at pan rail.
14. Lower vehicle and support transmission and flywheel or converter housing with a jack.
15. Attach engine lifting hooks to brackets and carefully lift engine out of engine compartment.

CYLINDER HEAD
REPLACE

On Mustang SVO models, loosen and disconnect intercooler clamps from intercooler air ducts.

1. Drain cooling system, then remove air cleaner assembly.
2. Remove heater hose-to-rocker arm cover retaining screw.
3. Remove distributor cap and ignition wires.
4. Remove spark plugs.
5. Disconnect all vacuum hoses necessary for cylinder head removal.
6. Remove engine oil dipstick.
7. Remove rocker arm cover attaching bolts and the cover.
8. Remove intake manifold attaching bolts, then the intake manifold and carburetor as an assembly.
9. Remove alternator drive belt, then the alternator mounting bracket attaching bolts.
10. Removing timing belt cover attaching bolts and the cover.
11. Loosen cam idler attaching bolts. Move idler to the unloaded position and retighten attaching bolts.
12. Remove timing belt from camshaft and auxiliary sprockets.
13. Remove heat stove from exhaust manifold.
14. Remove exhaust manifold, then the timing belt idler and two bracket bolts.
15. Remove timing belt idler spring stop from cylinder head, then disconnect oil sending unit electrical connector.
16. Remove cylinder head attaching bolts and the cylinder head.
17. Reverse procedure to install. Torque cylinder head bolts to specifications in sequence shown in **Fig. 3** and intake manifold attaching bolts in sequence shown in **Fig. 4. When installing cylinder head, position camshaft in the 5 o'clock position, Fig. 3, allowing minimum protrusion of valves from cylinder head.**

INTAKE MANIFOLD
REPLACE

1983–86

1. Disconnect battery ground cable.
2. Drain cooling system.
3. Remove air cleaner assembly.
4. Disconnect accelerator cable.
5. Label, then disconnect vacuum hoses and electrical connectors as required.
6. Remove dipstick.
7. Disconnect heat tube at EGR valve.
8. Disconnect fuel line at fuel rail.
9. Remove dipstick tube attaching bolt.
10. Remove PCV valve from intake manifold.
11. Remove distributor attaching bolts.
12. Remove intake manifold attaching bolts, then the intake manifold.
13. Reverse procedure to install. Torque intake manifold bolts in sequence shown in **Fig. 5**. Torque bolts in two steps first to 11-12.5 ft. lbs., then to 14-21 ft. lbs.

1987–88

Upper Intake Manifold & Throttle Body Assembly

1. Disconnect battery ground cable.
2. Label, then disconnect all electrical connectors and vacuum lines from manifold assembly.

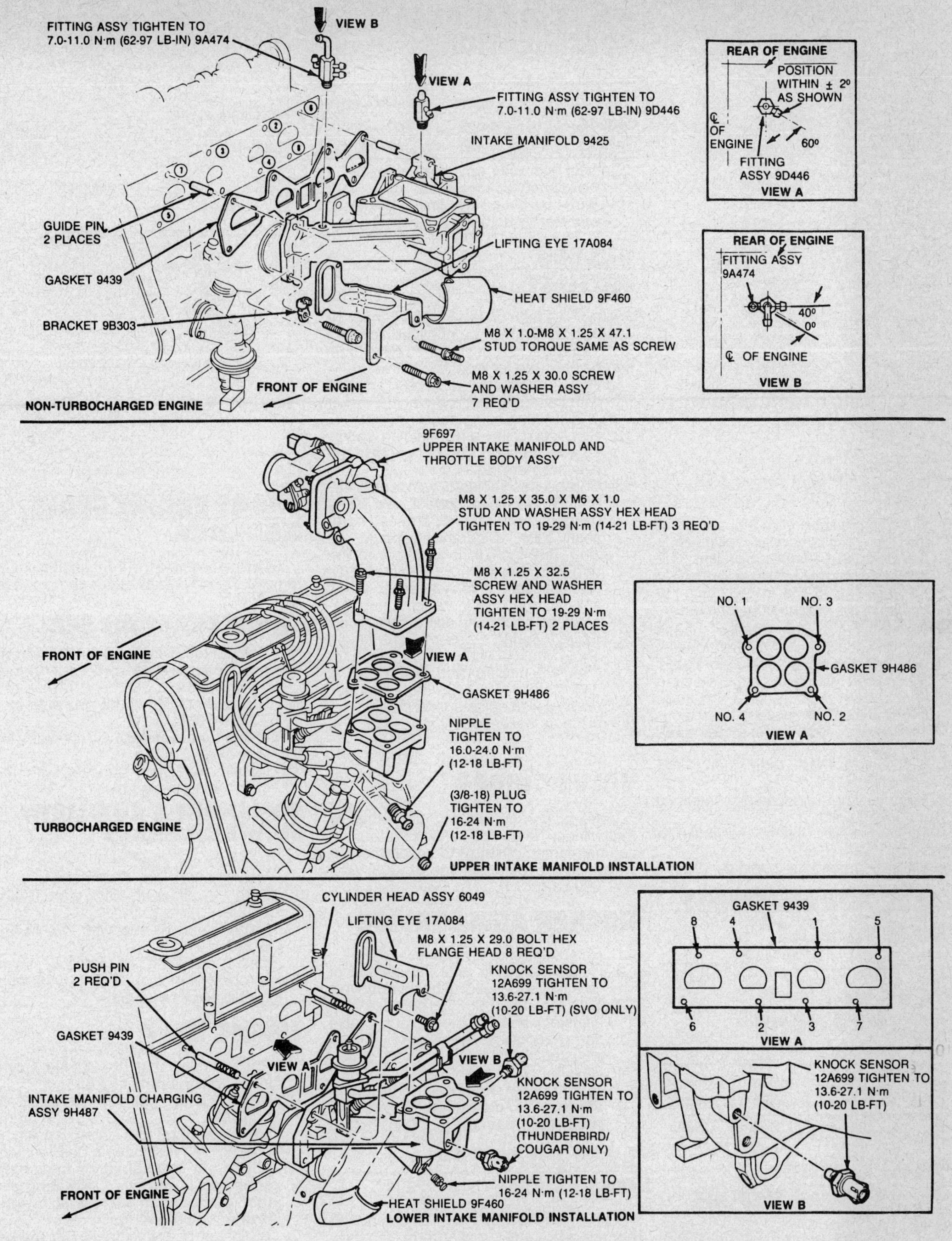

FITTING ASSY TIGHTEN TO
7.0-11.0 N·m (62-97 LB-IN) 9A474
VIEW B
VIEW A
FITTING ASSY TIGHTEN TO
7.0-11.0 N·m (62-97 LB-IN) 9D446
INTAKE MANIFOLD 9425
GUIDE PIN
2 PLACES
GASKET 9439
LIFTING EYE 17A084
HEAT SHIELD 9F460
BRACKET 9B303
M8 X 1.0-M8 X 1.25 X 47.1
STUD TORQUE SAME AS SCREW
M8 X 1.25 X 30.0 SCREW
AND WASHER ASSY
7 REQ'D
FRONT OF ENGINE
NON-TURBOCHARGED ENGINE
REAR OF ENGINE
POSITION
WITHIN ± 2°
AS SHOWN
℄ OF ENGINE
60°
FITTING
ASSY 9D446
VIEW A
REAR OF ENGINE
FITTING ASSY
9A474
40°
0°
℄ OF ENGINE
VIEW B
9F697
UPPER INTAKE MANIFOLD AND
THROTTLE BODY ASSY
M8 X 1.25 X 35.0 X M6 X 1.0
STUD AND WASHER ASSY HEX HEAD
TIGHTEN TO 19-29 N·m (14-21 LB-FT) 3 REQ'D
M8 X 1.25 X 32.5
SCREW AND WASHER
ASSY HEX HEAD
TIGHTEN TO 19-29 N·m
(14-21 LB-FT) 2 PLACES
FRONT OF ENGINE
VIEW A
GASKET 9H486
NIPPLE
TIGHTEN TO
16.0-24.0 N·m
(12-18 LB-FT)
(3/8-18) PLUG
TIGHTEN TO
16-24 N·m
(12-18 LB-FT)
TURBOCHARGED ENGINE
UPPER INTAKE MANIFOLD INSTALLATION
NO. 1
NO. 3
GASKET 9H486
NO. 4
NO. 2
VIEW A
CYLINDER HEAD ASSY 6049
LIFTING EYE 17A084
M8 X 1.25 X 29.0 BOLT HEX
FLANGE HEAD 8 REQ'D
PUSH PIN
2 REQ'D
KNOCK SENSOR
12A699 TIGHTEN TO
13.6-27.1 N·m
(10-20 LB-FT) (SVO ONLY)
GASKET 9439
VIEW A
VIEW B
INTAKE MANIFOLD CHARGING
ASSY 9H487
KNOCK SENSOR
12A699 TIGHTEN TO
13.6-27.1 N·m
(10-20 LB-FT)
(THUNDERBIRD/
COUGAR ONLY)
NIPPLE TIGHTEN TO
16-24 N·m (12-18 LB-FT)
FRONT OF ENGINE
HEAT SHIELD 9F460
LOWER INTAKE MANIFOLD INSTALLATION
GASKET 9439
8
4
1
5
6
2
3
7
VIEW A
KNOCK SENSOR
12A699 TIGHTEN TO
13.6-27.1 N·m
(10-20 LB-FT)
VIEW B

Fig. 5 Intake manifold assembly. EFI models

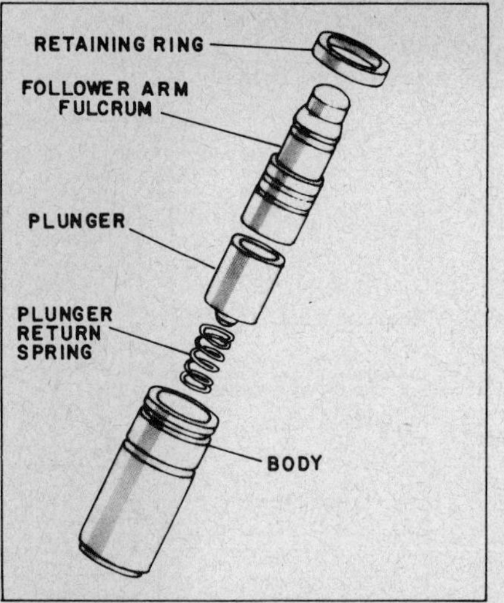

Fig. 6 Valve lash adjuster, Type I

3. Release pressure from fuel system at the fuel pressure relief valve using tool T80L-9974-B or equivalent. The fuel pressure relief valve is located on the fuel line in the upper righthand corner of the engine compartment.
4. Disconnect throttle linkage, cruise control and kickdown cables. Loosen, then position aside accelerator cable.
5. Disconnect air hose from crankcase vent hose.
6. Disconnect PCV system by disconnecting hose from upper intake manifold fitting.
7. Disconnect EGR tube from EGR valve.
8. Remove four upper intake manifold mounting bolts.
9. Remove upper intake manifold assembly.
10. Reverse procedure to install.

VALVE ARRANGEMENT

FRONT TO REAR

4-140 Engine............ E-I-E-I-E-I-E-I

VALVE LIFT SPECIFICATIONS

Engine	Year	Intake	Exhaust
4-140	1982-83	.3997	.3997
4-140	1984-88	.3900	.3900

VALVE TIMING

INTAKE OPENS BEFORE TDC

Engine	Year	Degrees
4-140	1982-86	22

VALVE CLEARANCE SPECIFICATIONS

Year	Engine	Valve Lash
1982-86	4-140	.070-.170①
1987-88	4-140	.040-.050②

①—With hydraulic valve lash adjuster completely collapsed.
②—With hydraulic valve lash adjuster completely collapsed, taken at cam.

VALVES

ADJUST

The valve lash on this engine cannot be adjusted due to the use of hydraulic valve lash adjusters. However, the valve train can be checked for wear as follows:

1. Crank engine to position camshaft with flat section of lobe facing rocker arm of valve being checked.
2. Remove rocker arm retaining spring. **Late models do not incorporate the retaining spring.**
3. Collapse lash adjuster with tool T74P-6565B and insert correct size feeler gauge between rocker arm and camshaft lobe. Clearance should be .040-.050 inch. If not, remove rocker arm and check for wear and replace as necessary. If rocker arm is found satisfactory, check valve spring assembled height and adjust as needed. Valve spring assembled height should be 167 ft. lbs. at 1.16 inch for 1982-83 models, and 154 ft. lbs. at 1.16 inch on 1984-88 models. If not, remove lash adjuster and clean or replace as necessary.

VALVE GUIDES

Valve guides consist of holes bored in the cylinder head. For service the guides can be reamed oversize to accommodate valves with oversize stems of .003, .015 and .030 inch.

ROCKER ARM SERVICE

1. Remove rocker arm cover.
2. Rotate camshaft until flat section of lobe faces rocker arm being removed.
3. With tool T74P-6565B, collapse lash adjuster and, if necessary, valve spring and slide rocker arm over lash adjuster.
4. Reverse procedure to install. **Before rotating camshaft, ensure that lash adjuster is collapsed to prevent valve train damage.**

LASH ADJUSTER

REPLACE

The hydraulic valve lash adjusters can be removed after rocker arm removal. There are two types of lash adjusters available, Type 1, being the standard lash adjuster, **Fig. 6**, and Type II, having a .020 inch oversize outside diameter, **Fig. 7.**

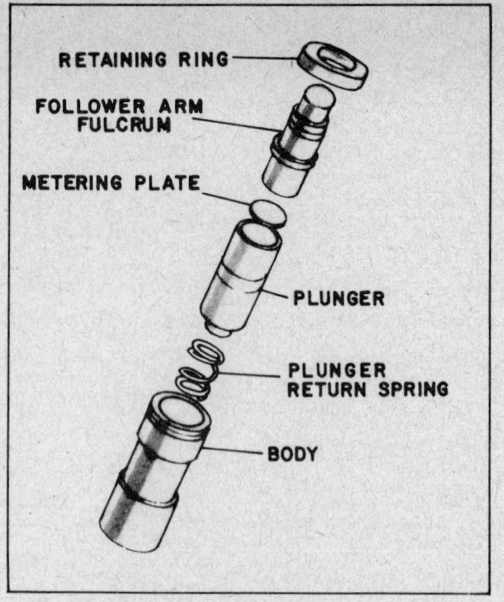

Fig. 7 Valve lash adjuster, Type II

FRONT ENGINE SEALS

REPLACE

To gain access to the front engine seals, remove the timing belt cover and proceed as follows:

CRANKSHAFT OIL SEAL

1. Without removing cylinder front cover, remove crankshaft sprocket with tool T74P-6306A.
2. Remove crankshaft oil seal with tool T74P-6700B.
3. Install a new crankshaft oil seal with tool T74P-6150A.
4. Install crankshaft sprocket with recess facing engine block.

CAMSHAFT & AUXILIARY SHAFT OIL SEALS

1. Remove camshaft or auxiliary shaft sprocket with tool T74P-6256A.
2. Remove oil seal with tool T74P-6700B.
3. Install a new oil seal with tool T74P-6150A.
4. Install camshaft or auxiliary shaft sprocket with tool T74P-6256A with center arbor removed.

TIMING BELT

1. Position crankshaft at TDC, No. 1 cylinder compression stroke.
2. Remove timing belt cover, loosen belt tensioner, and remove belt from sprockets, **Fig. 8.** Tighten tensioner bolt, holding tensioner in position. **Do not rotate crankshaft or camshaft after belt is removed. Rotating either component will result in improper valve timing.**
3. To install belt, ensure timing marks are aligned, **Fig. 9,** and place belt over sprockets.
4. Loosen tensioner bolt, allowing tensioner to move against belt.

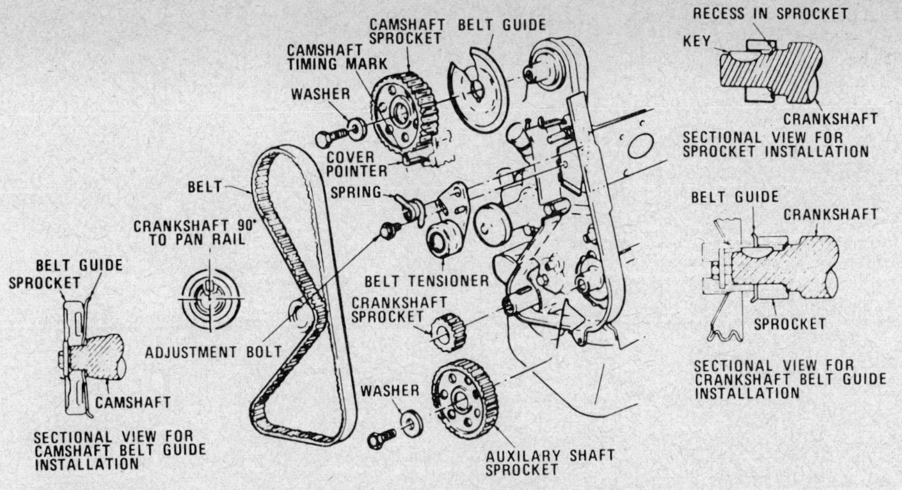

Fig. 8 Drive belt & sprockets installation. 4-140 engine

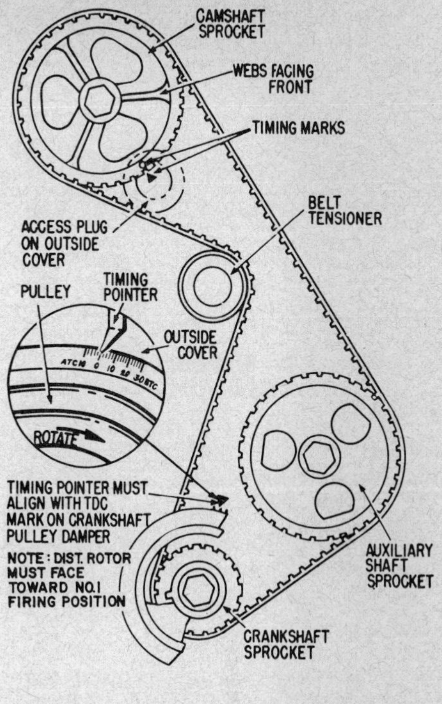

Fig. 9 Valve timing marks

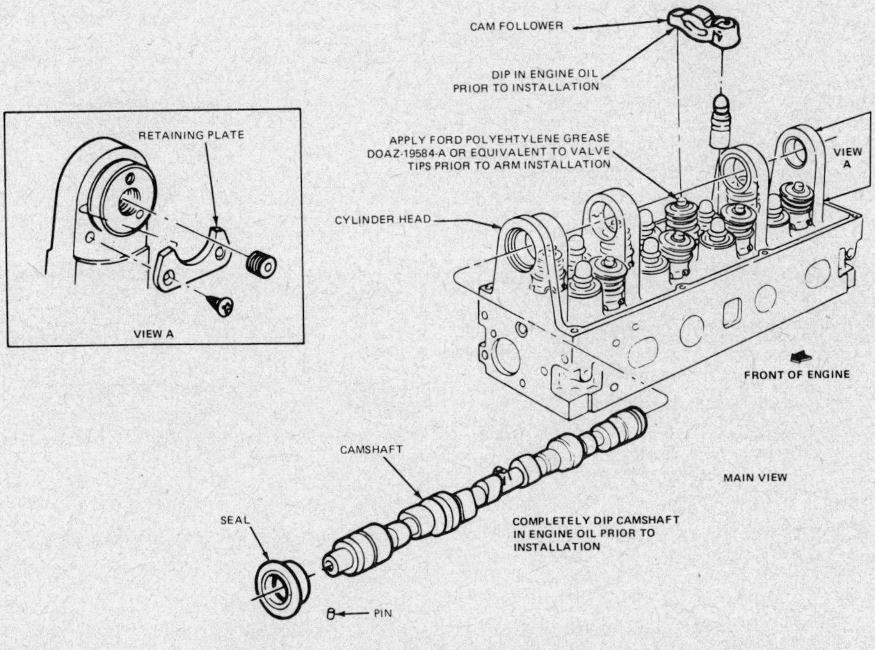

Fig. 10 Camshaft replacement

5. Rotate crankshaft two complete turns, removing slack from belt. Torque tensioner adjustment and pivot bolts and check alignment of timing marks, **Fig. 9.**
6. Install timing belt cover.

CAMSHAFT REPLACE

1. Drain cooling system, then remove air cleaner assembly.
2. Disconnect ignition wires from spark plugs and rocker arm cover and position aside.
3. Disconnect all vacuum hoses necessary for camshaft removal.
4. Remove rocker arm cover attaching bolts and the cover.
5. Remove alternator drive belt.
6. Remove alternator mounting bracket attaching bolts and position bracket aside.
7. Remove upper radiator hose and disconnect lower hose.
8. Remove fan shroud. On models equipped with electric fan, remove fan and shroud as an assembly.
9. Remove timing belt cover attaching bolts and the cover.
10. Loosen cam idler attaching bolts. Move idler to the unloaded position and retighten attaching bolts.
11. Remove timing belt from camshaft and auxiliary sprockets.
12. Raise and support vehicle.
13. Remove right and left engine mount nuts and washers.
14. Raise engine as far as possible using a suitable transmission jack with a block of wood positioned between jack and engine. Install wood blocks between No. 2 crossmember pedestals and engine mounts, then remove jack and lower vehicle.
15. Depress valve springs using tool No. T74P-6565-A or equivalent and remove camshaft followers.
16. Remove camshaft sprocket attaching bolt, then the sprocket using tool No. T-74P-6565-A, or equivalent.
17. Remove seal using tool No. T74P-6700-A, or equivalent.
18. Remove camshaft retainer attaching screws, then retainer.
19. Remove camshaft from cylinder head, **Fig. 10.**
20. Reverse procedure to install. **The camshaft sprocket attaching bolt should be replaced. If a new bolt is not available, coat threads of original bolt with D8AZ-19554-A sealer or equivalent, or wrap Teflon tape around threads prior to installation.**

PISTON & ROD ASSEMBLE

Assemble the rod to the piston with the arrow or notch on top of piston facing front of engine, **Fig. 11.**

Checkside clearance between connecting rods at each connecting rod crankshaft journal. Clearance should be .0035-.0105 in.

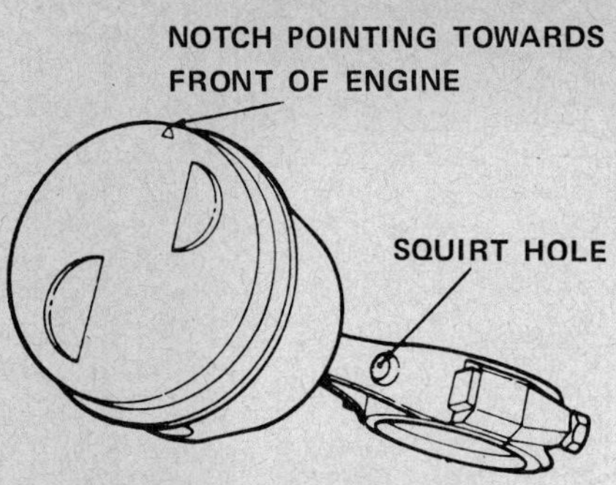

Fig. 11 Piston & rod assembly

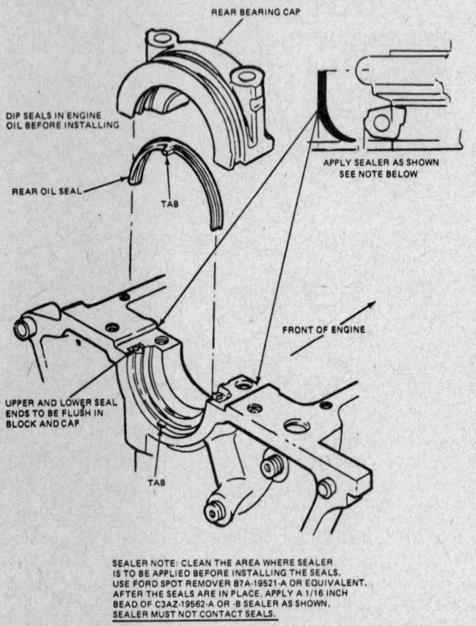

Fig. 13 Crankshaft rear oil seal installation. 1982 4-140 engine

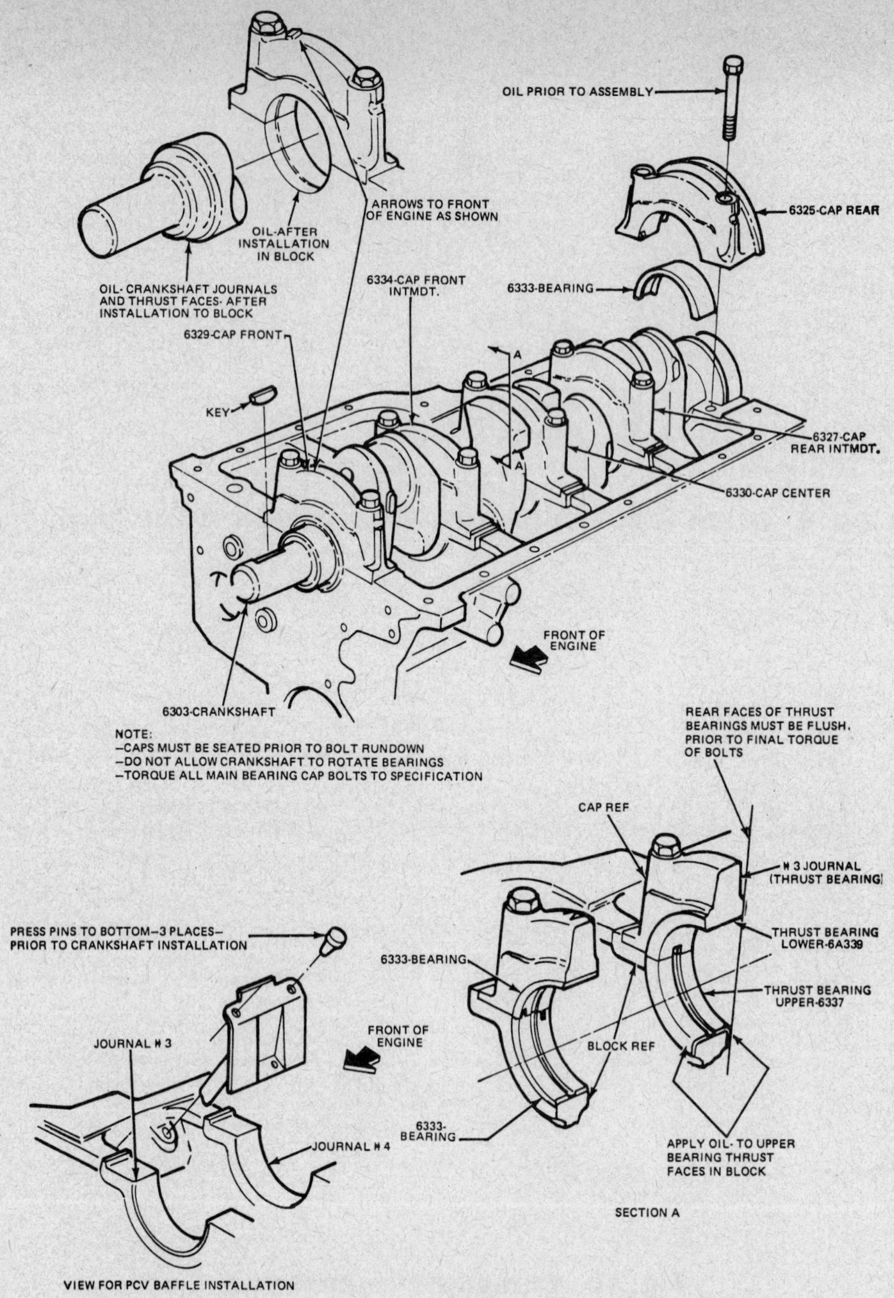

Fig. 12 Crankshaft & main bearing installation

PISTONS, PINS & RINGS

Oversize pistons are available in oversizes of .003 inch, .020 inch, .030 inch and .040 inch. Oversize rings are available in .020 inch, .030 inch and .040 inch oversizes. Oversize pins are not available.

MAIN & ROD BEARINGS

Undersize main bearings are available in .002 inch, .020 inch, .030 inch and .040 inch undersizes. Undersize rod bearings are available in undersizes of .002 inch, .010 inch, .020 inch, .030 inch and .040 inch.

The crankshaft and main bearings are installed with arrows on main bearing caps facing front of engine, **Fig. 12.** Install PCV baffle between bearing journals No. 3 and 4.

CRANKSHAFT OIL SEAL

1982

1. Remove oil pan.
2. Remove rear main bearing cap.
3. Loosen remaining bearing caps, allowing crankshaft to drop down about 1/32 inch.
4. Install a sheet metal screw into seal and pull screw to remove seal.
5. Carefully clean seal groove in block with a brush and solvent. Also clean seal groove in bearing cap.
6. Dip seal halves in clean engine oil.
7. Carefully install upper seal half in its groove with locating tab toward rear of engine, **Fig. 13,** by rotating it on shaft journal of crankshaft until approximately 3/8 inch protrudes below the parting surface. Be sure no rubber has been shaved from outside diameter of seal by bottom edge of groove.
8. Retighten main bearing caps and torque to specifications.
9. Install lower seal in main bearing cap with undercut side of seal toward front of engine, and allow seal to protrude about 3/8 inch above parting surface to mate with upper seal upon cap installation.

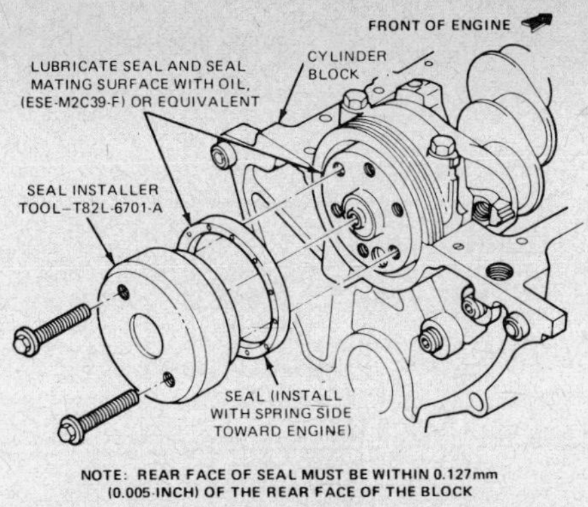

Fig. 14 Crankshaft rear oil seal installation. Except 1982 4-140 engine

10. Apply suitable sealer to parting faces of cap and block. Install cap and torque to specifications. **If difficulty is encountered in installing the upper half of the seal in position, lightly lap (sandpaper) the side of the seal opposite the lip side using a medium grit paper. After sanding, the seal must be washed in solvent, then dipped in clean engine oil prior to installation.**

EXCEPT 1982

1. Remove oil pump, if necessary, as described under "Oil Pump, Replace."
2. Punch one hole into metal surface between seal and block using a sharp awl.
3. Screw the threaded end of slide hammer, tool No. T77L-9533-B or equivalent, into seal and remove seal. Use care to avoid damaging oil seal mating surface.
4. Apply suitable sealer to seal and block mating surfaces.
5. Position seal on tool No. T82L-6701-A or equivalent, **Fig. 14,** and install seal. Tighten bolts alternately to ensure proper seating of the seal.
6. Install oil pump if previously removed.

OIL PAN
REPLACE

1. Disconnect battery ground cable.
2. Remove fan shroud. If equipped with electric fan, remove fan and shroud as an assembly.
3. On except 1982 models, drain cooling system, then disconnect upper and lower hoses from radiator.
4. On all models, raise and support vehicle.
5. Drain engine oil, then remove right and left engine mount nuts and bolts or washers.
6. Raise engine as far as possible using a suitable jack with a block of wood positioned between jack and engine. Install wood blocks between mounts and chassis brackets or No. 2 crossmember pedestals, then remove jack.
7. Remove shake brace, then the sway bar attaching bolts and lower the sway bar.
8. Remove starter motor.
9. Remove steering gear attaching bolts and lower the gear.
10. Remove oil pan attaching bolts and the oil pan. **The number four piston must be in the up position to allow clearance between crankshaft and rear of oil pan for oil pan removal.**
11. Reverse procedure to install.

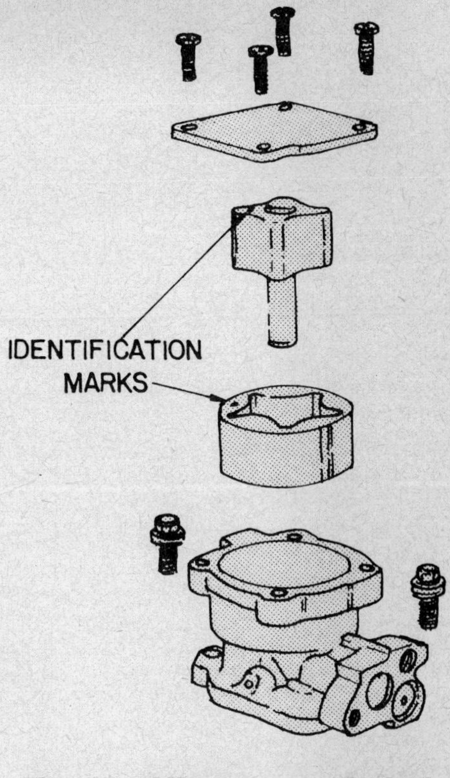

Fig. 15 Oil pump exploded view

OIL PUMP
REPLACE

The oil pump, **Fig. 15,** can be removed after oil pan removal, **Fig. 16.**

OIL PUMP REPAIRS

1. Remove end plate and withdraw O-ring from groove in body.

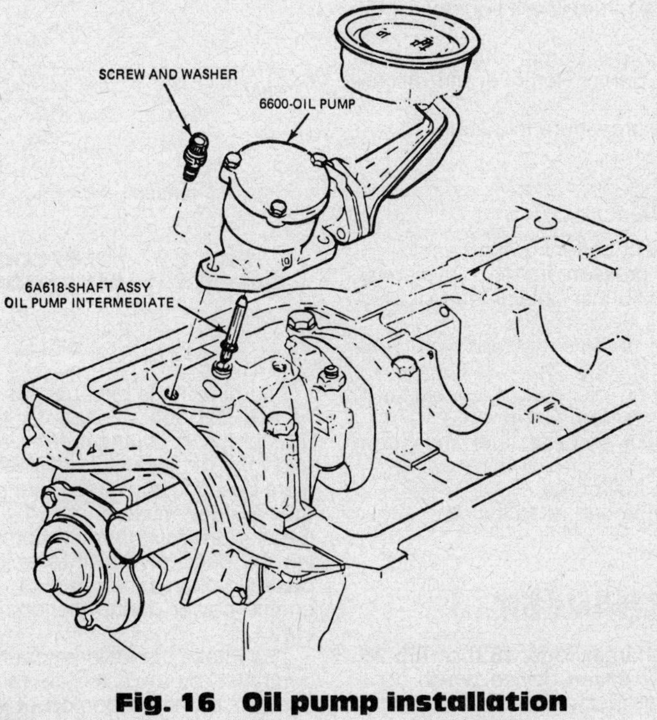

Fig. 16 Oil pump installation

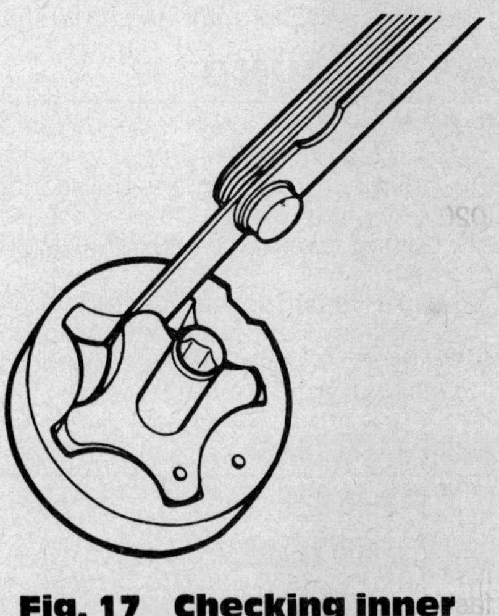

Fig. 17 Checking inner rotor tip clearance

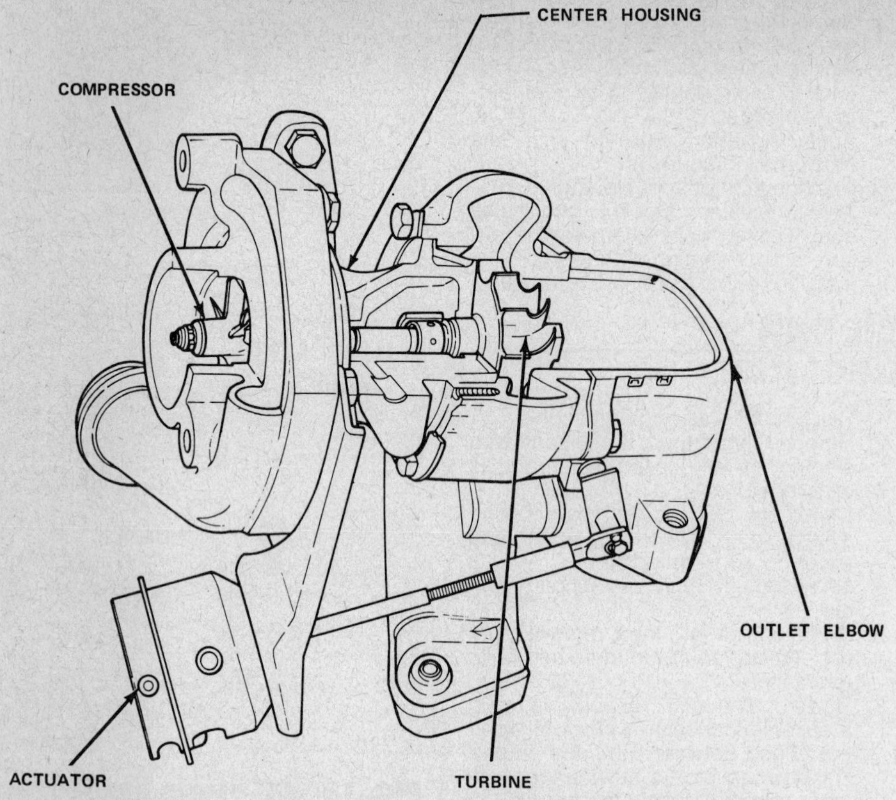

Fig. 18 Turbocharger

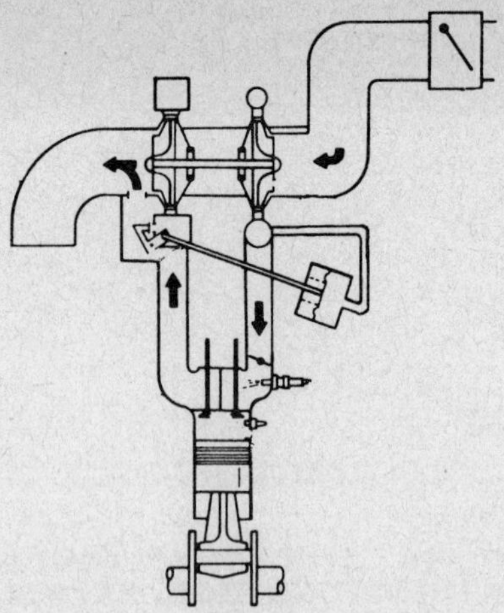

Fig. 19 Turbocharger air flow

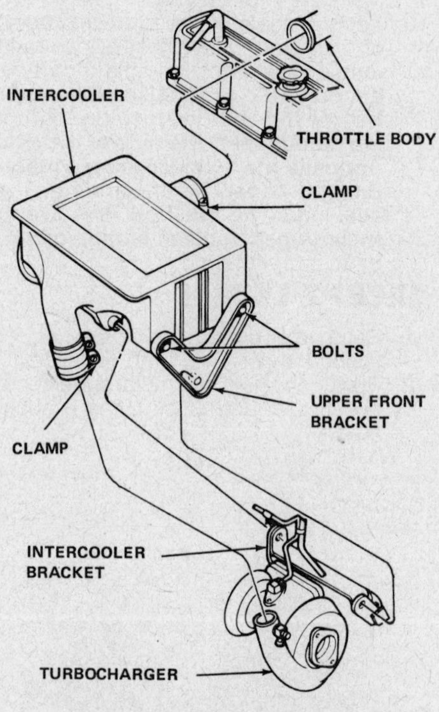

Fig. 20 Intercooler assembly. Mustang SVO

2. Check clearance between inner rotor tip and outer rotor lobe, **Fig. 17.** This should not exceed .012 inch. Rotors are supplied only in a matched pair.
3. Check clearance between outer rotor and the housing. This should not exceed .013 inch.
4. Place a straightedge across face of pump body. Clearance between face of rotors and straightedge should not exceed .004 inch.
5. If necessary to replace rotor or drive shaft, remove outer rotor and then drive out retaining pin securing the skew gear to drive shaft and pull off the gear.
6. Withdraw inner rotor and drive shaft.

WATER PUMP REPLACE

1. Drain cooling system and disconnect hoses from pump.
2. Loosen alternator and remove drive belt.
3. Remove fan, spacer and pulley.
4. Remove water pump attaching bolts and water pump after removing drive belt cover.

FUEL PUMP REPLACE

MECHANICAL

1. Loosen fuel line connectors, then retighten hand tight. Do not disconnect lines at this time.
2. Loosen fuel pump attaching bolts one or two turns. Apply hand force to break pump free from gasket.
3. Rotate engine slightly until pump cam lobe is near it's lowest position.
4. Disconnect inlet and outlet lines and the vapor return line, if equipped, from pump.
5. Remove fuel pump attaching bolts and the pump. Remove and discard gasket.
6. Reverse procedure to install.

ELECTRIC

1. Disconnect battery ground cable.
2. Release pressure from fuel system as described under "Intake Manifold, Replace."
3. Lower or remove fuel tank from vehicle.
4. Label, then disconnect all electrical connectors from pump.
5. Disconnect and cap fuel lines from pump.
6. Remove fuel pump.
7. Reverse procedure to install.

TURBOCHARGER

The turbocharger, **Figs. 18 through 20,** is an exhaust driven device which compresses the air-fuel mixture that is used to increase engine power on a demand basis, allowing a smaller, more economical engine to be used.

A turbine in the exhaust gas flow is connected through a shaft to the impeller (compressor). During normal, steady operation, the turbine does not rotate with sufficient speed to boost pressure to compress the air-fuel mixture. As the speed increases, the mixture is compressed, allowing the denser mixture to enter the combustion chambers and develop more engine power during the combustion cycle.

The intake manifold pressure (boost) is controlled by a wastegate valve which is used to bypass a portion of the exhaust gasses around the turbine at a predetermined point in the cycle, limiting the boost pressure.

A green light on the instrument panel indicates that the turbocharger is in a safe boost condition. A red light and buzzer are used to indicate a malfunction or if boost pressure exceeds a predetermined level.

Some models are equipped with a charge air cooler (intercooler) mounted between the turbocharger and throttle body assemblies. The intercooler cools the air flowing out of the turbocharger. The Mustang SVO also uses a turbo boost control system which along with the intercooler, allows higher turbo boost pressures, increased combustion efficiency, engine horsepower and torque.

The turbocharger boost control system used on some models, is designed to provide electronic variable boost control. The boost control system provides regulation of the wastegate actuator signal allowing up to 14 psi of turbo boost pressure. The system includes a control module, solenoid/hose assembly, calibrated T-fitting and a relay/switch assembly.

Turbochargers are lubricated from the engine oil system. These turbochargers operate at speeds up to 120,000 RPM which makes the lubrication of the bearings which support the shaft important for cooling as well as friction.

The oil enters the turbocharger through an inlet fitting in the center housing. This inlet fitting directs oil to the center housing bearings, the oil then drains from the turbocharger through a return hole in the center housing. When changing oil and filter on a turbocharged engine disconnect the ignition switch connector from the distributor then crank engine several times until the oil light goes out. Reconnect the ignition wire to the distributor. This procedure will aid in the filling of the oil system before starting engine.

BELT TENSION DATA

Belt	New Lbs.	Used Lbs.
Exc. 1/4 inch	140	110
1/4 inch	65	40
4 Ribs Exc. Air Pump	130	115
4 Ribs Air Pump	110	105
5 Ribs	150	135
6 Ribs①	113	110
6 Ribs②	160	145

①—W/tensioner.
②—Fixed.

6-200 (3.3L) Engine Section

NOTE: Refer to the Ford & Mercury—Compact & Intermediate chapter for service procedures on this engine not included in this section.

INDEX

Page No.

OIL PAN, REPLACE

1. If equipped with automatic transmission, disconnect transmission oil cooler lines from radiator, then remove the radiator top support.
2. Remove dipstick, then raise and support vehicle and drain crankcase.
3. Remove the four bolts and nuts retaining sway bar to chassis and allow sway bar to hang down.
4. Remove K-brace, then lower the rack and pinion steering gear.
5. Remove starter motor, then remove the two engine mounts to support bracket nuts and loosen the two rear insulator to crossmember retaining bolts.
6. Raise engine and place a 1¼ inch wooden block between each engine support insulator and chassis bracket, then lower engine onto wood blocks.
7. Using floor jack, raise transmission slightly, then remove the oil pan retaining bolts and lower oil pan onto crossmember.
8. Position transmission oil cooler lines aside and remove oil pan. If necessary, rotate engine so crankshaft throws clear oil pan rail.
9. Reverse procedure to install.

V6-232 (3.8L) Engine Section

NOTE: Refer to Ford & Mercury—Compact & Intermediate chapter for service procedures on this engine.

V8-255 (4.2L) & V8-302 (5.0L) Engine Section

NOTE: Refer to the Ford & Mercury—Compact & Intermediate chapter for service procedures on this engine not included in this section.

INDEX

Page No.

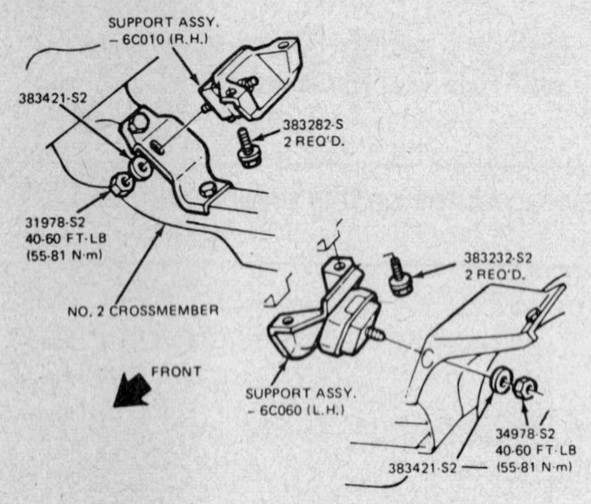

Fig. 1 Engine mounts

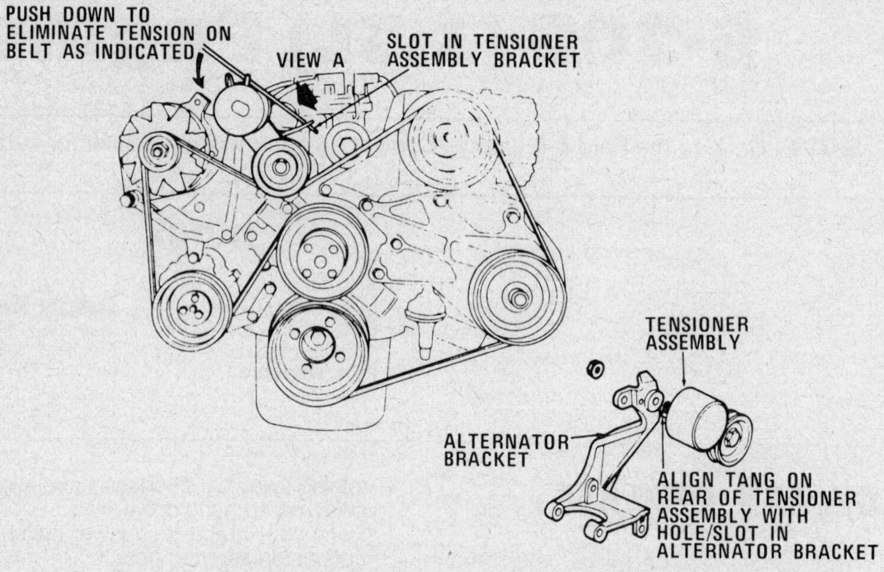

Fig. 2 Serpentine drive belt

ENGINE MOUNTS

REPLACE

Late 1985 and 1986-88 models, use viscous type engine mounts.

1. Remove fan shroud attaching screws, if necessary.
2. Remove nuts attaching insulators to lower bracket, **Fig. 1.**
3. Raise engine with a suitable jack and a block of wood placed under oil pan.
4. Remove insulator to engine block attaching bolts.
5. Remove insulator from vehicle.
6. Reverse procedure to install.

VALVE CLEARANCE SPECIFICATIONS

Year	Engine	Valve Lash
1982	V8-255	.096-.146
1982-88	V8-302	.096-.146
1983-88	V8-302 H.O.	.123-.146

VALVES

ADJUST

When adjusting valves on these engines, refer to the procedure for the V8 engines in the "Ford & Mercury—Compact & Intermediate" chapter.

OIL PAN

REPLACE

1. Disconnect battery cables.
2. Remove fan shroud retaining bolts and position fan shroud over fan.
3. Remove dipstick and tube assembly.
4. On all models, raise and support vehicle, then drain crankcase. **Some oil pans have dual oil sumps. Make sure to remove both drain plugs to thoroughly drain oil.**
5. Remove the two bolts retaining steering gear to main crossmember and allow steering gear to rest on frame away from oil pan.
6. Remove engine mount retaining bolts, then raise engine and place a 2 x 4 inch wooden block between each engine mount and vehicle frame.
7. Remove rear K-braces.
8. Remove oil pan retaining bolts and lower oil pan onto frame.
9. Remove oil pump retaining bolts and the inlet tube retaining nut from No. 3 main bearing cap stud. Lower the oil pump assembly into the oil pan.
10. Remove oil pan. If necessary, rotate engine so that crankshaft throws clear oil pan rail.
11. Reverse procedure to install.

SERPENTINE DRIVE BELT

Some engines are equipped with a serpentine drive belt, **Fig. 2**, to drive the accessories in place of the usual arrangement. This "V" ribbed belt drives the fan/water pump, alternator, secondary air pump, optional A/C compressor and optional power steering pump.

The tensioner arm should be checked to ensure that the top edge of the arm is located between the two index marks scribed on the circumference next to the slot of the tensioner housing, **Fig. 3.** If the tensioner arm is not properly aligned, the drive belt and pulleys should be inspected for wear and binding. If the drive belt and pulleys are satisfactory, the tensioner must be replaced as outlined in the following procedure:

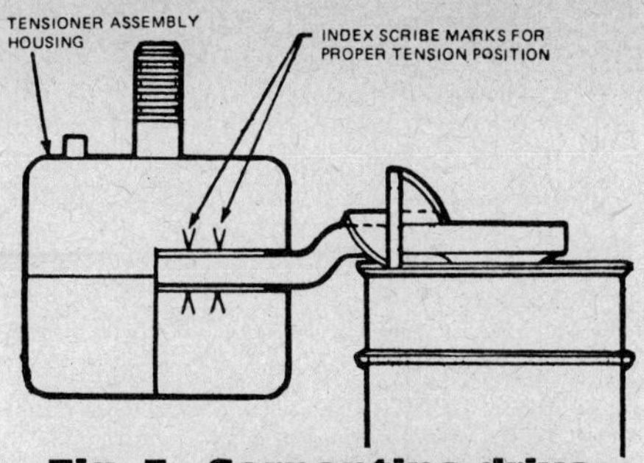

Fig. 3 Serpentine drive belt tensioner alignment marks

1. Insert a 16 inch pry bar or equivalent in the slot of the tensioner bracket, and using the tensioner housing as a fulcrum, push the pry bar downward to force the tensioner pulley upward, relieving tension on belt, **Fig. 2.**
2. Remove drive belt.
3. Remove bolt securing tensioner assembly to alternator bracket.
4. Remove tensioner assembly.
5. Position tensioner assembly so the tang, located on the rear of the assembly, is placed to fit in the hole or slot in alternator bracket.
6. Install the tensioner assembly bolt through the hole in the alternator bracket and torque bolt to 55-80 ft. lbs.
7. Install drive belt by inserting the pry bar as outlined in Step 1. Refer to decal located on top of the windshield washer/coolant expansion reservoir for proper belt routing.
8. Remove pry bar.
9. The drive belt is automatically tensioned when the tensioner arm is located between the two index marks, **Fig. 3.**

Clutch & Transmission Section

INDEX

CLUTCH PEDAL ADJUST

A self adjusting type clutch mechanism is used. The adjust mechanism consists of a spring loaded rachet quadrant attached to the clutch cable. To accomplish this adjustment, grasp clutch pedal and pull upward, then slowly depress clutch pedal. If a click is heard during the procedure, an adjustment was necessary and has been accomplished. This procedure should be performed at least every 5000 miles.

CLUTCH & TRANSMISSION REPLACE

Prior to installing throw-out bearing, apply a light film of lithium base lubricant part No. C1AZ-19590-B or equivalent to transmission front bearing retainer outside diameter, the clutch release fork and anti-rattle spring where they contact the release bearing hub and to the throw-out bearing where the bearing contacts the pressure plate release fingers. In addition, fill the throw-out bearing grease groove with the same lubricant. Wipe off all excess lubricant.

EXCEPT MUSTANG SVO

Lift clutch pedal upward to disengage clutch cable self adjuster pawl and quadrant. Push quadrant forward, then detach cable from quadrant and allow quadrant to slowly swing rearward.

1. Loosen clutch cable adjusting nut to allow slack in cable. Disconnect cable from release lever.
2. Position gear shift lever in neutral, then remove lever attaching screws and the lever.
3. Raise and support vehicle.
4. On all models, remove dust shield.
5. On all models, remove driveshaft. Cover extension housing to prevent leakage.
6. Disconnect electrical leads and speedometer cable from transmission.
7. Support rear of engine and remove crossmember, then lower engine as necessary and remove transmission attaching bolts and transmission.
8. Disconnect clutch release cable from lever and flywheel housing.
9. Disconnect starter cable and remove starter motor.
10. On models with V6 engine, remove number 2A crossmember. This crossmember is located behind the number 2 crossmember which supports the engine.
11. On all models, remove flywheel housing.
12. Evenly loosen and remove pressure plate attaching screws to prevent distortion of pressure plate. If pressure plate is to be reused, mark pressure plate and flywheel to assure correct assembly.

MUSTANG SVO

1. Lift clutch pedal to its uppermost position, then disconnect pawl and quadrant. Push quadrant forward, disconnect cable from quadrant and allow quadrant to slowly swing rearward.
2. Raise and support vehicle, then disconnect shift linkage assembly from transmission.
3. Remove retainer and clevis pins from lower end of bellcrank.
4. Separate clevis from cable end.
5. Remove retaining clip and cable from flywheel housing.
6. Remove starter cable and starter motor from flywheel housing.
7. Remove engine rear plate attaching bolts from front lower portion of flywheel housing.
8. Disconnect drive shaft from U-joint flange and slide drive shaft from

transmission output shaft. Insert output shaft cap tool onto transmission output shaft.

9. Position a suitable jack under transmission, then remove transmission to bellhousing attaching bolts. Disconnect speedometer cable and electrical connectors from transmission.
10. Lower transmission assembly from vehicle.
11. Remove housing to cylinder block attaching bolts. Pull housing rearward to clear pressure plate, then remove housing.
12. Disconnect the short cable from release lever by pushing cable and release lever boot approximately 1/2 inch toward release bearing. Pull cable rearward through release lever boot hole.
13. Remove release lever boot from flywheel housing.
14. Remove clutch release lever from housing by pulling lever through housing window until retainer spring is disengaged from pivot.
15. Remove release bearing from release lever.
16. Loosen the six pressure plate cover attaching bolts evenly to gradually release spring tension and avoid damaging the pressure plate cover.
17. If the same pressure plate and cover are to be reused, mark pressure plate cover and flywheel so pressure plate can be installed in its original position.
18. Remove pressure plate and clutch disc assembly from flywheel.
19. Reverse procedure to install.
20. During installation of pressure plate assembly, proceed as follows:
    a. Using a suitable clutch alignment tool, align clutch disc.
    b. Alternately tighten the bolts a few turns at a time, until bolts are tight.
    c. Torque the six pressure plate cover bolts to 12-24 ft. lbs., then remove clutch alignment tool.
    d. Apply a light film of grease part No. C1AZ-19590-B or equivalent, onto the outside diameter of transmission front bearing retainer, release lever fork and anti-rattle spring where they contact the release bearing hub, release bearing surface, release lever ball pivot and lever pocket.

Rear Axle, Propeller Shaft & Brakes

INDEX

REAR AXLE

This rear axle, **Fig. 1** is an integral design hypoid with the center line of the pinion set below the center line of the ring gear. The semi-floating axle shafts are retained in the housing by ball bearings and bearing retainers at axle ends.

The differential is mounted on two opposed tapered roller bearings which are retained in the housing by removable caps. Differential bearing preload and drive gear backlash is adjusted by nuts located behind each differential bearing cup.

The drive pinion assembly is mounted on two opposed tapered roller bearings. Pinion bearing preload is adjusted by a collapsible spacer on the pinion shaft. Pinion and ring gear tooth contact is adjusted by shims between the rear bearing cone and pinion gear.

REAR AXLE REPLACE

1. Raise vehicle and support at rear frame members.
2. Drain lubricant from axle.
3. Mark drive shaft and pinion flanges for reassembly, then disconnect drive shaft at rear axle U-joint and remove drive shaft from transmission exten-

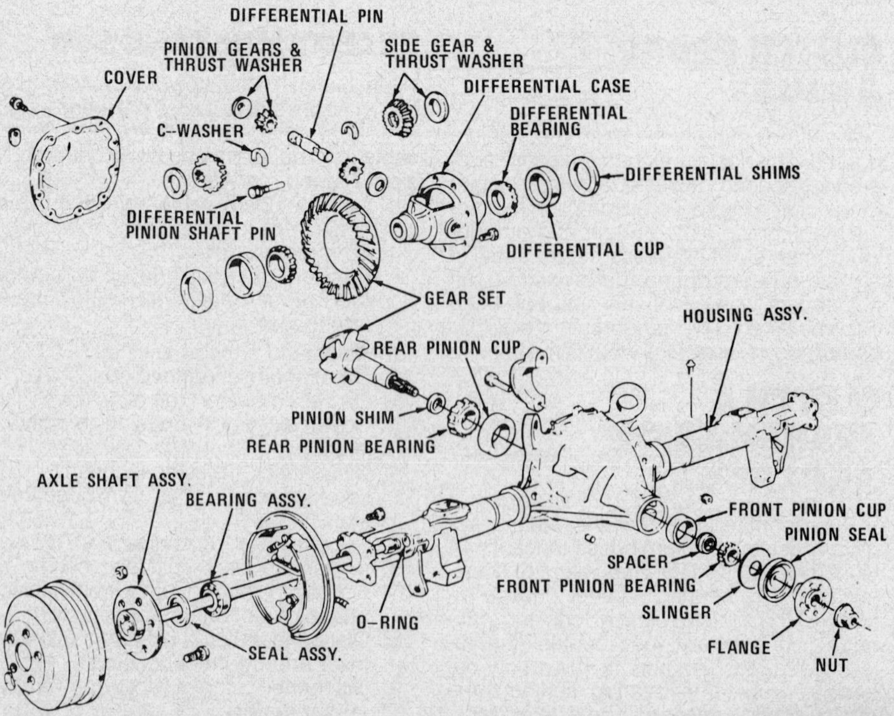

Fig. 2 Disassembled integral rear axle. 8.8 inch ring gear

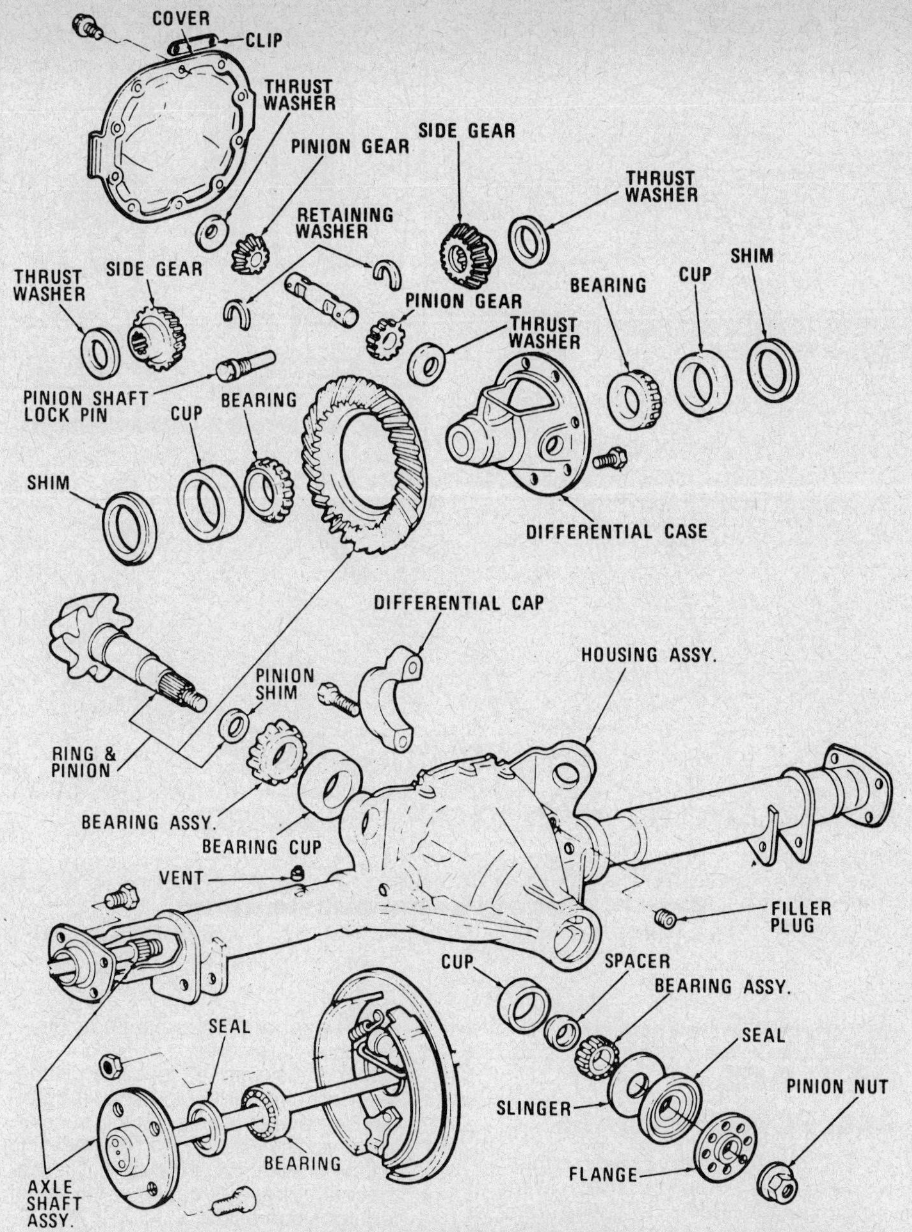

Fig. 1 Disassembled integral rear axle. 7½ inch ring gear (6¾ axle similar)

sion housing. Install seal replacer tool in extension housing to prevent leakage.

4. Disconnect shock absorbers at lower mountings.
5. Remove rear wheels and brake drums, then disconnect brake lines at wheel cylinders.
6. Disconnect vent hose from vent tube, then remove vent tube from brake junction and axle housing.
7. Remove clips retaining brake lines to axle housing.
8. Support rear axle housing using a suitable jack.
9. On models with coil springs, disconnect upper control arms from mountings on axle housing, then carefully lower axle assembly until spring tension is relieved and remove coil springs. Disconnect lower control arms from axle housing.
10. On models with leaf springs, remove U-bolts and plates.
11. Lower rear axle and remove from vehicle.
12. Reverse procedure to install.

AXLE SHAFT, BEARING & OIL SEAL REPLACE

6¾ INCH RING GEAR

1. Remove wheel and tire from brake drum.
2. Remove attaching nuts that secure brake drum to axle flange and remove brake drum.
3. Working through hole in each axle flange, remove nuts that secure wheel bearing retainer plate. Then pull the axle shaft assembly out of the housing being careful not to cut or rough up the seal. **The brake backing plate must not be dislodged. Replace one nut to hold the plate in place after shaft is removed.**
4. If wheel bearing is to be replaced, loosen inner retainer ring by nicking it deeply with a chisel in several places. It will then slide off.
5. Remove bearing from shaft.

7½ INCH RING GEAR

1. Raise and support vehicle.
2. Remove wheel and tire assembly, then the brake drum.
3. Clean all dirt from carrier cover area.
4. Remove housing cover to drain lubricant from rear axle.
5. Remove differential pinion shaft lock bolt and the shaft.
6. Move flanged end of axle shafts toward center of vehicle and remove "C" clip from button end of shaft.
7. Remove axle shaft from housing. Use care to avoid damaging the oil seal.
8. Remove bearing and seal as an assembly using a suitable slide hammer.
9. Reverse procedure to install. Lubricate new bearing with rear axle lubricant prior to installation. Apply suitable grease between lips of oil seal. **The bearing should be installed using tool No. T78P-1225-A or equivalent, and the seal using tool No. T78P-1177-A or equivalent. If proper tools are not used, early bearing or seal failure may result. If seal becomes cocked in the bore during installation, it must be removed and replaced with a new one.**

8.8 INCH RING GEAR

1. Raise and support vehicle, then remove rear wheel and tire assembly.
2. Clean all dirt from carrier cover area with a wire brush and/or cloth.
3. Remove axle housing cover and drain lubricant from axle, **Fig. 2.**
4. Remove differential pinion shaft lock bolt and differential pinion shaft.
5. Push flanged end of axle shaft toward center of the vehicle, then remove C-lock from button end of axle shaft assembly.
6. Remove axle shaft from housing. Ensure not to damage oil seal.
7. Insert tool 1175-AC or equivalent, into housing bore and position it behind bearing so tangs on tool engage bearing outer race. Using slide hammer tool T50T-100-A or equivalent, remove bearing and seal as a unit.
8. Reverse procedure to install, noting the following:
   a. Lubricate new bearing with lubricant E0AZ-19580-A or equivalent, and install bearing into housing bore using tool T78P-1225-A or equivalent.
   b. Install axle shaft seal using tool T78P-1177-A or equivalent. Apply lubricant C1AZ-19590-B or equivalent, between the lips of the seal. **Installation of bearing or seal assembly without proper tool may result in an early bearing or seal failure. If seal becomes cocked**

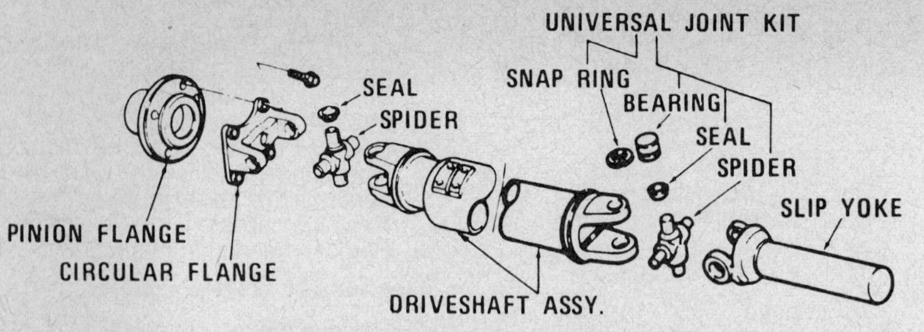

Fig. 3 Drive shaft and universal joints disassembled. Single Cardan type U-joint

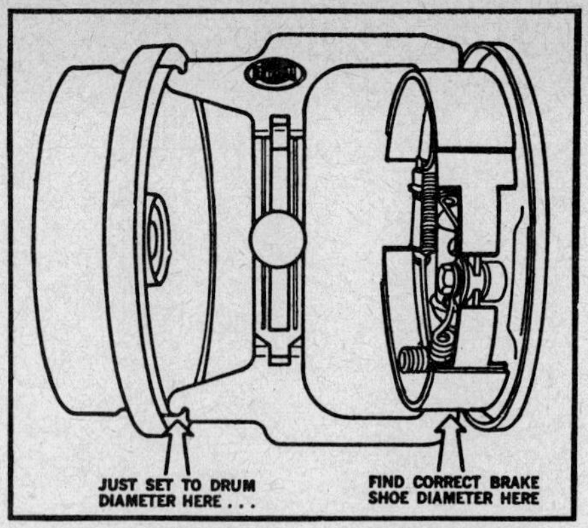

Fig. 4 Brake adjustment

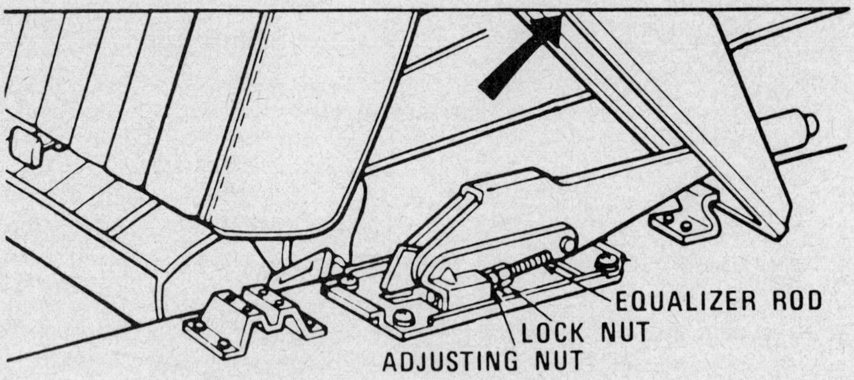

Fig. 5 Parking brake adjustment

in bore during installation, remove it and install a new one.

c. Check for presence of axle shaft O-ring on the spline end of the shaft and install if not present.

PROPELLER SHAFT
REPLACE

1. To maintain balance, mark relationship of rear drive shaft yoke and the drive pinion flange of the axle if alignment marks are not visible.
2. Disconnect rear U-joint from companion flange, **Fig. 3.** Wrap tape around loose bearing caps to prevent them from falling off spider. Pull drive shaft toward rear of car until slip yoke clears transmission extension housing and the seal. Install tool in extension housing to prevent lubricant leakage.

BRAKE ADJUSTMENTS

The hydraulic drum brakes, **Fig. 4,** are self-adjusting and require a manual adjustment only after brake shoes have been replaced. The adjustment is made as follows:

1. Using tool No. 11-0001 on 1982 models, or tool No. D81L-1103-A on except 1982 models, determine inside diameter of brake drum, **Fig. 5.**
2. Reverse tool and adjust brake shoes to fit the gauge. Hold automatic adjusting lever out of engagement while rotating adjusting screw, to prevent burring slots in screw.

PARKING BRAKE
ADJUST

1. Release parking brake.
2. Place transmission in Neutral and raise vehicle until rear wheels clear floor.
3. Tighten adjusting nut on equalizer rod at the control, **Fig. 5,** to cause the rear wheel brakes to drag.
4. Loosen adjusting nut until rear brakes are just free.

MASTER CYLINDER
REPLACE
EXC. POWER BRAKES

1. Disconnect battery ground cable.
2. Disconnect stoplight switch wires at connector. Remove spring retainer and slide stop light switch off brake pedal pin just far enough to clear end of pin, then lift switch straight upward from the pin.
3. Slide master cylinder pushrod and nylon washers and bushings off brake pedal pin.
4. Remove brake tubes from master cylinder ports.
5. Loosen and remove master cylinder by lifting forward and upward from vehicle.

POWER BRAKES

Disconnect brake tubes from master cylinder, then remove attaching nuts and slide master cylinder forward and upward from vehicle.

POWER BRAKE UNIT
REPLACE
EXC. 1985–88 4-140

1. Remove stop light switch and slide booster pushrod, bushing and inner nylon washer from brake pedal pin.
2. Remove air cleaner.
3. On models with V8 engine, disconnect accelerator cable from carburetor. Remove screws securing accelerator cable bracket to engine and rotate bracket toward engine. Disconnect inlet hose of choke water cover and position aside.
4. Disconnect vacuum hose from power brake unit.
5. Disconnect hydraulic lines from master cylinder and cap open lines and ports.
6. Remove master cylinder.
7. From inside vehicle, remove power brake unit to dash panel attaching nuts.
8. On models with speed control, remove control amplifier which is mounted on the lower outboard booster stud and set aside.
9. On all models, work from engine compartment and move booster forward until booster studs clear the dash panel, then raise front of unit and remove from vehicle.

1985–88 4-140

1. Disconnect battery ground cable, then remove air cleaner.
2. Disconnect accelerator cable from carburetor.
3. Remove screw that secures accelera-

tor cable to shaft bracket, then remove cable from bracket.
4. Remove two screws that secure accelerator shaft bracket to manifold, and rotate bracket toward engine.
5. Remove RPO horn, if equipped.
6. Release fuel system pressure, then disconnect the two manifold injector connectors located near oil dipstick retaining bracket. Disconnect two fuel lines to fuel supply manifold assembly.
7. Remove engine oil dipstick tube and bracket.
8. Remove windshield wiper motor.
9. Disconnect vacuum lines located over brake booster at dash panel vacuum tee.
10. Remove bolt securing clutch cable stand, then move bracket to side rail at fender inner panel.
11. On models equipped with speed control, move speed control cable to one side to clear booster.
12. On all models, disconnect manifold booster line from booster check valve.
13. Disconnect brake lines from master cylinder, remove master cylinder attaching nuts, then the master cylinder.
14. Working under instrument panel, disconnect electrical connector from stop lamp switch.
15. Remove hairpin type retainer and outer nylon washer from brake pedal pin, then slide stop lamp switch off brake pedal pin just enough for outer arm to clear pin.
16. On models equipped with speed control, unfasten control amplifier from lower outboard booster stud and position aside. Slide booster pushrod, bushing, and inner nylon washer off brake pedal pin.
17. Move booster forward in engine compartment until booster studs clear dash panel, then rotate front of booster toward engine and remove booster.
18. Reverse procedure to install.

Rear Suspension

INDEX

SHOCK ABSORBER REPLACE

On hatchback models, the upper shock absorber upper mounting is accessible from the luggage compartment. On hatchback and fastback models, remove side panel trim covers to gain access to the upper shock absorber mounting.

1. Disconnect shock absorber from upper mounting.
2. Raise vehicle and support rear axle.
3. Compress shock absorber to clear hole in upper shock absorber tower.
4. Disconnect shock absorber from lower mounting and remove shock absorber from vehicle.
5. Reverse procedure to install.

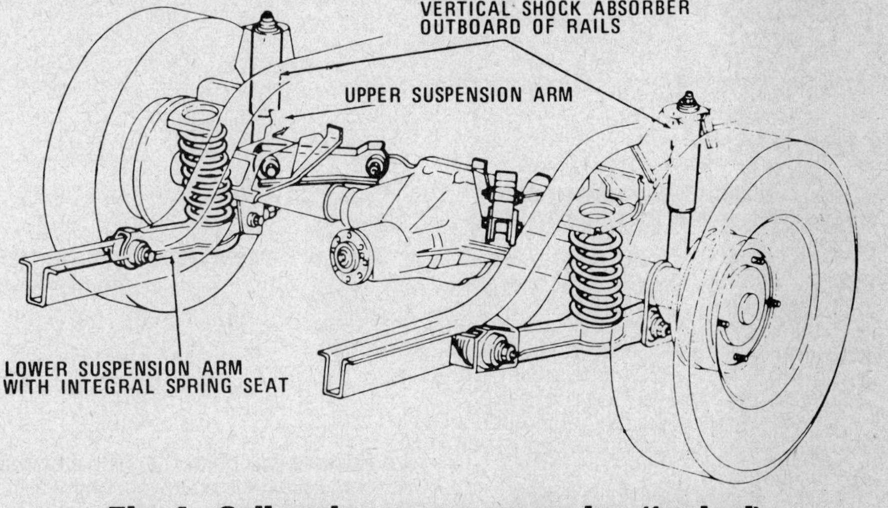

Fig. 1 Coil spring rear suspension (typical)

COIL SPRING REPLACE

1. Raise rear of vehicle and support at rear body crossmember.
2. Remove stabilizer bar, if equipped, **Fig. 1.**
3. Lower axle housing until shock absorbers are fully extended. **The axle housing must be supported with a suitable jack.**
4. Position a suitable jack under lower control arm rear pivot bolt to support control arm, then remove pivot bolt.
5. Carefully lower the lower control arm until spring tension is relieved, then remove coil spring and insulator.
6. Reverse procedure to install. Torque lower control arm pivot bolt to 70-100 ft. lbs. on except 1982 models, or 90-100 ft. lbs. on 1982 models, with suspension at curb height.

CONTROL ARMS & BUSHINGS REPLACE

UPPER CONTROL ARM

1. Raise rear of vehicle and support at rear body crossmember.
2. Remove upper control arm rear and front pivot bolts, then remove control arm.
3. If control arm axle bracket bushings are to be replaced, refer to **Figs. 2 and 3.**
4. Position upper control arm into side rail bracket, then install front pivot bolt. Do not tighten bolt at this time.
5. Raise rear axle until upper control arm rear pivot bolt hole is aligned with hole in axle housing, then install rear pivot bolt. Do not tighten bolt at this time.
6. Position suspension at curb height.

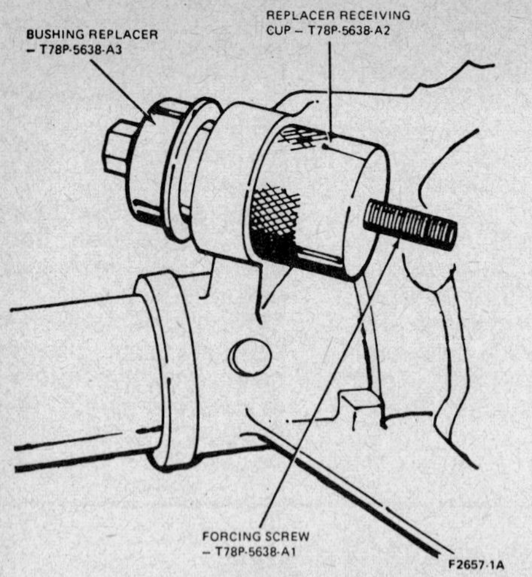

Fig. 2 Upper control arm axle bracket bushing installation

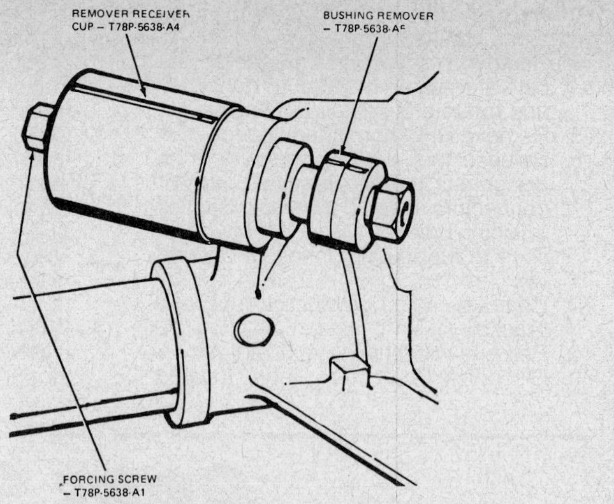

Fig. 3 Upper control arm axle bracket bushing removal

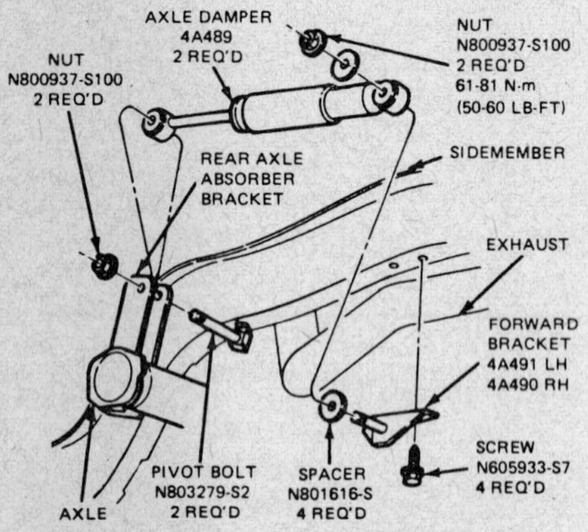

Fig. 4 Axle damper assembly. Mustang GT, Capri RS, GS & Mustang SVO

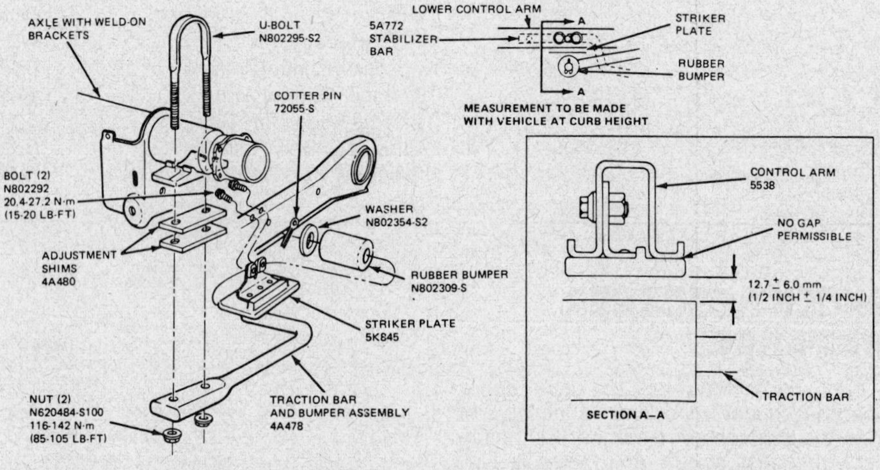

Fig. 5 Traction bar assembly. 4-140 turbocharged or V8-302 H.O. engines

Torque front pivot bolt to 70-100 ft. lbs. on except 1982 models, or 100 ft. lbs. on 1982 models. Torque rear pivot bolt to 100 ft. lbs. on 1982 models, or 80-104 ft. lbs. on except 1986 models.

LOWER CONTROL ARMS

1. Remove coil spring as described under "Coil Spring, Replace."
2. Remove lower control arm front pivot bolt and nut, then remove control arm.
3. Reverse procedure to install. Torque front pivot bolt to 100 ft. lbs. on 1982 models, or 80-104 ft. lbs. on except 1982 models. Torque rear pivot bolt to 70-100 ft. lbs. except 1982 models, or 100 ft. lbs. on 1982 models.

STABILIZER BAR REPLACE

1. Raise and support rear of vehicle.
2. Remove four bolts attaching stabilizer bar to brackets on lower control arms.
3. Remove stabilizer bar from vehicle.
4. Reverse procedure to install. Torque all bolts to 45-50 ft. lbs.

AXLE DAMPERS REPLACE

1. Raise vehicle and support rear axle.
2. Remove rear wheel, then the axle damper rear attaching nut and pivot bolt, **Fig. 4.**
3. Remove axle damper forward attaching nut, the axle damper and spacer.
4. Reverse procedure to install. Torque attaching bolts to 50-60 ft. lbs.

TRACTION BAR REPLACE

1. Raise vehicle and support rear axle.
2. Remove traction bar to rear axle attaching bolts, then the traction bar, adjusting shims and "U" bolt, **Fig. 5.**
3. Remove cotter pin and washer, then the rubber bumper if necessary.
4. Reverse procedure to install, noting the following:
   a. If rubber bumper is replaced, use tire mounting solution ESAM-1B6B or equivalent to ease installation.
   b. Torque traction bar attaching nuts to 85-105 ft. lbs.
   c. Adjust traction bar, as needed, by adding or subtracting shims.

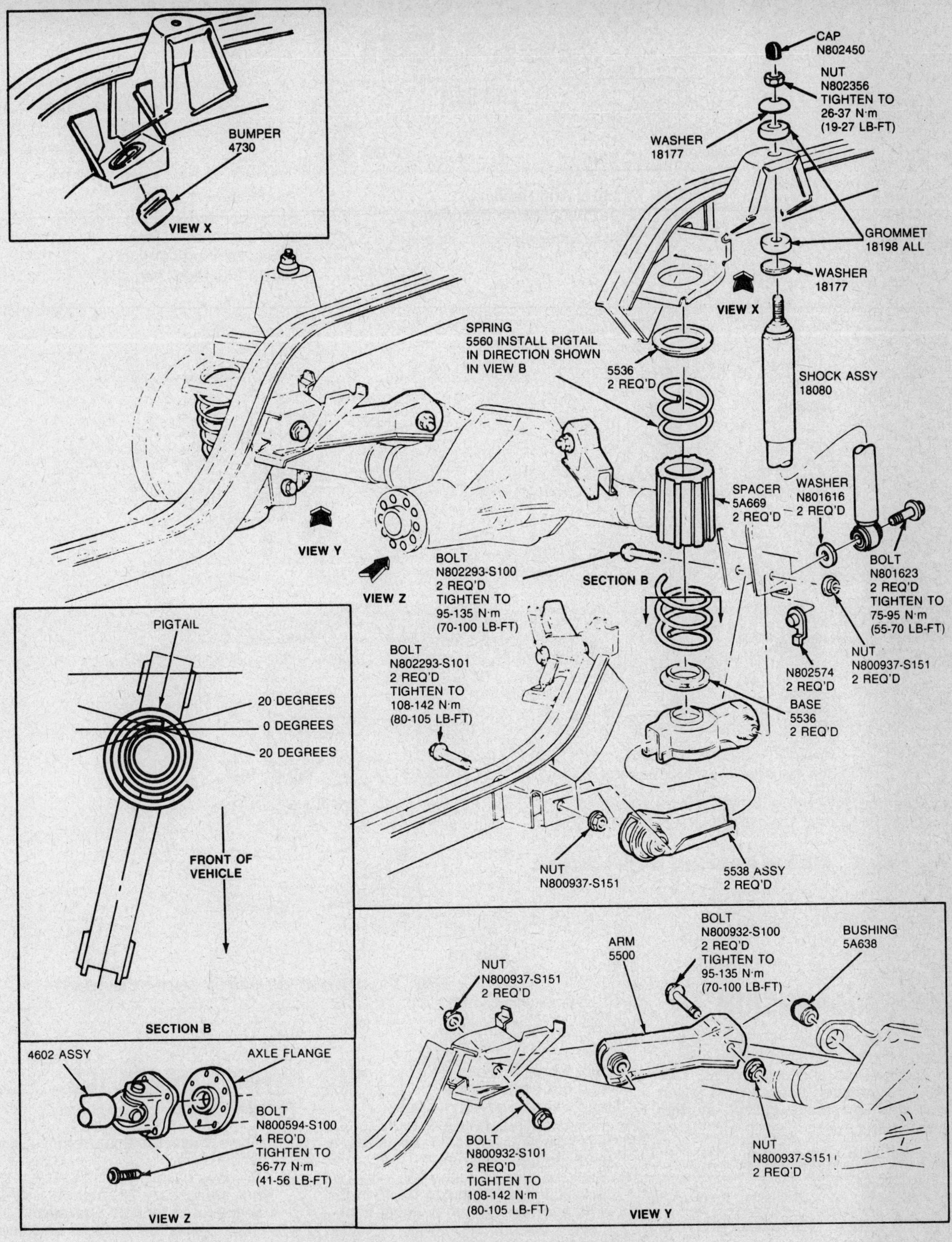

Fig. 6 Typical rear suspension

Front Suspension & Steering Section

INDEX

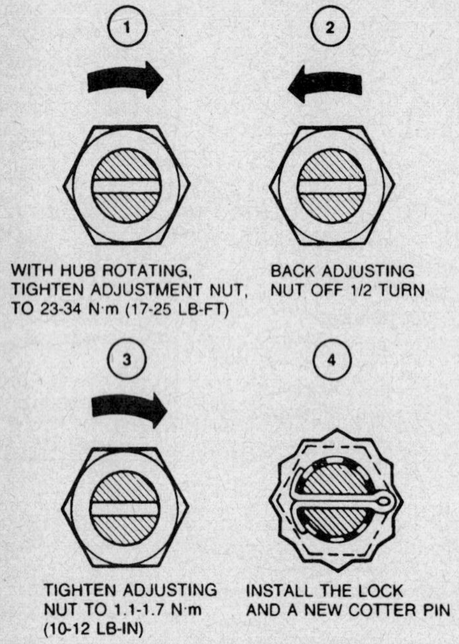

Fig. 2 Wheel bearing adjustment

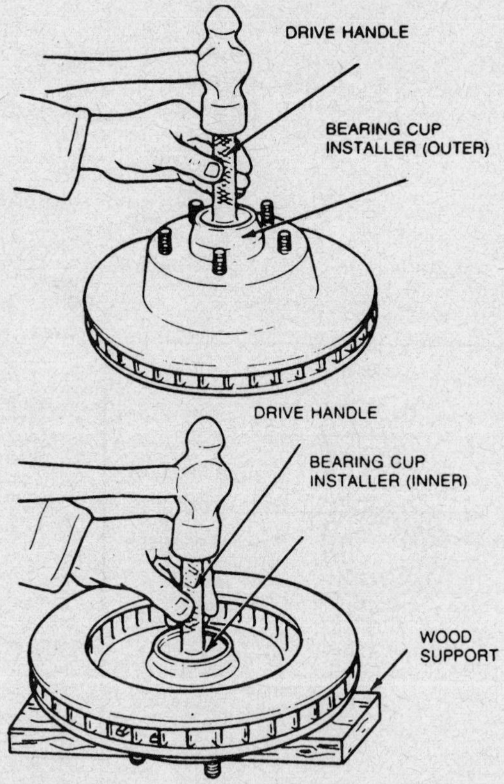

Fig. 3 Wheel bearing replacement

FRONT SUSPENSION

The front suspension, **Fig. 1,** is of the modified MacPherson strut design, which uses shock struts and coil springs. The springs are mounted between the lower control and a spring pocket in the crossmember.

WHEEL BEARINGS
ADJUST

1. Raise vehicle until wheel and tire clear floor.
2. Remove wheel cover and dust cap from hub.
3. Remove cotter pin and locknut.
4. Loosen adjusting nut 3 turns, then rock wheel, hub and rotor assembly in and out several times to move shoe and linings away from rotor.
5. While rotating wheel assembly, torque the adjusting nut to 17-25 ft. lbs. to seat the bearings, Fig. 2.
6. Back off the adjusting nut one half turn. Retighten the nut to 10-15 in. lbs. with a torque wrench or finger tight.
7. Locate the nut lock on the adjusting nut so the castellations on the lock are aligned with the cotter pin hole in the spindle.
8. Install new cotter pin and replace dust cap and wheel cover.

WHEEL BEARINGS
REPLACE

1. Raise vehicle and remove front wheels.
2. Remove caliper mounting bolts. **It is not necessary to disconnect the brake lines for this operation.**
3. Slide caliper off of disc, inserting a clean spacer between the shoes to hold them in their bores after the caliper is removed. Position caliper out of the way. **Do not allow caliper to hang by brake hose.**

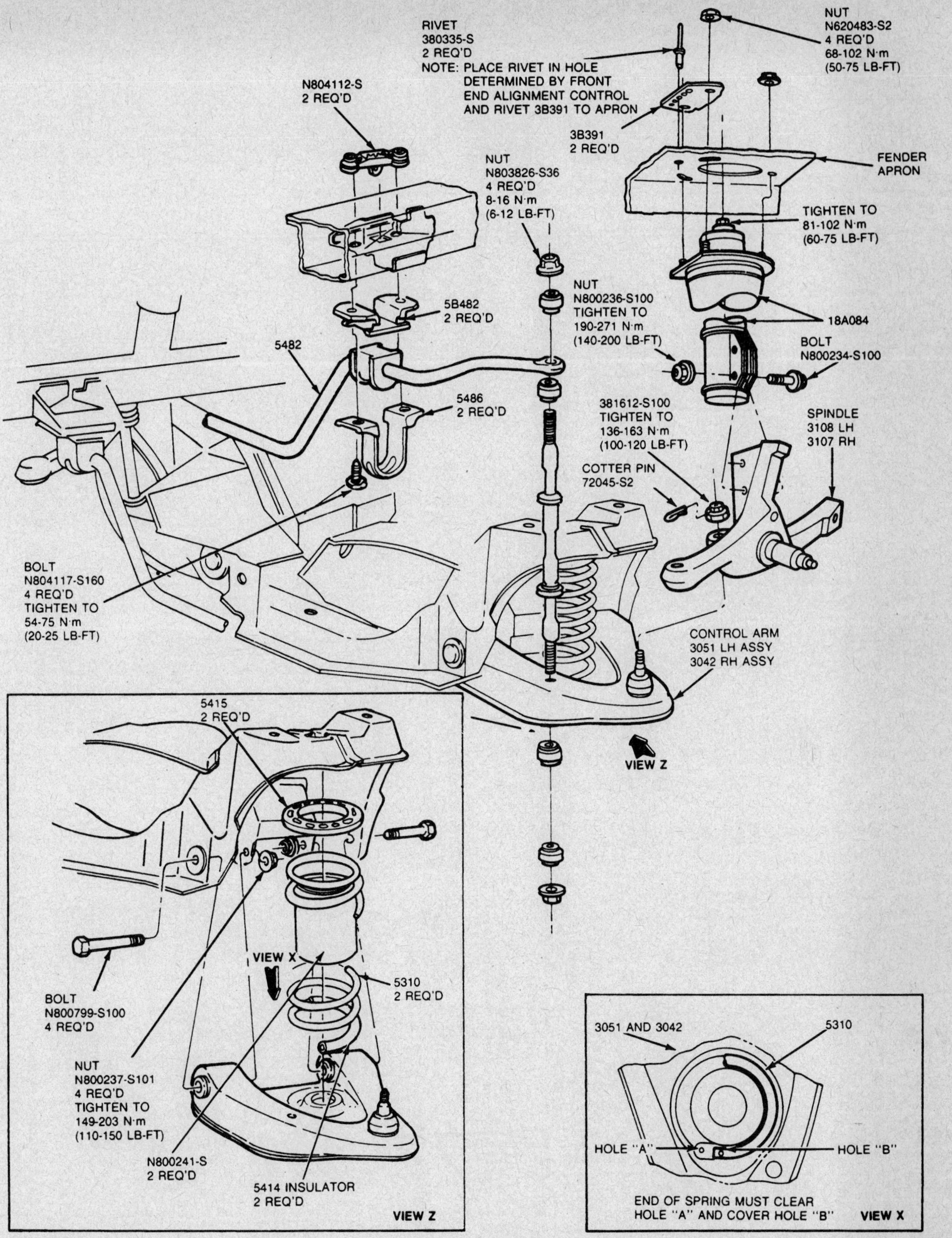

Fig. 1 Front suspension assembly

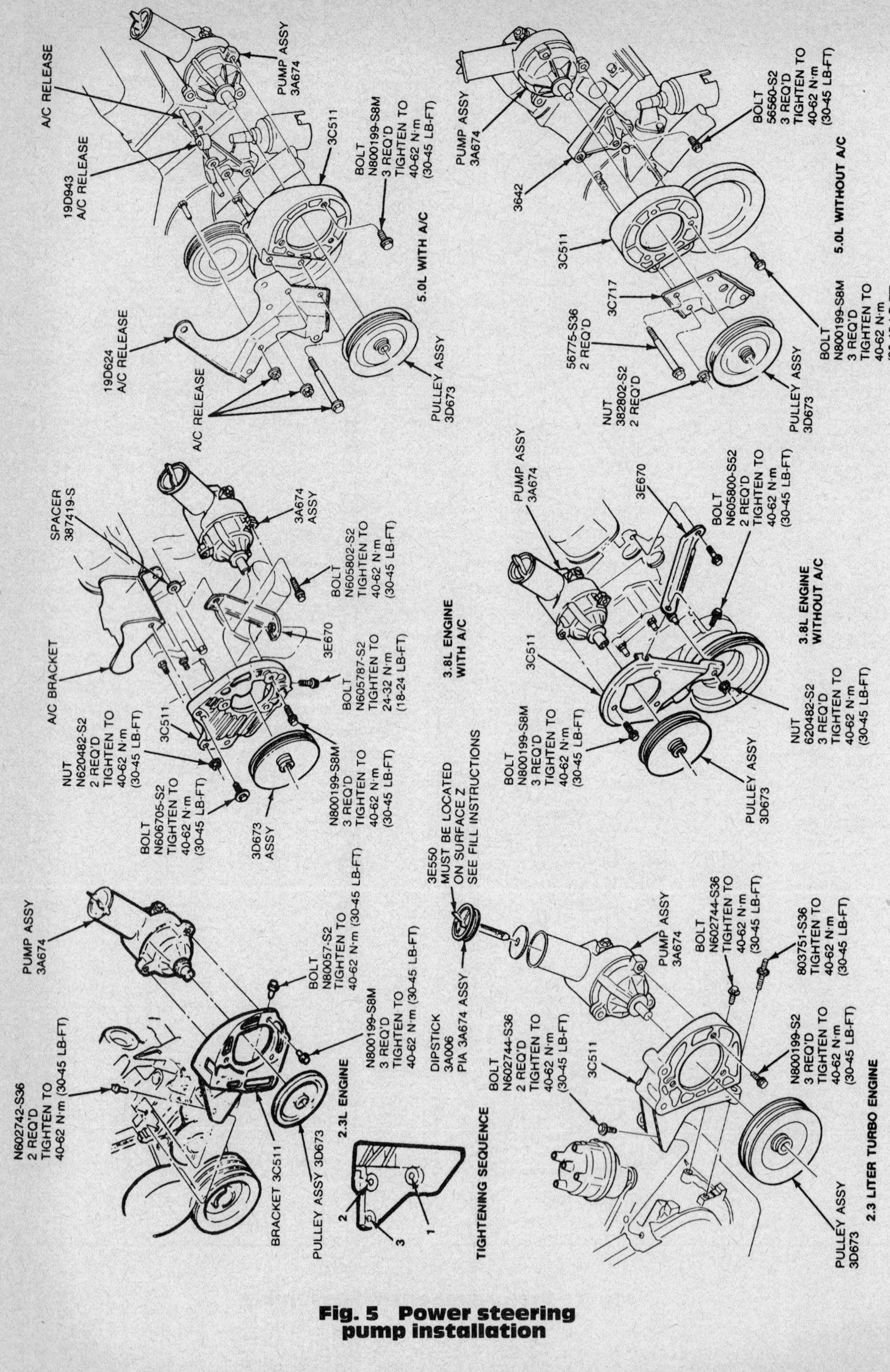

Fig. 5 Power steering pump installation

4. Remove hub and disc assembly. Grease retainer and inner bearing can now be removed, **Fig. 3.**
5. Reverse procedure to install.

CHECKING BALL JOINTS FOR WEAR

Support vehicle in normal driving position with both ball joints loaded. Clean area around grease fitting and checking surface. The checking surface is the round boss into which the grease fitting is installed. The checking surface should project outside the ball joint cover, **Fig. 4.** If checking surface is inside the cover replace the lower control arm assembly.

SHOCK STRUT
REPLACE

1. Place ignition switch in the unlocked position.
2. From engine compartment, remove upper shock absorber mounting nut.
3. Raise front of vehicle and support lower control arms. Position safety stands under frame jacking pads located rearward of wheels.
4. Remove wheel and tire assembly.
5. Remove caliper, rotor and dust shield.
6. Remove two bolts attaching shock absorber to spindle.
7. Lift strut upward from spindle to compress rod, then pull downward and remove shock absorber.
8. Remove jounce bumper, if equipped.
9. Reverse procedure to install. Torque upper mounting nut to 60-75 ft. lbs. on 1983-88 models. Torque lower mounting nuts to 150-180 ft. lbs. on 1982 models, or 120-179 ft. lbs. on except 1983-88 models. .

COIL SPRING
REPLACE

1. Raise front of vehicle and place safety stands under jack pads located rearward of wheels, then remove wheel and tire assembly.
2. Disconnect stabilizer bar link from lower control arm.
3. Remove steering gear attaching bolts and position gear out of way.
4. Using tool 3290-C, disconnect tie rod from spindle.
5. Install spring compressor T82P-5310A on 1982-88 models and compress coil spring until it is free of the spring seat. **Ensure spring compressor is properl y installed before compressing spring. Also ensure spring is sufficiently compressed to permit removal of lower control arm pivot bolts.**
6. Remove two lower control arm pivot bolts, then disengage lower control arm and remove spring assembly, **Fig. 1. Measure compressed length of spring and amount of curvature to aid in compressing and installing spring.**

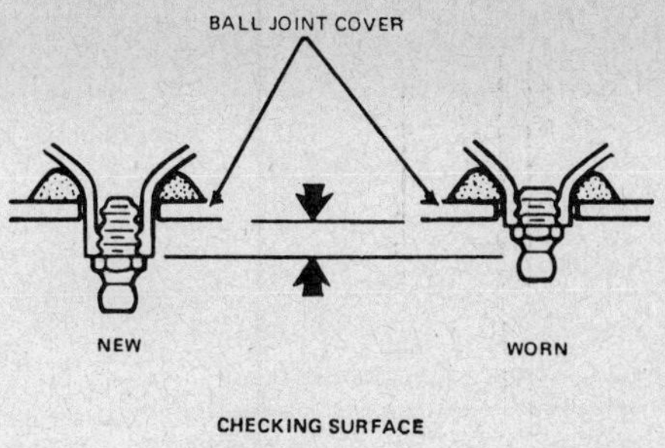

Fig. 4 Checking lower ball joint for wear

7. Reverse procedure to install. Ensure lower spring end is positioned between two holes in lower control arm spring pocket. Torque stabilizer bar to lower arm to 9 ft. lbs., steering gear to No. 2 crossmember to 35 ft. lbs.

BALL JOINTS
REPLACE

The lower ball joint and lower control arm must be replaced as an assembly.

CONTROL ARM
REPLACE

1. Raise and support vehicle, allowing control arm to hang freely.
2. Remove brake caliper, rotor and dust shield, then disconnect tie rod from spindle using suitable tool.
3. If necessary, remove steering gear attaching bolts and position gear as necessary to gain access to control arm attaching bolts.
4. Remove cotter pin, then loosen ball joint stud nut approximately two turns. **Do not remove stud nut at this time.**
5. Tap spindle boss with suitable mallet to disengage bail joint stud from spindle, then compress coil spring using suitable tool.
6. Remove ball joint stud nut, then raise strut and spindle assembly and wire in place to gain increased working area for control arm removal.
7. Remove control arm to crossmember pivot bolts and nuts, then the control arm.
8. Reverse procedure to install, noting the following:
   a. When installing coil spring, ensure lower spring end is positioned between the two holes in control arm spring pocket as shown in **Fig. 1.**
   b. Torque control arm attaching nuts to 130 ft. lbs., steering gear to crossmember attaching nuts to 95 ft. lbs., ball joint stud nut to 110 ft. lbs. and tie rod to spindle attaching nut to 35 ft. lbs.

STABILIZER BAR & INSULATOR
REPLACE

1. Raise and support vehicle.
2. Disconnect stabilizer bar from each link, the remove insulator attaching clamps, insulators and stabilizer bar from vehicle.
3. Reverse procedure to install. Torque attaching clamp to side rail retaining bolts to 48 ft. lbs. and stabilizer bar to link attaching nuts to 9 ft. lbs.

STEERING GEAR
REPLACE

1. Disconnect battery ground cable.
2. Remove bolt attaching flexible coupling to input shaft.
3. Place ignition switch in the On position, then raise and support front of vehicle.
4. Remove cotter pins and nuts from tie rod ends, then using a suitable tool separate tie rods from spindle arms.
5. Support steering gear, then remove two nuts, bolts and washers attaching steering gear to crossmember. On power steering gears, lower gear slightly and disconnect pressure and return lines. Cap lines and fittings to prevent entry of dirt.
6. Remove steering gear from vehicle.
7. Reverse procedure to install. Torque flexible coupling to input shaft bolt to 20-30 ft. lbs., tie rod to spindle arm nuts to 35-47 ft. lbs. and steering gear to crossmember bolts to 80-100 ft. lbs. Torque pressure line fitting at gear housing to 10-15 ft. lbs.

POWER STEERING PUMP
REPLACE

1. Disconnect return hose from power steering pump reservoir and allow fluid to drain into a suitable container.
2. Disconnect pressure hose from power steering pump fitting, then remove pump mounting bracket and disconnect drive belt from pulley.
3. On 2.3L, 3.8L and 5.0L engines which incorporate a fixed pump system, remove the belt from the pulley, and remove the pulley, **Fig. 5.**
4. On all models, remove power steering pump.
5. Reverse procedure to install. Torque pump to mounting bracket bolts to 30-45 ft. lbs. and pressure hose to pump tube nut to 10-15 ft. lbs. **Endplay of pressure hose to pump fitting is normal and does not indicate a loose fitting. Do not overtorque.**

Wheel Alignment Section

INDEX

FRONT WHEEL ALIGNMENT

CASTER

The caster angle of this suspension is factory pre-set and cannot be adjusted.

CAMBER

1. Remove pop rivet from camber plate.
2. Loosen 3 camber plate-to-body apron nuts.
3. Move top of shock strut as needed to bring camber angle within specifications, then tighten nuts. **It is not necessary to replace the pop rivet.**

TOE-IN, ADJUST

1. Check to see that steering shaft and steering wheel marks are in alignment and in the top position.
2. Loosen clamp screw on the tie rod bellows and free the seal on the rod to prevent twisting of the bellows, **Fig. 1.**
3. Loosen tie rod jam nut.
4. Use suitable pliers to turn the tie rod inner end to correct the adjustment to specifications. Do not use pliers on tie rod threads. Turning to reduce number of threads showing will increase toe-in. Turning in the opposite direction will reduce toe-in. On 1981 models, torque tie rod jam nuts to 35-50 ft. lbs. On 1982-86 models, torque to 43-50 ft. lbs.

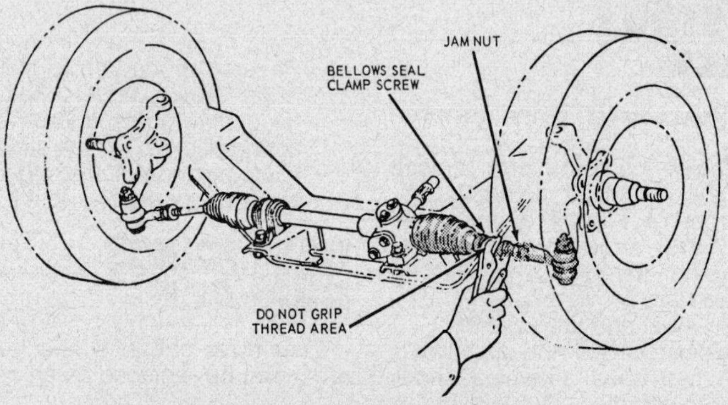

Fig. 1 Toe-in adjustment

FORD TAURUS & MERCURY SABLE

INDEX OF SERVICE OPERATIONS

NOTE: Refer to the rear of this manual for vehicle manufacturer's special service tools.

Specifications

GENERAL ENGINE SPECIFICATIONS

Year	Engine CID①/Liter	Engine VIN Code②	Fuel System	Bore & Stroke	Compression Ratio	Net H.P. @ RPM ③	Maximum Torque Ft. Lbs. @ RPM	Normal Oil Pressure Pounds
1986-88	4-153 (2.5L)	D	C.F.I.④	3.7 x 3.3	9.0	86 @ 4000	124 @ 2800	55-60⑥
	V6-182 (3.0L)	U	E.F.I.⑤	3.5 x 3.1	9.2	140 @ 4800	160 @ 3000	55-60⑥
1988	V6-232 (3.8L)	—	E.F.I.	3.8 x 3.4	9.0	140 @ 3800	215 @ 2200	40-60⑥

①—CID-Cubic inch displacement.
②—The eighth digit of the V.I.N. denotes engine code.
③—Ratings are net-as installed in vehicle.
④—Central (single point) Fuel Injection.
⑤—Electronic (multi-point) Fuel Injection.
⑥—At 2000 RPM.

ENGINE TIGHTENING SPECIFICATIONS*

*Torque specifications are for clean and lightly lubricated threads only. Dry or dirty threads produce increased friction which prevents accurate measurement of tightness.

Year	Engine/VIN	Spark Plugs Ft. Lbs.	Cylinder Head Bolts Ft. Lbs.	Intake Manifold Ft. Lbs.	Exhaust Manifold Ft. Lbs.	Rocker Arm Ft. Lbs.	Rocker Arm Cover Ft. Lbs.	Connecting Rod Cap Nuts Ft. Lbs.	Main Bearings Cap Bolts Ft. Lbs.	Flywheel to Crankshaft Ft. Lbs.	Vibration Damper or Pulley Ft. Lbs.
1986-88	4-153/D	5-10	①	15-23	②	③	7-10	21-26	51-66	54-64	140-170
	V6-182/U	5-11	④	⑤	15-22	⑥	⑦	⑧	65-81	54-64	140-170
1988	V6-232/	5-11	—	—	—	⑦	—	—	—	—	—

①—First step, tighten to 52-59 ft. lbs.; second step, tighten to 70-76 ft. lbs.
②—First step, tighten to 5-7 ft. lbs.; second step, tighten to 20-30 ft. lbs.
③—First step, tighten to 4.5-7.5 ft. lbs.; second step, tighten to 19.5-26.5 ft. lbs.
④—First step, tighten to 48-54 ft. lbs.; second step, tighten to 63-80 ft. lbs.
⑤—First step, tighten to 11 ft. lbs.; second step, 18 ft. lbs.; third step, 24 ft. lbs.
⑥—First step, 5-11 ft. lbs.; second step, 18-26 ft. lbs.
⑦—80-106 inch lbs.
⑧—Tighten to 20-28 ft. lbs.; then back off at least two complete turns and retighten to 20-25 ft. lbs.

ALTERNATOR & REGULATOR SPECIFICATIONS

Year	Stamp Color Code	Current Rating Amperes	Current Rating Volts	Voltage Regulator
1986-88	①	70	15	External
	①	100	15	External
	Orange, Red① ②	40	15	Internal
	Green① ②	60	15	Internal
	Black① ②	65	15	Internal

①—Side terminal alternator.
②—Stamp color code.

STARTING MOTOR APPLICATIONS

Year	Engine/V.I.N.	Ident. No.
1986-88	4-153/D	—
	V6-182/U	—

FRONT WHEEL ALIGNMENT SPECIFICATIONS

Year	Model	Caster Angle, Degrees		Camber Angle, Degrees				Toe-In Inch
				Limits		Desired		
		Limits	Desired	Left	Right	Left	Right	
1986-87	Sable Sedan	+2⅞ to 5⅞	+3⅞	−1 1/16 to +1/16	−1 1/16 to +1/16	−½	−½	−3/32
	Taurus Sedan	+3 to +6	+4	−1 1/16 to +1/16	−1 1/16 to +1/16	−½	−½	−3/32
	Wagon	+2 13/16 to +5 13/16	+3 13/16	−1 1/32 to +5/32	−1 1/32 to +5/32	−7/16	−7/16	−3/32
1988	Sedan	+3.0 to +6.0	+4.5	—	—	−.50	−.50	.10
	Wagon	+2.8 to +5.8	+3.8	—	—	−.44	−.50	.10

REAR WHEEL ALIGNMENT SPECIFICATIONS

Year	Model	Camber Angle, Degrees		Toe-In Inch
		Limits	Desired	
1986-87	Sable Sedan	−1 9/16 to −3/16	−⅞	1/16
	Taurus Sedan	−1⅝ to −¼	−15/16	1/16
	Wagon	−1 5/16 to 1/16	−⅝	1/16
1988	Sedan	−.24 to −1.64	−.94	+.06
	Wagon	−.2 to −.16	−.9	+.06

COOLING SYSTEM & CAPACITY DATA

Year	Model	Engine/VIN	Cooling Capacity, Qts.		Radiator Cap Relief Pressure, Lbs.	Thermo. Opening Temp.	Fuel Tank Gals.	Engine Oil Refill, Qts.	Transaxle Capacity	
			Less A/C	With A/C					Manual Pts.	Automatic Qts.①
1986-88	Sedan	4-153/D	8.3	8.3	16	192	16	4②	6.1	8.1
	Sedan	V6-182/U	11.0	11.0	16	197	16	4②	—	10.4
	Wagon	V6-182/U	11.8	11.8	16	197	16	4②	—	10.4
1988	Sedan	V6-232/	12	12	16	197	16	4②	—	—
	Wagon	V6-232/	12	12	16	197	16	4②	—	—

①—Approximate, make final check with dipstick.
②—Add ½ qt. with filter change.

Electrical Section

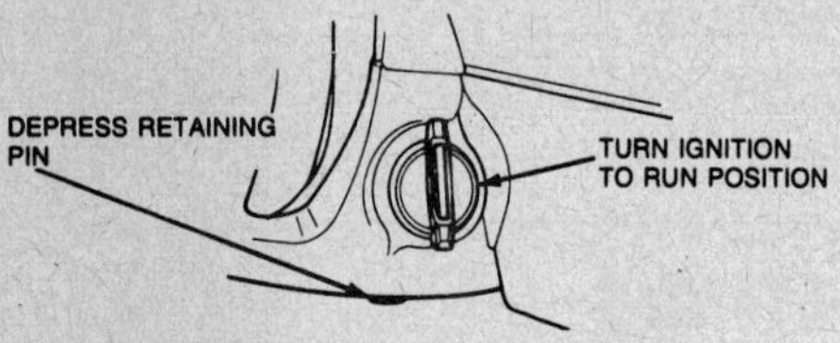

Fig. 1 Ignition lock cylinder removal

STARTER
REPLACE

If the starter motor is noisy or if it locks up, before condemning the starter, loosen the mounting bolts enough to hand fit the starter properly into the pilot plate. Tighten the mounting bolts, starting with the top one.

1. Disconnect battery ground cable, then the starter electrical cable.
2. Remove cable support and ground cable connection from upper starter stud bolt.
3. Remove starter brace from cylinder block and starter.
4. Remove starter mounting bolts, then on models equipped with auto. trans., remove starter from between sub-frame and radiator. On models equipped with man. trans., remove starter from between sub-frame and engine.
5. Reverse procedure to install.

IGNITION LOCK
REPLACE

1. Disconnect battery ground cable.
2. Rotate ignition switch to the Run position, then working through steering column lower shroud, **Fig. 1,** depress lock cylinder retaining pin with suitable 1/8 inch drill.
3. Pull ignition lock cylinder from housing.
4. Install replacement lock cylinder in housing, then rotate ignition switch through travel.
5. Install battery ground cable, then ensure ignition lock operates properly.

IGNITION SWITCH
REPLACE

1. Remove ignition lock as outlined elsewhere in this section.
2. On models equipped with tilt columns, remove tilt release lever attaching screw then the lever.
3. Remove lower instrument panel attaching screws, then the panel.
4. Remove steering column shroud attaching screws, then the shroud.
5. Remove steering column to support bracket attaching nuts and bolts, then lower steering column.
6. Disconnect ignition switch electrical connector, **Fig. 2.**
7. Remove lock actuator cover plate attaching bolt, **Fig. 3,** then the cover plate. **The lock actuator assembly is free to slide out of cylinder housing.**
8. Remove ignition switch attaching screws, then the ignition switch, **Fig. 4.**
9. Ensure replacement ignition switch is in the RUN position by fully rotating driveshaft clockwise to Start position and releasing.
10. Install lock actuator assembly to a depth of .46-.54 inch from the bottom of actuator assembly to bottom of lock cylinder housing.
11. While holding actuator at proper depth, install ignition switch and cover. Attach with two tamper-resistant Torx head screws. Torque screws to 30-48 inch lbs.
12. Install lock cylinder, then rotate ignition switch to the Lock position. Measure depth of actuator assembly as outlined in step 10 above. Actuator assembly must be .92-1.00 inch inside lock cylinder housing. If measurement is not within specifications, actuator assembly must be removed and reinstalled.
13. Install lock actuator cover plate with tamper-resistant Torx head screw. Torque screw to 30-48 inch lbs.
14. Install ignition switch electrical connector, then connect battery ground cable.
15. Ensure ignition switch works properly at all functions and the steering column locks functions properly.

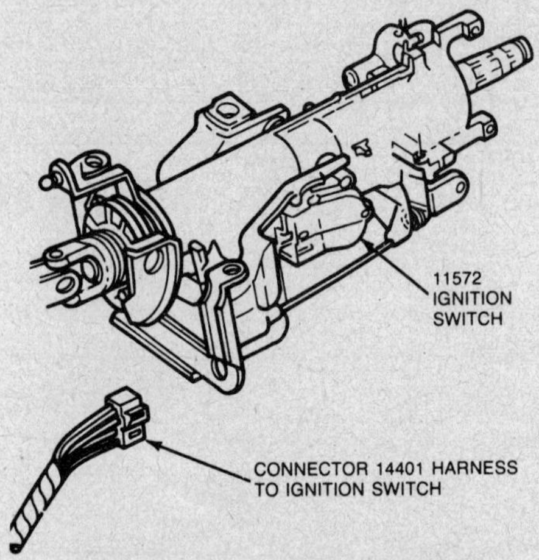

Fig. 2 Ignition switch electrical connector removal

16. Remove ignition lock cylinder as outlined elsewhere in this section.
17. Align steering column mounting bracket with steering column bracket and install mounting bolts and nuts. Torque to 15-25 ft. lbs.
18. Install steering column shrouds, then instrument panel lower cover.
19. On models equipped with tilt columns, install tilt lever and tilt lever mounting screw. Torque screw to 6.5-8.5 inch lbs.
20. Install ignition lock cylinder.

LIGHT SWITCH
REPLACE
SABLE

1. Disconnect battery ground cable.
2. Remove lower lefthand side finish panel.
3. Remove two headlight switch attaching screws, then disconnect switch electrical connector.
4. Remove light switch.
5. Reverse procedure to install.

TAURUS

1. Disconnect battery ground cable.
2. Pull off light switch knob.

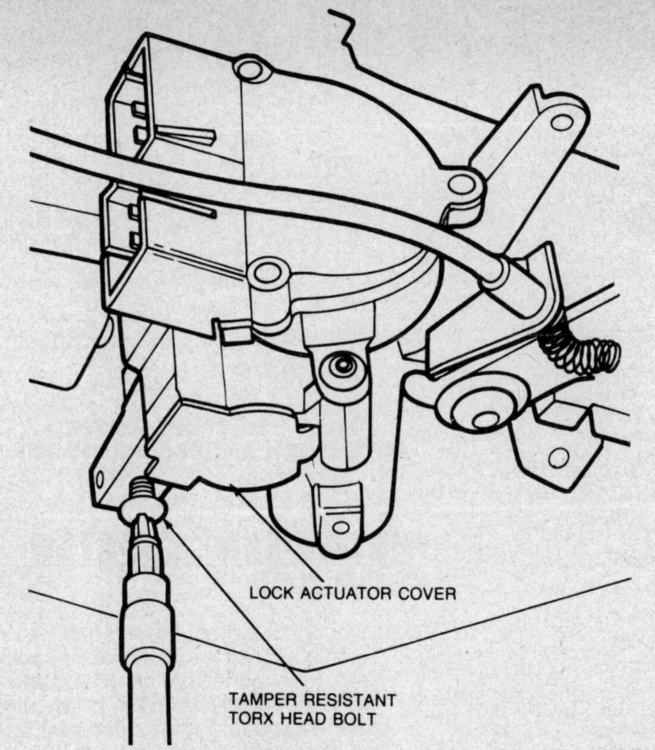

Fig. 3 Lock actuator cover plate removal

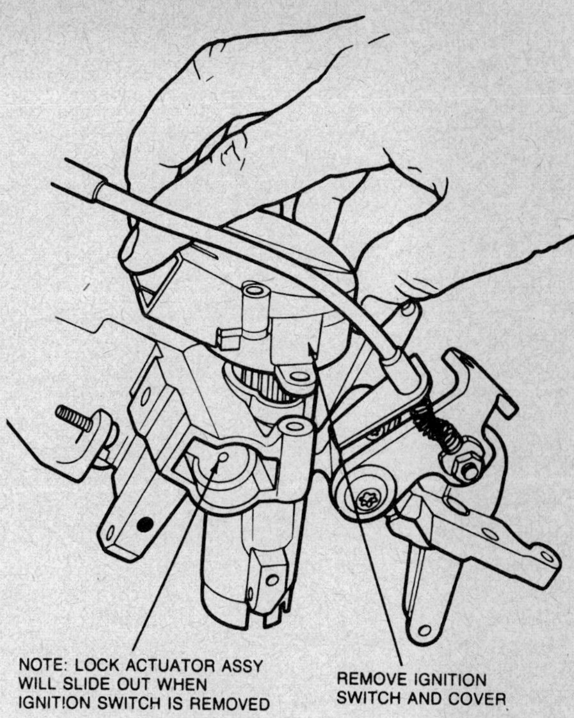

Fig. 4 Ignition switch removal

3. Remove bezel retaining nut, then the bezel.
4. Remove instrument cluster finish panel.
5. Remove two headlight switch attaching screws, then pull switch out of instrument panel and disconnect electrical connector. Remove switch.
6. Reverse procedure to install.

STOP LIGHT SWITCH
REPLACE

1. Lift stop light switch wire harness connector locking tab, then remove wire connector.
2. Remove hairpin retainer and white nylon washer, then slide switch and pushrod assembly away from brake pedal. Remove switch by sliding up and/or down. **Since switch side plate nearest switch is slotted, it is not necessary to remove master cylinder pushrod, black bushing or one white bushing, nearest the brake pedal from brake pedal pin, Fig. 5.**
3. Position switch so U-shaped side is nearest brake pedal and directly over brake pedal pin. **The black bushing must be in position in pushrod eyelet with washer face on side away from pedal arm.**
4. Slide switch up and down as necessary to trap black plastic bushing and pushrod between the two side plates of the switch, then push switch and pushrod assembly towards brake pedal arm.
5. Install white nylon washer on pedal pin, then the hairpin retainer. **Do not**

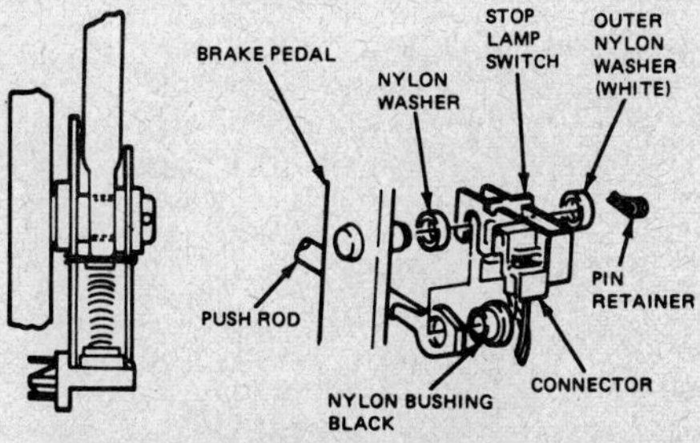

Fig. 5 Brake light switch installation

substitute other types of pin retainers. Replace only with production type hairpin retainer.

6. Connect wire harness connector to switch, then check stop lights for proper operation. The brake lights should illuminate with less than 6 lbs. of force applied at the brake pedal pad.

MULTI-FUNCTION SWITCH
REPLACE

1. Disconnect battery ground cable.
2. On models equipped with tilt steering column, move column to lowest position and remove tilt lever attaching screw and the lever.
3. On all models, remove ignition lock as outlined elsewhere in this section.
4. Remove upper and lower steering column shrouds.
5. Remove wiring harness retainer, then the three multi-function switch wiring connectors, **Fig. 6.**
6. Remove multi-function switch attaching screws, then disengage switch from casting and remove.
7. Reverse procedure to install, noting the following:
   a. Torque multi-function attaching screws to 18-27 ft. lbs.
   b. Torque tilt lever attaching screw (if equipped) to 6-8.5 inch lbs.

STARTER/CLUTCH INTERLOCK SWITCH
REPLACE
MAN. TRANS. VEHICLES ONLY

1. Disconnect battery ground cable.
2. Remove panel above clutch pedal, then disconnect starter/clutch interlock switch wiring.
3. Remove starter/clutch interlock switch attaching screw and hairpin clip, then remove switch.
4. Depress barb at end of rod, then pull rod from clutch pedal.
5. Install switch with self-adjusting clip about one inch from end of rod. **During installation of switch, the clutch pedal must be fully up, otherwise the switch may become misadjusted.**
6. Insert eyelet end of rod over clutch pedal pin, then install hairpin clip, **Fig. 7.**
7. Align switch mounting hole with mounting bracket hole, then install and tighten attaching screw.
8. Adjust starter/clutch interlock switch by pressing clutch pedal to floor.
9. Connect wiring connector, then install

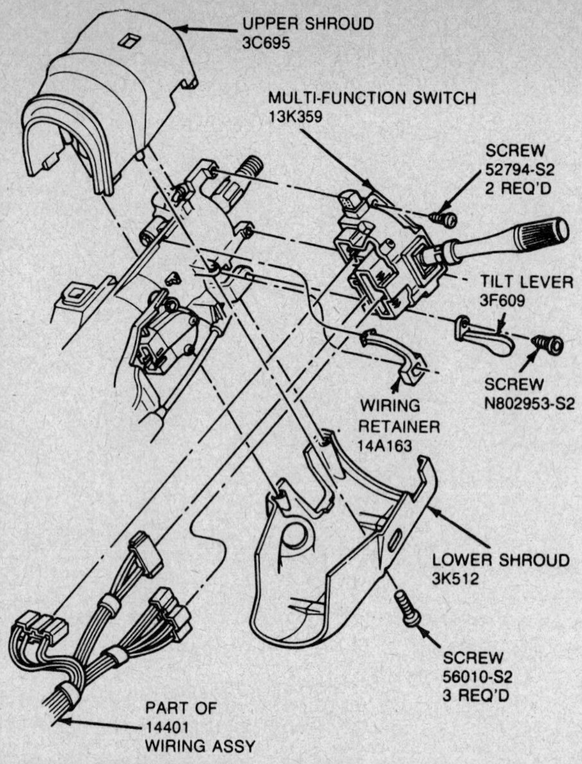

Fig. 6 Multi-function switch replacement

panel above clutch pedal.
10. Connect battery ground cable, then check switch for proper operation.

NEUTRAL SAFETY SWITCH
REPLACE

1. Disconnect battery ground cable.
2. Set shift lever in Neutral position.
3. Remove linkage from transmission manual shift lever.
4. Disconnect neutral safety switch wiring connector.
5. Remove neutral safety switch attaching bolts, then the switch.
6. Install replacement switch on manual shaft.
7. Install neutral safety switch attaching bolts. Do not tighten at this time.
8. Insert a No. 43 (.089 inch) drill bit through hole provided in switch.
9. Torque attaching bolts to 7-9 inch lbs., then remove drill bit.
10. Connect neutral safety switch wiring connector, then battery negative terminal.
11. Ensure starter operates in Neutral and Park positions only.

HORN SOUNDER
REPLACE

1. Disconnect battery ground cable.
2. Remove two screws from back of steering wheel spokes.
3. Pull hub cover from steering wheel, then disconnect wires. Remove steering wheel hub cover and horn switch assembly.
4. Reverse procedure to install.

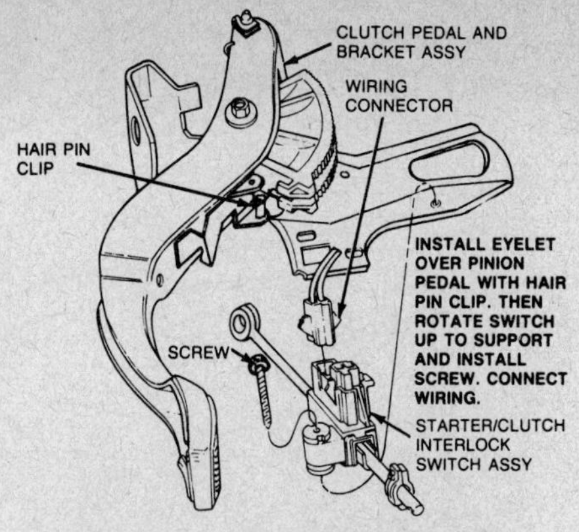

Fig. 7 Starter/clutch interlock switch removal

INSTRUMENT CLUSTER
REPLACE

1. Disconnect battery ground cable.
2. To gain access to speedometer cable, drop fuse panel on its hinge, then reach behind instrument panel and disengage cable from cluster by depressing cable latch.
3. Remove instrument cluster finish panel retaining screws, then the panel, Fig. 8.

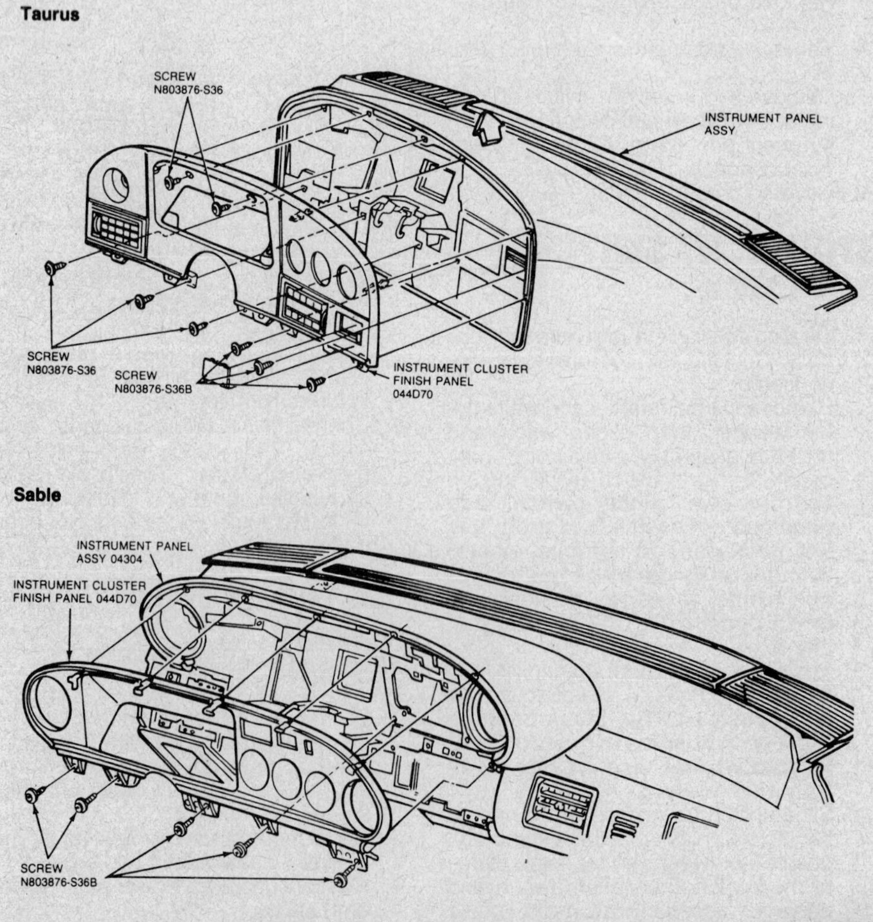

Fig. 8 Instrument cluster removal

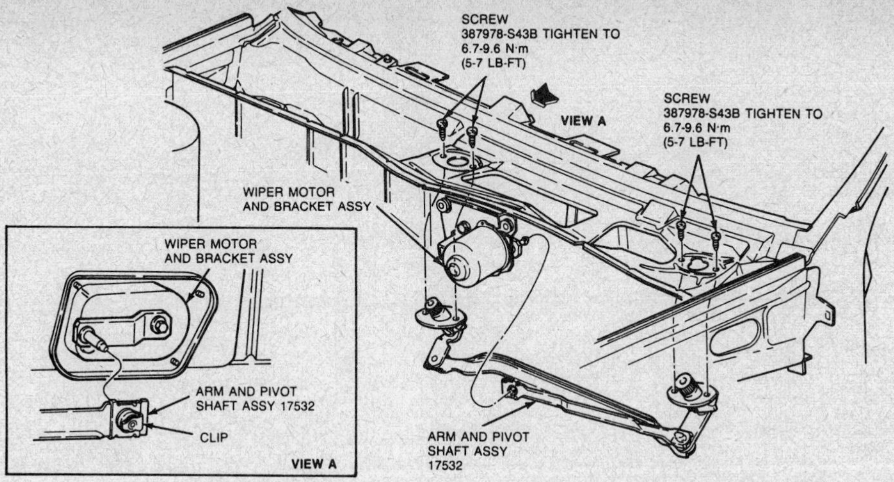

Fig. 9 Windshield wiper transmission removal

4. Remove steering column shroud.
5. On Sable models with tachometer cluster, remove lower trim panel attaching screws, then the panel.
6. On all models, remove lens and mask mounting screws, then the lens and mask assembly.
7. On Sable models with tachometer cluster, remove two lower floodlamp bulb and socket assemblies.
8. Pull main dial assembly from backplate. Due to quick disconnect wiring connectors, some e effort may be required to pull dial assembly.
9. On models equipped with column shift auto. trans., remove trans. selector indicator attaching screws, then the indicator.
10. Remove instrument cluster attaching screws, then the instrument cluster.
11. Reverse procedure to install.

WINDSHIELD WIPER MOTOR

REPLACE

FRONT

1. Disconnect battery ground cable.
2. Disconnect wiper motor electrical connector.
3. Remove left side wiper arm. Lift water shield cover from passenger side cowl.
4. Remove linkage retaining clip from wiper motor arm.
5. Remove wiper motor attaching bolts, then the wiper motor.
6. Reverse procedure to install. Torque wiper motor attaching bolts to 60-85 inch lbs.

REAR

1. Disconnect battery ground cable, then remove wiper arm and blade.
2. Remove pivot shaft attaching nut and washers, then disconnect wiper motor electrical connector. **Pull connector only. Do not pull wires.**
3. Remove wiper motor attaching nut, then the motor.
4. Reverse procedure to install.

WINDSHIELD WIPER SWITCH

REPLACE

FRONT

The Windshield wiper switch is an integral part of the multi-function switch. For replacement procedures, refer to "Multi-Function Switch, Replace."

REAR

1. Remove four instrument cluster finish panel attaching screws, then remove by rocking upper edge of finish panel towards drivers seat.
2. Disconnect rear washer switch wiring connector.
3. Remove washer switch from instrument panel.
4. Reverse procedure to install.

WINDSHIELD WIPER TRANSMISSION

REPLACE

1. Disconnect battery ground cable.
2. Remove wiper arm and blade assemblies from windshield wiper pivot arms.
3. Remove leaf screens from both sides of cowl.
4. Remove linkage drive arm-to-motor crank arm retaining clip, then separate linkage drive arm from motor crank arm, **Fig. 9.**
5. Remove pivot arm-to-cowl attaching screws, then withdraw windshield wiper transmission from cowl chamber.
6. Reverse procedure to install. Torque pivot arm attaching screws to 60-84 inch lbs.

RADIO

REPLACE

1. Disconnect battery ground cable.
2. On Taurus models, remove radio opening finish panel attaching screw (in lower part of panel), then, on Taurus and Sable models, remove radio finish panel by snapping out.
3. Remove radio bracket-to-instrument panel attaching screws, then push radio to front and raise back end of radio slightly so rear support bracket clears clip in instrument panel. Carefully remove radio from instrument panel.
4. Disconnect radio wiring connector and antenna lead.
5. Reverse procedure to install.

HEATER CORE

REPLACE

1. Disconnect battery ground cable.
2. Drain cooling system into suitable container.
3. Disconnect heater hoses from heater core, then plug heater core tubes.
4. Disconnect vacuum supply hose from inline check valve located in engine compartment.
5. On Taurus models, proceed as follows:
   a. Remove steering column opening cover attaching screws, then the cover.
   b. Remove round insulator in cowl area.
   c. Remove steering column trim shrouds, then disconnect steering column switches electrical connectors.
   d. Remove steering column mounting bracket mounting screws, then lower steering column.
   e. Remove radio opening finish panel attaching screw (in lower part of panel), then, remove radio finish panel by snapping out.
   f. Remove seven cluster opening finish panel retaining screws, one jam nut behind headlamp switch knob and one screw behind clock or clock cover. Remove finish panel by rocking its upper edge towards driver's seat.
   g. Swing fuse panel downward to provide access to speedometer cable, then press on speedometer cable connector flat to release cable.
   h. Using glove compartment and steering column openings for access, disconnect electrical connections, vacuum hoses, heater and A/C (if equipped) control cables and radio antenna cable.
   i. Remove two lower instrument panel-to-cowl side retaining screws both both sides of instrument panel.
   j. Disconnect under hood connectors from main wiring harness. Disengage main harness rubber grommet from dash panel, then

feed wiring harness and its connector halves into instrument panel area.
k. Remove two instrument panel brace attaching screws located near bottom of radio.
l. Snap out left and right front speaker opening covers, then remove upper instrument panel attaching screws.
m. Remove instrument panel and lay it on front seat.
6. On Sable models, proceed as follows:
a. Disconnect battery ground cable.
b. Remove steering column opening cover attaching screws, then the cover.
c. Remove steering column trim shrouds, then disconnect steering column switches electrical connectors.
d. Remove one bolt and nut at lock pillar U-joint and steering column mounting bracket mounting screws, then lower steering column.
e. Snap out lower finish panels, then remove cluster opening finish panel attaching screws. Remove finish panel by disengaging five hidden retainers located along upper edge. Free panel by rocking upper edge towards driver, then remove panel with instrument cluster attached.
f. Pivot glove compartment assembly downward by depressing side of glove compartment tray.
g. Using glove compartment and steering column openings for access, disconnect electrical connections, vacuum hoses, heater and A/C (if equipped) control cables and radio antenna cable.
h. Disconnect under hood connectors from main wiring harness. Disengage main harness rubber grommet from dash panel, then feed wiring harness and its connector halves into instrument panel area.
i. Remove two lower instrument panel-to-cowl side attaching screws from right and left sides of instrument panel.
j. Remove two instrument panel brace attaching screws located near bottom of radio.
k. Snap out left and right front speaker opening covers, then remove upper instrument panel attaching screws.
l. Remove instrument panel and lay it on front seat.
7. On all models, remove instrument panel to heater case shake brace attaching screw, then the instrument panel shake brace.
8. Remove floor register to heater case attaching bolts, then the floor register.
9. Remove heater case-to-dash panel attaching nuts located in engine compartment.

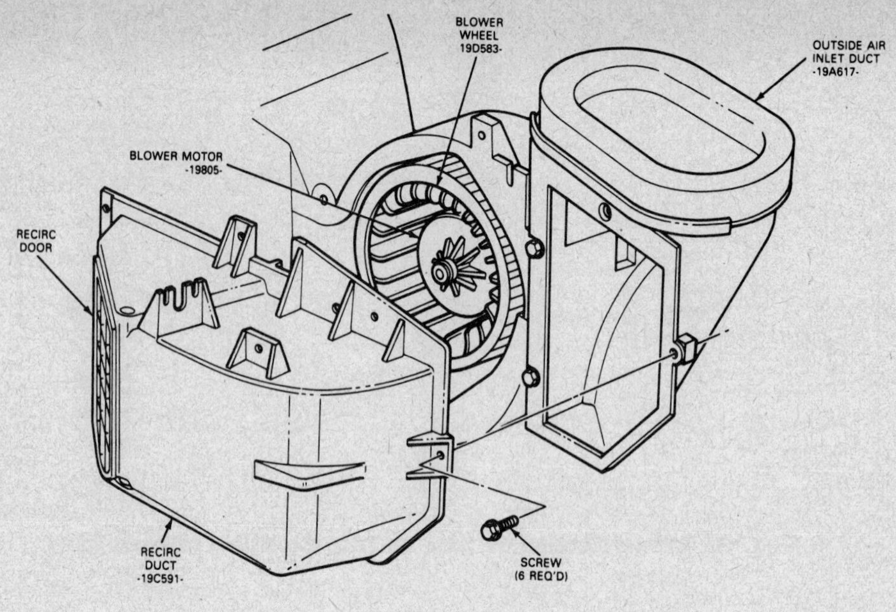

Fig. 10 Blower motor removal

when the brake pedal is not depressed and opens when the brake pedal is depressed.
10. Remove screws attaching top brackets to cowl top panel, then carefully pull heater assembly from dash panel and remove from vehicle.
11. Remove vacuum source line from heater core tube seal, then remove heater core tube seal.
12. Remove heater core access cover attaching screws, then the access cover.
13. Remove heater core and seals from heater case.
14. Reverse procedure to install.

BLOWER MOTOR REPLACE

1. Disconnect battery ground cable.
2. Open glove compartment door, then release retainers and allow glove box door to swing downward. Remove recirculation duct support bracket-to-cowl attaching screw, then the recirculation door motor vacuum connection.
3. Remove six recirculation duct-to-heater case attaching screws, **Fig. 10**, then lower duct from between instrument panel and heater case and remove.
4. Disconnect blower motor electrical connection.
5. Remove blower wheel attaching clip and the blower wheel.
6. Remove blower motor attaching bolts, then the blower motor from the evaporator case.
7. Reverse procedure to install.

SPEED CONTROLS

ACTUATOR ADJUSTMENT

4-153 Engine

1. Remove locking pin.
2. Pull bead chain through adjuster.
3. Insert locking pin in adjuster hole that provides a tight bead chain without opening throttle plate.

V6-182 Engine

1. Remove speed control actuator cable locking clip.
2. Push actuator cable through adjuster until a slight tension is felt.
3. Install cable locking clip and snap into place.

CLUTCH SWITCH, ADJUST

This adjustment is for vehicles equipped with man. trans. and cruise control.
1. Prop clutch pedal in full up position with pawl fully released from the sector.
2. Loosen clutch switch mounting screw.
3. Slide switch as necessary to establish a dimension of .030 inch between switch plunger cap and contacting switch housing, then tighten mounting screw.
4. Test drive vehicle to ensure cancellation of speed control when clutch pedal is depressed.

VACUUM DUMP VALVE

The vacuum dump valve is mounted on a movable mounting bracket. The valve should be adjusted so that it is closed

4-153 (2.5L) Engine Section

INDEX

ENGINE MOUNTS

REPLACE

LH INSULATOR & SUPPORT ASSEMBLY

Models Equipped W/Auto. Trans.

1. Raise and support vehicle, then remove left front wheel and tire assembly.
2. Support transmission with suitable jack and block of wood positioned near insulator.
3. Remove insulator-to-support assembly attaching nuts, **Fig. 1**.
4. Remove insulator-to-frame through bolts, then using jack, raise transmission enough to unload insulator.
5. Remove support assembly-to-transmission attaching bolts, then remove insulator and/or transmission support assembly.
6. Reverse procedure to install, noting the following:
   a. Torque support assembly-to-transmission attaching bolts to 40-55 ft. lbs.
   b. Torque insulator-to-frame and insulator-to-support attaching bolts to 70-96 ft. lbs.

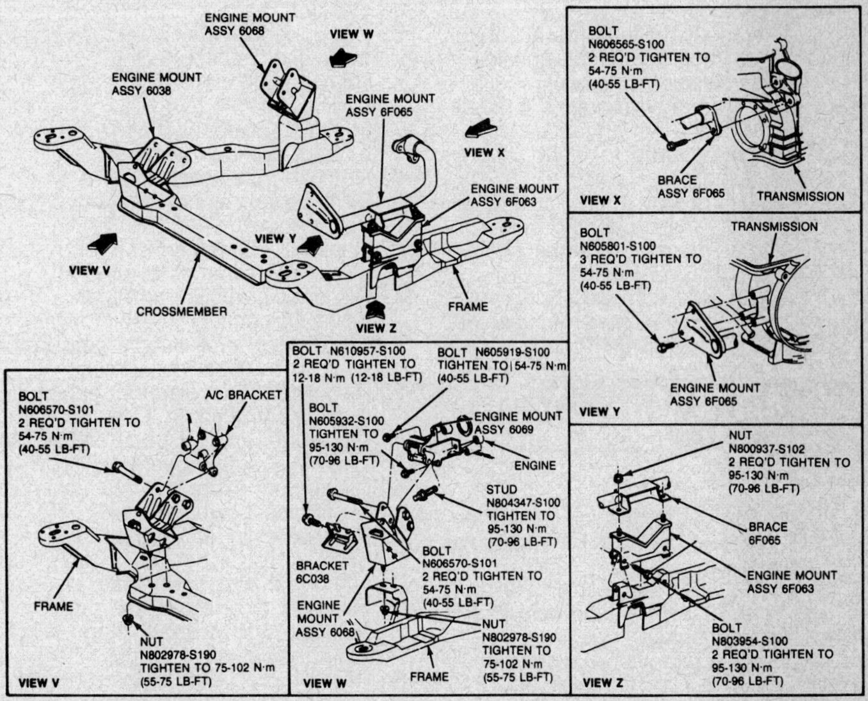

Fig. 1 Engine mounts. Models equipped w/auto. trans.

Models Equipped W/Man. Trans.

1. Raise and support vehicle, then remove left front wheel and tire assembly.
2. Support transmission with suitable jack and block of wood positioned near insulator.
3. Remove insulator-to-frame attaching bolts, **Fig. 2**, then using jack, raise transmission enough to unload insulator.
4. Remove insulator-to-transmission attaching bolts, then the mount.
5. Reverse procedure to install. Torque attaching bolts to 70-96 ft. lbs.

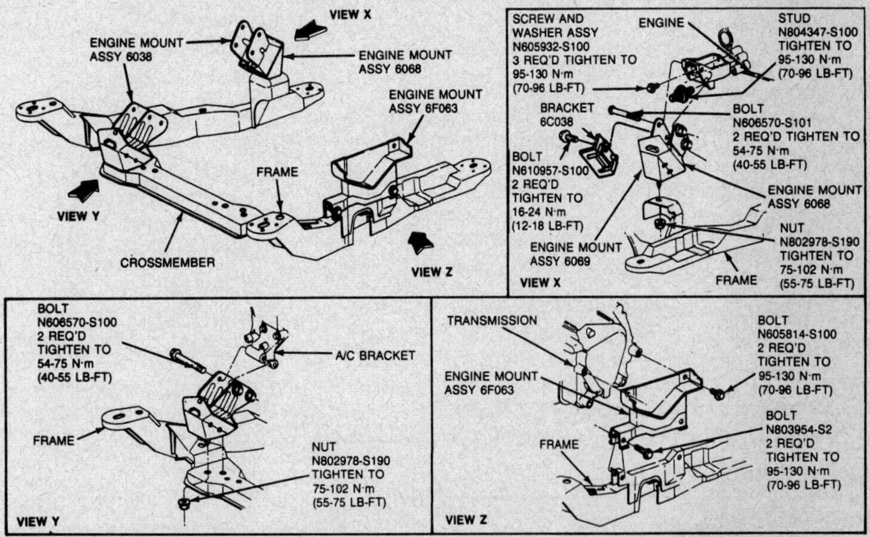

Fig. 2 Engine mounts. Models equipped w/man. trans.

RH FRONT OR REAR INSULATOR

1. On models equipped with man. trans.,

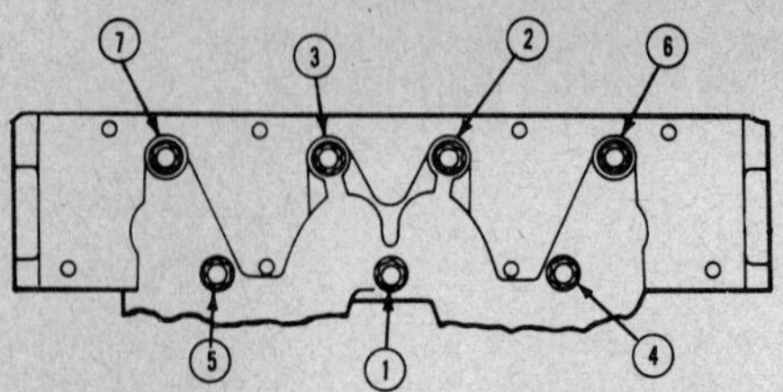

Fig. 3 Exhaust manifold bolt tightening sequence

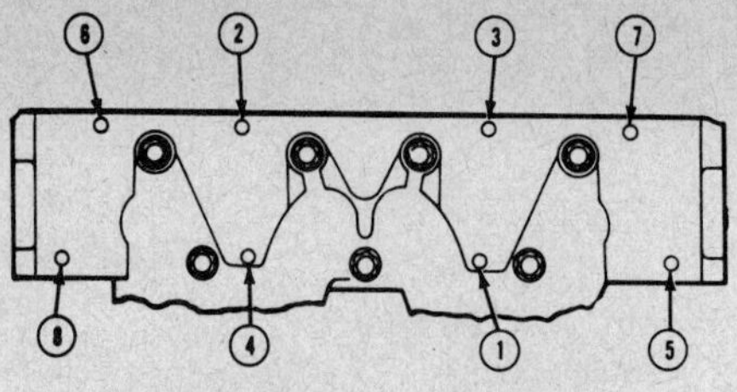

Fig. 4 Intake manifold bolt tightening sequence

remove damper nut from right side of engine.

2. On all models, raise and support vehicle, then support engine with suitable jack and block of wood positioned near insulator.
3. Remove insulator-to-frame attaching nut, **Figs. 1 and 2**, then raise engineenough to unload insulator.
4. Remove insulator-to-engine bracket attaching bolts, then the insulator.
5. Reverse procedure to install, noting the following:
   a. Torque insulator-to-engine bracket attaching bolts to 40-55 ft. lbs.
   b. Torque insulator-to-frame attaching nut to 55-75 ft. lbs.
   c. On models equipped with man. trans., torque damper-to-engine attaching nut to 8-12 ft. lbs.

INTAKE & EXHAUST MANIFOLDS
REPLACE

1. Disconnect battery ground cable, then drain cooling system into suitable container.
2. Remove accelerator cable, then the air cleaner assembly and heat stove tube at heat shield.
3. Identify, then remove necessary vacuum lines.
4. Remove Thermactor belt, hose and pump assembly.
5. Remove exhaust pipe-to-exhaust manifold nuts, then the manifold heat shroud.
6. Disconnect Exhaust Gas Oxygen (EGO) sensor wire connector.
7. Disconnect Thermactor check valve hose at tube assembly, then remove bracket-to-EGR valve attaching nuts.
8. Disconnect water inlet hose at intake manifold, then the EGR tube at EGR valve.
9. Remove intake manifold attaching bolts, then the intake manifold and gasket.
10. Remove exhaust manifold attaching bolts, then the exhaust manifold.
11. Reverse procedure to install. Refer to Engine Tightening Specifications for torque values and **Figs. 3 and 4**, for tightening sequence.

CYLINDER HEAD
REPLACE

1. Disconnect battery ground cable.
2. Remove lower radiator hose and drain coolant from engine.
3. Disconnect heater hose from fitting located under intake manifold.
4. Disconnect upper radiator hose from cylinder head.
5. Disconnect electric cooling fan switch from electrical connector.
6. Remove air cleaner assembly from engine.
7. Mark and disconnect all vacuum hoses from cylinder head.
8. Remove rocker arm cover.
9. Remove all accessory drive belts from engine.
10. Remove distributor cap and spark plug wires as an assembly.
11. Disconnect EGR tube from EGR valve. Disconnect choke cap wire.
12. Disconnect fuel supply and return lines from rubber connector.
13. Disconnect accelerator cable and speed control cable, if equipped.
14. Loosen thermactor pump belt pulley.
15. Raise and support vehicle.
16. Disconnect exhaust system from exhaust pipe. Lower vehicle.
17. Remove cylinder head bolts, cylinder head and gasket with thermactor pump, exhaust and intake manifolds attached. **Do not lay cylinder head flat. Damage to spark plugs or gasket surfaces may result.**
18. Reverse procedure to install. Refer to Engine Tightening Specifications for torque values and **Fig. 5**, for tightening sequence.

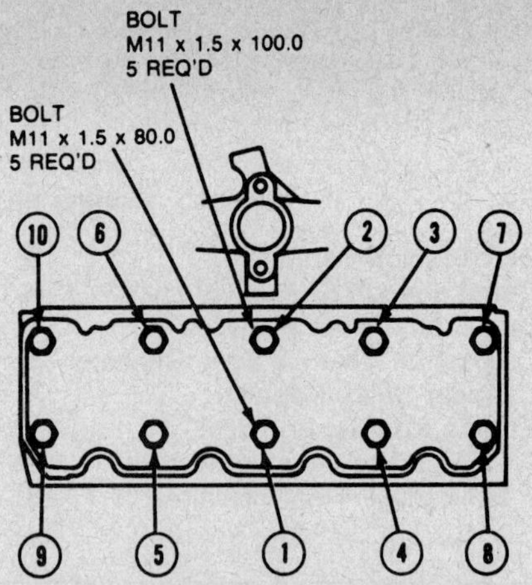

Fig. 5 Cylinder head bolt tightening sequence

VALVE ARRANGEMENT
FRONT TO REAR

4-153 .... I-E-I-E-E-I-E-I

CAM LOBE LIFT SPECIFICATIONS

Exhaust .... .239 inch
Intake .... .249 inch

VALVE LIFT SPECIFICATIONS

Exhaust .... .377 inch
Intake .... .392 inch

VALVES
ADJUST

Hydraulic valve lifters are used. No adjustment is required. To check intake and exhaust valve stem-to-rocker arm tip clearance, refer to "Hydraulic Valve Lifters, Replace."

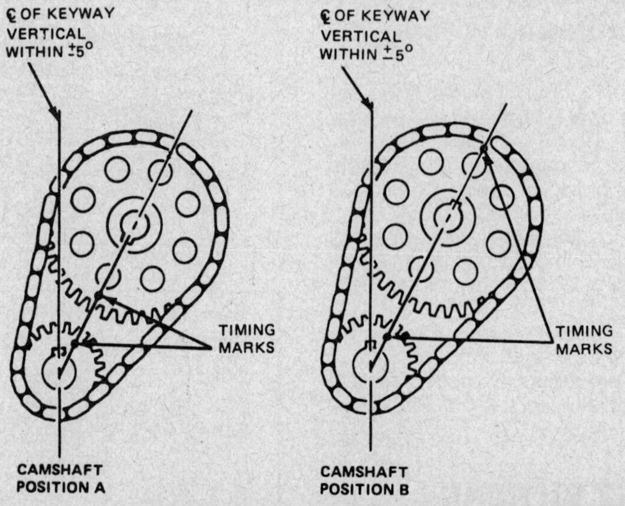

Fig. 6 Positioning camshaft to check for collapsed tappet gap

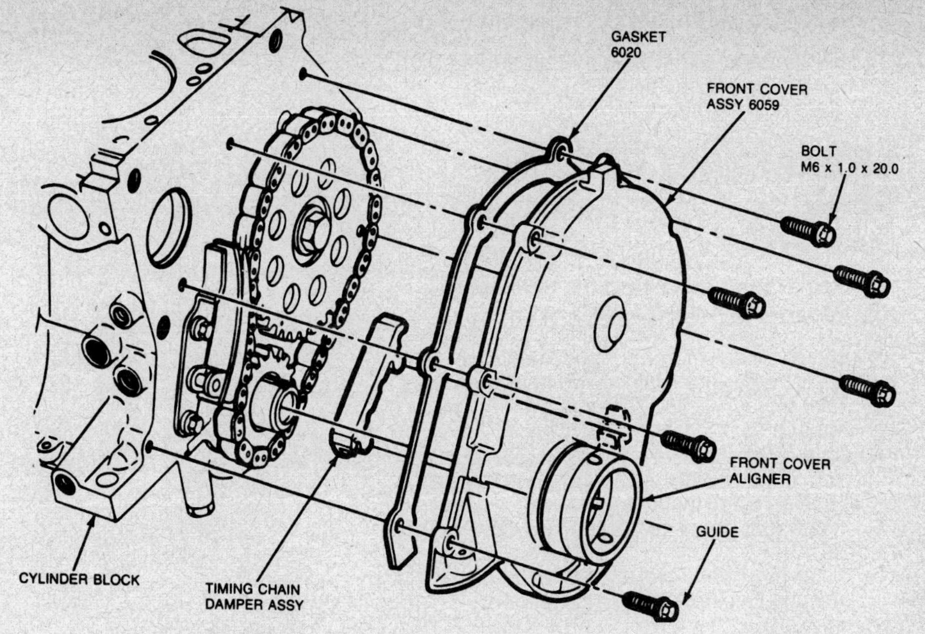

Fig. 7 Front cover removal

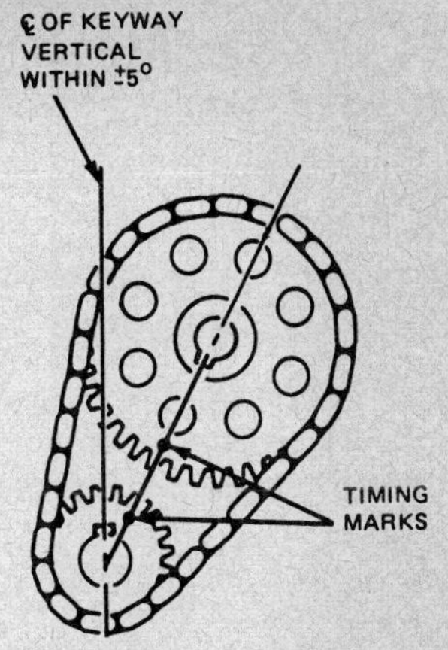

Fig. 8 Valve timing marks

HYDRAULIC VALVE LIFTERS

REPLACE

Before replacing a hydraulic valve lifter for noisy operation, ensure the noise is not caused by improper collapsed tappet gap, worn rocker arms, pushrods or valve tips.

To check for collapsed tappet gap, proceed as follows:

1. Rotate camshaft to position A as shown in **Fig. 6.**
2. Check intake and exhaust valve stem-to-rocker arm tip clearance on compression stroke under camshaft position A. With camshaft in position A, gap should be .072-.174 inch with tappet collapsed on base circle. Check No. 1 cylinder intake and exhaust valves. Check No. 2 cylinder intake valve. Check No. 3 cylinder exhaust valve. Tighten fulcrum bolts to specifications.
3. Rotate camshaft 180 degrees to position B as shown in **Fig. 6.** Check No. 2 cylinder exhaust valve. Check No. 3 cylinder intake valve. Check No. 4 cylinder intake and exhaust valve. Tighten fulcrum bolts to specification.

Remove lifters as follows:

1. Remove cylinder head as described previously.
2. Using a suitable magnet, remove lifters from lifter bores.
3. Place valve lifters in a rack so they can be installed in their original positions. **If the lifters are stuck in their bores by excessive varnish or gum buildup, use tool No. T70L-6500-A or equivalent to remove valve lifters.**
4. Reverse procedure to install.

ROCKER ARM COVER

REPLACE

1. Disconnect battery ground cable.
2. Remove oil filler cap.
3. Disconnect PCV hose from PCV valve.
4. Disconnect throttle linkage cable from rocker arm cover.
5. Disconnect speed control cable from rocker arm cover, if equipped.
6. Remove rocker arm cover bolts and cover.
7. Reverse procedure to install.

FRONT COVER OIL SEAL

REMOVAL

The following removal and installation procedure can only be performed with the engine removed from the vehicle.

1. Remove bolt and washer from crankshaft pulley.
2. Using tool No. T77F-4220-B1 or equivalent, remove crankshaft pulley.
3. Using tool No. T74P-6700-A or equivalent, remove front cover oil seal.

INSTALLATION

1. Coat new front cover oil seal with a suitable lubricant.
2. Using tool No. T83T-4676-A or equivalent, install oil seal into front cover. Drive oil seal in until it is fully seated into front cover recess. Check oil seal after installation to ensure spring is properly positioned in oil seal.
3. Lubricate, then install crankshaft pulley, washer and bolt. Torque crankshaft pulley bolt to specifications.

FRONT COVER, TIMING CHAIN & SPROCKETS

REPLACE

The following procedure can only be performed with the engine removed from the vehicle.

1. Remove dipstick, accessory drive pulley (if equipped), crankshaft pulley bolt, washer and pulley.
2. Using front cover seal remover T74P-6700-A, remove front seal, then front cover attaching bolts and front cover, **Fig. 7.**
3. Align camshaft and crankshaft sprocket timing marks as shown in **Fig. 8.**
4. Remove camshaft sprocket bolt and washer.
5. Remove sprockets and timing chain from engine as an assembly. Check timing chain vibration damper (located inside front cover) for wear. Replace if necessary.
6. Remove oil pan.
7. Install sprockets and timing chain. Align timing marks as shown in **Fig. 8.** Oil timing chain, sprockets and tensioner after installation.
8. With front cover seal removed, position front cover on engine.
9. Position front cover alignment tool T84P-6019-C or equivalent onto end of crankshaft. Ensure crankshaft pulley key is aligned with key way in tool.
10. Install front cover bolts. Torque bolts to 6-9 ft. lbs., then remove front cover alignment tool.
11. Coat new front cover oil seal with a suitable lubricant.
12. Using tool No. T83T-4676-A or equivalent, install oil seal into front cover. Drive oil seal in until it is fully seated into front cover recess. Check oil seal after installation to ensure spring is properly positioned in oil seal.
13. Lubricate, then install crankshaft pulley. Do not install washer and bolt at this time.
14. Install oil pan and accessory drive pulley (if equipped).

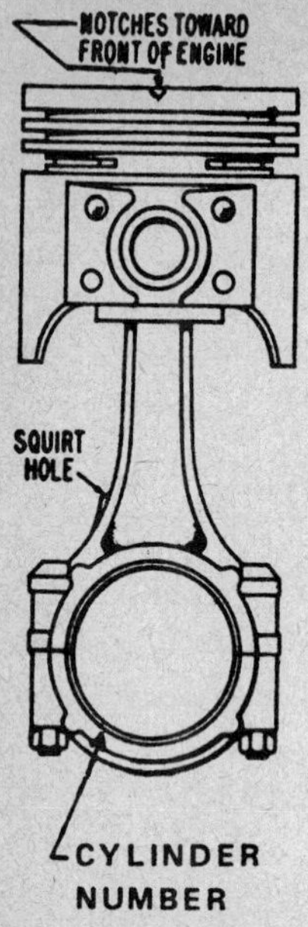

Fig. 9 Piston & rod assembly

15. Install crankshaft pulley bolt and washer. Torque crankshaft pulley bolt to specifications.

CAMSHAFT

REPLACE

The following procedure can only be performed with the engine removed from the vehicle.

1. Remove dipstick. Drain coolant and oil from engine.
2. Remove accessory drive belts and pulleys.
3. Position No. 1 piston at TDC with distributor rotor at No. 1 firing position, then remove distributor.
4. Remove cylinder head as described under "Cylinder Head, Replace."
5. Using a suitable magnet, remove hydraulic tappets and position in order so that they can be installed in their original locations. If tappets are stuck in their bores, use tool No. T70L-6500A or equivalent to remove tappets.
6. Remove crankshaft pulley bolt, washer and pulley.
7. Remove front cover as described under "Front Cover, Timing Chain & Sprockets, Replace."
8. Remove fuel pump, gasket and fuel pump pushrod.
9. Remove timing chain, sprockets and timing chain tensioner as described under "Front Cover, Timing Chain & Sprockets, Replace."
10. Remove camshaft thrust plate. Carefully remove camshaft from engine to avoid damaging camshaft bearings, journals and lobes.
11. Reverse procedure to install. Lubricate camshaft with suitable oil before installing. Ensure No. 1 piston is at TDC with distributor rotor at No. 1 firing position.

MAIN BEARINGS

Main bearings are available in standard sizes and undersizes of .001, .002, .010, .020, .030 and .040 inch.

CRANKSHAFT REAR OIL SEAL

REPLACE

1. Remove transaxle, then the flywheel.
2. Remove rear cover plate.
3. Using a suitable tool, punch a hole into the seal metal surface between the lip and block. Using slide hammer, Tool No. T77L-9533-B or equivalent, remove seal.
4. Coat crankshaft seal area and seal lip with engine oil, then using tool No. T81P-6701-A, install seal.
5. Install rear cover plate and two dowels.
6. Install flywheel. Torque bolts to values given in Engine Tightening Specifications.

PISTON & ROD ASSEMBLE

Assemble the rod to the piston with the notch on top of piston facing front of engine, **Fig. 9.**

After installation, check connecting rod big end side clearance. Clearance should be .0035-.0105 inch.

OIL PAN

REPLACE

1. Disconnect battery ground cable.
2. Raise and support vehicle.
3. Drain engine coolant and oil into suitable container.
4. On models equipped with manual transaxle, remove roll restrictor.
5. Remove starter from engine.
6. Disconnect exhaust pipe from oil pan.
7. Remove engine coolant tube located at the lower radiator hose, at the water pump and from tabs on oil pan. On models equipped with A/C, position A/C line off to side.
8. Remove oil pan bolts and oil pan, **Fig. 10,** from engine.
9. Clean oil pan and cylinder block surfaces with Dupont Freon TF or equivalent.
10. Remove oil pump screen and pickup tube and clean thoroughly, then reinstall.
11. Reverse steps 1-9 to assemble, noting the following. Torque oil pan-to-transaxle attaching bolts to 30-39 ft. lbs. to align oil pan, then loosen bolts 1/2 turn. Tighten oil pan-to-cylinder block attaching bolts to 6-9 ft. lbs., then the oil pan-to-transaxle attaching bolts to 30-39 ft. lbs.

OIL PUMP

REPLACE

1. Disconnect battery ground cable.

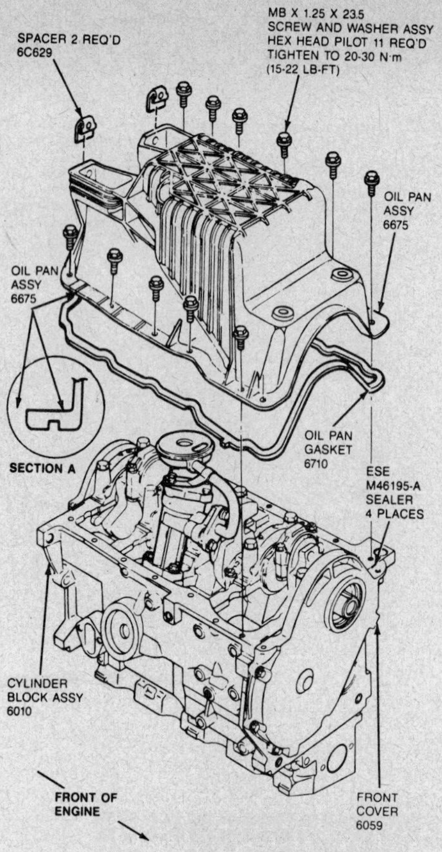

Fig. 10 Oil pan removal

2. Remove oil pan as described under "Oil Pan, Replace."
3. Remove oil pump bolts and oil pump from engine. Remove intermediate driveshaft from oil pump.
4. Reverse procedure to install.

WATER PUMP

REPLACE

1. Disconnect battery ground cable and drain coolant from engine.
2. Loosen thermactor pump adjusting bolt and remove belt.
3. Remove thermactor air pump hose clamp, thermactor pump bracket bolts, pump and bracket assembly from engine.
4. Loosen water pump idler pulley bolt and remove belt from water pump pulley.
5. Remove water pump inlet tube.
6. Remove water pump bolts and water pump.
7. Reverse procedure to install.

FUEL PUMP

REPLACE

Fuel supply lines will remain pressurized for long periods of time after engine shutdown. This pressure must be relieved before any service is attempted. A valve is provided on the fuel rail assembly for this purpose. To relieve system pressure, remove air cleaner assembly and connect pressure gauge tool No. T80L-9974-A or equivalent onto fuel valve on fuel rail assembly.

1. Disconnect battery ground cable.
2. Depressurize fuel system as described previously.
3. Remove fuel from fuel tank by pumping fuel out of fuel filler neck.
4. Raise and support vehicle.
5. Disconnect then remove fuel filler neck.
6. Support fuel tank, then remove tank support straps. Lower fuel tank partially and remove fuel lines, electrical connectors and vent lines from tank. Remove tank and place on suitable workbench.
7. Turn fuel pump locking ring counterclockwise and remove locking ring.
8. Remove fuel pump, bracket and gasket assembly.
9. Reverse procedure to install. To pressurize fuel system, proceed as follows:
   a. Install pressure gauge tool No. T80L-9974-A or equivalent onto fuel rail pressure fitting.
   b. Turn ignition switch to ON position for 3 seconds, repeatedly 5 to 10 times until pressure gauge indicates 13 psi.

BELT TENSION DATA

Belt tension is automatically maintained on these models by an automatic tensioner. Therefore, no adjustment is necessary.

V6-182 (3.0L) Engine Section

INDEX

ENGINE MOUNTS
REPLACE

Refer to **Fig. 1**, for engine mount replacement.

ENGINE
REPLACE

1. Disconnect battery ground cable.
2. Drain engine coolant and oil into suitable containers.
3. Discharge A/C system (if equipped).
4. Remove air filter assembly, battery, battery tray, integrated relay controller, cooling fan assembly and bounce damper bracket.
5. Disconnect radiator hoses from radiator, then remove radiator.
6. Disconnect evaporative emission control hose.
7. Disconnect starter brace, then exhaust pipes from manifolds.
8. disconnect power steering hoses, fuel lines and vacuum hoses.
9. Disconnect engine ground strap, heater hoses, accelerator cable linkage, throttle valve linkage (if equipped w/auto. trans.) and speed control linkage (if equipped).
10. Remove engine mount through bolts, **Fig. 1.**
11. Disconnect the following wire connectors:
    a. Ignition coil.
    b. Radio frequency suppressor.
    c. Cooling fan voltage resistor.
    d. Engine coolant temperature sensor.
    e. TFI module.
    f. Fuel injector wiring harness.
    g. Oil pressure sending switch.
    h. Ground wire.
    i. Block heater (if equipped).
    j. Knock sensor.
    k. EGO sensor.
    l. Oil level sensor.
12. Install suitable engine lifting equipment and remove engine assembly.

INTAKE MANIFOLD
REPLACE

1. Disconnect battery ground cable.
2. Drain engine cooling system into suitable container.
3. Remove throttle body, then disconnect fuel lines.
4. Remove fuel injector wiring harness.
5. Disconnect upper radiator hose, then the heater hose from water outlet.
6. Mark distributor rotor and body reference marks, then remove distributor assembly.
7. Remove intake manifold attaching bolts, then the intake manifold.
8. Reverse procedure to install. Torque bolts to specifications in sequence shown in **Fig. 2.**

EXHAUST MANIFOLD
REPLACE
LEFT SIDE

1. Remove dipstick support bracket and power steering pressure and return hoses.
2. Remove exhaust pipe-to-manifold attaching nuts.
3. Remove exhaust manifold-to-cylinder head attaching bolts, then the manifold.
4. Reverse procedure to install. Prior to installation, lightly lubricate nuts and bolts with suitable oil.

RIGHT SIDE

1. Remove heater hose support bracket, then disconnect heater hoses.
2. Using suitable back-up wrench on EGR tube lower adapter, remove EGR tube from exhaust manifold.
3. Remove exhaust pipe-to-manifold attaching nuts.
4. Remove exhaust manifold-to-cylinder head attaching bolts, then the manifold.

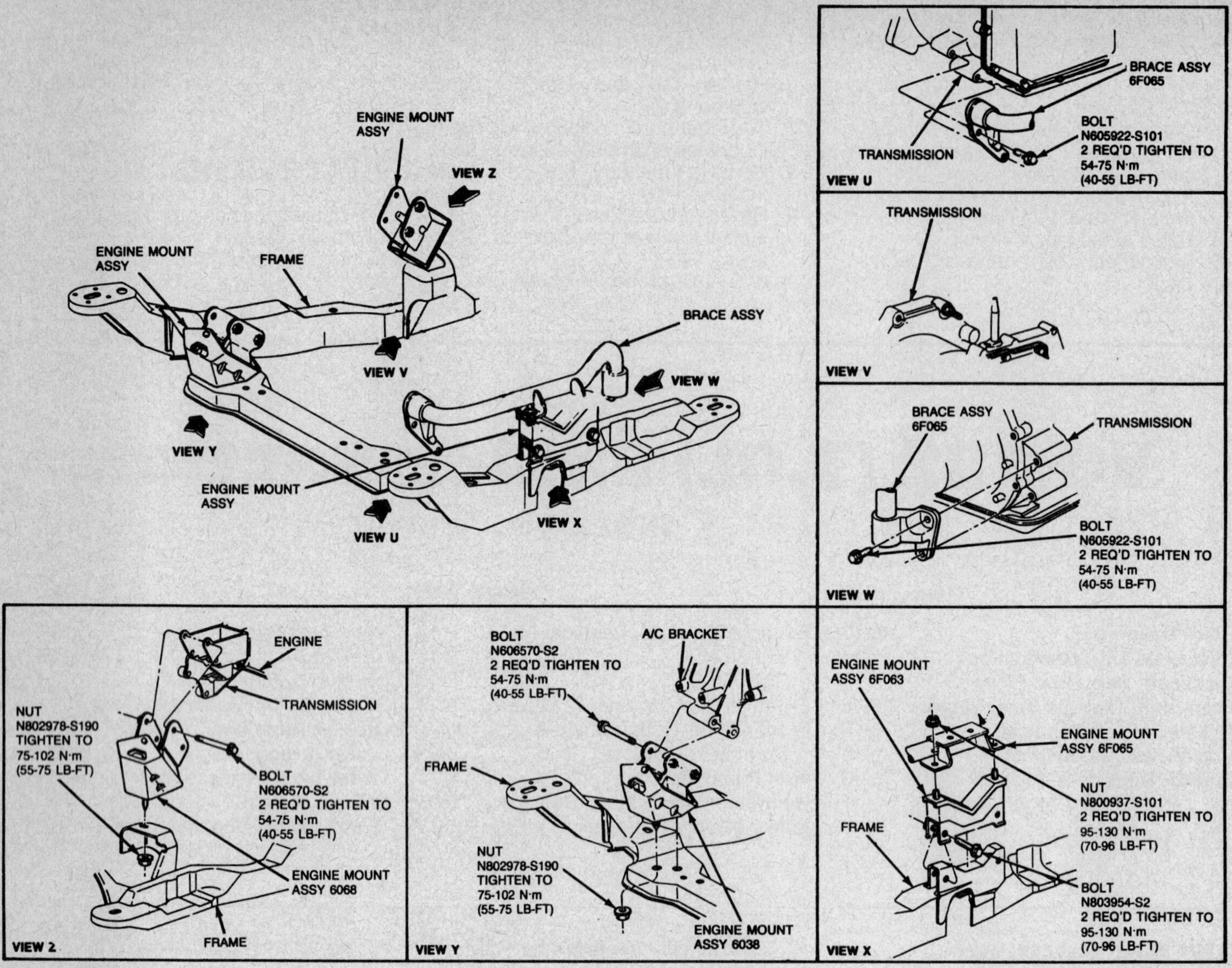

Fig. 1 Engine mounts

5. Reverse procedure to install. Prior to installation, lightly lubricate nuts and bolts with suitable oil.

CYLINDER HEAD
REPLACE

1. Disconnect battery ground cable.
2. Drain engine cooling system into suitable container.
3. Remove air cleaner outlet tube.
4. Remove intake manifold. Refer to Intake Manifold, Replace for procedure.
5. Remove accessory drive belt. If right side head is being removed, remove accessory belt idler. If left side head is being removed, remove alternator adjusting arm.
6. On models equipped w/power steering, remove pump bracket attaching bolts, then the pump and bracket as an assembly with hoses attached. Position pump and bracket assembly aside in an upright position to prevent leakage of fluid.
7. If left side head is being removed, remove coil bracket and dipstick tube. If right side head is being removed, remove ground strap and throttle cable support bracket.
8. Remove exhaust manifold(s), then the PCV valve and valve cover(s).
9. Remove rocker arm fulcrum bolts enough to allow the rocker arms to be swung aside and the pushrods removed. Keep pushrods in order of removal.
10. Remove cylinder head attaching bolts, then the cylinder head(s) and gasket(s). Discard gaskets(s).
11. Reverse procedure to install, noting the following:
    a. Refer to Engine Tightening Specifications for torque valves and to **Fig. 3,** for torque sequence.
    b. Lightly oil bolt threads prior to installation.
    c. If gasket alignment dowels are damaged, they should be replaced.
    d. Prior to installation, dip each pushrod end in oil conditioner D9AZ-19579-C or other suitable heavy engine oil.
    e. Lubricate rocker arm assemblies with oil conditioner D9AZ-19579-C or other suitable heavy engine oil.

VALVE ARRANGEMENT
FRONT TO REAR

Right Side	I-E-I-E-I-E
Left Side	E-I-E-I-E-I

CAM LOBE LIFT SPECIFICATIONS

Exhaust	.260 inch
Intake	.260 inch

VALVE LIFT SPECIFICATIONS

Exhaust	.419 inch
Intake	.419 inch

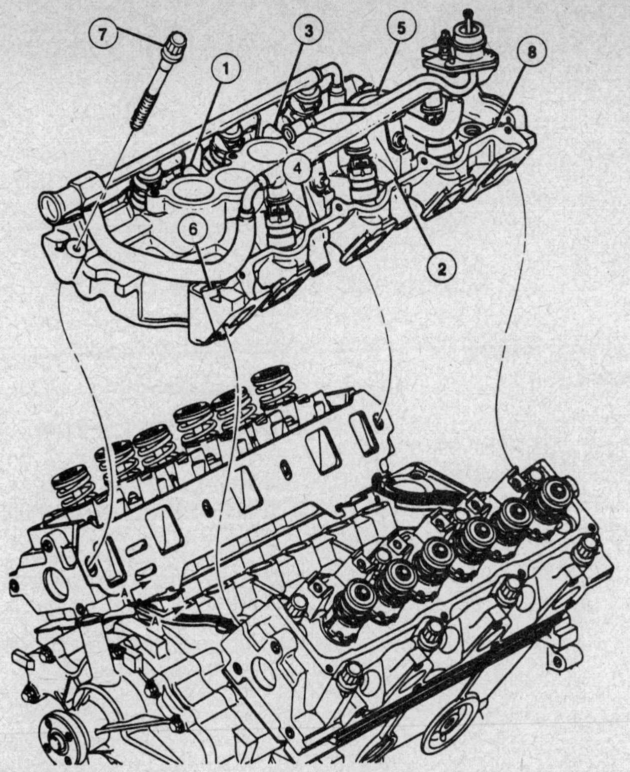

Fig. 2 Intake manifold bolt tightening sequence

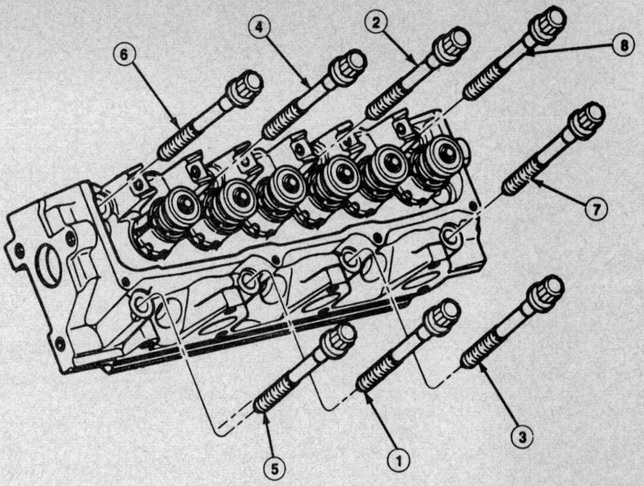

Fig. 3 Cylinder head bolt tightening sequence

VALVES
ADJUST

Hydraulic valve lifters are used. No adjustment is required.

HYDRAULIC VALVE LIFTERS
REPLACE

Before replacing a hydraulic valve lifter for noisy operation, ensure the noise is not caused by improper rocker arm-to-stem clearance, worn rocker arms, pushrods or valve tips.

1. Disconnect battery ground cable, then drain engine coolant.
2. Remove throttle body, then the spark plug wire routing clips mounted on valve cover attaching bolt studs. Lay spark plug wires with the routing clips attached towards rear of engine.
3. Remove rocker arm covers and intake manifold as outlined elsewhere in this section.
4. Loosen rocker arm fulcrum attaching bolt(s) a sufficient amount to swing rocker arm aside to allow the pushrod(s) to be removed, then remove pushrod(s). Keep pushrods in order so they can be returned to their original position.
5. Using a suitable magnet, remove lifter(s) from lifter bores. **If the lifters are stuck in their bores by excessive varnish or gum buildup, use tool No. T70L-6500-A or equivalent to remove valve lifters.**
6. Place valve lifters in a rack so they can be installed in their original positions.
7. Reverse procedure to install, noting the following:
   a. Lubricate lifter(s), lifter bores, rocker arms and pushrod(s) with oil conditioner D9AZ-19579-A or suitable heavy engine oil.
   b. Torque bolts to specifications given in Engine Tightening Specifications.

ROCKER ARM COVER
REPLACE

1. Disconnect secondary ignition cables from spark plugs.
2. Remove secondary cable separators from rocker arm cover attaching bolt studs.
3. If left side rocker arm cover is being removed, disconnect crankcase breather hose and remove oil filler cap.
4. If right side rocker arm cover is removed, disconnect EGR tube and heater hoses, then remove PCV valve.
5. Remove rocker arm cover attaching bolts, then the cover.
6. Reverse procedure to install, noting the following:
   a. Lightly oil bolt and stud threads prior to installation.
   b. Apply bead of RTV sealant at cylinder head to intake manifold rail step.
   c. Torque EGR tube to 25-36 ft. lbs. For other torque specifications, refer to Engine Tightening Specifications.

FRONT OIL SEAL
REPLACE

1. Loosen accessory drive belts, then remove right front wheel.
2. Remove four crankshaft pulley-to-damper attaching bolts, then remove accessory drive belt and the pulley.
3. Remove vibration damper attaching bolt, then using suitable puller, remove vibration damper.
4. Using flat bladed screwdriver or other suitable tool, pry seal from front timing cover. Use caution not to damage front cover or crankshaft.
5. Lubricate replacement seal lip with clean engine oil, then install seal with suitable seal installer.
6. Lubricate inner hub surface of vibration damper with clean engine oil, then apply RTV sealant to keyway of inner hub surface of vibration damper.
7. Install vibration damper. Torque attaching bolt to 140-170 ft. lbs.
8. Install crankshaft pulley. Torque bolts to 15-22 ft. lbs.
9. Install accessory drive belts, then install right front wheel.
10. Start engine and check for oil leaks.

FRONT COVER, TIMING CHAIN & SPROCKETS
REPLACE

1. Remove idler pulley and bracket assembly, then the drive and accessory belts.
2. Remove water pump as described elsewhere in this section.
3. Remove crankshaft pulley and damper. Refer to Front Oil Seal, Replace.
4. Remove lower radiator hose, then the oil pan-to-timing cover bolts.
5. Remove front cover-to-cylinder block attaching bolts, then remove front cover, **Fig. 4.**

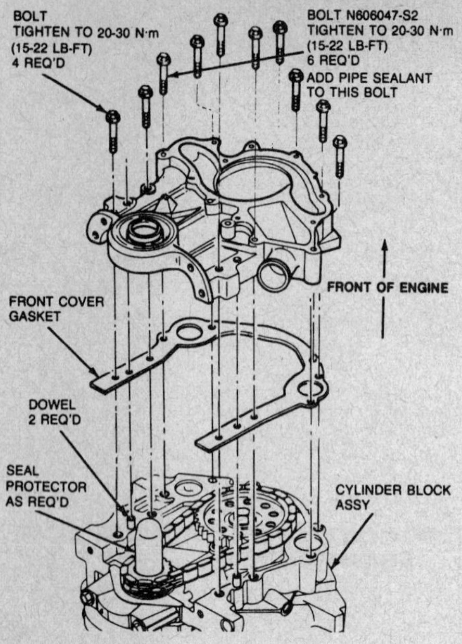

Fig. 4 Front cover removal & installation

6. Cover oil pan opening to prevent dirt entry, then rotate crankshaft until No. 1 piston is at TDC compression stroke and timing marks are aligned as shown, **Fig. 5.**
7. Remove camshaft sprocket attaching bolt and washer, then slide crankshaft sprocket, timing chain and camshaft sprocket from engine as an assembly.
8. Install replacement camshaft sprocket, timing chain and crankshaft sprocket as an assembly with timing marks aligned, **Fig. 5.**
9. Carefully cut, then remove exposed portion of oil pan gasket. Coat oil pan gasket surface with sealing compound B54-19554-A or equivalent. Cut and position necessary gaskets on oil pan gasket surface and apply sealing compound above, at the corners and on gasket surface.
10. Lubricate replacement seal lip with clean engine oil, then install seal with suitable seal installer. Install front cover, refer to **Fig. 4,** for torque specifications. **Use suitable sealant on front cover bolt which extends through water jacket.**
6. Lubricate inner hub surface of vibration damper with clean engine oil, then apply RTV sealant to keyway of inner hub surface of vibration damper.
7. Reverse steps 1 through 4 to complete installation.

CAMSHAFT

REPLACE

1. Remove engine from vehicle and mount in suitable work stand.
2. Remove front cover and timing chain as outlined under Front Cover, Timing Chain & Sprockets, Replace.

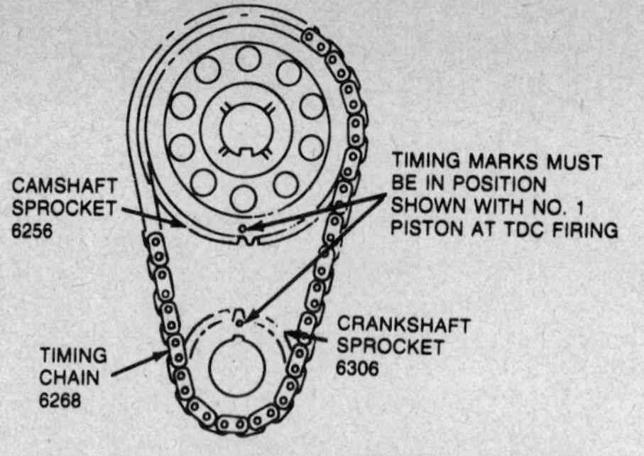

Fig. 5 Valve timing mark alignment

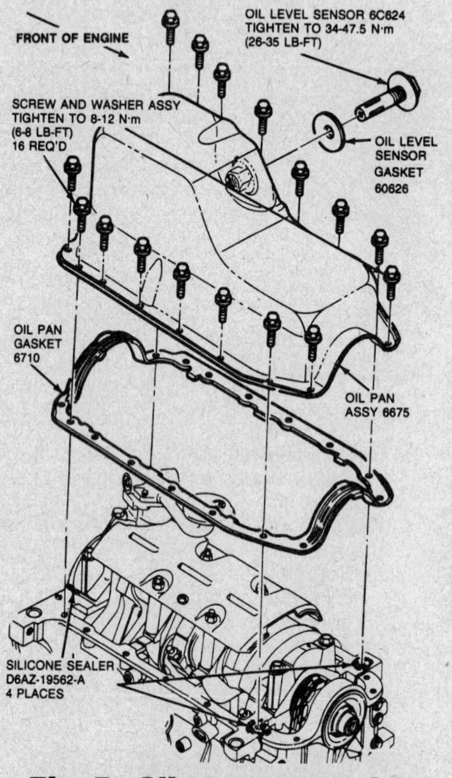

Fig. 7 Oil pan removal & installation

3. Remove intake manifold and hydraulic valve lifters as outlined under Hydraulic Valve Lifters, Replace.
4. Remove camshaft thrust plate, then carefully pull camshaft from cylinder block. Use caution to avoid damaging bearings, journals and lobes.
5. Reverse procedure to install, noting the following:
   a. Prior to installation, lubricate camshaft lobes and journals with SAE 50 weight oil.
   b. Torque camshaft thrust plate attaching screws to 6-8 ft. lbs.
   c. Lubricate lifters, lifter bores, rocker arms and pushrods with oil conditioner D9AZ-19579-A or suitable heavy engine oil.

MAIN BEARINGS

Main bearings are available in standard sizes and undersizes of .001, .002, .010, .020, .030 and .040 inch.

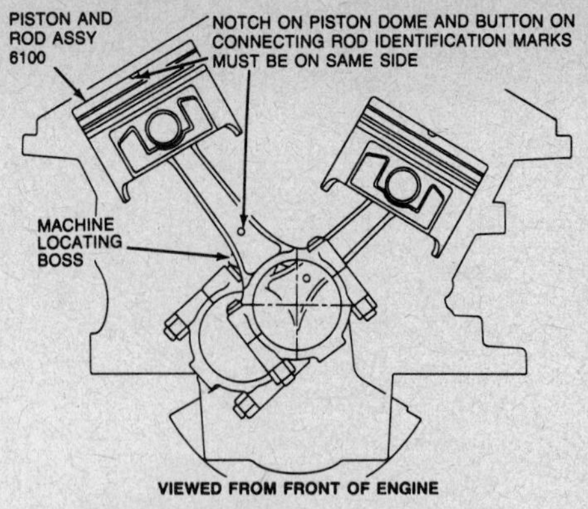

Fig. 6. Piston & rod assembly

CRANKSHAFT REAR OIL SEAL

REPLACE

1. Remove transaxle, then the flywheel.
2. Remove rear cover plate.
3. Using a suitable tool, punch a hole into the seal metal surface between the lip and block. Using slide hammer, Tool No. T77L-9533-B or equivalent, remove seal.
4. Coat crankshaft seal area and seal lip with engine oil, then using tool No. T82L-6701-A, install seal.
5. Install rear cover plate and two dowels.
6. Install flywheel. Torque bolts to values given in Engine Tightening Specifications.

PISTON & ROD ASSEMBLE

Assemble the rod to the piston with the notch on the piston dome on the same side as the button on the connecting rod identification marks. Assemble piston and rod assembly in engine with notch in dome facing front of engine, **Fig. 6.**

After installation, check connecting rod big end side clearance. Clearance should be .006-.014 inch.

OIL PAN

REPLACE

1. Disconnect battery ground cable, then remove oil dipstick.
2. Raise and support vehicle. On models equipped with low oil level sensor, remove retainer clip at sensor, then disconnect sensor electrical connector.
3. Drain engine oil into suitable container.
4. Remove starter motor, then disconnect Exhaust Gas Oxygen (EGO) sensor electrical connector.
5. Remove head pipe and catalytic converter assembly.
6. Remove lower engine/flywheel dust cover from converter/flywheel housing.
7. Remove oil pan-to-cylinder block and front cover attaching screws, **Fig. 7,**

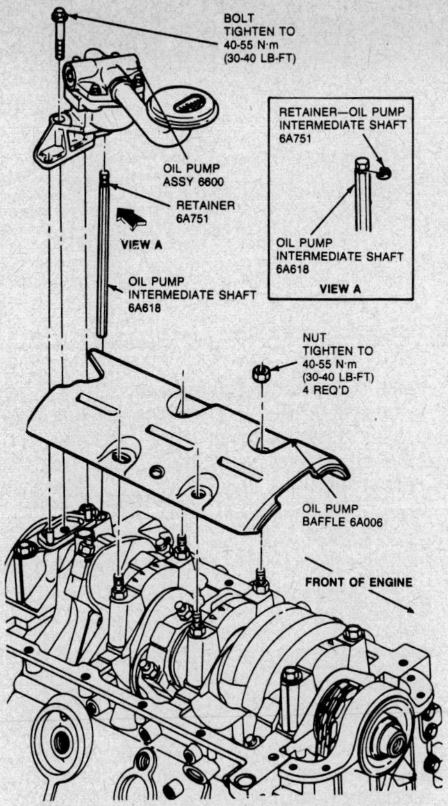

Fig. 8 Oil pump removal

then the oil pan and gasket.

8. Reverse procedure to install, noting the following:
   a. Apply 1/8inch bead of suitable silicone sealer to junction of front and rear main bearing caps with cylinder block, prior to installing new gasket.
   b. Torque oil pan bolts to 71-106 inch lbs. and low oil level sensor (if equipped) to 26-35 ft. lbs.

OIL PUMP REPLACE

1. Remove oil pan. Refer to Oil Pump, Replace for procedure.
2. Remove oil pump attaching bolts, **Fig. 8.**
3. Remove oil pump and intermediate shaft.
4. If necessary, pull intermediate from oil pump.
5. If removed, install intermediate shaft into replacement pump until shaft retainer clicks into position.
6. Install oil pump. Torque attaching bolts to 30-40 ft. lbs.
7. Install oil pan.

WATER PUMP REPLACE

1. Drain cooling system into suitable container.
2. Loosen accessory drive belt idler, then remove drive belts.
3. Remove accessory drive belt idler bracket from engine.
4. Disconnect heater hose from water pump.
5. Remove water pump pulley-to-pump hub attaching bolts. **The pump pulley cannot be removed at this time due to insufficient clearance between body and pump.**
6. Remove eleven water pump attaching bolts, **Fig. 9,** then lift the water pump and pulley assembly up and out of vehicle and remove pulley.
7. Lightly lubricate all bolts and stud threads with oil.
8. Position pulley on replacement pump, then install pump/pulley assembly. Torque attaching bolts as shown in **Fig. 9.**
9. Install water pump pulley-to-pump hub attaching bolts and torque to 15-22 ft. lbs.
10. Reverse steps 1 through 4 to complete installation.

FUEL PUMP REPLACE

Fuel supply lines will remain pressurized for long periods of time after engine shutdown. This pressure must be relieved before any service is attempted. A valve is provided on the fuel rail assembly for this purpose. To relieve system pressure, remove air cleaner assembly and connect pressure gauge tool No. T80L-9974-A or equivalent onto fuel valve on fuel rail assembly.

1. Disconnect battery ground cable.
2. Depressurize fuel system as described previously.
3. Remove fuel from fuel tank by pumping fuel out of fuel filler neck.

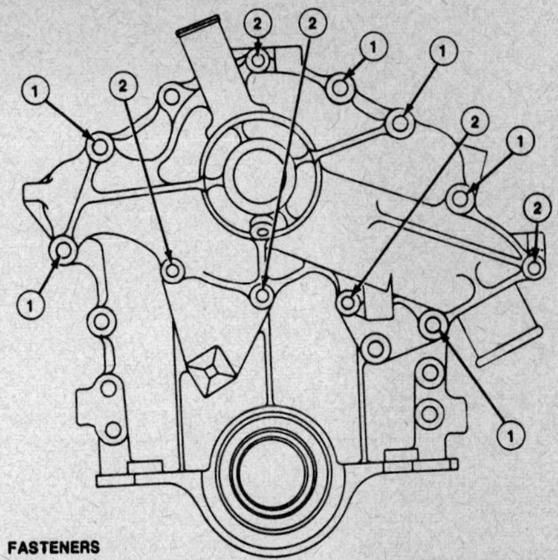

FASTENERS

REF NO.	PART NO.	SIZE	N·m	LB-FT
1	N606047-S2	M8 x 70.0	20-30	15-22
2	N605774-S2	M6 x 1.0 x 25.0	8-12	6-8

Fig. 9 Water pump removal & installation

4. Raise and support vehicle.
5. Disconnect then remove fuel filler neck.
6. Support fuel tank, then remove tank support straps. Lower fuel tank partially and remove fuel lines, electrical connectors and vent lines from tank. Remove tank and place on suitable workbench.
7. Turn fuel pump locking ring counterclockwise and remove locking ring.
8. Remove fuel pump, bracket and gasket assembly.
9. Reverse procedure to install. To pressurize fuel system, proceed as follows:
   a. Install pressure gauge tool No. T80L-9974-A or equivalent onto fuel rail pressure fitting.
   b. Turn ignition switch to ON position for 3 seconds, repeatedly 5 to 10 times until pressure gauge indicates 13 psi.

BELT TENSION DATA

Using belt tension gauge 0210028 or equivalent, set belt tensions as follows: On new belts; alternator belt, 100-140 lbs., A/C and power steering belt, 150-190 lbs. On used belts; alternator belt, 80-100 lbs., A/C and power steering belt, 140-160 lbs.

V6-232 (3.8L) Engine Section

INDEX

DESCRIPTION

The V6-232 engine is used on 1988 Taurus and Sable models. This engine is basically the same design used on previous models for the exception of a balance shaft assembly. In conjunction with the balance shaft assembly, the cylinder block, camshaft, pistons and oil pump have been revised.

CYLINDER BLOCK & BALANCE SHAFT

The cylinder block incorporates a specially designed, cast iron balance shaft. In addition, this counter-rotating shaft offsets noise, vibration and harshness qualities for improved driving and vehicle operation.

Geared to the engine's camshaft, the balance shaft operates in the cylinder block at engine speed and uses special bearings with an added lubrication notch.

CAMSHAFT

The full circumference design camshaft and balance shaft thrust plates are incorporated for balance shaft accommodation. In addition, a steel gear balance drive has been incorporated.

PISTONS

Revised dish pistons are incorporated for a 9.0:1 compression ratio. These pistons utilize new, low tension design compression piston rings and a reduced tension oil control ring spacer for improved performance. A shrouded valve design is used to enhance fast burn combustion.

OIL PUMP

A special design gear and gear shaft oil pump is used to provide oil cooling, and also, uses separate, die cast aluminum housing for the oil pump gears. Special oil drain-back passages, gasket cover and an oil pan which uses stiffer ribs to reduce resonance is used.

Clutch & Manual Transmission Section

INDEX

CLUTCH

ADJUST

These models incorporate a self-adjusting clutch mechanism. The self-adjust mechanism consists of a spring loaded ratchet quadrant attached to the clutch cable. During clutch cable replacement or whenever clutch adjustment is necessary, grasp the clutch pedal and pull upwards, then slowly depress clutch pedal several times.

Whenever the clutch cable is disconnected for any reason, the clutch pedal assembly must be restrained in the uppermost position during both removal and replacement of the components. After the clutch cable is installed and the clutch allowed to rest in its normal position, adjust clutch by slowly depressing clutch several times.

CLUTCH

REPLACE

On 5 speed models built prior to April 11, 1986, a clutch chatter condition may occur while releasing the clutch pedal in reverse gear. The chatter is caused by the clutch cable being pulled away from the clutch bracket on quick engagements due to the clutch cable being to short.

To correct this condition, inspect clutch cable at the transmission end. If the cable is color coded green, it should be replaced with a longer cable that is color coded tan, part No. E6DZ-7K553-B.

1. Remove transaxle as described under "Manual Transaxle, Replace" procedure.
2. Loosen pressure plate attaching bolts evenly to avoid distortion. If pressure plate is to be reused, scribe reference marks between plate and flywheel for reference during assembly.
3. Remove pressure plate and clutch disc from flywheel, **Fig. 2. These models do not use a pilot bearing.**
4. Position clutch disc and pressure plate onto flywheel with flatter side of clutch disc facing toward flywheel.

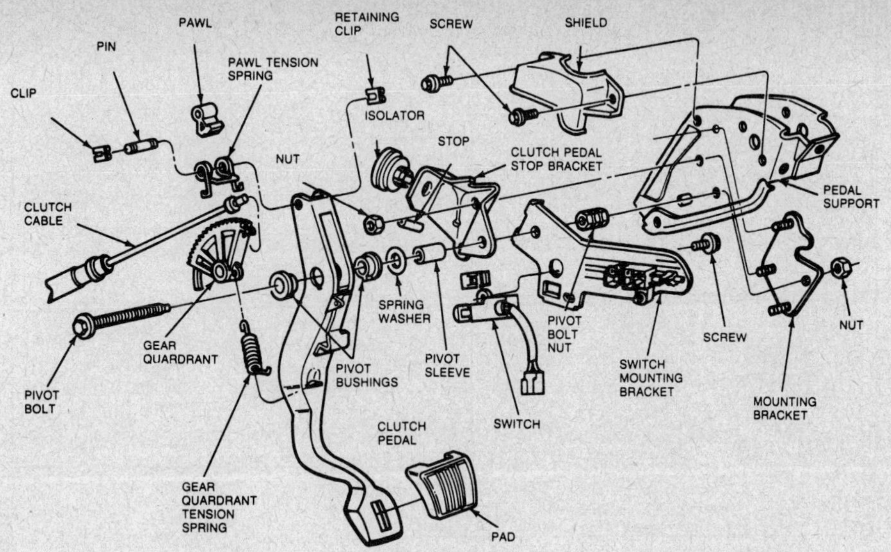

Fig. 1 Clutch pedal & self-adjusting mechanism

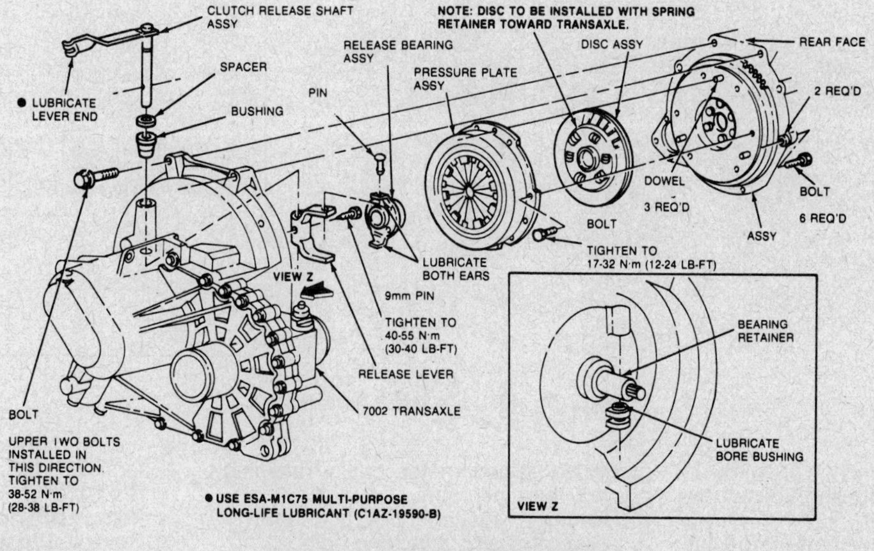

Fig. 2 Clutch assembly

5. Ensure three dowel pins on flywheel are aligned with holes in pressure plate, then install mounting bolts. Do not tighten at this time.
6. Using clutch alignment tool T81P-7550-A or equivalent, align clutch disc with flywheel. Alternately tighten pressure plate mounting screws until fully seated, then torque bolts to 12-24 ft. lbs.
7. Remove alignment tool, than install transaxle.

GEARSHIFT LINKAGE
ADJUST

Adjustment of the gearshift linkage is not necessary and no provision for adjustment is provided, **Fig. 3.**

MANUAL TRANSAXLE
REPLACE

1. Using block of wood, rope or other suitable method, restrain clutch pedal in its uppermost position.
2. Grasp clutch cable end with fingers and pull forward, disconnecting cable from clutch release shaft assembly, then remove clutch cable casing from rib on top of transaxle case.
3. Remove top transaxle-to-engine mounting bolts, then raise and support front of vehicle.
4. Remove both lower control arm ball joint-to-steering knuckle attaching nuts and bolts, then using suitable tool, pry lower control arms away from steering knuckles. **Use caution not to cut or damage the ball joint boot. Do not allow pry bar to contact lower control arm. Pry control arm from stabilizer bar.**
5. Using suitable tool, pry left side inboard Constant Velocity (CV) joint from transaxle, then remove CV joint from transaxle by grasping left side steering knuckle and swinging the knuckle and halfshaft assembly outward from the transaxle. Repeat procedure on other side. **When prying CV joints from transaxle, use caution not to damage the differential seals.**
6. Wire halfshafts in a near level position away from transaxle.
7. Disconnect back-up lamp switch connector from the transmission mount-

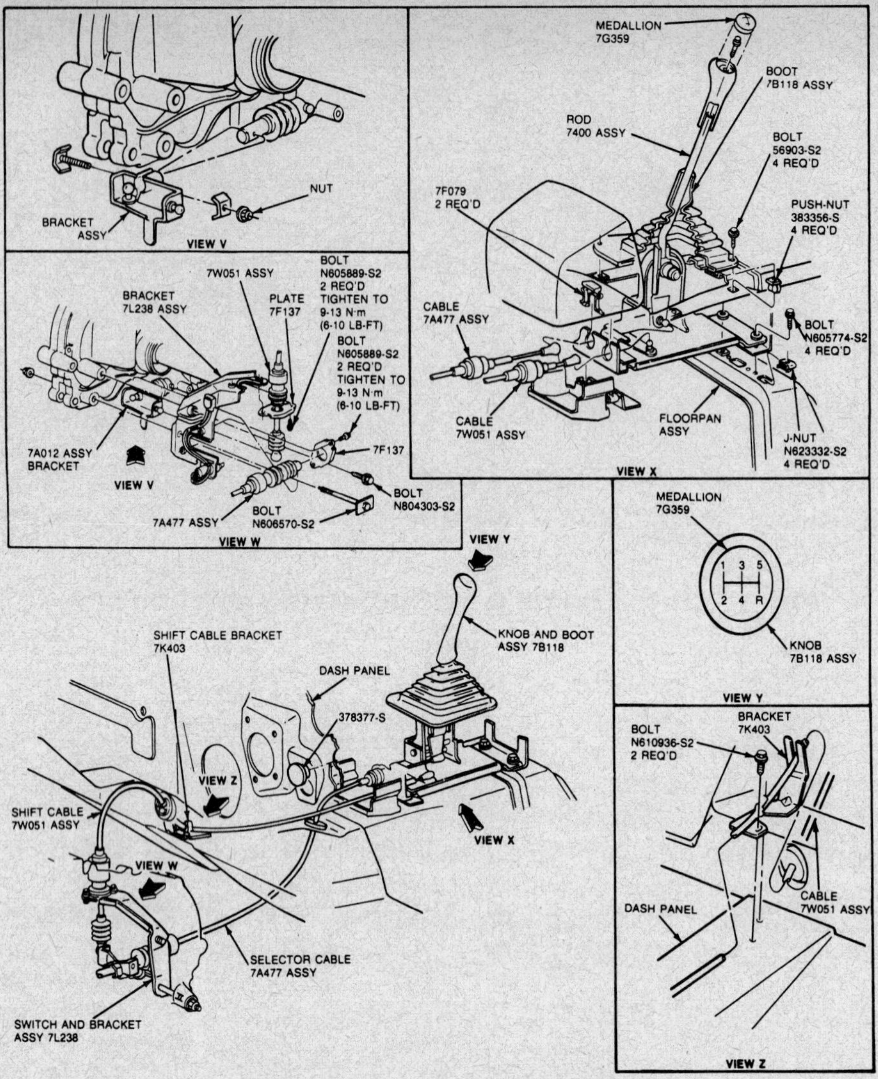

Fig. 3 Gearshift linkage

ed back up light switch.

8. Remove starter mounting bolts, then the starter.
9. Remove shift mechanism-to-shift shaft attaching nut and bolt and control selector indicator switch arm, then the shift shaft.
10. Using suitable crows foot wrench, remove speedometer cable retaining nut, then the cable.
11. Remove stiffener brace-to-lower clutch housing attaching bolts.
12. Position suitable transmission jack under transaxle and support transaxle.
13. Remove lower transaxle-to-engine attaching bolts, then slide transmission rearward to disengage input shaft from clutch plate and lower transaxle.
14. Reverse procedure to install. After installation is complete, allow clutch pedal to hang in its normal position, then depress pedal several times to adjust clutch pedal.

Rear Suspension & Brakes Section

INDEX

DESCRIPTION

SEDAN MODELS

These models utilize an independent rear suspension. Each side consists of a MacPherson strut, an upper mount and washers, two parallel lower control arms, a tension strut, a spindle and a stabilizer bar mounted on the strut.

The top of the MacPherson strut is attached to the inner body side panel, while the lower end of the strut is attached to the spindle with a pinch clamp and bolt. The parallel lower control arms attach to the underbody with nuts and bolts. The tension strut attaches to the lower part of the spindle and to the underbody, **Fig. 1**.

WAGON MODELS

These models also utilize an independent rear suspension. Each side consists of an upper and lower control arm, a shock absorber, a two piece spindle tension control strut and a coil spring.

The top of the shock absorber is attached to the body side panel by a rubber insulated top mount assembly and to the lower control arms by two nuts. The upper control arm attaches to the crossmember and the upper part of the spindle. The lower control arm attaches to the underbody and lower part of the spindle. The coil spring operates against the lower control arm and is located inboard of the shock absorber, **Fig. 2**.

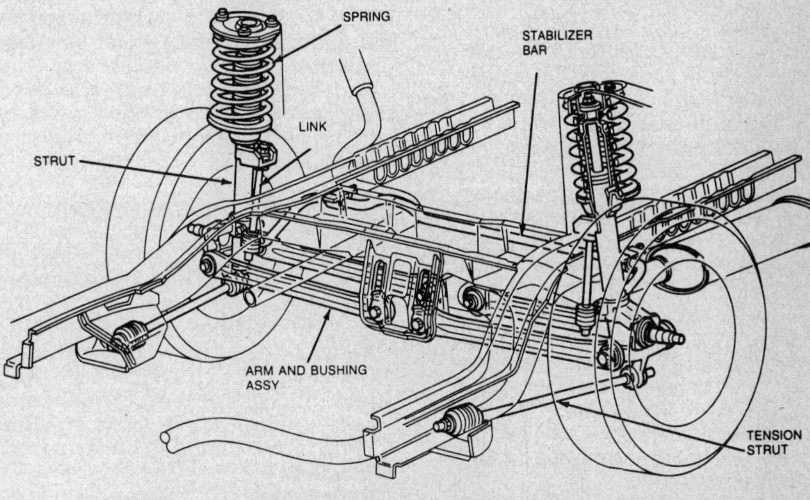

Fig. 1 Rear suspension. Sedan models

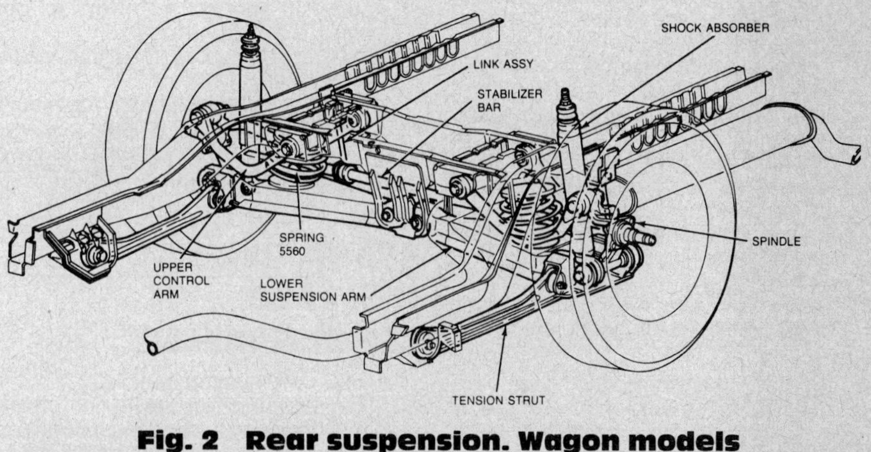

Fig. 2 Rear suspension. Wagon models

STRUT, UPPER MOUNT & SPRING

REPLACE

SEDAN MODELS

1. Position suitable jack or hoist under vehicle, then raise just enough to contact body.
2. Working in trunk, loosen, but do not remove, the three strut-to-inner body attaching nuts.
3. Raise and support vehicle, then remove tire and wheel assembly from side being worked on.
4. Remove brake differential valve-to-control arm attaching bolt.
5. Using suitable wire suspend control arm to body to ensure proper support after strut removal.
6. Remove brake hose-to-shock strut bracket attaching clip and position

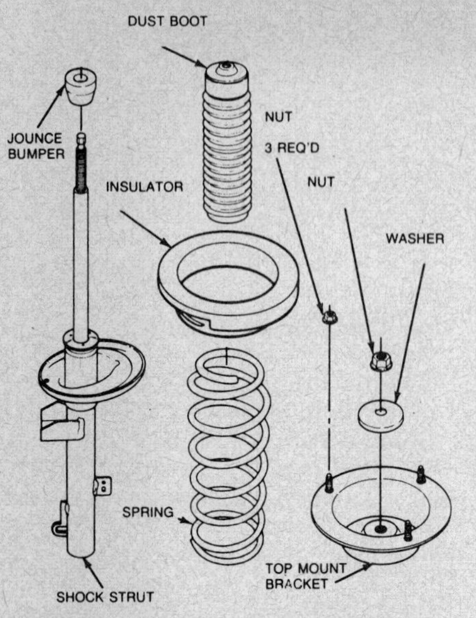

Fig. 3 MacPherson strut components. Sedan models

hose aside.

7. If equipped with stabilizer bar, remove U-bracket from body, then the stabilizer bar attaching nut, washer and insulator. Separate stabilizer bar from link.
8. Remove tension strut-to-spindle attaching nut, washer and insulator, then move spindle rearward enough to separate it from tension strut.
9. Remove strut-to-spindle pinch bolt, then using a pry bar or other suitable tool, separate pinch joint as necessary to allow for strut removal.
10. Remove strut from pinch joint, then lower vehicle as necessary to allow removal of bolts loosened in step 2. Remove strut from vehicle. **During strut removal, use care not to stretch the rear brake hose or kink the steel brake line.**
11. Remove link attaching nut, washer and insulator, then the link from the strut.
12. Mark location of insulator to top mount, then place strut, spring and upper mount assembly in suitable spring compressor and compress spring.
13. While restraining strut shaft from turning, remove strut upper shaft mounting nut. **If strut is to be reused, do not use vise grips or pliers to hold strut shaft as damage will result.**
14. Carefully loosen spring compressor tool, then remove top mount bracket assembly, spring insulator and spring, **Fig. 3.**
15. Using new attaching parts, reverse procedure to install, noting the following:
    a. When installing spring on strut, ensure spring is properly located in upper and lower spring seats. Refer to **Fig. 4**, for spring end placement.
    b. When tightening strut nut, restrain strut shaft from turning. Torque strut nut to 35-50 ft. lbs.
    c. Torque stabilizer link-to-strut attaching nut to 6-12 ft. lbs.
    d. Torque strut pinch bolt to 55-81 ft. lbs.
    e. Torque tension strut-to-spindle attaching nut to 52-74 ft. lbs.
    f. Torque stabilizer link-to-stabilizer bar attaching nut to 6-12 ft. lbs.
    g. Torque stabilizer bar U-bracket attaching bolt to 15-25 ft. lbs.
    h. Tighten strut top mount-to-body attaching nuts to 19-26 ft. lbs.

SHOCK ABSORBER REPLACE

WAGON MODELS

These models use gas filled shock absorbers.

1. Remove rear compartment access panels.
2. While restraining shock absorber shaft, loosen, but do not remove top mounting nut. **If shock absorber is to be reused, do not use vise grips or pliers to hold shock absorber shaft as damage will result.**
3. Raise and support rear of vehicle, then remove tire and wheel assembly. **If a frame contact hoist is used, support lower control arm with floor jack. If a twin post lift is used, support body with floor jacks on lifting pads forward of tension strut body bracket.**
4. Loosen shock absorber-to-lower control arm attaching nuts. Do not remove nuts at this time.
5. Lower vehicle, then remove shock absorber top mounting nut, washer and insulator.
6. Raise and support rear of vehicle. **If a frame contact hoist is used, support lower control arm with floor jack. If a twin post lift is used, support body with floor jacks on lifting pads forward of tension strut body bracket.**
7. Remove shock absorber-to-lower control arm attaching nuts, then remove shock absorber from vehicle. **The shock absorbers are gas filled and will require an effort to collapse them for removal.**
8. Reverse procedure to install, noting the following:
    a. Torque shock absorber top mounting nut to 19-27 ft. lbs.
    b. Torque shock absorber-to-lower control arm mounting nuts to 12-20 ft. lbs.

STABILIZER BAR REPLACE

SEDAN MODELS

1. Raise and support vehicle.
2. Remove stabilizer bar-to-link attaching nuts, washers and insulators from both sides. Remove U-bracket attaching bolts, then the stabilizer bar.
3. Remove link-to-strut attaching nuts, washers and insulators.
4. Inspect attaching parts for damage and replace as necessary.
5. Using new attaching parts, reverse procedure to install, noting the following:
    a. Torque link-to-strut attaching nuts to 6-12 ft. lbs.
    b. Torque U-bracket attaching bolts to 15-25 ft. lbs.
    c. Torque stabilizer bar-to-link attaching nuts to 6-12 ft. lbs.

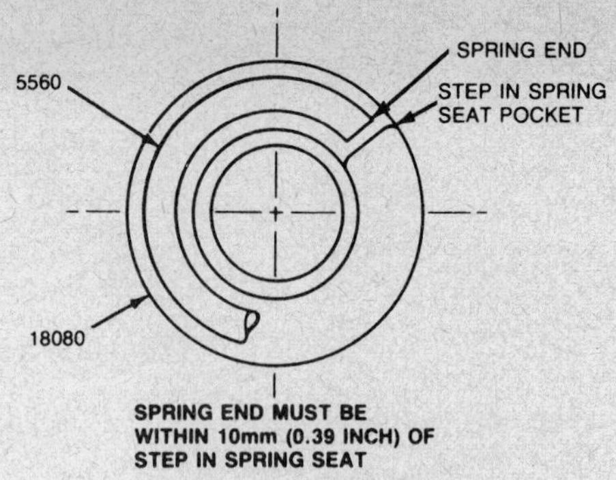

Fig. 4 Coil spring installation

WAGON MODELS

1. Raise and support vehicle.
2. Remove U-bracket retaining nuts and bolts from either side, then slide U-brackets and insulators from stabilizer bar.
3. Remove link-to-body bracket attaching nuts and bolts, then the stabilizer and link assemblies.
4. Slide link assemblies from stabilizer bar.
5. Inspect attaching parts for damage and replace as necessary.
6. Reverse procedure to install, noting the following:
    a. Install new nuts and bolts, then torque link-to-body bracket attaching nuts and bolts to 40-55 ft. lbs.
    b. Install new nuts and bolts, then torque U-bracket attaching nuts and bolts to 20-30 ft. lbs.

TENSION STRUT REPLACE

SEDAN MODELS

1. Raise vehicle on frame contact hoist using lift pads located rearward of front wheels and forward of rear wheels. Raise hoist only enough to contact body.
2. Working inside trunk, loosen, but do not remove, three strut-to-inner body attaching nuts.
3. Raise vehicle, then remove tire and wheel assembly.
4. Remove tension strut-to-spindle attaching nut.
5. Remove tension strut-to-body attaching nut.
6. While moving spindle rearward, remove tension strut.
7. Install new inner washers and bushings on both ends of tension strut. Refer to **Fig. 5**, for bushing and washer identification.
8. Install tension strut end into body bracket, then install outer bushing,

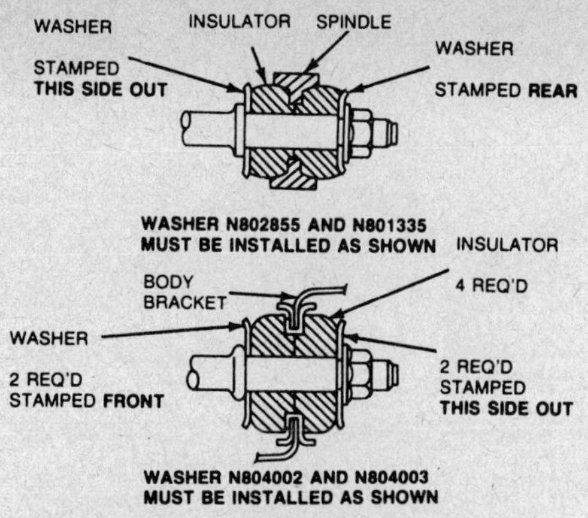

Fig. 5 Tension strut bushing installation. Sedan models

washers and nut. Do not tighten nut at this time.

9. While moving spindle rearward, install tension strut in spindle, then install outer bushing, washer and nut.
10. Ensure bushings are correctly seated in mountings, **Fig. 5**, then torque attaching nuts 52-74 ft. lbs.
11. Support spindle with suitable jack stand, then working inside trunk, remove three strut-to-inner body attaching nuts. Install new nuts and torque to 19-26 ft. lbs.
12. Remove jack stand, then install tire and wheel assembly.
13. Lower vehicle.

WAGON MODELS

1. Raise vehicle on frame contact hoist, then position suitable jack under lower control arm and raise arm to normal curb height.
2. Remove wheel and tire assembly, then tension strut-to-lower control arm attaching nut and bolt.
3. Remove tension strut-to-body bracket attaching nut and bolt, then the tension strut.
4. Insert front end of replacement torsion strut in body bracket, then install new attaching nut and bolt. Do not tighten at this time.
5. Position rear end of torsion strut in lower control arm, then install new attaching nut and bolt. Torque to 40-55 ft. lbs.
6. Torque torsion strut-to-body bracket attaching nut and bolt to 40-55 ft. lbs.
7. Install wheel and tire assembly, then remove jack and lower vehicle.

SPINDLE REPLACE

SEDAN MODELS

1. Raise and support vehicle, then remove tire and wheel assembly.
2. Remove brake drum, then the brake hose-to-strut retaining clip.
3. Remove brake backing plate attaching bolts, then the plate. Wire backing plate out of the way.
4. Remove control arm-to-spindle attaching bolts, washers and nuts, then the tension strut nut, washer and bushing.
5. Remove spindle-to-strut pinch bolt, then the spindle.
6. Position replacement spindle onto tension strut, then onto shock strut.
7. Install new strut-to-spindle pinch bolt. Do not tighten at this time.
8. Install tension strut bushing, washer and new nut. Do not tighten at this time.
9. Install new control arm-to-spindle attaching bolts.
10. Using suitable jack, raise lower control arm to normal curb height, then tighten nuts and bolts as follows:
    a. Torque spindle-to-strut bolt to 55-81 ft. lbs.
    b. Torque tension strut nut to 52-74 ft. lbs.
    c. Torque control arm-to-spindle attaching nuts to 52-74 ft. lbs.
11. Install brake backing plate and brake hose-to-strut retaining clip.
12. Install brake drum and wheel and tire assembly.
13. Lower vehicle.

WAGON MODELS

1. Raise and support vehicle, then remove tire and wheel assembly. **If vehicle is raised on frame contact hoist, position suitable jack under lower control arm to raise arm to normal curb height.**
2. Remove brake drum and wheel bearings, then the brake backing plate.
3. Remove upper control arms-to-crossmember attaching nuts and bolts.
4. Remove bolt, one washer, adjusting cam and nut attaching spindle to lower control arm.
5. Remove spindle and upper control arm as an assembly, then remove upper control arm-to-spindle attaching nut and the spindle.
6. Install upper control arms to spindle using a new nut. Do not tighten at this time.
7. Position spindle and upper control arm assembly on lower control arm. Install new nut and washer, existing adjusting cam and new nut. Do not tighten at this time.
8. Position front and rear upper control arms to body bracket, then install new nuts and bolts. Do not tighten at this time.
9. Ensure lower control arm is at normal curb height, then proceed as follows:
    a. Torque upper control arms-to-body bracket attaching bolts to 70-95 ft. lbs.
    b. Torque upper control arms-to-spindle attaching nut to 150-190 ft. lbs.
    c. Torque spindle-to-lower control arm attaching nut to 60-86 ft. lbs.
    d. Install brake backing plate, brake drum and wheel bearings.
    e. Install tire and wheel assembly, then remove jack assembly and lower vehicle.

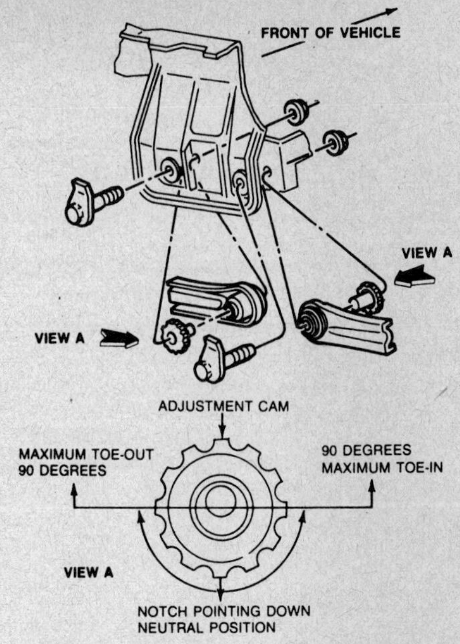

Fig. 6 Lower control arm bushing & cam installation. Sedan models

LOWER CONTROL ARM REPLACE

SEDAN MODELS

1. Raise and support vehicle.
2. Disconnect brake proportioning valve from left side front control arm, then the parking brake cable from control arms.
3. Remove control arm-to-spindle attaching bolt, nut and washer.
4. Remove control arm-to-body bracket attaching bolt and nut, then the control arm.
5. Position control arm (and cam where required, **Fig. 6**) at body bracket, then install new nut and bolt. Do not tighten at this time. **When installing control arms, the offset must face up (the arms are stamped "bottom" on lower edge). The flange edge of the right side rear arm stamping must face the front of the vehicle. The other three must face the rear of the vehicle. During installation, note that the control arms have two adjustment cams that fit inside the bushings at the control arm-to-body attachment. The cam is installed from the rear on the left arm and from the front on the right arm, Fig. 6.**
6. Position outer end of arm at spindle, then install new bolt, washer and nut. Torque nut to 52-74 ft. lbs.
7. Torque control arm-to-body bracket attaching nut to 52-74 ft. lbs.
8. Attach parking brake cables and brake proportioning valve to control arms.
9. Lower vehicle, then check rear toe and reset as necessary.

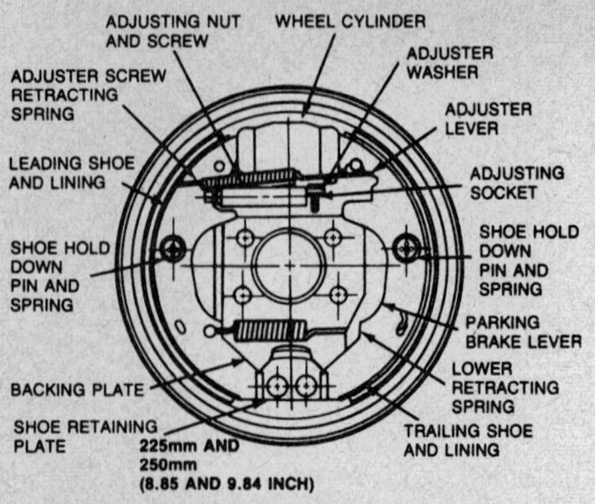

Fig. 7 Exploded view of rear hub & bearing assembly

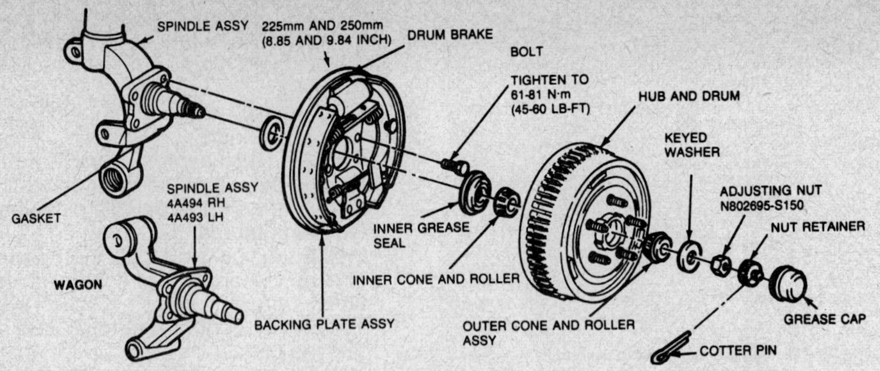

Fig. 8 Rear brake assembly

WAGON MODELS

1. Raise and support rear of vehicle, then remove tire and wheel assembly.
2. Remove rear spring. Refer to Spring, Replace for procedure.
3. Remove lower control arm-to-body bracket attaching bolt, then the control arm.
4. Position lower control arm in body bracket, then install new nut and bolt with bolt head toward front of vehicle. Do not tighten at this time.
5. Install rear spring. Refer to Spring, Replace for procedure.
6. Using suitable jack, support lower control arm at normal curb height, then torque control arm-to-body bracket attaching bolt to 40-55 ft. lbs.
7. Torque lower control arm-to-spindle attaching bolt to 60-86 ft. lbs.
8. Install tire and wheel assembly, then lower vehicle.

SPRING
REPLACE
WAGON MODELS

1. Raise vehicle on frame contact hoist, then using suitable floor jack, raise lower control arm to normal curb height.
2. Remove tire and wheel assembly.
3. Remove brake hose bracket from body, then the stabilizer bar U-bracket from lower control arm.
4. Remove shock absorber-to-lower control arm attaching nuts, then the parking brake cable and clip from lower control arm.
5. Remove tension strut-to-lower control arm attaching nut and bolt, then wire upper control arms and spindle to keep them from dropping down.
6. Remove lower control arm-to-spindle attaching nut, bolt and toe adjusting cam.
7. Carefully lower control arm with floor jack until spring can be removed.
8. Remove spring and insulators.
9. Install lower spring insulator on control arm. Ensure insulator is seated properly.
10. Position upper insulator on spring, then install spring on lower control arm. Ensure spring is properly seated.
11. Using floor jack, raise lower control arm and spring while guiding upper spring insulator onto upper spring seat.
12. Position spindle in lower control arm and install new bolt, nut and existing toe adjusting cam. Install bolt with head facing front of vehicle. Do not tighten at this time.
13. Remove wire from upper control arms and spindle assembly, then position tension strut in lower control arm and install new nut and bolt. Do not tighten at this time.
14. Install parking brake cable and clip to lower control arm, then install lower end of shock absorber. Torque nuts to 12-20 ft. lbs.
15. Install stabilizer bar and U-bracket. Install new bolt and torque to 20-30 ft. lbs.
16. Install brake hose bracket. Torque attaching bolt to 8-12 ft. lbs.
17. Using floor jack, raise lower control arm to normal curb height, then torque lower control arm-to-spindle nut to 60-86 ft. lbs. and tension strut-to-body bracket bolt to 40-55 ft. lbs.
18. Install tire and wheel assembly, then remove floor jack and lower vehicle.
19. Check rear end alignment.

UPPER CONTROL ARMS
REPLACE
WAGON MODELS

1. Raise vehicle on frame contact hoist, then using suitable floor jack, raise lower control arm to normal curb height.
2. Remove wheel and tire assembly, then brake hose bracket from body.
3. Loosen spindle-to-upper control arms attaching nut.
4. Loosen spindle-to-lower control arm attaching nut.
5. Remove upper control arms-to-body brackets attaching nuts and bolts. Ensure spindle does not fall outward.
6. Carefully tilt upper part of spindle outward until upper control arms are clear of body brackets. Wire spindle in this position.
7. Remove spindle-to-upper control arms attaching nut, then the upper control arms.
8. Install upper control arms on spindle and install new nut. Do not tighten at this time.
9. Position upper control arms in body brackets, then install new nuts and bolts. Torque to 70-95 ft. lbs. Remove wire from spindle.
10. Torque upper control arms-to-spindle attaching nut to 150-190 ft. lbs.
11. Torque lower control arm-to-spindle attaching nut to 60-86 ft. lbs.
12. Install brake hose bracket on body, then the tire and wheel assembly.
13. Remove floor jack and lower vehicle.
14. Check rear wheel alignment and correct as necessary.

BRAKE ADJUSTMENTS

Although the brakes are self-adjusting, **Fig. 7**, an initial adjustment will be required after a brake repair. The initial adjustment is performed as follows:

1. Determine inside diameter of brake drum surface using brake shoe gauge tool D81L-1103-A or equivalent. Adjust brake shoe diameter to fit gauge. Hold automatic adjusting lever out of engagement while rotating adjusting screw and ensure that screw rotates freely.
2. Install brake drum, **Fig. 8**, then tire and wheel assembly.
3. Adjust wheel bearings. Refer to Wheel Bearings, Adjust for procedure.

WHEEL BEARINGS
ADJUST

1. Raise and support rear of vehicle, then remove grease cap.
2. Remove cotter pin and nut retainer.
3. Back of adjusting nut one full turn, then while rotating hub and drum assembly to seat bearings, torque ad-

justing nut to 17-25 ft. lbs.
4. Loosen adjusting nut one-half turn, then re-torque to 10-15 inch lbs.
5. Install nut retainer and cotter pin. Bend over ends of cotter pin over retainer flange. **Properly adjusted wheel bearings may have a slightly loose feel which is considered normal.**

PARKING BRAKE
ADJUST

1. Ensure parking brake is released.
2. With transmission in Neutral, raise and support vehicle.
3. Tighten parking brake nut against brake equalizer until rear brakes drag, then loosen nut until rear brakes are fully released.
4. Lower vehicle, then check parking brake operation.

MASTER CYLINDER
REPLACE

1. Remove brake tubes from primary and secondary fluid outlet ports. On wagon models, remove brake tubes from pressure control valves. **Sedan models do not use master cylinder mounted pressure control valves. Instead, a floor pan mounted brake differential control valve is used. This valve utilizes a mechanical linkage to the lower control arm to vary rear brake hydraulic pressure according to vehicle load.**
2. Disconnect brake warning light connector.
3. Remove brake booster-to-master cylinder attaching bolts, then slide master cylinder upward from vehicle.
4. Reverse procedure to install. After installation is complete, fill master cylinder with heavy duty brake fluid and bleed brakes.

POWER BRAKE BOOSTER
REPLACE

1. Disconnect battery ground cable.
2. Remove master cylinder. Refer to Master Cylinder, Replace for procedure.
3. Disconnect booster vacuum hose from check valve.
4. Remove stop lamp switch. Refer to Stop Light Switch, Replace in "Electrical Section" for procedure.
5. Remove brake booster-to-dash panel attaching nuts, then slide booster pushrod and pushrod bushing off brake pedal pin.
6. Remove vacuum tee attaching bolts, then position tee aside.
7. Position wiring harness aside.
8. Remove transmission shift cable and bracket.
9. Move booster assembly forwards until it clears dash panel, then remove booster.
10. Reverse procedure to install.

Front Suspension & Steering Section

INDEX

DESCRIPTION

This suspension is of the gas filled MacPherson strut type, **Fig. 1.** The strut top mount consists of a rubber insulated bearing and seat and coil spring insulator. The top mount is attached to the body side apron by three bolts. The lower part of the strut is mounted in the steering knuckle and is retained by a pinch bolt. A forged lower control arm is attached to the subframe and to the steering knuckle. A tension strut is connected to the lower control arm and to the forward part of the subframe.

STRUT ASSEMBLY
REPLACE

1. Place ignition switch in Off position and ensure steering wheel is not locked.
2. Remove hub nut and loosen three strut attaching nuts, then raise and support vehicle. Do nut raise vehicle with lower control arm.

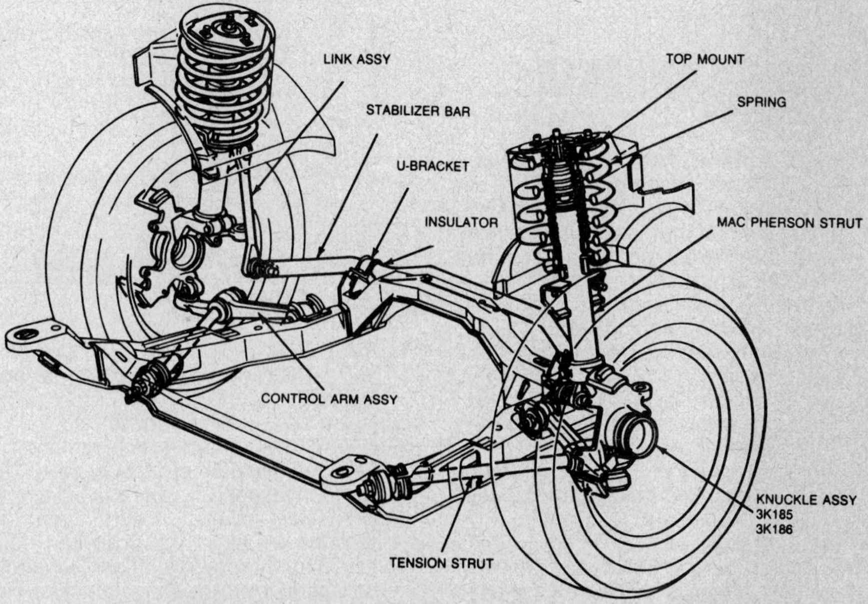

Fig. 1 Front suspension assembly

3. Remove wheel and tire assembly.
4. Remove brake caliper and wire it aside.
5. Remove brake rotor and tie rod end.
6. Remove stabilizer bar link nut, then remove link from strut.
7. Remove lower control arm-to-steering knuckle pinch nut and bolt, then slightly spread joint and remove lower control arm.
8. Using suitable hub remover/installer, press axle from hub. Wire axle shaft to body to maintain level position. **Do not allow axle shaft to move outward. Over extension of the constant velocity (CV) joint could result in separation of internal parts, which could cause CV joint failure.**
9. Remove strut-to-steering knuckle pinch bolt, then spread joint slightly and remove steering knuckle and hub assembly.
10. Remove strut attaching nuts, then remove strut assembly from vehicle.
11. Compress strut spring with coil spring compressor D85P-7178-A or equivalent.
12. Using a 10 mm box wrench, restrain strut shaft, then remove strut mounting nut with suitable 21 mm crow foot socket. **Do not allow strut shaft to rotate.**
13. Loosen compressor tool, then remove strut top mount bracket assembly, bearing and seat assembly and spring, **Fig. 2.**
14. Reverse procedure to install, noting the following:
    a. Torque strut-to-steering knuckle pinch bolt to 70-95 ft. lbs.
    b. Torque lower control arm-to-steering knuckle pinch bolt to 40-55 ft. lbs.
    c. Torque stabilizer bar assembly-to-strut to 35-48 ft. lbs.
    d. Torque tie rod end attaching nut to 23-36 ft. lbs.
    e. Torque strut attaching nuts to 20-30 ft. lbs.
    f. With vehicle on ground, torque hub nut to 180-200 ft. lbs.

STEERING KNUCKLE
REPLACE

1. Place ignition switch in Off position and ensure steering wheel is not locked.
2. Remove hub nut and loosen three strut attaching nuts, then raise and support vehicle. Do nut raise vehicle with lower control arm.
3. Remove wheel and tire assembly.
4. Remove brake caliper and wire it aside.
5. Remove brake rotor and tie rod end.
6. Remove stabilizer bar link nut, then remove link from strut.
7. Remove lower control arm-to-steering knuckle pinch nut and bolt, then slightly spread joint and remove lower control arm.
8. Using suitable hub remover/installer, press axle from hub. Wire axle shaft to body to maintain level position. **Do not allow axle shaft to move outward. Over extension of the constant velocity (CV) joint could result in separation of internal parts, which could cause CV joint failure.**

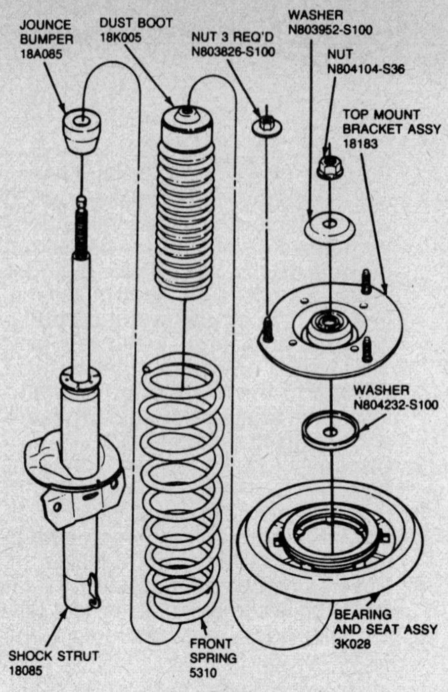

Fig. 5 MacPherson strut assembly

9. Remove rotor splash shield (if equipped).
10. Remove strut-to-steering knuckle pinch bolt, then spread joint slightly and remove steering knuckle and hub assembly.
11. Reverse procedure to install, noting the following:
    a. Torque strut-to-steering knuckle pinch bolt to 70-95 ft. lbs.
    b. Torque lower control arm-to-steering knuckle pinch bolt to 40-55 ft. lbs.
    c. Torque stabilizer bar assembly-to-strut to 35-48 ft. lbs.
    d. Torque tie rod end attaching nut to 23-36 ft. lbs.
    e. Torque strut attaching nuts to 20-30 ft. lbs.
    f. With vehicle on ground, torque hub nut to 180-200 ft. lbs.

LOWER CONTROL ARM
REPLACE

1. Place ignition switch in Off position and ensure steering wheel is not locked.
2. Raise and support vehicle.
3. Remove wheel and tire assembly.
4. Remove tension strut nut, then the dished washer.
5. Remove lower control arm-to-steering knuckle pinch nut and bolt, then slightly spread joint and separate ball joint from steering knuckle. **Do not use a hammer to separate suspension pieces.**
6. Remove lower control arm inner pivot bolt and nut, then the control arm.
7. Reverse procedure to install, noting the following:
    a. Torque lower control arm pivot bolt to 70-95 ft. lbs.
    b. Torque lower control arm-to-steering knuckle attaching bolt to 40-55 ft. lbs.
    c. Torque tension strut nut to 70-95 ft. lbs.

STABILIZER BAR
REPLACE

1. Raise and support vehicle.
2. Remove stabilizer bar link-to-strut attaching nuts.
3. Remove stabilizer bar link-to-stabilizer bar attaching nuts.
4. Remove steering gear-to-sub-frame attaching bolts, then move steering gear off sub-frame.
5. Support sub-frame with suitable safety stands, then remove rear sub-frame attaching bolts. Lower rear part of sub-frame to gain access to stabilizer bar mounting brackets.
6. Remove mounting brackets, then the stabilizer bar.
7. Reverse procedure to install, noting the following:
    a. Torque stabilizer bar mounting brackets to 21-32 ft. lbs.
    b. Torque sub-frame attaching bolts to 85-100 ft. lbs.
    c. Torque stabilizer bar link attaching nuts to 35-48 ft. lbs.

STEERING GEAR
REPLACE

1. Disconnect battery ground cable.
2. Remove steering shaft weather boot-to-dash panel attaching bolts.
3. Remove intermediate shaft-to-steering column shaft attaching bolts.
4. Move weather boot aside, then remove steering gear input shaft pinch bolt and remove intermediate shaft.
5. Raise and support vehicle.
6. Remove left front wheel and heat shield.
7. Remove bundling strap retaining lines to gear.
8. Remove tie rod ends from steering knuckles.
9. Place suitable drain pan under steering gear, then remove pressure and return lines from gear and allow to drain into pan.
10. Remove nuts from gear mounting bolts. **The gear mounting bolts are pressed into the steering gear housing and should not be removed during normal service procedures.**
11. Push weather boot end into vehicle and lift steering gear out of mounting holes. Rotate gear as necessary so input shaft passes between brake booster and floorpan. Carefully start working steering gear out through left front fender apron opening.
12. Rotate input shaft as necessary so it clears left front fender apron opening

and remove steering gear from vehicle.

13. Reverse procedure to install, noting the following:
    a. Prior to installing hydraulic hoses, install new plastic seals on fittings.
    b. Torque steering gear attaching nuts to 85-100 ft. lbs.
    c. Torque hydraulic pressure hose fitting to 20-25 ft. lbs. Torque hydraulic return hose fitting to 15-20 ft. lbs. **When hydraulic fittings are properly installed, the hoses are free to swivel.**
    d. Fill power steering system with automatic transmission fluid type F.
    e. Set toe-in to specifications.

POWER STEERING PUMP REPLACE

4-153 ENGINE

1. Disconnect battery ground cable.
2. Using suitable 1/2 inch drive socket wrench, rotate tensioner pulley clockwise and remove alternator and power steering belts.
3. Position suitable drain pan under pump, then disconnect pressure and return lines and allow fluid to drain.
4. Using hub puller T69L-10300-B or equivalent, remove pulley from shaft.
5. Remove three pump-to-bracket attaching bolts, then the pump.
6. Reverse procedure to install.

V6 ENGINE

1. Disconnect battery ground cable.
2. Loosen idler pulley, then remove power steering belt.
3. Using hub puller T69L-10300-B or equivalent, remove pulley from shaft.
4. Position suitable drain pan under pump, then disconnect return line and allow fluid to drain.
5. Completely back off pressure line fitting. Line will separate during pump removal.
6. Remove three pump-to-bracket attaching bolts, then the pump.
7. Reverse procedure to install.

Wheel Alignment Section

INDEX

FRONT WHEEL ALIGNMENT

CASTER & CAMBER

1. Prior to aligning the front end, the sub-frame alignment must be checked using the following procedure.
    a. Loosen sub-frame to body attaching bolts.
    b. Install a 3/4 inch outside diameter pipe or similar tool into left front sub-frame and body alignment holes, **Fig. 1.**
    c. Align left front sub-frame and body alignment holes, then slightly tighten left front sub-frame attaching bolt.
    d. Repeat steps b and c on right front alignment holes, then recheck left front alignment.
    e. Torque sub-frame attaching bolts to 65-100 ft. lbs.
2. Center punch spot welds on both strut alignment plates, then loosen strut attaching nuts, **Fig. 2.**
3. Using Rotunda Spot-Eze or equivalent, remove spot welds. **Do not drill deeper than thickness of alignment plates.**
4. Remove strut attaching nuts, then the alignment plates.

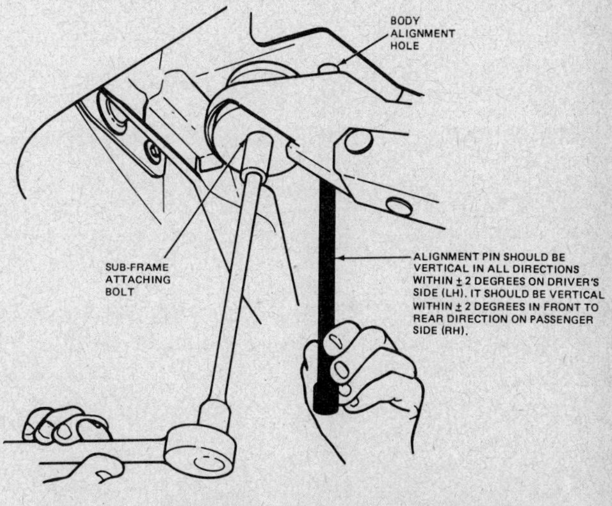

Fig. 1 Aligning front suspension

5. Remove burrs from strut towers and alignment plates, then paint all exposed metal on strut towers and alignment plates.
6. Install alignment plates, then loosely install strut attaching nuts.
7. Align front end, then torque strut attaching nuts to 20-30 ft. lbs.
8. Drill three 1/8 inch holes as indicated in **Fig. 3,** through alignment plates and strut towers, then paint exposed metal. **Do not drill deeper than 3/8 inch into strut tower.**
9. Install three 1/8 inch diameter pop rivets with a grip range of 1/4 inch into alignment plate/strut tower.

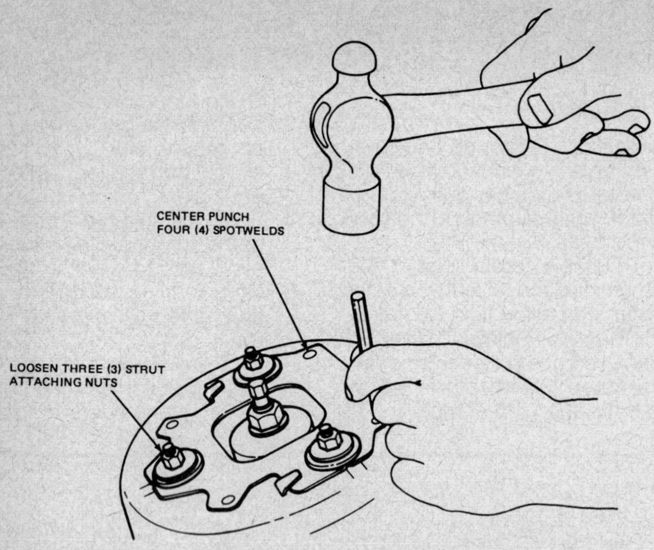

Fig. 2 Loosening alignment plate

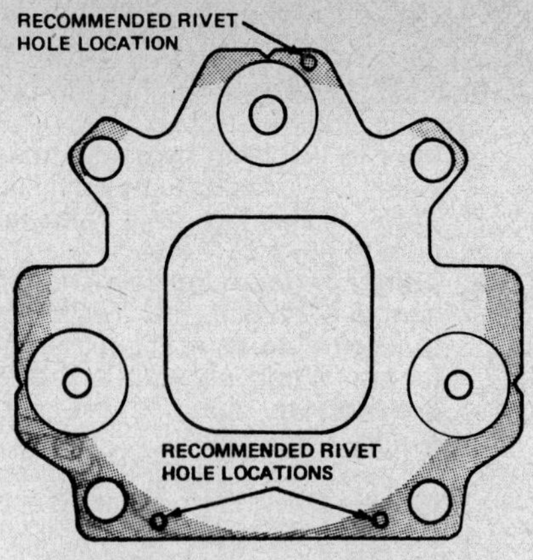

Fig. 3 Rivet hole location

TOE-IN

To adjust toe-in, lock steering wheel in straight ahead position using suitable steering wheel holder. Loosen and slide off small outer clamps from steering boot to prevent boot from twisting during adjustment procedure. Loosen tie rod adjusting, then adjust left and right tie rods until each wheel has 1/2 the desired total toe specification. Tighten tie rod adjusting nuts and install clamps. Remove steering wheel holding tool.

REAR WHEEL ALIGNMENT

CASTER & CAMBER

The caster and camber angles are factory set and cannot be adjusted.

TOE-IN

On sedan models, toe-in is adjusted by rotating the cams located inside the rear inner lower control arm bushings.

On wagon models, toe-in is adjusted by rotating the cams located inside the outer lower control arm bushings.

AIR CONDITIONING

TABLE OF CONTENTS

System Testing

INDEX

GENERAL PRECAUTIONS

The Freon refrigerant used is also known as R-12 or F-12. It is colorless and odorless both as a gas and a liquid. Since it boils (vaporizes) at −21.7°F, it will usually be in a vapor state when being handled in a repair shop. But if a portion of the liquid coolant should come in contact with the hands or face, note that its temperature momentarily will be at least 22° below zero.

Protective goggles should be worn when opening any refrigerant lines. If liquid coolant does touch the eyes, bathe the eyes quickly in cold water, then apply a bland disinfectant oil to the eyes. See an eye doctor.

When checking a system for leaks with a torch type leak detector, do not breathe the vapors coming from the flame. Do not discharge refrigerant in the area of a live flame. A poisonous phosgene gas is produced when R-12 or F-12 is burned. While the small amount of this gas produced by a leak detector is not harmful unless inhaled directly at the flame, the quantity of refrigerant released into the air when a system is purged can be extremely dangerous if allowed to come in contact with an open flame. Thus, when purging a system, be sure that the discharge hose is routed to a well ventilated place where no flame is present. Under these conditions the refrigerant will be quickly dissipated into the surrounding air.

Never allow the temperature of refrigerant drums to exceed 125°F. The resultant increase in temperature will cause a corresponding increase in pressure which may cause the safety plug to release or the drum to burst.

If it is necessary to heat a drum of refrigerant when charging a system, the drum should be placed in water no hotter than 125°F. Never use a blow torch or other open flame. If possible, a pressure release mechanism should be attached before the drum is heated.

When connecting and disconnecting service gauges on A/C systems, ensure that gauge hand valves are fully closed and that compressor service valves, if equipped, are in the back-seated (fully counterclockwise) position. Do not disconnect gauge hoses from service port adapters, if used, while gauges are connected to A/C system. To disconnect hoses, always remove adapter from service port. Do not disconnect hoses from gauge manifold while connected to A/C system, as refrigerant will be rapidly discharged.

After disconnecting gauge lines, check the valve areas to be sure service valves are correctly seated and Schraeder valves, if used, are not leaking.

EXERCISE SYSTEM

An important fact most owners ignore is that A/C units must be used periodically. Manufacturers caution that when the air conditioner is not used regularly, particularly during cold months, it should be turned on for a few minutes once every two or three weeks while the engine is running. This keeps the system in good operating condition.

Checking out the system for the effects of disuse before the onset of summer is one of the most important aspects of A/C servicing.

First clean out the condenser core, mounted in all cases at the front of the radiator. All obstructions, such as leaves, bugs and dirt, must be removed, as they will reduce heat transfer and impair the efficiency of the system. Make sure the space between the condenser and the radiator also is free of foreign matter.

Make certain the evaporator water drain is open. The evaporator cools and dehumidifies the air before it enters the passenger compartment; there, the refrigerant is changed from a liquid to a vapor. As the core cools the air, moisture condenses on it but is prevented from collecting in the evaporator by the water drain.

PERFORMANCE TEST

The system should be operated for at least 15 minutes to allow sufficient time for all parts to become completely stabilized. Determine if the system is fully charged by the use of test gauges and sight glass if one is installed on system. Head pressure will read from 180 psi to 220 psi or higher, depending upon ambient temperature and the type unit being tested. The sight glass should be free of bubbles if a glass is used in the system. Low side pressures should read approximately 15 psi to 30 psi, again depending on the ambient temperature and the unit being tested. It is not feasible to give a definite reading for all types of systems used, as the type control and component installation used on a particular system will directly influence the pressure readings on the high and low sides, **Fig. 1.**

The high side pressure will definitely be affected by the ambient or outside air temperature. A system that is operating normally will indicate a high side gauge reading between 150-170 psi with an 80°F ambient temperature. The same system will register 210-230 psi with an ambient temperature of 100°F. No two systems will register exactly the same, which requires that allowance for variations in head pressures must be considered. Following are the most important normal readings likely to be encountered during the season.

Ambient Temp.	High Side Pressure
80	150-170
90	175-195
95	185-205
100	210-230
105	230-250
110	250-270

RELATIVE TEMPERATURE OF HIGH & LOW SIDES

The high side of the system should be uniformly hot to the touch throughout. A

Evaporator Pressure Gauge Reading	Evaporator Temperature F°	High Pressure Gauge Reading	Ambient Temperature
0	-21°	45	20°
0.6	-20°	55	30°
2.4	-15°	72	40°
4.5	-10°	86	50°
6.8	- 5°	105	60°
9.2	0°	126	70°
11.8	5°	140	75°
14.7	10°	160	80°
17.1	15°	185	90°
21.1	20°	195	95°
22.5	22°	220	100°
23.9	24°	240	105°
25.4	26°	260	110°
26.9	28°	275	115°
28.5	30°	290	120°
37.0	40°	305	125°
46.7	50°	325	130°
57.7	60°		
70.1	70°		
84.1	80°		
99.6	90°		
116.9	100°		
136.0	110°		
157.1	120°		
179.0	130°		

Fig. 1 Pressure-temperature relationship (Typical). Conditions equivalent to 30 mph or 1750 engine RPM

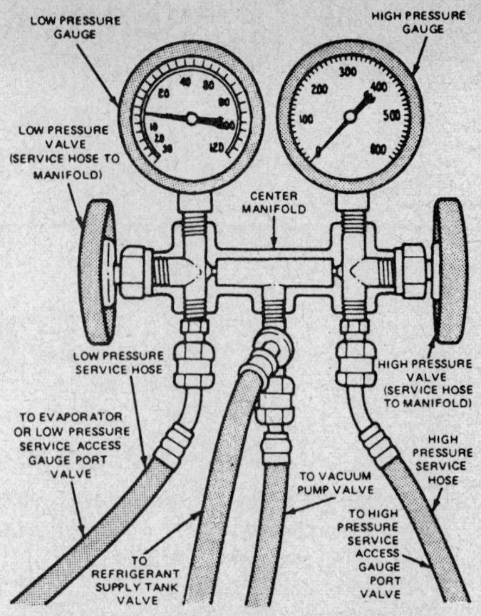

Fig. 2 Manifold gauge set hose connections (Typical)

difference in temperature will indicate a partial blockage of liquid or gas at this point.

The low side of the system should be uniformly cool to the touch with no excessive sweating of the suction line or low side service valve. Excessive sweating or frosting of the low side service valve usually indicates an expansion valve is allowing an excessive amount of refrigerant into the evaporator.

EVAPORATOR OUTPUT

At this point, provided all other inspection tests have been performed, and components have been found to operate as they should, a rapid cooling down of the interior of the vehicle should result. The use of a thermometer is not necessary to determine evaporator output. Bringing all units to the correct operating specifications will insure that the evaporator performs as intended.

DISCHARGING & EVACUATING SYSTEM

DISCHARGING SYSTEM

1. Connect gauges into system, Fig. 2, and adjust controls for maximum cooling. This is necessary when the system has not been operating to return excess oil to the compressor.
2. Operate engine for 10 to 15 minutes to stabilize the system at 1500-1750 RPM.
3. Adjust engine speed to slow idle, then shut off engine and controls.
4. Open low side hand manifold valve slightly, using a container to catch oil and refrigerant. Do not discharge the refrigerant near an open flame as a toxic gas (phosgene) can result.
5. When the system is nearly discharged, slowly open the high pressure gauge valve. **Open hand valve(s) only enough to bleed refrigerant from system. Too rapid purging will draw excessive oil from compressor and system.**
6. As soon as the system is completely discharged, close both high and low pressure valves to prevent moisture from entering the system.

EVACUATE SYSTEM WITH VACUUM PUMP

Vacuum pumps suitable for removing air and moisture from A/C systems are commercially available. A specification for system pump-down used here is 28 to 29 1/2 inches vacuum. This reading can be attained at or near sea level only. For each 1000 feet of altitude this operation is being performed, the reading will be 1 inch vacuum lower. For example, at 5000 feet elevation, only 23-24 1/2 inch of vacuum can be obtained. **The system must be completely discharged before it can be evacuated. Damage to vacuum pump may result if pressurized refrigerant is allowed to enter.**

1. With gauges connected into system, remove cap from vacuum hose connector. Install center hose from gauge manifold to vacuum pump connector. Mid-position high and low side compressor service valves (if used). Open high and low side gauge manifold hand valves.
2. Operate vacuum pump a minimum of 20-30 minutes for air and moisture removal. Watch compound gauge that system pumps down into a vacuum. System will reach 28-29 1/2 inches vacuum in not over 5 minutes. If system does not pump down, check all connections and leak test if necessary.
3. Close gauge manifold hand valves and shut off vacuum pump.
4. Check ability of system to hold vacuum. Watch compound gauge to see that gauge does not rise at a faster rate than 1 inch vacuum every 4 or 5 minutes. If compound gauge rises at too rapid a rate, install partial charge and leak test. Then evacuate system as outlined above.
5. If system holds vacuum, charge system with refrigerant.

EVACUATE SYSTEM USING CHARGING STATION

A vacuum pump is built into the charging station and is constructed to withstand repeated and prolonged use without damage. Complete moisture removal from the system is possible only with a vacuum pump constructed for the purpose.

The system must be completely discharged before it can be evacuated. Damage to the vacuum pump may result if pressurized refrigerant is allowed to enter.

1. Connect hose to vacuum pump if sys-

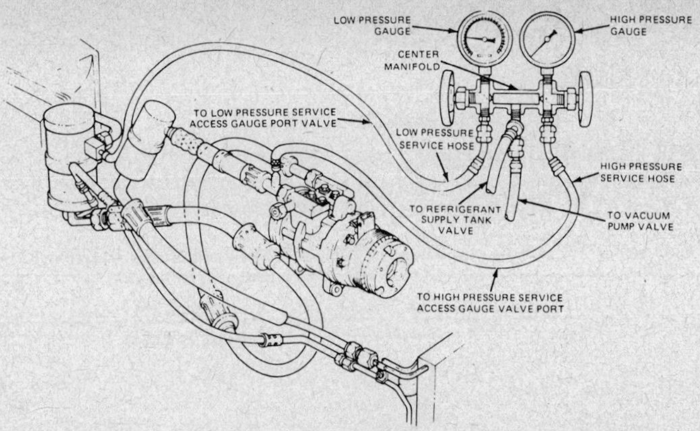

Fig. 3 Refrigerant system service connections

tem was discharged through charging station.

2. Open high and low side gauge valves of charging station.
3. Connect station into 110-volt current.
4. Engage "Off-On" switch to vacuum pump according to directions of specific station being used.
5. System should pump down into a 28-29½ inch vacuum in not more than 5 minutes. If system fails to meet this specification, repair as necessary.
6. Operate pump a minimum of 30 minutes to remove all air and moisture.
7. Close high and low side gauge valves. Open switch to turn off pump.
8. Check ability of system to hold vacuum by watching compound gauge to see that it does not rise at a rate higher than 1 inch of vacuum every 4 or 5 minutes: If rise rate is not within specifications, repair system as necessary. If rise rate is within specifications, charge system with refrigerant.

SYSTEM CHARGING

CHARGING FROM SMALL CONTAINERS

When charging from small cans, do not open manifold gauge set high pressure (discharge) gauge valve, as this can cause containers to explode.

1. Connect a suitable refrigerant dispensing valve and valve retainer such as Motorcraft tool YT-280 or equivalent to the refrigerant can.
2. Connect manifold gauge set to system, **Fig. 3.** Connect hose normally connected to R-12 tank to special valve on small can adapter. Make sure valve is closed (full clockwise position).
3. When can is connected, charge system according to procedure under "Charging From Drum." When can is empty, close valve and remove can. Connect new can open valve and continue charging until correct weight of refrigerant has entered system. Note capacity of refrigerant cans. When specifications require use of a portion of a can, weigh it to ensure proper amount of refrigerant is installed.

CHARGING FROM DRUM

1. With manifold gauge set valves closed to center hose, disconnect vacuum pump from manifold gauge set.
2. Connect center hose of manifold gauge set to refrigerant drum.
3. Purge air from center hose by loosening hose at manifold gauge set and open refrigerant drum valve. When refrigerant escapes from hose, tighten center hose connection at manifold gauge set.
4. On vehicles so equipped, disconnect wire harness connector at clutch cycling pressure switch. Install jumper wire across terminals of connector.
5. On all models, open manifold gauge set low side valve and allow refrigerant to enter system. Refrigerant can must be kept upright if vehicle low pressure service gauge port is not on suction accumulator/drier or suction accumulator fitting.
6. When system stops drawing refrigerant in, start engine and set control lever to A/C position and blower switch to "Hi" position to draw remaining refrigerant into system.
7. When specified weight of refrigerant is in system, close gauge set low pressure valve and refrigerant supply valve.
8. On vehicles so equipped, remove jumper wire from clutch cycling pressure switch connector and connect connector to pressure switch.
9. On all models, operate system until pressures stabilize to check operation and system pressures. During high ambient temperatures, a high volume fan may be necessary to blow air through the radiator and condenser to cool engine and prevent excessive refrigerant system pressures.
10. When charging is complete and system operating pressures are normal, disconnect manifold gauge set from vehicle and install protective caps on service gauge port valves.

LEAK TEST SYSTEM

The propane torch Halide Leak Detector is the most widely used of the detection devices. Therefore, only the procedure for this device will be given. The procedure is the same for any electronic detector, except that the pickup device registers the presence of refrigerant by a flashing light or high pitched squeal instead of changing the color of the flame. All other steps in preparing the system and leak testing are the same and can be followed as outlined below:

1. Stabilize system at 1500-1750 RPM. If system is empty of refrigerant, it will be necessary to install a partial charge before continuing. With gauges connected into system, adjust A/C controls for maximum cooling. Operate for 10 to 15 minutes, then shut off car engine.
2. Light leak detector. Open valve to a low flame that will not blow itself out. Warm up until copper element turns cherry red. Lower flame until flame tip is even with or slightly below center of element. For electronic tester, follow preparation procedure as given in operating instructions.
3. Move leak detector pickup under hoses, joints, seals, and any possible place for a leak to occur. **Freon 12 refrigerant is heavier than air and will move downward. If concentration of refrigerant is located, move pickup upward to locate leak. Do not inhale fumes produced by burning refrigerant.**
4. Watch for color change of flame: Pale blue, no refrigerant; yellow, small amount of refrigerant; purplish-blue, large amount of refrigerant. Repair system as necessary if leaks are located.
5. Check sensitivity of reaction plate: Pass pickup hose over empty can or crack open refrigerant container; flame should show violent reaction. If no color change, replace reaction plate, following instructions accompanying leak detector. Too high a flame will result in short life to reaction plate and poor reaction and will soon burn out element.
6. Charge system if repairs were necessary.

System Servicing

INDEX

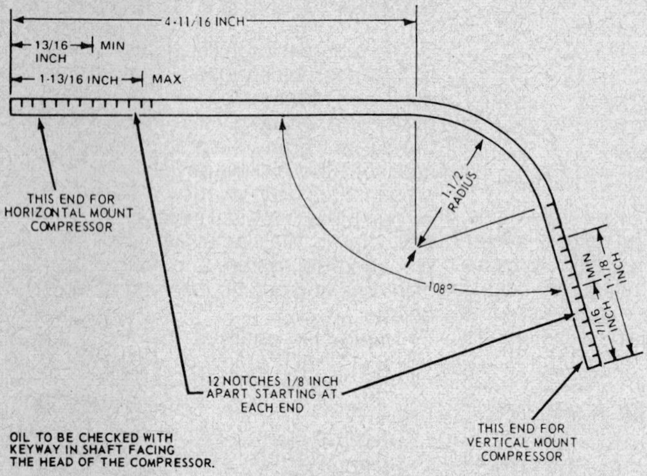

Fig. 1 York compressor oil level dipstick fabrication

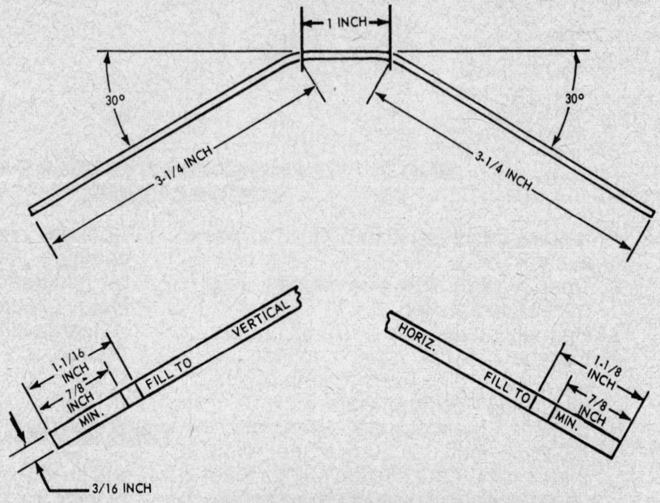

Fig. 2 Tecumseh compressor oil level dipstick fabrication

OIL CHARGE

MOTORCRAFT AXIAL 6 CYL. COMPRESSOR

Compressor Replacement

1. Idle engine for 10 minutes at approximately 1250 RPM at maximum cooling and high blower speed to distribute oil in system.
2. Remove compressor from vehicle.
3. Remove plug and allow oil to drain from compressor into a container calibrated in ounces.
4. Drain oil from new compressor.
5. If amount drained from original compressor is more than four ounces, add the same amount of new refrigerant oil to the new compressor plus amount lost during discharge.
6. If amount of oil drained from original compressor is less than 4 ounces, add 6 ounces of new refrigerant oil to the new compressor plus amount lost during discharge.

Component Replacement

Whenever a component of the A/C system is replaced, if not pre-charged by factory, measured quantities of refrigeration oil should be added to the component to assure that the total oil charge in the system is correct before the unit is placed into operation.

The oil is poured directly into the replacement component. If an evaporator is installed, pour oil into the inlet pipe with the pipe held vertically so the oil will drain into the evaporator core. No additional oil is required if valves and hoses are replaced.

Add additional oil as specified if any of the following components are replaced.

Evaporator	3 ounces
Condenser	1 ounce
Receiver	1 ounce
Condenser & Receiver Assembly	2 ounces

FORD FS6 COMPRESSOR

1. If compressor is not seized, operate engine at 1000 to 1500 RPM with A/C on maximum cooling and high blower for approximately 10 minutes.
2. Discharge refrigerant system, then remove compressor from vehicle.
3. Remove drain plug from compressor and pour refrigerant oil into a calibrated container.
4. If oil drained is less than 3 ounces, add 6 ounces of new refrigerant oil to compressor.
5. If oil drained is between 3 and 6 ounces, add the same amount of new refrigerant oil to the compressor.
6. If oil drained is more than 6 ounces, only add six ounces to compressor. **Replacement compressors are charged with 10 ounces of refrigerant oil. Before installing a replacement compressor, the oil must be drained and only 6 ounces of oil reinstalled into the replacement compressor. When certain other refrigerant system components are replaced, the oil level must be adjusted to compensate for oil retained in these components. When installing a replacement evaporator core, add 3 ounces of oil to evaporator. When installing a replacement condenser or accumulator, add 1 ounce of oil to the component.**

FORD HR-980 RADIAL 4 CYLINDER & 6P148 AXIAL 6 CYL. COMPRESSORS

A new service replacement 4 cylinder compressor contains 8 fluid ounces of refrigerant oil. Before installing replacement compressor, drain 4 fluid ounces of oil from compressor in order to maintain total system oil charge within specified limits, and a 6 cylinder compressor contains 10 ounces of oil.

When other air conditioning system components are replaced, measured amounts of 500 viscosity oil should be added to the component to ensure total oil charge is correct. Clean refrigerant oil should be added as follows:

Evaporator core.......... 3 fluid ounces
Condenser .... 1 fluid ounces
Accumulator: Drain oil from accumulator through pressure switch fitting and measure. Add equal amount plus 1 ounce clean refrigerant oil to new accumulator.

Replacement of other components such as valves or hoses does not require the addition of any refrigerant oil.

OIL LEVEL CHECK

The oil level of these compressors should be checked whenever refrigerant has been lost due to leakage or through normal system servicing.

A/C Data Table

			Refrigeration Oil			
Year	Model	Refrigerant Capacity, Lbs.	Viscosity	Total System Capacity, Ounces	Compressor Oil Level Check, Inches	Compressor Clutch Air Gap Inch
FORD & MERCURY FULL SIZE						
1982	All	$3\frac{1}{4}$	500	13	①	.021-.036
1983-87	All	$3\frac{1}{4}$	500	10	①	.021-.036
FORD & MERCURY COMPACT & INTERMEDIATE (EXC. CAPRI & MUSTANG)						
1982	Ford FS-6 Comp.	$2\frac{1}{2}$	500	13	①	.021-.036
1982-83	York Comp.	$2\frac{1}{2}$	②	10	③ ④	—
	Tecumseh 2 Cyl. Comp.	$2\frac{1}{2}$	②	11	③ ④	—
1983-85	Ford FS-6 Comp.	$2\frac{1}{2}$	500	10	①	.021-.036
	Tecumseh HR-980 Comp.	$2\frac{1}{2}$	500	8	①	.021-.036
1986-87	Ford FS-6 Comp.	$2\frac{1}{2}$	500	10	①	.021-.036
	Nippondenso 6P148 Comp.	$2\frac{1}{2}$	500	10	①	.021-.036
	Tecumseh HR-980 Comp.	$2\frac{1}{2}$	500	8	①	.009-.041
FORD ESCORT, EXP & TEMPO; MERCURY LYNX, LN7 & TOPAZ						
1982	All	$2\frac{9}{16}$	500	10	①	.021-.036
1983	Escort & Lynx	$2\frac{9}{16}$	500	10	①	.021-.036
	EXP & LN7	$2\frac{5}{16}$	500	10	①	.021-.036
1984	All	$2\frac{9}{16}$	500	10	①	.021-.036
1985	Exc. EXP	$2\frac{9}{16}$	500	10	①	.021-.056
	EXP	$2\frac{5}{16}$	500	10	①	.021-.036
1986-87	All	$2\frac{5}{16}$	500	10	①	.021-.036
FORD MUSTANG & MERCURY CAPRI						
1982-83	York Comp.	$2\frac{1}{2}$	②	10	①	—
	Tecumseh 2 Cyl. Comp.	$2\frac{1}{2}$	②	11	①	—
1983-87	Nippondenso 6P148 Comp.	$2\frac{1}{2}$	500	10	①	.021-.036
	Tecumseh HR-980 Comp.	$2\frac{1}{2}$	500	8	①	⑤
	Ford FS-6 Comp.	$2\frac{1}{2}$	500	10	①	.021-.036
LINCOLN						
1982	Exc. Continental	3	500	13	①	.021-.036
	Continental	$2\frac{1}{2}$	500	13	①	.021-.036
1983	Continental	$2\frac{1}{2}$	500	10	①	.021-.036
	Exc. Continental	3	500	10	①	.021-.036
1984-87	Continental & Mark VII	$2\frac{1}{2}$	500	10	①	.021-.036
	Town Car	3	500	10	①	.021-.036

①—Note that "Oil Level Inches" cannot be checked. Refer to total capacity in ounces. See text for procedure.

②—Suniso 5G or Capella E.

③—Dipstick reading with compressor installed.

④—York comp.: vertical mount, $\frac{7}{8}$-$1\frac{1}{8}$; horizontal mount, $\frac{13}{16}$-$1\frac{3}{16}$. Tecumseh comp.: vertical mount, $\frac{7}{8}$-$1\frac{3}{8}$; horizontal mount, $\frac{7}{8}$-$1\frac{5}{8}$.

⑤—1983-84, .021-.036"; 1985-87, .009-.041".

TECUMSEH & YORK

1. Connect manifold gauge set, then operate system for approximately 10 minutes or until system pressures stabilize. This will allow oil in the system to return to compressor sump.
2. Discharge entire refrigerant system.
3. Slowly loosen compressor oil filler plug to relieve any internal pressures in compressor. **A face shield should be worn when loosening or removing oil filler plug.**
4. Insert clean dipstick into filler plug hole until it bottoms in sump, **Figs. 1 and 2. On York compressors ensure keyway in shaft faces head of compressor before checking oil level.**
5. Remove dipstick and measure oil level. Refer to "A/C Data Table" and add refrigerant oil as necessary. Install filler plug and O-ring.
6. Evacuate and recharge system.

NIPPONDENSO

1. Operate compressor for 10 to 15 minutes at maximum cooling to stabilize system.
2. Discharge system and remove compressor from vehicle. Remove drain plug and measure amount of oil drained from compressor.
3. If less than three ounces of oil were drained from compressor, add six ounces of refrigerant oil to drained service replacement compressor.
4. If between three and six ounces of oil were drained from compressor, oil is properly distributed throughout system. Add an equal amount of refrigerant oil to drained service replacement compressor.
5. Never add more than six ounces of refrigerant oil to a replacement compressor and never install a replacement compressor containing more than six ounces of refrigerant oil. Clean refrigerant oil should be added to the following replacement components:

Evaporator .... 3 ounces
Condenser .... 1 ounce
Accumulator .... 1 ounce

Charging Valve Location

Model	High Pressure Fitting	Low Pressure Fitting
Ford & Mercury Exc. Full Size	High Pressure Line From Compressor	Low Pressure Line From Compressor
Ford & Mercury Full Size	High Pressure Line From Compressor	Accumulator
Lincoln Exc. Continental	High Pressure Line From Compressor	Accumulator
Continental	High Pressure Line From Compressor	Low Pressure Line From Compressor

ENGINE COOLING FANS

TABLE OF CONTENTS

Variable Speed Fans

INDEX

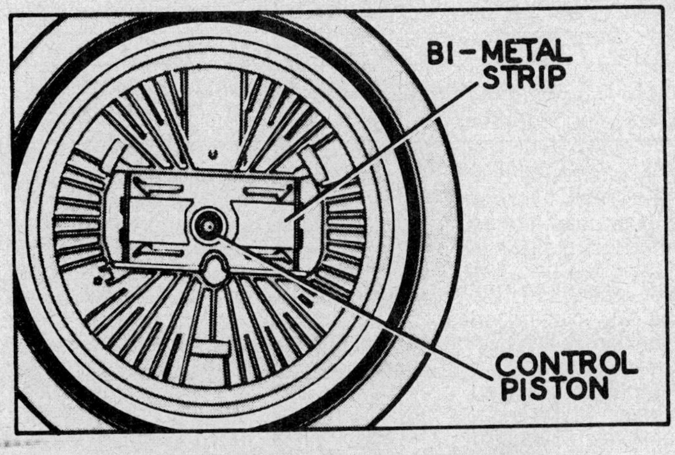

Fig. 1 Variable-speed fan with flat bi-metal thermostatic spring

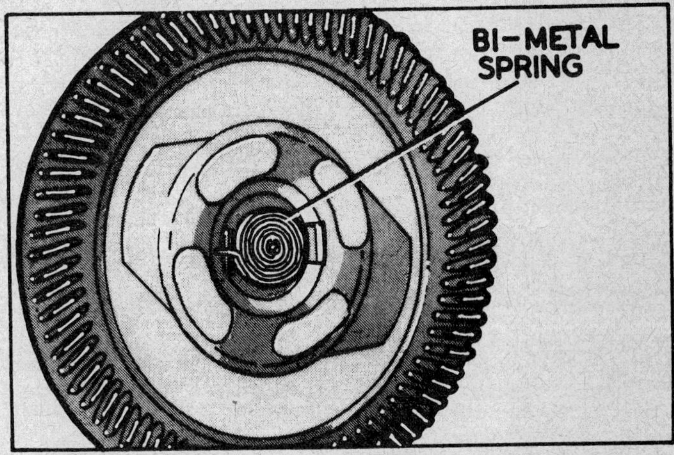

Fig. 2 Variable-speed fan with coiled bi-metal thermostatic spring

DESCRIPTION

The fan drive clutch is a fluid coupling containing silicone oil. Fan speed is regulated by the torque-carrying capacity of the silicone oil. The more silicone oil in the coupling the greater the fan speed, and the less silicone oil the slower the fan speed.

Two types of fan drive clutches are in use. On one, **Fig. 1,** a bi-metallic strip and control piston on the front of the fluid coupling regulates the amount of silicone oil entering the coupling. The bi-metallic strip bows outward with an increase in surrounding temperature and allows a piston to move outward. The piston opens a valve regulating the flow of silicone oil into the coupling from a reserve chamber. The silicone oil is returned to the reserve chamber through a bleed hole when the valve is closed.

On the other type of fan drive clutch, **Fig. 2,** a heat-sensitive, bi-metal spring connected to an opening plate brings about a similar result. Both units cause the fan speed to increase with a rise in temperature and to decrease as the temperature goes down.

In some cases a Flex-Fan is used instead of a Fan Drive Clutch. Flexible blades vary the volume of air being drawn through the radiator, automatically increasing the pitch at low engine speeds.

FAN DRIVE CLUTCH TEST

Do not operate the engine until the fan has been first checked for possible cracks and separations.

Run the engine at a fast idle speed (1000 RPM) until normal operating temperature is reached. This process can be speeded up by blocking off the front of the radiator with cardboard. Regardless of temperatures, the unit must be operated for at least five minutes immediately before being tested.

Stop the engine and, using a glove or a cloth to protect the hand, immediately check the effort required to turn the fan. If considerable effort is required, it can be assumed that the coupling is operating satisfactorily. If very little effort is required to turn the fan, it is an indication that the coupling is not operating properly and should be replaced.

If the clutch fan is the coiled bi-metal spring type, it may be tested while the vehicle is being driven. To check, disconnect the bi-metal spring and rotate 90° counterclockwise. This disables the temperature-controlled free-wheeling feature and the clutch performs like a conventional fan. If this cures the overheating condition, replace the clutch fan.

SERVICE PROCEDURE

To prevent silicone fluid from draining into fan drive bearing, do not store or place drive unit on bench with rear of shaft pointing downward.

The removal procedure for either type of fan clutch assembly is generally the same for all cars. Merely unfasten the unit from the water pump and remove the assembly from the car.

The variable speed fan with flat bi-metal thermostatic spring may be partially disassembled for inspection and cleaning. Remove screws holding the assembly together and separate the fan from the drive clutch. Next remove the metal strip on the front by pushing one end of it toward the fan clutch body so it clears the retaining bracket. Then push the strip to the side so that its opposite end will spring out of place. Now remove the small control piston underneath it.

Check the piston for free movement of the coupling device. If the piston sticks, clean it with emery cloth. If the bi-metal strip is damaged, replace the entire unit. These strips are not interchangeable.

When reassembling, install the control piston so that the projection on the end of it will contact the metal strip. Then install the metal strip. After reassembly, clean the clutch drive with a cloth soaked in solvent. Avoid dipping the clutch assembly in any type of liquid. Install the assembly in the reverse order of removal.

The coil spring type of fan clutch cannot be disassembled, serviced or repaired. If it does not function properly it must be replaced with a new unit.

Electric Cooling Fans

INDEX

CAUTION: On models equipped with electric engine cooling fans, the battery ground cable should be disconnected whenever under hood service is performed.

DESCRIPTION

EXC. CONTINENTAL & MARK VII W/6-146 DIESEL ENGINE

The cooling fan is activated by the thermal switch when engine coolant temperature reaches approximately 210-220 degrees F. The fan will continue to operate until coolant temperature drops to approximately 185 to 193 degrees F, at which time the thermal switch opens, releasing the relay contacts which supply current to the fan motor. On models equipped with A/C, the fan motor will continue to operate whenever the compressor clutch is operating regardless of coolant temperature. On some models, two fuses are used to protect the fan motor and thermal switch. A 16 amp fuse is located in the fan motor relay at the left hand dash panel near the steering column. There is also an 8 amp fuse located in the fuse panel. Cycling of the cooling fan will cause the temperature gauge to read between mid and upper range of the gauge range.

CONTINENTAL & MARK VII W/6-146 DIESEL ENGINE

These vehicles have an electric pusher fan mounted behind the grille, in addition to the belt driven engine cooling fan attached to the water pump.

The electric cooling fan system consists of a fan and an electric motor mounted on the fan shroud, an ambient temperature switch and a cooling fan relay.

The electric cooling fan is wired to operate only when the A/C compressor is operating and the ambient temperature is above 70°F. The cooling fan relay is energized by power from the A/C blower motor speed controller which then allows battery current to flow to the electric cooling fan. The cooling fan relay is energized only when the A/C compressor clutch field coil is engaged and the ambient temperature switch, located on the hood lock support, is closed. The electric cooling fan will only operate when the ignition switch is in the "Run" position, since the A/C system can only operate when the ignition switch is in "Run."

The A/C clutch field coil is powered through the A/C cutout relay, which is energized to turn off power to the clutch field coil in one of two ways.

With EGR vacuum below 7 inches Hg and turbo boost pressure below 2 psi the A/C cutout switch and the A/C turbo boost switch are closed, providing a ground to energize the A/C cutout relay. With the relay energized, the current to the A/C clutch field coil is turned off.

With engine coolant temperature above 233°F, the coolant temperature switch closes, providing the ground to energize the A/C cutout relay.

TROUBLESHOOTING

For troubleshooting procedures refer to **Fig. 1,** to determine which electric engine cooling fan system applies to a particular model.

TYPES 1 & 2

Refer to **Figs. 2 and 3,** during the following procedures.

1. Check cooling fan fusible link. If fusible link is not blown, go to step 2. If blown, repair and retest.
2. Disconnect fan motor electrical connector, then connect a jumper wire from motor ground connection to a known good ground and a jumper wire from battery positive to motor B+ connection. If motor does not run, replace motor. If motor runs, reconnect electrical connector and proceed to step 3.
3. On type 2 systems, turn ignition "On." On both systems disconnect coolant temperature switch connector, then connect a jumper wire from connector to ground. If motor runs, check switch ground. If ground is satisfactory, replace coolant temperature switch. If motor does not run, proceed to step 4.
4. Using an ohmmeter, check continuity of wire 197 from temperature switch to fan relay. If no continuity exists, check circuit 197 for opens. If continuity exists, connect a jumper wire from coolant temperature switch connector to ground and proceed to step 5.
5. Disconnect fan relay wire connector then, connect a jumper wire from wire terminal 37 to 228. If motor runs, replace fan relay. If motor does not run, check circuit 37 for opens.

TYPE 3

Refer to **Fig. 4,** during the following procedures.

1. Check cooling fan fusible link. If fusible link is not blown, go to step 2. If blown, repair and retest.
2. Disconnect coolant temperature switch connector, then connect a jumper wire from connector to ground and turn ignition "On." If fan motor does not run, proceed to step 3. If fan motor does run, primary system is operating satisfactory. If complaint is overheating, replace coolant temperature switch.
3. Connect coolant temperature switch connector. Set A/C controls on maximum and turn ignition "On." If fan motor does not run, proceed to step 4. If fan motor runs, system is satisfactory.
4. Disconnect fan motor electrical connector, then connect a jumper wire from motor ground connection to a known good ground and a jumper wire from battery positive to motor

Year	Engine	Models	With Fuel Economy Package	With Auto. Trans.	With Power Brakes	With Air Conditioning	With High Output Engine	With Fuel Injection	System Type
1982	1.6L	Escort, EXP, LN7 & Lynx	—	—	—	No	—	—	1
	1.6L	Escort, EXP, LN7 & Lynx	—	—	No	Yes	—	—	3
	1.6L	Escort, EXP, LN7 & Lynx	—	—	Yes	Yes	—	—	4
	2.3L	Fairmont & Zephyr	Yes	—	—	No	—	—	1
	2.3L	Capri & Mustang	—	—	—	—	—	—	5
	2.3L	Cougar, Fairmont, Granada & Zephyr	No	—	—	Yes	—	—	5
1983	1.6L	Escort, EXP, LN7 & Lynx	No	Yes	—	No	No	No	1
	1.6L	Escort, EXP, LN7 & Lynx	Yes	No	—	No	No	No	2
	1.6L	Escort, EXP, LN7 & Lynx	No	Yes	Yes	Yes	—	No	9
	1.6L	Escort, EXP, LN7 & Lynx	No	No	—	Yes	No	No	11
	1.6L	Escort, EXP, LN7 & Lynx	No	No	—	Yes	Yes	No	13
	1.6L	Escort, EXP, LN7 & Lynx	No	—	—	Yes	No	Yes	10
	2.3L	All	Yes	—	—	No	—	—	2
	2.3L	All	No	—	—	No	—	—	1
	2.3L, 3.3L	All	No	—	—	Yes	—	—	6
	3.8L	Exc. Capri & Mustang	No	—	—	Yes	—	—	6
	3.8L	Capri & Mustang	No	—	—	Yes	—	—	5
1984	1.6L ①	Escort, EXP & Lynx	—	No	—	Yes	No	No	14
	1.6L ①	Escort, EXP & Lynx	—	No	—	Yes	Yes	No	15
	1.6L ①	Escort, EXP & Lynx	—	Yes	—	Yes	No	No	17
	1.6L ①	Escort, EXP & Lynx	—	—	—	Yes	No	Yes	18
	1.6L ①	Escort, EXP & Lynx	—	—	—	No	No	No	26
	1.6L ②	Escort, EXP & Lynx	—	—	—	Yes	Yes	Yes	20
	2.0L ③	Escort, EXP, Lynx, Tempo & Topaz	—	—	—	Yes	—	Yes	19
	2.3L ①	Exc. Tempo & Topaz	—	—	—	Yes	—	—	7
	2.3L ②	Exc. Tempo & Topaz	—	—	—	Yes	Yes	Yes	5
	—	Tempo & Topaz	—	—	—	—	—	—	25
	2.3L	Tempo & Topaz	Yes	—	—	—	No	—	2
	2.3L	Tempo & Topaz	No	—	—	—	Yes	—	12
1985	1.6L	Escort, EXP & Lynx	Yes	No	—	Yes	No	—	14
	1.6L	Escort, EXP & Lynx	No	No	—	Yes	Yes	—	16
	1.6L	Escort, EXP & Lynx	—	Yes	—	Yes	—	No	21
	1.6L	Escort, EXP & Lynx	—	—	—	Yes	—	Yes	22
	1.6L	Escort, EXP & Lynx	—	—	—	No	—	—	26
	2.0L	Escort, EXP, Lynx, Tempo & Topaz	—	—	—	Yes	—	Yes	23
	2.3L	Tempo & Topaz	—	—	—	Yes	—	—	24
	2.3L	Tempo & Topaz	—	—	—	No	—	—	27
	2.3L	Exc. Tempo & Topaz	—	—	—	Yes	—	—	28
	2.4L ③	Continental & Mark VII	—	—	—	Yes	—	Yes	29
1986-87	1.9L	Escort & Lynx	—	No	—	Yes	—	—	30
	1.9L	Escort & Lynx	—	—	—	No	—	—	31
	1.9L	Escort & Lynx	—	Yes	—	Yes	—	—	32
	1.9L	Escort & Lynx	—	—	—	Yes	—	Yes	33
	2.0L ③	Escort, Lynx, Tempo & Topaz	—	—	—	Yes	—	Yes	34
	2.3L	Tempo & Topaz	—	—	—	Yes	—	—	35
	2.3L	Tempo & Topaz	—	—	—	No	—	—	36
	2.3L	Exc. Tempo & Topaz	—	—	—	Yes	—	—	28
1987	2.0L	Tempo & Topaz	—	—	—	Yes	—	—	8

①—Exc. Turbocharged.
②—Turbocharged.
③—Diesel.

Fig. 1 Electric engine cooling fan system application chart

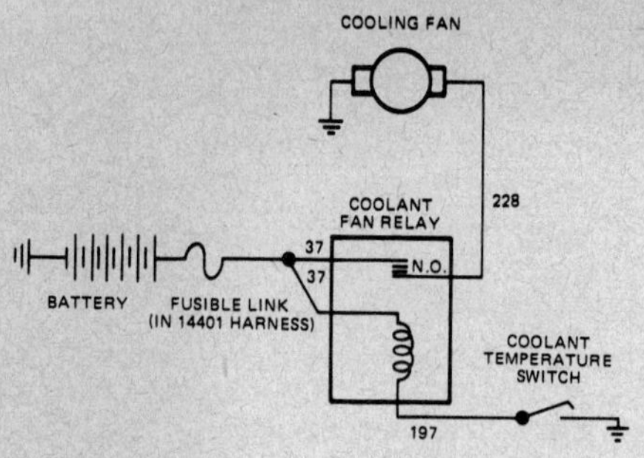

COLOR CODES

CIRCUIT NUMBER	COLOR
37	Y
197	T/O HASH
228	BR/Y

Fig. 2 Electric engine cooling fan wiring diagram. Type 1

B+ connection, **Fig. 5.** If motor does not run, replace motor. If motor runs, reconnect electrical connection and proceed to step 5.

5. Disconnect cooling fan relay connector and turn ignition "On." Using a test light, check for voltage at terminals 37 and 354, **Fig. 6.** If there is no voltage at one or both terminals, service relay feed circuits. If voltage at both terminals, proceed to step 6.
6. Connect jumper wire between terminals 354 and 228, **Fig. 6.** If fan motor does not run, repair wiring from relay connector to motor connector. If motor runs, disconnect jumper wire and proceed to step 7.
7. Using an ohmmeter, check continuity of wire 228 from relay connector to coolant temperature switch connector. If no continuity exists, repair wires and/or connectors. If continuity exists, replace cooling fan relay and recheck step 2.
8. Disconnect A/C relay connector. Using an ohmmeter, check continuity of wire 228 from relay to motor. If no continuity exists, repair wires and/or connectors. If continuity exists, proceed to step 9.
9. Reconnect fan motor connector, then disconnect A/C relay connector. Set A/C controls on maximum and turn ignition "On." Using a test light, check for voltage at terminals 37 and 321, **Fig. 7.** If there is no voltage at one or both terminals, service relay feed circuits or A/C control and recheck step 3. If there is voltage at both terminals, go to step 10.
10. Connect jumper wire to base of relay and connect to known good ground. If fan motor does not run, replace relay and recheck step 3. If fan motor runs, clean relay ground.

TYPE 4

Refer to **Fig. 8,** during the following procedures.

1. Check cooling fan fuse and fusible link. If fuse or fusible link is not blown, proceed to step 2. If fuse or fusible link is blown, repair or replace as necessary and retest.
2. Disconnect coolant temperature switch connector, then connect a jumper wire from connector to ground and turn ignition "On." If fan motor does not run, proceed to step 5. If fan motor runs, primary system is operating satisfactory. If complaint is overheating, replace coolant temperature switch.
3. Reconnect coolant temperature switch connector. Set A/C controls on maximum and turn ignition "On." If fan motor does not run, proceed to step

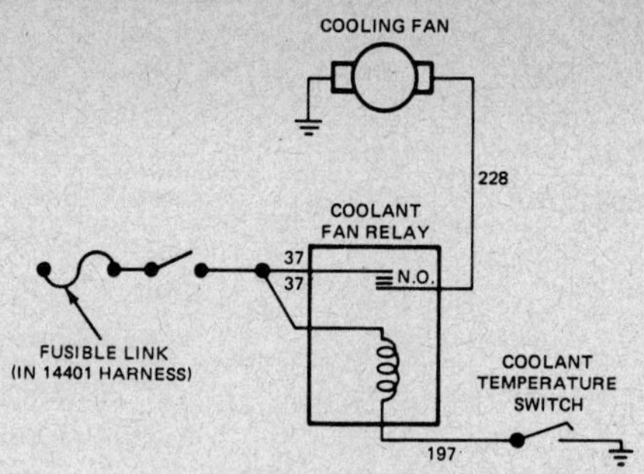

COLOR CODES

CIRCUIT NUMBER	COLOR
37	Y
197	T/O HASH
228	BR/Y

Fig. 3 Electric engine cooling fan wiring diagram. Type 2

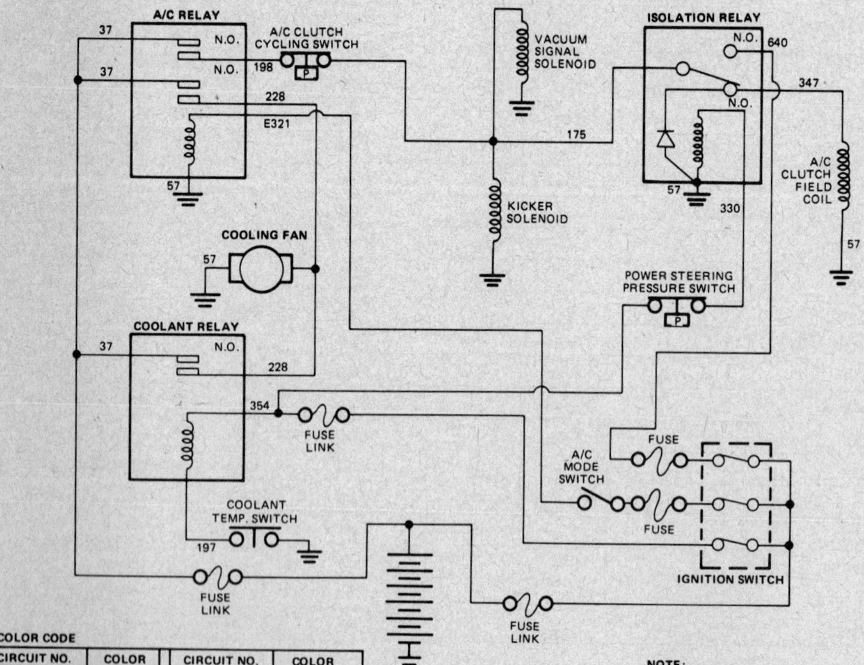

COLOR CODE

CIRCUIT NO.	COLOR	CIRCUIT NO.	COLOR
37	Y	197	T/O HASH
198	T/Y DOT	175	B/Y DOT
228	B/Y	330	Y/LG
E321	G/W	640	R/YHASH
57	B	347	B/YHASH
354	LG/Y		

Fig. 4 Electric engine cooling fan wiring diagram. Type 3

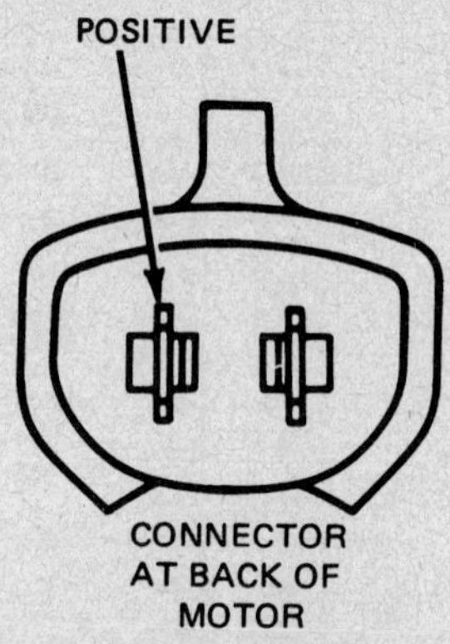

Fig. 5 Fan motor terminal identification

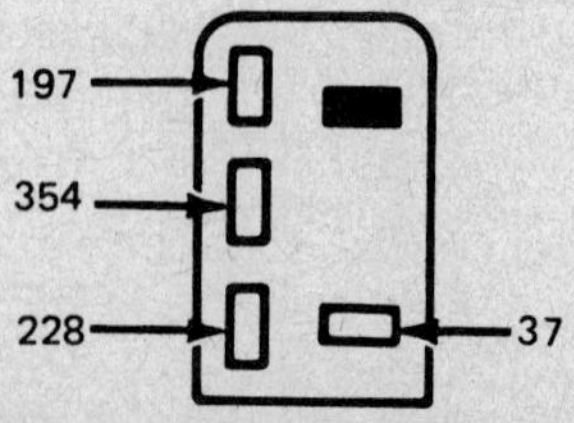

Fig. 6 Cooling fan relay wire connector terminal identification. Exc. type 4

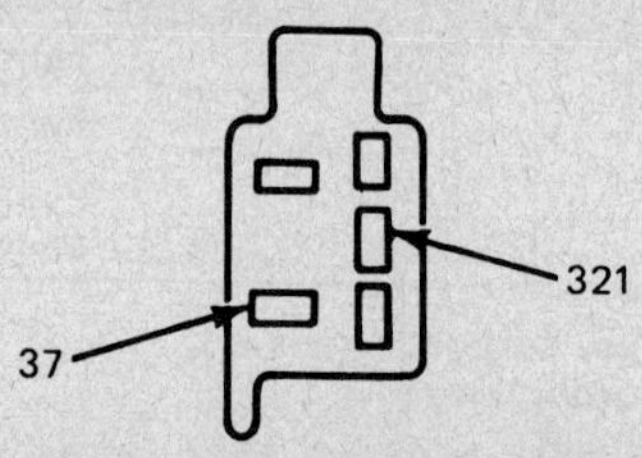

Fig. 7 A/C relay wire connector terminal identification

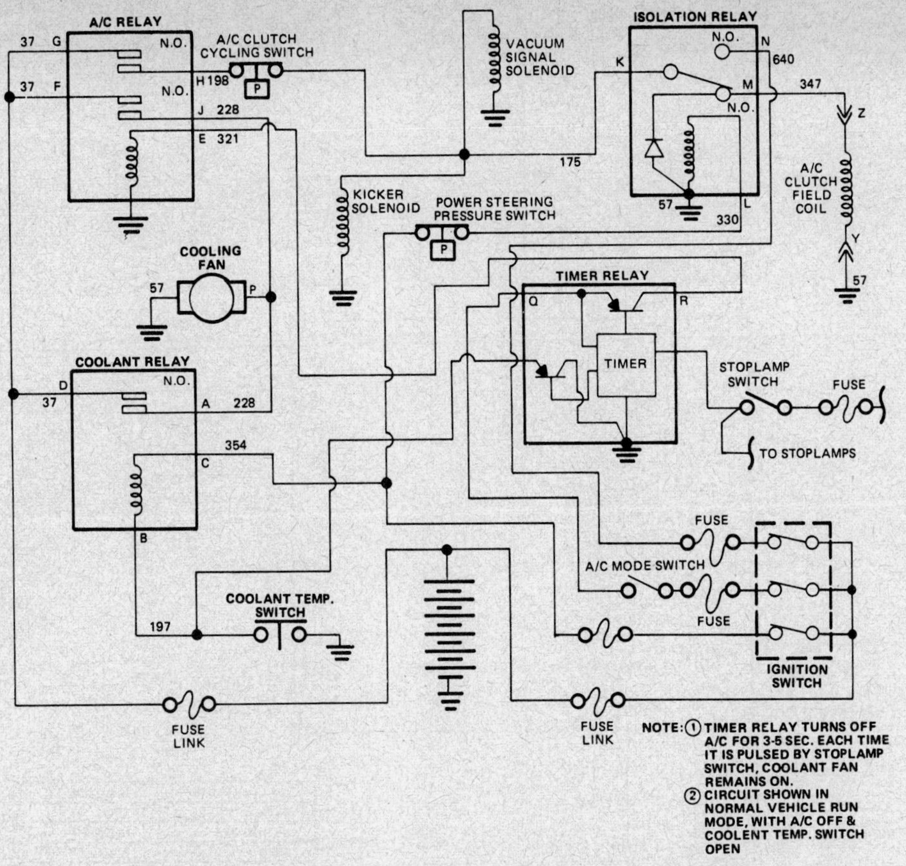

Fig. 8 Electric engine cooling fan wiring diagram. Type 4

10. If fan motor does run, secondary system is operating satisfactorily, except possibly the coolant temperature switch. If complaint is overheating, proceed to step 4.
4. Using an ohmmeter, check coolant temperature switch body to thermostat housing for continuity. If no continuity exists, tighten switch until continuity exists. Start engine and allow to warm up thoroughly. If fan motor runs, system is satisfactory. If fan motor does not run, replace coolant temperature switch.
5. Disconnect cooling fan motor connector, then connect a jumper wire from motor ground connection to a known good ground and a jumper wire from battery positive to motor B+ connection, **Fig. 5.** If fan motor does not run, replace motor. If fan motor runs, proceed to step 6.
6. Using an ohmmeter, check fan motor ground. If continuity exists, proceed to step 7. If continuity does not exist, repair ground.
7. Remove jumper wires, then reconnect fan motor connector. Disconnect cooling fan relay connector and switch ignition "On." Using a test light, check for voltage at terminals 37 and 354, **Fig. 9.** If there is no voltage at one or both terminals, repair relay feed circuits. If there is voltage at both terminals, proceed to step 8.
8. Jump terminals 37 to 228 of cooling fan relay connector, **Fig. 9.** If fan motor does not run, repair wiring from relay connector to fan motor connector. (Check capacitor, if equipped.) If fan motor runs, proceed to step 9.
9. Remove jumper wires. Using an ohmmeter, check continuity of wire 354 from relay connector to coolant temperature switch connector, **Fig. 9.** If continuity does not exist, repair wires and/or connectors. If continuity does exist, replace cooling fan relay and retest.
10. Disconnect A/C relay connector. Using an ohmmeter, check continuity of wire 228 from relay to motor. If continuity does not exist, repair wires and/or connectors. If continuity does exist, proceed to step 11.
11. Reconnect fan motor connector, then disconnect A/C relay connector. Set A/C controls on maximum and turn ignition "On." Using a test light, check for voltage at terminals 37 and 321, **Fig. 7.** If there is no voltage at terminal 37, repair relay connector feed circuit. If there is no voltage at terminal 321, proceed to step 13. If there is voltage at both terminals, proceed to step 12.
12. Reconnect A/C relay connector. Connect jumper wire to base of relay to a known good ground. If fan motor does not run, replace relay and retest step 4. If fan motor runs, clean relay ground.
13. Using a test light, test for voltage at circuit 296 of A/C function control harness. If voltage exists, proceed to step 14. If no voltage exists, repair feed wire from fuse box.

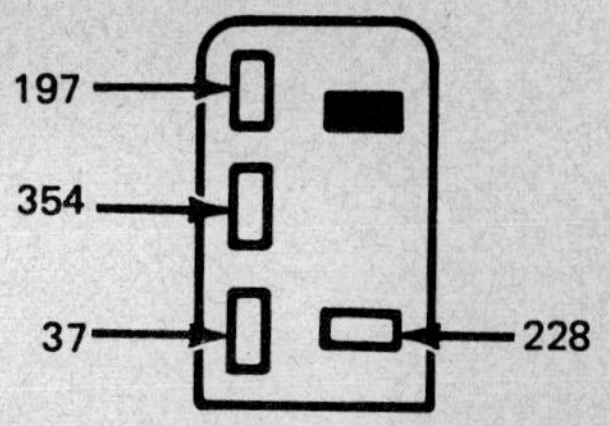

Fig. 9 Cooling fan relay connector terminal identification. Type 4

14. Using an ohmmeter, check continuity of terminals 296 to 321 in A/C function control. Continuity should only exist in the following positions: A/C Max., A/C Norm. and Defrost. If continuity is not satisfactory, replace A/C function control. If continuity is satisfactory, proceed to step 15.
15. Using an ohmmeter, check continuity of circuit 321 from A/C function control to A/C relay. If continuity does not exist, repair wiring and/or connectors. If continuity does exist, repeat step 11.

TYPES 5, 6 & 7

Refer to **Figs. 10, 11 and 12**, during the following procedures.

Fan Motor Inoperative

1. Check cooling fan fuses and fusible link. If fuses or fusible link are not blown, proceed to step 2. If fuses or fusible link are blown, repair or replace as necessary, and retest.
2. Disconnect fan motor electrical connector, then connect a jumper wire from motor ground connection to a known good ground and a jumper wire from battery positive to motor B+ connection. If motor does not run, replace motor. If motor runs, reconnect electrical connector and proceed to step 3.
3. Disconnect coolant temperature switch connector, then connect a jumper wire from connector to ground and turn ignition "On." If fan motor does not run, proceed to step 4. If motor does run, check switch ground, and if satisfactory, replace coolant temperature switch.
4. Turn ignition "Off," then remove jumper wire installed in step 3. Using an ohmmeter, check continuity of circuit 45 from cooling fan controller terminal 1 to coolant temperature switch. The controller, **Fig. 13,** is located under instrument panel. If continuity does not exist, check wire circuit 45 for opens. If continuity does exist, jump coolant temperature switch to ground and proceed to step 5.
5. Without disconnecting wiring connector from controller, **Fig. 13,** connect battery positive to circuit 68 at controller (terminal 8). If fan motor runs, check ignition feed circuits for opens. If fan motor does not run, remove jumper wire and proceed to step 6.
6. Disconnect cooling fan wiring connector at controller, **Fig. 13.** Using a jumper wire, connect battery positive current to circuit 228 (terminal 5). If

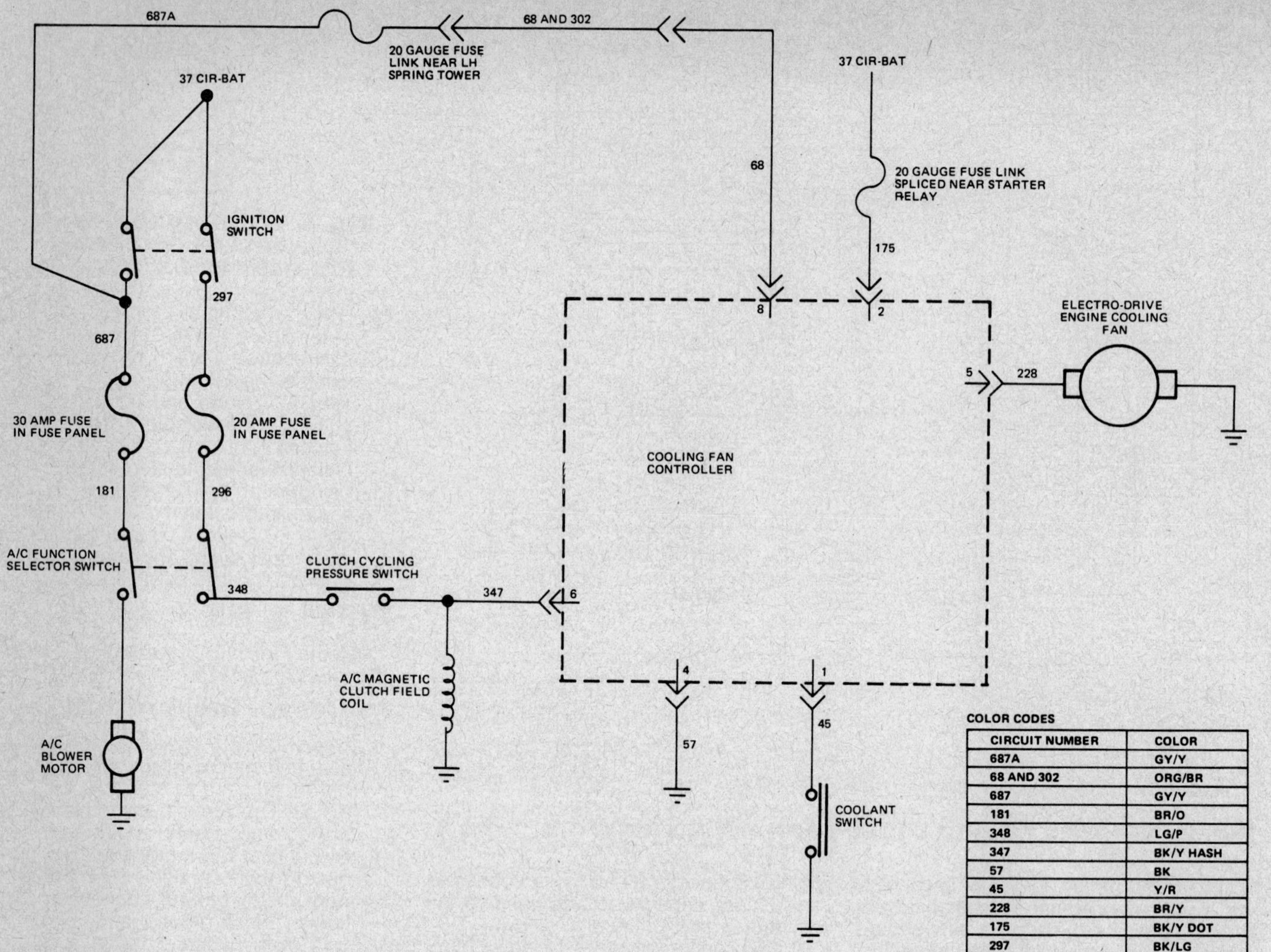

COLOR CODES

CIRCUIT NUMBER	COLOR
687A	GY/Y
68 AND 302	ORG/BR
687	GY/Y
181	BR/O
348	LG/P
347	BK/Y HASH
57	BK
45	Y/R
228	BR/Y
175	BK/Y DOT
297	BK/LG
296	W/P

Fig. 10 Electric engine cooling fan wiring diagram. Type 5

fan motor does not run, check circuit 228 for opens. If motor runs, remove jumper and proceed to step 7.

7. Using a jumper wire, connect circuit 175 to 228 (terminals 2 and 5) at the cooling fan motor controller connector. If motor does not run, check circuit 175 for opens. If motor does run, replace cooling fan controller, then remove jumper wire from temperature switch and reconnect connector.

Fan Motor Operates When Engine Overheats, Does Not Operate With A/C On

1. Set A/C controls selector lever in A/C position and turn ignition "On." If A/C clutch does not engage, proceed to step 2. If A/C clutch does engage, proceed to step 7.
2. Check fuse in fuse panel. If blown, replace. If fuse is not blown, proceed to step 3.
3. Disconnect A/C clutch cycle pressure switch. Use a jumper wire to jump across connector. If A/C clutch does not engage, proceed to step 5. If A/C clutch does engage, proceed to step 4.
4. Check A/C system for low refrigerant charge. If charge is insufficient, leak test, service and charge system. If charge is satisfactory, replace clutch cycling pressure switch.
5. Using a test light, check for voltage on 348 circuit at clutch cycling pressure switch. If there is no voltage, proceed to step 6. If there is voltage, repair open 347 circuit to A/C clutch.
6. Using a test light, test for voltage on 296 and 348 circuits at A/C function selector switch in instrument panel. If there is voltage on 296 but not on 348, replace A/C control assembly. If there is no voltage on 296 circuit, trace circuits 296 and 297 toward ignition switch.
7. Using a test light, check for voltage on 347 or 883 circuit (terminal 6) of cooling fan controller, **Fig. 13.** If there is no voltage, repair open 347 or 883 circuit. If voltage does exist, proceed to step 8.
8. Leaving connector attached to controller, ground 57 circuit (terminal 4) of controller. If fan motor runs, repair ground circuit. If fan does not run, replace controller.

TYPE 8

Refer to **Fig. 14** during the following procedures.

With A/C

1. Check fuse and fuse link. Replace blown fuse. If fuse is satisfactory, proceed to step 2.
2. Determine when fan operates or does not operate. If cooling fan operates with A/C on, proceed to step 3. If cooling fan does not operate with A/C on or during high engine coolant temperatures, proceed to step 11. If cooling fan operates during high engine coolant temperature only, proceed to step 6.
3. Turn ignition switch to RUN position, then disconnect electrical connector from coolant temperature switch. With A/C off, connect and jumper wire from connector to ground. If cooling fan operates, proceed to step 4. If cooling fan does not operate, proceed to step 5.
4. Verify the coolant switch is grounded by checking for continuity from switch body to thermostat housing. If not grounded, tighten switch until continu-

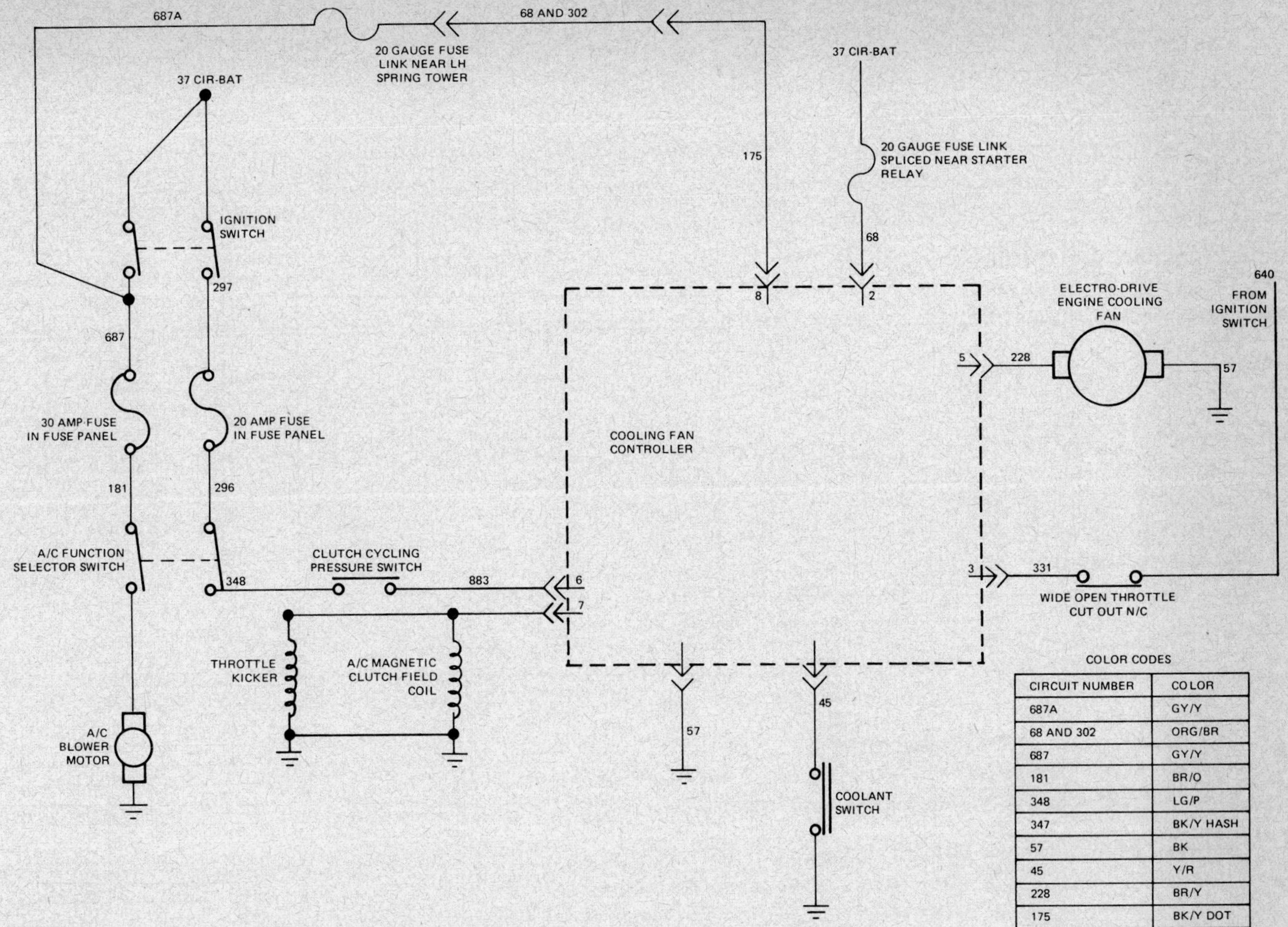

COLOR CODES

CIRCUIT NUMBER	COLOR
687A	GY/Y
68 AND 302	ORG/BR
687	GY/Y
181	BR/O
348	LG/P
347	BK/Y HASH
57	BK
45	Y/R
228	BR/Y
175	BK/Y DOT
297	BK/LG
296	W/P

Fig. 11 Electric engine cooling fan wiring diagram. Type 6

ity exists. Verify engine coolant has exceeded 210°F, by idling (a cold) engine for approximately 25 minutes. Vehicles equipped with temperature gauge should indicate toward the high end of the normal band. If cooling fan operates, cooling fan system is satisfactory. If cooling fan does not operate, replace coolant temperature switch.

5. Disconnect electrical connector from cooling fan controller and check continuity of circuit 197 from controller coolant temperature switch. If continuity exists, replace cooling fan controller. If no continuity exists, repair circuit.
6. Check fan controller system ground at terminal 5 of fan controller. If ground is satisfactory, proceed to step 7. If ground is not satisfactory, repair ground.
7. Disconnect electrical connector from cooling fan controller and check voltage at circuits 198 and 348. If no voltage is indicated at one or both circuits, proceed to step 8. If voltage indication is satisfactory, replace fan controller.
8. Disconnect electrical connector from clutch cycling pressure switch, then using a jumper wire, jump across the connector and check if fan motor engages. If fan motor engages, proceed to step 9. If fan motor does not engage, proceed to step 10.
9. Check A/C system for refrigerant charge. If no refrigerant charge, leak test, service and charge system. If refrigerant pressure is above 50 psi, replace clutch cycling pressure switch.
10. Disconnect electrical connector from A/C control assembly. Using a suitable jumper wire, jump circuits 294 and 348 and check for voltage. If voltage indication is satisfactory, replace A/C push button switch. If no voltage is indicated, service open circuits.
11. Disconnect electrical connector at cooling fan motor. Then jump B+ and ground to motor. If fan operates, proceed to step 12. If fan motor does not operate, replace motor.
12. Remove jumper wires and connect harness connector to fan motor. Disconnect electrical connector from cooling fan controller and turn ignition switch to RUN position. Check for voltage at circuits 37, 687, 198 and 348 and fan controller ground. If no voltage is indicated at one or both circuits, service circuits. If voltage and ground are satisfactory, proceed to step 13.
13. Using a suitable jumper wire, jump circuit 37 to 228A at the cooling fan controller. If fan operates, proceed to step 14. If fan motor does not operate, service fan motor ground.
14. Using a suitable jumper wire, jump circuit 37 to circuit 228. If fan motor operates, replace fan controller. If fan motor does not operate, proceed to step 15.
15. Disconnect 5 way electrical connector (mounted on fan relay). Using a suitable jumper wire, jump circuit 37 to circuit 228A. If fan motor operates, proceed to step 16. If fan motor does not operate, service circuit 37A.
16. Using a suitable jumper wires, jump circuit 57 to fan relay terminal 1 and circuit 37 to circuit 228. If fan motor operates, service circuits. If fan motor does not operate, replace fan relay.

Less A/C

1. Disconnect electrical connector from motor. Using a suitable jumper wire, jump motor negative terminal to ground and motor positive terminal to

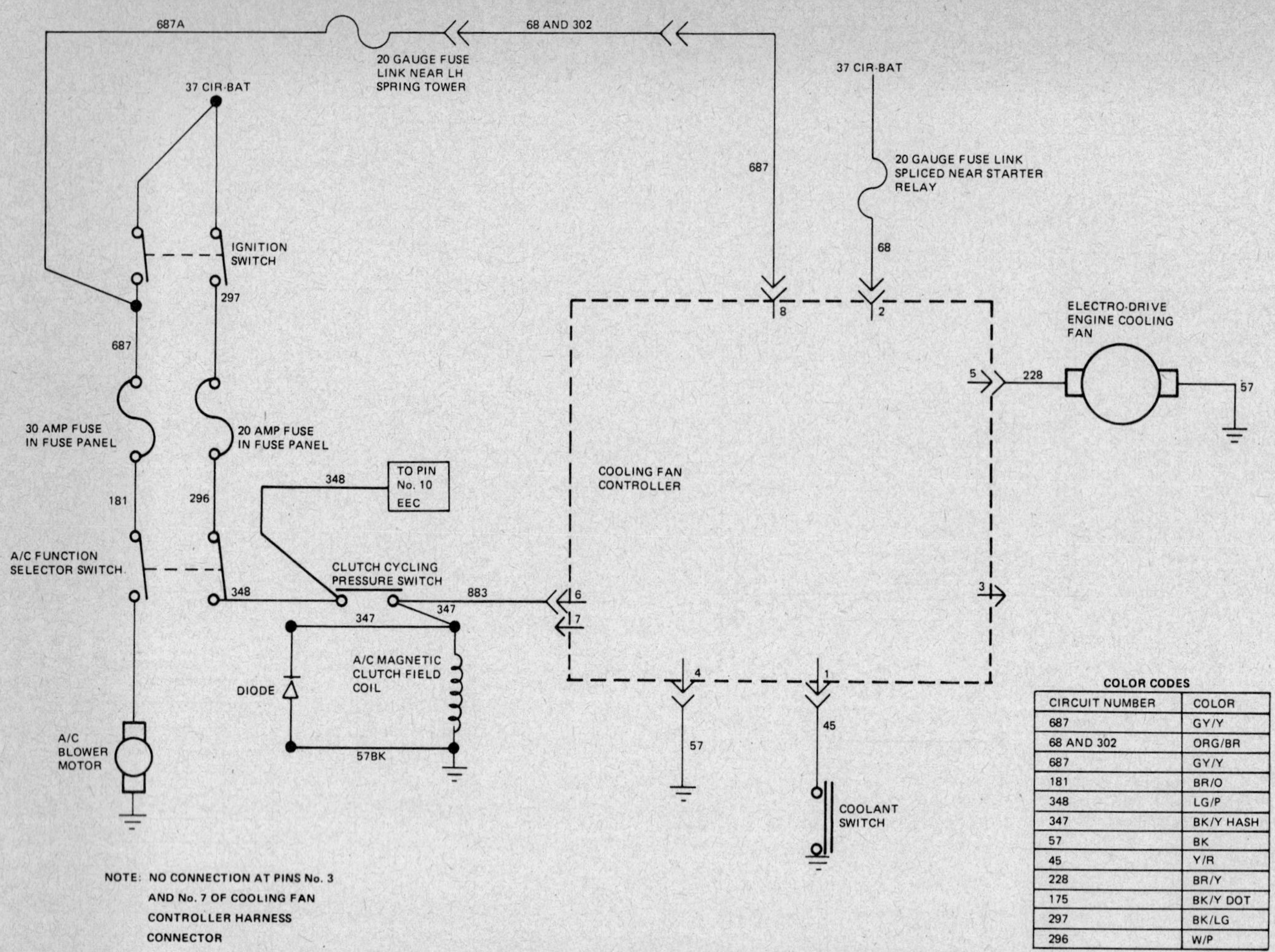

COLOR CODES

CIRCUIT NUMBER	COLOR
687	GY/Y
68 AND 302	ORG/BR
687	GY/Y
181	BR/O
348	LG/P
347	BK/Y HASH
57	BK
45	Y/R
228	BR/Y
175	BK/Y DOT
297	BK/LG
296	W/P

Fig. 12 Electric engine cooling fan wiring diagram. Type 7

B+. If motor does not operate, replace motor. If motor operates, connect motor lead and proceed to step 2.

2. Disconnect electrical connector at cooling fan temperature switch. With ignition switch in the RUN position check for voltage at circuit 197. Voltage reading should equal battery voltage. If voltage obtained is satisfactory, proceed to step 3. If not, check for open or short circuit in circuit 197 and/or fuse link.
3. Using a suitable jumper wire, jump cooling fan temperature switch connector pins together. With ignition switch in the RUN position, cooling fan motor should operate. If motor operates, replace cooling fan temperature switch. If motor does not operate leave jumper wire connected and proceed to step 4.
4. Disconnect electrical connector at fan motor. Check for voltage at circuit 228. With ignition switch in the RUN position and cooling fan temperature switch connector terminals jumped. Battery voltage should be indicated at circuit 228. If battery voltage is indicated, proceed to step 5. If not, check circuit 228 for open. Service wiring between fan motor and temperature switch.
5. Check ground, circuit 57 for continuity. If continuity exists, replace cooling fan motor. If not, service open in circuit 57.

TYPES 9, 10, 11 & 12

Refer to **Figs. 15, 16, 17 and 18,** during the following procedures.

1. Check cooling fan fuse and fusible link. If satisfactory, proceed to step 2. If fuse or fusible link is blown, repair or replace as necessary and retest.
2. Bring engine to operating temperature and above while operating A/C to determine when cooling fan does or does not operate. If cooling fan operates during A/C operation only, proceed to step 3. If cooling fan does not operate at any time, proceed to step 13. If cooling fan operates only during high engine temperature, proceed to step 6.
3. Disconnect coolant temperature switch connector, then connect a jumper wire from connector to ground. If fan motor operates, proceed to step 4. If fan motor does not operate, proceed to step 5.
4. Using a suitable ohmmeter, check temperature switch body to thermostat housing continuity. If continuity does not exist (poor ground), tighten switch until continuity exists, then recheck operation. If continuity does exist between switch and thermostat housing, replace temperature switch.
5. Disconnect cooling fan controller connector, then using a suitable ohmmeter, check continuity of 197 circuit from controller to temperature switch. If continuity exists, replace controller.

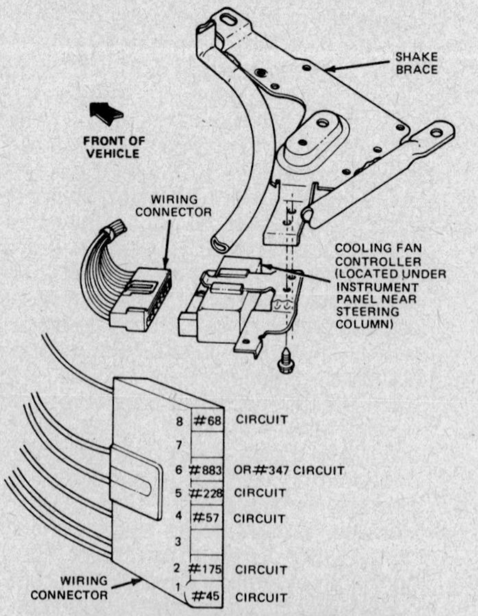

Fig. 13 Cooling fan controller terminal identification. Types 5, 6 & 7

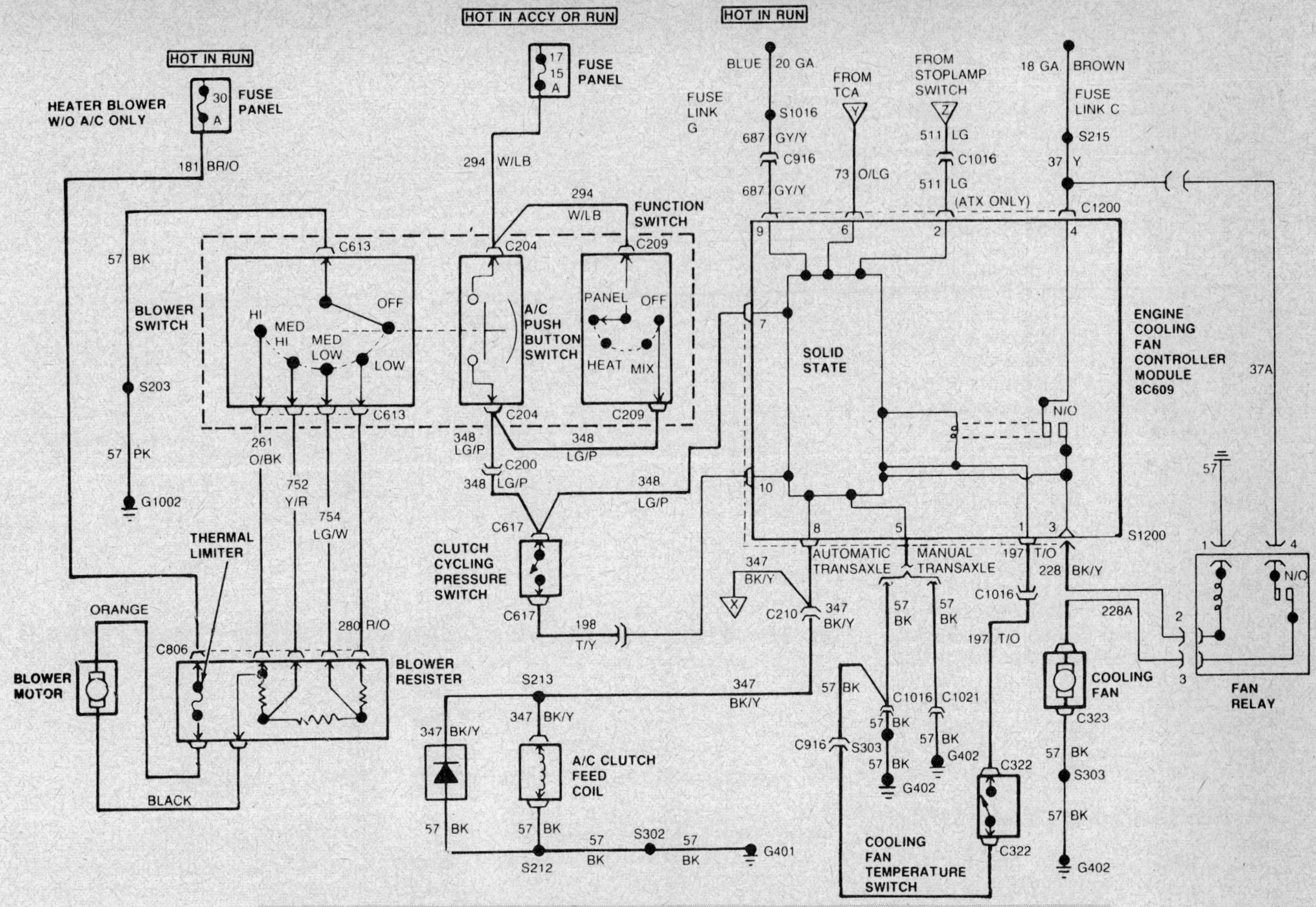

Fig. 14 Electric engine cooling fan wiring circuit. Type 8

If no continuity exists, service 197 circuit.

6. With engine running, engage A/C clutch. If clutch engages, proceed to step 7. If clutch does not engage, check fuse. If satisfactory, proceed to step 9.
7. Inspect wide open throttle switch to determine position. If switch is open, replace or adjust as necessary. If switch is closed, proceed to step 8.
8. Disconnect cooling fan controller connector, then check for voltage at 354 circuit. If no voltage exists, service 354 circuit as necessary. If voltage exists, replace cooling fan controller.
9. Disconnect cooling fan controller connector, then turn ignition and A/C "On." Check for voltage at 198 circuit. If voltage exists, replace cooling fan controller. If voltage does not exist, proceed to step 10.
10. Disconnect A/C clutch cycling pressure switch, then using a suitable jumper wire, jump across connector. Check again for voltage at 198 circuit. If voltage exists, proceed to step 11. If voltage does not exist, proceed to step 12.
11. Check A/C system for sufficient charge. If charge is sufficient, replace clutch cycling pressure switch.
12. Disconnect A/C control assembly connector, then jump 296 circuit to 321 circuit and check for voltage at 198 and 348 circuits at cooling fan controller connector. If voltage exists at both circuits, replace function selector switch. If voltage exists at 198 circuit only, service 348 circuit.
13. Disconnect fan motor electrical connector, then connect a jumper wire from motor ground connection to a known good ground and a jumper wire from battery positive to motor B+ connection. If fan motor does not run, replace motor. If fan motor runs, proceed to step 14.
14. Remove jumper wire, then reconnect fan motor connector. Disconnect fan motor controller connector. With ignition "On," check for voltage at controller connector 37 and 354 circuits. If voltage exists at both circuits, proceed to step 15. If no voltage exists at one or both circuits, service circuit(s).
15. Using a jumper wire, jump circuit 37 to 228 circuit at cooling fan controller connector. If fan motor runs, replace cooling fan controller. If fan motor does not run, service motor ground.

TYPE 13

Refer to **Fig. 19,** during the following procedures.

1. Refer to steps 1 through 5 of Types 9, 10, 11 and 12 electric engine cooling fan systems, then continue using the following procedures.
2. With engine running, engage A/C clutch. If clutch engages, proceed to step 3. If clutch does not engage, check fuse. If satisfactory, proceed to step 4.
3. Disconnect cooling fan controller connector, then check for voltage at 640 and 37 circuits. If voltage exists at both circuits, replace controller. If voltage does not exist at one or both circuits, service circuits as necessary.
4. Disconnect A/C clutch cycling pressure switch, then using a suitable jumper wire, jump across connector. Check to see if A/C clutch engages. If clutch engages, proceed to step 5. If clutch does not engage, proceed to step 6.
5. Check A/C system for sufficient charge. If charge is insufficient, leak test, repair and recharge system, then retest. If charge is sufficient, replace clutch cycling pressure switch.
6. Disconnect A/C control assembly connector, then jump 296 circuit to 321 circuit and check for voltage at black/yellow wire of clutch connector. If voltage exists, replace function selector switch. If voltage does not exist, service 321, 347 or 348 circuit.
7. Remove jumper wire from A/C clutch cycling pressure switch connector

and connect to pressure switch.

TYPES 14, 15 & 16

Refer to **Figs. 20, 21 and 22,** during the following procedures.

1. Check fuse and fusible link. If satisfactory, proceed to step 2. If not satisfactory, repair or replace as required.
2. Bring engine to operating temperature while operating A/C to determine when cooling fan does or does not operate. If cooling fan operates only during A/C operation, proceed to step 3. If cooling fan does not operate at any time, proceed to step 11. If cooling fan operates only during high engine temperature, proceed to step 6.
3. With A/C off and ignition on, disconnect coolant temperature switch connector. Connect a jumper wire from connector to ground. If fan motor operates, proceed to step 4. If fan motor does not operate, proceed to step 5.
4. Using a suitable ohmmeter, check temperature switch body to thermostat housing continuity. If continuity does not exist (poor ground), tighten switch until continuity exists, then recheck operation. If continuity does exist between switch and thermostat housing, replace temperature switch.
5. Disconnect cooling fan controller connector, then using a suitable ohmmeter, check continuity of 197 circuit from controller to temperature switch. If continuity exists, replace controller. If no continuity exists, service 197 circuit.
6. With engine running, engage A/C clutch. If clutch engages, proceed to step 7. If clutch does not engage, check fuse. If satisfactory, proceed to step 8.
7. Disconnect cooling fan controller connector, then check for voltage at 37 and 640 circuits on type 14 or 37 and 354 circuits on type 15. If no voltage exists at one or both circuits, service circuit(s) as necessary. If voltage exists at both circuits, replace controller.
8. Disconnect A/C clutch cycling pressure switch, then using a suitable jumper wire, jump across connector. If clutch engages, proceed to step 9. If clutch does not engage, proceed to step 10.
9. Check A/C system for sufficient charge. If charge is insufficient, leak test, repair and recharge system, then retest. If charge is sufficient, replace clutch cycling pressure switch.
10. Disconnect A/C control connector. Using a jumper wire, connect 321 circuit to 296 circuit, then check for voltage at yellow/black A/C connector.
11. If voltage exists, replace A/C function selector switch. If voltage does not exist, service 321, 347 or 348 circuits as necessary. Reconnect all removed wiring.
12. Disconnect fan motor electrical connector, then connect a jumper wire from motor ground connection to a known good ground and a jumper wire from motor B+ connection to battery positive terminal. If fan motor does not run, replace motor. If fan motor runs, proceed to step 13.
13. Remove jumper wires, then reconnect fan motor electrical connector to fan motor. Disconnect cooling fan controller connector and turn ignition On. Check for voltage at 37 and 640 circuits on types 14 and 16, or 37 and 354 circuits on type 15. If no voltage exists at one or both circuits, service circuit(s) as necessary. If voltage exists at both circuits, proceed to step 14.
14. Using a jumper wire connect circuit 37 to circuit 228 at cooling fan controller. If fan motor runs, replace cooling fan controller. If fan motor does not run, service motor ground.

TYPES 17 THROUGH 24

Refer to **Figs. 23 through 30,** during the following procedures.

1. Check fuse and fusible link. If satisfactory, proceed to step 2. If not satisfactory, repair or replace as required.
2. Bring engine to operating temperature while operating A/C to determine when cooling fan does or does not operate. If cooling fan operates only during A/C operation, proceed to step 3. If cooling fan does not operate at

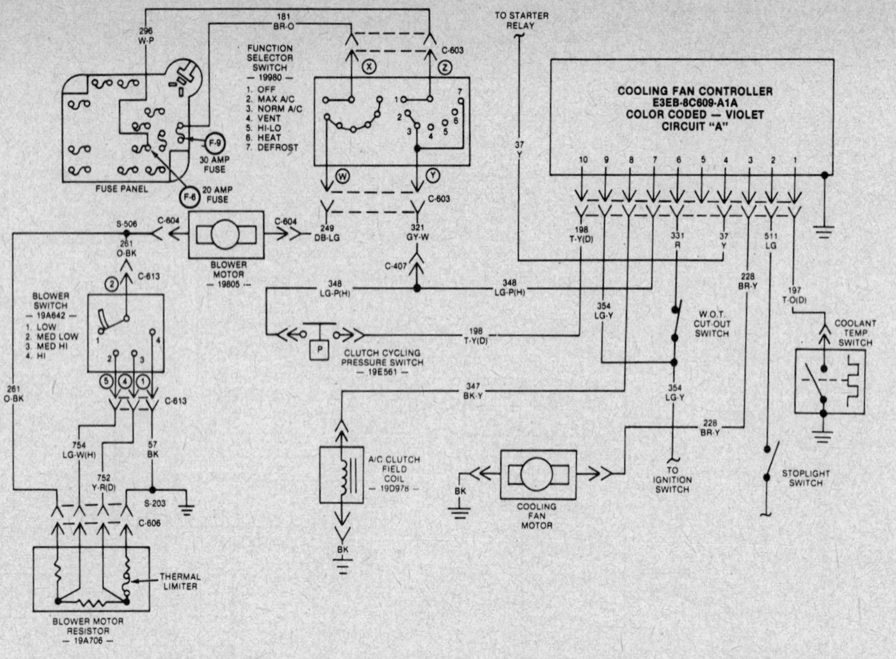

Fig. 15 Electric engine cooling fan wiring circuit. Type 9

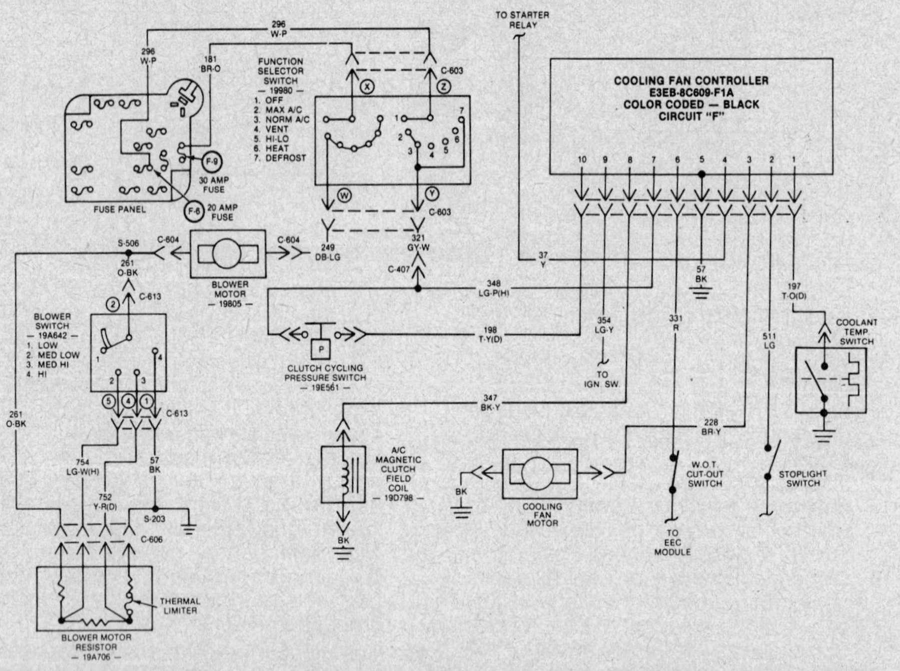

Fig. 16 Electric engine cooling fan wiring diagram. Type 10

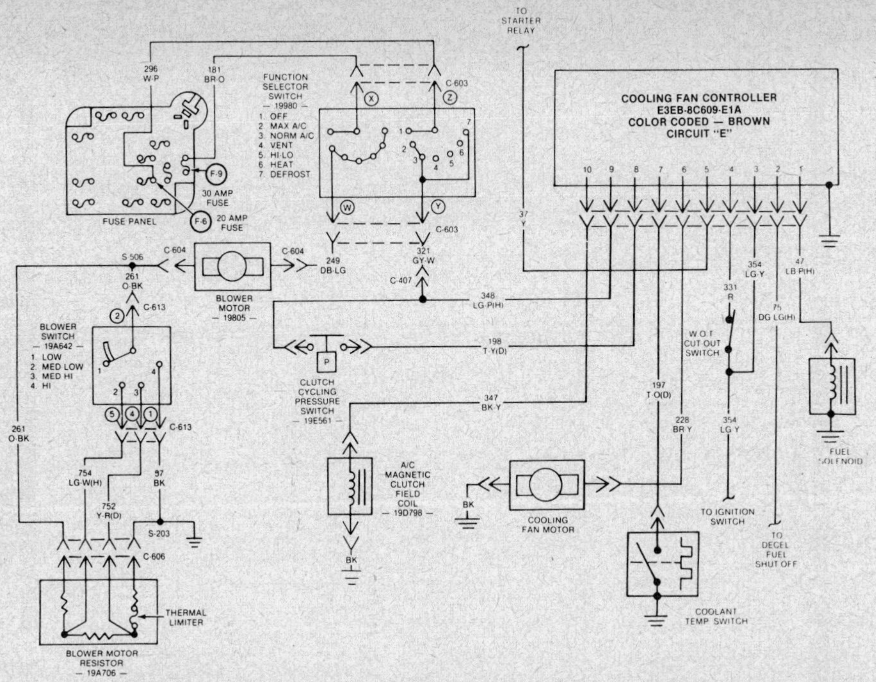

Fig. 17 Electric engine cooling fan wiring diagram. Type 11

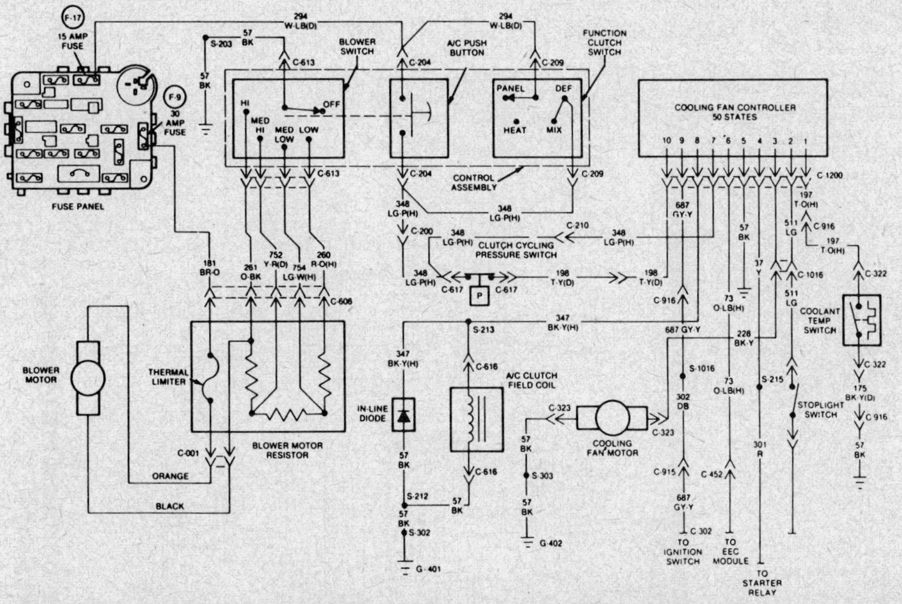

Fig. 18 Electric engine cooling fan wiring circuit. Type 12

any time, proceed to step 13. If cooling fan operates only during high engine temperature, proceed to step 6.

3. With A/C off and ignition on, disconnect coolant temperature switch connector. Connect a jumper wire from connector to ground. If fan motor operates, proceed to step 4. If fan motor does not operate, proceed to step 5.
4. Using a suitable ohmmeter, check temperature switch body to thermostat housing continuity. If continuity does not exist (poor ground), tighten switch until continuity exists, then recheck operation. If continuity does exist between switch and thermostat housing, replace temperature switch.
5. Disconnect cooling fan controller connector, then using a suitable ohmmeter, check continuity of 197 circuit from controller to temperature switch. If continuity exists, replace controller. If no continuity exists, service 197 circuit.
6. With engine running, engage A/C clutch. If clutch engages, proceed to step 7. If clutch does not engage, check fuse. If satisfactory, proceed to step 9.
7. Check wide open throttle switch to determine if switch is opened or closed. If switch is open, adjust or replace switch as necessary. If switch is closed, proceed to step 8.
8. Disconnect cooling fan controller connector, then check for voltage at 354 circuit. If no voltage exists, service circuit as necessary. If voltage exists, replace controller.
9. With cooling fan controller connector disconnected and A/C on, check for voltage at 198 circuit. If no voltage exists, proceed to step 10. If voltage exists, replace cooling fan controller.
10. Disconnect A/C clutch cycling pressure switch, then using a suitable jumper wire, jump across connector. Again check for voltage at 198 circuit. If voltage exists, proceed to step 11. If voltage does not exist, proceed to step 12.
11. Check A/C system for sufficient charge. If charge is insufficient, leak test, repair and recharge system. If charge is sufficient, replace clutch cycling pressure switch.
12. Disconnect A/C control connector. Using a jumper wire, connect 321 circuit to 296 circuit. Check for voltage at 198 circuit and 348 circuit at cooling fan controller connector. If voltage exists at both circuits, replace A/C function selector switch. If voltage exists at 198 circuit only, service 348 circuit.
13. Disconnect fan motor electrical connector, then connect a jumper wire from motor ground connection to a known good ground and a jumper wire from motor B+ connection to battery positive terminal. If fan motor runs, proceed to step 14. If fan motor does not run, replace motor.
14. Remove jumper wires, then reconnect fan motor electrical connector to fan motor. Disconnect cooling fan controller connector and turn ignition On. Check for voltage at 37 circuit and 354 circuit. If no voltage exists at one or both circuits, service circuit(s) as necessary. If voltage exists at both circuits, proceed to step 15.
15. Using a jumper wire connect circuit 37 to circuit 228 at cooling fan controller. If fan motor runs, replace cooling fan controller. If fan motor does not run, service motor ground.

TYPE 25

Refer to **Fig. 31,** during the following procedures.

1. Check cooling fan fusible link, if satisfactory, proceed to step 2. If not satisfactory, repair and retest.
2. With ignition On, disconnect coolant temperature switch connector, then jump both connector terminals to ground. If fan motor runs, service fan motor ground circuit. If fan motor does not run, proceed to step 3.
3. Disconnect fan motor electrical connector, then connect a jumper wire from motor ground connection to a known good ground and a jumper wire from battery positive terminal to motor B+ connection, **Fig. 5.** If fan motor runs, proceed to step 4. If fan motor does not run, replace motor.

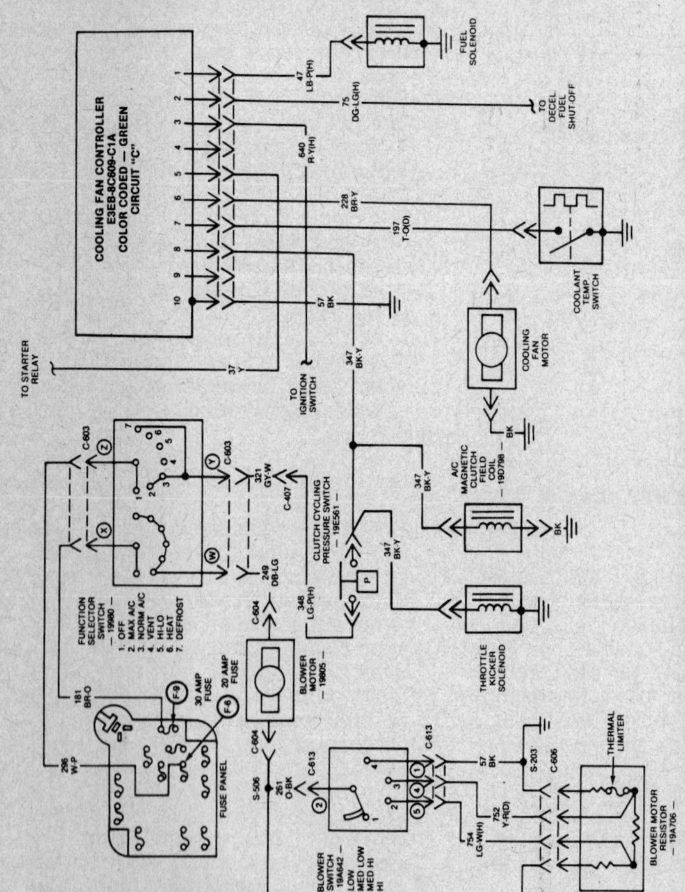

Fig. 19 Electric engine cooling fan wiring diagram. Type 13

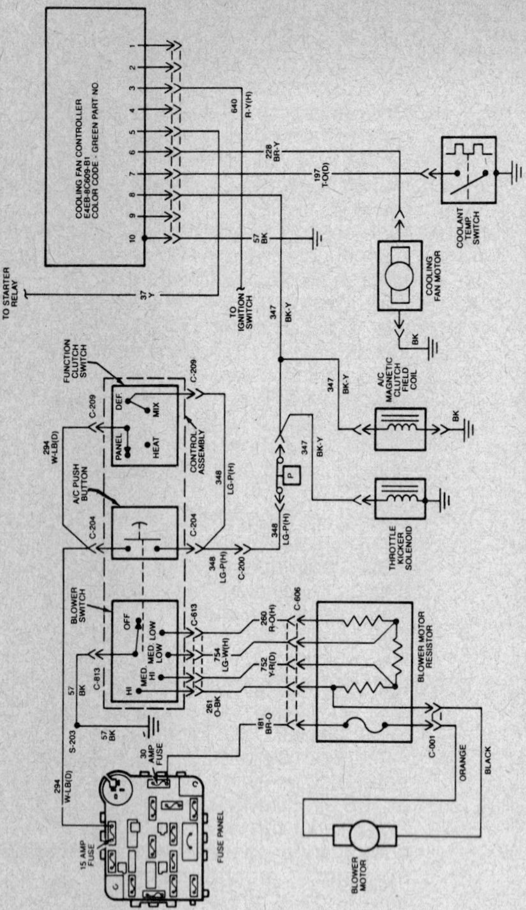

Fig. 20 Electric engine cooling fan wiring diagram. Type 14

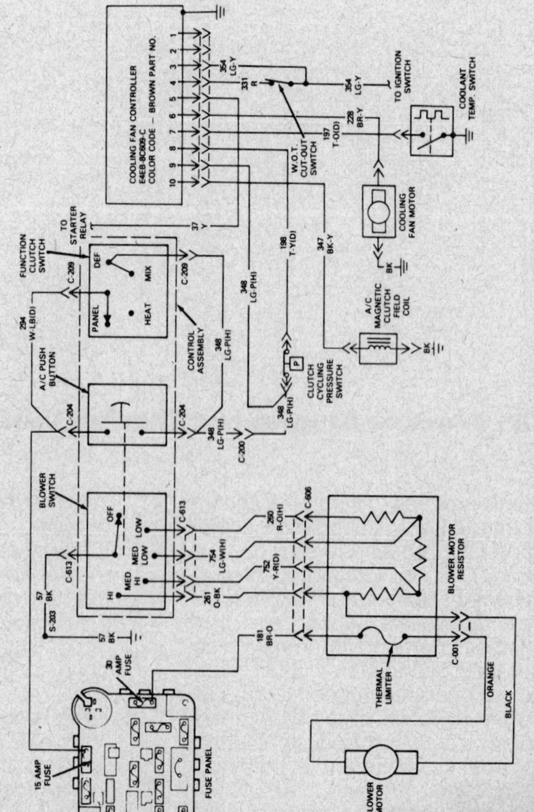

Fig. 21 Electric engine cooling fan wiring diagram. Type 15

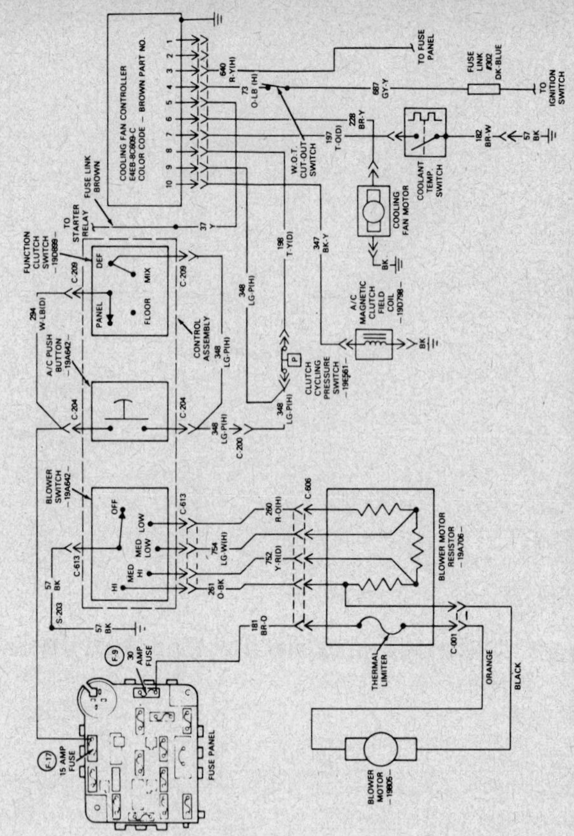

Fig. 22 Electric engine cooling fan wiring diagram. Type 16

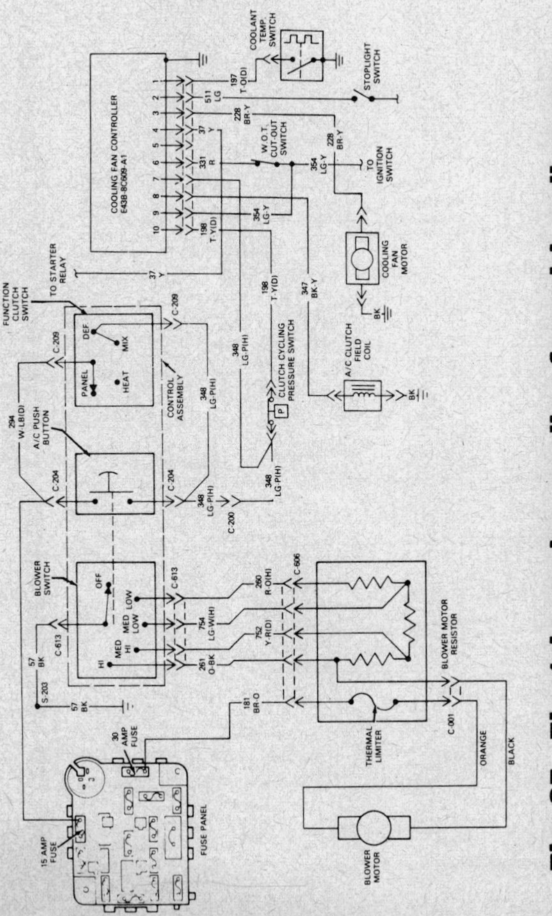

Fig. 23 Electric engine cooling fan wiring diagram. Type 17

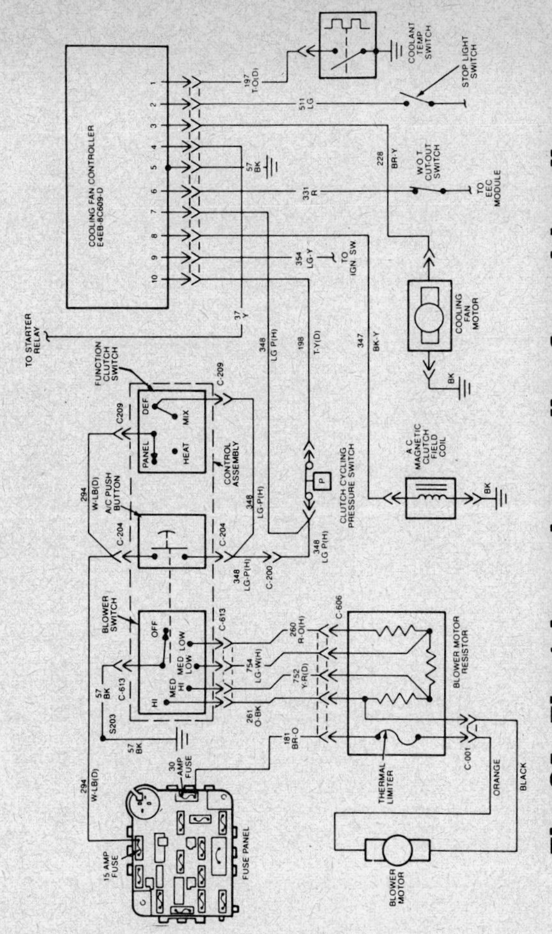

Fig. 24 Electric engine cooling fan wiring diagram. Type 18

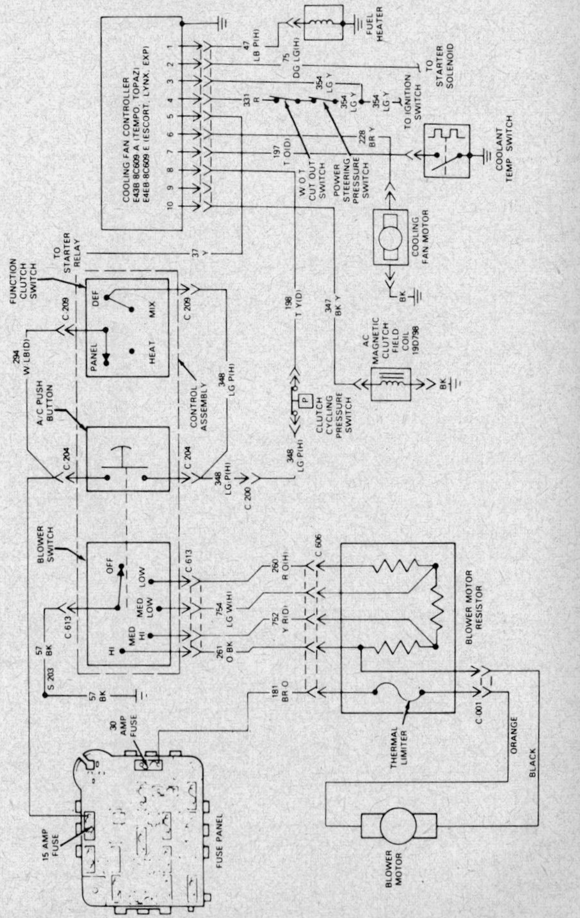

Fig. 25 Electric engine cooling fan wiring diagram. Type 19

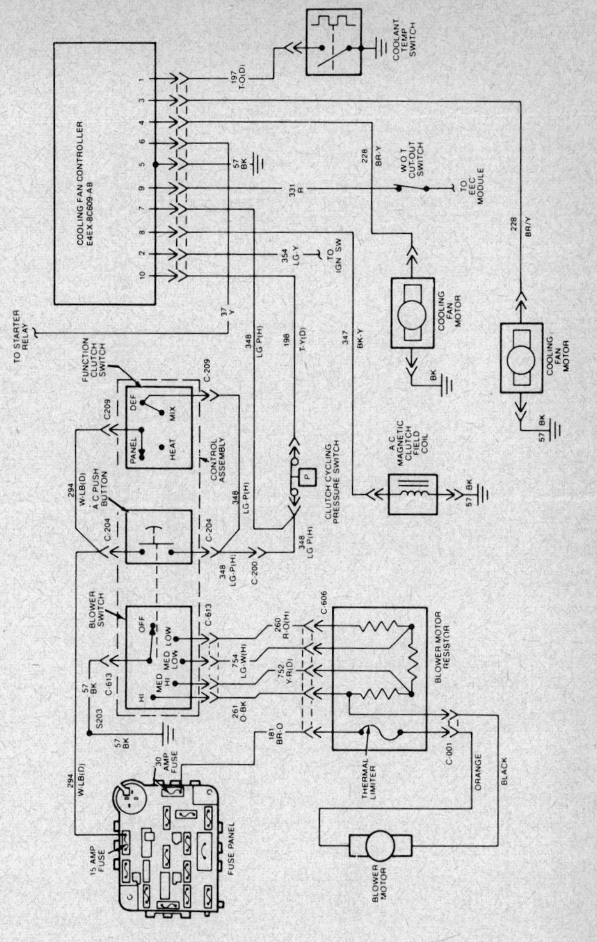

Fig. 26 Electric engine cooling fan wiring diagram. Type 20

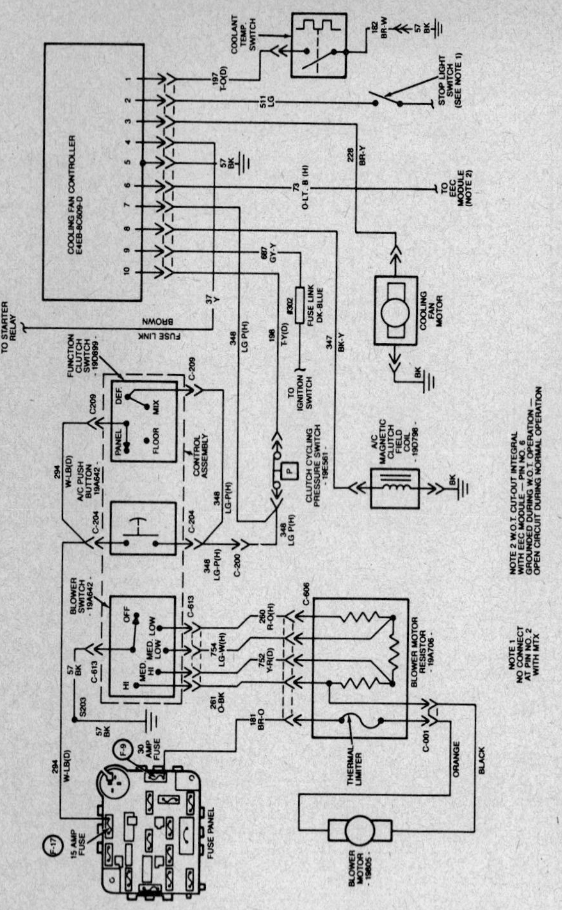

Fig.28 Electric engine cooling fan wiring diagram. Type 22

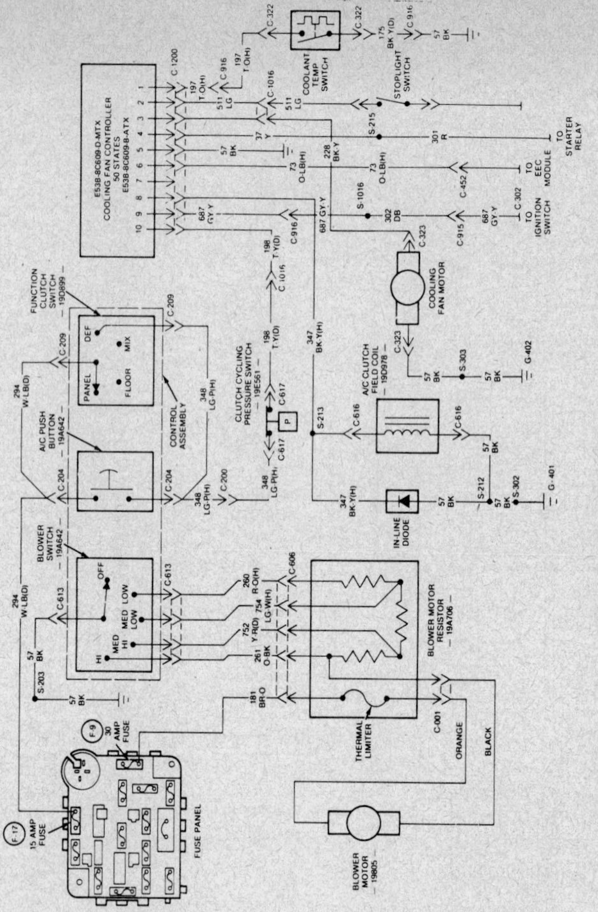

Fig. 30 Electric engine cooling fan wiring diagram. Type 24

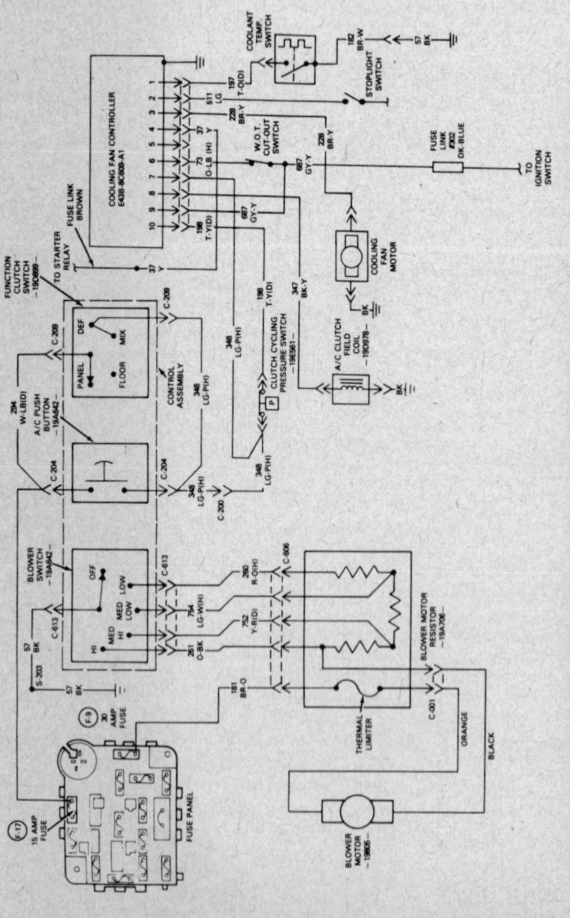

Fig. 27 Electric engine cooling fan wiring diagram. Type 21

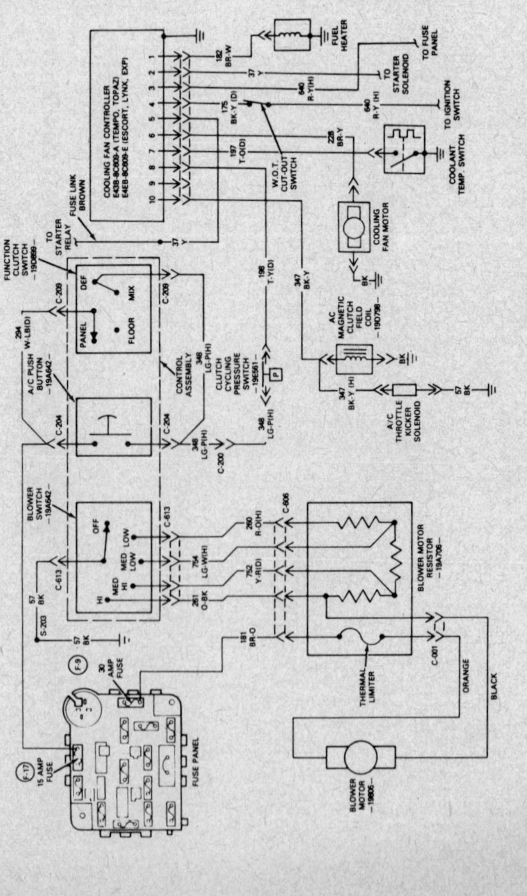

Fig. 29 Electric engine cooling fan wiring diagram. Type 23

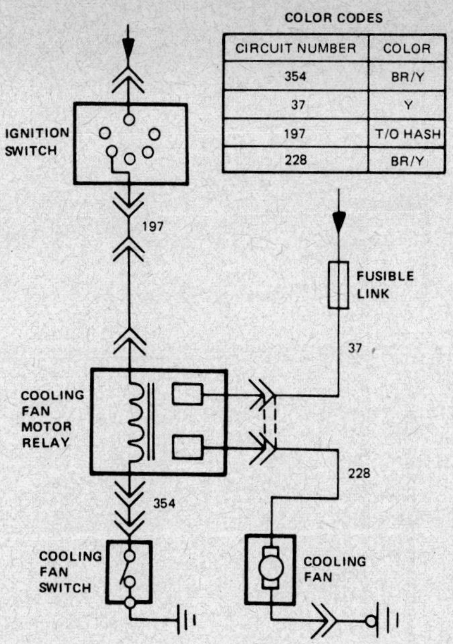

Fig. 31 Electric engine cooling fan wiring diagram. Type 25

4. Remove jumper wires and reconnect fan motor connector. Disconnect cooling fan relay connector, then turn ignition On. Check for voltage at relay connector terminals 37 and 197, **Fig. 6.** If no voltage exists at either terminal, service feed circuits. If voltage exists at both terminals, proceed to step 5.
5. Jump terminals 37 and 228 of cooling fan relay connector, **Fig. 6.** If fan motor runs, proceed to step 6. If fan motor does not run, service wiring from relay connector to motor connector 228.
6. Reconnect cooling fan relay connector. Turn ignition On, then jump terminal 354 to ground (with connector attached to relay). If fan motor runs, service 354 circuit. If fan motor does not run, replace relay.

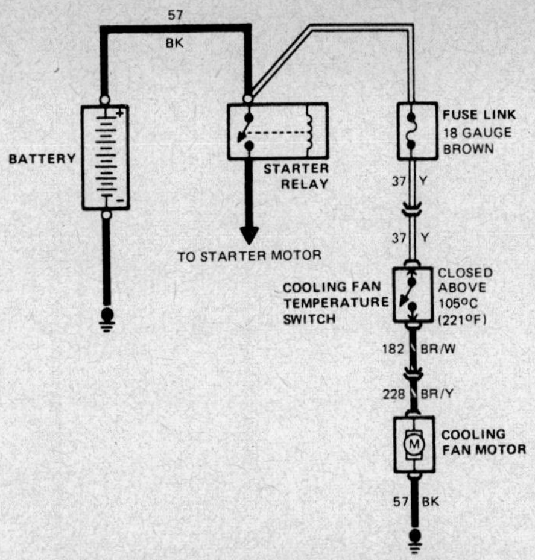

Fig. 32 Electric engine cooling fan wiring diagram. Type 26

TYPES 26 & 27

Refer to **Figs. 32 and 33,** during the following procedures.

1. Disconnect fan motor electrical connector, then connect a jumper wire from motor ground connection to a known good ground and a jumper wire from battery positive terminal to motor B+ connection. If fan motor runs, proceed to step 2. If fan motor does not run, replace motor.
2. Disconnect cooling fan temperature switch connector, then check for battery voltage on 37 (Y) circuit for Type 26 or 197 (T/OH) circuit for Type 27. If battery voltage exists, proceed to step 3. If battery voltage does not exist, check for opens or shorts in 37 or 197 circuits.

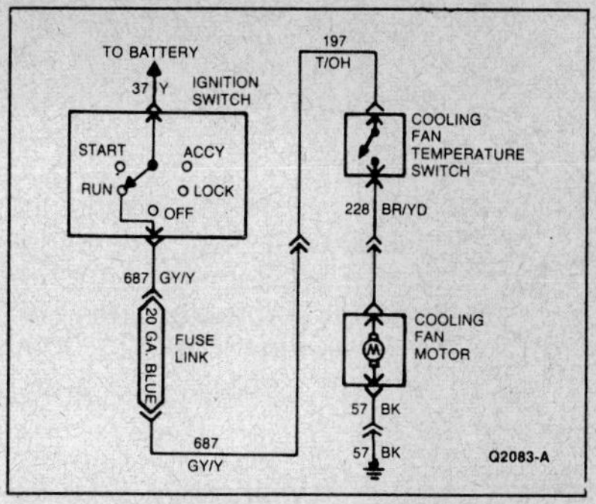

Fig. 33 Electric engine cooling fan wiring diagram. Type 27

3. Jump cooling fan temperature switch connector pins together. If fan motor runs, replace temperature switch. If fan motor does not run, proceed to step 4.
4. Disconnect fan motor connector, then check for voltage at 228 (BR/Y) terminal with cooling fan temperature switch jumped. If battery voltage is indicated, proceed to step 5. If battery voltage is not indicated, check 228 and 182 circuits for opens and repair as necessary. Recheck cooling fan operation.
5. Check ground circuit (57) for continuity. If continuity exists, replace cooling fan motor and recheck cooling fan operation. If continuity does not exist, service open in ground circuit (57) and recheck cooling fan operation.

TYPES 28 & 29

Refer to **Figs. 34 and 35,** during the following procedures.

Fan Motor Inoperative

1. Disconnect electrical connector at fan motor and connect jumper wires between negative terminal and ground and between positive terminal and B+ at motor. If motor does not run, replace motor. If motor runs, connect electrical connector at motor and proceed to step 2.
2. Disconnect electrical connector at coolant temperature switch, connect jumper wire between connector and ground on circuit 45 and turn ignition switch to "Run." If motor runs, check switch ground. If ground is satisfactory, replace coolant temperature switch. If motor does not run, proceed to step 3.
3. Turn ignition switch to "Off" and remove jumper wire installed in step 2, then check continuity of circuit 45 from cooling fan controller (terminal 1) to coolant temperature switch. If there is no continuity, check for open in circuit 45. If there is continuity, connect jumper wire between coolant temperature switch connector to ground and proceed to step 4.
4. Connect jumper wire between B+ and circuit 687 at cooling fan controller (terminal 8) without disconnecting

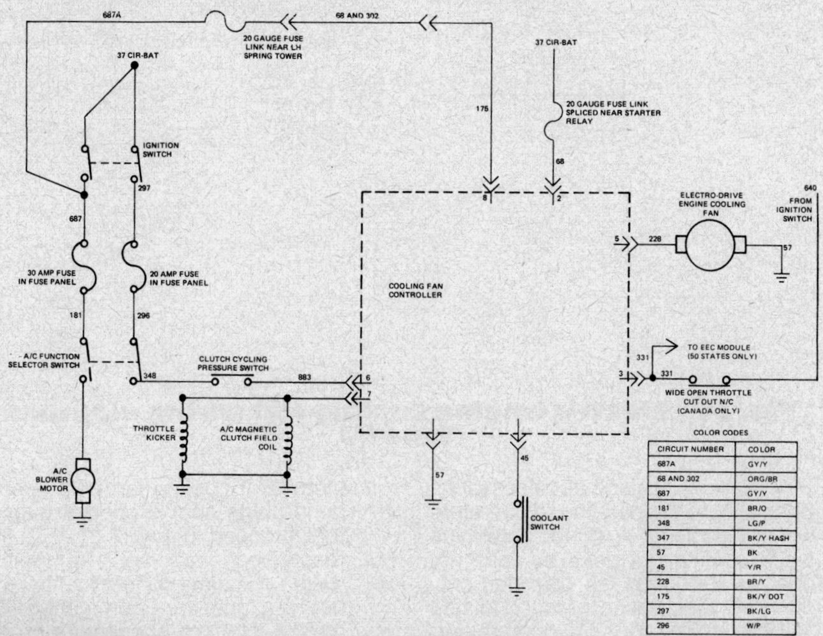

Fig. 34 Electric engine cooling fan wiring diagram. Type 28

electrical connector from controller. If motor runs, check for open in ignition feed circuits 68 and 687. If motor does not run, remove jumper wire and proceed to step 5.

5. Disconnect electrical connector at cooling fan controller, then connect jumper wire between B+ and circuit 228 (terminal 5). If motor does not run, check for open in circuit 228. If motor runs, remove jumper wire and proceed to step 6.
6. Connect jumper wire between circuits 68 and 228 (terminals 2 and 5) at the cooling fan controller connector. If motor does not run, check for open in circuit 68. If motor runs, replace cooling fan controller and remove jumper wire from temperature switch electrical connector.

Fan Motor Operates When Engine Overheats But Does Not Operate With The A/C Compressor Clutch

1. Place selector switch in A/C position and turn ignition switch "On." If A/C clutch does not engage, proceed to step 2. If A/C clutch engages, proceed to step 8.
2. Check 20 amp fuse in fuse panel. If fuse is not blown, proceed to step 3.
3. Disconnect A/C clutch cycle pressure switch and connect jumper wire across connector terminals. If A/C clutch engages, proceed to step 4. If A/C clutch does not engage, proceed to step 6.
4. Check A/C system for loss of refrigerant charge. If there is no refrigerant charge, leak test, repair and charge system. If refrigerant system has charge with low pressure above 50 psi, proceed to step 5.
5. Check wide open throttle signal from EEC. If there is no continuity, repair linkage or EEC signal. If there is continuity, replace clutch cycling pressure switch.
6. Check for voltage in circuit 348 at A/C clutch cycling pressure switch. If there is voltage, repair open in circuit 347 to A/C clutch. If there is no voltage, proceed to step 7.
7. Check for voltage in circuits 296 and 348 at function selector switch in instrument panel. If there is voltage in circuit 296 but not in circuit 348, replace A/C control assembly. If there is no voltage in circuit 296, trace circuits 296 and 297 toward ignition switch.
8. Check for voltage in circuit 883 at pin 6 of cooling fan controller. If there is voltage, proceed to step 9. If there is no voltage, repair open in circuit 883 to controller.
9. Ground circuit 57 at pin 4 of controller without disconnecting controller electrical connector. If fan runs, repair ground circuit. If fan does not run, replace controller.

TYPE 30

Refer to **Fig. 36,** during the following procedures.

1. Check fuse and fusible link. If satisfactory, proceed to step 2. If not satisfactory, repair or replace as necessary.
2. Bring engine to operating temperature while operating A/C to determine when cooling fan does or does not operate. If cooling fan operates only during A/C operation, proceed to step 3. If cooling fan does not operate during A/C operation or during high engine coolant temperatures, proceed to step 12. If cooling fan only operates during high engine coolant temperature, proceed to step 7.
3. Disconnect coolant temperature switch electrical connector, then connect a jumper wire from connector to ground. If fan motor operates, proceed to step 4. If fan motor does not operate, proceed to step 5.

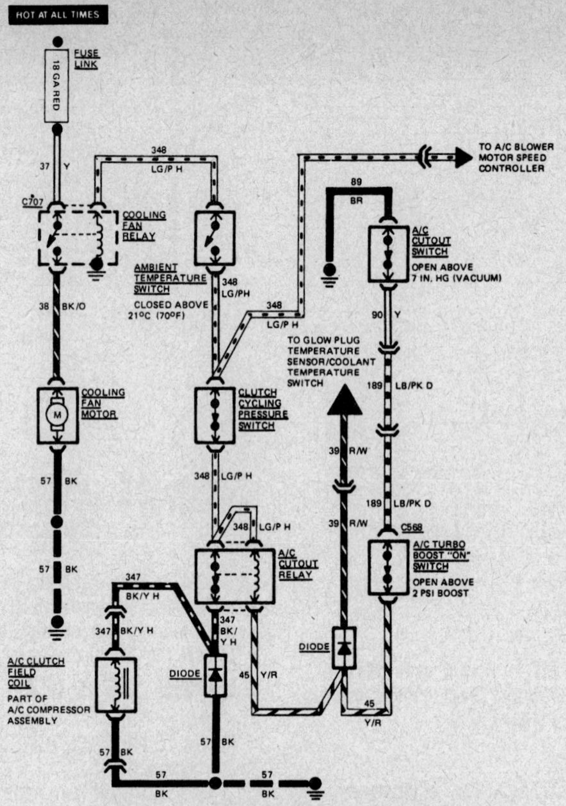

Fig. 35 Electric engine cooling fan wiring diagram. Type 29

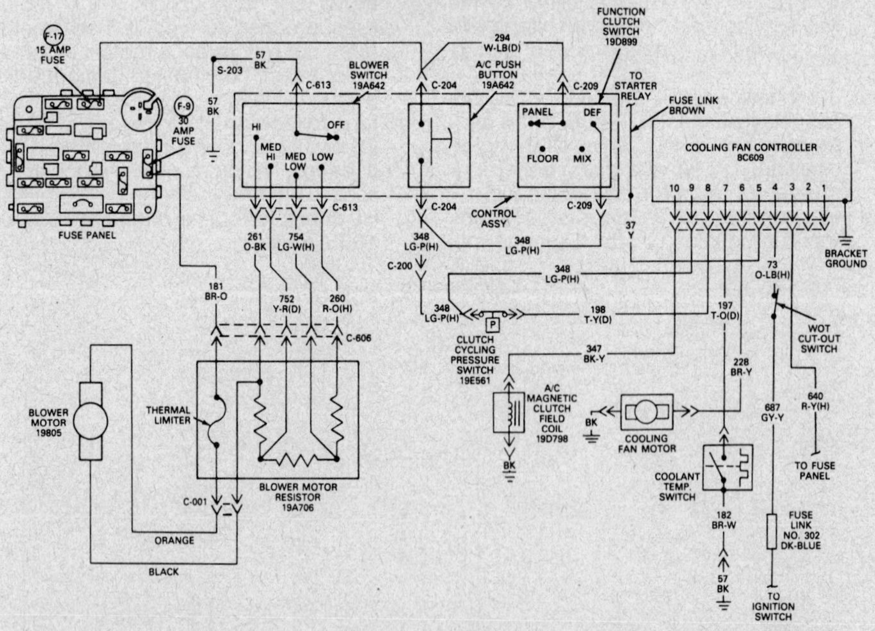

Fig. 36 Electric engine cooling fan wiring diagram. Type 30

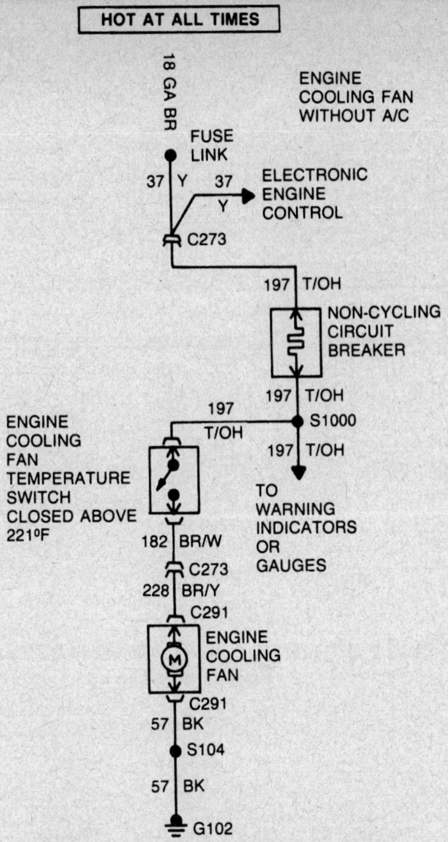

Fig. 37 Electric engine cooling fan wiring diagram. Type 31

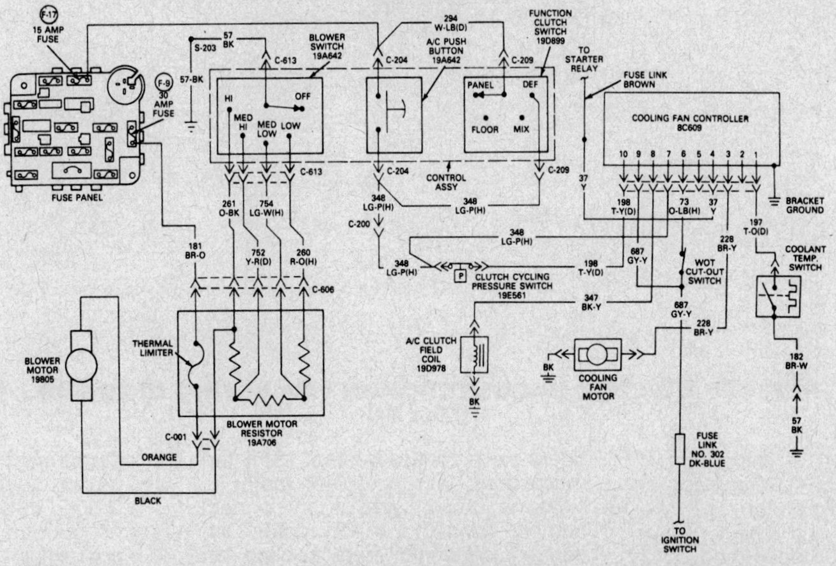

Fig. 38 Electric engine cooling fan wiring diagram. Type 32

4. Using a suitable ohmmeter, check continuity from switch body to thermostat housing. If continuity is not present, tighten switch until continuity is achieved, then recheck operation. Ensure coolant temperature has exceeded 221 degrees F, by operating engine for approximately 25 minutes. If fan motor runs, cooling fan system is operational. If fan motor does not operate, replace coolant temperature switch.
5. Disconnect fan controller electrical connector, then check circuit 197 from controller to coolant temperature switch. If continuity exists, replace cooling fan controller. If no continuity exists, service 197 circuit.
6. Check wide open throttle cut-out switch to determine if switch is open or closed. If switch is open, adjust or replace switch. If switch is closed, proceed to step 7.
7. Remove connector from cooling fan controller, then check for voltage at circuits 354, 687, 640, 348 and 198. If no voltage is present, service circuit, then go to step 10. If voltage is satisfactory, proceed to step 10.
8. Disconnect connector from clutch cycling pressure switch, then install jumper wire across connector. Check for voltage at circuit 198 of cooling fan controller. If voltage is satisfactory, proceed to step 9. If no voltage is present, proceed to step 11.
9. Check A/C system for satisfactory refrigerant charge. If no refrigerant charge is present, leak test, service

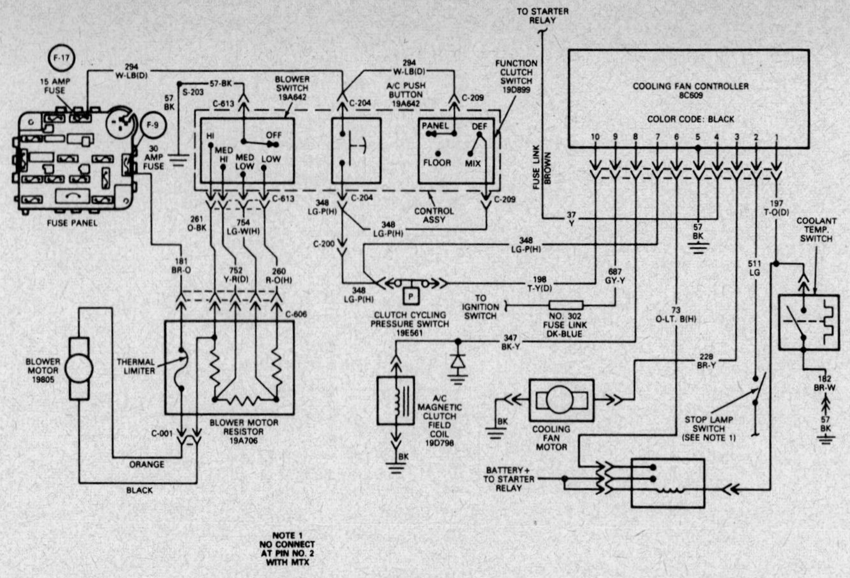

Fig. 39 Electric engine cooling fan wiring diagram. Type 33

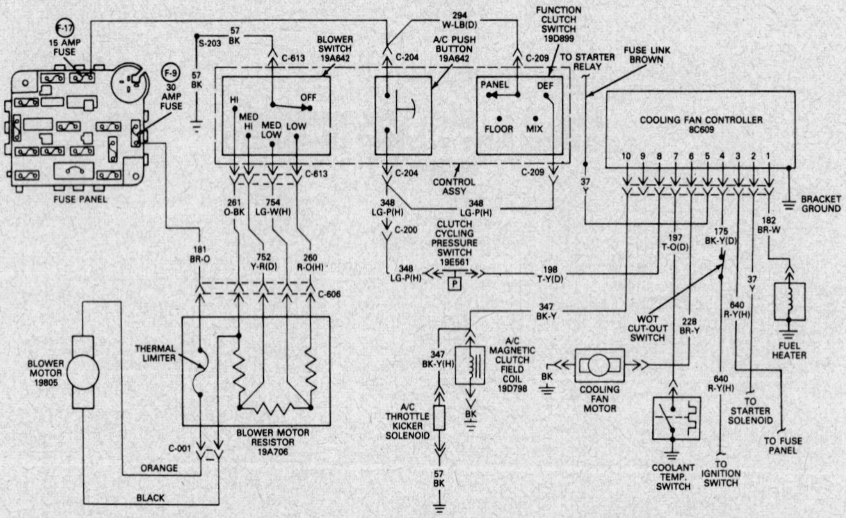

Fig. 40 Electric engine cooling fan wiring diagram. Type 34

and recharge system. If refrigerant pressure is above 50 psi, replace clutch cycling pressure switch.

10. Remove connector and check for ground at circuit 57 or loose module attachment. If ground is not satisfactory, repair as necessary. If ground is satisfactory, replace fan controller.
11. Remove connector from A/C control assembly. Connect a jumper from circuit 296 to circuit 321 and check for voltage at circuit 198 and 348, at cooling fan controller connector. If voltage is available at both circuits, replace A/C push button switch. If voltage is present at circuit 198 only, service circuit 348.
12. Disconnect connector at cooling fan motor, then connect a jumper from B+ and ground to motor. If fan motor operates, proceed to step 13. If fan motor does not run, replace motor.
13. Remove jumper wires, then connect harness connector to fan motor. Disconnect connector from cooling fan controller, then turn ignition switch "On" and check for voltage at circuits 37 and 354. If no voltage exists on bracket ground at 1 or all circuits, service as necessary. If voltage is satisfactory, proceed to step 14.
14. Jumper circuit 37 to 228 at cooling fan controller. If fan motor operates, replace cooling fan controller. If fan motor does not operate, service circuit 228.

TYPE 31

Refer to **Fig. 37**, during the following procedures.

1. Disconnect fan motor electrical connector, then install a jumper from ground to B+ terminal. If motor does not operate, replace. If motor operates, connect motor lead, then proceed to step 2.
2. Disconnect electrical connector at cooling fan temperature switch, then check for voltage at circuit 37. If battery voltage is present, proceed to step 3. If battery voltage is not present, check for open or short circuit in circuit 37 and or fusible link. Service as necessary, then check operation of cooling fan.
3. Jumper cooling fan temperature switch connector pins together and check that cooling fan motor is operating. If motor is operating, replace

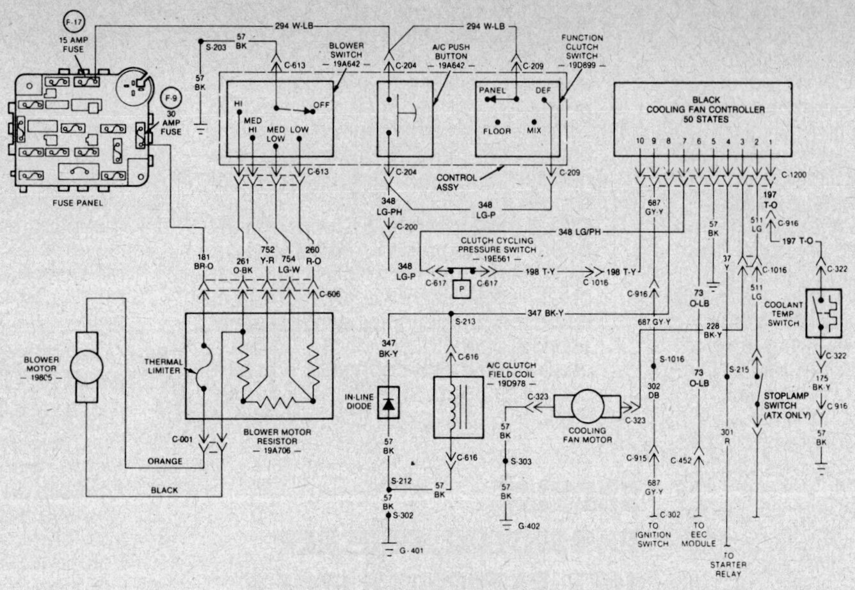

Fig. 41 Electric engine cooling fan wiring diagram. Type 35

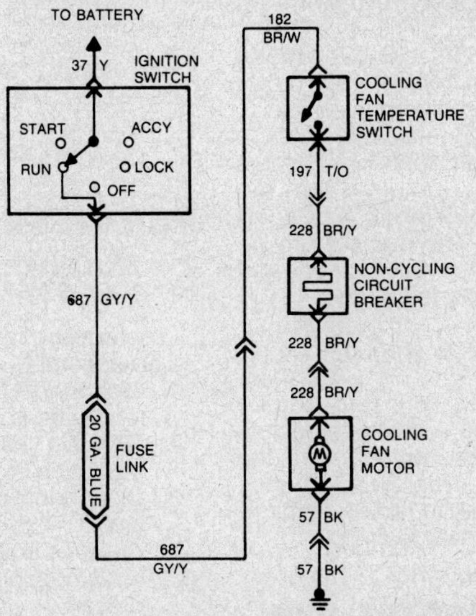

Fig. 42 Electric engine cooling fan wiring diagram. Type 36

temperature switch and recheck operation. If motor is not operating, leave jumper and proceed to step 4.

4. Disconnect fan motor connector, then check for battery voltage at circuit 228. If battery voltage is present, proceed to step 5. If battery voltage is not present, check for open in circuits 228 and 182. Service wiring between fan motor and cooling fan temperature switch. Connect temperature switch, then recheck operation.
5. Check ground circuit 57 for continuity. If continuity is present, replace cooling fan motor, connect cooling fan temperature switch connector, then check operation. If continuity is not present, service open in circuit 57. Connect cooling fan motor connector and temperature switch, then recheck fan operation.

TYPES 32 THROUGH 35

Refer to **Figs. 38 through 41,** during the following procedures.

1. Check fuse and fusible link. If satisfactory, proceed to step 2. If not satisfactory, repair or replace as necessary.
2. Bring engine to operating temperature while operating A/C to determine when cooling fan does or does not operate. If cooling fan operates only during A/C operation, proceed to step 3. If cooling fan does not operate during A/C operation or during high engine coolant temperatures, proceed to step 12. If cooling fan only operates during high engine coolant temperature, proceed to step 6.
3. Turn ignition switch "On," then disconnect connector at coolant temperature switch and jumper connector to ground with A/C off. If fan motor runs, proceed to step 4. If fan motor does not run, proceed to step 5.
4. Using a suitable ohmmeter, check continuity from switch body to thermostat housing. If continuity is not present, tighten switch until continuity is achieved, then recheck operation. Ensure coolant temperature has exceeded 221 degrees F, by operating engine for approximately 25 minutes. If fan motor runs, cooling fan system is operational. If fan motor does not operate, replace coolant temperature switch.
5. Disconnect fan controller electrical connector, then check circuit 197 from controller to coolant temperature switch. If continuity exists, replace cooling fan controller. If no continuity exists, service 197 circuit.
6. Check A/C clutch engagement. If clutch engages, proceed to step 8. If clutch does not engage, check fuse. If fuse is satisfactory, proceed to step 9.
7. Check fan controller bracket to ground. If ground is satisfactory, proceed to step 8. If ground is not satisfactory, repair as necessary.
8. Remove connector from cooling fan controller, then check for voltage at circuits 640, 37 and 175. If no voltage is present, service circuits as necessary. If voltage is satisfactory, proceed to step 9.
9. Disconnect connector from clutch cycling pressure switch, then install jumper wire across connector. Check that A/C clutch engages. If clutch engages, replace fan controller. If clutch does not engage, proceed to step 11.
10. Check A/C system for satisfactory refrigerant charge. If no refrigerant charge is present, leak test, service and recharge system. If refrigerant pressure is above 50 psi, replace clutch cycling pressure switch.

11. Remove connector from A/C control assembly. Connect a jumper from circuit 296 to circuit 321 and check for voltage at black/yellow wire of clutch connector. If voltage is available, replace A/C push button switch. If no voltage is present, service open in circuits 321, 347 or 348. Remove jumper 5 and connect to pressure switch.
12. Disconnect connector at cooling fan motor, then connect a jumper from B+ and ground to motor. If fan motor operates, proceed to step 13. If fan motor does not run, replace motor.
13. Remove jumper wires, then connect harness connector to fan motor. Disconnect connector from cooling fan controller, then turn ignition switch "On" and check for voltage at circuits 37, 640, 175, 198, 348 and fan controller bracket ground. If no voltage exists on bracket ground at 1 or all circuits, service as necessary. If voltage is satisfactory, proceed to step 14.
14. Jumper circuit 37 to 228 at cooling fan controller. If fan motor operates, replace cooling fan controller. If fan motor does not operate, service circuit 228.

TYPE 36

Refer to **Fig. 42**, during the following procedures.

1. Disconnect fan motor electrical connector, then install a jumper from ground to B+ terminal. If motor does not operate, replace. If motor operates, connect motor lead, then proceed to step 2.
2. Disconnect electrical connector at cooling fan temperature switch, then check for voltage at circuit 197. If battery voltage is present, proceed to step 3. If battery voltage is not present, check for open or short circuit in circuit 137 and or fusible link. Service as necessary, then check operation of cooling fan.
3. Jumper cooling fan temperature switch connector pins together and check that cooling fan motor is operating with ignition switch in "On" position. If motor is operating, replace temperature switch and recheck operation. If motor is not operating, leave jumper and proceed to step 4.
4. Disconnect fan motor connector, then check for battery voltage at circuit 228. If battery voltage is present, proceed to step 5. If battery voltage is not present, check for open in circuit 228. Service wiring between fan motor and cooling fan temperature switch. Connect temperature switch, then recheck operation.
5. Check ground circuit 57 for continuity. If continuity is present, replace cooling fan motor, connect cooling fan temperature switch connector, then check operation. If continuity is not present, service open in circuit 57. Connect cooling fan motor connector and temperature switch, then recheck fan operation.

SERVICE

FAN MOTOR, REPLACE

1982–83 ESCORT & LYNX & 1982–83 EXP & LN7

1. Disconnect battery ground cable, then disconnect fan motor wire connector and detach wire loom clip from fan shroud.
2. Remove two nuts attaching fan motor and shroud, then remove fan motor and shroud assembly from vehicle.
3. Remove nut or clip retaining fan blade to fan motor shaft, then remove fan blade. **The nut retaining the fan blade to the motor shaft has a left handed thread. The nut should be rotated clockwise to loosen and counterclockwise to tighten.**
4. Remove three nuts and washers attaching fan motor to shroud, then remove fan motor.
5. Reverse procedure to install. Torque fan motor to fan shroud attaching nuts to 6.6 to 9.6 ft. lbs., fan blade to fan motor retaining nut to 30 to 40 inch lbs. and fan shroud to radiator attaching nuts to 80 to 100 inch lbs.

1982–83 EXC. ESCORT, EXP, LN7 & LYNX & 1984–87 EXC. ESCORT, EXP, LYNX, TEMPO & TOPAZ

1. Disconnect battery ground cable, then remove wiring from routing clip.
2. Disconnect fan motor wiring connector.
3. Remove four screws securing mounting bracket and remove fan assembly from vehicle.
4. Remove fan blade retaining clip, then remove fan.
5. Remove nuts securing fan motor to mounting bracket.
6. Reverse procedure to install. Torque fan motor attaching nuts to 70-95 in. lbs., fan shroud to radiator attaching bolts, 70-95 in. lbs.

1984–87 ESCORT, EXP, LYNX, TEMPO & TOPAZ

1. Disconnect battery ground cable.
2. Disconnect electrical connector at fan motor, then disconnect wire loom from clip on shroud.
3. Remove two nuts retaining fan motor and shroud assembly and remove from vehicle.
4. Remove retaining clip from motor shaft and remove fan.
5. Remove three nuts and washers and withdraw fan motor from shroud.
6. Reverse procedure to install, torquing motor to shroud attaching nuts and washers to 44-66 inch lbs. and the fan, motor, shroud assembly retaining nuts to 35-45 inch lbs. on Escort, EXP and Lynx, or 23-33 inch lbs. on Tempo and Topaz.

ELECTRO-DRIVE COOLING FAN, REPLACE

Continental & Mark VII W/6-146 Diesel Engine

The cooling fan and motor are replaced as an assembly on these vehicles.

1. Disconnect battery ground cable, then raise and support vehicle.
2. Remove nuts and bolts attaching mounting brackets to radiator support.
3. Disconnect electrical connector at fan.
4. Remove bolts attaching hood latch to radiator support and position latch out of way.
5. Remove nuts and bolts attaching mounting brackets to fan and motor assembly, then remove fan and motor assembly from vehicle.
6. Reverse procedure to install, torquing all nuts and bolts to 4-5 ft. lbs.

DASH GAUGES

INDEX

TESTING

Gauge failures are often caused by defective wiring or grounds. The first step in locating trouble should be a thorough inspection of all wiring, terminals and printed circuits. If wiring is secured by clamps, check to see whether the insulation has been severed thereby grounding the wire. In the case of a fuel gauge installation, rust may cause failure by corrosion at the ground connection of the tank unit.

CONSTANT VOLTAGE REGULATOR TYPE (CVR)

The Constant Voltage Regulator (CVR) type indicator is a bi-metal resistance type system consisting of an Instrument Voltage Regulator (IVR), an indicator gauge, and a variable resistance sending unit. Current to the system is applied to the gauge terminals by the IVR, which maintains an average pulsating value of 5 volts.

The indicator gauge consists of a pointer which is attached to a wire-wound bimetal strip. Current passing through the coil heats the bi-metal strip, causing the pointer to move. As more current passes through the coil, heat increases, moving the pointer farther.

The circuit is completed through a sending unit which contains a variable resistor. When resistance is high, less current is allowed to pass through the gauge, and the pointer moves very little. As resistance decreases due to changing conditions in system being monitored, more current passes through gauge coil, causing pointer to move farther.

OPERATIONAL TEST

1. Disconnect wiring harness connector at sending unit. Connect a test lamp or voltmeter between terminal in wiring harness connector and ground.
2. With ignition switch in ON position, light should pulse or meter reading should fluctuate.
3. If lamp lights but does not pulse, or if meter reading remains steady, check ground to IVR. If ground is satisfactory, IVR is defective.
4. If lamp fails to light, or if meter reads 0 volts, check for open circuit across IVR terminals, indicator gauge terminals, or open circuit in wiring harness and printed circuit between components.
5. Connect test lamp or voltmeter ground lead to ground terminal in sending unit wiring harness connector. Light should pulse or meter reading should fluctuate as in step 2. If not, locate open in ground circuit. **Do not apply battery voltage to system or ground output terminals of IVR, as damage to system components or wiring circuits may result.**

DASH GAUGE TEST

1. Disconnect battery ground cable and remove gauge from vehicle.
2. Connect ohmmeter between gauge terminals and read coil winding resistance.
3. An upward movement of ohmmeter needle from 10 ohms to 14 ohms is normal, as test current of ohmmeter causes a temperature rise in gauge coil windings.
4. If ohmmeter reads below 10 ohms or above 14 ohms, gauge is defective.

SENDING UNIT TEST

Fuel Tank Gauge

1. Disconnect wiring harness connector at sending unit and connect ohmmeter between ground terminal and resistor terminal on sending unit.
2. Meter should read 8-86 ohms. If reading shows no continuity (infinite reading), check ground connection to tank gauge.
3. If ground is satisfactory, but reading is not within specification, tank unit is defective.
4. If reading is within specification, remove fuel tank gauge from vehicle and connect ohmmeter between resistor terminal and ground terminal (metal housing on single terminal units).
5. Observe meter while slowly moving float rod between empty and full stops. Meter should read 60-86 ohms at empty stop and 8-12 ohms at full stop. Change in readings should be smooth, without hesitation or jumping.
6. If tank unit fails to operate as outlined, unit is defective. **Before installing fuel tank gauge, connect wiring harness connector to gauge and move float rod from empty to full position with ignition key in ON position. If dash gauge reading is incorrect, check IVR and dash gauge. If system tests prove satisfactory, but system still does not operate correctly, check that tank gauge rod is not bent or binding and that float is not damaged, loose or filled with fuel.**

Oil & Temperature Sending Units

1. Test dash gauge and IVR as outlined above.
2. If system is satisfactory, start engine and allow it to reach operating temperature.
3. If no reading is indicated on the gauge, check the sending unit-to-gauge wire by removing the wire from the sending unit and momentarily ground this wire to a clean, unpainted portion of the engine.
4. If the gauge still does not indicate, the wire is defective. Repair or replace the wire.
5. If grounding the new or repaired wire causes the dash gauge to indicate, the sending unit is faulty.

AMMETERS

The ammeter is an instrument used to indicate current flow into and out of the battery. When electrical accessories in the vehicle draw more current than the alternator can supply, current flows from the battery and the ammeter indicates a discharge (−) condition. When electrical loads of the vehicle are less than alternator output, current is available to charge the battery, and the ammeter indicates a charge (+) condition. If battery is fully charged, the voltage regulator reduces alternator output to meet only immediate vehicle electrical loads. When this happens, ammeter reads zero.

CONVENTIONAL AMMETER

A conventional ammeter must be connected between the battery and alternator in order to indicate current flow. This type ammeter, **Fig. 1**, consists of a frame to which a permanent magnet is attached. The frame also supports an armature and pointer assembly. Current in this system flows from the alternator through the ammeter, then to the battery or from the battery through the ammeter into the vehicle electrical system, depending on vehicle operating conditions.

When no current flows through the ammeter, the magnet holds the pointer armature so that the pointer stands at the center of the dial. When current passes in either direction through the ammeter, the resulting magnetic field attracts the armature away from the effect of the permanent magnet, thus giving a reading proportional to the strength of the current flowing.

Troubleshooting

When the ammeter apparently fails to register correctly, there may be trouble in the wiring which connects the ammeter to the alternator and battery or in the alternator or battery itself.

To check the connections, first tighten the two terminal posts on the back of the ammeter. Then, following each wire from the ammeter, tighten all connections on the ignition switch, battery and alternator. Chafed, burned or broken insulation can be found by following each ammeter wire from end to end.

All wires with chafed, burned or broken insulation should be repaired or replaced. After this is done, and all connections are tightened, connect the battery cable and turn on the ignition switch. The needle should point slightly to the discharge (−) side.

Start the engine and speed it up a little above idling speed. The needle should then move to the charge side (+), and its movement should be smooth.

If the pointer does not behave correctly, the ammeter itself is out of order and a new one should be installed.

SHUNT TYPE AMMETER

The shunt type ammeter is actually a specially calibrated voltmeter. It is connected to read voltage drop across a resistance wire (shunt) between the battery and alternator. The shunt is located either in the vehicle wiring or within the ammeter itself.

When voltage is higher at the alternator end of the shunt, the meter indicates a charge (+) condition. When voltage is higher at the battery end of the shunt, the meter indicates a discharge (−) condition. When voltage is equal at both ends of the shunt, the meter reads zero.

Troubleshooting

Ammeter accuracy can be determined by comparing reading with an ammeter of known accuracy.

1. With engine stopped and ignition switch in RUN position, switch on headlamps and heater fan. Meter should indicate a discharge (−) condition.
2. If ammeter pointer does not move, check ammeter terminals for proper connection and check for open circuit in wiring harness. If connections and wiring harness are satisfactory, ammeter is defective.
3. If ammeter indicates a charge (+) condition, wiring harness connections are reversed at ammeter.

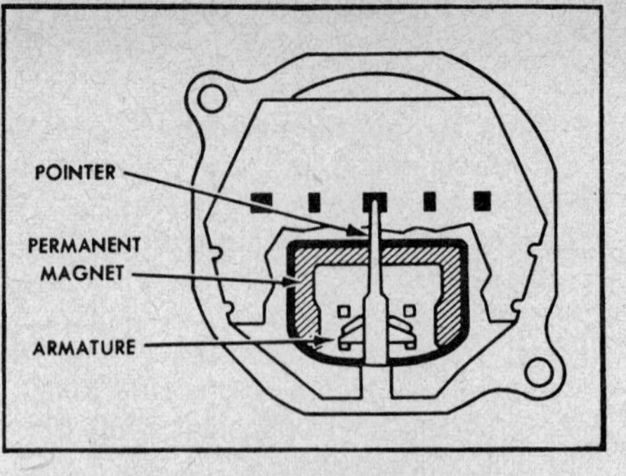

Fig. 1 Conventional type ammeter (typical)

ALTERNATOR INDICATOR LIGHT

The indicator lamp glows when field relay fails to close. When ignition is in the On position, battery current flows through the charge indicator lamp and a parallel resistor, and through regulator to field, and the lamp comes on. Vehicles with electronic voltage regulator have a 500 ohm resistor. On all others the resistor is 15 ohms. When the alternator builds up enough voltage to close the field relay the charge indicator lamp will go out. Place ignition switch in the Run position with the engine stopped. The lamp should light. If not, the bulb is burned out or indicator lamp has an open circuit.

On vehicles with electro-mechanical or transistorized regulators, an open resistor wire in the alternator charging circuit will usually cause the indicator lamp to remain on until engine speed is increased to approximately 2000 RPM. In some cases the lamp will remain on above 2000 RPM. The charge indicator lamp may be tested using a test light containing a No. 67 or 1155 bulb. Disconnect regulator wire connector from regulator, then place ignition switch in the Run position. Place one test lamp lead on regulator wire connector "I" terminal and other lead on regulator base. Test lamp will light if circuit is in proper working order. If 15 ohm resistor or circuit is open, indicator lamp will operate at full brightness and test lamp will not light.

VOLTMETER

The voltmeter is a gauge which measures the electrical flow from the battery to indicate whether the battery output is within tolerances. The voltmeter reading can range from 13.5-14.0 volts under normal operating conditions. If an undercharge or overcharge condition is indicated for an extended period, the battery and charging system should be checked.

TROUBLESHOOTING

To check voltmeter, turn key and headlights on with engine off. Pointer should move to 12.5 volts. If no needle movement is observed, check connections from battery to circuit breaker. If connections are tight and meter shows no movement, check wire continuity. If wire continuity is satisfactory, the meter is inoperative and must be replaced.

ELECTRICAL TEMPERATURE GAUGES

This temperature indicating system consists of a sending unit, located on the cylinder head, electrical temperature gauge and an instrument voltage regulator. As engine temperature increases or decreases, the resistance of the sending unit changes, in turn controlling current flow to the gauge. When engine temperature is low, the resistance of the sending unit is high, restricting current flow to the gauge, in turn indicating low engine temperature. As engine temperature increases, the resistance of the sending unit decreases, permitting an increased current flow to the gauge, resulting in an increased temperature reading.

TROUBLESHOOTING

Troubleshooting for the electrical temperature indicating system is the same as for the electrical oil pressure indicating system.

ELECTRIC OIL PRESSURE GAUGES

This oil pressure indicating system incorporates an instrument voltage regulator, electrical oil pressure gauge and a sending unit which are connected in series. The sending unit consists of a diaphragm, contact and a variable resistor. As oil pressure increases or decreases, the diaphragm actuated the contact on the variable resistor, in turn controlling current flow to the gauge. When oil pressure is low, the resistance of the variable resistor is high, restricting current flow to the gauge, in turn indicating low oil pressure. As oil pressure increases, the resistance of the variable resistor is lowered, permitting an increased current flow to the gauge, resulting in an increased gauge reading.

TROUBLESHOOTING

Disconnect the oil pressure gauge lead from the sending unit, connect a 12 volt test lamp between the gauge lead and the ground and turn ignition ON. If test lamp flashes, the instrument voltage regulator is functioning properly and the gauge circuit is not broken. If the test lamp remains lit, the instrument voltage regulator is defective and must be replaced. If the test lamp does not light, check the instrument voltage regulator for proper ground or an open circuit. Also, check for an open in the instrument voltage regulator to oil pressure gauge wire or in the gauge itself.

If test lamp flashes and gauge is not accurate, the gauge may be out of calibration, requiring replacement.

OIL PRESSURE INDICATOR LIGHT

Many cars utilize a warning light on the instrument panel in place of the conventional dash indicating gauge to warn the driver when the oil pressure is dangerously low. The warning light is wired in series with the ignition switch and the engine unit—which is an oil pressure switch.

The oil pressure switch contains a diaphragm and a set of contacts. When the ignition switch is turned on, the warning light circuit is energized and the circuit is completed through the closed contacts in the pressure switch. When the engine is started, build-up of oil pressure compresses the diaphragm, opening the contacts, thereby breaking the circuit and putting out the light.

TROUBLESHOOTING

The oil pressure warning light should go on when the ignition is turned on. If it does not light, disconnect the wire from the engine unit and ground the wire to the frame or cylinder block. Then if the warning light still does not go on with the ignition switch on, replace the bulb.

If the warning light goes on when the wire is grounded to the frame or cylinder block, the engine unit should be checked for being loose or poorly grounded. If the unit is found to be tight and properly grounded, it should be removed and a new one installed. (The presence of sealing compound on the threads of the engine unit will cause a poor ground).

If the warning light remains lit when it normally should be out, replace the engine unit before proceeding further to determine the cause for a low pressure indication.

The warning light sometimes will light up or will flicker when the engine is idling, even though the oil pressure is adequate. However, the light should go out when the engine is speeded up. There is no cause for alarm in such cases; it simply means that the pressure switch is not calibrated precisely correct.

TEMPERATURE INDICATOR LIGHT

TROUBLESHOOTING

If the red light is not lit when the engine is being cranked, check for a burned out bulb, an open in the light circuit, or a defective ignition switch.

If the red light is lit when the engine is running, check the wiring between light and switch for a ground, temperature switch defective, or overheated cooling system.

As a test circuit to check whether the red bulb is functioning properly, a wire which is connected to the ground terminal of the ignition switch is tapped into its circuit. When the ignition is in the "Start" (engine cranking) position, the ground terminal is grounded inside the switch and the red bulb will be lit. When the engine is started and the ignition switch is in the "On" position, the test circuit is opened and the bulb is then controlled by the temperature switch.

BOOST/OVERBOOST WARNING SYSTEM

Two calibrated pressure switches provide the driver visual indication that turbo boost pressure is satisfactory and visual and audible indication when turbo boost pressure is unsatisfactory. One switch will illuminate the green Turbo lamp located on the instrument panel when turbo boost pressure levels are within satisfactory limits. The second pressure switch will turn off the green Turbo lamp and illuminate the red engine warning lamp and sound the audible buzzer when excessive turbo boost pressure or high engine oil temperatures are encountered. When the red engine lamp is constant and buzzer sounds, the turbocharger is in an overboost condition, reduce engine speed immediately until buzzer ceases and warning lamp goes off. When the red engine warning light flashes on and off with no buzzer, this indicates excessive engine oil temperature, reduce engine speed to approximately 2500 RPM. The engine warning lamp should go out within 5 minutes. When the red engine warning lamp flashes on and off and buzzer sounds simultaneously, excessive turbo overboost and/or high engine oil temperatures are occuring, reduce engine speed immediately.

Whenever the engine warning lamp has illuminated or the audible buzzer sounds, the vehicle should be inspected as soon as possible to determine the cause.

With ignition switch in start position and engine not operating, the warning lamps should glow and the buzzer should sound to indicate the electrical circuits are operating properly. If warning lamps do not glow or if buzzer does not sound, the boost/overboost electrical system should be checked as soon as possible.

SPEEDOMETERS

The following material covers only that service on speedometers which can be performed by the average service man. Repairs on the units themselves are not included as they require special tools and extreme care when making repairs and adjustments and only an experienced speedometer mechanic should attempt such servicing.

The speedometer has two main parts—the indicator head and the speedometer drive cable. When the speedometer fails to indicate speed or mileage, the cable or housing is probably broken.

SPEEDOMETER CABLE

Most cables are broken due to lack of lubrication or a sharp bend or kink in the housing.

A cable might break because the speedometer head mechanism binds. If such is the case, the speedometer head should be repaired or replaced before a new cable or housing is installed.

A "jumpy" pointer condition, together with a sort of scraping noise, is due, in most instances, to a dry or kinked speedometer cable. The kinked cable rubs on the housing and winds up, slowing down the pointer. The cable then unwinds and the pointer "jumps."

To check for kinks, remove the cable, lay it on a flat surface and twist one end with the fingers. If it turns over smoothly the cable is not kinked. But if part of the cable flops over as it is twisted, the cable is kinked and should be replaced.

LUBRICATION

The speedometer cable should be lubricated with special cable lubricant every 10,000 miles.

Fill the ferrule on the upper end of the housing with the cable lubricant. Insert the cable in the housing, starting at the upper end. Turn the cable around carefully while feeding it into the housing. Repeat filling the ferrule except for the last six inches of cable. Too much lubricant at this point may cause the lubricant to work into the indicating hand.

INSTALLING CABLE

During installation, if the cable sticks when inserted in the housing and will not go through, the housing is damaged inside or kinked. Be sure to check the housing from one end to the other. Straighten any sharp bends by relocating clamps or elbows. Replace housing if it is badly kinked or broken. Position the cable and housing so that they lead into the head as straight as possible.

Check the new cable for kinks before installing it. Use wide, sweeping, gradual curves when the cable comes out of the transmission and connects to the head so the cable will not be damaged during its installation.

If inspection indicates that the cable and housing are in good condition, yet pointer action is erratic, check the speedometer head for possible binding.

The speedometer drive pinion should also be checked. If the pinion is dry or its teeth are stripped, the speedometer may not register properly.

The transmission mainshaft nut must be tight or the speedometer drive gear may slip on the mainshaft and cause slow speed readings.

ELECTRIC CLOCKS

Regulation of electric clocks used on automobiles is accomplished automatically by merely resetting the time. If the clock is running fast, the action of turning the hands back to correct the time will automatically cause the clock to run slightly slower. If the clock is running slow, the action of turning the hands forward to correct the time will automatically cause the clock to run slightly faster (10 to 15 seconds day).

A lock-out feature prevents the clock regulator mechanism from being reset more than once per wind cycle, regardless of the number of times the time is reset. After the clock rewinds, if the time is then reset, automatic regulation will take place. If a clock varies over 10 minutes per day, it will never adjust sufficiently, and must be repaired or replaced.

WINDING CLOCK WHEN CONNECTING BATTERY OR CLOCK WIRING

The clock requires special attention when reconnecting a battery that has been disconnected for any reason, a clock that has been disconnected, or when replacing a blown clock fuse. It is very important that the initial wind be fully made. The procedure is as follows:

1. Make sure that all other instruments and lights are turned off.
2. Connect positive cable to battery.
3. Before connecting the negative cable, press the terminal to its post on the battery. Immediately afterward strike the terminal against the battery post to see if there is a spark. If there is a spark, allow the clock to run down until it stops ticking, and repeat as above until there is no spark. Then immediately make the permanent connection before the clock can again run down. The clock will run down in approximately two minutes.
4. Reset clock after all connections have been made. The foregoing procedure should also be followed when reconnecting the clock after it has been disconnected, or if it has stopped because of a blown fuse. Be sure to disconnect battery before installing a new fuse.

TROUBLESHOOTING

If clock does not run, check for blown "clock" fuse. If fuse is blown check for short in wiring. If fuse is not blown check for open circuit.

With an electric clock, the most frequent cause of clock fuse blowing is voltage at the clock which will prevent a complete wind and allow clock contacts to remain closed. This may be caused by any of the following: discharged battery, corrosion on contact surface of battery terminals, loose connections at battery terminals, at junction block, at fuse clips, or at terminal connection of clock. Therefore, if in reconnecting battery or clock it is noted that the clock is not ticking, always check for blown fuse, or examine the circuits at the points indicated above to determine and correct the cause.

FIBER OPTIC MONITORING SYSTEM

Fiber optics are non-electric light conductors made up of coated strands which, when exposed to a light source at one end, will reflect the light through their entire length, thereby illuminating a monitoring lens on the instrument panel or fender without the use of a bulb when the exterior lights are turned on.

LOW FUEL WARNING SYSTEM

The switch type consists of an indicator light and a low fuel warning switch located on the instrument panel.

The warning switch contacts are closed by the difference in voltage potential between the fuel gauge terminals. This voltage differential will activate the warning switch when the fuel tank is less than 1/4 full and, in turn, cause the indicator to light.

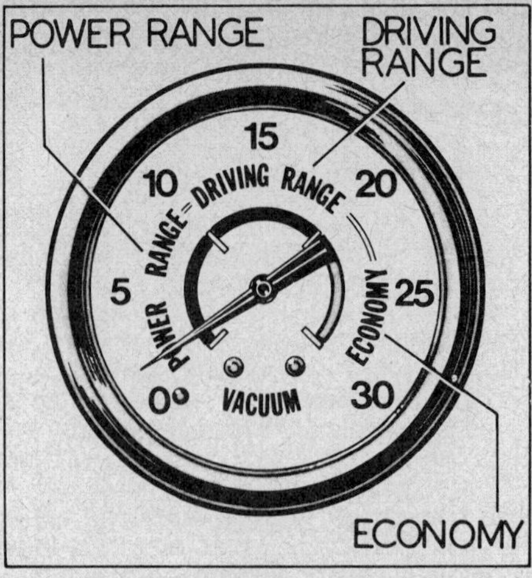

Fig. 2 Typical vacuum gauge

TROUBLESHOOTING

This system incorporates an indicator light. With ignition switch turned to "On", the indicator should light. If not, check bulb and all electrical connections.

Improper operation of the warning switch will be indicated when the light remains "ON" when tank is more than 1/4 full. To test system, disconnect connector on warning switch and turn ignition "ON". Starting with the terminal on the end opposite the blank position, connect a jumper wire between the battery positive terminal and connector terminal. The indicator on instrument panel should light. If not, replace warning switch. Skip the next connector terminal and connect a test lamp between the battery positive terminal and connector terminal. The test lamp should light. If not, trace wire from ignition switch for an open circuit. Test the remaining connector terminals with the test lamp making connections between ground and terminal connectors. If lamp fails to light, trace particular wire for an incomplete circuit.

VACUUM GAUGE

This gauge, **Fig. 2,** measures intake manifold vacuum. The intake manifold vacuum varies with engine operating conditions, carburetor adjustments, valve timing, ignition timing and general engine condition.

Since the optimum fuel economy is directly proportional to a properly functioning engine, a high vacuum reading on the gauge relates to fuel economy. For this reason some manufacturers call the vacuum gauge a "Fuel Economy Indicator." Most gauges have colored sectors the green sector being the "Economy" range and red the "Power" range. Therefore, the vehicle should be operated with gauge registering in the green sector or a high numerical number, **Fig. 2,** for maximum economy.

GRAPHIC DISPLAY WARNING INDICATOR SYSTEM

1982–87 FORD/MERCURY

Operation

This system is equipped with five L.E.D. (light emitting diodes) located on console, which will indicate running lamp failure, headlamp failure, brake lamp or low windshield washer fluid or fuel level. If lamp is burned out, L.E.D. will illuminate, indicating bulb failure. Application of emergency flasher or rear turn signal when turn signal/stop lamp bulb is burned out will cause L.E.D. to flash. When windshield washer fluid or fuel is below a predetermined level, corresponding L.E.D. will illuminate. If circuit is inoperative refer to **Figs. 3 through 9.**

LAMP-OUT WARNING SYSTEM

1982–87 THUNDERBIRD, COUGAR & XR-7; 1982 LINCOLN CONTINENTAL; 1983–87 LTD & MARQUIS

The lamp-out warning system monitors low-beam headlamps, tail lamps and brake lamps. The system consists of a warning module, a wiring harness and a set of three indicator lamps located on the upper tier of the instrument panel.

The wiring harness used with the system uses special resistance wire to ensure proper system operation. To prevent malfunctioning of the system, the lengths of these wires should never be altered.

The warning module contains a printed circuit board and logic circuitry. Normal operating voltage is 10-15 volts, however the unit will withstand up to 24 volts for a period of 15 minutes.

The lamp-out warning system operates when the ignition is in ACC or RUN position.

If one or more low beam lamps are burned out when headlamps are energized in low beam mode, the low beam Out indicator will illuminate. The tail lamp Out indicator will illuminate when running lamps are energized and one or more tail lamps are burned out. The brake lamp Out indicator will light when brake lights are energized and one or more brake lamps are burned out.

When ignition key is in START position, all three warning lights should illuminate.

1982–87 LINCOLN TOWN CAR & 1982–83 MARK VI

The lamp-out warning system monitors low beam headlamps, tail lamps and brake lamps. Each assembly is equipped with three outputs connected to the electronic message center module which displays the appropriate warning message.

Lamp outages are sensed by measuring change in voltage drop across a section of wiring harness by a transistor-diode bridge which provides logic level signals to external message center.

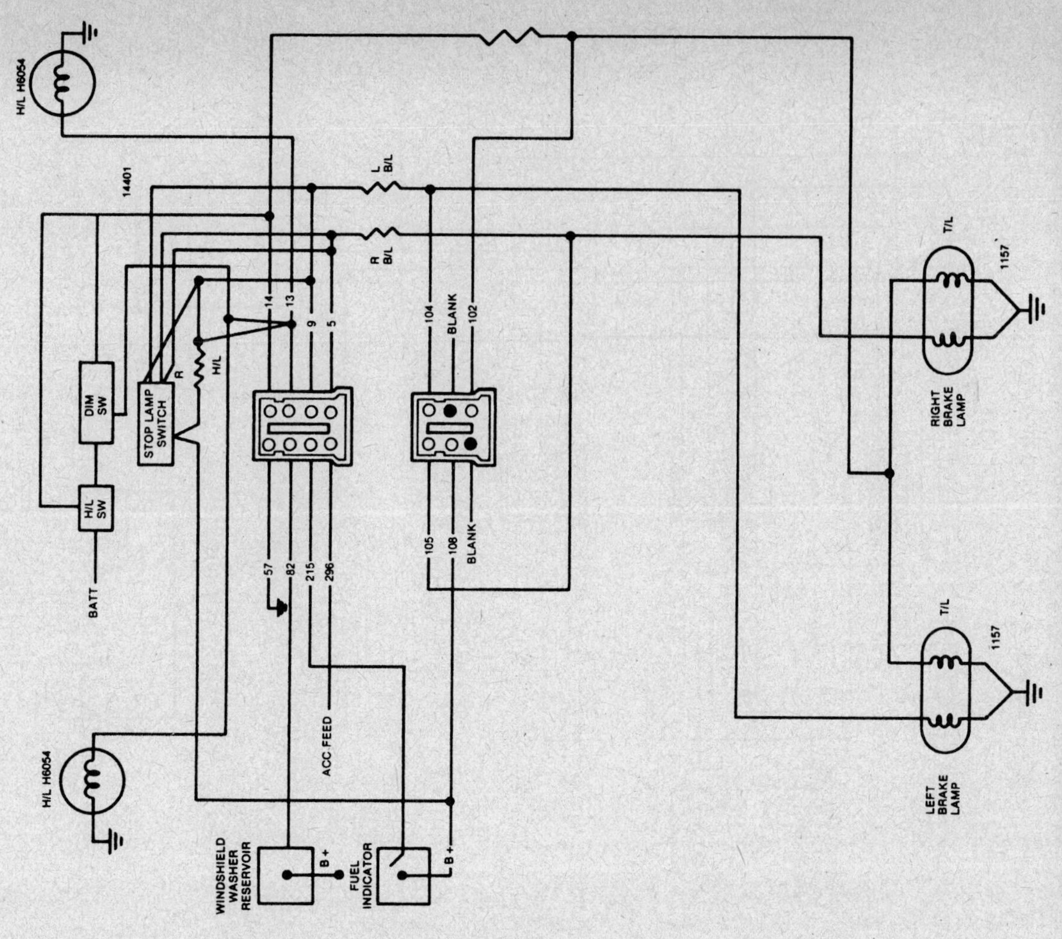

Fig. 4 Graphic display warning indicator wiring diagram. 1982–83 Escort & Lynx base model

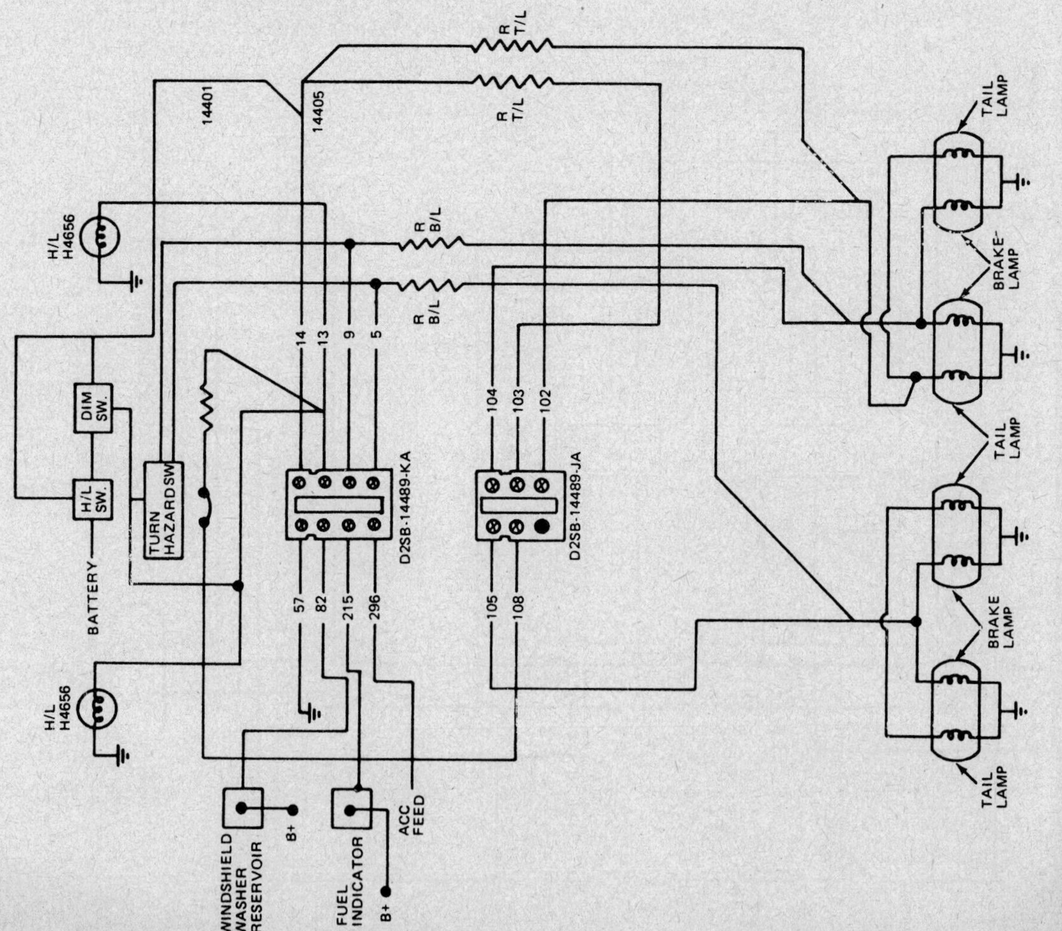

Fig. 3 Graphic display warning indicator wiring diagram. 1982–87 Ford & Mercury Exc. Escort & Lynx (Mustang/Capri & Fairmont/Zephyr sedan shown, typical of other models)

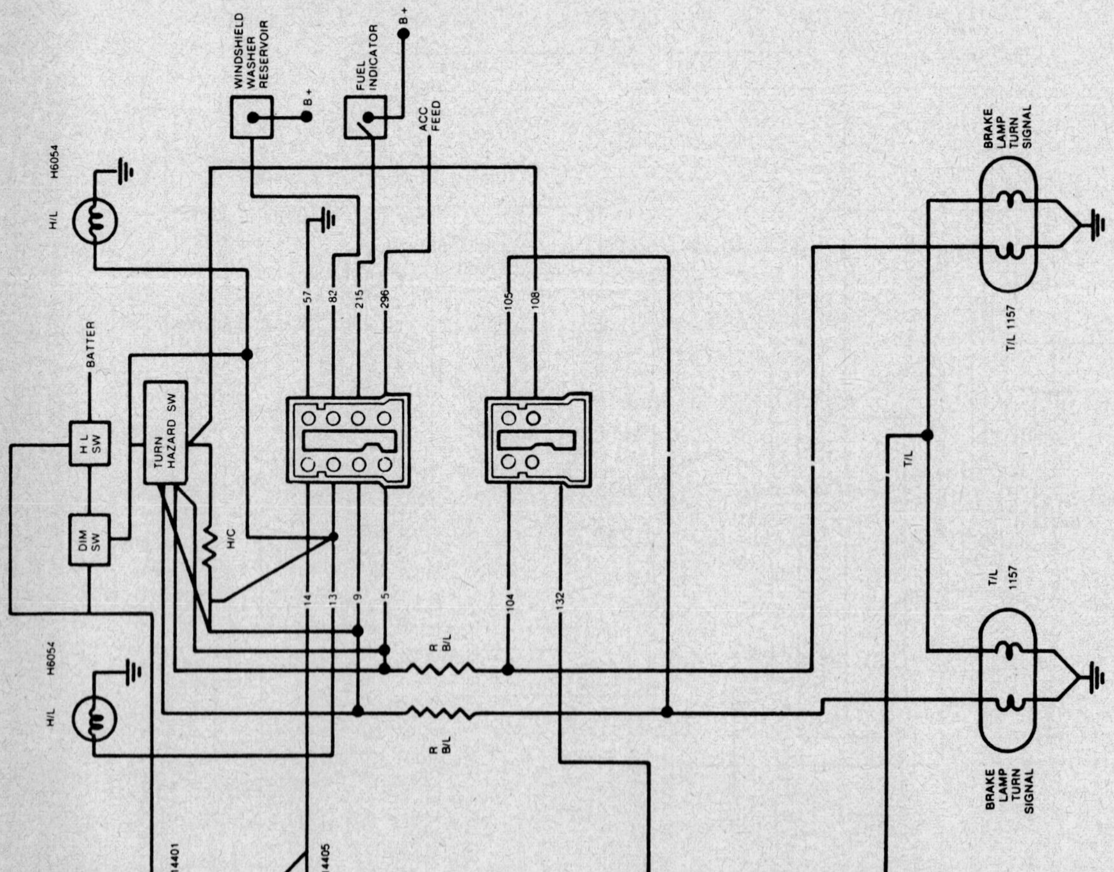

Fig. 5 Graphic display warning indicator wiring diagram. 1982–83 Escort & Lynx exc. base model

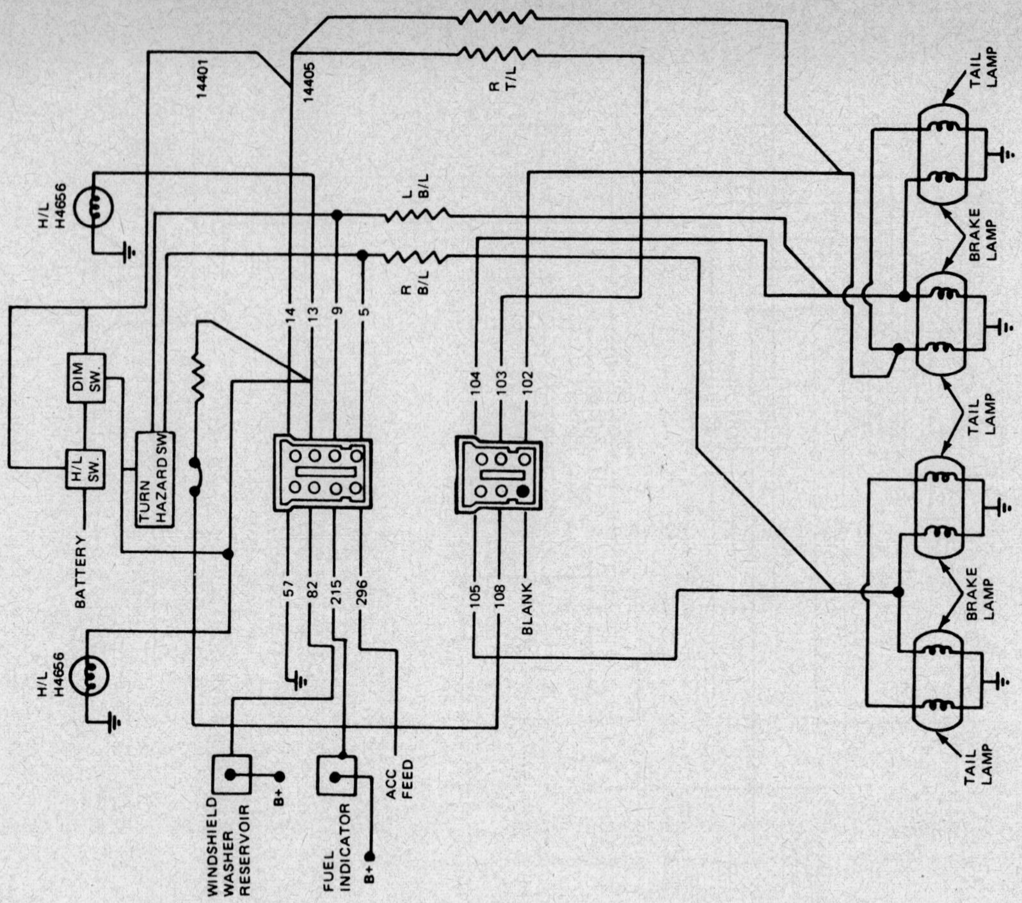

Fig. 6 Graphic display warning indicator wiring diagram. 1984–86 Escort & Lynx & 1984–87 Tempo & Topaz

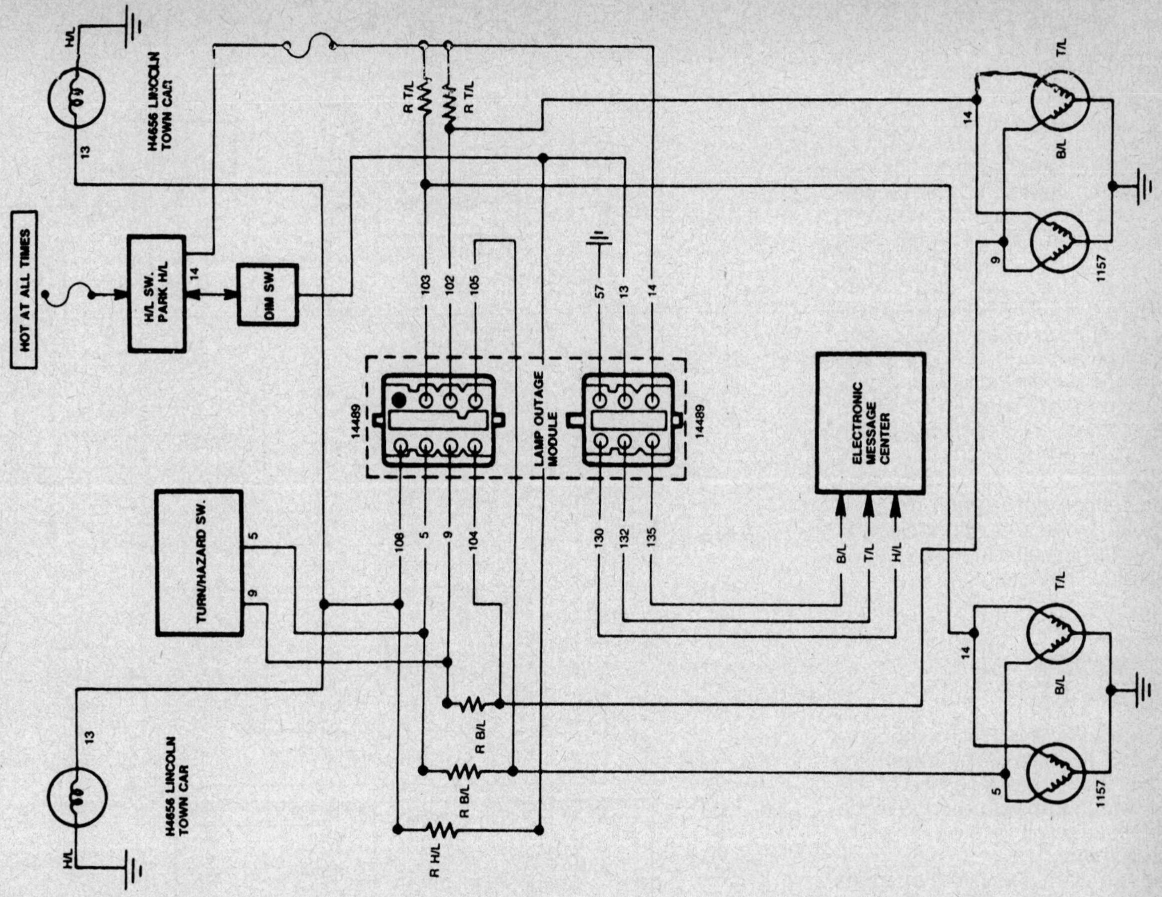

Fig. 8 Graphic display warning indicator wiring diagram. 1987 Town Car

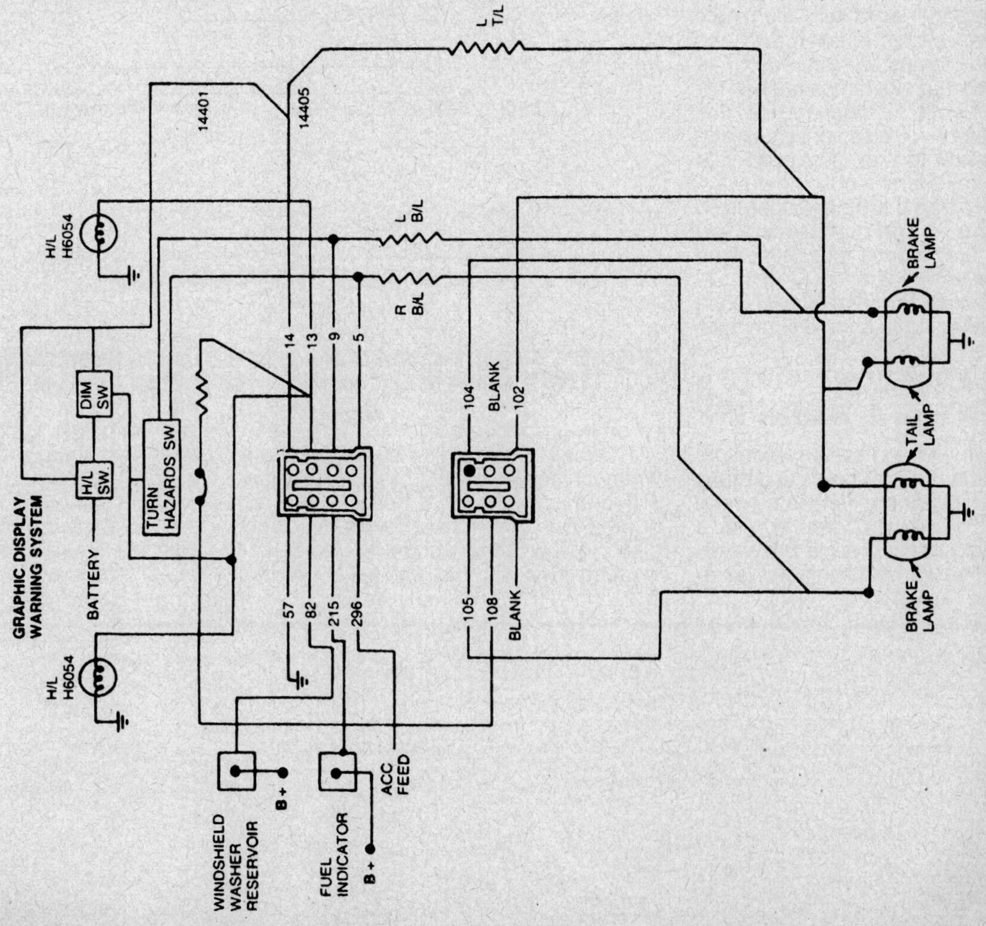

Fig. 7 Graphic display warning indicator wiring diagram. 1987 Escort, EXP & Lynx

The lamp-out warning module contains a printed circuit board and logic circuitry. Normal operating voltage is 10-15 volts, however the unit will withstand up to 24 volts for a period of 15 minutes.

The lamp-out warning system operates when ignition is in ACC or RUN position.

If one or more low beam lamps are burned out when headlamps are energized in low beam mode, the headlamp outage message will flash. The tail lamp outage indicator will flash when headlamp switch is energized and one or more tail lamps are burned out. The brake lamp outage indicator will flash when brake or turn signal is applied and one or more brake lamps are burned out. The brake lamp indicator will also be illuminated if turn signal or emergency flasher is activated with message center on and one or more lamps burned out.

When the "check out" button on message center is depressed with ignition in ACC or RUN position, all lamp-out warning displays should illuminate.

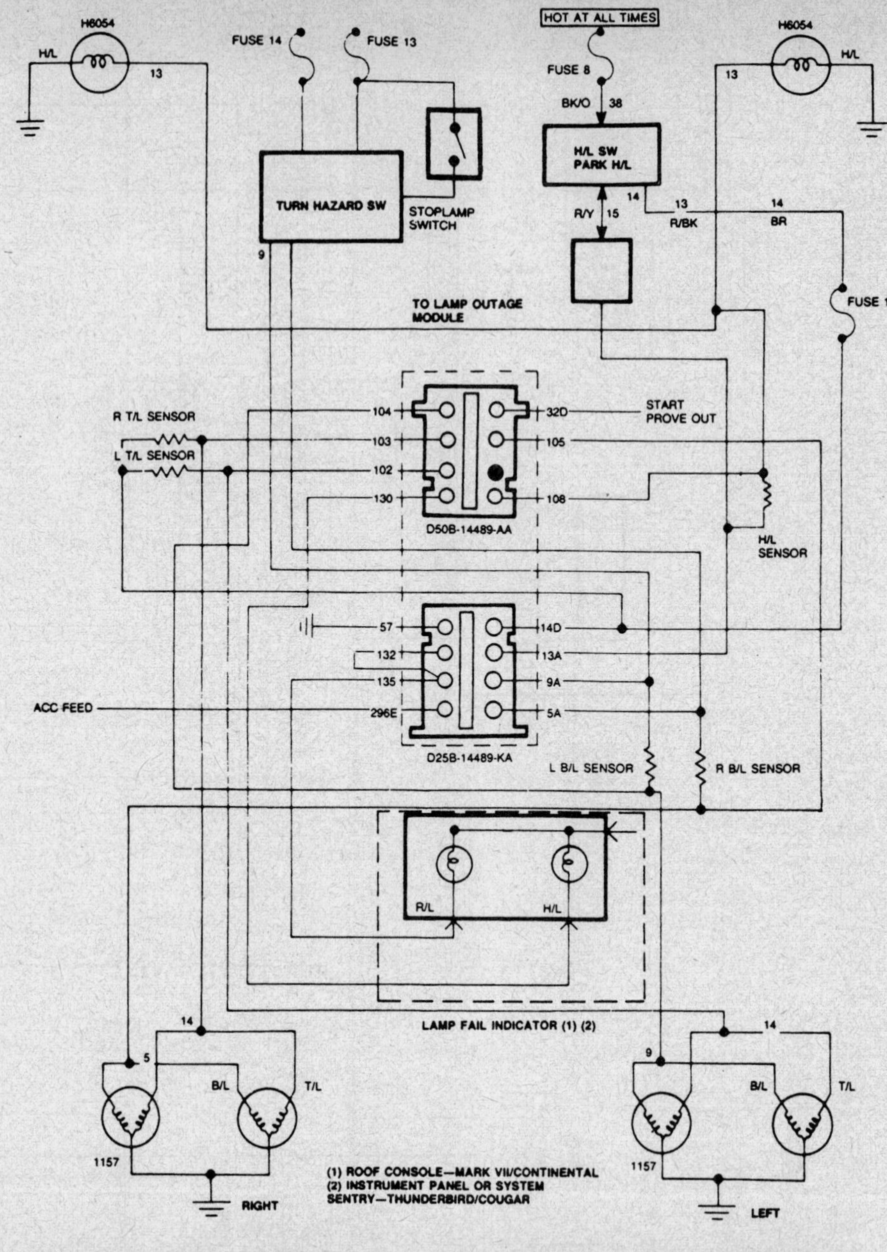

Fig. 9 Graphic display warning indicator wiring diagram. 1987 Cougar, Continental, Mark VII & Thunderbird

1983 LINCOLN CONTINENTAL

The lamp-out warning system monitors rear lamps and headlamps by measuring change in voltage across a section of wiring harness with a transistor-bridge diode. Warning indicators are located on either side of the tripminder.

The lamp-out warning system operates when ignition is in ACC or RUN position.

The rear outage light will illuminate when headlamp switch is energized and one or more tail lamps are burned out, or when one or more brake lamps are burned out and brake or turn signal is applied. The rear lamp indicator will also light if turn signal or emergency flasher is applied with one or more brake lamps out.

When the headlamp switch is energized in low beam mode and one or more low beam lamps are burned out, headlamp outage light will illuminate.

When the ignition key is in START position, both warning lights should illuminate.

1984–87 LINCOLN CONTINENTAL & MARK VII

The lamp-out warning system monitors low beam headlamps, tail lamps and brake lamps. Lamp outages are sensed by measuring change in voltage drop across a section of wiring harness by a transistor-diode bridge. The warning lights are located on the roof console.

The lamp-out warning system operates when ignition is in ACC or RUN position.

If one or more low beam lamps are burned out when headlamps are energized in low beam mode, the headlamp warning lamp will light. The tail lamp warning lamp will light when the headlamp switch is energized and one or more tail lamps are burned out. The brake lamp warning lamp will light when brakes are applied or the turn signal or emergency flashers are activated and one or more brake lamps are burned out.

STARTER MOTORS & SWITCHES

TABLE OF CONTENTS

General Information

INDEX

STARTER TROUBLE CHECK OUT

When trouble develops in the starting motor circuit, and the starter cranks the engine slowly or not at all, several preliminary checks can be made to determine whether the trouble lies in the battery, in the starter, in the wiring between them, or elsewhere. Many conditions besides defects in the starter itself can result in poor cranking performance.

To make a quick check of the starter system, turn on the headlights. They should burn with normal brilliance. If they do not, the battery may be run down.

If the battery is in a charged condition so that lights burn brightly, operate the starting motor. Any one of three things will happen to the lights: (1) They will go out, (2) dim considerably or (3) stay bright without any cranking action taking place.

IF LIGHTS GO OUT

If the lights go out as the starter switch is closed, it indicates that there is a poor connection between the battery and starting motor. This poor connection will most often be found at the battery terminals. Correction is made by removing the cable clamps from the terminals, cleaning the terminals and clamps, replacing the clamps and tightening them securely. A coating of corrosion inhibitor (petroleum jelly will do) may be applied to the clamps and terminals to retard the formation of corrosion.

IF LIGHTS DIM

If the lights dim considerably as the starter switch is closed and the starter operates slowly or not at all, the battery may be run down, or there may be some mechanical condition in the engine or starting motor that is throwing a heavy burden on the starting motor. This imposes a high discharge rate on the battery which causes noticeable dimming of the lights.

Check the battery state of charge. If it is charged, the trouble probably lies in either the engine or starting motor itself. In the engine, tight bearings or pistons or heavy oil place an added burden on the starting motor. Low temperatures also hamper starting motor performance since it thickens engine oil and makes the engine considerably harder to crank and start. Also, a battery is less efficient at low temperatures.

In the starting motor, a bent armature, loose pole shoe screws or worn bearings, any of which may allow the armature to drag, will reduce cranking performance and increase current draw.

In addition, more serious internal damage is sometimes found. Thrown armature windings or commutator bars, which sometimes occur on over-running clutch drive starting motors, are usually caused by excessive overrunning after starting. This is the result of such conditions as the driver keeping the starting switch closed too long after the engine has started, the driver opening the throttle too wide in starting, or improper carburetor fast idle adjustment. Any of these subject the overrunning clutch to extra strain so it tends to seize, spinning the armature at high speed with resulting armature damage.

Another cause may be engine backfire during cranking which may result, among other things, from ignition timing being too far advanced.

To avoid such failures, the driver should pause a few seconds after a false start to make sure the engine has come completely to rest before another start is attempted. In addition, the ignition timing should be checked if engine backfiring has caused the trouble.

LIGHTS STAY BRIGHT, NO CRANKING ACTION

This condition indicates an open circuit at some point, either in the starter itself, the starter switch or control circuit. The solenoid control circuit can be eliminated momentarily by placing a heavy jumper lead across the solenoid main terminals to see if the starter will operate. This connects the starter directly to the battery and, if it operates, it indicates that the control circuit is not functioning normally. The wiring and control units must be checked to locate the trouble.

If the starter does not operate with the jumper attached, it will probably have to be removed from the engine so it can be examined in detail.

CHECKING CIRCUIT WITH VOLTMETER

Excessive resistance in the circuit between the battery and starter will reduce cranking performance. The resistance can be checked by using a voltmeter to measure voltage drop in the circuits while the starter is operated. There are three checks to be made:

1. Voltage drop between car frame and grounded battery terminal post (not cable clamp).
2. Voltage drop between car frame and starting motor field frame.
3. Voltage drop between insulated battery terminal post and starting motor terminal stud (or the battery terminal stud of the solenoid).

Each of these should show no more than one-tenth (0.1) volt drop when the starting motor is cranking the engine. Do not use the starter for more than 30 seconds at a time to avoid overheating it.

If excessive voltage drop is found in any of these circuits, make correction by disconnecting the cables, cleaning the connections carefully, and then reconnecting the cables firmly in place. A coating of petroleum jelly on the battery cables and terminal clamps will retard corrosion.

On some cars, extra long battery cables may be required due to the location of the battery and starter. This may result in somewhat higher voltage drop than the above recommended 0.1 volt. The only means of determining the normal voltage drop in such cases is to check several of these vehicles. Then when the voltage drop is well above the normal figure for all cars checked, abnormal resistance will be indicated and correction can be made as already explained.

SOLENOID SWITCHES

The solenoid switch on a cranking motor not only closes the circuit between the battery and the cranking motor but also shifts the drive pinion into mesh with the engine flywheel ring gear. This is done by means of a linkage between the solenoid switch plunger and the shift lever on the cranking motor.

There are two windings in the solenoid; a pull-in winding and a hold-in winding. Both windings are energized when the external control switch is closed. They produce a magnetic field which pulls the plunger in so that the drive pinion is shifted into mesh, and the main contacts in the solenoid switch are closed to connect the battery directly to the cranking motor. Closing the main switch contacts shorts out the pull-in winding since this winding is connected across the main contacts. The magnetism produced by the hold-in winding is sufficient to hold the plunger in, and shorting out the pull-in winding reduces drain on the battery. When the control switch is opened, it disconnects the hold-in winding from the battery. When the hold-in winding is disconnected from the battery, the shift lever spring withdraws the plunger from the solenoid, opening the solenoid switch contacts and at the same time withdrawing the drive pinion from mesh. Proper operation of the switch depends on maintaining a definite balance between the magnetic strength of the pull-in and hold-in windings.

This balance is established in the design by the size of the wire and the number of turns specified. An open circuit in the hold-in winding or attempts to crank with a discharged battery will cause the switch to chatter.

STARTING MOTOR SERVICE

To obtain full performance data on a starting motor or to determine the cause of abnormal operation, the starting motor should be submitted to a no-load and torque test. These tests are best performed on a starter bench tester with the starter mounted on it.

From a practical standpoint, however, a simple torque test may be made quickly with the starter in the car. Make sure the battery is fully charged and that the starter circuit wires and terminals are in good condition. Then operate the starter to see if the engine turns over normally. If it does not, the torque developed is below standard and the starter should be removed for further checking.

STARTER DRIVE TROUBLES

Starter drive troubles are easy to diagnose and they usually cannot be confused with ordinary starter difficulties. If the starter does not turn over at all or if it drags, look for trouble in the starter or electrical supply system. Concentrate on the starter drive or ring gear if the starter is noisy, if it turns but does not engage the engine, or if the starter won't disengage after the engine is started. After the starter is removed, the trouble can usually be located quickly.

Worn or chipped ring gear or starter pinion are the usual causes of noisy operation. Before replacing either or both of these parts try to find out what caused the damage. With the Bendix type drive, incomplete engagement of the pinion with the ring gear is a common cause of tooth damage. The wrong pinion clearance on starter drives of the over-running clutch type leads to poor meshing of the pinion and ring gear and too rapid tooth wear.

A less common cause of noise with either type of drive is a bent starter armature shaft. When this shaft is bent, the pinion gear alternately binds and then only partly meshes with the ring gear. Most manufacturers specify a maximum of .003 inch radial run-out on the armature shaft.

WHEN CLUTCH DRIVE FAILS

The over-running clutch type drive seldom becomes so worn that it fails to engage since it is directly activated by a fork and lever. The only thing that is likely to happen is that, once engaged, it will not turn the engine because the clutch itself is worn out. A much more frequent difficulty and one that rapidly wears ring gear and teeth is partial engagement. Proper meshing of the pinion is controlled by the end clearance between the pinion gear and the starter housing or pinion stop, if used.

On some starters, the solenoids are completely enclosed in the starter housing and the pinion clearance is not adjustable. If the clearance is not correct, the starter must be disassembled and checked for excessive wear of solenoid linkage, shift lever mechanism, or improper assembly of parts.

Failure of the over-running clutch drive to disengage is usually caused by binding between the armature shaft and the drive. If the drive, particularly the clutch, shows signs of overheating it indicates that it is not disengaging immediately after the engine starts. If the clutch is forced to overrun too long, it overheats and turns a bluish color. For the cause of the binding, look for rust or gum between the armature shaft and the drive, or for burred splines. Excess oil on the drive will lead to gumming, and inadequate air circulation in the flywheel housing will cause rust.

Over-running clutch drives cannot be overhauled in the field so they must be replaced. In cleaning, never soak them in a solvent because the solvent may enter the clutch and dissolve the sealed-in lubricant. Wipe them off lightly with kerosene and lubricate them sparingly with SAE 10 or 10W oil.

WHEN BENDIX DRIVE FAILS

When a Bendix type drive doesn't engage the cause usually is one of three things: either the drive spring is broken, one of the drive spring bolts has sheared off, or the screwshaft threads won't allow the pinion to travel toward the flywheel. In the first two cases, remove the drive by unscrewing the set screw under the last coil of the drive spring and replace the broken parts. Gummed or rusty screwshaft threads are fairly common causes of Bendix drive failure and are easily cleaned with a little kerosene or steel wool, depending on the trouble. Here again, as in the case of over-running clutch drives, use light oil sparingly, and be sure the flywheel housing has adequate ventilation. There is usually a breather hole in the bottom of the flywheel housing which should be open.

The failure of a Bendix drive to disengage or to mesh properly is most often caused by gummed or rusty screwshaft threads. When this is not true, look for mechanical failure within the drive itself.

STARTING MOTOR SPECIFICATIONS

Starter Make	Starter Model Number	Brush Spring Tension, Ounces	Free Speed Test			Solenoid	
			Amps	Volts	RPM	Hold-In Windings	Pull-In Windings
Motorcraft	D5AF-EA	80	80	12	—	—	—
	D6AF-AA	40	70	12	—	—	—
	D6BF-AA	80	80	12	—	—	—
	D6BF-BA	80	80	12	—	—	—
	D6DF-AA	80	80	12	—	—	—
	D6EF-AA	40①	70	12	—	—	—
	D6EF-BA	40①	70	12	—	—	—
	D6OF-AA	80	80	12	—	—	—
	D8AF-AA	80	80	12	—	—	—
	D8AF-BA	80	80	12	—	—	—
	D8BF-AA	40	70	12	—	—	—
	D8DF-AA	80	80	12	—	—	—
	D8ZF-AA	40①	70	12	—	—	—
	E1AF-BA	40-80	85	12	—	—	—
	E1BF-AA	40-80	85	12	—	—	—
	E1BF-BA	40-80	85	12	—	—	—
	E1EF-AB	80	80	12	—	—	—
	E1EF-AD	80	80	12	—	—	—
	E1EFF-11001-BA	—	67	12	7380-9356	—	—
	E1ZF-AA	80	80	12	—	—	—
	E1ZF-BA	80	80	12	—	—	—
	E2BF-AA	80	80	12	—	—	—
	E25F-AA	40-80	85	12	—	—	—
	②	80	80	12	—	—	—
	③	40-80	85	12	—	—	—
	④	208	190	12	—	—	—
	3212235	40	65	12	9250	—	—
	3229844	40	65	12	9250	—	—
	3231371	—	77	12	8900-9600	—	—
	3231372	—	67	12	7380-9356	—	—
	3238665	—	67	12	7380-9356	—	—
	3250032	—	69	12	6709-10843	—	—
	⑤	80	80	12	—	—	—
	⑥	80	85	12	—	—	—
	⑦	—	190	12	—	—	—

①—Minimum.
②—1983-85 four cylinder Ford models.
③—1983-85 six and eight cylinder Ford models.
④—1984-85 diesel Ford models.
⑤—1986-87 gasoline engine models w/4 inch diameter starter.
⑥—1986 gasoline engine models w/4.5 inch diameter starter.
⑦—1986-87 diesel engine models.

Ford Motorcraft Starters

INDEX

FORD MOTORCRAFT STARTER WITH INTEGRAL POSITIVE ENGAGEMENT DRIVE

DESCRIPTION

This type starting motor, **Figs. 1 and 2,** is a four pole, series parallel unit with a positive engagement drive built into the starter. The drive mechanism is engaged with the flywheel by lever action before the motor is energized.

When the ignition switch is turned on to the start position, the starter relay is energized and supplies current to the motor. The current flows through one field coil and a set of contact points to ground. The magnetic field given off by the field coil pulls the moveable pole, which is part of the lever, downward to its seat. When the pole is pulled down, the lever moves the drive assembly into the engine flywheel, **Fig. 3.**

When the moveable pole is seated, it functions as a normal field pole and opens the contact points. With the points open, current flows through the starter field coils, energizing the starter. At the same time, current also flows through a holding coil to hold the movable pole in its seated position.

When the ignition switch is released from the start position, the starter relay opens the circuit to the starting motor. This allows the return spring to force the lever back, disengaging the drive from the flywheel and returning the movable pole to its normal position.

DIAGNOSIS

When diagnosing this starter motor, refer to **Fig. 4.**

IN-VEHICLE TESTING

Disconnect vacuum line to thermactor bypass valve before performing any cranking tests. After tests, run engine 3 minutes before connecting vacuum line.

Starter Cranking Circuit Test

1. Make test connections as shown in **Fig. 5.**
2. Disconnect ignition coil and crank engine.
3. Connect remote control starter switch from battery terminal of starter relay to S terminal of relay.
4. Maximum allowable voltage drop should be as follows:

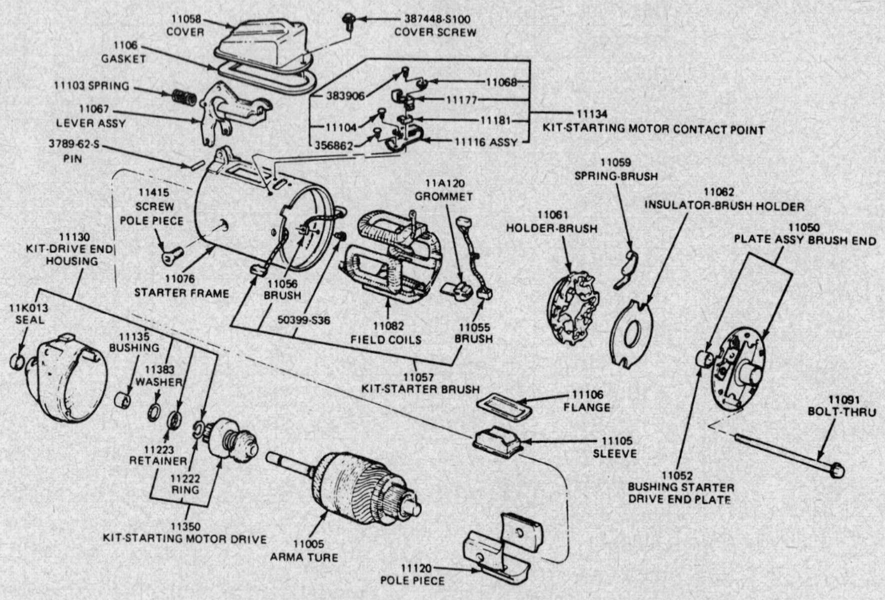

Fig. 1 Ford Motorcraft positive engagement starting motor. 4-140 & 4-97.6 engines (Typical)

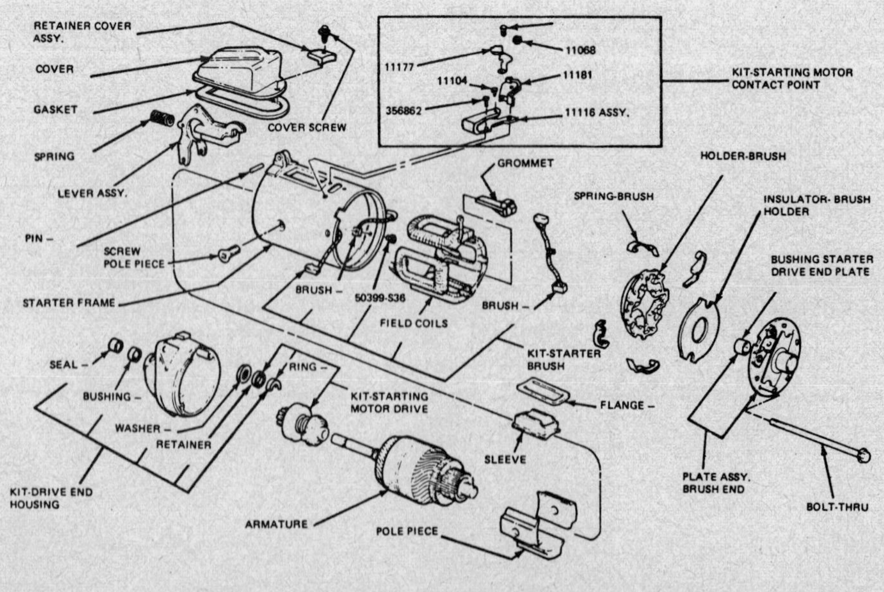

Fig. 2 Ford Motorcraft positive engagement starting motor. Except 4-140 & 4-97.6 (Typical)

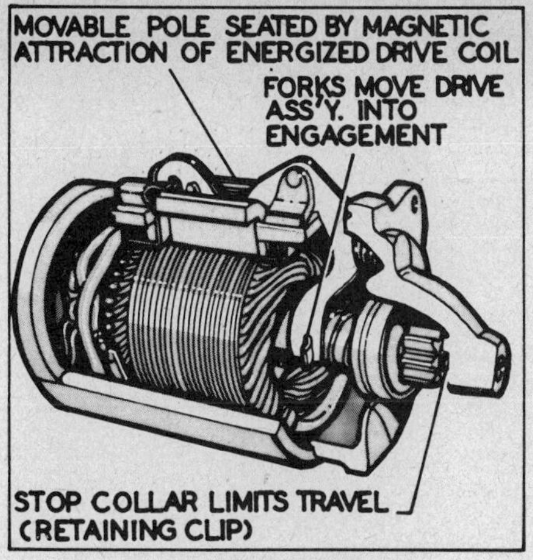

Fig. 3 Starter drive engaged

CONDITION	POSSIBLE CAUSE	RESOLUTION
Engine will not crank — starter spins.	1. Starter motor. 2. Flywheel ring gear.	1. Remove starter, inspect for broken or worn starter drive components. Repair or replace as required. 2. Inspect ring gear teeth. Replace flywheel and ring gear if necessary.
Engine will not crank.	1. Loose or corroded battery cables. 2. Undercharged battery. 3. Burned fusible link in main wire feed to ignition switch. 4. Starter relay. 5. Loose or broken cables. 6. Loose or open wiring through neutral switch to relay. 7. Starter motor.	1. Clean and tighten cable connections. 2. Check battery. Charge or replace. 3. Check fusible link — correct wiring problem. 4. Replace starter relay. 5. Tighten or replace cable. 6. Repair, adjust or replace as required. 7. Repair or replace as required.
Engine cranks slowly.	1. Loose connections or corroded battery cables. 2. Undercharged battery. 3. Starter motor.	1. Clean and tighten cable connections. 2. Check battery. Charge or replace. 3. Repair or replace as required.

Fig. 4 Diagnosis chart

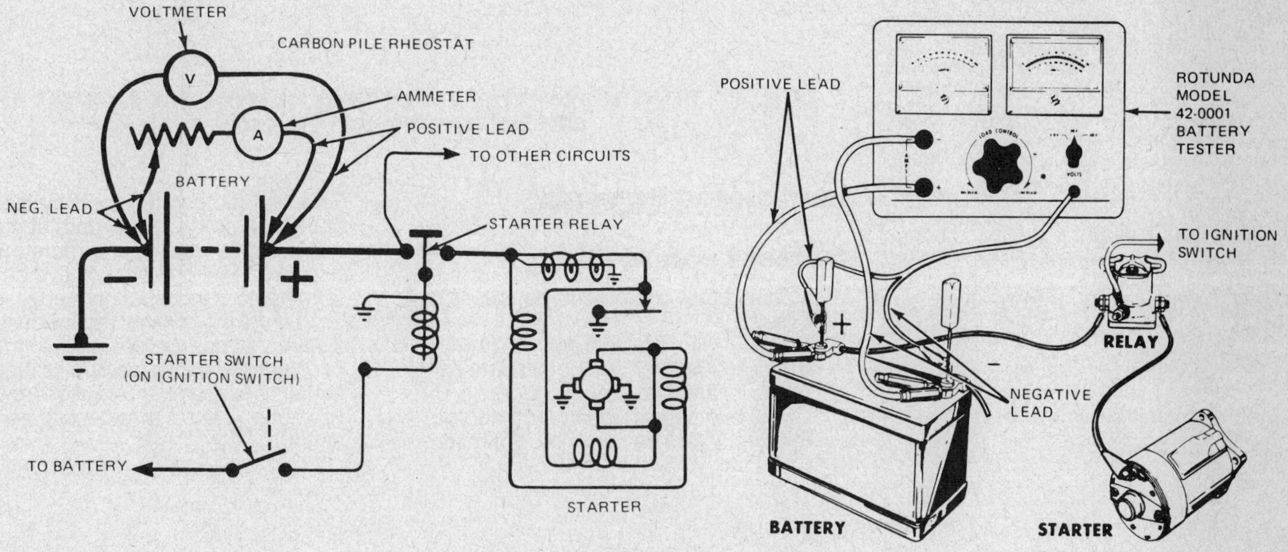

Fig. 5 Starter cranking circuit test connections

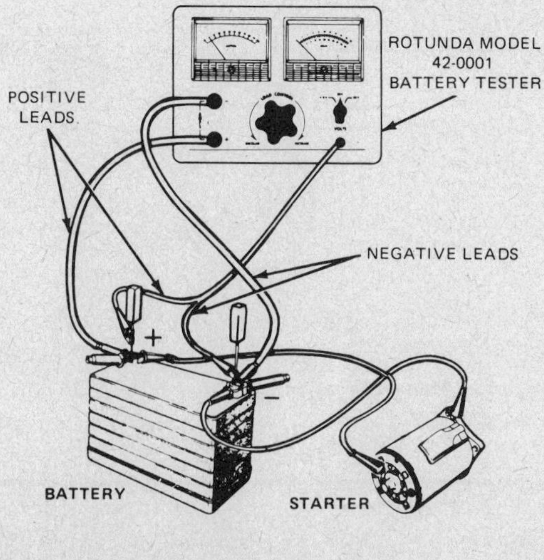

Fig. 6 Starter load test connection. Positive engagement starter

a. .5 volt with voltmeter negative lead connected to starter terminal and positive lead connected to battery positive terminal.
b. .1 volt with voltmeter negative lead connected to starter relay (battery side) and positive lead connected to positive terminal of battery.
c. .3 volt with voltmeter negative lead connected to starter relay (starter side) and positive lead connected to positive terminal of battery.
d. .3 volt with voltmeter negative lead connected to negative terminal of battery and positive lead connected to engine ground.

Starter Load Test

1. Connect test equipment as shown in **Fig. 6.**
2. Ensure that no current is flowing through ammeter and heavy duty carbon pile rheostat portion of circuit.
3. Crank engine with ignition off and determine exact reading on voltmeter.

This test is accomplished by disconnecting push-on connector S at starter relay and by connecting a remote control starter switch from positive battery terminal to S terminal of starter relay.

4. Stop cranking engine and reduce resistance of carbon pile until voltmeter indicates same reading as that obtained while starter cranked engine. Ammeter should read 150-250 amps.

FORD MOTORCRAFT 4-122 & 6-149 DIESEL STARTER

DESCRIPTION

This type starting motor, **Fig. 7,** has the solenoid mounted on the starter housing. When the starter relay contacts are closed, the solenoid is energized and the starter drive is engaged to start the engine. During the engine starting, the starter is protected from excessive speed by an overrunning clutch in the drive. Current flows through the solenoid energizing coil until the solenoid plunger reaches the end of its travel, at which time the plunger closes a set of contacts that bypass the energizing coil. The holding coil keeps the starter drive engaged and passes current to the starting motor.

DIAGNOSIS

When diagnosing this starter motor, refer to **Fig. 4.**

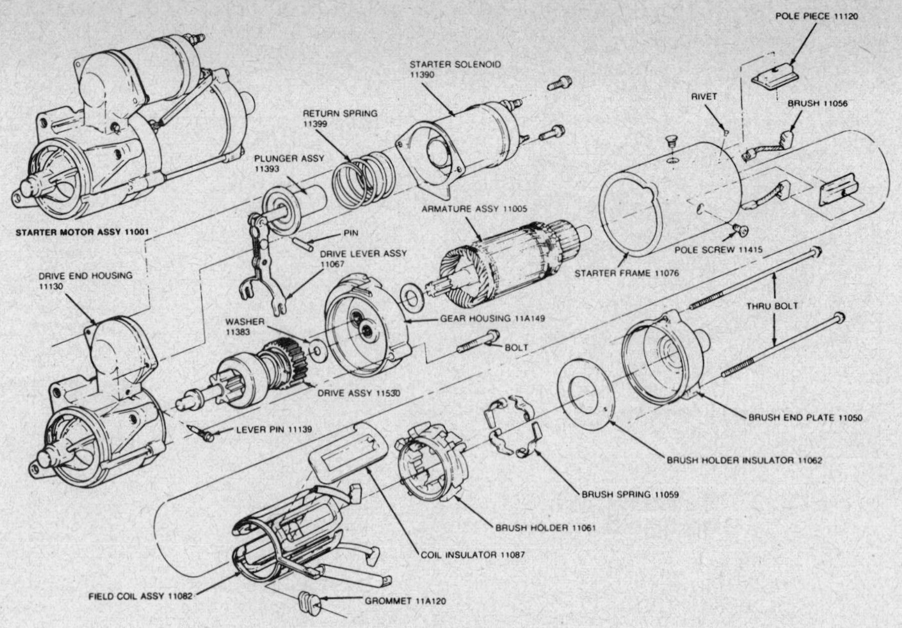

Fig. 7 Ford Motorcraft starting motor. 4-122 & 6-149 diesel engines (Typical)

IN-VEHICLE TESTING

Starter Load Test

1. Connect test equipmemt as shown in **Fig. 8.**
2. Ensure that no current is flowing through ammeter and heavy duty carbon pile rheostat portion of circuit.
3. Crank engine with ignition off and determine exact reading on voltmeter.

This test is accomplished by disconnecting push on connectors at starter relay and by connecting remote control starter switch from positive battery terminal to S terminal on starter relay.

4. Stop cranking engine, then reduce resistance at carbon pile until voltmeter indicates the same reading as that obtained while starter cranked engine. Ammeter should read less than 375 amps.

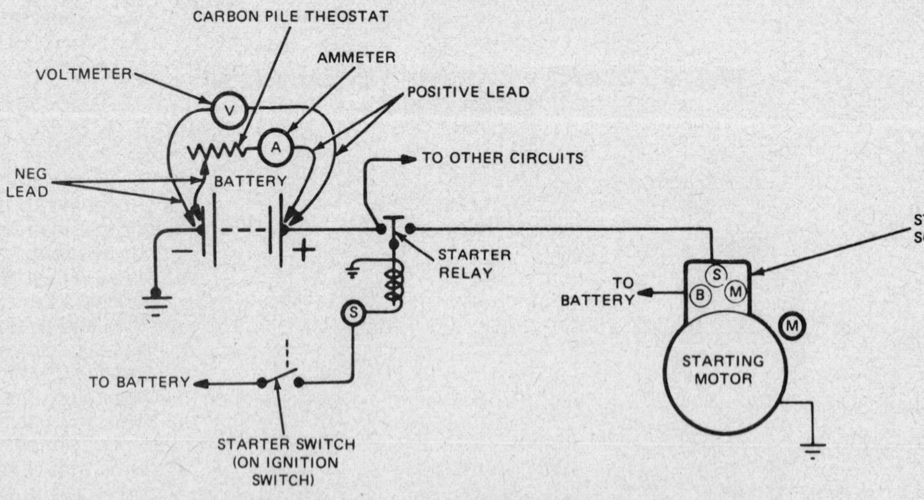

Fig. 8 Starter load test connections. Diesel starter

ALTERNATOR SYSTEMS

TABLE OF CONTENTS

General Information

INDEX

INTRODUCTION

Alternators are composed of the same functional parts as the conventional D.C. generator but they operate differently: The field is called a rotor and is the turning portion of the unit. A generating part, called a stator, is the stationary member, comparable to the armature in a D.C. generator. The regulator, similar to those used in a D.C. system, regulates the output of the alternator-rectifier system.

The power source of the system is the alternator. Current is transmitted from the field terminal of the regulator through a slip ring to the field coil and back to ground through another slip ring. The strength of the field regulates the output of the alternating current. This alternating current is then transmitted from the alternator to the rectifier where it is converted to direct current.

These alternators employ a three-phase stator winding in which the phase windings are electrically 120 degrees apart. The rotor consists of a field coil encased between interleaved sections producing a magnetic field with alternate north and south poles. By rotating the rotor inside the stator the alternating current is induced in the stator windings. This alternating current is rectified (changed to D.C.) by silicon diodes and brought out to the output terminal of the alternator.

DIODE RECTIFIERS

Six silicon diode rectifiers are used and act as electrical one-way-valves. Three of the diodes have ground polarity and are pressed or screwed into a heat sink which is grounded. The other three diodes (ungrounded) are pressed or screwed into and insulated from the end head; these diodes are connected to the alternator output terminal.

Since the diodes have a high resistance to the flow of current in one direction and a low resistance in the opposite direction, they may be connected in a manner which allows current to flow from the alternator to the battery in the low resistance direction. The high resistance in the opposite direction prevents the flow of current from the battery to the alternator. Because of this feature no circuit breaker is required between the alternator and battery.

SERVICE PRECAUTIONS

1. Be certain that battery polarity is correct when servicing units. Reversed battery polarity will damage rectifiers and regulators.
2. If booster battery is used for starting, be sure to use correct polarity in hook up.
3. When a fast charger is used to charge a vehicle battery, the vehicle battery cables should be disconnected unless the fast charger is equipped with a special Alternator Protector, in which case the vehicle battery cables need not be disconnected. Also the fast charger should never be used to start a vehicle as damage to rectifiers will result.
4. Unless the system includes a load relay or field relay, grounding the alternator output terminal will damage the alternator and/or circuits. This is true even when the system is not in operation since no circuit breaker is used and the battery is applied to the alternator output terminal at all times. The field or load relay acts as a circuit breaker in that it is controlled by the ignition switch.
5. When adjusting the voltage regulator, do not short the adjusting tool to the regulator base as the regulator may be damaged. The tool should be insulated by taping or by installing a plastic sleeve.
6. Before making any "on vehicle" tests of the alternator or regulator, the battery should be checked and the circuit inspected for faulty wiring or insulation, loose or corroded connections and poor ground circuits.
7. Check alternator belt tension to be sure the belt is tight enough to prevent slipping under load.
8. The ignition switch should be off and the battery ground cable disconnected before making any test connections to prevent damage to the system.
9. The vehicle battery must be fully charged or a fully charged battery may be installed for test purposes.

Ford Motorcraft Alternator

INDEX

GENERAL DESCRIPTION

A charge indicator lamp or ammeter can be used in charging system.

If a charge indicator lamp is used in the charging system, **Figs. 1 and 2,** the system operation is as follows: when the ignition switch is turned ON, a small electrical current flows through the lamp filament (turning the lamp on) and through the alternator regulator to the alternator field. When the engine is started, the alternator field rotates and produces a voltage in the stator winding. When the voltage at the alternator stator terminal reaches about 3 volts, the regulator field relay closes. This puts the same voltage potential on both sides of the charge indicator lamp causing it to go out. When the field relay has closed, current passes through the regulator A terminal and is metered to the alternator field.

If an ammeter is used in the charging system, **Figs. 2 and 3,** the regulator 1 terminal and the alternator stator terminal are not used. When the ignition switch is turned ON, the field relay closes and electrical current passes through the regulator A terminal and is metered to the alternator field. When the engine is started, the alternator field rotates causing the alternator to operate.

Some vehicles are equipped with electronic voltage regulators. These solid state regulators are used in conjunction with other components in the charging system such as an alternator with a high field current requirement, a warning indicator lamp shunt resistor (500 ohms) and a wiring harness with a regulator connector. Some 1985-87 vehicles are equipped with Integral Alternator/Regulator (IAR) charging system. This system has a solid state voltage regulator located in the rear of the alternator.

When replacing system components, note the following precautions:

1. Always use the proper alternator in the system.
2. Do not use an electro-mechanical regulator in the system since the wiring harness connector will not index properly with this type of regulator.
3. On models with external voltage regulator, the electronic regulators are color coded for proper installation. The black color coded unit is installed in systems equipped with a warning indicator lamp. The blue color coded regulator is installed in systems equipped with an ammeter.
4. The systems use a 500 ohm resistor on the rear of the instrument cluster

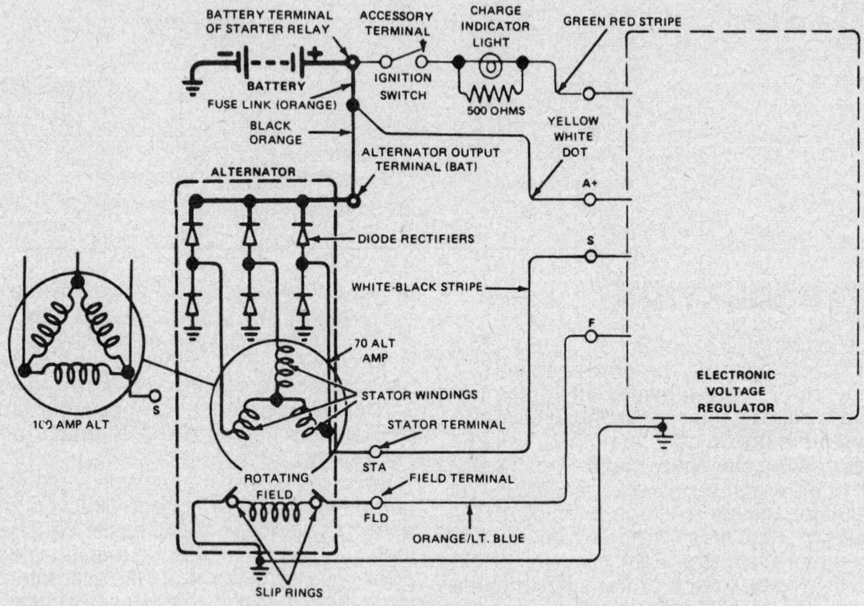

Fig. 1 Typical indicator light charging circuit. Exc. 1985–87 alternator w/integral regulator

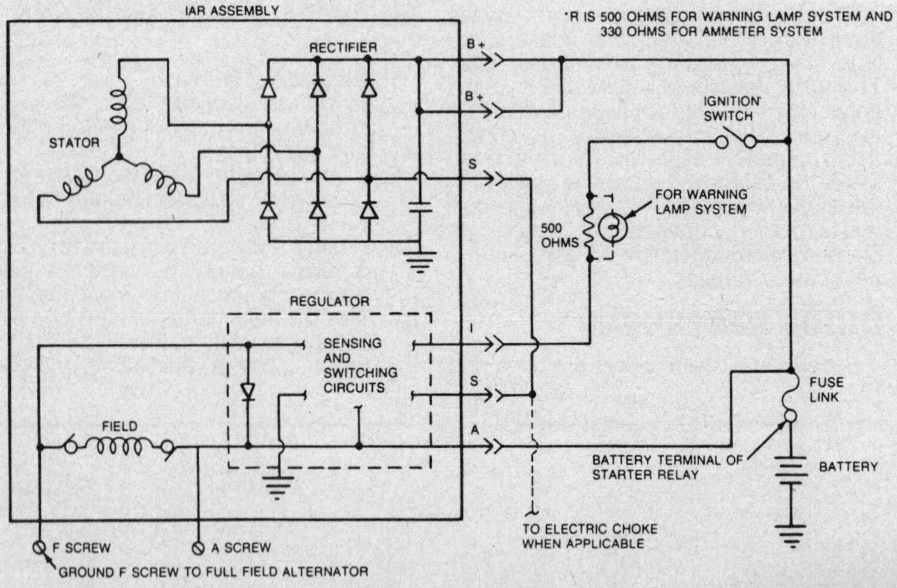

Fig. 2 Alternator charging circuit. 1985–87 alternator w/integral regulator

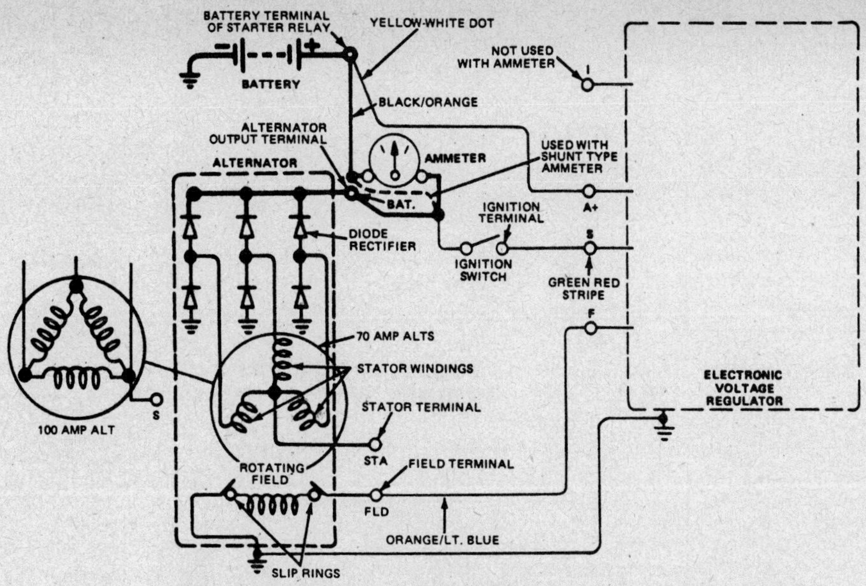

Fig. 3 Ammeter charging circuit. Exc. 1985–87 alternator w/integral regulator

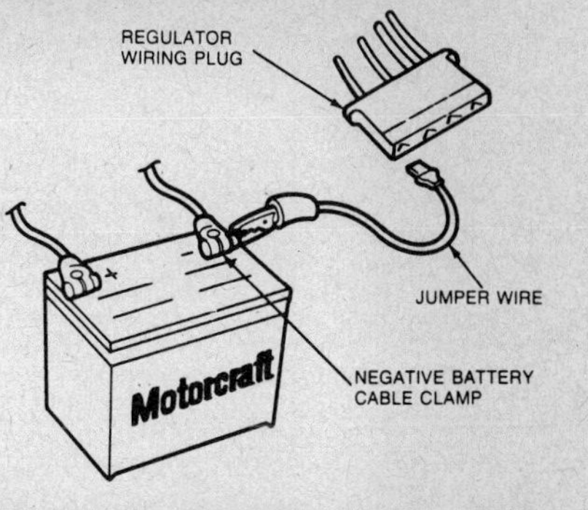

Fig. 4 Indicator lamp test. External Voltage Regulator (EVR)

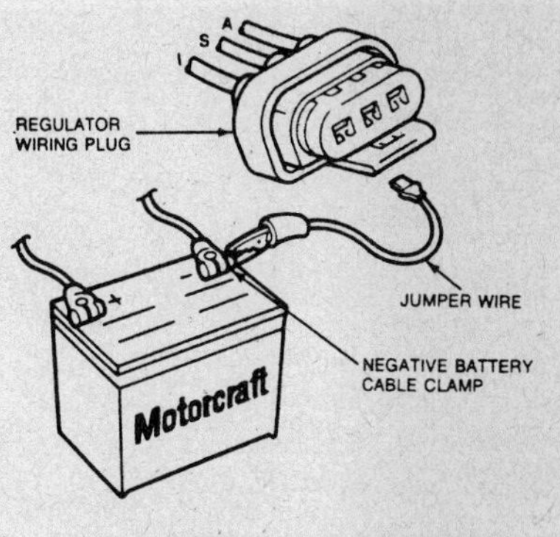

Fig. 5 Indicator lamp test. Integral Alternator Regulator (IAR)

on vehicles equipped with a warning indicator lamp.

On systems with an indicator lamp, closing the ignition switch energizes the warning lamp and turns on the regulator output stage. The alternator receives maximum field current and is ready to generate an output voltage. As the alternator rotor speed increases, the output and stator terminal voltages increase from zero to the system regulation level determined by the regulator setting. When the ignition switch is turned off, the solid state relay circuit turns the output stage off, interrupting current flow through the regulator so there is not a current drain on the battery.

On vehicles equipped with an ammeter, the operating principle is similar.

The ammeter indicates current flow into (charge) or out of (discharge) the vehicle battery.

IN-VEHICLE TESTING

The operations and on vehicle test procedures for the side terminal alternator are same as for rear terminal alternator. However, the internal wiring and bench test procedures differ.

INDICATOR LAMP SYSTEM

External Voltage Regulator (EVR) System

1. If charge indicator lamp does not come with the ignition key in the run position and engine not running, check the I wiring circuit (ignition switch to regulator I terminal) for open circuit or burned out charge indicator lamp.
2. If charge indicator lamp does not come on, disconnect electrical connector from regulator and connect a jumper wire **Fig. 4** from the I terminal of the regulator wiring plug to negative battery post cable clamp.
3. Charge indicator lamp should go on with ignition key turned to RUN position.
4. If charge indicator lamp does not go on, check for presence of bulb socket resistor. If resistor is missing, replace bulb socket. If resistor is present, check for contact of bulb socket leads to the flexible printed circuit. If satisfactory, check indicator bulb for continuity and replace if burned out.
5. If bulb and socket are satisfactory and socket leads are in contact with the flexible circuit, open circuit exists between ignition switch and regulator.
6. Check 500 ohm resistor across indicator lamp.

Integral Alternator Regulator (IAR) System

The Integral Alternator Regulator (IAR) has a circuit in the regulator that will indicate a high battery voltage condition. With the IAR system, three conditions can cause the charge indicator to come on during vehicle operation: no alternator output, over-voltage condition or under-voltage condition.

1. If charge indicator does not come on, disconnect wiring connector from regulator **Fig. 5** and connect a jumper wire from wiring connector I to battery post cable clamp.
2. Turn ignition to run position with engine off. If indicator lamp does not light, check for presence of bulb socket resistor. If resistor is missing, replace bulb socket. If resistor is present, check for contact of bulb contact leads to the flexible printed circuit. If satisfactory, check indicator bulb for continuity and replace bulb if burned out. If bulb is satisfactory, perform regulator I circuit test.
3. If indicator lamp does light, remove jumper wire and reconnect electrical connector to regulator. Connect voltmeter negative lead to battery negative post cable clamp and contact voltmeter positive lead to regulator A terminal screw. Battery voltage should be indicated. If battery voltage is not indicated, service A wiring circuit.

CHARGING SYSTEM TEST

All lights and electrical systems in the off position, parking brake applied, transmission in neutral and a charged battery (at least 1.200 specific gravity).

1. Connect the negative lead of the voltmeter to the negative battery cable clamp (not bolt or nut).
2. Connect the positive lead of the voltmeter to the positive battery cable clamp (not bolt or nut).
3. Record the battery voltage reading shown on the voltmeter scale.
4. Connect the red lead of a tachometer to the distributor terminal of the coil and the black tachometer lead to a good ground.
5. Then, start and operate the engine at approximately 1500 RPM. With no other electrical load (foot off brake pedal and car doors closed), the voltmeter reading should increase but not exceed (2 volts) above the first recorded battery voltage reading. The reading should be taken when the voltmeter needles stops moving.
6. With the engine running, turn on the heater and/or air conditioner blower motor to high speed and headlights to high beam.
7. Increase the engine speed to 2000 RPM. The voltmeter should indicate a minimum reading of 0.5 volts above the battery voltage, **Fig. 6. If the above tests indicate proper volt-**

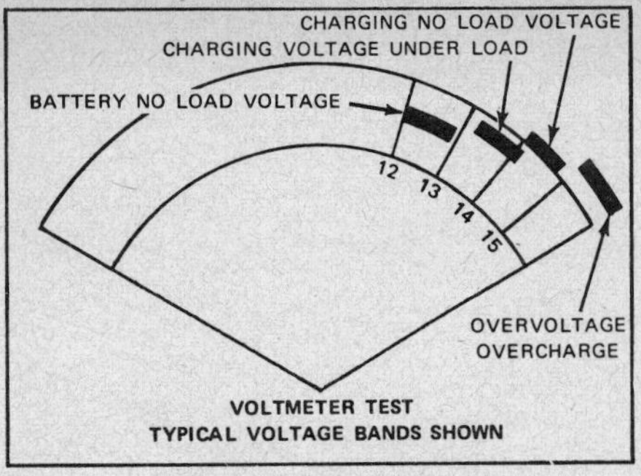

Fig. 6 Voltmeter test scale

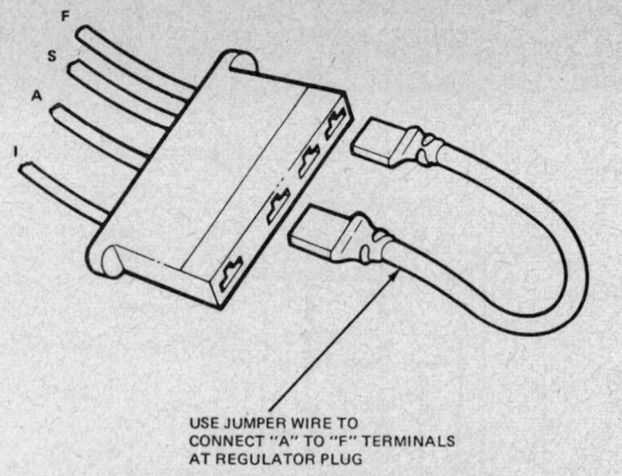

Fig. 7 Regulator plug jumper wire connection

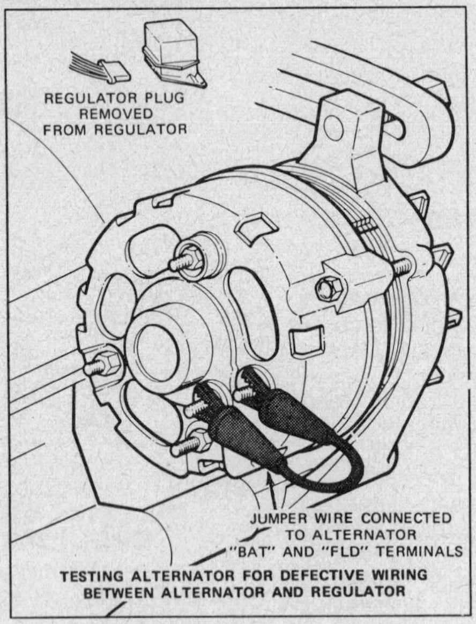

Fig. 8 Rear terminal alternator. Typical jumper wire connection

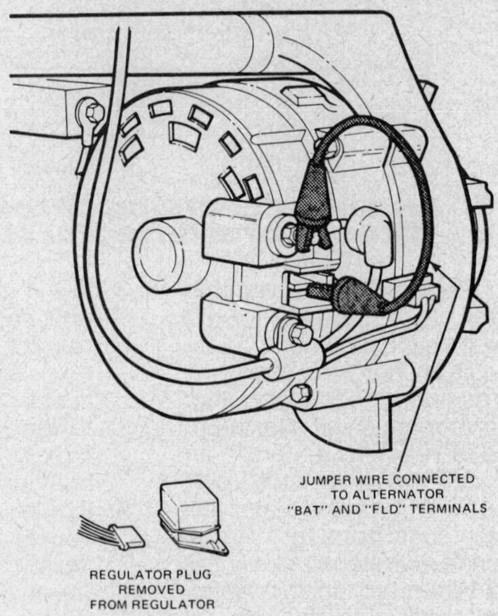

Fig. 9 Side terminal alternator. Typical jumper wire connection.

age readings, the charging system is operating normally. Proceed to "Test Results" if a problem still exists.

TEST RESULTS

Exc. Alternators W/Integral Regulators

1. If voltmeter reading indicates 2 volts over battery voltage (over voltage), proceed as follows:
   a. Stop the engine and check the ground connections between the regulator and alternator and/or regulator to engine. Clean and tighten connections securely and repeat the Charging System Test Procedures.
   b. If over voltage condition still exists, disconnect regulator wiring plug from regulator and repeat the Charging System Test Procedures.
   c. If over voltage still exists with the regulator wiring plug disconnected, repair the short in the wiring harness between the alternator and regulator. Then, replace the regulator and connect the regulator wiring plug to the regulator and repeat the Charging System Test Procedures.
2. If voltmeter does not indicate more than 1/2 volt above battery voltage, proceed as follows:
   a. Disconnect voltage regulator wire connector and connect an ohmmeter between wire connector "F" terminal and ground. If reading is less than 3 ohms on 1983-83 models, or 2.4 ohms on 1984-87 models, repair grounded field circuit and repeat Charging System Test procedure.
   b. If ohmmeter reading is more than 3 ohms on 1982-83 models, or 2.4 ohms on 1984-87 models, connect a jumper wire between voltage regulator wire connector terminals A and F, **Fig. 7**, then repeat Charging System Test procedure. If voltmeter reading is now more than 1/2 volt above battery voltage, the voltage regulator or wiring is defective, refer to Regulator Test.
   c. If voltmeter still indicates less than 1/2 volt, disconnect jumper wire from voltage regulator wire connector and leave connector disconnected from regulator. Connect a jumper wire between alternator FLD and BAT terminals, **Figs. 8 and 9,** then repeat Charging System Test procedures.
   d. If voltmeter reading now indicates 1/2 volt or more above battery voltage, repair alternator to regulator wiring harness.
   e. If voltmeter still indicates less than 1/2 volt above battery voltage, stop engine and move voltmeter positive lead to alternator BAT terminal.
   f. If voltmeter now indicates battery voltage, the alternator should be removed, inspected and repaired. If zero volts is indicated, repair BAT terminal wiring.

Alternators W/Integral Regulators

1. If voltmeter reading indicates 2 volts or over battery voltage (over voltage), proceed as follows:
   a. Stop engine and place ignition switch in the "On" position, then connect voltmeter negative lead to the alternator rear housing.

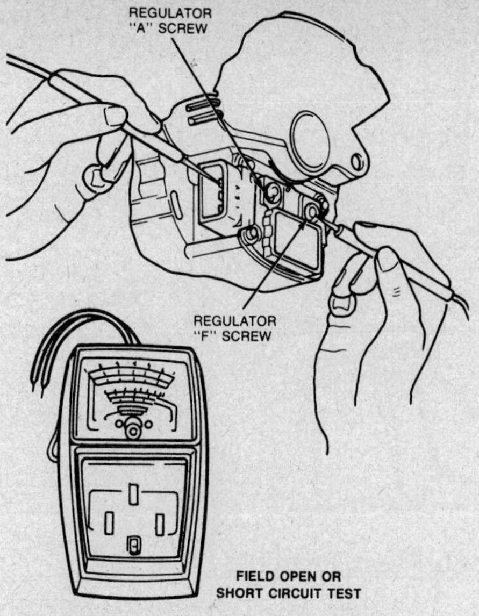

Fig. 10 Charging circuit test points. Alternator w/integral regulator

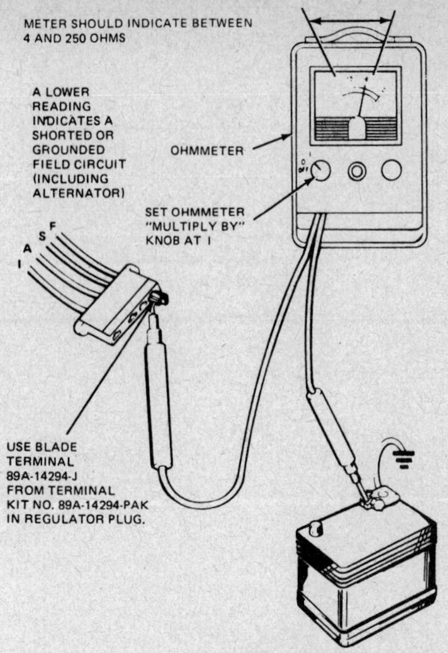

Fig. 11 Regulator plug voltage test

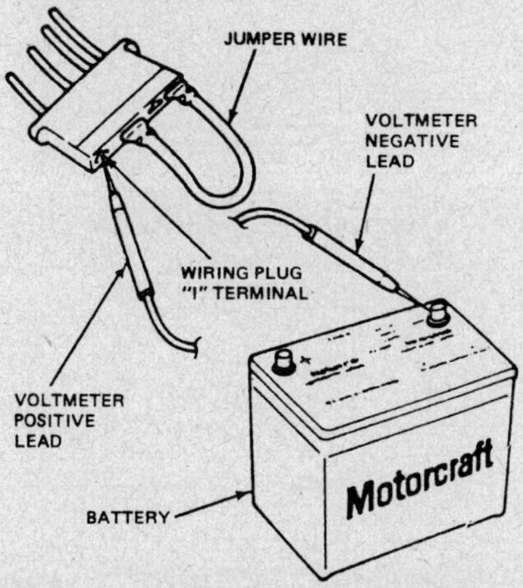

Fig. 12 Testing regulator S and/or I circuit. External Voltage Regulator (EVR)

b. Connect voltmeter positive lead first to the alternator output connection at the starter solenoid, then to the regulator "A" screw head, **Fig. 10.**

c. If the voltage difference between the two locations is greater than .5 volts, repair the "A" wiring circuit to eliminate the high resistance condition indicated by the excessive voltage drop.

d. If over voltage condition still exists, check for loose regulator to alternator grounding screws. Torque regulator grounding screws to 15-26 inch lbs.

e. If over voltage condition still exists, connect voltmeter negative lead to the alternator rear housing.

f. Place ignition switch in the "Off" position, then connect voltmeter positive lead first to the regulator "A" screw head and then to the regulator "F" screw head, **Fig. 10.**

g. Different voltage readings at the two screw heads in step 1f indicates a defective regulator, grounded brush lead or grounded rotor coil. Repair or replace as required.

h. If battery voltage is obtained at both screw heads in step 1f, replace regulator.

2. If voltmeter does not indicate more than .5 volts over battery voltage, proceed as follows:

a. Disconnect wiring plug from regulator, then connect an ohmmeter between regulator "A" and "F" terminal screws, **Fig. 10.** Meter should indicate more than 2.4 ohms.

b. If meter indicates less than 2.4 ohms in step 2a, check integral alternator/regulator unit for a defective regulator, then check the alternator for a shorted rotor or field circuit. Perform Charging System Test procedure after servicing alternator. **Do not replace the regulator until a shorted rotor coil or field circuit has been serviced.**

c. If meter indicates greater than 2.4 ohms in step 2a, reconnect regulator wiring plug. Connect voltmeter ground lead to the alternator rear housing and voltmeter positive lead to the regulator "A" terminal screw.

d. Meter should read battery voltage. If battery voltage is not present, repair "A" wiring circuit, then perform Charging Circuit Test procedure. If battery voltage is present, connect the voltmeter ground lead to the alternator rear housing.

e. Place ignition switch in the "Off" position, then connect voltmeter positive lead to the regulator "F" terminal screw. Meter should indicate battery voltage.

f. If voltage is not present, check integral alternator/regulator unit for an open field circuit. Repair as required, then perform Charging Circuit Test procedure. If voltmeter indicates battery voltage, connect voltmeter negative ground lead to alternator rear housing.

g. Turn ignition switch to the "On" position and connect voltmeter positive probe lead to the regulator "F" terminal screw. Voltmeter should indicate 1.5 volts or less.

h. If more than 1.5 volts is present, proceed to "I Circuit Test." If "I Circuit" is satisfactory, replace the regulator and preform Charging Circuit Test procedure. If 1.5 volts or less is present, disconnect alternator wiring plug and connect suitable jumper wires between the alternator B(+) terminal and mating wiring connector terminals.

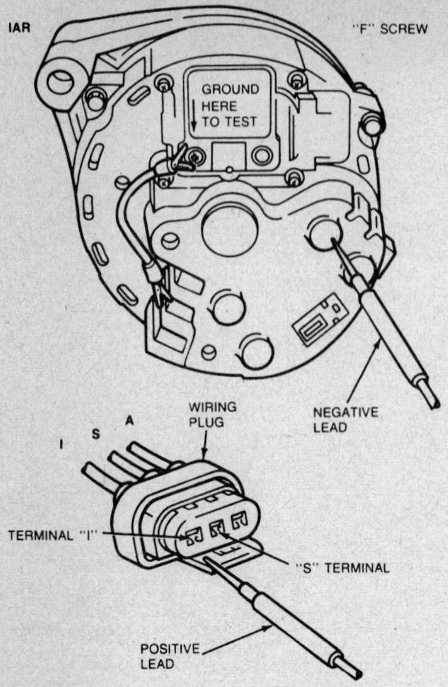

Fig. 13 Testing regulator S and/or I circuit. Integral Alternator Regulator (IAR)

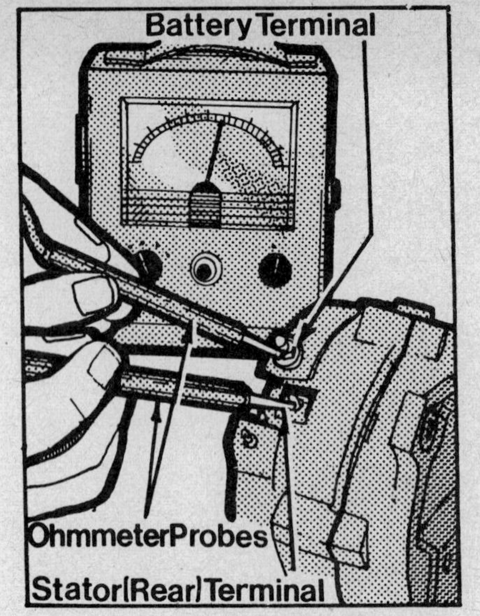

Fig. 14 Side terminal alternator rectifier short or grounded & stator grounded test

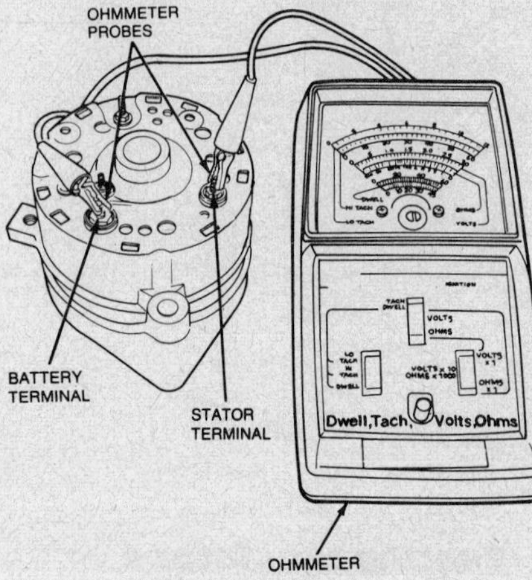

Fig. 15 Rear terminal alternator rectifier short or grounded & stator grounded test

i. Perform Charging System Test procedure, but connect voltmeter positive terminal to one of the B(+) jumper wire terminals.

j. If voltage rises more than .5 volts above battery voltage, check alternator and starter relay wiring, then repeat Charging System Test procedure, measuring voltage at battery cable clamps.

k. If voltage does not rise more than .5 volts above battery voltage, connect jumper wire from alternator rear housing to the regulator "F" terminal.

l. Repeat Charging System Tests procedure with voltmeter positive lead connected to one of the jumper wire terminals.

m. If voltage rises more than .5 volts, replace regulator. If voltage does not rise more than .5 volts, service the alternator.

REGULATOR TESTS

S CIRCUIT TEST—WITH AMMETER

Exc. Alternators W/Integral Regulator

1. Connect the positive-lead of the voltmeter to the S terminal of the regulator wiring plug **Fig. 11.** Turn the ignition switch to the "On" position. Do not start the engine.
2. The voltmeter reading should indicate battery voltage.
3. If there is no voltage reading, disconnect the positive voltmeter lead from the positive battery clamp and repair the S wire lead from the ignition switch to the regulator wiring plug.
4. Connect the positive voltmeter lead to the positive battery cable terminal and repeat the Charging System Test Procedures.

Alternators W/Integral Regulator

For test procedures, refer to "S and I Circuit Test-With Indicator Light."

S AND I CIRCUIT TEST—WITH INDICATOR LIGHT

Exc. Alternators W/Integral Regulator

1. Disconnect regulator wiring plug, then install a suitable jumper wire between connector "A" and "F" terminals, **Fig. 12.**
2. With the engine idling and negative voltmeter lead connected to battery ground, connect positive lead of voltmeter to S terminal and then to I terminal of regulator wiring plug, **Fig. 11.** Voltage of S circuit should read approximately 1/2 of the I circuit. If voltage readings are as specified, remove jumper wire, replace regulator and connect wiring plug.
3. If no voltage is present, the wiring is at fault. Service the faulty circuit.

Alternators W/Integral Regulator

1. Disconnect electrical connector from regulator. Connect a jumper wire from the regulator A lead to connector plug A lead. Add a jumper wire from the regulator F screw to the alternator rear housing, **Fig. 13.**
2. With engine idling and voltmeter negative lead connected to alternator rear

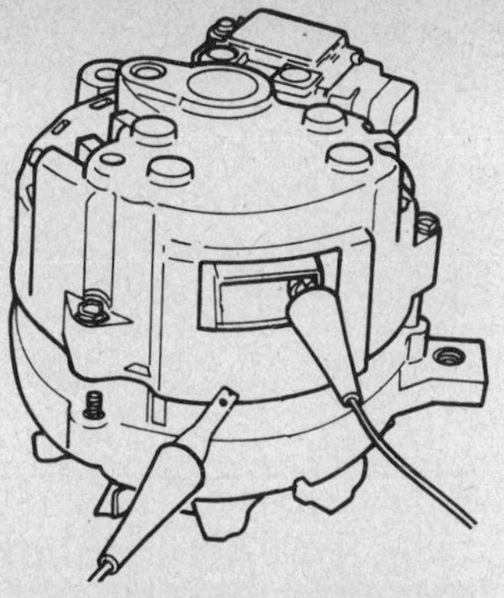

Fig. 16 Alternator w/integral regulator rectifier short or grounded & stator grounded test

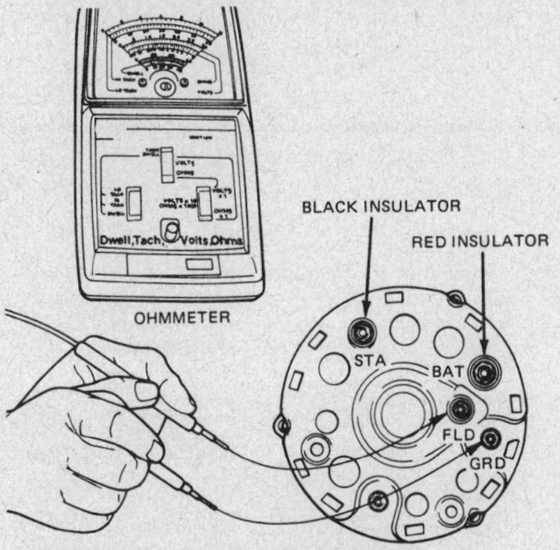

Fig. 18 Rear terminal alternator field open or short circuit test

housing, connect voltmeter positive lead to S terminal and then to I terminal of regulator electrical connector. Voltage at S circuit should read approximately one-half of the I circuit. If voltage readings are normal, remove jumper wire. Replace regulator and connect electrical connector to regulator.

3. If no voltage is present, remove jumper wires and service faulty circuit or alternator.
4. Connect voltmeter positive lead to positive battery terminal.
5. Connect electrical connector to regulator and replace bulb, if equipped.

FIELD CIRCUIT DRAIN TEST

Alternators W/Integral Regulator

Connect voltmeter negative lead to the alternator rear housing for all of the following voltage readings.

1. Turn ignition switch to the "Off" position, then connect voltmeter positive lead to the regulator "F" terminal screw. Battery voltage should be present.
2. If less than battery voltage is present, disconnect regulator electrical connector and connect voltmeter positive lead to connector I terminal. No voltage should be present.
3. If voltage is present, repair circuit between I lead and ignition switch. If no voltage is present, proceed to step 4.
4. Connect voltmeter positive lead to the connector S terminal.
5. No voltage should be present. If voltage is present, disconnect alternator electrical connector. Again, connect voltmeter positive lead to the regulator connector S terminal.
6. If voltage is still present, repair circuit between S lead and alternator connector. If no voltage is present, replace alternator rectifier assembly.

BENCH TESTS

RECTIFIER SHORT OR GROUNDED & STATOR GROUNDED TEST

Using a suitable ohmmeter, connect one probe to the alternator BAT or B+ terminal, **Figs. 14, 15 and 16,** the other probe to the STA terminal (rear blade terminal). Then, reverse the ohmmeter probes and repeat the test. A reading of about 6-6.5 ohms should be obtained in one direction

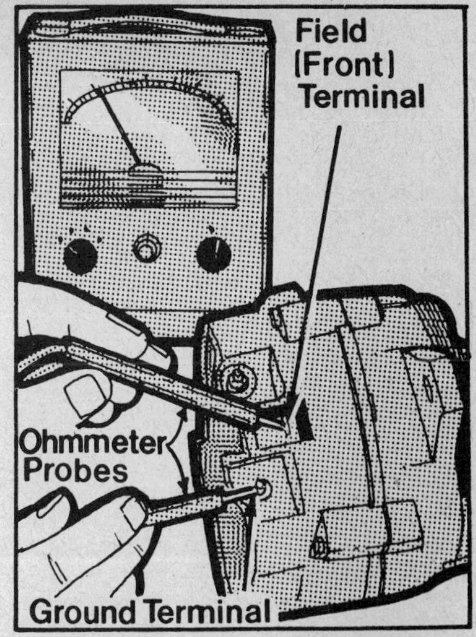

Fig. 17 Side terminal alternator field open or short circuit test

and no needle movement with the probes reversed. A reading in both directions indicates a bad positive diode, a grounded positive diode plate, grounded BAT or B+ terminal or a shorted radio suppression capacitor, if equipped.

Perform the same test using the STA and GND (ground) terminals of the alternator. A reading in both directions indicates either a bad negative diode, a grounded stator winding, a grounded stator terminal, a grounded positive diode plate, or a shorted radio capacitor, if equipped.

Infinite readings (no needle movement) in all four probe positions in the proceeding tests indicates an open terminal lead connection inside the alternator.

FIELD OPEN OR SHORT CIRCUIT TEST

Exc. Alternators W/Integral Regulators

Using a suitable ohmmeter, connect the alternator field terminal with one probe and the ground terminal with the other probe, **Figs. 17 and 18.** Then, spin the alternator pulley. The ohmmeter reading should be 2.4 and 100 ohms, and should fluctuate while the pulley is turning. An infinite reading (no meter movement) indicates an open brush lead, worn or stuck brushes, or a bad rotor assembly. An ohmmeter reading less than 2.4 ohms indicates a grounded brush assembly, a grounded field terminal or a bad rotor.

Regulators W/Integral Regulator

1. Using a suitable ohmmeter, connect regulator A blade terminal with one probe and the regulator "F" screw head with the other probe, **Fig. 19.**
2. Spin the alternator pulley and note meter reading, then reverse probes and repeat step 1. In one probe direction ohmmeter reading should be between 2.2 and 100 ohms and may fluctuate while pulley is turning. In the other direction, reading should fluctu-

ate between 2.2 and approximately 9 ohms.

3. An infinite reading, no meter movement, in one direction and approximately 9 ohms in the other, indicates an open brush lead, worn or stuck brushes, defective rotor or a loose regulator to brush holder attaching screw.
4. An ohmmeter reading less than 2.2 ohms in both directions indicates a shorted or defective regulator.
5. An ohmmeter reading significantly over 9 ohms in both directions indicates a defective regulator or loose "F" terminal screw.
6. Connect alternator rear housing with one ohmmeter probe and touch the other probe first to regulator "A" blade terminal and then to the regulator "F" screw head.
7. If ohmmeter reads less than infinite at either point, a grounded brush lead, grounded rotor or defective regulator is indicated.

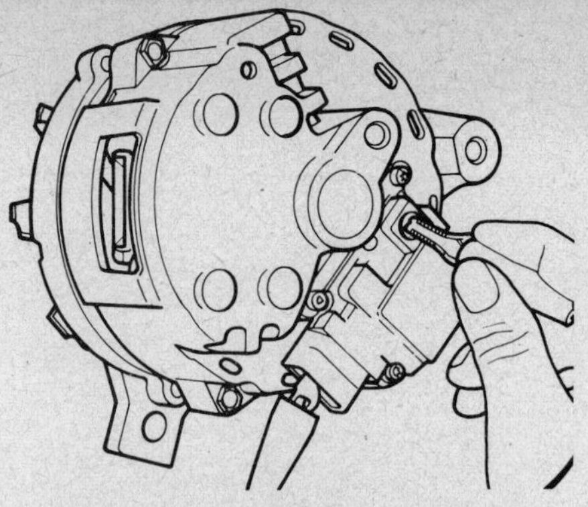

Fig. 19 Alternator w/integral regulator field open or short circuit test

REGULATOR ADJUSTMENTS

These regulators are factory calibrated and sealed and no adjustment is possible. If regulator calibration values are not within specifications, the regulator must be replaced.

DISC BRAKES

NOTE: Refer to "Application" to determine which type brakes are used on vehicle being serviced.

TABLE OF CONTENTS

APPLICATION

General Information

INDEX

BRAKE SHOES, LININGS & CALIPERS

Remove wheels and inspect brake disc, caliper and linings. The wheel bearings should be inspected at this time and repacked if necessary. Do not get any grease on the linings.

The brake shoe and lining assemblies should be replaced if the lining is worn to within 1/32 inch of rivet heads (riveted linings) or brake shoe (bonded linings). It is recommended that both front and/or rear wheel sets be replaced whenever a respective shoe and lining assembly is replaced.

If a visual inspection does not adequately determine the condition of the linings, the brake shoe and lining assemblies should be removed and inspected. If shoes do not require replacement, reinstall them in their original positions. Brake shoes and linings should also be replaced if cracked or damaged.

If the caliper is cracked or fluid leakage through the casting is evident, it must be replaced as a unit.

BRAKE ROUGHNESS

The most common cause of brake chatter on disc brakes is a variation in thickness of the disc. If roughness or vibration is encountered during highway operation or if pedal pumping is experienced at low speeds, the disc may have excessive thickness variation. To check for this condition, measure the disc at 12 points with a micrometer at a radius approximately one inch from edge of disc. If thickness measurements vary by more than .0005 inch, the disc should be replaced with a new one.

Excessive lateral runout of braking disc may cause a "knocking back" of the pistons, possibly creating increased pedal travel and vibration when brakes are applied.

Before checking the runout, wheel bearings should be adjusted. The readjustment is very important and will be required at the completion of the test to prevent bearing failure. Be sure to make the adjustment according to the recommendations given under "Front Wheel Bearings, Adjust" in the car chapters.

BRAKE DISC SERVICE

Servicing of disc brakes is extremely critical due to the close tolerances required in machining the brake disc to in-

Fig. 1 Checking rotor for lateral runout

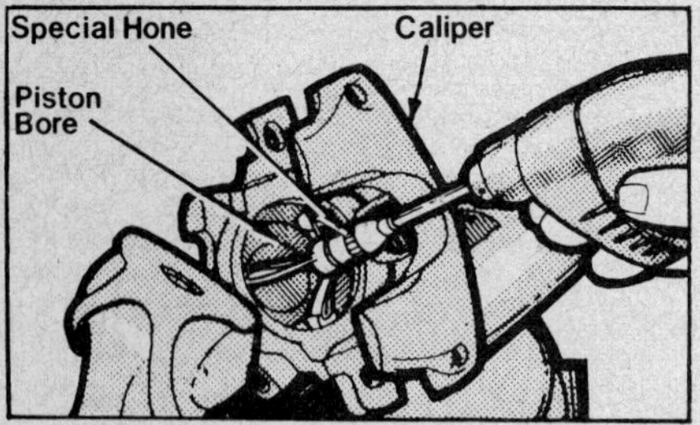

Fig. 3 Honing caliper piston bore

sure proper brake operation.

The maintenance of these close controls of the shape of the rubbing surfaces is necessary to prevent brake roughness. In addition, the surface finish must be non-directional and maintained at a micro inch finish. This close control of the rubbing surface finish is necessary to avoid pulls and erratic performance and promote long lining life and equal lining wear of both left and right brakes.

In light of the foregoing remarks, refinishing of the rubbing surfaces should not be attempted unless precision equipment, capable of measuring in micro inches (millionths of an inch) is available.

To check lateral runout of a disc, mount a dial indicator on a convenient part (steering knuckle, tie rod, disc brake caliper housing) so that the plunger of the dial indicator contacts the disc at a point one inch from the outer edge, **Fig. 1.** If the total indicated runout exceeds specifications, install a new disc.

To check parallelism (thickness variation), mount dial indicators, **Fig. 2,** so the plunger contacts rotor approximately 1 inch from outer edge. If parellelism exceeds specifications, replace rotor.

GENERAL PRECAUTIONS

1. Grease or any other foreign material must be kept off the caliper, surfaces of the disc and external surfaces of the hub, during service procedures. Handling the brake disc and caliper should be done in a way to avoid deformation of the disc and nicking or scratching brake linings.
2. If inspection reveals rubber piston seals are worn or damaged, they should be replaced immediately.
3. During removal and installation of a wheel assembly, exercise care so as not to interfere with or damage the caliper splash shield, or bleeder screw.
4. Front wheel bearings should be adjusted to specifications.
5. Be sure vehicle is centered on hoist before servicing any of the front end components to avoid bending or damaging the disc splash shield on full right or left wheel turns.
6. Before the vehicle is moved after any brake service work, be sure to obtain a firm brake pedal.
7. The assembly bolts of the two caliper housings should not be disturbed unless the caliper requires service.

INSPECTION OF CALIPER

Should it become necessary to remove the caliper for installation of new parts, clean all parts in alcohol, wipe dry using lint free cloths. Using an air hose, blow out drilled passages and bores. Check dust boots for punctures or tears. If punctures or tears are evident, new boots should be installed upon reassembly.

Inspect piston bores in both housings for scoring or pitting. Bores that show light scratches or corrosion can usually be cleaned with crocus cloth. However, bores that have deep scratches or scoring may be honed, provided the diameter of the bore is not increased more than .002 inch. If the bore does not clean up within this specification, a new caliper housing should be installed (black stains on the bore walls are caused by piston seals and will do no harm).

When using a hone, **Fig. 3,** be sure to install the hone baffle before honing bore. The baffle is used to protect the hone stones from damage. Use extreme care in cleaning the caliper after honing. Remove all dust and grit by flushing the caliper with alcohol. Wipe dry with clean lint free cloth and then clean a second time in the same manner.

BLEEDING DISC BRAKES

Pressure bleeding is recommended for all hydraulic disc brake systems.

The disc brake hydraulic system can be bled manually or with pressure bleeding equipment. On vehicles with disc brakes the brake pedal will require more pumping and frequent checking of fluid level in master cylinder during bleeding operation.

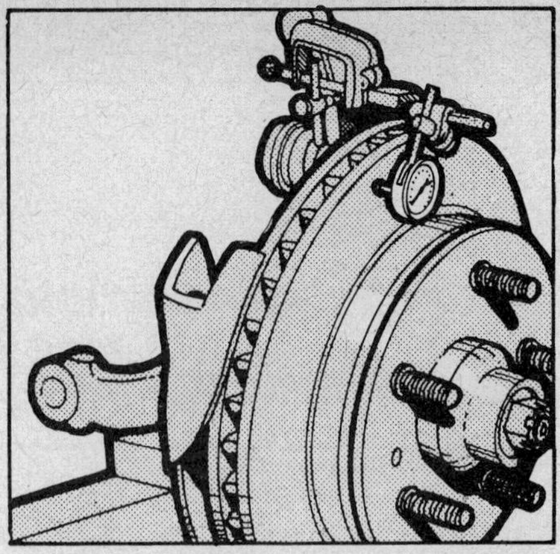

Fig. 2 Checking rotor parallelism (thickness variation)

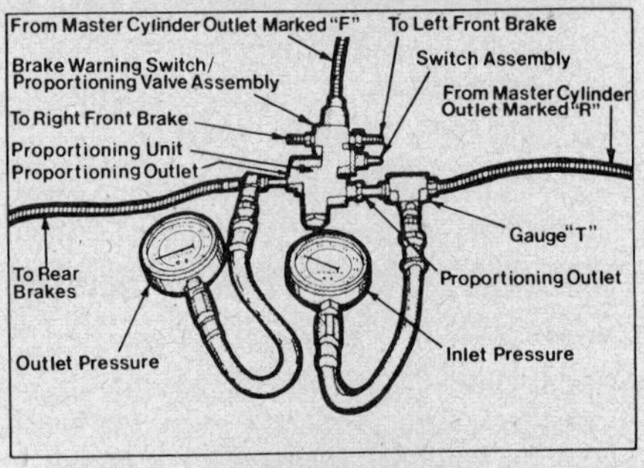

Fig. 4 Gauge hook-up for testing proportioning valve (typical)

Never use brake fluid that has been drained from hydraulic system when bleeding the brakes. Be sure the disc brake pistons are returned to their normal positions and that the shoe and lining assemblies are properly seated. Before driving the vehicle, check brake operation to be sure that a firm pedal has been obtained.

PROPORTIONING VALVE

The proportioning valve (when used), **Fig. 4,** provides balanced braking action between front and rear brakes under a wide range of braking conditions. The valve regulates the hydraulic pressure applied to the rear wheel cylinders, thus limiting rear braking action when high pressures are required at the front brakes. In this manner, premature rear wheel skid is prevented.

TESTING PROPORTIONING VALVE

When a premature rear wheel slide is obtained on a brake application, it usually is an indication that the fluid pressure to the rear wheels is above the 50% reduction ratio for the rear line pressure and that malfunction has occured within the proportioning valve.

To test the valve, install gauge set shown in **Fig. 4** in brake line between master cylinder and proportioning valve, and at output end of proportioning valve and brake line as shown. Be sure all joints are fluid tight.

Have a helper exert pressure on brake pedal (holding pressure). Obtain a reading on master cylinder output of approximately 700 psi. While pressure is being held as above, reading on valve outlet should be 550-610 psi. If the pressure readings do not meet these specifications, the valve should be removed and a new valve installed.

Kelsey-Hayes Pin Slider Caliper

INDEX

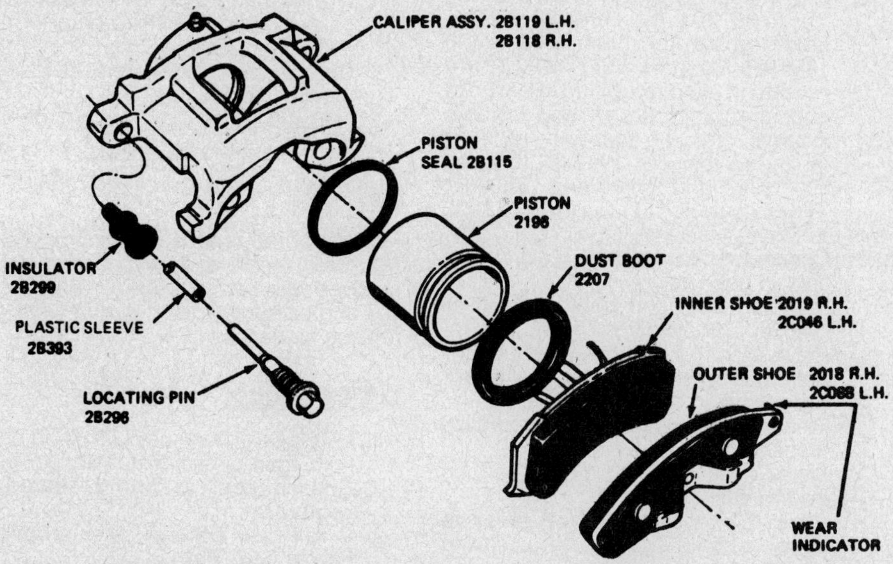

Fig. 1 Kelsey-Hayes pin slider disc brake caliper (Typical)

OPERATION

The caliper assembly consists of a pin slider caliper housing, inner and outer shoe and lining assemblies and a single piston, **Fig. 1.** The caliper slides on two pins which also act as attaching bolts between caliper and the combination anchor plate and spindle. The outer brake shoe and lining assembly is longer than the inner brake shoe and lining assembly. Inner and outer shoe and lining assemblies are attached to the caliper by spring clips riveted to the shoe surfaces. The inner shoe is attached to the caliper by installing the spring clip to the inside of the caliper piston. The outer shoe clips directly to the caliper housing. A wear indicator is incorporated which emits a noise when the lining is worn to a point when replacement is necessary. Inner and outer shoes are of left and righthand and are not interchangeable.

The inner shoe and lining on Capri, Fairmont, Mustang, and Zephyr with V8-302 engine has a replaceable single finger anti-rattle clip and an insulator held in position by the clip. The shoe is slotted to accept the snap on clip which loads the assembly against the caliper bridge. The inner shoe on the Capri and Mustang with 2300cc engine has a single finger anti-rattle clip similar to the Fairmont and Zephyr inner shoe, holding the shoe down against the spindle ledge. The clip does not lock into the piston. The insulator is also riveted to the shoe and is not replaceable.

BRAKE SHOE & LINING REPLACE

REMOVAL

1. Remove brake fluid until reservoir is half full.
2. Raise and support front of vehicle, then remove wheel and tire assembly.
3. Remove caliper locating pins.
4. Lift caliper assembly from spindle and adapter plate, then remove outer shoe from caliper assembly. **On some models, slip shoe down caliper leg until clip is disengaged.**
5. Remove inner shoe and lining assembly. **On some models, pull shoe straight out of piston. This ould require a force as high as 20-30 lbs.**
6. Suspend caliper from inner fender housing with wire to avoid damaging brake hose.
7. Remove and discard locating pin insulators and plastic sleeves.

INSTALLATION

1. Using a 4 in. C-clamp and a block of wood 2³/₄ x 1 in. and approximately ³/₄ in. thick, seat caliper piston in bore, then remove C-clamp and wooden block. **On some models, the piston is made of phenolic material. Do not seat piston in bore by applying C-clamp directly to piston. Extra care must be taken during this procedure to prevent damage to the piston. Metal or sharp objects cannot come into direct contact with the piston or damage may result.**
2. Install locating pin insulators and plastic sleeves on caliper housing. Ensure insulators and sleeves are properly positioned.
3. Install inner shoe and lining assembly on caliper piston, **Fig. 2. Inner brake shoes are marked LH (lefthand) and RH (righthand) and must be installed on the proper caliper. Use care to not bend spring clips too far during installation in piston, otherwise distortion and rattles may result.**
4. Install outer brake shoe and lining assembly, **Fig. 3.** Ensure that shoes are installed on proper caliper. Make sure that clip and buttons on shoe are properly seated. **The outer shoe can**

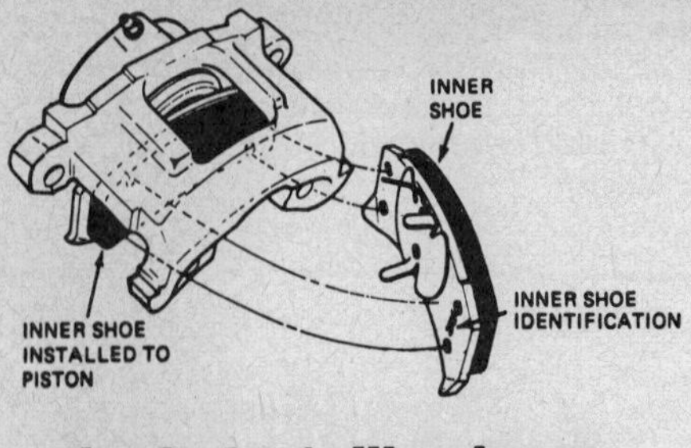

Fig. 2 Installing inner brake shoe on caliper

be identified as lefthand and righthand by the wear indicator which must be installed toward front of vehicle.

5. Install locating pins and torque to 30-40 ft. lbs. **On 1982-87 Lincoln Continental, 1984-87 Mark VII, 1987 Thunderbird Turbo, 1984-86 Mustang SVO and 1982-87 Ford and Mercury full size models, torque locating pins to 40-60 ft. lbs. On 1982-87 Escort, EXP, LN7 and Lynx, 1984-87 Tempo and Topaz and 1986-87 Sable and Taurus torque to 18-25 ft. lbs. On 1982-87 models except Lincoln Continental, 1984-87 Mark VII, 1987 Thunderbird Turbo & Mustang SVO ensure that two round torque buttons are firmly seated in the two holes of outer caliper leg and that shoe is held tightly against housing by spring clip. A temporary loss of brakes may occur if buttons are not properly seated.**
6. Refill master cylinder, then install wheel and tire assembly and lower vehicle.
7. Pump brake pedal several times to position brake linings before moving vehicle.

CALIPER

REPLACE

REMOVAL

Before removing calipers, mark left and righthand calipers so they can be installed in the same position.

1. Raise and support front of vehicle, then remove wheel and tire assembly.
2. Loosen brake tube fitting which connects brake tube to fitting on frame and plug brake tube. Remove retaining clip from brake hose and bracket, then disconnect brake hose from caliper.
3. Remove caliper locating pins.
4. Lift caliper from rotor and spindle anchor plate assembly. **On equipped with phenolic caliper piston, do not pry directly against the piston or damage may result.**

INSTALLATION

1. Install caliper assembly over rotor with outer shoe against rotor braking surface during installation on spindle and anchor plate to prevent pinching of piston boot between inner brake shoe and piston. **Ensure calipers are installed in the correct position.**
2. Install locating pins. Torque locating pins to 30-40 ft. lbs. **On 1982-87 Lincoln Continental, 1984-87 Mark VII, 1984-86 Mustang SVO, 1987 Thunderbird Turbo and 1982-87 Ford and Mercury full size and Lincoln models, torque locating pins to 40-60 ft. lbs. On 1982-87 Escort, EXP LN7 and Lynx and 1984-87 Tempo and Topaz, torque to 18-25 ft. lbs.**
3. Connect brake hose to caliper and tighten hose fitting.
4. Position upper end of brake hose in bracket and install retaining clip. Remove plug from brake line, then connect brake hose fitting to brake line. Torque fitting to 10-18 ft. lbs.
5. Bleed brake system and centralize pressure differential valve.
6. Install wheel and tire assembly, then lower vehicle.
7. Pump brake pedal several times to position brake shoes before moving vehicle.

CALIPER OVERHAUL

DISASSEMBLE

1. Remove caliper assembly from vehicle as described under "Caliper, Replace."
2. Position fiber block and shop towels between caliper piston and caliper housing, then apply compressed air to caliper brake line fitting bore to force piston from caliper.
3. Remove dust boot from caliper assembly, **Fig. 1.**
4. Remove pistol seal from cylinder and discard.

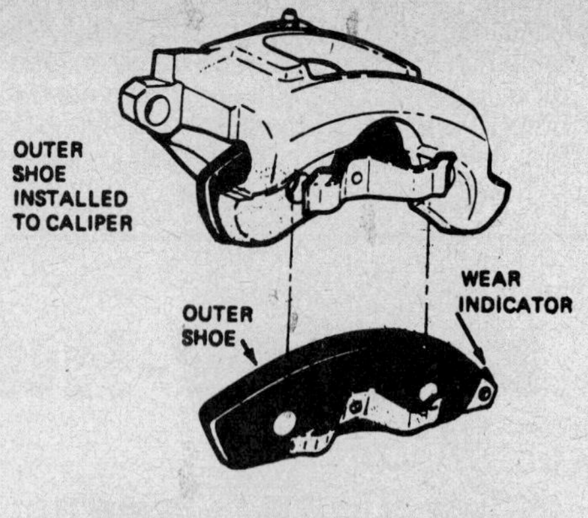

Fig. 3 Installing outer brake shoe on caliper

INSPECTION

Clean all metal parts with isopropyl alcohol, then clean and dry passages and grooves with compressed air. Check caliper and piston for damage and wear and replace as necessary.

ASSEMBLE

1. Lubricate piston seal with clean brake fluid, then install seal in caliper bore. **Ensure seal is firmly seated in groove.**
2. Install dust boot in outer groove of caliper bore, **Fig. 1.**
3. Coat piston with clean brake fluid and install piston in caliper bore. Spread dust boot over piston as it is installed. Seat dust boot in piston groove.
4. Install caliper assembly as described under "Caliper, Replace."

Ford Rear Wheel Disc Brake & Parking Brake

INDEX

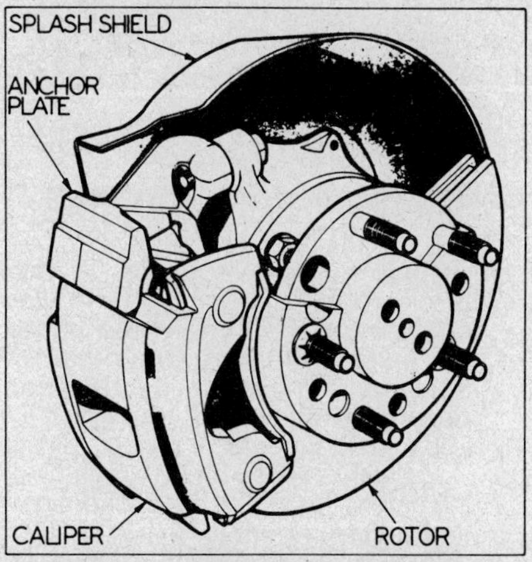

Fig. 1 Rear disc brake

Fig. 3 Parking lever & cable installation

OPERATION

Sliding caliper rear disc brakes are used on 1982-87 Lincoln Continental, 1984-87 Mark VII, 1987 Thunderbird Turbo & 1984-86 Mustang SVO, **Fig. 1.** The caliper is basically the same as the larger front wheel caliper, however, a parking brake mechanism and a larger inner brake shoe anti-rattle spring have been added, **Fig. 2.** A hydraulically powered brake booster (Hydroboost) provides the power assist for this four wheel disc brake system.

The parking brake lever, located at the rear of the caliper, is actuated by a cable system similar to rear drum brake applications. When the parking brake is applied, the cable rotates the lever and operating shaft. Three steel balls, placed in pockets between the opposing heads of the operating shaft and thrust screw, roll between ramps formed in the pockets and force the thrust screw away from the operating shaft, in turn, driving the caliper piston and brake shoe assembly against the rotor. An automatic adjuster in the assembly compensates for lining wear and maintains proper clearance in the parking brake mechanism.

The cast iron rotors are ventilated by curved fins located between the braking surfaces and are designed to cause the rotor to act as an air pump when the vehicle is traveling forward. The rotors are not interchangeable and are identified by a Right or Left marking cast inside the hat section of the rotor. The rotor is secured to the axle flange in the same manner as a rear brake drum. A splash shield is bolted to a forged axle adapter to protect the inboard rotor surface.

The 1984 Mustang SVO four wheel disc brake system is the same as the Continental and Mark VII brake system, except that the Mustang SVO incorporates a vacuum booster.

CALIPER REMOVAL

After performing any service work, obtain a firm brake pedal before moving vehicle.

1. Raise vehicle and support on safety stands, then remove tire and wheel assemblies.
2. Disconnect fitting on rear brake tube from hose end fitting at frame mounted bracket and plug end of brake tube to prevent loss of fluid and entry of dirt. Remove horseshoe retaining clip from hose fitting and disengage hose from bracket.
3. Disconnect parking cable from lever, **Fig. 3**, using care to avoid kinking or cutting cable or return spring, then remove retaining screw from caliper retaining key, **Fig. 4**, then remove caliper locating pins.
4. Slide caliper retaining key and support spring from anchor plate, **Fig. 4.** If necessary, use a hammer and brass drift, being careful to avoid damaging key on sliding ways or hitting parking brake lever. **If caliper cannot be removed due to rust build-up on outer edge of rotor, scrape off loose scale, being careful not to damage braking surfaces. If rotor wear or scoring prevents removal of caliper, it will be necessary to loosen caliper end retainer 1/2 turn maximum, to allow piston to be forced back into its bore. To loosen end retainer, remove parking brake lever and mark or scribe end retainer and caliper housing to be sure that end retainer is not loosened more than 1/2 turn, then force piston back in its bore, Fig. 2, and move caliper back and forth to center rotor and remove caliper. If retainer must be**

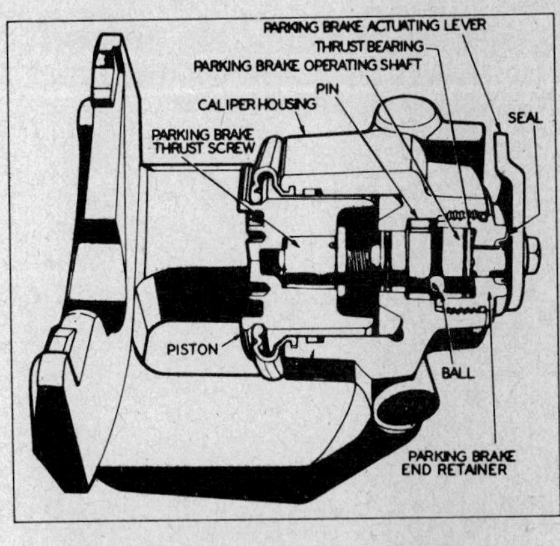

Fig. 2 Caliper housing cutaway to show parking brake mechanism

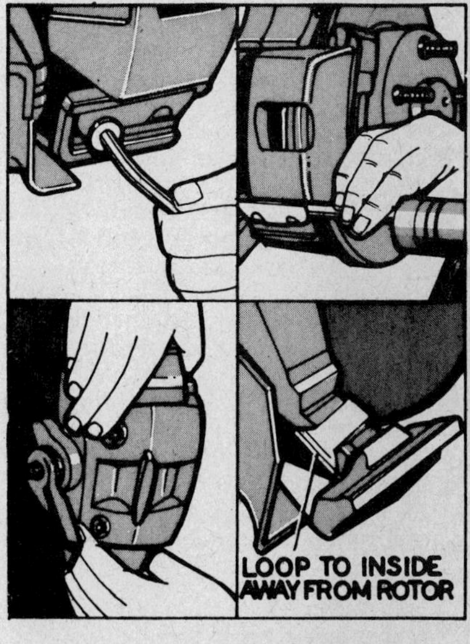

Fig. 4 Removing rear caliper assembly

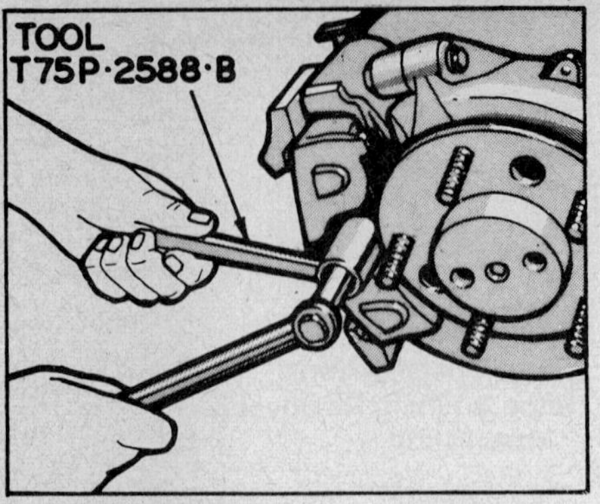

Fig. 5 Adjusting piston depth for lining installation

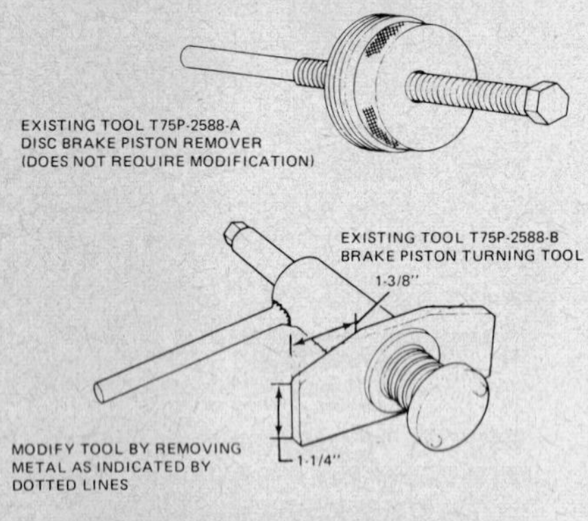

Fig. 6 Disc brake tool modification

loosened more than 1/2 turn, use caution, as the seal between the thrust screw and housing may be broken and brake fluid will enter parking brake mechanism chamber. In this case, the end retainer must be removed and the internal parts cleaned and lubricated.

5. Remove outer shoe and lining assembly from anchor plate, then remove rotor retainer nuts and rotor from axle shaft.
6. Remove inner brake shoe and lining assembly from anchor plate and mark each shoe for identification if they are to be reused.
7. Remove anti-rattle clip from anchor plate, then remove flexible hose from caliper by removing hollow retaining bolt.

CLEANING & INSPECTION

Clean caliper, anchor plate and rotor assembly and inspect for signs of brake fluid leakage, excessive wear or damage. The caliper must be inspected for leakage both in piston boot area and operating shaft seal area. Lightly sand or wire brush any rust or corrosion from caliper and anchor plate sliding surfaces and inner brake shoe abutment surfaces in anchor plate. Inspect brake shoes for wear. Linings must not be worn to within less than 1/8 inch of shoe surface.

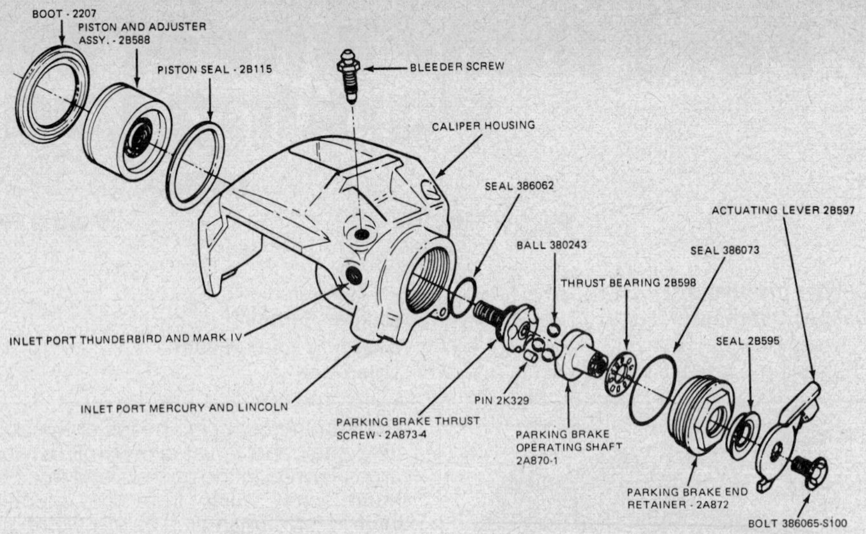

Fig. 7 Rear disc brake caliper assembly (Typical)

CALIPER INSTALLATION

1. If end retainer has been loosened only 1/2 turn, reinstall caliper in anchor plate using key. Do not install shoe and lining assembly. Torque end retainer to 75-95 ft. lbs. and install parking brake actuating lever on its keyed spline. Lever arm must point down and rearward so that parking brake cable will pass freely under axle. Torque retainer screw to 16-22 ft. lbs. **Parking brake lever must rotate freely after torquing retainer screw.**
2. Remove caliper from anchor plate. If new shoe and lining assemblies are to be installed, the piston must be bottomed in caliper bore using tool T75P-2588-B to provide clearance. Remove rotor and install caliper without lining and shoe assemblies in anchor plate using key only. Install tool and while holding shaft, rotate tool handle counterclockwise until the tool seats firmly against piston, **Fig. 5.** Loosen handle about 1/4 turn, and while holding handle rotate tool shaft clockwise until piston is fully bottomed in bore (piston will continue to turn even after it is bottomed). Turn tool handle until there is no further inward movement of piston and there is a firm seating force, then remove caliper from mounting plate and reinstall rotor. **For use on some vehicles, tool T75P-2588-B must be slightly modified, Fig. 6.**
3. Making certain that brake shoe anti-rattle clip is in place in lower inner brake shoe support on anchor plate with loop of clip toward inside of anchor plate, **Fig. 4,** position inner brake shoe and lining assembly on anchor plate, then install rotor and two retaining nuts.
4. Install outer brake shoe with lower flange ends against caliper abutments and brake shoe upper flanges over shoulders on caliper legs. The shoe upper flanges fit tightly against machined shoulder surfaces. **If old brake shoes and lining assemblies are reused, be certain the shoes are installed in their original positions as marked for identification during removal.**
5. Lubricate caliper and anchor sliding ways with D7AE-019590 grease, using care to prevent lubricant from getting on braking surfaces, then position caliper housing lower V-groove on anchor plate lower abutment surfaces.
6. Rotate caliper until it is completely over rotor, being careful not to damage piston dust boot, then pull caliper outboard until inner shoe and lining is firmly seated against rotor. Measure clearance between outer lining and rotor, clearance must be between 1/32 and 3/32 inch. If it is greater, remove caliper and move piston outward to narrow gap. Follow procedure in step 2 and note that 1/4 turn of the shaft counterclockwise, moves piston about 1/16 inch. **A clearance greater than specified limit may allow adjuster to be pulled out of piston when service brake is applied, causing parking brake to fail to adjust. It will then be necessary to replace piston/adjuster assembly.**
7. While holding caliper against anchor plate upper abutment surfaces, center caliper over lower anchor plate abutment, then position caliper support spring and key in slot and slide them into opening between lower end of caliper and lower anchor plate abutment until key semi-circular slot is centered over retaining screw threaded hole in anchor plate.
8. Install key retaining screw and torque to 12-16 ft. lbs., then reinstall brake hose on caliper. Place a new gasket on each side of the fitting outlet, then install the attaching bolt through the washers and fitting and torque to 20-30 ft. lbs.
9. Lubricate pins and inside of insulator with D7AZ-19A331-A or equivalent silicone grease and add one drop of

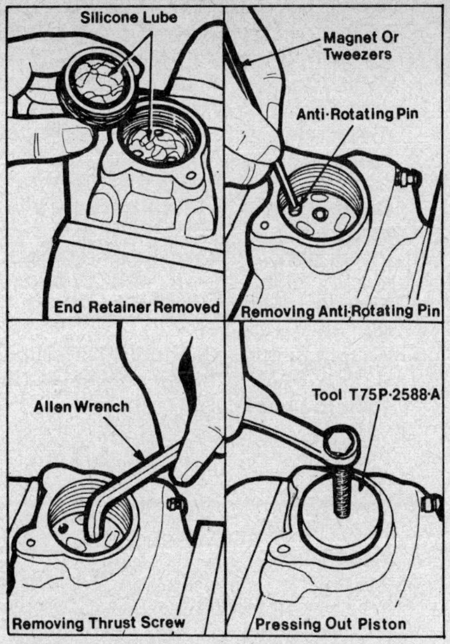

Fig. 8 Disassembling rear disc brake caliper

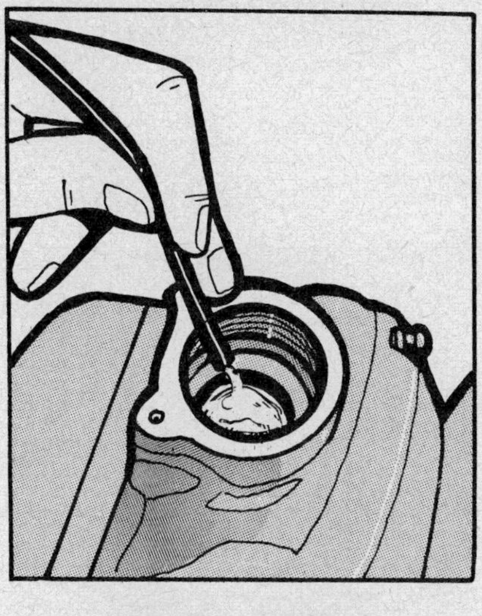

Fig. 10 Filling piston/adjuster assembly

Loctite EOAC-19554-A, or equivalent, to locating pin threads. Install locating pins through caliper insulators and into anchor plate and torque to 29-37 ft. lbs.

11. Connect parking brake lever to lever on caliper.
12. Bleed brake system, then with engine running pump brake pedal lightly about 40 times allowing 1 second between pedal applications. An alternate with engine off is to pump brake pedal lightly about 10 times to discharge accumulator, then pump brake pedal firmly about 30 times. Check parking brake for excessive travel or very light effort, if so, repeat pumping brake pedal, and if necessary check parking brake cable tension.
13. Install wheel and torque nuts to 70-115 ft. lbs. **Before moving vehicle, make certain that a firm brake pedal has been obtained.**

SHOE & LINING REMOVAL & INSTALLATION

To remove shoe and lining assemblies, follow "Caliper Removal" procedure and omit step 2 as it is not necessary to disconnect brake hose. After removing caliper, support it with a length of wire to avoid damaging brake hose. To install shoe and lining assemblies, follow "Caliper Installation" procedure, making certain that proper parking brake adjustment is obtained.

CALIPER OVERHAUL

DISASSEMBLE

1. Remove caliper assembly as described previously.
2. Remove caliper end retainer, operating shaft, thrust bearing and balls, **Fig. 7.**
3. Remove thrust screw anti-rotation pin with a magnet or tweezers. If pin cannot be removed with a magnet or tweezers, proceed with the following procedure:
   a. With tool T75P-2588B, force piston approximately one inch from caliper bore.
   b. Push piston back into caliper housing with tool, then with tool in position, hold tool shaft in place and rotate handle counterclockwise until thrust screw clears anti-rotation pin. Remove thrust screw and anti-rotation pin.
4. Remove thrust screw by rotating with 1/4 inch Allen wrench.
5. Install tool T75P-2588-A through back of caliper housing and remove piston assembly, **Fig. 8. Use care not to damage polished surface in thrust screw bore and do not attempt to remove or press adjuster can, as it is a press fit in piston.**
6. Remove and discard piston seal, boot, thrust O-ring seal, end retainer, O-ring and end retainer lip seal.

CLEANING & INSPECTION

1. Clean all metal parts with alcohol, then using clean, dry compressed air, blow out and dry all grooves and passages making sure the caliper bore and component parts are free of any foreign material.
2. Inspect caliper bore for damage or excessive wear. The thrust screw must be smooth and free of pits. If piston is pitted, scored or chrome plating is worn, replace piston and adjuster assembly.
3. Adjuster can must be bottomed in piston to be properly seated and provide consistent brake operation. If adjuster can is loose, appears high in piston, is damaged, or if brake adjustment is usually too tight, too loose or not functioning, replace piston/adjuster assembly. Check adjuster operation by assembling thrust screw into piston/adjuster assembly, then pull the two parts apart about 1/4 inch and release them, **Fig. 9.** When pulling on the two parts, the brass drive ring must remain stationary causing the nut to rotate. When releasing the two parts, the nut must remain stationary and drive ring must rotate. If action does not follow this pattern, replace piston/adjuster assembly.
4. Inspect ball pockets, threads, grooves, bearing surfaces of thrust screw, operating shaft, balls and anti-rotation pin for wear, brinnelling or pitting. Replace operating shaft, balls, thrust screw and anti-rotation pin if any of these parts are worn or damaged. A polished appearance on the ball paths is acceptable if there is no sign of wear into the surface.
5. Inspect thrust bearing for corrosion, pitting or wear and replace as necessary.
6. Inspect end plug bearing surface for wear or brinnelling and replace as necessary. A polished appearance on bearing surface is acceptable if there is no sign of wear into surface.
7. Inspect operating lever for damage and replace as necessary.

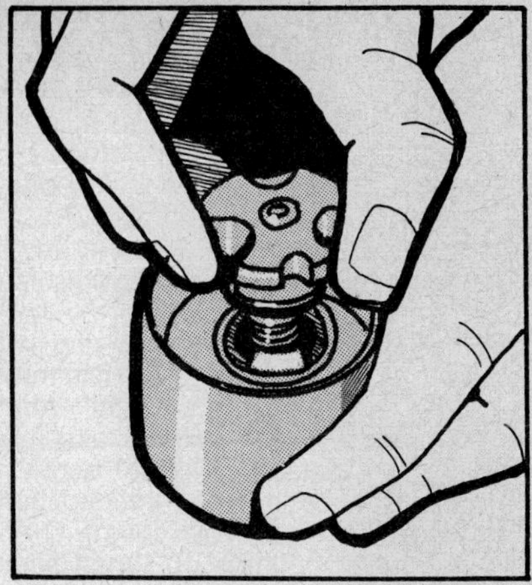

Fig. 9 Checking parking brake adjuster operation

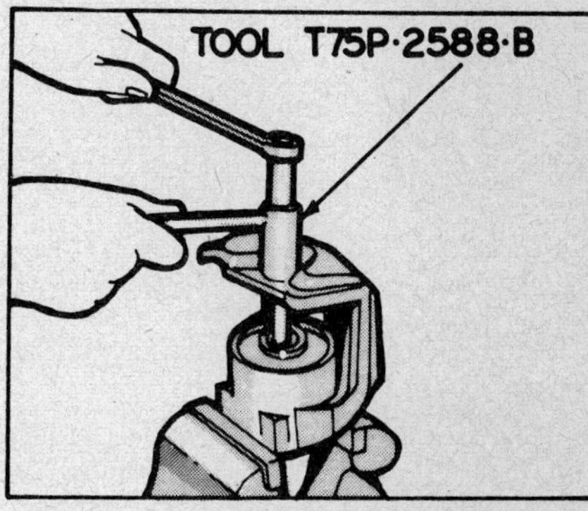

Fig. 11 Bottoming piston in caliper

ASSEMBLE

1. Coat new caliper piston seal with clean brake fluid and install it in caliper making certain that seal is not twisted and is fully seated in groove.

2. Install new dust boot by seating flange squarely in outer groove of caliper bore, then coat piston/adjuster assembly with clean brake fluid and install it in caliper bore. Spread dust boot over piston as it is installed and seat dust boot in piston groove.
3. Install caliper in vise, **Fig. 10,** and fill piston/adjuster assembly with clean brake fluid.
4. Coat new thrust screw O-ring with clean brake fluid and install it in thrust screw groove, then install thrust screw into piston adjuster assembly until top surface of thrust screw is flush with bottom of threaded bore, being careful to avoid cutting O-ring seal. Index notches on thrust screw and caliper housing and install anti-rotation pin. **The thrust screw and operating shafts are not interchangeable from side to side since the ramp direction in the ball pockets are different. The pocket surfaces of the operating shaft and thrust screws are stamped "R" (Right) and "L" (Left).**
5. Place a ball in each of three pockets of thrust screw and apply a liberal amount of silicone grease M1C-169-A on parking brake components, then install operating shaft on balls.
6. Coat thrust bearing with silicone grease and install it on operating shaft, then install a new lip seal and O-ring on end retainer.
7. Lightly coat O-ring seal and lip seal with silicone grease and install end retainer in caliper. Firmly hold operating shaft against internal mechanism while installing end retainer to prevent mislocation of balls. If lip seal moves out of position, reseat seal. Torque end retainer to 75-95 ft. lbs. **Parking brake lever must rotate freely after torquing.**
8. Install parking brake lever on keyed spline facing down and rearward. Torque retaining screw to 16-22 ft. lbs.
9. Bottom piston using tool T75P-2588-B, **Fig. 11,** and install caliper as described previously.

Rotor Specifications

Car	Year	Nominal Thickness	Minimum Refinish Thickness	Thickness Variation (Parallelism)	Lateral Runout (T.I.R.)	Finish (Microinch)
FORD MOTOR COMPANY						
Ford & Mercury Full Size	1982-87	1.030	.972	.0005	.003	10-80
Ford & Mercury Intermediate	1982-87 ①	.870	.810	.0005 ⑥	.003	15-125 ⑦
Granada	1982	.870	.810	.0005	.003	15-125
Mark VI & Town Car	1982-83	1.030	.972	.0005	.003	10-80
Town Car	1984-87	1.030	.972	.0005	.003	10-80
Continental, Mark VII, Thunderbird Turbo & Mustang SVO	1982-87	1.030 ②	.972 ③	.0005	.003 ④	15-125 ⑤
Capri, Mustang, (Exc. SVO)	1982-87	.870	.810	.0005	.003	15-125
Fairmont & Zephyr	1982-83	.870	.810	.0005	.003	15-125
Escort, EXP, LN7 & Lynx	1982-84	.945	.882	.0004	.003 ⑥	16-79
	1985-87	.945	.882	.0004	.002	20-140
Tempo & Topaz	1984	.945	.882	.0005	.003	15-80
	1985-87	.945	.882	.0005	.003	10-80
Sable & Taurus	1986-87	.945	.896	.0005	.003	10-80

①—Cougar, Cougar XR-7, Thunderbird Exc. Turbo & 1983-87 LTD & Marquis.
②—Rear disc, .945.
③—Rear disc, .895.
④—Rear disc, .004.
⑤—Rear disc, 15-80.
⑥—1984-87 LTD & Marquis, .0003.
⑦—1984-87, 10-81.

Caliper Specifications

Year	Model	Caliper Bore Dia. In.
FORD & MERCURY: Full Size Models		
1982-87	All	2.88 ①
FORD & MERCURY: Compact & Intermediate Models		
1982-87	Exc. Sable & Taurus	2.36 ③
1986-87	Sable & Taurus	2.59
FORD MUSTANG & MUSTANG SVO & MERCURY CAPRI		
1982-87	All	2.36 ② ④
FORD ESCORT, EXP & TEMPO • MERCURY LN7. LYNX & TOPAZ		
1982-83	All	2.125
1984-87	All	2.36
LINCOLN		
1982-83	Exc. Continental	2.88
	Continental	2.38 ②
1984-87	Continental & Mark VII	2.87 ②
	Town Car	2.88

①—Rear disc brake caliper bore, 2.6".
②—Rear disc brake caliper bore, 2.1".
③—Rear disc brake caliper bore, 1.77".
④—Mustang W/5.0 L, 2.87".

DRUM BRAKES

NOTE: Refer to "Brake Usage Chart" to determine which type brakes are used on vehicle being serviced.

TABLE OF CONTENTS

Brake Usage Chart

	Type No.
Ford & Mercury Full Size & Lincoln	1
1982-86 Capri	2
1982 Cougar Exc. Station Wagon	2
1982 Cougar Station Wagon	1
1983-84 Cougar	2
1985-87 Cougar Less Heavy Duty Brakes	2
1985-87 Cougar W/Heavy Duty Brakes	1
1982 Cougar XR-7 Less V8 Engine	2
1982 Cougar XR-7 W/V8 Engine	1
1982-84 Escort 2 & 3 Door Hatchback	3
1982-84 Escort Exc. 2 & 3 Door Hatchback	4
1985 Escort 3 Door Less Styled Steel Wheels	3
1985 Escort Exc. 3 Door Less Styled Steel Wheels	4
1986-87 Escort 2 Door Less Styled Steel Wheels	3
1986-87 Escort Exc. 2 Door Less Styled Steel Wheels	4
1982-85 EXP	4
1982-83 Fairmont	2
1982 Granada Station Wagon	1
1982-83 LN7	4
1983-84 LTD Exc. Station Wagon	2
1983-84 LTD Station Wagon	1
1985-87 LTD Exc. Station Wagon & Touring Sedan	1
1982-84 Lynx 2 & 3 Door Hatchback	3
1982-84 Lynx Exc. 2 & 3 Door Hatchback	4
1985 Lynx 3 Door Less Styled Steel Wheels	3
1985 Lynx Exc. 3 Door Less Styled Steel Wheels	4
1986-87 Lynx 2 Door Less Styled Steel Wheels	3
1986-87 Lynx Exc. 2 Door Less Styled Steel Wheels	4
1983-84 Marquis Exc. Station Wagon	2
1983-84 Marquis Station Wagon	1
1985-87 Marquis Exc. Station & Touring Sedan	2
1985-87 Marquis Station Wagon & Touring Sedan	1
1982-87 Mustang	2
1986-87 Sable	5
1986-87 Taurus	5
1984-87 Tempo	4
1984-87 Topaz	4
1982 Thunderbird Less V8 Engine	2
1982 Thunderbird Less V8 Engine	2
1982 Thunderbird W/V8 Engine	1
1983-84 Thunderbird	2
1985-87 Thunderbird Less Heavy Duty Brakes	2
1985-87 Thunderbird W/Heavy Duty Brakes	1
1982-83 Zephyr	2

General Information

INDEX

SERVICE PRECAUTIONS

When working on or around brake assemblies, care must be taken to prevent breathing asbestos dust, as many manufacturers incorporate asbestos fibers in the production of brake linings. During routine service operations the amount of asbestos dust from brake lining wear is at a low level, due to a chemical breakdown during use and a few precautions will minimize exposure. **Do not sand or grind brake linings unless suitable local exhaust ventilation equipment is used to prevent excessive asbestos exposure.**

1. Wear a suitable respirator approved for asbestos dust use during all repair procedures.
2. When cleaning brake dust from brake parts, use a vacuum cleaner with a highly efficient filter system. If a suitable vacuum cleaner is not available, use a water soaked rag. **Do not use compressed air or dry brush to clean brake parts.**
3. Keep work area clean using same equipment as for cleaning brake parts.
4. Properly dispose of rags and vacuum cleaner bags by placing them in plastic bags.
5. Do not smoke or eat while working on brake systems. **Never use gasoline, kerosene, alcohol, motor oil, transmission fluid, or any fluid containing mineral oil to clean brake system components. These fluids will damage the rubber caps and seals. If system contamination is suspected, check brake fluid in the reservoir for dirt, discoloration, or separation (breakdown) of the brake fluid into distinct layers. Drain and flush the hydraulic system with clean brake fluid if contamination is suspected.**

GENERAL INSPECTION

BRAKE DRUMS

Any time the brake drums are removed for brake service, the braking surface diameter should be checked with a suitable brake drum micrometer at several points to determine if they are within the safe oversize limit stamped on the brake drum outer surface. If the braking surface diameter exceeds specifications, the drum must be replaced. If the braking surface diameter is within specifications, drums should be cleaned and inspected for cracks, scores, deep grooves, taper, out of round and heat spotting. If drums are cracked or heat spotted, they must be replaced. Minor scores should be removed with sandpaper. Grooves and large scores can only be removed by machining with special equipment, as long as the braking surface is within specifications stamped on brake drum outer surface. Any brake drum sufficiently out of round to cause vehicle vibration or noise while braking or showing taper should also be machined, removing only enough stock to true up the brake drum.

After a brake drum is machined, wipe the braking surface diameter with a denatured alcohol soaked cloth. If one brake drum is machined, the other should also be machined to the same diameter to maintain equal braking forces.

BRAKE LININGS & SPRINGS

Inspect brake linings for excessive wear, damage, oil, grease or brake fluid contamination. If any of the above conditions exists, brake linings should be replaced. Do not attempt to replace only one set of brake shoes. They should be replaced as an axle set only to maintain equal braking forces. Examine brake shoe webbing, hold-down and return springs for signs of overheating indicated by a slight blue color. If any component exhibits overheating signs, replace hold-down and return springs with new ones. Overheated springs lose their pull and could cause brake linings to wear out prematurely. Inspect all springs for sags, bends and external damage and replace as necessary.

Inspect hold-down retainers and pins for bends, rust and corrosion. If any of the above is found, replace as required.

BACKING PLATE

Inspect backing plate shoe contact surface for grooves that may restrict shoe movement and cannot be removed by lightly sanding with emery cloth or other suitable abrasive. If backing plate exhibits above condition, it should be replaced. Also inspect for signs of cracks, warpage and excessive rust, indicating need for replacement.

ADJUSTER MECHANISM

Inspect all components for rust, corrosion, bends and fatigue. Replace as necessary. On adjuster mechanism equipped with adjuster cable, inspect cable for kinks, fraying or elongation of eyelet and replace as necessary.

PARKING BRAKE CABLE

Inspect parking brake cable end for kinks, fraying and elongation and replace as necessary. Use a small hose clamp to compress clamp where it enters backing plate to remove.

Types 1 & 2

INDEX

REMOVAL

1. Raise and support rear of vehicle, then remove tire and wheel assembly.
2. Remove brake drum. If brake lining is dragging on brake drum, back off brake adjustment by rotating adjustment screw. Refer to individual car chapter for procedure. **If brake drum is rusted or corroded to axle flange and cannot be removed, lightly tap axle flange to drum mounting surface with a suitable hammer.**
3. Install suitable wheel cylinder clamp over ends of wheel cylinder to retain pistons in bore.
4. On type 1 brakes, **Fig 1,** remove parking brake lever retaining clip.
5. On both types, **Figs. 1 and 2,** remove adjuster lever spring, primary and secondary shoe return springs using a suitable pair of brake spring pliers.
6. Remove shoe guide plate, if equipped and adjuster cable and guide plate.
7. Using suitable tool, compress hold-down springs, then remove spring retainers, hold-down springs and pins.
8. Separate springs and remove from backing plate.
9. On type 2 brake, disengage parking brake lever from secondary shoe.
10. On all types, remove parking brake lever from cable.
11. Separate all components from brake shoes.
12. Clean dirt from brake drum, backing plate and all other components. **Do not use compressed air or dry brush to clean brake parts. Many brake parts contain asbestos fibers which, if inhaled, can cause serious injury. Clean brake parts with a water soaked rag or a suitable vacuum cleaner to minimize airborne dust.**

INSPECTION

1. Inspect components for damage and unusual wear. Replace as necessary.
2. Inspect wheel cylinders. Boots which are torn, cut, or heat damaged indicate need for wheel cylinder replacement. Fluid spilling from boot center hole, or wetness around wheel cylinder ends indicates cup leakage and need for wheel cylinder replacement. **A small amount of fluid is always present and is considered normal, acting as a lubricant for the cylinder pistons.**
3. Inspect backing plate for evidence of seal leakage. If leakage exists, refer to individual car chapters for axle seal replacement procedure.
4. Inspect backing plate attaching bolts and ensure they are tight.
5. Check adjuster screw operation. If satisfactory, lightly lubricate adjusting screw and washer with suitable brake lube. If operation is unsatisfactory, replace.
6. Using fine emery cloth or other suitable abrasive, clean rust and dirt from shoe contact surfaces on backing plate.

INSTALLATION

1. Lightly lubricate backing plate shoe contact surfaces with suitable brake lube.
2. On type 1 brakes, assemble parking brake lever to secondary shoe and secure with spring washer and retaining clip. Crimp ends of clip with suitable pliers. On type 2 brakes, engage parking brake lever tang with secondary shoe.
3. Position brake shoes on backing plate, primary (short lining) shoe facing front of vehicle and secondary (long lining) facing rear. Secure brake shoes with hold-down springs, pins and retainers.
4. Install parking brake link and spring between shoes.
5. Loosen parking brake adjustment nut,

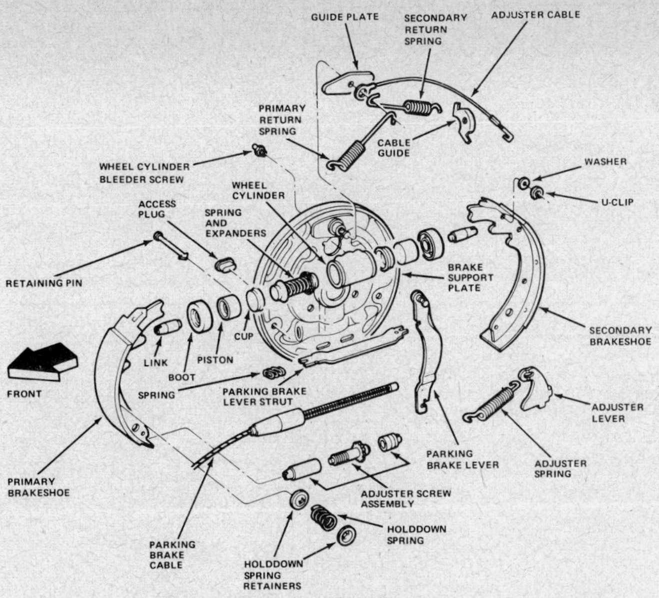

Fig. 1 Drum brake assembly. Type 1

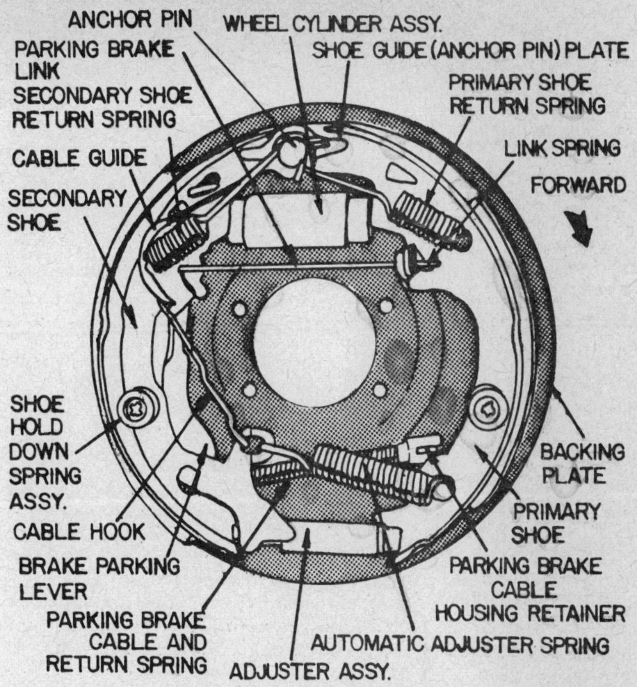

Fig. 2 Drum brake assembly. Type 2

then install parking brake cable on parking brake lever.

6. Install shoe guide plate and adjuster cable eyelet on anchor. Ensure adjuster cable crimp faces out.
7. Ensure parking brake link is properly positioned between brake shoes and wheel cylinder links are engaged in shoe web.
8. Using suitable brake spring pliers, install primary return spring from brake shoe to anchor, then secondary return spring from brake shoe to anchor.
9. On all types, remove wheel cylinder clamp installed during removal of brake shoes.
10. Tighten adjuster screw assembly to thread limit and back off 1/2 turn.
11. Install adjuster screw assembly between shoes. Ensure toothed wheel is on secondary shoe side. **Adjuster screw assemblies are stamped R (right) and L (left). To ensure proper adjuster operation, they must be installed on their respective sides.**
12. Hook adjuster cable hook into adjuster lever hole, then position adjuster spring hook in large hole in primary shoe web. Using suitable brake spring pliers, install adjuster spring in adjuster lever hole.
13. Ensure adjuster cable is properly seated in cable guide, then pull adjuster lever, cable and adjuster spring down and towards the rear, engaging lever pivot hook in the large hole of secondary shoe web.

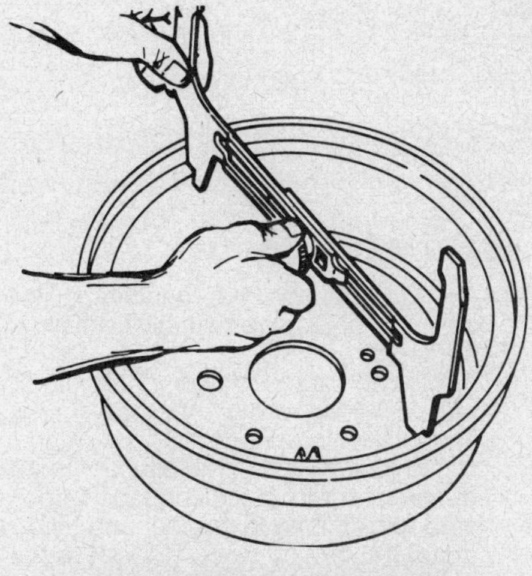

Fig. 3 Measuring brake drum inside diameter

14. After installation, check adjuster operation by pulling adjuster cable between cable guide and adjuster lever towards secondary shoe sufficiently to lift adjuster lever past one tooth on adjuster screw assembly. The adjuster lever should snap into position behind the next tooth, then upon release of adjuster cable, rotate toothed wheel one notch. If operation is not satisfactory, recheck installation.
15. Ensure brake shoe upper ends are seated against anchor pin and shoe assemblies are centered on backing plate. If not, back off parking brake adjustment.
16. Using suitable brake drum to shoe gauge, **Fig. 3,** measure brake drum inside diameter. Adjust brake shoes to dimension obtained on outside portion of gauge using adjuster screw.
17. Install brake drum, wheel and tire assembly.
18. If any hydraulic brake connections have been opened, bleed brake system.
19. Adjust parking brake. Refer to individual car chapter for procedures.
20. Inspect all hydraulic lines and connections for leakage and repair as necessary.
21. Check master cylinder fluid level and replenish as necessary.
22. Check brake pedal for proper feel and return.
23. Lower vehicle and road test. **Do not severely apply brakes immediately after installation of new brake linings or permanent damage may occur to linings, and/or brake drums may become scored. Brakes must be used moderately during first several hundred miles of operation to ensure proper burnishing of linings.**

Type 3

INDEX

Page No.

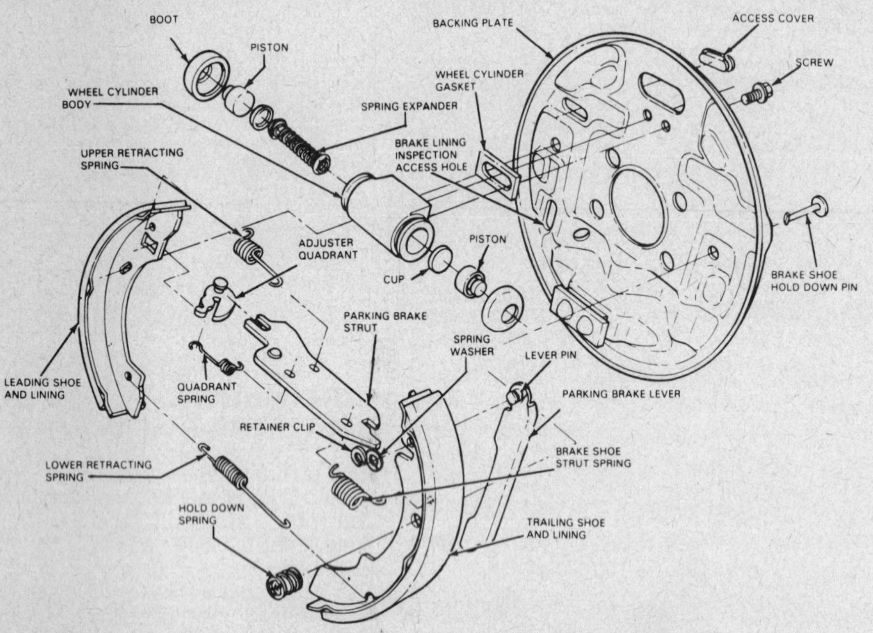

Fig. 1 Drum brake assembly. Type 3

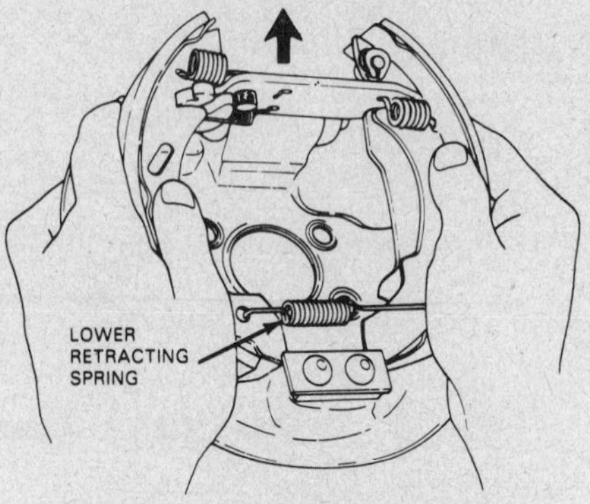

Fig. 2 Removing brake shoe and adjuster assemblies. Type 3

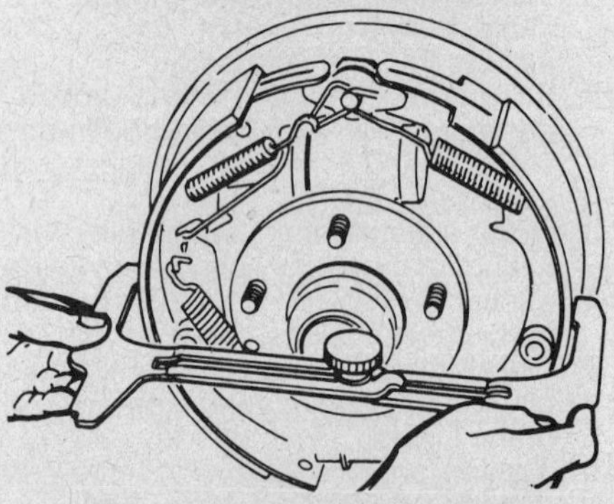

Fig. 3 Adjusting brake shoes to brake drum inside diameter. Type 3

REMOVAL

1. Raise and support rear of vehicle, then remove tire and wheel assembly.
2. Remove brake drum. If brake lining is dragging on brake drum, back off brake adjustment. Refer to individual car chapters for procedure.
3. Using suitable tool, remove hold-down retainers, springs and pins, **Fig. 1.**
4. Remove brake shoe and adjuster assemblies from backing plate by lifting up and away from anchor block and shoe guide, **Fig. 2. When removing brake shoe and adjuster assemblies, use care not to damage wheel cylinder boots.**
5. Remove parking brake cable from parking brake lever.
6. Remove lower retracting spring from leading and trailing shoes.
7. While holding brake shoe and adjuster assemblies, remove leading shoe upper retracting spring by rotating leading shoe over adjuster quadrant until spring is slack, then remove spring. Remove leading shoe from adjuster assembly.
8. Remove parking brake strut from trailing shoe by pulling strut outward from shoe assembly, then twisting strut downward until spring tension is released. Unhook brake shoe strut spring, then remove parking brake strut and adjuster assembly from trailing shoe.
9. If adjuster disassembly is required, pull adjuster quadrant away from knurled pin in parking brake strut and rotate quadrant in either direction until quadrant teeth are disengaged from strut pin. Remove spring and slide quadrant out of strut. **Do not over stress quadrant spring during removal.**
10. Remove parking brake lever retaining clip and spring washer, then the parking brake lever.
11. Clean dirt from brake drum, backing plate and all other components. **Do not use compressed air or dry brush to clean brake parts. Many brake parts contain asbestos fibers which, if inhaled, can cause serious injury. Clean brake parts with a water soaked rag or a suitable vacuum cleaner to minimize airborne dust.**

INSPECTION

1. Inspect components for damage and unusual wear. Replace as necessary.
2. Inspect wheel cylinders. Boots which are torn, cut or heat damaged indicate need for wheel cylinder replacement. Peel back lower edge of boot. If fluid spills out, cup leakage is indicated and wheel cylinder should be replaced. **A slight amount of fluid is always present and is considered normal, acting as a lubricant for the cylinder pistons.**
3. Inspect backing plate attaching bolts and ensure they are tight.
4. Using fine emery cloth or other suitable abrasive, clean rust and dirt from shoe contact surfaces on backing plate.

INSTALLATION

1. Lightly lubricate backing plate shoe contact surfaces with suitable brake lube.
2. Remove brake drum hub grease seal and bearings, then clean and repack bearings and reinstall. Install new grease seal.
3. Lightly lubricate strut to adjuster quadrant contact surfaces with suitable brake lube.
4. Position adjuster quadrant pin in strut slot and install quadrant spring, then

pivot quadrant until it engages with strut knurled pin in third or fourth notch of outboard end of quadrant.

5. Assemble parking brake lever to trailing shoe, then install spring washer and retaining clip. Using suitable pliers, crimp retaining clip until securely fastened.
6. Assemble parking brake strut to trailing shoe by attaching brake shoe strut spring to slots in shoe web and strut, and pivoting strut into position, tension spring and holding assembly in place. **Ensure end of spring with hook parallel to the center line of spring coils is installed in shoe web hole. Installed spring should be flat against shoe web and parallel to parking brake strut.**
7. Install lower retracting spring between shoes. Ensure spring hook with longest straight piece fits into trailing shoe hole, **Fig. 1.**
8. Install upper retracting spring by installing hooks in leading shoe web and other end in parking brake strut, then pivot leading shoe over adjuster quadrant and into position.
9. Spread shoe and strut assemblies sufficiently to fit over anchor plate and wheel cylinder piston inserts, and install onto backing plate. **When installing brake shoe and adjuster assemblies, use care not to damage wheel cylinder boots.**
10. Connect parking brake cable to parking brake lever.
11. Using suitable tool, install hold-down springs, retainers and pins.
12. Using suitable brake drum to shoe gauge, measure brake drum inside diameter. Adjust brake shoes to dimension obtained on outside portion of gauge, **Fig. 3.**
13. Install brake drum. Refer to individual car chapters for wheel bearing adjustment procedure.
14. Install tire and wheel assembly.
15. If any hydraulic connections have been opened, bleed brake system.
16. Adjust parking brake. Refer to individual car chapters for procedure.
17. Inspect all hydraulic lines and connections for leakage and repair as necessary.
18. Check master cylinder fluid level and replenish as necessary.
19. Check brake pedal for proper feel and return.
20. Lower vehicle and road test. **Do not severely apply brakes immediately after installation of new brake linings or permanent damage may occur to lining, and/or brake drums may become scored. Brakes must be used moderately during first several hundred miles of operation to ensure proper burnishing of linings.**

Type 4

INDEX

Page No.

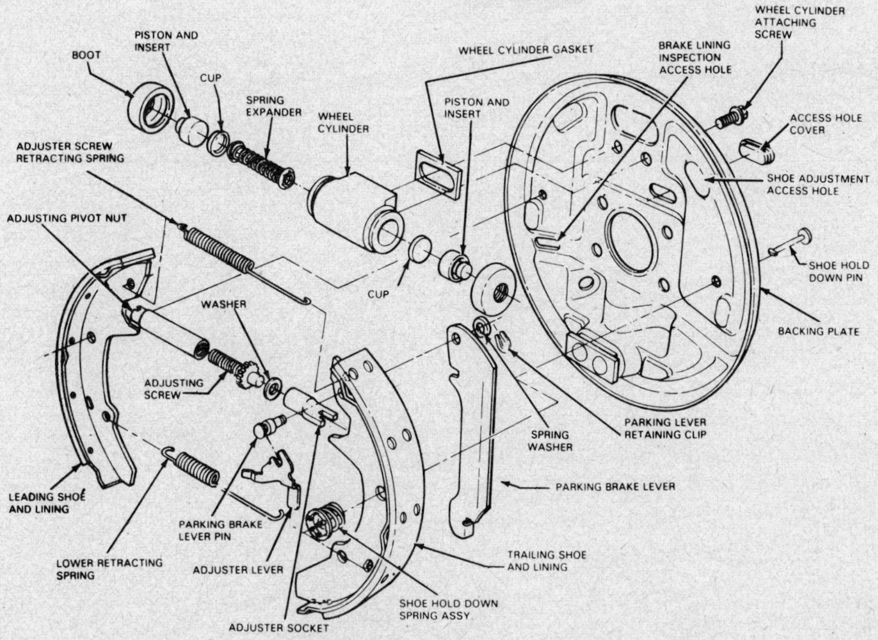

Fig. 1 Drum brake assembly. Type 4

REMOVAL

1. Raise and support rear of vehicle, then remove tire and wheel assembly.
2. Remove brake drum. If brake lining is dragging on brake drum, back off brake adjustment. Refer to individual car chapters for procedure.
3. Using suitable tool, remove hold-down retainers, springs and pins, **Fig. 1.**
4. Remove brake shoes and adjuster assemblies from backing plate by lifting up and away from wheel cylinder assembly. **When removing brake shoe and adjuster assemblies, use care not to bend adjusting lever.**
5. Remove parking brake cable from parking brake lever.
6. Remove lower retracting spring, adjuster screw retracting spring and adjuster lever.
7. Separate brake shoes, then remove parking brake lever retaining clip and spring washer and slide lever off parking brake lever pin on the trailing shoe.
8. Clean dirt from brake drum, backing plate and all other components. **Do not use compressed air or dry brush to clean brake parts. Many brake parts contain asbestos fibers which, if inhaled, can cause serious injury. Clean brake parts with a water soaked rag or a suitable vacuum cleaner to minimize airborne dust.**

INSPECTION

1. Inspect components for damage and unusual wear. Replace as necessary.
2. Inspect wheel cylinders. Boots which are torn, cut or heat damaged indicate need for wheel cylinder replacement. Peel back lower edge of boot. If fluid spills out, cup leakage is indicated and wheel cylinder should be replaced. **A small amount of fluid is always present and is considered normal, acting as a lubricant for the cylinder pistons.**
3. Inspect backing plate attaching bolts and ensure they are tight.
4. Using fine emery cloth or other suitable abrasive, clean rust and dirt from shoe contact surfaces on backing plate.
5. Check adjuster screw operation. If satisfactory, lightly lubricate adjusting screw and washer with suitable brake lube. If operation is unsatisfactory, replace.

INSTALLATION

1. Lightly lubricate backing plate shoe contact surfaces with suitable brake lubrication.
2. Remove brake drum hub grease seal and bearings, then clean and repack bearings and reinstall. Install new grease seal.
3. Assemble parking brake lever to trailing shoe, then install spring washer and retaining clip. Using suitable pliers, crimp retaining clip until securely fastened.
4. Attach parking brake cable to parking brake lever.
5. Assemble lower retracting spring to leading and trailing shoe assemblies, then spread lower part of shoes and install on backing plate.
6. Using suitable tool, install hold-down springs.
7. Tighten adjuster assembly, then back off 1/2 turn. Install adjuster assembly between leading shoe slot and trailing shoe/parking brake lever slot. The adjuster socket end slot must fit into trailing shoe/parking brake lever. **Adjuster assemblies are stamped R (right) and L (left). To ensure proper adjuster operation, they must be installed on their respective sides. The letter must be installed in the upright position, facing wheel cylinder to ensure the deeper of the two slots in the adjuster socket fits in the parking brake lever.**
8. Install adjuster lever in the parking brake lever groove and into the adjuster socket slot.
9. Using suitable brake spring pliers, install adjusting screw retracting spring from leading shoe slot to adjuster lever notch.
10. Install brake drum. Refer to individual car chapters for wheel bearing adjustment procedure.
11. Install tire and wheel assembly.
12. If any hydraulic connections have been opened, bleed brake system.
13. Adjust parking brake. Refer to individual car chapters for procedure.
14. Inspect all hydraulic lines and connection for leakage, and repair as necessary.
15. Check master cylinder fluid level and replenish as necessary.
16. Check brake pedal for proper feel and return.
17. Lower vehicle and road test. **Do not severely apply brakes immediately after installation of new brake linings or permanent damage may occur to linings, and/or brake drums may become scored. Brakes must be used moderately during first several hundred miles of operation to ensure proper burnishing of linings.**

Type 5

INDEX

Page No.

REMOVAL

1. Raise and support rear of vehicle, then remove tire and wheel assembly.
2. Remove brake drum. If brake lining is dragging on brake drum, back off brake adjustment. Refer to individual car chapters for procedures.
3. Using suitable tool, remove shoe hold-down springs and pins, **Fig. 1.**
4. Lift brake shoes, springs and adjuster assembly off backing plate and wheel cylinder assembly, being careful not to bend adjusting lever.
5. Remove parking brake cable from parking brake lever.
6. Remove retracting springs from lower brake shoe attachments and upper shoe to adjusting lever attachment points, then separate shoes and disengage adjuster mechanism.
7. Clean dirt from brake drum, backing plate and all other components. **Do not use compressed air or dry brush to clean brake parts. Many brake parts contain asbestos fibers which, if inhaled, can cause serious injury. Clean brake parts**

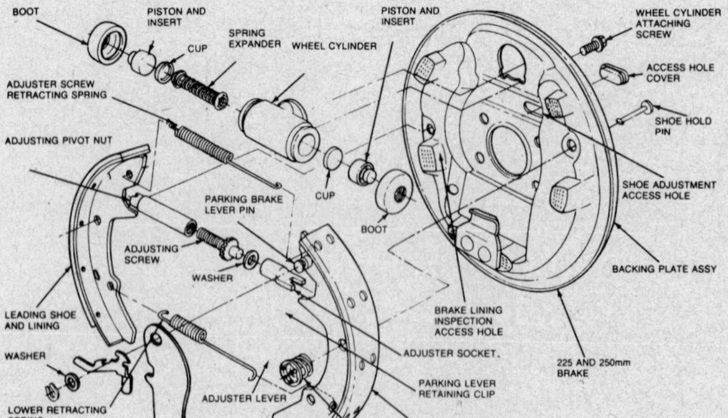

Fig. 1 Drum brake assembly. Type 5

with a water soaked rag or a suitable vacuum cleaner to minimize airborne dust.

INSPECTION

1. Inspect components for damage and unusual wear. Replace as necessary.
2. Inspect wheel cylinders. Boots which are torn, cut or heat damaged indicate need for wheel cylinder replacement. Peel back lower edge of boot. If fluid spills out, cup leakage is indicated and wheel cylinder should be replaced. **A small amount of fluid is always present and is considered normal, acting as a lubricant for the cylinder pistons.**
3. Inspect backing plate attaching bolts and ensure they are tight.
4. Using fine emery cloth or other suitable abrasive, clean rust and dirt from shoe contact surfaces on backing plate.
5. Check adjuster screw operation. If satisfactory, lightly lubricate adjusting screw and washer with suitable brake lube. If operation is unsatisfactory, replace.

INSTALLATION

1. Lightly lubricate backing plate shoe contact surfaces with suitable brake lubrication.
2. Apply a thin uniform coat of suitable brake lube to adjuster screw threads and socket end of adjusting screw.
3. Install stainless steel washer over socket end of adjusting screw and install socket, then turn adjusting screw fully into adjusting pivot nut and back off 1/2 turn.
4. Assemble parking brake lever to trailing shoe and lining assembly by installing spring washer and a new horseshoe retaining clip. Crimp the clip until it retains lever to shoe securely.
5. Attach parking brake cable to parking brake lever.
6. Attach lower shoe retracting spring to leading and trailing shoe assemblies and install on backing plate. It will be necessary to stretch retracting spring as shoes are installed downward over anchor plate to inside of shoe retaining plate.
7. Install adjuster screw assembly between leading shoe slot and the slot in the trailing shoe and parking brake lever. The adjuster socket end slot must fit into the trailing shoe and parking brake lever. **The adjuster socket blade is marked "R" or "L" for right and left side brake assemblies. The R or L adjuster blade must be installed with the letter R or L in the upright position (facing wheel cylinder) on the correct side to ensure that the deeper of two slots in adjuster sockets fits into the parking brake lever.**
8. Assemble adjuster lever in groove located in parking brake lever pin and into slot of adjuster socket that fits into trailing shoe web.
9. Attach upper retracting spring to leading shoe slot and, using suitable tool, stretch other end of spring into notch on adjuster lever. **If adjuster lever does not contact star wheel after installing spring, adjuster socket may be improperly installed.**
10. Install brake drum. Refer to individual car chapters for wheel bearing adjustment procedure.
11. Install tire and wheel assembly.
12. If any hydraulic connections have been opened, bleed brake system.
13. Adjust parking brake. Refer to individual car chapters for procedure.
14. Inspect all hydraulic lines and connections for leakage, repairing as necessary.
15. Check master cylinder fluid level and replenish as necessary.
16. Check brake pedal for proper feel and return.
17. **Lower vehicle and road test. Do not severely apply brakes immediately after installation of new brake linings or permanent damage may occur to linings and/ or brake drums may be come scored. Brakes must be used moderately during first several hundred miles of operation to ensure proper burnishing of linings.**

SPECIFICATIONS

Year	Model	Brake Drum Inside Dia. In.
FORD & MERCURY: Full Size Models		
1982-84	All ①	10.00
	All ② ③	11.03
1985-87	All ②	10.00
	All ①	11.03
FORD & MERCURY: Compact & Intermediate Models		
1982	Cougar & Granada	④
	Cougar XR-7 & Thunderbird	③
	Fairmont & Zephyr	9
1983	Cougar & Thunderbird	9
	Fairmont & Zephyr	9
	LTD & Marquis	④
1984	Cougar & Thunderbird	9.0
	LTD & Marquis	④
1985-87	Cougar & Thunderbird	⑤
	LTD & Marquis	⑥
FORD MUSTANG • MERCURY CAPRI		
1982-87	All	9.0
FORD ESCORT, EXP & TEMPO • MERCURY LN7, LYNX & TOPAZ		
1982-83	Escort & Lynx	⑦
	EXP & LN7	8
1984	Tempo & Topaz	8
	Escort, Lynx & EXP	⑦
1985	EXP, Tempo & Topaz	8
	Escort & Lynx	⑧
1986-87	Escort & Lynx	⑨
	Tempo & Topaz	8
FORD TAURUS • MERCURY SABLE		
1986-87	All	⑪
LINCOLN		
1982-83	All	10.00
1984	Continental & Mark VII	⑩
1985-86	Lincoln	10.00

①—Station wagon, police, taxi & trailer tow.
②—Sedan exc. police taxi & trailer tow.
③—With 6 cyl. engine, 9"; w/V8 engine, 10".
④—Exc. sta. wag., 9"; sta. wag., 10".
⑤—Standard brakes, 9"; heavy duty Brakes, 10".
⑥—Exc. Touring Sedan & sta. wag., 9"; Touring SEdan & sta. wag., 10".
⑦—Exc. 2 & 3 door hatchback, 8"; 2 & 3 door hatchback, 7".
⑧—3 door models less styled steel wheels, 7"; exc. 3 door models less styled steel wheels, 8".
⑨—2 door models less styled steel wheels, 7"; exc. 2 door models less styled steel wheels, 8".
⑩—With 4¾" bolt circle, 9.5"; with 5" bolt circle, 11".
⑪—Sedan, 8.85"; station wagon, 9.84".

AUTOMATIC TRANSMISSIONS/TRANSAXLES

TABLE OF CONTENTS

Ford A4LD Automatic Overdrive Transmission

INDEX

TRANSMISSION IDENTIFICATION

This transmission may be identified by the tag attached to the lower lefthand extension attaching bolt. The tag includes model prefix and suffix, a service identification number and a build data code, **Fig. 1.**

DESCRIPTION

The A4LD, **Fig. 2,** is a 4 speed overdrive automatic transmission with a lockup torque converter.

The hydraulic lockup and unlock function of the torque converter is electronically controlled by the EEC-IV system.

The EEC-IV system controls a converter clutch solenoid in the main control which hydraulically operates a piston/plate clutch in the converter to provide a solid drive transmission function.

The electronics also prevents the clutch application in engine modes where noise, vibration or harness concerns are most evident in solid drive transmissions.

TROUBLESHOOTING

CONVERTER CLUTCH DOES NOT ENGAGE

1. Converter clutch solenoid not energized electrically.
2. Wires to solenoid shorted or circuit open.
3. Transmission case connector not seated.
4. Open or shorted circuit inside solenoid.
5. Malfunctioning engine coolant temperature sensor.
6. Malfunctioning throttle position sensor.
7. Malfunctioning manifold absolute pressure (MAP) sensor.
8. Disconnected vacuum line disconnected from MAP sensor.
9. Malfunctioning brake switch.
10. Malfunctioning EEC-IV processor.
11. Converter clutch shuttle valve stuck in the unlock position.
12. Torque converter internal malfunction.

CONVERTER CLUTCH ALWAYS ENGAGED

1. Converter clutch shift valve stuck in lock position.
2. Converter clutch shuttle valve stuck in locked position.
3. Lockup piston in torque converter will not disengage.

CONVERTER CLUTCH WILL NOT DISENGAGE DURING COAST DOWN

1. Malfunctioning throttle position sensor.
2. Converter clutch solenoid sticking.

SLOW INITIAL ENGAGEMENT

1. Incorrect fluid level.
2. Damaged or incorrectly adjusted manual linkage.
3. Contaminated fluid.
4. Incorrect clutch and band application, or low main control pressure.

ROUGH INITIAL ENGAGEMENT IN FORWARD OR REVERSE

1. Incorrect fluid level.
2. High engine idle.
3. Automatic choke on.
4. Loose driveshaft U-joints.
5. Incorrect clutch or band application.
6. Sticking or dirty valve body.
7. Converter clutch not disengaging.

HARSH ENGAGEMENT W/ENGINE WARM

1. Incorrect fluid level.
2. Engine curb idle speed too high.
3. Loose or tight valve body bolts.
4. Sticking or dirty valve body valves.

NO/DELAYED FORWARD ENGAGEMENT

1. Incorrect fluid level.

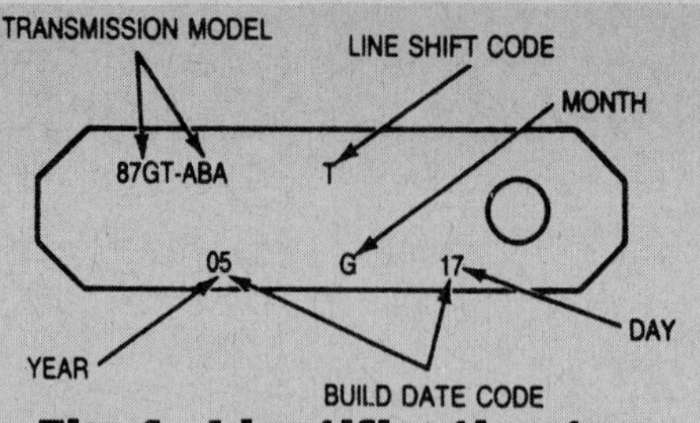

Fig. 1 Identification tag

2. Incorrect adjusted manual linkage.
3. Low main control pressure.
4. Damaged forward clutch assembly.
5. Loose or tight valve body bolts.
6. Sticking or dirty valve body valves.
7. Restricted transmission filter.
8. Leaking or damaged pump.

NO/DELAYED REVERSE ENGAGEMENT

1. Incorrect fluid level.
2. Incorrectly adjusted manual linkage.
3. Low main control pressure in reverse.
4. Damaged reverse clutch assembly.
5. Loose valve body bolts.
6. Sticking or dirt valve body valves.
7. Damaged pump.
8. Leaking reverse servo piston seal.

NO ENGAGEMENT OR DRIVE IN FORWARD

1. Incorrect fluid level.
2. Low main control pressure.
3. Mechanical damage.

NO ENGAGEMENT/DRIVE IN DRIVE

1. Incorrectly adjusted manual linkage.
2. Damaged rear one-way clutch.
3. Dirty or contaminated transmission fluid.

VEHICLE CREEPING IN NEUTRAL

1. Forward clutch failing to disengage.

NO ENGINE BRAKING IN MANUAL SECOND GEAR

1. Incorrectly adjusted intermediate band.
2. Incorrect band or clutch application.
3. Leaking intermediate servo.
4. Overdrive clutch, overdrive one-way clutch damaged.
5. Glazed band.

FORWARD ENGAGEMENT SLIPS/SHUDDERS/CHATTERS

1. Incorrect fluid level.
2. Incorrectly adjusted manual linkage.
3. Low main control pressure.
4. Loose or tight valve body bolts.
5. Sticking or dirty valve body valves.
6. Incorrectly seated or leaking forward clutch piston ball.
7. Worn or damaged forward clutch piston seals.
8. Overdrive one-way clutch damaged.
9. Rear one-way clutch damaged.

REVERSE SHUDDER/CHATTER/SLIPPING

1. Incorrect fluid level.
2. Low main control pressure in reverse.
3. Overdrive and/or rear one-way clutch damaged.
4. Overdrive and/or rear reverse high clutch drum bushing damaged.
5. Overdrive and/or rear reverse high clutch center support seal rings and ring grooves damaged.
6. Low reverse servo piston damaged.
7. Low reverse band out of adjustment.

NO 1–2 UPSHIFT

1. Incorrect fluid level.
2. Damaged kickdown system.
3. Incorrectly adjusted manual linkage.
4. Sticking governor valve.
5. Incorrectly adjusted intermediate band.
6. Vacuum leak to diaphragm unit.

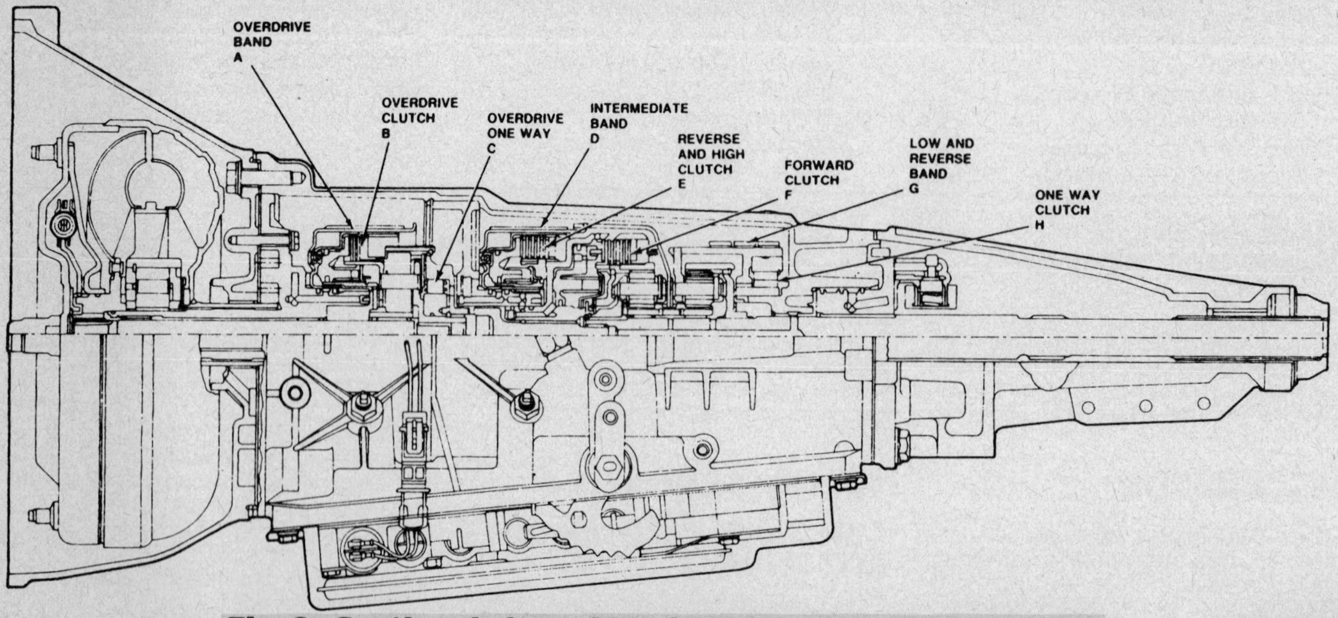

Fig. 2 Sectional view of Ford A4LD Automatic Overdrive Transmission

7. Loose or tight valve body bolts.
8. Sticking or dirty valve body valves.
9. Damaged intermediate band and/or servo.

ROUGH/HARSH/DELAYED 1–2 UPSHIFT

1. Incorrect fluid level.
2. Poor engine output.
3. Incorrectly adjusted kickdown linkage.
4. Incorrectly adjusted intermediate band.
5. Excessively high main control pressure.
6. Damaged intermediate servo.
7. Engine vacuum leak.
8. Loose or tight valve body bolts.
9. Vacuum leak to diaphragm unit.
10. Leaking or damaged vacuum diaphragm.

NO 2–3 UPSHIFT

1. Incorrect fluid level.
2. Damaged kickdown system.
3. Low main control pressure to reverse high clutch.
4. Loose or tight valve body bolts.
5. Sticking or dirty valve body valves.
6. Sticking governor valve.
7. Damaged intermediate servo or band.

HARSH/DELAYED 2–3 UPSHIFT

1. Poor engine output.
2. Engine vacuum leak.
3. Damaged kickdown system.
4. Damaged or worn intermediate servo.
5. Loose or tight valve body bolts.
6. Sticking or dirty valve body valves.
7. Damaged vacuum diaphragm.
8. Stuck throttle valve.

ERRATIC SHIFTS

1. Poor engine performance.
2. Damaged vacuum line.
3. Loose or tight valve body bolts.
4. Stuck governor valve.
5. Damaged output shaft collector body seal rings.

SHIFTS 1–3 IN OVERDRIVE OR DRIVE

1. Incorrectly adjusted intermediate band.
2. Damaged intermediate servo and/or internal leaks.
3. Incorrect band or clutch application.
4. Glazed band or drum.
5. Stuck governor valve.
6. Incorrectly adjusted kickdown linkage.

ENGINE OVERSPEEDS ON 2–3 SHIFT

1. Damaged kickdown system.
2. Incorrect band or clutch application.
3. Damaged or worn reverse high clutch and/or intermediate servo piston.
4. Damaged intermediate servo piston seals.
5. Dirty or sticking valve body.
6. Stuck throttle valve.
7. Damaged vacuum diaphragm.

ROUGH/SHUDDER 3–2 SHIFT AT CLOSED THROTTLE IN DRIVE

1. Incorrect engine idle.
2. Incorrect kickdown linkage adjustment.
3. Incorrect clutch or band application.
4. Incorrect governor operation.
5. Dirty or sticking valve body.

NO 3–4 UPSHIFT, MUSTANG ONLY

1. Damaged kickdown system.
2. Damaged vacuum line.
3. Damaged vacuum diaphragm.
4. Sticking throttle valve.
5. Damaged overdrive servo.
6. Glazed overdrive band.
7. Dirty of sticking valve body.

NO 3–4 OR 4–3 SHIFT, THUNDERBIRD ONLY

1. 3-4 solenoid is not being energized.
2. Dirty or sticking solenoid valve.
3. 3-4 shift valve stuck.

SLIPPING 4TH GEAR

1. Overdrive servo damaged or leaking.
2. Glazed overdrive band or drum.

ENGINE STALL SPEEDS EXCEEDED IN OVERDRIVE, DRIVE OR REVERSE

1. Faulty vacuum system.
2. Low main control pressure.

ENGINE STALL SPEED EXCEEDED IN REVERSE

1. Low/reverse servo/band damaged.
2. Reverse and high clutch damaged.

ENGINE STALL SPEED EXCEEDED IN OVERDRIVE OR DRIVE

1. Overdrive one-way clutch or rear one-way clutch damaged.

1–2 UPSHIFT IS ABOVE 40 MPH AT MODERATE ACCELERATION

1. Faulty vacuum system.
2. Faulty main control pressure.
3. Worn or damaged governor.
4. Dirty or sticking valve body.

KICKDOWN SHIFT SPEEDS TOO EARLY

1. Kickdown system damaged.
2. Faulty main control pressure.
3. Damaged or worn governor.

NO KICKDOWN INTO 2ND GEAR BETWEEN 40–60 MPH IN OVERDRIVE OR DRIVE

1. Damaged kickdown system.
2. Faulty main control pressure.
3. Dirty or sticking valve body.

NO SHIFT INTO 2ND GEAR W/ACCELERATOR 3/4 DEPRESSED AT 25 MPH IN OVERDRIVE OR DRIVE

1. Faulty main control pressure.
2. Damaged or worn governor.
3. Dirty or sticking valve body.

NO FORCED DOWNSHIFTS

1. Damaged kickdown cable.
2. Damaged internal kickdown linkage.
3. Incorrect clutch or band application.
4. Dirty or sticking governor.
5. Dirty or sticking valve body.

ENGINE OVERSPEEDS ON 3–2 DOWNSHIFT

1. Incorrectly adjusted linkage.
2. Incorrectly adjusted intermediate band.
3. Damaged or worn intermediate servo.
4. Glazed band or drum.
5. Dirty or sticking valve body.

SHIFT EFFORT HIGH

1. Manual shaft linkage damaged.
2. Inner manual lever nut loose.
3. Manual retainer pin damaged.

TRANSMISSION OVERHEATS

1. Incorrect fluid level.
2. Poor engine output.
3. Restriction in cooler or lines.
4. Seized converter one-way clutch.
5. Dirty or sticking valve body.

LEAKING TRANSMISSION

1. Restricted case breather vent.
2. Leaking gaskets and seals.

POOR VEHICLE ACCELERATION

1. Poor engine output.
2. Torque converter one-way clutch locked.

NOISY TRANSMISSION/VALVE RESONANCE

1. Incorrectly fluid level.
2. Incorrectly adjusted linkage.
3. Incorrect band or clutch application.
4. Cooler lines grounding.
5. Dirty or sticking valve body.
6. Internal leakage or pump cavitation.

IN-VEHICLE ADJUSTMENTS

MANUAL LINKAGE, ADJUST

Thunderbird Turbo Coupe

1. Position transmission selector lever in Overdrive against stop. **When adjusting hold lever against overdrive stop.**
2. Raise and support vehicle, then loosen manual lever shift cable attaching nut, **Fig. 3.**
3. Move transmission manual lever to

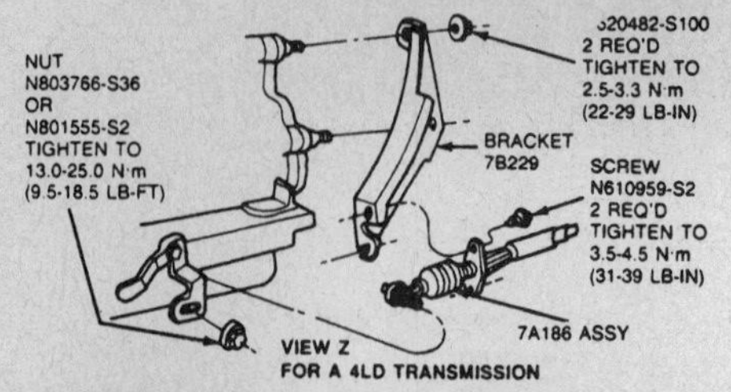

Fig. 3 Manual linkage, adjust. Thunderbird Turbo Coupe models

the Overdrive position, third detent position from the full counterclockwise position.

4. With transmission selector and manual levers in the Overdrive position, tighten attaching nut to 9.5-18.5 ft. lbs.
5. Check transmission operation.

Mustang W/4-140 Engine

1. Position transmission selector lever into Overdrive. Ensure that the lever is held tightly against rearward overdrive stop.
2. Raise and support vehicle, then loosen manual lever shift rod retaining nut, **Fig. 4.**
3. Move transmission manual lever to the Overdrive position, third detent position from the full counterclockwise position.
4. With transmission selector lever and manual lever in the Overdrive position, tighten attaching nut to 10-20 ft. lbs.
5. Check transmission operation.

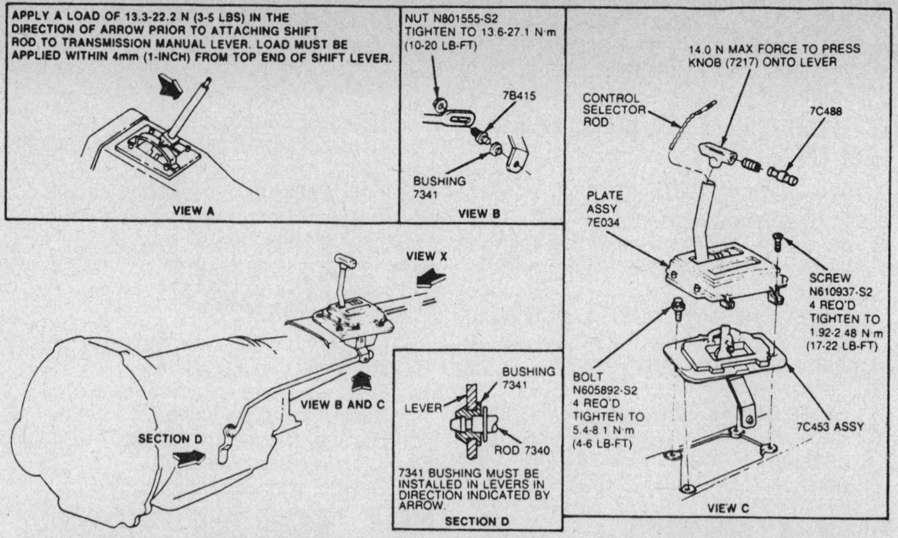

Fig. 4 Manual linkage, adjust. Mustang w/4-140 engine

IN-VEHICLE REPAIRS

SHIFT LINKAGE GROMMET, REPLACE

1. Place a suitable tool, between lever and rod, **Fig. 5.**
2. Position stop pin against end of rod and force rod out of grommet.
3. Remove grommet from the lever by cutting off the large shoulder with a sharp knife.
4. Adjust the stop to 1/2 and coat the outside of the grommet with lubricant. Place a new grommet on the stop pin and force it into the lever hole.
5. Turn grommet several times to ensure it is properly seated.
6. Squeeze rod into bushing until the stop washer seats against the grommet.

CONTROL VALVE BODY, REPLACE

1. Raise and support vehicle.
2. Loosen pan attaching bolts, then drain fluid from transmission.
3. Remove attaching bolts, pan and gasket.
4. Remove filter screen and O-ring.
5. Remove low/reverse servo cover, piston, spring and gasket.
6. Disconnect electrical connectors from converter clutch solenoid on Mustang models and two additional electrical connectors at 3-4 shift solenoid on Thunderbird models.
7. Remove bolts from control valve body.
8. Reverse procedure to install.

LOW/REVERSE SERVO

1. Raise and support vehicle.
2. Loosen pan attaching bolts and allow transmission fluid to drain.
3. Remove all pan attaching bolts except two bolts at the front to allow fluid to drain further.
4. Remove oil filter screen and gasket.
5. Remove retaining screws, low/reverse servo cover, piston and spring and gasket.
6. Reverse procedure to install.

EXTENSION HOUSING, REPLACE

1. Raise and support vehicle.
2. Remove driveshaft.
3. Support transmission with a suitable jack.
4. Disconnect speedometer cable from extension housing.
5. Remove rear support to crossmember attaching bolts or nuts.
6. Raise transmission slightly and remove rear support from extension housing.
7. Loosen extension housing attaching bolt and allow transmission fluid to drain.
8. Remove extension housing attaching bolts.

GOVERNOR, REPLACE

1. Remove extension housing.
2. Remove governor body to coil collector body attaching bolts.
3. Remove governor body, valve, spring and weight from collector body.
4. Reverse procedure to install.

TRANSMISSION REPLACE

1. Disconnect battery ground cable.
2. Raise and support vehicle.
3. Drain fluid from transmission.
4. Remove converter access cover and adapter plate attaching bolts from lower lefthand side of converter housing.
5. Rotate crankshaft pulley clockwise (as viewed from the front) to gain access to each attaching bolt, then remove flywheel to converter attaching bolts. **On belt driven overhead cam engines, never rotate the pulley in a counterclockwise direction (as view from the front).**
6. Place an alignment mark on driveshaft and rear axle flange, then remove driveshaft. **Do not use a sharp tool to place alignment mark.**
7. Disconnect and remove speedometer sensor from extension housing.
8. Disconnect shift rod from transmission on Mustang models or shift cable from transmission on Thunderbird models.
9. Remove starter motor.
10. Label, then disconnect all electrical connectors, vacuum lines and fluid cooler lines from transmission.
11. Position a suitable jack under transmission.
12. Remove crossmember to frame side support attaching bolts. Remove crossmember insulator support and damper.
13. Lower jack carefully and slightly and allow transmission to hang.
14. Position a jack to front of engine. Raise engine to gain access to the two upper converter housing to engine attaching bolts.
15. Support transmission again, then remove lower converter housing to engine attaching bolts.
16. Remove transmission filler tube.
17. Remove two upper converter housing to engine attaching bolts. Move transmission rearward, disengaging it from the dowel pins. Disengage converter from flywheel.
18. Lower transmission from vehicle.
19. Reverse procedure to install. **Proper installation of the converter re-**

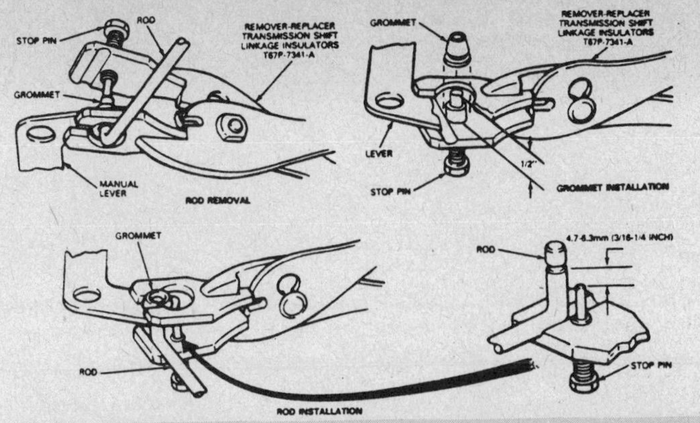

Fig. 5 Shift linkage grommet removal & installation

quires full engagement of the converter hub in the pump gear. To accomplish this, the converter must be pushed and at the same time rotated through what feels like two "notches" or bumps. When completely seated, rotation of the converter will usually result in a clicking noise, caused by the converter surface touching the housing to case attaching bolts. This should not be a concern, but an indication of correct converter installation. The converter should rotate without binding. For reference a properly installed converter will have a pilot nose from face to converter housing outer face dimension of 7/16 inch minimum to 9/16 inch maximum.

Ford Automatic Overdrive Transmission

INDEX

TRANSMISSION IDENTIFICATION

This transmission may be identified by the tag attached to the upper right hand extension housing to transmission case bolt. The tag includes model prefix and suffix, a service identification number and a build date code, Fig. 1. The service identification number indicates changes in service details which affect interchangeability when the transmission model is not changed. For interpretation of this number the Ford Master Parts Catalog should be consulted.

DESCRIPTION

This unit is a 4 speed automatic transmission incorporating an integral overdrive

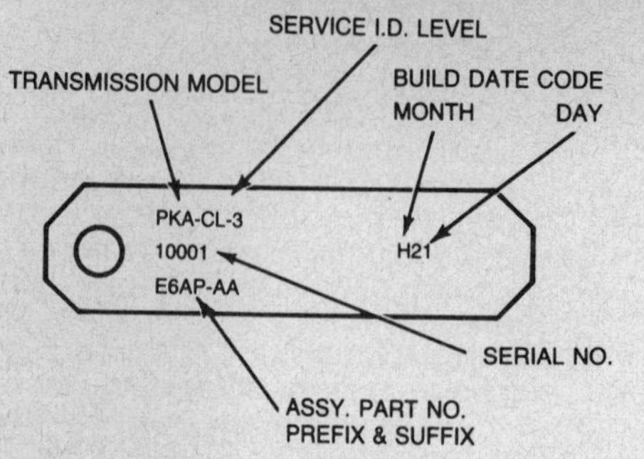

Fig. 1 Identification tag

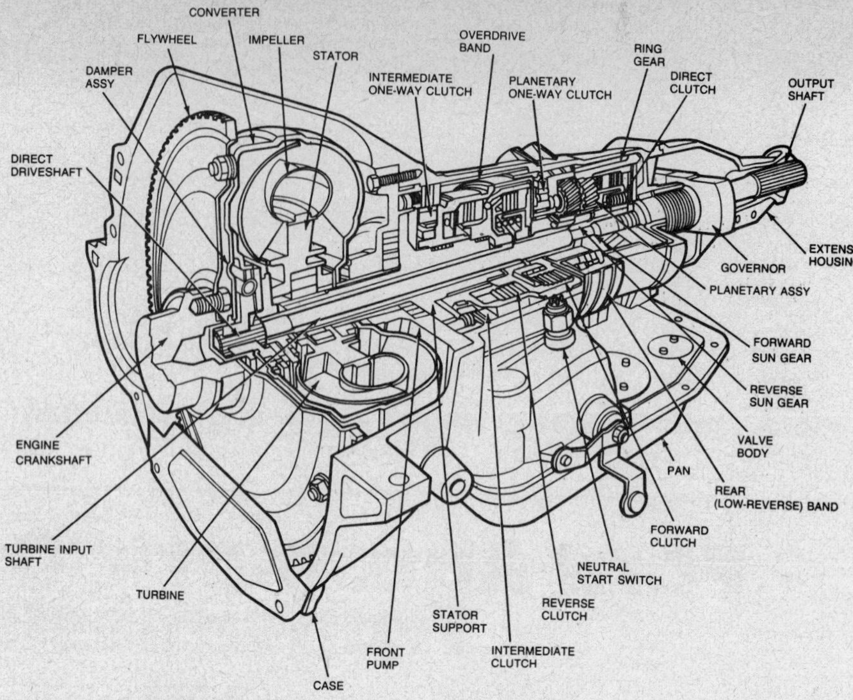

Fig. 2 Sectional view of Ford Automatic Overdrive Transmission

feature. With selector lever in 1 position, the transmission will start and remain in first gear until the selector lever is moved to another position. In 3 position, the transmission will automatically shift through 1-2-3 range, but will not engage overdrive. In D position, the transmission will automatically select the appropriate time to shift into overdrive (4th gear). The design of the transmission features a split torque path in third gear, where 40% of the engine torque is transmitted hydraulically through the torque converter and 60% is transmitted mechanically through solid connections (direct drive input shaft) to the driveshaft. When transmission is in overdrive (4th gear), 100% of engine torque is transmitted through the direct drive input shaft.

The transmission consists essentially of a torque converter assembly, compound planetary gear train and a hydraulic control system, **Fig. 2.** For gear control the transmission has four friction clutches, two one-way roller clutches and two bands. Overdrive is accomplished by the addition of a band to lock the reverse sun gear while driving the planet carrier. The torque converter operation is similar to other types of automatic transmission, but has an added damper assembly and input shaft for 3rd gear and overdrive. The direct drive input shaft couples the engine directly to the direct clutch. This shaft is driven by the torque converter cover through the damper assembly which cushions engine shock to the transmission.

TROUBLESHOOTING

ROUGH INITIAL ENGAGEMENT IN FORWARD OR REVERSE

1. Improper fluid level.
2. High engine idle.
3. Loose driveshaft, engine mounts or U-joints.
4. Sticking or dirty valve body.
5. Improper clutch or band application, or low oil control pressure.
6. Incorrectly adjusted automatic choke.

SLOW INITIAL ENGAGEMENT

1. Improper fluid level.
2. Damaged or improperly adjusted linkage.
3. Contaminated fluid.
4. Low main control pressure or improper clutch and band application.

HARSH ENGAGEMENTS W/WARM ENGINE

1. Improper fluid level.
2. Damaged or improperly adjusted linkage.
3. High engine idle.
4. Sticking or dirty valve body.
5. Throttle linkage return spring disconnected.
6. Valve body bolts improperly torqued.

NO OR DELAYED FORWARD ENGAGEMENT

1. Improper fluid level.
2. Damaged or improperly adjusted linkage.
3. Low main control pressure.
4. Forward clutch stator support seal rings Nos. 3 and/or 4 leaking.
5. Burnt and/or damaged forward clutch assembly.
6. Forward clutch cylinder check ball and/or piston seal rings leaking.
7. Valve body bolts improperly torqued.
8. Valve body dirty or valves sticking.
9. Clogged transmission filter.
10. Damaged or leaking pump.

NO OR DELAYED REVERSE ENGAGEMENT

1. Improper fluid level.
2. Damaged or improperly adjusted linkage.
3. Low main control pressure.
4. Leaking high reverse clutch or reverse clutch stator support seal rings Nos. 1 and/or 2.
5. Burnt or worn reverse clutch assembly.
6. Leaking reverse clutch piston check ball and/or piston seal rings.
7. Valve body bolts improperly torqued.
8. Valve body dirty or valves sticking.
9. Clogged transmission filter.
10. Damaged pump.

NO OR DELAYED REVERSE ENGAGEMENT AND/OR NO ENGINE BRAKING IN MANUAL LOW

1. Improper fluid level.
2. Damaged or improperly adjusted linkage.
3. Leaking low reverse servo piston seal.
4. Burnt or worn low reverse servo piston.
5. Damaged planetary low one-way clutch.
6. Endplay clearance too tight.

NO ENGINE BRAKING IN MANUAL 2ND

1. Improper fluid level.
2. Damaged or improperly adjusted linkage.
3. Improper clutch or band application.
4. Improper control system pressure.
5. Leaking intermediate servo.
6. Damaged intermediate one-way clutch.

FORWARD ENGAGEMENT SLIPS, SHUDDERS AND/OR CHATTERS

1. Improper fluid level.
2. Incorrectly adjusted or damaged linkage.
3. Low main control pressure.
4. Valve body bolts improperly torqued.
5. Valve body dirty or valves sticking.
6. Forward clutch piston check ball leaking and/or not seating.
7. Cut and/or worn forward clutch piston seal.

8. Leaking forward clutch stator support seal rings Nos. 3 and 4.
9. Damaged low one-way clutch (planetary).

REVERSE SHUDDERS, CHATTERS AND/OR SLIPS

1. Improper fluid level.
2. Low main control pressure in reverse.
3. Leaking low reverse servo.
4. Damaged planetary low one-way clutch.
5. Damaged reverse clutch drum bushing.
6. Worn or damaged reverse clutch stator support seal rings or grooves.
7. Cut and/or worn reverse clutch piston.
8. Damaged reverse band.
9. Loosen driveshaft, engine mounts or U-joints.

NO DRIVE, SLIPS OR CHATTERS IN 1ST GEAR IN DRIVE OR OVERDRIVE

1. Damaged planetary low one-way clutch.

NO DRIVE, SLIPS OR CHATTERS IN 2ND GEAR

1. Worn or damaged friction clutch or one-way clutch.
2. Intermediate clutch piston belled hole clogged or not positioned at 12 o'clock.
3. Control pressure or improper band or clutch application.
4. Internal leakage.
5. Dirty valve body or sticking valves.

INITIAL DRIVE IN 2ND OR 3RD

1. Improper fluid level.
2. Damaged or improperly adjusted linkage.
3. Oil pressure control system or improper clutch and/or band application.
4. Intermediate clutch pack clearance too tight.
5. Damaged, worn or sticking governor.
6. Sticking or dirty valve body.
7. Valve body bolts too loose.
8. Cross leaks between valve body and case mating surface.

IMPROPER SHIFT POINTS

1. Improper fluid level.
2. Damaged or improperly adjusted linkage.
3. Improper speedometer gear installed.
4. Improper clutch or band application.
5. Improper control system pressure.
6. Damaged or worn governor.
7. Sticking or dirty valve body.

HARSH, DELAYED OR NO UPSHIFTS

1. Improper fluid level.
2. Damaged or improperly adjusted linkage.
3. Throttle return spring disconnected.
4. Damaged or incorrectly adjusted manual linkage.
5. Governor sticking.
6. High main control pressure.
7. Valve body bolts improperly torqued.
8. Sticking or dirty valve body.

MUSHY AND/OR EARLY UPSHIFTS OR UPSHIFT PILEUP

1. Improper fluid level.
2. Damaged or improperly adjusted linkage.
3. Low main control pressure.
4. Sticking throttle control valve or valve body.
5. Sticking governor valve.
6. Valve body bolts improperly torqued.

NO 1–2 UPSHIFTS

1. Improper fluid level.
2. Damaged or improperly adjusted linkage.
3. Low main control pressure to intermediate friction clutch.
4. Sticking, leaking or bent diaphragm unit.
5. Sticking or dirty valve body.
6. Burnt intermediate clutch, band or servo.
7. Valve body bolts improperly torqued.

ROUGH, HARSH AND/OR DELAYED 1–2 UPSHIFT

1. Improper fluid level.
2. Poor engine performance.
3. Incorrectly adjusted or damaged throttle linkage.
4. Main control pressure too high.
5. Sticking governor valve.
6. Valve body bolts improperly torqued.
7. Valve body dirty or valves sticking.

MUSHY, EARLY, SOFT AND/OR SLIPPING 1–2 UPSHIFT

1. Improper fluid level.
2. Improperly tuned engine.
3. Damaged or improperly adjusted linkage.
4. Incorrect main control pressure.
5. Sticking governor valve.
6. Valve body bolts improperly torqued.
7. Valve body dirty or valves sticking.
8. Worn or burnt intermediate friction clutch.
9. Damaged intermediate servo.

NO 2–3 UPSHIFTS

1. Improper fluid level.
2. Low main control pressure to direct clutch.
3. Valve body bolts improperly torqued.
4. Sticking or dirty valve body.
5. Burnt or worn direct or reverse-high clutch assembly.
6. Broken weld on converter damper hub.

HARSH AND/OR DELAYED 2–3 UPSHIFT

1. Incorrect engine performance.
2. Incorrectly adjusted, sticking or damaged throttle linkage.
3. Plugged or missing 2-3 accumulator apply passage.
4. Cut or worn 2-3 accumulator piston seals.
5. Damaged 2-3 accumulator.
6. Valve body bolts improperly torqued.
7. Valve body dirty.
8. Sticking 2-3 capacity modulator valve.
9. Bent, sticking or leaking vacuum diaphragm or TV control rod.

SOFT, EARLY AND/OR MUSHY 2–3 UPSHIFT

1. Improper fluid level.
2. Improperly tuned engine.
3. Damaged or improperly adjusted linkage.
4. Valve body bolts improperly torqued.
5. Burnt or worn direct clutch assembly or reverse/high clutch.
6. Damaged accumulator.
7. Dirty or sticking valve body.
8. Bent, sticking or leaking vacuum diaphragm or TV control rod.

NO 3–4 UPSHIFTS

1. Low fluid level.
2. Damaged or improperly adjusted linkage.
3. Direct clutch circuit leakage.
4. Sticking or dirty valve body.
5. Distorted main control gasket.
6. Distorted case.
7. Leaking governor.

HARSH AND/OR DELAYED 3–4 UPSHIFT

1. Improper fluid level.
2. Damaged or improperly adjusted linkage.
3. Throttle return spring disconnected.
4. Valve body bolts improperly torqued.
5. Valve body dirty or valves sticking.
6. Incorrect engine performance.
7. Cut or worn 3-4 accumulator piston seals.
8. Clogged 3-4 accumulator piston drain passage.

SLIPPING IN 4TH GEAR

1. Overdrive circuit leakage or blocked passage.
2. Overdrive servo piston and/or band not applying.
3. Overdrive band incorrectly located.
4. Converter damper plate and hub damaged.
5. Distorted direct driveshaft splines.

ERRATIC SHIFTS

1. Improper fluid level.
2. Improperly tuned engine.
3. Damaged or improperly adjusted linkage.
4. Dirty or sticking valve body.
5. Sticking governor valve.
6. Damaged output shaft collector body seal rings.
7. Valve body bolts improperly torqued.

SHIFTS 1–3 IN OVERDRIVE

1. Improper fluid level.
2. Damaged or burnt intermediate friction clutch.
3. Damaged intermediate one-way clutch.
4. Improper control system pressure or clutch application.
5. Sticking or dirty valve body.

6. Sticking governor valve.

ENGINE OVERSPEEDS ON 2–3 SHIFT

1. Improper fluid level.
2. Damaged or improperly adjusted linkage.
3. Improper control system pressure or clutch application.
4. Damaged or worn high clutch or intermediate servo.
5. Sticking or dirty valve body.
6. Broken converter damper hub.
7. Cut or leaking intermediate servo piston seals.

SHIFT HUNTING 3–4 OR 4–3

1. Improperly tuned engine.
2. Damaged or improperly adjusted linkage.
3. Worn or damaged EGR solenoid.

NO FORCED DOWNSHIFTS

1. Improper fluid level.
2. Damaged or improperly adjusted linkage.
3. Improper control system pressure or clutch application.
4. Sticking or dirty valve body.
5. Sticking or dirty governor.

ROUGH SHUTTER 3–1 SHIFT AT CLOSED THROTTLE IN OVERDRIVE

1. Improper fluid level.
2. Improperly tuned engine.
3. Damaged or improperly adjusted linkage.
4. Improper control system pressure or clutch application.
5. Improper governor operation.
6. Sticking or dirty valve body.

ROUGH OR MUSHY 4–2 OR 3–1 SHIFT

1. Improper fluid level.
2. Improperly tuned engine.
3. Damaged or improperly adjusted linkage.
4. Improper application of intermediate friction and one-way clutch.
5. Sticking or dirty valve body.

HIGH SHIFT EFFORT

1. Damaged or improperly adjusted linkage.
2. Loose manual lever nut.
3. Damaged manual lever retainer pin.

TRANSMISSION OVERHEATS

1. Improper fluid level.
2. Improperly tuned engine.
3. Improper control system pressure or clutch application.
4. Restricted cooler or lines.
5. Seized converter one-way clutch.
6. Sticking or dirty valve body.

CLUNK OR SQUAWK IN 1–2 OR 2–3

1. Blocked intermediate bleed hole or bleed hole not at 12 o'clock position.
2. Incorrectly aligned anti-clunk spring.

HARSH DOWNSHIFT COASTING CLUNK

1. Improperly seated anti-clunk spring.
2. Damaged or improperly adjusted linkage.

TRANSMISSION LEAKS

1. Case breather vent.
2. Leakage at gaskets or seals.

POOR VEHICLE ACCELERATION

1. Improperly tuned engine.
2. Seized torque converter one-way clutch.

SLIPPING SHIFT FOLLOWED BY SUDDEN ENGAGEMENT

1. Throttle valve linkage set too short.

TRANSMISSION NOISY (VALVE RESONANCE)

1. Improper fluid level.
2. Damaged or improperly adjusted linkage.
3. Improper control system pressure or clutch application.
4. Cooler lines contacting frame, floor pan or other components.
5. Sticking or dirty valve body.
6. Internal leakage or pump cavitation.

TRANSMISSION NOISY (OTHER THAN VALVE RESONANCE)

1. Improper fluid level.
2. Damaged or improperly adjusted linkage.
3. Contaminated fluid.
4. Loose converter to flywheel housing bolts or nuts.
5. Loose or worn speedometer driven gear.
6. Damaged or worn extension housing bushing seal or driveshaft.
7. Damaged or worn front or rear planetary and/or one-way clutch.

HARSH COASTING DOWNSHIFT CLUNK

1. Improperly seated anti-clunk spring.
2. Incorrectly adjusted throttle linkage.
3. Sticking throttle linkage return spring.

INITIAL ENGAGEMENT CLUNK W/ENGINE WARM

1. Engine idle speed incorrect.
2. Incorrectly adjusted throttle linkage.
3. Worn, damaged or loose universal joints, slip yoke, rear axle or suspension.
4. Excessive transmission endplay.

VEHICLE WILL NOT START

1. Incorrectly adjusted ignition switch.
2. Defective ignition switch.
3. Defective neutral start switch.

THROTTLE VALVE LINKAGE DIAGNOSIS

Refer to the following for TV linkage conditions and subsequent shift troubles.

TV CONTROL LINKAGE ADJUSTED TOO SHORT

1. Early or soft upshifts.
2. Harsh light throttle shift into and out of overdrive.
3. No forced downshift at proper speeds.

TV CONTROL LINKAGE ADJUSTED TOO LONG

1. Harsh idle engagement after engine warm up.
2. Clunking when throttle is released after heavy acceleration.
3. Harsh coasting downshifts out of overdrive.

INTERFERENCE PREVENTING RETURN OF TV CONTROL ROD

1. Delayed or harsh upshifts.
2. Harsh idle engagement.

BINDING GROMMETS PREVENTING TV LINKAGE RETURN

1. Delayed or harsh upshifts.
2. Harsh idle engagement.

TV CONTROL ROD DISCONNECTED

1. Delayed or harsh upshifts.
2. Harsh idle engagement.

CLAMPING BOLT ON TRUNNION AT LOWER END OF TV CONTROL ROD LOOSE

1. Delayed or harsh upshifts.
2. Harsh idle engagement.

LINKAGE LEVER RETURN SPRING BROKEN OR DISCONNECTED

1. Delayed or harsh upshifts.
2. Harsh idle engagements.

MAINTENANCE

CHECKING OIL LEVEL

1. With transmission at operating temperature, park vehicle on level surface.
2. Operate engine at idle speed with parking brake applied and move selector lever through each detent position. Return selector lever to Park.
3. With engine idling, remove dipstick and check fluid level. Fluid level should be between arrows on dipstick.
4. Add fluid as necessary to bring fluid to proper level. Use only fluid meeting Ford Qualification No. M2C-138-CJ or Dexron II.

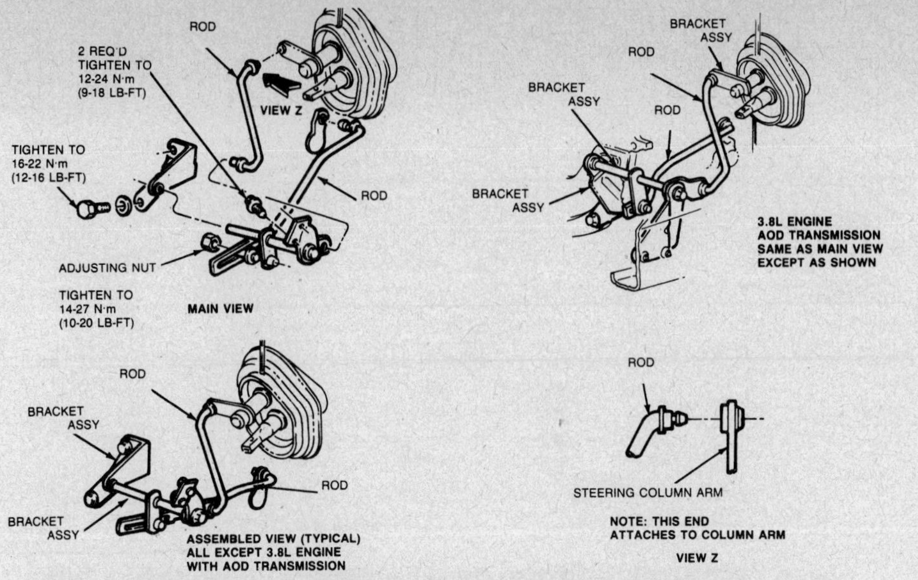

Fig. 3 Manual linkage. 1982 Cougar, XR-7, 1983–87 Cougar, LTD & Marquis

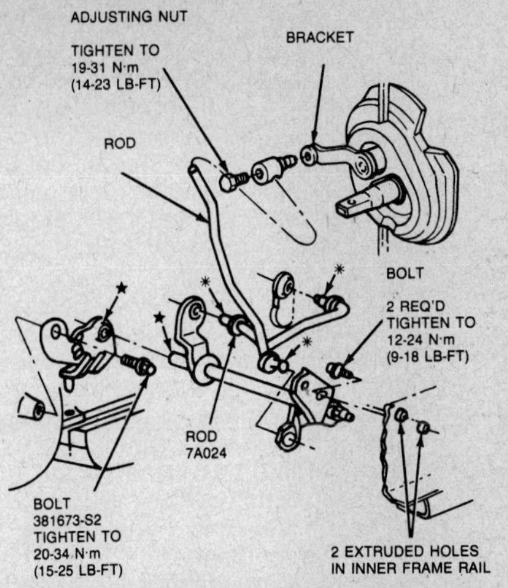

∗ LUBRICATE WITH ESE-M2C96-E ENGINE OIL
★ LUBRICATE ID OF BEARING LIBERALLY WITH ESA-MIC75-B

Fig. 5 Manual linkage. 1982–87 Ford, Lincoln Town Car, Mark VI & Mercury

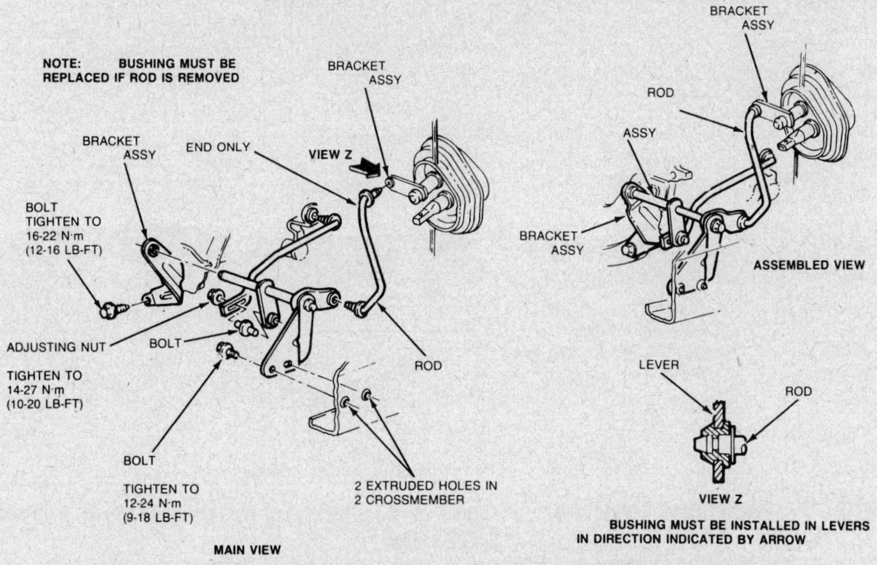

Fig. 4 Manual linkage. 1982–87 Continental & Thunderbird, 1983–87 Cougar

IN-VEHICLE ADJUSTMENTS

MANUAL LINKAGE, ADJUST

Column Shift

1. Place selector lever in overdrive position, tight against overdrive stop, and hang 8 lb. weight from selector lever to ensure lever remains in overdrive.
2. Raise and support vehicle as necessary and loosen adjusting bolt or nut, **Figs. 3 through 5.**
3. Shift transmission into overdrive, ensure that selector lever has not moved from overdrive and tighten adjusting bolt or nut, then check transmission operation in all selector positions.

Floor Shift

1. Place transmission selector lever in overdrive position.
2. Raise and support vehicle and loosen manual lever shift rod retaining nut, **Figs. 6 through 9.**
3. Move transmission manual lever to overdrive position and torque attaching nut to 10-15 ft. lbs.
4. Check transmission operation in all selector lever positions.

THROTTLE VALVE LINKAGE, ADJUST

On 1986-87 models equipped with V8-302 engine, adjustments can be made only by using throttle valve pressure as described further on.

At Transmission, 1982–83 Models

1. Set engine curb idle speed, with and without throttle solenoid position, to specification.
2. With engine off, de-cam fast idle cam on carburetor so that throttle lever is against idle stop or throttle solenoid positioner stop, then place shift lever in Neutral and apply parking brake.
3. Set linkage lever adjustment screw at approximately mid-range.
4. If a new TV control rod assembly is being installed, connect rod to linkage lever at carburetor.
5. Raise and support vehicle.
6. Loosen bolt on sliding trunnion block on TV control rod assembly, removing any corrosion from control rod and freeing up trunnion block so that it slides freely on control rod.
7. Push up on lower end of control rod to ensure that linkage lever at carburetor is firmly against throttle lever, then release force on rod and ensure rod stays up.
8. Push TV control lever on transmission up against its internal stop with a force of approximately 5 lbs. and tighten bolt on trunnion block. Do not relax force on lever until bolt is tightened.
9. Lower vehicle and ensure that throttle lever is still against stop and, if not, repeat steps 2 through 9.

At Transmission, 1984–87 Models

1. On vehicles without idle speed control (ISC), proceed as follows:
   a. Check and adjust curb idle speed to specifications with and without throttle solenoid positioner (anti-dieseling solenoid energized, if equipped).
   b. Shut off engine and remove air cleaner.
   c. De-cam fast idle cam on carburetor so that throttle lever is against

idle stop or throttle solenoid positioner stop.

2. On vehicles w/idle speed control, proceed as follows:
   a. Locate self test connector and self test input connector in engine compartment. These connectors are generally located in the area of the righthand fender apron, adjacent to each other.
   b. Connect a jumper wire between self test input connector and signal return ground on self test connector, **Fig. 10.**
   c. Turn ignition key to RUN position without starting engine and wait approximately 10 seconds for ISC plunger to fully retract.
   d. Shut off key and remove jumper wire and air cleaner.
3. On all vehicles, place shift lever in Neutral and apply parking brake.
4. Perform steps 3 through 9 as described for 1982-83 models.

At Carburetor Or Throttle Body

1. Position throttle lever at idle stop, place shift lever in Neutral and apply parking brake (engine off).
2. Turn linkage lever adjusting screw counterclockwise until end of screw is flush with throttle lever face.
3. Turn adjusting screw clockwise to provide .005 inch clearance between end of screw and throttle lever. Continue turning adjusting screw an additional three turns. If screw travel is limited, one turn is acceptable.
4. If adjusting screw cannot be turned at least one turn, refer to "At Transmission" procedure. **Whenever idle speed is adjusted by more than 50 RPM, the adjustment screw on the linkage lever at the carburetor should also be adjusted as listed in the "Idle Speed/Throttle Valve Linkage Adjustment Chart", Fig. 11. If idle speed was adjusted, ensure that .005 inch clearance exists between linkage lever adjusting screw and the throttle lever. The throttle lever should be at the idle stop and the shift lever in Neutral.**

THROTTLE VALVE PRESSURE ADJUSTMENT

Vehicles W/TV Rod Linkage

1. Check curb idle speed, adjusting as necessary. Ensure curb idle speed is set to specification with and without throttle solenoid positioner (anti-diesel solenoid) energized, if equipped.
2. Using adapter fitting D80L-77001-A or equivalent, attach suitable pressure gauge to TV port on transmission, using enough flexible hose so that gauge can be read while operating engine.
3. Obtain TV control pressure gauge block No. D84P-70332-A or fabricate a block .390-.404 inch thick, **Fig. 12.**
4. Run engine until it reaches normal operating temperature and the throttle lever is off fast idle, or the idle speed

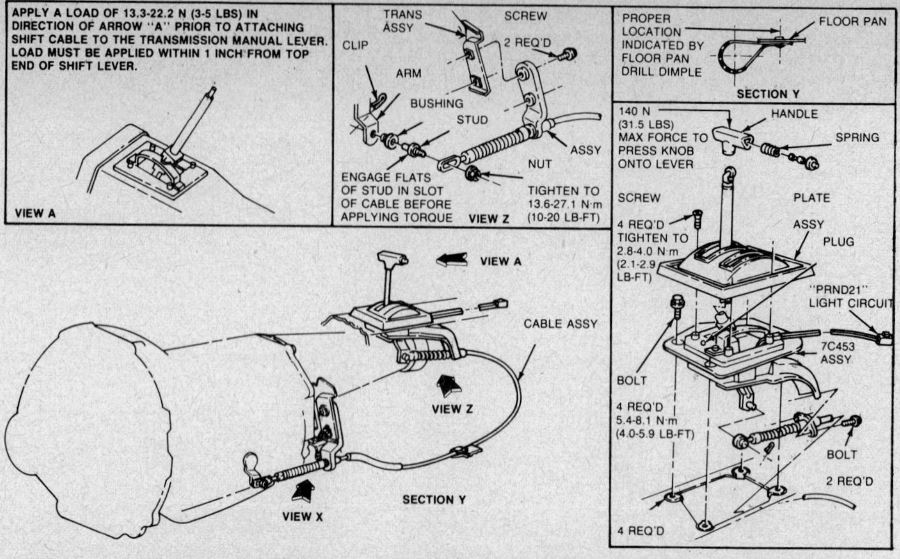

Fig. 6 Manual linkage. Capri & Mustang w/cable type linkage

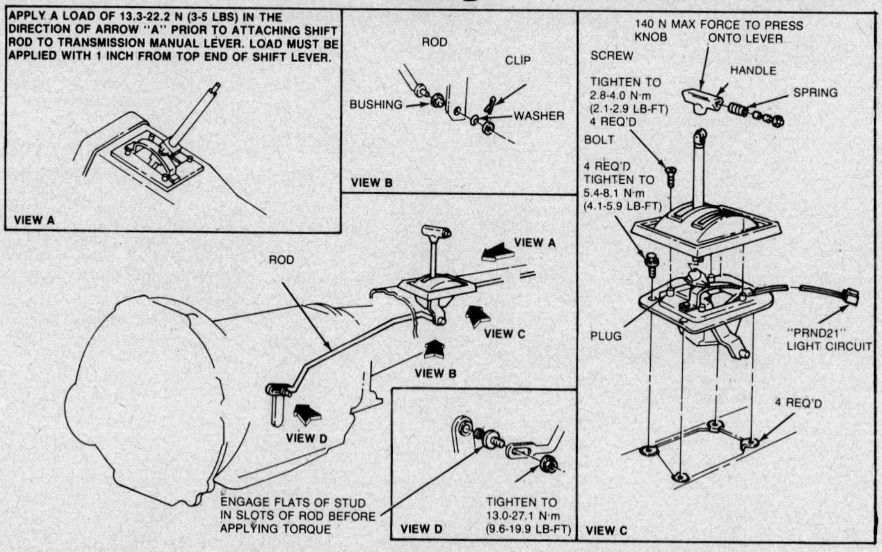

Fig. 7 Manual linkage. Capri & Mustang w/solid link type linkage

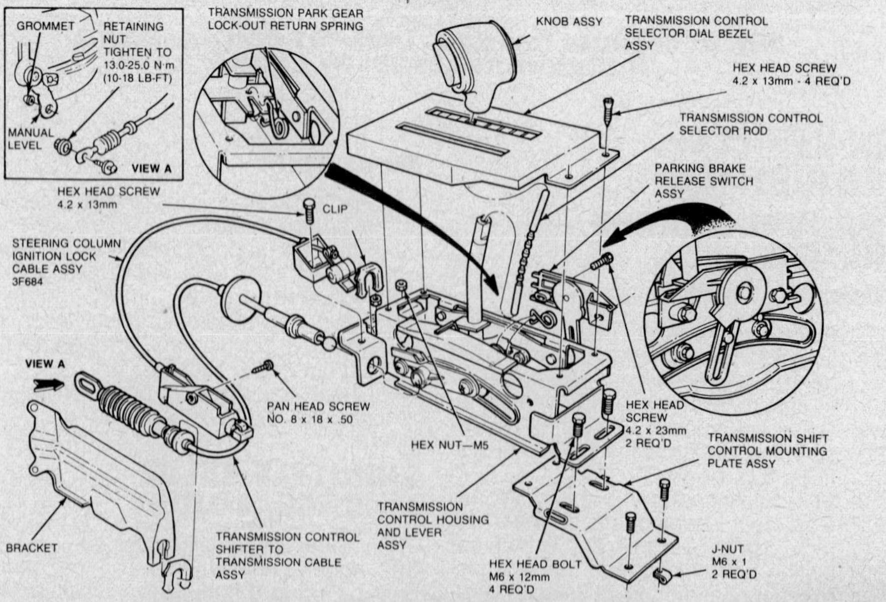

Fig. 8 Manual linkage. Mark VII

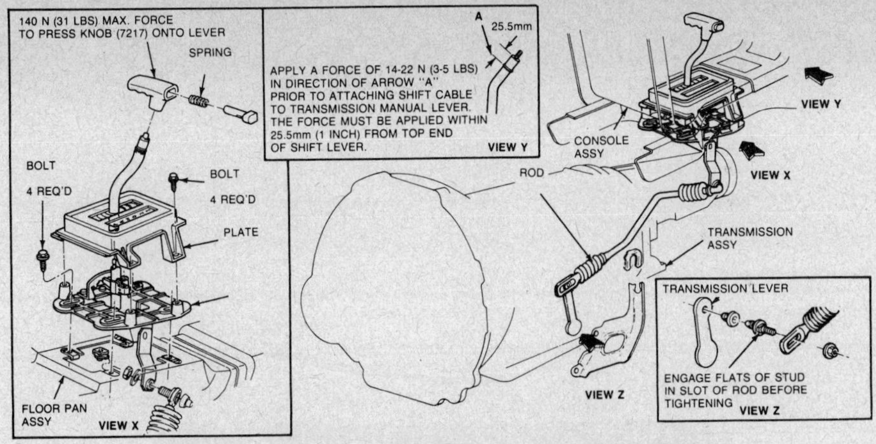

Fig. 9 Manual linkage. Thunderbird

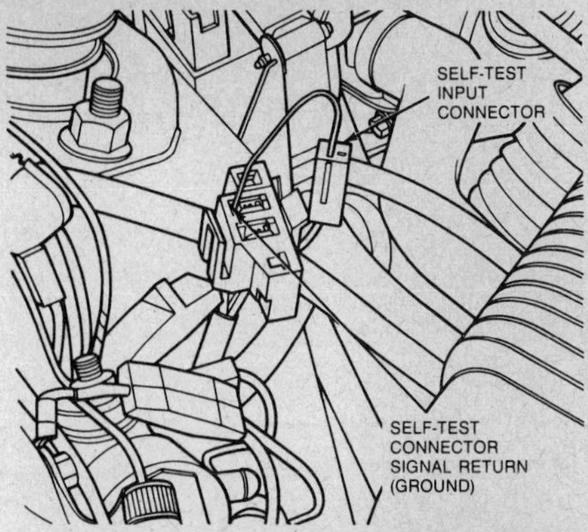

Fig. 10 Connecting jumper wire between self test input connector & signal return ground

Change on Linkage Lever Adj. Screw	Idle Speed Change
No change.	Less than 50 RPM
1½ turns counterclockwise	50–100 RPM increase
1½ turns clockwise	50–100 RPM decrease
2½ turns counterclockwise	100–150 RPM increase
2½ turns clockwise	100–150 RPM decrease

Fig. 11 Idle Speed/Throttle Valve Linkage Adjustment Chart

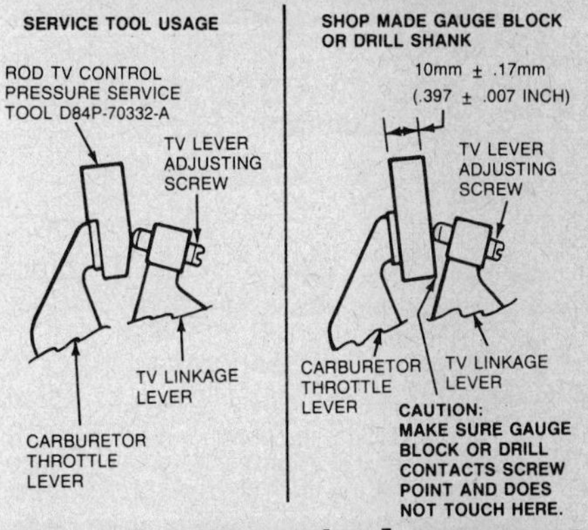

Fig. 12 TV control pressure gauge block

control (ISC) plunger, if equipped, is at its normal idle position. Ensure transmission fluid temperature is approximately 100-150°F.

5. Apply parking brake, place shift selector in Neutral, remove air cleaner and shut off air conditioner. If equipped with a vacuum operated throttle modulator, disconnect and plug vacuum line to this unit. If equipped with a throttle solenoid positioner or an idle speed control, do not disconnect either of these units.
6. With engine idling in Neutral and no accessory load on engine, insert gauge block between carburetor throttle lever and adjustment screw on the TV linkage lever at the carburetor, **Fig. 12.** The TV pressure should be 30-40 psi. For optimum setting, use adjusting screw to set pressure as close to 35 psi as possible. Turning the screw in will raise the pressure 1.5 psi per turn and backing out the screw will lower the pressure. If equipped with idle speed control, some "hunting" may occur and an average pressure reading will have to be determined. If the adjusting screw does not have enough adjustment range to bring TV pressure within specification, first adjust rod at transmission as previously described.
7. Remove gauge block, allowing TV lever to return to idle. With engine still idling in Neutral, TV pressure must be less than 5 psi. If not, back out adjusting screw until TV pressure is less than 5 psi, then reinstall gauge block and ensure TV pressure is still 30-40 psi.

Vehicles w/TV Cable Linkage

1. Attach TV pressure gage with hose, No. T86L-70002-A, or equivalent, to TV port on transmission, using enough hose to make gage accessible while operating engine.
2. If necessary, remove air cleaner cover and inlet tube from throttle body inlet.
3. Insert tapered end of cable TV gage tool No. T86L-70332-A or equivalent between crimped slug on end of cable and plastic cable fitting that attaches to throttle lever, **Fig. 13.**
4. Push gage tool in, forcing the crimped slug away from the plastic fitting, ensuring gage block is pushed in as far as it will go.
5. Run engine until it reaches normal operating temperature and temperature of transmission fluid is 100-150°F.
6. Apply parking brake and place shift selector in Neutral. TV pressure should be 30-40 psi. For best results, set TV pressure as close to 35 psi as possible as follows:
   a. Using suitable tool, pry up white toggle lever on cable adjuster located immediately behind throttle body cable mounting bracket. The adjuster preload spring should cause the adjusting slider to move away from the throttle body and TV pressure should increase.
   b. Push on slider from behind bracket until TV pressure is 35 psi and, while still holding slider, push down on toggle lever as far as it will go, locking slider in position.
7. Remove gage tool, allowing cable to return to its normal idle position.
8. If TV pressure is not less than 5 psi, reinstall gage block and repeat step 6, setting TV pressure to a pressure of less than 35 psi but not less than 30 psi.
9. Remove gage block and ensure TV pressure is less than 5 psi.

IN-VEHICLE REPAIRS

MANUAL SHIFT LINKAGE GROMMET, REPLACE

The automatic transmission linkage system incorporates a polyurethane plastic grommet to connect the various rods, levers and adjusting stud. Whenever a rod is disconnected from a grommet type connector, the old grommet must be removed and a new one installed.

1. Place lower jaw of shift linkage insulator tool T67P-7341-A, or equivalent, between lever and rod, **Fig. 14. For limited work space applications, use tool T84P-7341-A or equivalent, Fig. 15.**
2. Position stop pin against end of control rod and force rod out of grommet.
3. Remove grommet from lever by cutting off large shoulder with sharp knife.
4. Adjust stop pin to ½ inch and coat outside of grommet with suitable lubricant.
5. Place a new grommet on the stop pin and force it into the lever hole, then turn grommet several times to ensure it is properly seated.
6. Readjust stop pin to proper height, **Fig. 14,** coating ends of rods with suitable lubricant.
7. With pin height properly adjusted, position rod on tool and force rod into grommet until groove in rod seats on inner retaining lip of grommet. **Use**

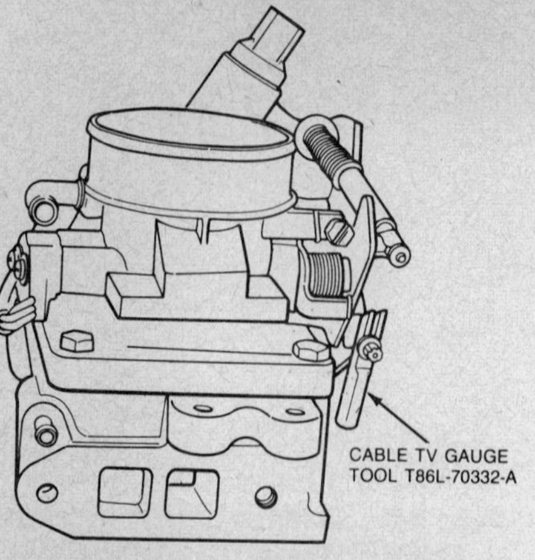

Fig. 13 Installing cable TV gauge tool. 1986–87 models

tool T84P-7341-B for limited work space applications, Fig. 15.

CONTROL VALVE BODY, REPLACE

1. Raise and support vehicle, drain transmission fluid, then remove transmission pan, gasket and filter.
2. Remove detent spring attaching bolt, then the spring.
3. Remove valve body to case attaching bolts, then the valve body.
4. Reverse procedure to install. Use suitable guide pins to align valve body to case.

OVERDRIVE SERVO ASSEMBLY, REPLACE

1. Remove valve body as previously described.
2. Compress overdrive servo piston cover with a suitable tool, then remove snap ring retainer.
3. Apply compressed air to servo piston release passage and remove the overdrive servo piston cover and spring. Remove piston from cover, then the rubber seal from piston and cover.
4. Install new servo piston and cover seals on the servo piston and cover.
5. Lubricate all seals, piston and piston bore with transmission fluid.
6. Install servo piston into cover, then the return spring into servo piston.
7. Install overdrive piston assembly into overdrive servo bore.
8. Compress overdrive piston using suitable tool, then install snap ring retainer.
9. Install valve body, filter, pan and gasket. Refill transmission to proper fluid level.

REVERSE SERVO ASSEMBLY, REPLACE

1. Refer to "Overdrive Servo Assembly" procedure for replacement. Apply compressed air to the servo piston release passage to remove servo piston from case. **Reverse servo piston is under spring pressure. Use caution when removing servo piston cover.**

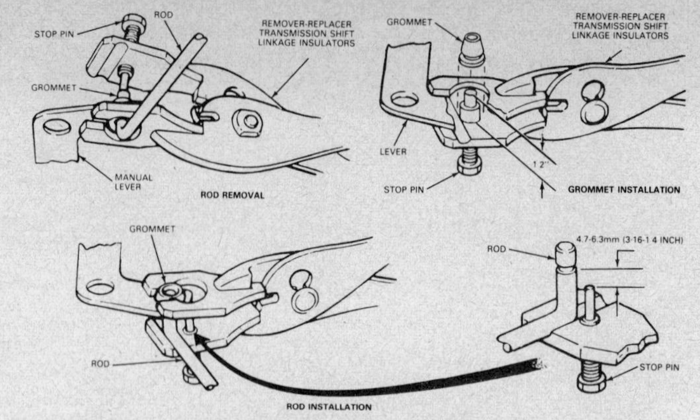

Fig. 14 Removing or installing shift linkage grommet.

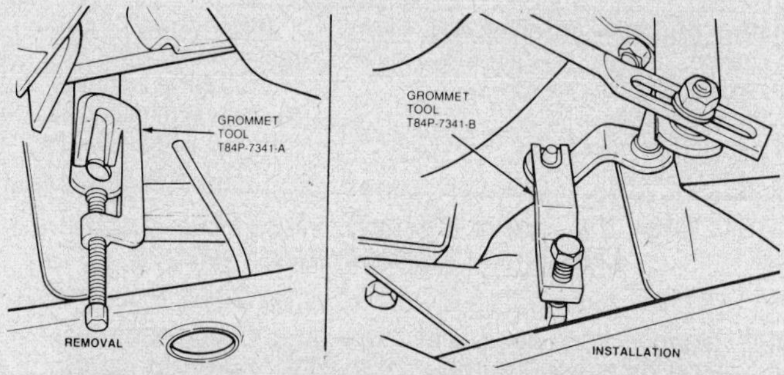

Fig. 15 Removing or installing shift linkage grommet in limited space situations

3–4 ACCUMULATOR PISTON, REPLACE

1. Remove valve body as previously described.
2. Compress 3-4 accumulator piston cover, then remove snap ring retainer.
3. Release cover slowly, then remove piston cover, return spring and piston. Some models do not use a spring.
4. Remove seal from 3-4 accumulator cover and piston and inspect for damage and wear.
5. Install new seals on 3-4 accumulator cover, if necessary. Lubricate cover pocket of case with transmission fluid.
6. Install 3-4 accumulator piston and return spring into case, then the cover.
7. Compress cover using suitable tool, then install snap ring. Ensure cover is reseated snugly against snap ring.
8. Install valve body, filter, pan and gasket. Refill transmission pan to proper fluid level.

2–3 ACCUMULATOR PISTON, REPLACE

1. Refer to "3-4 Accumulator Piston" procedure for replacement.

EXTENSION HOUSING, REPLACE

1. Raise and support vehicle.
2. Disconnect parking brake cable from equalizer, if necessary.
3. Disconnect driveshaft from rear axle flange, then remove driveshaft from transmission.
4. Disconnect speedometer cable from extension housing.
5. Remove engine rear support to extension housing attaching bolts, then the reinforcement plate if equipped.
6. Support transmission with suitable jack and raise transmission enough to remove weight from rear engine support.
7. Remove engine rear support from crossmember, then lower transmission and remove extension housing attaching bolts. Slide extension housing from output shaft and allow fluid to drain.
8. Reverse procedure to install.

GOVERNOR, REPLACE

1. Remove extension housing as described above. **If governor body only is being removed, proceed to step 4.**
2. Remove governor to output shaft retaining snap ring.
3. Remove governor assembly from output shaft using suitable tool. Remove governor driveball.
4. Remove governor to counterweight attaching screws. Remove governor from counterweight.
5. Reverse procedure to install.

INTERNAL & EXTERNAL SHIFT LINKAGE, REPLACE

1982–83 Vehicles

1. Raise and support vehicle.
2. Drain transmission fluid from pan, then remove pan and gasket.

3. Disconnect shift rod at transmission manual lever, then the throttle valve linkage at transmission.
4. Disconnect inner throttle lever spring. Remove detent spring.
5. Hold outer throttle lever, then loosen outer throttle lever attaching nut. Remove attaching nut and lock washer.
6. Remove outer throttle lever seal, then the manual lever roll pin.
7. Remove outer manual lever attaching bolt, then the outer manual lever.
8. Remove inner throttle lever and spring.
9. Remove inner manual lever and park pawl actuating rod.
10. Remove manual lever oil seal.
11. Reverse procedure to install. Adjust transmission manual linkage and throttle linkage as outlined previously.

1984–87 Vehicles

It may be necessary to remove fan shroud attaching bolts and position shroud out of way on models that necessitate lowering transmission to gain access to manual lever.

1. Raise and support vehicle.
2. Remove interfering exhaust components and/or lower transmission as necessary.
3. Apply penetrating oil to outer throttle lever attaching nut to prevent breaking inner throttle lever.
4. Grasp outer throttle lever and hold firmly, then remove outer throttle lever attaching nut and lock washer and position lever and TV rod or cable assembly out of way.
5. Carefully disconnect manual rod from transmission manual lever at transmission using shift linkage grommet removal tool T84P-7341-A or equivalent.
6. Remove oil pan, gasket and filter.
7. Remove manual lever detent spring and roller assembly.
8. Remove manual lever retaining pin by carefully prying with sharp narrow screwdriver.
9. Note assembled position of TV lever torsion spring, then remove spring.
10. Slide a 5/8 inch box wrench over inner manual lever close to bottom of lever, not allowing wrench to contact "rooster comb" area, and, using 21 mm wrench, remove manual lever attaching nut. Hold inner manual lever securely with box wrench while applying break torque to manual lever attaching nut.
11. Remove outer manual lever from case.
12. Remove inner throttle lever and shaft assembly.
13. Remove inner manual lever and park pawl actuating rod assembly.
14. Disconnect park pawl actuating rod from inner manual assembly.
15. Remove and discard manual lever oil seal.
16. Reverse procedure to install, then adjust manual and throttle linkages.

TRANSMISSION REPLACE

1. Raise and support vehicle.
2. Starting at rear of oil pan and working toward the front, loosen bolts and allow fluid to drain. Remove remaining oil pan bolts except for two at front of oil pan. After fluid has been drained, install two bolts onto rear side of pan.
3. Remove converter drain plug access cover from lower end of converter housing.
4. Remove converter to flywheel attaching nuts.
5. Turn converter until drain plug is accessible. Remove plug and drain fluid.
6. Install converter drain plug.
7. Remove driveshaft.
8. Position a suitable plug into extension housing to prevent fluid leakage.
9. Remove starter motor and disconnect neutral start switch electrical connector.
10. Remove rear mount-to-crossmember and two crossmember-to-frame bolts.
11. Remove engine rear support-to-extension housing bolts, then disconnect T.V. linkage rod from transmission T.V. lever and manual rod from manual lever at transmission.
12. Remove bolts securing bellcrank bracket to converter housing.
13. Using a suitable jack, raise transmission and remove crossmember from side supports.
14. Lower transmission and disconnect oil cooler lines from transmission.
15. Disconnect speedometer cable from extension housing.
16. Remove bolt and transmission filler tube from transmission.
17. Secure transmission to jack using a suitable chain.
18. Remove converter housing to cylinder block bolts.
19. Carefully move transmission and converter assembly away from engine and at the same time, lower jack to permit the transmission to clear the underside of vehicle.
20. Reverse procedure to install.

Ford C3 & C4 Automatic Transmission

INDEX

TRANSMISSION IDENTIFICATION

Each transmission may be identified by the tag attached to the low-reverse servo cover bolt. The tag includes the model prefix and suffix, a service identification number and a build date code. The service identification number indicates changes to

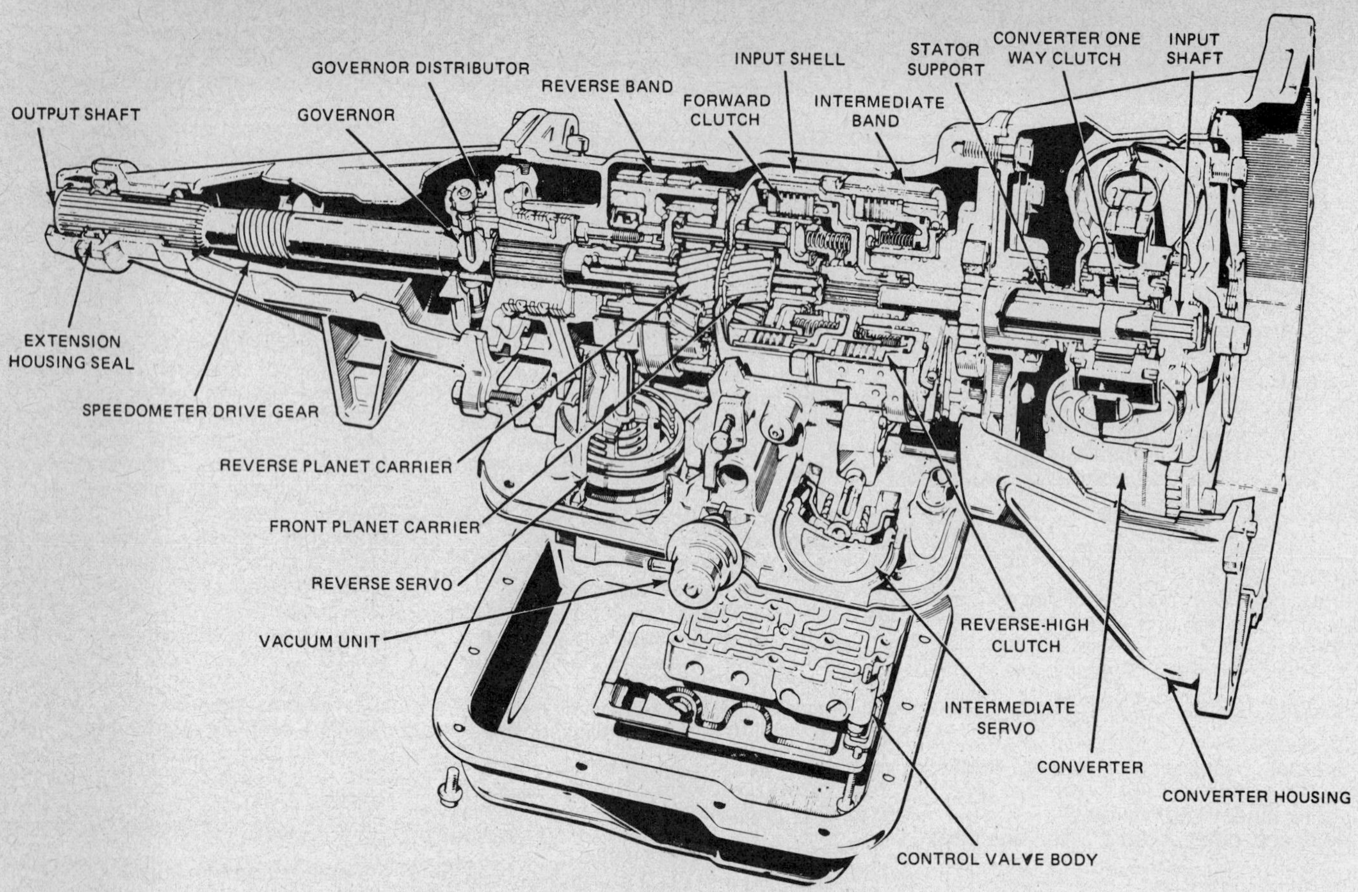

Fig. 1 C3 Dual Range Automatic

service details which affect interchangeability when the transmission model is not changed. For interpretation of this number the Ford Master Parts Catalog should be consulted.

DESCRIPTION

The main control incorporates a manually selective first and second gear range. The transmission features a drive range that provides for fully automatic upshifts and downshifts, and manually selected low and second gears.

The transmission consists essentially of a torque converter, a compound planetary gear train, two multiple disc clutches, a one-way clutch and a hydraulic control system, **Figs. 1 and 2.**

For all normal driving the selector lever is moved to the green dot under Drive on the selector quadrant on the steering column or on the floor console. As the throttle is advanced from the idle position, the transmission will upshift automatically to intermediate gear and then to high.

The driver can force downshift the transmission from high to intermediate at speeds up to 65 mph. A detent on the downshift linkage warns the driver when the carburetor is wide open. Accelerator pedal depression through the detent will bring in the downshift.

With the throttle closed the transmission will downshift automatically as the car speed drops to about 10 mph. With the throttle open at any position up to the detent, the downshifts will come in automatically at speeds above 10 mph and in proportion to throttle opening. This prevents engine lugging on steep hill climbing, for example.

When the selector lever is moved to "L" with the transmission in high, the transmission will downshift to intermediate or to low depending on the road speed. At speed above 25 mph, the downshift will be from high to intermediate. At speeds below 25 mph, the downshift will be from high to low. With the selector lever in the "L" position the transmission cannot upshift.

TROUBLESHOOTING

ROUGH INITIAL ENGAGEMENT IN D1 OR D2

1. Engine idle speed.
2. Vacuum diaphragm unit or tubes restricted, leaking or incorrectly adjusted.
3. Check control pressure.
4. Pressure regulator.
5. Valve body.
6. Forward clutch.

1–2 OR 2–3 SHIFT POINTS ERRATIC

1. Check fluid level.
2. Vacuum diaphragm unit or tubes restricted, leaking or incorrectly adjusted.
3. Immediate servo.
4. Manual linkage adjustment.
5. Governor.
6. Check control pressure.
7. Valve body.
8. Make air pressure check.

ROUGH 1–2 UPSHIFTS

1. Vacuum diaphragm unit or tubes restricted, leaking or incorrectly adjusted.
2. Intermediate servo.
3. Intermediate band.
4. Check control pressure.
5. Valve body.
6. Pressure regulator.

ROUGH 2–3 UPSHIFTS

1. Vacuum diaphragm unit or tubes restricted, leaking or incorrectly adjusted.
2. Intermediate servo.
3. Check control pressure.
4. Pressure regulator.
5. Intermediate band.
6. Valve body.
7. Make air pressure check.
8. Reverse-high clutch.
9. Reverse-high clutch piston air bleed valve.

DRAGGED OUT 1–2 SHIFT

1. Check fluid level.
2. Vacuum diaphragm unit or tubes restricted, leaking or incorrectly adjusted.
3. Intermediate servo.
4. Check control pressure.

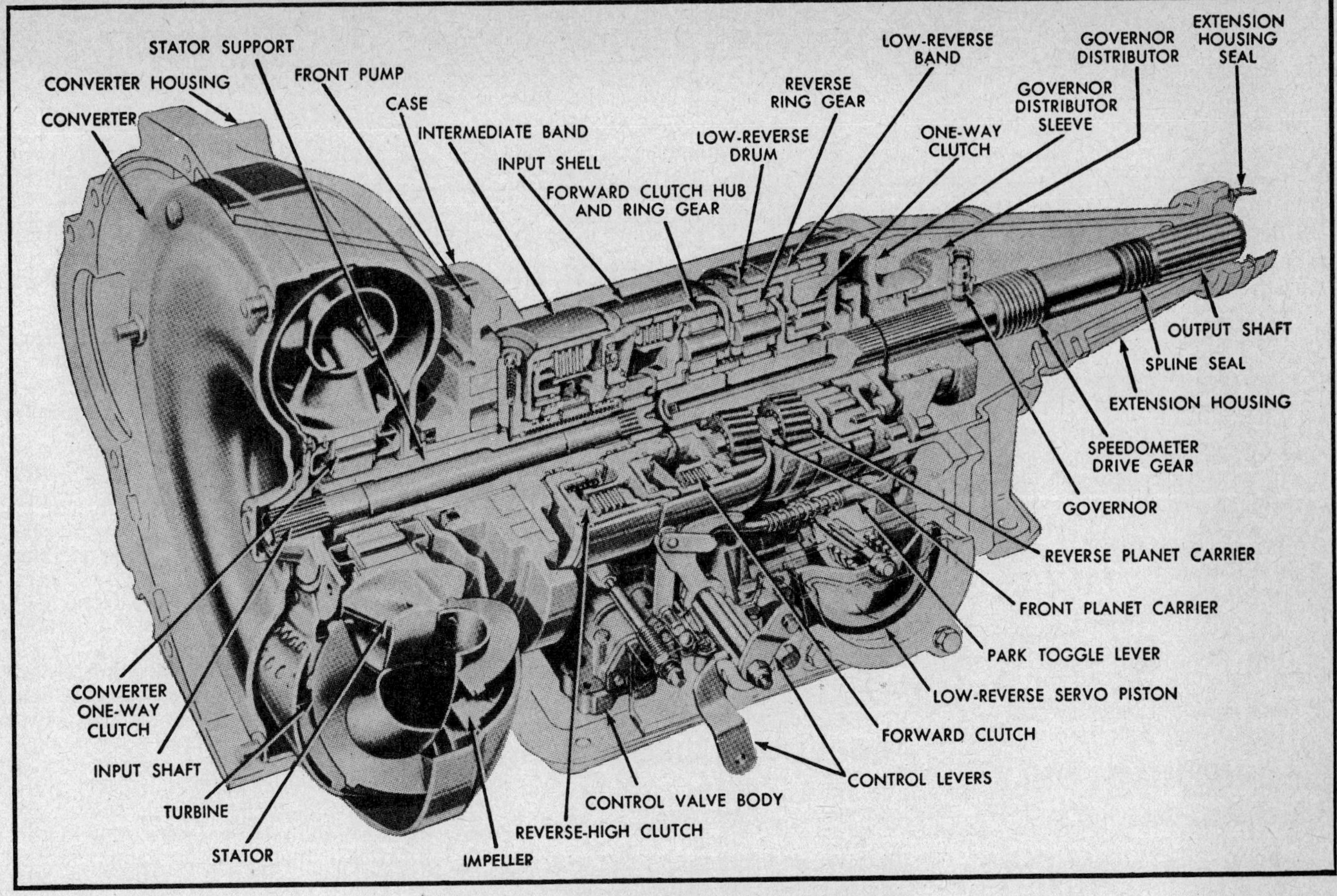

Fig. 2 C4 Dual Range Automatic

5. Intermediate band.
6. Valve body.
7. Pressure regulator.
8. Make air pressure check.
9. Leakage in hydraulic system.

ENGINE OVERSPEEDS ON 2–3 SHIFT

1. Manual linkage.
2. Check fluid level.
3. Vacuum diaphragm unit or tubes restricted, leaking or incorrectly adjusted.
4. Reverse servo.
5. Check control pressure.
6. Valve body.
7. Pressure regulator.
8. Intermediate band.
9. Reverse-high clutch.
10. Reverse-high clutch piston air bleed valve.

NO 1–2 OR 2–3 SHIFT

1. Manual linkage.
2. Downshift linkage, including inner lever position.
3. Vacuum diaphragm unit or tubes restricted, leaking or incorrectly adjusted.
4. Governor.
5. Check control pressure.
6. Valve body.
7. Intermediate band.
8. Intermediate servo.
9. Reverse-high clutch.
10. Reverse-high clutch piston air bleed valve.

NO 3–1 SHIFT IN D1 OR 3–2 SHIFT IN D2

1. Governor.
2. Valve body.

NO FORCED DOWNSHIFTS

1. Downshift linkage, including inner lever position.
2. Valve body.
3. Vacuum diaphragm unit or tubes restricted, leaking or incorrectly adjusted.

RUNAWAY ENGINE ON FORCED 3–2 DOWNSHIFT

1. Check control pressure.
2. Intermediate servo.
3. Intermediate band.
4. Pressure regulator.
5. Valve body.
6. Vacuum diaphragm unit or tubes restricted, leaking or incorrectly adjusted.
7. Leakage in hydraulic system.

ROUGH 3–2 OR 3–1 SHIFT AT CLOSED THROTTLE

1. Engine idle speed.
2. Vacuum diaphragm unit or tubes restricted, leaking or incorrectly adjusted.
3. Intermediate servo.
4. Valve body.
5. Pressure regulator.

SHIFTS 1–3 IN D1 AND D2

1. Intermediate band.
2. Intermediate servo.
3. Vacuum diaphragm unit or tubes restricted, leaking or incorrectly adjusted.
4. Valve body.
5. Governor.
6. Make air pressure check.

NO ENGINE BRAKING IN 1ST GEAR—MANUAL LOW

1. Manual linkage.
2. Reverse band.
3. Reverse servo.
4. Valve body.
5. Governor.
6. Make air pressure check.

SLIPS OR CHATTERS IN 1ST GEAR—D1

1. Check fluid level.
2. Vacuum diaphragm unit or tubes restricted, leaking or incorrectly adjusted.
3. Check control pressure.
4. Pressure regulator.
5. Valve body.
6. Forward clutch.
7. Leakage in hydraulic system.
8. Planetary one-way clutch.

SLIPS OR CHATTERS IN 2ND GEAR

1. Check fluid level.
2. Vacuum diaphragm unit or tubes restricted, leaking or incorrectly adjusted.
3. Intermediate servo.
4. Intermediate band.
5. Check control pressure.
6. Pressure regulator.
7. Valve body.
8. Make air pressure check.
9. Forward clutch.
10. Leakage in hydraulic system.

SLIPS OR CHATTERS IN REVERSE

1. Check fluid level.
2. Vacuum diaphragm unit or tubes restricted, leaking or incorrectly adjusted.
3. Reverse band.
4. Check control pressure.
5. Reverse servo.
6. Pressure regulator.
7. Valve body.
8. Make air pressure check.
9. Reverse-high clutch.
10. Leakage in hydraulic system.
11. Reverse-high piston air bleed valve.

NO DRIVE IN D1 ONLY

1. Check fluid level.
2. Manual linkage.
3. Check control pressure.
4. Valve body.
5. Make air pressure check.
6. Planetary one-way clutch.

NO DRIVE IN D2 ONLY

1. Check fluid level.
2. Manual linkage.
3. Check control pressure.
4. Intermediate servo.
5. Valve body.
6. Make air pressure check.
7. Leakage in hydraulic system.
8. Planetary one-way clutch.

NO DRIVE IN LOW ONLY

1. Check fluid level.
2. Manual linkage.
3. Check control pressure.
4. Valve body.
5. Reverse servo.
6. Make air pressure check.
7. Leakage in hydraulic system.
8. Planetary one-way clutch.

NO DRIVE IN REVERSE ONLY

1. Check fluid level.
2. Manual linkage.
3. Reverse band.
4. Check control pressure.
5. Reverse servo.
6. Valve body.
7. Make air pressure check.
8. Reverse-high clutch.
9. Leakage in hydraulic system.
10. Reverse-high clutch piston air bleed valve.

NO DRIVE IN ANY SELECTOR POSITION

1. Check fluid level.
2. Manual linkage.
3. Check control pressure.
4. Pressure regulator.
5. Valve body.
6. Make air pressure check.
7. Leakage in hydraulic system.
8. Front pump.

LOCKUP IN D1 ONLY

1. Reverse-high clutch.
2. Parking linkage.
3. Leakage in hydraulic system.

LOCKUP IN D2 ONLY

1. Reverse band.
2. Reverse servo.
3. Reverse-high clutch.
4. Parking linkage.
5. Leakage in hydraulic system.
6. Planetary one-way clutch.

LOCKUP IN LOW ONLY

1. Intermediate band.
2. Intermediate servo.
3. Reverse-high clutch.
4. Parking linkage.
5. Leakage in hydraulic system.

LOCKUP IN REVERSE ONLY

1. Intermediate band.
2. Intermediate servo.
3. Forward clutch.
4. Parking linkage.
5. Leakage in hydraulic system.

PARKING LOCK BINDS OR WON'T HOLD

1. Manual linkage.
2. Parking linkage.

MAXIMUM SPEED TOO LOW, POOR ACCELERATION

1. Engine performance.
2. Brakes bind.
3. Converter one-way clutch.

NOISY IN NEUTRAL OR PARK

1. Check fluid level.
2. Pressure regulator.
3. Front pump.
4. Planetary assembly.

NOISY IN ALL GEARS

1. Check fluid level.
2. Pressure regulator.
3. Planetary assembly.
4. Forward clutch.
5. Front pump.
6. Planetary one-way clutch.

CAR MOVES FORWARD IN NEUTRAL

1. Manual linkage.
2. Forward clutch.

MAINTENANCE

Ford Motor Company recommends the use of an automatic transmission fluid with the specification No. ESP-MC138-CJ or Dexron II series D be used. Use of a fluid other than specified above may result in transmission malfunction or failure.

CHECKING OIL LEVEL

1. With transmission at operating temperature, park vehicle on a level surface.
2. Run engine at idle speed with service and parking brakes applied and move selector lever through each range. Return selector lever to Park.
3. With engine idling, remove dipstick and check fluid level. Fluid level should be between the Add and Full marks.
4. Add specified fluid as required to bring the fluid to the proper level.

DRAIN & REFILL

Normal maintenance and lubrication requirements do not necessitate periodic fluid changes. If a major failure has occurred in the transmission, it will have to be removed for service. At this time the converter must be thoroughly flushed to remove any foreign matter.

When filling a dry transmission and converter, install five quarts of specified fluid. Start engine, shift the selector lever through all ranges and place it at P position. Check fluid level and add enough to raise the level in the transmission to the "F" (full) mark on the dipstick. When a partial drain and refill is required due to front band adjustment or minor repair, proceed as follows:

1. Loosen and remove all but two oil pan bolts and drop one edge of the pan to drain the oil. **Some models of the C4 transmission can be drained by removing the filler tube from the pan.**
2. Remove and clean pan and screen.
3. Place a new gasket on pan and install pan and screen.
4. Add three quarts of specified fluid to transmission.
5. Run engine at idle speed for about two minutes.
6. Check oil level and add oil as necessary.
7. Run engine at a fast idle until it reaches normal operating temperature.
8. Shift selector lever through all ranges and then place it in P position.
9. Add fluid as required to bring the level to the full mark.

IN-VEHICLE ADJUSTMENTS

MANUAL LINKAGE, ADJUST

FLOOR SHIFT

Except V8-255

1. Place transmission selector lever in Drive position against rearward stop. Shift lever should be held against rearward drive stop when linkage is adjusted.
2. Raise vehicle and loosen manual lever shift rod retaining nut. Move transmission manual lever to Drive posi-

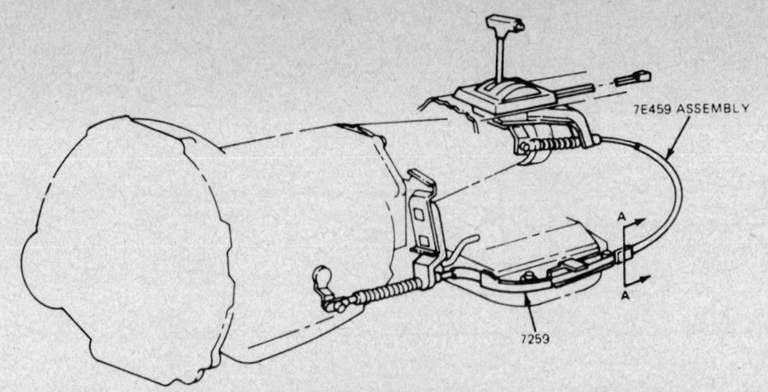

Fig. 3 Floorshift linkage adjustment. V8-255 engine

tion, second detent position from rear of transmission.

3. With transmission selector lever and manual lever in Drive position, torque attaching nut to 10-15 ft. lbs.

V8-255

1. Place transmission selector lever in Drive against rearward drive stop. Shift lever should be held against rearward drive stop when linkage is adjusted.
2. Raise vehicle and loosen manual lever shift cable retaining nut, **Fig. 3.** Move transmission manual lever to Drive position, third detent position from rear of transmission.
3. With transmission selector lever and manual lever in Drive position, torque attaching nut to 10-15 ft. lbs.

COLUMN SHIFT

1. Place selector lever in Drive position. Use suitable force on the lever to keep it against the Drive stop during adjustment.
2. Raise vehicle and loosen shift rod adjusting nut at point A, **Figs. 4 and 5.**
3. Shift transmission manual lever into drive position, second detent from the full counterclockwise position.
4. On models equipped with shift cable, place cable end on transmission manual lever stud. Align flats on stud with flats on cable, then install adjustment nut.
5. On all models, tighten adjustment at point A. Ensure selector lever is against D stop when tightening adjustment nut.
6. Check transmission for proper operation in all selector lever detent positions.

THROTTLE & DOWNSHIFT LINKAGE, ADJUST

1. Apply parking brake and place selector lever in Neutral.
2. Run engine at normal idle speed.
3. Connect tachometer to engine.
4. Adjust engine idle speed to specified RPM with selector lever in either Drive position. **The carburetor throttle lever must be against the hot idle speed adjusting screw at specified idle speed.**
5. Proceed with adjustments as outlined below.

1984–86 Cougar & Thunderbird W/4-140 Turbocharged Engine

1. Ensure cable and kickdown return spring are installed at transmission kickdown lever.
2. Remove clip in cable adjuster located at accelerator bracket fitting.
3. Rotate throttle lever to wide open throttle (WOT) position.
4. While holding throttle at WOT, install clip in kickdown cable adjuster.

1983–86 Exc. Cougar & Thunderbird W/4-140 Turbocharged Engine

Refer to **Figs. 6 through 9** for adjustment procedure.

1982 All W/4-140

1. Remove downshift retracting spring and hold throttle in wide open position.
2. Depress downshift rod with 6 lbs. weight positioned against through detent stop.
3. Turn downshift adjusting screw to obtain .01-.08 inch clearance between screw and throttle arm.
4. Return system to idle and install downshift retracting spring.

1982 Capri, Fairmont, Mustang, Zephyr, W/V8-255

1. Hold throttle in wide open position.
2. Depress downshift rod with 4.25 lb. weight positioned against through detent stop.
3. Turn downshift adjusting screw to obtain .01-.08 inch clearance between screw and throttle arm.
4. Return system to idle.

1982 All W/6-200

1. Remove downshift retracting spring and hold throttle in wide open position.
2. Depress downshift rod with 4.25 lb. weight positioned against through detent stop, **Figs. 10 and 11.**
3. Turn downshift adjusting screw to obtain .01-.08 inch clearance between screw and throttle arm.
4. Return system to idle and install downshift retracting spring.

BANDS, ADJUST

The intermediate and low-reverse bands adjusting screw locknut must be

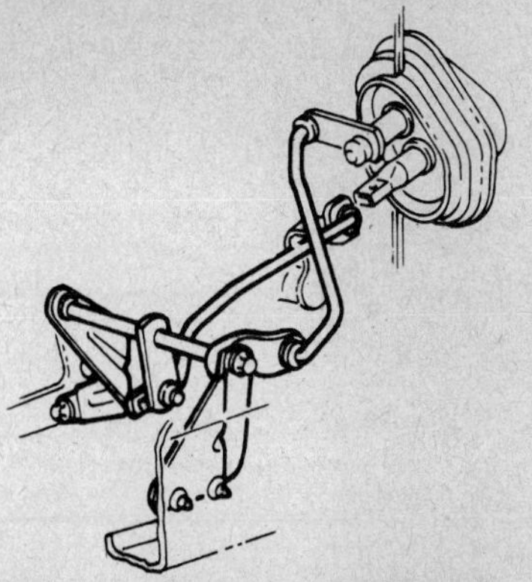

Fig. 4 Manual linkage. 1982 Fairmont, Zephyr & 1982 Cougar & Granada (typical)

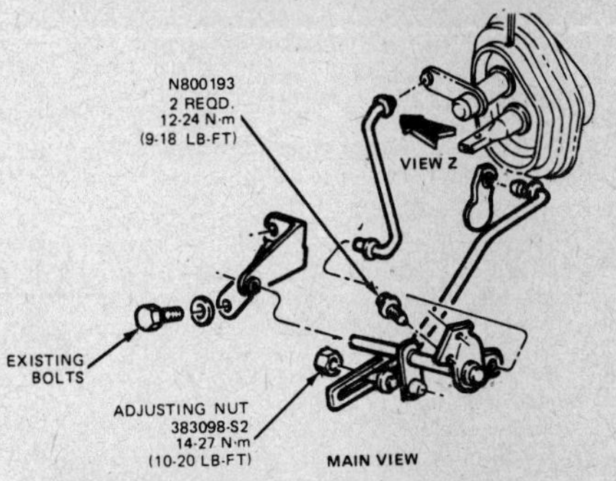

Fig. 5 Manual linkage. 1983–86 Fairmont, Futura, LTD, Marquis, Thunderbird, XR-7 & Zephyr column shift

discarded and a new one installed each time a band is adjusted.

INTERMEDIATE BAND

C3

1. Disconnect downshift linkage from transmission lever.
2. Discard adjusting screw locknut and install a new locknut.
3. With tools shown in **Figs. 12 and 13,** tighten adjusting screw until tool handle clicks. This tool is a pre-set torque wrench which clicks and overruns when the torque on the adjusting screw reaches 10 ft. lbs.
4. Back off adjusting screw 2 turns.
5. Hold adjusting screw from turning and tighten locknut.
6. Connect downshift linkage to transmission lever.

C4

C4 transmissions are equipped with an intermediate band adjuster screw and nut using a fine pitch 1/2-28 thread. When performing band adjustment, on these models, use the following procedure:

1. Remove and discard locknut.
2. Install new locknut on adjusting screw and torque to 10 ft. lbs.
3. Back off adjusting screw exactly three turns.
4. Hold adjusting screw from turning and torque locknut to 40 ft. lbs. This procedure applies to model cases with yellow trademark. The fine adjusting

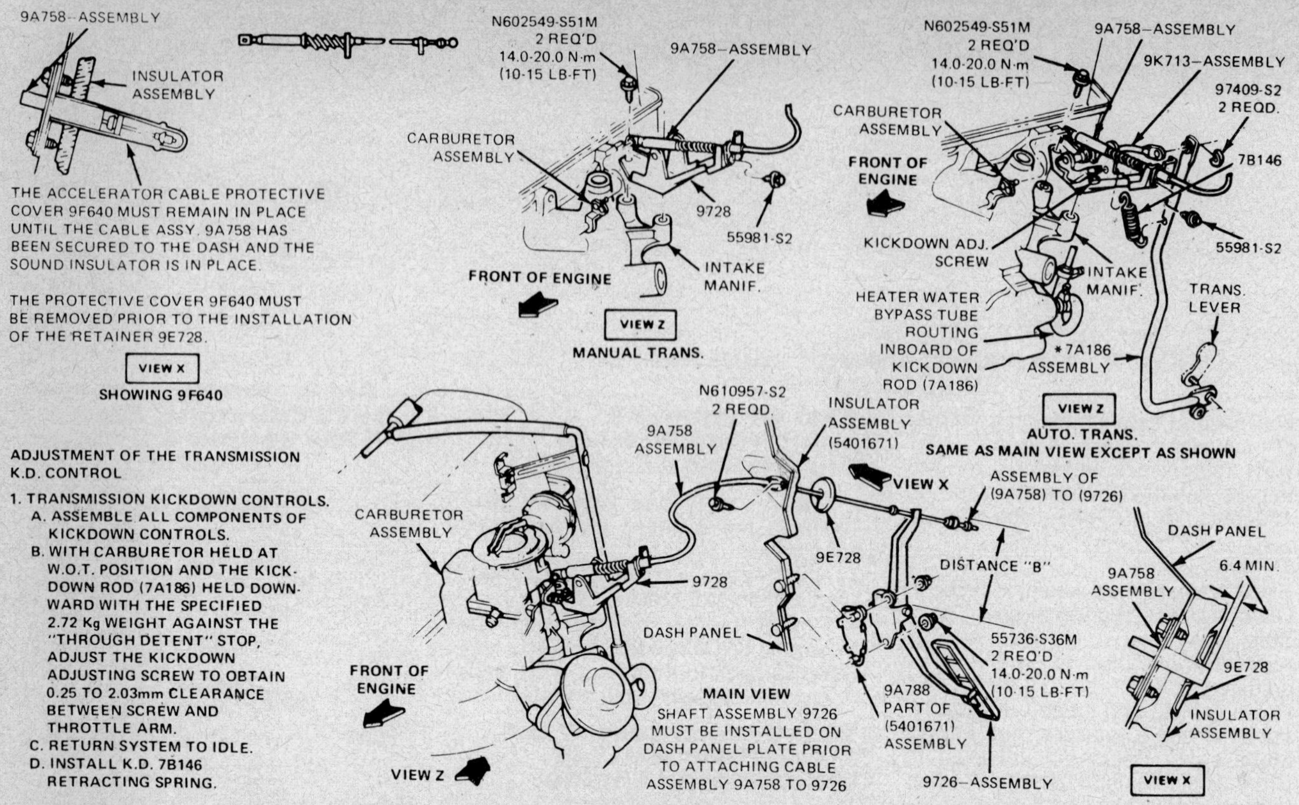

ADJUSTMENT OF THE TRANSMISSION K.D. CONTROL

1. TRANSMISSION KICKDOWN CONTROLS.
   A. ASSEMBLE ALL COMPONENTS OF KICKDOWN CONTROLS.
   B. WITH CARBURETOR HELD AT W.O.T. POSITION AND THE KICK-DOWN ROD (7A186) HELD DOWNWARD WITH THE SPECIFIED 2.72 Kg WEIGHT AGAINST THE "THROUGH DETENT" STOP, ADJUST THE KICKDOWN ADJUSTING SCREW TO OBTAIN 0.25 TO 2.03mm CLEARANCE BETWEEN SCREW AND THROTTLE ARM.
   C. RETURN SYSTEM TO IDLE.
   D. INSTALL K.D. 7B146 RETRACTING SPRING.

Fig. 6 Throttle & downshift linkage adjustment. Capri, LTD, Marquis & Mustang w/4-140 engine

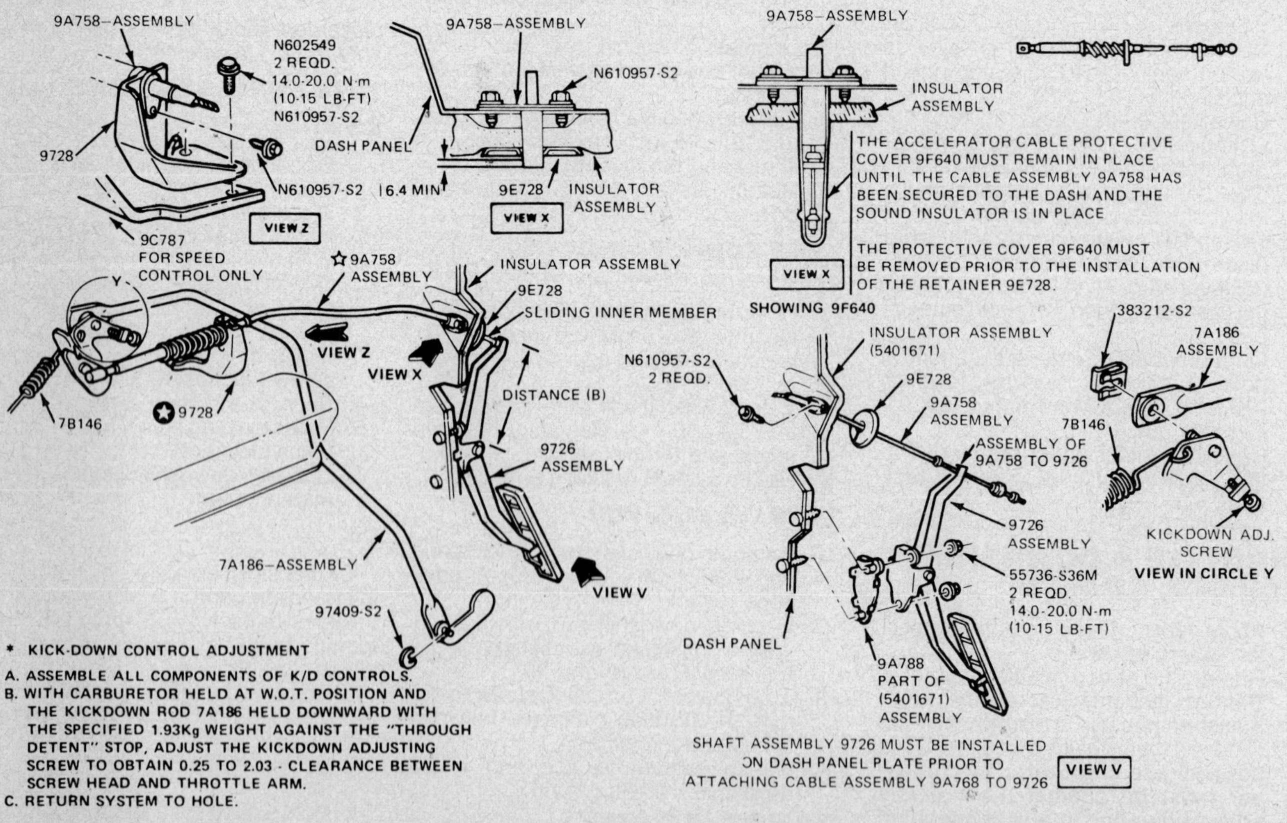

* KICK-DOWN CONTROL ADJUSTMENT

A. ASSEMBLE ALL COMPONENTS OF K/D CONTROLS.
B. WITH CARBURETOR HELD AT W.O.T. POSITION AND THE KICKDOWN ROD 7A186 HELD DOWNWARD WITH THE SPECIFIED 1.93Kg WEIGHT AGAINST THE "THROUGH DETENT" STOP, ADJUST THE KICKDOWN ADJUSTING SCREW TO OBTAIN 0.25 TO 2.03 - CLEARANCE BETWEEN SCREW HEAD AND THROTTLE ARM.
C. RETURN SYSTEM TO HOLE.

Fig. 7 Throttle & downshift linkage adjust. Capri & Mustang w/V6-232 engine

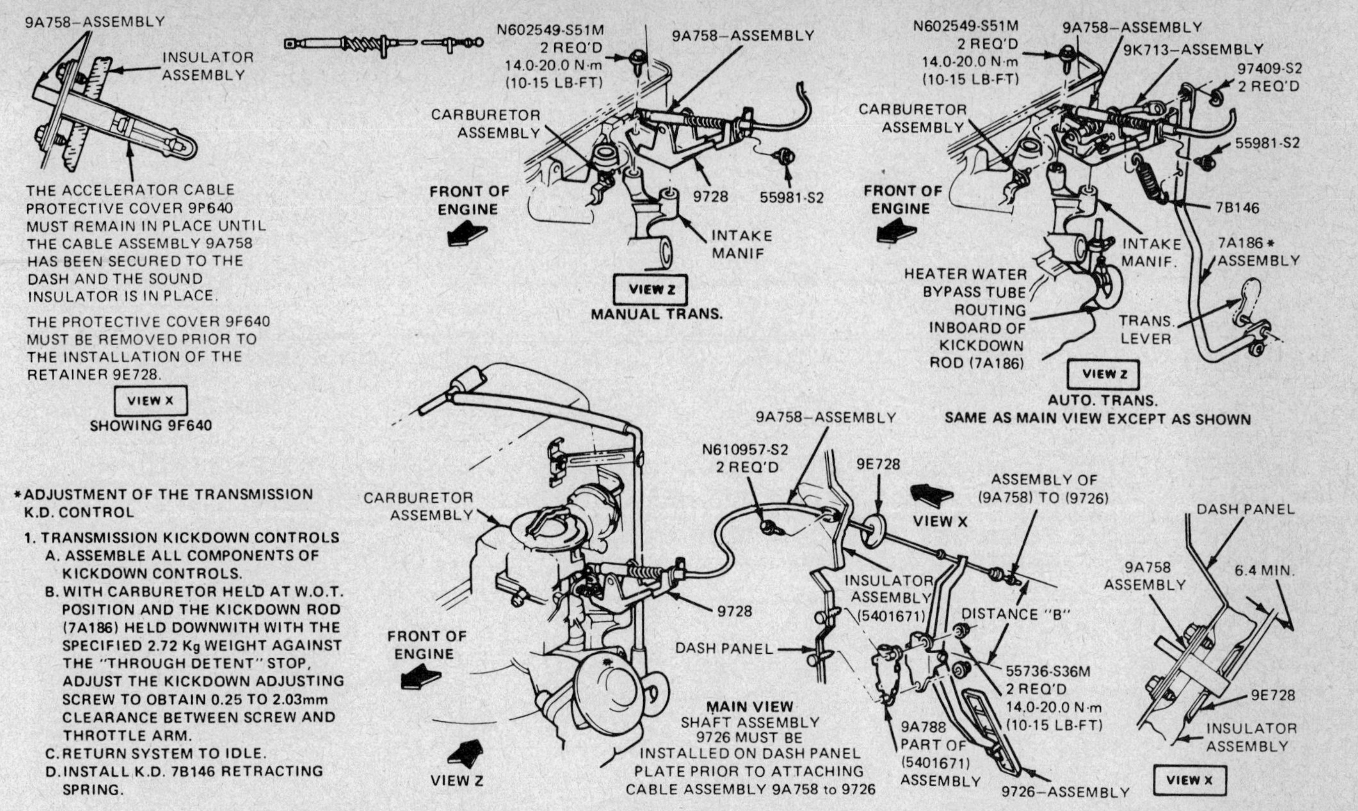

Fig. 8 Throttle & downshift linkage adjust. Fairmont Futura & Zephyr w/4-140 engine

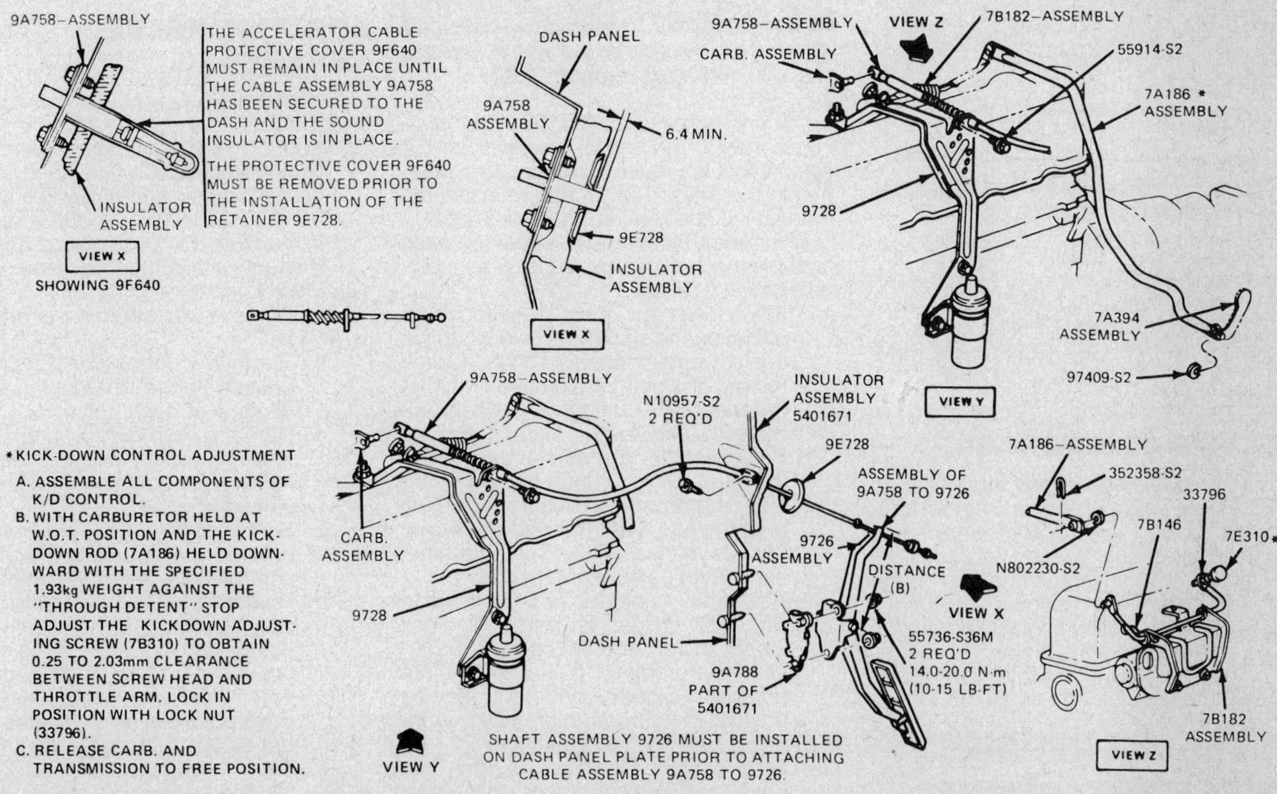

Fig. 9 Throttle & downshift linkage adjust. Fairmont Futura & Zephyr w/6-200 engine

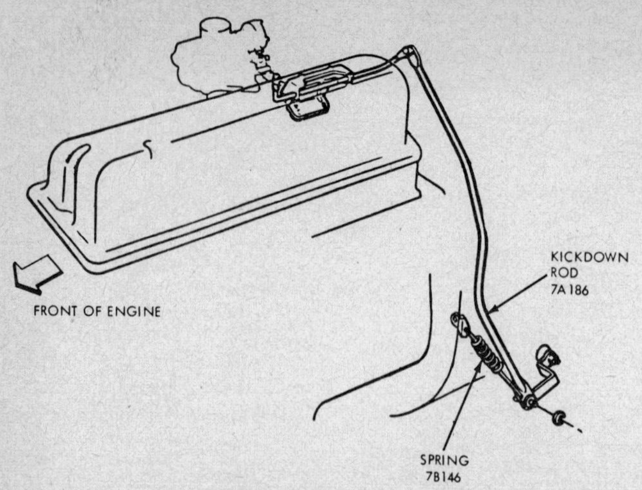

Fig. 10 Downshift linkage 6 cyl. (typical). 1982 Capri, Fairmont, Granada, Monarch, Mustang & Zephyr

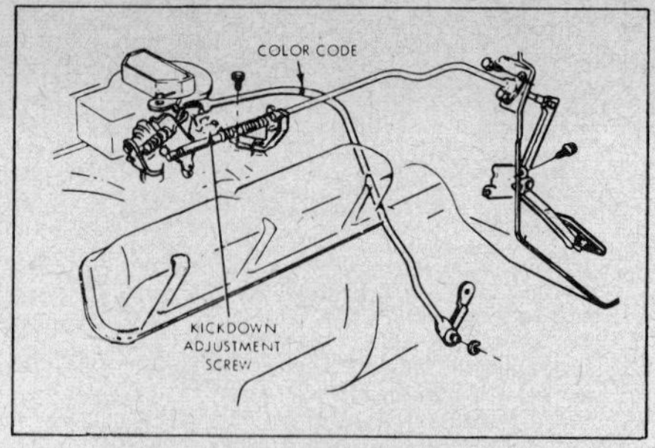

Fig. 11 Throttle & downshift linkage V8 (typical). 1982 Capri & Mustang

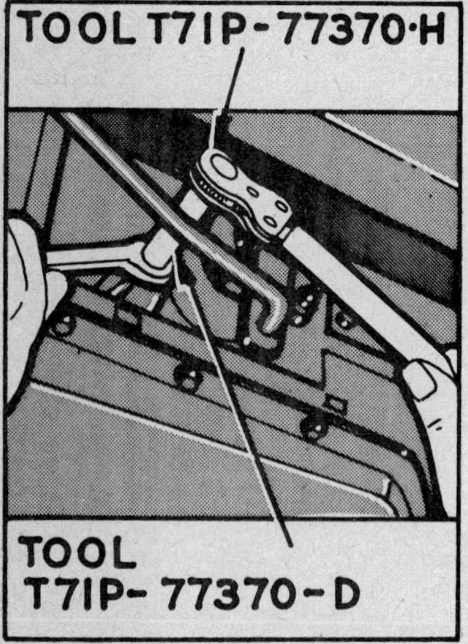

Fig. 12 Intermediate band adjustment. C4

screw can be identified by an identification rib on strut end. New models numbers affected are: PEJ-AC4, AD4, PEA-CP1, CE10, PEB-N11, P9, Z1, U5, PEE-FL6, GB1, PEN-A1, B1, PEM-W1, C6, D6, E6 AC1, AD1, AE1, AL1, AM1, AN1, AK1.

C4 LOW-REVERSE BAND

1. Loosen locknut several turns.
2. Tighten adjusting screw until tool handle clicks, **Fig. 14.** Tool shown is a pre-set torque wrench which clicks and overruns when the torque on the adjusting screw reaches 10 ft. lbs.
3. Back off adjusting screw exactly 3 full turns.
4. Hold adjusting screw from turning and tighten locknut.

IN-VEHICLE REPAIRS

SHIFT LEVER GROMMET, REPLACE

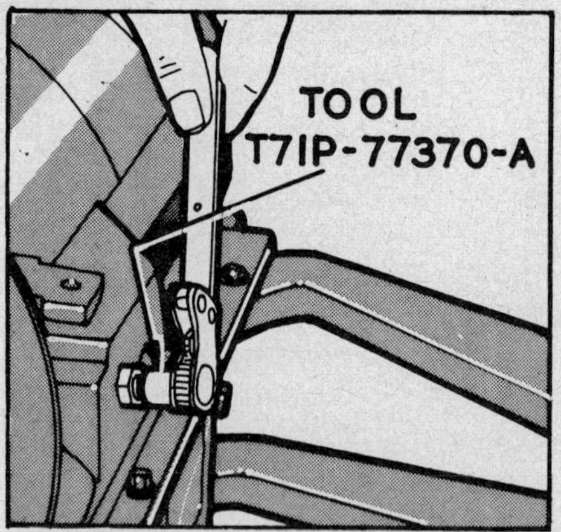

Fig. 13 Intermediate band adjustment. C3

On some shift lever assemblies, **Fig. 15,** an oil impregnated plastic grommet is incorporated in the end of the lever arm. A special tool is required to install the grommet in the manual lever, and to install the manual linkage rod into the grommet.

This grommet should be replaced each time the manual linkage rod is disconnected from shift lever.

1. Place lower jaw of tool between manual lever and shift rod. Position stop in against end of control rod and force rod out of grommet. Remove grommet from lever by cutting off large shoulder with a knife.
2. Before installing a new grommet, adjust stop pin to 1/2 inch and coat outside of grommet with lubricant. Place grommet on stop pin and force into hole in manual lever. Turn grommet several times to seat properly.
3. Adjust height of stop pin as shown in **Fig. 15.** Height is determined by length of rod end which is to be installed in grommet. If pin height is not adjusted properly, control rod may be pushed to far through grommet, damaging grommet and retaining lip.
4. With proper alignment of stop pin height, position control rod on tool and force rod into grommet until groove on rod seats on inner retainer lip of grommet.

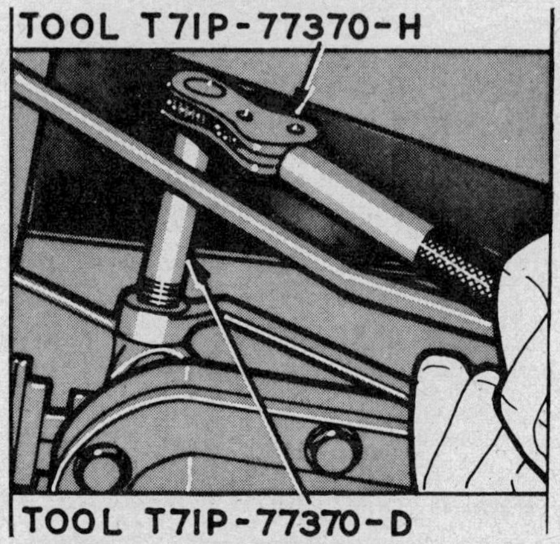

Fig. 14 Low-reverse band adjustment. C4

CONTROL VALVE, REPLACE

All fasteners used on C3 transmissions are designed to metric specifications.

1. Support vehicle on jack stands.
2. Drain transmission fluid, then remove oil pan, fluid screen, gasket and on early C3 units, remove three spacers. **If fluid is to be reused, filter it through a 100 mesh screen.**
3. On C3 units:
   a. Remove rear servo cover and gasket.
   b. Remove control valve attaching bolts. Note the different length and location of each bolt.
   c. Carefully remove control valve while unlocking and detaching selector lever connecting rod.
4. On C4 units:
   a. Shift selector lever into Park and remove the two detent spring to control valve and case bolts.
   b. Remove remaining control valve to case bolts, then while holding manual valve inward, remove control valve. **Failure to hold manual valve inward, while removing control valve, could cause manual valve to become damaged.**
5. After installing valve, torque attaching bolts to 72-96 in. lbs. on C3 units and 89-120 in. lbs. on C4 units. Torque rear servo cover attaching bolts to 84-120 inch lbs.

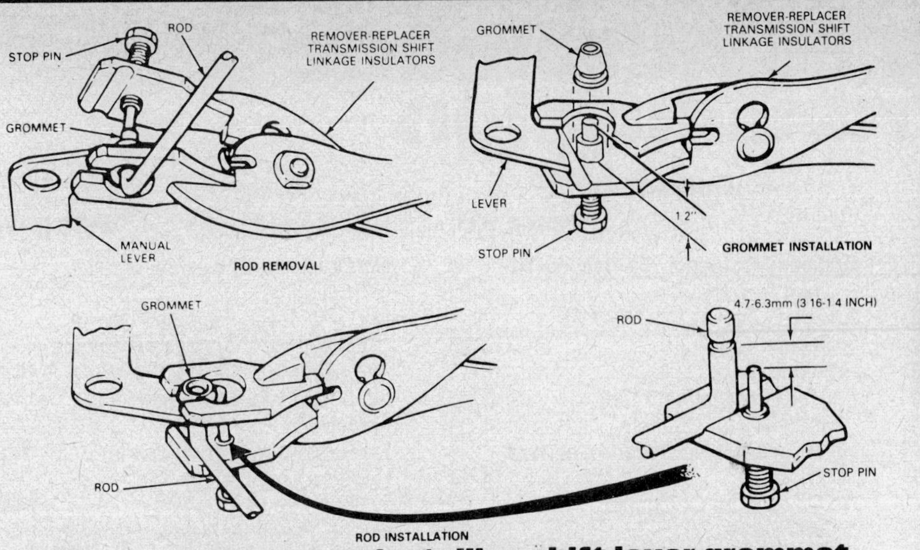

Fig. 15 Removing or installing shift lever grommet

Fig. 16 Rear servo removal C3

SERVO REPAIR

C4 Intermediate Servo

1. Support vehicle on jack stands.
2. On some models, it is necessary to remove crossmember to gain access to the servo.
3. Remove servo cover attaching screws, servo cover, gasket, piston and piston return spring.
4. Replace piston seals. Lubricate new seals with transmission fluid before installation.
5. Reverse procedure to install.

C4 Low-Reverse Servo

1. Support vehicle on jack stands.
2. Loosen reverse band adjusting screw locknut and torque adjusting screw to 10 ft. lbs. With adjusting screw torqued, the band strut is forced against case, preventing the strut from falling out of position when removing servo piston.
3. Remove servo cover retaining bolts, servo cover, seal and servo piston from case.
4. On some models, the piston seal is bonded to the piston, requiring piston replacement. To remove piston from stem, insert a small screwdriver through hole in stem and remove piston from stem, insert a small screwdriver through hole in stem and remove piston retaining nut, piston, accumulator spring and spacer.
5. On all other models, replace piston seals. Lubricate new seals with transmission fluid before installation.
6. Reverse procedure to install making sure to readjust low-reverse band. **If the band cannot be adjusted, the low-reverse band struts are not in position. Remove the fluid pan and valve body to install the struts into position. Adjust the band.**

C3 Rear Servo

1. Support vehicle on jack stands, then drain transmission.
2. Remove oil filter screws, gasket and on early models, three spacers.
3. Remove servo cover retaining screws, servo cover, piston and spring, **Fig. 16.**
4. Reverse procedure to install.

EXTENSION HOUSING, REPLACE

1. Support vehicle on jack stands and remove driveshaft. **Scribe marks on driveshaft yoke and companion flange, to insure proper positioning of driveshaft during assembly.**
2. Support transmission with suitable jack and disconnect speedometer cable. **On some models, it will be necessary to disconnect the exhaust system from the exhaust manifolds to perform the following step.**
3. Remove engine rear support to crossmember attaching bolts or nuts, then raise transmission slightly and remove rear support from extension housing. **On some models, it will be necessary to remove crossmember in order to remove rear support from extension housing.**
4. Loosen extension housing bolts and allow transmission fluid to drain and remove extension housing.

GOVERNOR, REPLACE

1. Remove extension housing as described previously.
2. Remove governor to governor housing retaining bolts and slide governor off output shaft.
3. Reverse procedure to install. Torque governor retaining bolts to 7 to 10 ft. lbs.

TRANSMISSION REPLACE

1. Support vehicle on jack stands and remove converter housing lower cover.
2. Drain transmission oil pan and the converter. Use a wrench on crankshaft pulley nut to rotate crankshaft and converter to gain access to drain plug. **Do not rotate overhead camshaft engines in opposite direction of normal rotation.**
3. Remove converter to flywheel bolts or nuts.
4. Remove propeller shaft.
5. Remove vacuum line hose from transmission vacuum unit. Disconnect vacuum line from clip.
6. If equipped, disconnect TRS switch wire.
7. Remove two extension housing to crossmember bolts.
8. Remove speedometer cable from extension housing.
9. Disconnect exhaust system if necessary. **On some models with C3 transmission, remove rear engine support.**
10. Disconnect oil cooler lines from transmission.
11. Remove the manual and kickdown linkage rods from transmission shift levers.
12. Where necessary disconnect the neutral start switch wires.
13. Remove starter.
14. Remove transmission fluid filler tube.
15. Support transmission with suitable jack and remove crossmember.
16. Remove converter housing to engine bolts and lower transmission from vehicle.
17. Reverse procedure to install. **Flywheel assemblies used with C3 transmissions have a pilot hole to ensure proper flywheel to converter alignment. During installation, the flywheel must be indexed with the pilot hole in the six o'clock position. Because the flywheel has only one converter drain plug access hole, it is necessary to rotate the converter so the drain plug is located at 4 o'clock position with a 2.3 liter engine, and 8 o'clock position with a 2.8 Liter engine. On some models with C4 transmission, align dyed converter drive stud into painted flywheel hole to maintain initial engine to transmission balance.**

Ford C5 Automatic Transmission

INDEX

TRANSMISSION IDENTIFICATION

Each transmission is identified by a tag, **Fig. 1,** located under the lower front intermediate servo cover bolt. The tag indicates model prefix and suffix, assembly part numbers, and the build date code. The service identification number indicates changes to service details which affect interchangeability within the same transmission model line.

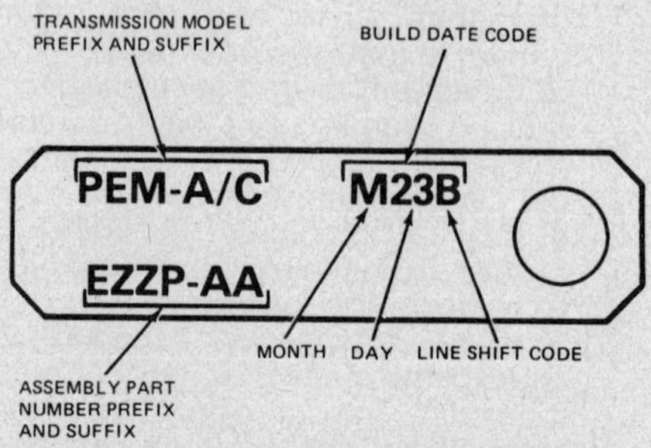

Fig. 1 C5 identification tag

DESCRIPTION

The C5 transmission, **Fig. 2,** is a three speed fully automatic unit. First and second gear can be selected manually. The transmission consists of a welded torque converter assembly, a two-unit planetary gear train, and a hydraulic system which controls gear selection and automatic shifts. Larger displacement engines use a 12-inch torque converter which has a converter clutch. The planetary gear train, which is the same as that used in the C4 with minor changes, is a Simpson design with two gear sets in series and common sun gear. Gear operation is controlled by two friction clutches and two bands.

In spite of some similarities to the C4, the C5 incorporates major differences in the hydraulic system. The valve body is different and the converter relief valve has been moved from the reactor support in the pump assembly to the timing valve body. As a result C4 oil pump assemblies cannot be used when servicing the C5.

With the selector in Park position the transmission is in neutral and the output shaft is locked to the case by the parking pawl. In Reverse the transmission is in reverse gear. In Neutral the engine is in neutral and the output shaft is not locked to the case. Drive is the normal driving range in which the vehicle starts in low with automatic upshifts to second (intermediate) and high (direct drive). With throttle closed, the transmission downshifts from high to low, when vehicle speed drops to 10 mph. In 2 (intermediate), the transmission shifts to second gear and remains there regardless of speed. In 1 (low), the transmission stays in low and does not upshift. If placed in 1 above 25 mph, the transmission will shift to second and downshift to low, once vehicle speed has dropped below 25 mph. At speeds below 25 mph, the transmission shifts to low immediately.

TROUBLESHOOTING

SLOW INITIAL ENGAGEMENT

1. Improper fluid level.
2. Damaged or improperly adjusted linkage.
3. Contaminated fluid.
4. Improper clutch and band application or low main control pressure.

ROUGH INITIAL ENGAGEMENTS IN EITHER FORWARD OR REVERSE

1. Improper fluid level.
2. High engine idle.
3. Automatic choke on (warm temp.).
4. Looseness in the driveshaft U-joint or engine mount.
5. Incorrect linkage adjustment.
6. Improper clutch or band application, or oil control pressure.

NO OR DELAYED FORWARD ENGAGEMENT

1. Improper fluid level.
2. Manual linkage, incorrectly adjusted or damaged.
3. Low main control pressure.
4. Valve body bolts, loose or too tight.
5. Valve body, dirty or sticking valve.
6. Forward clutch assembly burnt or damaged.
7. Forward clutch assembly piston seals worn or cut.
8. Forward clutch assembly cylinder ball check not seating.
9. Forward clutch assembly stator support seal ring grooves, damaged or worn.

NO OR DELAYED REVERSE ENGAGEMENT

1. Improper fluid level.

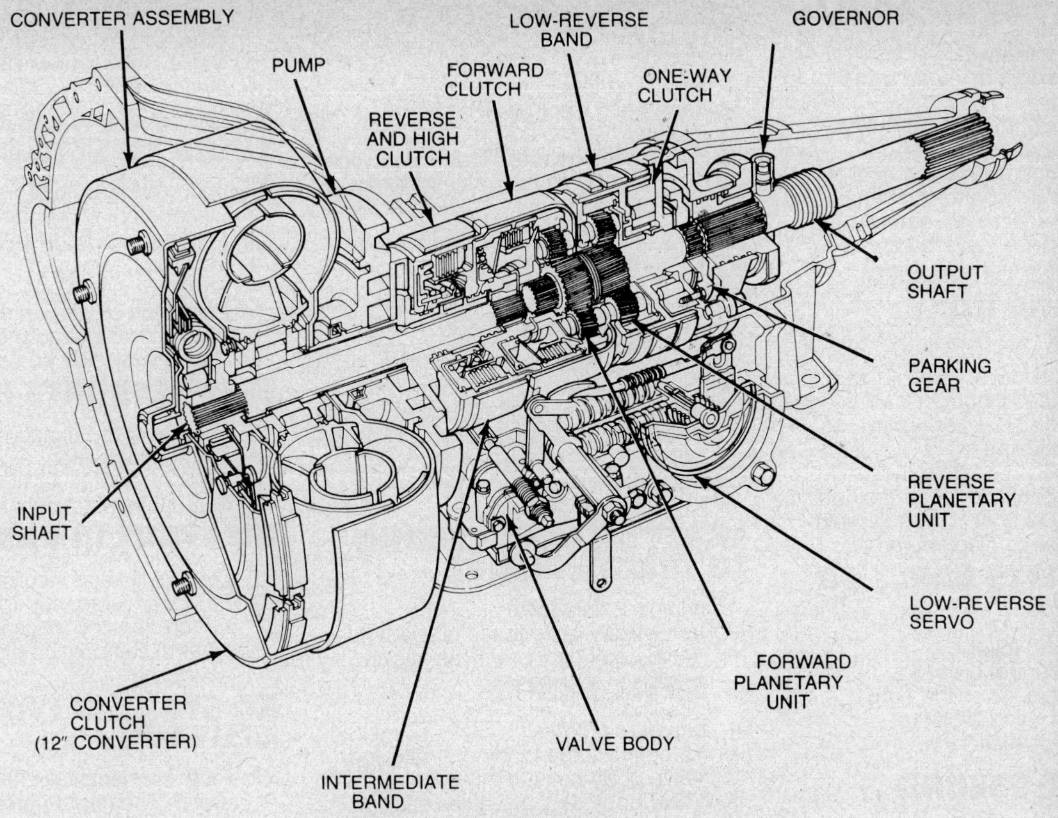

Fig. 2 Ford C5 transmission

2. Low main control pressure in reverse.
3. Manual linkage incorrectly adjusted or damaged.
4. Valve body, dirty or sticking valve.
5. Valve body bolts loose or too tight.
6. Reverse clutch assembly, burnt or worn.
7. Reverse clutch assembly piston seals, worn or cut.
8. Reverse clutch assembly piston ball not seating.
9. Reverse clutch assembly stator support seal rings or ring grooves, worn or damaged.

NO OR DELAYED REVERSE ENGAGEMENT AND/OR NO ENGINE BRAKING IN MANUAL LOW (1)

1. Low reverse band or servo piston burnt or worn.
2. Low reverse servo seal worn or cut.
3. Low reverse servo bore damaged.
4. Low reverse servo piston sticking in bore.
5. Low reverse band, line pressure low.
6. Low reverse bands out of adjustment.
7. Polished or glazed band or drum.

NO ENGINE BRAKING IN MANUAL SECOND GEAR

1. Improper fluid level.
2. Linkage out of adjustment.
3. Intermediate band out of adjustment.
4. Improper band or clutch application, or oil pressure control system.
5. Intermediate servo leaking.
6. Polished or glazed band or drum.

NO ENGAGEMENT FORWARD AND REVERSE

1. Pump gear damaged.
2. Output shaft broken.
3. Turbine shaft or input shaft broken.

FORWARD ENGAGEMENT SLIP, SHUDDERS OR CHATTERS

1. Improper fluid level.
2. Manual linkage incorrectly adjusted or damaged.
3. Low main control pressure.
4. Valve body bolts, loose or too tight.
5. Valve body dirty or sticking valve.
6. Forward clutch piston ball check not sealing.
7. Forward clutch piston seal cut or worn.
8. Contamination blocking forward clutch feed hole.
9. Low (planetary) one-way clutch damaged.

REVERSE ENGAGEMENT SLIP, SHUDDERS OR CHATTERS

1. Improper fluid level.
2. Low main control pressure in reverse.
3. Reverse servo or servo bore damaged.
4. Low (planetary) one-way clutch damaged.
5. Reverse clutch drum bushing damaged.
6. Reverse clutch stator support seal rings or ring grooves worn or damaged.
7. Reverse clutch piston seal cut or worn.
8. Reverse band out of adjustment or damaged.
9. Looseness in the driveshaft U-joints or engine mounts.

NO DRIVE, SLIPS OR CHATTERS IN FIRST GEAR DRIVE

1. Damaged or worn one-way clutch.

NO DRIVE, SLIPS OR CHATTERS IN SECOND

1. Improper fluid level.
2. Damaged or improperly adjusted linkage.
3. Intermediate band out of adjustment.
4. Improper band or clutch application, or oil pressure control.
5. Damaged or worn servo and/or internal leaks.
6. Dirty or sticking valve body.
7. Polished or glazed intermediate band or drum.

START UP IN SECOND OR THIRD

1. Improper fluid level.
2. Damaged or improperly adjusted linkage.
3. Improper band and/or clutch application, or oil pressure control system.
4. Damaged or worn governor, governor sticking.
5. Valve body loose.
6. Dirty or sticking valve body.
7. Cross leaks between valve body and case mating surface.

SHIFT POINTS INCORRECT

1. Improper fluid level.
2. Improper vacuum hose routing or leaks.
3. Improper operation of EGR system.
4. Throttle out of adjustment.
5. Improper clutch or band application, or oil pressure control system.
6. Damaged or worn governor.
7. Dirty or sticking valve body.

ALL UPSHIFTS HARSH, DELAYED OR NO UPSHIFTS

1. Improper fluid level.
2. Manual linkage incorrectly adjusted or damaged.
3. Governor sticking.
4. Main control pressure too high.
5. Valve body bolts loose or too tight.
6. Valve body dirty or valves sticking.
7. Vacuum leak to diaphragm unit.

ALL UPSHIFTS EARLY OR SLUGGISH

1. Improper fluid level.
2. Low main control pressure.
3. Valve body loose or too tight.
4. Valve body valve sticking.
5. Governor valve sticking.

NO LOW TO SECOND UPSHIFT

1. Improper fluid level.
2. Manual linkage incorrectly adjusted or damaged.
3. Governor valve sticking.
4. Valve body bolts loose or too tight.
5. Valve body dirty or sticking valves.
6. Intermediate clutch or band and/or servo assembly burnt.
7. Intermediate piston seals worn or cut.
8. Intermediate piston not positioned properly.
9. Intermediate clutch in improper stack up.
10. Low line pressure in intermediate clutch or band.

ROUGH, HARSH, OR DELAYED UPSHIFT LOW TO SECOND

1. Governor valve sticking.
2. Improper fluid level.
3. Poor engine performance.
4. Main control pressure too high.
5. Valve body bolts loose or too tight.
6. Valve body dirty or valves sticking.
7. Intermediate band out of adjustment.
8. Damaged intermediate servo.
9. Engine vacuum leak.

EARLY, SOFT OR SLIPPING LOW TO SECOND UPSHIFT

1. Improper fluid level.
2. Low main control.
3. Valve body bolts loose or too tight.
4. Valve body dirty or valves sticking.
5. Governor valve sticking.
6. Incorrect engine performance.
7. Intermediate band out of adjustment.
8. Damaged intermediate servo or band.
9. Polished or glazed band or drum.

NO SECOND TO THIRD UPSHIFT

1. Low fluid level.
2. Low main control pressure to direct clutch.
3. Valve body bolts too loose or too tight.
4. Valve body dirty or valves sticking.
5. Converter damper hub weld broken.

HARSH OR DELAYED SECOND TO THIRD UPSHIFT

1. Low fluid level.
2. Valve body bolts loose or too tight.
3. Valve body dirty or valves sticking.
4. Damaged or worn intermediate servo release and high clutch piston check ball.
5. Incorrect engine performance.
6. Engine vacuum leak.

EARLY OR SOFT SECOND TO THIRD UPSHIFT

1. Improper fluid level.
2. Valve body bolts loose or too tight.
3. Valve body dirty or valves sticking.

ERRATIC SHIFTS

1. Improper fluid level.
2. Throttle linkage binding or sticking.
3. Valve body bolts loose or too tight.
4. Valve body dirty or valves sticking.
5. Governor valve sticking.
6. Output shaft collector body seal rings (large cast iron) worn or cut.

SHIFTS FROM LOW TO THIRD IN DRIVE

1. Improper fluid level.
2. Intermediate band out of adjustment.
3. Damaged intermediate servo and/or internal leaks.
4. Polished or glazed band or drum.
5. Improper band or clutch application, or oil pressure control system.
6. Valve body dirty or valves sticking.

ENGINE OVERSPEEDS ON SECOND TO THIRD UPSHIFT

1. Improper fluid level.
2. Linkage out of adjustment.
3. Improper band or clutch application, or oil pressure control system.
4. Damaged or worn high clutch and/or intermediate servo.
5. Valve body dirty or valves sticking.

ROUGH OR SHUDDER THIRD TO LOW SHIFT AT CLOSED THROTTLE

1. Improper fluid level.
2. Incorrect engine idle or performance.
3. Improper linkage adjustment.
4. Improper clutch or band application, or oil pressure control system.
5. Improper governor operation.
6. Valve body dirty or valves sticking.

NO FORCED DOWNSHIFT

1. Improper fluid level.
2. Kickdown linkage out of adjustment.
3. Damaged internal kickdown linkage.
4. Damaged or incorrectly adjusted (short) throttle linkage.
5. Valve body dirty or valves sticking.
6. Dirty or sticking governor.

ENGINE RUNAWAY ON THIRD TO SECOND SHIFT

1. Improper fluid level.
2. Linkage out of adjustment.
3. Intermediate band out of adjustment.
4. Improper band or clutch application, or oil pressure control system.
5. Damaged or worn intermediate servo.
6. Polished or glazed band or drum.
7. Valve body dirty or valves sticking.

SHIFT EFFORTS HIGH

1. Manual shift linkage damaged or incorrectly adjusted.
2. Inner manual lever nut loose.
3. Manual level retainer pin damaged.

NO START IN PARK

1. Manual linkage incorrectly adjusted.
2. Plug connector for the neutral start switch does not fit properly.
3. Neutral start switch plunger travel, inadequate.

NO START IN PARK AND NEUTRAL

1. Plug connector for the neutral start switch does not fit properly.

TRANSMISSION OVERHEATS

1. Improper fluid level.
2. Incorrect engine idle or performance.
3. Improper band or clutch application, or oil pressure control system.
4. Restriction in cooler or lines.
5. Seized converter one-way clutch.
6. Valve body dirty or valves sticking.

MAINTENANCE

CHECKING OIL LEVEL

1. With engine idling, foot brake applied and vehicle on level surface, move selector lever through each range, pausing in each position.
2. Place selector in Park and apply parking brake. Leave engine running during fluid level check.
3. Clean dirt from transmission fluid dipstick cap and remove dipstick. Wipe dipstick and push back into tube making sure it is fully seated.
4. Pull dipstick out and check fluid level. With transmission at operating temperature, fluid level should be between arrows. With transmission cool, fluid level should read between inner holes. Use only Type H fluid, Ford spec. ESP M2C166-H. Do not overfill.
5. Insert dipstick, making sure it is fully seated.

IN-VEHICLE ADJUSTMENT

MANUAL LINKAGE, ADJUST

1. Locate slotted rod in linkage and loos-

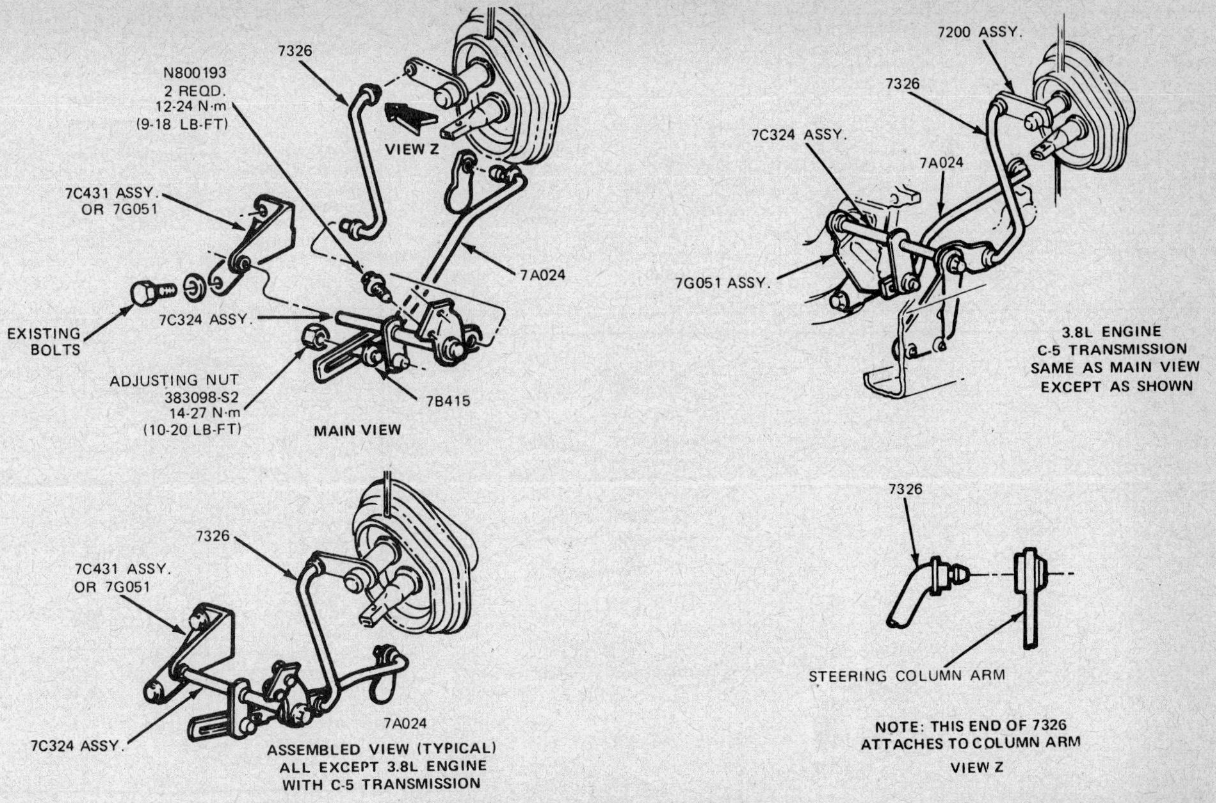

Fig. 3 Column shift manual linkage. Cougar, Fairmont, Granada, LTD, Marquis, Thunderbird & Zephyr

en nut or screw, **Figs. 3 through 6.**

2. Place selector in Drive firmly against gate stop.
3. Move manual shift lever on transmission to Drive position, three detents away from Park.
4. Tighten nut securely.
5. Move shift lever through all ranges. Check to see that detents agree with markings on shift lever. Make sure that lever cannot be moved from Drive position to 2, without moving lever.

DOWNSHIFT LINKAGE, ADJUST

1982

1. Hold throttle lever wide open against stop.
2. Push rod down so down shift valve is forced to bottom in valve body.
3. Measure clearance between tip of adjusting screw and throttle lever, **Fig. 7.** Clearance should be .050-.070 inch.
4. Turn screw, if necessary, to obtain this clearance.

1983–87

Refer to **Fig. 8** for adjustment procedure on 1983 models or **Fig. 9** for adjustment procedures on 1984-87 models.

BANDS, ADJUST

To determine the need for adjustments, the bands can be checked as follows:

Make sure oil level is correct. Then shift selector to Reverse and 2, checking for firm engagement. If engagement in Reverse is delayed or mushy, adjust rear band, **Fig. 10.** If engagement in 2 is delayed or mushy, adjust front band, **Fig. 11.** Adjust bands as follows:

1. Loosen adjuster stop, remove and discard locknut. Install new locknut loosely.
2. Torque screw to 10 ft. lbs.
3. Back screw off exactly 4 1/4 turns for the front (intermediate) band; 3 turns for the rear (low-reverse) band.
4. Hold adjustment and torque new locknut to 35-45 ft. lbs.

IN-VEHICLE REPAIRS

VALVE BODY, REPLACE

1. Raise and support vehicle.
2. Loosen pan bolts and drain transmission fluid.
3. Remove oil pan bolts, pan, and gasket.
4. Shift transmission lever to Park, and remove two bolts attaching detent spring to valve body and case.
5. Remove filter.
6. Remove remaining valve body bolts. Hold manual valve in valve body and remove valve body from case. Manual valve must be held to prevent it from being bent or damaged.
7. Clean and remove all gasket material from pan and pan mounting face. Remove and discard nylon shipping plug, if found in pan.
8. Position valve body in case. Make sure inner downshift lever is between downshift lever stop and downshift valve. The two lands on end of manual valve must engage actuating pin on manual detect lever. Install seven valve body bolts.
9. Position detent spring on lower valve body and install spring-to-case bolt.
10. Hold detent spring roller in center of manual detent lever and install detent spring-to-lower valve body bolt. Torque bolt to 80-120 inch lbs.
11. Torque valve body bolts to 80-120 inch lbs.
12. Position filter and torque bolt to 30 inch lbs.
13. Install pan using new gasket and torque bolts to 12-16 ft. lbs.
14. Lower vehicle and fill transmission with fluid. Check pan area for leakage.

EXTENSION HOUSING, REPLACE

1. Raise and support vehicle and remove driveshaft.
2. Using suitable jack, support transmission.
3. Remove speedometer cable from extension housing.
4. Remove engine rear support to crossmember nuts.
5. Raise transmission and remove rear support bolts. Remove crossmember.
6. Loosen extension housing bolts and let transmission drain.
7. Remove the six extension housing bolts and vacuum tube clip and remove extension housing.
8. Reverse procedure to install, noting the following torques: extension housing bolts, 28-40 ft. lbs; crossmember nuts, 35-50 ft. lbs.; rear support bolts, 25-35 ft. lbs.

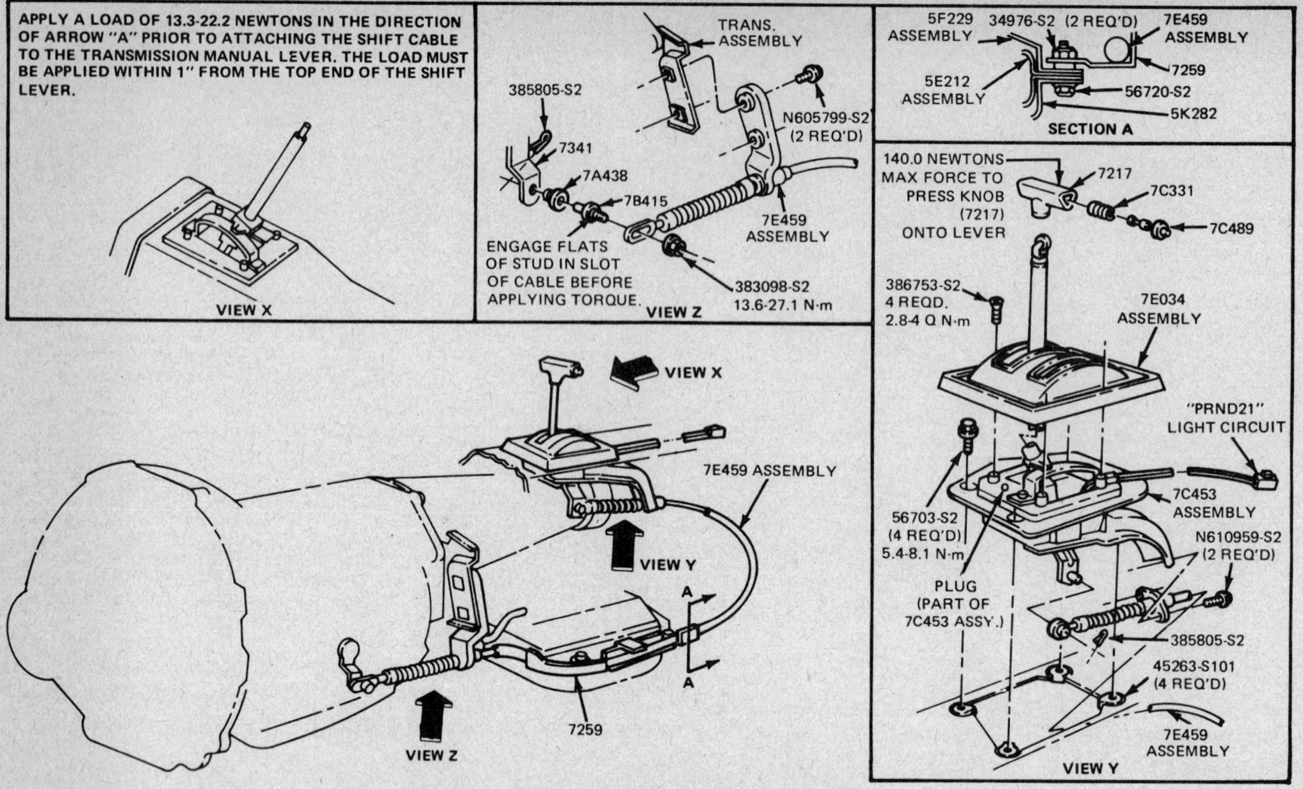

Fig. 4 Floor shift manual linkage. Capri, Cougar, Fairmont, Granada, Mustang & Zephyr w/V6-232 & V8-255 engines

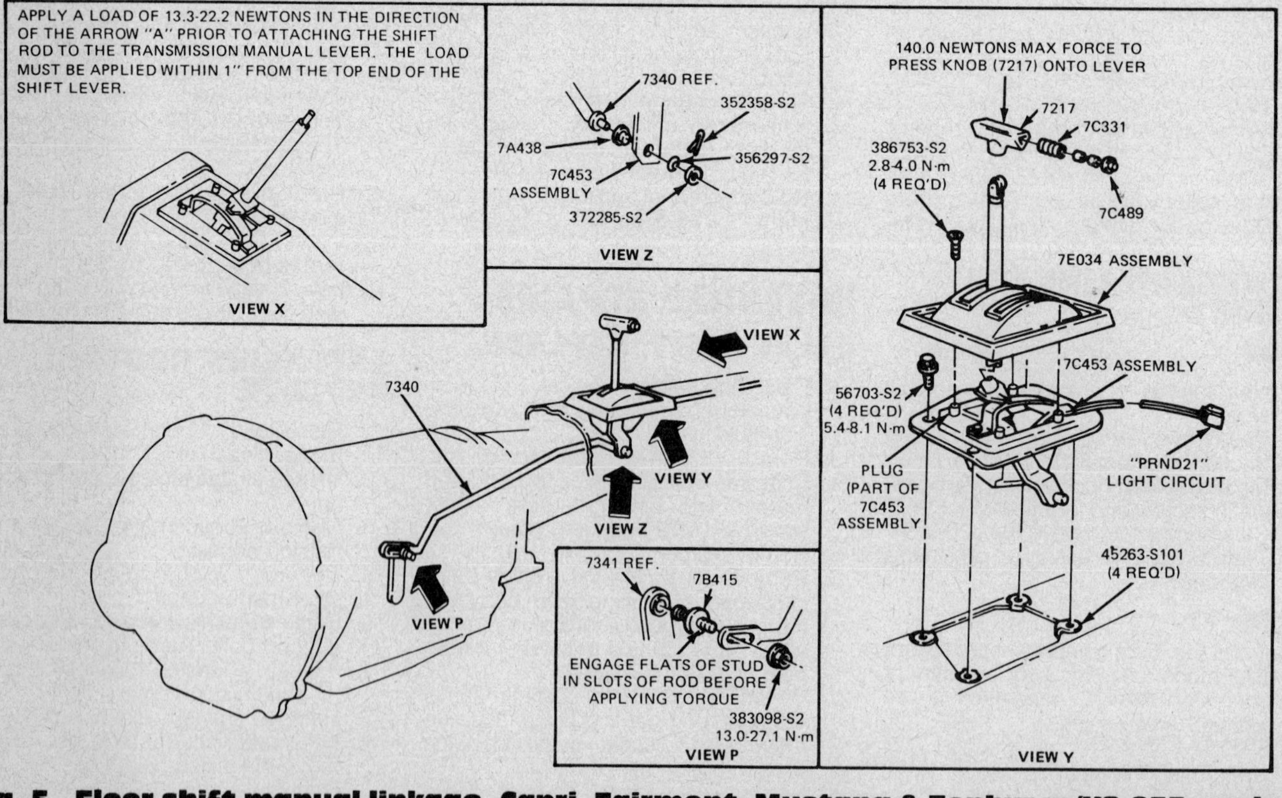

Fig. 5 Floor shift manual linkage. Capri, Fairmont, Mustang & Zephyr w/V8-255 engine

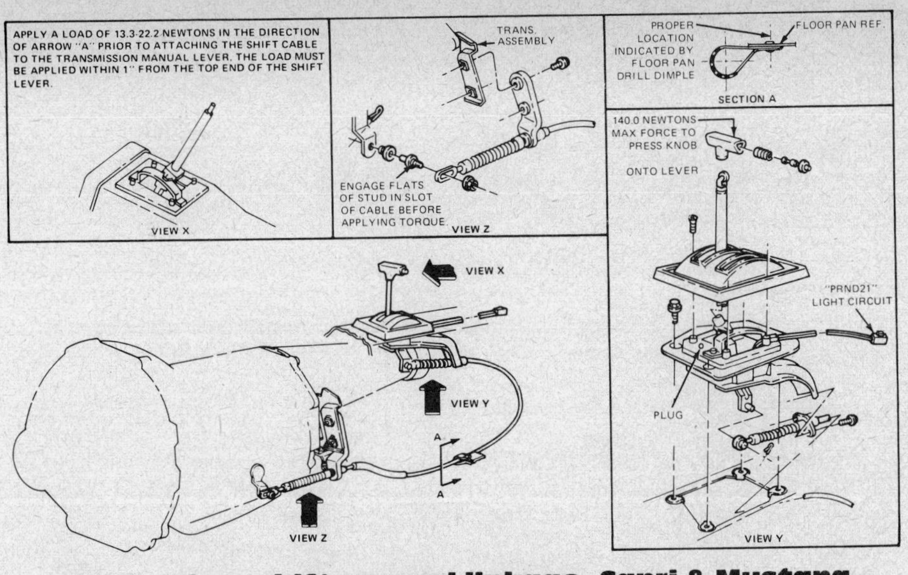

Fig. 6 Floor shift manual linkage. Capri & Mustang w/V6-232 engine

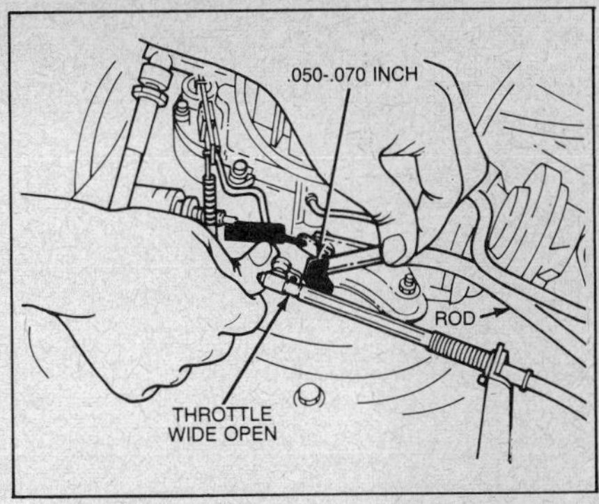

Fig. 7 Downshift rod adjustment

GOVERNOR, REPLACE

1. Refer to "Extension Housing, Replace" and remove extension housing.
2. Remove bolts holding governor housing to governor distributor.
3. Slide governor away from distributor body and off output shaft.
4. Reverse procedure to install. Torque governor bolts to 80-120 inch lbs.

LOW-REVERSE SERVO, REPLACE

Exc. Mustang & Capri W/V8-255 Engine

1. Raise and support vehicle.
2. Loosen low-reverse band adjusting screw locknut. Torque band adjusting screw to 10 ft. lbs. to prevent band strut from falling when reverse servo piston assembly is removed.
3. Disengage neutral switch harness from clips on servo cover.
4. Remove servo cover bolts, servo cover, and seal from case.
5. Remove servo piston from case. If seal is bad, piston must be replaced.
6. Install piston in case. Install cover with new seal. Use two 5/16-18 x 1 1/4 bolts to position cover against case. Install two cover bolts, remove two locating bolts and install remaining bolts. Torque to 12-20 ft. lbs.

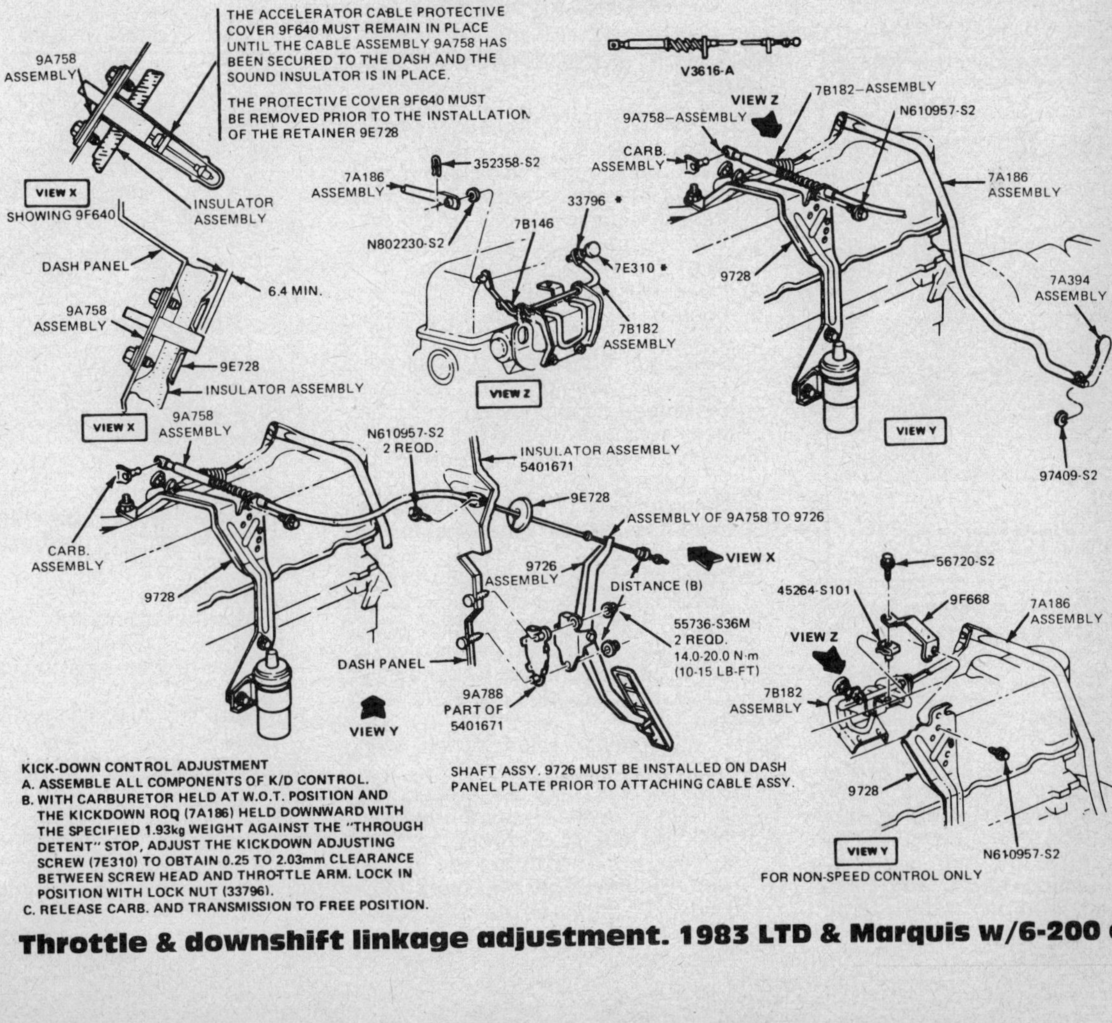

Fig. 8 Throttle & downshift linkage adjustment. 1983 LTD & Marquis w/6-200 engine

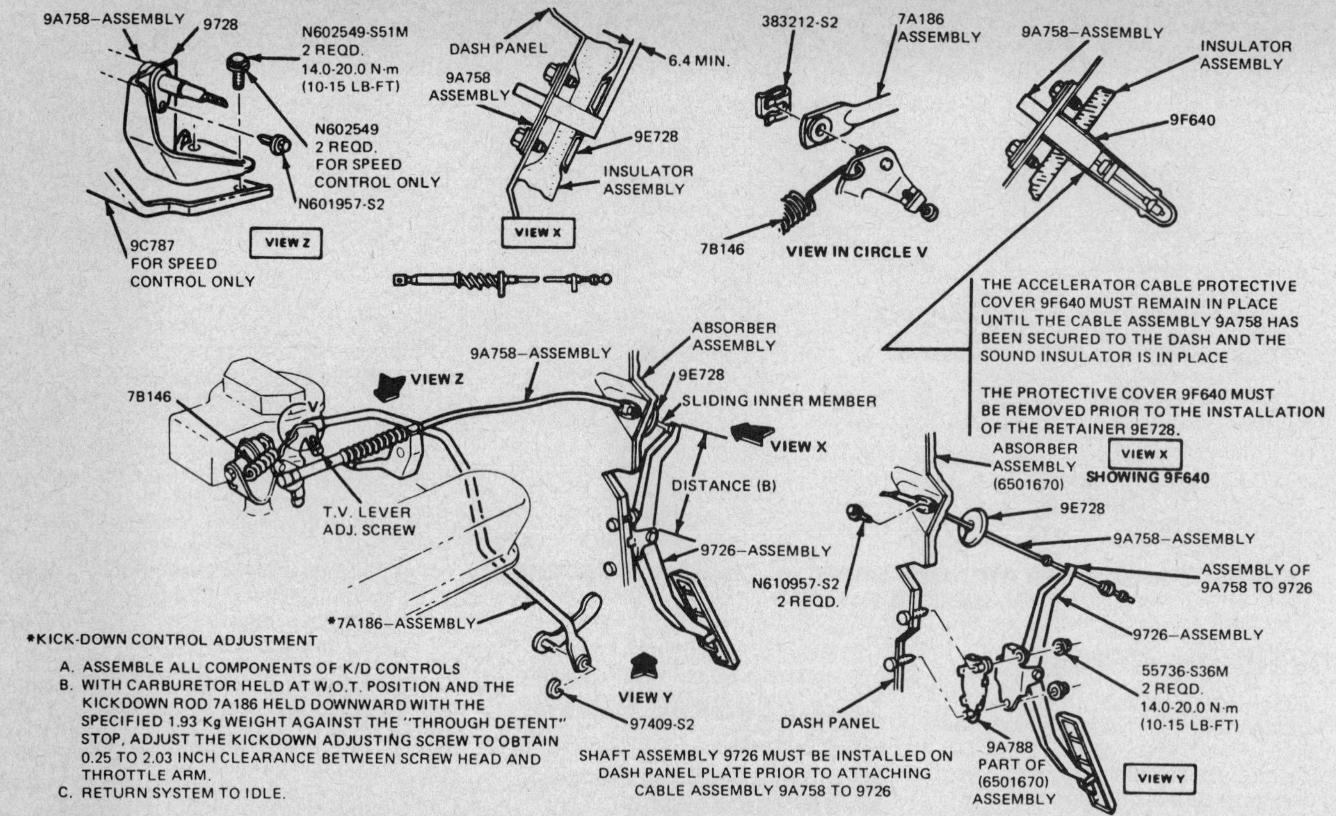

Fig. 9 Throttle & downshift linkage adjustment. 1984–87 Cougar & Thunderbird W/V6-232 engine

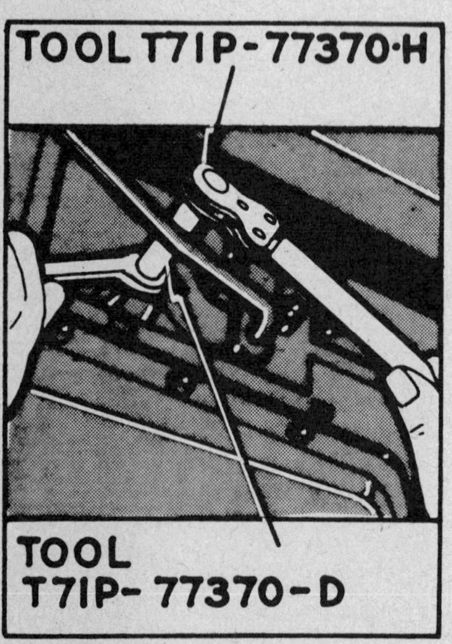

Fig. 10 Low-Reverse band adjustment

7. Position neutral switch harness in clips.
8. Adjust low-reverse band. Refer to "Bands, Adjust" procedure. **If band cannot be adjusted properly, low-reverse band struts are not in position. Remove oil pan and valve body. Position struts and install valve body and pan. Adjust band.**
9. Lower vehicle and check transmission fluid level.

Mustang & Capri W/V8-255 Engine

1. Disconnect fan shroud and position against engine.
2. Raise and support vehicle and position suitable transmission jack under transmission.
3. Remove transmission crossmember bolts.
4. Lower transmission.
5. Loosen low-reverse band adjusting screw locknut. Torque band adjusting screw to 10 ft. lbs. to prevent band strut from falling down.
6. Disengage neutral switch wiring harness from clips on servo cover.
7. Remove servo cover bolts, servo cover, and seal from case.
8. Remove servo piston and spring from case. If piston seal is bad, piston must be replaced.
9. Install piston and return spring in case. Install cover with new seal. Use two 5/16-18 x 1 1/4 bolts to position cover. Install two cover bolts, remove two locating bolts and install remaining two cover bolts. Torque bolts to 12-20 ft. lbs.
10. Position neutral start switch wiring harness in clips.
11. Refer to "Bands, Adjust" procedure to adjust low-reverse band. **If band cannot be adjusted properly, low-reverse band struts are not in position. Remove oil pan and valve body. Position struts and install valve body and pan. Adjust band.**
12. Raise transmission into position and install crossmember bolts. Torque nuts to 35-50 ft. lbs.
13. Remove transmission jack and lower vehicle.
14. Install fan shroud and check transmission fluid.

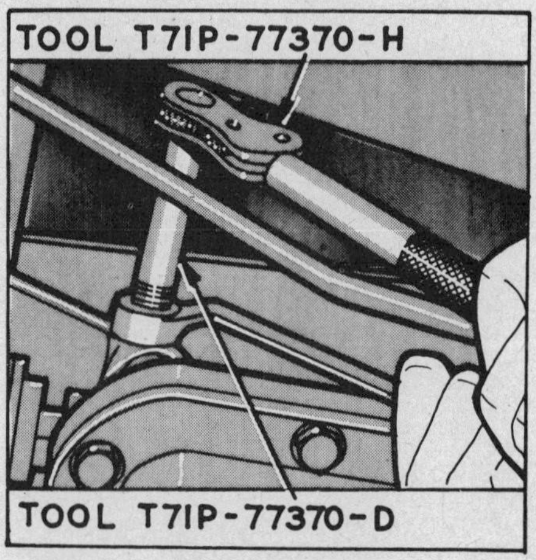

Fig. 11 Intermediate band adjustment

INTERMEDIATE SERVO, REPLACE

1. Disconnect fan shroud from radiator and push shroud back against engine.
2. Raise and support vehicle.
3. Support transmission with suitable jack and remove crossmember bolts.
4. Lower transmission.

5. On models with V6-232 engine, except 1982 Thunderbird and XR7, disconnect oil cooler line.
6. On all models, remove servo cover bolts.
7. Remove servo cover/piston assembly and return spring from case.
8. Remove and discard servo cover gasket.
9. Position new gasket on servo cover so notch aligns with fluid passage in case.
10. Install piston return spring and servo cover/piston assembly in case. Use two 5/16-18 x 1 1/4 bolts to position cover against case. Install two cover bolts, remove locating bolts and install remaining cover bolts. Torque bolts to 12-20 ft. lbs.
11. Refer to "Bands, Adjust" and adjust intermediate band. **If band cannot be adjusted properly, intermediate band strut is not in position. Remove oil pan and valve body. Position struts and install valve body and oil pan. Adjust band.**
12. On Granada and Cougar models with V6-232 engine, connect transmission oil cooler line.
13. On all models, raise transmission into position and install crossmember bolts. Torque nuts to 35-50 ft. lbs.
14. Remove jack and lower vehicle.
15. Position fan shroud bolt to radiator. Check transmission fluid level.

TRANSMISSION REPLACE

1. Disconnect battery ground cable.
2. On models with V6-232 engine, remove air cleaner assembly if necessary.
3. On all models, remove fan shroud bolts and position shroud back over fan.
4. On models with V6-232 and V8-255, loosen clamp and disconnect thermactor air injection hose at catalytic converter check valve.
5. On models with V6-232 engine, except 1982 Thunderbird and XR7, remove the top two engine-to-transmission bolts.
6. On all models, remove driveshaft after raising vehicle.
7. Disconnect muffler inlet pipe from catalytic converter outlet pipe. Support muffler pipe assembly.
8. Disconnect exhaust pipes from exhaust manifolds.
9. Release catalytic converter hangers from bracket by pulling back on converter.
10. Remove speedometer cable clamp bolt and pull cable out of extension housing.
11. Disconnect neutral start switch harness connector.
12. Disconnect kickdown rod at transmission lever.
13. Disconnect shift linkage at bellcrank. On vehicles with floor shifts, remove shift cable routing bracket bolts and disconnect cable at transmission lever.
14. Remove converter dust shield.
15. Remove torque converter drive plate nuts. Crankshaft can be turned by using socket and ratchet handle on crankshaft pulley bolt.
16. Remove starter.
17. Loosen nuts attaching rear support to No. 3 crossmember.
18. Position suitable jack under transmission oil pan.
19. Remove bolt attaching No. 3 crossmember to body brackets.
20. Lower transmission enough to allow access to cooler line fittings. Disconnect cooler lines.
21. Remove all transmission-to-engine bolts.
22. Pull transmission back to clear converter studs. Lower transmission.
23. Reverse procedure to install. Note the following torque values: engine-to-transmission bolts, 40-50 ft. lbs.; no. 3 crossmember bolts, 20-30 ft. lbs.; rear support nuts, 30-50 ft. lbs.; torque converter-to-drive-plate nuts, 20-30 ft. lbs.; linkage bellcrank bracket, 12-16 ft. lbs.; speedometer cable clamp, 36-54 inch lbs.

ZF 4HP-22 Automatic Transmission

INDEX

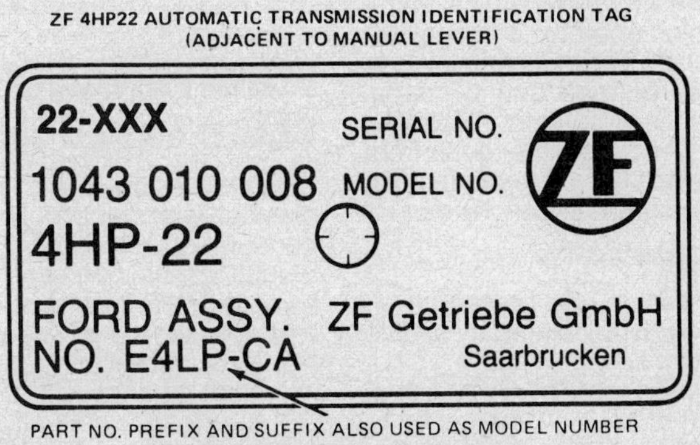

Fig. 1 Transmission identification tag

TRANSMISSION IDENTIFICATION

The ZF automatic transmission is used on Continental and Mark VII models equipped with 2.4 liter diesel engines, and can be identified by a tag attached to the housing adjacent to the manual shift lever, **Fig. 1.**

DESCRIPTION

The 4HP-22 is a 4 speed transmission that provides automatic upshifts and downshifts through 4 forward gear ratios. While selector lever positions are the same as for the Automatic Overdrive (AOD) units, the 4HP-22 uses an entirely different gear train and includes a torque converter lockup feature.

The drivetrain consists of a front compound planetary gear set that operates in first, second, third and reverse speeds, and a separate overdrive gear set which provides fourth gear and remains locked for direct (through) drive in all other operating ranges. Drive train operation and gear selection is controlled by seven disc clutches and 3 one-way clutches. The output shaft is housed in a conventional Ford type extension housing which is fitted with a bushing and slip yoke seal common with C-3 transmissions.

The torque converter operates as a conventional torque multiplier and fluid coupling in all gears except fourth (overdrive). When fourth gear is engaged, a specific combination of road speed and accelerator position will signal the converter to lockup to mechanical drive. When converter lockup is signaled, the valve body applies fluid pressure to a hydraulic clutch in the converter, locking the impeller to the turbine.

The valve body is controlled by the manual selector, a centrifugal governor on the output shaft and a cable operated throttle valve which signals throttle lever position. The throttle valve (kickdown) cable is attached to a bracket and operated by the injection pump control lever.

SHIFT SELECTOR POSITION & OPERATION

The 4HP-22 is fully automatic when the selector lever is in either the overdrive or overdrive lockout position. Manual upshifting and downshifting is available through all forward drive ranges.

Overdrive

This is the selector lever position for normal operating conditions. In this range, the transmission starts in first gear and automatically upshifts to second, third and fourth gears as the vehicle accelerates; and the transmission automatically downshifts as vehicle speed decreases. When the transmission is operating in fourth gear and load and road speed are within specified limits, the torque converter clutch will be engaged and the converter will be locked. However, the transmission will not shift into or remain in fourth gear when the accelerator is fully depressed.

Overdrive Lockout

With the selector in this position, the transmission operates as in the overdrive mode except there is no shift into fourth (overdrive) gear and no converter clutch lockup. This position is used to provide increased performance and greater engine braking than is available in the overdrive position. The transmission can be shifted between overdrive and overdrive lockout positions at any vehicle speed.

Low (L Or 1)

This selector position is used when maximum engine braking is desired. At vehicle speeds above 20 mph, moving the selector to the low position will cause the transmission to shift to second gear until vehicle speed drops below 20 mph, then shift into and remain in first gear. When the low position is selected for initial driveaway, the transmission will remain in the selected range until the selector is moved to another gear position. Upshifts from the low position can be made manually by moving the selector to the overdrive or overdrive lockout positions.

CONDITION	POSSIBLE SOURCE	ACTION
1. **Position P**		
1.1 Transmission does not engage Park	• Improperly adjusted linkage	• Adjust linkage
	• Excessive friction in Park mechanism	• Replace parts (cam and connection rod, eventually pawl)
1.2 Transmission does not hold Park	• Improperly adjusted linkage	• Adjust linkage
1.3 Engine cannot be started	• Improperly adjusted linkage	• Adjust linkage
	• Neutral start switch malfunctioning	• Replace switch
2. **Position R**		
2.1 No or delayed Reverse gear engagement	• Improperly adjusted linkage	• Adjust linkage
	• Transmission filter plugged	• Replace filter
	• Body dirty/sticking valves	• Replace valve body
	• Clutch burnt/worn, in this case no 3rd gear	• Replace transmission
	• Clutch burnt/worn, no engine braking in Position 1, 1st gear	• Replace transmission
	• Clutch burnt/worn, no engine braking in 2nd + 3rd gear, also in Position 1, 1st gear	• Replace transmission
2.2 Slipping or chatter at start in Reverse gear	• Clutches damaged, burnt or worn	• Replace transmission
2.3 Harsh engagement P-R or N-R, or distinct double jerk at P-R or N-R (below 1500 rpm engine speed)	• Valve body malfunction (will give the same symptoms when changing from 2nd to 3rd gear)	• Replace valve body
2.4 Backup lamp does not illuminate (bulbs, fuses and cables OK)	• Go to 1.3	• Go to 1.3
3. **Position N**		
3.1 Engine cannot be started	• Go to 1.3	• Go to 1.3
3.2 Vehicle moves in Position N	• Improperly adjusted linkage	• Adjust linkage
	• Clutch seized	• Replace transmission
4. **Position Ⓓ**		
4.1 No Drive	• Improperly adjusted linkage	• Adjust linkage
	• Transmission filter plugged	• Replace filter
	• Clutch burnt/worn	• Replace transmission
	• One way clutch 1st gear slips	• Replace transmission
4.2 Slipping or chatter at driveaway	• Clutch burnt/worn	• Replace transmission
4.3 Stroke jerk N-D (below 1500 rpm engine speed)	• Clutch damper malfunction	• Replace valve body
	• Clutch burnt/worn	• Replace transmission

Fig. 2 Transmission troubleshooting chart (Part 1 of 4)

Reverse Inhibitor

The transmission operates in a conventional manner when the selector lever is placed in reverse position during normal operation. However, a reverse inhibitor is used which prevents reverse gear from being engaged when the vehicle is moving forward at speeds greater than 19 mph.

Forced Downshifts

Normal transmission shifting can be altered by changes in accelerator (throttle lever) position as follows:

1. At vehicle speeds of 20-50 mph when the selector lever is in overdrive or overdrive lockout, the transmission will downshift to second gear when the accelerator pedal is fully depressed.
2. At vehicle speeds below 20 mph, the transmission will downshift into first gear when the accelerator pedal is fully depressed.
3. When the selector is in overdrive range, the transmission will downshift from fourth to third gear at most vehicle speeds when the accelerator pedal is depressed to provide moderate to heavy acceleration.

MAINTENANCE

FLUID LEVEL CHECK

Transmission fluid level should be checked with unit at normal operating temperature of 150-170° F (dipstick hot to touch). Normal operating temperature may be obtained by operating vehicle for 15-20 miles of city type driving with ambient temperatures above 50° F.

1. Start engine, set parking brake securely and ensure that curb idle speed is within specifications.
2. Firmly apply service brakes and move transmission selector through all ranges, allowing transmission time to

CONDITION	POSSIBLE SOURCE	ACTION
4.4 No or erratic shifts		
— No 1-2/2-1	• Governor valve sticking	• Replace governor
	• Shift valve 1-2 sticking	• Replace valve body
— No 1-2	• Clutches burnt/worn	• Replace transmission
— No 2-3/3-2	• Governor valve sticking	• Replace governor
	• Shift valve 2-3 sticking	• Replace valve body
— No 2-3	• Clutch burnt/worn	• Replace transmission
— No 3-4/4-3	• Governor valve sticking	• Replace governor
	• Shift valve 3-4 sticking	• Replace valve body
— No 3-4	• Clutch burnt/worn	• Replace transmission
4.5 Vehicle starts in 2nd gear	• Sticking governor	• Replace governor
	• 1-2 Shift valve sticking	• Replace valve body
Vehicle starts in 3rd gear	• Sticking governor	• Replace governor
	• 1-2, 2-3 Shift valves sticking	• Replace valve body
Shifts 1-3 in Ⓓ, D ranges	• 2-3 Shift valve sticking	• Replace valve body
4.6 Shift Speeds		
— No upshifts	• Stuck governor	• Replace governor
	• Shift valves sticking	• Replace valve body
— Shift points incorrect at full throttle	• Throttle cable setting incorrect	• Re-adjust throttle cable
— No 1-2/2-1 shift at kickdown	• Throttle cable setting incorrect	• Re-adjust throttle cable
— No 2-3/3-2 shift at kickdown	• Throttle cable setting incorrect	• Re-adjust throttle cable
— No 4-3 shift at kickdown	• 4-3 Kickdown valve sticking	• Replace valve body
4.7 Shift quality		
— Harsh shifts at light throttle	• Valve body malfunction	• Replace valve body
— Harsh shifts at full throttle and kickdown	• Valve body malfunction	• Replace valve body
— Soft shifts at full throttle and kickdown	• Clutch plates burnt/worn	• Replace transmission
	• Valve body malfunction	• Replace valve body
	• Clutch plates burnt/worn	• Replace transmission
5. Position D		
3rd Gear		
5.1 No engine braking	• Clutch burnt/worn	• Replace transmission
6. **Position L**		
6.1 No manual 2-1 downshift	• Dirty/sticking valve body	• Replace valve body
	• Governor sticking	• Replace governor
6.2 No engine braking	• Clutch burnt/worn	• Replace transmission

Fig. 2 Transmission troubleshooting chart (Part 2 of 4)

CONDITION		POSSIBLE SOURCE	ACTION
7.	Torque Converter **Lockup Clutch**		
7.1	Lockup points incorrect	• Valve body malfunction	• Replace valve body
		• Governor pressure incorrect	• Replace governor
7.2	Shift too harsh	• Damper malfunction	• Replace valve body
		• Torque converter malfunction	• Replace transmission
7.3	No lockup	• Valve body malfunction	• Replace valve body
		• Torque converter malfunction	• Replace transmission
8.	**General**		
8.1	Throttle cable sticking	• Too much friction in sleeve of throttle cable	• Replace cable
		• Throttle pressure valve sticking	• Replace valve body
8.2	Noisy and no Drive after long journey	• Oil filter on valve body dirty	• If there is no burnt clutch plate lining in oil sump, then replace filter, otherwise replace transmission
8.3	Very noisy and no Drive	• Flex plate is damaged	• Replace flex plate or transmission
		• Pump drive worn	• Replace transmission
9.	**Oil Leaks**		
9.1	Oil dripping from converter housing	• Seal ring in pump housing damaged	• Replace seal
		• Pump housing porous	• Replace transmission
		• Converter leaking from welded seam	• Replace transmission
9.2	Leakage between transmission and oil pan	• Incorrect torque of bolts	• Tighten bolts
		• Pan gasket damaged	• Replace gasket
9.3	Leakage between intermediate plate and main housing (especially at pump pressure point)	• Converter housing bolts have worked loose	• Tighten bolts
9.4	Oil loss at speedo	• Damaged O-ring on speedo	• Replace O-ring
9.5	Oil leak at throttle connection cable	• O-ring connection damaged	• Replace O-ring or complete cable
9.6	Oil leak at extension housing	• Output oil seal damaged	• Replace seal
9.7	Loss of oil through breather	• Oil level too high	• Check and correct oil level
		• No breather cap	• Replace cap or change breather
		• O-ring breather damaged	• Remove extension housing and replace O-ring
		• Securing clip broken/damaged	• Replace clip

Fig. 2 Transmission troubleshooting chart (Part 3 of 4)

CONDITION	POSSIBLE SOURCE	ACTION
9.8 Leakage in cooler lines	• Loose connections	• Re-tighten
9.9 Oil leak at intermediate plate	• Plugs loose	• Tighten plugs • Replace washers
9.10 Leakage between main case and extension housing	• Loose bolts • Gasket damaged	• Re-tighten • Replace gasket
10. **Noises** 10.1 High pitched noise in all positions, especially if oil is cold	• Low oil level • Leaking valve body	• Top off as required • Replace valve body
10.2 High-pitched squeaking noise (dependent on engine rpm) in all gears when oil is warm, accompanied by intermittent no drive after long journey	• Dirty filter	• If no debris in sump, just replace filter, otherwise replace transmission
10.3 Loud noise when in lockup	• Torsional damper malfunction	• Replace transmission
10.4 Torsional vibrations from engine when in lockup	• Engine rpm is too low; lockup shift point incorrect	• Replace valve body

Fig. 2 Transmission troubleshooting chart (Part 4 of 4)

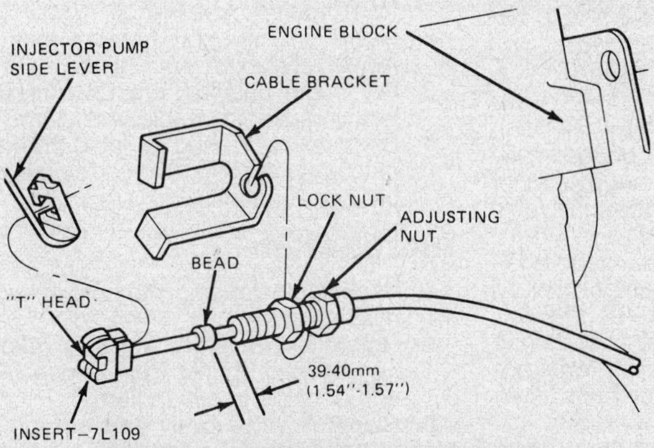

Fig. 3 Kickdown (throttle lever) cable installation at injection pump

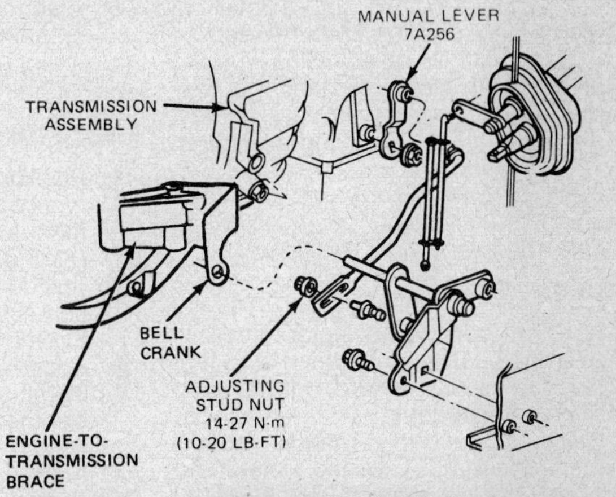

Fig. 4 Manual shift linkage assembly. Models w/column shift

engage in each range, then return selector to Park.

3. Clean dirt from around transmission dipstick cap, withdraw dipstick and wipe it clean, then push dipstick back into tube ensuring that it is fully seated.
4. With engine running at normal curb idle speed, withdraw dipstick from tube and check fluid level against reference marks on dipstick.
5. If transmission is at normal operating temperature (150-170° F), fluid level should be within cross hatched area on dipstick. If fluid is at room temperature (70-90° F), fluid level should be between middle and top holes in dipstick.
6. If fluid level is not within specifications, add a sufficient quantity of Dexron II type fluid through dipstick tube to bring fluid to specified level. **Do not overfill transmission as this may cause foaming and loss of fluid through vent. If transmission is overfilled, remove sufficient fluid to lower level using suitable suction pump.**

TROUBLESHOOTING

Refer to **Fig. 2** when troubleshooting this transmission.

IN-VEHICLE ADJUSTMENT

KICKDOWN (THROTTLE VALVE) CABLE, ADJUST

1. Ensure that injection pump linkage is properly adjusted.
2. Set injection pump top lever in full throttle position.
3. Loosen cable locknut, then tighten adjusting nut, **Fig. 3,** until gap between end of cable housing and bead on cable is 1.54-1.57 inches.
4. Torque locknut to 80-106 inch lbs., ensure that gap between end of housing and bead on cable is still within specifications, then release injection pump lever.

MANUAL SHIFT LINKAGE, ADJUST

Column Shift

1. Place selector lever on column in overdrive position, ensuring that lever is tight against stop. **Hang an 8 lb. weight from column shift lever to ensure that lever remains against stop during adjustment.**
2. Raise and support vehicle as needed, then loosen adjusting stud nut secur-

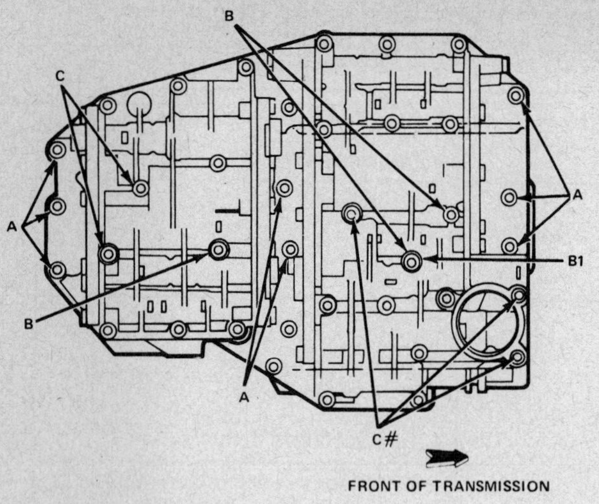

POSITION	LENGTH	QUANTITY
A	30MM (1.20")	8
B	60MM (2.40")	3
C	65MM (2.60")	5

INSTALLED AFTER OIL SCREEN IS IN PLACE

Fig. 5 Valve body retaining bolt identification

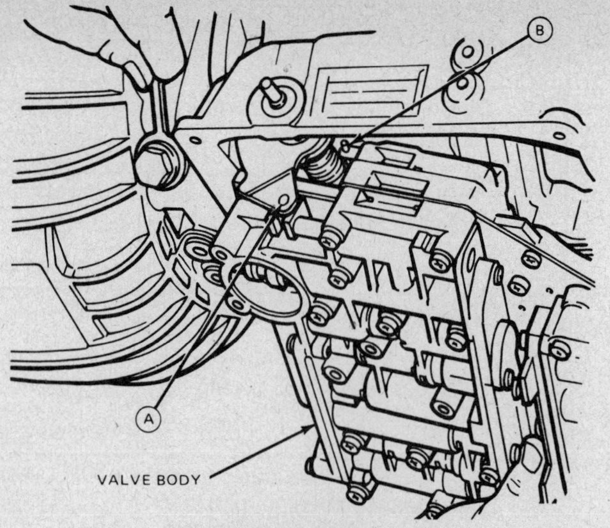

Fig. 6 Valve body installation

ing slotted end of transmission control rod, **Fig. 4.**

3. Rotate manual lever on transmission fully rearward, then return lever to third detent position from the rear.
4. Ensure that flats on adjusting stud are aligned with slot in rod and that column shift lever is still tight against stop, then torque adjusting stud nut to 10-20 ft. lbs.
5. Remove weight from shift lever and check transmission operation in all selector lever detent positions.

Console Shift

1. Position console selector lever in overdrive position and secure so that lever is held rearward against stop during adjustment.
2. Raise and support vehicle as needed, then loosen nut securing slotted end of shift cable to manual lever on transmission.
3. Position transmission lever in third detent position from rear (overdrive position), then torque cable retaining nut to 10-18 ft. lbs.
4. Check operation of transmission in all selector lever positions.

IN-VEHICLE REPAIR

VALVE BODY, REPLACE

Removal

1. Raise and support vehicle, place suitable drain pan under transmission oil pan and drain transmission.
2. Disconnect oil filler tube from oil pan.
3. Remove bolts and clamps securing oil pan, the oil pan and gasket.
4. Remove bolts securing filter screen and O-ring.
5. Support valve body and remove remaining 13 retaining bolts, **Fig. 5,** then lower valve body from case. Note position of bolts for installation. **Remove only large head retaining bolts, using Torx drive D79P-2100-T27 or equivalent.**
6. Clean case and valve body mating surfaces, then inspect for burrs or distortion of surfaces.

Installation

1. Position valve body under case mounting surface and engage inner manual lever pin with manual valve (A), **Fig. 6.**
2. Pull down on kickdown cable to position accelerator cam so that roller on throttle lever clears cam (B), **Fig. 6.**
3. Support valve body against case and install 13 retaining bolts in proper positions, **Fig. 5,** then tighten bolts finger tight.
4. Align valve body by inserting gauge T84P-77003-A or equivalent between throttle lever pin and valve body housing, **Fig. 7. If throttle valve pin position interferes with alignment gauge, use notch on gauge handle to grip pin and draw throttle valve further from its bore.**
5. Push valve body forward toward converter until alignment gauge is held snug, then tighten bolt, **Fig. 7,** firmly to hold valve body in position.
6. Torque valve body bolts to 71 inch lbs., then recheck position with gauge. Light pressure should be required to move gauge up and down.
7. Clean filter screen, insert new O-ring into screen inlet, install screen assembly on valve body and torque retaining bolts to 71 inch lbs.
8. Install oil pan, new gasket retaining bolts and clamps, installing long radiused clamps on corners, and torque retaining bolts to 53 inch lbs.
9. Lower vehicle and fill transmission to specified level with Dexron II type transmission fluid.
10. Road test transmission in all operating ranges and check for leaks.

KICKDOWN (THROTTLE VALVE) CABLE, REPLACE

Removal

1. Disconnect cable from injection pump lever and bracket, **Fig. 3.**
2. Raise and support vehicle and remove valve body as outlined.
3. Pry cable casing from transmission housing using suitable levers.
4. Disconnect "T" end of cable from accelerator cam, **Fig. 8,** then remove cable from transmission.

Installation

1. Push cable housing into bore in transmission case.
2. Rotate accelerator cam one revolution to load spring, then engage "T" end of cable in slot in cam.
3. Reinstall valve body and oil pan as outlined, lower vehicle and fill transmission to specified level with Dexron II type transmission fluid.
4. If new cable is being installed, spin rear adjusting nut back to end of housing and insert cable housing into slot in cable bracket, **Fig. 3.** If used cable is being installed, proceed to step 9.
5. Pull cable housing into bracket, install front locknut and set adjusting nuts so that threaded barrel of cable housing is centered in bracket.
6. Pull cable out of housing just until detent step is felt (approximately 0.25 inch before maximum cable travel) and hold in position.
7. Slide bead stop along cable until bead is 1.54-1.57 inches from end of cable housing, then crimp bead to cable to secure position.
8. Remove cable and housing assembly from bracket.
9. Slip cable through slot in injection pump lever insert with "T" head toward trunnion side and pull cable through insert.

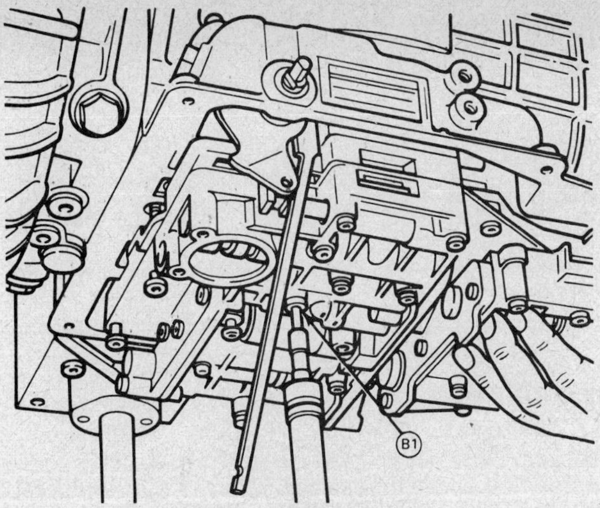

Fig. 7 Valve body alignment

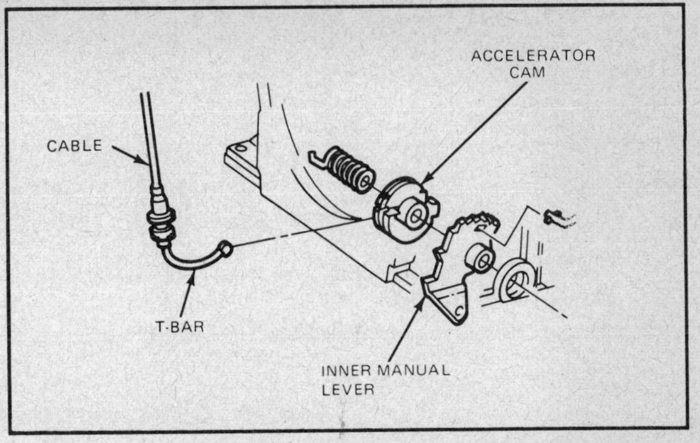

Fig. 8 Kickdown (throttle valve) cable installation at transmission

10. Snap "T" head into insert trunnions, thread cable through slot in injection pump lever and snap insert into rectangular hole in lever.
11. Spin cable adjusting nuts to opposite ends of threaded portion on cable housing, then mount cable housing in bracket.
12. Adjust cable as outlined in "Kickdown (Throttle Lever) Cable, Adjust."

EXTENSION HOUSING, BUSHING & SEAL, REPLACE

Removal

1. Place transmission selector lever in Neutral, then raise and support vehicle.
2. Mark position of propeller shaft yoke and rear axle companion flange, disconnect shaft from companion flange and remove propeller shaft.
3. If only seal and/or bushing is to be replaced, proceed as follows:
   a. Remove seal and bushing as needed, using suitable pullers, taking care not to damage extension housing or output shaft.
   b. Inspect counterbores in extension housing for burrs and damage, removing burrs as needed with crocus cloth.
   c. Install replacement bushing and/or seal using suitable drivers.
   d. Inspect propeller shaft yoke for damage and scoring, and replace as needed.
   e. Reinstall driveshaft as outlined under "Installation."
4. Disconnect speed sensor electrical connector from extension housing.
5. Remove position sensor from converter housing.
6. Remove bolts securing rear mount to extension housing, then raise and support transmission just enough to remove weight from rear mount.
7. Remove nuts securing rear mount to crossmember, then the rear mount.
8. Lower transmission to gain clearance, remove 9 bolts securing extension housing, then remove extension housing and gasket.

Installation

1. Position new extension housing gasket on transmission housing.
2. Ensure that alignment pins are properly seated in extension housing, slide housing over output shaft and position against case, then install retaining bolts.
3. Evenly torque extension housing bolts to 17 ft. lbs.
4. Raise transmission and install rear support on extension housing.
5. Lower transmission, install nuts securing rear mount to crossmember, then remove support.
6. Insert propeller shaft into transmission, align matching marks between propeller shaft yoke and companion flange, then secure yoke to companion flange.
7. Install position sensor in converter housing and connect speed sensor electrical connector.
8. Lower vehicle and ensure that transmission is filled to specified level, then road test vehicle and check for leaks.

GOVERNOR, REPLACE

Removal & Disassembly

1. Remove extension housing as outlined.
2. Remove interlocking snap ring from output shaft, **Fig. 9.**
3. Remove parking gear, governor assembly and split drive rings from output shaft.
4. Remove 2 bolts securing governor housing to governor hub.
5. Remove 2 bolts securing governor hub to parking gear.
6. Remove counterweight and clamp from governor hub, noting installation position.
7. Remove O-ring, snap ring and seal rings.

Assembly & Installation

1. Lubricate and install seal rings, snap ring and new O-ring, **Fig. 9.**
2. Insert counterweight into governor hub and secure with clamp.
3. Install governor housing on hub and torque bolts to 7 ft. lbs.
4. Install parking gear on governor hub and torque bolts to 7 ft. lbs.
5. Lubricate O-ring on output shaft and slide parking gear with split drive ring and governor assembly onto shaft until assembly reaches stop.
6. Install interlocking snap ring onto output shaft.
7. Reinstall extension housing assembly as outlined.
8. Road test vehicle and check for leaks.

SELECTOR LINKAGE, ACCELERATOR CAM & PARKING PAWL ROD, REPLACE

Removal

1. Place transmission in neutral, then raise and support vehicle.
2. Remove outer manual lever.
3. Remove transmission oil pan, filter and valve body as outlined in "Valve body, Replace."
4. Remove "T" bar end of kickdown cable from the accelerator cam.
5. Remove roll pin securing manual lever to manual lever shaft.
6. Slide out shaft to remove the spring, cam and inner manual lever.
7. Unhook parking pawl rod and remove from case.
8. Remove shaft seal.

Installation

1. Install new shaft seal flush with case.
2. Hook park rod to the inner manual lever and install in case. Ensure that the rod protrudes through the guide plate in rear of case.
3. Install manual lever shaft through the case and inner manual lever.
4. Insert spring into cam.
5. Install spring and cam into end of shaft, then push cam into case until it stops.
6. Align shaft and inner manual lever holes to accept new roll pin.

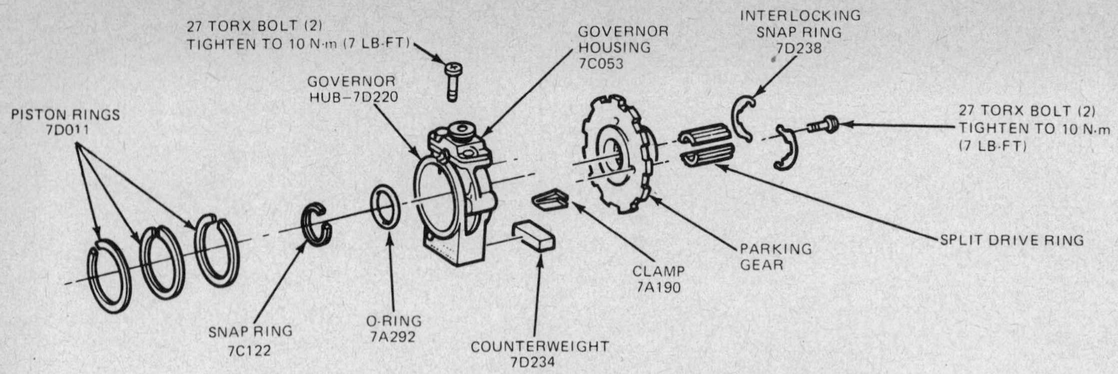

Fig. 9 Governor assembly exploded view

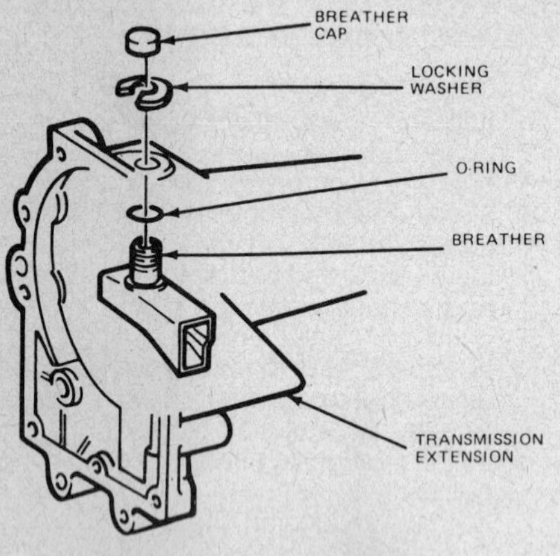

Fig. 10 Breather components

7. Install new roll pin with slot facing rear of transmission.
8. Rotate cam to set spring load, then install "T" bar end of cable in the cam.
9. Reinstall valve body, filter and pan, using new transmission pan gasket.

BREATHER ASSEMBLY, REPLACE

Removal

1. Remove extension housing as outlined in "Extension Housing, Bushing & Seal, Replace."
2. Remove breather cap from breather.
3. Remove locking washer securing breather to housing using suitable pliers, **Fig. 10.**
4. Remove breather assembly.

Installation

1. Replace O-ring and install breather assembly into extension housing.
2. Install new lockwasher to secure breather assembly into housing.
3. Snap breather cap onto breather assembly.
4. Reinstall extension housing.

PARKING PAWL, SHAFT & SPRING, REPLACE

Removal

1. Remove extension housing as outlined in "Extension Housing, Bushing & Seal, Replace."
2. Remove guide plate attaching bolt,

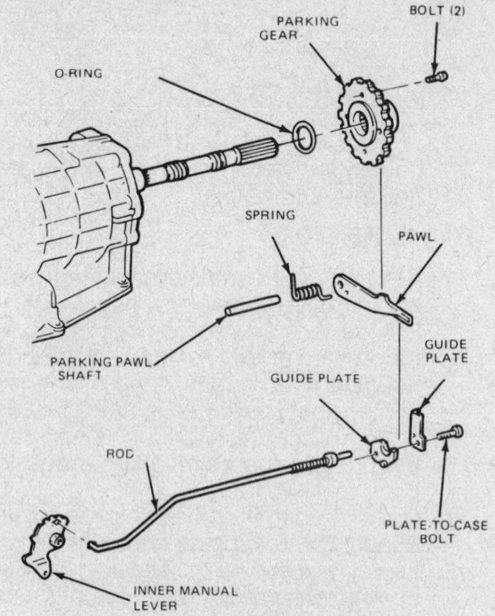

Fig. 11 Parking pawl components

then the plates from transmission case, **Fig. 11.**

3. Remove parking pawl, shaft and spring from transmission case, **Fig. 11.**

Installation

1. Install parking pawl, shaft and spring into transmission case, **Fig. 12.**
2. Install parking pawl onto the shaft, then place leg of spring into hole in pawl.
3. Set spring load by turning pawl clockwise, **Fig. 12.**
4. Install guide plate and tighten attaching bolt to 7 ft. lbs.
5. Reinstall extension housing.

TRANSMISSION REPLACE

REMOVAL

1. Disconnect kickdown cable from bracket and injection pump lever.
2. Place transmission selector lever in Neutral, then raise and support vehicle.
3. Remove nut securing outer manual lever and lever from manual lever shaft.
4. Remove position sensor from con-

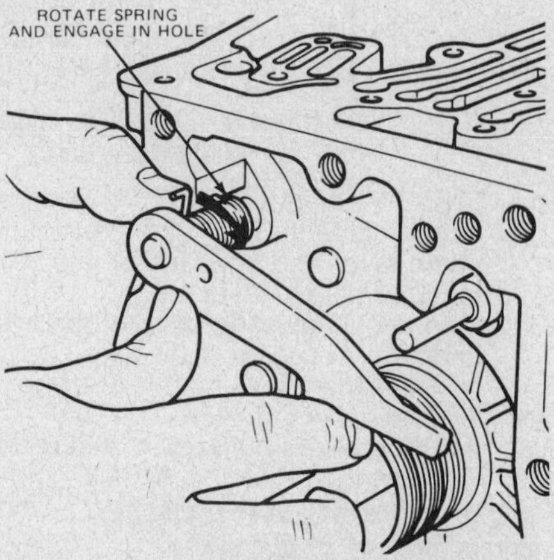

Fig. 12 Installing parking pawl spring

verter housing.

5. Disconnect brace from lower end of converter housing and engine block and remove brace.
6. Place suitable jack under transmission.
7. Rotate engine as needed using crankshaft pulley nut and remove nuts securing torque converter to flex plate.
8. Mark position of propeller shaft yoke and rear axle companion flange, then remove propeller shaft.
9. Disconnect neutral start switch electrical connector and remove extension housing damper.
10. Support transmission and remove rear support to crossmember nuts and two crossmember to side support bolts.
11. Remove bolts securing rear support to extension housing, the rear exhaust system support and the crossmember assembly. **It may be necessary to remove exhaust system components to facilitate crossmember and transmission removal.**
12. On models with column shift, remove bolts securing linkage bell crank bracket to the engine/transmission brace.
13. On all models, disconnect oil cooler lines from transmission using push connect tool T82L-9500-AH or equivalent.
14. Disconnect electrical connector to speed sensor and remove bolts se-

curing starter motor to converter housing.
15. Ensure that transmission is properly secured to jack, then lower jack slightly.
16. Remove 4 bolts securing converter housing to engine block.
17. Disconnect and remove filler tube and dipstick assembly, draining fluid into suitable container.
18. Move transmission and torque converter assembly away from engine, lowering jack as needed to provide clearance.

INSTALLATION

1. Mount transmission and converter assembly on suitable jack and secure transmission with safety chain.
2. Position transmission assembly under vehicle, and rotate converter until converter studs are aligned with holes in flex plate, ensuring that converter is properly seated.
3. Mount transmission assembly on rear of engine, ensuring that converter face is seated squarely against face plate.
4. Install filler tube and dipstick assembly and insert converter housing retaining bolt through tube bracket and converter housing flange.
5. Install 3 remaining converter housing bolts, then torque bolts to 38-48 ft. lbs.
6. Remove chain from around transmission.
7. Connect oil cooler lines by pushing them into fittings located on intermediate shaft.
8. Connect speed sensor electrical connector, then install extension housing damper, torquing retaining bolts to 18-25 ft. lbs.
9. Install rear support on exhaust system.
10. Raise transmission assembly as needed, then install crossmember assembly and side mounting bolts.
11. Align extension housing with rear support, install bolts securing rear mount to extension housing and ensure that all crossmember and mount bolts are properly tightened. Install exhaust system components, if removed.
12. Insert nuts securing torque converter to flex plate and torque nuts to 20-34 ft. lbs.
13. Install brace between engine block and lower end of converter housing, torquing bolts to 15-18 ft. lbs.
14. On models equipped with column shift, mount linkage bellcrank bracket on engine/transmission brace and torque retaining bolts to 10-20 ft. lbs.
15. On all models, lower and remove transmission jack.
16. Guide kickdown cable up into engine compartment, mount transmission manual lever on manual shaft, ensuring that linkage is properly aligned and torque retaining nut to 10-20 ft. lbs.
17. Connect neutral start switch harness and install position sensor in converter housing.
18. Insert propeller shaft yoke into transmission, align rear yoke with rear axle companion flange and secure yoke to flange.
19. Lower vehicle, fill transmission to specified level with Dexron II type fluid, adjust manual linkage and kickdown cable, then road test vehicle.

Ford Automatic Transaxle

INDEX

TRANSAXLE IDENTIFICATION

The transaxle identification tag, **Fig. 1**, is located near the valve body (upper) cover.

DESCRIPTION

This transaxle, **Fig. 2**, combines a three speed automatic transaxle with a front wheel driving axle into a single unit.

The transaxle section uses a torque converter with a planetary gear set, one band and three friction elements. The planetary gear set is used to split input power between mechanical and hydraulic in some gears. On Sable and Taurus models, the torque converter is also equipped with a centrifugal locking clutch (CLC).

Other unique features of this transmission are that there are two input shafts

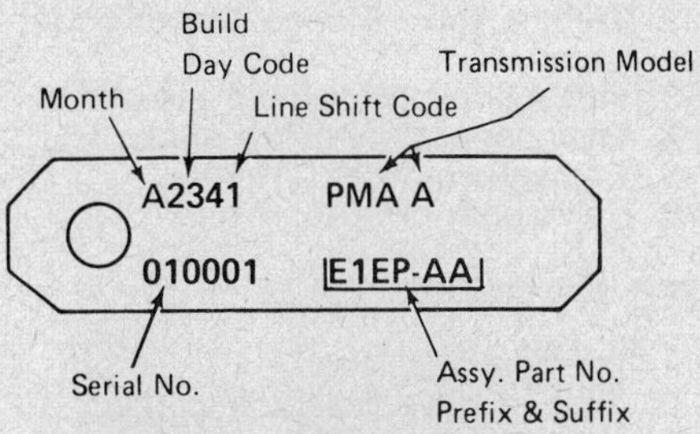

Fig. 1 Transaxle identification tag

from the converter to the gear train, the valve body is mounted on top of the case, the oil pump is installed at the end opposite the converter and the parking gear is installed in the final drive.

Output from the transmission goes through a final drive assembly to the differential to drive the front axle shafts. The final drive consists of an input gear, idler gear and final drive gear (ring) gear.

TROUBLESHOOTING

SLOW INITIAL ENGAGEMENT

1. Improper fluid level.
2. Damaged or improperly adjusted manual linkage.
3. Incorrect throttle valve linkage adjustment.
4. Contaminated fluid.
5. Improper clutch or band application or oil control pressure.
6. Dirt in valve body.

ROUGH INITIAL ENGAGEMENT IN FORWARD OR REVERSE

1. Improper fluid level.

2. Engine idle too high.
3. Automatic choke closed on warm engine.
4. Play in halfshafts, constant velocity joints or engine mounts.
5. Improper clutch or band application or oil control pressure.
6. Incorrect throttle valve linkage adjustment.
7. Dirt in valve body.

NO DRIVE, ANY GEAR

1. Improper fluid level.
2. Damaged or improperly adjusted manual linkage.
3. Improper clutch or band application or oil control pressure.
4. Internal leak.
5. Loose valve body.
6. Damaged or worn clutches or bands.
7. Valve body sticking or dirty.

NO DRIVE IN 1, 2 OR D

1. Improper fluid level.
2. Damaged or improperly adjusted manual linkage.
3. Improper one-way clutch or band application.
4. Incorrect oil pressure.
5. Damaged or worn band, servo or clutches.
6. Loose valve body.
7. Valve body sticking or dirty.

NO REVERSE OR SLIPS IN REVERSE

1. Improper fluid level.
2. Damaged or improperly adjusted manual linkage.
3. Play in halfshafts, constant velocity joints or engine mounts.
4. Improper oil pressure control.
5. Damaged or worn reverse clutch.
6. Loose valve body.
7. Valve body sticking or dirty.

NO START IN PARK OR NEUTRAL

1. Neutral start switch improperly adjusted.
2. Neutral start wire damaged.
3. Manual linkage improperly adjusted.

NO DRIVE OR SLIPS IN D

1. Damaged or worn one way clutch.
2. Improper fluid level.
3. Damaged or worn band.
4. Incorrect throttle valve linkage adjustment.

NO DRIVE OR SLIPS IN 2

1. Improper fluid level.
2. Incorrect throttle valve linkage adjustment.
3. Damaged or worn intermediate friction clutch.
4. Improper clutch application.
5. Internal leakage.
6. Valve body dirty or sticking.
7. Band or drum glazed.

TAKE OFF IN 2ND OR 3RD

1. Improper fluid level.
2. Damaged or improperly adjusted manual linkage.

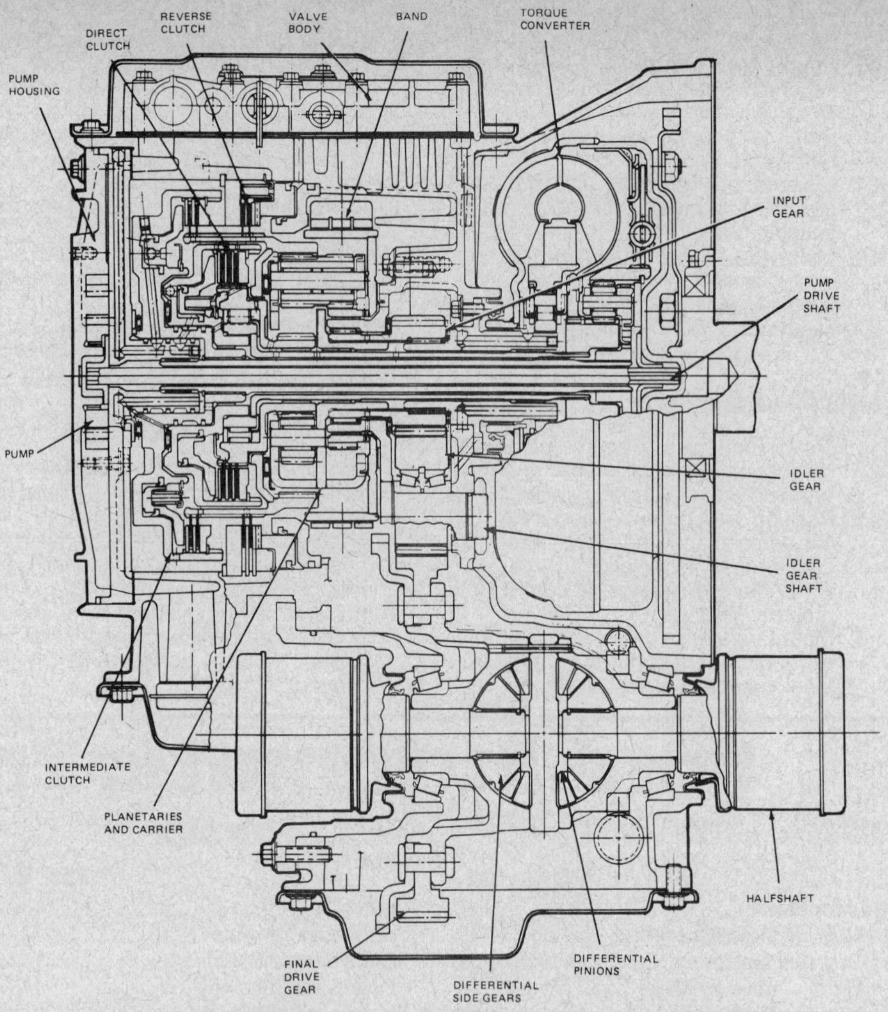

Fig. 2 Sectional view of automatic transaxle

3. Improper band or clutch application.
4. Damaged or worn governor.
5. Loose valve body.
6. Valve body sticking or dirty.
7. Leaks between valve body and case mating surface.

INCORRECT SHIFT POINTS

1. Improper fluid level.
2. Throttle valve linkage improperly adjusted.
3. Improper clutch or band application.
4. Improper oil control pressure.
5. Damaged or worn governor.
6. Valve body dirty or sticking.

NO UPSHIFT IN D

1. Improper fluid level.
2. Throttle valve linkage improperly adjusted.
3. Improper band or clutch application.
4. Improper oil control pressure.
5. Damaged or worn governor.
6. Valve body sticking or dirty.

SHIFT 1–3 IN D

1. Improper fluid level.
2. Damaged or worn intermediate friction clutch.
3. Improper clutch application.
4. Improper oil control pressure.
5. Valve body sticking or dirty.

RUNAWAY UPSHIFTS

1. Improper fluid level.
2. Improper band or clutch application.
3. Improper oil pressure.
4. Damaged or worn direct clutch or servo.
5. Valve body sticking or dirty.

DELAYED 1–2 SHIFT

1. Improper fluid level.
2. Improper engine performance.
3. Improper throttle valve linkage adjustment.
4. Improper intermediate clutch application.
5. Improper oil control pressure.
6. Damaged intermediate clutch.
7. Valve body sticking or dirty.

ROUGH 1–2 UPSHIFT

1. Improper fluid level.
2. Improper throttle valve linkage adjustment.
3. Incorrect engine idle or performance.
4. Improper intermediate clutch application.
5. Improper oil control pressure.
6. Valve body sticking or dirty.

ROUGH 2–3 UPSHIFT

1. Improper fluid level.
2. Incorrect engine performance.
3. Improper band release or direct clutch application.
4. Improper oil control pressure.
5. Valve body sticking or dirty.
6. Damaged or worn servo release and direct clutch piston check ball.
7. Improper throttle valve linkage adjustment.

ROUGH 3–2 DOWNSHIFT AT CLOSED THROTTLE IN D

1. Improper fluid level.
2. Incorrect engine idle or performance.
3. Improper throttle valve linkage adjustment.
4. Improper band or clutch application.
5. Improper oil control pressure.
6. Improper governor operation.
7. Valve body sticking or dirty.

NO FORCED DOWNSHIFTS

1. Improper fluid level.
2. Improper clutch or band application.
3. Improper oil control pressure.
4. Damaged internal kickdown linkage.
5. Throttle valve linkage improperly adjusted.
6. Valve body sticking or dirty.
7. Dirty or sticking governor.

DOWNSHIFT RUNAWAY

1. Improper fluid level.
2. Throttle valve linkage improperly adjusted.
3. Band improperly adjusted.
4. Improper band or clutch application.
5. Improper oil control pressure.
6. Damaged or worn servo.
7. Glazed band or drum.
8. Valve body sticking or dirty.

NO ENGINE BRAKING IN 1

1. Improper fluid level.
2. Throttle valve linkage improperly adjusted.
3. Damaged or improperly adjusted manual linkage.
4. Improperly adjusted band or clutch.
5. Improper oil control pressure.
6. Glazed band or drum.
7. Valve body sticking or dirty.

NO ENGINE BRAKING IN 2

1. Improper fluid level.
2. Throttle valve linkage improperly adjusted.
3. Manual linkage improperly adjusted.
4. Improper band or clutch application.
5. Improper oil control system.
6. Leaking servo.
7. Glazed band or drum.

MAINTENANCE

ADDING OIL

To check fluid level, apply parking brake, operate engine at idle speed with vehicle on level surface and transmission in Park position. Add fluid as necessary to bring mark on dipstick between "Add" and "Full" marks.

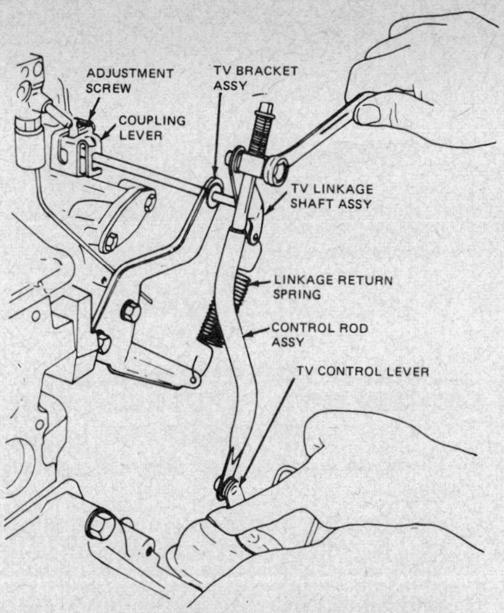

Fig. 3 Adjusting throttle valve control linkage

CHANGING OIL

Fluid and filter changes are not required for average passenger car use. Severe usage such as commercial use or prolonged periods of idling require fluid and filter be changed every 20,000 miles on 1982-83 models or every 30,000 miles on 1984-87 models. Whenever fluid is changed only fluid labeled Dexron II should be used.

1. Raise and support vehicle.
2. Loosen transaxle oil pan attaching bolts and allow fluid to drain.
3. Remove oil pan and clean thoroughly.
4. Install new gasket onto pan, then the pan onto transaxle.
5. Fill transaxle to correct fluid level, then operate engine at idle. With parking brake applied, move selector lever to each position. Place lever in Park position and check fluid level with engine at operating temperature. Add fluid as necessary.

IN-VEHICLE ADJUSTMENTS

GEARSHIFT LINKAGE

1. Position selector lever in Drive position against rearward stop.
2. Raise and support vehicle, then loosen manual lever to control cable retaining nut or adjusting bolt.
3. Position transmission manual lever at second detent from most rearward position. This is Drive position.
4. Torque attaching nut to 10-15 ft. lbs. (7-11 Nm) on all models except Sable and Taurus or 16-27 ft. lbs. (12-20) on Sable and Taurus.
5. Lower vehicle and check for proper operation of transmission in each selector lever position.

THROTTLE VALVE LINKAGE

Except CFI Engines

1. Operate engine at curb idle speed, then turn engine Off. Ensure that carburetor throttle lever is against hot engine curb idle stop with choke off. **Ensure throttle lever is not on choke fast idle cam.**
2. On 1982 models, position coupling lever adjustment screw at its midpoint, then ensure throttle valve linkage shaft assembly is seated fully upward into coupling lever, **Fig. 3.**
3. On all models, loosen sliding trunnion block bolt on throttle valve control rod assembly at least one turn.
4. Rotate transaxle throttle valve control lever upward to ensure throttle valve lever is against its internal idle stop. Maintain force on throttle control lever, then torque bolt on trunnion block to 24-36 inch lbs. (2.7-4.1 Nm) on 1982 models or 7-11 ft. (9-14 Nm) on 1983-87 models.
5. Check that carburetor throttle lever is still against hot engine curb idle stop. If not, repeat steps 1 through 6.

CFI Engines

1. Simultaneously hold throttle open to maintain 1000 RPM while pressing lightly on the ISC motor shaft.
2. After the shaft retracts completely, release throttle and quickly disconnect ISC motor electrical connector.
3. Loosen bolt on sliding trunnion block on TV control rod assembly. A minimum of one turn is necessary.
4. Remove any surface corrosion from the control rod and ensure trunnion block moves freely on control rod assembly.
5. With ISC plunger retracted and trunnion block loosened, rotate transaxle TV control lever upward, using approximately a one lb. force to ensure TV control lever is completely against its internal idle stop. Without releasing force on TV control lever, tighten trunnion block attaching bolt to 7-11 ft. lbs.

IN-VEHICLE REPAIRS

VALVE BODY, REPLACE

1. Remove battery and battery tray.
2. On all models except Sable and Taurus, remove ignition coil.
3. On Sable and Taurus models, remove air cleaner assembly.
4. On all models, remove transaxle oil dipstick.
5. On all models except Sable and Taurus, disconnect all hoses and lines from air management valve, then remove the valve from transaxle valve body cover. Also, disconnect fuel evaporator hose from frame rail.
6. On all models, disconnect neutral safety switch electrical connector.
7. Disconnect fan motor and temperature sending unit electrical connectors.
8. Remove valve body cover bolts, then the valve body cover and gasket.
9. Remove valve body bolts, then the valve body and gaskets.
10. Reverse procedure to install. Install guide pins to properly align valve body before tightening attaching

bolts. One alignment pin may have to be temporarily removed to allow attachment of manual valve. Ensure roller on end of throttle valve plunger engages cam on end of throttle lever shaft. Torque valve body bolts to 6-8 ft. lbs. (8-11 Nm) and valve body cover bolts to 7-9 ft. lbs. (9-12 Nm).

GOVERNOR, REPLACE

1. Disconnect battery ground cable, and on carbureted engines, all hoses and lines from air management valve.
2. On 4-97.6 carbureted engines, remove managed air valve supply hose band to intermediate shift control bracket attaching screw.
3. On all models, remove air cleaner, then using a long screwdriver, remove governor cover retaining clip.
4. Remove governor cover and governor.
5. Reverse procedure to install.

SERVO

1. Disconnect battery ground cable.
2. Disconnect electrical connectors from fan motor and temperature sending unit.
3. Disconnect FM capacitor wiring, if equipped.
4. Remove two fan shroud to radiator attaching nuts, then the fan and fan shroud.
5. Remove filler tube to case attaching bolt, then the filler tube and dipstick.
6. Remove lower left side mount to case attaching bolt.
7. Remove servo cap and snap ring using tool T81P-70027A or equivalent.
8. Reverse procedure to install.

TRANSAXLE REPLACE

ESCORT & LYNX, LN7, EXP & 1986–87 TEMPO & TOPAZ

Due to case configuration, righthand halfshaft assembly must be removed first. The lefthand inboard CV joint assembly is then driven from case by inserting tool No. T81P-4026-A or equivalent into transaxle.

1. Position vehicle on hoist, then disconnect battery ground cable.
2. Disconnect managed air valve from transaxle valve body cover, if equipped.
3. On 1986-87 models, remove air cleaner assembly, then back out thermactor hose attaching bolts and position valve and hoses aside.
4. On all models, disconnect electrical connector from neutral safety switch.
5. Disconnect throttle valve linkage and manual lever cable from levers.
6. On 1986-87 models, disconnect ground strap located above upper engine mount, then remove ignition coil and bracket assembly.
7. On all models, remove two transaxle-to-engine upper bolts located below and to either side of distributor.
8. Raise and support vehicle.

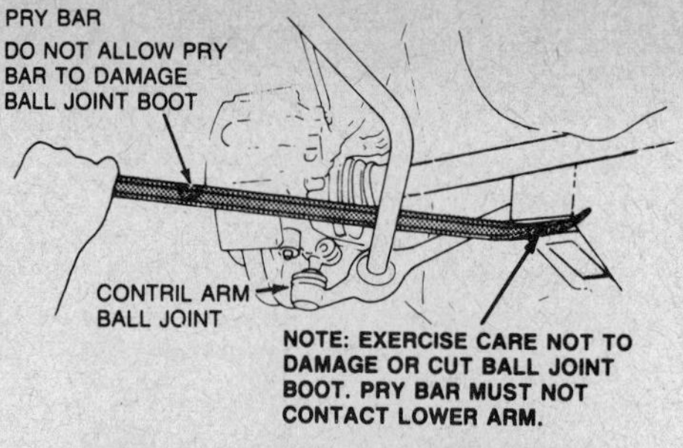
PRY BAR
DO NOT ALLOW PRY BAR TO DAMAGE BALL JOINT BOOT
CONTRIL ARM BALL JOINT
NOTE: EXERCISE CARE NOT TO DAMAGE OR CUT BALL JOINT BOOT. PRY BAR MUST NOT CONTACT LOWER ARM.

Fig. 4 Disengaging control arm form steering knuckle

9. Remove front wheel and tire assemblies.
10. Remove nut from control arm to steering knuckle bolt, on both sides of vehicle, then drive bolts out using punch and hammer. **The bolts and nuts must be discarded.**
11. Disengage control arm from steering knuckle, on both sides of vehicle, using a suitable pry bar, **Fig. 4. Use care to avoid damaging ball joint boot. Pry bar must not contact lower arm. Do not use hammer on knuckle to remove ball joints. Plastic splash shield behind rotor has pocket into which lower ball joint fits. When disconnecting lower control arm from knuckle, shield should be bent back to clear ball joint and avoid damaging the shield.**
12. Remove and discard stabilizer bar bracket bolts from both sides of vehicle.
13. Remove and discard stabilizer-to-control arm nut and washer from both side of vehicle, then slide stabilizer bar out of control arms.
14. Remove brake hose routing clip attaching bolts from suspension strut bracket on both sides of vehicle.
15. Disconnect tie rod from steering knuckle on both sides of vehicle.
16. Pry halfshaft out of right side of transaxle and position shaft on transaxle housing. **If difficulty is encountered when prying halfshaft, remove transaxle oil pan and discard gasket. Insert a large blade screwdriver between differential pinion shaft and inboard CV joint stub shaft. Tap screwdriver handle to dislodge circlip from side gear and free halfshaft from differential. Prior to installation of the halfshaft, install a new circlip on inboard stub shaft. Also, use a new gasket when installing oil pan.**
17. Disconnect left halfshaft from differential side gear using driver No. T81P-4026-A or equivalent.
18. Slide halfshaft out of transaxle and support end of shaft. **Do not allow end of driveshaft to hang unsupported, as damage to outboard CV joint may result.**
19. Install seal plugs T81P-1177-B or equivalent into differential seals.
20. Unfasten starter support bracket, then disconnect starter cable and remove starter from vehicle. **On some fuel injected models, it will be necessary to disconnect hoses from starter motor.**
21. Remove transaxle support bracket, then the torque converter housing dust cover.
22. Remove torque converter-to-flywheel attaching nuts. Rotate crankshaft as necessary to provide access to each nut.
23. Position a suitable jack under transaxle and remove rear support bracket attaching nuts.
24. Remove left front body bracket attaching nuts and bolts and the bracket.
25. On 1982-83 models, remove left rear insulator bracket attaching nut.
26. On all models, disconnect cooler lines from transaxle.
27. Remove manual lever bracket attaching bolts from transaxle case.
28. Ensure engine is properly supported, then position a suitable jack under transaxle and remove remaining transaxle-to-engine attaching bolts.
29. Insert a screwdriver between flywheel and torque converter and carefully move transaxle and converter away from engine. When converter studs clear flywheel, lower transaxle several inches and disconnect speedometer cable.
30. Lower transaxle and remove from vehicle.
31. Reverse procedure to install, noting the following:
    a. Replace circlip on CV joint stub shaft, **Fig. 5.** Avoid spreading the circlip any more than necessary.
    b. When inserting halfshaft in transaxle, push CV joint into differential until circlip seats in side gear, **Fig. 6.** A rubber mallet may be used to tap the outboard CV joint stub shaft, if necessary.
    c. When attaching lower ball joint to steering knuckle, use care to avoid damaging ball joint boot. Install new pinch bolt and nut and torque nut to 37-44 ft. lbs. Do not torque bolt.

1984–85 TEMPO & TOPAZ

On these models, the engine and transaxle is removed as an assembly.

1. Mark position of hood hinges, then remove hood.
2. Disconnect battery ground cable, then remove air cleaner assembly.
3. Remove lower radiator hose and drain coolant from engine. Remove upper radiator hose from engine.
4. Disconnect transaxle cooler lines from rubber hoses below radiator.
5. Remove coil assembly from cylinder head. Disconnect coolant fan electrical connector.
6. Remove radiator shroud, cooling fan and radiator.
7. Carefully discharge refrigerant from air conditioning system, if equipped. Remove inlet and outlet lines from compressor.
8. Mark and disconnect all electrical and vacuum lines from engine.

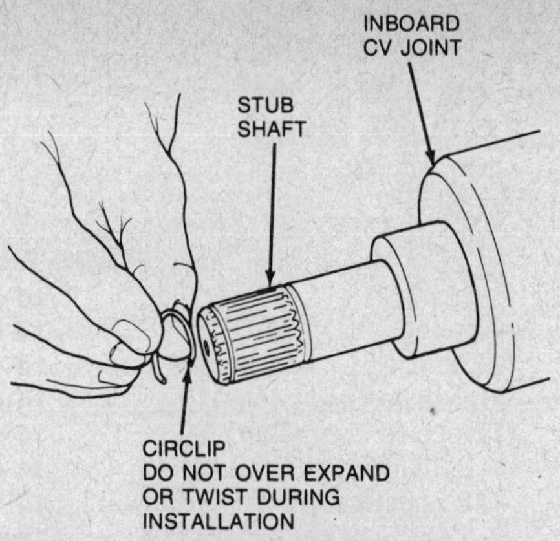

Fig. 5 Replacing circlip on CV stub shaft

9. Disconnect TV linkage from transaxle.
10. Disconnect accelerator linkage, fuel supply and return lines from engine.
11. Disconnect air pump discharge hose.
12. Disconnect power steering pressure and return lines from pump, if equipped. Remove power steering line bracket from cylinder head.
13. Install engine support tool No. D79P-6000-A or equivalent, to engine lifting eye.
14. Raise and support vehicle.
15. Remove starter cable from starter.
16. Remove air hose from catalytic converter.
17. Remove bolt securing exhaust pipe bracket to oil pan. Remove two exhaust pipes to exhaust manifold nuts, then pull exhaust pipe out of rubber insulating grommets and position aside.
18. Disconnect speedometer cable from transaxle.
19. Remove water pump inlet hose from engine.
20. Remove bolts securing control arms to body. Remove stabilizer bar bracket bolts and brackets.
21. Remove halfshaft assembly from transaxle.
22. Disconnect manual shift cable clip from transaxle shift lever. Remove manual shift linkage bracket bolts and bracket from transaxle.
23. Remove nuts and lefthand rear No. 4 insulator mount bracket from body bracket.
24. Lower vehicle and install suitable lifting hoist to engine. **Do not allow front wheels to touch floor.**
25. Remove engine support tool No. D79L-6000-A or equivalent from engine.
26. Remove righthand No. 3 insulator intermediate bracket to engine bracket bolts and intermediate bracket to insulator nuts. Remove nut on the bottom of double ended stud which secures intermediate bracket to engine bracket. Remove bracket.
27. Carefully lower engine and transaxle assembly from vehicle.
28. Reverse procedure to install.

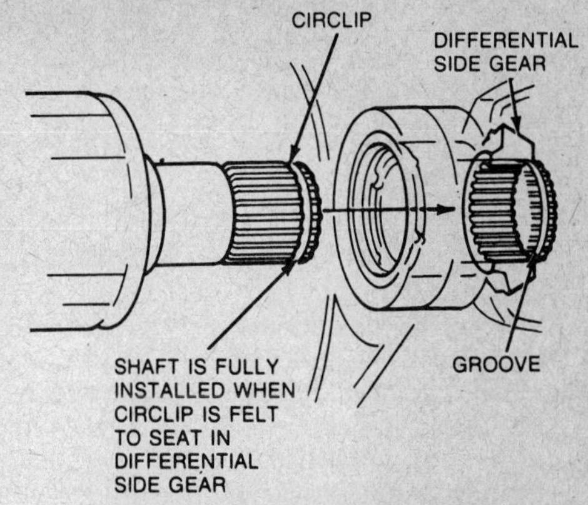

Fig. 6 Seating half shaft

FORD AXOD AUTOMATIC OVERDRIVE TRANSAXLE

INDEX

TRANSAXLE IDENTIFICATION

The identification tag, **Fig. 1**, located on top of the converter housing, includes transaxle assembly number, serial number and build date. For interpretation of these numbers, refer to Ford Master Parts Catalog.

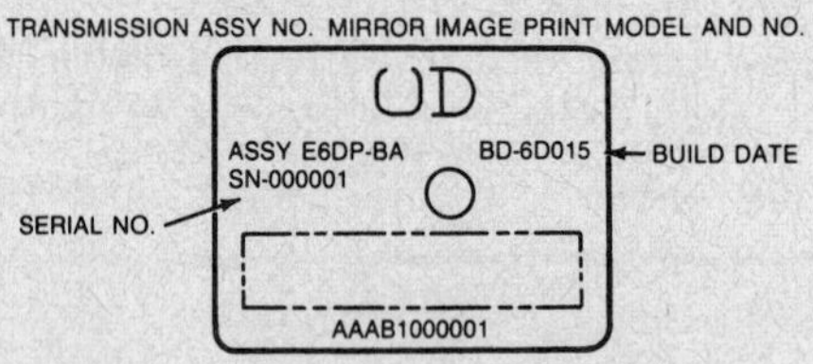

Fig. 1 Identification tag

DESCRIPTION

The AXOD transaxle, **Fig. 2**, has two planetary gear sets and a combination planetary/differential gear set. Four multiple plate clutches, two band assemblies and two one-way clutches act together for proper operation of the planetary gear sets.

A lockup torque converter is coupled to the engine crankshaft and transmits engine power to the gear train by means of a drive link assembly (chain) that connects the drive and driven sprockets. Converter clutch application is controlled through an electronic control integrated in the onboard EEC-IV system. These controls, along with the hydraulic controls in the valve body, operate a piston plate clutch in the torque converter to provide improved fuel economy by eliminating converter slip when applied.

MAIN COMPONENTS & FUNCTIONS

TORQUE CONVERTER

Converter

The torque converter couples the engine to the turbine shaft. It also provides torque multiplication and absorbs engine shock of gear shifting.

Piston Plate Clutch & Damper Assembly

The piston plate clutch and damper assembly transmit engine power to the turbine from the converter cover during lockup.

Converter Cover

The converter cover transmits power from the engine into the converter. Also, the oil pump driveshaft is splined to the converter cover.

Turbine

The turbine is splined to the drive sprocket turbine shaft and driven by fluid by the impeller.

Impeller

The impeller is driven by the converter cover. Together with the reactor it supplies torque multiplication.

Reactor

The reactor, also called the stator, contains a one-way clutch to hold it stationary only when "reaction" is required. It also causes hydraulic reaction during torque multiplication.

GEAR TRAIN

Forward Clutch

The forward clutch locks the driven sprocket to the low one-way clutch.

Low One-Way Clutch

The low one-way clutch transmits torque from the driven sprocket to the sun gear of the forward planetary gear set in first gear. It also provides engine braking in third gear in connection with the forward clutch.

Overdrive Band

The overdrive band holds the sun gear of the forward planetary gear set stationary in fourth gear (overdrive).

Direct Clutch

The direct clutch locks the sun gear of the planetary assembly of the forward planetary gear set to the direct one-way clutch in third gear.

Direct One-Way Clutch

The direct one-way clutch transmits torque from the driven sprocket to the sun gear of the forward planetary gear set in third gear, and provides engine braking in manual low.

Intermediate Clutch

The intermediate clutch locks the driven sprocket to the planetary assembly of the forward planetary gear set in second and third gear.

Reverse Clutch

The reverse clutch holds the planetary assembly of the forward planetary gear set, and the ring gear of the rear planetary gear set stationary in reverse gear.

Planetary Gears

Two planetary gear sets are used to provide four forward speeds, including reverse, depending upon clutch and/or band applications.

Parking Gear

The parking gear allows the output (axle) shaft to be mechanically locked by the parking pawl anchored in the case.

Low Intermediate Band

The low intermediate band holds the sun gear of the rear planetary gear set stationary in low, first and second gears.

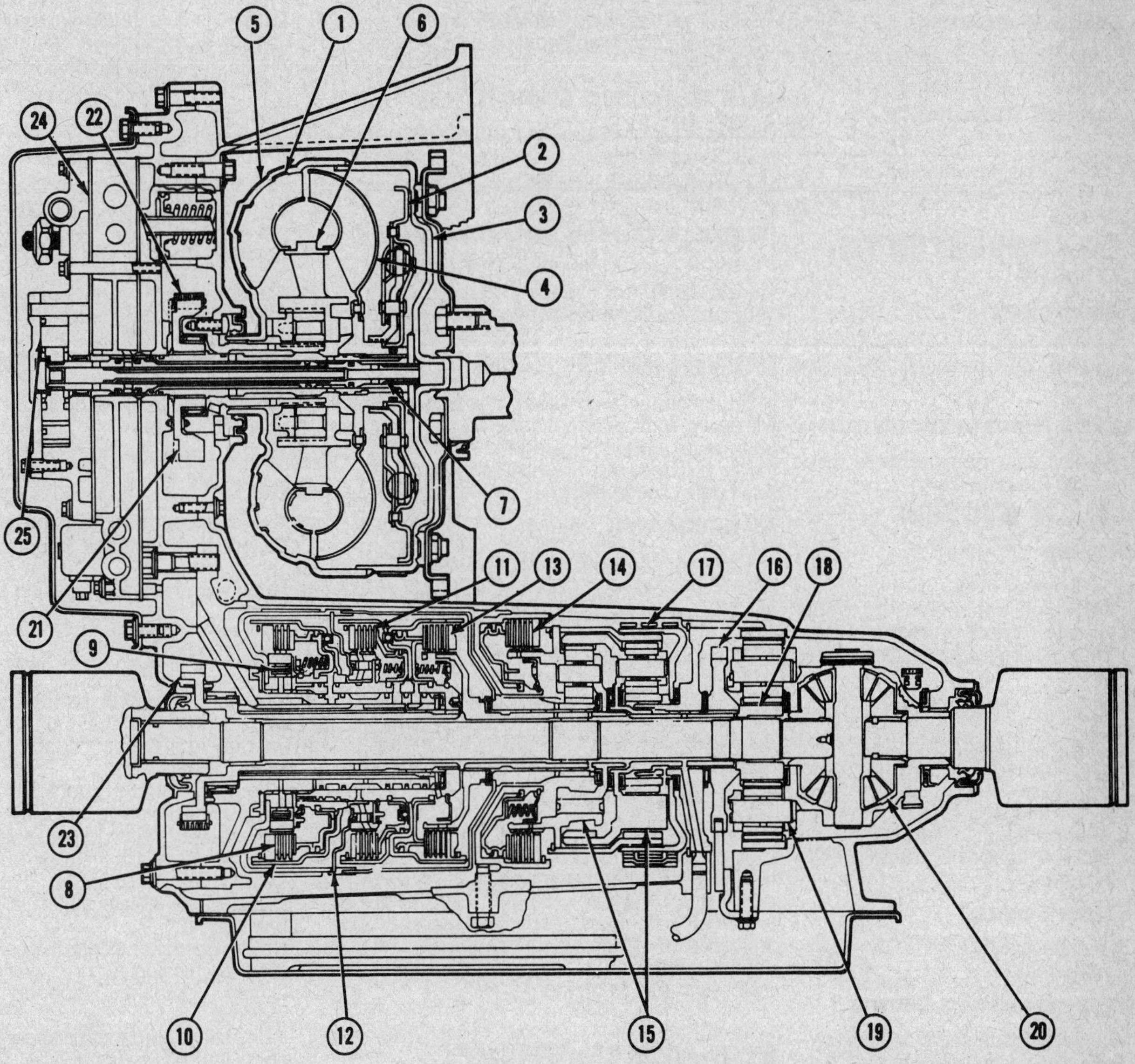

1. TORQUE CONVERTER
2. CONVERTER CLUTCH (PISTON PLATE CLUTCH AND DAMPER ASSEMBLY)
3. CONVERTER COVER
4. TURBINE
5. IMPELLER
6. REACTOR
7. OIL PUMP DRIVESHAFT
8. FORWARD CLUTCH
9. LOW ONE-WAY CLUTCH
10. OVERDRIVE BAND
11. DIRECT CLUTCH
12. DIRECT ONE-WAY CLUTCH
13. INTERMEDIATE CLUTCH
14. REVERSE CLUTCH
15. PLANETARY GEARS
16. PARKING GEAR
17. LOW-INTERMEDIATE BAND
18. FINAL DRIVE SUN GEAR
19. FINAL DRIVE PLANET
20. DIFFERENTIAL ASSEMBLY
21. DRIVE SPROCKET
22. DRIVE LINK ASSEMBLY (CHAIN)
23. DRIVEN SPROCKET
24. VALVE BODY (MAIN CONTROL ASSEMBLY)
25. OIL PUMP

Fig. 2 Sectional view of Ford AXOD automatic transaxle

Final Drive Sun Gear

The final drive sun gear transfers torque from the transmission output to the final drive planetary assembly.

Final Drive Planet

The final drive planet drives the differential assembly.

Differential Assembly

The differential assembly drives the front axle shafts and provides the differential action if driving wheels are turning at different speeds.

TORQUE CONVERTER TO GEAR TRAIN

Drive Sprocket

The drive sprocket transmits power from the converter to the drive link assembly (chain).

Drive Link Assembly (Chain)

The drive link assembly transmits converter power to the gear train.

HYDRAULIC SYSTEM

Valve Body

The valve body or main control assembly directs fluid (oil) under pressure to the torque converter, band servos, clutches and governor to control transaxle operation.

Oil Pump

The oil pump provides a supply of fluid (oil) under pressure to operate, lubricate and cool the transaxle. The pump is a variable capacity vane and rotor pump with output flow proportional to demand. It is located within the transaxle control valve and pump assembly.

Overdrive Servo

The overdrive servo applies overdrive band in fourth gear.

Low-Intermediate Servo

The low-intermediate servo applies low-intermediate band in manual, low, first and second gears.

Governor

The governor provides a "road speed" signal to the hydraulic control system for shift control, and is driven by a gear on the differential assembly.

Reservoir

Two reservoir areas are used to control oil level, dependent on fluid temperature. Along with the lower sump, a fluid reservoir is located in the lower section of the valve body cover. As fluid temperature in the reservoir increases, a thermostatic element closes, retaining fluid in the upper reservoir.

ELECTRICAL COMPONENT FUNCTION

Neutral Pressure Switch (NPS)

The NPS signals the EEC-IV of transaxle engagement shift into "Reverse" or "Drive" for engine control functions.

3/2 Pressure Switch

The 3/2 pressure switch signals the EEC-IV of hydraulic transaxle gear shifts for bypass clutch solenoid control. Detects 3-2 shift.

4/3 Pressure Switch

The 4/3 pressure switch signals the EEC-IV of hydraulic transaxle gear shifts for bypass clutch solenoid control. Detects 4-3 shift.

Bypass Clutch Solenoid

The bypass clutch solenoid applies the torque converter bypass clutch when energized or releases it when de-energized.

DOWNSHIFTS

Under certain conditions the transaxle will downshift automatically to a lower gear range without moving the shift selector lever. There are three different types of downshift categories:

Coastdown

The coastdown downshift occurs when vehicle is coasting down to a stop.

Torque Demand

The torque demand downshift occurs during part throttle acceleration when demand for torque is greater than the engine can provide at that gear ratio. The axle will disengage the converter clutch to provide added acceleration, if applied.

Kickdown

The kickdown downshift occurs when the accelerator pedal is depressed fully to the floor. A forced downshift into second gear is possible below 55 mph. Below approximately 25 mph a forced kickdown to first gear will occur. All shift speed specifications will vary due to tire size and engine calibration requirements.

TROUBLESHOOTING

The transaxle electrical system is controlled by the EEC-IV computerized engine control system. Diagnosis involves the use of specialized testing equipment.

OIL LEAK

1. Side or bottom pan attaching bolts incorrectly torqued.
2. Side or bottom pan gasket or pan rail damaged.
3. Side or bottom pan distorted.
4. TV cable, fill tube or electrical connector loose or damaged.
5. Manual shaft seal damaged.
6. Governor or servo cover O-ring seal damaged.
7. Cooler fittings or pressure taps incorrectly torqued or damaged.
8. Converter weld seal leaking.
9. Cooler or converter seal damaged or garter spring missing.
10. Halfshaft seals damaged or garter spring missing.
11. Speedometer cable or speed sensor O-ring seal damaged.

OIL VENTING OR FOAMING

1. Transaxle overfilled.
2. Transaxle fluid contaminated with antifreeze or engine overheating.
3. Bi-metallic element stuck open.
4. Oil filter O-ring damaged.

HIGH OR LOW OIL PRESSURE

1. Incorrect oil level.
2. TV cable/linkage stuck or damaged.
3. Pressure regulator spring damaged.
4. Pressure regulator valve or valve bore nicked or scored.
5. Pressure relief valve damaged or relief valve ball and/or spring missing.
6. Oil pump slide stuck.
7. Oil pump seals and/or vanes damaged.
8. Oil pump driveshaft broken or damaged.

NO 1–2 SHIFT (FIRST GEAR ONLY)

1. Governor assembly weights binding.
2. Governor assembly springs and gears damaged.
3. Governor shaft seal missing or damaged.
4. Governor valve (ball) stuck or missing.
5. Governor tube leaking or damaged.
6. Intermediate clutch plates damaged or missing.
7. Intermediate clutch assembly piston or seals damaged.
8. Intermediate clutch check ball assembly stuck or missing.
9. Intermediate clutch cylinder damaged.
10. Direct/intermediate clutch hub seals damaged or missing.
11. Direct/intermediate clutch hub holes blocked.
12. Driven sprocket support seals damaged or missing.
13. Driven sprocket support holes blocked.
14. 1-2 shift valve stuck, nicked or damaged.
15. 1-2 throttle delay valve stuck, nicked or damaged.
16. 1-2 accumulator capacity modulator valve stuck, nicked or damaged.
17. Number 9 check ball missing.
18. Control assembly attaching bolts incorrectly torqued.
19. Carrier damaged.
20. Intermediate clutch tap plug loose or missing.

1–2 SHIFT FEELS HARSH OR SOFT

1. Incorrect oil pressure.
2. 1-2 accumulator regulator valve stuck, nicked or damaged.
3. 1-2 accumulator regulator valve spring missing or damaged.
4. 1-2 accumulator capacity modulator valve stuck, nicked or damaged.
5. 1-2 accumulator capacity modulator valve spring missing or damaged.
6. 1-2 accumulator assembly piston stuck or damaged.

7. 1-2 accumulator assembly seal damaged or missing.
8. 1-2 accumulator assembly springs damaged or missing.

1–2 SHIFT SPEED HIGH OR LOW

1. Governor weights binding.
2. Governor springs and gear damaged.
3. Governor shaft seal or valve stuck or missing.
4. Governor tube leaking or damaged.
5. TV control valve, TV plunger, TV line modulator valve and 1-2 throttle delay valve stuck, nicked or damaged.
6. TV control valve, TV plunger, TV line modulator valve and 1-2 throttle delay valve springs missing or damaged.

NO 2–3 SHIFT (1–2 SHIFT OK)

1. Governor weights binding.
2. Governor springs and gear damaged.
3. Governor shaft seal or valve stuck or missing.
4. Governor tube leaking or missing.
5. Low/intermediate servo apply rod too long.
6. Low/intermediate servo bore or piston damaged.
7. Low/intermediate piston seals damaged or missing.
8. Low/intermediate servo return spring or retaining clip missing or broken.
9. Direct clutch plates damaged or missing.
10. Direct clutch piston or seals damaged.
11. Direct clutch check ball assembly stuck or missing.
12. Direct clutch cylinder damaged.
13. Direct/intermediate clutch hub seals damaged or missing.
14. Direct/intermediate clutch hub holes blocked.
15. Driven sprocket support seals damaged or missing.
16. Driven sprocket support holes blocked.
17. Direct one-way clutch assembly cage, rollers or springs damaged.
18. Direct one-way clutch assembly rollers missing.
19. Direct one-way clutch assembly inner race incorrectly assembled.
20. Control assembly attaching bolts incorrectly torqued.
21. 2-3 shift valve stuck, nicked or damaged.
22. Number 4 check ball missing.
23. Bypass solenoid not energized during wide open throttle upshift.
24. Case servo release passage blocked.
25. Servo release tube leaking or improperly installed.
26. Direct clutch pressure tap plug loose or missing.

2–3 SHIFT FEELS HARSH OR SOFT

1. Low oil pressure.
2. Low/intermediate servo apply rod length incorrect.
3. Low/intermediate servo piston, seal, springs and rod damaged.
4. 2-3 servo regulator valve stuck, nicked or damaged.
5. 2-3 servo regulator valve spring damaged.
6. Backout valve stuck, nicked or damaged.
7. Backout valve spring damaged.

2–3 SHIFT SPEED HIGH OR LOW

1. Governor weights binding.
2. Governor springs and gear damaged.
3. Governor shaft seal or valve damaged or missing.
4. Governor tube leaking or damaged.
5. TV cable damaged or disconnected.
6. TV control valve, TV plunger, TV line modulator valve and 2-3 throttle modulator valve stuck, nicked or damaged.
7. TV control valve, TV plunger, TV line modulator valve and 2-3 throttle modulator valve springs missing or damaged.
8. Governor tube leaking.

NO 3–4 SHIFT

1. Governor weights binding.
2. Governor springs and gear damaged.
3. Governor shaft seal or valve leaking or missing.
4. Overdrive band assembly not holding.
5. Overdrive servo assembly apply rod too long.
6. Overdrive servo bore or piston damaged.
7. Overdrive servo assembly piston seals damaged or missing.
8. Overdrive servo assembly return spring or retaining clip missing or broken.
9. Forward clutch assembly return springs and piston damaged.
10. Front ring gear damaged.
11. Control assembly attaching bolts incorrectly torqued.
12. 3-4 shift valve stuck, nicked or damaged.
13. 3-4 shift valve spring damaged.
14. 3-4 modulator valve stuck, nicked or damaged.
15. 3-4 modulator valve spring missing.
16. 4-3 scheduling valve stuck, nicked or damaged.
17. 4-3 scheduling valve spring missing.

3–4 SHIFT FEELS HARSH OR SOFT

1. Incorrect oil pressure.
2. 3-4 accumulator piston stuck or damaged.
3. 3-4 accumulator piston seal missing or damaged.
4. 3-4 accumulator springs missing or damaged.
5. Number 14 check ball missing.

3–4 SHIFT SPEED HIGH OR LOW

1. Governor weights binding.
2. Governor springs and gear damaged.
3. Governor shaft seal or valve missing or damaged.
4. Governor tube leaking.
5. TV cable damaged or disconnected.
6. TV control valve, TV plunger, TV line modulator valve and 3-4 modulator valve stuck, nicked or damaged.
7. TV control valve, TV plunger, TV line modulator valve and 3-4 modulator valve springs missing or damaged.

NO CONVERTER CLUTCH APPLY

1. No lockup signal to the electronic engine control.
2. Bypass solenoid damaged or inoperative.
3. Transaxle bulkhead electrical connector damaged or electrical system wires pinched.
4. 3-2 or 4-3 pressure switch inoperative.
5. Converter clutch blowoff check ball not seating or damaged.
6. Turbine shaft seals damaged.
7. Bypass clutch control valve stuck.
8. Bypass clutch control valve plunger stuck.
9. Pump shaft seals missing or damaged.
10. Valve body pilot sleeve damaged or incorrectly aligned.

CONVERTER CLUTCH DOES NOT RELEASE

1. No unlock signal to the electronic engine control.
2. Bypass solenoid damaged or inoperative.
3. Bypass clutch control valve or plunger valve stuck, nicked or damaged.

2–1 OR 3–1 DOWNSHIFT HARSH

1. Low/intermediate servo piston or seal damaged.
2. Low/intermediate servo assembly springs missing or damaged.
3. Low/intermediate servo apply rod length incorrect.
4. Number 9 check ball missing (3-1 only).

3–2 DOWNSHIFT HARSH

1. Low/intermediate servo assembly springs missing or damaged.
2. Low/intermediate servo apply rod length incorrect.
3. 3-2 control valve stuck, nicked or damaged.
4. Number 5 check ball missing.

4-3 DOWNSHIFTS HARSH

1. Overdrive servo assembly apply rod length incorrect.
2. Overdrive servo piston or seal damaged.
3. Overdrive servo assembly springs missing or damaged.

NO DRIVE IN DRIVE RANGE

1. Low oil level.
2. Low oil pressure.
3. Linkage misadjusted, disconnected, damaged, broken or bent.
4. TV linkage disconnected or missing.
5. Oil pump worn or damaged.
6. Oil pump driveshaft damaged.
7. Drive chain assembly damaged or broken.
8. Drive sprocket shaft to converter turbine spline damaged.
9. Driven sprocket shaft to direct/intermediate clutch hub damaged.
10. Forward clutch plates burned or missing.
11. Forward clutch piston seals or pistons damaged.
12. Forward clutch check ball assembly missing or damaged.
13. Forward clutch driven sprocket support seals damaged or missing.
14. Forward clutch oil holes blocked.
15. Forward clutch direct intermediate hub seals damaged or missing.
16. Low one-way clutch improperly assembled or damaged sprag.
17. Front sun gear/shell damaged.
18. Front and rear carrier pistons/lugs to rear ring gear damaged.
19. Rear ring gear/lugs to forward carrier damaged.
20. Low/intermediate band assembly burned or broken.
21. Low/intermediate servo assembly apply rod too short.
22. Low/intermediate servo assembly piston, seal or rod damaged.
23. Low/intermediate servo oil tubes damaged.
24. Final drive assembly or final drive sun gear shaft pistons or gears damaged.
25. Output shaft incorrectly aligned with axles or damaged shaft splines.
26. Halfshaft disengaged from transaxle or damaged shaft splines.

NO REVERSE

1. Low oil level or pressure.
2. Linkage misadjusted, disconnected, damaged, broken or bent.
3. TV linkage disconnected or missing.
4. Oil pump worn or damaged.
5. Oil pump driveshaft damaged.
6. Drive chain assembly damaged or broken.
7. Drive sprocket shaft to converter turbine spline damaged.
8. Driven sprocket shaft to direct/intermediate clutch hub damaged.
9. Reverse clutch plates missing or burned.
10. Forward clutch plates missing or burned.
11. Forward clutch piston seals or pistons damaged.
12. Forward clutch check ball assembly missing or damaged.
13. Forward clutch driven sprocket support seals damaged or missing.
14. Forward clutch oil holes blocked.
15. Forward clutch direct intermediate hub seals damaged or missing.
16. Low one-way clutch improperly assembled or damaged sprag.
17. Front and rear carrier pistons/lugs to rear ring gear damaged.
18. Reverse apply tube leaking or improperly installed.

NO PARK RANGE

1. Chipped or broken parking pawl or park gear.
2. Broken park pawl return spring.
3. Bent or broken actuating rod.
4. Manual linkage misadjusted.

HARSH NEUTRAL TO REVERSE OR HARSH NEUTRAL TO DRIVE

1. Low/intermediate servo assembly springs damaged or missing.
2. Low/intermediate servo apply rod length incorrect.
3. 3-2 control valve stuck, nicked or damaged.
4. Number 5 ball missing.
5. Neutral/drive accumulator piston stuck.
6. Neutral/drive accumulator seal damaged or missing.
7. Neutral/drive accumulator springs damaged or missing.
8. Number 1 check ball missing.
9. Main control separator plate thermal elements do not close when warm.

TRANSAXLE OVERHEATS

1. Excessive tow loads.
2. Incorrect fluid level.
3. Incorrect engine idle or performance.
4. Incorrect clutch or band application or oil pressure control system.
5. Restriction in cooler or lines.
6. Seized converter one-way clutch.
7. Dirty or sticking valve body.

TRANSAXLE FLUID LEAKS

1. Incorrect oil level.
2. Defective gaskets, seals, etc.

MAINTENANCE

CHECKING OIL LEVEL

1. Start engine and allow to reach normal operating temperature.
2. Move transaxle selector lever through each range, allowing enough time in each range for transaxle to engage. Return selector lever to the Park position and apply parking brake. **Do not turn engine off during fluid level check.**
3. Clean all dirt from transaxle fluid dipstick cap before removing dipstick from filler tube.
4. Remove dipstick from tube and wipe it clean, then push it all the way back into the tube. Ensure dipstick is fully seated.
5. Pull dipstick out of tube and check fluid level. Fluid should be between the arrows.
6. If necessary, add Motorcraft Type H, XT-4-H or equivalent fluid through the filler tube to raise level to the correct position. **Adding approximately 8 ounces of fluid will raise level from bottom arrow to top arrow. Use caution not to overfill transaxle.**

DRAIN & REFILL

Normal maintenance and lubrication requirements do not necessitate periodic fluid change. If vehicle is operated under abnormal conditions, fluid should be changed every 30,000 miles. If major failure has occurred in the transaxle, it will have to be removed for service. At this time, the converter should be thoroughly flushed to remove any foreign matter. Use of fluid other than Motorcraft Type H, XT-4-H or equivalent fluid could result in transaxle malfunction or failure.

1. Raise and support vehicle, then position a suitable drain pan under transaxle.
2. Loosen pump and valve body cover attaching bolts and drain oil.
3. Loosen lower oil pan attaching bolts and drain fluid from transaxle.
4. When fluid has drained ot the level of the oil pan flange, remove pan attaching bolts working from the RH side, allowing pan to drop and drain slowly.
5. When fluid has stopped draining, remove and clean pan and screen. Discard pan gasket.
6. Install pan using a new gasket.
7. Tighten pump and valve body cover attaching bolts, then refill transaxle to correct level.

IN-VEHICLE ADJUSTMENTS

MANUAL LINKAGE, ADJUST

1. Position selector lever in the OVERDRIVE position against rearward stop, Fig. 3. **Shift lever should be held in the rearward position while linkage is being adjusted.**
2. Loosen manual lever to control cable attaching nut.
3. Place transaxle lever in the OVERDRIVE position, second detent from most rearward position, then torque cable attaching nut to 10-15 ft. lbs.
4. Check operation of transaxle in each selector position. Ensure park and neutral switch operates satisfactorily.

THROTTLE VALVE (TV) CABLE, ADJUST

The TV cable normal does not require adjustment. The only time cable should be adjusted is if one of the following compo-

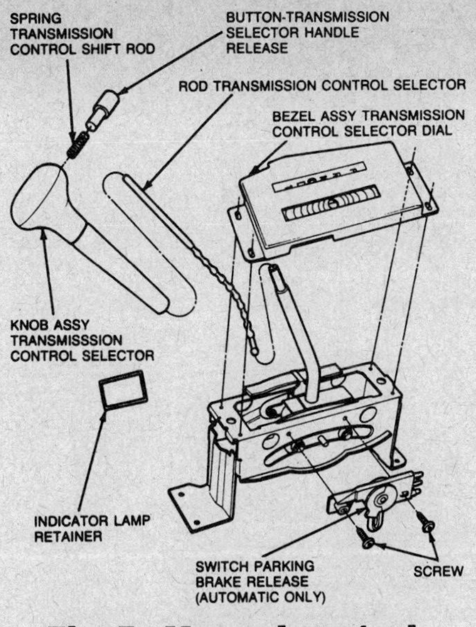

Fig. 3 Manual control linkage adjustment

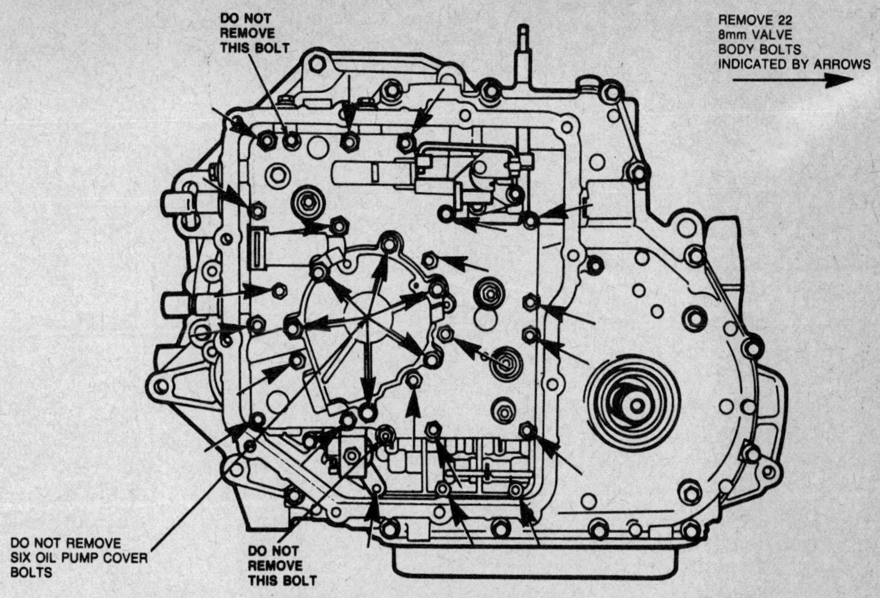

Fig. 5 Removing oil pump & valve body attaching bolts

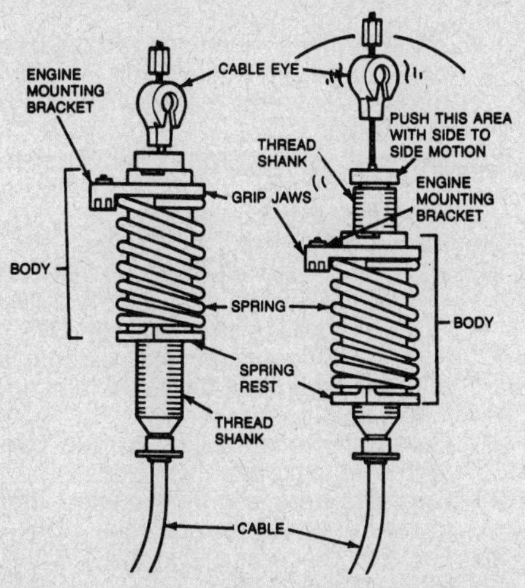

Fig. 4 TV cable adjustment

nents is replaced: main control assembly, TV cable, TV cable engine mounting bracket, throttle control lever link or lever assembly, engine throttle body or transaxle assembly.

1. Connect TV cable eye, **Fig. 4,** then attach cable boot to chain cover.
2. With TV cabie mounted in engine bracket, ensure threaded shank is fully retracted. To retract shank, hold spring rest and wiggle top of thread shank while pressing shank toward spring.
3. Attach end of TV cable to throttle body.
4. Rotate throttle lever to WOT position and release.
5. Threaded shank should show movement or "ratchet" out of grip jaws. If movement is not present, inspect TV cable system for broken or disconnected components and repeat procedure as required.

IN-VEHICLE REPAIRS

OIL PUMP & VALVE BODY ASSEMBLY

Removal

1. Disconnect battery ground cable, then remove battery and battery tray.
2. Remove air cleaner assembly, then position all hoses, vacuum lines and wiring away from pump and valve body cover.
3. Raise and support vehicle, then support engine and transaxle assembly using a suitable jack.
4. Remove LH engine mounts and supports.
5. Loosen pump and valve body cover attaching bolts and drain transaxle fluid. After fluid has drained, remove cover and gasket.
6. Remove 22 pump and valve body attaching bolts, **Fig. 5.**
7. Pull pump and valve body assembly out enough to clear throttle valve bracket, then rotate valve body clockwise and disconnect manual valve link, **Fig. 6.**
8. Remove pump and valve body assembly from vehicle.

Installation

1. Install new pump and valve body to chain cover guide.
2. Slide pump and valve body assembly into oil pump shaft.
3. Rotate pump and valve body assembly toward dash panel, then engage manual valve link with manual valve.
4. Rotate or jiggle pump and valve body assembly to engage spline on oil pump shaft with splines on oil pump rotor. Valve body should slide flush onto chain cover without force. If full engagement of the pump and valve body is not obtained, perform one of the two following methods:
   a. Rotate engine using 7/8 inch deep well socket on the crankshaft pulley to complete engagement of the pump shaft to pump.
   b. Remove manual valve from valve body, then rotate assembly as necessary to allow full engagement of pump shaft to pump.
5. Using valve body alignment pin T86P-70100-C or equivalent to position valve body, install pump and valve body attaching bolts. Torque attaching bolts to 7-9 ft. lbs. in the sequence shown in **Fig. 7. Use caution not to using attaching bolts to draw pump and valve body into position.**
6. Install pump, valve body cover and new gasket. Torque cover attaching bolts to 7-9 ft. lbs.
7. Install LH engine mounts and supports, then remove engine and transaxle supporting jack and lower vehicle.
8. Reconnect all hoses and electrical connectors, then install air cleaner, battery and battery tray.
9. Fill transaxle with suitable oil, then start engine and ensure transaxle operates properly.

TRANSAXLE

REPLACE

1. Disconnect battery ground cable, then remove air cleaner, hoses and tubes.
2. Remove shift cable and bracket assembly attaching bolt from transaxle.
3. Remove two shift cable bracket attaching bolts and bracket from transaxle.
4. Disconnect neutral safety switch electrical connector, then the bulkhead electrical connector from rear of transaxle.
5. Remove throttle valve cable from throttle body lever.
6. Remove one throttle valve cable to

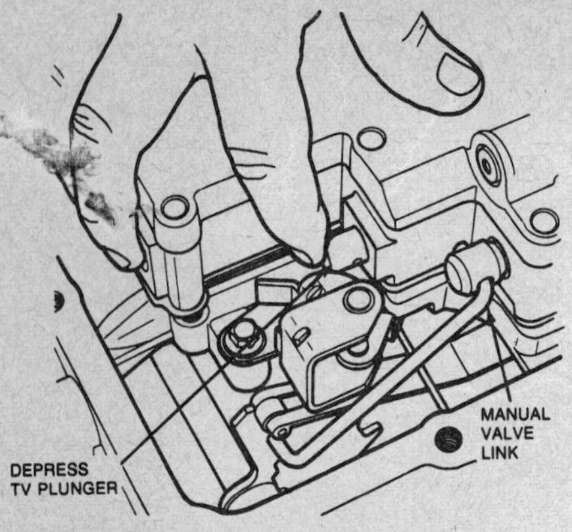

Fig. 6 Disconnecting manual valve link

transaxle case attaching bolt.

7. Pull up on throttle valve cable, then disconnect cable from link. **Use care to avoid bending internal throttle valve bracket.**
8. Remove LH engine support strut attaching bolt, then the four torque converter housing attaching bolts from top of transaxle.
9. Install suitable engine support fixture to three engine lift points, then raise engine slightly to relieve weight from engine mounts.
10. Raise and support vehicle, then remove both front wheels.
11. Remove each tie rod end from its spindle.
12. Remove both lower ball joint attaching bolts, then the lower ball joint.
13. Remove lower control arms from each spindle, then the stabilizer bar attaching nuts.
14. Remove two rack and pinion-to-subframe attaching bolts.
15. Remove two engine mount attaching bolts, then disconnect exhaust gas oxygen (EGO) sensor.
16. Remove exhaust Y-pipe from engine and rear portion of exhaust system.

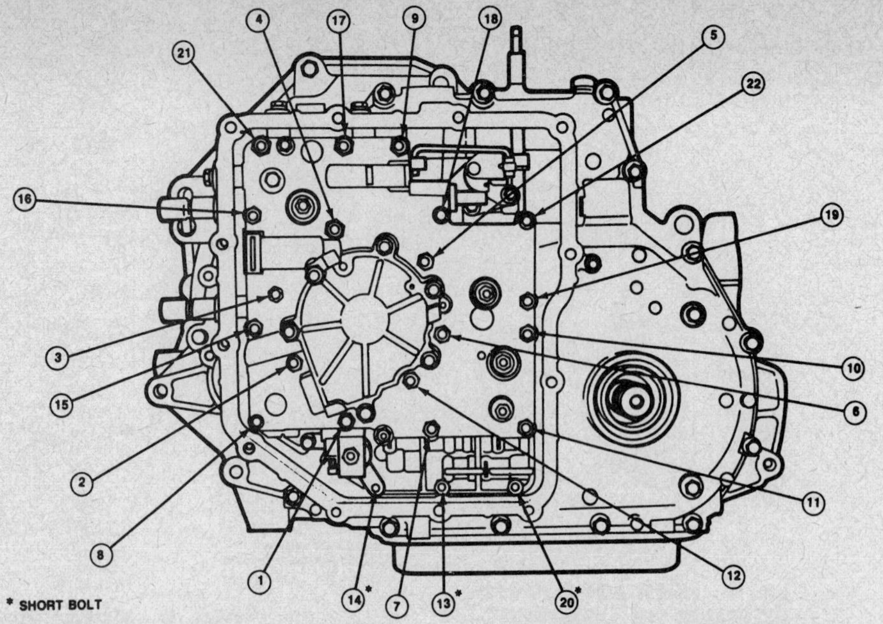

Fig. 7 Installing oil pump & valve body attaching bolts

17. Remove four bolts from sub-frame attaching points, then two bolts from LH engine support mount. Lower subframe from vehicle.
18. Position suitable jack under transaxle oil pan, then remove vehicle speed sensor from transaxle. **Vehicles with electronic instrument clusters do not use a speedometer cable.**
19. Remove two transaxle mount attaching bolts.
20. Remove four LH engine support attaching bolts, then the support.
21. REmove separator plate attaching bolts.
22. Remove two starter attaching bolts and position starter aside.
23. Remove separator plate.
24. Rotate engine with a $1/2$ inch drive socket and a $7/8$ inch deep well socket on crankshaft pulley bolt to align torque converter bolts with starter drive hole.
25. Remove four torque converter-to-flywheel attaching nuts, then disconnect transaxle cooler lines.
26. Remove halfshafts as follows:
    a. Screw extension T86P-3514-A2 into CV joint puller T86P-3514-A1 and install slide hammer D79P-100-A or equivalent into extension.
    b. Position puller behind CV joint and remove joint.
27. Remove two remaining torque converter housing attaching bolts.
28. Separate transaxle from engine, then lower transaxle from vehicle.
29. Reverse procedure to install.

FRONT DRIVE AXLES

TABLE OF CONTENTS

Exc. Sable & Taurus

INDEX

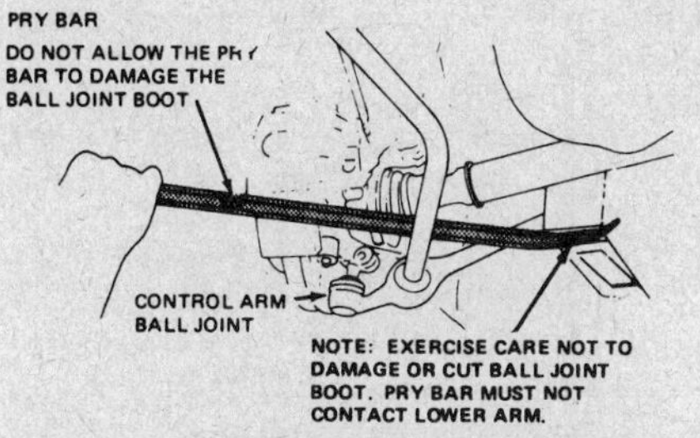

PRY BAR
DO NOT ALLOW THE PR
BAR TO DAMAGE THE
BALL JOINT BOOT
CONTROL ARM
BALL JOINT
NOTE: EXERCISE CARE NOT TO DAMAGE OR CUT BALL JOINT BOOT. PRY BAR MUST NOT CONTACT LOWER ARM.

Fig. 1 Separating ball joint from steering knuckle

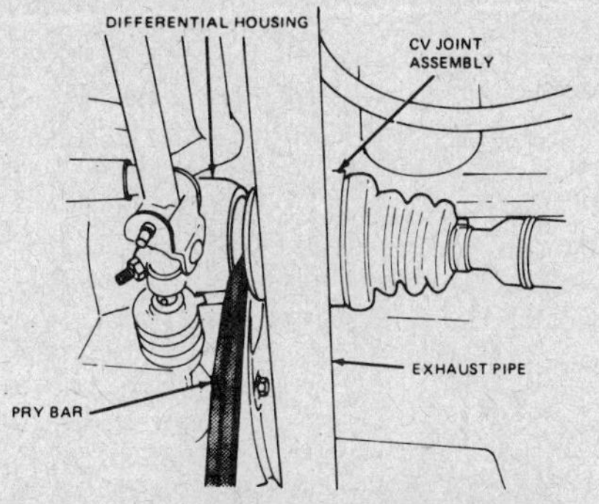

DIFFERENTIAL HOUSING
CV JOINT ASSEMBLY
EXHAUST PIPE
PRY BAR

Fig. 2 Removing halfshaft from differential housing

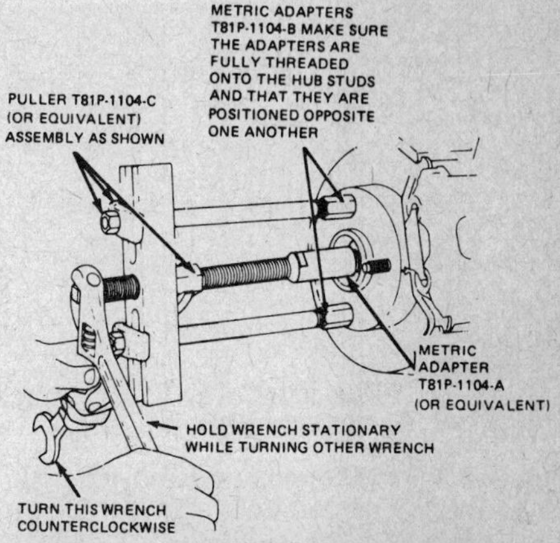

METRIC ADAPTERS T81P-1104-B MAKE SURE THE ADAPTERS ARE FULLY THREADED ONTO THE HUB STUDS AND THAT THEY ARE POSITIONED OPPOSITE ONE ANOTHER
PULLER T81P-1104-C (OR EQUIVALENT) ASSEMBLY AS SHOWN
METRIC ADAPTER T81P-1104-A (OR EQUIVALENT)
HOLD WRENCH STATIONARY WHILE TURNING OTHER WRENCH
TURN THIS WRENCH COUNTERCLOCKWISE

Fig. 3 Separating outer constant velocity joint from hub

DRIVESHAFTS REPLACE

If removing both right and left side halfshafts, plugs T81P-1177B or equivalent must be installed. Failure to do so may result in dislocation of differential side gears, necessitating transaxle disassembly to realign the gears. Also, halfshaft removal and installation procedures are the same for manual and automatic transaxles except for the following: due to automatic transaxle case configuration the right side halfshaft assembly must be removed first. Tool T81P-4026A or equivalent is then inserted into transaxle to remove left side inner constant velocity joint assembly from transaxle. If only the left side halfshaft is to be removed from the vehicle, remove right side halfshaft assembly from the transaxle case only and secure to underside of vehicle, then remove left side halfshaft assembly. The hub nut and lower control arm to steering knuckle attaching bolt and nut must be discarded after removal and new nuts and bolts installed.

1. Loosen hub nut without unstaking. Use of a chisel or similar tool to unstake nut may damage spindle threads.
2. Raise and support vehicle and remove wheel assemblies.
3. Remove bolt attaching brake hose routing clip to suspension strut.
4. Remove nut from ball joint to steering knuckle attaching bolt, then drive bolt from knuckle using suitable punch and hammer.
5. Separate ball joint from steering knuckle using pry bar, **Fig. 1. Lower ball joints fit into a pocket formed in the plastic disc brake shield. The shield must be positioned away from the ball joint while removing ball joint from steering knuckle.**
6. Remove halfshaft from differential housing using suitable pry bar. Use caution not to damage dust deflector located between shaft and case, **Fig. 2.** If an automatic transaxle halfshaft assembly cannot be removed from differential by using a pry bar, insert a large bladed screwdriver between differential pinion shaft and inboard constant velocity joint stub shaft. Sharply tap on screwdriver handle, to free halfshaft from differential. **Use caution not to damage differential oil seal, constant velocity joint boot or constant velocity joint dust deflector.**
7. Separate outer constant velocity joint from hub using puller T81P-1104C or equivalent, **Fig. 3,** and adapters T81P-1104B and T81P-1104A or equivalent. **Do not use a hammer to separate outboard constant velocity joint stub shaft from hub as damage to internal components may result.**
8. Reverse procedure to install. Install new circlip on inboard constant velocity joint stub shaft. Align splines of inboard constant velocity joint stub shaft with splines in differential. Push joint into differential until circlip seats in side gear, **Fig. 4.** Torque new control arm to steering knuckle nut to 40 ft. lbs. Torque new hub nut to 180-200 ft. lbs., and stake nut, **Fig. 5. If the hub nut cracks or splits during staking, remove and replace hub nut.**

CONSTANT VELOCITY JOINT SERVICE

Replacement

1982 & EARLY 1983 MODELS

REMOVAL

Service is the same for both inner and outer constant velocity joints.

1. Place halfshaft in suitable vice. Use caution not to damage boot or clamp.
2. Cut large boot clamp and remove from boot, **Fig. 6,** then position boot upward on shaft. If boot only is being replaced due to damage, check joint grease for contamination. If joints were operating satisfactorily and grease is not contaminated, add grease and install new boot. If grease is contaminated, joint must be completely disassembled.
3. Separate constant velocity joint from shaft using tool T81P-3514A or equivalent, **Fig. 7.** If necessary, boot may be removed from shaft by cutting

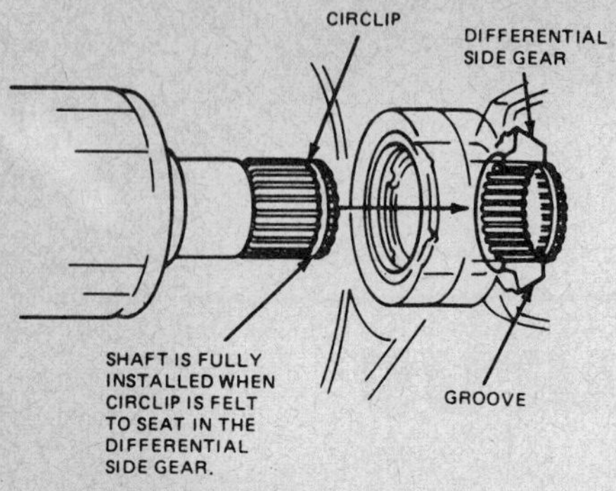

Fig. 4 Installing inner constant velocity joint into differential side gear

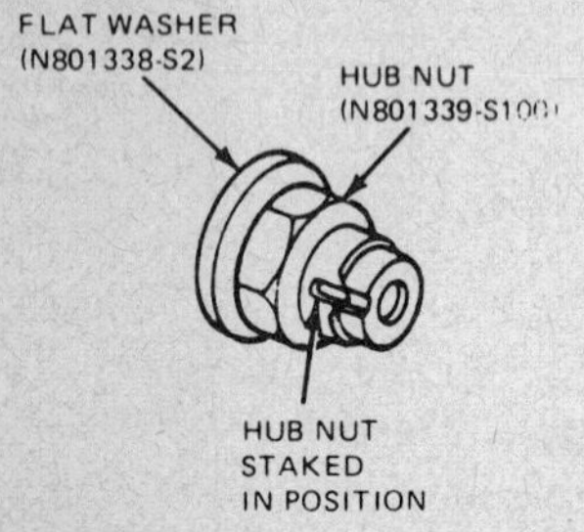

Fig. 5 Hub nut staking tool fabrication

remaining clamp and removing boot.

4. Remove circlip from end of shaft and discard. Inspect stop ring for damage and replace as necessary, **Fig. 8.**

INSTALLATION

1. Inspect splines at each end of shaft for damage and wear. Inner constant velocity joint must be installed onto longer splines, **Fig. 9.**
2. Ensure stop ring is in proper position, then install new circlip into groove nearest end of shaft.
3. Install joint boot until it seats in its groove, then install clamp. Tighten clamp securely but do not damage boot or cut clamp bridge, **Fig. 10.**
4. Position boot upward towards end of shaft, then position constant velocity joint onto shaft and tap into position using plastic mallet. Joint is fully seated when circlip locks in groove cut into joint bearing inner race. Check for proper seating by trying to pull joint from shaft.
5. Lubricate joints with lubricant packs supplied with service kit. On outer joint, fill boot with 2/3 packet and pack joint with 1 1/3 packet of lubricant. On inner joint, fill boot with one packet and pack joint with one packet of lubricant. Use lubricant D8RZ-19590A or equivalent only.
6. Position boot over joint, then pry end of boot upward to release any trapped air.
7. Position joint inward or outward as necessary to adjust halfshaft to length shown in **Fig. 11.**
8. Ensure boot is seated in groove, then refer to step 3 for clamp installation.

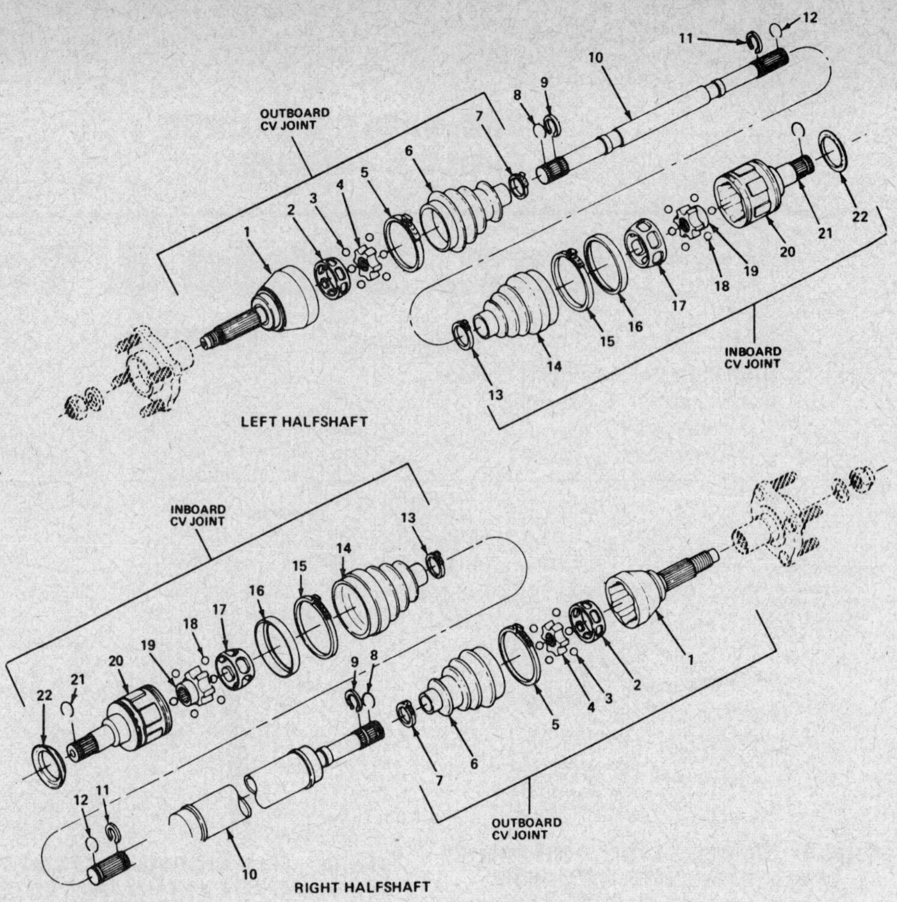

LEGEND:

1. OUTER BEARING RACE AND STUB SHAFT ASSEMBLY
2. BEARING CAGE
3. BALL BEARINGS (6)
4. INNER BEARING RACE
5. BOOT CLAMP (LARGE)
6. BOOT
7. BOOT CLAMP (SMALL)
8. CIRCLIP
9. STOP RING
10. INTERCONNECTING SHAFT
11. STOP RING
12. CIRCLIP
13. BOOT CLAMP (SMALL)
14. BOOT
15. BOOT CLAMP (LARGE)
16. BEARING RETAINER
17. BEARING CAGE
18. BALL BEARINGS (6)
19. INNER BEARING RACE
20. OUTER BEARING RACE AND STUB SHAFT ASSEMBLY
21. CIRCLIP
22. DUST DEFLECTOR

Fig. 6 Halfshaft assemblies. 1982 & 1983 Early Models

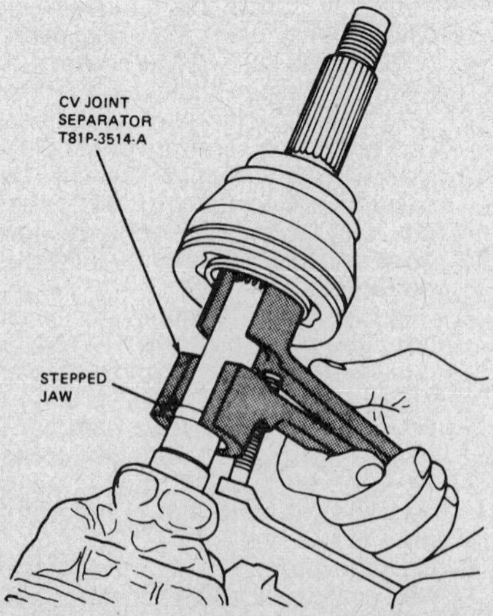

Fig. 7 Separating constant velocity joint from shaft. 1982 & 1983 Early Models

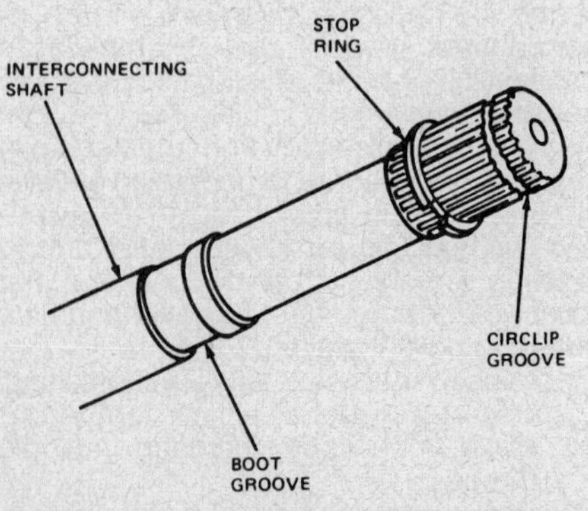

Fig. 8 Stub shaft stop ring

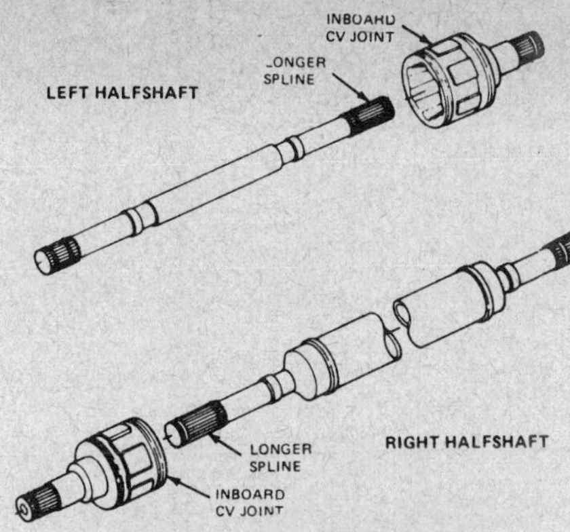

Fig. 9 Assembling constant velocity joints onto halfshafts

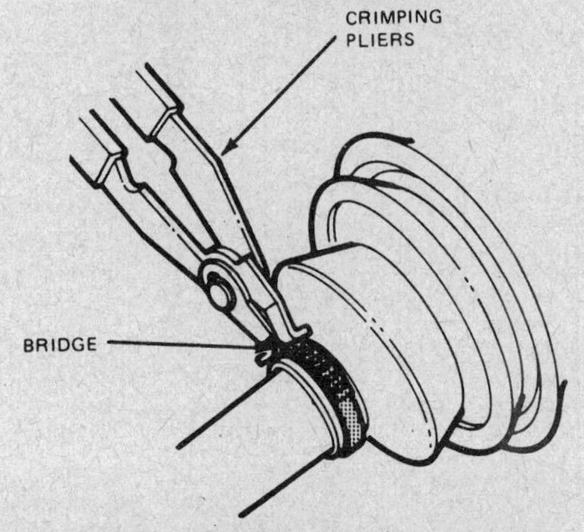

Fig. 10 Installing constant velocity joint clamp

LATE 1983 & 1984–87 MODELS

REMOVAL

Except Inboard Constant Velocity Joint & Boot, 5 Speed Manual Transaxle

1. Place halfshaft in suitable vise. Use caution not to damage boot or clamp.
2. Cut large boot clamp and remove from boot, **Figs. 12 through 14,** then position boot upward on shaft. If boot only is being replaced due to damage, check joint grease for contamination. If joints were operating satisfactorily and grease is not contaminated, add grease and install new boot. If grease is contaminated, joint must be completely disassembled.
3. Place interconnecting shaft in a suitable vise and angle constant velocity joint so that inner bearing race is exposed, **Fig. 15.**
4. Using suitable drift and hammer, tap inner bearing race to dislodge internal circlip and separate constant velocity joint from interconnecting shaft, being careful not to drop joint.
5. Remove boot from shaft, cutting remaining clamp as necessary.
6. Remove circlip from end of shaft and discard. Inspect stop ring for damage and replace as necessary, **Fig. 8.**

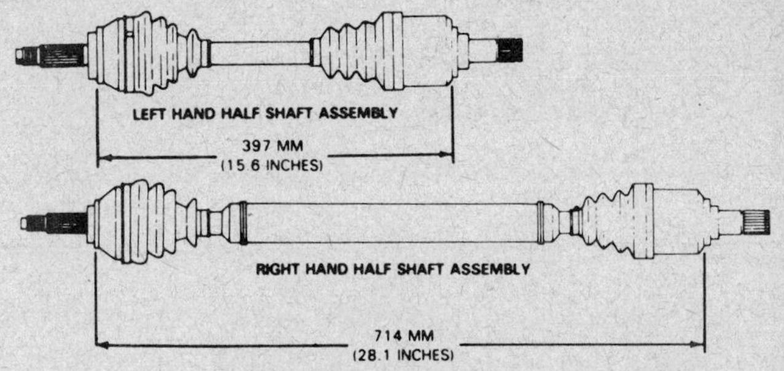

Fig. 11 Halfshaft assembled length. 1982 & 1983 Early Models

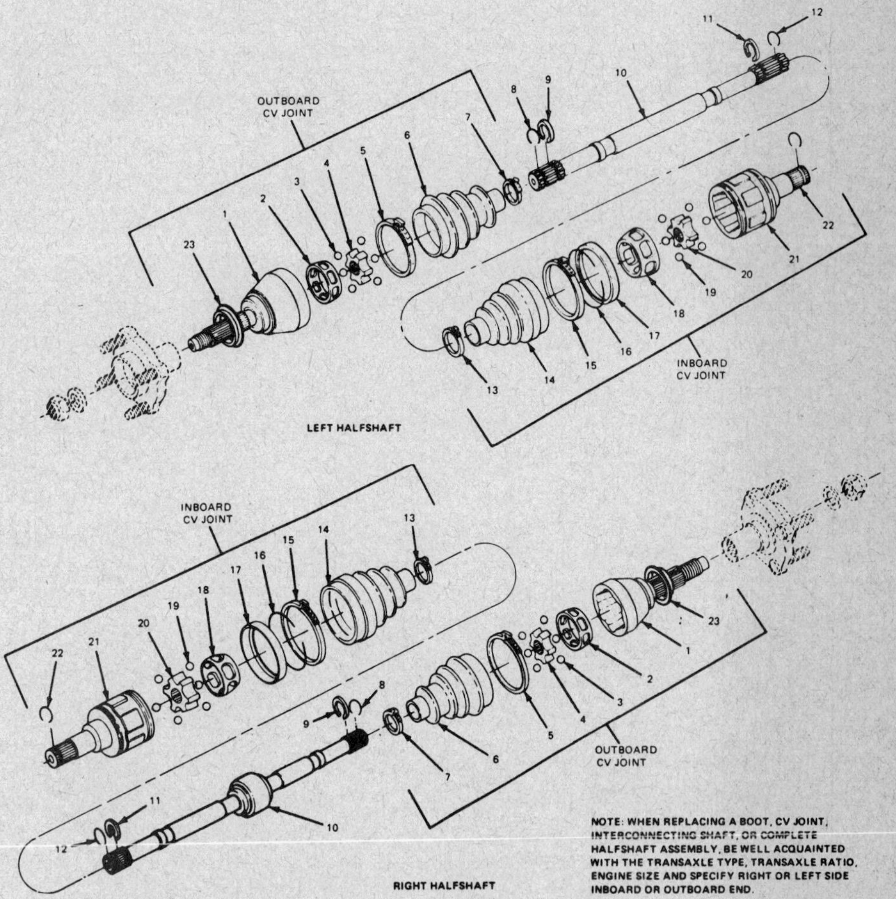

LEGEND:

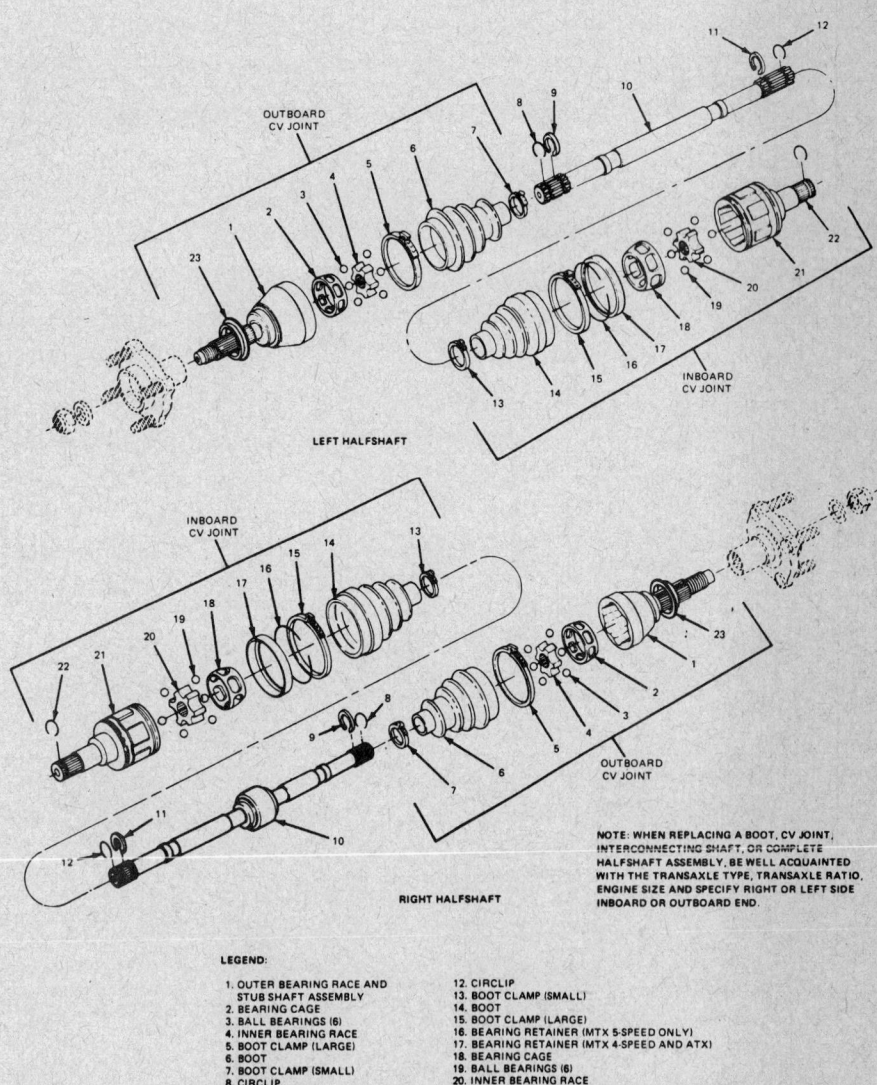

1. OUTER BEARING RACE AND STUB SHAFT ASSEMBLY
2. BEARING CAGE
3. BALL BEARINGS (6)
4. INNER BEARING RACE
5. BOOT CLAMP (LARGE)
6. BOOT
7. BOOT CLAMP (SMALL)
8. CIRCLIP
9. STOP RING
10. INTERCONNECTING SHAFT
11. STOP RING
12. CIRCLIP
13. BOOT CLAMP (SMALL)
14. BOOT
15. BOOT CLAMP (LARGE)
16. BEARING RETAINER (MTX 5-SPEED ONLY)
17. BEARING RETAINER (MTX 4-SPEED AND ATX)
18. BEARING CAGE
19. BALL BEARINGS (6)
20. INNER BEARING RACE
21. OUTER BEARING RACE AND STUB SHAFT ASSEMBLY
22. CIRCLIP
23. DUST SEAL

Fig. 12 Halfshaft assemblies. Late 1983 & 1984–85 models

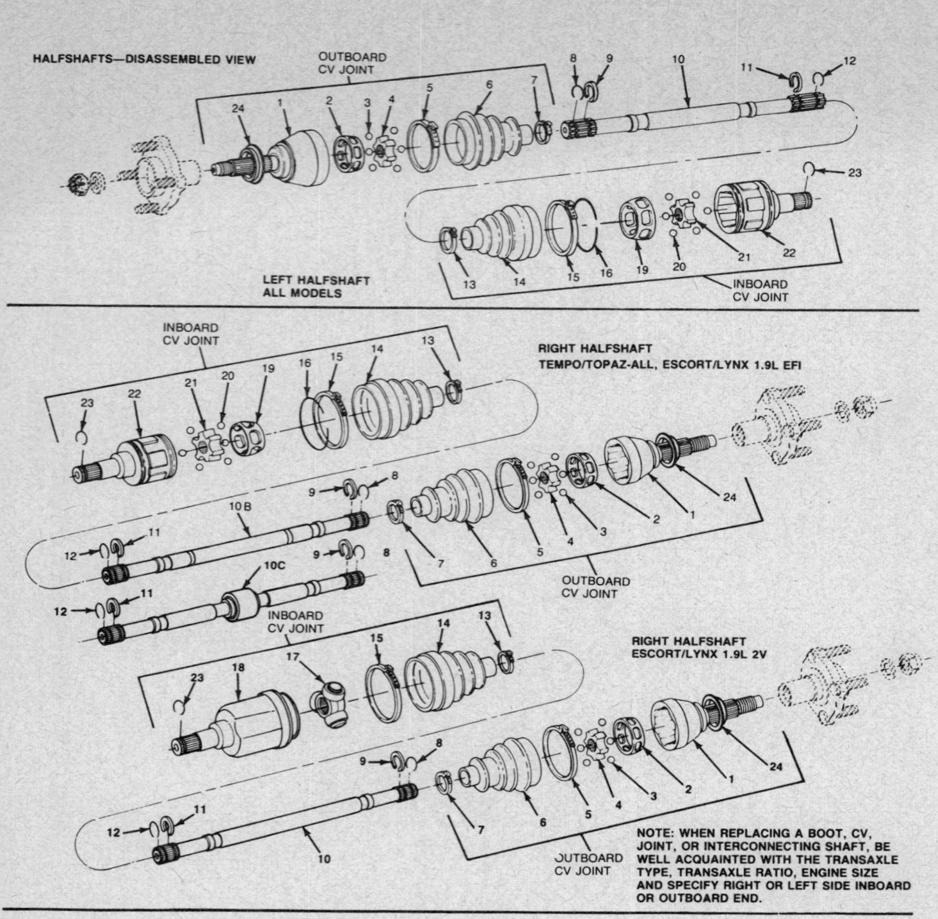

LEGEND:

1. OUTBOARD JOINT OUTER RACE AND STUB SHAFT
2. BALL CAGE
3. BALLS (SIX)
4. OUTBOARD JOINT INNER RACE
5. BOOT CLAMP (LARGE)
6. BOOT
7. BOOT CLAMP (SMALL)
8. CIRCLIP
9. STOP RING
10A. INTERCONNECTING SHAFT
10B. INTERCONNECTING SHAFT TEMPO/TOPAZ (MTX) ESCORT/LYNX (ALL)
10C. INTERCONNECTING SHAFT TEMPO/TOPAZ (ATX)
11. STOP RING
12. CIRCLIP
13. BOOT CLAMP (SMALL)
14. BOOT
15. BOOT CLAMP (LARGE)
16. WIRE RING BALL RETAINER
17. TRIPOD ASSY
18. TRIPOD OUTER RACE
19. BALL CAGE
20. BALLS (SIX)
21. INBOARD JOINT INNER RACE
22. INBOARD JOINT OUTER RACE AND STUB SHAFT
23. CIRCLIP
24. DUST SEAL

Fig. 13 Halfshaft assemblies. 1986 models

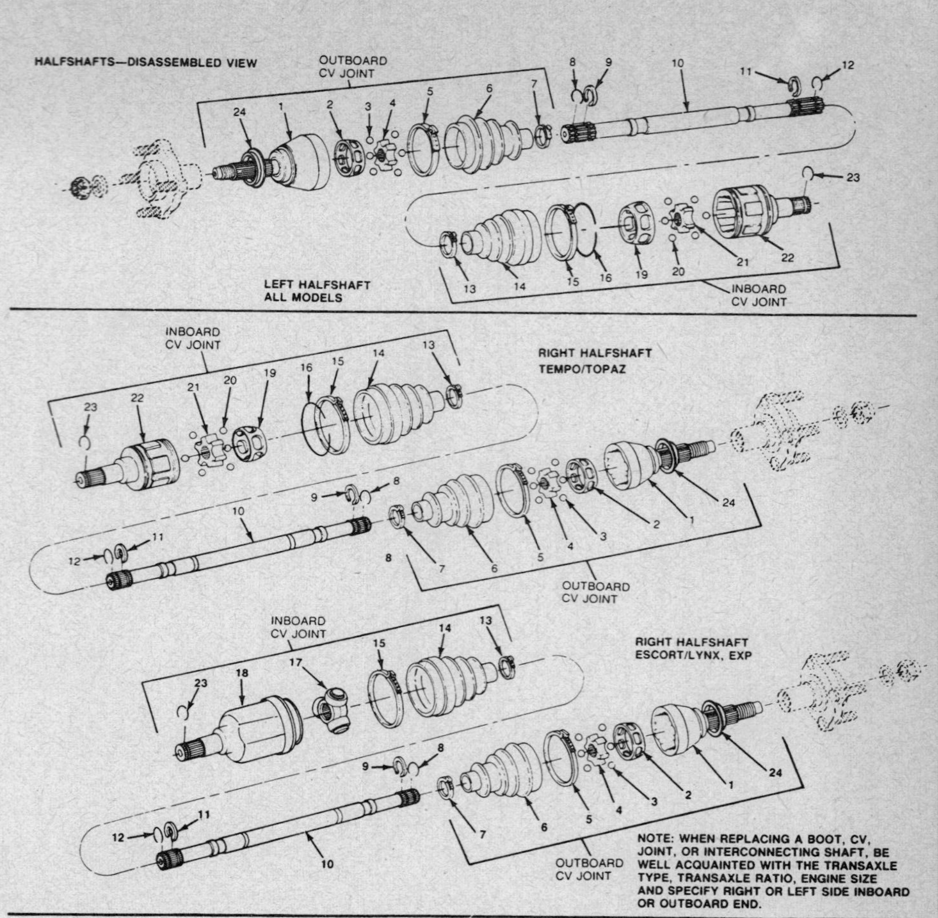

LEGEND:

1.	OUTBOARD JOINT OUTER RACE AND STUB SHAFT	13.	BOOT CLAMP (SMALL)
2.	BALL CAGE	14.	BOOT
3.	BALLS (SIX)	15.	BOOT CLAMP (LARGE)
4.	OUTBOARD JOINT INNER RACE	16.	WIRE RING BALL RETAINER
5.	BOOT CLAMP (LARGE)	17.	TRIPOD ASSY
6.	BOOT	18.	TRIPOD OUTER RACE
7.	BOOT CLAMP (SMALL)	19.	BALL CAGE
8.	CIRCLIP	20.	BALLS (SIX)
9.	STOP RING	21.	INBOARD JOINT INNER RACE
10.	INTERCONNECTING SHAFT	22.	INBOARD JOINT OUTER RACE AND STUB SHAFT
11.	STOP RING	23.	CIRCLIP
12.	CIRCLIP	24.	DUST SEAL

Fig. 14 Halfshaft assemblies. 1987 models

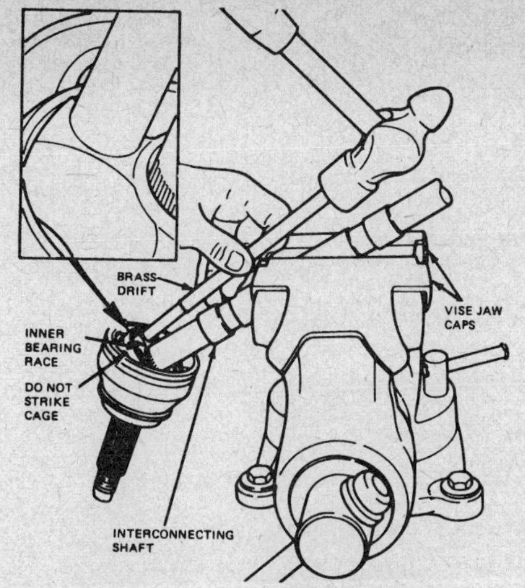

Fig. 15 Separating constant velocity joint from shaft. Late 1983 & 1984–87 models

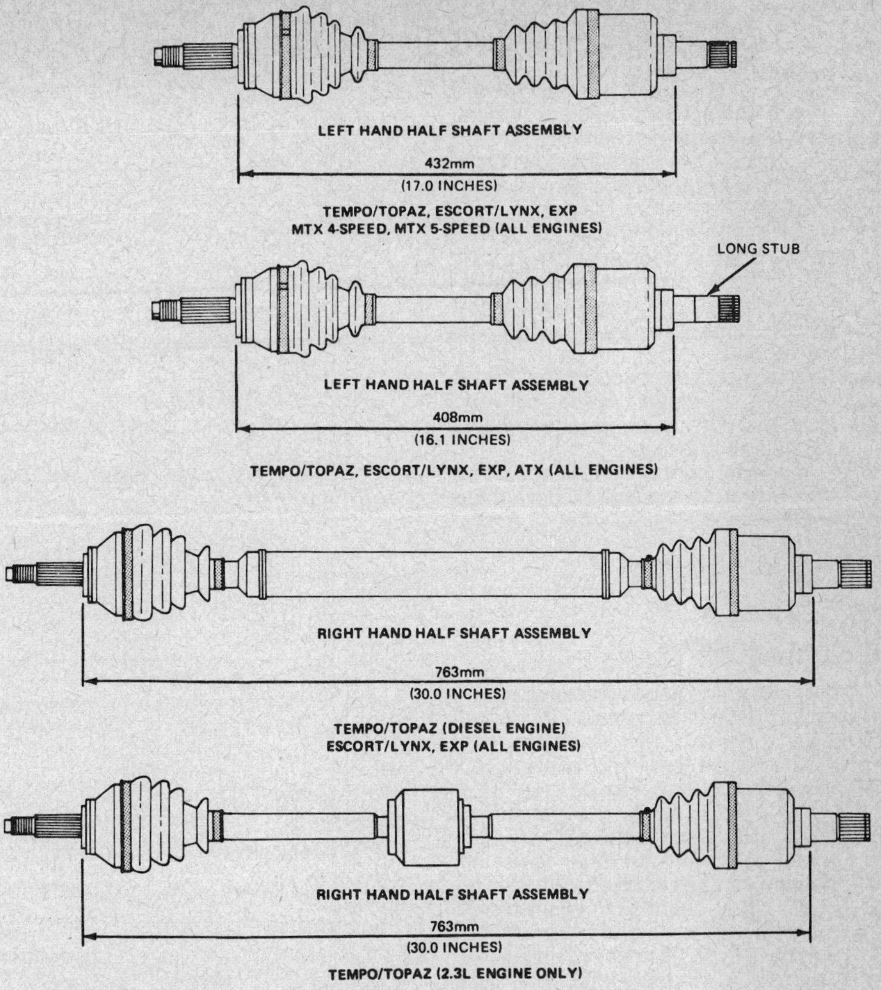

Fig. 16 Halfshaft assembled lengths. Late 1983 & 1984–85 models

Inboard Constant Velocity Joint & Boot, 5 Speed Manual Transaxle

1. Remove large boot clamp, roll boot back, and wipe away excess grease.
2. Remove wire ring bearing retainer from outer race, then remove outer race.
3. Pull inner race and bearing assembly out until it rests on circlip, then, using suitable pliers, spread stop ring and move it back on shaft.
4. Slide inner race and bearing assembly down shaft to expose circlip, then remove circlip.
5. Remove inner race and bearing assembly and, if necessary, remove boot.

INSTALLATION

Except Inboard Constant Velocity Joint & Boot, 5 Speed Manual Transmission

1. Install new stop ring, if removed. Ensure that stop ring is properly seated in groove.
2. Install new circlip in groove nearest end of shaft. To avoid over-expansion or twisting of circlip, start one end in groove and work circlip over stub shaft end and into groove. **Interconnecting shafts are different depending on application. These shafts are non-symmetrical. Outboard end is approximately 1/4 inch longer, from end of shaft to end of boot groove, than inboard end. Be careful to install inboard and outboard constant velocity joints to proper ends of shaft.**
3. Install constant velocity joint boot, if removed, ensuring that boot is seated in groove. Tighten clamp securely, but not too tight.
4. Before positioning boot over constant velocity joint, pack joint and boot as follows:
   a. On inboard constant velocity joint, fill boot with 45 grams of grease and pack joint with 90 grams of grease.
   b. On outboard constant velocity joint, fill boot with 45 grams of grease and pack joint with 45 grams of grease. **Use only lubricant E2FZ-19590-A or equivalent.**
5. Position boot upward toward end of shaft, then position constant velocity joint onto shaft and tap into position using plastic mallet. Joint is fully seated when circlip locks in groove cut into joint bearing inner race. Check for proper seating by trying to pull joint from shaft.
6. Remove all excess grease from external surfaces of constant velocity joint, then position boot over constant velocity joint and move joint in or out to adjust to proper length, **Figs. 16 through 18.**
7. Before installing boot clamp, insert dulled screwdriver blade between boot and outer bearing race to allow trapped air to escape.
8. Ensure that boot is seated in groove, then install clamp securely but not too tight.

Inboard Constant Velocity Joint & Boot, 5 Speed Manual Transmission

1. Move circlip and stop ring back into their respective grooves on shaft. **Lefthand interconnecting shaft is symmetrical and inboard and outboard constant velocity joints may be installed on either end. Righthand interconnecting shaft is non-symmetrical and care must be taken so that inboard and outboard constant velocity joints are correctly installed, Figs. 19 and 20.**
2. Install constant velocity joint boot, if removed. Ensure that boot is seated in groove, then install clamp securely but not too tight.
3. Install new circlip in groove nearest end of shaft. To avoid over-expansion or twisting of circlip, start one end in groove and work circlip over stub shaft end and into groove.
4. Fill boot with 45 grams of grease and fill outer race with 90 grams of grease. Use only lubricant E2FZ-19590-A or equivalent.
5. Push inner race and bearing assem-

bly into outer race by hand.

6. Install ball retainer into groove inside outer race.
7. With boot positioned upward toward end of shaft, install constant velocity joint using suitable hammer. Ensure that splines are aligned before hammering constant velocity joint onto shaft.
8. Remove all excess grease from external surfaces of constant velocity joint, then position boot over constant velocity joint and move joint in or out to adjust to proper length, **Figs. 16 through 18.**
9. Before installing boot clamp, insert dulled screwdriver blade between boot and outer bearing race to allow trapped air to escape.
10. Ensure that boot is seated in groove, then install clamp securely but not too tight.

Disassembly & Assembly

OUTER JOINT

Different bearing cages are used on the outer joints. One type contains four equal sized windows and two elongated windows while the other type contains six windows of equal size, **Fig. 21.**

1. Position stub shaft in suitable vise with bearing facing upward.
2. Press downward on inner race until bearing can be removed, **Fig. 22.** Remove all six bearings in this manner.
3. Pivot bearing cage and inner race assembly into position shown in **Fig. 23.** Align cage windows with outer race lands while pivoting cage, **Fig. 24,** then remove from outer race.
4. To separate inner race from cage, determine cage design and proceed as follows: on cages with six equal windows rotate inner race upward and remove from cage. On cages with two elongated windows, pivot inner race until it is in position shown in **Fig. 23,** then align one inner race band with one elongated window and position race through the window. Rotate inner race upward and remove from cage, **Fig. 25.**
5. Reverse procedure to assemble. Refer to **Fig. 26** for ball groove and window alignment and proper counterbore positioning.

INNER JOINT

Roll Crimp Ball Retainer Type, Fig. 27

On late 1983 and 1984-87 models with 5 speed manual transmission, disassembly of inboard constant velocity joint, **Fig. 28,** is performed during removal. Assembly of inboard constant velocity joint is performed during installation as previously described.

1. Remove circlip from end of joint stub shaft, then using suitable cutters, cut and remove ball retainer, **Fig. 29.** Discard retainer since a new retainer is not required for assembly.
2. Gently tap joint on work surface until

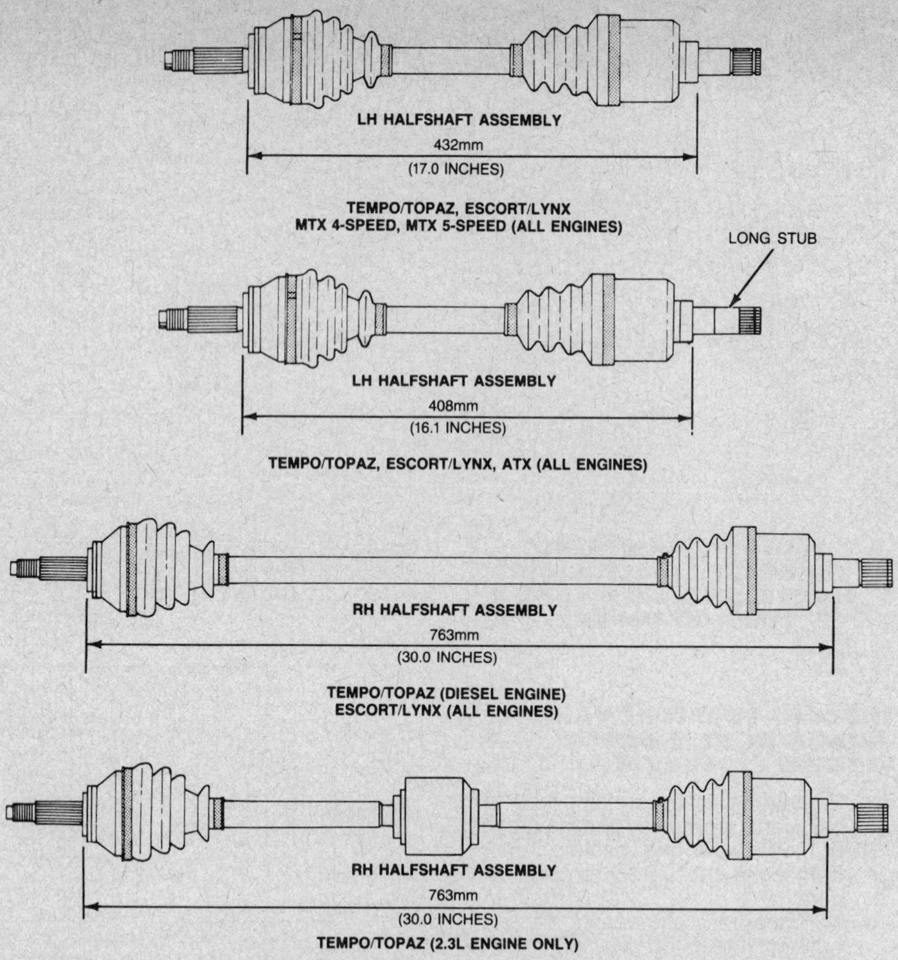

Fig. 17 Halfshaft assembled lengths. 1986 models

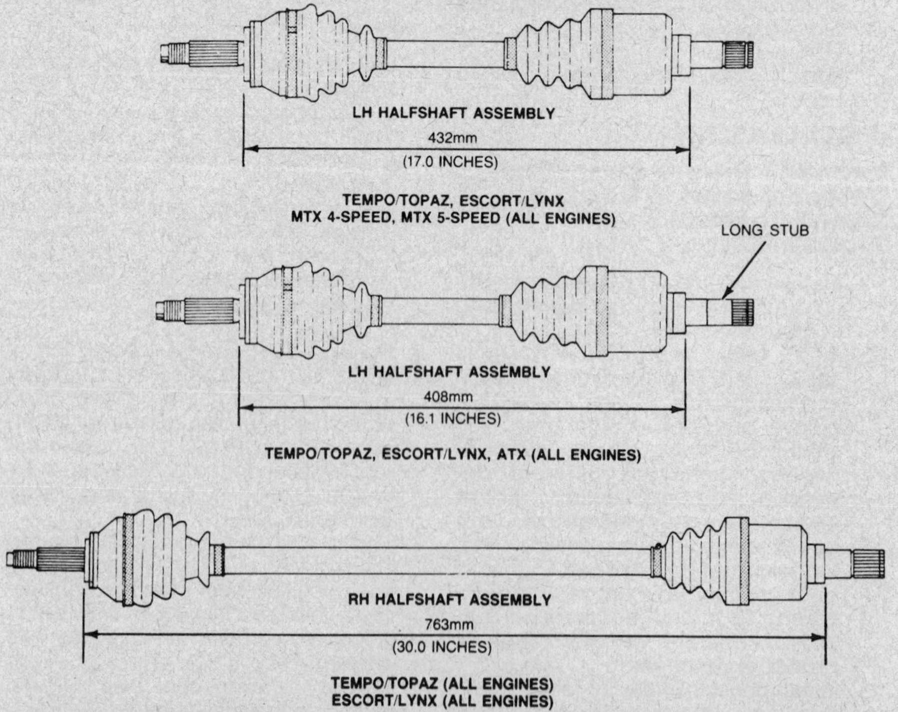

Fig. 18 Halfshaft assembled lengths. 1987 models

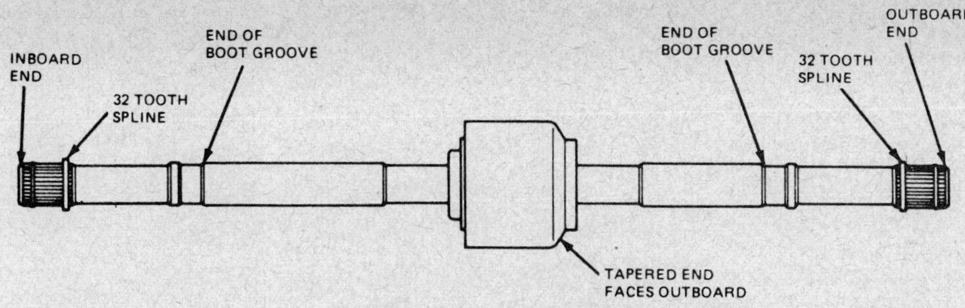

Fig. 19 Righthand interconnecting shaft. Late 1983 & 1984–86 models

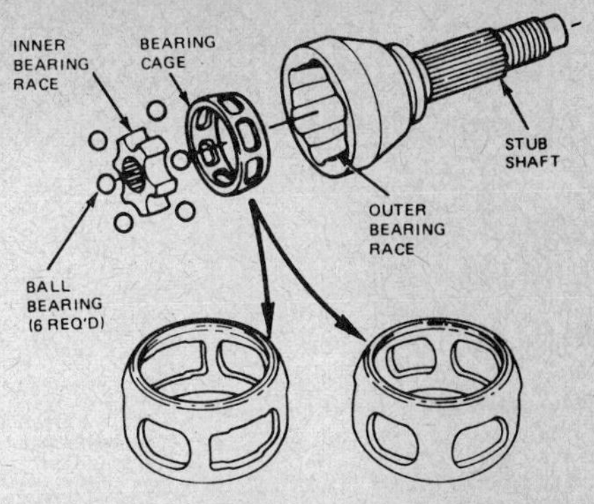

Fig. 21 Outer constant velocity joint bearing cage configuration

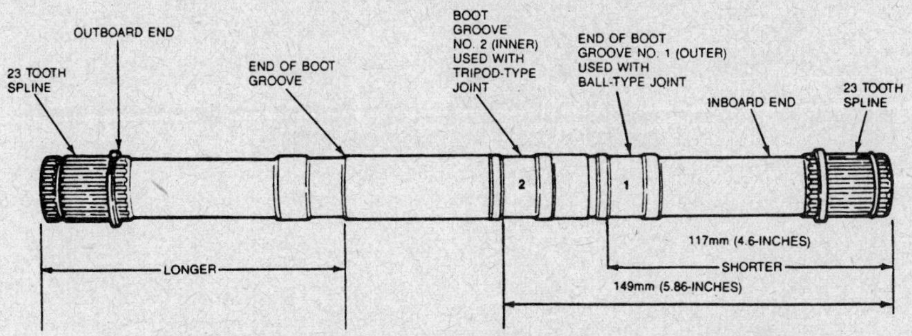

Fig. 20 Interconnecting shaft. 1987 models

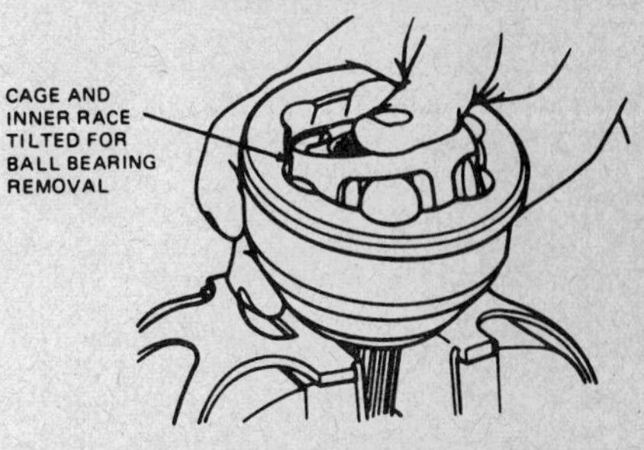

Fig. 22 Removing outer constant velocity joint bearings

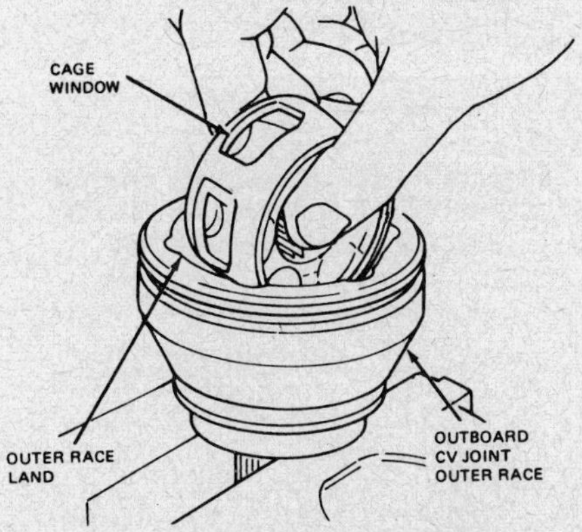

Fig. 23 Removing bearing cage and inner race assembly from outer constant velocity joint

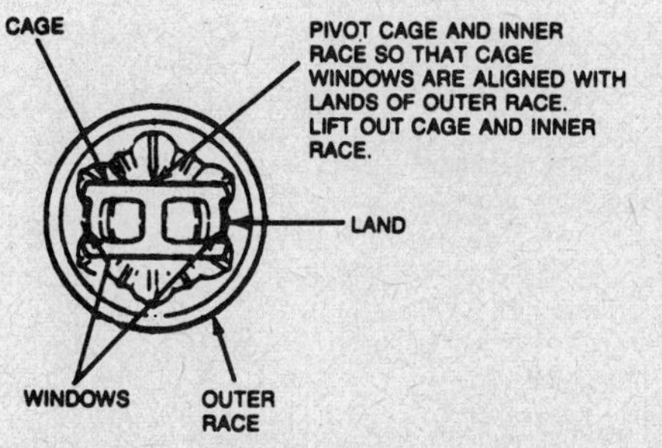

Fig. 24 Aligning inner cage and bearing race

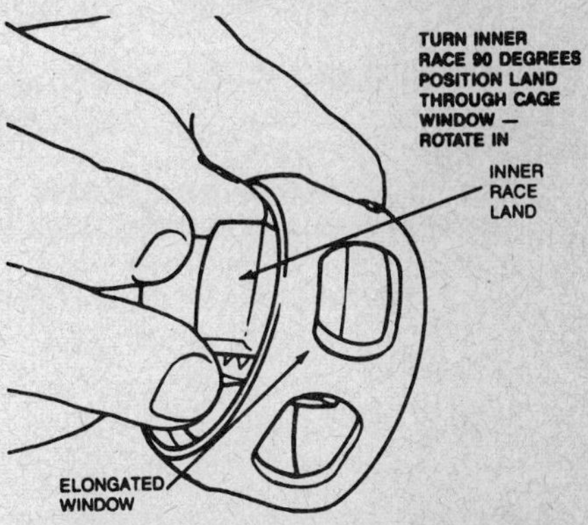

Fig. 25 Removing inner race from bearing cage

assembly can be removed by hand, **Fig. 30.**

3. Remove bearings from cage by prying with a dulled screwdriver. Use caution not to damage or scratch any components, **Fig. 31.**
4. Rotate inner race to align lands with cage windows, then remove race from bearing cage through wider end of cage, **Fig. 32.**
5. Reverse procedure to assemble.

Wire Ring Ball Retainer Type

1. Remove large clamp, then slide boot back and wipe excess grease.
2. Using a suitable tool, remove wire ring ball retainer from race.
3. Remove outer race.
4. Pull inner race and bearing assembly out until race contacts snap ring.
5. Using suitable pliers, spread then slide snap ring back onto shaft.
6. Slide inner race and bearing assembly down the shaft to allow access to the snap ring.
7. Using a suitable screwdriver, remove snap ring.
8. Remove inner race and bearing assembly.
9. Reverse procedure to assemble.

Tripod CV Joint, RH Side, 1986 Escort & Lynx & 1987 Escort, Lynx & EXP

1. Remove large clamp, then slide boot back and wipe off excess grease. **Inspect CV joint grease for contamination by rubbing a small amount between two fingers. Any gritty feeling indicates contamination. If grease is contaminated, proceed with disassembly. If grease is not contaminated and joint was operating satisfactorily, add grease and replace boot.**
2. Using suitable pliers, bend retaining tabs back and separate outer race from tripod assembly.
3. Using suitable snap ring pliers, slide snap ring back on shaft, **Fig. 33.**
4. Push tripod assembly back on shaft, to gain access to circlip, then remove circlip from shaft.
5. Remove tripod assembly from shaft, and boot if necessary.
6. Reverse procedure to install noting the following:
   a. Fill CV joint outer race with 3.5 ounces of grease and CV boot with 2.1 ounces of grease. Use Ford Constant Velocity Joint Grease/High Temperature E43Z-19590-A or equivalent.

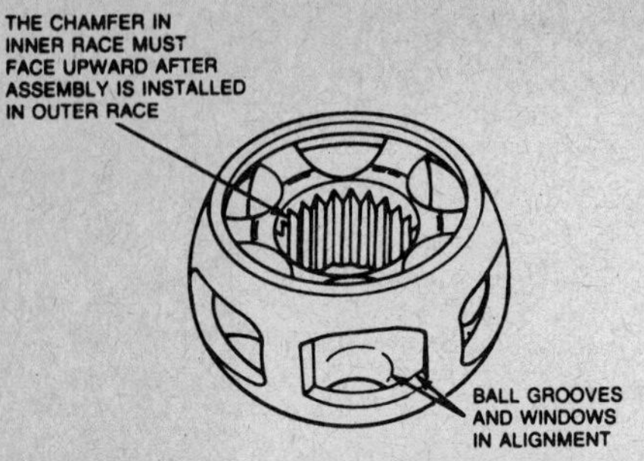

Fig. 26 Counterbore positioning and ball groove & window alignment

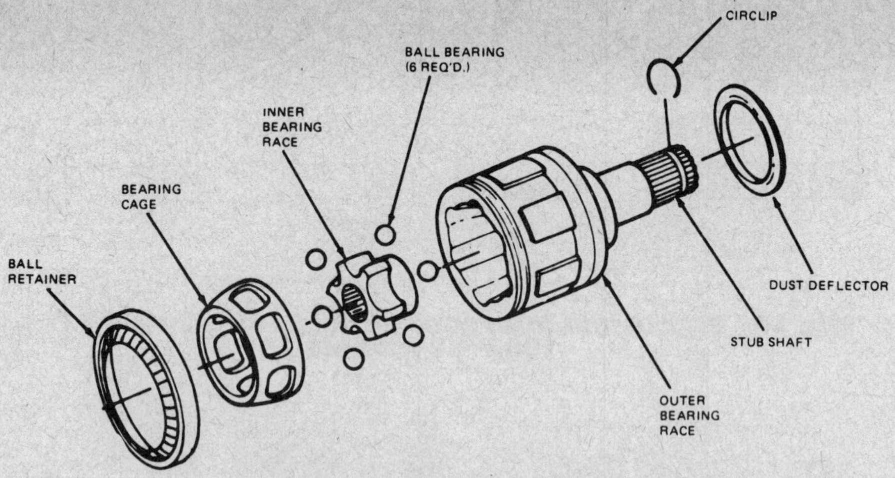

Fig. 27 Inner constant velocity joint assembly. Roll crimp ball retainer type

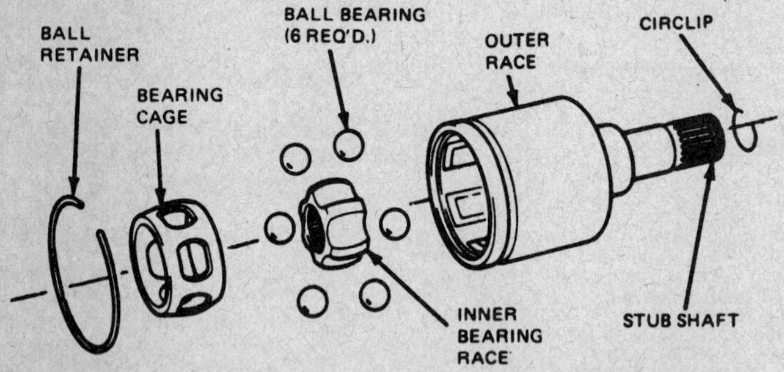

Fig. 28 Inner constant velocity joint assembly. Wire ring ball retainer type

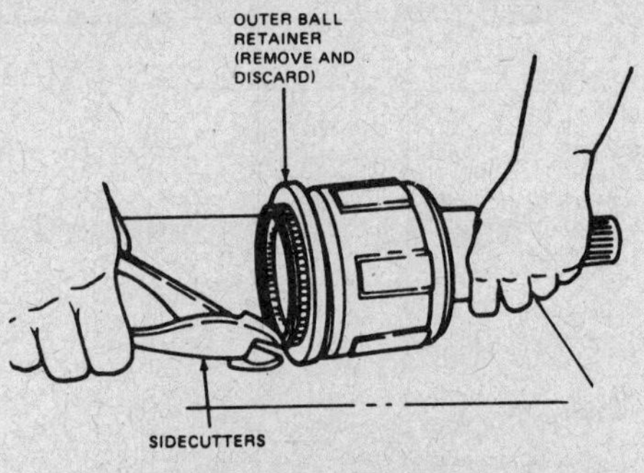

Fig. 29 Removing inner constant velocity joint outer ball retainer

Fig. 30 Removing inner constant velocity joint inner race and bearing assembly

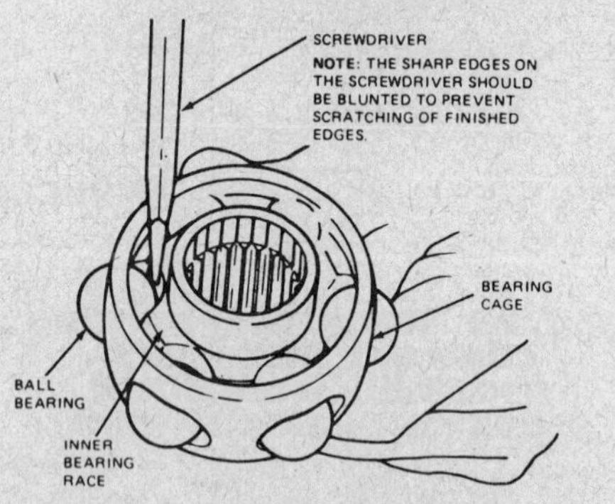

Fig. 31 Removing bearings from cage

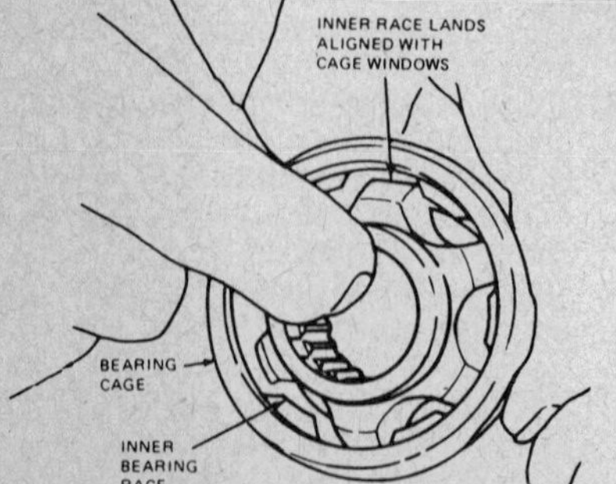

Fig. 32 Removing inner race from bearing cage

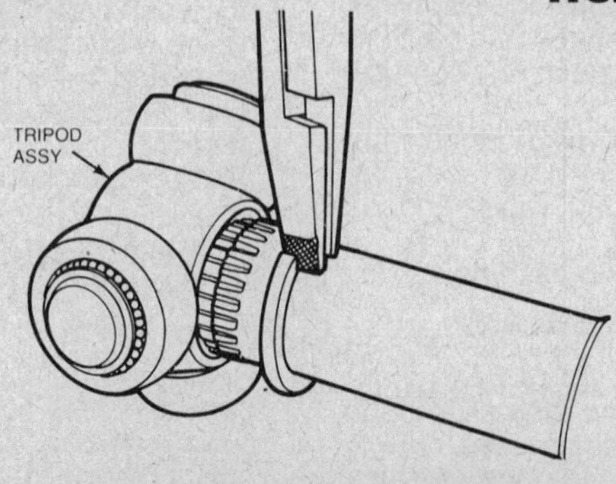

Fig. 33 Removing snap ring from shaft

Sable & Taurus

INDEX

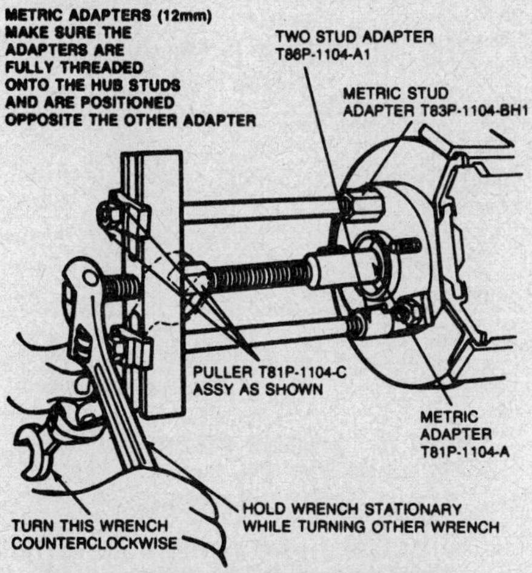

Fig. 1 Separating front hub from outer CV joint

DRIVESHAFTS REPLACE

If removing both right and left side halfshafts, plugs T81P-1177-B or equivalent must be installed. Failure to do so may result in dislocation of differential side gears, necessitating transaxle disassembly to realign the gears. Also, halfshaft removal and installation procedures are the same for automatic and manual transaxles except for the following: due to the automatic transaxle case configuration, the right side halfshaft and linkshaft must be removed first. Tool T81P-4026-A or equivalent is then inserted into transaxle to remove left side inner Constant Velocity (CV) joint assembly from transaxle. If only the left side halfshaft is being removed from the vehicle, remove right side halfshaft assembly from the transaxle case and secure it in a horizontal position to the underside of vehicle, then remove left side halfshaft assembly.

Whenever removed, the hub nut, lower control arm-to-steering knuckle attaching nut and bolt and inboard CV joint stub shaft circlip must be replaced as their torque holding ability is destroyed during removal.

1. Loosen hub nut and lug nuts, then raise and support front of vehicle.
2. Remove wheel and tire assemblies, then remove hub nut and washer and discard nut.
3. Remove and discard lower ball joint-to-steering knuckle attaching nut and pinch bolt, then using suitable pry bar, separate ball joint from steering knuckle. **When separating ball joint from steering knuckle, use caution to avoid cutting or damaging ball joint boot.**

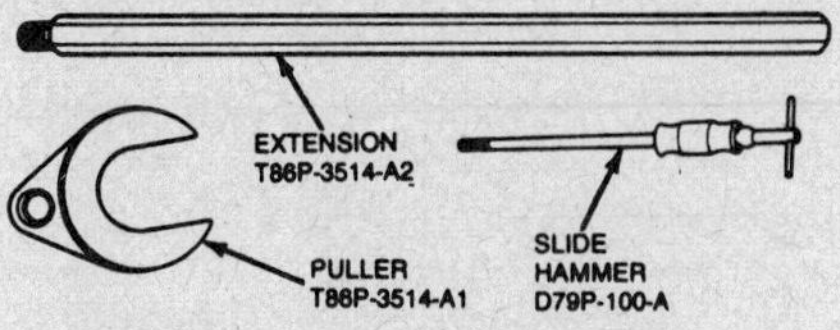

Fig. 2 Inboard CV joint removal tools. Exc. models equipped w/AOD

4. Remove stabilizer bar link at stabilizer bar.
5. To remove right side halfshaft and linkshaft from all except models equipped with Automatic Overdrive Transaxle (AOD), proceed as follows:
   a. Remove bearing support-to-bracket attaching bolts, then slide link shaft out of transaxle. Support end of shaft in horizontal position with suitable wire. **Do not allow shaft to hang unsupported as damage to the outboard CV joint can result.**
   b. Separate hub assembly from outer CV joint using hub remover T81P-1104-C, adapters T83P-1104-BH, T86P-1104-A1 and T81P-1104-A or equivalent, **Fig. 1. Never use a hammer to separate hub assembly from outer CV joint as damage to the CV joint threads and internal components may result.**
   c. Remove right side halfshaft and linkshaft from vehicle as an assembly.
6. To remove both halfshafts on models equipped with Automatic Overdrive Transaxle (AOD) or left side halfshaft on models equipped with manual transaxle, proceed as follows:
   a. Turn steering hub to one side or wire and/or wire strut assembly aside.
   b. Using puller tools shown in **Fig. 2,** attached to the inboard side of the inboard CV joint, remove CV joint from transaxle.
   c. Support end of shaft in horizontal position with suitable wire. **Do not allow shaft to hang unsupported as damage to the outboard CV joint can result.**
   d. Separate hub assembly from outer CV joint using hub remover T81P-1104-C, adapters T83P-1104-BH, T86P-1104-A1 and T81P-1104-A or equivalent, **Fig. 1. Never use a hammer to separate hub assembly from outer CV joint as damage to the CV joint threads and internal components may result.**
   e. Remove halfshaft from vehicle.

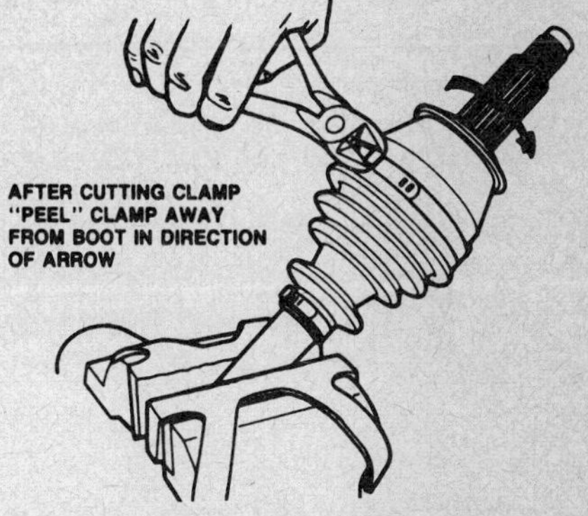

Fig. 3 Boot clamp removal

7. To remove left side halfshaft from models equipped with automatic transaxle (exc. AOD), proceed as follows. **If removing both right and left side halfshafts, plugs T81P-1177-B or equivalent must be installed. Failure to do so may result in dislocation of differential side gears, necessitating transaxle disassembly to realign the gears.**
   a. Remove right side halfshaft assembly from the transaxle case and secure it in a horizontal position to the underside of vehicle, then remove left side halfshaft by inserting driver T81P-4026-A or equivalent into right side halfshaft opening and driving left side halfshaft and CV joint from transaxle.
   b. Support end of shaft in horizontal position with suitable wire. **Do not allow shaft to hang unsupported as damage to the outboard CV joint can result.**
   c. Separate hub assembly from outer CV joint using hub remover T81P-1104-C, adapters T83P-1104-BH, T86P-1104-A1 and T81P-1104-A or equivalent, **Fig. 1. Never use a hammer to separate hub assembly from outer CV joint as damage to the CV joint threads and internal components may result.**
   d. Remove halfshaft from vehicle.
8. On all models, prior to installation install new circlip on inboard CV joint stub shaft and/or linkshaft. **The original circlip cannot be reused.**
9. Align CV joint splines with transaxle differential splines, then push CV joint into differential splines until circlip is felt to seat inside side gears. **Some force may be necessary to insert CV joints. Ensure differential oil seal is not damaged during installation. If difficulty is encountered**

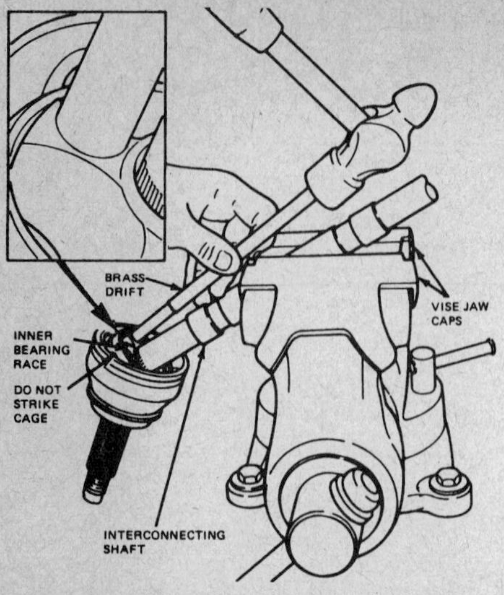

Fig. 4 Removing internal snap ring

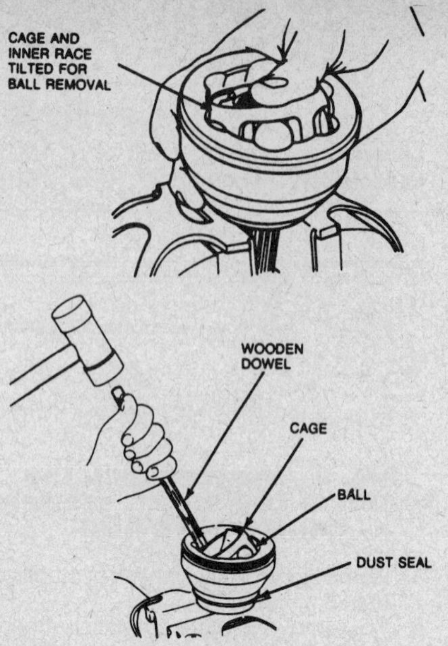

Fig. 5 CV joint ball removal

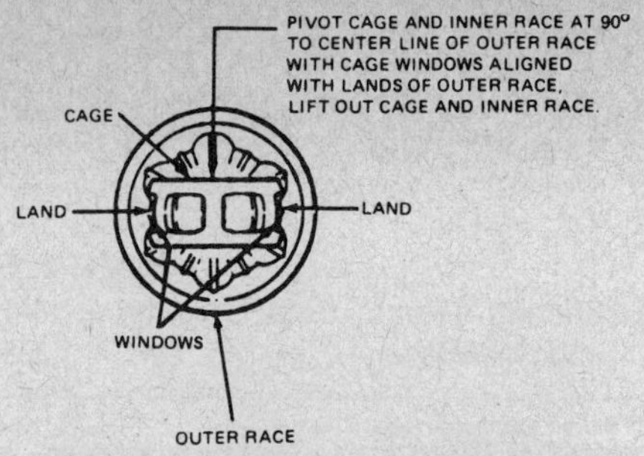

Fig. 6 Cage & inner race removal

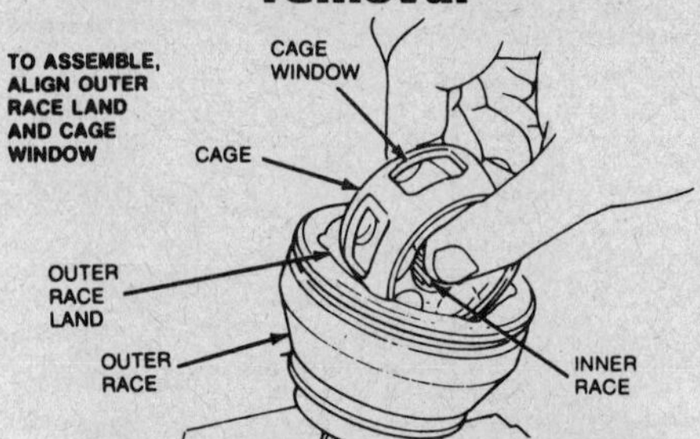

Fig. 9 Inner race & cage assembly to outer race installation

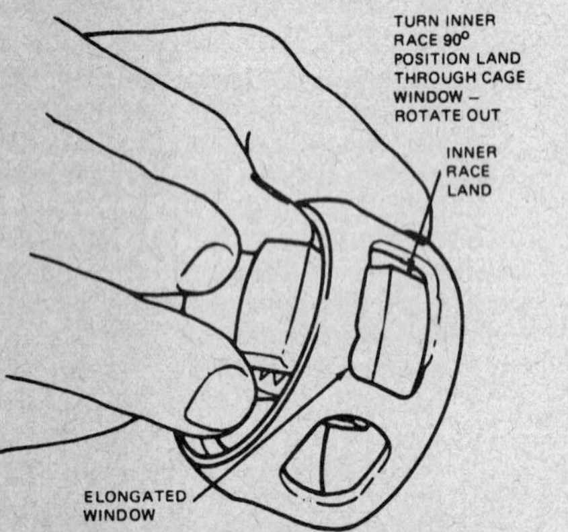

Fig. 7 Inner race removal & installation

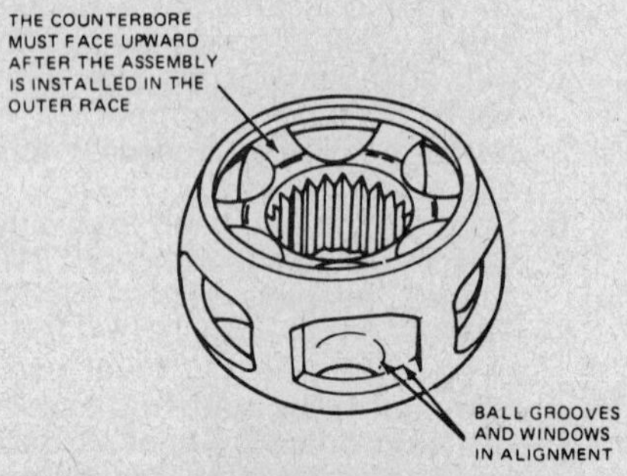

Fig. 8 Inner race & cage assembly

installing CV joints, a non-metallic mallet may be used on the outside joint CV joint stub shaft.

10. Align CV joint splines with hub splines, then install stub shaft in hub as far as possible.
11. Temporarily fasten rotor to hub with two lug nuts and suitable washers. Install steel rod between lug nuts and use to prevent rotor from turning.
12. Install hub washer and new hub nut, then manually thread nut onto CV joint stub shaft as far as possible.
13. Connect steering knuckle to lower ball joint stud, then install new nut and bolt and torque 37-44 ft. lbs.
14. Connect stabilizer bar to stabilizer bar link.
15. Install wheel and tire assembly, then lower vehicle to ground. Torque hub nut to 180-200 ft. lbs.
16. Top off transaxle with lubricants listed below:
    a. On Automatic Overdrive Transaxle (AOD), use Motorcraft Type H XT-4-H.
    b. On automatic (exc. AOD) and manual transaxle, use Dexron II.

CONSTANT VELOCITY JOINT SERVICE

OUTBOARD CV JOINT & BOOT

Disassembly

During manufacture, CV joints components are matched and cannot be interchanged with components of other CV joint. If a CV joint component is defective, the entire CV joint should be replaced.

1. Install soft vise jaw caps in vise to prevent damage to halfshaft, then position halfshaft in vise. Do not allow the vise to contact the CV joint boot or clamps.
2. Using suitable side cutting pliers, cut large boot clamp and peel away from boot. Roll boot back over halfshaft, **Fig. 3.**
3. Turn halfshaft over in vise, then angle CV joint so that inner bearing race is exposed, **Fig. 4.** Using suitable brass drift and hammer, give a sharp rap to inner bearing race to dislodge internal snap ring. Separate CV joint from halfshaft. Take care not to drop the CV joint. Remove CV boot from shaft.
4. Inspect CV joint grease for contamination. If grease is contaminated, proceed with disassembly. If grease is not contaminated and joint was operating satisfactorily, add grease and replace boot.
5. Remove and discard circlip from end of shaft. Inspect stop ring located below circlip, if it is worn or damaged, replace it.
6. Clamp CV joint stub axle in vise with soft vise jaw caps. Be careful not to damage dust seal.
7. Push down on CV joint inner race until it tilts enough to allow ball removal, **Fig. 5. If inner race is tight, it can be tilted by tapping inner race with wooden dowel and hammer. Do not hit cage.**
8. Remove balls from cage. If balls are tight, use blunt screwdriver to pry balls from cage.
9. Pivot cage and inner race assembly until its straight up, **Fig. 6.** Align cage windows with outer race lands while pivoting bearing cage, then lift out cage and inner race.
10. Rotate inner race up and out of cage, **Fig. 7.**

Inspection

During manufacture, CV joints components are matched and cannot be interchanged with components of other CV joint. If a CV joint component is defective, the entire CV joint should be replaced.

Inspect all parts. If any parts are cracked, broken, severely pitted, worn or otherwise unserviceable, replace CV joint. If any parts appear polished, do not replace CV joint as this is a normal condition.

Assembly

1. Apply light coating of Ford constant velocity joint grease No. E2FZ-19590-A or equivalent on inner and outer

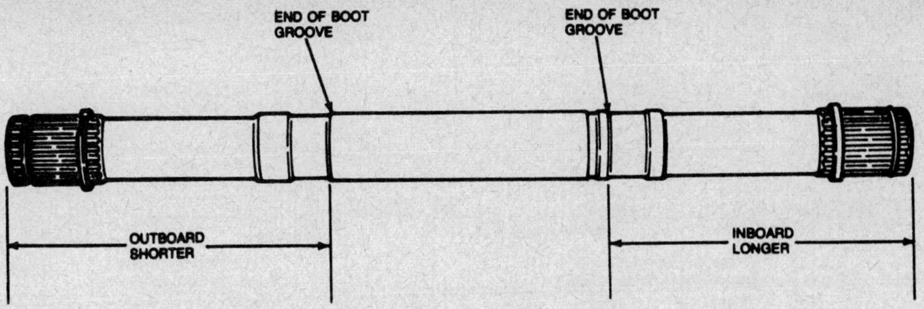

Fig. 10 Halfshaft end identification

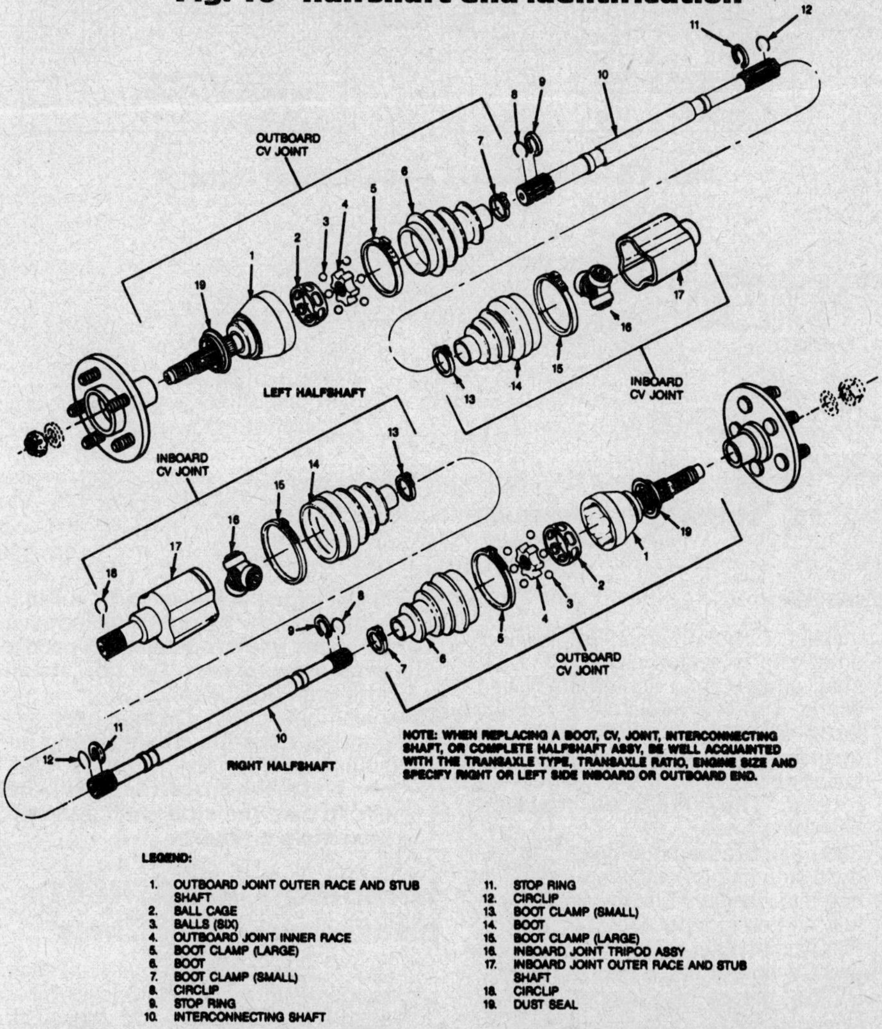

Fig. 11 Exploded view of halfshaft assemblies

races, then install inner race in bearing cage, **Fig. 7.**

2. Install inner race and cage assembly in outer race land, **Fig. 8.**
3. Install CV joint assembly into outer race and pivot 90 degrees into position, **Fig. 9.**
4. Align bearing cage and inner race with outer race, then tilt inner race and install a ball, followed by remaining five balls.
5. Determine which end of halfshaft is for outboard CV joint. The outboard joint side has a shorter end of boot groove to end of shaft dimension, **Fig. 10.**
6. Install CV joint boot and small boot clamp. If stop ring was removed, install at this time. If stop ring was not removed, ensure it is seated properly in groove.
7. Install new circlip, **Fig. 11. Do not over expand or twist the circlip during installation. To install properly, start one end in the groove and work the circlip over the stub shaft and into the circlip groove.**
8. Pack CV joint with Ford CV joint grease No. E2FZ-19590-A or equivalent. Correct quantity is 3.17 ounces. Any remaining grease is to be spread evenly inside CV boot.
9. With boot peeled back, position CV joint on halfshaft and tap into position with suitable plastic hammer. The CV joint is properly seated when the circlip locks into position. Check for proper retention by attempting to pull off CV joint.
10. Remove all excess grease from CV external surfaces, then position boot over CV joint. Ensure boot is seated in its groove and install clamp.

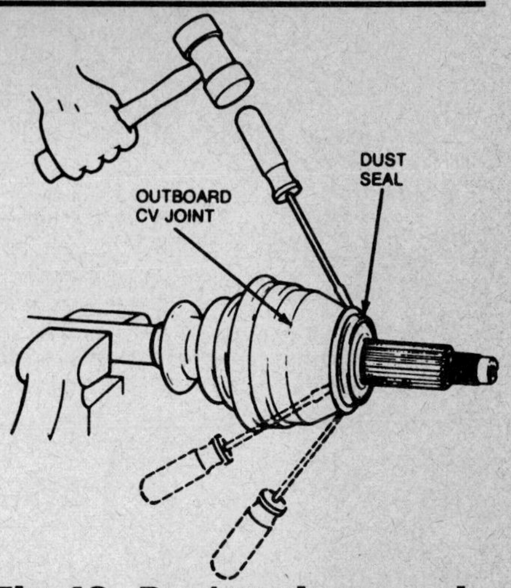

Fig. 12 Dust seal removal

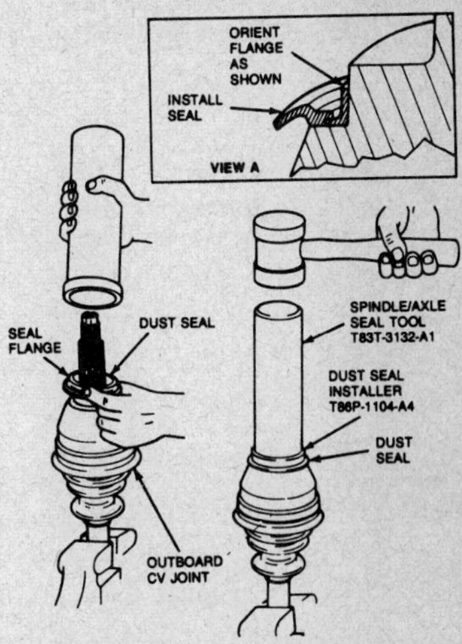

Fig. 13 Dust seal installation

OUTBOARD CV JOINT DUST SEAL

Disassembly

1. With halfshaft removed, use a light duty hammer and screwdriver to tap evenly around seal until unseated and remove seal, **Fig. 12.**

Assembly

Using spindle/axle seal tool T83T-3132-A1 and dust seal installer tool T83P-3425-AH or equivalent, install dust seal, **Fig. 13.** The dust seal flange must face outboard.

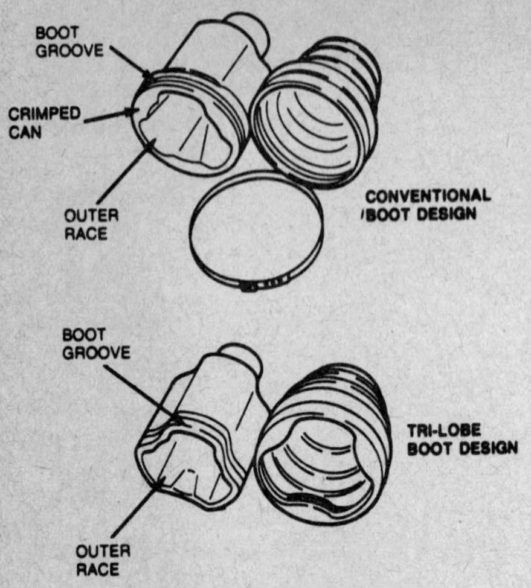

Fig. 14 CV joint identification

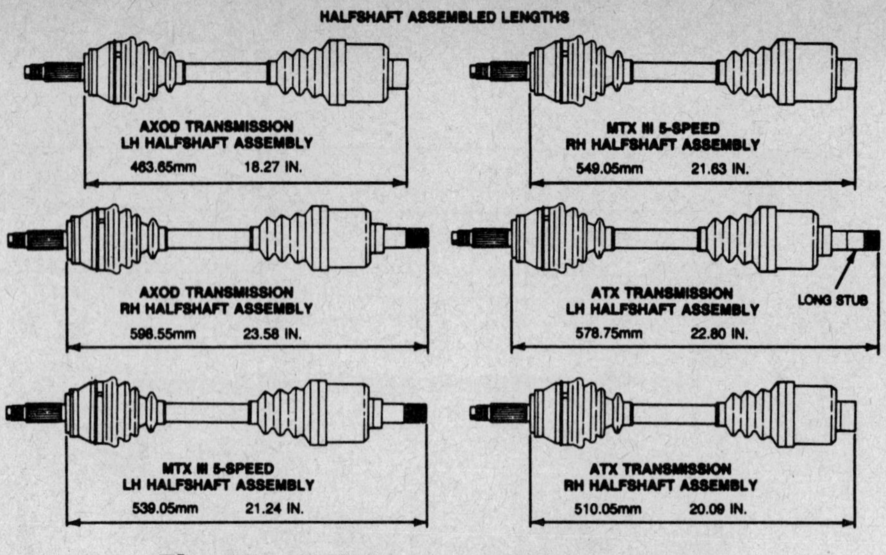

Fig. 15 Halfshaft assembled length

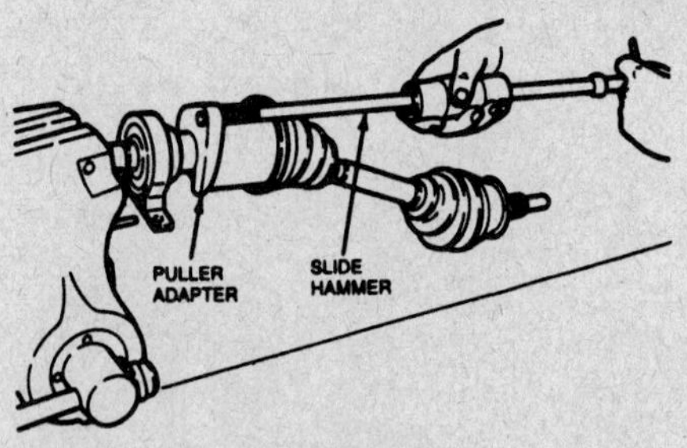

Fig. 16 Linkshaft removal

INBOARD CV JOINT

Disassembly

These models use two different types of inboard CV joints and boots, **Fig. 14.** The first one is of a conventional boot design that uses a crimped can on the large end. The other is a tri-lobe design CV joint that does not require a crimped can on the large end. Although both designs are similar, there is no interchangeability between them.

1. Cut and remove both large and small boot clamps from CV joint, then slide boot back on shaft. **All right side inboard CV joints use a reusable low profile large boot clamp. Do not cut this clamp as it will be re-used.**
2. Slide outer race off tripod assembly. Inspect CV joint grease for contamination by rubbing a small amount between two fingers. Any gritty feeling indicates contamination. If grease is contaminated, proceed with disassembly. If grease is not contaminated and joint was operating satisfactorily, add grease and replace boot.
3. Using suitable snap ring pliers, slide stop ring back on shaft.
4. Slide tripod assembly back on shaft to provide clearance to circlip, then remove circlip, tripod assembly and boot.

Assembly

1. Install CV boot on shaft. Ensure boot small end is seated properly in halfshaft groove, then tighten small end clamp.
2. Install tripod assembly on shaft with chamfered side toward stop ring, then install new circlip. **Circlips cannot be reused. They must be replaced with new ones.**
3. Slide tripod assembly forward to expose stop ring groove, then slide stop ring into position. Ensure stop ring is fully seated in groove.
4. Fill CV joint outer race with 3.5 ounces and CV boot with 2.5 ounces of Ford CV joint grease-high temperature No. E43Z-19590-A or equivalent.
5. Install outer race over tripod assembly, then position boot over outer race. Ensure boot is properly seated in its groove.
6. Remove excess grease from boot exterior. Move CV joint in or out as necessary to adjust halfshaft to length as shown in **Fig. 15.** After halfshaft length has been determined, expel any built up air pressure from boot by inserting a dull screwdriver between boot and outer bearing and allowing air to escape.
7. Install large boot clamp with suitable crimping pliers. **All right side inboard CV joints use a reusable low profile large boot clamp. Do not install with crimping pliers.**
8. Install new circlip. **Do not over expand or twist the circlip during installation. To install properly, start one end in the groove and work the circlip over the stub shaft and into the circlip groove.**

LINKSHAFT/HALFSHAFT

Disassembly & Assembly

1. Clamp linkshaft in vise with halfshaft supported on workbench. Using puller adapter T86P-3514-A or equivalent and slide hammer D79P-100-A or equivalent, separate linkshaft from halfshaft, **Fig. 16.**
2. Pry seal from linkshaft with screwdriver.
3. Position linkshaft in suitable arbor press, then press off bearing.
4. Press on new bearing and bearing seal with arbor press.
5. Coat shaft splines with Ford CV joint grease No. E2FZ-19590-A or equivalent, then assemble linkshaft to halfshaft.

UNIVERSAL JOINTS

INDEX

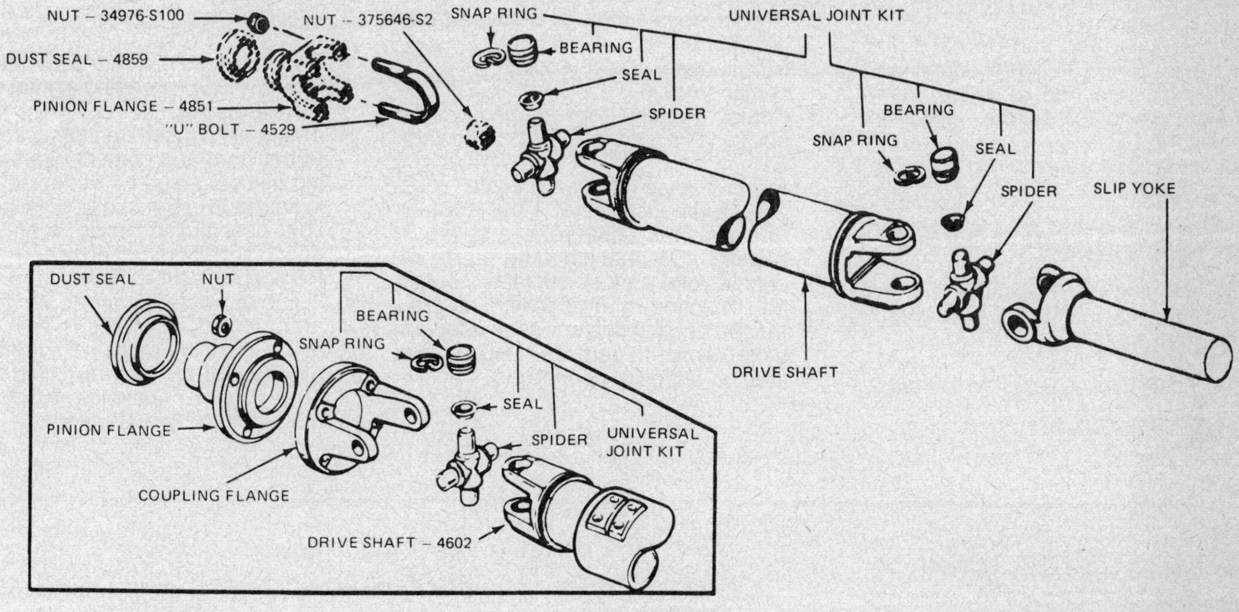

Fig. 1 Single Cardan type universal joint & propeller shaft (Typical)

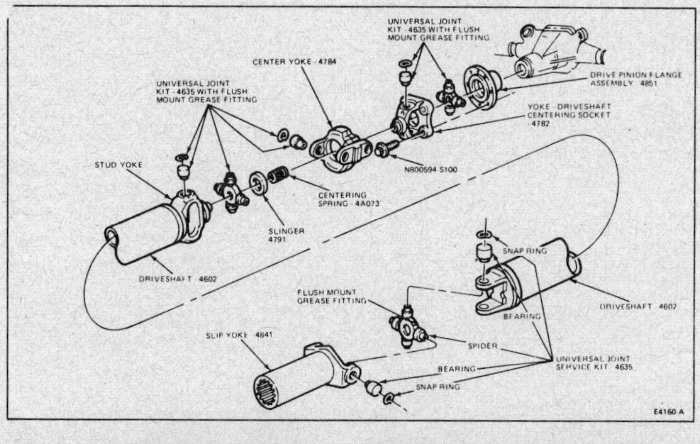

Fig. 2 Drive shaft & double Cardan type universal joint exploded view

SERVICE PRECAUTIONS

Before disassembling any universal joint, examine the assembly carefully and note the position of the grease fitting (if used). Also, be sure to mark the yokes with relation to the propeller shaft so they may be reassembled in the same relative position. Failure to observe these precautions may produce rough vehicle operation which results in rapid wear and failure of parts, and place an unbalanced load on transmission, engine and rear axle.

When universal joints are disassembled for lubrication or inspection, and the old parts are to be reinstalled, special care must be exercised to avoid damage to universal joint spider or cross and bearing cups.

SINGLE CARDAN TYPE

DISASSEMBLY

1. Place driveshaft on suitable workbench, being careful not to damage tube.
2. Remove snap rings retaining bearing cups, **Fig. 1.**
3. Position tool T74P-4635-C or equivalent on slip yoke and press out bearing. If bearing cup cannot be pressed all the way out of the slip yoke, remove it with vise grip or channel lock pliers.
4. Position tool 180° to press on spider and remove remaining bearing cup from opposite side.
5. Remove slip yoke from spider.
6. Remove remaining bearing cups and spiders from driveshaft as previously described.
7. Clean all foreign matter from yoke area at each end of driveshaft.

ASSEMBLY

1. Start a new bearing cup into yoke at rear of driveshaft.
2. Position new spider in rear yoke and press bearing cup 1/4 inch below yoke surface using spacer CJ-912 or equivalent.
3. Remove spacer CJ-912 and install a new snap ring.
4. Start a new bearing cup into opposite side of yoke.
5. Position tool T74P-4635-C or equivalent and press on bearing cup until opposite bearing cup contacts snap ring.

6. Remove tool and install a new snap ring. It may be necessary to grind surface of snap ring to facilitate installation.
7. Position driveshaft and install remaining new bearing cups and spider as previously described.
8. Check joints for freedom of movement. If binding has resulted from misalignment during assembly, a sharp rap on the yokes with a brass hammer will seat bearing needles. Take care to support shaft end and do not strike bearings during this procedure. Ensure joints are free to rotate easily without binding before installing driveshaft.
9. Lubricate joint assemblies with suitable lubricant.

DOUBLE CARDAN TYPE

When rear U-joint disassembly is required, new U-joints should be installed.

DISASSEMBLY

1. Mark position of all yokes so that original position can be maintained during assembly.
2. Support driveshaft in suitable vise.
3. Remove two snap rings that secure rear spider bearing to center yoke.
4. Install tool T74P-4635-C onto joint. Tighten tool until bearing cup extends approximately 3/8 inch from yoke.
5. Remove driveshaft from vise and grip bearing cup in vise. Tap on center yoke to free bearing from yoke, **Fig. 2.**
6. Repeat steps 2 through 5 on opposite bearing.
7. Pull flanged center socket yoke off center stud.
8. Remove spider from flanged center socket yoke following steps 2 through 5.
9. Remove snap rings from center yoke and studs. Install tool T74P-4635-C on driveshaft stud yoke and press bearing cup outward until inside of center yoke almost contacts slinger ring attached to stud yoke. Grip protruding bearing cup in vise and tap on yoke center to remove. Repeat this step on opposite bearing.

ASSEMBLY

1. Install front spider in driveshaft stud yoke. Press in bearing cups using tool T74P-4635-C and install snap rings.
2. Install center yoke over spider ends and press in bearing cup assemblies using tool T74P-4635-C. Install snap rings.
3. Install rear spider in flanged center socket yoke and press in bearing cup assemblies using tool T74P-4635-C. Install snap rings.
4. Pack inside of ball with ESW-MIC147-A and place centering spring inside ball stud yoke.
5. Assemble flanged center socket yoke to ball stud and center yoke by guiding ball onto stud while flexing spider in flange. Press in center yoke bearing cup assemblies using tool T74P-4635-C. Install snap rings.
6. Rap center yoke to free joint.
7. Remove grease plug from each spider and lubricate all U-joints with ESW-M1C147-A. Install plugs. **Flush type grease fittings are required to insure proper clearance during normal vehicle operation.**

FORD UNIT REPAIR ELECTRONIC IGNITION SYSTEMS

TABLE OF CONTENTS

1982–86 Dura Spark II Ignition System, Less EEC

INDEX

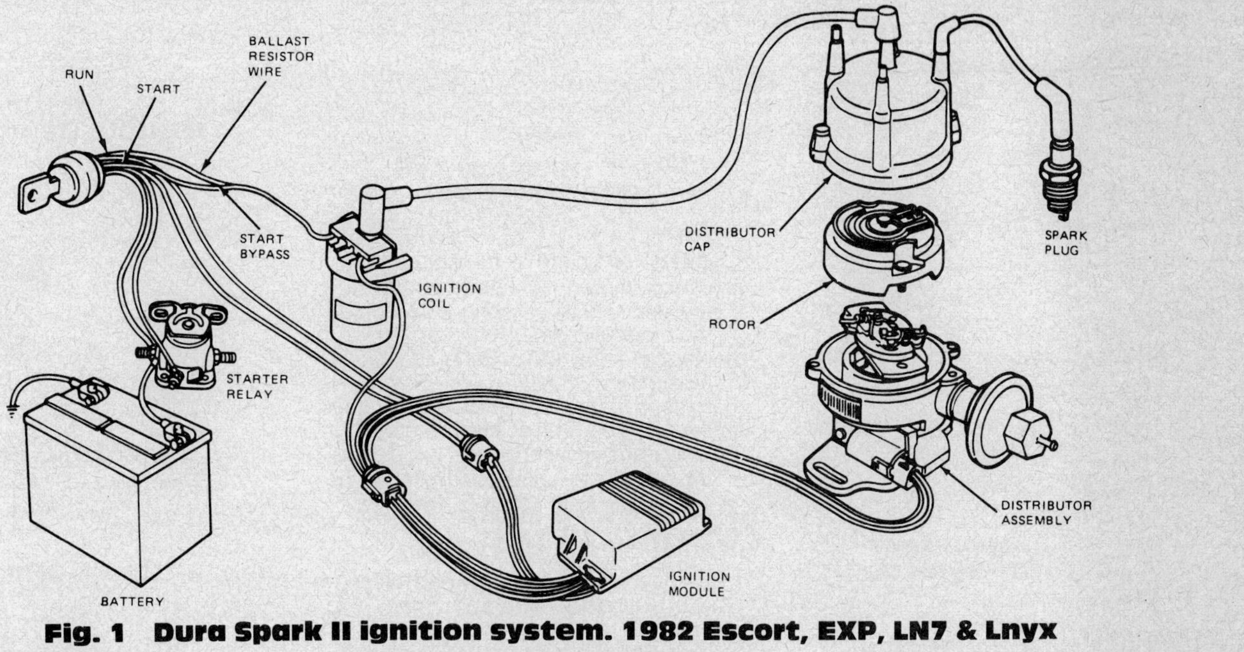

Fig. 1 Dura Spark II ignition system. 1982 Escort, EXP, LN7 & Lnyx

DESCRIPTION

This system, **Figs. 1 and 2,** is controlled by an electronic module. The Dura Spark systems produce higher spark plug voltages, permitting the use of wider spark plug gaps required to ignite the leaner air/fuel mixtures.

The distributor shaft and armature rotation, **Fig. 3,** causes the armature poles to pass by the core of the magnetic pickup assembly. As an armature tooth approaches the pole piece, it reduces the reluctance of the magnetic circuit, thus increasing field strength. The resulting alternating voltage is applied to the ignition module at a rate proportional to engine speed. The ignition module shuts off the primary circuit each time it receives a pulse from the magnetic pickup. The timing circuitry in the module leaves the circuit "Off" just long enough for the coil to discharge into the secondary circuit, then turns the primary circuit "On" again. Maximum time is allowed for the coil to discharge.

Special low resistance ignition coils are used, therefore, conventional ignition coils are not to be used with these systems. The ignition coil can be identified by its blue color and the terminals are marked differently, **Fig. 4.**

The electronic module, **Fig. 5,** is the brain of this system and is well protected from outside elements such as heat and shock. The heat sink containing all the electronic devices is sealed in a mixture of epoxy and sand. This module cannot be disassembled and must be replaced if malfunctioning.

The ignition system is protected against electrical current produced during normal vehicle operation and against reverse polarity or high voltage accidentally applied if vehicle is jump started.

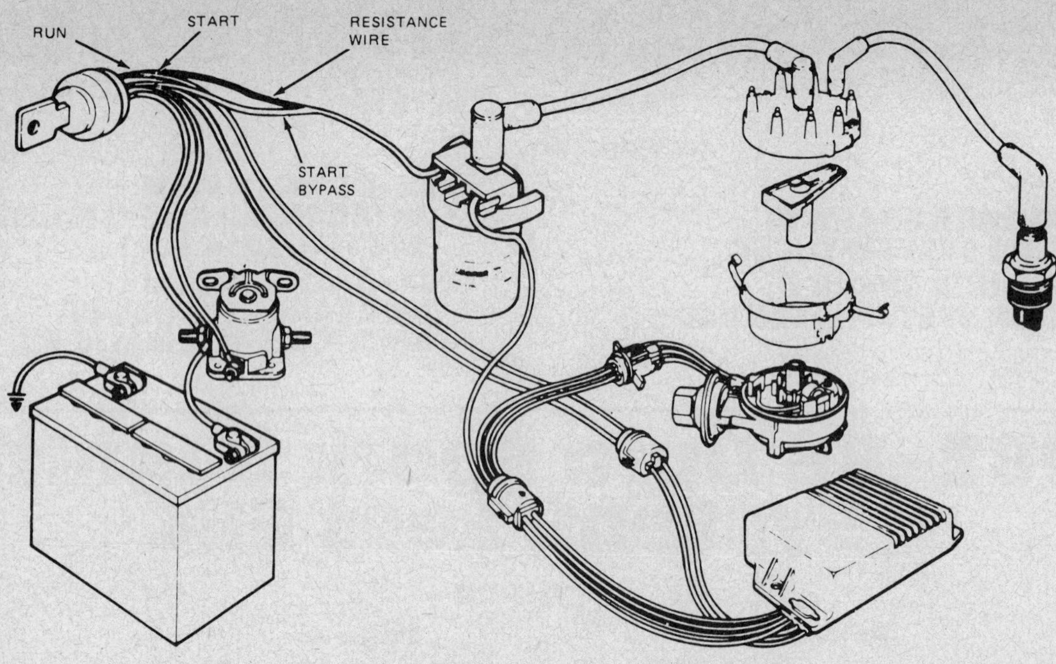

Fig. 2 Dura Spark II ignition system. Exc. 1982 Escort, EXP, LN7 & Lynx

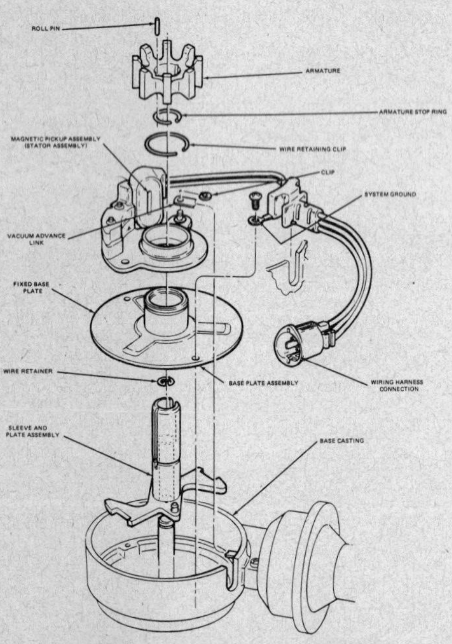

Fig. 3 Breakerless distributor (typical)

SYSTEM DIAGNOSIS

When performing diagnostic or service procedures on models equipped with Dura-Spark II, the ignition switch should remain in the "Off" position unless otherwise stated in the procedure. On these units, a spark will be generated when the ignition switch is placed from the "On" position to "Off," which may inadvertently cause the engine to rotate, resulting in personal injury.

SPARK PLUG FIRING VOLTAGE TEST

1. Connect an oscilloscope with voltage pickup on coil to distributor cable.
2. Check for firing spikes which are appreciably lower or higher (5 KV) than the other cylinders.
3. Normal firing spikes should be approximately 15 KV.
4. Expand pattern to inspect individual firing spikes. If all spikes are above or below specifications, check rotor, distributor cap or coil to distributor cable.

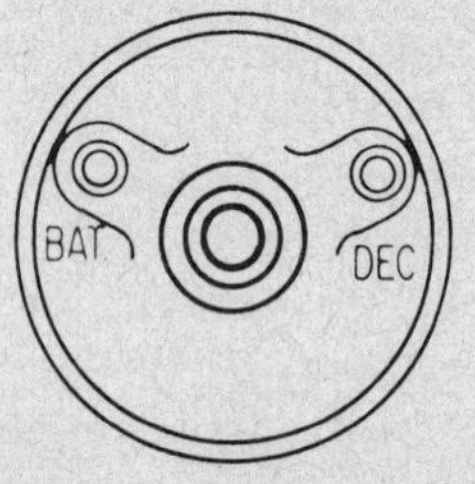

Fig. 4 Ignition coil identification

SPARK PLUG WIRE CONTINUITY TEST

1. Remove distributor cap and disconnect suspected wire from spark plug or coil.
2. Using an ohmmeter, check wire resistance through distributor cap. Resistance should be 5000 ohms per inch on 1982-85, or 7000 ohms per foot on 1986 models. If reading is greater than as specified, replace wire.

SPARK PLUG WIRE INSPECTION

1. Clean off any deposits of dirt from wires, boots, distributor cap and coil using mild soap and water solution.
2. Inspect wires and boots for cuts, punctures or other damage.
3. Inspect wire terminals for corrosion and clean with fine sandpaper.
4. Coat all boots with silicone grease before installing.

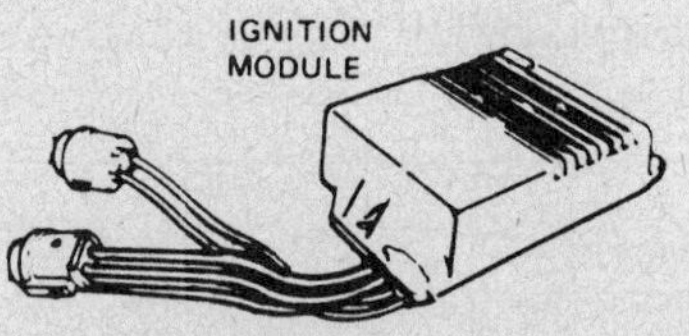

Fig. 5 Electronic control module (typical)

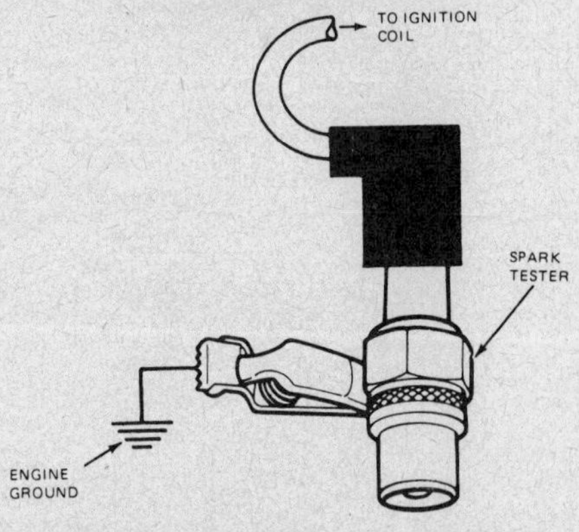

Fig. 6 Spark plug tester

CIRCUIT TESTS

TEST 1, START CIRCUIT

1. Connect a suitable spark tester between coil wire and a suitable ground, **Fig. 6.**
2. While cranking engine, check for sparks.
3. If spark is observed, start circuit is satisfactory. If spark does not occur, measure coil wire resistance. If resis-

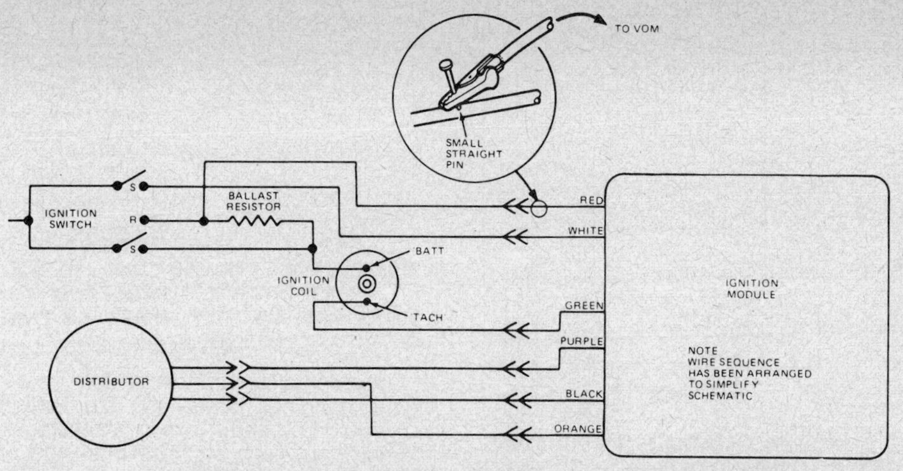

Fig. 7 Dura Spark II ignition system module voltage test connections

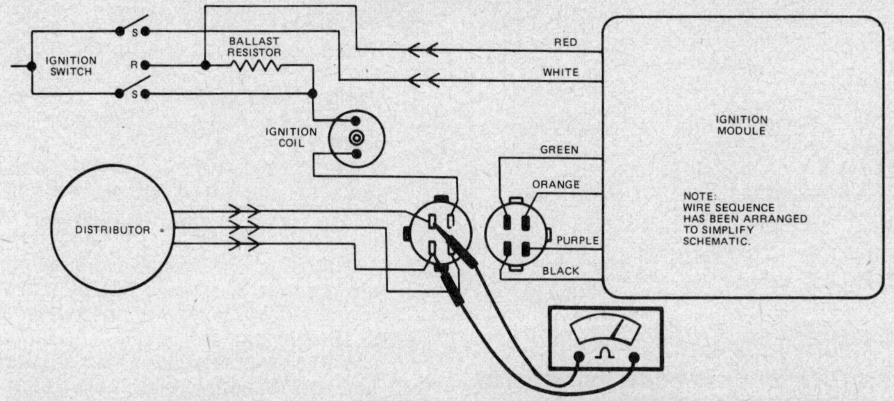

Fig. 8 Dura Spark II ignition system stator assembly & wiring harness test connections

tance exceeds 5000 ohms per inch on 1982-85 models or 7000 ohms on 1986 models. Replace wire.

4. If coil wire is satisfactory, inspect coil for signs of carbon tracking or external damage and inspect distributor shaft with engine cranking to ensure distributor shaft rotation. Proceed to test 5.

TEST 2, RUN CIRCUIT

1. While observing spark tester, cycle ignition switch from "Off" to "Run" position several times (a spark should be generated at the spark tester each time the ignition switch is turned "Off").
2. If spark is observed:
   a. Inspect distributor cap, rotor and adapter for signs of carbon tracking and cracks, replace as necessary.
   b. Ensure armature to sleeve roll pin is correctly installed, repair as necessary.
   c. Ensure orange and purple wires are not crossed between distributor and ignition module.
   d. Check ignition timing, adjust as necessary.
3. If spark does not occur, proceed to test 3.

TEST 3, MODULE VOLTAGE

1. With ignition "Off," install a straight pin into module red wire, **Fig. 7.** Connect a suitable voltmeter positive lead to straight pin and ground negative lead to distributor base. Turn ignition "On" and measure voltage. **Do not allow straight pin to contact engine ground.**
2. If reading obtained is 90% of battery voltage or greater, module voltage is satisfactory. Proceed to test 4.
3. If reading obtained is less than 90% of battery voltage, inspect ignition switch and wiring between ignition switch and module, repair as necessary.

TEST 4, BALLAST RESISTOR

1. Disconnect module connector with red and white wires then, ignition coil connector.
2. Using a suitable ohmmeter, measure resistance between Batt. terminal of ignition coil connector and wiring harness connector wire that joins red wire in module connector.
3. If resistance is 0.8-1.6 ohms, ballast resistor is satisfactory. If resistance is less than 0.8 ohms or greater than 1.6 ohms, replace ballast resistor.

TEST 5, SUPPLY VOLTAGE CIRCUIT

1. Connect coil wire to distributor cap (if still removed), and note the following:
   a. If starter relay is equipped with an I terminal, disconnect starter cable from starter relay.
   b. If starter relay is equipped with a S terminal, disconnect S wire from relay.
2. With ignition "Off," install straight pins into module red and white wires. **Do not allow straight pins to contact engine ground.**
3. Using a suitable voltmeter, connect negative lead to ground at distributor base.
   a. With ignition in "On" position, measure voltage at red wire pin.
   b. Place ignition in "Start" position, measure voltage at white wire pin and at coil Batt. terminal. **When measuring voltages, wiggle wires to simulate any open circuits that might exist.**
4. If readings obtained are 90% of battery voltage or greater, supply circuits are satisfactory. Proceed to test 6.
5. If readings obtained are less than 90% of battery voltage, note the following:
   a. Defective wiring harness or connectors in supply voltage circuits.
   b. Defective ignition switch.
   c. Defective radio interference capacitor on ignition coil.

TEST 6, IGNITION COIL SUPPLY VOLTAGE

1. Connect positive lead of voltmeter to coil Batt. terminal and negative lead to ground at distributor base.
2. Turn ignition switch to "On" position.
3. Observe voltmeter reading. If 6-8 volts, proceed to test 7. If less than 6 volts or more than 8 volts, proceed to test 12.

TEST 7, DISTRIBUTOR STATOR ASSEMBLY & WIRING HARNESS

1. Disconnect module 4 wire connector. Inspect connectors for dirt and corrosion.
2. Using a suitable ohmmeter, measure resistance of stator and wiring harness between wiring harness terminals joining orange and purple wires of module connector, **Fig. 8. When measuring resistance, wiggle wires to simulate any open circuits that might exist.**
3. If resistance is 400-1300 ohms, test results are satisfactory. Proceed to test 8. If resistance is less than 400 ohms or more than 1300 ohms, proceed to test 11.

TEST 8, IGNITION MODULE TO DISTRIBUTOR STATOR ASSEMBLY WIRING HARNESS

1. Disconnect module 4 wire connector. Inspect connectors for dirt and corrosion.
2. Using a suitable ohmmeter, connect one lead to ground at distributor base.

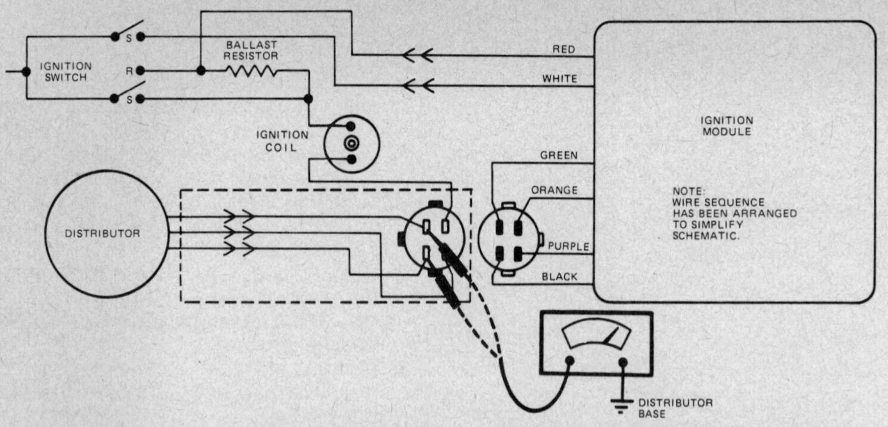

Fig. 9 Dura Spark II ignition system module to stator wiring harness test connections

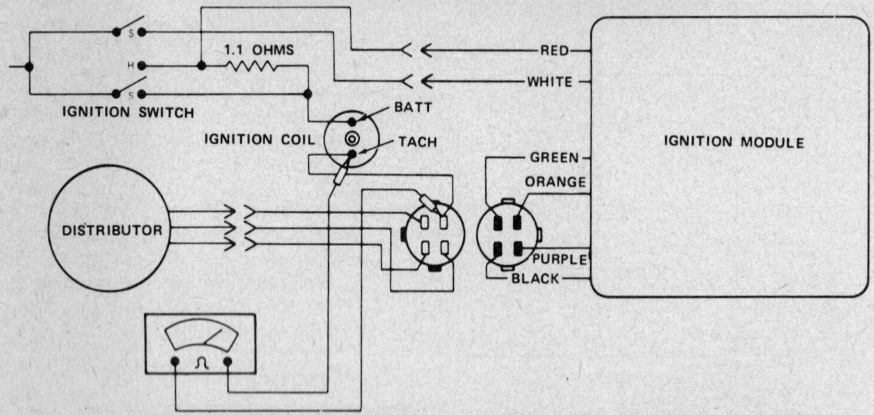

Fig. 10 Dura Spark II ignition system coil tach terminal to module connector circuit test connections

Using other lead, alternately measure resistance of harness wiring which connects to orange and purple wires of module connector and ground, **Fig. 9.**

3. If test results are greater than 70,000 ohms, circuits are satisfactory. If test results are less than 70,000 ohms, inspect and repair as necessary wiring harness between module connector and distributor. Also inspect distributor grommet.

TEST 9, IGNITION COIL SECONDARY RESISTANCE

1. Disconnect and inspect ignition coil electrical connector.
2. Using a suitable ohmmeter, measure resistance between coil Batt. terminal and high tension lead terminal.
3. If resistance is between 7700-10,500 ohms, coil is satisfactory. If not between limits, replace coil.

TEST 10, COIL TACH TERMINAL TO MODULE CONNECTOR CIRCUIT

1. Disconnect module 4 wire connector. Inspect connectors for dirt and corrosion.
2. Using a suitable ohmmeter, measure resistance between coil connector tach wire and the terminal in the wiring harness connector that joins the green wire of the module connector, **Fig. 10.**
3. If resistance is greater than 1 ohm on 1982-85 models, or greater than 100 ohms on 1986 models, replace ignition module. If resistance is one ohm or less on 1982-85 models or 100 ohms or less on 1986 models, inspect wiring harness between ignition coil and module and repair as necessary.

TEST 11, DISTRIBUTOR STATOR ASSEMBLY

Escort, EXP, LN7 & Lynx

1. Disconnect distributor electrical connector. Inspect connectors for dirt and corrosion.
2. Using a suitable ohmmeter, measure resistance across black/orange stripe wire and black/purple stripe wire in distributor connector, **Fig. 11. The distributor stator assembly wire connector wire colors cannot be seen without removal of connector hold-down plate or distributor cap.**
3. If readings obtained are within 650-1300 ohms, circuit is satisfactory. If readings are less than 650 or more than 1300 ohms, replace stator assembly.

Exc. Escort, EXP, LN7 & Lynx

1. Disconnect distributor electrical connector. Inspect connections for dirt or corrosion.
2. Using a suitable ohmmeter, measure resistance across orange and purple

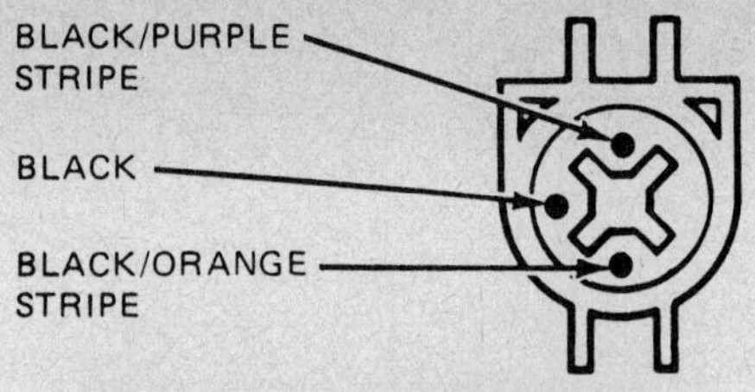

Fig. 11 Distributor electrical connector. 1982 Dura Spark II ignition system. Escort, EXP, LN7 & Lynx

wires in distributor connector.

3. If readings obtained are within 400-1000 ohms, circuit is satisfactory. If readings are less than 400 or more than 1000 ohms, replace stator assembly.

TEST 12, IGNITION COIL PRIMARY RESISTANCE

1. Disconnect ignition coil electrical connector.
2. Using a suitable ohmmeter, measure resistance between coil Batt. terminal and Tach terminal.
3. If reading obtained is 0.8-1.6 ohms, coil is satisfactory. If not, replace coil.

TEST 13, PRIMARY CIRCUIT

1. With ignition "Off," install a straight pin into module green wire, **Fig. 12.** Connect a suitable voltmeter positive lead to straight pin and ground negative lead to distributor base. Turn ignition "On" and measure voltage. **Do not allow straight pin to contact engine ground.**
2. If voltage obtained is more than 1.5 volts, circuit is satisfactory. Proceed to test 14.
3. If voltage obtained is less than 1.5 volts, inspect wiring harness and connectors between ignition coil and module. Repair as necessary.

TEST 14, GROUND CIRCUIT

1. With ignition "Off," install a straight pin into module black wire, **Fig. 13.** Connect a suitable voltmeter positive lead to straight pin and ground negative lead to distributor base. Turn ignition "On" and measure voltage.
2. If voltage obtained is more than 0.5 volts, circuit is satisfactory. Proceed to test 15.
3. If voltage obtained is less than 0.5 volts, replace ignition module.

TEST 15, DISTRIBUTOR GROUND CIRCUIT

Escort, EXP, LN7 & Lynx

1. Disconnect distributor electrical connector. Inspect connections for dirt and corrosion.
2. Using a suitable ohmmeter, measure resistance between distributor base and black wire in distributor connector, **Fig. 11. The distributor stator assembly wire connector wire colors cannot be seen without removal of connector hold-down or distributor cap.**

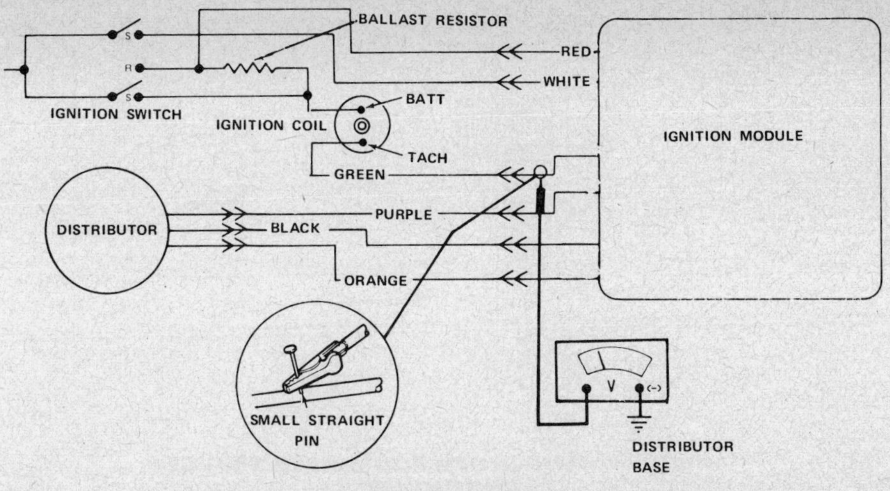

Fig. 12 Dura Spark II ignition system coil primary circuit test connections

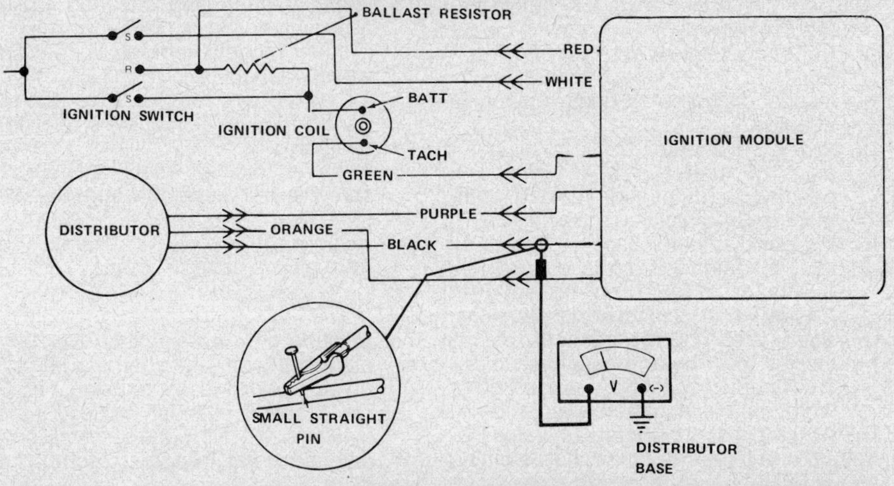

Fig. 13 Dura Spark II ignition system ground circuit test connections

3. If reading obtained is less than 1 ohm, circuit is satisfactory. If reading is more than 1 ohm, inspect and repair distributor ground screw.

Exc. Escort, EXP, LN7 & Lynx

1. Disconnect distributor electrical connector. Inspect connections for dirt or corrosion.
2. Using a suitable ohmmeter, measure resistance between distributor base and black wire in distributor connector. **When measuring resistance, wiggle wires to simulate any open circuits which might exist.**
3. If reading obtained is less than 1 ohm, circuit is satisfactory. If reading is more than 1 ohm, inspect and repair distributor ground screw.

DISTRIBUTOR REPLACE

ESCORT, EXP, LN7 & LYNX

Removal

1. Disconnect primary circuit connector from distributor.
2. Disconnect vacuum hose from distributor vacuum advance.
3. Remove distributor cap, then mark relationship of rotor to distributor housing and relationship of distributor housing to engine for reference during installation.
4. Remove rotor, then remove distributor retaining bolts and the distributor.

Installation

1. Check to ensure that distributor base O-ring is in place.
2. Install distributor into engine checking to ensure that marks made during removal align. Also check that offset tang of drive coupling seats into camshaft groove.
3. Install retaining bolts, rotor, vacuum and electrical connectors and cap.
4. Start engine and adjust ignition timing as specified in the individual car chapters.

EXC. ESCORT, EXP, LN7 & LYNX

Removal

On some 4 and 6 cylinder models, it may be necessary to position thermactor air pump aside to gain access to distributor. It may also be necessary to disconnect the thermactor air filter.

1. Disconnect distributor wiring connector from the engine wiring harness.
2. Disconnect vacuum advance hose, then remove distributor cap and position aside.
3. Remove rotor and adapter if equipped, then reinstall rotor.
4. Mark position of distributor in engine and position of rotor on the distributor housing to aid installation.
5. Remove distributor hold-down and clamp, then lift distributor out of engine. **Do not crank engine after the distributor has been removed.**

Installation

1. If engine was not cranked after distributor was removed from engine, proceed as follows:
   a. Position the distributor in the engine, aligning the housing to block marks and rotor to housing marks made before removal.
   b. Install the distributor hold-down and clamp but do not tighten bolt until timing has been adjusted.
   c. Install distributor cap and wires, then connect distributor wiring connector to engine wiring harness and attach vacuum advance hose.
   d. Adjust ignition timing to specifications.
2. If engine was cranked after distributor was removed from engine, proceed as follows:
   a. Remove No. 1 spark plug and crank engine until compression pressure is felt in No. 1 cylinder. Slowly rotate engine until the correct initial timing mark on the crankshaft damper aligns with the timing pointer.
   b. Position the distributor in the engine with rotor at number one firing position and armature tooth aligned with stator as shown, **Fig. 14. Ensure oil pump intermediate shaft properly engages the distributor shaft. It may be necessary to crank the engine with the starter after the distributor drive gear is partially engaged in order to engage the oil pump intermediate shaft.**
   c. Install distributor hold-down bolt and clamp but do not tighten bolt until timing has been adjusted.
   d. Install distributor cap and wires, then connect distributor wiring connector to engine wiring harness and attach vacuum advance hose.
3. Adjust ignition timing to specifications. **Due to higher ignition system voltage, a timing light specifically designed for this system should be**

used when checking ignition timing. If a timing light designed for this system is not available, an inductive pickup type timing light may operate satisfactorily if a piece of split vacuum hose is first placed around the spark plug wire.

COMPONENT REPLACEMENT

ESCORT, EXP, LN7 & LYNX

Vacuum Advance Unit, Replace

1. Remove distributor cap and position aside with ignition wires attached.
2. Disconnect vacuum advance vacuum hose.
3. Remove diaphragm retaining screws, then partially remove diaphragm assembly until it clears distributor base.
4. Tilt diaphragm assembly to disconnect rod from stator pivot pin, then remove vacuum advance assembly.
5. Check diaphragm O-ring for damage, then align threaded hole in advance assembly housing with screw hole in base.
6. Rotate stator assembly clockwise to position stator pivot pin.
7. Insert vacuum advance assembly through base until rod engages stator pivot pin.
8. Continue seating advance assembly into base until threaded hole in diaphragm casting aligns with hole in base.
9. Install diaphragm retaining screw, connect vacuum hose and install distributor cap.

Stator Assembly, Replace

1. Remove distributor and vacuum advance assembly.
2. Using a small screwdriver or other suitable tool, remove drive coupling spring. Use care not to damage parts.
3. Clean distributor drive end then, using paint, make reference marks on distributor drive coupling and shaft to aid in reassembly.
4. Position distributor in a suitable holding device. Using a suitable drift and hammer, drive pin out of shaft and remove coupling.
5. Inspect end of shaft assembly and in area of drive pin hole for burrs. If necessary, use fine emery paper to polish shaft. Wipe shaft clean prior to removal to prevent damage to seal and bushing in distributor base.
6. Remove shaft assembly by gently pulling out of distributor base.
7. Inspect distributor shaft and centrifugal advance assembly. Centrifugal advance assembly should advance freely and return to original position. If binding occurs, the entire distributor should be replaced.
8. Remove screws securing stator connector to distributor housing then screws securing the stator retainer in distributor housing.

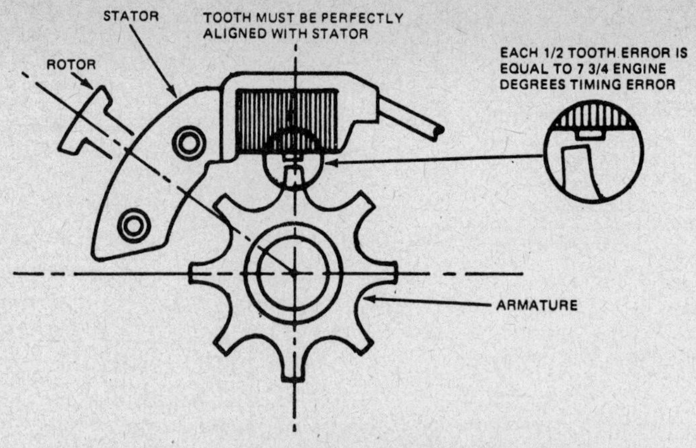

Fig. 14 Armature tooth and stator alignment

9. Gently lift stator assembly out of distributor housing.
10. Pull stator retainer assembly from stator.
11. Inspect distributor O-rings, replace as necessary.
12. Inspect distributor base bushing for signs of wear and heat damage. If bushing is damaged, replace complete distributor.
13. Inspect distributor shaft oil seal. If oil seal is damaged, replace complete distributor. **If seal spring retainer (inside seal) is missing or damaged, it can be replaced.**
14. Inspect distributor base casting for cracks and wear. If base is cracked or worn, replace complete distributor.
15. Assemble stator retainer to stator. Position retainer so horseshoe opening of retainer is at the vacuum advance diaphragm rod pivot point.
16. Install stator assembly in distributor base with vacuum advance diaphragm pivot point positioned approximately in front of diaphragm mounting hole.
17. Install stator securing screws, ensure stator is free to rotate. If not, disassemble and check parts. Position wire connector and install securing screws.
18. Lightly lubricate distributor shaft and install. **Do not over lubricate.**
19. Reverse steps 1 through 4 to complete assembly.

EXC. ESCORT, EXP, LN7 & LYNX

MAGNETIC PICKUP ASSEMBLY, REPLACE

Removal

1. Remove distributor cap and rotor, then disconnect distributor wiring harness plug, **Fig. 3.**
2. Using two screwdrivers, pry armature from advance plate sleeve and remove roll pin.
3. Remove snap ring securing pickup assembly to base plate. On 4 and 6 cylinder models, remove washer and wave washer.
4. On all models, remove snap ring securing vacuum advance link to pickup assembly.
5. Remove pickup assembly ground screw and lift assembly from distributor.
6. Disconnect vacuum advance link from pickup assembly post.

Installation

1. Position pickup assembly over base plate and slide wiring harness into slot on side of distributor housing, **Fig. 3.**
2. On 4 and 6 cylinder models, install washers. On all models, install snap ring securing pickup assembly to base plate.
3. Position vacuum advance link on pickup assembly post and install snap ring.
4. Insert ground screw through wiring harness tab and install on base plate.
5. Install armature on advance plate sleeve, ensuring roll pin is engaged in slot.
6. Install distributor rotor and cap, then connect distributor wiring harness plug to vehicle wiring harness.

VACUUM ADVANCE UNIT, REPLACE

1. Remove distributor cap and rotor.
2. Disconnect vacuum lines, then remove snap ring that secures vacuum advance link to pickup assembly.
3. Remove vacuum advance attaching screws, then tilt unit downward to disconnect link.
4. Carefully remove unit from distributor.
5. Reverse procedure to install.

FIXED BASE PLATE, REPLACE

1. Remove distributor cap and rotor.
2. Remove vacuum advance unit and magnetic pickup assembly.
3. Remove attaching screws and lift base plate from distributor.
4. Reverse procedure to install.

1982–86 Thick Film Integrated I (TFI-I) Ignition System, Less E.F.I.

INDEX

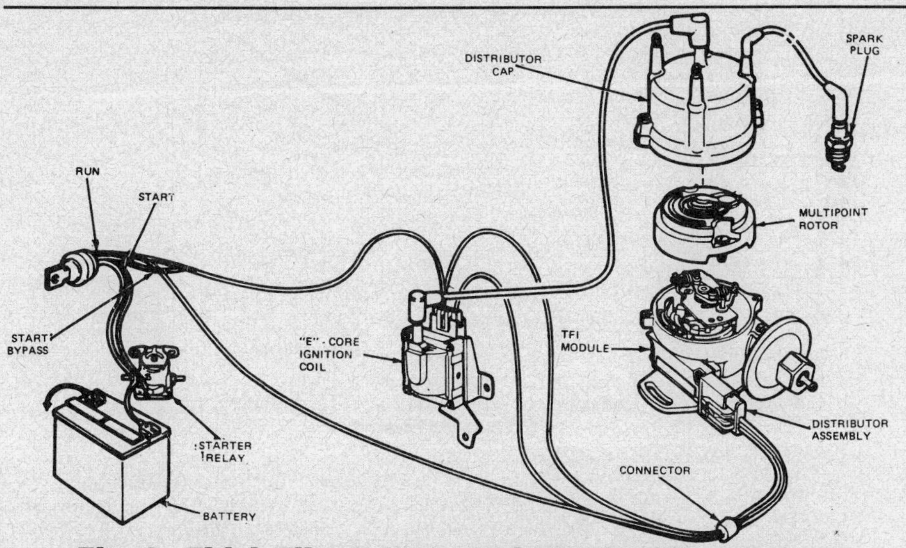

Fig. 1 Thick Film Integrated (TFI) ignition system. 1982–86 Escort, EXP, LN7 & Lynx

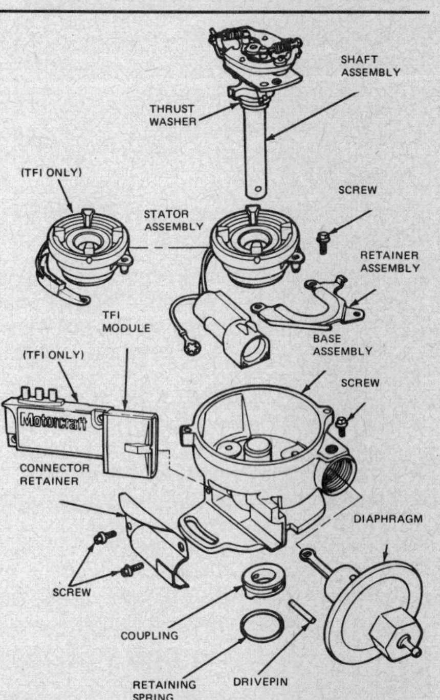

Fig. 2 Exploded view of TFI ignition system distributor. 1982–86 Escort, EXP, LN7 & Lynx

DESCRIPTION

On this system the ignition module is mounted on a mounting pad located on the distributor bowl, **Figs. 1 and 2.** The ignition coil is potted in plastic and has external laminations similar to a transformer.

On these units, do not reapply or remove any of the silicone coating from the distributor cap electrodes. Also when installing a replacement single point distributor rotor, apply a coating, approximately 1/32 inch thick, of silicone dielectric compound D7AZ-19A331-A or equivalent to the brass rotor electrode. When installing a replacement multi-point distributor rotor, do not apply any silicone dielectric compound to any part of the rotor.

SYSTEM DIAGNOSIS

Concerns of no start, slow start, misfire, lower power output at part throttle and/or poor fuel economy may be caused by spark tracking and crossfire in the distributor cap and/or a cracked diaphragm in the distributor vacuum advance assembly. When troubleshooting these problems, the "Spark Plug Firing Voltage Test" should be performed. If the display is not satisfactory, the distributor cap, rotor and vacuum advance diaphragm should be replaced. Only a vented cap (part No. E5FZ-12106-C), blade rotor (part No. E5FZ-12200-A) and a vented diaphragm assembly of the same calibration code should be used.

SPARK PLUG FIRING VOLTAGE TEST

1. Connect an oscilloscope with voltage pickup on coil to distributor cable.
2. Check for firing spikes which are appreciably lower or higher (5 KV) than the other cylinders.
3. Normal firing spikes should be approximately 15 KV.
4. Expand pattern to inspect individual firing spikes. If all spikes are above or below specifications, check rotor, distributor cap or coil to distributor cable.

SPARK PLUG WIRE CONTINUITY TEST

1. Remove distributor cap and disconnect suspected wire from spark plug or coil.
2. Using an ohmmeter, check wire resistance through distributor cap. Resistance should be 5000 ohms per inch on 1982-85 models or 7000 ohms per foot on 1986 models. If reading is greater than as specified, replace wire.

SPARK PLUG WIRE INSPECTION

1. Clean off any deposits of dirt from wires, boots, distributor cap and coil using mild soap and water solution.
2. Inspect wires and boots for cuts, punctures or other damage.
3. Inspect wire terminals for corrosion and clean with fine sandpaper.
4. Coat inside of boots with silicone grease before installing.

CIRCUIT TESTS

Test 1, Start Circuit

1. Connect a suitable spark tester between coil wire and a suitable ground, **Fig. 3.**
2. While cranking engine, check for sparks.
3. If spark is observed, start circuit is satisfactory. If spark does not occur, measure coil wire resistance. If resistance exceeds 5000 ohms per inch on 1982-85 models or 7000 ohms per foot on 1986 models, replace wire.
4. If coil wire is satisfactory, inspect coil for signs of carbon tracking or external damage and inspect distributor shaft with engine cranking to ensure

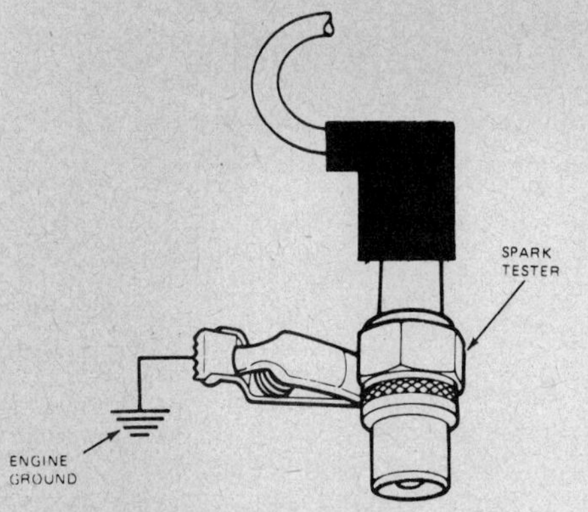

Fig. 3 Spark plug tester

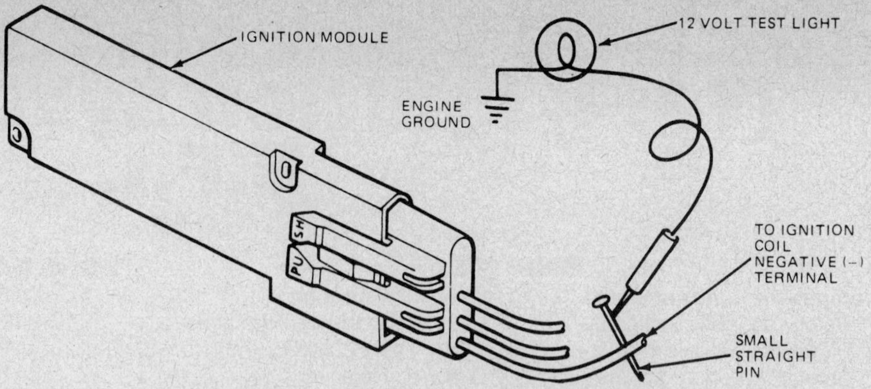

Fig. 4 TFI ignition system ignition coil primary circuit switching test connections

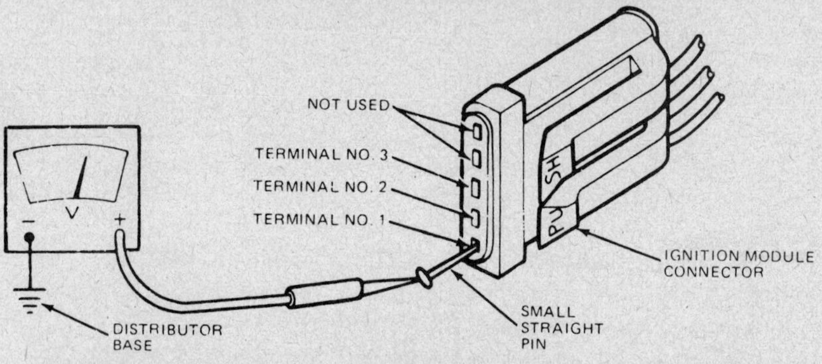

Fig. 5 TFI ignition system wiring harness test connections

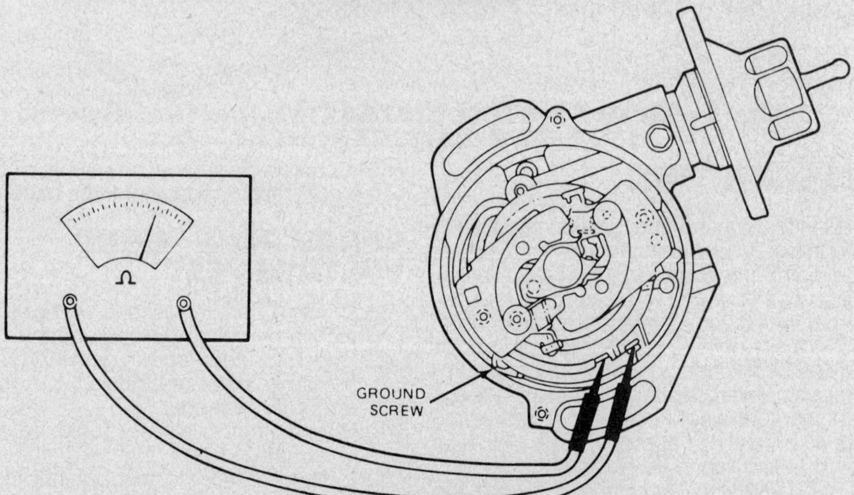

Fig. 6 TFI ignition system stator assembly test connections

distributor shaft rotation. Proceed to test 2.

Test 2, Ignition Coil Primary Circuit Switching

1. With ignition "Off," install a straight pin in ignition coil negative wire 1 inch from connector, **Fig. 4. Do not allow straight pin to contact engine ground.**
2. Connect a suitable 12 volt test light between ground and straight pin. While observing test light, crank engine.
3. If test light flashes, circuit is satisfactory. Proceed to test 3. If test light glows but does not flash, proceed to test 5 on 1982-84 models or test 3 on 1985-86 models. If light does not glow or flash, proceed to test 7.

Test 3, Ignition Coil Primary Resistance

1. With ignition "Off," disconnect ignition coil connector. Inspect connector for dirt and corrosion.
2. Using a suitable ohmmeter, measure resistance between coil positive to negative terminals.
3. If reading is 0.3-1.0 ohm, coil is satisfactory. Proceed to test 4. If reading is less than 0.3 ohm or more than 1.0 ohm, replace coil.

Test 4, Ignition Coil Secondary Resistance

1. Disconnect and inspect ignition coil electrical connector.
2. Using a suitable ohmmeter, measure resistance between coil negative terminal and high tension lead terminal.
3. If resistance is between 8000-11,500 ohms, coil is satisfactory. If not between limits, replace coil.

Test 5, Wiring Harness

1. Disconnect wiring harness connector from distributor ignition module. Inspect connector for dirt and corrosion. **To remove distributor connector, push connector tabs.**
2. Disconnect wire at "S" terminal of starter relay.
3. Connect the negative lead of a suitable voltmeter to distributor base. Connect positive lead to a straight pin to serve as a probe.
4. Turn ignition "On," probe terminals 1 and 2, **Fig. 5,** and record voltages.
5. Turn ignition to "Start" position and probe terminals 2 and 3, **Fig. 5.** Record voltage.
6. If voltages obtained are 90% of battery voltage, circuit is satisfactory. If obtained voltages are less than 90% of battery voltage, a defective wiring harness or ignition switch is indicated.

Test 6, Stator Assembly & Module

1. Remove distributor, then remove ignition module.
2. Inspect stator wiring, wire connections and ground screw.
3. Using a suitable ohmmeter, measure stator resistance, **Fig. 6.**
4. If resistance is 650-1300 ohms, stator is satisfactory. Replace ignition module. If readings are out of specifications, ignition module is satisfactory. Replace stator assembly.

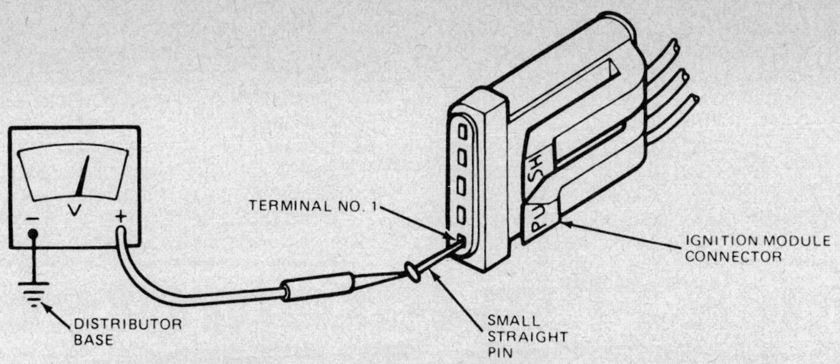

Fig. 7 TFI ignition system primary system test connections

Test 7, Primary Circuit

1. Disconnect wiring harness connector from distributor ignition module. Inspect connector for dirt and corrosion. **To remove distributor connector, push connector tabs.**
2. Connect the negative lead of a suitable voltmeter to distributor base. Connect positive lead to a straight pin to serve as a probe.
3. Turn ignition "On" and note voltage at terminal 1 of connector, **Fig. 7.**
4. If reading is within 90% of battery voltage, circuit is satisfactory. If reading is not within 90% of battery voltage, proceed to test 8.

Test 8, Ignition Coil Primary Voltage

1. Connect the negative lead of a suitable voltmeter to distributor base. Connect positive lead to ignition coil negative terminal.
2. Turn ignition "On" and note voltage.
3. If reading is within 90% of battery voltage, circuit is satisfactory. If reading is not within 90% of battery voltage, a defective wiring harness between ignition module and ignition coil negative terminal is indicated.

Test 9, Ignition Coil Supply Voltage

1. Connect the negative lead of a suitable voltmeter to distributor base. Connect positive lead to ignition coil positive terminal.
2. Turn ignition "On" and note voltage.
3. If reading is within 90% of battery voltage, circuit is satisfactory. If reading is not within 90% of battery voltage, a defective wiring harness or ignition switch is indicated.

DISTRIBUTOR REPLACE

REMOVAL

1. Disconnect primary wire connector from distributor and vacuum hose from vacuum advance unit.
2. Using a screwdriver, remove distributor cap and position aside with wires attached. **Mark position of rotor to distributor housing and position of distributor housing to engine for reference during installation.**
3. Remove rotor attaching screws, then remove rotor.
4. Remove distributor hold-down bolts, then remove distributor. **Some models use special distributor hold-down bolts. To remove these bolts, tool No. T82L-12270-A or equivalent must be used.**

INSTALLATION

1. Check to ensure that distributor base O-ring is in position.
2. Install distributor into engine, checking to ensure that marks made during removal are aligned. Also check to ensure that offset tang of drive coupling is seated in camshaft groove.
3. Install retaining bolts, rotor, vacuum advance hose, primary wire connector and distributor cap.
4. Start engine and adjust ignition timing.

COMPONENT REPLACEMENT

VACUUM ADVANCE UNIT, REPLACE

1. Remove distributor cap and position aside with ignition wires attached.
2. Disconnect vacuum advance vacuum hose.
3. Remove diaphragm retaining screw, then partially remove diaphragm assembly until it clears distributor base, **Fig. 2.**
4. Tilt diaphragm assembly to disconnect rod from stator pivot pin, then remove vacuum advance assembly.
5. Check diaphragm O-ring for damage, then align threaded hole in advance assembly housing with screw hole in base.
6. Rotate stator assembly clockwise to position stator pivot pin.
7. Insert vacuum advance assembly through base until rod engages stator pivot pin.
8. Continue seating advance assembly into base until threaded hole in diaphragm casting aligns with hole in base.
9. Install diaphragm retaining screw, connect vacuum hose and install distributor cap.

TFI IGNITION MODULE, REPLACE

Removal

1. Remove distributor as described under "Distributor, Replace."
2. Remove two screws attaching TFI module to distributor housing, **Fig. 2.**
3. Pull righthand side of module downward toward distributor mounting flange, then up to disengage module terminals from connector in distributor base. Pull toward flange and away from distributor.

Installation

1. Apply a 1/32 inch thick coating of silicone grease D7A2-19A331-A or equivalent to metal base of TFI module.
2. Position TFI module on distributor mounting flange.
3. Carefully position TFI module toward distributor base to securely engage the three distributor connector pins.
4. Install two TFI module attaching screws and torque to 9 to 16 inch lbs. on 1982-84 models, or 16-35 inch lbs. on 1985-86 models.
5. Install distributor as described under "Distributor, Replace."

STATOR ASSEMBLY, REPLACE

1. Remove distributor and vacuum advance assembly, **Fig. 2.**
2. Using a small screwdriver or other suitable tool, remove drive coupling spring. Use care not to damage parts.
3. Clean distributor drive and then, using paint, make reference marks on distributor drive coupling and shaft to aid in reassembly.
4. Position distributor in a suitable holding device. Using a suitable drift and hammer, drive pin out of shaft and remove coupling.
5. Inspect end of shaft assembly and in area of drive pin hole for burrs. If necessary use fine emery paper to polish shaft. Wipe shaft clean prior to removal to prevent damage to seal and bushing in distributor base.
6. Remove shaft assembly by gently pulling out of distributor base.
7. Inspect distributor shaft and centrifugal advance assembly. Centrifugal advance assembly should advance freely and return to original position. If binding occurs, the entire distributor should be replaced.
8. Remove screws securing stator connector to distributor housing then screws securing the stator retainer in distributor housing. Remove connector from top of module.
9. Gently lift stator assembly out of distributor housing.
10. Pull stator retainer assembly from stator.
11. Inspect distributor O-rings, replace as necessary.
12. Inspect distributor base bushing for signs of wear and heat damage. If bushing is damaged, replace complete distributor.

13. Inspect distributor shaft oil seal. If oil seal is damaged, replace complete distributor. **If seal spring retainer (inside seal) is missing or damaged, it can be replaced.**
14. Inspect distributor base casting for cracks and wear. If base is cracked or worn, replace complete distributor.
15. Assemble stator retainer to stator. Position retainer so horseshoe opening of retainer is at the vacuum advance diaphragm rod pivot point.
16. Install stator assembly in distributor base with vacuum advance diaphragm pivot point positioned approximately in front of diaphragm mounting hole.
17. Install stator securing screws, ensure stator is free to rotate. If not, disassemble and check parts. Install wire connector securing screws.
18. Position module connector on top of three pins and press down to seat the connector.
19. Lightly lubricate distributor shaft and install. **Do not over lubricate.**
20. Reverse steps 1 through 4 to complete assembly.

1983–87 Thick Film Integrated IV (TFI-IV) Ignition System, W/E.F.I.

INDEX

DESCRIPTION

On this system, the ignition module is attached to a mounting pad located on the distributor bowl, **Fig. 1.** The ignition coil is potted in plastic and has external laminations similar to a transformer.

On these units, do not reapply or remove any of the silicone coating from the distributor cap electrodes. Also, when installing a replacement single point distributor rotor, apply a coating approximately 1/32 inch thick of silicone dielectric compound D7AZ-19A331-A or equivalent to the brass rotor electrode. When installing a replacement multi-point distributor rotor, do not apply any silicone dielectric compound to any part of the rotor.

SYSTEM DIAGNOSIS

SPARK PLUG FIRING VOLTAGE TEST

1. Connect an oscilloscope with voltage pickup on coil to distributor cable.
2. Check for firing spikes which are appreciably lower or higher (5 KV) than the other cylinders.
3. Normal firing spikes should be approximately 15 KV.
4. Expand pattern to inspect individual firing spikes. If all spikes are above or below specifications, check rotor, distributor cap or coil to distributor cable.

SPARK PLUG WIRE CONTINUITY TEST

1. Remove distributor cap and disconnect suspected wire from spark plug or coil.
2. Measure wire resistance through distributor cap using a suitable ohmmeter. Resistance should measure 5000 ohms per inch on 1983-85 models or 7000 ohms per foot on 1986-87 models. If resistance is greater than 5000 ohms per inch, replace wire.

SPARK PLUG WIRE INSPECTION

1. Clean off any dirt deposits from wires, boots, distributor cap and coil using mild soap and water solution.
2. Inspect wires and boots for cuts, punctures, or other damage.
3. Inspect wire terminals for corrosion, and clean with fine sandpaper.
4. Coat all boots with silicone grease before reinstalling.

CIRCUIT TESTS

The primary winding if the ignition coil may be damaged if there is a short to ground in the wiring harness containing the tachometer circuit. Before replacing the ignition coil due to a no start condition, measure and record battery voltage as well as voltage between coil negative terminal and ground with ignition Key in the ON position. If there is more than a 1 volt difference between the readings, inspect tachometer circuit for a short to ground and repair as necessary. If a short to ground is caused by a failed TFI-IV module, the ignition coil primary winding may be damaged. Because this type of malfunction will not be identified using standard testing procedures, the following steps should be taken when servicing a weak or no spark condition: check for spark as described in "Test 1"; if there is no spark test coil primary resistance as described in "Test 3"; if coil primary resistance is satisfactory, continue with diagnostic procedure described in step "Test 1"; if coil primary resistance is not satisfactory, replace coil and check for weak or no spark; if spark is satisfactory, the problem no longer exists; if spark is still not satisfactory, continue with diagnostic procedure described in "Test 1."

Test 1, Ignition Coil Secondary Voltage

1. Connect a suitable spark plug tester between coil wire and engine ground, Fig. 2.
2. Crank engine and check for sparks.
3. If no sparks occur, proceed to step 4. If sparks are observed, coil secondary voltage is satisfactory. Proceed to step 5.
4. Measure coil wire resistance using a suitable ohmmeter. If resistance exceeds 5000 ohms per foot, replace wire. If resistance is less than 5000 ohms per foot on 1983-85 models, or 7000 ohms on 1986-87 models, inspect coil for damage or signs of carbon tracking, and replace as needed. If coil is satisfactory, check distributor shaft rotation while cranking engine. If shaft rotates properly, proceed to "Test 2."
5. Inspect distributor cap and rotor for damage or signs of carbon tracking, and service as needed. If engine still will not start, proceed to "Test 5."

Test 2, Ignition Coil Primary Circuit Switching

1. Disconnect electrical connector from ignition module by depressing tabs.
2. Clean any corrosion or dirt buildup on connector, then connect to module.
3. Connect a suitable 12 volt test lamp between coil tach terminal and ground, **Fig. 3.** Observe test lamp while cranking engine.
4. If test lamp flashes, proceed to "Test 3." If test lamp lights continuously, proceed to "Test 5" on 1983-84 models, or "Test 3" on 1985-87 models. If test lamp does not light or lights dimly, proceed to "Test 10."

Test 3, Ignition Coil Primary Resistance

1. Turn ignition off, then disconnect ignition coil electrical connector.
2. Inspect connector for dirt and corrosion, and clean as necessary.
3. Measure resistance between ignition coil positive and negative terminals, **Fig. 4.**

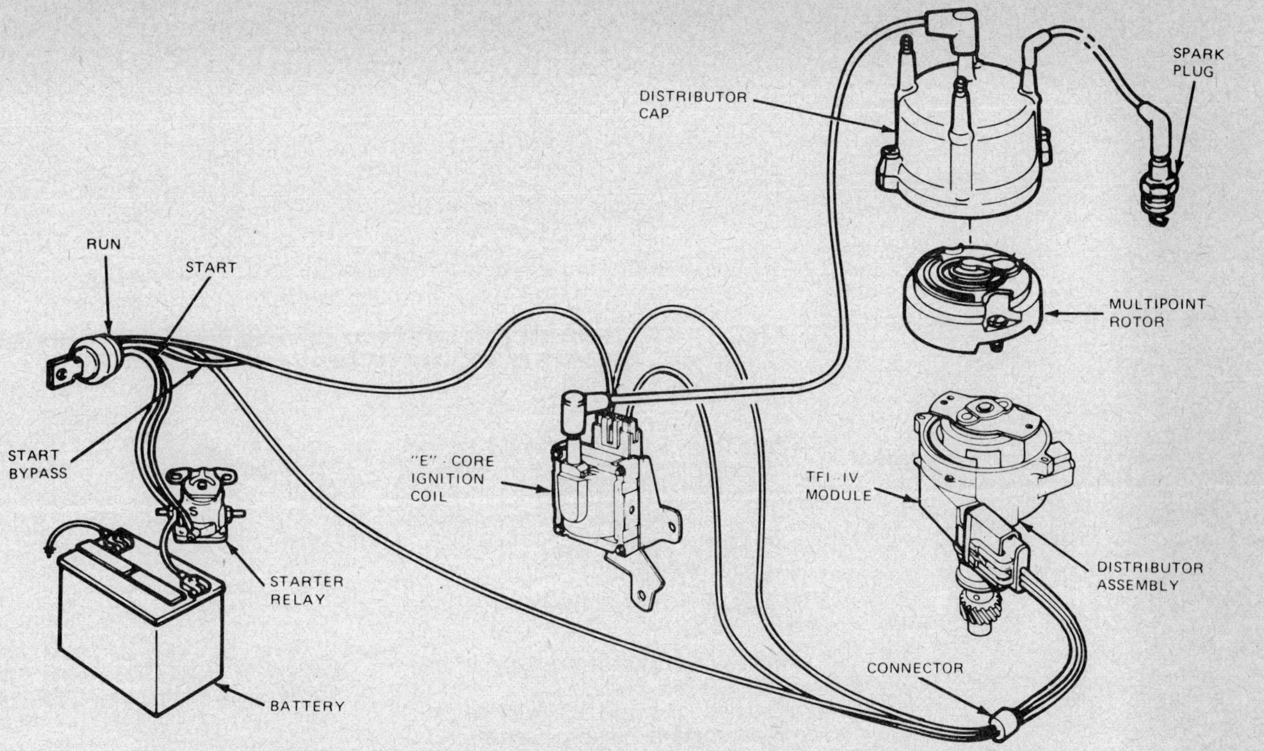

Fig. 1 Thick film integrated (TFI) IV ignition system (Typical)

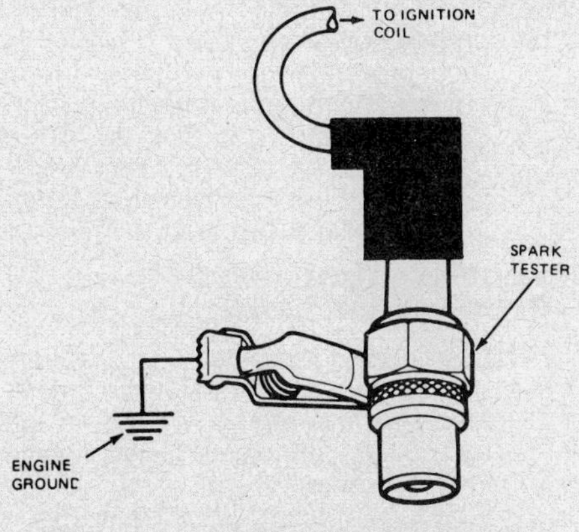

Fig. 2 Spark plug tester

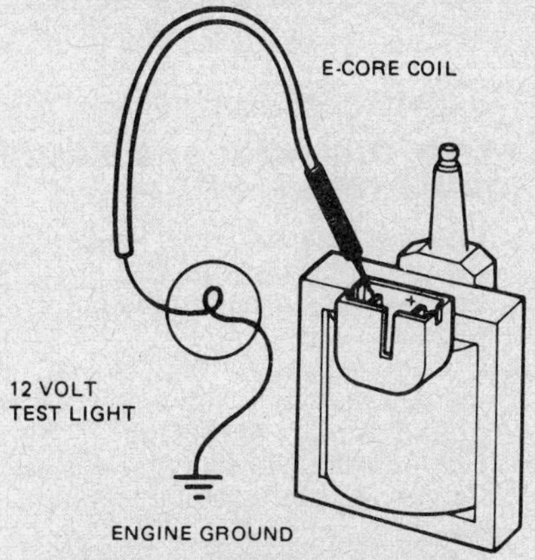

Fig. 3 TFI IV ignition system ignition coil primary circuit switching test connections

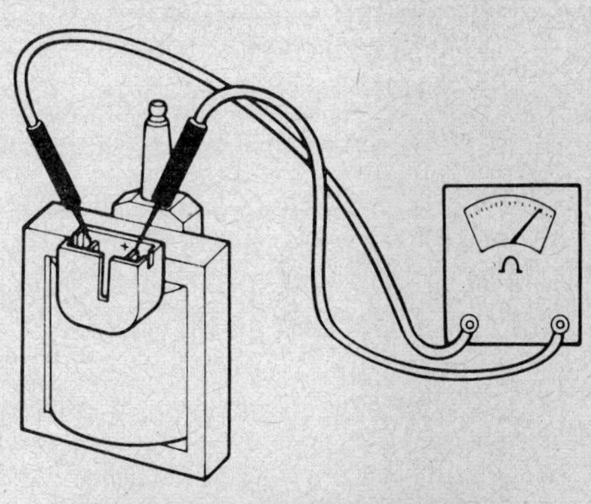

Fig. 4 TFI IV ignition system ignition coil primary resistance test connections

4. If resistance is .3-1 ohm, coil is satisfactory. Proceed to "Test 4."
5. If resistance is greater than 1 ohm or less than .3 ohm, replace ignition coil.

Test 4, Ignition Coil Secondary Resistance

1. Measure resistance between ignition coil negative and high voltage terminals, **Fig. 5.**
2. If resistance is 8,000-11,500 ohms, coil is satisfactory. Proceed to "Test 5."
3. If resistance is less than 8,000 ohms or greater than 11,500 ohms, replace ignition coil.

Test 5, Wiring Harness

1. Disconnect electrical connector from ignition module by depressing tabs.
2. Inspect connector for dirt or corrosion and clean as necessary.
3. Disconnect electrical connector at starter relay "S" terminal.
4. Connect negative lead of a suitable voltmeter to distributor base. Connect positive lead to a straight pin to serve as a probe, **Fig. 6.**

A high impedance voltmeter will not draw sufficient current to indicate a voltage drop when testing ignition power circuits for resistive connections. To ensure accurate test results, connect a test lamp between circuit being tested and ground as shown in **Fig. 6.** The lamp will draw current from the connection and permit measurement of the voltage drop so a resistive connection may be identified. Because the test lamp draws more current than the signal circuit can supply, the lamp must only be used on power circuits.

5. Measure and record voltage at terminal No. 2 with ignition in Run position.
6. Measure and record voltage at terminal No. 3 with ignition in Run and Start positions.
7. Measure and record voltage at terminal No. 4 with ignition in Start position.
8. If all voltage readings are 90% or more of battery voltage, wiring harness is satisfactory. Proceed to "Test 6."
9. If any or all voltage readings are less than 90% of battery voltage, inspect harness and electrical connectors, and repair or replace as necessary.

Test 6, EEC-IV to TFI-IV Circuit Continuity (1983–85)

1. Disconnect electrical connector from ignition module by depressing tabs.
2. Inspect connector for dirt or corrosion and clean as necessary, then connect to module.
3. Disconnect pin inline connector, then check for spark.

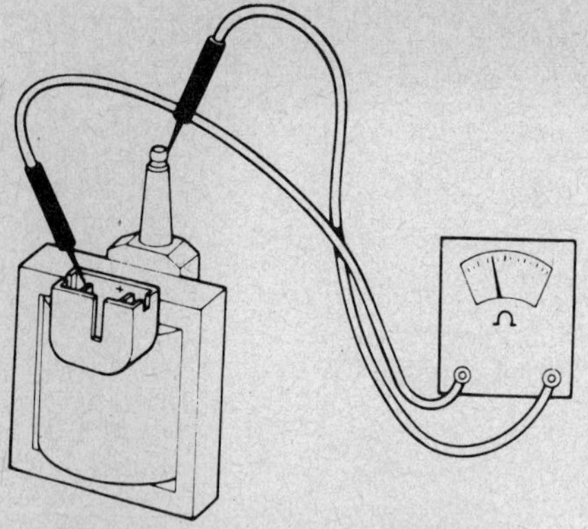

Fig. 5 TFI IV ignition system ignition coil secondary resistance test connections

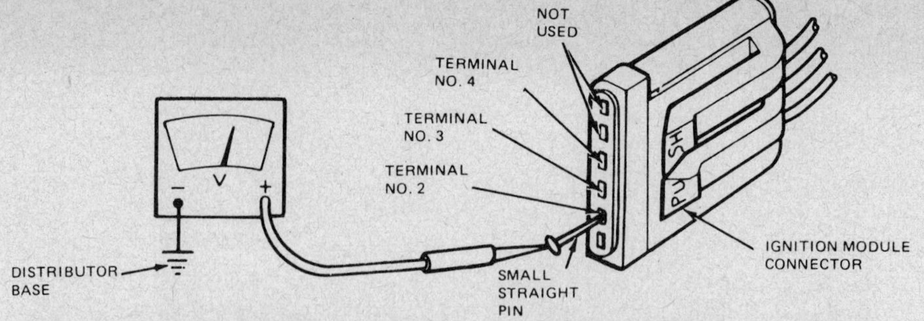

Fig. 6 TFI IV ignition system wiring harness & primary circuit continuity test connections

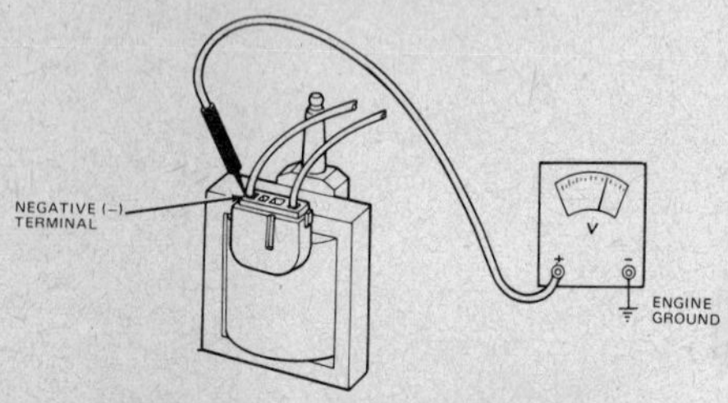

Fig. 7 TFI IV ignition system ignition coil primary voltage test connections

4. If no sparks occur, proceed to "Test 7."
5. If sparks are observed, check IMS wire for continuity. If wire is satisfactory, problem is not in ignition system.

Test 7, Stator (1986–87)

1. Turn ignition switch to OFF position, then disconnect and ground ignition coil wire.
2. Attach volt-ohmmeter negative lead to distributor base.
3. Disconnect pin inline connector near distributor and attach volt-ohmmeter positive lead to TFI module side of connector.
4. Turn ignition switch to ON position, then bump starter and note voltage levels with engine not moving. Record all values for future reference. **Allow enough time for reading to stabilize before taking measurements.**
5. If highest value is less than 90% of battery voltage, replace stator assembly.
6. If highest value is greater than 90% of battery voltage, and lowest value is greater than .5 volt, proceed as follows:
   a. Remove distributor from engine.
   b. Remove TFI module from distributor.
   c. Inspect stator connector terminals and TFI terminals for incorrect alignment and correct as necessary.
   d. If terminals are satisfactory, replace stator assembly.
7. If highest value is greater than 90% of battery voltage and lowest value is less than .5 volt and values were recorded between these two extremes, replace stator assembly.
8. If all values recorded were either lower than .5 volt or higher than 90% of battery voltage, proceed to "Test 8."

Test 8, EEC-IV/TFI-IV (1986–87)

1. Connect spark tester between ignition coil wire and ground.
2. Crank engine and check for spark.
3. If no spark is present, replace TFI-IV module.
4. If spark is present, check PIP and ignition ground wires for continuity and correct as necessary. If ground wires are satisfactory, the EEC-IV system must be diagnosed.

Test 9, Distributor & TFI-IV Module (1983–85)

1. Remove distributor and ignition module assembly from vehicle.
2. Install a new ignition module on distributor.
3. Connect electrical connector to module. Ground unit with a jumper wire from distributor to ground.
4. Rotate distributor by hand and check for sparks using a suitable spark tester.
5. If sparks are observed, reinstall original distributor with new ignition module.
6. If no sparks occur, sensor is faulty. Replace distributor with original ignition module.

Test 10, Primary Circuit Continuity

1. Disconnect electrical connector from ignition module by depressing tabs.
2. Inspect connector for dirt or corrosion, and clean as necessary.
3. Connect negative lead of a suitable voltmeter to distributor base. Connect positive lead to a straightpin inserted into connector terminal No. 2, **Fig. 6.**

A high impedance voltmeter will not draw sufficient current to indicate a voltage drop when testing ignition power circuits for resistive connections. To ensure accurate test results, connect a test lamp between circuit being tested and ground as shown in **Fig. 6.** The lamp will draw current from the connection and permit measurement of the voltage drop so a resistive connection may be identified. Because the test lamp draws more current than the signal circuit can supply, the lamp must only be used on power circuits.

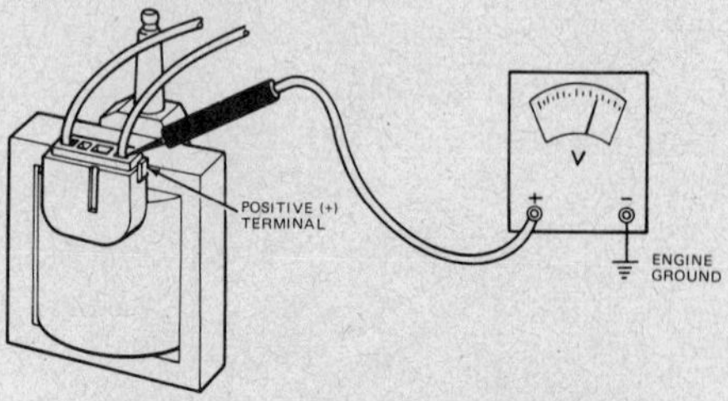

Fig. 8 TFI IV ignition system ignition coil supply voltage test connections

4. Measure and record voltage at terminal No. 2 with ignition in Run position.
5. If voltage reading is at least 90% of battery voltage, refer to "Test 5."
6. If voltage reading is less than 90% of battery voltage, proceed to "Test 11."

Test 11, Ignition Coil Primary Voltage

1. Connect negative lead of a suitable voltmeter to distributor base, **Fig. 7.**
2. Measure and record voltage at ignition coil negative terminal with ignition in Run position.
3. If voltage reading is at least 90% of battery voltage, inspect wiring harness between ignition module and coil negative terminal, and repair as necessary.
4. If voltage reading is less than 90% of battery voltage, inspect wiring harness between ignition module and coil negative terminal. If wiring is satisfactory, proceed to "Test 12."

Test 12, Ignition Coil Supply Voltage

1. Disconnect electrical connector from ignition coil.
2. Connect negative lead of a suitable voltmeter to distributor base, **Fig. 8.**
3. Measure and record voltage at ignition coil positive terminal with ignition in Run position.
4. If voltage reading is at least 90% of battery voltage, inspect ignition coil terminals and electrical connectors for dirt, corrosion and damage. If satisfactory, replace coil.
5. If voltage reading is less than 90% of battery voltage, repair circuit between ignition coil and ignition switch.

DISTRIBUTOR REPLACE

ESCORT, EXP, LN7, LYNX, TEMPO & TOPAZ

Removal

1. Disconnect primary wire connector from distributor.
2. Using a screwdriver, remove distributor cap and position aside with wires attached. **Before removing distributor cap, mark position of No. 1 tower on distributor base for assembly reference.**
3. Remove distributor rotor, then disconnect ignition module electrical connector.
4. Remove distributor hold-down bolt(s) and clamp, and the distributor. **Some models use special distributor hold-down bolts. To remove these bolts, use tool No. T82L-12270-A or equivalent.**

Installation

1. Rotate engine until No. 1 piston is on compression stroke.
2. Align timing marks for correct initial timing.
3. Rotate distributor shaft until center rod on rotor is pointing toward mark made on distributor base during removal. Continue to rotate shaft slightly until leading edge of vane is centered in vane switch stator assembly.
4. Rotate distributor in block until leading edge and vane stator switch assembly are aligned, and rotor is pointing to No. 1 cap terminal. **If vane and switch stator cannot be aligned by rotating distributor in block, slide distributor out of block just enough to disengage distributor gear. Rotate distributor shaft to engage a different gear tooth, then repeat steps 1 through 4 as needed.**
5. Install distributor clamp and hold-down bolt. Do not tighten bolt at this time.
6. Connect distributor to wiring harness.
7. Install distributor cap, rotor and ignition wires. Ensure ignition wires are attached securely to distributor cap and spark plugs.
8. Torque distributor attaching screws to 18-23 inch lbs. and the rotor screws to 23-35 inch lbs.
9. Adjust ignition timing to specifications.
10. Torque distributor hold-down bolt to 17-25 ft. lbs.

EXC. ESCORT, EXP, LN7, LYNX, TEMPO & TOPAZ

Removal

1. Disconnect primary wire connector from distributor.
2. Using a screwdriver, remove distributor cap, and position aside with wires attached.
3. Remove distributor rotor.
4. Note position of shaft plate, armature and rotor locating holes for assembly reference, then remove distributor hold-down bolt and clamp and the distributor. **Some models use special distributor hold-down bolts. To remove these bolts, use tool No. T82L-12270-A or equivalent.**

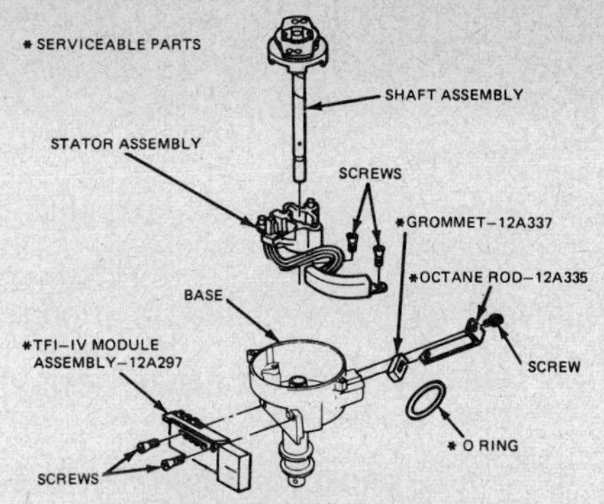

Fig. 9 Exploded view of TFI IV ignition system distributor

Installation

1. Rotate distributor by hand to ensure free rotation.
2. Ensure base O-ring is in place, then position rotor locating holes in original locations.
3. Install distributor, ensuring TFI-IV module is in same position relative to engine as when it was removed.
4. Install hold-down bolt and tighten until distributor can just barely be rotated.
5. Install distributor and torque screws to 25-35 inch lbs.
6. Connect wiring harness to distributor, then install distributor cap and torque screws to 17-23 inch lbs.
7. Adjust ignition timing to specifications, then torque distributor hold-down bolt to 6-8.5 ft. lbs.

COMPONENT REPLACEMENT

TFI-IV IGNITION MODULE, REPLACE

Removal

1. Remove distributor as described under "Distributor, Replace."
2. Remove 2 module attaching screws, **Fig. 9.**
3. Slide right side of module down distributor mounting flange, then back up to disengage module terminals from connector in distributor base. Remove module from distributor. **Do not attempt to remove module before moving toward distributor flange, as connector pins will be damaged.**

Installation

1. Apply a 1/32 inch coating of silicone grease D7ZA-19A331-A or equivalent to metal base of module.
2. Position module on distributor mounting flange.
3. Carefully position module toward distributor base to securely engage the 3 distributor attaching screws.
4. Install 2 module attaching screws and torque to 9-16 inch lbs. on 1983-84 front wheel drive models, 16-35 inch lbs. on 1985-87 front wheel drive models or 20-30 inch lbs. on 1984-87 rear wheel drive models.
5. Install distributor as described under "Distributor, Replace."

OCTANE ROD, REPLACE

1. Remove distributor cap and rotor.
2. Remove octane rod attaching rod from octane adjustment boss.
3. Slide octane rod and grommet out and disengage from stator retaining post, **Fig. 9.**
4. Reverse procedure to install. Torque attaching screw to 15-35 inch lbs. on front wheel drive models, or 20-30 inch lbs. on rear wheel drive models.

STATOR, REPLACE

ESCORT, EXP, LN7, LYNX, TEMPO & TOPAZ

Removal

1. Remove distributor cap and position aside, leaving wires attached.
2. Disconnect TFI module from harness, then remove distributor from engine block.
3. Remove rotor, then carefully pry drive coupling spring out with a small screwdriver.
4. Thoroughly clean drive end of distributor using compressed air.
5. Mark relationship between drive coupling and shaft for assembly reference.
6. Secure drive end coupling in a suitable vise. Ensure drive pin aligns with slot in base, then drive pin out of shaft.
7. Remove distributor and drive coupling from vise.
8. Remove any burrs from end of shaft using emery cloth, then remove shaft assembly by gently pulling up on the shaft plate.
9. Remove module-to-base attaching screws and the module. Remove grease from module and base.
10. Remove octane rod attaching screw and the octane rod.
11. Remove stator attaching screws and the stator. Retain screws for assembly.
12. Inspect base bushing for wear or signs of excess heat concentration and the shaft oil seal and base casting for wear. Replace complete distributor assembly if any damage is noted.
13. Inspect spring retainer that holds shaft oil seal against shaft and replace if necessary.
14. Inspect base O-ring and replace if necessary.

Installation

1. Position stator over bushing and press down until properly seated.
2. Position stator connector, ensuring tab fits in notch on base and fastening eyelets align with screw holes.

3. Ensure wires are positioned away from moving components, then install stator screws and torque to 25-35 inch lbs.
4. Install octane rod and torque attaching screw to 25-35 inch lbs.
5. Clean module mating surfaces, then apply silicone compound D7AZ-19A331-A or equivalent to back of module.
6. Invert distributor base and install module, ensuring pins are inserted into stator connector and against base.
7. Install module attaching screws and torque to 25-35 inch lbs.
8. Apply a light coat of clean engine oil to distributor shaft below the armature. **On 1.6 liter engines, synthetic oil should be used.**
9. Slide shaft assembly through base bushing.
10. Position drive coupling over shaft with reference marks aligned, then start pin into drive coupling and shaft.
11. Secure distributor in a suitable vise and drive pin into shaft until end of pin is flush with step in drive coupling.
12. Check for free movement of drive coupling on pin and ensure pin does not extend beyond step in coupling in either direction.
13. Remove distributor from vise and check for free rotation.
14. Install drive coupling spring in groove on the coupling.
15. Install distributor, cap and rotor.
16. Connect TFI module connector.

EXC. ESCORT, EXP, LN7, LYNX, TEMPO & TOPAZ

Removal

1. Remove distributor cap and position aside, leaving wires attached.
2. Disconnect TFI module from harness, then remove distributor from engine block.
3. Mark positions of armature, gear and collar, if equipped, for assembly reference.
4. Remove and discard pins in gear and collar, if equipped.
5. Remove gear and collar or thrust washer, as equipped.
6. Polish shaft with emery cloth, then slide shaft assembly out of distributor base.
7. Remove thrust washer from from distributor shaft.
8. Remove octane rod attaching screw and the 2 module attaching screws.
9. Remove module and octane rod.
10. Remove stator assembly from top of bowl.
11. Inspect base bushing for wear or signs of excess heat concentration and the base for wear or damage. Replace complete distributor assembly if any damage is noted.
12. Inspect base O-ring and replace if necessary.

Installation

1. Position stator over bushing and press down until properly seated.
2. Position stator connector, ensuring tab fits in notch on base and fastening eyelets align with screw holes.
3. Ensure wires are positioned away from moving components, then install stator screws and torque to 25-35 inch lbs.
4. Install octane rod and torque attaching screw to 25-35 inch lbs.
5. Clean module mating surfaces, then apply suitable grease to back of module.
6. Invert distributor base and install module, ensuring pins are inserted into stator connector. Fully seat module into connector and against base.
7. Install module attaching screws and torque to 25-35 inch lbs.
8. Install thrust washer, if equipped, on top of bushing.
9. Apply suitable lubricant to distributor shaft below the armature, then slide shaft assembly through base bushing.
10. On units equipped with collar, position collar over shaft, aligning mark on armature with original drill hole. Insert new roll pin through collar and shaft until pin is flush with both sides of collar.
11. On all units, position gear over shaft, aligning mark on armature with original drill hole. Insert new roll pin through gear and shaft until pin is flush shaft.
12. Verify free rotation of distributor, then install distributor, cap and rotor.

1982–84 Dura Spark III Ignition System W/EEC

INDEX

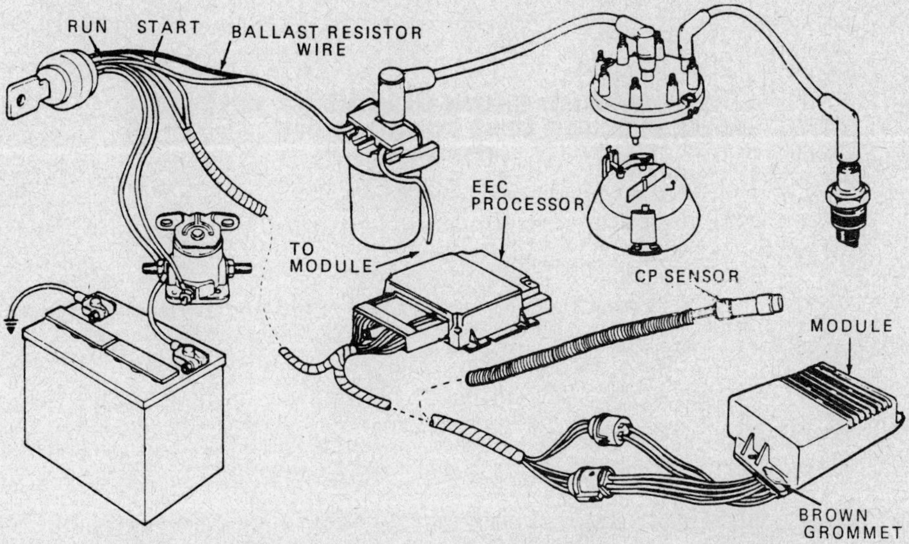

Fig. 1 Dura Spark III ignition system (typical)

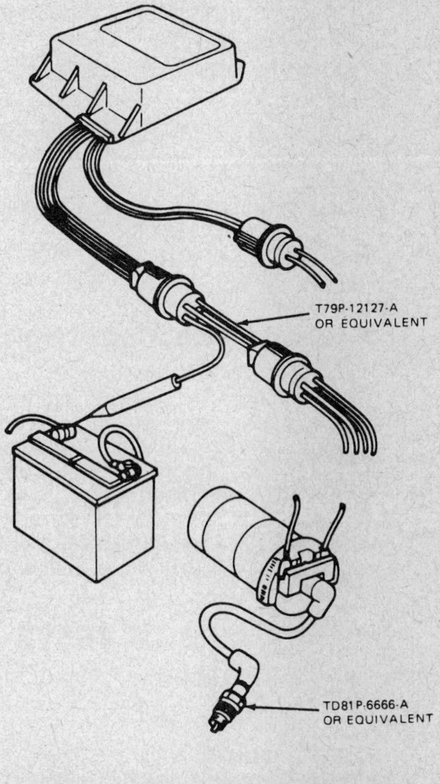

Fig. 2 Installing ignition diagnostic test adapter

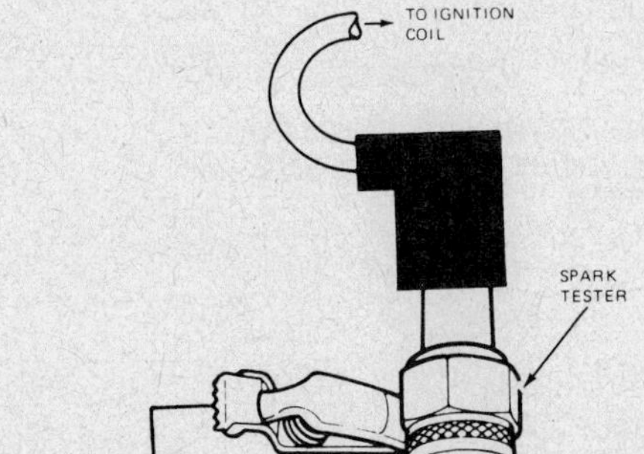

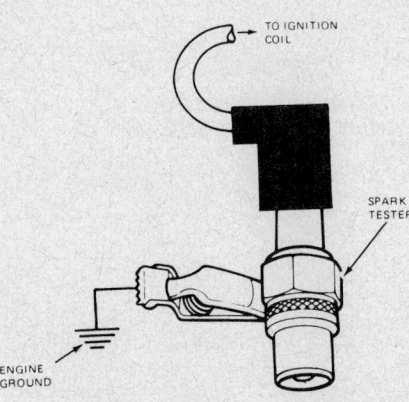

Fig. 3 Spark tester

DESCRIPTION

The Dura Spark III system, **Fig. 1**, is used on engines equipped with Electronic Engine Control (EEC). The system primary side consists of the battery, ignition switch, primary wiring, EEC system input and an ignition module. The secondary side consists of a distributor, distributor cap, adapter and rotor, spark plug cables and spark plugs. When the ignition switch is in the On position, the primary circuit and the ignition coil are energized. The EEC system provides a signal which tells the ignition module to turn off the coil primary circuit. The off and on times of the primary circuit are controlled by the EEC computer. When the circuit is turned Off, the magnetic field built up in the ignition coil collapses, inducing a high voltage into the coil secondary windings. This high voltage is then delivered to the spark plugs by the rotor and secondary ignition wires.

SYSTEM DIAGNOSIS

Before proceeding with system diagnosis, ensure battery is fully charged and all accessories are "Off." Inspect all vacuum hoses and spark plug wires for proper routing and secure connections. Inspect engine compartment ignition wiring harness and connectors for signs of insulation damage, burning, overheating and loose or broken connections. Repair as necessary.

SECONDARY CIRCUIT TESTS

Spark Plug Firing Voltage Test

1. Connect an oscilloscope with voltage pickup on coil to distributor wire. Set oscilloscope to parade pattern.
2. Start engine, then while slowly increasing engine RPM from idle to 2000 RPM, observe scope pattern. If the average spark plug firing voltage is 15 KV and the spark plug firing voltages do not vary more than 5 KV, the system is operating properly.
3. If the spark plug firing voltages do not vary more than 5 KV and the average spark plug firing voltage is more than 15 KV, check the following:
   a. Ignition coil wire for proper installation and resistance. Resistance should be less than 5000 ohms per inch. If more, replace.
   b. Spark plugs for wide gaps.
   c. Distributor cap and rotor for excessive clearance.
   d. Distributor cap and rotor for lack of silicone compound on rotor.
   e. Distributor rotor alignment. See "Distributor Rotor, Replace."
4. If the spark plug firing voltages vary more than 5 KV, check the following:
   a. Spark plug gap(s) or worn electrodes.
   b. Correct distributor cap, adapter and rotor installation.
   c. Distributor rotor alignment. See "Distributor Rotor, Replace."
5. If one or more spark plug firing voltages are unusually high, check the following:
   a. Disconnected spark plug wire(s).

b. Spark plug gap(s) or open plug wire(s).
6. If one or more spark plug firing voltages are unusually low, check the following:
a. Spark plug(s) for fouling or narrow gap(s).
b. Spark plug wires for grounding.
c. Distributor cap and adapter for tracking.
7. If spark plug firing voltages are inverted, check the following:
a. Ignition coil primary connector for improper installation. If installation is satisfactory, replace coil.

Spark Plug Wire Continuity Test

1. Remove distributor cap and disconnect suspected wire from spark plug or coil.
2. Using an ohmmeter, check wire resistance through distributor cap.
3. Resistance should be 5000 ohms per inch. If reading is greater than specified, replace wire.

Spark Plug Wire Inspection, All Models

1. Clean off any deposits of dirt from wires, boots, distributor cap and coil using mild soap and water solution.
2. Inspect wires, boots for cuts, punctures or other damage.
3. Inspect wire terminals for corrosion and clean with fine sandpaper.
4. Coat all boots with silicone grease before installing.

PRIMARY CIRCUIT TESTS

1982–84 MODELS

Test 1, Run Circuit

1. Disconnect ignition module three wire connector and install ignition diagnostic test adapter into wiring circuit, **Fig. 2.**
2. Connect spark tester, **Fig. 3,** between ignition coil and ground.
3. Turn ignition "On," then, while observing spark tester, touch diagnostic test lead to battery positive terminal. Spark should occur every time lead touches battery.
4. If spark occurs, circuit is satisfactory. If not, proceed to Test 2.

Test 2, Start Circuit

1. Remove diagnostic test adapter installed in Test 1, but leave spark tester attached.
2. While cranking over engine with ignition switch, observe spark tester for sparks.
3. If sparks occur, circuit is satisfactory. If not, proceed to Test 3.

Test 3, Start Voltage

1. Connect coil wire to distributor cap, noting the following:
a. If starter relay is equipped with an I terminal, disconnect starter cable from starter relay.
b. If starter relay is equipped with S terminal, disconnect S wire from relay.

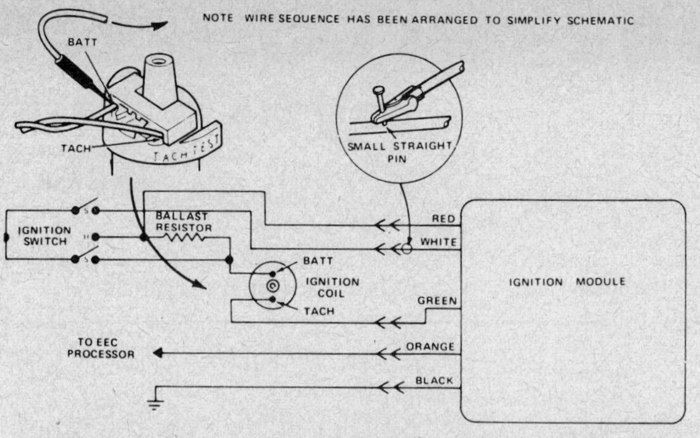

Fig. 4 Dura Spark III ignition system start voltage test connections. 1982–84 models

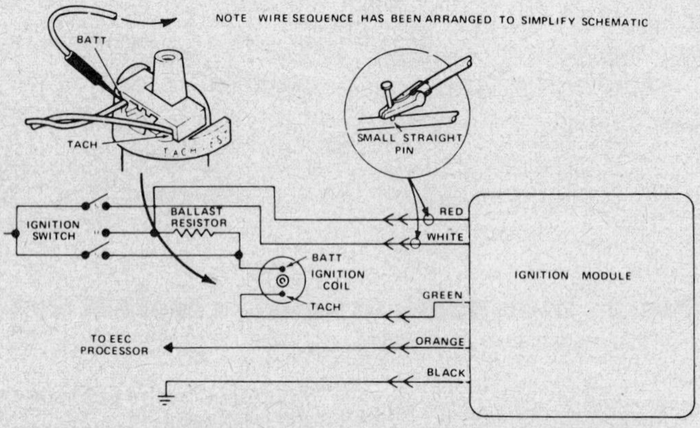

Fig. 5 Dura Spark III ignition system supply voltage test connections. 1982–84 models

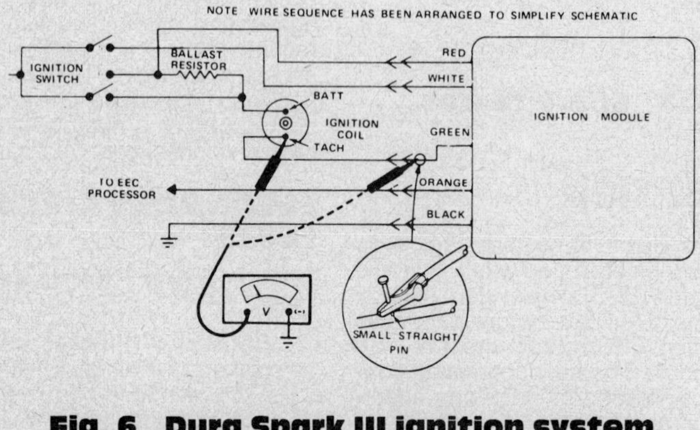

Fig. 6 Dura Spark III ignition system module to coil wire test connections. 1982–84 models

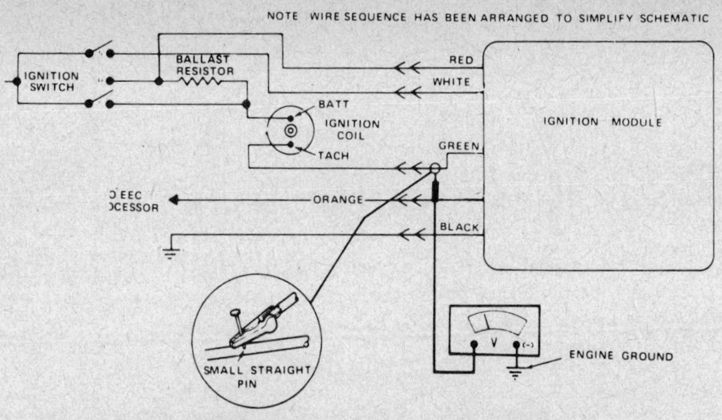

Fig. 7 Dura Spark III ignition system primary circuit continuity test connections. 1982–84 models

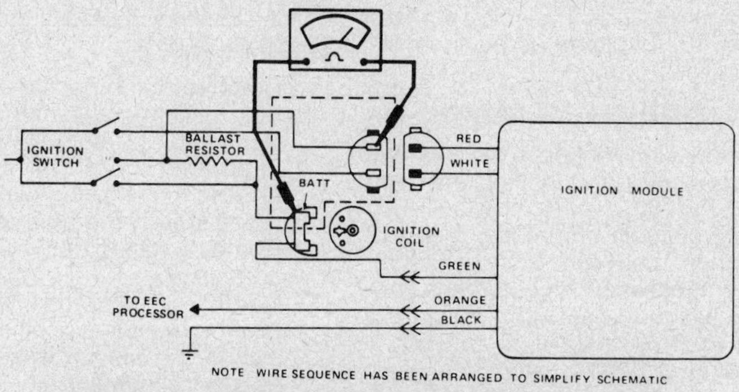

Fig. 8 Dura Spark III ignition system ballast resistor test connections. 1982–84 models

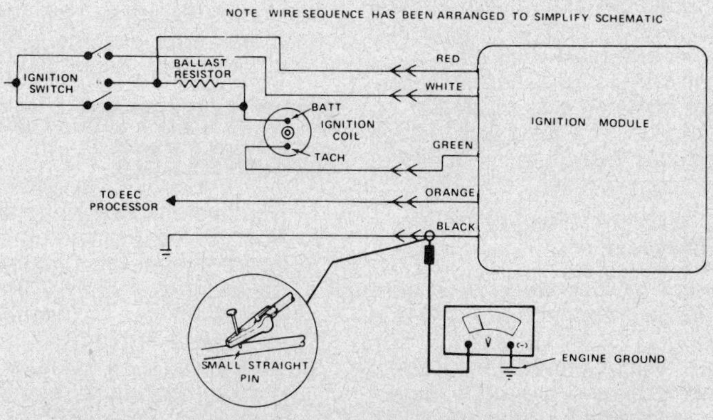

Fig. 9 Dura Spark III ignition system ground circuit test connections. 1982–84 models

2. With ignition "Off," install straight pin into module white wire, **Fig. 4.**
3. Connect a suitable voltmeter between ground and straight pin.
4. Turn ignition switch to "Start" position and note voltage.
5. Move voltmeter positive lead to coil Batt. connector and note voltage with ignition switch in start "position."
6. If voltage obtained is 90% of battery voltage, circuit is satisfactory. If voltage obtained is less than 90% of battery voltage, a defective ignition switch or wiring harness is indicated.

Test 4, Ignition Coil Primary Circuit Switching

1. Disconnect ignition module three wire connector and install ignition diagnostic test adapter into wiring circuit, **Fig. 2.**
2. Connect a suitable test light between coil Tach terminal and engine ground.
3. Turn ignition "On", then while observing test light, touch diagnostic test lead to battery positive terminal. Test light should flash every time lead touches battery.
4. If test light flashes, circuit is satisfactory. If not, proceed to Test 6.

Test 5, Ignition Coil Secondary Resistance

1. Disconnect and inspect ignition coil electrical connector.
2. Using a suitable ohmmeter, measure resistance between coil Batt. terminal and high tension lead terminal.
3. If resistance is between 7700-10,500 ohms, coil is satisfactory. If not between limits, replace coil.

Test 6, Supply Voltage Circuits

1. Remove diagnostic test adapter installed in Test 4 and test light, then note the following:
   a. If starter relay is equipped with an I terminal, disconnect starter cable from starter relay.
   b. If starter relay is equipped with S terminal, disconnect S wire from relay.
2. With ignition "Off," install straightpins into module red and white wires, **Fig. 5. Do not allow straightpins to contact engine ground.**
3. Using a suitable voltmeter, connect negative lead to ground and note the following:
   a. With ignition in "On" position, measure voltage at red wire pin.
   b. Place ignition in "Start" position, measure voltage at white wire pin and at coil Batt. terminal. **When measuring voltages, wiggle wires to simulate any open circuits that might exist.**
4. If readings obtained are 90% of battery voltage, supply circuits are satisfactory. Proceed to Test 7.
5. If readings obtained are less than 90% of battery voltage, check for:
   a. Defective wiring harness or connectors in supply voltage circuits.
   b. Defective ignition switch.
   c. Defective radio interference capacitor on ignition coil.

Test 7, Ignition Coil Supply Voltage

1. Connect positive lead of voltmeter to coil Batt. terminal and negative lead to ground.
2. Turn ignition switch to "On" position.
3. Observe voltmeter reading. If 6-8 volts, circuit is satisfactory. If less than 6 volts or more than 8 volts, proceed to Test 9.

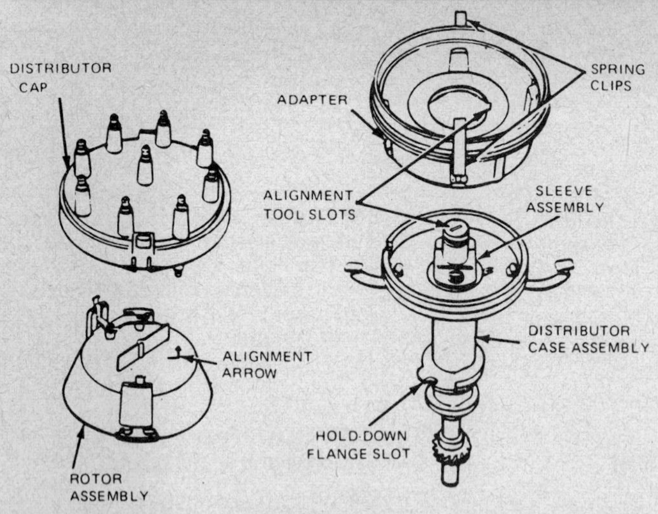

Fig. 10 1982–84 Dura Spark III distributor (typical)

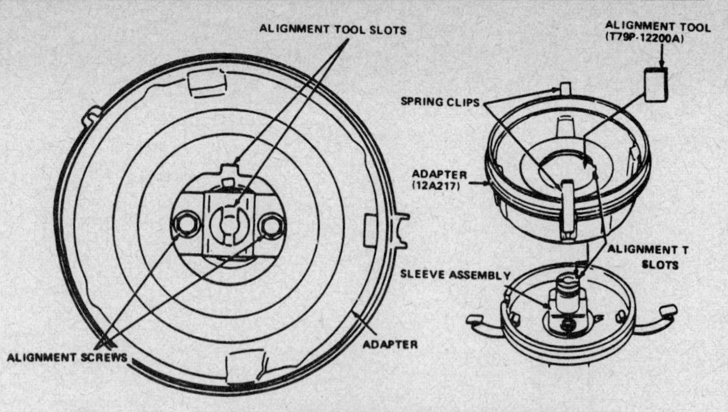

Fig. 11 1982–84 Dura Spark III rotor alignment

Test 8, Testing Tach Wire

1. Disconnect and inspect module three wire connector and coil connector.
2. Using a suitable ohmmeter, connect one lead to ground and the other to the coil connector Tach. terminal. Measure resistance.
3. If readings obtained are one ohm or less, circuit is satisfactory. If readings are more than one ohm, repair short in tach wire.

Test 9, Ignition Coil Primary Resistance

1. Disconnect and inspect ignition coil connector.
2. Using a suitable tachometer, measure resistance between coil Batt. and Tach. terminals.
3. If readings are 0.8-1.6 ohms, circuit is satisfactory. If readings are out of specifications, replace coil.

Test 10, Module to Coil Wire

1. With ignition "Off," insert straightpin in module green wire, **Fig. 6. Do not allow straightpin to contact engine ground.**
2. Using a suitable voltmeter, connect negative lead to ground.
3. Turn ignition "On," then measure voltage at green wire pin and Tach. terminal of ignition coil, **Fig. 6.**
4. If voltmeter shows less than 1/2 volt difference, circuit is satisfactory. If more than 1/2 volt difference, inspect and repair wiring harness between coil and module.

Test 11, Primary Circuit Continuity

1. Leave straight pin in green wire as outlined in Test 10.
2. Turn ignition "On," then using a suitable voltmeter connected to ground, measure voltage at green wire pin, **Fig. 7.**
3. If voltage exceeds 1 1/2 volts, proceed to Test 13. If voltage obtained is 1 1/2 volts or less, proceed to Test 12.

Test 12, Ballast Resistor

1. Disconnect and inspect module two wire connector and ignition coil connector, **Fig. 8.**
2. Using a suitable ohmmeter, measure resistance between coil connector Batt. terminal and wiring harness connector which mates with module red wire, **Fig. 8.**
3. If reading is 0.8-1.6 ohms, circuit is satisfactory. If reading is less than 0.8 ohms or more than 1.6 ohms, replace ballast resistor.

Test 13, Ground Circuit

1. With ignition "Off," install straightpin in module black wire, **Fig. 9. Do not allow straightpin to touch engine ground.**
2. Using a suitable ohmmeter, connect negative lead to engine ground and positive lead to black wire pin.
3. Turn ignition "On," measure voltage.
4. If voltage obtained was more than 1/2 volts, proceed to Test 14. If voltage obtained was less than 1/2 volts, replace ignition module.

Test 14, Wiring Harness Ground Circuit

1. Disconnect module three wire connector, inspect connector for dirt and corrosion.
2. Using a suitable ohmmeter, connect one lead to engine ground. Connect other lead to wiring harness terminal which mates with black module wire terminal. Measure resistance. **When measuring resistances, wiggle wires to simulate any open circuits that might exist.**
3. If resistance is less than one ohm, inspect wiring harness connector and module black wire. If no problem is found, it is either intermittent or not in ignition system.
4. If resistance is greater than one ohm, inspect and repair wiring harness between ignition module and ground connection.

DISTRIBUTOR REPLACE

1. Remove distributor cap and rotor, **Fig. 10.** Position crankshaft as outlined in Distributor Rotor Alignment. **The alignment slot in the adapter should be aligned with the alignment slot in the sleeve assembly.**
2. Remove distributor hold-down bolt and clamp.
3. Carefully remove distributor from engine block, noting position of the large slot in the sleeve in relation to the adapter alignment slot as distributor drive gear is felt to disengage with cam gear. **Do not rotate engine after distributor has been removed.**
4. Install distributor in engine block. Ensure the distributor hold-down flange slot is aligned with the clamp bolt hole and adapter alignment slot is aligned with the large sleeve alignment slot.
5. Install distributor hold-down bolt and clamp. Torque to 17 ft. lbs.
6. Check rotor alignment. Refer to Distributor Rotor Alignment procedure.

DISTRIBUTOR ROTOR ALIGNMENT

1. Remove distributor cap and rotor.
2. Position No. 1 piston on compression stroke, then rotate crankshaft until rotor alignment tool, T79P-12200-A or equivalent, can be inserted into alignment slots, **Fig. 11.**
3. Check vibration damper and timing pointer alignment marks. If timing pointer is within $\pm$ 4° of TDC, alignment is satisfactory. If alignment is out of specifications, position vibration damper at TDC with cylinder No. 1 at TDC. Loosen sleeve assembly adjustment screws and rotate sleeve until rotor alignment tool can be inserted into alignment slots, **Fig. 11.** Torque adjustment screws to 25-35 in. lbs. and remove tool.
4. Replace rotor and distributor cap.

CARBURETOR SECTION

TABLE OF CONTENTS

Carter YFA 1 Barrel Carburetor

INDEX

ADJUSTMENT SPECIFICATIONS

Year	Carb. Model	Float Level	Float Drop	Fast Idle Cam Setting	Dechoke Or Unloader Setting	Pulldown Setting	Choke Setting
1983	E3ZE-ABA	21/32	—	.140	.220	.260	①
	E3ZE-ACA	21/32	—	.140	.220	.260	①
	E3ZE-ADA	21/32	—	.140	.220	.260	①
	E3ZE-AEA	21/32	—	.140	.220	.260	①
	E3ZE-ASA	21/32	—	.160	.220	.260	①
	E3ZE-ATA	21/32	—	.160	.220	.260	①
	E3ZE-LA	21/32	—	.140	.220	.260	①
	E3ZE-MA	21/32	—	.140	.220	.260	①
	E3ZE-TB	21/32	—	.140	.220	.260	①
	E3ZE-TC	21/32	—	.140	.220	.240	①
	E3ZE-UA	21/32	—	.140	.220	.260	①
	E3ZE-UB	21/32	—	.140	.220	.240	①
	E3ZE-VA	21/32	—	.140	.220	.260	①
	E3ZE-YA	21/32	—	.140	.220	.260	①
1984	E4ZE-DB	21/32	—	.140	.270	.260	①
	E4ZE-HC	21/32	—	.140	.270	.260	①
	E4ZE-MA	21/32	—	.140	.270	.240	①
	E4ZE-NA	21/32	—	.140	.270	.240	①
	E4ZE-PA	21/32	—	.140	.270	.260	①
	E4ZE-PB	21/32	—	.140	.270	.240	①
	E4ZE-RA	21/32	—	.140	.270	.260	①
	E4ZE-RB	21/32	—	.140	.270	.260	①
1985	E5ZE-AA	21/32	—	.140	.270	.260	①
	E52E-CA	21/32	—	.140	.270	.260	①
1986	E6ZE-DA	21/32	—	.140	.220	.260	①
	E6ZE-EA	21/32	—	.140	.220	.260	①

①—Tamper-resistant.

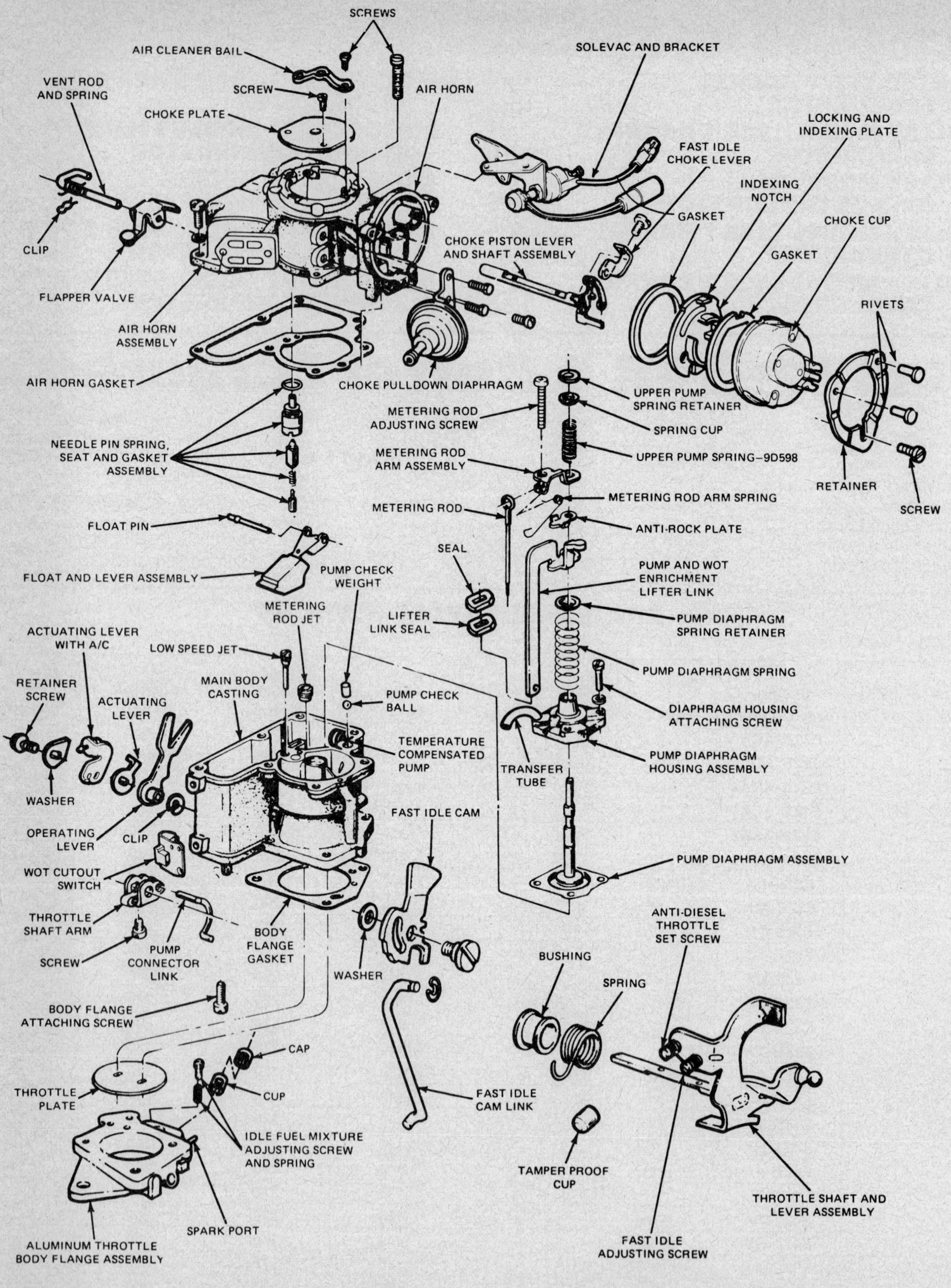

Fig. 1 Exploded view of Carter Model YF Series carburetor. 1983–86 model less feedback solenoid. 1983 shown, 1984–86 similar

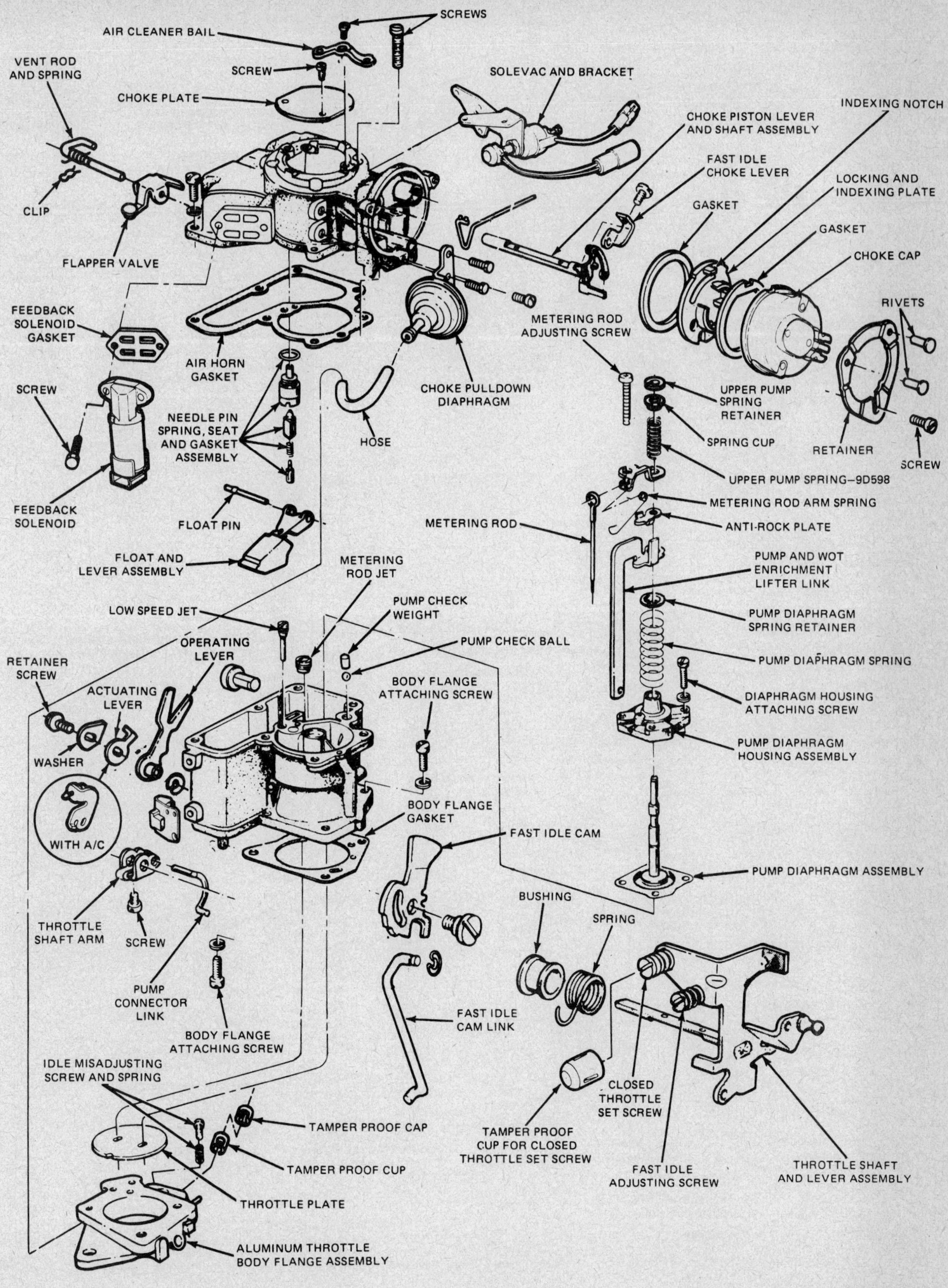

Fig. 2 Exploded view of Carter Model YF Series carburetor. 1983 model with feedback solenoid

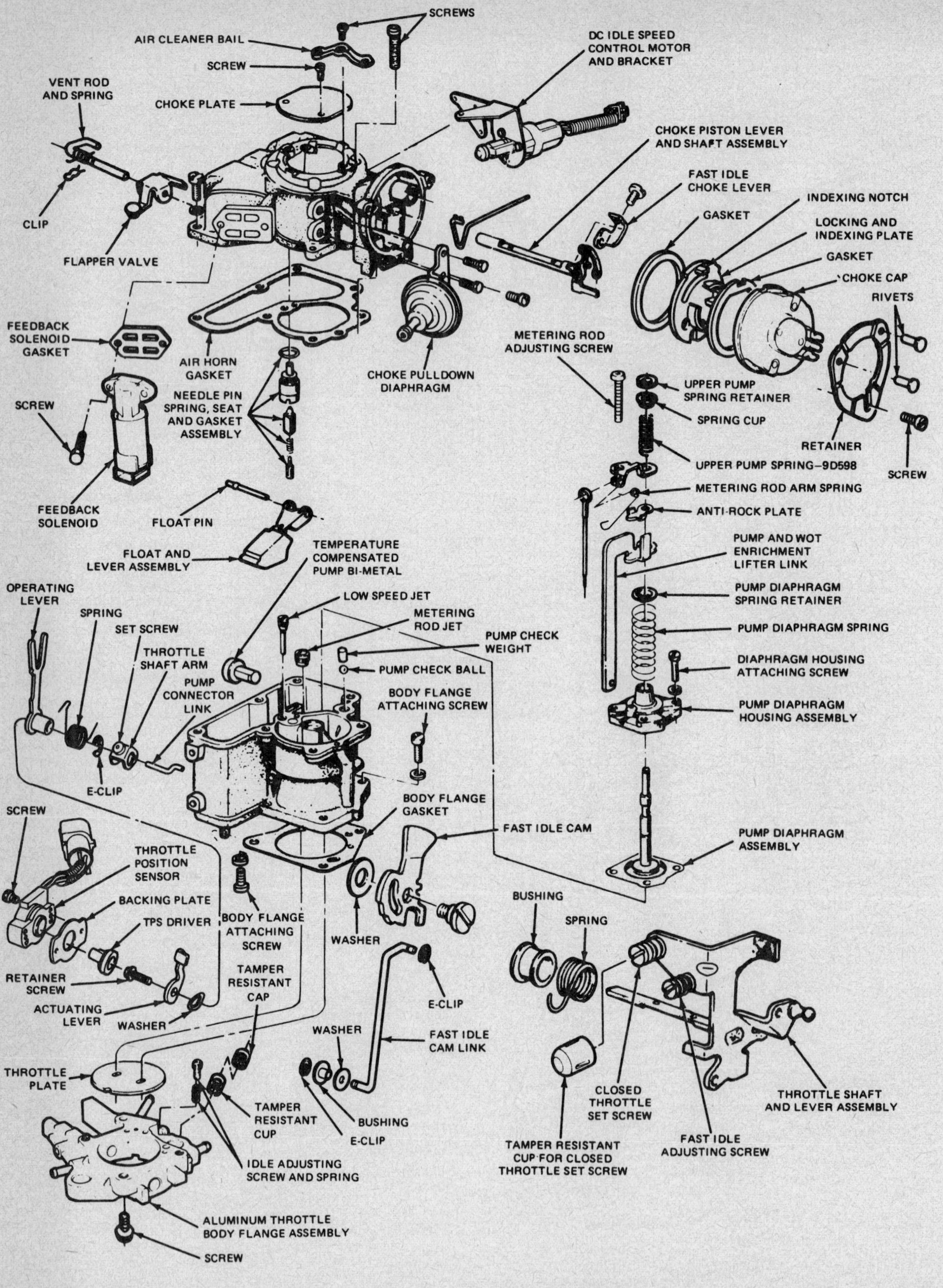

Fig. 3 Exploded view of Carter Model YF series carburetor. 1984–86 model with feedback solenoid. 1984 shown, 1985–86 similar

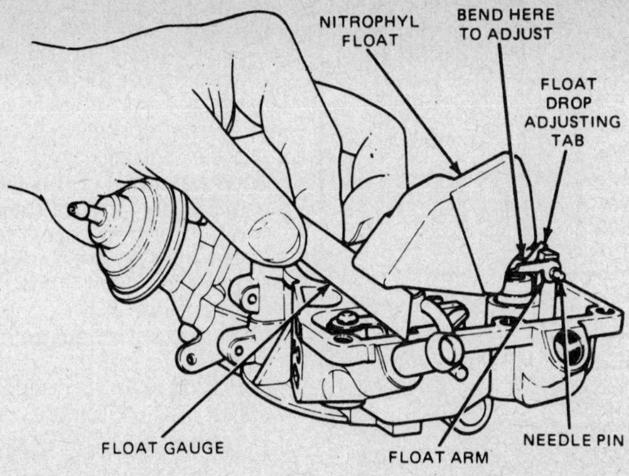

Fig. 4 Float level adjustment. YF series carburetor

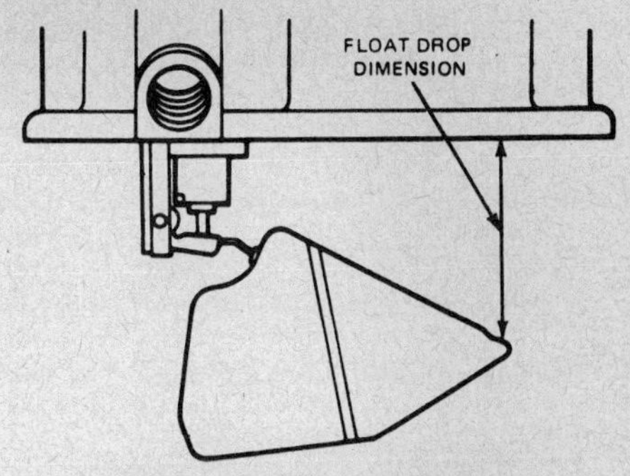

Fig. 5 Float drop adjustment. YF series carburetor

IDENTIFICATION LOCATION

The carburetor identification number is located on a tag attached to the carburetor by one of the fuel bowl cover attaching screws.

DESCRIPTION

The YF Series carburetor, **Figs. 1 thru 3,** is a single-barrel, downdraft unit combining the fundamental features of other Carter carburetors. In addition, it features a diaphragm-type accelerating pump. It also has a diaphragm-operated metering rod, both vacuum and mechanically controlled.

ON-VEHICLE ADJUSTMENTS

CURB IDLE SPEED

1983 4-140

1. Place transmission into Neutral or Park.
2. Install a suitable tachometer onto engine as per manufacturer's instructions.
3. Start and allow engine to reach operating temperature.
4. Place A/C selector switch to OFF position.
5. Check curb idle speed. If curb idle speed obtained is not as specified, turn curb idle speed adjusting screw until specified speed is obtained.

1984–86 4-140 Turbocharged Engine

1. Place transmission into Neutral, then turn A/C-Heat selector switch to OFF position.
2. Start and allow engine to reach normal operating temperature, then switch ignition OFF. Install a suitable tachometer on engine per manufacturer's instructions.
3. Disconnect electrical connector from idle speed control air bypass valve.
4. Start and operate engine at 2000 RPM for approximately 1 1/2 minutes. **If electric cooling fan comes ON during idle speed adjustment procedure, disconnect electrical connector from fan assembly.**
5. Allow engine to idle and check specified curb idle speed. If curb idle speed is not as specified, turn throttle plate stop screw until correct idle speed is obtained.

FAST IDLE SPEED

1983 4-140

1. Place transmission into Neutral or Park.
2. Install a suitable tachometer onto engine as per manufacturer's instructions.
3. Start and allow engine to reach normal operating temperature, then turn ignition switch to OFF position.
4. Place A/C selector switch to OFF position.
5. Disconnect and plug EGR valve vacuum lines.
6. Disconnect electrical connector from PVS, if equipped.
7. Place fast idle adjusting screw onto specified step of cam.
8. Check fast idle speed. If fast idle speed obtained is not as specified, turn fast idle speed screw until correct speed is obtained.

FLOAT LEVEL

Invert the air horn assembly, and check the clearance from the top of the float to the bottom of the air horn with the float level gauge, **Fig. 4.** Hold the air horn at eye level when gauging the float level. The float arm (lever) should be resting on the needle pin. Do not load the needle when adjusting the float. Bend the float arm as necessary to adjust the float level (clearance). Do not bend the tab at the end of the float arm. It prevents the float from striking the bottom of the fuel bowl when empty.

FLOAT DROP

Hold air horn upright and measure maximum clearance from top of float to bottom of air horn with float drop gauge, **Fig. 5.** Bend tab at end of float arm to obtain specified setting listed under Adjustment Specifications.

METERING ROD

If equipped, cut off the tamper-proof cup covering the adjusting screw. Back out the idle speed adjusting screw until the throttle plate is closed tight in the throttle bore. Press down on upper end of diaphragm shaft until diaphragm bottoms in vacuum chamber. Metering rod should contact bottom of metering rod well, and metering rod should contact lifter link at the outer end nearest the springs and at supporting lug. For models not equipped with metering rod adjusting screw, adjust by bending lip of metering rod arm to which metering rod is attached, up or down as required. For models equipped with a metering rod adjusting screw, turn the adjusting screw until metering rod just bottoms in the body casting. For final adjustments turn metering rod adjusting screw in (clockwise) one additional turn.

FAST IDLE CAM LINKAGE

Position fast idle screw on second step of fast idle cam and against shoulder of highest step. Using a drill of specified size, check clearance between lower edge of choke plate and bore. Refer to Adjustment Specifications. To adjust, bend choke connector rod as required.

CHOKE PLATE PULLDOWN

Bend a 0.026 in. diameter wire gauge at a 90 degree angle approximately 1/8 inch from one end. Insert the bent end of the gauge between the choke piston slot and the righthand slot in choke housing. Rotate the choke piston lever counterclockwise until gauge is snug in the piston slot. Exert a light pressure on choke piston lever to hold the gauge in place, then use a drill with a diameter equal to the specified pulldown clearance between the lower edge of choke plate and carburetor bore to check clearance.

To adjust the choke plate pulldown clearance, bend the choke piston lever as required to obtain specified setting.

When bending the lever, be careful not to distort the piston link. Install the choke thermostatic spring housing and gasket. Set the housing to specifications.

DECHOKE

Hold the throttle plate fully open and close the choke plate as far as possible without forcing it. Use a drill of specified diameter to check the clearance between choke plate and air horn. If clearance is not within specification, adjust by bending arm on choke trip lever of the throttle lever. Bending the arm downward will decrease the clearance, bending it upward will increase the clearance.

If the choke plate clearance and fast idle cam linkage adjustment was performed with the carburetor on the engine, adjust the engine idle speed and fuel mixture. Adjust dash pot (if so equipped).

DASH POT

With the engine idle speed and mixture properly adjusted, and the engine at normal operating temperature, loosen the antistall dash pot locknut. Hold the throttle in the curb idle position and depress the dash pot plunger. Measure the clearance between the throttle lever and plunger tip. Turn the antistall dash pot to provide 7/64 inch ± 1/64 inch clearance between the tip of the plunger and the throttle lever. Tighten the locknut to secure the adjustment.

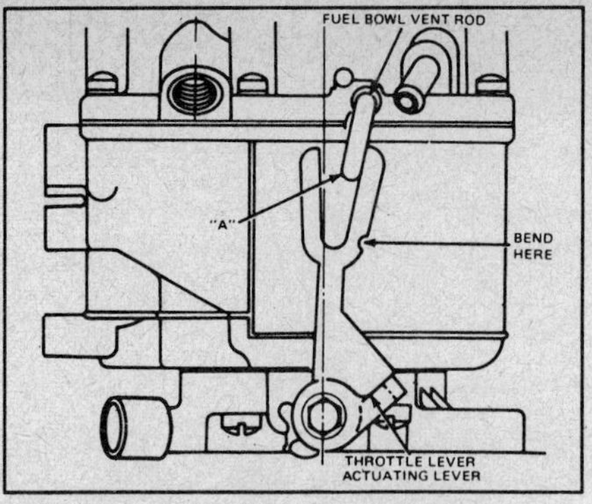

Fig. 6 YF mechanical fuel bowl vent adjustment

MECHANICAL FUEL BOWL VENT

To perform this adjustment, engine idle must be set to specifications and must be at normal operating temperature.

Open throttle lever so actuating lever does not make contact with fuel bowl vent rod, **Fig. 6.** Close throttle lever to idle set position and measure travel of fuel bowl vent rod at point "A," **Fig. 6.** This distance represents vent rod travel from point where there is no contact with actuating lever to point where actuating lever moves vent rod to idle set position. Bend throttle actuating lever as needed until travel measures .100-.150 inch.

AUTOMATIC CHOKE

Loosen choke cover retaining screws and turn choke cover so that line or Index mark on cover lines up with the specified mark listed in Adjustment Specifications on choke housing.

Holley Model 1946 1 Barrel Carburetor

INDEX

ADJUSTMENT SPECIFICATIONS

Year	Carb. No.	Float Level	Fuel Bowl Vent Setting	Accelerator Pump: Pump Hole No.	Accelerator Pump: Pump Setting	Fast Idle Cam	Choke Pulldown	Dechoke	Choke Setting
1982	E1BE-AGA	.690	—	2	—	.086	.120	.150	2 Rich
	E2BE-BA	.690	—	2	—	.078	.110	.150	2 Rich
	E2BE-CA	.690	—	2	—	.078	.110	.150	2 Rich
	E2BE-HA	.690	—	2	—	.078	.110	.150	2 Rich
	E2BE-JA	.690	—	2	—	.078	.110	.150	2 Rich
	E2BE-SA	.690	—	2	—	.078	.110	.150	2 Rich
	E2BE-TA	.690	—	2	—	.078	.110	.150	2 Rich
1983	E2BE-BA	.690	—	2	—	.078	.110	.150	2 Rich
	E2BE-CA	.690	—	2	—	.078	.110	.150	2 Rich
	E2BE-SA	.690	—	2	—	.078	.110	.150	2 Rich
	E2BE-TA	.690	—	2	—	.078	.110	.150	2 Rich
	E3BE-CA	.690	—	2	—	.078	.100	.150	2 Rich
	E3BE-DA	.690	—	2	—	.078	.100	.150	2 Rich
	E3SE-AA	.690	—	2	—	.078	.095	.150	2 Rich
	E3SE-BA	.690	—	2	—	.078	.095	.150	2 Rich
	E3SE-CA	.690	—	2	—	.078	.105	.150	2 Rich
	E3SE-DA	.690	—	2	—	.078	.105	.150	2 Rich

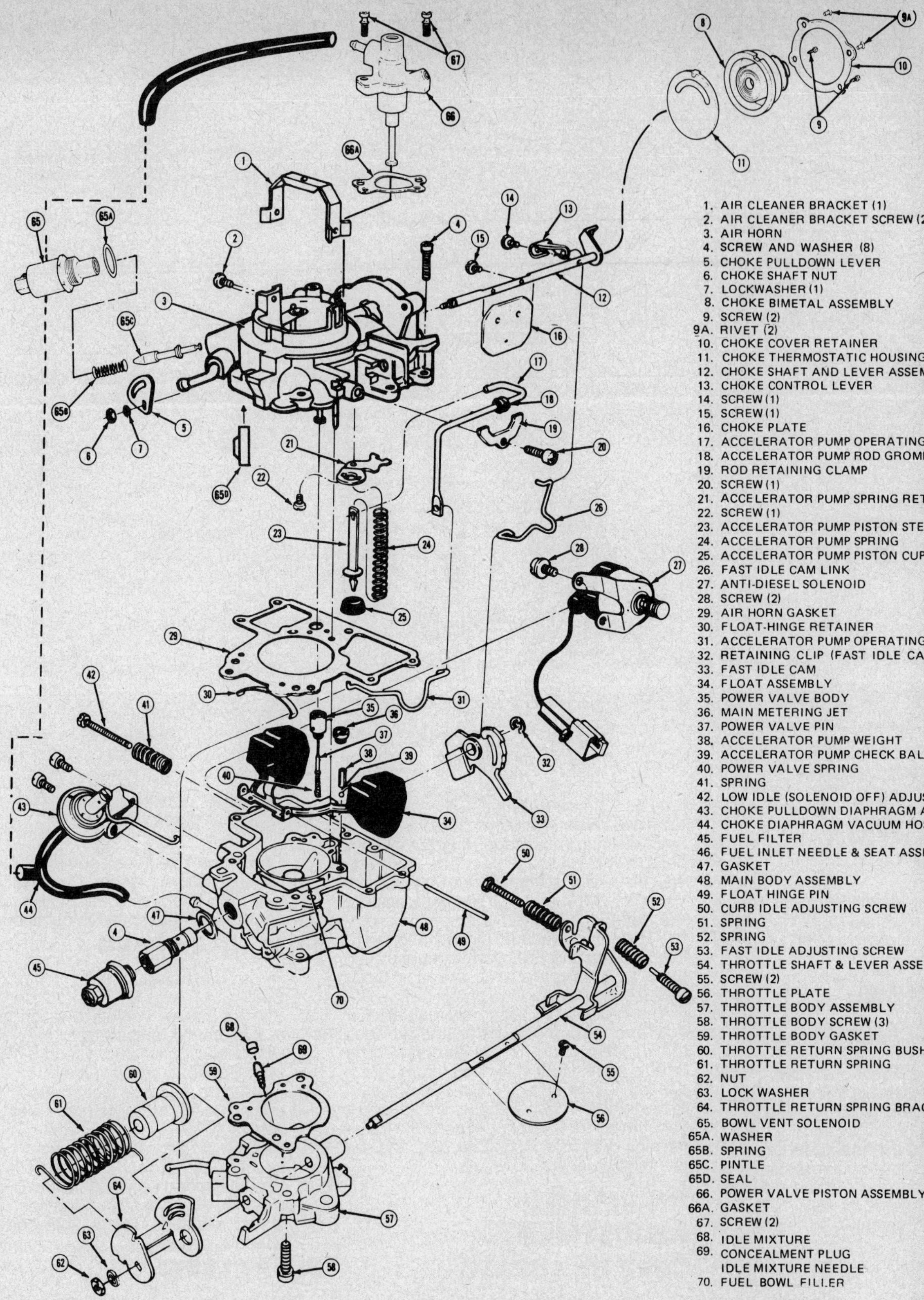

1. AIR CLEANER BRACKET (1)
2. AIR CLEANER BRACKET SCREW (2)
3. AIR HORN
4. SCREW AND WASHER (8)
5. CHOKE PULLDOWN LEVER
6. CHOKE SHAFT NUT
7. LOCKWASHER (1)
8. CHOKE BIMETAL ASSEMBLY
9. SCREW (2)

9A. RIVET (2)

10. CHOKE COVER RETAINER
11. CHOKE THERMOSTATIC HOUSING LOCATING DISC
12. CHOKE SHAFT AND LEVER ASSEMBLY
13. CHOKE CONTROL LEVER
14. SCREW (1)
15. SCREW (1)
16. CHOKE PLATE
17. ACCELERATOR PUMP OPERATING ROD
18. ACCELERATOR PUMP ROD GROMMET
19. ROD RETAINING CLAMP
20. SCREW (1)
21. ACCELERATOR PUMP SPRING RETAINING PLATE
22. SCREW (1)
23. ACCELERATOR PUMP PISTON STEM
24. ACCELERATOR PUMP SPRING
25. ACCELERATOR PUMP PISTON CUP
26. FAST IDLE CAM LINK
27. ANTI-DIESEL SOLENOID
28. SCREW (2)
29. AIR HORN GASKET
30. FLOAT-HINGE RETAINER
31. ACCELERATOR PUMP OPERATING LINK
32. RETAINING CLIP (FAST IDLE CAM)
33. FAST IDLE CAM
34. FLOAT ASSEMBLY
35. POWER VALVE BODY
36. MAIN METERING JET
37. POWER VALVE PIN
38. ACCELERATOR PUMP WEIGHT
39. ACCELERATOR PUMP CHECK BALL
40. POWER VALVE SPRING
41. SPRING
42. LOW IDLE (SOLENOID OFF) ADJUSTING SCREW
43. CHOKE PULLDOWN DIAPHRAGM ASSEMBLY
44. CHOKE DIAPHRAGM VACUUM HOSE
45. FUEL FILTER
46. FUEL INLET NEEDLE & SEAT ASSEMBLY
47. GASKET
48. MAIN BODY ASSEMBLY
49. FLOAT HINGE PIN
50. CURB IDLE ADJUSTING SCREW
51. SPRING
52. SPRING
53. FAST IDLE ADJUSTING SCREW
54. THROTTLE SHAFT & LEVER ASSEMBLY
55. SCREW (2)
56. THROTTLE PLATE
57. THROTTLE BODY ASSEMBLY
58. THROTTLE BODY SCREW (3)
59. THROTTLE BODY GASKET
60. THROTTLE RETURN SPRING BUSHING
61. THROTTLE RETURN SPRING
62. NUT
63. LOCK WASHER
64. THROTTLE RETURN SPRING BRACKET
65. BOWL VENT SOLENOID

65A. WASHER

65B. SPRING

65C. PINTLE

65D. SEAL

66. POWER VALVE PISTON ASSEMBLY

66A. GASKET

67. SCREW (2)
68. IDLE MIXTURE
69. CONCEALMENT PLUG

IDLE MIXTURE NEEDLE

70. FUEL BOWL FILLER

Fig. 1 Disassembled view of Holley Model 1946 one barrel carburetor (Typical)

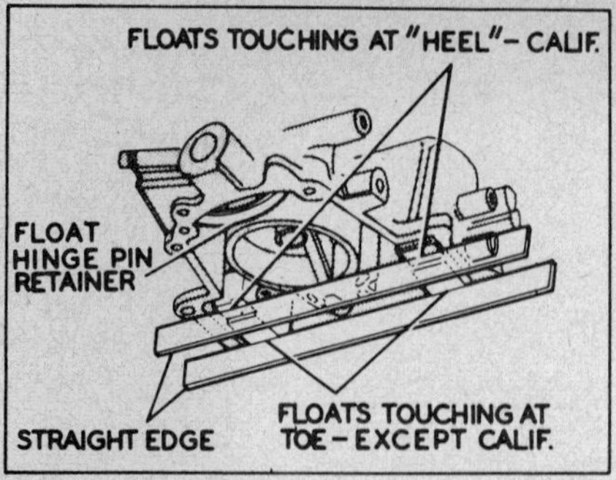

Fig. 2 Float adjustment

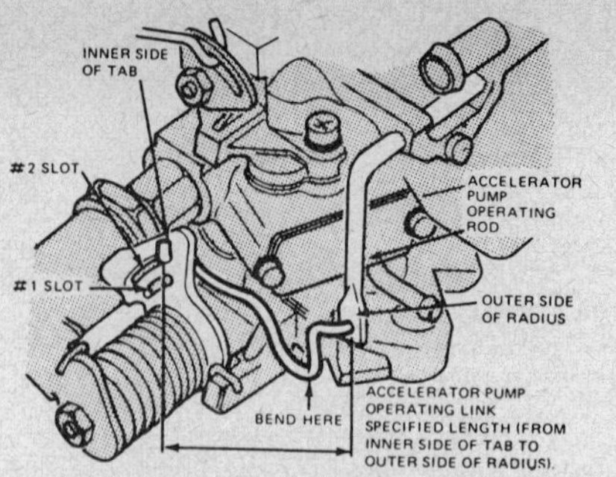

Fig. 3 Accelerator pump adjustment

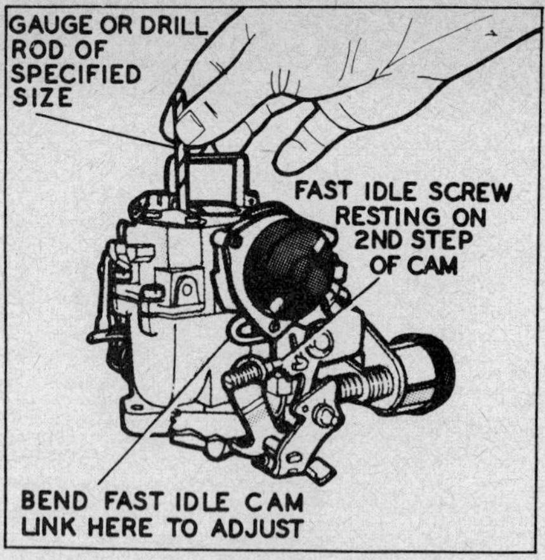

Fig. 4 Fast idle cam adjustment

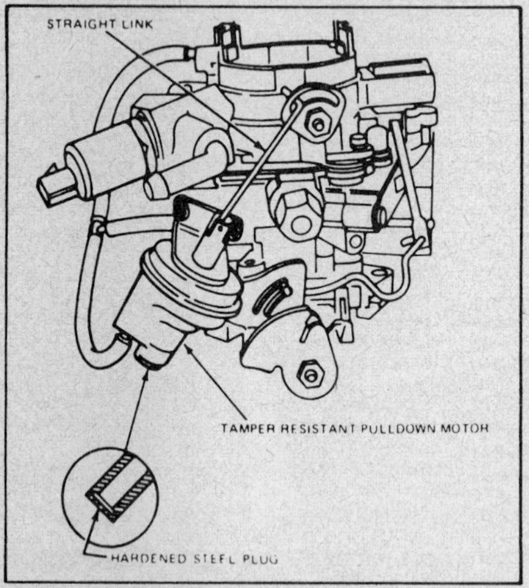

Fig. 5 Choke pulldown adjustment

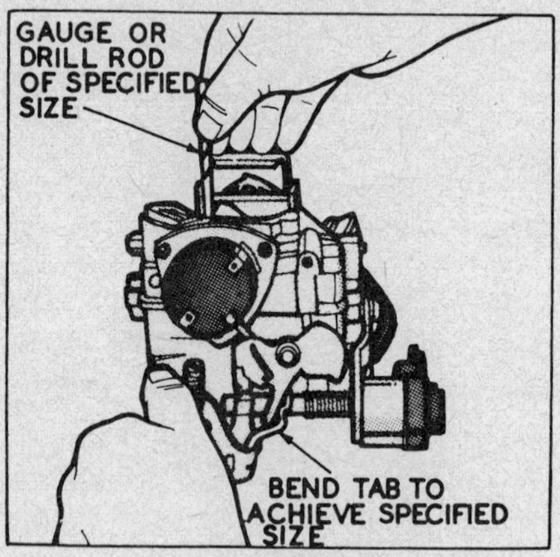

Fig. 6 Dechoke adjustment

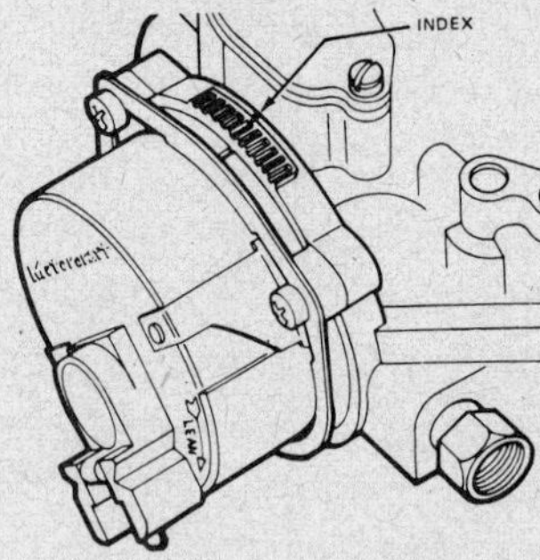

Fig. 7 Choke setting adjustment

IDENTIFICATION LOCATION

The carburetor identification number is located on a tag attached to the carburetor by one of the fuel bowl cover attaching screws.

DESCRIPTION

This carburetor, **Fig. 1,** uses seven basic systems to provide the correct air/fuel mixture under various operating conditions. The systems are as follows: fuel inlet system, idle system, main metering system, power enrichment system, accelerator pump system, external fuel bowl vent system and automatic choke system. The carburetor is divided into three main assemblies which are the air horn assembly, the main body assembly and the throttle body assembly.

The air horn assembly contains the fuel bowl vent, enrichment valve piston and the accelerator pump piston, cup, spring and operating lever. Also contained in the air horn is the choke plate, shaft, lever, housing and choke cap. The idle air bleed and the high speed bleed restrictors are also found in the air horn assembly.

The main body assembly contains the fuel inlet system including the needle and seat assembly, the float, float hinge pin and retainer. The centrally located venturi contains two venturi vacuum boosters and the main discharge passage. The accelerator pump well, passages, check ball and weight, main metering jet, enrichment valve, idle tube and hot idle compensator are also located in the main body assembly. The venturi vacuum pickup tube, manifold vacuum and EGR port vacuum pickup tubes are incorporated in the main body assembly.

The throttle body assembly regulates air flow through the carburetor and provides the mounting flange for the carburetor. The throttle plate, shaft lever and return spring assemblies regulate air flow. Also located in the throttle body assembly are the spark vacuum port, EGR vacuum port, idle transfer slot, curb idle discharge port and the idle mixture adjusting screw.

ON-VEHICLE ADJUSTMENTS

CURB IDLE SPEED

1. Place transmission into Neutral or Park.
2. Start and allow engine to reach normal operating temperature.
3. Place A/C-Heat selector to OFF position, if equipped.
4. Connect suitable tachometer onto engine as per manufacturer's instructions.
5. Check curb idle speed obtained. If idle speed obtained is not as specified, turn curb idle speed adjusting screw until correct idle speed is obtained.

FAST IDLE SPEED

1. Place transmission into Neutral or Park.
2. Start and allow engine to reach normal operating temperature.
3. Disconnect and plug vacuum lines from EGR and purge valves.
4. Connect a suitable tachometer onto engine as per manufacturer's instructions.
5. Place fast idle cam adjustment onto second step of fast idle cam. Check fast idle speed obtained. If speed obtained is not as specified, turn fast idle speed adjusting screw until correct speed is obtained.

FLOAT LEVEL

With air horn removed, place a finger over float hinge pin retainer and invert main body, **Fig. 2.** Do not lose accelerator pump check ball and weight. Using a straightedge, check position of floats. The floats should touch the straightedge at points shown in illustration. On all units, the floats should touch straightedge at the heel. To adjust, bend float tang.

ACCELERATOR PUMP

With the accelerator pump operating link in the specified slot, measure the length of the rod from inner side of tab to outer side of radius. To adjust, bend rod at U-joint, **Fig. 3.**

FAST IDLE CAM POSITION

With fast idle adjusting screw contacting second highest step of fast idle cam, move choke plate toward closed position, **Fig. 4.** Insert specified gauge between upper edge of choke valve and air horn wall. To adjust, bend fast idle cam link.

CHOKE PULLDOWN

The carburetor must be removed from the vehicle to remove the rivets retaining the choke cap to the choke housing. Using a 1/8 inch or No. 30 drill, remove rivet heads, then drive out rivet using a 1/8 inch diameter punch.

Remove choke thermostatic housing, retainer ring and screws, then temporarily remove choke thermostatic housing index spacer. Reinstall choke thermostatic housing, retainer and screws. Loosen choke cover screw, rotate housing 90 degrees in the rich direction and tighten screws. Using an external vacuum source, apply sufficient vacuum to retract vacuum diaphragm. Push on small metal plate in the bottom of the linkage slot to ensure that the diaphragm is fully retracted. Insert specified gauge between upper edge of choke valve and air horn wall. Drill a 3/32 inch hole through pull down motor adjusting screw plug, then remove plug using an easy out, **Fig. 5.** Turn adjusting screw inward or outward as necessary. After completing adjustment, install a replacement plug in adjusting screw access hole.

DECHOKE

With throttle held in wide open position, insert specified gauge between upper edge of choke valve and air horn wall, **Fig. 6.** With light pressure against choke shaft lever, a slight drag should be felt when removing the gauge. To adjust, bend unloader tang on throttle lever.

CHOKE SETTING

Loosen choke cover retaining screws and rotate cover to align mark on cover with specified mark on housing, **Fig. 7.** Tighten choke cover retaining screws.

Holley Model 4180-C 4 Barrel Carburetor

INDEX

ADJUSTMENT SPECIFICATIONS

Year	Carb. Part No.	Float Level (Dry)	Fuel Level (Wet)	Dechoke Clearance	Pulldown Setting	Choke Setting
1983	E3ZE-AUA	①	②	.300	.205	3 Rich
	E3ZE-AUB	①	②	.300	.205	3 Rich
	E3ZE-BGA	①	②	.300	.205	3 Rich
	E3ZE-BGB	①	②	.300	.205	3 Rich
1984	E43ZE-SA	①	②	.300	.205	1 Lean
	E4ZE-YA	①	②	.300	.199	2 Lean
1985	E5ZE-GA	①	②	.300	.178	2 Lean
1986	All	①	②	.300	—	—

①—Refer to text.
②—Bottom of sight plug.

IDENTIFICATION LOCATION

The carburetor identification number is located on a tag attached to the carburetor at the choke shield screw.

DESCRIPTION

The Holley Model 4180-C, **Figs. 1 and 2,** is a four barrel, downdraft, two-stage carburetor. This unit can be considered as two dual carburetors, one which supplies an air/fuel mixture throughout the entire engine operating range (primary stage), and the other which functions only when a greater quantity of air/fuel mixture is needed (secondary stage).

The primary stage contains a fuel bowl, metering block and accelerating pump assembly. Each primary barrel contains a primary and booster venturi, throttle plate, main fuel discharge nozzle and idle fuel passage.

The secondary stage contains a fuel bowl, metering body and secondary throttle operating diaphragm assembly. The secondary barrels each contain a primary and booster venturi, throttle plate, idle fuel passages, main secondary fuel discharge nozzle and a transfer system fuel passage from the primary fuel bowl.

A constant fuel supply is provided to fuel metering systems by a fuel inlet system for both primary and secondary stages. A fuel balance tube is not used.

ON-VEHICLE ADJUSTMENTS

CURB IDLE SPEED

1. Place transmission into Neutral or Park.
2. Start and allow engine to reach normal operating temperature.
3. Place A/C-Heat selector switch to OFF position.

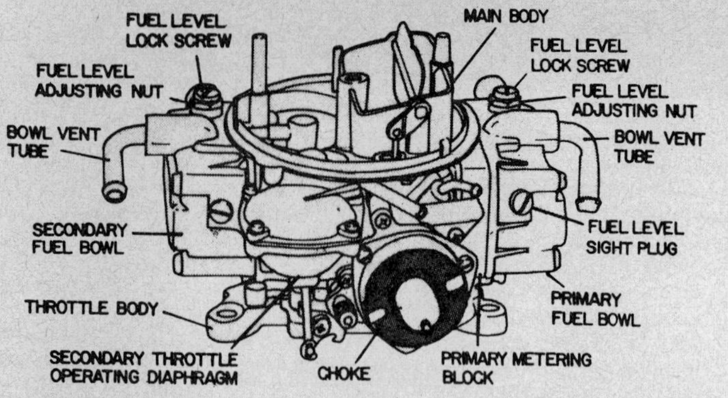

Fig. 1 Right side view of Holley model 4180-C carburetor. 1983 shown, 1984–86 similar

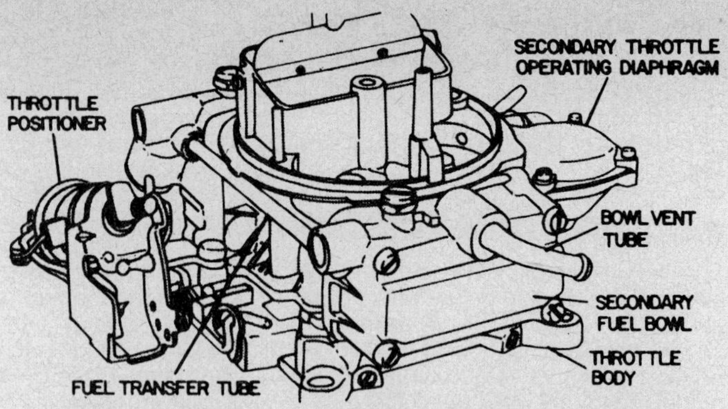

Fig. 2 Left side view of Holley model 4180-C carburetor. 1983 shown, 1984–86 similar

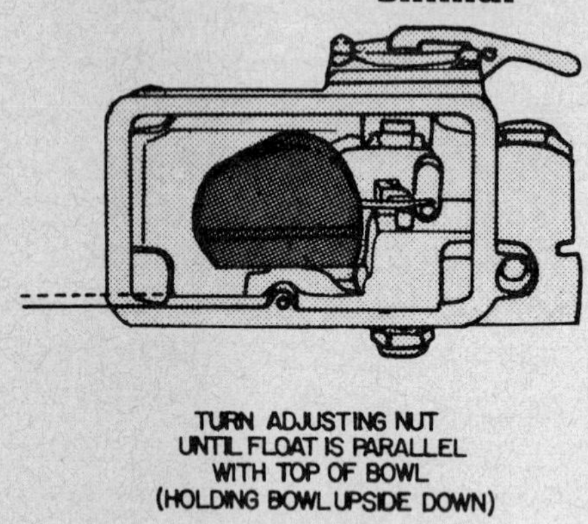

Fig. 3 Dry float level adjustment

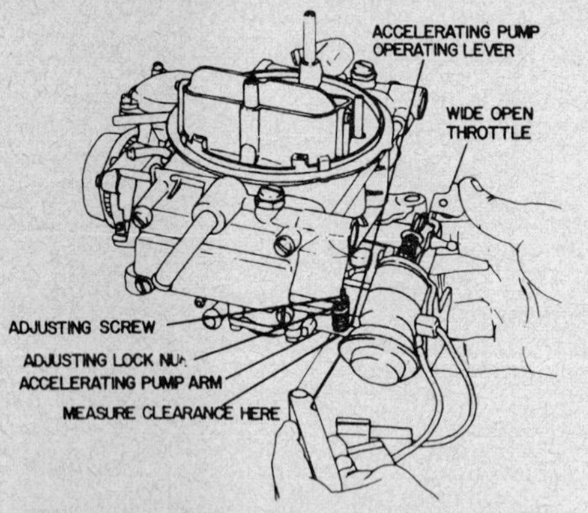

Fig. 5 Accelerating pump lever adjustment

4. Connect a suitable tachometer onto engine as per manufacturer's instructions.
5. Check curb idle speed obtained. If curb idle speed obtained is not as specified, turn curb idle speed adjusting screw.

FAST IDLE SPEED

1. Place transmission into Neutral or Park.
2. Start and allow engine to reach normal operating temperature.
3. Connect a suitable tachometer onto engine as per manufacturer's instructions.
4. Disconnect and plug vacuum hose from EGR or EGR/PVS valve.
5. Place fast idle adjustment onto specified step of fast idle cam. Check fast idle speed obtained. If fast idle speed obtained is not as specified, turn fast idle speed adjusting screw until specified speed is obtained.

FLOAT LEVEL (DRY)

This is a preliminary adjustment only, and final adjustment must be made after carburetor is installed on engine.

With float assemblies and fuel bowls removed, adjust floats so they are parallel to the fuel bowls with the tops of the fuel bowls inverted, **Fig. 3.**

FUEL LEVEL (WET)

1. With vehicle resting on a flat surface, operate engine until normal operating temperature is reached.
2. Remove air cleaner, then operate engine at approximately 1000 RPM for 30 seconds to stabilize fuel level.
3. Stop engine, then remove sight plug from side of primary carburetor bowl.
4. Fuel level should be at bottom of sight plug hole. If fuel level is below sight plug hole, raise fuel level. If fuel overflows when plug is removed, lower fuel level. **Never loosen lock screw or nut or attempt to adjust fuel level with sight plug removed or engine running, as this will create a potential fire hazard.**
5. Adjust fuel level as necessary by loosening lock screw, then turning adjusting nut clockwise to lower fuel level or counterclockwise to raise fuel level, **Fig. 4.** Tighten lock screw and install sight plug, using old gasket, then run engine at 1000 RPM for approximately 30 seconds to stabilize fuel level. **Each 1/6 turn of the adjusting nut will change fuel level approximately 1/32 inch.**
6. Stop engine, remove sight plug and recheck fuel level. Repeat step 5 until fuel level is at bottom of sight plug hole, then reinstall sight plug using a new gasket.
7. Perform steps 3 through 6 for secondary fuel bowl. **To stabilize fuel level in the secondary fuel bowl, the secondary throttle must be used.**

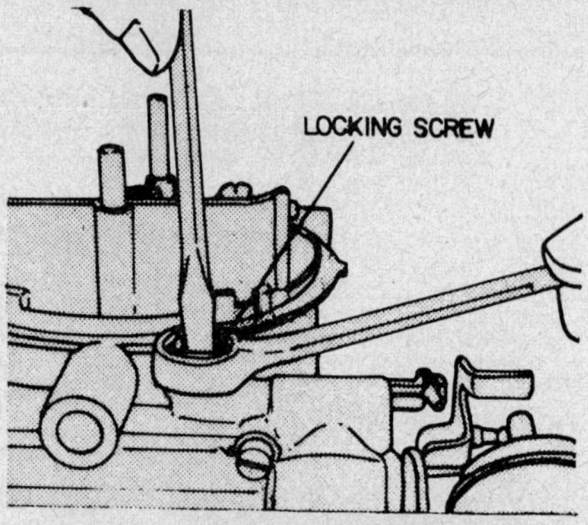

Fig. 4 Wet fuel level adjustment

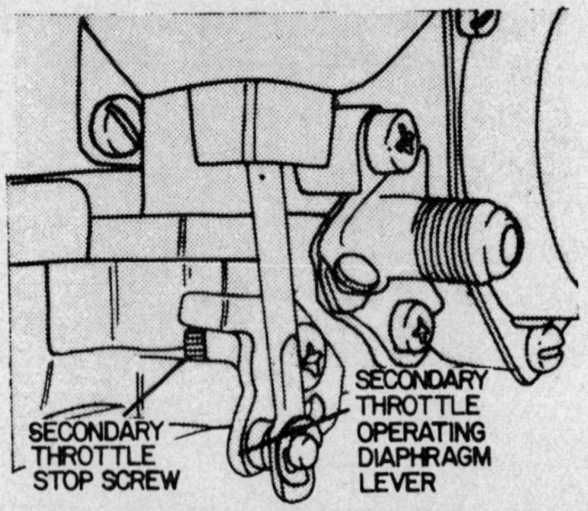

Fig. 6 Secondary throttle plate adjustment

ACCELERATING PUMP LEVER

With throttle plates in the wide open position, and pump arm manually depressed, insert a feeler gauge of the specified thickness between operating lever adjustment screw head and pump arm, **Fig. 5.** Adjust clearance as necessary by loosening the lock screw, then turning the adjusting nut while holding the screw. Turn the adjusting nut in to increase clearance or out to decrease clearance. When proper clearance is obtained, hold nut and tighten screw. Note that 1/2 turn of the adjusting nut is equal to approximately .015 inch.

SECONDARY THROTTLE PLATE

With carburetor removed from engine, hold secondary throttle plates closed, then turn secondary throttle shaft lever adjusting screw out until throttle plates seat in throttle bores, **Fig. 6.** Turn adjusting screw in until it just makes contact with secondary lever, then turn screw in an additional 1/4 turn.

CHOKE PULLDOWN

Remove choke thermostat housing, gasket and retainer, then insert specified gauge into choke piston bore. While holding choke valve toward closed position, measure choke pulldown clearance between air horn wall and lower edge of choke valve. Adjust by turning screw, clockwise to decrease clearance or counterclockwise to increase clearance.

CHOKE

Loosen choke thermostat cover retaining screws, rotate cover to align mark on cover with specified mark on housing, and tighten cover screws.

Holley Model 6149 1 Barrel Carburetor

INDEX

ADJUSTMENT SPECIFICATIONS

Year	Model No.	Choke Pulldown Setting	Fast Idle Cam Index	Dechoke Setting	Choke Setting	Float Level
1984	E43E-VA	.095-.135①	.020-.030	.180-.220	2 Rich	②
	E43E-VB	.140-.180①	.020-.030	.180-.220	2 Rich	②
	E43E-ZA	.100-.140①	.020-.030	.180-.220	2 Rich	②
	E43E-ZG	.140-.180①	.020-.030	.180-.220	2 Rich	②
	E43E-ZH	.140-.180①	.020-.030	.180-.220	2 Rich	②

①—With modulator spring compressed.
②—Both float pontoons at outboard edge flush with surface of main body casting less gasket.

IDENTIFICATION LOCATION

The carburetor identification number is located on a tag attached to the carburetor by one of the fuel bowl cover attaching screws.

DESCRIPTION

The model 6149 carburetor, **Fig. 1**, is a single barrel, booster type, feedback unit. The carburetor uses twelve basic systems to provide the correct air/fuel mixture under various operating conditions. The systems are: fuel inlet system, idle system, idle transfer system, main metering system, feedback system, auxiliary main metering system, wide open throttle (WOT) pullover enrichment system, accelerator pump system, choke system, throttle position sensor (TPS) system, hot idle compensator (HIC) valve system and mechanical fuel bowl vent system.

ON-VEHICLE ADJUSTMENTS

CURB IDLE SPEED

1. Place transmission into Neutral or Park.
2. Disconnect and plug throttle kicker vacuum line.
3. Install a suitable tachometer onto engine as per manufacturer's instructions.
4. Start and allow engine to reach normal operating temperature. Ensure cooling fan is On.
5. Place A/C selector switch to OFF position.
6. Using a suitable jumper wire, activate cooling fan by grounding control wire.
7. Check curb idle speed obtained. If curb idle speed obtained is not as specified, turn idle speed adjusting screw until specified speed is obtained.

FAST IDLE SPEED

1. Place transmission into Neutral or Park.
2. Install a suitable tachometer onto engine as per manufacturer's instructions.
3. Place fast idle adjustment onto second step of fast idle cam, then start and allow engine to reach normal operating temperature.
4. Return throttle to normal position.
5. Place A/C selector switch to OFF position.
6. Disconnect and plug EGR valve vacuum line.
7. Place fast idle screw onto specified step of fast idle cam.
8. Check fast idle speed. If fast idle speed is not as specified, turn fast idle speed screw until specified speed is obtained.

FLOAT LEVEL

With air horn removed, place a finger over float hinge pin retainer and invert main body. Use care not to lose accelerator pump check ball and weight. Using a straightedge, **Fig. 2**, check position of floats. The extreme outside edge of floats should be flush with surface of main body casting without gasket. Adjust as necessary by bending float tabs to raise or lower float level. After completing adjustment, invert main body and ensure float moves freely without contacting fuel bowl walls.

ACCELERATOR PUMP

Measure length of accelerator pump operating stroke from inside edge at pump operating rod to inside edge at throttle lever hole, **Fig. 3.** Adjust as necessary by bending loop in operating link.

MECHANICAL FUEL BOWL VENT

Off Vehicle

With choke plate secured wide open, set

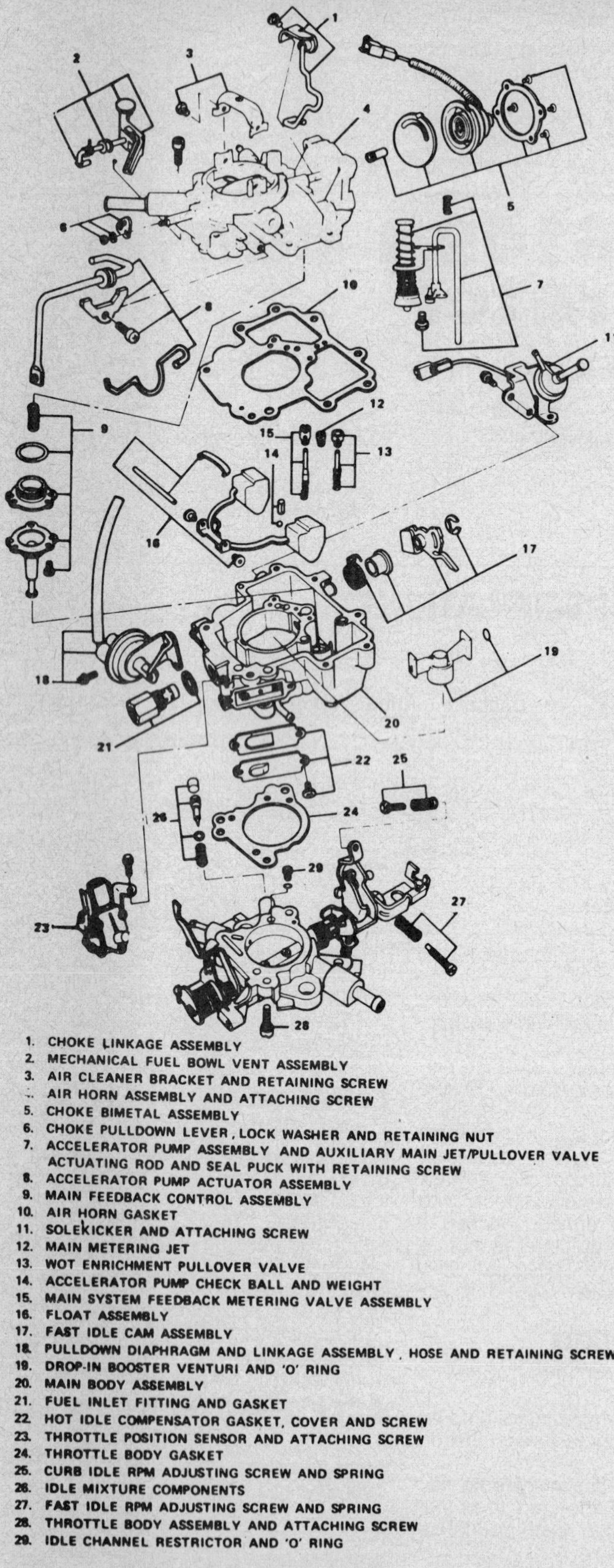

1. CHOKE LINKAGE ASSEMBLY
2. MECHANICAL FUEL BOWL VENT ASSEMBLY
3. AIR CLEANER BRACKET AND RETAINING SCREW
4. AIR HORN ASSEMBLY AND ATTACHING SCREW
5. CHOKE BIMETAL ASSEMBLY
6. CHOKE PULLDOWN LEVER, LOCK WASHER AND RETAINING NUT
7. ACCELERATOR PUMP ASSEMBLY AND AUXILIARY MAIN JET/PULLOVER VALVE ACTUATING ROD AND SEAL PUCK WITH RETAINING SCREW
8. ACCELERATOR PUMP ACTUATOR ASSEMBLY
9. MAIN FEEDBACK CONTROL ASSEMBLY
10. AIR HORN GASKET
11. SOLEKICKER AND ATTACHING SCREW
12. MAIN METERING JET
13. WOT ENRICHMENT PULLOVER VALVE
14. ACCELERATOR PUMP CHECK BALL AND WEIGHT
15. MAIN SYSTEM FEEDBACK METERING VALVE ASSEMBLY
16. FLOAT ASSEMBLY
17. FAST IDLE CAM ASSEMBLY
18. PULLDOWN DIAPHRAGM AND LINKAGE ASSEMBLY, HOSE AND RETAINING SCREW
19. DROP-IN BOOSTER VENTURI AND 'O' RING
20. MAIN BODY ASSEMBLY
21. FUEL INLET FITTING AND GASKET
22. HOT IDLE COMPENSATOR GASKET, COVER AND SCREW
23. THROTTLE POSITION SENSOR AND ATTACHING SCREW
24. THROTTLE BODY GASKET
25. CURB IDLE RPM ADJUSTING SCREW AND SPRING
26. IDLE MIXTURE COMPONENTS
27. FAST IDLE RPM ADJUSTING SCREW AND SPRING
28. THROTTLE BODY ASSEMBLY AND ATTACHING SCREW
29. IDLE CHANNEL RESTRICTOR AND 'O' RING

Fig. 1 Exploded view of Holley Model 6149 carburetor

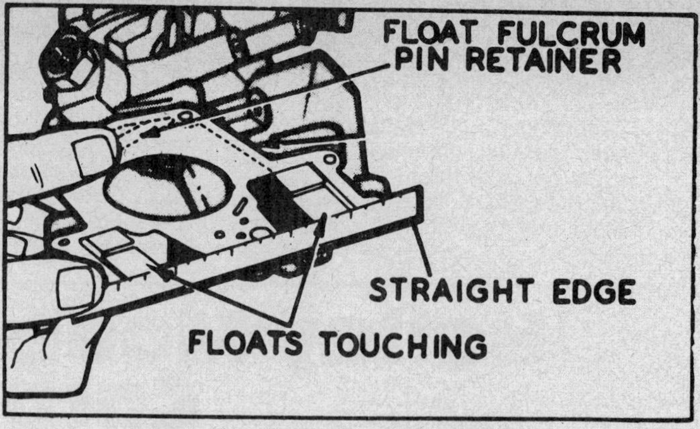

Fig. 2 Float adjustment

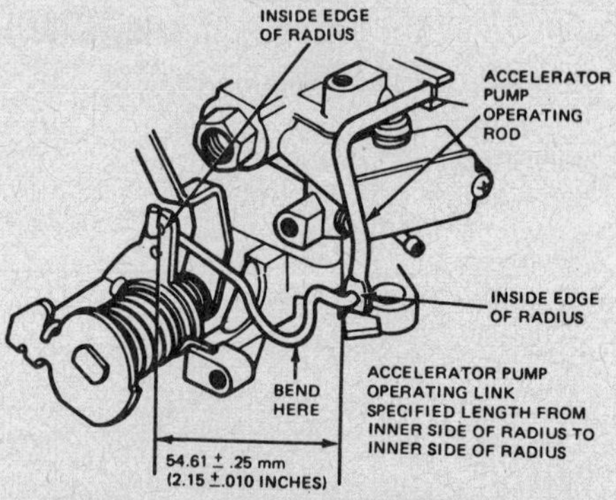

Fig. 3 Accelerator pump adjustment

throttle at TSP Off position. Turn TSP Off adjustment screw counterclockwise until throttle plate is closed in throttle bore. Adjust as necessary by bending fuel bowl vent actuator lever until specified clearance is obtained, **Fig. 4.** Do not bend fuel bowl vent arm and/or adjacent part of actuator lever.

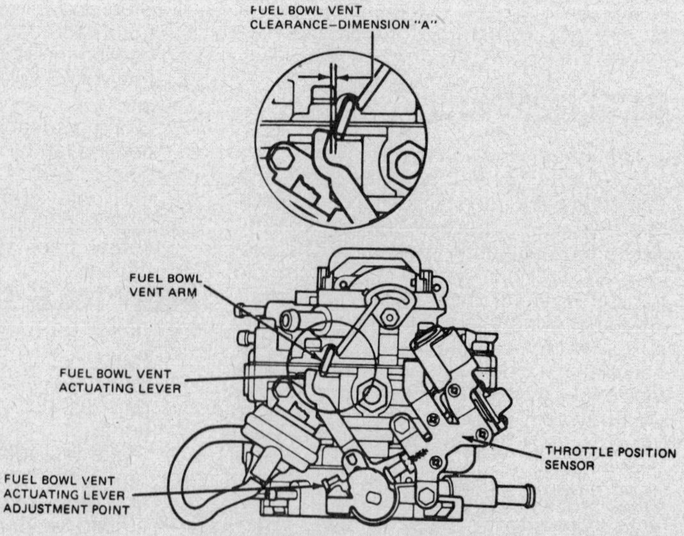

Fig. 4 Mechanical fuel bowl vent adjustment

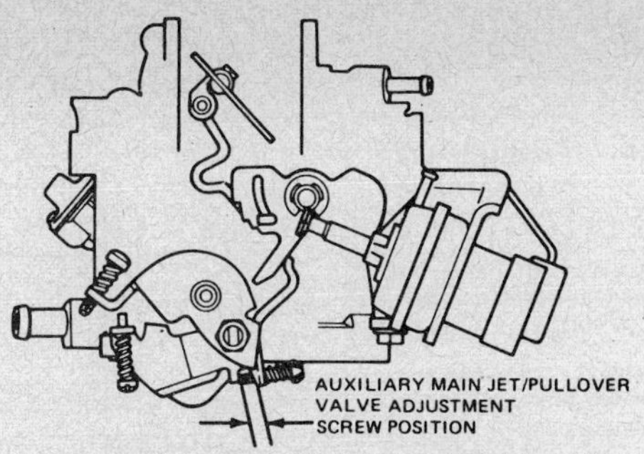

Fig. 5 Auxiliary main jet/pullover valve timing adjustment

On Vehicle

Curb idle speed must be adjusted to specifications before performing this adjustment.

With choke plate secured wide open, turn ignition On to activate TSP (engine not running). Open throttle to extend TSP plunger and ensure throttle is in idle set position, contacting TSP plunger. Measure clearance between fuel bowl vent arm and bowl vent actuating lever, **Fig. 4.** Adjust as necessary by bending bowl vent actuator until specified clearance is obtained. Do not bend fuel bowl vent arm and/or adjacent part of actuator lever.

AUXILIARY MAIN JET/PULLOVER VALVE TIMING

Measure protrusion of adjustment screw at rear of throttle pickup lever, **Fig. 5.** Adjust as necessary by turning screw until protrusion measures .335-.355 inch.

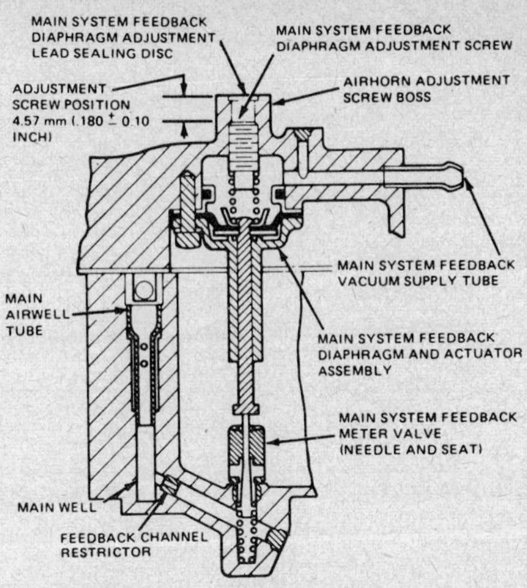

Fig. 6 Feedback controlled main system diapragm adjustment

FEEDBACK CONTROLLED MAIN SYSTEM DIAPHRAGM

Drill a 3/32 inch hole through lead sealing disc on diaphragm adjustment screw, then pry disc off using a suitable punch. Adjust as necessary by turning adjustment screw until top of screw is .170-.190 inch below top of air horn adjustment screw boss, **Fig. 6.** On carburetors with an "S" stamped on top of air horn, adjust to .240-.260 inch. Install a new lead sealing disc and secure by staking with a suitable punch. After completing adjustment, apply a maximum vacuum of 10 inches Hg and ensure diaphragm does not leak.

Holley Model 6500 2 Barrel Carburetor

INDEX

IDENTIFICATION LOCATION

The carburetor identification number is located on a tag attached to the carburetor by one of the fuel bowl cover attaching screws.

DESCRIPTION

The Holley Model 6500 carburetor, **Fig. 1,** is used with the Ford Feedback Electronic Engine Control System. This carburetor is basically the same as the Motorcraft Model 5200 as described elsewhere in this chapter. The Model 6500 is equipped with an externally variable auxiliary fuel metering system in place of the enrichment valve used on the Motorcraft Model 5200. The auxiliary system consists of a metering valve assembly, metering valve operating piston and a diaphragm.

The feedback metering valve supplements fuel entering the main well through the conventional metering jet and channel. The amount of fuel entering the main well through the metering valve depends on the position of the tapered metering rod in the orifice, **Fig. 2.** The position of the metering rod depends on the metering rod operation piston assembly.

Control vacuum from the vacuum regulator solenoid is transmitted to the cavity above the metering rod diaphragm. When no vacuum is present, the valve spring causes the valve to move to the lowest (richest) position and maximum fuel can pass through the orifice. As vacuum is applied to the diaphragm, spring pressure is overcome and the metering rod rises, reducing the orifice area and less fuel passes through the orifice. The metering valve is calibrated so the maximum vacuum signal supplied by the vacuum regulator solenoid raises the rod to the highest (leanest) position.

ON-VEHICLE ADJUSTMENTS

All adjustments for the Model 6500 are the same as the Motorcraft Model 5200 as described elsewhere in this chapter, however, the choke plate vacuum pulldown adjustment is different.

CHOKE PLATE VACUUM PULLDOWN ADJUSTMENT

It is necessary to remove the carburetor from the vehicle to remove rivets retaining the choke cover to choke housing. Using a 1/8 inch or No. 30 drill bit, remove rivet heads, then drive rivets out using a 1/8 inch diameter punch.

ADJUSTMENT SPECIFICATIONS

Year	Carb. Model	Float Level	Pump Level Hole No.	Choke Plate Pulldown	Fast Idle Cam Clearance	Dechoke	Choke Setting
1982	E2ZE-ACA	15/32	3	.276	.118	.394	—
	E2ZE-ADA	15/32	3	.276	.118	.394	—
	E2ZE-APA	15/32	2	.276	.118	.394	—
	E2ZE-ARA	15/32	2	.276	.118	.394	—
	E2ZE-UA	15/32	3	.276	.118	.394	—
	E2ZE-VA	15/32	3	.276	.118	.394	—

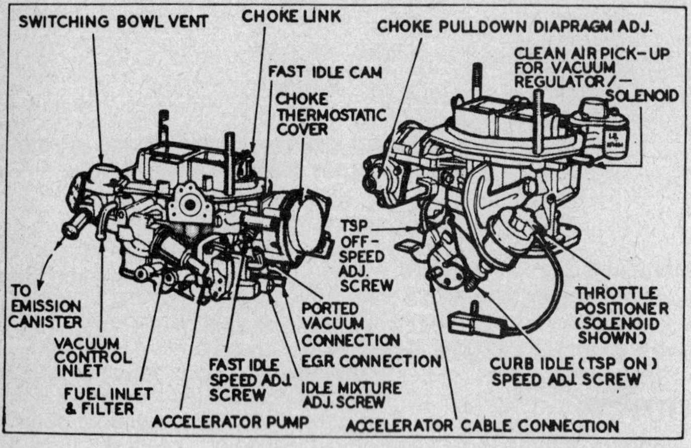

Fig. 1 Model 6500 carburetor

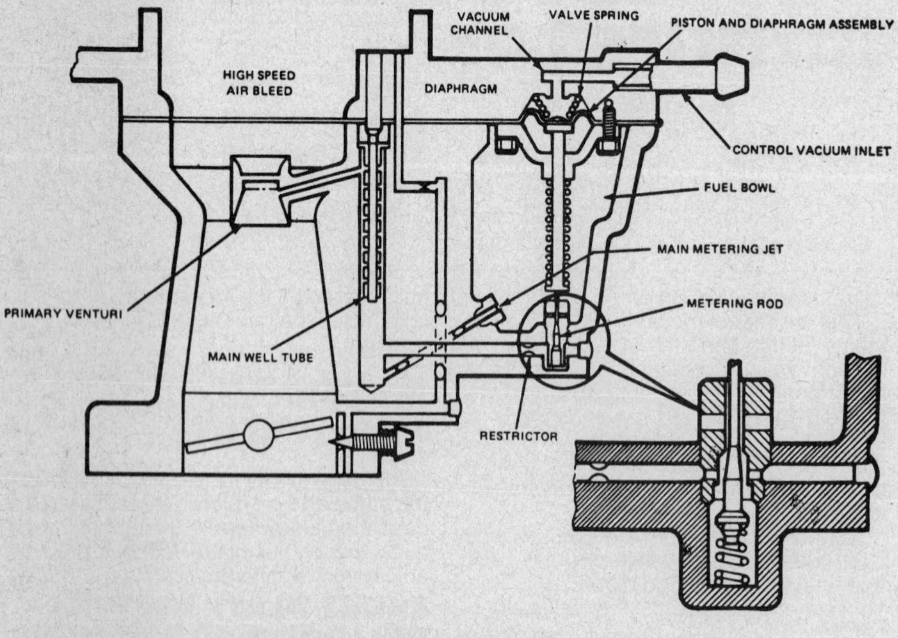

Fig. 2 Fuel metering system

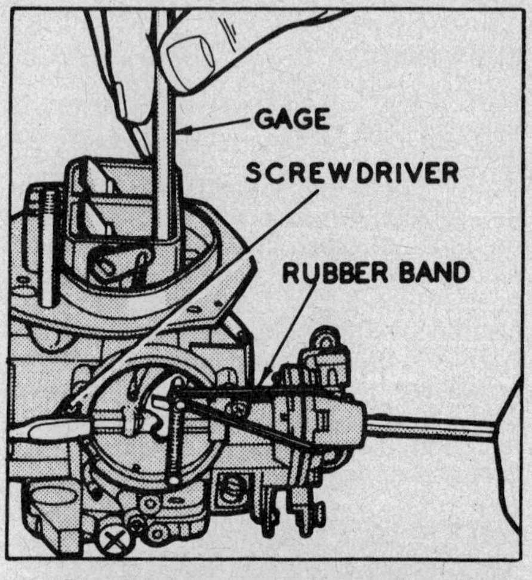

Fig. 3 Measuring choke plate vacuum pulldown

1. Remove choke cap, bi-metal heater assembly and plastic shield.
2. Place fast idle speed adjusting screw on top step of fast idle cam.
3. Using a suitable screwdriver, push diaphragm stem back against stop and place specified gauge between lower edge of choke valve and air horn wall, **Fig. 3.**
4. Remove slack from choke linkage by attaching a rubber band to choke operating lever, **Fig. 3.**
5. To adjust, rotate vacuum diaphragm adjusting screw as required to obtain proper setting, **Fig. 4.**

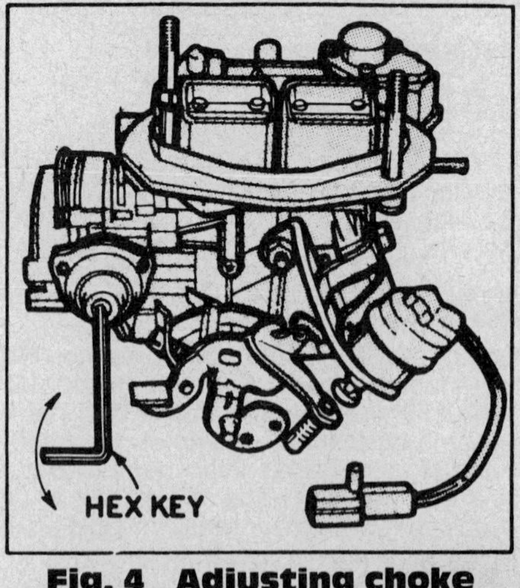

Fig. 4 Adjusting choke plate vacuum pulldown

Motorcraft Model 740 2 Barrel Carburetor

INDEX

IDENTIFICATION LOCATION

The carburetor identification number is located on a tag attached to the carburetor by one of the fuel bowl cover attaching screws.

DESCRIPTION

The Motorcraft Model 740 carburetor, **Fig. 1**, consists of five basic systems: choke system, idle system, main metering system, acceleration system and power enrichment system.

The choke system is used for cold engine starting and consists of a bi-metallic spring and an electric heater. The idle system is adjustable and provides for the proper air/fuel ratio for both idle and low speed operation. The main metering system provides the correct air/fuel ratio for normal cruising speeds. A main metering system is used for primary and secondary stage operation. The acceleration system consists of a diaphragm type pump that is mechanically operated by the primary throttle linkage. This system provides fuel-to the primary stage during acceleration. The power enrichment system consists of a vacuum operated power valve and a secondary stage pull over system that is regulated by air flow. This system is used together with the main metering system to provide proper vehicle operation during periods of moderate to heavy acceleration. The distributor and EGR vacuum ports are located in the primary venturi area of the carburetor.

FUEL INLET SYSTEM

The fuel inlet system maintains a specified fuel level in the fuel bowl, allowing the fuel metering system to deliver the correct air/fuel mixture to the engine. The fuel inlet needle position is controlled by a float and lever assembly hinged on the float pin. The amount of fuel entering the bowl is regulated by the distance the inlet needle is moved off its seat. When the float drops, it causes the inlet needle to drop and this allows additional fuel to enter the bowl. As the fuel level reaches a specified level, the inlet needle is raised to a position that will allow only enough fuel to enter to replace that being used by the metering systems. The float bowl uses a solenoid valve to operate the dual venting system, **Fig. 2.** When the ignition is On, the bowl is vented internally to the air cleaner. This balances the bowl with carburetor inlet air. When the ignition is Off, the bowl is vented externally, and fuel vapors are stored in the carbon canister to be drawn into the engine when the engine is started.

IDLE SYSTEM

Fuel for idle and off idle operation flows from the bowl through the primary main metering jet into the main well. Fuel then flows through an idle fuel restriction and is mixed with air entering through the primary idle air bleed. This air/fuel mixture travels past the idle transfer holes which serve asadditional air bleeds during curb idle. The air/fuel mixture then moves past the idle mixture screw tip which controls the amount of mixture discharged into the engine from below the throttle plate. At speeds slightly above idle, the idle transfer holes begin discharging additional air/fuel mixture. This occurs because the increased opening of the throttle plates exposes the idle transfer holes to intake manifold vacuum. As the throttle opening and engine speed increase, air flow through the carburetor is increased. This creates a vacuum in the venturi causing the main metering system to begin operation.

FUEL SHUT-OFF SYSTEM

When the ignition switch is in the On position, the fuel shut off system solenoid is in the operational position. This allows fuel to flow through the idle system of the carburetor. When the ignition switch is in the Off position, the solenoid releases, stopping the flow of fuel to the carburetor idle system.

Fuel flow through the idle system is shut off during deceleration as vehicle and engine sensors provide a signal to deenergize the idle fuel solenoid. The solenoid is automatically energized by the sensors to allow the engine to idle when necessary.

MAIN METERING SYSTEM

As engine speed increases, air velocity through the booster venturi creates a vacuum in the venturi. Fuel begins to flow through the main metering system due to high pressure in the bowl and low pressure at the main discharge nozzle. Fuel flows from the fuel bowl through the main jet and into the main well. Then the fuel travels up the main well tube where it is mixed with air. Air, supplied through the high speed air bleed, mixes with the fuel through small holes in the sides of the main well tubes. The proper air fuel ratio is maintained because the high speed air bleed meters an increased amount of air whenever venturi vacuum increases. As the air/fuel mixture moves to the discharge port, it is discharged into the booster venturi.

SECONDARY PROGRESSION

When the primary throttle plate is opened approximately 45°, the secondary throttle plate begins to open, **Fig. 3.** The air/fuel mixture begins flowing from the secondary transfer holes as they are exposed to manifold vacuum. As the throttle plates are opened further, the secondary main metering system begins to operate. This system is similar to the primary main metering system.

ACCELERATOR PUMP SYSTEM

When the throttle plates are opened quickly, air flows through the carburetor almost immediately. Because fuel is heavier than air, there is a brief time lag before fuel flow can gain enough speed to maintain proper air/fuel ratio. During this lag, the accelerator pump system supplies the necessary extra fuel to maintain correct air/fuel ratio until the other metering systems can respond. When the throttle plates are opened, the diaphragm rod is pushed upward, forcing fuel from the pump chamber into the discharge passage. Fuel under pressure moves the discharge check ball off its seat. This fuel then travels through the pump discharge valve where it enters the primary venturi through the pump discharge nozzle.

PRIMARY POWER ENRICHMENT SYSTEM

The air/fuel ratio must be increased during periods of heavy acceleration or high speed operation. The power enrichment system, controlled by intake manifold vacuum, supplies extra fuel during these operating conditions. Manifold vacuum is applied to the power valve diaphragm from an opening in the carburetor base where it is connected by passages in the main

ADJUSTMENT SPECIFICATIONS

Year	Carb. Model ①	Float Level (Dry)	Float Drop	Choke Pulldown Clearance	Fast Idle Cam Clearance	Dechoke Clearance	Dash Pot Clearance	Choke Setting ②
1982	E1EE-ALA, APA	.250	—	.157	.079	.138	.157	1 Lean
	E1EE-NA, ZA	.250	—	.157	.079	.138	.157	1 Lean
	E1GE-CA, DA	.250	—	.118	.079	.138	.138	Index
	E1GE-EA, GA	.250	—	.157	.079	.138	.157	1 Lean
	E2EE-AGA, AHA	.250	—	.138	.079	.138	.157	Index
	E2EE-JA, LC	.250	—	.138	.079	.138	.059	Index
	E2EE-JC	.295	—	.256	.079	.138	.157	Index
	E2EE-GA	.250	—	.138	.079	.138	.059	Index
	E2EE-GC	.250	—	.138	.079	.138	.138	Index
	E2EE-LA, MA	.250	—	.138	.079	.138	.157	Index
	E2EE-LC	.250	—	.177	.079	.138	.157	Index
	E2EE-MC, NC	.250	—	.177	.079	.138	.157	Index
	E2EE-NA, PA	.250	—	.138	.079	.138	.157	Index
	E2EE-PC	.250	—	.177	.079	.138	—	Index
	E2EE-SA	.250	—	.138	.079	.138	.059	Index
	E2EE-VA	.250	—	.138	.079	.138	.157	1 Lean
	E2EE-YA	.250	—	.138	.079	.138	.157	1 Lean
	E2EE-ZA	.250	—	.156	.079	.138	.157	1 Lean
	E2GE-AA	.250	—	.167	.079	.138	.157	Index
1983	E3EE-AA	.295	1.693	.138	.079	.138	.157	—
	E3EE-BA	.295	1.693	.295	.079	.138	.157	—
	E3EE-CA	.295	1.693	.315	.079	.138	.098	—
	E3EE-DA	.295	1.693	.335	.079	.138	.079	—
	E3EE-EA	.295	1.693	.315	.079	.138	.098	—
	E3EE-GB	.295	1.693	.256	.079	.138	.138	—
	E3EE-JA	.295	1.693	.138	.079	.138	.157	—
	E3EE-KA	.295	1.693	.295	.079	.138	.157	—
	E3EE-NA	.295	1.693	.295	.079	.138	—	—
	E3EE-PA	.295	1.693	.295	.079	.138	.157	—
	E3GE-DA	.295	1.693	.325	.079	.138	—	—
	E3GE-DC	.295	1.693	.325	.079	.138	—	—
	E3GE-FA	.295	1.693	.325	.079	.138	—	—
	E3GE-FC	.295	1.693	.325	.079	.138	—	—
	E3GE-HA	.295	1.693	.325	.079	.138	—	—
	E3GE-HC	.295	1.693	.325	.079	.138	—	—
	E3GE-JA	.295	1.693	.325	.079	.138	.157	—
	E3GE-JC	.295	1.693	.325	.079	.138	—	—
	E3GE-KB	.295	1.693	.295	.079	.138	.157	—
	E3GE-KD	.295	1.693	.295	.079	.138	.157	—
	E3GE-LA	.295	1.693	.295	.079	.138	.157	—
	E3GE-LC	.295	1.693	.295	.079	.138	.157	—
	E3GE-MA	.295	1.693	.276	.098	.138	.157	—
	E3GE-NA	.295	1.693	.276	.098	.138	.157	—
	E3GE-PA	.295	1.693	.256	.079	.138	.157	—
	E3GE-RA	.295	1.693	.256	.079	.138	.157	—
	E3GE-SA	.295	1.693	.256	.079	.138	.157	—
	E3GE-UA	.295	1.693	.276	.098	.138	.157	—

ADJUSTMENT SPECIFICATIONS—Continued

Year	Carb. Model ①	Float Level (Dry)	Float Drop	Choke Pulldown Clearance	Fast Idle Cam Clearance	Dechoke Clearance	Dash Pot Clearance	Choke Setting ②
1984	E4EE-AAA	.295	1.693	.315	.098	.138	.098	—
	E4EE-ABA	.295	1.693	.315	.098	.138	.098	—
	E4EE-ACA	.295	1.693	.315	.079	.138	.079	—
	E4EE-ADA	.295	1.693	.256	.079	.138	.138	—
	E4EE-AFA	.295	1.693	.216	.079	.138	—	—
	E4EE-YA	.295	1.693	.315	.098	.138	.098	—
	E4GE-AAA	.295	1.693	.256	.106	.138	—	—
	E4GE-KA	.295	1.693	.295	.079	.138	.157	—
	E4GE-LA	.295	1.693	.295	.079	.138	.157	—
	E4GE-MA	.295	1.693	.295	.177	.138	.157	—
	E4GE-RA	.295	1.693	.325	.128	.138	—	—
	E4GE-SA	.295	1.693	.276	.098	.138	.157	—
	E4GE-TA	.295	1.693	.295	.128	.138	—	—
	E4GE-UA	.295	1.693	.325	.079	.138	—	—
	E4GE-ZA	.295	1.693	.256	.106	.138	—	—
1985	E4EE-AAA	.295	1.693	.315	.098	.138	.098	—
	E4EE-ABA	.295	1.693	.315	.098	.138	.098	—
	E4EE-ACA	.295	1.693	.315	.098	.138	.079	—
	E4EE-YA	.295	1.693	.315	.098	.138	.098	—
	E4GE-AAA	.295	1.693	.256	.106	.138	—	—
	E4GE-ACA	.295	1.693	.285	.130	.138	—	—
	E4GE-KA	.295	1.693	.295	.138	.138	.157	—
	E4GE-LA	.295	1.693	.295	.138	.138	.157	—
	E4GE-MA	.295	1.693	.295	.177	.138	.157	—
	E4GE-ZA	.295	1.693	.256	.106	.138	—	—

①—Stamped on tag attached to bowl cover.

②—Tamper-resistant.

body to the diaphragm. During idle and light load conditions, high manifold vacuum overcomes the force of the power valve spring and the valve is held closed. When the throttle opening is increased and intake manifold vacuum drops, the valve opens and fuel flows from the bowl through the power valve into the primary main well. This extra fuel is then added to the main metering system fuel to provide the increased air/fuel ratio necessary for high speed or heavy load operation.

SECONDARY POWER ENRICHMENT SYSTEM

The secondary system is provided with an air velocity operated power system for fuel enrichment, **Fig. 4**. As the secondary throttle plate nears wide open position, air velocity through the secondary venturi creates a low pressure area at the discharge opening in the air horn. Fuel flows from the bowl through a vertical channel. During this time, air enters through a calibrated air bleed and mixes with the fuel, and this mixture is discharged through the opening.

ON-VEHICLE ADJUSTMENTS

CURB IDLE SPEED

1982

1. Place transmission into Neutral or Park.
2. Start and allow engine to reach normal operating temperature.
3. Install a suitable tachometer onto engine as per manufacturer's instructions.
4. Position fast idle adjustment onto second step of fast idle cam, then operate engine until cooling fan comes ON.
5. Depress throttle slightly to allow fast idle cam to rotate, and check curb idle speed.
6. If curb idle speed is not as specified, turn idle speed adjusting screw until correct idle speed is obtained. **The engine cooling fan must be operating when checking curb idle speed.**

1983–85

1. Place transmission into Neutral or Park.
2. Start and allow engine to reach normal operating temperature.
3. On models with vacuum operated throttle modulator (VOTM), proceed as follows:
   a. Position A/C heater selector in heat and blower switch on high.
   b. Disconnect vacuum hose from VOTM, then plug.
   c. Install slave vacuum hose from intake manifold vacuum to VOTM.
4. Disconnect and plug vacuum hose from thermactor air control valve bypass.
5. Install a suitable tachometer onto engine as per manufacturer's instructions.
6. On models with VOTM, run engine until cooling fan comes on.
7. On models less VOTM, position fast idle adjustment onto the second highest step of fast idle cam, then operate engine until cooling fan comes ON.
8. Depress throttle slightly to allow fast idle cam to rotate, then check curb idle speed.
9. On models without idle speed control, proceed as follows:
   a. If curb idle speed is not as specified, turn idle speed adjusting screw until specified idle speed is obtained.
   b. Position transmission into Neutral or Park and recheck curb idle speed.
10. On models with mechanical vacuum idle speed control, proceed as follows:

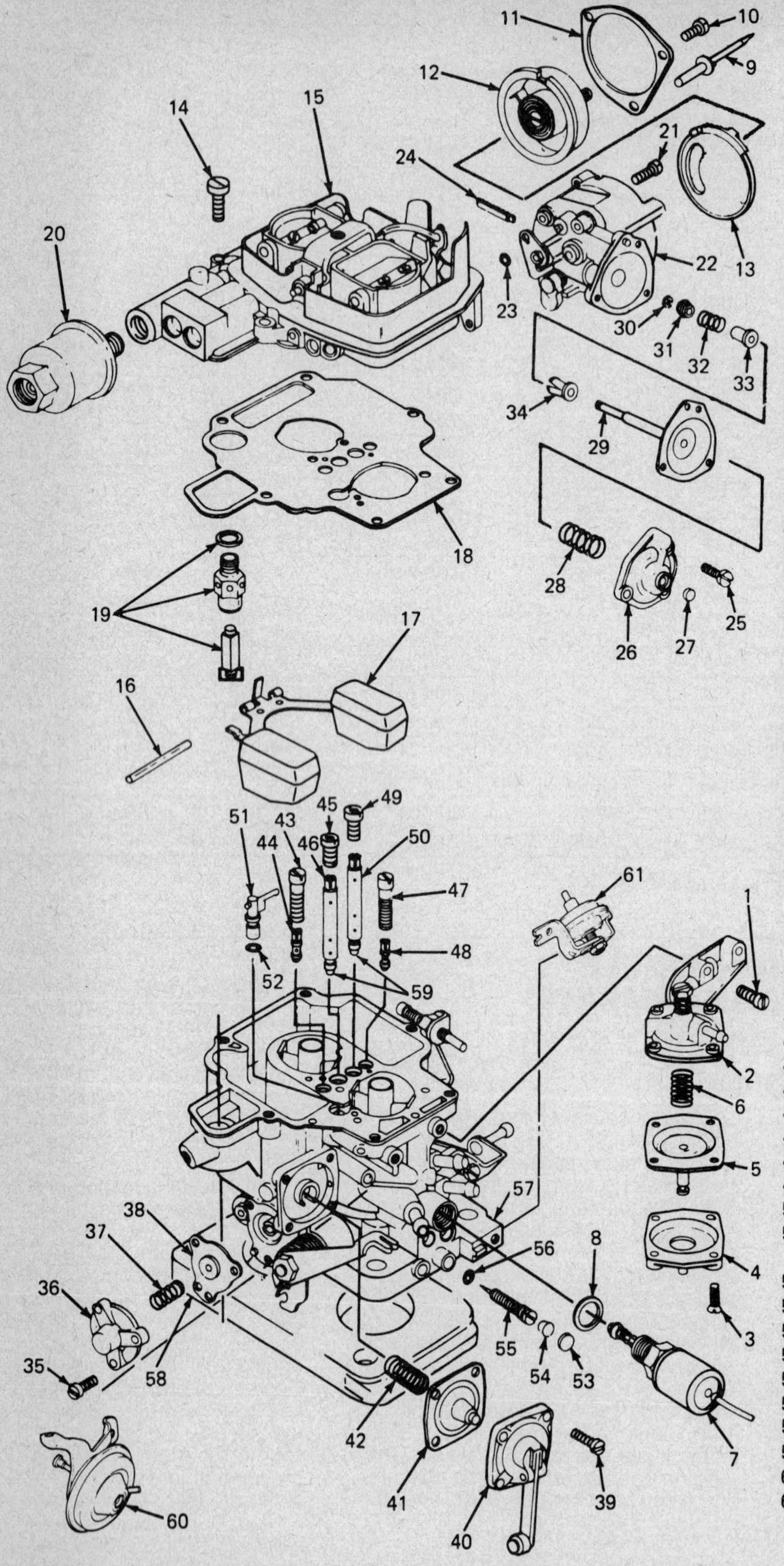

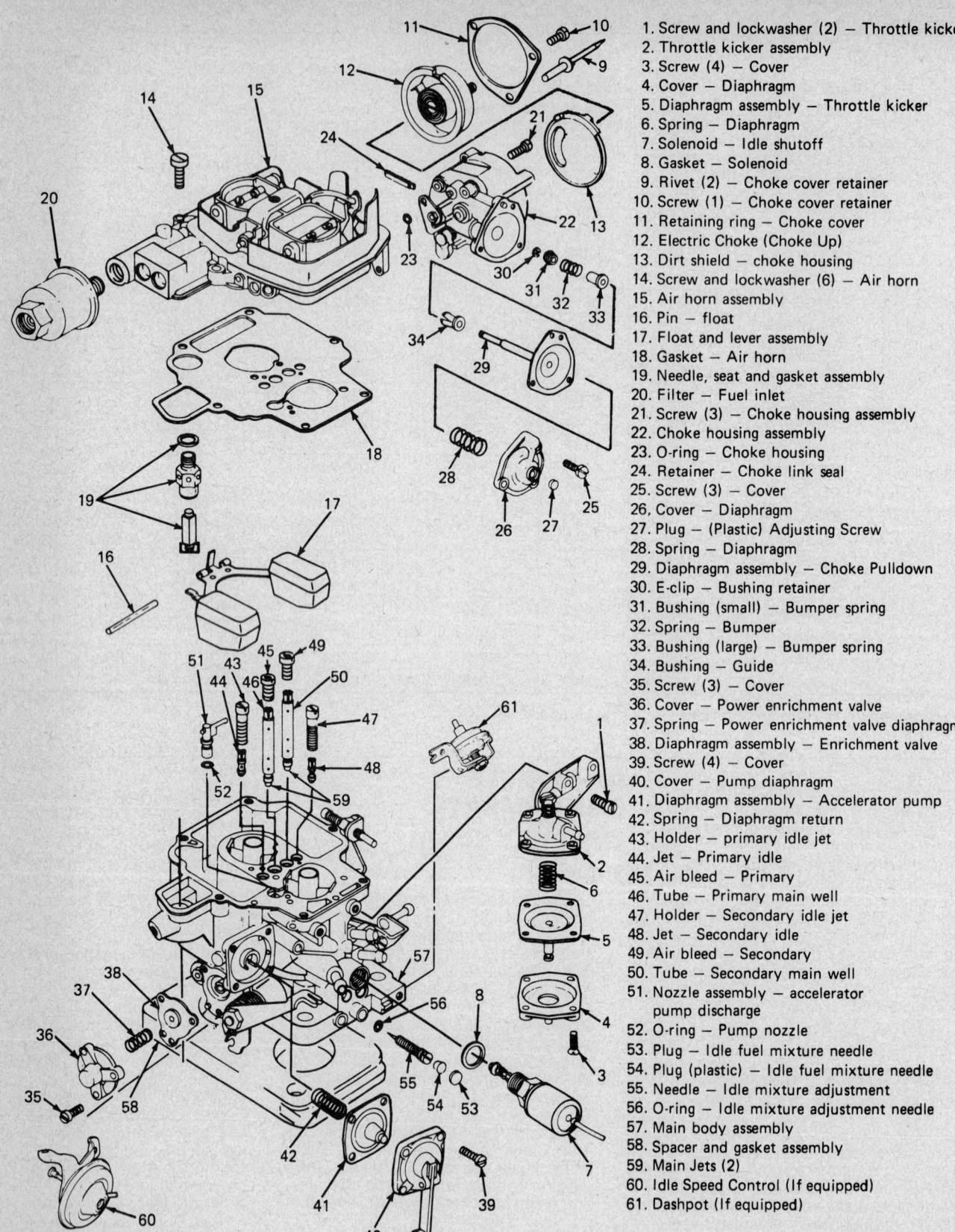

1. Screw and lockwasher (2) – Throttle kicker
2. Throttle kicker assembly
3. Screw (4) – Cover
4. Cover – Diaphragm
5. Diaphragm assembly – Throttle kicker
6. Spring – Diaphragm
7. Solenoid – Idle shutoff
8. Gasket – Solenoid
9. Rivet (2) – Choke cover retainer
10. Screw (1) – Choke cover retainer
11. Retaining ring – Choke cover
12. Electric Choke (Choke Up)
13. Dirt shield – choke housing
14. Screw and lockwasher (6) – Air horn
15. Air horn assembly
16. Pin – float
17. Float and lever assembly
18. Gasket – Air horn
19. Needle, seat and gasket assembly
20. Filter – Fuel inlet
21. Screw (3) – Choke housing assembly
22. Choke housing assembly
23. O-ring – Choke housing
24. Retainer – Choke link seal
25. Screw (3) – Cover
26, Cover – Diaphragm
27. Plug – (Plastic) Adjusting Screw
28. Spring – Diaphragm
29. Diaphragm assembly – Choke Pulldown
30. E-clip – Bushing retainer
31. Bushing (small) – Bumper spring
32. Spring – Bumper
33. Bushing (large) – Bumper spring
34. Bushing – Guide
35. Screw (3) – Cover
36. Cover – Power enrichment valve
37. Spring – Power enrichment valve diaphragm
38. Diaphragm assembly – Enrichment valve
39. Screw (4) – Cover
40. Cover – Pump diaphragm
41. Diaphragm assembly – Accelerator pump
42. Spring – Diaphragm return
43. Holder – primary idle jet
44. Jet – Primary idle
45. Air bleed – Primary
46. Tube – Primary main well
47. Holder – Secondary idle jet
48. Jet – Secondary idle
49. Air bleed – Secondary
50. Tube – Secondary main well
51. Nozzle assembly – accelerator pump discharge
52. O-ring – Pump nozzle
53. Plug – Idle fuel mixture needle
54. Plug (plastic) – Idle fuel mixture needle
55. Needle – Idle mixture adjustment
56. O-ring – Idle mixture adjustment needle
57. Main body assembly
58. Spacer and gasket assembly
59. Main Jets (2)
60. Idle Speed Control (If equipped)
61. Dashpot (If equipped)

Fig. 1 Exploded view of Motorcraft Model 740 carburetor. 1982–83 shown, 1984-85 similar

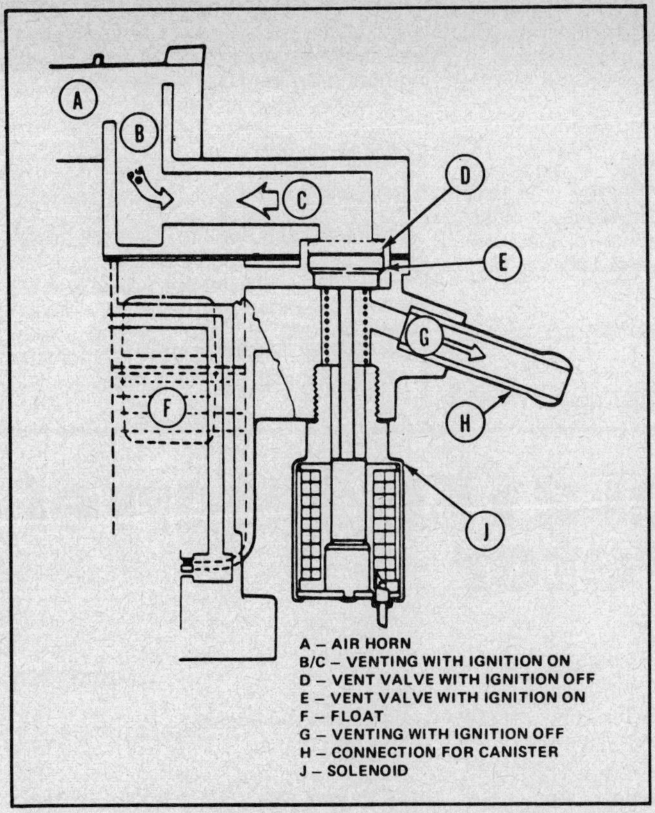

Fig. 2 Carburetor fuel bowl vent system

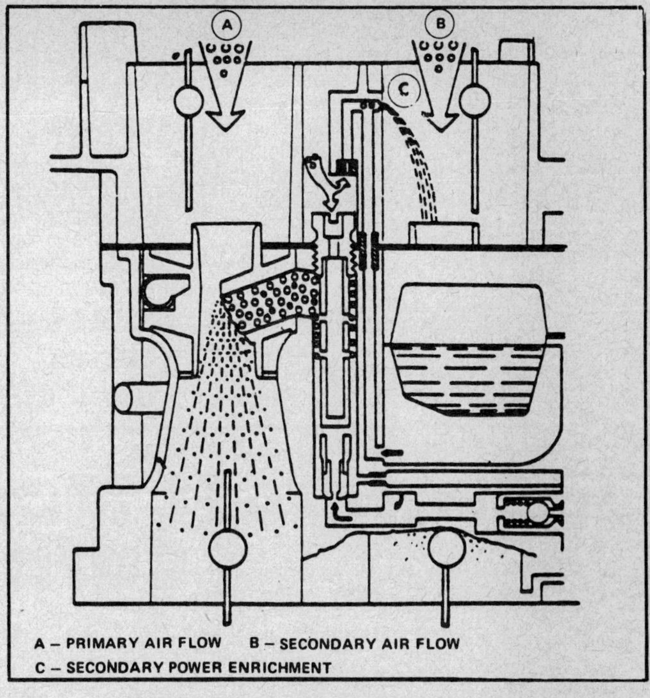

Fig. 3 Carburetor secondary progression system

a. If curb idle speed is not as specified, position transmission into Park and deactivate ISC by disconnecting and plugging ISC vacuum hose.
b. Turn ISC adjusting screw until ISC plunger is clear from throttle lever.
c. Adjust curb idle speed by turning throttle stop adjusting screw.

11. On models with VOTM, proceed as follows:
    a. If VOTM RPM is not as specified, adjust by turning screw on VOTM.
    b. Remove plug and connect vacuum hoses.

FAST IDLE SPEED

1. Place transmission into Neutral or Park.
2. Install a suitable tachometer onto engine as per manufacturer's instructions.
3. Start and allow engine to reach normal operating temperature.
4. Disconnect and plug EGR valve vacuum hose.
5. Place fast idle adjustment screw onto second step of fast idle cam.
6. Operate engine until cooling fan comes ON.
7. Check fast idle speed. If fast idle speed is not as specified, turn fast idle speed screw until specified speed is obtained.

CHOKE PLATE PULLDOWN

On these units, it is necessary to remove the carburetor to remove the three rivets retaining the choke housing cover. Using a 1/8 inch or No. 30 drill bit, remove rivet head, then drive rivet out using a 1/8 inch diameter punch.

Position fast idle adjusting screw on high step of fast idle cam. Using an external vacuum source, apply 17 inches Hg of

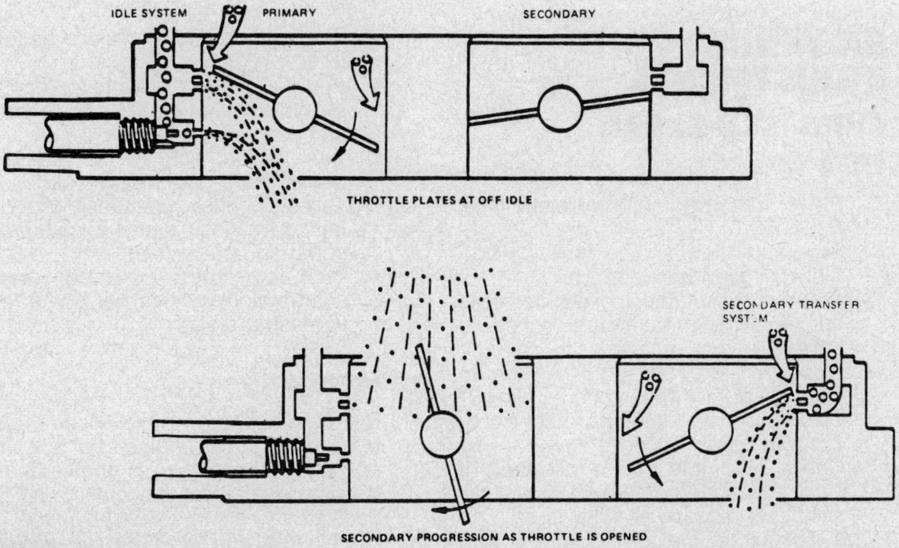

Fig. 4 Carburetor secondary power enrichment system

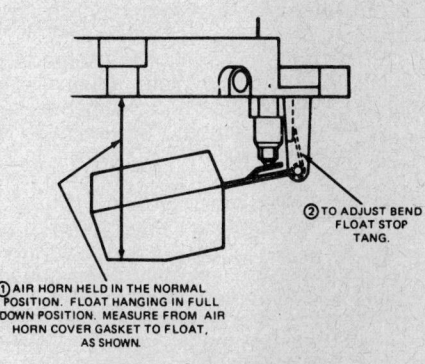

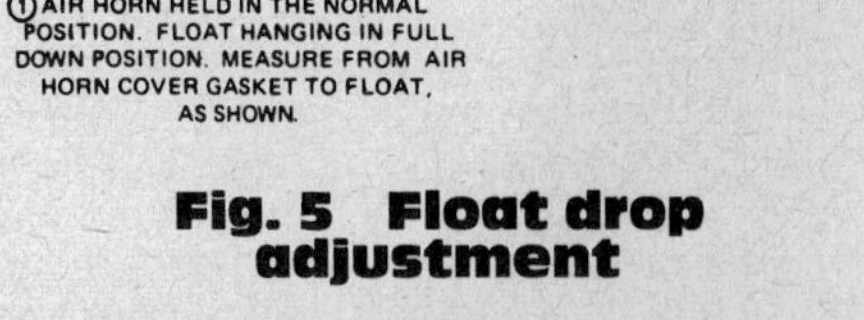

Fig. 5 Float drop adjustment

vacuum to vacuum channel adjacent to the primary bore on the base of the carburetor. The modulator spring should not be compressed. Using the specified drill, check clearance between choke plate and air horn wall. If clearance is not within limits as listed in Adjustment Specifications, remove choke pulldown motor adjusting screw cover and adjust as required.

FAST IDLE CAM KICKDOWN

Position fast idle screw on kickdown of fast idle cam against shoulder of top step. Manually close the primary choke plate and measure distance between choke plate and air horn wall. To obtain specified clearance, adjust right fork of choke bimetal shaft, which engages the fast idle cam, by bending upward or downward.

FLOAT LEVEL

1982–85

Invert air horn with gasket in place and hold at a 45° angle so that the float tang rests lightly on inlet needle. Measure clearance at end of float. Adjust to specifications by removing float and bending float level adjusting tang as needed.

FLOAT DROP

1983–85

Hold air horn in normal position with gasket in place. Measure distance from air horn gasket to bottom of float. Adjust to specifications by removing float and bending float drop tang as needed, **Fig. 5.**

DASH POT

1983–85

Depress dash pot into dash pot assembly. Measure distance between accelerator lever pad and dash pot. Adjust to specifications by loosening dash pot adjusting screw on end of dash pot and rotating dash pot as needed. Torque adjusting screw to 53 inch lbs. and recheck clearance.

Motorcraft Model 2150 2 Barrel Carburetor

INDEX

IDENTIFICATION LOCATION

The carburetor identification number is located on a tag attached to the carburetor by one of the fuel bowl cover attaching screws.

DESCRIPTION

The Holley 2150 carburetor, **Fig. 1,** has two main bodies—the air horn and the throttle body. The air horn assembly, which serves as a cover for the throttle body, contains the choke plate and vents for the fuel bowl. On 2150 units installed on V-6 engines, the air horn assembly contains a fuel deceleration system which consists of a metered pickup orifice in the fuel bowl and air/fuel mixing orifices and bleeds.

An electric choke system is incorporated which opens choke plate within 1-1½ minutes when underhood temperatures are above approximately 55° to 60°. The electric choke system is supplied current to open the choke when underhood temperatures are between 54 and 74°F.

Some 2150 units are equipped with an altitude compensation aneroid to improve high altitude emission control and driveability. Intake air entering the bypass valve is metered into the air flow above the throttle plates, leaning the mixture for high altitude operation. Air flow is controlled by a valve activated by an aneroid attached to the rear of the carburetor main body. Also, these units are equipped with a choke in the bypass air intake, linked to the main choke.

The throttle plate, accelerating pump, power (enrichment) valve and fuel bowl are in the throttle body. The choke housing is attached to the throttle body.

The two bodies each contain a main and booster venturi, main fuel discharge, accelerating pump discharge, idle fuel discharge, and a throttle plate. On some units, an antistall dash pot is attached to the carburetor when the vehicle is equipped with an automatic transmission.

ON-VEHICLE ADJUSTMENTS

CURB IDLE SPEED

1982 V6

1. Place transmission into Neutral or Park.
2. Start and allow engine to reach normal operating temperature.
3. Connect a suitable tachometer onto engine as per manufacturer's instructions.
4. Place A/C-Heat selector switch to OFF position, if equipped.
5. Disconnect and plug throttle kicker vacuum hose.
6. Check curb idle speed obtained. If curb idle speed obtained is not as specified, proceed as follows:
   a. On except California models, turn idle speed adjusting screw until specified curb idle speed is obtained.
   b. On California models, turn saddle bracket adjusting screw until specified curb idle speed is obtained.
7. Place transmission into Neutral or Park.
8. Momentarily increase engine speed, then recheck curb idle speed.
9. On California models, connect vacuum hose onto throttle kicker.
10. On except California models, without A/C and all California models, check and, if necessary, adjust dash pot clearance. Clearance should be .090-.140 inch.
11. On California models, proceed as follows:
    a. Apply light pressure onto top of nylon nut located on the accelerator pump.
    b. Turn nylon nut on accelerator pump rod clockwise until a .005-.015 inch clearance is obtained between top of accelerator pump and pump lever.
    c. Turn accelerator pump rod 1 turn counterclockwise to set pump lever lash preload.

1982 V8-255

1. Place transmission into Neutral or Park and operate engine until normal operating temperature is obtained.
2. Position A/C-Heat selector to OFF position.
3. Disconnect and plug throttle kicker vacuum hose.
4. Place transmission into specified gear.

ADJUSTMENT SPECIFICATIONS

Year	Carb. Model ①	Float Level (Dry)	Fuel Level (Wet)	Pump Setting Hole No. ②	Choke Plate Clearance (Pulldown)	Fast Idle Cam Linkage Clearance	Dechoke Clearance ③	Dash Pot Setting	Choke Setting
1982	E2AE-SA	7/16	13/16	No. 2	.172	—	.250	—	V-Notch
	E2BE-AAA, ABA	7/16	13/16	No. 2	.110	—	.250	.0045	V-Notch
	E2BE-ACA, ADA	7/16	13/16	No. 2	.113	—	.250	—	V-Notch
	E2BE-AGA, AHA	7/16	13/16	No. 2	.113	—	.250	.0041	V-Notch
	E2BE-AJA, AKA	7/16	13/16	No. 2	.110	—	.250	.0045	V-Notch
	E2BE-ALA, AMA	7/16	13/16	No. 2	.113	—	.250	—	V-Notch
	E2BE-UA	7/16	13/16	No. 2	.110	—	.250	.0045	V-Notch
	E2BE-VA	7/16	13/16	No. 2	.113	—	.250	.0045	V-Notch
	E2DE-JA	7/16	13/16	No. 2	.137	—	.250	.0045	V-Notch
	E2DE-KA	7/16	13/16	No. 2	.137	—	.250	.0045	V-Notch
	E2DE-LA	7/16	13/16	No. 2	.137	—	.250	.0045	V-Notch
	E2DE-MA	7/16	13/16	No. 2	.137	—	.250	.0045	V-Notch
	E2KE-AA, BA	7/16	13/16	No. 2	.140	—	.250	.0045	V-Notch
	E2KE-CA, DA	7/16	13/16	No. 2	.140	—	.250	.0045	V-Notch
	E2VE-CA	7/16	13/16	No. 2	.113	—	.250	.0045	V-Notch
	E2WE-EA	7/16	13/16	No. 2	.137	—	.250	.0045	V-Notch
	E2WE-FA	7/16	13/16	No. 2	.137	—	.250	.0045	V-Notch
	E2ZE-BAA, BBA	13/32	25/32	No. 2	.172	—	.250	.045	V-Notch
	E2ZE-BCA, BDA	13/32	25/32	No. 2	.172	—	.250	.0045	V-Notch
	E2ZE-BGA, BHA	13/32	25/32	No. 2	.190	—	.250	.0045	V-Notch
	E24E-AA, BA	7/16	13/16	No. 2	.110	—	.250	.0045	V-Notch
	E24E-CA, DA	7/16	13/16	No. 2	.110	—	.250	.0045	V-Notch
	E24E-EA, FA	7/16	13/16	No. 2	.110	—	.250	.0045-	V-Notch
	E24E-GA, HA	7/16	13/16	No. 2	.110	—	.250	—	V-Notch
	E24E-JA, KA	7/16	13/16	No. 2	.110	—	.250	—	V-Notch
	E25E-CA	7/16	13/16	No. 2	.137	—	.250	—	V-Notch
	E25E-DA	7/16	13/16	No. 2	.144	—	.250	.0045	V-Notch
1983	E3AE-ABA, ACA	7/16	13/16	No. 3	.103	—	.250	—	V-Notch
	E3AE-ADA, AEA	7/16	13/16	No. 3	.103	—	.250	—	V-Notch
	E3AE-AFA, AGA	7/16	13/16	No. 3	.103	—	.250	—	V-Notch
	E3AE-AKA, ALA	7/16	13/16	No. 3	.103	—	.250	—	V-Notch
	E3AE-EA	7/16	13/16	No. 2	—	—	.250	—	V-Notch
	E3AE-RA, SA	7/16	13/16	No. 3	.103	—	.250	—	V-Notch
	E3AE-TA, UA	7/16	13/16	No. 3	.103	—	.250	—	V-Notch
	E3CE-AA, BA	7/16	13/16	No. 3	.103	—	.250	.0045	V-Notch
	E3CE-EA, FA	7/16	13/16	No. 3	.113	—	.250	—	V-Notch
	E3CE-GA, HA	7/16	13/16	No. 3	.103	—	.250	—	V-Notch
	E3CE-JA, KA	7/16	13/16	No. 3	.103	—	.250	—	V-Notch
	E3CE-LA, MA	7/16	13/16	No. 3	.103	—	.250	—	V-Notch
	E3CE-NA, PA	7/16	13/16	No. 3	.120	—	.250	—	V-Notch
	E3SE-ALA, AMA	7/16	13/16	No. 3	.107	—	.250	—	V-Notch
	E3SE-ANA, APA	7/16	13/16	No. 3	.101	—	.250	—	V-Notch
	E3SE-ATA, AA	7/16	13/16	No. 3	.113	—	.250	—	V-Notch
	E3SE-BDA, BEA	7/16	13/16	No. 3	.107	—	.250	—	V-Notch
	E3SE-BFA, BGA	7/16	13/16	No. 3	.107	—	.250	—	V-Notch
	E3SE-EA, FA	7/16	13/16	No. 3	.113	—	.250	—	V-Notch
	E3SE-GA, HA	7/16	13/16	No. 3	.120	—	.250	—	V-Notch
	E3SE-JA, KA	7/16	13/16	No. 3	.101	—	.250	—	V-Notch
	E3SE-LA, MA	7/16	13/16	No. 3	.107	—	.250	—	V-Notch
	E3SE-NA, PA	7/16	13/16	No. 3	.107	—	.250	—	V-Notch

①—Stamped on left side of fuel bowl or on tag attached to bowl cover.

②—With link in inboard hole in pump lever.

③—Minimum clearance between choke plate and air horn wall with throttle plates wide open.

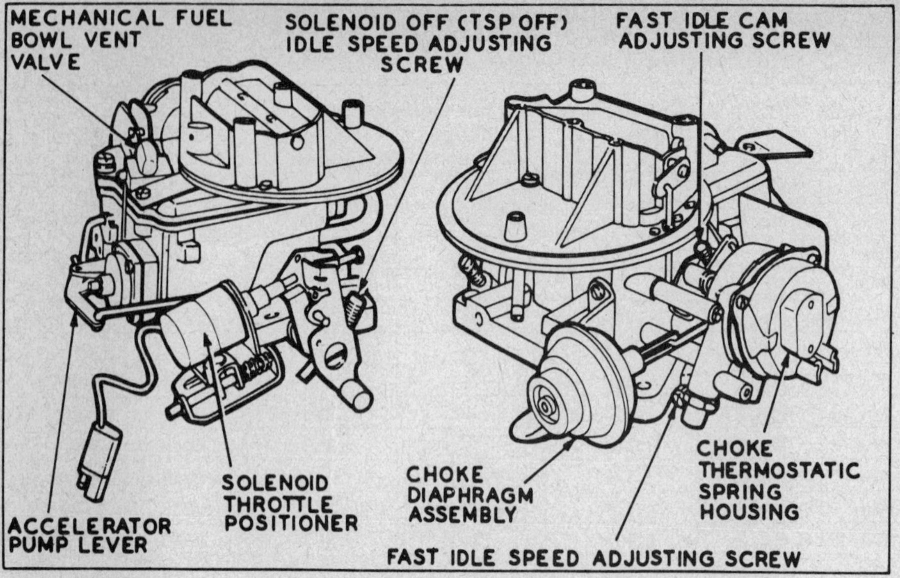

Fig. 1 Typical Motorcraft 2150 carburetor

5. Check and adjust curb idle speed to specification as follows:
   a. Adjust curb idle speed screw.
   b. Adjust saddle bracket adjusting screw.
6. Place transmission in Neutral or Park and momentarily increase engine speed. Place transmission into specified gear, and check curb idle speed. Adjust, if necessary.
7. Check and adjust dash pot clearance.
8. Remove plug and connect throttle kicker vacuum hose.
9. Switch engine OFF. Turn throttle lever to wide open throttle position and release, allowing throttle plates to snap shut. Ensure that no excessive force is needed to open throttle lever.

1982 V8-302

1. Place transmission into Neutral or Park and operate engine until normal operating temperature is obtained.
2. Position A/C-Heat selector to OFF position.
3. Disconnect and plug throttle kicker vacuum hose.
4. Place transmission in specified gear as indicated on the engine emission decal.
5. Check and adjust curb idle speed to specification as follows:
   a. On vehicles without air conditioning, adjust curb idle speed.
   b. On vehicles equipped with air conditioning, adjust saddle bracket screw.
6. Place transmission into Neutral or Park and momentarily increase engine speed. Place transmission into specified gear, and check curb idle speed. Adjust if necessary.
7. On vehicles without air conditioning, adjust dash pot clearance.
8. Remove plug and connect throttle kicker vacuum hose.

1983 V6

If carburetor is equipped with a VOTM/TSP, set A/C-ON RPM prior to adjusting curb idle speed. Refer to steps 1 through 7 to set A/C-ON RPM.

1. Place transmission into Neutral or Park.
2. Start and allow engine to reach normal operating temperature.
3. Place A/C-Heat selector switch to OFF position.
4. Connect a suitable tachometer onto engine as per manufacturer's instructions.
5. Disconnect and plug vacuum hose from VOTM kicker.
6. Connect a suitable vacuum pump onto VOTM kicker.
7. Check and adjust VOTM kicker ON RPM. VOTM ON speed should be 650 RPM, if not, turn saddle bracket adjusting screw until specified speed is obtained.
8. To check and, if necessary, adjust curb idle speed, proceed as follows:
   a. Repeat steps 1 through 4, if necessary.
   b. Check curb idle speed obtained.
   c. If curb idle speed obtained is not as specified, turn saddle bracket adjusting screw on except A/C models or hex head screw protruding from rear of the TSP on A/C models.
9. Place transmission into Neutral or Park.
10. Momentarily increase engine speed and recheck curb idle speed. Adjust, if necessary.
11. Disconnect TSP feed wire electric connector.
12. Check and, if necessary, adjust TSP-OFF speed. TSP-OFF speed should be 450 RPM. If speed obtained is not as specified, turn TSP-OFF adjusting screw until specified speed is obtained.

1983 V8-302

1. Place transmission into Neutral or Park.

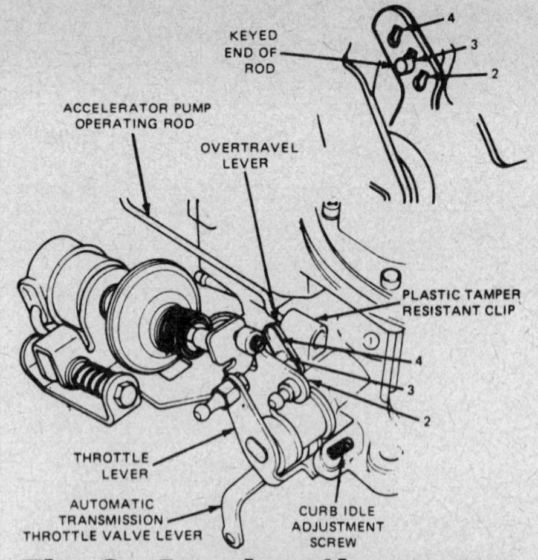

Fig. 2 Accelerating pump stroke adjustment. (Typical)

2. Start and allow engine to reach normal operating temperature.
3. Place A/C-Heat selector switch to OFF position.
4. Connect a suitable tachometer onto engine as per manufacturer's instructions.
5. Disconnect and plug vacuum hose from throttle kicker.
6. Check curb idle speed obtained. If curb idle speed obtained is not as specified, turn curb idle speed adjusting screw. Adjust saddle bracket adjusting screw.

FAST IDLE SPEED

1982 V6

1. Place transmission into Neutral or Park.
2. Connect a tachometer onto engine as per manufacturer's instructions.
3. Start and allow engine to reach normal operating temperature.
4. Disconnect and plug vacuum hose from EGR valve.
5. On except California models, disconnect and plug vacuum hose from purge valve.
6. Check fast idle speed obtained. If fast idle speed obtained is not as specified, turn adjusting screw until specified speed is obtained.

1983 V6

1. Place transmission into Neutral or Park.
2. Start and allow engine to reach normal operating temperature.
3. Connect a suitable tachometer onto engine as per manufacturer's instructions.
4. Disconnect and plug vacuum hose from EGR valve.
5. Check fast idle speed obtained.
6. If fast idle speed obtained is not as specified, turn fast idle speed adjusting screw until specified speed is obtained.

V8 Engines

1. Place transmission into Neutral or Park.
2. Start and allow engine to reach normal operating temperature.

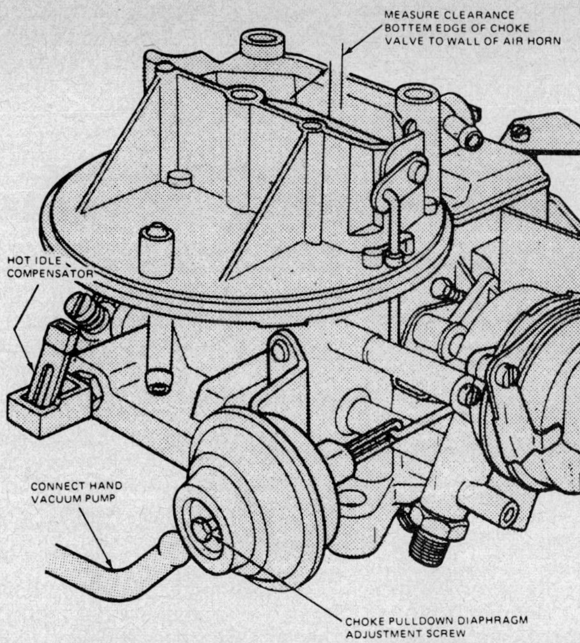

Fig. 3 Choke plate pulldown adjustment. (Typical)

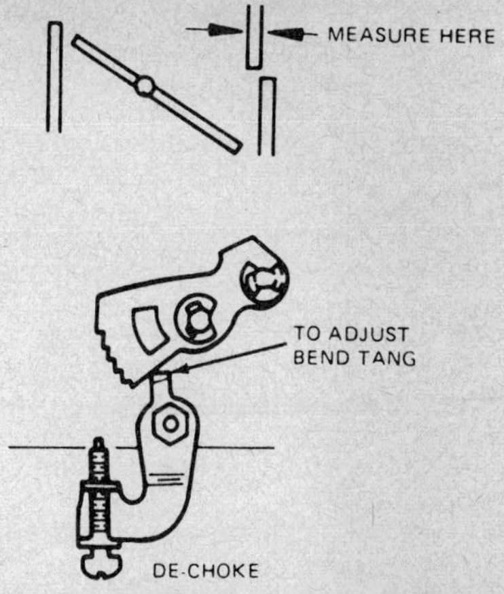

Fig. 4 Dechoke clearance adjustment

3. Connect a suitable tachometer onto engine as per manufacturer's instructions.
4. Disconnect and plug vacuum hose from EGR or EGR/PVS valve.
5. Place fast idle adjustment onto specified step of fast idle cam. Check fast idle speed obtained. If fast idle speed obtained is not as specified, turn fast idle speed adjusting screw until specified speed is obtained.

FLOAT LEVEL (DRY)

1983 units used on Thunderbird and XR-7 car models incorporate a spring loaded fuel inlet needle. The ball must not be compressed when checking float level. Seat the needle by raising the float with light finger pressure applied to the float tab, then lower the float until a light step is felt, and check the setting. Repeat this procedure several times before making final adjustment.

This is a preliminary adjustment; the final adjustment must be made after the carburetor is mounted on the engine.

With air horn removed, float raised and fuel inlet needle seated, measure distance between top surface of throttle body and top surface of float. Take measurement near center of float at a point 1/8 inch from free end of float.

If a cardboard float gauge is used, place the gauge in the corner of the enlarged end section of the fuel bowl as shown. The gauge should touch the float near the end but not on the end radius.

Depress the float tab to seat the fuel inlet needle. The float height is measured from the gasket surface of the throttle body with gasket removed. If the float height is not as listed in the Adjustment Specifications, bend tab on float as required to achieve the desired setting.

FUEL LEVEL (WET)

With vehicle on a level surface, operate engine until normal temperature is reached, then stop engine and check fuel level as follows:

1. Remove carburetor air cleaner.
2. Remove air horn retaining screws and carburetor identification tag.
3. Temporarily leave air horn and gasket in position on throttle body and start engine.
4. Allow engine to idle for several minutes, then rotate air horn and remove air horn gasket to gain access to float or floats.
5. While engine is idling, use a standard depth gauge to measure vertical distance from top machined surface of the throttle body to level of fuel in bowl. The measurement must be made at least 1/4 inch away from any vertical surface to assure an accurate reading.
6. If the fuel level is not as listed in the Specifications chart, stop the engine to avoid any fire hazard due to fuel spray when float setting is disturbed.
7. To adjust fuel level, bend float tab (contacting fuel inlet needle) upward in relation to original position to raise the fuel level, and downward to lower it.
8. Each time an adjustment is made to the float tab to alter the fuel level, the engine must be started and permitted to idle for at least three minutes to stabilize the fuel level. Check fuel level after each adjustment until the specified level is achieved.
9. Assemble carburetor with a new air horn gasket. Then adjust idle speed and mixture, and anti-stall dash pot, if so equipped.

ACCELERATING PUMP

The primary throttle shaft lever (Overtravel lever) has four holes on most units. However, some units have three holes. On units with three holes in the overtravel lever, the holes are numbered as shown in **Fig. 2** with the No. 1 hole omitted. The accelerator pump hole has two holes, inboard and outboard. **The stroke should not be changed from the specified setting.**

1. Support accelerator pump housing at roll pin connection.
2. Using a suitable punch, tap retainer pin from accelerator pump cover and lever.
3. Rotate lever and rod assembly upward until key on rod end is aligned with key hole on pump overtravel lever.
4. Remove rod, clip and pin assembly from overtravel lever.
5. Position rod, clip and pin assembly in the specified hole, then reassemble pump link and rod assembly.

CHOKE PLATE CLEARANCE (PULLDOWN)

Do not attempt to turn the diaphragm adjusting screw without first loosening the Loctite which has been applied to the threads of the screw. The Loctite can be softened by heating the area around the screw with an electric soldering gun or by applying Loctite to the screw. When the Loctite has softened enough, the screw can be turned without causing any damage.

1. Remove carburetor from engine, then, using a suitable punch, center punch choke retaining cap screw heads.
2. Using a 1/4 inch drill bit, drill screw heads deep enough to remove retainer from cap, then remove choke cap by inserting a flat chisel between cap and gasket.
3. Remove remaining portion of choke cap retaining screws using pliers. Also clean epoxy sealer and gasket from choke cap and housing mating surfaces.
4. Rotate choke thermostatic housing to lightly close choke plate, then rotate housing an additional 90°.
5. Using the edge of a file, file a 1/8 inch deep groove on pulldown motor tamper resistance cover 1/4 inch from rear edge of pulldown motor. **On 1982-83 models, a tamper resistance cover is not used on the pulldown motor.**

6. Using a suitable awl inserted in filed groove, carefully tap plug from pulldown motor.
7. Activate pulldown motor using an external vacuum source or by manually forcing the diaphragm to the retracted position.
8. Using a drill bit of the specified size, measure clearance between choke plate and carburetor air horn wall, **Fig. 3.**
9. Loosen pulldown motor adjusting screw as described in Caution above, then remove adjusting screw and clean remaining thread locking compound.
10. Reinstall adjusting screw and adjust. Rotate adjusting screw clockwise to decrease pulldown and counterclockwise to increase pulldown.
11. After completing adjustment, use Loctite 240 or equivalent to lock adjusting screw in position, then tap tamper resistance cover into place on pulldown motor. Apply epoxy sealer MT13 or equivalent to edge and groove on cover. **After completing choke plate clearance adjustment, leave choke thermostatic housing in the full rich position and check fast idle cam setting as described under Fast Idle Cam Position Adjustment.**

FAST IDLE CAM POSITION

1. With choke thermostatic housing in the rich position, cycle throttle to set fast idle cam.
2. Activate pulldown by applying an external vacuum source.
3. Cycle throttle and observe fast idle cam. Fast idle cam should drop to the kickdown step and fast idle speed screw should be opposite the V notch on the cam.
4. Align screw with notch on fast idle cam by rotating screw on fast idle cam lever.
5. Reconnect vacuum hose to choke pulldown motor.
6. Reset choke thermostatic housing to specification listed in Adjustment Specifications. **Apply three 1/2 inch beads of MT-13 sealant to each side of choke cap gasket adjacent to choke housing screw bosses, then position gasket to housing. Position choke cap and retainer to housing, then install breakaway screws finger tight. Tighten each screw until head breaks off, then reinstall carburetor.**

DECHOKE (CHOKE UNLOADER) CLEARANCE

1. Hold throttle in the wide open position and measure clearance between lower edge of choke plate and air horn wall using the specified size drill. Refer to Adjustment Specifications.
2. To adjust clearance, bend metal tang on fast idle speed lever attached to throttle shaft, **Fig. 4.**
3. Rotate throttle lever to ensure minimum throttle effort during dechoke tang engagement.

AUTOMATIC CHOKE VALVE TENSION

Turn thermostatic spring cover against spring tension until index mark on cover is aligned with mark specified in the Adjustment Specifications on choke housing.

Motorcraft Models 2700 & 7200 VV Carburetors

INDEX

ADJUSTMENT SPECIFICATIONS

Year	Carb Model (Code 9510)	Float Level (Dry)	Float Drop	Internal Vent	Venturi Valve Limiter	Fast Idle Cam	Control Vacuum Regulator	Choke Setting
1982	E1AE-ACA	$1\frac{3}{64}$	$1\frac{15}{32}$	—	①	③	.245-.255	Index
	E1AE-AGA	$1\frac{3}{64}$	$1\frac{15}{32}$	—	①	③	.245-.255	Index
	E1AE-SA	$1\frac{3}{64}$	$1\frac{15}{32}$	—	②	③	.245-.255	1 Rich
	E2AE-ABA, RA	$1\frac{3}{64}$	$1\frac{15}{32}$	—	①	③	.245-.255	Index
	E2AE-AGA, AHA	$1\frac{3}{64}$	$1\frac{15}{32}$	—	②	③	.245-.255	1 Rich
	E2AE-LB, LC	$1\frac{3}{64}$	$1\frac{15}{32}$	—	①	③	.295-.305	Index
	E2AE-MA, MB	$1\frac{3}{64}$	$1\frac{15}{32}$	—	②	③	.245-.255	1 Rich
	E2AE-TA	$1\frac{3}{64}$	$1\frac{15}{32}$	—	②	③	.245-.255	Index
	E2AE-TB	$1\frac{3}{64}$	$1\frac{15}{32}$	—	②	③	.245-.255	Index
	E2DE-NA, SA, TA, UA	$1\frac{3}{64}$	$1\frac{15}{32}$	—	①	③	.295-.305	Index
	E2SE-DA, DB, FA	$1\frac{3}{64}$	$1\frac{15}{32}$	—	①	③	.070-.080	Index
	E25E-ABA	$1\frac{3}{64}$	$1\frac{15}{32}$	—	①	③	.245-.255	Index
	E25E-AC, YA	$1\frac{3}{64}$	$1\frac{15}{32}$	—	①	③	.070-.080	Index
	E25E-FA, GA, SA, UA	$1\frac{3}{64}$	$1\frac{15}{32}$	—	①	③	.245-.255	Index
	E25E-GB, TA	$1\frac{3}{64}$	$1\frac{15}{32}$	—	①	③	.245-.255	Index

①—Limiter adjusting screw setting, .39-.41 inch; limiter stop screw setting, .99-1.01 inch.

②—Limiter adjusting screw setting, .74-.76 inch; limiter stop screw setting, .99-1.01 inch.

③—.355-.365 inch on second step.

IDENTIFICATION LOCATION

The carburetor identification number is stamped on the upper body casting over the fuel bowl.

DESCRIPTION

The Motorcraft model 2700 and 7200 carburetors, **Figs. 1 through 4,** are two bore, variable venturi units. The model 7200 carburetor is used in conjunction with EEC system. The variable venturis, located at the top of the throttle bores, are small oblong castings that slide across the throttle bores. The venturis are positioned by a spring loaded diaphragm valve regulated by a vacuum signal obtained below the venturis in the throttle bores. As the throttle is opened, the vacuum signal increases, thereby opening the venturis and permitting more air to enter the carburetor while maintaining approximately the same venturi air velocity.

Tapered metering rods are attached to the venturi valves and fit into the metering jets. As the venturis are positioned in response to air demand, the metering rods slide in the jets to provide the proper air-fuel mixture during all modes of engine operation. By the use of the variable venturi principle, the only auxiliary fuel metering systems required are the accelerator pump, idle trim, starting enrichment and cold running enrichment.

ON-VEHICLE ADJUSTMENTS

CURB IDLE SPEED

1982 V6-232

1. Place transmission into Neutral or Park.
2. Start and allow engine to reach normal operating temperature.
3. Connect a suitable tachometer onto engine as per manufacturer's instructions.
4. Place A/C-Heat selector switch to OFF position, if equipped.
5. Disconnect and plug throttle kicker vacuum hose.
6. Check curb idle speed obtained. If curb idle speed obtained is not as specified, proceed as follows:
   a. On except California models, turn idle speed adjusting screw until specified curb idle speed is obtained.
   b. On California models, turn saddle bracket adjusting screw until specified curb idle speed is obtained.
7. Place transmission into Neutral or Park.
8. Momentarily increase engine speed, then recheck throttle kicker.
9. On California models, connect vacuum hose onto throttle kicker.
10. On except California models without A/C and all California models, check and, if necessary, adjust dash pot clearance. Clearance should be .090-.140 inch.
11. On California models, proceed as follows:
    a. Apply light pressure onto top of nylon nut located on the accelerator pump.
    b. Turn nylon nut on accelerator pump rod clockwise until a .005-.015 inch clearance is obtained between top of accelerator pump and pump lever.
    c. Turn accelerator pump rod 1 turn counterclockwise to set pump lever lash preload.

1982 V8-255

1. Place transmission into Neutral or Park and operate engine until normal operating temperature is obtained.
2. Position A/C-Heat selector to OFF position.
3. Disconnect and plug throttle kicker vacuum hose.
4. Place transmission into specified gear.
5. Check and adjust curb idle speed to specification by turning curb idle speed adjusting screw.
6. Adjust saddle bracket adjusting screw.
7. Place transmission in Neutral or Park and momentarily increase engine speed. Place transmission into specified gear and check curb idle speed. Adjust if necessary.
8. Check and adjust dash pot clearance.
9. Apply pressure on top of accelerator pump nylon nut.
10. Turn nylon nut clockwise until a .010 inch clearance is obtained between top of accelerator pump and pump lever.
11. Turn accelerator pump rod 1 turn counterclockwise to set lever lash preload.
12. Remove plug and connect throttle kicker vacuum hose.
13. Switch engine OFF. Turn throttle lever to wide open throttle position and release, allowing throttle plates to snap shut. Ensure that no excessive force is needed to open throttle lever.

1982 V8-302 & 351W

1. Place transmission into Neutral or Park and operate engine until normal operating temperature is obtained.
2. Position A/C-Heat selector to OFF position.
3. Disconnect and plug throttle kicker vacuum hose.
4. Place transmission in specified gear as indicated on engine emission decal.
5. Check and adjust curb idle speed by adjusting curb idle speed adjusting screw and the saddle bracket adjusting screw.
6. Place transmission in Neutral or Park and momentarily increase engine speed. Place transmission into specified gear and check curb idle speed. Adjust if necessary.
7. Check and adjust throttle position sensor TPS.
8. Apply pressure to accelerator pump nylon nut.
9. Turn nylon nut clockwise until a .010 inch clearance is obtained between top of the accelerator pump and pump lever.
10. Turn accelerator pump rod 1 turn counterclockwise to set lever lash preload.
11. Remove plug and connect throttle kicker vacuum hose.

FAST IDLE SPEED

1982 V6-232

1. Place transmission into Neutral or Park.
2. Connect a tachometer onto engine as per manufacturer's instructions.
3. Start and allow engine to reach normal operating temperature.
4. Disconnect and plug vacuum hose from EGR valve.
5. On California Granada and Cougar models, disconnect and plug vacuum hose from triple vacuum switch.
6. Check fast idle speed obtained. If fast idle speed obtained is not as specified, turn adjusting screw until specified speed is obtained.

V8 Engines

1. Place transmission into Neutral or Park.
2. Start and allow engine to reach normal operating temperature.
3. Connect a suitable tachometer onto engine as per manufacturer's instructions.
4. Disconnect and plug vacuum hose from EGR or EGR/PVS valve.
5. Place fast idle adjustment onto specified step of fast idle cam. Check fast idle speed obtained. If fast idle speed obtained is not as specified, turn fast idle speed adjusting screw until specified speed is obtained.

FUEL LEVEL

Remove upper body assembly and replace the upper body gasket. With the upper body inverted, measure vertical distance from the upper body cast surface and the bottom of float. To adjust, bend float operating lever away from the fuel inlet needle to decrease the setting or toward the needle to increase the setting, **Fig. 5.** After adjustment, the float pontoon must be parallel with the gasket surface. Check and adjust float drop, if necessary.

FLOAT DROP

With upper body held in upright position, measure vertical distance between the cast surface of the upper body and the bottom of float. To adjust, bend stop tab on float lever away from hinge pin to increase setting or toward the hinge pin to decrease setting, **Fig. 6.**

COLD ENRICHMENT METERING ROD

On some vehicles, it is necessary to remove the carburetor to remove the rivets on the choke housing. Remove the top two rivets with a 1/8 inch diameter twist drill. The third bottom rivet is located in a "Blind" hole and is removed by lightly tapping the rear of the retainer ring using a

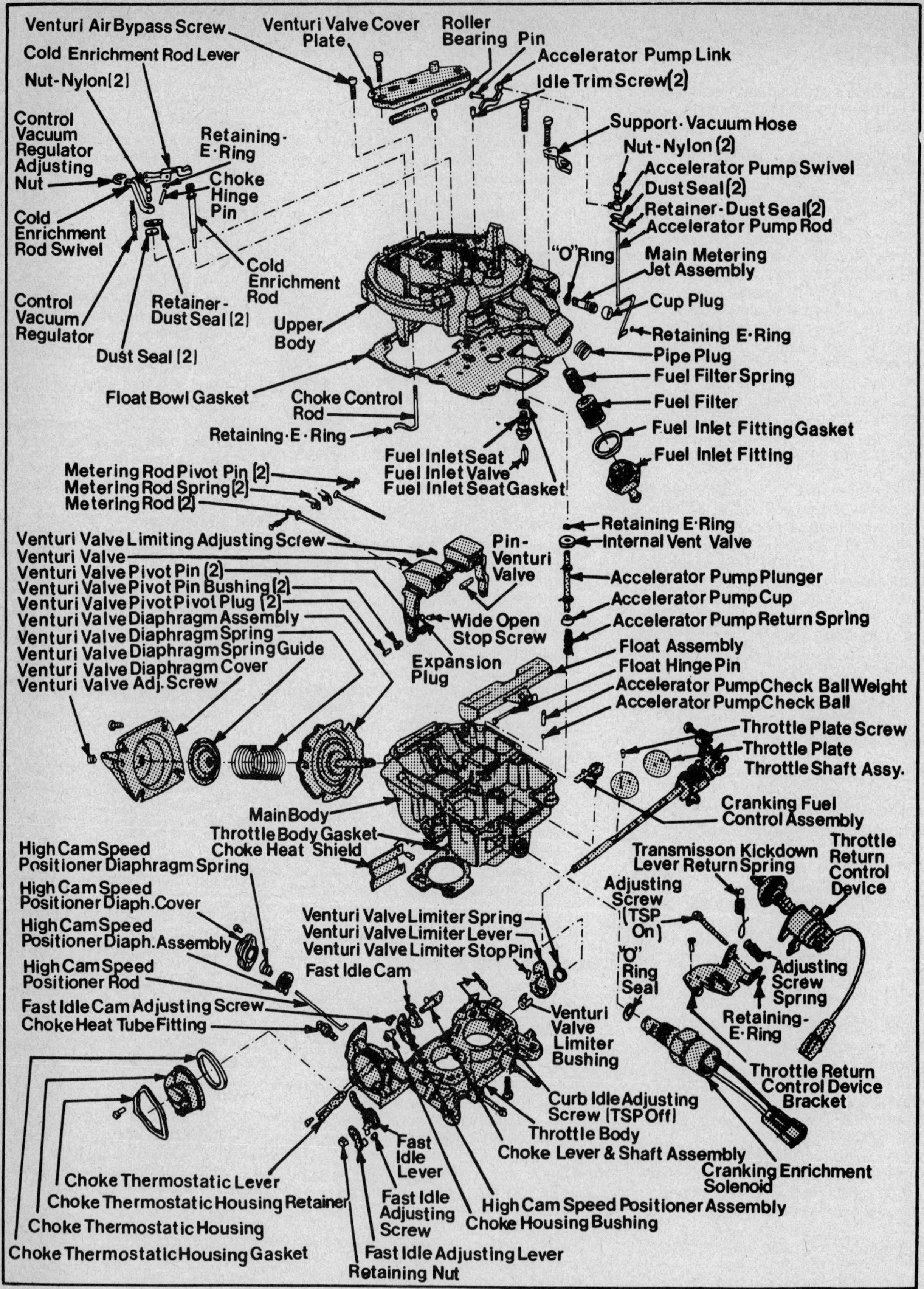

Fig. 1 Motorcraft model 2700 variable venturi carburetor, disassembled

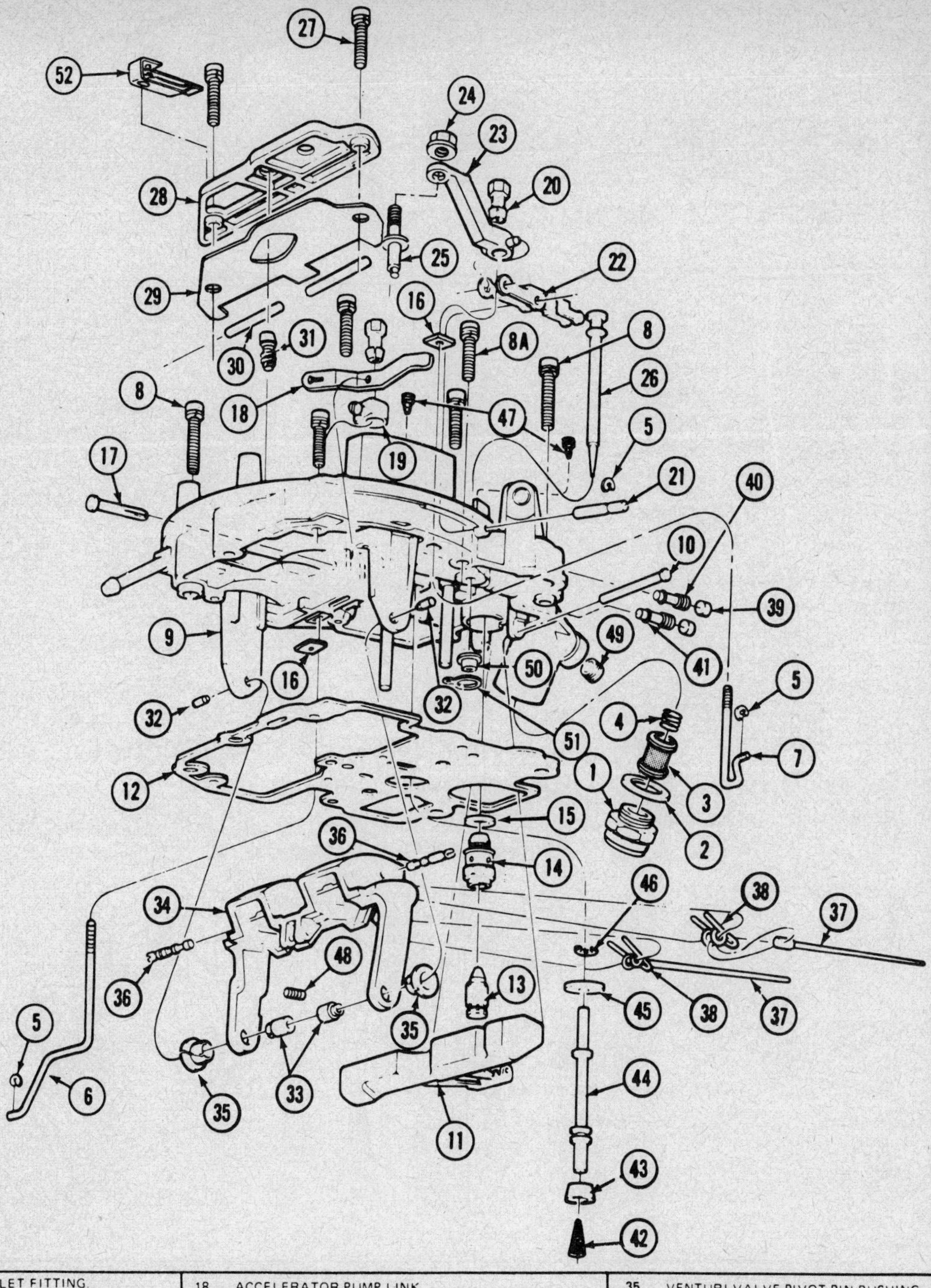

1.	FUEL INLET FITTING.	18.	ACCELERATOR PUMP LINK.	35.	VENTURI VALVE PIVOT PIN BUSHING.
2.	FUEL INLET FITTING GASKET.	19.	ACCELERATOR PUMP SWIVEL.	36.	METERING ROD PIVOT PIN.
3.	FUEL FILTER.	20.	NUT - NYLON.	37.	METERING ROD.
4.	FUEL FILTER SPRING.	21.	CHOKE HINGE PIN.	38.	METERING ROD SPRING.
5.	1/8 RETAINING E-RING.	22.	COLD ENRICHMENT ROD LEVER.	39.	CUP PLUG.
6.	ACCELERATOR PUMP ROD.	23.	COLD ENRICHMENT ROD SWIVEL.	40.	MAIN METERING JET ASSEMBLY.
7.	CHOKE CONTROL ROD	24.	CONTROL VACUUM REGULATOR ADJUSTING NUT	41.	"O" RING.
8.	SCREW (2). 8-32 X .88	25.	CONTROL VACUUM REGULATOR.	42.	ACCELERATOR PUMP RETURN SPRING.
8A.	SCREW (5) 8-32 X .75	26.	COLD ENRICHMENT ROD.	43.	ACCELERATOR PUMP CUP.
9.	UPPER BODY	27	SCREW (2) 8-32 X .75	44.	ACCELERATOR PUMP PLUNGER.
10.	FLOAT HINGE PIN.	28.	VENTURI VALVE COVER PLATE.	45.	INTERNAL VENT VALVE.
11.	FLOAT ASSEMBLY.	29.	GASKET	46.	3/16 RETAINING E-RING.
12.	FLOAT BOWL GASKET.	30.	ROLLER BEARING	47.	IDLE TRIM SCREW.
13.	FUEL INLET VALVE.	31.	VENTURI AIR BYPASS SCREW AND TORQUE RETENTION SPRING	48.	VENTURI VALVE LIMITER ADJUSTING SCREW.
14.	FUEL INLET SEAT.	32.	VENTURI VALVE PIVOT PLUG.	49.	PIPE PLUG.
15.	FUEL INLET SEAT GASKET.	33.	VENTURI VALVE PIVOT PIN.	50.	COLD ENRICHMENT ROD SEAL
16.	DUST SEAL.	34.	VENTURI VALVE	51.	SEAL RETAINER
17.	PIN 12 X .69			52.	HOT IDLE COMPENSATOR

Fig. 2 Upper body exploded view. Model 7200

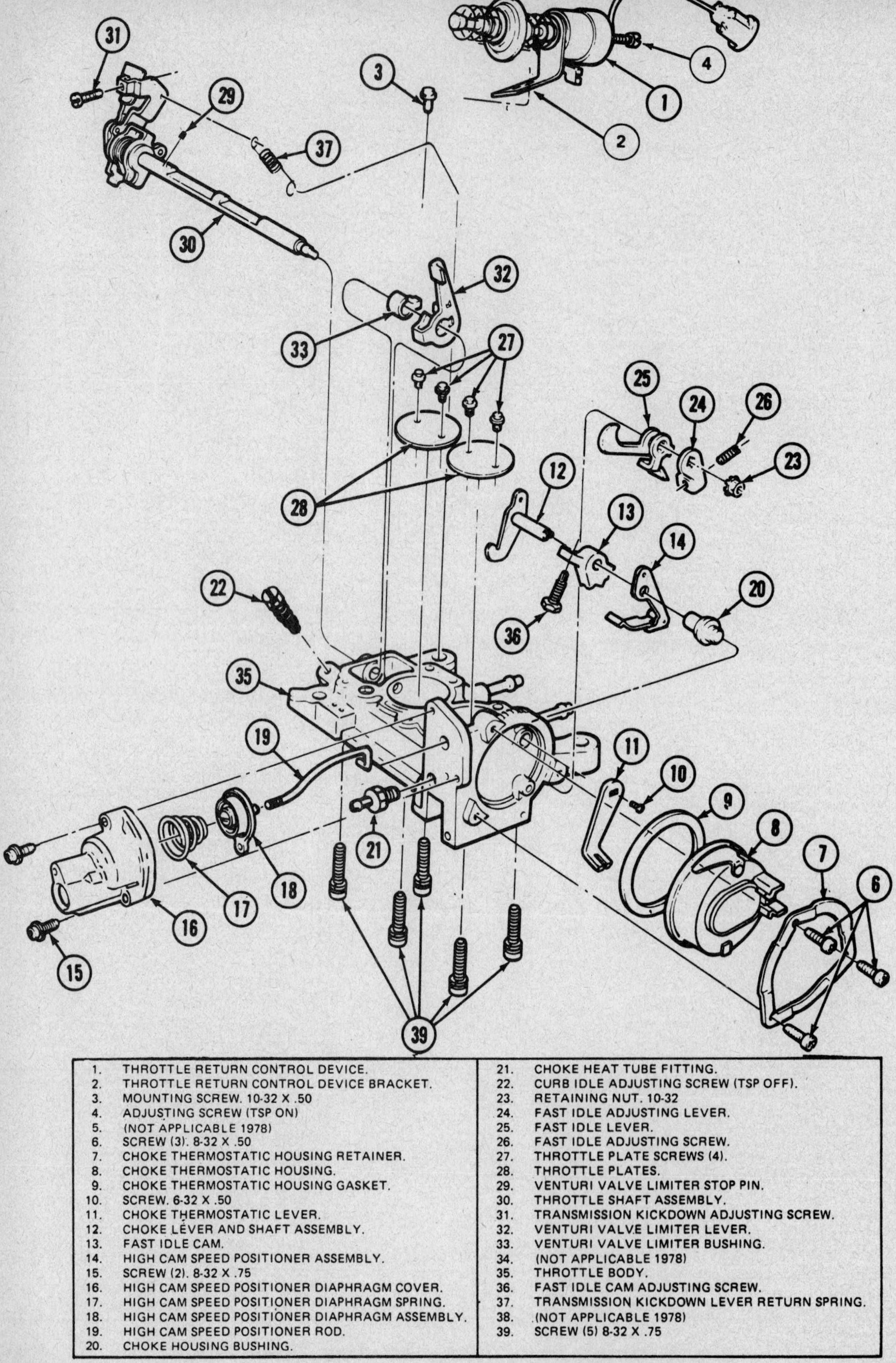

1. THROTTLE RETURN CONTROL DEVICE.
2. THROTTLE RETURN CONTROL DEVICE BRACKET.
3. MOUNTING SCREW. 10-32 X .50
4. ADJUSTING SCREW (TSP ON)
5. (NOT APPLICABLE 1978)
6. SCREW (3). 8-32 X .50
7. CHOKE THERMOSTATIC HOUSING RETAINER.
8. CHOKE THERMOSTATIC HOUSING.
9. CHOKE THERMOSTATIC HOUSING GASKET.
10. SCREW. 6-32 X .50
11. CHOKE THERMOSTATIC LEVER.
12. CHOKE LEVER AND SHAFT ASSEMBLY.
13. FAST IDLE CAM.
14. HIGH CAM SPEED POSITIONER ASSEMBLY.
15. SCREW (2). 8-32 X .75
16. HIGH CAM SPEED POSITIONER DIAPHRAGM COVER.
17. HIGH CAM SPEED POSITIONER DIAPHRAGM SPRING.
18. HIGH CAM SPEED POSITIONER DIAPHRAGM ASSEMBLY.
19. HIGH CAM SPEED POSITIONER ROD.
20. CHOKE HOUSING BUSHING.
21. CHOKE HEAT TUBE FITTING.
22. CURB IDLE ADJUSTING SCREW (TSP OFF).
23. RETAINING NUT. 10-32
24. FAST IDLE ADJUSTING LEVER.
25. FAST IDLE LEVER.
26. FAST IDLE ADJUSTING SCREW.
27. THROTTLE PLATE SCREWS (4).
28. THROTTLE PLATES.
29. VENTURI VALVE LIMITER STOP PIN.
30. THROTTLE SHAFT ASSEMBLY.
31. TRANSMISSION KICKDOWN ADJUSTING SCREW.
32. VENTURI VALVE LIMITER LEVER.
33. VENTURI VALVE LIMITER BUSHING.
34. (NOT APPLICABLE 1978)
35. THROTTLE BODY.
36. FAST IDLE CAM ADJUSTING SCREW.
37. TRANSMISSION KICKDOWN LEVER RETURN SPRING.
38. (NOT APPLICABLE 1978)
39. SCREW (5) 8-32 X .75

Fig. 3 Lower body exploded view. Model 7200

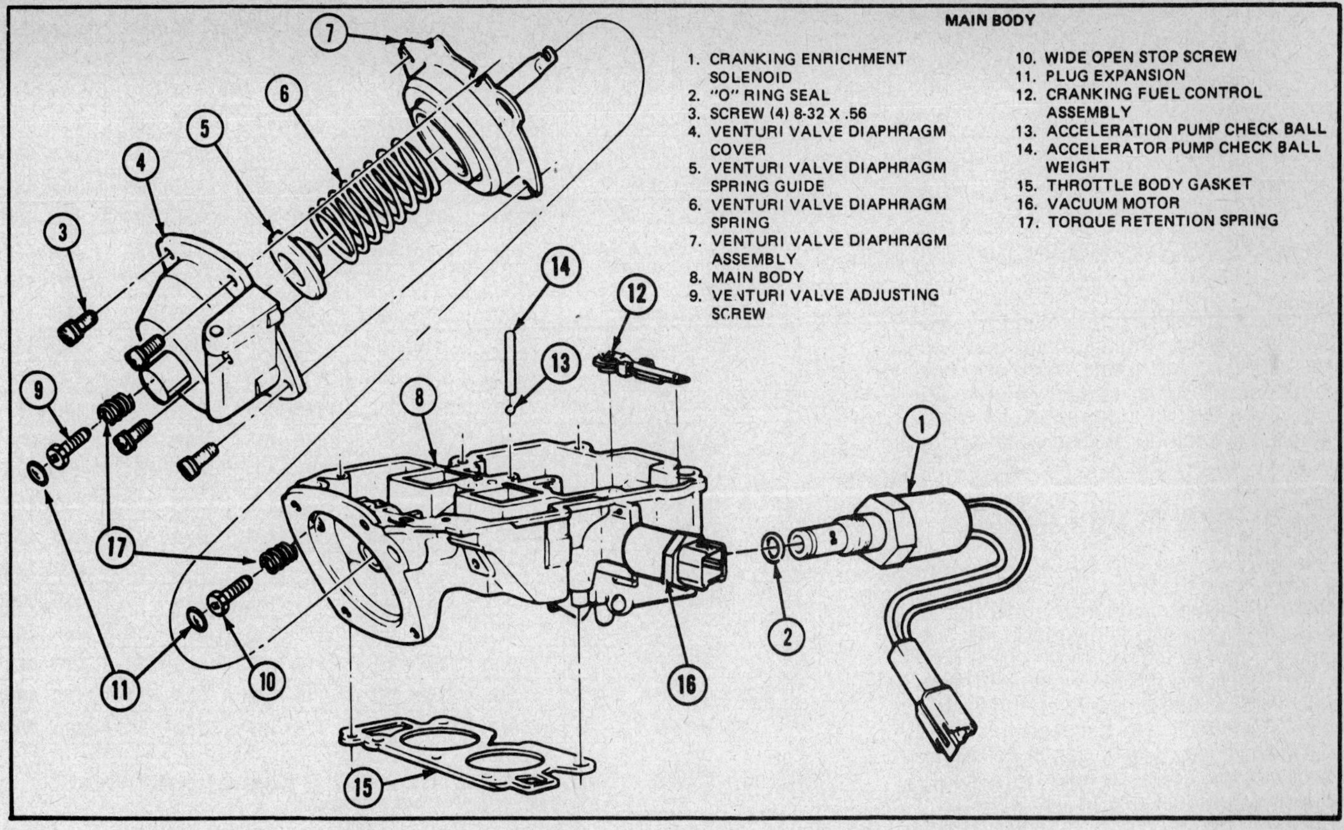

Fig. 4 Main body exploded view. Model 7200

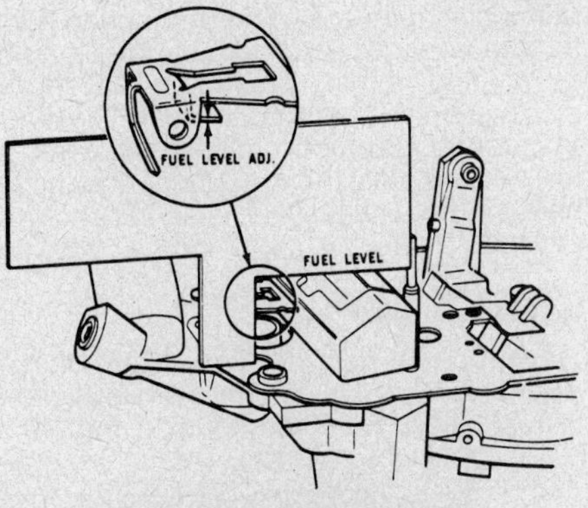

Fig. 5 Fuel level adjustment

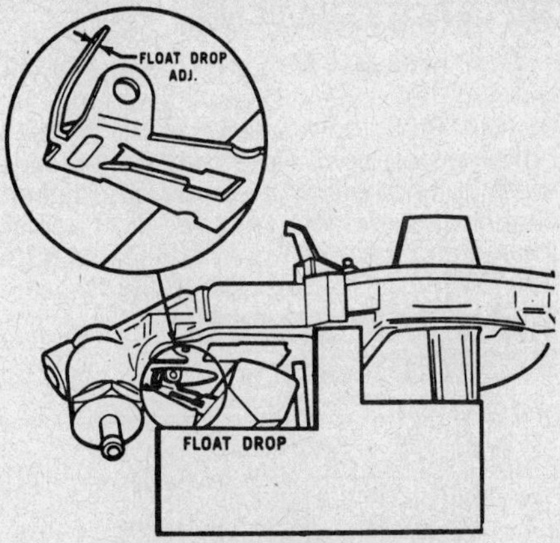

Fig. 6 Float drop adjustment

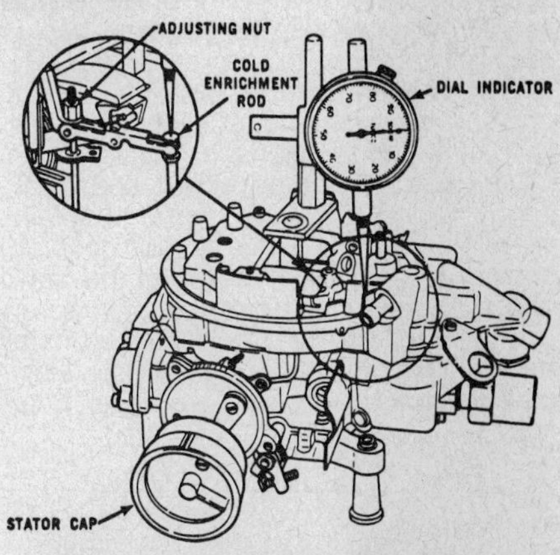

Fig. 7 Cold enrichment metering rod adjustment

punch and hammer. The rivet, retainer ring, choke housing and gasket can then be removed.

1982 Units

Remove carburetor from vehicle, then remove choke cap. Install choke weight tool T77L-9848-A7 on choke bi-metal lever, then install dial indicator, **Fig. 7,** with contact positioned on top of cold enrichment metering rod and zero indicator. Install stator cap and rotate to index, then note indicator reading. Reading should be between as indicated in **Fig. 8,** under the run position 75°F column. If reading is not within limits, adjust by turning the choke enrichment adjusting nut until reading is within limits. Do not remove or reset dial indicator to check the start position 0°F adjustment. To check this adjustment, rotate thermostat lever clockwise until cold enrichment metering rod travel stop screw is bottomed against the upper body and note indicator reading. If reading is not within limits listed in **Fig. 8,** under start position 0°F column, adjust by turning the travel stop screw. Without removing or resetting dial indicator, perform control vacuum regulator adjustment as described under Control Vacuum-Regulator (CVR) Adjustment, then recheck cold enrichment metering rod run position 75°F adjustment. Remove adjustment limiting diaphragm cover, then seat diaphragm using finger and note dial indicator reading, **Fig. 9.** If reading is not within limits listed in **Fig. 8,** under start position 75°F column, rotate diaphragm until dial indicator reads within specifications. Align holes on diaphragm and casting, then install diaphragm cover. Push inward on diaphragm rod until diaphragm is seated, then rotate thermostat lever clockwise until choke shaft lever pin touches fast idle intermediate lever and note indicator reading, **Fig. 10.** If reading is not within limits listed in **Fig. 8,** under run position 0°F column, remove lead ball from choke diaphragm cover and rotate adjusting screw clockwise to increase or counterclockwise to decrease height, **Fig. 10.** After completing adjustment, install lead ball and choke cover.

FAST IDLE CAM

On some California vehicles, it is necessary to remove the carburetor to remove the rivets on the choke housing. Remove the top two rivets with a 1/8 inch diameter twist drill. The third bottom rivet is located in a "Blind" hole and is removed by lightly tapping the rear of the retainer ring using a punch and hammer. The rivet, retainer ring, choke housing and gasket can then be removed.

Remove choke cap and place the fast idle lever in the corner of the specified step of the fast idle cam with the high cam speed positioner retracted, **Fig. 11.** If adjustment is performed on the bench, hold throttle closed with a rubber band to maintain cam position. Install stator cap, tool T77L-9848-A, and rotate clockwise until lever contacts adjusting screw. Rotate adjusting screw until index mark on stator cap aligns with the specified notch on the choke casting. Remove stator cap and reinstall choke cap.

VENTURI VALVE LIMITER

Remove venturi valve cover and roller bearings, then the expansion plug located at rear of main body on the throttle side of carburetor. With an Allen wrench, **Fig. 12**, remove venturi valve wide open stop screw. Block the throttle wide open, then apply light closing pressure on the venturi valve and check gap between the valve and the air horn wall. If gap is not within specifications, adjust as follows: manually open the venturi valve to the wide open position and insert appropriate Allen wrench into the hole from which the stop screw was removed. Rotate limiter adjusting screw clockwise to increase gap or counterclockwise to decrease gap. Remove Allen wrench, apply light closing pressure to valve and recheck gap. If gap is within specifications, reinstall venturi valve wide open stop screw and rotate screw clockwise until screw contacts valve. Push venturi valve to wide open position and check gap between the valve and air horn wall, then rotate stop screw until gap is within specifications. Install new expansion plug in access hole. Reinstall venturi valve cover and roller bearings.

Year	Carb. Ident. No.	Carb. Model	Cold Enrichment Metering Rod Adjustment			
			Run Position		Start Position	
			0°F	75°F	0°F	75°F
1982	E1AE-ACA	7200	.345-.355	.115-.135	.485-.495	.430-.460
	E1AE-AGA	7200	.345-.355	.115-.135	.485-.495	.440-.480
	E1AE-SA	7200	.345-.355	.115-.135	.485-.495	.440-.480
	E2AE-ABA, RA	7200	.345-.355	.115-.135	.485-.495	.430-.460
	E2AE-AGA, AHA	7200	.345-.355	.115-.135	.485-.495	.440-.480
	E2AE-LB	7200	.345-.355	.115-.135	.520-.530	.430-.460
	E2AE-LC	7200	.345-.355	.115-.135	.520-.530	.430-.460
	E2AE-MA	7200	.345-.355	.115-.135	.485-.495	.440-.480
	E2AE-MB	7200	.345-.355	.115-.135	.485-.495	.440-.480
	E2AE-NA, SA	7200	.345-.355	.115-.135	.520-.530	.430-.460
	E2AE-TA	7200	.345-.355	.115-.135	.485-.495	.430-.460
	E2AE-TB	7200	.345-.355	.115-.135	.485-.495	.430-.460
	E2DE-NA, SA, TA, UA	7200	.345-.355	.115-.135	.485-.495	.440-.480
	E2SE-DA, FA	7200	.345-.355	.115-.135	.520-.530	.460-.490
	E2SE-DB	7200	.345-.355	.115-.135	.520-.530	.460-.490
	E25E-ABA	7200	.345-.355	.115-.135	.485-.495	.430-.460
	E25E-AC, YA	7200	.345-.355	.115-.135	.520-.530	.460-.490
	E25E-FA	7200	.345-.355	.115-.135	.520-.530	.430-.460
	E25E-GA, SA, UA	7200	.345-.355	.115-.135	.520-.530	.430-.460
	E25E-GB, TA	7200	.345-.355	.115-.135	.520-.530	.430-.460

Fig. 8 Cold enrichment metering rod adjustment specification chart

CONTROL VACUUM REGULATOR (CVR)

With the dial indicator installed, **Fig. 13**, remove the stator cap with tool T77L-9848-A. Press downward on CVR rod until bottomed on seat. Note the dial indicator reading. If not within specifications, place a 3/8 inch box end wrench over CVR adjusting nut and, using a 3/32 inch Allen wrench, turn CVR rod to adjust the travel.

HIGH CAM SPEED POSITIONER

Place high cam speed positioner in the corner of the specified cam step, **Fig. 14.** Then, place the fast idle lever in the corner of the high cam speed positioner and hold throttle firmly closed. Remove diaphragm cover and rotate diaphragm assembly clockwise until lightly bottomed on casting, then rotate assembly counterclockwise 1/2 to 1 1/2 turns, until the vacuum port and diaphragm hole align. Reinstall diaphragm cover.

CHOKE CAP

With choke cap installed, rotate choke cap clockwise until notch on cap is aligned with specified notch on housing, **Fig. 15.**

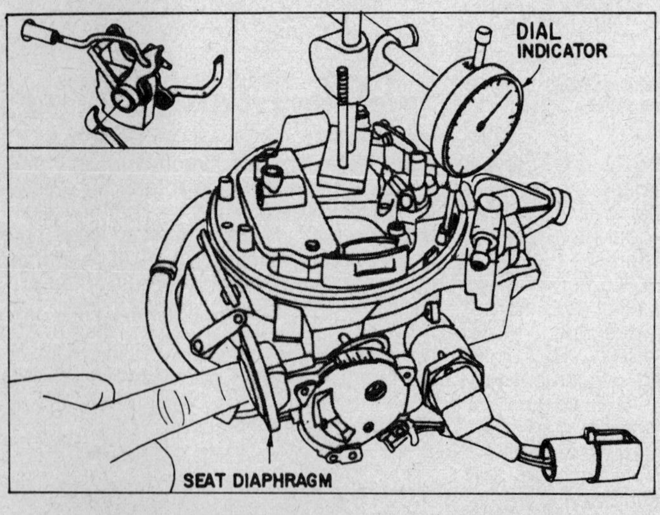

Fig. 9 Checking cold enrichment metering rod Start 75°F position adjustment

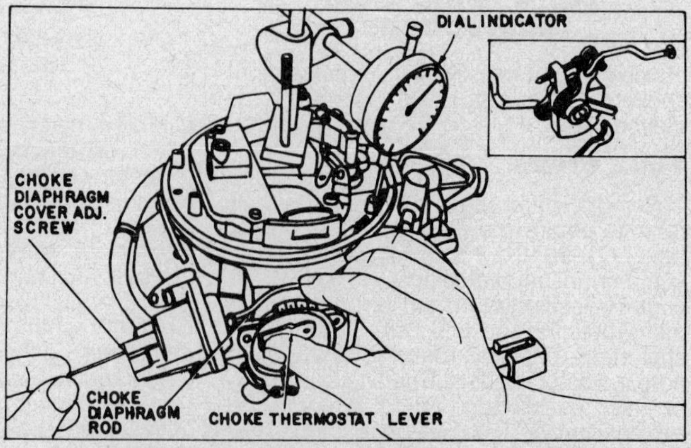

Fig. 10 Adjusting cold enrichment metering rod Run 0°F position

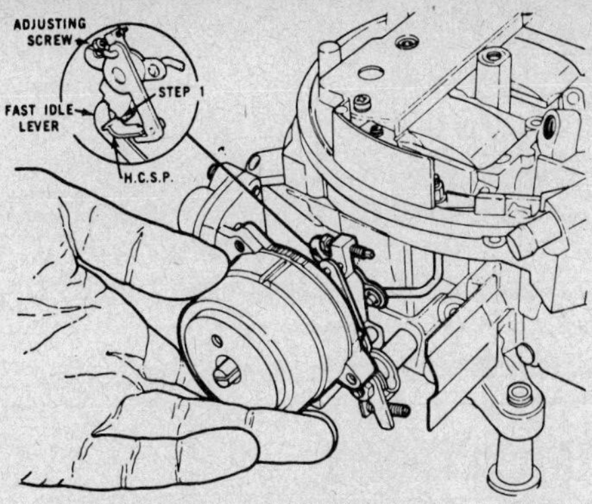

Fig. 11 Fast idle cam adjustment

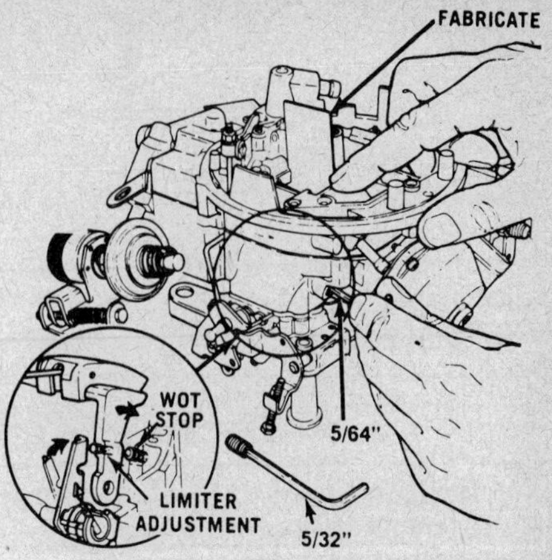

Fig. 12 Venturi valve limiter adjustment

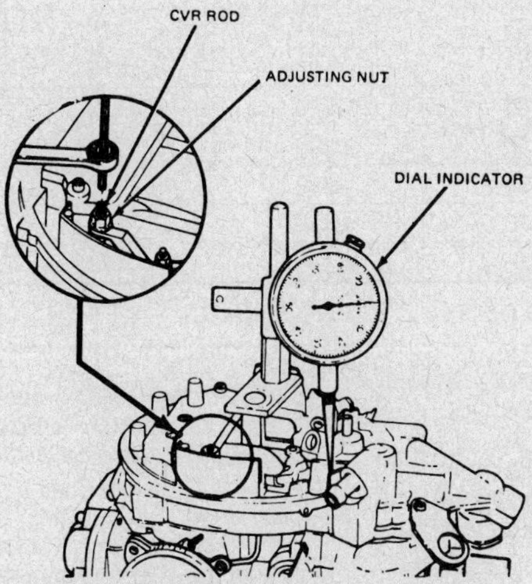

Fig. 13 Control vacuum regulator (CVR) adjustment

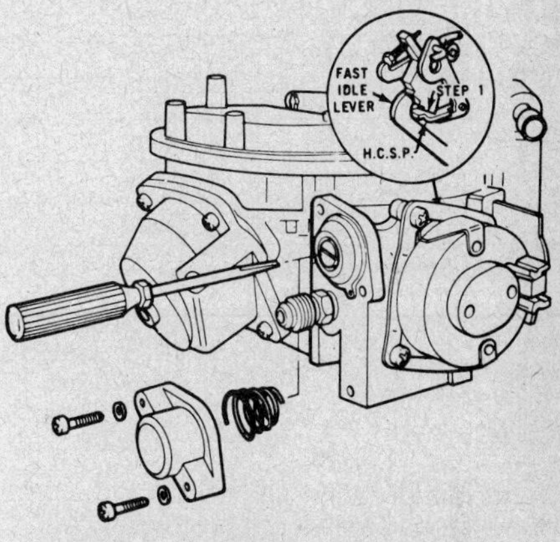

Fig. 14 High cam speed positioner adjustment

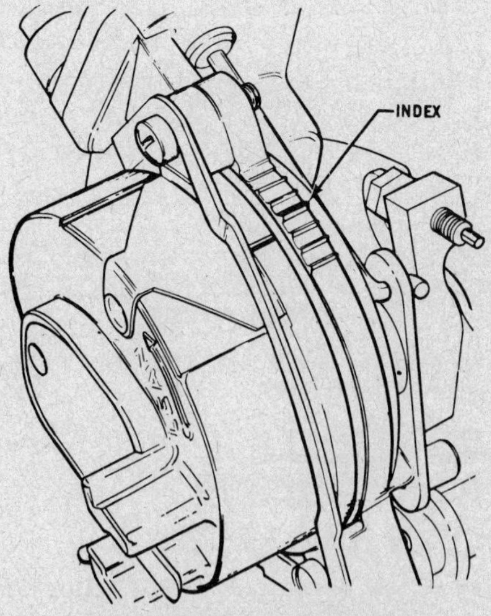

Fig. 15 Choke cap adjustment

Motorcraft Model 5200 2 Barrel Carburetor

INDEX

ADJUSTMENT SPECIFICATIONS

Year	Carb. Model (9510) ①	Float Level	Pump Setting (Hole)	Choke Pulldown	Dechoke Clearance	Fast Idle Cam Clearance	Choke Setting
1982	E1BE-RA	15/32	2	.197	.197	.079	—
	E1ZE-ACA	15/32	2	.197	.197	.079	—
	E1ZE-ADB	15/32	3	.276	.394	.236	—
	E1ZE-VA	15/32	2	.197	.197	.079	—
	E1ZE-YA	15/32	2	.197	.197	.079	—
	E2ZE-AAA	15/32	2	.236	.236	.118	—
	E2ZE-ABA	15/32	2	.236	.236	.118	—
	E2ZE-AFA	15/32	2	.236	.236	.118	—
	E2ZE-AGA	15/32	2	.236	.236	.118	—
	E2ZE-AHA	15/32	2	.236	.236	.118	—

①—Tag attached to carburetor.

IDENTIFICATION LOCATION

The carburetor identification number is located on a tag attached to the carburetor by one of the fuel bowl cover attaching screws.

DESCRIPTION

This carburetor is a two stage, two venturi carburetor, **Fig. 1.** The primary stage or venturi is smaller than the secondary venturi. The secondary is operated by mechanical linkage.

The primary stage includes a curb idle system, accelerator pump system, idle transfer system, main metering system and power enrichment system.

The secondary stage includes a transfer system, main metering system, and power system. Both the primary and secondary systems draw fuel from a common fuel bowl.

All units are equipped with a vacuum operated, solenoid assisted fuel bowl vent which is called a "Switching Bowl Vent." With the engine "Off," a spring holds the external vent open, closing the internal vent passage. In this position, the fuel bowl vapors pass to the evaporative emission canister. When the engine is started, manifold vacuum acting on the diaphragm overcomes the spring pressure and pulls the external vent to the seated position, uncovering the internal vent passage. A holding solenoid, connected to the ignition circuit, holding the vent closed to prevent the vent opening under low vacuum conditions. The vent will close only when the ignition is turned "Off."

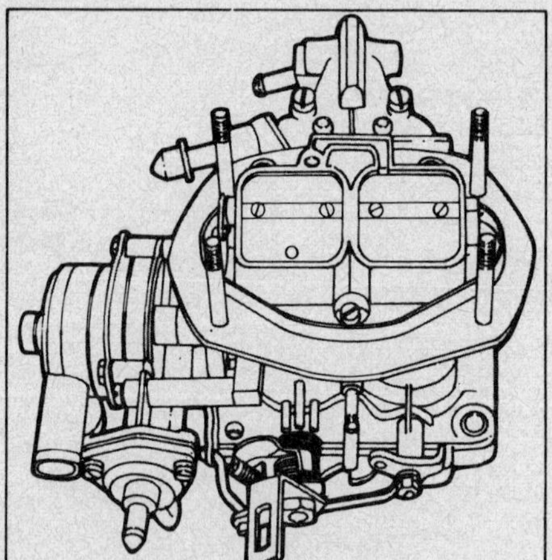

Fig. 1 Model 5200-2V carburetor

ON-VEHICLE ADJUSTMENTS

CURB IDLE SPEED

1. Place transmission into Neutral or Park.
2. Install a suitable tachometer onto engine as per manufacturer's instructions.
3. Start and allow engine to reach normal operating temperature.
4. Place A/C-Heat selector switch to OFF position, if equipped.
5. Check curb idle speed. If curb idle speed obtained is not as specified, turn curb idle speed adjusting screw until specified speed is obtained.

FAST IDLE SPEED

1. Place transmission into Neutral or Park.
2. Install a suitable tachometer onto engine as per manufacturer's instructions.
3. Start and allow engine to reach normal operating temperature.
4. Disconnect and plug EGR and purge valve(s) vacuum lines.
5. On feedback carburetor models, disconnect electrical connector from PVS.
6. Disconnect electrical connector from cooling fan, if equipped.
7. Place fast idle adjustment onto second step of fast idle cam.
8. Check fast idle speed. If fast idle speed obtained is not as specified, turn fast idle speed adjusting screw until specified speed is obtained.

DRY FLOAT SETTING

With the bowl cover held in an inverted position and the float tang resting lightly on the spring loaded fuel inlet needle, **Fig.2,** measure the clearance between the edge of the float and the bowl cover. Adjust clearance by bending the float tang up or down as required, **Fig. 3. Do not scratch or damage the tang. Adjust both floats equally.**

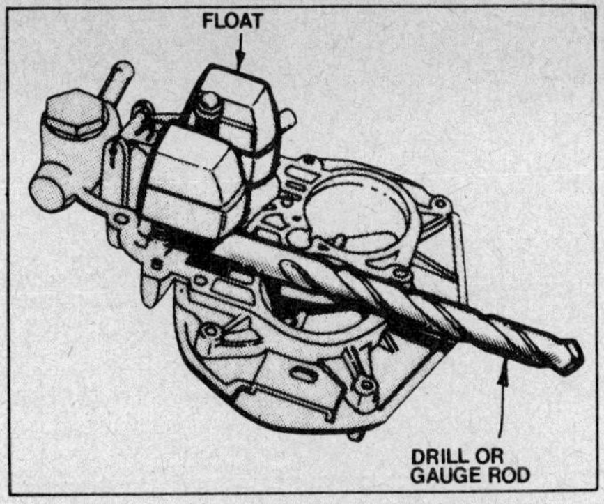

Fig. 2 Dry float setting

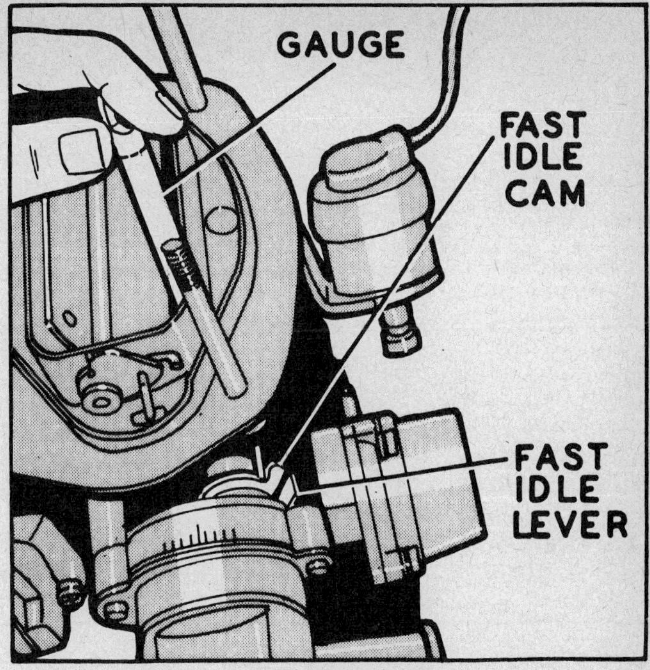

Fig. 4 De-choke adjustment

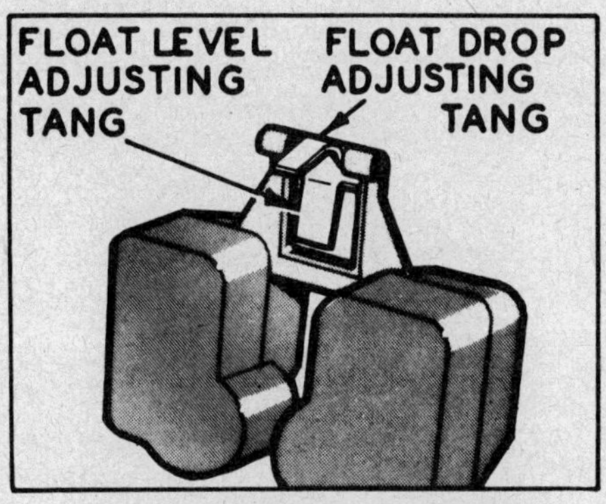

Fig. 3 Float adjusting point

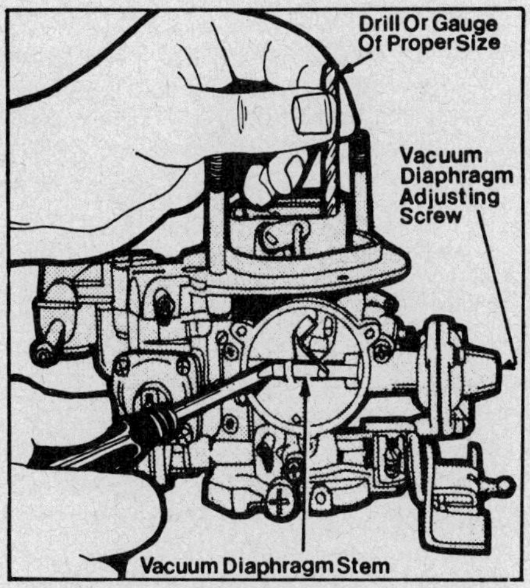

Fig. 5 Choke plate pull-down

DECHOKE CLEARANCE

Hold throttle lever in wide open position and take slack out of choke linkage by applying finger pressure to top edge of choke plate. Measure clearance between lower edge of choke plate and air horn wall, **Fig. 4.** Adjust by bending tab on fast idle lever where it touches the fast idle cam.

CHOKE PLATE VACUUM PULLDOWN

It is necessary to remove the carburetor to remove rivets retaining choke cover to choke housing. Using a 1/8 inch or No. 30 drill bit, remove rivet heads, then drive rivet out using a 1/8 inch diameter punch.

Remove the three screws and ring retaining choke spring cover and pull the water cover and/or choke spring cover from carburetor. Place fast idle cam on high step. Push the diaphragm stem back against its stop, **Fig. 5.** Place gauge rod or drill between the lower edge of the choke plate and the air horn wall. Remove the slack from the choke linkage by applying finger pressure to the top edge of the choke plate. Adjust the choke plate-to-air horn clearance by removing the plug from the diaphragm and turning the adjusting screw in or out as required.

FAST IDLE CAM CLEARANCE

Insert specified drill or gauge between the lower edge of the choke plate and the air horn wall, **Fig. 6.** With the fast idle screw held on the second step of the fast idle cam, measure the clearance between the tang of the choke lever and the arm on the fast idle cam. Adjust clearance by bending choke lever tang up or down as required. Refer to Adjustment Specifications.

SECONDARY THROTTLE STOP SCREW

Back off the secondary throttle stop screw until the secondary throttle plate seats in its bore, **Fig. 7.** Turn the screw in until it touches the tab on the secondary throttle lever. On all units except when used on 2800 cc engines, turn the screw inward an additional 1/4 turn. On units used on 2800 cc engines, turn screw inward an additional 3/4 turn.

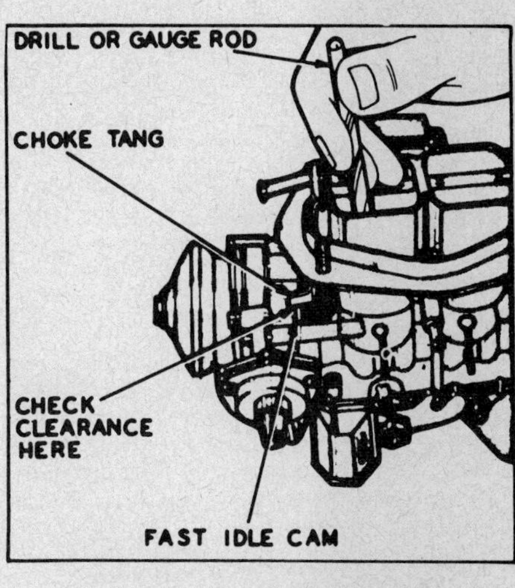

Fig. 6 Fast idle cam clearance

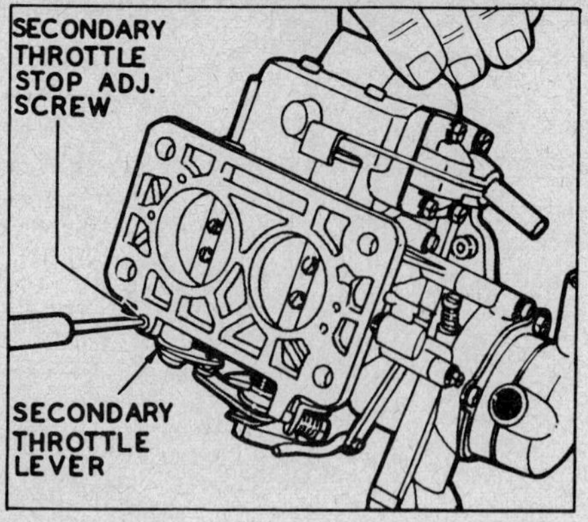

Fig. 7 Secondary throttle stop adjustment

Motorcraft Model 5740 2 Barrel Carburetor

INDEX

ADJUSTMENT SPECIFICATIONS

Year	Model	Float Level	Float Drop	Fast Idle Cam Setting	Pulldown Setting	Dash Pot
1985	All	.246	1.71	—	—	①
1986	E5G-AEC, AFC	.295	.171.	.079	.276	①

①—Auto. trans., .059 inch; man. trans., .079 inch.

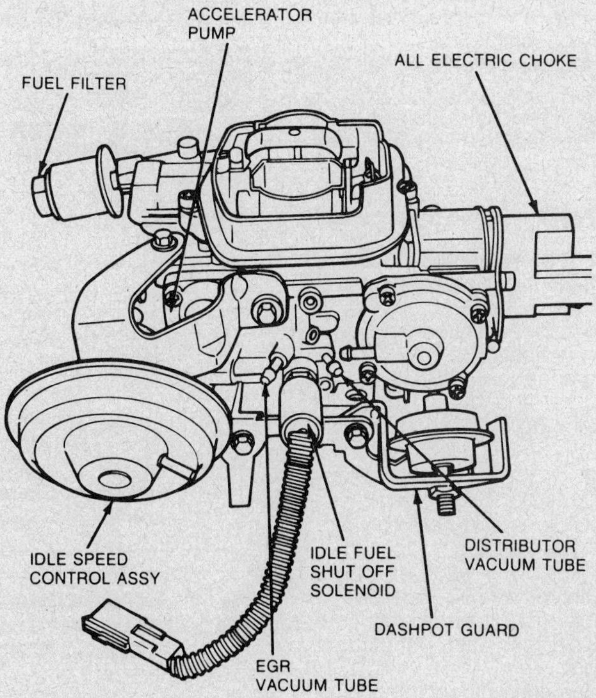

Fig. 1 Motorcraft model 5740 2 barrel carburetor

IDENTIFICATION LOCATION

The carburetor identification number is located on a tag attached to the carburetor by one of the fuel bowl cover attaching screws.

DESCRIPTION

This carburetor, **Fig. 1,** is a two barrel unit having four basic metering systems: choke system, main metering system, acceleration system and idle system. On some applications, a power enrichment system is also used to provide improved performance during moderate to heavy acceleration.

An idle fuel shutoff solenoid system, **Fig. 2,** is used to eliminate dieseling when the engine is shut off. When the ignition switch is in the On position, the idle fuel shutoff solenoid is energized, allowing fuel to flow through idle system of carburetor. When the ignition switch is turned to the Off position, the solenoid is de-energized and fuel flow through the carburetor idle system is blocked.

A dash pot, mounted on the carburetor, helps to control hydrocarbon emissions during deceleration by slowing the closing of the throttle plates. As the throttle plates close, the throttle lever applies pressure on the dash pot plunger. This causes air in the dash pot chamber to escape, allowing the throttle plates to slowly return to the idle position.

The altitude compensation system is used to improve driveability and reduce emissions at high altitude. The system consists of an altitude barometric switch, a bleed solenoid and associated wiring to the carburetor. The system operates only when the vehicle is operated at altitudes above approximately 4000 feet.

On certain applications, a Wide Open Throttle (WOT) A/C cutout switch is used to electrically disengage the A/C compressor clutch at WOT position.

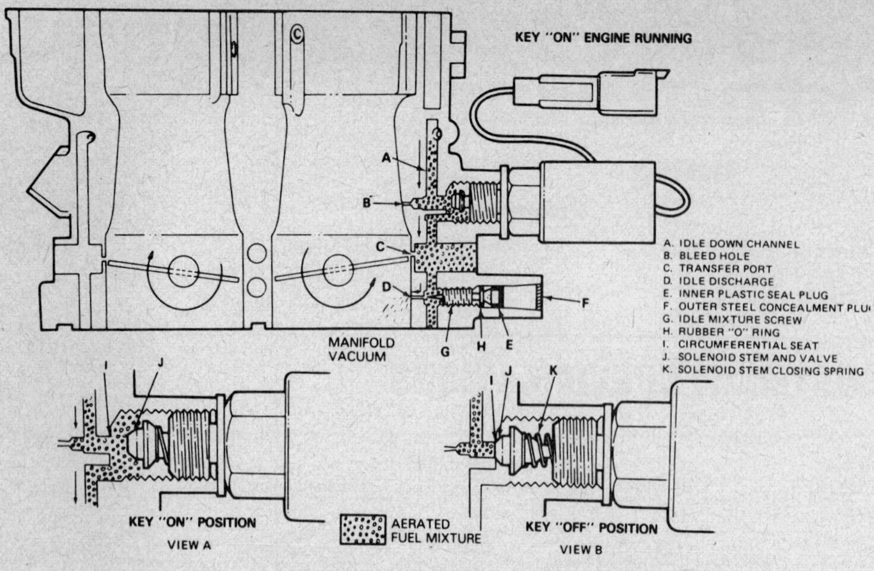

Fig. 2 Idle fuel shutoff solenoid system

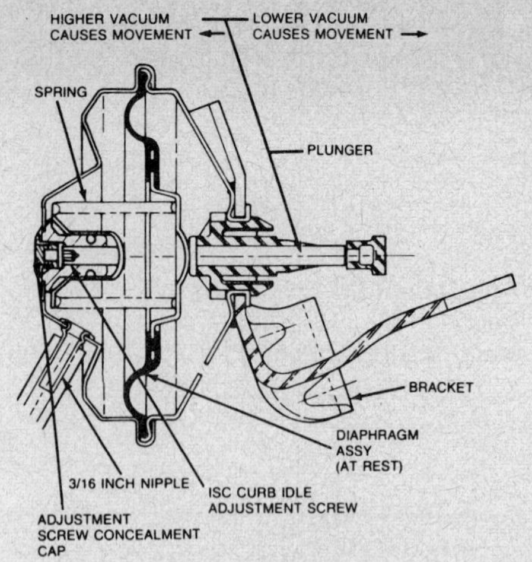

Fig. 3 Idle Speed Control (ISC) assembly

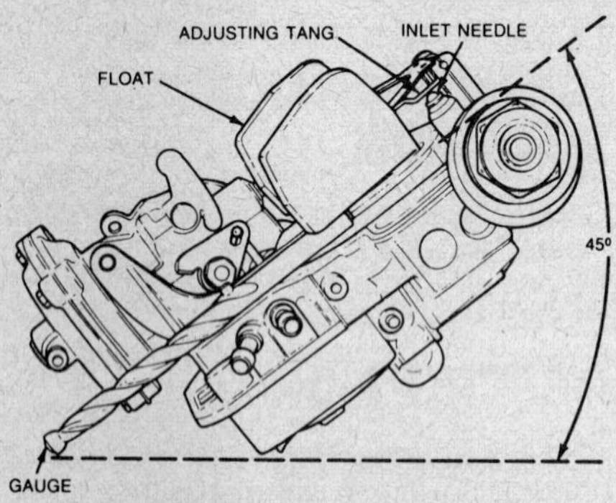

Fig. 4 Float level adjustment

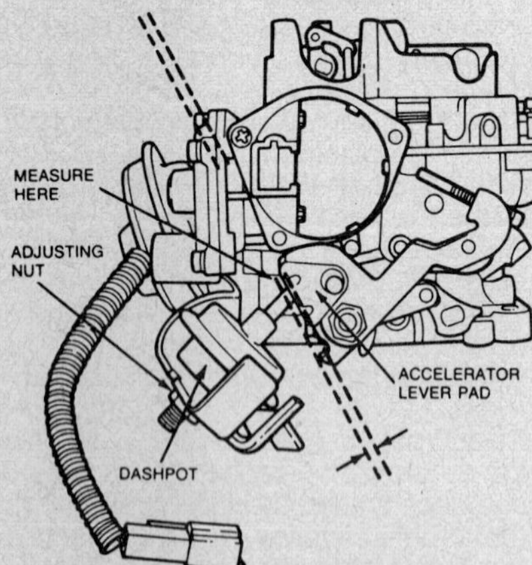

Fig. 5 Float drop adjustment

The carburetor-mounted Idle Speed Control (ISC), **Fig. 3**, is a throttle positioner which uses direct manifold vacuum to maintain a specified idle speed for various engine loading conditions. As manifold vacuum decreases, the ISC plunger moves outward to increase carburetor throttle plate opening and return engine to a specified speed.

ON-VEHICLE ADJUSTMENTS

FLOAT LEVEL

1. Invert air horn assembly and hold at a 45 degree angle with air horn gasket removed, **Fig. 4.** Ensure float tank rests lightly on inlet needle.
2. Measure clearance at end of float, **Fig. 4.**
3. Adjust clearance to specifications by removing float and bending float level adjusting tank up or down as necessary.

FLOAT DROP

1. Suspend air horn assembly in normal position with air horn gasket removed, **Fig. 5.**
2. Measure distance between air horn and bottom of float, **Fig. 5.**
3. Adjust clearance to specifications by removing float and bend float level adjusting tank up or down as necessary.

DASH POT

1. Disconnect idle speed control vacuum line from ISC motor.
2. Apply 22 inches Hg vacuum to ISC motor to fully retract ISC plunger.
3. With engine off and throttle at curb idle speed, depress dash pot plunger into dash pot.
4. Measure clearance between accelerator lever pad and dash pot, **Fig. 6.**
5. Adjust clearance to specifications by loosening adjusting nut, turning dash pot as necessary and retightening nut. Torque nut to 53 inch lbs. after adjustment.
6. Recheck clearance and adjust as necessary.
7. Connect ISC vacuum line to ISC motor.

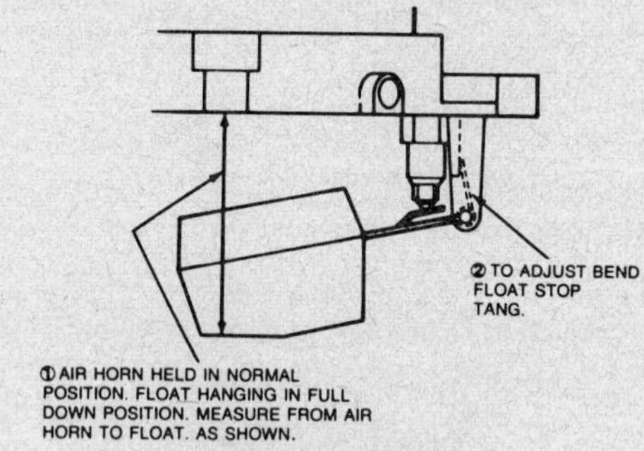

Fig. 6 Dash pot adjustment

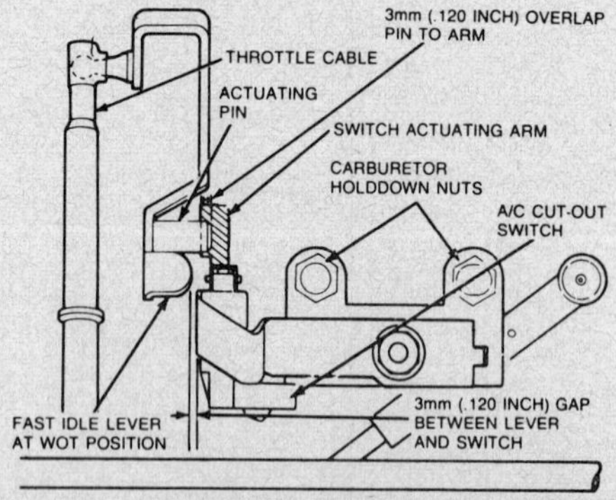

Fig. 7 Wide Open Throttle (WOT) A/C cutout switch adjustment

WIDE OPEN THROTTLE (WOT) A/C CUTOUT SWITCH

1. With carburetor linkage in the WOT position, ensure adequate pin and actuating arm overlap, **Fig. 7.**
2. Bend switch support bracket outward as necessary to provide a .120 inch minimum overlap.

FUEL INJECTION, GASOLINE

TABLE OF CONTENTS

Multi-Point EFI System

INDEX

DESCRIPTION

The system used on 1983-85 4-97.6 engines, 1983-87 4-140 turbocharged engines and 1986-87 V6-182 and 4-116 engines, is a multi-point, pulse time, mass air flow fuel injection system. Fuel is metered into the intake air stream through either four or six injectors mounted on a tuned intake manifold.

The system used on 1986-87 V8-302 engines is a sequential, multi-point, pulse time, speed density control fuel injection system. Fuel is metered into the intake air stream through eight injectors mounted on a tuned intake manifold.

The system used on 1987 4-140 Mustang models, is a multi-point, pulse time, speed density fuel injection system. Fuel is metered into the intake air stream in accordance with the engine demand through four injectors mounted on a tuned intake manifold.

All three systems use an electronic control unit (ECU, part of the EEC-IV system) which receives signals from various engine sensors and computes the required rate of fuel flow to maintain an optimum air/fuel ratio throughout the entire range of engine operation. The ECU then sends a command to the fuel injectors to meter the appropriate quantity of fuel.

The EFI system can be divided into four basic sub-systems: fuel delivery, air induction, sensors and ECU.

On four and six cylinder engine applications, the fuel delivery system consists of a chassis-mounted (four cylinder) or tank-mounted (six cylinder), high pressure electric fuel pump which delivers fuel from the fuel tank through a fuel filter to the fuel charging manifold assembly.

On eight cylinder engine applications, the fuel delivery system consists of a low pressure tank-mounted fuel pump, a fuel filter/reservoir combination and a high pressure electric fuel pump which delivers fuel from the fuel tank through a fuel filter to the fuel charging manifold assembly.

The fuel charging manifold assembly, **Figs. 1 through 6,** houses the injectors which are mounted directly above each of the engine's intake ports. When energized, the injectors spray a metered quantity of fuel into the intake air stream.

SYSTEM COMPONENTS & OPERATION

FUEL INJECTORS

The fuel injectors, **Fig. 7,** are electromechanical devices which meter and atomize fuel for combustion. The injectors, located in the lower intake manifold, are installed so fuel is directed just ahead of the intake valves. The injector solenoid receives an electrical control signal from the ECU which causes the pintle to move off its seat, allowing fuel to flow. Because the fuel pressure drop across the injector tip is constant and the injector orifice is fixed, fuel flow is regulated by the length of time the solenoid is energized.

FUEL PRESSURE REGULATOR

The fuel pressure regulator, **Fig. 8,** is located on the fuel supply manifold and regulates fuel pressure supplied to the injectors. One side of the diaphragm in the regulator senses fuel pressure, while intake manifold pressure is applied to the other side. Nominal fuel pressure is established by spring tension applied to the diaphragm. A constant fuel pressure drop across the injectors is maintained by balancing one side of the diaphragm with manifold pressure. Excess fuel is bypassed through the regulator and returned to the fuel tank.

AIR VANE METER

The following system components are either used on mass air flow or speed density systems.

Four Cylinder Engines

On 4-97.6 and 4-116 engines, the air vane meter, located between the throttle body and air cleaner, is mounted on a bracket near the left side shock tower. On 1983-86 4-140 turbocharged engines, the air vane meter, located between air cleaner and turbocharger, is mounted on a bracket below air cleaner in lower righthand corner of engine compartment. On 1987 4-140 turbocharged engines, the air vane meter is located between the air cleaner and the turbocharger and is mounted on a bracket immediately below the air cleaner in the lower righthand corner of the engine compartment.

The air vane meter, located between the throttle body and air cleaner, is mounted on a bracket near the left side shock tower. Housed in the air vane meter are the vane air flow and vane air temperature sensors. The air flow sensor measures the mass of air flow to the engine and the temperature sensor measures incoming air temperature. These two signals are sent to the ECU to compute mass air flow. This value is used to determine necessary fuel flow to the injectors to provide the optimum air/fuel ratio.

THROTTLE BODY

Air flow to the engine is controlled by the throttle body through a single butterfly-type valve. Throttle position is controlled by a cable/cam throttle linkage. The throttle body has a single bore with an air bypass channel around the throttle plate. The bypass channel controls both cold and warm engine idle air flow which is regulated by an air bypass valve assembly mounted on the throttle body. The air bypass valve is controlled by the ECU and incorporates a linear actuator which positions a variable area metering valve.

FUEL SUPPLY MANIFOLD

The fuel supply manifold, **Figs. 9, 10 and 11,** delivers high pressure fuel from the fuel supply line to the injectors. The

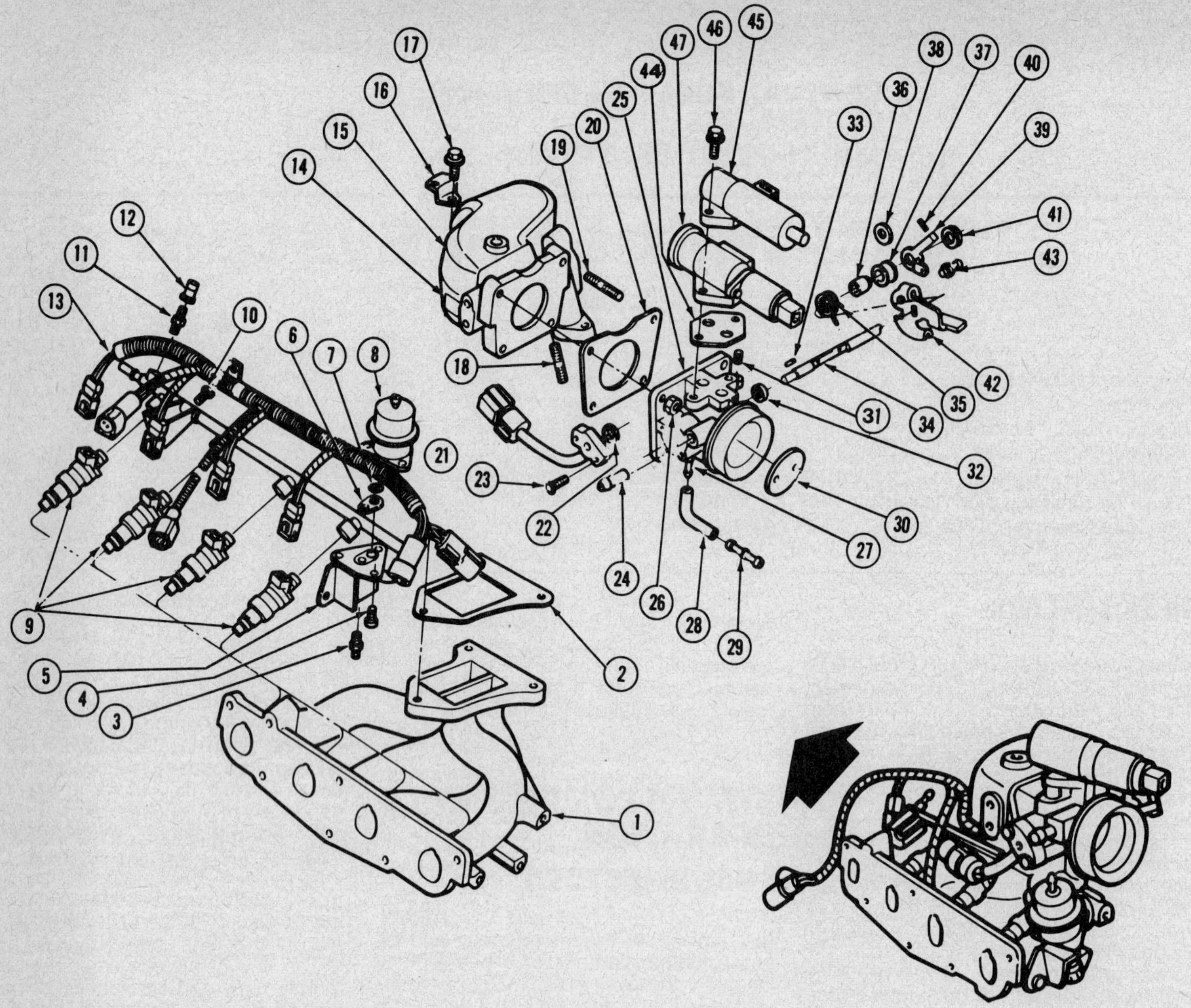

ITEM	PART NAME
1.	MANIFOLD – INTAKE LOWER
2.	GASKET – INTAKE MANIFOLD UPPER
3.	CONNECTOR
4.	SCREW
5.	MANIFOLD ASSEMBLY – FUEL INJECTION FUEL SUPPLY
6.	GASKET – FUEL PRESSURE REGULATOR
7.	SEAL
8.	REGULATOR ASSEMBLY – FUEL PRESSURE
9.	INJECTOR ASSEMBLY – FUEL
10.	BOLT
11.	VALVE ASSEMBLY – FUEL PRESSURE RELIEF
12.	CAP – FUEL PRESSURE RELIEF
13.	WIRING HARNESS – FUEL CHARGING
14.	DECAL – CARBURETOR IDENTIFICATION
15.	MANIFOLD – INTAKE UPPER
16.	RETAINER – WIRING HARNESS
17.	BOLT
18.	STUD
19.	STUD
20.	GASKET – AIR INTAKE CHARGE TO INTAKE MANIFOLD
21.	SENSOR – THROTTLE POSITION
22.	BUSHING – CARBURETOR THROTTLE SHAFT
23.	SCREW AND WASHER ASSEMBLY
24.	TUBE – EMISSION INLET

ITEM	PART NAME
25.	BODY – AIR INTAKE CHARGE THROTTLE
26.	NUT
27.	TUBE
28.	HOSE – VACUUM
29.	CONNECTOR
30.	PLATE – AIR INTAKE THROTTLE CHARGE
31.	SCREW
32.	SEAL – THROTTLE CONTROL SHAFT
33.	PIN – SPRING COILED
34.	SHAFT
35.	SPRING – THROTTLE RETURN
36.	BUSHING – ACCELERATOR PUMP OVERTRAVEL SPRING
37.	BEARING – THROTTLE CONTROL LINKAGE
38.	SPACER – THROTTLE CONTROL TORSION SPRING (MAN. TRANS. ONLY)
39.	LEVER – CARBURETOR TRANSMISSION LINKAGE
40.	SCREW
41.	SPACER – CARBURETOR THROTTLE SHAFT
42.	LEVER – CARBURETOR THROTTLE
43.	BALL – CARBURETOR THROTTLE LEVER
44.	GASKET – AIR BYPASS VALVE
45.	VALVE ASSEMBLY – THROTTLE AIR BYPASS (ALT.)
46.	BOLT
47.	VALVE ASSEMBLY – THROTTLE AIR BYPASS

Fig. 1 Exploded view of fuel charging assembly. 4-97.6 engine

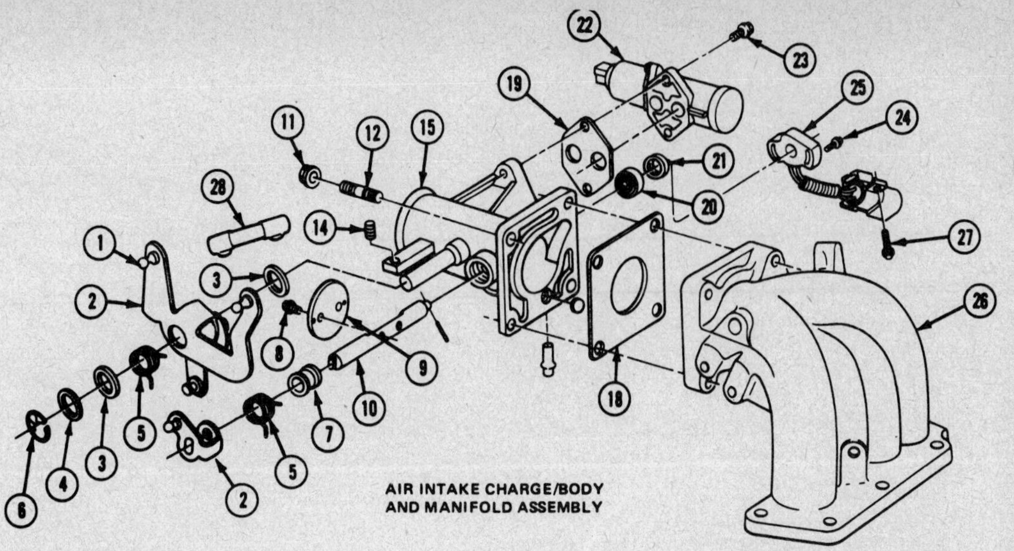

ITEM	PART NAME	ITEM	PART NAME
1	BALL – THROTTLE LEVER	15	BODY – AIR INTAKE CHARGE THROTTLE
2	LEVER – THROTTLE – PRIMARY	18	GASKET – AIR CHARGE CONTROL TO INTAKE MANIFOLD
3	SPACER – THROTTLE SHAFT	19	GASKET – AIR BYPASS VALVE
4	SPACER – THROTTLE CONTROL TORSION SPRING	20	SEAL – THROTTLE CONTROL SHAFT
5	SPRING – THROTTLE RETURN	21	BUSHING – CARBURETOR THROTTLE SHAFT
6	CLIP – THROTTLE SHAFT	22	VALVE ASSEMBLY – THROTTLE AIR BYPASS
7	BUSHING	23	BOLT – M6x1.0x20 HEX HEAD FLANGE
8	SCREW M4x.7x8	24	SCREW AND WASHER ASSEMBLY M4x22
9	PLATE – AIR INTAKE CHARGE THROTTLE	25	POTENTIOMETER THROTTLE POSITION
10	SHAFT – AIR INTAKE CHARGE THROTTLE	26	MANIFOLD – INTAKE UPPER
11	NUT – M8	27	SCREW – M4x0.7x14.0 HEX WASHER TAP
12	STUD – M8x42.5	28	LINK – ROD ASSEMBLY THROTTLE CONTROL
14	SCREW – M5x.8x16.25 SLOT HEAD	29	LEVER – THROTTLE SECONDARY

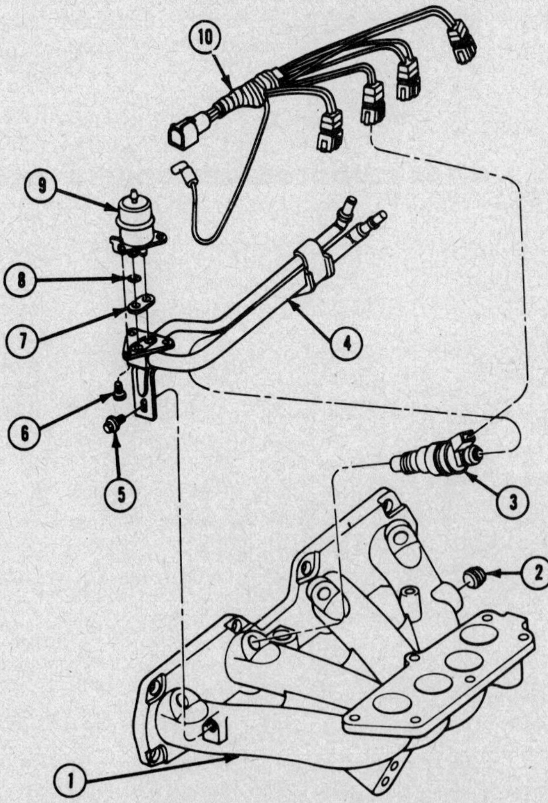

ITEM	PART NAME
1	MANIFOLD – INTAKE LOWER
2	PLUG – 3/8
3	INJECTOR ASSEMBLY – FUEL
4	MANIFOLD ASSEMBLY – FUEL INJECTION FUEL SUPPLY
5	BOLT – M6x1.0x18 HEX HEAD
6	SCREW – M5x.8x10 SOCKET HEAD
7	GASKET – FUEL PRESSURE REGULATOR
8	SEAL – 5/16x.070 O-RING
9	REGULATOR ASSEMBLY – FUEL PRESSURE
10	WIRING HARNESS – FUEL CHARGING

FUEL CHARGING MANIFOLD ASSEMBLY

Fig. 2 Exploded view of fuel charging assembly. 4-140 turbocharged engine (Mustang SVO)

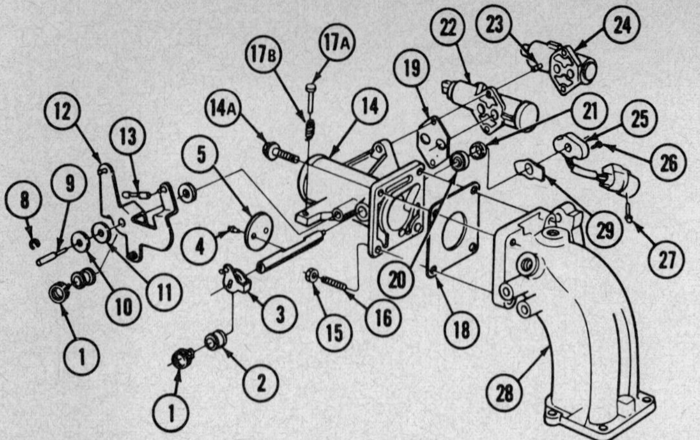

ITEM	PART NAME
1	SPRING — CARBURETOR THROTTLE RETURN
2	BUSHING — ACCELERATOR PUMP OVERTRAVEL SPRING (2)
3	LEVER — ENGINE THROTTLE
4	SCREW — M4 X .7 X 8
5	PLATE — AIR INTAKE CHARGE THROTTLE
6	SHAFT — AIR INTAKE CHARGE THROTTLE
7	SPRING — SECONDARY THROTTLE RETURN
8	E-RING
9	HUB — THROTTLE CONTROL
10	SPACER
11	WASHER — NYLON (2)
12	LEVER — THROTTLE CONTROL
13	ROD — ENGINE SECONDARY THROTTLE CONTROL
14	BODY — AIR INTAKE CHARGE THROTTLE
14A	BOLT M8 X 1.25 X 30 HEX FLANGE HEAD (2 REQ'D)
15	NUT — M8 (2 REQ'D)
16	STUD — M8 X 42.5 (2 REQ'D)
17A	SCREW THROTTLE STOP
17B	SPRING — THROTTLE RETURN CONTROL
18	GASKET — AIR CHARGE CONTROL TO INTAKE MANIFOLD
19	GASKET — AIR BYPASS VALVE
20	SEAL — THROTTLE CONTROL SHAFT
21	BUSHING — CARBURETOR THROTTLE SHAFT
22	VALVE ASSEMBLY — THROTTLE AIR BYPASS
23	BOLT — M6 X 1.0 X 20 HEX HEAD FLANGE
24	VALVE ASSEMBLY — THROTTLE AIR BYPASS (ALT.)
25	POTENTIOMETER THROTTLE POSITION
26	SCREW AND WASHER ASSEMBLY M4 X 22
27	SCREW — M4 X 0.7 X 14.0 HEX. WASHER TAP
28	MANIFOLD — INTAKE UPPER
29	GASKET T.P.S.

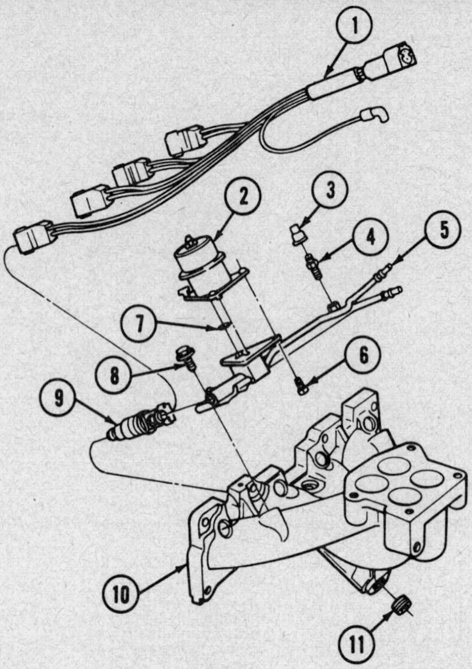

ITEM	PART NAME
1	WIRING HARNESS — FUEL CHARGING
2	REGULATOR ASSEMBLY — FUEL PRESSURE
3	CAP — FUEL PRESSURE RELIEF
4	VALVE ASSEMBLY — FUEL PRESSURE RELIEF
5	MANIFOLD ASSEMBLY — FUEL INJECTION FUEL SUPPLY
6	SCREW — M5 X 0.8 X 10 SOCKET HEAD (3 REQ'D)
7	SEAL — 5/16 X .070 O-RING
8	BOLT (2 REQ'D)
9	INJECTOR ASSEMBLY — FUEL (4 REQ'D)
10	MANIFOLD — INTAKE LOWER
11	PLUG

Fig. 3 Exploded view of fuel charging assembly. 4-140 turbocharged engine (exc. Mustang SVO)

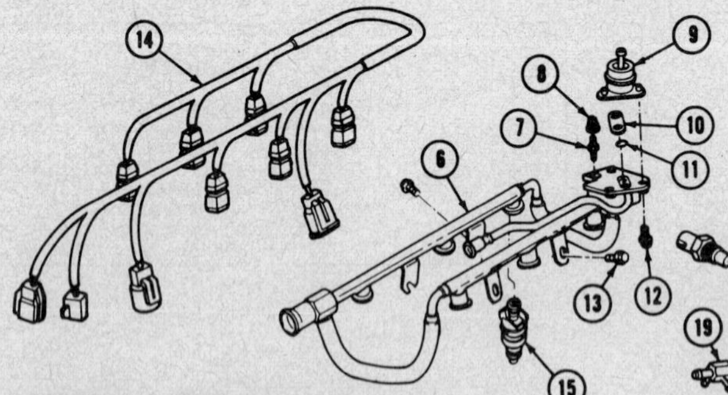

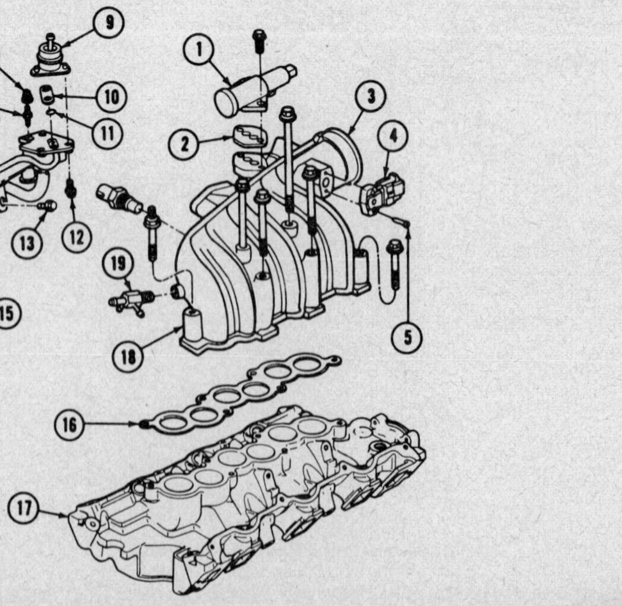

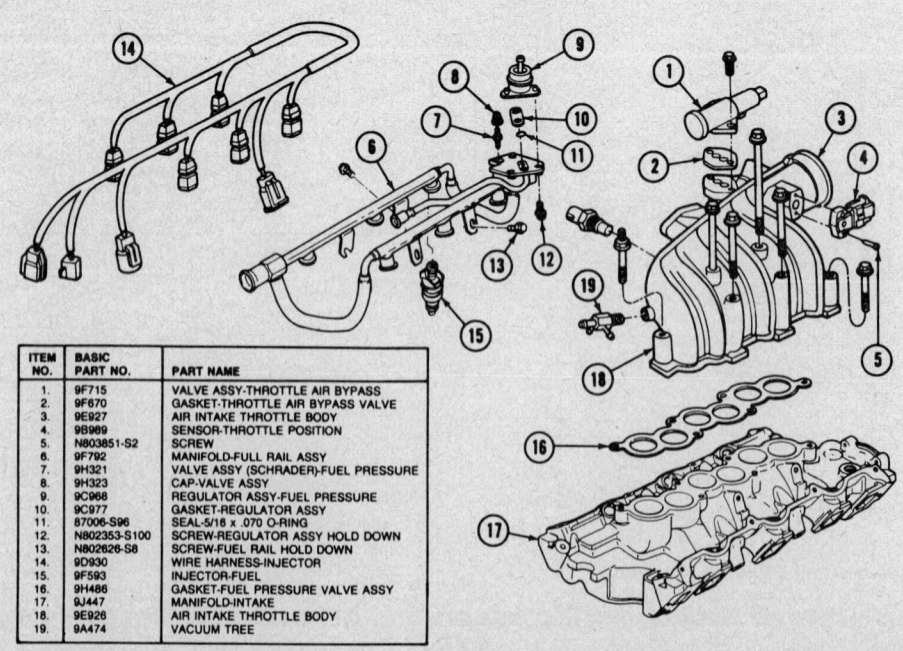

ITEM NO.	BASIC PART NO.	PART NAME
1.	9F715	VALVE ASSY-THROTTLE AIR BYPASS
2.	9F670	GASKET-THROTTLE AIR BYPASS VALVE
3.	9E927	AIR INTAKE THROTTLE BODY
4.	9B989	SENSOR-THROTTLE POSITION
5.	N803851-S2	SCREW
6.	9F792	MANIFOLD-FULL RAIL ASSY
7.	9H321	VALVE ASSY (SCHRADER)-FUEL PRESSURE
8.	9H323	CAP-VALVE ASSY
9.	9C968	REGULATOR ASSY-FUEL PRESSURE
10.	9C977	GASKET-REGULATOR ASSY
11.	87006-S96	SEAL-5/16 x .070 O-RING
12.	N802353-S100	SCREW-REGULATOR ASSY HOLD DOWN
13.	N802626-S8	SCREW-FUEL RAIL HOLD DOWN
14.	9D930	WIRE HARNESS-INJECTOR
15.	9F593	INJECTOR-FUEL
16.	9H486	GASKET-FUEL PRESSURE VALVE ASSY
17.	9J447	MANIFOLD-INTAKE
18.	9E926	AIR INTAKE THROTTLE BODY
19.	9A474	VACUUM TREE

Fig. 5 Exploded view of fuel charging assembly. V6-182 engine

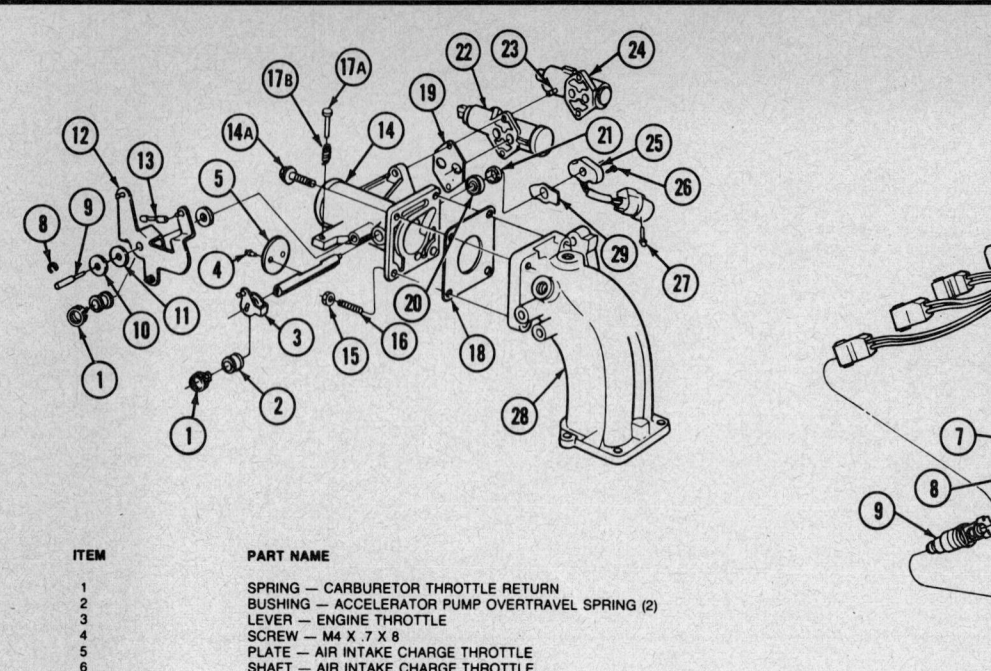

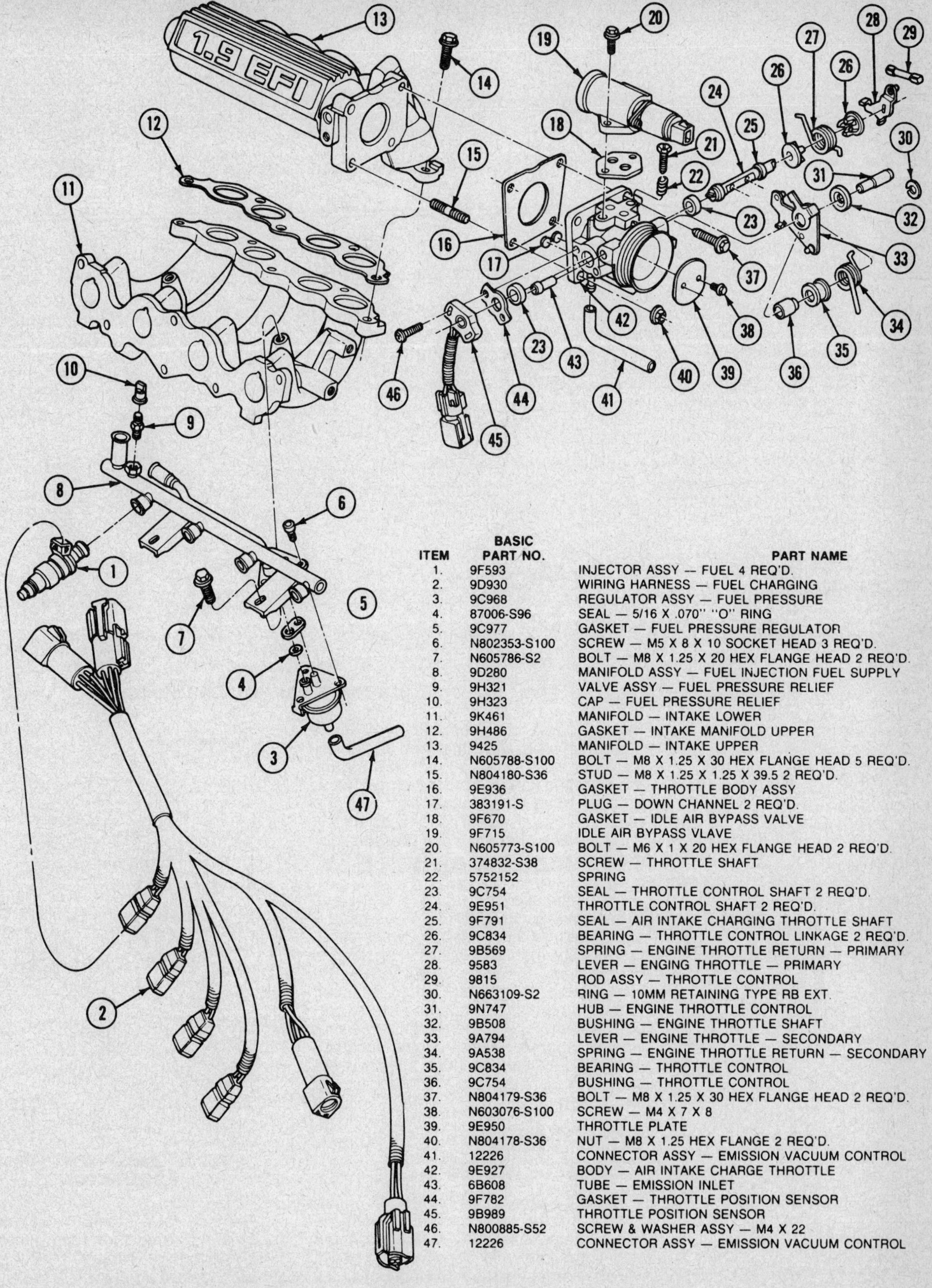

ITEM	BASIC PART NO.	PART NAME
1.	9F593	INJECTOR ASSY — FUEL 4 REQ'D.
2.	9D930	WIRING HARNESS — FUEL CHARGING
3.	9C968	REGULATOR ASSY — FUEL PRESSURE
4.	87006-S96	SEAL — 5/16 X .070" "O" RING
5.	9C977	GASKET — FUEL PRESSURE REGULATOR
6.	N802353-S100	SCREW — M5 X 8 X 10 SOCKET HEAD 3 REQ'D.
7.	N605786-S2	BOLT — M8 X 1.25 X 20 HEX FLANGE HEAD 2 REQ'D.
8.	9D280	MANIFOLD ASSY — FUEL INJECTION FUEL SUPPLY
9.	9H321	VALVE ASSY — FUEL PRESSURE RELIEF
10.	9H323	CAP — FUEL PRESSURE RELIEF
11.	9K461	MANIFOLD — INTAKE LOWER
12.	9H486	GASKET — INTAKE MANIFOLD UPPER
13.	9425	MANIFOLD — INTAKE UPPER
14.	N605788-S100	BOLT — M8 X 1.25 X 30 HEX FLANGE HEAD 5 REQ'D.
15.	N804180-S36	STUD — M8 X 1.25 X 1.25 X 39.5 2 REQ'D.
16.	9E936	GASKET — THROTTLE BODY ASSY
17.	383191-S	PLUG — DOWN CHANNEL 2 REQ'D.
18.	9F670	GASKET — IDLE AIR BYPASS VALVE
19.	9F715	IDLE AIR BYPASS VLAVE
20.	N605773-S100	BOLT — M6 X 1 X 20 HEX FLANGE HEAD 2 REQ'D.
21.	374832-S38	SCREW — THROTTLE SHAFT
22.	5752152	SPRING
23.	9C754	SEAL — THROTTLE CONTROL SHAFT 2 REQ'D.
24.	9E951	THROTTLE CONTROL SHAFT 2 REQ'D.
25.	9F791	SEAL — AIR INTAKE CHARGING THROTTLE SHAFT
26.	9C834	BEARING — THROTTLE CONTROL LINKAGE 2 REQ'D.
27.	9B569	SPRING — ENGINE THROTTLE RETURN — PRIMARY
28.	9583	LEVER — ENGING THROTTLE — PRIMARY
29.	9815	ROD ASSY — THROTTLE CONTROL
30.	N663109-S2	RING — 10MM RETAINING TYPE RB EXT.
31.	9N747	HUB — ENGINE THROTTLE CONTROL
32.	9B508	BUSHING — ENGINE THROTTLE SHAFT
33.	9A794	LEVER — ENGINE THROTTLE — SECONDARY
34.	9A538	SPRING — ENGINE THROTTLE RETURN — SECONDARY
35.	9C834	BEARING — THROTTLE CONTROL
36.	9C754	BUSHING — THROTTLE CONTROL
37.	N804179-S36	BOLT — M8 X 1.25 X 30 HEX FLANGE HEAD 2 REQ'D.
38.	N603076-S100	SCREW — M4 X 7 X 8
39.	9E950	THROTTLE PLATE
40.	N804178-S36	NUT — M8 X 1.25 HEX FLANGE 2 REQ'D.
41.	12226	CONNECTOR ASSY — EMISSION VACUUM CONTROL
42.	9E927	BODY — AIR INTAKE CHARGE THROTTLE
43.	6B608	TUBE — EMISSION INLET
44.	9F782	GASKET — THROTTLE POSITION SENSOR
45.	9B989	THROTTLE POSITION SENSOR
46.	N800885-S52	SCREW & WASHER ASSY — M4 X 22
47.	12226	CONNECTOR ASSY — EMISSION VACUUM CONTROL

Fig. 4 Exploded view of fuel charging assembly. 4-116 engine

ITEM	PART NUMBER	PART NAME
1.	9H321	SCHRADER VALVE
2.	9H323	CAP-SCHRADER VALVE
3.	9F792	FUEL RAIL ASSY
4.	87006-S96	SEAL O-RING 5/16 -18 x 6.07 INCH
5.	9C977	GASKET, FUEL PRESSURE REGULATOR
6.	9C968	FUEL PRESSURE REGULATOR
7.	9E434	COVER, UPPER MANIFOLD
8.	57357	SCREW
9.	390397-S8	BOLT 5/16-18 x 6.07 INCH
10.	9E464	GASKET, EGR SPACER
11.	9H474	EGR SPACER
12.	14A464	CONNECTOR, TP SENSOR (PIA TPS)
13.	N804221-S52	SCREW
14.	9B989	SENSOR, THROTTLE POSITION
15.	9F715	THROTTLE AIR BYPASS VALVE
16.	9F670	GASKET, THROTTLE AIR BYPASS VALVE
17.	9E926	THROTTLE BODY ASSY
18.	9E933	GASKET, THROTTLE BODY
19.	9D476	GASKET, EGR VALVE
20.	9F483	EGR VALVE ASSY
21.	6A666	PCV VALVE ASSY
22.	6K780	PCV GROMMET
23.	6A631	ELEMENT, CRANKCASE VENT
24.	9K461	LOWER INTAKE MANIFOLD
25.	8255	GASKET, THERMOSTAT HOUSING
26.	8575	THERMOSTAT
27.	56132	BOLT 5/16-18 x 3.50 INCH
28.	8592	CONNECTOR ASSY, ENGINE COOLANT OUTLET
29.	9D424	TUBE, HEATER WATER SUPPLY AND RETURN
30.	12A648	SENSOR, EEC COOLANT TEMPERATURE
31.	9H486	GASKET, UPPER TO LOWER MANIFOLD
32.	390358-S8	BOLT 5/16-18 x 1.62 INCH
33.	9S434	COVER, DECORATIVE END
34.	376043-S36	PLUG-CAP 1.75 INCH DIA.
35.	9425	UPPER INTAKE MANIFOLD
36.	N802353-S100	SCREW-SOCKET HEAD 5.0 x 0.8 x 1.0
37.	N802626-S8	BOLT, ATT RAIL ASSY TO LOWER MANIFOLD
38.	9F593	FUEL INJECTOR

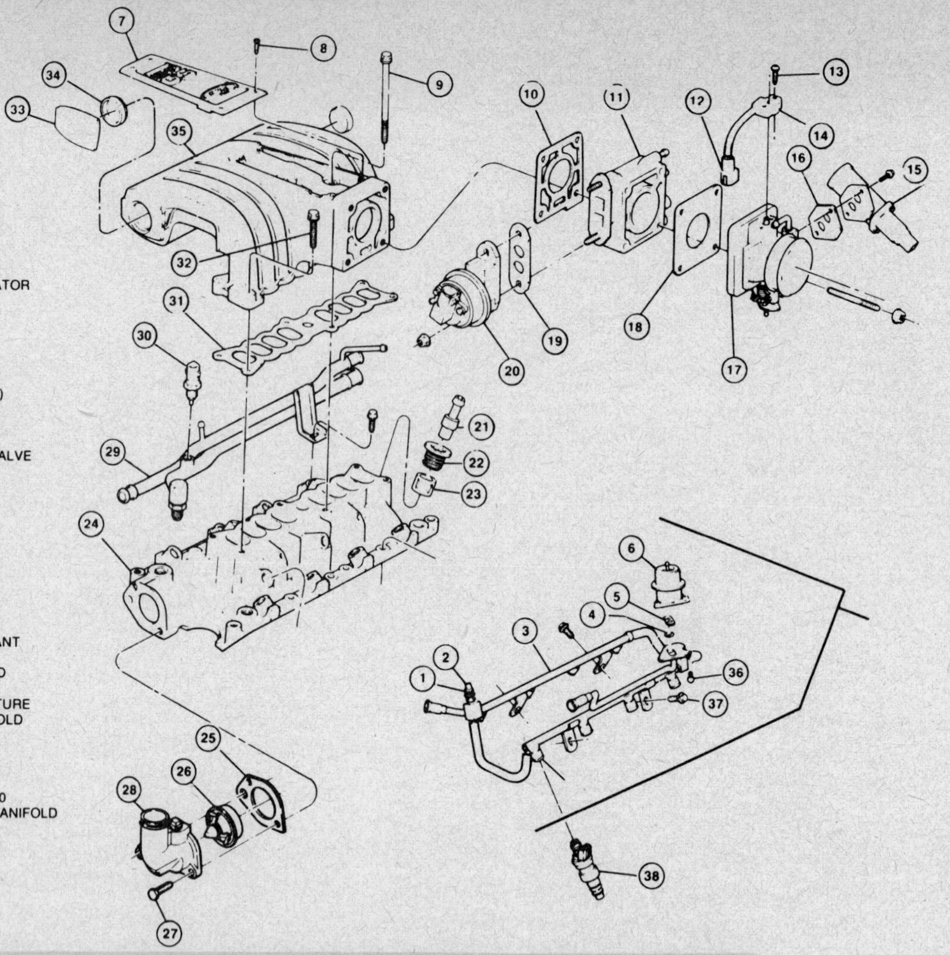

Fig. 6 Exploded view of fuel charging assembly. V8-302 engine

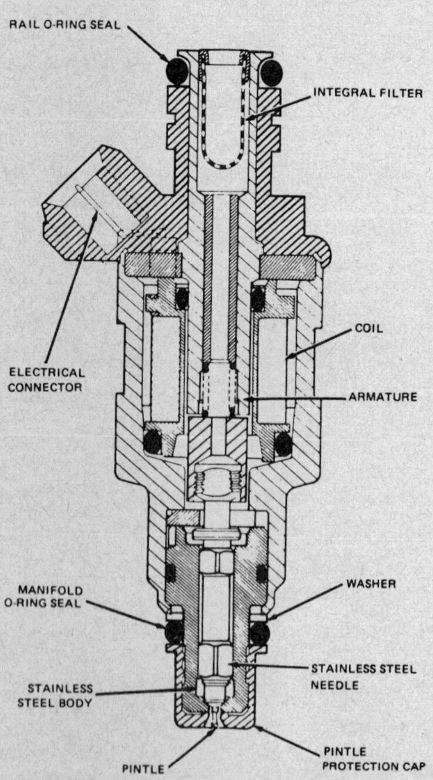

Fig. 7 Fuel injector

manifold assembly consists of a single preformed tube with either four or eight injector connectors, a fuel pressure regulator mounting flange, a pressure relief valve and mounting attachments. The pressure relief valve is used for diagnostic testing and bleeding of fuel system pressure.

AIR INTAKE MANIFOLD

The air intake manifold is a two-piece aluminum casting which provides mounting flanges for the throttle body assembly, fuel supply manifold, accelerator control brackets and the EGR valve and supply tube. Runner lengths are precisely tuned to optimum engine torque and power output. Vacuum taps in the manifold are provided to support various engine accessories. Cutouts for the fuel injectors are specially machined to prevent both air and fuel leakage.

COMPONENT REPLACEMENT

If any subassemblies of the system are to be serviced and/or replaced with the fuel charging assembly installed on the engine, the following steps must be taken:

1. Disconnect battery ground cable.
2. On four cylinder engines, drain engine coolant from radiator.
3. On all models, remove gas cap to release residual fuel pressure in the tank.

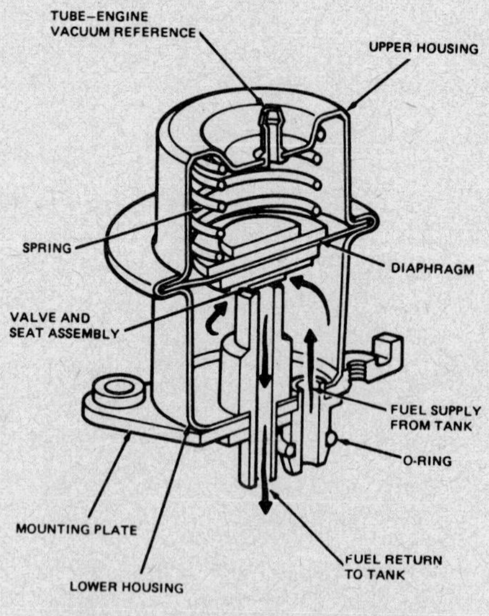

Fig. 8 Fuel pressure regulator

4. Remove valve cap from fuel pressure relief valve on fuel supply manifold. Using tool No. T80L-9974-A or equivalent, release fuel system pressure at the valve.
5. On 4-97.6 engines, proceed as follows:
   a. Disconnect the push/connect fuel supply line. Insert screwdriver un-

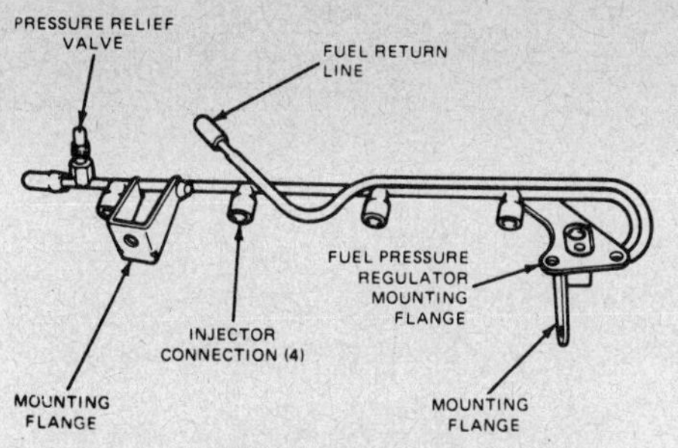

Fig. 9 Four cylinder fuel supply manifold (Typical)

der hairpin clip and disengage clip from fitting, **Fig. 12.**

b. Tag and disconnect fuel return lines and vacuum connections. **When disconnecting fuel lines, wrap a clean towel around fittings to avoid spillage.**

c. Disconnect sensor in heater supply tube under lower intake manifold, then the electronic engine control and injector electrical connectors.

d. Disconnect air bypass electrical connector from electronic engine control harness.

6. On 4-116 engines, proceed as follows:
   a. Disconnect fuel supply and return lines using tool No. T81P-19623-G or G1 or equivalent.
   b. Disconnect injector wiring harness by disconnecting ECT sensor in heater supply tube below lower intake manifold and EEC harness.
   c. Disconnect air bypass electrical connector from EEC harness.
7. On V6-182 engines, proceed as follows:
   a. Disconnect fuel supply and return lines using tool No. T81P-19623-G or equivalent.
   b. Disconnect electrical connectors from injectors.
   c. Disconnect electrical connectors from throttle position sensor, air bypass valve and air charge temperature sensor.

FUEL CHARGING ASSEMBLY, REPLACE

4-97.6 Engine

1. Remove air cleaner outlet tube between throttle body and vane air meter.
2. Remove accelerator and speed control cables, if equipped, from accelerator mounting bracket and throttle lever.
3. Disconnect top manifold vacuum fitting connections.
4. Disconnect vacuum lines from two large connectors on throttle body and intake manifold.
5. Disconnect throttle body port hose.
6. Disconnect canister purge line at straight plastic connector, then the PCV line from rocker cover.
7. Disconnect vacuum line at EGR valve.

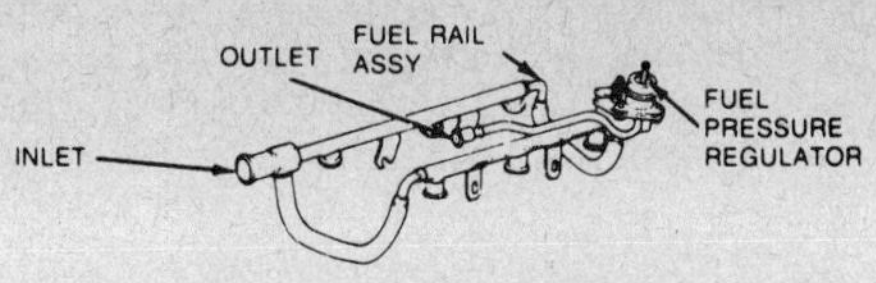

Fig. 10 V6-182 engine fuel supply manifold

8. Disconnect EGR vacuum line from upper intake manifold by removing two flange nuts.
9. Remove dipstick and dipstick tube, then the fuel return line.
10. Remove manifold attaching nuts, then the manifold with gasket and electrical connector.
11. Reverse procedure to install, noting the following:
    a. Ensure that mating surfaces of fuel charging assembly and cylinder head are clean and not damaged.
    b. Clean and lubricate manifold stud threads prior to installation of the assembly.
    c. Install charging assembly using a new gasket and secure with top middle nut finger tight only. Install fuel return line to fuel manifold, then two manifold nuts finger tight.
    d. Install dipstick tube and tighten bracket nut finger tight. Install remaining three manifold nuts and tighten all nuts to 12-15 ft. lbs.
    e. Torque EGR tube flange nuts to 6-8.5 ft. lbs.

4-116 Engine

1. Remove air cleaner outlet tube between throttle body and vane air meter.
2. Remove accelerator and speed control cables, as equipped, from accelerator mounting bracket and throttle lever.
3. Disconnect top manifold vacuum fitting connections.
4. Disconnect hoses from PCV valve at intake manifold connection.
5. Disconnect vacuum line from EGR valve, then the EGR tube from upper intake manifold.
6. Remove top bolt and disconnect upper support manifold bracket.
7. Disconnect electrical connectors from main engine harness and ECT sensor located in heater supply tube.
8. Disconnect fuel supply and return lines, then remove manifold attaching nuts.
9. Remove top bolt and disconnect lower support manifold bracket.
10. Remove manifold assembly with wiring harness and gasket.
11. Reverse procedure to install, noting the following:
    a. Ensure mating surfaces of fuel charging assembly and cylinder head are clean and not damaged.
    b. Clean and lubricate manifold stud threads prior to installation of assembly.
    c. Install charging assembly using a new gasket and secure with top middle nut finger tight only. Install fuel return line to fuel manifold,

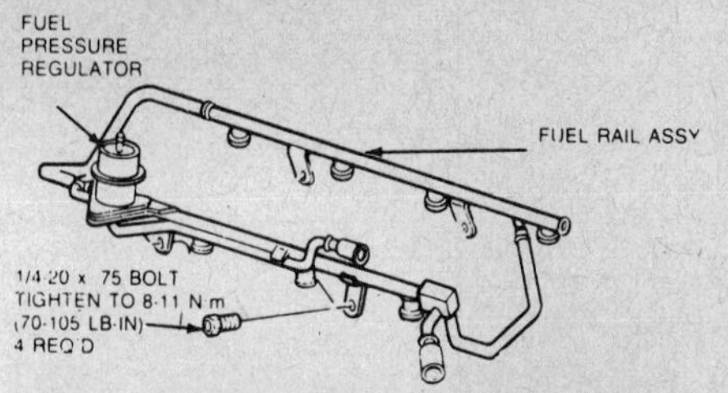

Fig. 11 V8-302 engine fuel supply manifold

then two manifold nuts finger tight. Install remaining three nuts, then torque all six to 12-15 ft. lbs.

    d. Torque upper and lower manifold support bracket bolts to 15-22 ft. lbs.
    e. Lubricate EGR tube compression nut and torque to 29.5-40.5 ft. lbs.
    f. Torque air supply tube clamps to 12-20 inch lbs.

4-140 Turbocharged Engine

1. Disconnect the following electrical connectors:
   a. Air bypass valve.
   b. Throttle position sensor.
   c. Injector wiring harness.
   d. Knock sensor and air charge temperature sensor, if equipped.
   e. Fan and coolant temperature sensor.
2. Disconnect top manifold vacuum connections.
3. Disconnect throttle linkage.
4. On 1986 Mustang SVO models, remove air cooler assembly.
5. On all models except 1986 Mustang SVO, remove two cast tube assembly to turbocharger assembly attaching bolts.
6. On all models, remove four air throttle body to fuel charging assembly attaching nuts or two nuts and two bolts.
7. On all models except 1986 Mustang SVO, separate cast tube from turbocharger assembly and remove gasket.
8. On all models, remove throttle body and cast tube, then disconnect PCV hose from fitting on underside of upper intake manifold.
9. Disconnect water bypass hose at lower intake manifold.
10. Disconnect EGR tube from EGR valve, then remove upper intake manifold attaching nuts.
11. Remove upper intake manifold assembly.
12. Disconnect fuel return line from fuel supply manifold using tool No. T82L-9500-AH or equivalent.
13. Remove oil dipstick/fuel injector wiring harness bracket attaching bolt.
14. Disconnect all four fuel injector electrical connectors and position harness to one side.
15. Remove fuel supply manifold attaching bolts, then the fuel supply manifold.
16. Remove lower intake manifold attaching bolts, then the lower intake manifold assembly.
17. Reverse procedure to install, noting the following:

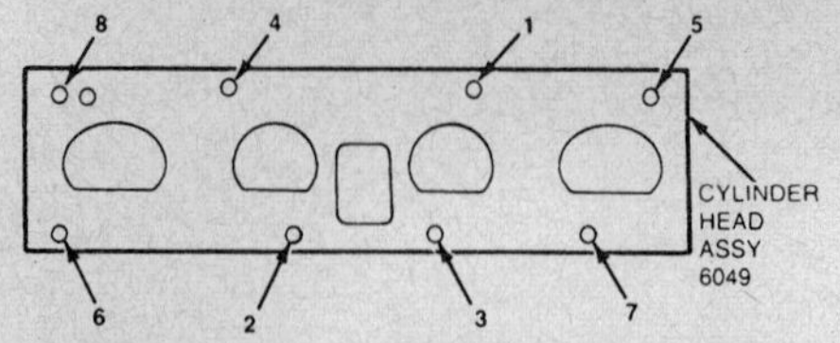

Fig. 12 Throttle body bolt tightening sequence. 1987 4-140

a. Ensure that mating surfaces of fuel charging assembly and cylinder head are clean and not damaged.
b. Clean and lubricate manifold stud threads before installation.
c. Install new gasket on lower intake manifold assembly.
d. Torque EGR tube flange nuts to 6-8.5 ft. lbs.
e. Install new gasket on fuel charging assembly air throttle body mounting flange.
f. Torque two cast tube attaching bolts to 14-21 ft. lbs.
g. Torque four air throttle body/cast tube assembly to fuel charging assembly attaching nuts and/or bolts to 12-15 ft. lbs.

1987 4-140

1. Disconnect the following electrical connectors:
   a. Throttle position sensor.
   b. Injector wiring harness.
   c. Knock sensor.
   d. Air charge temperature sensor.
   e. Engine coolant temperature sensor.
   f. Air bypass valve.
   g. Fan switch.
   h. EGR valve.
2. Disconnect upper intake manifold vacuum fitting connections.
3. Disconnect vacuum lines from upper intake manifold vacuum tee.
4. Disconnect vacuum line from fuel pressure regulator.
5. Remove throttle linkage shield and disconnect throttle linkage, cruise control and kickdown cable. Loosen accelerator cable from bracket and position aside.
6. Disconnect air intake hose.
7. Disconnect PCV hose from upper intake manifold.
8. Loosen hose clamp on water bypass line at lower intake manifold.
9. Disconnect EGR valve line.
10. Remove engine oil dipstick bracket attaching screw.
11. Remove four upper intake manifold attaching nuts.
12. Remove upper intake manifold and air throttle body assembly.
13. Disconnect the push/connect fitting at the fuel supply manifold and fuel lines.
14. Label, then disconnect all electrical connectors from the four fuel injectors and position harness aside.
15. Remove two fuel supply manifold attaching bolts. Carefully remove fuel supply manifold and injectors.
16. Remove four bottom attaching bolts from lower manifold.
17. Remove four upper attaching bolts from lower manifold.
18. Reverse procedure to install. Torque manifold attaching bolts to 12-15 ft. lbs. Torque bolts in sequence shown in **Fig. 12.**

UPPER INTAKE MANIFOLD, REPLACE

4-97.6 Engine

1. Remove fuel charging assembly as previously described.
2. Disconnect throttle position sensor and air bypass valve electrical connectors from wiring harness.
3. Remove manifold attaching bolts and manifold.
4. Remove and discard gasket from manifold.
5. Reverse procedure to install, using a new gasket. Torque manifold attaching bolts to 15-22 ft. lbs.

4-116 Engine

1. Remove fuel charging assembly as previously described.
2. Disconnect engine air cleaner outlet tube from throttle body.
3. Disconnect throttle position sensor electrical connector from wiring harness.
4. Disconnect vacuum lines from upper manifold and throttle body.
5. Disconnect EGR tube from manifold connection.
6. Disconnect air bypass valve electrical connector, then remove top bolt from manifold upper support bracket.
7. Remove five upper manifold attaching bolts, then the manifold assembly.
8. Remove and discard gasket from lower manifold.
9. Reverse procedure to install, noting the following:
   a. Torque manifold attaching bolts and upper support bracket bolt to 15-22 ft. lbs.
   b. Lubricate EGR tube compression nut and torque to 29.5-40.5 ft. lbs.
   c. Torque engine air cleaner outlet tube clamp to 12-20 inch lbs.

4-140 Turbocharged Engine

1. Perform steps 1 through 8 under "Fuel Charging Assembly, Replace" procedure.
2. Disconnect EGR hose from EGR valve.
3. On 1983-84 models, disconnect fuel supply and return lines using tool No. T82L-9500-AH or equivalent.
4. On 1985-87 models, remove oil dipstick/fuel injector pulse dampener mounting bracket.
5. On all models, remove six upper intake manifold attaching bolts, then the manifold assembly.
6. Reverse procedure to install. Torque manifold attaching bolts to 15-22 ft. lbs.

UPPER INTAKE MANIFOLD & THROTTLE BODY, REPLACE

V8-302 Engine

1. Disconnect electrical connectors from throttle position sensor, air bypass valve and EGR position sensor.
2. Disconnect throttle linkage from ball and transmission linkage from throttle body. Remove two throttle cable bracket-to-intake manifold attaching bolts and position bracket and cables aside.
3. Disconnect upper intake manifold vacuum connections. Disconnect all lines to vacuum tree, EGR valve and fuel pressure regulator.
4. Disconnect PCV hose from rear of upper manifold.
5. Disconnect two canister purge lines from throttle body.
6. Remove flange nut and disconnect EGR tube from EGR valve.
7. Remove upper intake support bracket-to-upper manifold attaching bolt.
8. Remove upper intake manifold attaching bolts, then the upper intake manifold and throttle body as an assembly from lower intake manifold.
9. Reverse procedure to install, noting the following:
   a. Install new gasket on lower intake manifold mating surface.
   b. Torque upper intake manifold attaching bolts to 15-22 ft. lbs.
   c. Torque throttle cable bracket attaching bolts to 8-10 ft. lbs.

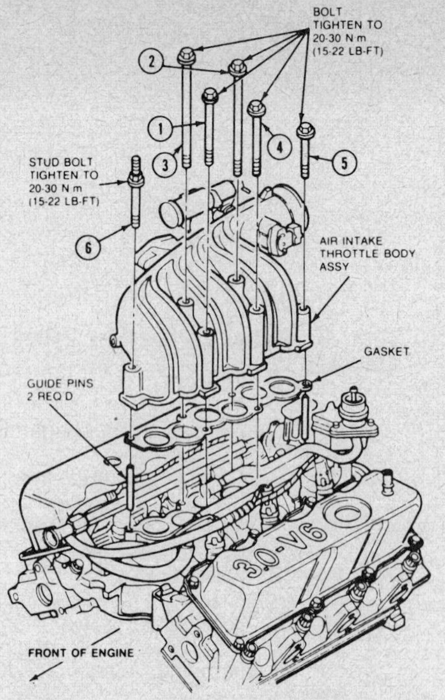

Fig. 13 Throttle body bolt tightening sequence. V6-182

THROTTLE BODY, REPLACE

4-97.6 Engine

1. Remove fuel charging assembly as previously described.
2. Disconnect throttle position sensor and air bypass valve electrical connectors from wiring harness.

3. Remove four throttle body attaching nuts.
4. Tag and disconnect vacuum lines from throttle body.
5. Remove throttle body bracket.
6. Remove throttle body from upper intake manifold.
7. Remove and discard throttle body gasket.
8. Reverse procedure to install, using new gasket. Torque throttle body attaching nuts and bracket nuts to 12-15 ft. lbs.

4-116 Engine

1. Remove two throttle body attaching bolts and two nuts.
2. Disconnect throttle position sensor and air bypass valve electrical connectors from wiring harness.
3. Disconnect air cleaner outlet tube, then the vacuum hose from throttle body.
4. Disconnect throttle control cable and speed control cable, if equipped, from throttle body.
5. Remove throttle body bracket, then carefully separate throttle body from upper intake manifold.
6. Remove and discard gasket from manifold.
7. Reverse procedure to install. Torque throttle body and bracket retaining bolts and nuts to 12-15 ft. lbs.

4-140 Turbocharged Engine

1. Remove fuel charging assembly as previously described.
2. On 1986 Mustang SVO models, remove air cooler assembly.
3. On all models, remove four throttle body nuts or two bolts and two nuts, as equipped.
4. Disconnect throttle position sensor and air bypass valve electrical connectors from wiring harness.
5. Separate throttle body assembly from upper intake manifold.
6. Remove and discard gasket from manifold.
7. Reverse procedure to install. Torque retaining nuts and/or bolts to 12-15 ft. lbs.

V6-182 Engine

1. Remove air cleaner outlet tube between air cleaner and throttle body.
2. Remove snow shield retaining nut and bolts and the shield, if necessary.
3. Disconnect vacuum hoses from intake manifold.
4. Disconnect accelerator cable and speed control cable, if equipped, from accelerator mounting bracket and throttle lever.
5. On models equipped with automatic transmission, disconnect transmission valve linkage from throttle lever.
6. Remove throttle body attaching bolts and the throttle body.
7. Remove and discard gasket from lower intake manifold.
8. Reverse procedure to install. Torque attaching bolts to 15-22 ft. lbs. in sequence shown, **Fig. 13.**

V8-302 Engine

1. Disconnect throttle position sensor and throttle air bypass valve electrical connectors.
2. Remove PCV vent closure hose from throttle body.
3. Remove four throttle body attaching nuts, then separate throttle body from intake manifold.
4. Remove and discard gasket between throttle body and EGR spacer.
5. Reverse procedure to install, using a new gasket. Torque throttle body attaching nuts to 12-18 ft. lbs.

AIR BYPASS VALVE, REPLACE

1. Disconnect air bypass valve electrical connector from wiring harness.
2. Remove two air bypass attaching screws and valve.
3. Remove and discard gasket.
4. Reverse procedure to install, using new gasket. Torque valve attaching screws to 71-102 inch lbs.

THROTTLE POSITION SENSOR, REPLACE

1. Disconnect sensor electrical connector from wiring harness.
2. On 1985-87 models, scribe alignment marks on throttle body and throttle position sensor for installation reference.
3. On all models, remove two sensor attaching screws and the sensor.
3. Reverse procedure to install. Ensure rotary tangs on sensor are properly aligned, then torque sensor attaching screws to 11-16 inch lbs. **When installing sensor on 1985-87 models, slide rotary tangs over throttle shaft blade, then rotate sensor clockwise to installed position. Failure to perform this operation may result in incorrect idle speeds.**

PRESSURE RELIEF VALVE, REPLACE

Four & Six Cylinder Engines

If pressure relief valve is to be removed with fuel charging assembly installed on engine, release fuel system pressure as previously described.

1. Remove pressure relief valve from fuel injection manifold using suitable tool.
2. Install valve and cap into manifold. Torque valve to 48-84 inch lbs. and cap to 4-6 inch lbs.

FUEL MANIFOLD, REPLACE

Four Cylinder Engines

1. Release fuel system pressure as previously described.
2. Disconnect fuel supply and return lines from manifold.
3. Disconnect injector wiring harness.
4. Disconnect vacuum line from pressure regulator valve.
5. Remove two manifold attaching bolts and manifold.
6. Reverse procedure to install. Torque manifold attaching bolts to 15-22 ft. lbs.

V6-182 Engine

1. Remove throttle body assembly as previously described.
2. Disconnect fuel supply and return lines using tool No. T81P-19623-G or equivalent.
3. Disconnect injector wiring harness.
4. Disconnect vacuum line from pressure regulator valve.
5. Remove four fuel manifold attaching bolts and the manifold.
6. Reverse procedure to install. Install one side of fuel manifold with bolts finger tight, then complete installation of other side and torque all bolts to 6-8 ft. lbs.

V8-302 Engine

1. Remove upper intake manifold assembly as previously described.
2. Disconnect fuel crossover hose from fuel supply manifold using tool No. T81P-19623-G or G1 or equivalent.
3. Disconnect fuel supply and return line connections from fuel supply manifold, then remove fuel supply manifold attaching bolts.
4. Remove manifold and fuel injectors as an assembly.
5. Reverse procedure to install. Torque manifold attaching bolts to 6-8 ft. lbs.

FUEL PRESSURE REGULATOR, REPLACE

If pressure relief valve is to be removed with fuel charging assembly installed on engine, release fuel system pressure as previously described.

1. Disconnect vacuum line from regulator.
2. Remove three pressure regulator attaching screws and regulator.
3. Remove and discard gasket and inspect O-ring for wear or damage.
4. Reverse procedure to install, using new gasket. Torque regulator attaching screws to 27-40 inch lbs.

FUEL INJECTOR, REPLACE

1. Remove fuel manifold as previously described.
2. Remove electrical connectors from injectors as required.
3. Pull injector(s) out of manifold.
4. Remove O-rings and pintle protective cap and inspect for wear or damage. Replace as necessary.
5. Reverse procedure to install. Lubricate O-rings with suitable light oil.

VANE AIR METER, REPLACE

4-97.6 Engine

1. Disconnect air outlet hose from air meter and position aside.
2. Remove air intake and outlet hoses from air cleaner.
3. Disengage four spring clamps, then remove air cleaner front cover and filter panel.
4. Remove four air cleaner-to-air meter attaching screws.
5. Separate air cleaner base from air meter. Remove gasket and discard if

worn or damaged.
6. Disconnect electrical connector from air meter.
7. Remove two air meter attaching screws and the air meter.
8. Reverse procedure to install. Torque attaching screws to 6-9 ft. lbs.

4-116 Engine

1. Disconnect outlet hose from vane air meter and position aside.
2. Remove air intake tube from air cleaner.
3. Unfasten two spring clamps and position air cleaner front cover and filter away from rear tray.
4. Remove four air cleaner tray flange-to-air meter attaching screws, then move tray away from air meter. Remove and replace gasket, if necessary.
5. Disconnect electrical connector from air meter.
6. Remove air meter attaching screws and the air meter.
7. Reverse procedure to install. Torque air cleaner tray attaching screws to 33-49 inch lbs. and air meter attaching screws to 6-9 ft. lbs.

4-140 Turbocharged Engine

1. Remove air cleaner cover and air cleaner element.
2. Disconnect carbon canister hose, then the vane air meter electrical connector.
3. Loosen hose clamp on turbocharger air inlet hose, then disconnect hose at vane air meter.
4. Remove four vane air meter bracket attaching screws, then the vane air meter and air cleaner housing bracket.
5. Loosen vane air meter inlet hose clamp, then remove hose from meter.
6. Remove three vane air meter attaching screws, then the vane air meter.
7. Reverse procedure to install. Torque vane air meter attaching screws to 15-22 ft. lbs.

Central Fuel Injection (CFI) System

INDEX

DESCRIPTION

This system, used on 1982-85 V8-302, 1984-87 V6-232, 1985-87 4-140 high swirl combustion (HSC) and 1986-87 4-153 engines, is a single point, pulse timed modulated injection system and uses a fuel charging assembly instead of a carburetor, **Figs. 1 and 2.** The fuel charging assembly contains two injectors, a fuel pressure regulator and a throttle body. Fuel is metered into the intake air stream according to engine demands by the two injectors.

An in-tank high pressure fuel pump supplies the fuel to the system. The fuel is filtered and sent to the air throttle where the regulator maintains fuel pressure at a constant 39 psi. Excess fuel supplied by the pump but not used by the engine, is returned to the fuel tank by a fuel return line, **Fig. 3.**

This system consists of the following four sub-systems: 1) Fuel Delivery, 2) Air and Fuel Control, 3) Engine Sensors and 4) Electronic Control Unit (ECU).

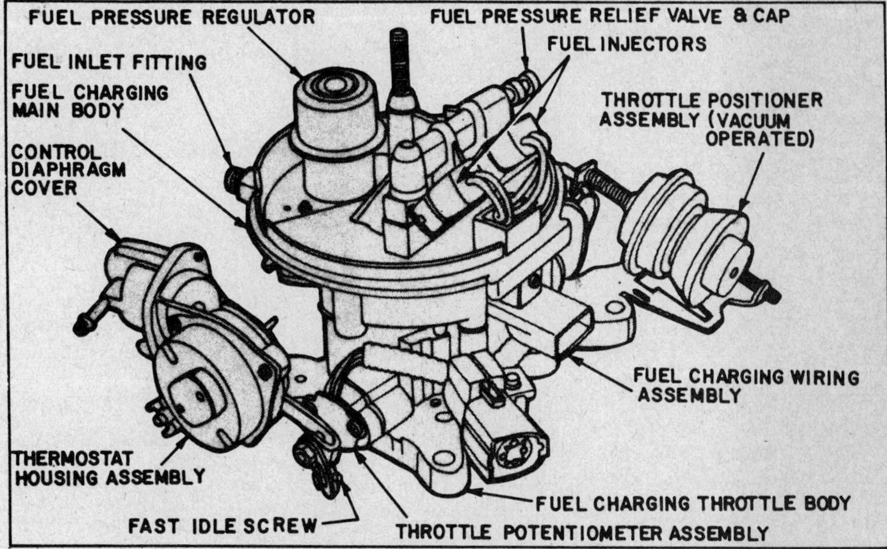

Fig. 1 Front view of fuel charging assembly

SYSTEM COMPONENTS & OPERATION

FUEL PUMP

All 1982–83 Models; 1984–85 Crown Victoria, Grand Marquis & Town Car; 1985 Continental & Mark VII; 1985–87 Cougar & Thunderbird; 1986 Capri & Mustang

The in-tank fuel pump, **Fig. 4**, is a high pressure unit capable of maintaining a working pressure of 39 psi and an overpressure protection feature that opens an internal relief valve when pressure reaches 80-120 psi. The pump is protected at its inlet by a nylon filter that filters out dirt and contaminants which could damage the pump, while permitting passage of small quantities of water that may accumulate within the fuel tank sump.

The electrical system has a single fuel pump control relay, **Fig. 5,** controlled by the EEC module, which provides power to the fuel pump under various operating conditions.

When the ignition switch is off, the contacts of all three relays are open. When ignition switch is initially turned to "On", the EEC power relay is energized, closing its contacts. Power is provided to both the fuel pump relay and EEC module. If ignition switch is not turned to "Crank," the timing device in the EEC module will open the ground circuit after about one second and shut power off at the fuel pump. When ignition switch is turned to "Crank" position, the starter relay is energized supplying power to both starter motor and fuel pump. After engine starts and ignition switch is returned to the "On" position, power to fuel pump is again supplied through the resistance wire and fuel pump relay.

The EEC module senses engine speed and shuts off the pump by opening the EEC controlled relay when the engine stops, or speed is below 120 RPM.

In case of a collision, the inertia switch opens and shuts off the fuel pump even if the engine does not stop running. The engine will stop moments thereafter and cannot be restarted unless the switch is reset manually. On 1984-85 Crown Victoria Wagon and Grand Marquis Wagon the inertia switch is located in the left side storage compartment. On all other models, the inertia switch is located in the luggage compartment, **Fig. 6.**

The inertia switch must not be reset until after the vehicle has been inspected for fuel leaks and the necessary repairs made.

1984 Continental, Cougar, Mark VII & Thunderbird; 1984–85 Capri & Mustang; 1984–86 LTD & Marquis

The electric fuel pump system uses a low pressure in-tank mounted electric fuel pump and an externally mounted high pressure inline electric fuel pump, **Figs. 7 through 9.**

The low pressure electric fuel pump provides pressurized fuel to the inlet of the high pressure pump. The inlet of the low pressure pump has a nylon filter to prevent dirt and other foreign particles from entering the system. The low pressure pump has an external resistor in the electrical circuit to reduce operating voltage to 11 volts.

The externally mounted high pressure pump is capable of maintaining a working pressure of 39 psi and has an overpressure protection feature that opens an internal relief valve when pressure reaches 138 psi.

The electrical system has a fuel pump control relay controlled by the EEC module, which provides power to the fuel pump under various operating conditions, **Fig. 10.**

When ignition switch is in the "Off" position, contacts of EEC power and fuel pump relays are open. When ignition switch is

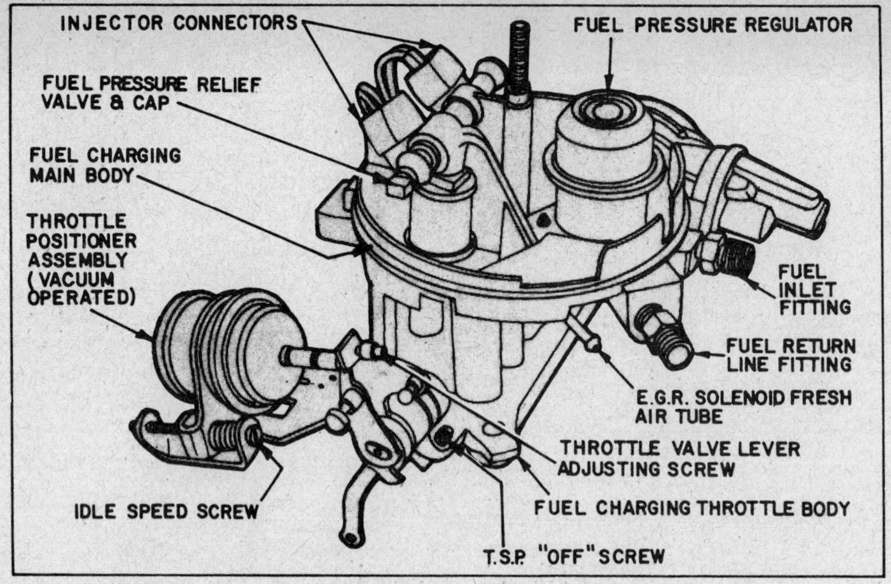

Fig. 2 Rear view of fuel charging assembly

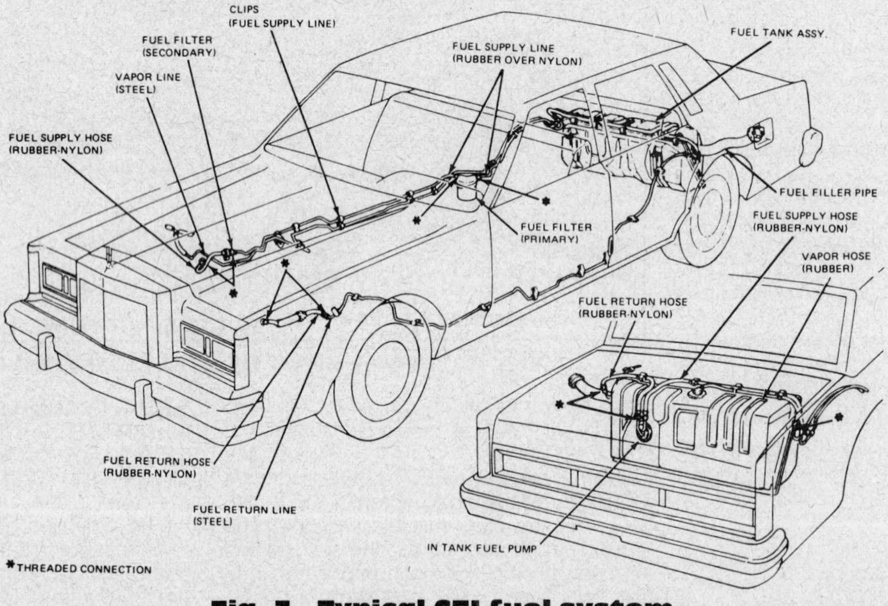

Fig. 3 Typical CFI fuel system

first turned to the "On" position, the EEC power relay is energized, closing its contacts. Power is provided to both fuel pump relay and to a timing device in the EEC module. If ignition switch is not turned to the "Crank" position, a timing device in the EEC module will open the ground circuit and shut power off to the fuel pump. When ignition switch is turned to the "Crank" position, the EEC module operates fuel pump relay to provide fuel for starting engine while cranking. After engine starts and ignition switch is returned to the "On" position, power to fuel pump is supplied to fuel pump relay.

The EEC module senses engine speed and shuts off the pump by opening the EEC control relay when engine stops, or speeds below 120 RPM.

In case of a collision, the inertia switch opens and shuts off the fuel pump even if the engine does not stop running. The engine will stop moments thereafter and cannot be restarted unless the switch is reset manually. On 1984 Mustang and Capri Hatchback models, the inertia switch is located in the lefthand corner of the spare tire well, **Fig. 11.** On 1985-86 Capri and Mustang Hatchback models, the switch is located near the lefthand tail lamp. On all other models, the switch is located in the luggage compartment, **Fig. 6.**

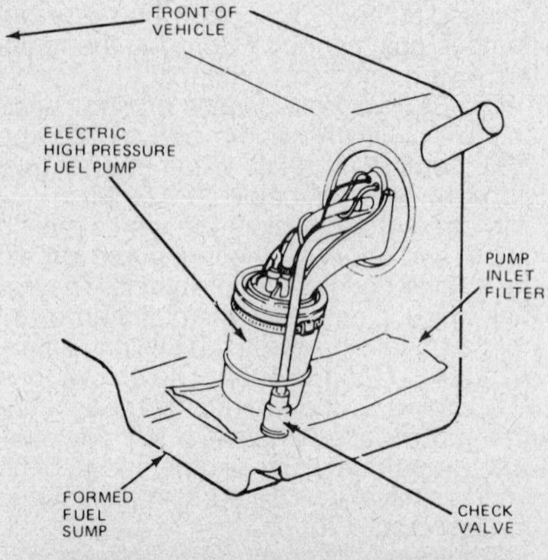

Fig. 4 In-tank fuel pump assembly (Typical)

1985–87 Tempo & Topaz & 1986–87 Sable & Taurus

The fuel tank on these models has an internal pump cavity in which the fuel pump and sender assembly rest. This design provides satisfactory operation during ex-

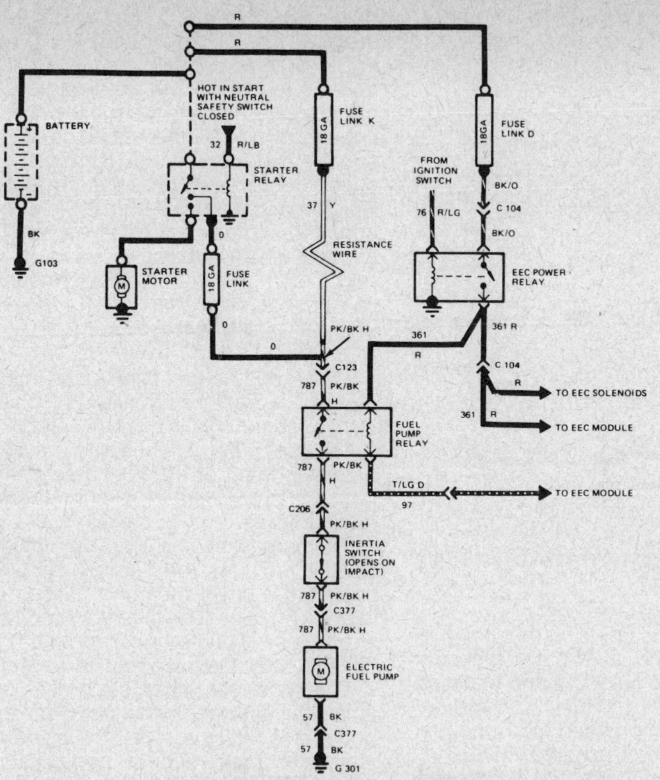

Fig. 5 High pressure fuel pump wiring circuit (Typical)

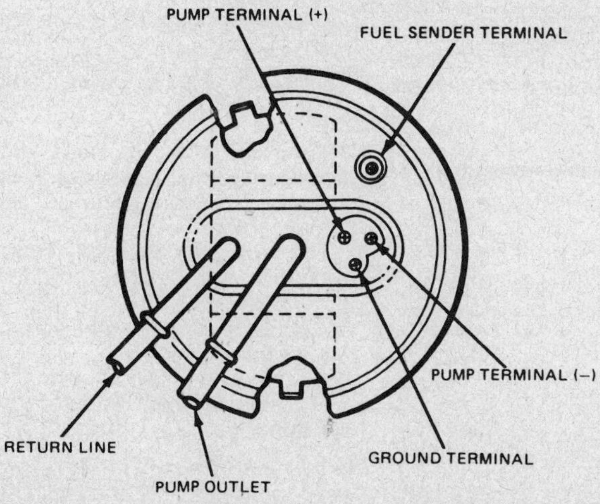

Fig. 8 Low pressure in-tank fuel pump assembly. Exc. Capri & Mustang

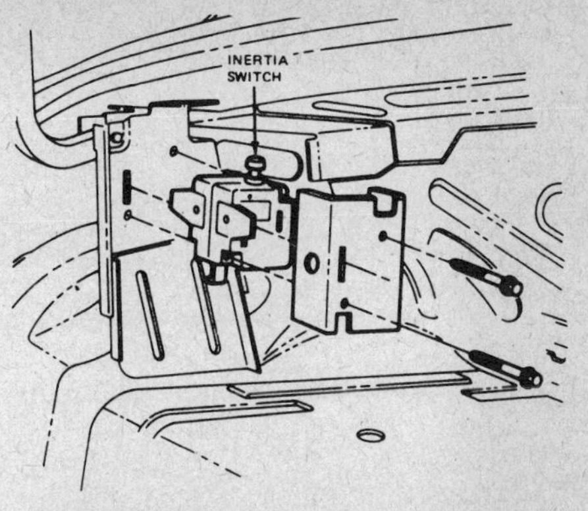

Fig. 6 Fuel pump inertia switch. Exc. 1984 Capri & Mustang (Typical)

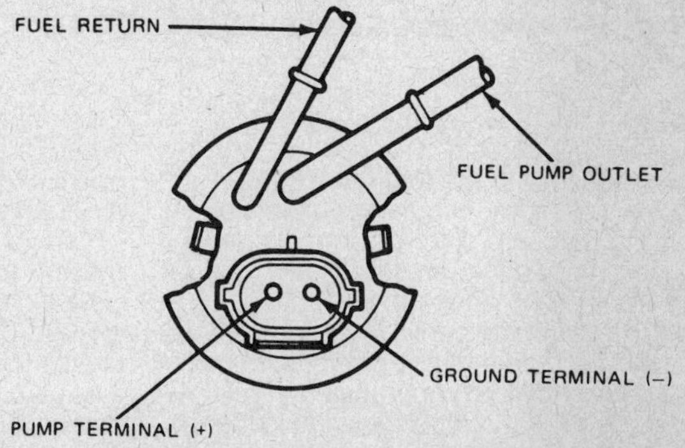

Fig. 7 Low pressure in-tank fuel pump assembly. Capri & Mustang

treme vehicle operation.

The fuel pump is mounted on the fuel sender assembly within the fuel tank. This assembly includes a check valve which is located between the fuel pump and the outlet tube of the assembly. The function of this valve is to maintain pressure in the system after the vehicle is shut down. The fuel pump is protected at its inlet by a nylon pickup element. This nylon element filters dirt and contaminants which could plug or damage the internal pump components, while at the same time allowing passage of small quantities of water which may accumulate within the fuel tank sump. The electrical system has a fuel pump control relay which is controlled by the EEC-IV module, which provides power to the fuel pump under various engine operating conditions. When the ignition switch is in the OFF position, the contacts of the EEC-IV power and fuel pump relays are open. When the ignition switch is first turned to the ON position, the EEC-IV power relay is energized, closing its contacts. Power is provided to both the fuel pump relay and a timing device within the EEC-IV module assembly. When the ignition switch is turned to the START position, the EEC-IV module operates the fuel pump relay to provide fuel for starting the engine. After the engine starts, the ignition switch is returned to the ON position, power to the fuel pump is again supplied through the fuel pump relay. The EEC-IV module senses engine speed and shuts off the fuel pump by opening the ground circuit to the fuel pump relay when the engine stops, or when engine speed is below 120 RPM.

AIR & FUEL CONTROL

The throttle body consists of six separate components which perform the fuel and air metering to the engine. The throttle body is mounted on the intake manifold and provides a housing for the 1) Air Control Butterfly Valves, 2) Injector Nozzles, 3) Fuel Pressure Regulator, 4) Cold Engine Speed Control), 5) Throttle Position Sensor and 6) Fuel Pressure Diagnostic Valve.

The air flow is controlled by two butterfly valves which are mounted on the throttle body and are similar in design and operation to those of a carburetor.

The fuel injector nozzles are mounted vertically above the throttle plates. They are electro-mechanical units that meter and atomize the fuel delivered to the engine, **Figs. 1, 2 and 5.** The injector consists of a solenoid actuated pintle and needle valve assembly. An electrical control signal from the EEC electronic processor actuates the solenoid causing the pintle to move off its seat allowing fuel flow. The injector flow orifice is fixed and the fuel supply pressure is constant, therefore fuel flow to the engine is determined by the amount of time the solenoid is energized.

The pressure regulator, **Figs. 1 and 2,** is mounted on the fuel charging main body near the rear of the air horn. The regulator is located so as to offset the affects of

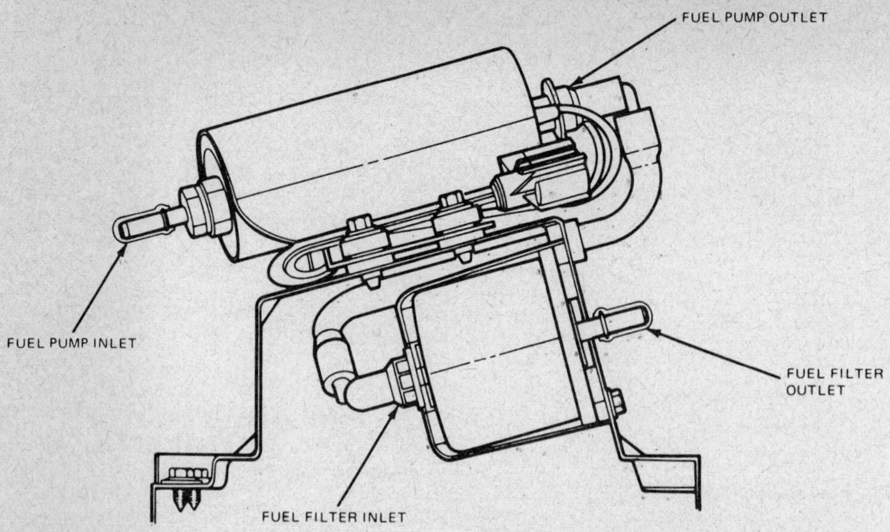

Fig. 9 High pressure inline electric fuel pump assembly

pressure fluctuations in the fuel system. It is designed so that it is not affected by back pressure in the fuel return line.

The pressure regulator maintains a working pressure of 39 psi and also maintains a fuel supply pressure after engine and fuel pump turn off, by acting as a check valve between itself and the fuel pump. This maintenance of pressure helps to prevent fuel line vapor lock and permits rapid restarts and stable engine idling immediately thereafter.

The diagnostic pressure valve located at the top of the fuel metering body provides a convenient point to monitor fuel pump pressure and allows for bleeding down of the system pressure and bleeding air during service.

Do not apply compressed air to the fuel system through the diagnostic valve.

Cold engine speed control is accomplished by a throttle stop cam positioner similar to that used on carburetors, **Fig. 12.** The cam is positioned by a bi-metal spring and an electric positive temperature heating element. The electrical source for the heating element is 7.3 volts from the alternator which provides voltage only when the engine is running. The heating element provides the necessary warm up according to starting temperature (cold engine) and the length of time after starting. Multiple positions on the cam allow for a decreasing cold engine speed to curb idle speed during warm up. The cold engine speed control also provides an automatic kickdown from high cam (fast idle) engine speed to some intermediate speed. This is accomplished through a vacuum motor and bleed which physically moves the cam a short time after starting the engine.

FUEL FILTERS

There are four fuel filters used in the CFI system: 1) Fuel pump inlet, 2) Primary filter, 3) Secondary filter and 4) Injector filter.

The fuel pump inlet filter is a nylon element mounted at the inlet inside the fuel tank and protects the fuel pump from contaminants.

The primary filter is an inline replaceable type. It provides the filtration required to protect the small metering orifices of the injector nozzles. The filter is located downstream of the pump and is mounted to the chassis near the right rear wheelwell.

The secondary filter is a small serviceable filter located inline near the throttle body. This filter protects the injector nozzles from contaminants purged through the system during initial assembly and service. This filter should never need replacement.

The injector filter is located at the top of each injector, **Fig. 13,** and is not serviceable.

ELECTRONIC CONTROL UNIT (ECU)

The ECU is a solid state preprogrammed micro-processor which consists of a processor assembly and calibration assembly.

The processor assembly contains electronic circuitry capable of performing the following:

1. Choose one of eight sensor signals for calculations.
2. Convert the chosen signal to a form usable by the computer for calculations.

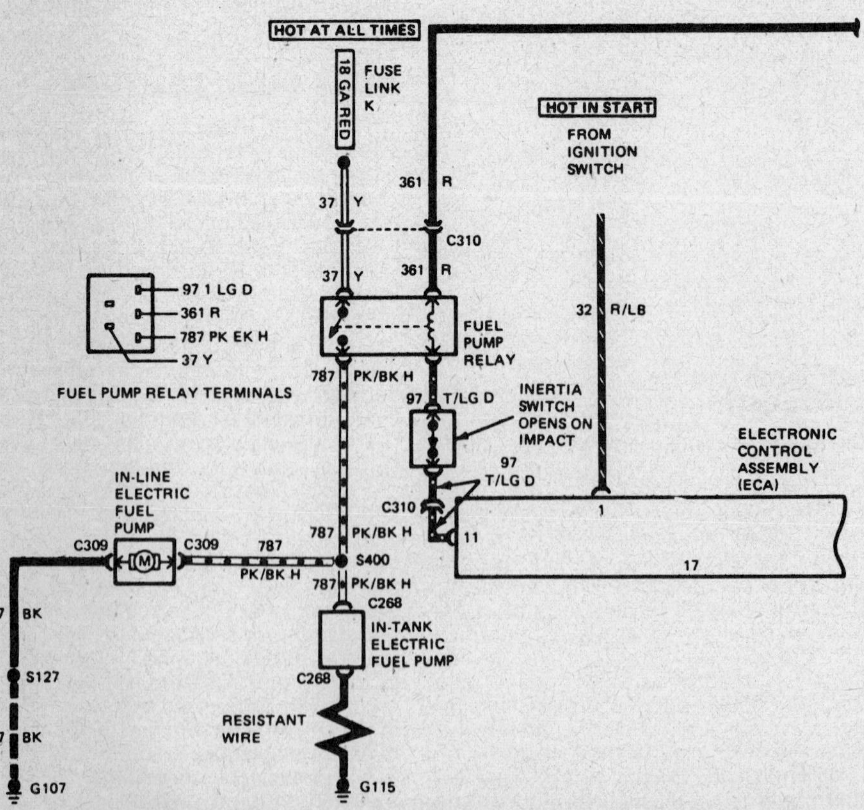

Fig. 10 Low pressure fuel pump wiring circuit (Typical)

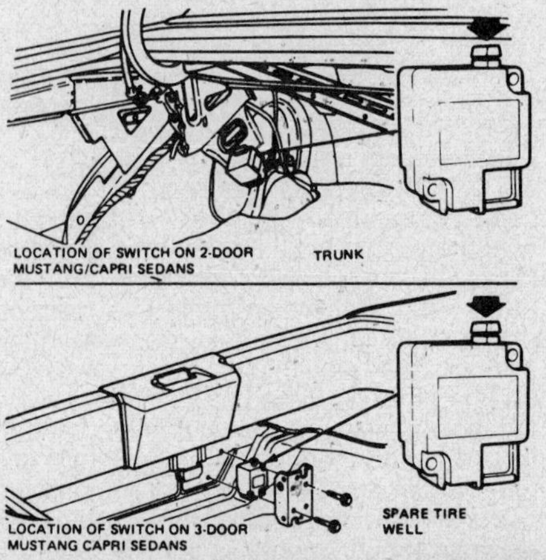

Fig. 11 Fuel pump inertia switch. 1984 Capri & Mustang

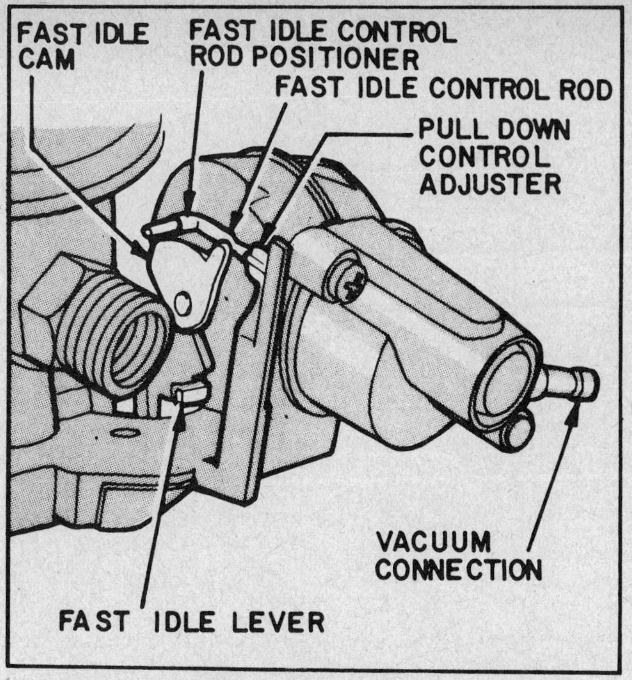

Fig. 12 Cold engine speed control

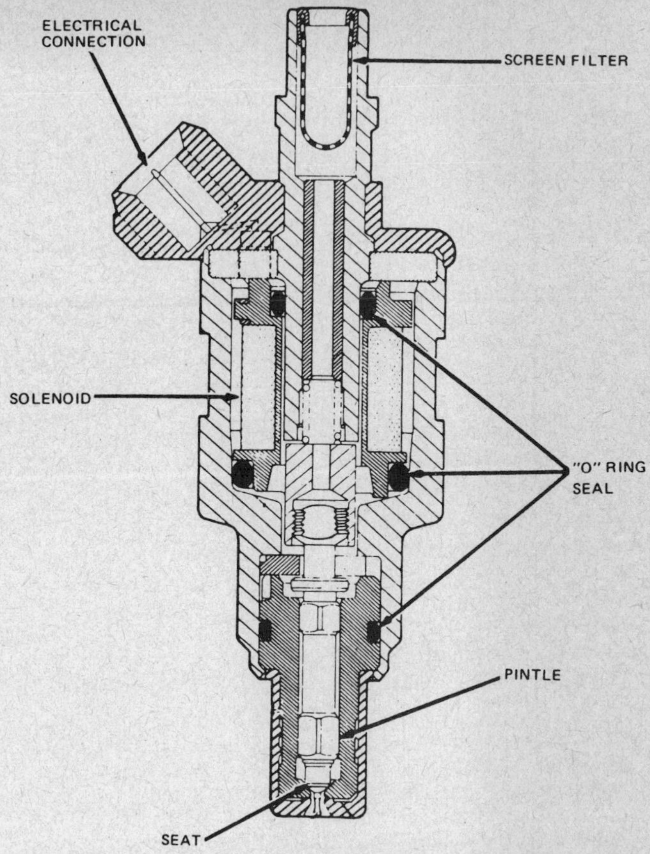

Fig. 13 Fuel injector

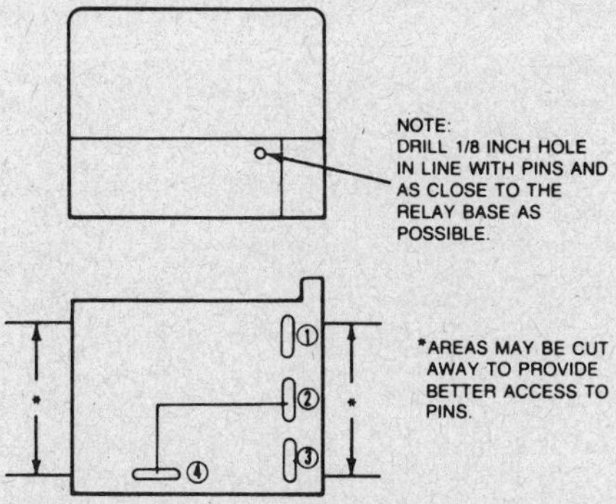

Fig. 14 Fuel pump relay modification

3. Choose the proper operating mode for the operating conditions.
4. Perform spark, EGR, air/fuel ratio, canister purge, throttle kicker and other calculations.
5. Send electrical output control signals to the ignition module and control solenoids to adjust timing and dwell, EGR flow rate, thermactor air mode and throttle kicker mode.

The calibration assembly contains the electronic circuitry that provides calibration equations necessary for specific vehicle application for use by the processor assembly.

SYSTEM DIAGNOSIS

FUEL PUMP

The following tests can be used to determine if the fuel pump is operating properly.

All 1982–83 Models & 1984–85 Crown Victoria, Grand Marquis & Town Car

1. Check for adequate supply of fuel.
2. Check for fuel leakage at all lines and fittings.
3. Check continuity to fuel pump as follows:
   a. Disconnect electrical connector just forward of fuel tank, then connect a voltmeter to body wiring harness connector.
   b. Turn ignition key to "On" while observing voltmeter. Voltmeter should indicate battery voltage, then return to zero after one second.
   c. Turn ignition switch to Start position momentarily while observing voltmeter. Voltmeter should indicate approximately eight volts while cranking.
   d. If voltages are not as specified, check electrical system and make necessary repairs.
4. Check fuel pump operation as follows:
   a. Disconnect return fuel line at throttle body, then connect hose from throttle body fitting to a calibrated container of at least 1 quart capacity.
   b. Connect pressure gauge T80L-9974-A or equivalent to fuel diagnostic valve on fuel charging assembly.
   c. Disconnect electrical connector to fuel pump just forward of fuel tank, then connect an auxiliary wiring harness to fuel pump connector.
   d. Energize pump for 10 seconds by connecting auxiliary wiring harness to a fully charged 12 volt battery. Observe pressure while pump is energized.
   e. Allow fuel to flow into container while observing capacity. The fuel pressure reached should be 35-45 psi and the fuel capacity should be a minimum of 1/3 quart in 10 seconds. Fuel pressure should remain steady at 30 psi immediately after de-energizing the fuel pump. The fuel pump is operating normally if the above conditions are met.
   f. If specified pressure in step 4e is obtained, but volume is below specifications, check for obstructions in fuel filters or supply lines. After making the necessary corrections, repeat steps d and e. If fuel volume is not as specified, replace pump.
   g. If specified volume in step e is obtained, but pressure is below specifications, check for damaged or worn pressure regulator.
   h. If both pressure and volume are as specified in step e, but pressure is not maintained after de-energizing, check for leaking injector valve and/or pressure regulator. If both are satisfactory, replace fuel pump.

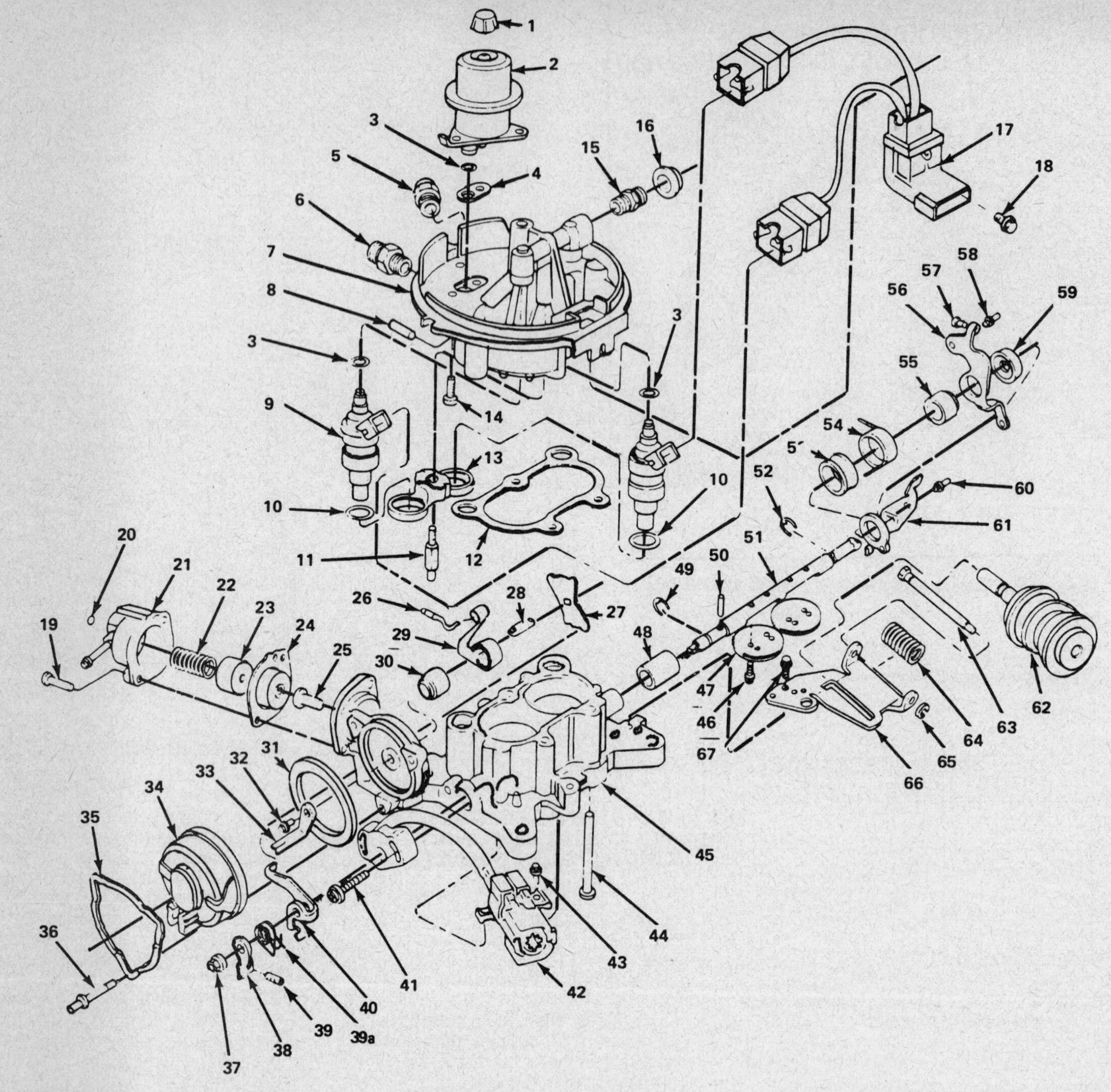

Legend:

1. PLUG – FUEL PRESSURE REGULATOR ADJUSTING SCREW
2. REGULATOR ASSEMBLY – FUEL PRESSURE
3. SEAL – 5/16 x .070 "O" RING
4. GASKET – FUEL PRESSURE REGULATOR
5. CONNECTOR – 1/4 PIPE TO 1/2-20
6. CONNECTOR – 1/8 PIPE TO 9/16-16
7. BODY – FUEL CHARGING MAIN
8. PLUG – 1/16 x 27 HEADLESS HEX
9. INJECTOR ASSEMBLY – FUEL
10. SEAL – 5/8 x .103 "O" RING
11. SCREW – FUEL INJECTOR RETAINING
12. GASKET – FUEL CHARGING BODY
13. RETAINER – FUEL INJECTOR
14. SCREW M5.0 x 20.0 PAN HEAD
15. VALVE ASSEMBLY – DIAGNOSTIC VALVE
16. CAP – FUEL PRESSURE RELIEF VALVE
17. WIRING ASSEMBLY – FUEL CHARGING
18. SCREW – M3.5 x 1.27 x 12.7 PAN HEAD
19. SCREW & WASHER – M4 x 7.0 20.00
20. BALL – LEAD SHOT .26 - .24 DIA.
21. COVER ASSEMBLY – CONTROL DIAPHRAGM
22. SPRING – CONTROL MODULATOR
23. RETAINER – PULLDOWN DIAPHRAGM
24. DIAPHRAGM – PULLDOWN CONTROL
25. ADJUSTER – PULLDOWN CONTROL
26. ROD – FAST IDLE CONTROL
27. CAM – FAST IDLE
28. SHAFT – CHOKE HOUSING
29. POSITIONER – FAST IDLE CONTROL ROD
30. BUSHING – CHOKE HOUSING
31. GASKET – THERMOSTAT HOUSING
32. SCREW & WASHER – M3.5 x 0.6 x 6 PAN HEAD
33. LEVER – CHOKE THERMOSTAT
34. HOUSING ASSEMBLY – THERMOSTAT
35. RETAINER – HOUSING ASSEMBLY
36. POP RIVET – 1/8 x .517
37. NUT & WASHER ASSEMBLY – .7-6H HEX
38. LEVER – FAST IDLE CAM ADJUSTER
39. SCREW – NO. 10 - 32 x .50 SET SLOTTED HEAD

39a. FAST IDLE PICK-UP LEVER RETURN SPRING

40. LEVER – FAST IDLE
41. SCREW & WASHER – M4.07 x 22.0 PAN HEAD
42. THROTTLE POSITION SENSOR
43. SCREW – M4 x .7 x 14.0 HEX WASHER TAP
44. SCREW – M5 x .7 x 55.0
45. BODY – FUEL CHARGING – THROTTLE
46. SCREW – M3 x 0.5 x 7.4 HEX WASHER HEAD
47. PLATE – THROTTLE
48. BEARING – THROTTLE CONTROL LINKAGE
49. "E" RING – 7/32 RETAINING
50. PIN – SPRING COILED
51. SHAFT – THROTTLE
52. "C" RING – THROTTLE SHAFT BUSHING
53. BEARING – THROTTLE CONTROL LINKAGE
54. SPRING – THROTTLE RETURN
55. BUSHING – ACCELERATOR PUMP OVER TRAVEL SPRING
56. LEVER – TRANSMISSION LINKAGE
57. SCREW – M4 x 0.7 x 7.6
58. PIN – TRANSMISSION LINKAGE LEVER
59. SPACER – THROTTLE SHAFT
60. BALL – THROTTLE LEVER
61. LEVER – THROTTLE
62. POSITIONER ASSEMBLY – THROTTLE
63. SCREW – 1/4 - 28 x 2.53 HEX HEAD ADJUSTING
64. SPRING – THROTTLE POSITIONER RETAINING
65. "E" RING – RETAINING
66. BRACKET – THROTTLE POSITIONER
67. SCREW – M5 x 8 x 14.0 HEX WASHER TAP

Fig. 15 Fuel charging assembly exploded view. V8 engine units shown, V6 engine units similar

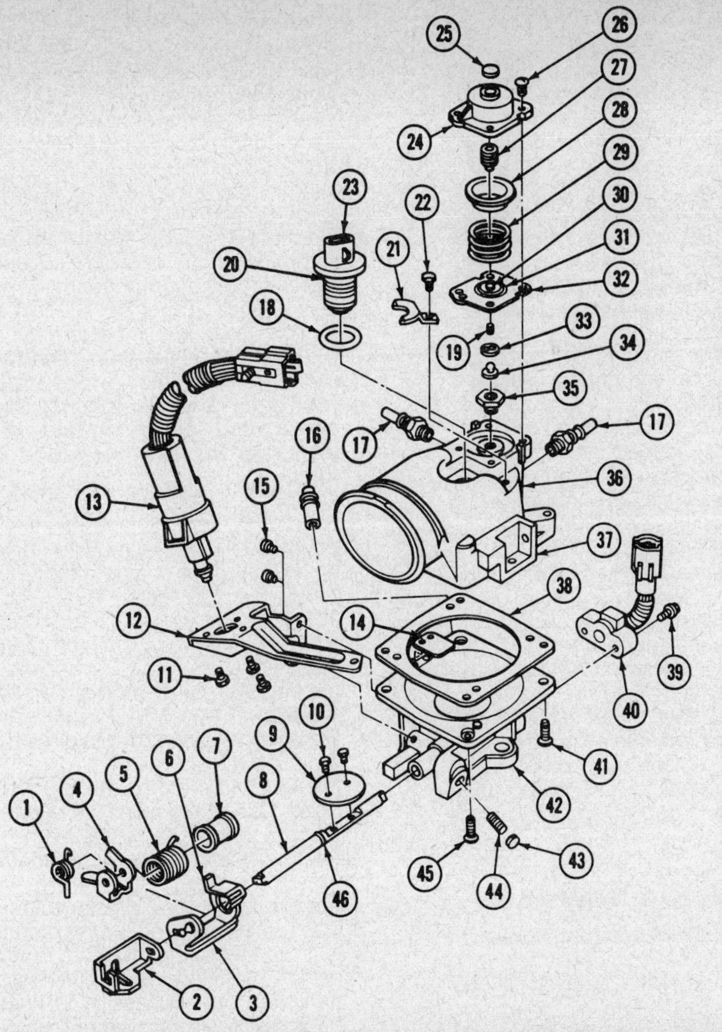

ITEM	PART NAME
1	SPRNG — ENGINE IDLE SPEED-UP CONTROL ACTUATOR
2	LEVER — CARB. TRANSMISSION LINKAGE
3	BALL — CARB. THROTTLE LEVER
4	LEVER — CARB. IDLE SPEED-UP CONTROL
5	SPRING — CARBURETOR THROTTLE RETURN
6	LEVER — CARBURETOR THROTTLE
7	BEARING — THROTTLE CONTROL LINKAGE
8	SHAFT — AIR INTAKE CHARGE THROTTLE
9	PLATE — AIR INTAKE CHARGE THROTTLE
10	SCREW — M4 X .7 X 8.0
11	SCREW — M4.2 X 1.41 X 15.9 (SELF TAPPING)
12	BRACKET — ENGINE THROTTLE POSITIONER
13	ACTUATOR ASSY. — THROTTLE CONTROL
14	PLATE — ENGINE AIR DISTRIBUTION
15	SCREW — M5 X .8 X 14.0
16	TUBE — CARBURETOR EMISSION INLET
17	CONNECTOR — QUICK CONNECT FUEL INJECTION (5/16 X 1/4 NPTF)
18	O-RING — 20.4 I.D. X 1.78 WIDE
19	SPRING — FUEL PRESSURE REGULATOR VALVE
20	O-RING — 18.6 I.D. X 3.50 WIDE
21	RETAINER — FUEL INJECTOR
22	SCREW — M4 X .7 X 12.0
23	INJECTOR ASSY. — FUEL
24	COVER — FUEL PRESSURE REGULATOR
25	PLUG — EXPANSION
26	SCREW — M4 X .7 X 16.0
27	SCREW — FUEL PRESSURE REGULATOR ADJUSTING
28	CUP — FUEL PRESSURE REGULATOR DIAPHRAGM
29	SPRING — FUEL PRESSURE REGULATOR DIAPHRAGM
30	BODY — FUEL PRESSURE REGULATOR VALVE
31	RETAINER — FUEL PRESSURE REGULATOR DIAPHRAGM
32	DIAPHRAGM — FUEL PRESSURE REGULATOR
33	RETAINER — FUEL PRESSURE REGULATOR VALVE
34	VALVE ASSY. — FUEL PRESSURE REGULATOR
35	TUBE — FUEL PRESSURE REGULATOR OUTLET
36	BODY ASSY. — FUEL CHARGING MAIN
37	BODY — FUEL CHARGING MAIN
38	GASKET — FUEL CHARGING BODY
39	SCREW — M4 X .7 X 22.0
40	POTENTIOMETER ASSY. — CARBURETOR THROTTLE
41	SCREW — M5 X .8 X 25.0
42	BODY — FUEL CHARGING THROTTLE
43	PLUG — EXPANSION
44	SCREW — M5 X .8 X 19.0
45	SCREW — M5 X .8 X 30.0
46	SEAL — FUEL CHARGING SHAFT

Fig. 16 Fuel charging assembly exploded view. 1985 Tempo & Topaz shown, 1986–87 Sable, Taurus, Tempo & Topaz similar

1984 Continental, Cougar, Mark VII & Thunderbird; 1984–85 Capri & Mustang; 1984–86 LTD & Marquis

1. Check for adequate fuel supply. **Tank must be at least half full.**
2. Check for fuel leakage at all lines and fittings.
3. Check continuity to fuel pump as follows:
   a. Disconnect electrical connector to fuel pumps at high pressure pump module, then connect voltmeter to body wiring harness connector.
   b. Turn ignition switch to the "On" position, while watching voltmeter.
   c. Voltage should rise to battery voltage, then return to zero voltage after approximately one second. If voltage is not as specified, check inertia switch and electrical system for proper operation.
   d. Connect ohmmeter to pump wiring harness connector. If no continuity is present, check continuity directly at pump terminals.
   e. If continuity is not present at pump terminals, replace pump. If continuity is present at the terminals but not at pump wiring harness connector, repair or replace wiring harness.
   f. Connect ohmmeter across body wiring harness connector. If continuity is approximately 5 ohms, low pressure pump circuit is satisfactory. If no continuity is present, check for continuity at fuel pump sender flange terminals. If continuity is not present, replace assembly.
4. Check electric fuel pump operation as follows:
   a. Disconnect return line at fuel rail, then connect hose from fuel rail fitting to a calibrated container of at least one quart capacity.
   b. Connect pressure gauge T80L-9974-A or equivalent to fuel diagnostic valve on fuel rail.
   c. Disconnect fuel pump electrical connector located forward of pump outlet.
   d. Connect auxiliary wiring harness to the electrical connector to fuel pump.
   e. Energize fuel pump for 10 seconds by connecting auxiliary wiring harness to a fully charged 12 volt battery and note pressure. If no pressure is present, check polarity of wiring harness and terminal connectors at fuel pump.
   f. Allow fuel to flow into container while observing capacity. The fuel pressure reached should be 35-45 psi and the fuel capacity should be a minimum of 9.5 oz. in 10 seconds. Fuel pressure should remain steady at 30 psi immediately after de-energizing the fuel pump. The fuel pump is operating normally if the above conditions are met.
   g. If specified pressure in step 4f is obtained, but volume is below specifications, check for obstructions in fuel filters or supply lines. After making necessary corrections, repeat steps 4e and 4f. If volume is not as specified, replace pump.
5. If hot fuel problems exist or system is noisy, check low pressure in-tank fuel pump as follows:
   a. Remove inlet push connect fitting and line from high pressure pump assembly. **Raise end of fitting above level of fuel in tank to prevent siphon action.**
   b. Connect hose from fuel tank to a calibrated container of at least one quart.
   c. Place ignition switch in "Run" posi-

tion for approximately one second until fuel pump relay stops operation.

d. Check container for a minimum fuel flow of 1.5 oz. If no fuel is present, repeat steps c and d two or three times. If fuel is still not present, check for pinched line between fuel tank and fitting.

e. Connect voltmeter to chassis electrical connector to fuel pump, then turn ignition switch to "On" position. Voltage should rise to battery voltage for approximately one second, then return to zero volts.

f. If voltage is as specified and electrical connector at pump is satisfactory, replace fuel pump assembly and repeat test. If no voltage is present, check vehicle electrical circuit.

1985 Continental & Mark VII; 1985–87 Cougar & Thunderbird; 1986 Capri & Mustang

1. Check for adequate fuel supply.
2. Check for fuel leakage at all lines and fittings.
3. Check for electrical continuity to fuel pump as follows:
   a. Locate 14 gauge (pink/black) fuel pump power feed wire at grommet in trunk or at fuel pump relay and connect a suitable volt-ohmmeter between that point and ground.
   b. Measure resistance to ground with ignition key in the Off position.
   c. If resistance measures 5 ohms or less, proceed to step 3d. If resistance measures more than 5 ohms, check for continuity of the pump ground circuit. If satisfactory, check body ground or wiring between fuel pump and body ground. If resistance is still more than 5 ohms, remove fuel tank and check for poorly mated fuel pump electrical connection or faulty pump. Measure resistance across fuel pump terminals. If resistance is within limits, check wiring and repair as needed. if resistance is not within limits, replace fuel pump and proceed to step 3d.
   d. Set meter to indicate voltage, then turn ignition switch to the On position. Voltage should rise to 10 volts or more for one second, then return to zero. If voltage reading is not as specified, inspect wiring and repair as necessary.
   e. Ensure inertia switch is set by depressing white button on top of switch.
4. Check electric fuel pump operation as follows:
   a. Connect pressure gauge T80L-9974-A or equivalent to fuel diagnostic valve on fuel rail.
   b. Turn ignition key to On position and ensure gauge indicates 30-40 psi pressure.
   c. Carefully disconnect fuel return line from fuel rail and position the fuel line in a calibrated container with a capacity of at least one quart.
   d. Locate fuel pump relay and replace with a modified relay, **Fig. 14.**
   e. Energize fuel pump for ten seconds, then allow fuel to drain into container.
   f. The fuel pump is operating properly if fuel pressure reaches 35-45 psi, the fuel flow is a minimum of 5.6 ounces in ten seconds and fuel remains at a minimum of 30 psi immediately after shutdown.
   g. If all three conditions are met, the fuel pump is operating properly. Check for engine and/or electrical malfunctions.
   h. If pressure condition is met, but flow is not, inspect filters and fuel lines for obstructions and correct as necessary. If, after making necessary repairs, flow conditions are still not met, replace fuel pump.
   i. If both flow and pressure conditions are met, but pressure drops off immediately after shutdown, check for leaking injectors or regulator. If injectors and regulator are satisfactory, replace fuel pump.
   j. If no fuel flow or pressure is observed, repeat step 4h. If no trouble is found, replace fuel pump.
   k. Replace modified fuel pump relay with original relay.

1985–87 Tempo & Topaz & 1986–87 Sable & Taurus

1. Check fuel tank for adequate fuel supply.
2. Check for fuel leakage at all fittings and lines.
3. Check for electrical continuity to fuel pump as follows:
   a. Locate inertia switch. Switch is located in the luggage compartment.
   b. Disconnect electrical connector from switch and connect a suitable ohmmeter to one of the leads at the wiring harness.
   c. Check for continuity between wire and ground. If no continuity is detected, switch to the other wire and recheck.
   d. If continuity is not present at either lead, remove fuel tank and check continuity between wiring harness and switch leads. If the leads are satisfactory, check for continuity across pump terminals. If no continuity, replace fuel pump. If continuity is present across terminals, check ground circuit or connections to the pump from the body connector.
   e. Connect electrical connector to switch and install a voltmeter to the wiring harness on the pump side of the switch.
   f. Turn ignition key while checking voltage to the fuel pump. Voltmeter should read 10 or more volts for one second and then return to zero.
   g. If voltage is not as specified, check switch to ensure that it is not open. Check electrical circuit.
4. Check electric fuel pump operation as follows:
   a. Disconnect electrical connector from inertia switch.
   b. Crank vehicle for a minimum of 15 seconds to reduce fuel pressure in the lines.
   c. Disconnect fuel return line from throttle body.
   d. Connect a suitable hose from fuel return fitting to a calibrated container of at least one quart.
   e. Disconnect jumper hose between throttle body and the fuel filter in the engine compartment. **The fuel system contains pressurized fuel after the vehicle is shut down and will maintain this pressure for a long period of time.**
   f. Connect a pressure gauge between throttle body and fuel filter.
   g. Locate fuel pump relay, located behind the glove compartment on 1985 Tempo and Topaz and 1986-87 Sable and Taurus models, or on lefthand side of instrument panel near the EEC IV module on 1986-87 Tempo and Topaz models.
   h. Remove relay and replace with a modified relay, **Fig. 14.**
   i. Energize fuel pump for 10 seconds. Check pressure while energized. If there is no pressure, monitor the voltage past the inertia switch to determine whether the pump is getting the proper voltage.
   j. The fuel pump is operating properly if the fuel pump pressure reaches 13-16 psi and the fuel flow is a minimum of 6 ounces in ten seconds and fuel pressure remains at a minimum of 11.6 psi after engine shut down.
   k. If pressure condition is met, but flow is not, inspect filters and fuel lines for obstructions and correct as necessary. If, after making necessary repairs, flow conditions are still not met, replace fuel pump sender assembly.
   l. If both flow and pressure conditions are met, but pressure drops off immediately after shutdown, check for leaking injectors or regulator. If injectors and regulator are satisfactory, replace fuel pump sender assembly.
   m. If no fuel flow or pressure is observed, repeat step 4k. If no trouble is found, replace fuel pump sender assembly.
   n. Replace modified fuel pump relay with original relay.

COMPONENT REPLACEMENT

FUEL CHARGING ASSEMBLY

Exc. 1985–87 Tempo & Topaz & 1986–87 Sable & Taurus

Rich or lean conditions during accel-

eration or other driving conditions can be caused by water, dirt or other foreign material in the fuel charging assembly.

To remove, proceed as follows:

1. Remove air cleaner, then release pressure from fuel system at diagnostic valve on fuel charging assembly using tool T80L-9974-A or equivalent.
2. Disconnect throttle cable and transmission throttle valve lever.
3. Disconnect fuel, vacuum and electrical connections.
4. Remove fuel charging assembly retaining nuts, then remove fuel charging assembly.
5. Remove mounting gasket spacer (if used) and lower gasket from intake manifold.

To install, proceed as follows:

1. Clean gasket mounting surfaces on spacer and fuel charging assembly.
2. Place spacer between two new gaskets and place spacer and gaskets on intake manifold.
3. Position fuel charging assembly on spacer and gasket, then install retaining nuts and torque to 120 inch lbs. **To avoid distortion, tighten nuts evenly and in a criss-cross pattern.**
4. Reconnect fuel line, throttle cable, vacuum lines and electrical connections.
5. Start engine and check for leaks. Adjust engine idle speed if necessary.

1985–87 Tempo & Topaz & 1986–87 Sable & Taurus

To remove, proceed as follows:

1. Remove air tube clamp from fuel charging assembly air inlet.
2. Disconnect electrical connector from inertia switch in luggage compartment.
3. Crank engine for 15 seconds to release fuel system pressure.
4. Disconnect throttle cable and throttle valve lever, if equipped, from fuel charging assembly.
5. Disconnect fuel, vacuum and electrical connections from fuel charging assembly.
6. Remove two fuel charging assembly retaining nuts and the assembly.
7. Remove and discard mounting gasket from intake manifold.

To install, proceed as follows:

1. Clean mating surfaces and position new gasket on intake manifold.
2. Position fuel charging assembly on manifold, then install retaining nuts and torque to 14-16 ft. lbs.
3. Reconnect fuel lines, electrical connectors and vacuum lines.
4. Install air tube and clamp, then start engine and check for leaks. Adjust engine idle speed if necessary.

COMPONENT OVERHAUL

FUEL CHARGING ASSEMBLY

Exc. 1985–87 Tempo & Topaz & 1986–87 Sable & Taurus

To prevent damage to the throttle plates, the fuel charging assembly should be supported on a work stand. If stand is not available, use four bolts 5/16 x 2 1/2 inches as stands. Install nuts on bolts above and below the throttle body.

To disassemble, proceed as follows: **Any screws painted blue are metric.**

1. Remove air cleaner stud, then invert assembly and remove the four screws in throttle body, **Fig. 15.**
2. Separate upper body from throttle body and remove gasket (12).
3. Remove upper body screws (14) and pressure regulator (2).
4. Disconnect wiring from injector (17), then remove injector retaining screw (11) and injector retainer (13).
5. Loosen wiring harness retaining screw (18), then pinch on tabs and remove wiring harness from upper body.
6. Remove injectors by pulling them out. **Identify each injector as to choke side or throttle side.**
7. Remove fuel diagnostic valve cap (16) and valve assembly (15).
8. Drill out choke cap retaining rivets, then remove retaining ring (35), choke cap (34) and gasket (31). **On 1983 units, the choke cap is retained by three screws.**
9. Remove thermostat lever screw (32) and lever (33), then remove fast idle cam assembly (27, 28).
10. Remove fast idle control and rod positioner (26).
11. Remove screws (19), control diaphragm cover assembly (21), control modulator spring (22) and pulldown control diaphragm (24).
12. Remove fast idle retaining nut (37), fast idle cam adjuster lever (38) fast idle lever (40), fast idle return spring (39a) on 1982 units, if equipped and E-ring (49).
13. Scribe a mark on potentiometer (42) and throttle body (45) and remove connector bracket retaining screws (43).
14. Remove potentiometer retaining screws (41) and potentiometer (42).
15. Remove throttle positioner retaining screw (67) and throttle positioner assembly.
16. Using a 1/16 inch punch, carefully drive out roll pin (50).
17. Remove throttle plate retaining screws (46) and throttle plate. **Note exact location of throttle plates as to choke side and throttle plate side.**
18. Remove C-ring, if used, and slide throttle shaft assembly while disengaging throttle return spring (54).

To assemble, proceed as follows:

1. Install fuel pressure valve assembly (15) and torque to 48-84 inch lbs. Install valve cap (16) and torque to 5-10 inch lbs., **Fig. 15.**
2. Install wiring harness (17) and screw (18) into upper body. Torque to 8-10 inch lbs.
3. Lubricate O-rings (3) on injectors (9) with light oil and push injectors into upper body. Make sure to install in their original positions.
4. Install injector retainer (13) and retainer screw (11). Torque to 36-60 inch lbs.
5. Connect fuel charging connectors to injectors.
6. Lubricate fuel pressure regulator O-ring with light oil, then install O-ring (3) and gasket (4) on fuel pressure regulator (2).
7. Install pressure regulator on upper body and install screws (14). Torque to 27-40 inch lbs.
8. Install throttle shaft assembly and secure throttle shaft to proper boss, then install throttle plates (47) and retaining screws (46) in their original locations. Torque screws to 10-15 inch lbs. After installing throttle plate, cycle throttle shaft several times to insure freedom of operation.
9. Install roll pin (50), an equal distance through throttle shaft. **Use care not to damage throttle shaft when installing pin. Cycle shaft several times to insure freedom of operation.**
10. Position potentiometer on throttle shaft with its scribe mark at 12 o'clock position. Hold potentiometer firmly against throttle body and rotate potentiometer clockwise until its scribe mark aligns with scribe mark on throttle body, then install retaining screws.
11. Install E-ring (49), fast idle lever (40), fast idle return spring (39a), if equipped, fast idle adjustment lever (38) and fast idle retaining nut (37). Torque nut to 16-20 inch lbs.
12. Install pulldown control diaphragm (24), control modulator spring (22) and retaining screws (19). Torque retaining screws to 13-19 inch lbs.
13. Install fast idle cam assembly (27), thermostat lever (33) and screw (32). Torque screw to 13-19 inch lbs. **Thermostatic lever should be straight down when properly installed.**
14. Install gasket (31), choke cap (34), retaining ring (35) and rivets (36). On 1983 units, install choke cap retaining screws and torque to 13-18 inch lbs.
15. Install gasket (12) on throttle body, then place upper body on throttle body.
16. Holding upper body and throttle body in place, invert and install the four retaining screws (44) and air cleaner stud. **Install all screws and stud before tightening.**

1985–87 Tempo & Topaz & 1986–87 Sable & Taurus

To prevent damage to the throttle plates, the fuel charging assembly should be positioned on a suitable stand or pad.

To disassemble, proceed as follows:

1. Invert fuel charging assembly and remove four throttle body-to-main body attaching screws, **Fig. 16.**
2. Separate throttle body from main body, then remove and discard gasket.
3. Carefully remove four fuel pressure regulator attaching screws. **Fuel pressure regulator cover is spring loaded. Apply downward pressure**

to regulator when removing attaching screws to prevent personal injury.

4. Remove cover assembly, cup, spring and diaphragm.
5. Remove regulator valve seat, then the fuel injector retaining screw and retainer.
6. Remove injector assembly and O-ring.
7. Remove fuel fittings and filter screen from fuel inlet channel.
8. Remove TPS attaching screws and the TPS from throttle body.
9. Remove ISC motor and bracket assembly from throttle body. Remove ISC motor from bracket, if necessary.

To assemble, proceed as follows:

1. If previously removed, attach ISC motor to bracket and torque retaining screws to 44-50 inch lbs.
2. Install ISC motor and bracket assembly to throttle body. Torque retaining screws to 38-44 inch lbs.
3. Position TPS with connector toward main body. Rotate sensor counterclockwise to align screw holes, then install retaining screws and torque to 14-16 ft. lbs. **To ensure correct idle speeds, the TPS must be turned counterclockwise only when installing.**
4. Position new gasket on main body, then mount throttle body on main body. Install retaining screws and torque to 38-44 inch lbs.
5. Lubricate new lower O-ring and injector seat with clean engine oil, then position the O-ring on injector.
6. Lubricate upper O-ring, then clean and lubricate throttle body O-ring seat.
7. Center injector and apply a steady downward pressure with a slight rotational force to install injector. Install injector retainer and screw and torque screw to 18-22 inch lbs.
8. Install fuel pressure regulator valve seat, diaphragm, spring and spring cup cover.
9. Apply downward pressure to cover and install four retaining screws. Torque screws to 28-32 inch lbs.
10. Clean and install fuel filter screen in fuel inlet channel.
11. Remove any debris from fuel fittings and apply suitable locking compound to the fittings.
12. Install fuel fittings and torque to 14-17 ft. lbs.

EMISSION CONTROL SYSTEMS

INDEX

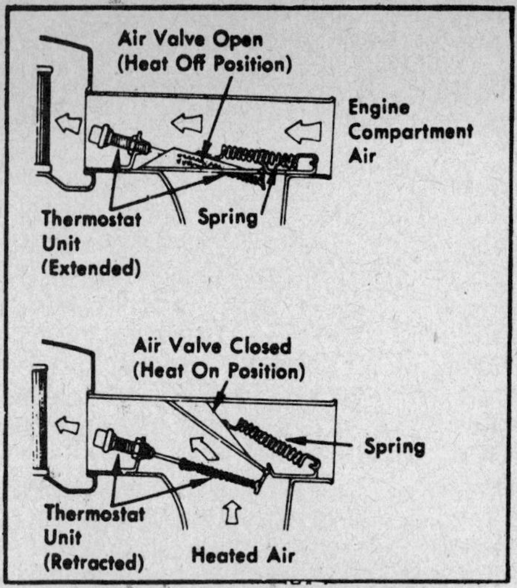

Fig. 1 Mechanically controlled thermostatic assembly

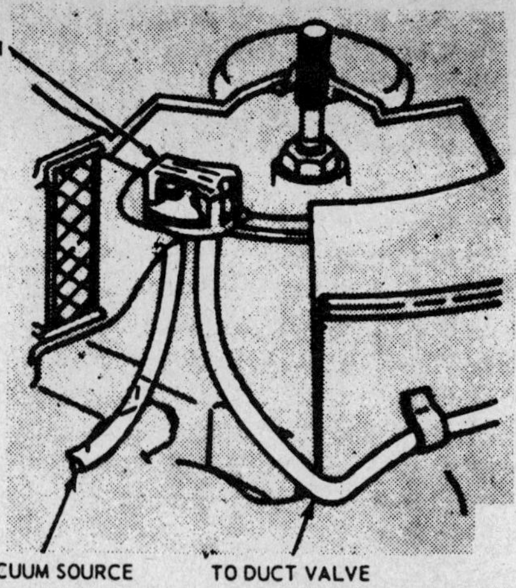

Fig. 2 Bi-metal switch

AIR CLEANER AIR TEMPERATURE INLET CONTROL

MECHANICALLY CONTROLLED THERMOSTATIC

Carburetor air temperature is thermostatically controlled by the air duct and valve assembly. Air from the engine compartment, or heated air from the shrouded exhaust manifold is supplied to the engine, **Fig. 1.**

During the engine warm-up period when the air temperature entering the air duct is less than 105°F, the thermostat is in the retracted position and the air valve is held in the closed position by the air valve spring, thus shutting off the air from the engine compartment. Air is then drawn from the shroud at the exhaust manifold.

As the temperature of the air passing the thermostat unit rises, the thermostat starts to open and pulls the air valve down. This allows cooler air from the engine compartment to enter the air cleaner. When the temperature of the air reaches 130°F, the air valve is in the open position so that only engine compartment air is allowed to enter the air cleaner.

VACUUM OPERATED THERMOSTATIC

A vacuum operated duct valve with a thermostatic bi-metal control, **Fig. 2,** is used. The valve in the duct assembly is in an open position when the engine is not operating. When the engine is operating at below 75°F, manifold vacuum is routed through the bi-metal switch to the vacuum motor to close the duct valve, allowing only heated air to enter the air cleaner. When the engine reaches normal operating temperature the bi-metal switch opens an air-bleed which eliminates the vacuum and the duct valve opens, allowing only cold air to enter the air cleaner. During periods of acceleration the duct valve will open regardless of temperature due to the loss of manifold vacuum.

COLD WEATHER MODULATOR

This modulator, **Fig. 3,** is used on some models to prevent the air cleaner door from opening when outside air is below a predetermined temperature. At higher ambient temperatures, the modulator is inoperative. During acceleration, with outside air below the preset temperature, the modulator will close off the vacuum to the motor and hold the duct open. The modulator is located inline between the air temperature control sensor and the vacuum duct motor.

AUXILIARY AIR INLET VALVE

The auxiliary air inlet valve is mounted on the outside of the air cleaner housing and serves to allow outside air to bypass the heated air inlet system when the engine is under load. When manifold vacuum is low, a spring in the vacuum motor allows the valve to open, providing an additional flow of air into the air cleaner housing, **Fig. 4.**

Testing

MECHANICALLY CONTROLLED THERMOSTATIC

Preferred Method

1. Remove air cleaner cover and components necessary to observe position of duct door.
2. With engine cold and ambient air temperature less than 105°F, the duct valve should be closed in the heat on position (closed). If duct valve is open, cool thermostat by spraying with Refrigerant 12. **Do not spray refrigerant with engine running, as any refrigerant drawn into the carburetor and burned in the engine will produce poisonous phosgene gas. Conduct this procedure in well ventilated area.**
3. Place a magnetic based thermometer (Rotunda T75L-9601-A or equivalent) as near as possible to the thermostat and reinstall air cleaner cover without wing nut. Start engine and allow to idle.
4. As engine warms up, observe duct valve door. When duct valve door opens (heat off position), remove air cleaner cover and note temperature reading.
5. Temperature reading should be about 130-150°F. If not, repair or replace components as necessary.

Alternate Method

1. With duct assembly installed, engine cold and ambient temperature below 100°F, the valve plate should be in the heat on position.
2. If plate is not in the heat on position, check for interference of plate and duct which may cause plate to bind.
3. Remove duct and valve assembly. Immerse assembly in cool (below 75°F) water so that thermostat capsule is covered with water.
4. Raise water temperature to 100°F, allowing 5 minutes for stabilization, and observe valve position. The correct position should be in the heat on position.
5. Increase water temperature to 135°F, allowing 5 minutes for stabilization and observe valve plate. The plate should be in the heat off position.

VACUUM OPERATED THERMOSTATIC

This test must be performed with ambient air temperature below 60°F. **Do not immerse any part of the vacuum operated duct and valve assembly in water.**

1. On systems with Cold Weather Modulator, bypass the modulator by connecting the two vacuum lines from the modulator.
2. Apply parking brake and block wheels, then remove air cleaner cover and element. Check heat riser tube and zip tube for proper installation or

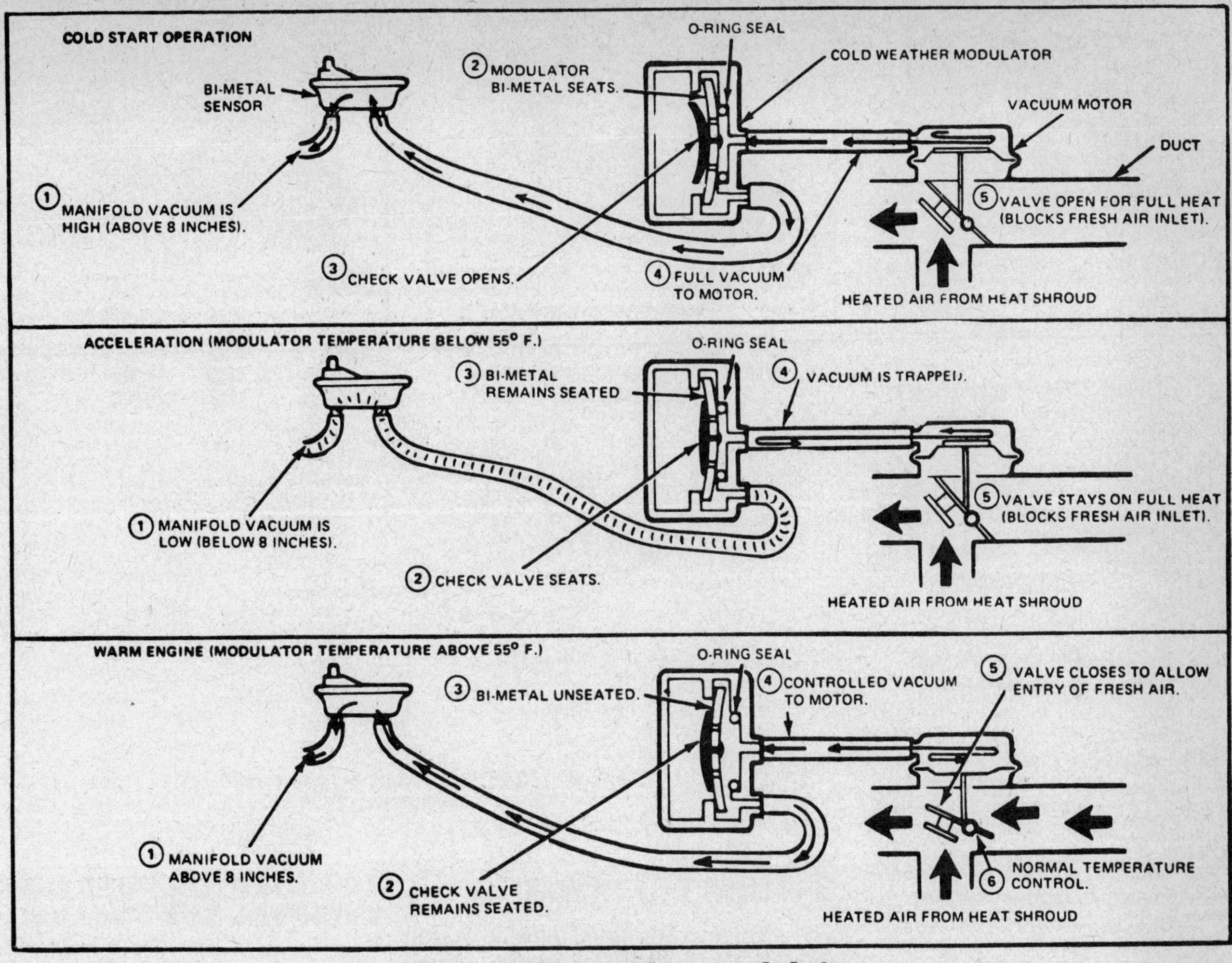

Fig. 3 Cold weather modulator

damage. Repair or replace as necessary.

3. Remove components necessary to observe position of duct door. On vacuum operated units, disconnect vacuum line at duct and valve. Check that duct door is in the open (fresh air side) position. If not, check for binding or sticking. Repair or replace as necessary.
4. Place a magnetic based thermometer as near as possible to temperature sensor on inlet side. If air cleaner housing is aluminum, use tape to secure thermometer. **Do not allow magnet to touch temperature sensor.**
5. Start engine. If duct door is in the heat on position, proceed to step 7. If duct door is in the heat off position, turn engine off. Cool sensor temperature by spraying with Refrigerant 12 for 20 seconds. **Do not spray refrigerant with engine running, as any refrigerant drawn into the carburetor and burned in the engine will produce poisonous phosgene gas. Conduct this procedure in well ventilated area.**
6. Restart engine. If duct door is in the heat off position during idle, check vacuum hoses.
7. Reinstall air cleaner cover without wing nut. With engine running, observe duct door. When door starts to open, remove air cleaner cover and note temperature reading on thermometer. Temperature reading should not exceed the following specifications:
   a. For brown color coded sensors, temperature should not exceed 75°F.
   b. For black or pink color coded sensors, temperature should not exceed 90°F.
   c. For blue or yellow or green color coded sensors, temperature should not exceed 105°F.
   d. If temperatures are greater than those specified above, replace sensor.
8. If duct door does not start to open within 5 minutes after performing step 7, remove air cleaner cover and note temperature. If temperature is less than specified above, the temperature is insufficient to operate the duct door. Reinstall air cleaner cover without wing nut and continue to run engine until specified temperature is reached. If duct door has not started to open by then, replace sensor.

COLD WEATHER MODULATOR

1. Cool modulator to below the following temperatures by spraying with Refrigerant 12: black modulator, 20°F; blue modulator, 40°F; green modulator, 50°F; yellow modulator, 65°F. Allow sufficient time for modulator temperature to stabilize and modulator valve to close. **Do not spray refrigerant with engine running, as any refrigerant drawn into the carburetor and burned in the engine will produce poisonous phosgene gas. Conduct test in well ventilated area.**
2. Use a 24 inch length of 1/4 inch hose between cold weather modulator and vacuum gauge. Using an external vacuum source, apply at least 16 inches Hg vacuum to vacuum motor side of modulator and trap vacuum by pinching hose. The modulator must hold at least 5 inches Hg vacuum for 30 seconds. If not, replace modulator.

CATALYTIC CONVERTERS

The catalytic converter, **Figs. 5 and 6**, is an emission control device added to the

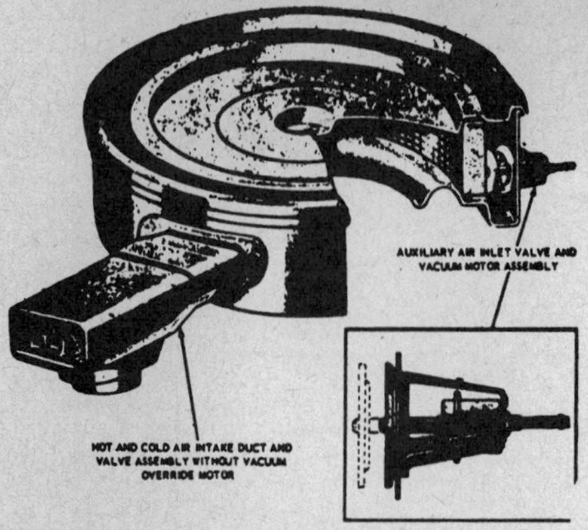

Fig. 4 Auxiliary air inlet valve

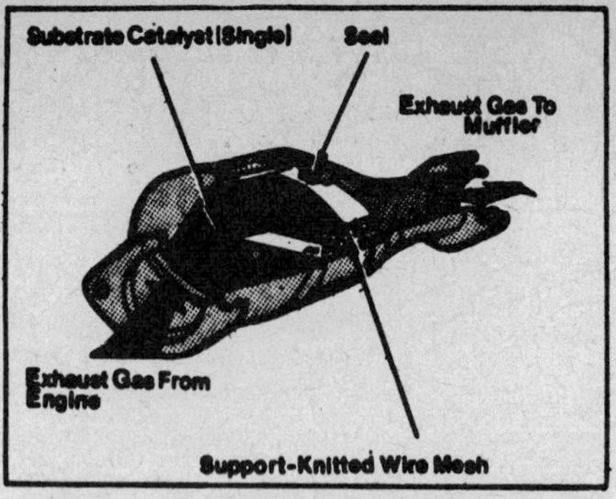

Fig. 5 Catalytic converter with single substrate catalyst

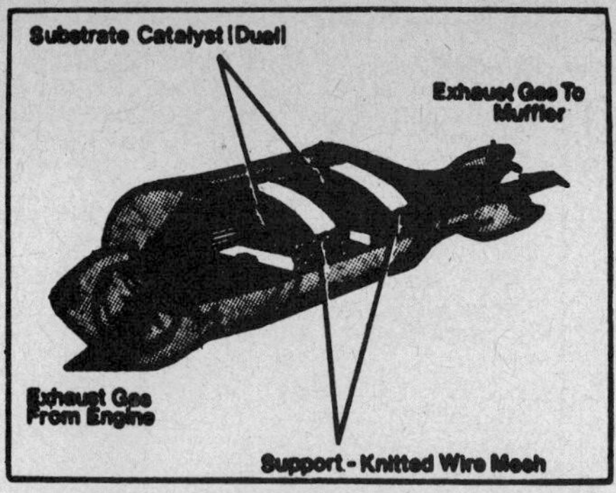

Fig. 6 Catalytic converter with dual substrate catalyst

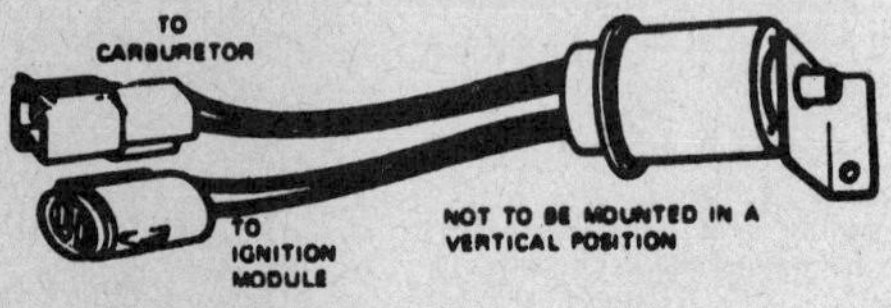

Fig. 7 Electrical type altitude compensator

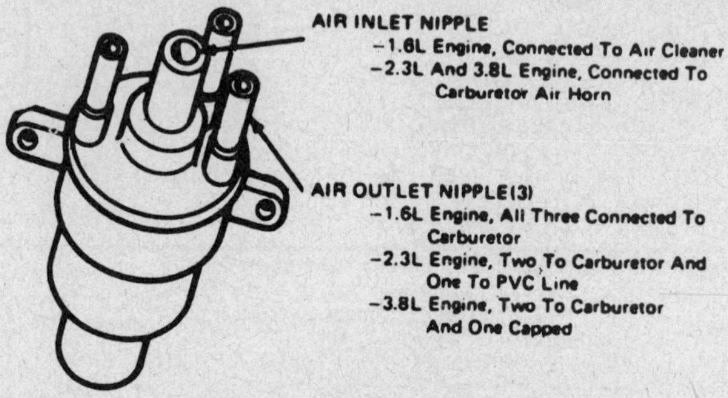

Fig. 8 Mechanical type altitude compensator

exhaust system to effectively reduce the levels of carbon monoxide (CO), hydrocarbons (HC), and in some cases oxides of nitrogen (NOx), entering the atmosphere. The converter permits a faster chemical reaction to take place and, although it enters into the chemical reaction, it remains unchanged, ready to repeat the process.

The catalyst in these converters is structured in the form of a honeycomb monolithic composition, **Figs. 5 and 6.** The catalyst consists of a porous substrate of an inert material, coated with platinum and other noble metals (the catalytically active materials).

During engine operation, all of the exhaust gases flow through the converter where a chemical change takes place. This change causes the temperature inside the converter to be higher than the temperature of the exhaust gases when they leave the engine. Due to this increase in heat, the converter is insulated so that its outside temperature is about the same temperature as the muffler. However, due to its solid mass, the converter remains hot much longer than the muffler.

The body of the catalytic converter is made of stainless steel designed to last the life of the vehicle. Excessive heat can bulge or distort the converter. Since excessive heat built up is not the fault of the converter, the carburetion or ignition system should be checked whenever a converter is damaged by overheating.

Although all vehicles with catalytic converter must use unleaded fuel, small amounts of leaded fuel can be used in case of an emergency. To prevent adding leaded fuel, the fuel tank filler nozzle has a built-in restrictor.

Heat shields are used on some vehicles to protect chassis components, passenger compartment, and other areas from heat damage that may be caused by the catalytic converter.

System Servicing

The catalytic converters used in these vehicles are not serviceable. After determining that the catalyst has lost its effectiveness, the catalytic converter assembly must be replaced.

CONTROL SWITCHES & VALVES

ALTITUDE COMPENSATOR

Electrical

The electrical type altitude compensator, **Fig. 7**, is mounted on the ignition module. The compensator improves emissions and aids engine performance at altitudes above 4000 ft. by advancing the timing and leaning the air/fuel mixture.

Mechanical

The mechanical type altitude compensator, **Fig. 8**, is mounted on the bulkhead. The compensator leans the air/fuel mixture at altitudes above 3000 ft. by supplying additional filtered air to the carburetor.

CARBURETOR FUEL BOWL SOLENOID VENT VALVE

This valve, **Fig. 9**, is a normally open valve located in the fuel bowl vent line. When the engine is running, the valve closes off the fuel bowl vent line. When the engine is shut off, the vent line returns to the normally open position.

CARBURETOR FUEL BOWL THERMAL VENT VALVE

The thermal vent valve, **Fig. 10**, used on some 1984-87 vehicles, is a temperature actuated on/off valve that is inserted in the carburetor to canister vent line. This valve is closed when the engine compartment is cold, preventing fuel tank vapors, generated when the fuel tank heats up before the engine compartment, from being vented through the carburetor bowl.

COLD START SPARK HOLD (CSSH)

This system, used on some, provides momentary spark advance hold during acceleration when the engine is cold, to provide improved cold engine acceleration.

When engine coolant temperature is less than 128°F, the CSSH PVS is closed and the distributor vacuum signal travels through the restrictor, **Fig. 11.**

When the engine is started cold, high vacuum acts on the vacuum advance unit to provide maximum advance. During acceleration, the high vacuum in the vacuum advance unit is slowly bled down through the restrictor, providing a modified vacuum advance during the initial stage of acceleration.

DASH POT THROTTLE STOP

The dash pot, **Fig. 12,** is mounted on the carburetor and aids in controlling hydrocarbon emissions by slowing the closing of the throttle plates. As the throttle is opened, a spring extends the dash pot

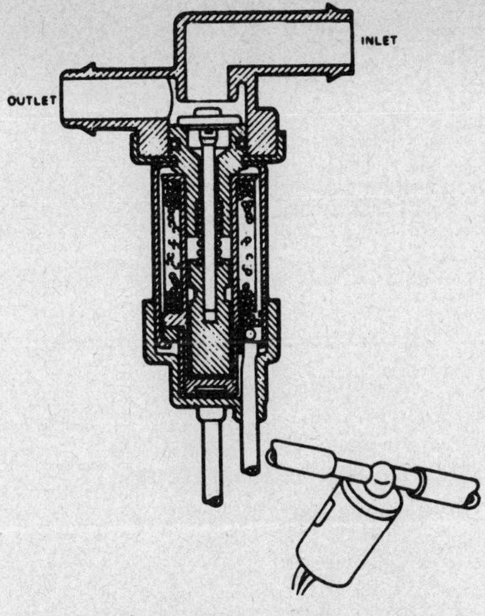

Fig. 9 Carburetor fuel bowl solenoid vent valve

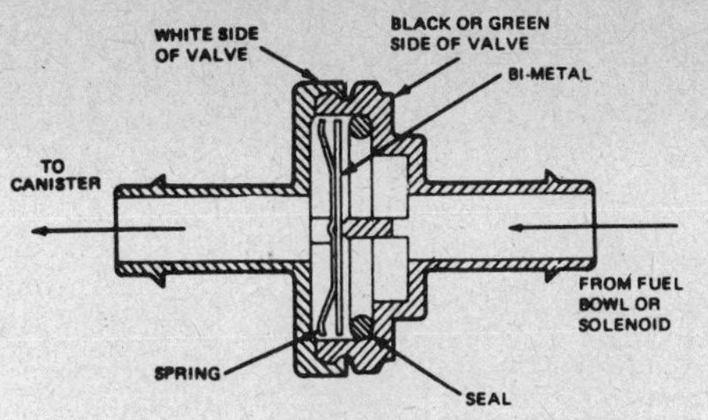

Fig. 10 Carburetor fuel bowl thermal vent valve

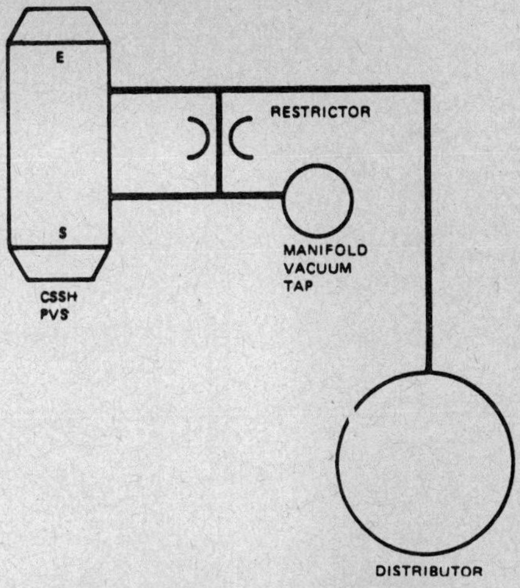

Fig. 11 Cold start hold system—CSSH

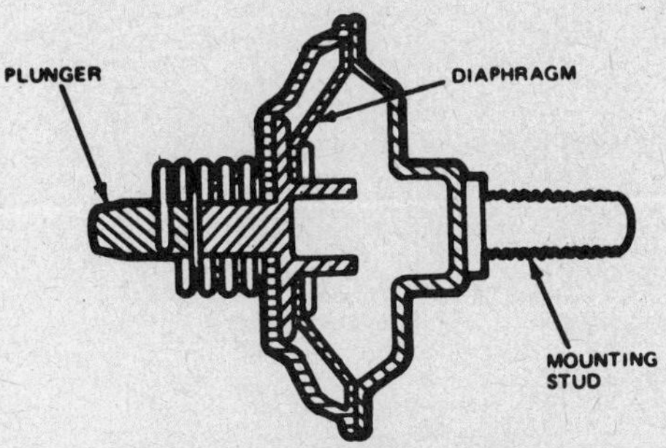

Fig. 12 Dash pot

plunger. As the throttle plates close, the throttle lever applies pressure to the dash pot plunger. This causes the air in the dash pot chamber to leak out slowly, allowing the throttle plates to return slowly to the idle position.

DISTRIBUTOR MODULATOR VALVE

This valve is used in the Throttle Kicker system and has three ports. Port A which is common, is open to Port B and closed to Port C when the solenoid is de-energized. When energized, Port A is opened to Port C and closed to Port B.

DISTRIBUTOR VACUUM VENT VALVE

This valve, **Fig. 13,** is used on some vehicles equipped with a variable venturi carburetor. The primary functions of this valve are to control exhaust emissions, and to prevent fuel migration to the distributor and act as a delay valve.

This valve controls exhaust emissions by delaying vacuum spark advance during light acceleration and eliminating vacuum spark advance during heavy acceleration, deceleration and idle.

When spark port vacuum is applied to the vent valve, the dump valve closes, the check valve opens and the distributor vacuum advance unit begins to evacuate through the sintered metal restrictor which acts as a spark delay valve. When spark port vacuum decreases, the check valve closes and the dump valve opens the distributor vacuum line to atmosphere. Venting the distributor vacuum line to atmosphere prevents fuel migration to the distributor diaphragm and returns the distributor to zero vacuum advance.

HOT IDLE COMPENSATOR

The hot idle compensator, **Fig. 14,** cools the engine during hot idle operation. The compensator may be integral with the carburetor or mounted separately. When open, the compensator bleeds air into the manifold, leaning out the air/fuel mixture at idle. This increased air intake causes an increase in engine idle speed, resulting in cooling of the engine. Temperature rise on the bi-metal sensor lifts the normally closed valve and opens the air passage. A valve that does not fully close will cause high idle speed and excessive exhaust emission.

IDLE SPEED CONTROLLER WITH INTEGRAL TRACKING SWITCH

This switch, **Fig. 15,** used on some 1982 models, is used on vehicles with an electronic processor. It can serve as a throttle positioner switch at idle and off idle and/or maintain a given idle speed with various engine loads. This switch also incorporates a vacuum decel control of the dash pot type.

IGNITION BAROMETRIC PRESSURE SWITCH

1983

At low altitudes, this switch, **Fig. 16,** signals the ignition module to retard spark timing. Calibration resistors inside the switch control the amount of retard.

1984–87

This switch, **Fig. 17,** controls spark timing and/or other electrical devices according to altitude. Calibration resistors in the switch assembly cause the ignition module to vary the spark timing. Spark timing is advanced for vehicle operation above a predetermined altitude and retarded for vehicle operation below a predetermined altitude. Some switch assemblies control both spark timing and another device while other switch assemblies control only one or the other.

IGNITION TIMING VACUUM SWITCH

Below vacuum setting, this switch, **Fig. 18,** is open and signals the ignition module to retard spark timing. The switch is closed above the vacuum setting and the ignition module is in the non-retard spark timing mode. Calibration resistors inside the switch control the amount of retard.

INERTIA SWITCH

This switch, **Fig. 19,** is used on 1984-87 vehicles with electric fuel pumps. This switch shuts off the fuel pump in the event of an accident. The switch consists of a steel ball held in place by a magnet. Upon sharp impact, the ball breaks loose from the magnet, rolls up a conical ramp, and strikes a target plate that opens the switch electrical contacts and shuts off the fuel pump. Once the switch is open, it must be manually reset before starting the vehicle.

PORTED VACUUM SWITCHES (PVS)

These switches, **Fig. 20,** control vacuum to emission components during engine warmup. The 2-port and 4-port types open when coolant temperature reaches a predetermined value. The 3-port type switches vacuum from the center to the top or bottom ports. Electrical switches can be opened or closed until the PVS is fully cycled. All PVS units are temperature-activated and have a specific opening and closing temperature.

SPARK DELAY VALVE (SDV)

This unit is used in conjunction with some of the other Ford systems. Its purpose is to further reduce emissions by delaying the spark advance during rapid acceleration and by cutting off advance immediately upon deceleration, **Fig. 21.**

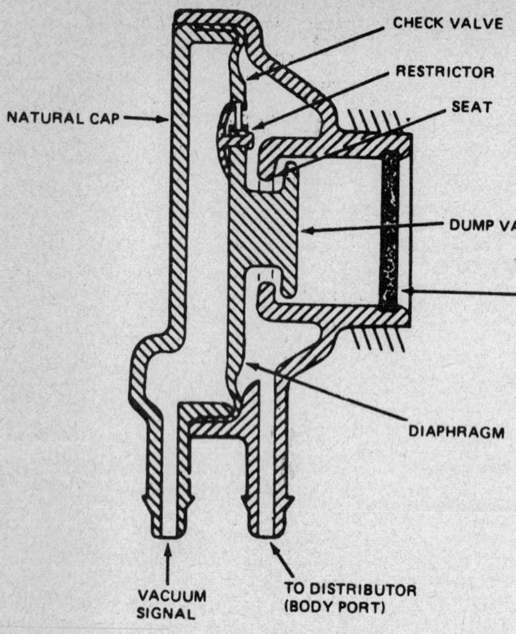

Fig. 13 Distributor vacuum vent valve

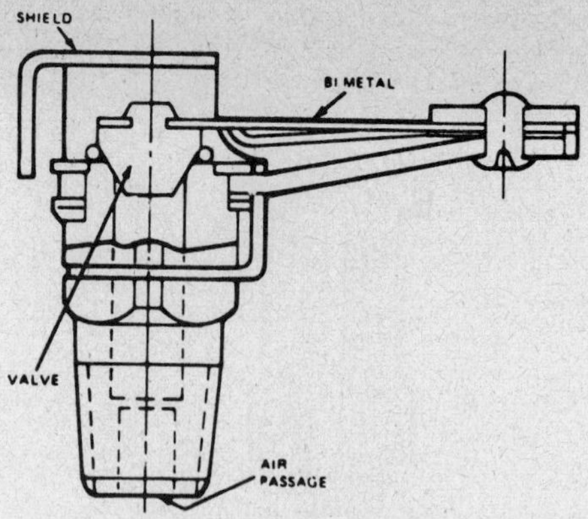

Fig. 14 Hot idle compensator

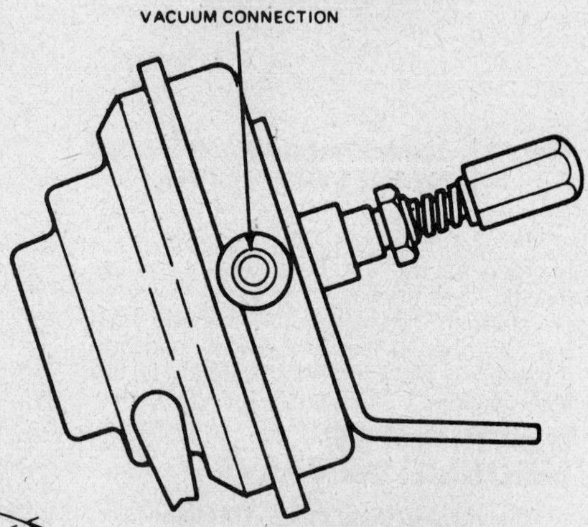

Fig. 15 Idle speed controller with integral tracking switch

This plastic disc-shaped valve is installed in the carburetor vacuum line at the distributor advance diaphragm. It is a one way valve and will not operate if installed backwards. The black side of the valve must be toward the carburetor. This valve cannot be repaired. **On all systems which employ the dual diaphragm distributor the line which has high vacuum at idle (normally operating temperature) is connected to the secondary (retard) side of the distributor vacuum advance unit. This is the connection closest to the distributor cap.**

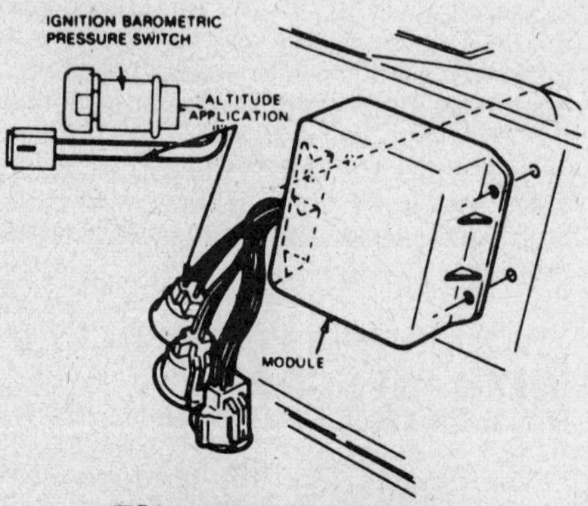

Fig. 16 Ignition barometric pressure switch. 1983

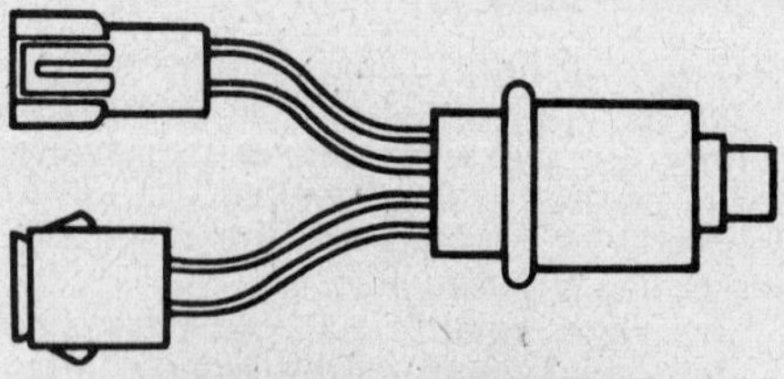

Fig. 17 Ignition barometric pressure switch. 1984–87

TEMPERATURE VACUUM SWITCH (TVS)

This switch, **Fig. 22,** has a bi-metal disc which locates itself in one of two positions, depending on its temperature. One position allows free air flow in the vacuum line; and the other blocks air flow by sealing itself against the O-ring. The switching temperature is below the range of normal engine operating temperature.

The TVS may be used to control the vacuum signal to the thermactor dump valve, to reduce emissions.

The normally open TVS may block the purge vacuum signal to provide satisfactory cold driveability and reduce cold engine emissions. It may be also used to hold off EGR operation during cold engine operation.

The normally closed TVS may allow cold spark advance to provide satisfactory cold engine driveability.

THROTTLE SOLENOID POSITIONER (TSP)

With Dash Pot

The TSP with dash pot, **Fig. 23,** acts as

Fig. 18 Ignition timing vacuum switch

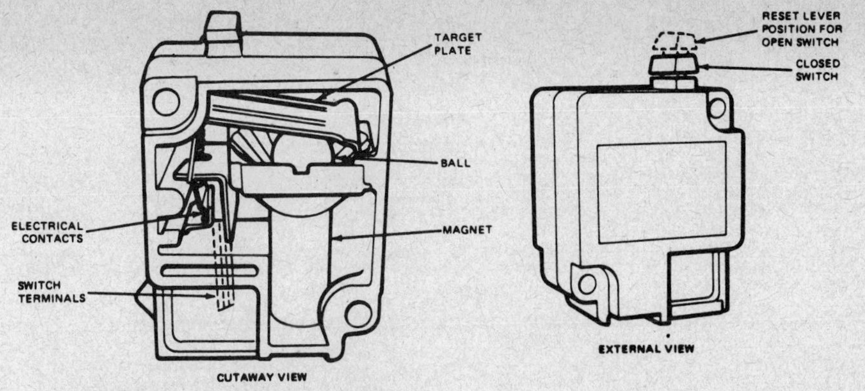

Fig. 19 Inertia switch

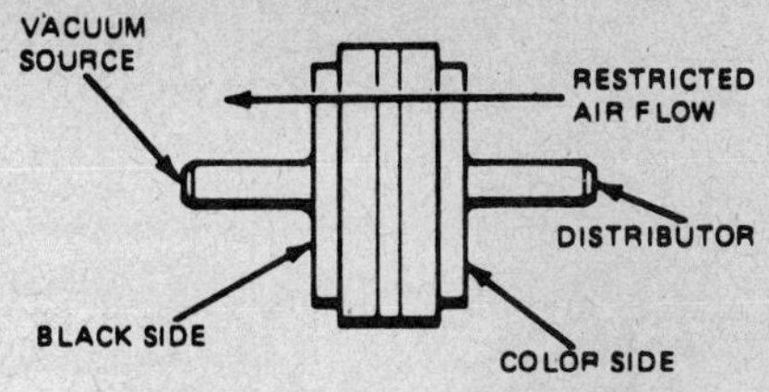

Fig. 21 Spark delay valve—SDV

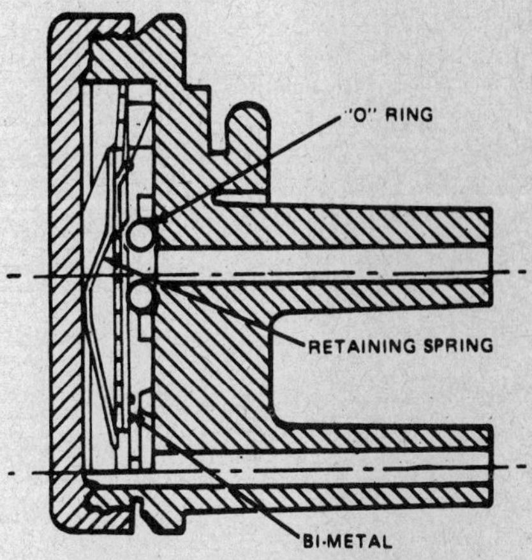

Fig. 22 Temperature vacuum switch—TVS

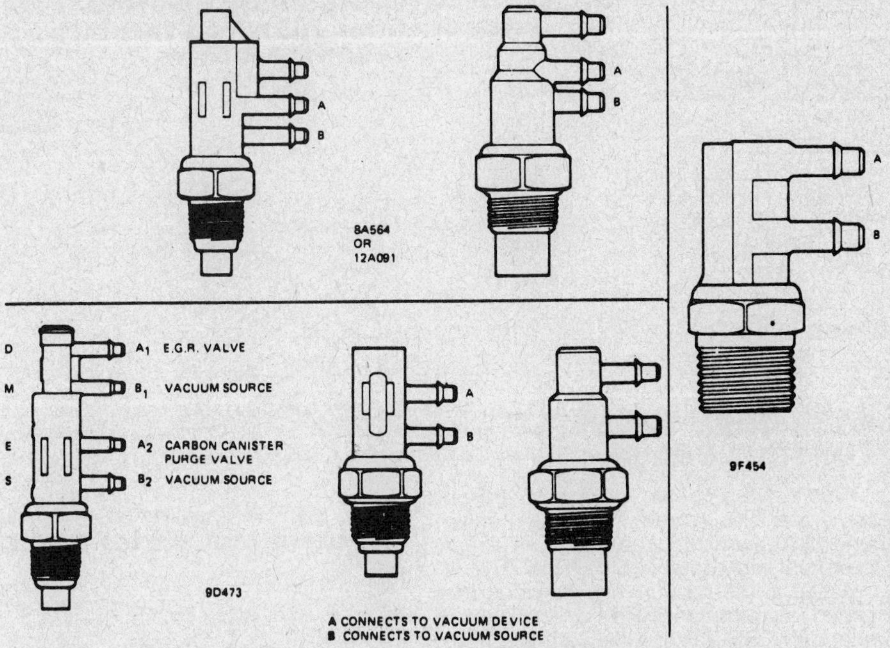

Fig. 20 Ported vacuum switches—PVS

a variable throttle stop by extending its plunger when the solenoid is activated and retracting the plunger when the solenoid is de-energized. When energized, the TSP holds the throttle at an idle position. When de-energized, the TSP functions as an anti-dieseling device by retracting its plunger and fully closing the throttle. A TSP may also be used to increase throttle opening when the A/C is in operation.

Two types of TSPs with dash pot are used: the adjustable plunger rod length type and the fixed plunger rod length type. The TSP with dash pot does not exert sufficient force to open the throttle, however, it will hold throttle open after it has been mechanically opened.

With Vacuum Operated Throttle Modulator (VOTM)

The solenoid portion of the TSP with VOTM, **Fig. 24,** may be used as an anti-dieseling TSP or an A/C TSP. The vacuum portion can be used for maintaining a cold idle RPM or as an A/C VOTM. The VOTM, operating the throttle through a connecting lever, may be activated by an electric vacuum solenoid or other vacuum control device.

VACUUM DELAY VALVE (VDV)

This valve, **Fig. 25,** further reduces emissions by delaying the spark advance during rapid acceleration and by cutting off advance immediately upon deceleration. This is a one-way valve and will not operate if installed backwards. **On all systems which employ the dual diaphragm distributor, the line which has high vacuum at idle (normal operating temperature) is connected to the secondary (retard) side of the distributor vacuum advance unit. This is the connection closest to the distributor cap.**

VACUUM OPERATED THROTTLE MODULATOR (VOTM)

The VOTM, **Fig. 26,** acts as a variable carburetor stop. The plunger extends when vacuum is applied.

VACUUM REGULATOR

Three port, **Fig. 27,** regulators and four port, **Fig. 28,** regulators are used to control the vacuum advance to the distributor. During engine idle conditions, the manifold vacuum signal is reduced to a constant output signal. Off idle, the output signal equals the spark port.

VACUUM REGULATOR/SOLENOID

This regulator, **Fig. 29,** is used to control vacuum to the 6500 feedback carburetor on 2.3 liter engines. During engine operation, the manifold vacuum signal is reduced to a variable vacuum output signal. The vacuum output signal is varied in response to an electric input from the MCU module. The vacuum signal from the vacuum regulator/solenoid varies the air fuel ratio in the carburetor.

VACUUM RESERVOIR

The vacuum reservoir, **Fig. 30,** acts as an accumulator and prevents sudden drops or rapid fluctuations in a vacuum signal during acceleration. If vacuum in the reservoir leaks more than 1/2 inch Hg in 1 minute, the reservoir is defective and must be replaced.

VACUUM RESTRICTOR

The orifice type flow restrictor, **Fig. 31,** is used on some systems to control the flow rate and or timing characteristics to the following systems:

a. EGR valve timing (opening and closing).

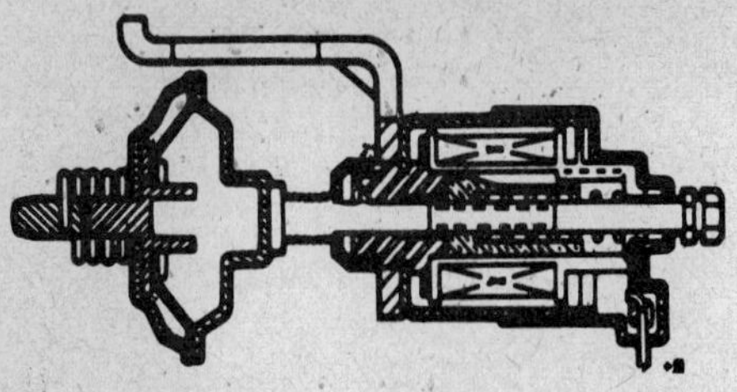

Fig. 23 Throttle solenoid positioner (TSP) with dash pot

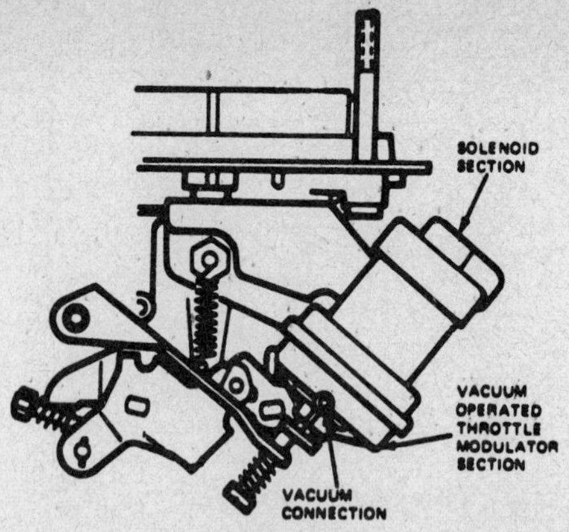

Fig. 24 Throttle solenoid positioner (TSP) with vacuum operated throttle modulator (VOTM)

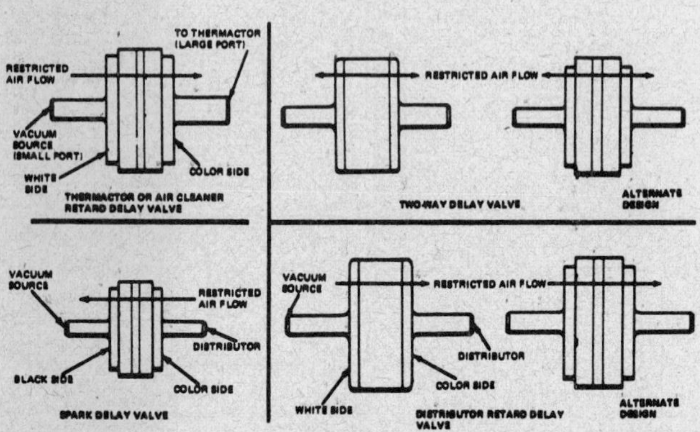

Fig. 25 Vacuum delay valves

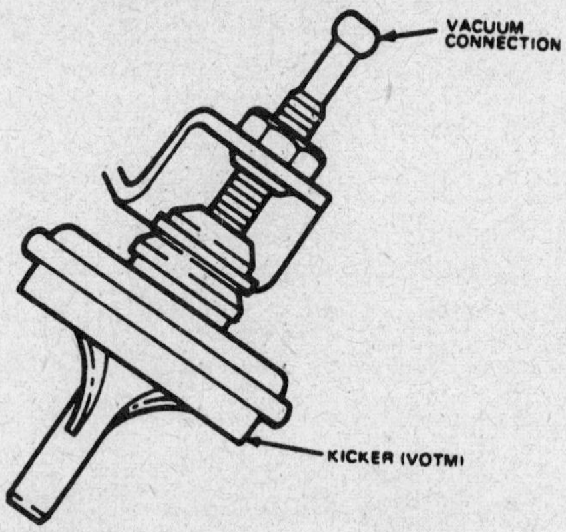

Fig. 26 Vacuum operated throttle modulator (VOTM)

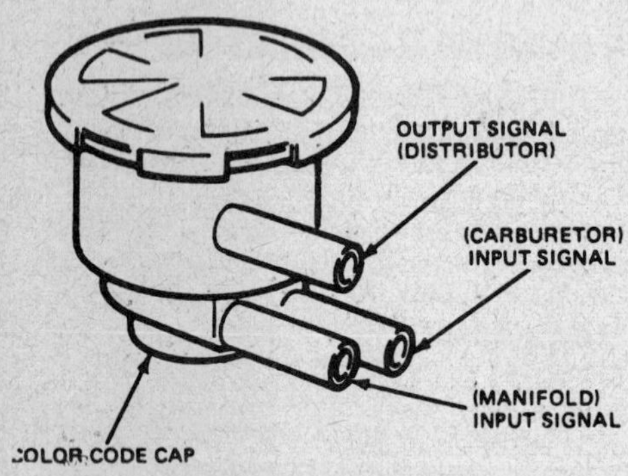

Fig. 27 Three port vacuum regulator

b. Part throttle spark advance.
c. Purge system.
d. Thermactor system.

The flow rate through the restrictor is the same in both directions. If blocked, it should be replaced.

VACUUM VENT VALVES

Vacuum vent valves, **Figs. 32 and 33,** control the induction of fresh air into a vacuum system to prevent chemical decay of vacuum diaphragms that can occur on contact with fuel vapors. Two types of valves are used. The black color coded valve is a vent valve only, while the natural color coded valve is a combination vent and delay valve. **These valves should be installed with ports pointing downward. The vacuum source should be connected to the cap port, and the system or device operated by the valve to the body port.**

WIDE OPEN THROTTLE CONTROL VALVE

This valve, **Fig. 34,** which is used on some vehicles, closes the EGR valve when the engine requires maximum power at or near wide open throttle. This valve is installed in the vacuum line between the ported vacuum connection on the carburetor and EGR valve. A vacuum line from the carburetor venturi vacuum tap is connected to the top port on the valve and provides control for the valve. When venturi vacuum signal is at a predetermined level near wide open throttle, it is strong enough to overcome the calibration spring pressure and unseat the diaphragm valve, diverting EGR source vacuum to the atmosphere and causing the EGR valve to close. Normal EGR flow is resumed when there is a reduction in engine load from the wide open throttle position.

Testing

ALTITUDE COMPENSATOR

Electrical

1. Check and record engine timing.
2. Disconnect compensator from ignition module and connect suitable jumper wire across module connectors. Recheck engine timing.
3. At altitudes of 3000 ft. or lower, timing should change as follows: Ford & Mercury full size models, with V8-302, advance 6°; all other models, advance 8°.
4. At altitudes of 4000 ft. or higher, there should be no change in timing.

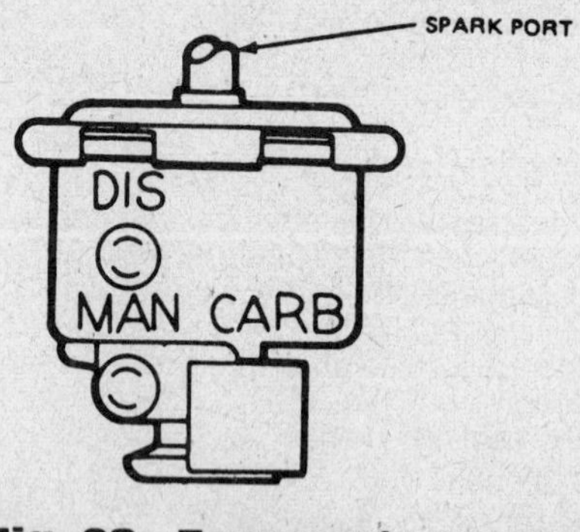

Fig. 28 Four part vacuum regulator

Mechanical

1. Connect a suitable vacuum gauge to air inlet nipple, **Fig. 8,** and check for vacuum with engine running.
2. On 4-140 engine, there should be no vacuum at altitudes of 2500 ft. or lower and vacuum should be present at altitudes of 3000 ft. or higher.
3. On 4-97 and V6-232 engines, there should not be vacuum at altitudes of 3500 ft. or lower and vacuum should be present at altitudes of 4000 ft. or higher.

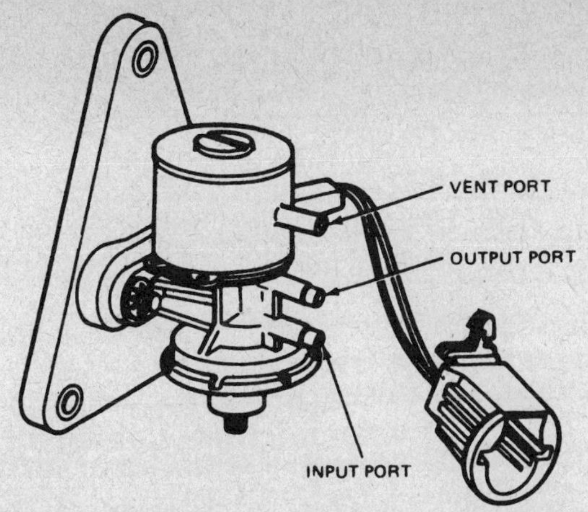

Fig. 29 Vacuum regulator solenoid

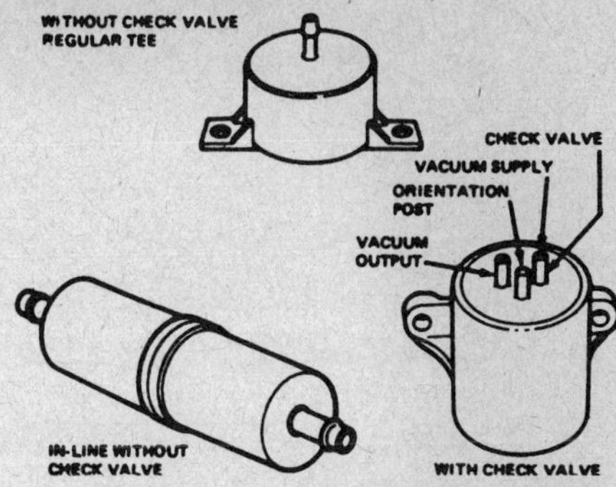

Fig. 30 Vacuum reservoirs

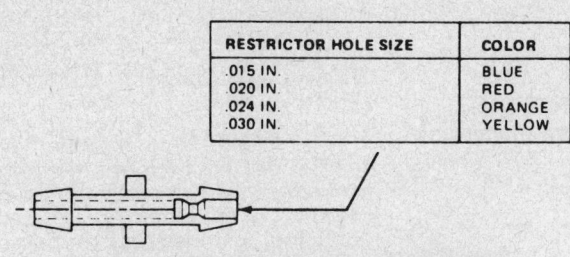

RESTRICTOR HOLE SIZE	COLOR
.015 IN.	BLUE
.020 IN.	RED
.024 IN.	ORANGE
.030 IN.	YELLOW

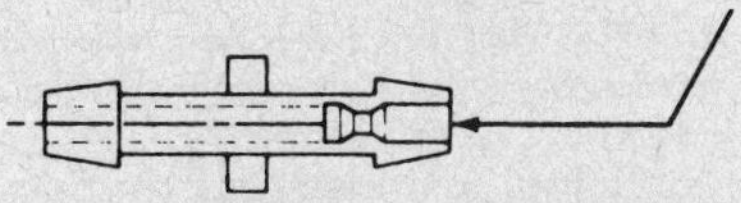

Fig. 31 Vacuum restrictor

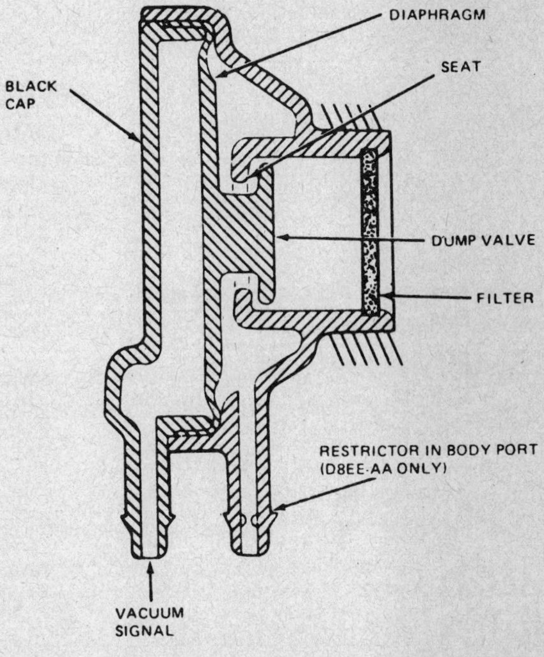

Fig. 32 Typical distributor vent valve installation

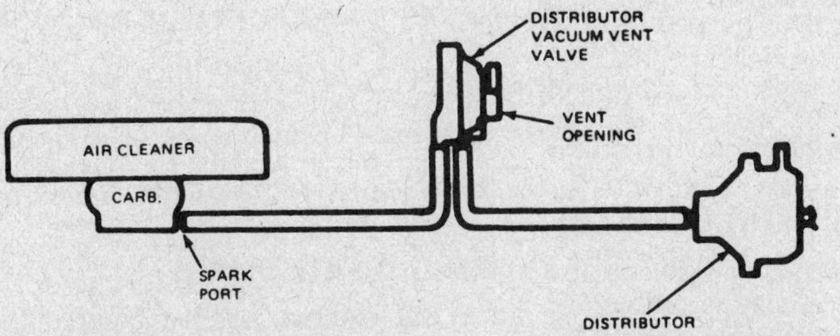

Fig. 33 Typical vent valve installation

CARBURETOR FUEL BOWL SOLENOID VENT VALVE

1. Apply 12 volts to valve and ensure valve closes to block air passage.
2. Replace valve if it does not close when energized.

CARBURETOR FUEL BOWL THERMAL VENT VALVE

1. With ambient temperature at or below 90°F, ensure that valve is fully closed.
2. With ambient temperature at or above 120°F, ensure that valve is fully open.

DASH POT THROTTLE STOP

1. Depress plunger inward, toward collapsed position.
2. If excessive force is required to bottom the plunger, or there is no resistance, replace the assembly.

DELAY VACUUM BYPASS (DVB)

1. Remove air cleaner.
2. Remove spark delay valve. (Refer to Spark Delay Valve section for test procedure for this unit.) Replace spark delay valve with a connector. Remove vacuum line at distributor and install a T-fitting and a vacuum gauge.
3. With transmission in neutral and engine idling at normal operating temperature, open throttle to 1/2 open position.
4. Open and close throttle as noted in Step 3 while watching vacuum reading. A quick rise and fall should be noted. If vacuum is indicated, proceed to next step. If no vacuum is indicated, check the vacuum lines, evaporative canister purge valve, T-fitting, and carburetor vacuum port for blockage. Correct as necessary.
5. Turn off engine and replace the spark delay valve (tested before reinstalling as noted in Step 2). Remove vacuum gauge and T-fitting and replace vacuum hoses.
6. Remove vacuum check valve and test. (Refer to Spark Delay Valve section for test procedure for this unit). Replace if defective. Reinstall valve.
7. Install a T-fitting between the check valve and the PVS. Connect a vacuum gauge at this point.
8. With transmission in neutral and engine idling at normal operating temperature, open throttle to 1/2 position. Note vacuum reading at steady 1/2 throttle. If reading is 2 inches Hg or less, PVS unit is good. If more than 2 inches Hg is indicated, PVS is defective and must be replaced.
9. Remove vacuum gauge and return all vacuum lines to original location. Reinstall air cleaner assembly.

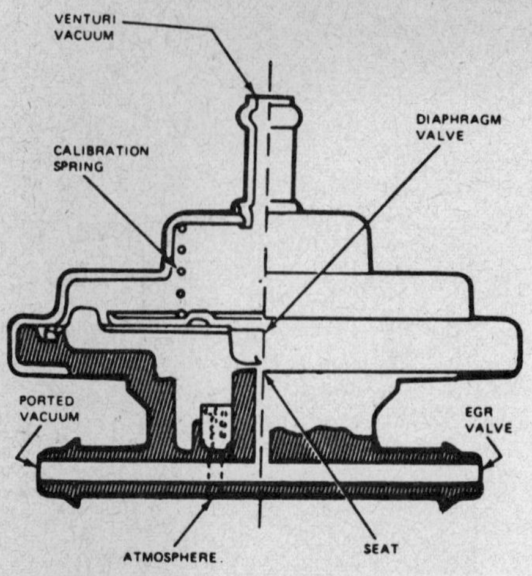

Fig. 34 EGR wide open throttle control valve

Part Number	Resistance (Ohms) Below 3,000 Feet	Resistance (Ohms) Above 4,600 Feet
E2AE-12A243-AA	Greater Than 200,000	0
E2SE-12A243-AA	3,350 - 3,990	1,750 - 1,850
E2TE-12A243-AA	2,560 - 2,660	1,750 - 1,850
E2TE-12A243-BA	2,820 - 2,920	1,750 - 1,850
E2TE-12A243-CA	3,250 - 3,390	1,750 - 1,850

Fig. 35 Ignition barometric pressure switch resistance chart. 1983

DISTRIBUTOR MODULATOR VALVE ASSEMBLY

1. Turn ignition key to "On" and check resistance at solenoid terminals.
2. If solenoid resistance is not 51-108 ohms, replace solenoid.

IDLE SPEED CONTROLLER WITH INTEGRAL TRACKING SWITCH

To check idle speed controller portion, connect a hand operated vacuum pump to vacuum connection. With vacuum applied, the switch should extend and hold, and must take longer than 10 seconds for vacuum to drop from 20 inches Hg to 10 inches Hg.

To check idle tracking switch portion, check for continuity at electrical connection, when throttle stop lever is against switch, and switch is open. There should be no continuity.

IGNITION BAROMETRIC PRESSURE SWITCH

1. Disconnect switch from ignition module.
2. Connect suitable ohmmeter across switch terminals and compare resistance measured to values in chart, **Figs. 35 and 36.**
3. Replace switch if resistance is not within specifications.

IGNITION TIMING VACUUM SWITCH

1. Disconnect switch from ignition module, **Fig. 18.**
2. Connect suitable ohmmeter across switch terminals and compare resistance measured to "less than" values in chart, **Fig. 37.**
3. Apply vacuum to switch, using an outside vacuum source. Compare resistance now measured across switch terminals to "greater than" values in chart, **Fig. 37.**
4. Replace switch if resistance is not within specifications.

INERTIA SWITCH

Special testing equipment is required to test the inertia switch. Follow manufacturer's instructions.

Reset Instructions

1. Turn ignition switch to "Off."
2. Check for leaking fuel in engine compartment, fuel lines, and tank(s).
3. If no fuel leak is apparent, reset switch by pushing reset button on top of switch. **Switch is located behind instrument panel.**
4. Turn ignition switch to "Start" momentarily, then back to "Off."
5. Check for leaking fuel in engine compartment, fuel lines, and tank(s). **If gasoline can be seen or smelled other than during refueling, do not reset switch.**

PORTED VACUUM SWITCH

1. Connect a vacuum gauge to port A and a vacuum source to port B, **Fig. 20. On the 4-port valve, check A1, B1 and A2, B2 separately.**
2. With engine cold, check that no vacuum flows from port A to port B.
3. Allow engine to reach normal operating temperature. Gauge should show a reading.
4. If conditions in steps 2 and 3 are not met, replace valve.
5. On 3 port valve, connect a vacuum gauge into hose A using a T-fitting. Leave the other hoses connected. When engine temperature reaches 35°F, the gauge must read full manifold vacuum.

THROTTLE SOLENOID POSITIONER (TSP)

With Dash Pot

1. Ensure plunger extends with throttle open and solenoid energized.
2. Depress plunger in toward collapsed position and ensure resistance is felt but not enough to make it difficult to bottom the plunger.

With Vacuum Operated Throttle Modulator (VOTM)

1. Check that plunger extends and holds when solenoid is energized.
2. Apply 20 inches Hg vacuum to VOTM section using a hand vacuum pump and check that plunger extends and holds. Vacuum must not decrease to 10 inches Hg in less than 10 seconds.

VACUUM DELAY VALVE (VDV)

Refer to **Fig. 38,** for number value by color code. **To perform the following procedure, an external vacuum source capable of maintaining a minimum constant 10 inches Hg is required.**

Mono Delay Valve

1. Set external vacuum source to 10 inches Hg and connect black side of delay valve to vacuum source.
2. Connect a vacuum gauge with a 24 inch hose to colored side of delay valve.
3. Apply 10 inches Hg vacuum and observe time in seconds for gauge to read 0-8 inches Hg. The minimum and maximum time for gauge to read 8 inches Hg should be as shown in **Fig. 39.**

Dual Delay Valve

1. Set external vacuum source to 10 inches Hg and connect vacuum gauge with a 24 inch hose to DIST nipple of delay valve.
2. Connect black side of delay valve and CARB nipple of delay valve to vacuum source. **Avoid applying vacuum to CARB nipple while applying vacuum to black side of valve.**
3. Apply 10 inches Hg of vacuum and observe time in seconds for gauge to read from 0-8 inches Hg. The minimum and maximum time for gauge to read 8 inches Hg should be as shown in **Fig. 39.**

Retard Delay Valve

1. Set external vacuum source to 10 inches Hg and connect colored side of delay valve to vacuum source.
2. Connect a vacuum gauge with a 24 inch hose to white side of delay valve.
3. Apply 10 inches Hg of vacuum and observe time in seconds for gauge to read from 0-8 inches Hg. The minimum and maximum time for gauge to read 8 inches Hg should be as shown in **Fig. 39.**

Part Number	Resistance (OHMS) Below 3,000 Feet	Resistance (OHMS) Above 4,600 Feet
E2AE-12A243-AA	Greater Than 200,000	Less Than 1
E2TE-12A243-BA	2,820–2,920	1,750–1,850
E37E-12A243-AA	Greater Than 200,000	Less Than 1
E43E-12A243-AA	2,820–2,920	1,750–1,850
E4DE-12A243-AB	2,560–2,660	1,960–2,060
E4EE-12A243-AA	Greater Than 200,000	Less Than 1

Fig. 36 Ignition barometric pressure switch resistance chart. 1984–87

Color	Number Value
White	5
Yellow	10
Blue	15
Green	20
Red	30

Fig. 38 SDV & VDV valve color coding

Part Number	Vacuum Setting ± 1.7 kPa (Inches Hg ± 0.5 In.)	Resistance Value (Ohms)
E1AE-12A265-BA	Less than 11.8 (3.5)	3,200 - 3,350
	Greater than 11.8 (3.5)	2,150 - 2,250
E1SE-12A265-BA	Less than 30 (9)	3,250 - 3,370
	Greater than 30 (9)	2,150 - 2,250
E1TE-12A265-CA	Less than 10 (3)	2,800 - 2,870
	Greater than 10 (3)	2,150 - 2,250
E25E-12A265-AA	Less than 13.5 (4)	2,800 - 2,870
	Greater than 13.5 (4)	2,150 - 2,250

Fig. 37 Ignition timing vacuum switch test chart

Color	I.D. No.	Time in Seconds	
		Min.	Max.
Black/Gray	1	.6	1.6
Black/Brown	2	1	3
Black/White	5	2.7	9.3
Black/Yellow	10	4.5	13.2
Black/Blue	15	6.8	18.8
Black/Green	20	8	26
Black/Orange	30	11.6	38
Black/Red	40	14	47.2
White/Pink①	5	2.7	9.3
White/Brown①	2	1	3
White/Green①	20	8	26
White/Yellow①	10	4.5	13.2
White/Gray①	1	.6	1.6
White/Blue①	20	8	26
White/Red①	40	14	47.2

①—Retard Delay Valve Only

Fig. 39 Vacuum & spark delay valve specifications chart

VACUUM OPERATED THROTTLE MODULATOR (VOTM)

1. Apply 20 inches Hg vacuum to VOTM using a hand vacuum pump and check that plunger extends and holds.
2. Vacuum must not decrease to 10 inches Hg in less than 10 seconds.

SPARK DELAY VALVE (SDV)

Refer to **Fig. 38**, for number value by color code. **To perform the following procedure, an external vacuum source capable of maintaining a minimum constant 10 inches Hg is required.**

Mono Delay Valve

1. Set external vacuum source to 10 inches Hg and connect black side of delay valve to vacuum source.
2. Connect a vacuum gauge with a 24 inch hose to colored side of delay valve.
3. Apply 10 inches Hg vacuum and observe time in seconds for gauge to read 0-8 inches Hg. The minimum and maximum time for gauge to read 8 inches Hg should be as shown in **Fig. 39**.

Dual Delay Valve

1. Set external vacuum source to 10 inches Hg and connect vacuum gauge with a 24 inch hose to DIST nipple of delay valve.
2. Connect black side of delay valve and CARB nipple of delay valve to vacuum source. **Avoid applying vacuum to CARB nipple while applying vacuum to black side of valve.**
3. Apply 10 inches Hg of vacuum and observe time in seconds for gauge to read from 0-8 inches Hg. The minimum and maximum time for gauge to read 8 inches Hg should be as shown in **Fig. 39**.

Retard Delay Valve

1. Set external vacuum source to 10 inches Hg and connect colored side of delay valve to vacuum source.
2. Connect a vacuum gauge with a 24 inch hose to white side of delay valve.
3. Apply 10 inches Hg of vacuum and observe time in seconds for gauge to read from 0-8 inches Hg. The minimum and maximum time for gauge to read 8 inches Hg should be as shown in **Fig. 39**.

TEMPERATURE VACUUM SWITCH (TVS)

1982–83

1. Apply 16 inches Hg to motor side of valve and trap. Cool to test temperature. Switch should hold vacuum as follows:
   a. White TVS—normally open. At 40°F must hold 5 inches Hg for 30 seconds. Should not hold vacuum above 80°F.
   b. Brown TVS—normally open. At 5°F must hold 5 inches Hg for 30 seconds. Should not hold vacuum above 40°F.
   c. Purple TVS—normally open. At 30°F must hold 5 inches Hg for 30 seconds. Should not hold vacuum above 60°F.
   d. Red TVS—normally closed. At 80°F must hold 5 inches Hg for 30 seconds. Should not hold vacuum below 40°F.

1984–87

1. Apply 16 inches Hg vacuum to motor side of valve and trap. Cool to test temperature. Switch should hold vacuum as follows:
   a. White TVS—normally open. At 50°F must hold 5 inches Hg vacuum for 30 seconds. Should not hold vacuum above 76°F.
   b. Brown TVS—normally open. At 15°F must hold 5 inches Hg vacuum for 30 seconds. Should not hold vacuum above 30°F.
   c. Purple TVS—normally open. At 40°F must hold 5 inches Hg vacuum for 30 seconds. Should not hold vacuum above 55°F.
   d. Red TVS—normally closed. At 60°F must hold 5 inches Hg vacuum for 30 seconds. Should not hold vacuum at or below 50°F.

VACUUM REGULATOR

1. Disconnect vacuum line from distributor port and connect a vacuum gauge.
2. With engine at idle, the vacuum gauge reading should be within 1 inch Hg vacuum of the calibration point. The calibration point of each valve can be identified according to color code as follows: Black, 6 inches Hg; green, 7 inches Hg; red, 8 inches Hg.
3. Replace valve if not within specifications.

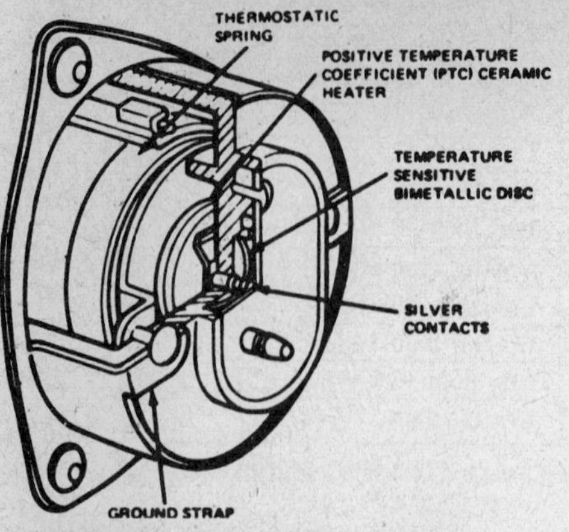

Fig. 40 Electric assist choke

VACUUM REGULATOR/SOLENOID

1. Disconnect vacuum line from output (middle) port, and connect a vacuum gauge to port.
2. With engine at idle, the vacuum gauge reading should average between 1.9 and 3.15 inches. The fluctuation of vacuum between the higher and lower limits is normal, but the average should be within specifications.

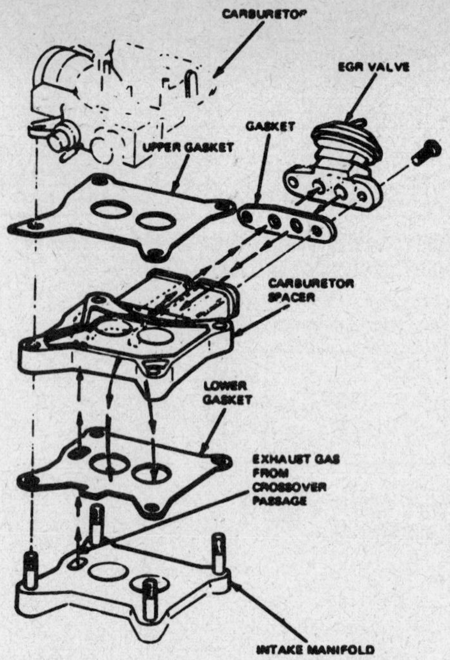

Fig. 41 Spacer entry EGR connection. 8 cyl. engines

ELECTRIC ASSIST CHOKE

Most vehicles are equipped with an electric assist choke. This device aids in reducing emissions of hydrocarbons (HC) and carbon monoxide (CO) during starting and warm-up (choke on) period. The electric assist choke is designed to give a more rapid choke opening at temperatures of about 54°F to 74°F, or higher. It also provides a slower choke opening at temperatures below this point.

The electric assist choke system does not change any carburetor service procedures and cannot be adjusted. If system is found out of calibration the heater control switch and/or choke unit must be replaced.

The electric choke system, **Fig. 40**, consists of a choke cap, thermostatic spring, a bi-metal temperature sensing disc (switch), and a ceramic positive temperature coefficient (PTC) heater. The choke is powered from terminal or tap of the alternator. Current is constantly supplied to the ambient temperature switch. The system is grounded through a ground strap connected to the carburetor body. At temperatures below approximately 60°F, the switch opens and no current is supplied to the ceramic heater located within the thermostatic spring. Normal thermostatic spring choking action then occurs. At temperatures above approximately 54°-74°F the temperature sensing switch closes and current is supplied to the ceramic heater. As the heater warms, it causes the thermostatic spring to pull the choke plates open within 1-1½ minutes.

Testing

1. Disconnect stator lead at connector leading from choke cap and connect a test light in series with stator lead and ground.
2. With engine running, test light should glow.
3. If light does not glow, repair or replace either the alternator or choke wire.
4. With engine running at normal operating temperature, place test light in series with choke terminal and alternator lead. If light does not glow, replace choke cap assembly.

EXHAUST GAS RECIRCULATION (EGR)

In this system the exhaust gases are metered through the EGR valve to a passage in the carburetor spacer, thereby diluting the air fuel mixture entering the combustion chambers. Dilution of the incoming mixture lowers peak flame temperatures during combustion and thus limits the formation of nitrogen oxides (NOx).

Eight cylinder engines use the "Spacer Entry" EGR System which has the EGR valve mounted on the rear of the carburetor spacer, **Fig. 41.** The exhaust gases are taken from a drilled passage in the exhaust crossover of the intake manifold. The exhaust gas is then routed through a metered EGR valve to a passage in the carburetor spacer and fed into the primary bore.

On four and six cylinder engines, the EGR system is basically the same as the Spacer Entry EGR System except that exhaust gas is routed directly from the exhaust manifold, **Fig. 42.**

Two variables control the operation of the EGR system, 1) engine coolant temperature and 2) carburetor vacuum. When engine coolant temperature is below the specified level the EGR system is locked out by a temperature controlled vacuum switch. The vacuum switch is installed in series with the EGR valve. This valve receives vacuum from a port in the carburetor body. When the valve is closed due to lower coolant temperature, no vacuum is applied to the EGR valve and no exhaust gas is fed to the air-fuel mixture. When the engine coolant temperature reaches the specified level, the valve opens, allowing vacuum to be applied to the EGR valve. Exhaust gas is then fed to the air-fuel mixture.

The second factor controlling EGR operation is carburetor vacuum. The location of the EGR port in the carburetor determines at what point vacuum is sent to the EGR valve. Vacuum should be fed to the EGR vacuum control valve when the primary throttle plate reaches a position corresponding to a road speed of approximately 20 mph under light acceleration.

A Venturi Vacuum Amplifier, **Fig. 43,** uses a weak venturi-vacuum signal to produce a strong intake manifold vacuum to operate the EGR valve, thereby achieving an accurate, repeatable and almost exact proportion between venturi air flow and EGR flow. This assists in controlling oxides of nitrogen with minimal sacrifice in driveability.

There are three basic types of EGR valves: the ported type, the back pressure type and the electronic-sonic type.

The electronic-sonic type valve is used with the EEC system. Information on this valve can be found in the "EEC" section of this chapter.

Ported type valves, **Fig. 44,** may be of the poppet or tapered stem design and can have base or side entry. The two passages connecting the exhaust system to intake manifold are blocked by a valve which is opened by vacuum and closed by spring

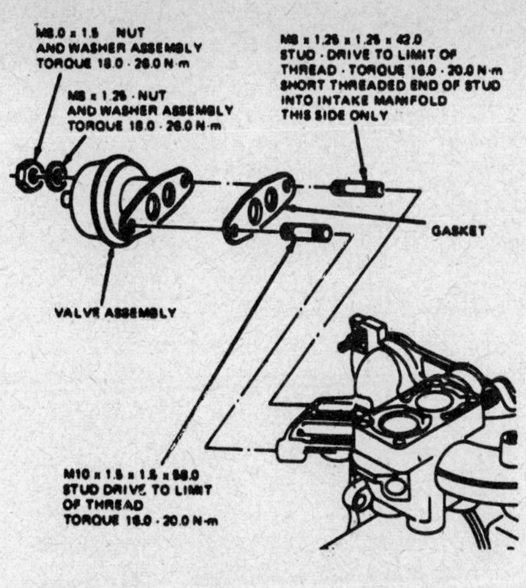

Fig. 42 EGR connection. 4 & 6 cyl. engines

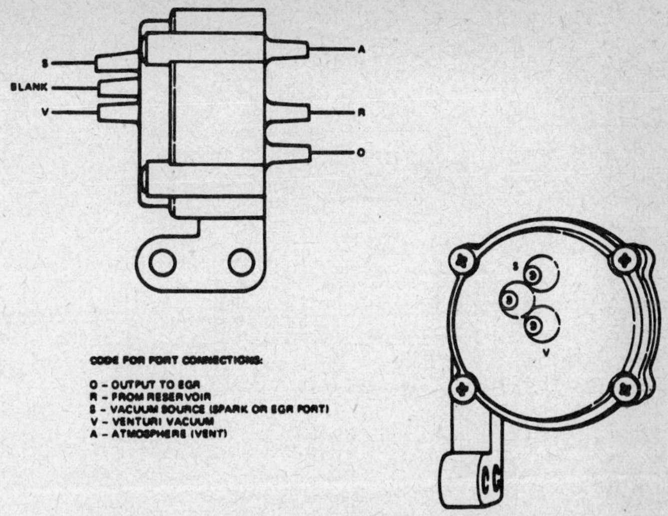

Fig. 43 Venturi vacuum amplifier

pressure.

Two types of back pressure valves are used. The integral back pressure transducer valve, **Fig. 45,** cannot be opened by vacuum until the bleed hole is closed by exhaust back pressure. When open, the valve oscillates at a level dependent on the exhaust back pressure flowing through the orifice. Valve opening increases as signal vacuum and exhaust back pressure increases.

Some vehicles use an EGR valve with a remote back pressure transducer, **Fig. 47.** This assembly operates the same as the EGR valve with integral back pressure transducer valve and is serviced only as an assembly.

Testing

EXC. BACK PRESSURE TRANSDUCER TYPE

1982

Single Response Tests

1. Check all system vacuum lines for proper routing and secure connections.
2. Inspect vacuum lines for wear or damage and replace as necessary.
3. Ensure there is no vacuum to valve at idle. Recheck hose routing if vacuum is present.
4. Make sure there is vacuum at valve at kickdown RPM with engine at operating temperature. If there is no vacuum, trace system vacuum lines back from EGR valve and replace components as necessary. **Refer to vehicle emission decal for kickdown RPM specification.**

Diaphragm Test

1. Cycle valve through full travel, using finger pressure on diaphragm. If valve sticks, clean or replace as necessary.
2. Apply 8 inches Hg vacuum to valve with engine at idle. Ensure valve stem moves and engine idle roughens.
3. Trap vacuum and hold in valve. Vacuum must not drop more than 1 inch Hg in 30 seconds.
4. If vacuum test is satisfactory but engine idle does not roughen, clean air passages.

Seat Test

This test should be performed when the valve is suspected of leaking in the closed position, indicated by rough engine operation.

1. Install blocking gasket (no flow holes) between mounting and valve, then retighten valve.
2. Improved engine operation indicates a defective valve. Clean or replace as necessary.

1983–87

Single Response Tests

1. Check all system vacuum lines for proper routing and secure connections.
2. Inspect vacuum lines for wear or damage and replace as necessary.
3. Ensure there is no vacuum to valve at idle. Recheck hose routing if vacuum is present.
4. Ensure that there is vacuum at valve at 3000 RPM on 4-140 engine, or kickdown RPM on other engines, with engine at operating temperature. If there is no vacuum, trace system vacuum lines back from EGR valve and replace components as necessary. **Refer to vehicle emission decal for kickdown RPM specification.**

Valve Function Test

1. Run engine at idle and apply 8 inches Hg vacuum to valve. Valve stem should move, opening valve, and engine should roughen.
2. If valve stem moves but engine does not roughen, remove valve and clean inlet and outlet ports with fine wire brush. **Do not use sand blasting or gasoline to clean EGR valve.**
3. Run engine at idle and trap and hold 4 inches Hg vacuum.
4. If vacuum drops more than 1 inch Hg vacuum in 30 seconds, replace valve.

Seat Test

This test should be performed when the valve is suspected of leaking, indicated by rough engine operation.

1. Install blocking gasket (no flow holes) between mounting and valve, then retighten valve.
2. Improved engine operation indicates a defective valve. Clean or replace as necessary.
3. Replace blocking gasket with conventional gasket.

WITH BACK PRESSURE TRANSDUCER

1982

Single Response Tests

1. Check all system vacuum lines for proper routing and secure connections.
2. Inspect vacuum lines for wear or damage and replace as necessary.
3. Ensure air flows freely with vacuum applied and valve at rest. If valve holds vacuum, clean or replace as necessary.
4. Ensure there is no vacuum to valve at idle. Recheck hose routing if vacuum is present.
5. Make sure there is vacuum to valve with engine at operating temperature at the following speeds: 4-97 engine, 4000 RPM; 4-140 engine, 3000 RPM; all other engines, kickdown RPM. If there is no vacuum, trace system vacuum lines back from EGR valve and replace components as necessary. **Refer to vehicle emission decal for kickdown RPM specification.**

Diaphragm Test

1. Cycle valve through full travel using finger pressure on diaphragm. If valve sticks, clean or replace as necessary.
2. Clamp a socket wrench, with an outside diameter approximately 1/16 inch less than inside diameter of tailpipe, into tailpipe. **Socket drive hole must be covered and socket installed with open-end facing out to achieve proper back pressure. Do**

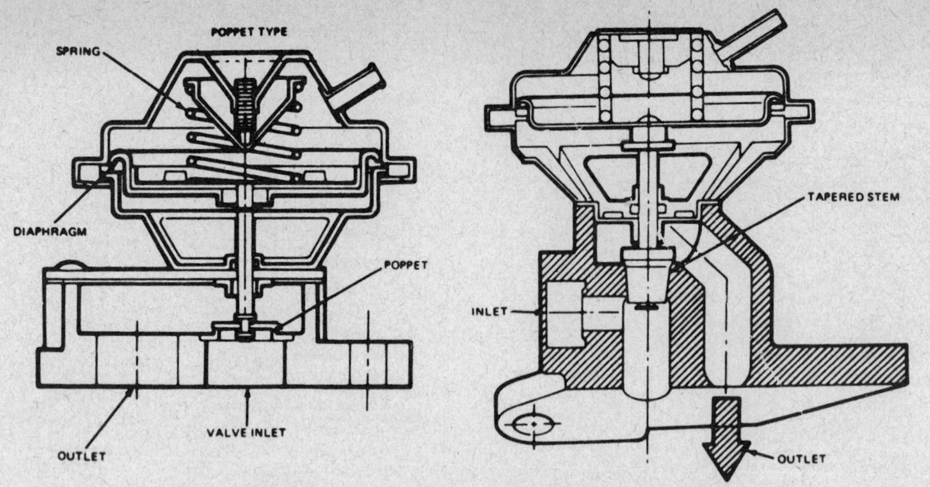

BASE ENTRY, POPPET TYPE   SIDE ENTRY, TAPERED STEM

Fig. 44 Ported type EGR valves

not completely block tailpipe and do not run engine faster than idle or for prolonged periods of time. Also, be sure to remove socket from tailpipe when test is completed.

3. Idle engine and gradually apply vacuum to valve. Ensure valve stem/diaphragm moves and engine idle roughens.
4. Trap 6 inches Hg vacuum in valve and hold. Vacuum must not drop more than 1 inch Hg in 30 seconds.
5. If vacuum test is satisfactory but engine idle does not roughen, clean air passages.
6. If conditions in steps 3 and 4 are not met, replace valve.

1983–87

Signal Response Test

1. Check all systems vacuum lines for proper routing and secure connections.
2. Inspect vacuum lines for wear or damage and replace as necessary.
3. Disconnect and plug vacuum line to EGR valve, then connect vacuum pump to valve.
4. Run engine at idle and apply 6 inches Hg vacuum to valve.
5. If vacuum holds and valve opens and stays open, replace valve.
6. Ensure that there is no vacuum to valve at idle. If there is, check hose routing.
7. Ensure that there is no vacuum to valve or valve operation when engine is cold. If there is, check ported vacuum switch and thermal vacuum switch, replacing as necessary.
8. Ensure that there is vacuum to valve at 3000 RPM on 4-140 engine, or kickdown RPM on all other engines, with engine at operating temperature. If there is no vacuum, trace system vacuum lines back from EGR valve and replace components as necessary. **Refer to vehicle emission decal for kickdown RPM specification.**

Valve Function Test

1. Select drive socket wrench with O. D. of approximately 1/16 inch less than I. D. of tailpipe.
2. Cover drive socket hole and insert socket in tailpipe with open end facing out. **Do not block tailpipe fully and do not run engine faster than idle or for prolonged periods of time. Be sure to remove socket from tailpipe at end of test.**
3. Run engine at idle and gradually apply vacuum. Valve stem/diaphragm should move smoothly and engine should roughen.
4. Trap 6 inches Hg of vacuum and hold. Vacuum should drop more than 1 inch Hg in 30 seconds.
5. If valve stem/diaphragm moves smoothly but engine does not roughen, clean valve passages.
6. If conditions in steps 3 and/or 4 are not met, replace valve.
7. If valve is suspected of sticking, remove valve from engine and cycle valve by pressing carefully with fingers against lower transducer plate.
8. If valve sticks open when fingers are released, replace valve.
9. If valve does not stick, clean inlet and outlet ports with wire brush. **Do not use sand blasting or gasoline to clean the valve.**

EGR VENTURI VACUUM AMPLIFIER

Idle must be set to specifications, engine must be at normal operating temperature and manifold vacuum must be adequate for this test.

1. Connect a vacuum gauge hose at EGR valve (port O). **The gauge may read as high as 2 inches Hg at idle.**
2. Disconnect venturi hose at carburetor and increase engine speed to 2000 RPM on all except 4-97 and 4-140 engines, 4000 RPM on 4-97 engines and 3000 on 4-140 engines.
3. Connect venturi hose. Gauge should read 4 inches Hg.
4. Return engine to idle. Gauge should return to initial reading.
5. If operation is not as described previously, replace VVA.

VACUUM LOAD CONTROL VALVE

1. Run engine at normal operating temperature and set throttle on high cam on 4-140 engine or on kickdown step on other engines.
2. Connect vacuum gauge to EGR side of load control valve and note reading.
3. Apply a vacuum of at least 6 inches Hg to venturi port of valve. If gauge does not drop to zero, replace valve.

System Diagnosis

1. If vehicle idles rough or stalls, proceed as follows:
   a. Check if EGR valve receives vacuum at idle. If so, check vacuum hose routing and correct as necessary.
   b. EGR valve may be stuck open or not closing fully. Remove valve and inspect for proper closing and seating of valve components, cleaning or replacing valve as necessary.
   c. EGR valve gasket may be blown or valve may be loose. Check valve attaching bolts for tightness and inspect gasket, tightening valve or replacing gasket as necessary.
   d. On back pressure type valves, air bleed may be plugged. Check if valve holds vacuum with engine off. If so, replace valve.
2. If vehicle runs rough, surges, hesitates, or shows general poor performance at part throttle with cold engine, proceed as follows:
   a. Check if EGR valve is receiving vacuum. If so, check vacuum hose routing, correcting as necessary.
   b. EGR valve may be stuck open or not closing fully. Remove valve and inspect for proper closing and

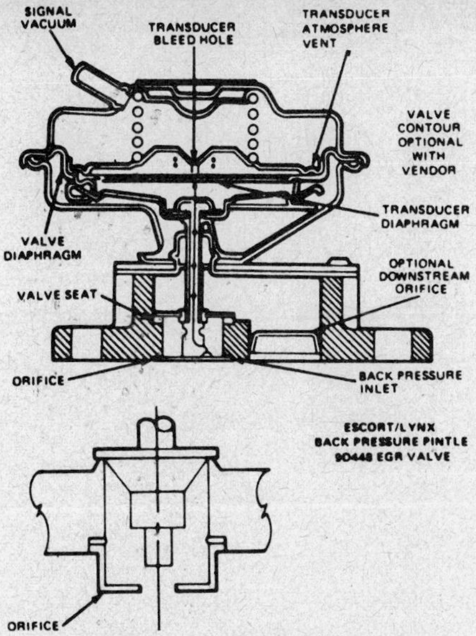

Fig. 45 EGR valve with integral back pressure transducer

seating of valve components, cleaning or replacing valve as necessary.

c. EGR valve gasket may be blown or valve may be loose. Check valve attaching bolts for tightness and inspect gasket, tightening valve or replacing gasket as necessary.
d. On back pressure type valves, air bleed may be plugged. Check if valve holds vacuum with engine off. If so, replace valve.
e. TVS or PVS may be opening too early. Check TVS or PVS at outlet port to EGR for vacuum with engine cold. If there is vacuum, replace damaged switch.

3. If vehicle runs rough, surges, hesitates, or shows general poor performance at part throttle regardless of engine temperature, EGR valve may be stuck wide open. Remove EGR valve and inspect for proper freedom of movement of valve components, cleaning or replacing as necessary.
4. If engine stalls on deceleration, EGR valve may be sticking open or not closing fully. Remove valve and inspect for proper closing and seating of valve components, cleaning or replacing valve as necessary.
5. If vehicle exhibits part throttle engine detonation, proceed as follows:
   a. EGR valve may be stuck closed. Check EGR valve for freedom of operation by pressing and releasing valve diaphragm to stroke valve mechanism. Clean or replace valve if not operating smoothly.
   b. Leaky valve diaphragm may not be actuating valve. Check valve by applying vacuum. If valve leaks vacuum, replace valve. **On back pressure type valve, block tailpipe as described under "Valve Function Test" for 1983-87 vehicles.**
   c. Vacuum to EGR valve may be restricted. Check vacuum hoses, fittings, routing, and supply for blockage.
   d. EGR valve may be disconnected. Check connections and reconnect as required.
   e. TVS and/or PVS may not be opening. Check TVS or PVS at outlet to EGR valve for vacuum. If there is no vacuum present at part throttle with engine at operating temperature, replace damaged switch. Ensure that vacuum supply is not restricted.
   f. The load control valve may be venting. Check for vacuum at load control valve vacuum port to EGR valve. If there is no vacuum, replace load control valve.
   g. EGR passages may be blocked. Check passages for restrictions or blockage.
   h. On back pressure type valves, there may be insufficient exhaust back pressure. Check for exhaust leaks ahead of muffler/catalyst or for blown out muffler/catalyst. Check for blockage to EGR valve.
   i. Vacuum hoses may be leaking. Check all hoses for damage or faulty connections, repairing or replacing as necessary.
6. If there is abnormally low power at wide open throttle, the load control valve may not be venting. Check for vacuum at vacuum port to EGR valve at wide open throttle or heavy load. If there is vacuum, replace load control valve.
7. If engine starts but stalls immediately when cold, proceed as follows:
   a. EGR valve may be receiving vacuum with engine cold. Check vacuum hose routing, correcting as necessary.
   b. EGR valve may not be closing fully. Remove valve and inspect for proper closing and seating of valve components, cleaning or replacing as necessary.
8. If engine is hard to start or will not start, proceed as follows:
   a. EGR valve may be receiving vacuum with engine cold. Check vacuum hose routing, correcting as necessary.
   b. EGR valve may be stuck open. Remove EGR valve and inspect for proper closing and seating of valve components, cleaning or replacing valve as necessary.
9. If vehicle exhibits poor fuel economy, it may be caused by detonation or other symptom of restricted or no EGR flow. Refer to step 5.

FUEL EVAPORATIVE EMISSION CONTROLS

These models use a manifold purge system. The charcoal canister media has been changed with a more efficient carbon, and a purge control valve situated atop the charcoal canister controls the evaporative system.

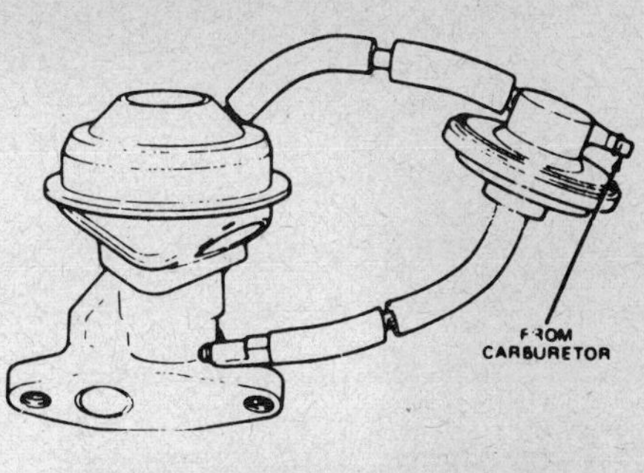

Fig. 46 EGR valve with remote back pressure transducer

The purge signal (EGR port, spark port or manifold vacuum), actuates the purge valve to allow purging of the canister through the purge line. When the engine is off, the purge valve directs fuel vapors from the fuel tank and carburetor bowl to the canister. An exception to this would be when the engine compartment is below the temperature where sufficient gasoline vaporization occurs. During this time the thermal vent valve (on some models) closes, stopping flow in either direction in the bowl vent line. The purpose of the thermal bowl vent valve is to prevent fuel tank vapors from migrating up the bowl vent line and out the internal vent of the carburetor when the fuel bowl is not vaporizing. When the fuel bowl is vaporizing, the thermal valve is open, allowing flow to the canister. Also, the internal fuel bowl vent valve must be open (at idle) and/or the solenoid vent valve must be open (ignition off) to allow flow into the canister.

Auxiliary Fuel Bowl Vent Tube

Used on some vehicles, this auxiliary vent tube, **Fig. 47**, is teed into the primary fuel bowl vent tube to vent the fuel bowl when the internal vent is closed (external vent is closed) and the solenoid or thermal vent valves are closed. This tube is vented to the air cleaner.

Canister Purge Solenoid

This valve, **Fig. 48** used on some vehicles, controls the flow of vapors from the carbon canister to the intake manifold during various engine operating modes. This is a normally closed valve that is opened by a signal from the electronic control assembly to control carbon canister purging.

Carbon Canister

The carbon canister, **Fig. 49**, stores fuel vapors from the fuel tank and carburetor bowl until the engine is started. At this time, fuel vapors are purged from the canister into the engine for combustion. Depending on application, either a 925ml or 1400ml canister is used.

On vehicles equipped with a dual canister system, two canisters are linked together and the second canister is used for "spill over" fuel vapors.

Fuel Tank Vapor Valve

All fuel tank vapor valves, **Fig. 50**, use a small orifice which allows only vapor and not fuel to pass into the line going to the

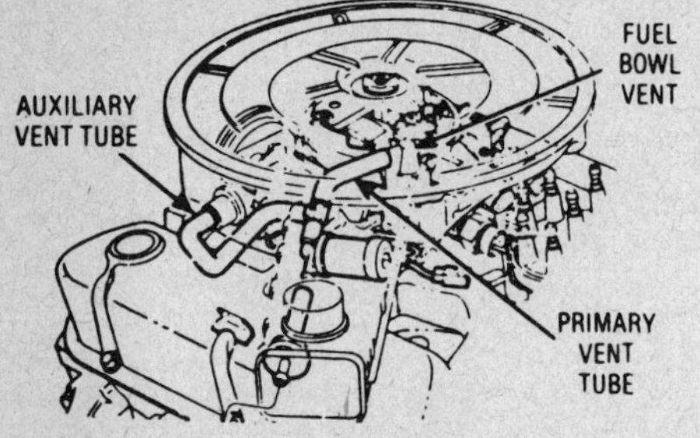

Fig. 47 Auxiliary fuel bowl vent tube

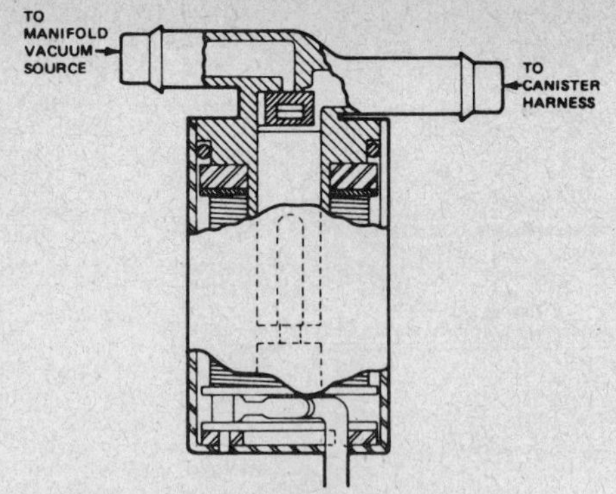

Fig. 48 Canister purge solenoid

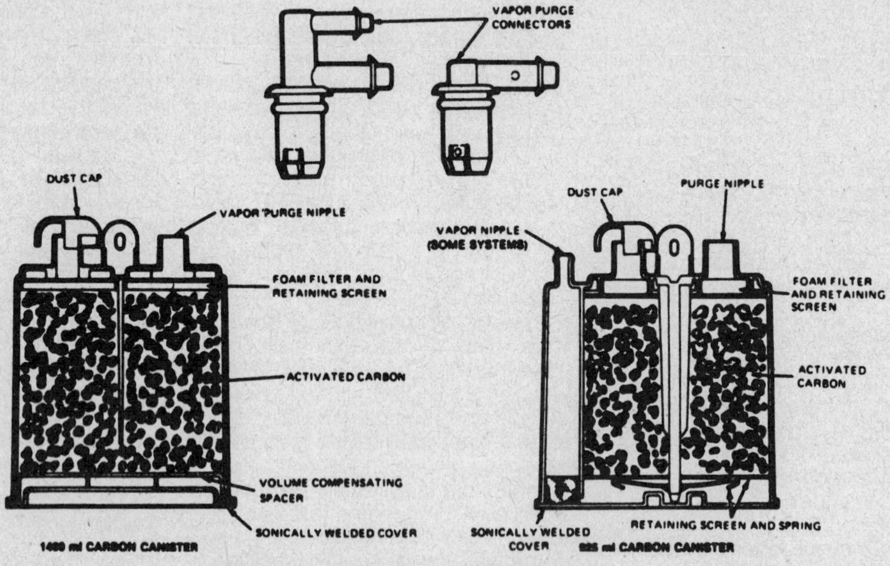

Fig. 49 Charcoal canister

vapor storage canister. This assembly is mounted on the fuel tank. Fuel vapors trapped in the sealed fuel tank are vented through the vapor valve assembly. The vapors leave the valve assembly through a single vapor line and continue to the charcoal canister for storage, until they are purged into the engine. On vehicles equipped with fuel/vapor return lines, vapors created in the fuel line is continuously vented back to the fuel tank. This prevents engine surging from fuel enrichment.

In Tank Venting

This system provides a vapor space above the gasoline surface in the fuel tank. This area is enough to permit breathing space for the tank vapor valve assembly under all static and most dynamic conditions. Horizontally mounted tanks accomplish this by a raised mounting section for the valve assembly which is centrally located on the upper surface of the tank. Vertically mounted tanks use a centrally mounted vapor valve assembly on the uppermost surface of the fuel tank.

Purge Control Valve

This valve, **Fig. 51**, is installed in line with the carbon canister and controls the flow of fuel vapors during various engine operating modes. The control is provided by a vacuum signal from either the spark port, EGR port or intake manifold and opens or closes the valve accordingly.

When the engine is off, the vapors from the fuel tank and carburetor fuel bowl are routed through the purge control valve and into the carbon canister for storage.

During normal cruise conditions, spark port or EGR vacuum is strong enough to open the orifice in the purge control valve to allow fuel vapors to flow from the carburetor canister through the purge line to a connection in the PCV tube or into the carburetor spacer. At the same time, the vapors from the fuel tank are also directed into the purge line.

At idle and low speed cruise conditions, spark port or EGR port vacuum is not strong enough to open the orifice in the purge control valve so that the fuel vapors are then routed to the carbon canister.

On some vehicles fuel vapors are not purged during low engine speeds because the additional fuel vapors will affect the fuel air mixture, resulting in a reduction of idle quality and an increase in exhaust emissions. On vehicles not affected by this purging, manifold vacuum is used to actuate the purge control valve and control the purging of fuel vapors since spark port or EGR port vacuum is too weak.

Ported Vacuum Switch Valve

The PVS (ported vacuum switch) valve allows vacuum to open the purge control valve as the engine warms up. The purge control valve closes as soon as the engine is turned off and vacuum drops off.

The evaporative emission system may be equipped with either a 2 or 4 port PVS. The 4 port PVS valve is actually two vacuum valves in one, and performs the same function as two 2 port valves.

Solenoid Vent Valve

The purpose of this valve, **Fig. 52**, is to close off the fuel bowl vent line when the engine is operating. It is a normally open valve located in the fuel bowl vent to canister line. This valve is on carburetors which do not have a built-in fuel bowl vent valve.

When the ignition switch is turned on, the coil energizes and the plunger is pulled against the valve seat to the closed position to prevent purge vacuum from reaching the carburetor fuel bowl and upsetting the balanced air pressure.

When the ignition switch is turned off,

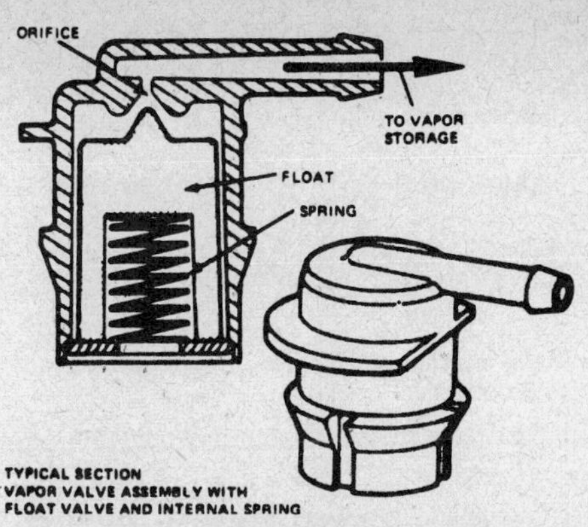

Fig. 50 Fuel tank vapor valve

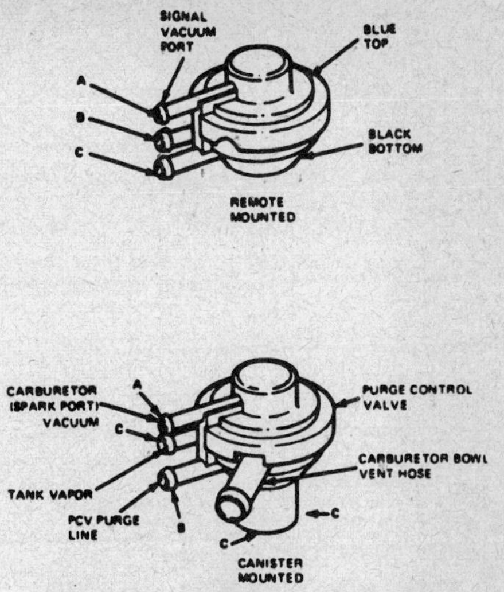

Fig. 51 Purge control valve

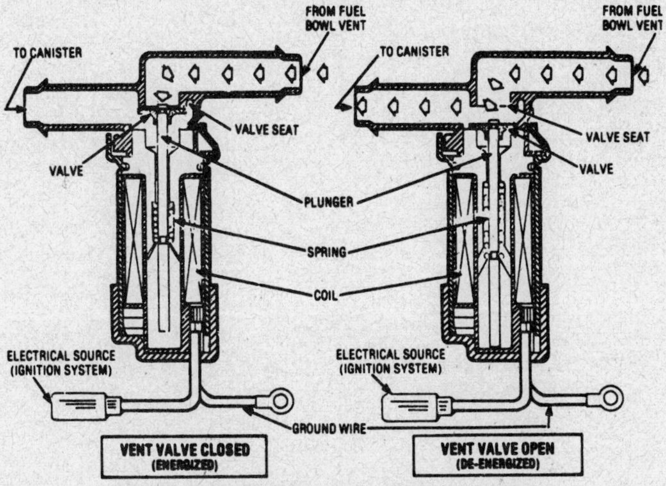

Fig. 52 Solenoid vent valve

the coil de-energizer and spring pressure unseats the plunger to allow fuel vapors to flow to the carbon canister where they are stored until purged when the engine is started.

If vacuum from the purge control valve does reach the fuel bowl vent line, the resultant low air pressure in the bowl will cause a lean fuel mixture condition. When diagnosing a driveability problem associated with a lean fuel mixture, check the solenoid vent valve and/or the built-in fuel bowl vent. The vent valves must be closed when the engine is operating.

Thermal Vent Valve

This valve, **Fig. 53,** is used on some vehicles and is located in the fuel bowl vent to canister line. This valve is normally closed.

When underhood temperatures are low, the bi-metal contracts to close the valve. This prevents fuel tank vapors from venting through the carburetor fuel bowl during periods of fuel tank heat build-up.

When underhood temperatures are high, the bi-metal expands to open the valve and allow fuel bowl vapors to flow through the thermal vent valve. Also, the engine must be turned off so that the solenoid vent valve is open to allow this passage of fuel vapors through the thermal vent valve.

Vacuum Bowl Vent Valve

This valve, **Fig. 54,** used on some 1983-87 vehicles, is a vacuum operated on/off valve. This valve controls vapor flow from the carburetor bowl to the carbon canister. When the engine is running, manifold vacuum closes the flow path from the carburetor bowl to the carbon canister.

Vacuum/Thermostatic Bowl Vent Valve

This valve, **Fig. 55,** used on some 1983-87 vehicles, is a vacuum/temperature operated on/off valve. This valve controls vapor flow from the carburetor bowl to the carbon canister. When the engine is running, manifold vacuum closes the flow path from the carburetor bowl to the carbon canister. This valve also closes the bowl to canister flow path when the temperature of the valve is less than 90°F even if there is no manifold vacuum. When the temperature of the valve exceeds 120°F, the valve is open except when closed by manifold vacuum.

Testing

1982 MANIFOLD PURGE SYSTEM

If engine will not start, proceed to step 1. If it does start and run, proceed to step 2.

1. Disconnect purge line, **Fig. 56,** from purge control valve and plug line, then attempt to start engine. If engine does not start, the problem is not in the evaporative control system.
2. With engine idling, disconnect vacuum signal line, **Fig. 56,** from purge control valve and plug hose, then remove valve from canister. If a strong hissing sound is heard at purge control valve, replace valve. **A slight hissing sound is normal due to small orifice in valve.**
3. Reconnect vacuum signal line, **Fig. 56,** to purge control valve which remains separated from canister, then accelerate engine to about 2000 RPM so that ported vacuum is applied to purge control valve. If strong hissing sound is heard at purge control valve, system is performing properly. Proceed to step 4. If not, check for vacuum at source port, and operation of PVS valve, PCV valve, and retard delay valve(s). Repair or replace components as necessary.
4. Return engine to idle. Strong hissing sound at purge control valve should stop if there is a port vacuum signal at valve. If strong hissing sound does not stop, check for vacuum at source port and check operation of retard delay valve(s). Repair or replace components as necessary.
5. Reconnect purge control valve to canister. **Make sure that carburetor fuel bowl vent line has a continuous downward slope to the carbon canister.**

Canister Purge Solenoid

Apply 12 volts to valve. The valve should open and allow air to pass.

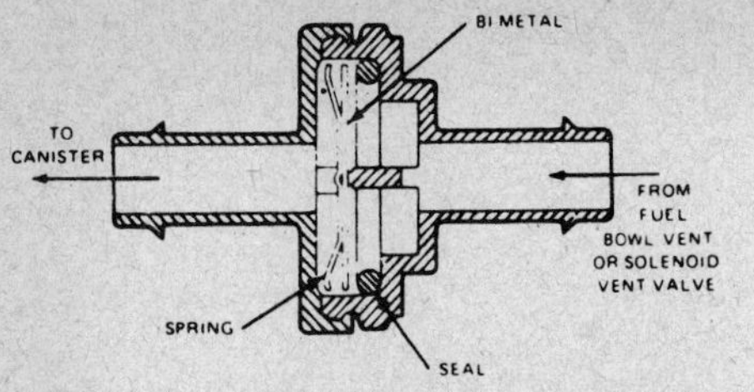

Fig. 53 Thermal vent valve

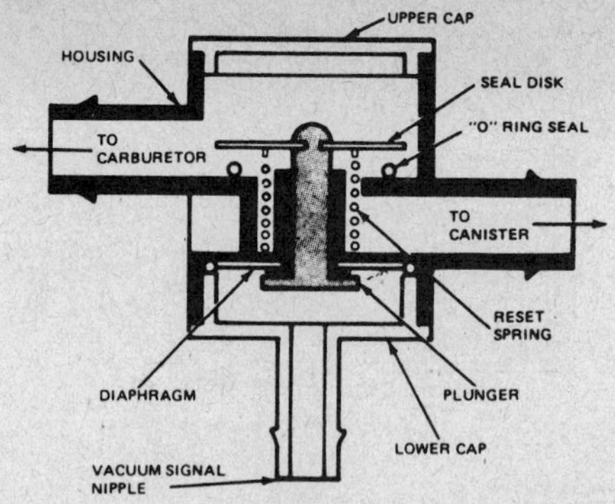

Fig. 54 Vacuum bowl vent valve

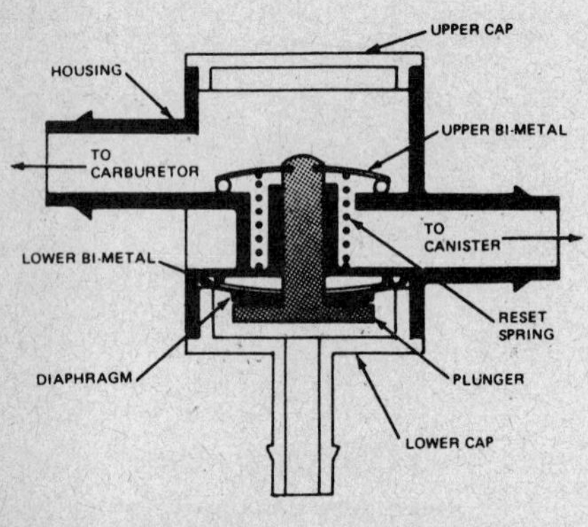

Fig. 55 Vacuum/thermostatic bowl vent valve

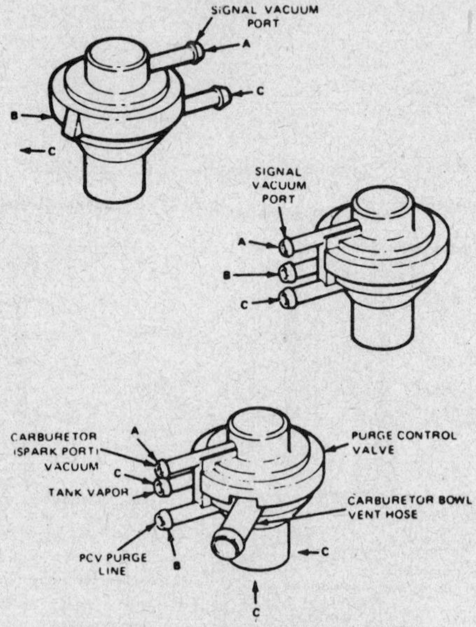

Fig. 56 Testing purge control valves. 1982

Canister Purge Valve

Apply 16 inches Hg vacuum to port A. Air should pass between ports B and C.

Carburetor Fuel Bowl Solenoid Vent Valve

Apply 12 volts to valve. The valve should close, allowing no air to pass.

If a lean fuel mixture is suspected of causing a problem, inspect either the solenoid vent valve or the fuel bowl vent valve for proper closing during engine operation. If the valve opens, allowing purged vacuum to affect fuel bowl balanced air pressure, the carburetor will give a leaner air/fuel mixture. On EEC equipped engines with a 7200 VV feedback carburetor (back-suction type only), the opposite (rich mixture) will result from an open or leaking valve.

The utmost care should be exercised when using a torch in the area of the fuel evaporation system as an open flame near these hoses may cause a fire and ultimate explosion.

Vapor line hoses used in these systems are made from a special rubber material. Bulk service hoses are available for service and will be marked "EVAP". Ordinary fuel hoses should not be used, as they are subject to deterioration and may clog system.

Installation of a fill cap from a non-emission fuel tank will render the system inoperative, since the non-emission fill cap is vented and the system must be sealed to function properly. Also if a non-vented fill cap is installed on a conventional tank, the result will be a serious deformation or a total collapse of the fuel tank.

COMPONENT TESTING, 1983–87

Carbon Canister

There are no moving parts or nothing to wear in the canister. Check for loose, missing, cracked, or broken connections and parts.

Purge Control Valve

1. Apply vacuum to port B, **Fig. 57.** If there is vacuum flow, replace valve.
2. Apply and maintain 16 inches Hg vacuum to port A, then apply vacuum to port B. If air does not flow, replace valve. **Never apply vacuum to port(s) C.**

Ported Vacuum Switches

1. With engine cold, ensure that passage A to B is closed and passage A to C is open, **Fig. 58.**
2. Start engine and run until it reaches normal operating temperature, then ensure that passage A to B is open and passage A to C is closed. **On 4-port valve, check A1 to B1 and A2 to B2 separately.**
3. If valve does not operate as described, replace valve.

Solenoid Vent Valve

Apply 9-14 volts DC to valve. If valve does not close, replace valve.

Thermal Vent Valve

Ensure that valve is fully closed when valve temperature is 90°F or below and that valve is fully open when valve temperature is 120°F or above.

Vacuum Bowl Vent Valve

1. Ensure that air flows between carburetor port and canister port when no vacuum is applied to vacuum signal nipple.
2. Apply vacuum to vacuum signal nipple and ensure that air does not flow between carburetor port and canister port.

Vacuum/Thermostatic Bowl Vent Valve

1. With valve temperature at or above 120°F, ensure that air flows between carburetor port and canister port when no vacuum is applied to vacuum signal nipple.
2. With valve temperature at or above 120°F, apply vacuum to vacuum signal nipple and ensure that air does not

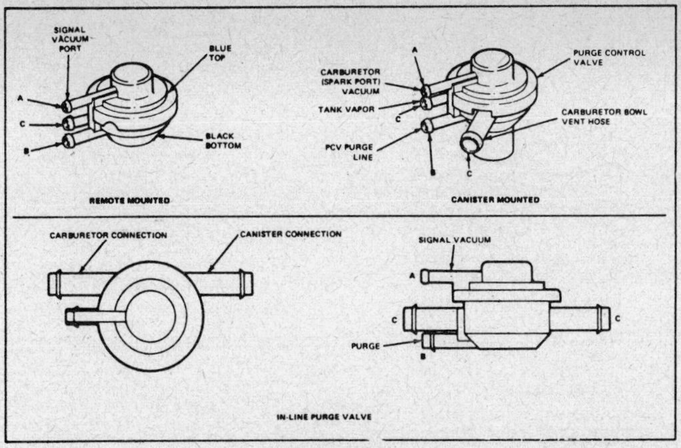

Fig. 57 Testing purge control valves. 1983–87

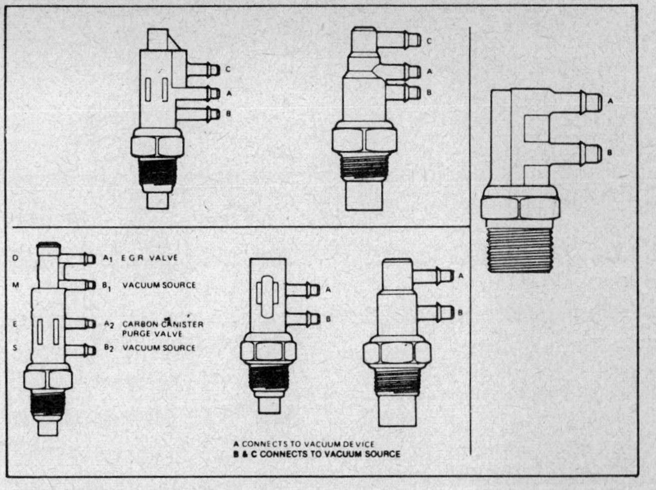

Fig. 58 Testing ported vacuum switches

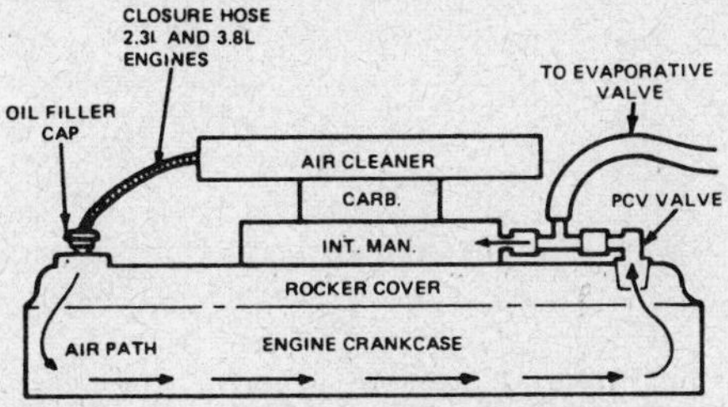

Fig. 59 Typical PCV system

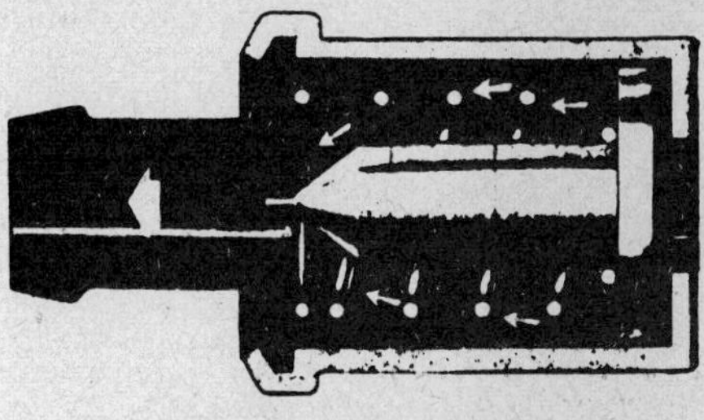

Fig. 60 PCV valve

flow between carburetor port and canister port.

3. With valve temperature at or below 90°F, ensure that there is no or very little air flow between carburetor port and canister port, whether or not vacuum is applied to vacuum signal nipple.

POSITIVE CRANKCASE VENTILATION (PCV) SYSTEM

All engines produce small amounts of blow-by gases which seep past the piston rings and into the crankcase. These blow-by gases are the result of the high pressures developed within the combustion chamber during the combustion process, and contain undesirable pollutants. To prevent blow-by gases from entering the atmosphere while allowing proper crankcase ventilation, all engines use a PCV system, **Fig. 59.**

The PCV system prevents blow-by gases from escaping by routing them through a vacuum controlled ventilating valve and a hose into the intake manifold. The blow-by gases mix with the air/fuel mixture and are burned in the combustion chambers. When the engine is running, fresh air is drawn into the crankcase through a tube or hose connected to the air cleaner housing.

The PCV valve, **Fig. 60,** consists of a needle valve, spring and housing. When the engine is off, the spring holds the needle valve closed to stop vapors from entering the intake manifold. When the engine is running, manifold vacuum unseats the valve, allowing crankcase vapors to enter the intake manifold. In case of a backfire in the intake manifold the valve closes, stopping the backflow and preventing ignition of fumes in the crankcase. During certain engine conditions, more blow-by gases are created than the ventilator valve can handle. The excess is returned through the air intake tube to the air cleaner and carburetor where it is burned in the engine.

Testing

1. Pull end of PCV valve out of valve cover. If valve rattles when shaken, proceed to step 2. If not, replace valve.
2. Disconnect vacuum hose from air cleaner and feel for vacuum at hose with engine at idle. If vacuum is felt, system is satisfactory. If no vacuum is felt, check for obstructions in PCV system or a leaking evaporative valve.
3. Disconnect evaporative hose, then cap the T-fitting and retest. If vacuum is now felt, PCV system is satisfactory. Check evaporative system. If no vacuum is felt, check for vacuum back through the system and inspect rocker cover gasket for leaks. Repair or replace components as necessary.
4. Some vehicles may experience a "hoot" noise which is heard within the driving compartment. This noise is caused by a resonating PCV valve and hose assembly. The "hoot" noise can be minimized by replacing the PCV valve and hose assembly with a new service assembly part. The new PCV valve and hose assembly relocates the valve away from the A/C lines, reducing resonating potential.

THERMACTOR

This system is used to reduce carbon monoxide and hydrocarbon emissions by adding a controlled amount of air to the exhaust gases through the exhaust ports. This causes oxidation of gases and an appreciable reduction of carbon monoxide and hydrocarbon emissions.

Although a properly operating system will effectively reduce emissions, if any system component or engine component operating in conjunction with the system should malfunction, emissions may be increased.

The basic Thermactor Air Injection System consists of an air injection pump, a centrifugal filter, an air bypass valve, check valves, air manifolds, tubes and hoses necessary to connect the various components.

Carburetors, distributors, and air pump system components on Thermactor equipped vehicles are designed for specific engine applications and should not be interchanged with units from other vehicles.

AIR BYPASS VALVES

1982

The air bypass system services the same purpose as earlier types, but three different types of bypass valves are used, depending on application. These are: normally closed bypass valve, normally open bypass valve with vacuum vent and normally open bypass valve without vacuum vent. They are mounted "inline," or on the air pump, **Figs. 61, 62 and 63.**

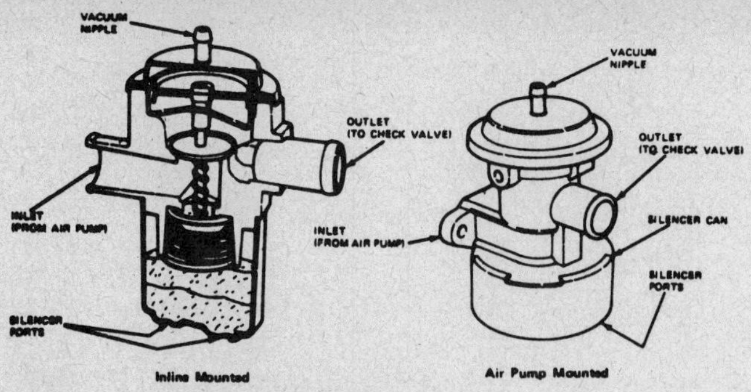

Fig. 61 Normally closed timed air bypass valve

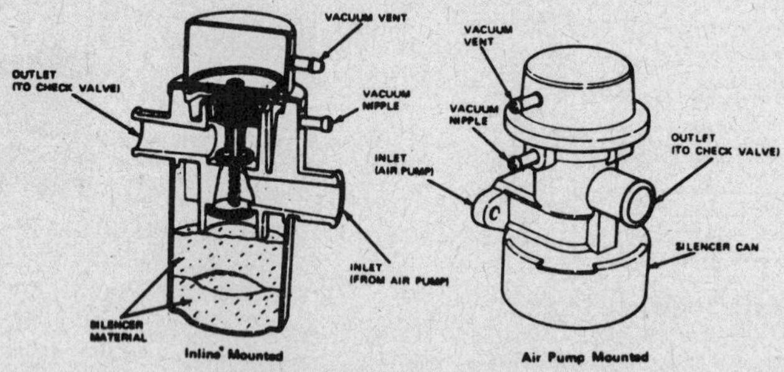

Fig. 62 Normally open timed air bypass valve with vacuum vent

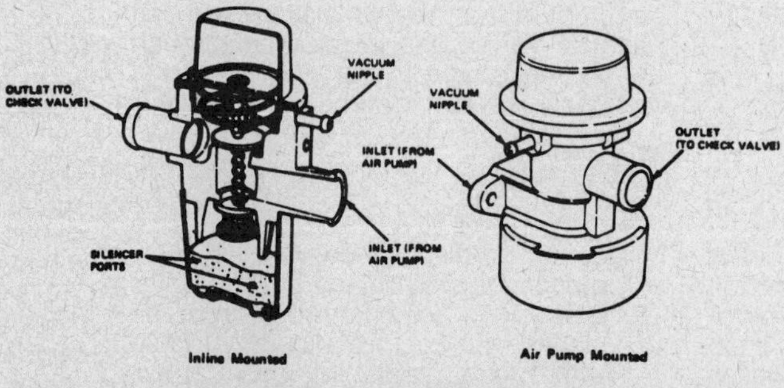

Fig. 63 Normally open timed air bypass valve less vacuum vent

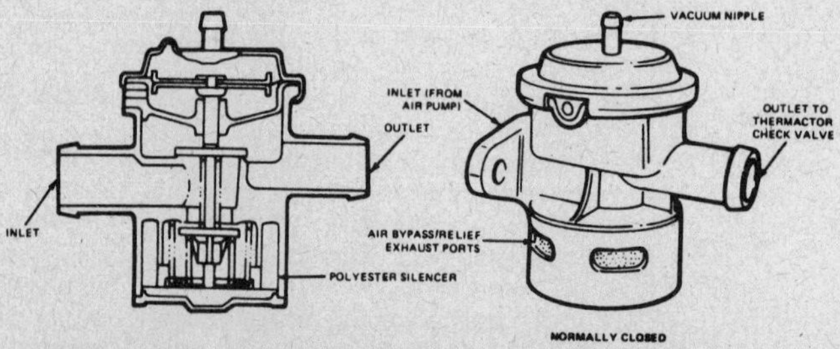

Fig. 64 Normally closed air bypass valves. 1983–87

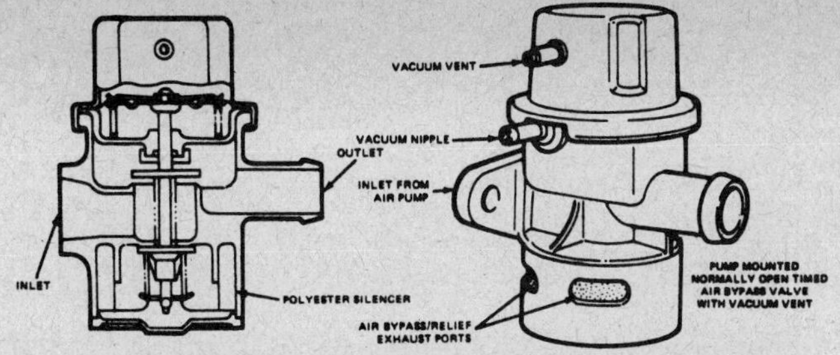

Fig. 65 Normally open air bypass valves with vacuum vents. 1983–87

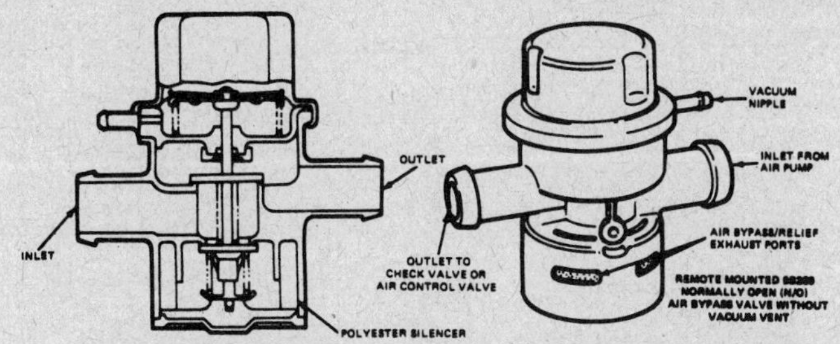

Fig. 66 Normally open air bypass valves without vacuum vents. 1983–87

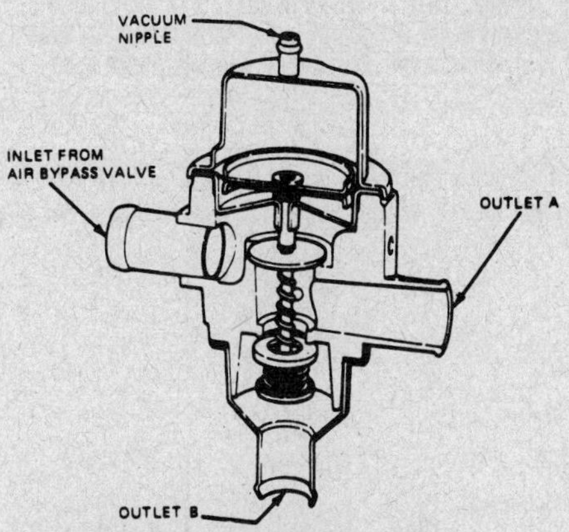

Fig. 67 Standard air control valve. 1982

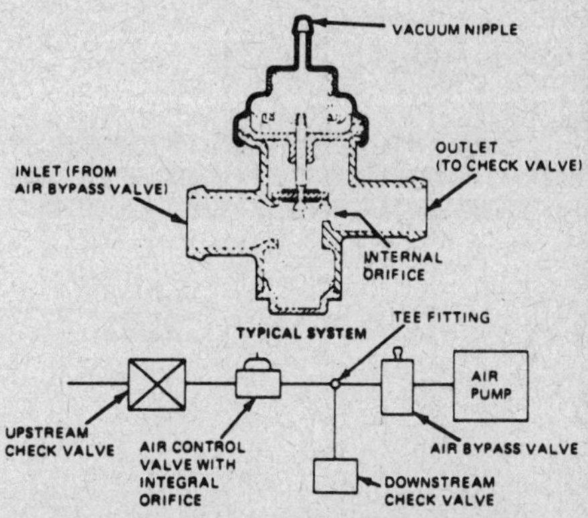

Fig. 68 Air control & shut off valve with orifice

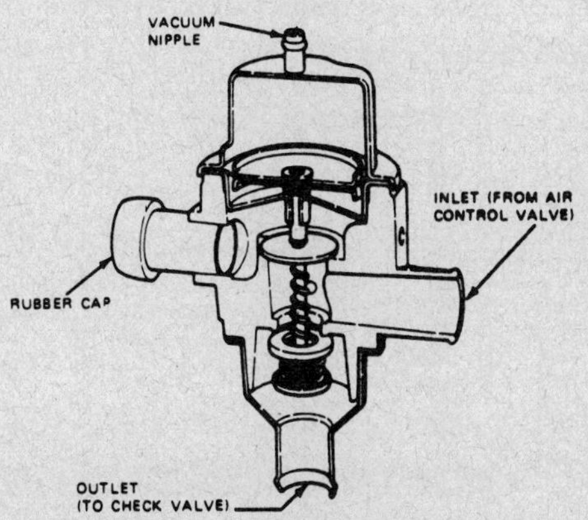

Fig. 69 Air control & shut off valve. 1982

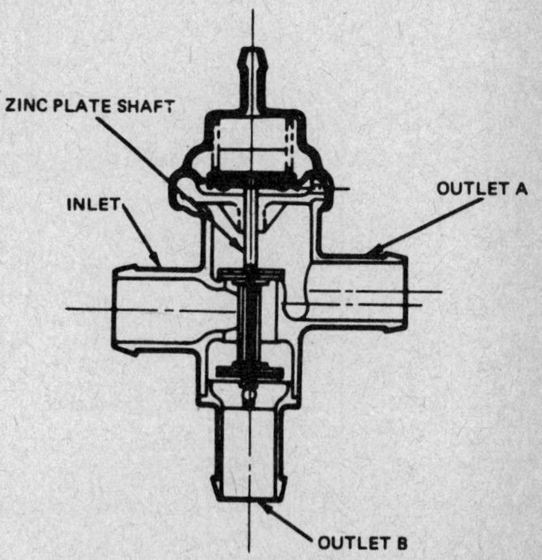

Fig. 70 Standard air control valve. 1983–87

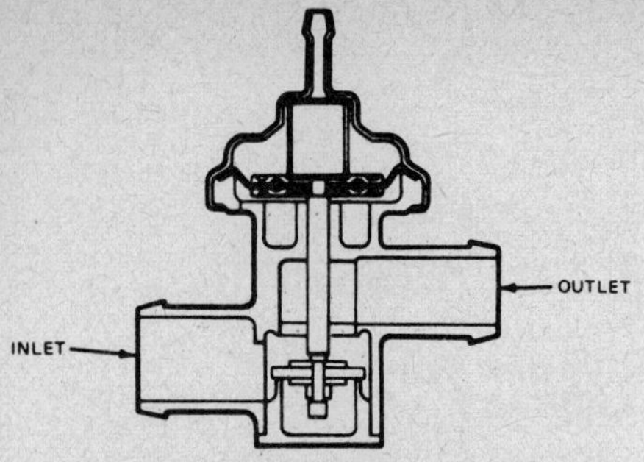

Fig. 71 Air control/shut-off valve. 1983

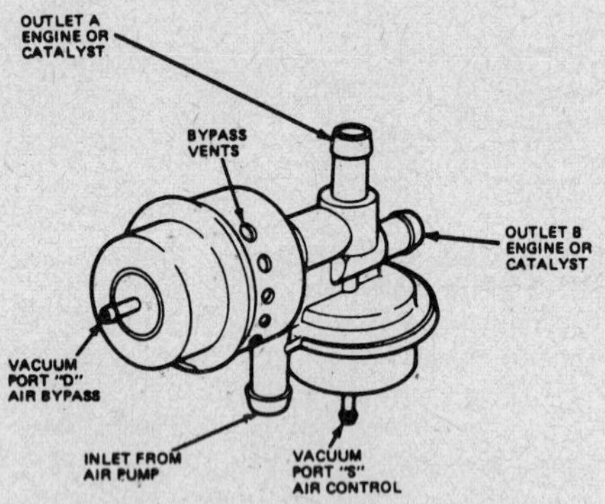

Fig. 72 Normally open combination air bypass/air control valve less bleed

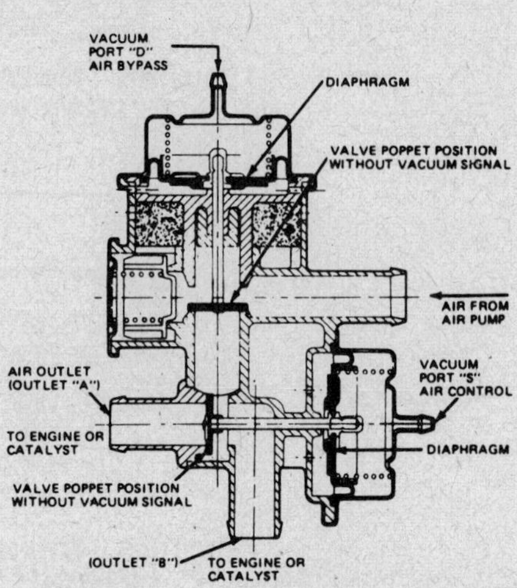

Fig. 73 Normally closed combination air bypass/air control valve less bleed

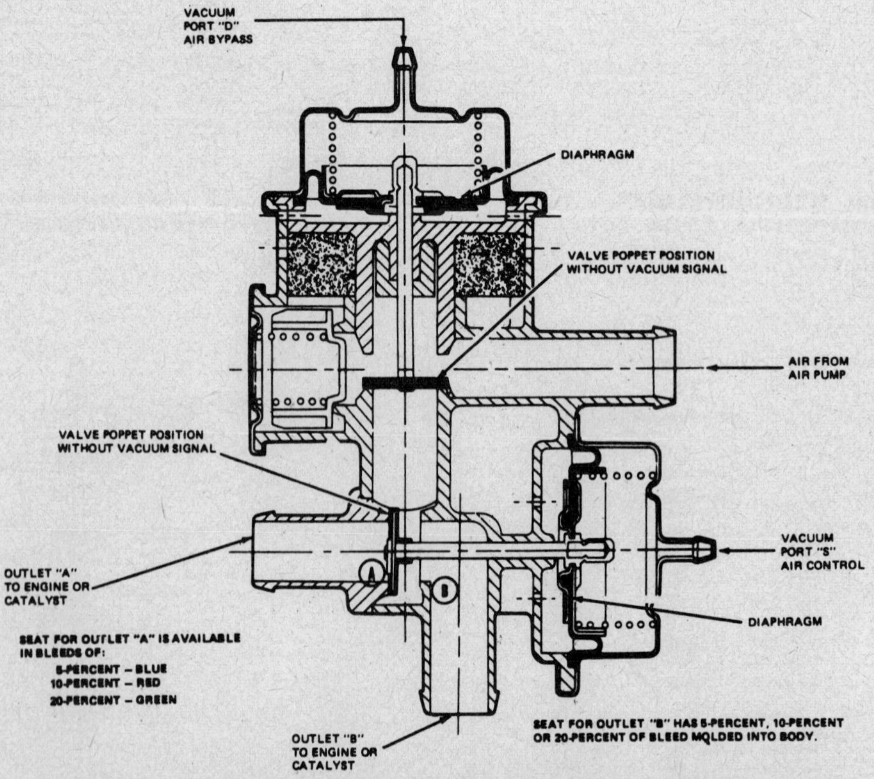

Fig. 74 Normally closed combination air bypass/air control valve less bleed

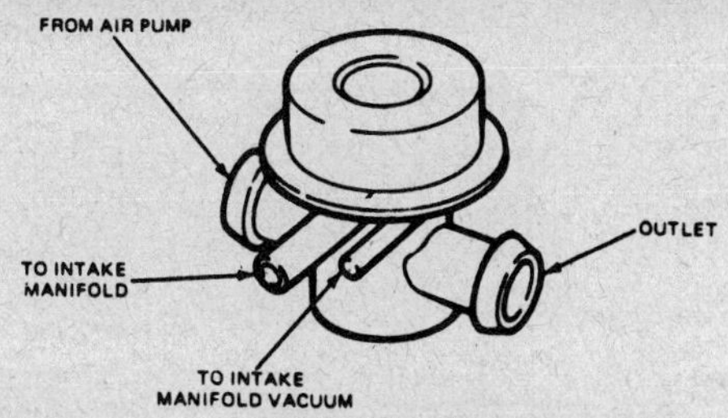

Fig. 75 Anti-backfire gulp valve

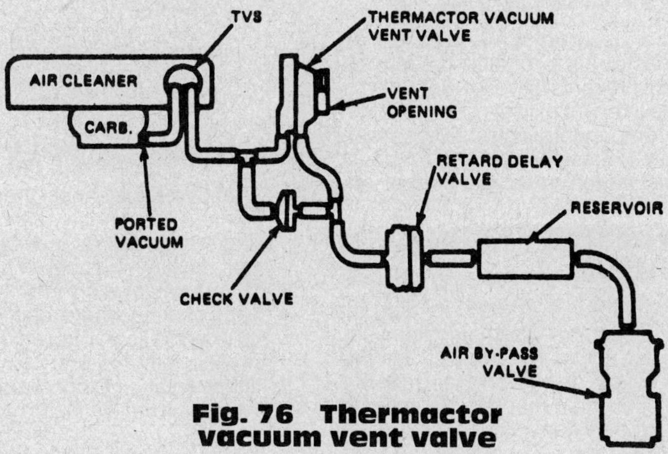

Fig. 76 Thermactor vacuum vent valve

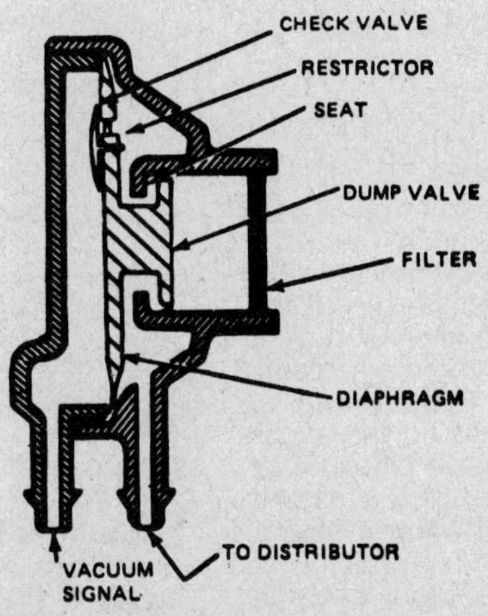

Fig. 77 Thermactor vacuum vent valve schematic (typical)

The normally closed timed bypass valve, **Fig. 61,** is used on vehicles with catalytic converter. During normal operation, engine manifold vacuum applied through the vacuum differential valve (VDV) holds the valve upward, allowing thermactor air to flow to the exhaust manifolds and blocking the vent port. When intake manifold vacuum rises or drops sharply, the VDV operates and momentarily cuts off the vacuum to the bypass valve. The spring pulls the stem down, seating the valve to cut off pump air to the exhaust manifolds and dumping the dump valve to momentarily divert the air to atmosphere. If air pump pressure becomes excessive or there is a restriction in the system, the excess pressure will unseat the valve in the lower portion of the bypass valve and allow a partial flow of pump air to the atmosphere, while at the same time, the valve in the upper part of the bypass is still unseated, allowing a partial flow of pump air to the exhaust manifold to meet system requirements.

The normally open timed bypass valve with vacuum vents, **Fig. 62,** provides a timed air dump during deceleration and when differences in vacuum pressure between the signal port and vent port occur. The signal port must have 3 inches Hg more vacuum than the vent port to prevent the valve from dumping. The valve is used to protect catalyst overheating.

The normally open timed bypass valve without vacuum vents supplies air to the exhaust system with a higher than normal vacuum signal during cold start, short idles and acceleration. When low or no vacuum is applied, pump air is dumped though the silencer ports of the valve, **Fig. 63.**

1983–87

There are two general groups of bypass valves, normally open and normally closed. Both groups are available in both remote and pump-mounted versions.

Normally closed valves, **Fig. 64,** supply air to the exhaust system with medium and high applied vacuum signals during normal modes (engine operating at normal operating temperature), short idles, and some accelerations. With low or no vacuum applied to pump, air is dumped through silencer ports of valve.

Normally open valves with a vacuum vent, **Fig. 65,** provide a timed air dump during decelerations and also dump when a vacuum pressure difference is maintained between the signal port and the vent port. The signal port must have 3 inches Hg more vacuum than the vent port to hold the dump. This mode is used to protect the catalyst from overheating.

Normally open valves without a vacuum vent, **Fig. 66,** provide a timed dump of air for 1.1 or 2.8 seconds when a sudden high vacuum of about 20 inches Hg is applied to the signal port. This prevents backfire during deceleration.

AIR SUPPLY CONTROL VALVES

1982

These valves are used to direct air pump output to the exhaust manifold or

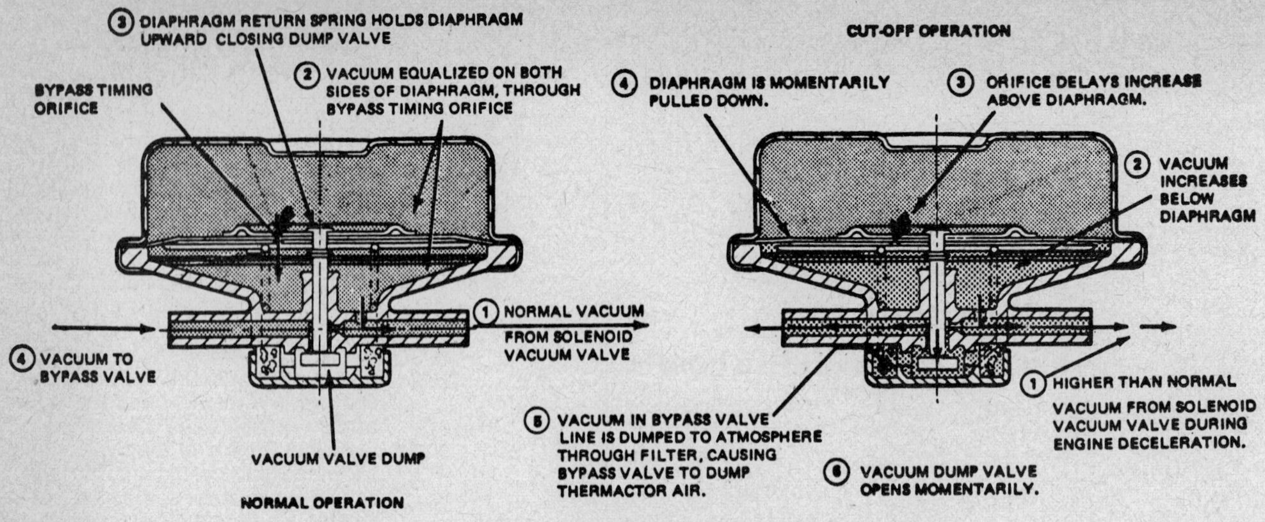

Fig. 78 Vacuum differential valve (VDV)

downstream to the catalyst system depending on the engine control modes.

Three types of valves are used, the standard air control valve, **Fig. 67,** the air control/shut off valve with orifice, **Fig. 68,** and the air control/shut off valve, **Fig. 69.**

1983–87

These valves are used to direct air pump output to the exhaust manifold or downstream to the catalyst system depending on the engine control modes.

Three types of valves are used on 1983 vehicles, the standard air control valve, **Fig. 70,** the air control/shut off valve, **Fig. 71,** and the air control/shut off valve with orifice, **Fig. 68.** 1984-87 vehicles use the standard air control valve, **Fig. 70.**

COMBINATION AIR BYPASS/AIR CONTROL VALVES

These valves, used on some vehicles, combine the function of the air bypass valve, and the air control valve.

Three types of valves are used, a normally open valve, **Fig. 72,** a normally closed valve without bleed, **Fig. 73,** and a normally closed valve with bleed, **Fig. 74.**

ANTI-BACKFIRE GULP VALVE

The anti-backfire gulp valve, used on some vehicles, routes a portion of thermactor air to the intake manifold and is activated by intake manifold vacuum signal, **Fig. 75.** This valve is located downstream from the air bypass valve and functions only during periods of sudden decrease in manifold pressure.

DIFFERENTIAL VALVE DELAY VALVE (DVDV)

This delay valve, used on some vehicles, delays air bypass during periods of low engine manifold vacuum. During sudden drops in manifold vacuum, DVDV delays operation of vacuum differential valve (VDV). A sudden rise in manifold vacuum will open check in delay valve.

EXHAUST CHECK VALVE

This valve, used on some vehicles, allows thermactor air to enter exhaust port drillings, but prevents reverse flow of exhaust gases in event of improper operation of system components. This valve is located between bypass valve and exhaust port drillings, either on air manifold or engine.

THERMACTOR VACUUM VENT VALVE

This valve, **Figs. 76 and 77,** is used on some engines equipped with variable venturi carburetor. It provides the air for the thermactor retard delay valve and air bypass valve during idle modes to deactivate the thermactor system after a controlled period of time. Application of vacuum from the carburetor to both ports of the thermactor vacuum vent causes the dump valve to seat and vacuum to be applied to the rest of the system. Removal of vacuum during idle modes results in unseating of the dump valve, opening of the vent and allowing air to enter the system to reduce the vacuum previously applied to the retard delay valve.

VACUUM DIFFERENTIAL VALVE (VDV)

On some vehicles with the Thermactor system and catalytic converters, a (VDV), **Fig. 78,** is used to control the operation of the air bypass valve. Under normal operation, vacuum applied through the VDV holds the valve upward, blocking the vent port and allowing Thermactor air flow. During acceleration or deceleration or in case of system failure, the VDV momentarily cuts off vacuum flow to the bypass valve, diverting the Thermactor air flow to atmosphere. In case of excessive pressure or system restriction, the excess pressure will unseat the valve in the lower part of the bypass valve, allowing a partial flow of air to atmosphere. At the same time, the valve in the upper part of the valve remains unseated, allowing a partial flow of air to the exhaust manifold.

Diagnosis

Engine tune up should be checked whenever the air pump system seems to be malfunctioning, especially items affecting air/fuel ratio.

AIR PUMP SUPPLY TEST

1. Remove air cleaner, then inspect all hoses and hose connections for leaks. Correct as necessary. Check belt tension and correct as necessary.
2. With transmission in Park or Neutral with parking brake applied, start engine and allow it to reach normal operating temperature.
3. Stop engine. Disconnect air supply hose(s) from air pump to air bypass valve.
4. Install suitable thermactor test gauge in end of hose disconnected from bypass valve. Secure hose with clamp to prevent it from blowing out. On side or cover mounted bypass valves, install an elbow and hose adapter, then install test gauge. **Position air pump supply tester so that air blast emitted will be harmlessly dissipated.**
5. Connect tachometer to engine and start engine. Slowly increase engine speed to 1000 RPM while observing pressure at gauge. Air pump pressure should be at least 2¼ psi. If thermactor test gauge is not used, increase engine speed to 1500 RPM and place hand over open hose. Air flow should be heard and felt.
6. If air pump output pressure is not at least 2¼ psi, or if air flow is not heard and felt, replace pump and repeat test.

Air Manifold, Hose and Tube

1. Inspect all hoses and tubes for deterioration or cracks.
2. Check hose and tube routing as interference may cause wear.
3. Check all hose and tube connections.
4. Check the pressure side of the system for leaks with a soapy water solution. With the pump running, bubbles

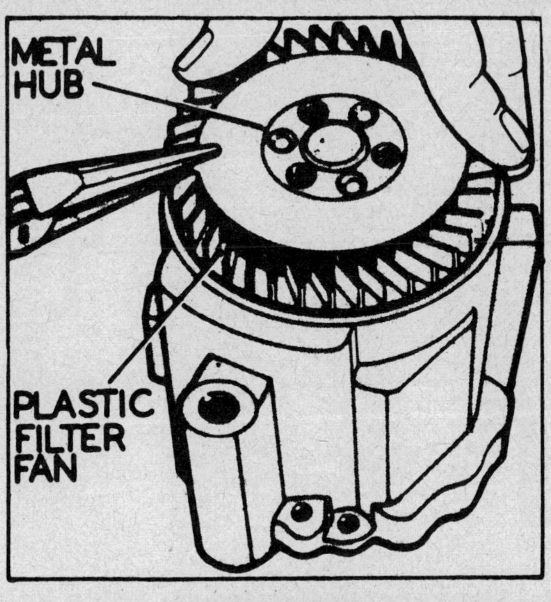

Fig. 79 Removing centrifugal type air pump filter

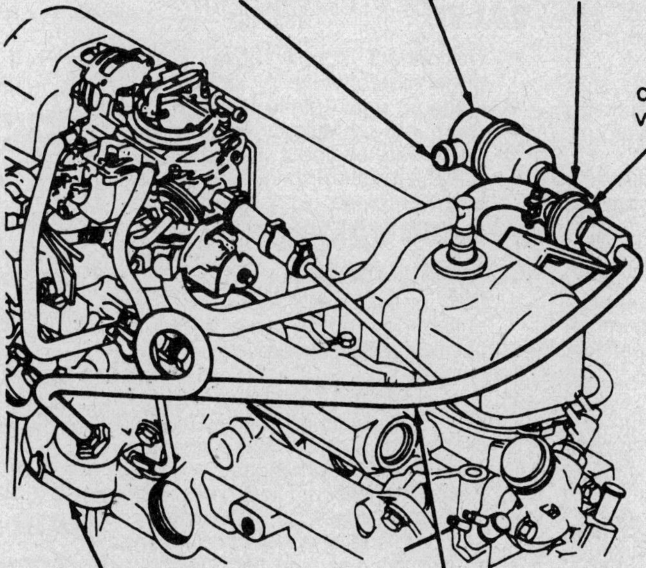

Fig. 80 Thermactor II system (typical)

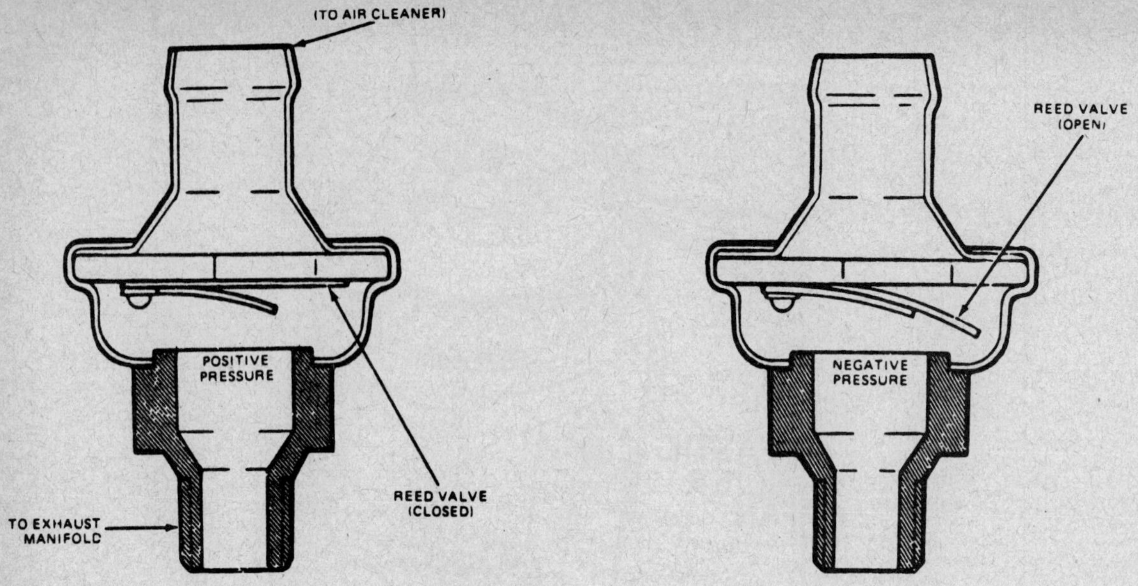

Fig. 81 Thermactor II pulse air valve operation

will form if a leak exists.

5. When replacing any hose or tube, note routing before removal. **The hoses used with this system are made of special material to withstand high temperature. No other type should be used.**

Exhaust Check Valves

1. Check valves should be inspected whenever the hose is disconnected from the valve or check valve failure is suspected. **Any indication of exhaust gases in the air pump indicates check valve failure.**
2. Orally blow through the check valve (toward air manifold) then attempt to suck back. Flow should be toward air manifold only.
3. When replacing a check valve, be careful not to bend or twist the air manifold.

AIR BYPASS SYSTEMS

1. Start engine and allow to reach normal operating temperature with transmission in Park or Neutral and parking brake applied.
2. Stop engine and remove air check valve hoses at bypass valve. On engines with two check valves, disconnect both hoses connecting bypass valve to check valves.
3. Connect tachometer to engine. Accelerate engine to 1500 RPM. Check that air is flowing from air bypass valve hose connection(s) by placing hand over valve connection. Air should be heard and felt.
4. Disconnect vacuum hose from bypass valve and plug vacuum hose. With engine speed at 1500 RPM and hand placed over bypass valve connection, there should be very little air flow heard or felt. Air should be discharged through the exhaust vents in the end of the air bypass valve silencer cover. If air flow is felt or heard through the bypass valve connection, the valve is defective and should be replaced.
5. Stop engine. Remove plug from vacuum hose and connect hose to bypass valve sense vacuum nipple.

Testing

ANTI-BACKFIRE GULP VALVE

1. Disconnect supply hose from air pump side of valve.
2. Observe valve pintle by looking into valve through disconnected port.
3. Accelerate engine to 3000 RPM, then release throttle. Pintle should be open and then close.

BYPASS VALVES

Normally Closed

1. Disconnect air supply hose at valve outlet, then remove vacuum line and check if vacuum is present at vacuum nipple.
2. Remove any restrictors or delay valves in vacuum line. Before proceeding to step 3, ensure vacuum is present at vacuum nipple.
3. Reconnect vacuum line to nipple, then accelerate engine to 1500 RPM.
4. Air pump supply should be present at air bypass valve outlet. Disconnect vacuum line, air at outlet should stop and air pump supply air should be present at silencer port.
5. If above step proves incorrect, check air pump, then bypass valve.

Normally Open With Vacuum Vents

1. Disconnect air pump supply line at outlet, then vacuum lines from vacuum nipple and vacuum vent.
2. Accelerate engine to 1500 RPM, air pump supply air should be present at outlet.
3. Using suitable vacuum hose, connect vacuum nipple to intake manifold vacuum. No air should be present at valve outlet, all air should bypass through silencer ports.
4. Using the same vacuum hose as above step, cap vacuum vent and accelerate engine to 2000 RPM. Air pump supply air should be interrupted when throttle is released.
5. If above steps prove incorrect, check air pump, then bypass valve.

Normally Open Without Vacuum Vent

1. Disconnect air supply line at valve outlet, then vacuum line at vacuum nipple.
2. Accelerate engine to 1500 RPM, air pump supply air should be present at outlet.
3. Using suitable vacuum hose, connect vacuum nipple to intake manifold vacuum. Air at outlet should decrease or shut off.
4. Air pump supply air should be present at silencer ports.
5. If above steps prove incorrect, check air pump, then bypass valve.

AIR CONTROL VALVE

Standard Air Control Valve

1. Run engine at 1500 RPM and disconnect air supply hose at inlet, **Figs. 67 and 68.** There should be air flow at hose. Reconnect air supply hose at valve inlet.
2. Disconnect air supply hoses at outlets A and B and the vacuum line at the vacuum nipple.
3. Run engine at 1500 RPM. There should be air flow at outlet B but little

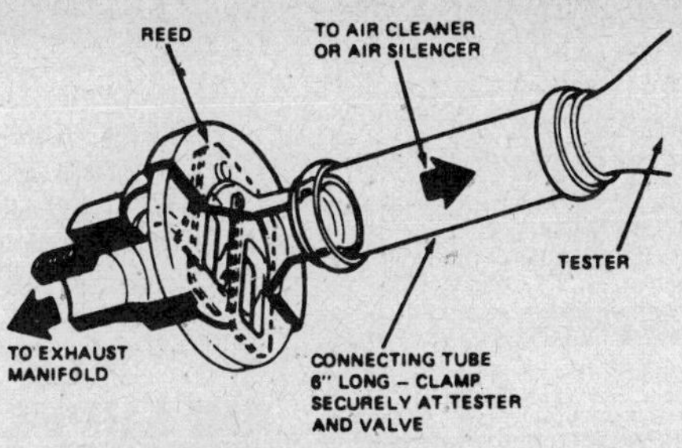

Fig. 82 Thermactor II pulse air valve test

or no air flow at outlet A.
4. Run engine at 1500 RPM and connect a direct vacuum line from any manifold vacuum fitting to air control valve vacuum nipple. There should be air flow at outlet A but little or no air flow at outlet B.
5. Connect all vacuum hoses at original positions. If valve does not function correctly, replace valve.

Air Control/Shut-Off Valve

1. Start engine and run at idle, disconnect vacuum supply hose from vacuum nipple, and disconnect inlet hose from valve. Suction should be felt at valve opening.
2. Apply manifold vacuum to vacuum nipple. No suction should be felt at valve inlet opening.

Air Control/Shut-Off Valve With Orifice

1. Disconnect valve inlet supply hose and ensure that there is air flow to valve inlet, **Fig. 68,** then reconnect air supply hose.
2. Run engine at 1500 RPM and disconnect air supply hose at valve outlet and the vacuum hose at vacuum nipple. There should be air flow at valve outlet.
3. Connect a direct vacuum line from any manifold fitting to valve vacuum nipple. There should be a noticeable increase in air flow at valve outlet.
4. Connect all vacuum hoses at original positions.

COMBINATION AIR BYPASS/AIR CONTROL VALVES

Normally Closed Valves

1. Disconnect hose from outlets A and B, **Figs. 73 and 74.**
2. Disconnect and plug vacuum line to port D.
3. Run engine at 1500 RPM. There should be air flow at bypass vents.
4. Reconnect vacuum line to port D and disconnect and plug vacuum line to port S, then ensure that vacuum is present in line to vacuum port D.
5. Run engine at 1500 RPM. There should be air flow at outlet B but no air flow at outlet A.
6. Apply 8-10 inches Hg vacuum to port S and run engine at 1500 RPM. There should be air flow at outlet A.
7. On bleed type valve, some lesser amount of air will flow from outlet A or B and the main discharge will change when vacuum is applied to port S. **If there is a small air tap attached to the inlet tube from the air pump, air flow should be present during engine operation.**

Normally Open Valves

1. Disconnect hoses from outlets A and B, **Fig. 72.**
2. Disconnect and plug vacuum lines to ports D and S.
3. Run engine at 1500 RPM. There should be air flow at outlet B.
4. Apply 8-10 inches Hg vacuum to port S and run engine at 1500 RPM. There should be air flow at outlet A.
5. Reconnect vacuum line to port D and ensure that vacuum is present.
6. Run engine at 1500 RPM. Air should flow out of bypass vents.
7. Reconnect vacuum hoses to original positions.

ELECTRIC PVS HIGH TEMP COOLANT LOCK OUT VACUUM CHECK

1. Disconnect vacuum line from air bypass valve to PVS valve at air bypass valve and connect to vacuum gauge.
2. With transmission in Park or Neutral and parking brake applied, start engine and allow to idle.
3. With engine at normal operating temperature, there should be a vacuum reading. If not, PVS is defective and should be replaced.

NORMALLY CLOSED (TYPE 1) SOLENOID VACUUM VALVE

A type 1 solenoid vacuum valve is used in conjunction with a type 1 air cleaner temperature switch.

1. Start engine and allow to reach normal operating temperature. Make sure that ambient air around air cleaner is above 65°F.
2. With engine idling, disconnect vacuum hose to thermactor air bypass valve. Thermactor air should exhaust in atmosphere through exhaust ports in end of valve silencer cover. Reconnect vacuum hose. **Vacuum supply hose must always be connected to bottom vacuum fitting on solenoid vacuum valve.**
3. Disconnect vacuum supply hose at solenoid valve, and check for vacuum by placing finger over end of hose. There should be vacuum with engine idling. If not, check vacuum hose and vacuum source for leaks or obstructions.
4. Disconnect solenoid vacuum valve wiring connector and determine which terminal has 12 volts with ignition in the run position. Use a test light; connect one end to terminal and other end to ground.
5. Connect wire with 12 volts battery voltage to solenoid vacuum valve. With engine idling, ground other exposed terminal on solenoid vacuum valve to chassis ground. Thermactor air should not be dumped.
6. Reconnect wire disconnected in step 4 to solenoid vacuum valve. Thermactor air should not be dumped.
7. Replace solenoid vacuum valve if operation is not as specified in steps 5 and 6.

NORMALLY OPEN (TYPE 2) SOLENOID VACUUM VALVE

A type 2 solenoid vacuum valve is used in conjunction with a type 2 air cleaner temperature switch.

1. Start engine and allow to reach normal operating temperature. Make sure that ambient air around air cleaner is above 65°F.
2. With engine idling, disconnect vacuum hose to thermactor air bypass valve. Thermactor air should exhaust to atmosphere through exhaust ports in end of valve silencer cover. Reconnect vacuum hose. **Vacuum hose must be connected to black input nozzle on solenoid valve.**
3. Disconnect wiring to solenoid valve and determine which wire has 12 volts when ignition switch is in the run position. Use a test light; connect one end to wire and other end to ground.
4. Connect wire power supply wire to solenoid vacuum valve, then, with engine at normal idle, ground other exposed terminal on solenoid vacuum valve to ground. Thermactor air should be exhausted to atmosphere.
5. Reconnect other wire to solenoid vacuum valve. Thermactor air should not be dumped to atmosphere.
6. Replace solenoid vacuum valve if operation is not as specified in steps 4 and 5.

THERMACTOR PVS (WITH 2 CONNECTORS)

1. Disconnect both vacuum hoses at PVS valve. Connect vacuum gauge to bottom connector on PVS.
2. Using an external vacuum source, apply at least 10 inches Hg vacuum to top connector. With engine cold, there should be no vacuum reading. If there

is, replace PVS.

3. Start engine and allow to reach normal operating temperature. With 10 inches Hg vacuum applied, there should be a vacuum reading. If not, PVS is defective and should be replaced.

THERMACTOR VACUUM VENT VALVE

1. If necessary, remove air cleaner assembly.
2. Disconnect vacuum tubing or connector block from valve, noting location of tubing. **It may be necessary to remove valve from bracket or air cleaner tray to gain access to vacuum ports on valve.**
3. Connect the black vacuum port to a manifold vacuum source.
4. Connect an external vacuum source to white body vacuum port.
5. With engine idling in neutral, apply 10 inches Hg vacuum to white port and trap. If vacuum cannot be obtained, replace valve.
6. Remove manifold vacuum source line from black port. The trapped vacuum should drop to zero. If not, replace valve.

VACUUM DIFFERENTIAL VALVE (VDV)

1. Start engine and allow to reach normal operating temperature with transmission in Park or Neutral and parking brake applied.
2. Stop engine and remove air bypass valve to air manifold check valve hose and bypass valve. On systems with two check valves, remove both hoses. Connect tachometer to engine.
3. Start engine, then, with hand placed over bypass valve outlet connections, accelerate engine to 2500 RPM and release throttle, allowing engine to return to normal idle. During deceleration, the air flow in the valve outlet should be felt or heard to momentarily diminish or stop and then resume to normal air flow. Air flow will be discharged through the exhaust ports in the end of the bypass valve silencer cover.
4. If bypass valve does not function as described in step 3, check to make sure that decel valve is receiving a vacuum signal. If it is, the decel valve is defective and should be replaced.

VACUUM RESERVOIR CHECK VALVE

This valve is used on some vehicles equipped with catalytic converter.

1. Disconnect vacuum hose on reservoir which connects to electric solenoid valve vacuum nipple.
2. Connect a 0-30 inch Hg vacuum gauge to reservoir using a suitable length of hose.
3. Disconnect manifold vacuum hose from reservoir and connect an external vacuum source to the nipple. Apply 14 inches Hg vacuum to reservoir and trap. Vacuum reading on gauge should not drop more than 1 inch Hg in one minute. If it does, replace reservoir.

Service

AIR INJECTION PUMP, REPLACE

1. Disconnect air inlet and outlet hoses from air pump.
2. Remove drive belt and mounting bolts from pump and remove the pump.
3. Reverse procedure to install.

CENTRIFUGAL FILTER FAN, REPLACE

1. Remove drive pulley and outer disc from air pump.
2. Remove filter fan from pump, **Fig. 79. Do not attempt to remove the metal drive hub.**
3. Install new filter fan using the pulley and bolts. Alternately tighten bolts to draw fan down evenly. **A slight interference between the fan and housing is normal. A new fan may make noise during initial operation, until its outer diameter sealing lip has worn in, after approximately 20-30 miles of operation.**

CHECK VALVE, REPLACE

1. Disconnect air supply valve from hose and, using a 1¼ inch crow-foot wrench, remove check valve.
2. Clean threads on air manifold adapter using a wire brush, then install new check valve.

AIR PUMP RELIEF VALVE, REPLACE

The air pump does not have to be disassembled to replace the relief valve, however, it must be removed from the engine.

1. Install Tool T66L-9A486-D on air pump and remove relief valve using a suitable slide hammer.
2. To install relief valve, use Tool T66L-9A486-B and lightly hammer the valve until it is seated.

RELIEF VALVE PRESSURE SETTING PLUG, REPLACE

1. Compress shoulders of pressure setting plug together and pull plug out of relief valve.
2. Install new valve into relief valve hole by pressing against its center with a suitable tool.

AIR BYPASS OR BACKFIRE SUPPRESSOR VALVE, REPLACE

1. Disconnect air and vacuum hoses from valve, then remove the valve.
2. Reverse procedure to install.

AIR MANIFOLD, REPLACE

1. Disconnect air supply hose from check valve and position hose aside.
2. Unscrew air manifold to cylinder head coupling nuts until free of the cylinder head, then remove air manifold.
3. Reverse procedure to install.

AIR SUPPLY TUBES, REPLACE

The air supply tubes, or air nozzles, will normally be replaced during cylinder head overhaul, however, they may be replaced without removing the cylinder head by removing the air manifold and using a hooked tool to pull the tube.

THERMACTOR II

Some vehicles are equipped with this type of exhaust air injection system, **Fig. 80,** which does not have an air pump. The system uses the natural pulses of the exhaust system to draw air into the exhaust manifold. The system is regulated by a pulse air valve. The valve, **Fig. 81,** is connected to the air cleaner with a hose and to the exhaust manifold with a metal tube. Some pulse air valves closely resemble the standard Thermactor check valves, but are not interchangeable with them.

When pressure inside the exhaust manifold is more than the pressure in the air cleaner, the reed in the pulse air valve is closed. When pressure in the exhaust manifold is lower than in the air cleaner, the reed opens and allows air to be drawn into the exhaust manifold.

Testing

1. Check to see that air flows freely through air cleaner or silencer to pulse air valve.
2. Check all hoses, tubes, and pulse air valves for leaks.
3. Disconnect hose at air cleaner side of pulse air valve and connect tester T75L-9487-A or equivalent to valve, **Fig. 82.** A 6 inch length of hose, clamped at either end, should be used between tester and valve.
4. Squeeze bulb as flat as possible, then release it. Bulb should remain flat for at least 8 seconds. If not, valve is defective.
5. If tester is not available, disconnect hose as in Step 3 and blow air through valve toward exhaust manifold side, then attempt to suck air back through valve. If air flows back through valve, the valve is defective.

GENERAL MOTORS CORPORATION

BUICK

CADILLAC

CHEVROLET

OLDSMOBILE

PONTIAC

GENERAL SERVICE

BUICK REAR WHEEL DRIVE MODELS & 1982–85 RIVIERA

INDEX OF SERVICE OPERATIONS

NOTE: Refer to rear of this manual for vehicle manufacturer's special service tool suppliers.

Specifications

GENERAL ENGINE SPECIFICATIONS

Year	Engine CID ①/Liter	Engine VIN Code ②	Fuel System	Bore & Stroke	Compression Ratio	Net H.P. @ RPM ③	Maximum Torque Lbs. Ft. @ RPM	Normal Oil Pressure Pounds
1982	V6-231, 3.8L	A	E2ME, 2 Bbl. ④	3.80 x 3.40	8.0	110 @ 3800	190 @ 1600	37
	V6-231, 3.8L ⑩	3	E4ME, 4 Bbl. ④	3.80 x 3.40	8.0	⑭	⑮	37
	V6-252, 4.1L	4	E4ME, 4 Bbl. ④	3.97 x 3.40	8.0	125 @ 4000	205 @ 2000	37
	V6-262, 4.3L ⑤ ⑬	V	Fuel Injection	4.057 x 3.385	21.6	85 @ 3600	165 @ 1600	35
	V8-307, 5.0L ⑤	Y	E4ME, 4 Bbl. ④	3.80 x 3.385	8.5	140 @ 3600	240 @ 1600	35
	V8-350, 5.7L ⑤ ⑬	N	Fuel Injection	4.057 x 3.385	22.5	105 @ 3200	200 @ 1600	35
1983	V6-231, 3.8L	A	2 Bbl. ④	3.80 x 3.40	8.0	110 @ 3800	190 @ 1600	37
	V6-231, 3.8L ⑩	8	4 Bbl. ④	3.80 x 3.40	8.0	180 @ 4000	⑧	37
	V6-252, 4.1L	4	4 Bbl. ④	3.965 x 3.40	8.0	125 @ 4000	205 @ 2000	37
	V6-262, 4.3L ⑤ ⑬	V	Fuel Injection	4.057 x 3.385	22.5	85 @ 3600	165 @ 1600	30-45
	V8-307, 5.0L ⑤	Y	4 Bbl. ④	3.80 x 3.385	8.0	140 @ 3600	240 @ 1600	30-45
	V8-350, 5.7L ⑤ ⑬	N	Fuel Injection	4.057 x 3.385	22.5	105 @ 3200	200 @ 1600	30-45
1984	V6-231, 3.8L	A	2 Bbl. ④	3.80 x 3.40	8.0	110 @ 3800	190 @ 1600	37
	V6-231, 3.8L ⑩	9	Fuel Injection	3.80 x 3.40	8.0	⑪	190 @ 4000	37
	V6-252, 4.1L	4	4 Bbl. ④	3.965 x 3.40	8.0	125 @ 4000	205 @ 2000	37
	V6-262, 4.3L ⑤ ⑬	V	Fuel Injection	4.057 x 3.385	21.6	85 @ 3600	165 @ 1600	30-45
	V8-307, 5.0L ⑤	Y	4 Bbl. ④	3.800 x 3.385	8.0	140 @ 3600	240 @ 1600	30-45
	V8-350, 5.7L ⑤ ⑬	N	Fuel Injection	4.057 x 3.385	21.6	105 @ 3200	200 @ 1600	30-45
1985	V6-231, 3.8L	A	2 Bbl. ④	3.800 x 3.400	8.0	110 @ 3800	190 @ 1600	37 ⑥
	V6-231, 3.8L ⑩	9	Fuel Injection	3.800 x 3.400	8.0	⑪	300 @ 2400	37 ⑥
	V6-262, 4.3L ⑤ ⑬	V	Fuel Injection	4.057 x 3.385	21.6	85 @ 3600	165 @ 1600	30 ⑦
	V8-307, 5.0L ⑤	Y	4 Bbl. ④	3.800 x 3.385	8.0	140 @ 3600	240 @ 1600	30 ⑦
	V8-350, 5.7L ⑤ ⑬	N	Fuel Injection	4.057 x 3.385	22.5	105 @ 3200	200 @ 1600	30 ⑦
1986-87	V6-231, 3.8L	A	2 Bbl. ④	3.800 x 3.400	8.01	110 @ 3800	190 @ 1600	37
	V6-231, 3.8L	7	Fuel Injection	3.800 x 3.400	8.01	235 @ 4400	330 @ 2800	37
	V8-307, 5.0L	Y	4 Bbl. ④	3.800 x 3.385	8.00	140 @ 3200	255 @ 2000	30
1988	V8-307, 5.0L	Y	4 Bbl. ④	3.800 x 3.385	8.0	140 @ 3200	255 @ 2000	30

①—CID-cubic inch displacement.
②—The eighth digit in the V.I.N. denotes engine code on these vehicles.
③—Ratings are net-as installed in the vehicle.
④—Rochester.
⑤—See Oldsmobile chapter for service procedures on this engine.
⑥—At 2400 RPM.
⑦—Minimum at 1500 RPM.
⑧—Regal, 280 @ 2400; Riviera, 290 @ 2400.
⑨—See Chevrolet chapter for service procedures on this engine.
⑩—Turbocharged engine.
⑪—Regal, 200 @ 4000; Riviera, 190 @ 4000.
⑫—Riviera.
⑬—Diesel.
⑭—Regal, 170 @ 4000; Riviera, 180 @ 4000.
⑮—Regal, 275 @ 2400; Riviera, 270 @ 2400.

ALTERNATOR SPECIFICATIONS

Year	Model	Rated Hot Output Amps.
1982	1100110	42
	1100111	63
	1100121	63
	1100156	55
	1100164	55
	1100165	60
	1100190	76
	1100194	70
	1100198	38
	1100281	63
	1100284	85
	1101037	70
	1101045	85
	1101056	—
	1101082	70
	1101084	85
	1101088	70
	1101098	70
	1103119	63
1983	1100200	78
	1100230	42
	1100239	55
	1100240	63
	1100260	78
	1100297	42
	1100300	63
	1105022	78
	1105025	63
	1105034	63
	1105040	85
	1105198	85
	1105250	70
1984	1100200	78
	1100239	56
	1100260	78
	1105028	78
	1105041	78
	1105197	70
	1105250	70
	1105443	94
	1105444	94
	1105493	94
	1105547	94
	1105548	85
	1105549	108
	1105561	94
	1105562	94
	1105564	66
	1105565	78
	1105566	66
	1105567	78
1985	1100200	78
	1100206	56
	1100208	66
	1100217	78
	1100239	56
	1100247	66
	1100257	78
	1100260	78
	1104446	94
	1105028	78
	1105085	108
	1105197	70
	1105200	85
	1105329	85
	1105428	94
	1105441	94
	1105443	94
	1105444	94
	1105447	94
	1105493	94
	1105494	78
	1105496	94
	1105497	108
	1105509	108
	1105541	94
	1105548	85
	1105552	85
	1105553	97
	1105562	66
	1105592	94
	1105617	94
1986-87	1100200	78
	1100239	55
	1105197	70
	1105444	94
	1105493	94
	1105546	85
	1105565	78
	1105685	120
1988	1100200	78

STARTING MOTOR APPLICATIONS

Year	Engine/VIN	Starter Number
1982	V6-231/3③	1998234
	V6-231/3④	1998237
1982-83	V6-231/A	1998234
	V6-252/4③	1998234
	V6-252/4④	1998237
	V8-262/V	1998552
	V8-307/Y③	1109544
	V8-307/Y④	1998237
	V8-350/N②③	1998552
	V8-350/N②④	1109495
1983	V6-231/8③	1998234
	V6-231/8④	1998237
1984	V6-231/A,9③	1998236
	V6-231/9①④	1998237
	V6-252/4③	1998234
	V6-252/4④	1998237
	V6-262/V②	1998556
		22511854
	V8-307/Y③	1109544
	V8-307/Y④	1998237
	V8-350/N②③	1998553
		22523207
	V8-350/N②④	1109495
1985	V6-231/A	1998236
	V6-231/9③	1998236
	V6-231/9④	1998237
	V6-262/V	22511854
	V8-307/Y③	1109544
	V8-307/Y④	1998237
	V8-350/N③	1998553
	V8-350/N④	1109495
1986-87	V6-231/A	1998516
	V6-231/7	—
	V8-307/Y	1998536
1988	V8-307/Y	1998536

①—Distributor at rear of engine, counter-clockwise rotation.
②—Diesel engine.
③—Exc. Riviera.
④—Riviera.

ENGINE TIGHTENING SPECIFICATIONS*

*Torque specifications are for clean and lightly lubricated threads only. Dry or dirty threads produce increased friction which prevents accurate measurement of tightness.

Year	Engine/VIN	Spark Plugs Ft. Lbs.	Cylinder Head Bolts Ft. Lbs.	Intake Manifold Ft. Lbs.	Exhaust Manifold Ft. Lbs.	Rocker Arm Shaft Bracket Ft. Lbs.	Rocker Arm Cover Ft. Lbs.	Connecting Rod Cap Bolts Ft. Lbs.	Main Bearing Cap Bolts Ft. Lbs.	Flywheel to Crankshaft Ft. Lbs.	Vibration Damper or Pulley Ft. Lbs.
1982-83	V6-231⑭	15	80	45	25	30	4	40	100	60	225
	V8-265,301⑭	15	95	40	35	20⑪	6	35	②	95	160
	V8-305⑭	22	65	30	20	—	4	45	70	60	60
	V8-350/L⑥	22	65	30	20	—	4	45	70	60	60
	V8-350/X⑤	15	80	45	25	30	4	40	100	60	225
	V8-350/R⑦	25	130⑩	40⑩	25	28④	⑫	42	③	⑧	255
1982-83	V6-252/4	15	80	45	25	30	4	40	100	60	225
	V8-307/Y⑦	25	130⑩	40⑩	25	28④	⑫	42	③	60	200-310
	V8-350/N⑨	—	130⑩	40⑩	25	28④	⑫	42	120	60	200-310
	V6-262/V⑨	—	⑬	41	29	29④	⑫	42	①	65	160-350
1984	V6-231/A,9	15	80	45	25	30	4	40	100	60	225
	V6-252/4	15	80	45	25	30	4	40	100	60	225
	V6-262/V⑨	—	⑬	41	31	28④	—	42	105	57	203-350
1984-85	V8-307/Y⑦	25	125⑩	40⑩	25	28④	—	42	③	60	200-310
	V8-350/N⑨	—	130⑩	40⑩	25	28④	—	42	120	60	200-310
1985	V6-231/A,9	15	80	47	25	25	6	40	100	60	200
	V6-262/V	—	⑬	41	28	28④	6	42	⑮	57	203-350
1986	V6-231/A,7	20	⑰	45	20	25	44⑯	40	100	60	219
	V8-307/Y	25	125⑩	40⑩	25	25④	90⑯	42	③	60	200-310
1987	V6-231/A,7	20	⑰	45	20	25	44⑯	40	100	60	°219
	V8-307/Y	25	130⑩	40⑩	25	25	90⑯	48	③	60	200-310
1988	V8-307/Y	25	130⑩	40⑩	25	25	90⑯	48	③	60	200-310

①—1982, 107 ft. lbs.; 1983, 89 ft. lbs.
②—Rear main 100 ft. lbs.; all others, 70 ft. lbs.
③—Nos. 1, 2, 3, 4-80 ft. lbs., No. 5-120 ft. lbs.
④—Rocker arm pivot bolt to head.
⑤—Buick built engine. Distributor located at front of engine.
⑥—Chevrolet built engine. Distributor located at rear of engine, clockwise rotation.
⑦—Oldsmobile built engine. Distributor located at rear of engine, counter-clockwise rotation.
⑧—Auto. trans. 60 ft. lbs.; man. trans., 90 ft. lbs.
⑨—Oldsmobile built diesel engine.
⑩—Clean and dip entire engine bolt in engine oil before installing and tightening.
⑪—Rocker arm to stud nut.
⑫—Fully driven, seated and not stripped.
⑬—Torque inner 8 bolts to 142 ft. lbs. Torque outer 6 bolts (bolts nearest intake & exhaust manifolds to cylinder head mating surfaces) to 59 ft. lbs.
⑭—For VIN code identification refer to the General Engine Specifications at the beginning of the chapter.
⑮—Engines w/2 bolt caps, 89 ft. lbs. Engines w/4 bolt main caps: Exc. caps 2 & 3 outer, 89 ft. lbs.; caps 2 & 3 outer, 52 ft. lbs.
⑯—Inch pounds.
⑰—See text.

DRIVE AXLE SPECIFICATIONS

Year	Model	Carrier Type	Ring Gear & Pinion Backlash		Pinion Bearing Preload			Differential Bearing Preload		
						Adjustment			Adjustment	
			Method	Adjustment	Method	New Bearings Inch Lbs.	Used Bearings Inch Lbs.	Method	New Bearings Inch Lbs.	Used Bearings Inch Lbs.
1982-84	Exc. Riviera	Integral	Shims	.006-.008	Spacer	20-25①	10-15①	Shims	35-40②	20-25②
1982-85	Riviera	Integral	Shims	.005-.009	Spacer	18-24	③	Shims	④	④
1985-88	Exc. Riviera	Integral	Shims	.005-.009	Spacer	20-25①	10-15①	Shims	35-40②	20-25②

①—Measured with torque wrench at pinion flange nut.
②—Total preload measured with torque wrench at pinion flange nut with new seal installed.
③—Pre-check reading plus 5 inch lbs.
④—Slip fit plus .003 inch preload on each side.

FRONT WHEEL ALIGNMENT SPECIFICATIONS

Year	Model	Caster Angle, Degrees		Camber Angle, Degrees				Toe-In Inch
				Limits		Desired		
		Limits	Desired	Left	Right	Left	Right	
1982	Regal	+2.5 to +3.5	+3	0 to +1	0 to +1	+.5	+.5	1/16 to 3/16
	Riviera	+2 to +3	+2.5	−.5 to +.5	−.5 to +.5	Zero	Zero	①
	Others	+2.5 to +3.5	+3	+.3 to +1.3	+.3 to +1.3	+.8	+.8	1/16 to 3/16
1983-84	Regal	+2.5 to +3.5	+3	0 to +1	0 to +1	+.5	+.5	1/16 to 3/16
	Riviera	+2 to +3	+2.5	−.5 to +.5	−.5 to +.5	Zero	Zero	①
	Others	+2.5 to +3.5	+3	+.3 to +1.3	+.3 to +1.3	+.8	+.8	1/16 to 3/16
1985	Regal	+2 to +4	+3	−.3 to +1.3	−.3 to +1.3	+1/2	+1/2	1/16 to 1/4
	Riviera	+1.5 to +3.5	+2.5	−.8 to +.8	−.8 to +.8	0	0	−1/8 to +1/8
	Others	+2 to +4	+3	0 to +1.6	0 to +1.6	+.8	+.8	1/16 to 1/4
1986	Regal	+2 to +4	+3	−.3 to +1.3	−.3 to +1.3	+1/2	+1/2	1/16 to 1/4
	Estate Wagon	+2 to +4	+3	0 to +1.6	0 to +1.6	+.8	+.8	1/16 to 1/4
1987	Regal	+1.8 to +3.8	+2.8	−.3 to +1.3	−.3 to +1.3	+.5	+.5	.05 to .1②
	Estate Wagon	+1.8 to +3.8	+2.8	0 to +1.6	0 to +1.6	+.8	+.8	.05 to .1②
1988	Estate Wagon	+1.8 to +3.8	+2.8	0 to +1.6	0 to +1.6	+.8	+.8	.05 to .1②

①—1/16" toe-in to 1/16" toe-out.
②—Degrees per wheel.

REAR WHEEL ALIGNMENT SPECIFICATIONS

Year	Model	Camber Angle, Degrees		Toe-In Inch①
		Limits	Desired	
1982	Riviera	−.8 to +.8	0	0 to 3/16
1983-85	Riviera	−.8 to +.8	0	0 to 3/32

①—Per wheel.

COOLING SYSTEM & CAPACITY DATA

Year	Model or Engine/V.I.N.	Cooling Capacity, Qts.		Radiator Cap Relief Pressure, Lbs.	Thermo. Opening Temp.	Fuel Tank Gals.	Engine Oil Refill Qts. ①	Auto. Trans. Qts.	Rear Axle Oil Pints
		Less A/C	With A/C						
1982	V6-231/A⑱	12.98	13.02	15	195	18	4	⑮	⑥
	V6-231/A⑧	13	13	15	195	25③	4	⑮	⑥
	V6-231 Turbo/3⑱	13.44⑳	13.44⑳	15	195	25③	4	⑮	⑥
	V6-231 Turbo/3⑪	13.6㉑	13.6㉑	15	195	21	4	⑮	3.2⑦
	V6-252/4⑱	12.98	13.02	15	195	18	4	⑮	⑥
	V6-252/4⑧ ⑫	13	13	15	195	25③	4	⑮	⑥
	V6-252/4⑪	13	13	15	195	21	4	⑮	3.2⑦
	V6-262 Diesel/V⑯	14.8	14.8	15	195	20	6.5⑰	⑮	⑥
	V8-307/Y⑥ ⑫	18.9	18.9	15	195	25③	4	⑮	⑥
	V8-307/Y⑪	18.8	18.95	15	195	21	4	⑮	3.2⑦
	V8-350 Diesel/N⑯	17.33	17.33	15	195	20	7⑰	⑮	⑥
	V8-350 Diesel/N⑧ ⑫	17	17	15	195	27③	7⑰	⑮	⑥
	V8-350 Diesel/N⑪	18.2	18.2	15	195	23	7⑰	⑮	3.2⑦

Continued

COOLING SYSTEM & CAPACITY DATA—Continued

Year	Model or Engine/V.I.N.	Cooling Capacity, Qts. Less A/C	Cooling Capacity, Qts. With A/C	Radiator Cap Relief Pressure, Lbs.	Thermo. Opening Temp.	Fuel Tank Gals.	Engine Oil Refill Qts. ①	Auto. Trans. Qts.	Rear Axle Oil Pints
1983	V6-231/A ⑯	12.9	13	15	195	⑩	4	⑮	⑥
	V6-231/A ⑧	12.9	13	15	195	25 ③	4	⑮	⑥
	V6-231 Turbo/8 ⑱	13.4	13.4 ⑳	15	195	19.8	4	⑮	⑥
	V6-231 Turbo/8 ⑪	—	13.6 ㉑	15	195	21.1	4	⑮	3.2 ⑦
	V6-252/4 ⑯	12.9	13	15	195	⑩	4	⑮	⑥
	V6-252/4 ⑧ ⑫	12.9	13	15	195	25 ③	4	⑮	⑥
	V6-252/4 ⑪	—	13	15	195	21.1	4	⑮	3.2 ⑦
	V6-262 Diesel/V ⑯	—	14.7	18.5	195	⑩	6.5 ⑰	⑮	⑥
	V8-307/Y ⑧ ⑫	15.4 ⑭	16 ⑭	15	195	25 ③	4	⑮	⑥
	V8-307/Y ⑪	—	16 ⑭	15	195	21.1	4	⑮	3.2 ⑦
	V8-350 Diesel/N ⑯	—	17.3	15	195	⑩	6.5 ⑰	⑮	⑥
	V8-350 Diesel/N ⑧ ⑫	—	17.9	15	195	26 ③	6.5 ⑰	⑮	⑥
	V8-350 Diesel/N ⑪	—	18	15	195	22.8	6.5 ⑰	⑮	3.2 ⑦
1984	V6-231/A ⑯	12.9	13	15	195	19.8	4	⑮	3.5
	V6-231/A ⑧	13	13	15	195	25 ③	4	⑮	⑥
	V6-231 Turbo/9 ⑯	13	13	15	180	19.8	5	⑮	3.5
	V6-231 Turbo/9 ⑪	—	12.9 ⑳	15	180	21.1	5	⑮	3.3 ⑦
	V6-252/4 ⑯	13	13	15	195	19.8	4	⑮	3.5
	V6-252/4 ⑧ ⑫	13	13	15	195	25 ③	4	⑮	⑥
	V6-252/4 ⑪	—	12.6	15	195	21.1	4	⑮	3.3 ⑦
	V6-262 Diesel/V ⑯	13.6	14.4	15	195	⑩	6 ⑰	⑮	3.5
	V8-307/Y ⑧ ⑫	15.4	16	15	195	25 ③	4	⑮	⑥
	V8-307/Y ⑪	—	16	15	195	21.1	4	⑮	3.3 ⑦
	V8-350 Diesel/N ⑧ ⑫	18.3	17.9	15	195	26 ③	7 ⑰	⑮	⑥
	V8-350 Diesel/N ⑪	18.2	18.2	15	195	22.8	7 ⑰	⑮	3.3 ⑦
1985	V6-231/A ⑧	13.0	13.0	15	195	25 ③	4	⑮	⑥
	V6-231/A ⑯	12.9	13.0	15	195	18.1	4	⑮	⑥
	V6-231/9 ⑯	13.0	13.0	15	180	18.1	5	⑮	⑥
	V6-231/9 ⑪	—	12.9 ⑳	15	180	21.1	5	⑮	3.3 ⑦
	V6-262 Diesel/V	13.6 ⑲	14.4	16-18.5	195	19.8	6 ⑰	⑮	⑥
	V8-307/Y ⑬	15.4 ⑭	16.0	15	195	25 ③	4	⑮	⑥
	V8-307/Y ⑪	—	16.0	15	195	21.1	4	⑮	3.3 ⑦
	V8-350 Diesel/N ⑬	18.0	18.3	15	195	26 ③	7 ⑰	⑮	⑥
	V8-350 Diesel/N ⑪	18.2	18.2	15	195	22.8	7 ⑰	⑮	3.3 ⑦
1986-87	V6-231/A	12.9	13.0	15	195	18.1	4	⑮	⑥
	V6-231/7	13.0	13.0 ⑨	15	180	18.1	5	⑮	⑥
	V8-307/Y	15.4 ⑭	16.0	15	195	22	4	⑮	⑥
1988	V8-307/Y	—	16.3	15	195	22	4	⑮	5.4

①—Add one quart with filter change.
②—Approximate. Make final check with dipstick.
③—Estate Wagon 22 gallons.
④—With heavy duty cooling system, 14.5 qts.
⑤—With heavy duty cooling system, 21.6 qts.
⑥—7½ inch axle, 3.5 pts.; 8½ inch axle, 4.25 pts.; 8¾ inch axle, 5.4 pts.
⑦—Final drive.
⑧—LeSabre.
⑨—With heavy duty cooling, 13.5 qts.
⑩—Exc. wagon, 19.8 gals.; wagon, 18.2 gals.
⑪—Riviera.
⑫—Electra.
⑬—Exc. Riviera.
⑭—With heavy duty cooling, 16.0 qts.
⑮—THM 200C-total 9.4 qts., pan only 3.48 qts. THM 200-4R-total 11.05 qts., pan only, 3.48 qts. THM 250C-total 10.04 qts., pan only 4.0 qts. THM325-4L-total 11.75 qts., pan only 4.86 qts. THM 350C-total 10.04 qts., pan only 3.17 qts.
⑯—Regal.
⑰—Includes oil filter.
⑱—Regal.
⑲—With heavy duty cooling, 14.4 qts.
⑳—With heavy duty cooling, 13.7 qts.
㉑—With heavy duty cooling, 14.1 qts.

Electrical Section

INDEX

STARTER REPLACE

To remove the starter, disconnect ground cable from battery. Disconnect cable and solenoid lead wire from solenoid switch. Remove flywheel inspection cover. Remove starter attaching bolts and remove starter.

LIGHT SWITCH REPLACE

1982–84 ELECTRA & LESABRE; 1985 LESABRE & ALL ESTATE WAGONS

1. Disconnect battery ground cable.
2. Remove left lower instrument panel trim and A/C ducts as required.
3. Pull headlamp switch to full on position.
4. Depress retainer through slot in rear of knob and pull knob from stem.
5. Remove switch stem escutcheon and instrument cluster bezel.
6. Remove nut securing switch, lower switch from rear of instrument panel, then disconnect electrical connector from switch.
7. Reverse procedure to install.

1982–85 RIVIERA & 1982–83 REGAL

1. Disconnect battery ground cable.
2. Depress retainer through slot in rear of switch knob, then pull knob from stem.
3. Remove switch escutcheon, then the instrument cluster bezel.
4. Remove screws securing switch to instrument panel, then pull switch away from panel. **Disconnect twilight sentinel harness, if equipped, prior to pulling switch from instrument panel.**
5. On Regal models, disconnect electrical connector from switch.
6. On all models, reverse procedure to install.

1984–87 REGAL

1. Disconnect battery ground cable.
2. Remove instrument cluster bezel by carefully pulling it away from instrument panel. **Place column mounted gear selector lever in low position and lower tilt wheel, if equipped, to aid removal of bezel.**
3. Remove 3 retaining screws, then pull switch assembly from instrument panel.
4. Reverse procedure to install, ensuring that switch is properly seated in instrument panel socket.

COLUMN-MOUNTED DIMMER SWITCH REPLACE

1. Disconnect battery ground cable.
2. Remove instrument panel lower trim and on models with A/C, remove A/C duct extension at column.
3. Disconnect shift indicator from column and remove toe-plate cover screws.
4. Remove two nuts from instrument panel support bracket studs and lower steering column, resting steering wheel on front seat.
5. Remove dimmer switch retaining screw(s) and the switch. Tape actuator rod to column and separate switch from rod.
6. Reverse procedure to install. To adjust switch, depress dimmer switch slightly and install a 3/32 inch twist drill to lock the switch to the body. Force switch upward to remove lash between switch and pivot. Torque switch retaining screw(s) to 35 inch lbs. and remove tape from actuator rod. Remove twist drill and check for proper operation.

IGNITION LOCK REPLACE

1. Remove steering wheel as described under Horn Sounder and Steering Wheel, Replace.
2. Remove turn signal switch as described under Turn Signal Switch, Replace, then remove buzzer switch.
3. Place ignition switch in Run position, then remove lock cylinder retaining screw and lock cylinder.
4. To install, rotate lock cylinder to stop while holding housing, **Fig. 1.** Align cylinder key with keyway in housing, then push lock cylinder assembly into housing until fully seated.
5. Install lock cylinder retaining screw. Torque screw to 40 in. lbs. for standard columns. On adjustable columns, torque retaining screw to 22 in. lbs.
6. Install buzzer switch, turn signal switch and steering wheel.

IGNITION SWITCH REPLACE

The ignition switch is located on the top of the steering column under the instrument panel. To replace it, the steering column must be lowered.

1. Lower steering column as outlined in "Column Mounted Dimmer Switch, Replace" procedure.
2. Remove column mounted dimmer switch, if equipped.
3. Disconnect electrical connector from switch. On models equipped with standard column and key release feature or tilt column except key release, ensure switch is in "Accessory" position. On models equipped with standard column except key release or tilt

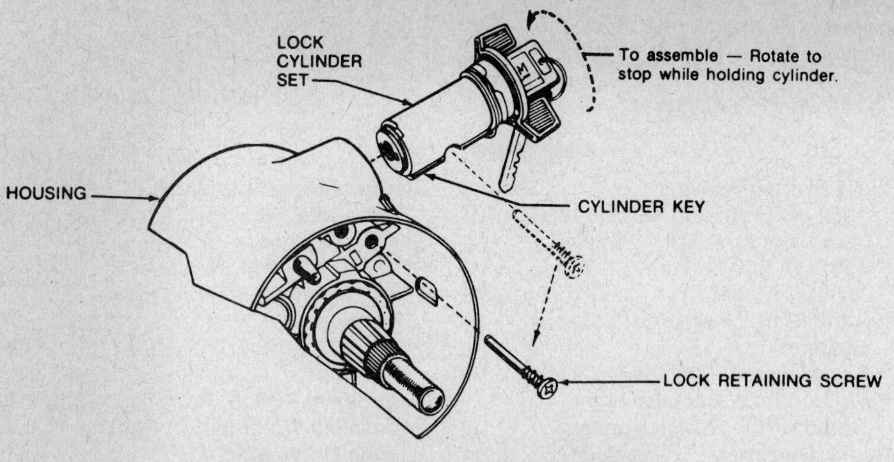

Fig. 1 Ignition lock removal

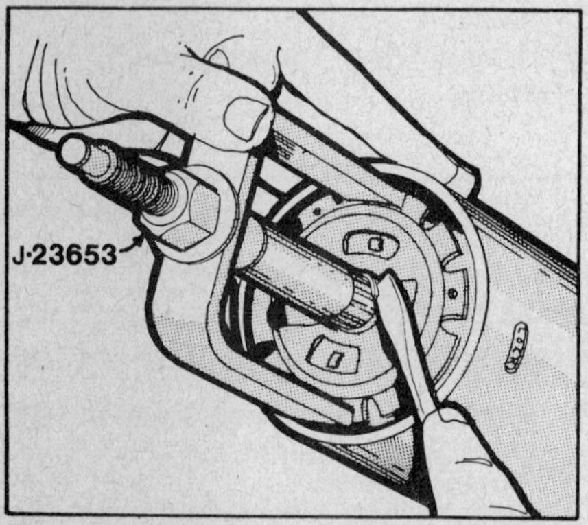

Fig. 3 Lock plate retainer removal

column with key release, ensure switch is in "Off-Unlock" position.

4. Remove two screws securing switch, then remove switch.
5. On models equipped with standard column and key release feature or tilt column except key release, position switch slider and lock in the "Accessory" position. On models equipped with standard column except key release or tilt column with key release, position switch slider and lock at "Accessory" position, then move slider and lock two detents to the "Off-Unlock" position.
6. Fit actuator rod into switch and assemble to column.
7. Complete assembly in reverse of removal procedure.

STOP LIGHT SWITCH

REPLACE

The stop lights are controlled by a mechanical switch mounted on the brake pedal bracket. This spring loaded switch makes contact whenever the brake pedal is applied. When the brake pedal is released it depresses the switch to open the contacts and turn brake lights off.

TURN SIGNAL SWITCH

REPLACE

As shown in **Fig. 2,** the assembly is a turn signal switch and hazard warning switch. It is mounted in a housing at the upper end of the steering column mast jacket, just below the steering wheel. Therefore to get at the switch the steering wheel will have to be removed.

Also, on models equipped with tilt steering columns, it will be necessary to lower the column assembly from instrument panel.

1. Disconnect battery ground cable.
2. Remove steering wheel and lock plate cover. On tilt columns, remove tilt lever.
3. With a suitable compressor, compress lock plate and spring, then remove snap ring from shaft, **Fig. 3.**
4. Remove lock plate cover with a suitable screwdriver.
5. Remove lock plate, cancelling cam, preload spring and thrust washer.
6. Remove turn signal lever and hazard warning switch knob.
7. Disconnect switch wiring connector and wrap a piece of tape around connector upper end and wiring harness, preventing snagging when removing switch.
8. Remove three switch retaining screws and switch.
9. Reverse procedure to install.

NEUTRAL START/MECHANICAL LOCKOUT SYSTEM

EXC. MODELS W/KEY RELEASE LEVER

Actuation of the ignition switch is prevented by a mechanical lockout system, **Figs. 4 and 5,** which prevents the lock cylinder from rotating when the selector lever is out of Park or Neutral. When the selector lever is in Park or Neutral, the slots in the bowl plate and the finger on the actuator rod align allowing the finger to pass through the bowl plate in turn actuating the ignition switch, **Fig. 6.** If the selector lever is in any position other than Park or Neu-

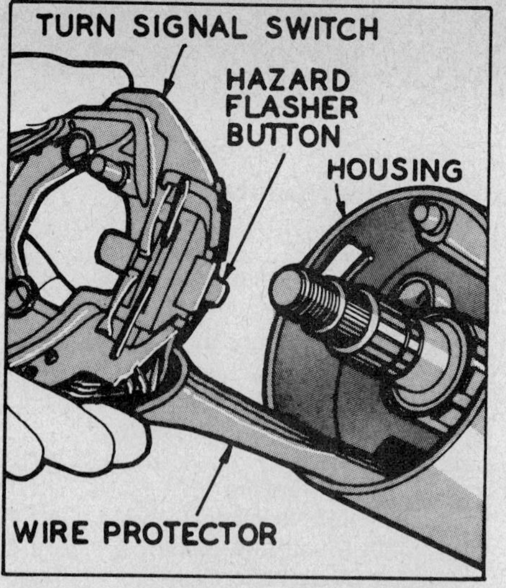

Fig. 2 Turn signal & hazard warning switch assembly

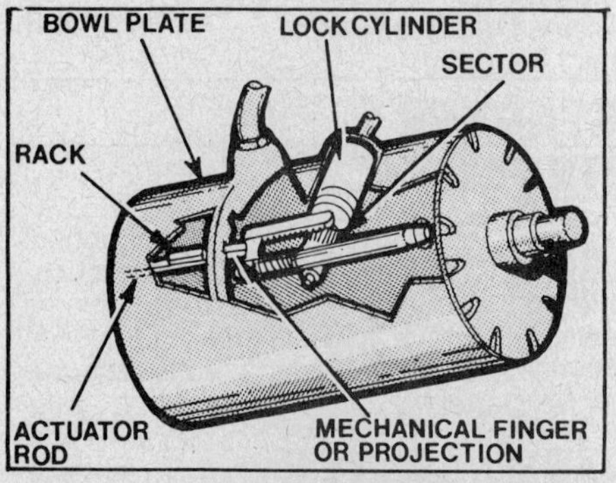

Fig. 4 Mechanical neutral start mechanism. Standard column

tral, the finger contacts the bowl plate when the lock cylinder is rotated, thereby preventing full travel of the lock cylinder.

PARK/NEUTRAL & BACK-UP LIGHT COMBINATION SWITCH

REPLACE

Some models use a combination neutral start & back-up light switch, while other models use a separate back-up light switch. The combination switch indicates to the ECM when the transmission is in Park or Neutral, and also activates the back-up lights when the transmission is placed in Reverse. Both type switches are serviced by the following procedures.

1. Place gear selector in "Neutral."
2. Gently rock switch out of steering column.
3. Disconnect wiring connectors. Connect wiring connectors to new switch.
4. Align switch actuator with hole in shift tube, **Fig. 7.**
5. Position connector side of switch into lower jacket cut out.
6. Push down front of switch, ensuring switch tangs snap into holes in steering column jacket.

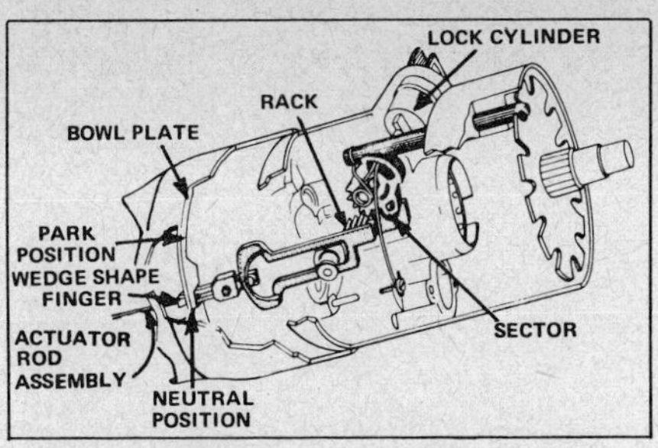

Fig. 5 Mechanical neutral start mechanism. Tilt column

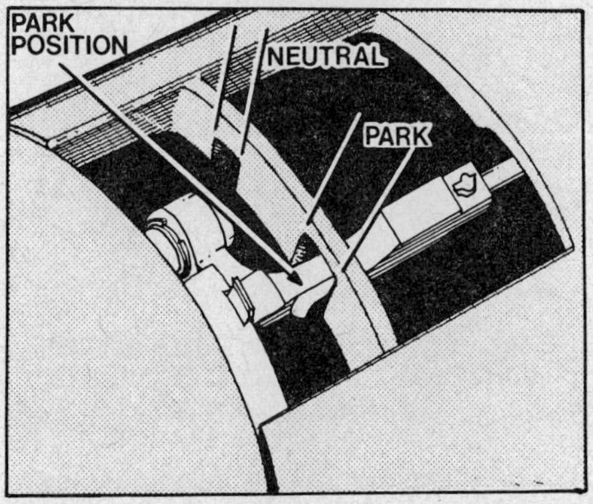

Fig. 6 Mechanical neutral start mechanism. Shown in park position

7. Adjust switch by placing gear selector in "Park" position. The switch main housing and housing back should ratchet, providing proper adjustment.

STANDARD HORN SOUNDER & STEERING WHEEL

REPLACE

1. Remove horn cap or actuator bar.
2. Remove steering wheel nut retainer, if used.
3. On all models, back off nut until flush with top of steering shaft.
4. Use a suitable puller to remove wheel.

TILT & TELESCOPE STEERING WHEEL

REPLACE

REMOVAL

1. Disconnect battery ground cable.
2. Remove screws, **Fig. 8**, and lift pad assembly up, then disconnect horn wiring electrical connector by pushing in and turning counterclockwise.
3. Push locking lever counterclockwise until full release position is obtained.
4. Scribe plate assembly where the two screws secure plate assembly to locking lever.
5. Remove screws and plate assembly.
6. Remove steering wheel nut retainer and nut.
7. Using tool No. J185903, remove steering wheel assembly. **Use of a steering wheel puller other than the one recommended in Step 7, or a sharp blow on the end of the steering shaft or shift lever, could shear or loosen the plastic fasteners which maintain steering column rigidity.**

INSTALLATION

1. Install a suitable setscrew into upper shaft at the full extended position and lock.
2. Align scribe mark on steering wheel hub with mark on end of shaft and install steering wheel. Ensure unsecured end of horn upper contact assembly is completely seated against top of horn contact carrier assembly.
3. Install nut onto upper steering shaft and torque to 30 ft. lbs. Install nut retainer.
4. Remove setscrew and install plate assembly and screws. Tighten screws finger tight.
5. Position locking lever in vertical position and move lever counterclockwise until plate holes align with holes in lever. Install plate securing screws.
6. Align pad assembly with holes in steering wheel and install screws.
7. Connect battery ground cable. Ensure locking lever securely locks steering wheel travel and that steering wheel travel is free in the unlocked position.

INSTRUMENT CLUSTER

REPLACE

1982 RIVIERA

1. Disconnect ground cable from battery and speedometer cable from transaxle or cruise control transducer.
2. Disconnect parking brake release cable and lap cooler hose, as equipped, then remove left lower instrument panel trim.
3. Remove headlamp switch knob, escutcheon and instrument cluster bezel, **Fig. 9.**
4. Disconnect shift indicator cable from steering column, remove 2 nuts securing column bracket, then lower steering column.
5. Remove cluster retaining screws, then pull cluster from instrument panel.
6. Disconnect speedometer cable and electrical connectors from cluster, then remove cluster.
7. Reverse procedure to install.

1983–85 RIVIERA

Standard Cluster

1. Disconnect ground cable from battery and speedometer cable at transaxle, cruise control transducer or union in engine compartment.
2. Remove center trim bezel, headlamp switch knob and escutcheon, and left (cluster) trim bezel, **Fig. 9**, pulling bezels straight away from instrument panel.

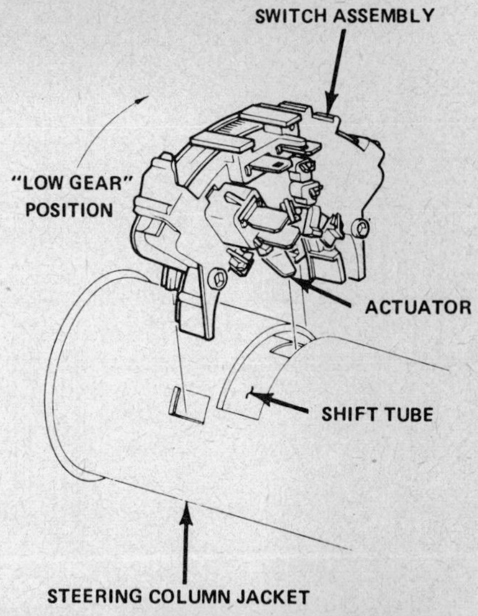

Fig. 7 Park/Neutral start & back-up lamp switch installation

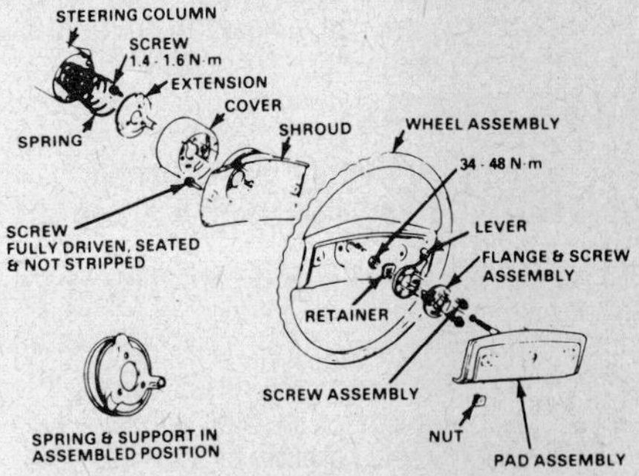

Fig. 8 Tilt & telescoping steering wheel assembly exploded view

3. Remove 2 screws securing leading edge of lower instrument panel cover, then disconnect shift indicator cable from steering column.
4. Remove 4 screws securing cluster, then tilt top of cluster away from instrument panel.
5. Remove "Check Engine" bulb and socket from cluster and disconnect speedometer cable.
6. Place gear selector lever in low, then pull cluster away from instrument panel just far enough to gain access to Vehicle Speed Sensor (VSS).
7. Remove screw securing VSS optic head and the optic head, then lift cluster from instrument panel.
8. Reverse procedure to install.

Digital Cluster

1. Perform steps 1-5 as outlined for "Standard Cluster."
2. Disconnect wiring harness from cluster by depressing lock tab on connector and pulling connector away from cluster.
3. Remove screw securing cluster ground strap to instrument panel brace.

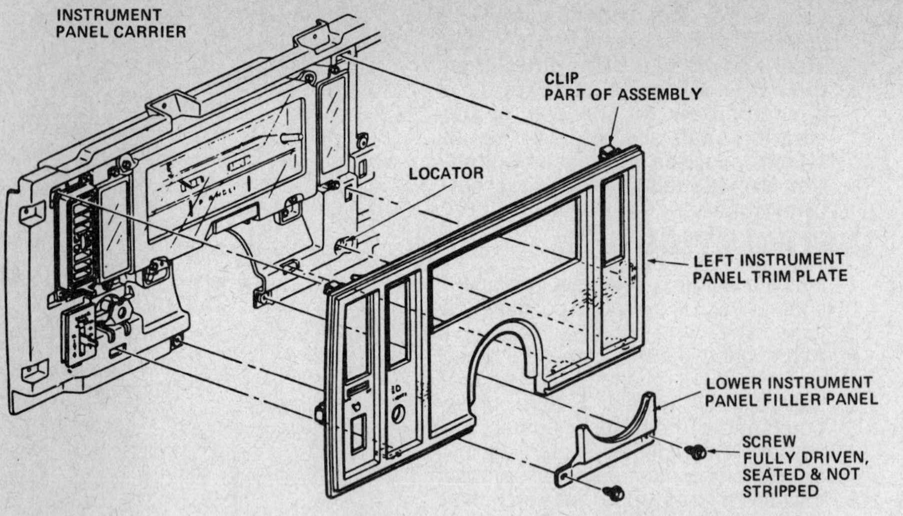

Fig. 9 Instrument cluster trim cover. 1982–85 Riviera

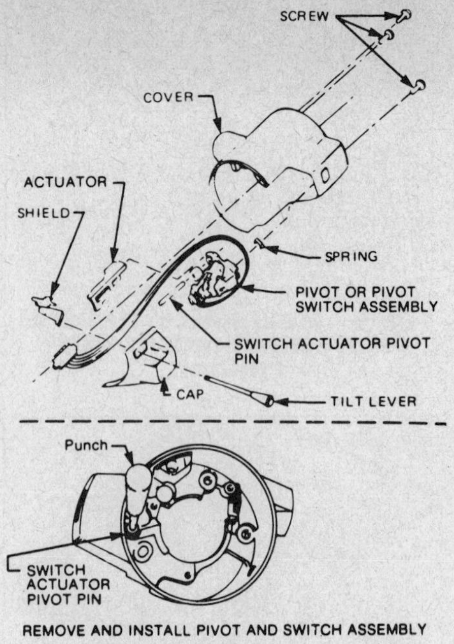

Fig. 10 Windshield wiper switch removal. Models w/tilt column

4. Place gear selector lever in low, pull cluster out just enough to gain access to Vehicle Speed Sensor (VSS), then remove screw securing VSS optic head and the optic head from cluster.
5. Reverse procedure to install.

1982 REGAL

1. Disconnect battery ground cable.
2. Remove headlamp switch knob and escutcheon.
3. Carefully pry out and remove cluster trim plate.
4. Remove five cluster lens attaching screws, then remove cluster lens.
5. To remove speedometer, remove two speedometer retaining screws. Disconnect speedometer cable and wire connector, then lift speedometer from instrument cluster.
6. To replace fuel gauge or clock, remove attaching screws, then slide gauge or clock from cluster and disconnect wire connector.

1983 REGAL

1. Disconnect ground cable from battery and speedometer cable from transmission or cruise control transducer.
2. Remove headlamp switch knob and pull knob from rear defogger switch, if equipped.
3. Remove left (cluster) bezel, grasping bezel with both hands and pulling it straight away from instrument panel.
4. Remove 5 screws securing cluster lens, trip odometer knob and the lens assembly.
5. Remove clock and fuel gauge.
6. Remove speedometer retaining screws and withdraw speedometer just enough to gain access to Vehicle Speed Sensor (VSS).
7. Disconnect speedometer cable, remove screw securing VSS optic head, then withdraw speedometer head from cluster.
8. Remove steering column cover, then disconnect shift indicator cable from steering column.
9. Remove 4 cluster retaining screws and the cluster.
10. Reverse procedure to install.

1984–87 REGAL

1. Disconnect ground cable from battery and speedometer cable from transmission or cruise control transducer.
2. Place gear selector lever in low and lower tilt wheel if equipped, then grasp left (cluster) trim bezel with both hands and pull bezel straight away from instrument panel.
3. Remove steering column lower cover, then disconnect shift indicator cable from steering column.
4. Remove 2 nuts securing column bracket, then lower steering column.
5. Remove 4 cluster retaining screws, then disconnect speedometer cable and any "hard wired" bulb sockets from cluster.
6. Pull cluster away from instrument panel just enough to gain access to Vehicle Speed Sensor (VSS), then remove screw securing VSS optic head to speedometer.
7. On models with digital cluster, release harness connector, then disconnect connector from cluster and remove screw securing cluster ground strap.
8. On all models, remove cluster.
9. Reverse procedure to install.

FULL SIZE MODELS EXC. RIVIERA

On these models, the speedometer and fuel gauge are removed from the instrument panel carrier as separate assemblies.

1. Disconnect battery ground cable.
2. If speedometer is to be removed, disconnect speedometer cable from transmission, cruise control transducer or union in engine compartment.
3. Pull steering column filler forward and remove headlamp switch knob as outlined previously.
4. Remove left (cluster) trim bezel, grasping bezel on both sides and pulling straight away from instrument panel.
5. Remove fuel gauge as follows:
   a. Remove 4 screws securing gauge.
   b. Withdraw gauge assembly from carrier, then remove bulb sockets and disconnect electrical connector from gauge.
6. Remove speedometer as follows:
   a. Remove 4 screws securing speedometer.
   b. Withdraw speedometer just far enough to gain access to cable and electrical connections.
   c. Remove bulb sockets and disconnect cable from speedometer.
   d. Remove screws securing speed sensor optic head and disconnect sensor from speedometer.
   e. Remove speedometer.
7. Reverse procedure to install components.

WINDSHIELD WIPER MOTOR

REPLACE

1. Disconnect battery and remove cowl screen.
2. Loosen nuts on wiper drive link to motor cranking arm and slip drive link off cranking arm.
3. Disconnect washer hoses and electrical connections.
4. Unfasten motor and remove. **On models with round motor, the motor must be in "Park" position when assembling crank arm to transmission drive link.**

WINDSHIELD WIPER TRANSMISSION

REPLACE

1. Disconnect battery ground cable and remove cowl vent screen or grille.
2. Disconnect wiper motor electrical connector.

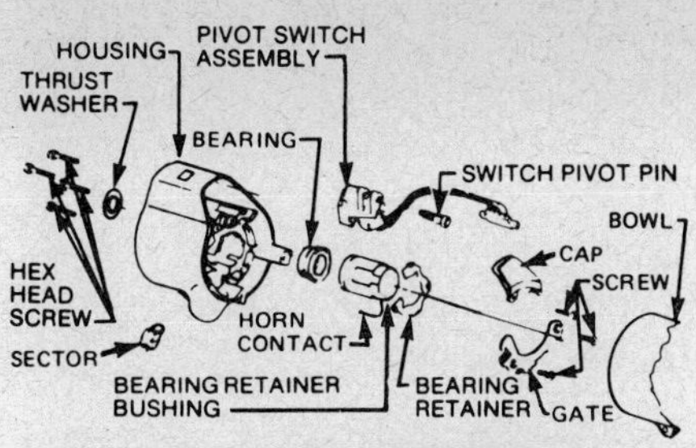

Fig. 11 Windshield wiper switch removal. Models w/standard column

3. Remove wiper arm and blade assemblies.
4. Loosen transmission drive link to motor crank arm attaching nuts, then disconnect drive link from crank arm.
5. Remove right and left transmission to body retaining screws and guide transmission and linkage through cowl opening. **On full size models equipped with round motor, remove transmission retaining screws from transmission being removed.**
6. Reverse procedure to install.

WINDSHIELD WIPER SWITCH

REPLACE

MODELS W/COLUMN MOUNTED SWITCH

1. Remove steering wheel as described under "Horn Sounder and Steering Wheel, Replace."
2. Remove turn signal switch as described under "Turn Signal Switch, Replace."
3. Remove ignition lock and buzzer as described under "Ignition Lock, Replace."
4. Remove and install cover and wiper switch as shown in **Figs. 10 & 11.**
5. Reverse remaining procedure to install.

MODELS LESS COLUMN MOUNTED SWITCH

1. Remove headlamp switch knob and escutcheon.
2. Remove trim plate.
3. Remove two switch attaching screws, then disconnect wire connector and remove switch.
4. Reverse procedure to install.

RADIO

REPLACE

When installing radio, be sure to adjust antenna trimmer for peak performance.

1982–85 RIVIERA

1. Disconnect battery ground cable.
2. Remove center trim plate by grasping firmly and pulling rearward.
3. Remove six screws from radio mounting bracket.
4. Remove six screws from instrument panel lower cover assembly, then pull cover assembly out from instrument panel enough to gain access to two screws attaching radio bracket to instrument panel lower tie bar. Remove screws.
5. Carefully pull radio assembly rearward to remove.
6. Disconnect radio harness connectors and antenna lead.
7. Reverse procedure to install.

1982–87 REGAL

1. Disconnect battery ground cable.
2. Remove cigar lighter, then the radio control knobs and escutcheons, as needed.
3. Remove center trim plate by grasping firmly and pulling rearward. **A flat blade screwdriver or putty knife can be used to pry up a corner of the center trim plate to aid in removal.**
4. Remove four screws attaching radio bracket to instrument panel.
5. Open glove box door and release spring retainers, then allow door to open fully.
6. Working through glove box door, loosen holding bracket nut on right rear side of radio, then remove antenna lead.
7. Carefully pull radio assembly rearward to remove.
8. Disconnect radio harness connectors, then remove bracket.
9. Reverse procedure to install.

1982–88 FULL SIZE MODELS EXC. RIVIERA

1. Disconnect battery ground cable.
2. Remove radio knobs, escutcheons and if equipped with rear defogger, rear defogger knob.
3. Remove lefthand instrument panel trim plate by removing headlight knob, then place gear selector in low. Using a suitable flat bladed screwdriver or putty knife, remove trim plate by gently prying edge, then lifting straight out.
4. Remove center trim plate attaching screws, then trim plate.
5. Remove screws attaching radio to radio bracket, then carefully pull radio rearward out of instrument panel.
6. Disconnect radio harness connectors and antenna lead.
7. Reverse procedure to install.

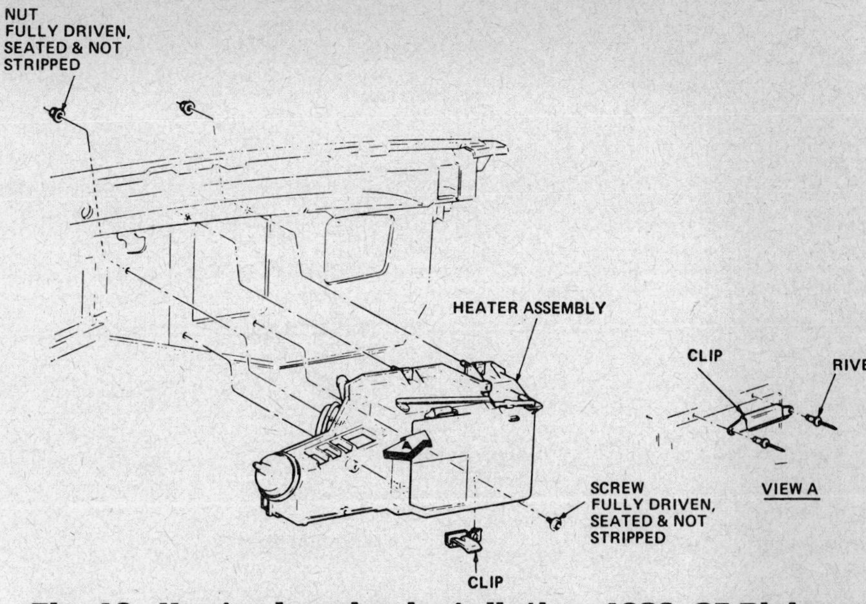

Fig. 12 Heater housing installation. 1982–85 Riviera

HEATER CORE

REPLACE

1982–85 RIVIERA

1. Disconnect battery ground cable and drain cooling system.
2. Disconnect heater hoses from heater core and install plugs in heater core outlets.
3. Remove instrument panel sound absorbers, then lower steering column.
4. Remove instrument cluster as described under Instrument Cluster, Replace.
5. Remove radio front speakers.
6. Remove screws attaching manifold to heater case.
7. Remove upper and lower instrument panel attaching screws.
8. Disconnect parking brake release cable.
9. Disconnect instrument panel wiring harness from dash wiring harness.
10. Disconnect righthand remote control mirror cable from instrument panel pad.
11. Disconnect speedometer cable and temperate control cable at heater case.
12. Disconnect radio, A/C wiring and vacuum lines, and all wiring necessary to remove instrument panel assembly. If equipped with pulse wiper, remove wiper switch, unlock wire connector from cluster carrier and separate pulse wiper jumper harness from wiper switch wire connector.

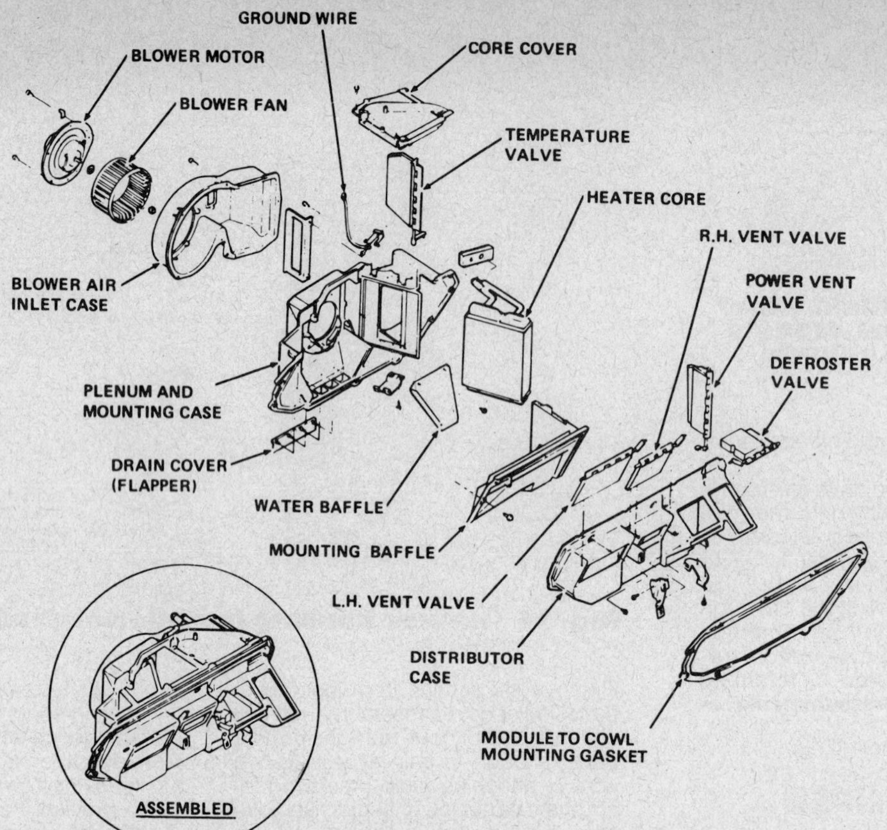

Fig. 13 Heater module assembly exploded view. 1982–87 Regal less A/C

13. Remove instrument panel and harness assembly.
14. Remove defroster ducts, then remove blower motor resistor.
15. Remove A/C-heater housing to dash panel nuts, **Fig. 12.**
16. Remove housing to dash screw and clip from inside vehicle, then remove housing assembly from dash.
17. Remove heater core from housing assembly.

1982–87 REGAL

Less Air Conditioning

1. Disconnect battery ground cable and partially drain cooling system.
2. Disconnect hoses from heater core, then the electrical connectors.
3. Remove front module retaining screws and module cover.
4. Remove heater core, **Fig. 13.**
5. Reverse procedure to install.

W/Air Conditioning

1. Disconnect battery ground cable and partially drain cooling system.
2. Disconnect hoses from heater core, then the electrical connectors from module.
3. Remove retaining bracket, ground strap, module rubber seal and screen.
4. Remove righthand windshield wiper arm.
5. Remove retaining screws from diagnostic connector, hi-blower relay and thermostatic switch.
6. Remove module top cover, then heater core, **Fig. 14.**
7. Reverse procedure to install.

1982–88 FULL SIZE MODELS EXC. RIVIERA

Less Air Conditioning

1. Disconnect battery ground cable and drain radiator.
2. Disconnect heater hoses from module, then the electrical connections from module front case.
3. Remove module front case attaching screws, then the heater core, **Fig. 15.**
4. Reverse procedure to install.

W/Air Conditioning

1. Disconnect battery ground cable and drain radiator.
2. Disconnect heater hoses from module.
3. Remove diagnostic connector and thermostatic switch from module.
4. Remove weather seal from top of module cover, then the cowl screen and windshield washer nozzle.
5. Remove module cover attaching screws.
6. Remove heater core retaining clip and the heater core from vehicle, **Fig. 16.**
7. Reverse procedure to install.

BLOWER MOTOR REPLACE

RIVIERA

1. Disconnect battery ground cable.
2. Remove right fender skirt to provide clearance for blower motor removal.
3. Disconnect wire connector and cooling hose.
4. Remove blower motor attaching screws and blower motor.

EXC. RIVIERA

1. Disconnect blower motor wiring.
2. Remove blower motor attaching screws and the blower motor, **Figs. 13, 14, 15 and 16.**

SPEED CONTROL ADJUSTMENTS

POWER UNIT, ADJUST

Units With Bead Chain

1. Make sure that engine hot idle speed is properly adjusted, then shut off engine and set carburetor choke to hot idle position.

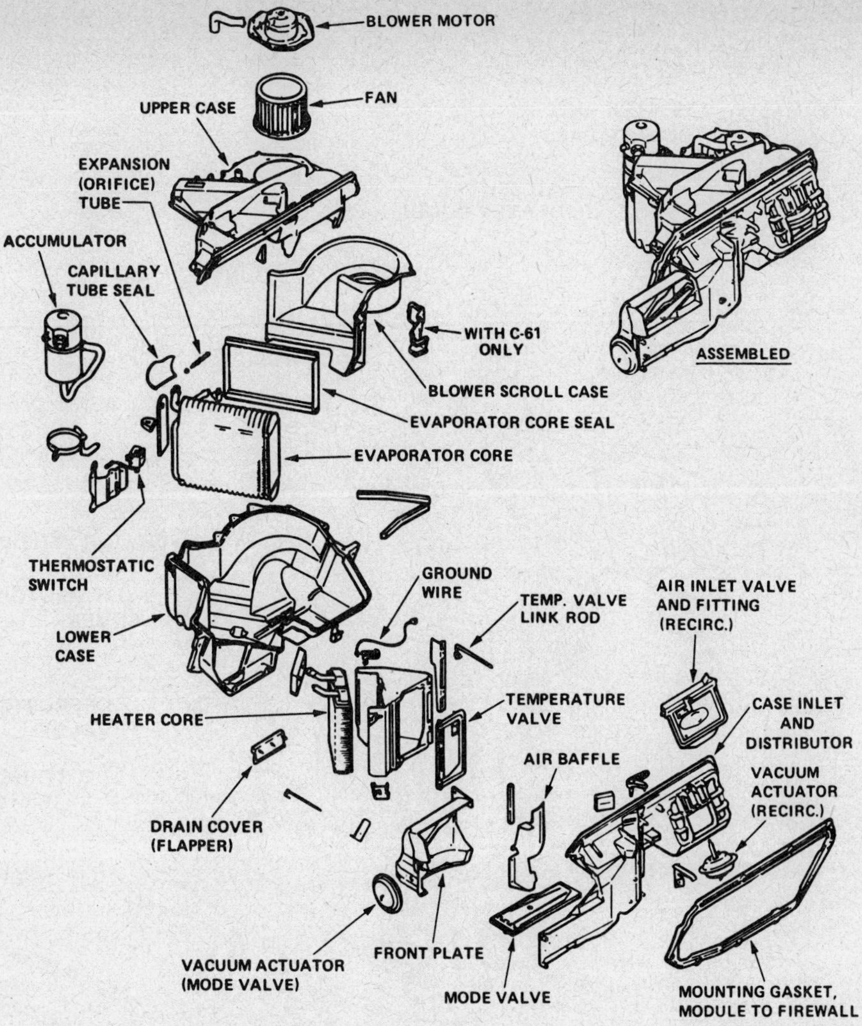

Fig. 14 Heater module assembly exploded view. 1982–87 Regal with A/C

2. Check slack in chain by disconnecting swivel from ball stud and holding chain taut at ball stud. Center of swivel should extend 1/8 inch beyond center of ball stud.
3. To adjust bead chain slack, remove retainer from swivel and chain assembly, then place chain into swivel cavities which permits chain to have slight slack.
4. Install retainer over swivel and chain assembly.

Units With Servo Rod

1. Make sure that engine hot idle speed is properly adjusted, then shut off engine and set carburetor choke to hot idle position.
2. Remove servo rod retainer, then adjust rod and install retainer in hole which provides some clearance between retainer and servo bushing. Clearance must not exceed width of one hole.

Units With Cable

1. Make sure that engine hot idle speed is properly adjusted, then shut off engine and set carburetor choke to hot idle position.
2. Remove cable pin retainer, then pull power unit end of cable toward power unit as far as it will go. If one of four holes in power unit tab aligns with cable pin, connect pin to tab with retainer.
3. If tab does not align with pin, move cable away from power unit until next closest tab hole aligns and connect pin to tab with retainer. **Do not force cable to make adjustment, as this will prevent engine from returning to idle.**

CRUISE SPEED ADJUSTMENT

1982

The cruise speed adjustment can be set as follows:

1. If car cruises below engagement speed, screw orifice tube on transducer outward.
2. If car cruises above engagement speed, screw orifice tube inward. **Each 1/4 turn of the orifice tube will change cruise speed about one mile per hour. Snug up locknut after each adjustment.**

BRAKE RELEASE SWITCH ADJUSTMENT

Fully depress brake pedal, then push switch and valve forward to contact bracket or arm. Pull pedal rearward with approximately 15 to 20 pounds of force to adjust switch and valve properly.

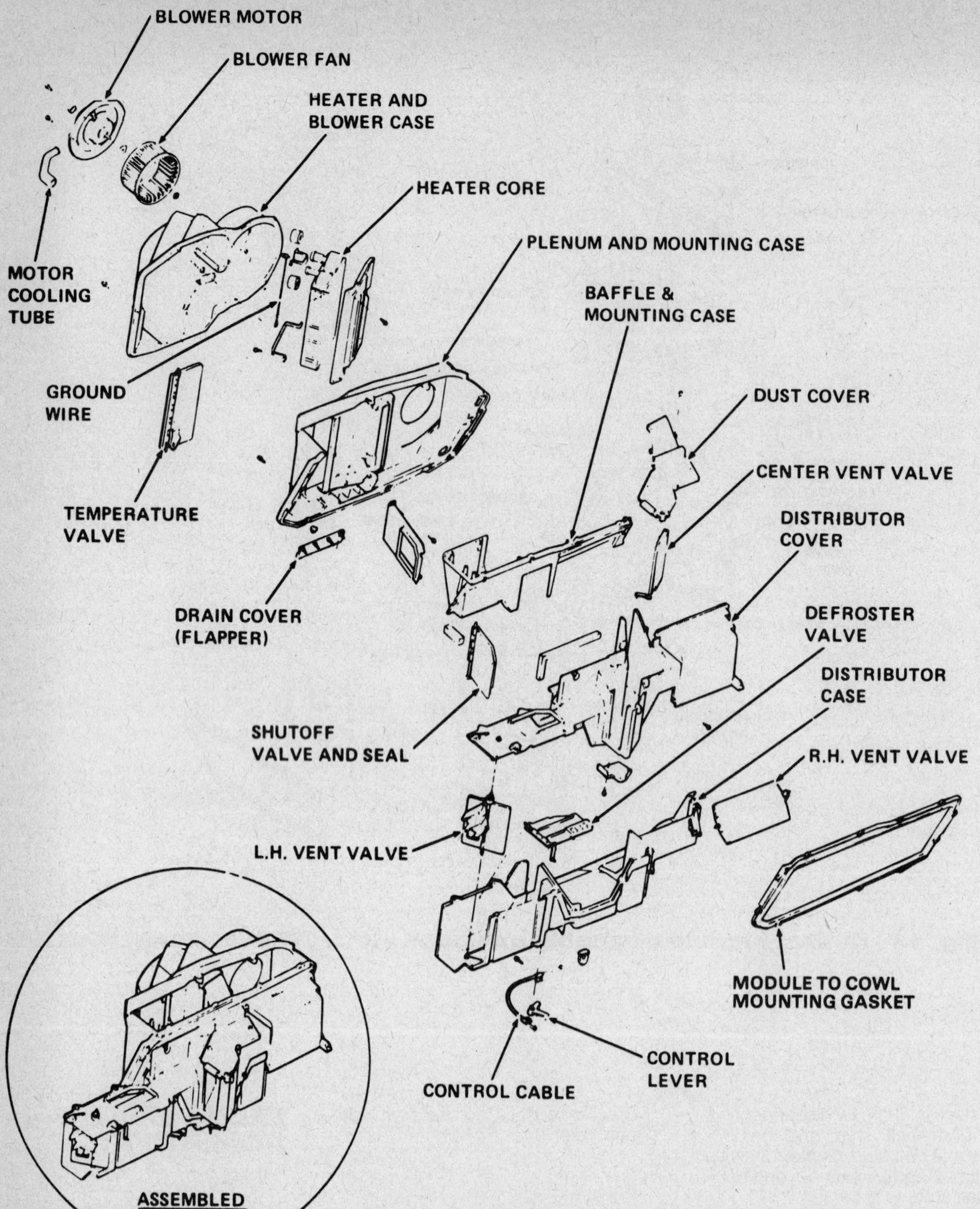

Fig. 15 Heater module assembly exploded view. 1982–88 Full Size exc. Riviera & models with A/C

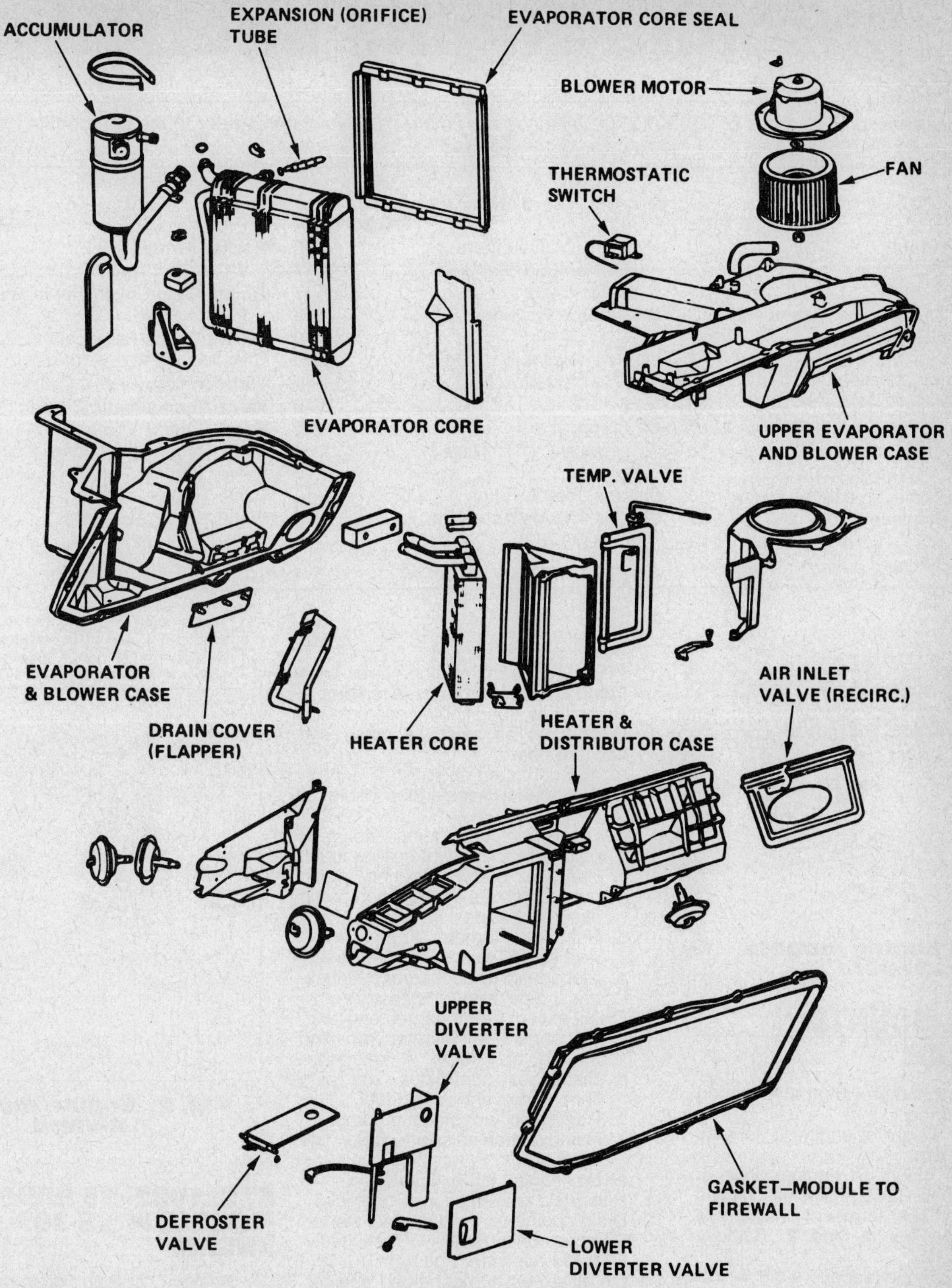

Fig. 16 Heater module assembly exploded view. 1982–88 Full Size with A/C exc. Riviera

Gasoline Engine Section

NOTE: For service procedures on V8-307 (5.0L) engines not covered in this chapter, refer to the appropriate Oldsmobile chapter.

INDEX

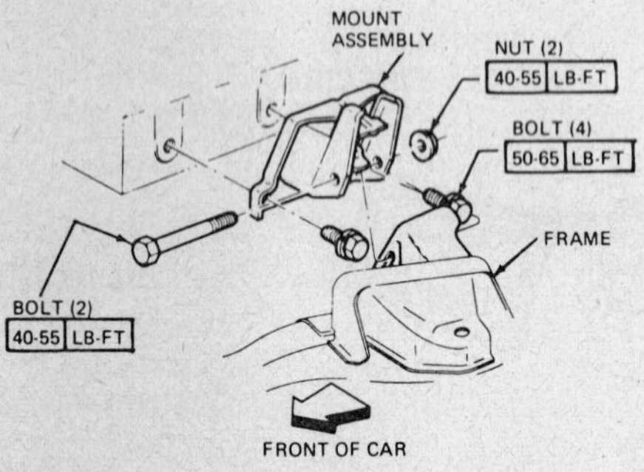

Fig. 1 Engine mounts. Riviera

ENGINE MOUNTS
REPLACE

1. Raise car and provide frame support at front of car.
2. Support weight of engine at forward edge of pan.
3. Remove mount to engine block or frame bolts. Raise engine slightly and remove mount to mount bracket bolt and nut, **Figs. 1 and 2.** Remove mount.
4. Reverse above procedureto install.

ENGINE
REPLACE
1982–85 RIVIERA

1. Remove hood. Scribe alignment marks on hood around hinge areas for alignment during installation.
2. Disconnect battery ground cable and remove air cleaner.
3. Drain cooling system and disconnect heater hoses.
4. Remove fan, pulleys and belts.
5. Remove upper and lower radiator hoses and fan shroud.
6. Disconnect transmission cooler lines from radiator, then remove radiator.
7. Remove air conditioning compressor.
8. Disconnect all electrical wires and vacuum hoses.
9. On turbocharged engines:
   a. Disconnect accelerator cable at carburetor.
   b. Disconnect fuel pump lines and plug lines to prevent spilling fuel.
   c. Remove power steering pump mounting bolts and position pump assembly aside.
   d. Remove alternator, then disconnect engine to body ground straps.
   e. Disconnect turbocharger outlet exhaust pipe from turbocharger.
10. On all except turbocharged engines:
    a. Disconnect accelerator rod and throttle valve cable.
    b. Disconnect fuel lines and plug lines to prevent spilling fuel.
    c. Remove power steering pump.
    d. Remove transmission cooler line bracket.
    e. Disconnect left exhaust pipe.
11. Raise and properly support vehicle.
12. Drain engine oil, then remove starter.
13. Remove converter shield, then the flywheel to converter bolts.
14. On all except turbocharged engines, disconnect right exhaust pipe and remove splash shield.
15. Remove the right transmission to engine bolts.
16. Remove right output shaft support bolts, then lower vehicle.
17. Support the final drive using a chain, then remove the remaining transmission to engine bolts.
18. Remove front motor mount support bolts.
19. Remove final drive to engine bracket.
20. Remove engine using a suitable hoist.
21. Reverse procedure to install.

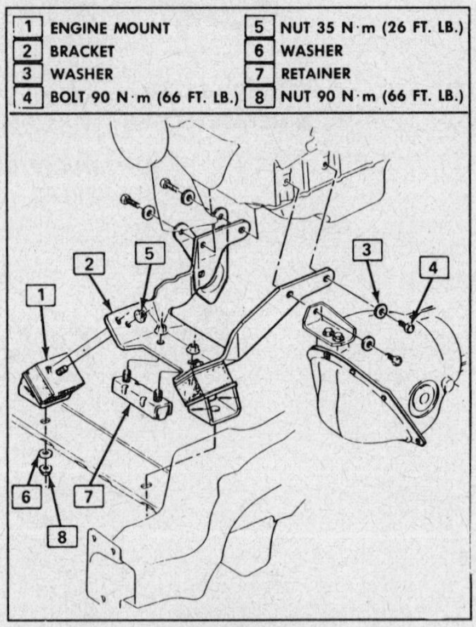

Fig. 2 Engine mounts. Riviera

EXC. 1982–85 RIVIERA & MODELS W/V8-307 ENGINE

1. Remove hood and drain radiator.
2. Disconnect battery ground cable and remove air cleaner.
3. Remove fan shroud, fan, pulleys and belts.
4. If equipped with A/C, disconnect compressor brackets and position compressor aside.
5. Remove power steering pump from bracket and position aside, then remove alternator.
6. Disconnect all hoses, linkages and electrical connections from engine.
7. Disconnect exhaust pipes and remove converter cover.

8. Remove flywheel to converter or pressure plate bolts, engine to transmission bolts and motor mount bolts.
9. Support transmission and remove engine using suitable hoist.
10. Reverse procedure to install.

MODELS W/V8-307 ENGINE

1. Disconnect battery ground cable and drain cooling system.
2. Remove air cleaner and hot air pipe, then scribe alignment marks and remove hood.
3. Remove all electrical connections, hoses and lines that will interfere with engine removal.
4. Remove upper radiator support, fan and drive belts, then disconnect transmission cooling lines and remove radiator.
5. Disconnect power steering pump and A/C compressor, if equipped, and position aside. **Do not disconnect hoses from pump or compressor.**
6. Disconnect throttle cable, then remove AIR pipe from catalytic converter.
7. Raise and support vehicle, then disconnect exhaust pipes from manifolds.
8. Remove converter cover, scribe alignment marks on converter and flywheel, then remove converter attaching bolts.
9. Remove engine mount attaching bolts, then the starter motor.
10. Remove all engine to transmission attaching bolts except the lower left hand bolt.
11. Attach suitable chain and hoist to engine, then lift transmission slightly and remove remaining transmission to engine bolt.
12. Lift engine slowly and remove from vehicle.
13. Reverse procedure to install.

INTAKE MANIFOLD REPLACE

V6-231 & 252

1. On fuel injected engines, relieve fuel pressure as follows:
   a. Disconnect fuel tank harness connector.
   b. Start engine and allow to run until engine stalls. Engage starter for approximately 3 seconds to completely clear lines of any remaining pressure.
2. On all engines, disconnect battery ground cable and remove air cleaner assembly.
3. Disconnect accelerator cable, fuel lines and cruise control cable or rod.
4. Drain cooling system, then remove upper radiator, heater and bypass hoses.
5. Disconnect all wiring and remove all accessory mounting brackets that will interfere with manifold removal.
6. If applicable, remove distributor cap and rotor to gain access to lefthand intake manifold torx head bolt. Use tool J-24394 to remove torx head bolt.

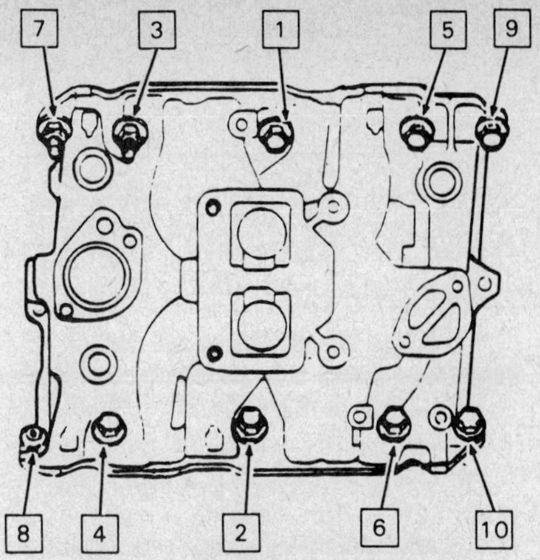

Fig. 3 Intake manifold tightening sequence. V6-231 & 252

7. Remove remaining attaching bolts and the intake manifold.
8. Reverse procedure to install. Refer to **Fig. 3** for bolt tightening sequence.

CYLINDER HEAD REPLACE

V6-231 & 252

Prior to reinstalling cylinder head bolts, coat the head bolts with a suitable heavy body thread sealer. This is to prevent coolant leakage, as the head bolt holes extend into the water jacket.

An accurate torque wrench should be used when installing head bolts. Uneven tightening of the head bolts can distort the cylinder bores, causing compression loss and excessive oil consumption.

1. Drain coolant and disconnect battery.
2. Remove intake manifold as outlined previously.
3. When removing right cylinder head, remove alternator and/or A/C compressor with mounting bracket and position aside. Do not disconnect hoses from A/C compressor.
4. When removing left cylinder head, remove oil dipstick and power steering pump, and secure pump aside leaving hoses connected.
5. Disconnect exhaust manifold from head to be removed.
6. Remove rocker arm shaft and lift out pushrods.
7. Remove cylinder head.
8. On 1982-85 engines, reverse procedure to install and tighten bolts gradually and evenly in the sequence shown, **Figs. 4 and 5.**
9. On 1986-87 V6-231, reverse procedure to install and note the following:
   a. Install cylinder head, then apply a suitable sealant to bolt threads.
   b. Insert cylinder head bolts, then torque to 25 ft. lbs. in sequence shown, **Fig. 5.**
   c. Torque each bolt an additional 1/4 turn in tightening sequence. **If 60 ft. lbs. of torque is obtained during above step, stop, do not complete 90° turn.**
   d. Again torque each bolt an additional 1/4 turn in tightening sequence. **If 60 ft. lbs. of torque is obtained during above step, stop, do not complete 90° turn.**

ROCKER ARMS

V6-231 & 252

A nylon retainer is used to retain the rocker arm. To remove them, break them below their heads with a chisel, or pry out with channel locks, **Fig. 6.** Production rocker arms can be installed in any sequence since the arms are identical.

Replacement rocker arms for all engines are identified with a stamping, right (R) and left (L), **Fig. 7** and must be installed as shown in **Fig. 8.**

To install rocker arms, position arm on rocker shaft, centering it over the 1/4 inch hole in the rocker shaft. Install new rocker arm retainers in the provided holes using a 1/2 inch or larger drift to seat them.

VALVE ARRANGEMENT

FRONT TO REAR

V6-231 & 252:
Right .... E-I-I-E-I-E
Left .... E-I-E-I-I-E

VALVE LIFT SPECIFICATIONS

Engine	Year	Intake	Exhaust
V6-231①	1982-84	.3570	.3660
V6-252	1982-84	.3570	.3660

①—Exc. turbocharged engine.

VALVE TIMING

INTAKE OPENS BEFORE TDC

Engine	Year	Degrees
V6-231	1982-84	16
V6-252	1982-84	16

VALVES ADJUST

V6-231 & 252

These engines are equipped with hydraulic valve lifters, which have zero lash clearance. No provision for adjustment is provided.

VALVE GUIDES

The valve guides are an integral part of the cylinder head and cannot be replaced.

If valve stem clearance is excessive, the valve guide must be reamed and an oversize valve installed. Valves are available in the oversize of .010 inch.

Abnormal oil consumption or detonation on some 1982 V6-252 engines may be caused by intake valve seals

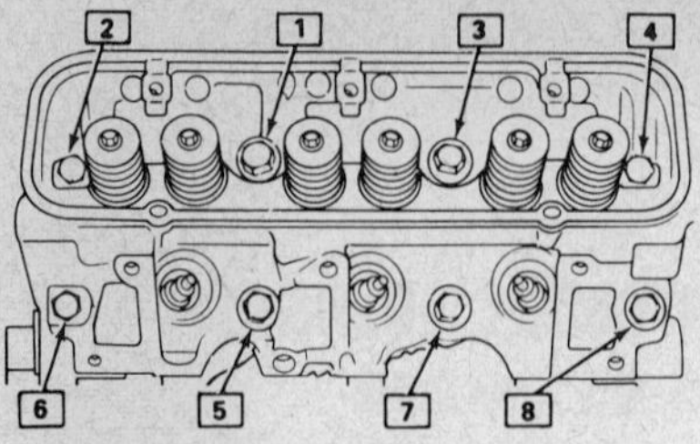

Fig. 4 Cylinder head tightening sequence. 1982–83 V6-231 & 252

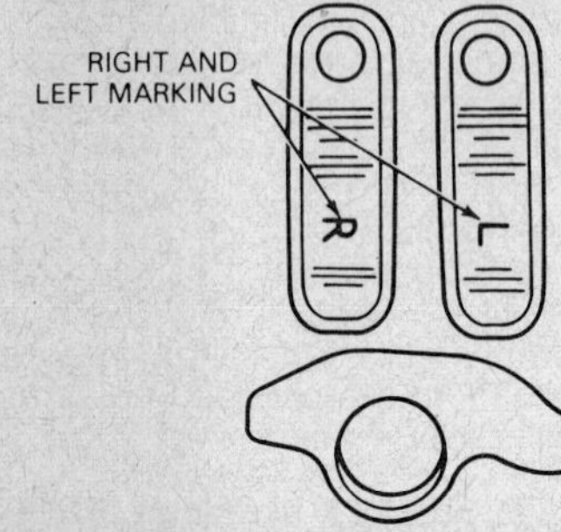

Fig. 7 Service rocker arm identification. V6-231 & 252

that have lifted off the valve guide. To correct this condition, a smaller replacement seal, Part No. 25516279, should be installed onto valve guide. Since valve guide outside diameter must be reduced from .605 to .552 to accept the new seal, it will be necessary to rework the valve guides prior to seal installation. Using valve guide cutting tool KL1440, or equivalent, perform the following operation.

1. Remove cylinder head as outlined in "Cylinder Head, Replace" procedure.
2. Remove all intake and exhaust valves from cylinder head to prevent metal chips from lodging in exhaust guide mechanism.
3. Insert cutting tool into chuck of low speed drill, oil tool pilot, then insert pilot into intake valve guide.
4. Applying steady pressure to cutting tool, machine valve guide until small cutter block in tool has cut chamfer on top of valve guide.
5. Thoroughly clean cylinder head and guides, then remove any burrs from valve stem and guides with a fine stone.
6. Oil valves and install them into guides.
7. Install new seals onto valve guides, then reassemble cylinder head assembly.
8. Install cylinder head.

HYDRAULIC VALVE LIFTERS

Failure of hydraulic valve lifters is generally caused by an inadequate oil supply or dirt. An air leak at the intake side of the oil pump or too much oil in the engine will cause air bubbles in the oil supply to the lifters, causing them to collapse. This is a probable cause of trouble if several lifters fail to function, but air in the oil is an unlikely cause of failure of a single unit.

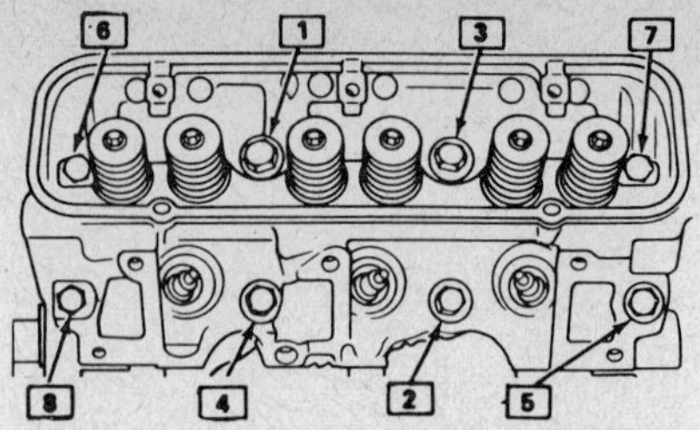

Fig. 5 Cylinder bolt tightening sequence. 1984 V6-252 & 1984–87 V6-231

The valve lifters may be lifted out of their bores after removing the rocker arms, pushrods and intake manifold. Adjustable pliers with taped jaws may be used to remove lifters that are stuck due to varnish, carbon or dirt.

TIMING CASE COVER REPLACE

V6-231 & 252

1. Drain cooling system and remove radiator and heater return hose.
2. Remove fan, pulleys and belts.
3. Remove crankshaft pulley and balancer.
4. If equipped with power steering, remove any pump bracket bolts attached to timing chain cover and loosen and remove any other bolts necessary that will allow pump and brackets to be positioned aside.
5. Remove fuel pump.
6. Remove alternator and brackets.
7. Remove distributor cap and pull spark plug wire retainers off brackets on rocker arm cover. Swing distributor cap with wires attached aside.
8. Disconnect distributor wiring, then remove distributor. If chain and sprockets are not to be disturbed, note position of distributor rotor for installation in the same position.
9. Loosen and slide clamp on thermostat bypass hose rearward.
10. Remove bolts attaching chain cover to block.
11. Remove two oil pan-to-chain cover bolts and remove cover.
12. Reverse procedure to install, noting data shown in **Fig. 9.** Remove the oil pump cover and pack the space around the oil pump gears completely full of petroleum jelly. There must be no air space left inside the pump. Reinstall the cover using a new gasket. This step is very important as the oil pump may lose its prime whenever the pump, pump cover or timing chain cover is disturbed. If the pump is not packed it may not begin to pump oil as soon as the engine is started.

TIMING CHAIN REPLACE

V6-231 & 252

1. With the timing case cover removed as outlined above, temporarily install

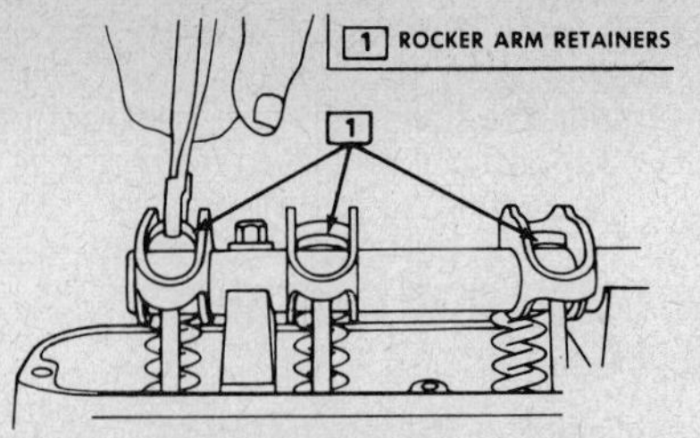

Fig. 6 Rocker arm retainer removal. V6-231 & 252

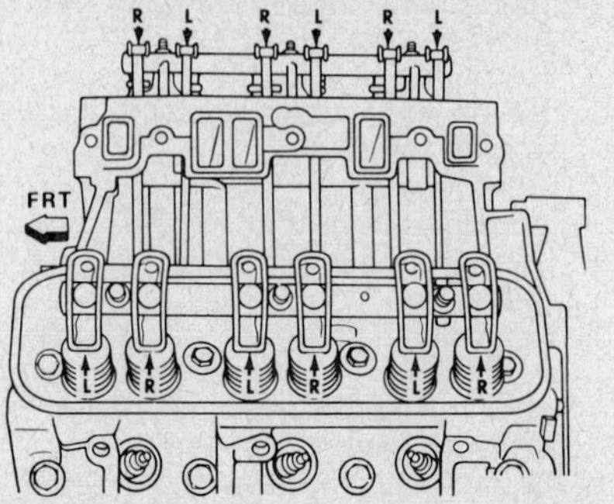

Fig. 8 Service rocker arms installation. V6-231 & 252

the vibration damper bolt and washer in end of crankshaft.
2. Turn crankshaft so sprockets are positioned as shown in **Fig. 10.** Use a sharp rap on a wrench handle to start the vibration damper bolt out without disturbing the position of the sprockets.
3. Remove oil slinger.
4. Remove distributor drive gear, fuel pump eccentric, and chain dampener, if applicable.
5. Use two large screwdrivers to alternately pry the camshaft sprocket then the crankshaft sprocket forward until the camshaft sprocket is free. Then remove camshaft sprocket and chain, and pull crankshaft sprocket off crankshaft.
6. To install, assemble chain on sprockets and slide sprockets on their respective shafts with the "O" marks on the sprockets lined up as shown, **Fig. 10.**
7. Complete the installation in the reverse order of removal.

CAMSHAFT REPLACE

V6-231 & 252

Rods and pistons should be assembled and installed as shown in **Fig. 11.**

Measure connecting rod side clearance using a suitable feeler gauge. Clearance obtained should be .006-.023 for 1982-84 engines, or .003-.015 inch for 1985-87 engines.

If engine is in the car, the radiator, grille and A/C components will have to be removed. If engine is out of car, proceed as follows:

1. To remove camshaft, remove intake manifold, rocker arm/shaft assemblies, pushrods and valve lifters.
2. Remove timing chain and sprockets.
3. Slide camshaft out of engine, using care not to mar the bearing surfaces.

Fig. 9 Timing chain cover installation. V6-231 & 252

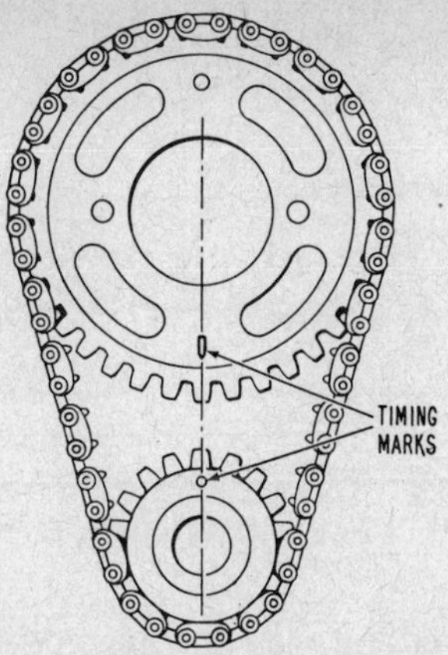

Fig. 10 Valve timing mark alignment. V6-231 & 252

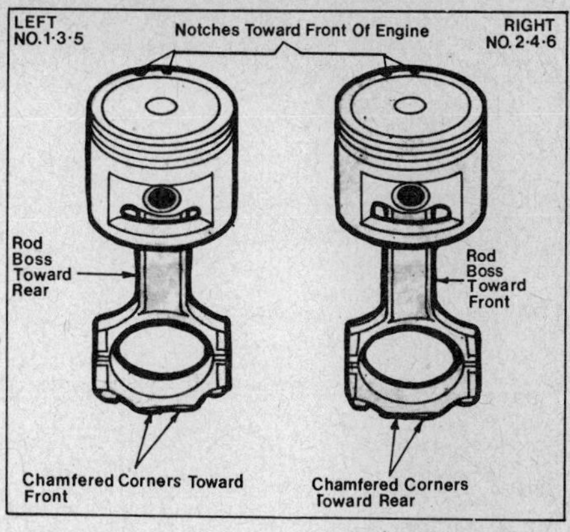

Fig. 11 Piston and connecting rod installation. V6-231 & 252

PISTONS & RODS ASSEMBLE

V6-231 & 252

Rods and pistons should be assembled and installed as shown in **Fig. 11.**

Measure connecting rod side clearance using a suitable feeler gauge. Clearance obtained should be .006-.023 for 1982-84 engines, or .003-.015 inch for 1985-87 engines.

Some 1982 V6-231 (Vin A) and V6-252 engines may exhibit engine noise just above idle with transmission in gear. The noise can best be described as a light ticking sound, similar to overhead valve noise, but appears to come from the bottom portion of the engine and is most pronounced at the rear of the front wheel opening. This noise may be caused by excessive side clearance between the connecting rod and the crankshaft journal thrust surfaces on the number one, three or five cylinder. The clearance should be checked using a dial indicator or feeler gauge. If a feeler gauge is used, the gauge should be placed next to the thrust surface on the counterweight and not next to the thin wall section between two adjacent rods. Make sure the feeler gauge is fully seated on the journal and not on top of the narrow raised thrust surface. Clearance measurements should be made at several places around the journal. If rod clearance exceeds .015 inch on the above mentioned cylinders, the rod should be replaced. A new rod, Part No. 25516444, is available which is .010 inch thicker than the original. The new rod will reduce the clearance to the low side of the specified limits.

PISTONS, PINS & RINGS

V6-231 & 252

Pistons are available in standard sizes and oversizes of .005, .010 and .030 inch.

Rings are furnished in standard sizes and oversizes of .010 and .030 inch.

Piston pins are supplied in standard sizes only.

OIL PAN REPLACE

V6-231 & 252

Exc. 1982–85 Riviera

1. Raise and support front of vehicle.
2. Remove flywheel cover and exhaust crossover pipe. Remove engine mount retaining bolts, then raise engine with a suitable lifting device to gain clearance.
3. Drain engine oil into a suitable container.
4. Remove oil pan bolts, then pan.
5. Reverse procedure to install. **Some engines use R.T.V. silicone sealer instead of a gasket for oil pan to crankcase sealing. When replacing the oil pan, either R.T.V. sealer or a gasket can be used during reassembly. If R.T.V. sealer is used, the pan rail and block sealing surfaces should be cleaned thoroughly and a 1/4 inch bead of sealant applied evenly to the pan rail, avoiding any breaks or gaps in the sealer during application.**

1982–85 Riviera

1. Disconnect battery ground cable.
2. Remove one final drive to transmission bolts.
3. Install suitable engine support fixture.
4. Raise and support vehicle.
5. Remove idler arm bracket from frame, then position steering wheel at left lock.
6. Disconnect drive axles from output shafts, then battery cable support from output shaft support.
7. Disconnect output shaft support from engine block.
8. Remove remaining final drive to transmission bolts.
9. Position suitable transmission jack under final drive, then remove final drive cover and final drive unit.
10. Remove starter, then flywheel cover.
11. Remove oil pan bolts, then oil pan.
12. Reverse procedure to install. **Some engines use R.T.V. silicone sealer instead of a gasket for oil pan to crankcase sealing. When replacing the oil pan, either R.T.V. sealer or a gasket can be used during reassembly. If R.T.V. sealer is used, the pan rail and block sealing surfaces should be cleaned thoroughly and a 1/4 inch bead of sealant applied evenly to the pan rail, avoiding any breaks or gaps in the sealer during application.**

V8-307

1. Disconnect battery ground cable, then remove oil level indicator.
2. Remove fan shroud, then raise and support vehicle.
3. Drain engine oil, then remove flywheel cover and disconnect crossover pipe.
4. Remove starter motor.
5. Support engine using tools BT-6501 and BT-7109, or equivalents, then remove motor mount to engine block retaining bolts.
6. Raise engine as high as possible, using tools mentioned in previous step, then remove oil pan attaching bolts and the oil pan.
7. Reverse procedure to install and note the following:
   a. Apply sealer 1050026 or equivalent to pan side gaskets, then position gaskets onto pan side rails.
   b. Install front and rear rubber seals, then apply a bead of RTV sealant at points where seals meet side gaskets.

MAIN & ROD BEARINGS

V6-231 & 252

Main bearings are available in standard sizes and undersizes of .001, .002, and .010 inch.

Rod bearings are furnished in standard sizes and undersizes of .001, .002 and .010 inch, **Fig. 12.**

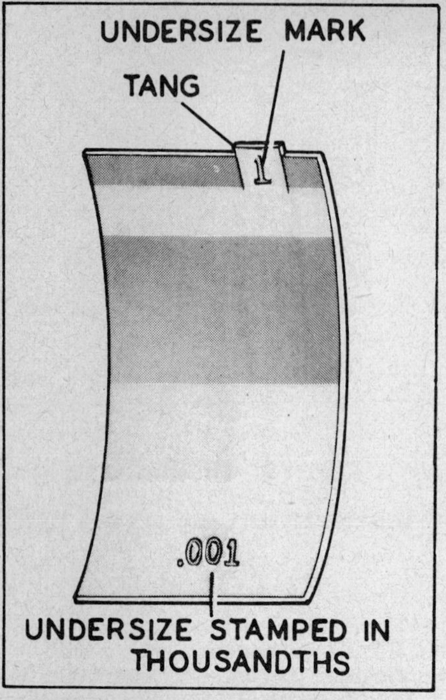

Fig. 12 Connecting rod and main bearing insert identification

CRANKSHAFT REAR OIL SEAL REPAIR

Since the braided fabric seal used on these engines can be replaced only when the crankshaft is removed, the following repair procedure is recommended.

1. Remove oil pan and bearing cap.
2. Drive end of old seal gently into groove, using a suitable tool, until packed tight. This may vary between 1/4 and 3/4 inch depending on amount of pack required.
3. Repeat previous step for other end of seal.
4. Measure and note amount that seal was driven up on one side. Using the old seal removed from bearing cap, cut a length of seal the amount previously noted plus 1/16 inch.
5. Repeat previous step for other side of seal.
6. Pack cut lengths of seal into appropriate side of seal groove. A guide tool, J-21526-1, and packing tool, J-21526-2, may be used since these tools have been machined to provide a built-in stop.
7. Install new seal in bearing cap.
8. Apply thin coat of suitable sealer to block contact surfaces of bearing cap, then install cap and torque bolts to specifications.

OIL PUMP

REMOVAL

1. To remove pump, take off oil filter.
2. Disconnect wire from oil pressure indicator switch in filter bypass valve cap (if so equipped).
3. Remove screws retaining oil pump cover to timing chain cover. Remove cover and slide out pump gears. Replace any parts not serviceable.
4. Check relief valve in its bore in cover, **Fig. 13**. Valve should have no more clearance than an easy slip fit. If any perceptible side shake can be felt, the valve and/or cover should be replaced.
5. The filter bypass valve should be flat and free of nicks and scratches.

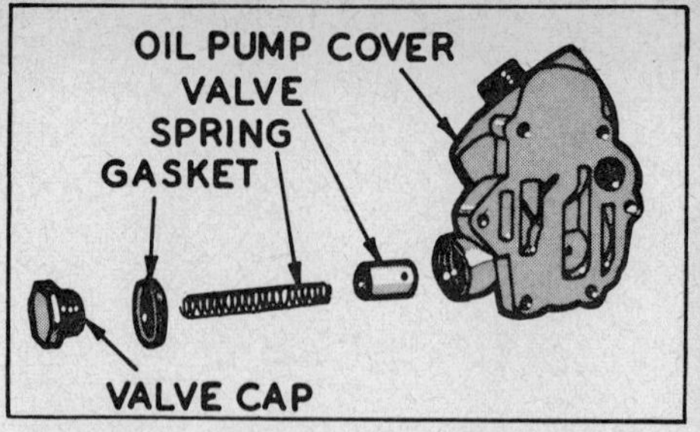

Fig. 13 Oil pump cover and relief valve exploded view

ASSEMBLY & INSTALLATION

1. Lubricate and install pressure relief valve and spring in bore of pump cover. Install cap and gasket. Torque cap to 30-35 ft. lbs.
2. Install pump gears and shaft in pump body section of timing chain cover to check gear end clearance. Check clearance as shown in **Fig. 14.** If clearance is less than .002 inch, check timing chain cover for evidence of wear.
3. If gear end clearance is satisfactory, remove gears and pack gear pocket full of petroleum jelly, not chassis lube.
4. Reinstall gears so petroleum jelly is forced into every cavity of gear pocket and between teeth of gears. Unless pump is properly packed, it may not prime when engine is started.

Fig. 14 Checking oil pump gear and cover clearance

5. Install cover and tighten screws alternately and evenly. Final tightening is 10-15 ft. lbs. torque. Install filter on nipple.

BELT TENSION DATA

Belt	New Lbs.	Used Lbs.
5/16 inch	80	50
3/8 inch less cogs	140	70
3/8 inch w/cogs	—	60
15/32 inch	165	90

WATER PUMP REPLACE

V6-231 & 252

Drain cooling system, being sure to drain into a clean container if antifreeze solution is to be saved. Remove the fan belt and disconnect all hoses from water pump. Remove water pump.

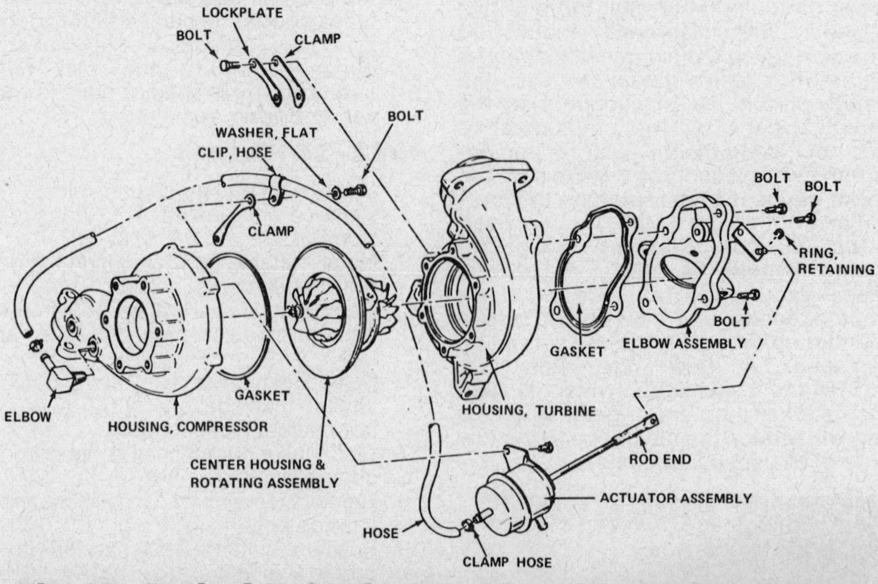

Fig. 15 Typical turbocharger assembly exploded view

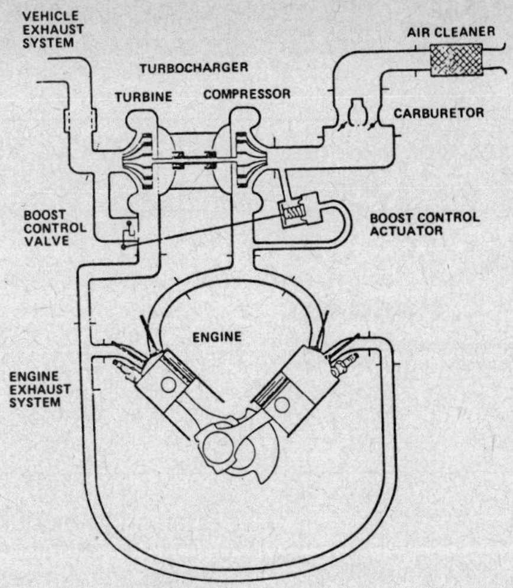

Fig. 16 Turbocharger system schematic. V6-231

FUEL PUMP REPLACE

ELECTRIC PUMP

The fuel system on models with fuel injected engines is under high pressure, which must be relieved prior to opening the system. To relieve system pressure: remove "Fuel Pump" fuse from fuse block, start and run engine until fuel remaining in lines is consumed, crank engine for approximately 3 seconds to ensure complete pressure relief, then turn off ignition and reinstall fuse.

1. Disconnect battery ground cable.
2. Raise and support vehicle. **If vehicle is raised on center post type hoist, place suitable supports under front of vehicle to aid stability when fuel tank is removed.**
3. Support fuel tank, then remove retaining straps and screw securing ground strap to chassis.
4. Lower tank, disconnect fuel and vapor lines and electrical connectors from sending unit, then remove tank from under vehicle.
5. Release cam lock retainer securing sending unit using a J-24187 or equivalent, then withdraw sending unit/pump assembly from tank.
6. Slide pump up into connector hose and separate pump from bottom retainer.
7. When pump clears bottom retainer, pull pump from connecting hose to remove.
8. Reverse procedure to install.

MECHANICAL PUMP

Before installing the pump, it is good practice to crank the engine so that the nose of the camshaft eccentric is out of the way of the fuel pump rocker arm when the pump is installed. In this way there will be the least amount of tension on the rocker arm, thereby easing the installation of the pump.

1. Disconnect fuel lines from fuel pump.
2. Remove fuel pump mounting bolts and the fuel pump.
3. Remove all gasket material from the pump and block gasket surfaces. Apply sealer to both sides of new gasket.
4. Position gasket on pump flange and hold pump in position against its mounting surface. Make sure rocker arm is riding on camshaft eccentric.
5. Press pump tight against its mounting. Install retaining screws and tighten them alternately.
6. Connect fuel lines. Then operate engine and check for leaks.

TURBOCHARGER

The turbocharger, **Fig. 15,** is used to increase engine power on a demand basis, therefore allowing a smaller, more economical engine to be used. The turbocharged V6-231 is available with either two or four barrel carburetion on 1982-83 models and with sequential port fuel injection on 1984-87 models.

As engine load increases and the throttle opens, more air-fuel mixture is drawn into the combustion chambers. As the increased volume is burned, a larger volume of high energy exhaust gasses enters the engine exhaust system and is directed through the turbocharger turbine housing, **Fig. 16.** Some of the exhaust gas energy is used to increase the speed of the turbine wheel which is connected to the compressor wheel. The increased speed of the compressor wheel compresses the air-fuel mixture and delivers the compressed air-fuel mixture to the intake manifold, **Fig. 16.** The high pressure in the intake manifold allows a denser charge to enter the combustion chambers, in turn developing more engine power during the combustion cycle.

The intake manifold pressure (Boost) is controlled to a maximum value by an exhaust gas bypass valve (Wastegate). The wastegate allows a portion of the exhaust gas to bypass the turbine wheel, thereby not increasing turbine speed. On 1982-83 models, the wastegate is operated by a spring loaded diaphragm device sensing the pressure differential across the compressor. When intake manifold pressure reaches a set value above ambient pressure, the wastegate begins to bypass the exhaust gas. On 1984-87 models, an electronic wastegate is used. In this system, a pulse width modulated solenoid has been positioned between the manifold and wastegate diaphragm. Information regarding air flow, engine RPM, transmission gear and detonation is collected and analyzed by the Electronic Control Module. If the engine will tolerate additional boost, the solenoid signals the wastegate accordingly. Inside the wastegate, the exhaust divert valve is normally closed, allowing boost pressure to rise until the mass air flow called for by the ECM is satisfied. When air flow reaches this level, the exhaust divert valve opens, allowing the exhaust gas to divert around the turbine and flow directly into the exhaust system.

Diesel Engine Section

NOTE: Refer to the Oldsmobile Diesel Engines chapter for service procedures on V6-262 (4.3L) & V8-350 (5.7L) diesel engines not found in this section.

INDEX

ENGINE REPLACE

V8-350 ENGINE

Exc. Riviera

1. Disconnect ground cable from batteries and drain cooling system.
2. Remove air cleaner.
3. Scribe hood hinge locations and remove hood.
4. Disconnect ground wires at inner fender and the engine ground strap at right cylinder head.
5. Disconnect radiator hoses, oil cooler lines, heater hoses, vacuum hoses, power steering hoses from gear, A/C compressor with brackets and hoses attached, fuel pump hose from fuel pump and the wiring.
6. Remove hairpin clip from bellcrank.
7. Remove throttle and throttle valve cables from intake manifold brackets and position cables aside.
8. Remove upper radiator support and the radiator.
9. Raise and support vehicle.
10. Disconnect exhaust pipes from exhaust manifold.
11. Remove torque converter cover and the three bolts securing torque converter to flywheel.
12. Remove engine mount bolts or nuts.
13. Remove three engine to transmission bolts on the right side.
14. Disconnect starter wiring and remove starter.
15. Lower vehicle.
16. Attach suitable engine lifting equipment to engine. Support transmission with a suitable jack.
17. Remove the three engine to transmission bolts on the left side.
18. Remove engine from vehicle.
19. Reverse procedure to install.

Riviera

1. Disconnect battery ground cable and drain cooling system.
2. Remove radiator upper support.
3. Remove air cleaner assembly.
4. Scribe hood hinge locations and remove hood.
5. Disconnect engine ground strap.
6. Disconnect upper and lower radiator hoses from engine.
7. Disconnect transmission oil cooler lines from radiator.
8. Disconnect heater hoses from water pump and water control valve.
9. Remove radiator, fan and the shroud.
10. Disconnect power steering pump bracket from engine and position aside without disconnecting lines.
11. Disconnect A/C compressor bracket from engine and position aside without disconnecting lines.
12. Disconnect fuel lines.
13. Disconnect throttle cable, vacuum hoses and electrical connections.
14. Disconnect lefthand exhaust pipe from manifold.
15. On left side of engine, remove through bolt and bracket securing final drive to engine.
16. Raise and support engine.
17. Remove flywheel shield.
18. Disconnect righthand exhaust pipe from manifold.
19. Disconnect starter motor wiring and remove starter motor.
20. Remove converter to flywheel bolts. Mark location of converter on flywheel for alignment during installation.
21. Remove splash shield.
22. Remove engine front mounting attaching nuts.
23. Remove two bolts securing righthand output shaft support brackets. Using a sharp tool, scribe a mark around the washers as far as possible. Use these scribe marks to position bracket upon installation.
24. Remove lower righthand transmission to engine attaching bolts. One bolt retains the modulator line clip.
25. Use a suitable length of chain to retain final drive in vehicle.
26. Lower vehicle and attach suitable engine lifting equipment to engine.
27. Remove the remaining transmission to engine bolts. It may be necessary to raise or lower transmission with a suitable jack to facilitate bolt removal.
28. Raise engine and remove from vehicle.
29. Reverse procedure to install.

V6-262 ENGINE

1. Disconnect battery ground cable and drain cooling system.
2. Scribe reference marks, then remove hood from vehicle.
3. Disconnect all hoses, lines and electrical connectors from engine. **Do not disconnect wires from the starter.**
4. Disconnect throttle cable, transmission T.V. or detent cable at injection pump and engine brackets.
5. Remove upper radiator support and radiator from vehicle.
6. Raise and support vehicle.
7. Disconnect exhaust pipes at exhaust manifold.
8. Remove torque converter flywheel cover and three torque converter to flywheel bolts.
9. Remove starter and two engine mount bolts.
10. From the right side of the vehicle, remove three engine to transmission bolts.
11. Lower vehicle and position suitable lifting equipment onto engine.
12. Using a suitable jack, raise transmission enough to gain access to the other three transmission to engine bolts. Remove bolts and lift engine from vehicle.
13. Reverse procedure to install. Torque flywheel to torque converter bolts to 35 ft. lbs. Torque two engine mount bolts to 55 ft. lbs.

Rear Axle, Propeller Shaft & Brakes

INDEX

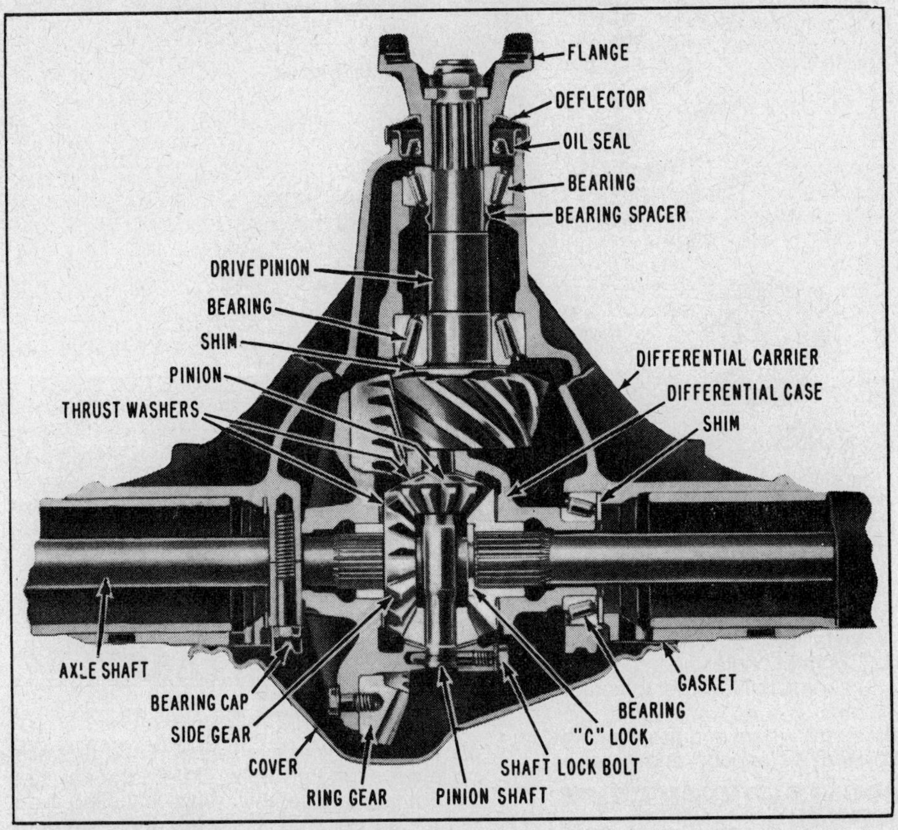

Fig. 1 Differential assembly cross sectional view

REAR AXLE DESCRIPTION

Fig. 1 illustrates the type rear drive axle assembly used on Buicks. When necessary to overhaul any of these units, refer to the Rear Axle Specifications table in this chapter.

In this rear axle, **Fig. 1,** the drive pinion is mounted in two tapered roller bearings which are preloaded by a collapsible spacer. The pinion is positioned by shims located between a shoulder on the drive pinion and the rear bearing. The front bearing is held in place by a large nut.

The differential is supported in the carrier by two tapered roller side bearings. These are preloaded by inserting shims between the bearings and the pedestals. The differential assembly is positioned for proper ring gear and pinion backlash by varying these shims. The ring gear is bolted to the case. The case houses two side gears in mesh with two pinions mounted on a pinion axle which is anchored in the case by a spring pin. The pinions and side gears are backed by thrust washers.

REAR AXLE ASSEMBLY REPLACE

It is not necessary to remove the rear axle assembly for any normal repairs, but if the housing must be replaced, the assembly may be removed as follows:

1. Raise vehicle and support using jack stands under both frame side rails.
2. Mark rear universal joint and flange for proper reassembly and disconnect rear joint.
3. Push propeller shaft as far forward as possible and wire up out of way.
4. Disconnect parking brake cables and rear brake hose. Cover brake hose opening to prevent entrance of dirt.
5. Support axle with jack and disconnect shock absorbers at lower ends.
6. Disconnect upper control arms at axle housing, then lower axle and remove coil springs.
7. Disconnect lower control arms and remove axle assembly.

AXLE SHAFT REPLACE

Design allows for axle shaft endplay of .025 inch on "C", "G", "K", "O" and "P" (7½ inch) axles, and .032 inch on "P" (except 7½ inch). These axles may be identified by the third letter located on the right rear tube on the forward side. This endplay can be checked with the wheel and brake drum removed by measuring the difference between the end of the housing and the axle shaft flange while moving the axle shaft in and out by hand.

Endplay over this is excessive. Compensating for all the endplay by inserting a shim inboard of the bearing in the housing is not recommended since it ignores the endplay of the bearing itself, and may result in improper seating of the gasket or backing plate against the housing. If endplay is excessive, the axle shaft and bearing assembly should be removed and the cause of the excessive endplay determined and corrected.

REMOVING AXLE SHAFT

1. Remove wheels and brake drums.
2. Remove bolts and differential cover and allow lubricant to drain.
3. Remove pinion shaft lock bolt and pinion shaft then push axle shafts inward, remove C-lock and axle shaft.

REPLACING AXLE SHAFT BEARINGS & SEALS

1. Using a suitable pry bar, remove seal from housing. **Do not damage axle housing.**

2. Position tool No. J-23689 or equivalent behind bearing bore so tangs on tool engage bearing outer race, then using a suitable slide hammer attached to tool No. J-23689, remove bearing.
3. Using suitable gear lubricant, lubricate bearing. Then, using axle bearing installer J-23690 or equivalent, install bearing. Bearing is properly seated when tool bottoms against housing shoulder.
4. Lubricate seal with suitable gear lubricant, then using seal installer J-21128 or equivalent, tap seal into position until seal is flush with axle tube.
5. Install axle.

AXLE SHAFT INSTALLATION

1. Apply a coat of wheel bearing grease in wheel bearing and seal recess.
2. Install axle shaft through seal and bearing and through side gear as far in as possible. **Do not let shaft drag across seal lip, and always apply grease between seal lips.**
3. Install C-lock and move axle shaft outward to bottom C-lock in recess of side gear.
4. Install pinion shaft and torque lock bolt to 20 ft. lbs.
5. Install gasket and cover and torque bolts to 30 ft. lbs. After 20 minutes, retorque bolts to 30 ft. lbs.
6. Install correct type and amount of lubricant.
7. Install brake drum and wheel.

REAR WHEEL BEARING & SPINDLE

REPLACE

1982–85 RIVIERA

The rear wheel bearing is a sealed unit. This bearing is not serviceable for repacking or adjustment. The bearing must not be subjected to heat or early bearing failure may result.

MODELS W/REAR DISC BRAKES

Removal

1. Raise and support rear of vehicle.
2. Remove tire and wheel assembly.
3. Mark a wheel stud and a corresponding place on the rotor to assist in installation if bearing is not replaced.
4. Disconnect brake line at bracket on control arm.
5. Remove caliper and rotor assembly.
6. Remove four nuts and bolts securing the spindle to the control arm and remove bearing assembly, **Fig. 2.**

Installation

Before installing bearing, remove all rust and corrosion from bearing mounting surfaces. Lack of a flat surface may result in early bearing failure. A slip fit must exist between the bearing and the control arm assembly.

1. Install rear spindle, shield and plate to lower control arm. Torque nuts to 35 ft. lbs., **Fig. 2.**

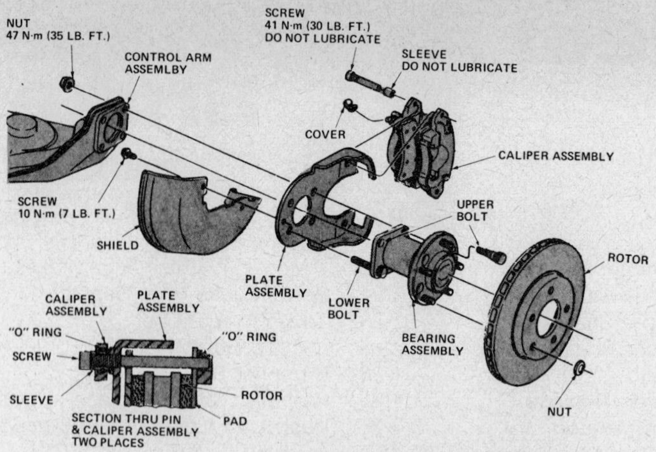

Fig. 2 Rear wheel bearing. Riviera w/rear disc brakes

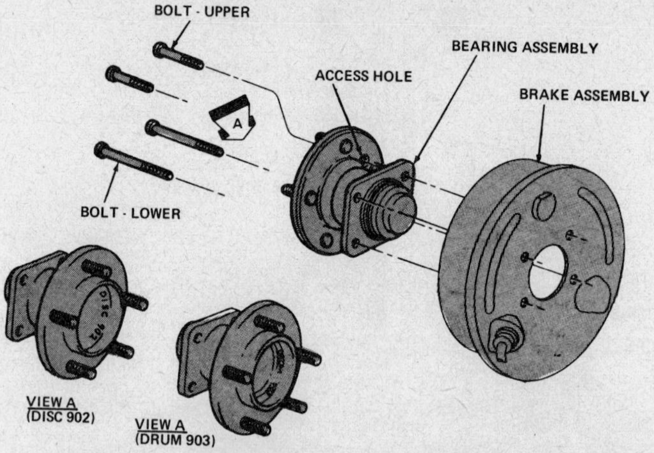

Fig. 3 Rear wheel bearing. Riviera w/rear drum brakes

2. If bearing was not replaced, install rotor using reference marks made at time of removal.
3. Install brake caliper assembly.
4. Connect brake line at bracket on control arm, tighten, then bleed brake system.
5. Install wheel and tire assembly.
6. Remove support and lower car.

MODELS W/REAR DRUM BRAKES

Removal

1. Raise and support rear of vehicle.
2. Remove tire and wheel assembly.
3. Remove brake drum.
4. Remove four nuts attaching rear wheel bearing assembly to control arm.
5. Remove wheel bearing and four attaching bolts, **Fig. 3.**

Installation

Before installing bearing, remove all rust and corrosion from bearing mounting surfaces. Lack of a flat surface for any reason may result in early bearing failure. A slip fit must exist between the bearing and the control arm assembly.

1. Install four nuts and bolts attaching wheel bearing to rear control arm assembly, **Fig. 3.** Torque nuts to 35 ft. lbs.
2. Install brake drum.
3. Install wheel and tire assembly.
4. Remove supports and lower car.

PROPELLER SHAFT

REPLACE

When service is required, the propeller shaft must be removed from the car as a complete assembly. While handling it out of the car, the assembly must be supported on a straight line as nearly as possible to avoid jamming or bending any of the parts.

Two attachment methods are used to secure the propeller shaft to the pinion flange or end yoke, a pair of bolted straps or a set of bolted flanges.

1. Scribe alignment marks between propeller shaft and pinion flange or end yoke to aid reassembly.
2. Remove strap or flange bolts at rear of propeller shaft. Tape bearing cups to prevent loss of needle bearings.
3. Slide shaft assembly rearward, disengaging front yoke from transmission output shaft splines and lower from vehicle.
4. Reverse procedure to install. **Prior to installing propeller shaft, lubricate all shaft splines with engine oil. When installing propeller shaft, do not attempt to drive in place with**

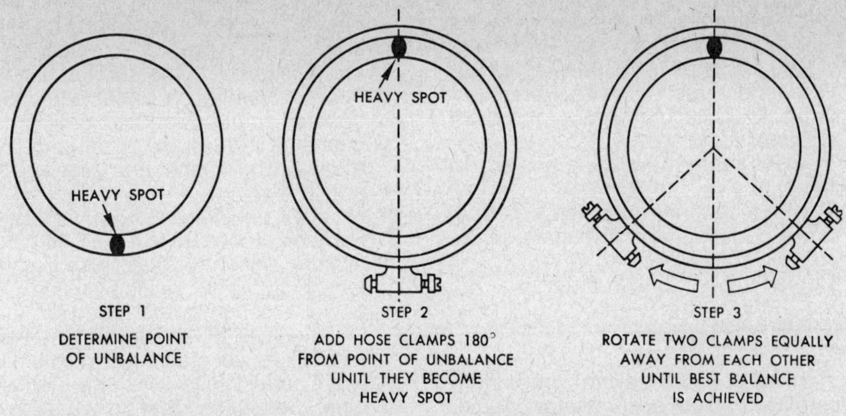

Fig. 4 Positioning clamps to balance propeller shaft

Fig. 5 Typical drum brake adjustment

hammer. If shaft will not slip into place, inspect for burrs on transmission output shaft splines, twisted slip yoke splines or the wrong U-joint yoke. Repair as necessary.

PROPELLER SHAFT BALANCE

A wheel balancer of the type equipped with a strobe light can be used to facilitate balancing of the driveshaft. The pickup unit should be placed directly under the nose of the rear axle carrier and as far forward as possible.

1. Place car on twin post lift so rear of car is supported on the rear axle housing and rear wheels are free to rotate.
2. Remove both rear wheels and tire assemblies and reinstall wheel lug nuts with flat side next to drum.
3. Mark and number driveshaft at four points 90° apart at rear of shaft just forward of balance weights.
4. Place strobe light pickup under nose of differential.
5. With car running in gear at car speed where unbalance is at its peak, allow driveline to stabilize by holding at constant speed. Point strobe light at spinning shaft and note position of one of the reference marks.
6. Shut off engine and position shaft so reference mark will be in position noted when car was running. **Do not run car on hoist for extended periods due to danger of overheating transmission or engine.**
7. When strobe light flashed, the heaviest point of the shaft was down. To balance shaft it will be necessary to apply weight 180° away. Screw type hose clamps can be used as weights as shown in **Fig. 4.**

SERVICE BRAKE ADJUSTMENTS

SELF-ADJUSTING DRUM BRAKES

These brakes have self-adjusting shoe mechanisms that assure correct lining-to-drum clearances at all times. The automatic adjusters operate only when the brakes are applied as the car is moving rearward.

Although the brakes are self-adjusting, an initial adjustment is necessary after the brake shoes have been relined or replaced, or when the length of the adjusting screw has been changed during some other service operation.

Frequent usage of an automatic transmission forward range to halt reverse vehicle motion may prevent the automatic adjusters from functioning, thereby inducing low pedal heights. Should low pedal heights be encountered, it is recommended that numerous forward and reverse stops be made until satisfactory pedal height is obtained. **If a low pedal condition cannot be corrected by making numerous reverse stops (provided the hydraulic system is free of air) it indicates that the self-adjusting mechanism is not functioning. Therefore, it will be necessary to remove the brake drum, clean, free up and lubricate the adjusting mechanism. Then adjust the brakes as follows, being sure the parking brake is fully released.**

Adjustment

1. Remove adjusting hole cover from backing plate. Turn brake adjusting screw to expand shoes until wheel can just be turned by hand.
2. Using suitable tool to hold actuator away from adjuster, **Fig. 5,** and back off adjuster 30 notches. If shoes still drag, back off one or two additional notches. **Brakes should be free of drag when adjuster has been backed off approximately 12 notches. Heavy drag at this point indicates tight parking brake cables.**
3. Install adjusting hole cover and check parking adjustment. **If finger movement will not turn the screw, free it up. If this is not done, the actuator will not turn the screw during subsequent vehicle operation. Lubricate the screw with oil and coat with wheel bearing grease. Any other adjustment procedure may cause damage to the adjusting screw with consequent self-adjuster problems.**
4. Install wheel and drum, and adjusting hole cover. Adjust brakes on remaining wheels in the same manner.
5. If pedal height is not satisfactory, drive the vehicle and make sufficient reverse stops until proper pedal height is obtained.

PARKING BRAKE ADJUST

MODELS W/REAR DISC BRAKES

1. Lubricate parking brake cables at equalizer and underbody rub points. Check all cables for freedom of operation.
2. Fully release parking brake and raise vehicle.
3. Hold cable stud from turning and tighten equalizer nut until cable slack is removed and levers are against stops on caliper housing. If levers are off stops, loosen cable until levers return to stop.
4. Operate parking brake several times to check adjustment. When properly adjusted, the parking brake pedal should move 5¹/₄ inch to 6³/₄ inch when a force of approximately 125 pounds is applied on all except Riviera. On Riviera, the parking brake pedal should move ¹/₄ inch to 5¹/₂ inch when a force of approximately 125 pounds is applied.

MODELS W/REAR DRUM BRAKES

Need for parking brake adjustment is indicated if the service brake operates with good pedal reserve but the parking brake pedal can be depressed a minimum of 9 ratchet clicks but not more than 16 under heavy foot pressure. After making sure that the service brakes are properly adjusted, adjust the parking brake as follows:

1. Depress parking brake exactly three ratchet clicks on 1985-88 models or two ratchet clicks on 1982-84 models.
2. Loosen jam nut and tighten adjusting nut until rear wheels can just be

turned rearward using both hands, but are locked when forward motion is attempted.

3. Tighten jam nut and release parking brake. Rear wheels should turn freely in either direction with no brake drag.

MASTER CYLINDER REPLACE

1. Disconnect brake pipes from master cylinder and tape end of pipes to prevent entrance of dirt.
2. On manual brakes, disconnect brake pedal from master cylinder pushrod.
3. Remove two nuts holding master cylinder to dash or power cylinder and remove master cylinder from car.

POWER BRAKE UNIT REPLACE

EXC. HYDRO-BOOST

1. Remove two nuts attaching master cylinder to brake unit, then position master cylinder away from brake unit with brake lines attached. **Use care not to bend or kink brake lines.**
2. Disconnect vacuum hose from check valve. Plug vacuum hose to prevent dirt from entering.
3. Remove four nuts holding power unit to dash.
4. Remove retainer and washer from brake pedal pin and disengage push-rod eye or clevis.
5. Remove power unit from car.

HYDRO-BOOST

Pump brake pedal several times with engine off to deplete accumulator of fluid.

1. Remove two nuts attaching master cylinder to booster, then move master cylinder away from booster with brake lines attached.
2. Remove three hydraulic lines from booster. Plug and cap all lines and outlets.
3. Remove retainer and washer securing booster pushrod to brake pedal arm.
4. Remove four nuts attaching booster unit to dash panel.
5. From engine compartment, loosen booster from dash panel and move booster pushrod inboard until it disconnects from brake pedal arm. Remove spring washer from brake pedal arm.
6. Remove booster unit from vehicle.
7. Reverse procedure to install. To purge system, disconnect feed wire from injection pump or ignition system. Fill power steering pump reservoir, then crank engine for several seconds and recheck power steering pump fluid level. Connect feed wire and start engine, then cycle steering wheel from stop to stop twice and stop engine. Discharge accumulator by depressing brake pedal several times, then check fluid level. Start engine, then turn steering wheel from stop to stop and turn engine off. Check fluid level and add fluid as necessary. If foaming occurs, stop engine and wait for approximately one hour for foam to dissipate, then recheck fluid level.

Rear Suspension Section

INDEX

SHOCK ABSORBER REPLACE

1. With the rear axle supported properly, disconnect shock absorber from lower mounting bracket. On models equipped with automatic level control, disconnect air hose from shock absorber.
2. Disconnect shock absorber upper end from underbody attachment.
3. Reverse procedure to install.

COIL SPRINGS REPLACE

1982–85 RIVIERA

1. Raise and support rear of vehicle.
2. Using a suitable jack support lower control arm.
3. Disconnect automatic level control air hose from shock absorber. If removing spring from lefthand side of vehicle, disconnect level control link from control arm.
4. Disconnect shock absorber from upper mounting.
5. Lower the control arm until all spring tension is relieved, then remove spring.
6. Reverse procedure to install. Locate spring as shown in **Fig. 1.**

EXC. 1982–85 RIVIERA

1. Support vehicle at frame and support rear axle with a suitable jack.
2. Disconnect shock absorbers from lower mounting brackets, **Fig. 2,** then the brake hose from the axle housing.
3. Disconnect upper control arms at differential.
4. Lower jack fully, extending springs, then remove springs. **Do not allow the brake hose to become kinked or stretched.**
5. Reverse procedure to install. Refer to **Fig. 3,** for correct coil spring staggering. After installation, bleed brakes.

CONTROL ARMS REPLACE

Remove and replace one control arm at a time as axle assembly may slip sideways, making installation difficult.

1982–85 RIVIERA

1. Raise and support rear of vehicle, then remove wheel and tire assembly.
2. Disconnect brake line at bracket on control arm.
3. Remove stabilizer bar. Refer to "Stabilizer Bar, Replace."
4. Remove rear wheel bearing and spindle. Refer to "Rear Wheel Bearing And Spindle, Replace" procedure as outlined in the Rear Axle, Propeller Shaft and Brakes Section.
5. If removing lefthand control arm, disconnect automatic level control link from control arm.
6. Using a suitable jack, support control arm.
7. Disconnect air hose from shock absorber, then detach shock absorber from upper and lower mountings.
8. Lower control arm until all spring tension is relieved, then remove spring and insulators.
9. Remove two bolts attaching control arm to frame and remove control arm, **Fig. 4.**

EXC. 1982–85 RIVIERA

Upper Control Arms

1. Support vehicle at frame and rear axle.
2. Remove control arm mount bolts from frame and axle housing attachments, **Fig. 2.**
3. Reverse procedure to install. **Control arm bolts must be tightened with vehicle at curb height.**

Lower Control Arm

Lower control arms may be removed and replaced using the "Upper Control Arms" procedure. However, it may be necessary to reposition the jack farther forward under carrier to aid in removing rear mount bolt. Also, a brass drift may be needed to remove mount bolts.

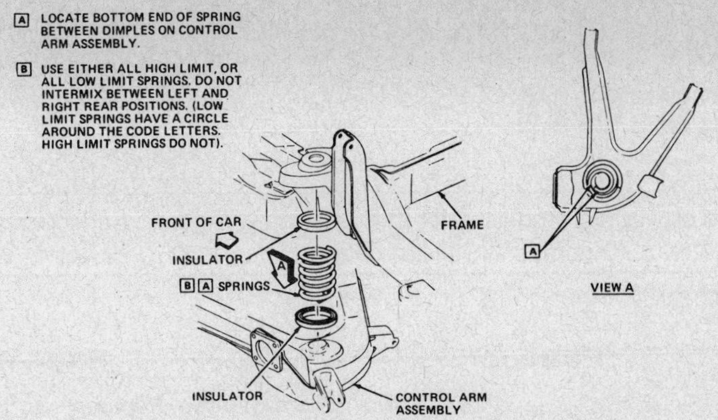

Fig. 1 Coil spring installation. Riviera

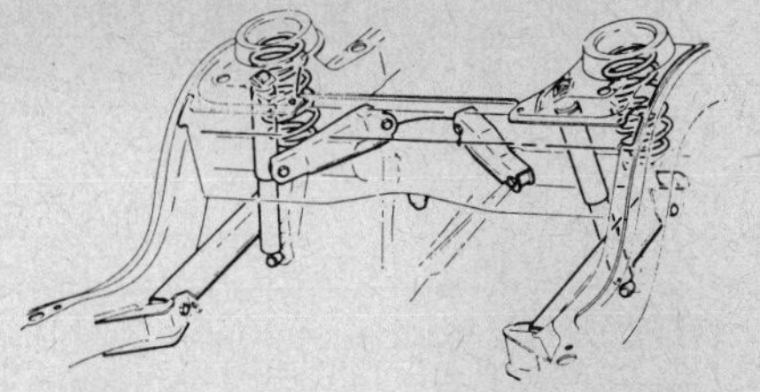

Fig. 2 Typical coil spring suspension. Exc. Riviera

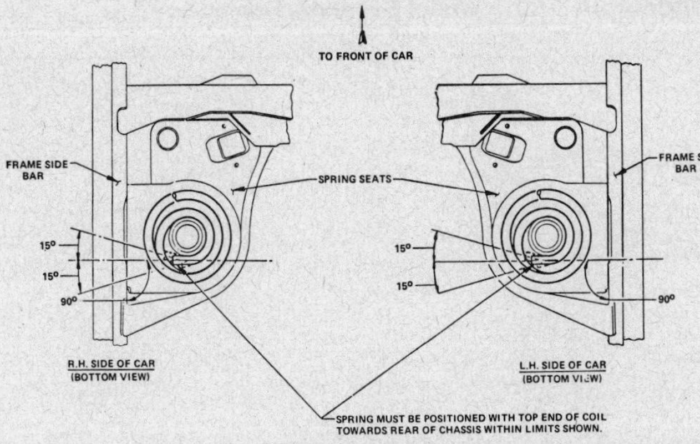

Fig. 3 Coil spring installation. Exc. Riviera

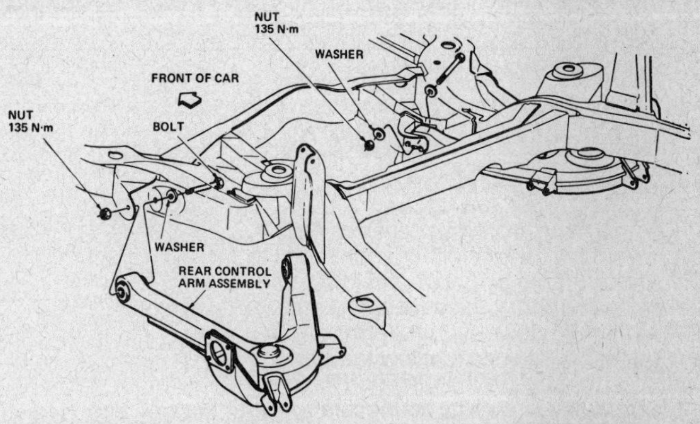

Fig. 4 Control arm assembly. Riviera

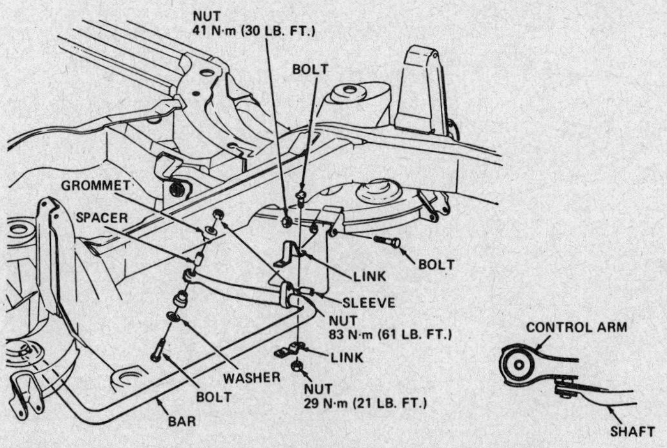

Fig. 5 Rear stabilizer installation. Riviera

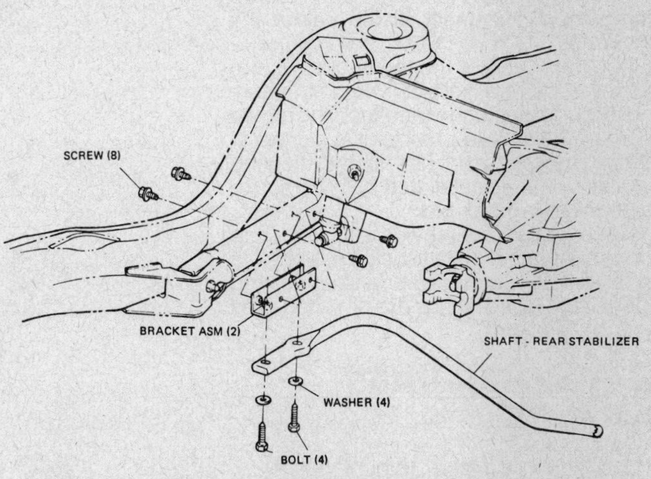

Fig. 6 Rear stabilizer installation. Exc. Riviera

STABILIZER BAR REPLACE

1982–85 RIVIERA

1. Raise and support rear of vehicle.
2. Remove bolts attaching front of stabilizer bar to control arms, **Fig. 5.**
3. Remove inside nut and bolt from each side of stabilizer bar link, then loosen nut and bolt on outside of link.
4. Rotate bottom parts of link to one side and slide stabilizer bar out of bushings.

EXC. 1982–85 RIVIERA

1. Support vehicle at rear axle.
2. Remove stabilizer bar attaching bolts from brackets on lower control arms, **Fig. 6.**
3. Reverse procedure to install.

Front Suspension & Steering Section

NOTE: For front suspension & steering service procedures on Riviera models, refer to Front End & Steering Section in the "Cadillac Rear Wheel Drive & 1982-85 Eldorado & Seville" chapter.

INDEX

FRONT SUSPENSION DESCRIPTION

On this type front suspension, **Fig. 1**, each wheel is connected independently to the vehicle frame by upper and lower control arms, ball joints and a steering knuckle. The upper and lower control arms are designed and positioned to allow the steering knuckles to move in a prescribed three dimensional arc. Tie rods, connected to the steering knuckles, ensure the front wheels are held in the proper relationship to each other.

A ball joint is riveted to the outer end of the upper arm and is spring loaded to insure proper alignment of the ball in the socket.

The inner end of the lower control arm has pressed-in bushings. Two bolts, passing through the bushings, attach the arm to the frame. The lower ball joint is a press fit in the arm and attaches to the steering knuckle with a castellated nut that is retained with a cotter pin.

Rubber seals are provided on upper and lower shafts and at ball socket assemblies to exclude dirt and moisture from bearing surfaces. Grease fittings are provided at all bearing locations.

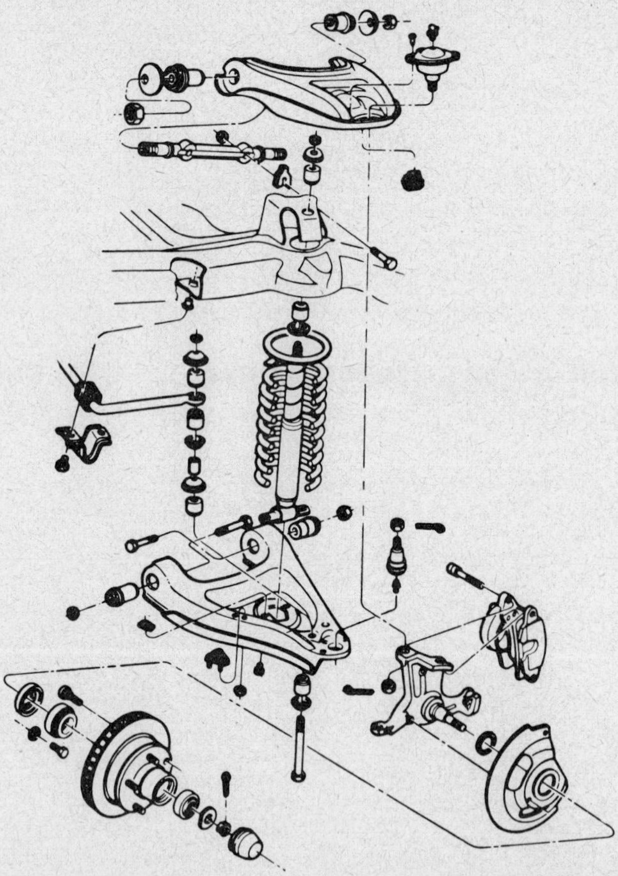

Fig. 1 Typical front suspension exploded view

WHEEL BEARINGS

ADJUST

1. Raise and support front of vehicle.
2. Remove wheel hub dust cap.
3. Remove spindle nut cotter pin, then while rotating wheel assembly forward, torque spindle nut to 12 ft. lbs. to seat bearings.
4. Loosen spindle nut slightly to "the just loose" position.
5. Hand tighten spindle nut, then install cotter pin. If cotter pin cannot be installed, loosen spindle nut until hole in the spindle lines up with a slot in the nut. Do not loosen more then 1/2 flat of the nut.
6. With wheel bearings properly adjusted, endplay should be .001 to .005 inch.

WHEEL BEARINGS

REPLACE

1. Raise and support vehicle and remove front wheels.
2. Remove brake tube support bracket bolt. Do not disconnect hydraulic tube or hose.
3. Remove caliper to mounting bracket bolts. Hang caliper from upper suspension. **Do not place strain on brake line.**
4. Remove spindle nut, hub and disc assembly and outer wheel bearing.
5. Pry out grease retainer using suitable tool, then remove inner bearing.

CHECKING BALL JOINTS FOR WEAR

If loose ball joints are suspected, first be sure front wheel bearings are properly adjusted and that control arms are tight, then check ball joints as outlined below.

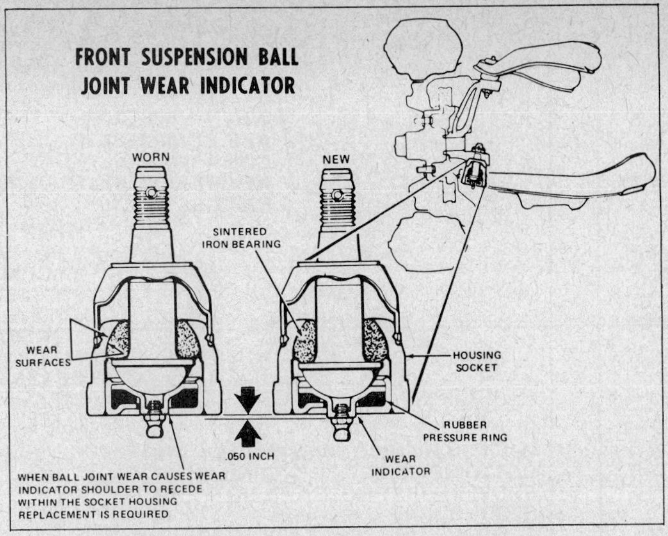

Fig. 2 Lower ball joint check

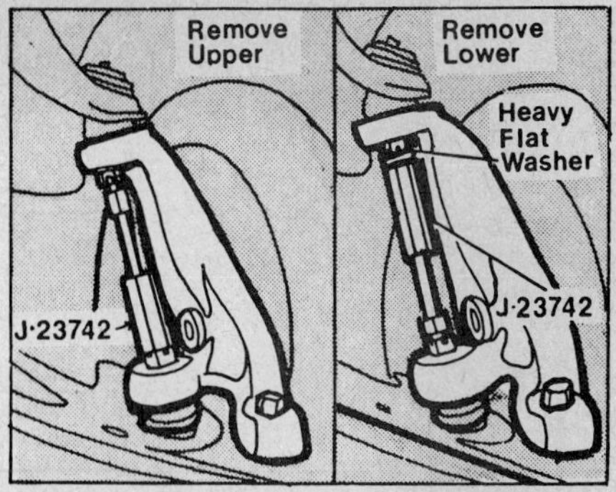

Fig. 3 Removing ball joint stud from steering knuckle

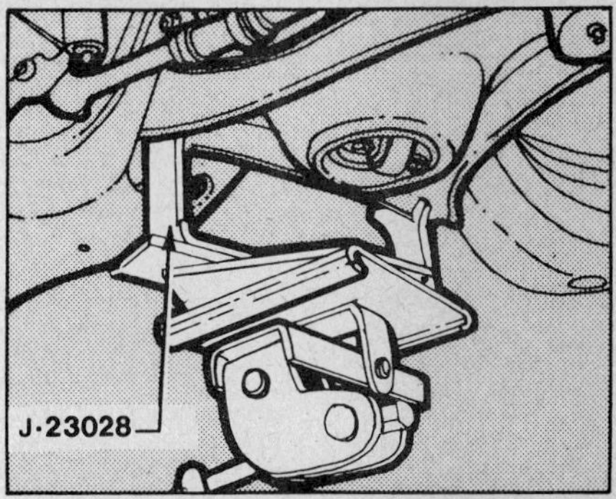

Fig. 4 Removing front coil spring

UPPER BALL JOINT

1. Raise front of vehicle with jacks placed between coil spring pockets and ball joint of lower control arm.
2. Position suitable dial indicator at top of wheel rim, then grasp wheel top and bottom, while pulling out top, push in bottom and read dial indicator. Reverse the push-pull procedure and read dial indicator.
3. If dial indicator reading exceeds .125 inch, the upper ball joint should be replaced.

LOWER BALL JOINT

A wear indicator is built into the ball joint. Remove dirt deposits around service plug and observe position of nipple. Refer to **Fig. 2** for wear tolerance.

BALL JOINTS
REPLACE

On all models the upper ball joint is spring-loaded in its socket. If the ball stud has any perceptible shake or if it can be twisted with the fingers, the ball joint should be replaced.

On all models, the lower ball joint is not spring-loaded and depends upon car weight to load the ball. The lower ball joint should never be replaced merely because it "feels" loose when in an unloaded condition.

Upper ball joints on all models are riveted to the control arm and can be replaced.

Lower ball joints on all models are pressed into the control arm and can be replaced with a suitable ball joint tool. **When servicing lower ball joints, be sure to support lower control arm with a suitable jack. If lower control arm is not supported and steering knuckle is disconnected from control arm, the heavily compressed front spring will be completely released.**

UPPER BALL JOINT

1. Support vehicle at frame and remove wheel assembly.
2. Remove cotter pin from upper ball joint stud, loosen nut approximately 2 turns, do not remove nut.
3. Position tool as shown in **Fig. 3,** turn threaded end of tool until stud disengages knuckle.
4. Position jack under lower control arm at spring seat, raise jack until compression is relieved from upper control arm bumper.
5. Remove stud nut, lift control arm from steering knuckle and place a block of wood between control arm and frame.
6. On all models:
   a. Center punch rivet head as close to center as possible.
   b. Using a 1/8 inch twist drill, drill through center of rivet approximately 1/2 rivet length deep.
   c. Remove rivet head using a 1/2 inch drill.
   d. Using a chisel, remove rivet heads, then drive rivets out using a suitable punch.
7. Position ball joint on upper control arm. Install bolts through bottom of control arm with nuts on top, torque to 8 ft. lbs.
8. On all models, position ball joint stud so cotter pin hole is facing forward and remove wooden block from between control arm and frame.
9. Place wheels in straight ahead position, raise jack under lower control until ball joint stud can be installed in steering knuckle.
10. Install castellated nut on ball joint stud. Torque nut to 65 ft. lbs. **If cotter pin holes do not align, do not loosen nut, however, tighten until cotter pin can be installed.**
11. Install wheel assembly and lower vehicle.

LOWER BALL JOINT

1. Support vehicle under frame side rails. **Position jack under lower control at outboard end, raise jack until it is 1/2 inch below control arm.**
2. Remove cotter pin, loosen ball joint stud nut approximately 2 turns, do not remove nut.
3. Position tool as shown in **Fig. 3,** turn threaded end of tool until ball joint stud is disengaged from steering knuckle.
4. Position jack under lower control arm at spring seat and raise jack until compression is removed from upper control arm bumper.
5. Remove lower ball joint stud nut and position steering knuckle aside.
6. Using tool No. J-9519-10, remove ball joint from lower control arm.
7. Position ball joint on control arm with bleed vent on rubber boot facing inward.
8. Install tool J-9519-10 and turn threaded end of tool until ball joint is fully seated in lower control arm.
9. Position new ball joint stud so cotter pin hole is facing forward.
10. Place wheels in the straight ahead position and install ball joint stud on steering knuckle.
11. Install stud nut and torque to 81 ft. lbs., then install cotter pin. **If cotter pin holes do not align do not loosen stud nut, tighten nut until cotter pin can be installed.**
12. Install wheel assembly.

SHOCK ABSORBER
REPLACE

Unfasten shock absorber at top and bottom and remove it through the spring seat. Check shock absorber for obvious physical damage or oil leakage. Push and pull shock absorber in an upright position. If smooth hydraulic resistance is not present in both directions, replace shock absorber.

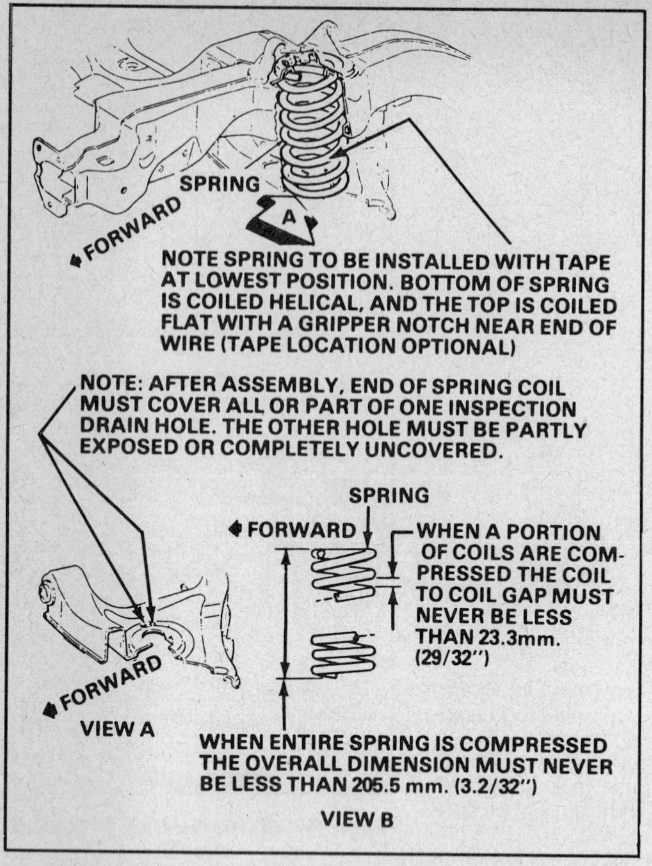
SPRING
FORWARD
A
NOTE SPRING TO BE INSTALLED WITH TAPE AT LOWEST POSITION. BOTTOM OF SPRING IS COILED HELICAL, AND THE TOP IS COILED FLAT WITH A GRIPPER NOTCH NEAR END OF WIRE (TAPE LOCATION OPTIONAL)
NOTE: AFTER ASSEMBLY, END OF SPRING COIL MUST COVER ALL OR PART OF ONE INSPECTION DRAIN HOLE. THE OTHER HOLE MUST BE PARTLY EXPOSED OR COMPLETELY UNCOVERED.
SPRING
FORWARD
WHEN A PORTION OF COILS ARE COMPRESSED THE COIL TO COIL GAP MUST NEVER BE LESS THAN 23.3mm. (29/32")
FORWARD
VIEW A
WHEN ENTIRE SPRING IS COMPRESSED THE OVERALL DIMENSION MUST NEVER BE LESS THAN 205.5 mm. (3.2/32")
VIEW B

Fig. 5 Coil spring installation. Exc. full size models

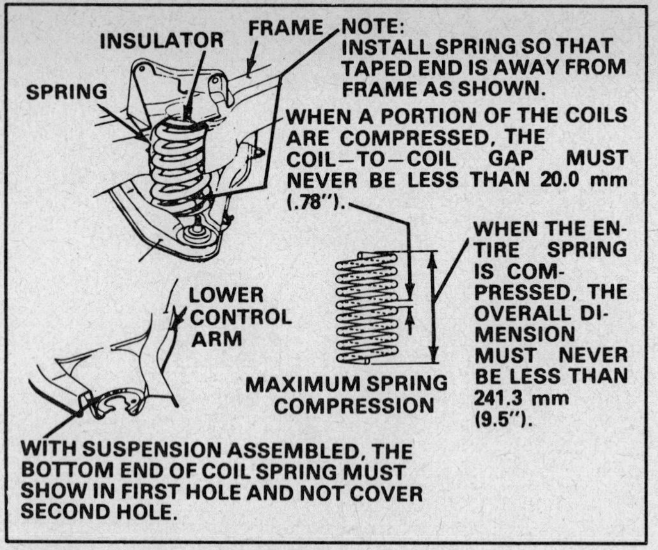

Fig. 6 Coil spring installation. Full size models

COIL SPRING
REPLACE

1. Raise and support vehicle at frame.
2. Remove shock absorber lower mount, then push shock up through control arm and into spring.
3. Remove stabilizer bar from lower control arm. Refer to "Stabilizer Bar, Replace."
4. Position a tool No. J-23028 at lower control arm pivot bolts, **Fig. 4.**
5. Position a suitable jack under tool installed in step 4 and chain together, then raise jack slightly to remove tension from lower control arm pivot bolts.
6. Using a suitable chain, secure lower control arm and coil spring together.
7. Remove rear lower control arm pivot bolt, then front bolt.
8. Slowly lower jack with lower control arm and spring attached.
9. When spring compression is relieved, remove spring.
10. Reverse procedure to install. Refer to **Figs. 5 and 6,** for proper installation.

STABILIZER BAR
REPLACE

1. Raise and support front of vehicle.
2. Remove nut, link bolt, retainers, grommets, spacer and stabilizer linkage from lower control arms.
3. Remove bracket to frame bolts, then remove stabilizer shaft, rubber bushings and brackets. On Regal models, use tool No. J-25359-20 to remove stabilizer shaft bolt.
4. Reverse procedure to install and note the following:
   a. When installing rubber bushings, bushings should be positioned squarely in the brackets with the bushing slit facing front of vehicle.
   b. Torque stabilizer link nut to 13 ft. lbs. and bracket bolts to 25 ft. lbs.

MANUAL STEERING GEAR
REPLACE

1. Remove two nuts or pinch bolt securing lower coupling to steering shaft flange.
2. Use a suitable puller to remove pitman arm.
3. Unfasten gear (3 bolts) from frame and remove from vehicle.
4. Reverse procedure to install.

POWER STEERING GEAR
REPLACE

1. Disconnect pressure and return line hoses at steering gear and elevate ends of hoses higher than pump to prevent oil from draining out of pump.
2. Remove pinch bolt securing coupling to steering gear.
3. Jack up car and remove pitman shaft nut, then use a suitable puller to remove pitman arm.
4. On full size models, remove sheet metal baffle that covers frame-to-gear attaching bolts, if equipped.
5. Loosen the three frame-to-steering gear bolts and remove steering gear.
6. Reverse procedure to install.

POWER STEERING PUMP
REPLACE

1. Disconnect battery ground cable.
2. Remove steering pump belt, alternator belt and air conditioning compressor belt, if equipped.
3. On all models disconnect steering pump hoses from pump and plug all open lines and fittings to prevent entry of dirt.
4. Remove pump or pump with brackets from engine.
5. Reverse procedure to install.

Wheel Alignment Section

INDEX

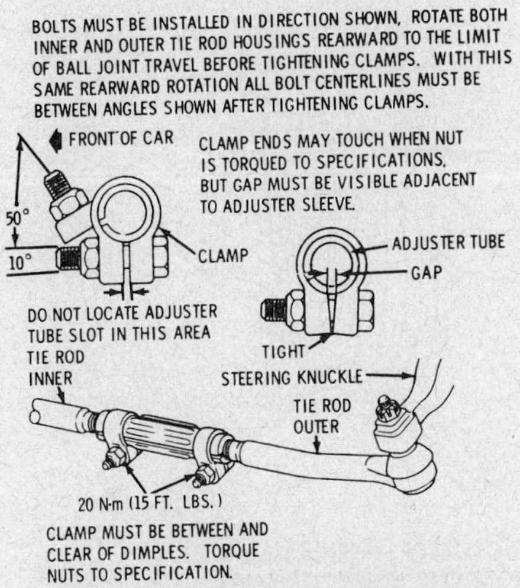
BOLTS MUST BE INSTALLED IN DIRECTION SHOWN, ROTATE BOTH INNER AND OUTER TIE ROD HOUSINGS REARWARD TO THE LIMIT OF BALL JOINT TRAVEL BEFORE TIGHTENING CLAMPS. WITH THIS SAME REARWARD ROTATION ALL BOLT CENTERLINES MUST BE BETWEEN ANGLES SHOWN AFTER TIGHTENING CLAMPS.
FRONT OF CAR
CLAMP ENDS MAY TOUCH WHEN NUT IS TORQUED TO SPECIFICATIONS, BUT GAP MUST BE VISIBLE ADJACENT TO ADJUSTER SLEEVE.
50°
10°
CLAMP
ADJUSTER TUBE
GAP
DO NOT LOCATE ADJUSTER TUBE SLOT IN THIS AREA
TIGHT
TIE ROD INNER
STEERING KNUCKLE
TIE ROD OUTER
20 N·m (15 FT. LBS.)
CLAMP MUST BE BETWEEN AND CLEAR OF DIMPLES. TORQUE NUTS TO SPECIFICATION.

Fig. 1 Tie rod adjustment sleeve & clamp installation. Exc. Riviera

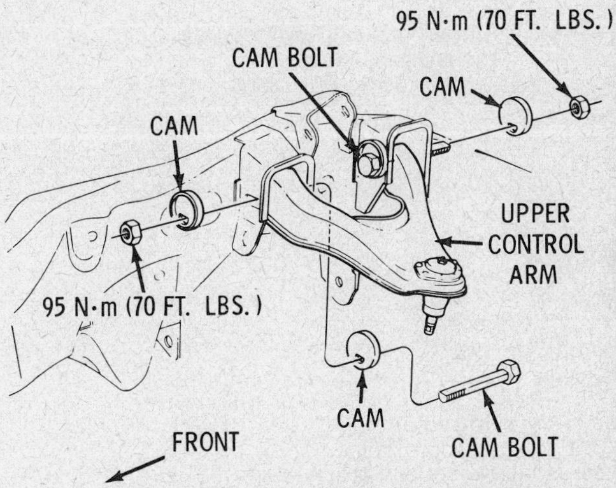
95 N·m (70 FT. LBS.)
CAM BOLT
CAM
CAM
UPPER CONTROL ARM
95 N·m (70 FT. LBS.)
CAM
CAM BOLT
FRONT

Fig. 2 Caster & camber adjustment. Riviera

FRONT WHEEL ALIGNMENT

EXC. RIVIERA

Caster & Camber

Prior to checking or resetting caster and camber angles, bounce the front end at least twice to allow vehicle to return to normal trim height.

Caster and camber are adjusted by shimming at the upper control arm shaft attaching points.

Adding shims at the front locations will change caster toward negative with practically no change in camber. Adding shims at the rear locations will change caster toward positive and camber toward negative. Adding equal shims at both front and rear locations will not change caster but will change camber.

To adjust, loosen both front and rear nuts to free shims for removal or addition. After installing or removing shims, torque shaft nuts to 75 ft. lbs. on all except Regal models, or 46 ft. lbs. for Regal.

A normal service shim pack should leave at least two threads exposed beyond the shaft nuts after final tightening. The difference between front and rear shim packs should not exceed .40 inch.

Toe-In

Prior to checking or resetting toe-in, bounce the front end at least twice to allow vehicle to return to normal trim height.

1. Ensure wheel bearings are adjusted properly.
2. Using suitable alignment equipment, with steering wheel in the straight ahead position, check toe-in.
3. If toe-in is not within specifications, loosen tie rod adjustment sleeve clamp bolts.
4. Turn tie rod adjustable sleeves an equal amount of turns but in opposite directions to bring toe-in within specifications.
5. Ensure tie rod end housings are at right angles to the steering arm, then position and torque tie rod adjustable sleeve clamps as shown in **Fig. 1.**

RIVIERA

Camber

While holding cam bolt in position, loosen cam bolt nut, **Fig. 2.** Rotate cam bolt to obtain a change in camber equal to 1/2 the needed correction, then hold cam bolt in position and tighten cam bolt nut to 70 ft. lbs. To obtain the remaining 1/2 of needed correction, apply the same procedure to other cam bolt.

Caster

Record camber reading, then hold front cam bolt and loosen nut, **Fig. 2.** Turn front cam bolt to obtain 1/4 of the desired caster change. At front cam bolt, a positive camber change produces a positive caster change, while a negative camber change produces a negative caster change. Hold cam bolt in position and tighten nut. Loosen rear cam bolt nut and rotate cam bolt to return camber to setting recorded earlier. Recheck caster and repeat procedure, if necessary. When adjustment is completed, hold rear cam bolt, then torque nut to 70 ft. lbs.

Toe-In

Prior to checking or resetting toe-in, bounce the front end at least twice to allow vehicle to return to normal trim height.

1. Ensure wheel bearings are adjusted properly.
2. Using suitable alignment equipment, with steering wheel in the straight ahead position, check toe-in.
3. If toe-in is not within specifications, loosen tie rod adjustment sleeve clamp bolts.
4. Turn tie rod adjustable sleeves an equal amount of turns but in opposite directions to bring toe-in within specifications.
5. Ensure tie rod end housings are at right angles to the steering arm, then position and torque tie rod adjustable sleeve clamps as shown in **Fig. 3.**

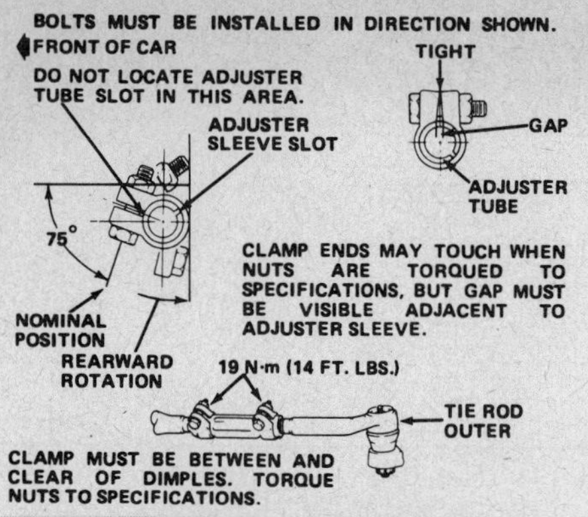

Fig. 3 Tie rod adjustment sleeve & clamp installation. Riviera

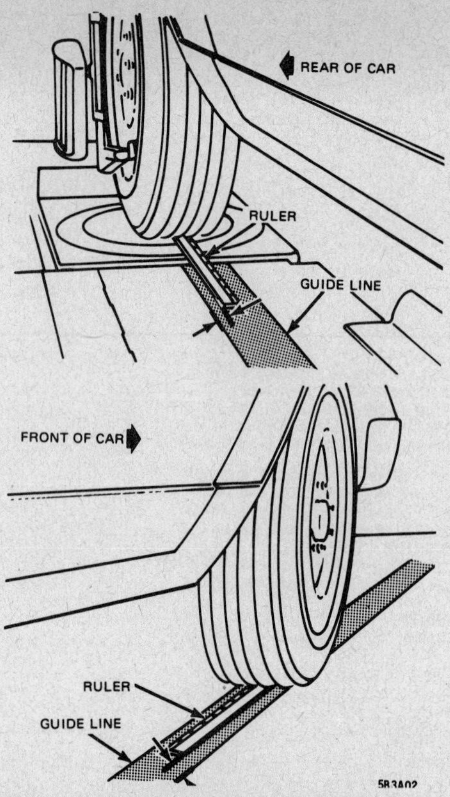

Fig. 4 Checking vehicle for squareness on alignment rack

REAR WHEEL ALIGNMENT

RIVIERA

Camber & Toe-In

Camber and toe-in are checked at the same time following the procedure outlined below. Camber is factory set and is not adjustable. If camber deviates from specified settings, check for a bent control arm or frame, or for a improperly mounted hub and bearing assembly.

1. Check front and rear trim heights.
2. Check automatic level control system, if equipped, for proper operation.
3. Position vehicle on alignment rack as follows:
   a. Place masking tape on floor from wheel plate to rear of vehicle to use as a guide to square vehicle on alignment rack.
   b. Back rear of vehicle onto rack, positioning wheels on wheel plates.
   c. Place a ruler at same rib of tire at front and rear of vehicle, then measure distance from inside edge of ruler to edge of guide line, **Fig. 4.** When vehicle is square, measurement from guide line to ruler should be greater at rear tire by approximately 5/8 inch.
4. Attach alignment mirrors to rear wheels, then check camber and toe settings and compare to specifications. **When vehicle is backed onto alignment rack, toe-in and toe-out are reversed. That is, toe-in will be read as toe-out, while toe-out will be read as toe-in.**
5. As stated previously, camber is not adjustable. To adjust toe-in, loosen inner pivot bushing retaining nut and bolt. Move control arm rearward to increase toe-in, or toward front of vehicle to decrease toe-in. A pry bar can be used to facilitate adjustment. After adjustment is completed, torque bushing retaining nut to 70 ft. lbs.

CADILLAC—REAR WHEEL DRIVE MODELS & 1982–85 ELDORADO & SEVILLE

INDEX OF SERVICE OPERATIONS

NOTE: Refer to the rear of this manual for vehicle manufacturer's special special service tool suppliers.

Specifications

GENERAL ENGINE SPECIFICATIONS

Year	Engine CID①/Liter	Engine VIN Code②	Carburetor	Bore and Stroke	Compression Ratio	Net H.P. @ RPM③	Maximum Torque Lbs. Ft. @ RPM	Normal Oil Pressure Pounds
1982	V6-252/4.1L⑥	4	E4ME, 4 Bbl. ④	3.96 x 3.40	8.0	125 @ 4000	205 @ 2000	37
	V8-250/4.1L	8	Fuel Injection	3.465 x 3.307	8.5	135 @ 4600	200 @ 1600	30
	V8-350/5.7L⑤	N	Fuel Injection	4.06 x 3.38	22.5	105 @ 3200	200 @ 1600	30-45
1983	V8-250/4.1L	8	Fuel Injection	3.465 x 3.307	8.5	135 @ 4200	200 @ 2200	30
	V8-350/5.7L⑤	N	Fuel Injection	4.06 x 3.38	22.5	105 @ 3200	200 @ 1600	30-45
1984-85	V8-250/4.1L	8	Fuel Injection	3.465 x 3.307	8.5	135 @ 4400	200 @ 2200	30
	V8-350/5.7L⑤	N	Fuel Injection	4.06 x 3.38	22.7	105 @ 3200	200 @ 1600	30-45
1986	V8-307/5.0L	Y	E4MC, 4 Bbl. ④	3.8 x 3.4	8.0	140 @ 3200	255 @ 2000	30-45
1987	V8-307/5.0L	Y	E4MC, 4 Bbl. ④	3.8 x 3.4	8.0	140 @ 3200	255 @ 2000	30-45
1988	V8-307/5.0L	Y	E4MC, 4 Bbl. ④	3.8 x 3.4	8.0	140 @ 3200	255 @ 2000	30-45

①—CID-Cubic inch displacement.
②—The eighth digit in the VIN denotes the engine code.
③—Net rating-as installed in the vehicle.
④—Rochester.
⑤—Oldsmobile built diesel engine.
⑥—Buick built engine.

ENGINE TIGHTENING SPECIFICATIONS*

*Torque specifications are for clean and lightly lubricated threads only. Dry or dirty threads produce increased friction which prevents accurate measurement of tightness.

Year & Engine/VIN	Spark Plugs Ft. Lbs.	Cylinder Head Bolts Ft. Lbs.	Intake Manifold Ft. Lbs.	Exhaust Manifold Ft. Lbs.	Rocker Arm Shaft Bracket Ft. Lbs.	Rocker Arm Cover Ft. Lbs.	Connecting Rod Cap Bolts Ft. Lbs.	Main Bearing Cap Bolts Ft. Lbs.	Flex Plate to Crankshaft Ft. Lbs.	Vibration Damper or Pulley Ft. Lbs.
1982-85 V8-350/N④	—	130⑤	40⑤	25	28⑥	3	42	120	60	200-310
1982 V6-252/4⑦	15	80	45	25	30	4	40	100	60	225
1982-85 V8-250/8	10	⑧	③	20	20⑥	50①	20	85	35	20
1986 V8-307/Y	25	125⑤	40⑤	25	25⑥	90①	42	②	60	200-310
1987 V8-307/Y	25	130⑤	40⑤	25	25⑥	90①	48	②	60	200-310
1988 V8-307/Y	25	130⑤	40⑤	25	25⑥	90①	48	②	60	200-310

①—Inch pounds. Retorque after engine has been run.
②—Exc. No. 5, 80 ft. lbs.; No. 5, 120 ft. lbs.
③—Refer to text for procedure.
④—Diesel engine.
⑤—Clean and dip entire bolt in engine oil before tightening.
⑥—Rocker arm pivot bolt to head.
⑦—Buick built engine.
⑧—Torque bolts in 3 steps: First-torque all bolts to 38 ft. lbs. Second-torque all bolts to 74 ft. lbs. Third-torque bolts, 1, 3 and 4 to 90 ft. lbs. Refer to text for tightening sequence.

ALTERNATOR SPECIFICATIONS

Year	Alternator Model	Rated Hot Output Amps.	Field Current 12 Volts @ 80°F.
1982-85	1101044	70	4.0-4.6
	1101046	80	4.4-4.9
	1101050	100	4.4-4.9
1986	—	94	—
1987	—	94	—
1988	—	94	—

STARTING MOTOR APPLICATIONS

Year	Engine/VIN	Starter Number
1982	V8-250/8②	1109531
	V6-252/4①	1109062
	V8-350/N⑥	1109216
1983	V8-250/8② ④	1109531
	V8-250/8② ③ ⑤	1998233
	V8-350/N④ ⑥	1109216
	V8-350/N③ ⑤ ⑥	1109495
1984-85	V8-250/8② ④	—
	V8-250/8② ③ ⑤	—
	V8-350/N④ ⑥	—
	V8-350/N③ ⑤ ⑥	—
1986	V8-307/Y④	—
1987	V8-307/Y	—
1988	V8-307/Y	—

①—4 Bbl.
②—Fuel injected.
③—Seville.
④—Exc. Eldorado & Seville.
⑤—Eldorado.
⑥—Diesel engine.

DRIVE AXLE SPECIFICATIONS

			Ring Gear Pinion Backlash		Pinion Bearing Preload			Differential Bearing Preload		
Year	Model	Carrier Type	Method	Adjustment	Method	Adjustment New Bearings Inch Lbs.	Adjustment Used Bearings Inch Lbs.	Method	Adjustment New Bearings Inch Lbs.	Adjustment Used Bearings Inch Lbs.
1982	Exc. Eldorado & Seville	Integral	Shims	.005-.009①	Collapsible Spacer	24-32	8-12	Shims	②	②
	Eldorado & Seville	Integral	Shims	.005-.009①	Collapsible Spacer	18-24	5	Shims	③	③
1983-85	Exc. Eldorado & Seville	Integral	Shims	.006-.008①	Collapsible Spacer	20-25	10-15	Shims	②	②
	Eldorado & Seville	Integral	Shims	.005-.009①	Collapsible Spacer	18-24	5	Shims	③	③
1986	Brougham	Integral	Shims	.005-.009①	Collapsible Spacer	20-25	10-15	Shims	②	②
1987	Brougham	Integral	Shims	.005-.009①	Collapsible Spacer	20-25	10-15	Shims	②	②
1988	Brougham	Integral	Shims	.005-.009①	Collapsible Spacer	20-25	10-15	Shims	②	②

①—New gears.
②—Slip fit plus .008" (.004" added to each side).
③—Slip fit plus .006".

FRONT WHEEL ALIGNMENT SPECIFICATIONS

Year	Model	Caster Angle, Degrees		Camber Angle, Degrees				Toe-In Inch
				Limits		Desired		
		Limits	Desired	Left	Right	Left	Right	
1982-85	Eldorado & Seville	+2 to +3	+2 1/2	— –1/2 to +1/2	–1/2 to +1/2	Zero	Zero	–1/16 to +1/16
	Others	+2 1/2 to +3 1/2	+3	—+.1 to +.9	+.1 to +.9	+1/2	+1/2	1/8
1986	Brougham	+2 1/2 to +3 1/2	+3	—+.1 to +.9	+.1 to +.9	+1/2	+1/2	1/8
1987	Brougham	+2 to +4	+3	–1/2 to +1/2	–1/2 to +1/2	0	0	0
1988	Brougham	+2 to +4	+3	–1/2 to +1/2	–1/2 to +1/2	0	0	0

REAR WHEEL ALIGNMENT SPECIFICATIONS

Year	Model	Camber Angle, Degrees		Toe-In Inch ①
		Limits	Desired	
1982-84	Eldorado & Seville	—	0②	0 to +3/10
1985	Eldorado & Seville	—	0②	0 to + 1/5

①—Per wheel. ②—Not adjustable.

COOLING SYSTEM & CAPACITY DATA

Year	Model or Engine/VIN	Cooling Capacity Qts.	Radiator Cap Relief Pressure, Lbs.	Thermo. Opening Temp.	Fuel Tank Gals.	Engine Oil Refill Qts. ①	Auto. Trans. Qts. ②	Rear Axle Oil Pints
1982	Eldorado V6-252/4	13.1	15	195	21.1	4	⑤	3 1/5⑥
	Seville V6-252/4	13.1	15	195	21.1	4	⑤	3 1/5⑥
	Others V6-252/4	18.2	15	195	25	4	⑨	4 1/4
	Eldorado V8-250/8	11.8	15	195	20.3	5③	⑤	3 1/5⑥
	Seville V8-250/8	11.8	15	195	20.3	5③	⑤	3 1/5⑥
	Others V8-250/8	10.8	15	195	25	4③	⑨	4 1/4
	Eldorado V8-350 Diesel/N	18.4	15	195	22.8	7⑧	⑤	3 1/5⑥
	Seville V8-350 Diesel/N	18.4	15	195	22.8	7⑧	⑤	3 1/5⑥
	Others V8-350 Diesel/N	23.7	15	195	27	7⑧	⑨	4 1/4
1983	Eldorado V8-250/8	10.9	15	195	20.3	5③	④	3 1/5⑥
	Seville V8-250/8	10.9	15	195	20.3	5③	④	3 1/5⑥
	Others V8-250/8	11.0	15	195	24.5	4③	⑦	4 1/4
	Eldorado Diesel/N	18.4	15	195	22.8	7⑦	④	3 1/5⑥
	Seville Diesel/N	18.4	15	195	22.8	7⑧	④	3 1/5⑥
	Others Diesel/N	23.7	15	195	26	7⑧	⑦	4 1/4
1984-85	Eldorado V8-250/8	—	15	195	20.3	5③	—	3 1/5⑥
	Seville V8-250/8	—	15	195	20.3	5③	—	3 1/5⑥
	Others V8-250/8	—	15	195	24.5	4③	—	4 1/4
	Eldorado Diesel/N	—	15⑥Y°195	22.8	7⑧		—	3 1/5
	Seville Diesel/N	—	15	195	22.8	7⑧	—	3 1/5⑥
	Others Diesel/N	—	15	195	26	7⑧	—	4 1/4
1986	Brougham	—	15	195	24.5	4③	⑦	4 1/4
1987	Brougham	—	15	195	20.7	4.6③	⑦	3.5
1988	Brougham	—	15	195	25.0	4.5③	⑦	3.5

①—Add one quart with filter change.
②—Approximate. Make final check with dipstick.
③—Includes filter.
④—Oil pan 5 qts. Total capacity 13 qts.
⑤—Oil pan 5 qts. Total capacity 11 3/4 qts.
⑥—Front drive axle.
⑦—Oil pan, 5 qts. Total capacity, 11 qts.
⑧—Includes oil filter. Recommended diesel engine oil-use oil designated SF/CD, SF/CC or SE/CC on all except 1982-85 models or SF/CD, SF/CC on 1982-85 models.
⑨—Oil pan 3 1/2 qts. Total capacity 11 qts.

Electrical Section

INDEX

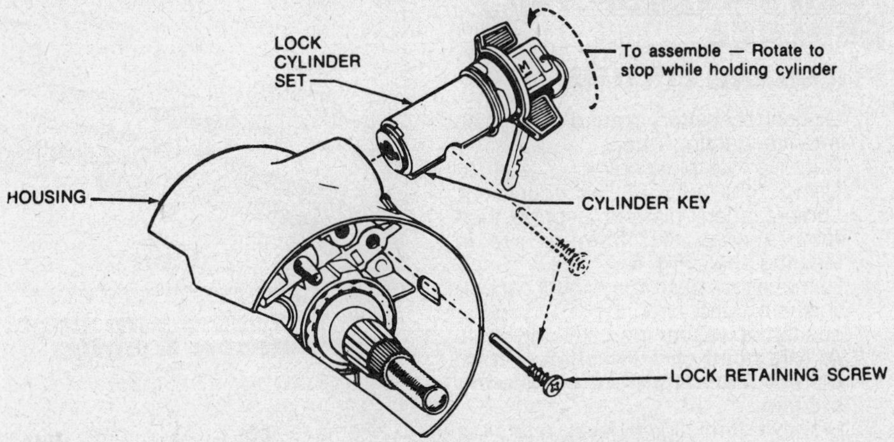

Fig. 1 Ignition lock removal

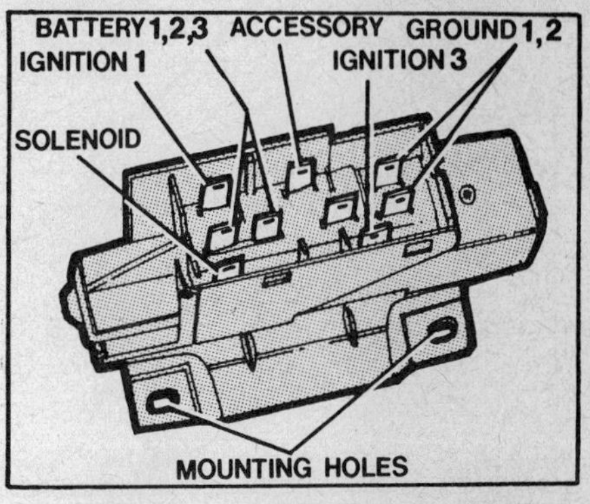

Fig. 2 Ignition switch

STARTER
REPLACE

1. Disconnect battery ground cable (two ground cables on diesel engines).
2. Raise and support front of vehicle.
3. Remove starter braces, shields, brackets and clips that may interfere with starter removal.
4. Remove starter attaching bolts, then lower starter.
5. Disconnect wiring harness from starter and remove starter.
6. Reverse procedure to install.

IGNITION LOCK
REPLACE

1. Remove steering wheel as described under Horn Sounder and Steering Wheel, Replace.
2. Remove turn signal switch as described under Turn Signal Switch, Replace, then remove buzzer switch.
3. Place ignition switch in Run position, then remove lock cylinder retaining screw and lock cylinder.
4. To install, rotate lock cylinder to stop while holding housing, **Fig. 1.** Align cylinder key with keyway in housing, then push lock cylinder assembly into housing until fully seated.
5. Install lock cylinder retaining screw. Torque screw to 40 in. lbs. for standard columns. On adjustable columns, torque retaining screw to 22 in. lbs.
6. Install buzzer switch, turn signal switch and steering wheel.

IGNITION SWITCH
REPLACE

1. Disconnect battery cable and position ignition key in "Lock."
2. Remove steering column lower cover.
3. Loosen two upper column support nuts and allow column to drop as far as possible without removing the nuts. **Do not remove nuts as column may bend under its own weight.**
4. Disconnect switch connector and remove switch, **Fig. 2.**
5. When reassembling, make sure the ignition key is in the "Lock" position. Assemble switch on actuator rod. Hold rod stationary and move switch towards bottom of column, then back off one detent on standard steering column models. On models with tilt column, move switch toward upper end of column, then back off one detent.

LIGHT SWITCH
REPLACE

ELDORADO & SEVILLE

1. Disconnect battery ground cable.
2. Remove instrument cluster trim panel.
3. Remove two screws attaching switch to cluster carrier, then pull switch rearward to remove.
4. Reverse procedure to install.

EXC. ELDORADO & SEVILLE

1. Disconnect battery ground cable.
2. Remove lefthand instrument panel insert.
3. Remove three screws attaching light switch to instrument panel.
4. On vehicles equipped with Cruise Control and Twilight Sentinel, remove two screws retaining Cruise Control switch to instrument panel.
5. Slide Cruise Control switch forward to remove headlamp switch.
6. Disconnect electrical connector from headlamp switch, then if used, disconnect Guidematic connector from under instrument panel.
7. Remove switch.
8. Reverse procedure to install.

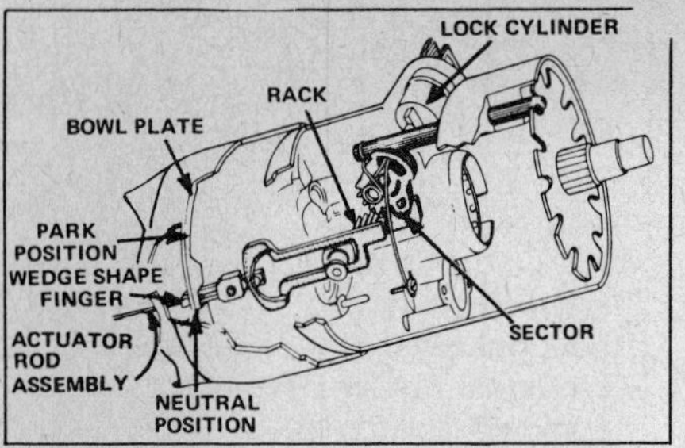

Fig. 3 Mechanical neutral switch system with Tilt-Telescope column

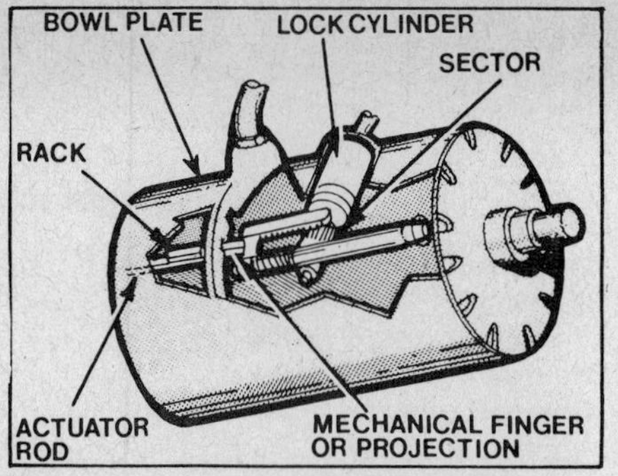

Fig. 4 Mechanical neutral start system with standard column

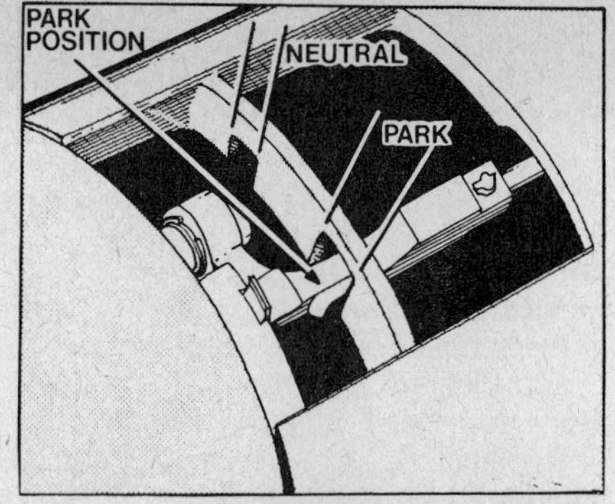

Fig. 5 Mechanical neutral start system in Park position

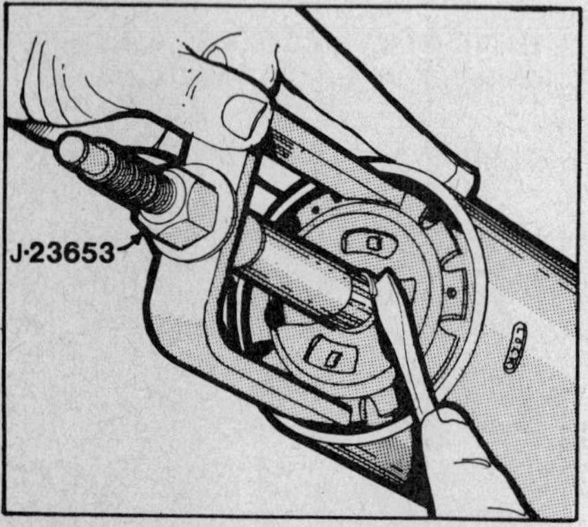

Fig. 6 Compressing lock plate & removing snap ring

STOP LIGHT SWITCH

The stop light switch is retained to the brake pedal bracket. To adjust, pull the brake pedal fully up to its stop. This action automatically adjusts the switch.

NEUTRAL START SWITCH

Actuation of the ignition switch is prevented by a mechanical lockout system, **Figs. 3 and 4,** which prevents the lock cylinder from rotating when the selector lever is out of Park or Neutral. When the selector lever is in Park or Neutral, the slots in the bowl plate and the finger on the actuator rod align, allowing the finger to pass through the bowl plate in turn actuating the ignition switch, **Fig. 5.** If the selector lever is in any position other than Park or Neutral, the finger contacts the bowl plate when the lock cylinder is rotated, thereby preventing full travel of the lock cylinder.

On all models incorporating an electric neutral start switch, this switch plus the back-up light switch and parking brake vacuum release valve are combined into one unit. This unit is mounted on the steering column under the instrument panel.

TURN SIGNAL SWITCH REPLACE

STANDARD COLUMN

1. Disconnect battery ground cable, then remove steering wheel.
2. Remove lock plate cover.
3. Using tool J-23653 or equivalent, compress lock plate and spring, then remove snap ring from groove in steering shaft, **Fig. 6.**
4. Remove lock plate, turn signal cancelling cam, upper bearing preload spring and thrust washer from steering shaft. **At this point steering shaft is free. Do not slide shaft out of steering column.**
5. Remove turn signal lever attaching screw, then signal lever.
6. On vehicles equipped with cruise control, proceed as follows:
   a. Attach a long piece of piano wire to cruise control switch harness connector.
   b. Pull cruise control harness up through and out of column.
   c. Remove piano wire from harness connector. Do not remove wire from column.
7. On all models, remove turn signal switch attaching screws, then slide switch wire connector off bracket.
8. Remove mounting bracket to steering column attaching bolts, then bracket.
9. Disconnect switch connector from wire harness.
10. Wrap a piece of tape around switch connector and harness to facilitate removal, **Fig. 7.**
11. Pull turn signal straight up with wire protector attached, and remove switch harness and connector from column.
12. Reverse procedure to install.

TILT & TELESCOPE WHEEL

1. Disconnect battery cable.
2. Remove steering wheel and slide rubber sleeve from steering shaft.
3. Remove plastic retainer from C-ring.
4. With a suitable compressor, thread bolt into steering shaft lock hole.
5. Compress preload spring and remove C-ring, **Fig. 6.**

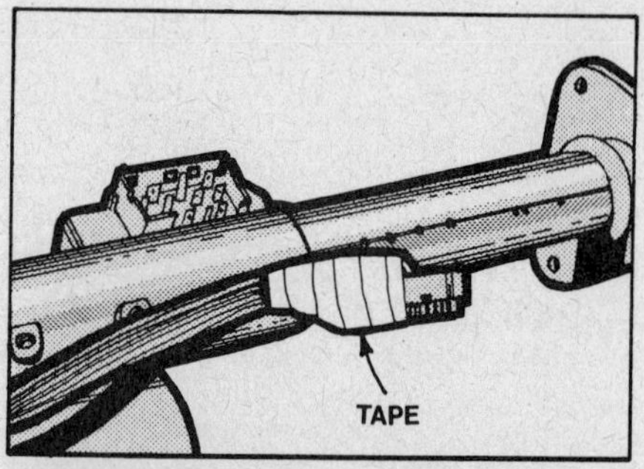

Fig. 7 Taping turn signal connector & wiring

6. Remove compressor and remove lock plate, horn contact carrier and preload spring.
7. Remove steering column lower cover and the signal lever.
8. On cars equipped with cruise control proceed as follows:
   a. Disconnect cruise control wire from harness.
   b. Remove harness protector from cruise control.
   c. Wrap wire around turn signal lever until lever is disconnected. Do not remove wire from column.
9. On all models remove bolts at upper support.
10. Remove four screws securing upper mounting bracket to column and remove bracket.
11. Disconnect turn signal harness and remove wires from plastic protector. Wrap a piece of tape around connector and harness to facilitate removal, **Fig. 7.**
12. Remove screw securing turn signal switch to column and pull switch out.
13. Reverse procedure to install.

HORN SOUNDER & STEERING WHEEL REPLACE

1. Disconnect battery ground cable.
2. Remove attaching screws from back of spokes and lift pad assembly from wheel.

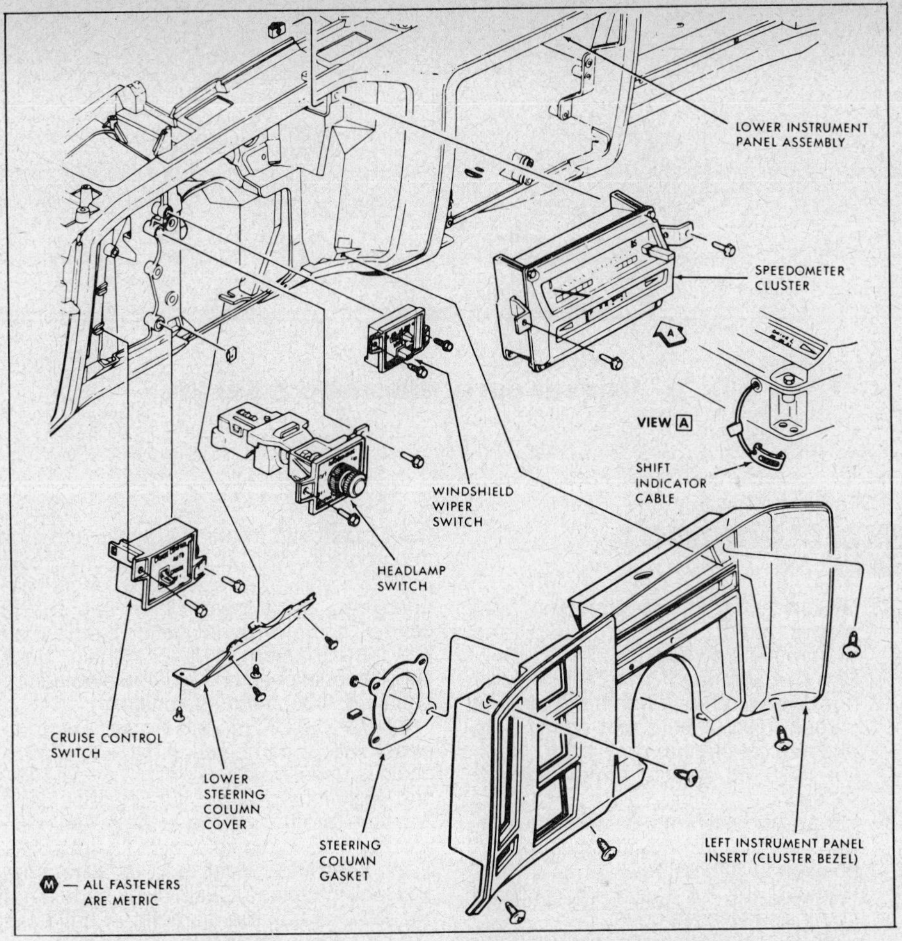

Fig. 8 Instrument cluster. Exc. Eldorado & Seville

3. Remove horn contact wire from plastic tower.
4. On tilt and telescope models, remove three screws securing lever assembly to adjuster, then adjuster from steering shaft.
5. On standard models, remove locking lever assembly.
6. On all models, scribe an alignment mark on wheel hub in line with slash mark on steering shaft to be used upon installation.
7. Loosen steering shaft nut, then using a suitable puller, remove nut and wheel.
8. Reverse procedure to install.

INSTRUMENT CLUSTER REPLACE

ELDORADO & SEVILLE

1. Disconnect battery ground cable.
2. Remove instrument cluster trim panel.
3. Remove headlamp and windshield wiper switches.
4. Unlock headlamp, windshield wiper and cruise control wire connectors from cluster carrier.
5. Disconnect speedometer cable and instrument cluster wiring.
6. Remove instrument cluster attaching screws and remove cluster assembly.
7. Reverse procedure to install.

EXC. ELDORADO & SEVILLE

1. Disconnect battery ground cable.
2. Remove cluster bezel, then with shift lever in "Park" remove screw securing shift indicator cable to steering column.
3. Remove four screws securing cluster to instrument horizontal support, **Fig. 8. On vehicles equipped with speed control sensor, disconnect sensor from cluster before completely removing cluster assembly. This will prevent connector from damaging cluster during removal.**
4. Disengage speedometer cable at neck by pulling cluster straight out and depressing retaining spring. **To remove cluster, place shift lever in low range and on cars with tilt wheel, place wheel in lowest position.**
5. Rotate cluster downward, disconnect printed circuit connector and remove cluster.
6. Reverse procedure to install.

RADIO REPLACE

When installing radio, be sure to adjust antenna trimmer for peak performance.

ELDORADO & SEVILLE

1. Disconnect battery ground cable.
2. Remove center applique retaining screws, radio knobs, and hex nuts, then remove center applique.
3. Remove radio mounting screws, then pull radio rearward. Disconnect electrical connectors and antenna lead from radio, then remove radio.
4. Reverse procedure to install.

EXC. ELDORADO & SEVILLE

1. Remove center instrument panel insert.
2. Remove screws retaining radio to lower instrument panel.
3. Disconnect electrical connectors and antenna leads(s) and remove radio.

WINDSHIELD WIPER MOTOR REPLACE

1. Raise hood and remove cowl screen. On Eldorado and Seville, remove cowl panel prior to removing cowl screen.
2. Loosen transmission drive link to crank arm attaching nuts.
3. Remove transmission drive link from motor crank arm.
4. Disconnect motor electrical connectors and hoses.
5. Remove motor attaching screws, then remove motor while guiding crank arm through hole.
6. Reverse procedure to install. **Check to ensure wiper motor is in Park position before assembling crank arm to transmission drive link.**

WINDSHIELD WIPER TRANSMISSION REPLACE

1. Raise hood and remove cowl vent screen. On Seville it is first necessary to remove cowl panel.
2. Loosen attaching nuts securing transmission drive link to motor crank arm.
3. Disconnect transmission drive link from crank arm.
4. Remove attaching screws securing transmission to body.
5. Remove transmission and linkage assembly through plenum chamber opening.

WINDSHIELD WIPER SWITCH REPLACE

ELDORADO & SEVILLE

1. Disconnect battery ground cable.
2. Remove instrument cluster trim panel.
3. Remove two screws attaching switch to cluster carrier, then pull switch rearward to remove.
4. Reverse procedure to install.

EXC. ELDORADO & SEVILLE

1. Disconnect battery ground cable.
2. Remove lefthand climate control outlet grille.
3. Remove screw securing switch to instrument panel.
4. Pull control switch and electrical connector out and disconnect from panel.

HEATER CORE REPLACE

After draining radiator and disconnecting heater hoses and battery ground cable proceed as follows:

ELDORADO & SEVILLE

1. Plug heater core outlets to prevent spillage when removing heater core.
2. Remove instrument panel sound absorbers, then lower steering column.
3. Remove instrument cluster trim panel and instrument cluster as described under Instrument Cluster, Replace.
4. Remove radio front speakers.
5. Remove screws attaching manifold to heater case.
6. Remove instrument panel upper and lower attaching screws, then disconnect parking brake release cable.
7. Disconnect instrument panel wiring harness from dash wiring assembly.
8. Disconnect righthand remote control mirror cable from instrument panel pad.
9. Disconnect speedometer cable from clip and temperature control cable from heater case.
10. Disconnect radio and A/C wiring, vacuum lines and all necessary wiring to remove instrument panel. If equipped with pulse wipers, remove wiper switch, and then disconnect wire connector from instrument cluster carrier and separate pulse wiper jumper harness from wiper switch wire connector.
11. Remove instrument panel and wiring harness assembly.
12. Remove four screws retaining defroster nozzle to cowl and one screw at heater case, then remove defroster nozzle.
13. Disconnect vacuum hoses to programmer and vacuum actuators.
14. Disconnect wire connector from programmer.
15. From engine side of dash, remove four nuts retaining heater case to cowl, **Fig. 9.**
16. From passenger compartment side of dash, remove one screw retaining heater case to cowl, and remove heater case.
17. Remove four screws securing heater core to case and remove heater core.
18. Reverse procedure to install.

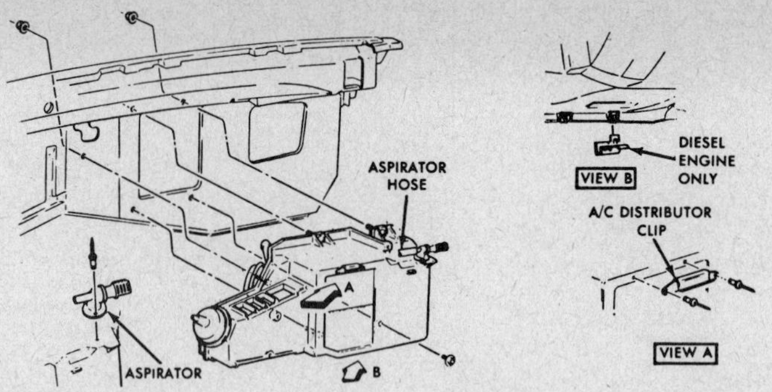

Fig. 9 Heater core. Eldorado & Seville

EXC. ELDORADO & SEVILLE

1. Disconnect electrical connectors from blower motor, blower resistors and thermostatic cycling switch.
2. Remove righthand windshield washer nozzle and remove righthand air inlet screen from plenum and cover plate at center of plenum opening.
3. On 1983-88 models, remove blower motor.
4. On all models, remove screws retaining thermostatic cycling switch and position switch aside.
5. Remove the 16 fasteners retaining cover and remove cover.
6. Remove one screw and retainer holding heater core to frame at top.
7. Place temperature door in the max. heat position and reach through temperature housing and push lower forward corner of heater core away from housing, then rotate core parallel to housing. This will cause core to snap out of lower clamp. Remove heater core from temperature housing.
8. Reverse procedure to install.

BLOWER MOTOR REPLACE

1. Disconnect battery ground cable.
2. Disconnect wire connector and cooling hose.
3. Remove five blower motor attaching screws and remove blower motor.
4. Reverse procedure to install.

SPEED CONTROL ADJUST

BEAD CHAIN ADJUSTMENT

On 1982 V6-252 models except Eldorado and Seville, a bead chain is used. Install bead chain into throttle lever clip and lock into position. With throttle lever in hot idle position and idle control solenoid de-energized, place bead chain into swivel cavity. The ball swivel must be installed on the inboard side of lever. Chain slack should not exceed one half the diameter of ball stud. Cut off excess chain.

On V8-250 DFI models except Eldorado and Seville, a combination cable and bead chain is used. Install cable into throttle clip and lock into position. Chain should be taut with throttle body lever in hot idle position and idle speed solenoid fully retracted. Place bead into swivel, then install retainer and lock into place. Chain slack should not exceed one half the diameter of ball stud. Cut off excess chain.

On Eldorado and Seville models, a rod assembly is used. Install rod into servo assembly bushing, then assemble plastic end of rod to ball stud on throttle body lever. Adjust by rotating rod assembly to obtain minimum slack with idle speed control screw fully retracted and engine stopped.

On 1986-88 models, a rod assembly is used to control cruise control speed. Adjustment is made with engine Off, carburetor lever on slow idle screw and Idle Load Control (ILC) fully retracted. Adjust rod length to obtain the least amount of slack.

BRAKE RELEASE SWITCH ADJUSTMENT

With brake pedal depressed, push cruise control/stoplight switch fully into retainer and pull brake pedal fully back to rest position. Switch will back out of retainer and adjust automatically.

VACUUM DUMP VALVE ADJUSTMENT

With brake pedal depressed, push vacuum valve switch all the way into the retaining clip. Pull the brake pedal to the stop to automatically adjust the valve.

Engine Section

NOTE: The following engines are covered in this section; V6-252 (4.1L), V8-250 (4.1L) and V8-368 (6.0L). Refer to appropriate Buick Section for service procedures on V6-252 engine not included in this section. Refer to appropriate Oldsmobile Section for service procedures on V8-307 gasoline engine and V8-350 diesel engine.

INDEX

ENGINE MOUNTS REPLACE

1982–85 V8-250

Engine Mount, Replace

1. Open hood, then remove screws securing strut support rod and position rods aside, **Fig. 1.**
2. Position upper radiator shroud so that it will not be damaged when engine is raised.
3. Raise and support vehicle, then remove engine mount through bolt.
4. Raise engine slightly using suitable jack until engine mount bracket is free from mount.
5. Remove nuts securing engine mount, then remove engine mount.

1982 V6-252

Removal

1. Remove front engine mount to cylinder block bolts, **Fig. 2.**
2. Raise and support vehicle.
3. Using a suitable jack, raise and support engine weight at front edge of oil pan.
4. Remove rear engine mount to cylinder block bolts.
5. Raise engine slightly and remove engine mount through bolts.
6. Remove mount.

Installation

1. Install rear engine mount to cylinder block bolts and torque to 55 ft. lbs.
2. Lower engine until mounts rest on crossmember bracket.
3. Install and tighten engine mount through bolts.
4. Lower vehicle. Install front engine mount bolts and torque to 55 ft. lbs.

ENGINE REPLACE

1982–85 V8-250

1. Disconnect battery ground cable and drain cooling system.
2. Remove screws securing strut support rods and position rods aside.
3. Remove radiator shroud to radiator support screws. Remove staples securing upper and lower fan shrouds.
4. Remove radiator cover from radiator support.
5. Remove power steering reservoir from upper fan shroud, then position reservoir aside and remove fan shroud.
6. Mark hood hinge outlines on hood, then remove hood.
7. Remove air cleaner and duct assembly.
8. Disconnect upper radiator hose from thermostat housing.
9. Disconnect following electrical connectors:
   a. Coolant temperature sensor.
   b. Engine metal temperature switch.
   c. MAT sensor.
   d. Idle speed control motor.
   e. Throttle position sensor.
   f. EGR solenoid.
   g. AIR management valve.
   h. Oxygen sensor.
   i. Ignition timing connector.
   j. Distributor and A/C compressor.
   k. Alternator, cruise control servo and right side cylinder head ground wires.
10. Disconnect wiring harness support clips and position harness aside.
11. Disconnect brake vacuum hose from pipe, throttle linkage, and vapor canister hose.
12. Remove clutch fan assembly, then disconnect lower radiator hose.
13. Remove A/C compressor mounting bolts and position compressor aside with all lines attached.
14. Disconnect coolant reservoir hose and remove water nipple from rear of intake manifold.
15. Disconnect fuel inlet and return lines.
16. On Brougham and DeVille models, raise and support vehicle, then proceed as follows:
    a. Disconnect oil cooler lines from filter adapter, then remove filter adapter.

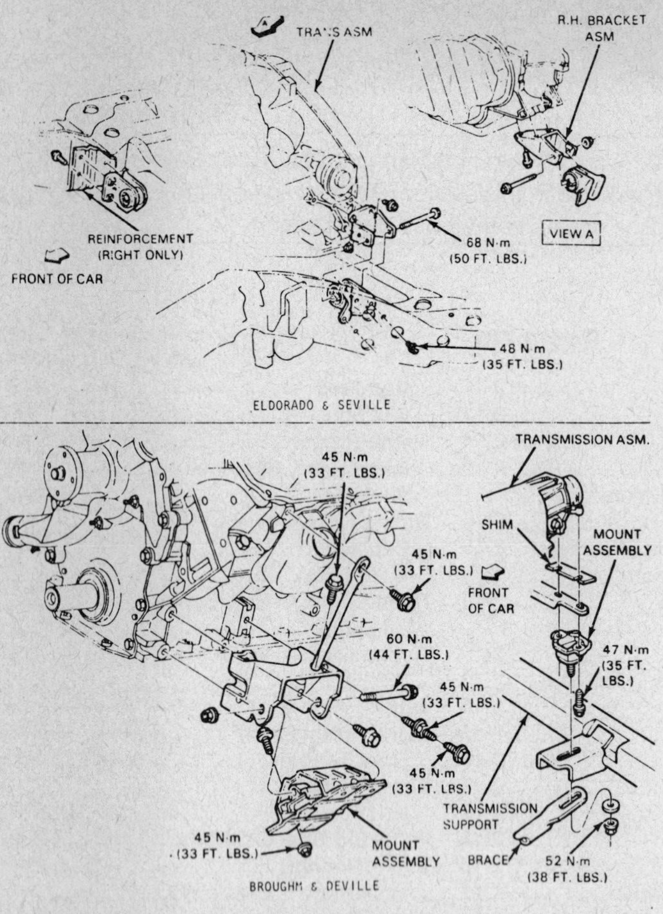

Fig. 1 Engine mounts. 1982–85 models with V8-250 engine

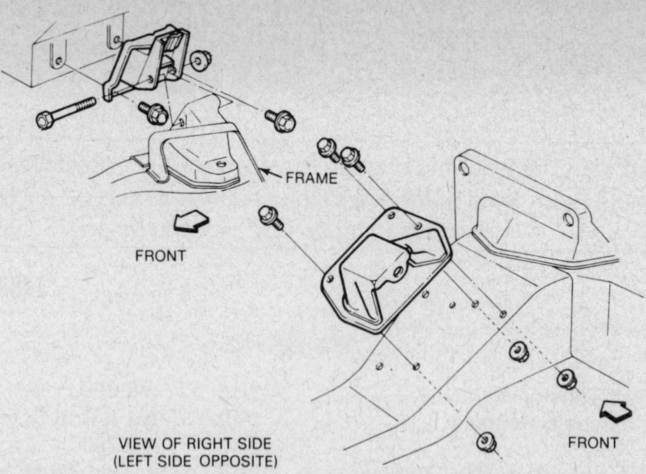

Fig. 2 Front engine mounts. 1982 models with V6-252 engine

b. Remove strut rods connecting engine mounts to flywheel cover.
c. Remove flywheel cover.
d. Remove six engine to transmission screws, then remove motor mount through bolts.
e. Remove screws securing flywheel to converter.
f. Disconnect starter motor electrical connectors, then disconnect exhaust pipes from exhaust manifold.
g. Lower vehicle to ground, then support transmission with suitable jack.
h. Attach suitable lifting equipment to engine lift brackets, then raise engine slowly and position forward to disengage from transmission.
i. Remove engine from vehicle.
j. Reverse procedure to install.

7. On Eldorado and Seville models, raise and support vehicle, then proceed as follows:
   a. Disconnect oil cooler lines from junction at righthand side of engine compartment.
   b. Remove six engine to transaxle screws, then remove nuts securing engine mount brackets to transmission.
   c. Remove flywheel cover and screws securing flywheel to converter.
   d. Disconnect starter motor electrical connectors, then disconnect exhaust pipes from exhaust manifold.
   e. Lower vehicle, then support transaxle with suitable jack.
   f. Attach suitable lifting equipment to engine lift brackets, then raise engine slowly and pull forward to disengage from transmission.
   g. Remove engine from vehicle.
   h. Reverse procedure to install.

1982 V6-252, EXC. ELDORADO & SEVILLE

Removal

1. Mark hood hinge and hinge bracket for installation alignment, then remove hood.
2. Remove battery ground cable.
3. Drain engine coolant, remove air cleaner, then disconnect A/C compressor ground wire from mounting bracket.
4. Disconnect compressor clutch connector.
5. Remove compressor from mounting bracket and position out of the way.
6. Remove fan, pulley and belts.
7. Disconnect radiator and heater hoses and position aside, then remove radiator and fan shroud.
8. Remove power steering pump from bracket and position aside.
9. Disconnect and plug fuel pump hose.
10. Disconnect vacuum feed hose from carburetor, then the vacuum modulator and power brake vacuum hoses from engine.
11. Disconnect the three evaporative canister to carburetor hoses.
12. Disconnect throttle and TV cable from carburetor.
13. Disconnect Cruise Control servo cable at mounting bracket, if equipped.
14. Disconnect all sending unit switch connections from engine. Remove alternator, then disconnect engine wiring harness at engine.
15. Raise and support vehicle, then disconnect engine wiring harness at starter and remove starter.
16. Disconnect exhaust pipes from exhaust manifold.
17. Remove lower flywheel cover, then mark flywheel and converter for reassembly alignment. Remove converter to flywheel bolts.
18. Remove engine to transmission bolts and engine mount through bolts.
19. Lower vehicle and support transmission. Using a suitable lifting device, raise engine. Ensure wiring harness, vacuum hoses and other parts are clear of engine before removal.
20. Lift engine just enough to clear engine mounts, then lift transmission support evenly and alternately until engine is separated from transmission and can be removed.

Installation

1. Lower engine into vehicle, engaging transmission. Align flywheel and converter marks, then install and torque flywheel bolts to 35 ft. lbs.
2. Install and tighten engine mount through bolts and nuts.
3. Raise and support vehicle, then install transmission to engine bolts and torque to 35 ft. lbs.
4. Install starter, then install flywheel cover. Connect starter electrical leads.
5. Connect exhaust pipes to exhaust manifolds.
6. Lower vehicle, then connect engine wiring harness, throttle cable, vacuum and water hoses, emission control line from canister to air cleaner and the transmission cooler line clip to exhaust manifold stud.

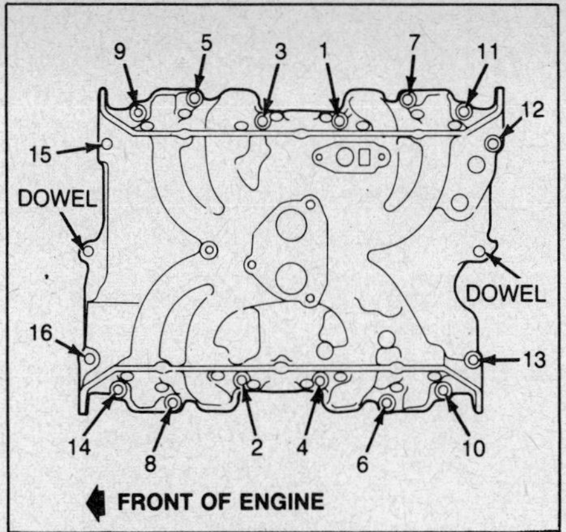

BOLT TIGHTENING SEQUENCE

1. TIGHTEN BOLTS 1, 2, 3, & 4 IN SEQUENCE TO 15.0-20.0 N•m (11-15 FT-LBS).
2. TIGHTEN BOLTS 5 THRU 16 IN SEQUENCE TO 24.5-30.0 N•m (18-22 FT-LBS).
3. RETIGHTEN ALL BOLTS IN SEQUENCE TO 24.5-30.0 N•m (18-22 FT-LBS).

Fig. 3 Intake manifold bolt tightening sequence. V8-250

7. Connect battery ground cable to A/C compressor bracket.
8. Connect fuel line to fuel pump.
9. Install power steering pump into bracket. Adjust power steering belt tension.
10. Install fan shroud and radiator assembly. Attach radiator hoses and transmission cooler lines.
11. Install pulley, fan and belts. Adjust belt tension.
12. Install A/C compressor into bracket and connect wiring.
13. Install alternator to bracket and connect wiring.
14. Install air cleaner.
15. Install engine coolant; ensure proper level is attained after engine reaches operating temperature.
16. Connect negative battery cable to battery.
17. Install hood, aligning marks made at removal.

INTAKE MANIFOLD REPLACE

V8-250

Some vehicles equipped with V8-250 engine may have oil leakage at the intake manifold to block seal. This may be caused by a split intake manifold seal. To correct this problem, new silicone end seals were put into production during 1984.

The seals, which can be identified by their gray color are part of gasket set 3634619 and can be used to service older model engines.

1. Drain coolant from radiator, then disconnect radiator hose from thermostat housing.
2. Disconnect electrical connectors from coolant sensor, MAT sensor, throttle position sensor, distributor, ISC motor and fuel injectors.
3. Disconnect heater hoses from manifold.
4. Disconnect fuel lines from throttle body and remove distributor.
5. Remove both rocker arm covers.
6. Remove rocker arm support and rocker arms as an assembly.
7. Remove bolts securing A/C compressor, then position compressor aside with all hoses and lines attached.
8. Remove vacuum harness connectors from rear of manifold.
9. Remove intake manifold bolts and lower thermostat housing to front cover bolts. **Engine lift brackets must be bent or positioned aside for intake manifold removal.**
10. Remove intake manifold by lifting straight up off dowels.
11. Reverse procedure to install. Refer to **Fig. 3** for intake manifold bolt tightening sequence and torque procedure.

The V8-250 engine uses three different intake manifolds, all using different intake manifold to cylinder head bolts. To determine which manifold and bolts are used, an identification mark is located next to the manifold air temperature sensor.

The first type manifold has no identification mark. Bolt location, Fig. 3, and size are as follows: locations 1, 2, 3, 4, 12, 13 and 16; 1.57 inch (40 mm) bolts; locations 5, 6, 7, 8, 9, 10, 11 and 14; 1.18 inch (30 mm) bolts; and location 15; 2.36 inch (60 mm) bolt.

The second type manifold is identified by an X. Bolt location, Fig. 3, and sizes are as follows: locations 1, 2, 3 and 4; 2.16 inch (55 mm) bolts; locations 5, 6, 7, 8, 9, 10, 11 and 14; 1.18 inch (30 mm) bolts; locations 12, 13 and 16; 1.57 inch (40 mm) bolts; and location 15, 2.36 inch (60 mm) bolt.

The third type manifold is identified by a circled X. This manifold uses the same bolts in the same location as the manifold with the X identification mark, with the exception of bolt 12. In this manifold a 2.16 inch (55 mm) bolt is used, Fig. 3.

V6-252

1. Disconnect battery ground cable, then drain cooling system.
2. Remove air cleaner.
3. Disconnect the following:
   a. Upper radiator hose and heater hose at manifold.
   b. Accelerator linkage at carburetor, linkage bracket at manifold and cruise control chain if equipped.
   c. Booster vacuum pipe at manifold.
   d. Fuel line at carburetor.
   e. Transmission vacuum modulator line.

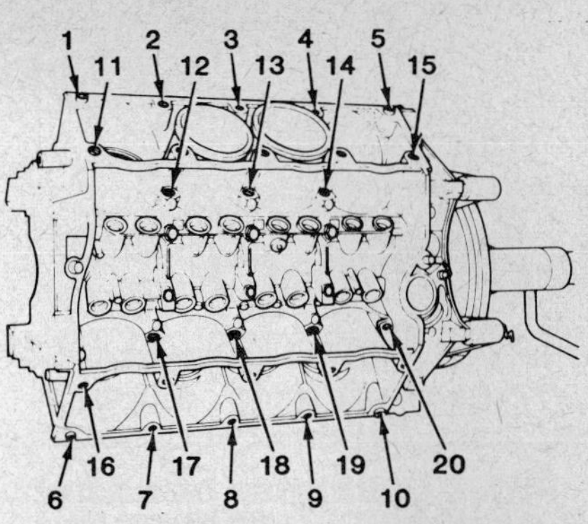

Fig. 4 Cylinder head bolt hole locations. V8-250

   f. Idle stop solenoid wire, if equipped.
   g. Distributor wires and temperature sending unit wire.
   h. Vacuum hoses from, distributor TVS and EFE valve pipe, from carburetor to vacuum manifold.
   i. Fuel economy and load leveler hose, if equipped.
   j. Coolant bypass hose at manifold.
4. Remove distributor cap and rotor to gain access to left intake manifold torx head bolt. Use Tool J-24394 or equivalent to remove torx head bolt.
5. Remove accelerator linkage springs.
6. Remove compressor upper bracket, if equipped.
7. Remove intake manifold.
8. Reverse procedure to install.

CYLINDER HEAD REPLACE

V8-250

Some V8-250 engine blocks may exhibit casting porosity, indicated by oil leakage around the threads of cylinder head bolts. This leakage is caused by porosity between a pressurized oil passage and the threaded bolt hole. This condition occurs between an oil gallery and holes 11, 12, 13, 14, 17, 18, 19 or 20, **Fig. 4.** An internal oil leak will occur around these bolts and will rarely be detected. However, when this condition is experienced at bolt holes 1, 2, 3, 4, 5, 6, 7, 8, 9, 10, 15, or 16, **Fig. 4,** an external oil leak may result. To provide a permanent repair for this condition, remove the bolt and clean both the bolt and hole with a suitable cleaner. With compressed air, blow out the bolt hole and apply a suitable two-part epoxy to the lower 5 or 6 threads of the bolt. Install the bolt and torque to 90 ft. lbs.

1. Remove valve covers, then remove intake manifold as described under "Intake Manifold, Replace."
2. On righthand side cylinder head removal, remove alternator and AIR pump.
3. For lefthand side cylinder head removal, remove vacuum pump and bracket. Remove bolts and position power steering pump aside.
4. Remove exhaust manifold from cylinder head, then bolt securing AIR pipe to cylinder head.

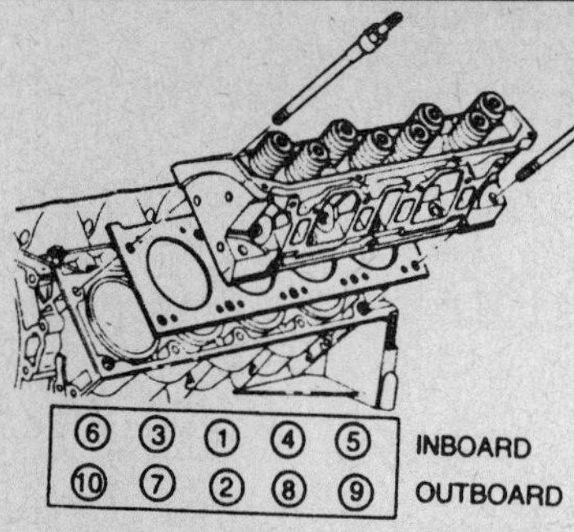

Fig. 5 Cylinder head bolt tightening sequence. V8-250

5. Remove cylinder head bolts, then remove cylinder head.
6. Reverse procedure to install. Refer to **Fig. 5** for cylinder head bolt tightening sequence.

VALVES, ADJUST

These engines use hydraulic valve lifters. No provision for adjustment is provided.

VALVE ARRANGEMENT

FRONT TO REAR

V6-252. . . . . E-I-I-E-I-E
V8-250. . . . . I-E-I-E-E-I-E-I

VALVE LIFT SPECIFICATIONS

Engine	Year	Intake	Exhaust
V6-252①	1982	.357	.366
V8-250	1982-85	.384	.396

①—Refer to Buick Chapter for service procedures.

VALVE TIMING

INTAKE OPENS BEFORE TDC

Engine	Year	Degrees
V6-252①	1982	16
V8-250	1982-85	37

①—Refer to Buick Chapter for service procedures.

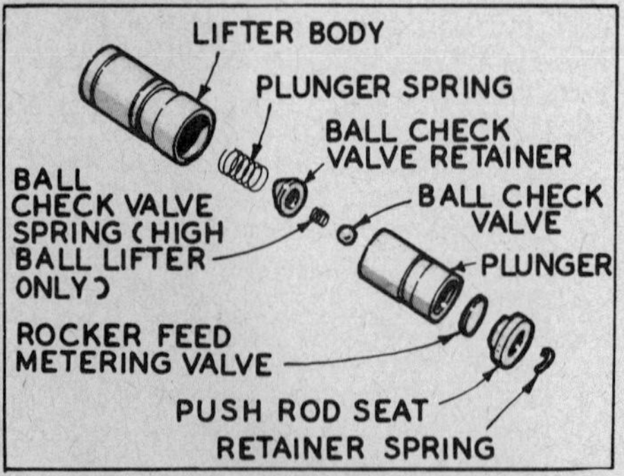

Fig. 7 Hydraulic valve lifter

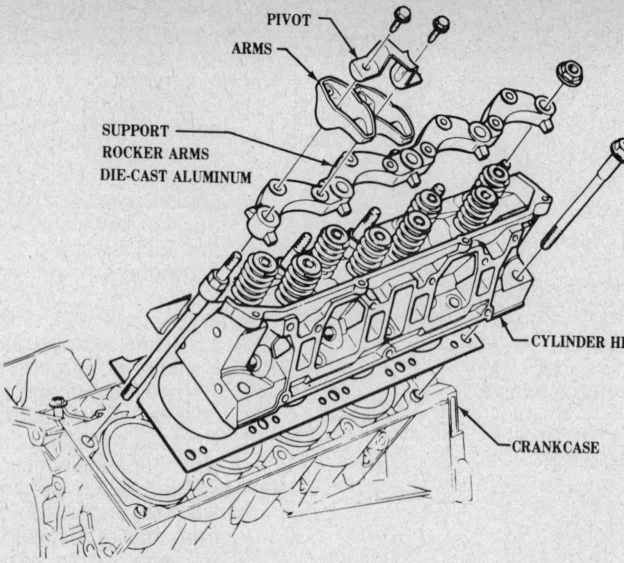

Fig. 6 Rocker arm assembly exploded view. V8-250

ROCKER ARMS REPLACE

V8-250

1. Remove valve cover.
2. Remove nuts from stud headed cylinder head bolts, then remove valve train support with rocker arms and pivots as an assembly, **Fig. 6. Pivot assemblies may be damaged unless rocker arms and pivots are removed as an assembly.**
3. Position rocker arm support in suitable vise and remove rocker arms and pivots.
4. Install rocker arms and pivots into valve train support and tighten pivot bolts.
5. Position valve train support over mounting studs and snug tighten retaining nuts.
6. Check pushrods for correct positioning, then tighten nuts alternately and evenly.

VALVE GUIDES

V8-250

Check valve stem to valve guide clearance, clearance should be no more than .005 inch. Service valves are available in standard (.343 inch) and .003, .006 and .013 inch oversizes. If clearance is found to be excessive, valve guide should be reamed out to next oversize using appropriate reamer, and a corresponding oversize valve installed. On some engines, valves with a .003 inch oversize diameter and .003 inch oversize valve guides are installed at the factory. Engines so fitted will be identified by a "3" stamped on the cylinder head gasket surface inline with the oversize valve.

HYDRAULIC VALVE LIFTERS REPLACE

The valve lifters may be lifted out of their bores after removing the rocker arms, pushrods and intake manifold. Adjustable pliers with taped jaws may be used to remove lifters that are stuck due to varnish, carbon, etc., **Fig. 7**, illustrates the type of lifter used.

On 1982-83 V8-250 engines, if valve lifter replacement is required, replacement should be made with the new design type. The new design type lifter foot is more convex in shape and is identified by two machined grooves on the lifter body, Fig. 8. If camshaft replacement is necessary, all 16 lifters should be replaced with the new design type.

TIMING CASE COVER REPLACE

V8-250

1. Disconnect battery ground cable and drain cooling system.
2. On Brougham and DeVille models,

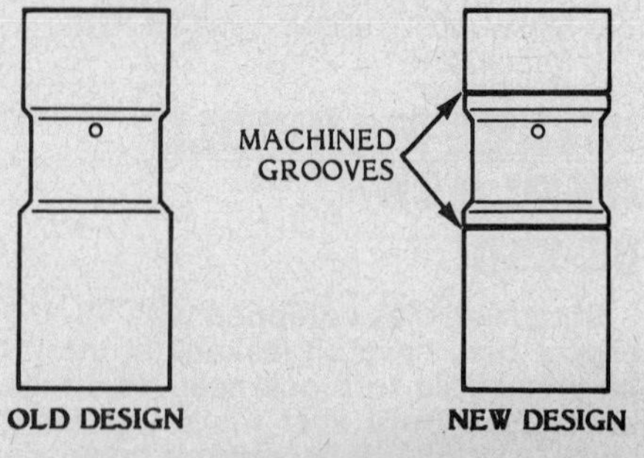

Fig. 8 New design valve lifter. V8-250

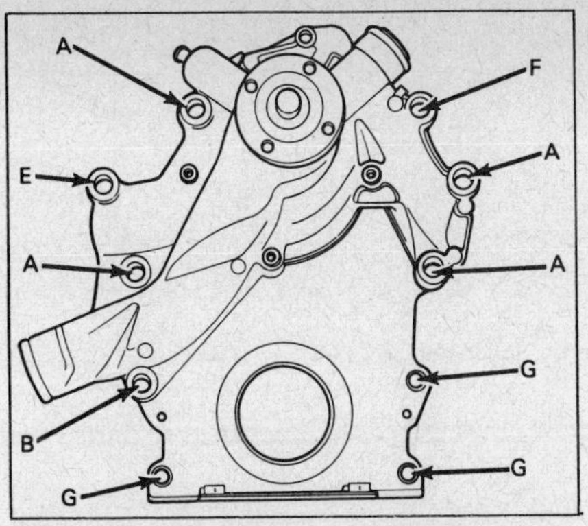

Fig. 9 Engine front cover attaching screws. V8-250

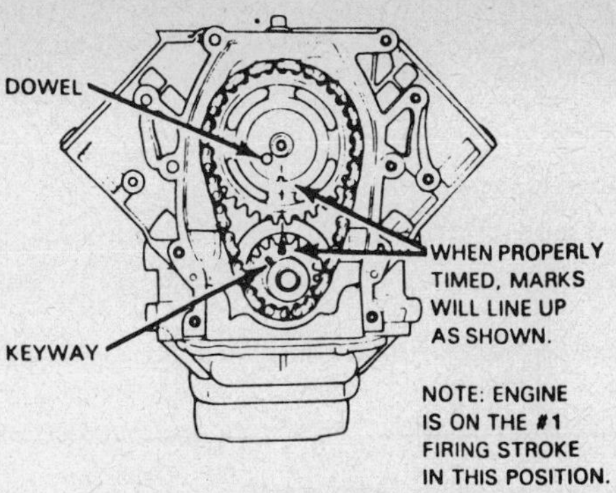

Fig. 10 Timing gear location marks. V8-250

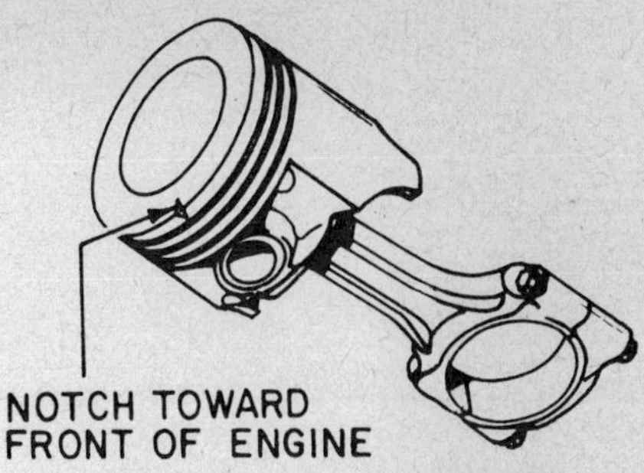

Fig. 11 Piston & rod assembly. V8-250

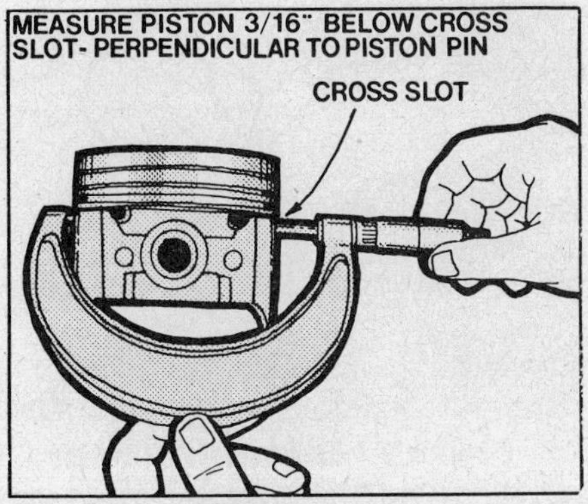

Fig. 12 Measuring piston diameter

position support rods aside.

3. Disconnect wiring harness from upper fan shroud clamps.
4. Remove power steering pump reservoir from upper fan shroud, then remove upper fan shroud.
5. Remove clutch fan, then loosen alternator and AIR pump mounting bolts and remove drive belts.
6. Loosen power steering pump retaining bolts and remove vacuum pump drive belts.
7. Remove A/C compressor mounting bolts, then remove drive belt and position compressor aside with all hoses and lines attached.
8. Remove alternator and support bracket, then disconnect coolant reservoir hose at water pump.
9. Disconnect hoses from water pump.
10. Remove water pump and crankshaft pulleys.
11. Remove A/C compressor bracket from engine.
12. Remove timing mark tab from front cover, then remove crankshaft vibration damper.
13. Remove bolts securing front cover to cylinder block, then remove cover, water pump and lower thermostat housing as an assembly.
14. Reverse procedure to install. Coat oil pan front lip with suitable sealer. Refer to **Fig. 9** and torque bolts "A," "E" and "F" to 30 ft. lbs. and bolts "B" and "G" to 15 ft. lbs.

TIMING CASE COVER OIL SEAL

REPLACE

V8-250

1. Remove crankshaft pulley and vibration damper.
2. Remove front cover oil seal using tools J-1859-03 and J-23129 or equivalents.
3. Lubricate new seal with engine oil, then install using tool J-29662 or equivalent.
4. Install vibration damper and crankshaft pulley.

TIMING CHAIN

REPLACE

V8-250

1. Remove engine timing case cover as described under "Timing Case Cover, Replace."
2. Remove oil slinger from crankshaft.
3. Rotate crankshaft to align camshaft and crankshaft sprocket timing marks, **Fig. 10.**
4. Remove screw attaching camshaft sprocket to camshaft, then remove camshaft and crankshaft sprockets with timing chain attached.
5. Reverse procedure to install. Ensure that timing marks are aligned as shown in **Fig. 10.**

CAMSHAFT

REPLACE

V8-250

1. Remove timing chain as described previously.
2. Remove valve lifters as described under "Valve Lifters, Replace."
3. Remove radiator, then remove camshaft from engine. Use caution not to damage camshaft bearings when removing camshaft.
4. Reverse procedure to install.

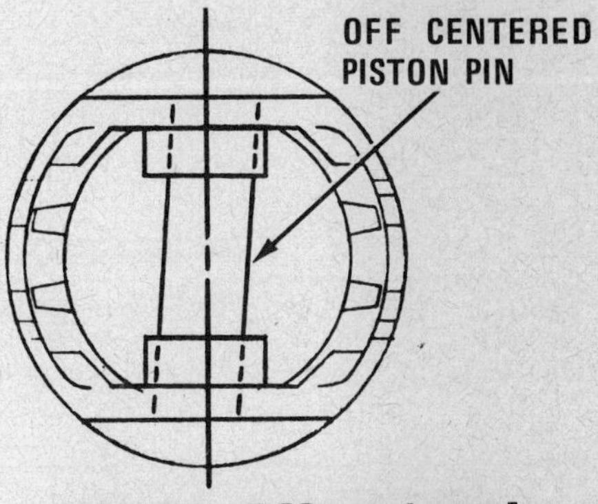

Fig. 13 Off centered piston pin. V8-250

PISTONS & RODS ASSEMBLE

V8-250

Assemble and install the piston and rod assemblies as shown in **Fig. 11.**

Measure connecting rod side clearance using a suitable feeler gauge. Clearances should be .008-.020 inch.

PISTONS

V8-250

When measuring piston diameter, place micrometer 3/16 inch below cross slot or 3/8 inch below oil ring groove, **Fig. 12.** Cylinder liner diameter is measured by placing a micrometer two inches down from top of liner and perpendicular to cylinder center line. The difference between the two readings should be .0010-.0018 inch. Cylinder bore out-of-round should not exceed .0008 inch and piston bore taper should not exceed .0005-.002 inch. If any reading is not as specified, piston and cylinder liner assembly must be replaced. No attempt should be made to rebore or hone cylinder liners. Refer to "Cylinder Liner, Replace" for procedure.

On some 1982 V8-250 engines a minor to severe internal metallic knock may be encountered. This may be caused by close piston to counterbalance tolerance on cylinder Nos. 1, 2, 3, 6, 7 and 8 and is usually heard when engine is at operating temperature between 800-1400 RPM.

The following procedure should be used

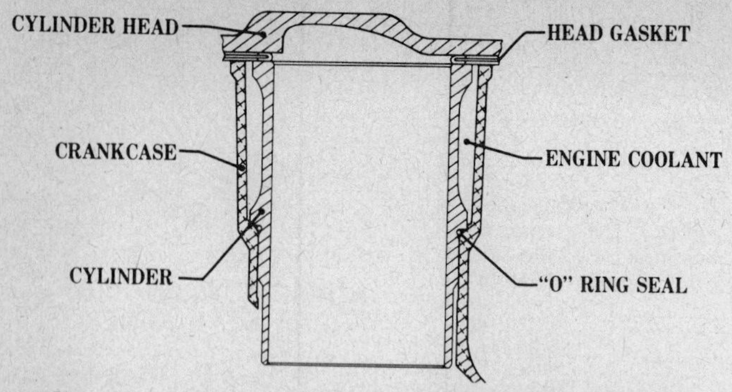

Fig. 14 Cylinder liner assembly. V8-250

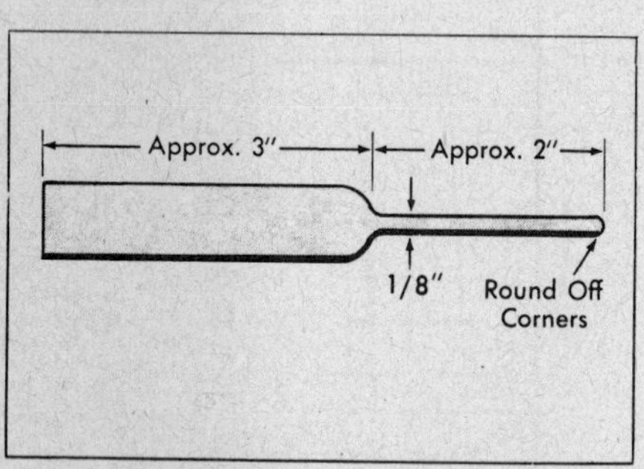

Fig. 16 Main bearing oil seal tool. V8-250

to correct this problem:

1. Remove engine oil pan and cylinder heads as previously described.
2. Inspect all pistons for correct installation.
3. Using a wax pencil, mark right and left sides of outboard piston skirts which rotate next to crankshaft counterbalance weights on piston Nos. 1, 2, 3, 6, 7 and 8.
4. Remove and inspect all pistons for off-centered piston wrist pins, **Fig. 13.** If off-centered piston pins are encountered, replace piston and liner assembly.
5. Using a suitable file, remove a small amount of material from piston skirt edges marked in step 3. All surfaces must be smooth and free of all file marks after reworking. If interference marks are evident in the piston skirts and filing does not remove marks, replace piston and liner assembly.
6. Reinstall pistons into block.
7. Check piston skirt to crankshaft counterweight clearance by placing an index card between skirts and counterweights while rotating crankshaft. No drag should be felt on card. If drag is felt, crankshaft should be replaced.
8. Reinstall cylinder heads and oil pan.

PISTON RINGS

Replacement rings are available on all except V8-250 engines in standard size and .010 inch oversize. On V8-250 engine, replacement rings are available in standard size only. If piston ring clearance is excessive on this engine, new piston and cylinder liner must be installed. Refer to "Cylinder Liner, Replace."

PISTON PINS

V8-250

Piston pins are a matched fit with the piston and are not available separately. Piston pins are pressed in the connecting rods and will not become loose enough to cause a knock or tapping until after very high mileages. In such cases a new piston and pin assembly should be installed.

CYLINDER LINER REPLACE

V8-250

The cylinder heads, pistons, connecting rods, bearings and crankshaft must be removed from engine before replacing cylinder liners.

1. If original liners, **Fig. 14,** are to be reinstalled, mark position of liner in cylinder block and keep piston with original liner for reference during installation.
2. Use tool J-29775 or equivalent to remove liners from cylinder block. Discard O-ring from bottom of cylinder liner.
3. Check cylinder liner and block mating surfaces to ensure they are free of nicks and burrs.
4. If original liners are to be installed into original block, it is not necessary to gauge their height. Install new O-ring seal onto liner, align reference marks made during removal, then install liner into block using tool J-29775 or equivalent.
5. If new liner and piston assembly is to be installed, or if original block experienced overheating, then cylinder liner height must be gauged.
6. Position new liner into block without O-ring.
7. Position gauge J-29776 or equivalent onto cylinder liner. Check to ensure that spring loaded guide pins fit into liner with machined pads resting on edge of liner and dial indicator contacting block deck face. Apply moderate pressure to gauge until dial indicator stops moving.
8. Record this reading. If reading is on + side of dial indicator, cylinder liner is higher than block face by indicated amount. If reading is on − side, cylinder liner is below block face.

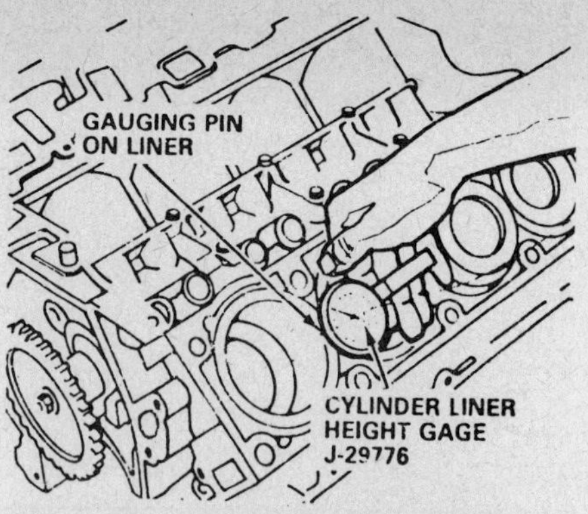

Fig. 15 Measuring liner to liner height. V8-250

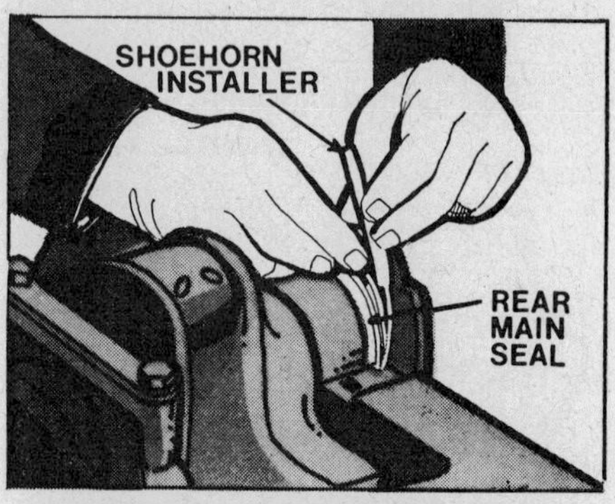

Fig. 17 Installing rear main bearing oil seal. V8-250

9. Repeat steps 7 and 8 at two other locations. Take average of three readings as actual liner height.
10. Specified liner height is .01-.08 mm above block deck face. If specified height cannot be obtained, replace liner with new one. Liners may be rotated in block to obtain specified height.
11. If liner height is satisfactory, then liner-to-liner height must be checked. Install adjacent liners into cylinder block without O-ring. Using gauge J-29766 or equivalent, measure height between liners while second liner is held firmly in place, **Fig. 15.** Liner-to-liner height should be ±.05 mm. Mark liners in this position.
12. When installing liners into block, check to ensure that liners are installed in marked position. Install O-ring onto liner, then install liner into block using tool J-29775 or equivalent.

MAIN & ROD BEARINGS

V8-250

Main and rod bearings are supplied by Cadillac in standard sizes only.

CRANKSHAFT OIL SEAL REPLACE

V8-250

Rear main bearing installation tool can be made from shim stock or a metal banding strap using dimensions in **Fig. 16.**

The two seal halves are identical and can be used in either the lower or upper location. However, both seal halves are prelubricated with a film of wax for break-in. Do not remove or damage this film.

To install the lower half of the seal into the bearing cap, slide either end of seal into position at one end of bearing cap and place tool on seal land at other end of bearing. Make sure seal is positioned over bearing ridge and lip of seal is facing forward (car position).

Hold thumb over end of seal that is flush with split line to prevent it from slipping upward, and push seal into seated position by applying pressure to the other end. Make sure seal is pressed down firmly and is flush on each side to avoid possibility of a leak at seal split line. Avoid pressing on lip as damage to sealing edge could result.

To install upper half of seal in cylinder block (with crankshaft in car), position "shoehorn" tool on land of block, **Fig. 17.** Start seal into groove in block with lip facing forward and rotate seal into position. Do not press on lip or sealing edge may be damaged. Both ends of seal must be flush at seal split line to avoid leaks. If necessary, Lubriplate or its equivalent may be used to facilitate installation of both upper and lower seal halves. Do not use silicone or a leak may result.

OIL PAN

REPLACE

1982–85 V8-250 EXC. ELDORADO & SEVILLE

1. Disconnect battery ground cable, then raise and support vehicle.
2. Drain engine oil and remove oil filter.
3. Remove flywheel cover and support struts.
4. Disconnect exhaust pipe from manifold and remove catalytic converter bracket bolt.
5. Remove oil pan nuts and bolts, then lower exhaust pipe and remove oil pan from vehicle.
6. Reverse procedure to install. Use suitable RTV sealer in sufficient quantities when installing pan. Torque pan attaching bolts and nuts to 11 ft. lbs. on 1982 models and 15 ft. lbs. on 1983-85 models.

1982–85 V8-250 ELDORADO & SEVILLE

1. Raise and support vehicle and drain engine oil. Remove oil filter.
2. Remove flywheel cover, then remove final drive assembly.
3. Disconnect exhaust pipe from manifold, then remove front suspension stone shield.
4. Remove bolts securing engine mount to frame crossmember.
5. Remove oil pan bolts and nuts, then lower exhaust pipe and remove oil pan from vehicle. **To facilitate oil pan removal, place suitable jack under cylinder head ledge of crankcase or against cylinder head, and raise engine just enough to remove oil pan.**

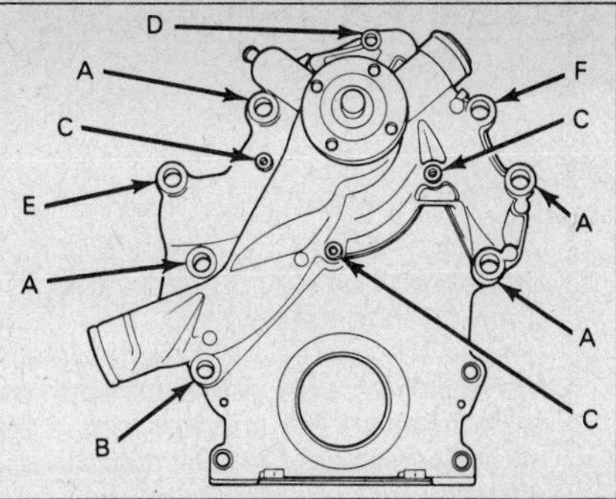

KEY	NO.	SIZE	TORQUE N·M	TORQUE FT. LBS.
A	4	M10 X 1.50 X 45	40	30
B	1	M8 X 1.25 X 35	20	15
C	3	M6 X 1.0 (NUT)	7	5
D	1	(1620262)	10	7
E	1	M10 X 1.50 (NUT)	40	30
F	1	M10 X 1.50 X 50 (STUD HEAD)	40	30

Fig. 18 Water pump attaching screws. V8-250

6. Reverse procedure to install. Use suitable RTV sealer in sufficient quantities when installing pan. Torque pan attaching bolts to 10 to 11 ft. lbs.

1982 V6-252 EXC. ELDORADO & SEVILLE

Removal

1. Raise and support vehicle. Drain oil.
2. Remove flywheel cover.
3. Remove exhaust crossover pipe.
4. Remove oil pan attaching bolts and the oil pan.

Installation

1. Reverse procedure to install. Ensure oil pan and cylinder block mating surfaces are clean. **These engines use RTV silicone sealer in place of a cork gasket for oil pan to crankcase sealing. If replacement of the oil pan or gasket is necessary, either RTV sealer or a cork gasket may be used for reassembly. If RTV sealer is used, the pan rail and block mating surfaces should be thoroughly cleaned and a 1/4 inch bead of sealant applied evenly to the pan rail. Use caution to avoid any breaks or gaps in the sealer during application.**
2. Torque oil pan bolts to 14 ft. lbs.
3. Torque flywheel cover bolts to 4 ft. lbs.
4. Lower vehicle and add oil.

1982 V6-252 ELDORADO & SEVILLE

1. Disconnect battery ground cable.
2. Remove one final drive to transmission bolt.
3. Install engine support and hoist car, then install jack stands and lower hoist.
4. Disconnect idler arm bracket at frame.
5. Lock steering wheel in full left position.
6. Disconnect drive axles from output shafts and disconnect battery cable bracket from output shaft support, then disconnect shaft support from engine block.
7. Remove remaining final drive to transmission bolts and place transmission jack under final drive.
8. Remove final drive cover and final drive unit.
9. Remove splash shield, then disconnect starter wires and remove starter.
10. Remove flywheel cover and drain oil pan.
11. Remove oil pan attaching bolts and remove oil pan.
12. Reverse procedure to install. Apply suitable RTV sealer when installing pan.

1982 EXC. V6-252 & ELDORADO & SEVILLE

1. Disconnect battery ground cable.
2. Remove two screws on each side securing radiator cover to strut rods, support rods and loosen two screws at strut. Position support rods aside.
3. Remove two screws securing upper radiator shroud to radiator and one screw securing upper radiator hose clamp to shroud.
4. Drill out the six rivets securing the upper shroud to the lower shroud and remove shroud.
5. Loosen drive belts and remove crankshaft pulleys.
6. Raise vehicle and drain oil pan.
7. Remove exhaust "Y" pipe at exhaust manifold and converter.
8. Remove through bolts from engine mounts.
9. Remove starter motor.
10. Remove transmission lower cover.
11. Using a suitable jack, raise engine to gain clearance for oil pan removal.
12. Remove nuts and screws securing oil pan to cylinder block.
13. Reverse procedure to install.

OIL PUMP

REPLACE

V8-250

1. Remove oil pan as described previously.
2. Remove bolts securing oil pump to engine, then remove pump.
3. Reverse procedure to install.

OIL PUMP SERVICE

V8-250

1. Remove screws securing pump cover to housing.
2. Remove drive shaft, drive gear and driven gear from pump housing.
3. Remove oil pressure regulator valve and spring from bore in housing assembly. Inspect oil pressure regulator for nicks and burrs.
4. Check for free length of 2.57 inches on regulator spring. Check that spring can be compressed to 1.46 inches under 9.3-10.5 lbs. load.

5. Inspect drive gear and driven gear for nicks and burrs.
6. Inspect pump housing for excessive wear.
7. Check pump cover interior surface for scoring. Check pump housing cover surface for wear.
8. Check drive shaft for damage and wear.
9. To assemble, install pump drive gear over drive shaft so that retaining ring is inside gear. Position drive gear over pump housing shaft closest to pressure regulator bore.
10. Position driven gear over remaining shaft in pump housing, meshing driven gear with drive gear.
11. Install oil pressure regulator spring and valve in bore of housing.
12. install pump cover over drive shaft and install retaining screws. Torque to 5 ft. lbs.

BELT TENSION DATA

Belt	New Lbs.	Used Lbs.
Exc. V8-250		
Air Conditioning	168	67
AIR Pump	78	45
Generator	145	90
Power Steering	168	67
1982 V8-250		
A/C-Steering Pump	202	90
AIR Pump	180	67
Generator	147	56
Vacuum Pump	49	25
1983–85 V8-250		
A/C-Steering Pump	191	146
AIR Pump	169	135
Generator	135	90
Vacuum Pump	45	34

WATER PUMP REPLACE

V8-250

1. Disconnect battery ground cable, then drain cooling system.
2. On DeVille and Brougham models, remove two screws, one from each side at radiator end of support rods. Loosen screws at strut end of support rods and move support rods aside.
3. Remove screws from upper fan shroud, then remove wiring harness from upper fan shroud clamps.
4. Remove screws securing power steering pump reservoir to upper fan shroud, then remove reservoir.
5. Remove staples securing upper fan shroud to lower shroud and remove upper shroud.
6. Remove fan assembly.
7. Loosen generator mounting screws and remove drive belt.
8. Remove AIR pump drive belt.
9. Remove lower power steering pump mounting bolt and loosen the remaining bolt. Remove the vacuum pump drive belt.
10. Remove A/C compressor drive belt.
11. Remove air conditioning compressor from engine mounting brackets and position aside. Do not remove high and low pressure lines from compressor.
12. Remove generator and support bracket from engine.
13. Loosen clamp and disconnect coolant reservoir to water pump hose at pump.
14. Loosen clamps and disconnect water pump inlet and outlet hoses at pump.
15. Remove water pump and crankshaft pulleys.
16. Remove A/C compressor bracket.
17. Remove timing mark tab.
18. Remove screws and nuts securing water pump, **Fig. 18,** to engine front cover and remove pump. Discard gasket and clean gasket surfaces.
19. Reverse procedure to install.

FUEL PUMP REPLACE

WITH FUEL INJECTION

In-Tank Fuel Pump

1. Drain and remove fuel tank.
2. Remove locknut(s) securing wiring to fuel gauge pump unit, then fuel pump feed and gauge wires to tank unit.
3. Using tool J-24187, disengage lock ring from fuel tank. Remove tool, then lift gauge pump unit from tank and separate components.
4. Reverse procedure to install.

Chassis Mounted Fuel Pump

1. Remove fuel inlet and outlet hoses.
2. Pull back rubber boot and remove nuts from electrical terminals, then electrical leads.
3. Remove fuel pump to mounting bracket screws, then fuel pump assembly.
4. Reverse procedure to install. Torque fuel pump mounting screws to 25 inch lbs. Connect 14 dark green wire to positive terminal and 14 black wire to negative terminal.

LESS FUEL INJECTION

1. Raise vehicle and disconnect fuel inlet line at pump and plug line.
2. Disconnect fuel outlet pipe at pump.
3. Disconnect vapor return hoses.
4. Remove upper pump flange mounting screws.
5. Remove nut from mounting stud at lower pump flange.
6. Tipping pump upward, pull pump straight out from engine and remove.
7. Reverse procedure to install.

Rear Axle, Propeller Shaft & Brakes

INDEX

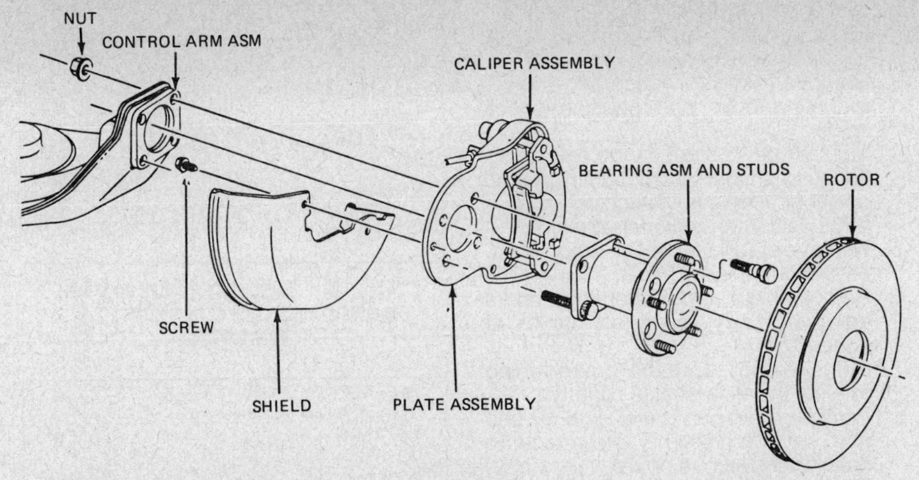

Fig. 1 Rear wheel spindle disassembled. Eldorado & Seville

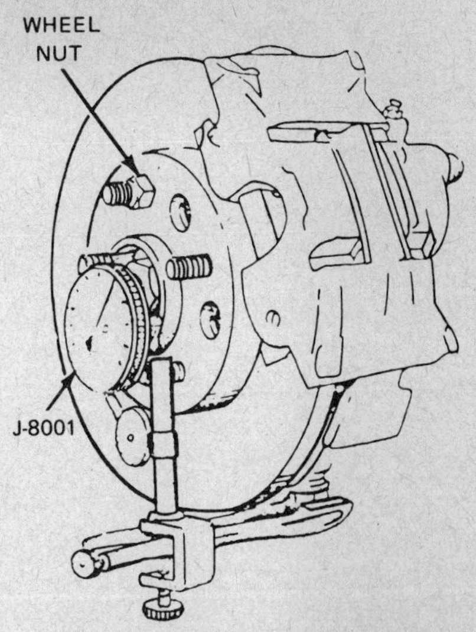

Fig. 2 Checking wheel bearing for looseness. Eldorado & Seville

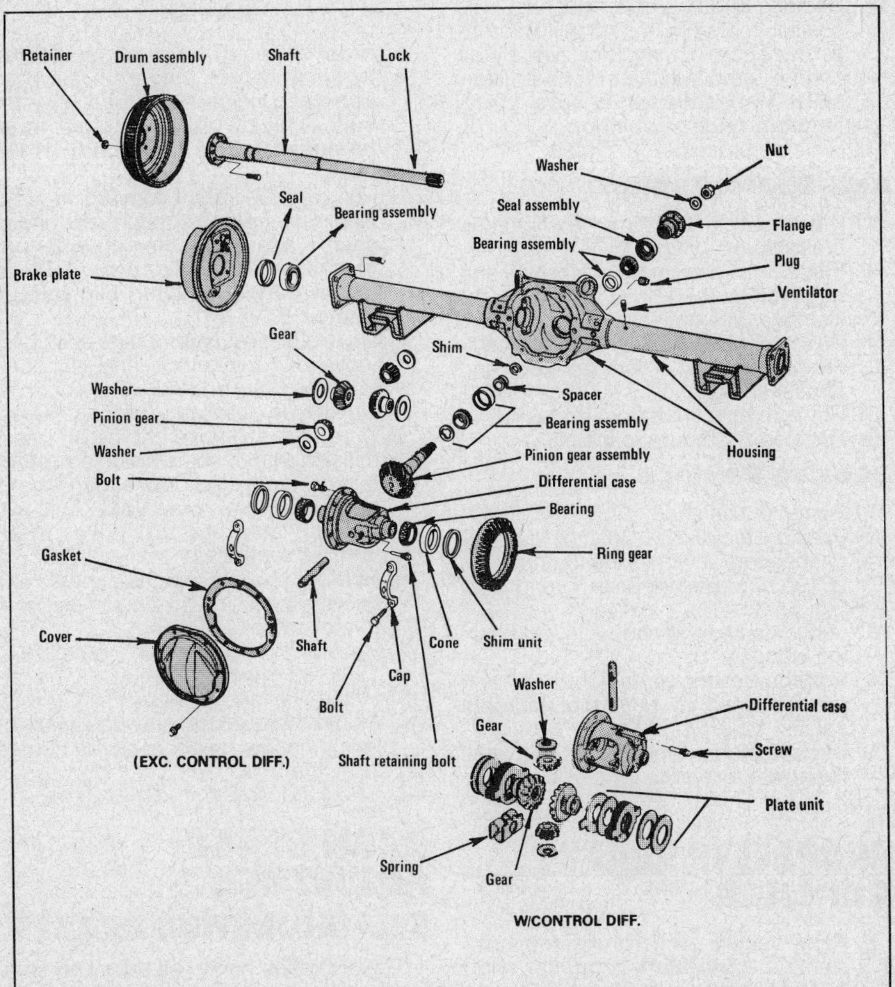

Fig. 3 Rear axle assembly. Brougham & Deville (Typical)

REAR AXLE

ELDORADO & SEVILLE

The spindle and wheel bearing is a unitized assembly which eliminates the need for periodic maintenance and adjustments. The spindle and wheel bearing assembly is bolted to the rear suspension control arm, **Fig. 1.**

Wheel Bearing Inspection

1. Raise and support rear of vehicle, then remove wheel and tire assembly.
2. Free disc brake shoes from disc or remove calipers, then reinstall two wheel nuts to secure disc to bearing.
3. Mount dial indicator as shown in **Fig. 2,** then grasp rotor and check inward and outward movement of spindle assembly. Movement should be less than .020 in.
4. Remove dial indicator and rotate spindle by hand to check for roughness or grinding within the spindle.
5. Replace spindle and bearing assembly if out of specifications or roughness or grinding is present.

Spindle & Bearing Assembly, Replace

1. Raise vehicle and remove wheel and tire assembly.
2. Remove brake caliper assembly.
3. Mark wheel stud and corresponding place on rotor for use during installation, then remove rotor.
4. Remove four nuts and bolts attaching spindle and bearing assembly to control arm, **Fig. 1.**
5. Reverse procedure to install. Torque spindle to lower control arm attaching bolts to 34 ft. lbs.

BROUGHAM & DEVILLE

In this axle, **Fig. 3,** the rear axle housing and differential carrier are cast into an integral assembly. The drive pinion assembly is mounted in two opposed tapered roller

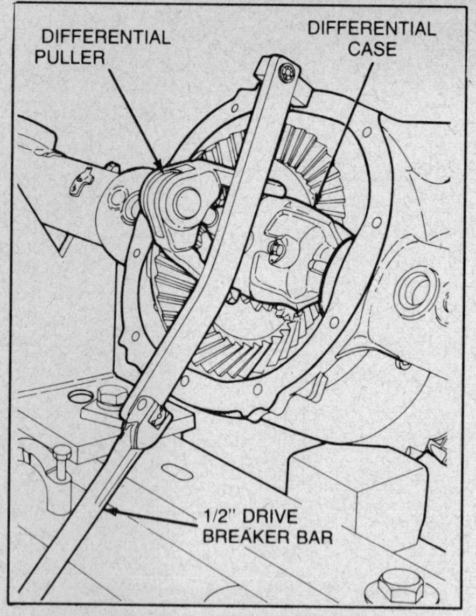

Fig. 4 Removing differential. Brougham & DeVille

bearings. The pinion bearings are preloaded by a collapsible spacer behind the front bearing. The pinion is positioned by a washer between the head of the pinion and the rear bearing.

The differential is supported in the carrier by two tapered roller side bearings. These bearings are preloaded by spacers located between the bearings and carrier housing. The differential assembly is positioned for proper ring gear and pinion backlash by varying these spacers. The differential case houses two side gears in mesh with two pinions mounted on a pinion shaft which is held in place by a lock pin. The side gears and pinions are backed by thrust washers.

Rear Axle, Replace

1. Raise vehicle and support rear axle and frame, then remove rear wheels and brake drums.
2. Disconnect emergency brake overtravel lever from link.
3. Remove shock absorbers from lower mount.
4. Place jack under front differential to relieve tension on lower control arm.
5. Remove upper and lower control arms as outlined under "Control Arms and Bushings, Replace" procedure in Rear Suspension Section.
6. Disconnect propeller shaft from axle flange and support with wire.
7. Remove brake hose at differential housing and plug. **If axle is allowed to wind up as it is lowered, springs may snap from their seats and could cause injury or damage. Use extreme caution to prevent wind-up condition.**
8. Lower axle shaft and remove springs from vehicle.
9. Reverse procedure to install.

Differential, Replace

1. Raise vehicle and support so axle can be raised and lowered.
2. Disconnect leveling control lever from link and hold lever down until shock absorbers are deflated.
3. Remove shock absorber lower mounting bolts and position shock aside.
4. Mark propeller shaft flange and pinion flange to ensure installation in original position. Remove attaching screws and position propeller shaft aside.
5. Remove stabilizer bar link nuts, retainer and bushings.
6. Remove nut from parking brake equalizer, then disconnect cables at connectors.
7. Remove clips securing brake tubing to axle, then lower axle slightly.
8. Position drain pan under axle, loosen rear cover bolts and allow axle to drain, then remove cover.
9. Remove wheel and brake drum.
10. Remove differential cross shaft through bolt, then the shaft. Push in on axle shafts, then remove "C" locks and pull axle shafts out about 1 inch.
11. Install cross shaft and bolt, then remove side bearing cap and bearing. **Mark bearing caps to ensure installation in original position.**
12. Remove one ring gear attaching bolt, position tools, **Fig. 4,** and pull differential case from housing until side shims can be removed, then remove differential. **Mark shims to ensure installation in original position.**
13. Reverse procedure to install.

Axle Shaft, Replace

1. Raise vehicle and remove wheel and brake drum.
2. Place drain pan under differential and remove cover.
3. Remove differential cross shaft.
4. Push axle shaft toward center of vehicle and remove "C" lock from butt end of axle shaft.
5. Remove axle shaft from housing.
6. Reverse procedure to install.

Bearing Replace

1. Remove axle shaft.
2. Position tool J-22813-01 or J-23689 on bearing, attach slide hammer J-2619, then remove bearing and seal, **Fig. 5.**
3. Lubricate bearing and seal with bearing lubricant.
4. Position bearing on tool J-23690 and drive bearing in until tool bottoms against tube, **Fig. 6.**
5. Using suitable tool, tap seal in until flush with axle tube.

PROPELLER SHAFT REPLACE

1. Raise vehicle on hoist with transmission in neutral. **Mark propeller shaft relationship to axle pinion flange to maintain balance.**
2. On 1982-83 models, remove propeller shaft flange retaining bolts. On 1984-88 models, remove rear universal joint-to-pinion flange attaching clamp nuts and clamps. **Do not allow propeller shaft to be supported by front or center universal joint, as damage to universal joint may result. Rear of propeller shaft must be supported to underbody of vehicle.**
3. Pull propeller shaft forward to clear pinion flange and support rear end of shaft. **Place a suitable container under transmission, to catch any fluid which may leak when slip joint is removed.**
4. On two piece type propeller shafts, remove the two center bearing supports to frame bolts and nuts.
5. On all types, slide propeller shaft rearward until slip yoke comes off transmission output shaft. **Place a protective device such as a cardboard shipping cover, over yoke. This will prevent damage to yoke when shaft is removed.**
6. Remove shaft and install a spare yoke into transmission extension housing to prevent loss of oil.
7. Reverse procedure to install. On 1982-83 models, torque flange attaching bolts to 70 ft. lbs. On 1984-88 models, torque rear universal joint-to-pinion flange attaching clamp nuts to 16 ft. lbs.
8. Check transmission oil.

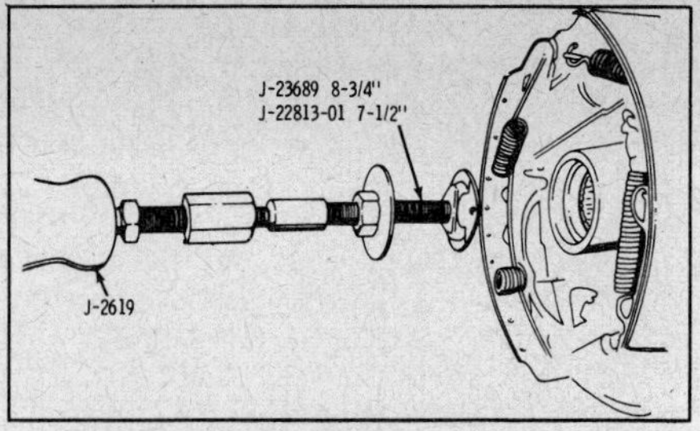

Fig. 5 Removing axle bearing. Brougham & Deville

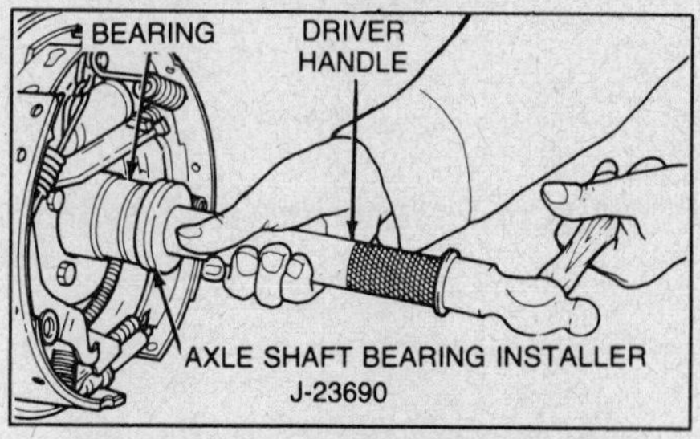

Fig. 6 Installing axle bearing. Brougham & Deville

DRUM BRAKE ADJUSTMENTS

SELF-ADJUSTING BRAKES

These brakes have self-adjusting shoe mechanisms that assure correct lining-to-drum clearances at all times. The automatic adjusters operate only when the brakes are applied as the car is moving rearward.

Although the brakes are self-adjusting, an initial adjustment is necessary after the brake shoes have been relined or replaced, or when the length of the star wheel adjuster has been changed during some other service operation.

Frequent usage of an automatic transmission forward range to halt reverse vehicle motion may prevent the automatic adjusters from functioning, thereby inducing low pedal heights. Should low pedal heights be encountered, it is recommended that numerous forward and reverse stops be made with a moderate pedal effort until satisfactory pedal height is obtained.

If a low pedal height condition cannot be corrected by making numerous reverse stops (provided the hydraulic system is free of air) it indicates that the self-adjusting mechanism is not functioning. Therefore, it will be necessary to remove the brake drum, clean, free up and lubricate the adjusting mechanism. Then adjust the brakes, being sure the parking brake is fully released.

The recommended method of adjusting the brakes is by using the Drum-to-Brake Shoe Clearance Gauge to check the diameter of the brake drum inner surface. Turn the tool to the opposite side and fit over the brake shoes by turning the star wheel until the gauge just slides over the linings. Rotate the gauge around the brake shoe lining surface to assure proper clearance.

PARKING BRAKE

ADJUST

W/REAR DISC BRAKES

1. Lubricate parking brake cables at equalizer and underbody rub points. Check all cables for freedom of operation.
2. Fully release parking brake and raise vehicle.
3. Hold cable stud from turning and tighten equalizer nut until cable slack is removed and levers are against stops on caliper housing. If levers are off stops, loosen cable until levers return to stop.
4. Operate parking brake several times to check adjustment. When properly adjusted, the parking brake pedal should move 5¼-6¾ inches on all except Seville and Eldorado or 4-5½ inches on Eldorado and Seville.

W/REAR DRUM BRAKES

1. With service brakes properly adjusted, lubricate parking brake linkage at equalizer and cable stud with heat-resistant lubricant, and check for free movement of cables.
2. Depress parking brake pedal about 1½ inch from full released position.
3. Raise rear wheels off floor.
4. Hold brake cable and stud from turning and tighten equalizer nut until a slight drag is felt on either wheel (going forward). After each turn of equalizer nut, check to see if either wheel begins to drag.
5. Release parking brake. No brake drag should be felt at either rear wheel. Operate several times to check adjustment. When properly adjusted, the parking brake pedal should move 5¼ to 6¾ inches.

VACUUM RELEASE PARKING BRAKE

The foot-operated parking brake is mounted on the cowl to the left of the steering column. It incorporates a vacuum release, operated by a vacuum diaphragm that is connected to the parking brake mechanism. When the transmission selector is moved into any Drive position, a vacuum valve in the neutral safety switch opens, allowing the diaphragm to be actuated by engine vacuum.

The diaphragm is connected by a link to a release mechanism on the parking brake. Vacuum acting on the diaphragm unlocks the parking brake pedal, permitting it to return to the release position by spring action. Any abnormal leaks in the vacuum release system will prevent proper brake release. A manual release is provided and may be used if the automatic release is inoperative or if manual release is desired at any time.

Under some conditions, aided by cold weather, the parking brake vacuum release valve (integral with the back-up light switch on steering column) may not release the parking brake automatically. Although when the brake is applied, the "Brake" indicator light will go on, brake can be released manually. If this condition is present the back-up light switch must be replaced.

TESTING VACUUM RELEASE

1. If the mechanism is inoperative, first check for damaged or kinked vacuum hoses and for loose hose connections at the diaphragm, vacuum release valve at neutral safety switch, and at engine manifold connection.
2. Check adjustment of neutral safety switch and operation of vacuum release valve.
3. Check diaphragm piston travel by running engine and moving transmission selector lever from drive to neutral. The manual release lever should move up and down as vacuum is applied and released. If no movement is observed, or if movement is slow (more than 1 or 2 seconds to complete the full stroke) diaphragm is leaking and should be replaced.
4. Check brake release with vacuum applied. If diaphragm piston completes full stroke but does not release brake, a malfunction of the pedal assembly is indicated, and the complete parking brake assembly should be replaced.
5. Check operation of parking brake with engine off. Parking brake should remain engaged regardless of transmission selector lever position. If not, replace parking brake assembly.

MASTER CYLINDER

REPLACE

1. Remove brake lines from master cylinder. Plug lines and ports.
2. Remove booster to master cylinder attaching nuts, then remove master cylinder.
3. Reverse procedure to install. Torque master cylinder attaching nuts to 28 ft. lbs. Torque brake line to master cylinder nuts to 18 ft. lbs.

POWER BRAKE UNIT

REPLACE

A sign of brake fluid dampness below the master cylinder at the power brake unit or on wheel cylinders at the bottom of the boot, does not necessarily indicate that these cylinders are leaking.

A small amount of fluid leakage at these areas can occur due to the creeping action of a very light film of fluid on the cylinder bores around the seals. This action provides proper seal lubrication. In addition, normal brake heat will produce a slight escape of lubricant from the impregnated, porous-metal wheel cylinder pistons.

Normal dampness at the master cylinder or wheel cylinders is not easily distinguishable from a definite leak. Therefore, this condition must be checked carefully.

If there is sufficient dampness to form a "teardrop" of fluid at the bottom of the master cylinder or on the bottom of the wheel cylinders at the boot area, the rate of fluid seepage is too high and the cause should be determined and corrected.

HYDRO-BOOST

1. With engine off pump brake pedal several times to empty accumulator of fluid.
2. Remove master cylinder to booster attaching nuts, then move master cylinder away from booster with brakes lines attached.
3. Remove three hydraulic lines from booster, cap all ports and lines to prevent entry of dirt and loss of fluid.
4. Remove retainer and washer securing booster pedal rod to brake pedal arm.
5. Remove four booster to firewall attaching nuts.
6. Loosen booster from firewall and move booster pedal rod inboard until it disconnects from brake arm.
7. Remove spring washer from brake pedal arm and remove booster.
8. Reverse procedure to install. To purge system, disconnect feed wire from injection pump. Fill power steering pump reservoir, then crank engine for several seconds without starting and recheck power steering pump fluid level. Connect injection pump feed wire and start engine, then cycle steering gear wheel from stop to stop twice and turn off engine. Discharge accumulator by depressing brake pedal several times, then check fluid level. Start engine, then turn steering wheel from stop to stop and turn off engine. Check fluid level and add fluid if necessary. If foaming occurs, turn off engine and wait for approximately one hour for foam to dissipate, then recheck fluid level.

VACUUM BOOSTER

1. Remove master cylinder to booster attaching nuts, then move master cylinder away from booster with brake lines attached. **On some models, it may be necessary to remove brake lines from master cylinder. If lines must be removed, cover exposed ends of brake lines to prevent contamination.**
2. Remove vacuum hose from check valve on booster.
3. Remove nuts attaching brake unit to cowl and pedal support bracket.
4. From inside of vehicle, disconnect power brake push rod from brake pedal and remove vacuum booster.
5. Reverse procedure to install.

Rear Suspension

INDEX

SHOCK ABSORBER REPLACE

1. If equipped with Automatic Level Control, disconnect air lines from shock absorber fittings.
2. With the rear axle supported properly disconnect shock absorber at upper and lower mountings. **Use care not to damage brake hoses or lines when removing shock absorber.**
3. Reverse procedure to install, noting the following:
   a. When installing shocks equipped with automatic level control, air ports should face front of vehicle.
   b. Extend shocks completely before installation.

COIL SPRINGS REPLACE

ELDORADO & SEVILLE

1. Raise and support rear of vehicle, then remove wheel and tire assembly.
2. Remove stabilizer bar as described under Stabilizer Bar, Replace.
3. Using a suitable jack support lower control arm.
4. Disconnect automatic level air line at shock absorber. If removing lefthand spring from vehicle, disconnect automatic level control link from ball pivot at control arm.
5. Disconnect shock absorber from upper and lower mountings and remove shock absorber.
6. Carefully lower control arm until spring tension is relieved, then remove spring and insulator, **Fig. 1.**
7. Reverse procedure to install. Locate bottom end of spring between dimples on lower control arm assembly, **Fig. 2.**

EXC. ELDORADO & SEVILLE

1. Support vehicle at frame and support rear axle using a suitable jack.
2. Remove shock absorbers.
3. If equipped with Automatic Level Control, remove bolts attaching stabilizer bar to lower control arms and remove stabilizer bar.
4. Remove bolt attaching brake line junction block to rear axle housing, then disconnect brake lines from clips on rear axle housing.
5. If equipped with Automatic Level Control, disconnect link from leveling valve arm.
6. Position a jack stand under nose of differential carrier to relieve tension on lower control arm to axle housing bolts, then remove bolts, **Fig. 3.**
7. Disconnect drive shaft from pinion flange and support from frame with wire.
8. Remove jack stand from under nose of differential carrier, then remove upper control arm pivot bolts at rear axle housing.
9. Disconnect lefthand parking brake cable at equalizer and cable at frame by removing clip.
10. Disconnect parking brake cable from clip at center of rear crossmember and cable at "C" connector located at lefthand side of frame.
11. Lower axle assembly to a point where springs can be pryed out, using care not to stretch brake lines or parking brake cables. **When lowering axle and prying out springs, use care to prevent axle assembly from rotating, as springs may snap from seats.**
12. Reverse procedure to install. Note spring positions, **Fig. 4.**

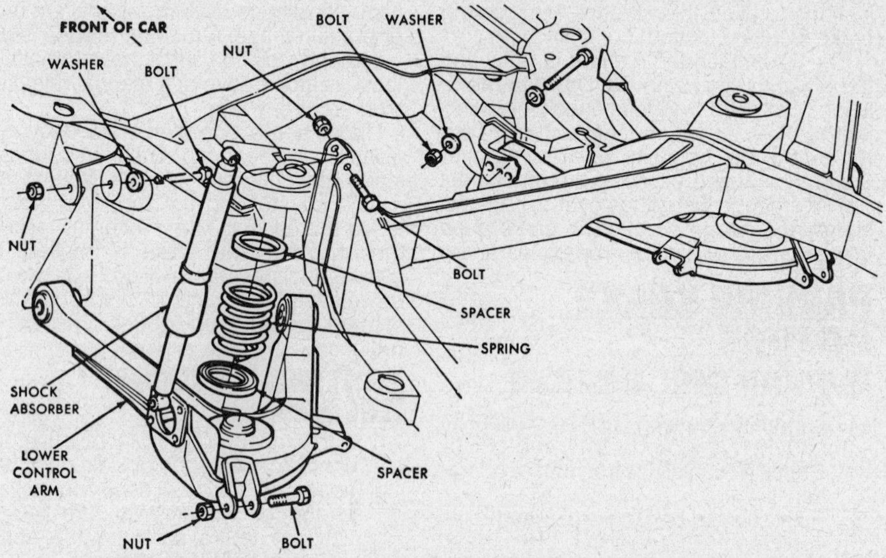

Fig. 1 Eldorado & Seville rear suspension

CONTROL ARMS & BUSHINGS REPLACE

Replace one control arm at a time as axle assembly may slip sideways, making installation difficult.

UPPER CONTROL ARMS

Exc. Eldorado & Seville

1. Support vehicle at frame and support rear axle using a suitable jack.
2. If vehicle is equipped with Automatic Level Control, remove bolt attaching height control link to right upper control arm. Position overtravel lever in center position.

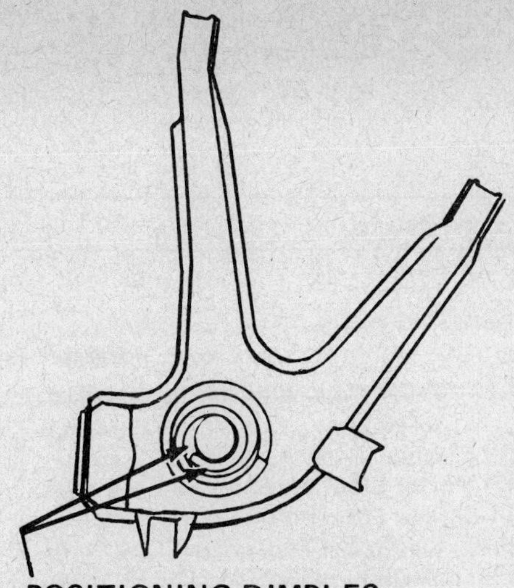

Fig. 2 Coil spring installation. Eldorado & Seville

3. Position a jack stand under differential pinion retainer.
4. Remove both control arm pivot bolts and control arm.
5. Reverse procedure to install. Tighten control arm pivot bolts with vehicle curb weight applied to axle.

LOWER CONTROL ARMS

Eldorado & Seville

1. Raise and support rear of vehicle, then remove wheel and tire assembly.
2. Remove stabilizer bar as described under Stabilizer Bar, Replace.
3. Disconnect brake line bracket from control arm, then remove caliper assembly.
4. Mark a wheel stud and a corresponding point on the rotor for alignment, then remove rotor.
5. If lefthand control arm is to be removed, disconnect automatic level control link from ball pivot on control arm.
6. Using a suitable jack, support control arm.
7. Disconnect air line from shock absorber, then disconnect shock absorber from upper and lower mountings and remove shock absorber.
8. Carefully lower the control arm until spring tension is relieved, then remove spring and insulator.
9. Remove two bolts mounting control arm to frame and remove control arm, **Fig. 1.**
10. Reverse procedure to install. Torque control arm to frame mounting bolts to 75 ft. lbs.

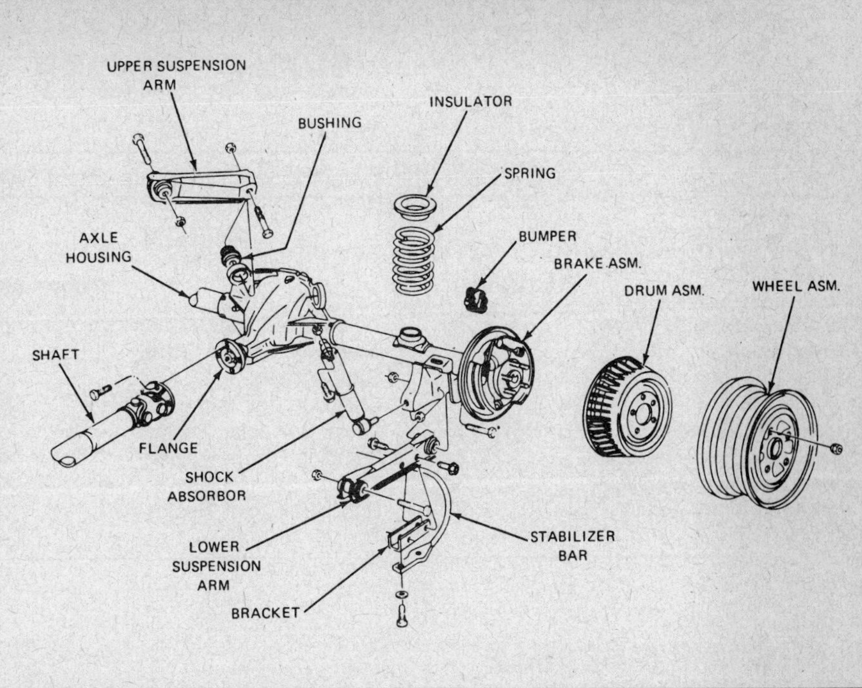

Fig. 3 Rear suspension (typical). Exc. Eldorado & Seville

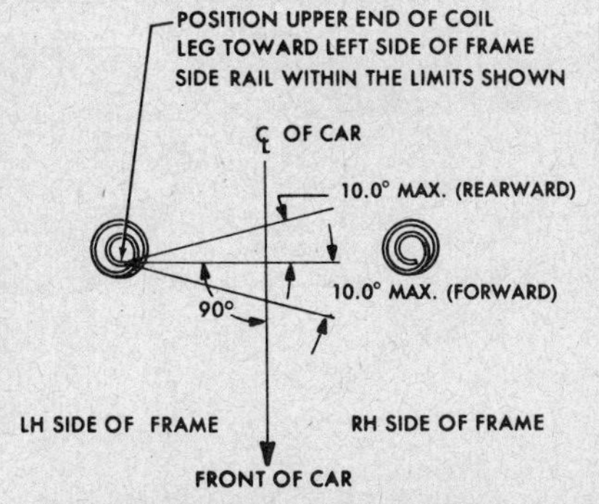

Fig. 4 Coil spring installation. Exc. Eldorado & Seville

Exc. Eldorado & Seville

1. Support vehicle at frame and support rear axle using a suitable jack.
2. If equipped with Automatic Level Control, remove two bolts securing stabilizer bar to control arm being removed.
3. Remove front and rear lower control arm nuts.
4. Position a suitable jack under front of differential carrier to relieve tension on lower control arm bolts.
5. Remove front and rear lower control arm bolts and lower control arm. **Lower control arm bushings are not serviceable.**
6. Reverse procedure to install. Tighten control arm bolts with vehicle at curb height.

STABILIZER BAR REPLACE

ELDORADO & SEVILLE

1. Raise and support rear of vehicle.
2. Remove nuts and bolts securing front of stabilizer bar to control arms.
3. Remove inside nut and bolt from each side of stabilizer bar link, then loosen outside nut and bolt on the stabilizer link.
4. Rotate bottom parts of link to one side and slip stabilizer out of bushings.

EXC. ELDORADO & SEVILLE

1. Raise and support rear of vehicle.
2. Remove bolts securing stabilizer bar to lower control arms, then remove stabilizer bar from vehicle.

Front Suspension & Steering Section

NOTE: Refer to appropriate section for Front Drive Axle Service.

INDEX

BROUGHAM & DEVILLE FRONT SUSPENSION

The front suspension consist of two upper and lower control arm assemblies, steel coil springs, shock absorbers, stabilizer bar, two integral steering arms, and knuckles, **Fig. 1.**

Ball joints are used at outer ends of upper and lower control arms. The upper ball joints is riveted to the upper control arm. The lower ball joint is pressed into the lower control arm.

A stabilizer bar is mounted in rubber bushings to the front frame side rails and is attached to the lower control arms by means of steel links.

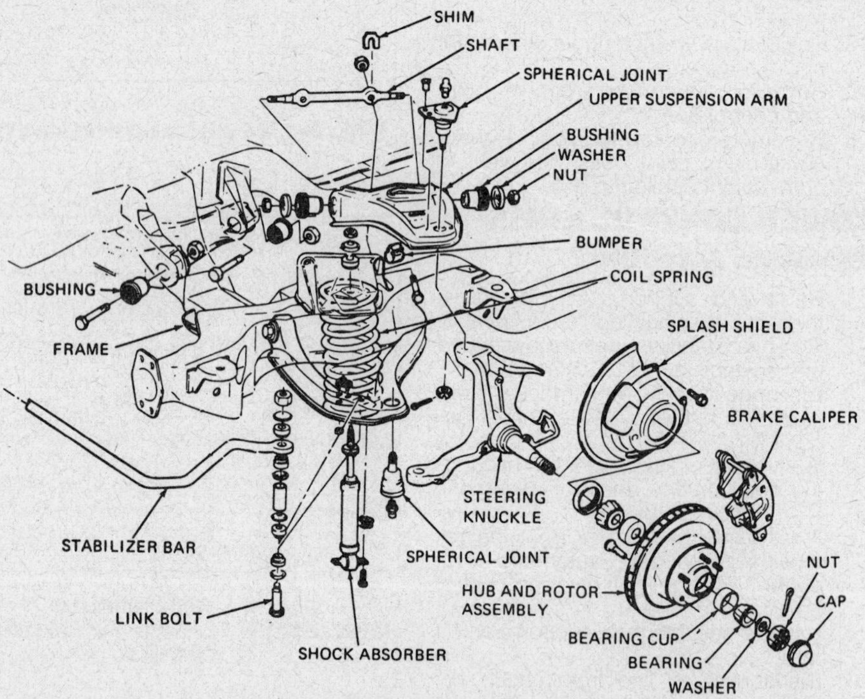

Fig. 1 Front suspension disassembled. Brougham & DeVille

WHEEL BEARINGS, ADJUST

Looseness at a front wheel does not necessarily indicate worn bearings or a loose spindle nut, since the tapered roller bearings used on front wheels of all standard Cadillacs should not be preloaded and normally can have up to .004 inch endplay.

1. While rotating wheel and tire assembly, tighten spindle nut to 12 ft. lbs. making certain that hub is fully seated on spindle.
2. Back off spindle nut until free, and tighten nut finger tight.
3. Install new cotter pin. If pin cannot be installed, back off nut to next hole and install pin. **Cotter pin must be tight after installation, as vibration can break pin.**

WHEEL BEARINGS, REPLACE

1. Remove caliper retaining bolts, then slide caliper off disc and using a length of wire, attach caliper to upper control arm. **Never allow caliper to hang from brake hose.**
2. Remove dust cap, cotter pin, spindle nut, washer and outer bearing assembly.
3. Remove hub and disc assembly, being careful to avoid damage to spindle threads or grease seal.
4. Remove inner bearing grease seal and bearing assembly. **Inner and outer bearing cups are press fit in hub and can be driven out from the opposite side using a brass drift. Tap alternately on opposite sides to prevent cocking cup and damaging hub.**

CHECKING BALL JOINTS FOR WEAR

Upper Ball Joint

If ball joint has any noticeable lateral movement or can be twisted within its socket using finger pressure, the joint must be replaced.

Lower Ball Joint

A wear indicator is built in the ball joint. Remove dirt deposits around service plug and observe position of nipple. Refer to **Fig. 2**, for wear tolerance.

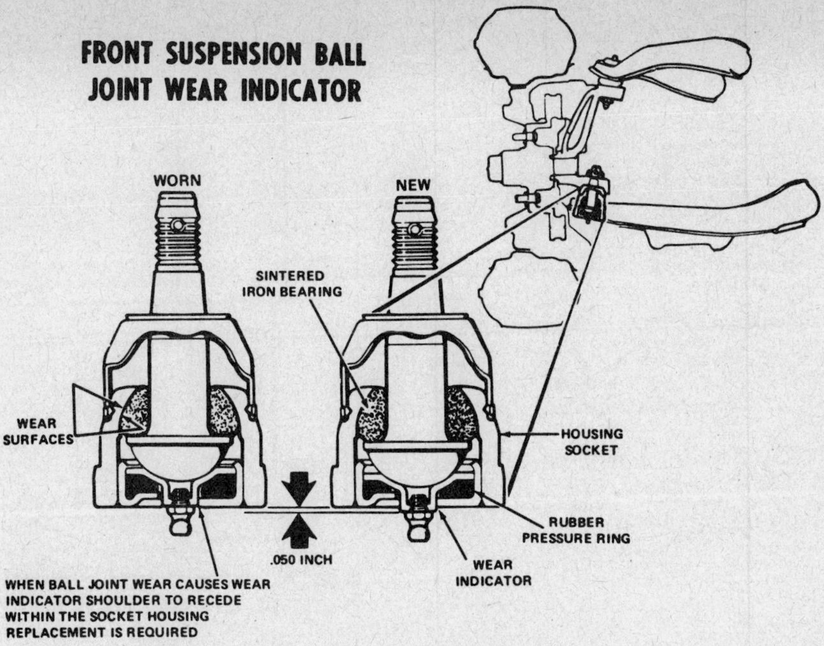

Fig. 2 Ball joint wear indicator

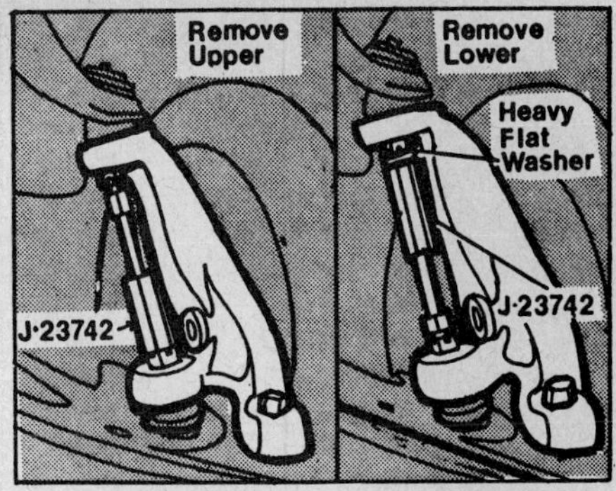

Fig. 3 Removing ball joint studs from steering knuckle. Brougham & DeVille

UPPER BALL JOINT, REPLACE

1. Raise vehicle and remove wheel.
2. Remove cotter pin from upper ball joint stud.
3. Remove caliper and position aside. **When removing caliper use care not to damage brake tubing or hose. Secure caliper to frame with wire.**
4. Loosen stud nut, however, not more than one turn.
5. Using tool No. J-23742, free ball joint stud from steering knuckle, **Fig. 3. The lower control arm must be supported so spring cannot force arm down.**
6. Remove upper ball joint stud nut, allow steering knuckle to swing out of way and place block of wood between frame and upper control arm.
7. To remove rivets securing ball joint to upper control arm, grind rivet heads off, then, using a punch, drive rivets out. **Use care not to damage ball joint seat or upper control arm when removing rivets.**
8. Remove ball joint.
9. Install new ball joint in control arm and attach with bolt and nut assembly provided with new joint. Install bolts from bottom and torque nuts to 20 ft. lbs.
10. Remove block of wood from between frame and upper control arm, position upper ball stud to steering knuckle, install and torque nut to 60 to 61 ft. lbs. Install cotter pin. **If cotter pin hole is not aligned do not back nut off. Nut may be torqued to a maximum of 100 ft. lbs. (1/6 additional turn) to align cotter pin hole.**
11. Install caliper, lubricate ball joint and install wheel.
12. Check wheel alignment.

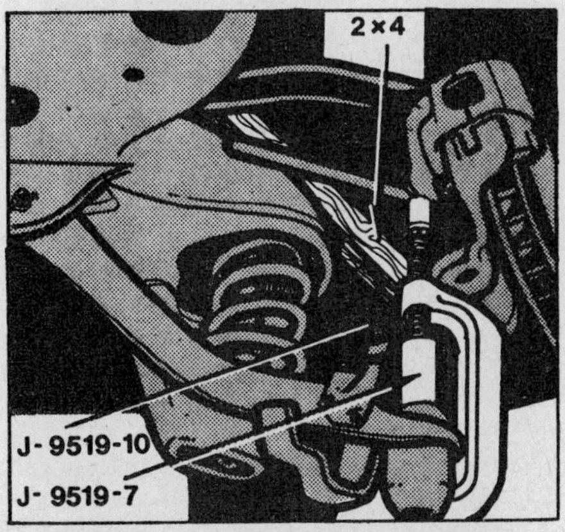

Fig. 4 Removing ball jointfrom lower control arm. Brougham & DeVille

LOWER BALL JOINT, REPLACE

1. Raise vehicle and remove wheel.
2. Remove cotter pin from lower ball joint stud and loosen nut one turn.
3. Using tool No. J-23742, free ball joint stud from steering knuckle, **Fig. 3. Lower control arm must be supported so spring cannot force arm down.**
4. Remove lower stud nut and pull upward and outward on bottom of brake disc to free ball joint stud from steering knuckle.
5. Lift upper control arm up with steering knuckle and hub attached and place a block of wood between frame and upper control arm. **It may be necessary to remove tie rod from steering knuckle.**
6. Using tools J-9519-10 and J-9519-7 or equivalent, remove ball joint from lower control arm, **Fig. 4.**
7. Install ball joint in lower control arm using tools J-9519-9 and J-9519-10 or equivalent. **Position bleed vent in ball joint rubber boot to face inward and the stud cotter pin hole to face forward.**
8. Remove block of wood from between frame and upper control arm, then install lower ball joint stud in steering knuckle. Install and torque nut to 80 to 83 ft. lbs. and install cotter pin. **Some models are equipped with prevailing torque fasteners, and therefore no cotter pins are used. On models with fasteners that use cotter pins as locking devices, nut may be torqued to a maximum of 92 ft. lbs. to align cotter pin holes.**
9. Lubricate ball joint and install tie rod, if removed. Torque tie rod nut to 40 ft. lbs. on 1982 models, or 30 ft. lbs. on 1983-88 models. **Some models are equipped with prevailing torque fasteners, and therefore no cotter pins are used.**
10. Install wheel and check wheel alignment.

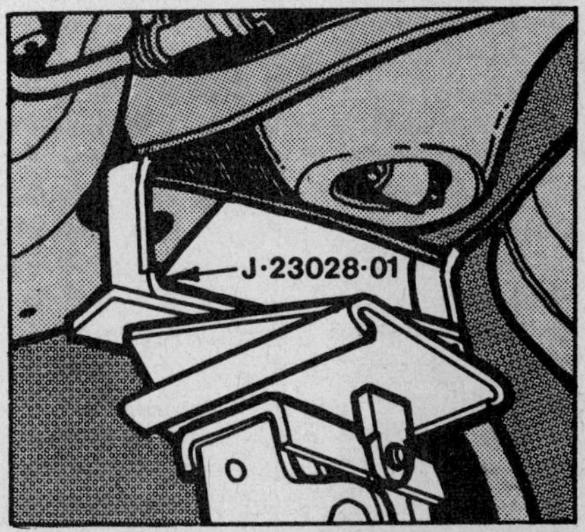

Fig. 5 Removing and instal ling front spring. Brougham & DeVille

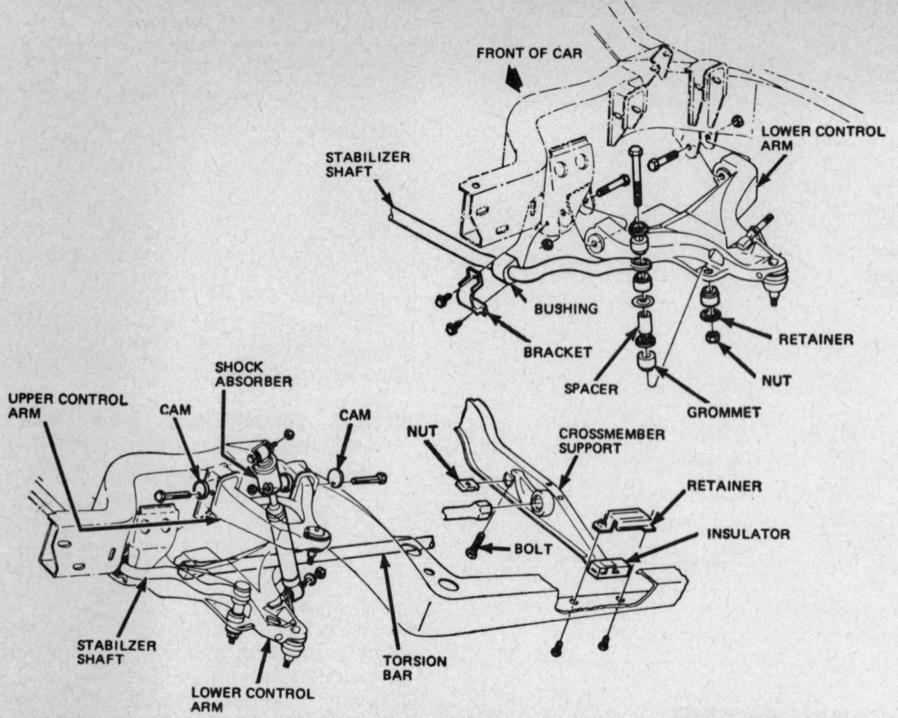

Fig. 6 Front suspension disassembled. Eldorado & Seville

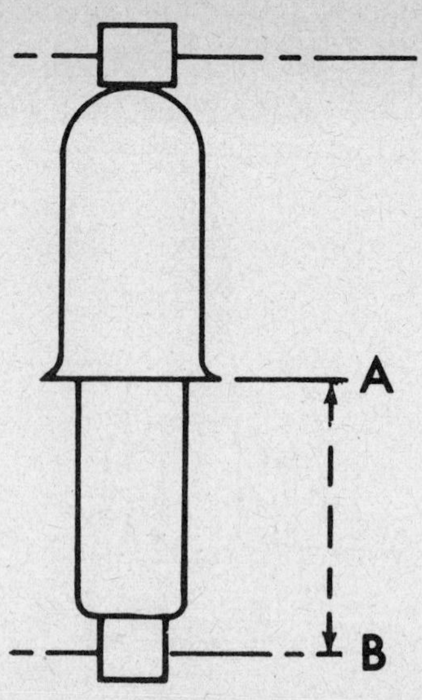

Fig. 7 Checking standing height. Eldorado & Seville

SHOCK ABSORBER, REPLACE

The shock absorbers are removed through the bottom of the lower control arm after unfastening it at the top and bottom.

To install, place the retainer and rubber grommet on the upper stem and fully extend the shock absorber rod. Insert the shock absorber up into the coil spring and guide the stem through the tower in the crossmember. Then place the lower end in position on the lower control arm. Install bolts and torque to 20 to 22 ft. lbs. Install shock stud retaining nut and tighten to end of threads on stud (about 1 1/8 inch).

COIL SPRING, REPLACE

1. Raise vehicle on hoist, remove shock absorber lower mounting bolts and push shock through control arm up into spring.
2. Support vehicle so control arms hang free and disconnect stabilizer bar from lower control arm.
3. Secure tool No. J-23028-01 to a suitable jack, position tool so lower control arm is supported by inner bushings, **Fig. 5.**
4. Raise jack to relieve spring tension from lower control arm pivot and install a safety chain around spring and through lower control arm.
5. Remove bolt from rear of lower control arm, then remove other bolt and slowly lower control arm until all spring tension is relieved.
6. Remove safety chain, spring and spring insulator.
7. Reverse procedure to install. **When installing spring, bottom coil must cover all or part of one inspection hole on the lower control arm. The other inspection hole must be fully or partially uncovered.**

ELDORADO & SEVILLE FRONT SUSPENSION

The front suspension consists of two upper and two lower control arms, a stabilizer bar, shock absorbers and a right and left torsion bar, **Fig. 6.** Torsion bars are used instead of the conventional coil springs. The front end of the torsion bar is attached to the lower control arm. The rear of the torsion bar is mounted into an adjustable arm in the torsion bar crossmember. The standing height of the car is controlled by this adjustment.

STANDING HEIGHT, ADJUST

Before standing height adjustment is performed, vehicle should be on a flat, level surface, with front seat all the way back, fuel tank full and tires inflated to proper pressure. Air lines must be loosened at shock absorbers, if equipped with electronic level control, and system must be depressurized.

The standing height must be checked and adjusted if necessary before checking and adjusting front wheel alignment. The standing height is controlled by the adjustment setting of the torsion bar adjusting bolt, **Fig. 6.** Clockwise rotation of the bolt increases standing height: counterclockwise rotation decreases standing height.

To check vehicle height, measure from lower edge of front shock absorber dust tube (A) to center line of lower attachment (B), **Fig. 7.** This dimension between (A) and (B) should be 5 1/2-6 inches.

WHEEL BEARING INSPECTION

The front wheel bearing is a sealed unit bearing. The bearing cannot be adjusted or repacked. There are darkened areas on the bearing assembly. These darkened areas are from a heat treatment process and do not indicate need for bearing replacement, **Fig. 8.**

To check wheel bearing assembly for looseness, free brake pads from disc or remove calipers. Install two lug nuts to secure disc to bearing. Mount dial indicator as shown in **Fig. 9,** then rock disc and note indicator reading. If looseness exceeds .005 in. replace hub and bearing assembly.

WHEEL BEARING & STEERING KNUCKLE, REPLACE

1. Raise and support vehicle under lower control arms.
2. Remove drive axle nut and washer and remove wheel and tire assembly.
3. Remove brake hose clip from ball joint and replace nut, then remove brake caliper off disc, and using a length of wire support caliper on suspension. **Do not allow caliper to hang from brake hose as this could cause damage and premature failure of hose.**
4. Mark hub and disc assembly for alignment during assembly and remove disc, then strike steering knuckle in area of upper ball joint until upper ball joint is loose. **Use extreme care to prevent striking and damaging brake hose or ball joint seal.**
5. Place a short length of rubber hose over lower control arm torsion bar connector to avoid damage to inboard tri-pot joint seal when hub and knuckle are removed.
6. Using appropriate puller, disconnect tie rod end, upper and lower ball joints and remove steering knuckle and hub assembly, **Fig. 10.**

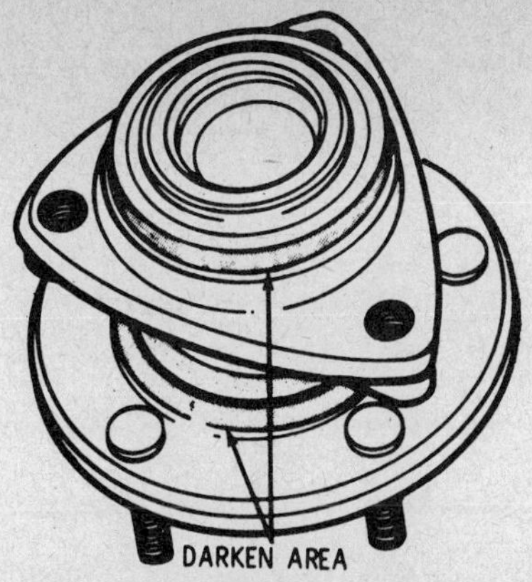

Fig. 8 Sealed wheel bearing assembly. Eldorado & Seville

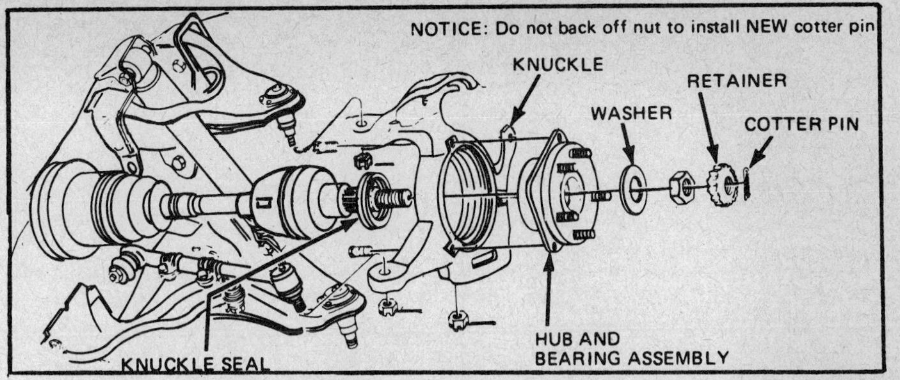

Fig. 10 Wheel bearing & steering knuckle assembly. Eldorado & Seville

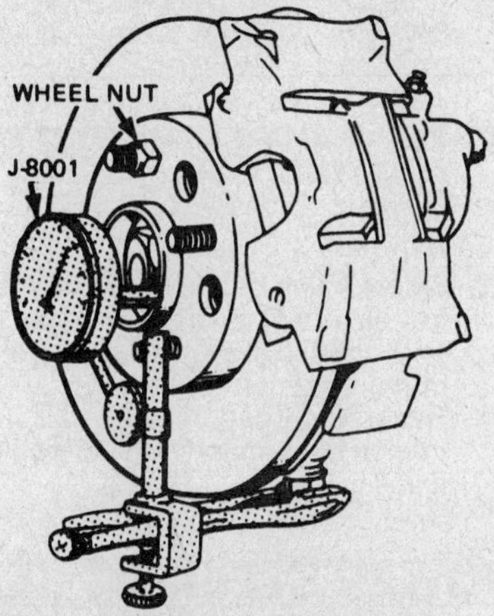

Fig. 9 Checking wheel bearing for looseness. Eldorado & Seville

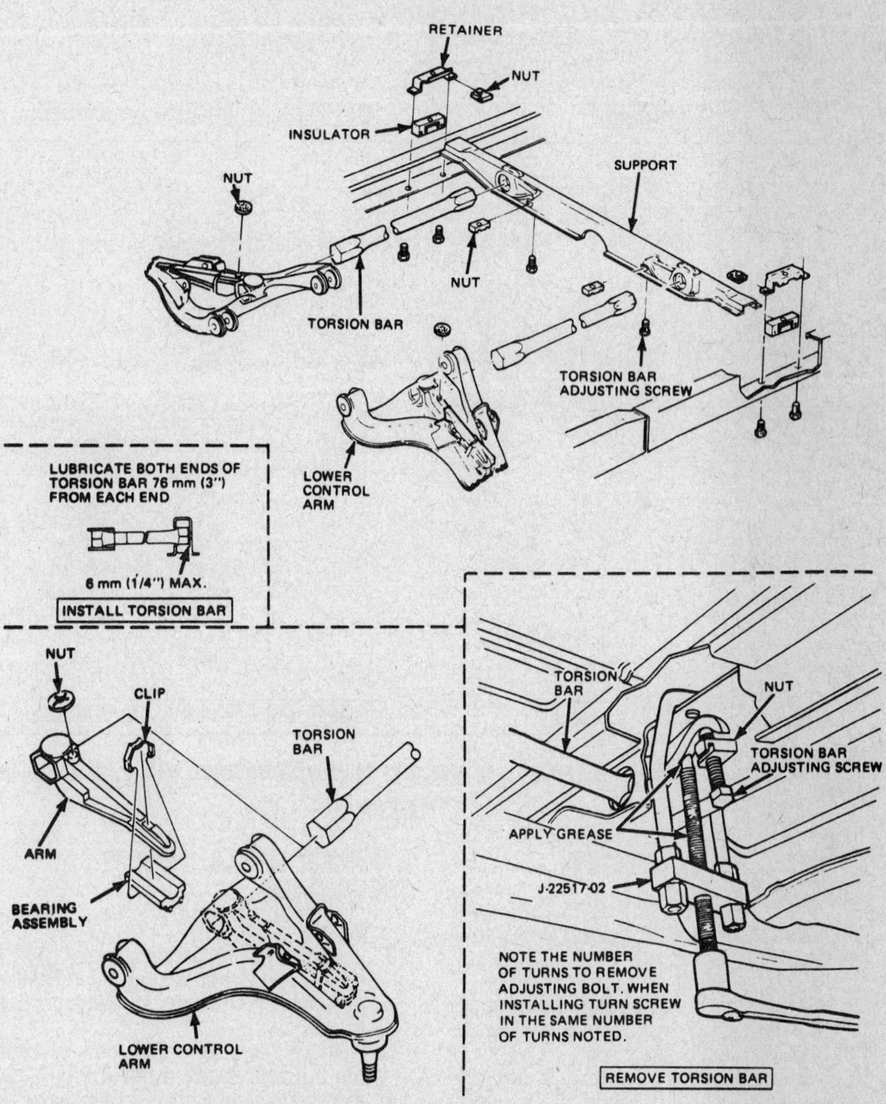

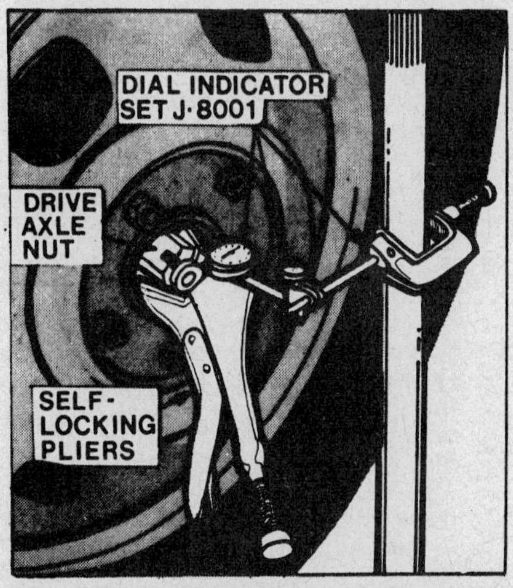

Fig. 11 Checking ball joints for wear. Eldorado & Seville

Fig. 12 Torsion bar removal. Eldorado & Seville

7. Reverse procedure to install, noting the following torque values: drive axle nut to hub and bearing, 175 ft. lbs.; lower ball joint nut, 83 ft. lbs.; upper ball joint nut, 61 ft. lbs.; tie rod to steering knuckle nut, 40 ft. lbs.; hub and bearing to knuckle bolts, 75 ft. lbs.

CHECKING BALL JOINTS FOR WEAR

1. Raise car and position jack stands under lower control arms as near as possible to each ball joint.
2. Clamp vise grips on end of drive axle and position a dial indicator so that dial indicator ball rests on vise grip, **Fig. 11.**
3. Place a pry bar between lower control arm and outer race and pry down on bar. Reading must not exceed 1/8 inch.

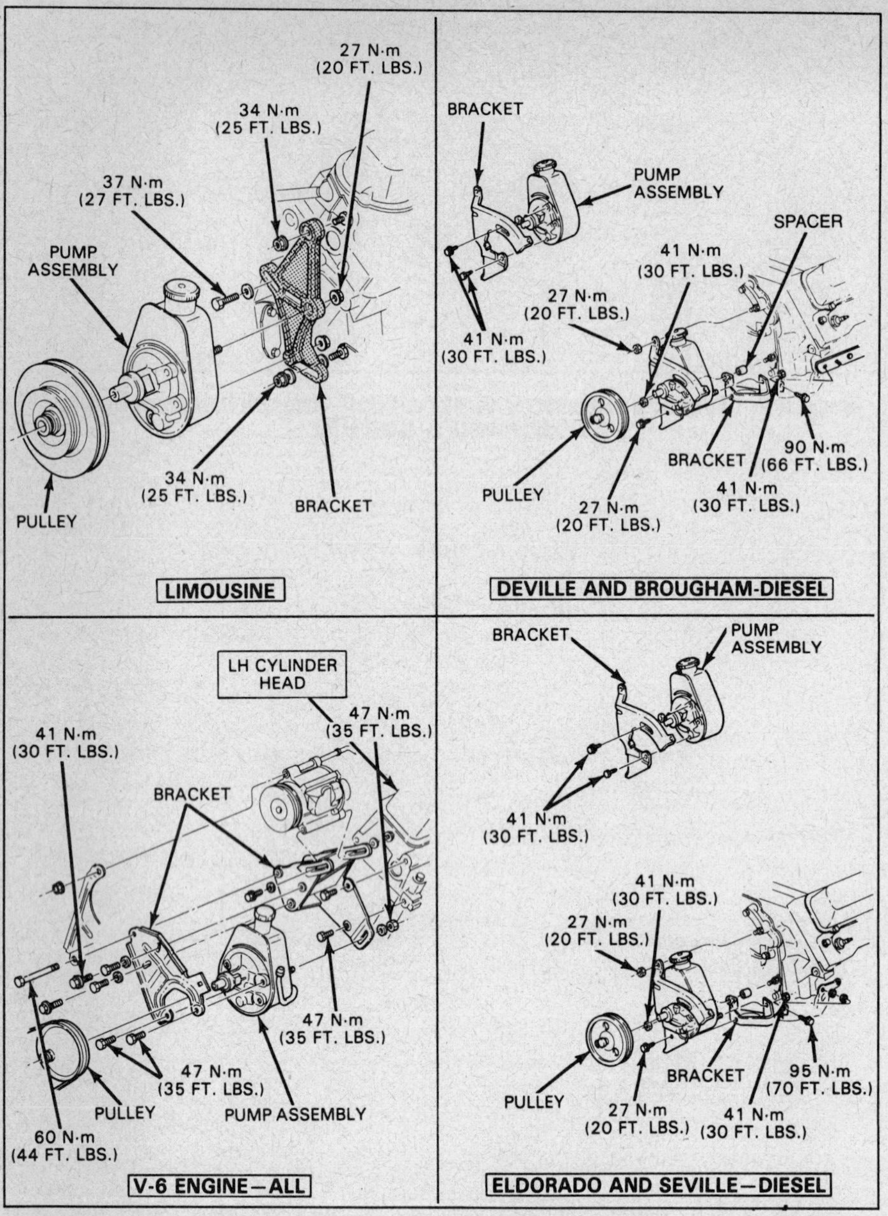

Fig. 13 Power steering pump installation. Exc. V8-250 (Typical)

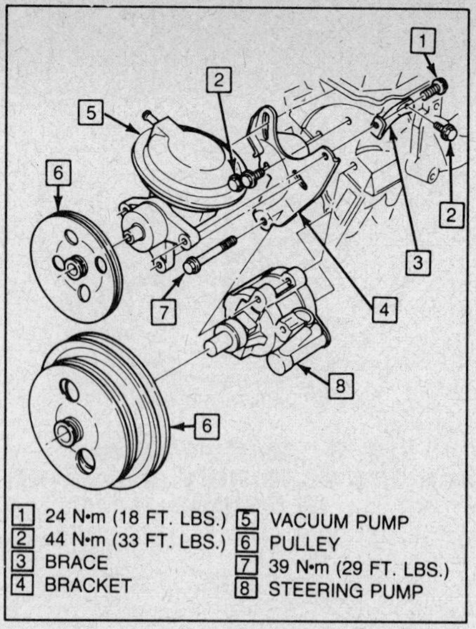

Fig. 14 Power steering pump installation. V8-250

UPPER BALL JOINT, REPLACE

1. Raise vehicle and support under lower control arms.
2. Remove wheel and tire assembly.
3. Remove cotter pin and nut from upper ball joint stud, then disconnect brake hose clip from stud.
4. Using a hammer and brass drift, disengage ball joint stud from steering knuckle.
5. Place a block of wood between control arm and frame, then drill rivets with a 1/8 in. drill bit 1/4 in. deep from top side of control arm.
6. Drill rivet heads off using a 1/2 inch drill bit. Do not drill into control arm.
7. Using a hammer and punch, drive rivets out and remove ball joint.
8. Install ball joint into control arm and torque nuts and bolts to 8 ft. lbs.

LOWER BALL JOINT, REPLACE

1. Remove knuckle.
2. Using 1/8 in. drill bit, drill center of rivets 1/4 in. deep, then using 1/2 in. drill bit, drill deep enough to remove rivet heads.
3. Using a hammer and punch, drive rivets out and remove ball joint.
4. Install ball joint into control arm and torque nuts and bolts to 8 ft. lbs.

TORSION BAR, REPLACE

1. Raise and support vehicle, then remove parts as shown in **Fig. 12.**
2. Remove torsion bar adjusting screw as shown in **Fig. 12. Count number of turns when removing screw. When installing, turn screw in the same number of turns to return vehicle to proper height.**
3. Slide torsion bar forward in lower control arm until torsion bar clears support, then pull down on bar and remove from control arm.
4. Reverse procedure to install. Torque torsion bar support retainer bolts to 20 ft. lbs.

POWER STEERING GEAR REPLACE

1. Disconnect pressure and return lines from gear and plug all lines and openings.
2. Remove stone shield, if equipped.
3. Remove pinch bolt, then flex coupling from gear.
4. Raise and support vehicle.
5. On all models except 1983-85 Eldorado and Seville, remove pitman arm nut and lock washer, then using a suitable puller remove pitman arm from steering gear.
6. Remove steering gear to side rail retaining bolts, then steering gear.
7. On 1983-85 Eldorado and Seville, remove pitman arm from steering shaft.
8. Reverse procedure to install, noting the following torque values: steering gear to side rail retaining bolts, 70 ft. lbs.; pitman arm to pitman shaft nut, 185 ft. lbs.; flex coupling pinch bolt, 30 ft. lbs.; steering gear pressure lines, 20 ft. lbs.

POWER STEERING PUMP REPLACE

V6-252

1. Disconnect pressure and return lines from pump.
2. Loosen adjusting screws on front and rear bracket, then remove drive belt.

3. Remove adjusting screws securing front of mounting bracket, **Fig. 13.**
4. Remove adjusting nut securing pump to rear mounting bracket.
5. Remove pivot screw, then remove steering pump and bracket as an assembly.
6. Reverse procedure to install.

V8-250

1. Loosen A/C mounting bracket and vacuum pump bracket, then remove belts from pulley.
2. Disconnect pressure and return lines from pump and plug all openings.
3. Remove two bolts holding pump to engine block through access holes in pulley, then remove pump, **Fig. 14.**
4. Reverse procedure to install.

Wheel Alignment Section

INDEX

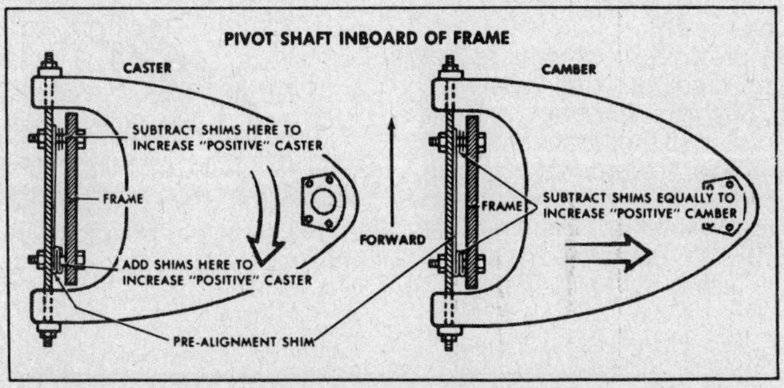

Fig. 1 Caster and camber adjustment. Brougham & DeVille

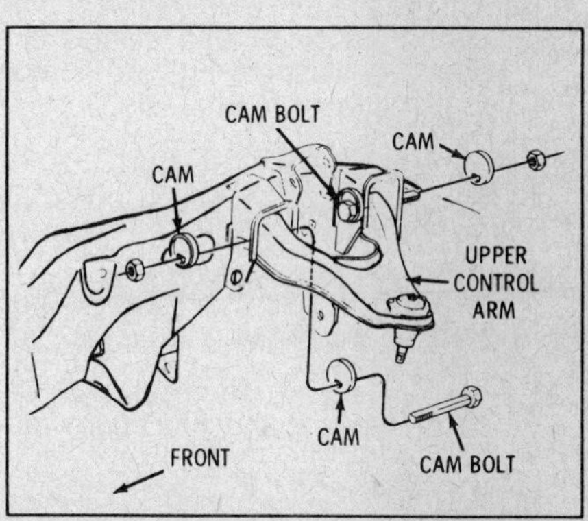

Fig. 2 Caster-camber cam locations. Eldorado & Seville

FRONT WHEEL ALIGNMENT

BROUGHAM & DEVILLE

Caster & Camber

Caster and camber are adjusted by adding or removing shims from between the upper control arm and frame bracket, **Fig. 1.** Caster is adjusted by transfering shims from front to rear and rear to front. Transfering shims from front bolt to rear bolt will increase positive caster, from rear bolt to front bolt will increase negative caster.

Camber is adjusted by adding or removing an equal number of shims from the front and rear bolts. To increase positive camber remove an equal amount of shims from front and rear bolts, to increase negative camber add an equal amount of shims to front and rear bolts.

After adjusting caster and camber torque nut to 70-80 ft. lbs. Tighten bolt with the least amount of shims first. After adjusting caster and camber toe-in must be adjusted.

The difference in thickness between front and rear shim packs should not exceed .40 inch. If difference is greater than .40 inch check arms, frame and related parts for damage.

Toe-In, Adjust

Toe-in is adjusted by loosening the clamp bolts at each end of each tie rod and turning each tie rod to increase or decrease its length as necessary until proper toe-in is achieved and the steering gear is on the high point for straight-ahead driving.

ELDORADO & SEVILLE

Prior to checking caster and camber settings, check front end standing height. Refer to "Standing Height, Adjust" under Front Suspension & Steering Section for procedure.

Caster

Record camber reading, then hold front cam bolt and loosen nut, **Fig. 2.** Turn front cam bolt to obtain 1/4 of the desired caster change. At front cam bolt a positive camber change produces a positive caster change and a negative camber change produces a negative caster change. Hold cam bolt in position and tighten nut. Loosen rear cam bolt nut and rotate cam bolt to return camber to setting recorded previously, **Fig. 2.** When adjustment has been completed hold rear cam bolt and torque nut to 70 ft. lbs.

Camber

While holding cam bolt in position, loosen cam bolt nut, **Fig. 2.** Rotate cam bolt to obtain a change in camber equal to 1/2 the needed correction. Hold cam bolt in position and tighten cam bolt nut. To obtain the remaining 1/2 of needed correction apply the above procedure to the other cam bolt.

Toe-In, Adjust

Toe-in is adjusted by turning the tie rod adjusting tubes at outer ends of each tie rod after loosening clamp bolts. Readings should be taken only when front wheels

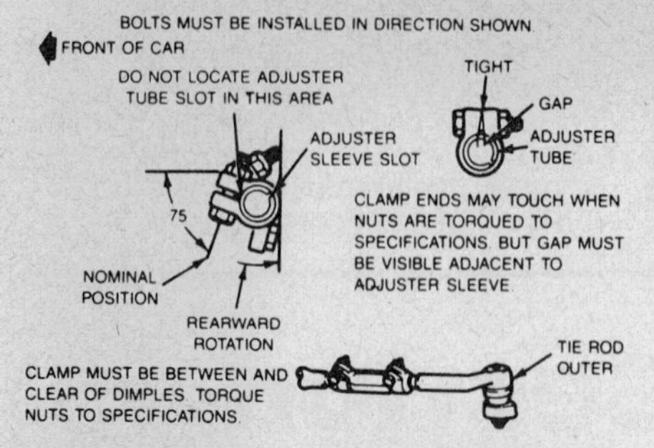

Fig. 3 Tie rod clamp and sleeve positioning

are straight ahead and steering gear is on its high spot.

1. Loosen clamp bolts at each end of tie rod adjusting sleeve.
2. Turn tie rod adjusting sleeve to obtain the proper toe-in adjustment.
3. After completing adjustment, check to ensure that the number of threads at each end of sleeve are equal and tie rod end housings and clamps are properly positioned, **Fig. 3.** Torque clamp bolt to 14 to 15 ft. lbs.

REAR WHEEL ALIGNMENT

ELDORADO & SEVILLE

Camber & Toe-In

Camber and toe-in are checked at the same time following the procedure outlined below. Camber is factory set and is not adjustable. If camber deviates from specified settings, check for a bent control arm or frame, or for a improperly mounted hub and bearing assembly.

1. Check front and rear trim heights.
2. Check automatic level control system, if equipped, for proper operation.
3. Position vehicle on alignment rack as follows:
   a. Place masking tape on floor from wheel plate to rear of vehicle to use as a guide to square vehicle on alignment rack.
   b. Back rear of vehicle onto rack, positioning wheels on wheel plates.
   c. Place a ruler at same rib of tire at front and rear of vehicle, then measure distance from inside edge of ruler to edge of guide line, **Fig. 4.** When vehicle is square, measurement from guide line to ruler should be greater at rear tire by approximately 5/8 inch.
4. Attach alignment mirrors to rear wheels, then check camber and toe settings and compare to specifications. **When vehicle is backed onto alignment rack, toe-in and toe-out are reversed. That is, toe-in will be read as toe-out, while toe-out will be read as toe-in.**
5. As stated previously, camber is not adjustable. To adjust toe-in, loosen inner pivot bushing retaining nut and bolt. Move control arm rearward to increase toe-in, or toward front of vehicle to decrease toe-in. A pry bar can be used to facilitate adjustment. After adjustment is completed, torque bushing retaining nut to 70 ft. lbs.

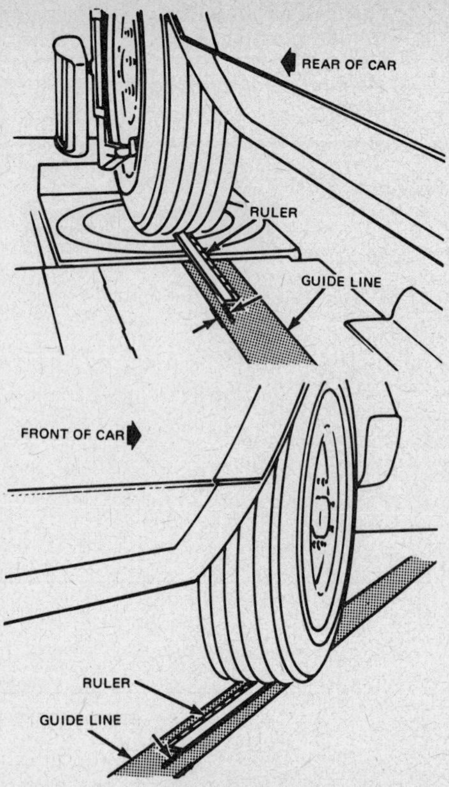

Fig. 4 Checking vehicle for squareness on alignment rack

CAMARO, CHEVROLET, CORVETTE, MALIBU & MONTE CARLO

INDEX OF SERVICE OPERATIONS

NOTE: Refer to rear of this manual for vehicle manufacturer's special tool suppliers.

Specifications

GENERAL ENGINE SPECIFICATIONS

Year	Engine CID①/Liter	Engine VIN Code②	Fuel System	Bore & Stroke	Com-presseion Ratio	Net Brake H.P. @ RPM③	Maximum Torque Ft. Lbs. @ RPM	Normal Oil Pressure Pounds
1982	4-151, 2.5L⑭	2	Fuel Injection	4.00 x 3.00	8.2	90 @ 4000	132 @ 2800	37.5
	V6-173, 2.8L	1	E2SE, 2 Bbl.④	3.50 x 2.99	8.5	102 @ 4800	142 @ 2400	50-65
	V6-229, 3.8L⑪	K	E2ME, 2 Bbl.④	3.736 x 3.480	8.6	110 @ 4200	170 @ 2000	50-65
	V6-231, 3.8L⑤	A	E2ME, 2 Bbl.④	3.80 x 3.40	8.0	110 @ 3800	190 @ 1600	50-65
	V8-262, 4.3L⑨⑩	V	Fuel Injection	4.057 x 3.385	22.5	85 @ 3600	165 @ 1600	30-45
	V8-267, 4.4L⑪	J	E2ME, 2 Bbl.④	3.50 x 3.48	8.3	115 @ 4000	200 @ 2400	45
	V8-305, 5.0L	H	E4ME, 4 Bbl.④	3.736 x 3.480	8.6	145 @ 4000	240 @ 2400	50-65
	V8-305, 5.0L	7	Fuel Injection	3.736 x 3.480	9.5	165 @ 4200	240 @ 2400	50-65
	V8-350, 5.7L	6	Fuel Injection	4.00 x 3.48	9.0	200 @ 4200	285 @ 2800	45
	V8-350, 5.7L⑨⑩	N	Fuel Injection	4.057 x 3.385	22.5	105 @ 3200	200 @ 1600	30-45
1983	4-151, 2.5L⑭	2	Fuel Injection	4.00 x 3.00	8.2	90 @ 4000	134 @ 2800	37.5
	V6-173, 2.8L	1	E2SE, 2 Bbl.④	3.50 x 2.99	8.5	107 @ 4800	145 @ 2100	50-65
	V6-229, 3.8L	9	E2ME, 2 Bbl.④	3.736 x 3.480	8.6	110 @ 4200	170 @ 2000	50-65
	V6-231, 3.8L⑤	A	E2ME, 2 Bbl.④	3.80 x 3.40	8.0	110 @ 3800	190 @ 1600	45
	V6-262, 4.3L⑨⑩	V	Fuel Injecton	4.057 x 3.385	21.6	85 @ 3600	165 @ 1600	30-45
	V8-305, 5.0L	H	E4ME, 4 Bbl.④	3.736 x 3.480	8.6	150 @ 3800	240 @ 2400	50-65
	V8-305, 5.0L	S	Fuel Injection	3.736 x 3.480	9.5	175 @ 4200	250 @ 2800	45
	V8-350, 5.7L⑨⑩	N	Fuel Injection	4.057 x 3.385	21.6	105 @ 3200	200 @ 1600	30-45
1984	4-151, 2.5L⑭	2	Fuel Injection	4.00 x 3.00	9.0	90 @ 4000	132 @ 2800	37.5
	V6-173, 2.8L	1	E2SE, 2 Bbl.④	3.50 x 2.99	8.5	112 @ 5100	148 @ 2400	50-65
	V6-229, 3.8L	9	E2ME, 2 Bbl.④	3.736 x 3.480	8.6	110 @ 4200	170 @ 2000	50-65
	V6-231, 3.8L⑤	A	E2ME, 2 Bbl.④	3.80 x 3.40	8.0	110 @ 3800	190 @ 1600	45
	V6-262, 4.3L⑨⑩	V	Fuel Injecton	4.057 x 3.385	21.6	85 @ 3600	165 @ 1600	30-45
	V8-305, 5.0L	H	E4ME, 4 Bbl.④	3.736 x 3.480	8.6	150 @ 3800	240 @ 2400	50-65
	V8-305 H.O. 5.0L	G	E4ME, 4 Bbl.④	3.736 x 3.480	9.5	190 @ 4800	240 @ 3200	50-65
	V8-350, 5.7L	8	Fuel Injection	4.00 x 3.48	9.0	205 @ 4300	290 @ 2800	50-65
	V8-350, 5.7L⑨⑩	N	Fuel Injection	4.057 x 3.385	21.6	105 @ 4200	200 @ 1600	30-45
1985	4-151/2.5L⑭	2	Fuel Injection	4.00 x 3.00	9.0	88 @ 4400	132 @ 2800	37.5
	V6-173/2.8	S	Fuel Injection	3.50 x 2.99	8.9	135 @ 5100	165 @ 3600	50-65
	V6-262/4.3L	Z	Fuel Injection	4.00 x 3.48	9.3	130 @ 3600	210 @ 2000	50-65
	V8-305/5.0L	F	Fuel Injection	3.74 x 3.48	9.5	215 @ 4400	275 @ 3200	—
	V8-305/5.0L⑮	G	E4ME, 4 Bbl.④	3.74 x 3.48	9.5	190 @ 4800	240 @ 3200	50-65
	V8-305/5.0L⑯	G	E4ME, 4 Bbl.④	3.74 x 3.48	9.5	180 @ 4800	235 @ 3200	50-65
	V8-305/5.0L⑮	H	E4ME, 4 Bbl.④	3.74 x 3.48	8.6	165 @ 4400	250 @ 2000	50-65
	V8-305/5.0L⑦	H	E4ME, 4 Bbl.④	3.74 x 3.48	8.6	150 @ 4000	240 @ 2000	50-65
	V8-305/5.0L⑧	H	E4ME, 4 Bbl.④	3.74 x 3.48	8.6	165 @ 4200	245 @ 2400	50-65
	V8-350/5.7L⑫	8	Fuel Injection	4.00 x 3.48	9.0	230 @ 4000	330 @ 3200	50-65
	V8-350/5.7L	N	Fuel Injection	4.00 x 3.39	22.1	105 @ 3200	200 @ 1600	30-45

Continued

GENERAL ENGINE SPECIFICATIONS—Continued

Year	Engine		Fuel System	Bore & Stroke	Com-presseion Ratio	Net Brake H.P. @ RPM ③	Maximum Torque Ft. Lbs. @ RPM	Normal Oil Pressure Pounds
	CID ①/Liter	VIN Code ②						
1986	4-151/2.5L ⑭	2	Fuel Injection	4.00 x 3.48	9.0	88 @ 4800	132 @ 2800	37.5
	V6-173/2.8L	S	Fuel Injection	3.50 x 2.99	8.9	135 @ 5100	160 @ 3900	50-65
	V6-262/4.3L	Z	Fuel Injection	4.00 x 3.48	9.3	140 @ 4000	225 @ 2000	50-65
	V8-305/5.0L	F	Fuel Injection	3.74 x 3.48	9.5	190 @ 4000	285 @ 2800	50-65
	V8-305/5.0L ⑮	G	E4ME, 4 Bbl. ④	3.74 x 3.48	9.5	190 @ 4800	240 @ 3200	50-65
	V8-305/5.0L ⑯	G	E4ME, 4 Bbl. ④	3.74 x 3.48	9.5	180 @ 4400	225 @ 3200	50-65
	V8-305/5.0L ⑮	H	E4ME, 4 Bbl. ④	3.74 x 3.48	9.5	⑬	⑥	50-65
	V8-305/5.0L ⑧	H	E4ME, 4 Bbl. ④	3.74 x 3.48	9.5	165 @ 4200	245 @ 2400	50-65
	V8-305/5.0L ⑦	H	E4ME, 4 Bbl. ④	3.74 x 3.48	9.5	150 @ 4000	240 @ 2000	50-65
	V8-350/5.7L ⑫	8	Fuel Injection	4.00 x 3.48	9.5	230 @ 4000	330 @ 3200	50-65
1987	V6-173/2.8L	S	Fuel Injection	3.50 x 2.99	8.9	135 @ 4900	160 @ 3900	50-65
	V6-262/4.3L	Z	Fuel Injection	4.00 x 3.43	9.3	140 @ 4200	225 @ 2000	50-65
	V8-305/5.0L	F	Fuel Injection	3.74 x 3.48	9.5	—	—	50-65
	V8-305/5.0L	G	E4ME, 4 Bbl. ④	3.74 x 3.48	9.5	—	—	50-65
	V8-305/5.0L	H	E4ME, 4 Bbl. ④	3.74 x 3.48	8.6	—	—	50-65
	V8-307/5.0L	Y	E4MC, 4 Bbl. ④	3.80 x 3.40	8.0	140 @ 3200	255 @ 2000	50-65
	V8-350/5.7L	6	E4ME, 4 Bbl. ④	4.00 x 3.48	8.2	—	—	50-65
	V8-350/5.7L ⑮	8	Fuel Injection	4.00 x 3.48	9.0	225 @ 4400	300 @ 2800	50-65
	V8-350/5.7L ⑫	8	Fuel Injection	4.00 x 3.48	9.5	240 @ 4000	345 @ 3200	50-65
1988	V6-173/2.8L	S	Fuel Injection	3.50 x 2.99	8.9	—	—	50-65
	V6-262/4.3L	Z	Fuel Injection	4.00 x 3.48	9.3	140 @ 4000	225 @ 2000	50-65
	V8-305/5.0L	F	Fuel Injection	3.74 x 3.48	9.3	—	—	50-65
	V8-305/5.0L	G	4 Bbl. ④	3.74 x 3.48	9.3	200 @ 4800	225 @ 3200	50-65
	V8-305/5.0L	H	4 Bbl. ④	3.74 x 3.48	9.3	180 @ 4000	240 @ 2000	50-65
	V8-307/5.0L	Y	4 Bbl. ④	3.80 x 3.40	8.0	—	—	50-65
	V8-350/5.7L ⑮	8	Fuel Injection	4.00 x 3.48	9.3	—	—	50-65
	V8-350/5.7L ⑫	8	Fuel Injection	. 4.00 x 3.48	9.5	—	—	50-65

①—CID-Cubic inch displacement.
②—V.I.N.-On 1982-88 vehicles, the 8th digit in the V.I.N. denotes engine code.
③—Ratings are net-As installed in the vehicle.
④—Rochester.
⑤—For service procedures on this engine, see Buick chapter.
⑥—Exc. IROC-Z & Z28, 245 @ 2000; IROC-Z & Z28, 250 @ 2000.
⑦—Monte Carlo.
⑧—Caprice/Impala.
⑨—For service procedures on this engine, see Oldsmobile chapter.
⑩—Diesel.
⑪—Exc. Calif.
⑫—Corvette.
⑬—Exc. IROC-Z & Z28, 155 @ 4200; IROC-Z & Z28, 165 @ 4400.
⑭—For service procedures on this engine, refer to Pontiac chapter.
⑮—Camaro.
⑯—Monte Carlo SS.

ENGINE TIGHTENING SPECIFICATIONS*

*Torque specifications are for clean and lightly lubricated threads only. Dry or dirty threads produce increased friction which prevents accurate measurement of tightness.

Year	Engine Model/ VIN	Spark Plugs Ft. Lbs.	Cylinder Head Bolts Ft. Lbs.	Intake Manifold Ft. Lbs.	Exhaust Manifold Ft. Lbs.	Rocker Arm Stud Ft. Lbs.	Rocker Arm Cover Ft. Lbs.	Connecting Rod Cap Bolts Ft. Lbs.	Main Bearing Cap Bolts Ft. Lbs.	Flywheel to Crankshaft Ft. Lbs.	Vibration Damper or Pulley Ft. Lbs.
1982-83	4-151/⑩ ⑮	7-15	85	29	44	20⑥	6	32	70	44	160
1984-85	4-151/⑩ ⑮	7-15	92	29	44	20⑥	7.5	32	70	44	160
1986	4-151/2	7-15	⑩	⑰	⑱	20⑥	6	32	70	55	162
1982-85	V6-173⑮	7-15	70	23	25	46	8	37	69	②	75
1986-87	V6-173/S	7-15	65-90	13-25	19-31	—	7-15	34-45	63-83	—	67-85
1982-84	V6-229⑮	22	65	30	20	—	45③	45	70	60	60
1982-84	V6-231/A⑦	15	80	45	25	30④	4	40	100	60	225
1982-83	V6-262/V⑪ ⑫	15⑤	⑬ ⑭	41⑬	29	28⑥	9	42	107	48	160-350
1985-87	V6-262/Z	22	65	30	20	—	45③	45	70	60	60
1982	V8-267/J	22	65	30	20	—	45③	45	70	60	60
1982-84	V8-305⑮	22	65	30	20	—	45③	45	70	60	60
1985-87	V8-305/F,G,H	22	60-75	25-45	⑲	—	23	42-47	60-75	63-85	65-75
1982	V8-350⑨ ⑮	22	65	30	20①	⑧	45③	45	70	60	60
1984-85	V8-350/8⑨	22	65	35	20①	50	50③	45	80	60	60
1986-87	V8-350/6, 8⑨	22	⑯	35	20①	50	50③	45	80	60	60
1982-85	V8-350/N⑪ ⑫	12⑤	130⑬	40⑬	25	28⑥	70③	42	120	60	200-310
1987	V8-307/Y	25	125	40	25	25	90③	42	㉑	60	200-310

①—Inside bolts 30 ft. lbs.
②—Auto. trans., 25-35 ft. lbs.; manual trans., 45-55 ft. lbs.
③—Inch lbs.
④—Rocker arm shaft to cylinder head bolts.
⑤—Glow plug torque.
⑥—Rocker arm pivot bolt.
⑦—Refer to Buick Chapter for service procedures on this engine.
⑧—Corvette, 50 ft. lbs.
⑨—Gasoline engine.
⑩—Refer to Pontiac chapter for service procedures.
⑪—Diesel engine.
⑫—Refer to Oldsmobile Section for service procedures on this engine.
⑬—Clean & dip bolt in engine oil before tightening to obtain correct torque reading.
⑭—Bolts 5, 6, 11, 12, 13 & 14, 59 ft. lbs.; All others, 142 ft. lbs.
⑮—For V.I.N. code, refer to the General Engine Specifications at the beginning of the chapter.
⑯—Long & medium bolts, 65 ft. lbs.; short bolts, 60 ft. lbs.
⑰—Torque stud bolts except front upper to 25 ft. lbs.; torque front upper stud bolt to 37 ft. lbs. Torque hex bolts to 28 ft. lbs.
⑱—Torque four outer manifold attaching bolts to 31 ft. lbs.; torque three center manifold attaching bolts to 37 ft. lbs.
⑲—Outer four bolts, 14-26 ft. lbs.; inner two bolts, 20-32 ft. lbs.
⑳—Studs 10 inch lbs. min.; nuts, 50-65 inch lbs.
㉑—Bolts 1, 2, 3 & 4, 80 ft. lbs.; bolt 5, 120 ft. lbs.

ALTERNATOR SPECIFICATIONS

Year	Model	Rated Hot Output Amps	Field Current 12 Volts @ 80°F
1982	1103060	42	4-4.5
	1101040	70	4-4.5
	1100195	70	4-4.5
	1100294	63	4-4.5
	1101097	85	4-4.5
	1100285	85	4-4.5
1983	1105360	42	4-4.5
	1100250	63	4-4.5
	1101040	70	4-4.5
	1105360	37	4-4.5
	1103061	42	4-4.5
	1105357	63	4-4.5
1984	1100200	78	4-4.5
	1100226	37	4-4.5
	1100228	37	4-4.5
	1100230	40	4-4.5
	1100237	55	4-4.5
	1100239	55	4-4.5
	1100246	63	4-4.5
	1100247	63	4-4.5
	1100260	78	4-4.5
	1100263	78	4-4.5
	1100264	78	4-4.5
	1100270	78	4-4.5
	1100297	42	4-4.5
	1100300	63	4-4.5
	1105022	78	4-4.5
	1105025	63	4-4.5
	1105041	78	4-4.5
	1105513	97	4-4.5
1985	1100200	78	4.5-5.0
	1100226	37	4.0-5.0
	1100237	56	4.5-5.0
	1100239	56	4.5-5.0
	1100246	66	4.5-5.0
	1100260	78	4.5-5.0
	1100270	78	4.5-5.0

Year	Model	Rated Hot Output Amps	Field Current 12 Volts @ 80°F
	1105521	78	4.5-5.0
	1105522	37	4.0-5.0
	1105523	56	4.5-5.0
	1105555	66	4.5-5.0
	1105564	66	4.5-5.0
	1105565	78	4.5-5.0
	1105566	66	4.5-5.0
	1105567	78	4.5-5.0
1986	1100254	66	—
	1100272	78	—
	1105521	78	—
	1105545	94	—
	110555	66	—
	110556	42	—
	1105587	97	—
	1105588	78	—
	1105600	66	—
	1105639	108	—
1987	1100200	78	—
	1100239	56	—
	1101137	85	—
	1101138	100	—
	1101139	85	—
	1101140	100	—
	1101141	105	—
	1105197	70	—
	1105565	78	—
	1105650	78	—
	1105651	94	—
	1105652	78	—
	1105662	78	—
	1105673	56	—
	1105674	66	—
	1105697	74	—
	1105701	85	—
	1998527	105	4-4.5

STARTING MOTOR APPLICATIONS

Year	Engine/VIN	Starter Number
1982	4-151/F②	1109533
	V6-173/1	1109535
	V6-229/K⑨	1109524
	V6-229/K⑦	1109534
	V6-231/A	1109524
	V6-262 Diesel/V	1998552
	V8-267/J⑨	1109064
	V8-267/J⑦	1109534
	V8-305/H⑨	1109064
	V8-305/H⑦	1109534
	V8-350/8①	1998241
	V8-350/N	1998552
1983	4-151/2②	1109556
	V6-173/1	1109535
	V6-229/9	1998236
	6-231/A	1998236
	V6-262 Diesel/V	1998554
	V8-305/H, G	1109534
	V8-305/S	1109534
	V8-350 Diesel/N	1998554
1984	4-151/2②	1109556
	V6-173/1	1109535
	V6-229/9	1998236

①—Corvette.
②—Refer to Pontiac chapter for service procedures.
③—With auto. trans.
④—With manual trans.

Year	Engine/VIN	Starter Number
	V6-231/A	1981109
	V6-262 Diesel/V	1981104
	V8-305/H⑧	1981102
	V8-305/S & H⑤	1109534
	V8-350/8①	1998435
	V8-350 Diesel/N	1981104⑥
1985-86	4-151/2②	1998450
	V6-173/S	1998427
	V6-262/Z	1998435
	V8-305/H③	1998435
	V8-305/G, H④	1998466
	V8-305/F	1998452
	V8-350/8	1998435
1987	V6-173/S	1998427
	V6-262/Z	1998557
	V8-305/F③	1998452
	V8-305/G	1998564
	V8-305/H③ ⑤	1998435
	V8-305/H, 7④ ⑤	1998466
	V8-305/H⑧	1998557
	V8-307/Y	1998536
	V8-350/6	1998558
	V8-350/8	1998527

⑤—Camaro.
⑥—With heavy duty battery, 1981106.
⑦—Exc. Malibu & Monte Carlo.
⑧—Exc. Camaro.
⑨—Malibu & Monte Carlo.

REAR AXLE SPECIFICATIONS

Year	Model	Carrier Type	Ring Gear Pinion Backlash		Pinion Bearing Preload			Differential Bearing Preload		
			Method	Adjustment	Method	New Bearings Inch Lbs.	Used Bearings Inch Lbs.	Method	New Bearings	Used Bearings
1982	③	Integral	Shims	.005-.008	Spacer	20-25①	10-15①	Shims	.008② ④	.008② ④
	Camaro	Integral	Shims	.005-.009	Spacer	24-32①	8-12①	Shims	.008	.008
1982	Corvette	Integral	Shims	.005-.009	Shims	15-35①	—	Shims	.008②	.008②
1983-86	Exc. Corvette	Integral	Shims	.005-.008	Spacer	24-32①	8-12①	Shims	.008②	.008②
1984	Corvette	Integral	Shims	.005-.008	Shims	15-35	—	Shims	.008②	.008②
1985-87	Corvette⑤	Integral	Shims	.006-.009	Shims	15-35	—	Shims	.015-.020	—
1985-87	Corvette⑥	Integral	Shims	.006-.009	Shims	20-30	—	Shims	.008-.012	—
1987	Camaro	Integral	Shims	.004-.007	Shims	12-25	6-12	Shims	.008②	—
1987	③	Integral	Shims	.005-.008	Spacers	15-30	10	Shims	.008②	—

①—Use inch-pound torque wrench on pinion shaft nut.
②—Slip fit plus 0.004 inch additional preload per side.
③—Exc. Camaro & Corvette.
④—Total preload measured with torque wrench at pinion flange nut with new seal installed. 35-40 inch lbs., new bearings; 20-25 inch lbs., used bearings.
⑤—Model 36 (auto. trans.).
⑥—Model 44 (manual trans.).

WHEEL ALIGNMENT SPECIFICATIONS

Year	Model	Caster Angle, Degrees		Camber Angle, Degrees				Toe-In Inch		
				Limits		Desired				
		Limits	Desired	Left	Right	Left	Right			
CAMARO										
1982-84	All	+2 to +4	+3	+.2 to +1.8	+.2 to +1.8	+1	+1	①		
1985	Exc. IROC-Z	+2 to +4	+3	+.2 to +1.8	+.2 to +1.8	+1	+1	①		
	IROC-Z	+3 to +5	+4	+.2 to +1.8	+.2 to +1.8	+1	+1	+.05 to .25②		
1986	Exc. Z-28	+2½ to +3½	+3	+½ to +1½	+½ to +1½	+1	+1	+.15②		
	Z-28	+3 to +4	+3½	+½ to +1½	+½ to +1½	+1	+1	+.15②		
1987	All	0 to +1	+½	+½ to +1½	+½ to +1½	+1	+1	+.05②		
1988	Exc. IROC-Z	0 to +1	+½	+½ to +1½	+½ to +1½	+1	+1	+.05②		
	IROC-Z	+3 to +4	+3.5	+½ to +1½	+½ to +1½	+1	+1	+.05②		
MALIBU & MONTE CARLO										
1982-86	Manual Steering	0 to +2	+1	−.3 to +1.3	−.3 to +1.3	+.5	+.5	+1/16 to +¼		
	Power Steering	+2 to +4	+3	−.3 to +1.3	−.3 to +1.3	+.5	+.5	+1/16 to +¼		
1987	Manual Steering	−.2 to +1.8	+.8	−.3 to +1.3	−.3 to +1.3	+.5	+.5	+.05②		
	Power Steering	+2 to +4	+3	−.3 to +1.3	−.3 to +1.3	+.5	+.5	+.05②		
1988	Manual Steering	0 to +2	+1	−.3 to +1.3	−.3 to +1.3	+.5	+.5	+.05②		
	Power Steering	+2 to +4	+3	−.3 to +1.3	−.3 to +1.3	+.5	+.5	+.05②		
CHEVROLET										
1982-86	Caprice, Impala	+2 to +4	+3	0 to +1.6	0 to +1.6	+.8	+.8	+1/16 to +¼		
1987-88	Caprice	+1.8 to +3.8	+2.8	0 to +1.6	0 to +1.6	+.8	+.8	+.05②		
CORVETTE										
1982	Front Whl. Align.	+1¼ to +3¼	+2¼	0 to +1½	0 to +1½	+¾	+¾	+⅛ to +⅜		
	Rear Whl. Align.	—	—	−½ to +½	−½ to +½	0	0	+.06②		
1984	Front Whl. Align.	+2.2 to +3.8	+3	+.3 to +1.3	+.3 to +1.3	+.8	+.8	0 to +.3②		
	Rear Whl. Align.	—	—	−.5 to +.5	−.5 to +.5	0	0	+.15②		
1985-86	Front Whl. Align.	+2.2 to +3.8	+3	+.3 to +1.3	+.3 to +1.3	+.8	+.8	0 to +.15		
	Rear Whl. Align.	—	—	+.1 to +.9	+.1 to +.9	+.4	+.4	+.15		
1987-88	Front Whl. Align.	+4.7 to +6.3	+5.5	+.3 to +1.3	+.3 to +1.3	+.8	+.8	0		
	Rear Whl. Align.	—	—	−.1 to +.9	−.1 to +.9	+.4	+.4	0		

①—Exc. Z-28, +.1 to +.3 degrees per wheel; Z-28, +.05 to +.25 degrees per wheel.

②—Degrees per wheel.

COOLING SYSTEM & CAPACITY DATA

Year	Model or Engine/ VIN	Cooling Capacity, Qts.		Radiator Cap Relief Pressure, Lbs.	Thermo. Opening Temp.	Fuel Tank Gals.	Engine Oil Refill Qts. ①	Transmission Oil			Rear Axle Oil Pints
		Less A/C	With A/C					4 Speed Pints	5 Speed Pints	Auto. Trans. Qts. ②	
CAMARO											
1982	4-151/2	8.8	9.1	15	195	16	3⑯	3½	—	㉗	3½
	V6-173/1	12½	12½	15	195	16	4⑯	3½	—	㉗	3½
	V8-305/H,7	15	15	15	195	16	4	3½	—	㉗	3½
1983	4-151/2	8.8	9.1	15	195	16	3⑯	4.3	5.3	⑧	3½
	V6-173/I	12½	12½	15	195	16	4⑯	4.3	5.3	⑧	3½
	V8-305/H,G	15	15	15	195	16	4	4.3	5.3	⑧	3½
	V8-305 E.F.I./7	15	15	15	195	16	4	4.3	5.3	⑧	3½
1984	4-151/2	8.8	9.1	15	195	16	3⑯	4.3	5.3	⑥	3½
	V6-173/I	12.5	12.5	15	195	16	4⑯	4.3	5.3	⑥	3 ½
	V8-305/H,G	15	15	15	195	16	4	4.3	5.3	⑥	3½
1985	4-151/2	⑤	⑤	15	195	15.5	3⑯	2.4	6.9	⑥	3.5
	V6-173/S	㉑	㉒	15	195	15.5	4⑯	—	6.9	⑥	3.5
	V8-305/F	—	—	15	195	15.5	4	—	—	⑥	3.5
	V8-305/G	15.8	16.8	15	195	16.2	4	—	6.9	—	3.5
	V8-305/H	15.2⑨	15.7⑨	15	195	16.2	4	—	6.9	⑥	3.5
1986	4-151/2	9.8	9.8	15	195	15.5	3⑯	—	6.6	⑥	3.5
	V6-173/S	12½	12.5	15	195	15.5	4⑯	—	6.6	⑥	3.5
	V8-305/F	17	17	15	195	15.5	4	—	6.6	⑥	3.5
	V8-305/G	15.6	15.6	15	195	16.2	4	—	6.6	⑥	3.5
	V8-305/H	15.3	15.6	15	195	16.2	4	—	6.6	⑥	3.5
1987	V6-173/S	12½	12½	15	195	15.5	4⑯	—	6.6	⑥	3.6
	V8-305/F	17	17	15	195	15.5	4	—	6.6	⑥	3.6
	V8-305/G	17	17	15	195	16.2	4	—	6.6	⑥	3.6
	V8-305/H	15.3	15.6	15	195	16.2	4	—	6.6	⑥	3.6
	V8-350/8	17	17	15	195	15.5	4	—	6.6	⑥	3.6
1988	V6-173S	—	—	15	195	15.5	4⑯	—	6.9	4.75	1.7
	V8-305/F	—	—	15	195	15.5	5	—	6.9	4.75	1.7
	V8-350/8	—	—	15	195	15.5	5	—	6.9	4.75	1.7
MALIBU & MONTE CARLO											
1982	V6-229/K	18½	18½	15	195	18.1	4⑯	—	—	⑪	③
	V6-231/A	15½	15½	15	195	18.1	4⑯	—	—	⑪	③
	V8-267/J	21	21	15	195	18.1	4	—	—	⑪	③
	V8-305/H	19	19	15	195	18.1	4	—	—	⑪	③
1983	V6-229/9	18½	18½	15	195	18.1	4⑯	—	—	⑪	3½
	V6-231/A	15½	15½	15	195	18.1	4⑯	—	—	⑪	3½
	V6-262/V	13.4	13.4	15	195	19.8	6⑫	—	—	⑪	3½
	V8-305/H	19	19	15	195	18.1	4	—	—	⑪	3½
	V8-350/N⑱	18.3	18.4	15	195	19.8	7⑫	—	—	⑪	3½
1984	V6-229/9	14¼	14¼	15	195	25⑮	4⑯	—	—	⑦	③
	V6-231/A	11¾	11¾	15	195	25⑮	4⑯	—	—	⑦	③
	V8-305/H, G	⑰	⑰	15	195	25⑮	4	—	—	⑦	③
	V8-350/N⑱	18.3	18.3	15	195	27⑮	7⑫	—	—	⑦	③
1985	V6-262/Z	13.0㉓	13.1㉓	15	195	17.6	—	—	—	㉔	㉕
	V8-305/G	15.9	16.7	15	195	18.1	4	—	—	㉔	㉕
	V8-305/H	16.4	15.9	15	195	18.1	4	—	—	㉔	㉕
1986	V6-262/Z	12	12	15	195	17.6	4⑯	—	—	㉔	㉕
	V8-305/H	16.3	16.3	15	195	18.1	4	—	—	㉔	㉕
	V8-305/G	16.6	16.6	15	195	18.1	4	—	—	㉔	㉕
1987	V6-262/Z	13.1	13.1	15	195	17.6	4	—	—	㉔	㉕
	V8-305/G	16.7	16.7	15	195	18.1	5	—	—	㉔	㉕
	V8-305/H	16.5	16.5	15	195	18.1	5	—	—	㉔	㉕

COOLING SYSTEM & CAPACITY DATA—Continued

Year	Model or Engine/VIN	Cooling Capacity, Qts.		Radiator Cap Relief Pressure, Lbs.	Thermo. Opening Temp.	Fuel Tank Gals.	Engine Oil Refill Qts. ①	Transmission Oil			Rear Axle Oil Pints
		Less A/C	With A/C					4 Speed Pints	5 Speed Pints	Auto. Trans. Qts. ②	
1988	V6-262/Z	13	13.1	15	195	17.6	4	—	—	㉔	—
	V8-305/G	16.4	15.9	15	195	18.1	5	—	—	㉔	—
	V8-305/H	16.4	15.9	15	195	18.1	5	—	—	㉔	—
CHEVROLET											
1982	V6-229/K	14¼	14¼	15	195	25⑮	4⑯	—	—	⑪	③
	V6-231/A	11¾	11¾	15	195	25⑮	4⑯	—	—	⑪	③
	V8-267/J	⑰	⑰	15	195	25⑮	4	—	—	⑪	③
	V8-305/H	15½	15½	15	195	25⑮	4	—	—	⑪	③
	V8-350/N⑱	18.3	18	15	195	25⑮	7④	—	—	⑪	③
1983	V6-229/K	14¼	14¼	15	195	25⑮	4⑯	—	—	⑦	③
	V6-231/A	11¾	11¾	15	195	25⑮	4⑯	—	—	⑦	③
	V8-305/H	15½	15½	15	195	25⑮	4	—	—	⑦	③
	V8-350/N⑱	18.3	18.3	15	195	27⑮	7⑫	—	—	⑦	③
1984	V6-229/K	18½	18½	15	195	25⑮	4⑯	—	—	⑦	③
	V6-231/A	15½	15½	15	195	25⑮	4⑯	—	—	⑦	③
	V8-305/H	19	19	15	195	25⑮	4	—	—	⑦	③
	V8-350/N⑱	18.1㉖	18.2㉖	15	195	25⑮	7.0⑫	—	—	⑦	③
1985	V6-262/Z	12	12	15	195	25	—	—	—	㉔	㉕
	V8-305/H	16.5	16.5	15	195	25⑮	4	—	—	㉔	㉕
	V8-350/N	18	18	15	195	25⑮	7.0⑫	—	—	㉔	㉕
1986	V6-262/Z	12	12	15	195	25⑮	4⑯	—	—	㉔	㉕
	V8-305/H	16½	16½	15	195	25⑮	4	—	—	㉔	㉕
1987	V6-262/Z	12.2	12.6	15	195	25⑮	4⑯	—	—	㉔	㉕
	V8-305/H	16.8	17.4	15	195	25⑮	4	—	—	㉔	㉕
	V8-307/Y	17.1	17.6	15	195	25⑮	4	—	—	㉔	㉕
	V8-350/6	—	—	15	195	25⑮	4	—	—	㉔	㉕
1988	V6-262/Z	12.2	12.6	15	195	25⑮	4	—	—	—	—
	V8-305/H	15.9	16.6	15	195	25⑮	5	—	—	—	—
	V8-307/Y	15.6	16.1	15	195	25⑮	4	—	—	—	—
CORVETTE											
1982	V8-350/6	21	21	15	195	23.7	4	—	3	10	4
1984	V8-350/8	14.5⑳	14.5⑳	15	195	20	4	—	⑲	10	4
1985	V8-350 TPI/8	14	14	15	195	20	4	—	⑲	㉙	4
1986-88	V8-350 TPI/8	—	14	15	195	20	4	—	⑲	㉙	4

①—Add one quart with filter change.

②—Approximate. Make final check with dipstick.

③—7½" ring gear, 3½ pts.; 8½" ring gear, 4¼ pts.; 8¾" ring gear, 5.4 pts.

④—Includes filter. Use recommended diesel engine oil, designated SF/CC, SF/CD or SE/CC.

⑤—Std. cooling: auto. trans., 9.1 qts.; manual trans., 9.3 qts. Heavy duty cooling, 9.25 qts.

⑥—Oil pan only, 4.95 qts.; total capacity, 11½ qts.

⑦—THM 200C, oil pan only 3½ qts.; total capacity, 9½ qts.; THM 200-4R, oil pan only, 3.48 qts.; total capacity, 11.05 qts. THM 250C & 350C, oil pan only, 3.15 qts.; total capacity, 10 qts. THM 700-R4, oil pan only, 4.95 qts.; total capacity, 11½ qts.

⑧—THM 200c, oil pan only, 3½ qts.; total capacity 5 qts. THM 700-R4, oil pan only, 4.95 qts.; total capacity, 11½ qts.

⑨—Heavy duty cooling, 15.8 qts.

⑩—3¼ pts. for 7½" ring gear. 4 pts. for 8½" and 8¾" ring gears.

⑪—THM 200 oil pan only, 3½ qts. Total capacity, 5 qts., THM350 oil pan only, 3 qts. Total capacity, 10 qts.

⑫—Includes filter. Use recommended diesel engine oil, designated SF/CC or SF/CD.

⑬—With heavy duty cooling system, add 1 qt.

⑭—With auto. trans., add 1 qt.

⑮—Sta. Wag., 22 gals.

⑯—With or without filter change.

⑰—Exc. Sta. Wag. Standard cooling, 16.75 qts.; Sta. Wag. with standard cooling, 15.5 qts.

⑱—Diesel.

⑲—4 spd., 2 pts.; over drive, 4 pts.

Electrical Section

INDEX

STARTER REPLACE

If shims are used between starter and engine block, they should be placed in their original location during installation. If starter is noisy during cranking, remove one .015 inch double shim or add one .015 single shim to the outer bolt. If starter makes a high pitched whine after firing, add .015 inch double shims until noise ceases.

1. Disconnect battery ground cable.
2. Raise and support vehicle.
3. Remove starter to engine brace and starter heat shields, if equipped.
4. Remove starter mounting bolts and lower starter. Note position of shims, if used.
5. Disconnect solenoid wires and the battery cable.
6. Remove starter from vehicle.
7. Reverse procedure to install.

IGNITION LOCK REPLACE

1. Remove steering wheel as described under Horn Sounder and Steering Wheel.
2. Remove turn signal switch as described under Turn Signal Switch, Replace, then remove buzzer switch.
3. Place ignition switch in "Run" position, then remove lock cylinder retaining screw and lock cylinder.

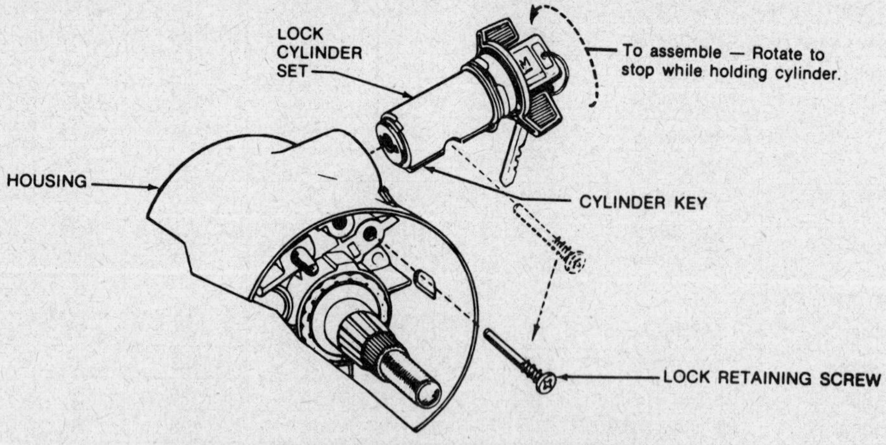

Fig. 1 Ignition lock installation

4. On 1987-88 Corvette, cut wire at lock cylinder assembly, then attach remaining wire extending from steering column cover to back of connector body of new lock cylinder. Pull original wire through column while feeding through new wire.
5. On all models, install by rotating lock cylinder to stop while holding housing, **Fig. 1.** Align cylinder key with keyway in housing, then push lock cylinder assembly into housing until fully seated.
6. Install lock cylinder retaining screw. Torque screw to 35 in. lbs.
7. Install buzzer switch, turn signal switch and steering wheel.

IGNITION SWITCH REPLACE

The ignition switch is mounted on top of the mast jacket inside the brake pedal support and is actuated by a rod and rack assembly.

1. Disconnect battery cable.
2. Disconnect and lower steering column. **It may be necessary, on some models, to remove the upper column mounting bracket if it hinders servicing of switch. Use extreme care when lowering steering column to prevent damage to column**

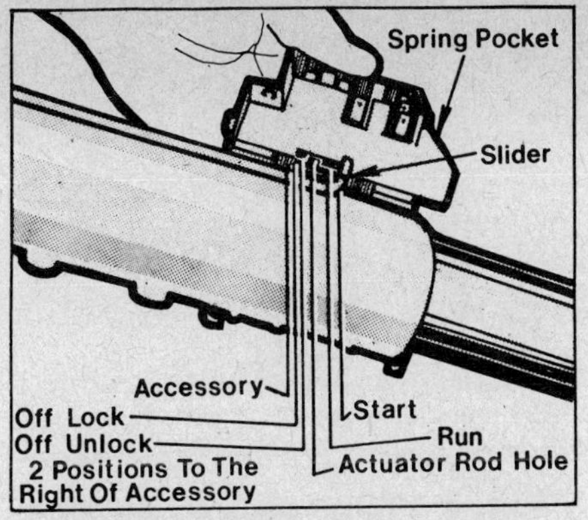

Fig. 2 Ignition switch

assembly. Only lower steering column a sufficient distance to perform ignition switch service.

3. Rotate ignition lock to "Off" unlocked position.
4. If lock cylinder has been removed, pull switch actuator rod up to stop, then push rod down to second detent to place switch in "Off" unlocked position, **Fig. 2.**
5. Remove column mounted dimmer switch, if equipped, then remove switch retaining screws and switch.
6. Reverse procedure to install, noting the following:
   a. Place gear shift lever in neutral.
   b. Place lock cylinder and switch in "Off" unlocked position, **Fig. 2.**
   c. Fit actuator rod into hole in switch slider and secure switch with retaining screws, ensuring switch does not move out of detent.
   d. Install and adjust dimmer switch, if removed, as outlined in "Dimmer Switch, Replace."
   e. Torque retaining screws to 35 inch lbs., then check switch operation.

LIGHT SWITCH REPLACE

MALIBU & MONTE CARLO

1. Disconnect battery ground cable.
2. Remove instrument panel bezel.
3. Pull switch knob to "On" position.
4. Remove three screws attaching windshield wiper/light switch mounting plate to cluster and pull assembly rearward.
5. Depress shaft retainer button on switch and pull knob and shaft assembly from switch, **Fig. 3.**
6. Remove ferrule nut and switch assembly from mounting plate.
7. Reverse procedure to install.

CORVETTE

1982

1. Disconnect battery ground cable.
2. Remove left air distribution duct.
3. Remove instrument cluster to instrument panel attaching screws and pull cluster rearward.
4. Disconnect speedometer cable and electrical connectors and remove cluster.

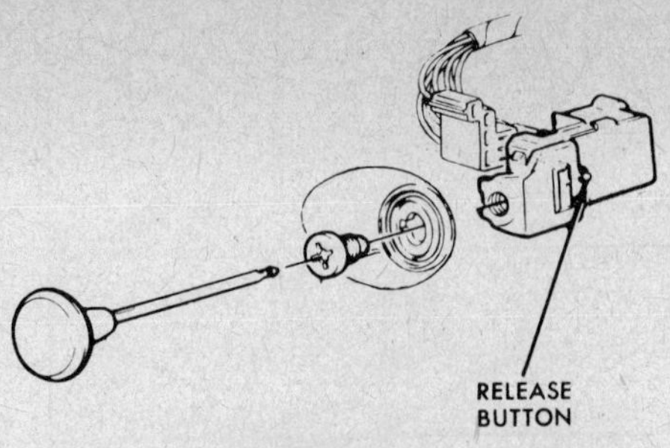

Fig. 3 Headlamp switch knob removal

5. Remove two instrument panel to left door pillar attaching screws and pull left side of instrument panel slightly rearward.
6. Pull switch knob to "On" position, depress release button on switch and remove shaft and knob assembly, **Fig. 3.** Remove bezel nut securing switch to instrument panel.
7. Disconnect vacuum hoses from switch and the electrical connector.
8. Remove light switch from vehicle.
9. Reverse procedure to install.

1984–88

1. Disconnect battery ground cable.
2. Remove hush panel from under left side of instrument panel.
3. Pull switch knob to "On" position, reach up under dash and depress release button on switch, and remove shaft and knob assembly, **Fig. 3.**
4. Remove cluster bezel and nut securing switch to instrument panel and lower switch.
5. Disconnect electrical connectors and remove switch.
6. Reverse procedure to install.

CHEVROLET

1. Disconnect battery ground cable.
2. Pull switch knob to "On" position, reach up under instrument panel and depress switch shaft retainer, then pull knob and shaft assembly from switch, **Fig. 3.**
3. Remove windshield wiper switch.
4. Remove light switch ferrule nut and remove switch from panel.
5. Disconnect electrical connector from switch and remove switch from vehicle.
6. Reverse procedure to install.

CAMARO

1982–84 Exc. 1984 Berlinetta

1. Disconnect battery ground cable.
2. Remove left and right lower instrument panel trim plates.
3. Pull light switch to On position, depress release button on switch frame, then remove knob and stem from switch, **Fig. 3.**
4. Remove switch bezel and retaining nut.
5. Depress switch retaining tabs, if equipped, pull switch from instrument cluster and disconnect electrical connector.
6. Reverse procedure to install.

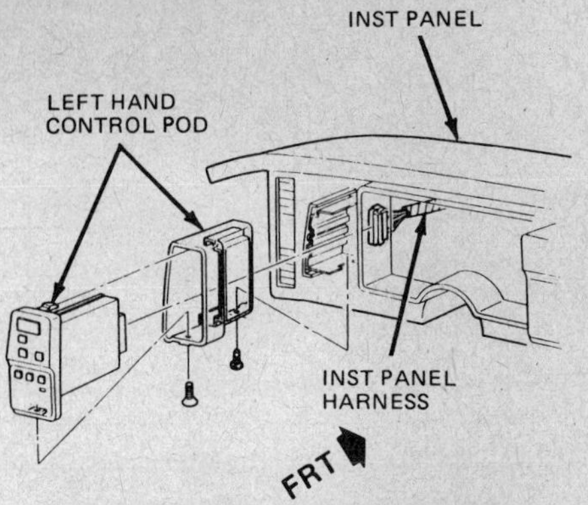

Fig. 4 Left control pod removal. 1984–86 Berlinetta

1. Disconnect battery ground cable.
2. Remove instrument panel close-out panel and lower steering column cover.
3. Remove bottom front screw securing left control pod, then release pod retainer.
4. Disconnect left control pod electrical connector below instrument panel, **Fig. 4.**
5. Remove pod housing and screw securing control assembly to track.
6. Slide control assembly from track.
7. Reverse procedure to install.

1985–88 Exc. 1984–86 Berlinetta

1. Disconnect battery ground cable.
2. Remove right and lefthand lower trim plates and the instrument panel cluster trim plate.
3. Remove 2 switch attaching screws, then depress side tangs and remove switch from instrument panel.
4. Reverse procedure to install.

STOP LIGHT SWITCH REPLACE

EXC. CORVETTE

1. On Camaro, remove hush panel.
2. On all models, disconnect wiring connector at switch.
3. Remove retaining nut, if so equipped, and unscrew switch from bracket.
4. To install: Depress brake pedal and push new switch into clip until shoulder bottoms out.
5. Plug connector onto switch and check operation. Electrical contact should be made when pedal is depressed 3/8 to 5/8 from fully released position.

CORVETTE

1982

1. Disconnect wiring connector at switch.
2. Remove retaining nut and unscrew switch from bracket.
3. Upon installation, check for proper operation. Electrical contact should be made when pedal is depressed 1/4 to 5/8. Switch bracket has a slotted screw hole for adjustment.

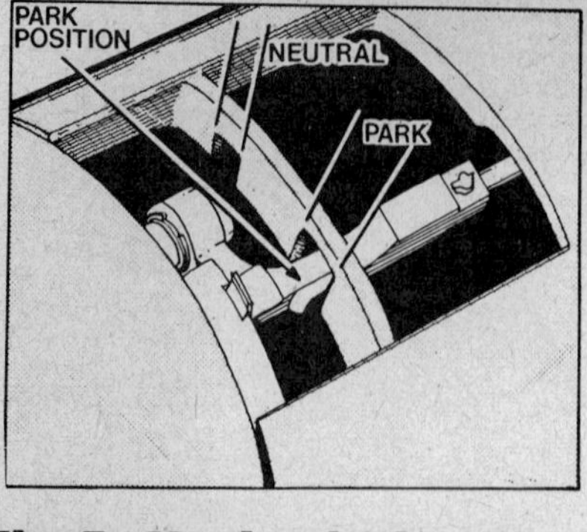

Fig. 5 Mechanical neutral start system. Chevrolet, Malibu & Monte Carlo

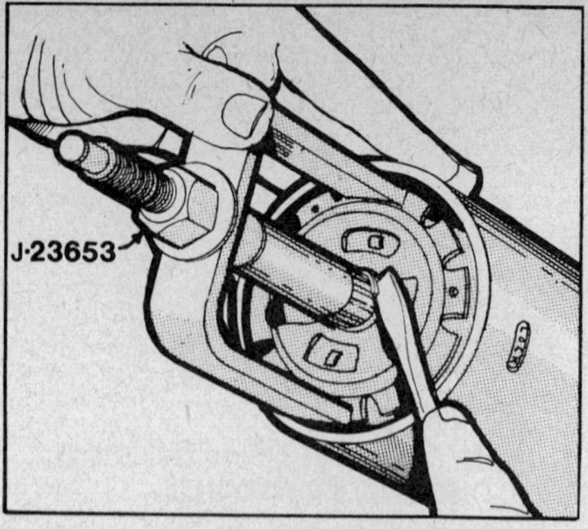

Fig. 6 Lock plate retaining ring removal

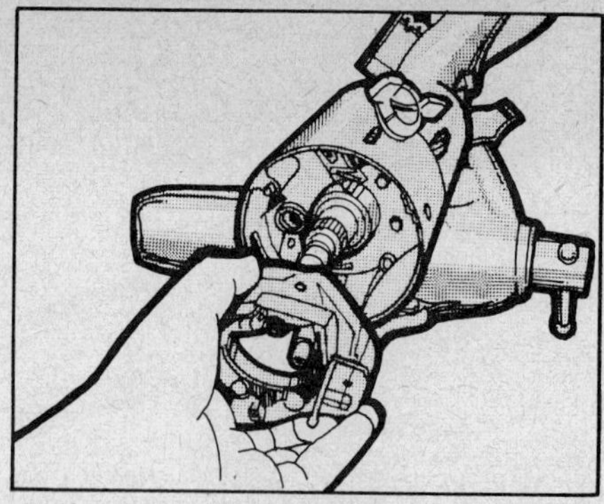

Fig. 7 Turn signal switch assembly

1984–88

1. Remove hush panel from under left side of instrument panel.
2. Disconnect electrical connectors from switch and pull switch out of retaining clip on brake pedal support.
3. Depress brake pedal and push replacement switch into retainer until switch shoulder is bottomed against bracket.
4. Adjust switch by pulling brake pedal back against stop.
5. Ensure switch has continuity when pedal is depressed .53 inch from normal rest position, and pedal fully returns to rest position.
6. Reconnect electrical connectors and install hush panel.

CLUTCH START SWITCH

REPLACE

CAMARO

1. Disconnect wire connector at switch.
2. Remove retaining nut, if so equipped and unscrew switch from bracket.
3. To install: depress clutch pedal, then insert and push switch into clip until shoulder bottoms out.
4. Plug connector on switch and check for proper operation.

CORVETTE

1982

1. Disconnect wiring connector from switch.
2. Remove retainer from pins or link on clutch pedal arm.
3. Remove retaining screw and switch.

1984–88

1. Disconnect battery ground cable and set parking brake.
2. Remove retaining screw and switch from clutch pedal bracket, rotate switch slightly, and pull switch actuating lever from hole in pedal arm.
3. Disconnect electrical connector and remove switch.
4. Position replacement switch with actuating lever installed in hole in pedal arm, then secure switch to bracket with retaining screw.
5. Connect electrical connector to switch and adjust by fully depressing clutch pedal. **If readjustment is necessary, depress detent on switch adjusting block and slide block fully forward on switch rod. Fully depress clutch pedal to complete adjustment.**

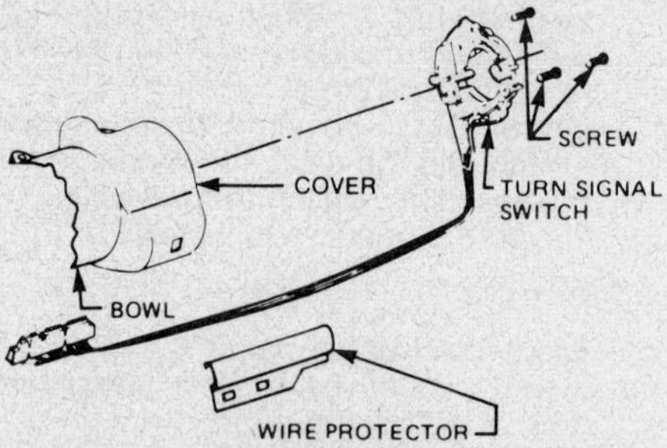

Fig. 8 Turn signal switch removal

EXC. CORVETTE & CAMARO

1. Disconnect wiring connector from switch.
2. Compress switch actuating shaft retainer and remove shaft with switch attached from switch bracket.

NEUTRAL SAFETY SWITCH

REPLACE

CHEVROLET, MALIBU & MONTE CARLO

Actuation of the ignition switch is prevented by a mechanical lockout system, **Fig. 5,** which prevents the lock cylinder from rotating when the selector lever is out of Park or Neutral. When the selector lever is in Park or Neutral, the slots in the bowl plate and the finger on the actuator rod align allowing the finger to pass through the bowl plate in turn actuating the ignition switch, **Fig. 5.** If the selector lever is in any position other than Park or Neutral, the finger contacts the bowl plate when the lock cylinder is rotated, thereby preventing full travel of the lock cylinder.

1982 CORVETTE

1. Disconnect shift control lever arm from transmission control rod.
2. Remove shift control knob.
3. Remove trim plate.
4. Remove control assembly from seal and disconnect switch wiring.
5. Remove switch from control assembly.
6. To install, position gearshift in Drive position, align hole in contact support with hole in switch and insert a pin (3/32 inch) to hold support in place.
7. Place contact support drive slot over drive tang and tighten switch mounting screws.
8. Connect wiring harness to switch wiring.
9. Install trim plate control knob and connect shift lever arm to transmission control rod.

CAMARO & 1984–88 CORVETTE

1. Remove floor console cover, then disconnect electrical connectors from switch.
2. Place shift lever in "Neutral" position of detent plate, then remove switch attaching screws and switch.
3. To install, ensure that the shift lever is in "Neutral," then position switch on shift lever making sure pin on shaft is in slot of switch.
4. Install attaching screws and torque to 16 inch lbs.
5. Move shift lever out of "Neutral" to shear pin which is part of new switch.
6. Reconnect electrical connectors to switch, then apply parking brake and start engine. Check back-up lights and seat belt warning system for proper operation and ensure that engine will start only in "Park" or "Neutral."
7. Turn ignition off and install floor console.

TURN SIGNAL SWITCH

REPLACE

1. Disconnect battery cable, then remove steering wheel and column to instrument panel trim cover.

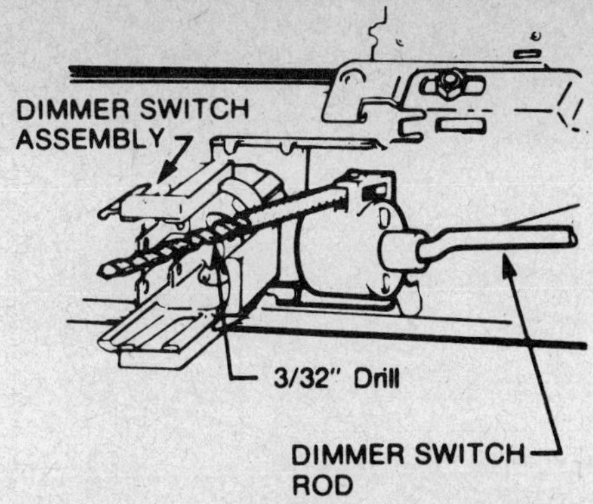

Fig. 9 Column mounted dimmer switch installation

2. On models with telescoping column, remove bumper spacer and snap ring retainer. On all other models, remove cover from lockplate.
3. Using a suitable tool, compress lock plate (horn contact carrier on tilt models) and remove snap ring (C-ring on tilt models), **Fig. 6.** On 1982 Corvette models with tilt-telescopic column, place a 5/16 inch nut under each leg of puller.
4. Remove lock plate, cancelling cam, upper bearing preload spring, thrust washer and signal lever.
5. Remove turn signal lever or actuating arm screw, if equipped, or on models with column mounted wiper switch, pull lever straight out of detent. Depress hazard warning button, then unscrew button.
6. Pull connector from bracket and wrap upper part of connector with tape to prevent snagging the wires during removal. On Tilt models, position shifter housing in "Low" position. Remove harness cover.
7. Remove retaining screws and remove switch, **Figs. 7 and 8.**
8. Reverse procedure to install.

COLUMN-MOUNTED DIMMER SWITCH
REPLACE

1. Disconnect battery ground cable.
2. Remove instrument panel lower trim and on models with A/C, remove A/C duct extension at column.
3. Disconnect shift indicator from column and remove toe plate cover screws.
4. Remove two nuts from instrument panel support bracket studs and lower steering column, resting steering wheel on front seat.
5. Remove dimmer switch retaining screws and the switch. Tape actuator rod to column and separate switch from rod.
6. Reverse procedure to install. To adjust switch, depress dimmer switch slightly and install a 3/32 inch twist drill to lock the switch to the body, **Fig. 9.** Force switch upward to remove lash between switch and pivot. Torque switch retaining screw to 35 inch lbs. and remove tape from actuator rod. Remove twist drill and check for proper operation.

HORN SOUNDER & STEERING WHEEL
REPLACE

Mark position of steering wheel in relation to shaft prior to removal to ensure correct installation.

CUSHIONED RIM WHEEL

1. Disconnect battery ground cable.
2. Pry off horn button cap.
3. Remove three spacer screws, spacer, plate and belleville spring.
4. Remove steering wheel nut, washer and snap ring.
5. Using a suitable puller, remove steering wheel.
6. Reverse procedure to install.

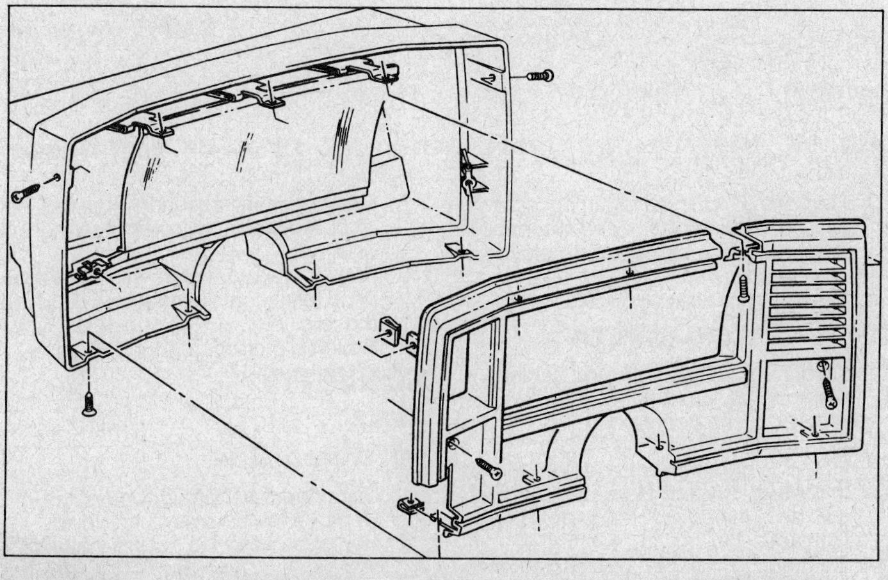

Fig. 11 Instrument cluster bezel removal (Typical). Malibu & Monte Carlo

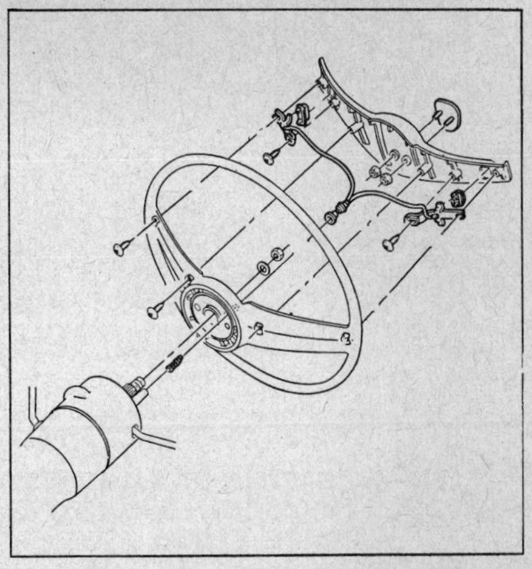

Fig. 10 Steering wheel and horn contact (Typical). Standard wheel

STANDARD WHEEL

1. Disconnect battery ground cable.
2. Remove attaching screws on underside of the steering wheel, **Fig. 10.**
3. Lift steering wheel shroud and pull horn wires from cancelling cam tower.
4. Remove steering wheel nut, washer and snap ring.
5. Using a suitable puller, remove steering wheel.
6. Reverse procedure to install.

1982 CORVETTE

1. Disconnect battery ground cable.
2. Remove horn button cap, 3 screws securing upper horn contact, and upper contact.
3. Remove shim, if used, then the screw securing the center star screw and the star screw and lever.
4. Remove snap ring and nut from shaft.
5. Using a suitable puller, remove steering wheel assembly.
6. To disassemble the steering wheel assembly, remove three screws securing wheel and separate, then remove four screws retaining extension to wheel and separate.
7. Reverse procedure to install.

1984–88 CORVETTE

1. Disconnect battery ground cable.
2. Pry up horn button cap, disconnect contact from steering wheel, and remove cap.
3. Remove screws securing center star screw, star screw, and adjusting lever.
4. Remove snap ring and nut from steering shaft.
5. Remove steering wheel using a suitable puller.
6. Reverse procedure to install.

INSTRUMENT CLUSTER
REPLACE

MONTE CARLO & 1982–83 MALIBU

1. Disconnect battery ground cable.

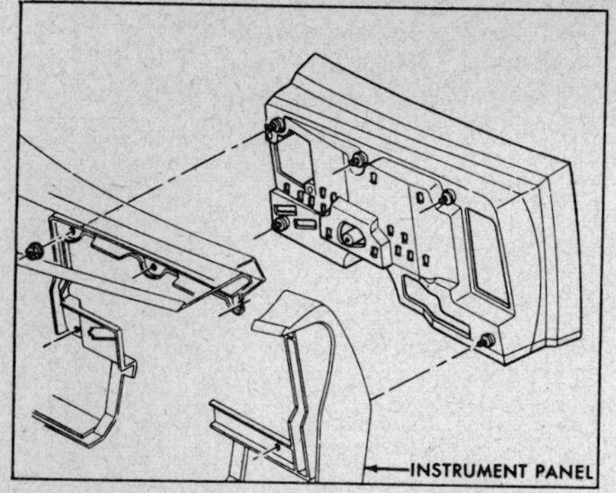

Fig. 12 Instrument cluster removal (Typical). Malibu & Monte Carlo

2. Remove radio knobs and clock set stem knob.
3. Remove instrument bezel retaining screws, **Fig. 11.**
4. Pull bezel rearward slightly and disconnect the rear defogger switch and remote control mirror control, if equipped.
5. Remove bezel, **Fig. 11.**
6. Remove speedometer retaining screws, pull speedometer from cluster slightly, disconnect speedometer cable and remove speedometer.
7. Remove fuel gauge or tachometer retaining screws, disconnect electrical connectors and remove fuel gauge or tachometer.
8. Remove clock or voltmeter retaining screws, disconnect electrical connectors and remove clock or voltmeter.
9. Disconnect transmission shift indicator cable from steering column.
10. Disconnect all wiring connectors and remove cluster case, **Fig. 12.**
11. Reverse procedure to install.

CHEVROLET

1. Disconnect battery ground cable.
2. Remove four steering column lower cover screws and the cover.
3. If equipped with automatic transmission, disconnect shift indicator cable from steering column.
4. Remove two steering column to instrument panel screws and lower steering column. **Use extreme care when lowering steering to prevent damage to column assembly.**
5. Remove six screws and the three snap-in fasteners from perimeter of instrument cluster lens, **Fig. 13.**
6. Remove two screws from upper surface of gray sheet metal trim plate.
7. Remove two stud nuts from lower corner of cluster.
8. Disconnect speedometer cable and pull cluster from instrument panel.
9. Disconnect electrical connectors from cluster and remove from vehicle.
10. Reverse procedure to install.

CAMARO

1982–88 Exc. 1984–86 Berlinetta

1. Disconnect battery ground cable.
2. Remove instrument cluster bezel, **Fig. 14.**

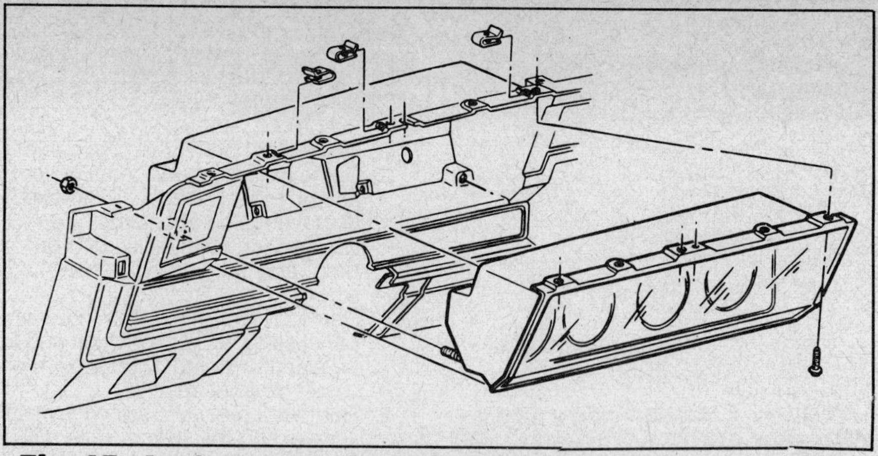

Fig. 13 Instrument cluster, exploded view. Chevrolet Full Size

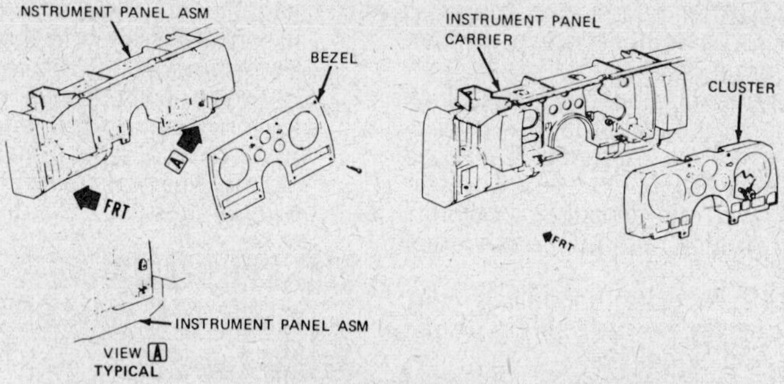

Fig. 14 Instrument cluster, exploded view. 1982–88 Camaro exc. 1984–86 Berlinetta

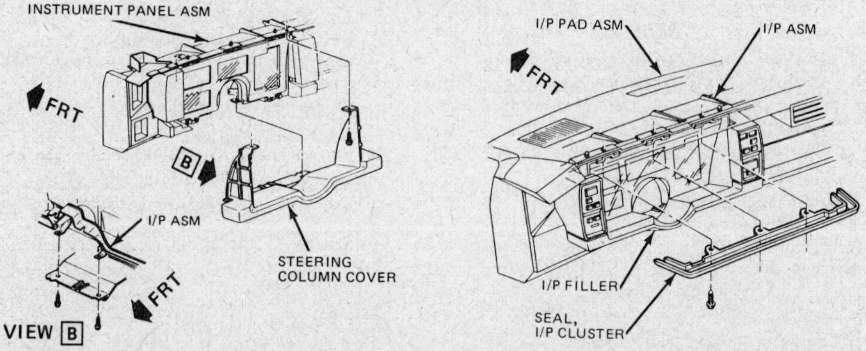

Fig. 15 Instrument cluster removal. 1984–86 Berlinetta

3. Remove 6 cluster retaining screws, then pull cluster back and disconnect speedometer cable and electrical connectors.
4. Reverse procedure to install.

1984–86 BERLINETTA

1. Disconnect battery ground cable.
2. Remove close out panel, 8 screws securing steering column cover and the cover, **Fig. 15.**
3. Remove right control pod as outlined in "Wiper Switch, Replace," and left pod as outlined in "Headlamp Switch, Replace."
4. Remove 3 cluster bezel retaining screws and the bezel; 5 cluster lens retaining screws and the lens.
5. Remove nuts securing steering column bracket and lower steering column.
6. Pull cluster away from carrier, disconnect electrical connectors and remove cluster.
7. Reverse procedure to install.

CORVETTE

1982

Lefthand Side

1. Disconnect battery ground cable.
2. Remove left air distribution duct.
3. Remove lens to bezel attaching screws and the lens.
4. Remove cluster to instrument panel attaching screws.

5. Pull cluster rearward slightly, then disconnect speedometer cable and electrical connectors.
6. Remove cluster from vehicle.
7. Reverse procedure to install.

Center Cluster

1. Disconnect battery ground cable.
2. Remove console tunnel side panels.
3. Remove radio knobs.
4. Remove two screws securing console trim plate to instrument cluster, **Fig. 16.**
5. Remove rear window defogger switch, if equipped, from console trim plate.
6. Remove five screws from upper perimeter of instrument cluster.
7. Pull instrument cluster outward slightly and disconnect electrical connectors.
8. Remove cluster from vehicle.
9. Reverse procedure to install.

1984–88

1. Disconnect battery ground cable.
2. Remove left hush panel, lower instrument panel pad, and steering column cover.
3. Remove light switch knob and shaft, and bezel nut securing switch
4. Remove nuts securing steering column to instrument panel brace and lower column.
5. Remove cluster bezel retaining screws and bezel.
6. Remove cluster retaining screws and pull cluster away from dash.
7. Release metal retainers securing electrical connectors, disconnect electrical connectors from cluster, and remove cluster assembly.

FRONT WIPER MOTOR REPLACE

EXC. CORVETTE

1. Raise hood and remove cowl screen or grille.
2. Disconnect wiring and washer hoses.
3. Reaching through cowl opening, loosen transmission drive link attaching nuts to motor crankarm.
4. Disconnect drive link from motor crankarm.
5. Remove motor attaching screws.
6. Remove motor while guiding crankarm through hole.
7. Reverse procedure to install.

CORVETTE

1982

1. Make sure wiper motor is in "Park" position.
2. Disconnect washer hoses and electrical connectors from assembly.
3. Remove the air intake screen.
4. Remove the nut which retains the crank arm to the motor.
5. Remove the ignition shield and distributor cap to gain access to the motor retaining screws or nuts. **Remove left bank spark plug wires from the cap and mark both cap and wires for aid in reinstallation.**

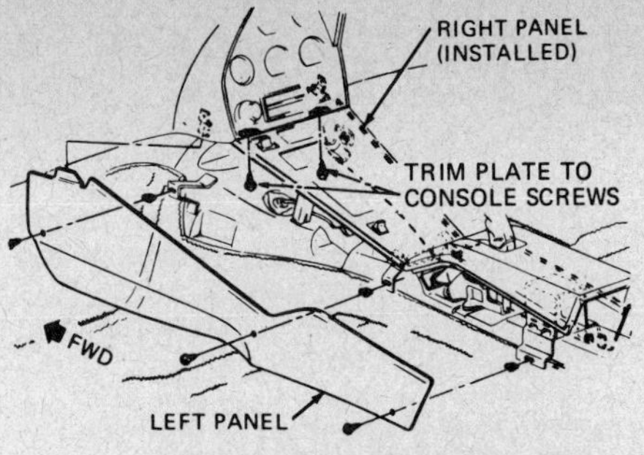

Fig. 16 Center cluster bezel removal. 1982 Corvette

6. Remove three motor retaining screws or nuts and remove motor. **Wiper motor must be in the "Park" position prior to installation on the cowl. Do not install a motor that was dropped or hung by the drive link.**

1984–88

1. Open hood, then remove wiper arms and air inlet screen.
2. Turn ignition on and operate motor. Stop motor with crank arm pointing to a position between 4 and 5 o'clock (viewed from passenger compartment) by turning ignition off.
3. Disconnect battery ground cable.
4. Disconnect upper electrical connector from wiper motor.
5. Remove motor retaining bolts, and remove motor after disconnecting lower electrical connector and linkage.
6. Reverse procedure to install.

REAR WIPER MOTOR REPLACE

CAMARO

1. Remove wiper arm using tool No. J-8966 or equivalent.
2. Remove nut and spacer from wiper motor shaft, then raise lid and remove lift window trim panel.
3. Disconnect wire connectors from motor, then remove rivets securing motor support to trim panel and remove assembly from vehicle.
4. Remove motor attaching screws and motor.
5. Reverse procedure to install.

FRONT WIPER TRANSMISSION REPLACE

CAMARO, 1982-83 CHEVROLET, MALIBU & MONTE CARLO, 1984-88 CORVETTE

1. Ensure that motor is in park position.
2. Raise hood and remove wiper arm assemblies.
3. Remove cowl vent screen.
4. Loosen nuts securing pivot at motor crankarm, then disconnect transmission rod from crankarm.
5. Remove retaining nuts or screws securing transmission to body, then withdraw transmission assembly through cowl opening.
6. Reverse procedure to install.

1982 CORVETTE

1. Make sure motor is in "Park" position.
2. Disconnect battery ground cable.
3. Open hood and remove chamber screen.
4. Loosen nuts retaining ball sockets to crankarm and detach drive rod from crankarm.
5. Remove transmission nuts, then lift rod assemblies from chamber.
6. Remove transmission linkage from chamber.
7. Reverse procedure to install.

1984–88 CHEVROLET & MONTE CARLO

1. Raise hood and remove wiper arm assemblies.
2. Remove lower windshield reveal molding and cowl vent screen.
3. Place suitable lever between drive link and motor crankarm, then pry drive link from crankarm.
4. Remove screws securing transmission pivot retainers to body, then withdraw transmission assembly through plenum opening.
5. Reverse procedure to install.

REAR WIPER TRANSMISSION REPLACE

CAMARO

1. Remove three mounting grommets from transmission housing cover and cover.
2. Remove drive link retainer, then disengage drive link from cam drive pin and position so that cam retainer is accessible. **When reassembling drive link to cam, a new retainer must be used.**
3. Remove cam retainer and washer, then cam from shaft. **During assembly, if cam does not seat fully when pushed onto drive shaft, rotate cam 180 degrees.**
4. Drill out three rivets attaching housing to wiper gearbox, and remove transmission.
5. Reverse procedure to install. **A service kit is available for installation of the transmission. The kit includes screw, nuts and washers to replace the rivets.**

WINDSHIELD WIPER SWITCH REPLACE

CORVETTE

1982

1. Disconnect battery ground cable.
2. Remove left air distribution duct.
3. Remove instrument cluster attaching screws and pull cluster rearward.

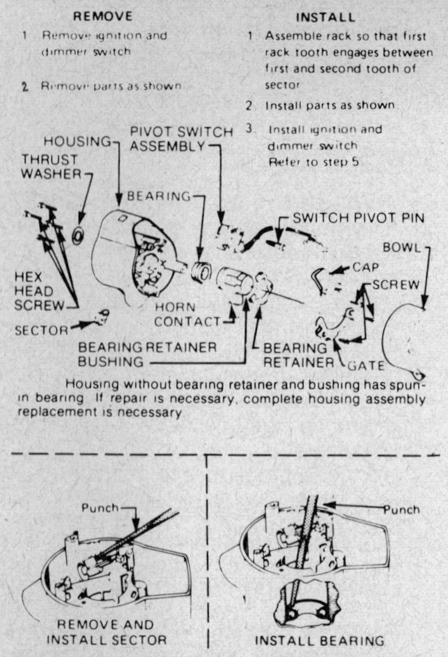

Fig. 17 Column mounted wiper switch removal. 1982–88 w/standard column

4. Disconnect speedometer cable and all electrical connectors, then remove cluster.
5. Remove two instrument panel to left door pillar attaching screws and pull left side of instrument panel rearward for access.
6. Remove wiper switch to mounting plate screws, disconnect electrical connector and remove switch.
7. Reverse procedure to install.

1984–88

1. Disconnect battery ground cable.
2. Remove 2 screws securing left armrest, push inward to release armrest from door trim and remove armrest.
3. Remove screws securing accessory trim plate to door panel, including screw behind handle, and remove lock button.
4. Pull accessory plate away from door panel and disconnect electrical connectors to panel switches.
5. Remove wiper switch from trim plate.
6. Reverse procedure to install.

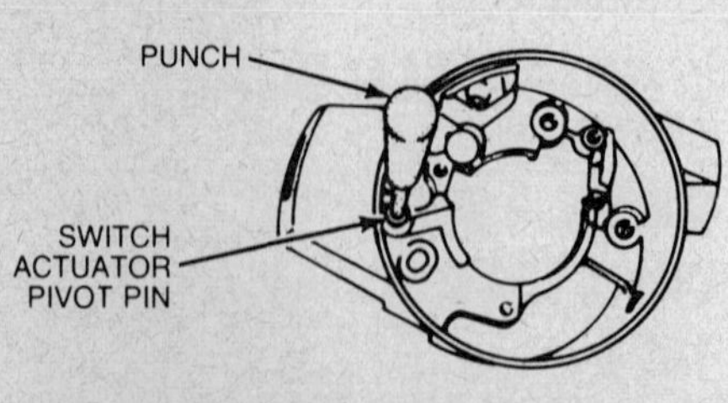

Fig. 19 Wiper switch pivot removal. Models w/column mounted switch

1982 MALIBU & MONTE CARLO

1. Disconnect battery ground cable.
2. Remove instrument panel bezel.
3. Remove screws securing wiper switch mounting plate to cluster and pull assembly rearward.
4. Disconnect electrical connector and remove wiper switch.
5. Reverse procedure to install.

1982–83 CHEVROLET

1. Disconnect battery ground cable.
2. Remove screws securing control shroud on instrument panel. (One screw is hidden above headlight switch shaft and one is hidden above cigarette lighter knob.)
3. Lift off shroud and remove remaining screws.
4. Unplug wiper switch and remove.
5. Reverse procedure to install.

CAMARO EXC. 1984-86 BERLINETTA, 1983 MALIBU, 1983-88 MONTE CARLO, 1984-88 CHEVROLET

1. Disconnect battery ground cable and remove turn signal switch as outlined.
2. Remove ignition lock, ignition switch and dimmer switch as outlined.
3. Remove ignition lock housing retaining screws and housing, **Figs. 17 and 18.**
4. Remove pivot bolt and wiper switch from lock housing, **Fig. 19.**
5. Reverse procedure to install.

1984–86 BERLINETTA

1. Disconnect battery ground cable.
2. Remove retaining screw from bottom front of right control pod housing, then release retaining tab.
3. Disconnect electrical connector, then slide right pod assembly from track, **Fig. 20.**
4. Reverse procedure to install.

RADIO

REPLACE

When installing radio, be sure to adjust antenna trimmer for peak reception. Also, be sure to connect speaker before applying power to radio.

MALIBU & MONTE CARLO

1. Disconnect battery ground cable.
2. Remove control knobs from control shafts.
3. Remove trim plate attaching screws and trim plate.
4. Disconnect antenna lead and wire connector from radio.
5. Remove stud nut at right side of bracket attachment.
6. Remove control shaft nuts and washers.
7. Remove instrument panel bracket screws and bracket.
8. Remove radio through opening in instrument panel.
9. Reverse procedure to install.

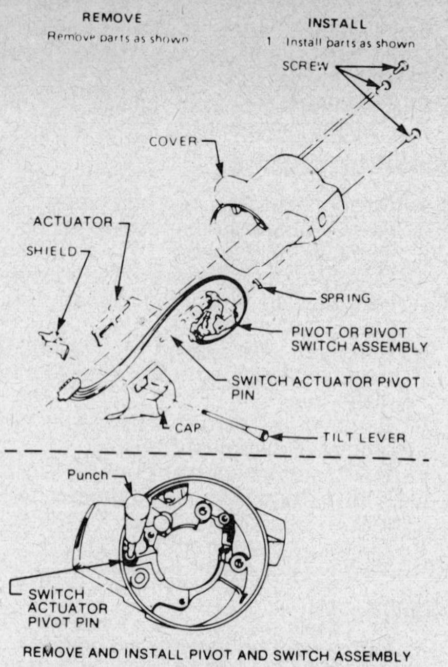

Fig. 18 Column mounted wiper switch removal. 1982–88 w/tilt column

CHEVROLET

1982–84 & 1987–88

1. Disconnect battery ground cable.
2. Remove control knobs from control shafts.
3. Remove three radio trim plate attaching screws.
4. Remove two screws and bottom nut attaching radio bracket to instrument panel.
5. Disconnect antenna lead and wire connector from radio.
6. Remove radio with mounting bracket attached from instrument panel.
7. Remove bracket from radio.
8. Reverse procedure to install.

1985–86

1. Disconnect battery ground cable.
2. Remove glove box to provide access to temperature control cable.

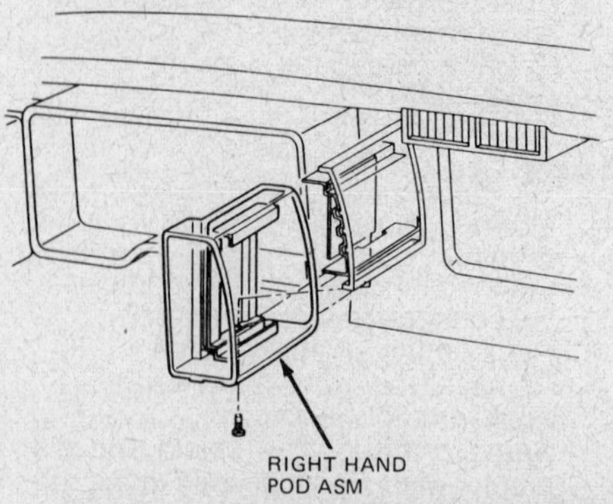

Fig. 20 Right control pod removal. 1984–86 Berlinetta

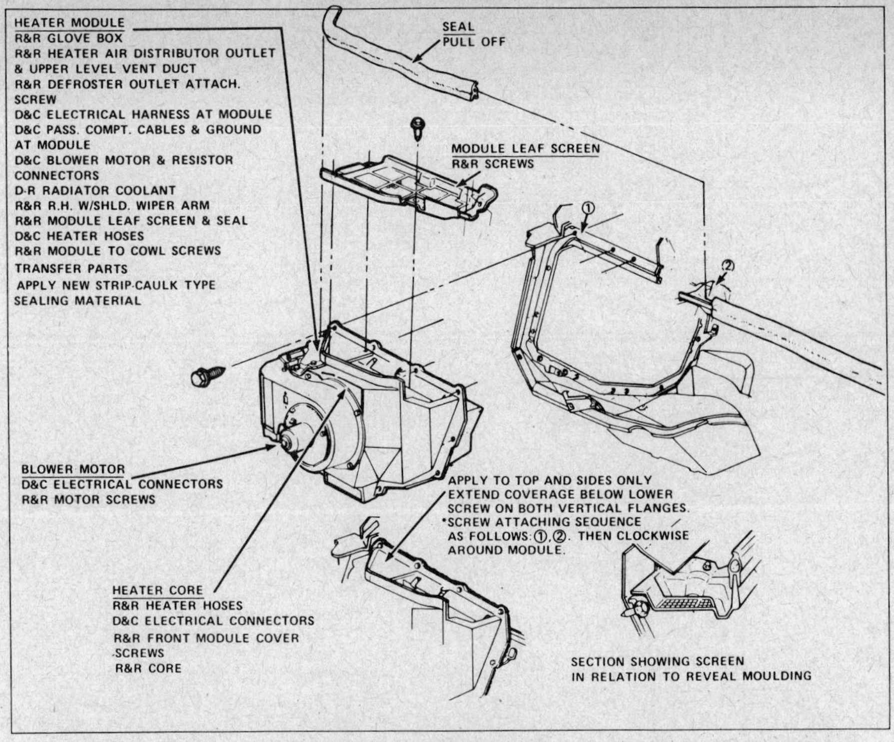

Fig. 21 Blower motor & heater core. Malibu & Monte Carlo less A/C

3. Disconnect temperature cable from temperature door.
4. Remove radio/heater A/C control panel fasteners.
5. Pull control panel out of dash and disconnect vacuum and electrical connectors.
6. Remove A/C control trimplate with knobs, then the radio from bracket.
7. Reverse procedure to install.

CORVETTE

1982

1. Disconnect battery ground cable.
2. Remove control knobs from control shafts.
3. Remove instrument cluster as described under "Instrument Cluster, Replace."
4. Remove screw attaching radio mounting bracket to reinforcement on floor pan.
5. Pull radio outward and disconnect antenna lead and wire connector from rear of radio.
6. Remove mounting bracket from radio.
7. Reverse procedure to install.

1984–88

1. Disconnect battery ground cable and remove instrument cluster as outlined.
2. Remove accessory trim plate retaining screws and trim plate.
3. Remove screws securing radio and bracket, and pull radio away from dash.
4. Disconnect electrical connectors and antenna lead, then remove radio.
5. Reverse procedure to install, ensuring A/C center outlet seal is properly positioned.

CAMARO

1982–88 Exc. 1984–86 Berlinetta

1. Disconnect battery ground cable.
2. Remove three console bezel and four radio to console attaching screws.
3. Pull radio outward and disconnect electrical connector, then remove radio.
4. Reverse procedure to install.

1984–86 Berlinetta

1. Disconnect battery ground cable.
2. Remove 4 retaining screws from console trim plate, raise shift lever trim panel and position aside, leaving electrical connectors connected.
3. Remove 4 screws securing radio control head to bracket.
4. Remove control head, pulling back on spring pawl while lifting control, then disconnect electrical connector to control.
5. Remove screws securing radio receiver.
6. Disconnect antenna and electrical connectors, then remove receiver.
7. Reverse procedure to install.

BLOWER MOTOR REPLACE

CHEVROLET, MALIBU, MONTE CARLO

1. Disconnect battery ground cable.
2. Disconnect blower motor lead wire, then the cooling tube, if equipped.
3. Remove blower motor to case attaching screws, then remove blower motor, **Figs. 21 through 25.**
4. Reverse procedure to install.

CAMARO

1. Disconnect battery ground cable.
2. Disconnect blower motor and resistor wires.
3. Disconnect cooling tube, if equipped.
4. Remove blower motor retaining screws and motor/cage assembly from case.
5. While holding blower motor cage, remove cage retaining screw and slide cage from motor shaft.
6. Reverse procedure to install.

CORVETTE

1982

1. Disconnect battery ground cable.
2. Remove A/C compressor mounting bolts and position compressor aside with refrigerant lines attached.
3. Remove air cleaner from front and right side inlet ducts, then position air cleaner out of way.
4. Remove engine coolant recovery bottle.
5. Disconnect hose and electrical connections from blower motor.
6. Remove blower motor mounting flange attaching screws, then remove blower with impeller from vehicle, **Fig. 25.**

1984–88

1. Disconnect battery ground cable.
2. Remove right front wheel housing rear panel, and push housing aside.
3. Remove motor cooling tube and screws securing relay, and set relay aside.
4. Remove motor retaining screws, motor and impeller.
5. Reverse procedure to install.

HEATER CORE REPLACE

LESS A/C

Camaro

1. Disconnect battery ground cable and drain cooling system.
2. Remove right lower hush panel and instrument panel trim panel.
3. Remove ESC module, if equipped.
4. Remove lower right instrument panel carrier to cowl screw.
5. Remove heater case cover attaching screws and cover. To gain access to the upper left screw, position a long 3/8 inch socket extension through the opening exposed by removal of the trim panel. Carefully lift lower right corner of instrument panel to align socket extension.
6. Remove support plate and baffle screws, then heater core, support plate and baffle from case.

Malibu & Monte Carlo

1. Disconnect battery ground cable and drain cooling system.
2. Disconnect heater hoses from heater core. Plug core outlets to prevent

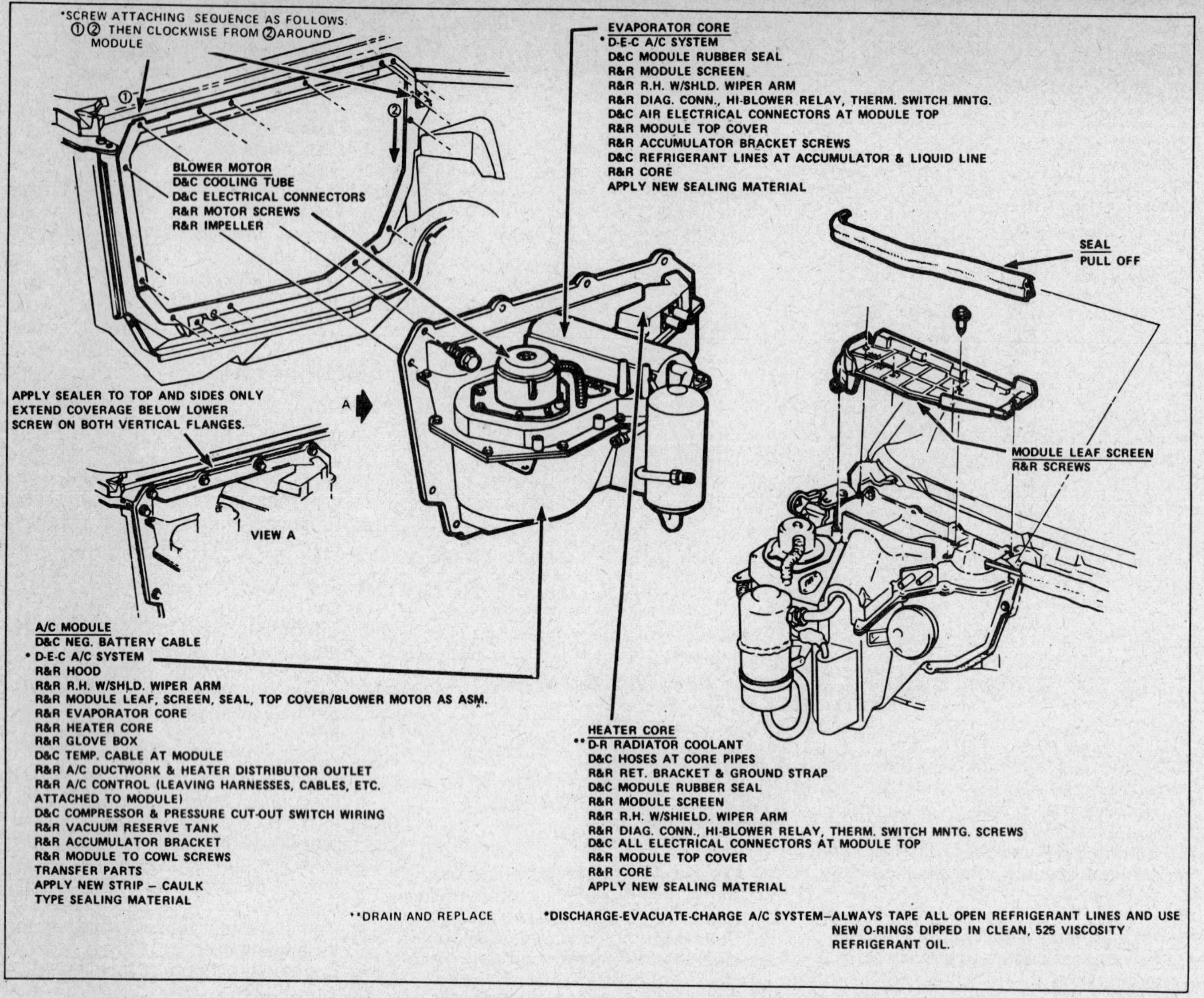

Fig. 22 Blower motor & heater core. Malibu & Monte Carlo with A/C

coolant spillage.

3. Disconnect wire connectors, then remove front module cover attaching screws and cover.
4. Remove heater core from module, **Fig. 21.**
5. Reverse procedure to install.

Chevrolet

1. Disconnect battery ground cable and drain cooling system.
2. Disconnect heater hoses from heater core. Plug core outlets to prevent coolant spillage.
3. Remove attaching screws from around perimeter of heater core cover on engine side of dash panel.
4. Pull heater core cover from dash panel mounting.
5. Remove heater core from module assembly, **Fig. 23.**
6. Reverse procedure to install.

1982 Corvette

1. Disconnect battery ground cable.
2. Drain radiator, disconnect heater hoses at core and plug openings to prevent spillage of water.
3. Remove nuts from air distributor duct studs on engine side of firewall, **Fig. 26.**
4. Remove right instrument panel pad, righthand dash braces, center dash console duct and floor outlet duct, radio and center dash console.
5. Pull distributor duct from firewall being careful not to bend cable.
6. Remove core assembly from duct.
7. Reverse procedure to install.

WITH A/C

CAMARO

1982–88

For removal procedure, refer to "Heater Core, Replace" less air conditioning.

MALIBU & MONTE CARLO

1. Disconnect battery ground cable and drain cooling system.
2. Disconnect heater hoses at heater core.
3. Remove retaining bracket and ground strap.
4. Remove module rubber seal and module screen, **Fig. 22.**
5. Remove righthand windshield wiper arm.
6. Remove high blower relay and thermostatic switch mounting screws.
7. Disconnect wire connector at top of module, then remove module top cover.
8. Remove heater core from module.
9. Reverse procedure to install.

CHEVROLET

1. Disconnect battery ground cable and drain cooling system.
2. Disconnect heater hoses at heater core. Cap core outlets to prevent coolant spillage.
3. Remove diagnosis connector to upper case attaching screws.
4. Disconnect wire connectors from blower motor, resistor, blower relay and thermostatic switch.
5. Remove wiring harness retainer from blower case shroud.
6. Remove module screen to cowl attaching screws and remove screen.

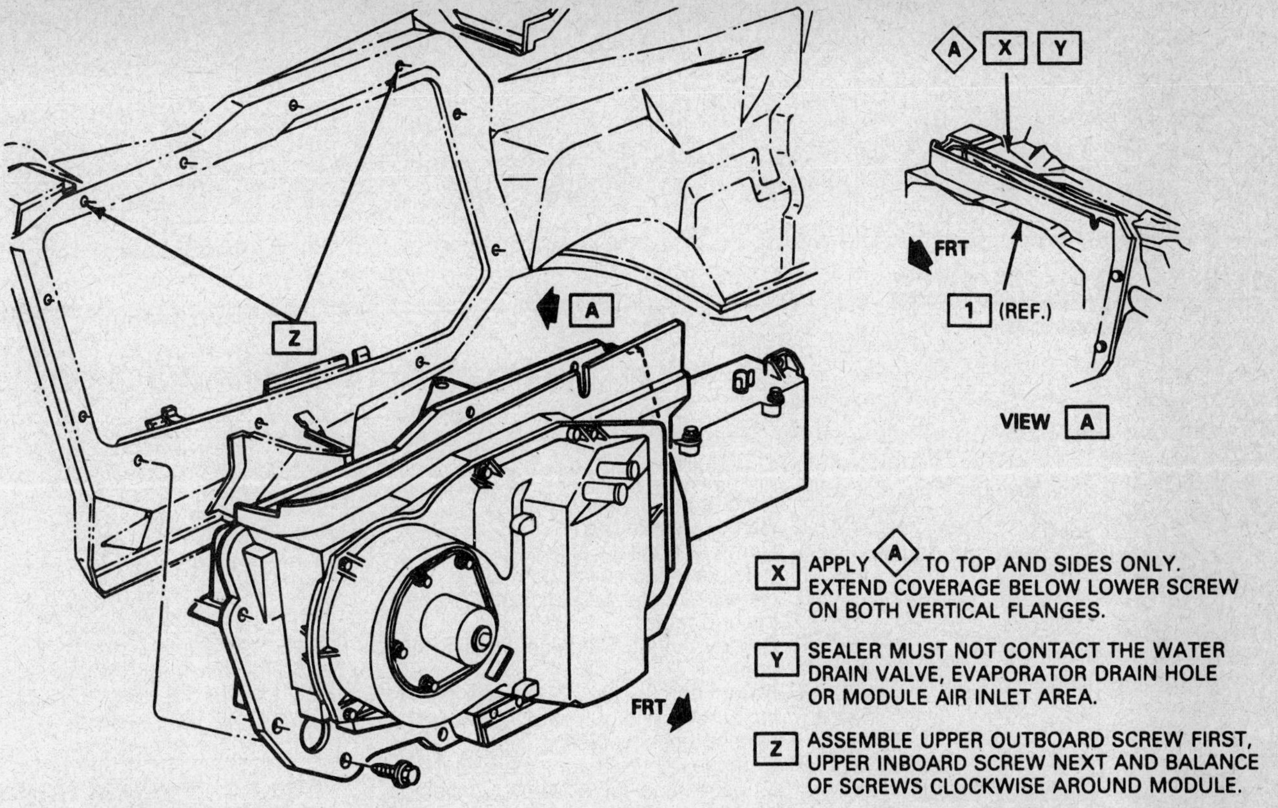
A
X
Y
Z
A
FRT
1 (REF.)
VIEW A
FRT
X APPLY A TO TOP AND SIDES ONLY. EXTEND COVERAGE BELOW LOWER SCREW ON BOTH VERTICAL FLANGES.
Y SEALER MUST NOT CONTACT THE WATER DRAIN VALVE, EVAPORATOR DRAIN HOLE OR MODULE AIR INLET AREA.
Z ASSEMBLE UPPER OUTBOARD SCREW FIRST, UPPER INBOARD SCREW NEXT AND BALANCE OF SCREWS CLOCKWISE AROUND MODULE.

Fig. 23 Blower motor & heater core. Chevrolet Full Size less A/C

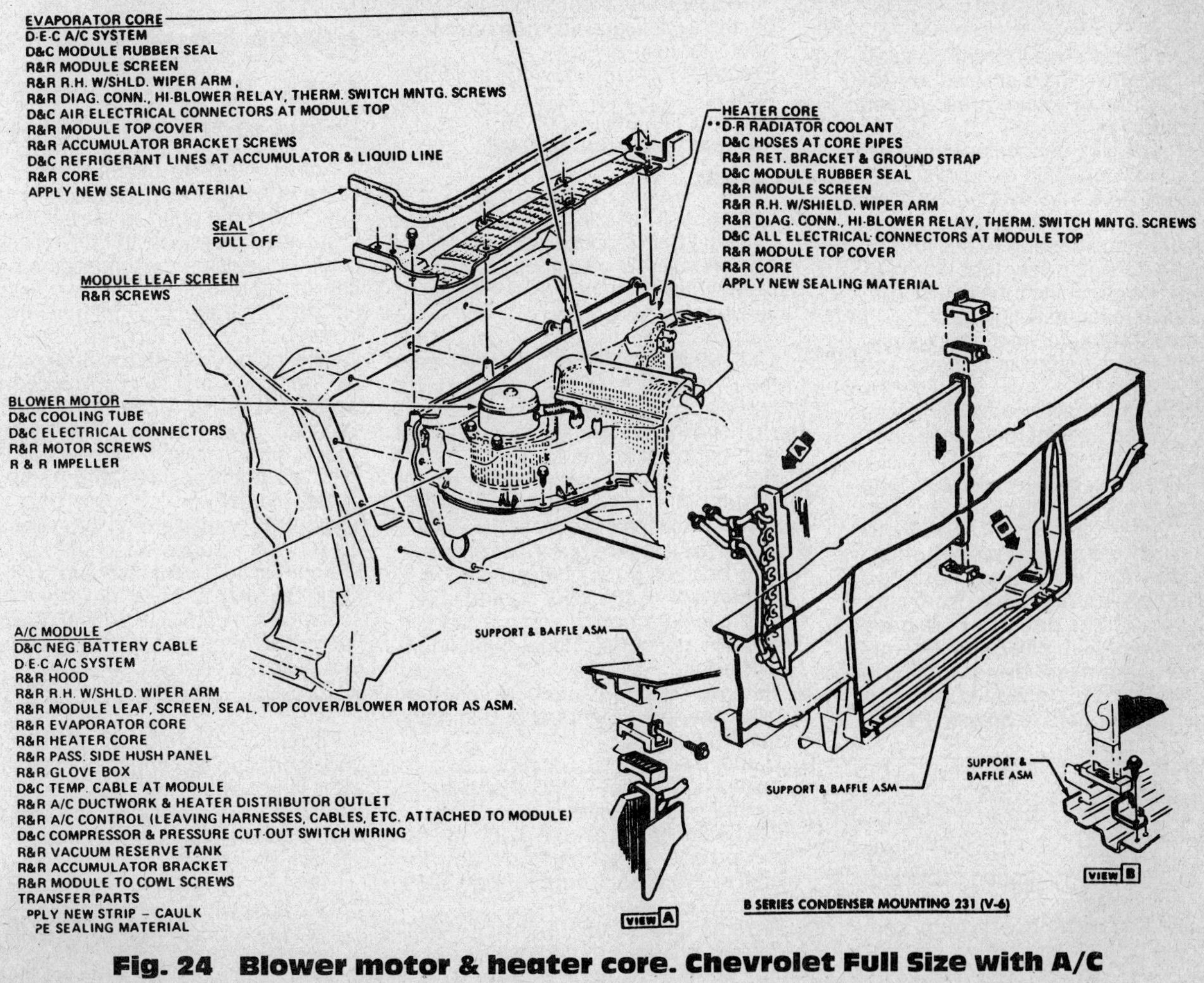

Fig. 24 Blower motor & heater core. Chevrolet Full Size with A/C

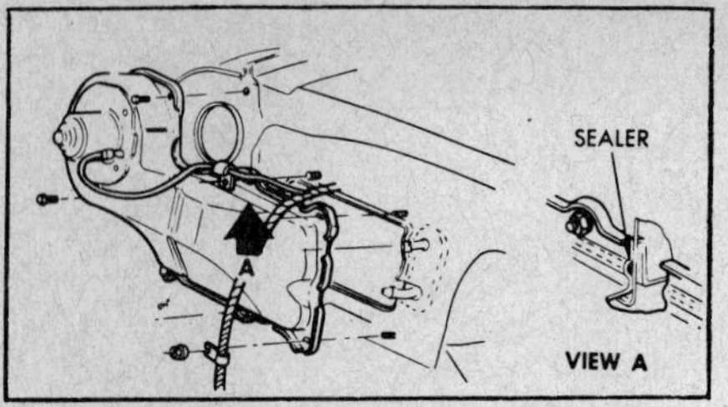

Fig. 25 Typical blower motor installation. 1982 Corvette

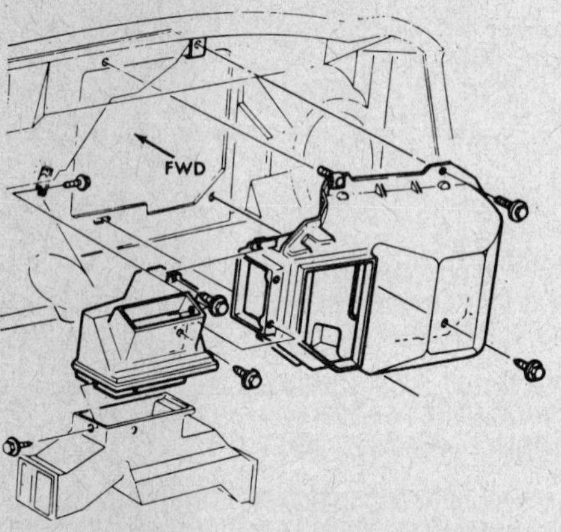

Fig. 26 Heater core installation. 1982 Corvette

7. Remove upper case to lower case attaching screws. **Two screws are located inside air intake area at case separation point.**
8. Disconnect wire connector from thermostatic switch, then remove screws attaching switch to evaporator case. Carefully remove insulation and loosen two clamps enough to pull formed end of switch capillary tube from under clamps attaching tube to evaporator inlet pipe for installation.
9. Remove evaporator inlet pipe support bracket to case attaching screws and remove bracket.
10. Remove heater-evaporator core case cover, using care not to damage sealer.
11. Remove heater core to case attaching screws at top of heater core, then remove heater core, **Fig. 24. The heater core is held in position at bottom by a spring clip. Pull up firmly on heater core to disengage from clip. When installing, position core base in alignment with clip before lowering core into case. Upper retaining bracket will line up with hole at top of core when core is properly seated.**
12. Reverse procedure to install.

CORVETTE

1982

1. Disconnect battery ground cable and drain radiator.
2. Disconnect heater hoses from core and plug hoses and core openings.

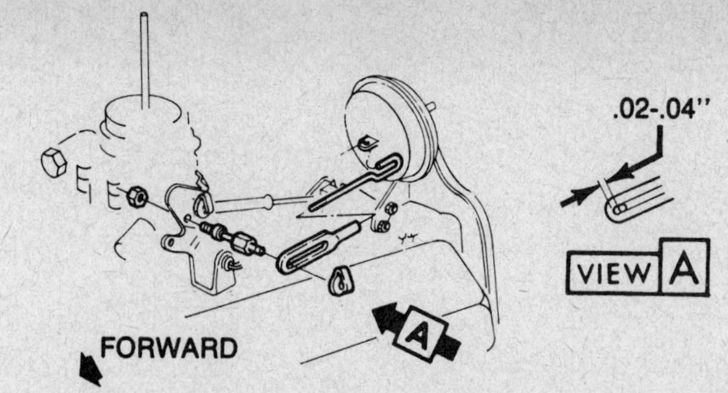

Fig. 27 Servo unit rod adjustment. 1982–83

3. Remove heater case retaining nut from top of blower case.
4. Remove glove box.
5. Remove console side panels retaining screw and swing both sides out.
6. Remove center gauge cluster assembly and radio.
7. Remove right windshield pillar trim panel.
8. Remove right side dash panel retaining screws and pull panel rearward to release upper retaining clip.
9. Remove right side vent, main vent distribution, and lower heater deflector ducts.
10. Remove heater-defroster distribution duct assembly, then disconnect temperature cable and vacuum hose from heater housing.
11. Remove heater housing assembly from vehicle and heater core from housing, **Fig. 26.**
12. Reverse procedure to install.

1984–88

1. Disconnect battery ground cable, place heater control in warm position, and drain cooling system.
2. Remove instrument cluster bezel and tilt wheel control lever.
3. Remove instrument panel upper trim pad retaining screws and trim pad, then remove A/C distribution ducts and disconnect flex hoses.
4. Remove right lower hush panel and side defroster flex hose.
5. Remove screws securing side defroster outlet to heater cover, and disconnect extension.
6. Remove temperature control cable and bracket from heater cover and disconnect heater door control shaft.
7. Remove electronic control module and disconnect electrical connectors to module.
8. Remove support brace between door pillar and instrument panel reinforcement brace.
9. Remove screws securing heater core cover, heater pipe bracket and water control valve bracket.
10. Cut heater hoses at core pipes and remove heater core. **Measure and install replacement heater hose links during reassembly.**
11. Reverse procedure to install. Refill cooling system and check for leaks.

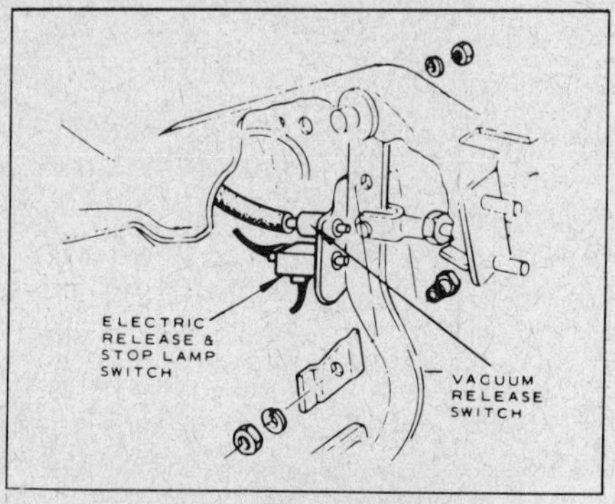

Fig. 28 Typical release switch installation. 1982–83

SPEED CONTROLS

1982–83 CRUISE MASTER

Servo Unit Adjustment

Adjust the bead chain cable or rod so that it is as tight as possible without holding the throttle open when the carburetor is set at its lowest idle throttle position. The cable is adjusted by turning the hex portion of servo. The bead chain or cable is adjusted so there is 1/16 inch of lost motion in servo cable. The rod is adjusted by turning link onto rod. With rod hooked through tab, on power unit, turn link onto rod until dimension in **Fig. 27** is obtained, then install link and retainer. This adjustment should be made with ignition off and fast idle cam in off position with throttle completely closed.

When connecting the bead chain or cable (engine stopped) manually set the fast idle cam at its lowest step and connect the chain so that it does not hold the idle screw off the cam. If the chain needs to be cut, cut it three beads beyond the bead that pulls the linkage.

Regulator Unit Adjustment

To remove any difference between engagement and cruising speed, one adjustment is possible. However, no adjustment should be made until the following items have been checked or serviced.

1. Bead chain or cable properly adjusted.
2. All hoses in good condition, properly attached, not leaking, pinched or cracked.

3. Regulator air filter cleaned and properly oiled.
4. Electric and vacuum switches properly adjusted.

Engagement—Cruising Speed Zeroing

If the cruising speed is lower than the engagement speed, loosen the orifice tube locknut and turn the tube outward; if higher turn the tube inward. Each 1/4 turn will alter the engagement-cruising speed difference one mph. Tighten locknut after adjustment and check the system operation at 50 mph.

Brake Release Switch

The electric brake switch is actuated when the brake pedal is depressed .38-.64 inch, **Fig. 28.** The vacuum release switch is actuated when brake pedal is moved 5/16 inch on all units.

1984–88

SERVO ADJUSTMENT

Units With Cable

With throttle closed, ignition and fast idle cam off, adjust cable until freeplay is removed from cable sleeve without holding throttle open.

Units With Bead & Chain

With servo cable installed on bracket, place ball of cable chain on cable end. With throttle completely closed (ignition and fast idle control off), adjust cable housing jam nuts until cable is tight, but not holding throttle open. Tighten jam nuts and check system operation.

Units With Servo Rod

With curb idle speed properly adjusted and carburetor in curb idle position with engine off, install servo rod retainer in hole that provides clearance between retainer and servo bushing. Some clearance is required, however, do not exceed width of one hole.

Gasoline Engine Section

NOTE: This section includes service procedures for V6-173/2.8L, 229/3.8L, 262/4.3L, V8-267/4.4L, 305/5.0L & 350/5.7L engines. Refer to "Pontiac Exc. Fiero, 1000 & Front Wheel Drive" section for service procedures on 4-151/2.5L engines. Refer to "Buick Rear Wheel Drive Models & 1982-85 Riviera" section for service procedures on V6-231/3.8L engines. Refer to "Oldsmobile Rear Wheel Drive & 1982-85 Toronado" section for service procedures on V8-307/5.0L engines.

INDEX

ENGINE MOUNTS REPLACE

V6-173

1. Disconnect battery ground cable.
2. Remove upper half of fan shroud.
3. Raise and support vehicle.
4. Remove engine mount through bolt, then raise front of engine to release weight from mount.
5. Remove mount to engine bolts and mount. **Raise engine only enough to provide sufficient clearance for mount removal. Check for interference between rear of engine and cowl panel which could result in distributor damage.**
6. Reverse procedure to install.

V6-229, 262 & ALL V-8 ENGINES EXC. 1984–88 CORVETTE

1. Remove mount retaining bolt from below frame mounting bracket, **Figs. 1 and 2.**
2. Raise front of engine and remove mount to engine bolts and mount. On models equipped with V6 engines, the

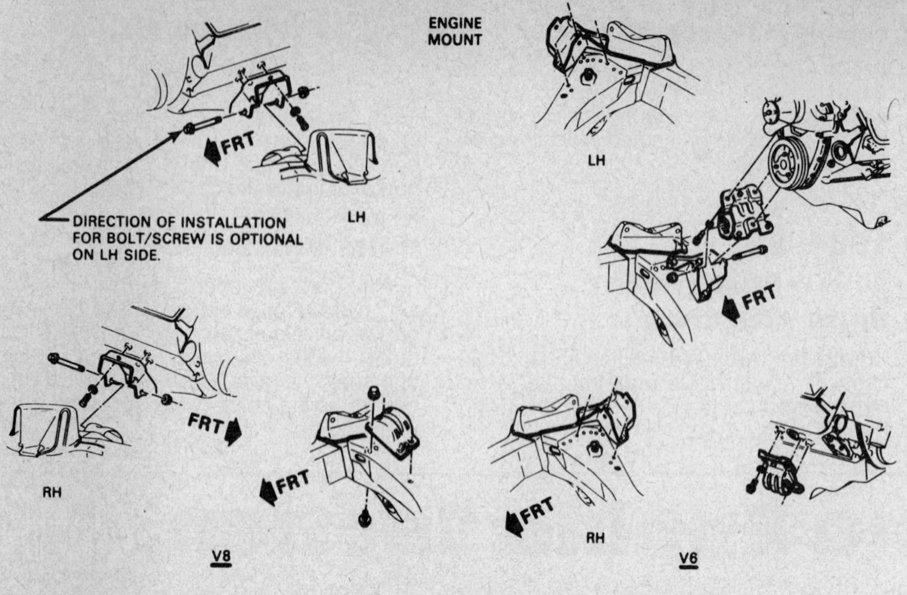

Fig. 1 Engine mounts. V6-229, 262 & V8 engines exc. Corvette

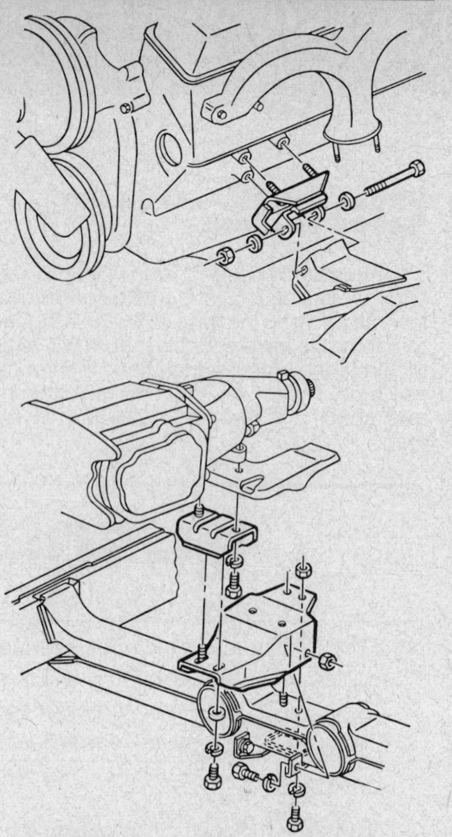

Fig. 2 Engine mounts. 1982 Corvette

righthand mount may be removed by loosening the through bolt. **Raise engine only enough to provide sufficient clearance for mount removal. Check for interference between rear of engine and cowl panel which could result in distributor damage.**

3. Reverse procedure to install.

1984–88 CORVETTE

1. Disconnect battery ground cable, then raise and support vehicle.
2. Support engine and remove mount through bolt, **Fig. 3.**
3. Disconnect AIR injection pipe at manifold, exhaust pipe and catalytic converter.
4. Raise engine sufficiently to provide clearance for mount bolt removal.
5. Remove bolts securing engine mount to block and the mount.
6. Position replacement mount on engine, lower engine into position and install retaining bolts.
7. Reverse procedure to install.

ENGINE REPLACE

EXC. CAMARO & 1984–88 CORVETTE

1. Disconnect battery ground cable and remove air cleaner.
2. Mark position of hinges for reassembly, then remove hood.
3. Drain cooling system, remove radiator hoses, and disconnect heater hoses from engine.
4. On models with A/C, disconnect electrical connector from compressor clutch and ground wire from bracket, remove compressor and secure aside.
5. On V6-231 engines, remove fan blade, pulleys and shroud. On all other engines, remove fan shroud and radiator. **On models with automatic transmission, disconnect and plug cooler lines.**

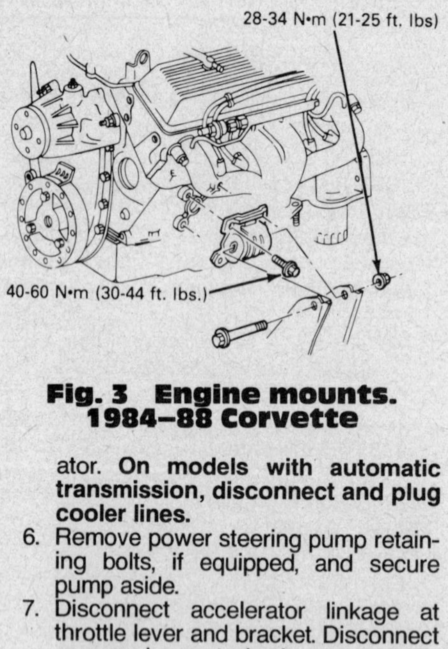

Fig. 3 Engine mounts. 1984–88 Corvette

6. Remove power steering pump retaining bolts, if equipped, and secure pump aside.
7. Disconnect accelerator linkage at throttle lever and bracket. Disconnect vacuum hoses to body mounted accessories and fuel hoses at fuel pump, then plug fuel hoses.
8. Disconnect battery and chassis ground straps from engine.
9. Disconnect electrical connectors from alternator, distributor or remote mounted coil and all engine mounted switches and accessories.
10. Remove engine harness from retaining clips and secure aside.
11. Raise and support vehicle and drain crankcase.
12. Disconnect exhaust pipes and AIR pipe from manifolds, and remove front exhaust and cruise control brackets, if equipped.
13. Disconnect electrical connectors and battery cable from starter, or remove starter.
14. Remove flywheel shield and remove bolts securing torque converter to flex plate, if equipped. **Mark position of converter in relation to flex plate for reassembly.**
15. Remove motor mount through bolts and bolts securing bellhousing to engine.
16. Lower vehicle and support transmission with suitable floor jack.
17. Attach suitable lifting equipment to engine lifting brackets, raise engine and transmission, and remove motor mount to engine brackets.
18. Separate engine and transmission while supporting transmission with jack. **On automatic transmission models, ensure converter remains with transmission during engine removal and is properly seated prior to engine installation.**
19. Lift and remove engine after disconnecting any remaining harness connectors.
20. Reverse procedure to install.

CAMARO

1. Disconnect battery ground cable and remove air cleaner and fresh air hoses.
2. Disconnect electrical connectors from hood lamp or air door, if equipped, mark position of hood hinges for reassembly, and remove hood.
3. Drain cooling system, remove radiator hoses, and disconnect heater hoses from engine.

4. If equipped with A/C, disconnect electrical connector from compressor clutch and ground wire from bracket, remove compressor and secure aside.
5. Disconnect and plug transmission cooler lines at radiator, if equipped, then remove fan blade, shroud and radiator. **On 4-151 engines with manual transmission, only fan blade and upper shroud should be removed.**
6. On V6 and V8 engines, remove power steering pump retaining bolts and secure pump aside. On 4-151 engines, disconnect and plug power steering hoses at pump.
7. Disconnect accelerator and cruise control linkage at throttle and brackets, then the vacuum hoses from all body mounted accessories, and secure cables and hoses.
8. Disconnect and plug fuel supply and return hoses. **On models with EFI, relieve fuel system pressure before disconnecting hoses.**
9. On V6 and V8 engines, proceed as follows:
   a. Remove distributor cap and lay wiring aside.
   b. Disconnect electrical connectors to alternator, distributor and all other engine mounted switches and accessories.
   c. Release engine harness from retaining clips and secure harness aside.
10. On 4-151 engines, proceed as follows:
    a. Disconnect engine electrical harness at bulkhead connector.
    b. From inside vehicle, lower right hush panel and remove ECM harness from main ECM connector.
    c. Remove splash shield from right inner fender and carefully pull ECM harness into engine compartment.
    d. Secure harnesses to engine.
11. Disconnect battery and chassis ground straps from engine, then raise and support vehicle.
12. Disconnect exhaust pipes from manifolds, and on 4-151 engines, remove exhaust pipe assembly.
13. On V6 and V8 engines, disconnect electrical connectors and battery cable from starter and remove wiring shields. On 4-151 engines, disconnect electrical connectors from transmission and remove starter.
14. Remove flywheel shield and bolts securing converter to flex plate, if equipped. **Mark position of converter in relation to flex plate for reassembly.**
15. On models with manual transmission, remove clutch linkage.
16. Remove motor mount through bolts and bolts securing bellhousing to engine.
17. Lower vehicle and support transmission with suitable floor jack.
18. Attach suitable lifting equipment to engine lifting brackets, remove bracket securing AIR injection pipe, then raise engine and transmission assembly.
19. Separate engine and transmission, and lift engine from vehicle after removing bracket from rear of left cylinder head (V6 and V8). **On automatic transmission models, ensure that converter remains with transmission during engine removal, and that it is properly seated prior to engine installation.**
20. Reverse procedure to install.

1984 CORVETTE

1. Disconnect battery ground cable, remove air cleaner and fresh air ducts, and drain cooling system.
2. Disconnect AIR pump inlet and outlet hoses at check valves.
3. Rotate belt tensioner counterclockwise to release tension, then remove drive belt.
4. Remove A/C compressor rear brackets and disconnect electrical connectors to compressor.
5. Remove pulley and air management valves from AIR pump, then remove pump.
6. Remove upper radiator hose and bolt securing power steering reservoir brace to thermostat housing.
7. Disconnect electrical connectors to alternator, then remove alternator and brace.
8. Remove bolt securing AIR pipe and steering reservoir bracket to intake manifold.
9. Disconnect power steering hoses at rack and plug open fittings, remove power steering pump lower bracket, then secure pump, reservoir and A/C harness toward front of vehicle.
10. Disconnect and plug fuel supply and return lines. **Relieve fuel system pressure before disconnecting hoses.**
11. Remove nuts securing A/C bracket to water pump and lower compressor mounting bolt, move bracket forward and remove upper mounting bolt, then secure compressor aside.
12. Remove fuel line, detent cable and idler pulley brackets, disconnect hoses from water pump and secure hoses and fuel lines aside.
13. Disconnect accelerator, cruise control and downshift cables from TBI and brackets.
14. Disconnect brake booster and PCV hoses from intake cover and vacuum hoses between engine and body mounted components.
15. Disconnect electrical connectors from TBI, front ground stud, coolant sensor and EGR solenoid.
16. Release clips securing wiring to valve cover, then move harness, AIR pipe and air management valves toward rear of engine.
17. Remove tach filter and ground wire from intake stud, and disconnect electrical connectors to distributor.
18. Remove distributor cap and spark plug wires after removing shields, then disconnect heater hose from manifold.
19. Mark and remove distributor, then remove oil pressure sensor and bolt securing ground strap to engine.
20. Remove crankshaft damper, raise and support vehicle.
21. Disconnect crossover pipe and AIR pipe from manifolds and converter, and remove crossover pipe brace.
22. Disconnect electrical connectors from block, coolant, oil, and oxygen sensors and starter, remove wiring shields and release harness clips, and secure harness aside.
23. Disconnect battery and chassis ground straps from above oil filter.
24. Remove flywheel shield and bolts securing converter to flex plate, if equipped. **Mark position of converter in relation to flex plate for reassembly.**
25. Remove right lower and upper bellhousing bolts, then remove right center and left side bolts.
26. Support engine and remove bolts securing right and left motor mounts to block.
27. Lower vehicle and support transmission with suitable floor jack.
28. Attach suitable lifting equipment to engine lifting brackets, then separate engine and transmission.
29. Lift and remove engine assembly after disconnecting wiring from rear of left cylinder head. **On automatic transmission models, ensure that converter remains with transmission during engine removal, and that it is properly seated prior to engine installation.**
30. Reverse procedure to install.

1985–86 CORVETTE

1. Disconnect battery ground cable.
2. Drain cooling system, then remove air cleaner assembly.
3. Remove serpentine drive belt.
4. Remove rear A/C compressor brackets, then disconnect electrical connectors from compressor.
5. Relieve fuel system pressure, then disconnect and plug fuel supply and return lines.
6. Remove A/C compressor mounting bracket nuts and bolts.
7. Disconnect heater hoses, then the upper radiator hose from thermostat outlet.
8. Disconnect fuel line clip from fuel pump cover plate.
9. Unfasten A/C compressor from mounting bracket, then position compressor aside and remove bracket.
10. Disconnect fuel injection wiring harness from engine.
11. Disconnect cruise, detent and accelerator cables, then remove distributor shield and cap.
12. Disconnect electrical connector from distributor.
13. Disconnect detent cable bracket from intake manifold, then remove distributor.
14. Disconnect electrical connector from oil pressure sending unit, then remove the sending unit.
15. Disconnect all vacuum lines necessary for engine removal.
16. Disconnect power steering hoses from rack and pinion.
17. Remove crankshaft pulley.

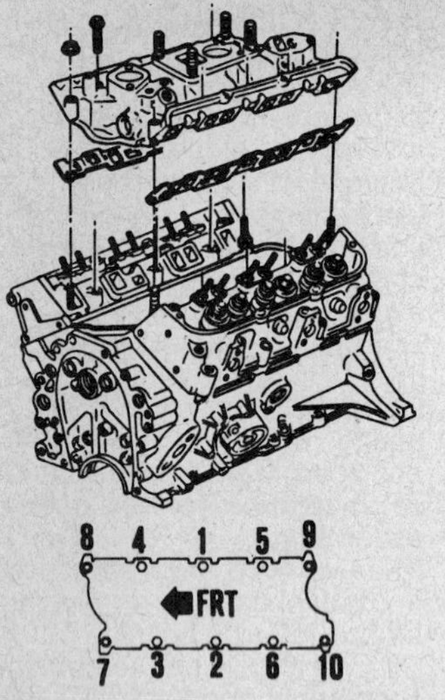

Fig. 4 Intake manifold tightening sequence. V6-173

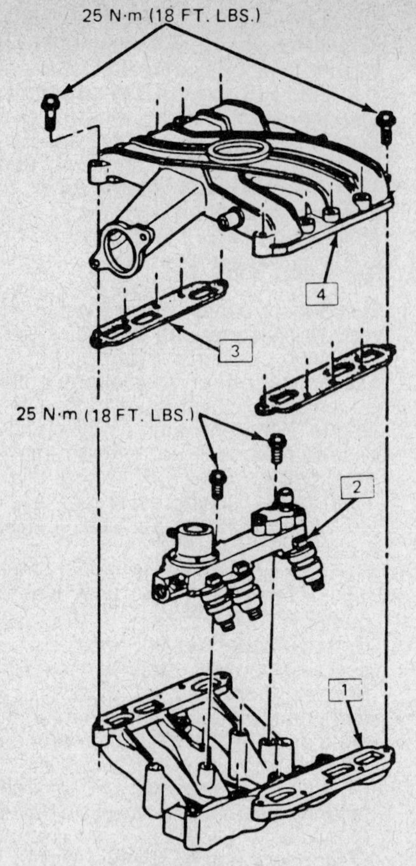

1 INTAKE MANIFOLD	3 GASKET
2 FUEL RAIL ASSEMBLY	4 PLENUM

Fig. 5 Manifold plenum & fuel rail installation. 1985–88 V6-173

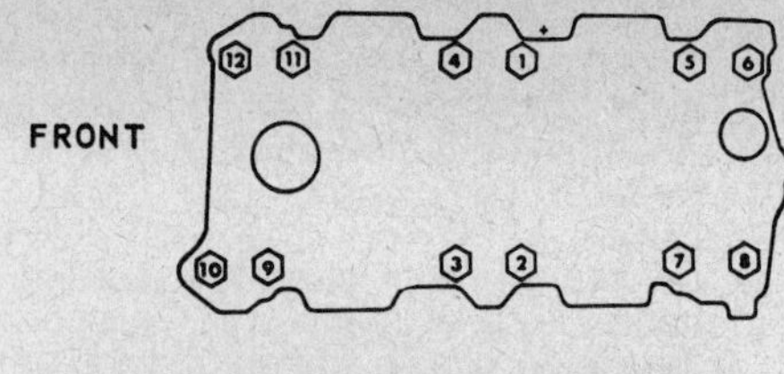

Fig. 6 Intake manifold tightening sequence. 1982–84 V6-229 & 1982–88 V8 carbureted engines

18. Disconnect bulkhead connector and all other electrical connectors necessary for engine removal.
19. Disconnect air injection hose from converter check valve.
20. Position fuel lines aside as necessary.
21. Disconnect radiator hose from water pump and the upper radiator hose from power steering reservoir bracket.
22. Raise and support vehicle.
23. Disconnect air injection pipe from exhaust manifold, then remove converter air pipe.
24. Disconnect exhaust pipe hanger, then remove heat shields from exhaust pipe and converter.
25. Disconnect oxygen sensor electrical connector, then remove exhaust pipe.
26. Remove flywheel cover, then the torque converter attaching bolts.
27. Loosen motor mount through bolts and remove motor mount-to-engine bolts.
28. Remove bellhousing bolts, then lower vehicle.
29. Disconnect knock sensor electrical connector.
30. Disconnect ground cable from block, then the positive battery cable from battery and harness.
31. Remove right rear intake manifold bolt and install suitable lifting hook.
32. Support transmission with suitable jack, then attach lifting equipment to engine and lift engine from vehicle after disconnect wires from rear of left cylinder head.
33. Reverse procedure to install.

1987–88 CORVETTE

1. Disconnect battery ground cable.
2. Disconnect accelerator and cruise control cables at engine, then remove plenum extension.
3. Disconnect plug wires at distributor cap, then remove distributor cap and distributor.
4. Remove cowl screen, then the wiper motor arm attaching nut.
5. Disconnect wiper motor electrical connectors, then remove wiper motor cover and motor.
6. Remove air intake duct with MAF sensor, then disconnect all necessary vacuum hoses and electrical connectors at engine.
7. Disconnect injection harness at intake.
8. Drain engine oil and cooling system, then disconnect heater and radiator hoses.
9. Remove serpentine belt.
10. Relieve fuel pressure, then disconnect fuel lines at fuel rail.
11. Disconnect AIR switching valve at A/C compressor, then the catalytic converter AIR pipe.
12. Disconnect A/C brace at exhaust manifold, then remove A/C bracket attaching nuts at water pump.
13. Loosen upper bracket attaching bolts, then the lower A/C mount bolt.
14. Disconnect accumulator at fan shroud and brace, then the fuel lines at block.
15. Remove fuel lines from A/C bracket and position compressor aside.
16. Remove alternator, then the AIR pump with bracket.
17. Disconnect power steering reservoir at fan shroud and brace.
18. Disconnect power steering pump and position aside.
19. Remove water pump and crankshaft pulley, then raise and support vehicle.
20. Disconnect ground wires at block.
21. Disconnect catalytic converter AIR pipe at manifold, then the transmission cooler lines at flywheel cover.
22. Disconnect starter motor electrical connectors, then remove starter motor from engine.
23. Disconnect exhaust pipe at manifold, then remove oil filter and oil cooler adapter.
24. Remove flywheel cover, then the oil cooler line at oil pan.
25. Disconnect exhaust at converter hanger.
26. Remove engine mount through bolts, then the engine mount to block attaching bolts.
27. Remove bellhousing attaching bolts, then lower vehicle.
28. Support transmission using a suitable jack, then lift engine out of vehicle.
29. Reverse procedure to install.

INTAKE MANIFOLD REPLACE

V6-173

1982–84

1. Disconnect battery ground cable, remove air cleaner and drain cooling system.
2. Disconnect necessary electrical connectors and vacuum hoses, noting position for installation.
3. Disconnect fuel line and accelerator, cruise control and transmission cables, as equipped.
4. Disconnect high tension leads from spark plugs and disconnect wiring from coil.
5. Remove distributor cap and plug wire assembly.
6. Rotate crankshaft until No. 1 cylinder is at TDC on compression stroke, mark position of distributor rotor and remove distributor.
7. Remove air injection hoses, disconnect canister hose and remove pipe bracket from left valve cover.
8. Remove left valve cover and air management bracket, then remove right valve cover.
9. Disconnect upper radiator and heater hoses from manifold.

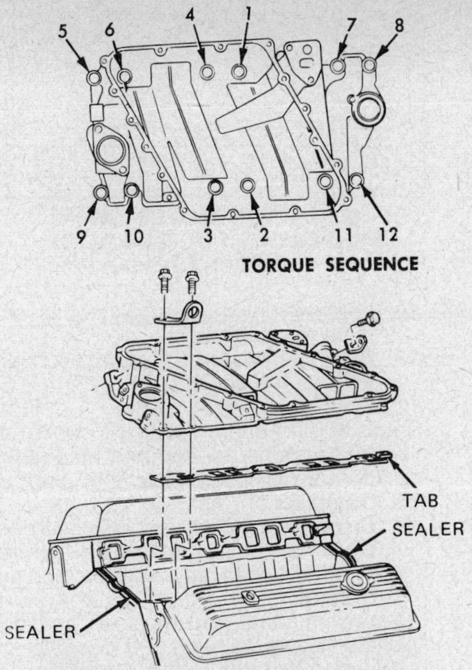

Fig. 7 Intake manifold installation. 1982 & 1984 Corvette

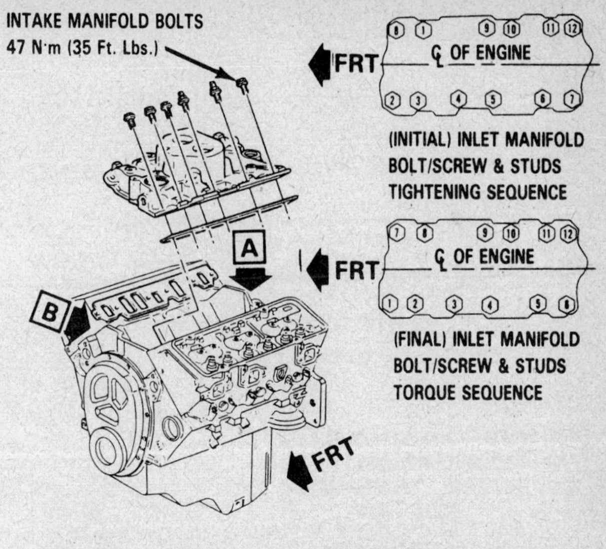

Fig. 8 Intake manifold tightening sequence. 1985–88 V6-262 engine

10. Disconnect coolant switches and remove manifold retaining bolts.
11. Remove manifold and thoroughly clean old gasket and sealer from mating surfaces.
12. Ensure surfaces are clean and dry, then apply 3/16 bead of RTV sealer on each block ridge, install gaskets and secure gasket position by extending bead of sealer approximately 1/4 inch onto gasket ends. **New gaskets must be cut to fit behind pushrods. When installing gaskets, note left and right side markings.**
13. Install manifold and retaining bolts, ensuring areas between case ridges and manifold are completely sealed.
14. Torque manifold bolts to specifications in sequence shown in **Fig. 4**, then reverse remaining procedure to complete installation.

1985–88

1. Disconnect battery ground cable, remove air cleaner and drain cooling system.
2. Connect pressure gauge J-34730-1 or equivalent to fuel rail pressure valve, position bleed hose in suitable container and relieve fuel system pressure. **Failure to relieve fuel pressure prior to disconnecting fuel system connections may cause fire or personal injury.**
3. Disconnect air inlet duct, electrical connectors, coolant hoses and vacuum hoses from throttle body, noting position for installation.
4. Disconnect accelerator, cruise control and transmission cables, as equipped.
5. Remove throttle body retaining bolts and the throttle body.
6. Remove EGR pipe retaining bolts and throttle cable bracket.
7. Remove bolts securing plenum to manifold and the plenum, **Fig. 5.**
8. Disconnect fuel lines from fuel rail and remove cold start valve.
9. Disconnect vacuum hose from pressure regulator and remove fuel rail retaining bolts.
10. Disconnect injector harness connectors and remove fuel rail assembly, **Fig. 5.**
11. Disconnect high tension leads from spark plugs and disconnect wiring from coil.
12. Remove distributor cap and plug wire assembly.
13. Rotate crankshaft until No. 1 cylinder is at TDC on compression stroke, mark position of distributor rotor and remove distributor.
14. Remove air injection hose, if equipped, disconnect canister hoses and remove pipe bracket from front of left valve cover.
15. Remove left valve cover and air management bracket, then remove right valve cover.
16. Disconnect upper radiator and heater hoses from manifold.
17. Disconnect coolant switches and remove manifold retaining bolts.
18. Remove manifold and thoroughly clean old gasket and sealer from mating surfaces.
19. Ensure surfaces are clean and dry, then apply 3/16 bead of RTV sealer on each block ridge, install gaskets and secure gasket position by extending bead of sealer approximately 1/4 inch onto gasket ends. **New gaskets must be cut to fit behind pushrods. When installing gaskets, note left and right side markings.**
20. Install manifold and retaining bolts, ensuring areas between case ridges and manifold are completely sealed.
21. Torque manifold bolts to specifications in sequence shown in **Fig. 4**, then reverse remaining procedure to complete installation.

V6-229, 262 & ALL V8 ENGINES EXC. 1984–88 CORVETTE & 1985–88 V8-305 W/EFI

1. Disconnect battery ground cable, drain cooling system and remove air cleaner.
2. Disconnect accelerator, transmission and cruise control linkages, as equipped.
3. Disconnect fuel line from carburetor or TBI unit and remove fuel line clips as needed.
4. Disconnect necessary vacuum hoses and electrical connectors, noting position for installation.
5. Disconnect upper radiator and heater hoses from manifold.
6. Disconnect high tension leads from spark plugs in right side of engine and remove distributor cap, rotate crankshaft until No. 1 cylinder is at TDC on compression stroke, mark position of distributor rotor, then remove distributor.
7. Remove ignition coil, AIR pump, cruise control servo and brackets, as needed.
8. Remove generator upper mounting bracket and EGR solenoids.
9. Remove manifold retaining bolts and the manifold. **It may be necessary to remove carburetor, EGR valve and/or idle control solenoid to provide clearance for manifold bolt removal.**
10. Ensure surfaces are clean and dry, then apply 3/16 bead of RTV sealer on each block ridge and apply suitable sealer around water outlets, install

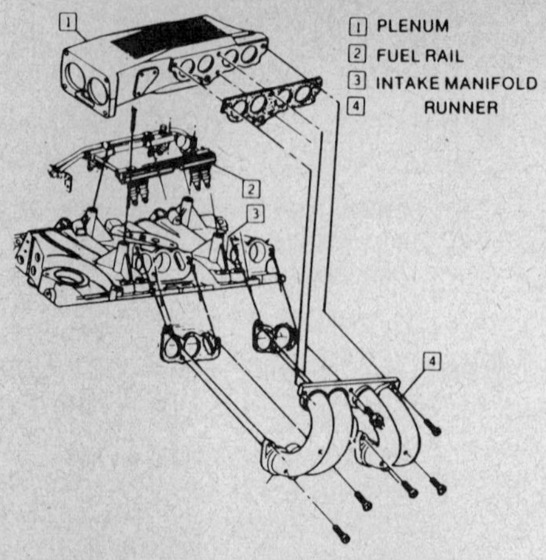

Fig. 9 Plenum, runner & fuel line installation. 1985–88 Corvette, 1985–88 V8-305 W/EFI similar

gaskets and secure gasket position by extending bead of sealer approximately 1/2 inch onto gasket ends.

11. Install manifold and retaining bolts, ensuring areas between case ridges and manifold are completely sealed.
12. Torque manifold bolts to specifications in sequence shown in **Figs. 6, 7 and 8,** then reverse remaining procedure to complete installation.

1984 CORVETTE

1. Disconnect and plug fuel supply and return lines. **Relieve fuel system pressure before disconnecting fuel hoses.**
2. Disconnect electrical connectors and vacuum hoses as needed, and secure wiring and hoses aside.
3. Disconnect accelerator, cruise control and downshift cables from TBI unit and brackets.
4. Rotate belt tensioner counterclockwise to release tension, and remove drive belt.
5. Remove AIR pump pulley, air management valve adapter and AIR pump.
6. Disconnect upper radiator and heater hoses, and remove bolts securing accessory mounting brackets to manifold.
7. Disconnect spark plug wires, remove distributor cap, and lay cap and wire assembly aside.
8. Mark position of distributor rotor and remove distributor.
9. Remove intake cover and TBI assembly.
10. Remove intake manifold bolts and manifold.
11. Ensure surfaces are clean and dry, then apply 3/16 bead of RTV sealer on each block ridge and apply suitable sealer around water outlets, install gaskets and secure gasket position by extending bead of sealer approximately 1/2 inch onto gasket ends.
12. Install manifold and retaining bolts, ensuring areas between case ridges and manifold are completely sealed.

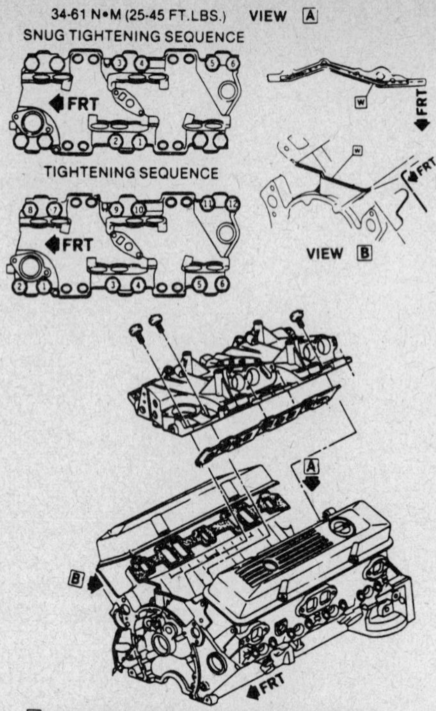

W AT TIME OF INSTALLATION SURFACE AREA MUST BE FREE OF OIL AND SEALING COMPOUND MUST BE WET TO TOUCH WHEN BOLT/SCREWS ARE TORQUED. APPLY SEALING COMPOUND .12 THICK.

Fig. 10 Intake manifold installation. 1985–88 Corvette & V8-305 W/EFI

13. Torque manifold bolts to specifications in sequence shown in **Fig. 7,** then reverse remaining procedure to complete installation.

1985–88 V8-305 W/EFI

1. Disconnect battery ground cable, drain cooling system and remove air intake duct.
2. Disconnect accelerator, cruise control and transmission cables, as equipped.
3. Disconnect coolant hoses, electrical connectors, and the vacuum and breather hoses from throttle body, noting position for installation.
4. Remove throttle body from plenum, then remove distributor shield.
5. Disconnect brake booster and vacuum hoses from plenum, noting position for installation.
6. Connect pressure gauge J-34370-1 or equivalent to pressure tap on fuel rail, position bleed hose in suitable container and slowly relieve fuel system pressure. **Failure to relieve system pressure prior to disconnecting fuel system components may cause fire or personal injury.**
7. Disconnect canister control valve pipe, remove right side runners and plenum bolt, then remove plenum, **Fig. 9.**
8. Disconnect fuel line to cold start valve and remove valve.
9. Disconnect fuel lines from fuel rail and electrical connectors from injectors.

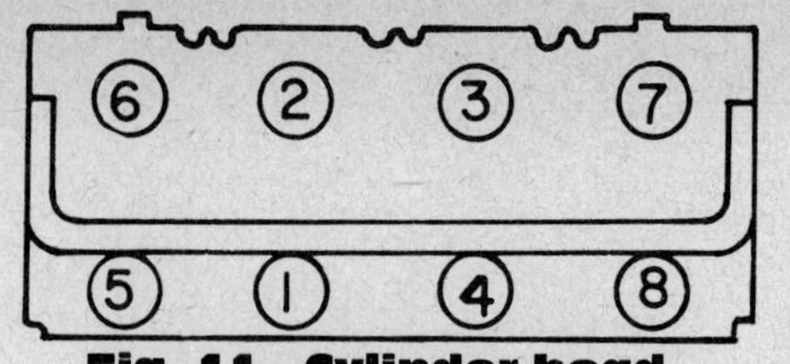

Fig. 11 Cylinder head tightening sequence. V6-173

10. Loosen fuel rail retaining bolts and raise rail assembly.
11. Remove remaining manifold runners and the fuel rail assembly.
12. Rotate crankshaft until No. 1 cylinder is at TDC on compression stroke, remove distributor cap and mark position of distributor rotor, then remove distributor.
13. Disconnect EGR solenoid and all necessary electrical connectors, then remove manifold retaining bolts and the manifold.
14. Ensure surfaces are clean and dry, then apply 3/16 bead of RTV sealer on each block ridge and apply suitable sealer around water outlets, install gaskets and secure gasket position by extending bead of sealer approximately 1/2 inch onto gasket ends.
15. Install manifold and retaining bolts, ensuring areas between case ridges and manifold are completely sealed.
16. Torque manifold bolts to specifications in sequence shown in **Fig. 10,** then reverse remaining procedure to complete installation.

1985–88 CORVETTE

1. Disconnect battery ground cable, drain cooling system and remove air intake duct and mass air flow sensor assembly.
2. Disconnect accelerator, cruise control and transmission cables, as equipped, and remove cable bracket.
3. Disconnect electrical connectors, coolant hoses and vacuum hoses, then remove throttle body from plenum.
4. Disconnect brake booster and vacuum hoses from plenum, noting position for installation.
5. Remove right intake runners, plenum retaining bolts and the plenum, **Fig. 9.**
6. Connect pressure gauge J-34370-1 or equivalent to pressure tap on fuel rail, position bleed hose in suitable container and slowly relieve fuel system pressure. **Failure to relieve system pressure prior to disconnecting fuel system components may cause fire or personal injury.**
7. Disconnect cold start valve fuel line and remove cold start valve.
8. Disconnect fuel lines and injector harness connectors.
9. Loosen fuel rail bolts and raise fuel rail assembly.
10. Remove remaining manifold runners, then the fuel rail assembly.
11. Disconnect electrical connectors and vacuum hoses necessary to allow manifold removal, noting position for installation.

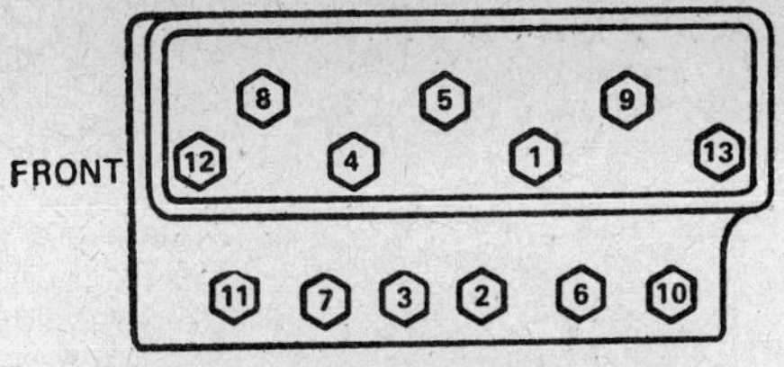

Fig. 12 Cylinder head tightening sequence. V6-229 & 262

12. Disconnect wires from spark plugs, then remove distributor cap assembly.
13. Rotate crankshaft until No. 1 cylinder is at TDC on compression stroke, mark position of distributor rotor, then remove distributor.
14. Disconnect upper radiator hose from thermostat housing and remove air injection pump brace.
15. Disconnect EGR pipe and heater control vacuum hose from intake.
16. Remove thermostat housing, then the manifold retaining bolts and manifold.
17. Ensure gasket surfaces are clean and dry, then install gaskets on cylinder head with blocked openings toward rear of engine.
18. Bend gasket tabs flush with rear face with cylinder head, then apply a 3/16 inch bead of RTV sealer to front and rear ridges of cylinder block.
19. Apply Loctite 1052624 or equivalent to manifold bolts.
20. Install manifold and torque bolts to specifications in sequence shown in **Fig. 10**, then reverse remaining procedure to complete installation.

CYLINDER HEAD

REPLACE

V6-173

1. Remove intake manifold.
2. Raise and support vehicle.
3. Disconnect exhaust pipe from manifold, then drain engine block.
4. If lefthand cylinder head is to be removed, remove dipstick tube attachment.
5. Lower vehicle, then remove serpentine belt, as required.
6. Loosen rocker arms until pushrods can be removed.
7. If right hand cylinder head is to be removed, remove alternator bracket and AIR bracket, then the A/C compressor and power steering pump, as required.
8. Remove cylinder head bolts and cylinder head.
9. Reverse procedure to install. Coat cylinder head bolts with sealer. Torque cylinder bolts in sequence shown in **Fig. 11.**

V6-229, 262 & ALL V8 ENGINES EXC. 1984–88 CORVETTE

1. Disconnect battery ground cable, then drain cooling system and engine block.
2. Remove intake manifold and exhaust manifolds.
3. Remove alternator lower mounting bolt and position alternator aside.
4. If equipped with A/C, remove compressor and forward mounting bracket and position aside.
5. Remove rocker arm cover, rocker arms and pushrods. **Keep rocker arm, rocker arm balls and pushrods in order so they can be installed in the same position.**
6. On all except 1982 Corvette, remove diverter valve.
7. Remove cylinder head bolts and cylinder head.
8. Reverse procedure to install. Apply suitable sealer to cylinder head bolts and gradually torque bolts to specifications in sequence shown in **Figs. 12 and 13.**

1984–88 CORVETTE

1. Disconnect battery ground cable and remove air cleaner.
2. Drain cooling system and engine block, then remove intake manifold.
3. Disconnect AIR hose from exhaust manifold check valve, and if right cylinder head is to be removed, disconnect AIR hose from converter pipe.
4. If right cylinder head is to be removed, remove A/C compressor as follows:
   a. Remove lower compressor mounting bolt and nuts securing bracket to water pump.
   b. Move compressor assembly forward, remove upper mounting bolt and disconnect electrical connector, and secure compressor aside.
   c. Disconnect electrical connectors to high pressure switch, then remove high pressure switch and EGR solenoid.
   d. Disconnect EFI harness from rocker cover clamp.
5. If left cylinder head is to be removed, remove alternator and brace.
6. Remove valve cover retaining bolts, bend plug wire bracket away from cover for clearance, and remove cover.
7. Remove spark plugs and temperature sending unit from cylinder head.
8. Raise and support vehicle, and disconnect exhaust pipe from manifold. If right cylinder head is to be replaced, remove 2 rear manifold bolts and dipstick tube bolt.
9. Lower vehicle and remove exhaust manifold.
10. If left cylinder head is to be removed, remove AIR pump upper bracket and power steering reservoir, and set aside.
11. Remove spark plug wire bracket and bolts securing ground straps to cylinder head.
12. Loosen rocker arm nuts and remove pushrods.
13. Remove head bolts and cylinder head.
14. Reverse procedure to install, noting the following:
    a. Ensure gasket surfaces are clean and free of nicks or deep scratches, and bolt and block threads are clean.
    b. Coat both sides of head gasket with a thin even coat of sealer, and ensure gasket is properly positioned over dowel pins.
    c. Coat cylinder head bolt threads with GM sealer No. 1052080 or equivalent, then install all bolts finger tight.
    d. Torque cylinder head bolts to specifications in sequence shown in **Fig. 13.**
    e. Install intake manifold gaskets on head with blocked openings toward rear, bend gasket tabs flush with rear face of cylinder head, and apply a 3/16 inch bead of RTV sealer on front and rear cylinder block ridges, **Fig. 10.**
    f. Install manifold, apply Loctite No. 1052624 or equivalent to manifold bolts, and torque bolts to 35 ft. lbs. in sequence shown in **Fig. 10.**

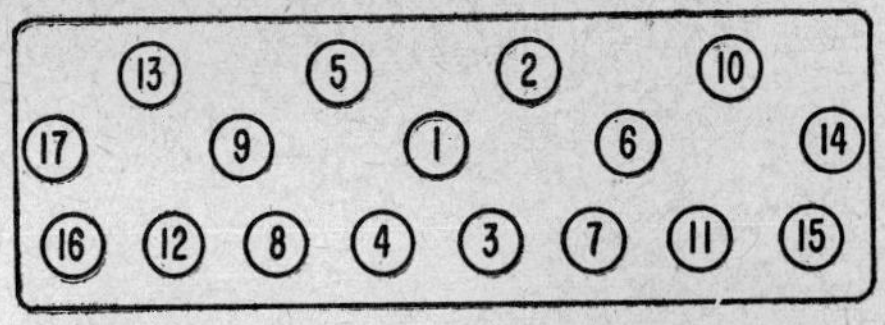

Fig. 13 Cylinder head tightening sequence. V8 engines

VALVES

ADJUST

After the engine has been thoroughly warmed up the valves may be adjusted with the engine shut off as follows: With engine in position to fire No. 1 cylinder the following valves may be adjusted: V6-173, Exhaust 1-2-3, intake 1-5-6. V6-229 and 262, Exhaust 1-5-6, intake 1-2-3. V8's, Exhaust 1-3-4-8, intake 1-2-5-7. Then crank the engine one more complete revolution which will bring No. 4 cylinder on V6-173, V6-229 and 262, engine and No. 6 cylinder on V8 engines, to the firing position at which time the following valves may be adjusted: V6-173, Exhaust 4-5-6, intake 2-3-4. V6-229 and 262, Exhaust 2-3-4, intake 4-5-6. V8's, Exhaust 2-5-6-7, intake 3-4-6-8.

The following procedure, performed with the engine running, should be done only in case readjustment is required.

1. After engine has been warmed up to operating temperature, remove valve cover and install a new valve cover gasket.
2. With engine running at idle speed, back off valve rocker arm nut until rocker arm starts to clatter.
3. Turn rocker arm nut down slowly until the clatter just stops. This is the zero lash position.
4. Turn nut down 1/4 additional turn and pause 10 seconds until engine runs smoothly. Repeat additional 1/4 turns, pausing 10 seconds each time, until

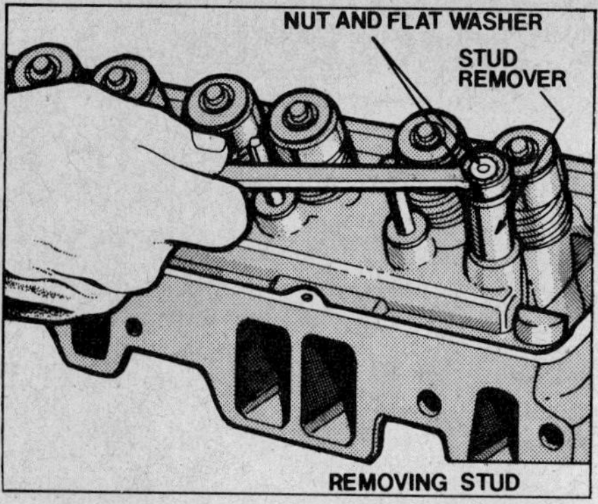

Fig. 14 Rocker arm stud removal. Press type studs

nut has been turned down the number of turns listed in the Valve Clearance Specifications Chart from the zero lash position. **This preload adjustment must be done slowly to allow the lifter to adjust itself to prevent the possibility of interference between the intake valve head and top of piston, which might result in internal damage and/or bent pushrods. Noisy lifters should be replaced.**

VALVE CLEARANCE SPECIFICATIONS

Year	Engine/VIN	Valve Lash
1982	V6-173/1	1½ Turns①
	V6-229/K	1 Turn①
	V8-267/J	1 Turn①
	V8-305/H & 7	1 Turn①
	V8-350/6	1 Turn①
1983	V6-173/1	1½ Turns①
	V6-229/9	1 Turn①
	V8-305/G, H & S	1 Turn①
1984	V6-173/1	1½ Turns①
	V6-229/9	1 Turn①
	V8-305/G & H	1 Turn①
	V8-350/8	1 Turn①
1985	V6-173/S	1½ Turns①
	V6-262/Z	1 Turn①
	V8-305/F	1 Turn①
	V8-305/G & H	1 Turn①
	V8-350/8	1 Turn①
1986	V6-173/S	1½ Turns①
	V6-262/Z	1 Turn①
	V8-305/F	1 Turn①
	V8-305/G & H	1 Turn①
	V8-350/8	1 Turn①
1987	V6-173/S	1½ Turns①
	V6-262/Z	1 Turn①
	V8-305/F	1 Turn①
	V8-305/G & H	1 Turn①
	V8-350/6, 8	1 Turn①
1988	V6-173/S	1½ Turns①
	V6-262/Z	1 Turn①
	V8-305/F	1 Turn①
	V8-305/G & H	1 Turn①
	V8-350/8	1 Turn①

①—Turn rocker arm stud nut until all lash is eliminated, then tighten nut the additional turn listed.

ROCKER ARM STUDS
REPLACE

If studs are loose in cylinder head, .003 inch or .013 inch oversize studs may be installed on all engines with pressed-in type studs, after reaming holes with a proper size reamer. On engines with threaded rocker studs, looseness can be corrected by installing the proper size Heli-Coil insert, or by replacing cylinder head. Replace damaged pressed-in rocker arm studs using the following procedure:

1. Remove the old stud by placing a suitable spacer, **Fig. 14**, over stud. Install nut and flat washer and remove stud by turning nut.
2. Ream hole for oversize stud.
3. Coat press-fit area of stud with rear axle lube. Then install new stud, **Fig. 15.** If tool shown is used, it should bottom on the head.

PUSHRODS

On engines that use pushrods with a hardened insert at one end, the hardened end is identified by a color stripe and should always be installed toward the rocker arm during assembly.

VALVE GUIDES

On all engines valves operate in guide holes bored in the head. If clearance becomes excessive, use the next oversize valve and ream the bore to fit. Valves with oversize stems are available in .003, .015 and .030 inch.

VALVE ARRANGEMENT
FRONT TO REAR

V6-173

Right . . . . E-I-E-I-I-E
Left. . . . . E-I-I-E-I-E

V6-229, 262

Right . . . . E-I-I-E-I-E
Left. . . . . E-I-E-I-I-E

Small V8

All. E-I-I-E-E-I-I-E

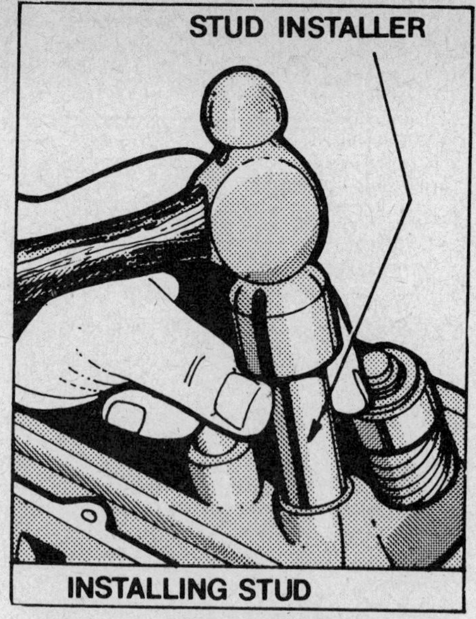

Fig. 15 Rocker arm stud installation. Press type studs

VALVE LIFT SPECIFICATIONS

Engine	Year	Int.	Exh.
V6-173	1982–84	.3466	.3938
V6-173	1985	.3500	.3850
V6-173	1986–88	.2626⑩	.2732⑩
V6-229	1982	.5355	.5355
V6-229	1983–84	.3510	.3855
V6-262	1985	.3500	.3850
V6-262	1986–88	.2340⑩	.2570⑩
V8-267	1982	.3570	.3900
V8-305①	1982	.4000	.3726
V8-305②③	1982	.3570	.3900
V8-305④	1982	.3900	.4095
V8-305③	1983–84	.3510	.3855
V8-305④	1983–84	.3855	.4035
V8-305⑨	1985	.3510	.3855
V8-305③⑥	1985	.4035	.4140
V8-305③	1986–88	.2340⑩	.2570⑩
V8-305④	1986–88	.2690⑩	.2760⑩
V8-350⑤	1982	.3900	.4100
V8-350⑦	1982 & 84	.4100	.4230
V8-350⑧	1983–84	.3855	.4035
V8-350⑦	1985	.4040	.4150
V8-350②⑦	1986–88	.2733⑩	.2820⑩
V8-350⑧	1987–88	.2570⑩	.2690⑩

①—Exc. Camaro.
②—Camaro.
③—Exc. EFI.
④—EFI.
⑤—Exc. Corvette high performance.
⑥—High performance VIN code G.
⑦—Corvette.
⑧—Exc. Corvette.
⑨—VIN code H.
⑩—Camshaft lobe lift.

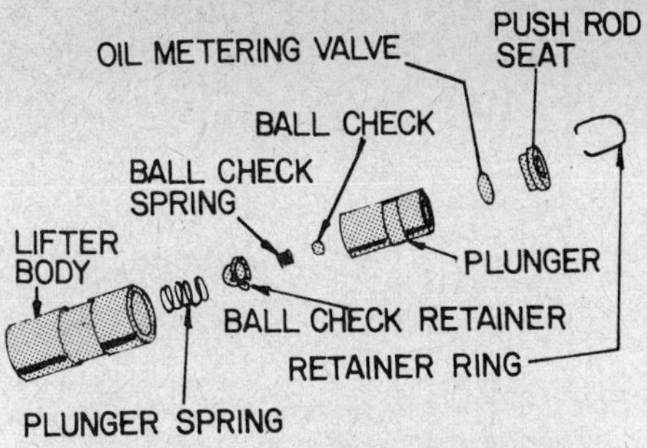

Fig. 16 Standard type hydraulic lifter exploded view

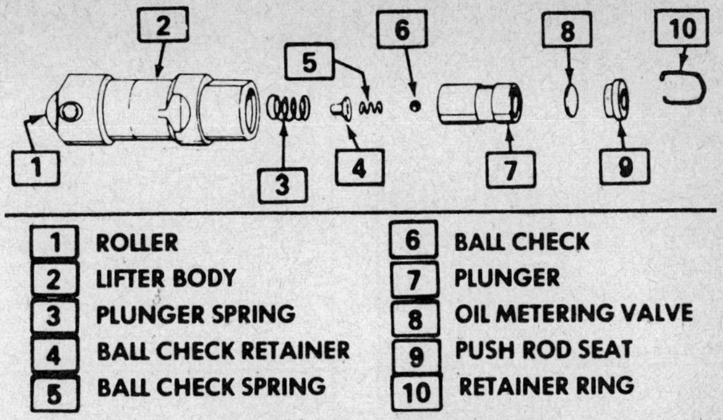

Fig. 17 Roller type hydraulic lifter exploded view

VALVE TIMING

INTAKE OPENS BEFORE TDC

Engine	Year	Degrees
V6-173	1982	25
V6-229	1982	42
V6-231	1982-84	16
V8-267	1982	44
V8-305①	1982	38
V8-305	1982	44
V8-350②	1982	32

①—Fuel injected engine.
②—Corvette high performance engine.

HYDRAULIC LIFTERS

REPLACE

Valve lifters can be lifted from their bores after removing rocker arms and pushrods and intake manifold. Adjustable pliers with protected jaws may be used to remove lifters which are stuck due to carbon or varnish deposits. **Figs. 16 and 17** illustrate the two types of valve lifters used.

TIMING CASE COVER

REPLACE

On all engines the cover oil seal may be replaced without taking off the timing gear cover. After removing the vibration damper, pry out the old seal with a screwdriver. Install the new seal with the lip or open end toward inside of cover and drive it into position.

V6-173

1. Remove water pump, then, on vehicles equipped with A/C, remove compressor and mounting bracket and position aside.
2. Remove vibration damper, then disconnect lower radiator hose from cover and heater hose from water pump.
3. Remove cover retaining bolts and cover.
4. Thoroughly clean sealing surfaces of front cover and engine block, then apply a continuous thin bead of anerobic sealant 1052357 or equivalent to front cover sealing surface.

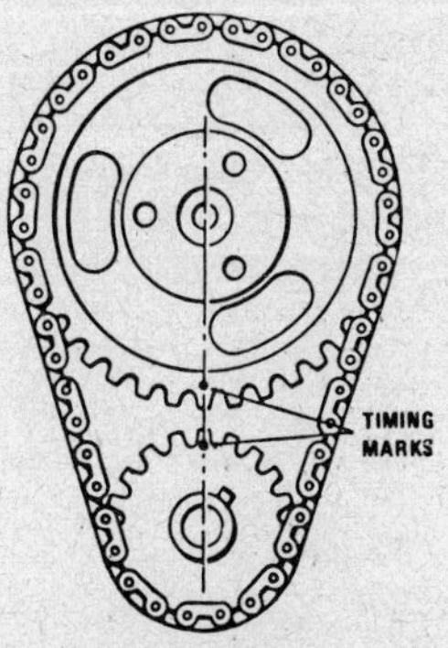

Fig. 18 Timing gear locating marks. V6 & V8 engines

5. Install front cover and water pump on engine, then install retaining bolts and nut and torque to specifications. **Final torquing of bolts must be completed within five minutes of installing the cover.**
6. Reconnect hoses and install vibration damper.
7. Install A/C compressor and mounting bracket.
8. Service cooling system as required.

1982–85 V6 & V8 ENGINES EXC. V6-173

1. Remove vibration damper and water pump.
2. Remove cover retaining screws and cover.
3. Clean gasket surface of block and timing case cover.
4. Remove any excess oil pan gasket material that may be protruding at the oil pan to engine block junction.
5. Apply a thin bead of RTV 1052366 sealer or equivalent to the joint formed at oil pan and block.
6. Coat new gasket with sealer and position it on cover, then install cover to oil pan seal on cover and coat bottom of seal with engine oil.
7. Position cover on engine and loosely install the upper bolts.
8. Tighten screws alternately and evenly while pressing downward on cover so that dowels are aligned with holes in cover. Do not force cover over dowels as cover can be distorted.
9. Install remaining cover screws, vibration damper and water pump. **Late production 1985 and all 1986-88 V6-262 and V8 engines use a one-piece oil pan gasket. On these models the oil pan and gasket must be removed in order to replace the timing cover.**

1986–88 EXC. V6-173

1. Disconnect battery ground cable and drain cooling system.
2. Remove vibration damper and water pump.
3. Remove oil pan and gasket as outlined.
4. Remove timing cover retaining screws and the timing cover.
5. Reverse procedure to install.

TIMING CHAIN

REPLACE

V6 & V8 ENGINES

1. Remove timing chain cover as outlined previously.
2. Remove crankshaft oil slinger.
3. Crank engine until timing marks on sprockets are in alignment, **Fig. 18.**
4. Remove three camshaft-to-sprocket bolts.
5. Remove camshaft sprocket and timing chain together. Sprocket is a light press fit on camshaft for approximately 1/8 inch. If sprocket does not come off easily, a light blow with a plastic hammer on the lower edge of the sprocket should dislodge it.
6. If crankshaft sprocket is to be replaced, remove it with a suitable gear puller. Install new sprocket, aligning key and keyway.
7. Install chain on camshaft sprocket. Hold sprocket vertical with chain hanging below and shift around to align the timing marks on sprockets.
8. Align dowel in camshaft with dowel hole in sprocket and install sprocket on camshaft. Do not attempt to drive sprocket on camshaft as welch plug at rear of engine can be dislodged.
9. Draw sprocket onto camshaft, using the three mounting bolts. Tighten to 20 ft. lb. torque.
10. Lubricate timing chain and install cover.

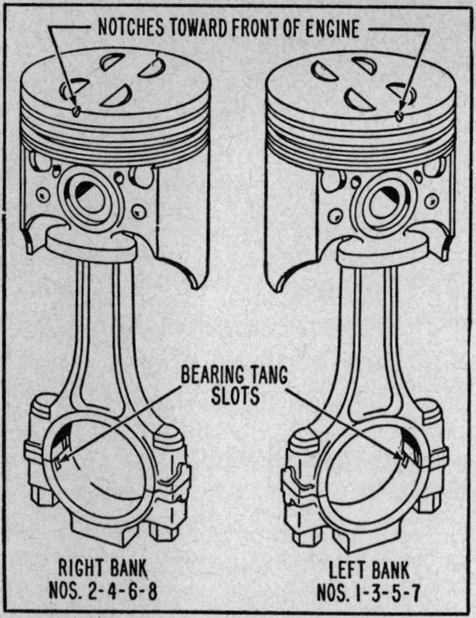

Fig. 19 Piston & rod assembly. V8 engines exc. V8-350 high performance

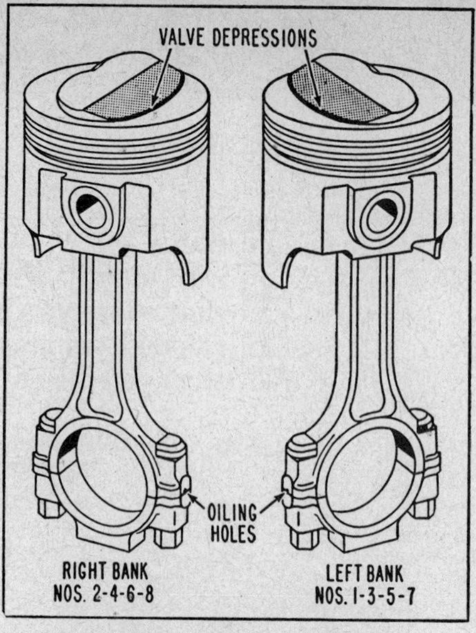

Fig. 20 Piston & rod assembly. V8-350 high performance

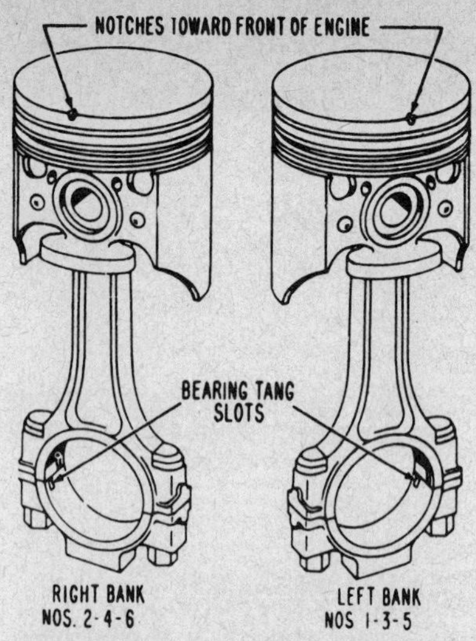

Fig. 21 Piston & rod assembly. V6-229 & 262

CAMSHAFT

REPLACE

1. Remove valve lifters and engine front cover.
2. Remove grille, radiator and condenser.
3. Remove fuel pump and the pushrod, as required.
4. Remove timing chain as outlined previously.
5. On all except V6-173, install two 5/16-18x4 bolts in camshaft bolt holes, then remove camshaft.
6. Reverse procedure to install.

PISTONS & RODS

ASSEMBLE

Assemble pistons to connecting rods as shown in **Figs. 19 through 22.**

Upon installation, measure the connecting rod side clearance using a suitable feeler gauge. Refer to "Engine Rebuilding Specifications" for connecting rod side clearance.

PISTONS, PINS & RINGS

Pistons are available in standard and oversizes of .010 and .030 inch.

Piston rings are available in standard and oversizes of .030 inch.

MAIN & ROD BEARINGS

Connecting rod bearings are available in standard and undersizes of .001, .002, .010 and .020 inch.

Main bearings are available in standard and undersizes of .001, .002, .009, .010 and .020 inch.

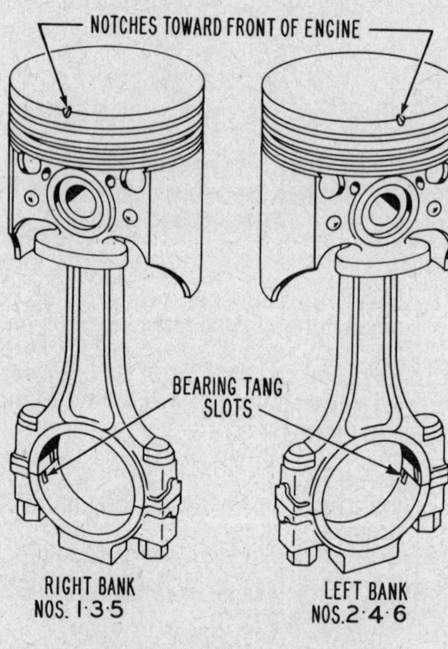

Fig. 22 Piston & rod assembly. V6-173

CRANKSHAFT REAR OIL SEAL

REPLACE

1982–85 EXC. V6-173

These engines are equipped with two-piece, helix type rear seal. A seal starting tool, **Fig. 23,** must be used to prevent the upper seal half from coming into contact with the sharp edge of the block.

When necessary to correct an oil leak due to a defective seal, always replace the upper and lower seal halves as a unit. When installing either half, lubricate the lip portion only with engine oil, keeping oil off the parting line surface as this is treated with glue. Always clean crankshaft surface before installing a new seal.

1. To replace the lower seal, remove seal from groove in bearing cap, using a small screwdriver to pry it out.
2. Insert new seal and roll it in place with finger and thumb.
3. To replace the upper seal (with engine in car) use a small hammer and tap a brass pin punch on one end of the seal until it protrudes far enough to be removed with pliers.
4. Position tip of tool, **Fig. 23,** between crankshaft and seal seat in cylinder block.
5. Position seal between crankshaft and tip of tool with seal bead contacting tip of tool. Ensure oil seal lip is facing toward front of engine.
6. Roll seal around crankshaft, using tool as a "shoehorn" to protect seal bead from sharp corner of seal seat surface in cylinder block. **Tool must remain in position until seal is properly seated with both ends flush with block.**
7. Remove tool, using care not to dislodge seal.
8. Install new seal into bearing cap with tool as outlined previously.
9. Install bearing cap with sealant applied to the cap to case interface, **Fig. 24.** Do not apply sealant to seal ends. Torque rear main bearing cap bolts to specifications.

1986–88 EXC. V6-173

These engines are equipped with a one-piece, lip type seal mounted in a separate seal retainer. Seal replacement requires removal of the transmission.

1. Raise and support vehicle, then remove transmission, clutch assembly and flywheel, as equipped.
2. Pry seal from retainer, inserting screwdriver in notches provided in seal retainer.

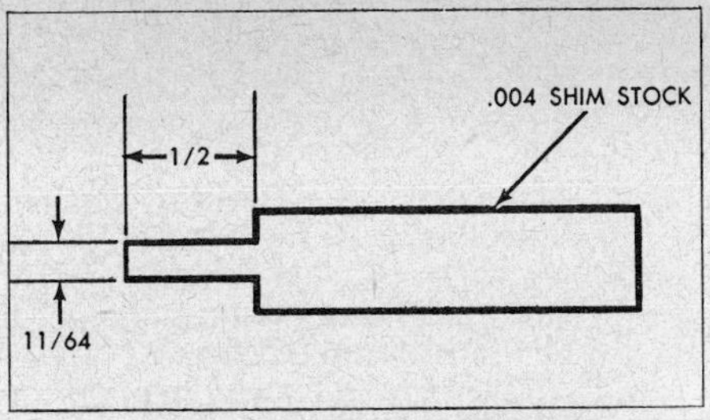

Fig. 23 Rear main seal installation tool. 1982–85 V6 & V8 exc. V6-173

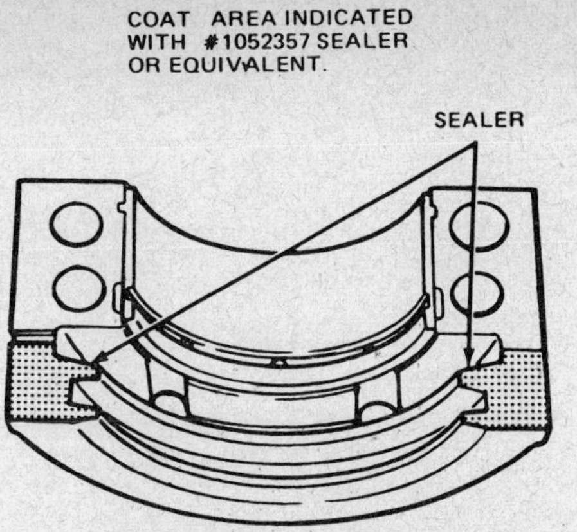

Fig. 24 Rear main bearing cap sealing areas

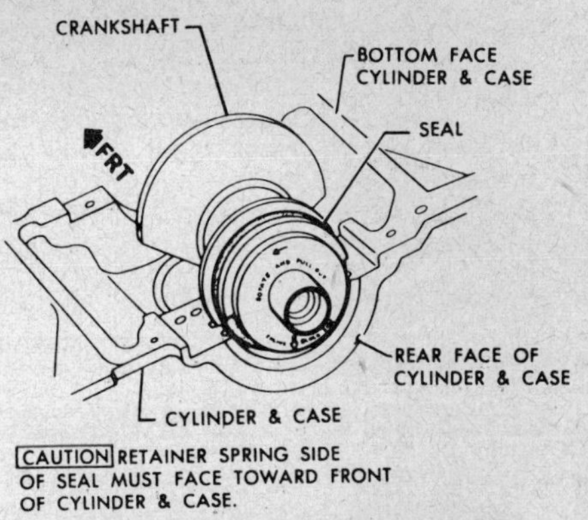

Fig. 25 Rear main seal installation. 1982–84 & early production 1985 V6-173

3. Lubricate inner and outer diameters of replacement seal with engine oil, then mount seal on tool J-35621 or equivalent.
4. Mount tool on rear of crankshaft, tightening screws snugly to ensure seal will be installed squarely on crankshaft.
5. Tighten wing nut on tool until it bottoms, then remove tool from crankshaft.
6. Reverse remaining procedure to complete installation.

V6-173

When rear main oil seal replacement is required on 1982-84 models, the existing seal should be replaced with the thin, one piece, lip type seal used on early production 1985 models. This seal, available as kit part No. 14081761, should be used to replace the rope type seal used on early production engines and the two piece rubber seal released for service on 1982-84 models, both for oil leak correction and during engine service. In addition, a redesigned crankshaft has been recommended for use on 1982-84 engines where installation of the one piece seal alone does not correct oil leakage at the rear main seal. This new crankshaft, part No. 14089826, has had the knurling removed from the rear seal area to improve sealing and oil retention.

Early production engines installed in 1985 models use the thin lip seal designated for service on 1982-84 engines (part No. 14081761, thin seal), while late production 1985 and all 1986 engines have been modified to use a thicker lip type seal (part No. 14077817). This type seal used can be determined by referring to the engine date code, stamped on the horizontal machined block surface just forward of the intake manifold between the cylinder heads. Engines with the code A050723 through A050829 and beginning with code K0730 use the thin seal. Engines beginning with code A050901 and T0730 use the thick seal. Models that use the thin type rear seal require engine and crankshaft removal for seal replacement, while the crankshaft need not be removed for seal replacement on models using the thick type seal.

1985-88 models use an O-ring to seal oil pump transfer passage from rear main bearing cap to cylinder block. The O-ring fits into a machined groove in the cylinder block and must be replaced whenever the rear main bearing cap is removed. In addition to the O-ring, the rear main bearing cap must also be sealed to the block using suitable sealing compound.

1982–84 & Early Production 1985

1. Remove engine as outlined previously.
2. Remove clutch assembly, if equipped, and flywheel or flex plate, drain engine oil and mount engine in suitable holding fixture.
3. Remove crankshaft as follows:
   a. Remove spark plugs, crankshaft pulley and damper.
   b. Remove oil pan and oil pump.
   c. Remove water pump, front cover, camshaft sprocket and timing chain, referring to "Timing Chain, Replace" procedure.
   d. Note position of connecting rod caps, remove caps and place in order for assembly, then push pistons to tops of bores, taking care not to mar crankshaft.
   e. Note installation position of main bearing caps, loosen main bearing bolts and remove main caps, keeping them in order for assembly.
   f. Lift crankshaft from block and set aside, taking care not to damage bearing surfaces.
4. Remove old oil seal and clean all sealant and foreign material from seal groove, engine case and bearing cap, and crankshaft sealing surface.
5. Inspect seal groove and crankshaft for wear, nicks, burrs and machining defects, and repair as needed.
6. Leaving seal on installation tool, coat outer diameter of seal with anaerobic sealer such as Loctite 515 or equivalent.
7. Push seal and tool assembly onto crankshaft as far as it will go, positioning tool so that arrow points toward cylinder case as shown in **Fig. 25.**
8. Ensure that main bearings in block are properly positioned and lubricated, then set crankshaft into engine, aligning oil seal with case groove.
9. Lightly lubricate crankshaft journals, and ensure that bearing shells are properly installed in main caps and that rear main cap sealing surfaces are clean and free from oil.
10. Apply a 1-2 mm bead of anaerobic sealer (Loctite 515 or equivalent) to rear main cap as shown in **Fig. 24,** install cap and torque retaining bolts to specifications. **It is important that cap joint be properly sealed to prevent oil leakage. Do not substitute RTV sealer for the specified anaerobic sealer, and do not apply an excessive amount of sealer to the cap, as this will cause oil leaks.**
11. Install remaining main bearing caps and torque to specifications.
12. Ensure that connecting rod bearings are properly seated in rods and caps, lightly lubricate bearings and crankpin journals, then reconnect rods to crankpins, install caps and torque cap nuts to specifications.
13. Complete engine reassembly and installation as outlined in appropriate service procedures.

Late Production 1985 & 1986–88 All (Thick Seal)

1. Raise and support vehicle.
2. Support engine as needed, then remove transmission.
3. Remove clutch and pressure plate, if equipped, then remove flywheel or flex plate.
4. Insert screwdriver through seal lip and pry seal from bore, taking care not to damage crankshaft.
5. Clean seal bore and crankshaft, then inspect for burrs, nicks and wear, and repair as needed.
6. Lightly lubricate replacement seal lip, mount seal on installer J-34686 or equivalent and seat dust lip of seal squarely against collar.
7. Lubricate outer diameter of seal, align dowel pin of tool with dowel pin hole in crankshaft, mount tool on crankshaft and torque retaining bolts to 2-5 ft. lbs.
8. Rotate "T" handle of tool clockwise, pressing seal into bore until collar is

tight against engine case to ensure that seal is fully seated.
9. Rotate "T" handle of tool counterclockwise to stop, then remove tool and ensure that seal is seated squarely in bore.
10. Reverse remaining procedure to complete installation.

OIL PAN

REPLACE

CAMARO V6-173 & V8-305

1. Disconnect battery ground cable, then remove fan shroud.
2. Raise and support vehicle, then drain crankcase.
3. Remove AIR pipe and hanger bolts from catalytic converter.
4. Remove starter motor attaching bolts and position starter motor aside.
5. Remove engine mount through bolts, then raise engine.
6. Remove oil pan attaching bolts and oil pan. **If oil pan removal is hampered by the forward crankshaft throw and/or counterweight extending downward, turn crankshaft as needed to put throw in a horizontal position.**
7. Reverse procedure to install, using a new gasket and seals, as equipped. If RTV sealer is used to seal pan, apply a 1/8 inch wide bead of sealant 1052366 or equivalent to pan sealing flange. **If M6 x 1.0 bolts are used, torque to 8 ft. lbs. If M8 x 1.25 bolts are used, torque to 18 ft. lbs.**

1982–84 V6-229

1. Disconnect battery ground cable, then remove upper half of fan shroud.
2. On models equipped with cruise control, remove cruise control servo bracket.
3. Raise vehicle and drain crankcase.
4. Disconnect exhaust crossover pipe from exhaust manifold.
5. Remove torque converter cover, if equipped.
6. Remove starter motor attaching bolts and position starter motor aside.
7. Remove lefthand engine mount through bolt, then loosen righthand engine mount through bolt.
8. Raise engine and reinstall through bolt. Do not tighten through bolt.
9. Remove oil pan attaching bolts and remove oil pan.
10. Reverse procedure to install. Torque oil pan attaching bolts to 80 inch lbs. Torque engine mount attaching bolts to 50 ft. lbs.

V8 ENGINES EXC. CORVETTE & CAMARO

1. Disconnect battery ground cable.
2. Remove air cleaner and snorkle.
3. On models with 2 piece fan shroud, remove upper half of shroud. On models with one piece shroud, remove retaining screws and release shroud from lower retaining clips.
4. Remove distributor cap to prevent breakage and lay cap aside, leaving spark plug wires connected.

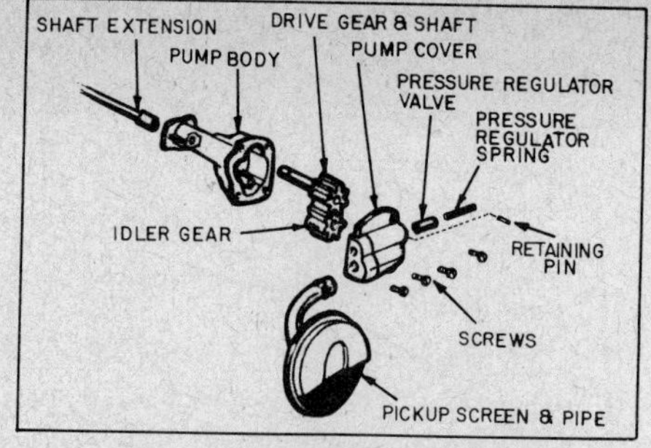

Fig. 26 Oil pump exploded view V6 & V8 engines

5. On models equipped with cruise control, remove cruise control servo bracket.
6. On all models, raise and support vehicle, then drain oil pan.
7. Disconnect exhaust crossover pipe at exhaust manifold and catalytic converter.
8. Remove flywheel cover or torque converter cover. **If equipped with manual transmission, remove starter motor before the flywheel cover.**
9. Support engine with a suitable jack and remove engine mount through bolts.
10. Remove oil pan bolts and lower oil pan. Check that the forward crankshaft throw and/or counterweight is not extending downward as to block removal of oil pan. Rotate crankshaft as necessary to position crankshaft to permit pan removal.
11. Raise engine and install engine mount through bolts.
12. Remove oil pan.
13. Reverse procedure to install. Torque oil pan bolts to 80 inch lbs.

CORVETTE

1982

1. Disconnect battery ground cable.
2. Raise and support vehicle, then drain oil pan.
3. Remove engine oil dipstick and tube.
4. Disconnect idler arm and lower steering linkage.
5. Remove flywheel splash shield.
6. Remove oil pan bolts and oil pan.
7. Reverse procedure to install. Torque oil pan bolts to 80 inch lbs.

1984–86

1. Disconnect battery ground cable.
2. Raise and support vehicle, then drain crankcase.
3. Remove starter brace and retaining bolts, and secure starter aside.
4. Remove flywheel cover.
5. Remove oil pan bolts and oil pan.
6. Reverse procedure to install. Torque oil pan retaining bolts to 80 inch lbs.

1987–88

1. Disconnect battery ground cable.
2. Raise and support vehicle, then drain crankcase.
3. Disconnect transmission oil cooler lines at flywheel cover.
4. Disconnect catalytic converter AIR pipe clamps at manifold and exhaust pipe.
5. Disconnect starter motor electrical connectors, then remove starter motor.
6. Remove oil filter, then disconnect oil cooler adapter at block.
7. Remove flywheel cover, then disconnect oil cooler line at oil pan.
8. Remove ESC shield, then the front crossmember braces.
9. Remove oil pan attaching bolts, then rotate crankshaft and remove oil pan.
10. Reverse procedure to install. Torque oil pan retaining bolts to 80 inch lbs.

OIL PUMP

OIL PUMP, REPLACE

1. Remove oil pan as described previously.
2. Remove pump to rear main bearing cap bolt and remove pump and extension shaft.
3. Reverse procedure to install. Make sure that installed position of oil pump screen is with bottom edge parallel to oil pan rails.

OIL PUMP SERVICE

1. Remove oil pump as described previously.
2. Remove pump cover screws and pump cover, **Fig. 26.**
3. Mark gear teeth so they can be reassembled with same teeth indexing, then remove drive gear, idler gear and shaft.
4. Remove pressure regulator valve retaining pin, pressure regulator valve and related parts.
5. If pickup screen and pipe require replacement, mount pump in a soft-jawed vise and extract pipe from pump.
6. Wash all parts in cleaning solvent and dry with compressed air.
7. Inspect pump body and cover for cracks and excessive wear.
8. Inspect pump gears for damage or excessive wear.
9. Check drive gear shaft for looseness in pump body.
10. Inspect inside of pump cover for wear that would allow oil to leak past the ends of the gears.
11. Inspect pickup screen and pipe assembly for damage to screen, pipe or relief grommet.
12. Check pressure regulator valve for fit in pump housing.
13. Reverse procedure to assemble. Turn drive shaft by hand to check for smooth operation. **The pump gears and body are not serviced separately. If the pump gears or body are damaged or worn, the pump assembly should be replaced. Also, if the pickup screen and pump assembly was removed, it should be replaced with a new one as loss of the press fit condition could result in an air leak and loss of oil pressure.**

BELT TENSION DATA

Belt	New Lbs.	Used Lbs.
1982–83		
V8-350 Diesel	110-140	70-80
Power Steering Pump Exc. V6-231 & V8-350 Diesel	120-130	70-80
V6-231	165	100
V8-350 Diesel	110-140	70-80
A/C Compressor 4-151	135-165	65
V6-133 & 229; V8-267, 305, 350	145	65-80
V6-231	165	100
V6-262 Diesel & V8-350 Diesel	135-165	85-95
AIR Pump 4-151	120-150	55
V6-173	100	45
V6-229, V8-267, 305 & 350	130	65-80
Alternator 4-151	120-150	55
V6-173	145	65-80
V6-229, V8-267, 305 & 350	130	65-80
V6-231	145	80
V6-262 Diesel & V8-350 Diesel	110-140	70-80
Power Steering Pump 4-151	120-150	55
V6-173 & 229; V8-267, 305 & 350	135	65-80
V6-231	165	100
V6-262 Diesel & V8-350 Diesel	110-140	70-80
1984 Exc. Corvette		
A/C Compressor 4-151	135-165	65
V6-173 & 229; V8-305 & 350	135-145	85-95
V6-231	165	100
V8-350 Diesel	135-165	85-95
AIR Pump 4-151	120-150	55
V6-173	100	45
V6-229, V8-305 & 350	120-130	70-80

Belt	New Lbs.	Used Lbs.
1982–83		
Alternator 4-151	120-150	55
V6-173	145	65-80
V6-229, V8-305 & V8-350	120-130	70-80
V6-231	145	80
V8-350 Diesel	110-140	70-80
Power Steering Pump 4-151	120-150	55
V6-173	135	65-80
V6-229, V8-305 & V8-350	120-130	70-80
V8-350 Diesel	110-140	70-80
1984–88 Corvette		
Serpentine Drive Belt	120-140 ①	120-140 ①
1985–86 Exc. Corvette		
A/C Compressor V6-262 & V8-305	135-145	85-95
V8-350 Diesel	135-165	85-95
AIR Pump, Alternator & Power Steering Pump V6-262 & V8-305	120-130	70-80
V8-350 Diesel	110-140	70-80
1987–88 Exc. Corvette		
A/C Compressor Exc. V6-173	135-145	85-95
AIR Pump, Alternator & Power Steering Pump Exc. V6-173	120-130	70-80
Serpentine Drive Belt V6-173	②	②

①—Checked between alternator & AIR Pump.

②—Indicator mark on moveable portion of tensioner must be within limits of slotted area on stationary portion of tensioner.

WATER PUMP REPLACE

EXC. 1984–88 CORVETTE

1. Disconnect battery ground cable and drain cooling system.
2. Remove fan shroud or upper radiator support, as applicable, then remove accessory drive belts.
3. Remove fan and pulley from water pump hub.
4. Remove upper and lower alternator brackets. On Camaro, remove AIR brace and bracket.
5. If equipped with power steering, remove power steering lower bracket from water pump and position aside.
6. Remove radiator lower hose and heater hose from water pump.
7. Remove water pump attaching bolts and pump, noting position of bolts for assembly.
8. Reverse procedure to install.

1984–88 CORVETTE

1. Disconnect battery ground cable, and drain cooling system.
2. Rotate belt tensioner counterclockwise to release tension, and remove drive belt.
3. Remove water pump and AIR pump pulleys, and disconnect air management valve adapter from AIR pump.
4. Remove AIR pump, then disconnect fuel supply and return lines. **Relieve fuel system pressure before disconnecting fuel hoses.**
5. Remove A/C compressor rear braces and lower mounting bolt.
6. Remove nuts securing A/C compressor and idler pulley bracket to water pump and disconnect electrical connector from compressor.
7. Move compressor bracket forward, remove upper mounting bolt and compressor, and secure aside.
8. Disconnect AIR hoses at check valves and AIR pipe at intake manifold and power steering bracket.
9. Remove power steering reservoir bracket and upper alternator mounting bolt.
10. Remove lower AIR pump bracket, then disconnect hoses from water pump.
11. Remove mounting bolts and water pump.
12. Reverse procedure to install.

FUEL PUMP REPLACE

CARBURETED ENGINES

1. Disconnect fuel lines from pump.
2. Disconnect vapor return line, if so equipped.
3. Remove fuel pump attaching bolts and pump.
4. Reverse procedure to install.

Diesel Engine Section

NOTE: Refer "Oldsmobile Diesel Engine Section" for service procedures on the V6-262 and V8-350 Diesel engines.

Clutch & Manual Transmission Section

INDEX

CLUTCH PEDAL

ADJUST

1982–83 EXCEPT CORVETTE

1. Disconnect return spring at clutch fork.
2. Rotate clutch lever and shaft assembly until pedal is against rubber bumper on dash brace.
3. Push outer end of clutch fork rearward until throwout bearing lightly contacts pressure plate fingers.
4. Install pushrod in gauge hole and increase length until all lash is removed, **Fig. 1.**
5. Remove swivel or rod from gauge hole and insert into lower hole on lever. Install retainer and tighten locknut being careful not to change rod length.
6. Reinstall return spring and check pedal free travel, which should be 1/2 to 1 inch.

1984–88 CAMARO

The hydraulic clutch release mechanism on these models consists of a clutch master cylinder, slave cylinder and connecting hose which is serviced as a complete assembly. The hydraulic system is supplied filled with fluid, and no adjustment or bleeding is required. Before removing release mechanism for service, verify that a malfunction exists as follows:

1. Remove clutch housing dust shield and note position of slave cylinder plunger.
2. Depress clutch pedal fully and measure slave cylinder plunger travel.
3. If plunger moves release lever a minimum of .57 inch, check clutch disc, pressure plate, release fork and bearing for damage and repair as needed.
4. If plunger does not move lever at least .57 inches, check fluid level in clutch master cylinder with pedal depressed, and fill to step in reservoir. **Do not overfill. Upper portion of reservoir must be open to accept fluid displaced in slave cylinder due to clutch wear.**
5. Recheck plunger travel and check hydraulic components for leaks.
6. If plunger travel is still less than .57 inch, or if excessive leakage is noted, replace hydraulic system as an assembly.

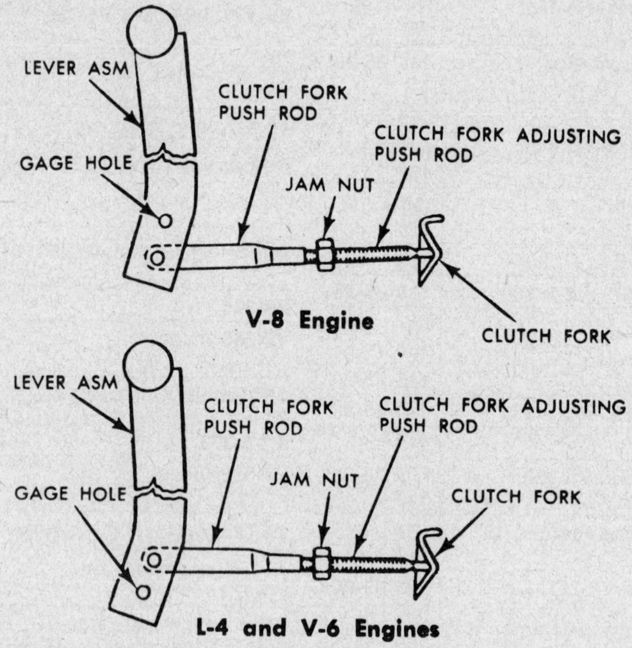

Fig. 1 Clutch linkage adjustment. 1982–83 Camaro

1984–88 CORVETTE

The clutch release mechanism on these models is hydraulically operated, and is not adjustable. When the clutch pedal is depressed, the pedal pushrod contacts a plunger in the clutch master cylinder bore. The plunger first closes off the master cylinder fluid return port, then when moved further, forces fluid under pressure into the clutch slave cylinder. As pressure is applied to the slave cylinder, the slave cylinder piston is forced outward activating the clutch release fork. To diagnose malfunctions in the clutch release system, proceed as follows:

Inspection

1. With engine running at normal operating temperature and brakes applied, hold clutch pedal approximately 1/2 inch from fully depressed position and move transmission selector between 1st and reverse several times.
2. If transmission selector can be moved without binding or gear clash, clutch is releasing properly.
3. If shifter cannot be moved or if gear clash is evident, inspect linkage, fork and ball stud for damage and wear, and replace as needed.
4. If linkage is satisfactory, check clutch pedal and slave cylinder travel.
5. Clutch pedal travel should be 7 3/8 inch, and slave cylinder plunger travel should be .70 inch, measured at the clutch fork.
6. If pedal travel is not within specifications, repair as needed. If plunger travel is not as specified, bleed or repair hydraulic system.

Bleeding

1. Fill master cylinder reservoir with specified fluid.
2. Raise and support vehicle.
3. Remove slave cylinder attaching bolts and secure cylinder at 45° angle with bleeder screw at highest point.
4. Fully depress and hold clutch pedal, then open bleeder.
5. Close bleeder then release clutch pedal.

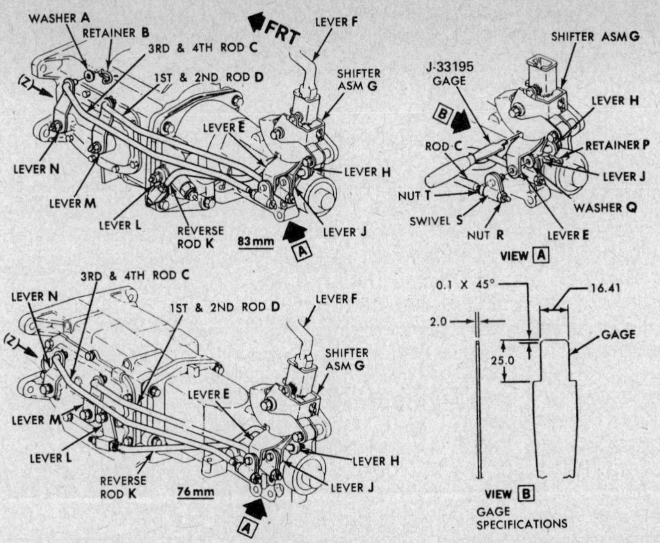

Fig. 2 Four speed shift linkage adjustment. 1982–84 Camaro

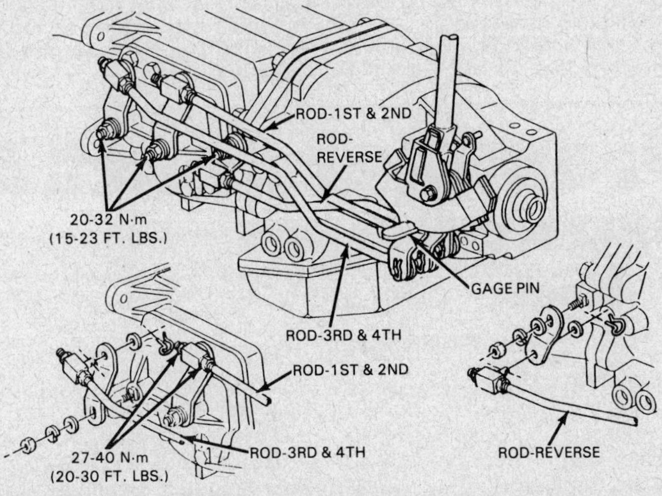

Fig. 3 Four speed shift linkage adjustment. 1984–88 Corvette

6. Repeat steps 4 and 5 until all air has been purged from system, remount slave cylinder and repeat inspection. **Check and fill master cylinder reservoir, as needed, to ensure that no air is drawn into system during bleeding.**

CLUTCH
REPLACE

1. Support engine and remove transmission as outlined further on.
2. On all except 1984-88 Camaro and Corvette, disconnect clutch fork pushrod and return spring. On 1984-88 Camaro and Corvette, remove slave cylinder heat shield and cylinder from flywheel housing. **Prior to removing slave cylinder on 1984-88 Camaro and Corvette, disconnect pushrod from clutch master cylinder.**
3. Remove flywheel housing.
4. Slide clutch fork from ball stud and remove fork from dust boot. **Look for "X" mark on flywheel and on clutch cover. If "X" mark is not evident, prick punch marks on flywheel and clutch cover for indexing purposes during installation.**
5. Loosen clutch-to-flywheel attaching bolts evenly one turn at a time until spring pressure is released. Then remove bolts and clutch assembly.
6. Reverse procedure to install, using suitable pilot tool to center clutch disc. Tighten clutch cover bolts evenly and gradually to avoid distorting cover.

MANUAL TRANSMISSION
REPLACE

It may be necessary to remove the catalytic converter and its support bracket to facilitate transmission removal.

CAMARO
Four Speed

1. Raise and support vehicle, then drain transmission fluid.
2. Remove torque arm and propeller shaft.
3. Disconnect speedometer cable and all electrical connectors at transmission, then remove exhaust brace.
4. Remove shifter support attaching bolts from transmission and disconnect shift linkage from shifter.
5. Support transmission with a suitable jack, then remove crossmember and transmission mount attaching bolts and the crossmember and mount.
6. Remove transmission attaching bolts and the transmission.
7. Reverse procedure to install.

Five Speed

1. Disconnect battery ground cable, remove shifter boot retaining screws and slide boot up lever.
2. Remove shift lever retaining bolts and lever, then raise and support vehicle.
3. Remove torque arm and propeller shaft, and on 1983 models disconnect clutch cable.
4. Disconnect speedometer cable and electrical connectors from transmission.
5. Support transmission and remove transmission mount retaining bolts and catalytic converter bracket.
6. Remove crossmember retaining bolts, crossmember and bolts securing flywheel cover.
7. Remove bolts securing transmission to engine, transmission and flywheel cover.
8. Reverse procedure to install.

1984–88
CORVETTE

1. Disconnect battery ground cable and remove air cleaner assembly.
2. Disconnect overdrive throttle valve cable from throttle linkage.
3. Remove distributor cap to prevent damage and lay cap aside, leaving plug wires connected.
4. Raise and support vehicle.
5. Remove complete exhaust system as follows:
   a. Disconnect AIR pipe from converter and remove AIR pipe clamps from manifold.
   b. Disconnect electrical connector to oxygen sensor.
   c. Remove bolts securing exhaust hangers to mufflers and hanger bracket from converter.
   d. Disconnect exhaust system from manifolds and remove system as an assembly.
   e. Remove exhaust hanger from transmission.
6. Support transmission with suitable jack.
7. Remove bolts securing driveline beam to transmission and axle housings, then the driveline beam.
8. Mark installation position of propeller shaft, then remove shaft assembly. **Tape bearing cups to universal**

joints to prevent loss of needle bearings.

9. Disconnect oil cooler lines and throttle valve cable from overdrive unit.
10. Disconnect shift linkage at transmission side cover, noting position for installation.
11. Disconnect electrical connectors from transmission and overdrive unit.
12. Lower transmission and support engine.
13. Remove bolts securing transmission to bellhousing, slide transmission rearward until input shaft clears housing, then lower transmission from vehicle.

FOUR SPEED SHIFT LINKAGE

ADJUST

1982–84 CAMARO

1. Place levers (L), (M) and (N) in neutral position, **Fig. 2.** To obtain neutral position, move levers counterclockwise to forward detent, then clockwise one detent.
2. Move lever (F) to neutral position. Align holes of levers (E), (H) and (J) with notch in lever and bracket assembly, then insert Gauge J-33195 or equivalent to secure levers in neutral position.
3. Attach rod (C) to lever (N) with washer (A) and retainer (B).
4. Loosely assemble nuts (R) and (T) and swivel (S) on rod (C).
5. Insert swivel (S) into lever (E), then attach washer (Q) and secure with retainer (P). Apply a load on lever (N) in direction of arrow (Z). At the same time, finger tighten nuts (T) and (R) against swivel, then torque nuts to 25 ft. lbs.
6. Repeat steps 3, 4 and 5 for rod (D) and levers (J) and (M).
7. Repeat steps 3, 4 and 5 for rod (K) and levers (H) and (L).
8. Remove gauge and check that center lines of shift levers are aligned to provide free crossover motion.

1984–88 CORVETTE

1. Disconnect battery ground cable.
2. Remove left seat, disconnecting electrical connectors as needed.
3. Remove shift knob, console cover and glove box lock.
4. Remove left console side panel and shifter cover.
5. Loosen front and rear adjuster nut on each shift rod.
6. Ensure that transmission is in neutral, align shifter levers in neutral position, then insert gauge pin through lever alignment holes, **Fig. 3.**
7. Equalize swivels on each shift rod, hand tightening front and rear adjuster nuts simultaneously.
8. Simultaneously torque front and rear adjuster nuts on each shift rod to 20-30 ft. lbs.
9. Remove gauge pin and check shifter operation.
10. Reinstall components removed to gain access to shifter.

FIVE SPEED SHIFT LINKAGE

ADJUST

1985–88 CAMARO

The gear shift lever assembly is floor mounted and located on top of extension housing. The shift assembly does not require adjustment.

Rear Axle, Propeller Shaft & Brakes

INDEX

REAR AXLE

CORVETTE

These models are equipped with Positraction differentials.

In this axle, the drive pinion is mounted in two tapered roller bearings that are preloaded by a spacer. The pinion is positioned by a shim located between the head of the drive pinion and the rear pinion bearing. The front bearing is held in place by a large washer and a locking pinion nut.

The differential is supported in the carrier by two tapered roller side bearings.

The differential side bearings are preloaded by shims between the bearings and carrier housing. The differential assembly is positioned for proper ring gear and pinion backlash by varying the position and thickness of these shims.

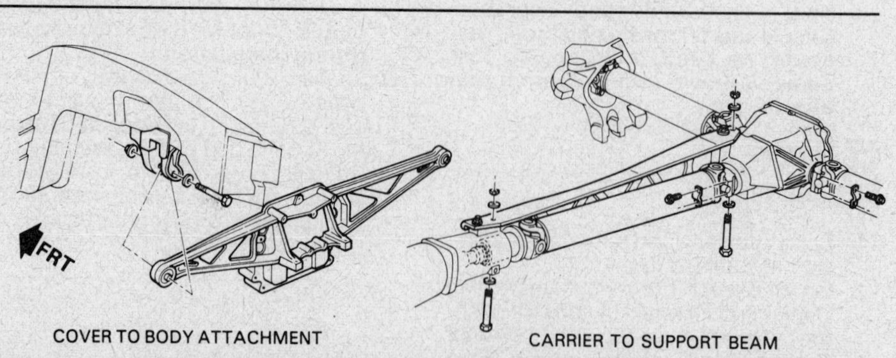

Fig. 1 Rear axle assembly mounting. 1984–88 Corvette

The ring gear is bolted to the case. The case houses two side gears in mesh with two pinions mounted on a pinion shaft which is held in place by a lock screw. The side gears are backed by thrust washers.

The differential side gears drive two splined yokes which are retained by snap rings located on the yoke splined end. The yokes are supported on caged needle bearings pressed into the carrier, adjacent to the differential bearings. A lip seal, pressed into the carrier outboard of the bearing, prevents oil leakage and dirt entry.

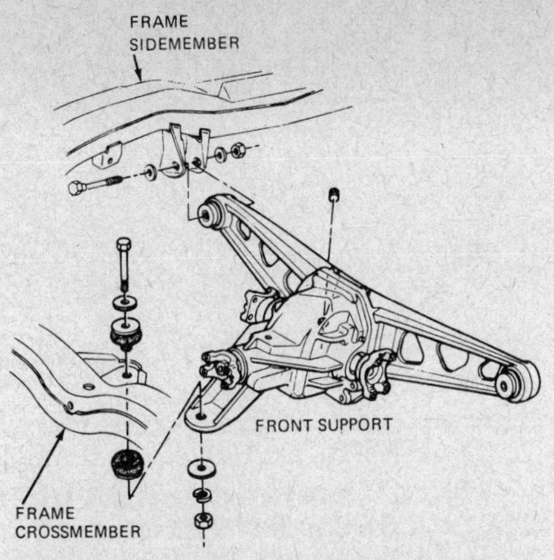

Fig. 2 Rear axle assembly mounting. 1982 Corvette

EXC. CORVETTE

In these rear axles, the rear axle housing and differential carrier are cast into an integral assembly. The drive pinion assembly is mounted in two opposed tapered roller bearings. The pinion bearings are preloaded by a spacer behind the front bearing. The pinion is positioned by a washer between the head of the pinion and the rear bearing.

The differential is supported in the carrier by two tapered roller side bearings. These bearings are preloaded by spacers located between the bearings and carrier housing. The differential assembly is positioned for proper ring gear and pinion backlash by varying these spacers. The differential case houses two side gears in mesh with two pinions mounted on a pinion shaft which is held in place by a lock pin. The side gears and pinions are backed by thrust washers.

A limited slip rear axle, available on most models, uses disc or cone type clutches which are splined to the side gears to "lock" the axle shafts to the case, or in effect to each other. Therefore, if one drive wheel is on a slippery surface, the other wheel must develop more torque than on a standard type differential before the differential case will allow wheel spin. However, axle shaft torques produced during cornering are sufficient to overcome the clutch action, allowing axles to rotate at different speeds.

REAR AXLE

REPLACE

CORVETTE

1984–88

1. Remove air cleaner and distributor shields, then disconnect cap from distributor.
2. Raise and support vehicle, and remove spare tire, tire cover and under body braces, as required.
3. Remove exhaust system assembly as follows:
   a. Disconnect AIR pipe at converter and AIR pipe clamps at manifold.
   b. Disconnect electrical connector from oxygen sensor.
   c. Support exhaust system, remove bolts securing mufflers to hangers, and remove converter bracket.
   d. Disconnect exhaust pipes at manifolds and remove exhaust system.
4. Disconnect leaf spring from spindle support knuckles, then remove bolts securing spring to differential carrier and spring as outlined in "Rear Suspension Section."
5. Scribe mark between cam bolts and brackets, then remove cam bolts and mounting bracket from carrier.
6. Disconnect tie rods from left and right spindle support knuckles.
7. Remove straps securing driveshaft universal joints to differential side yokes, push wheel and tire assemblies outward, and disconnect drive shafts from side yokes. **Tape bearing cups to universal joint yokes to prevent loss of needle bearings.**
8. Remove straps securing propeller shaft universal joint to pinion flange, push propeller shaft forward into transmission and tie shaft to support beam.
9. Support transmission and remove bolts securing differential carrier beam to frame brackets, **Fig. 1.**
10. Remove mounting bolts at front of differential carrier and carrier assembly.
11. Reverse procedure to install, then check rear suspension alignment.

1982

1. Raise vehicle and remove spare tire.
2. Remove spare tire cover by removing support hooks attached to carrier cover.
3. Remove exhaust system, then position jack stands under front control arms to support vehicle.
4. Remove heat shield.
5. Using a suitable jack and C-clamp, raise spring to relieve tension, then disconnect spring from spindle support.
6. Remove rear spring cover plate.
7. Place alignment marks on cam bolt for reassembly, then remove cam bolt from bracket.
8. Remove bolts attaching strut bracket to carrier, then lower strut rods by pushing outward on wheel and tire assembly.
9. Mark propeller shaft and pinion flange, then disconnect propeller shaft.
10. Remove differential carrier to frame crossmember mount bolt, **Fig. 2.**
11. Position jack stand under carrier, then remove carrier to body attaching bolts, **Fig. 2.**
12. Lower differential to gain access to cover bolts.
13. Drain differential and remove cover.
14. Disconnect drive shaft at spindle at companion flange.
15. Lower and remove differential assembly.
16. Remove drive shafts from side yokes.
17. Reverse procedure to install.

EXC. CORVETTE

Construction of the axle assembly is such that service operations may be performed with the housing installed in the vehicle or with the housing removed and installed in a holding fixture. The following procedure is necessary only when the housing requires replacement.

1. Raise and support vehicle, then support rear axle with a suitable jack.
2. Disconnect shock absorbers from lower mountings.
3. Remove propeller shaft.
4. Disconnect upper control arms from axle housing attachments, if equipped with coil springs.
5. Disconnect brake line from axle housing junction block and the parking brake cable.
6. Disconnect lower control arms from axle housing attachments, if equipped with coil springs.
7. On models equipped with coil springs, lower axle slowly until springs can be moved. Roll axle assembly out from under vehicle.
8. On models equipped with leaf springs, remove leaf springs as outlined under "Leaf Springs & Bushings, Replace" in Rear Suspension Section. Roll axle assembly out from under vehicle.
9. Reverse procedure to install.

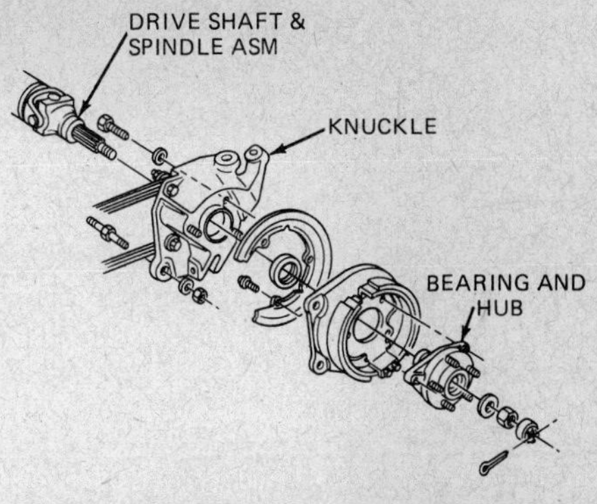

Fig. 3 Rear hub & spindle assembly, exploded view. 1984–88 Corvette

AXLE SHAFT

REPLACE

EXC. CORVETTE

1. Raise vehicle and remove wheel and brake drum or rotor.
2. Drain lube from carrier and remove cover.
3. Remove differential pinion shaft lock screw and remove differential pinion shaft.
4. Push flanged end of axle shaft toward center of vehicle and remove C-lock from button end of shaft.
5. Remove axle shaft from housing, being careful not to damage seal.
6. Reverse procedure to install the axle shaft.

1982 CORVETTE

1. Raise and support vehicle.
2. Disconnect inboard driveshaft trunnion from side gear yoke.
3. Remove plastic splash shields attaching screws and the shields.
4. Remove bolts securing shaft flange to spindle drive flange.
5. Scribe a mark on the camber adjust-

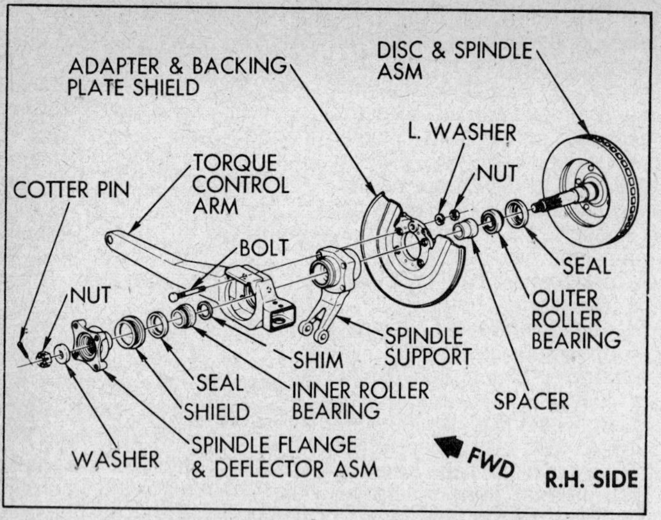

Fig. 4 Rear hub & spindle assembly, exploded view. 1982 Corvette

ing cam and mounting bracket for alignment during assembly.

6. Loosen camber adjusting nut and rotate cam so the high point of the cam faces inboard. This pushes the control arm outboard providing spindle-driveshaft clearance.
7. Remove driveshaft by withdrawing outboard end first.
8. Reverse procedure to install, then check rear suspension alignment.

1984–88 CORVETTE

1. Remove center cap from wheel.
2. Remove cotter pin, spindle nut and washer from spindle, **Fig. 3.**
3. Raise and support vehicle, and remove wheel and tire.
4. Disconnect tie rod and spring from spindle support knuckle as outlined in "Rear Suspension Section."
5. Scribe a reference mark between cam bolt and bracket, remove cam bolt and separate spindle support rod from bracket.
6. Remove straps securing inner universal joint to drive yoke, pull knuckle assembly outward, and disconnect driveshaft from yoke. **Tape bearing cups to universal joint yoke to prevent loss of needle bearings.**
7. Pull spindle out of hub and remove driveshaft.
8. Reverse procedure to install, torquing cam bolt to 158-213 ft. lbs. and spindle nut to 151-177 ft. lbs., then check rear suspension alignment.

REAR SPINDLE & BEARINGS

REPLACE

1982 CORVETTE

1. Raise and support vehicle, and remove wheel and tire.
2. Remove axle driveshaft as outlined in "Drive Axle, Replace."
3. Set parking brake to prevent spindle from turning, and remove cotter pin and nut from spindle, **Fig. 4.**
4. Release parking brake and remove spindle flange and deflector.
5. Remove 2 brake caliper mounting bolts and secure caliper assembly aside.
6. Disconnect shock absorber and strut rod from spindle support.
7. Install thread protector over end of spindle, and puller J-22602 or equivalent on strut rod stud, **Fig. 5. Ensure puller is installed vertically on spindle support before tightening puller screw.**
8. Tighten puller screw and remove spindle and outer bearing.
9. Remove outer bearing from spindle using a suitable puller, then the outer seal.
10. Remove spacer tube, endplay shim, inner bearing, race, seal and outer bearing race from spindle support.
11. Clean and inspect all components, and replace as needed.
12. Install bearing races in spindle support using driver J-7827 or equivalent, and pack bearings with EPB-2 bearing lube or equivalent.
13. Check endplay prior to spindle installation as follows:
    a. Mount outer bearing, spacer and endplay shim on gauging tool J-24626, and insert assembly into spindle support.
    b. Install inner bearing, washer and nut on gauging tool, ensure bearings are properly seated in races, and torque nut to 100 ft. lbs.
    c. Mount dial indicator on control arm with pointer bearing on outer end of gauging tool.
    d. Move gauging tool in and out while observing endplay on indicator.
    e. Endplay should be .001 to .008 inch. If endplay is not within specifications, replace shim as needed to provide proper clearance. **If gauging tool is not available, install spindle and bearings as outlined, then check endplay at spindle flange. If endplay is not within specifications, note dial indicator reading, press out spindle, and replace shim with one which will provide .001 to .008 inch clearance.**

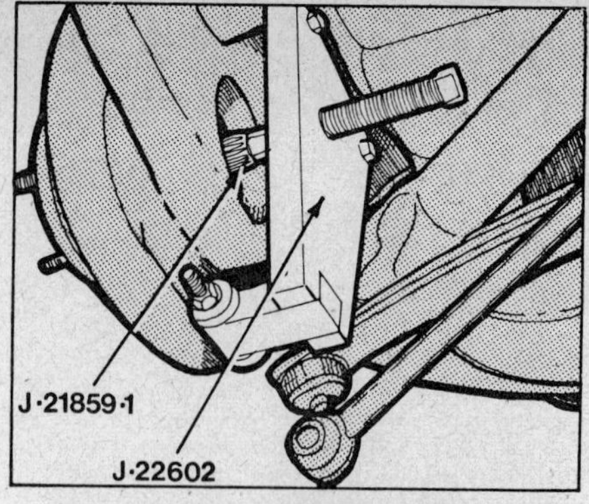

Fig. 5 Spindle removal. 1982 Corvette

14. Remove gauging tool, bearings, spacer and shim.
15. Install outer bearing in race, then seat outer seal in bore of spindle support using a suitable driver.
16. Insert spindle through outer seal and bearing, taking care not to damage seal.
17. Install spacer, shim and inner bearing over end of spindle.
18. Install threaded shaft J-24490-1 on end of spindle.
19. Install sleeve J-24490-2, washer and nut on threaded shaft, then tighten nut to draw spindle into final installed position.
20. Remove installation tool, install inner seal and reverse remaining procedure to complete installation. Torque spindle nut to 100 ft. lbs., and check rear suspension alignment. **If specified nut does not allow insertion of cotter pin, tighten spindle flange nut to next flat, then install pin.**

1984–88 CORVETTE

1. Remove drive shaft assembly as outlined in "Drive Axle, Replace."
2. Remove 2 bolts securing brake caliper bracket to support knuckle, secure caliper aside, then remove brake rotor.
3. Remove hub and bearing retaining bolts using a No. 45 Torx driver, **Fig. 3.**
4. Remove hub and bearing assembly.
5. Reverse procedure to install, torquing hub retaining bolts to 59-73 ft. lbs., then check rear suspension alignment.

PROPELLER SHAFT

REPLACE

EXC. 1984–88 CORVETTE

1. With transmission in neutral and parking brake released, raise and support vehicle.
2. Mark position of shaft in relation to pinion flange for reassembly.
3. Remove straps securing universal

joint to pinion flange, then disconnect shaft from flange. **Tape bearing cups to universal joint to prevent loss of needle bearings.**
4. Slide yoke out of transmission and remove propeller shaft. Insert suitable plug in transmission to prevent fluid loss.
5. Reverse procedure to install.

1984–88 CORVETTE

1. With transmission in neutral and parking brake released, raise and support vehicle, then remove under body braces, as required.
2. Remove exhaust system as follows:
   a. Disconnect AIR pipe from catalytic converter and exhaust pipe.
   b. Disconnect electrical connector to oxygen sensor.
   c. Remove bolts securing muffler to hangers, disconnect exhaust pipes from manifolds and remove exhaust system as an assembly.
3. Support transmission, remove support beam retaining bolts and support beam.
4. Mark position of shaft in relation to pinion flange for installation.
5. Remove straps securing universal joint to pinion flange, then disconnect shaft from flange. **Tape bearing cups to universal joint to prevent loss of needle bearings.**
6. Slide yoke out of transmission and remove propeller shaft. Insert suitable plug in transmission to prevent fluid loss.
7. Reverse procedure to install.

SERVICE BRAKES

ADJUST

These brakes, have self-adjusting shoe mechanisms that assure correct lining-to-drum clearances at all times. The automatic adjusters operate only when the brakes are applied as the car is moving rearward or when the car comes to an uphill stop.

Although the brakes are self-adjusting, an initial adjustment is necessary after the brake shoes have been relined or replaced, or when the length of the adjusting screw has been changed during some other service operation.

Frequent usage of an automatic transmission forward range to halt reverse vehicle motion may prevent the automatic adjusters from functioning, thereby inducing low pedal heights. Should low pedal heights be encountered, it is recommended that numerous forward and reverse stops be made until satisfactory pedal height is obtained.

If a low pedal condition cannot be corrected by making numerous reverse stops (provided the hydraulic system is free of air) it indicates that the self-adjusting mechanism is not functioning. Therefore it will be necessary to remove the brake drum, clean, free up and lubricate the adjusting mechanism. Then adjust the brakes, being sure the parking brake is fully released.

1. Using a suitable punch, knock out lanced area in backing plate or drum.

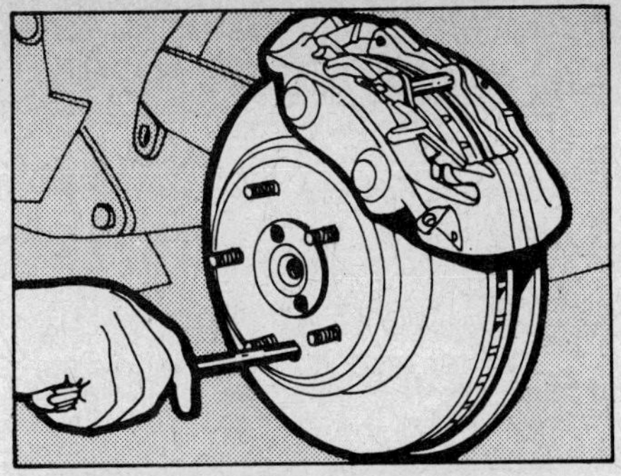

Fig. 6 Parking brake shoe adjustment. Corvette

If drum is installed on vehicle when this is done, remove drum and clean brake compartment of all metal. **When adjustment is completed, a new hole cover must be installed in the backing plate.**
2. Using Tool J-6166 or equivalent, turn brake adjusting screw to expand brake shoes at each wheel until wheel can just be turned by hand. Drag should be equal on all wheels.
3. On all except Camaro, back off adjusting screw at each wheel 30 notches.
4. On Camaro, back off screw 12 notches.
5. If shoe still drags slightly on drum, back off adjusting screw an additional one or two notches.
6. When adjusting screw has been backed off approximately 12 notches, brakes should be free of drag. Heavy drag at this point indicates tight parking brake cables.
7. Install adjusting hole cover in brake backing plate.
8. Check parking brake for proper adjustment.

PARKING BRAKE

ADJUST

EXC. CORVETTE & CAMARO W/REAR DISC BRAKES

1. Jack up both rear wheels.
2. Apply parking brake two to three notches.
3. Tighten adjusting nut until left rear wheel can just be rotated rearward but is locked when forward rotation is attempted.
4. Release parking brake and check to ensure that rear wheels rotate freely in either direction with no brake drag.

CAMARO W/REAR DISC BRAKES

1. Lubricate parking brake cables at underbody rub points and at equalizer hooks and ensure free movement of all cables.
2. With parking brake fully released, jack up both rear wheels.
3. Remove slack from cable by holding brake cable stud and tightening equalizer nut. **After tightening nut, check that caliper levers are against stops on caliper housing. If not, loosen cable until levers return to stops.**
4. Actuate parking brake several times to check adjustment.

1982 CORVETTE

1. Release parking brake lever, then raise and support vehicle.
2. Loosen parking brake cable adjusting nut at equalizer until brake shoe actuating levers move freely to the released position with slack in cables.
3. Remove rear wheels and turn each brake rotor until parking brake shoe star adjuster is visible through hole in rotor hub.
4. Insert a suitable adjusting tool through hole in rotor, and tighten adjusters by moving hand away from floor, **Fig. 6.**
5. Adjust one side at a time, tightening adjuster until rotor cannot be turned by hand, then backing star wheel off 6 to 8 notches.
6. Install rear wheels and pull parking brake lever up 13 notches to the applied position.
7. Tighten cable adjusting nut at equalizer until 80 lbs. pull is required to lift parking brake lever to the 14th notch, then secure adjustment with locknut.
8. Release parking brake lever and check adjustment. Rear wheels should turn freely in both directions with no brake drag.

1984–88 CORVETTE

1. Release parking brake lever, then raise and support vehicle.
2. Remove rear wheels, then install lug nuts on 2 opposite wheel studs to hold brake rotor in position.
3. Back caliper pistons into bores.
4. Loosen parking brake cable adjusting nut until there is no tension on parking brake shoes.
5. Turn each brake rotor until parking brake shoe star adjuster is visible through hole in rotor.
6. Adjusting one side at a time, tighten adjuster until rotor cannot be turned by hand, then back star wheel off 5 to 7 notches. **Adjust parking brake shoes by inserting a suitable tool through hole in rotor. On driver's side, tighten adjuster by moving handle of tool upwards. On passenger side, tighten adjuster by moving handle of tool downwards.**
7. Install rear wheels and pull parking brake lever up 2 notches.
8. Tighten cable adjusting nut at equalizer until there is drag on wheels.
9. Release parking brake lever and check adjustment. No drag should be felt when rotating wheels.

MASTER CYLINDER

REPLACE

1. Disconnect brake pipes from master cylinder. Plug lines and master cylinder ports to prevent entry of foreign material.

2. Disconnect brake pedal from master cylinder pushrod, if equipped with manual brakes.
3. Remove master cylinder attaching nuts and the master cylinder.
4. Reverse procedure to install.

POWER BRAKE UNIT

HYDRO-BOOST

Pump brake pedal several times with engine off to deplete accumulator of fluid.

1. Remove two nuts attaching master cylinder to booster, then move master cylinder away from booster with brake lines attached.
2. Remove three hydraulic lines from booster. Plug and cap all lines and outlets.
3. Remove retainer and washer securing booster pushrod to brake pedal arm.
4. Remove four nuts attaching booster unit to dash panel.
5. From engine compartment, loosen booster from dash panel and move booster pushrod inboard until it disconnects from brake pedal arm. Remove spring washer from brake pedal arm.
6. Remove booster unit from vehicle.
7. Reverse procedure to install. To purge system, disconnect feed wire from injection pump. Fill power steering pump reservoir, then crank engine for several seconds and recheck power steering pump fluid level. Connect injection pump feed wire and start engine, then cycle steering wheel from stop to stop twice and stop engine. Discharge accumulator by depressing brake pedal several times, then check fluid level. Start engine, then turn steering wheel from stop to stop and turn engine off. Check fluid level and add fluid as necessary. If foaming occurs, stop engine and wait for approximately one hour for foam to dissipate, then recheck fluid level.

EXC. HYDRO-BOOST

1. Remove vacuum hose from check valve and master cylinder retaining nuts.
2. Pull master cylinder forward so it clears mounting studs and move to one side. Support cylinder to avoid stress on hydraulic lines.
3. Remove power unit to dash nuts.
4. Remove brake pedal pushrod retainer and disconnect pushrod from pin.
5. Remove power unit from vehicle.
6. Reverse procedure to install.

Rear Suspension

INDEX

SHOCK ABSORBER

REPLACE

1. If equipped with Superlift shock absorbers, disconnect air lines from shock absorber fittings.
2. With rear axle properly supported, disconnect shock absorber from upper and lower mountings, **Figs. 1 through 4.**
3. Reverse procedure to install.

COIL SPRINGS

REPLACE

CHEVROLET, MALIBU & MONTE CARLO

1. Support vehicle at frame and rear axle.
2. Disconnect shock absorbers at lower mountings.
3. Disconnect upper control arms from axle housing.
4. If equipped with a stabilizer bar, disconnect bar from either right or left-hand side of control arm.
5. On all models, remove brake hose support bolt and support without disconnecting the brake lines.

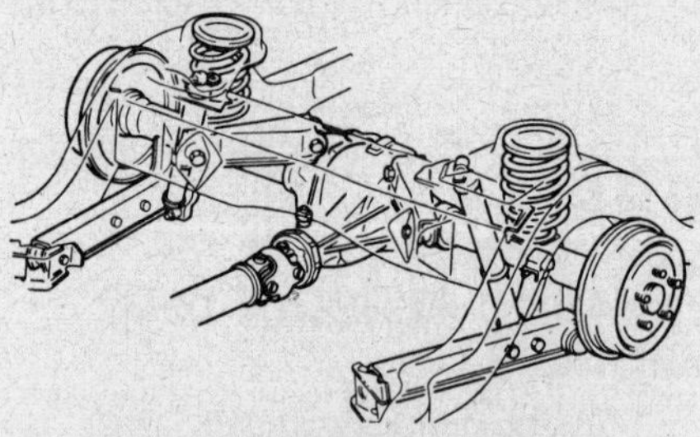

Fig. 1 Typical rear suspension. Exc. Camaro & Corvette

6. Lower axle until it reaches end of its travel and using a suitable tool, pry lower pigtail over retainer on axle bracket. Remove spring and insulator.
7. Reverse procedure to install. Springs must be installed with an insulator between upper seat and spring and positioned properly, **Fig. 5.**

CAMARO

1. Raise and support vehicle and support rear axle with a suitable adjustable jack.
2. Remove track bar mounting bolt from axle and loosen track bar bolt at body brace.
3. Disconnect rear brake hose clip at underbody, then disconnect shock absorbers at lower mountings.
4. On models equipped with 4-151 engine, remove propeller shaft.
5. Lower rear axle and remove springs and insulators.
6. Reverse procedure to install.

LEAF SPRINGS & BUSHINGS

REPLACE

1982 CORVETTE

1. Support vehicle at frame and remove rear wheels.
2. Install a C-clamp approximately 9 inches from end of spring.
3. Place a suitable jack under spring, **Fig. 6,** and place a wooden block between C-clamp and jack pad.
4. Raise jack until load is off spring link, then remove cotter pin, link nut and spring cushion, **Fig. 7.** Lower jack, removing tension from spring.
5. Repeat steps 2, 3 and 4 on opposite side of spring.

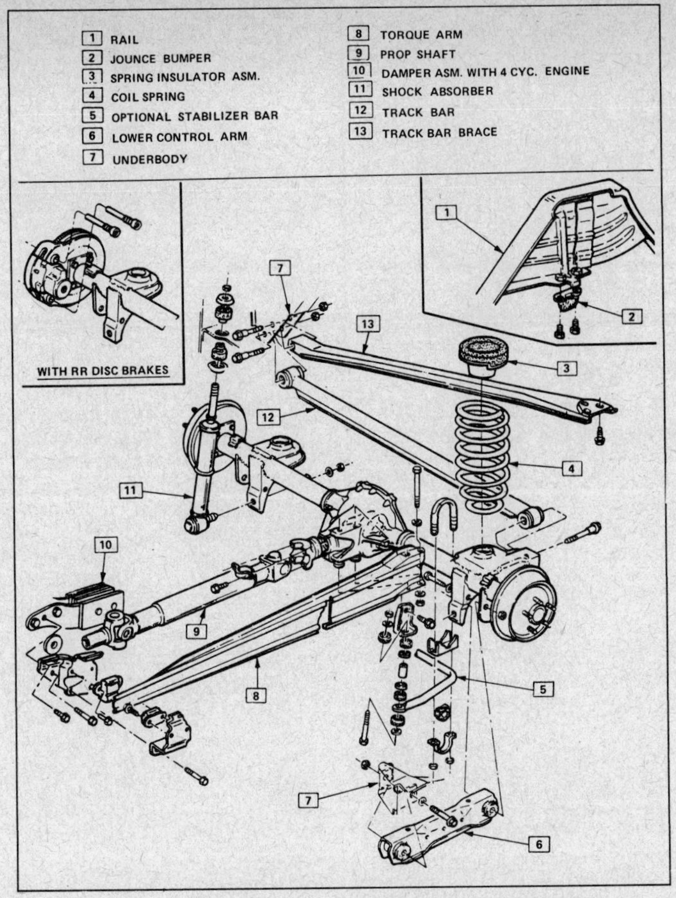

Fig. 2 Rear suspension. Camaro

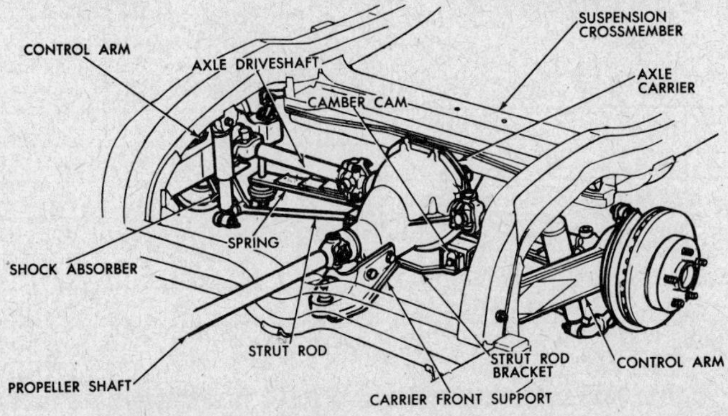

Fig. 3 Typical rear suspension. 1982 Corvette

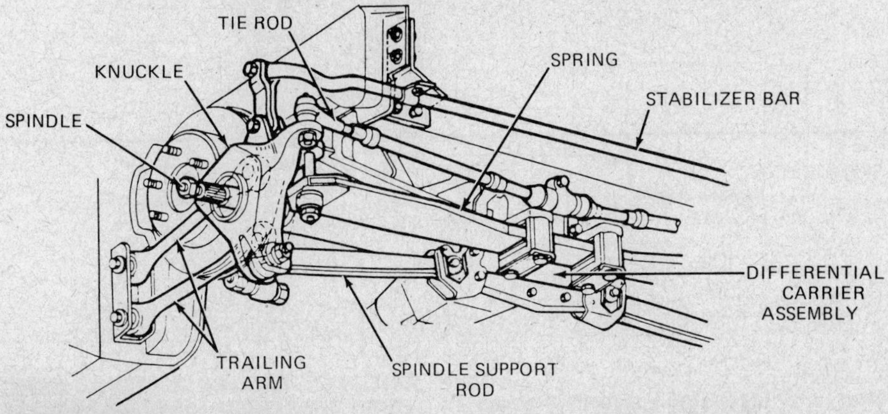

Fig. 4 Rear suspension. 1984–88 Corvette

6. Remove bolts from spring center clamp plate, then remove clamp plate.
7. Remove spring from vehicle.
8. Reverse procedure to install.

1984–88 CORVETTE

1. Raise and support vehicle and remove one wheel and tire assembly.
2. Remove cotter pin, retaining nuts, bushings and link bolts securing spring to spindle support knuckles, **Fig. 8.**
3. Remove bolts securing spring to cover beam, spacers, insulators and spring, **Fig. 9.**
4. Reverse procedure to install. Torque bolts securing spring to cover beam to 29-44 ft. lbs.

LEAF SPRING SERVICE

The spring leaves are not serviced separately, however, the spring leaf inserts may be replaced.

1. Clamp spring in a vise and remove spring clips.
2. File peened end of center bolt to permit nut removal, remove nut and open vise slowly, allowing spring to expand.
3. Replace spring leaves or leaf inserts.
4. Use a drift to align center bolt holes, compress spring in vise and install new center bolt and nut. Peen end of bolt to retain nut.
5. Align springs and bend spring clips into position. **Over tightening of spring clips will cause spring binding.**

CONTROL ARMS & BUSHINGS REPLACE

EXC. CORVETTE

If more than one control arm is being replaced, remove and install one arm at a time to prevent axle assembly from slipping or twisting out of position.

CONTROL ARMS, REPLACE

1. Raise vehicle and support at frame pads. Support nose of axle housing to prevent assembly from twisting when control arm is removed.
2. If lower control arm is being replaced, remove bolts securing stabilizer bar to control arm, if equipped.
3. Remove bolts securing control arm to chassis and rear axle, and the control arm.
4. Reverse procedure to install, lower vehicle and torque control arm bolts to specifications, **Fig. 10,** with vehicle at normal ride height. **All torque prevailing type fasteners must be torqued at the nut, not at the bolt, to ensure proper clamping force.**

BUSHING REPLACEMENT

Differential Carrier Bushings (Upper Control Arm Rear Bushing)

The upper control arm rear bushing, which is pressed into the differential carri-

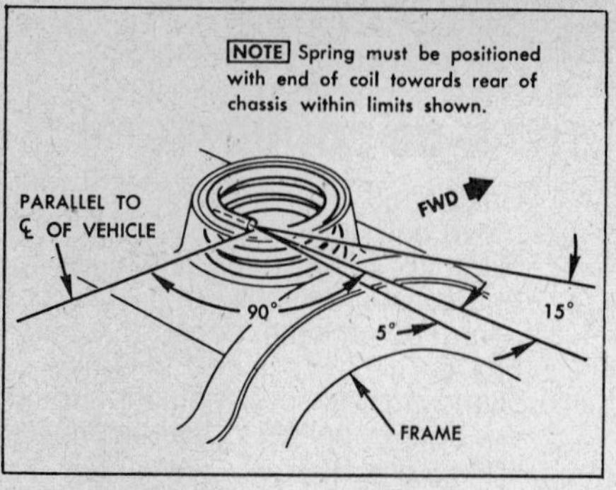

Fig. 5 Coil spring installation

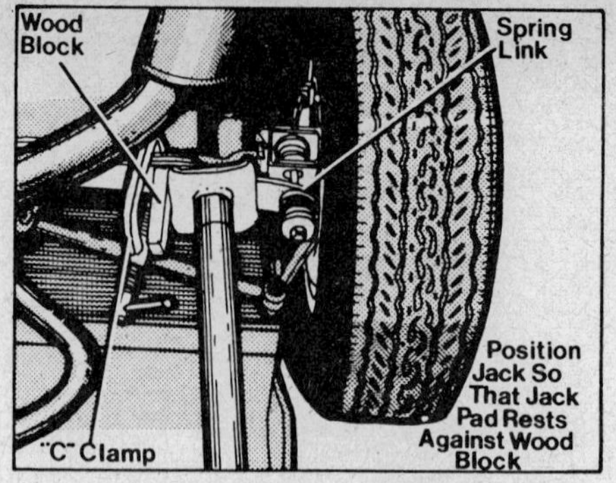

Fig. 6 Supporting leaf spring. 1982 Corvette

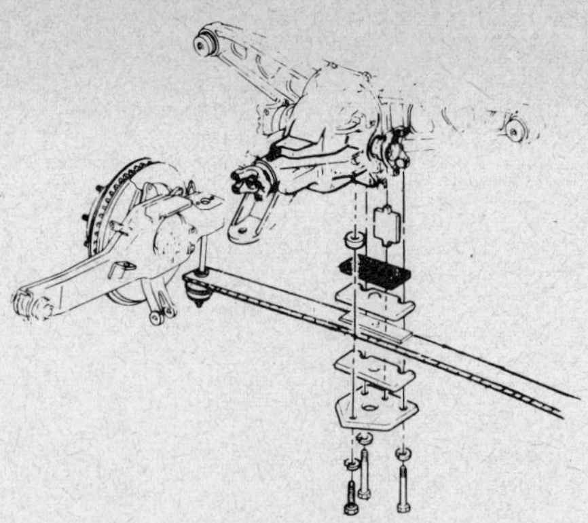

Fig. 7 Transverse leaf spring mounting. 1982 Corvette

er, can be replaced using the following procedure:

1. Raise vehicle and support at frame pads, and support nose of axle housing to prevent assembly from twisting.
2. Lower rear axle to obtain clearance, disconnect upper control arm from axle and position aside.
3. Install suitable bushing removal tool as shown in **Fig. 11**, tighten puller screw and press bushing out of housing.
4. To install replacement bushing, reverse position of removal tool and pull bushing into position by tightening screw, **Fig. 12.**

Control Arm Bushings

1. Raise and support vehicle and remove control arm as outlined previously.
2. Press bushings out of control arm using suitable tools as shown in **Fig. 13.**
3. Reverse procedure to install, ensuring bushing is properly seated in control arm, **Fig. 14. If replacement bushing fits loosely in control arm, or if mounting areas are damaged or deformed, control arm must be replaced.**

1984–88 CORVETTE

Control Arms, Replace

1. Raise and support vehicle, and remove wheel and tire assembly.
2. Remove shock absorber. Use a back-up wrench on lower mounting stud when removing retaining nut.
3. Remove bolts securing control arm to spindle support knuckle.
4. Remove control arm bolt at mounting bracket and control arm.
5. Reverse procedure to install. Torque control arm to bracket bolt to 55-70 ft. lbs., and control arm to knuckle bolt to 125-154 ft. lbs.

STABILIZER BAR REPLACE

CHEVROLET, MALIBU & MONTE CARLO

1. Support vehicle at rear axle.
2. Remove bolts securing stabilizer bar to lower control arms, Fig. 15.

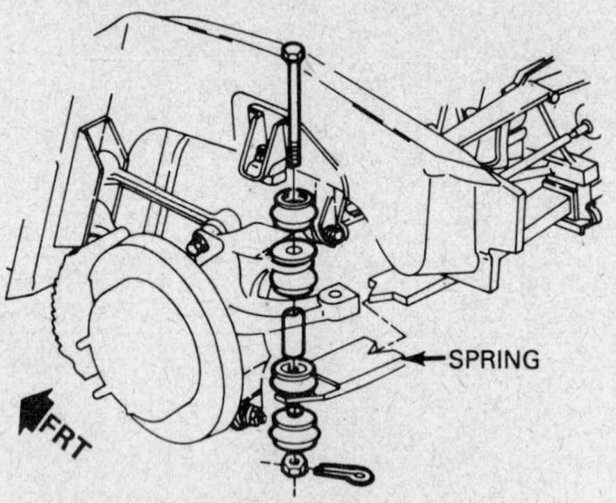

Fig. 8 Transverse leaf spring link assembly. 1984–88 Corvette

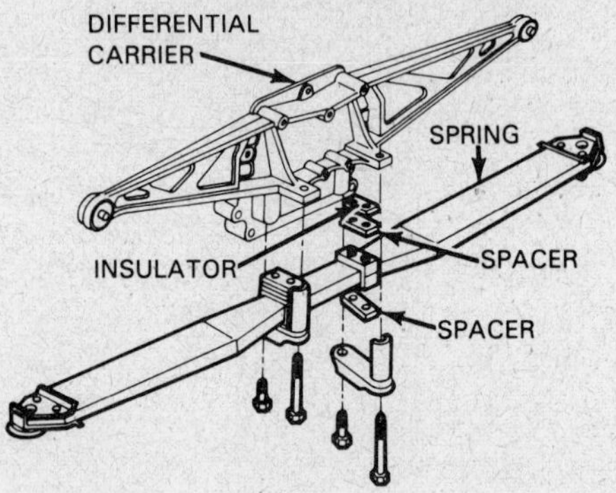

Fig. 9 Transverse leaf spring mounting. 1984–88 Corvette

Year	Model	Upper F	Upper R	Lower F	Lower R
1982-83	Malibu & Monte Carlo	to	73	70	73①
1982-88	Chevrolet	92	70	92	92
1982-88	Camaro	—	—	68	68
1984-88	Monte Carlo	70	73	70	73①

①—Bolt torque.

Fig. 10 Control arm retaining nut torque specifications

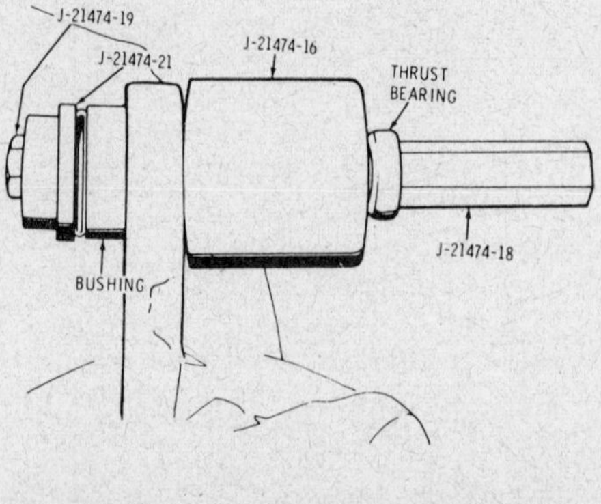

Fig. 11 Upper control arm rear bushing (differential carrier bushing) removal

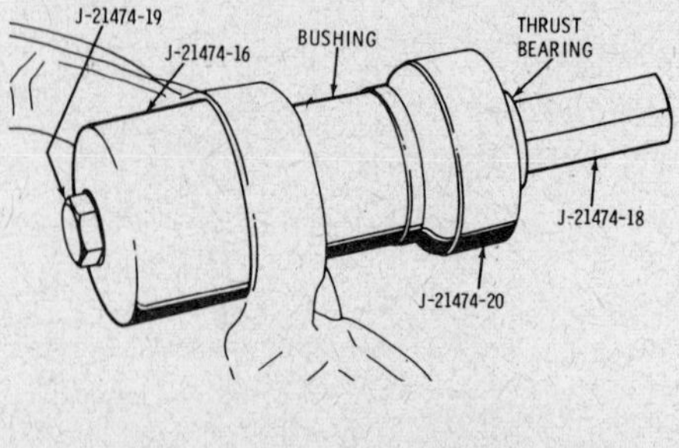

Fig. 12 Upper control arm rear bushing (differential carrier bushing) installation

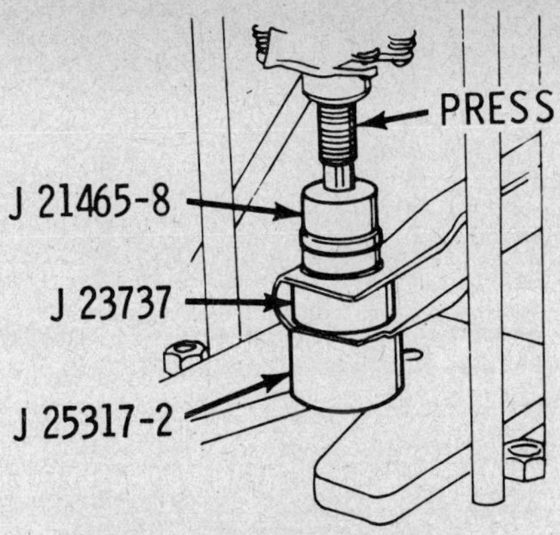

Fig. 13 Control arm bushing removal. Exc. Corvette

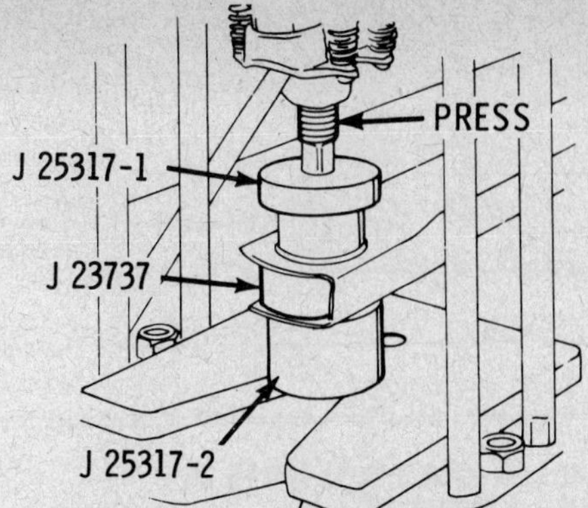

Fig. 14 Control arm bushing installation. Exc. Corvette

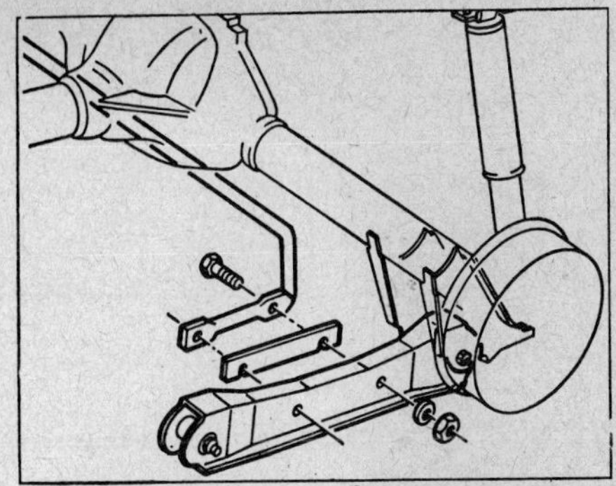

Fig. 15 Stabilizer bar installation. Chevrolet, Malibu & Monte Carlo

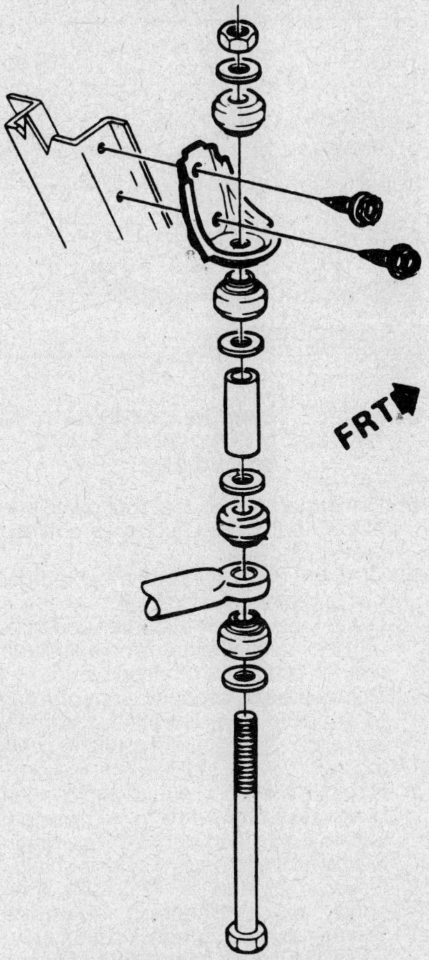

Fig. 16 Stabilizer link assembly. Camaro

3. Reverse procedure to install. Use spacer shims, if needed, placed equally on each side of stabilizer bar. Tighten attaching bolts with vehicle at curb height.

CAMARO

1. Raise and support vehicle.
2. Remove link bolt nuts, washers, bushings, spacers and link bolts securing stabilizer to chassis, **Fig. 16.**
3. Remove clamps securing stabilizer shaft to rear axle and stabilizer shaft.
4. Reverse procedure to install. Torque link bolts to 12 ft. lbs., and U-bolt nuts to 20 ft. lbs.

1982 CORVETTE

1. Disconnect stabilizer bar from torque control arms and remove stabilizer bar frame brackets, **Fig. 17.**
2. Replace bushings as necessary, **Fig. 17.**
3. Reverse procedure to install.

1984–88 CORVETTE

1. Raise and support vehicle.
2. Remove spare tire and carrier.
3. Disconnect stabilizer links from spindle support knuckles.
4. Remove retainers securing shaft bushings to crossmember, bushings and stabilizer shaft.
5. Reverse procedure to install. Torque bushing retaining nuts and bolts securing stabilizer links to knuckles to 14-22 ft. lbs., and bolts securing links to stabilizer bar to 25-35 ft. lbs.

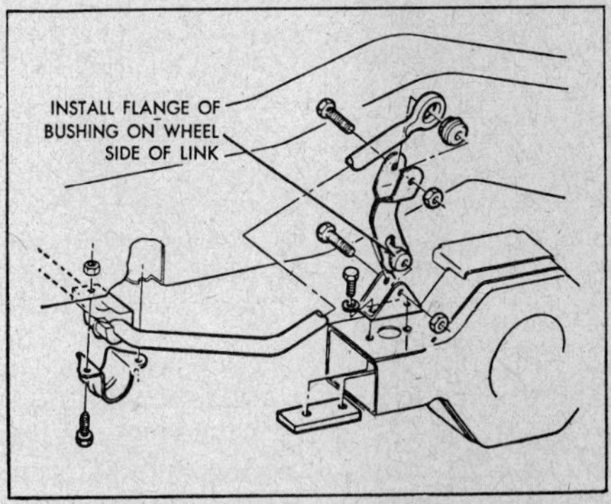

Fig. 17 Stabilizer bar installation. 1982 Corvette

TRACK BAR & BRACE REPLACE

CAMARO

1. Raise vehicle and support rear axle at curb height.
2. Remove track bar mounting bolt and nut from rear axle and from body

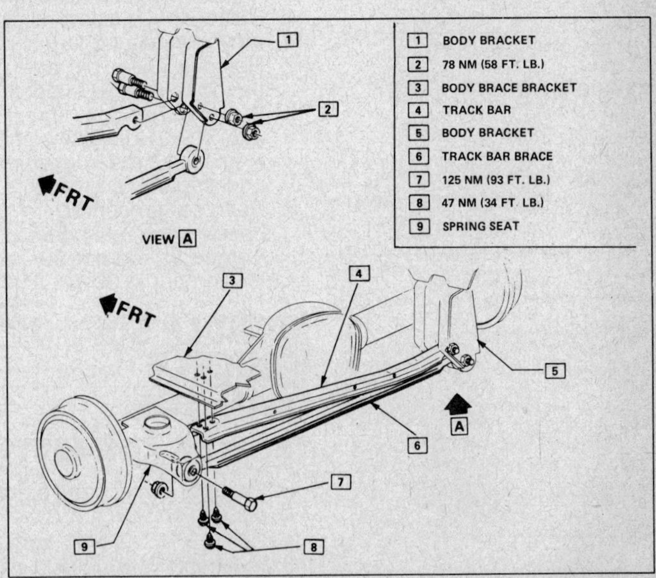

Fig. 18 Track bar & brace installation. Camaro

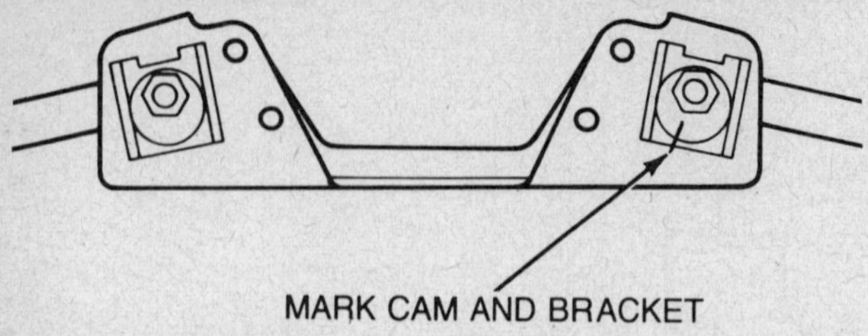

Fig. 19 Indexing adjustment cam bolt & bracket (Typical). Corvette

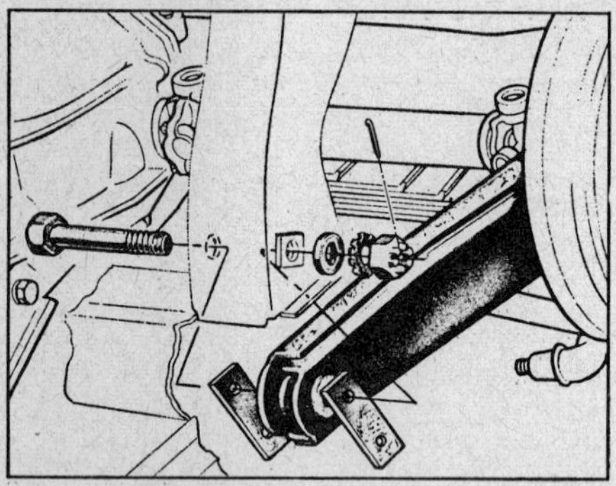

Fig. 21 Torque control arm installation. 1982 Corvette

bracket, then remove track bar, **Fig. 18.**
3. Remove heat shield attaching screws from track bar brace.
4. Remove three track bar brace to body brace screws.
5. Remove nut and bolt from body bracket, then remove track bar brace.
6. Reverse procedure to install.

STRUT ROD, SPINDLE SUPPORT ROD & TIE ROD

REPLACE

1982 CORVETTE

Strut Rod

1. Support vehicle at frame.
2. Disconnect shock frame from lower mounting.

Fig. 23 Torque control arm bushing installation. 1982 Corvette

3. Remove cotter pin and nut from strut rod shaft. Pull shaft toward front of vehicle and remove from bracket.
4. Mark position of camber adjusting cam to ensure proper installation, **Fig. 19** and loosen camber bolt nut.
5. Remove bolts securing strut rod bracket to carrier.
6. Remove camber bolt and nut, pull strut rod out of bracket and remove bushing caps.
7. Replace bushings as necessary, **Fig. 20.**
8. Reverse procedure to install.

1984–88 CORVETTE

Spindle Support Rod

1. Raise and support vehicle, and remove wheel and tire.
2. Scribe mark between cam bolt and bracket for reassembly, **Fig. 19.**
3. Remove cam bolt and disconnect support rod from bracket.
4. Remove bolt securing spindle support rod to knuckle and rod.
5. Reverse procedure to install, then check rear suspension alignment. Torque retaining bolt at knuckle to 95-118 ft. lbs., and cam bolt to 158-213 ft. lbs.

Tie Rod

1. Raise and support vehicle, and remove wheel and tire.
2. Remove cotter pin and nut securing tie rod to spindle support knuckle.
3. Press tie rod from knuckle using tool J-24319-01 or equivalent.
4. Remove tie rod from adjusting sleeve, counting number of turns necessary.
5. Reverse procedure to install, then check rear suspension alignment. Torque tie rod nut 29-36 ft. lbs., and locking nut to 39-53 ft. lbs.

SPINDLE SUPPORT KNUCKLE

REPLACE

1984–88 CORVETTE

1. Remove center cap from wheel, cotter pin and spindle nut.
2. Raise and support vehicle, and remove wheel and tire.
3. Remove 2 bolts securing brake caliper to knuckle, brake caliper assembly and brake rotor.

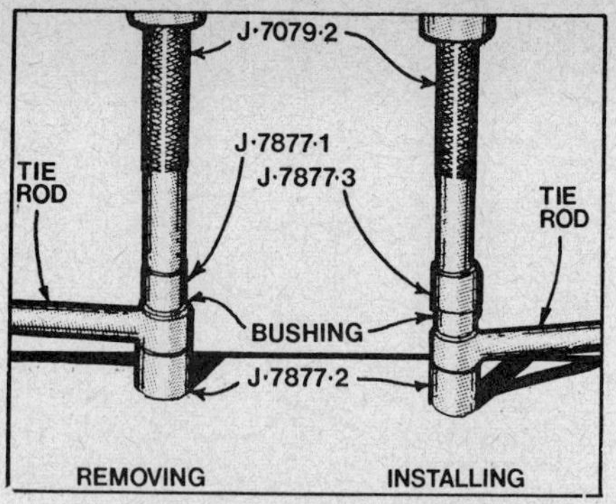

Fig. 20 Strut rod bushing replacement. 1982 Corvette

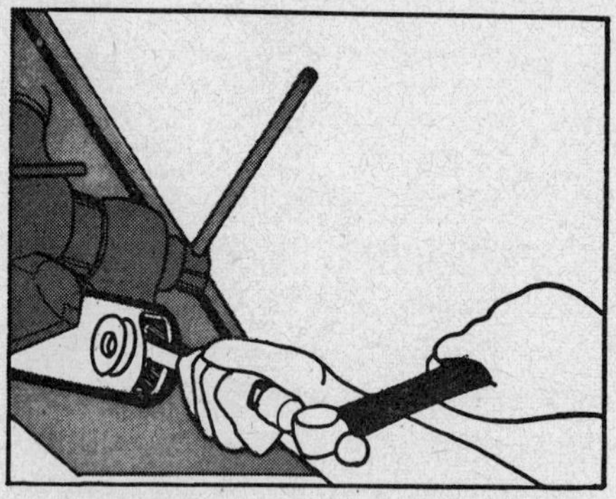

Fig. 22 Torque control arm bushing removal. 1982 Corvette

4. Disconnect tie rod, leaf spring and stabilizer shaft from knuckle as outlined previously.
5. Disconnect parking brake cable from backing plate and bracket.
6. Disconnect shock absorber and support rod from knuckle, using a back-up wrench on shock mounting stud.
7. Remove bolts securing control arms to knuckle, lower knuckle assembly and slide spindle out of hub and bearing.
8. Remove hub and bearing and parking brake assembly from knuckle, using a No. 45 Torx bit to remove hub retaining bolts, then remove splash shield.
9. Reverse procedure to install, then check rear suspension alignment. Torque all bolts to specifications given in individual component replacement procedures.

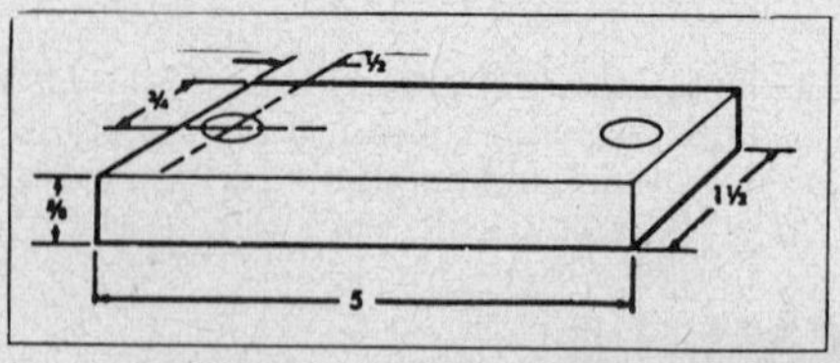

Fig. 24 Flaring tool back-up plate

TORQUE CONTROL ARMS & BUSHINGS REPLACE

1982 CORVETTE

1. Perform steps 1 thru 4 as outlined under "Leaf Spring Replace" 1982 Corvette procedure.
2. If equipped with a stabilizer shaft, disconnect shaft at torque arms.
3. Disconnect shock absorber at lower mounting.
4. Disconnect and lower strut rod shaft.
5. Disconnect axle drive shaft from spindle flange by removing attaching bolts. **It may be necessary to force torque arm outboard providing clearance to lower axle drive shaft.**
6. Disconnect brake line from caliper and from torque arm. Disconnect parking brake cable.
7. Remove torque arm forward mounting bolt and toe-in shims, **Fig. 21,** and pull torque arm out of frame attachment.

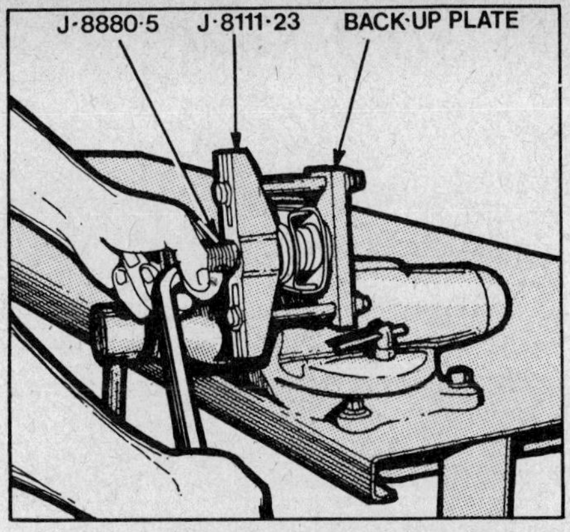

Fig. 25 Flaring torque control arm bushing retainer. 1982 Corvette

8. Replace bushings if necessary as described under "Torque Control Arm Bushing Service."
9. Reverse procedure to install.

Torque Control Arm Bushing Service

1. Using an 11/16 inch twist drill, drill out flared end of bushing retainer, remove retainer plate and retainer from bushing.
2. Spread bushing with a chisel, **Fig. 22,** and tap bushing from arm. **If bushing is rusted in torque arm, torque arm may spread during bushing removal. Install a C-clamp torque arm, preventing torque arm spreading.**
3. Oil steel portion of new bushing and press bushing into arm, **Fig. 23.**
4. Place retainer plate over flared portion of bushing retainer and insert retainer into bushing.
5. Make a flaring tool back-up plate, **Fig. 24,** with 1/2 inch bolt holes.
6. Place back-up plate on flared end of bushing retainer and assemble tool to plate, **Fig. 25,** with 1/2 x 5 inch bolts. Center threaded hole in tool J-8111-23 over unflared end of bushing retainer. Also center chamfered retainer plate over retainer tube.
7. Lubricate end of tool J-8880-5 and thread screw into tool, flaring retainer.

Front Suspension & Steering Section

INDEX

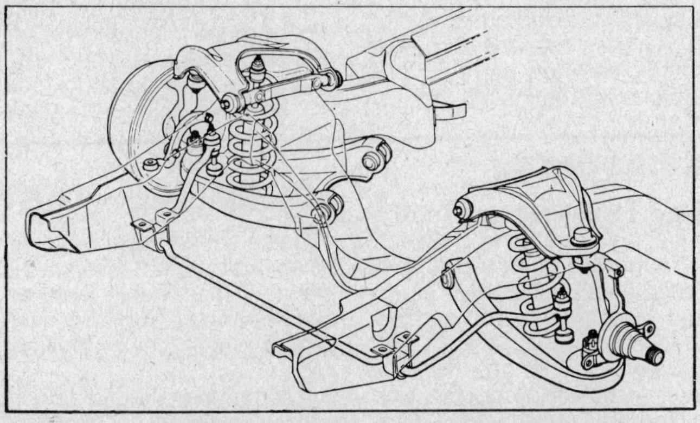

Fig. 1 Typical front suspension. Exc. Camaro & 1984–88 Corvette

DESCRIPTION

All models except Camaro and 1984-88 Corvette use a Short-Long Arm (SLA) type front suspension with independent coil springs riding on lower control arms, **Fig. 1.** Ball joints link upper and lower control arms to a spindle assembly, and tubular shock absorbers are used to dampen spring action. On some models, a spring steel stabilizer shaft is connected between the chassis and lower control arms to control side roll.

A modified strut type suspension is used on Camaro, **Fig. 2.** Each wheel is independently connected to the chassis by a lower control arm, spindle and a strut assembly which locates the spindle and controls ride

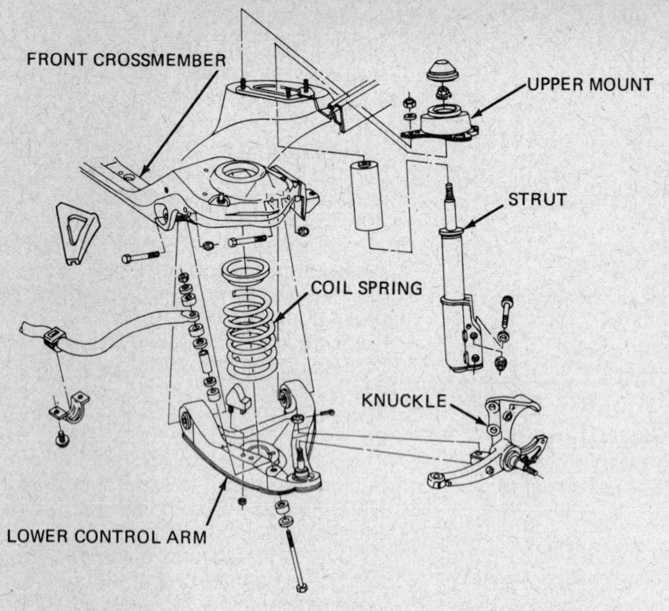

Fig. 2 Front suspension exploded view. Camaro

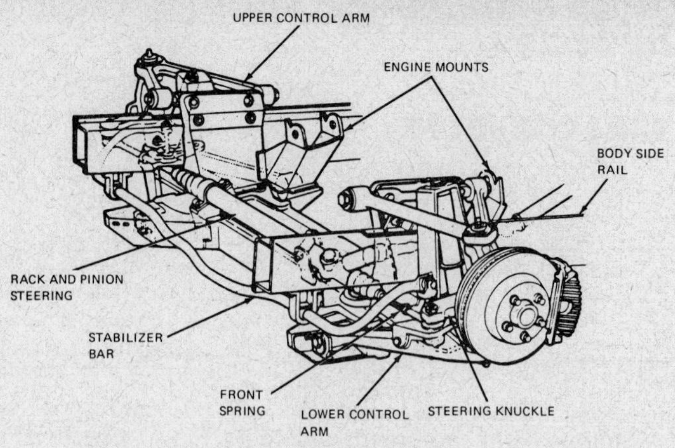

Fig. 3 Front suspension. 1984–88 Corvette

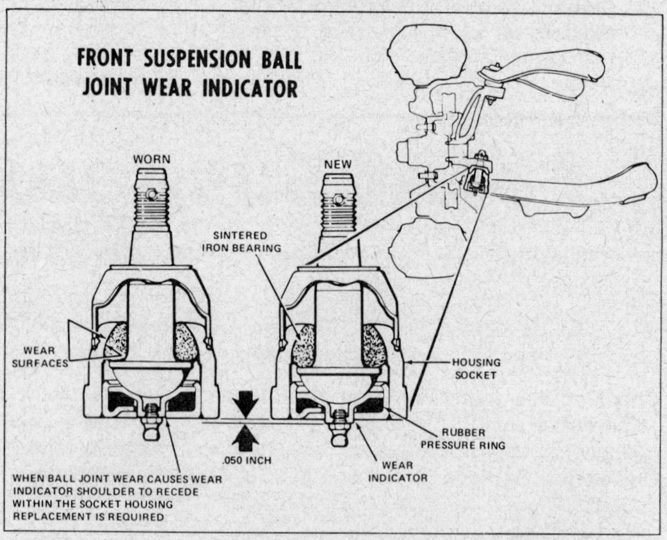

Fig. 4 Lower ball joint wear indicator

by dampening spring action. Coil springs are mounted between the lower control arm and crossmember, and a stabilizer shaft is connected between the chassis and control arms to control side roll.

The front suspension used on 1984-88 Corvette consists of forged aluminum upper and lower control arms and steering knuckle, a fiberglass mono-leaf spring, shock absorbers and stabilizer bar, **Fig. 3.** The front spring is transverse mounted on the crossmember and bears against lower control arms. The stabilizer bar and shock absorbers are connected between the chassis and lower control arms, and control side roll and dampen spring action respectively. Upper and lower control arms are connected through the knuckle, which is specially designed to move the wheel center line rearward of the conventional ball joint center line.

WHEEL BEARINGS
ADJUST
EXC. 1984–88 CORVETTE

1. While rotating wheel forward, torque spindle nut to 12 ft. lbs.
2. Back off nut until "just loose" then hand tighten nut and back it off again until either hole in spindle lines up with hole in nut. **Do not back off nut more than 1/2 flat.**
3. Install new cotter pin. With wheel bearing properly adjusted, there will be .001-.005 inch endplay.

WHEEL BEARINGS
REPLACE
EXC. 1984–88 CORVETTE

1. Raise car and remove front wheels.
2. Remove bolts holding brake caliper to its mounting and insert a fabricated block (1 1/16 x 1 1/16 x 2 inches in length) between the brake pads as the caliper is being removed. Once removed, the caliper can be wired or secured in some manner away from the disc.
3. Remove spindle nut and hub and disc assembly. Grease retainer and inner wheel bearing can now be removed.
4. Reverse procedure to install.

1984–88 CORVETTE

The wheel bearing and hub assembly is a sealed unit. If endplay exceeds .005 inch, or if noise or roughness is detected, unit must be replaced as an assembly.

1. Raise and support vehicle, and remove wheel and tire.
2. Remove 2 bolts securing brake caliper bracket to steering knuckle, and secure caliper assembly aside.
3. Remove brake rotor, bolts securing hub to knuckle and hub assembly.
4. Reverse procedure to install.

CHECKING BALL JOINTS FOR WEAR
UPPER BALL JOINT

1. Raise front of vehicle with jacks placed between the coil spring pocket and ball joint of lower control arm.
2. Shake top of wheel in and out. Observe steering knuckle for any movement relative to the control arm.
3. Replace upper ball joint if looseness is indicated.

LOWER BALL JOINT

Raise car and support lower control arm so spring is compressed in the same manner as if the wheels were on the ground and check axial (up and down) play at ball joint. If play exceeds 1/8 inch, replace the joint.

Another indication of lower ball joint excessive wear is when difficulty is experienced when lubricating the joint. If the liner has worn to the point where the lubrication grooves in the liner have been worn away,

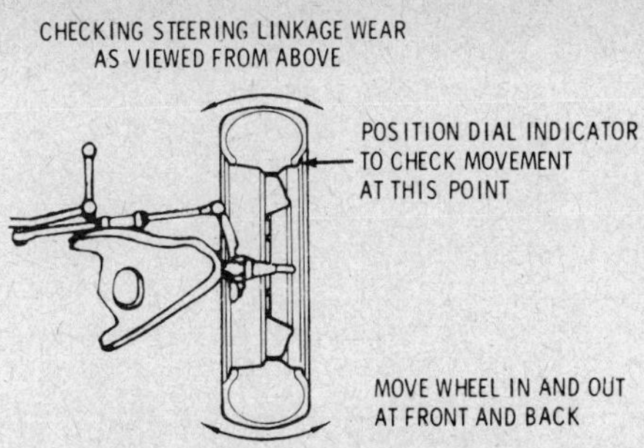

Fig. 5 Suspension & steering linkage check

then abnormal pressure is required to force lubricant through the joint. Should this condition be evident, replace both lower ball joints.

All models except 1982 Corvette and Camaro have a wear indicator built into the lower ball joint, **Fig. 4.** When inspecting wear indicator, vehicle must be supported normally on wheels to properly load ball joint.

SUSPENSION & STEERING LINKAGE CHECK

1. Raise vehicle with jack placed under frame torque box behind front wheel.
2. Lock steering wheel with wheels in straight ahead position, then mount dial indicator on a suitable stand with pointer bearing against outer rim of wheel, **Fig. 5.**
3. Move wheel in and out at front and rear, without moving steering wheel, while observing gauge.
4. If gauge reading exceeds .108 inches, check steering linkage and suspension for excessive wear or damage.

UPPER BALL JOINT REPLACE

EXC. 1982 CORVETTE

1. Raise vehicle and support with stands at outer ends of lower control arms.
2. Remove wheel and tire.
3. Remove cotter pin and retaining nut, then separate ball joint stud from knuckle using a suitable tool, **Fig. 6.**
4. Support upper control arm in a raised position.
5. Remove heads of rivets securing joint to arm, then drive out rivets to remove joint.
6. Position replacement joint on top of control arm, insert retaining bolts supplied with joint from under arm, install nuts and torque to 13 ft. lbs.
7. Remove upper control arm support, assemble ball joint to steering knuckle, install washer, if equipped, and retaining nut. **On 1982 models, seat ball joint stud in knuckle before installing nut. Install tool J-29293 on stud, torque tool to 40 ft. lbs., then remove tool and install nut.**

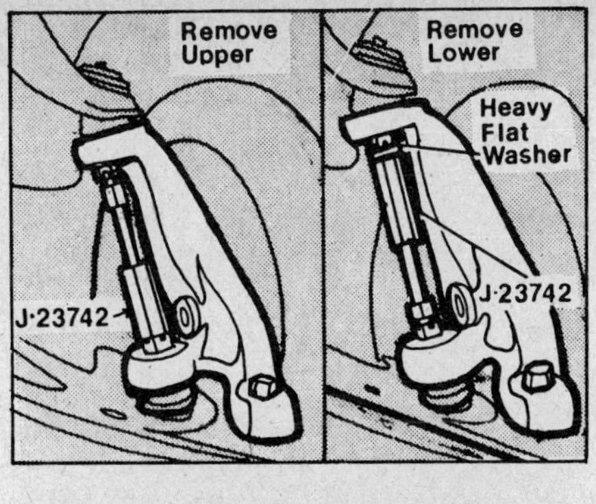

Fig. 6 Disconnecting ball joints from steering knuckle (Typical). Exc. 1982 Corvette & Camaro

8. Torque retaining nut to 60 ft. lbs. on 1982 models, 65 ft. lbs. on 1983-88 models except Corvette, and 32 ft. lbs. on 1984-88 Corvette.
9. Tighten retaining nut up to an additional 1/16 turn, if necessary, to align hole in ball stud with nut, then install cotter pin. **On 1982 Malibu and Monte Carlo, install cotter pin from rear.**

1982 CORVETTE

1. Raise and support vehicle, and remove wheel and tire.
2. Remove cotter pin and loosen but do not remove ball joint retaining nut. **Nut should not be loosened more than one full turn.**
3. To release ball stud from knuckle, tap on boss of knuckle with hammer using another heavy hammer or similar tool as a drift.
4. Support lower control arm at outer end to release spring tension on upper control arm, remove retaining nut and support upper control arm in raised position.
5. Remove heads of rivets securing joint to arm, then drive out rivets to remove joint.
6. Position replacement joint on top of control arm, insert retaining bolts supplied with joint from under arm, install nuts and torque to 25 ft. lbs.
7. Remove upper control arm support, assemble ball joint to steering knuckle, install retaining nut and torque to 50 ft. lbs.
8. Tighten nut up to an additional 1/16 of a turn, if necessary, to align hole in ball stud with nut, then install cotter pin.

LOWER BALL JOINT REPLACE

EXC. 1982 CORVETTE

1. Raise vehicle and support at frame, and remove wheel and tire.
2. Position a suitable jack under lower control arm spring seat, and raise jack to compress coil spring. **Jack must remain in place during ball joint replacement to hold spring and lower control arm in position.**

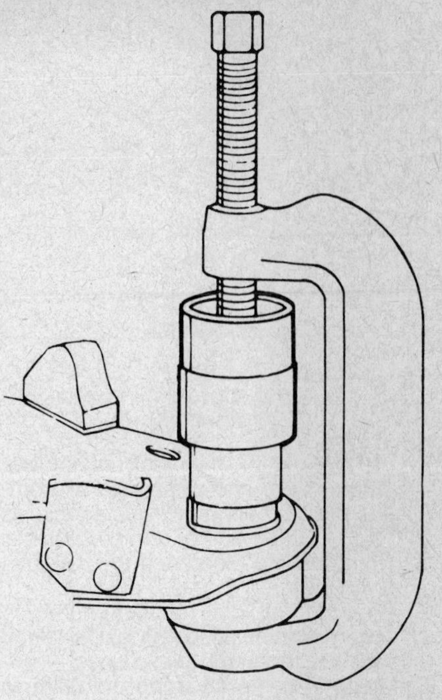

Fig. 7 Pressing ball joint from lower control arm (Typical)

3. Remove cotter pin and nut securing ball joint stud to steering knuckle, then disconnect joint from knuckle using a suitable tool, **Fig. 6.**
4. Lift knuckle assembly from ball stud, guiding control arm out of splash shield, then support knuckle aside to allow clearance for joint removal.
5. Remove grease fitting, then press ball joint assembly out of lower control arm using a suitable tool, **Fig. 7.**
6. Press replacement joint into arm by reversing removal tools, fit spindle over ball stud, install washer, if equipped, and retaining nut. **On 1982 models except 1982 Camaro, seat ball stud in steering knuckle before installing nut. Install tool J-29194 over stud, torque tool to 40 ft. lbs., then remove tool and install nut.**
7. Torque retaining nut to 90 ft. lbs. on 1982-88 models except 1984-88 Corvette and 48 ft. lbs. on 1984-88 Corvette.
8. Tighten nut up to an additional 1/16 turn, if necessary, to align hole in ball stud with nut, then install cotter pin. **On 1982 Malibu and Monte Carlo, install cotter pin from rear.**

1982 CORVETTE

1. Raise vehicle and support at frame, and remove wheel and tire.
2. Remove cotter pins from upper and lower joints and loosen but do not remove retaining nuts. **Do not loosen nuts more than one full turn.**
3. To release ball studs from knuckle, tap on boss of knuckle with a hammer, using another heavy hammer or similar tool as a drift.

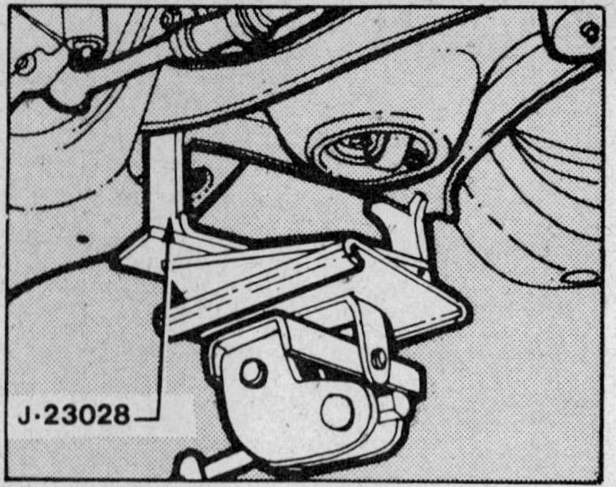
J-23028

Fig. 8 Coil spring removal (Typical)

4. Place a suitable floor jack under lower control arm, and raise jack to compress coil spring. Position jack as close to outer end of arm as possible, while leaving clearance for ball joint removal.
5. Remove ball joint retaining nuts and secure spindle assembly aside, taking care not to stretch brake hose.
6. Remove rivets securing ball joint to control arm and ball joint.
7. Position replacement joint on control arm, install retaining bolts and nuts, and torque to 25 ft. lbs.
8. Install spindle assembly and ball joint retaining nuts, then torque upper nut to 50 ft. lbs. and lower nut to 80 ft. lbs.
9. Tighten nuts up to an additional 1/16 turn, if necessary, to align holes in ball studs with nuts, then install cotter pins.

SHOCK ABSORBER REPLACE

On Camaro, refer to "Strut, Replace" procedure.

1. Raise and support vehicle as needed, and remove wheel and tire.
2. Hold shock absorber shaft with a suitable wrench and remove upper retaining nut, washer and bushing.
3. Remove lower retaining bolts and shock absorber. On Corvette, remove shock mounting bracket, if necessary, to provide clearance for shock absorber removal.
4. Reverse procedure to install. Torque upper retaining nut to 90 inch lbs. on 1982 Corvette; 8 ft. lbs. on all 1982-88 models except Corvette, and 19 ft. lbs. on 1984-88 Corvette. Torque lower mounting bolts to 20 ft. lbs. on all models except Corvette; 150 inch lbs. on 1982 Corvette, and 22 ft. lbs. on 1984-88 Corvette.

STRUT REPLACE

CAMARO

1. Raise and support vehicle.
2. Remove wheel and support lower control arm with a suitable jack.
3. Remove brake hose bracket and two strut to knuckle bolts, Fig. 2.
4. Remove upper mounting assembly cover.
5. Remove nut from upper end of strut, then the strut and shield.
6. Reverse procedure to install. Tighten strut to knuckle bolts to 195 ft. lbs., and strut to upper mount nut to 50 ft. lbs.

COIL SPRING REPLACE

EXC. CAMARO

1. Disconnect shock absorber from lower mounting, push shock absorber through hole in lower control arm and compress into spring.
2. Support vehicle by frame so control arms hang free.
3. Install a safety chain through spring and lower control arm.
4. Install tool J-23028 onto a suitable jack and position jack so control arm is supported by bushings seated in grooves of tool, **Fig. 8.**
5. Remove stabilizer to lower control arm attachment.
6. Raise jack to relieve tension on control arm bolts and remove bolts.
7. Lower jack until tension is removed from spring, remove chain and spring from vehicle.
8. Reverse procedure to install, installing front pivot bolt first. **To ensure adequate suspension clearance, install front pivot bolt from front, with nut toward rear of vehicle. Rear bolt can be installed from either direction.**
9. Torque pivot bolts to specifications:

1982 Corvette front	70 ft. lbs.
1982 Corvette rear	95 ft. lbs.
1982-83 Malibu	65 ft. lbs.
1982-88 Chevrolet	90 ft. lbs.
1982-88 Monte Carlo	65 ft. lbs.

CAMARO

1. Raise and support vehicle and remove wheel.
2. Remove stabilizer link and bushings from lower control arm.
3. Remove pivot bolt nuts, leaving the bolts installed.
4. Install tool J-23028 onto a suitable jack and position so that tool supports bushings, **Fig. 8.**
5. Raise jack to relieve tension on pivot bolts and remove bolts.
6. Carefully lower jack until tension is removed from spring and remove spring from vehicle.
7. Reverse procedure to install. Torque pivot bolt nuts to 65 ft. lbs. and stabilizer link nut to 20 ft. lbs. **The spring force under compression is very great. Exercise every safety precaution when performing this operation to see that individuals and materials subject to damage are removed from the path of the spring when the control arm is being lowered. Also, the compressed spring should be relaxed immediately after lowering the control arm to reduce the time of exposure to the great compressive force.**

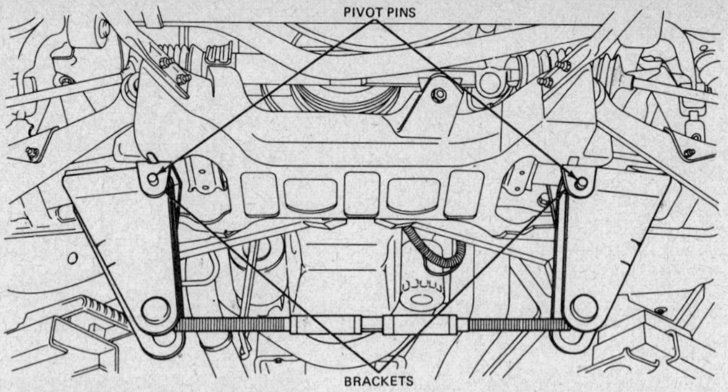
PIVOT PINS
BRACKETS
NOTE: PIVOT PINS ARE REMOVED SO THAT THE BRACKET MAY BE PLACED OVER THE TOP OF THE SPRING.

Fig. 9 Leaf spring removal. 1984–88 Corvette

LEAF SPRING REPLACE

1984–88 CORVETTE

1. Raise and support vehicle, and remove front wheels.
2. Remove both spring protectors.
3. Install spring compressor J-33432 or equivalent, **Fig. 9.**
4. Disconnect lower ball joints from steering knuckles.
5. Compress spring by rotating turnbuckle on spring compressor.
6. Remove bolts securing shock brackets to lower control arms and spring mounting bolts.
7. Release tension on spring compressor and remove compressor.
8. Remove spring.
9. Reverse procedure to install. Torque spring mounting bolts to 46 ft. lbs. with vehicle on ground.

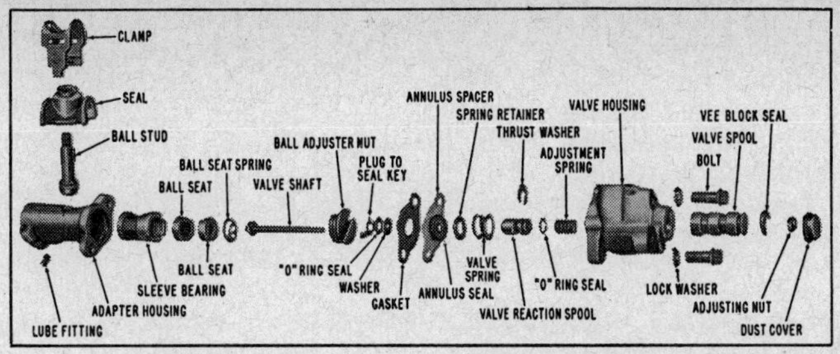

Fig. 10 Power steering control valve and adapter, exploded view. 1982 Corvette

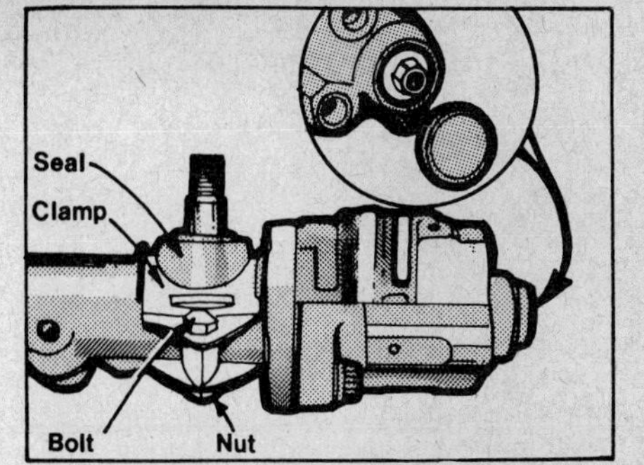

Fig. 11 Control valve ball stud seal replacement. 1982 Corvette

MANUAL STEERING GEAR

REPLACE

On models where shield is installed, remove shield from coupling.

1. Remove nuts, washers and bolts at steering coupling.
2. Remove pitman arm nut and washer from sector shaft and mark relation of arm position to shaft.
3. Use a suitable puller to remove pitman arm.
4. Unfasten gear from frame and remove assembly.
5. Reverse procedure to install. Torque gear mounting bolts to 30 ft. lbs. on 1982 Corvette, 80 ft. lbs. on 1982 models except Corvette or 70 ft. lbs. on 1983-88 models except Corvette. Torque shaft coupling nuts to 30 ft. lbs. Torque pitman arm retaining nut to 185 ft. lbs.

INTEGRAL POWER STEERING

REPLACE

EXC. CORVETTE

To remove gear assembly, disconnect pressure and return hoses from gear housing and cap both hoses and steering gear outlets to prevent foreign material from entering system, then follow procedure as outlined under Steering Gear, Replace.

LINKAGE TYPE POWER STEERING

1982 CORVETTE

Power steering equipment consists of a recirculating ball type steering gear and linkage to which a hydraulic power mechanism has been added as part of the steering linkage. The hydraulic mechanism furnishes additional power to assist the manual operation so that the turning effort at the steering wheel is greatly reduced. The hydraulic mechanism consists of three basic units: a hydraulic pump and reservoir, a control valve, and a power cylinder.

CONTROL VALVE, ADJUST

1. Disconnect cylinder rod from frame bracket.
2. With car on a hoist, start the engine. One of the following two conditions will exist:
   a. If piston rod remains retracted, turn the adjusting nut clockwise until the rod begins to move out. Then turn the nut counterclockwise until the rod just begins to move in. Now turn the nut clockwise to exactly one half the rotation needed to change the direction of shaft movement.
   b. If the rod extends upon starting the pump, move the nut counterclockwise until the rod begins to retract, then clockwise until the rod begins to move out again. Now turn the rod to exactly one half the rotation needed to change the direction of shaft movement. **Do not turn the nut back and forth more than is absolutely necessary to balance the valve.**
3. Restart engine. Front wheels should not turn from center if valve has been properly balanced.

POWER CYLINDER REPAIRS

Removal

1. Disconnect two hydraulic lines at power cylinder.
2. Unfasten power cylinder rod from brace at frame.
3. Unfasten power cylinder from relay rod bracket.
4. Remove power cylinder from car.

Inspection

1. Inspect seals for leaks around cylinder rod and if leaks are present, replace seals as follows:
   a. Use a hook tool to remove retaining ring. Remove wiper ring, backup washer, back-up ring and seal. Piston rod seal should not be removed unless there are signs of leakage along the piston shaft at shaft seal.
   b. Examine brass fitting hose connection seats for cracks or damage and replace if necessary.
   c. For service other than seat or seal replacement, replace the power cylinder.

Installation

1. Install power cylinder on car by reversing removal procedure. Torque the frame bracket to rod nut to 23 ft. lbs. and the relay rod bracket nut to 45 ft. lbs. Additional torque may be applied to align castellation with hole in stud, not to exceed 30 ft. lbs. on frame bracket to rod nut and 50 ft. lbs. on relay rod bracket nut.
2. Reconnect two hoses, fill system with fluid and bleed system as outlined below.

Filling & Bleeding System

1. Fill reservoir to proper level with Automatic Transmission Fluid and let fluid remain undisturbed for about two minutes.
2. Raise front wheels off floor.
3. Run engine at idle for two minutes.
4. Increase engine speed to about 1500 RPM.
5. Turn wheels from one extreme to the other, lightly contacting stops.
6. Lower wheels to floor and turn wheels right and left.
7. Recheck for leaks.
8. Check oil level and refill as required. Pump pressure should be 870 lbs.

CONTROL VALVE REPAIRS

Replace

1. Loosen relay rod-to-control valve clamp.
2. Disconnect hose connections at control valve.
3. Disconnect control valve from pitman arm.
4. Unscrew control valve from relay rod, **Fig. 10.**
5. Remove control valve from car.
6. Reverse procedure to install. Torque relay rod clamp bolt to 25 ft. lbs. Torque pitman arm nut to 45 ft. lbs. plus additional torque required to align castellation with hole in stud not to exceed 50 ft. lbs.

Ball Stud Seal, Replace

In servicing the control valve, refer to **Fig. 10.** To replace the ball stud seal, refer to **Fig. 11** and proceed as follows:

1. Remove pitman arm with a suitable puller.
2. Remove clamp by removing nut, bolt and spacer. If crimped type clamp is used, straighten clamp end and pull clamp and seal off end of stud.
3. Install new seal and clamp over stud so lips on seal mate with clamp. (A nut and bolt attachment type clamp replaces the crimped type for service).
4. Center the ball stud, seal and clamp in

opening in adapter housing, then install spacer, bolt and nut.

RACK & PINION STEERING GEAR REPLACE

1984–88 CORVETTE

1. Raise and support vehicle, and remove left wheel and tire.
2. Disconnect hoses at steering gear, and plug lines and open ports.
3. Disconnect outer tie rods from steering knuckles.
4. Remove upper and lower mounting bolts on right side and single mounting bolt on left side.
5. Disconnect intermediate shaft universal joint from steering gear.
6. Remove stabilizer shaft and electric fan to provide clearance.
7. Remove steering gear.
8. Reverse procedure to install. Torque bolts securing right bracket to 18 ft. lbs., and bolt securing gear to crossmember to 25 ft. lbs.
9. Top off fluid reservoir, bleed system and check for leaks.

POWER STEERING PUMP REPLACE

EXC. 1984–88 CORVETTE

1. Disconnect hoses at power steering pump, then plug pump parts and hoses.
2. Loosen pump adjusting bolt and remove pump drive belt.
3. Remove pump to support bracket attaching bolts and the pump.
4. Reverse procedure to install. Torque attaching bolts to the following specifications: 1982 Corvette, 25 ft. lbs., 1982-88 all except Corvette, 35 ft. lbs.

1984–88 CORVETTE

1. Rotate belt tensioner counterclockwise, and remove serpentine drive belt.
2. Remove AIR pump pulley.
3. Remove bolts securing power steering reservoir bracket and bolts securing reservoir brace to intake manifold.
4. Disconnect power steering hoses between pump and steering gear, then plug hoses and open fittings.
5. Remove pump mounting bolts, pump and reservoir.
6. Reverse procedure to install, torquing pump and bracket bolts to 18 ft. lbs.

Wheel Alignment Section

INDEX

FRONT WHEEL ALIGNMENT

Prior to checking or adjusting front suspension alignment, inspect suspension components for damage or excessive wear, and replace as needed. Ensure tire pressures and wheel bearings are properly adjusted, then raise and release front bumper several times to allow vehicle to assume normal ride height.

CASTER, ADJUST

Chevrolet, Corvette, Malibu & Monte Carlo

Caster adjustments are performed by moving, adding or subtracting the shims that are located between the upper control arm support shaft and the support bracket on the frame. Refer to **Figs. 1 and 2** and note the effect of shim placement. Although all models utilize the same basic type of front suspension, the movement of shims on Corvette models is opposite that

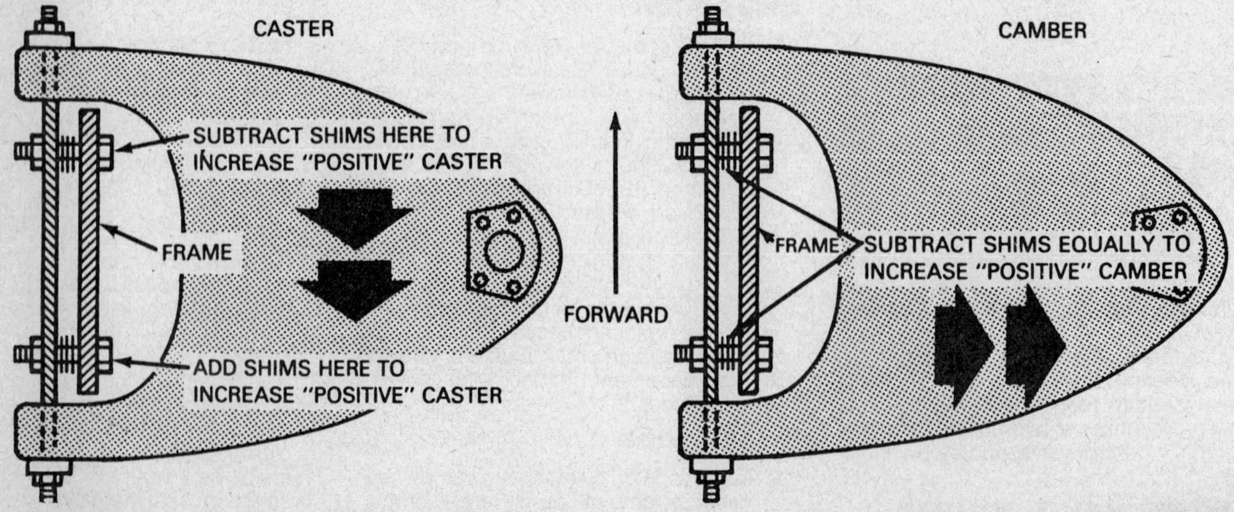

Fig. 1 Caster & camber adjustments. Chevrolet, Malibu & Monte Carlo

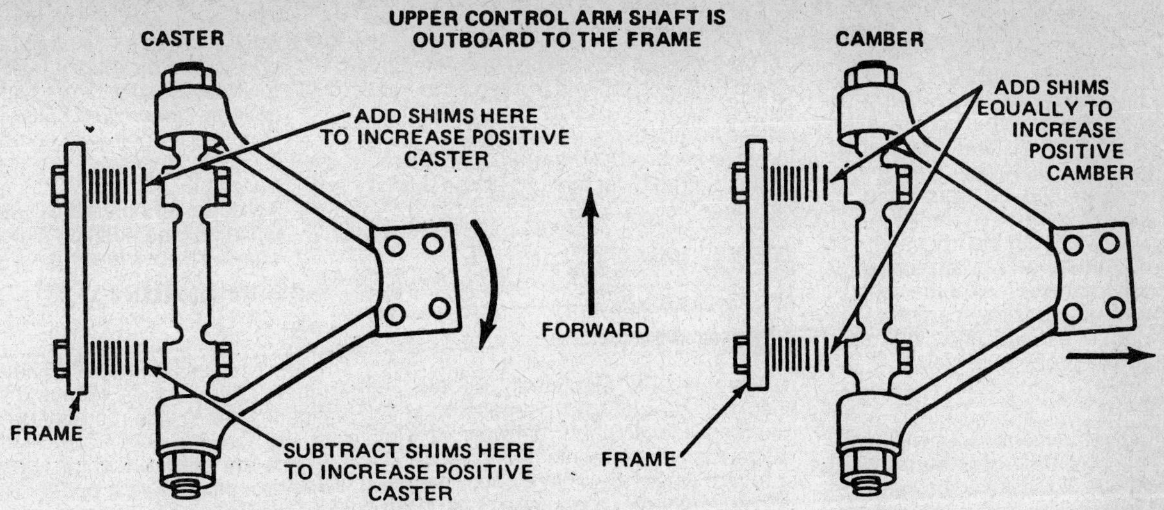

Fig. 2 Caster & camber adjustments. Corvette

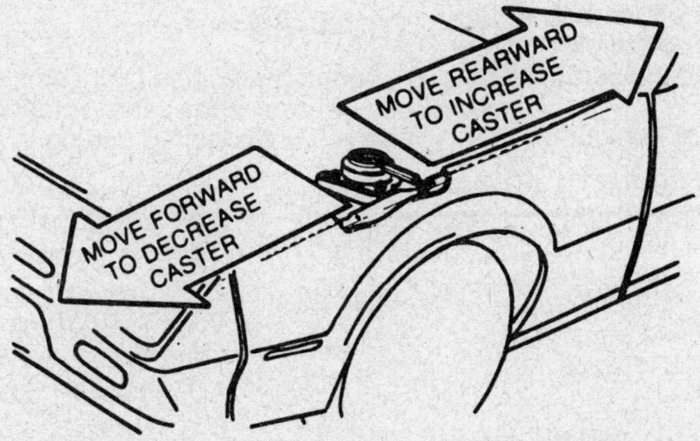

Fig. 3 Caster adjustment. Camaro

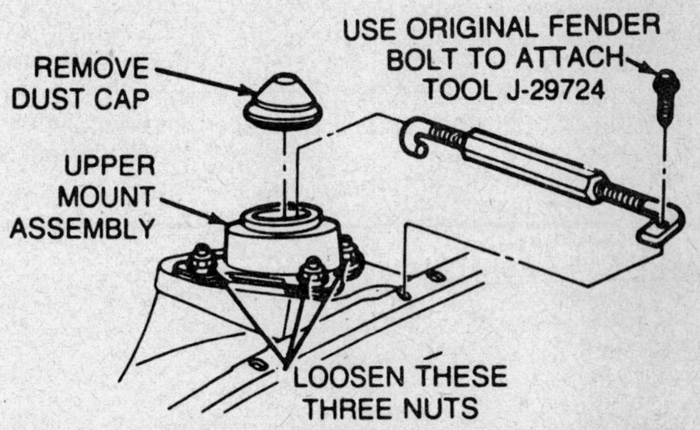

Fig. 4 Caster & camber adjustment tool installation. Camaro

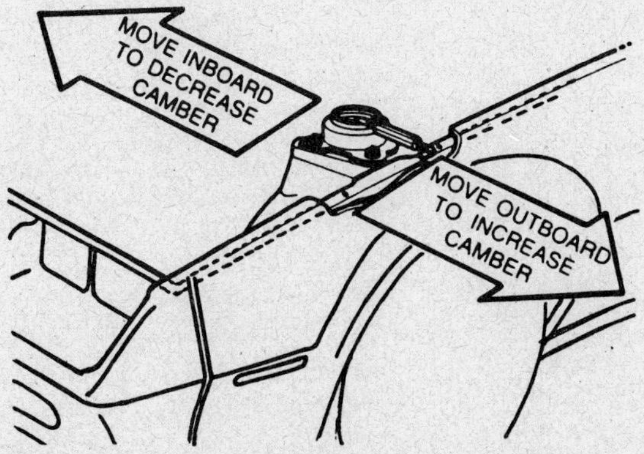

Fig. 5 Camber adjustment. Camaro

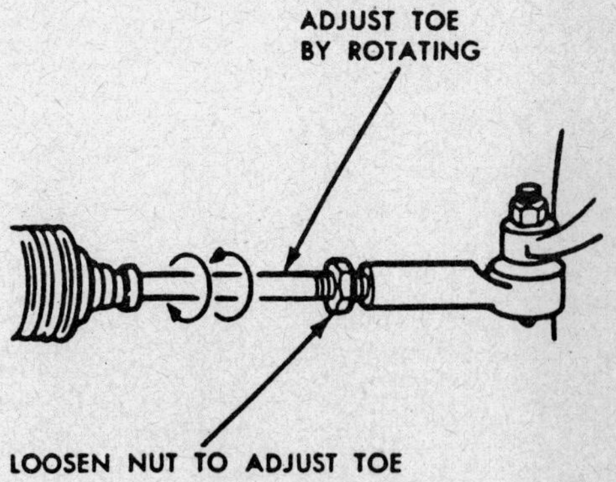

Fig. 6 Toe-in adjustment

of the Chevrolet, Malibu and Monte Carlo since the upper control arm shaft is outboard of the frame (compare **Figs. 1 and 2.**).

Camaro

Caster adjustments are made by moving the position of the upper strut mount assembly, **Fig. 3.** To make adjustment, remove dust cap and fender bolt and attach tool J-29724 to original fender bolt, **Fig. 4.** Tighten the turnbuckle and loosen the three strut mount attaching nuts.

Adjust caster by lightly tapping the mount assembly forward or rearward. Move mount forward to decrease caster, or rearward to increase caster, **Fig. 3.**

When adjustments are completed, torque the three strut mount attaching nuts to 20 ft. lbs.

CAMBER, ADJUST

Exc. Camaro

Camber adjustments are made by means of shims between the upper control arm inner support shaft and the support bracket attached to the frame. Shims may be added, subtracted or transferred to change the readings.

Change shims at both the front and rear of the shaft. Adding an equal number of shims at both front and rear of the support shaft will decrease positive camber. One shim (1/32 inch) at each location will move camber approximately 1/6 degree.

Camaro

Camber adjustments are made by moving the position of the upper strut mount assembly, **Fig. 5.** To make adjustment, remove dust cap and fender bolt and attach tool J-29724 to original fender bolt, **Fig. 4.** Tighten the turnbuckle and loosen the three strut mount attaching nuts.

Adjust camber by rotating the turnbuckle to move mount assembly inward or outward. Move mount inboard to decrease camber, or outboard to increase camber, **Fig. 5**.

When adjustments are completed, torque the three strut mount attaching nuts to 20 ft. lbs.

TOE-IN, ADJUST

Toe-in can be adjusted by loosening the clamp bolts at each end of each tie rod and turning each tie rod to increase or decrease its length as necessary until proper toe-in is secured and the steering gear is on the high point for straight-ahead driving, **Fig. 6**.

REAR WHEEL ALIGNMENT

CORVETTE

Rear wheel alignment should be checked and adjusted periodically, when rear tires indicate abnormal wear, or when suspension components are replaced. Prior to rear wheel alignment, check suspension components for damage or excessive wear and repair as needed. Also ensure tires are properly inflated, and wheel bearing endplay is within specifications.

Camber, Adjust

Wheel camber is adjusted by rotating the eccentric cam and bolt located at the inboard end of the strut rod or spindle support rod. To check and adjust camber, proceed as follows:

1. Place rear wheels of vehicle on suitable alignment equipment following manufacturer's instructions, then check camber reading.
2. If wheel camber is not within specifications, loosen cam bolt retaining nut.
3. Rotate cam bolt until camber reading is within specifications listed at the front of this chapter.
4. Torque cam bolt nut to specifications while holding position of bolt, then recheck camber reading.

TOE-IN ADJUST

1982

Rear wheel toe-in is adjusted by inserting slotted shims of varying thickness inside the frame side member on both sides of the torque control arm pivot bushing. Shims are available in thicknesses of 1/64 inch, 1/32 inch, 1/8 inch and 1/4 inch.

To adjust, loosen torque arm pivot bolts until shims are free enough to remove. Position torque arm assembly until toe-in is within specifications listed in the front of this chapter. Shim gap toward vehicle centerline between end of control arm bushing and frame side inner wall.

1984–88

Toe-in is adjusted by loosening locknuts on tie rod ends and rotating adjuster sleeves until desired setting is obtained.

OLDSMOBILE—REAR WHEEL DRIVE & 1982–85 TORONADO

INDEX OF SERVICE OPERATIONS

NOTE: Refer to the rear of this manual for vehicle manufacturer's special service tool suppliers.

Specifications

GENERAL ENGINE SPECIFICATIONS

Year	Engine		Fuel System	Bore & Stroke	Compression Ratio	Net H.P. @ RPM③	Maximum Torque Ft. Lbs. @ RPM	Normal Oil Pressure Pounds
	CID①/Liter	VIN Code ②						
1982	V6-231, 3.8L⑤	A	E2ME, 2 Bbl.④	3.80 x 3.40	8.0	110 @ 3800	190 @ 1600	37
	V6-252, 4.1L⑤	4	E4ME, 4 Bbl.④	3.96 x 3.40	8.0	125 @ 4000	205 @ 1600	37
	V6-262, 4.3L⑧	V	Fuel Injection	4.05 x 3.38	21.6	85 @ 3600	165 @ 1600	30-45
	V8-260, 4.3L	8	E2ME, 2 Bbl.④	3.50 x 3.38	7.5	100 @ 3600	190 @ 1600	35
	V8-307, 5.0L	Y	E4ME, 4 Bbl.④	3.80 x 3.38	8.0	140 @ 3600	240 @ 1600	35
	V8-350, 5.7L⑧	N	Fuel Injection	4.05 x 3.38	22.5	105 @ 3200	200 @ 1600	30-45
1983	V6-231, 3.8L⑤	A	2 Bbl.④	3.80 x 3.40	8.0	110 @ 3800190 @ 1600	37	
	V6-252, 4.1L⑤	4	4 Bbl.④	3.96 x 3.40	8.0	125 @ 4000	205 @ 2000	37
	V6-262, 4.3L⑧	V	Fuel Injection	4.05 x 3.38	22.5	85 @ 3600	165 @ 1600	30-45
	V8-307, 5.0L⑥	Y	4 Bbl.④	3.80 x 3.38	8.0	140 @ 3600	240 @ 1600	30-45
	V8-307, 5.0L⑦	9	E4MC, 4 Bbl.④	3.80 x 3.38	—	180	245	30-45
	V8-350, 5.7L⑧	N	Fuel Injection	4.05 x 3.38	22.5	105 @ 3200	200 @ 1600	30-45
1984	V6-231, 3.8L⑤	A	E2ME, 2 Bbl.④	3.80 x 3.40	8.0	110 @ 4000	190 @ 1600	37
	V6-252, 4.1L⑤	4	E4ME, 4 Bbl.④	3.96 x 3.40	8.0	125 @ 4000	205 @ 2000	37
	V6-262, 4.3L⑧	V	Fuel Injection	4.05 x 3.38	22.8	85 @ 3600	165 @ 1600	30-45
	V8-307, 5.0L⑥	Y	E4MC, 4 Bbl.④	3.80 x 3.38	8.0	140 @ 3600	240 @ 1600	30-45
	V8-307, 5.0L⑦	9	4 Bbl.	3.80 x 3.38	—	180 @ 4000	245 @ 3200	30-45
	V8-350, 5.7L⑧	N	Fuel Injection	4.05 x 3.38	22.7	105 @ 3200	200 @ 1600	30-45
1985	V6-231, 3.8L⑤	A	E2ME, 2 Bbl.④	3.80 x 3.40	8.0	110 @ 3800	190 @ 1600	—
	V6-262, 4.3L⑧	V	Fuel Injection	4.05 x 3.38	22.8	85 @ 3600	165 @ 1600	30-45
	V8-307, 5.0L	Y	E4MC, 4 Bbl.④	3.80 x 3.38	8.0	140 @ 3200	255 @ 2000⑨	30-45
	V8-350, 5.7L⑧	N	Fuel Injection	4.05 x 3.38	22.7	105 @ 3200	200 @ 1600	30-45
1986	V6-231, 3.8L⑦	A	E2ME, 2 Bbl.④	3.80 x 3.40	8.0	110 @ 3800	190 @ 1600	37
	V8-307, 5.0L	Y	E4MC, 4 Bbl.④	3.80 x 3.38	8.0	140 @ 3200	255 @ 2000	30-45
	V8-307, 5.0L	9	4 Bbl.	3.80 x 3.38	8.0	—	—	30-45
1987	V6-231, 3.8L	A	E2ME, 2 Bbl.④	3.80 x 3.40	8.0	110 @ 3800	190 @ 1600	37
	V8-307, 5.0L	Y	E4MC, 4 Bbl.④	3.80 x 3.38	8.0	140 @ 3200	255 @ 2000	30-45
	V8-307, 5.0L	9	E4MC, 4 Bbl.④	3.80 x 3.38	8.0	—	—	30-45
1988	V8-305, 5.0L	H	E4ME, 4 Bbl.④	3.74 x 3.48	9.3	180 @ 4000	240 @ 2000	50-65
	V8-307, 5.0L	Y	E4ME, 4 Bbl.④	3.80 x 3.38	8.0	140 @ 3200	255 @ 2000	30-45

①—CID-cubic inch displacement.
②—The eighth digit in the VIN denotes engine code.
③—All ratings are net-as installed in vehicle.
④—Rochester.
⑤—Bulck built engine. Distributor located at front of engine.
⑥—Exc. Hurst option.
⑦—Hurst option.
⑧—Diesel.
⑨—88 & Custom Cruiser 240 @ 1600.

ENGINE TIGHTENING SPECIFICATIONS*

*Torque specifications are for clean and lightly lubricated threads only. Dry or dirty threads produce increased friction which prevents accurate measurement of tightness.

Year	Engine Model/VIN	Spark Plugs Ft. Lbs.	Cylinder Head Bolts Ft. Lbs.	Intake Manifold Ft. Lbs.	Exhaust Manifold Ft. Lbs.	Rocker Arm Shaft Bracket Ft. Lbs.	Rocker Arm Cover Ft. Lbs.	Connecting Rod Cap Bolts Ft. Lbs.	Main Bearing Cap Bolts Ft. Lbs.	Flywheel to Crankshaft Ft. Lbs.	Vibration Damper or Pulley Ft. Lbs.
1982-83	V6-231/A ⑦	15	80	45	25	30	4	40	100	60	225
	V6-252/4 ⑦	15	80	45	25	30	4	40	100	60	225
	V6-262/V ⑤	—	②	41	29	28 ①	—	42	④	48	160-350
	V8-260/8	25	85 ③	40 ③	25	28 ①	—	42	80 ④	60 ⑧	200-310
	V8-307/Y,9	25	125 ③	40 ③	25	28 ①	—	42	80 ④	60 ⑧	200-310
	V8-350/N ⑤	—	130 ③	40 ③	25	28 ①	—	42	120	60	210-300
1984	V6-231/A ⑦	15	80	45	25	30	4	40	100	60	225
	V6-252/4 ⑦	15	80	45	25	30	4	40	100	60	225
	V6-262/V ⑤	—	②	41	31	28 ①	—	42	89	57	200-350
	V8-307/Y,9	25	125 ③	40 ③	25	28 ①	—	42	80 ⑥	60	200-310
	V8-350/N ⑤	—	130 ③	40 ③	25	28 ①	—	42	120	60	200-310
1985	V6-231/A ⑦	15	80	45	25	30	4	40	100	60	225
	V6-262/V ⑤	—	②	41	28	28 ①	—	42	89 ⑨	57	203-350
	V8-307/Y	25	125 ③	40 ③	25	28 ①	—	42	80 ⑥	60	200-310
	V8-350/N ⑤	—	130 ③	40 ③	25	28 ①	—	42	120	60	200-310
1986	V6-231	15	②	45	25	30	4	40	100	60	225
	V8-307	25	125 ③	40 ③	25	25	—	42	80 ⑥	60	200-310
1987	V6-231	20	②	45	37	25	4	40	100	60	200
	V8-307	25	130 ③	40 ③	25	25	—	48	80 ⑥	60	200-310

①—Rocker arm pivot bolt to head.
②—See text for procedure.
③—Clean and dip entire bolt in engine oil before tightening.
④—1982, 107 ft. lbs.; 1983, 89 ft. lbs.
⑤—Oldsmobile built diesel engine.
⑥—Rear 120 ft. lbs.
⑦—Buick built engine.
⑧—With automatic transmission.
⑨—Type II bolts at Nos. 2 and 3 outer positions.

DRIVE AXLE SPECIFICATIONS

Year	Model	Carrier Type	Ring Gear & Pinion Backlash		Pinion Bearing Preload			Differential Bearing Preload		
			Method	Adjustment	Method	New Bearings Inch Lbs.	Used Bearings Inch Lbs.	Method	New Bearings Inch Lbs.	Used Bearings Inch Lbs.
1982-85	Exc. Toronado	Integral	Shims	.005-.009	Spacer	24-32	8-12	Shims	①	①
	Toronado	Integral	Shims	.005-.007	Spacer	22	5	Shims	①	①
1986-87	All	Integral	Shims	.005-.009	Spacer	20-25	10-15	Shims	①	①

①Slip fit plus .004 inch clearance on each side.

ALTERNATOR SPECIFICATIONS

Year	Model	Rated Hot Output Amps.	Field Current 12 Volts @ 80°F
1982	1100110	42	4-5
	1100121	63	4-5
	1100164	55	4-5
	1100165	63	4-5
	1100190	85	4.0-4.6
	1100194	70	4.0-4.6
	1100195	85	4.0-4.6
	1100198	42	4-5
	1101037	70	4.0-4.6
	1101045	85	4.0-4.6
	1101084	85	4.0-4.6
	1101088	70	4.0-4.6
	1103151	63	4-5
1983	1100200	78	4.5-5.0
	1100230	42	4-5
	1100239	55	4.5-5.0
	1100247	63	4.5-5.0
	1100260	78	4.5-5.0
	1100263	78	4.5-5.0
	1100297	42	4-5
	1100298	55	4.5-5.0
	1100300	63	4.5-5.0
	1101264	78	—
	1105022	78	4.5-5.0
	1105025	63	4.5-5.0
	1105027	63	4.5-5.0
	1105029	63	4.5-5.0
	1105032	78	4.5-5.0
	1105041	78	4.5-5.0
	1105042	78	4.5-5.0
	1105194	78	4.5-5.0
	1105198	85	4.0-4.6
	1105250	70	4.0-4.6
	1105343	85	4.0-4.6
1984	1100200	78	4.5-5.0
	1100239	55	4.5-5.0
	1100260	78	4.5-5.0
	1105025	66	4.5-5.0
	1105028	78	4.5-5.0
	1105041	78	4.5-5.0
	1105197	70	4.0-4.6
	1105548	70	4.0-4.6
	1105564	66	4.5-5.0
	1105565	78	4.5-5.0
	1105566	66	4.5-5.0
	1105567	78	4.5-5.0
	1105568	78	4.5-5.0
	1105569	78	4.5-5.0
1985	1100200	78	4.5-5.0
	1100239	55	4.5-5.0
	1100260	78	4.5-5.0
	1105197	70	4.0-4.6
	1105562	94	—
	1105565	78	4.5-5.0
	1105569	78	4.5-5.0
1986-87	1100200	78	—
	1100239	55	—
	1105197	70	—
	1105565	78	—
1988	—	—	—

STARTING MOTOR APPLICATIONS

Year	Model/VIN	Starter Number
1982	V6-231/A	1998236
	V6-252/4 ②	1998234
	V6-252/4 ③	1998237
	V6-262 Diesel/V	1998552
	V8-260/8	1109544
	V8-307/Y ① ②	1109544
	V8-307/Y ③	1998237
	V8-350 Diesel/N ① ②	1998552
	V8-350 Diesel/N ③	1109495
1983	V6-231/A	1998236
	V6-252/4 ②	1998234
	V6-252/4 ③	1998237
	V6-262 Diesel/V	1998554
	V8-307/Y,9 ① ②	1109544
	V8-307/Y ③	1998237
	V8-350 Diesel/N ① ②	1998554
	V8-350 Diesel/N ③	1109495
1984	V6-231/A	1998236
	V6-252/4	1998237
	V6-262 Diesel/V	1998556
		22511854
	V8-307/Y,9 ① ②	1109544
	V8-307/Y ③	1998237
	V8-305 Diesel/N ① ②	1998553
		22511854
	V8-350 Diesel/N ③	1109495
1985	V6-231/A	1998236
	V6-262 Diesel/V	1998556
		22511854
	V8-307/Y ① ④	1109544
	V8-307/Y ③	1998237
	V8-350 Diesel/N ① ④	1998553
		22523207
	V8-350 Diesel/N ③	1109495
1986	V6-231	1998516
	V8-307	1998536
1987	V6-231	1998516
	V8-307	1998536
1988	V8-305	—
	V8-307	—

①—Cutlass.
②—88 & 98.
③—Toronado.
④—88.

FRONT WHEEL ALIGNMENT SPECIFICATIONS

Year	Model	Caster Angle, Degrees		Camber Angle, Degrees				Toe-In. Inch
				Limits		Desired		
		Limits	Desired	Left	Right	Left	Right	
1982-83	Cutlass②	+1/2 to +1 1/2	+1	0 to +1	0 to +1	+1/2	+1/2	+1/16 to +3/16
	Cutlass①	+2 1/2 to +3 1/2	+3	0 to +1	0 to +1	+1/2	+1/2	+1/16 to +3/16
	88, 98	+2 1/2 to +3 1/2	+3	+1/4 to +1 1/4	+1/4 to +1 1/4	+3/4	+3/4	+1/16 to +3/16
	Toronado	+2 to +3	+2 1/2	−1/2 to +1/2	−1/2 to +1/2	0	0	−1/16 to +1/16
1984-85	Cutlass	+2 1/2 to +3 1/2	+3	0 to +1	0 to +1	+1/2	+1/2	+1/10 to +2/10
	88, 98	+2 1/2 to +3 1/2	+3	+3/10 to +1 3/10	+3/10 to +1 3/10	+4/5	+4/5	+1/10 to +2/10
	Custom Cruiser	+2 1/2 to 3 1/2	+3	+3/10 to 1 3/10	+3/10 to +1 3/10	+4/5	+4/5	+1/10 to +2/10
	Toronado	+2 to +3	+2 1/2	−1/2 to +1/2	−1/2 to +1/2	0	0	−1/20 to +1/20
1986	Cutlass	+2 to +4	+3	−3/10 to +1 3/10	−3/10 to +1 3/10	+1/2	+1/2	1/16 to +1/4
	Custom Cruiser	+1 4/5 to +3 4/5	+2 4/5	0 to 1 3/5	0 to 1 3/5	+4/5	+4/5	−1/20 to +1/20
1987	Cutlass	+1 4/5 to +3 4/5	+2 4/5	−3/10 to +1 3/10	−3/10 to +1 3/10	+1/2	+1/2	−1/10 to +3/10
	Custom Cruiser	+1 4/5 to +3 4/5	+2 4/5	0 to +1 3/5	0 to +1 3/5	+4/5	+4/5	−1/10 to +3/10
1988	Cutlass	—	—	—	—	—	—	—
	Custom Cruiser	—	—	—	—	—	—	—

①—Power Steering.
②—Manual Steering.

REAR WHEEL ALIGNMENT SPECIFICATIONS

Year	Model	Camber Angle, Degrees				Toe-In Inch
		Limits		Desired		
		Left	Right	Left	Right	
1982-83	Toronado	−.4 to +.4	−.4 to +.4	0	0	0 to 5/32
1984-85	Toronado	−.4 to +.4	−.4 to +.4	0	0	0 to +3/32

COOLING SYSTEM & CAPACITY DATA

Year	Model or Engine/V.I.N.	Cooling Capacity, Qts.		Radiator Cap Relief Pressure Lbs.	Thermo. Opening Temp.	Fuel Tank Gals.	Engine Oil Refill Qts. ①	Auto. Trans. Qts. ②	Rear Axle Oil Pints
		Less A/C	With A/C						
1982	V6-231/A Cutlass ⑦	13 ⑳	13 ⑳	15	195	18	4		⑤
	V6-231/A 88 ⑦	13	13	15	195	25 ⑨	4	⑤	④
	V6-252/4 98	12.8	12.8	15	195	25	4	⑤	3¼ ③
	V6-252/4 Toronado	13.1	13.1	15	195	21	4	⑤	3¼ ③
	V6-262/V ⑬	14.5	15.3	15	195	19.75	7 ⑥ ⑰	⑤	④
	V8-260/8	16.5 ⑪	16.2 ⑪	15	195	25 ⑨	4	⑤	④
	V8-307/Y Cutlass	14.9 ⑲	15.6	15	195	25 ⑨	4	⑤	④
	V8-307/Y 88 & Custom Cruiser	15.6 ⑫	15.3 ⑫	15	195	25 ⑨	4	⑤	④
	V8-307/Y 98	16.2	16.2	15	195	25	4	⑤	④
	V8-307/Y Toronado	16.5	16.5	15	195	21	4	⑤	3¼ ③
	V8-350/N Cutlass ⑬	17.4	17.3	15	195	19.75 ⑮	7 ⑥ ⑰	⑤	④
	V8-350/N 88 & 98 ⑬	18	18	15	195	26.5 ⑨	7 ⑥ ⑰	⑤	④
	V8-350/N Toronado ⑬	18.1	18.1	15	195	22.75	7 ⑥ ⑰	⑤	3¼ ③
1983	V6-231/A Cutlass	13 ⑩	13 ⑩	15	195	18	4	⑤	④
	V6-231/A 88	13	13	15	195	25 ⑨	4	⑤	④
	V6-252/4 98	12.5	12.5	15	195	25	4	⑤	④
	V6-252/4 Toronado	13.25	13.25	15	195	21	4	⑤	3¼ ③
	V6-262/V ⑬	13.75	14.25	15	195	19.8	6 ⑥ ⑰	⑤	④
	V8-307/Y Cutlass	14.75	15.5	15	195	18	4	⑤	④
	V8-307/Y 88	15.5 ⑭	15.3 ⑭	15	195	25	4	⑤	④
	V8-307/Y 98	15.25 ⑭	15.25 ⑭	15	195	25	4	⑤	④
	V8-307/Y Toronado	16.25	16.25	15	195	21	4	⑤	3¼ ③
	V8-350/N Cutlass	17.5	17.5	15	195	19.8	7 ⑥ ⑰	⑤	④
	V8-350/N 88 & 98	18.25	18	15	195	26	7 ⑥ ⑰	⑤	④
	V8-350/N Toronado	18.25	18.25	15	195	22.8	7 ⑥ ⑰	⑤	3¼ ③
1984	V6-231/A Cutlass	13 ⑩	13 ⑩	15	195	18.2	4	⑤	④
	V6-231/A 88	13	13	15	195	25 ⑨	4	⑤	④
	V6-252/4 Toronado	—	12.5	15	195	21	4	⑤	3¼ ③
	V6-262/V ⑬ Cutlass	13.6	14.4	15	195	19.8	6 ⑥ ⑰	⑤	④
	V8-307/Y Cutlass	14.9	15.6	15	195	18.2	4	⑤	④
	V8-307/Y 88 & 98	15.6 ⑭	15.3 ⑭	15	195	25	4	⑤	④
	V8-307/Y Toronado	—	16.4	15	195	21	4	⑤	3⅓ ③
	V8-350/N Cutlass	17.4	17.3	15	195	19.8	7 ⑥ ⑰	⑤	④
	V8-350/N 88 & 98	18.3	18	15	195	27 ⑨	7 ⑥ ⑰	⑤	④
	V8-350/N Toronado	—	18.2	15	195	22.8	7 ⑥ ⑰	⑤	3⅓ ③
1985	V6-231/A Cutlass	13	13.5	15	195	18	4	⑧	④
	V6-231/A 88	13	13	15	195	25 ⑨	4	⑧	④
	V6-262/V ⑬ Cutlass	13.6	14.4	15	195	19.8	6 ⑥ ⑰	⑧	④
	V8-307/Y Cutlass	14.9	15.5	15	195	18	4	⑧	④
	V8-307/Y 88	15.5	15.3 ⑭	15	195	25 ⑨	4	⑧	④
	V8-307/Y Toronado	—	16.5 ⑱	15	195	21	4	⑧	3½ ③
	V8-350/N ⑬ Cutlass	17.4	17.4	15	195	19.8	4	⑧	④
	V8-350/N ⑬ 88	18.3	18	15	195	26 ⑨	7 ⑥ ⑰	⑧	④
	V8-350/N ⑬ Toronado	—	18.3	15	195	22.8	7 ⑥ ⑰	⑯	3½ ③

Continued

COOLING SYSTEM & CAPACITY DATA—Continued

Year	Model or Engine/V.I.N.	Cooling Capacity, Qts. Less A/C	Cooling Capacity, Qts. With A/C	Radiator Cap Relief Pressure Lbs.	Thermo. Opening Temp.	Fuel Tank Gals.	Engine Oil Refill Qts. ①	Auto. Trans. Qts. ②	Rear Axle Oil Pints
1986	V6-231 Cutlass	13	13.5	15	195	18	4	4.2	3.5③
	V8-307 Cutlass	14.9	15.6	15	195	18	4	4.2	3.4③
	V8-307 Custom Cruiser	㉑	15.3㉑	15	195	22	4	⑧	④
1987	V6-231 Cutlass	13	13.5	15	195	18	4	⑧	④
	V8-307 Cutlass	14.9	15.6	15	195	18	4	⑧	④
	V8-307 Custom Cruiser	㉑	15.3㉑	15	195	22	4	⑧	④
1988	V8-305 Cutlass	16.4	15.9	15	195	18	5	—	—
	V8-307 Cutlass	—	—	15	195	22	4	—	3½③
	V8-307 Custom Cruiser	㉑	15.3㉑	15	195	22	4	—	5 ⅖

①—Add one quart with filter change.
②—Approximate; make final check with dipstick.
③—Final drive.
④—7.5 inch ring gear, 3.5 pints; 8.5 inch ring gear, 4.25 pints.
⑤—T.H.M. 200C, oil pan 4⅛ qts.; total capacity, 10½ qts. T.H.M. 2004R, oil pan 5 qts.; total capacity, 11 qts. T.H.M. 250C & 350C, oil pan 3⅛ qts.; total capacity 10 qts. T.H.M. 325-4L, oil pan 5½ qts.; total capacity 13 qts.
⑥—Recommended diesel engine oil, use oil designation SF/CC or SF/CD.
⑦—Buick built engine.
⑧—T.H.M. 200C, oil pan only, 3.5 qts.; total capacity, 9.5 qts. T.H.M. 250-4R, oil pan only, 3.5 qts.; total capacity, 11 qts. T.H.M. 325-4L, oil pan only 3.25 qts.; total capacity, 10 qts.
⑨—Custom Cruiser, 22 gals.
⑩—With high capacity cooling, 13.25 qts.
⑪—Trailer towing, 17.0 qts.; Heavy duty, 17.25 qts.
⑫—Heavy duty & trailer towing, 16.25 qts.
⑬—Diesel engine.
⑭—High capacity cooling, 16.25 qts.; heavy duty trailer tow, 16 qts.
⑮—Cutlass Cruiser, 18.25 gals.
⑯—Oil pan only, 3¼ qts,; total capacity, 10 qts.
⑰—Includes filter.
⑱—Trailer Towing, 18.5 qts.
⑲—Heavy duty & trailer towing, 15.5 qts.
⑳—With heavy duty or trailer tow, 13.6 qts.
㉑—With high capacity cooling system, 16 qts.; With extra capacity cool ing system, 16.3 qts.

Electrical Section

INDEX

IGNITION LOCK
REPLACE

1. Remove steering wheel as described under Horn Sounder and Steering Wheel, Replace.
2. Remove turn signal switch as described under Turn Signal Switch. Replace, then remove buzzer switch.
3. Place ignition switch in Run position, then remove lock cylinder retaining screw and lock cylinder.
4. To install, rotate lock cylinder to stop while holding housing, **Fig. 1.** Align cylinder key with keyway in housing, then push lock cylinder assembly into housing until fully seated.
5. Install lock cylinder retaining screw. Torque screw to 40 inch lbs. for standard columns. On adjustable columns, torque retaining screw to 22 inch lbs.
6. Install buzzer switch, turn signal switch and steering wheel.

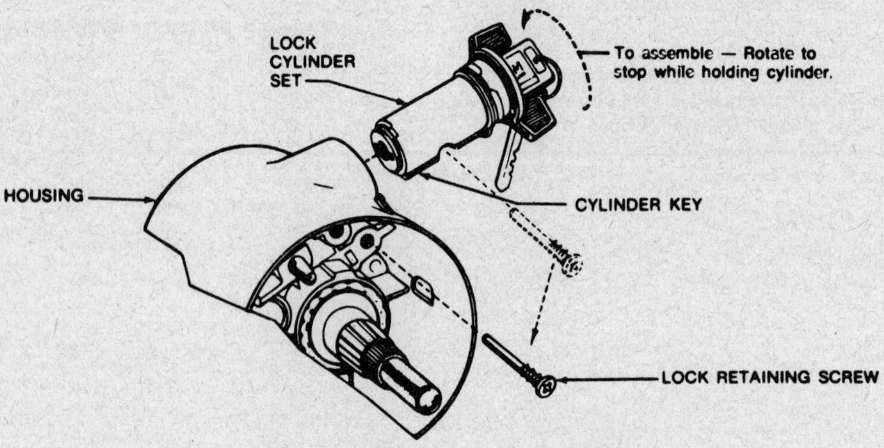

Fig. 1 Ignition lock removal

STARTER
REPLACE

Upon removal of starter, note if any shims are used. If shims are used, they should be reinstalled in their original location during installation.

If starter is noisy during cranking, remove one .015 inch double shim or add one .015 inch single shim to the outer bolt. If starter makes a high pitched whine after firing, add .015 inch double shims until noise ceases.

V6-231 & 252

1. Disconnect battery ground cable, then raise and support vehicle.
2. On vehicles with automatic transmission, disconnect exhaust crossover pipe and disconnect oil cooler lines at transmission, then remove flywheel housing cover.
3. On vehicles with manual transmission, remove front crossmember to body bolts, right and left brace to crossmember bolts, then remove crossmember.
4. Remove starter bolts, then lower the starter, disconnect electrical leads and remove starter.
5. Reverse procedure to install.

EXC. TORONADO, V6-231 & 252 & V8-260 DIESEL W/MANUAL TRANS.

1. Disconnect battery ground cable, then raise and support vehicle.
2. Proceed as follows:
   a. Remove upper support retaining bolts.
   b. On V8 engines, remove flywheel housing cover.
3. Remove starter retaining bolts, then lower starter, disconnect electrical leads and remove starter.
4. Reverse procedure to install.

TORONADO

1. Disconnect battery ground cable, then raise and support vehicle.
2. Remove starter attaching bolts and position starter so that starter wiring can be disconnected.
3. Disconnect starter wiring, then lower starter from vehicle.
4. Reverse procedure to install. If shims were removed, they must be installed in their original location.

IGNITION SWITCH
REPLACE

1. Disconnect battery ground cable.
2. On models with regular steering column, turn ignition lock to "Off-Unlock"

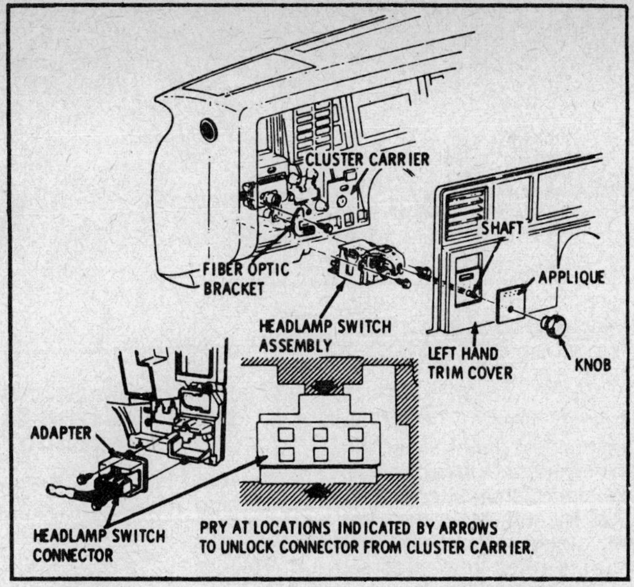

Fig. 2 Headlight switch. Toronado

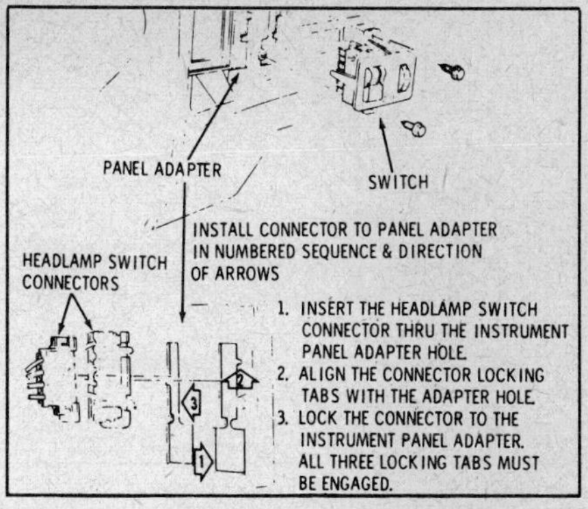

Fig. 3 Headlight switch. Cutlass

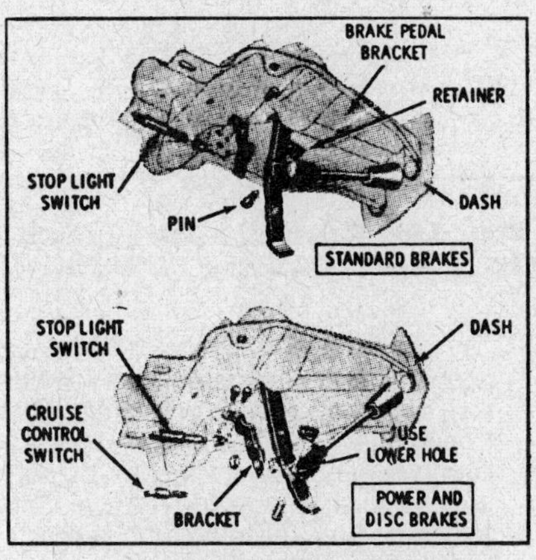

Fig. 4 Brake switch installation.

position. On models with tilt and telescope steering column, turn ignition lock to "Accessory" position.

3. Remove cover attaching bolts, loosen toe pan clamp bolts and remove trim cap from lower part of panel.
4. Remove bracket retaining nuts and lower steering column to the seat.
5. Disconnect and remove switch.
6. On models equipped with column mounted dimmer switch, remove two switch attaching screws, then remove switch and disconnect wire connector.
7. Be sure that lock is in same position as when switch was removed then install switch onto actuator and column.
8. Connect wiring and reinstall column. On models with column mounted dimmer switch, install and adjust dimmer switch as described under "Column Mounted Dimmer Switch."

LIGHT SWITCH REPLACE

TORONADO

1. Disconnect battery ground cable.
2. Remove headlamp switch knob, radio knobs and steering column trim cover.
3. Remove four screws from underside of lefthand trim cover, **Fig. 2.**
4. Remove lefthand sound absorber, then carefully pull lefthand trim cover from instrument panel. **It may be necessary to disconnect shift indicator cable clip and lower steering column slightly to remove lefthand trim cover.**
5. Remove two screws attaching switch to instrument cluster carrier, then pull switch rearward to remove.
6. To disconnect wire connector, remove two connector attaching screws, then pry connector at locations shown in **Fig. 2.**
7. Reverse procedure to install.

CUTLASS

1. Disconnect battery ground cable.
2. Remove cluster pad assembly.
3. Remove two headlight switch mounting screws, then pull switch away from panel adapter.
4. To disconnect wire connector, pry connector at locations indicated by arrows as shown in **Fig. 3.** Pull connector out, then slide to left and push forward to remove.
5. Reverse procedure to install. Refer to **Fig. 3,** to install wire connector.

88, 98 & CUSTOM CRUISER

1. Disconnect battery ground cable.
2. Remove steering column trim cover, gauge cluster and headlamp switch knob.
3. Remove two screws attaching left side trim cover to cluster carrier, then

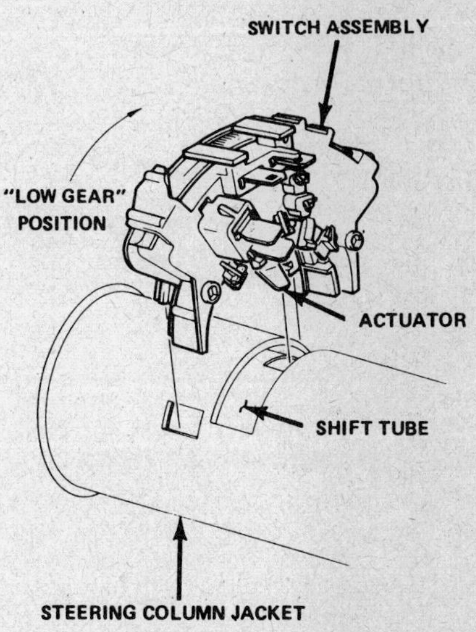

Fig. 5 Back-up light switch installation

remove trim cover by pulling rearward.

4. Remove two screws attaching mounting plate to cluster carrier.
5. Pull switch and mounting plate rearward and disconnect electrical connector.
6. Remove nut and separate mounting plate from switch.
7. Reverse procedure to install.

STOP LIGHT SWITCH

The stop light switch is attached to the brake pedal bracket and is actuated by the brake pedal arm, **Fig. 4.** When installing the switch, insert switch into tubular clip until switch body seats on tube clip. Pull brake pedal rearward until it contacts brake pedal stop. This moves the switch in the tubular clip providing proper adjustment.

BACK-UP LIGHT SWITCH REPLACE

1. Place gear selector in "Neutral."
2. Gently rock back-up light switch out of steering column.

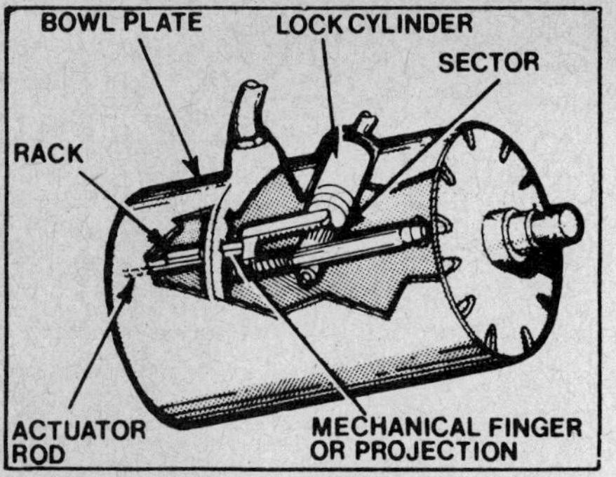

Fig. 6 Mechanical neutral start system w/standard column

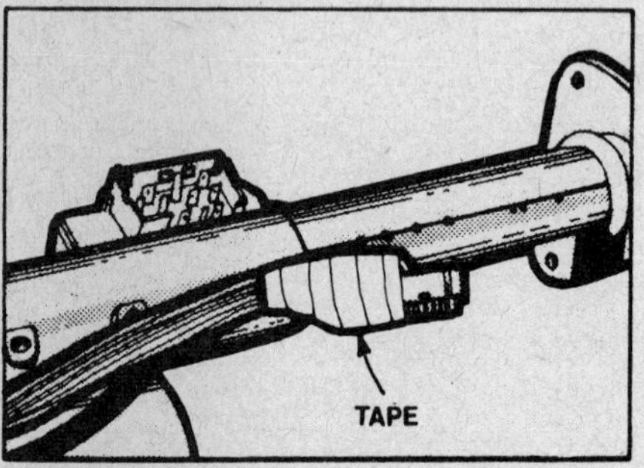

Fig. 9 Taping turn signal connector & wires

3. Disconnect wiring connectors. Connect wiring connectors to new switch.
4. Align switch actuator with hole in shift tube, **Fig. 5.**
5. Position connector side of switch into lower jacket cut out.
6. Push down front of switch, ensuring switch tangs snap into holes in steering column jacket.
7. Adjust switch by placing gear selector in "Park" position. The switch main housing and housing back should ratchet, providing proper adjustment.

NEUTRAL START SYSTEM

Actuation of the ignition switch is prevented by a mechanical lockout system, **Figs. 6 and 7,** which prevents the lock cylinder from rotating when the selector lever is out of Park or Neutral. When the selector lever is in Park or Neutral, the slots in the bowl plate and the finger on the actuator rod align allowing the finger to pass through the bowl plate in turn actuating the ignition switch, **Fig. 8.** If the selector lever is in any position other than Park or Neutral, the finger contacts the bowl plate when the lock cylinder is rotated, thereby preventing full travel of the lock cylinder.

TURN SIGNAL SWITCH

REPLACE

TILT & TELESCOPE

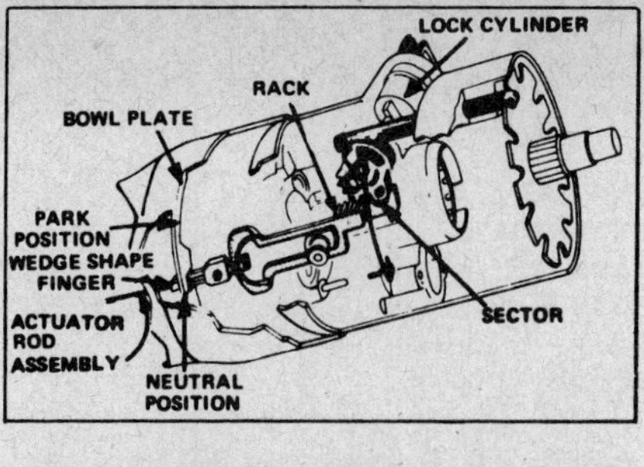

Fig. 7 Mechanical neutral start system w/tilt column

1. Disconnect battery ground cable and remove steering wheel.
2. Remove instrument panel lower trim panel, then disconnect turn signal harness connector. Remove connector from packet mounting bracket and wrap tape around connector and wires to prevent wires from snagging when removing switch, **Fig. 9.**
3. Remove four bolts securing column bracket assembly to mast jacket.
4. Disconnect shift indicator.
5. Hold column in position and remove two nuts securing column bracket assembly. Then, remove bracket and turn signal wiring connector. Loosely reinstall bracket to hold column in place.
6. Remove rubber bumper and plastic retainer.
7. Using a suitable compressor, **Fig. 10,** depress lock plate far enough to remove C-ring from shaft. **Compressor must be positioned on large lips of cancelling cam.**
8. Remove lock plate and carrier assembly, then the upper bearing spring.
9. On models less column mounted dimmer switch, place turn signal lever in right turn position and unscrew lever. Lift tilt lever and position in center position.
10. On models with column mounted dimmer switch, remove actuator arm screw and actuator arm, then remove turn signal lever by pulling straight out to disengage.
11. Push in hazard warning knob, then remove screw and hazard warning knob.
12. Remove turn signal switch attaching screws, then pull switch and wiring from top of column.

EXC. TILT & TELESCOPE

1. Disconnect battery ground cable.
2. Remove steering wheel.
3. Remove cover screws and cover.
4. Using suitable compressor, depress lock plate far enough to remove the C-ring from shaft.
5. Remove lock plate, cancelling cam, spring and signal lever.
6. Depress hazard warning knob then unscrew knob and remove.
7. On models less column mounted dimmer switch, position lever in right turn position and remove three switch attaching screws.
8. On models with column mounted dimmer switch, remove actuator arm screw and actuator arm, then remove turn signal lever by pulling straight out to disengage.
9. Remove panel lower trim cap, disconnect switch harness and remove bolts attaching bracket to column jacket.
10. Disconnect shift indicator if equipped.
11. Remove two nuts holding column in position, remove bracket and wire protector while holding column in position then loosely install bracket to hold column in place.
12. Tape switch wires at connector keeping wires flat, then carefully remove wires and switch.

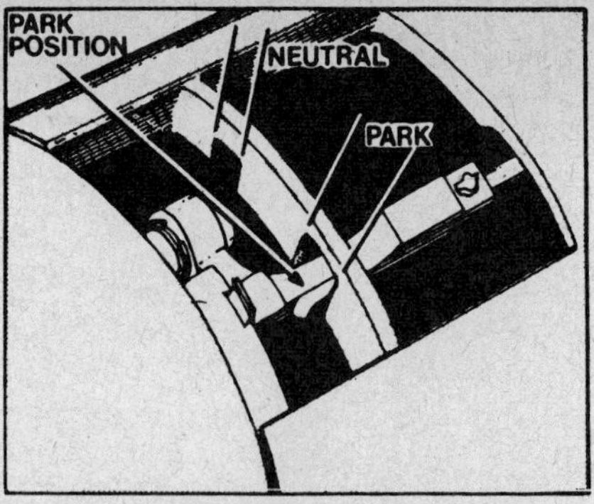

Fig. 8 Mechanical neutral start system in Park position

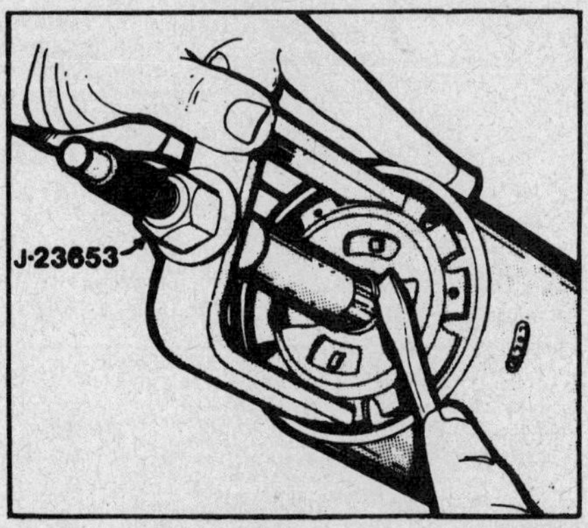

Fig. 10 Compressing lock plate & removing retaining ring

COLUMN-MOUNTED DIMMER SWITCH

REPLACE

1. Disconnect battery ground cable.
2. Remove instrument panel lower trim and on models with A/C, remove A/C duct extension at column.
3. Disconnect shift indicator from column and remove toe-plate cover screws.
4. Remove two nuts from instrument panel support bracket studs and lower steering column, resting steering wheel on front seat.
5. Remove dimmer switch retaining screw and the switch. Tape actuator

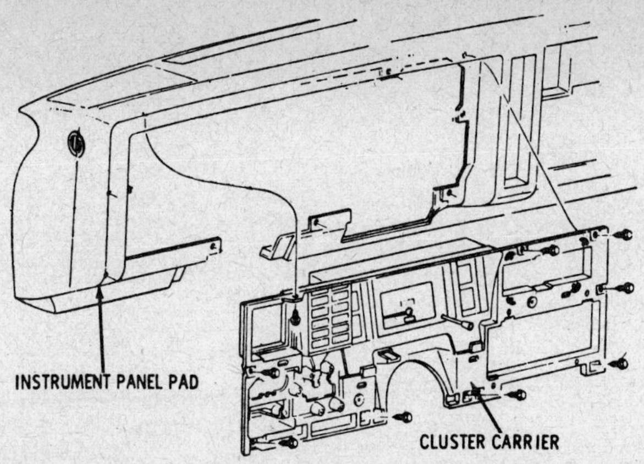

Fig. 11 Instrument cluster. Toronado

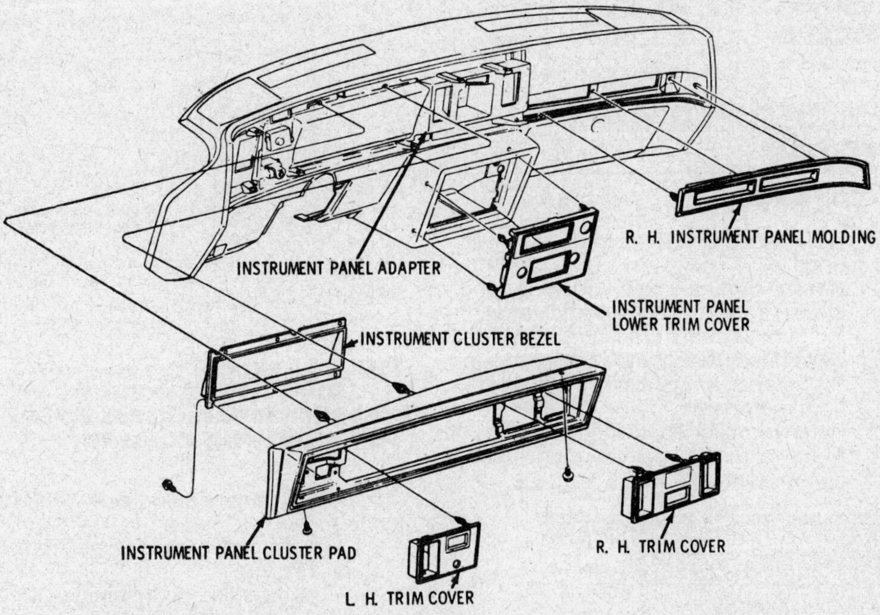

Fig. 12 Instrument panel cluster pad. Cutlass

rod to column and separate switch from rod. **Two screws are used to retain dimmer switch to steering column.**

6. Reverse procedure to install. To adjust switch, depress dimmer switch slightly and install a 3/32 inch twist drill to lock the switch to the body. Force switch upward to remove lash between switch and pivot. Torque switch retaining screw to 35 inch lbs. and remove tape from actuator rod. Remove twist drill and check for proper operation.

HORN SOUNDER & STEERING WHEEL REPLACE

1. Disconnect battery ground cable.
2. For tilt and telescope steering column proceed as follows:
   a. Remove pad assembly retaining screws, disconnect connector and remove pad assembly.
   b. Move locking lever counterclockwise until full release is obtained. Scribe a mark on the plate assembly where the two screws attach plate assembly to locking lever (for ease of installation) and remove the two screws.
   c. Unscrew and remove plate assembly.
3. For standard wheel, pull up on horn cap retainer assembly and disconnect horn contacts.
4. For deluxe wheel, remove three screws from pad assembly and disconnect connectors.
5. On sport wheel, pull up on and remove emblem and horn contact assembly from wheel.
6. On wood grain wheel, carefully pry horn cap assembly from wheel.
7. On all models, remove steering wheel nut and using a suitable puller, remove steering wheel. **Some vehicles have a snap ring on the end of the steering shaft which must be removed before removing steering wheel nut.**
8. Reverse procedure to install.

INSTRUMENT CLUSTER REPLACE

On some models, a yellow flag with the word emissions will rotate into the odometer window at 30,000 mile intervals indicating either a catalyst or oxygen sensor change is required. After performing the required maintenance, reset the emissions flag as follows:

a. On Cutlass models, remove cluster pad assembly. On 88, 98, Custom Cruiser and Toronado, remove lefthand trim cover.
b. On all models, remove trip odometer reset knob, if equipped.
c. Remove screws attaching cluster lens to cluster assembly and remove lens.
d. Using a pointed tool inserted at an angle to engage flag wheel detents, rotate flag wheel downward. When flag wheel is reset, the alignment mark will be in center of odometer window.

TORONADO

1. Disconnect battery ground cable.
2. Remove headlamp switch knob, radio knobs and steering column trim cover.
3. Remove four screws from underside of lefthand trim cover.
4. Remove lefthand sound absorber, then pull lefthand trim cover from instrument panel. **It may be necessary to disconnect shift indicator cable clip and lower steering column slightly to remove lefthand trim cover.**
5. Remove two screws attaching headlamp switch to cluster carrier, then pull switch from carrier.
6. Remove windshield wiper switch, then remove radio from instrument panel.
7. Remove four screws attaching heater-A/C control to cluster. Pull control out of cluster and disconnect wiring, vacuum lines and temperature control cable, then remove control assembly.
8. Unlock headlamp switch, windshield wiper, cruise control and defogger switch connectors from cluster carrier, then disconnect speedometer cable.
9. Remove nine cluster carrier attaching screws, then remove cluster carrier, **Fig. 11.**

CUTLASS

1. Disconnect battery ground cable.
2. Remove righthand and lefthand trim panels, **Fig. 12.**
3. Remove the 7 screws retaining cluster pad to panel adapter.
4. Pull panel pad to disengage it from retaining clips and remove pad assembly, **Fig. 12.**
5. Remove steering column trim cover, then disconnect shift indicator clip from shift bowl.

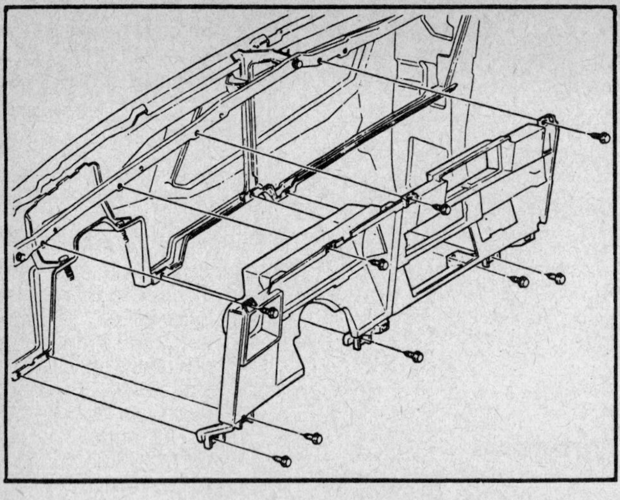

Fig. 13 Instrument cluster. 88, 98 & Custom Cruiser

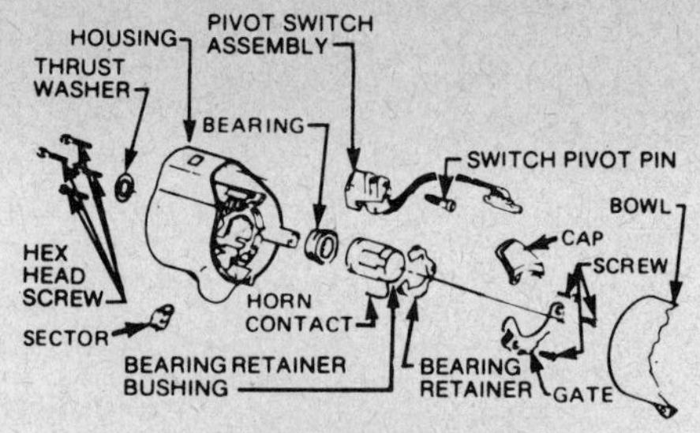

Fig. 14 Windshield wiper switch removal & installation. Models w/standard steering column

6. Remove the 4 screws retaining cluster assembly, then disconnect speedometer cable and electrical connectors and remove cluster assembly.
7. Reverse procedure to install.

88, 98 & CUSTOM CRUISER

1. Disconnect battery ground cable.
2. Rotate headlight switch so notch on switch faces downward. Bend a 1/8 inch hook on a piece of stiff wire. Use the wire hook in the notch to pull the knob retainer clip and pull knob off shaft.
3. Remove twilight sentinel knob.
4. Position steering column collar upward and remove column lower trim cover.
5. Remove two screws securing trim cover to cluster carrier, **Fig. 13.**
6. Pull trim cover from clips.
7. Remove radio knobs and cigar lighter.
8. Remove two screws securing to panel, **Fig. 13.**
9. Pull trim cover from panel clips.
10. Remove radio as outlined under "Radio, Replace."
11. Remove A/C-heater control attaching screws, pull control outward and disconnect control cables and electrical connectors.
12. Remove switches, clock and disconnect ashtray lamp.
13. Remove righthand outside remote mirror control screws.
14. Disconnect shift indicator cable clip.
15. Remove steering column bolts at floor pan and the nuts from the steering column bracket. Then, lower the steering column and rest steering wheel on seat.
16. Disconnect speedometer cable.
17. Remove instrument panel cluster carrier bolts and the two instrument panel screws, **Fig. 13.**
18. Remove center air duct screws.
19. Pull cluster outward to disconnect electrical connectors.
20. Remove cluster carrier, **Fig. 13.**

WINDSHIELD WIPER MOTOR

REPLACE

1. Raise hood and remove cowl screen or grille.
2. Reach through cowl opening and loosen transmission drive link attaching nuts to motor crankarm.
3. Disconnect wiring and washer hoses.
4. Disconnect transmission drive link from motor arm.
5. Remove motor attaching screws.
6. Remove motor while guiding crankarm through opening.

WINDSHIELD WIPER TRANSMISSION

REPLACE

RECTANGULAR MOTOR

1. Remove wiper arms and blades.
2. Raise hood and remove cowl vent screen or grille.
3. Disconnect wiring from motor.
4. Loosen, do not remove, transmission drive link to motor crankarm attaching nuts and disconnect drive link from crankarm.
5. Remove right and left transmission to body attaching screws and guide transmission and linkage out through cowl opening.

ROUND MOTOR

1. Raise hood and remove cowl vent screen.
2. On all except Toronado, remove right and left wiper arm and blade assemblies. On Toronado, remove arm and blade only from transmission to be removed.
3. Loosen, do not remove, attaching nuts securing transmission drive link to motor crankarm. **On Toronado, if only the left transmission is to be removed, it will not be necessary to loosen attaching nuts securing the right transmission drive link to the motor.**
4. Disconnect drive link from motor crankarm.
5. On all except Toronado, remove right and left transmission to body attaching screws. On Toronado, remove the attaching screws securing only the transmission to be removed.
6. Remove transmission and linkage by guiding it through opening.

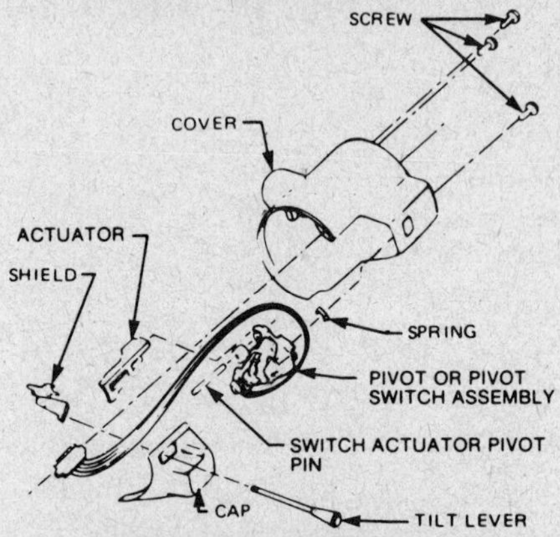

Fig. 15 Windshield wiper switch removal & installation. Models w/tilt steering column

WINDSHIELD WIPER SWITCH

REPLACE

1. Remove steering wheel as described under "Horn Sounder and Steering Wheel, Replace."
2. Remove turn signal switch as described under "Turn Signal Switch, Replace."
3. Remove ignition lock as described under "Ignition Lock, Replace."
4. Remove and install cover and wiper switch as shown in **Figs. 14 and 15.**
5. Reverse steps 1 through 3 to install.

RADIO

REPLACE

When installing radio, be sure to adjust antenna trimmer for peak performance.

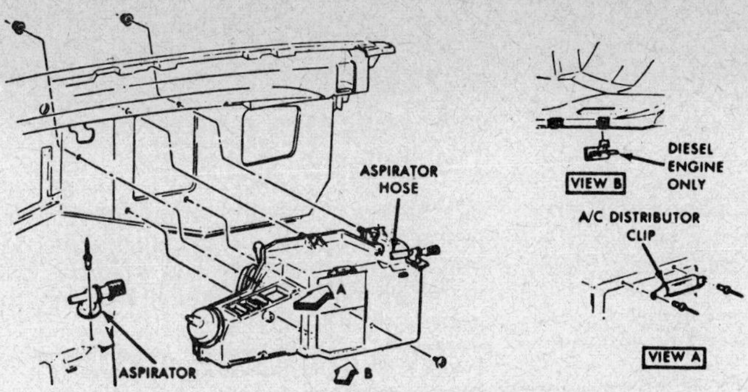

Fig. 16 Heater core. Toronado

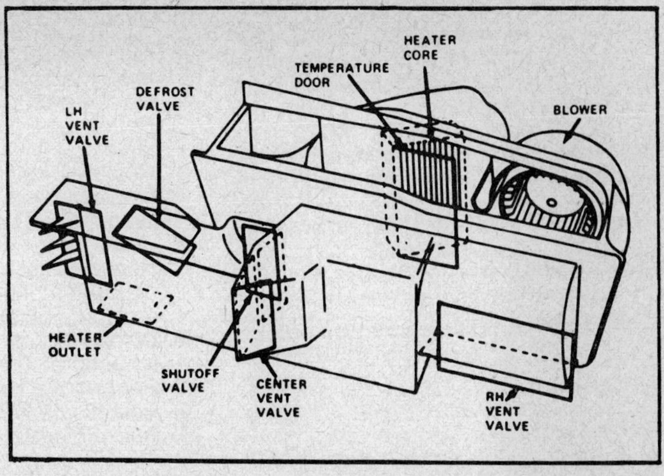

Fig. 17 Heater core & blower motor (less air conditioning). 88, 98 & Custom Cruiser

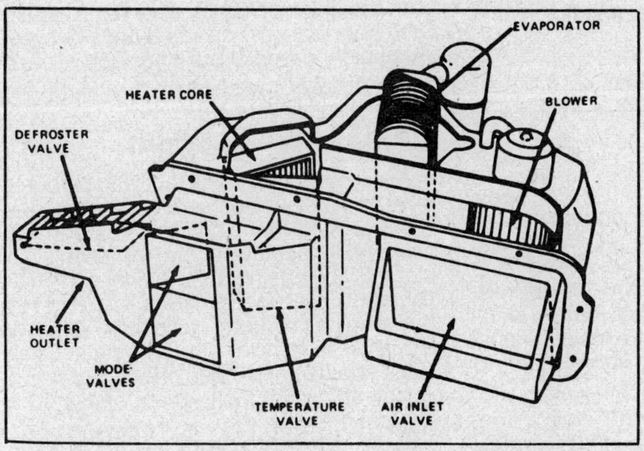

Fig. 18 Heater core & blower motor (w/air conditioning). 88, 98 & Custom Cruiser

TORONADO

1. Disconnect battery ground cable.
2. Remove headlamp switch knob, radio knobs and steering column trim cover.
3. Remove four screws from underside of lefthand trim cover.
4. Remove lefthand sound absorber, then pull lefthand trim cover from instrument panel. **It may be necessary to disconnect shift indicator cable clip and lower steering column slightly to remove lefthand trim cover.**
5. Remove righthand sound absorber.
6. Remove screw attaching instrument panel wiring harness to radio bracket and screw attaching radio to tie bar. Move tone generator aside, if equipped.
7. Remove four screws attaching radio mounting plate to cluster carrier.
8. Disconnect antenna lead and radio wiring.
9. Pull radio and mounting plate rearward to remove.

CUTLASS

1. Disconnect battery ground cable.
2. Remove instrument panel lower trim cover.
3. Remove the 4 radio mounting plate screws, and the screw from radio support bracket on lower instrument panel tie bar.
4. Pull radio outward, then disconnect antenna and electrical connectors and remove radio.
5. Reverse procedure to install.

88, 98 & CUSTOM CRUISER

1. Disconnect battery ground cable.
2. Remove radio knobs, cigar lighter and right hand trim panel cover.
3. Remove radio mounting plate attaching screws and nuts and the plate.
4. Remove ashtray, then the lefthand sound absorber, if equipped.
5. Remove lower center air duct attaching screw and the duct.
6. Remove radio support bracket attaching nut.
7. Pull radio rearward, then disconnect antenna lead and electrical connectors and remove radio assembly.
8. Reverse procedure to install.

HEATER CORE REPLACE

TORONADO

1. Disconnect battery ground cable, then drain cooling system.
2. Disconnect heater hoses at heater core, then install plugs in core outlets to prevent spillage.
3. Remove instrument panel sound absorbers, then lower steering column.
4. Remove instrument cluster as described under "Instrument Cluster, Replace."
5. Remove radio front speakers.
6. Remove three screws attaching manifold to heater case.
7. Remove four upper and three lower instrument panel attaching screws.
8. Disconnect parking brake release cable.
9. Disconnect instrument wiring harness from dash wiring assembly.
10. Disconnect righthand remote control mirror cable from instrument panel pad.
11. Disconnect speedometer cable from clip and temperate control cable at heater case.
12. Disconnect radio and A/C wiring, vacuum lines and all wiring necessary to remove instrument panel assembly. If equipped with pulse wiper, remove wiper switch and unlock wire connector from cluster carrier, then separate pulse wiper jumper harness from wiper switch wire connector.
13. Remove instrument panel and wiring harness assembly.
14. Remove defroster ducts, then disconnect lines from actuators.
15. Remove blower motor resistor.
16. From engine side of dash panel, remove three heater and A/C case retaining nuts.
17. From passenger compartment, remove screws and clip retaining heater and A/C case to dash panel.
18. Remove heater and A/C case, then remove heater core from case, **Fig. 16.**

88, 98 & CUSTOM CRUISER

Less A/C

1. Disconnect battery ground cable.
2. Disconnect blower resistor and blower motor wiring.
3. Drain cooling system into a suitable container, then remove heater hoses from heater core.
4. Remove seven screws attaching heater and blower case to plenum case, then remove case. **The heater**

temperature air valve can be removed at this time by disconnecting valve cable and tapping hinge pin down until it clears the upper pivot, then lift valve and hinge pin out of lower pivot, Fig. 17.

5. Remove four screws securing heater core shroud, then shroud and core, **Fig. 18.**
6. Remove core mounting screws and clamps, then separate core from shroud.
7. Reverse procedure to install. Replace sealer as necessary during installation to prevent air and water leaks.

With A/C

1. Disconnect battery ground cable.
2. Disconnect blower resistor and blower motor wiring.
3. Disconnect A/C wiring, then heater core ground strap.
4. Remove thermostatic switch and diagnostic connector (if equipped).
5. Remove right half of hood seal, then seven screws attaching air inlet screen. Remove screen.
6. Remove five bolts attaching case to dash, nine upper to lower case attaching screws around flange and two upper to lower case attaching screws located inside plenum.
7. Remove upper case by lifting straight up, then off, **Fig. 18.**
8. Remove accumulator bracket, then lift evaporator out of case.
9. Remove heater hoses, then lift heater core out of case.
10. Reverse procedure to install. Replace sealer as necessary during installation to prevent air and water leaks.

CUTLASS

Less A/C

1. Disconnect battery ground cable and drain cooling system.
2. Disconnect heater hoses.
3. Disconnect electrical connectors from heater module.
4. Remove module front cover screws.
5. Remove heater core from module.
6. Reverse procedure to install.

With A/C

1. Disconnect battery ground cable and drain cooling system.
2. Disconnect heater hoses from core.
3. Remove retention bracket and ground strap.
4. Remove module rubber seal and screen.
5. Removeright hand windshield wiper arm.
6. Remove attaching screws from the diagnostic connector, hi-blower relay and thermostatic switch.
7. Disconnect all electrical connectors from top of module.
8. Remove top cover from module.
9. Remove heater core from module.
10. Reverse procedure to install.

BLOWER MOTOR REPLACE

TORONADO

1. Disconnect battery ground cable.
2. Disconnect hi blower relay electrical connectors, then remove relay.
3. Remove screws securing blower motor, then remove blower motor.
4. Reverse procedure to install. Apply continuous bead of suitable sealer to blower motor mounting.

88, 98 & CUSTOM CRUISER

1. Disconnect battery ground cable.
2. Disconnect blower motor ground and feed wires.
3. Remove six blower motor attaching screws and blower motor, **Figs. 17 and 18.**

CUTLASS

1. Disconnect battery ground cable.
2. If equipped with air conditioning, disconnect cooling tube from blower motor, if necessary.
3. On all models, disconnect electrical connector from blower motor.
4. Remove blower motor retaining screws and the blower motor.
5. Reverse procedure to install.

CRUISE CONTROL ADJUST

SYSTEM RELEASE SWITCHES, ADJUST

Insert switches into tubular clip until the switch seats on clip. Then, pull brake pedal rearward against stop. The switches will be moved in the clip, thereby providing the proper adjustment.

SERVO LINKAGE, ADJUST

Units w/Servo Rod

With curb idle speed properly adjusted and the carburetor in curb idle position with the engine off, install servo rod retainer in hole that provides clearance between retainer and servo bushing. Some clearance is required, however, do not exceed the width of one hole.

Units w/Bead Chain

Assemble chain to be taut with carburetor in hot idle position and the idle solenoid de-energized. Place chain into swivel cavities which permits chain to have slight slack. Place retainer over swivel and chain assembly. Retainer must be made to rest between balls. Cut off chain flush with side of swivel to remove excess length. Chain slack should not exceed one half diameter of ball stud, .150 inch, when measured at hot idle position.

Units w/Cable

With throttle closed, ignition and fast idle cam off, adjust cable jam nuts until freeplay is removed from cable sleeve at carburetor without holding throttle open. Torque jam nuts to 50 inch lbs. Ensure servo boot is over cable washer.

ORIFICE TUBE ADJUSTMENT

Models w/Transducer Regulator

If the cruising speed is lower than the engagement speed, loosen the orifice tube locknut and turn the tube outward; if higher turn the tube inward. Each 1/4 turn will alter the engagement-cruising speed difference one mph. Tighten locknut after adjustment and check the system operation.

Gasoline Engine Section

NOTE: This section covers V8-260 (4.3L) and V8-307 (5.0L) Oldsmobile built engines. For service procedures on V6-231 (3.8L) and V6-252 (4.1L) engines, refer to chapter 1-1. For service procedures on V6-262 (4.3L) and V8-350 (5.7L) diesel engines, refer to chapter 5-1.

INDEX

ENGINE MOUNTS REPLACE

TORONADO

1. Raise and support vehicle.
2. Remove front splash shield.
3. Remove two screws from engine mount bracket to engine mount on each side, **Fig. 1.**
4. Place a suitable lifting device under the harmonic balancer and raise engine only enough to remove each mount.
5. Reverse procedure to install.

EXC. TORONADO

Removal or replacement of a motor mount can be accomplished by supporting the weight of the engine at the area of the mount to be replaced, **Figs. 2 and 3.**

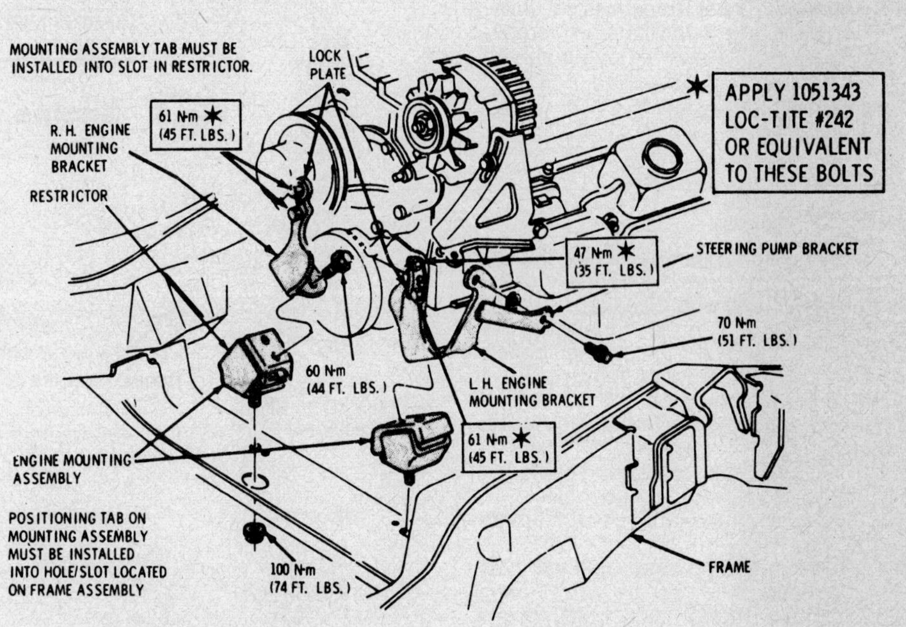

Fig. 1 Front engine mounts. Toronado

ENGINE REPLACE

EXC. TORONADO

1. Mark hood hinge before removing to aid in proper alignment upon reassembly.
2. Drain radiator and disconnect battery.
3. Disconnect radiator hoses, heater hoses, vacuum hoses, power steering pump hoses (if necessary), starter cable at junction block, engine-to-body ground strap, fuel hose from fuel line, wiring and accelerator linkage.
4. On 1986-87 models, disconnect AIR pipe, if equipped, from catalytic converter.
5. Remove fan blade and pulley, coil, upper radiator support and radiator, as necessary.
6. Raise car.
7. Disconnect exhaust pipes at manifolds.
8. Remove torque converter cover and the three bolts securing converter to flywheel.
9. Remove engine mount bolts, then three transmission to engine bolts on right side.
10. Remove starter with wiring attached and position aside.
11. Lower vehicle and support engine with suitable lifting equipment.
12. Support transmission with a suitable jack and remove three lefthand transmission to engine bolts.
13. Remove engine from vehicle.

TORONADO

1. Disconnect battery ground cable and drain cooling system.
2. Remove radiator upper support.
3. Remove air cleaner assembly.
4. Scribe hood hinge locations and remove hood.
5. Disconnect engine ground strap.
6. Disconnect upper and lower radiator hoses from engine.
7. Disconnect transmission oil cooler lines from radiator.
8. Disconnect heater hoses from water pump and water control valve.
9. Remove radiator, fan and the shroud.
10. Disconnect power steering pump bracket from engine and position aside without disconnecting lines.
11. Disconnect A/C compressor bracket from engine and position aside without disconnecting lines.
12. Disconnect fuel lines.
13. Disconnect throttle cable, vacuum hoses and electrical connections.
14. Disconnect lefthand exhaust pipe from manifold.
15. On left side of engine, remove through bolt and bracket securing final drive to engine.
16. Raise and support vehicle.
17. Remove flywheel shield.
18. Disconnect righthand exhaust pipe

from manifold.
19. Disconnect starter motor wiring and remove starter motor.
20. Remove converter to flywheel bolts. Mark location of converter on flywheel for alignment during installation.
21. Remove splash shield.
22. Remove engine front mounting attaching nuts.
23. Remove two bolts securing righthand output shaft support brackets. Using a sharp tool, scribe a mark around the washers as far as possible. Use these scribe marks to position bracket upon installation.
24. Remove lower righthand transmission to engine attaching bolts. One bolt retains the modulator line clip.
25. Use a suitable length of chain to retain final drive in vehicle.
26. Lower vehicle and attach suitable engine lifting equipment to engine.
27. Remove the remaining transmission to engine bolts. It may be necessary to raise or lower transmission with a suitable jack to facilitate bolt removal.
28. Raise engine and remove from vehicle.
29. Reverse procedure to install.

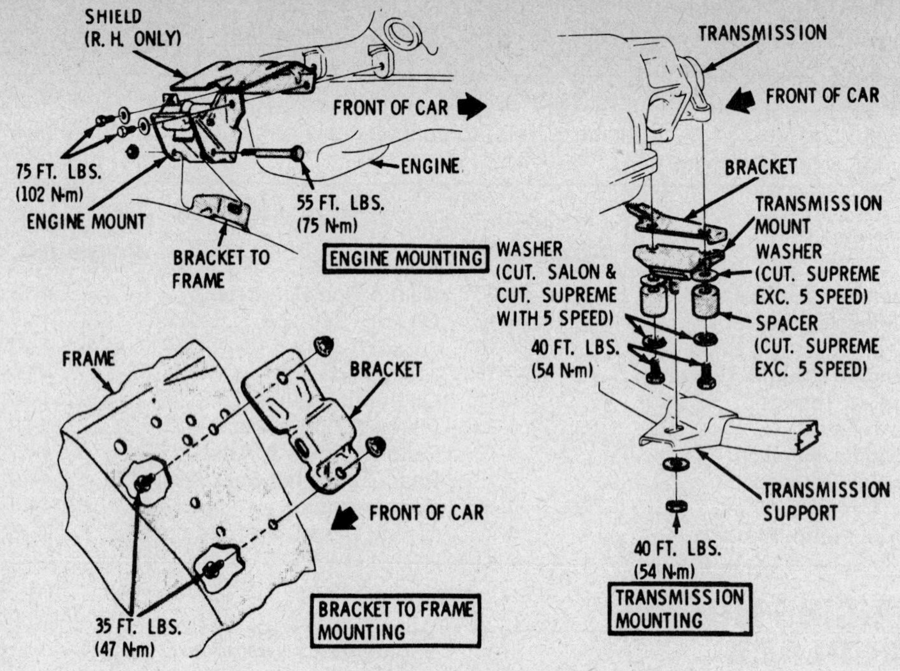

Fig. 2 Engine mounts. Cutlass

CYLINDER HEAD
REPLACE

Head gaskets used on these engines are of a special composition material that is not to be used with a sealer.

Prior to installation, clean the head bolts and dip in engine oil. Tighten head bolts in steps and in the sequence shown in **Fig. 4.** Final torquing should be to the specifications listed in "Engine Tightening Specifications."

1. Disconnect battery ground cable.
2. Drain radiator and cylinder block.
3. Remove intake and exhaust manifolds.
4. Remove ground strap from left cylinder head.
5. Remove rocker arm bolts, pivots, rocker arms and pushrods. Keep rocker arms, pivots and pushrods in order so they can be installed in the same position.
6. Remove cylinder head attaching bolts and remove cylinder head.
7. Reverse procedure to install. Torque cylinder head bolts in sequence shown in **Fig. 4** and torque intake manifold bolts in sequence shown in **Fig. 5.**

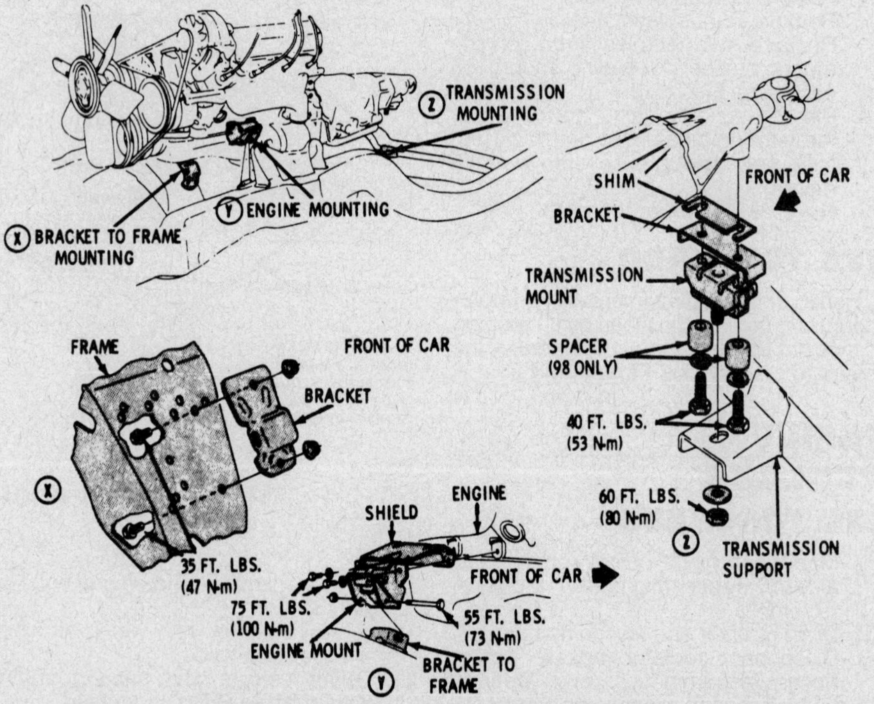

Fig. 3 Engine mounts. 88, 98 & Custom Cruiser

ROCKER ARMS

V8 engines use valve rotators, **Fig. 6.** The rotator operates on a sprag clutch principle utilizing the collapsing action of a coil spring to give rotation to the rotor body which turns the valve.

1. Remove valve cover.
2. Remove flanged bolts, rocker arm pivot and rocker arms, **Fig. 6.**
3. When installing rocker arm assemblies, lubricate wear surfaces with suitable lubricant. Torque flanged bolts to 25 ft. lbs.

VALVE ROTATORS

The rotator operates on a Sprag clutch principle utilizing the collapsing action of coil spring to give rotation to the rotor body which turns the valve, **Fig. 6.**

To check rotator action, draw a line across rotator body and down the collar. Operate engine at 1500 RPM, rotator body should move around collar. Rotator action can be in either direction. Replace rotator if no movement is noted.

When servicing valves, valve stem tips should be checked for improper wear pattern which could indicate a defective valve rotator, **Fig. 7.**

VALVES

Whenever a new valve is installed or after grinding valves, it will be necessary to measure valve stem height using the Special Tool shown in **Figs. 8 and 9.**

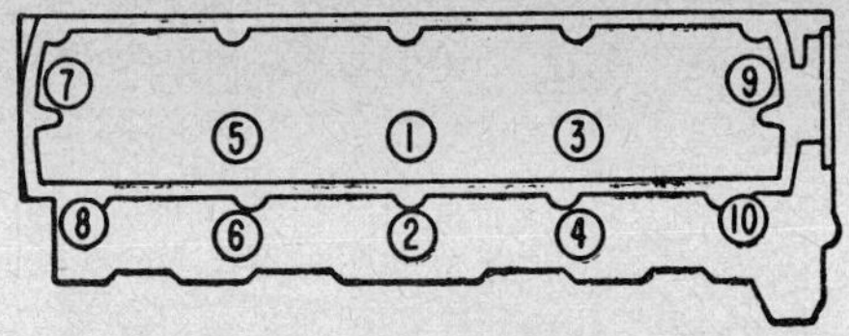

Fig. 4 Cylinder head tightening sequence

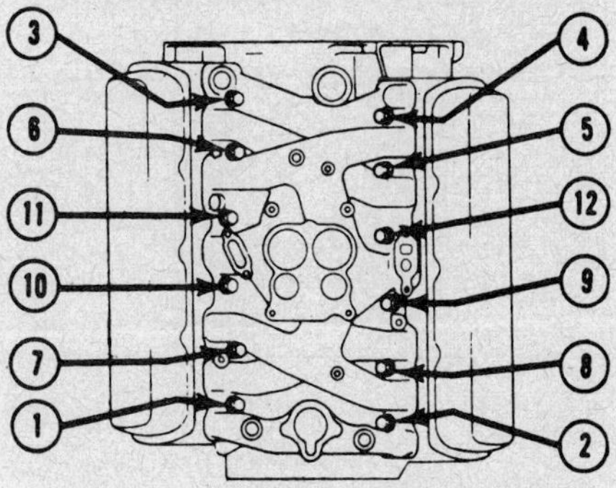

Fig. 5 Intake manifold tightening sequence

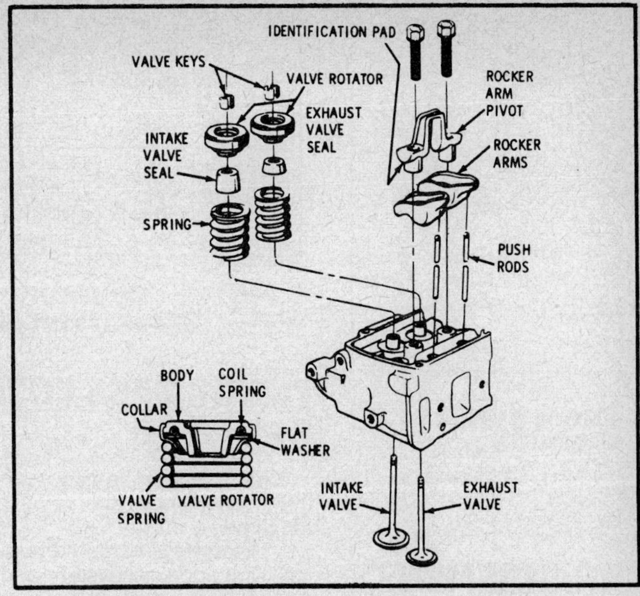

Fig. 6 Cylinder head exploded

There should be a minimum clearance of .015 inch between gauge surface and the valve stem, **Fig. 8.**

Check valve rotator height, **Fig. 9.** If valve stem tip extends less than .005 inch above rotator, replace the valve.

Lacking this tool the only alternative is to lay flat feeler gauges on the retainer and check the distance between the retainer and valve stem tip.

VALVES

ADJUST

V8-260 and V8-307 engines are equipped with hydraulic valve lifters. No provision for adjustment is made for these engines.

VALVE GUIDES

Valve stem guides are not replaceable, due to being cast in place. If valve guide bores are worn excessively, they can be reamed oversize.

If a standard valve guide bore is being reamed, use a .003 inch or .005 inch oversize reamer. For the .010 inch oversize valve guide bore, use a .013 inch oversize reamer. If too large a reamer is used and the spiraling is removed, it is possible that the valve will not receive the proper lubrication.

Occasionally a valve guide will be oversize as manufactured. These are marked on the cylinder head as shown in **Fig. 10.** If no markings are present, the guide bores are standard. If oversize markings are present, any valve replacement will require an oversize valve. Service valves are available in standard diameters as well as .003 inch, .005 inch, .010 inch and .013 inch oversize.

VALVE LIFTERS

Valve lifters are available in standard size and an oversize of .010 inch. An "O" is etched on the side of the .010 inch oversize lifter for identification. Also, the cylinder block near the valve lifter bore is marked with an "O." Ensure valve lifters are reinstalled in original bores.

Plungers are not interchangeable because they are fitted to the bodies at the factory.

If plunger and body appear satisfactory blow off with air to remove all particles of dirt. Install the plunger in the body without other parts and check for free movement. A simple test is to be sure that the plunger will drop of its own weight in the body, **Fig. 11.**

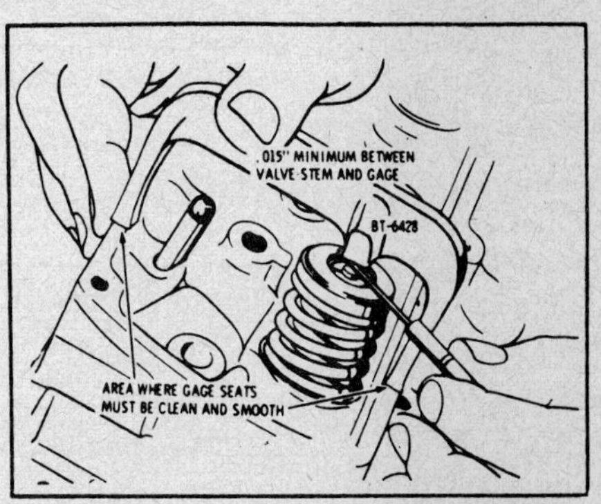

Fig. 8 Measuring valve stem height

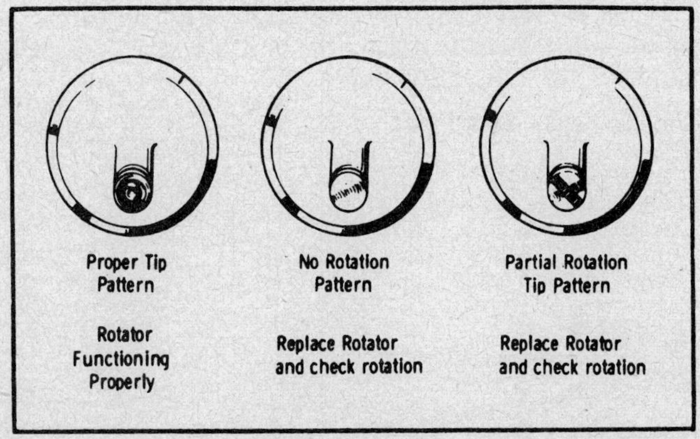

Fig. 7 Checking valve stems for rotator malfunction

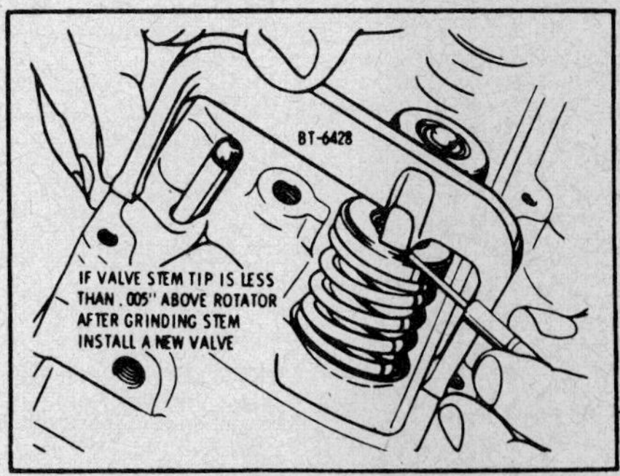

Fig. 9 Measuring valve retainer or valve rotator height

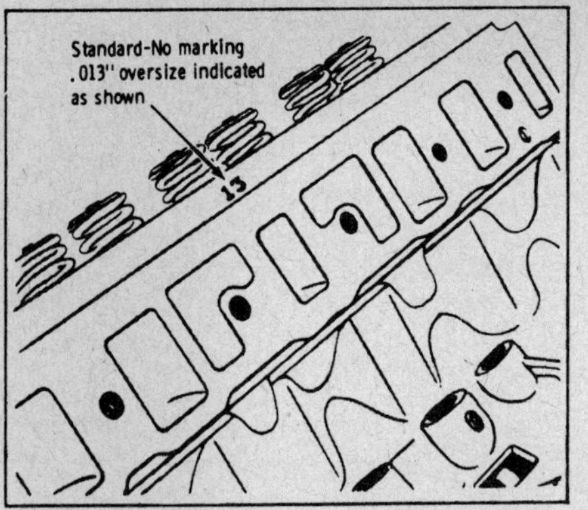

Fig. 10 Valve guide bore marking

VALVE ARRANGEMENT

FRONT TO REAR

V8-260, 307 .... I-E-I-E-E-I-E-I

VALVE TIMING

INTAKE OPENS BEFORE TDC

Engine	Year	Degrees
V8-260	1982	14
V8-307	1982-87	20

VALVE LIFT SPECIFICATIONS

Engine	Year	Intake	Exhaust
V8-260	1982	.395	.400
V8-307①	1982-87	.400	.400
V8-307②	1983-85	.440	.440

①—Exc. Hurst Olds.
②—Hurst Olds.

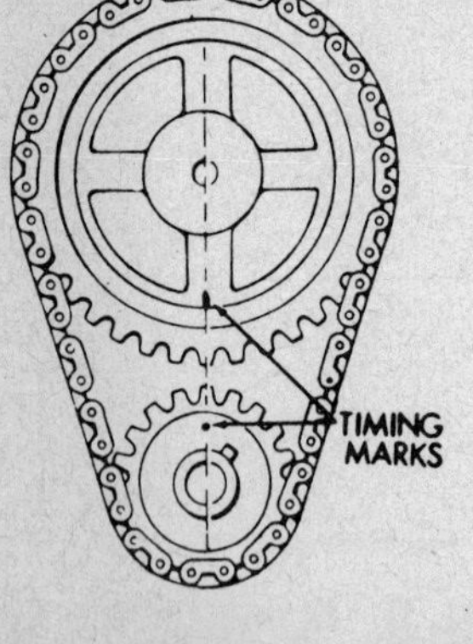

Fig. 13 Timing chain position

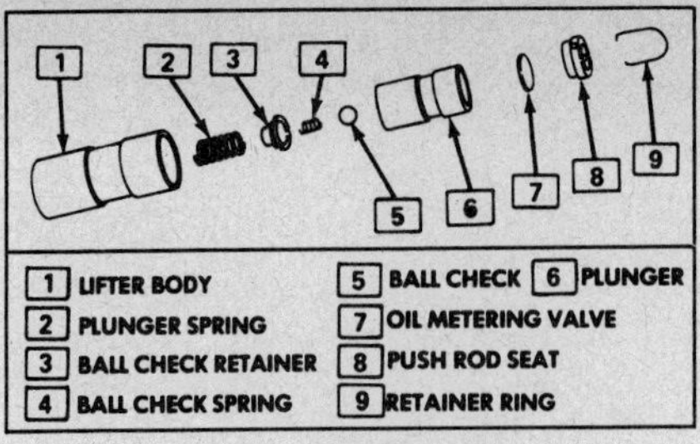

Fig. 11 Hydraulic valve lifter (typical)

TIMING CASE COVER

REPLACE

When it becomes necessary to replace the cover oil seal, the cover need not be removed.

1. Disconnect battery ground cable.
2. Drain cooling system and disconnect radiator hoses and bypass hose.
3. Remove all drive belts, fan and pulley, crankshaft pulley and harmonic balancer, and accessory brackets.
4. Remove timing indicator and water pump.
5. Remove remaining front cover attaching bolts and the front cover. Also, remove the dowel pins. It may be necessary to grind a flat on the dowel pin to provide a rough surface for gripping.
6. Grind a chamfer on one end of each dowel pin.
7. Cut excess material from front end of oil pan gasket on each side of cylinder block.
8. Trim approximately 1/8 inch from each end of new front pan seal.
9. Install new front cover gasket and apply suitable sealer to gasket around coolant holes.
10. Apply RTV sealer to mating surfaces of cylinder block, oil pan and front cover.
11. Place front cover on cylinder block and press downward to compress seal. Rotate cover right and left and guide oil pan seal into cavity with a small screwdriver.
12. Apply engine oil to bolts.
13. Install two bolts finger tight to retain cover.
14. Install the two dowel pins, chamfered end first.
15. Install timing indicator and water pump and torque bolts as shown in **Fig. 12.**
16. Install harmonic balancer and crankshaft pulley.
17. Install accessory brackets.
18. Install fan and pulley and drive belts.
19. Connect radiator hoses and bypass hose.
20. Connect battery ground cable.

TIMING CHAIN

REPLACE

1. After removing front cover, remove fuel pump eccentric, oil slinger, crankshaft sprocket, chain and camshaft sprocket.

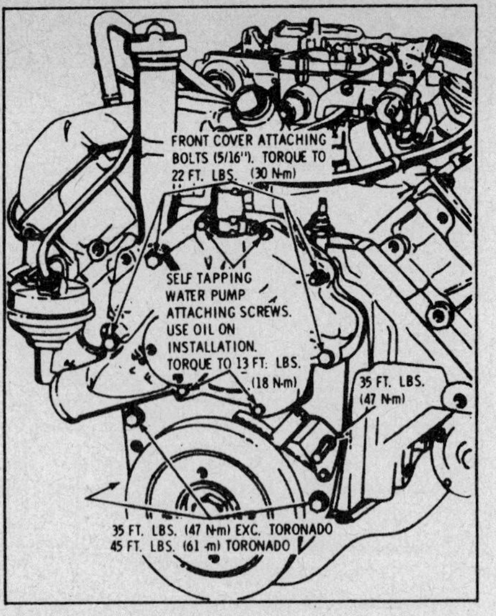

Fig. 12 Engine front cover bolts

2. Install camshaft sprocket, crankshaft sprocket and timing chain together, aligning timing marks as shown in **Fig. 13.**
3. Install fuel pump eccentric with flat side rearward, **Fig. 14.** Then install oil slinger and replace front cover. **The valve timing marks, Figs. 13 and 14,** do not indicate TDC compression stroke for No. 1 cylinder, which is used for distributor installation. If distributor was removed, install timing chain and sprockets, aligning timing marks, **Figs. 13 and 14,** then rotate engine until No. 1 cylinder is on compression stroke and camshaft timing mark is 180° from valve timing position shown in illustrations, then install distributor.

CAMSHAFT

REPLACE

1. Disconnect battery ground cable and drain radiator.

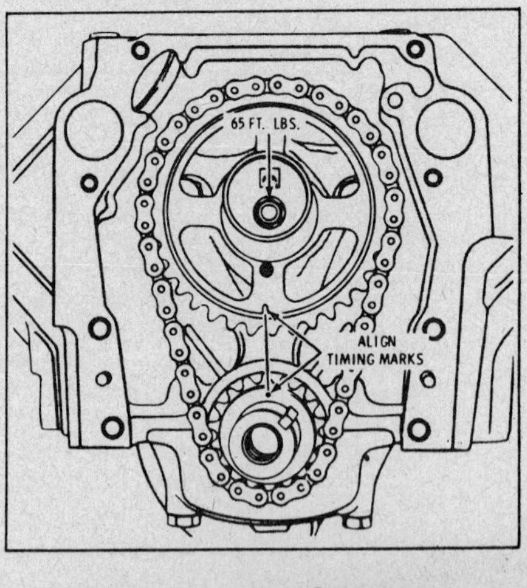

Fig. 14 Fuel pump eccentric

Fig. 15 Assembly of piston to rod

2. Remove upper radiator baffle and disconnect upper radiator hose from water outlet.
3. Disconnect transmission oil cooler lines at radiator.
4. Remove radiator fan shroud, then the radiator.
5. Disconnect fuel lines from fuel pump.
6. Remove air cleaner and disconnect throttle cable.
7. Remove all drive belts and position alternator, power steering pump and air conditioning compressor aside.
8. Disconnect bypass hose from water pump and all electrical and vacuum connections from engine.
9. Remove distributor.
10. Raise vehicle and drain oil pan.
11. Remove exhaust crossover pipe and the starter.
12. Disconnect exhaust pipe from manifold.
13. Install engine support bar.
14. Remove engine mount to bracket bolts, raise engine and remove engine mounts.
15. Remove flywheel cover and engine oil pan.
16. Place wood blocks between exhaust manifolds and crossmember to support engine, then remove engine support bar.

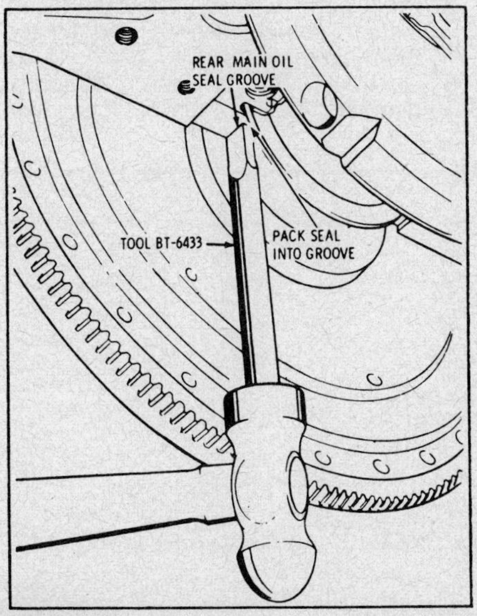

Fig. 18 Packing upper rear main bearing oil seal

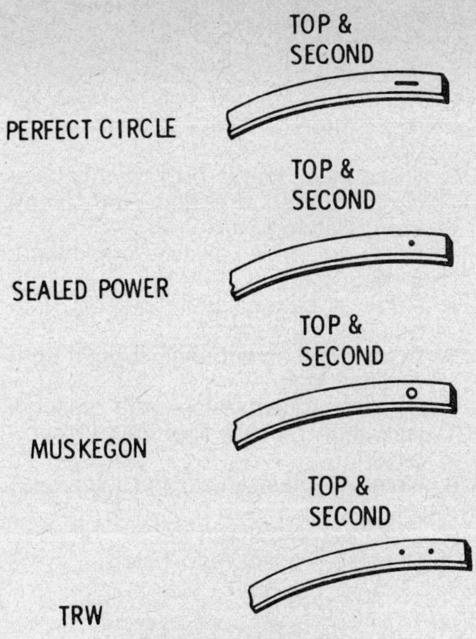

Fig. 16 Piston compression ring identification

17. Remove crankshaft pulley and balancer, then the engine front cover.
18. Lower vehicle and remove valve covers, intake manifold, rocker arms, pushrods and valve lifters. **Note position of the valve train components to ensure installation in original location.**
19. If equipped with A/C, discharge refrigerant and remove condenser.
20. Remove fuel pump eccentric, camshaft sprocket, oil slinger and timing chain.
21. Slide camshaft from front of engine.
22. Reverse procedure to install. **To insure proper camshaft installation, and to provide initial lubrication, it is extremely important that the camshaft be coated with GM Concentrate (Part No. 1051396).**

PISTON & ROD

ASSEMBLE

Lubricate the piston pin hole and piston pin to facilitate installation of pin, then position the connecting rod with its respective piston as shown in **Fig. 15.** Measure connecting rod side clearance using a suitable feeler gauge, clearance should be .006-.020 inch.

PISTONS, RINGS & PINS

Different types of piston compression rings are used, refer to **Fig. 16** for piston ring identification. On V8-260 engines, piston ring end gap should be .009-.019 inch for Sealed Power piston rings and .010-.020 inch for Perfect Circle and Muskegon piston rings. On V8-307 engines, piston ring end gap should be .009-.019 inch for Sealed Power piston rings and .010-.020 inch for TRW piston rings.

Pistons are available in standard sizes and oversizes of .010 and .030 inch. Rings are available in standard sizes and oversizes of .010 and .030 inch.

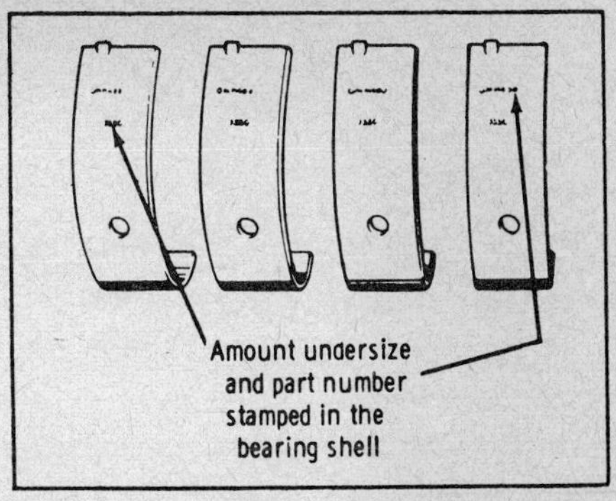

Fig. 17 Main bearing size location

MAIN & ROD BEARINGS

Main bearings are available in standard sizes and undersizes of .0005, .001, .0015, .002, .010 and .020 inch.

Rod bearings are available in standard sizes and undersizes of .001, .002, .005, .010, .012 and .020 inch.

Main bearing clearances not within specifications must be corrected by the use of selective upper and lower shells. **Fig. 17** illustrates the undersize identification marking on the bearing tang.

REAR CRANKSHAFT SEAL SERVICE

Since the braided fabric seal used on these engines can be replaced only when the crankshaft is removed, the following repair procedure is recommended.

1. Remove oil pan and bearing cap.
2. Drive end of old seal gently into groove, using a suitable tool, until packed tight. This may vary between 1/4 and 3/4 inch depending on amount of pack required.
3. Repeat previous step for other end of seal.

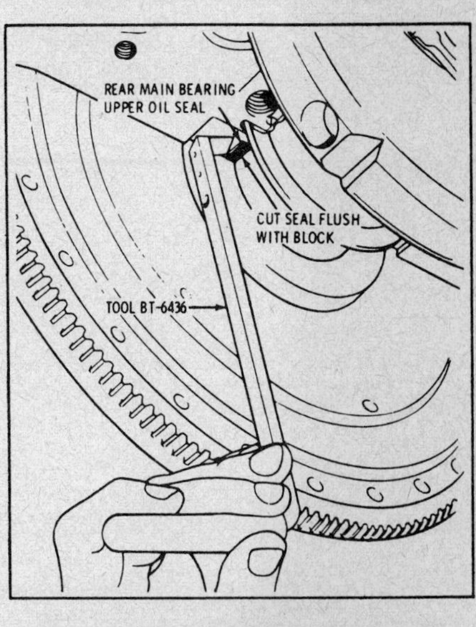

Fig. 19 Trimming upper rear main bearing oil seal

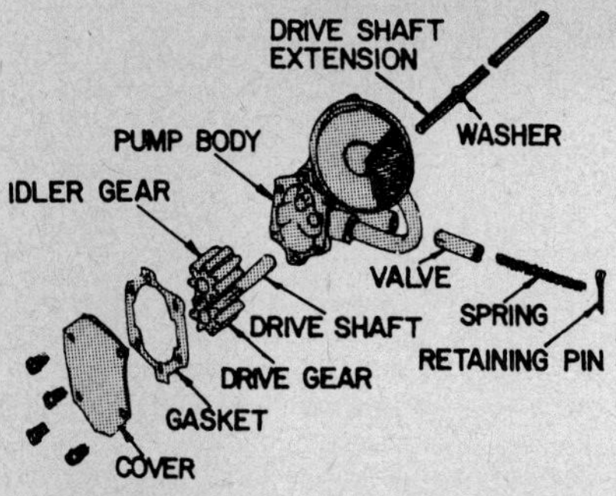

Fig. 20 Oil pump disassembled (Typical)

4. Measure and note amount that seal was driven up on one side. Using the old seal removed from bearing cap, cut a length of seal the amount previously noted plus 1/16 inch.
5. Repeat previous step for other side of seal.
6. Pack cut lengths of seal into appropriate side of seal groove. A packing tool, BT-6433, **Fig. 18**, may be used since the tool has been machined to provide a built-in stop. Use tool BT-6436 to trim the seal flush with block, **Fig. 19.**
7. Install new seal in lower bearing cap.

OIL PAN
REPLACE
EXC. TORONADO

1. Remove distributor cap and align rotor with No. 1 firing position.
2. Disconnect ground cable, remove dip stick and drain oil pan.
3. Remove upper radiator support and fan shroud attaching screws.
4. Remove flywheel cover and starter.
5. Disconnect exhaust pipes and crossover pipe on single exhaust models.
6. Disconnect engine mounts and raise engine.
7. Remove oil pan bolts and oil pan.
8. Reverse procedure to install. Torque oil pan bolts to 10 ft. lbs.

TORONADO

1. Disconnect battery ground cable.
2. Raise and support vehicle, then remove three final drive to transmission bolts.
3. Disconnect frame braces, then disconnect idler arm and pitman arm from relay rod.
4. Separate drive axles from output shafts.
5. Remove battery cable bracket from output shaft support.
6. Disconnect output shaft support from engine block.
7. Support transmission with suitable jack, then remove final drive assembly.
8. Remove splash shield and starter motor.
9. Drain engine oil and remove oil pan.
10. Reverse procedure to install.

OIL PUMP REPAIRS

1. Remove oil pan and pump baffle. Remove attaching screws and remove pump and driveshaft extension.
2. To service the pump, refer to **Fig. 20.**
3. To install, insert the driveshaft extension through the opening in the block until the shaft mates into the distributor drive gear. Position pump onto rear main bearing cap and torque the attaching bolts to 35 ft. lbs.
4. Install oil pump baffle and pan.

WATER PUMP
REPLACE

1. Drain cooling system and remove heater and lower hoses from pump.
2. Loosen pulley belts and remove fan and pulley. On air conditioned cars, remove clutch fan assembly and pulley.
3. Remove pump from front cover.

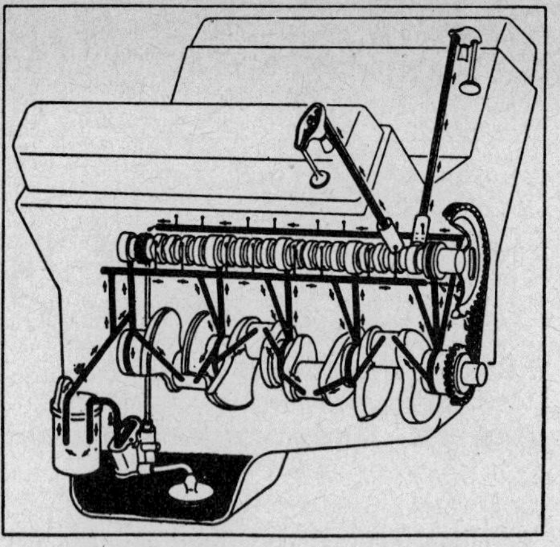

Engine lubrication (Typical)

BELT TENSION DATA

Belt	New Lbs.	Used Lbs.
Air Conditioning	170	90
A.I.R. Pump	80①	45①
Alternator	160②	80②
Power Steering	170	90
Vacuum Pump	125	55

①—3/8 inch belts; new, 145; used, 70.
②—Cogged belts; new, 145; used, 55.

FUEL PUMP
REPLACE

1. Disconnect fuel line from fuel pump.
2. Remove fuel pump mounting bolts and the fuel pump.
3. Remove all gasket material from the pump and block gasket surfaces. Apply sealer to both sides of new gasket.
4. Position gasket on pump flange and hold pump in position against its mounting surface. Make sure rocker arm is riding on camshaft eccentric.
5. Press pump tight against its mounting. Install retaining screws and tighten them alternately.
6. Connect fuel lines. Then operate engine and check for leaks.

Rear Axle, Propeller Shaft & Brakes

INDEX

REAR AXLE

Toronado

On these models the hub and wheel bearing is incorporated into one assembly which eliminates the need for wheel bearing adjustment and does not require periodic maintenance.

WHEEL BEARINGS & SPINDLE, REPLACE

REAR DISC BRAKES

Removal

1. Raise and support rear of vehicle.
2. Remove tire and wheel assembly.
3. Mark a wheel stud and a corresponding place on the rotor to assist in installation if bearing is not replaced.
4. Disconnect brake line at bracket on control arm.
5. Remove caliper and rotor assembly.
6. Remove four nut and bolts securing the spindle to the control arm and remove bearing assembly, **Fig. 1.**

Installation

Before installing bearing, remove all rust and corrosion from bearing mounting surfaces. Lack of a flat surface may result in early bearing failure. A slip fit must exist between the bearing and the control arm assembly.

1. Install rear spindle, shield and plate to lower control arm with four nut and bolt assemblies. Tighten to 32 ft. lbs., **Fig. 1.**
2. If bearing was not replaced install rotor using reference marks made at time of removal.
3. Install brake caliper assembly.
4. Connect brake line at bracket on control arm, tighten and bleed brake system.
5. Install wheel and tire assembly. Tighten to100 ft. lbs.
6. Remove support and lower car.

REAR DRUM BRAKES

Rem oval

1. Raise and support rear of vehicle.
2. Remove tire and wheel assembly.
3. Remove brake drum.

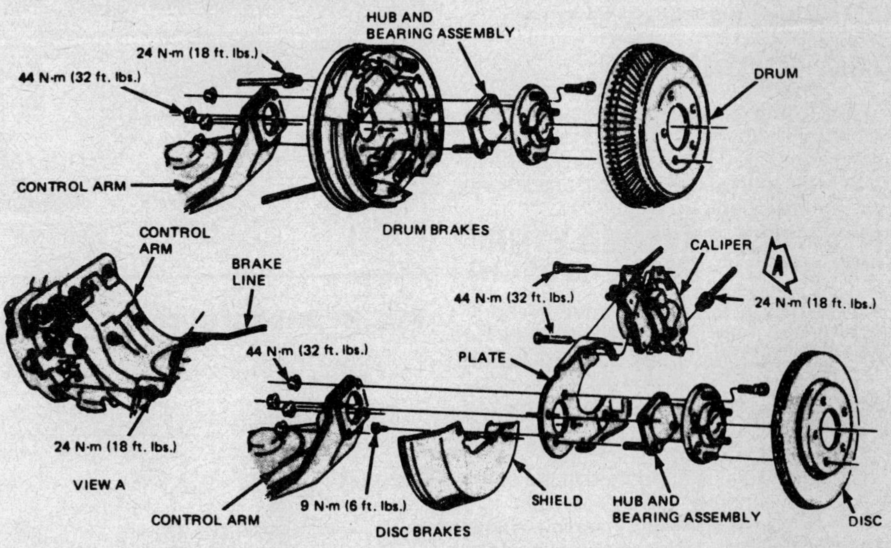

Fig. 1 Wheel bearing & hub assembly removal. Toronado

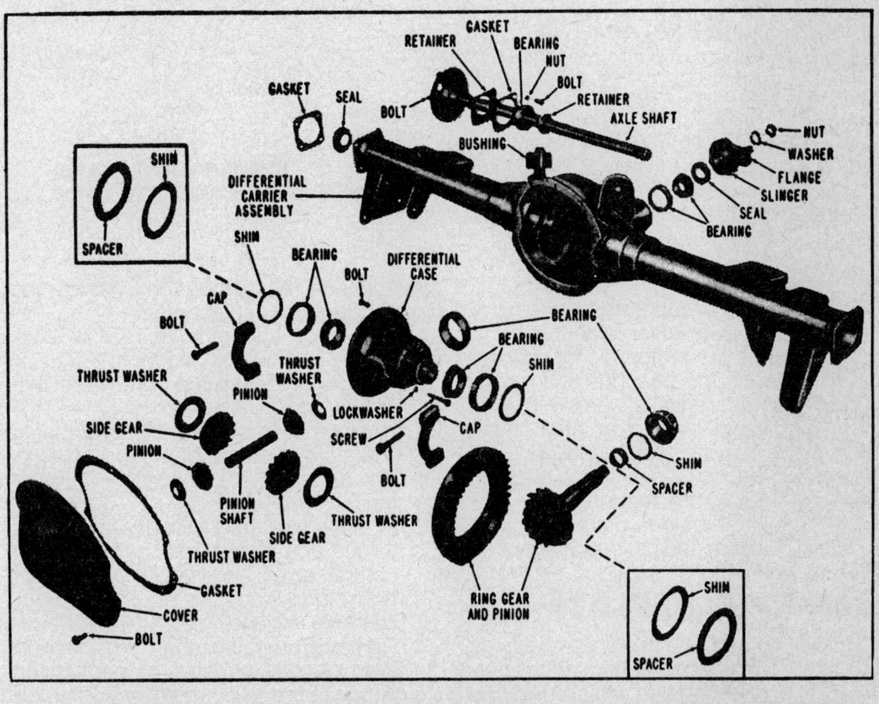

Fig. 2 Integral carrier type rear axle. Type B & O (exc. 7½ inch) axle

4. Remove four nuts attaching rear wheel bearing assembly to control arm.
5. Remove wheel bearing and four attaching bolts, **Fig. 1.**

Installation

Before installing bearing, remove all rust and corrosion from bearing mounting surfaces. Lack of a flat surface for any reason may result in early bearing failure. A slip fit must exist between the bearing and the control arm assembly.

1. Install four nuts and bolts attaching wheel bearing to rear control arm assembly, **Fig. 1.**
2. Install brake drum.
3. Install wheel and tire assembly, tighten to 100 ft. lbs.
4. Remove supports and lower car.

Exc. Toronado

Figs. 2 and 3 illustrate the rear axle assemblies used on conventional models. When necessary to overhaul any of these units, refer to the Rear Axle Specifications table in this chapter.

INTEGRAL CARRIER TYPE "B" & "O" (EXC. 7½ INCH)

As shown in **Fig. 2**, the drive pinion is mounted on two tapered roller bearings that are preloaded by two selected spacers. The drive pinion is positioned by shims located between a shoulder on the pinion and the rear bearing. The front bearing is held in place by a large nut.

The differential is supported in the carrier by two tapered roller side bearings. These are preloaded by inserting shims between the bearings and the pedestals. The differential assembly is positioned for ring gear and pinion backlash by varying these shims.

TYPE C, G, K, M, O (7½ INCH) & P

In these rear axles, **Fig. 3**, the rear axle housing and differential carrier are cast into an integral assembly. The drive pinion assembly is mounted in two opposed tapered roller bearings. The pinion bearings are preloaded by a spacer behind the front bearing. The pinion is positioned by a washer between the head of the pinion and the rear bearing.

The differential is supported in the carrier by two tapered roller side bearings. These bearings are preloaded by spacers located between the bearings and carrier housing. The differential assembly is positioned for proper ring gear and pinion backlash by varying these spacers. The differential case houses two side gears in mesh with two pinions mounted on a pinion shaft which is held in place by a lock pin. The side gears and pinions are backed by thrust washers.

REAR AXLE, REPLACE

Construction of the axle assembly is such that service operations may be performed with the housing installed in the vehicle or with the housing removed and installed in a holding fixture. The following procedure is necessary only when the housing requires replacement.

1. Raise car and remove rear wheels, drums and axle shafts.
2. Disconnect brake line from wheel cylinders.
3. Unfasten and support backing plates with wire hooks to frame kickup.
4. Disconnect shock absorbers at housing.
5. Position jack stands under frame rear torque boxes, then disconnect upper control arms and slowly lower axle housing to stands.
6. Remove springs.
7. Remove propeller shaft and support front of axle housing at companion flange to prevent assembly from rotating when the lower control arms are disconnected.
8. Remove lower control arm bolts at axle housing.
9. Remove support at companion flange and lower axle housing.
10. Remove assembly to bench and transfer parts tonew axle housing.
11. Reverse procedure to install.

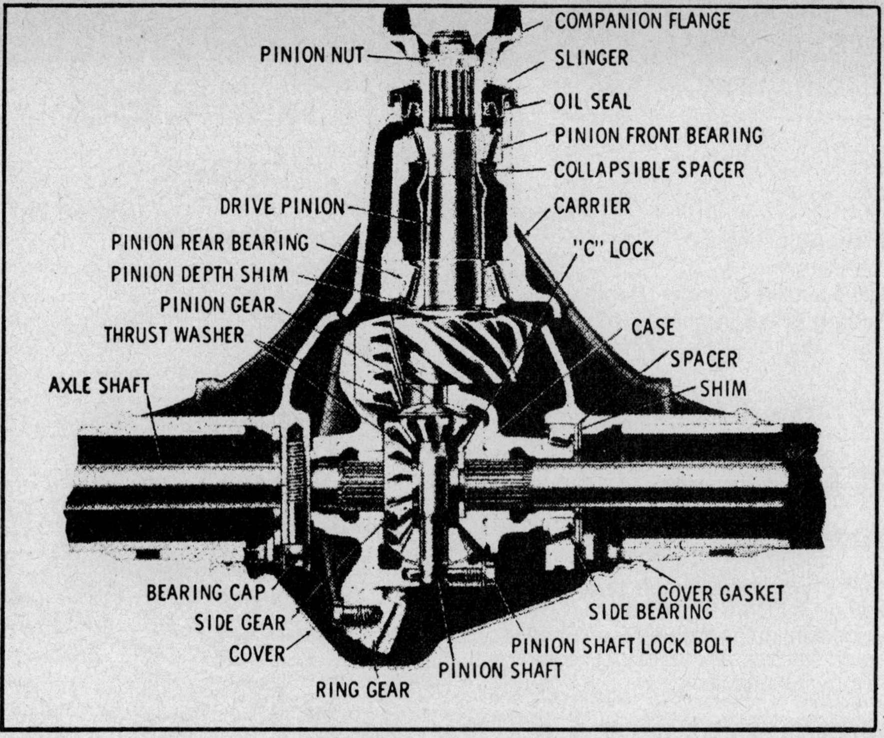

Fig. 3 Integral carrier type differential. Types C, G, K, M, O (7½ inch) & P axle

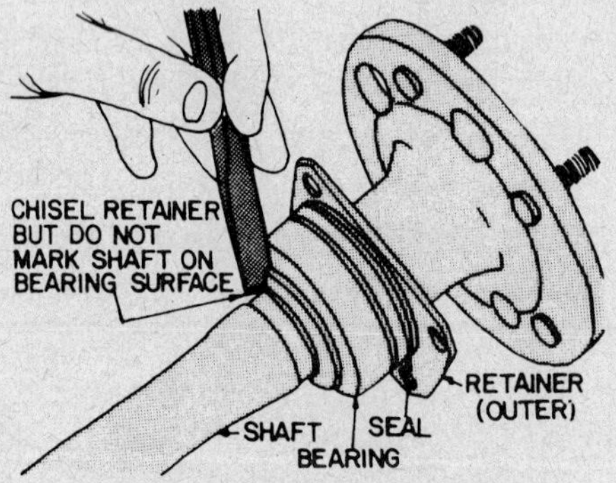

Fig. 4 Removing axle shaft bearing retainer

AXLE SHAFT, REPLACE

Type C, G, K, M, O (7½ Inch) & P

1. Raise vehicle and remove wheel and brake drum.
2. Clean all dirt from area of carrier cover.
3. Drain lubricant from carrier by removing cover.
4. Remove differential pinion shaft lock screw and shaft.
5. Push flanged end of axle shaft toward center of vehicle and remove "C" lock from button end of shaft.
6. Remove axle shaft from housing, being careful not to damage oil seal.
7. Reverse procedure to install.

Type B & O (Exc. 7½ Inch)

1. Remove wheel and brake drum.
2. Remove axle bearing retainer (4 nuts).
3. Pull axle shaft from housing. If bearing is a tight fit in housing, use a slide hammer-type puller. Do not drag shaft over seal as this may damage seal.
4. Attach one axle bearing retainer nut to hold brake backing plate in position.
5. Before installing axle shaft, examine oil seal. The seals have feathered edges which form a tight seal around the shaft. If these edges are damaged

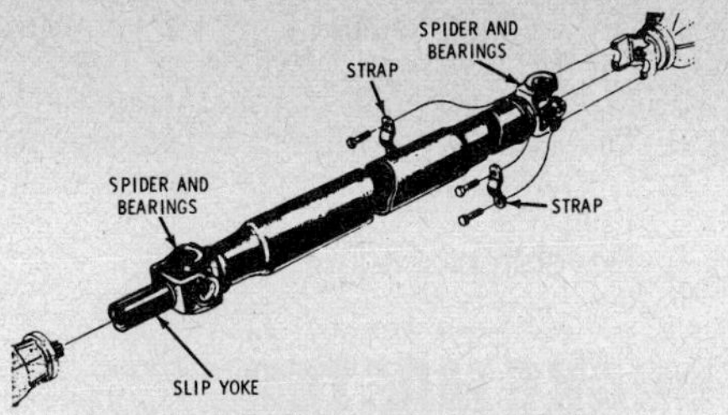

Fig. 5 Propeller shaft installation (Typical)

in any way, seal must be replaced. Examine seal surface on shaft; if it is not smooth, dress it down with very fine emery cloth.

6. Reverse removal procedure to install axle shaft, being sure to grease outside of axle bearing, seal surface on axle shaft and bore of axle housing with differential lubricant. Place new gasket and bearing retainer over studs, install nuts and tighten to 35 ft. lbs.
7. Bearings should be replaced if found to be rough or have greater than .020 inch endplay. Remove bearing only when new bearing is to be installed; once removed it must not be reused.
8. With axle shaft removed from housing, split bearing retainer with a chisel, **Fig. 4.**
9. Press bearing off shaft.
10. Press new bearing on shaft up against shoulder on shaft.
11. Press retainer on shaft up against bearing.
12. Reverse removal procedure to install axle shaft.

PROPELLER SHAFT

The propeller shaft is of one or two piece construction with a single or double U-joint securing the shaft to the companion flange, **Fig. 5.**

1. Mark propeller shaft and companion flange so they can be installed in the same position.
2. Remove strap bolts, **Fig. 5.** Use a piece of tape or wire to hold universal joint bearing caps in place.
3. Lower rear of shaft and slide rearward.
4. Reverse procedure to install. If driveshaft yokes do not have vent holes, lubricate internal splines with engine oil. If driveshaft yokes have vent holes apply lubricant No. 1050169 or equivalent to internal splines prior to installation. Torque strap bolts to 14-16 ft. lbs.

BRAKE ADJUSTMENTS

These brakes have self adjusting shoe mechanisms that assure correct lining-to-drum clearances at all times. The automatic adjusters operate only when the brakes are applied as the car is moving rearward.

Although the brakes are self-adjusting, an initial adjustment is necessary after the brake shoes have been relined or replaced, or when the length of the star wheel adjuster has been changed during

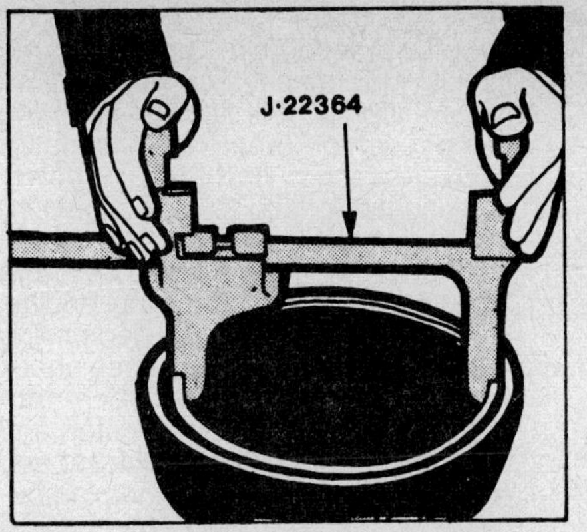

Fig. 6 Brake shoe gauge measuring inside diameter of brake drum

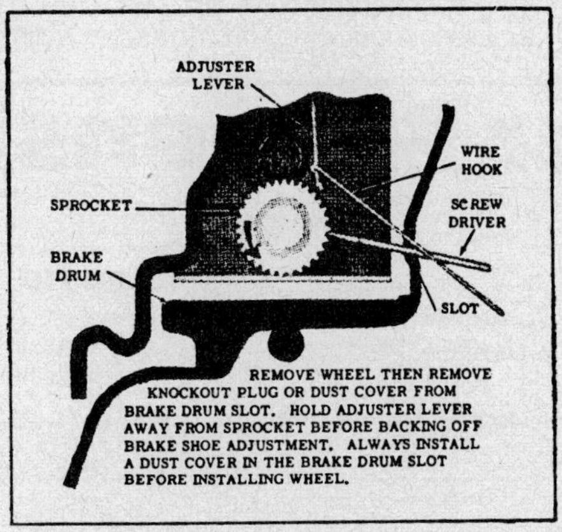

Fig. 8 Backing off brake shoe adjustment

some other service operation.

Frequent usage of an automatic transmission forward range to halt reverse vehicle motion may prevent the automatic adjusters from functioning, thereby inducing low pedal heights. Should low pedal heights be encountered, it is recommended that numerous forward and reverse stops be made until satisfactory pedal height is obtained.

If a low pedal height condition cannot be corrected by making numerous reverse stops (provided the hydraulic system is free of air) it indicates that the self-adjusting mechanism is not functioning. Therefore, it will be necessary to remove the brake drum, clean, free up and lubricate the adjusting mechanism. Then adjust the brakes as follows, being sure the parking brake is fully released.

ADJUSTMENT

Inasmuch as there is no way to adjust these brakes with the drums installed, the following procedure is mandatory after new linings are installed or if it becomes necessary to change the length of the brake shoe adjusting screw.

1. With brake drums removed, position the caliper shown in **Fig. 6** to the inside diameter of the drum and tighten the clamp screw.

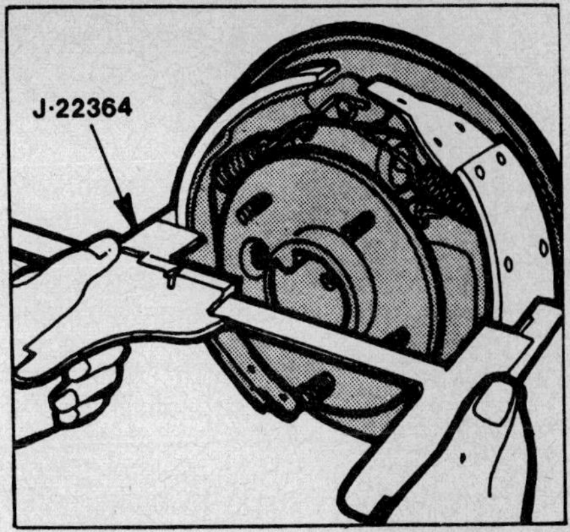

Fig. 7 Brake shoe gauge measuring outside diameter of brake shoes

2. Next position brake shoe end of the caliper tool over the brake shoes as shown in **Fig. 7.**
3. Rotate the gauge slightly around the shoes to insure that the gauge contacts the linings at the largest diameter.
4. Adjust brake shoes until the gauge is a snug fit on the linings at the point of largest lining diameter. **If it is necessary to back off the brake shoe adjustment, it will be necessary to hold the adjuster lever away from the adjuster screw, Fig. 8.**

PARKING BRAKE

ADJUST

EXC. MODELS W/REAR WHEEL DISC BRAKES

Depress parking brake pedal 2 clicks on 1982-86 models, or 3 clicks on 1987 models. Tighten adjusting nut until left rear wheel on 1982-86 models, or right rear wheel on 1987 models can just be rotated rearward using both hands and cannot be rotated forward. Release parking brake and ensure rear wheels turn freely in either direction with no brake drag.

MODELS W/REAR WHEEL DISC BRAKES

1. Lubricate parking brake cables at underbody contact points and equalizer hooks.
2. Raise and support rear of vehicle with parking brakes fully released.
3. Prevent cable stud from turning and tighten equalizer nut until cable slack is removed. Ensure caliper levers are against stops on caliper housing after tightening equalizer nut, otherwise, loosen cable until levers return to stops.
4. Operate parking brake several times to check adjustment. Pedal should travel 4-5½ inches with approximately 120 lbs. force applied to pedal.
5. Lower vehicle and ensure levers remain on caliper stops. If not, back off parking brake adjuster as necessary.

POWER BRAKE UNIT
REPLACE
HYDRO-BOOST

Pump brake pedal several times with engine off to deplete accumulator of fluid.

1. Remove two nuts attaching master cylinder to booster, then move master cylinder away from booster with brake lines attached.
2. Remove three hydraulic lines from booster. Plug and cap all lines and outlets.
3. Remove retainer and washer securing booster pushrod to brake pedal arm.
4. Remove four nuts attaching booster unit to dash panel.
5. From engine compartment, loosen booster from dash panel and move booster pushrod inboard until it disconnects from brake pedal arm. Remove spring washer from brake pedal arm.
6. Remove booster unit from vehicle.
7. Reverse procedure to install. To purge system, disconnect feed wire from injection pump. Fill power steering pump reservoir, then crank engine for several seconds and recheck power steering pump fluid level. Connect injection pump feed wire and start engine, then cycle steering wheel from stop to stop twice and stop engine. Discharge accumulator by depressing brake pedal several times, then check fluid level. Start engine, then turn steering wheel from stop to stop and turn engine off. Check fluid level and add fluid as necessary. If foaming occurs, stop engine and wait for approximately one hour for foam to dissipate, then recheck fluid level.

VACUUM BOOSTER

1. Disconnect vacuum hose from vacuum cylinder and cover openings to prevent entrance of dirt.
2. Disconnect pipes from master cylinder outlets and cover openings in master cylinder and end of pipes to prevent entrance of dirt.
3. Disconnect pushrod from brake pedal.
4. Unfasten and remove power brake unit.
5. Reverse procedure to install.

BRAKE MASTER CYLINDER
REPLACE

1. Be sure area around master cylinder is clean, then disconnect the hydraulic lines at master cylinder. Plug or tape end of line to prevent entrance of dirt or loss of brake fluid.
2. On Cutlass models with manual brakes, remove pushrod to brake pedal pin.
3. Remove master cylinder retaining nuts and the master cylinder.
4. Reverse procedure to install.

Rear Suspension

INDEX

SHOCK ABSORBER
REPLACE

1. With rear axle properly supported, disconnect shock absorber from upper mounting.
2. Disconnect shock absorber from lower mounting.
3. Reverse procedure to install.

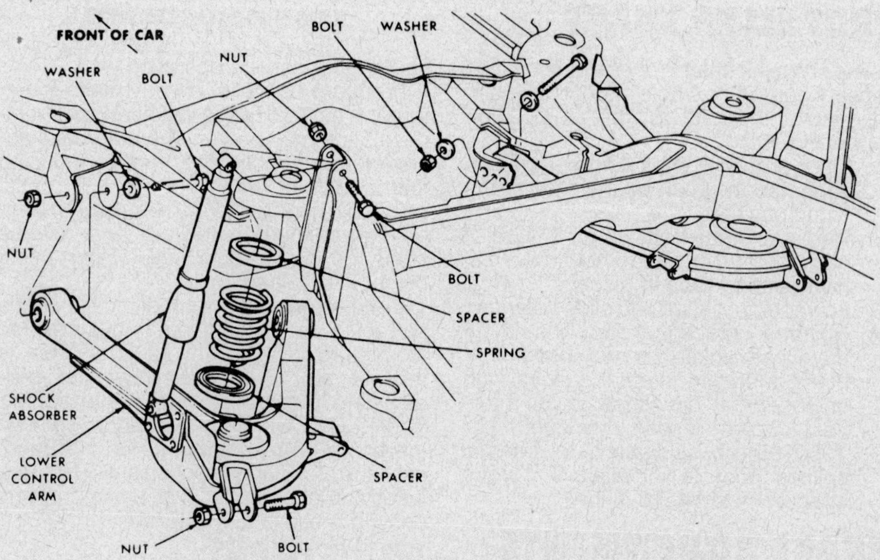

Fig. 1 Rear suspension. Toronado

COIL SPRING
REPLACE
EXC. TORONADO

1. Position a suitable jack under rear axle housing and raise rear of vehicle, then support frame side rails with support stands. Do not lower jack.
2. Disconnect brake line at axle housing.
3. Disconnect upper control arms at axle housing.
4. Disconnect shock absorber at lower mounting, then carefully lower rear axle assembly. **Use care not to stretch or kink brake hoses.**
5. Remove coil spring from vehicle.

TORONADO

1. Raise and support rear of vehicle, then remove wheel and tire assembly.
2. Remove stabilizer bar as described under Stabilizer Bar, Replace.
3. Using a suitable jack support lower control arm.
4. Disconnect automatic level air line at shock absorber. If removing lefthand spring from vehicle, disconnect automatic level control link from ball pivot at control arm.
5. Disconnect shock absorber from upper and lower mountings and remove shock absorber.

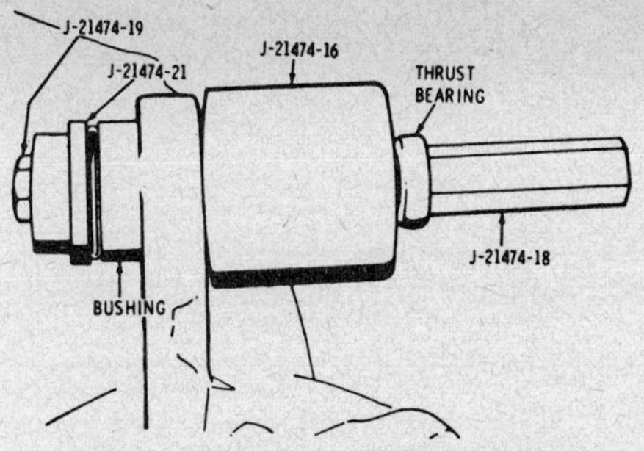

Fig. 2 Upper control arm axle bracket bushing removal

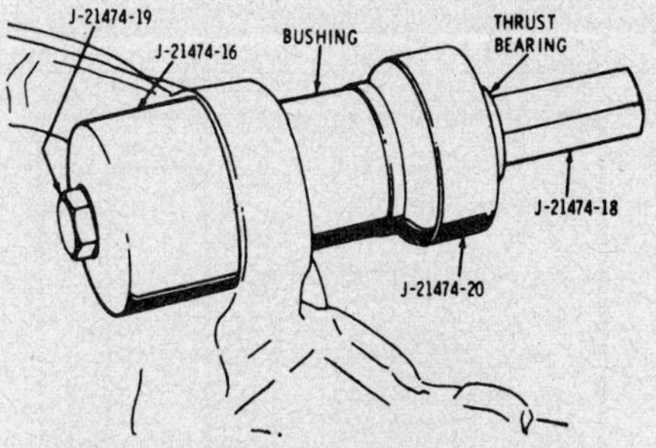

Fig. 3 Upper control arm axle bracket bushing installation

6. Carefully lower control arm until spring tension is relieved, then remove spring and insulator, **Fig. 1.**
7. Reverse procedure to install. Locate bottom end of spring between dimples on lower control arm assembly.

CONTROL ARMS & BUSHINGS

REPLACE

Replace control arms one at a time to prevent axle assembly misalignment, making installation difficult.

UPPER CONTROL ARMS

Exc. Toronado

1. Support vehicle at frame and rear axle.
2. Remove control arm front and rear mount bolts.
3. Remove bushings as necessary, **Figs. 2 and 3.**

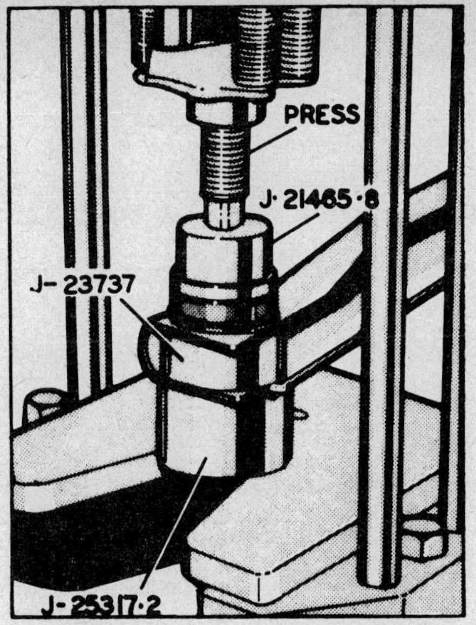

Fig. 4 Front & lower control arm rear bushing removal

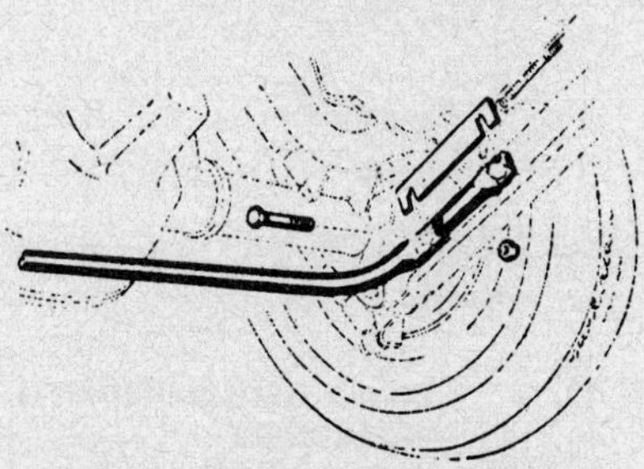

Fig. 6 Stabilizer bar installation (typical)

LOWER CONTROL ARMS

Exc. Toronado

Follow "Upper Control Arms" procedure for replacement of lower control arms. Replace control arm bushings as shown in **Figs. 4 and 5.**

Toronado

1. Raise and support rear of vehicle, then remove wheel and tire assembly.
2. Remove stabilizer bar as described under Stabilizer Bar, Replace.
3. Disconnect brake line bracket from control arm, then remove caliper assembly.
4. Mark a wheel stud and a corresponding point of the rotor for alignment, then remove rotor.
5. If lefthand control arm is to be removed, disconnect automatic level control link from ball pivot on control arm.
6. Using a suitable jack support control arm.
7. Disconnect air line from shock absorber, then disconnect shock absorber from upper and lower mountings and remove shock absorber.
8. Carefully lower the control arm until spring tension is relieved, then remove spring and insulator.
9. Remove two bolts mounting control arm to frame and remove control arm.
10. Reverse procedure to install.

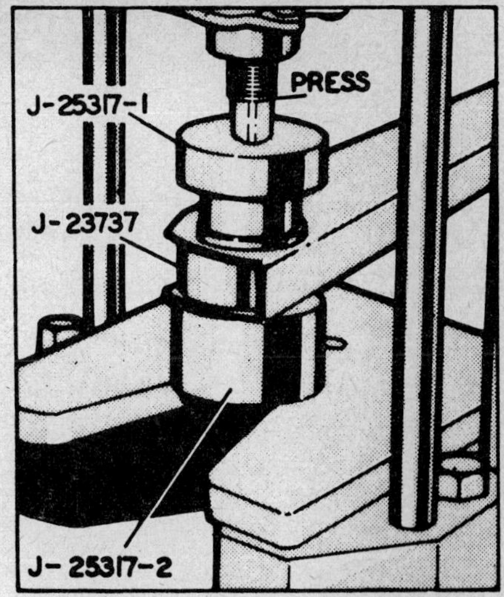

Fig. 5 Front & lower control arm rear bushing installation

STABILIZER BAR

REPLACE

EXC. TORONADO

1. Support vehicle at rear axle.
2. Remove bolts attaching stabilizer bar to the lower control arms, **Fig. 6.**
3. Reverse procedure to install.

TORONADO

1. Raise and support rear of vehicle.
2. Remove nuts and bolts securing front of stabilizer bar to control arms.
3. Remove inside nut and bolt from each side of stabilizer bar link, then loosen outside nut and bolt on the stabilizer link.
4. Rotate bottom parts of link to one side and slip stabilizer out of bushings.

Front Suspension & Steering Section

NOTE: For service procedures on Toronado, refer to chapter 2, "Front Suspension & Steering." Follow procedures pertaining to Eldorado & Seville.

INDEX

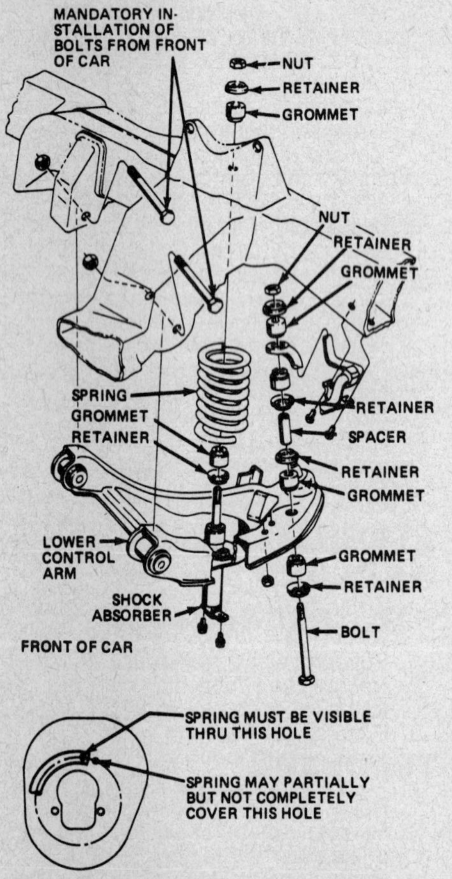

Fig. 1 Front suspension. Exc. Cutlass (Typical)

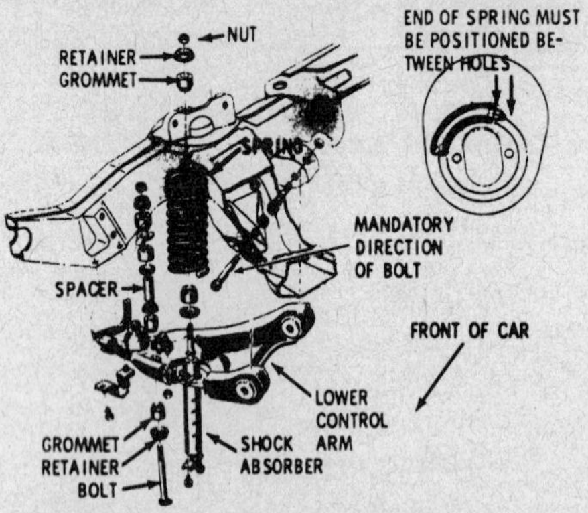

Fig. 2 Front suspension. Cutlass

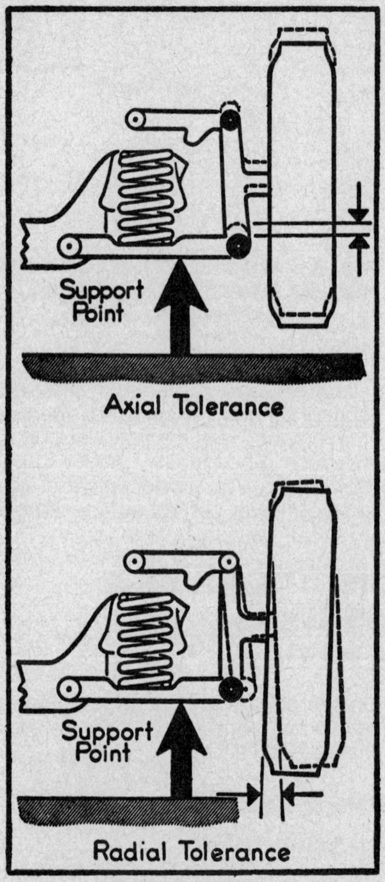

Fig. 3 Checking ball joints for wear

FRONT SUSPENSION

As shown in **Figs. 1 and 2**, the front suspension is of the conventional "A" frame design with ball joints. Double acting shock absorbers are mounted within the coil springs. Caster and camber are controlled by shims.

CHECKING BALL JOINTS FOR WEAR

If loose ball joints are suspected, first be sure the front wheel bearings are properly adjusted and that the control arms are tight. Then check ball joints for wear as follows:

Referring to **Fig. 3**, raise wheel with a jack placed under the lower control arm as shown. Then test by moving the wheel up and down to check axial play, and rocking it at the top and bottom to measure radial play.

CUTLASS

1. Upper ball joint should be replaced if looseness exceeds .125 inch. **A wear indicator is built into the lower ball joint, Fig. 4.**

EXC. CUTLASS

1. Upper ball joint should be replaced if looseness exceeds .125 inch. **A wear indicator is built into the lower ball joint. Refer to Fig. 4.**

BALL JOINTS REPLACE

On some models the ball joints are riveted to the control arms. All service ball joints, however, are provided with bolt, nut and washer assemblies for replacement purposes.

Some ball joints are pressed into the control arms, in which case they may be pressed out and new ones installed.

LOWER BALL JOINT

1. Raise vehicle and support at frame. Remove wheel.
2. Support lower control arm with a suitable jack.

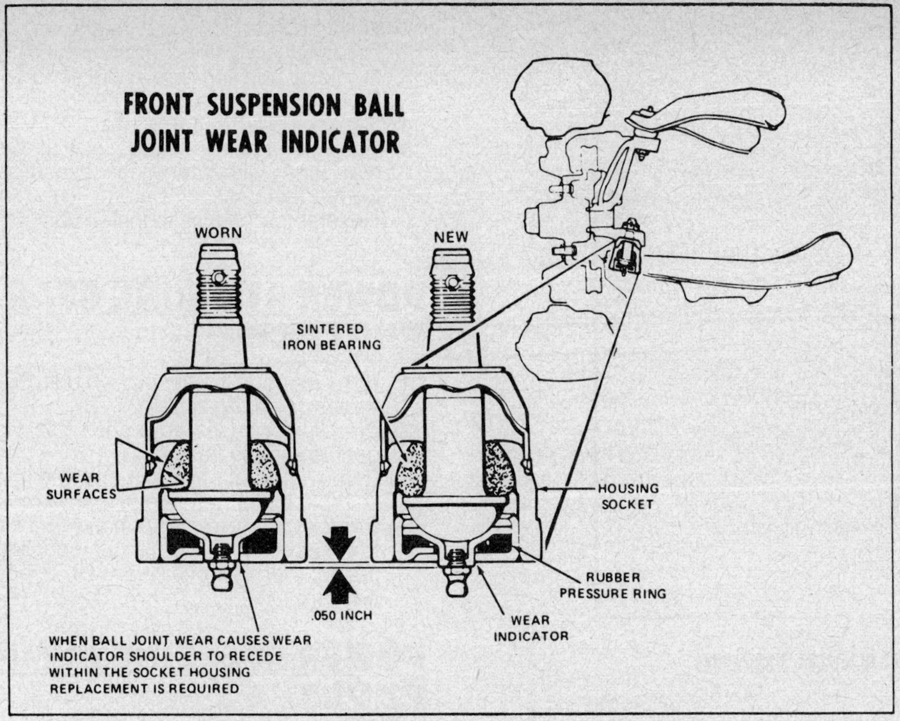

Fig. 4 Ball joint wear indicator

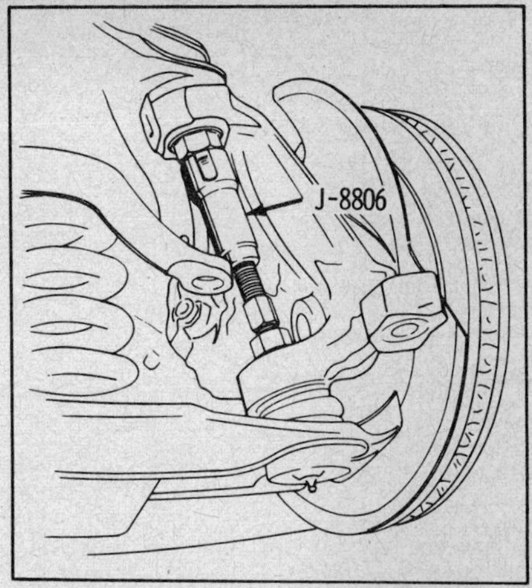

Fig. 5 Removing lower ball joint stud from knuckle

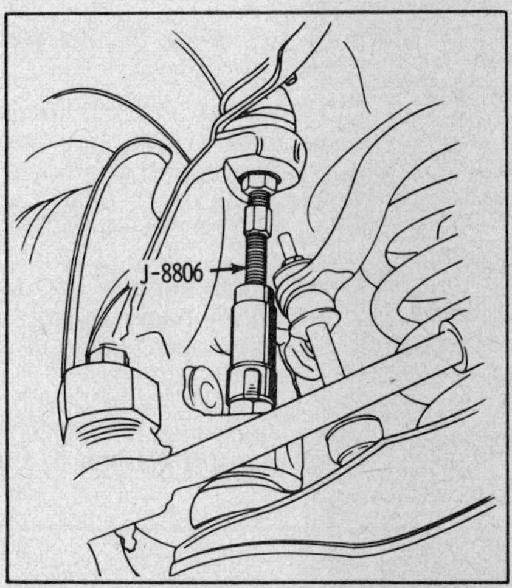

Fig. 6 Removing upper ball joint stud from knuckle

3. Remove cotter pin and loosen stud nut 2-3 turns. Using tool No. J-8806 or equivalent, break ball joint loose from the knuckle, **Fig. 5.**
4. Remove stud nut and lower the control arm. Position knuckle assembly aside.
5. Pry ball joint seal retainer from joint and remove seal.
6. Press ball joint from lower control arm with suitable tools.
7. Reverse procedure to install. Torque ball joint stud nut to 70 ft. lbs.

UPPER BALL JOINT

1. Raise vehicle and support at frame. Remove wheel.
2. Support lower control arm with suitable jack or jack stand.
3. Remove cotter pin and loosen stud nut 2-3 turns. Using tool No. J-8806 or equivalent, break ball joint loose from the knuckle, **Fig. 6.**
4. Remove stud nut and support knuckle assembly to prevent damage to brake hose.
5. Using a 1/8 inch twist drill, drill the 4 ball joint rivets approximately 1/4 inch. Then drill off rivets heads using a 1/2 inch twist drill.
6. Punch out rivets and remove lower ball joint.
7. Install new ball joint in lower control arm and torque attaching bolts to 8 ft. lbs.
8. Reverse procedure to assemble. Torque ball joint stud nut to 50 ft. lbs.

WHEEL BEARINGS
REPLACE

1. Raise car and remove front wheels.
2. Remove brake pads and caliper assembly but do not disconnect brake line. Suspend caliper from a wire loop or hook to avoid strain on the brake hose.
3. Remove grease cap, cotter pin and nut. Pull off hub and disc assembly. Grease retainer and inner bearing can now be removed.

WHEEL BEARINGS
ADJUST

1. While rotating hub assembly, tighten spindle nut to 12 ft. lbs. to insure bearings are properly seated.
2. Back off nut to the just loose position.
3. Hand tighten spindle nut, then loosen nut until either hole in spindle aligns with slot in nut. Do not back off more than 1/2 flat.
4. Install cotter pin, then measure hub assembly endplay. There will be .001 to .005 inch endplay when bearings are properly adjusted.

SHOCK ABSORBER
REPLACE

1. Remove upper attaching nut, retainer and grommet from shock absorber.
2. Remove two bolts and washers attaching shock absorber to lower control arm and remove shock absorber.
3. To install, position grommet and retainer over shock and slide shock up through spring and frame. Install and tighten attaching nut and lower capscrews.

COIL SPRING
REPLACE

Left and right coil springs should not be interchanged. Spring part number is stamped on outer side of end coil.

1. Place transmission in Neutral.
2. Disconnect shock absorber from upper mounting.
3. Raise vehicle and support at frame. Remove wheel.
4. Disconnect stabilizer bar from lower control arm.
5. Remove shock absorber.
6. Install lower plate BT-7408-1A or 1B, **Fig. 7,** with pivot ball seat facing downward into spring coils. Rotate plate to fully seat it in lower control arm spring seat.
7. Install upper plate BT-7408-1A or 1B, **Fig. 7,** with pivot ball seat facing upward into spring coils. Insert ball nut BT-7408-4 through spring coils and onto upper plate.

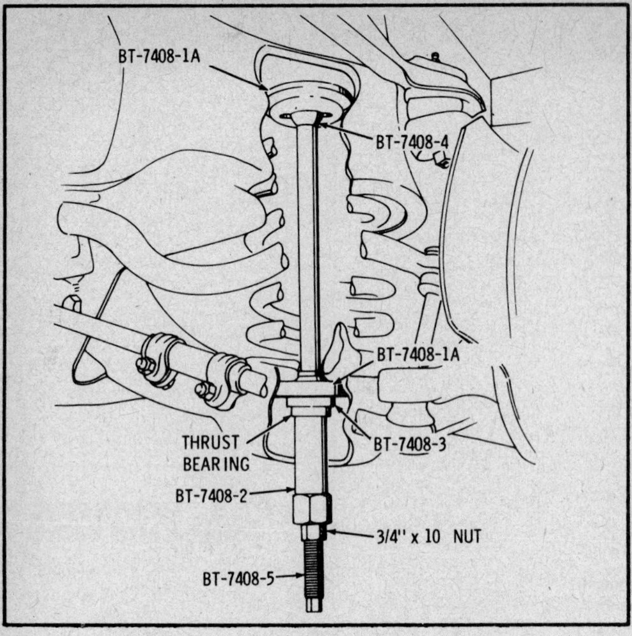

Fig. 7 Replacing coil spring

8. Install rod BT-7408-5 through shock absorber opening in lower control arm and through the upper and lower plates. Depress lock pin on shaft and thread into upper ball nut BT-7408-4. Ensure lock pin is fully extended above ball nut upper surface.
9. With ball nut tang engaged in slot in upper plate, rotate upper plate until it contacts upper spring seat.
10. Install lower pivot ball, thrust bearing and nut on rod and rotate nut until coil spring is compressed enough to be free in the seat.
11. Remove lower control arm pivot bolts. Move control arm rearward and remove coil spring.
12. Reverse procedure to install.

MANUAL STEERING GEAR
REPLACE

1. Remove two flex coupling flange nuts. **Remove coupling shield.**
2. Hoist and support car with stands under outer ends of lower control arms.
3. Remove nut and use a puller to remove pitman arm.
4. Remove gear-to-frame bolts.
5. Position steering linkage out of the way and withdraw gear assembly from under car.
6. Reverse procedure to install unit.

POWER STEERING GEAR
REPLACE

1. Remove coupling flange hub bolt. **Remove coupling shield.**
2. Disconnect hoses from gear and cap gear and hose fittings.
3. Remove pitman arm nut and, using a suitable puller, remove pitman arm.
4. Remove gear-to-frame bolts. Permit lower shaft to slide free of coupling flange, then remove gear with hoses attached.

POWER STEERING PUMP
REPLACE

To replace the power steering pump, loosen pump adjusting bolts and position pump so that drive belt can be removed from pump pulley. Disconnect hydraulic lines from pump and plug all lines and openings to prevent entry of dirt. Remove bolts securing pump or pump and bracket to engine and remove pump from vehicle. It may be necessary, depending on engine and vehicle model, to remove other accessories and components from front of engine to facilitate steering pump removal.

Wheel Alignment Section

INDEX

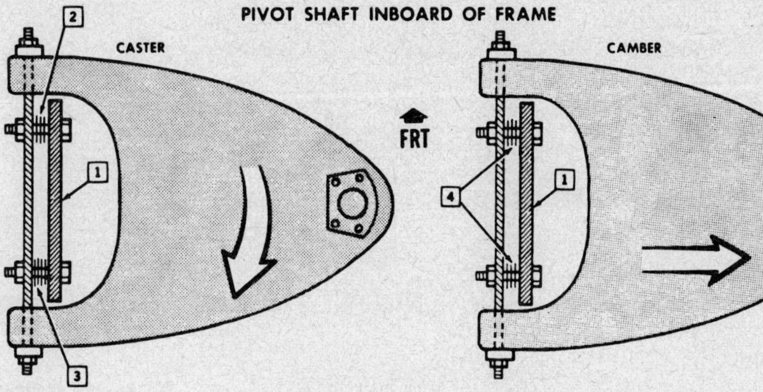

1. FRAME
2. SUBTRACT SHIMS HERE TO INCREASE "POSITIVE" CASTER
3. ADD SHIMS HERE TO INCREASE "POSITIVE" CASTER
4. SUBTRACT SHIMS EQUALLY TO INCREASE "POSITIVE" CAMBER

Fig. 1 Caster & camber adjustments. Exc. Toronado

FRONT WHEEL ALIGNMENT

CASTER & CAMBER ADJUSTMENT

EXC. TORONADO

Caster and camber angles can be adjusted by adding, subtracting or transferring shims between upper control arm shaft and frame bracket. Caster is adjusted by transferring shims from front to rear or rear to front, whereas camber is adjusted by changing shims at both the front and rear of the shaft. Caster and camber can be adjusted in one operation as follows:

1. Loosen upper control arm shaft-to-frame attaching nuts.
2. Add, subtract or transfer shims as needed, **Fig. 1.**
3. Tighten upper control arm shaft-to-frame attaching nuts. **Tighten nut on thinner shim pack first.**
4. Ensure shim pack has at least two bolt threads exposed past the nut and that difference between front and rear shim packs does not exceed .40 inch. If these requirements are not met after adjusting to specifications, check suspension and steering components for damage and repair as necessary.

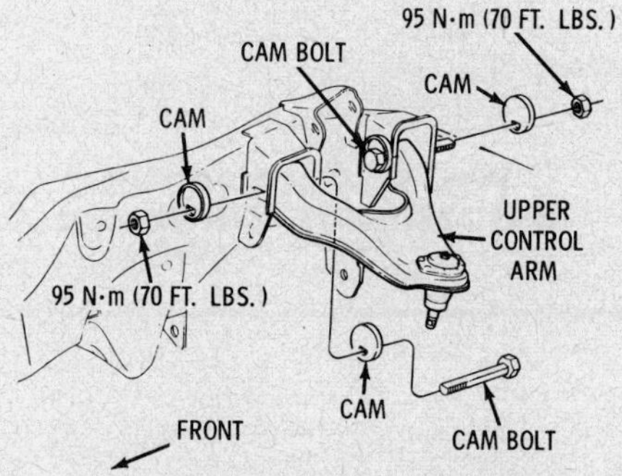

Fig. 2 Caster & camber adjustments. Toronado

TORONADO

Camber

1. Loosen nut while holding one cam bolt, **Fig. 2.**
2. Turn cam bolt to obtain change equal to 1/2 needed correction, then tighten nut while holding bolt in this position.
3. Repeat steps 1 and 2 on opposite side cam bolt.

Caster

1. Note camber reading, then loosen nut while holding front cam bolt, **Fig. 2.**
2. Turn front cam bolt to obtain change equal to 1/4 needed correction, then tighten nut while holding bolt in this position.
3. Loosen nut while holding rear cam bolt, then turn rear cam bolt to return camber to setting noted in step 1.
4. Ensure caster is within specifications, then tighten nut while holding bolt in position.

TOE-IN ADJUSTMENT

1. Loosen clamp bolts at each end of tie rod adjustable sleeves.
2. Set steering wheel in straight-ahead position and turn tie rods as necessary until toe-in is within specifications.
3. After adjustment is complete, ensure threads exposed on each end of sleeve are equal and tie rod end housings are at right angles to steering arm.
4. Position tie rod clamps and sleeves as shown, **Figs. 3 and 4,** then torque nuts to 15 ft. lbs.

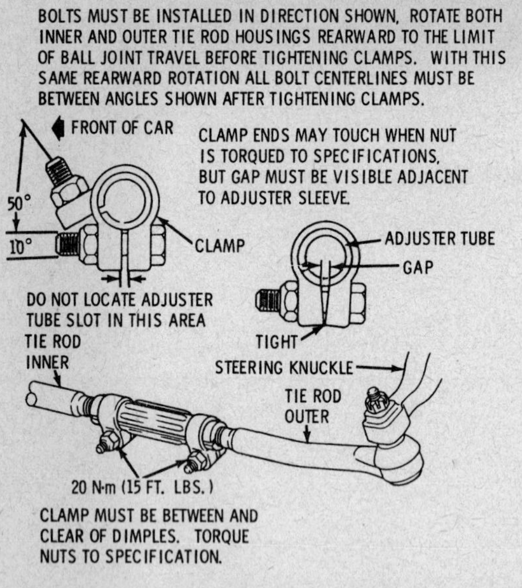
BOLTS MUST BE INSTALLED IN DIRECTION SHOWN. ROTATE BOTH INNER AND OUTER TIE ROD HOUSINGS REARWARD TO THE LIMIT OF BALL JOINT TRAVEL BEFORE TIGHTENING CLAMPS. WITH THIS SAME REARWARD ROTATION ALL BOLT CENTERLINES MUST BE BETWEEN ANGLES SHOWN AFTER TIGHTENING CLAMPS.
FRONT OF CAR
CLAMP ENDS MAY TOUCH WHEN NUT IS TORQUED TO SPECIFICATIONS, BUT GAP MUST BE VISIBLE ADJACENT TO ADJUSTER SLEEVE.
50°
10°
CLAMP
ADJUSTER TUBE
GAP
DO NOT LOCATE ADJUSTER TUBE SLOT IN THIS AREA
TIE ROD INNER
TIGHT
STEERING KNUCKLE
TIE ROD OUTER
20 N·m (15 FT. LBS.)
CLAMP MUST BE BETWEEN AND CLEAR OF DIMPLES. TORQUE NUTS TO SPECIFICATION.

Fig. 3 Tie rod clamp & sleeve positioning. Exc. Toronado

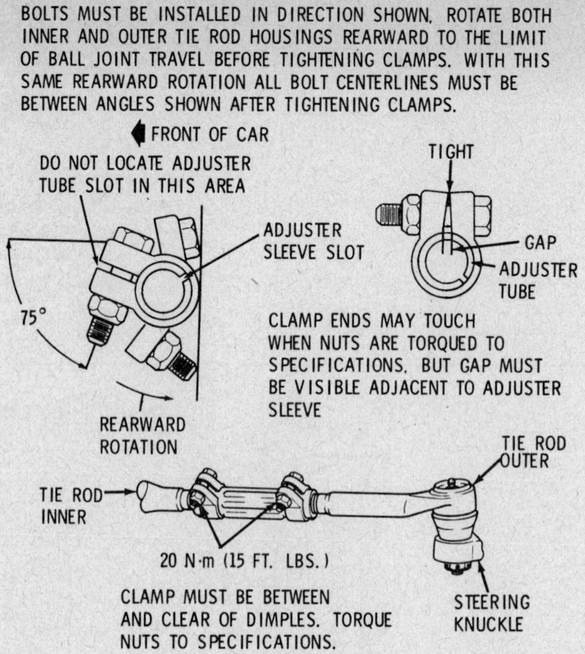
BOLTS MUST BE INSTALLED IN DIRECTION SHOWN. ROTATE BOTH INNER AND OUTER TIE ROD HOUSINGS REARWARD TO THE LIMIT OF BALL JOINT TRAVEL BEFORE TIGHTENING CLAMPS. WITH THIS SAME REARWARD ROTATION ALL BOLT CENTERLINES MUST BE BETWEEN ANGLES SHOWN AFTER TIGHTENING CLAMPS.
FRONT OF CAR
DO NOT LOCATE ADJUSTER TUBE SLOT IN THIS AREA
TIGHT
ADJUSTER SLEEVE SLOT
GAP
ADJUSTER TUBE
75°
CLAMP ENDS MAY TOUCH WHEN NUTS ARE TORQUED TO SPECIFICATIONS, BUT GAP MUST BE VISIBLE ADJACENT TO ADJUSTER SLEEVE
REARWARD ROTATION
TIE ROD OUTER
TIE ROD INNER
20 N·m (15 FT. LBS.)
CLAMP MUST BE BETWEEN AND CLEAR OF DIMPLES. TORQUE NUTS TO SPECIFICATIONS.
STEERING KNUCKLE

Fig. 4 Tie rod clamp & sleeve positioning. Toronado

REAR WHEEL ALIGNMENT

TORONADO

Camber Adjustment

Camber angle is not adjustable. If camber is found to be out of specifications, proceed as follows:

1. Inspect control arms for damage and replace as necessary.
2. Inspect frame for damage and repair as necessary.
3. Inspect hub and bearing assembly for improper seating and correct as necessary.

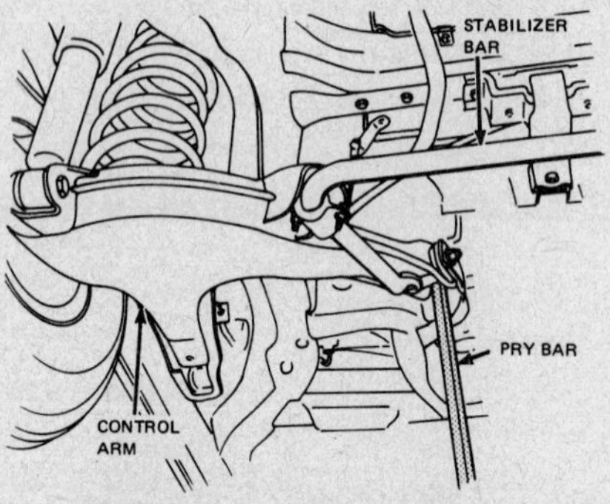
STABILIZER BAR
PRY BAR
CONTROL ARM

Fig. 5 Rear toe-in adjustment. Toronado

Toe-In Adjustment

Toe adjustments are made at the inner pivot bushings as follows:

1. Loosen inner bushing attaching nut and bolt.
2. Move control arm as necessary, **Fig. 5,** to bring toe within specifications. **Move control arm rearward to increase toe-in and outward to increase toe-out.**
3. If toe-in cannot be adjusted to specifications, proceed as follows:
   a. Ensure vehicle is properly centered on alignment equipment and correct as necessary.
   b. Inspect lower control arm for damage and replace as necessary.
   c. Inspect frame for damage and repair as necessary.

OLDSMOBILE DIESEL ENGINES V8-350 (5.7L) & V6-262 (4.3L) Rear Wheel Drive

INDEX OF SERVICE OPERATIONS

NOTE: This section covers all V8-350 diesel engines, and V6-262 diesel engines used in rear wheel drive vehicles. For other information not covered in this section, or for diesel engines used in front wheel drive vehicles, refer to the appropriate name chapter. Also, refer to rear of this manual for vehicle manufacturer's special service tool suppliers.

Specifications

GENERAL ENGINE SPECIFICATIONS

Year	Engine		Bore & Stroke	Compression Ratio	Net H.P. @ RPM ③	Maximum Torque Ft. Lbs. @ RPM	Normal Oil Pressure Lbs.
	CID ① Liter	VIN Code ②					
1982	V8-350, 5.7L	N	4.05 x 3.38	22.5	105 @ 3200	200 @ 1600	30-45
1983	V8-350, 5.7L	N	4.05 x 3.38	22.5	105 @ 3200	200 @ 1600	30-45
1984	V8-262, 4.3L	V	4.05 x 3.38	22.8	85 @ 3600	165 @ 1600	30-45
	V8-350, 5.7L	N	4.05 x 3.38	22.7	105 @ 3200	200 @ 1600	30-45
1985	V8-232, 4.3L	V	4.05 x 3.38	22.8	85 @ 3600	165 @ 1600	30-45
	V8-350, 5.7L	N	4.05 x 3.38	22.7	105 @ 3200	200 @ 1600	30-45

ENGINE TIGHTENING SPECIFICATIONS*

*Torque specifications are for clean and lightly lubricated threads only. Dry or dirty threads produced increased friction which prevents accurate measurement of tightness.

Year	Engine Model/VIN	Cylinder Head Belts Ft. Lbs.	Intake Manifold Ft. Lbs.	Exahust Manifold Ft. Lbs.	Rocker Arm Shaft Bracket Ft. Lbs.	Connecting Rod Cap Bolts Ft. Lbs.	Main Bearing Cap Bolts Ft. Lbs.	Flywheel to Crankshaft Ft. Lbs.	Vibration Damper or Pulley Ft. Lbs.
1982-83	V6-262/V	②	41	23	28 ①	42	④	48	160-350
	V8-350/N	130 ①	40 ③	25	28 ①	42	120	60	210-300
1984	V6-262/V	②	41	31	28 ①	42	80	57	203-350
	V8-350/N	130 ②	40 ③	25	28 ①	42	60	200-310	
1985	V6-262/V	②	41	28	28 ①	42	89 ⑤	57	203-350
	V8-350/N	130 ②	40 ③	25	28 ①	42	60	200-310	

①—Rocker arm pivot bolt to head.
②—See text for procedure.
③—Clean & dip entire bolt in engine oil before tightening.
④—1982, 107 ft. lbs.; 1983, 89 ft. lbs.
⑤—Type II bolts at Nos. 2 and 3 outer positions.
⑥—Rear, 120 ft. lbs.

STARTING MOTOR APPLICATIONS

Year	Model/VIN	Starter Number
1982	V6-262/V	1998552
	V8-350/N ① ②	1998552
	V8-350/N ③	1109545
1983	V6-262/V	1998554
	V8-350/N ① ②	1998554
	V8-350/N ③	1109495
1984	V6-262/V	1998556
		22511854
	V8-350/N ① ②	1998553
		22511854
V8-350/V ③	1109495	
1985	V6-262/V	1998556
		22511854
V8-350/N ① ④	1998553	
		22523207
	V8-350/N ③	1109495

①—Cutlass.
②—88 & 98.
③—Toronado.
④—88.

General Information

INDEX

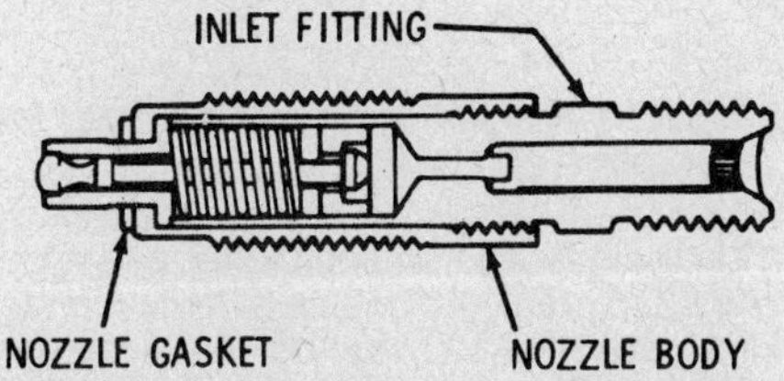

Fig. 1 Fuel injection nozzle

ENGINE CONSTRUCTION

The Oldsmobile four stroke cycle diesel engine is basically the same in construction as the Oldsmobile gasoline engine. The cylinders are numbered 1, 3, 5, 7 on the left bank and 2, 4, 6, 8 on the right bank on 8 cylinder engines or 1, 3 and 5 on the left bank and 2, 4 and 6 on the right bank on 6 cylinder engines. The firing order is 1-8-4-3-6-5-7-2 on 8 cylinder engines or 1-6-5-4-3-2 on 6 cylinder engines. The major differences between the diesel and gasoline versions is in the cylinder heads, combustion chamber, fuel distribution system, air intake manifold and method of ignition. The cylinder block, crankshaft, main bearings, connecting rods, pistons and pins are of heavy construction due to the high compression ratio required to ignite the diesel fuel. The diesel fuel is ignited when the heat developed in the combustion chamber during the compression stroke reaches a certain temperature.

The valve train operates the same as in the gasoline engine, but are of special design and material for diesel operation. The stainless steel pre-chamber inserts in the cylinder head combustion chambers are serviced separately from the cylinder head. With the cylinder head removed, these pre-chamber inserts can be driven from the cylinder head after removing the glow plugs or injection nozzles. The glow plugs are threaded into the cylinder head and the injection nozzles are retained by a bolt and clamp. The injection nozzles are spring loaded and calibrated to open at a specified fuel pressure.

FUEL SYSTEM

The fuel injection pump is mounted on top of the engine and is gear driven by the camshaft and rotates at camshaft speed. This high pressure rotary pump injects a metered amount of fuel to each cylinder at the proper time. Six or eight high pressure fuel delivery pipes from the injection pump to the injection nozzles, **Fig. 1,** are the same length to prevent any difference in timing from cylinder to cylinder. The fuel injection pump provides the required timing advance under all operating conditions. Engine speed is controlled by a rotary fuel metering valve, **Figs. 2 and 3.** When the accelerator is depressed, the throttle cable opens the metering valve and allows more fuel to be delivered to the engine. The injection pump also incorporates a low pressure transfer pump to deliver fuel to the fuel line to the high pressure pump, **Figs. 2 and 3.**

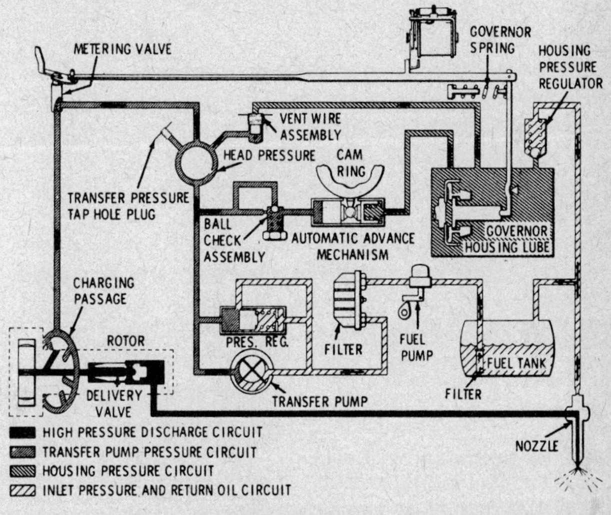

Fig. 2 Fuel injection pump circuit. V8 engine

The fuel filter is located between the mechanical fuel pump and the injection pump on 8 cylinder engines, or between the electric fuel pump and the injection pump on 6 cylinder engines. The diaphragm type mechanical fuel pump used on 8 cylinder engines is mounted on the righthand side of the engine and is driven by a cam on the crankshaft. The electric fuel pump used on 6 cylinder engines is mounted on the engine. The fuel tank at the rear of the vehicle is connected by fuel pipes to the mechanical fuel pump.

"WATER IN FUEL" SYSTEM

These vehicles have a "Water in Fuel" light mounted in the instrument panel. The "Water in Fuel" light has a bulb check feature and should light for 2 to 2½ seconds when the ignition is turned on. If not, the bulb is burned out or there is an open in the wiring circuit. When there is water in the fuel, the light will come back on and remain on after a 15 to 20 second delay.

A water sensing probe, mounted on the fuel sender, actuates the instrument panel light when it is partially covered with water. About 1 to 2½ gallons of water must be present in the fuel tank to cause the sensor light to activate.

If the "Water in Fuel" lamp goes on while the vehicle is being driven, the fuel system should be checked for water. If the lamp goes on immediately after refueling and before the vehicle is moved, there is a large quantity of water in the tank and should be removed immediately.

The water may be removed from the tank with a pump or by siphoning. The pump or siphon hose should be connected to the quarter inch fuel return hose (the smaller of the two hoses), located under the hood near the fuel pump. Refer to "Purging Water From Fuel Tank" procedure.

HOUSING PRESSURE COLD ADVANCE (HPCA)

This feature is used on all engines and advances the injection timing 3° during cold operation. This circuit is actuated by a temperature switch calibrated to open the circuit at 125°F. Below the switching point, housing pressure is decreased from 10 to 0 psi which advances the injection timing 3°. Above the switching point, the switch opens, de-energizing the solenoid and the housing pressure is returned to 10 psi. The fast idle solenoid is energized by the same switch and closes when the temperature falls below 95°F.

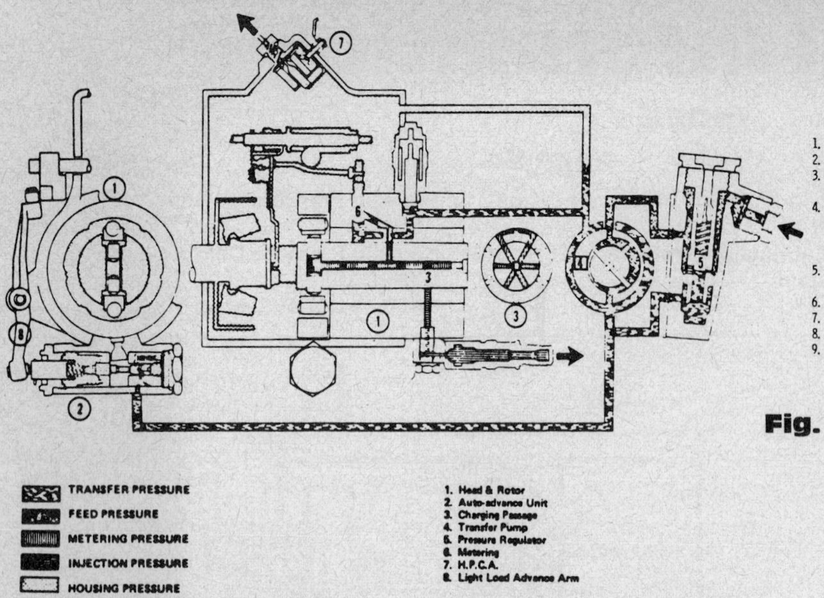

Fig. 3 Fuel injection pump circuit. V6 engine

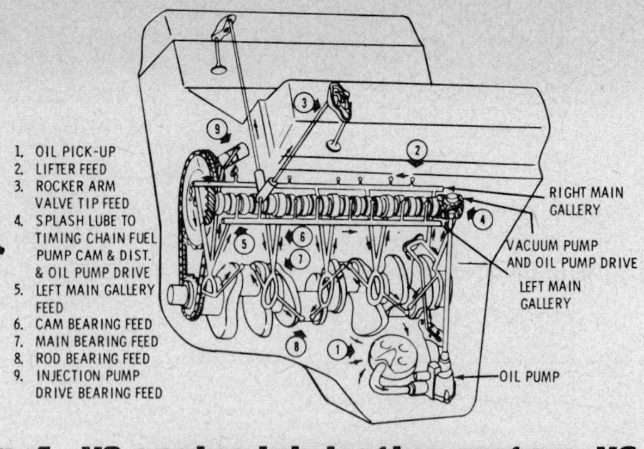

Fig. 4 V8 engine lubricating system, V6 engine similar

HOUSING PRESSURE ALTITUDE ADVANCE (HPAA)

Used on 1984-85 engines (exc. Calif.), the HPAA is used to meet emission standards at both low and high altitudes. Altitude compensation is achieved through timing changes and EGR modification and is controlled by an altitude sensitive switch.

Timing is controlled by two pressure regulators, the Housing Pressure Cold Advance, located in the injection pump, and the Housing Pressure Altitude Advance solenoid in the fuel return line.

The HPAA solenoid regulates housing pressure according to altitude. When the solenoid is activated, the glass check ball seats, regulating pressure at its calibrated value. When the solenoid is de-activated, the check ball moves off its seat, opening the fuel return line and preventing pressure regulation. It is possible for both the HPCA and the HPAA to regulate housing pressure at the same time. Likewise, it is also possible to have just the HPCA or the HPAA regulate pressure singularly. The HPCA must be energized and not regulating to allow the HPAA solenoid to regulate at its calibrated value.

ENGINE LUBRICATION SYSTEM

The diesel engine lubrication system is basically the same as the gasoline engine. The fuel injection pump driven gear is lubricated by oil directed through a passage from the top of the camshaft bearing, **Fig. 4.** An angled passage in the shaft portion of the driven gear directs the oil to the rear driven gear bearing. At the front of the right oil gallery, a small orifice sprays oil to lubricate the fuel pump eccentric cam on the crankshaft and timing chain. The recommended diesel engine oil is SF/CC or SF/CD.

ENGINE COOLING SYSTEM

The diesel engine cooling system is the same as the gasoline engine except the radiator incorporates two oil coolers. One cooler is used to cool the transmission fluid and the other cooler is used to cool the engine oil.

ENGINE ELECTRICAL SYSTEM

1982–83

Eight glow plugs are used to pre-heat the pre-chamber to aid in starting. The type 1 glow plugs are 12 volt heaters and are activated when the ignition switch is turned to the "Run" position. The type 1 system uses steady current applied to 12 volt glow plugs. The type 2 glow plug system uses 6 volt glow plugs with a controlled pulsating current applied to them for starting. The type 2 glow plug system uses an electromechanical controller to control glow plug temperature, pre-glow time, wait/start lights and after glow time. The Electronic Glow Plug Control System used on intermediate models uses an electronic module and a control sensor to control glow plug temperature, the glow plug relay and the wait light. On this system a coolant temperature switch controls the fast idle solenoid through a fast idle relay. The 6 volt and 12 volt glow plugs are not interchangeable and can be identified by the wire connector spade. The 6 volt glow plugs have a 5/16 in. wire connector spade, while the 12 volt glow plugs have a 1/4 in. wire connector spade. The glow plugs remain activated for a short time after starting then are automatically turned "Off." Two 12 volt batteries connected in parallel are required for the higher electrical load due to the glow plugs and starter motor. The diesel starter motor is larger than the gasoline engine starter and is designed to crank the engine at least the 100 RPM required for starting. An alternator supplies charging current to both batteries at the same time and there are no switches or relays in the charging circuit.

1984

The glow plug system features a self-limiting feature that regulates maximum temperature, while the glow plugs are programmed to shut off automatically should the vehicle not be started within the specified time period.

System Components

The glow plug control module, **Fig. 5,** is an integral assembly that includes the timer functions, lamp switch and glow plug relay. The control module serves the following functions:

1. Controls wait lamp operation, which varies according to system voltage and/or ambient temperature.
2. Controls system shutdown timing depending on voltage and ambient temperature.
3. An overvoltage function that protects the glow plugs from failure, should higher than normal voltages be incurred.
4. A thermal cutout function that disengages the glow plug system when module temperatures are greater than 113°F.
5. A power relay function that switches the voltage applied to the glow plugs.
6. A quick reset function that permits the module to recycle quickly, after initial shutdown time.

This control module can only be used with glow plugs that regulate their own temperature. The new glow plugs used have positive temperature coefficient properties, which mean they have low resistance values at low temperatures and high resistance values at high temperatures. The new plugs offer a fast temperature rise similar to past fixed resistance plugs, plus improved and simpler glow plug control.

System Operation

The glow plug control circuit, **Fig. 6,** operates the glow plug system in three steps: pre-glow, after-glow and off. During pre-glow, the circuit activates the wait lamp

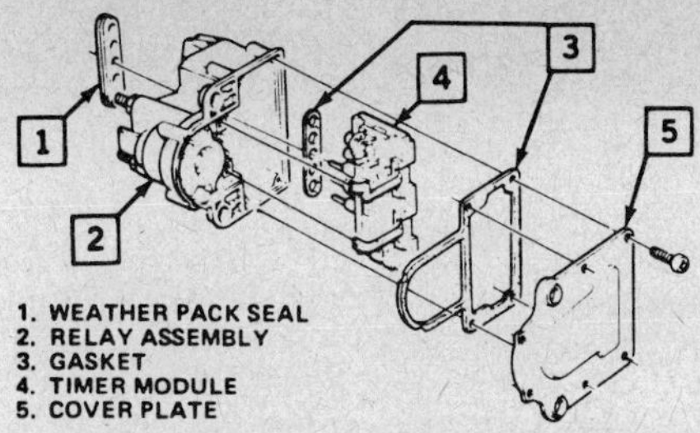

Fig. 5 Glow plug control module. 1984

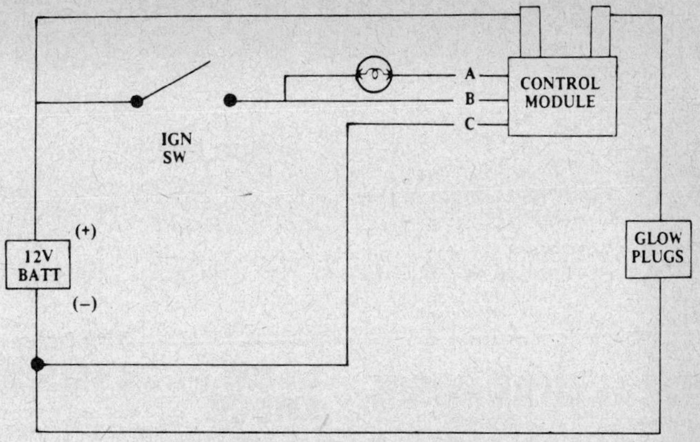

Fig. 6 Glow plug control circuit schematic. 1984

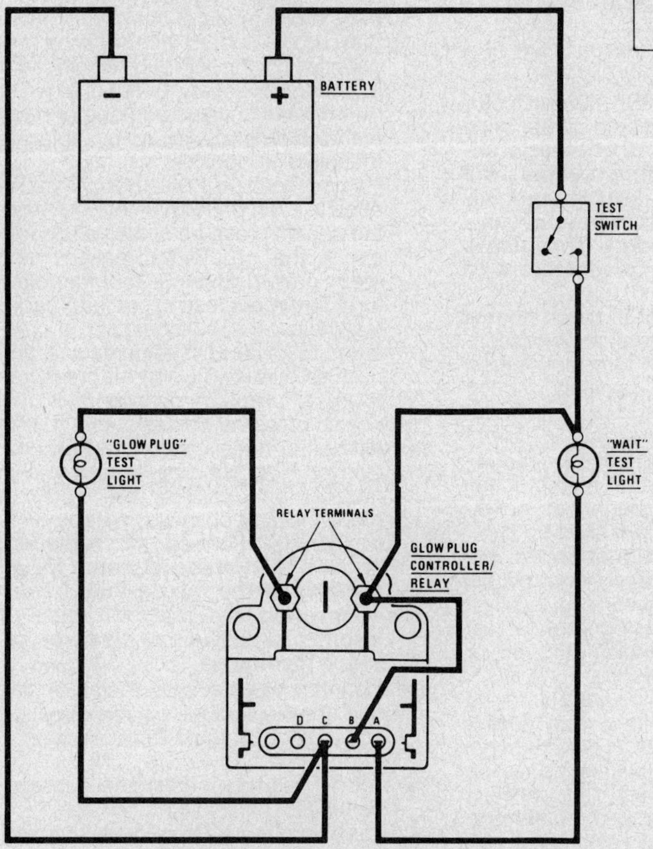

Fig. 7 Glow plug controller test connections. 1985

and heats the glow plugs until they are sufficiently warm to start the engine. During after-glow, the circuit deactivates the wait lamp, but continues to apply power to the glow plugs. During the Off cycle, the circuit removes power from the glow plugs and keeps it off until the engine is restarted.

As stated previously, the glow plug control module controls all circuit functions. The thermal controls open the pre-glow and after-glow switches to end the respective cycles, and are responsive to engine temperature. When the system is energized with the engine cold, both switches are in the "Cold" position. As time passes, current flow heats the thermal controls, moving both switches toward their "Hot" position. The time needed for each switch to reach its "Hot" position is dependent upon how cold the engine and control module were when the system was first energized. As the pre-glow switch reaches the "Hot" position, the wait lamp deactivates and the engine may now be started. The control module continues to operate, whether the engine is started or not, since the after-glow switch has not yet reached its "Hot" position. Current flow continues to heat the thermal control. When the thermal control reaches full temperature, the after-glow switch moves to "Hot," opening the path to ground from the coil of the glow plug relay. This allows current flow to bypass the coil of the reset relay. With the path to ground now open, current must flow to bypass the coil of the reset relay. With the path to ground now open, current must flow to ground through the reset relay coil. The glow plug relay de-energizes, removing power to the glow plugs. The reset relay now energizes, opening the contact of the relay and locking off the thermal controls. When the ignition switch is turned off, the reset relay contact closes, and the glow plug module is ready to repeat the cycle. If the engine is above 140°F when restarted, the thermal controls will be "Hot," energizing the reset relay and preventing glow plug operation.

The over-voltage protector protects the glow plugs should battery voltage rise above 14 volts. When the protector senses over 14 volts, it opens the circuit to the glow plug relay coil and prevents current from flowing to the glow plugs. After a short time, the protector closes the circuit. If battery voltage is still above 14 volts, it will reopen the circuit again. The protector continues to cycle in this way as long as the over-voltage condition exists and as long as glow plug operation is needed.

1985

A glow plug relay in the glow plug controller regulates the hearing of the glow plugs, **Fig. 7.** The relay is operated by the thermal controls in the controller. These thermal controls respond to engine temperature as well as the heating coil inside the thermal control unit.

When the ignition switch is turned to the Run position, battery voltage is applied to the "Wait" lamp. The "Wait" lamp switched is closed when cold and open when hot. When the lamp is on, battery voltage is applied to the glow plugs and they begin to heat. After approximately six seconds, when the glow plugs and engine are sufficiently heated, the "Wait" lamp goes out and the engine can be started. At this time, the glow plug relay remains closed continue heating the glow plugs to reduce exhaust smoke and improve cold driveability.

After approximately one minute of engine operation, the glow plug relay is opened and heating of the glow plugs is stopped. If the engine is restarted when hot, the thermal controller keeps both the lamp switch and relay open to prevent any further plug heating.

When the engine cools, the "Wait" lamp switch returns to the closed position and the glow plug relay remains open until battery voltage is applied to the thermal controls.

The thermal controls provide protection from overvoltage conditions by automatically de-energizing and energizing the glow plug relay. If the overvoltage surge remains present, voltage is cycled on and off to the glow plugs without damaging them.

Electrical & Engine Diagnosis

INDEX

ELECTRICAL DIAGNOSIS

1982–84

Refer to **Figs. 1 through 5** for diesel engine electrical diagnosis.

1985

Glow Plug Controller Diagnosis

1. If there is no voltage at the glow plugs, or a "Wait" lamp malfunction, disconnect electrical connector from glow plug controller.
2. Place ignition switch in Run position and check for voltage at connector terminals as well as controller relay stud terminals. Ensure terminal C (black) is grounded.
3. Battery voltage should be indicated at terminals A (dark blue) and B (pink/black) and the red relay terminal. No voltage should be indicated at terminal D (purple) or the green relay terminal.
4. If voltage is not present at terminal A, check "Wait" lamp bulb and associated wiring for an open. If voltage at any other terminal is incorrect, check circuit to that terminal.
5. If voltages at connector and relay terminals are correct, replace glow plug controller.

Glow Plug Controller Bench Test

1. Remove glow plug controller from vehicle and allow to cool below 122°F.
2. Connect test equipment to controller. Refer to **Fig. 7** in previous section.
3. Close test switch and observe test lamps. Both lamps should immediately go on when test switch is closed. After 5-7 seconds, "Wait" lamp should go off, followed by the "Glow Plug" lamp in 35-55 seconds. After 2 minutes, both lamps should remain off.
4. Open test switch, wait several seconds, then close switch. Both test lamps should immediately go on.
5. Replace controller if operation is not as described.

ROUGH IDLE DIAGNOSIS

Check for mechanical malfunctions such as incorrect idle speed or injection pump timing, or leaking nozzles or high pressure lines. If rough idle is still evident, refer to "Glow Plug Resistance Check."

GLOW PLUG RESISTANCE CHECK

1. Using multi-meter J-29125 (1982-83) or J-29125A (1984-85) set left selector switch to "OHMS," right selector switch to 200 ohms and center slide switch to "D.C. LO." **If another ohmmeter is used, different values will result. Tools J-29125 and J-29125A were used in the development of this procedure. Their use is required if similar readings are to be obtained.**
2. Start engine, allow it to reach normal operating temperature, then disconnect all feed wires from glow plugs. Turn heater to "On" position.
3. Disconnect alternator two wire connector.
4. Using tachometer J-26925, or equivalent, adjust idle speed screw to obtain worst engine idle roughness condition. Do not exceed 900 RPM.
5. Allow engine to run at worst idle speed for approximately one minute, then attach an alligator clip to black test lead of meter. Ground black test lead to fast idle solenoid (1983-85) or engine lift strap (1982).
6. Write down the engine firing order on a piece of paper, then with engine idling, probe each glow plug terminal and record the resistance values on each cylinder in the firing sequence. **If vehicle is equipped with an electric cooling fan, record resistance values with cooling fan inoperative. Do not disconnect cooling fan circuitry. The resistance values are dependent on the temperature in each cylinder, and therefore, can indicate cylinder output.**
7. If a resistance reading on any cylinder is 1.3-1.4 ohms for 1984-85 vehicles, or 1.2-1.3 for 1982-83 vehicles, check engine for a mechanical problem. Make a compression check of the lowest reading cylinder and the cylinders which fire before and after. Correct cause of low compression before proceeding to fuel system.
8. On 1984-85 vehicles, install glow plug luminosity probe, from tool J-33075, into cylinder with lowest resistance value. Observe combustion light flashes of probe. The flashes will usually be erratic and in sequence with the misfire. If not, move to the next lowest reading cylinder, until the misfire is found.
9. On all vehicles, observe the results of all glow plug resistance readings, looking for differences between cylinders. Rough engines will normally have a difference of .4 ohms or more between cylinders in the firing sequence. To correct rough engine idle, it will be necessary to raise or lower the resistance values on one or more of the offending cylinders by replacing the injection nozzles.
10. Remove nozzle from the cylinder(s) affecting idle performance. Determine the pop off pressure of the nozzle and check the nozzle for leakage and spray pattern. Refer to tool manufacturer for proper testing procedures. Install nozzles with higher pop off pressures to lower resistance values, and nozzles with lower pop off pressures to raise values. A change of 30 psi nozzle pressure will result in a .1 ohm difference in resistance. Use new nozzles on new vehicles and broken in nozzles on vehicles with 1500 or more miles, if possible. **Whenever a nozzle is cleaned or replaced, crank the engine and watch for air bubbles at the nozzle inlet before connecting the injection pipe. If bubbles are evident, clean or replace the nozzle.**
11. Connect injection pipe, restart engine and check idle quality. If idle quality is still not acceptable, repeat steps 6 through 10.
12. After making additional nozzle changes, check idle quality again.
13. If problem moves from cylinder to cylinder and resistance values do not change as nozzles are changed, the injection pump may be defective. **Always recheck cylinders at same engine RPM. Sometimes cylinder readings may not indicate that an improvement has been made, even though the engine may idle better. A nozzle with a tip leak can allow more fuel than required into a cylinder, raising the glow plug resistance value. This will steal fuel from the next nozzle in the firing order and will result in that glow plug having a lower resistance value. If this is evident, remove and check the nozzle with the high reading. If it is leaking, it may be responsible for the rough idle. If low readings are evident on a glow plug and it does not change with a nozzle change, switch glow plugs between the good and bad cylinder. If the reading of each cylinder is not the same as before the switch, then the glow plug cannot be used for rough idle diagnosis.**

1	2	3	4	5 (ENGINE RUNNING)	6 (ENGINE RUNNING)
IGN. SWITCH -"OFF"-	IGN. SWITCH -"RUN"-	IGN. SWITCH -"RUN"-	IGN. SWITCH -"START"-	IGN. SWITCH -"RUN"-	IGN. SWITCH -"RUN"-
WAIT LAMP-OFF	WAIT LAMP-ON	WAIT LAMP-OFF	WAIT LAMP-OFF	WAIT LAMP-OFF	WAIT LAMP-OFF
GLOW PLUGS-OFF	GLOW PLUGS-ON	GLOW PLUGS-ON	GLOW PLUGS-ON	GLOW PLUGS-ON	GLOW PLUGS-OFF
		SEE * 1		SEE * 2	

* 1: If the ignition is left in the "Run" position without starting the engine, the glow plugs will continue to pulse on/off until batteries run down. (About 4 hours when coolant switch is open.)

* 3: Do not manually energize or by-pass the glow plug relay as glow plugs will be damaged instantly.

* 2: Glow plugs will pulse on/off for about 30 seconds after engine starts. Then turn off and remain off as long as engine temperature is above about 120° F (49° C).

* 4: Diodes prevent glow plug operation when the engine is warm (above 120°) the engine is not running and key is in RUN.

IMPORTANT: Do Not use more than a 2–3 candle power test light when making circuit checks.

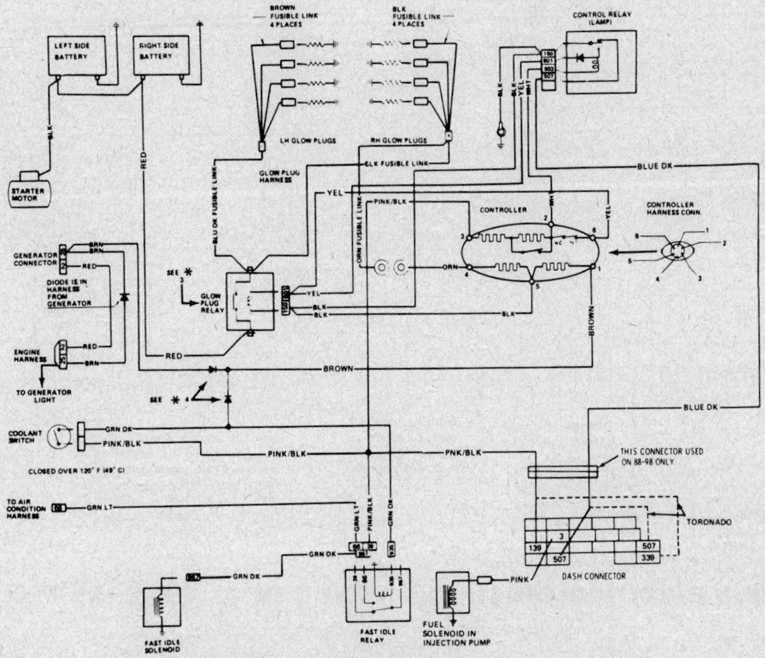

Fig. 1 Diesel engine electrical system (Part 1 of 2). 1982–83 Full Size Models Type 2

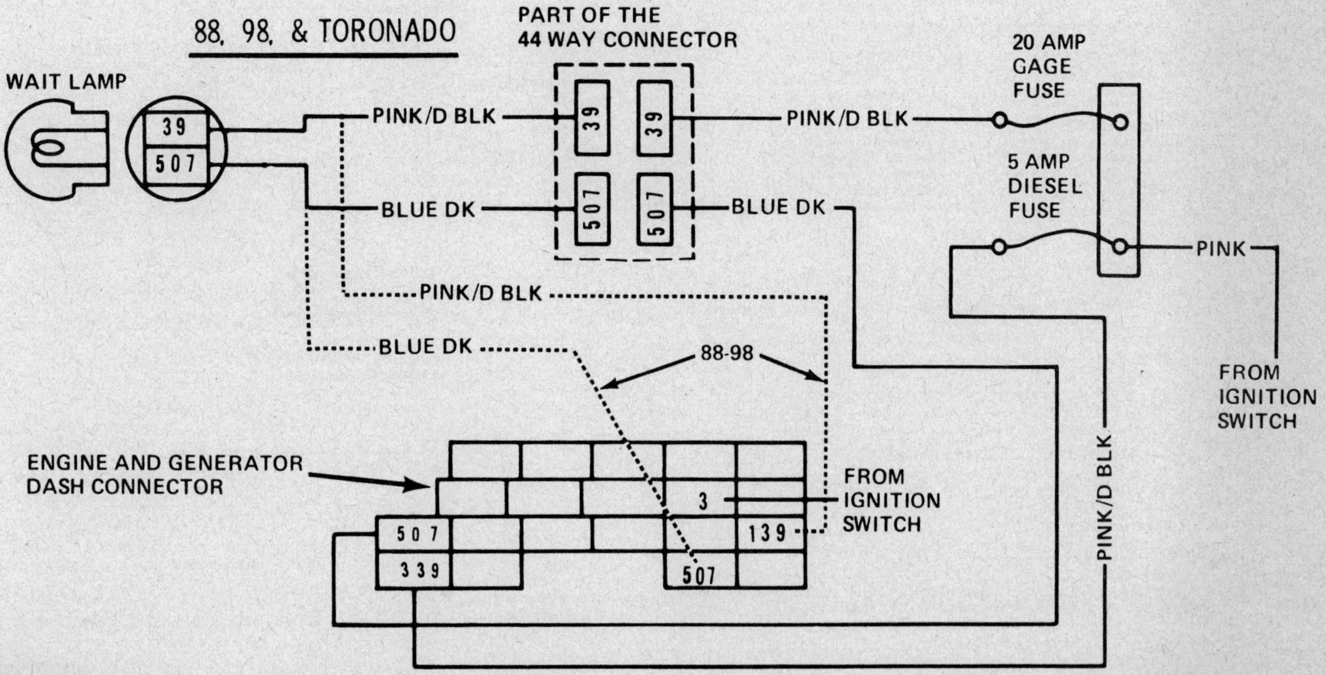

Fig. 1 Diesel engine electrical system (Part 2 of 2). 1982–83 Full Size Models Type 2

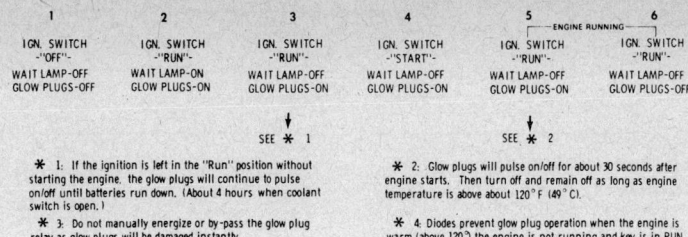

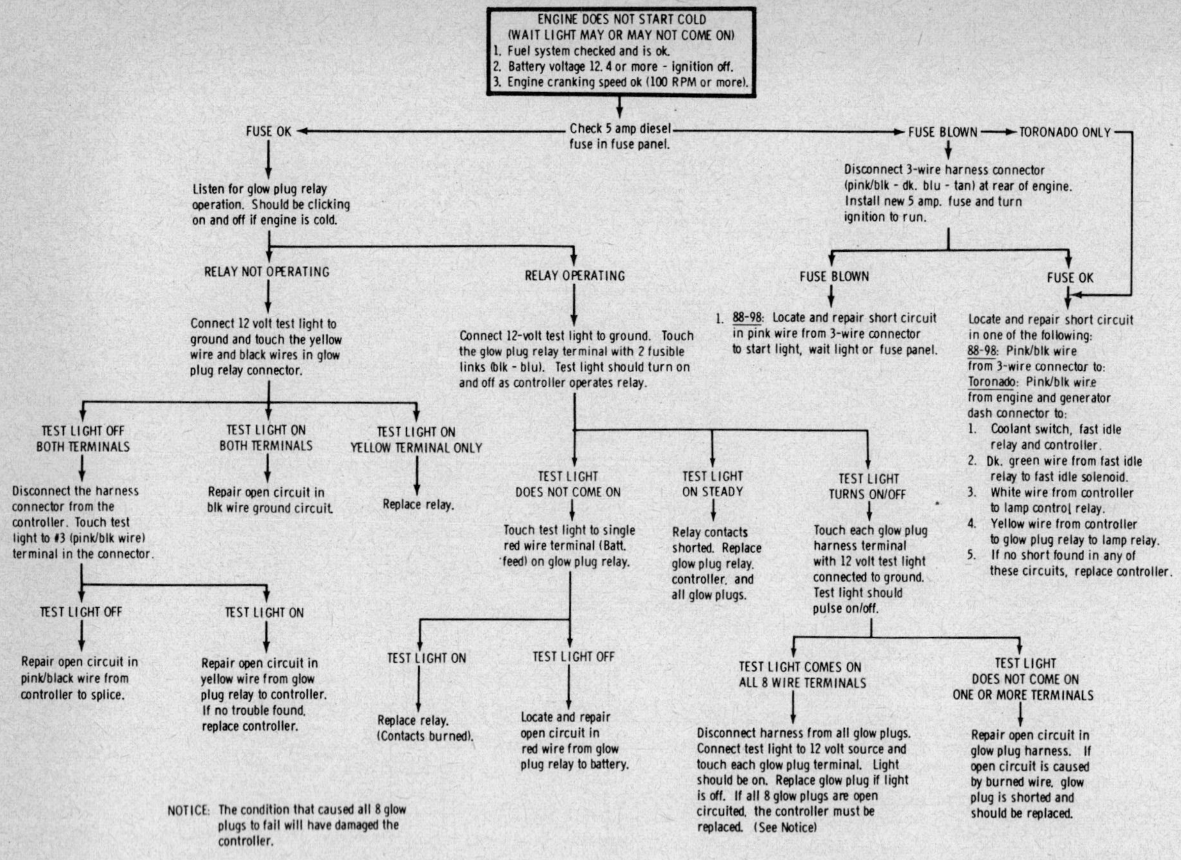

Fig. 2 Diesel engine electrical diagnosis (Part 1 of 4). 1982–83 Full Size Models Type 2

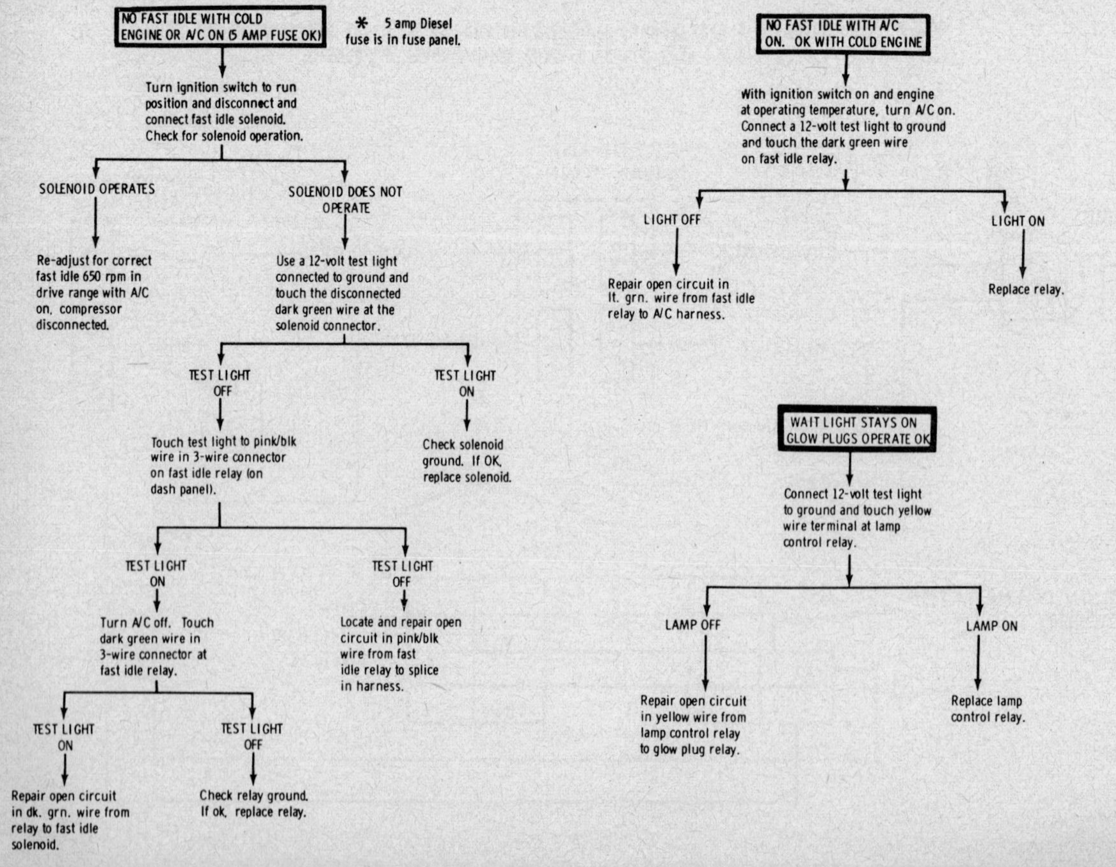

Fig. 2 Diesel engine electrical diagnosis (Part 2 of 4). 1982–83 Full Size Models Type 2

ENGINE CONTINUES TO RUN IGNITION KEY OFF

With ignition turned off and engine still running, disconnect 3 wire connector (2 brown-1 red) from generator.

- ENGINE CONTINUES TO RUN → Disconnect pink wire at injection pump solenoid.
  - ENGINE CONTINUES TO RUN → Remove injection pump for repair.
  - ENGINE STOPS → Check ignition switch adjustment. If OK, replace ignition switch.
- ENGINE STOPS → Check diode in brown wire from generator to lamp control relay for a short.

ENGINE STAYS ON FAST IDLE AT ALL TIMES

Turn A/C off, ignition on and disconnect fast idle solenoid - dark green wire.

- SOLENOID DOES NOT RETRACT → Check throttle linkage or solenoid plunger for binding. If linkage is OK, replace solenoid.
- SOLENOID RETRACTS → Connect solenoid wire. Open throttle slightly. Disconnect 3-wire connector at fast idle relay on dash panel in engine compartment.
  - SOLENOID RETRACTS → Connect 12-volt test light to ground and probe dk. green wire in single connector at fast idle relay.
    - TEST LIGHT OFF → Disconnect coolant switch connector and touch pink/blk wire terminal.
      - LIGHT ON → Connect jumper between pink/blk and dk. green wire in coolant switch connector.
        - FAST IDLE SOLENOID RETRACTS → Replace coolant switch.
        - FAST IDLE SOLENOID DOES NOT RETRACT → Repair open in dk. green wire from coolant switch to fast idle relay.
      - LIGHT OFF → Repair open in pink/blk wire from coolant switch to splice in harness.
    - TEST LIGHT ON → Check relay ground. If ok, replace relay.
  - SOLENOID DOES NOT RETRACT → Locate and repair shorted pink/blk to dk. grn. wire or terminals in connector.

ENGINE RUNS ROUGH ON COLD START (GLOW PLUGS NOT ON AFTER ENGINE STARTS - 5 AMP FUSE OK)

With cold engine and ignition on, connect a 12 volt test light to ground. Then touch each glow plug terminal. Test light should pulse on and off at each terminal.

- TEST LIGHT ON ALL TERMINALS → Turn ignition off and disconnect glow plug harness from all glow plugs. Connect 12 volt test light to a 12 volt source and touch each glow plug terminal. Replace any glow plugs that do not light test light.
- TEST LIGHT OFF ONE OR MORE TERMINALS → Repair open circuit in glow plug harness. If open is due to burnt wire, replace that glow plug. (Plug shorted.)

Fig. 2 Diesel engine electrical diagnosis (Part 3 of 4). 1982–83 Full Size Models Type 2

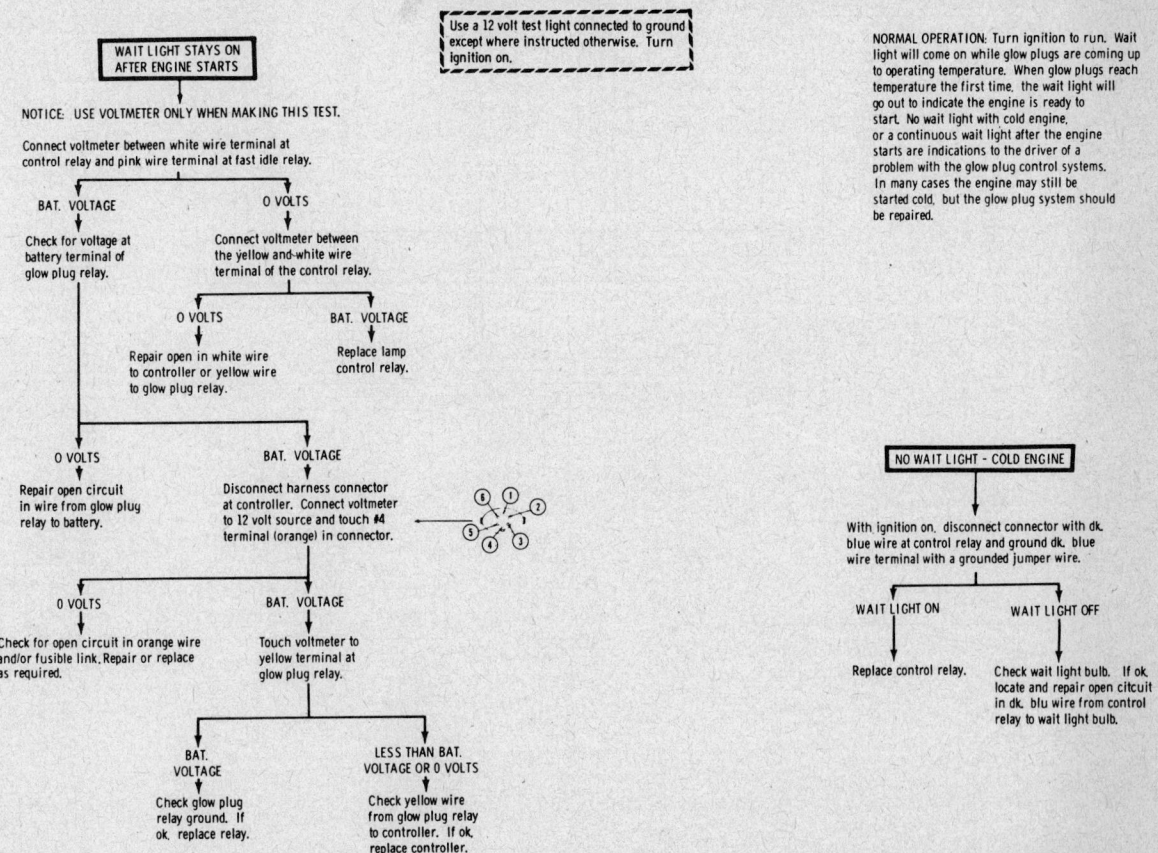

Use a 12 volt test light connected to ground except where instructed otherwise. Turn ignition on.

WAIT LIGHT STAYS ON AFTER ENGINE STARTS

NOTICE: USE VOLTMETER ONLY WHEN MAKING THIS TEST.

Connect voltmeter between white wire terminal at control relay and pink wire terminal at fast idle relay.

- BAT. VOLTAGE → Check for voltage at battery terminal of glow plug relay.
  - 0 VOLTS → Repair open circuit in wire from glow plug relay to battery.
  - BAT. VOLTAGE → Disconnect harness connector at controller. Connect voltmeter to 12 volt source and touch #4 terminal (orange) in connector.

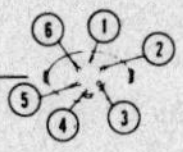

  - 0 VOLTS → Check for open circuit in orange wire and/or fusible link. Repair or replace as required.
  - BAT. VOLTAGE → Touch voltmeter to yellow terminal at glow plug relay.
    - BAT. VOLTAGE → Check glow plug relay ground. If ok, replace relay.
    - LESS THAN BAT. VOLTAGE OR 0 VOLTS → Check yellow wire from glow plug relay to controller. If ok, replace controller.
- 0 VOLTS → Connect voltmeter between the yellow and-white wire terminal of the control relay.
  - 0 VOLTS → Repair open in white wire to controller or yellow wire to glow plug relay.
  - BAT. VOLTAGE → Replace lamp control relay.

NORMAL OPERATION: Turn ignition to run. Wait light will come on while glow plugs are coming up to operating temperature. When glow plugs reach temperature the first time, the wait light will go out to indicate the engine is ready to start. No wait light with cold engine, or a continuous wait light after the engine starts are indications to the driver of a problem with the glow plug control systems. In many cases the engine may still be started cold, but the glow plug system should be repaired.

NO WAIT LIGHT - COLD ENGINE

With ignition on, disconnect connector with dk. blue wire at control relay and ground dk. blue wire terminal with a grounded jumper wire.

- WAIT LIGHT ON → Replace control relay.
- WAIT LIGHT OFF → Check wait light bulb. If ok, locate and repair open citcuit in dk. blu wire from control relay to wait light bulb.

Fig. 2 Diesel engine electrical diagnosis (Part 4 of 4). 1982–83 Full Size Models Type 2

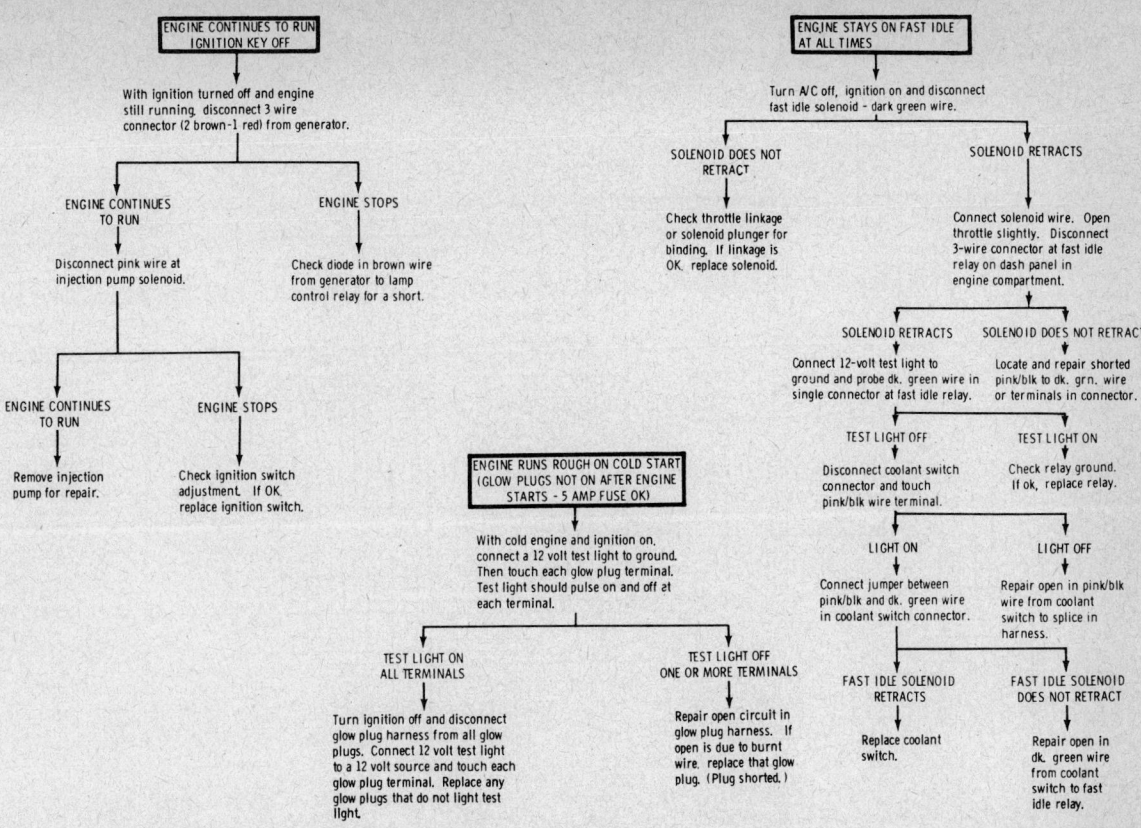

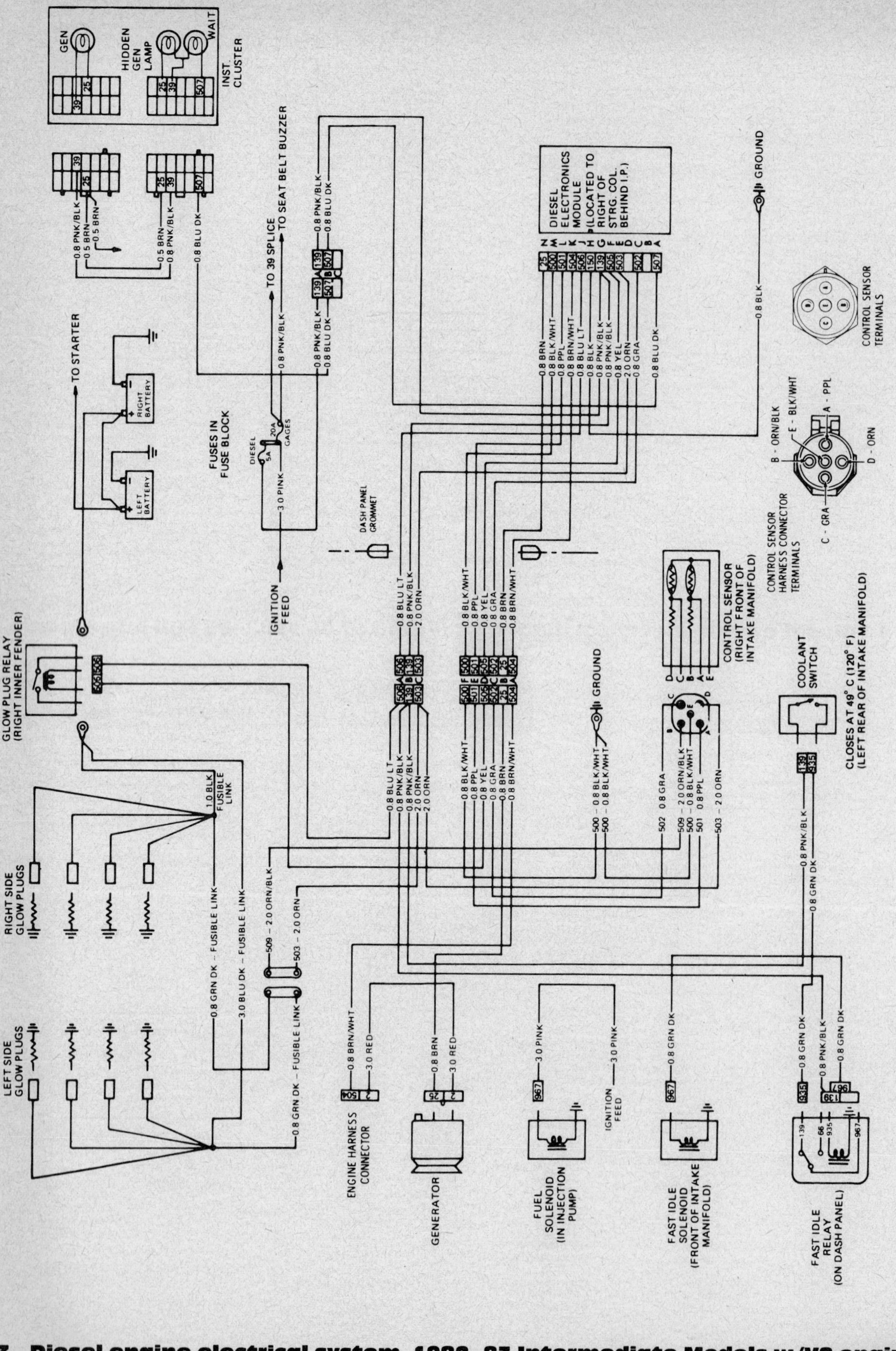

Fig. 3 Diesel engine electrical system. 1982–83 Intermediate Models w/V8 engine

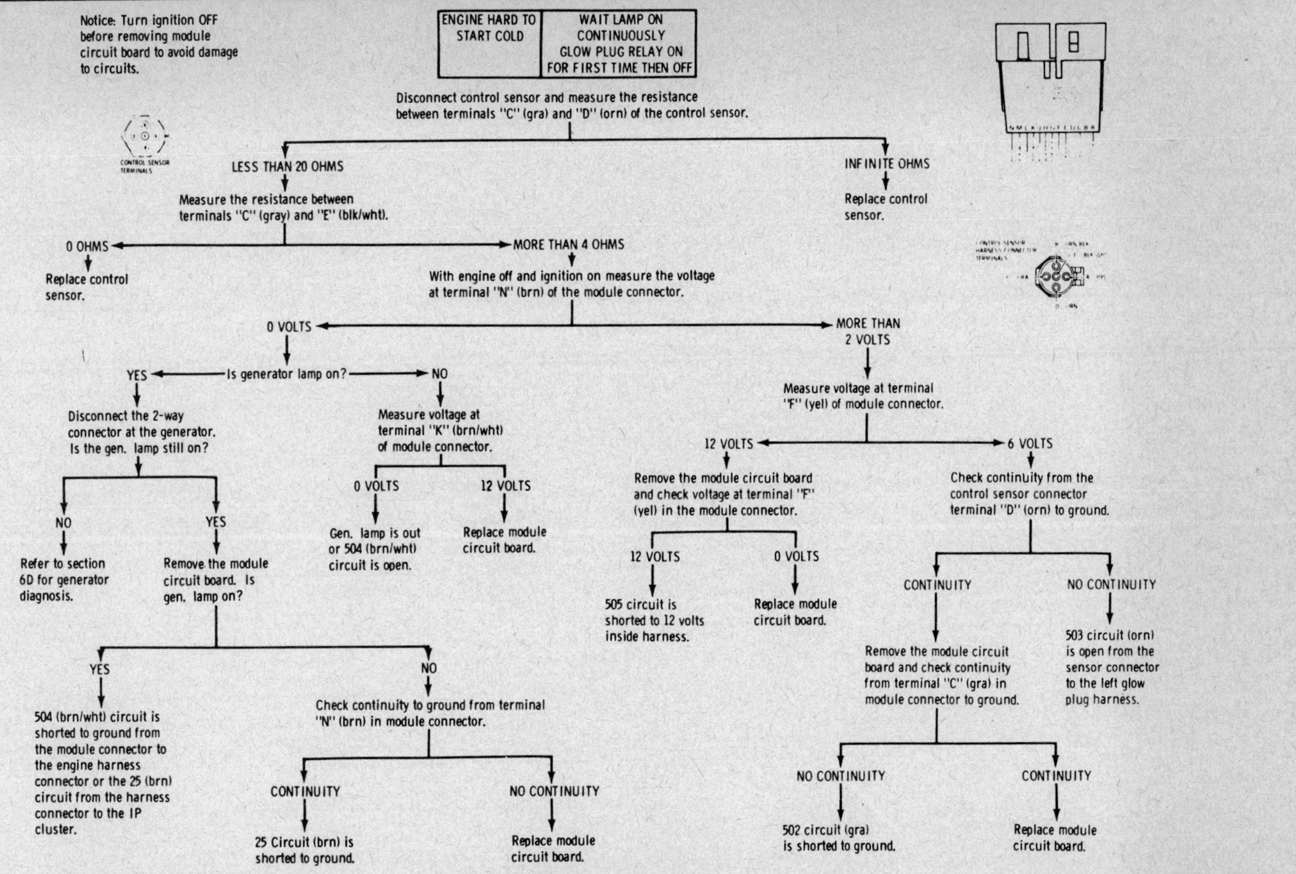

Fig. 4 Diesel engine electrical diagnosis (Part 1 of 10). 1982–83 Intermediate Models w/V8 engine

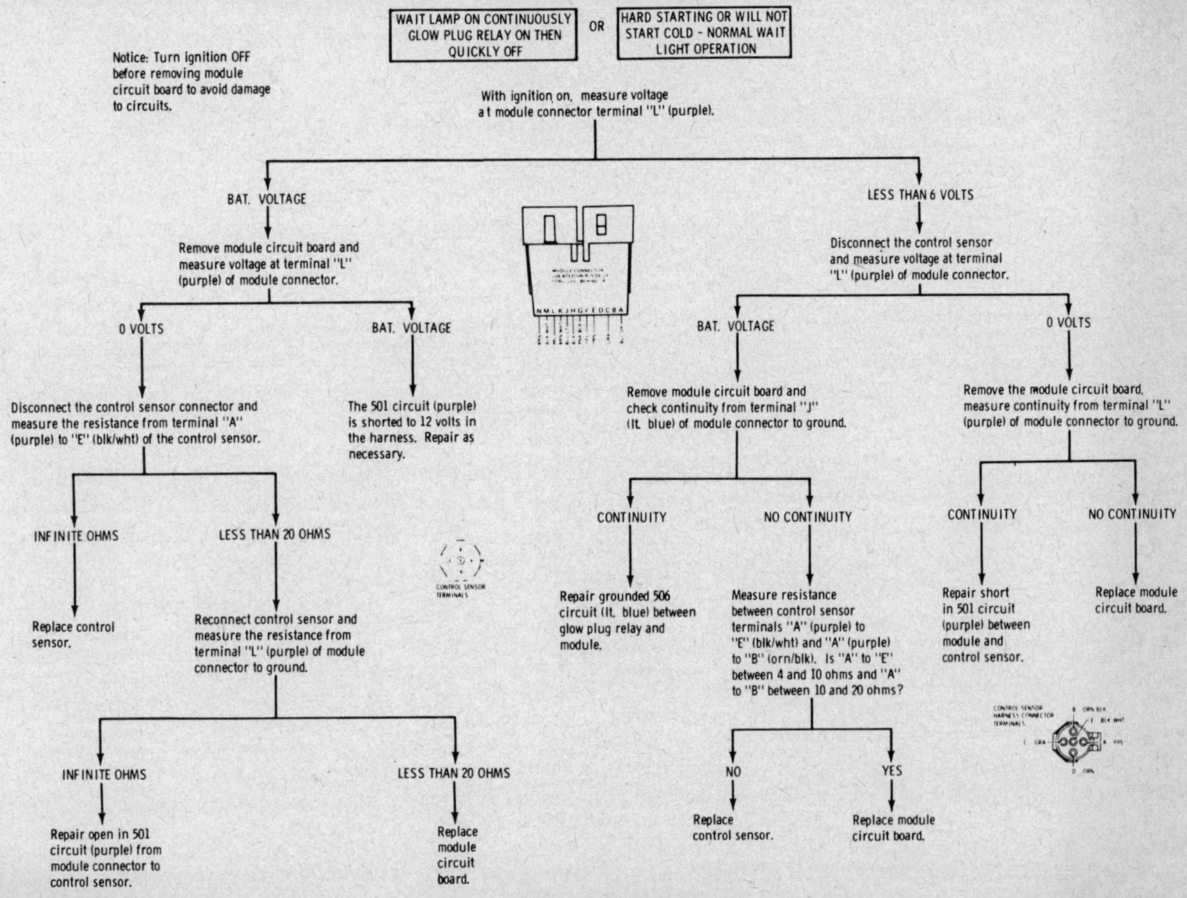

Fig. 4 Diesel engine electrical diagnosis (Part 2 of 10). 1982–83 Intermediate Models w/V8 engine

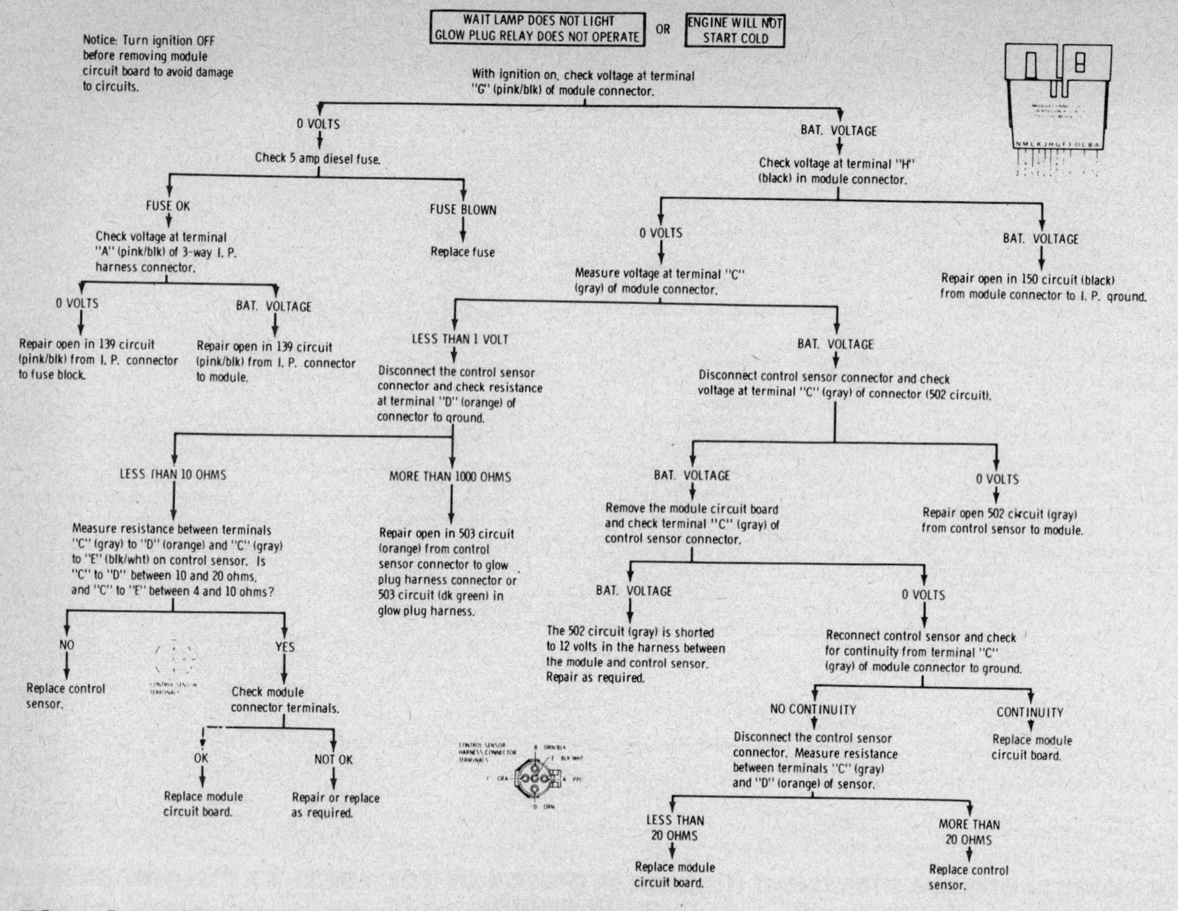

Fig. 4 Diesel engine electrical diagnosis (Part 3 of 10). 1982–83 Intermediate Models w/V8 engine

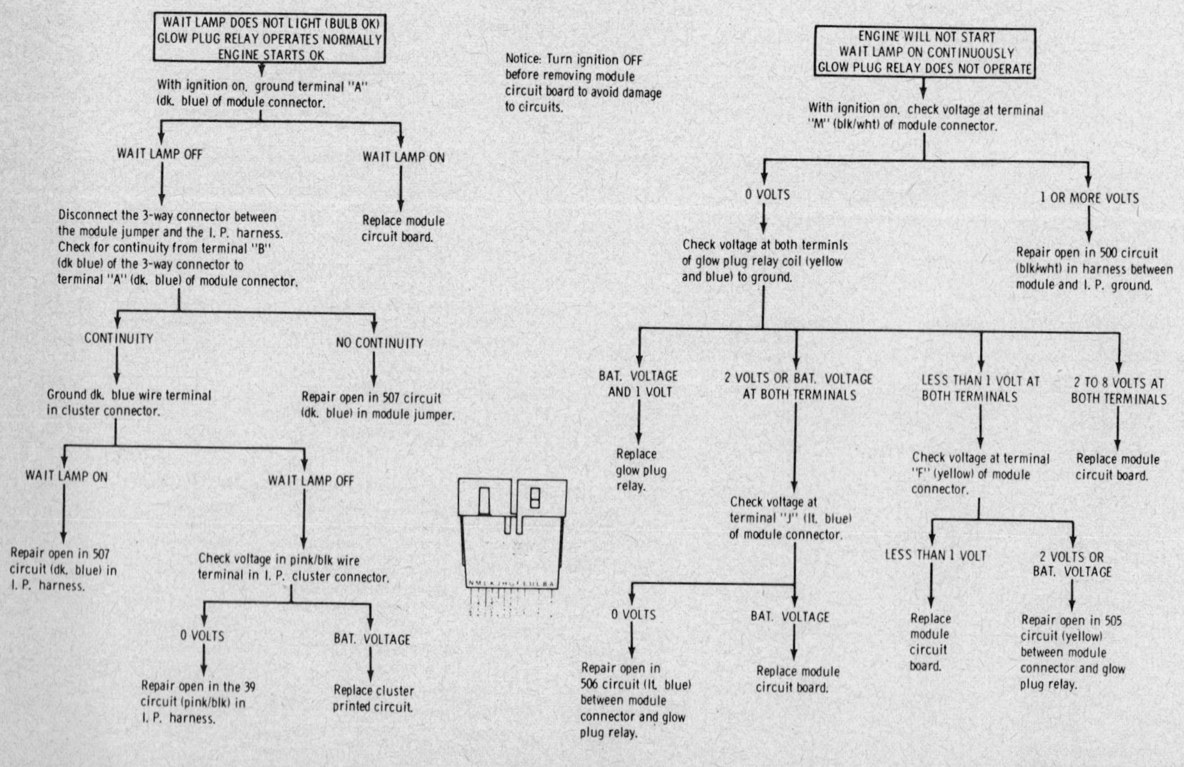

Fig. 4 Diesel engine electrical diagnosis (Part 4 of 10). 1982–83 Intermediate Models w/V8 engine

GENERATOR LAMP DOES NOT OPERATE WAIT LAMP AND GLOW PLUG RELAY OPERATE NORMAL (BULB OK)

Check connections to generator to see if they are properly connected.

- CONNECTED
  - With ignition on and engine off, ground terminal "K" (brn/wht) of module connector.
    - GENERATOR LAMP OFF
      - Repair open in 504 circuit (brn/wht) from module connector to engine harness and/or 25 circuit (brown) to cluster connector.
    - GENERATOR LAMP ON
      - Ground terminal "N" (brown) of module connector.
        - GENERATOR LAMP ON
          - Ground the 25 circuit (brown) at the generator connector.
            - GENERATOR LAMP ON
              - Repair generator.
            - GENERATOR LAMP OFF
              - Repair open in 25 circuit (brown) from module connector to generator connector.
        - GENERATOR LAMP OFF
          - Replace module circuit board.
- NOT CONNECTED
  - Repair connector.

Notice: Turn ignition OFF before removing module circuit board to avoid damage to circuits.

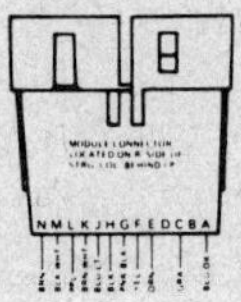

WAIT LAMP ON CONTINUOUSLY GLOW PLUG RELAY OPERATES NORMAL ENGINE STARTS AFTER NORMAL WAIT PERIOD

With ignition on, disconnect the 3-way connector between the module jumper and the I. P. harness.

- WAIT LAMP OFF
  - Reconnect 3-way connector and remove module circuit board.
    - WAIT LAMP OFF
      - Replace module circuit board.
    - WAIT LAMP ON
      - Repair short in 507 circuit (dk blue) between module jumper connector and module connector.
- WAIT LAMP ON
  - Disconnect the cluster printed circuit connector.
    - WAIT LAMP OFF
      - Repair short in 507 circuit (dk blue) from 3-way connector to cluster connector.
    - WAIT LAMP ON
      - Locate and repair short in cluster printed circuit or connector.

Fig. 4 Diesel engine electrical diagnosis (Part 5 of 10). 1982–83 Intermediate Models w/V8 engine

ENGINE STAYS ON FAST IDLE - ENGINE WARM

Turn ignition on and disconnect fast idle solenoid - dark green wire.

- SOLENOID DOES NOT RETRACT
  - Check throttle linkage or solenoid plunger for binding. If linkage is OK, replace solenoid.
- SOLENOID RETRACTS
  - Connect solenoid wire. Open throttle slightly. Disconnect 2-wire connector at fast idle relay on dash panel in engine compartment.
    - SOLENOID RETRACTS
      - Connect 12-volt test light to ground and probe dk. grn wire in single connector at fast idle relay.
        - TEST LIGHT OFF
          - Disconnect coolant switch connector and touch pink/blk wire terminal.
            - LIGHT ON
              - Connect jumper between pink/blk and dk. green wire in coolant switch connector.
                - FAST IDLE SOLENOID RETRACTS
                  - Replace coolant switch.
                - FAST IDLE SOLENOID DOES NOT RETRACT
                  - Repair open in dk. green wire from coolant switch to fast idle relay.
            - LIGHT OFF
              - Repair open in 139 circuit (pink/blk) from coolant switch to module.
        - TEST LIGHT ON
          - Check relay ground. If ok, replace relay.
    - SOLENOID DOES NOT RETRACT
      - Locate and repair shorted pink/blk to dk. grn wire or terminals in connector.

NO FAST IDLE WITH COLD ENGINE 5 AMP DIESEL FUSE OK

Turn ignition switch to run position and disconnect and connect fast idle solenoid. Check for solenoid operation.

- SOLENOID OPERATES
  - Re-adjust for correct fast idle 750 rpm in drive range.
- SOLENOID DOES NOT OPERATE
  - Use a 12-volt test light connected to ground and touch the disconnected dark green wire at the solenoid connector.
    - TEST LIGHT OFF
      - Touch test light to pink/blk wire in 2 wire connector on fast idle relay (on dash panel).
        - TEST LIGHT ON
          - Touch dark green wire in 2-wire connector at fast idle relay.
            - TEST LIGHT ON
              - Repair open in 967 circuit (dk. grn) from relay to fast idle solenoid.
            - TEST LIGHT OFF
              - Check relay ground. If ok, replace relay.
        - TEST LIGHT OFF
          - Locate and repair open in 139 circuit (pink/blk) from fast idle relay to module.
    - TEST LIGHT ON
      - Check solenoid ground. If OK, replace solenoid.

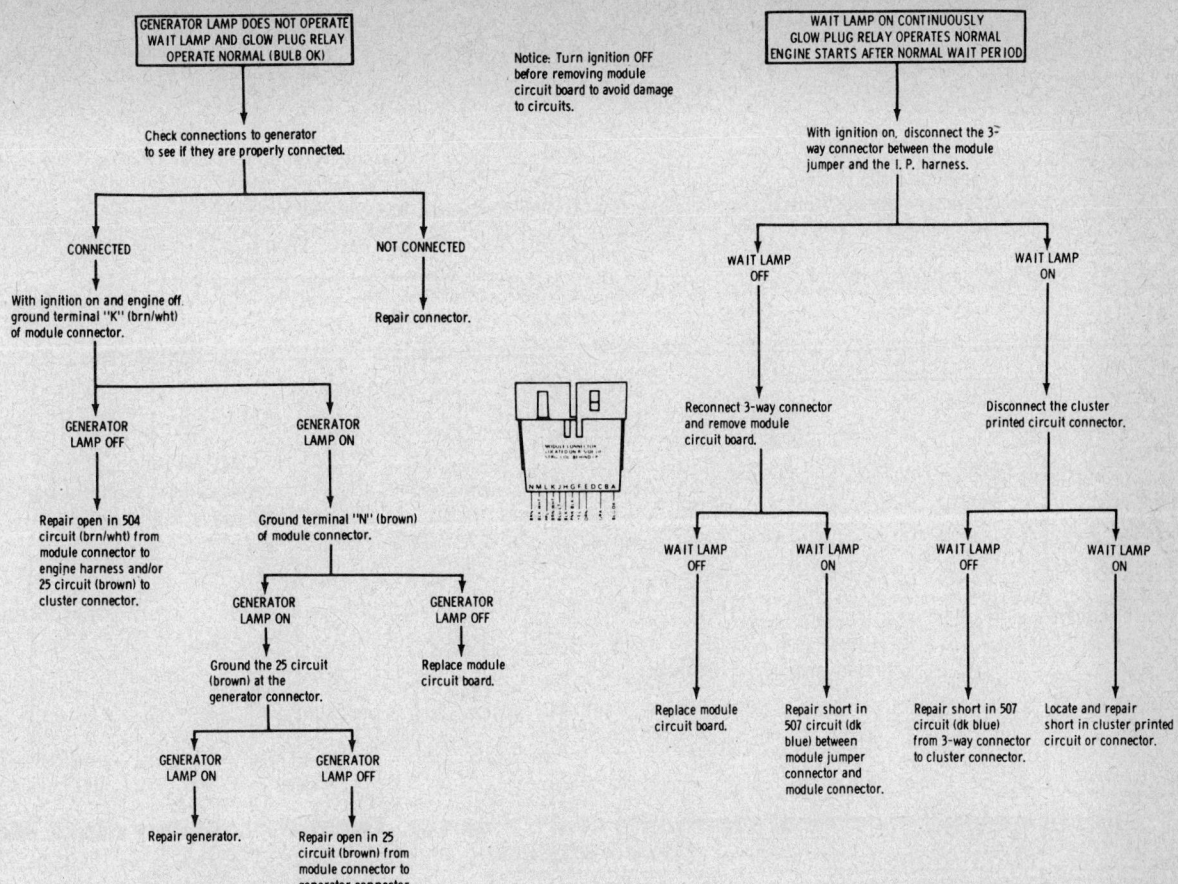

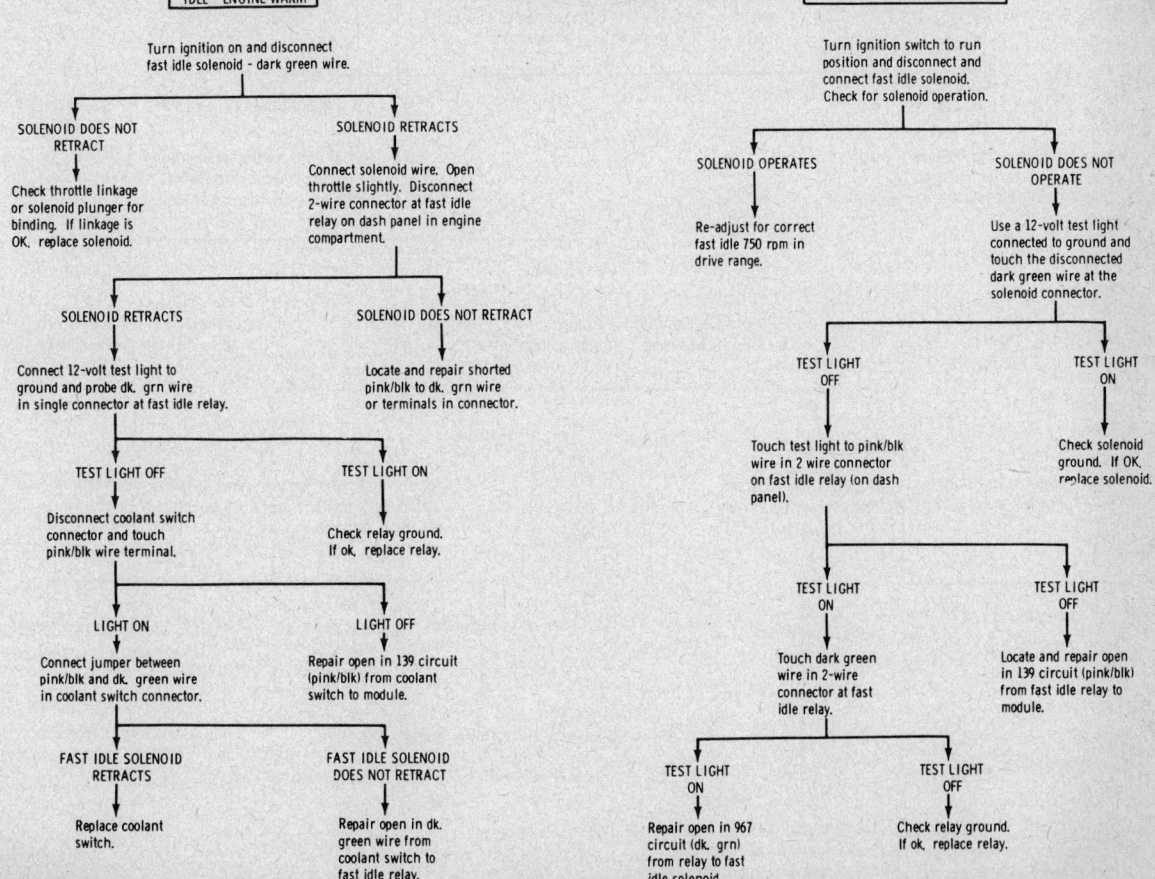

Fig. 4 Diesel engine electrical diagnosis (Part 6 of 10). 1982–83 Intermediate Models w/V8 engine

GLOW PLUG RELAY BUZZING

Disconnect the 3-way connector between control sensor harness and module jumper harness. Check for continuity between terminal "E" (orange) of module connector and terminal "C" (orange) of jumper connector.

- CONTINUITY → Replace module circuit board.
- NO CONTINUITY → Repair open in 503 circuit (orange) between module connector and jumper connector.

Notice: Turn ignition OFF before removing module circuit board to avoid damage to circuits.

WAIT LAMP AND GLOW PLUG RELAY NORMAL. CAR WON'T START

Disconnect connector from each glow plug and check continuity to ground from glow plug terminal.

- NO CONTINUITY → Replace bad glow plugs.
- CONTINUITY → Measure continuity from glow plug relay output to each glow plug connector.
  - CONTINUITY → Check fuel system.
  - NO CONTINUITY → Repair or replace glow plug harness.

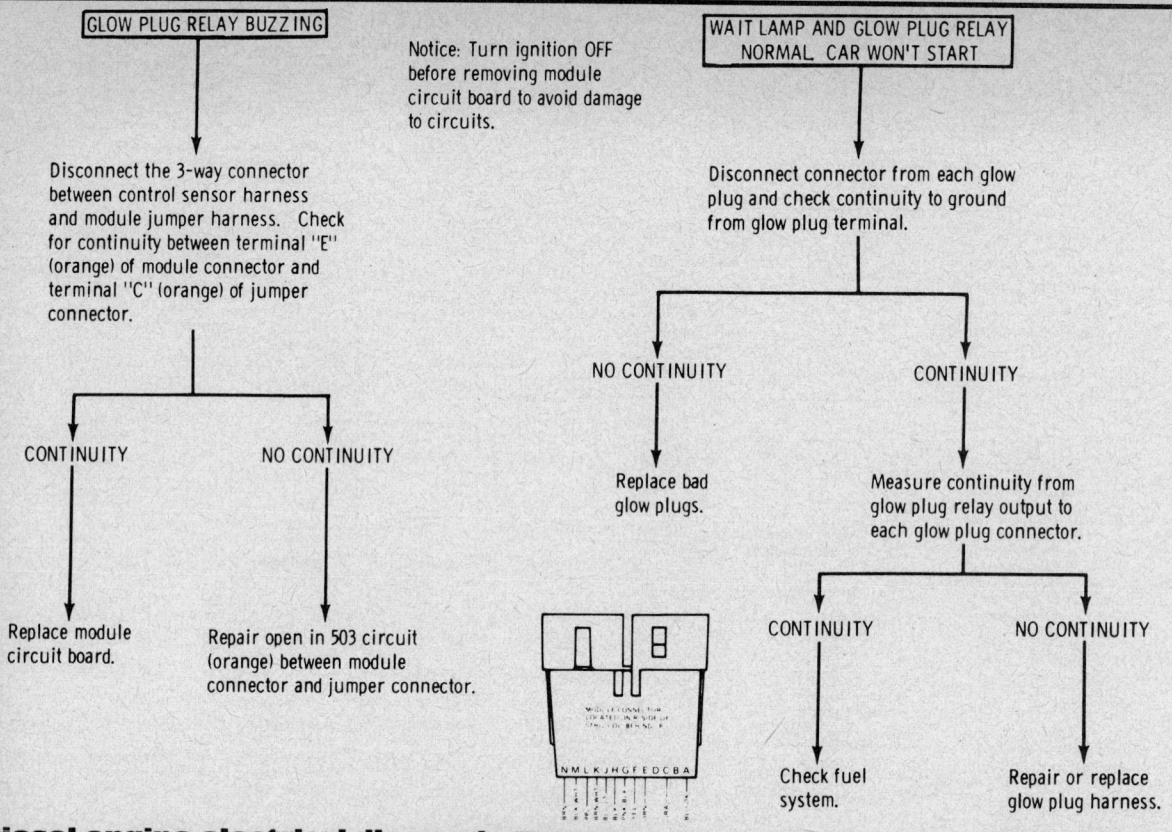

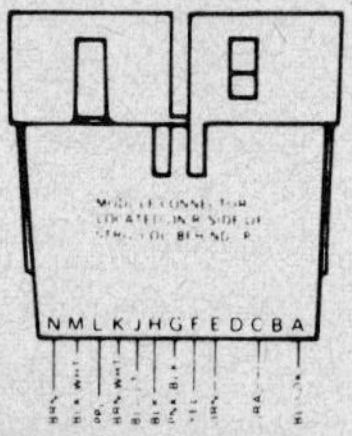

Fig. 4 Diesel engine electrical diagnosis (Part 7 of 10). 1982–83 Intermediate Models w/V8 engine

ENGINE STAYS ON FAST IDLE ENGINE WARM - A/C OFF

MAKE ALL CHECKS WITH AIR CONDITIONING OFF

With engine warm, turn ignition switch to run position. With 12V test light connected to ground, probe fast idle solenoid wire at solenoid.

- TEST LIGHT OFF → Check and make idle and fast idle adjustments as necessary. (Refer to emission label.) If fast idle solenoid will not adjust properly, replace solenoid.
- TEST LIGHT ON → Use a 12V test light connected to ground and probe the dark green wire (967) at the fast idle relay. Ignition switch in run.
  - TEST LIGHT ON → With one test light lead grounded, probe lt. grn/blk (936) wire at fast idle relay. Ignition switch in run.
    - TEST LIGHT OFF → With one test light lead grounded, probe lt. green wire (66) at fast idle relay. Ignition switch in run.
      - TEST LIGHT OFF → Replace fast idle relay.
      - TEST LIGHT ON → Check to make sure air conditioning is in off. If off, refer to air conditioning electrical schematics. Lt. green wire (66) has voltage applied only with A/C on.
    - TEST LIGHT ON → With one test light lead grounded, probe lt. green/blk wire (139) at engine temperature switch (left rear head bolt). Ignition in run.
      - TEST LIGHT OFF → Check for short in lt. green/blk wire (936) between engine temperature switch and fast idle relay.
      - TEST LIGHT ON → Check terminals of engine temperature switch for shorted connection. If OK, replace engine temperature switch.
  - TEST LIGHT OFF → Check for short in dark grn. Wire (967) from fast idle solenoid to fast idle relay.

Fig. 4 Diesel engine electrical diagnosis (Part 8 of 10). 1982–83 Intermediate Models w/V6 engine

NO FAST IDLE WITH COLD ENGINE
DIESEL FUSE OK

MAKE ALL CHECKS WITH AIR CONDITIONING OFF

With engine cold, turn ignition switch to run position. With 12V test light connected to ground, probe fast idle solenoid wire at solenoid.

TEST LIGHT ON

Check and make idle and fast idle adjustments as necessary. (Refer to emission label) If fast idle solenoid is not energizing, replace solenoid.

TEST LIGHT OFF

Use a 12V test light connected to ground and probe the dark green wire (967) at the fast idle relay. Ignition switch in run.

TEST LIGHT OFF

With one test light lead grounded, probe lt. grn/blk (936) wire at fast idle relay. Ignition switch in run.

TEST LIGHT ON

Check for open in dark grn. wire (967) from fast idle solenoid to fast idle relay.

TEST LIGHT ON

With one test light lead grounded, probe pnk/blk wire (139) at fast idle relay. Ignition switch in run.

TEST LIGHT OFF

With one test light lead grounded, probe pnk/blk wire (139) at engine temperature switch (left rear head bolt). Ignition in run.

TEST LIGHT OFF

Check for open in pnk/blk wire (139) between diesel fuse and engine temperature switch.

TEST LIGHT ON

Check terminals of engine temperature switch for good connection. If OK, replace engine temperature switch.

TEST LIGHT OFF

Check for open in pnk/blk wire (139) from diesel fuse to fast idle relay.

TEST LIGHT ON

With 12V test light connected to 12 volts, probe blk wire (150) at fast idle relay.

TEST LIGHT ON

Replace fast idle relay.

TEST LIGHT OFF

Repair open in blk wire (150) or clean and repair ground as necessary.

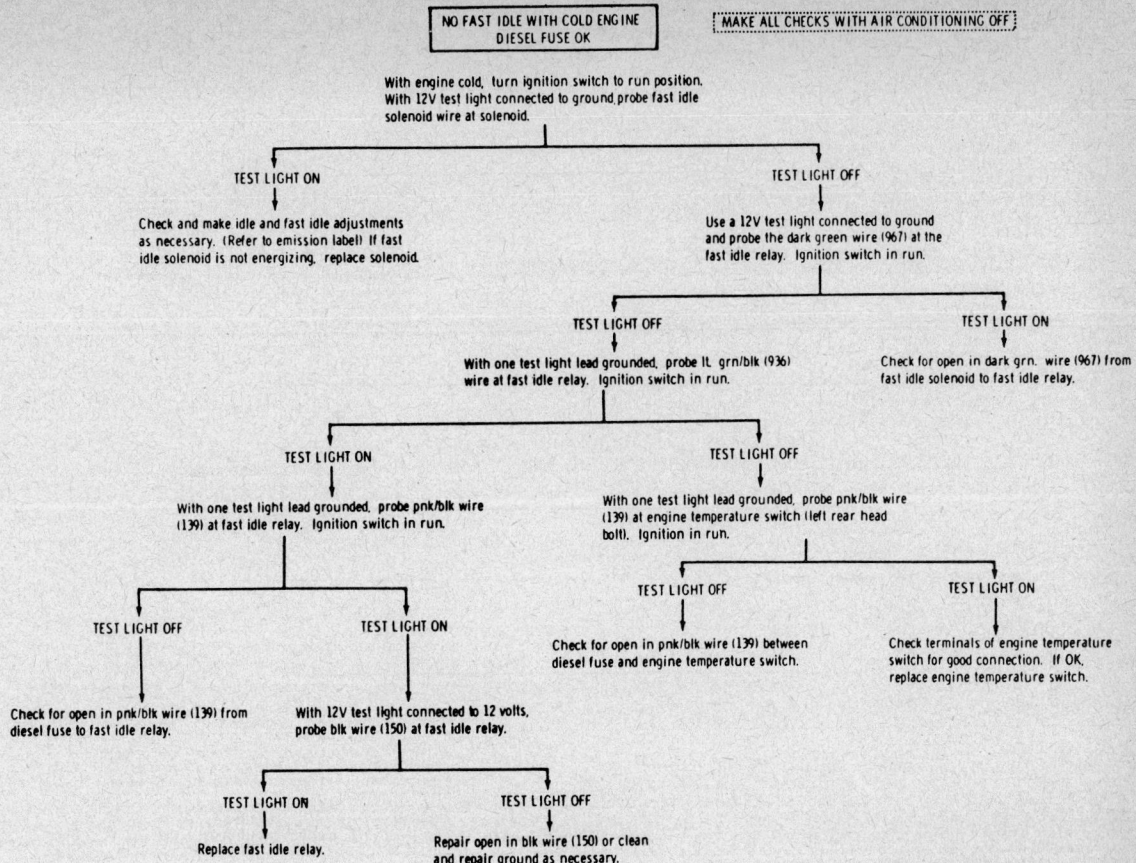

Fig. 4 Diesel engine electrical diagnosis (Part 9 of 10). 1982–83 Intermediate Models w/V6 engine

ENGINE WILL NOT START
GLOW PLUG RELAY BUZZING

Disconnect the 2 wire connector (orange/blk-orange wires) near the glow plug relay. Disconnect control sensor connector. Check for continuity between terminal "D" (orange wire) of sensor connector and terminal "E" (orange wire) of module connector.

CONTINUITY

Replace module circuit board.

NO CONTINUITY

Repair open in 503 circuit (orange) between module connector and control sensor connector.

Notice: Turn ignition OFF before removing module circuit board to avoid damage to circuits.

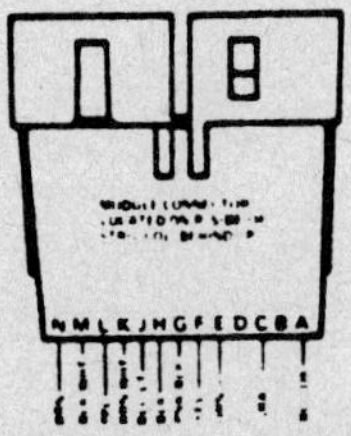

WAIT LAMP AND GLOW PLUG RELAY
NORMAL CAR WON'T START

Disconnect connector from each glow plug and check continuity to ground from each glow plug terminal.

NO CONTINUITY

Replace bad glow plugs.

CONTINUITY

Measure continuity from glow plug relay output to each glow plug connector.

CONTINUITY

Check fuel system.

NO CONTINUITY

Repair or replace glow plug harness.

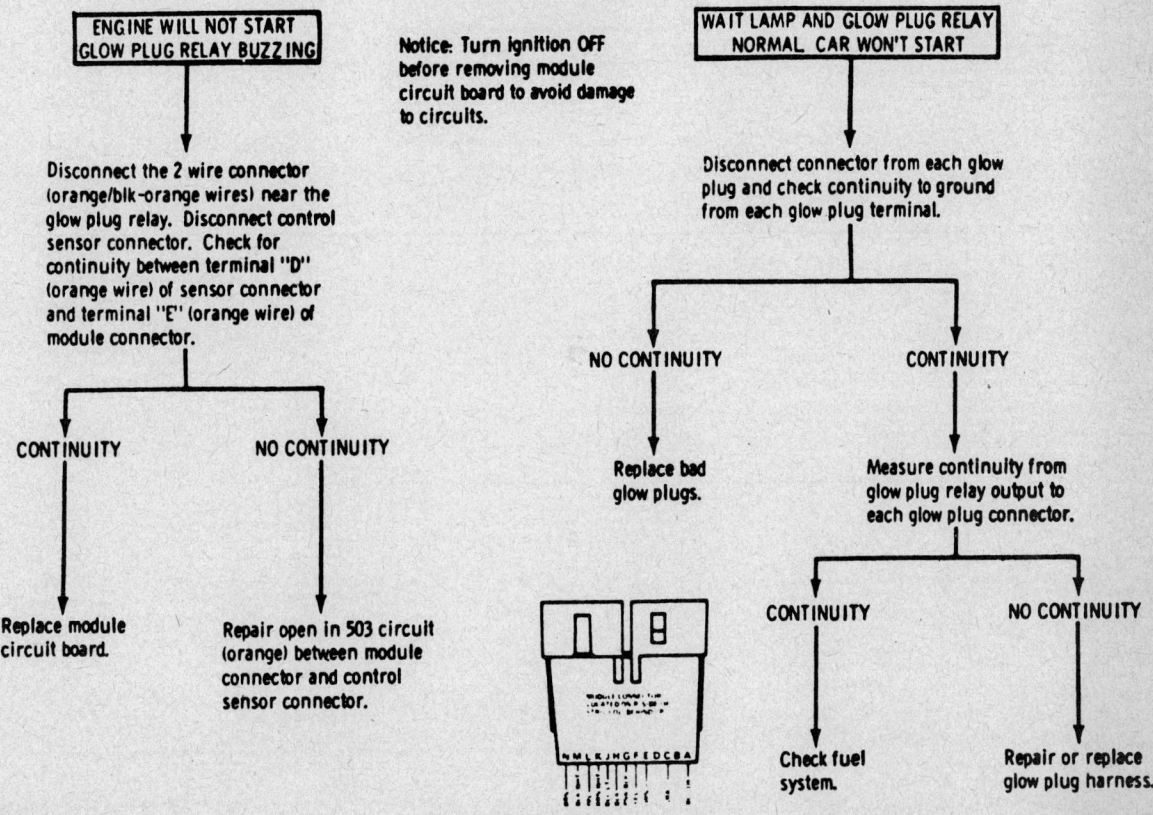

Fig. 4 Diesel engine electrical diagnosis (Part 10 of 10). 1982–83 Intermediate Models w/V6 engine

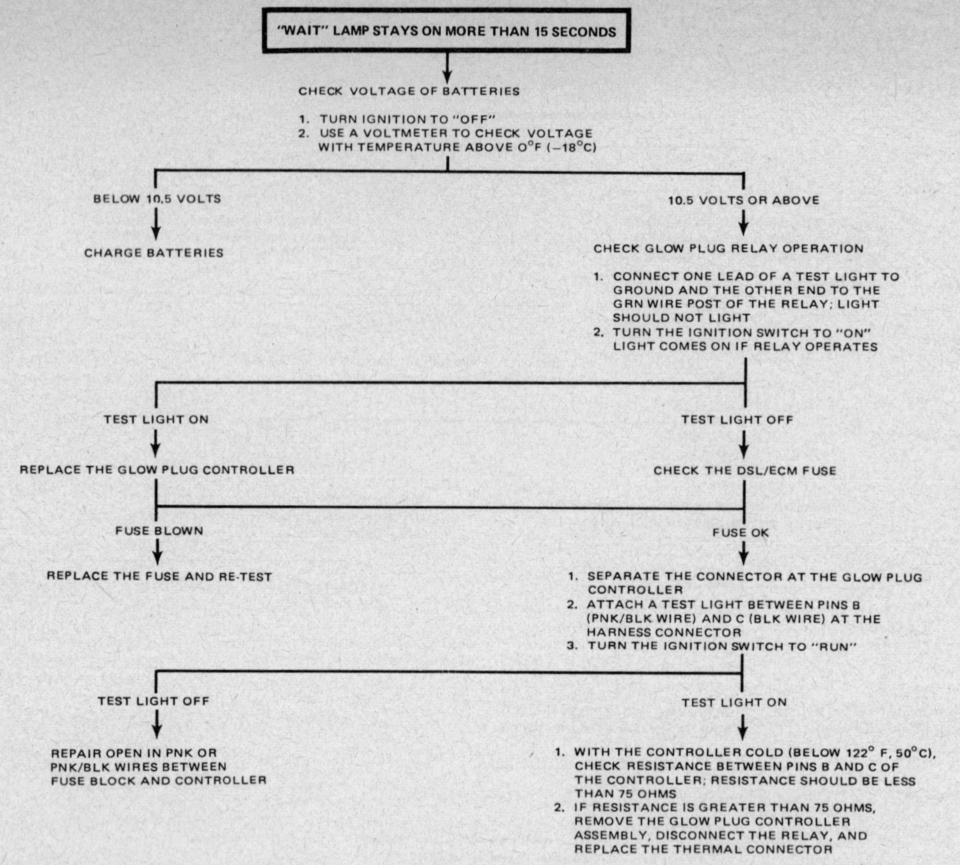

Fig. 5 Diesel engine electrical diagnosis (Part 1 of 3). 1984

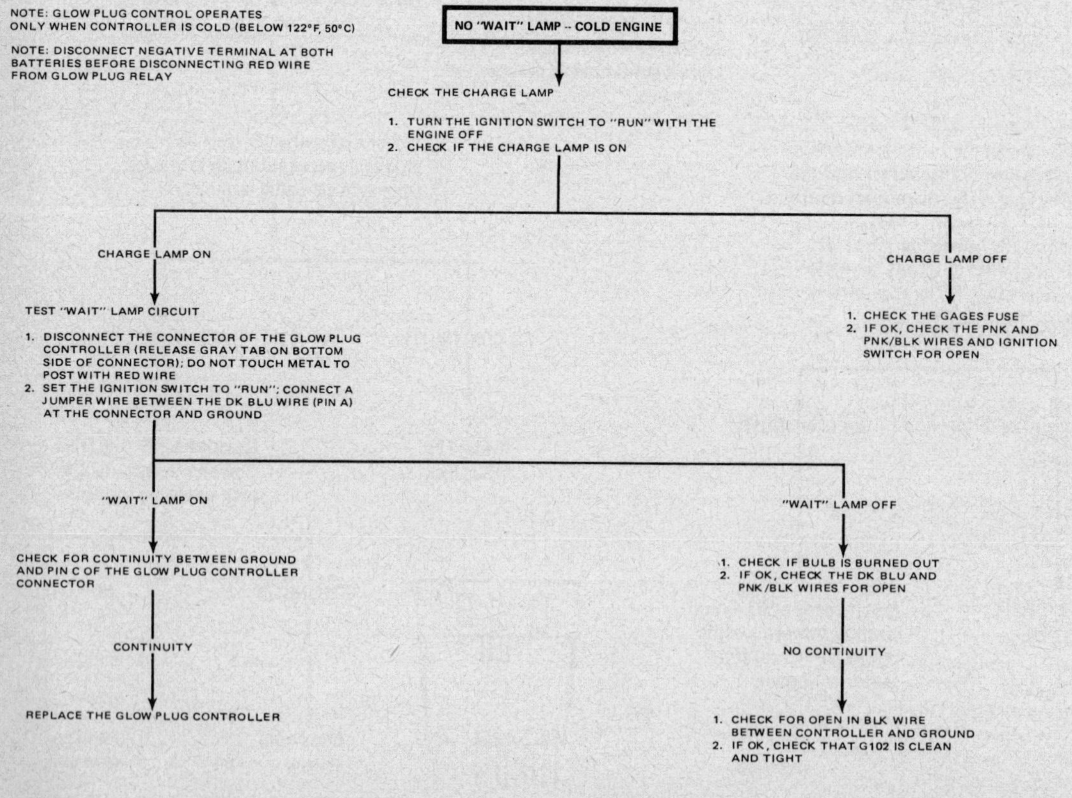

Fig. 5 Diesel engine electrical diagnosis (Part 2 of 3). 1984

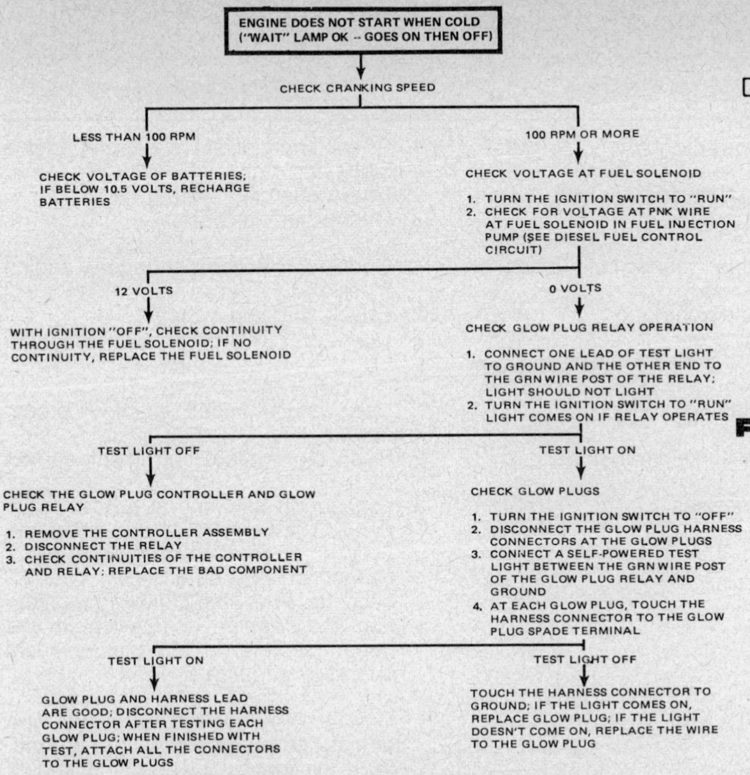

Fig. 5 Diesel engine electrical diagnosis (Part 3 of 3). 1984

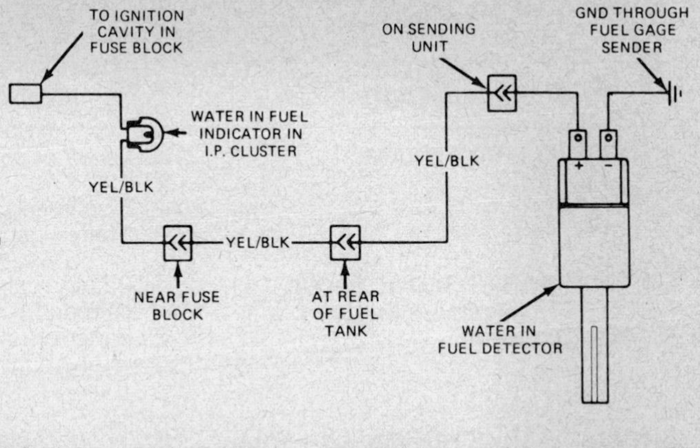

Fig. 6 Water in fuel system wiring circuit

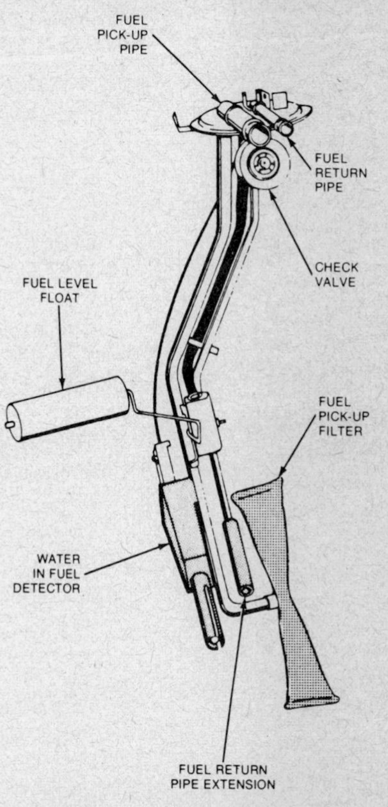

Fig. 7 Water in fuel system fuel level sender & water detector

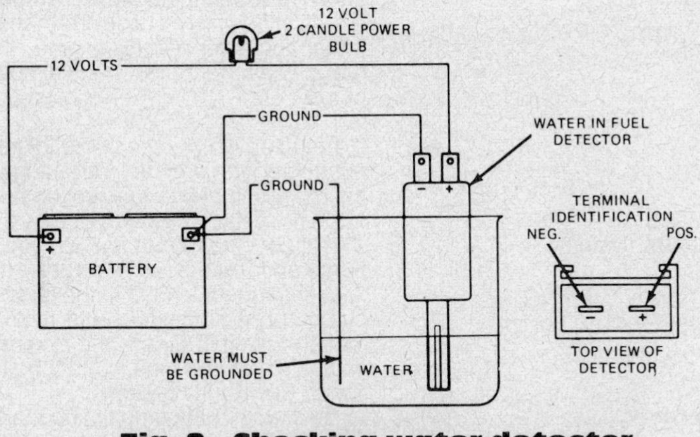

Fig. 8 Checking water detector operation

WATER IN FUEL SYSTEM DIAGNOSIS

WATER IN FUEL LAMP DOES NOT GO ON

If the likelihood of water in the fuel tank exists and the Water In Fuel lamp is off, siphon the fuel tank to check for water by connecting a pump to the fuel return line. If at least 3 gallons of water are siphoned from the tank, proceed as follows:

1. Disconnect Water In Fuel electrical lead at fuel tank and ground the lead. If lamp does not go on, proceed to step 4. If it does, check for at least 8 volts at the electrical lead. If no voltage is present, replace the Water In Tank light bulb.
2. Ground the Water In Tank electrical lead. If lamp does not go on, check for open circuit in wiring, **Fig. 6.**
3. Remove fuel level sender and Water in Fuel detector unit from fuel tank.
4. Check connections to "Water In Fuel." If satisfactory, check detector unit as follows:
   a. Remove detector from fuel sender unit, **Fig. 7.**
   b. Connect the detector to a bulb and power source as shown in **Fig. 8.** The lamp should go on when the detector probe is lowered into the container of water 3/8 inch or less. Make sure water is grounded to negative side of battery.

WATER IN FUEL LAMP STAYS ON

Under this condition, siphon the tank to check for water by connecting a pump to the fuel return line. If no water is present, proceed as follows:

1. Disconnect the Water In Fuel electrical lead near the fuel tank. If lamp does not go off, proceed to step 2. If lamp goes off, remove fuel level sender and check detector as described previously under "Water In Fuel Lamp Does Not Go On."
2. Check for short circuit in wire between the "Water In Fuel" connection at the fuel tank and the dash indicator lamp, **Fig. 6.**

DIESEL ENGINE DIAGNOSIS

Condition	Possible Cause	Correction
ENGINE WILL NOT CRANK	1. Loose or corroded battery cables	1. Check connections at battery, engine block and starter solenoid.
	2. Discharged batteries	2. Check charging system.
	3. Starter Inoperative	3. Check starting system.
ENGINE CRANKS SLOWLY—WILL NOT START (Minimum Engine Crank Speed—100 RPM)	1. Battery cable connections loose or corroded	1. Check connections at battery, engine block and starter.
	2. Batteries undercharged	2. Check charging system.
	3. Wrong engine oil	3. Drain and refill with recommended oil.
ENGINE CRANKS NORMALLY—WILL NOT START	1. Incorrect starting procedure	1. Use recommended starting procedure.
	2. Incorrect or contaminated fuel	2. Flush fuel system and install correct fuel.
	3. No fuel to nozzles	3. Loosen injection line at a nozzle. Do not disconnect. Use care to direct fuel away from sources of ignition. Wipe connection to be sure it is dry. Crank 5 seconds. Fuel should flow from injection line. Tighten connection. If fuel does not flow, check fuel solenoid operation as follows: Connect a 12 volt test lamp from wire at injection pump solenoid to ground. Turn ignition to "ON". Lamp should light. If lamp does not light, check wiring to solenoid.
	4. No fuel to injection pump	4. Remove line at inlet to injection pump fuel filter. Connect hose from line to metal container. Crank engine. If no fuel is discharged, test the fuel supply pump. If the pump is OK, check the injection pump fuel filter and replace if plugged. If filter and inlet line to injection pump are OK, replace injection pump.
	5. Plugged fuel return system	5. Disconnect fuel return line at injection pump and route hose to a metal container. Connect a hose to the injection pump connection and route it to the metal container. Crank the engine; if engine starts and runs, correct restriction in fuel return system.
	6. Pump timing incorrect	6. Make certain that pump timing mark is aligned with mark on adapter.
	7. Glow plug control system inoperative	7. Refer to Diesel Engine Electrical System Diagnosis.
	8. Glow plugs inoperative	8. Refer to Diesel Engine Electrical System Diagnosis.
	9. Internal engine problems	9. Correct as necessary.
	10. No voltage to fuel solenoid	10. Connect a 12 volt test lamp from injection pump solenoid to ground. Turn ignition to "On", lamp should light. If lamp lights, remove test lamp and connect and disconnect solenoid connector and listen for solenoid operation. If solenoid does not operate, remove injection pump for repairs. If lamp does not light, refer to Diesel Engine Electrical System Diagnosis.
	11. Restricted fuel tank filter.	11. Remove fuel tank and check filter.

Continued

DIESEL ENGINE DIAGNOSIS—Continued

Condition	Possible Cause	Correction
ENGINE STARTS BUT WILL NOT CONTINUE TO RUN AT IDLE	1. No fuel in tank	1. Install correct fuel in tank.
	2. Incorrect or contaminated fuel	2. Flush fuel system and install correct fuel.
	3. Limited fuel to injection pump	3. Test the fuel supply pump. Replace as necessary.
	4. Fuel solenoid disengaged with ignition switch in the "ON" position	4. Connect a 12 volt test lamp from wire at injection pump solenoid to ground. Turn ignition to "ON". Lamp should light. Turn ignition to "START". Lamp should light. If lamp does not light in both positions, check wiring to solenoid.
	5. Restricted fuel return system	5. Disconnect fuel return line at injection pump and route hose to a metal container. Connect a hose to injection pump connection and route to metal container. Crank engine; if engine starts and runs, correct restriction in fuel return system.
	6. Fast idle solenoid inoperative	6. With engine cold, start car; solenoid should move to support injection pump lever in "fast idle position" for about 5 seconds. If solenoid does not move, refer to Electrical System Diagnosis.
	7. Low idle incorrectly adjusted	7. Adjust idle screw to specification.
	8. Pump timing incorrect	8. Make certain that timing mark, on injection pump, is aligned with mark on adapter.
	9. Glow plug control system malfunction	9. Refer to Diesel Engine Electrical System Diagnosis.
	10. Injection pump malfunction	10. Install replacement pump.
	11. Internal engine problems	11. Correct as necessary.
ENGINE STARTS, IDLES ROUGH, WITHOUT ABNORMAL NOISE OR SMOKE	1. Low idle incorrectly adjusted	1. Adjust idle screw to specification.
	2. Injection line leaks	2. Wipe off injection lines and connections. Run engine and check for leaks. Correct leaks.
	3. Restricted fuel return system	3. Disconnect fuel return line at injection pump and route hose to a metal container. Connect a hose to the injection pump connection and route it to the metal container. Crank the engine; if engine starts and runs, correct restriction in fuel return system.
	4. Incorrect or contaminated fuel	4. Flush fuel system and install correct fuel.
	5. Nozzle(s) inoperative	5. With engine running, loosen injection line fitting at each nozzle in turn. Use care to direct fuel away from sources of ignition. Each nozzle should contribute to rough running. If nozzle is found that does not change idle quality, it should be replaced.
	6. Internal fuel leak at nozzle(s)	6. Disconnect fuel return system from nozzles on one bank at a time. With the engine running, observe the normal fuel seepage at the nozzles. Replace any nozzle with excessive fuel leakage.
	7. Fuel supply pump malfunctions	7. Test the fuel supply pump. Replace if necessary.
	8. Uneven fuel distribution to cylinders	8. Install new or reconditioned nozzles, one at a time, until condition is corrected as indicated by normal idle.

Continued

DIESEL ENGINE DIAGNOSIS—Continued

Condition	Possible Cause	Correction
ENGINE STARTS AND IDLES ROUGH WITH EXCESSIVE NOISE AND/OR SMOKE	1. Injection pump timing incorrect	1. Be sure timing mark on injection pump is aligned with mark on adapter.
	2. Nozzle(s) inoperative	2. With engine running, crack injection line at each nozzle, one at a time. Use care to direct fuel away from sources of ignition. Each nozzle should contribute to rough running. If a nozzle is found that does not affect idle quality or changes noise and/or smoke, it should be replaced.
	3. High pressure lines incorrectly installed	3. Check routing of each line. Correct as required.
ENGINE COLD, STARTS AND IDLES ROUGH WITH EXCESSIVE NOISE AND/OR SMOKE, BUT CLEARS UP AFTER WARM-UP	1. Incorrect starting procedure	1. Advise operator on correct procedure. (See owners manual.)
	2. Injection pump timing incorrect	2. Check timing with J-33075 timing meter and reset if needed.
	3. Insufficient engine break-in time	3. Break in engine 2000 miles or more.
	4. Air in system	4. Install a section of clear plastic tubing on the fuel return fitting from the engine. Evidence of bubbles in fuel when cranking or running indicates the presence of an air leak in the suction fuel line.
	5. Inoperative glow plug	5. Replace faulty glow plug.
	6. Nozzle(s) malfunction	6. Remove and clean or replace.
	7. Housing pressure cold advance inoperative	7. Check operation and repair.
ENGINE MISFIRES BUT IDLES CORRECTLY	1. Plugged fuel filter	1. Replace filter.
	2. Incorrect injection pump timing	2. Be sure that timing mark on injection pump and adapter are aligned.
	3. Incorrect or contaminated fuel	3. Flush fuel system and install correct fuel.
ENGINE WILL NOT RETURN TO IDLE	1. External linkage misadjustment or failure	1. Reset linkage or replace as required.
	2. Internal injection pump malfunction	2. Install replacement injection pump.
FUEL LEAKS ON GROUND—NO ENGINE MALFUNCTION	1. Loose or broken fuel line or connection	1. Examine complete fuel system, including tank, supply, injection and return system. Determine source and cause of leak and repair.
	2. Internal injection pump failure	2. Install replacement injection pump.
SIGNIFICANT LOSS OF POWER	1. Incorrect or contaminated fuel	1. Flush fuel system and install correct fuel.
	2. Pinched or otherwise restricted return system	2. Examine system for restriction and correct as required.
	3. Plugged fuel tank vent	3. Remove fuel cap. If "hissing" noise is heard, vent is plugged and should be cleaned.
	4. Restricted supply	4. Examine fuel supply system to determine cause of restriction. Repair as required.
	5. Plugged fuel filter	5. Remove and replace filter.
	6. External compression leaks	6. Check for compression leaks at all nozzles and glow plugs, using "Leak-Tec" or equivalent. If leak is found, tighten nozzle clamp or glow plug. If leak persists at a nozzle, remove it and reinstall with a new carbon stop seal and compression seal.
	7. Plugged nozzle(s)	7. Remove nozzles, check for plugging and have repaired or replaced.
	8. Internal engine problem	8. Correct as necessary.

DIESEL ENGINE DIAGNOSIS—Continued

Condition	Possible Cause	Correction
NOISE—"RAP" FROM ONE OR MORE CYLINDERS	1. Air in fuel system	1. Check for leaks and correct.
	2. Air in high pressure line(s)	2. Crack line at nozzle(s) and bleed air at each cylinder determined to be causing noise. Use care to direct fuel away from sources of ignition and be sure to carefully retighten lines.
	3. Nozzle(s) sticking open or with very low blowoff pressure	3. Replace the nozzle(s) causing the problem.
	4. Internal engine problem	4. Correct as necessary.
NOISE—SIGNIFICANT OVERALL COMBUSTION NOISE INCREASE WITH EXCESSIVE BLACK SMOKE	1. Timing not set to specification	1. Align timing marks on adapter and injection pump.
	2. Internal engine problem	2. Check for presence of oil in the air crossover. If present, determine cause and correct.
	3. Injection pump housing pressure out of specifications.	3. Check housing pressure. If incorrect, replace fuel return line connector assembly.
	4. Internal injection pump problem	4. Replace pump.
NOISE—INTERNAL OR EXTERNAL	1. Fuel supply pump, alternator, water pump, valve train, vacuum pump, bearings etc.	1. Inspect and correct as necessary.
ENGINE OVERHEATS	1. Coolant system leak or oil cooler system leak	1. Check for leaks and correct as required.
	2. Belt failure	2. Replace.
	3. Thermostat malfunction, head gasket failure or internal engine problem	3. Inspect and correct as necessary.
INSTRUMENT PANEL OIL WARNING LAMP "ON" AT IDLE	1. Oil cooler or oil cooler line restricted	1. Remove restriction in cooler or cooler line.
	2. Internal engine problem	2. Correct as necessary.
ODOR OR SMOKE—EXCESSIVE AND NOT PREVIOUSLY COVERED	1. Same as Gasoline Engines	1. Correct as necessary. Refer to Trouble-Shooting Chapter.
ENGINE WILL NOT SHUT OFF WITH KEY	1. Injection pump solenoid does not drop out	1. Refer to electrical diagnosis. If problem is determined to be internal with the injection pump, replace the injection pump.
NOTE: With engine at idle, pinch the fuel return line at the injection pump to shut off engine.	2. Injection pump solenoid return spring failed	2. Replace injection pump.

Engine Service

INDEX

ENGINE MOUNTS

Refer to **Figs. 1 through 4** for engine mount installation.

ENGINE

REPLACE

EXC. FULL SIZE FRONT WHEEL DRIVE MODELS

1. Disconnect ground cable from batteries and drain cooling system.
2. Remove air cleaner.
3. Scribe hood hinge locations and remove hood.
4. Disconnect ground wires at inner fender and the engine ground strap at right cylinder head.
5. Disconnect radiator hoses, oil cooler lines, heater hoses, vacuum hoses, power steering hoses from gear, A/C compressor with brackets and hoses attached, fuel pump hose from fuel pump and the wiring.
6. Remove hairpin clip from bellcrank, on all except 6 cylinder engine.
7. Remove throttle and throttle valve cables from intake manifold brackets and position cables aside.
8. Remove upper radiator support and the radiator on all except 6 cylinder engine.
9. Raise and support vehicle.
10. Disconnect exhaust pipes from exhaust manifold.
11. Remove torque converter cover and the three bolts securing torque converter to flywheel.
12. Remove engine mount bolts or nuts.
13. Remove three engine to transmission bolts on the right side.
14. Disconnect starter wiring and remove starter.
15. Lower vehicle.
16. Attach suitable engine lifting equipment to engine. Support transmission with a suitable jack.
17. Remove the three engine to transmission bolts on the left side.
18. Remove engine from vehicle.
19. Reverse procedure to install.

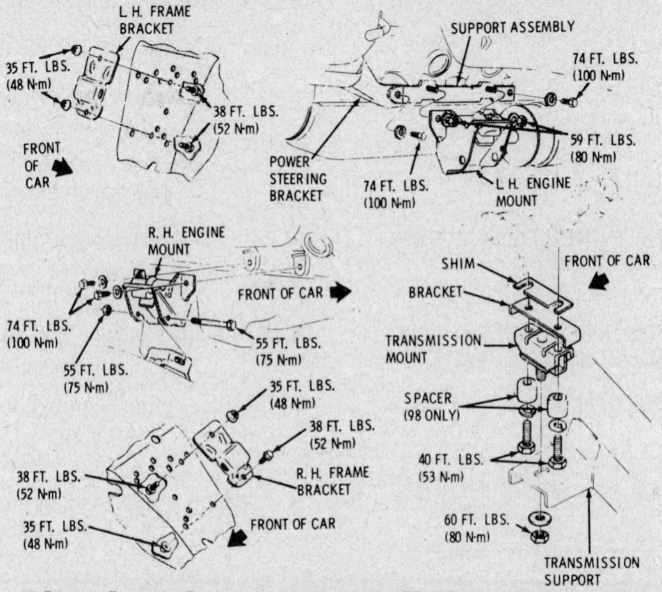

Fig. 1 Diesel engine mount. Full Size Rear Wheel Drive Models

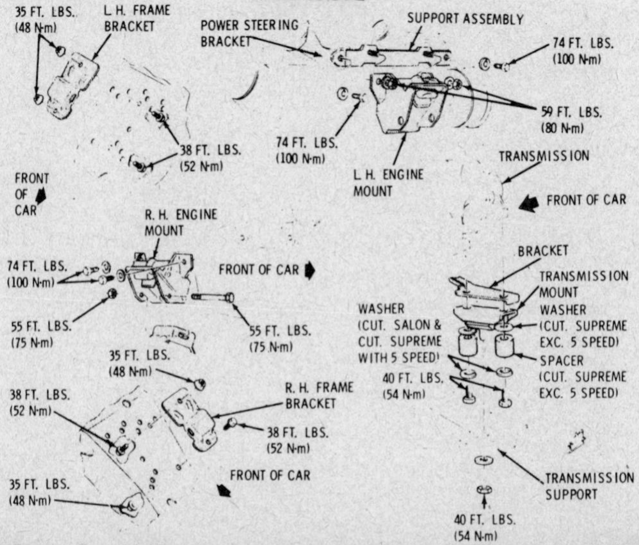

Fig. 2 Diesel engine mount. Intermediate Models w/V8 engine

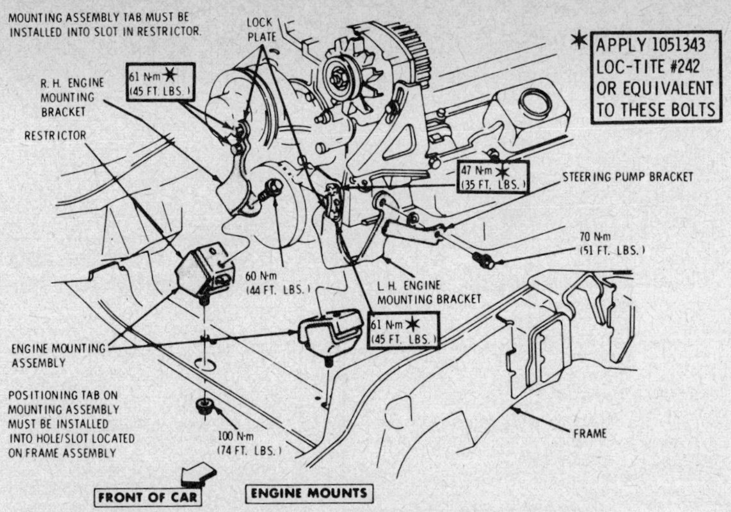

Fig. 3 Diesel engine mount. Full Size Front Wheel Drive Models (typical)

FULL SIZE FRONT WHEEL DRIVE MODELS

1. Disconnect battery ground cable and drain cooling system.
2. Remove radiator upper support.
3. Remove air cleaner assembly.
4. Scribe hood hinge locations and remove hood.
5. Disconnect engine ground strap.
6. Disconnect upper and lower radiator hoses from engine.
7. Disconnect transmission oil cooler lines from radiator.
8. Disconnect heater hoses from water pump and water control valve.
9. Remove radiator, fan and the shroud.
10. Disconnect power steering pump bracket from engine and position aside without disconnecting lines.
11. Disconnect A/C compressor bracket from engine and position aside without disconnecting lines.
12. Disconnect fuel lines.
13. Disconnect throttle cable, vacuum hoses and electrical connections.
14. Disconnect lefthand exhaust pipe from manifold.
15. On left side of engine, remove through bolt and bracket securing final drive to engine.
16. Raise and support vehicle.
17. Remove flywheel shield.
18. Disconnect righthand exhaust pipe from manifold.
19. Disconnect starter motor wiring and remove starter motor.
20. Remove converter to flywheel bolts. Mark location of converter on flywheel for alignment during installation.
21. Remove splash shield.
22. Remove engine front mounting attaching nuts.
23. Remove two bolts securing righthand output shaft support brackets. Using a sharp tool, scribe a mark around the washers as far as possible. Use these scribe marks to position bracket upon installation.
24. Remove lower righthand transmission to engine attaching bolts. One bolt retains the modulator line clip.
25. Use a suitable length of chain to retain final drive in vehicle.
26. Lower vehicle and attaching suitable engine lifting equipment to engine.
27. Remove the remaining transmission to engine bolts. It may be necessary to raise or lower transmission with a suitable jack to facilitate bolt removal.
28. Raise engine and remove from vehicle.
29. Reverse procedure to install.

INTAKE MANIFOLD REPLACE

V8 ENGINE

1. Disconnect ground cables from batteries.
2. Remove air cleaner assembly.
3. Drain cooling system, then disconnect upper radiator hose and thermostat bypass hose from water pump outlet. Disconnect heater hose and vacuum hose from water control valve.
4. Remove breather pipes from valve covers and air crossover, **Fig. 5.**
5. Remove air crossover and cap intake manifold, **Fig. 6.**
6. Disconnect throttle rod and return spring. If equipped with Cruise Control, remove servo.
7. Remove hairpin clip from bellcrank and disconnect the cables. Remove throttle and throttle valve cables from intake manifold brackets and position cables aside.
8. Disconnect wiring as necessary.
9. Disconnect or remove alternator and A/C compressor brackets as necessary.
10. Disconnect fuel line from fuel pump and filter and remove fuel filter and bracket.
11. Disconnect lines from injector nozzles and remove injection pump, refer to "Injection Nozzle Replace, Injection Pump & Lines." Cap all open fuel line lines and fittings.
12. Disconnect fuel return line from injection pump.
13. Disconnect vacuum lines at vacuum pump. Remove vacuum pump, if equipped with A/C, or oil pump drive assembly, if less A/C, **Fig. 7.**
14. Remove intake manifold drain tube, **Fig. 8.**
15. Remove intake manifold bolts and the intake manifold.
16. Remove adapter seal and injection pump adapter.
17. Reverse procedure to install. Torque intake manifold bolts in sequence, **Fig. 9,** to specifications.

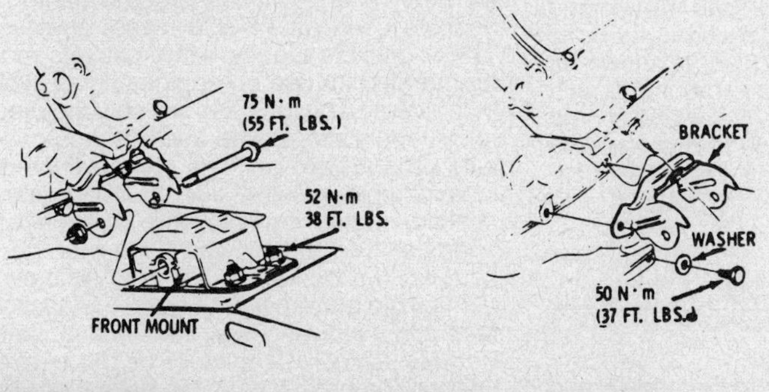

Fig. 4 Motor mounts. 1982–84 Intermediate Models w/V6 engine

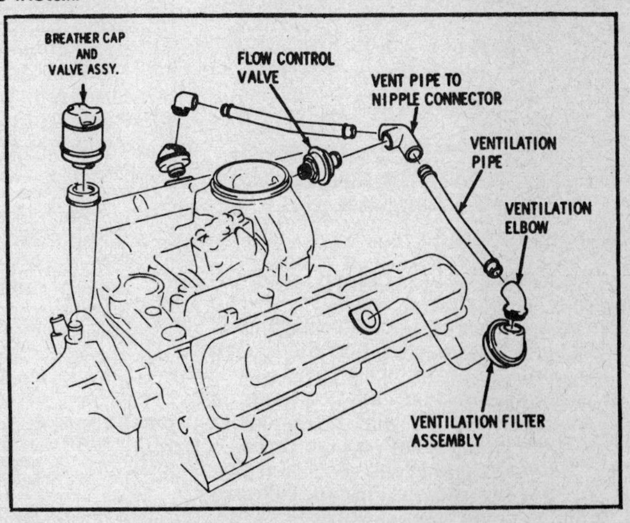

Fig. 5 Crankcase ventilation system. V8 engine

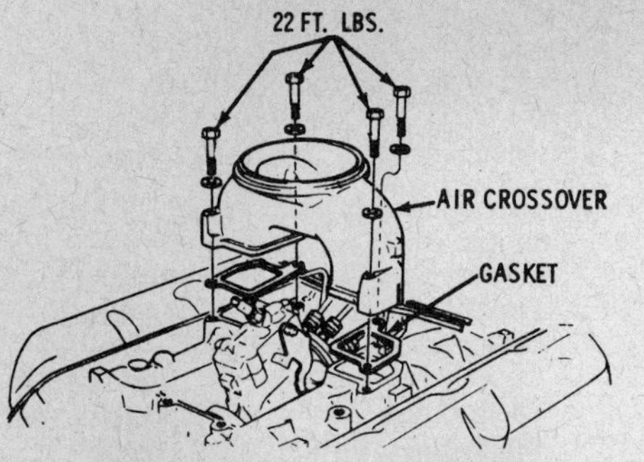

Fig. 6 Air crossover installation. Typical

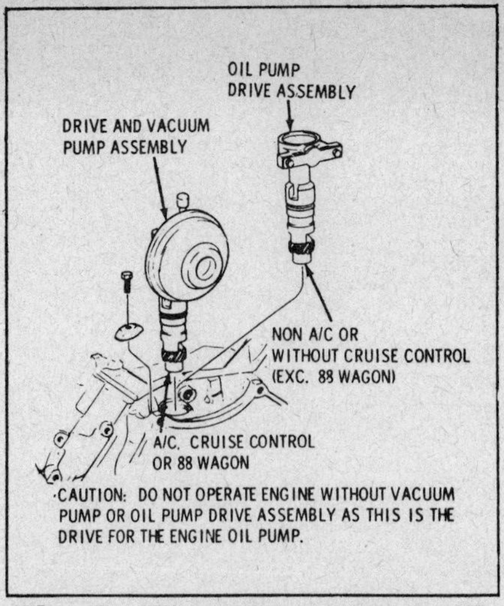

Fig. 7 Vacuum pump & oil pump drive assembly

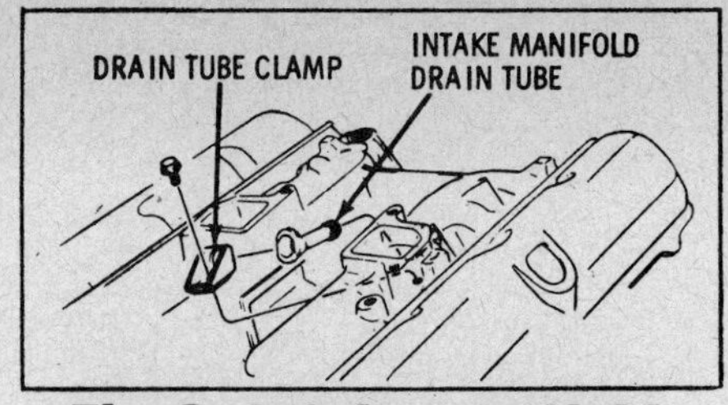

Fig. 8 Intake manifold drain tube installation

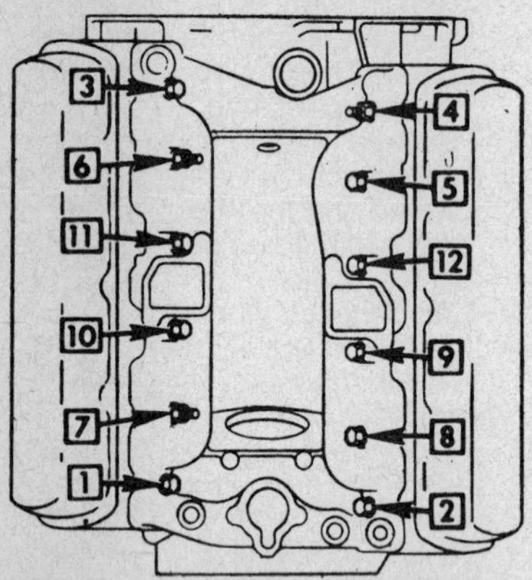

Fig. 9 Intake manifold tightening sequence. V8 engine

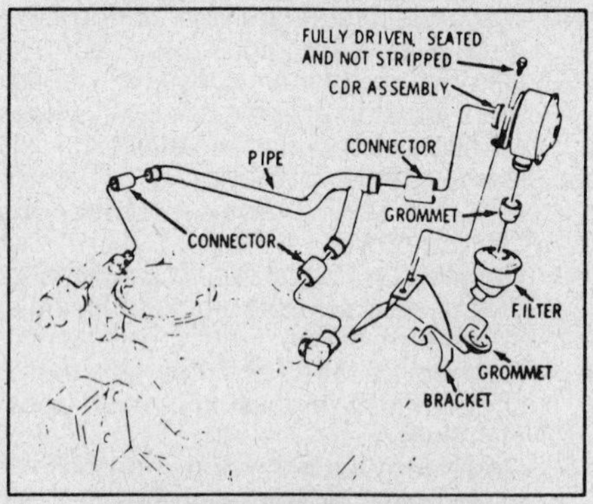

Fig. 10 Crankcase ventilation system. V6 engine

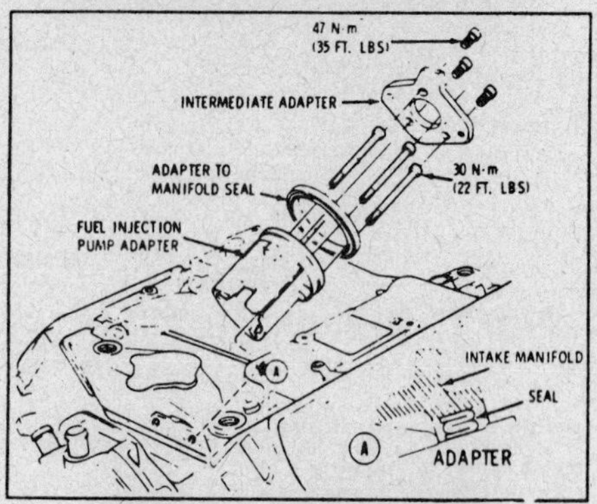

Fig. 11 Removing intermediate pump adapter. V6 engine

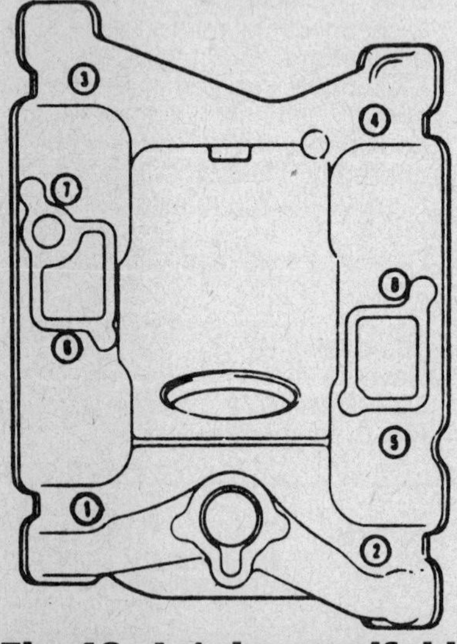

Fig. 12 Intake manifold bolt tightening sequence. V6 engine

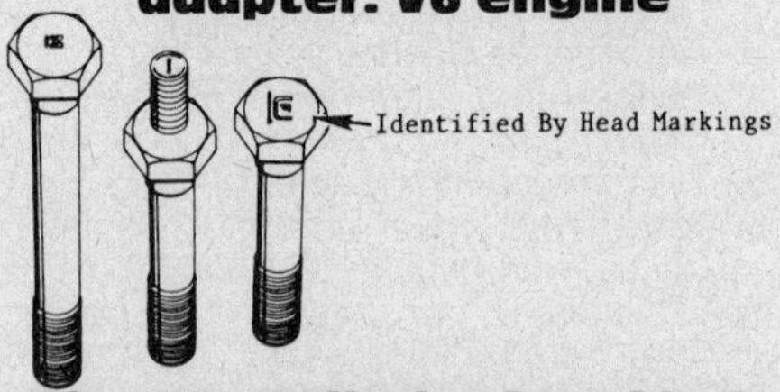

Fig. 13 Cylinder head bolt markings

V6 ENGINE

1. Disconnect battery ground cable and remove air cleaner.
2. Drain cooling system, then disconnect upper radiator hose and thermostat bypass hose from water outlet.
3. Disconnect heater inlet hose and on models equipped with air conditioning, the water valve vacuum line.
4. Disconnect crankcase ventilation pipe from air crossover, **Fig. 10.** Remove air crossover.
5. Remove fuel pump and plug all open lines and fittings.
6. Remove fuel injection pump as described under "Injection Pump, Replace."
7. Disconnect electrical connectors as necessary.
8. Remove cruise control servo, if equipped.
9. Disconnect fuel lines and position aside. Disconnect vacuum lines as necessary.
10. Remove drain tube, then remove intermediate pump adapter, **Fig. 11.**
11. Remove intake manifold bolts and the intake manifold.
12. Reverse procedure to install. Lubricate intake manifold bolts with engine oil before installing, then torque bolts as specified in sequence shown in **Fig. 12.** Apply chassis grease to seal area of intake manifold and pump adapter and to inside and outside diameter of seal and seal area of tool J-28425 or equivalent. Install seal onto tool, then install seal.

CYLINDER HEAD

REPLACE

New head bolts with increased torque capacity were introduced into production and are now available, **Fig. 13.**

When replacing a cylinder head, it is recommended new head bolts be used if they have not already been installed in the engine. When installing later production model head bolts, be sure to clean and oil the threads. Before installation of the cylinder head, ensure bolt holes are tapped deep enough into the block. Blow out any chips or liquid in the bolt holes. Then position cylinder head on cylinder block without the cylinder head gasket. Install bolt and tighten by hand until bolt head contacts the cylinder head. This will indicate that the holes are tapped deep enough into the block, allowing for proper torque. For cylinder head bolt location, part number and size, refer to **Fig. 14.**

New design he ad gaskets are available for service and will supersede previous gaskets used on V8-350 diesel engines. These gaskets are the same gaskets recommended for use on engines using .030 inch oversize pistons and will now be used for all applications. The use of these gaskets on standard engines should prevent loss of compression due to the gasket sealing ring falling into the combustion chamber. On 1983 engines, use new gasket, Part No. 22519416. This gasket is evident by the grey seal located on the gasket face. On 1982 engines, use new gasket, Part No. 22510719, evident by the purple seal on the gasket face. No gasket sealer should be used on either gasket during installation.

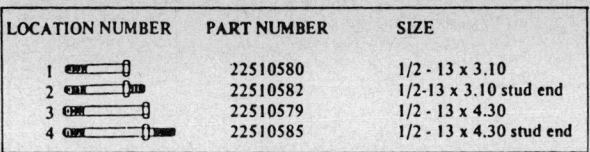

LOCATION NUMBER	PART NUMBER	SIZE
1	22510580	1/2 - 13 x 3.10
2	22510582	1/2-13 x 3.10 stud end
3	22510579	1/2 - 13 x 4.30
4	22510585	1/2 - 13 x 4.30 stud end

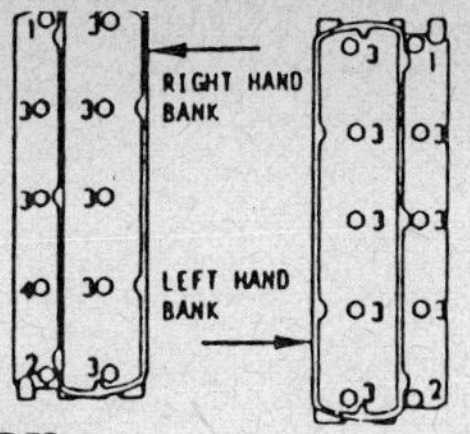

Fig. 14 Pre-chamber installation

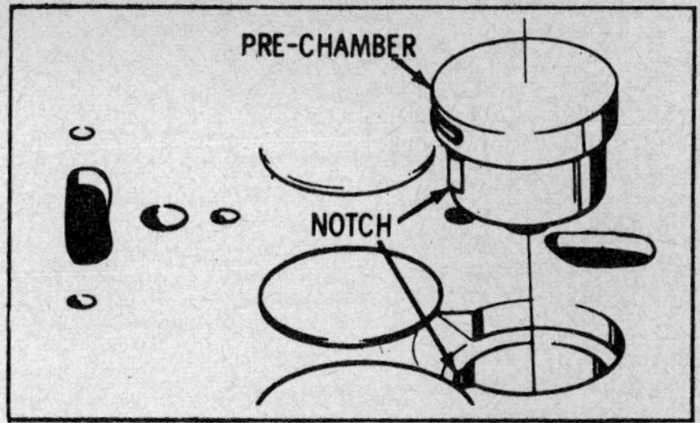

Fig. 15 Cylinder head bolt identification

Fig. 16 Cylinder head tightening sequence. V8 engine

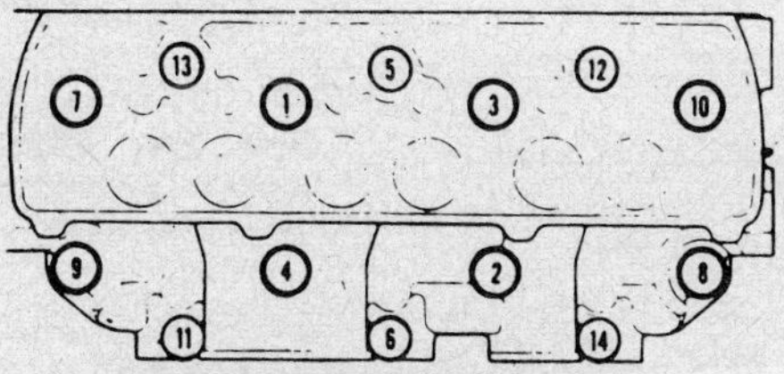

TORQUE ALL BOLTS (EXCEPT 5, 6, 11, 12, 13 & 14) TO 193 N·m (142 FT. LBS.). NUMBERS 5, 6, 11, 12, 13 & 14 TORQUE TO 80 N·m (59 FT. LBS.).

Fig. 17 Cylinder head bolt tightening sequence. V6 engine

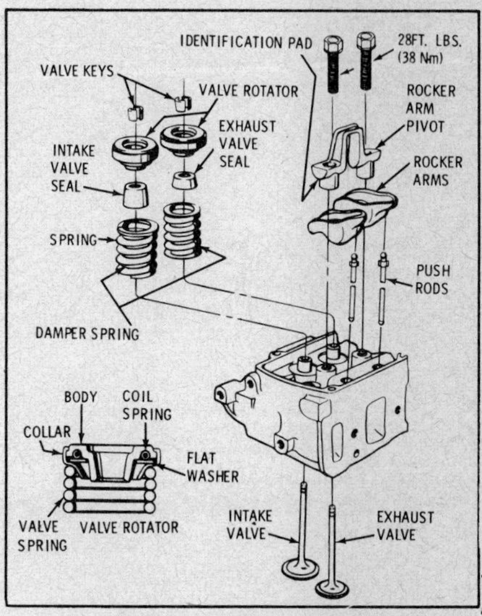

Fig. 18 Cylinder head exploded view

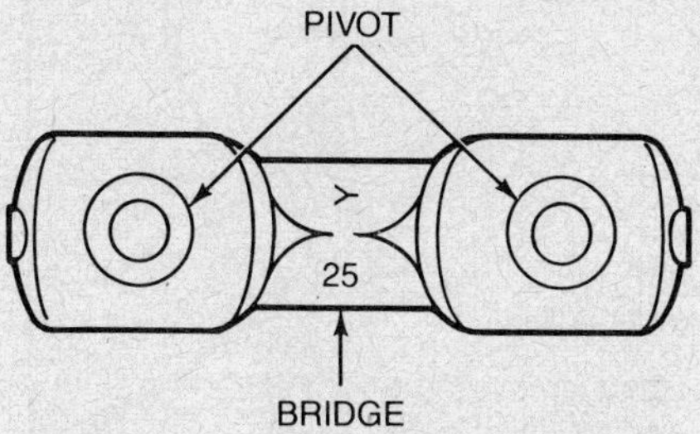

Fig. 19 Type 1 rocker arm pivot. 1982–83 V8 engine

When servicing cylinder head, ensure that prechambers are not recessed into cylinder head or protrude out of cylinder head more than .004 inch, since head gasket leakage may result. Measure the difference between flat or prechamber and the flat surface of cylinder head at two or more points around circumference of prechamber, using a straightedge and feeler gauge. If prechamber is recessed more than specified, replace prechamber or cylinder head, depending on which is at fault. If prechamber protrudes more than specified, grind top of prechamber for a flush fit, or replace as necessary.

1. Remove intake manifold as outlined previously.
2. Remove valve cover. It may be necessary to remove any interfering accessory brackets.
3. Disconnect glow plug wiring.
4. Remove ground strap from right cylinder head, if removing.
5. Remove rocker arm bolts, pivots, rocker arms and pushrod. Note locations of valve train components so they can be installed in original locations.
6. Remove fuel return lines from injection nozzles if equipped.
7. Remove exhaust manifold.
8. Remove engine block drain plug on side of block that cylinder head is being removed.
9. Remove cylinder head bolts and cylinder head. On 1982 V8 diesel remove TCC temperature switch located on exposed right rear cylinder head bolt.
10. If necessary to remove pre-chamber, remove a glow plug or injection nozzle, then tap out pre-chamber with a suitable drift, **Fig. 15.**
11. Reverse procedure to install. Do not use any sealing compound on cylinder head gasket. On 8 cylinder engines, torque cylinder head bolts in sequence, **Fig. 16,** to 100 ft. lbs., then to 130 ft. lbs. On 6 cylinder engines, torque cylinder head bolts except bolts 5, 6, 11, 12, 13 and 14, **Fig. 17,** to 142 ft. lbs. Torque bolts 5, 6, 11, 12, 13 and 14 to 59 ft. lbs.

ROCKER ARMS

This engine uses valve rotators, **Fig. 18.** The rotator operates on a sprag clutch principle utilizing the collapsing action of a coil spring to give rotation to the rotor body which turns the valve.

Some 1982-83 V8-350 diesel engines may experience valve train ticking noise and/or exhaust backfire. This condition may be caused by premature wear of the rocker arm pivots. Two types of rocker arm pivots were used on these engines. Type 1 pivot assemblies, Fig. 19, are the only ones showing premature wear. It is therefore recommended that only Type 2 pivot assemblies, Fig. 20, be used when servicing the engine for the above mentioned condition.

1. Remove valve cover.
2. Remove flanged bolts, rocker arm pivot and rocker arms, **Fig. 18.**
3. When installing rocker arm assemblies, lubricate wear surfaces with suitable lubricant. Torque flanged bolts to 25 ft. lbs. On 8 cylinder engines or 28 ft. lbs. on 6 cylinder engines.

VALVES

ADJUST

These engines are equipped with hydraulic valve lifters. No provision for adjustment is provided.

VALVE ROTATORS

The rotator operates on a sprag clutch principle utilizing the collapsing action of coil spring to give rotation to the rotor body which turns the valve, **Fig. 18.**

To check rotator action, draw a line across rotator body and down the collar. Operate engine at 1500 RPM, rotator body should move around collar. Rotator action can be in either direction. Replace rotator if no movement is noted.

When servicing valves, valve stem tips should be checked for improper wear pattern which could indicate a defective valve rotator, **Fig. 21.**

VALVE ARRANGEMENT

V8-260, 350 Diesel........ I-E-I-E-E-I-E-I
V6-262 Diesel .... I-E-E-I-E-I

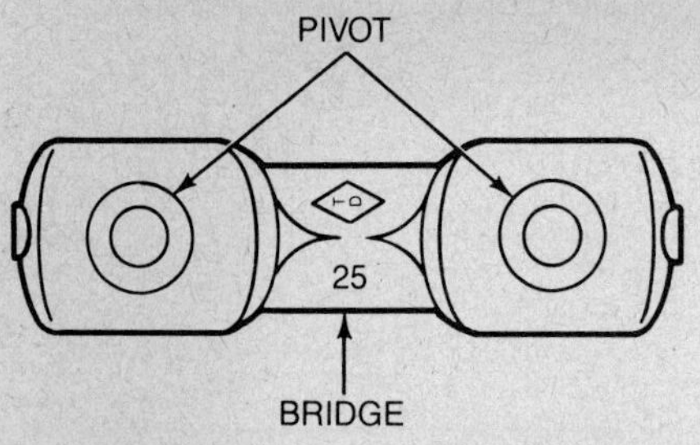

Fig. 20 Type 2 rocker arm pivot. 1982–83 V8 engine

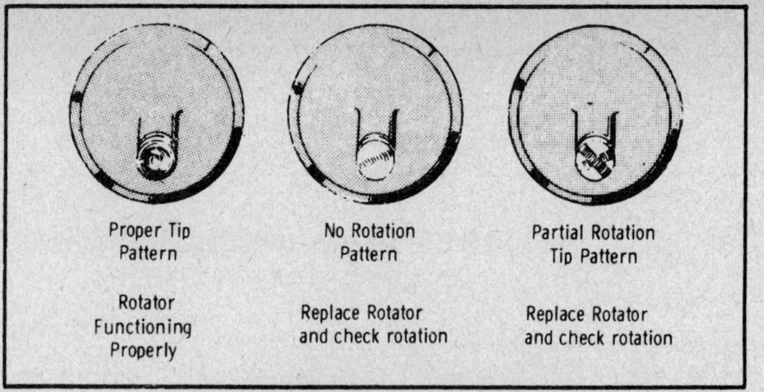

Fig. 21 Checking valve stem for rotator malfunction

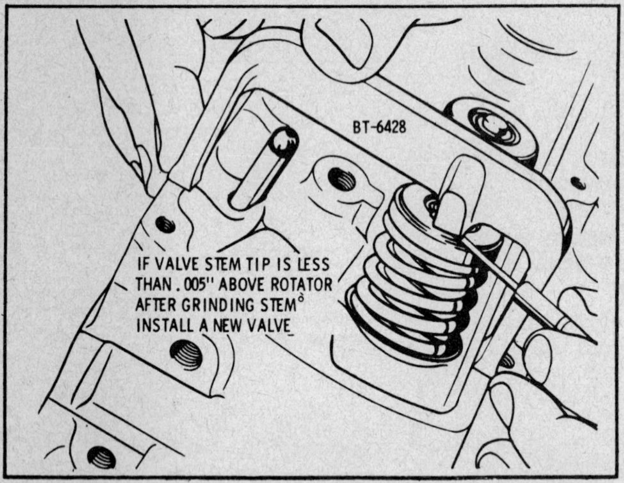

Fig. 22 Measuring valve stem height

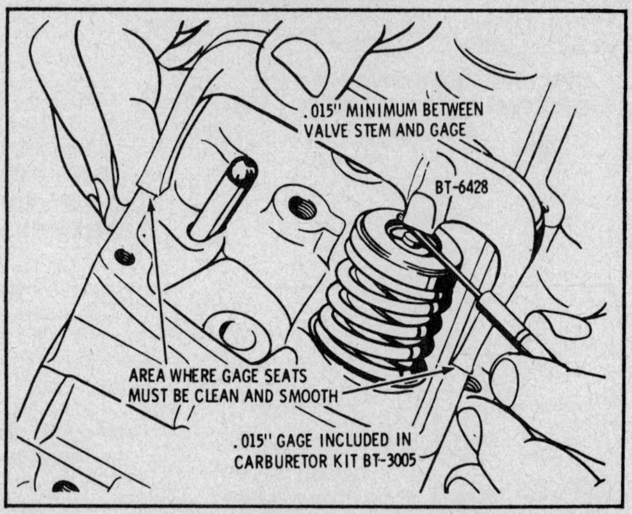

Fig. 23 Measuring valve rotator height

VALVE LIFT SPECIFICATIONS

Engine	Year	Intake	Exhaust
V8-350	1982-85	.375	.376
V6-262	1982-84	.375	.375

VALVE TIMING

INTAKE OPENS BEFORE TDC

Engine	Year	Degrees
V8-350 Diesel	1982-85	16
V6-262 Diesel	1982-84	16

VALVES

Whenever a new valve is installed or after grinding valves, it is necessary to measure the valve stem height with the special tool as shown in **Fig. 22.**

There should be at least .015 inch clearance between the gauge and end of valve stem. If clearance is less than .015 inch, remove valve and grind end of valve stem as required.

Check valve rotator height, **Fig. 23.** If valve stem end is less than .005 inch above rotator, the valve is too short and a new valve must be installed.

VALVE GUIDES

Valve stem guides are not replaceable, due to being cast in place. If valve guide bores are worn excessively, they can be reamed oversize.

If a standard valve guide bore is being reamed, use a .003 inch or .005 inch oversize reamer. For the .010 inch oversize valve guide bore, use a .013 inch oversize reamer. If too large a reamer is used and the spiraling is removed, it is possible that the valve will not receive the proper lubrication.

Occasionally a valve guide will be oversize as manufactured. These are marked on the cylinder head as shown in **Fig. 24.** If no markings are present, the guide bores are standard. If oversize markings are present, any valve replacement will require an oversize valve. Service valves are available in standard diameters as well as .003 inch, .005 inch, .010 inch and .013 inch oversize.

VALVE LIFTERS

REPLACE

Some engines have both standard and .010 inch oversize valve lifters. The .010 inch oversize valve lifters are etched with a "0" on the side of the lifter. Also, the cylinder block will be marked if an oversize lifter is used, **Fig. 25.**

1. Remove intake manifold as outlined previously.
2. Remove valve covers, rocker arm assemblies and pushrods. Note location of valve train components so they can be installed in original position.
3. Remove the hydraulic lifter retainer bolts, **Fig. 26.**
4. Remove valve lifters.
5. Reverse procedure to install. **Plungers are not interchangeable because they are selectively fitted to the bodies at the factory.**

VALVE LIFTER SERVICE

1. Remove valve lifters, refer to "Valve Lifters, Replace."
2. Using a small screwdriver, remove retainer ring, **Fig. 27.**
3. Remove pushrod seat, oil metering valve, plunger, and plunger spring.
4. Remove check ball retainer from plunger, then remove ball and spring.
5. Clean parts in a suitable solvent. **Do not interchange parts between lifters. If any parts are worn, replace lifter.**
6. Inspect all parts for nicks, burrs or scoring. If any parts are defective, replace lifter.
7. On roller lifters, inspect roller. It should rotate freely, but without excessive play. Also check for missing or broken needle bearing. If any parts are defective, replace lifter.
8. Apply a coating of light engine oil to all lifter surfaces.

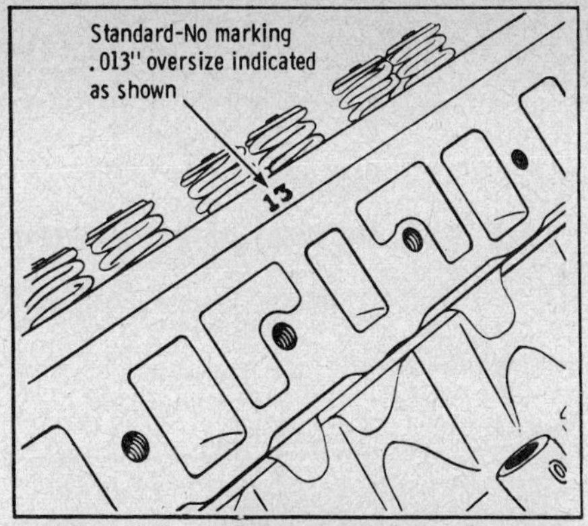

Fig. 24 Valve guide bore marking

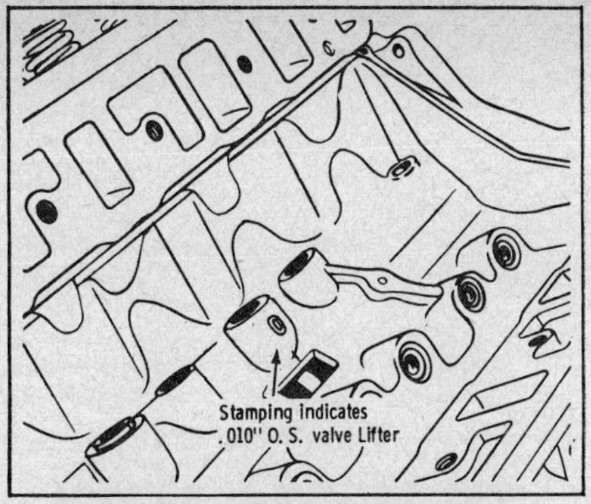

Fig. 25 Oversize valve lifter bore marking

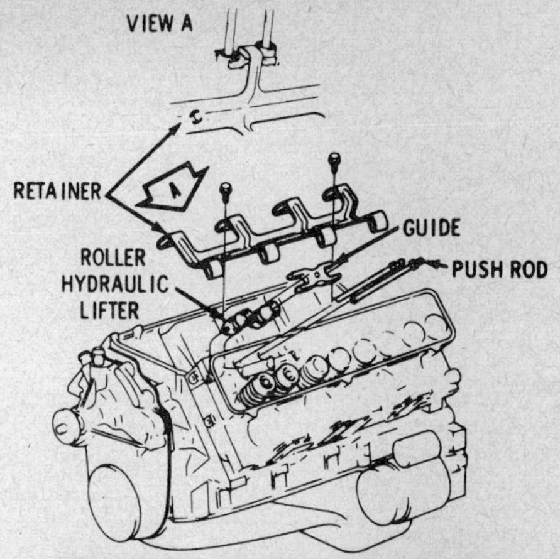

Fig. 26 Hydraulic roller lifter retainer & guide (Typical)

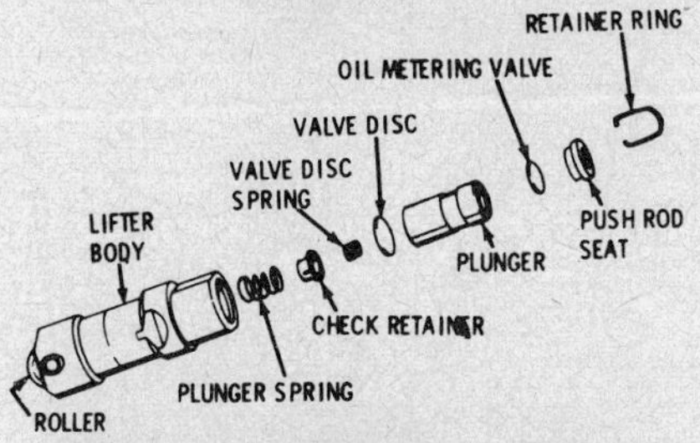

Fig. 27 Hydraulic roller lifter assembly exploded view

9. Install ball check spring and retainer into plunger. Ensure retainer flange is pressed tight against bottom of recess in plunger.
10. Install plunger spring over check retainer.
11. Hold plunger with spring up and insert in lifter body. Hold plunger vertically to prevent cocking spring.
12. Submerge lifter assembly in clean diesel fuel or kerosene, then install oil metering valve and pushrod seat into lifter and install retaining ring.

VALVE LIFTER BLEED DOWN

If the intake manifold has been removed and if any rocker arms have been removed or loosened, it will be necessary to remove those lifters, disassemble them, drain the oil from them and reassemble. Refer to "Valve Lifters, Service."

If the intake manifold has not been removed, but rocker arms have been loosened or removed, the valve lifters must be bled down to prevent possible valve to piston interference by using the following procedure:

1. Prior to installing rocker arms, rotate crankshaft pulley to a position 32° BTDC (before top dead center). This is approximately 2 inches counterclockwise from 0° pointer.
2. If the right side valve cover was removed only, remove cylinder No. 1 glow plug and determine if No. 1 piston is in the correct position, this can be determined by compression pressure.
3. If the left side valve cover was removed only, rotate crankshaft until No. 5 cylinder intake valve pushrod is .28 inch above the No. 5 cylinder exhaust valve pushrod.
4. If removed, install cylinder No. 5 pivot and rocker arms. Alternately torque the bolts until the intake valve begins to open and stop tightening. **When torquing rocker arms, use only hand wrenches to prevent engine damage.**
5. Install remaining rocker arms except No. 3 exhaust valve. Torque bolt to 28 ft. lbs.
6. If removed, install No. 3 exhaust rocker arm and pivot, but do not torque beyond the point that the valve would be fully opened. This is indicated by a strong resistance while turning the pivot retaining bolt. Going beyond this point would bend the pushrod. **While performing step 6, torque bolt slowly allowing the lifter to bleed down.**
7. Finish torquing No. 5 rocker arm pivot bolt slowly, allowing valve lifter to bleed down. Do not torque beyond the point that the valve would be fully opened. This is indicated by a strong resistance while turning the pivot retaining bolt. Going beyond this point would bend the pushrod.
8. Do not turn the crankshaft for at least 45 minutes while lifters bleed down. **Do not rotate the engine until the valve lifters have bled down, otherwise engine damage might occur.**

FRONT OIL SEAL REPLACE

1. Disconnect ground cables from batteries.
2. Remove accessory drive belts.
3. Remove crankshaft pulley and harmonic balancer.
4. Using tool BT-6406, remove front oil seal, **Fig. 28.**
5. Apply suitable sealer to outside diameter of new oil seal.
6. File .020 inch from flange of tool No. J-25264, **Fig. 29,** to prevent tool from contacting oil slinger before seal is properly seated in front cover.
7. Using tool BT-6611, install new oil seal, **Fig. 30.**
8. Install harmonic balancer and crankshaft pulley.
9. Install and tension accessory drive belts.

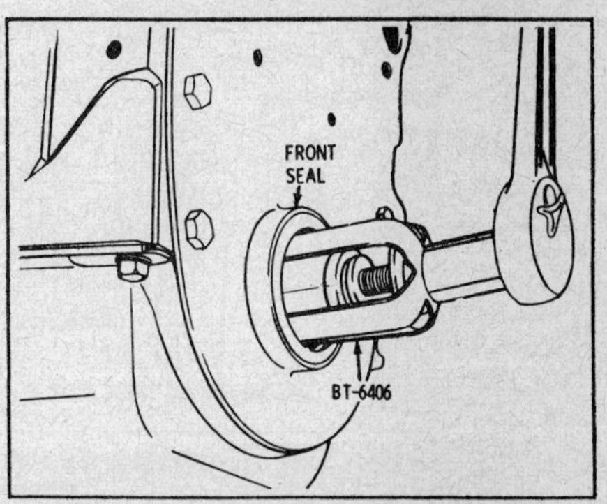

Fig. 28 Front oil seal removal

ENGINE FRONT COVER REPLACE

1. Disconnect ground cables from batteries.
2. Drain cooling system and disconnect radiator hoses and bypass hose.
3. Remove all drive belts, fan and pulley, crankshaft pulley and harmonic balancer, and accessory brackets.
4. Remove timing indicator and water pump.
5. Remove remaining front cover attaching bolts and the front cover. Also, remove the dowel pins. It may be necessary to grind a flat on the dowel pin to provide a rough surface for gripping.
6. Grind a chamfer on one end of each dowel pin, **Fig. 31.**
7. Cut excess material from front end of oil pan gasket on each side of cylinder block.
8. Trim approximately 1/8 inch from each end of new front pan seal.
9. Install new front cover gasket and apply suitable sealer to gasket around coolant holes.
10. Apply RTV sealer to mating surfaces of cylinder block, oil pan and front cover.
11. Place front cover on cylinder block and press downward to compress seal. Rotate cover right and left and guide oil pan seal into cavity with a small screwdriver.
12. Apply engine oil to bolts.

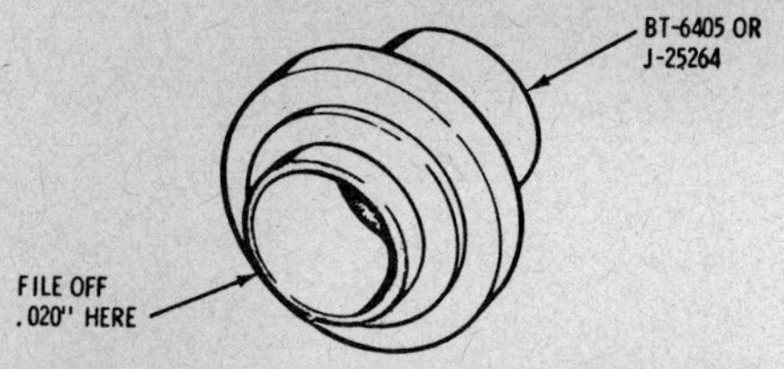

Fig. 29 Modifying tool for front oil seal installation

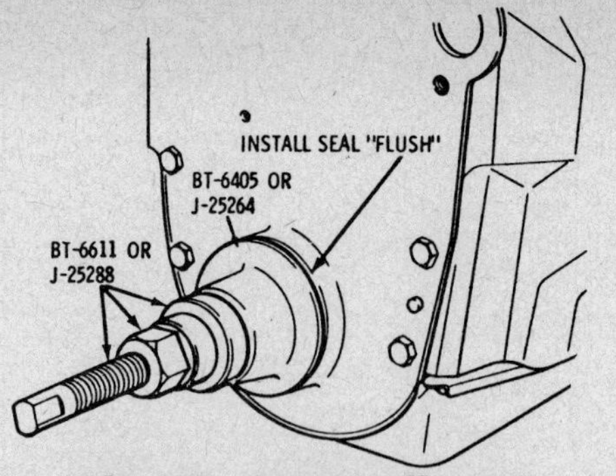

Fig. 30 Front oil seal installation

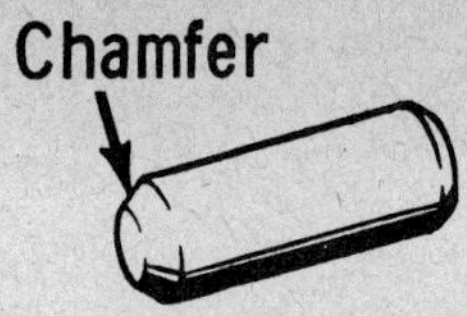

Fig. 31 Dowel pin chamfer

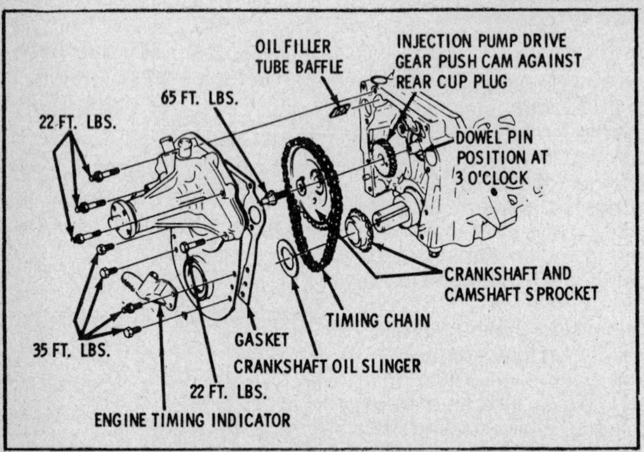

Fig. 32 Engine front cover installation. Typical

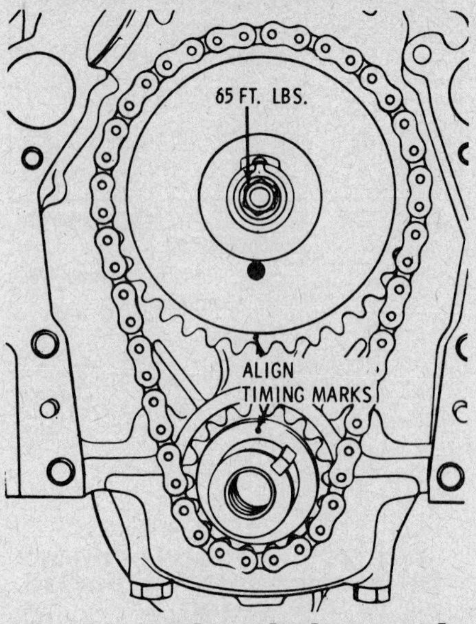

Fig. 33 Valve timing marks

13. Install two bolts finger tight to retain cover.
14. Install the two dowel pins, chamfered end first.
15. Install timing indicator and water pump and torque bolts as shown in **Fig. 32.**
16. Install harmonic balancer and crankshaft pulley.
17. Install accessory brackets.
18. Install fan and pulley and drive belts.
19. Connect radiator hoses and bypass hose.
20. Connect ground cables to batteries.

TIMING CHAIN & GEARS
REPLACE

1. Remove front cover as outlined previously. On 6 cylinder engines, loosen rocker arm pivot bolts evenly so that some lash is present between rocker arms and valves.
2. Remove oil slinger, cam gear, crank gear and timing chain.
3. Remove fuel pump eccentric from crankshaft.
4. Install key in crankshaft, if removed.
5. Install fuel pump eccentric, if removed.
6. Install cam gear, crank gear and timing chain with timing marks aligned, **Fig. 33. With the timing marks aligned in Fig. 33, No. 6 cylinder is in the firing position. To place No. 1 cylinder in the firing position, rotate crankshaft one complete revolution. This will bring the camshaft gear mark to top and No. 1 cylinder will be in the firing position.**
7. Install oil slinger.
8. Install front cover.

CAMSHAFT & INJECTION PUMP DRIVE & DRIVEN GEARS
REPLACE

1. Disconnect ground cables from batteries.
2. Drain cooling system.
3. Remove radiator upper baffle.
4. Disconnect upper radiator hose at water outlet and hose support clamp.
5. Disconnect cooler lines at radiator.
6. Remove fan shroud and radiator.
7. Remove intake manifold as outlined previously.
8. Remove engine front cover as outlined previously.
9. Remove valve covers.
10. Remove rocker arm bolts, pivots, rocker arms and pushrod. Note valve train component locations to install components in original locations.
11. If equipped with A/C, discharge refrigerant system and remove condenser.
12. On all models, remove timing chain and gears as outlined previously.
13. Position camshaft dowel pin at 3 o'clock position.
14. While holding the camshaft rearward and rocking the injection pump driven gear slide, slide the injection pump drive gear from camshaft.
15. Remove injection pump adapter, snap ring, selective washer, injection pump driven gear and spring, **Fig. 34.**
16. Slide camshaft from front of engine.
17. Reverse procedure to install. Check injection pump driven gear endplay. If endplay is not .002-.006 inch, replace selective washer, **Fig. 34.** Selective washers are available from .080 to .115 inch in increments of .003 inch.

PISTON & ROD ASSEMBLY

Install piston and rod assembly so that notch at top of piston is facing toward front of engine, **Fig. 35.** Check connecting rod side clearance. Clearance should be .006-.020 inch on V8 engines or .008-.021 on V6 engines.

PISTONS, RINGS & PINS

Some V8-350 diesel engines may exhibit excessive oil consumption, low compression and/or excessive blow-by. These conditions may be caused by stuck or frozen piston rings. To correct the above mentioned problem, proceed as follows:

1. With engine warm, remove all glow plugs from cylinders.
2. Using top engine cleaner Part No. 1050002, or equivalent, divide contents of can equally into each cylinder. Allow engine to soak for 24 hours.
3. Crank engine with glow plugs removed to expel excess cleaner.

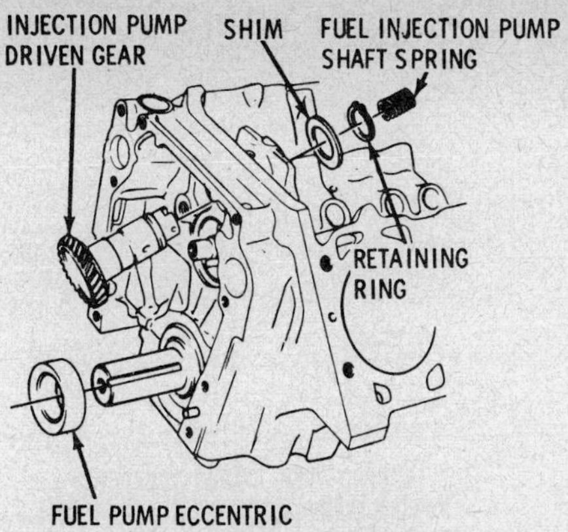

Fig. 34 Fuel injection pump driven gear installation

Fig. 35 Piston & rod assembly

4. Install glow plugs and start engine.

Pistons are available in standard sizes and oversizes of .010 and .030 inch on 8 cylinder engines or in standard size and oversize of .010 inch on 6 cylinder engines.

Rings are available in standard sizes and oversizes of .010 and .030 inch.

MAIN & ROD BEARINGS

Main bearings are available in standard sizes and undersizes of .0005, .0010 and .0015 inch. The amount of undersize and part number is stamped on the bearing shell, **Fig. 36.**

Rod bearings are available in standard sizes and an undersize of .010 inch.

CRANKSHAFT REAR SEAL SERVICE

Since the braided fabric seal used on these engines can be replaced only when the crankshaft is removed, the following repair procedure is recommended.

1. Remove oil pan and bearing cap.
2. Drive end of old seal gently into groove, using a suitable tool, until packed tight. This may vary between 1/4 and 3/4 inch depending on amount of pack required.
3. Repeat previous step for other end of seal.
4. Measure and note amount that seal was driven up on one side. Using the old seal removed from bearing cap, cut a length of seal the amount previously noted plus 1/16 inch.
5. Repeat previous step for other side of seal.
6. Pack cut lengths of seal into appropriate side of seal groove. A packing tool, BT-6433, **Fig. 37,** may be used since the tool has been machined to provide a built-in stop. Use tool BT-6436 to trim the seal flush with block, **Fig. 38.**
7. Install new seal in lower bearing cap.

OIL PAN

REPLACE

The recommended diesel engine oil is SF/CC or SF/CD.

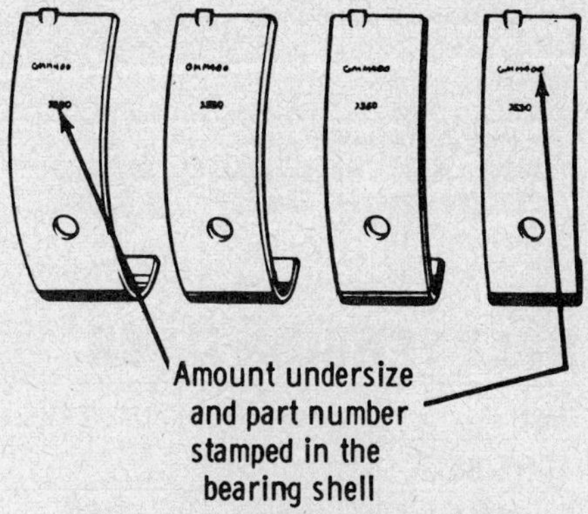

Fig. 36 Main bearing identification

FULL SIZE REAR WHEEL DRIVE MODELS

1. Disconnect ground cables from batteries.
2. Remove oil pump drive and vacuum pump, if equipped with A/C, or oil pump drive, if less A/C.
3. Remove oil dipstick.
4. Remove radiator upper support and fan shroud attaching screws.
5. Raise and support vehicle and drain oil pan.
6. Remove flywheel cover.
7. Disconnect exhaust and crossover pipes from exhaust manifold.
8. Remove oil cooler lines at filter base.
9. Disconnect starter wiring and remove starter.
10. Remove engine mounts from engine block, then raise front of engine with suitable equipment.
11. Remove oil pan attaching bolts and the oil pan.
12. Reverse procedure to install. Torque oil pan attaching bolts to 10 ft. lbs.

FULL SIZE FRONT WHEEL DRIVE MODELS

1. Disconnect battery ground cables.
2. Remove three final drive to transmission bolts, then raise and support vehicle.
3. Disconnect frame brace retaining bolts. Disconnect idler arm and pitman arm from relay rod.
4. Disconnect drive axles from output shafts.
5. Disconnect battery cable bracket from output shaft support.
6. Disconnect output shaft support from engine block.
7. Position suitable jack under final drive, then remove final drive.
8. Remove splash shield and starter motor.
9. Drain oil, then remove oil pan. **To remove oil pan, engine must be raised 1-1½ inch using tool No. BT-6501, or equivalent.**
10. Reverse procedure to install.

OIL PUMP

REPLACE & SERVICE

REPLACEMENT

1. Remove oil pan as outlined previously.
2. Remove oil pump to rear main bearing cap attaching bolts, **Fig. 39.**
3. Remove oil pump and driveshaft extension.
4. Reverse procedure to install. Torque attaching bolts to 35 ft. lbs.

SERVICE

Disassembly

1. Remove oil pump driveshaft extension, **Fig. 40.** Do not attempt to remove washers from driveshaft extension. The driveshaft extension and washers is serviced as an assembly.
2. Remove cotter pin, spring and pressure regulator valve. **Apply pressure on pressure regulator bore before removing cotter pin since the spring is under pressure.**
3. Remove oil pump cover attaching screws and the oil pump cover and gasket.
4. Remove drive gear and idler gear from pump body.

Inspection

1. Check gears for scoring or other damage, replace if necessary.
2. Proper end clearance is .0005-.0075 inch.
3. Check pressure regulator valve, valve spring and bore for damage. Proper

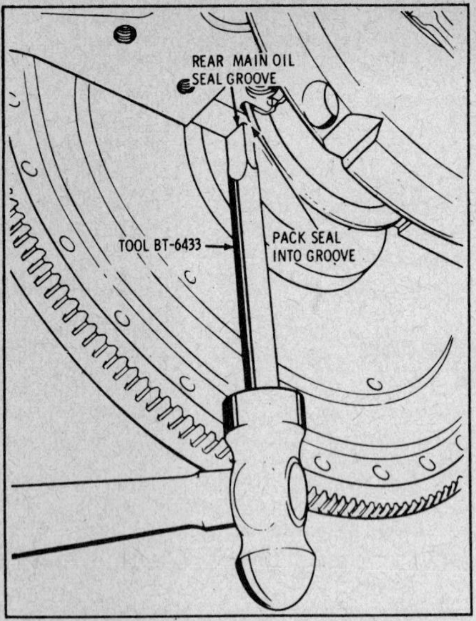

Fig. 37 Packing upper rear main bearing seal

bore to valve clearance is .0025-.0050 inch.

4. Check extension shaft ends for wear, Fig. 41.

Assembly

1. Install gears and shaft in oil pump body.
2. Check gear end clearance by placing a straightedge over the gears and measure the clearance between the straightedge and gasket surface. If end clearance is excessive, check for scores in cover that would bring the clearance over specified limits.
3. Install cover and torque attaching screws to 8 ft. lbs.
4. Install pressure regulator valve, closed end first, into bore, then the valve spring and cotter pin.

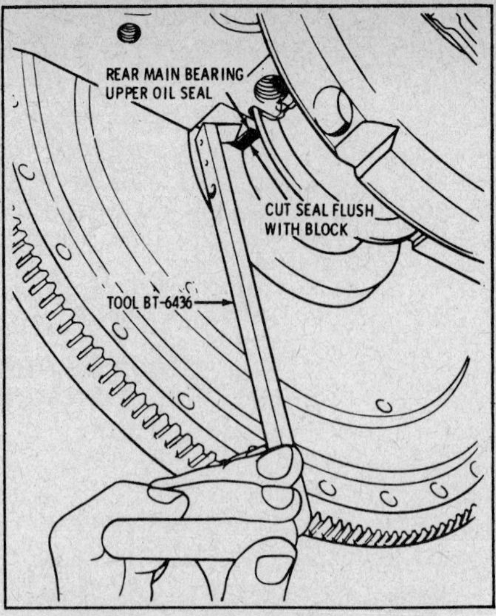

Fig. 38 Trimming upper rear main bearing seal

BELT TENSION DATA

Belt	New Lbs.	Used Lbs.
1982-85③		
3/8 inch①	160	80
3/8 inch②	145	55
7/16 inch	170	90

①—Except cogged belts.
②—Cogged belts.
③—V8 engine only. V6 engine serpentine drive belt is self adjusting.

WATER PUMP REPLACE

V6 ENGINE

1. Disconnect battery ground cables and drain cooling system.

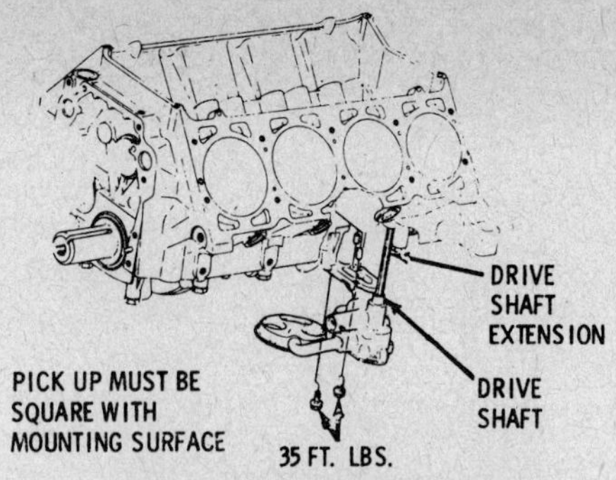

Fig. 39 Oil pump installation (Typical)

2. Remove fan clutch and fan, then disconnect radiator inlet hose at radiator.
3. Remove upper radiator support.
4. Remove drive belt and water pump pulley.
5. Remove vacuum pump and bracket assembly, then the cruise control servo mounting bracket, if equipped.
6. Remove power steering pump and brackets and position aside. Do not disconnect hoses from pump.
7. Disconnect heater and radiator outlet hoses at water pump, then loosen thermostat bypass hose clamp.
8. Remove water pump to front cover and water pump and front cover to block retaining bolts.
9. Remove water pump from front cover.
10. Reverse procedure to install. Coat gaskets with suitable sealer and water pump and front cover to block retaining bolts with primer and adhesive, Part No. 1052624, or equivalent. **Failure to use the above mentioned primer and adhesive may cause coolant leaks and/or loss of bolt torque.**

V8 ENGINE

1. Disconnect ground cables from batteries.
2. Drain cooling system.
3. Loosen drive belts and remove fan and pulley assembly.
4. Disconnect all hoses from water pump.
5. Remove water pump attaching screws and the water pump.
6. Reverse procedure to install.

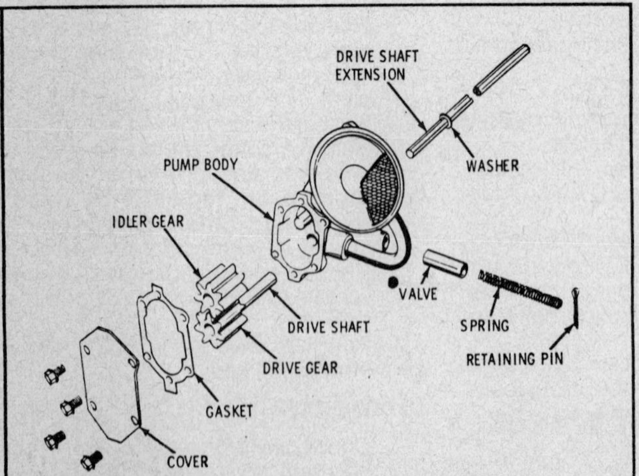

Fig. 40 Oil pump disassembled

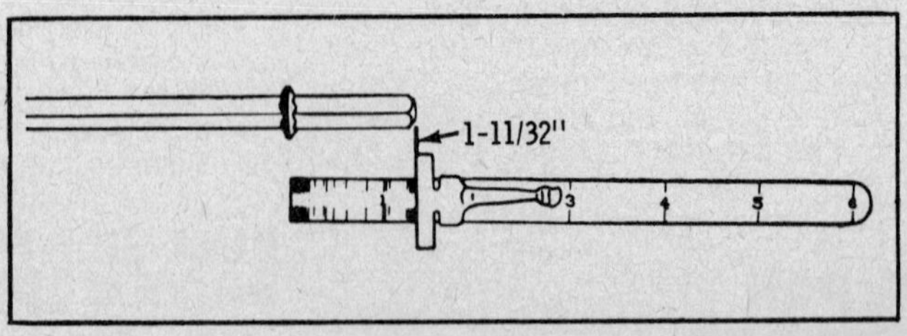

Fig. 41 Oil pump driveshaft extension. V8 engines

Fuel Injection Section

INDEX

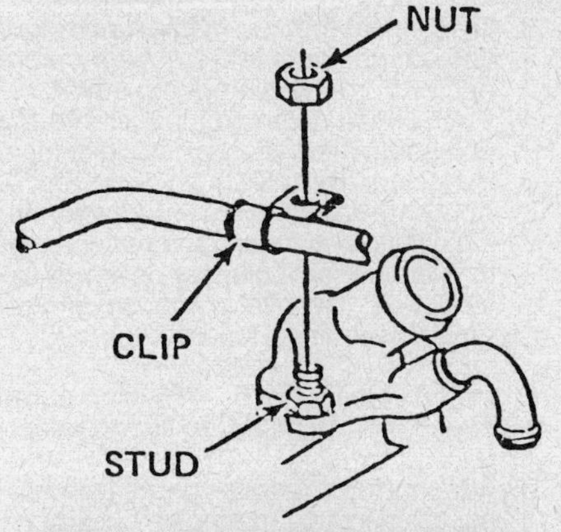

Fig. 1 Installing fuel line stud & clip assembly

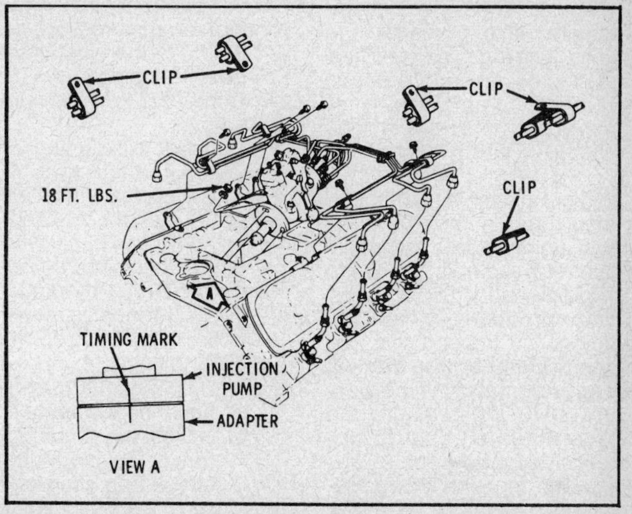

Fig. 2 Fuel injection pump timing marks. Typical

MECHANICAL FUEL PUMP

REPLACE

Some diesel engines may exhibit a condition of hard cold starts. If this condition exists, check the fuel pump housing for a crack in the area where the fuel line is connected to the fuel pump, which may allow air to enter the system. The cracked fuel pump housing could be caused by the fuel line vibrating.

To correct this condition, remove the righthand thermostat housing bolt and install stud, part No. 6270979. Disconnect fuel line at the fuel pump and install clip, part No. 343463 onto fuel line as shown in Fig. 1. Install washer face nut, part No. 10008001. Replace the fuel pump and connect the fuel line.

1. Disconnect fuel lines and electrical connectors from pump.
2. Remove fuel pump mounting bolts and the fuel pump.
3. Remove all gasket material from the pump and block gasket surfaces. Apply sealer to both sides of new gasket.
4. Position gasket on pump flange and hold pump in position against its mounting surface. Make sure rocker arm is riding on crankshaft eccentric.
5. Press pump tight against its mounting. Install retaining screws and tighten them alternately.
6. Connect fuel lines. Then operate engine and check for leaks. **Before installing the pump, it is good practice to crank the engine so that the nose of the crankshaft eccentric is out of the way of the fuel pump rocker arm when the pump is installed. In this way there will be the least amount of tension on the rocker arm, thereby easing the installation of the pump.**

INJECTION PUMP TIMING

LESS TIMING METER

1. The mark on the injection pump adapter must be aligned with the mark on the injection pump flange, **Fig. 2.**
2. To adjust:
   a. Loosen the injection pump retaining nuts with tool J-26987.
   b. Align the mark on the injection pump flange with the mark on the injection pump adapter, **Fig. 2.**
   c. Torque injection pump retaining nuts to 35 ft. lbs. (V6) or 18 ft. lbs. (V8).

WITH TIMING METER J-33075

Certain engine malfunctions can cause inaccurate timing readings. Engine malfunctions should be corrected before adjusting pump timing. The marks on the pump and pump adapter will normally be aligned within .030 (V8) or .050 (V6) inch.

1. Place transmission in Park, apply parking brake and block drive wheels.
2. Start engine and allow to reach normal operating temperature.
3. Shut engine off.
4. Remove air cleaner assembly, install cover J-26996-1 then disconnect EGR valve hose.
5. Clean dirt from engine probe holder and crankshaft balancer rim.
6. Clean lens on both ends of glow plug probe. Look through probe to ensure that it is clean.
7. Remove glow plug from No. 1 (V6) or No. 3 (V8) cylinder. Insert glow plug probe into glow plug opening and torque probe to 8 ft. lbs.
8. Set timing meter selector to A (V6) or B (V8), then connect meter battery leads.
9. Disconnect generator two lead connector, then start engine and adjust idle speed to specifications.

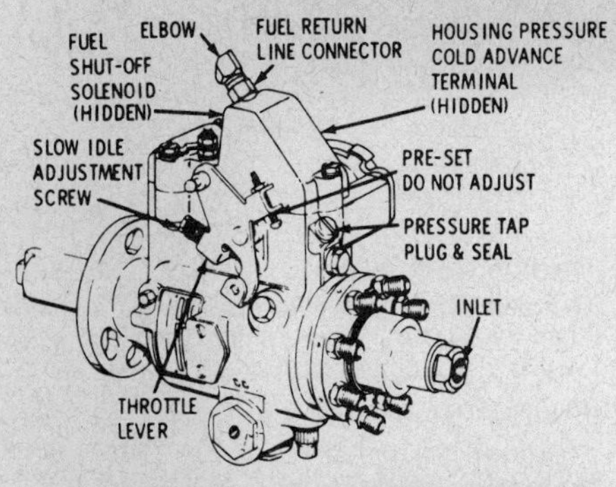

Fig. 3 Fuel injection pump connections. 1982–83 V8 engine

10. Observe timing meter, wait approximately two minutes, then observe timing meter again. When meter stabilizes, compare timing reading to specifications. If timing is as specified, proceed to step 16. If timing is not as specified, proceed to next step.
11. Turn engine off and note relative position of marks on pump flange and adapter.
12. Loosen nuts or bolts holding pump to adapter, then rotate pump to the left (advance) or right (retard) as necessary. Torque retaining nuts or bolts to 18 (V8) or 35 (V6 and 1985 V8) ft. lbs. **Move pump gradually when adjusting timing. On V8 engines, the width of the adapter timing mark is equal to approximately 1 degree. On V6 and 1985 V8 engines, the width of the mark is equal to approximately 2/3 of a degree.**
13. Start engine and recheck timing. Reset timing, if necessary.
14. On V8 engines, adjust pump rod.
15. On all engines, reset curb and fast idle speeds.
16. Disconnect timing meter and install removed glow plug. Torque glow plug to 12 (V8) or 15 (V6) ft. lbs.
17. Connect generator two lead connector, install air cleaner assembly and reconnect EGR valve hose.

The timing marks on the injection pump and adapter should be close to being lined up after timing the engine. If they are not, and the engine still exhibits poor performance, the timing may still be incorrect. A misfiring cylinder can result in incorrect timing. When this occurs, it is necessary that timing be checked in an alternate cylinder. Timing can be checked in cylinders 2 or 3 on V8 engines, or 1 or 4 on V6 engines. If a difference exists between cylinders, try both positions to determine which timing performs best.

If the engine continues to run poorly and excessive exhaust smoke is evident, check the housing pressure cold advance for proper operation. If the advance is operating properly, a stuck or frozen injection pump advance piston may be at fault. This piston can be checked by pushing in on the bottom of the face cam lever on the right side of the injection pump. If the piston is free, the timing will retard and cause the engine to run roughly. If no change is evident, the piston is sticking and must be repaired.

FUEL INJECTION PUMP HOUSING FUEL PRESSURE CHECK

1982–83

1. Remove air crossover and install screened covers J-29657 (V6 engines) or J-26996-10 (V8 engines) or equivalent.
2. Remove fuel return pressure tap plug or torque screw, **Figs. 3 and 4.** If equipped with torque screw, add second nut to locknut and back out screw with nuts attached to avoid disturbing the adjustment.
3. Install the seal from the pressure tap plug on the pressure tap adapter, tool J-28526, then install the adapter into pump housing.
4. Connect a low pressure gauge to the adapter.
5. Connect pickup tachometer, tool J-26925, to the engine.
6. Check pressure with engine operating at 1000 RPM in Park. The pressure should be 8-12 psi with no more than a 2 psi fluctuation.
7. If pressure reading is zero on 1982-83 models, check operation of housing pressure cold advance as follows:
   a. Disconnect housing cold pressure advance electrical connector.
   b. If pressure reading is still zero, remove injection pump cover and check operation of advance solenoid. Repair or replace as necessary.
   c. If pressure is as specified with housing cold pressure advance electrical connector disconnected, check operation of temperature switch located on cylinder head bolt.
8. If pressure is still low, replace fuel return line connector assembly. If pressure is too high, fuel return system or HPAA may be restricted. Remove return line at injection pump. Install fitting and short piece of hose to allow return flow to empty into a small container.
9. If pressure is lower than before, correct restriction in fuel line.
10. If pressure is still too high, replace fuel return line connector assembly. If assembly is replaced check injection pump timing and adjust if necessary.
11. If pressure remains too high, remove injection pump for repair.
12. Remove tachometer, pressure gauge and adapter.
13. Install a new pressure tap plug seal on the pressure tap plug and install plug into housing.
14. Remove screened covers and install air crossover.

1984

1. Ensure proper operation of temperature switch on EGR thermostatic vacuum switch.

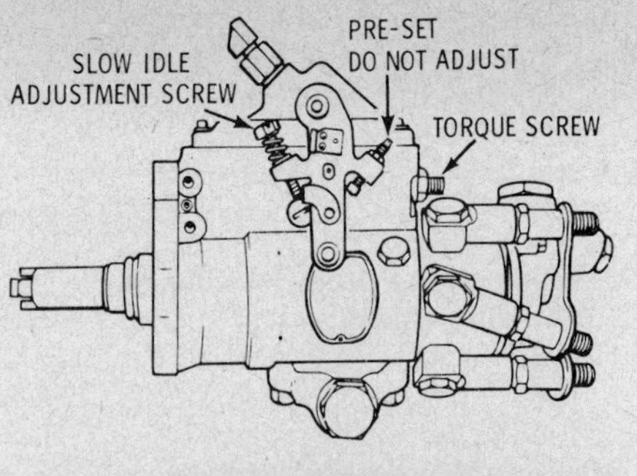

Fig. 4 Fuel injection pump housing torque screw. 1982–83 V6 engine

2. Remove air cleaner and install screened cover No. J-26996-1, or equivalent.
3. Disconnect fuel return line from return line connector, then remove the connector from injection pump cover.
4. Push HPCA solenoid plunger into the solenoid, then disconnect electrical connector from HPCA terminal, **Fig. 5.**
5. Apply 12 volts to HPCA terminal, using a suitable jumper, and observe solenoid plunger. If plunger does not extend fully, remove pump cover and repair or replace solenoid as necessary.
6. Install adapter No. J-34151 into pump cover and attach return line to adapter.
7. Attach a low pressure gauge to adapter, then install magnetic pickup tachometer No. J-26925 or equivalent.
8. Check housing pressure at 1000 RPM with transmission in Park, parking brake applied and drive wheels blocked. Compare recorded pressure to specifications in chart, **Fig. 6.**
9. If pressure is low, replace fuel return line connector assembly.
10. If pressure is high, proceed as follows:
    a. Disconnect return line from adapter pump.
    b. Install a suitable fitting and length of hose to allow return fuel flow to to drain into a small container, then recheck pressure.
    c. If pressure is lower than original reading, locate and correct restriction in fuel line.
    d. If pressure is still high, replace fuel return line connector assembly.
    e. If pressure remains high, remove injection pump and repair or replace as necessary.
11. Remove tachometer, pressure gauge and adapter.
12. Install fuel return line connector into pump cover, using a new O-ring.
13. Connect fuel return line to return line connector.
14. Start engine and check for leaks.
15. Remove screened covers and reinstall air cleaner.

1985

1. Block drive wheels, apply parking brake and shift transmission to Park.
2. Start engine and run until normal operating temperature is reached, then stop engine.

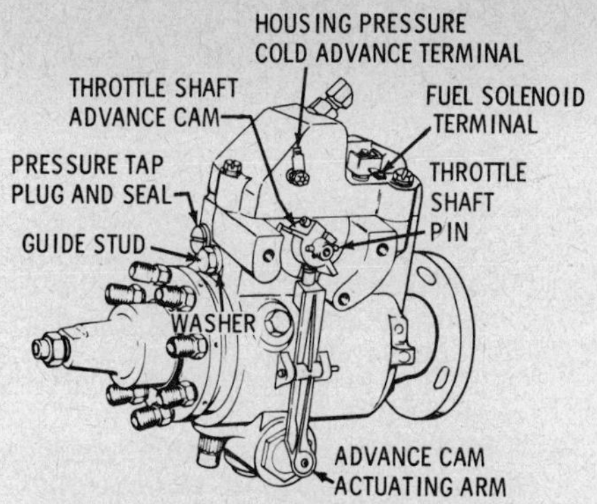

Fig. 5 Fuel injection pump connections. 1984

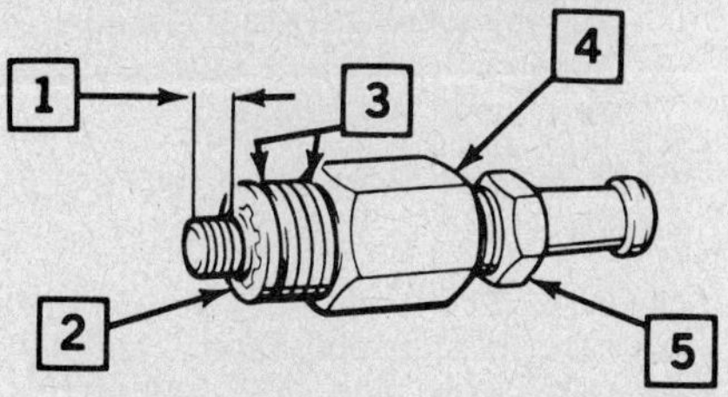

1. 3 MM (3/32")
2. PART NO. 561888 OR EQUIVALENT
3. FLAT WASHERS
4. J-28526
5. FITTING

Fig. 7 Housing pressure checking tool adapter. 1985

3. Remove air cleaner cover.
4. Remove MAP sensor retainer, then position sensor aside with leads and vacuum hose connected.
5. Remove air cleaner assembly and the air crossover.
6. Remove MVS adjustment hole plug.
7. Install washers onto adapter No. J-28526, **Fig. 7,** then attach a suitable pressure gauge to adapter.
8. Disconnect electrical connector from HPCA solenoid and the HPAA solenoid connector from engine harness.
9. Connect suitable tachometer to engine, then start engine. Check for fuel leaks and correct if necessary.
10. Raise engine speed to 1000 RPM and check housing pressure reading.
11. If pressure reading in step 10 is below 5 psi, proceed as follows:
    a. Remove pressure regulator from injection pump.
    b. Apply a minimum of 30 psi air pressure to regulator, first from pump side, then from outlet side. The check ball should seat when air is applied to outlet side.
    c. Replace pressure regulator if operation is not as described.
    d. Reconnect electrical connector to HPCA solenoid, ensuring wire colors are properly matched.
    e. Turn ignition switch to Run position and ensure solenoid plunger extends upward.
    f. Turn ignition switch to Off or Lock position and ensure plunger retracts automatically or can be made to do so with a light pressure applied.

	CONDITION: ALTITUDE	CONDITION: COOLANT	HPCA	HPAA	NOMINAL HOUSING PRESSURE kPa (psi)
FEDERAL PACKAGE	BELOW 1219m (4000 FT.)	COLD	ON	OFF	0
	BELOW 1219m (4000 FT.)	HOT	OFF	OFF	68.9 (10)
	ABOVE 1219m (4000 FT.)	COLD	ON	OFF	0
	ABOVE 1219m (4000 FT.)	HOT	ON	ON	48.3 (7)
ALTITUDE PACKAGE	ABOVE 1219m (4000 FT.)	COLD	ON	OFF	0
	ABOVE 1219m (4000 FT.)	HOT	OFF	OFF	68.9 (10)
	BELOW 1219m (4000 FT.)	COLD	ON	OFF	0
	BELOW 1219m (4000 FT.)	HOT	OFF	ON	89.6 (13)

HPCA = HOUSING PRESSURE COLD ADV. HPAA = HOUSING PRESSURE ALTITUDE ADV.
TIMING RETARDS WITH HIGHER HOUSING PRESSURE

Fig. 6 Injection pump housing pressure specifications. 1984

    g. Replace HPCA solenoid if operation is not as described.
12. If pressure reading in step 10 is 5-9 psi, proceed as follows:
    a. Stop engine, then remove line fitting from pressure regulator.
    b. Insert a suitable hex head key into pressure regulator and rotate adjustment screw as necessary to obtain 10 psi pressure reading.
    c. Check injection timing and adjust as necessary.
    d. Check operation of pressure regulator and HPCA solenoid as described in step 11.
13. If pressure reading in step 10 is 9-11 psi, proceed as follows:
    a. Reconnect HPCA and HPAA electrical connectors and recheck pressure. If pressure reading rises, proceed to step 13b. If pressure reading drops to below 6 psi or above 8 psi, proceed to step 13c. If pressure reading does not change, either the HPCA or HPAA is defective.
    b. Disconnect HPAA electrical connector. If pressure reading is now 9-11 psi, the HPCA is defective. If pressure reading drops to zero, check and adjust HPAA as described in steps 15 and 16.
    c. Disconnect HPAA electrical connector. If pressure drops or does not change, check and adjust HPAA as described in steps 15 and 16.
14. If pressure reading in step 10 is above 11 psi, proceed as follows:
    a. Disconnect fuel return line from HPAA inlet. Install a suitable hose over pipe outlet and position opposite end of hose in a small container.
    b. Start engine and observe pressure reading.
    c. If pressure reading does not change, perform step 12 above.
    d. If pressure reading is 9-11 psi, check for restriction in return line or HPAA and correct as necessary. If no restriction is found, proceed to step 14e.
    e. Reconnect pump return line to HPAA solenoid inlet and disconnect return line from HPAA solenoid outlet. Install a suitable hose over outlet and position opposite end of hose in a small container.
    f. Start engine and observe pressure. If pressure is still high, check and adjust HPAA as described in steps 15 and 16.

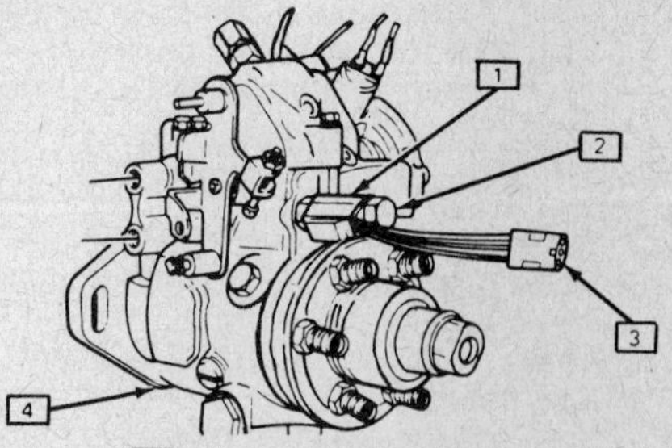

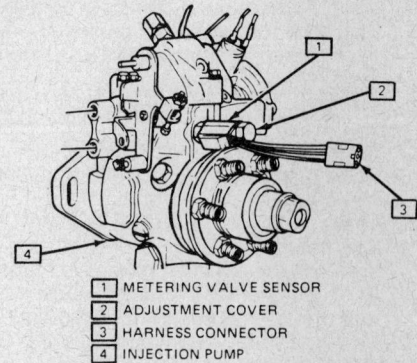

1 METERING VALVE SENSOR
2 ADJUSTMENT COVER
3 HARNESS CONNECTOR
4 INJECTION PUMP

Fig. 8 Metering valve sensor. 1984 V6 engine, Calif.

15. Check HPAA solenoid and pressure regulator operation as follows:
    a. Remove HPAA solenoid from engine.
    b. Apply a minimum of 30 psi air pressure to assembly, first from pump side, then from outlet side.
    c. If air does not flow freely in both directions, replace solenoid.
    d. Remove pressure regulator from solenoid. If solenoid plunger does not move freely, the solenoid must be replaced.
16. To adjust HPAA solenoid, proceed as follows:
    a. Install HPAA solenoid assembly.
    b. Disconnect electrical connector from MAP sensor.
    c. Start engine and note housing pressure, which should now read 6-8 psi.
    d. If pressure reading is not within specifications, remove HPAA assembly from engine and the line fitting from pressure regulator. Insert a suitable hex key into regulator and turn adjustment screw as necessary to bring reading within specifications.
    e. Install HPAA assembly and recheck housing pressure.

METERING VALVE SENSOR

Used on 1984 California V6-262 and 1985 V8-350 engines with Diesel Electronic Control System, the metering valve sensor, **Figs. 8 and 9,** is a variable type resistor that electrically signals the diesel ECM as to metering valve position.

TESTING

1984

1. Block drive wheels, apply parking brake and place transmission in Park.
2. Start engine, allow it to reach normal operating temperature, then shut engine off.
3. Remove air cleaner.
4. Remove air crossover, then install cover J-29657, or equivalent.
5. Disconnect metering valve sensor harness and attach test harness J-34678 or BT-8342 as shown, **Fig. 10.**
6. Install tachometer J-26925, or equivalent, then torque metering valve sensor to pump attaching bolts to 30 inch lbs.
7. Start engine, accelerate to 1500 RPM for 10-20 seconds to stabilize fuel flow, then return engine to idle.
8. Place transmission in Drive and set idle speed to 650 RPM.
9. Using voltmeter J-29124, or equivalent, set meter at 20V scale and measure voltage between terminals A and C of test harness, **Fig. 10.** Observe and record voltage (V-REF) reading.
10. Measure voltage between terminals B and C of test harness. Observe and record MVS voltage reading.
11. Shift transmission into Park, then compare voltages recorded in steps 9 and 10 with specifications in chart, **Fig. 11.** Voltages should be within ranges shown.
12. With gear selector in Park, measure voltage between terminals B and C as throttle is quickly opened to wide open throttle position. Voltage should range from less than 1 volt at idle to over 4 volts as throttle approaches wide open position.
13. If MVS voltage is as specified in steps 11 and 12, the sensor is operating properly. If voltage is not as specified, proceed to "Adjustment" procedure.
14. Connect sensor harness, start engine and adjust idle speed to specifications.
15. Install air crossover, then the air cleaner.

1985

1. Block drive wheels, apply parking brake and shift transmission to Park.

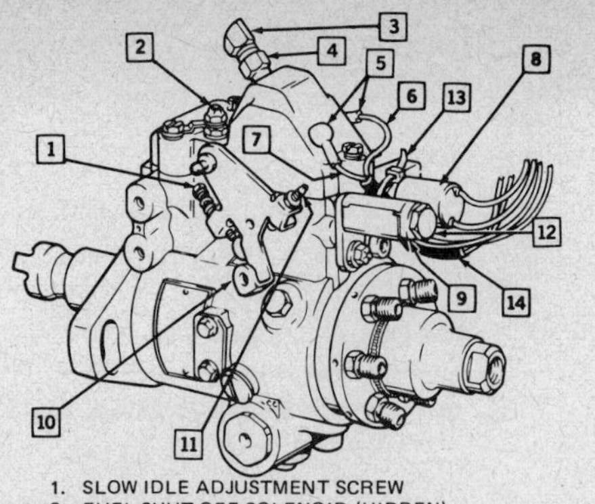

1. SLOW IDLE ADJUSTMENT SCREW
2. FUEL SHUT-OFF SOLENOID (HIDDEN)
3. TO FUEL RETURN LINE
4. FUEL RETURN LINE CONNECTOR
5. HOUSING PRESSURE COLD ADVANCE LEADS
6. PINK-BLACK
7. GREEN-BLACK
8. ALTITUDE FUEL LIMITER
9. METERING VALVE SENSOR (MVS)
10. THROTTLE LEVER
11. DO NOT ADJUST
12. MVS ADJ. HOLE PLUG
13. STRAP
14. PROTECTOR SLEEVE

Fig. 9 Metering valve sensor. 1985

2. Start engine and run until normal operating temperature is reached, then stop engine.
3. Remove air cleaner cover and MAP sensor retainer.
4. Position MAP sensor aside, leaving electrical connectors and vacuum line connected, then remove air cleaner assembly.
5. Remove air crossover and install screened covers No. J-26996-10.
6. Disconnect electrical connector from HPAA solenoid.
7. Disconnect MVS harness and install harness adapter, **Fig. 12.**
8. Connect suitable tachometer to engine.
9. Start engine and run at 1500 RPM for 10-20 seconds, then return to idle.
10. Ensure parking brake is still applied and drive wheels are blocked, then shift transmission to Drive.
11. Adjust idle speed to 600 RPM.
12. Measure and record voltage between terminals A and C, **Fig. 12.** This will be considered the V-Ref voltage.
13. Measure and record voltage between terminals B and C, **Fig. 12.** This is the MVS voltage.
14. Compare voltages recorded in steps 12 and 13 to specifications in chart, **Fig. 13.**
15. Shift transmission to Park and measure voltage between terminals B and C while quickly moving throttle between idle and wide open positions. Voltage should go from less than 1 volt at idle to more than 4 volts at wide open throttle.
16. If MVS voltages are within specifications, the sensor is operating properly. If voltages are not within specifications, proceed to adjustment procedure.
17. Reconnect HPAA solenoid connector and the MVS electrical connectors.
18. Install air crossover, MAP sensor and air cleaner assembly.

ADJUSTMENT

1984

1. With engine off, hold metering valve sensor assembly and carefully remove hole plug. Use caution to prevent sensor assembly from moving.
2. Using tool J-24182-2, or equivalent, turn adjustment screw clockwise to increase voltage reading, or counterclockwise to decrease reading. Turn adjustment screw in 1/8 turn increments. **It may be necessary to file tool J-24182-2, to enable it to enter sensor assembly.**
3. Install hole plug finger tight, then perform steps 7 through 11 of testing procedure. If voltages are not within chart specifications, readjust sensor as necessary.
4. Install hole plug using a new O-ring seal, then hold sensor assembly and torque hole plug to 30 inch lbs.
5. Connect sensor harness, start engine and check for fuel leaks.
6. Adjust idle speed to specifications, then install air crossover and air cleaner.

1985

1. With engine not running, remove MVS adjusting hole plug.
2. Using tool No. 34829, turn MVS adjustment screw clockwise to increase

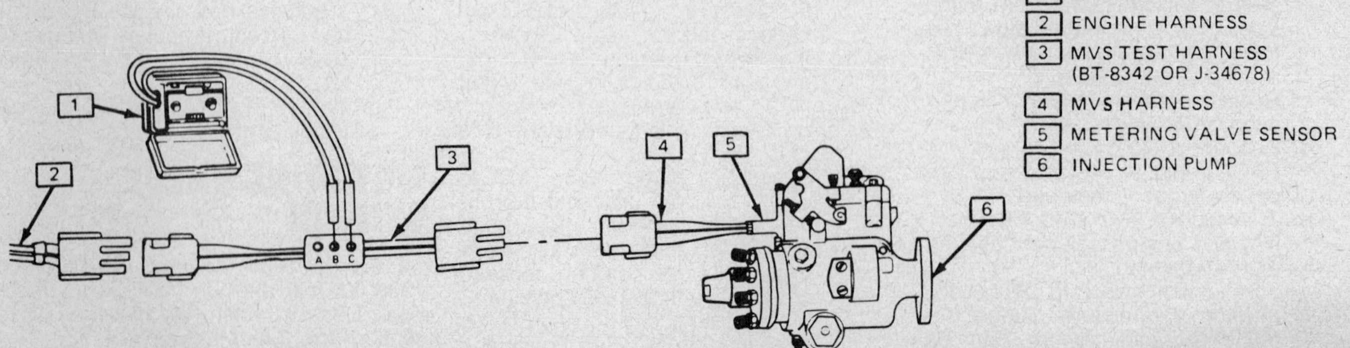

Fig. 10 Metering valve sensor test connections. 1984

MVS VOLTAGE TABLE

V-REF	4.5	4.6	4.7	4.8	4.9	5.0	5.1	5.2	5.3	5.4	5.5
MVS VOLTAGE (In "D" 650 RPM)	.53-.55	.54-.56	.55-.57	.57-.59	.58-.60	.59-.61	.60-.62	.61-.63	.63-.65	.64-.66	.65-.67

Fig. 11 Metering valve sensor voltage chart. 1984

MVS VOLTAGE TABLE

V-REF	4.0	4.1	4.2	4.3	4.4	4.5	4.6	4.7
MVS VOLTAGE	.47 - .49	.48 - .50	.49 - .51	.50 - .52	.51 - .54	.53 - .55	.54 - .56	.55 - .57
V-REF	4.8	4.9	5.0	5.1	5.2	5.3	5.4	5.5
MVS VOLTAGE	.57 - .59	.58 - .60	.59 - .61	.60 - .62	.61 -.63	.63 - .65	.64 - .66	.65 - .67

Fig. 13 Metering valve sensor voltage chart. 1985

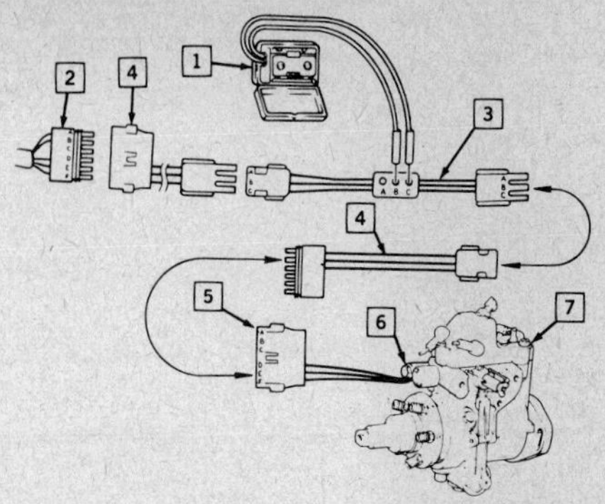

1. DIGITAL VOLTMETER
2. ENGINE HARNESS
3. MVS TEST HARNESS (BT-8342 OR J-34678)
4. MVS ADAPTER HARNESS (BT-8342-10 OR J-34678-50)
5. MVS HARNESS
6. METERING VALVE SENSOR (MVS)
7. INJECTION PUMP

Fig. 12 Metering valve sensor test connections. 1985

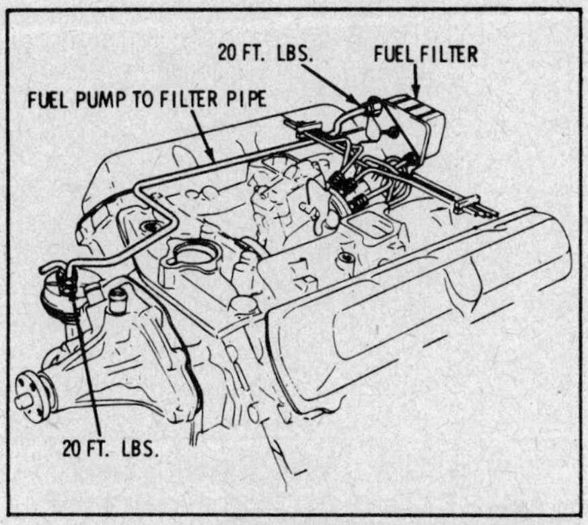

Fig. 14 Fuel filter & lines. V8 engine

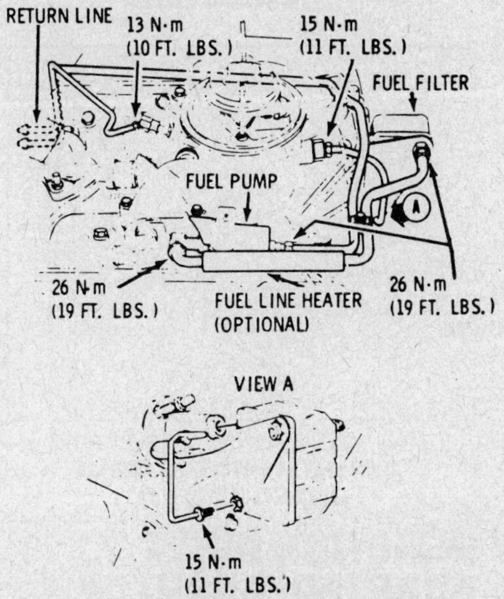

Fig. 15 Fuel filter & lines. V6 engine

voltage reading or counterclockwise to decrease voltage reading. Turn adjustment screw in 1/8 turn increments.

3. Install adjusting hole plug finger tight, then recheck voltages as described previously.
4. If voltages are not within specifications, readjust sensor as necessary.
5. Install hole plug using a new O-ring, then torque plug to 30 inch lbs.
6. Reconnect MVS electrical connector, then start engine and check for fuel leaks.
7. Install air crossover and air cleaner.

INJECTION PUMP REPLACE

INJECTION PUMP & LINES

Removal

1. Disconnect ground cables from batteries.
2. Remove air cleaner.
3. Remove filters and pipes from valve covers and air crossover.
4. Remove air crossover and plug intake manifold.
5. Disconnect throttle rod and return spring on V8 engines or throttle cable and TV detent cable from pump throttle lever.
6. Remove bellcrank.
7. Remove throttle and throttle valve cables from intake manifold brackets and position cables aside.
8. Remove fuel lines to fuel filter, then the fuel filter, **Figs. 14 and 15.**
9. Disconnect fuel line at fuel pump and remove fuel line. If equipped with A/C, remove rear compressor brace.
10. Disconnect fuel return line from injection pump, **Figs. 15 and 16.**
11. Slide clamp from fuel return lines at injector nozzles and remove fuel return lines from each bank.
12. Disconnect injection pump lines at injector nozzles, **Fig. 17.** It is necessary to use two wrenches.
13. Remove nuts retaining injection pump with tool No. J-26987.
14. Remove injection pump and cap all lines and fittings.

Installation

1. Align offset tang on pump driveshaft with pump driven gear, **Fig. 18,** and install injector pump.
2. Loosely install the injector pump retaining nuts and lock washers. Connect fuel lines to injector pump and torque line fittings to 25 ft. lbs., **Fig. 17.**
3. Connect fuel return lines to injector nozzles and injector pump.
4. Align mark on injection pump with line on adapter and torque retaining nuts to 18 ft. lbs. on V8 engines or 35 ft. lbs. on V6 engines.
5. Adjust throttle rod.
6. Install fuel line from fuel pump to fuel filter, **Figs. 14 and 15.** If equipped with A/C, install rear compressor brace.
7. Install bellcrank and hairpin clip.
8. Install throttle and throttle valve cables, to intake manifold brackets and attach to bellcrank. Adjust throttle valve cable.
9. Connect throttle rod and return spring on V8 engines or throttle cable and TV cable on V6 engines.
10. Crank engine and check for fuel leaks.
11. Remove plugs from intake manifold and install air crossover.
12. Install tubes in flow control valve in air crossover and ventilation filters in valve covers.
13. Install air cleaner.

INJECTION PUMP

Removal

1. Disconnect battery ground cable and remove air cleaner assembly.
2. Remove crankcase ventilation filters and pipes from the valve covers and air crossover.
3. Remove the air crossover and install intake manifold screened covers J-26996-10.
4. Disconnect the throttle rod and throttle return spring.
5. Remove bellcrank.
6. Remove throttle and TV detent cables from intake manifold brackets and position cables aside.
7. Remove fuel lines to fuel filter, then the fuel filter, **Figs. 14 and 15.**
8. Disconnect fuel line at fuel pump and remove fuel line. If equipped with A/C remove rear compressor brace.
9. Disconnect fuel return line from injection pump, **Figs. 15 and 16.**
10. Disconnect the injection line clamps closest to pump.
11. Disconnect the injection lines from pump and cap all openings.
12. Remove three nuts retaining injection pump, using tool No. J-26987.

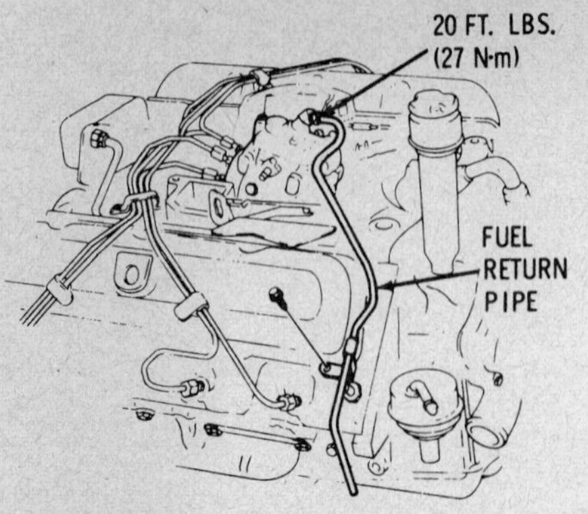

Fig. 16 Fuel return line

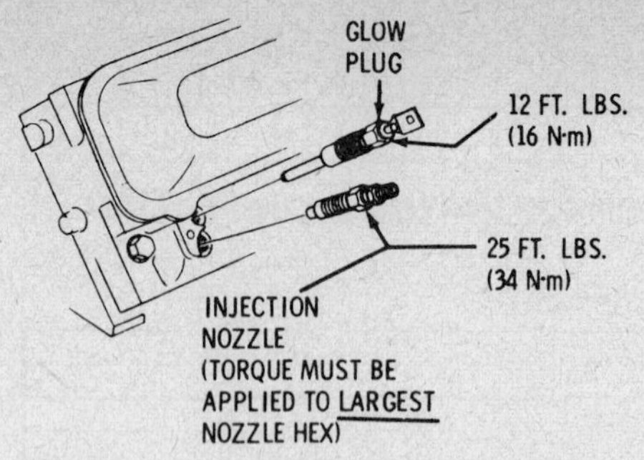

Fig. 17 Injection nozzle installation

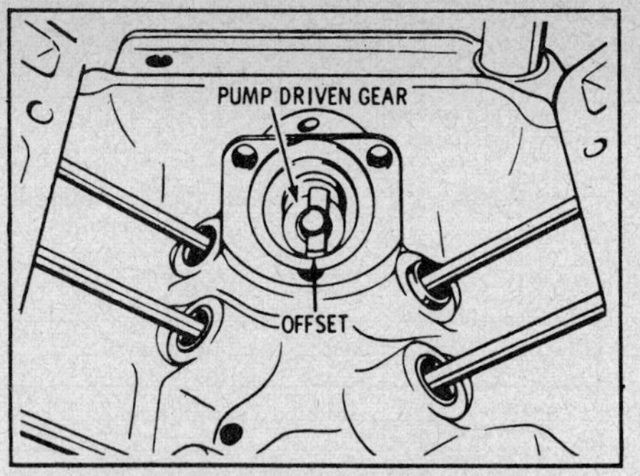

Fig. 18 Offset on fuel injection pump driven gear

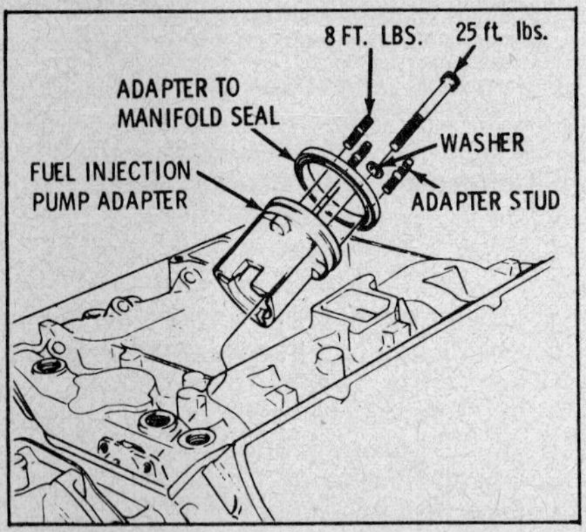

Fig. 19 Fuel injection pump adapter installation

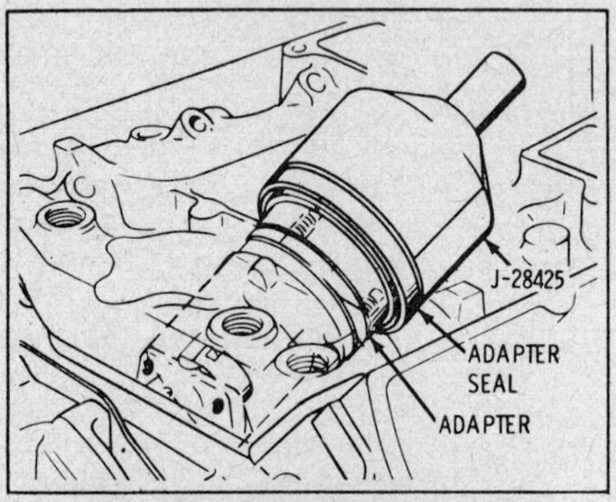

Fig. 20 Fuel injection pump adapter seal installation

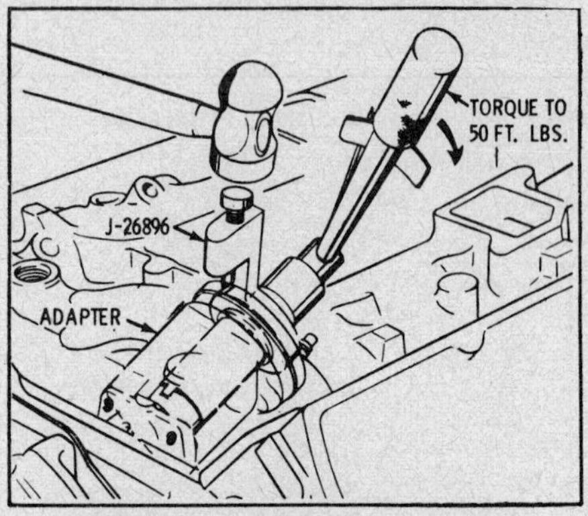

Fig. 21 Marking fuel injection pump adapter w/new timing mark

13. Remove pump and discard the pump to adapter O-ring.

Installation

1. Align offset tang on pump driveshaft with pump driven gear, **Fig. 18.**
2. Install new pump to adapter O-ring, then install the pump fully seating pump by hand.
3. Align mark on injection pump with line on adapter and torque retaining nuts to 18 ft. lbs.
4. Remove caps from the openings and connect the injection lines to the pump.
5. Install injection line clamps.
6. Connect the fuel return line.
7. Reconnect the fuel line at the fuel pump. If equipped with A/C, install the rear compressor brace.
8. Install the fuel filter and fuel filter to injection pump line.
9. Install throttle and TV detent cables on intake manifold.
10. Install bellcrank.
11. Install throttle rod and throttle return spring.
12. Remove screened covers from intake manifold, then install air crossover.
13. Install pipes and hoses in the air crossover and ventilation filters in valve covers.
14. Install air cleaner assembly and connect battery ground cable.

INJECTION PUMP ADAPTER, ADAPTER SEAL & NEW TIMING MARK

1. Remove injection pump as outlined previously.
2. Remove injection pump adapter, **Fig. 19.**
3. Remove seal from injection pump adapter.
4. File mark off injection pump adapter. Do not file mark from injection pump.
5. Position engine to No. 1 cylinder firing position. Align marks on balancer with zero mark on indicator. The injection pump driven gear should be offset to the right when No. 1 cylinder is at top dead center.
6. Loosely install injection pump adapter.
7. Install seal in injection pump adapter with tool J-28425, **Fig. 20.**
8. Torque injection pump adapter bolts to 25 ft. lbs.
9. Install timing tool J-26896 into injection pump adapter. Rotate torque wrench counterclockwise to obtain a 50 ft. lbs. reading, then mark injection pump adapter, **Fig. 21.**
10. Install injection pump as outlined previously.

INJECTION NOZZLE
REPLACE

Injection nozzle body leaks may be corrected by loosening the inlet fitting and re-torquing to 45 ft. lbs. on DED type injection nozzles, and 19 ft. lbs. on CAV type injection nozzles, Fig. 22. In the event this does not correct the leak, remove the inlet fitting. Using a piece of crocus cloth, press and rotate the end of the inlet fitting against the crocus cloth back and forth about six times. After polishing has been performed, flush inlet fitting using diesel fuel and install fitting onto pump.

1. Remove fuel lines, using a back-up wrench on upper injection nozzle hex.
2. Remove nozzle by applying torque to largest nozzle hex, **Fig. 17.**
3. Cap nozzle and lines to prevent entry of dirt. Also remove copper gasket from cylinder head if gasket did not remain with nozzle.
4. Reverse procedure to install. Torque nozzle to 25 ft. lbs. When tightening nozzle, torque must be applied to largest nozzle hex. Torque fuel line to 25 ft. lbs. using a back-up wrench on upper injection nozzle hex.

TRANSMISSION VACUUM VALVE
REPLACE

1. Note location of the valve vacuum hoses, then disconnect the vacuum hoses.
2. Remove the two valve attaching bolts and the valve.
3. Reverse procedure to install.

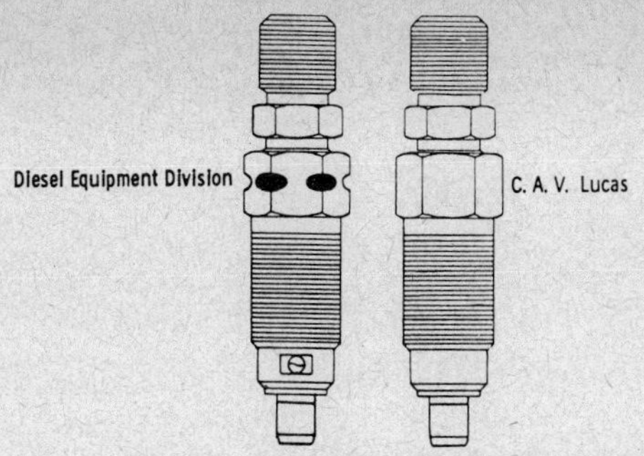

Fig. 22 Injection nozzle identification

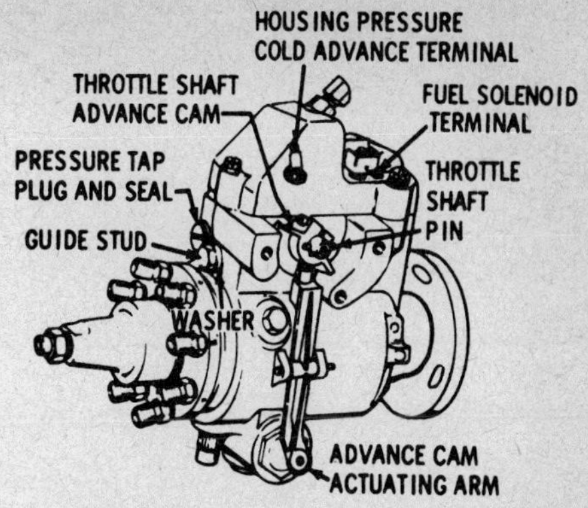

Fig. 23 Injection pump right side view. V8 engine

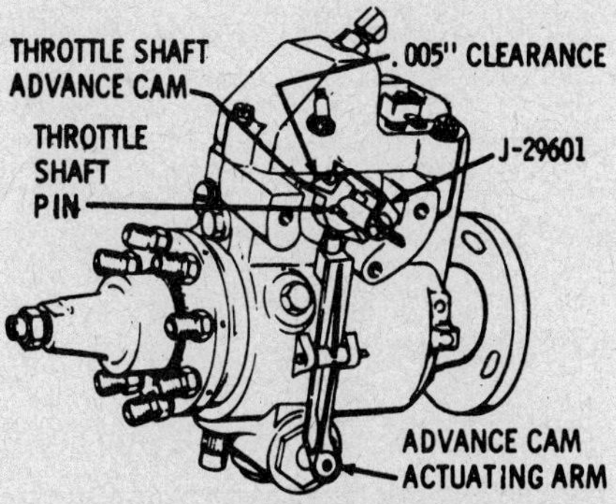

Fig. 24 Installing tool J-29601 on injection pump. V8 engine

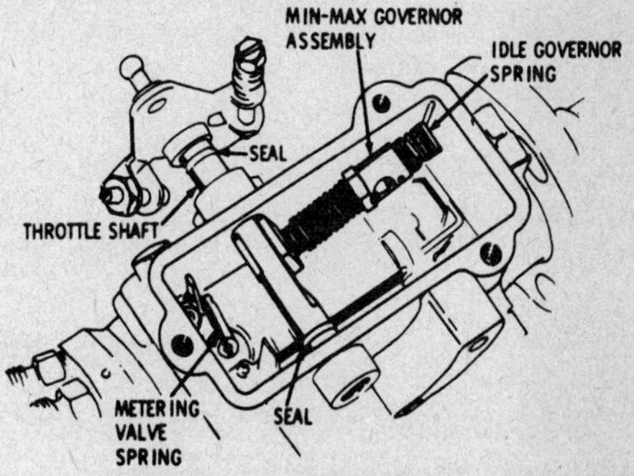

Fig. 25 Injection pump w/cover removed. V8 engine

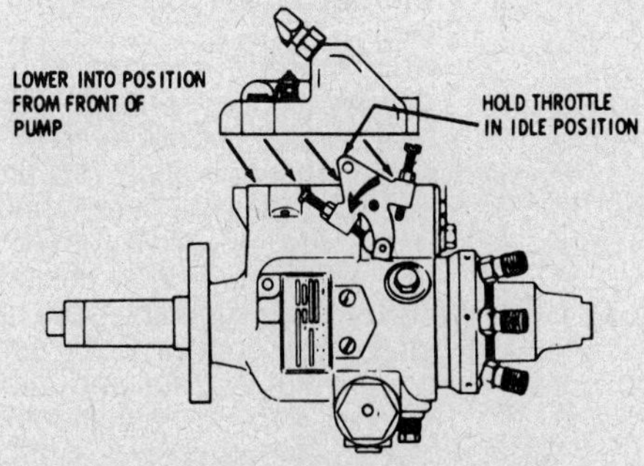

Fig. 26 Installing injection pump cover. V8 engine

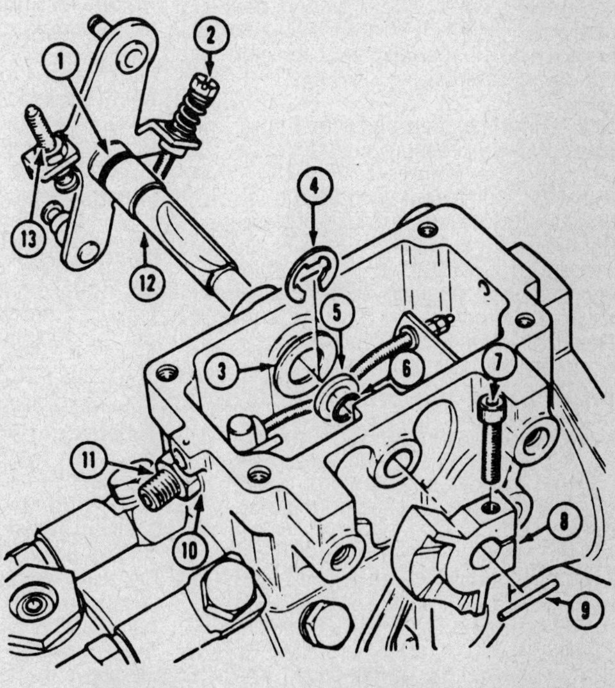

1. Rubber "O" ring
2. Idling adjuster screw
3. Thrust washer
4. "E" type circlip
5. Thrust washer
6. Rubber "O" ring
7. Clamp screw
8. Light load advance cam
9. Pin
10. Locknut and rubber "O" ring
11. Torque screw
12. Throttle shaft
13. Maximum speed adjustment screw (Do not adjust)

Fig. 27 Throttle shaft & seals. V6 engine

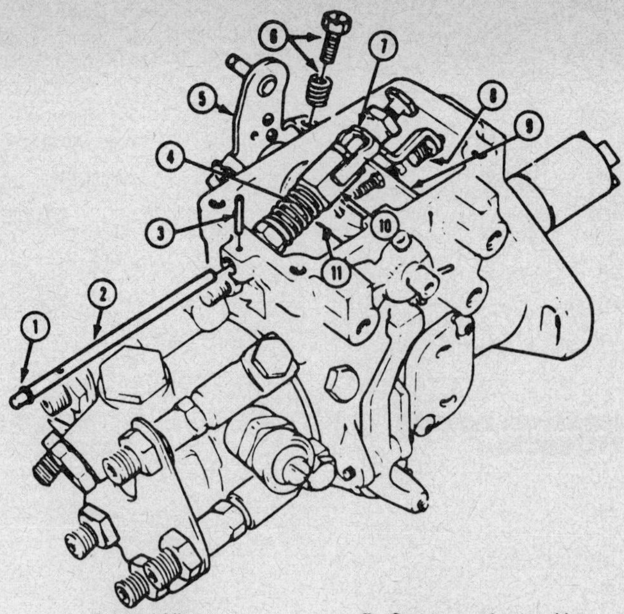

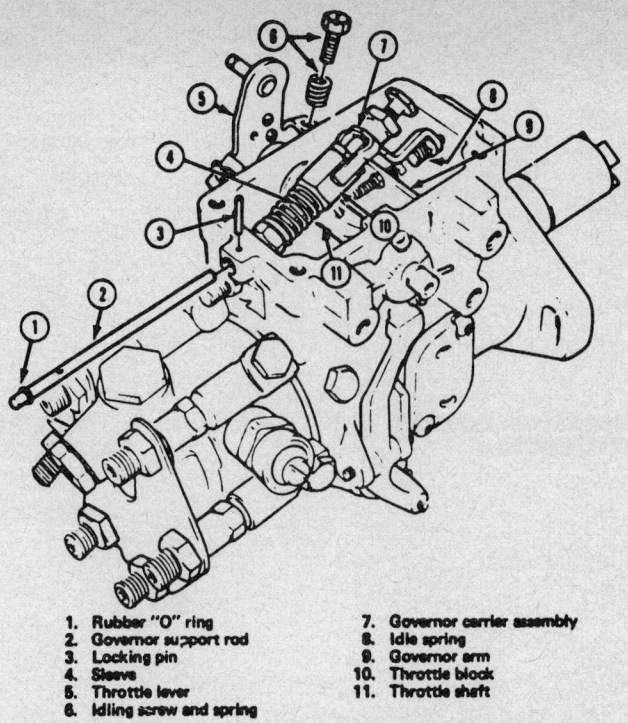

1. Rubber "O" ring
2. Governor support rod
3. Locking pin
4. Sleeve
5. Throttle lever
6. Idling screw and spring
7. Governor carrier assembly
8. Idle spring
9. Governor arm
10. Throttle block
11. Throttle shaft

Fig. 28 Governor assembly. V6 engine

THROTTLE SHAFT SEAL REPLACE

V8 ENGINE

1. Disconnect both battery ground cables.
2. Remove air cleaner and air crossover and install air screens J-26996-2 or J-26996-10.
3. Disconnect injection pump fuel solenoid, housing pressure cold advance wires and fuel return pipe, **Fig. 23.**
4. Remove throttle rod, vacuum regulator valve, return spring and throttle cable bracket.
5. Place tool J-29601 over throttle shaft and pin, then position spring clip of tool over throttle shaft advance cam and tighten wing nut. Without loosening wing nut, pull tool off shaft. This will provide proper alignment during reassembly, **Fig. 24.**
6. Drive pin from throttle shaft and remove shaft advance cam and fiber washer. Remove any burrs from shaft which may have resulted from pin removal.
7. Clean injection pump cover, upper portion of pump, throttle shaft and guide stud area. Position several shop cloths in engine valley area to absorb fuel.
8. Remove injection pump cover and screws. **Use care to avoid any foreign matter from entering pump when cover is removed. If any object or foreign matter enter pump, it must be removed before engine is started as injection pump damage or engine damage may occur.**
9. Note position of metering valve spring before removal as its position must be duplicated exactly during reassembly, **Fig. 25.**
10. Remove guide stud and washer, noting parts before removal.
11. Rotate min-max governor assembly up for clearance then remove it, **Fig. 25.** If idle governor spring becomes disengaged from throttle block, it must be reinstalled with tightly wound coils toward throttle block.
12. Remove throttle shaft assembly and inspect shaft for unusual wear or damage, replace if necessary. It may be necessary to loosen nuts at injection pump mounting flange and rotate pump slightly to allow throttle shaft to clear intake manifold.
13. Inspect throttle shaft bushings in pump housing for damage or unusual wear. If replacement of bushings is necessary, it must be performed by a qualified repair facility.
14. Remove throttle shaft seals. Do not cut seals to remove, as any nicks in the seal seat will cause leakage.
15. Install new shaft seals, lubricated with chassis grease. Use care to avoid cutting seals on sharp edges of shaft.
16. Carefully slide throttle shaft into pump to point where min-max governor assembly will slide back onto throttle shaft, **Fig. 25.**
17. Rotate min-max governor assembly downward, then hold in position and slide throttle shaft and governor into position.
18. Install new fiber washer, throttle shaft advance cam (do not tighten screw at this time) and a new throttle shaft drive pin, **Fig. 23.**
19. Align throttle shaft advance cam so tool J-20601 can be installed over throttle shaft, pins in slots and spring clip over advance cam.
20. Insert a .005 inch feeler gauge between cam and fiber washer, then tighten cam screw and remove tool J-29601.
21. Install guide stud with new washer, assuring that upper extension of metering valve spring slides on top of guide stud. Torque guide studs to 85 inch lbs. **Over torquing may strip the aluminum threads in the housing.**
22. Hold throttle in idle position and install new pump cover seal. Making sure that screws are not in cover, position cover about 1/4 inch forward toward shaft end and above 1/8 inch above pump, **Fig. 26.** Move cover rearward and downward into position, using care to avoid cutting seal, then reinstall cover screws. Each screw must have a flat washer and internal lock washer, with flat washer against pump cover. Torque screws to 37 inch lbs. and install vacuum regulator.
23. Reconnect both battery ground cables, then turn ignition switch to run position and touch pink solenoid wire to solenoid. A clicking noise should be heard as the wire is connected and disconnected. If not, the linkage may be jammed in the wide open position and the engine must not be started. Proceed to step 24. If clicking is heard, connect pump solenoid and housing pressure cold advance wires and proceed to step 25.
24. Remove cover, then ground solenoid lead (opposite hot lead) and connect

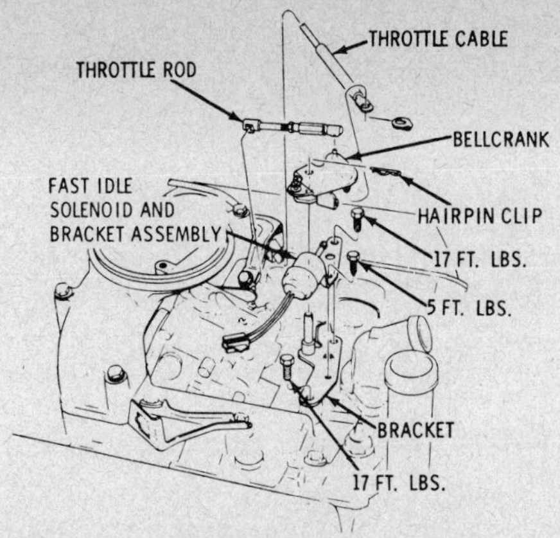

Fig. 29 Throttle linkage. V8 engine

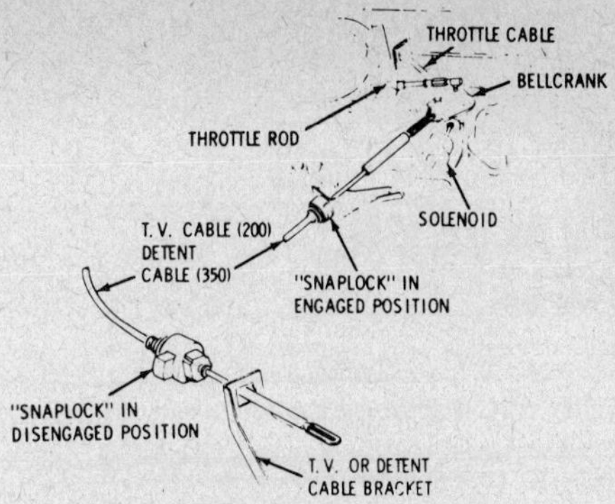

Fig. 30 Throttle valve or detent cable adjustment

pink wire. With ignition switch in run position, the solenoid in the cover should move the linkage. If not, the solenoid must be replaced. Minimum voltage across solenoid terminals must be 12 volts. Reinstall cover and repeat step 23.

25. Install throttle cable bracket, throttle rod, throttle cable and return springs. Make sure timing marks on pump and adapter are aligned and make sure nuts retaining pump are tight. Install fuel return pipe.
26. Start engine and check for fuel leaks. **Rough idle may be due to air in the pump. Allow sufficient time for air to purge by allowing engine to idle. It may be necessary to turn engine off to allow air bubbles to rise to top of pump where they will be purged.**
27. Adjust Transmission Vacuum Valve as described further on, then remove intake manifold screens and install air crossover and air cleaner.

V6 ENGINE

1. Remove air crossover and install cover J-29657 or equivalent.
2. Disconnect fuel return pipe, **Fig. 15**, then remove governor control cover screws and the cover.
3. Remove fast idle solenoid and vacuum regulator valve.
4. Disconnect throttle cable and TC detent cable.
5. Disconnect throttle return spring.
6. Install tool J-29601 or equivalent over throttle shaft with slots of tool engaging vacuum regulator valve lock pin. Place spring clip of tool over throttle shaft advance cam and tighten wing nut. Without loosening wing nut, pull tool off of shaft.
7. Remove lock pin from throttle shaft, **Fig. 27.**
8. Remove rollpin from pump housing and remove governor support rod.
9. Tilt governor carrier assembly by lifting end nearest drive end of pump and remove carrier from pump housing.
10. Remove clamping screw from light load cam, then remove cam.
11. Remove E-clip from throttle shaft, then remove throttle shaft from pump.
12. Remove and discard O-rings.
13. Check throttle shaft assembly and governor housing bores for damage and wear and replace as necessary.
14. Lubricate shaft and O-rings with oil and assemble larger O-rings onto shaft.
15. Install throttle shaft onto housing until thrust washers can be installed onto shaft in original positions. Install smaller O-ring onto shaft.
16. Assemble light load advance cam onto shaft and install but do not tighten clamping screw.
17. Install E clip into throttle shaft recess. If new throttle shaft is installed, shaft endplay must be checked and adjusted by selective fitting of thrust washers. Throttle shaft endplay should be .006-.012 inch.
18. Install new pin onto head of shaft. Align throttle shaft advance cam until tool J-29601 or equivalent can be installed over throttle shaft. Tighten cam screw, then remove tool J-29601.
19. Rotate throttle lever forward to the drive end of pump. Install governor carrier assembly onto pump housing and engage lug on underside of throttle block with cut away notch in throttle shaft.
20. Lubricate governor support rod and new O-ring, then install O ring onto support rod using tool J-33096 or equivalent.
21. Insert plain end of rod through rear of governor housing and into carrier assembly sleeve.
22. Install support rod into housing and install new new locking pin, **Fig. 28.**
23. Install governor cover and fuel return pipe.
24. Install throttle return springs and connect throttle cable.
25. Connect TV detent cable.
26. Install vacuum regulator valve and fast idle solenoid.
27. Start engine and check for leaks. Install air crossover and air cleaner.

PUMP COVER SEAL AND/OR GUIDE STUD
REPLACE

1. Disconnect both battery ground cables.
2. Remove air cleaner and air crossover and install air screens J-26996-2 or J-26996-10.
3. Disconnect injection pump fuel solenoid, housing pressure cold advance wires and fuel return pipe.
4. Clean injection pump cover, upper portion of pump and guide stud area. Position shop cloths to absorb fuel.
5. Remove injection pump cover, then remove screws from cover. **Use care to avoid any foreign matter from entering pump when cover is removed. If any object or foreign matter enter pump, it must be removed before starting engine as injection pump damage or engine damage may occur.**
6. Note position of metering valve spring before removal as its position must be duplicated exactly during reassembly, **Fig. 25.**
7. Remove guide stud and washer, noting location of parts before removal.
8. Refer to steps 21 thru 27 under "Throttle Shaft Seal, Replace" procedure for reassembly of "Pump Cover Seal And/Or Guide Stud."

THROTTLE ROD
ADJUST

1. If equipped with Cruise Control, remove clip from Cruise Control rod, then the rod from bellcrank.
2. Remove throttle valve cable from bellcrank, **Fig. 29.**
3. Loosen the throttle rod locknut and shorten the rod several turns.
4. Rotate the bellcrank to the full throttle stop, then lengthen the throttle rod until the injection pump lever contacts the injection pump full throttle stop. Release the bellcrank.
5. Tighten the throttle rod locknut.

6. Connect the throttle valve cable and Cruise Control rod, if equipped, to bellcrank.

THROTTLE VALVE OR DETENT CABLE

ADJUST

1. Remove throttle rod from bellcrank, **Fig. 30.**
2. Push snap lock to disengaged position.
3. Rotate bellcrank to full throttle stop position and push in snap lock until flush with cable end fitting. Release bellcrank.
4. Connect the throttle rod.

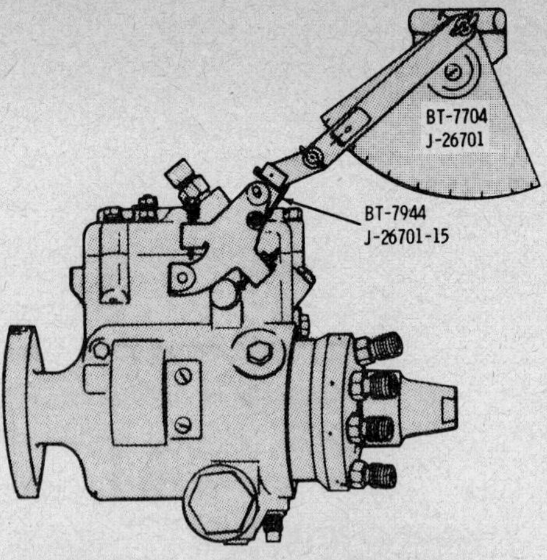

Fig. 31 Transmission vacuum valve adjustment (Typical)

TRANSMISSION VACUUM VALVE

ADJUST

1. Remove air crossover, then install screened covers J26996-2.
2. Remove throttle rod from throttle lever on V8 models or disconnect throttle cable and TV detent cable on V6 models, then loosen transmission vacuum valve injection pump bolts.
3. Install carburetor angle gauge J26701-15 and adapter on injection pump throttle lever, **Fig. 31.**
4. Rotate throttle lever to the wide open position and set angle gauge to zero degrees.
5. Center bubble in level, then set angle gauge to engines or 49° on V6 engines.
6. Rotate throttle lever so level bubble is centered.
7. Attach a suitable vacuum pump to center port of vacuum valve and install a vacuum gauge to outside port of vacuum valve, then apply 18-22 inches of vacuum.
8. Rotate vacuum valve clockwise to obtain 10.6 inches of vacuum, then tighten vacuum valve bolts. Remove vacuum gauge and vacuum pump.
9. Install throttle rod to bellcrank, on V8 models or connect throttle cable and TV detent cable on V6 models, then remove screened covers and install air crossover.

PURGING WATER FROM FUEL TANK

MODELS W/WATER IN FUEL DETECTOR

On these vehicles, any water in the fuel tank may be purged by siphoning or using a pump. The pump or siphon hose should be connected to the 1/4 inch fuel return hose (smaller of the two hoses) under the hood near the fuel pump. Purging should continue until all water is removed from the fuel tank. Also, remove fuel filler cap while purging, and replace cap when completed.

Use all safety precautions while handling the fuel/water mixture.

PONTIAC EXC. FIERO, 1000 & FRONT WHEEL DRIVE MODELS

INDEX OF SERVICE OPERATIONS

Specifications

GENERAL ENGINE SPECIFICATIONS

Year	Engine CID①/Liter	Engine VIN Code ②	Carburetor	Bore & Stroke	Compression Ratio	Net H.P. @ RPM③	Maximum Torque Ft. Lbs. @ RPM	Normal Oil Pressure Pounds
1982	4-151, 2.5L	2	T.B.I.	4.00 x 3.00	8.2	90 @ 4000	132 @ 2800	36-41
	V6-173, 2.8L④	1	E2SE, 2 Bbl.⑤	3.50 x 3.00	8.5	102 @ 4800	142 @ 2400	50-65
	V6-231, 3.8L⑦	A	E2ME, 2 Bbl.⑤	3.80 x 3.40	8.0	110 @ 3800	190 @ 1600	37
	V6-252, 4.1L⑦	4	E4ME, 4 Bbl.⑤	3.965 x 3.40	8.0	125 @ 3800	210 @ 2000	37
	V8-305, 5.0L④	H	E4ME, 4 Bbl.⑤	3.736 x 3.48	8.6	145 @ 4000	240 @ 2000	50-65
	V8-305, 5.0L④	7	T.B.I.	3.736 x 3.48	9.5	165 @ 4200	240 @ 2400	50-65
	V8-350, 5.7L⑥⑧	N	Fuel Injection	4.057 x 3.385	22.5	105 @ 3200	200 @ 1600	35
1983	4-151, 2.5L	2	T.B.I.	4.00 x 3.00	8.2	92 @ 4000	134 @ 2800	36-41
	V6-173, 2.8L④	1	E2SE, 2 Bbl.⑤	3.50 x 3.00	8.5	107 @ 4800	145 @ 2100	50-65
	V6-173 H.O., 2.8L④	L	E2SE, 2 Bbl.⑤	3.50 x 3.00	8.9	135 @ 5400	145 @ 2400	50-65
	V6-229, 3.8L④	9	E2ME, 2 Bbl.⑤	3.736 x 3.48	8.6	110 @ 4200	170 @ 2000	50-65
	V6-231, 3.8L⑦	A	E2ME, 2 Bbl.⑤	3.80 x 3.40	8.0	110 @ 3800	190 @ 1600	37
	V8-305, 5.0L④	H	E4ME, 4 Bbl.⑤	3.736 x 3.48	8.6	150 @ 4000	240 @ 2400	50-65
	V8-305, 5.0L④	S	T.B.I.	3.736 x 3.48	9.5	175 @ 4200	250 @ 2800	50-65
	V8-305 H.O., 5.0L④	G	E4ME, 4 Bbl.⑤	3.736 x 3.48	9.5	190 @ 4800	240 @ 3200	50-65
	V8-350, 5.7L⑥⑧	N	Fuel Injection	4.057 x 3.385	22.5	105 @ 3200	200 @ 1600	30-45
1984	4-151, 2.5L	2	T.B.I.	4.00 x 3.00	9.0	92 @ 4400	132 @ 2800	36-41
	V6-173, 2.8L④	1	E2SE, 2 Bbl.⑤	3.50 x 3.00	8.5	107 @ 4800	145 @ 2100	50-65
	V6-173 H.O., 2.8L④	L	E2SE, 2 Bbl.⑤	3.50 x 3.00	8.9	125 @ 5400	145 @ 2400	50-65
	V6-231, 3.8L⑦	A	E2ME, 2 Bbl.⑤	3.80 x 3.40	8.0	110 @ 3800	190 @ 1600	37
	V8-305, 5.0L④	H	E4ME, 4 Bbl.⑤	3.736 x 3.48	8.6	150 @ 4000	240 @ 2400	50-65
	V8-305, H.O., 5.0L④	G	E4ME, 4 Bbl.⑤	3.736 x 3.48	9.5	190 @ 4800	240 @ 3200	50-65
	V8-350, 5.7L⑥⑧	N	Fuel Injection	4.057 x 3.385	22.5	105 @ 3200	200 @ 1600	30-45
1985	4-151, 2.5L	2	T.B.I.	4.00 x 3.00	8.2	—	—	37.5
	V6-173, 2.8L④	S	M.F.I.	3.50 x 3.00	8.9	135 @ 5100	165 @ 3600	50-65
	V6-231, 3.8L⑦	A	E2ME, 2 Bbl.⑤	3.80 x 3.40	8.0	110 @ 3800	190 @ 1600	37
	V6-262, 4.3L④	Z	T.B.I.	4.00 x 3.48	9.3	130 @ 3600	210 @ 2000	50-65
	V8-305, 5.0L④	H	E4ME, 4 Bbl.⑤	3.736 x 3.48	9.5	165 @ 4200	245 @ 2400	50-65
	V8-305, H.O., 5.0L④	G	E4ME, 4 Bbl.⑤	3.736 x 3.48	9.5	—	—	50-65
	V8-305, TPI, 5.0L④	6	T.P.I.	3.736 x 3.48	9.5	215 @ 4400	275 @ 3200	—
	V8-350, 5.7L⑥⑧	N	Fuel Injection	4.057 x 3.385	21.6	105 @ 3200	200 @ 1600	30-45
1986	4-151, 2.5L	2	T.B.I.	4.00 x 3.00	9.0	88 @ 4400	132 @ 2800	37.5
	V6-173, 2.8L④	S	M.F.I.	3.50 x 3.00	8.5	140 @ 5200	170 @ 3600	50-65
	V6-231, 3.8L⑦	A	E2ME, 2 Bbl.⑤	3.80 x 3.40	8.0	110 @ 3800	190 @ 1600	37.5
	V6-262, 4.3L④	Z	T.B.I.	4.00 x 3.48	9.3	130 @ 3600	210 @ 2000	50-65
	V8-305, 5.0L④	H	E4ME, 4 Bbl.⑤	3.736 x 3.48	8.6	165 @ 4200	240 @ 2400	50-65
	V8-305, H.O. 5.0L④	G	E4ME, 4 Bbl.⑤	3.736 x 3.48	9.5	190 @ 4800	240 @ 3200	50-65
	V8-305, TPI, 5.0L④	F	T.P.I.	3.736 x 3.48	9.0	205 @ 4400	270 @ 3200	50-65
1987	V6-173, 2.8L④	S	M.F.I.	3.50 x 3.00	8.9	135 @ 5100	160 @ 3900	50-65
	V6-231, 3.8L⑦	A	E2ME, 2 Bbl.⑤	3.80 x 3.40	8.0	110 @ 3800	190 @ 1600	37
	V6-262, 4.3L④	Z	T.B.I.	4.00 x 3.48	9.3	—	—	50-65
	V8-305, 5.0L④	H	E4ME, 4 Bbl.⑤	3.736 x 3.48	8.6	165 @ 4400	250 @ 2400	50-65
	V8-305, TPI, 5.0L④	F	T.P.I.	3.736 x 3.48	9.5	—	—	50-65
	V8-307, 5.0L⑨	Y	E4MC, 4 Bbl.⑤	3.80 x 3.39	8.0	140 @ 3200	255 @ 2000	30-45
	V8-350, TPI, 5.7L④	8	T.P.I.	4.00 x 3.48	9.5	210 @ 4000	315 @ 3200	50-65
1988	V6-173, 2.8L④	S	M.F.I.	3.50 x 3.00	8.5	135 @ 4900	160 @ 3900	—
	V8-305, 5.0L④	—	T.B.I.	3.736 x 3.48	9.3	170 @ 4000	255 @ 2400	—
	V8-305, TPI, 5.0L④	F	T.P.I.	3.736 x 3.48	9.3	⑩	⑪	—
	V8-307, 5.0L⑨	Y	4 Bbl.	3.80 x 3.39	8.0	140 @ 3200	255 @ 2000	—
	V8-350, TPI, 5.7L④	—	T.P.I.	4.00 x 3.48	9.3	255 @ 4400	330 @ 3200	—

Continued

GENERAL ENGINE SPECIFICATIONS-Continued

① —CID-Cubic Inch displacement.
② —VIN Code-The eighth digit in the VIN denotes engine code.
③ —Ratings are net-as installed in vehicle.
④ —See Chevrolet chapter for service procedures on this engine.
⑤ —Rochester.
⑥ —See Oldsmobile Diesel Engine chapter for service procedures on this engine.
⑦ —See Buick chapter for service procedures on this engine.
⑧ —Diesel engine.
⑨ —See Oldsmobile chapter for service procedures on this engine.
⑩ —Auto. trans., 190 @ 4000; manual trans., 215 @ 4400.
⑪ —Auto. trans., 295 @ 2800; manual trans., 285 @ 3200.

ALTERNATOR SPECIFICATIONS

Year	Model	Rated Hot Output Amps	Field Current 12 Volts @ 80°F
1982	1100110	42	4.0-5.0
	1100179	42	4.0-5.0
	1103187	42	4.0-5.0
	1100121	63	4.0-5.0
	1103197	63	4.0-5.0
	1100199	63	4.0-5.0
	1101037	70	4.0-4.6
	1101088	70	4.0-4.6
	1100187	70	4.0-4.6
	1101449	70	—
	1101045	85	4.0-4.6
	1101443	85	4.0-4.6
1983	1100200	78	4.5-5.0
	1100226	37	4.0-5.0
	1100230	42	4.0-5.0
	1100239	55	4.5-5.0
	1100246	63	4.0-4.5
	1100247	55	4.0-4.5
	1100263	78	4.0-4.5
	1100270	78	4.0-4.5
	1100300	63	4.5-5.0
	1105022	78	4.0-4.5
	1105798	63	4.0-4.6
	1105343	85	—
1984	1100200	78	4.5-5.0
	1100239	56	4.5-5.0
	1100260	78	4.5-5.0
	1105197	70	4.0-4.6
	1105443	94	4.5-5.0
	1105444	94	4.5-5.0
	1105493	94	4.5-5.0
	1105548	85	4.0-4.6
	1105565	78	4.5-5.0
1985	1105555	66	4.5-5.0
	1100239	56	4.5-5.0
	1100270	78	4.5-5.0
	1105569	78	4.5-5.0
	1105548	85	4.0-4.6
	1105444	94	4.5-5.0
	1105523	56	4.5-5.0
	1105606	94	4.5-5.0
	1100237	56	4.5-5.0
	1100260	78	4.5-5.0
	1105521	78	4.5-5.0
	1100200	78	4.5-5.0
1986	1105548	85	—
	1100246	66	—
	1105651	94	—
	1105523	56	—
	1105444	94	—
	1105569	78	—
	1105676	56	—
	1105650	78	—
	1100237	56	—
	1105652	78	—
	1105673	56	—
	1100239	56	—
	1100200	78	—
	1105600	66	—
	1105556	42	—
	1105587	97	—
	1105588	78	—
	1105654	94	—
	1105675	66	—
	1101224	108	—
	1105662	85	—
1987-88	1101139	85	—
	1101140	100	—
	1101141	100	—
	1100200	81	—
	1100239	60	—
	1105444	103	—
	1105548	85	—
	1105651	103	—
	1105652	81	—
	1105654	103	—
	1105673	60	—
	1105674	70	—
	1105676	60	—

STARTING MOTOR APPLICATIONS

Year	Model/VIN	Starter Number
1982	4-151/2	1109533
	V6-173/1	1109535
	V6-231/A	1998236
	V6-252/4	1998234
	V8-305/H,7	④
	V8-350 Diesel/N	1998552
1983	4-151/2	1109556
	V6-173/L,1	1109535
	V6-229/9	1998236
	V6-231/A	1998236
	V8-305/G, H, S	1109534⑤
	V8-350 Diesel/N	1998554
1984	4-151/2	1998450
	V6-173/L,1	1998427
	V6-231/A⑥	1998236
	V6-231/A②	1998452
	V8-305/G, H	1998430⑤
	V8-350 Diesel/N	1998554
	V6-231/A	1998236
1985	4-151/2	—
	V6-173/S	1989453
	V6-231/A	—
	V6-262/Z	10496871
	V8-305/G	1988724
	V8-305/H①	10496871
	V8-305/H③	1988724
	V8-305/6	—
	V8-350/N	—
1986	4-151/2	—
	V6-173/S	—
	V6-231/A	—
	V6-262/Z	10496871
	V8-305/F	—
	V8-305/G	1988724
	V8-305/H	—
1987-88	V6-173/S	1998524
	V6-231/A	1998516
	V6-262/Z	1998557
	V8-305/F	⑦
	V8-305/H	1998557
	V8-307/Y	—
	V8-350/8	—

①—Except Firebird.
②—Parisienne.
③—Firebird.
④—Models less 4 spd. man. trans., No.1109534; models w/4 spd. man. trans., No.1998240.
⑤—With high output option, 1998466.
⑥—Exc. Parisienne.
⑦—Auto. trans., 1998564; manual trans., 1998527.

REAR AXLE SPECIFICATIONS

Year	Model	Carrier Type	Ring Gear & Pinion Backlash		Pinion Bearing Preload			Differential Bearing Preload		
			Method	Adjustment	Method	New Bearings Inch Lbs.	Used Bearings Inch Lbs.	Method	New Bearings Inch Lbs.	Used Bearings Inch Lbs.
1982 & 1986-88	All	Integral	Shims	.006-.008	①	20-25	10-15	Shims	35-40	20-25
1983-85	All	Integral	Shims	.005-.008	Spacer	15-30②	10-15②	Shims	—	—

①—Tighten pinion shaft nut with inch pound torque wrench.
②—Use inch pound torque wrench on pinion shaft nut.

ENGINE TIGHTENING SPECIFICATIONS*

*Torque specifications are for clean and lightly lubricated threads only. Dry or dirty threads produce increased friction which prevents accurate measurement of thickness.

Year	Model/VIN	Spark Plugs Ft. Lbs.	Cylinder Head Bolts Ft. Lbs.	Intake Manifold Ft. Lbs.	Exhaust Manifold Ft. Lbs.	Rocker Arm Ft. Lbs.	Rocker Arm Cover Ft. Lbs.	Connecting Rod Cap Bolts Ft. Lbs.	Main Bearing Cap Bolts Ft. Lbs.	Flywheel to Crankshaft Ft. Lbs.	Vibration Damper or Pulley Ft. Lbs.
1982	4-151/2	15	85⑫	29	⑬	20⑪	6	32	70	44	160
	V6-173/1③	7-15	65-75	20-25	22-28	43-49⑪	6-9	34-40	63-74	45-55	75
	V6-231/A⑨	15	80	45	25	30⑧	4	40	100	60	225
	V6-252/4⑨	15	80	45	20	30⑧	4	40	100	60	225
	V8-305/H,7③	22	65	30	20⑤	—	4	45	70	60	60
	V8-305 Diesel/ N⑥	—	130⑦	40⑦	25	28	—	42	120	60	200-310
1983	4-151/2	15	85⑫	29	⑬	20	6	32	70	⑩	200
	V6-173/1,L③	7-15	70	23	25	46⑪	8	37	69	50	75
	V6-229/9③	22	65	30	20	—	45④	45	70	60	60
	V6-231/A⑨	15	80	45	25	30⑧	4	40	100	60	225
	V8-305/G,H,S③	22	65	30	20⑤	—	45④	45	70	60	60
	V8-350/N⑥	—	130⑦	40⑦	25	28	—	42	120	60	200-310
1984	4-151/2	15	92⑫	29	⑬	20	6	32	70	44	200
	V6-173/1,L③	7-15	70	23	25	46⑪	8	37	69	50	66-84
	V6-231/A⑨	15	80	45	25	30⑧	4	40	100	60	225
	V8-305/G,H③	22	65	30	20⑤	—	45④	45	70	60	60
	V8-350/N⑥	—	130⑦	40⑦	25	28	—	42	120	60	200-310
1985	4-151/2	15	⑬	29	⑬	20	45④	32	70	44	200
	V6-173/S③	7-15	70	23	25	46⑪	8	37	69	50	66-84
	V6-231/A⑨	15	80	45	25	30⑧	4	40	100	60	225
	V6-262/2③	22	65	30	20	—	45④	45	70	60	60
	V8-305/G,H,6③	22	65	30	20	—	45④	45	70	60	60
	V8-350/N⑥	—	130⑦	40⑦	25	28	8	42	120	60	200-310
1986	4-151/2	15	⑬	29	⑬	20	6	32	70	55	162
	V6-173/S③	11	78	19	25	—	11	40	73	50	76
	V6-231/A⑨	20	⑬	45	20	25	44④	45	100	60	200
	V6-262/2③	22	68	35	20②	—	58④	45	78	60	70
	V8-305/F,G,H③	22	68	35	20②	—	65④	45	68①	74	70
1987	V6-173/S③	11	78	18	25	8	11	40	73	50	76
	V6-231/A⑨	20	⑬	45	37	25	44④	40	100	60	219
	V6-262/Z③	22	68	35	—	—	58④	44	78	60	70
	V8-305/F, H③	22	68	35	—	—	58④	44	78	60	70
	V8-307/Y⑮	25	130⑦	40⑦	25	25	90④	48	⑭	60	200-310
	V8-350/8③	22	68	35	—	—	58④	44	78	60	70
1988	V6-173/S③	11	78	18	25	8	11	40	73	50	76
	V8-305/F③	22	68	35	—	—	58④	44	78	60	70
	V8-307/Y⑮	25	130⑦	40⑦	25	25	90④	48	⑭	60	200-310
	V8-350/③	22	68	35	—	—	58④	44	78	60	70

①—Inside bolts, 78 ft. lbs.
②—Inside bolts, 26 ft. lbs.
③—For service on this engine, see Chevrolet Chapter.
④—Inch pounds.
⑤—Inside bolts 30 ft. lbs.
⑥—For service on this engine, see Oldsmobile Diesel Engine Chapter.
⑦—Clean & dip entire bolt in engine oil before tightening.
⑧—Rocker arm shaft to cylinder head.
⑨—See Buick chapter for service procedures.
⑩—Automatic transmission, 63; Manual transmission, 77.
⑪—Rocker arm stud.
⑫—Requires thread sealer on bolt heads & threads.
⑬—See text.
⑭—Exc. bearing No. 5, 80 ft. lbs.; bearing No. 5, 120 ft. lbs.
⑮—For service on this engine, see Oldsmobile chapter.

COOLING SYSTEM & CAPACITY DATA

Year	Model or Engine/VIN	Cooling Capacity, Qts.		Radiator Cap Relief Pressure, Lbs.	Thermo. Opening Temp.	Fuel Tank Gals.	Engine Oil Refill Qts. ①	Transmission Oil			Rear Axle Oil Pints
		Less A/C	With A/C					4 Speed Pints	5 Speed Pints	Auto. Trans. Qts. ②	
1982	4-151/2 Firebird	12.8	13	15	195	16	3⑬	3.5	—	⑮	3.5
	V6-173/1 Firebird	12.5	12.5	15	195	16	4⑬	3.5	—	⑮	3.5
	V6-231/A Bonneville	13	13	15	195	18	4	—	—	⑨	3.5
	V6-231/A Grand Prix	13	13	15	195	18	4	—	—	⑨	3.5
	V6-252/4 Bonneville	13	13	15	195	18	4	—	—	⑨	3.5
	V6-252/4 Grand Prix	13	13	15	195	18	4	—	—	⑨	3.5
	V8-305/H Firebird	15	15	15	195	16	4	—	—	⑮	3.5
	V8-305 E.F.I./7 Firebird	15	15	15	195	16	4	—	—	⑮	3.5
	V8-350 Diesel/N Bonneville	17.3	17.3	15	195	19.8④	7⑭	—	—	⑨	3.5
	V8-350 Diesel/N Grand Prix	17.3	17.3	15	195	19.8	7⑭	—	—	⑨	3.5
1983	4-151/2 Firebird	12.8	13	15	195	16	3⑬	4.3	5.3	⑦	3.5
	V6-173/1 Firebird	12.5	12.5	15	195	16	4⑬	—	5.3	⑦	3.5
	V6-173/L H.O. Firebird	12.5	12.5	15	195	16	4⑬	—	5.3	⑦	3.5
	V6-229/9 Parisienne	14.3	14.3	15	195	25⑧	4⑬	—	—	⑪	⑤
	V6-231/A Bonneville	13	13	15	195	17.5④	4	—	—	⑫	3.5
	V6-231/A Grand Prix	13	13	15	195	17.5	4	—	—	⑫	3.5
	V8-305/H Bonneville	15.3	15.9	15	195	17.5	4	—	—	⑫	3.5
	V8-305/G, H Firebird	15	15	15	195	16	4	—	5.3	⑦	3.5
	V8-305/H Grand Prix	15.3	15.9	15	195	17.5	4	—	—	⑫	3.5
	V8-305 TBI/S Firebird	15	15	15	195	16	4	—	—	⑦	3.5
	V8-305/H Parisienne	15.5	15.5	15	195	25⑧	4	—	—	⑪	5
	V8-350 Diesel/N Bonneville	17.3	17.3	15	195	19.8	7⑭	—	—	⑫	3.5
	V8-350 Diesel/N Grand Prix	17.3	17.3	15	195	19.8	7⑭	—	—	⑫	3.5
	V8-350 Diesel/N Parisienne	18.3	18.3	15	195	27⑧	7⑭	—	—	⑪	⑤
1984-85	4-151/2 Firebird	12.8	13	15	195	15.9	3⑬	4.3	5.3	⑦	3.5
	V6-173/1, L Firebird	12.5	12.5	15	195	15.9	4⑬	—	5.3	⑦	3.5
	V6-231/A Bonneville	13	13	15	195	18.1	4	—	—	⑥	3.5
	V6-231/A Grand Prix	13	13	15	195	18.1	4	—	—	⑥	3.5
	V6-231/A Parisienne	11.75	11.75	15	195	25⑧	4	—	—	⑥	⑤
	V8-305/H Bonneville	15.25	15.25	15	195	18.1	4	—	—	⑥	3.5
	V8-305/H Firebird	17.2	17.2	15	195	15.9	4	—	5.3	⑦	⑤
	V8-305/H Grand Prix	15.3	16.1	15	195	18.1	4	—	—	⑥	3.5
	V8-305/H Parisienne	15.25	15.25	15	195	25⑧	4	—	—	⑥	⑤
	V8-305 H.O./G Firebird	17.2	17.2	15	195	15.9	4	—	5.3	⑦	3.5
	V8-350 Diesel/N Bonneville	17.2	17.2	15	195	19.8	7⑭	—	—	⑥	3.5
	V8-350 Diesel/N Grand Prix	17.2	17.2	15	195	19.8	7⑭	—	—	⑥	3.5
	V8-350 Diesel/N Parisienne	18.3	18.3	15	195	27⑧	7⑭	—	—	⑥	⑤
1986	4-151/2 Firebird	12.8	13.0	15	195	15.9	3⑬	—	6.6	③	3.5
	V6-173/S Firebird	12.5	12.5	15	195	15.9	4⑬	—	6.6	③	3.5
	V6-231/A Bonneville	13.0	13.0	15	195	18.1	4	—	—	⑩	3.5
	6-231/A Grand Prix	13.0	13.0	15	195	18.1	4	—	—	⑩	3.5
	V6-262/Z Bonneville	13.0	13.1	15	195	18.1	4⑬	—	—	⑩	3.5
	V6-262/Z Grand Prix	13.0	13.1	15	195	18.1	4⑬	—	—° ⑩	3.5	
	V6-262/Z Parisienne	12.2	12.0	15	195	25.0⑧	4⑬	—	—	⑩	⑤
	V8-305/F Firebird	17.0	16.9	15	195	15.9	4	—	6.6	③	3.5
	V8-305/G Firebird	17.2	17.2	15	195	15.9	4	—	6.6	③	3.5
	V8-305/H Bonneville	15.3	16.1	15	195	18.1	4	—	6.6	⑩	3.5
	V8-305/H Firebird	17.2	17.2	15	195	16.1	4	—	6.6	③	3.5
	V8-305/H Grand Prix	15.3	16.1	15	195	18.1	4	—	—	⑩	3.5
	V8-305/H Parisienne	15.0	15.0	15	195	25.0⑧	4	—	—	⑩	3.5

COOLING SYSTEM & CAPACITY DATA - Continued

Year	Model or Engine/VIN	Cooling Capacity, Qts. Less A/C	Cooling Capacity, Qts. With A/C	Radiator Cap Relief Pressure, Lbs.	Thermo. Opening Temp.	Fuel Tank Gals.	Engine Oil Refill Qts. ①	Transmission Oil 4 Speed Pints	Transmission Oil 5 Speed Pints	Transmission Oil Auto. Trans. Qts. ②	Rear Axle Oil Pints
1987	V6-173/S Firebird	12.4	12.4	15	195	15.9	4⑬	—	6.6	③	3.5
	V6-231/A Grand Prix	13.1	13.1	15	195	17.5	4	—	—	⑩	3.5
	V6-262/Z Grand Prix	13.1	13.1	15	195	17.5	4⑬	—	—	⑩	3.5
	V8-305/F Firebird	17.2	17.2	15	195	15.9	4	—	6.6	③	3.5
	V8-305/H Firebird	17	17	15	195	15.9	4	—	6.6	③	3.5
	V8-305/H Grand Prix	15	16	15	195	17.5	4	—	—	⑩	3.5
	V8-307/Y Safari	15	15	15	195	22	4	—	—	⑩	4.25
	V8-350/ Firebird	15.7	15.7	15	195	15.9	4	—	6.6	③	3.5
1988	V6-173/S Firebird	12.4	12.4	15	195	15.9	4⑬	—	6.6	③	3.5
	V8-305/F Firebird	17.2	17.2	15	195	15.9	4	—	6.6	③	3.5
	V8-305/H Firebird	17	17	15	195	15.9	4	—	6.6	③	3.5
	V8-307/Y Safari	15	15	15	195	22	4	—	—	⑩	4.25
	V8-350/ Firebird	15.7	15.7	15	195	15.9	4	—	6.6	③	3.5

①—Add one quart with filter change.
②—Approximate. Make final check with dipstick.
③—Oil pan only, 5.0 qts.; after overhaul, 11.5 qts.
④—Station Wagons, 18 gals.
⑤—7 1/2 inch axle, 3.5 pints; 8 1/2 inch axle, pints; 8 3/4 inch axle, 5.4 pints.
⑥—T.H.M. 200C, oil pan only, 4 1/4 qts.; after overhaul, 10 1/2 qts. T.H.M. 200-4R, oil pan only, 3.48 qts.; after overhaul, 11.05 qts.; T.H.M. 250C, oil pan only, 3.15 qts.; after overhaul, 10.0 qts. T.H.M. 700-4R, oil pan only, 4.7 qts; after overhaul 11.5
⑦—T.H.M. 200C, oil pan only, 4 1/4 qts.; after overhaul, 10 1/2 qts.; T.H.M. 700-4R, oil pan only, 4.7 qts.; total capacity 11 1/2 qts.
⑧—Station Wagons, 22 gals.
⑨—T.H.M. 250C, oil pan only, 2.75 qts.; after overhaul, 10.25 qts. T.H.M. 350C, oil pan only, 3.15 qts.; after overhaul, 10.15 qts.
⑩—T.H.M. 200C, oil pan only, 4.3 qts.; after overhaul, 10.6 qts. T.H.M. 200-4R, oil pan only, 5.1 qts.; after overhaul, 11.1 qts. T.H.M. 700-4R, oil pan only, 5.0 qts.; after overhaul, 11.5 qts.
⑪—T.H.M. 200C, oil pan, 3.5 qts.; after overhaul, 5 qts. T.H.M. 350C, oil pan, 3 qts.; after overhaul, 10 qts.
⑫—T.H.M. 250C, oil pan only, 2.75 qts.; after overhaul, 10.25 qts. T.H.M. 350C, oil pan only, 3.25 qts.; after overhaul, 10.15 qts.
⑬—With or without filter change.
⑭—Includes filter. Recommended diesel engine oil on 1982-84 units, use oil designated SF/CD or SF/CC.
⑮—Oil pan only, 3.5 qts.; after overhaul, 5 qts.

WHEEL ALIGNMENT SPECIFICATIONS

Year	Model	Caster Angle, Degrees Limits	Caster Angle, Degrees Desired	Camber Angle, Degrees Limits Left	Camber Angle, Degrees Limits Right	Camber Angle, Degrees Desired Left	Camber Angle, Degrees Desired Right	Toe-In. Inch
1982	Firebird	+2.5 to +3.5	+3	+1/2 to + 1 1/2	+1/2 to +1 1/2	+1	+1	1/8 to 1/4
	Grand Prix	+2.5 to +3.5	+3	0 to +1	0 to +1	+.5	+.5	1/16 to 3/16
	Bonneville	+2.5 to +3.5	+3	0 to +1	0 to +1	+.5	+.5	1/16 to 3/16
1983-85	Firebird②	+2.5 to +3.5	+3	+.5 to +1.5	+.5 to +1.5	+1	+1	①
	Grand Prix	+2.5 to +3.5	+3	0 to +1	0 to +1	+.5	+.5	1/16 to 3/16
	Bonneville	+2.5 to +3.5	+3	0 to +1	0 to +1	+.5	+.5	1/16 to 3/16
	Parisienne	+2.5 to +3.5	+3	+.3 to +1.3	+.3 to +1.3	+.8	+.8	1/16 to 3/16
1986	Firebird	+3.0 to +4.0	+3.5	+.5 to +.5	+.5 to +1.5	+1	+1	③
	Grand Prix	④	⑤	−.3 to +1.3	−.3 to +1.3	+.5	+.5	③
	Bonneville	④	⑤	−.3 to +1.3	−.3 to +1.3	+.5	+.5	③
	Parisienne	+1.8 to +3.8	+2.8	0 to +1.6	0 to +1.6	+.8	+.8	③
1987	Firebird	+4.5 to +5.5	+5	+.5 to +1.5	+.5 to +1.5	+1	+1	⑥
	Grand Prix	④	⑤	−.3 to +1.3	−.3 to +1.3	+.5	+.5	⑦
	Safari	+1.8 to +3.8	+2.8	0 to +1.6	0 to +1.6	+.8	+.8	⑥
1988	Firebird	+4.5 to + 5.5	+5	+.5 to 1.5	+.5 to +1.5	+1	+1	⑥
	Safari	+1.8 to +3.8	+2.8	0 to +1.6	0 to + 1.6	+.8	+.8	⑥

①—Toe-in degrees per wheel, −.3° to +.7°.
②—Less WS6 suspension package.
③—Toe-in degrees per wheel, +.15.
④—Manual steering, −.2 to +1.8; power steering, +1.8 to +3.8.
⑤—Manual steering, +.8; power steering, +2.8.
⑥—Toe-in degrees per wheel, −.1° to +.3°.

Electrical Section

INDEX

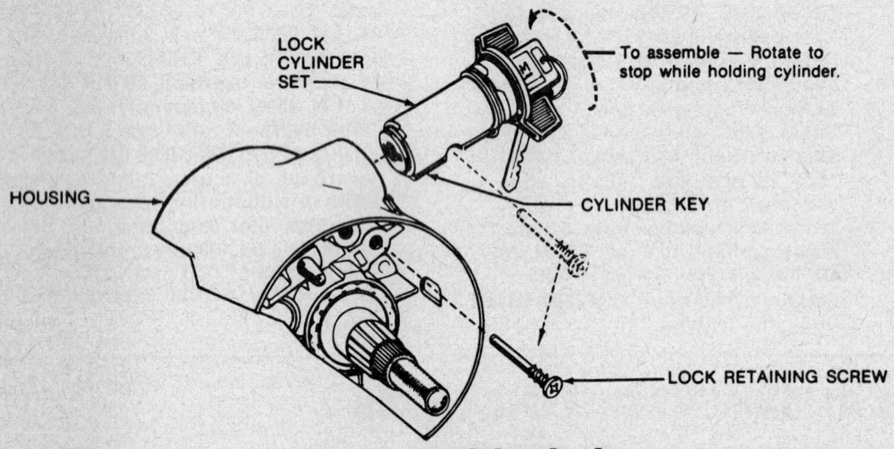

Fig. 1 Ignition lock replacement

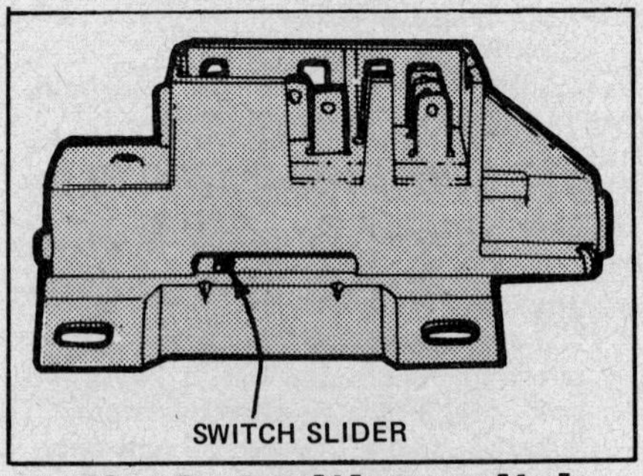

Fig. 2 Ignition switch (typical)

STARTER
REPLACE

Upon removal of starter, note if any shims are used. If shims are used, they should be reinstalled in their original location during installation.

If starter is noisy during cranking, remove one .015 inch double shim or add one .015 inch single shim to the outer bolt. If starter makes a high pitched whine after firing, add .015 inch double shims until noise ceases.

1. Disconnect battery ground cable.
2. Disconnect brace from starter and swing brace forward, then remove heat shields, if used.
3. On 4-151, disconnect wiring from starter, then remove retaining bolts and starter.
4. On all other engines, remove starter retaining bolts, then lower starter, disconnect wiring and remove starter.
5. Reverse procedure to install.

IGNITION LOCK
REPLACE

1. Remove steering wheel as described under Horn Sounder and Steering Wheel.
2. Remove turn signal switch as described under Turn Signal Switch, Replace, then remove buzzer switch.
3. Place ignition switch in "Run" position, then, remove lock cylinder retaining screw and lock cylinder.
4. To install, rotate lock cylinder to stop while holding housing, **Fig. 1.** Align cylinder key with keyway in housing, then push lock cylinder assembly into housing until fully seated.
5. Install lock cylinder retaining screw. Torque screw to 40 in. lbs. for standard columns. On adjustable columns, torque retaining screw to 22 in. lbs.
6. Install buzzer switch, turn signal switch and steering wheel.

IGNITION SWITCH
REPLACE

1. Disconnect battery ground cable.
2. Position ignition key in off-unlock position on standard columns, or ACC on tilt columns.
3. Remove lower portion of instrument panel, then toe-pan trim cover.
4. Remove shift indicator cable clip from shift bowl, if equipped with column shift.
5. Loosen toe-pan clamp bolts, then remove switch attaching screws.
6. Disconnect electrical wiring from switch, then remove switch from steering column.
7. Position new switch slider in same position as old switch slider, **Fig. 2.**
8. Install new switch.

LIGHT SWITCH
REPLACE
PARISIENNE & SAFARI

1. Disconnect battery ground cable.
2. Pull headlight knob to "On" position, then reach under instrument panel, depress switch shaft release button and pull knob and shaft assembly from switch.

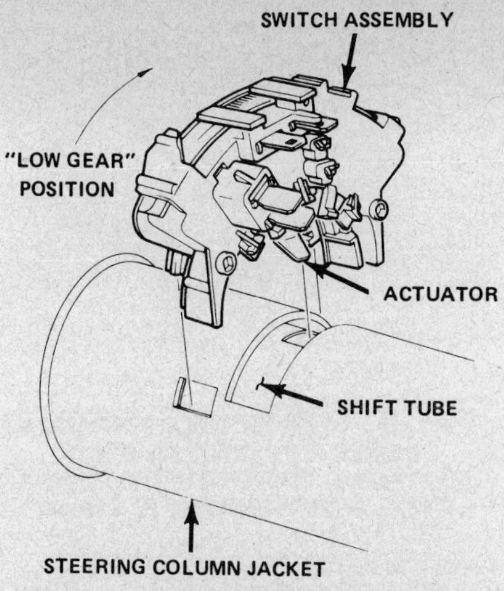

Fig. 3 Self-adjusting type neutral safety switch (typical)

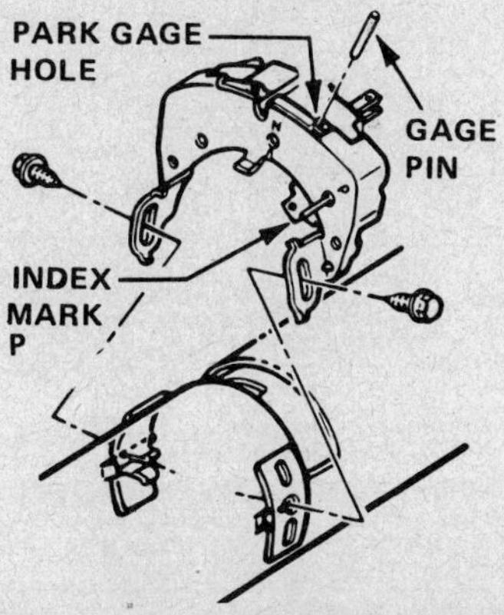

Fig. 5 Manual adjust type neutral safety switch. Automatic transmission (typical)

3. Remove switch retaining nut, wire connector and switch.
4. Reverse procedure to install.

BONNEVILLE & GRAND PRIX

1. Disconnect battery ground cable.
2. Remove left side lower trim panel.
3. Remove instrument panel bezel attaching screws, then bezel.
4. Pull headlight knob to "On" position, then remove light switch mounting plate to cluster attaching screws and pull assembly rearward.
5. Depress switch shaft retainer and pull out knob and shaft assembly.
6. Remove wiring connector from switch, then switch.
7. Disassemble light switch from bracket.
8. Reverse procedure to install.

FIREBIRD

1. Remove right and left lower trim plates.
2. Remove instrument panel cluster trim plate.
3. Remove two retaining screws from switch assembly.
4. Depress side tangs and pull switch assembly from instrument panel.
5. Reverse procedure to install.

STOP LIGHT SWITCH REPLACE

EXC. FIREBIRD

The stop light switch has a slip fit in the mounting sleeve which permits positive adjustment by pulling the brake pedal up firmly against the stop. The pedal arm forces the switch body to slip in the mounting sleeve bushing to position the switch properly.

1. Disconnect wires from switch and remove switch from bracket.
2. Position new switch in bracket and push into maximum distance. Brake pedal arm moves switch to correct distance on rebound. Check if pedal is in full return position by lifting slightly by hand.
3. Connect switch wires by inserting plug on switch.

FIREBIRD

1. Remove lefthand side hush panel.
2. Located under instrument panel, disconnect wire connector from switch at brake pedal support.
3. Remove switch from mounting bracket.
4. Depress brake pedal and install new switch into clip, until shoulder on switch bottoms out against clip.
5. If adjustment of the switch is necessary, the switch may be rotated or pulled in the clip. Electrical contact should be made when brake pedal is depressed .053 inch from its fully released position.

NEUTRAL SAFETY SWITCH REPLACE

Some models use a combination neutral start and back-up light switch, while others use a separate back-up light switch. Both switches are serviced in the following manner.

SELF-ADJUSTING TYPE

1. Place gear selector in "Neutral."
2. Gently rock switch out of steering column.
3. Disconnect wiring connectors. Connect wiring connectors to new switch.
4. Align switch actuator with hole in shift tube, **Fig. 3.**
5. Position connector side of switch into lower jacket cut out.
6. Push down front of switch, ensuring switch tangs snap into holes in steering column jacket.
7. Adjust switch by placing gear selector in "Park" position. Switch main housing and housing back should ratchet, providing proper adjustment.

MANUAL ADJUST TYPE

Exc. Firebird

1. Lock steering column in "Park" position for automatic transmissions and "Reverse" for manual transmissions, then remove screws attaching switch to steering column.
2. Remove switch electrical connectors, then switch.
3. Connect wiring connector to new switch.
4. Position new switch on steering column, aligning switch carrier tang in shift selector tube slot.
5. Install attaching screws and tighten. **The switch is held in the proper position with a plastic sheer pin. No additional pinning is required.**
6. Adjust switch by loosening attaching screws, then inserting a .096 inch gauge pin in gauge hole of switch, **Figs. 4 and 5.**
7. Rotate switch in clockwise direction until freeplay is eliminated and gauge pin slides in gauge hole to a depth of 3/8 inch.
8. Tighten attaching screws and remove gauge pin.

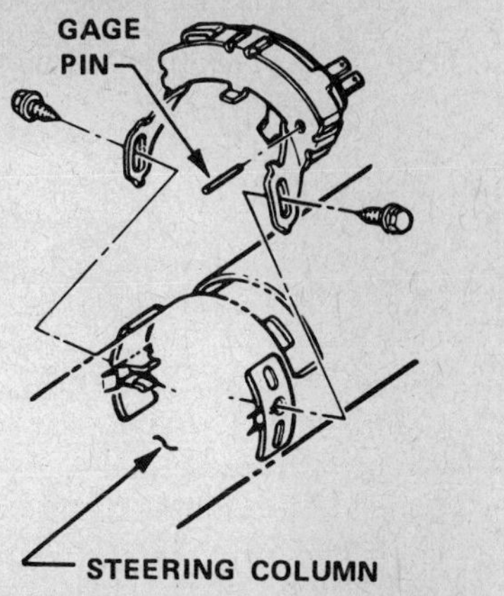

Fig. 4 Manual adjust type neutral safety switch. Manual transmission (typical)

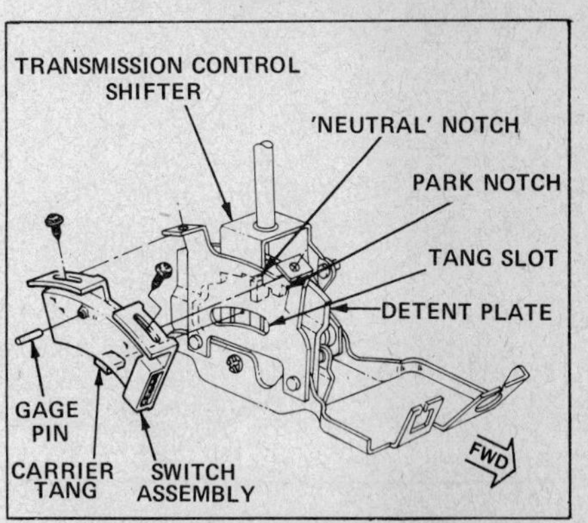

Fig. 6 Neutral safety switch. Firebird

Firebird

1. Remove floor console cover.
2. Disconnect wire connectors from back-up lamp/neutral start switch.
3. Position gear shift lever into Neutral position.
4. Remove two screws securing neutral starter switch, then remove switch.

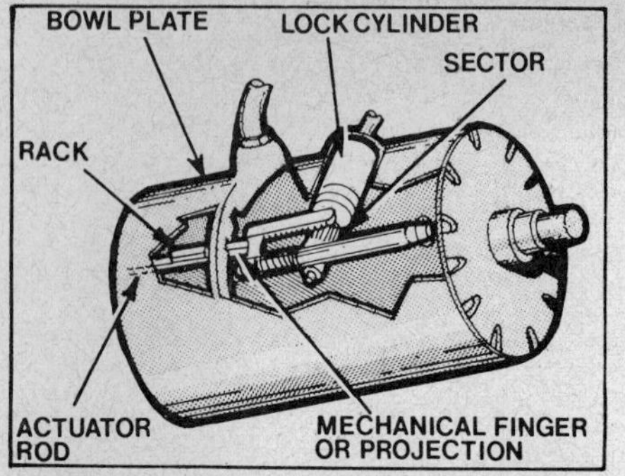

Fig. 7 Mechanical neutral start system w/standard column. Bonneville, Grand Prix, Parisienne & Safari

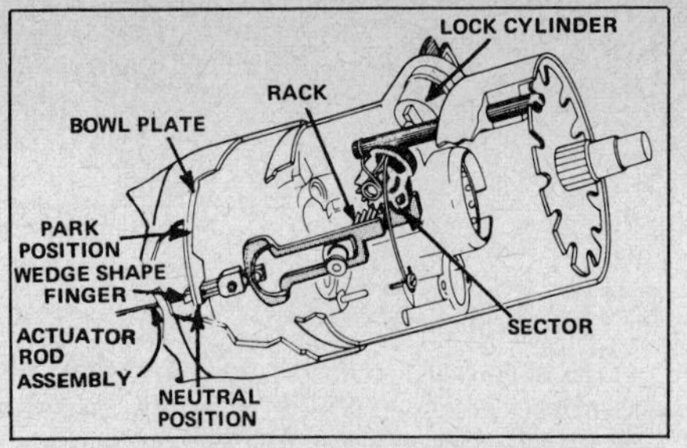

Fig. 8 Mechanical neutral start system w/tilt column. Bonneville, Grand Prix, Parisienne & Safari

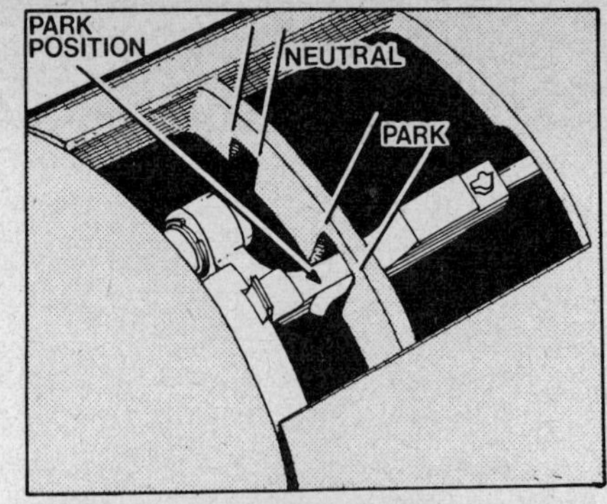

Fig. 9 Mechanical neutral start system in Park position. Bonneville, Grand Prix, Parisienne & Safari

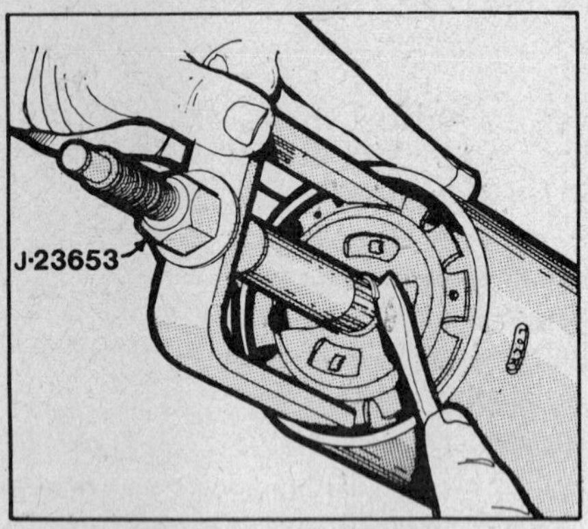

Fig. 10 Compressing lock plate and removing retaining ring

5. Ensure gear shift lever is in Neutral position before installing switch.
6. Install new switch in position on gear shift lever. Ensure pin on gear shift lever is in slot of switch. Tighten switch and torque to 14-19 inch lbs., **Fig. 6.**
7. Move gear shift lever out of Neutral position to break plastic shear pin.
8. Connect electrical connectors to switch. Apply parking brake and start vehicle. Ensure vehicle starts only in Park or Neutral positions.
9. Turn ignition off and install floor console cover.

MECHANICAL NEUTRAL START SYSTEM

EXC. FIREBIRD

Actuation of the ignition switch is prevented by a mechanical lockout system, **Figs. 7 and 8,** which prevents the lock cylinder from rotating when the selector lever is out of Park or Neutral. When the selector lever is in Park or Neutral, the slots in the bowl plate and the finger on the actuator rod align allowing the finger to pass through the bowl plate in turn actuating the ignition switch, **Fig. 9.** If the selector lever is in any position other than Park or Neutral, the finger contacts the bowl plate when the lock cylinder is rotated, thereby preventing full travel of the lock cylinder.

CLUTCH START SWITCH

All cars equipped with a manual transmission use a clutch start switch which is mounted on the pedal bracket. The switch closes when the clutch is depressed and completes solenoid connection. When installing switch, no adjustment is necessary.

TURN SIGNAL SWITCH

REPLACE

On tilt column, the column must first be lowered from panel.

1. Disconnect battery ground cable, then remove steering wheel using puller. **Do not hammer on end of shaft as hammering could collapse shaft or loosen plastic injections which maintain column rigidity.**
2. Remove cover by prying out with a screwdriver at slots provided in cover for this purpose.
3. Depress lock plate and pry round wire lock ring out of shaft groove, **Fig. 10.** Remove lock plate.
4. Slide upper bearing preload spring and turn signal cancelling cam off shaft.
5. Remove turn signal lever. **On models with column mounted dimmer switch, remove actuator arm screw and actuator arm before removing turn signal lever.**
6. Push hazard warning switch in and unscrew knob.
7. Pull turn signal wiring connector out of bracket on jacket and disconnect.
8. Remove three turn signal switch screws.
9. Remove shift indicator cable, if equipped.
10. Lower steering column from instrument panel and remove wire protector, then pull switch straight up with wire protector and remove housing. **Place tape around upper part of connector and wires to prevent snagging when switch is being removed, Fig. 11.**

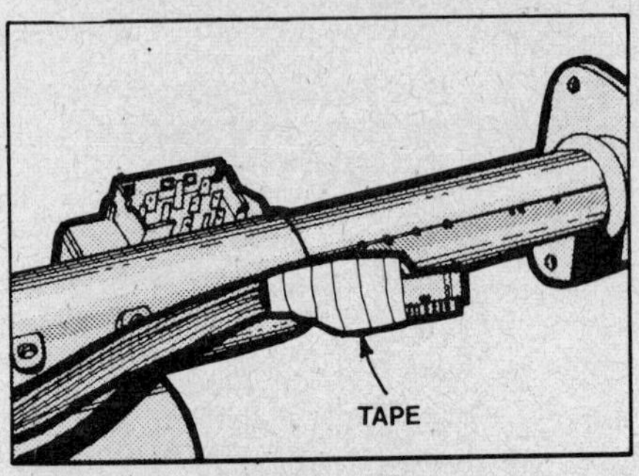

Fig. 11 Taping turn signal connector & wires

COLUMN-MOUNTED DIMMER SWITCH

REPLACE

1. Disconnect battery ground cable.
2. Remove instrument panel lower trim and on models with A/C, remove A/C duct extension at column.
3. Remove toe-plate cover screws.
4. Remove two nuts from instrument panel support bracket studs and lower steering column, resting steering wheel on front seat.
5. Remove dimmer switch retaining screw(s) and the switch. Tape actuator rod to column and separate switch from rod.
6. Reverse procedure to install. To adjust switch, depress dimmer switch slightly and install a 3/32 inch twist drill to lock the switch to the body. Force switch upward to remove lash. Torque retaining screws to 35 inch lbs. and remove tape from actuator rod. Remove twist drill and check for proper operation.

HORN SOUNDER & STEERING WHEEL

REPLACE

EXC. FIREBIRD

1. Disconnect battery ground cable.
2. Remove screws attaching horn pad assembly to steering wheel.

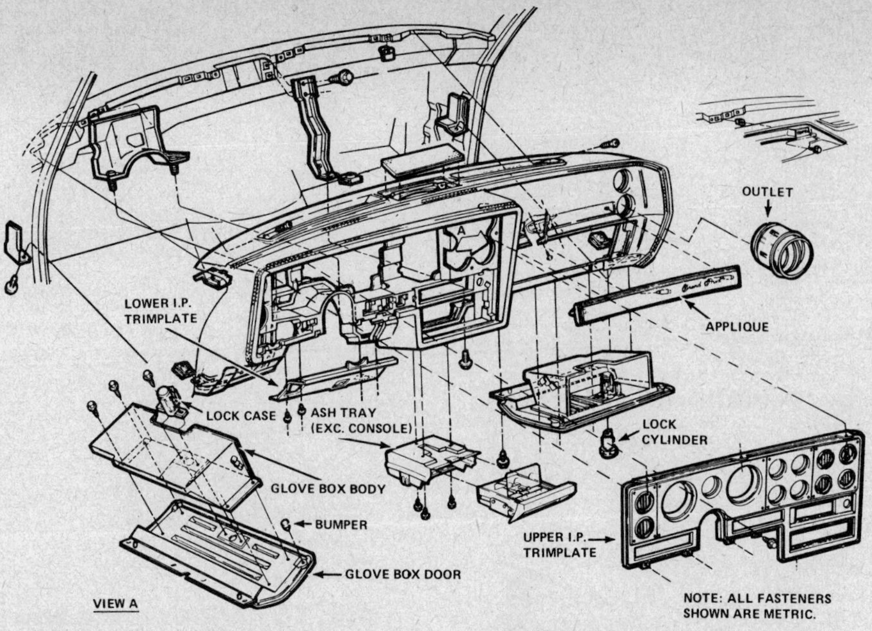

Fig. 12 Instrument panel. Bonneville & Grand Prix

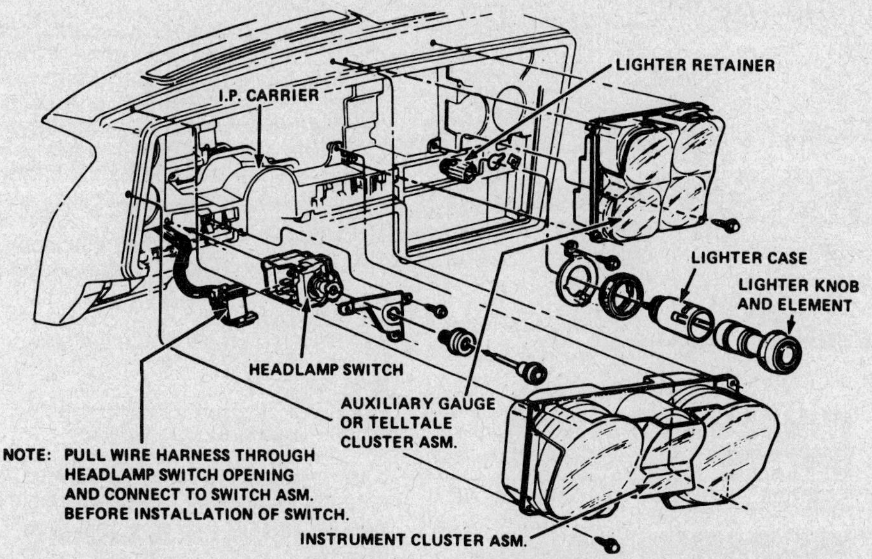

Fig. 13 Instrument cluster. Bonneville & Grand Prix

3. Disconnect horn contact from steering wheel.
4. Remove steering wheel nut retainer and attaching nut.
5. Using suitable steering wheel puller, remove steering wheel. Note position of steering wheel to shaft.
6. Reverse procedure to install.

FIREBIRD

1. Disconnect battery ground cable.
2. Remove steering wheel shroud screws on underside of steering wheel.
3. Remove steering wheel shroud and horn contact lead assembly from the steering wheel.
4. Remove snap ring and steering wheel nut.
5. Using steering wheel puller tool No. J-2927 or equivalent, remove steering wheel. Note position of steering wheel to shaft.
6. Reverse procedure to install.

INSTRUMENT CLUSTER REPLACE

EXC. FIREBIRD, PARISIENNE & SAFARI

1. Disconnect battery ground cable.
2. Remove upper and lower instrument panel trim plates, **Fig. 12.**
3. Remove instrument panel bezel attaching screws and bezel, if equipped.
4. On column mounted shift models, remove shift indicator cable.
5. On Firebird, loosen steering column nuts and lower column approximately $^{1}/_{2}$ inch.
6. On all models, remove cluster retaining screws, pull cluster outward and disconnect speedometer cable and printed circuit connector, if equipped.
7. Remove lower bezel anti-rattle clips, if equipped, then instrument cluster, **Fig. 13.**
8. Reverse procedure to install.

PARISIENNE & SAFARI

1. Disconnect battery ground cable.
2. Remove four steering column lower cover screws and cover.
3. If equipped with automatic transmission, disconnect shift indicator cable from steering column.
4. Remove two steering column to instrument panel screws and lower steering column. **Use extreme care when lowering steering to prevent damage to column assembly.**
5. Remove six screws and three snap-in fasteners from perimeter of instrument cluster lens, **Fig. 14.**
6. Remove two screws from upper surface of gray sheet metal trim plate.
7. Remove two stud nuts from lower corner of cluster.
8. Disconnect speedometer cable and pull cluster from instrument panel.
9. Disconnect electrical connectors from cluster and remove from vehicle.
10. Reverse procedure to install.

FIREBIRD

1. Disconnect battery ground cable, then remove right and left lower trim plates, **Fig. 15.**
2. Remove instrument cluster trim plate.
3. Remove six cluster attachment screws, pull cluster back and disconnect speedometer cable.
4. Disconnect necessary electrical connections.
5. Remove trip odometer and cluster lens.
6. Reverse procedure to install.

WINDSHIELD WIPER MOTOR REPLACE

1. Raise hood and remove cowl screen or grille.
2. Disconnect wiring and washer hoses.
3. Reaching through opening, loosen transmission drive link to crankarm attaching nuts.
4. Remove drive link from motor crankarm.
5. Remove three motor attaching screws and remove motor while guiding crankarm through opening.
6. Reverse procedure to install.

WINDSHIELD WIPER TRANSMISSION REPLACE

WITH RECTANGULAR MOTOR

1. Remove wiper arms and blades.
2. Raise hood and remove cowl vent screen or grille.

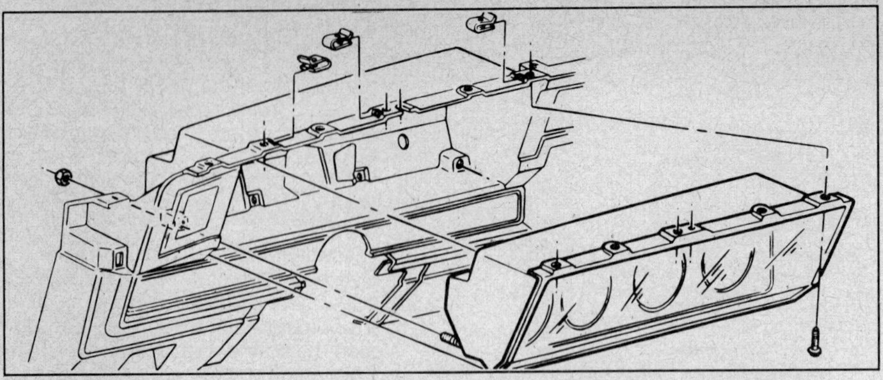

Fig. 14 Instrument cluster. Parisienne & Safari

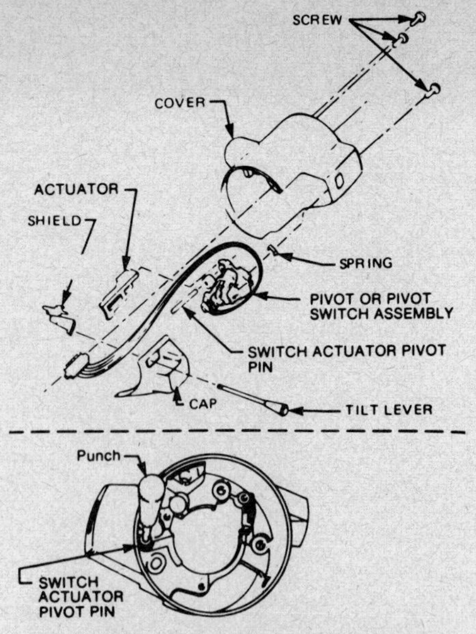

Fig. 16 Windshield wiper switch removal & installation. Models w/tilt wheel

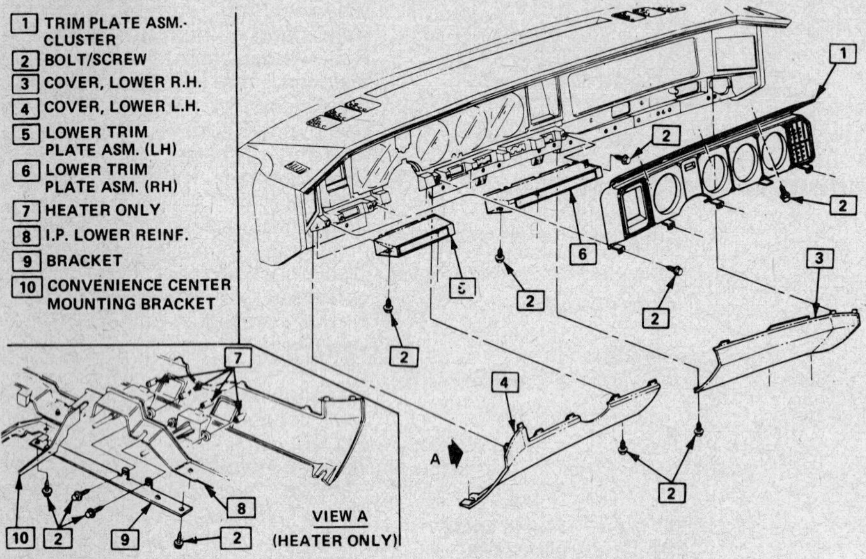

Fig. 15 Instrument cluster. Firebird

3. Disconnect wiring from motor.
4. Loosen, but do not remove, transmission drive link to motor crankarm attaching nuts and disconnect drive link from crankarm.
5. Remove right and left transmission to body attaching screws and guide transmission and linkage assembly out through opening. **When installing, motor must be in Park position.**

WITH ROUND MOTOR

1. Raise hood and remove cowl vent screen.
2. On Intermediates and full size models, remove right and left wiper arm and blade assemblies.
3. Loosen, but do not remove, attaching nuts securing transmission drive link to motor crankarm.
4. Disconnect transmission drive link from motor crankarm.
5. On Intermediate and full size models, remove right and left transmission to body attaching screws.
6. Remove transmission and linkage assembly by guiding it through opening. **When installing, motor must be in Park position.**

WINDSHIELD WIPER SWITCH

REPLACE

EXC. PARISIENNE & SAFARI

1. Remove steering wheel as described under Horn Sounder and Steering Wheel, Replace.
2. Remove turn signal switch as described under Turn Signal Switch, Replace.
3. Remove ignition lock and buzzer as described under Ignition Lock, Replace.
4. Remove and install cover and wiper switch as shown in **Fig. 16 and 17.**
5. Reverse remaining procedure to install.

PARISIENNE & SAFARI

1. Disconnect battery ground cable.
2. Pull headlight switch knob to ON position.
3. Reach up under instrument panel and depress headlight switch shaft release button, then pull out switch shaft and knob assembly.
4. Remove four screws securing control shroud to instrument panel. **When removing control shroud to instrument panel screws, one screw is hidden above cigar lighter knob while another is hidden above headlamp switch shaft location.**
5. Remove control shroud, then two remaining screws.
6. Remove wiper switch electrical connector, then light bulb and socket from rear of switch.
7. Remove switch.
8. Reverse procedure to install.

RADIO

REPLACE

When installing radio, be sure to adjust antenna trimmer for peak performance.

BONNEVILLE & GRAND PRIX

1. Disconnect battery ground cable.
2. Remove upper and lower trim plates.
3. If equipped with console, move shift lever fully rearward.
4. On all models, remove four radio attaching screws from front of radio.
5. Open glove box door and lower by releasing spring clip.
6. Loosen radio rear attaching nut and pull radio outward slightly.
7. Disconnect electrical leads from radio and remove radio from vehicle.
8. Reverse procedure to install.

FIREBIRD

1. Disconnect battery ground cable.
2. Remove radio and A/C heater console trim plate.
3. Remove four radio to console attaching screws, then pull radio outward and disconnect wire connectors and antenna lead.
4. Reverse procedure to install.

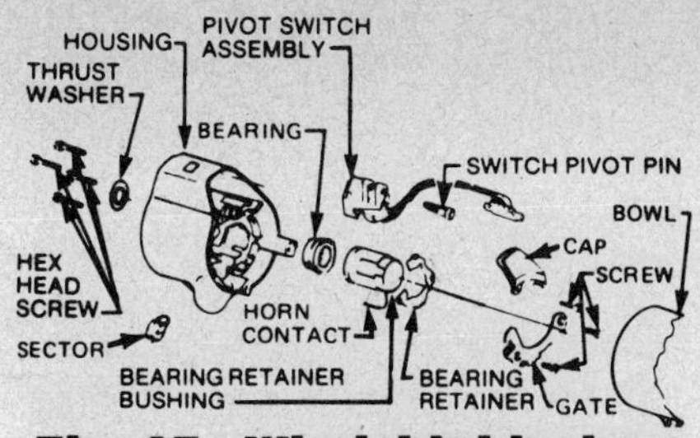

Fig. 17 Windshield wiper switch removal & installation. Models less tilt wheel

PARISIENNE & SAFARI

1. Disconnect battery ground cable.
2. Remove control knobs from control shafts.
3. Remove three radio trim plate attaching screws.
4. Remove two screws and bottom nut attaching radio bracket to instrument panel.
5. Disconnect antenna lead and wire connector from radio.
6. Remove radio with mounting bracket attached from instrument panel.
7. Remove bracket from radio.
8. Reverse procedure to install.

HEATER CORE REPLACE

LESS A/C

Bonneville & Grand Prix

1. Disconnect battery ground cable and drain cooling system.
2. Disconnect heater hoses.
3. Disconnect electrical connectors from heater module.
4. Remove module front cover screws.
5. Remove heater core from module.
6. Reverse procedure to install.

Firebird

1. Disconnect battery ground cable.
2. Drain radiator and remover heater hoses from heater core.
3. Remove right lower hush panel.
4. Remove right lower instrument trim panel.
5. Vehicles equipped with the V8-305 EFI engine, remove ESC module.
6. Remove lower right instrument panel carrier to cowl screw.
7. Remove four heater case cover screws.
8. Remove heater case cover.
9. Remove core support plate and baffle screws.
10. Remove heater core, support plate and baffle from case.
11. Reverse procedure to install.

Parisienne & Safari

1. Disconnect battery ground cable and drain cooling system.
2. Disconnect heater hoses from heater core. Plug core outlets to prevent coolant spillage.
3. Disconnect wire connectors from module cover, then remove front module cover attaching screws and

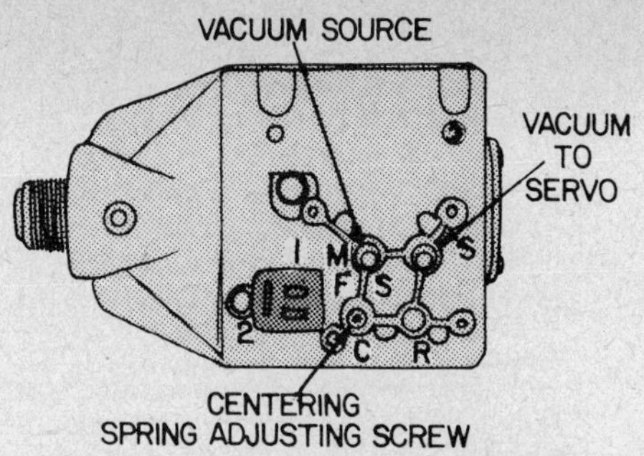

Fig. 18 Centering spring adjustment. Early model flyweight type regulator

cover.
4. Remove heater core from module.
5. Reverse procedure to install.

WITH A/C

Bonneville & Grand Prix

1. Disconnect negative battery cable.
2. Discharge air conditioning system and drain cooling system.
3. Remove both windshield wipers and wiper stops.
4. Remove cover windshield molding and leaf screens.
5. Remove lower windshield molding brackets, bolts from upper half of module case, all electrical connections and module cover.
6. Remove heater core clamp bolt and remove heater core.
7. Reverse procedure to install.

Firebird

1. Disconnect battery ground cable.
2. Drain radiator and remove heater hoses from heater core.
3. Remove right lower hush panel.
4. Remove right lower instrument trim panel.
5. Vehicles equipped with the V8-305 TBI engine, remove ESC module.
6. Remove lower right instrument panel carrier to cowl screw.
7. Remove four heater case cover screws.
8. Remove heater case cover.
9. Remove core support plate and baffle screws.
10. Remove heater core, support plate and baffle from case.
11. Reverse procedure to install.

Parisienne & Safari

1. Disconnect battery ground cable and drain cooling system.
2. Disconnect heater hoses from heater core. Plug core outlets to prevent coolant spillage.
3. Remove heater core retainer bracket and ground strap.
4. Remove module rubber seal and module screen.
5. Remove righthand windshield wiper arm.
6. Remove high blower relay, then thermostatic switch mounting screws.
7. Disconnect wire connector at top of module, then remove module top cover.

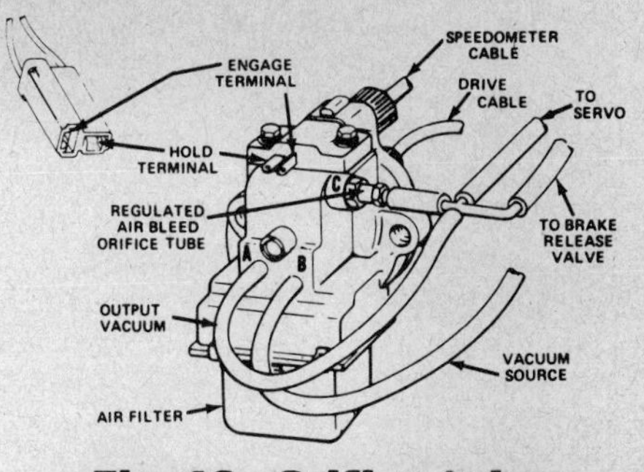

Fig. 19 Orifice tube adjustment. Late model transducer type regulator

8. Remove heater core from module.
9. Reverse procedure to install.

BLOWER MOTOR REPLACE

EXC. FIREBIRD

1. Disconnect battery ground cable.
2. If equipped with air conditioning, disconnect cooling tube from blower motor.
3. On all models, disconnect electrical connector from blower motor.
4. Remove blower motor retaining screws and the blower motor.
5. Reverse procedure to install.

FIREBIRD

1. Disconnect battery ground cable.
2. Disconnect wire connector. On models with A/C, disconnect cooling tube.
3. Remove motor attaching screws and nuts, then remove blower motor assembly from case.
4. Reverse procedure to install.

SPEED CONTROLS, ADJUST

1982–84

Brake Release Switches, Adjust

Apply brake pedal and push both switches forward as far as possible. Pull pedal forcibly rearward to adjust switches.

Centering Spring Adjustment, Exc. Cruise Master Units

If speed control holds speed three or more mph higher than selected speed, turn centering screw (C) clockwise 1/8 turn or less, **Fig. 18.**

If speed control holds speed three or more mph below selected speed, turn centering adjustment screw (C) counterclockwise 1/8 turn or less. Do not move adjustment screw (R).

Orifice Tube Adjustment, Cruise Master Units

To check engagement speed, engage the system at 55 mph. If vehicle cruises below the engagement speed, loosen the locknut and screw the orifice tube outward. If vehicle cruises above the engagement speed, loosen the locknut and screw the orifice tube inward, **Fig. 19.**

Approximately 1/4 turn of the orifice tube will change the cruise speed about 1 mph. Also, do not remove orifice tube as it cannot be reinstalled once removed.

Bead Chain Adjustment, Buick Built Engines

Assemble chain to be taut with carburetor in hot idle position and the idle solenoid de-energized. Place chain into swivel cavities which permits chain to have slight slack. Place retainer over swivel and chain assembly. Retainer must be made to rest between balls. Cut off chain flush with side of swivel to remove excess length. Chain slack should not exceed one half diameter of ball stud, .150 inch, when measured at hot idle position.

Cable Adjustment, Pontiac Built Engines

1. Set carburetor choke to hot idle position.
2. With cable connected to vacuum servo, pull steel tube of servo as far as it will go and check if one of the cross holes in the steel tube aligns with carburetor lever pin.
3. If one of the cross holes in the steel tube aligns with carburetor lever pin, install the tube, washer and cotter pin.
4. If none of the cross holes in the steel aligns with carburetor lever pin, move tube rearward to align the next closest hole and install cable, washer and cotter pin. Do not stretch cable to make adjustment, as this will prevent carburetor from returning to normal idle.

Cable Adjustment, Chevrolet Built Engines Less Electronic Fuel Injection

1. Assemble cable to cable bracket and throttle lever.
2. Install cable assembly onto servo bracket.
3. Place throttle in fully closed position. Attach servo chain to cable assembly with first two beads of servo chain hanging loose outside cable assembly clip.
4. Adjust cable assembly jam nuts until there is a .03 inch clearance between throttle lever stud pin and end of slot on throttle cable assembly. Torque jam nuts to 35-48 inch lbs. Pull rubber boot over washer on cable.

Cable Adjustment, Chevrolet Built Engines With Electronic Fuel Injection

1. Assemble cable to cable bracket and TBI lever and servo bracket.
2. Place throttle in fully closed position. Attach servo chain to cable assembly with first two beads of servo chain hanging loosely outside cable assembly clip.
3. Adjust cable jam nuts until cable sleeve at TBI unit is tight but not holding throttle open. Torque jam nuts to 35-48 inch lbs. Pull rubber boot over washer on cable.

Rod Adjustment, Oldsmobile Built Engines

Adjust length of rod to minimum slack with carburetor in hot idle position and the engine static.

Rod Adjustment, Chevrolet Built Engines

Screw rod into link with ignition "Off" and fast idle cam off and throttle closed. Hook rod through tab on servo. Adjust length so link assemblies over end of stud, then install retainer.

1986–88

CRUISE RELEASE SWITCHES, ADJUST

Grand Prix & Safari

1. With brake pedal fully depressed, insert valve into retainer until valve seats fully.
2. Pull brake pedal rearward against pedal stop until clicking sounds are no longer heard.
3. Release brake pedal, then repeat step 2 and ensure clicking is not present.

SERVO ROD, ADJUST

Adjust length of rod to minimum slack with carburetor lever on slow idle screw and engine not running. Ensure idle load control is fully retracted when retainer is installed.

SERVO CABLE, ADJUST

1. With cable connected to vacuum servo, pull servo end of cable assembly toward servo without moving lever.
2. If one of the holes in servo tab aligns with cable pin, connect pin to tab with retainer.
3. If none of the holes in servo tab aligns with cable pin, move cable away from servo until next closest hole aligns, then connect pin to tab with retainer. **Do not stretch cable to make adjustment, as the engine will not be able to return to idle.**

Gasoline Engine Section

NOTE: This section contains service information on the 4-151 (2.5L) Pontiac built engine. For service on V6-231 (3.8L) & V6-252 (4.1L) engines, refer to Section 1. For service on V6-173 (2.8L), V6-229 (3.8L), V8-305 (5.0L) & V8-350 (5.7L) engines, refer to Section 3. For service on V8-307 (5.0L) engine, refer to Section 4.

INDEX

ENGINE MOUNTS REPLACE

1. Disconnect battery ground cable.
2. Raise and support front of vehicle.
3. Remove mount through bolts on left and righthand side, **Fig. 1.**
4. Raise front of engine and remove mount to engine attaching bolts, then remove mounts.
5. Reverse procedure to install.

ENGINE REPLACE

1. Disconnect battery ground cable.
2. Drain cooling system.
3. Scribe alignment marks on hood, then remove hood from hinges.
4. Remove A/C compressor, brackets and position aside.
5. Remove upper and lower radiator hoses from engine.
6. Remove fan assembly.
7. On models with auto. trans., remove radiator and shroud assembly. On models with manual transmission, remove upper half of radiator shroud.
8. Disconnect power steering hoses, then remove power steering pump from mounting brackets.

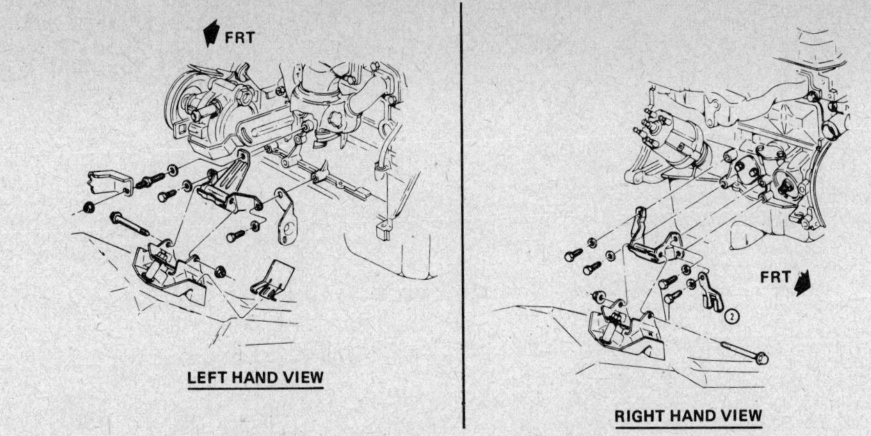

Fig. 1 Engine mounts

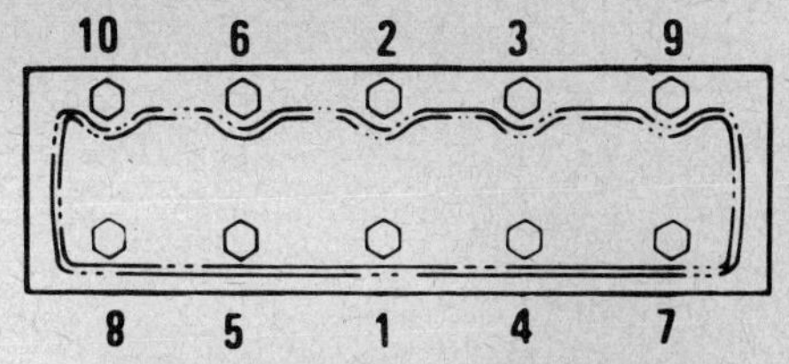

Fig. 2 Cylinder head tightening sequence

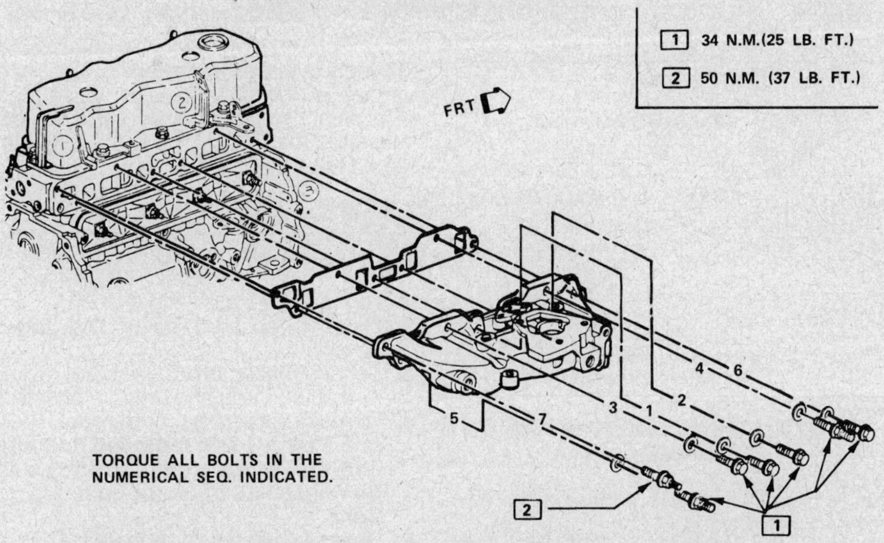

Fig. 3 Intake manifold tightening sequence

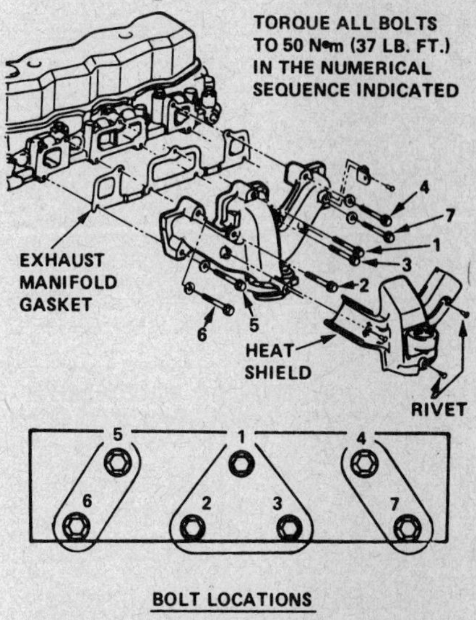

Fig. 4 Exhaust manifold tightening sequence. 1982–83

9. Disconnect engine wiring at bulkhead connection.
10. Disconnect inlet and return fuel lines at flex hoses.
11. Remove vacuum brake hose from filter.
12. Disconnect engine to body ground strap from rear of cylinder head.
13. From inside of vehicle, remove right-hand hush panel, then disconnect E.C.M. harness from E.C.M. unit.
14. Remove splash shield from right fender and feed E.C.M. harness from inside of vehicle.
15. Disconnect heater hoses from heater core.
16. Disconnect throttle linkage and canister hose from E.F.I. assembly.
17. Raise and support vehicle.
18. Disconnect electrical connectors from transmission.
19. Remove flywheel dust cover.
20. On models equipped with automatic transmission, remove torque converter to flywheel bolts.
21. Remove bellhousing to engine bolts.
22. Disconnect exhaust pipe at manifold, then remove exhaust pipe support at bellhousing.
23. Disconnect catalytic converter at tail pipe joint, then remove converter and exhaust pipe assembly.
24. Disconnect starter wiring, then remove starter assembly.
25. On models equipped with manual transmission, remove clutch fork return spring.
26. Remove motor mount through bolts.
27. Lower vehicle, then using a suitable jack and block of wood, support transmission.
28. Support weight of engine with suitable lifting device.
29. Remove engine from vehicle. On models equipped with manual transmission, swing engine slightly to the right to remove clutch swing arm from ball.

CYLINDER HEAD REPLACE

1. Drain cooling system and remove air cleaner.
2. Disconnect accelerator and fuel and vacuum lines at carburetor.
3. Remove intake and exhaust manifolds.
4. Remove bolts attaching alternator bracket to cylinder head.
5. If equipped with power steering or A/C, remove right side front bracket.
6. Disconnect temperature sending unit wiring harness, battery ground cable and radiator and heater hoses.
7. Disconnect spark plug wires and remove spark plugs.
8. Remove rocker cover, then back off rocker arm nuts.
9. Pivot rocker arms to clear pushrods and remove pushrods.
10. Remove cylinder head attaching bolts and cylinder head.
11. Reverse procedure to install. Coat cylinder head bolts with sealer. Torque bolts in sequence as shown in **Fig. 2.** When installing intake and exhaust manifolds, refer to **Figs. 3 through 6** for bolt tightening sequence. Note that on 1985 models, all exhaust manifold bolts are torqued to 44 ft. lbs. On 1986 models, bolts 1, 2, 6 and 7 are torqued to 32 ft. lbs. and bolts 3, 4 and 5 are torqued to 37 ft. lbs. **On 1985-86 models, torque cylinder head attaching bolts in the following sequence:**
    a. Torque all bolts in sequence, **Fig. 2,** to 18 ft. lbs.
    b. Torque bolt No. 9 to 29 ft. lbs. and all other bolts to 22 ft. lbs.
    c. Tighten bolt No. 9 an additional 90° and all other bolts an additional 120°.

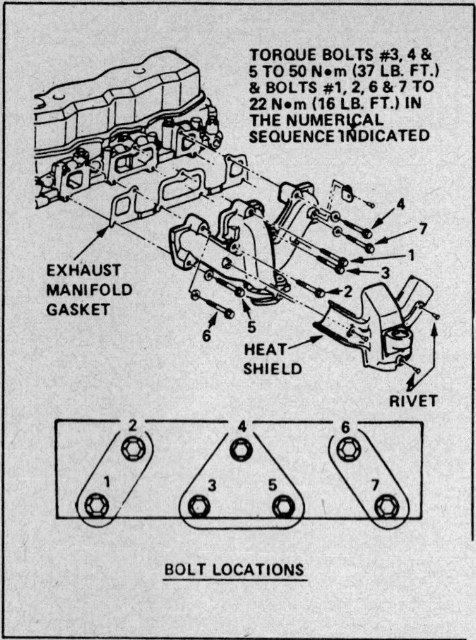

Fig. 5 Exhaust manifold tightening sequence. 1984

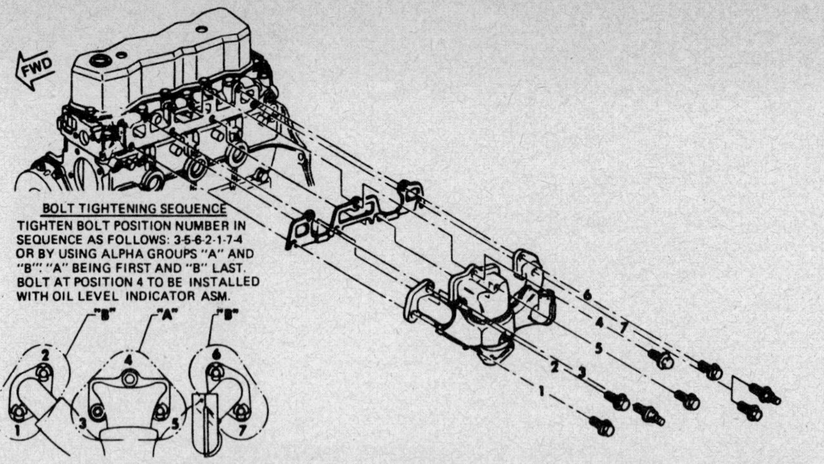

Fig. 6 Exhaust manifold tightening sequence. 1985–86

INTAKE MANIFOLD

REPLACE

1. Disconnect battery ground cable.
2. Remove air cleaner and heat stove pipe.
3. Remove PCV valve and disconnect hose from throttle body unit.
4. Drain cooling system, then disconnect fuel lines and vacuum hoses from intake manifold.
5. Disconnect electrical connectors and throttle linkage from throttle body unit.
6. Disconnect automatic transaxle downshift linkage and cruise control linkage, as applicable.
7. Disconnect throttle linkage and bellcrank and position aside.
8. Disconnect heater hose from intake manifold.
9. Remove alternator mounting bracket, then the ignition coil.
10. Remove intake manifold attaching bolts and the manifold.
11. Reverse procedure to install, using a new gasket. Torque attaching bolts to specifications in sequence, Fig. 3.

ROCKER ARM STUDS

REPLACE

1. Remove rocker arm cover.
2. Remove rocker arm and nut.
3. Using a deep socket, remove rocker stud.
4. Install new stud and tighten to 50 ft. lbs.
5. Install rocker arm and tighten nut to 20 ft. lbs.
6. Install rocker cover using new gasket.

VALVES

ADJUST

These engines are equipped with hydraulic valve lifters. No provision for adjustment is provided.

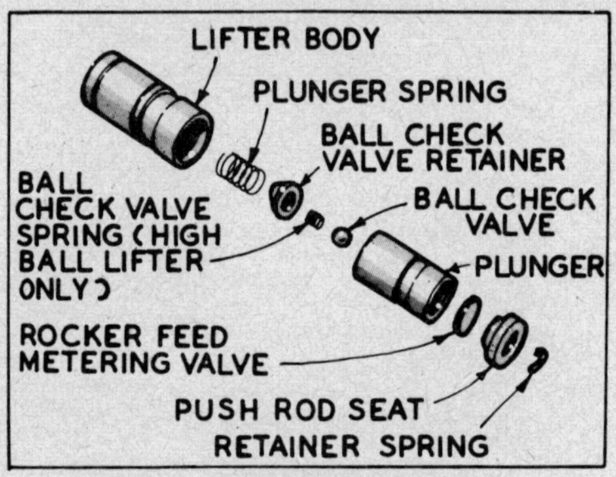

Fig. 7 Hydraulic valve lifter

VALVE ARRANGEMENT

FRONT TO REAR

4-151 .... E-I-I-E-E-I-I-E

CAM LOBE LIFT SPECIFICATIONS

Year	Engine	Int.	Exh.
1982-86	4-151	.398	.398

VALVE TIMING

INTAKE OPENS BEFORE TDC

Engine	Year	Degrees
4-151	1982	33

VALVE GUIDES

Valve guides are cast integral with the cylinder head. Valves with oversize stems are available in .001 inch, .003 inch and .005 inch larger than standard.

Oversize reamers are required to enlarge valve guide holes to fit the oversize stems. When installing a valve with a .005 inch oversize stem, ream valve guide to .003 inch oversize and then to .005 inch oversize. Always reface the valve and valve seat after reaming valve guide. Valves are marked .001, .003 or .005 with colored ink.

VALVE LIFTERS

REPLACE

1. Remove intake manifold.
2. Remove pushrod cover and valve cover.
3. Loosen rocker arm, then rotate rocker arm off pushrod and remove pushrod.
4. Remove lifter, Fig. 7. **If more than one lifter is to be removed, identify lifters and pushrods, so they can be reinstalled in their original locations.**
5. Reverse procedure to install. Torque rocker arm ball nut to 20 ft. lbs.

TIMING CASE COVER

REPLACE

If necessary to replace the cover oil seal it can be accomplished without removing the timing chain cover.

1. Disconnect battery ground cable.
2. Remove torsional damper and the two oil pan to front cover screws.
3. Remove front cover retaining screws.
4. Pull cover forward just enough to permit cutting of oil pan front seal, then cut oil pan front seal flush with cylinder block at both sides and remove front cover.
5. Reverse procedure to install.

CAMSHAFT

REPLACE

1. Disconnect battery ground cable.
2. Drain oil pan and radiator.
3. Remove radiator, fan and water pump pulley.
4. Remove distributor, spark plugs and fuel pump.
5. Remove pushrod cover and valve cover, then loosen rocker arms and rotate rocker arms off pushrods.
6. Remove pushrods and valve lifters. **Identify pushrods and lifters so**

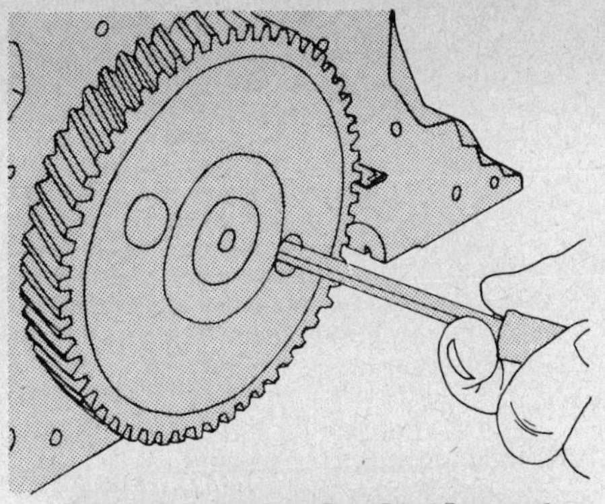

Fig. 8 Camshaft thrust plate screw removal

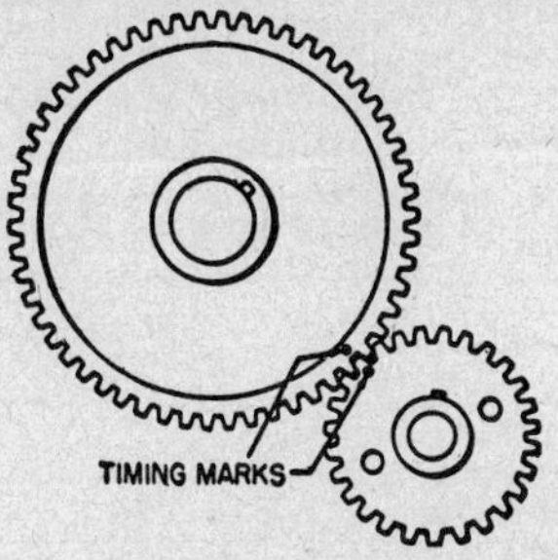

Fig. 11 Valve timing marks

they can be reinstalled in their original locations.

7. Remove harmonic balancer and timing gear cover.
8. Remove camshaft thrust plate retaining screws, **Fig. 8**, and carefully pull camshaft out of engine. **Use care to avoid damaging camshaft bearings.**
9. To remove gear, proceed as follows:
   a. Support gear on press using a suitable sleeve, **Fig. 9**, then press camshaft out of gear using a socket or other suitable tool. **Thrust plate must be positioned so that Woodruff key in shaft does not damage thrust plate when camshaft is pressed out.**
   b. To install gear, firmly support camshaft at back of front journal in press using plate adapters.
   c. Place gear spacer ring and thrust plate cover end of shaft and install Woodruff key.
   d. Press gear until it bottoms against the gear spacer ring. Check end clearance which should be .0015 to .0050 inch, **Fig. 10.** If clearance is less than specified, the spacer ring should be replaced. If clearance is greater than specified, the thrust plate should be replaced.
10. Carefully install camshaft making sure that marks are aligned as shown in **Fig. 11.** Torque thrust plate retaining screws to 75 inch lbs. **The valve timing marks shown in Fig. 11 do not indicate TDC compression stroke for No. 1 cylinder for use during distributor installation. Before installing distributor, turn crankshaft one complete revolution to firing position of No. 1 cylinder (TDC compression stroke), then install distributor in its original position and align shaft so that rotor points toward No. 1 cylinder in distributor cap.**
11. Reverse procedure to install remaining components.

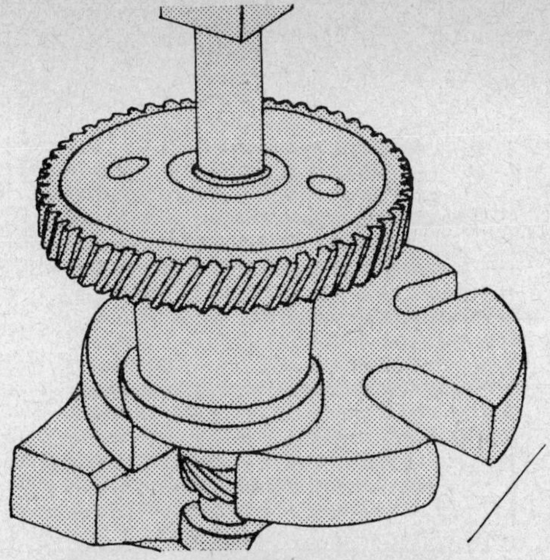

Fig. 9 Camshaft gear removal

PISTON & ROD ASSEMBLE

Assemble pistons and rods as indicated in **Fig. 12.**

The notch cast in the piston heads must face the front of the engine when the piston and connecting rod assemblies are installed.

Correct piston and connecting rod assembly installation is extremely important as incorrect installation could cause an engine knock.

Upon installation, measure the connecting rod side clearance using a suitable feeler gauge. Measurement obtained should be .006-.022 inch.

PISTONS, PINS & RINGS

Pistons and rings are available in standard sizes and oversizes of .005, .010, .020 and .030 inch.

Piston pins are available in oversizes of .001 and .003 inch.

MAIN & ROD BEARINGS

Main bearings are available in standard sizes and undersizes of .001 and .002 inch.

Rod bearings are available in standard sizes and undersizes of .001 and .002 inch.

CRANKSHAFT REAR OIL SEAL REPLACE

1. Disconnect battery ground cable.
2. Remove transmission.
3. Remove flywheel retaining bolts, then flywheel.
4. On all models, remove seal using suitable screwdriver.

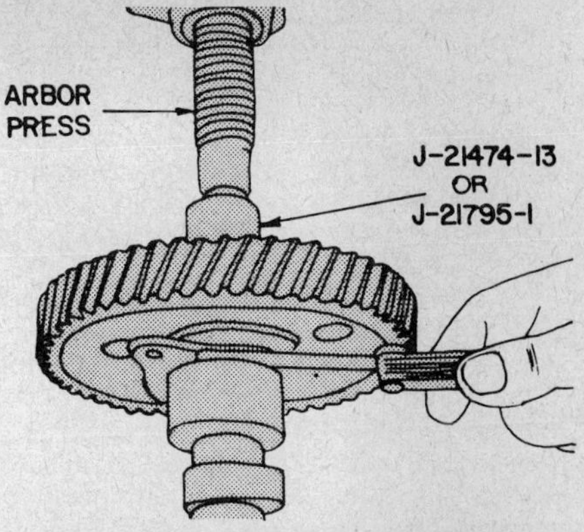

Fig. 10 Camshaft gear installation & thrust plate clearance check

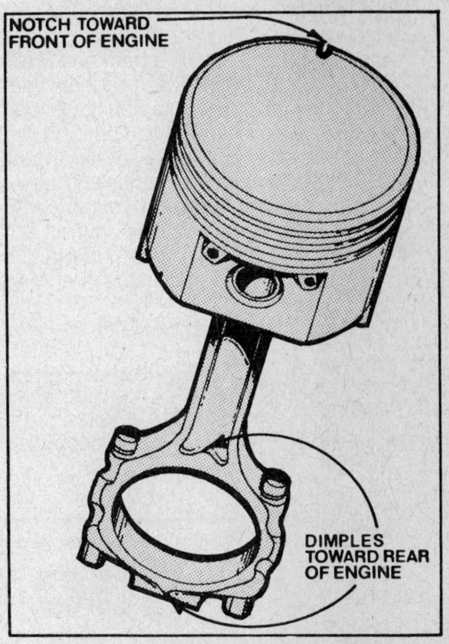

Fig. 12 Piston & rod assembly

5. Reverse procedure to install. **To facilitate installation, apply a light coat of engine oil to outside sealing surface of new seal, then evenly press seal into place.**

OIL PAN REPLACE

1. Disconnect battery ground cable and remove engine fan.
2. Raise vehicle and drain oil pan.
3. Disconnect exhaust pipe at manifold and loosen hanger bracket.
4. Remove starter and place aside, then remove flywheel housing inspection cover.
5. Raise engine slightly to remove weight from engine mounts and remove both brackets to engine mount bolts.
6. Remove oil pan bolts, then raise engine to allow oil pan removal and remove oil pan.
7. Reverse procedure to install.

OIL PUMP
REPLACE

Remove oil pan. Remove the two flange mounting bolts and nut and remove pump.

Remove the four cover retaining screws, cover, gears and shaft and regulator parts, Fig. 13.

Do not attempt to remove or disturb oil pickup tube.

Clean and inspect pump. If any of the following conditions are found, the oil pump should be replaced:

1. Inspect pump body for cracks or wear.
2. Inspect gears for excessive wear or damage.
3. Inspect shaft for looseness in housing.
4. Inspect inside of cover for wear which may permit oil to leak past the ends of the gears.
5. Inspect oil pickup screen.

To assemble, install drive gear and shaft in housing, then install idler gear with smooth side facing cover. Install cover and screws and torque screws to 105 inch lbs. Make sure that shaft turns freely. Install regulatory valve spring, retainer and pin.

To install pump, align driveshaft with distributor tang, then position pump on engine and install retaining bolts and nut. On 1982-84 models torque bolts and nuts to 20 to 22 ft. lbs.

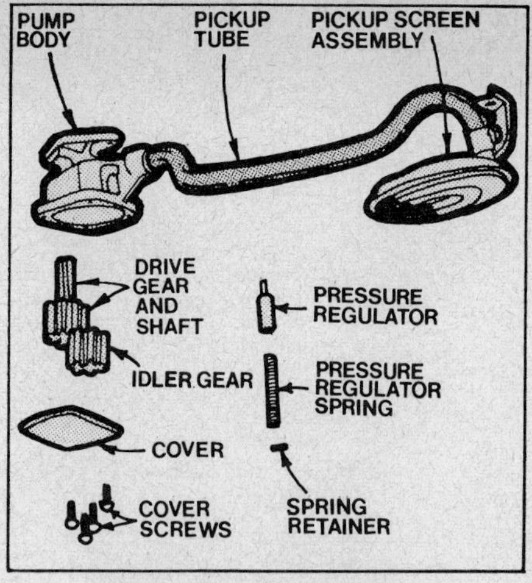

Fig. 13 Oil pump disassembled

WATER PUMP
REPLACE

Water pump is serviced as an assembly only .

1. Disconnect battery cable and drain cooling system.
2. Loosen alternator adjusting bolt and remove fan belt.
3. Remove fan and pulley.
4. Disconnect radiator and heater hose at pump, then remove water pump retaining bolts and pump.
5. Reverse procedure to install. Torque water pump retaining bolts to 15 ft. lbs.

FUEL PUMP
REPLACE

1. Disconnect fuel lines from pump.
2. Remove pump retaining bolts and pump.
3. Remove all gasket material from the pump and block gasket surfaces. Apply sealer on both sides of new gasket.
4. Position gasket on pump flange and hold pump in position against its mounting surface. Make sure rocker arm is riding on camshaft eccentric.
5. Press pump tight against its mounting. Install retaining screws and tighten them alternately.
6. Connect fuel lines. Then operate engine and check for leaks.

Before installing the pump, it is good practice to crank the engine so that the nose of the camshaft eccentric is out of the way of the fuel pump rocker arm when the pump is installed. In this way there will be the least amount of tension on the rocker arm, thereby easing the installation of the pump.

BELT TENSION DATA

Belt	New Lbs.	Used Lbs.
1982		
5/16 inch wide	80	50
3/8 inch wide	140	70
15/32 inch wide	165	90
7/16 inch wide	165	90
1983-86		
Air Conditioning	165	90
Generator With A/C	165	90
Less A/C	145	70
Power Steering	145	70

V8-350 (5.7L) Diesel Engine Section

NOTE: Refer to Section 5 for service procedures on this engine.

Clutch & Transmission Section

INDEX

CLUTCH PEDAL

ADJUST

1982–83

1. Disconnect return spring from clutch fork.
2. Rotate clutch lever and shaft assembly until clutch pedal is firmly seated against rubber bumper on dash brace.
3. Push outer end of clutch fork rearward until release bearing lightly contacts diaphragm spring fingers.
4. Disconnect lower pushrod from lever and shaft assembly and install it in gauge hole.
5. Rotate fork rod finger tight until all lash has been removed from linkage.
6. Remove swivel from gauge hole and install it in hole furthest from lever and shaft assembly.
7. Install washers and retainer, then tighten locknut being careful not to change length of rod.
8. Reconnect return spring and check pedal free travel. Free travel should be approximately 1.0 inch.

1984–88

The hydraulic clutch release mechanism consists of a clutch master cylinder, slave cylinder and connecting hose which is serviced as a complete assembly. The hydraulic system is supplied filled with fluid and no adjustment or bleeding is required. Before removing release mechanism for service, verify that a malfunction exists as follows:

1. Remove clutch housing dust shield and note position of slave cylinder plunger.
2. Depress clutch pedal fully and measure slave cylinder plunger travel.
3. If plunger moves release lever a minimum of .57 inch, check clutch disc, pressure plate, release fork and bearing for damage and repair as needed.
4. If plunger does not move at least .57 inch, check fluid level in clutch master cylinder with pedal depressed, and fill to step in reservoir. **Do not overfill. Upper portion of reservoir must be open to accept fluid displaced in slave cylinder due to clutch wear.**
5. Recheck plunger travel and check hydraulic components for leaks.
6. If plunger travel is still less than .57 inch, or if excessive leakage is noted, replace hydraulic system as an assembly.

CLUTCH

REPLACE

1. Remove transmission as described under "Transmission, Replace."
2. On 1982-83 models, disconnect clutch fork pushrod and spring.
3. On 1984-88 models, disconnect pushrod from clutch master cylinder, then remove slave cylinder heat shield and the slave cylinder from flywheel housing.
4. On all models, remove flywheel housing from engine.
5. Slide clutch fork from ball stud and remove fork from dust boot. **Look for an "X" mark on flywheel and clutch cover. If "X" mark is not evident, make punch marks on flywheel and clutch cover for indexing purposes during installation.**
6. Loosen clutch-to-flywheel attaching bolts evenly one turn at a time until spring pressure is released, then remove bolts and clutch assembly.
7. Reverse procedure to install, using suitable pilot tool to center clutch disc. Tighten clutch cover bolts evenly and gradually to avoid distorting cover.

FOUR SPEED TRANS.

REPLACE

1. Disconnect battery ground cable.
2. Raise vehicle and drain lubricant from transmission.
3. Remove torque arm as described in the "Rear Axle, Propeller Shaft & Brake Section" of this manual.
4. Scribe mark on companion flange and driveshaft yoke, then remove driveshaft.
5. Disconnect speedometer cable and back-up light switch electrical connector.
6. Remove shifter assembly to shifter support bolts and remove shifter assembly from transmission.
7. Remove crossmember to transmission mount bolts and catalytic converter to transmission bracket, if equipped, then remove crossmember to frame bolts.
8. Raise transmission and remove crossmember.
9. Remove transmission to clutch housing upper attaching bolts and install guide pins.
10. Remove transmission to clutch housing lower attaching bolts, then slide transmission straight back on guide pins until main drive splines are clear of clutch plate and remove transmission from vehicle.
11. Reverse procedure to install.

FOUR SPEED TRANS. SHIFT LINKAGE

ADJUST

1. Place selector lever in neutral.
2. Loosen trunnion nuts on transmission control rod.
3. Place transmission lever and bracket assembly in neutral and install a gauge pin through hole and slot provided in bracket.
4. Position lever on transmission in neutral.
5. Tighten trunnion nuts and remove gauge pin.
6. Position shift lever in Reverse, set steering column lever in Lock position and lock ignition. Push up on control rod to remove clearance and tighten nut of adjusting swivel.

FIVE SPEED TRANS.

REPLACE

1983–86

1. Disconnect battery ground cable.
2. From inside vehicle, remove screws attaching bezel to tunnel, then remove bezel by slipping over boot and shift lever.
3. With shift lever in neutral, hold boot out of way and remove four bolts attaching shift lever to transmission, then remove shift lever assembly.
4. Raise vehicle and scribe a mark on companion flange and driveshaft yoke, then remove driveshaft.
5. Remove bolts attaching catalytic converter support bracket to transmission.
6. Remove two bolts attaching transmission mount to support.
7. Raise transmission and remove two long end bolts, then remove transmission support.
8. Disconnect speedometer cable and back-up light switch wire connector.
9. Remove transmission to clutch housing upper attaching bolts and install guide pins.
10. Remove transmission to clutch housing lower attaching bolts, then slide transmission back on guide pins until main drive gear splines clear clutch plate and remove transmission from vehicle.
11. Reverse procedure to install.

1987–88

1. Disconnect battery ground cable.
2. Raise and support vehicle.

3. Remove shift lever attaching bolts from transmission. **The upper and lower levers are permanently bonded together and must not be separated.**
4. Remove torque arm and propeller shaft.
5. Disconnect speedometer cable and back-up lamp electrical connector from transmission.
6. Support transmission using a suitable jack, then remove transmission mount attaching bolts and catalytic converter hanger.
7. Remove crossmember attaching bolts and the crossmember.
8. Remove dust cover attaching bolts, then the transmission-to-engine attaching bolts and carefully lower transmission from vehicle.
9. Reverse procedure to install.

Rear Axle, Propeller Shaft & Brake Section

INDEX

REAR AXLES

Figs. 1 and 2 illustrate the rear axle assemblies used on conventional models. When necessary to overhaul either of these units, refer to the Rear Axle Specifications table in this chapter.

In this rear axle, **Fig. 1,** the rear axle housing and differential carrier are cast into an integral assembly. The drive pinion assembly is mounted in two opposed tapered roller bearings. The pinion bearings are preloaded by a spacer behind the front bearings. The pinion is positioned by a shim between the head of the pinion and the rear bearing.

The differential is supported in the carrier by two tapered roller side bearings. These bearings are preloaded by shims located between the bearings and carrier housing. The differential assembly is positioned for proper ring gear and pinion backlash by varying these shims. The differential case houses two side gears in mesh with two pinions mounted on a pinion shaft which is held in place by a lock screw. The side gears and pinions are backed by thrust washers.

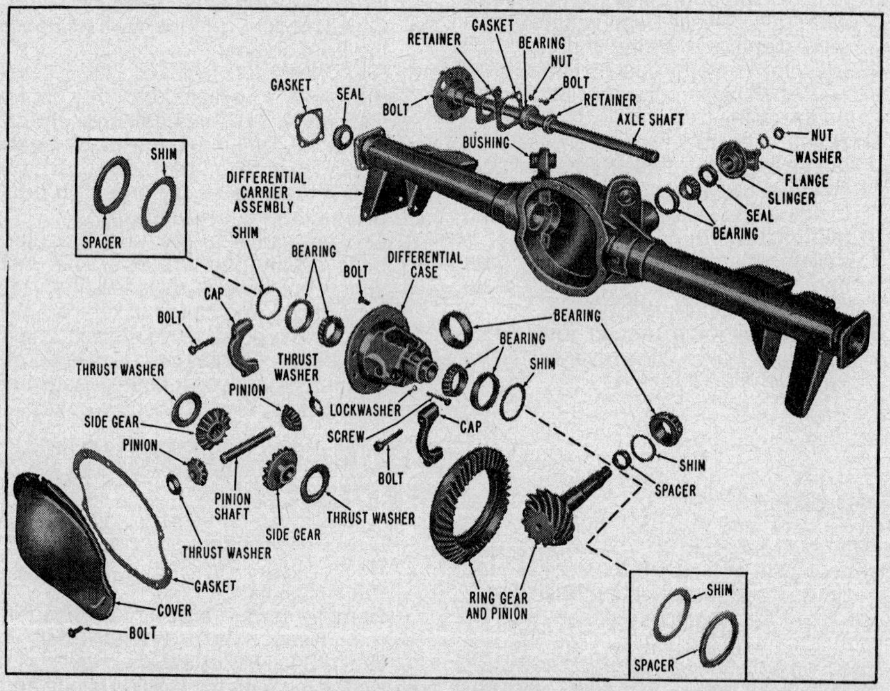

Fig. 1 Rear Axle assembly exploded. Exc. "C" lock axle retention

REAR AXLE, REPLACE

Exc. Firebird

It is not necessary to remove rear axle assembly from vehicle to perform any normal service operation. However, if any part of housing is damaged, rear axle assembly may be removed and installed using the following procedure.

1. Raise car and place a floor jack under center of axle housing so it starts to raise rear axle assembly. Place jack stands solidly under frame members on both sides.
2. Disconnect rear U-joint from drive pinion flange and support propeller shaft out of the way.
3. Remove both axle shafts.
4. Support both brake backing plates out of the way.
5. Disconnect rear brake hose bracket by removing top cover bolt. Remove brake line from housing by bending back tabs.
6. Loosen remaining cover bolts, break loose cover about 1/8 inch and allow lube to drain.
7. Disconnect shock absorbers at axle housing.
8. Disconnect upper control arms at axle housing.
9. Slowly lower jack until all spring tension is relieved and remove springs.
10. Disconnect lower control arms and remove axle assembly.

Firebird

1. Hoist car and support at frame and under rear axle housing.
2. Disconnect both shock absorbers and remove bolt from left side of track bar to axle.
3. Remove bolt from brake line junction block at axle housing and disconnect brake lines from junction block.
4. Lower rear axle assembly and remove springs.
5. Remove rear wheels and drums and remove rear axle cover and drain lube.
6. Disconnect brake lines from axle housing clips.
7. Remove axle shafts, brake backing plates, lower control arms and torque arm from axle housing.
8. Disconnect driveshaft from rear axle flange and place aside after marking for reinstallation.
9. Remove rear axle housing.
10. Reverse procedure to install.

AXLE SHAFT, REPLACE

The axle type identification marks for will be stamped on right rear axle tube, on forward side.

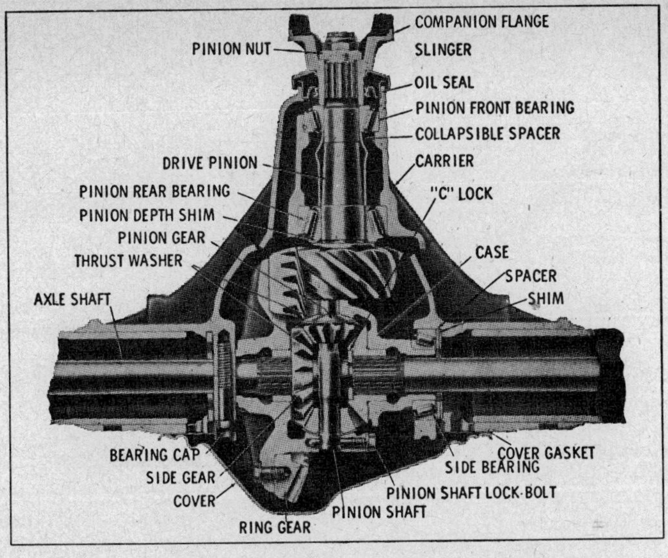

Fig. 2 Rear Axle assembly exploded. With "C" lock retention

TYPE "B & O" (EXC. 7½ inch)

1. To remove, take off wheels and brake drums.
2. Remove nuts holding retainer plates and brake backing plates. Pull retainers clear of bolts and reinstall two lower nuts finger tight to hold backing plate in position.
3. Use a slide hammer-type puller to remove axle shaft, **Fig. 3**.

Axle Shaft Bearing

1. Press axle shaft bearing off shaft.
2. Press new bearing against shoulder on shaft. **Outer retainer plate which retains bearing in housing must be on axle shaft before bearing is installed. A new outer retainer gasket can be installed after bearing. Use care not to wedge outer retainer between bearing and shoulder of shaft. Do not press bearing and inner retainer on in one operation.**
3. Press new inner retainer ring against bearing.

Axle Shaft Seal

1. Insert suitable tongs behind seal and pull straight out to remove seal.
2. Apply sealer to outside diameter of new seal.
3. Position seal over a suitable installer and drive straight into axle housing until tool bottoms on bearing shoulder in housing.

Axle Shaft, Install

1. Apply a coat of wheel bearing grease in bearing recess of housing. Also lightly lubricate the axle shaft with rear axle lube from the sealing surface to about 6 inch inboard.
2. Install new axle housing-to-brake backing plate gasket.
3. Install brake assembly with backing plate in proper position.
4. With a new outer retainer gasket in proper position, insert axle shaft until splines engage differential. Do not allow shaft to drag on seal.
5. Drive axle shaft into position.
6. Place new outer retainer gasket and retainer over studs and install nuts.
7. Install brake drums and wheels.

TYPE "C," "G," "K," "O" (7½ inch) & "P" AXLE

1. Raise and support car leaving the rear wheels and differential suspended.
2. Remove rear wheels and brake drums.
3. Remove differential cover and drain lubricant.
4. Remove pinion shaft lock bolt and pinion shaft.
5. Push axle shaft inward to permit removal of "C" locks then remove axle shaft.
6. Install axle shaft bearing and seal remover and remove the bearing and seal.

PROPELLER SHAFT REPLACE

One type of propeller shaft is used on all vehicles. The type being used is a one-piece shaft with two single cardan type U-joints.

Two methods of retention are used at the rear of the propeller shaft. The first method uses a pair of straps retained by bolts, while the second method uses a set of bolted flanges.

1. Raise and properly support vehicle, then mark relationship of propeller shaft to companion flange in order to insure correct alignment during reassembly.
2. Disconnect rear U-joint by removing strap bolts of flange bolts. **If U-joint bearing cups are loose, tape them together to avoid dropping and losing needle rollers.**
3. Remove propeller shaft by pulling rearward. **Support propeller shaft during removal. Do not allow propeller shaft to drop or allow universal joints to bend to an extreme angle.**

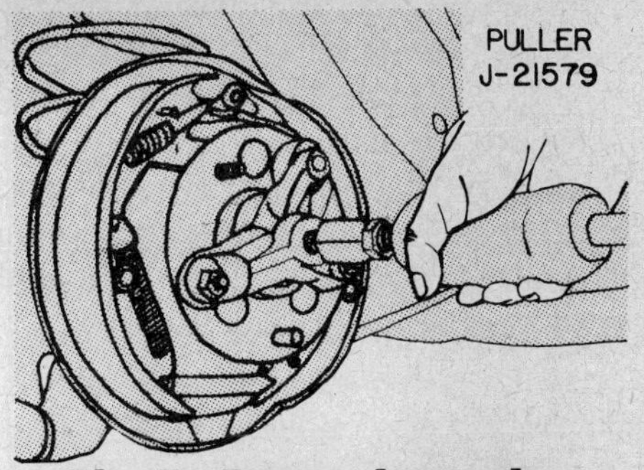

Fig. 3 Removing axle shaft with slide hammer-type puller

4. Reverse procedure to install, making sure that alignment marks are properly aligned. Torque strap retaining bolts to 15 ft. lbs. Torque flange bolts to 45 ft. lbs.

BRAKE ADJUSTMENTS

SELF-ADJUSTING BRAKES

These brakes have self-adjusting shoe mechanisms that assure correct lining-to-drum clearances at all times. The automatic adjusters operate only when the brakes are applied as the car is moving rearward.

Although the brakes are self-adjusting, an initial adjustment is necessary after the brake shoes have been relined or replaced, or when the length of the star wheel adjuster has been changed during some other service operation.

Frequent usage of an automatic transmission forward range to half reverse vehicle motion may prevent the automatic adjusters from functioning, thereby inducing low pedal heights. Should low pedal heights be encountered, it is recommended that numerous forward and reverse stops be made until satisfactory pedal height is obtained.

If a low pedal height condition cannot be corrected by making numerous reverse stops (provided the hydraulic system is free of air) it indicates that the self-adjusting mechanism is not functioning. Therefore, it will be necessary to remove the drum, clean, free up and lubricate the adjusting mechanism. Then adjust the brakes as follows, being sure the parking brake is fully released.

ADJUSTMENT

1. Knock out lanced area from brake backing plate with a suitable punch. **If this is done with drum installed on car, drum must be removed and brake area cleaned of all metal particles.**
2. Turn brake adjusting screw with tool J6166 or equivalent until brake shoes are expanded to where wheel can just be turned by hand. Amount of effort to turn wheels should be same at all four wheels.
3. While holding adjusting lever out of engagement with a suitable screwdriver, **Fig. 4**, back off adjusting screw several notches and check for drag. If brakes still drag, back off adjusting screw one or two more notches.

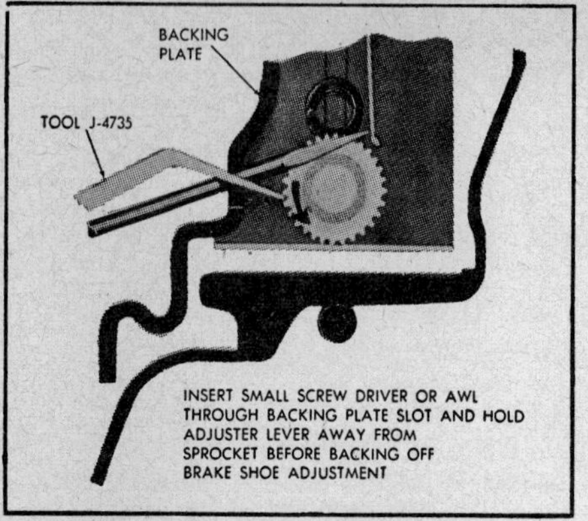

Fig. 4 Backing off adjusting screw

Brakes should be free of drag when screw has been backed off approximately 12 notches. Heavy drag at this point indicates tight parking brake cables.

4. Install new adjusting hole cover in brake backing plate cover.
5. Check parking brake adjustment. **The recommended method of adjusting the brakes is by using the Drum-to-Brake Shoe Clearance Gauge shown in Fig. 5 to check the diameter of the brake drum inner surface. Turn the tool to the opposite side and fit over the brake shoes by turning the star wheel until the gauge just slides over the linings, Fig. 6. Rotate the gauge around the brake shoe lining surface to assure proper clearance.**

PARKING BRAKE

ADJUST

LESS REAR DISC BRAKES

Adjustment of parking brake cable is necessary whenever rear brake cables are disconnected. The need for parking brake adjustment is indicated if parking brake pedal travel is less than 9 ratchet clicks or more than 17 ratchet clicks. It is also important that parking brake cables are not adjusted too tightly as brake drag will occur. Incorrect cable tension can damage brake system and cause premature wear to brake linings.

1. Raise and support rear of vehicle.
2. Apply parking brake pedal two to three ratchet clicks.
3. Tighten adjusting nut until left rear wheel on 1982-85 models, or right rear wheel on 1986-88 models, can just be rotated rearward but is locked when forward rotation is attempted.
4. Release parking brake and check to ensure that rear wheels rotate freely in either direction with no brake drag.

WITH REAR DISC BRAKES

1982–86

1. Lubricate parking brake cables at underbody rub points and at equalizer hooks. Check for free movement of all cables.
2. Ensure parking brake hand lever is in fully released position.

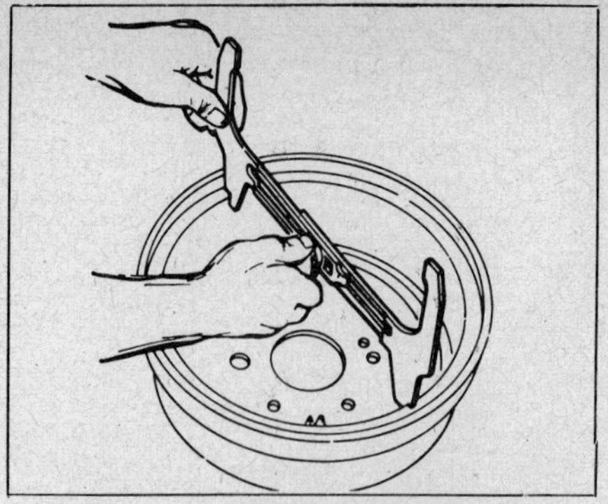

Fig. 5 Measuring brake drum inside diameter

3. Raise and support rear of vehicle.
4. Hold brake cable stud from turning and tighten equalizer nut until cable slack is removed.
5. Ensure caliper levers are against stops on caliper housing after tightening equalizer nut.
6. If levers are off the stops, loosen cable until levers return to stops.
7. Operate parking brake lever several times to check adjustment. After cable adjustment is performed, parking brake lever should travel 14 clicks with approximately 150 ± 20 pounds force of handle effort using tool J-28662.
8. Lower vehicle and ensure levers are against caliper stops. If necessary back off parking brake adjuster to keep levers against stops.

1987–88

1. Apply service brake pedal three times with a force of approximately 175 lbs.
2. Apply and release parking brake three times.
3. Raise and support vehicle.
4. Mark relationship of wheel to axle flange for installation reference.
5. Check parking brake lever for full release as follows:
   a. Turn ignition on and ensure "Brake" warning lamp is not lit.
   b. If warning lamp is lit and brake lever is completely released, remove slack from lever by pulling down on front parking brake cable.
   c. Turn ignition off.
6. Remove rear wheel and tire assemblies, then reinstall two lug nuts to retain rotors.
7. Pull parking brake lever back exactly four clicks.
8. Ensure parking brake levers on both calipers are contacting lever stops on caliper housings. If levers are not against stops, check for binding in rear cables and loosen cables at adjuster as necessary.
9. Tighten parking brake cable at adjuster until either right or left lever begins to move off stop, then back off until lever moves back just touching stop.
10. Apply and release parking brakes several times and check for proper operation. Parking brake lever should travel 14 clicks and rear wheels should not rotate forward when lever has been moved 8-14 clicks.

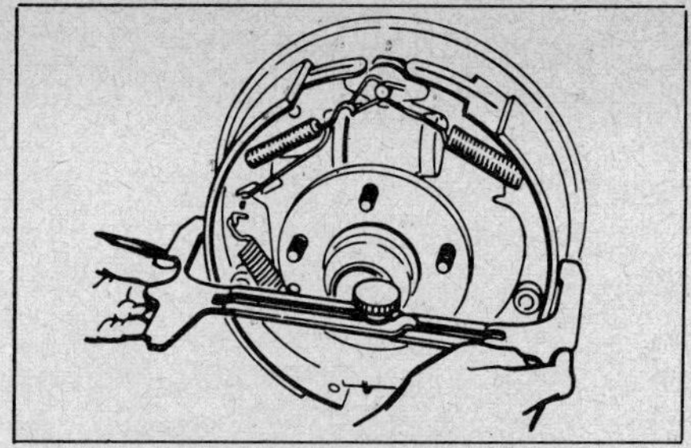

Fig. 6 Checking brake shoe lining clearance

POWER BRAKE UNIT

REPLACE

HYDRO-BOOST

Pump brake pedal several times with engine off to deplete accumulator of fluid.

1. Remove two nuts attaching master cylinder to booster, then move master cylinder away from booster with brake lines attached.
2. Remove three hydraulic lines from booster. Plug and cap all lines and outlets.
3. Remove retainer and washer securing booster pushrod to brake pedal arm.
4. Remove four nuts attaching booster unit to dash panel.
5. From engine compartment, loosen booster from dash panel and move booster pushrod inboard until it disconnects from brake pedal arm. Remove spring washer from brake pedal arm.
6. Remove booster unit from vehicle.
7. Reverse procedure to install. To purge system, disconnect feed wire from injection pump. Fill power steering pump reservoir, then crank engine for several seconds and recheck power steering pump fluid level. Connect injection pump feed wire and start engine, then cycle steering wheel from stop to stop twice and stop engine. Discharge accumulator by depressing brake pedal several times, then check fluid level. Start engine, then turn steering wheel from stop to stop and turn engine off. Check fluid level and add fluid as necessary. If foaming occurs, stop engine and wait for approximately one hour for foam to dissipate, then recheck fluid level.

VACUUM BOOSTER

1. Remove vacuum check valve.
2. If brake booster and master cylinder are being removed as an assembly, disconnect hydraulic lines and cover openings in master cylinder and lines to avoid entry of dirt. If only brake booster is to be removed, remove master cylinder retaining nuts and position master cylinder aside. **Be careful not to bend or kink hydraulic lines.**
3. Remove clevis pin retainer from brake pedal.
4. Remove brake booster retaining nuts and remove brake booster.
5. Reverse procedure to install.

MASTER CYLINDER REPLACE

1. Disconnect brake lines from two outlets on master cylinder and tape end of lines to prevent entrance of dirt.
2. On models less power brakes, disconnect master cylinder pushrod from brake pedal.
3. Remove two nuts attaching master cylinder to dash or power brake unit and remove master cylinder from vehicle.

Rear Suspension

INDEX

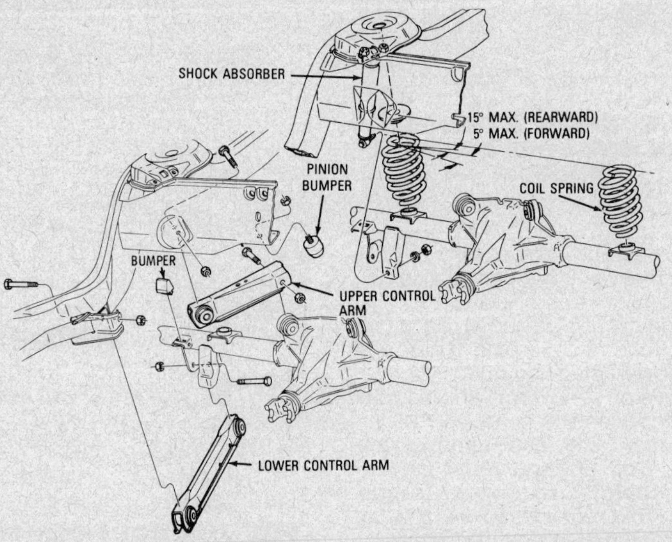

Fig. 1 Coil spring suspension (typical). Exc. Firebird

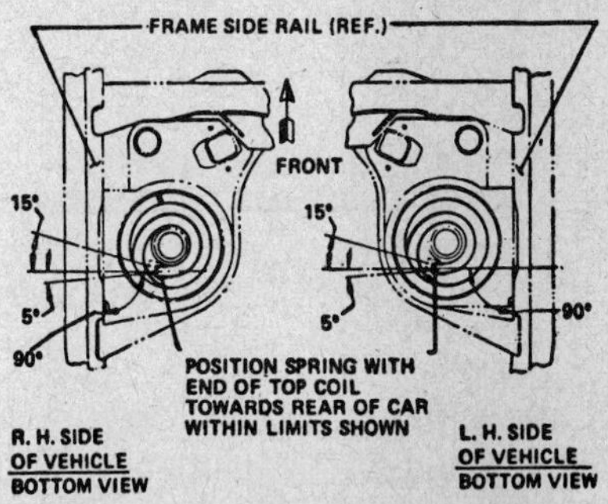

Fig. 2 Indexing coil springs. Exc. Firebird

SHOCK ABSORBER REPLACE

If vehicle is equipped with Superlift shock absorbers, bleed system air pressure through service valve before disconnecting lines at shock absorber fittings.

1. With rear axle supported properly, disconnect shock absorber from lower mounting nut. Use a wrench to prevent mounting stud rotation.
2. Disconnect shock absorber from upper mounting nut.
3. Reverse procedure to install.

COIL SPRING REPLACE

EXC. FIREBIRD

1. Support vehicle at frame rails and support rear axle with a suitable jack.
2. Remove brake line connector block bolt at axle housing.
3. Release brake line from clips on axle housing as necessary.
4. Disconnect upper control arms from axle housing, **Fig. 1.**
5. Disconnect shock absorbers from lower mountings.
6. Lower rear axle. Do not permit the rear brake hose to kink or stretch.
7. When the axle has been lowered sufficiently to provide clearance for coil spring removal, remove coil spring.
8. Reverse procedure to install. Ensure that coil springs are properly indexed, **Fig. 2.**

FIREBIRD

1. Raise car on suitable hoist and support rear axle on adjustable type lifting device.
2. Loosen track bar bolt at body brace and remove track bar mounting bolt at axle assembly, **Fig. 3.**
3. Disconnect rear brake hose clip at underbody and remove both shock absorber lower attaching nuts.
4. Remove prop shaft from vehicles with four cylinder engines.
5. Lower rear axle and remove coil spring and insulators.
6. Reverse procedure to install.

CONTROL ARMS & BUSHINGS REPLACE

Replace control arms one at a time to prevent axle misalignment, making installation difficult.

UPPER CONTROL ARMS

Firebird models use a single torque arm in place of upper control arms. Refer to "Torque Arm, Replace" and **Fig. 3.**

1. Support vehicle at frame and rear axle.
2. Remove control arm front and rear mounting bolts. **On some vehicles, disconnect the shock absorber lower mounting stud to provide clearance. Also, use a suitable jack under the nose of differential housing to aid bolt removal.**
3. Replace bushings as necessary, **Figs. 4 through 7.**
4. Reverse procedure to install. Tighten control arm bolts with vehicle at curb height.

LOWER CONTROL ARMS

Follow "Upper Control Arms" procedure for replacement of lower control arms. Lower control arm bushings are serviceable, **Figs. 4 and 5. On models equipped with a stabilizer bar, remove stabilizer bar outlined under "Stabilizer Bar & Bushings, Replace" procedure before removing lower control arm mounting bolts.**

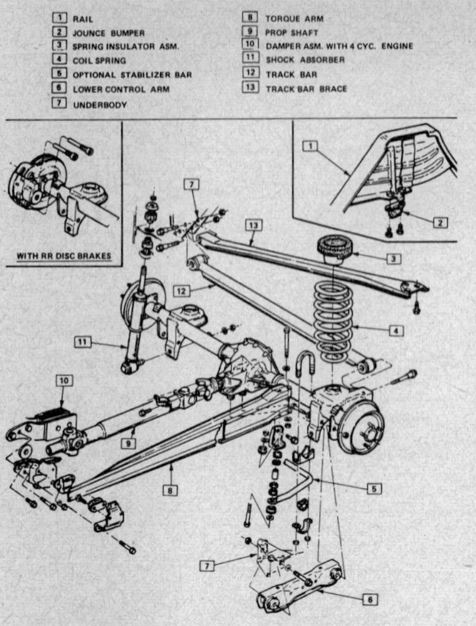

Fig. 3 Coil spring suspension. Firebird

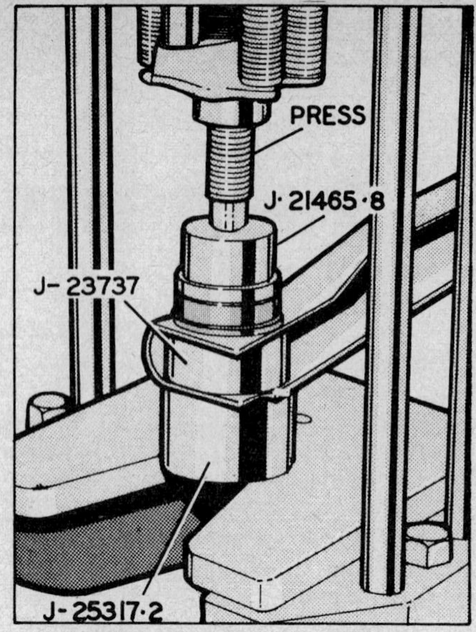

Fig. 4 Front & lower control arm rear bushing removal

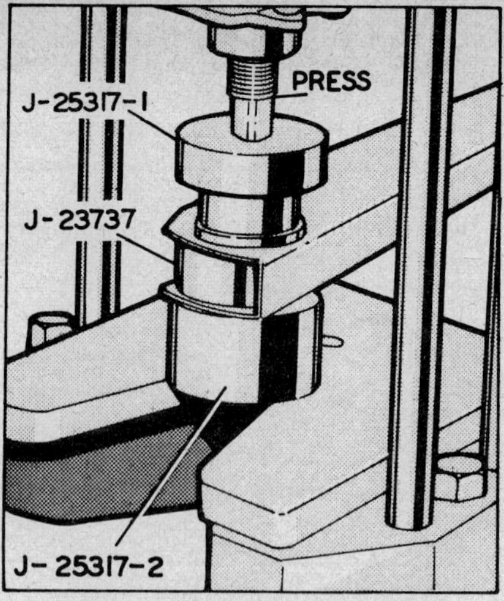

Fig. 5 Front & lower control arm rear bushing installation

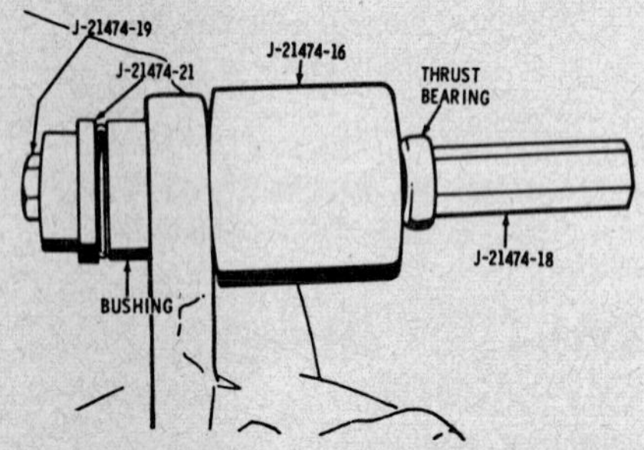

Fig. 6 Upper control arm rear bushing removal

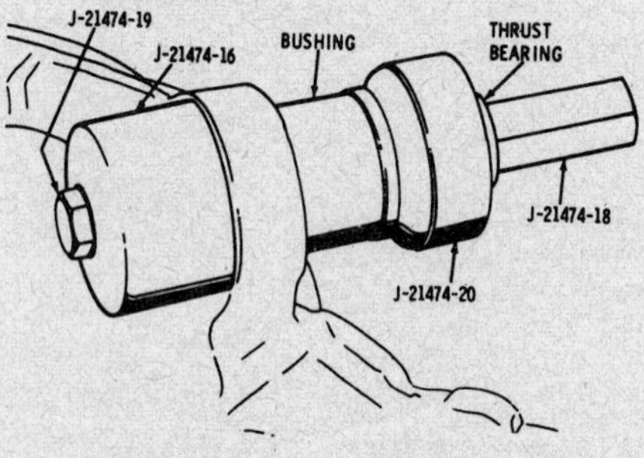

Fig. 7 Upper control arm rear bushing installation

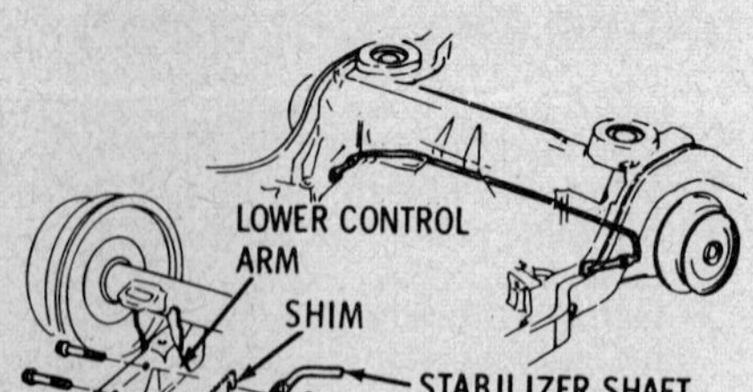

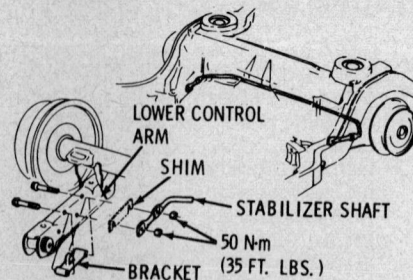

Fig. 8 Stabilizer bar installation. Bonneville & Grand Prix

TORQUE ARM
REPLACE

1. Raise vehicle on suitable hoist and support rear axle assembly with adjustable jack.
2. Loosen track bar bolt at body brace and remove track bar bolt at axle assembly.
3. Disconnect rear brake hose clip at underbody and remove both shock absorber lower attaching nuts.
4. Remove prop shaft from vehicles with four cylinder engine.
5. Lower rear axle and remove coil springs. **Coil springs must be removed before removing torque arm to avoid rear axle forward twist which may cause vehicle damage.**
6. Remove torque arm rear attaching bolts, front torque arm outer bracket and remove torque arm.
7. Reverse procedure to install. Torque track bar mounting nut at axle to 93 ft. lbs. and the track bar to body bracket nut to 58 ft. lbs.

STABILIZER BAR
REPLACE
EXC. FIREBIRD

1. With vehicle supported at rear axle, remove bolts attaching stabilizer bar to lower control arms, **Fig. 8.**
2. If equipped with shims, note number and location.
3. Reverse procedure to install. Tighten attaching bolts with vehicle at curb height.

FIREBIRD

Refer to **Fig. 9** for removal and installation procedures.

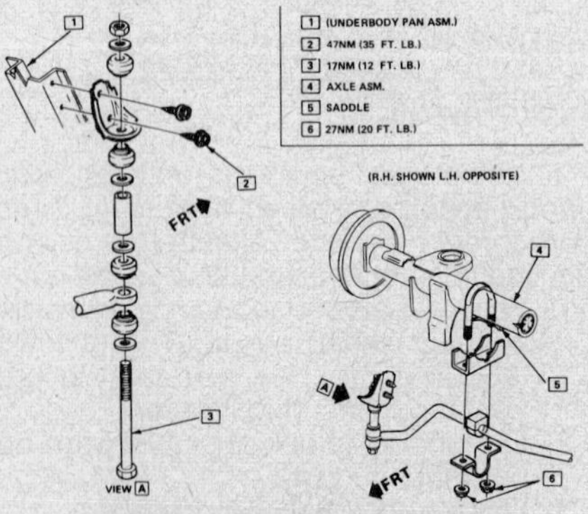

Fig. 9 Stabilizer bar installation. Firebird

Front Suspension & Steering Section

INDEX

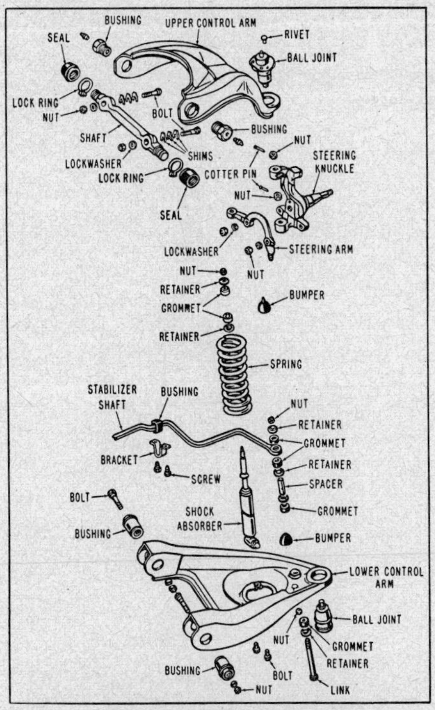

Fig. 1 Disassembled view of front suspension (typical). Exc. Firebird

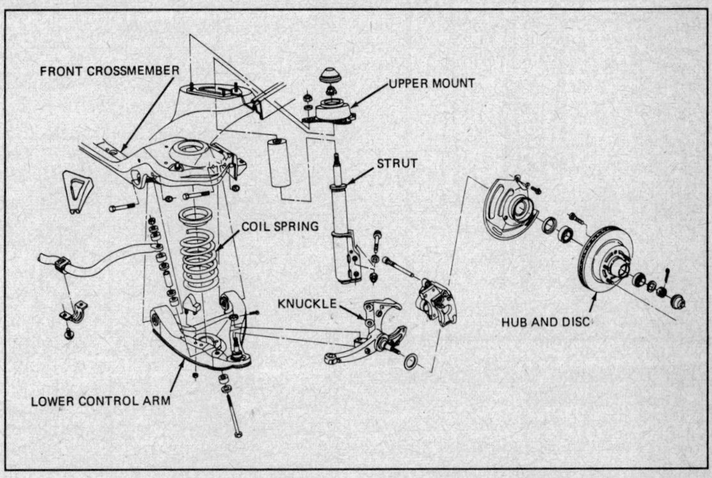

Fig. 2 Disassembled view of front suspension. Firebird

DESCRIPTION

EXC. FIREBIRD

The front suspension is of the conventional "A" frame design with coil springs and ball joints. The ball joints have a "fixed boot" grease seal for protection against the entry of dirt and water. The steering knuckles and spindles are of integral design.

On most models, an integral steering knuckle which is a combination steering knuckle, brake caliper support and steering arm is used. On other models, the steering knuckle is of the conventional type with a separate steering arm.

Rubber bushings at the inner ends of the upper control arms pivot on shafts attached to the car frame. Caster and camber adjustments are made with shims at this point, **Fig. 1.** Direct acting shock absorbers operate within the coil springs.

FIREBIRD

The front suspension is designed to allow each wheel to compensate for changes in the road surface level without appreciably affecting the opposite wheel. Each wheel is independently connected to the frame by a steering knuckle, strut assembly, ball joint, and lower control arm. The steering knuckles move in a prescribed three dimensional arc. The front wheels are held in proper relationship to each other by two tie rods which are connected to the steering knuckles and to a relay rod assembly.

Coil springs are mounted between the spring housings on the front crossmember and the lower control arms. The upper portion of each strut assembly extends through the fender well and attaches to the upper mount assembly with a nut, **Fig. 2.**

The inner ends of the lower control arm have pressed in bushings. Bolts, passing through the bushings, attach the arm to the suspension crossmember. The lower ball joint assembly is a press fit in the arm and attaches to the steering knuckle with a torque prevailing nut.

WHEEL BEARINGS ADJUST

1. While rotating wheel, torque spindle nut to 12 ft. lbs.
2. Back off spindle nut until just loose, then retighten by hand.
3. Loosen spindle nut until cotter pin can be inserted, however, do not loosen spindle nut more than $1/2$ flat.
4. With bearing properly adjusted, there should be .001-.005 inch endplay.

WHEEL BEARINGS REPLACE

1. Raise vehicle and remove front wheels.
2. Remove brake hose support to caliper mounting bracket screw.
3. Remove caliper to mounting bracket bolts. **Do not place strain on brake hose.**
4. Remove spindle nut, and disc and hub assembly. Grease retainer and inner bearing can now be removed.

CHECKING BALL JOINTS FOR WEAR

EXC. FIREBIRD

Before checking ball joints for wear, make sure the front wheel bearings are properly adjusted and that the control arms are tight.

Referring to **Fig. 3,** raise wheel with a jack placed under the lower control at the point shown. Then test by moving the

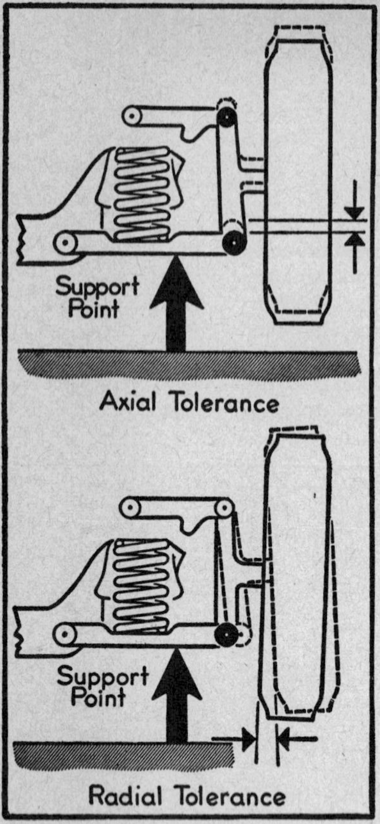

Fig. 3 Checking ball joints for wear

wheel up and down to check axial play, and rocking it at the top and bottom to measure radial play.

1. Upper ball joint should be replaced if there is any noticeable looseness at this joint. If the ball joint is the type using a built in rubber pre-load cushion it will be necessary to remove the ball stud from the knuckle. Then replace the ball joint retaining nut on the ball stud. Using a socket and torque wrench, measure amount of torque required to turn the ball stud in its socket. If any torque is required, the ball joint is satisfactory. If no torque is required, the ball joint must be replaced.
2. A visual wear indicator is built into the lower ball joint on all models, **Fig. 4.**

CHECKING FRONT SUSPENSION FOR WEAR

FIREBIRD

1. Raise vehicle with floor jack placed under frame torque box, located behind front wheel.
2. Place steering wheel in locked position, then place suitable dial indicator on outside perimeter of wheel.
3. Test by moving wheel back and forth without moving steering wheel. Gauge reading should not exceed .108 inch.
4. If gauge reading is not within specifications, a thorough front end inspection should be performed and parts replaced as necessary.

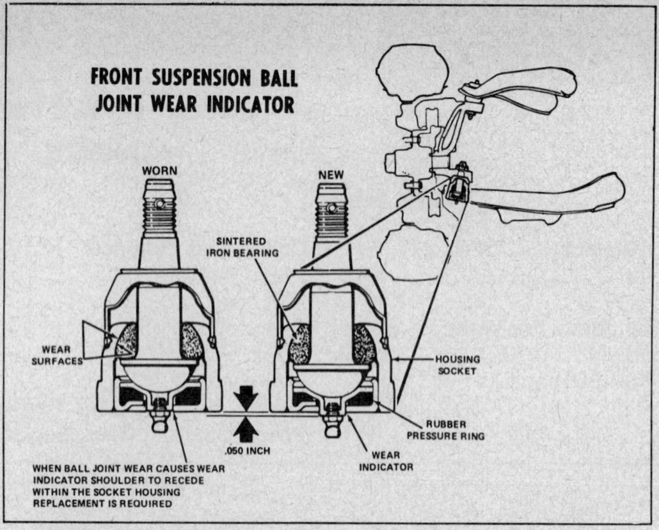

Fig. 4 Lower ball joint wear indicator. Exc. Firebird

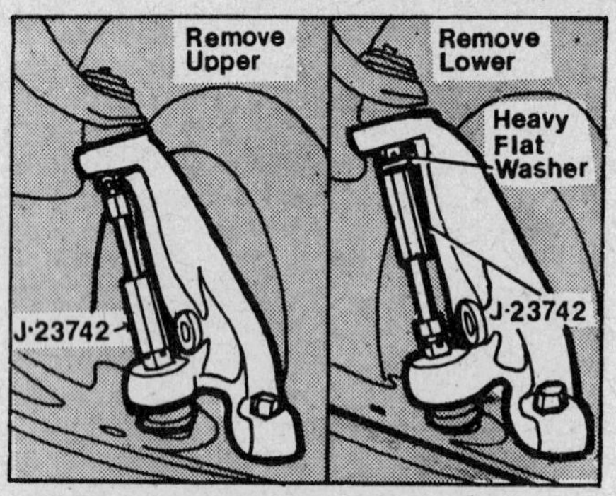

Fig. 5 Removing ball joint studs from steering knuckle

BALL JOINTS REPLACE

EXC. FIREBIRD

On all models the upper ball joint is riveted to the control arm. All service ball joints, however, are provided with bolt, nut and washer assemblies for replacement purposes.

The lower ball joint is pressed into the control arm. They may be pressed out and new joints pressed in.

Upper Ball Joint

1. Raise vehicle and support lower control arm.
2. Remove wheel assembly.
3. Remove upper ball joint stud from steering knuckle, **Fig. 5.**
4. Drill or chisel rivet heads from ball joint rivets. Then, drive rivets from control arm with a suitable punch.
5. Install new ball joint and torque retaining bolts to 9 ft. lbs. except on Parisienne and Safari, 13 ft. lbs. on Parisienne, or 8 ft. lbs. on Safari.
6. Install ball joint stud into steering knuckle and torque to 65 ft. lbs.
7. Install cotter pin.
8. Install wheel assembly and lower vehicle.

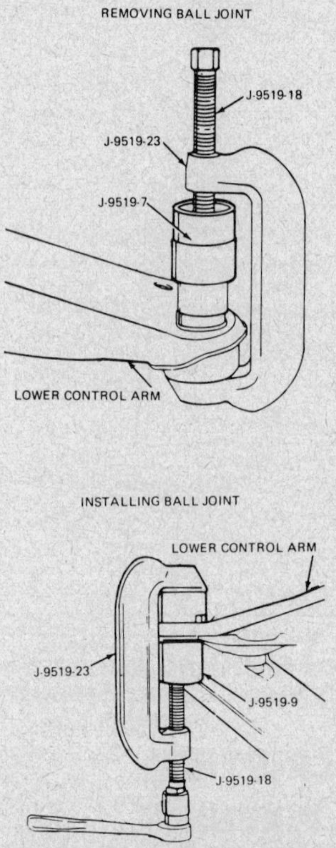

Fig. 6 Removing & installing ball joint. Firebird

Lower Ball Joint

1. Raise vehicle and support lower control arm under spring seats.
2. Remove brake drum and backing plate or caliper.
3. Remove lower ball joint stud from steering knuckle, **Fig. 5.**
4. With a screwdriver, pry ball joint seal and retainer from ball joint.
5. Press lower ball joint from control arm.
6. Press new ball joint into lower control arm.
7. Install ball joint stud into steering knuckle and torque nut to 90 ft. lbs.

8. Install cotter pin.
9. Install brake backing plate and drum or caliper, then the wheel assembly.

FIREBIRD

1. Raise and support vehicle.
2. Remove tire and wheel assembly.
3. Place a suitable floor jack under control arm spring seat. **Floor jack must remain under control arm spring seat during removal and installation to retain spring and control arm in position.**
4. Remove cotter pin and loosen nut. Use tool J-24292A to break ball joint loose from steering knuckle.
5. Remove tool and separate joint from knuckle.
6. Guide lower control arm out of opening in splash shield with a suitable tool.
7. Remove grease fittings, and install special tools as shown in **Fig. 6.**
8. Reverse procedure to install. Torque ball stud nut to 90 ft. lbs.

SHOCK ABSORBER REPLACE

EXC. FIREBIRD

Hold the shock absorber upper stem from turning with a suitable wrench and remove the nut and grommet. Remove the lower shock absorber pivot from the lower control arm and pull the shock absorber and mounting out at the bottom of the spring housing.

To install, reverse the removal procedure. Torque upper retaining nut to 10 ft. lbs. Torque shock absorber lower retaining bolts to 20 ft. lbs.

STRUT REPLACE

FIREBIRD

1. Raise and support vehicle.
2. Remove tire and wheel assembly.
3. Support lower control arm with jackstand.
4. Remove brake hose bracket.
5. Remove two strut-to-knuckle bolts.
6. Remove cover from upper mount assembly.
7. Remove nut from upper end of strut assembly.
8. Remove strut and shield.
9. Reverse procedure to install. Torque nuts to 52 ft. lbs.

COIL SPRING REPLACE

EXC. FIREBIRD

1. Support vehicle at frame and remove wheel.
2. Disconnect shock absorber from lower control arm and push shock absorber through hole in lower control arm up into spring.
3. Remove stabilizer link nut, link, spacer, grommets and retainer.
4. Support lower control arm with tool J-23028 bolted onto a suitable jack.
5. Install a safety chain through spring and lower control arm, remove the two lower control arm to frame crossmember pivot bolts. Lower jack, allowing spring to expand and remove spring.
6. Reverse procedure to install. Torque lower control arm to frame attaching nuts, with weight of vehicle on wheels, to 90 ft. lbs. on Parisienne and Safari, or 65 ft. lbs. on all other models.

FIREBIRD

1. Raise and support vehicle.
2. Remove tire and wheel assembly.
3. Remove stabilizer link and bushings at lower control arm.
4. Remove pivot bolt nuts. **Do not remove pivot bolts at this time.**
5. Install adapter tool No. J-23028 or equivalent adapter to floor jack and place into position with supporting bushings.
6. Install jack stand under outside frame on opposite side of vehicle.
7. Raise tool No. J-23028 enough to remove both pivot bolts.
8. Lower tool No. J-23028 carefully and remove spring.
9. Remove ball joint from steering knuckle using tool No. J-24292A or equivalent as outlined under "Ball Joint, Replace."
10. Replace bushings in lower control arm.
11. Reverse procedure to install. Torque nut to 70 ft. lbs.

MANUAL STEERING GEAR REPLACE

1. Use puller to remove pitman arm from steering gear shaft.
2. Remove flex coupling shield, if equipped, then scribe a mark on worm shaft flange and steering shaft and disconnect lower flange from steering shaft.
3. Unfasten gear housing from frame (3 bolts) and remove from car.

POWER STEERING GEAR REPLACE

1. Remove flex coupling shield if equipped, then scribe mark on worm shaft flange and steering shaft and disconnect lower flange from steering shaft.
2. Disconnect pressure and return hoses from gear housing.
3. Raise vehicle and disconnect pitman arm from shaft.
4. Remove gear housing to frame bolts and remove steering gear assembly.
5. Reverse procedure to install.

POWER STEERING PUMP REPLACE

1. Disconnect battery ground cable.
2. Remove power steering pump belt drive, then remove pulley from pump.
3. Disconnect pressure and return line from power steering pump. Cap lines and fittings to prevent entry of dirt.
4. Remove pump and bracket from engine as an assembly, then remove bracket from pump.
5. Reverse procedure to install.

Wheel Alignment Section

INDEX

CASTER & CAMBER ADJUST

EXC. FIREBIRD

Caster and camber adjustments are made by placing shims between the upper pivot shafts and frame, **Fig. 1.** Both adjustments can be made at the same time. In order to remove or install shims, raise car to remove weight from front wheel, then loosen control arm shaft-to-frame bolts.

Shim pack thickness should not exceed .40 inch. Also, difference between front and rear shim packs should not exceed 3/8 inch maximum.

1. To increase negative caster, add shims to front bolt or remove shims from rear bolt.
2. To decrease negative caster (increase positive caster), remove shims from front bolt or add shims to rear bolt.
3. To increase positive camber, remove

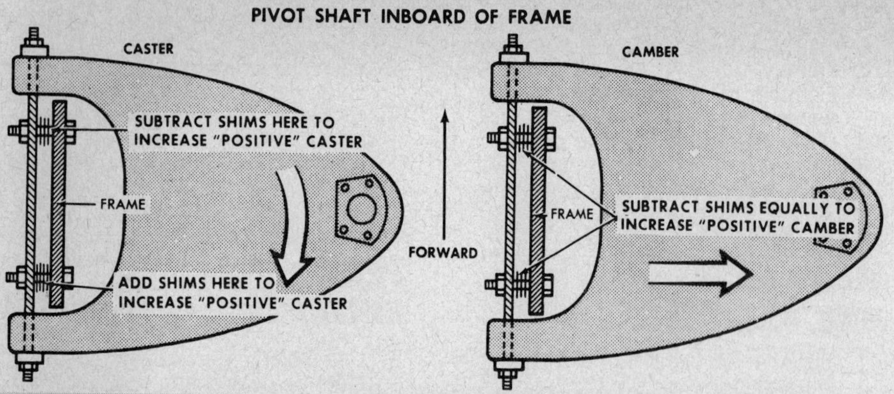

Fig. 1 Caster & camber shim location. Exc. Firebird

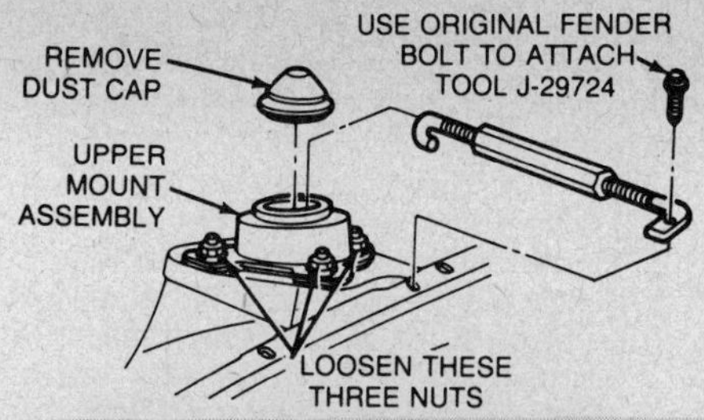

Fig. 2 Installing tool J-29724 for caster & camber adjustment. Firebird

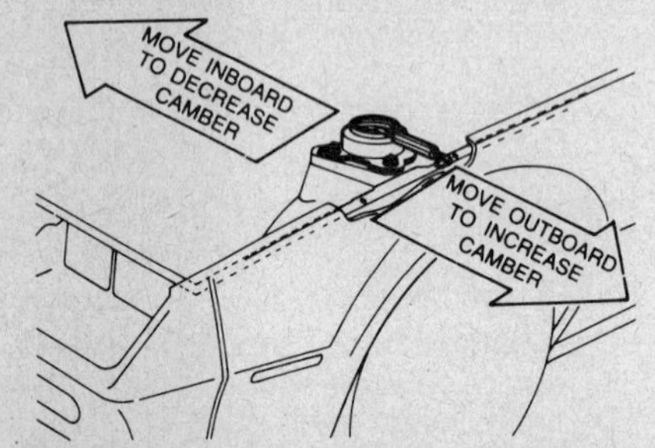

Fig. 3 Camber adjustment. Firebird

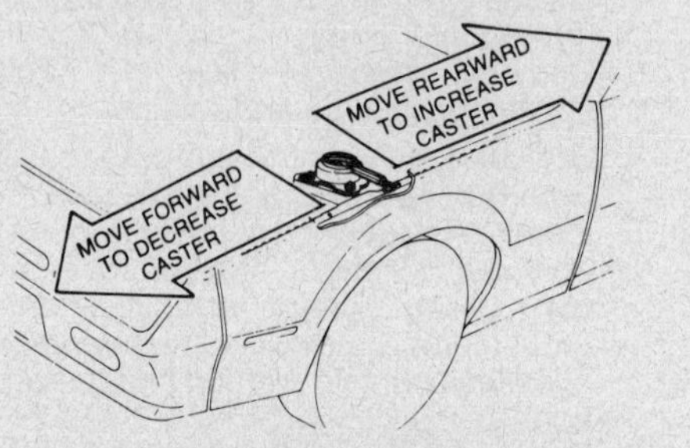

Fig. 4 Caster adjustment. Firebird

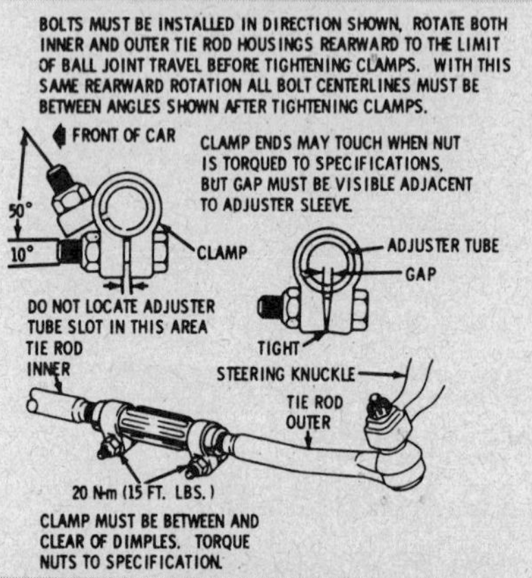

Fig. 5 Tie rod clamp & sleeve positioning. Exc. Firebird

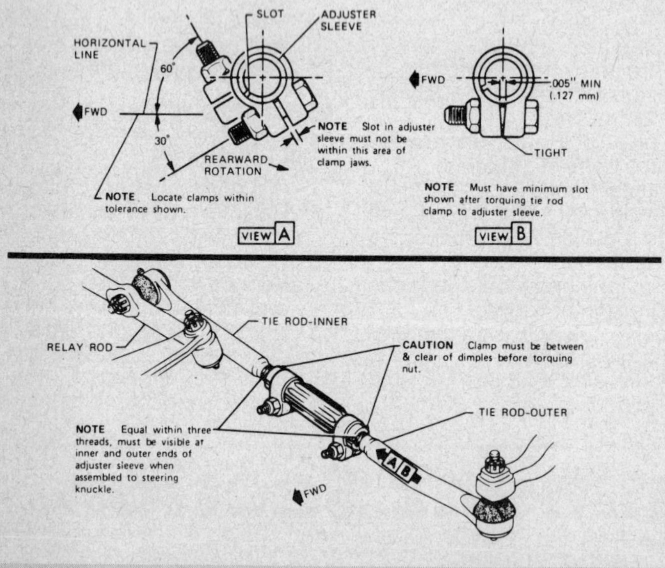

Fig. 6 Tie rod clamp & sleeve positioning. Firebird

shims from both front and rear bolts.

4. To decrease positive camber (increase negative camber), add shims to both front and rear bolts. **By adding or subtracting an equal amount of shims from front and rear bolts, camber will be changed without affecting caster.**
5. After proper shim pack has been installed, torque pivot shaft mounting bolts to 70 to 75 ft. lbs. on 1983-85 Parisienne, 45 ft. lbs. on 1982-85 Bonneville and Grand Prix, or 80 ft. lbs. on 1986-88 models.

FIREBIRD

Caster and camber can be adjusted by moving the position of the upper strut mount assembly.

1. Remove dust cap and fender bolt.
2. Attach J-29724, using original fender bolt and tighten the turnbuckle, **Fig. 2.**
3. Loosen three nuts attaching mount assembly.
4. Adjust camber by rotating the turnbuckle to allow the mount assembly to move inboard or outboard, **Fig. 3.**
5. Adjust the caster by lightly tapping the mount assembly forward or rearward, **Fig. 4.**
6. When correct camber and caster readings have been obtained to specifications, tighten the three nuts attaching the mount assembly to 20 ft. lbs.
7. Remove tool J-29724, and install fender bolt and dust cap.

TOE-IN

ADJUST

1. Remove steering wheel trim cover or horn button and set gear on high point by turning steering wheel until mark on end of shaft is exactly at top. This mark locates high point or middle travel of steering gear.
2. Loosen tie rod clamp bolts and turn both adjuster sleeves an equal amount until toe-in is set to specifications. To increase toe-in, turn left tie rod adjuster sleeve in direction of forward rotation of wheels. Turn right tie rod adjuster sleeve in opposite direction.
3. Make sure front wheels are straight ahead by measuring from a reference point at same place on each side of frame center to front of wheel rims. If measurements are unequal, turn both tie rod adjuster sleeves in same direction (so as not to change toe-in) until measurements become equal. Recheck toe-in and readjust as necessary.
4. Torque tie rod clamp bolts to 15 ft. lbs. **Open end clamps should be located to a vertical down position. Refer to Figs. 5 and 6.**

1982–88 CHEVROLET CELEBRITY • BUICK CENTURY • OLDS CUTLASS CIERA • PONTIAC 6000 • 1984–88 OLDS CUTLASS CRUISER

INDEX OF SERVICE OPERATIONS

NOTE: Refer to the rear of this manual for vehicle manufacturer's special service tool suppliers.

GENERAL ENGINE SPECIFICATIONS

Year	Engine		Fuel System	Bore & Stroke	Compression Ratio	Net H.P. @ RPM③	Maximum Torque Ft. Lbs. @ RPM	Normal Oil Pressure Pounds
	CID①/Liter	VIN Code ②						
1982	4-151, 2.5L	R	T.B.I	4.00 x 3.00	8.2	90 @ 4000	132 @ 2800	36-41
	V6-173, 2.8L	X	E2SE, 2 Bbl④	3.50 x 2.99	8.5	112 @ 5100	145 @ 2400	50-65
	V6-181, 3.0L	E	E2ME, 2 Bbl④	3.80 x 2.66	8.45	110 @ 4800	145 @ 2600	37
	V6-262, 4.3L⑤	T	Fuel Injection	4.05 x 3.385	21.6	85 @ 3600	165 @ 1600	30-45
1983	4-151, 2.5L	R	T.B.I	4.00 x 3.00	8.2	90 @ 4000	135 @ 2800	36-41
	V6-173, 2.8L	X	E2SE, 2 Bbl④	3.50 x 2.99	8.5	112 @ 4800	145 @ 2400	50-65
	V6-173 H.O., 2.8L⑥	Z	E2SE, 2 Bbl④	3.50 x 2.99	8.9	130 @ 5400	145 @ 2400	50-65
	V6-181, 3.0L	E	E2ME, 2 Bbl④	3.80 x 2.66	8.45	110 @ 4800	145 @ 2600	37
	V6-262, 4.3L⑤	T	Fuel Injection	4.05 x 3.385	21.6	85 @ 3600	165 @ 1600	30-45
1984	4-151, 2.5L	R	T.B.I	4.00 x 3.00	8.2	90 @ 4000	134 @ 2400	36-41
	V6-173, 2.8L	X	E2SE, 2 Bbl④	3.50 x 2.99	8.5	112 @ 5100	148 @ 2400	50-65
	V6-173 H.O., 2.8L⑥	Z	E2SE, 2 Bbl④	3.50 x 2.99	8.9	130 @ 5400	145 @ 2400	50-65
	V6-181, 3.0L	E	E2ME, 2 Bbl④	3.80 x 2.666	8.45	110 @ 4800	145 @ 2600	37
	V6-231 MFI, 3.8L	3	Fuel Injection	3.80 x 3.40	8.0	125 @ 4400	195 @ 2000	37
	V6-262, 4.3L⑤	T	Fuel Injection	4.05 x 3.385	21.6	85 @ 3600	165 @ 1600	30-45
1985	4-151, 2.5L	R	T.B.I	4.00 x 3.00	9.0	92 @ 4400	134 @ 2800	37.5
	V6-173, 2,8L	X	E2SE, 2 Bbl④	3.50 x 2.99	8.5	112 @ 4800	148 @ 2400	50-65
	V6-173 H.O. MFI, 2.8L⑥	W	Fuel Injection	3.50 x 2.99	8.9	125 @ 4500	145 @ 2400	50-65
	V6-181, 3.0L	E	E2ME, 2 Bbl④	3.80 x 2.666	8.45	110 @ 4800	145 @ 2600	37
	V6-231 MFI, 3.8L	3	Fuel Injection	3.80 x 3.40	8.0	125 @ 4400	195 @ 2000	37
	V6-262, 4.3L⑤	T	Fuel Injection	4.057 x 3.385	22.8	85 @ 3600	165 @ 1600	30-45
1986	4-151, 2.5L	R	T.B.I	4.00 x 3.00	9.0	92 @ 4400	134 @ 2800	37.5
	V6-173, 2.8L	X	E2SE, 2 Bbl	3.50 x 2.99	8.5	112 @ 4800	145 @ 2100	50-65
	V6-173 MFI, 2.8L	W	Fuel Injection	3.50 x 2.99	8.5	130 @ 4800	160 @ 3600	50-65
	V6-231 SFI, 3.8L	3, B	Fuel Injection	3.80 x 3.40	8.5	150 @ 4400	200 @ 2000	37
1987	4-151, 2.5L	R	T.B.I.	4.00 x 3.00	9.0	98 @ 4800	135 @ 4200	37.5
	V6-173, 2.8L	X	E2SE, 2 Bbl.	3.50 x 2.99	8.5	112 @ 4800	145 @ 2100	50-65
	V6-173 MFI, 2.8L	W	Fuel Injection	3.50 x 2.99	8.5	125 @ 4800	160 @ 3600	50-65
	V6-231 SFI, 3.8L	3	Fuel Injection	3.80 x 3.40	8.5	150 @ 4400	200 @ 2000	37
1988	4-151, 2.5L	R	T.B.I.	4.00 x 3.00	9.0	98 @ 4800	135 @ 3200	37.5
	V6-173 MFI, 2.8L	W	Fuel Injection	3.50 x 2.99	8.9	125 @ 4500	160 @ 3600	50-65
	V6-189 MFI, 3.1L	—	Fuel Injection	3.50 x 3.30	8.8	135 @ 4800	180 @ 3600	—
	V6-231 SFI, 3.8L	3	Fuel Injection	3.80 x 3.40	8.5	150 @ 4400	200 @ 2000	37

①—CID-cubic inch displacement.
②—The eighth digit denotes engine code.
③—Ratings are net-as installed in vehicle.
④—Rochester.
⑤—Diesel engine.
⑥—High output engine.

ENGINE TIGHTENING SPECIFICATIONS*

*Torque specifications are for clean and lightly lubricated threads only. Dry or dirty threads produce increased friction which prevents accurate measurement of tightness.

Year	Engine Model/VIN	Spark Plugs Ft. Lbs.	Cylinder Head Bolts Ft. Lbs.	Intake Manifold Ft. Lbs.	Exhaust Manifold Ft. Lbs.	Rocker Arm Stud Ft. Lbs.	Rocker Arm Cover Ft. Lbs.	Connecting Rod Cap Bolts Ft. Lbs.	Main Bearing Cap Bolts Ft. Lbs.	Flywheel to Crankshaft Ft. Lbs.	Vibration Damper or Pulley Ft. Lbs.
1982	4-151/R	15	85⑧	29	44	20⑥	6	32	70	44	200
	V6-173/X	7-15	65-75	20-25	22-28	43-49	6-9	34-40	63-74	44-55	66-84
	V6-181/E	15	80	45	25	30⑦	4	40	100	60	225
	V6-262/T①	—	②③	41	29	④	⑤	42	107	76	160-350
1983	4-151/R	15	85⑧	29	44	20⑥	6	32	70	63	200
	V6-173/X,Z	7-15	65-75	20-25	22-28	43-49	6-9	34-40	63-74	45-55	66-84
	V6-181/E	15	80	45	25	30⑦	4	40	100	60	225
	V6-262/T①	—	②③	41	29	④	⑤	42	89	76	160-350
1984	4-151/R	15	92⑧	29	44	20⑥	6	32	70	44	200
	V6-173/X,Z	7-15	65-75	20-25	22-28	43-49	6-9	34-40	63-74	45-55	66-84
	V6-181/E	15	80	45	25	30⑦	4	40	100	60	225
	V6-231/3	15	80	45	25	30⑦	4	40	100	60	225
	V6-262/T①	—	②③	41	31	④	⑤	42	89	76	203-350
1985	4-151/R	15	85⑧	29	44	20⑥	6	32	70	44	200
	V6-173/W,X	7-15	65-75	20-25	22-28	43-49	6-9	34-40	63-74	45-55	66-84
	V6-181/E	15	80	47	25	25⑦	6	40	100	60	200
	V6-231/3	15	80	47	25	25⑦	6	40	100	60	200
	V6-262/T①	—	②⑨	41	31	④	⑤	42	89	76	203-350
1986	4-151/R	15	85⑧	29	44	20⑥	6	32	70	44	200
	V6-173/W,X	11	65-90	20-25	22-28	43-49	6-9	34-40	63-74	40-52	67-85
	V6-231/3, B	20	⑩	32	37	43⑥	7	40	100	60	200
1987	4-151/R	15	⑨	25	31	24	4	32	70	⑪	162
	V6-173/W,X	17	33⑧⑫	25	15-23	15-20	6-9	34-40	63-83	44	66-85
	V6-231/3	20	⑩	32	37	43⑥	9	45	100	60	—
1988	4-151/R	—	—	—	—	—	—	—	—	—	—
	V6-173/W	—	—	—	—	—	—	—	—	—	—
	V6-189	—	—	—	—	—	—	—	—	—	—
	V6-231/3	—	—	—	—	—	—	—	—	—	—

①—Diesel engine.
②—Clean & dip entire bolt in engine oil before tightening to obtain a correct torque reading.
③—Torque inner 8 bolts to 142 ft. lbs. Torque outer 6 bolts (bolts nearest intake & exhaust manifold to cylinder block mating surfaces) to 59 ft. lbs.
④—Rocker arm pivot studs, 11 ft. lbs.; rocker arm nuts, 28 ft. lbs.
⑤—Fully driven, seated & not stripped.
⑥—Rocker arm bolt.
⑦—Rocker arm shaft.
⑧—Requires thread sealer on bolt threads and underside of bolt heads.
⑨—Refer to text for proper torque and sequence procedure.
⑩—Torque bolts in three steps: Step 1, torque all bolts to 25 ft. lbs.; Step 2, turn each bolt an additional 1/4 turn; Step 3, turn each bolt an additional 1/4 turn from that in Step 2. Should 60 ft. lbs. be reached in any step, do not complete balance of turn.
⑪—Auto. trans., 55 ft. lbs.; man. trans., 69 ft. lbs.
⑫—Torque bolts to specification, plus an additional 1/4 turn.

STARTING MOTOR APPLICATIONS

Year	Engine/VIN	Starter Ident. No.
1982	4-151, V6-173, V6-181①	1109530②
	V6-262 Diesel/T	1998553②
	V6-262 Diesel/T	22515863③
1983	4-151/R	1109556②
	V6-173/X,Z	1109533②
	V6-173/X,Z	1109564②
	V6-181	1109560②
	V6-262 Diesel/T	1998553②
	V6-262 Diesel/T	22515863③
1984	4-151/R	1109556②
	V6-173/X,Z	1109564②
	V6-181/E	1998448②
	V6-231 MFI/3	1998445②
	V6-262 Diesel/T	1998553②
	V6-262 Diesel/T	22515863③
1985	4-151/R	1998450②
	V6-173/X,W	1109564②
	V6-181/E	1998448②
	V6-231/3	1998445②
	V6-262 Diesel/T	2252209②
	V6-262 Diesel/T	22523207③
1986	4-151/R	1109564②
	V6-173/X,W	1109564②
	V6-231/3, B	1998521②
1987	4-151/R	1998530②
	V6-173/X,W	1998523②
	V6-231/3	1998544②

①—For VIN code, refer to the General Engine Specifications at the begining of chapter.
②—Delco-Remy.
②—Mitsubishi.

ALTERNATOR SPECIFICATIONS

Year	Model	Rated Hot Output Amps.
1982	1100113	63
	1100164	55
	1100166	63
	1100174	55
	1100192	85
	1100193	85
	1100196	63
	1101037	70
	1101039	70
	1101044	70
	1101067	70
	1101084	85
	1101086	85
	1101448	80
	1103197	63
1983	1100200	78
	1100208	63
	1100217	78
	1100231	42
	1100232	42
	1100233	42
	1100235	42
	1100239	55
	1100240	63
	1100243	63
	1100252	63
	1100254	63
	1100260	78
	1100272	78
	1105023	63
	1105189	85
	1105190	85
	1105196	85
	1105199	85
	1105200	85
	1105244	42
	1105245	78
1984	1100200	78
	1100206	56
	1100208	66
	1100217	78
	1100233	42
	1100235	42
	1100239	56
	1100243	66
	1100247	66
	1100252	66
	1100254	66
	1100268	78
	1100272	78
	1105425	94
	1105428	94
	1105441	94
	1105443	94
	1105444	94
	1105509	108
	1105542	94
	1105552	85
	1105553	97
	01100243	66
	01100247	66
	01105425	94
	01105428	94
	01105441	94
	01105444	94
	01105509	108
	01105552	85
	01105553	97
	01105587	97
	01105588	78
	01105590	56
	01105592	94
	01105600	66
	01105603	66
1985	01100200	78
	01100206	56
	01100208	66
	01100217	78
	01100239	56
1986	1100206	56
	1100208	63
	1100217	78
	1100666	85
	1101113	97
	1105588	78
	1105590	56
	1105592	94
	1105603	66
	1105610	66
	1105615	108
	1105667	100
1987	1101135	85
	1101136	100
	1101142	85
	1101143	100
	1101179	85
	1101181	105
	1101182	120

WHEEL ALIGNMENT SPECIFICATIONS

Year	Model	Caster Angle, Degrees		Camber Angle, Degrees				Toe-In Inch
		Limits	Desired	Left	Right	Left	Right	
1982-83	All	0°-+4°	+2°	-1/2° to +1/2°	-1/2° to +1/2°	0°	0°	0
1984-86	All	.9° to 2.9°	1.9°	-1/2° to +1/2°	-1/2° to +1/2°	0°	0°	0
1987-88	All	+.7° to +2.7°	+1.7°	−1/2° to +1/2° −1/2° to +1/2°	0°	0°	0	

COOLING SYSTEM & CAPACITY DATA

Year	Model & Engine/ VIN	Cooling Capacity, Qts.		Radiator Cap Relief Pressure, Lbs.	Thermo. Opening Temp.	Fuel Tank Gals.	Engine Oil Refill Qts.	Transaxle Oil	
		Less A/C	With A/C					Manual Transaxle Pts.	Auto. Transaxle Qts. (1)
1982	4-151/R	9.4	9.7	15	195	16	3 (2)	—	5
	V6-173/X	11.4	11.7	15	195	16	4 (2)	—	5
	V6-181/E	13.5	14.25	15	195	16	4 (3)	—	5
	V6-262/T (5)	13.2	13.7	15	195	16	6 (4)	—	5
1983	4-151/R	9.4 (6)	9.7 (6)	15	195	16	3 (2)	—	(7)
	V6-173/X,Z	11.9 (8)	12.4 (8)	15	195	16	4 (2)	—	(7)
	V6-181/E	13.5 (9)	14.4	15	195	16	4 (3)	—	(7)
	V6-262/T (5)	13 (10)	13.9	16-18.5	195	16	6 (4)	—	(7)
1984	4-151/R	9.4 (6)	9.7 (6)	15	195	15.7	3 (2)	6	(7)
	V6-173/X,Z	12.5 (13)	12.6 (13)	15	195	15.7	4 (2)	6	(7)
	V6-181/E	12.8 (11)	13.1 (11)	15	195	15.7	4 (3)	6	(7)
	V6-231 MFI/3	12.1	12.6	15	195	15.7	4 (3)	6	(7)
	V6-262/T (5)	12.4 (12)	12.6	16-18.5	185	16.4	6 (4)	6	(7)
1985	4-151/R	9.4 (6)	9.7 (6)	15	195	15.7	3 (2)	—	(7)
	V6-173/W,X	—	—	15	195	15.7	4 (2)	—	—
	V6-181/E	12.8 (11)	13.1 (11)	15	195	15.7	4 (3)	—	(7)
	V6-231/3	12.1	12.6	15	195	15.7	4 (3)	—	(7)
	V6-262/T (5)	12.4 (12)	12.6 (12)	16-18.5	185	16.4	6 (4)	—	(7)
1986	4-151/R	9.4	9.7	15	195	15.7	3.0 (2)	—	(7)
	V6-173/W,X	11.8	12	15	195	16.4	4.0 (2)	6	(7)
	V6-231/3, B	12	12.7	15	195	15.7	4.0 (3)	—	(7)
1987	4-151/R	9.4	9.7	15	195	15.7	3.0 (2)	—	(14)
	V6-173/W,X	12.5	12.7	15	195	16.4	4.0 (2)	4.1	(14)
	V6-231/3	12	12.7	15	195	15.7	4.0 (2)	—	(14)
1988	4-151/R	9.8	10	15	195	15.7	3.0 (2)	—	—
	V6-173/W	12.5	12.6	15	195	15.7	4.0 (2)	5.4	—
	V6-189	—	—	—	—	—	—	—	—
	V6-231/3	9.8	10	15	195	15.7	4.0 (2)	—	—

(1)—Approximate, make final check with dipstick.
(2)—With or without filter change.
(3)—Add 1 qt. with filter change.
(4)—Includes filter. Use recommended diesel engine oil, designated SF/CC or SF/CD.
(5)—Diesel Engine.
(6)—W/heavy duty cooling system, 12 qts.
(7)—Oil pan only, 4 qts.; total capacity, 6 qts.
(8)—W/heavy duty cooling system, 12.7 qts.
(9)—W/heavy duty cooling system, 14 qts.
(10)—W/heavy duty cooling system, 13.9 qts.
(11)—Heavy duty, 13.3 qts.
(12)—Heavy duty, 12.6 qts.
(13)—Heavy duty, 12.8 qts.
(14)—Oil pan only, 4 qts. w/125C trans. or 6 qts. w/440 trans.; total capacity, 6 qts. w/125C trans. or 10 qts. w/440 trans.

Electrical Section

INDEX

STARTER
REPLACE

Upon removal of starter, note if any shims are used. If shims are used, they should be reinstalled in their original location during installation.

If starter is noisy during cranking, remove one .015 inch double shim or add one .015 inch single shim to the outer bolt. If starter makes a high pitched whine after firing, add .015 inch double shims until noise ceases.

EXCEPT V6-262 DIESEL

1. Disconnect battery ground cable.
2. Raise and support vehicle.
3. From beneath vehicle, remove two starter motor to engine bolts and lower starter. On 4-151 engine remove nut securing starter bracket to rear of starter.
4. Disconnect solenoid wires and battery cable then, remove starter.
5. Reverse procedure to install.

V6-262 DIESEL

1. Disconnect battery ground cable. On engines with heavy duty option there will be two batteries. Install a suitable engine holding device.
2. Raise and support vehicle. Remove left and center engine mount stud nuts, then 2 front cradle mount bolts and lower cradle. Remove flywheel cover.
3. Remove starter lower shield nut and starter flex shield for removal accessibility.
4. Disconnect wires from starter noting position of wires for installation.
5. Remove starter attaching bolts, then remove starter.

STEERING WHEEL
REPLACE

1. Disconnect battery ground cable.

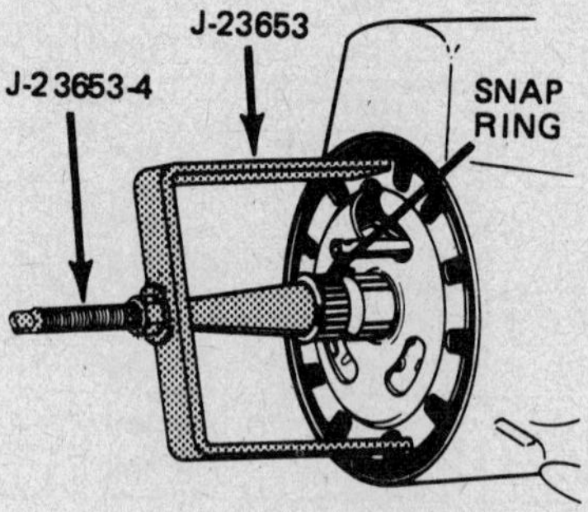

Fig. 1 Compressing lock plate

2. Remove horn button or pad.
3. Remove retainer and steering wheel retaining nut.
4. Remove steering wheel with a suitable puller (tool No. J-1859-03 or BT-61-9).
5. Reverse procedure to install.

IGNITION LOCK
REPLACE

1. Remove steering wheel as outlined under "Steering Wheel, Replace" procedure.
2. Remove turn signal switch as outlined under "Turn Signal Switch, Replace" procedure.
3. Remove buzzer switch and spring clip.
4. Turn lock cylinder to "Run" position, then remove lock cylinder retaining screw and the lock cylinder.
5. To install, rotate lock cylinder to the stop while holding housing. Align cylinder key with keyway in housing, then push lock cylinder into housing until fully seated.
6. Install lock cylinder retaining screw, then the buzzer switch, turn signal switch and steering wheel.

TURN SIGNAL SWITCH
REPLACE

1. Disconnect battery ground cable.
2. Remove steering wheel as outlined under "Steering Wheel, Replace" procedure.
3. Using a screwdriver, pry cover from housing.
4. Using lock plate compressing tool J-23653, compress lock plate, and pry snap ring from groove on shaft, **Fig. 1.** Slowly release lock plate compressing tool, then remove tool and lock plate from shaft end.
5. Slide canceling cam and upper bearing preload spring from end of shaft.
6. Remove turn signal (multi-function) lever.
7. Remove hazard warning knob retaining screw, button, spring and knob.
8. Remove pivot arm.
9. Wrap upper part of electrical connector with tape to prevent snagging of wires during switch removal.
10. Remove switch retaining screws and pull switch up from column, guiding wire harness through column.
11. Reverse procedure to install.

IGNITION & DIMMER SWITCHES
REPLACE

1. Remove turn signal switch as outlined under "Turn Signal Switch, Replace" procedure.
2. Refer to **Figs. 2 and 3** to remove ignition and dimmer switches. **On 1985-88 models with tilt column, position ignition switch slider to extreme right for key release feature, one detent to left for park lock**

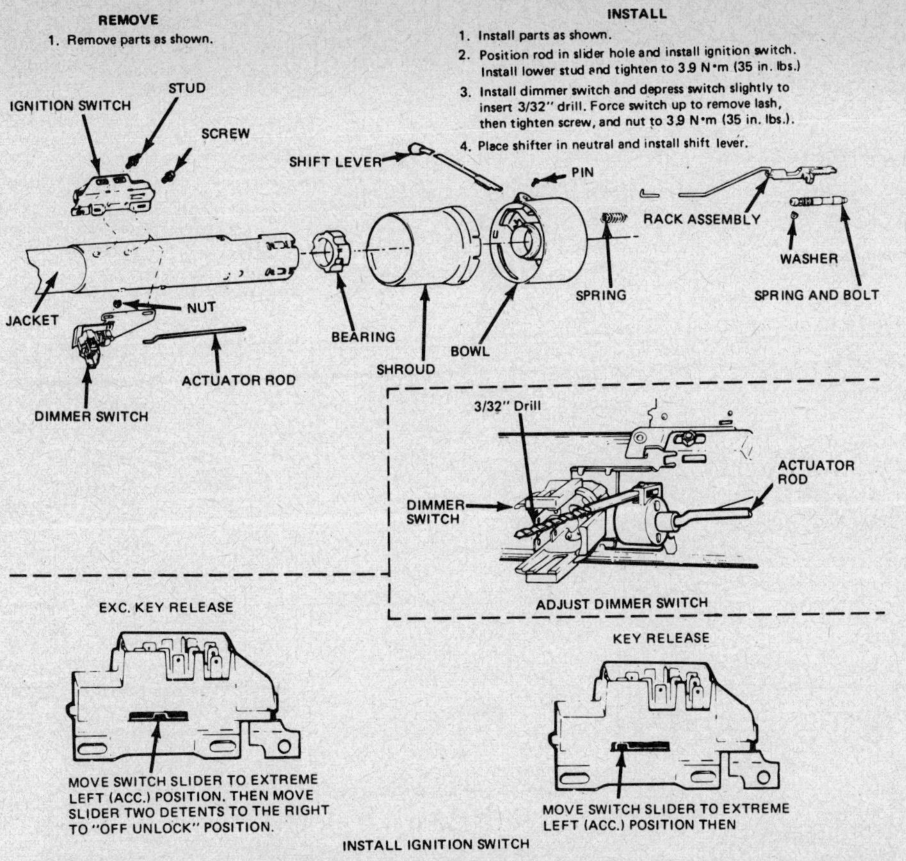
REMOVE
1. Remove parts as shown.
INSTALL
1. Install parts as shown.
2. Position rod in slider hole and install ignition switch. Install lower stud and tighten to 3.9 N•m (35 in. lbs.)
3. Install dimmer switch and depress switch slightly to insert 3/32" drill. Force switch up to remove lash, then tighten screw, and nut to 3.9 N•m (35 in. lbs.).
4. Place shifter in neutral and install shift lever.
IGNITION SWITCH
STUD
SCREW
SHIFT LEVER
PIN
RACK ASSEMBLY
WASHER
SPRING
SPRING AND BOLT
JACKET
NUT
BEARING
SHROUD
BOWL
ACTUATOR ROD
DIMMER SWITCH
3/32" Drill
ACTUATOR ROD
DIMMER SWITCH
ADJUST DIMMER SWITCH
EXC. KEY RELEASE
KEY RELEASE
MOVE SWITCH SLIDER TO EXTREME LEFT (ACC.) POSITION. THEN MOVE SLIDER TWO DETENTS TO THE RIGHT TO "OFF UNLOCK" POSITION.
MOVE SWITCH SLIDER TO EXTREME LEFT (ACC.) POSITION THEN
INSTALL IGNITION SWITCH

Fig. 2 Ignition & dimmer switch removal & installation (Typical). Except tilt column

feature or two detents to left for all other columns.

3. When installing dimmer switch, depress switch slightly to install a 3/32 inch twist drill. Force switch upward to remove lash and tighten retaining screw.

WIPER SWITCH

REPLACE

WINDSHIELD

1. Remove turn signal switch as outlined under "Turn Signal Switch, Replace" procedure.
2. Refer to **Figs. 4 and 5** for wiper switch replacement.

REAR WINDOW

1. Disconnect battery ground cable.
2. Remove left hand trim panel, then right side switch trim cover.
3. Remove switch attaching screws, then switch.
4. Reverse procedure to install.

STOPLAMP SWITCH

ADJUST

Insert switch into tubular clip until the switch body seats on the tube clip. Pull the brake pedal rearward against internal pedal stop. This will properly position switch in tubular clip.

NEUTRAL SAFETY SWITCH

REPLACE

MODELS WITH AUTO. TRANS. & KEY RELEASE

1. Disconnect battery ground cable.
2. Place gear selector in Neutral.
3. Gently rock switch out of steering column.
4. Disconnect electrical connectors, then remove switch from vehicle.
5. Connect electrical connectors to new switch.
6. Align switch actuator with hole in shift tube.
7. Position connector side of switch into lower jacket cutout.
8. Push down front of switch, ensuring switch tangs snap into holes in steering column jacket.
9. Adjust switch by placing gear selector in Park position. The switch main housing and housing back should ratchet, providing proper adjustment.
10. If readjustment is needed, move housing as far as possible toward Low gear position, then repeat step 9.

MODELS WITH AUTO. TRANS. LESS KEY RELEASE

These vehicles do not use a neutral safety switch. A mechanical block on the transmission gear selector prevents starting the engine when the transmission is in any gear other than Park or Neutral.

HEADLAMP SWITCH

REPLACE

CELEBRITY

1. Disconnect battery ground cable.
2. Remove headlamp switch knob.
3. Remove instrument cluster trim cover.
4. Remove screws attaching headlamp switch mounting plate to instrument cluster carrier.
5. Disconnect headlamp switch connector.
6. Remove headlamp switch from mounting plate.
7. Reverse procedure to install.

CENTURY

1982–84

1. Disconnect battery ground cable.
2. Pry trim panel and center trim cover outward using a suitable tool.
3. Remove three screws in steering column trim collar, then the collar.
4. Remove ashtray, then the six screws attaching trim pad to instrument panel.
5. Remove trim pad, then the three switch to instrument panel attaching screws.

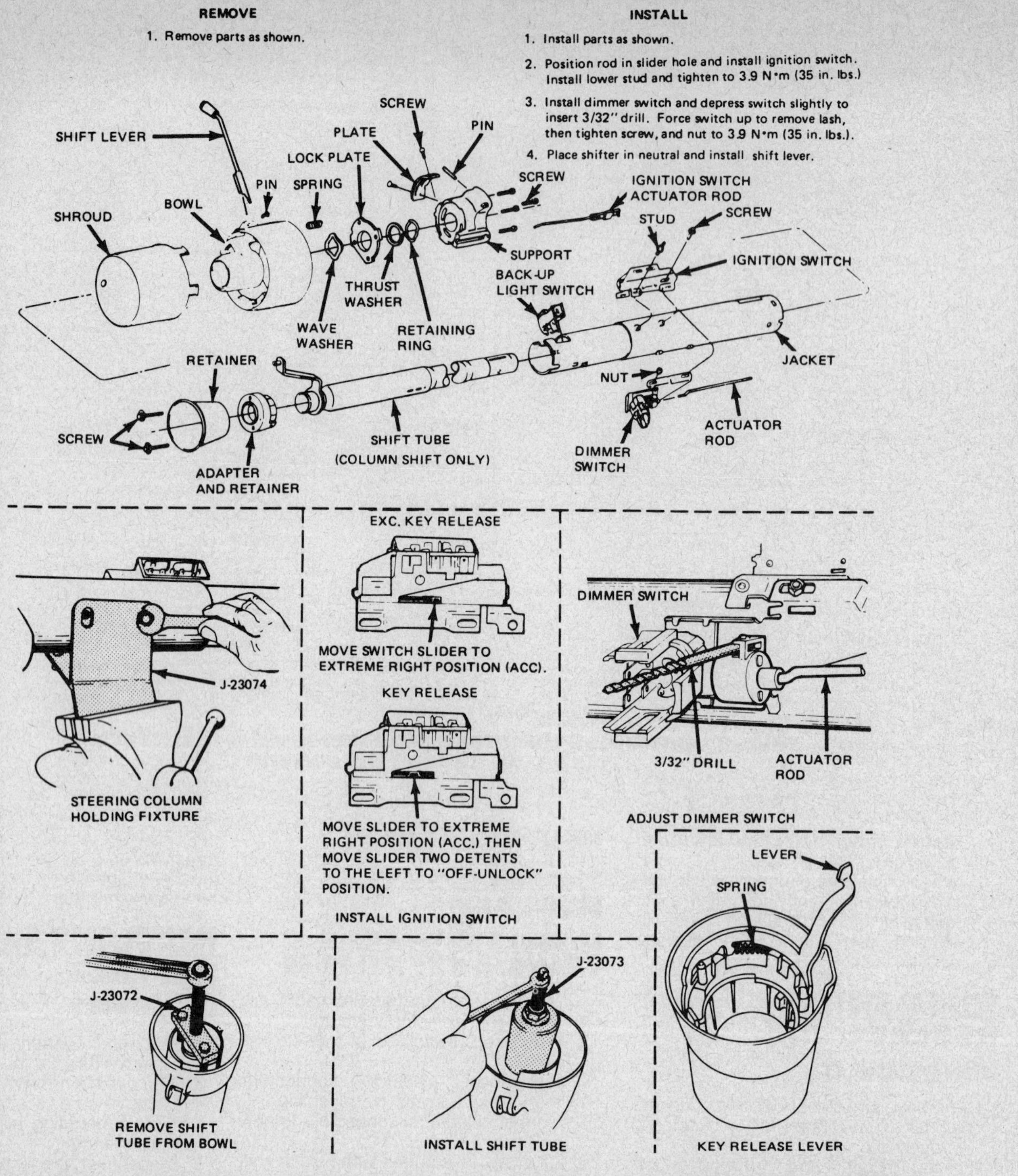
REMOVE
1. Remove parts as shown.
INSTALL
1. Install parts as shown.
2. Position rod in slider hole and install ignition switch. Install lower stud and tighten to 3.9 N•m (35 in. lbs.)
3. Install dimmer switch and depress switch slightly to insert 3/32" drill. Force switch up to remove lash, then tighten screw, and nut to 3.9 N•m (35 in. lbs.).
4. Place shifter in neutral and install shift lever.
SHIFT LEVER
SCREW
PLATE
PIN
LOCK PLATE
SCREW
IGNITION SWITCH ACTUATOR ROD
PIN
SPRING
BOWL
SHROUD
STUD
SCREW
SUPPORT
IGNITION SWITCH
BACK-UP LIGHT SWITCH
THRUST WASHER
WAVE WASHER
RETAINING RING
RETAINER
JACKET
NUT
SCREW
ACTUATOR ROD
SHIFT TUBE (COLUMN SHIFT ONLY)
DIMMER SWITCH
ADAPTER AND RETAINER
EXC. KEY RELEASE
MOVE SWITCH SLIDER TO EXTREME RIGHT POSITION (ACC).
J-23074
KEY RELEASE
DIMMER SWITCH
3/32" DRILL
ACTUATOR ROD
STEERING COLUMN HOLDING FIXTURE
ADJUST DIMMER SWITCH
MOVE SLIDER TO EXTREME RIGHT POSITION (ACC.) THEN MOVE SLIDER TWO DETENTS TO THE LEFT TO "OFF-UNLOCK" POSITION.
INSTALL IGNITION SWITCH
LEVER
SPRING
J-23073
J-23072
REMOVE SHIFT TUBE FROM BOWL
INSTALL SHIFT TUBE
KEY RELEASE LEVER

Fig. 3 Ignition & dimmer switch removal & installation (Typical). Tilt column

6. Pull switch rearward and remove.
7. Reverse procedure to install.

1985–88

1. Disconnect battery ground cable.
2. Pry steering column collar rearward, using a suitable tool, and remove.
3. Remove two outer ducts, then the two screws behind the ducts.
4. Remove screw from behind steering column collar.
5. On models less console, open ashtray and remove two screws.
6. On models with console, remove two screws from ashtray cover and trim plate.
7. On all models, pull trim plate rearward to release clips, then remove trim plate.
8. Remove switch to instrument panel attaching screws, then pull switch rearward and remove.
9. Reverse procedure to install.

6000

1. Disconnect battery ground cable.
2. Remove steering column trim cover, headlight rod and knob assembly.
3. Remove left trim plate.
4. Remove three screws attaching switch and bracket assembly to instrument panel, disconnect electrical connector and remove switch/bracket assembly.
5. Loosen bezel and remove switch from bracket.
6. Reverse procedure to install.

CUTLASS CIERA & CRUISER

1. Disconnect battery ground cable.
2. On 1982-84 models proceed as follows:
   a. Carefully insert a clean putty knife blade between the trim panel and left trim pad, then gently pry trim panel outward. Using same procedure, remove center trim cover.

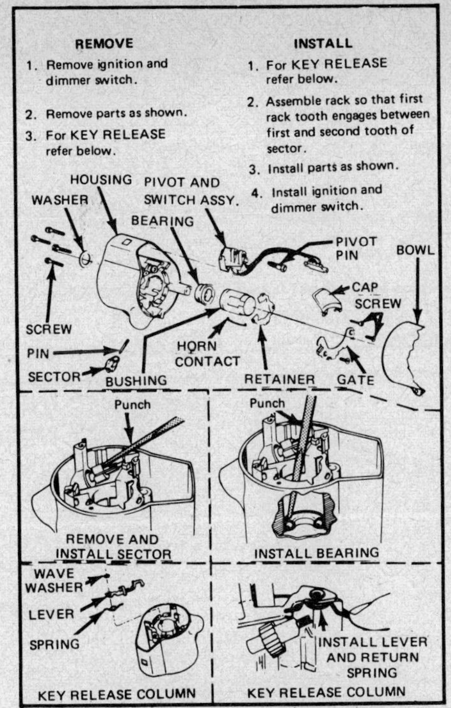

Fig. 4 Housing and wiper switch removal & installation. Standard steering column

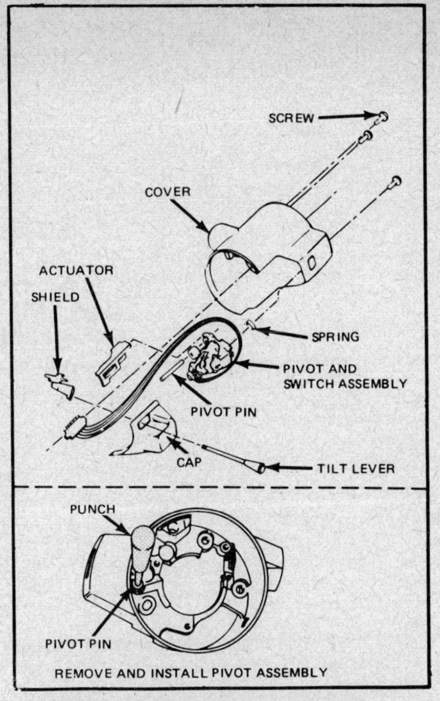

Fig. 5 Cover and wiper switch removal & installation. Tilt steering column

b. Remove three screws in steering column trim collar and remove collar, then remove ashtray.
c. Remove six screws attaching trim pad to instrument panel. Remove trim pad.

3. On 1985-88 models proceed as follows:
   a. Pry steering column collar rearward, using a suitable tool, and remove.
   b. Remove two outer ducts, then the two screws behind the ducts.
   c. Remove screw from behind steering column collar.
   d. On models less console, open ashtray and remove two screws.
   e. On models with console, remove two screws from ashtray cover and trim panel.
   f. On all models, pull trim plate rearward to release clips, then remove trim plate.
4. On all models, remove 3 switch to panel attaching screws.
5. Pull switch rearward and remove from panel.
6. Reverse procedure to install.

INSTRUMENT CLUSTER REPLACE

CELEBRITY

1. Disconnect battery ground cable.
2. Remove headlamp switch knob, then remove ten screws attaching trim plate to carrier and remove trim plate, **Fig. 6.**
3. Remove three screws at underside of trim pad, then remove upper screw at right of trim pad opening and two screws at right end of trim pad. Remove trim pad, **Fig. 7.**
4. Remove six cluster lens to carrier attaching screws, **Fig. 8.**
5. Tilt cluster rearward slightly and disconnect all electrical connectors and speedometer cable. Remove cluster.
6. Reverse procedure to install.

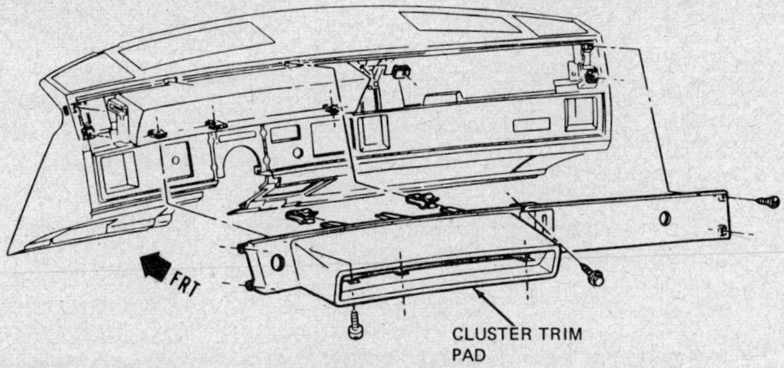

Fig. 6 Trim plate removal. 1982–88 Celebrity

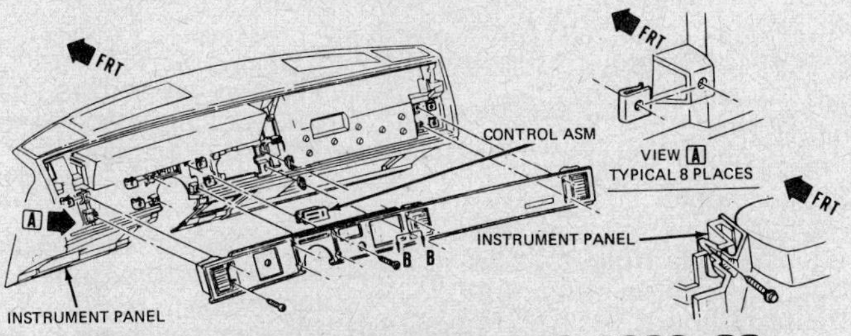

Fig. 7 Trim pad removal. 1982–88 Celebrity

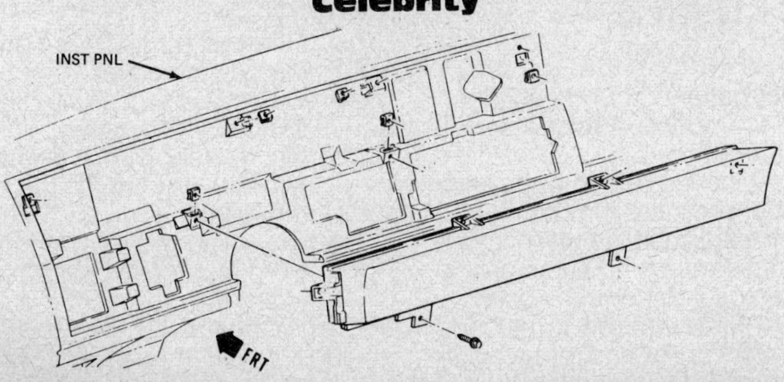

Fig. 8 Instrument cluster. 1982–88 Celebrity

CENTURY

1982

1. Disconnect battery ground cable.
2. Disconnect speedometer cable at cruise control transducer (if equipped). If not equipped with cruise control, disconnect cable at upper and lower cable connections.
3. Remove nine screws retaining trim plate to cluster, then put gear shift lever in low and gently pull on trim plate to remove.
4. Remove shift indicator cable clip from shift bowl.
5. Remove lap vent trim cover by removing two attaching screws.
6. Lower steering column by removing front two retaining bolts.
7. Pull instrument cluster outward three inches, and disconnect speedometer cable from cluster by pushing retaining clip toward cluster and pulling cable away from speedometer.
8. Pull cluster out remainder of the way, then remove one screw retaining

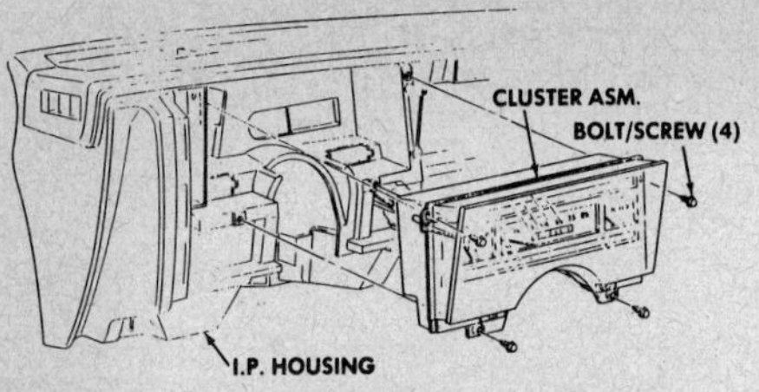

Fig. 9 Instrument cluster removal. 1982–88 Century

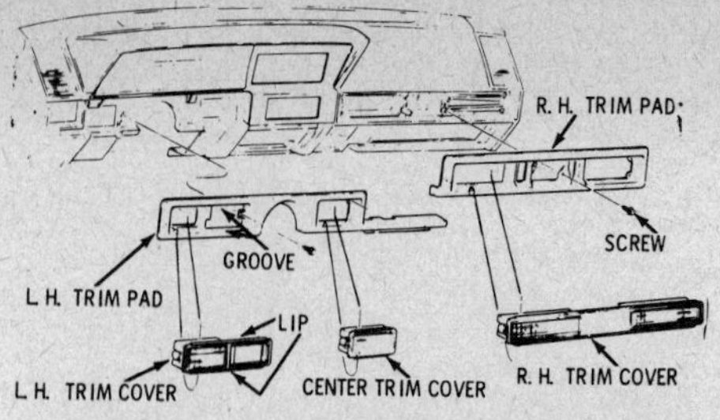

Fig. 10 Trim pad removal. 1982–84 Cutlass Ciera & Cruiser

electrical connector, **Fig. 9.**
9. Reverse procedure to install.

1983–88 Mechanical Cluster

1. Disconnect battery ground cable.
2. Remove steering column opening filler, then the ashtray.
3. Remove seven left hand trim panel attaching screws.
4. Place gear shift lever into low position and pull trim panel straight forward to release two retaining clips in center of panel, then remove panel.
5. Remove 4 screws attaching cluster assembly to instrument panel, **Fig. 9.**
6. Disconnect speedometer cable from transmission. If two piece cable is used, disconnect in engine compartment to ensure there is cable slack.
7. Remove shift indicator clip and position gear selector in low.
8. Pull cluster assembly out far enough to reach behind and disconnect speedometer cable.
9. To ease removal of cluster on vehicles equipped with tilt wheel, lower wheel, then unscrew tilt lever.
10. On all models, tilt top side of cluster assembly downward and remove cluster.
11. Reverse procedure to install.

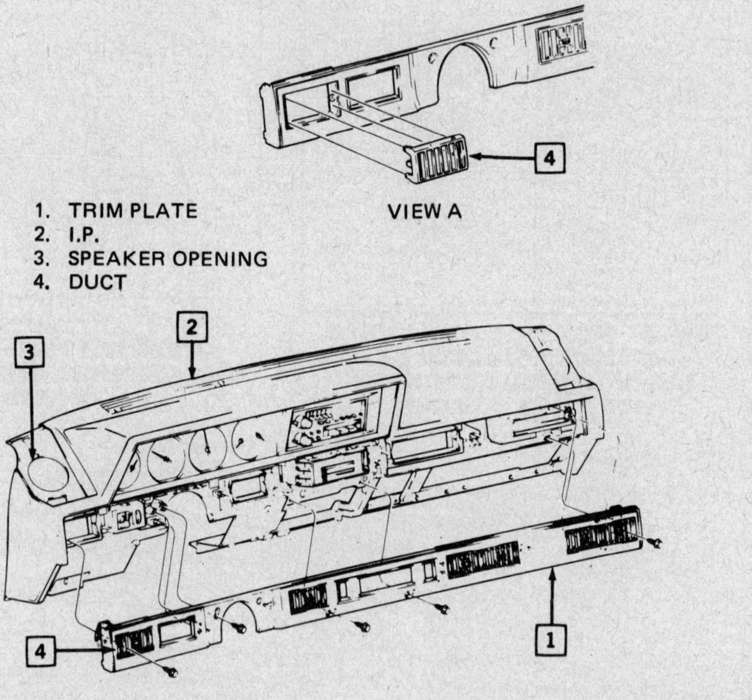

Fig. 11 Trim plate removal. 1985–88 Cutlass Ciera & Cruiser

1983–88 Digital Cluster

1. Disconnect battery ground cable.
2. Remove steering column opening filler, then the ashtray.
3. Remove seven lefthand trim panel attaching screws.
4. Place gear shift lever into low position and pull trim panel straight forward to release two retaining clips in center of panel, then remove panel.
5. Remove 4 screws attaching cluster assembly to instrument panel.
6. Disconnect speedometer cable from transmission. If two piece cable is used, disconnect in engine compartment to ensure there is cable slack.
7. Pull cluster assembly out far enough to disconnect optics head from vehicle speed sensor, then remove cluster assembly.
8. Disconnect 2 electrical connectors on printed circuit from the tube and circuit board assembly.
9. Remove cluster push buttons by pulling straight out.
10. Remove lens and bezel attaching screws, then lens and bezel.
11. Remove tube and circuit board to cluster attaching screws, then tube and circuit board.
12. Remove mechanical odometer from tube and circuit board.
13. Remove 2 telltale lenses and pads from face plate. **Shift indicator needle, spring and cable stay with tube and circuit board.**
14. Reverse procedure to install.

CUTLASS CIERA & CRUISER

1. Disconnect battery ground cable.
2. On 1982-84 models proceed as follows:
   a. Carefully insert a clean putty knife blade between the trim panel and left trim pad, then gently pry trim panel outward. Using same procedure, remove center trim cover.
   b. Remove three screws in steering column trim collar and remove collar, then remove ashtray.
   c. Remove six screws attaching trim pad to instrument panel, **Fig. 10.** Remove trim pad.
3. On 1985-88 models proceed as follows:
   a. Pry steering column collar rearward, using a suitable tool, and remove.
   b. Remove two outer ducts, then the two screws behind the ducts, **Fig. 11.**
   c. Remove screw from behind steering column collar.
   d. On models less console, open ashtray and remove two screws.
   e. On models with console, remove two screws from ashtray cover and trim panel.
   f. On all models, pull trim plate rearward to release clips, then remove trim plate.
4. On all models, remove screws attaching cluster trim cover to instrument panel, then remove cover.

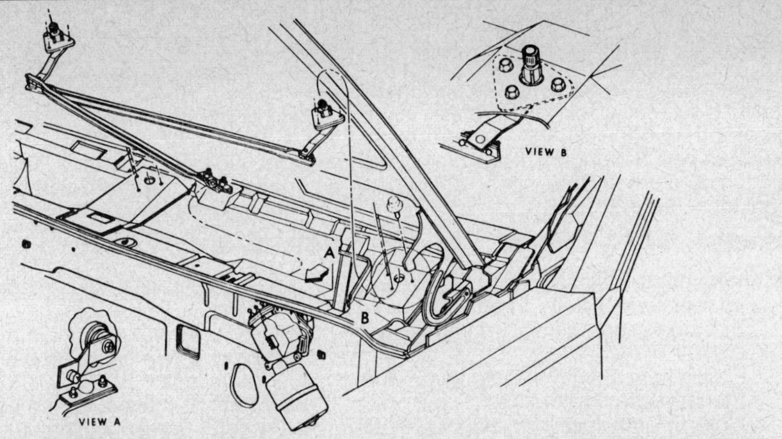

Fig.12 Windshield wiper transmission removal (typical)

5. Disconnect speedometer cable at transmission or cruise control transducer (if equipped).
6. Remove steering column trim cover.
7. Disconnect shift indicator clip from steering column shift bowl.
8. Remove 4 screws attaching cluster assembly to instrument panel.
9. Pull assembly out far enough to reach behind cluster and disconnect speedometer cable.
10. Remove cluster assembly.
11. Reverse procedure to install.

6000

1. Remove headlight rod knob assembly.
2. Using thin, flat tool carefully pry left side trim plate away from instrument panel.
3. Remove six screws attaching instrument cluster to instrument panel carrier.
4. Remove instrument panel cluster.
5. Reverse procedure to install.

RADIO
REPLACE
CENTURY

1. Disconnect battery ground cable.
2. On 1982-84 models, remove instrument panel trim plate.
3. On 1985-88 models, remove lefthand trim cover.
4. On all models, remove right side instrument panel switch trim panel by removing three screws and gently rocking panel out.
5. Remove four radio assembly attaching screws.
6. Disconnect antenna cable, power and speaker electrical connections.
7. Pull radio outward through instrument panel carrier housing.
8. Reverse procedure to install.

EXCEPT CENTURY
1982–84

1. Disconnect battery ground cable.
2. Remove instrument panel trim plate, except Cutlass Ciera, on Cutlass Ciera left side trim pad.
3. Remove three screws at radio bracket, except Cutlass Ciera, on Cutlass Ciera four screws.
4. Pull radio rearward and disconnect electrical connectors and antenna lead.
5. Remove radio.
6. Reverse procedure to install.

1985–88

1. Disconnect battery ground cable.
2. Loosen instrument panel insulator panel attaching screws, then remove steering column trim cover.
3. Remove ashtray, ashtray assembly and fuse block, separate fuse block and ashtray and push forward to gain access to cigar lighter and rear defogger switch electrical connectors.
4. Disconnect electrical connectors, then remove cigar lighter and glove box.
5. Remove instrument panel center trim panel retaining nuts, then pull trim panel outward to gain access to radio attaching screws.
6. Remove attaching screws, disconnect electrical and antenna connections, then remove radio from vehicle.
7. Reverse procedure to install.

WINDSHIELD WIPER MOTOR
REPLACE

1. Raise hood, then remove right and left wiper arm and blade assemblies.
2. Remove shroud grille to body attaching screws, then shroud grille.
3. Loosen, but do not remove nuts securing transmission drive link to motor crank arm, then disconnect drive link.
4. Disconnect wiring connectors and washer hoses.
5. Remove 3 screws attaching wiper motor to firewall.
6. Remove motor while guiding crank arm through hole.
7. Reverse procedure to install. Motor must be in "Park" position before assembling transmission drive link to crank arm. Torque transmission drive link to 48-75 in. lbs.

WINDSHIELD WIPER TRANSMISSION
REPLACE

1. Raise hood, then remove right and left wiper arm and blade assemblies.
2. Remove shroud grille to body attaching screws, then shroud grille.
3. Loosen, but do not remove nuts securing transmission drive link to motor crank arm, then disconnect drive link, **Fig. 12.**
4. Remove 6 screws attaching wiper transmission to body, **Fig. 12.**
5. Carefully guide transmission assembly through access hole in upper shroud panel to remove.
6. Reverse procedure to install. Torque transmission drive link nuts to 53-75 in. lbs.

HEATER CORE
REPLACE
LESS A/C
Exc. 1983–88 Century & Cutlass Ciera & 1984–88 Cutlass Cruiser

For service procedures on 1983-88 Century and Cutlass Ciera, refer to models with A/C.

1. Drain cooling system.
2. Remove heater inlet and outlet hoses.
3. Remove radio noise suppression strap.
4. Remove cover retaining screws and cover.
5. Remove heater core.
6. Reverse procedure to install.

WITH A/C

1. Drain cooling system.
2. On all except diesel engine models, disconnect heater inlet and outlet hoses. On diesel engine models, raise vehicle and disconnect heater inlet and outlet hoses, then lower vehicle.
3. On diesel engine models, remove instrument panel lower sound absorber. On all models, working inside vehicle, remove the heater ducts, then the heater case side cover.
4. Remove heater lower outlet.
5. Remove 2 housing cover to air valve housing clips, then the housing cover.
6. Remove heater core retaining straps, core tubing retainers, then the core.
7. Reverse procedure to install.

BLOWER MOTOR
REPLACE

1. Disconnect battery ground cable.
2. Disconnect blower motor electrical connections.
3. Remove blower motor attaching screws and the blower motor.
4. Reverse procedure to install.

CRUISE CONTROL

ADJUST

BRAKE RELEASE SWITCHES

Electrical & Vacuum Switches

Push switch fully into retaining clip, then pull brake pedal upward to adjust switch position. The electrical switch should break the electrical circuit when the brake pedal is depressed approximately .23-.51 inch.

SERVO, ADJUST

Models With Rod

Install pin retainer to provide minimum slack with throttle in slow idle position.

Models With Bead Chain

Assemble chain into swivel and install retainer so that slack in the chain is not greater than one half the diameter of the ball stud with the engine at normal operating temperature and idle speed solenoid, if equipped, de-energized.

Models With Cable

1. With cable installed in cable and servo brackets, rotate throttle lever so that stud aligns with hole in end of cable.
2. Engage cable with throttle lever stud, then release throttle lever.
3. Hold throttle lever position and pull cable taut from servo end.
4. Connect servo end of cable to servo actuator with pin, using hole which most closely aligns with cable end. **Do not stretch cable or open throttle to align cable, as this will not allow engine to return to idle.**

CRUISE SPEED, ADJUST

On 1984-88 vehicles, cruise speed is controlled by the electronic controller and is not adjustable.

1982–83

The cruise speed adjustment can be set as follows:

1. If vehicle cruises below engagement speed, screw orifice tube on transducer outward.
2. If vehicle cruises above engagement speed, screw orifice tube inward. **Each 1/4 turn of the orifice tube will change cruise speed approximately one mile per hour. Tighten locknut after each adjustment.**

4-151 (2.5L) & V6-173 (2.8L) Engine Section

INDEX

ENGINE MOUNTS

REPLACE

4-151

1. Raise and support front of vehicle, then remove chassis to mount attaching nuts, **Fig. 1.**
2. On models equipped with A/C, remove forward torque rod attaching bolts at radiator support panel.
3. Raise engine slightly using a suitable engine lifting device. Raise engine only enough to provide clearance for mount removal.
4. Remove two upper mount to engine support bracket attaching nuts and remove engine mount.
5. Reverse procedure to install.

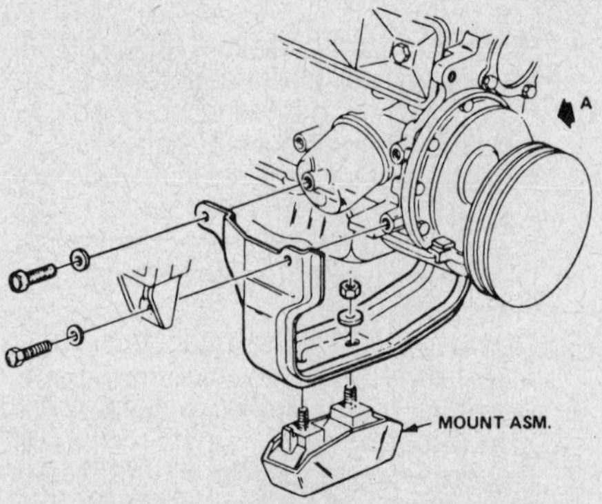

Fig. 1 Engine mounts. 4-151

V6-173

1. Remove mount retaining nuts from below cradle mounting bracket.
2. Raise engine and remove mount to engine attaching nuts, then remove mount, **Figs. 2 and 3.** Raise engine only enough to provide clearance for mount removal.
3. Reverse procedure to install, then lower engine into position. Install retaining nuts and torque to 35 ft. lbs. After engine mount is properly installed, check both transaxle mounts for prop-

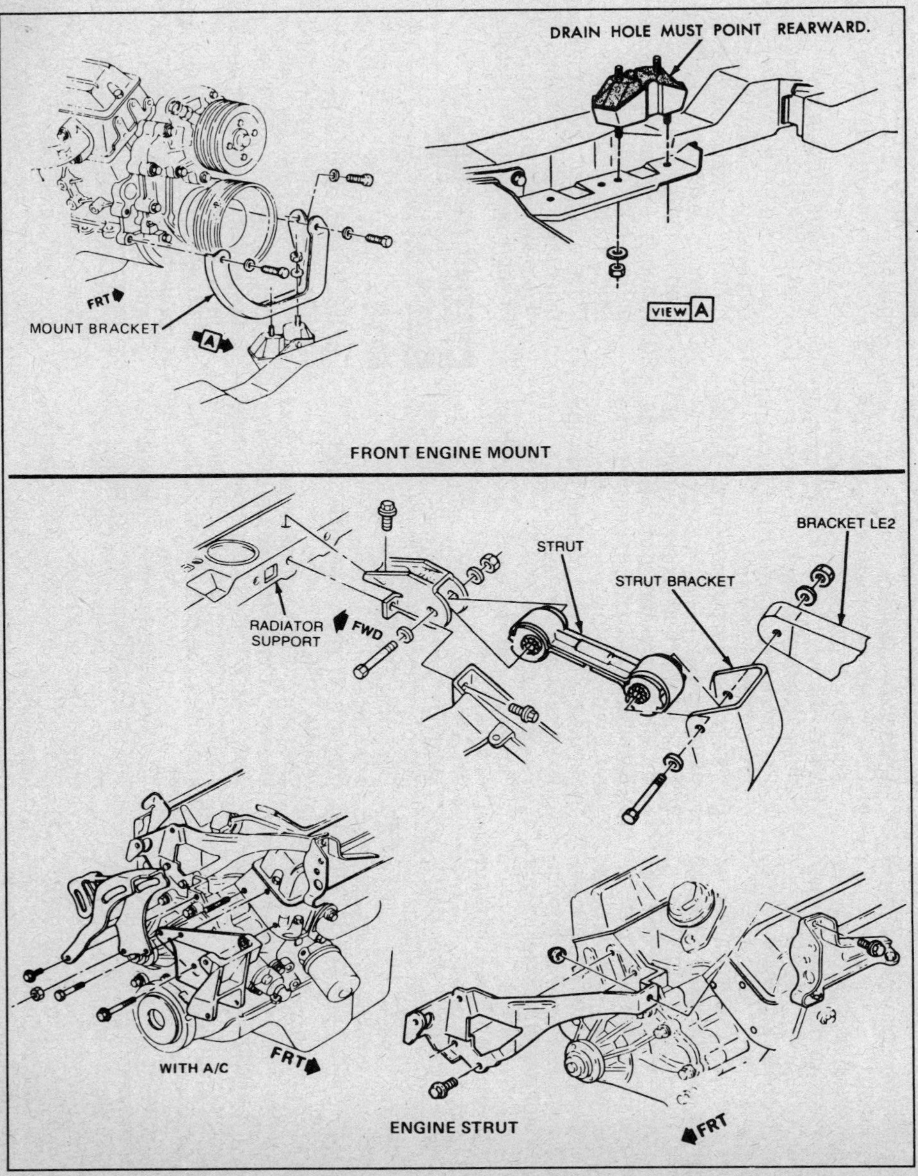

Fig. 2 Engine mounts. 1982–84 V6-173

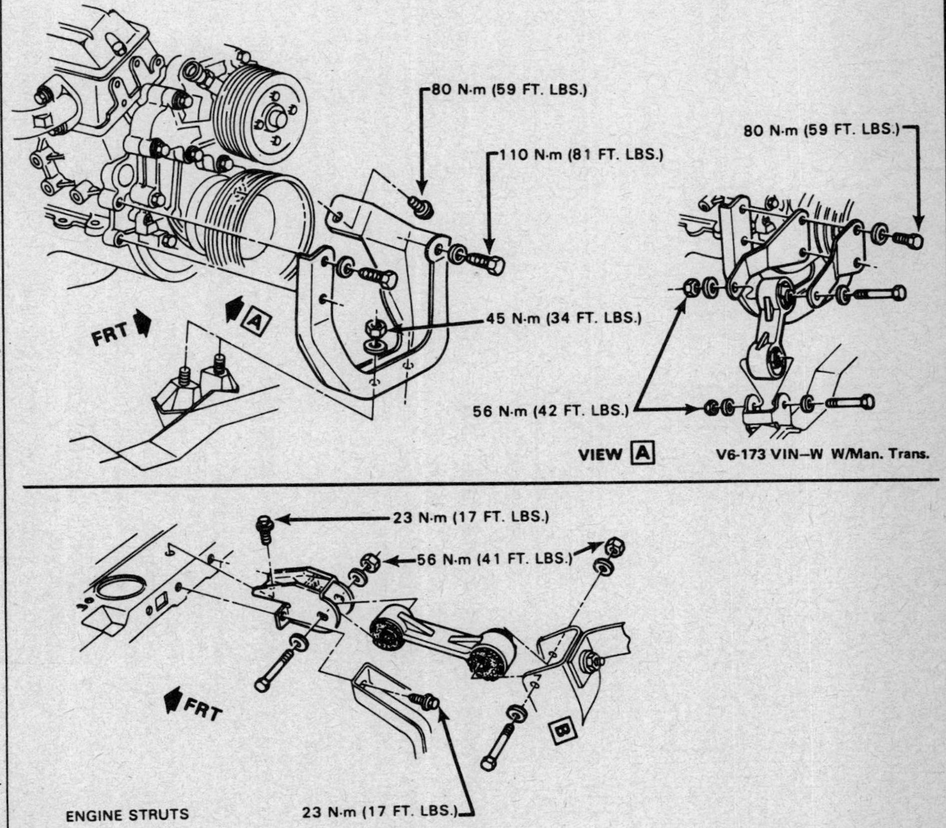

Fig. 3 Engine mounts. 1985–86 V6-173 (1987–88 V6-173 similar)

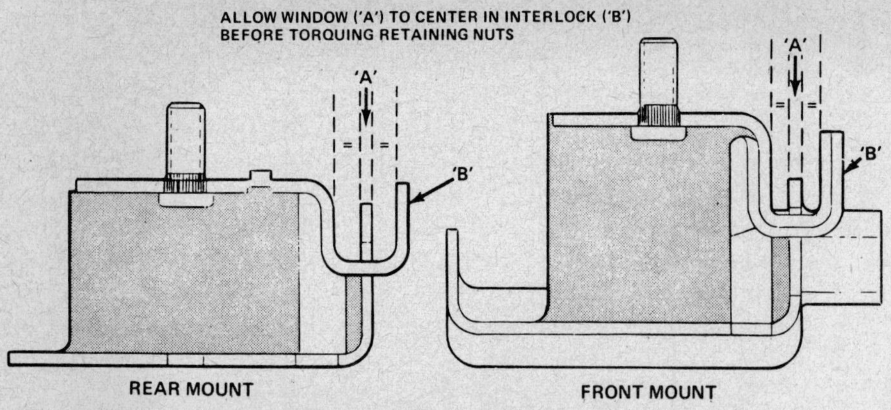

Fig. 4 Transaxle mount alignment. V6-173

er alignment. If window "A" is not properly located, **Fig. 4,** loosen mount to cradle retaining nuts and allow mount to reposition itself. If transaxle mount is allowed to remain out of position, damage to drive train components may result. Torque retaining nuts to 18 ft. lbs.

ENGINE REPLACE

4-151

Manual Transaxle

1. Disconnect cables from battery.
2. Raise and support vehicle.
3. Remove front engine mount-to-cradle attaching nuts.
4. Remove front exhaust pipe, then disconnect starter motor and position aside.
5. Remove flywheel inspection cover, then lower vehicle.
6. Remove air cleaner assembly.
7. Remove all bell housing attaching bolts.
8. Remove front torque reaction rod from engine and core support.
9. On models equipped with A/C, remove compressor drive belt, then disconnect compressor and position aside. Do not disconnect refrigerant lines from compressor.
10. Disconnect vacuum hoses from vapor canister.
11. On models equipped with power steering, disconnect power steering hose.
12. Disconnect all vacuum hoses and electrical connections needed for engine removal.
13. Remove heater blower motor as described under "Blower Motor, Replace" in the electrical section of this chapter.
14. Disconnect throttle cable.
15. Drain cooling system.
16. Disconnect heater hoses from engine and radiator hoses from radiator.
17. Disconnect engine electrical harness at bulkhead connector.
18. Install suitable engine lifting equipment and raise engine. Disconnect fuel line and the heater hose from intake manifold, then remove engine from vehicle.
19. Reverse procedure to install.

Automatic Transaxle

1. Disconnect cables from battery, then drain cooling system.
2. Remove air cleaner assembly and pre-heat tube.
3. Disconnect engine electrical harness connector.
4. Disconnect all external vacuum hose connections.
5. Remove throttle and transaxle linkages at the throttle body assembly and intake manifold.
6. On models equipped with A/C, disconnect compressor and position aside. Do not disconnect refrigerant lines from compressor.
7. Remove upper radiator hose and front engine strut assembly.
8. Disconnect heater hose from intake manifold.
9. Remove all transaxle-to-engine attaching bolts except the top two bolts.
10. Remove front engine mount-to-cradle nuts.
11. Remove front exhaust pipe, then the flywheel inspection cover.
12. Remove starter motor.
13. Remove torque converter-to-flywheel attaching bolts.
14. On models equipped with power steering, remove power steering pump and bracket and position aside.
15. Disconnect heater hose and lower radiator hose.
16. Remove 2 rear transaxle support bracket bolts.
17. Disconnect fuel feed line at fuel filter.
18. Using a suitable jack and a block of wood placed under transaxle, raise engine and transaxle until engine front mount studs clear cradle bracket.
19. Attaching suitable lifting equipment to engine. Put tension on engine and remove 2 remaining transaxle-to-engine attaching bolts.
20. Slide engine assembly forward and lift from vehicle.
21. Reverse procedure to install.

V6-173

1. Disconnect battery cables from battery and remove air cleaner.
2. Drain cooling system.
3. Remove engine strut bracket from radiator support and swing rearward, as required.
4. Remove AIR pump and bracket, then remove A/C compressor from mounting bracket and place aside, if so equipped.
5. Disconnect vacuum hosing to all non-engine mounted components.
6. Disconnect accelerator cable and detent cable, if so equipped.
7. Disconnect engine harness from ECM and pull connector through front of dash.
8. Disconnect engine harness from junction block at left side of dash panel.
9. Disconnect radiator and heater hoses from engine.
10. Remove power steering pump and bracket assembly from engine, if so equipped.
11. Disconnect fuel lines rubber hose connections at left side of engine compartment.
12. Raise vehicle, remove engine front mount-to-cradle and mount-to-engine bracket retaining nuts at right side of vehicle.
13. Disconnect battery cables from starter motor and transaxle case and remove starter.
14. Remove transaxle inspection cover and on automatic transaxle models, disconnect torque converter flex plate.
15. Remove crankshaft lower pulley and all belts.
16. Disconnect exhaust pipe.
17. Remove lower transaxle-to-engine bolt, located at back side of engine.
18. Disconnect power steering cut-off switch, if so equipped.
19. Remove exhaust cross over pipe, then lower vehicle.
20. Remove remaining transaxle-to-engine bolts. Make note of ground stud location.
21. Place a support under transaxle rear extension. Install suitable lifting device and remove engine.
22. Reverse procedure to install.

CYLINDER HEAD REPLACE

4-151

1. Raise and support front of vehicle, then drain cooling system and disconnect exhaust pipe from exhaust manifold.
2. Lower vehicle and remove oil dipstick tube and air cleaner.
3. Disconnect wire connectors and vacuum hoses from carburetor or TBI unit.
4. Remove EGR valve base plate from intake manifold, if applicable.
5. Disconnect heater hose from intake manifold, then remove AIR system discharge tube attaching bolt from intake manifold.

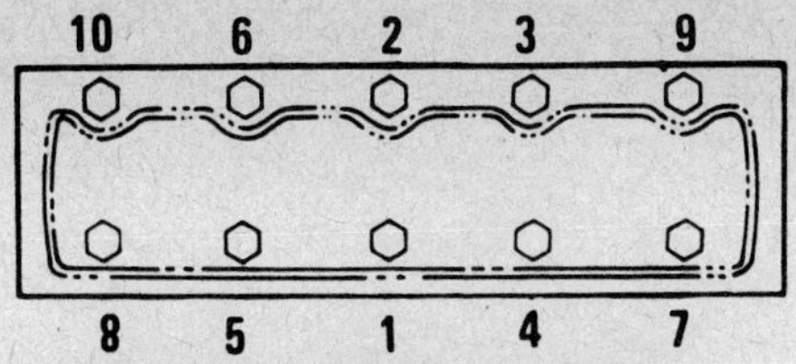

Fig. 5 Cylinder head tightening sequence. 4-151

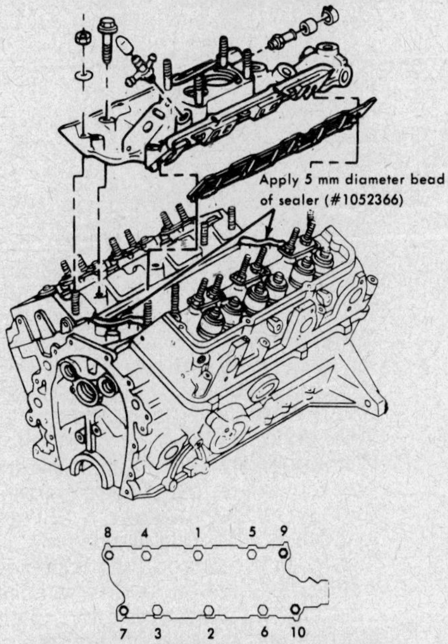

Fig. 8 Intake manifold installation. V6-173 exc. MFI

6. Remove ignition coil lower attaching bolt, then disconnect wiring from coil.
7. Disconnect all wiring from cylinder head and intake manifold, then remove engine upper support attaching bolt from engine strut.
8. Remove A/C compressor and position aside with refrigerant lines attached.
9. Remove alternator drive belt, then remove AIR pump bracket bolt from engine block, if equipped.
10. Disconnect throttle and throttle valve cables from throttle lever and intake manifold.
11. Disconnect upper radiator hose from cylinder head, then disconnect AIR hose from tube assembly, if equipped.
12. Remove rocker arm cover, then remove rocker arms and pushrods.
13. Remove cylinder head attaching bolts, then lift cylinder head and intake and exhaust manifolds as an assembly from cylinder block.
14. Reverse procedure to install. Coat heads and threads of cylinder bolts with a suitable sealing compound, then install bolts finger tight. On 1982-86 models, tighten cylinder head bolts in sequence shown in Fig.

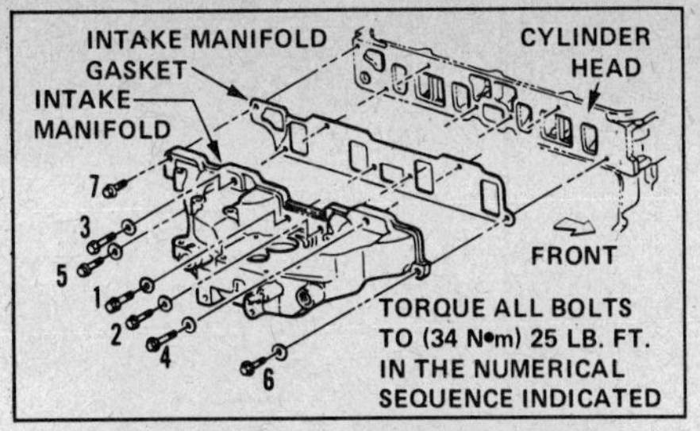

Fig. 6 Typical intake manifold tightening sequence. 4-151 engines

5. On 1987-88 models, tighten cylinder head bolts in sequence shown in **Fig. 5** to 18 ft. lbs., then repeat sequence increasing torque to 22 ft. lbs. on all bolts exc. No. 9. Torque No. 9 bolt to 29 ft. lbs. Repeat sequence again, turning all bolts exc. No. 9 an additional two flats and bolt No. 9 and additional 90 degrees. On all models, tighten intake manifold bolts in sequence shown in **Fig. 6,** if necessary.

V6-173

Right

1. Raise and support vehicle.
2. Drain cooling system.
3. Disconnect exhaust pipe, then lower vehicle.
4. On models equipped with cruise control, remove servo bracket.
5. Remove air management valve and hose.
6. Remove intake manifold, then disconnect exhaust crossover pipe.
7. Remove cover and loosen rocker arm stud nuts until pushrods can be removed.
8. Remove cylinder head attaching bolts and the cylinder head.
9. Reverse procedure to install. Coat cylinder head bolt threads with a suitable sealing compound. Torque cylinder head attaching bolts to specifications in sequence shown in **Fig. 7.** On 1987-88 models, turn cylinder head attaching bolts and additional 1/4 turn.

Left

1. Raise and support vehicle.
2. Drain cooling system.
3. Lower vehicle, then remove intake manifold and exhaust crossover pipe.
4. Remove alternator bracket, then the air injection pump and brackets.
5. Remove dipstick tube, then loosen rocker arm stud nuts until pushrods can be removed.
6. Remove cylinder head attaching bolts and the cylinder head.
7. Reverse procedure to install. Coat cylinder head bolt threads with suitable sealing compound. Torque cylinder head attaching bolts to specifications in sequence shown in **Fig. 7.** On 1987-88 models, turn cylinder head attaching bolts and additional 1/4 turn.

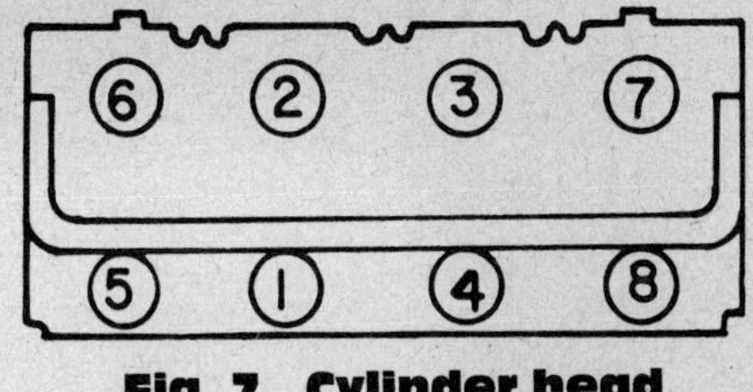

Fig. 7 Cylinder head tightening sequence. V6-173

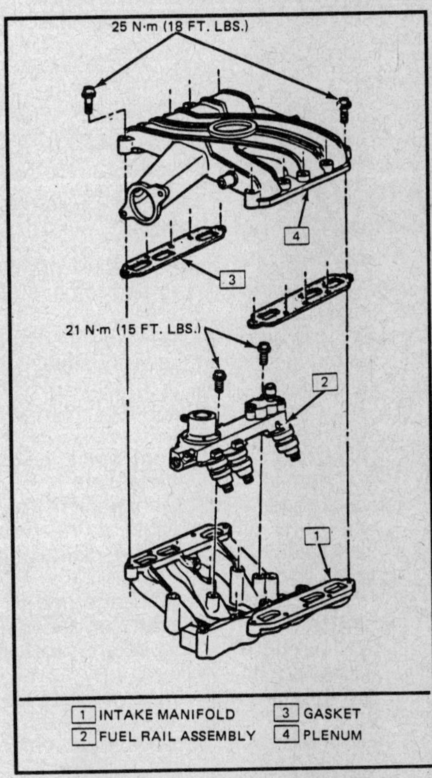

Fig. 9 Typical intake manifold installation. V6-173 w/MFI

INTAKE MANIFOLD REPLACE

4-151

1. Disconnect battery ground cable, then remove air cleaner and heat stove pipe.
2. Disconnect PCV valve and hose at TBI unit, then drain cooling system.
3. Disconnect fuel line and all vacuum hoses that will interfere with manifold removal.
4. Disconnect all electrical connections, then the throttle linkage from TBI unit.
5. Disconnect downshift and cruise control linkage, if applicable.
6. Disconnect throttle linkage and bellcrank and position aside.
7. Disconnect heater hose, then remove upper power steering pump bracket and ignition coil.
8. Remove intake manifold attaching bolts, then the intake manifold.

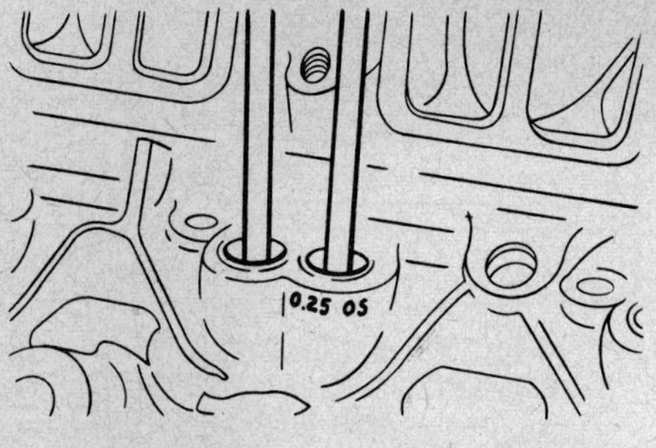

Fig. 10 Oversize valve lifter marking. V6-173

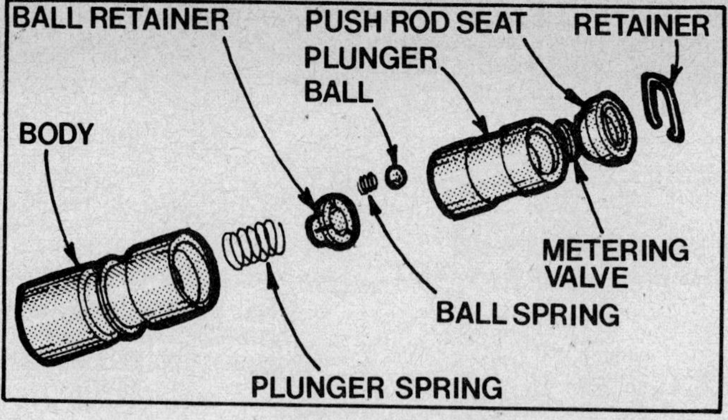

Fig. 11 Flat type hydraulic lifter exploded view

9. Reverse procedure to install. Torque bolts to specification in sequence shown in **Fig. 6.**

V6-173

Exc. EFI

1. Disconnect battery ground cable, drain cooling system and remove air cleaner.
2. Remove front engine strut, then the strut bracket from the cylinder head, if applicable.
3. Disconnect vacuum hoses and fuel lines as needed.
4. Disconnect wires from spark plugs and retainers on valve covers.
5. Disconnect electrical connectors from carburetor and manifold, as needed, then remove harness from clamps on valve cover.
6. Remove accelerator linkage and return springs from carburetor, and disconnect transmission detent cable, if equipped.
7. On models with cruise control, remove diaphragm actuator bracket.
8. On all models, remove both valve covers.
9. Remove AIR pump and bracket.
10. On all models, remove distributor cap and plug wire assembly.
11. Mark position of distributor rotor for installation, then remove distributor.
12. Disconnect heater, radiator and brake booster hoses from manifold.
13. On all models, remove manifold retaining bolts, manifold and gaskets.
14. Install replacement gaskets on cylinder heads, cutting gaskets only where needed to clear push rods. Hold gaskets in position by extending sealer bead approximately 1/4 inch past end of block end rails.
15. Install manifold and torque bolts in sequence as shown in **Fig. 8.**
16. Reverse remaining procedure to complete installation.

With EFI

1. Disconnect battery ground cable, drain cooling system and remove air duct between throttle body and air cleaner.
2. Disconnect vacuum hoses from plenum.
3. Remove bolts securing EGR pipe and throttle body to plenum.
4. Remove throttle cable bracket bolts and bracket.
5. Remove 10 plenum retaining bolts and the plenum, **Fig. 9.**
6. Connect gauge J-34730-1 or equivalent to fuel pressure regulator and bleed off pressurized fuel into a suitable container.
7. Disconnect cold start valve and fuel lines from fuel rail assembly.
8. Disconnect vacuum hose from regulator and electrical connectors from injectors.
9. Remove fuel rail retaining bolts and the fuel rail.
10. Remove intake manifold.
11. Reverse procedure to install, using new gaskets and injector seals.

ROCKER ARM STUDS

4-151

Rocker arm studs that are cracked or have damaged threads can be removed from the cylinder head using a deep well socket. Install and torque new rocker arm stud to 75 ft. lbs.

V6-173

Rocker arm studs that are cracked or have damaged threads can be replaced. If threads in cylinder head are damaged or stripped, the head can be retapped and a helical type insert added. When installing a new rocker arm stud, torque stud to 43 to 49 ft. lbs.

VALVE CLEARANCE SPECIFICATIONS

4-151 engines are equipped with hydraulic lifters, no provision for adjustment is provided.

On V6-173 engines, refer to "Valves, Adjust" procedure.

VALVES

ADJUST

V6-173

1. Crank engine until mark on torsional damper is aligned with TDC mark on timing tab. Check to ensure engine is in the No. 1 cylinder firing position by placing fingers on No. 1 cylinder rocker arms as mark on damper comes near TDC mark on timing tab. If valves are not moving, the engine is in the No. 1 firing position. If valves move as damper mark nears TDC mark on timing tab, engine is in the No. 4 cylinder firing position and should be rotated one revolution to reach the No. 1 cylinder firing position.
2. With engine in the No. 1 cylinder firing position, adjust the following valves: Exhaust-1, 2, 3; Intake-1, 5, 6. To adjust valves, back off adjusting nut until lash is felt at pushrod, then tighten adjusting nut until all lash is removed. This can be determined by rotating the pushrod while tightening the adjusting nut. When all lash has been eliminated, turn adjusting nut an additional 1 1/2 turns.
3. Crank engine one revolution until mark on torsional damper and TDC mark are again aligned. This is the No. 4 cylinder firing position. With engine in this position, the following valves can be adjusted: Exhaust-4, 5 & 6; Intake-2, 3 & 4.
4. Install rocker arm covers, then start engine and check timing and idle speed.

VALVE ARRANGEMENT

FRONT TO REAR

4-151 .... I-E-I-E-E-I-E-I
V6-173 Right .... E-I-E-I-I-E
V6-173 Left.................. E-I-I-E-I-E

CAM LOBE LIFT SPECIFICATIONS

Engine	Year	Int.	Exh.
4-151	1982-88	.398	.398
V6-173 2Bbl.	1982-87	.231	.262
V6-173 EFI	1985-88	.262	.273

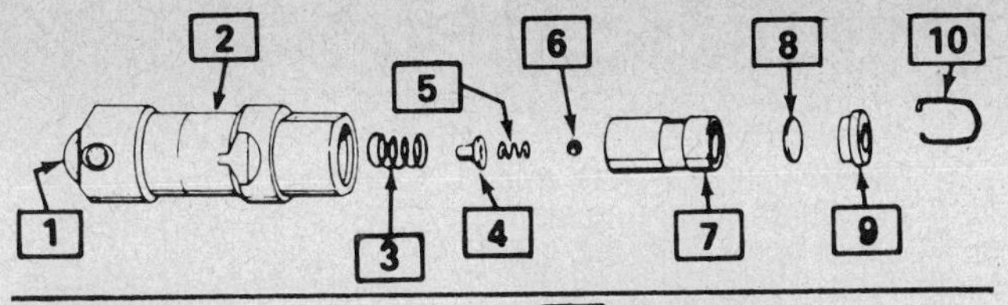

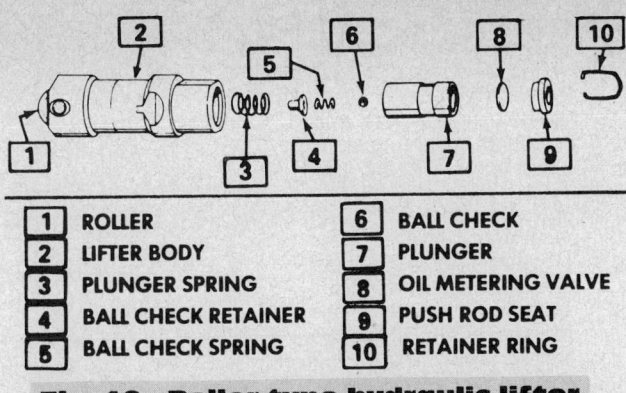

Fig. 12 Roller type hydraulic lifter exploded view

VALVE TIMING

INTAKE OPENS BEFORE TDC

Engine	Year	Degrees
4-151	1982-88	33
V6-173	1982-87	25
V6-173 H.O.	1982-84	31
V6-173 EFI	1985-88	31

VALVE GUIDES

Valve guides are an integral part of the cylinder head and are not removable. If valve stem clearance becomes excessive, the valve guide should be reamed to the next oversize and the appropriate oversize valves installed. Valves are available in .003 and .005 inch oversizes for 4-151 engine and .0035, .0155 and .0305 inch for V6-173 engines.

VALVE LIFTERS

Some V6-173 engines will be equipped with both standard and .25 mm oversize valve lifters. The cylinder case will be marked where the oversize valve lifters are installed with a dab of white paint and .25 mm. O.S. will be stamped on the valve lifter boss, **Fig. 10.**

Failure of a hydraulic valve lifter, **Figs. 11 and 12,** is generally caused by an inadequate oil supply or dirt. An air leak at the intake side of the oil pump or too much oil in the engine will cause air bubbles in the oil supply to the lifters, causing them to collapse. This is a probable cause of trouble if several lifters fail to function, but air in oil is an unlikely cause of failure of a single unit.

On 4-151 engines, valve lifters can be removed after removing rocker arm cover, intake manifold, pushrod cover and pushrod retainer and guide, if applicable. Loosen rocker arm stud nut and rotate rocker arm so that pushrod can be removed, then remove valve lifter. It may be necessary to use tool No. J-3049 to facilitate lifter removal.

On V6-173 engines, valve lifters can be removed after removing rocker arm covers, intake manifold, rocker stud nuts, rocker arm balls, rocker arms and pushrods.

ENGINE FRONT COVER REPLACE

4-151

1982–84

1. Remove drive belts, then remove right front inner fender splash shield.
2. Remove crankshaft pulley attaching bolt, then remove pulley and hub from shaft.
3. Remove alternator lower bracket.
4. Remove front engine mount to cradle nuts, then install suitable engine lifting equipment and raise engine.
5. Remove engine mount bracket to cylinder block bolts, then remove mount and bracket as an assembly.
6. Remove oil pan to front cover attaching screws. Pull front cover slightly forward to permit cutting of oil pan front seal.
7. Using a suitable cutting tool, cut oil pan front seal flush with cylinder block at both sides of cover.
8. Remove front cover and attached portion of oil pan front seal, then remove front cover gasket.
9. Clean gasket surfaces on cylinder block and front cover.
10. Cut tabs from a new oil pan front seal using a suitable cutting tool, then install seal to front cover, pressing tabs into holes provided on front cover.
11. Coat front cover gasket with gasket sealer, then position gasket on front cover.
12. Apply a 1/8 inch bead of RTV sealer to joint formed at oil pan and cylinder block.
13. Install centering tool No. J-23042 into front cover seal bore. It is important that the centering tool be used to align front cover, otherwise damage to seal may result when hub is installed.
14. Install front cover to block, then install and partially tighten the two oil pan to front cover screws.
15. Install front cover to cylinder block attaching screws. Torque all cover attaching screws to 90 inch lbs., then re-

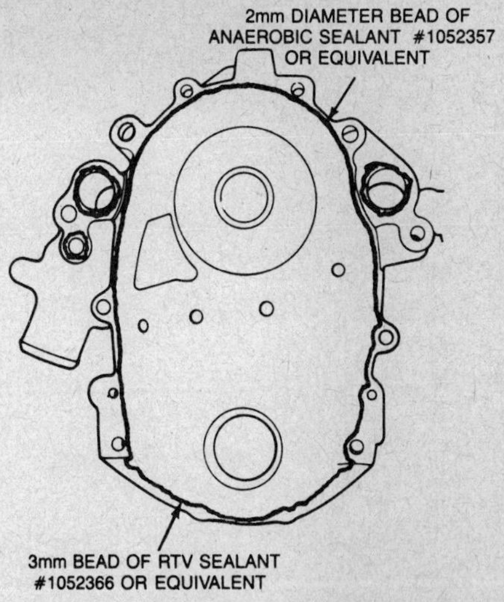

Fig. 13 Engine front cover installation. 1982–83 V6-173

16. Install front mount bracket assembly and alternator lower mounting bracket.
17. Lower engine and remove engine lifting equipment.
18. Install lower mount to cradle nuts, crankshaft pulley and hub, right front fender inner splash shield and drive belts. **Apply Drylock No. 299 or equivalent to threaded area of crankshaft pulley to hub bolts before installing bolts.**

1985–88

1. Remove drive belts, then the right front inner fender splash shield.
2. Remove crankshaft pulley attaching bolt, then the pulley and hub assembly.
3. Remove lower alternator bracket, then install engine support fixture J28467 or equivalent.
4. Remove engine mount bracket to cylinder block attaching bolts, then the mount and bracket as an assembly.
5. Remove front cover attaching screws, then the front cover.
6. Position oil pan front seal onto cover.
7. Apply a 3/8 inch bead of RTV sealer to joint where front cover meets oil pan, then a 1/4 inch bead of sealer to front cover to cylinder block mating surface.
8. Position centering tool J34995 into cover, then install and partially tighten two opposing cover screws.
9. Install remaining attaching screws, then torque all screws to 90 inch lbs.
10. Remove centering tool, then install engine mount and bracket.
11. Install alternator bracket, hub and pulley assembly and retaining bolt.

V6-173

1982–86

1. Disconnect battery ground cable.
2. Remove accessory drive belts.

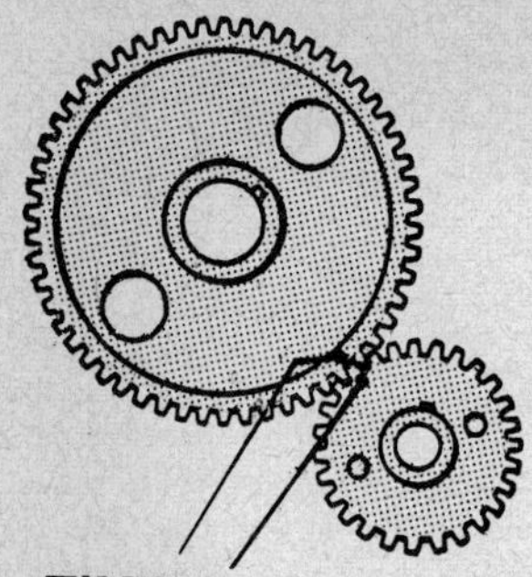

Fig. 14 Valve timing marks. 4-151

move centering tool J-23042.

3. On 1983-86 models equipped with A/C, remove air injection pump and pump bracket.
4. On all models, remove water pump as described under "Water Pump, Replace."
5. On 1982 models equipped with A/C, remove compressor from mounting bracket and position compressor aside, then remove bracket.
6. On all models, raise and support vehicle.
7. Remove inner fender splash shield, then the accessory drive pulley and damper retaining bolt.
8. Remove damper using tool No. J-23523, or equivalent.
9. On 1982 models, disconnect lower radiator hose from front cover and heater hose from water pump.
10. On 1983-86 models, remove oil pan-to-cover attaching bolts, then lower vehicle.
11. On all models, remove remaining front cover attaching bolts and the cover.
12. Reverse procedure to install. Apply sealant to mating surfaces as shown in **Fig. 13. On 1984-86 engines, it is only necessary to coat oil pan to front cover sealing surfaces since gasket is used in production.**

1987—88

1. Disconnect battery ground cable.
2. Drain cooling system, then remove belt tensioner.
3. Disconnect alternator and power steering pump and position aside.
4. Raise and support vehicle, then remove inner splash shield and damper.
5. Lower oil pan, then remove lower cover attaching bolts.
6. Lower vehicle, then remove radiator hose at water pump.
7. Remove bypass, overflow and canister purge hoses, then the heater coolant hose at cooling system fill pipe.
8. Remove upper front cover attaching bolts, then the front cover.
9. Reverse procedure to install. Coat oil pan to front cover sealing surfaces with suitable sealer.

TIMING GEARS

4-151

When necessary to install a new camshaft gear, the camshaft will have to be removed as the gear is a pressed fit on the camshaft. The camshaft is held in place by a thrust plate which is retained to the engine by two capscrews which are accessible through the two holes in the gear web.

To remove gear, use an arbor press and a suitable sleeve to properly support gear on its steel hub.

Before installing gear, assemble thrust plate and gear spacer ring, then press gear onto shaft until it bottoms against spacer ring. The thrust plate end clearance should be .0015-.0050 inch. If clearance is less than .0015 inch, the spacer ring should be replaced. If clearance is greater than .0050 inch, the thrust plate should be replaced.

The crankshaft gear can be removed using a puller and two bolts in the tapped holes of the gear.

When installing timing gears, make sure that the marks on the gears are properly aligned, **Fig. 14. The valve timing marks, Fig. 14, do not indicate TDC, compression stroke for No. 1 cylinder for use during distributor installation. When installing the distributor, rotate engine until No. 1 cylinder is on compression stroke and the camshaft timing mark is 180° from the valve timing position shown in Fig. 14.**

TIMING CHAIN REPLACE

V6-173

1. Remove front cover as described under "Engine Front Cover, Replace."
2. Place No. 1 piston at top dead center with marks on camshaft and crankshaft sprockets aligned, **Fig. 15.**
3. Remove camshaft sprocket bolts, then remove sprocket and timing chain. If sprocket does not come off easily, tap lower edge of sprocket with a plastic mallet.
4. If crankshaft sprocket is to be replaced, remove sprocket using a suitable puller. Install new sprocket, aligning key and keyway.
5. Install timing chain on camshaft sprocket. Hold sprocket vertically with chain hanging down and align marks on camshaft and crankshaft sprockets.
6. Align dowel pin hole in sprocket with dowel pin on camshaft, then install sprocket on camshaft.
7. Using camshaft sprocket attaching bolts, draw sprocket on camshaft. Torque bolts to 15 to 20 ft. lbs.
8. Lubricate timing chain with engine oil, then install front cover as outlined previously.

CAMSHAFT REPLACE

4-151

1. Remove engine from vehicle as described under "Engine, Replace."
2. Remove rocker arm cover, then loosen rocker arm stud nuts and pivot rocker arms clear of pushrods.
3. Remove distributor and fuel pump or

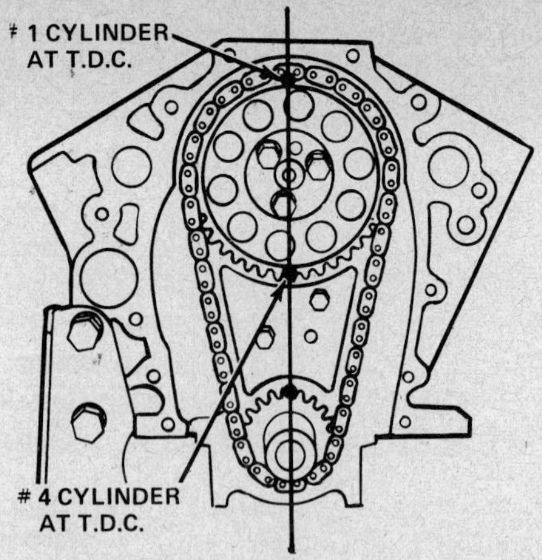

Fig. 15 Valve timing marks. V6-173

vacuum pump, if equipped.

4. Remove pushrod cover, pushrods and valve lifters.
5. Remove alternator, alternator lower mounting bracket and engine front mount bracket assembly.
6. Remove oil pump driveshaft and gear assembly.
7. Remove front pulley hub and front cover assembly.
8. Working through holes in camshaft sprocket, remove two camshaft thrust plate retaining screws.
9. Pull camshaft and gear assembly from engine block. Use care not to damage camshaft bearings.
10. Reverse procedure to install. When installing camshaft, align crankshaft and camshaft valve timing marks on gear teeth, **Fig. 14.** The valve timing marks does not indicate TDC compression stroke for No. 1 cylinder for use during distributor installation. When installing the distributor, rotate engine until No. 1 cylinder is on compression stroke and the camshaft timing mark is 180 degrees from valve timing position shown in **Fig. 14.**

V6-173

1. Remove engine from vehicle as described under "Engine, Replace."
2. Remove valve lifters and engine front cover as described previously.
3. Remove fuel pump and pushrod.
4. Remove timing chain and sprocket as described under "Timing Chain, Replace."
5. Withdraw camshaft from engine, using care not to damage camshaft bearings.
6. Reverse procedure to install. When installing timing chain, align valve timing marks as shown in **Fig. 15.**

BALANCE SHAFTS

1988 4-151

The crankshaft has been modified with the addition of a drive gear machined in the area next to the crankshaft timing disc, **Fig. 16.** This gear drives the combination in-sump oil pump and balance shafts.

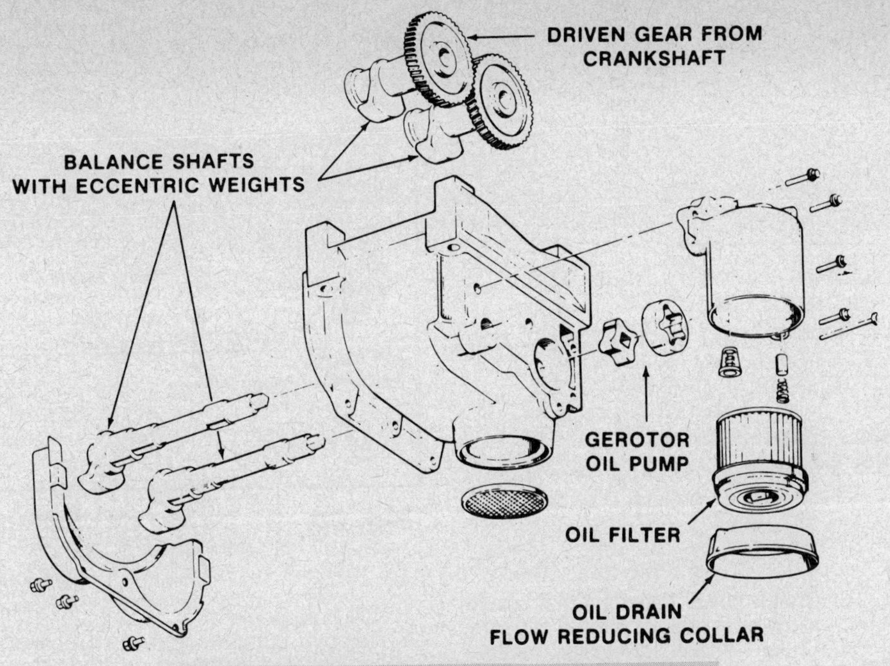

Fig. 16 Balance shafts. 1988 4-151

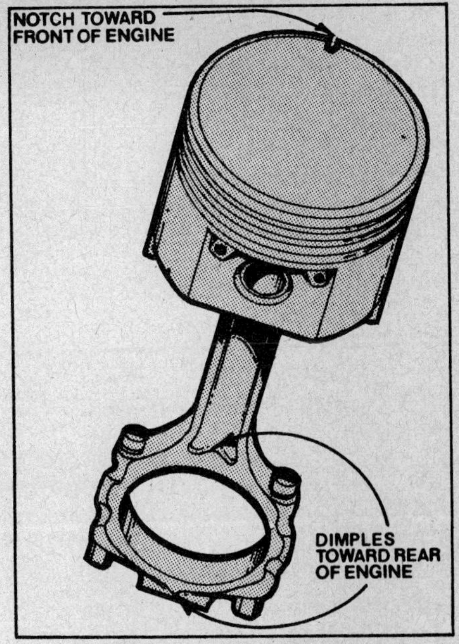

Fig. 17 Piston & rod assembly. 4-151

The balancer assembly consists of two eccentrically weighted shafts and gears which are counter rotated at twice the crankshaft speed by a concentric gear. These weights on the balance shafts reduce vibration at all engine speeds.

PISTONS & RODS ASSEMBLE

4-151

Assemble piston to rod with notch on piston facing toward front of engine and the raised notch side of rod at bearing end facing toward rear of engine, **Fig. 17.**

Upon installation, measure the connecting rod side clearance using a suitable feeler gauge. Clearance should be .006 to .022 inch.

V6-173

Assemble pistons to connecting rods as shown in **Fig. 18.**

Upon installation, measure the connecting rod side clearance using a suitable feeler gauge. Clearance should be .006 to .017 inch.

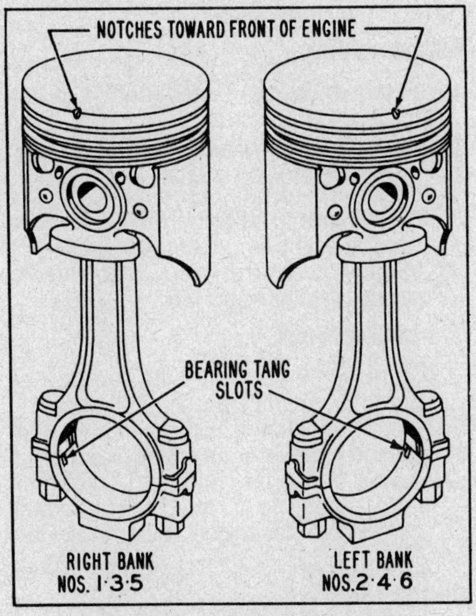

Fig. 18 Piston & rod assembly. V6-173

PISTONS, PINS & RINGS

4-151

Pistons and rings are available in standard and oversizes of .010, .020 and .030 inch. Piston pins are available in oversizes of .001 and .003 inch.

V6-173

Pistons and rings are available in standard size and oversizes of .05 and 1 mm.

MAIN & ROD BEARINGS

Main and rod bearings are available in standard size and undersizes of .001, .002 and .010 inch for the 4-151 engine. Main bearings are available in standard size and undersizes of .013 and .026 mm and connecting rod bearings are available in standard size and undersizes of .016 and .032 mm. for the V6-173 engine.

OIL PAN REPLACE

4-151

1982–87

1. Raise vehicle and drain crankcase.
2. Remove engine front mount to cradle attaching nuts.
3. Disconnect exhaust pipe at manifold and rear transaxle mount or converter.
4. Remove starter motor and flywheel housing cover, then the splash shield, if applicable.
5. Remove alternator upper mounting bracket and if equipped with power steering, the power steering pump and bracket.
6. Install a suitable engine lifting device and raise engine.
7. Remove lower alternator mounting bracket, engine strut and engine support bracket.
8. Remove oil pan attaching bolts and oil pan.
9. Clean engine block and oil pan gasket surfaces.
10. Reverse procedure to install, noting the following:
    a. On 1982-83 engines, apply a 1/8 inch by 1/4 inch bead of RTV sealant at split lines of front and side oil pan gaskets. Also apply a small amount of sealant in depressions where rear oil pan gasket engages engine block.
    b. On 1984-87 engines, apply RTV sealant as shown in **Fig. 19. When installing oil pan attaching bolts, the bolts attaching the oil pan to the front cover should be installed last. These bolts are installed at an angle and the bolt holes will only be aligned after the other oil pan bolts have been installed.**

1988

1. Remove engine from vehicle and place on suitable work stand.
2. Remove oil pan attaching bolts, then the oil pan.
3. Reveres procedure to install.

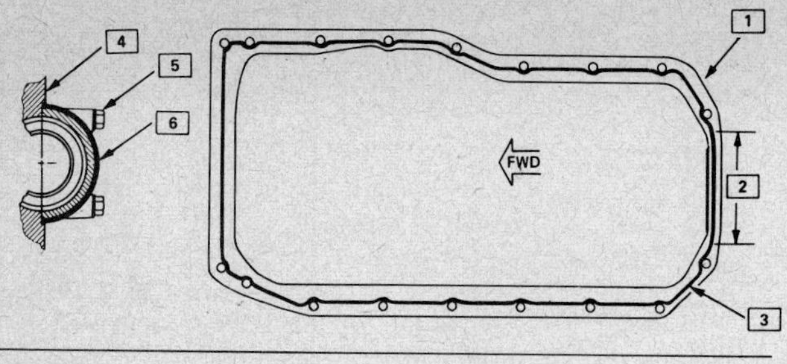

Fig. 19 Oil pan sealer application. 1984–88 V6-173

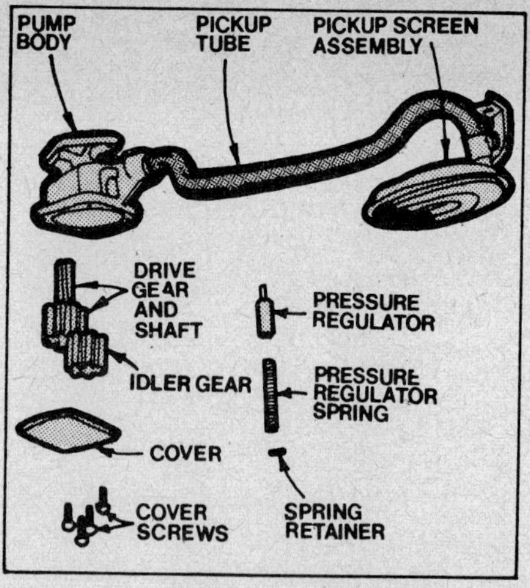

Fig. 20 Oil pump exploded view. 4-151

V6-173

1. Disconnect battery ground cable.
2. Remove serpentine belt and tensioner, if equipped.
3. Raise and support vehicle.
4. Drain engine oil from crankcase.
5. Remove flywheel housing shield or clutch housing cover as applicable.
6. Remove starter motor and air bracket, as required.
7. Attach suitable lifting equipment to engine. Remove engine mount bracket-to-engine attaching bolts and raise engine slightly.
8. On all models, remove oil pan attaching bolts and the oil pan.
9. Reverse procedure to install. Apply a 1/8 inch bead of RTV sealer to oil pan sealing flange.

OIL PUMP SERVICE

4-151

1982–87

Removal

1. Drain crankcase, then remove oil pan as described under "Oil Pan, Replace."
2. Remove two oil pump mounting bolts and nuts from main cap bolt and remove oil pump and screen as an assembly.

Disassemble

1. Remove four pump cover to body attaching screws, then remove cover, idler and drive gears and shaft, **Fig. 20.**
2. Remove pin, retainer, spring and pressure regulator valve.

Inspection

Inspect pump components and should any of the following conditions be found, the oil pump assembly should be replaced.

a. Inspect pump body for cracks and excessive wear.
b. Inspect oil pump gears for damage, cracks or excessive wear.
c. Check shaft for looseness in housing.
d. Check cover for wear that would allow oil to leak past ends of gears.
e. Check oil pick screen for damage to screen or relief grommet. Also remove any debris from screen surface.
f. Check pressure regulator valve for fit in body.

Assemble

1. Place drive gear and shaft in pump body, then install idler gear with smooth side of gear facing pump cover, **Fig. 20.**
2. Install and torque pump cover attaching screws to 105 inch lbs. Check to ensure that pump rotates freely.
3. Install pressure regulator valve, spring, retainer and pin.

Installation

1. Align oil pump shaft with tang on oil pump drive shaft, then install pump on block, positioning pump flange over oil pump drive shaft lower bushing.
2. Install oil pump mounting bolts and torque bolts to 20 ft. lbs., then install oil pan as described under "Oil Pan, Replace."

1988

Removal

1. Remove engine from vehicle.
2. Remove oil pan assembly, refer to "Oil Pan, Replace" procedure.
3. Remove balancer assembly, then the filter body.
4. Remove pump gears, then the pressure regulator valve.

Service

This engine uses a gerotor type oil pump. The oil pump is serviced only as an assembly with the balancer assembly.

Installation

Reverse removal procedure.

V6-173

Removal

1. Remove oil pan as described under "Oil Pan, Replace."
2. Remove pump to rear main bearing cap bolt and remove pump and extension shaft.

Disassembly

1. Remove pump cover attaching bolts and pump cover, **Fig. 21.**
2. Mark drive and idler gear teeth so they can be installed in the same position, then remove idler and drive gear and shaft from pump body.
3. Remove pin, spring and pressure regulator valve from pump cover.
4. If pickup tube and screen assembly are to be replaced, mount pump cover in a soft jawed vise and remove pickup tube from cover. Do not remove screen from pickup tube, these components are serviced as an assembly.

Inspection

1. Inspect pump body and cover for excessive wear and cracks.
2. Inspect pump gear for damage or excessive wear. If pump gears are damaged or worn, the entire pump assembly must be replaced.
3. Check drive gear shaft for looseness in pump body.
4. Inspect pump cover for wear that would allow oil to leak past gear teeth.
5. Inspect pickup tube and screen assembly for damage.
6. Check pressure regulator valve for fit in pump cover.

Assembly

1. If pickup tube and screen were removed, apply sealer to end of pickup tube, then mount pump cover in a soft jawed vise and using tool No. J-8369, tap pickup tube into position using a plastic mallet. **Whenever the pickup tube and screen assembly has been removed, a new pickup tube and screen assembly should be installed. Use care when installing pickup tube and screen assembly so that tube does not twist, shear or collapse. Loss of a press fit con-**

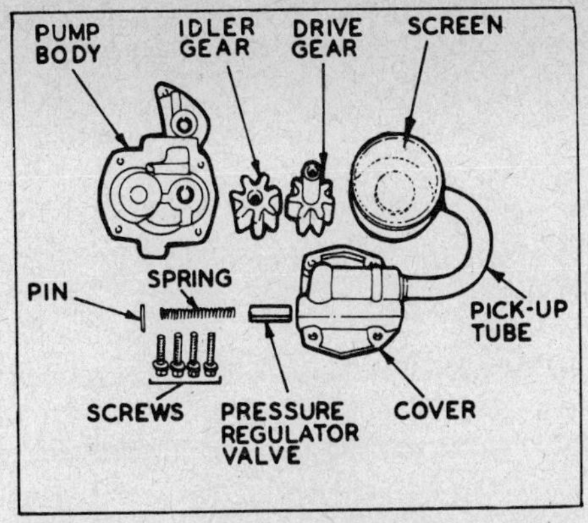

Fig. 21 Oil pump exploded view. V6-173

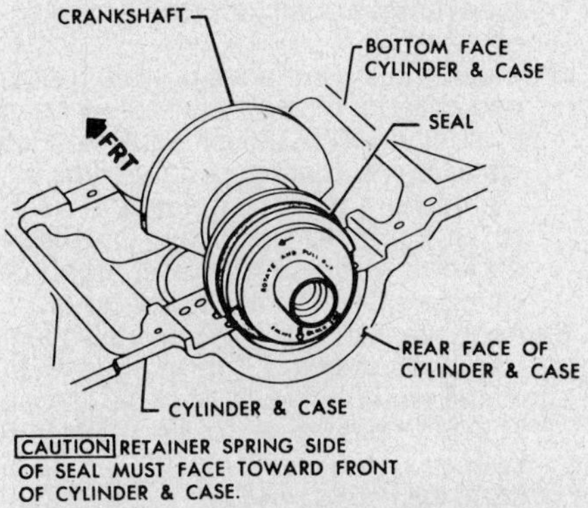

Fig. 24 Installing thin type seal. 1985–86 V6-173

dition could result in an air leak and a loss of oil pressure.

2. Install pressure regulator valve, spring and pin, **Fig. 21.**
3. Install drive gear and shaft in pump body.
4. Align marks made during disassembly, then install idler gear.
5. Install pump cover gasket, cover and attaching bolts. Torque bolts to 6 to 9 ft. lbs.
6. Rotate pump drive shaft by hand and check pump for smooth operation.

Installation

1. Assemble pump and extension shaft with retainer to rear main bearing cap, aligning top end of hexagon extension shaft with hexagon socket on lower end of distributor shaft.
2. Install pump to rear main bearing cap bolt.
3. Install oil pan as described under Oil Pan, Replace.

CRANKSHAFT REAR OIL SEAL

REPLACE

4-151

The rear main oil seal is a one piece unit and is replaced without removing the oil

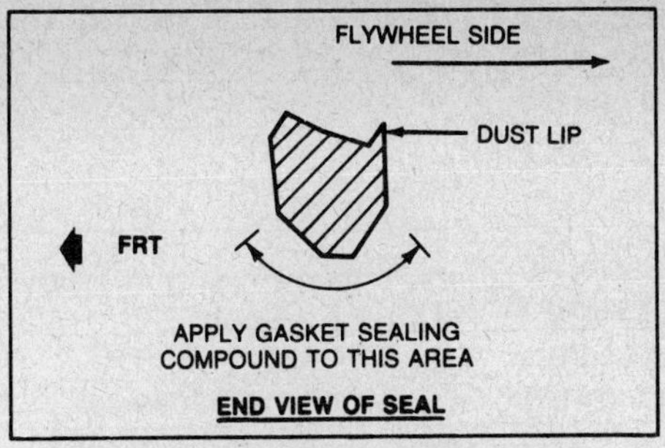

Fig. 22 Rear main seal installation. 1982–84 V6-173

pan or crankshaft.

1. Remove transaxle and flywheel.
2. Using a suitable screwdriver, remove rear main bearing oil seal. Use care not to scratch crankshaft.
3. Lubricate inside and outside diameters of replacement seal with engine oil. Install seal by hand onto rear crankshaft flange with helical lip side facing toward engine. Ensure seal is firmly and evenly seated.
4. Install flywheel and transaxle.

REAR MAIN BEARING OIL SEAL REPAIR

V6-173

1982–84

When replacement of the rear main seal is necessary, the rope type seal used during engine assembly should be replace with rubber split seal No. 14069889, or equivalent using the following procedure. Disregard instructions furnished with the replacement seal that refer to Cavalier models.

1. Remove oil pan and oil pump.
2. Remove rear main bearing cap.
3. Remove upper and lower rope seals, taking care not to damage crankshaft, then clean seal remnants and oil from seal channels. **It may be necessary to loosen No. 2 and 3 bearing cap bolts to allow removal of the rope type seal and installation of the upper split seal.**
4. Apply a thin coating of gasket sealing compound 1050026 or equivalent to outer circumference of replacement seal, **Fig. 22,** keeping sealer off seal lips.
5. Use a piece of shim stock to guide seal into block channel and roll seal into block by turning crankshaft. **Ensure that large seal lip is toward front of engine and that smaller dust lip faces the flywheel.**
6. Apply sealer to lower half of seal as in step 4, then install seal into bearing cap.
7. Apply a thin bead of anaerobic sealant to bearing cap surface as shown in **Fig. 23.** Keep sealant off ends of seal, main bearing, and out of drain slot.
8. Apply a thin film of motor oil to seal lip, install bearing cap and torque cap bolts to specifications. **If other main bearing cap bolts were loosened, retorque as needed.**

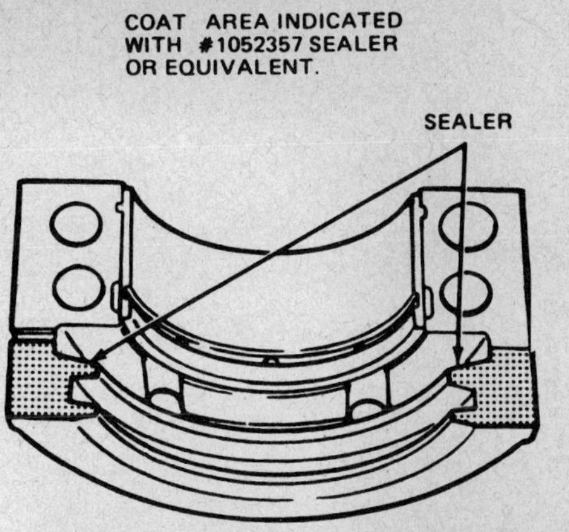

Fig. 23 Rear main bearing cap sealing areas. V6-173

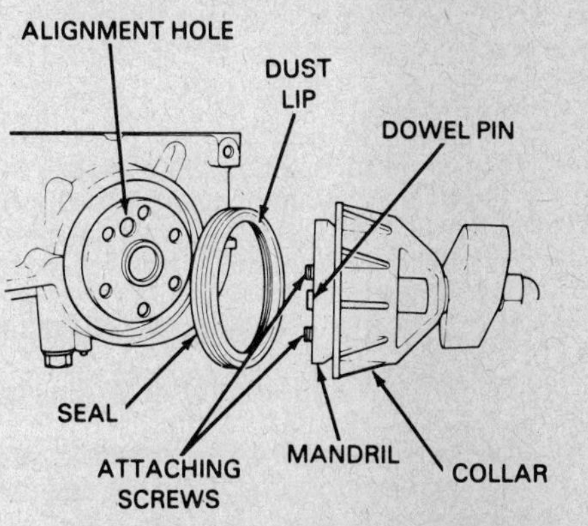

Fig. 25 Installing thick type seal. 1985–88 V6-173

9. Reinstall oil pump and pan as outlined.
10. Fill crankcase, start engine and check for leaks.

1985–88

Thin Seal

1. Remove engine as outlined under "Engine, Replace" procedure.
2. Remove oil pan and oil pump assembly.
3. Remove water pump and timing chain.
4. Remove connecting rod and main bearing caps, then the crankshaft and oil seal.
5. Coat outer diameter of new seal with sealant 1052756 or equivalent.
6. Position seal/tool assembly on rear of crankshaft, ensuring arrows on tool face toward cylinder and case assembly, **Fig. 24.**
7. Install crankshaft, discard tool, then coat crankshaft journals with engine oil.
8. Apply a 1 millimeter bead of anaerobic sealant to bearing cap surface as shown in **Fig. 23.**
9. Reinstall rear main cap, main bearing caps and connecting rod caps and torque to specifications.
10. Reverse removal procedure to complete installation.

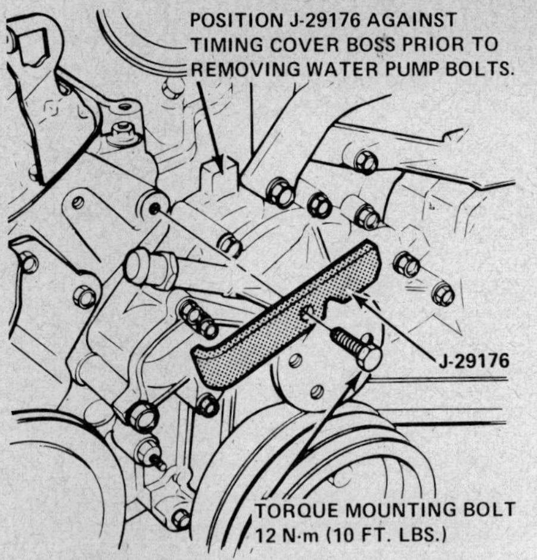

Fig. 26 Positioning tool J-29176 against timing cover boss. V6-173

Thick Seal

1. Remove transaxle and flex plate.
2. Using a screwdriver or similar tool, pry out old seal. Use care to avoid damaging crankshaft. File all burrs or nicks as required.
3. Install new seal using tool J34686 as follows:
   a. Apply a light coat of engine oil to I.D. of oil seal.
   b. Slide seal over tool mandril until dust lip bottoms squarely against collar of tool.
   c. Align dowel pin of tool with dowel pin hole in crankshaft, **Fig. 25,** then attach tool to crankshaft with screw provided.
   d. Turn handle of tool until seal is pushed into bore and collar is positioned firmly against case. Remove tool.
4. Install flywheel and transmission, then start engine and check for leaks.

BELT TENSION DATA

Belt	New Lbs.	Used Lbs.
Air Cond.		
4-151	135-165	65①
V6-173	145	65-80
A.I.R. Pump		
V6-173	100	45①
Alternator		
4-151	120-150	55①
V6-173	145	65-80
Power Steer.		
4-151	120-150	55①
V6-173	135	65-80

①—Minimum.

WATER PUMP REPLACE

4-151

Removal

1. Disconnect battery negative cable, then drain cooling system.
2. Remove accessory drive belts.
3. Using tool J 25034, remove pulley.
4. Remove water pump attaching bolts and remove pump.

Installation

1. With sealing surfaces cleaned, place a 1/8 inch bead of sealant, part number 1052289 or equivalent, on water pump sealing surface.
2. With sealing surfaces still wet, install pump and attaching bolts. Coat threaded area of bolts with part number 1052080 sealer or equivalent and torque bolts to 6 ft. lbs. on 1982-84 models or 20 ft. lbs. for 1985-88.
3. Using tool J-25033, install pulley on pump.
4. Install accessory drive belts and adjust to specifications.
5. Connect battery negative cable.

V6-173

1. Disconnect battery ground cable, then drain cooling system.
2. Disconnect heater hose at water pump, then remove drive belts and water pump pulley.
3. Using the existing tapped hole in the cylinder head, install tool No. J-29167 and torque mounting bolt to 10 ft. lbs., **Fig. 26.**

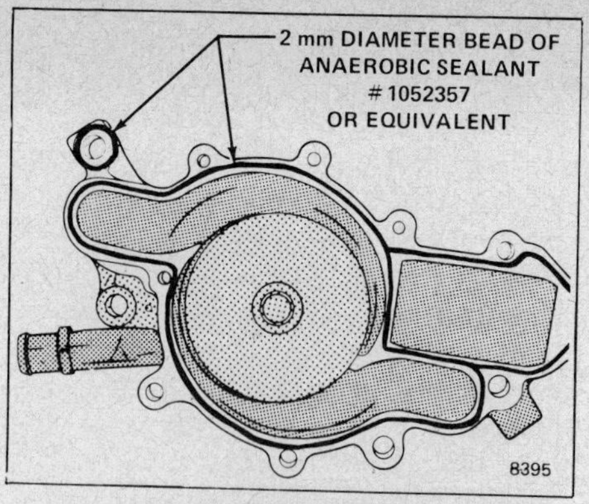

Fig. 27 Applying sealer to water pump mating surfaces. V6-173

4. Remove water pump attaching bolts, then remove pump assembly from engine.
5. Clean mating surfaces of water pump and cylinder block, then apply a bead of sealant 1052375 or equivalent to water pump mating surface, **Fig. 27. On some engines a gasket is used to seal mating surfaces. On these engines, replace gasket instead of using sealant mentioned above.**
6. Apply sealant 1052080 or equivalent to pump attaching bolt threads, then install water pump assembly. Torque M6x1.0 bolts to 8 ft. lbs., M8x1.25 bolts to 16 ft. lbs. and M10x1.5 bolts to 25 ft. lbs.
7. Remove tool J-29176, then install water pump pulley and drive belts and connect heater hose to pump.
8. Fill cooling system and connect battery ground cable, then start engine and check for leaks.

FUEL PUMP REPLACE

V6-173 LESS EFI

1. Disconnect fuel inlet and outlet lines from pump.
2. Disconnect vapor return hose if equipped.
3. Remove fuel pump attaching nuts and the fuel pump.
4. Reverse procedure to install, using a new gasket.
5. Start engine and check for leaks.

V6-181 (3.0L) & V6-231 (3.8L) Engine Section

INDEX

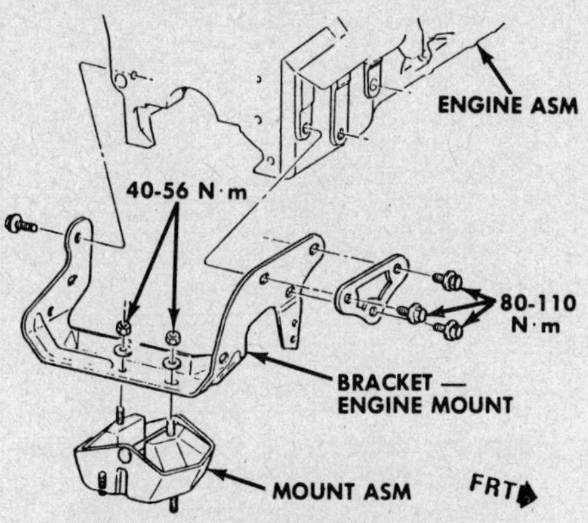

Fig. 1 Engine mount removal

ENGINE MOUNTS
REPLACE

1. Raise and support front of vehicle.
2. Attach suitable engine lifting fixture to engine.
3. Remove mount to engine mount bracket nuts. Raise engine slightly and remove mount to frame nuts. Remove mount, **Fig. 1.**
4. Reverse procedure to install.

ENGINE
REPLACE

1. Disconnect battery cables from battery and remove air cleaner.
2. Drain cooling system.
3. Disconnect vacuum hosing to all non-engine mounted components.
4. Disconnect detent cable from throttle lever.
5. Disconnect accelerator linkage.
6. Disconnect engine harness connector.
7. Remove alternator attaching bolts, then alternator.
8. Remove fan blower motor, then AIR pump and mounting bracket, if equipped.
9. Disconnect radiator hoses from radiator and heater hose from engine.
10. Remove power steering pump and bracket assembly from engine, if equipped.
11. Disconnect fuel lines at rubber hose connections.
12. Remove gas spring cylinder from hood, if equipped, then place hood in full open position.
13. Raise vehicle and disconnect exhaust pipe at manifold.
14. Remove engine front mount to cradle retaining nuts, located at right side of vehicle.
15. Disconnect battery cables from starter motor and transaxle case.
16. Remove flex plate cover, then disconnect torque converter form flex plate.
17. Remove transaxle case to cylinder case support bracket bolts, **Fig. 2.**
18. Lower vehicle. Place a support under transaxle rear extension.
19. Disconnect ground strap from engine at engine forward strut. Remove engine strut bracket from radiator support and swing rearward.
20. Remove transaxle to cylinder case retaining bolts. Make note of ground stud location.
21. If equipped with A/C, remove compressor and lay aside.
22. Using a suitable lifting device, remove engine.
23. Reverse procedure to install.

CYLINDER HEAD
REPLACE

1. Disconnect battery ground cable.
2. Remove intake manifold, then loosen and remove belts.
3. If left cylinder head is to be removed, remove dipstick, also remove air and vacuum pumps with mounting bracket if equipped, and position aside with hoses attached.
4. If right cylinder head is to be removed, remove alternator, also disconnect power steering gear pump and brackets attaching to cylinder head.
5. Disconnect wires from spark plugs, then remove spark plug wire clips from rocker arm cover studs.
6. Remove exhaust manifold bolts from head being removed.

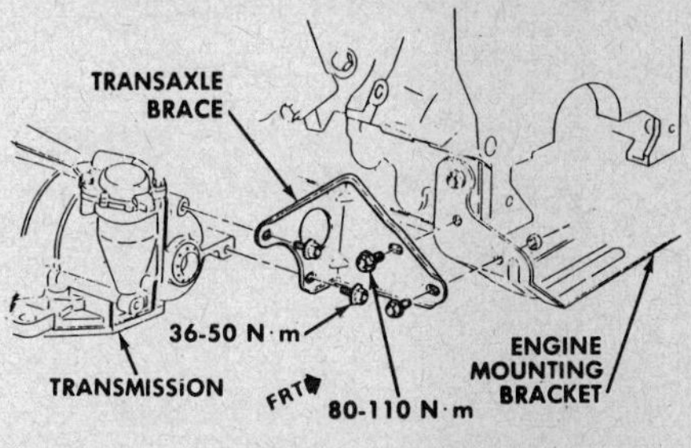

Fig. 2 Transaxle to engine case support bracket removal

7. Clean adjacent area to prevent dirt from entering engine, then remove intake manifold.
8. Remove rocker arm cover, then rocker arms and, if applicable, shaft assembly from cylinder head. Lift out pushrods, keeping them in order to ensure proper installation.
9. Loosen all cylinder head bolts, then remove bolts and lift off cylinder head.
10. Reverse procedure to install. Torque cylinder head bolts to specifications in sequence shown in **Figs. 3 or 3A.** On fuel injected engines, torque intake manifold bolts to specifications in sequence shown in **Fig. 4.**

ROCKER ARMS
MODELS W/NYLON RETAINERS

A nylon retainer is used to retain the rocker arm. Break them below their heads with a chisel, or pry out with channel locks **Fig. 5.** Production rocker arms can be installed in any sequence since the arms are identical.

Replacement rocker arms for all engines are identified with a stamping, right (R) and left (L), **Fig. 6** and must be installed as shown in **Fig. 7.**

To install rocker arms, position arm on rocker shaft, centering it over the 1/4 inch hole in the rocker shaft. Then, install new rocker arm retainers in the holes using a 1/2 inch drift to seat them.

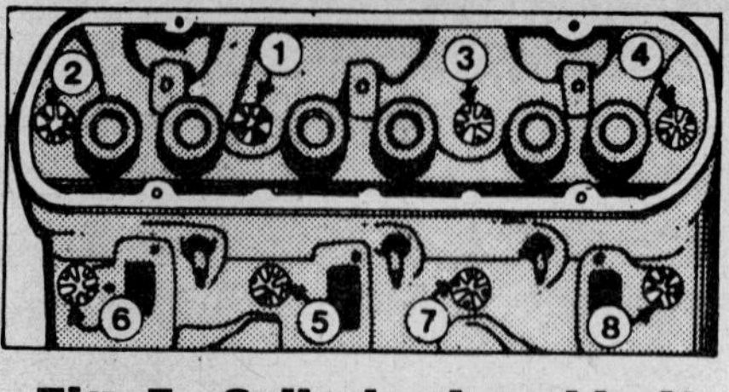

Fig. 3 Cylinder head bolt tightening sequence. 1982–83 models

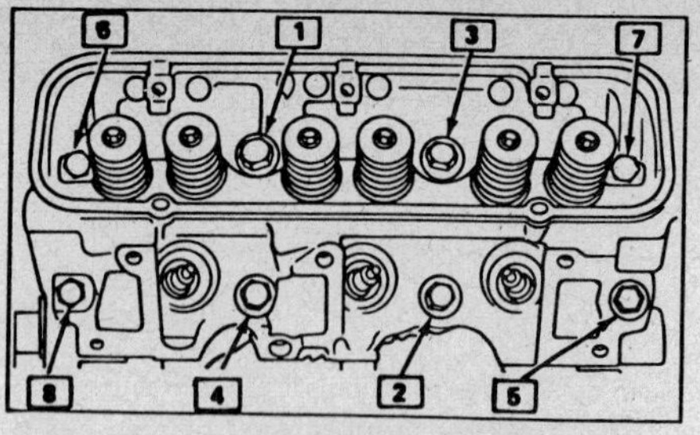

Fig. 3A Cylinder head bolt tightening sequence. 1984–88 models

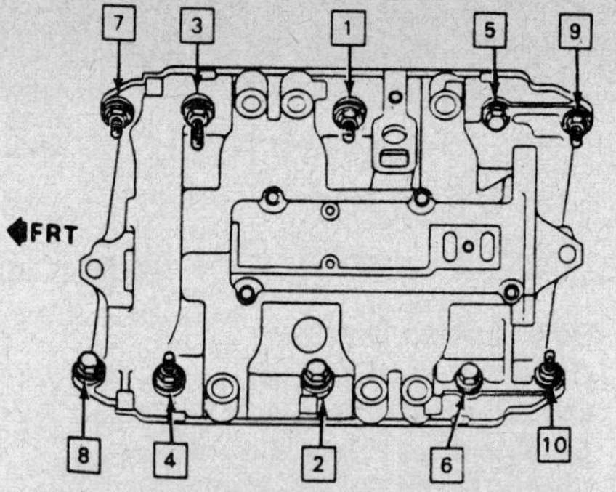

Fig. 4 Intake manifold tightening sequence. Fuel injected engines

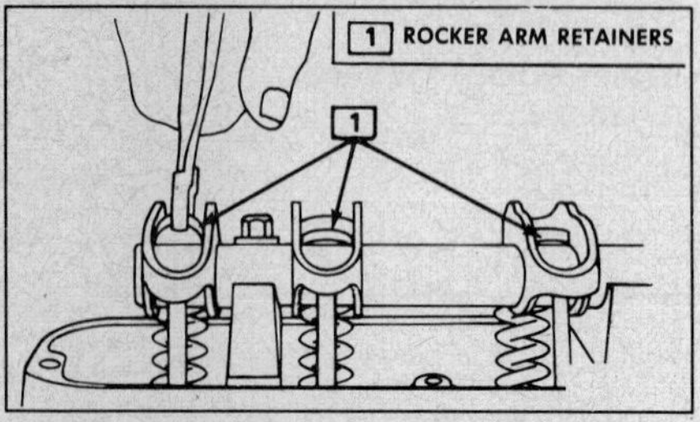

Fig. 5 Removing nylon retainer

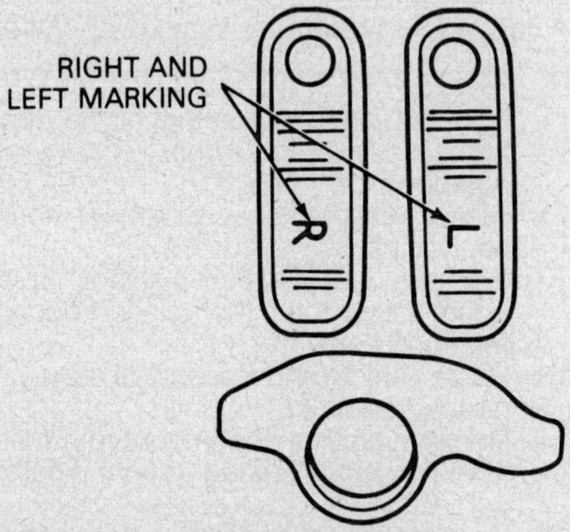

Fig. 6 Service rocker arm identification

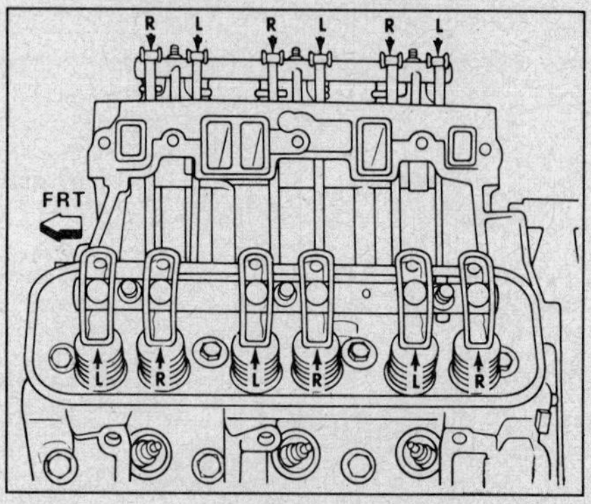

Fig. 7 Service rocker arm installation

MODELS LESS NYLON RETAINERS

Rocker arms are mounted to the cylinder head via individual iron pedestals and are retained by hardened steel bolts.

To install rocker arms, position pedestal retainer, rocker arm and pedestal onto cylinder head. Install retaining bolts and torque to specification.

VALVE ARRANGEMENT

FRONT TO REAR

V6-181 & V6-231 SFI

Left side .... E-I-E-I-I-E
Right side .... E-I-I-E-I-E

VALVE CLEARANCE SPECIFICATIONS

These engines are equipped with hydraulic lifters. No provision for adjustment is provided.

VALVE GUIDES

The valve guides are an integral part of the cylinder head and cannot be replaced.

If valve stem clearance is excessive, the valve guide must be reamed and an oversize valve installed. Valves are available in oversize of .010 inch.

VALVE LIFTERS

Failure of an hydraulic valve lifter, **Figs. 8 and 8A,** is generally caused by dirt or an inadequate oil supply. An air leak at the intake side of the oil pump or too much oil in the engine will cause air bubbles in the oil supply to the lifters, causing them to collapse. This is a probable cause of trouble if several lifters fail to function, but air in the oil is an unlikely cause of failure of a single unit.

The valve lifters may be lifted out of their bores after removing the rocker arms, pushrods and intake manifold. Adjustable pliers with taped jaws may be used to remove lifters that are stuck due to varnish, carbon, etc. **Fig. 8** illustrates flat type of lifter used. **Fig. 8A** illustrates roller type of lifter used. Roller type lifters are used to reduce friction and improve performance. The lifters are cylindrical with the exception of two parallel flats milled into the upper part of the body. Slotted guides which hold the lifters in pairs fit over the milled area to keep the lifters from turning in their bores.

ENGINE FRONT COVER

REPLACE

1. Drain engine coolant.
2. Disconnect upper and lower radiator hoses and heater return hose at water pump.
3. Remove nuts securing front engine mount to cradle, raise engine using suitable lifting device, then remove water pump pulley and drive belts.
4. Remove alternator bracket and alternator.
5. Remove distributor, if applicable. If timing chain and sprockets are not going to be disturbed, note position of distributor rotor for reinstallation in same position.
6. Remove balancer bolt and washer, then remove balancer assembly.
7. Remove bolts attaching engine front cover to cylinder block, **Fig. 9,** also remove two oil pan to engine front cover bolts.
8. Remove engine front cover assembly and gasket, **Fig. 9.**
9. Reverse procedure to install. On some engines, prior to reinstalling the engine front cover, remove the oil pump cover and pack the space around the oil pump drive gears completely full of petroleum jelly. Failure to do this may result in the pump losing its prime, causing a "dry" engine start.

When reinstalling engine front cover bolts, apply a suitable sealer to the threads to prevent leakage.

TIMING CHAIN

REPLACE

1. With front cover removed, as outlined in "Engine Front Cover, Replace", temporarily install balancer bolt and washer in end of crankshaft. Turn

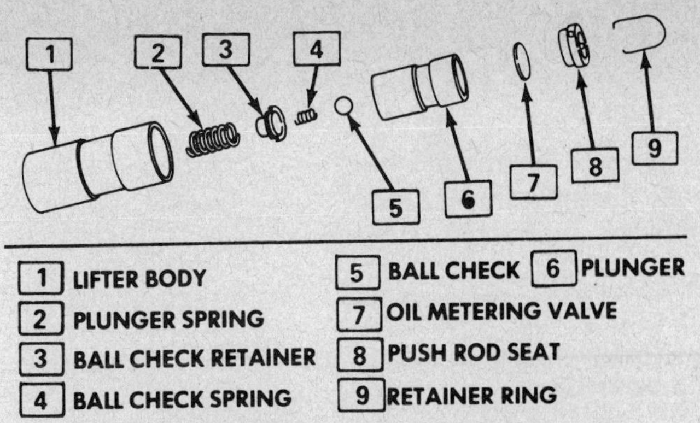

Fig. 8 Exploded view of flat type hydraulic valve lifter

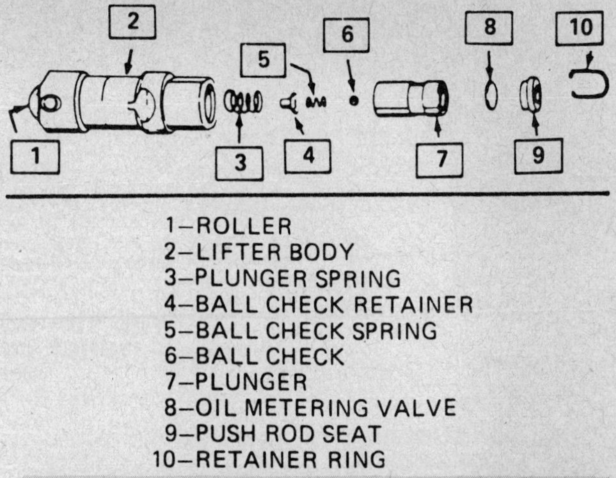

Fig. 8A Exploded view of roller type hydraulic valve lifter

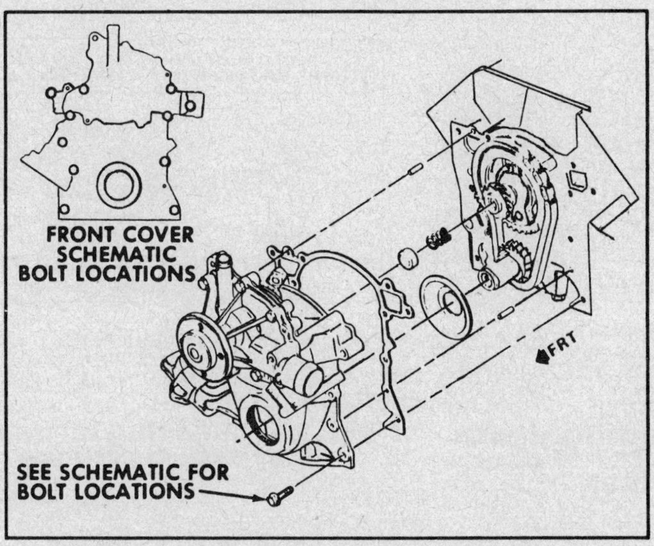

Fig. 9 Engine front cover removal & installation

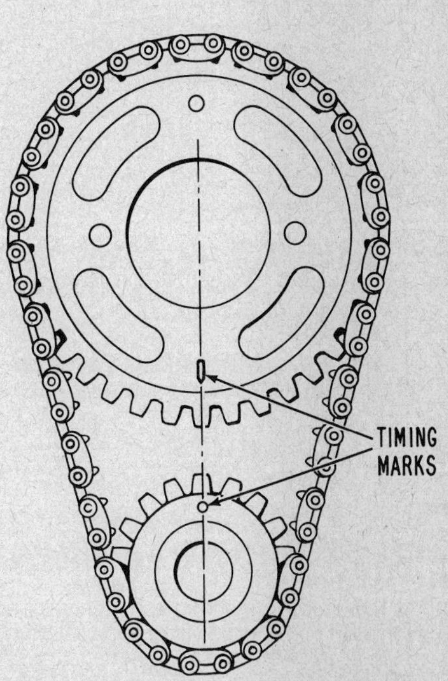

Fig. 10 Valve timing marks

crankshaft so timing marks on sprockets are as close together as possible. Remove balancer bolt and washer using a sharp blow on wrench handle, so bolt can be removed without changing position of sprockets.

2. Remove crankshaft oil slinger, timing chain dampener (if applicable) and camshaft sprocket bolts. On V6-231 SFI engines, remove cam sensor magnet assembly.
3. Using two large screwdrivers, alternately pry off sprockets and chain.
4. Thoroughly clean all parts that are to be reused.
5. Assemble timing chain on sprockets and slide sprockets and chain assembly onto camshaft and crankshaft with timing marks aligned as shown in **Fig. 10.**
6. Install cam sensor magnet assembly, if applicable, then the sprocket bolts.
7. Install oil slinger, camshaft thrust button, timing chain dampener, if equipped, and engine front cover.

CAMSHAFT REPLACE

1. Remove engine as outlined in "Engine, Replace."
2. Remove intake manifold.
3. Remove rocker arm covers.
4. Remove rocker arms, shaft assemblies (if applicable), pushrods and valve lifters.
5. Remove timing chain cover.
6. Align timing marks of camshaft and crankshaft sprocket. This avoids burring of camshaft journals by crankshaft during removal. Remove timing chain and sprocket and the cam sensor magnet assembly, if applicable.
7. Slide camshaft forward out of bearing bores, using care so as not to damage bearing surfaces.
8. Reverse procedure to install. When installing camshaft, align crankshaft and camshaft timing marks as shown in **Fig. 10.**

PISTON & ROD ASSEMBLE

Rods and pistons should be assembled and installed as shown in **Fig. 11.**

Measure connecting rod side clearance using a suitable feeler gauge. Clearance should be .003-.015 inch.

PISTONS, PINS & RINGS

Pistons are available in standard sizes and oversizes of .010 and .030 inch. Rings are available in standard sizes and oversizes of .010 and .030 inch. Piston pins are supplied with piston and available only in standard sizes.

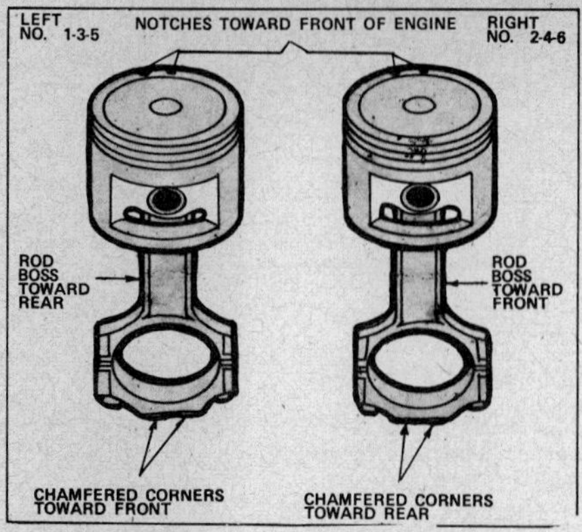

Fig. 11 Piston and rod assembly

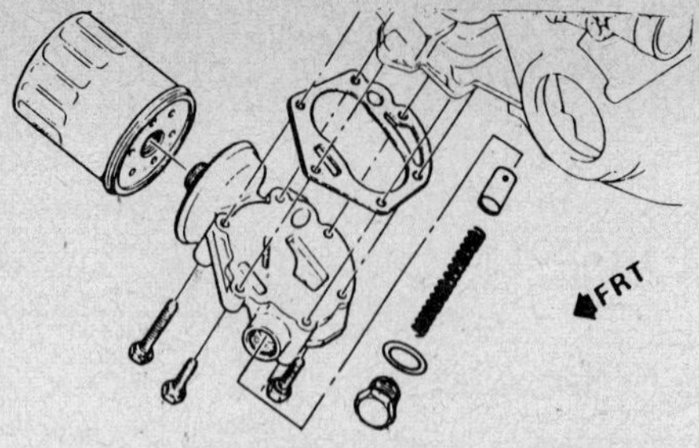

Fig. 12 Oil pump cover and relief valve and spring installation

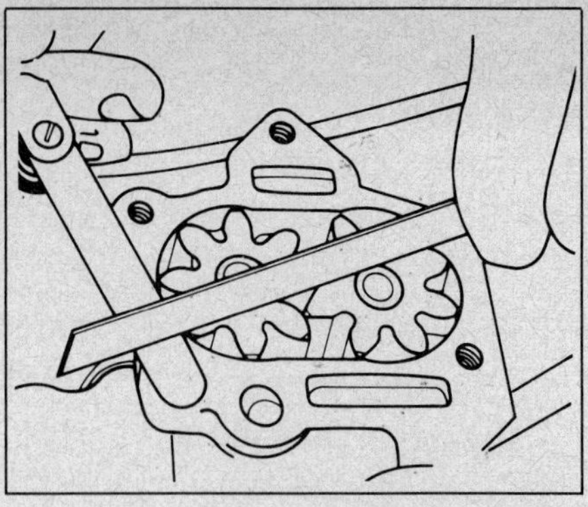

Fig. 13 Checking oil pump gear end clearance

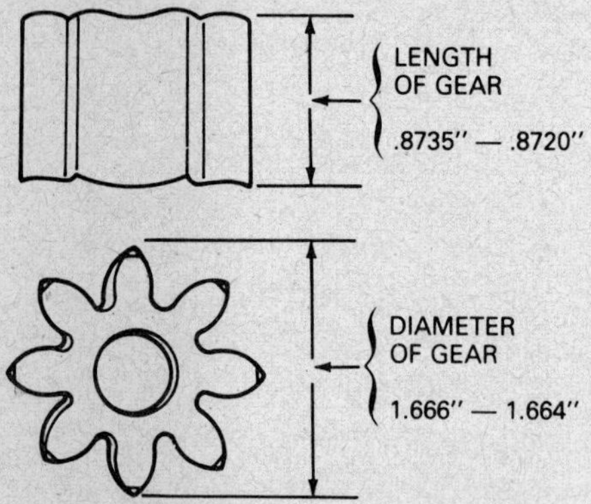

Fig. 14 Checking length and diameter of pump gear

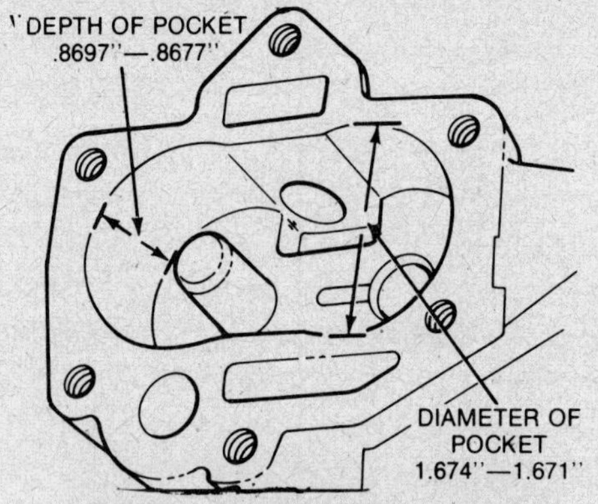

Fig. 15 Checking depth and diameter of gear pocket

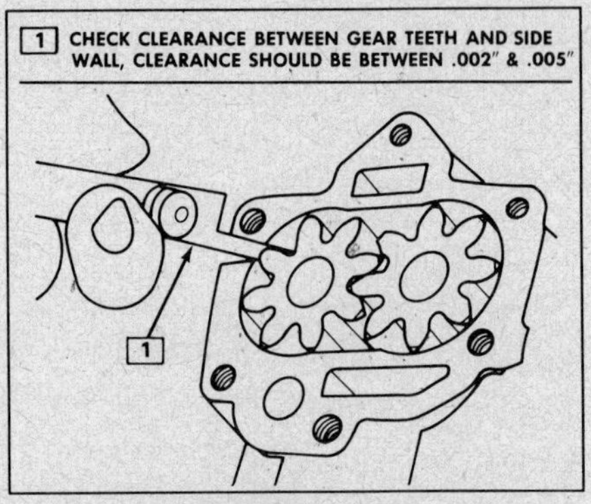

Fig. 16 Checking oil pump gear side clearance

MAIN & ROD BEARINGS

Main and connecting rod bearings are available in standard sizes and undersizes of .0005, .0010 and .0015 inch.

OIL PAN

REPLACE

1. Disconnect battery ground cable.
2. Raise and support vehicle.
3. Drain oil and remove flywheel cover.
4. Remove oil pan.
5. Reverse procedure to install. Apply RTV sealer to oil pan flange and torque oil pan bolts to 10 ft. lbs. **Late model vehicles use a formed rubber gasket. When replacing oil pan, clean oil pan flange, then install pan using new gasket.**

OIL PUMP SERVICE

EXC. GEROTOR TYPE PUMP

Removal & Inspection

1. Remove oil filter.
2. Remove screws attaching oil pump cover assembly to timing chain cover. Remove cover assembly and slide out oil pump gears.
3. Wash off gears and inspect for wear or scoring. Replace any gears not found serviceable.
4. Remove oil pressure relief valve cap, spring and valve, **Fig. 12.** Oil filter bypass valve and spring are staked in place and should not be removed.
5. Wash parts thoroughly, inspect relief valve for wear or scoring. Check relief valve spring to see that it is not worn on its side or collapsed. Replace any relief valve spring that is questionable.
6. Check relief valve in its bore in cover. The valve should have no more clearance than an easy slip fit. If any excessive clearance can be felt, valve and/or cover should be replaced.
7. Check relief bypass valve for cracks, or warping. Valve should be free of nicks or scratches.

Assembly & Installation

1. Lubricate and install pressure relief valve and spring in bore of oil pump cover, **Fig. 12.**
2. Install cap and gasket. Torque cap to 35 ft. lbs.
3. Install oil pump gears and shaft in oil pump body section of timing chain cover to check gear end clearance and side clearance.
4. Check oil pump end clearance by placing a straightedge over gears and measure clearance between straight edge and gasket surface, **Fig. 13.** Clearance should be between .002 and .006 inch. If clearance is less than .002 inch, measure gears and pocket to determine which is out of specification, **Figs. 14 and 15.**
5. Check oil pump side clearance, **Fig. 16.** Clearance should be between .002 and .005 inch. If clearance is greater than .0050 inch, measure gears and pocket to determine which is out of specification, **Figs. 14 and 15.**
6. Check oil pump cover flatness by placing a straightedge across cover face, using feeler gauge between straight edge and pump cover. If clearance is .001 or more pump cover must be replaced.
7. If gear clearance and oil pump cover is flat and side clearance is satisfactory remove gears and pack gear pocket full of petroleum jelly. **Never use chassis lube when reinstalling oil**

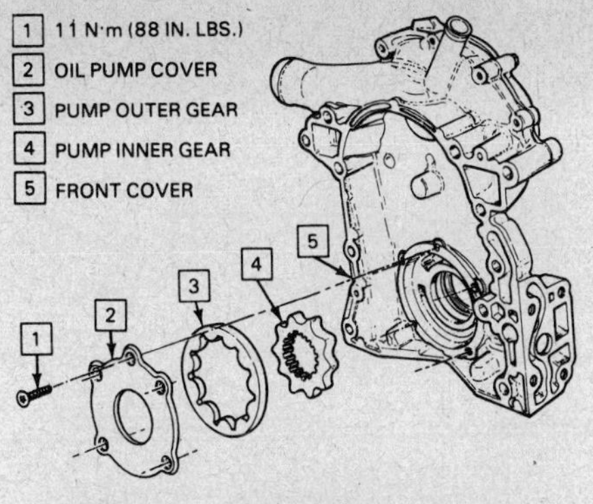

Fig. 17 Oil pump and housing assembly. Gerotor pump

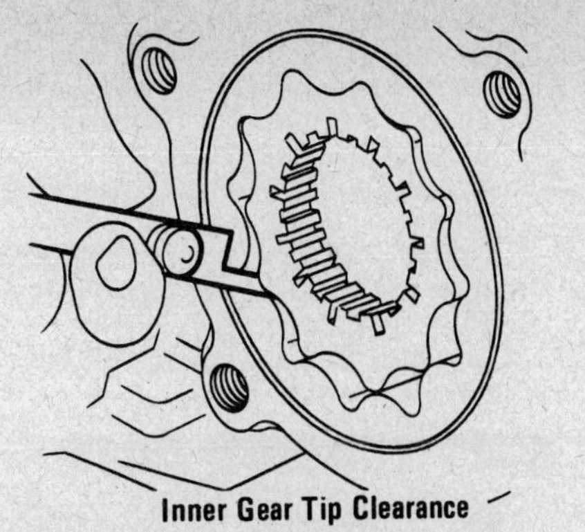

Fig. 18 Checking inner gear tip clearance. Gerotor pump

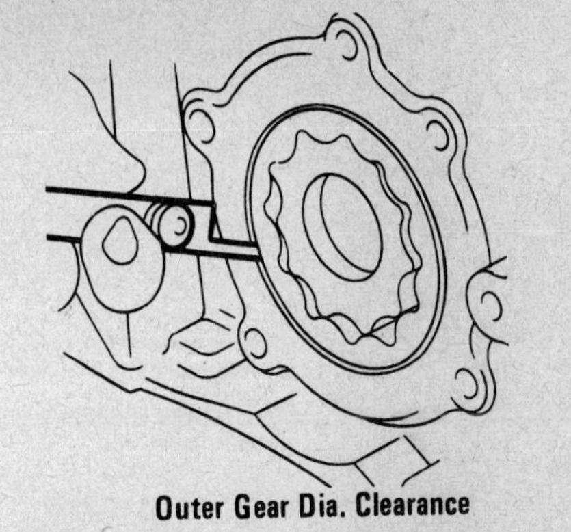

Fig. 19 Checking outer gear diameter clearance. Gerotor pump

pump gears.

8. Reinstall gears so petroleum jelly fills entire gear pocket and between teeth of gears. Place gasket in position. **Unless the pump is packed with petroleum jelly it may fail to prime itself when engine is started and damage to engine may result.**
9. Install cover assembly screws. To ensure proper seal of gasket, torque screws alternately and evenly to 10 ft. lbs.
10. Install filter on nipple.

GEROTOR TYPE PUMP

Removal & Inspection

1. Remove engine front cover, then the oil filter adapter, pressure regulator valve and valve spring.
2. Remove oil pump cover attaching screws, cover and gears, **Fig. 17.**
3. Inspect pump cover and housing for cracks, scoring, porosity and damaged threads, pressure regulator valve and spring for sticking, scoring or tension loss and gears for chipping, galling or excessive wear. Replace as necessary.
4. Check gear clearance as follows:
   a. Check inner gear tip clearance with feeler gauge as shown in **Fig. 18.** Maximum clearance should not exceed .006 inch.
   b. Check outer gear diameter clearance with feeler gauge as shown in **Fig. 19.** Clearance should be .008-.015 inch.
   c. Check gear end clearance (gear drop in housing) with suitable dial indicator as shown in **Fig. 20.** Clearance should be .001-.0035 inch.
5. Replace parts as necessary.

Assembly & Installation

1. Lubricate gears with motor oil, then install into oil pump housing.
2. Pack pump cavity with petroleum jelly, then install pump cover and attaching screws. Torque attaching screws to 88 inch lbs.
3. Install pressure regulator valve spring and valve.
4. Install oil filter adapter using new gasket. Torque adapter to 30 ft. lbs.
5. Reinstall front cover onto engine.

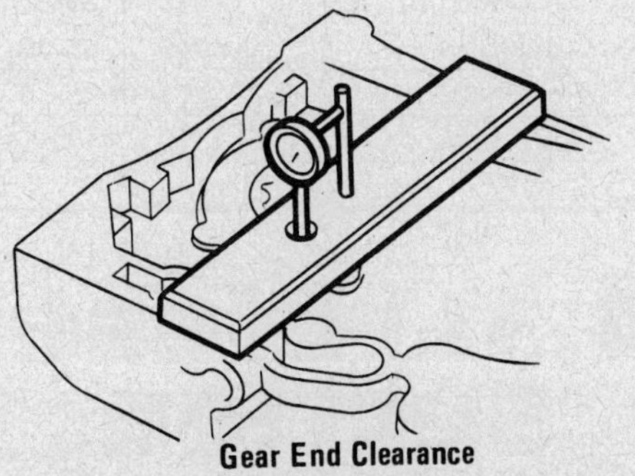

Fig. 20 Checking gear end clearance. Gerotor pump

REAR MAIN BEARING OIL SEAL REPAIR

1. Remove oil pan and oil pump (if applicable) as described previously.
2. Remove rear main bearing cap.
3. Using suitable tool, gently drive upper seal into groove approximately 1/4 in.
4. Repeat step 3 for other end of seal.
5. Measure the amount that was driven in on one side and add 1/16 in. Using a suitable cutting tool, cut this length from the old rear main bearing cap lower seal using the main bearing cap as a guide. Repeat this step for the other end of seal.
6. Place piece of cut seal into groove of seal installer tool guide and install tool guide onto engine block.
7. Using seal packing tool, drive piece of seal into block. Drive seal in until packing tool contacts machined stop.
8. Remove tool guide and repeat steps 6 and 7 for other end of seal.
9. Install new seal in bearing cap.
10. Install rear main bearing cap. Apply a thin film of sealant No. 1052357 or equivalent to rear main bearing cap and case interface. Use care not to allow sealant to contact crankshaft journal or main bearing.

ELECTRIC FUEL PUMP

REPLACE

1. Disconnect battery ground cable, then drain fuel tank.
2. Disconnect tank unit wire from connector in rear compartment.
3. Remove ground wire retaining screw from under body.
4. Disconnect hoses from tank unit.
5. Support fuel tank and disconnect the two fuel tank retaining straps.
6. Remove fuel tank from vehicle.
7. Remove fuel gage retaining cam, using tool J-24187, or other suitable tool.
8. Remove sending unit from tank.
9. Electric fuel pump can be unbolted from tank sending unit after sending unit has been removed.
10. Reverse procedure to install.

WATER PUMP

REPLACE

1982

1. Disconnect battery ground cable, then drain cooling system.
2. Remove accessory drive belts.
3. Remove water pump attaching bolts, **Fig. 21.**
4. Remove engine support strut.
5. Place jack under front crossmember and raise jack until vehicle just starts to raise.
6. Remove front two body mount bolts, (1 and 3), **Fig. 22,** also remove lower cushions and retainers.
7. Thread body mount bolts with retainers a minimum of three turns into cage nuts so bolts restrain cradle movement.
8. Release floor jack slowly until crossmember contacts body mount bolt retainers. As jack is being lowered watch and correct any interference with hose, lines, pipes and cables. **Do not lower the cradle without it being restrained as possible damage can occur to the body and underhood items.**
9. Remove water pump from engine.
10. Reverse procedure to install.

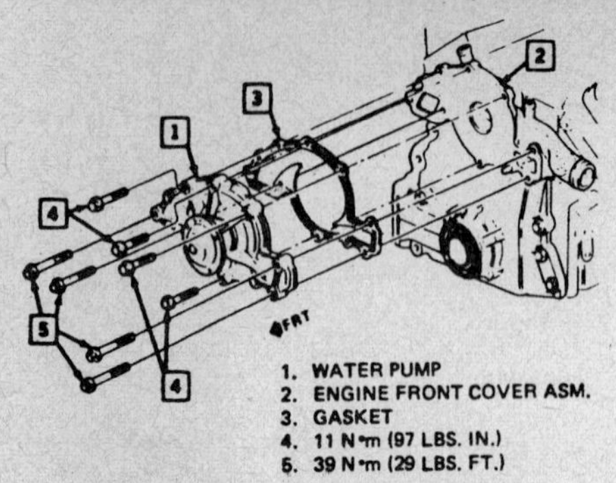

Fig. 21 Water pump removal & installation

1983–88

1. Disconnect battery ground cable.
2. Drain cooling system, then remove accessory drive belts.
3. Remove lower radiator hose and heater hose at pump.
4. On 1983 models, remove two nuts from front engine mount at cradle, then raise engine using a suitable lifting device and remove water pump pulley attaching bolts.
5. On 1984-88 models, remove water pump pulley attaching bolts. Long bolt is removed through access hole located in the body side rail.
6. On all models, remove water pump pulley.
7. Remove water pump attaching bolts, then the water pump, **Fig. 21.**
8. Reverse procedure to install.

BELT TENSION DATA

1986-88 vehicles use a serpentine drive belt to drive all engine mounted accessories. Drive belt tension is maintained by a spring loaded belt tensioner.

Belt	New Lbs.	Used Lbs.
1982		
Air Cond.	145	65-80
Alternator	145	65-80
Power Steer.	135	65-80
Air Pump	100	45
1983-85		
Air Cond.	165	90
Alternator	145	70
Power Steer.	165	90
AIR or Vacuum Pump	75	45

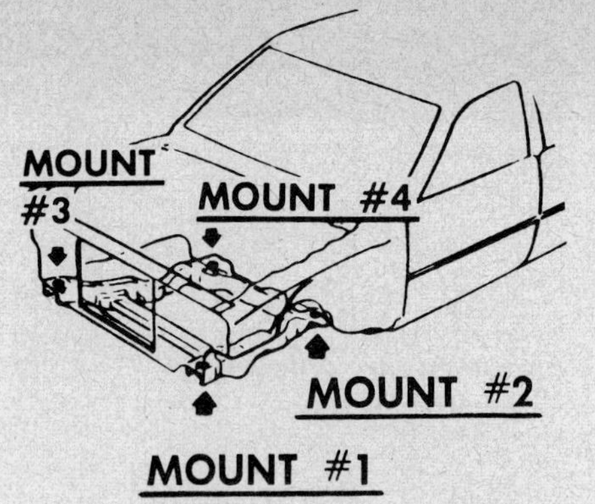

Fig. 22 Removing front body mounts

V6-262 (4.3L) Diesel Engine Section

INDEX

Condition	Possible Cause	Correction
ENGINE WILL NOT CRANK	1. Loose or corroded battery cables	1. Check connections at battery, engine block and starter solenoid.
	2. Discharged batteries	2. Check charging system.
	3. Starter Inoperative	3. Check starting system.
ENGINE CRANKS SLOWLY—WILL NOT START (Minimum Engine Crank Speed—100 RPM)	1. Battery cable connections loose or corroded	1. Check connections at battery, engine block and starter.
	2. Batteries undercharged	2. Check charging system.
	3. Wrong engine oil	3. Drain and refill with recommended oil.
ENGINE CRANKS NORMALLY—WILL NOT START	1. Incorrect starting procedure	1. Use recommended starting procedure.
	2. Incorrect or contaminated fuel	2. Flush fuel system and install correct fuel.
	3. No fuel to nozzles	3. Loosen injection line at a nozzle. Do not disconnect. Use care to direct fuel away from sources of ignition. Wipe connection to be sure it is dry. Crank 5 seconds. Fuel should flow from injection line. Tighten connection. If fuel does not flow, check fuel solenoid operation as follows: Connect a 12 volt test lamp from wire at injection pump solenoid to ground. Turn ignition to "ON". Lamp should light. If lamp does not light, check wiring to solenoid.
	4. No fuel to injection pump	4. Remove line at inlet to injection pump fuel filter. Connect hose from line to metal container. Crank engine. If no fuel is discharged, test the fuel supply pump. If the pump is OK, check the injection pump fuel filter and replace if plugged. If filter and inlet line to injection pump are OK, replace injection pump.
	5. Plugged fuel return system	5. Disconnect fuel return line at injection pump and route hose to a metal container. Connect a hose to the injection pump connection and route it to the metal container. Crank the engine; if engine starts and runs, correct restriction in fuel return system.
	6. Pump timing incorrect	6. Make certain that pump timing mark is aligned with mark on adapter.
	7. Glow plug control system inoperative	7. Refer to Diesel Engine Electrical System Diagnosis.
	8. Glow plugs inoperative	8. Refer to Diesel Engine Electrical System Diagnosis.
	9. Internal engine problems	9. Correct as necessary.
	10. No voltage to fuel solenoid	10. Connect a 12 volt test lamp from injection pump solenoid to ground. Turn ignition to "On", lamp should light. If lamp lights, remove test lamp and connect and disconnect solenoid connector and listen for solenoid operation. If solenoid does not operate, remove injection pump for repairs. If lamp does not light, refer to Diesel Engine Electrical System Diagnosis.
	11. Restricted fuel tank filter.	11. Remove fuel tank and check filter.

Fig. 1 Diesel engine diagnostic chart. (Part 1 of 4)

Condition	Possible Cause	Correction
ENGINE STARTS BUT WILL NOT CONTINUE TO RUN AT IDLE	1. No fuel in tank	1. Install correct fuel in tank.
	2. Incorrect or contaminated fuel	2. Flush fuel system and install correct fuel.
	3. Limited fuel to injection pump	3. Test the fuel supply pump. Replace as necessary.
	4. Fuel solenoid disengaged with ignition switch in the "ON" position	4. Connect a 12 volt test lamp from wire at injection pump solenoid to ground. Turn ignition to "ON". Lamp should light. Turn ignition to "START". Lamp should light. If lamp does not light in both positions, check wiring to solenoid.
	5. Restricted fuel return system	5. Disconnect fuel return line at injection pump and route hose to a metal container. Connect a hose to injection pump connection and route to metal container. Crank engine; if engine starts and runs, correct restriction in fuel return system.
	6. Fast idle solenoid inoperative	6. With engine cold, start car; solenoid should move to support injection pump lever in "fast idle position" for about 5 seconds. If solenoid does not move, refer to Electrical System Diagnosis.
	7. Low idle incorrectly adjusted	7. Adjust idle screw to specification.
	8. Pump timing incorrect	8. Make certain that timing mark, on injection pump, is aligned with mark on adapter.
	9. Glow plug control system malfunction	9. Refer to Diesel Engine Electrical System Diagnosis.
	10. Injection pump malfunction	10. Install replacement pump.
	11. Internal engine problems	11. Correct as necessary.
ENGINE STARTS, IDLES ROUGH, WITHOUT ABNORMAL NOISE OR SMOKE	1. Low idle incorrectly adjusted	1. Adjust idle screw to specification.
	2. Injection line leaks	2. Wipe off injection lines and connections. Run engine and check for leaks. Correct leaks.
	3. Restricted fuel return system	3. Disconnect fuel return line at injection pump and route hose to a metal container. Connect a hose to the injection pump connection and route it to the metal container. Crank the engine; if engine starts and runs, correct restriction in fuel return system.
	4. Incorrect or contaminated fuel	4. Flush fuel system and install correct fuel.
	5. Nozzle(s) inoperative	5. With engine running, loosen injection line fitting at each nozzle in turn. Use care to direct fuel away from sources of ignition. Each nozzle should contribute to rough running. If nozzle is found that does not change idle quality, it should be replaced.
	6. Internal fuel leak at nozzle(s)	6. Disconnect fuel return system from nozzles on one bank at a time. With the engine running, observe the normal fuel seepage at the nozzles. Replace any nozzle with excessive fuel leakage.
	7. Fuel supply pump malfunctions	7. Test the fuel supply pump. Replace if necessary.
	8. Uneven fuel distribution to cylinders	8. Install new or reconditioned nozzles, one at a time, until condition is corrected as indicated by normal idle.

Fig. 1 Diesel engine diagnostic chart. (Part 2 of 4)

Condition	Possible Cause	Correction
ENGINE STARTS AND IDLES ROUGH WITH EXCESSIVE NOISE AND/OR SMOKE	1. Injection pump timing incorrect	1. Be sure timing mark on injection pump is aligned with mark on adapter.
	2. Nozzle(s) inoperative	2. With engine running, crack injection line at each nozzle, one at a time. Use care to direct fuel away from sources of ignition. Each nozzle should contribute to rough running. If a nozzle is found that does not affect idle quality or changes noise and/or smoke, it should be replaced.
	3. High pressure lines incorrectly installed	3. Check routing of each line. Correct as required.
ENGINE COLD, STARTS AND IDLES ROUGH WITH EXCESSIVE NOISE AND/OR SMOKE, BUT CLEARS UP AFTER WARM-UP	1. Incorrect starting procedure	1. Advise operator on correct procedure. (See owners manual.)
	2. Injection pump timing incorrect	2. Check timing with J-33075 timing meter and reset if needed.
	3. Insufficient engine break-in time	3. Break in engine 2000 miles or more.
	4. Air in system	4. Install a section of clear plastic tubing on the fuel return fitting from the engine. Evidence of bubbles in fuel when cranking or running indicates the presence of an air leak in the suction fuel line.
	5. Inoperative glow plug	5. Replace faulty glow plug.
	6. Nozzle(s) malfunction	6. Remove and clean or replace.
	7. Housing pressure cold advance inoperative	7. Check operation and repair.
ENGINE MISFIRES BUT IDLES CORRECTLY	1. Plugged fuel filter	1. Replace filter.
	2. Incorrect injection pump timing	2. Be sure that timing mark on injection pump and adapter are aligned.
	3. Incorrect or contaminated fuel	3. Flush fuel system and install correct fuel.
ENGINE WILL NOT RETURN TO IDLE	1. External linkage misadjustment or failure	1. Reset linkage or replace as required.
	2. Internal injection pump malfunction	2. Install replacement injection pump.
FUEL LEAKS ON GROUND—NO ENGINE MALFUNCTION	1. Loose or broken fuel line or connection	1. Examine complete fuel system, including tank, supply, injection and return system. Determine source and cause of leak and repair.
	2. Internal injection pump failure	2. Install replacement injection pump.
SIGNIFICANT LOSS OF POWER	1. Incorrect or contaminated fuel	1. Flush fuel system and install correct fuel.
	2. Pinched or otherwise restricted return system	2. Examine system for restriction and correct as required.
	3. Plugged fuel tank vent	3. Remove fuel cap. If "hissing" noise is heard, vent is plugged and should be cleaned.
	4. Restricted supply	4. Examine fuel supply system to determine cause of restriction. Repair as required.
	5. Plugged fuel filter	5. Remove and replace filter.
	6. External compression leaks	6. Check for compression leaks at all nozzles and glow plugs, using "Leak-Tec" or equivalent. If leak is found, tighten nozzle clamp or glow plug. If leak persists at a nozzle, remove it and reinstall with a new carbon stop seal and compression seal.
	7. Plugged nozzle(s)	7. Remove nozzles, check for plugging and have repaired or replaced.
	8. Internal engine problem	8. Correct as necessary.

Fig. 1 Diesel engine diagnostic chart. (Part 3 of 4)

Condition	Possible Cause	Correction
NOISE—"RAP" FROM ONE OR MORE CYLINDERS	1. Air in fuel system	1. Check for leaks and correct.
	2. Air in high pressure line(s)	2. Crack line at nozzle(s) and bleed air at each cylinder determined to be causing noise. Use care to direct fuel away from sources of ignition and be sure to carefully retighten lines.
	3. Nozzle(s) sticking open or with very low blowoff pressure	3. Replace the nozzle(s) causing the problem.
	4. Internal engine problem	4. Correct as necessary.
NOISE—SIGNIFICANT OVERALL COMBUSTION NOISE INCREASE WITH EXCESSIVE BLACK SMOKE	1. Timing not set to specification	1. Align timing marks on adapter and injection pump.
	2. Internal engine problem	2. Check for presence of oil in the air crossover. If present, determine cause and correct.
	3. Injection pump housing pressure out of specifications.	3. Check housing pressure. If incorrect, replace fuel return line connector assembly.
	4. Internal injection pump problem	4. Replace pump.
NOISE—INTERNAL OR EXTERNAL	1. Fuel supply pump, alternator, water pump, valve train, vacuum pump, bearings etc.	1. Inspect and correct as necessary.
ENGINE OVERHEATS	1. Coolant system leak or oil cooler system leak	1. Check for leaks and correct as required.
	2. Belt failure	2. Replace.
	3. Thermostat malfunction, head gasket failure or internal engine problem	3. Inspect and correct as necessary.
INSTRUMENT PANEL OIL WARNING LAMP "ON" AT IDLE	1. Oil cooler or oil cooler line restricted	1. Remove restriction in cooler or cooler line.
	2. Internal engine problem	2. Correct as necessary.
ODOR OR SMOKE—EXCESSIVE AND NOT PREVIOUSLY COVERED	1. Same as Gasoline Engines	1. Correct as necessary. Refer to Trouble-Shooting Chapter.
ENGINE WILL NOT SHUT OFF WITH KEY	1. Injection pump solenoid does not drop out	1. Refer to electrical diagnosis. If problem is determined to be internal with the injection pump, replace the injection pump.
	2. Injection pump solenoid return spring failed	2. Replace injection pump.

Fig. 1 Diesel engine diagnostic chart. (Part 4 of 4)

DIESEL ENGINE DIAGNOSIS

Refer to diagnostic charts, **Fig. 1**, for general engine diagnosis.

DIESEL ENGINE ELECTRICAL TROUBLESHOOTING

1982–83

Engine Runs Rough On Cold Start

1. With ignition switch in Run position and engine off, disconnect electrical connector from engine temperature switch, **Fig. 2.**
2. Connect jumper wire between terminals on engine temperature switch electrical connector, and note if fast idle solenoid extends.
3. If solenoid extends, proceed to step 4. If solenoid does not extend, check throttle linkage or solenoid plunger for binding. If linkage is satisfactory, replace solenoid.
4. Connect tachometer J-26925 or equivalent to engine, then start engine and leave jumper wire attached to the engine temperature switch.
5. Disconnect electrical connector from cold advance solenoid. Engine speed should vary 30 RPM when connector is removed.
6. If there is no change in RPM, check solenoid and pump for proper operation and repair or replace as necessary.
7. Turn engine off, then check continuity of engine temperature switch using suitable self-powered test lamp.
8. Test lamp should not light above 120° F. If not satisfactory, replace switch.
9. Using suitable test lamp, ground one lead and connect other lead to dark green wire terminal at diode module A. If test lamp lights and engine is cold, replace coolant temperature switch.
10. Turn ignition OFF, then disconnect all glow plug wire connectors. Connect suitable self-powered test lamp between rear post of glow plug relay and ground.
11. At each glow plug, momentarily connect glow plug wire connector to plug spade terminal. Observe test light.
12. If test lamp lights, glow plug and wire connector are satisfactory. If test lamp does not light, touch wire connector to engine block or other ground. If test lamp lights, replace glow plug. If lamp does not light, replace wire to glow plug.

Engine Stays On Fast Idle

1. With ignition switch in Run position

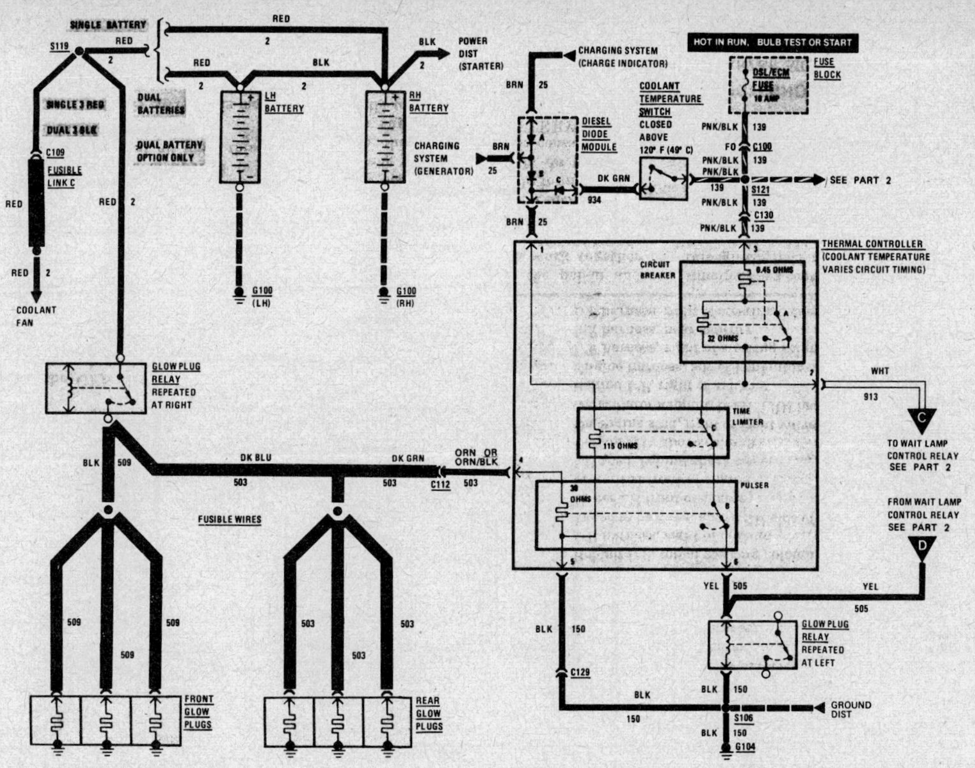

Fig. 2 Glow plug wiring schematic (Part 1 of 2). 1982–83 models

and engine not running, disconnect electrical connector from engine temperature switch, **Fig. 2.**

2. Connect jumper wire between terminals on engine temperature switch and note if fast idle solenoid extends.
3. If solenoid extends, proceed to step 4. If solenoid does not extend, check throttle linkage or solenoid plunger for binding. If linkage is satisfactory, replace solenoid.
4. Check continuity of engine temperature switch with suitable self-powered test lamp.
5. Lamp should light below 120° F and shut off above 120° F. If not satisfactory, replace switch.

Engine Continues To Run With Ignition Off

1. With ignition turned off and engine running, disconnect electrical connector from diode module, **Fig. 2.**
2. If engine stops, diode "C" is shorted. Replace diode module.
3. If engine continues to run, disconnect fuel solenoid pink wire connector.
4. If engine stops, repair or replace fuel solenoid.
5. If engine continues to run, stop engine by crimping flexible fuel return line near fuel supply pump, then repair or replace fuel solenoid.

No Fast Idle W/Cold Engine

1. With ignition switch in Run position and engine off, disconnect electrical connector from engine temperature switch, **Fig. 2.**
2. Connect jumper wire to both terminals on engine temperature switch connector.
3. Momentarily disconnect and connect fast idle solenoid electrical connector while noting if fast idle solenoid extends.
4. If solenoid does not extend, refer to step 5. If solenoid extends, readjust for correct fast idle operation.
5. Connect one end of suitable test lamp to ground and the other end to white/green lead on models without A/C, or black/pink lead at fast idle solenoid on models with A/C.
6. If test lamp lights, proceed as follows:
   a. Disconnect electrical connector from fast idle solenoid.
   b. Check continuity of fast idle solenoid using suitable self-powered test lamp.
   c. If lamp does not light, replace solenoid.
7. If test lamp does not light, proceed as follows:
   a. Momentarily connect test light lead to pink/black terminal of engine temperature switch.
   b. If test lamp lights, remove connector from switch and check switch for continuity using suitable self-powered test lamp.
   c. If test light shuts off below 120° F, replace engine temperature switch.

No Wait Lamp On Cold Engine

1. With ignition switch in Run position and engine off, observe "Charge" light, which should illuminate.
2. If "Charge" light is not lit, check condition of GAUGES fuse and replace if necessary.
3. If GAUGES fuse is satisfactory, confirm glow plug operation by listening for clicking noise from relay.
4. If relay operates, check pink/black wire between fuse block and splice S204 for a short or open and repair as necessary, **Fig. 2.** If wire is satisfactory, proceed to step 6.
5. If relay does not operate, check pink wires between ignition switch and fuse block for a short or open and repair as necessary. If wires are satisfactory, proceed to step 6.
6. Disconnect electrical connector from "Wait" lamp control relay. Connect jumper wire between ground and dark blue wire at connector, and observe "Wait" light, which should illuminate.
7. If "Wait" light is not lit, check condition of lamp bulb and replace if necessary.
8. If lamp bulb is satisfactory, check dark blue wire between "Wait" lamp control relay electrical connector and "Wait" lamp, and the pink/blue wire between "Wait" lamp and splice S204 for a short or open, and repair as necessary. If wires are satisfactory, proceed to step 9.

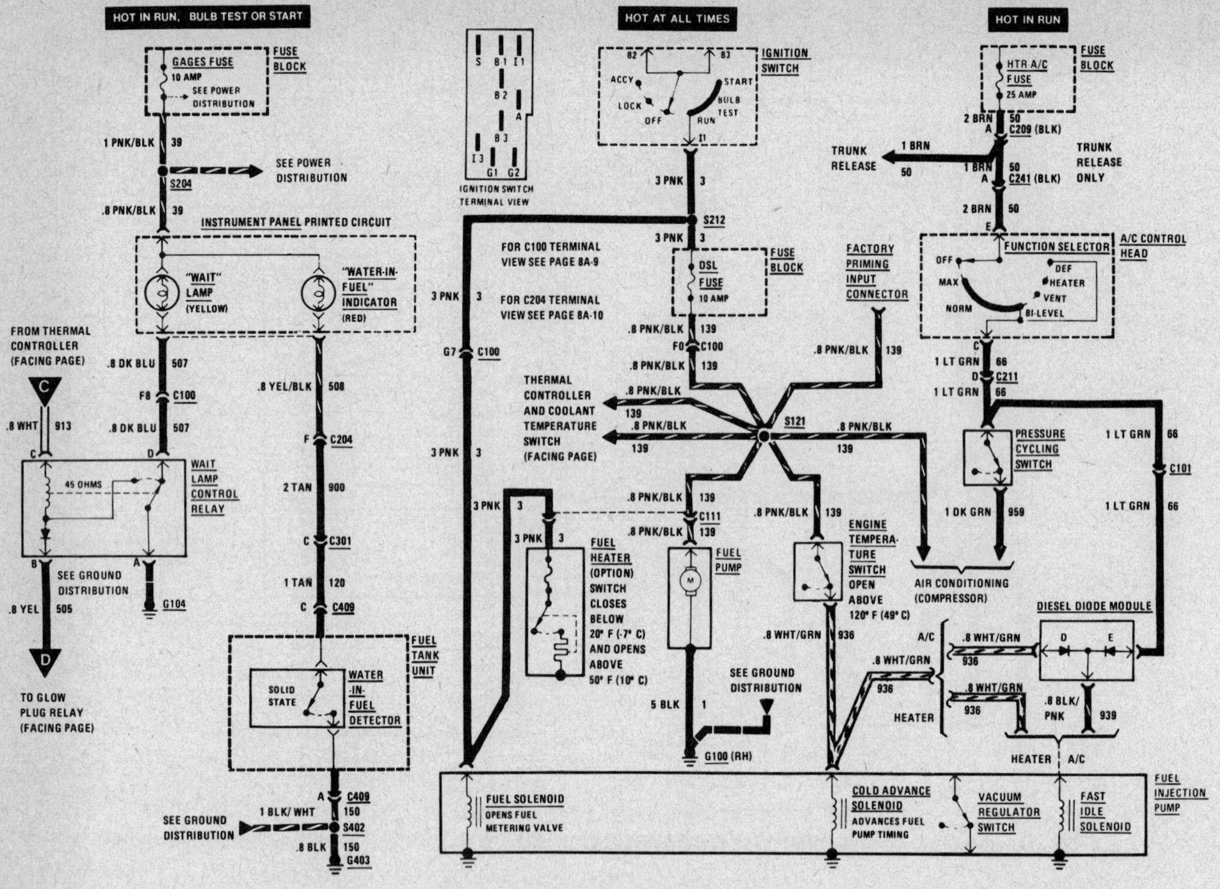

Fig. 2 Glow plug wiring schematic (Part 2 of 2). 1982–83 models

9. Using suitable test lamp, check ground connection at G104. Attach one end of test lamp to red wire terminal of Glow Plug Relay and the other end to the black wire lead of "Wait" lamp control relay.
10. If lamp does not light, circuit is satisfactory. If lamp lights, replace "Wait" lamp control relay.

Wait Lamp Pulses Slowly On & Off

1. With "Wait" lamp pulsing, connect suitable test lamp between white and yellow wires of wait lamp control relay, **Fig. 2.**
2. If test light is on when "Wait" lamp is off, and off when "Wait" lamp is on, replace "Wait" lamp control relay.
3. If test light does not turn on, connect test lamp between ground and orange or orange/black wires at thermal controller. With "Wait" lamp pulsing, confirm test light pulses on and off with "Wait" lamp.
4. If test lamp does not light, connect test lamp to front red wire and rear dark blue/black wire terminals of glow plug relay. Defect may be in red wire between battery and glow plug relay, or in black, dark blue, dark green, and orange or orange/black wires between relay and thermal controller or glow plug relay. Repair as necessary.
5. If test light flashes on and off with "Wait" lamp when connected to orange or orange/black wires at thermal controller, then connect test light between black wire at controller and ground.
6. If test lamp flashes on and off, repair black wire between controller and ground.
7. If test lamp does not light, replace controller.

Wait Lamp Stays On Longer Than 10 Seconds

1. Check glow plug relay operation. Disconnect connector at diesel diode module, **Fig. 2.** Connect one end of test lamp to ground and other end of test lamp to red (front) post of glow plug relay. Then touch test lamp to rear post (dark blue and black wires) of glow plug relay. Test lamp should light, indicating glow plug relay is operating properly.
2. If test lamp remains OFF, proceed as follows:
   a. Check ECM fuse and ground connection G104.
   b. Disconnect connector from thermal controller. Connect a suitable test lamp between pin 3 (pink/black wire) and pin 6 (yellow wire) of harness connector. If test lamp lights with ignition ON, check continuity between pins 3 and 6 of thermal controller. If test lamp remains ON, replace thermal controller.
   c. If test lamp remains OFF, connect a suitable ohmmeter to glow plug relay coil, and check resistance of coil. If ohmmeter indicates a high glow plug relay coil resistance, replace coil. Check continuity of pink/black, yellow and black wires.
3. If test lamp lights (glow plug relay is operating properly), proceed as follows:
   a. Disconnect "Wait" lamp control relay connector. "Wait" lamp should go OFF. Connect test lamp between white and yellow wires of connector. If test lamp lights, replace "Wait" lamp control relay.
   b. If test lamp remains OFF, turn ignition OFF. Connect a suitable ohmmeter to pins 4 and 5 of thermal controller, and check for 30 ohms resistance. If ohmmeter indicates more than 30 ohms, replace thermal controller. Check continuity of black, dark green, dark blue, orange or orange/black, white, yellow and black wires.

Engine Does Not Start When Cold (Wait Lamp OK-Goes On, Then Off)

1. If engine cranking speed is slow, turn ignition OFF, then, using a suitable

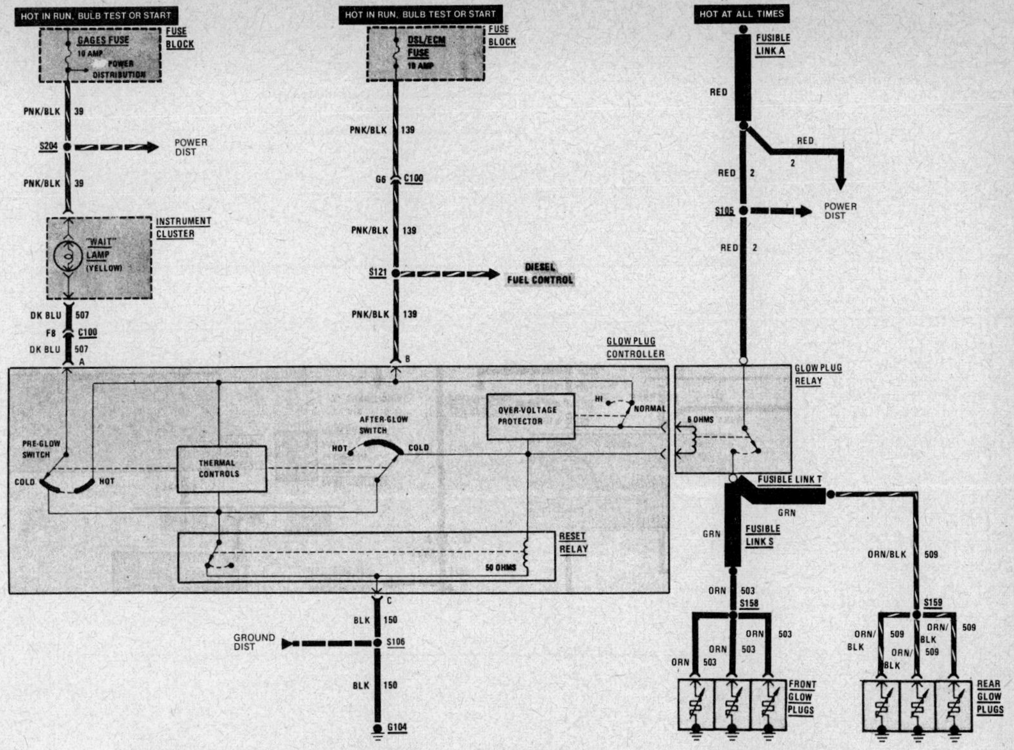

Fig. 3 Glow plug wiring schematic. 1984 models

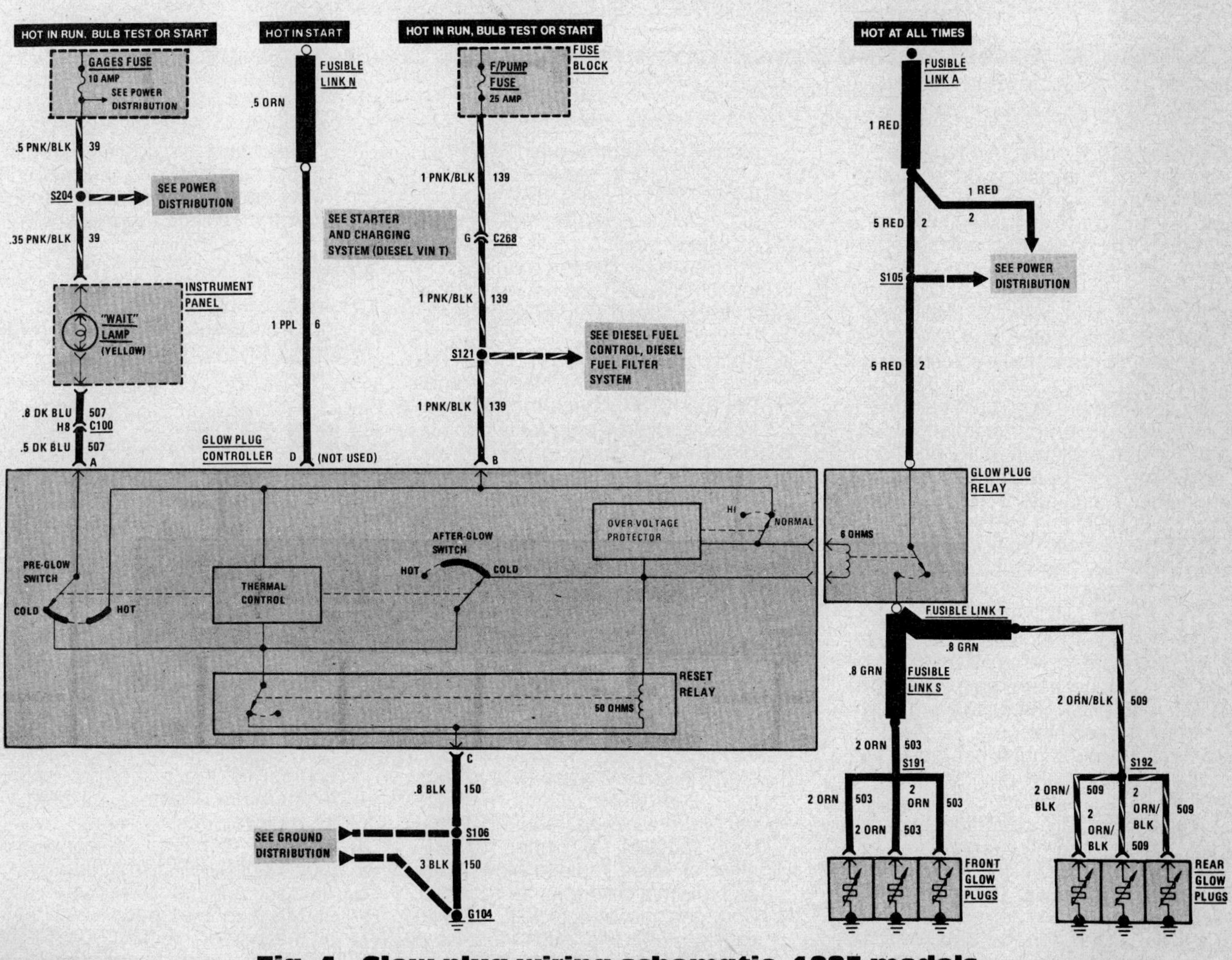

Fig. 4 Glow plug wiring schematic. 1985 models

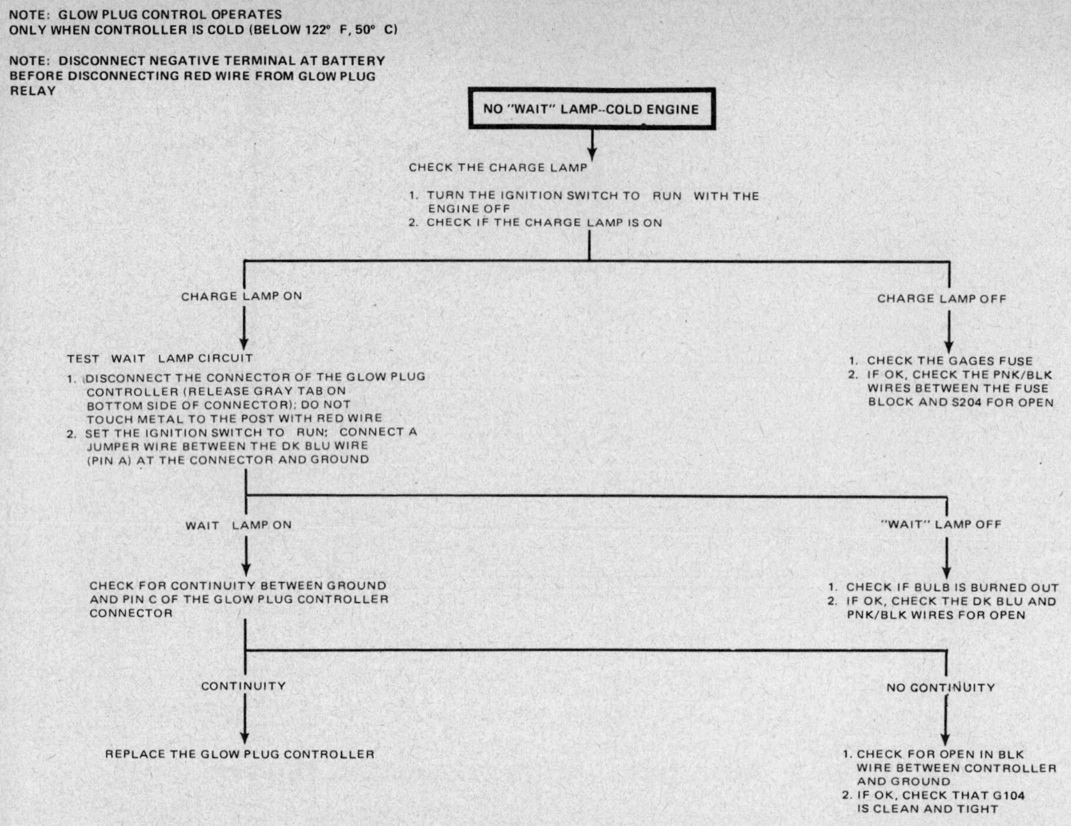

Fig. 5 Diesel engine electrical troubleshooting chart. 1984–85 Models

voltmeter, check battery voltage. Voltmeter should indicate approximately 12.4 volts.

2. Using a suitable test lamp and with ignition in RUN position, check voltage at pink wire at fuel injection pump solenoid, **Fig. 2.** If test lamp remains OFF, repair pink wire. If test lamp lights, turn ignition OFF and check for continuity through fuel solenoid to ground using test lamp KD-125 or equivalent. If there is no continuity, replace fuel injection pump solenoid.
3. With ignition switch in RUN position and engine not operating, check glow plug relay operation. Glow plug should click ON and OFF.
4. If glow plug relay operates as described in step 3, proceed as follows:
   a. Turn ignition OFF.
   b. Disconnect all glow plug harness connectors from glow plugs.
   c. Connect test lamp KD-125 or equivalent between rear post (dark blue and black wires) of glow plug relay and ground.
   d. At each glow plug, touch harness connector to glow plug spade terminal. If test lamp lights, glow plug and harness are operating properly. Connect harness connector to glow plugs. **Disconnect harness connector after testing each glow plug.**
   e. If test lamp does not light, touch harness connector to engine block. If test lamp lights, replace glow plug. If test lamp remains OFF, replace wire(s) to glow plug(s).
   f. If test lamp remains OFF for each glow plug tested after replacement of wires, replace glow plugs and thermal controller, as required.
5. If glow plug relay does not operate as described in step 3, proceed as follows:
   a. If glow plug relay does not click ON and OFF, and "Wait" lamp comes ON then OFF, check thermal controller and glow plug relay circuit.
   b. Disconnect connector at thermal controller. Connect one end of suitable test lamp to ground and turn ignition to RUN position. Connect other end of test lamp to brown wire and check for voltage. If test lamp lights, check coolant temperature switch. If coolant temperature switch is closed, replace switch.
   c. With one end of test lamp grounded, connect other end of test lamp to orange or orange/black wire. If test lamp lights, check for shorted glow plug relay wires (red to dark blue and black wires). Replace damaged wires as required. If test lamp remains OFF after replacement of wires, replace glow plugs and thermal controller as required.
   d. Connect one end of test lamp to battery. With other end of test lamp touch yellow wire between thermal controller and glow plug relay. If test lamp remains OFF, repair yellow wire between thermal controller and glow plug relay. If test lamp lights, replace thermal controller.

1984–85

Refer to wiring schematics, **Figs. 3 and 4,** and troubleshooting charts, **Figs. 5 through 7** for troubleshooting.

GLOW PLUG RESISTANCE TEST

1. On 1982-83 models, use a high impedance digital multimeter tool No. J-29125. On 1984-85 models, use high impedance digital multimeter tool No. J-29125A.
2. Position multimeter left hand switch to "OHMS," turn right hand switch counterclockwise to "200 OHMS" and slide center switch to the left "D.C. LO."
3. Start engine, turn heater ON and allow engine to reach normal operating temperature. Remove all feed wires from glow plugs.
4. On 1983-85 models, disconnect electrical connector from alternator.
5. Using magnetic tachometer No. J-26925, turn idle speed screw located on the side of injection pump until the roughest engine idle is obtained. Do not exceed 900 RPM.

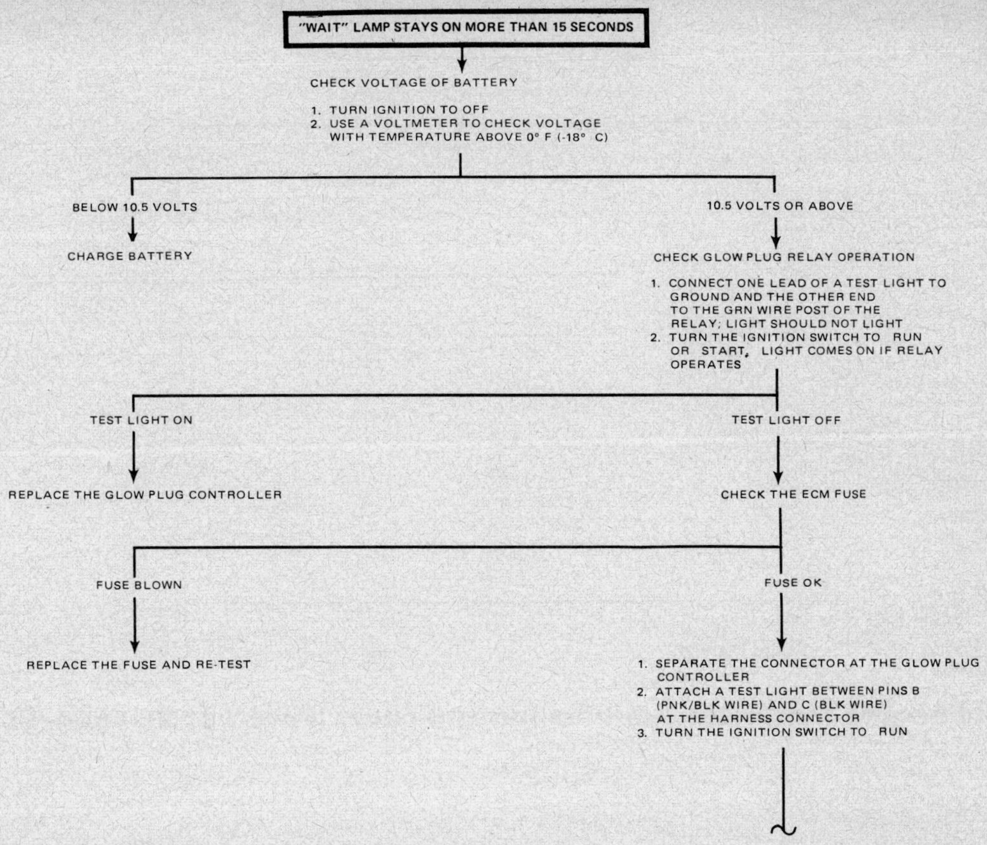

Fig. 6 Diesel engine electrical troubleshooting chart (Part 1 of 2). 1984–85 Models

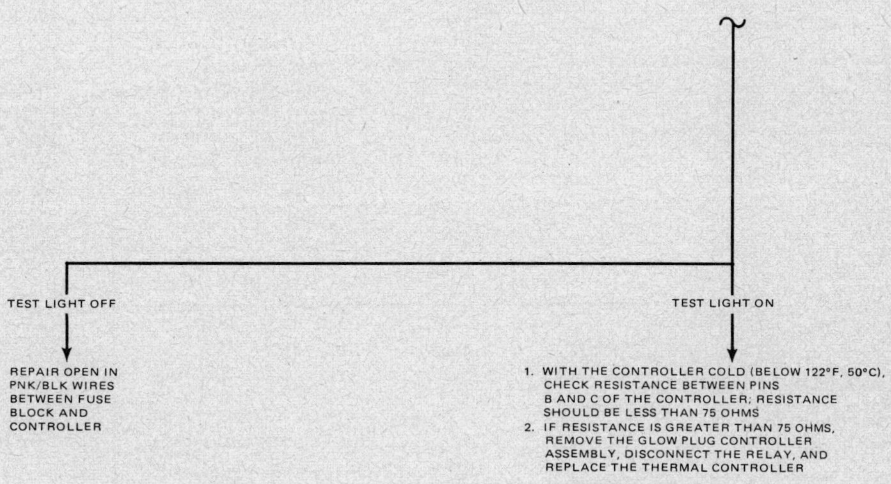

Fig. 6 Diesel engine electrical troubleshooting chart (Part 2 of 2). 1984–85 Models

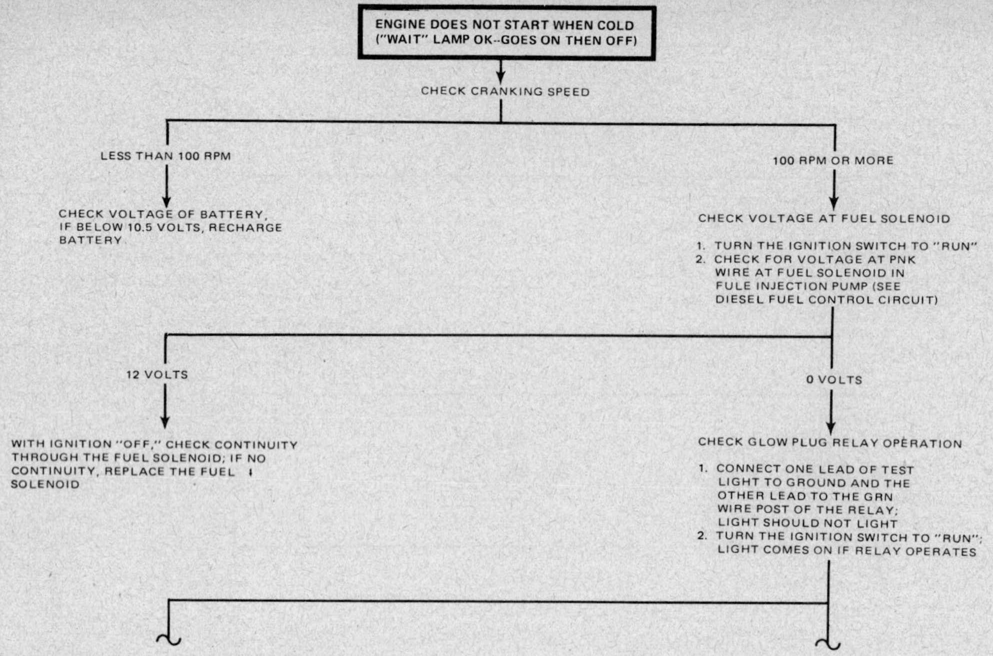

Fig. 7 Diesel engine electrical troubleshooting chart (Part 1 of 2). 1984–85 Models

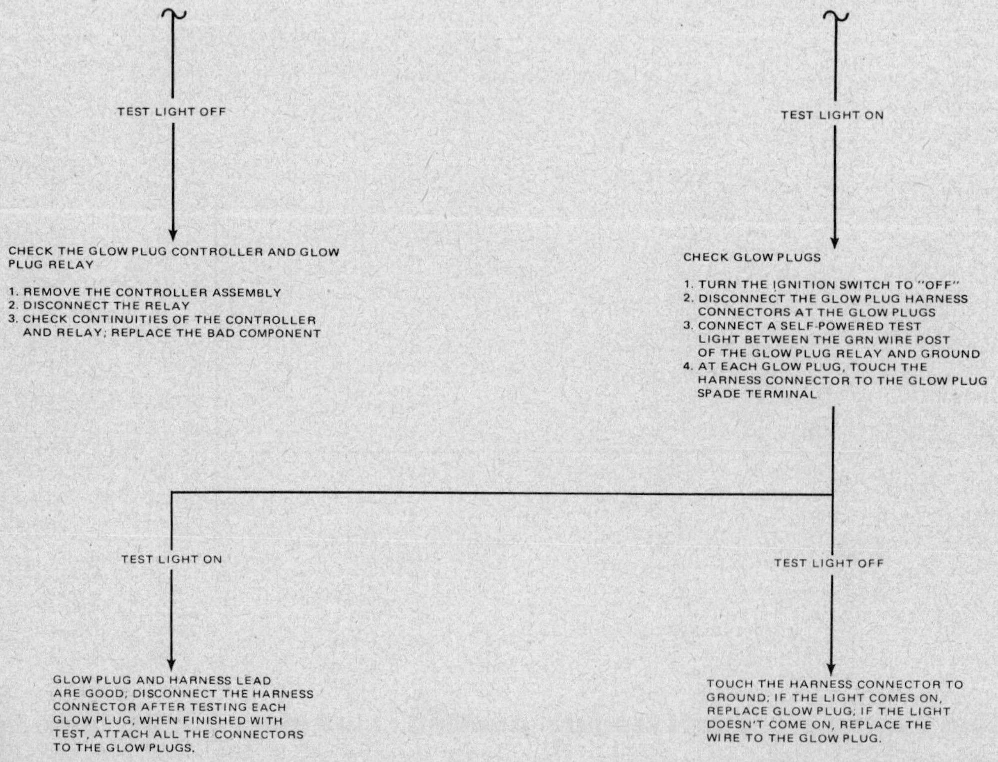

Fig. 7 Diesel engine electrical troubleshooting chart (Part 2 of 2). 1984–85 Models

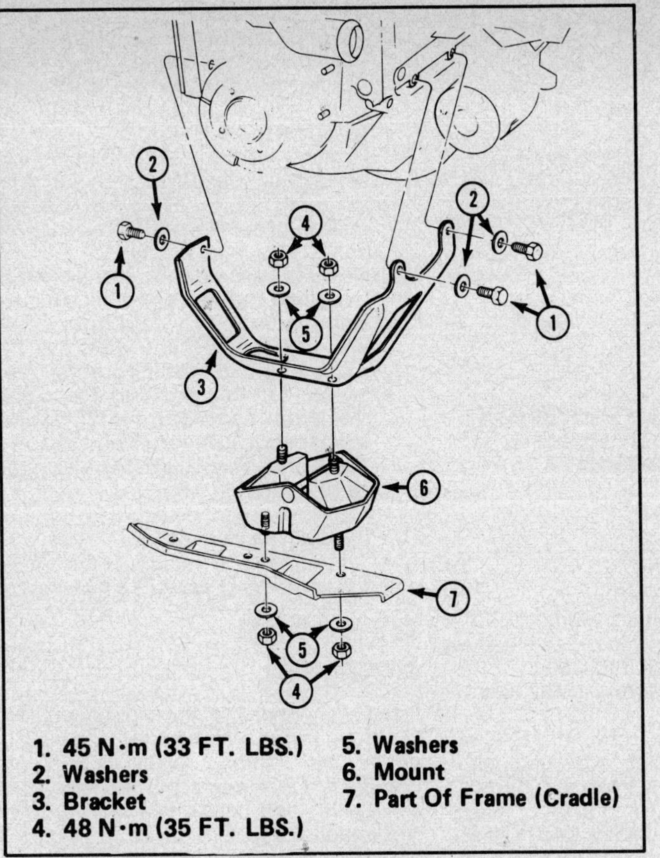

Fig. 8 Front engine mount removal and installation

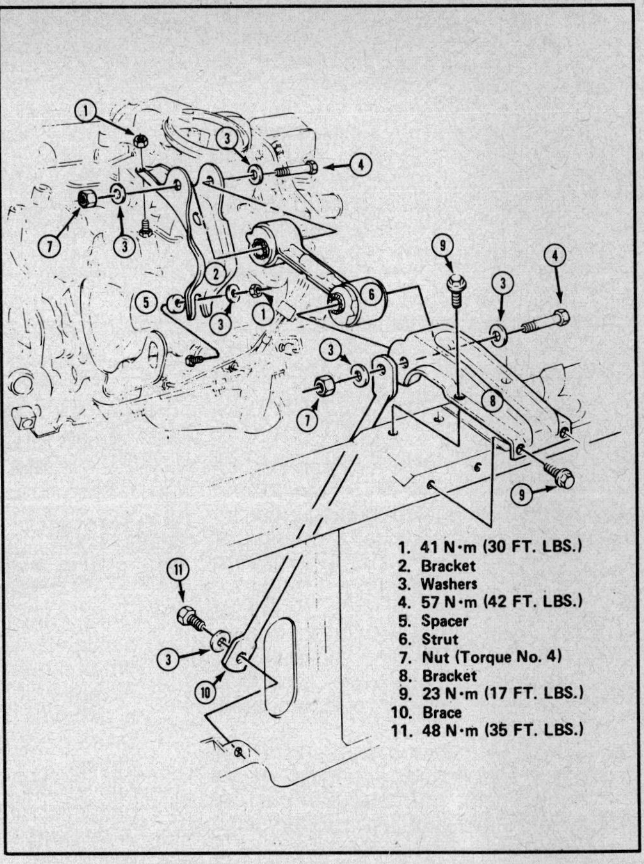

Fig. 9 Engine mount strut & bracket removal and installation. 1982–84 models

6. Allow engine to operate at its roughest idle speed for at least 1 minute. Thermostat must be open and upper radiator hose hot.
7. Connect a suitable clip to the black test lead of multimeter. The clip must be grounded to the fast idle solenoid and must remain grounded until all tests are completed.
8. With engine idling, probe each glow plug terminal and note resistance values on each cylinder in firing order. On 1982-83 models, reading will be between 1.8 and 3.4 ohms. If these readings are not obtained, turn engine OFF and check glow plugs. Resistance should be .7 or .8 ohms. If reading is not obtained, check multimeter for correct settings and for low or incorrect battery in multimeter. Check multimeter ground wire to engine. On 1984-85 models equipped with an electric cooling fan, note resistance values with cooling fan OFF. Do not disconnect electrical connector from fan. **The resistance values are dependent on the temperature in each cylinder, and indicate the output of each cylinder.**
9. If an ohm reading on any cylinder is approximately 1.2 or 1.3 ohms on 1982-83 models, or 1.3 or 1.4 ohms on 1984-85 models, check for engine mechanical problem. Check compression of the low reading cylinder and the cylinder which fires before and af-

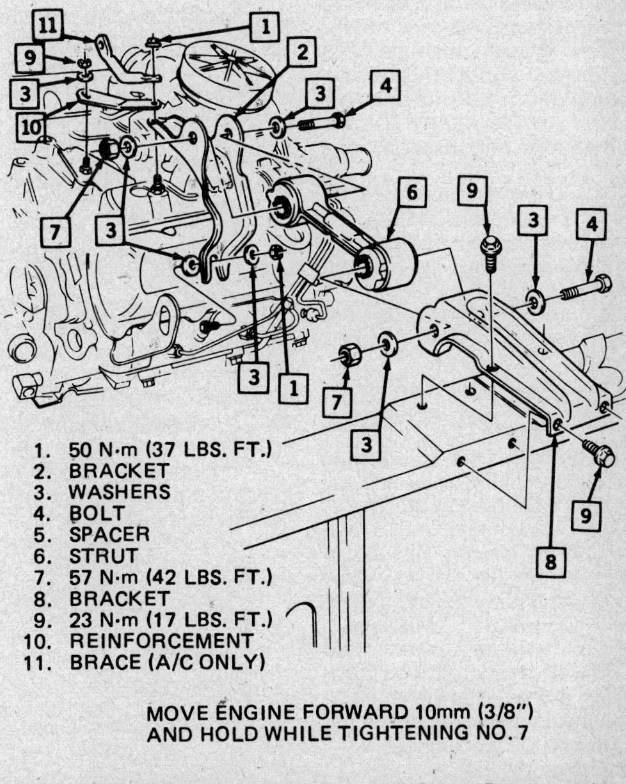

Fig. 10 Engine mount strut & bracket removal and installation. 1985 models

ter the low cylinder reading. **Correct the cause of the low compression cylinder before proceeding to the fuel system.**

10. Compare glow plug resistance readings, checking for differences between cylinders. Rough idle engines will normally vary .3 ohms on 1982-83 models, and on 1984-85 models, .4 ohms or more between cylinders in firing order. To compensate, it will be necessary to raise or lower the reading on one or more cylinders by selecting nozzles.
11. Remove nozzles from cylinders with the high or low ohm reading. Determine nozzle pop off pressure and check nozzle for leakage and spray pattern.
12. Install nozzles with a higher pop off pressure to lower ohm reading and nozzles with a lower pop off pressure to raise ohm readings. **A change of approximately 30 psi in pressure will change reading by .1 ohm.**
13. During cleaning or replacement of nozzle and before installation of injection pipe, crank engine and check for air bubbles at nozzle inlet. If bubbles are present, clean or replace nozzles as required.
14. Install injection tube, start engine and check idle speed. If engine idle is rough, check and note glow plug resistance values of each cylinder firing order.
15. Compare glow plug resistance readings, noting differences of .3 ohms on 1982-83 models, and on 1984-85 models, .4 ohms between cylinders. **It will be necessary to raise or lower resistance reading on one or more cylinders as described previously.**
16. After additional nozzle changes have been performed, check engine idle. **After completing two resistance checks and nozzle changes, correct engine idle can now be obtained.**
17. Injection pump replacement may be necessary if the following occurs:
    a. Problem cylinder moves from cylinder to cylinder as nozzle changes are made.
    b. Cylinder ohm readings do not change when nozzles are changed (replaced).

Always check cylinders at the same engine rpm. A nozzle with a tip leak can allow more fuel into the cylinder, which will raise glow plug ohm reading. This will rob fuel from the next nozzle in firing order, and will result in glow plug having a low ohm reading. Remove and check nozzle with a high reading. If nozzle is leaking, this could cause a rough engine idle. If a low glow plug resistance value is noted and it does not change with nozzle replacement, switch glow plugs between a known good cylinder and a bad cylinder. If resistance reading of each cylinder is not the same as before the switch, the glow plug cannot be used for rough engine idle diagnosis.

ENGINE MOUNTS
REPLACE

Refer to **Figs. 8, 9, and 10** for service procedures.

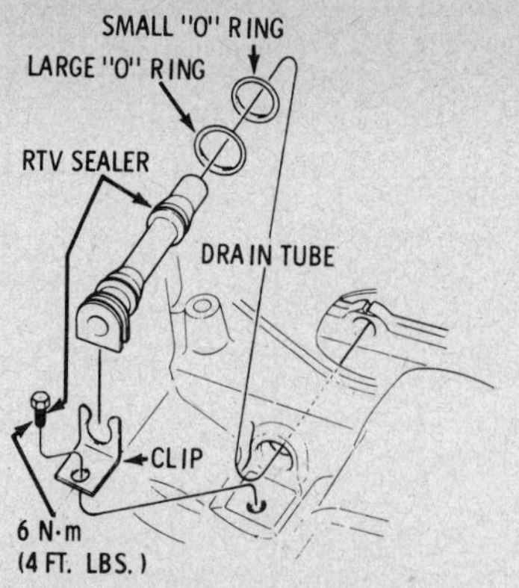

Fig. 11 Intake manifold drain tube removal & installation

ENGINE
REPLACE

1. Drain cooling system. Remove serpentine drive belt, also remove vacuum pump drive belt if equipped.
2. Remove air cleaner and install a suitable cover.
3. Disconnect battery ground cable at battery (on vehicles equipped with heavy duty system there will be two batteries), ground wires at inner fender and engine ground strap.
4. Raise vehicle. Remove flywheel cover.
5. Remove flywheel to torque converter attaching bolts.
6. Disconnect exhaust pipe from rear exhaust manifold.
7. Remove engine to transaxle brace.
8. Remove engine mount to cradle retaining nuts and washers.
9. Disconnect leads to starter motor, No. 2 cylinder glow plug and battery ground cable at transaxle to engine bolt.
10. Disconnect lower oil cooler hose and plug openings.
11. Remove accessible power steering pump bracket fasteners and lower vehicle.
12. Remove remaining power steering pump bracket/brace.
13. Remove heater outlet pipe.
14. Disconnect all remaining glow plug leads at glow plugs.
15. Disconnect all other leads at engine, disconnect engine harness at cowl connector and body mounted relays and position engine harness aside.
16. If equipped with A/C, disconnect compressor with brackets and lines attached and position aside.
17. Disconnect fuel and vacuum hoses, plug all fuel line openings.
18. Disconnect throttle and T.V. cables at injection pump and cable bracket. Position cables aside.
19. Disconnect upper oil cooler hose and plug openings. Remove exhaust crossover pipe heat shield.
20. Disconnect and position aside transaxle filler tube.
21. Remove exhaust crossover pipe.
22. Remove engine mounting strut and strut brackets.
23. Install a suitable engine lifting device. **When installing lifting chains to cylinder heads, ensure that washers are used under the chains and bolt heads and the bolts are torqued to 20 ft. lbs.**
24. Position a suitable support under transaxle rear extension. As engine is being removed it may be necessary to raise support. Remove engine to transaxle bolts, then engine.
25. Reverse procedure to install. **Before installing the flex plate to converter bolts, ensure the weld nuts on the converter are flush with the flex plate and converter rotates freely by hand in this position. Hand start the three bolts and finger tighten, then torque converter bolts to 35 ft. lbs. This ensures proper alignment of converter.**

INTAKE MANIFOLD
REPLACE
REMOVAL

1. Disconnect battery ground cable(s), then remove air cleaner.
2. Drain radiator coolant, then disconnect upper radiator hose from water outlet, and heater hoses from intake manifold.
3. Remove fuel injection pump. Refer to "Injection Pump, Replace."
4. Disconnect wiring from engine accessories.
5. If equipped with cruise control, remove servo.
6. If equipped with A/C, remove compressor and braces. Position aside.
7. Remove alternator assembly.
8. Disconnect engine mounting strut.
9. Remove fuel lines, filter and brackets. Plug all openings.
10. Disconnect glow plug controller and sending units wire connectors.
11. Disconnect heat shield from exhaust pipe crossover.
12. Using a suitable back-up wrench, remove left (forward) injection lines and plug all openings.
13. Disconnect T.V. and throttle cables from bracket.
14. Remove intake manifold drain tube, **Fig. 11.**
15. Remove injection pump intermediate adapter, pump adapter and seal, **Fig. 12.**
16. Remove intake manifold.

INSTALLATION

1. Thoroughly clean machined surfaces of cylinder head and intake manifold, ensuring neither surface becomes gouged or scratched. Clean all bolts and bolt holes.
2. Using a suitable sealer, coat both sides of the manifold to head sealing gasket surface, and place in position, **Fig. 13.**
3. Install end seals, ensure ends are positioned under cylinder heads. Apply RTV sealer to each end of seal, **Fig. 13. The end seals and mating sur-**

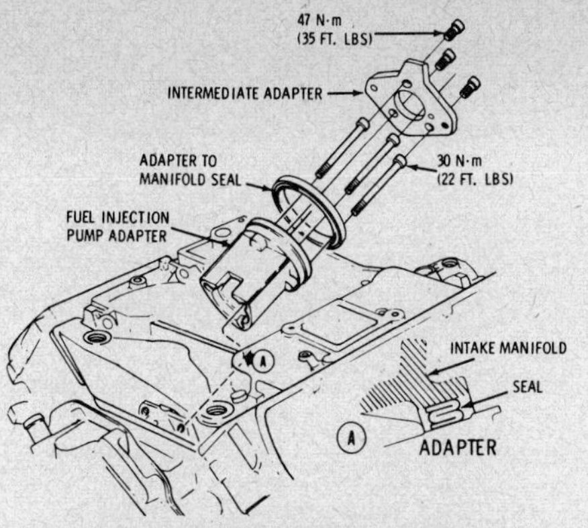

Fig. 12 Removal & installation of intermediate adapter, pump adapter & seal

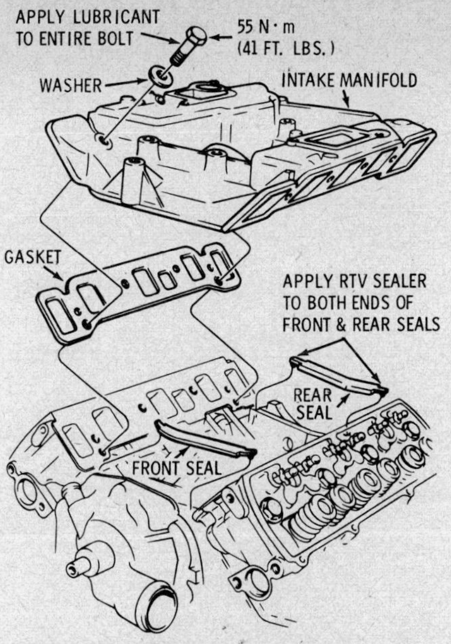

Fig. 13 Intake manifold installation

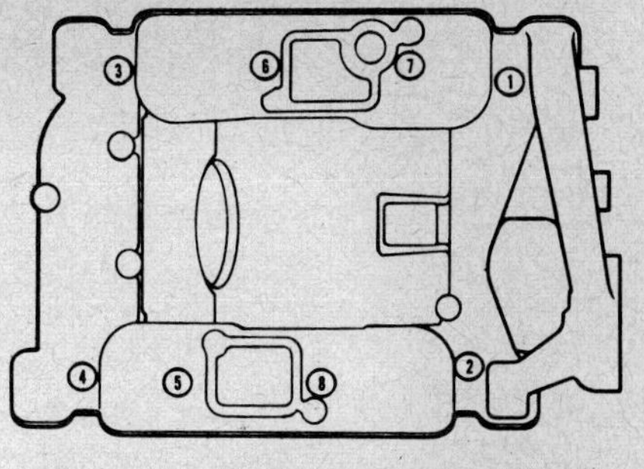

Fig. 14 Intake manifold torquing sequence

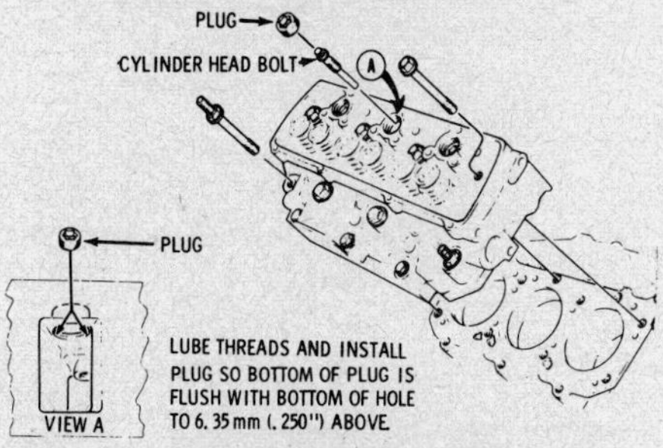

Fig. 15 Cylinder head pipe plug removal

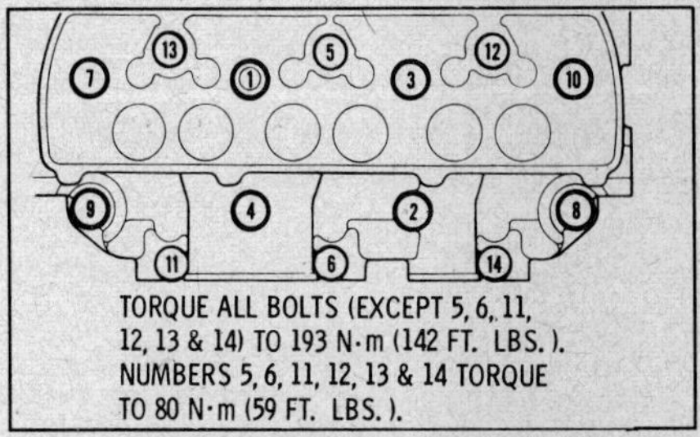

Fig. 16 Cylinder head bolt tightening sequence

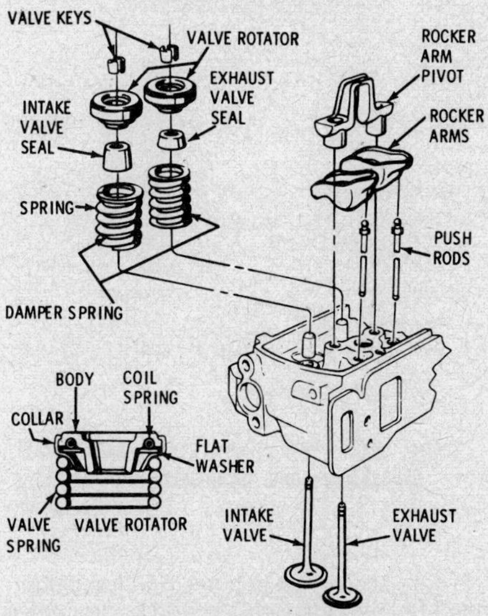

Fig. 17 Exploded view of cylinder head

faces must be dry to prevent gasket slippage.

4. Carefully position intake manifold on engine.
5. Lubricate intake manifold bolts entire length with lubricant 1052080 or equivalent.
6. Install bolts. Torque to specifications following sequence shown in **Fig. 14**, to 15 ft. lbs. Then retorque to specifications.
7. Reverse steps 1 through 15 of removal procedure to complete installation.

CYLINDER HEAD REPLACE

1. Remove intake manifold and valve cover.
2. Remove or loosen any accessory bracket or pipe that interferes with removal of cylinder head.
3. Disconnect glow plug wiring and block heater lead (if equipped).
4. Remove ground strap from right cylinder head.
5. Remove rocker arm nuts, pivots, rocker arms and pushrods. Scribe mark on pivots and separate so they may be easily identified and replaced in their original location.
6. Disconnect exhaust crossover pipe from exhaust manifold on side being removed and loosen it on opposite side.
7. Remove pipe plugs covering upper cylinder head bolts, **Fig. 15.**
8. Remove engine block drain plug, from side that is to be worked on.
9. Remove cylinder head bolts and cylinder head. If necessary to remove pre-chamber, remove glow plug and nozzle, then tap out with a small blunt 1/8 inch drift. Do not use tapered drift.
10. Reverse procedure to install. Refer to **Fig. 16** for correct torque sequence. Torque cylinder head bolts except bolts 5, 6, 11, 12, 13 and 14 to 100 ft. lbs. Torque bolts 5, 6, 11, 12, 13 and 14 to 41 ft. lbs. After original torquing, retorque bolts mentioned above to 142 and 59 ft. lbs. respectively. **The head gaskets used on this engine are composition type, and not to be used with a sealer of any kind. Any sealer applied may result in head gasket leakage.**

ROCKER ARMS

This engine uses valve rotators, **Fig. 17.** The rotator operates on a sprag clutch principle utilizing the collapsing action of a coil spring to give rotation to the rotor body which turns the valve.

1. Remove valve cover.
2. Remove flanged bolts, rocker arm pivot and rocker arms, **Fig. 18.**
3. When installing rocker arm assemblies, lubricate wear surfaces with suitable lubricant. Torque flanged bolts to 28 ft. lbs.

VALVE ROTATORS

The rotator operates on a Sprag clutch principle utilizing the collapsing action of coil spring to give rotation to the rotor body which turns the valve, **Fig. 17.**

To check rotator action, draw a line across rotator body and down the collar. Operate engine at 1500 RPM, rotator body should move around collar. Rotator action can be in either direction. Replace rotator if no movement is noted.

When servicing valves, valve stem tips should be checked for improper wear pattern which could indicate a defective valve rotator, **Fig. 19.**

VALVE LIFT SPECIFICATIONS

Engine	Year	Int.	Exh.
V6-262 Diesel	1982-85	.375	.375

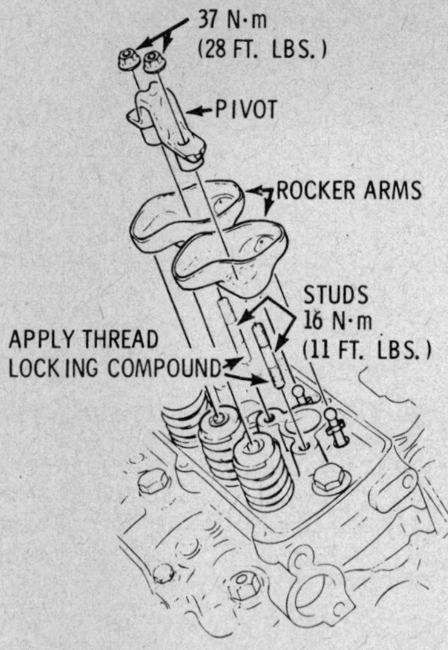

Fig. 18 Rocker arm assembly

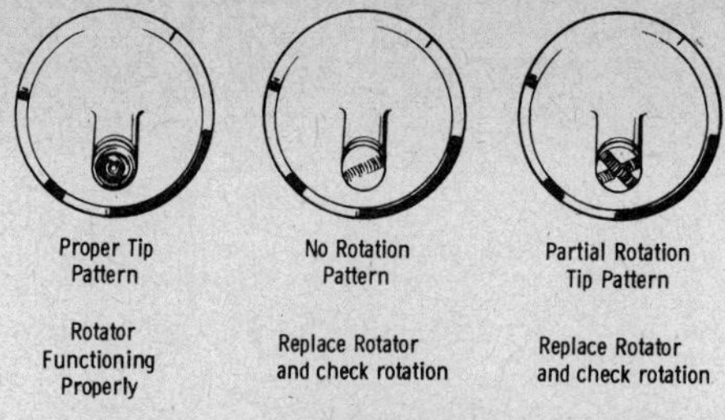

Fig. 19 Inspecting valve stem for rotator malfunction

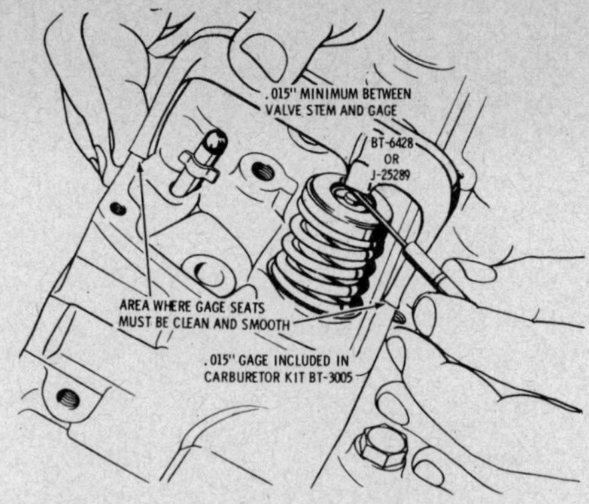

Fig. 20 Measuring valve stem height

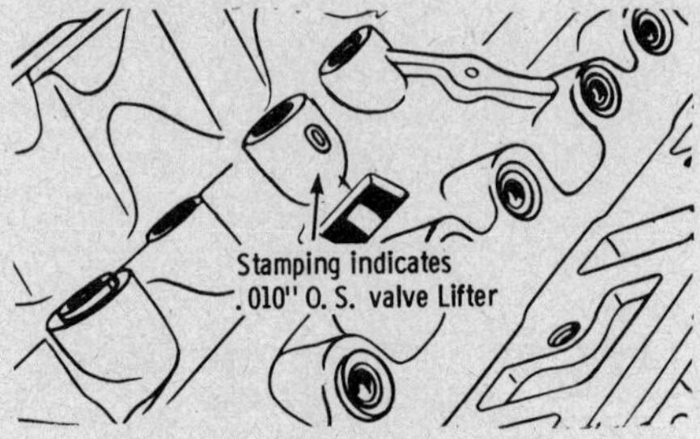

Fig. 22 Oversize valve lifter marking

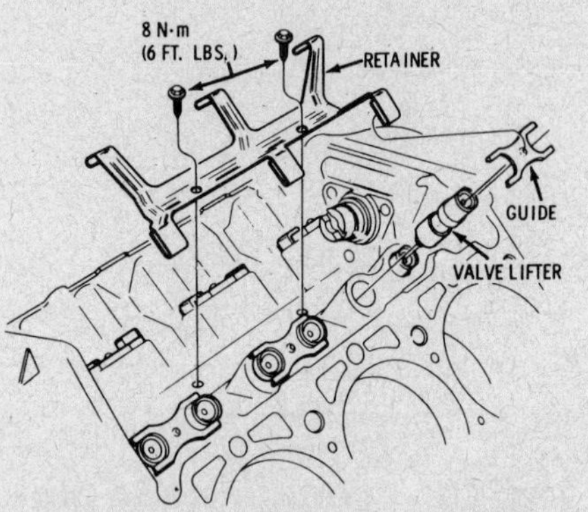

Fig. 23 Hydraulic roller lifter retainer and guide

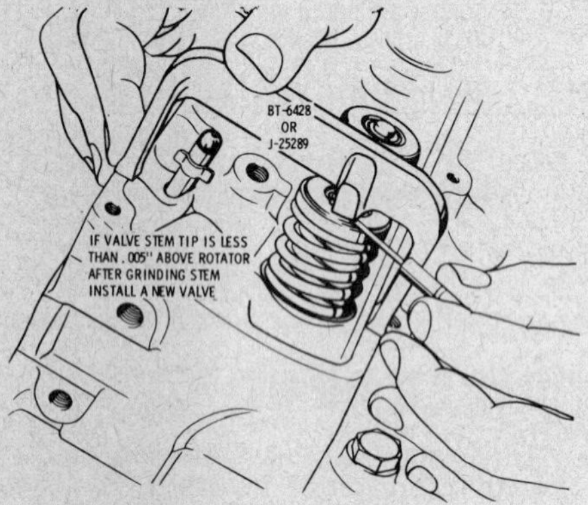

Fig. 21 Measuring valve rotator height

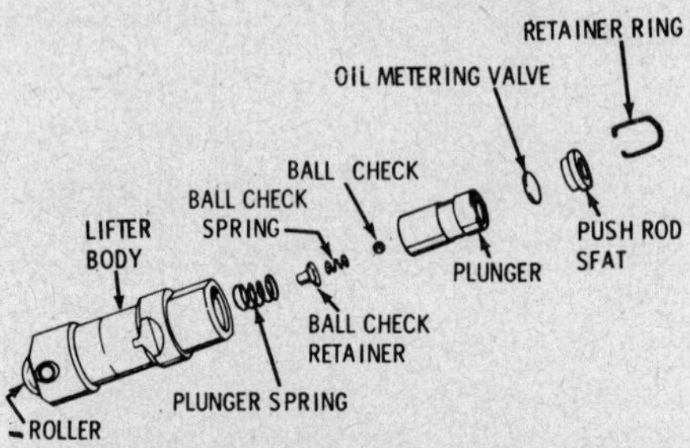

Fig. 24 Exploded view of hydraulic roller lifter

VALVE ARRANGEMENT

V6-262 Diesel . . . . I-E-E-I-E-I

VALVE TIMING

INTAKE OPENS BEFORE TDC

Engine	Year	Degrees
V6-262 Diesel	1982-85	16

VALVE CLEARANCE SPECIFICATIONS

These engines are equipped with hydraulic lifters, no provision for adjustment is provided.

VALVES

Whenever a new valve is installed or after grinding valves, it is necessary to measure the valve stem height with the special tool as shown in **Fig. 20.**

There should be at least .015 inch clearance between the gauge and end of valve stem. If clearance is less than .015 inch, remove valve and grind end of valve stem as required.

Check valve rotator height, **Fig. 21.** If valve stem end is less than .005 inch above rotator, the valve is too short and a new valve must be installed.

VALVE GUIDES

Valve stem guides are not replaceable, due to being cast in place. If valve guide bores are worn excessively, they can be reamed oversize.

If a standard valve guide bore is being reamed, use a .003 inch or .005 inch oversize reamer. For the .010 inch oversize valve guide bore, use a .013 inch oversize reamer. If too large a reamer is used and the spiraling is removed, it is possible that the valve will not receive the proper lubrication.

Occasionally a valve guide will be oversize as manufactured. These are marked on the cylinder head. If no markings are present, the guide bores are standard. If oversize markings are present, any valve replacement will require an oversize valve. Service valves are available in standard diameters as well as .003 inch, .005 inch, .010 inch and .013 inch oversize.

VALVE LIFTER

REPLACE

Some engines have both standard and .010 inch oversize valve lifters. The .010 inch oversize valve lifters are etched with a "0" on the side of the lifter. Also, the cylinder block will be marked if an oversize lifter is used, **Fig. 22.**

1. Remove intake manifold as outlined previously.
2. Remove valve covers, rocker arm assemblies and pushrods. Note location of valve train components so they can be installed in original position.
3. Remove hydraulic lifter retainer bolts, then retainer, **Fig. 23.**
4. Remove valve lifters, then disassemble, **Fig. 24.**
5. If plunger and body appear satisfactory, blow off air to remove all particles of dirt. Install the plunger in the body

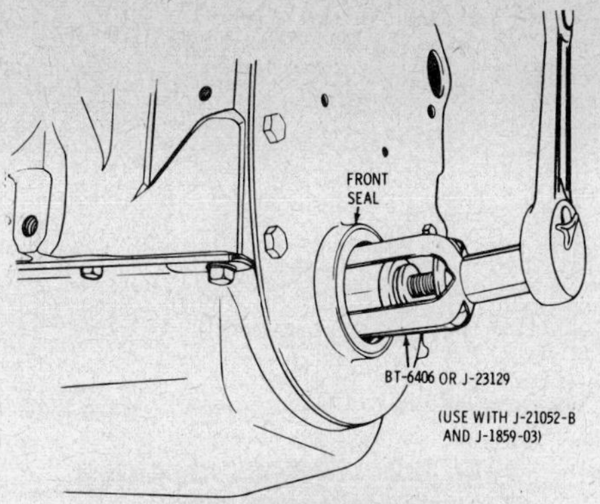

Fig. 25 Front oil seal removal

without other parts and check for free movement. A simple test is to be sure that the plunger will drop of its own weight in the body, **Fig. 24.**

6. Reverse procedure to install. **Before installation, prime new or reassembled lifters by working lifter plunger while submerged in kerosene or diesel fuel. Lifter could be damaged if installed dry when starting engine. When assembling lifters, do not interchange plungers, as they are specifically fitted to the bodies during manufacture.**

FRONT OIL SEAL REPLACE

1. Disconnect battery ground cables.
2. Remove accessory drive belts.
3. Remove crankshaft pulley and harmonic balancer.
4. Using tool BT-6406 or equivalent, remove front oil seal, **Fig. 25.**
5. Apply suitable sealant to outside diameter of new oil seal.
6. Using tool J-29659 or equivalent, install new oil seal, **Fig. 26.**
7. Install harmonic balancer and crankshaft pulley.
8. Install and tension accessory drive belts.

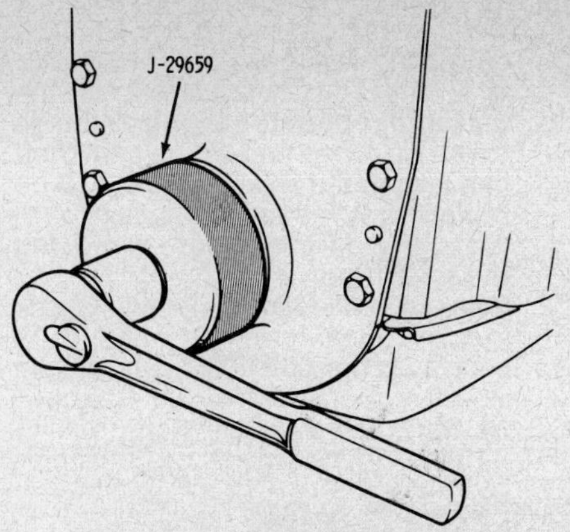

Fig. 26 Front oil seal installation

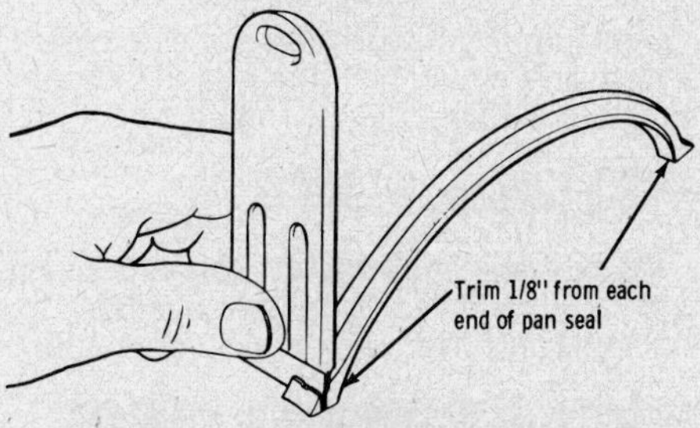

Fig. 28 Trimming oil pan seal

ENGINE FRONT COVER REPLACE

1. Disconnect battery ground cables.
2. Drain cooling system and disconnect lower radiator and heater hoses.
3. Remove drive belts, crankshaft pulley, harmonic balancer and accessory brackets.
4. Remove timing indicator.

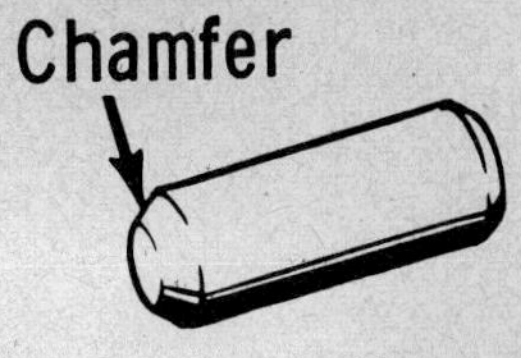

Fig 27 Dowel pin chamfer

5. Remove front cover attaching bolts, then the front cover. Also, remove the dowel pins. It may be necessary to grind a flat on the dowel pin to provide a rough surface for gripping.
6. Grind a chamfer on one end of each dowel pin, **Fig. 27.**
7. Cut excess material from front end of oil pan gasket on each side of cylinder block.
8. Trim approximately 1/8 inch from each end of new front pan seal, **Fig. 28.**
9. Install new front cover gasket and apply suitable sealer to gasket around coolant holes.
10. Apply RTV sealer to mating surfaces of cylinder block, oil pan and front cover.
11. Place front cover on cylinder block and press downward to compress seal. Rotate cover right and left and guide oil pan seal into cavity with a small screwdriver.
12. Apply engine oil to bolts.
13. Install two bolts finger tight to retain cover.
14. Install the two dowel pins, chamfered end first.
15. Install timing indicator and remaining bolts, **Fig. 29.** Torque bolts as follows: water pump bolts, 21 ft. lbs.; timing cover bolts, 41-42 ft. lbs. **Water pump and front cover to block attaching bolts must be coated with sealer 1052624 or equivalent, since coolant leaks and loss of bolt torque may result.**
16. Install harmonic balancer and crankshaft pulley, **Fig. 29.** Torque crankshaft bolt to 160-350 ft. lbs. and pulley bolts to 30 ft. lbs.

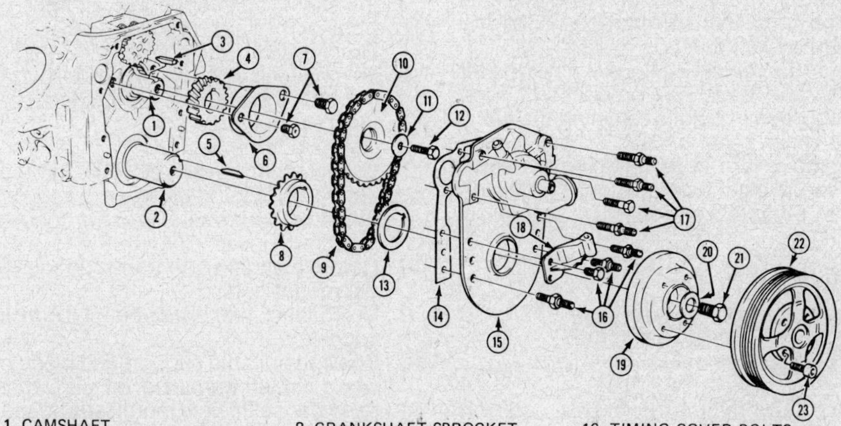

1. CAMSHAFT
2. CRANKSHAFT
3. CAMSHAFT SPROCKET KEY
4. INJECTION PUMP DRIVE GEAR
5. CRANKSHAFT SPROCKET KEY
6. FRONT CAMSHAFT BEARING RETAINER
7. RETAINER BOLT
8. CRANKSHAFT SPROCKET
9. TIMING CHAIN
10. CAMSHAFT SPROCKET
11. WASHER
12. CAMSHAFT SPROCKET BOLT
13. SLINGER
14. GASKET
15. FRONT COVER
16. TIMING COVER BOLTS
17. WATER PUMP BOLTS
18. PROBE HOLDER (RPM COUNTER)
19. CRANKSHAFT BALANCER
20. WASHER
21. CRANKSHAFT BOLT
22. PULLEY ASSEMBLY
23. PULLEY BOLTS

Fig. 29 Engine front cover installation

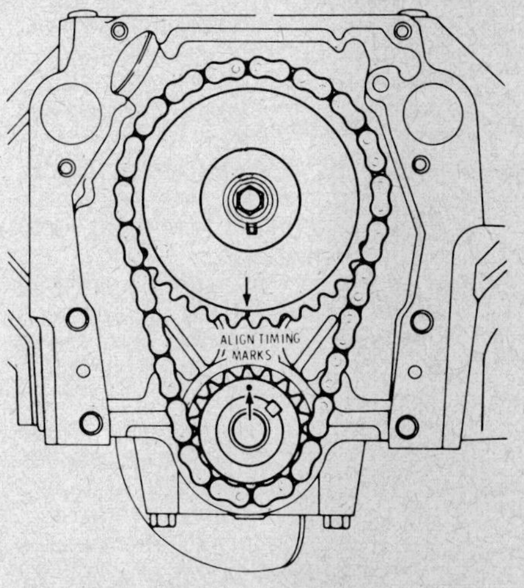

Fig. 30 Valve timing marks

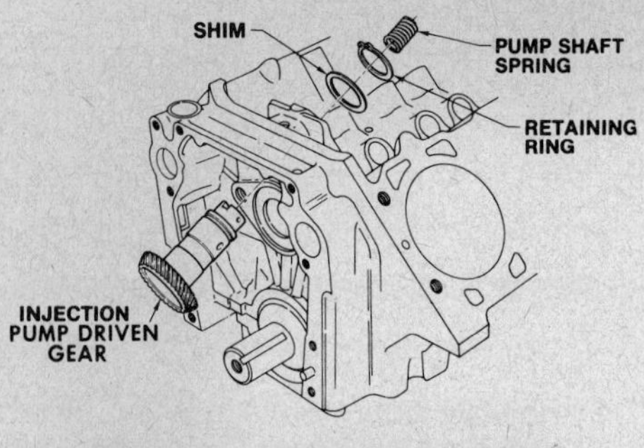

Fig. 31 Fuel injection pump driven gear removal and installation

17. Install accessory brackets.
18. Install drive belts.
19. Connect lower radiator and heater hoses.
20. Connect ground cables to batteries.

TIMING CHAIN & GEARS
REPLACE

1. Remove front cover as outlined previously. Loosen rocker arm pivot bolts evenly so that some lash is present between rocker arms and valves.
2. Remove oil slinger, cam gear, crank gear and timing chain.
3. Install key in crankshaft, if removed.
4. Install cam gear, crank gear and timing chain with timing marks aligned, **Fig. 30.** Torque cam gear bolt to 64 ft. lbs. on 1982 models, or 70 ft. lbs. on 1983-85 models.
5. Install oil slinger.
6. Install front cover.

CAMSHAFT & INJECTION PUMP DRIVE & DRIVEN GEARS
REPLACE

1. Remove engine assembly as previously outlined.
2. Remove intake manifold and gasket.
3. Remove oil pump drive assembly.
4. Remove front cover, then rotate crankshaft so that timing marks are in alignment.
5. Remove all rocker arms, pivots, pushrods, and lifters. Note valve train component location for proper location upon installation.
6. Remove bolt securing camshaft sprocket, then remove both cam and crank sprocket. If crank sprocket is tight on shaft, remove with a suitable puller.
7. Remove bolts retainingfront camshaft bearing retainer, then remove retainer.
8. Remove cam sprocket key.
9. Remove injection pump drive gear.
10. Remove intake manifold, intermediate pump adapter and pump adapter. Remove snap ring, selective washer, driven gear and spring, **Fig. 31.**
11. Install a long bolt into camshaft to act as a handle and carefully slide camshaft out of block. **Do not force the camshaft out of the block. Damage to the bearings and or the camshaft can result. If the bearings are to be replaced, it will be necessary to remove the oil pan before removing the bearings.**
12. Reverse procedure to install. Check injection pump driven gear endplay. If endplay is not .002-.006 inch, replace selective washer, **Fig. 31.** Selective washers are available from .080 to .115 inch in increments of .003 inch.

PISTON & ROD ASSEMBLE

The pistons must be installed with the notch in the top facing the front of the engine.

Measure the connecting rod side clearance using a suitable feeler gauge. Clearance should be .008-.021 inch.

PISTON & RINGS

Pistons are available in standard sizes and .010 oversizes. Rings are available in standard and oversizes of .010 and .030.

MAIN & ROD BEARINGS

Main bearings are available in standard sizes and undersizes of .0005, .0010 and .0015 inch. The amount of undersize is stamped on the bearing shell, **Fig. 32.**

Rod bearings are available in standard sizes and an undersize of .010 inch.

On 1982-84 vehicles, there are two different length main bearing cap-to-block bolts being used in production. Any given engine will use only one length cap bolt. A 3 15/16 inch (100 mm) long bolt is used on engines that have main bearing caps that have their locations in the engine cast into the cap. A 4 11/32 inch (110 mm) long bolt is used on engines that have main bearing caps that have their location in engine identified by the number of raised ribs cast into the cap. Use of improper bolts will cause the block threads to strip.

On 1985 vehicles, two distinct cylinder blocks are used in production. Type 1blocks have two bolts retaining the No. 2 and 3 main bearing caps, while Type 2 blocks have four bolts retaining the caps. On Type 2 blocks, torque outer retaining bolts to 52 ft. lbs. and inner bolts to 89 ft. lbs.

REAR CRANKSHAFTSEAL SERVICE

Since the braided fabric seal used on these engines can be replaced only when the crankshaft is removed, the following repair procedure is recommended.

1. Remove oil pan and bearing cap.
2. Drive end of old seal gently into groove, using a suitable tool, until packed tight. This may vary between 1/4 and 3/4 inch depending on amount

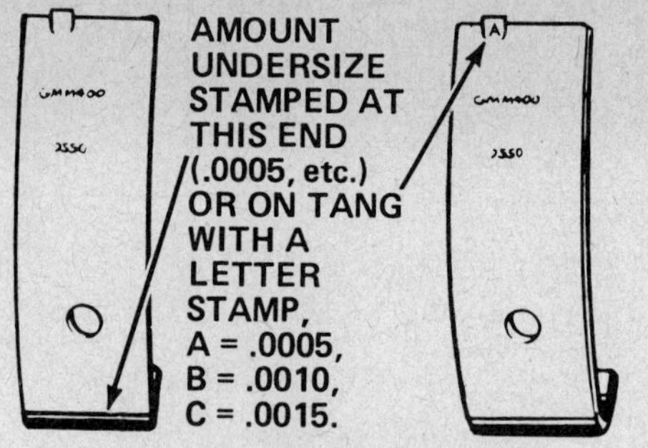

Fig. 32 Main bearing identification

of pack required.

3. Repeat previous step for other end of seal.
3. Repeat previous step for other end of seal.
4. Measure and note amount that seal was driven up on one side. Using the old seal removed from bearing cap, cut a length of seal the amount previously noted plus 1/16 inch.
5. Repeat previous step for other side of seal.
6. Pack cut lengths of seal into appropriate side of seal groove. A packing tool, BT-6433, **Fig. 33,** may be used since the tool has been machined to provide a built-in stop. Use tool BT-6436 to trim the seal flush with block, **Fig. 34.**
7. Install new seal in lower bearing cap.

OIL PAN
REPLACE

1. On 1983-85 models, rotate intermediate steering shaft until steering gear stub shaft clamp bolt is in the up position and remove clamp bolt, then disconnect the intermediate shaft from stub shaft. Install suitable engine lifting fixture on all models.
2. Raise vehicle but keep rear slightly lower than front.
3. Install suitable supports at front of body at forward lift points.
4. Drain engine oil.
5. Remove left side steering gear to cradle bolt, then loosen right side steering gear to cradle bolt.
6. Remove front stabilizer bar.
7. Using 1/2 inch drill bit, drill through spot weld located between rear holes at lefthand front stabilizer bar mounting.
8. Remove engine and transaxle to cradle mount nuts.
9. Disconnect left lower ball joint from knuckle.
10. Position suitable support and block of wood under transaxle oil pan, then raise transaxle until mount stud clears cradle.
11. Remove bolts securing front crossmember to right side of cradle.
12. Remove left side body mount bolts.
13. Remove left side and front crossmember assembly, then lower rear crossmember below left side by careful use of a pry bar.

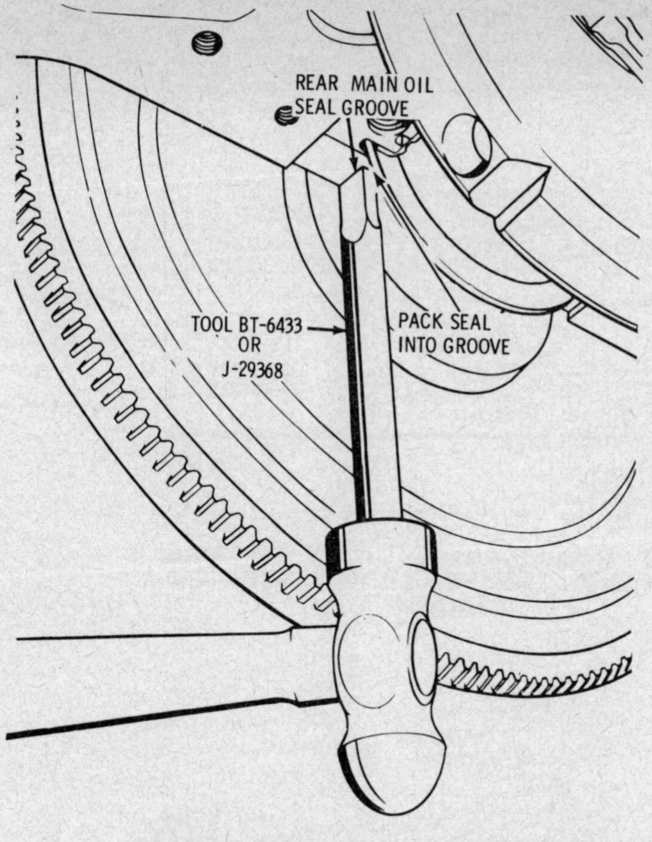

Fig. 33 Packing upper rear main bearing seal

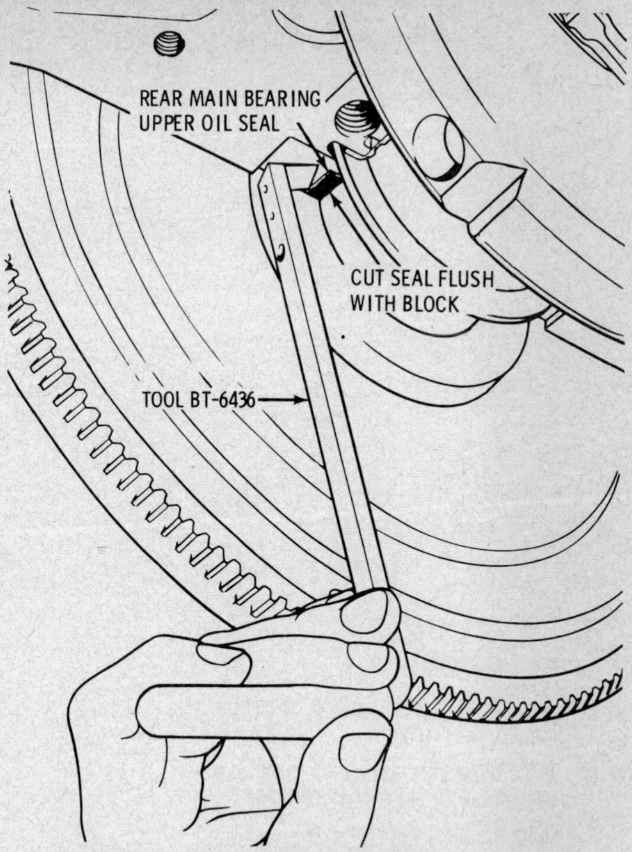

Fig. 34 Trimming upper rear main bearing seal

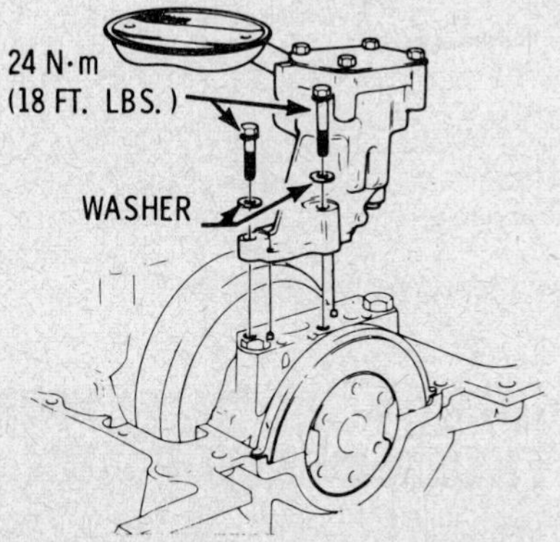

Fig. 35 Oil pump removal

14. Remove flywheel cover, starter assembly and engine mount bracket.
15. Remove oil pan attaching bolts and oil pan.
16. Reverse procedure to install.

OIL PUMP
REPLACE

1. Remove oil pan as outlined previously.
2. Remove oil pump to rear main bearing cap attaching bolts, **Fig. 35.**
3. Remove oil pump and drive shaft extension.
4. Reverse procedure to install. Torque attaching bolts to 18 ft. lbs.

OIL PUMP SERVICE
DISASSEMBLY

1. Remove oil pump drive shaft extension, **Fig. 36.** Do not attempt to remove washers from drive shaft extension. The drive shaft extension and washers are serviced as an assembly.
2. Remove cotter pin, spring and pressure regulator valve, **Fig. 36. Apply pressure on pressure regulator bore before removing cotter pin since the spring is under pressure.**
3. Remove oil pump cover attaching screws, then oil pump cover and gasket.
4. Remove drive gear and idler gear from pump body.

INSPECTION

1. Check gears for scoring or other damage, replace if necessary.
2. Proper end clearance is .0005-.0075 inch.
3. Check pressure regulator valve, valve spring and bore for damage. Proper bore to valve clearance is .0025-.0050 inch.
4. Check extension shaft ends for wear.

ASSEMBLY

1. Install gears and shaft in oil pump body.

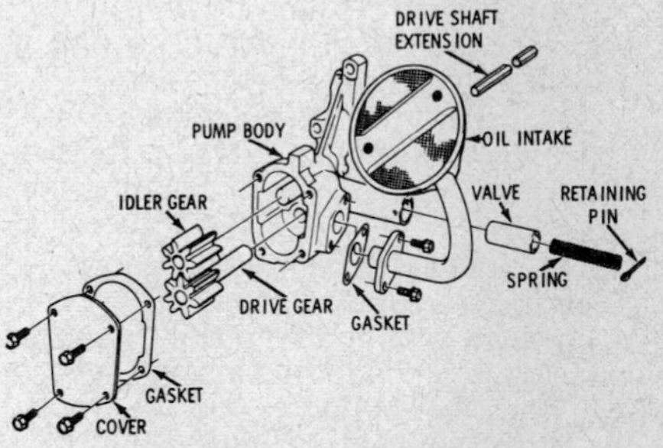

Fig. 36 Oil pump disassembled

2. Check gear end clearance by placing a straight edge over the gears and measure the clearance between the straight edge and gasket surface. If end clearance is excessive, check for scores in cover that would bring the clearance over specified limits.
3. Install cover and torque attaching screws to 7 ft. lbs.
4. Install pressure regulator valve, closed end first, into bore, then the valve spring and cotter pin.

WATER PUMP
REPLACE

1. Disconnect battery ground cable.
2. Drain radiator.

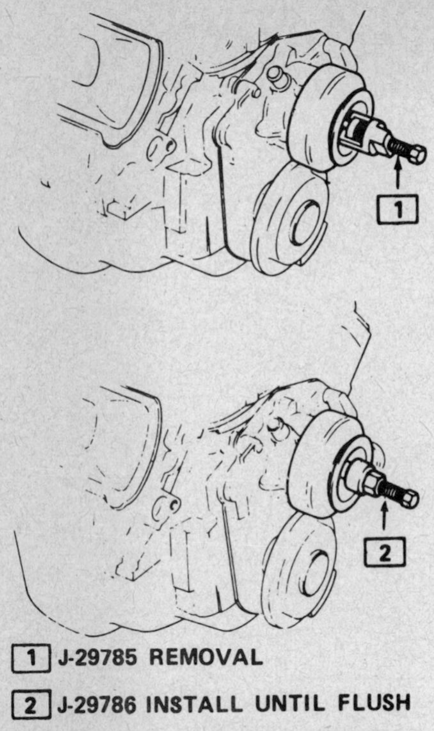

Fig. 37 Water pump pulley removal & installation

3. Disconnect heater return hose at water pump, then remove bolt retaining heater water return pipe to intake manifold and position aside.
4. Remove vacuum pump drive belt, if equipped with A/C.
5. Remove serpentine drive belt.
6. Remove alternator. Then, remove A/C compressor or vacuum pump brackets (if equipped).
7. Remove water pump attaching bolts and water pump assembly.
8. Remove water pump pulley, **Fig. 37.**
9. Reverse procedure to install.

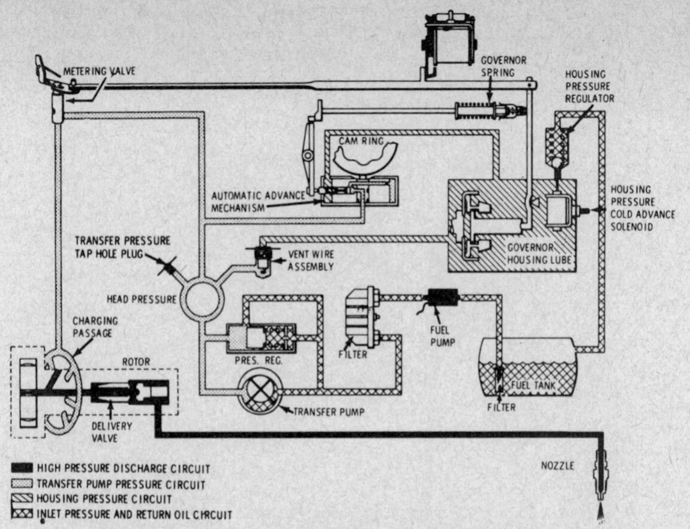

Fig. 38 Roosa-Master pump fuel flow schematic. 1982–83 shown, 1984–85 similar

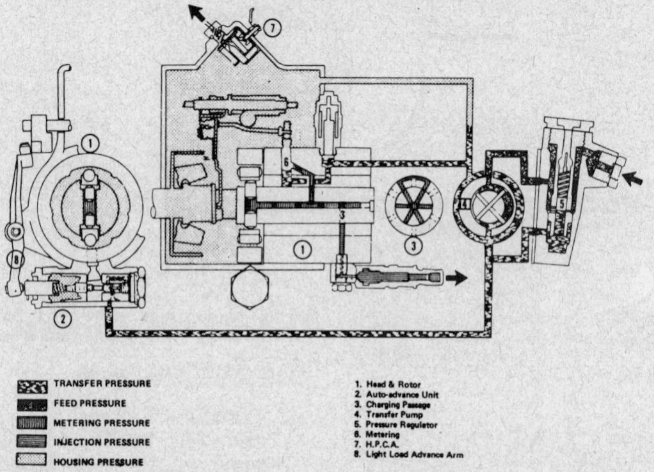

Fig. 39 CAV pump fuel flow schematic

FUEL PUMP

REPLACE

1. Ensure ignition switch is in "Off" position.
2. Remove air cleaner and disconnect 12 volt lead wire from pump.
3. Use 3/4 inch wrench to support the inlet fitting firmly, then with 5/8 inch wrench disconnect inlet tube and plug openings.
4. Repeat step three to disconnect outlet fitting. Place a suitable rag under pump outlet side to collect fuel since this line is slightly pressurized. **Do not overtwist pump outlet fitting; otherwise cover crimp may be loosened.**
5. Remove pump mounting bracket nut and pump.
6. Remove dust plugs from openings on new pump, then install pump and bracket assembly on engine. Torque pump mounting bracket nut to 18 ft. lbs. Torque inlet and outlet fuel line fittings to 19 ft. lbs. **In some instances, it may be necessary to adjust pump location by loosening the bracket screw and turning the pump to get the exact alignment between pump fittings and fuel lines. Be sure to torque bracket screw after the adjustment.**
7. After pump is installed, disconnect fuel line at fuel filter and turn ignition switch "On" in order to prime and bleed lines. Use a suitable container to catch fuel. If pump runs with a clicking sound or there are air bubbles in fuel, check for leaks in line. Check all connections to see that they are dry and that no fuel is leaking. When clicking sound disappears, tighten fuel line at filter.

BELT TENSION DATA

This engine is equipped with a serpentine drive belt that is self adjusting.

DIESEL FUEL INJECTION SYSTEM DESCRIPTION

The V6-262 diesel engine may be equipped with one of two fuel injection pumps: the Roosa Master which can be identified by a looped fuel inlet pipe, and CAV pump which can be identified by a straight fuel inlet pipe.

Injection timing is controlled by two pressure regulators. One regulator is the Housing Pressure Cold Advance (HPCA), located in the pump. The other pressure regulator, used on 1984 except California models and all 1985 models, is the Housing Pressure Altitude Advance (HPAA), located in the fuel return line. The HPCA is designed to advance injection timing about 4° during cold operation. The HPAA will regulate housing pressure according to altitude.

The Metering Valve Sensor (MVS), used on 1984 California models and all 1985 models with Diesel Electronic Control Sys-

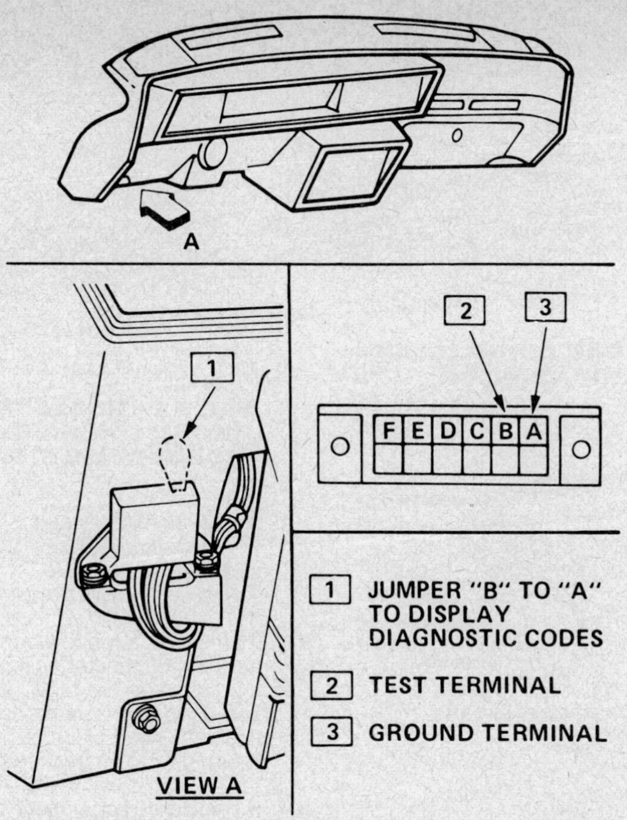

Fig. 40 Grounding ALCL diagnostic test ground terminal

tem, is a variable resistor which electronically signals the diesel ECM as to the position of the metering valve.

The injection pump is mounted on top of the engine. It is gear driven off the camshaft and turns at camshaft speed. It is a high pressure rotary pump that injects a metered amount of fuel to each cylinder at the proper time. The six high pressure delivery pipes from the pump to the injection nozzle in each cylinder are the same length to prevent any difference in timing, cylinder-to-cylinder. The fuel injection pump provides the required timing advance under all operating conditions. Engine RPM is controlled by a rotary fuel metering valve. Pushing down on the accelerator pedal moves the throttle cable to open the metering valve and allow more fuel to be delivered. The injection pump also has a low pressure transfer pump to deliver fuel from the fuel line to the high pressure pump.

The fuel filter is located between the electric fuel pump and the injection pump.

The fuel tank is at the rear of the vehicle, connected by fuel pipes and hoses to the fuel pump. Excess fuel returns from the fuel injection pump to the fuel tank through pipes and hoses.

The fuel flow schematics, **Figs. 38 and 39,** show the major components and their relationships and also provides a means of determining the differences in the two systems.

INJECTION PUMP TIMING

USING TIMING METER J-33075

Checking

1. Block drive wheels and apply parking brake.
2. Start engine, allow to reach normal operating temperature, then shut off.
3. On 1985 models, proceed as follows:
   a. Ground the instrument panel mounted Assembly Line Communication Link (ALCL) diagnostic test ground terminal, **Fig. 40.**
   b. Remove air cleaner cover, then remove MAP sensor retainer and position MAP sensor out of way with electrical connectors connected.
4. On all models, remove air cleaner assembly, then place suitable screen over intake manifold inlets. EGR valve hose must be disconnected.
5. Clean any dirt or oil from engine probe holder, crankshaft balancer rim, glow plug probe lens and lens in photoelectric pickup. **Retarded reading will result if probe of injection pump timing meter is not clean.**
6. Install RPM probe into crankshaft RPM counter.
7. Remove glow plug from number 1 cylinder, then install glow plug probe in glow plug opening. Torque probe to 8 ft. lbs.
8. Set timing meter selector to A (20), then connect meter battery leads.
9. Disconnect alternator electrical connector, then start engine and adjust engine RPM to specifications.
10. Observe timing reading at 2 minute intervals. When readings stabilize, compare to reading under "Tune Up Specifications" at beginning of chapter.
11. Disconnect timing meter, then apply suitable thread lubricant to glow plug.
12. Install glow plug and torque to 12 ft. lbs.
13. Connect alternator and install air cleaner.
14. On 1985 models, install MAP sensor and air cleaner cover, then remove jumper from ALCL.

Adjust

1. Loosen injection pump retaining nuts with tool J-25304.
2. Rotate pump to left to advance timing, and to right to retard timing.
3. Torque injection pump retaining nut to 35 ft. lbs.
4. Start engine and recheck timing as previously described. Reset as needed.

WITHOUT TIMING METER J-33075

Alignment of timing marks may be used in situations where timing meter J-33075 is not available. However for optimum engine operation, the timing should be adjusted with the meter. For adjustment of timing marks use following procedure.

1. The mark on the injection pump adapter must be aligned with the mark on the injection pump flange.
2. To adjust:
   a. Loosen the injection pump retaining nuts with tool J-25304.
   b. Align the mark on the injection pump flange with the mark on the injection pump adapter.
   c. Torque injection pump retaining nuts to 35 ft. lbs.

FUEL INJECTION PUMP HOUSING FUEL PRESSURE CHECK

1982–83

1. Remove air crossover and install screen covers J-29657 or other suitable covers.
2. On Roosa-Master pumps, remove pressure tap plug. On CAV pumps, remove torque screw, **Figs. 41 and 42.** If equipped with torque screw, to avoid disturbing adjustment add a second nut to locknut, then back out screw with nuts attached.
3. Attach low pressure gage to adapters.
4. Connect magnetic pickup tachometer.
5. With gear shift lever in park position and parking brake on, check pressure

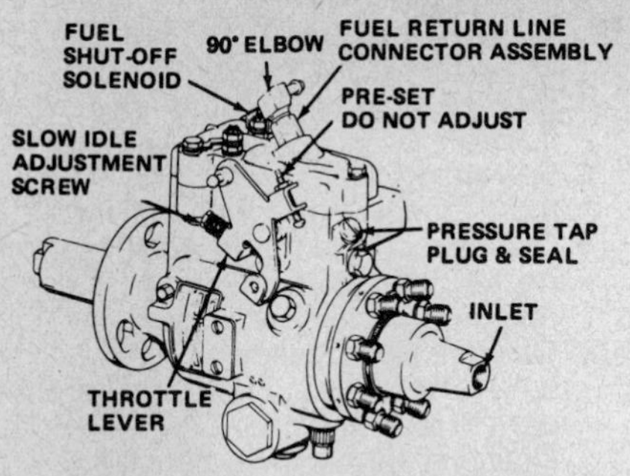

Fig. 41 Roosa-Master pump pressure tap plug location

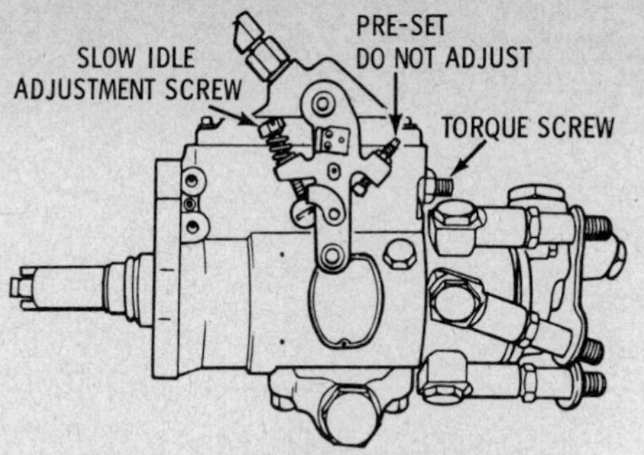

Fig. 42 CAV pump torque screw location

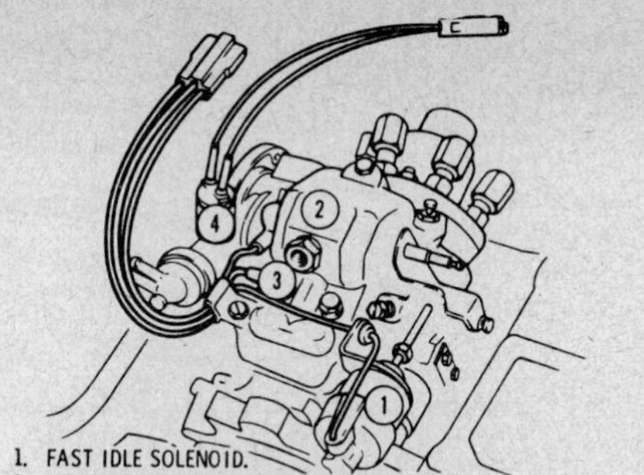

Fig. 43 Roosa Master pump solenoids and connectors location

with engine running at 1000 RPM. Pressure should be between 8-12 psi with no more than 2 psi fluctuation.

6. If pressure is at 0, check operation of housing pressure cold advance as follows:
   a. Remove electrical connector from housing pressure cold advance terminal, **Figs. 43 and 44.** If pressure remains at 0, remove injection pump cover and check operation of advance solenoid. If it is binding, repair or replace parts as necessary.
   b. If pressure is as specified with housing cold pressure advance electrical connector disconnected, check operation of temperature switch located in cylinder head bolt.
7. If pressure is not within specifications, replace fuel return line connector assembly or check for restricted HPAA, if equipped.
8. Remove tachometer, pressure gauge and adapter.
9. Install a new pressure tap plug seal on pressure tap plug and install plug into pump housing.
10. Remove screened covers and install air crossover.

1984

1. Ensure that temperature switch is functioning properly.
2. Remove air cleaner and install protective cover J-26996-1 or equivalent.
3. Disconnect fuel return line from return line connector.

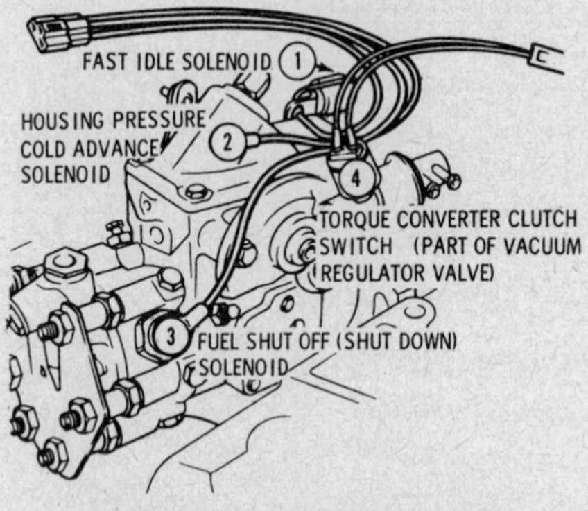

Fig. 44 CAV pump solenoids and connectors location

4. Remove return line connector from injection pump cover.
5. Push Housing Pressure Cold Advance (HPCA) solenoid plunger into solenoid.
6. Disconnect electrical connector at HPCA terminal and, using suitable jumper wire, apply 12 volts to HPCA solenoid.
7. If HPCA solenoid plunger does not extend fully, remove pump cover and repair or replace HPCA terminal.
8. Install suitable adapter in pump cover, connect return line to adapter, and attach low pressure gauge and suitable tachometer to adapter.
9. Apply parking brake, block drive wheels, place selector lever in "Park" and check pressure at 1000 RPM. Pressure should be as shown, **Fig. 45.**
10. If pressure is too low, replace fuel return line connector assembly.
11. If pressure is too high, remove return line at adapter pump and install a fitting with short piece of hose to allow return flow to empty into suitable container.
12. If pressure drops, clear restriction in fuel line.
13. If pressure does not drop in step 13, replace fuel return line connector assembly, then check timing, adjusting as necessary.
14. If pressure is still too high, repair or replace injection pump as necessary.
15. Remove tachometer, pressure gauge and adapter.
16. Using new O-ring, install fuel return line connector into pump cover.
17. Connect fuel return line to return line connector.
18. Start engine and check for leaks.
19. Remove protective cover and install air crossover.

1985

Refer to diagnostic chart, **Fig. 46,** to check housing fuel pressure. The following procedures are to be used in conjunction with letter references contained in the diagnostic chart.

	CONDITION		HPCA	HPAA	NOMINAL HOUSING PRESSURE kPa (psi)
	ALTITUDE	COOLANT			
FEDERAL PACKAGE	BELOW 1219m (4000 FT.)	COLD	ON	OFF	0
	BELOW 1219m (4000 FT.)	HOT	OFF	OFF	68.9 (10)
	ABOVE 1219m (4000 FT.)	COLD	ON	OFF	0
	ABOVE 1219m (4000 FT.)	HOT	ON	ON	48.3 (7)
ALTITUDE PACKAGE	ABOVE 1219m (4000 FT.)	COLD	ON	OFF	0
	ABOVE 1219m (4000 FT.)	HOT	OFF	OFF	68.9 (10)
	BELOW 1219m (4000 FT.)	COLD	ON	OFF	0
	BELOW 1219m (4000 FT.)	HOT	OFF	ON	89.6 (13)

HPCA = HOUSING PRESSURE COLD ADV. HPAA = HOUSING PRESSURE ALTITUDE ADV.
TIMING RETARDS WITH HIGHER HOUSING PRESSURE

Fig. 45 Injection pump housing fuel pressure specifications. 1984 models

INJECTION PUMP HOUSING PRESSURE DIAGNOSIS

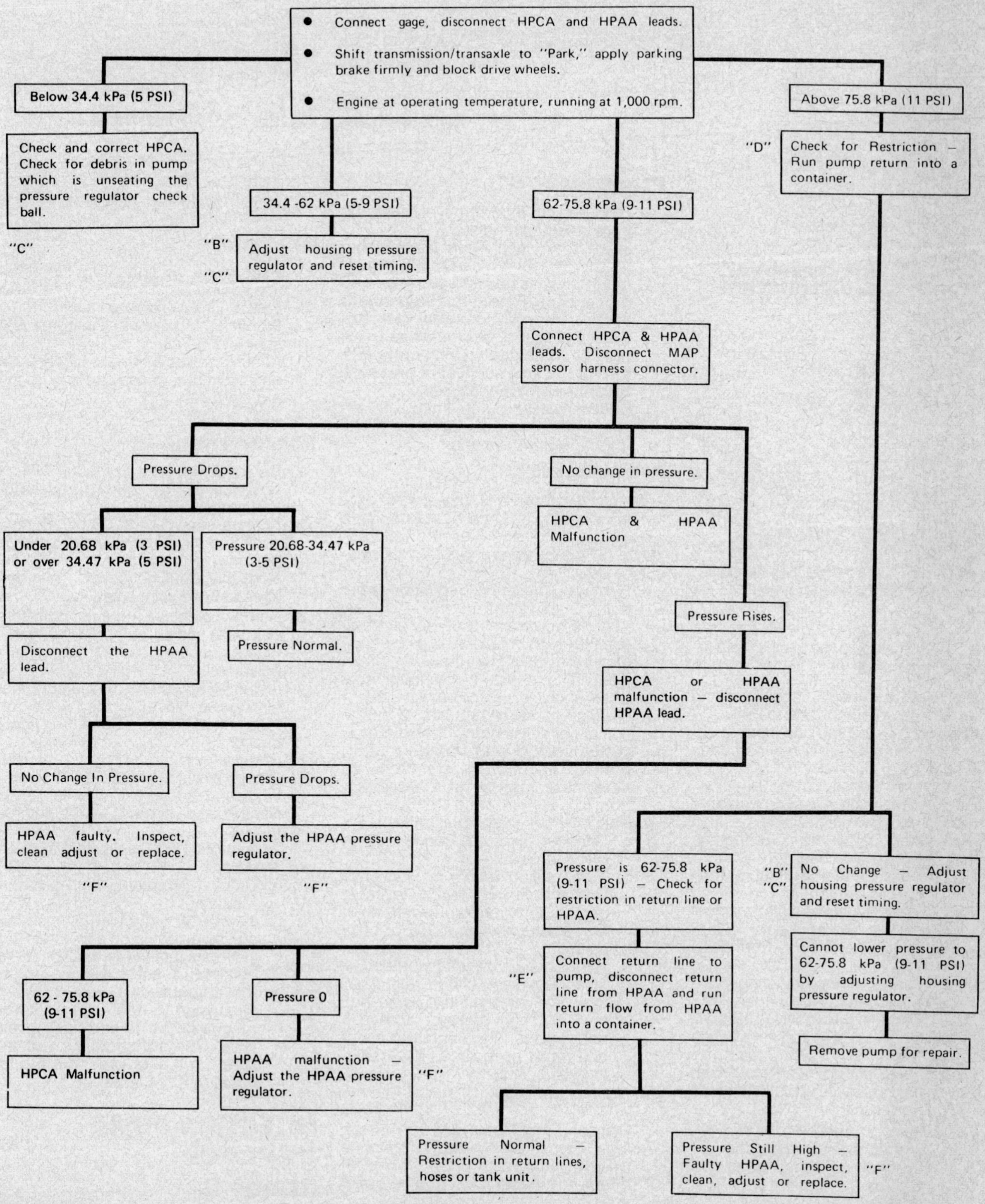

Fig. 46 Injection pump housing fuel pressure diagnostic chart. 1985 models

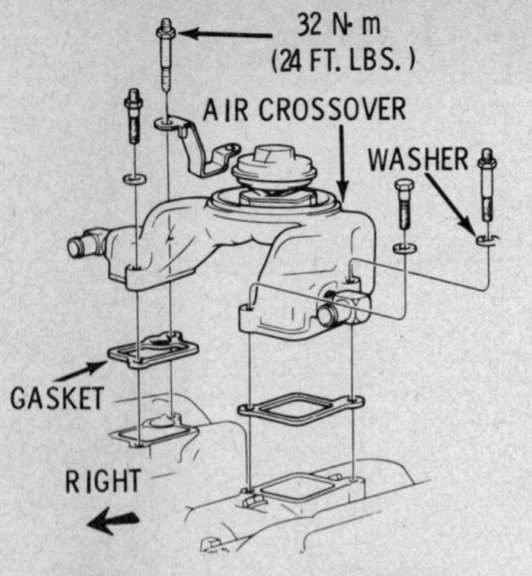

Fig. 47 Air crossover removal & installation

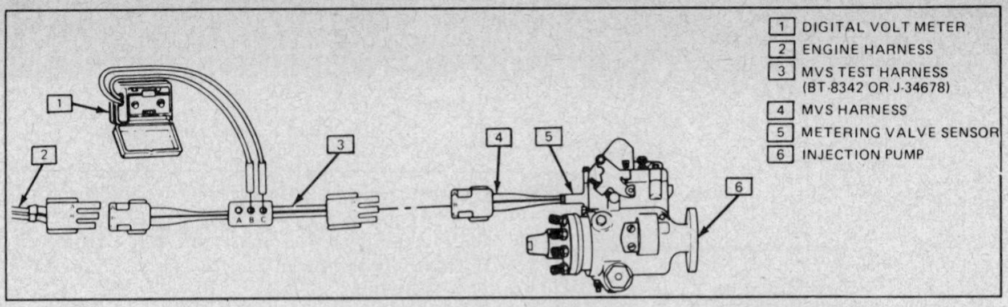

Fig. 49 MVS voltage check. 1984 models

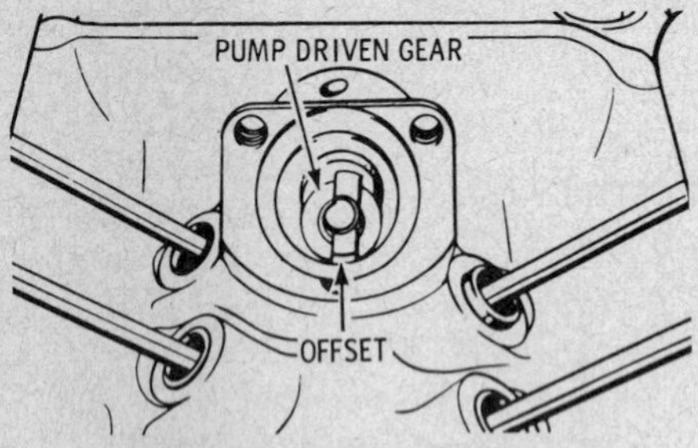

Fig. 48 Offset on fuel injection pump

Procedure "A"

1. Block drive wheels, apply parking brake and shift transaxle to Park.
2. Start engine and run until normal operating temperature is reached, then stop engine.
3. Remove air cleaner cover.
4. Remove Manifold Absolute Pressure (MAP) sensor retainer and position MAP sensor aside, leaving wiring and vacuum hose attached.
5. Remove air cleaner assembly, then the air crossover pipe.
6. On models equipped with external Exhaust Gas Recirculation (EGR), disconnect vacuum hose from EGR valve.
7. On all models, remove Metering Valve Sensor (MVS) adjustment hole plug.
8. Install washers onto tool No. J-28526, then attach a suitable pressure gauge to tool.
9. Disconnect electrical connectors from Housing Pressure Cold Advance (HPCA) solenoid.
10. Disconnect Housing Pressure Altitude Advance (HPAA) electrical connector from engine wiring harness.
11. Attach suitable tachometer to engine, then start engine.
12. Inspect for fuel leaks and correct as necessary.
13. Increase engine idle speed to 1000 RPM and note pressure reading.

Procedure "B"

1. Stop engine, then remove line fitting from pressure regulator.
2. Insert a 1/8 inch Allen wrench into pressure regulator and rotate adjustment screw as necessary to obtain 10 psi pressure. **Rotate the adjustment screw counterclockwise to decrease pressure or clockwise to increase pressure. One complete turn of the screw will alter pressure by approximately 3.2 psi.**
3. Check injection pump timing and adjust as necessary as described under "Injection Pump Timing."

Procedure "C"

If housing pressure is very low, or cannot be brought to 9-11 psi by adjusting the regulator, the Housing Pressure Cold Advance (HPCA) pressure regulator or solenoid is defective.

1. Remove pressure regulator from pump.
2. Apply a maximum of 30 psi air pressure through regulator at both ends (first from pump side, then from outlet side). The check ball should seat when applying air from outlet side.
3. Replace pressure regulator if operation is not satisfactory. **If regulator is contaminated with foreign matter, remove injection pump cover to determine source of contamination.**
4. Check HPCA solenoid as follows:
   a. Connect electrical connectors to HPCA solenoid.
   b. Turn ignition switch to Run position and ensure HPCA solenoid plunger is extended upward, then turn ignition switch to Off or Lock position.
   c. When ignition switch is turned Off, solenoid plunger should retract automatically or be able to be pushed back with light pressure applied. If not, remove injection pump cover and repair or replace HPCA solenoid as necessary.

Procedure "D"

1. Disconnect fuel return line from Housing Pressure Altitude Advance (HPAA) inlet.
2. Attach a suitable hose to pipe outlet and position opposite end of hose into a drain pan.
3. Start engine and observe pressure reading.
4. If housing pressure is now 9-11 psi, there is a restriction in HPAA solenoid assembly, hoses, tank unit, or other fuel return lines.

Procedure "E"

1. Reconnect injection pump fuel return line to Housing Pressure Altitude Advance (HPAA) solenoid inlet.
2. Disconnect fuel return line from HPAA solenoid outlet.
3. Attach a suitable hose to HPAA outlet and position opposite end of hose into a drain pan.
4. Start engine.

Procedure "F"

1. Remove Housing Pressure Altitude Advance (HPAA) solenoid assembly from engine.
2. Apply a maximum of 30 psi air pressure through both sides of solenoid (first from pump side, then from outlet side). If air does not flow freely in both directions, replace solenoid.
3. Remove pressure regulator from solenoid and check solenoid plunger. If plunger does not move freely, replace solenoid.
4. Install HPAA solenoid assembly, then disconnect electrical connector from Manifold Absolute Pressure (MAP) sensor.
5. Start engine and observe housing pressure, which should be 3-5 psi.
6. If housing pressure is not within specifications, adjust pressure regulator as follows:
   a. Remove HPAA assembly from engine.
   b. Remove line fitting from pressure regulator.
   c. Insert a 1/8 inch Allen wrench into pressure regulator and rotate adjustment screw as necessary to obtain 3-5 psi pressure. **Rotate the adjustment screw counterclockwise to decrease pressure or clockwise to increase pressure. One complete turn of the screw will alter pressure by approximately 3.2 psi.**

INJECTION PUMP REPLACE

REMOVAL

1. Remove air cleaner assembly.
2. Remove crankcase ventilation filter and pipes from valve cover and air crossover.

MVS VOLTAGE TABLE

V-REF	4.5	4.6	4.7	4.8	4.9	5.0	5.1	5.2	5.3	5.4	5.5
MVS VOLTAGE (IN "0" 650 RPM)	.53–.55	.54–.56	.55–.57	.57–.59	.58–.60	.59–.61	.60–.62	.61–.63	.63–.65	.64–.66	.65–.67

Fig. 50 MVS voltage chart

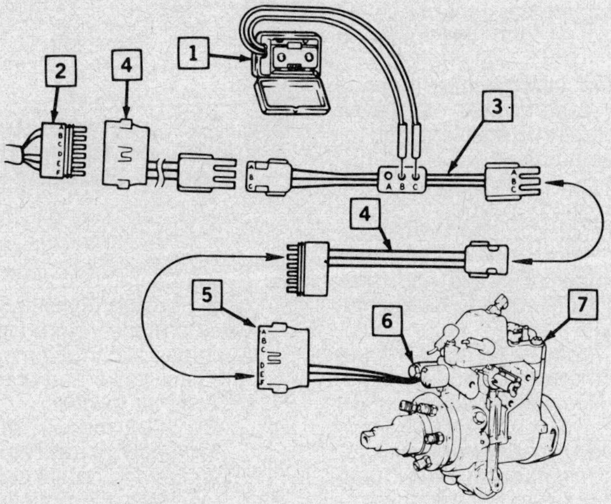

1. DIGITAL VOLTMETER
2. ENGINE HARNESS
3. MVS TEST HARNESS (BT-8342 OR J-34678)
4. MVS ADAPTER HARNESS (BT-8342-10 OR J-34678-50)
5. MVS HARNESS
6. METERING VALVE SENSOR (MVS)
7. INJECTION PUMP

Fig. 51 MVS voltage check. 1985 models

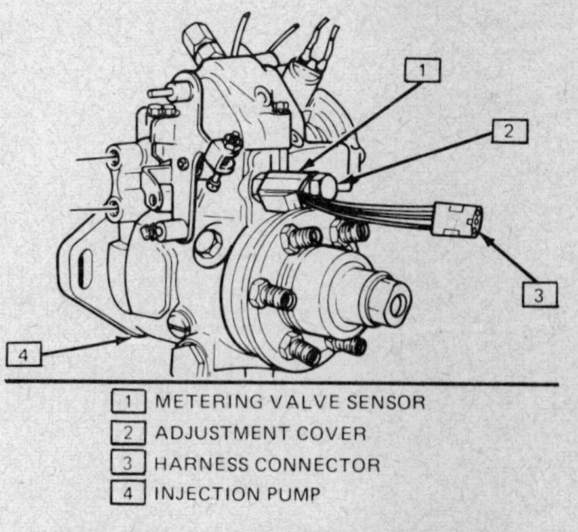

Fig. 52 MVS assembly

3. Remove air crossover, **Fig. 47**, and install suitable intake screen covers.
4. Remove fuel lines, filter and fuel pump as an assembly. Plug all openings.
5. Remove throttle and T.V. cables from intake manifold brackets and position aside.
6. Disconnect fuel return line from injection pump.
7. Disconnect injection line clamps that are closest to the pump.
8. Disconnect injection lines from pump and plug all openings. Then carefully reposition lines to gain enough clearance to remove pump.
9. Remove two bolts retaining injection pump.
10. Remove pump and discard pump to adapter O-ring.

INSTALLATION

1. Position No. 1 cylinder at firing position by aligning mark on balance with zero mark on indicator located at front of engine.
2. Align offset tang on pump drive shaft with pump driven gear, **Fig. 48.**
3. Install new pump to adapter O-ring, then install pump.
4. If a new intermediate adapter is installed, set injection pump at center of slots in pump mounting flange. If original intermediate adapter is being used, align pump timing mark with mark on intermediate adapter. Install two bolts and washers retaining pump and torque bolts to 35-37 ft. lbs.
5. Reverse steps 1 through 8 of removal procedure for remainder of installation. If necessary adjust T.V. cable, pump timing, vacuum regulator valve or idle speed.

METERING VALVE SENSOR (MVS)

CHECKING

1984

1. Block drive wheels and apply parking brake.
2. Start engine, allow it to reach normal operating temperature, then shut off.
3. Remove air cleaner and air crossover assembly, then place suitable screens over intake manifold openings, **Fig. 47.**
4. Disconnect MVS harness connector and install tool BT-8342 or T-34678 as shown, **Fig. 49.**
5. Install suitable tachometer.
6. Torque MVS assembly attaching bolts to 30 inch lbs. before attempting to check or adjust voltage.
7. Start engine in park, then raise engine speed to 1500 RPM for 10-20 seconds to stabilize fuel flow.
8. Return engine to idle and shift transmission to drive.
9. Set engine speed to 650 RPM.
10. Using suitable multi-meter set at 20 volt scale, measure V-REF voltage between terminals A and C, **Fig. 49.**
11. Measure MVS voltage between terminals B and C for given engine load.
12. Shift transmission into park, then compare voltage recorded in steps 10 and 11 with chart in **Fig. 50.**
13. Measure the voltage between terminals B and C as the throttle is moved from idle to wide open position. Voltage should range from zero to over 4 volts.
14. If MVS voltage is within specifications in steps 12 and 13, sensor is operating correctly. If not as specified, refer to "Adjust" procedure.
15. Connect MVS connectors, then start engine and adjust idle speed to specifications.
16. Remove screens from intake manifold openings, then install air crossover and air cleaner assembly, **Fig. 47.**

1985

1. Perform steps 1 and 2 as described for 1984.
2. Remove air cleaner cover, then the MAP sensor retainer, and position MAP sensor out of way with electrical connectors and vacuum hose attached.
3. Remove air cleaner assembly and the air crossover, disconnect vacuum hose to EGR valve and install suitable screened covers in intake manifold openings.

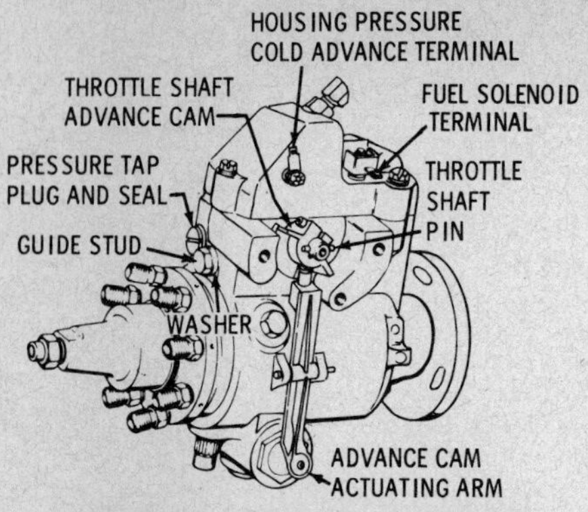

Fig. 53 Roosa-Master pump right side view

4. Disconnect electrical connector at HPAA solenoid.
5. Connect MVS test harness as shown, **Fig. 51.**
6. Install suitable tachometer.
7. Perform steps 7 through 14 as described for 1984, referring to **Fig. 51** instead of **Fig. 49.**
8. Connect HPAA solenoid connector and MVS connectors, then install air crossover, MAP sensor and air cleaner and connect EGR vacuum hose.

ADJUST

1984

1. With engine shut off, remove MVS hole plug, **Fig. 52.**
2. Using a file, resize metering valve sensor adjuster tool J-24182-2 so it enters into the MVS.
3. Turn the MVS adjustment screw clockwise to increase the voltage reading and counterclockwise to decrease voltage reading.
4. Install MVS hole plug finger tight, then proceed to steps 7 through 12 in MVS "Checking."
5. If voltage reading is not within chart specifications, readjust the MVS as necessary.
6. When the MVS voltage reading is within specifications, install MVS hole plug using new O-ring. Torque plug to 30 inch lbs.

1985

1. Shut off engine, then remove MVS adjusting hole plug, being careful not to move MVS assembly while removing cap nut.
2. Turn adjustment screw clockwise to increase voltage reading or counterclockwise to reduce voltage reading. Adjust in 1/8 turn increments.
3. Install adjusting hole plug finger tight.
4. Perform steps 7 through 12 in MVS "Checking," "1984."
5. If MVS voltage reading is not within specifications, readjust MVS as necessary.
6. When voltage reading is within specifications, install adjusting hole plug with new O-ring, torquing to 30 inch lbs.
7. Connect MVS connector, then start engine and check for leaks.
8. Install air crossover and air cleaner assembly.

INJECTION NOZZLES

REPLACE

1. Remove fuel lines, using a backup wrench on upper injection nozzle hex.
2. Plug nozzle and lines to prevent damage or contamination, then remove nozzles by applying torque to largest nozzle hex.
3. When working on rear bank, it may be necessary to perform the following procedures:
   a. Rotate the intermediate steering shaft so steering gear stub shaft clamp bolt is in up position, then remove clamp bolt.
   b. Disconnect intermediate shaft from stub shaft.
   c. Remove engine support strut.
   d. Place a floor jack under front crossmember of cradle and raise jack until it just starts to raise vehicle.
   e. Remove front two body mount bolts with lower cushions and retainers. Remove cushions from bolts.
   f. Thread body mount bolts with retainers a minimum of three turns into cage nuts so that the bolts restrain cradle movement.
   g. Release floor jack slowly until crossmember contacts body mount bolt retainers. As jack is being lowered watch and correct any interference with hose, lines, pipes and cables. **Do not lower cradle without it being restrained as possible damage may occur to the body and underhood items.**
4. Remove copper nozzle gasket from cylinder head if gasket did not remain on nozzle.
5. Reverse procedure to install. Apply suitable lubricant to nozzle threads, then torque nozzles to 25 ft. lbs. When tightening nozzle, torque must be applied to largest nozzle hex. Torque fuel line to 25 ft. lbs. using a backup wrench on upper injection nozzle hex. **Failure to apply the correct lubricant can cause engine damage. Use lubricant No. 9985462 or equivalent.**

VACUUM REGULATOR VALVE

REPLACE

1. Note location of valve vacuum hoses, then disconnect vacuum hoses.
2. Remove two valve attaching bolts, then valve.
3. Reverse procedure to install.

ROOSA-MASTER PUMP ON VEHICLE SERVICE

THROTTLE SHAFT SEAL, REPLACE

1. Disconnect battery ground cable.
2. Remove air cleaner and air crossover, **Fig. 47**, then install air screens.

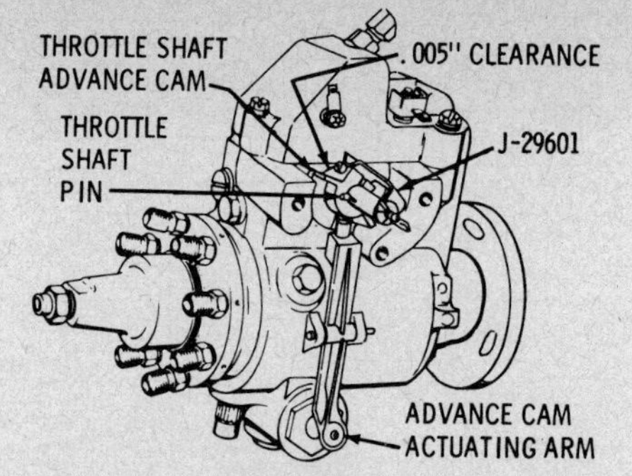

Fig. 54 Installation of tool J-29601 on injection pump. Roosa-Master pump

3. Disconnect injection pump fuel solenoid, housing pressure cold advance wires and fuel return pipe, **Fig. 53.**
4. Scribe an alignment mark on vacuum regulator valve and pump body, then proceed as follows:
   a. On 1982 models, remove throttle rod, vacuum regulator valve, return spring and detent cable.
   b. On 1983-85 models, remove vacuum regulator valve, then disconnect throttle and T.V. cables and return springs.
5. Place tool J-29601 over throttle shaft and pin, then position spring clip of tool over throttle shaft advance cam and tighten wing nut. Without loosening wing nut, pull tool off shaft. This will provide proper alignment during reassembly, **Fig. 54.**
6. Drive pin from throttle shaft and remove shaft advance cam and fiber washer. Remove any burrs from shaft which may have resulted from pin removal.
7. Clean injection pump cover, upper portion of pump, throttle shaft and guide stud area. Position several shop cloths in engine valley area to absorb fuel.
8. On 1984 California models only, remove MVS.
9. On all models, remove injection pump cover screws, then cover. **Use care to avoid any foreign matter from entering pump when cover is removed. If any object or foreign matter enter pump, it must be removed before engine is started as injection pump damage or engine damage may occur.**
10. Note position of metering valve spring before removal as its position must be duplicated exactly during reassembly, **Fig. 55.**
11. Remove guide stud and washer, noting parts before removal.
12. Rotate min-max governor assembly up for clearance then remove it, **Fig. 55.** If idle governor spring becomes disengaged from throttle block, it must be reinstalled with tightly wound coils toward throttle block.
13. Remove throttle shaft assembly and inspect shaft for unusual wear or damage, replace if necessary. It may

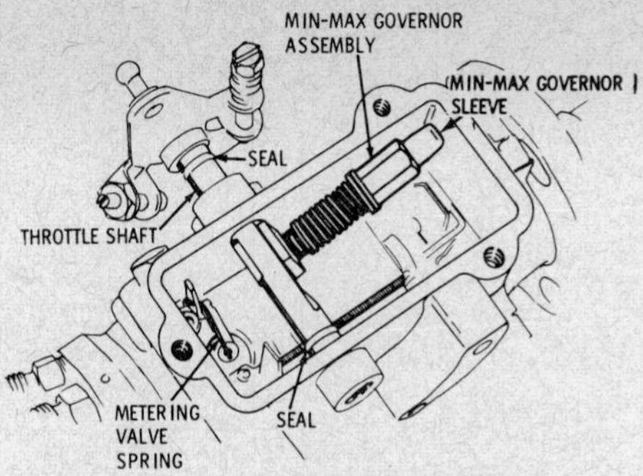

Fig. 55 Roosa-Master pump with cover removed

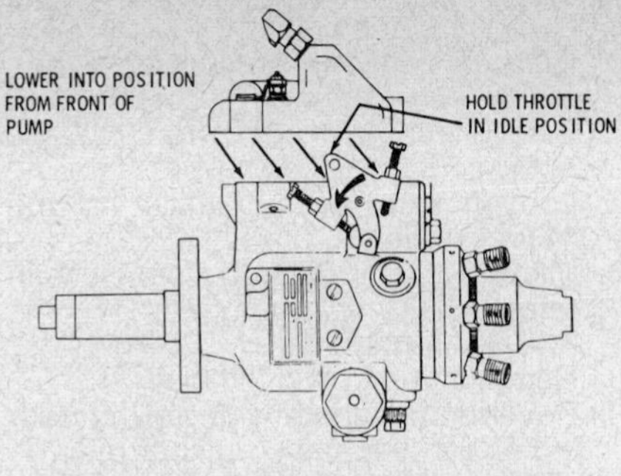

Fig. 56 Installation of pump cover. Roosa-Master pump

1. FUEL RETURN PIPE
2. CLIP
3. FULLY DRIVEN, SEATED & NOT STRIPPED
4. HOUSING PRESSURE ALTITUDE ADVANCE SOLENOID
5. 13 N·m (9.5 LBS. FT.)

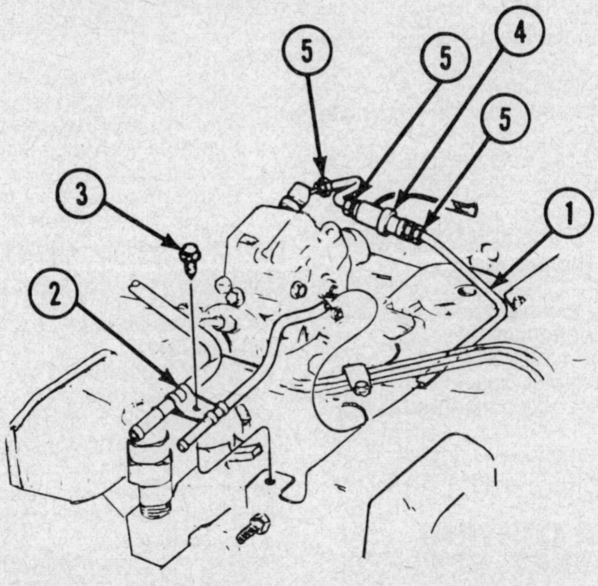

Fig. 57 HPAA removal & installation

be necessary to loosen nuts at injection pump mounting flange and rotate pump slightly to allow throttle shaft to clear intake manifold.

14. Inspect throttle shaft bushings in pump housing for damage or unusual wear. If replacement of bushings is necessary, it must be performed by a qualified repair facility.
15. Remove throttle shaft seals. Do not cut seals to remove, as any nicks in the seal seat will cause leakage.
16. Install new shaft seals, lubricated with chassis grease. Use care to avoid cutting seals on sharp edges of shaft.
17. Carefully slide throttle shaft into pump to point where min-max governor assembly will slide back onto throttle shaft, **Fig. 55.**
18. Rotate min-max governor assembly downward, then hold in position and slide throttle shaft and governor into position.
19. Install new fiber washer, throttle shaft advance cam (do not tighten screw at this time) and a new throttle shaft drive pin, **Fig. 53.**
20. Align throttle shaft advance cam so tool J-20601 can be installed over throttle shaft, pins in slots and spring clip over advance cam.
21. Insert a .005 inch feeler gauge between cam and fiber washer, then tighten cam screw and remove tool J-29601.
22. Install guide stud with new washer, assuring that upper extension of metering valve spring slides on top of guide stud. Torque guide studs to 85 inch lbs. **Over torquing may strip the aluminum threads in the housing.**
23. Hold throttle in idle position and install new pump cover seal. Making sure that screws are not in cover, position cover above 1/4 inch forward toward shaft end and about 1/8 inch above pump, **Fig. 56.** Move cover rearward and downward into position, using care to avoid cutting seal, then reinstall cover screws. Each screw must have a flat washer and internal lock washer, with flat washer against pump cover. Torque screws to 33 inch lbs. and install vacuum regulator.
24. On 1984 California models only, install the MVS using a new O-ring. Coat the threads using a suitable sealer and torque to 30 inch lbs.
25. On all models, reconnect both battery ground cables, then turn ignition switch to run position and touch pink solenoid wire to solenoid. A clicking noise should be heard as the wire is connected and disconnected. If not, the linkage may be jammed in the wide open position and the engine must not be started. Proceed to step 26. If clicking is heard, connect pump solenoid and housing pressure cold advance wires and proceed to step 26.
26. Remove cover, then ground solenoid lead (opposite hot lead) and connect pink wire. With ignition switch in run position, the solenoid in the cover should move the linkage. If not, the solenoid must be replaced. Minimum voltage across solenoid terminals must be 12 volts. Reinstall cover and repeat step 25.
27. Install throttle cable bracket, throttle rod, throttle cable and return springs. Make sure timing marks on pump and adapter are aligned and make sure nuts retaining pump are tight. Install fuel return pipe.
28. Start engine and check for fuel leaks. **Rough idle may be due to air in the pump. Allow sufficient time for air to purge by allowing engine to idle. It may be necessary to turn engine off to allow air bubbles to rise to top of pump where they will be purged.**
29. Adjust Vacuum Regulator Valve or MVS if equipped, then remove intake manifold screens and install air crossover and air cleaner, **Fig. 47.**

PUMP COVER SEAL AND/OR GUIDE STUD, REPLACE

1. Disconnect battery ground cable.
2. Remove air cleaner and air crossover, **Fig. 47,** and install air screen J-29657.
3. Disconnect injection pump fuel solenoid, housing pressure cold advance wires and fuel return pipe.
4. Clean injection pump cover, upper portion of pump and guide stud area. Position shop cloths to absorb fuel.
5. Remove injection pump cover screws, then cover. **Use care to avoid any foreign matter from entering pump when cover is removed. If any object or foreign matter enter pump, it must be removed before starting engine as injection pump damage or engine damage may occur.**

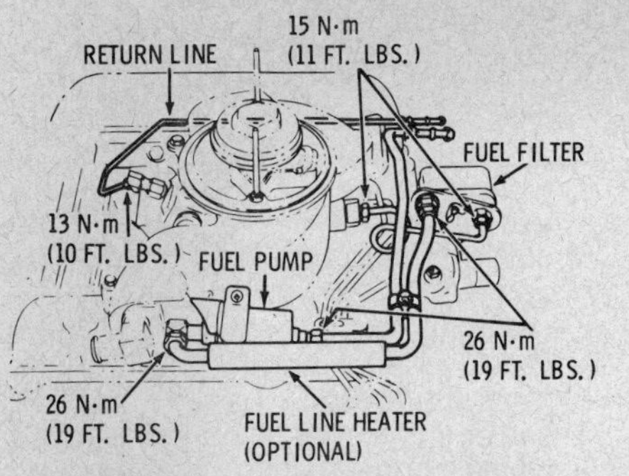

Fig. 58 CAV pump fuel inlet pipe removal

6. Note position of metering valve spring before removal as its position must be duplicated exactly during reassembly, **Fig. 55.**
7. Remove guide stud and washer, noting location of parts before removal.
8. Refer to steps 21 thru 27 under "Throttle Shaft Seal, Replace" procedure for reassembly of "Pump Cover Seal And/Or Guide Stud."

METERING VALVE SENSOR (MVS), REPLACE

1. Remove air cleaner and air crossover, **Fig. 47,** then install cover J-29657.
2. Disconnect sensor electrical connector, then remove sensor from pump, **Fig. 52.**
3. Install new O-ring on sensor, then coat threads with suitable sealer. Torque sensor to 30 inch lbs.
4. Remove cover J-29657, then install air cleaner and air crossover.

HOUSING PRESSURE COLD ADVANCE (HPCA) & SHUTDOWN SOLENOID, REPLACE

1. Remove pump cover.
2. Remove terminal contact nuts, then remove solenoid from cover noting position of any insulating washers.
3. Place solenoid in cover ensuring that shut-off solenoid linkage is free. Also, check that housing pressure cold advance solenoid plunger is centered so that it will contact fitting check ball, **Fig. 43.**
4. Place insulator washers on terminal studs and install terminal nuts. Torque nuts to 10-15 inch lbs. and replace pump cover.

HOUSING PRESSURE ALTITUDE ADVANCE (HPAA), REPLACE

Refer to **Fig. 57** for removal and installation procedures.

ALTITUDE FUEL LIMITER (AFL), REPLACE

1. Disconnect battery ground cable.
2. Remove air cleaner assembly and air crossover, then install suitable screened covers on manifold.
3. Disconnect AFL electrical wiring harness from engine wiring harness.
4. Remove pump cover.
5. Remove sufficient amount of fuel so fuel level is below AFL opening.
6. Disconnect AFL shaft from linkage hook.
7. Loosen AFL locknut while holding AFL assembly.
8. Mark AFL to facilitate assembly, then remove AFL, noting number of turns required for removal.
9. Remove O-ring and locknut.
10. Reverse procedure to install, threading AFL in the same number of turns required for removal, and align mark made during disassembly. Torque locknut to 85 inch lbs. while holding AFL in position.

CAV PUMP ON VEHICLE SERVICE

END PLATE ACCESS PLUG OR STOP PLUG WASHER, REPLACE

1. Remove air cleaner and install cover J-26996-1 or equivalent.
2. Clean any dirt from area.
3. Remove stop plug and/or end plate plug and discard washers.
4. Reverse procedure to install. Torque stop plug to 80 inch lbs. and end plate to 43 ft. lbs.

FUEL INLET CONNECTION WASHER, REPLACE

1. Remove air cleaner and install cover J-26996-1 or equivalent.
2. Clean any dirt from area.
3. Remove fuel inlet pipe, **Fig. 58.**
4. Remove inlet connection and discard washer.
5. Reverse procedure to install. Using new washer, install inlet to pump and torque to 33 ft. lbs.

GOVERNOR CONTROL COVER GASKET, REPLACE

1. Remove air crossover, **Fig. 47,** and install cover J-29657.
2. Clean any dirt from injection pump cover and upper area of pump.
3. Place several rags in engine valley to catch spilled fuel.
4. Remove fuel return pipe.
5. Remove control cover screws and cover, **Fig. 59,** discarding washers and gasket. **Extreme care must be exercised to keep foreign material out of the pump when the cover is off. If any objects are dropped into the pump, they must be removed before the engine is started or injection pump or engine damage may occur.**
6. Reverse procedure to install. Torque screws to 25 inch lbs.

HOUSING PRESSURE COLD ADVANCE SOLENOID, REPLACE

1. Remove governor control cover, see "Governor Control Cover Gasket, Replace."

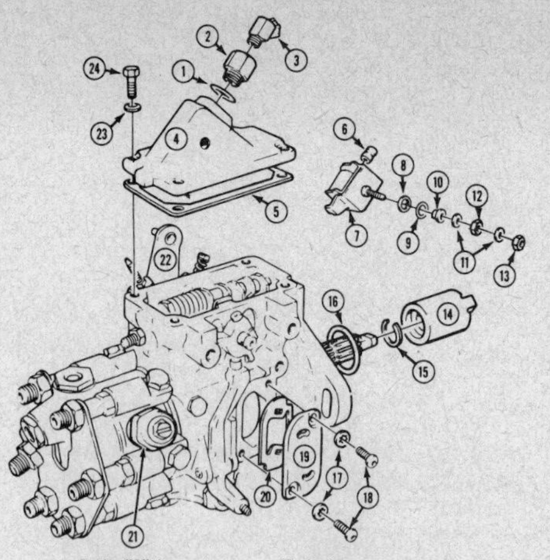

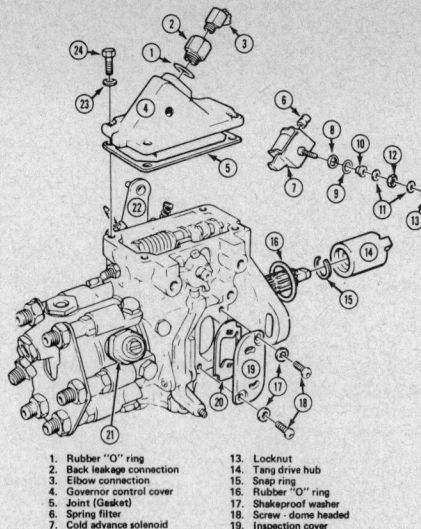

1. Rubber "O" ring
2. Back leakage connection
3. Elbow connection
4. Governor control cover
5. Joint (Gasket)
6. Spring filter
7. Cold advance solenoid
8. Backing washer
9. Rubber "O" ring
10. Insulating washer
11. Plain washer
12. Nut
13. Locknut
14. Tang drive hub
15. Snap ring
16. Rubber "O" ring
17. Shakeproof washer
18. Screw - dome headed
19. Inspection cover
20. Rubber sealing joint (Gasket)
21. Stop solenoid
22. Throttle lever
23. Shakeproof washer
24. Hexagon socket screw

Fig. 59 Exploded view of CAV pump

2. Remove solenoid terminal nut, spring filter, insulating washers and solenoid, **Fig. 59.** Discard gasket.
3. Reverse procedure to install. Torque terminal nut to 20 in. lbs. and ensure solenoid is centered in cover.

INSPECTION COVER PLATE GASKET, REPLACE

1. Remove air cleaner and install cover J-26996-1.
2. Place several shop rags in engine valley to catch spilled fuel.
3. Scribe a line on the vacuum regulator valve and pump body so valve can be reinstalled without readjusting.
4. Remove vacuum regulator valve from pump, then clean dirt from inspection plate area.
5. Remove inspection plate retaining screws, then inspection plate and gasket.
6. Reverse procedure to install. Using new gasket, torque inspection plate retaining screws to 20 inch lbs.

STOP SOLENOID, REPLACE

1. Remove air cleaner and install cover J-26996-1
2. Clean dirt from area around solenoid.
3. Remove electrical lead.
4. Remove solenoid and O-ring, **Fig. 59.** Discard O-ring.
5. Reverse procedure to install. Torque solenoid to 130 inch lbs.

THROTTLE SHAFT SEAL, REPLACE

1. Remove air crossover and install cover J-29657 or equivalent.
2. Disconnect fuel return pipe, then remove governor control cover screws and cover.
3. Remove fast idle solenoid and vacuum regulator valve.
4. Disconnect throttle cable and T.V. cable.

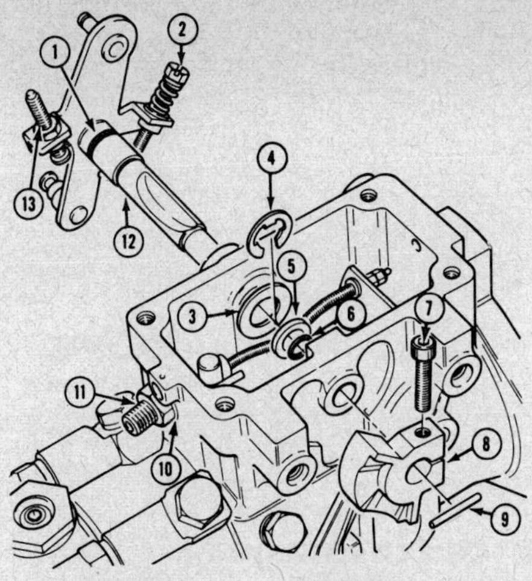

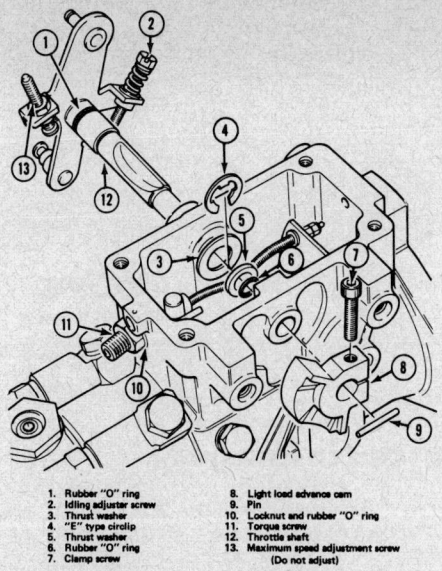

1. Rubber "O" ring
2. Idling adjuster screw
3. Thrust washer
4. "E" type circlip
5. Thrust washer
6. Rubber "O" ring
7. Clamp screw
8. Light load advance cam
9. Pin
10. Locknut and rubber "O" ring
11. Torque screw
12. Throttle shaft
13. Maximum speed adjustment screw (Do not adjust)

Fig. 60 Throttle shaft and seals. CAV pump

5. Disconnect throttle return spring.
6. Install tool J-29601 or equivalent over throttle shaft with slots of tool engaging vacuum regulator valve lock pin. Place spring clip of tool over throttle shaft advance cam and tighten wing nut. Without loosening wing nut, pull tool off of shaft.
7. Remove lock pin from throttle shaft, **Fig. 60.**
8. Remove roll pin from pump housing and remove governor support rod.
9. Tilt governor carrier assembly by lifting end nearest drive end of pump and remove carrier from pump housing.
10. Remove clamping screw from light load cam, then remove cam.
11. Remove E-clip from throttle shaft, then remove throttle shaft from pump.
12. Remove and discard O-rings.
13. Check throttle shaft assembly and governor housing bores for damage and wear and replace as necessary.
14. Lubricate shaft and O-rings with oil and assemble larger O-rings onto shaft.
15. Install throttle shaft into housing until thrust washers can be installed onto shaft in original positions. Install smaller O-ring onto shaft.
16. Assemble light load advance cam onto shaft and install but do not tighten clamping screw.
17. Install E-clip into throttle shaft recess. If new throttle shaft is installed, shaft endplay must be checked and adjusted by selective fitting of thrust washers. Throttle shaft endplay should be .006-.012 inch.
18. Install new pin onto head of shaft. Align throttle shaft advance cam until tool J-29601 or equivalent can be installed over throttle shaft. Tighten cam screw, then remove tool J-29601.
19. Rotate throttle lever forwards to the drive end of pump. Install governor carrier assembly onto pump housing and engage lug on underside of throttle block with cut away notch in throttle shaft.
20. Lubricate governor support rod and new O-ring, then install O-ring onto support rod using tool J-33096 or equivalent.

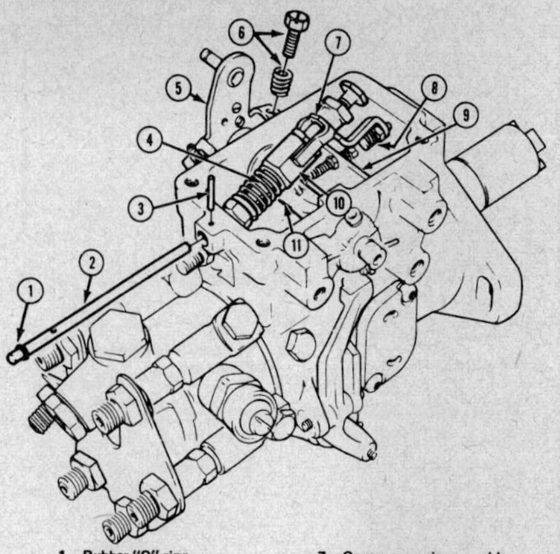

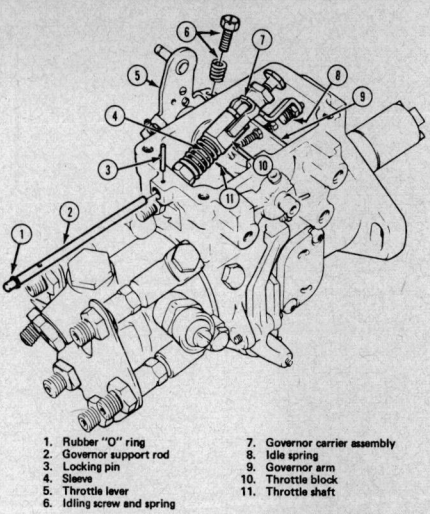

1. Rubber "O" ring
2. Governor support rod
3. Locking pin
4. Sleeve
5. Throttle lever
6. Idling screw and spring
7. Governor carrier assembly
8. Idle spring
9. Governor arm
10. Throttle block
11. Throttle shaft

Fig. 61 Governor assembly. CAV pump

21. Insert plain end of rod through rear of governor housing and into carrier assembly sleeve.
22. Install support rod into housing and install new locking pin, **Fig. 61.**
23. Install governor cover and fuel return pipe.
24. Install throttle return springs and connect throttle cable.
25. Connect TV detent cable.
26. Install vacuum regulator valve and fast idle solenoid.
27. Start engine and check for leaks. Install air crossover and air cleaner.

Clutch & Manual Transaxle Section

INDEX

CLUTCH PEDAL

ADJUST

1982–86

The clutch is automatically adjusted by a self-adjusting mechanism, **Fig. 1,** mounted to the clutch pedal and bracket assembly. The cable is a fixed length cable and cannot be shortened or lengthened, however, the position of the cable can be changed by adjusting the position of the quadrant in relation to the clutch pedal. The self-adjusting mechanism monitors clutch cable tension and adjusts the quadrant position, changing the effective cable length.

Inspection

1. With engine running and service and parking brakes applied, depress clutch pedal to approximately $1/2$ inch from floor mat.
2. Move shift lever between "First" and "Reverse" gears several times. If no

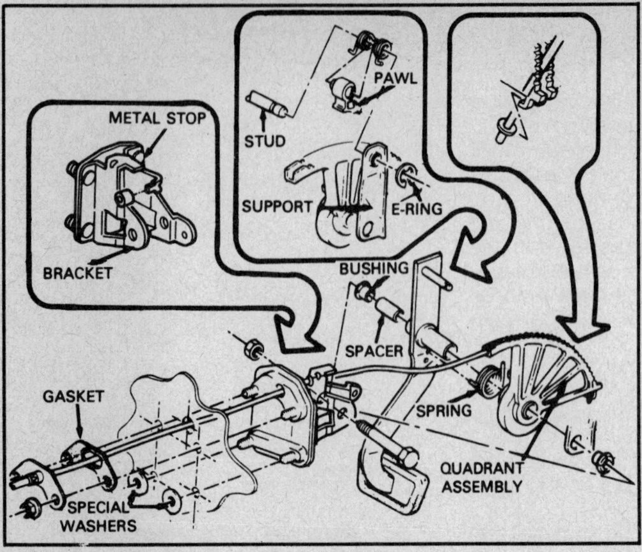

Fig. 1 Clutch self-adjusting mechanism

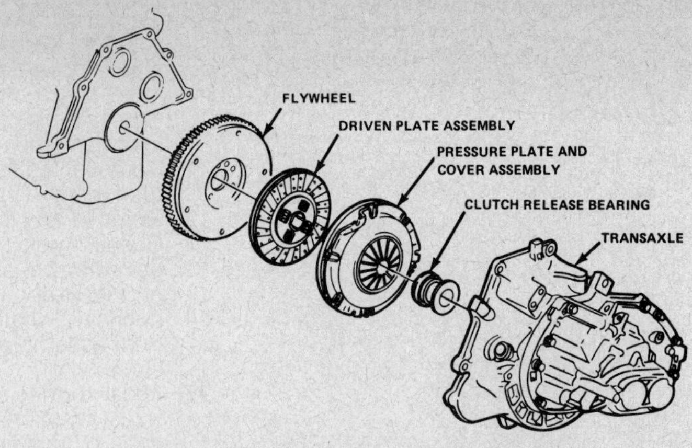

Fig. 2 Clutch assembly

clashing of the gears occur when going into "Reverse", the clutch is releasing fully.

3. If the shifting in Step 2 is not smooth, the clutch is not releasing fully and the linkage should be inspected and corrected as necessary.
4. Check clutch pedal bushings for sticking or excessive wear.
5. Have an assistant depress the clutch pedal to the floor and observe clutch fork lever travel at transaxle. The end of the clutch fork lever should have a total travel of approximately 1.5-1.7 inches.
6. To check the self-adjusting mechanism, proceed as follows:
   a. Depress the clutch pedal and observe if the pawl firmly engages the teeth of the quadrant.
   b. Release the clutch pedal and observe if the pawl is lifted off the quadrant teeth by the stop on the bracket.

1987–88

A hydraulic clutch operating mechanism in used on these models which provides automatic clutch adjustment. No adjustment of the clutch linkage or pedal position is required.

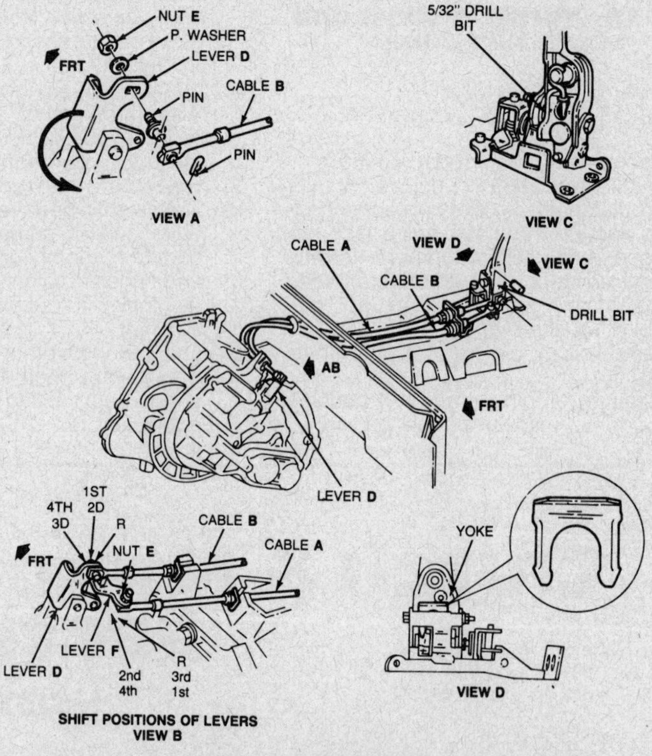

Fig. 3 Manual transaxle shift cable adjustment

CLUTCH REPLACE

1. On 1982-86 models, disconnect clutch cable from clutch release lever and transaxle as follows:
   a. Support clutch pedal upward against bumper stop to release pawl from quadrant.
   b. Disconnect cable from clutch release lever on transaxle. Use care to avoid cable from snapping toward rear of vehicle.
   c. Disconnect cable from quadrant. Lift the locking pawl away from quadrant, then slide cable out on right side.
2. On 1987-88 models, proceed as follows:
   a. Remove hush panel from inside of vehicle.
   b. Disconnect clutch master cylinder push rod from clutch pedal.
3. On all models, remove transaxle as described under "Manual Transaxle, Replace."
4. Mark position of pressure plate to flywheel to aid reassembly.
5. Gradually loosen pressure plate attaching bolts until spring pressure is relieved.
6. Support pressure plate and remove mounting bolts, pressure plate and driven disc, **Fig. 2.**
7. Clean pressure and flywheel mounting surfaces. Inspect bearing retainer outer surface of transaxle.
8. Place driven disc in relative installed position and support with a dummy shaft. **The driven disc is installed with the damper springs offset toward the transaxle. Stamped letters found on the driven disc identify the "Flywheel Side."**
9. Install and gradually tighten the pressure plate to flywheel bolts. Remove dummy shaft.
10. Lubricate the release bearing outside diameter groove and the inside diameter recess.
11. Install transaxle.

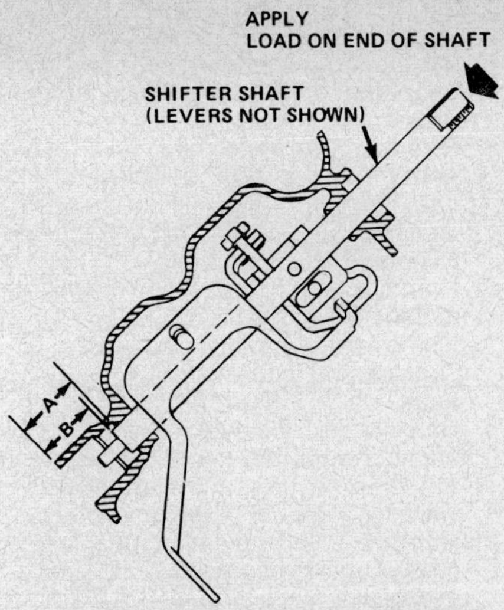

Fig. 4 Manual transaxle shifter shaft selective washer measurement

MANUAL TRANSAXLE SHIFT CABLE

ADJUST

1. Disconnect battery ground cable.
2. Shift transaxle into first gear.
3. Loosen shift cable attaching nuts "E" on transaxle lever "D" and "F," **Fig. 3.**
4. Remove console trim plate, then slide shifter boot up shifter handle and remove console.
5. Insert a yoke clip to hold lever as shown in view "D," **Fig. 3.**
6. Insert 5/32 inch or No. 22 drill bit into alignment hole on side of shifter assembly, view "C," **Fig. 3.**
7. Rotate lever "D" in direction of arrow while tightening nut "E," **Fig. 3,** to remove lash from transaxle.
8. Tighten nut "E" on lever "F," **Fig. 3.**
9. Remove drill bit and yoke from shifter assembly.
10. Reconnect battery ground cable.
11. Check for proper operation. If "hang-up" is encountered when shifting in the 1-2 gear range and shift cables are adjusted properly, it may be necessary to change shifter shaft selective washer.
12. Perform the following procedure to obtain correct washer thickness:
    a. Remove reverse inhibitor fitting spring and washer from end of housing.
    b. Place shifter shaft in "Second" gear.
    c. Measure dimension "A", **Fig. 4,** which is distance between end of housing and the shoulder just behind end of shaft.
    d. Apply a 9-13 pound load on opposite end of shaft, then measure dimension "B", **Fig. 4,** which is distance between end of housing and end of shifter shaft major diameter.
    e. Subtract dimension "B" from dimension "A" to obtain dimension "C".
    f. Refer to the following chart to obtain correct thickness shim:

Dimension "C" Inch	Shim Part No.
.07	14008235
.08	476709
.09	476710
.11	476711
.12	476712
.13	476713
.14	476714
.15	476715
.16	476716

MANUAL TRANSAXLE

REPLACE

1982

1. Disconnect battery ground cable from transaxle case and attach to upper radiator hose with wire or tape.
2. Remove two transaxle strut bracket bolts at transaxle, on left side of engine compartment, if so equipped.
3. Remove exhaust crossover pipe, if equipped.
4. Remove top four engine to transaxle bolts and one to rear of vehicle near cowl. The bolt nearer cowl is installed from engine side, **Fig. 5.**
5. Loosen but do not remove transaxle bolt near starter, at front of vehicle.
6. Disconnect speedometer cable at transaxle. On vehicles equipped with cruise control, remove transaxle speedometer cable at cruise control transducer.
7. Remove retaining clip and washer from transaxle shift linkage at transaxle.
8. Remove clips securing shift cables to mounting bosses on transaxle case.
9. Disconnect clutch cable. Install engine support fixture, **Fig. 6.**
10. Remove left hand side and crossmember assembly using following procedures:
    a. Rotate steering wheel so that intermediate shaft to steering gear stub shaft attaching bolt is in up position and remove bolt.
    b. Raise vehicle.
    c. Position jack under engine to act as a support during removal and installation.
    d. Remove left front tire and wheel assembly.
    e. Remove power steering pressure and return line brackets.
    f. Disconnect drive line vibration absorber and disconnect front stabilizer bar from left hand lower control arm.
    g. Disconnect left lower ball joint at knuckle then remove both front stabilizer bar reinforcement.
    h. Using a 1/2 inch drill bit, drill through spot weld located between rear holes of lefthand front stabilizer bar mounting.
    i. Disconnect engine and transaxle mounts from cradle.
    j. Remove side to crossmember bolts also bolts from left side body mounts.
    k. Remove left side and front crossmember assembly. It may be necessary to pull or gently pry crossmember loose.
10. Drain fluid from transaxle.
11. Install drive axle boot seal protectors. Disconnect drive axles from transaxle then swing left side drive axle outward from transaxle. Right side drive axle can be removed as transaxle is being removed from vehicle.
12. Remove flywheel and starter shield bolts. Remove shields.
13. Securely attach transaxle case to jack for removal.

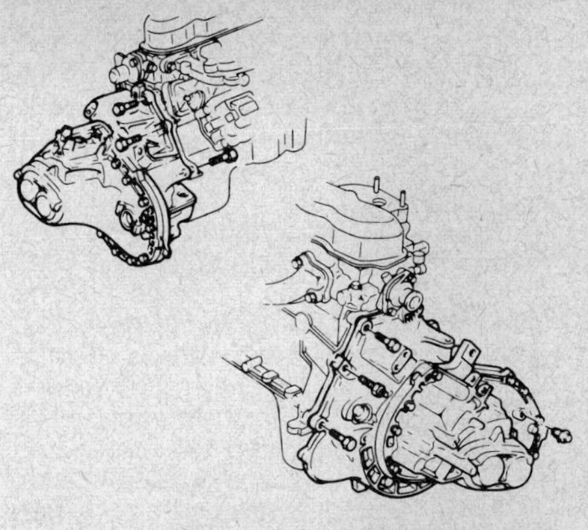

Fig. 5 Transaxle to engine attachment

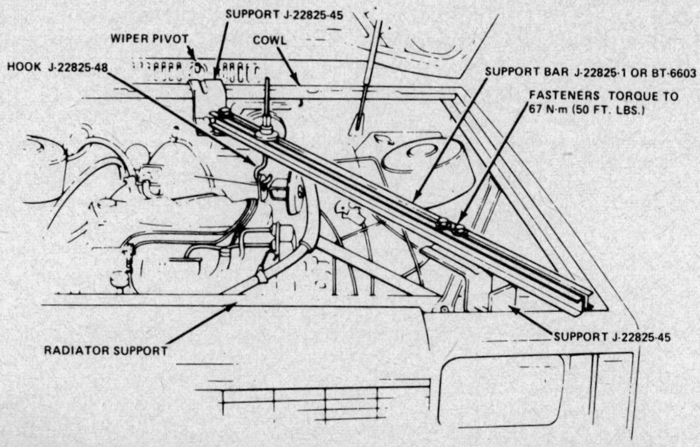

Fig. 6 Engine support tool installation

14. Remove last transaxle to engine bolt.
15. Remove transaxle by sliding to left side, away from engine. Carefully lower jack, and move transaxle to bench.
16. Reverse procedure to install and note the following:
   a. When installing the transaxle, position the right side drive axle shaft into its bore as transaxle is being installed. The righthand driveshaft cannot be readily installed after the transaxle is attached to the engine.
   b. After the transaxle is attached to the engine, swing the cradle into position and immediately install the cradle to body bolts. When swinging the cradle into the installed position, guide the left side driveshaft into the case bore.

1983–86

1. Disconnect battery ground cable from transaxle and attach to upper radiator hose with wire or tape.
2. Disconnect electrical connector from horn, then remove horn attaching bolt.
3. Remove air cleaner assembly.
4. Disconnect clutch cable as follows:
   a. Support clutch pedal upward against bumper stop to release pawl from quadrant.
   b. Disconnect cable from clutch release lever on transaxle. Use care to prevent cable from snapping toward rear of vehicle.
   c. Disconnect cable from quadrant. Lift locking pawl away from quadrant, then slide cable out on right side.
   d. Disconnect 2 upper nuts on engine side of cowl, holding cable retainer to upper studs.
   e. Disconnect cable from bracket on transaxle.
5. On models with V6 engine, disconnect fuel lines and fuel line clamps from clutch cable bracket.
6. On all models, remove clutch cable bracket from transaxle.
7. On models with V6 engine, remove exhaust crossover pipe.
8. On all models, remove retaining clips and washers from transaxle shift linkage at transaxle.
9. Remove shift cable to mounting boss retaining clips from transaxle case.
10. Disconnect speedometer cable from transaxle.
11. Remove 5 upper engine-to-transaxle attaching bolts.
12. Install engine support fixture, **Fig. 6.**
13. Raise and support vehicle.
14. Drain fluid from transaxle.
15. Install suitable drive axle boot seal protectors on both inner and outer seals.
16. Remove left front wheel assembly.
17. Remove left side cradle and crossmember assembly as follows:
   a. Position jack under engine to act as a support during removal and installation.
   b. Disconnect front ball joint.
   c. Disconnect front stabilizer bar from control arm.
   d. Remove front stabilizer bar plate and bushing from sidemember.
   e. Disconnect engine and transaxle mount from left sidemember.
   f. Remove sidemember-to-crossmember attaching bolts.
   g. Remove 2 left side body mount bolts.
   h. Remove left side and crossmember assembly.
18. Disconnect drive axles from transaxle, then swing left side drive axle outward from transaxle. Right side drive axle can be removed as transaxle is being removed from vehicle.
19. Remove flywheel and starter motor shield attaching bolts.
20. Securely attach transaxle case to jack for removal.
21. Remove remaining transaxle-to-engine attaching bolt.
22. Remove transaxle by sliding to left side away from engine and carefully lowering assembly from vehicle.
23. Reverse procedure to install, noting the following:
   a. When installing transaxle, position right side drive axle shaft into its bore, as driveshaft cannot be installed after transaxle is attached to engine.
   b. After transaxle is attached to engine, swing cradle into position and immediately install cradle-to-body attaching bolts.

1987–88

1. Disconnect battery ground cable from transaxle and attach to upper radiator hose with wire or tape.
2. Drain transaxle, then remove air cleaner assembly.
3. Disconnect hydraulic clutch slave cylinder and bracket from transaxle. Use caution not to allow manual clutch shaft to move while removing or installing clutch lever.
4. Remove clamp and nut from transaxle shift linkage at transaxle.
5. Disconnect speedometer electrical connector at permanent magnet generator.
6. Remove transaxle ball stud cable ends from transaxle shift levers and cables.
7. Remove one stud and five transaxle to engine attaching bolts.
8. Remove clutch inspection cover attaching screws.
9. Remove starter motor, then install engine support fixture J-28468 or equivalent.
10. Raise and support vehicle, then install suitable drive axle boot seal protectors on both inner and outer seals.
11. Remove left front wheel assembly.
12. Remove left side cradle and crossmember assembly as follows:
   a. Position jack under engine to act as a support during removal and installation.
   b. Disconnect front ball joint.
   c. Disconnect front stabilizer bar from control arm.
   d. Remove front stabilizer bar plate and bushing from sidemember.
   e. Disconnect engine and transaxle mount from left sidemember.
   f. Remove sidemember-to-crossmember attaching bolts.
   g. Remove 2 left side body mount bolts.
   h. Remove left side and crossmember assembly.
13. Disconnect drive axles from transaxle, then swing left side drive axle outward from transaxle. Right side drive axle can be removed as transaxle is being removed from vehicle.
14. Install suitable jack to transaxle, then remove rear transaxle mount to transaxle attaching studs and nuts.
15. Remove front transaxle mount attaching studs and nuts.
16. Remove remaining transaxle to engine attaching bolts.
17. Remove transaxle by sliding to left side away from engine and carefully lowering assembly from vehicle.
18. Reverse procedure to install, noting the following:
   a. When installing transaxle, position right side drive axle shaft into its bore, as driveshaft cannot be installed after transaxle is attached to engine.
   b. After transaxle is attached to engine, swing cradle into position and immediately install cradle-to-body attaching bolts.

Rear Axle, Rear Suspension & Brakes

INDEX

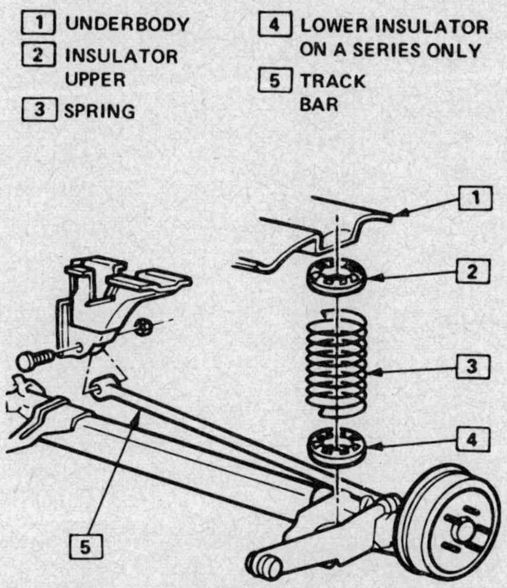

Fig. 1 Rear axle and suspension

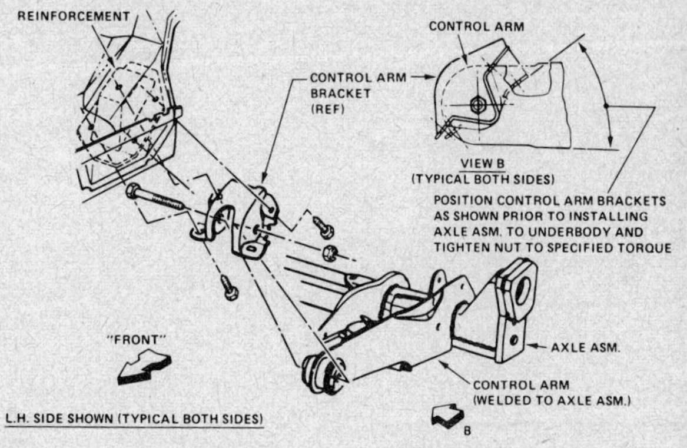

Fig. 2 Control arm bracket installation

DESCRIPTION

The rear suspension, **Fig. 1,** consists of a rear axle assembly, control arms, coil springs, shock absorbers and a track bar. The rear axle is trailing arm type design. A stabilizer bar is welded to the inside of the axle housing and is an integral part of the axle assembly. A single unit hub and bearing assembly is bolted to each end of the axle assembly. The hub and bearing assembly is a sealed unit and must be replaced as an assembly.

REAR AXLE
REPLACE

When removing rear axle assembly, do not use twin-post type hoist. The swing arc tendency of this axle may cause it to slip from hoist. Perform axle removal on floor if necessary.

1. Raise rear of vehicle and support rear axle using a suitable jack.
2. Remove rear wheel assembly and brake drum. Do not hammer on brake drum since damage to bearings may result.
3. Disconnect parking brake cable at equalizer, then remove brake line brackets from frame.
4. Disconnect shock absorber from lower mountings on axle housing.
5. Remove track bar attaching nut and bolt and disconnect track bar. **Do not suspend rear axle by brake hoses, otherwise damage to hoses may result.**
6. Carefully lower rear axle assembly and remove coil spring and insulators.
7. Disconnect brake lines from control arm attachments.
8. Remove parking brake cable from rear axle attachments.
9. Remove hub attaching bolts, then the hub and bearing assembly and position backing plate out of way.
10. Remove control arm bracket to underbody attaching bolts, then lower axle assembly and remove from vehicle.
11. Reverse procedure to install, noting the following:
    a. If control arm brackets were removed from control arms, torque attaching nuts to 78 ft. lbs.
    b. Install control arm bracket at a 40.5-44.5° angle as shown in **Fig. 2.**
    c. Torque control arm-to-underbody attaching bolts to 28 ft. lbs.
    d. Torque track bar attaching nut to 35 ft. lbs.

HUB & BEARING ASSEMBLY
REPLACE

1. Raise and support rear of vehicle, then remove wheel and tire assembly and brake drum. **Do not hammer on brake drum since damage to bearing may result.**
2. Remove four hub and bearing assembly to rear axle attaching bolts, then the hub and bearing assembly from axle.
3. Reverse procedure to install. Torque hub and bearing assembly to rear axle attaching bolts to 45 ft. lbs. **Use care not to drop hub and bearing assembly since damage to bearing may result.**

COIL SPRING
REPLACE

1. Raise rear of vehicle and support rear axle using a suitable jack.
2. Remove right and left brake line bracket attaching bolts from frame and allow brake lines to hang freely.
3. Remove track bar attaching nut and bolt, then disconnect track bar.
4. Disconnect shock absorbers at lower mountings. **Do not suspend rear axle by brake hoses since damage to hoses may result.**
5. Carefully lower rear axle assembly and remove springs and insulators.
6. Reverse procedure to install, **Fig. 3.**

CONTROL ARM BUSHING
REPLACE

1. Raise rear of vehicle and support rear

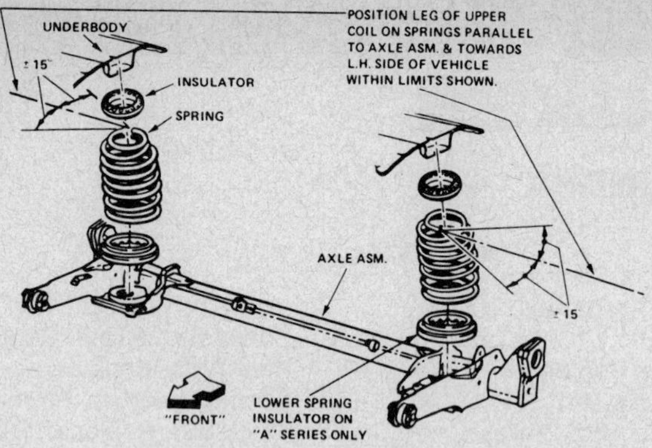

Fig. 3 Coil spring & insulator installation

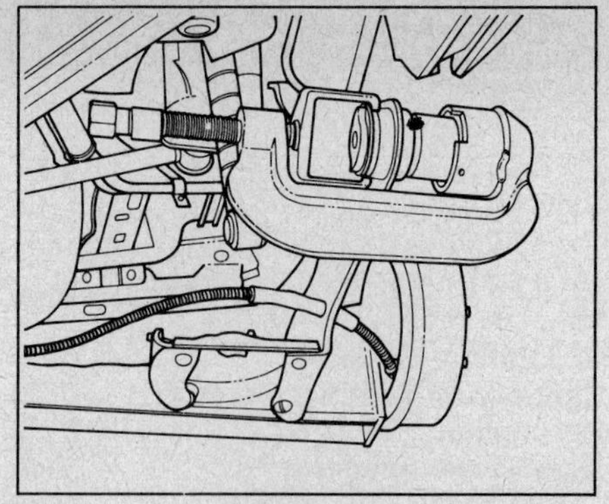

Fig. 4 Control arm bushing removal

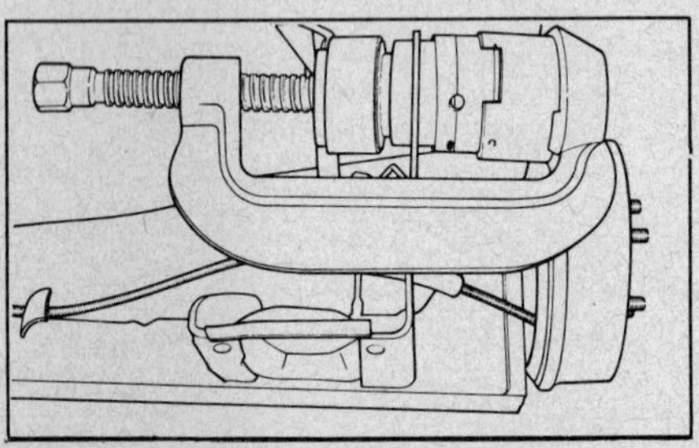

Fig. 5 Control arm bushing installation

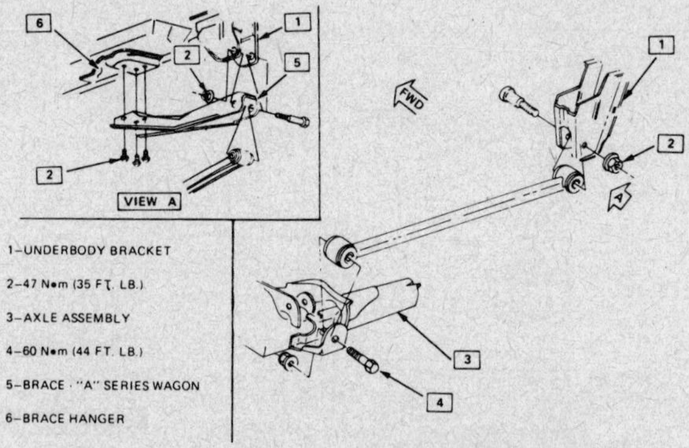

Fig. 6 Track bar installation

axle under front side of spring seat using a suitable jack.

2. If right hand side bushing is to be replaced, disconnect parking brake cable from equalizer.
3. Remove parking brake cables from bracket attachment and position out of way.
4. Disconnect brake line bracket from frame.
5. Disconnect shock absorber from lower mounting, then pull spring out of way.
6. Remove four control arm to underbody attaching bolts and allow control arm to rotate downward.
7. Remove nut and bolt from bracket attachment and remove bracket.
8. The bushing can now be replaced using tools shown in **Figs. 4 and 5.** When installing bushing, press bushing in until end of bushing is aligned with scribed line on tool J-28685-2, **Fig. 5.**
9. Reverse procedure to install control arm. Install bracket to control arm as shown in **Fig. 2.**

TRACK BAR
REPLACE

1. Raise rear of vehicle and support rear axle using a suitable jack.
2. Remove nut and bolt attaching track bar at axle housing and underbody and remove track bar, **Fig. 6.**
3. Reverse procedure to install, **Fig. 6.** Open side of track bar must face rear of vehicle. Also, nut must be at rear of attachments at both axle and underbody attachments.

SHOCK ABSORBER
REPLACE

1. Open deck lid and remove trim cover, then remove shock absorber upper attaching nut.
2. Raise rear of vehicle and support rear axle using a suitable jack.
3. Disconnect shock absorber at lower attachment and remove shock absorber from vehicle.
4. Reverse procedure to install. Torque shock absorber lower attaching nut to 43 ft. lbs. Torque shock absorber upper attaching nut to 13 ft. lbs.

DRUM BRAKE ADJUSTMENTS

These brakes have self adjusting shoe mechanisms that assure correct lining-to-drum clearances at all times. The automatic adjusters operate only when the brakes are applied as the car is moving rearward.

Although the brakes are self-adjusting, an initial adjustment is necessary after the brake shoes have been relined or replaced, or when the length of the star wheel adjuster has been changed during some other service operation.

Frequent usage of an automatic transmission forward range to halt reverse vehicle motion may prevent the automatic adjusters from functioning, thereby inducing low pedal heights. Should low pedal heights be encountered, it is recommended that numerous forward and reverse stops be made until satisfactory pedal height is obtained.

If a low pedal height condition cannot be corrected by making numerous reverse stops (provided the hydraulic system is free of air) it indicates that the self-adjusting mechanism is not functioning. Therefore, it will be necessary to remove the brake drum, clean, free up and lubricate the adjusting mechanism. Then adjust the brakes as follows, being sure the parking brake is fully released.

ADJUSTMENT

A lanced "knock out" area is provided in the web of the brake drum for servicing purposes on some models. When adjustment is required on models that do not have a lanced area on the brake drum, carefully drill a 1/2 in. hole into the round flat area on the backing plate opposite the parking brake cable. If lanced area of brake drum has been knocked out or if a hole was drilled in backing plate, ensure that all metal particles are removed from the brake compartment.

1. Turn brake adjusting screw to expand shoes until wheel can just be turned by hand.
2. Using a suitable tool to hold actuator from adjuster, back off adjuster 30 notches. If shoes still drag, back off one or two additional notches. **Brakes should be free of drag when adjuster has been backed off approximately 12 notches. Heavy drag at this point indicates tight parking brake cables.**
3. Install adjusting hole cover on brake drum or backing plate.
4. Check parking brake adjustment.

PARKING BRAKE

ADJUST

MODELS W/REAR DRUM BRAKES

Need for parking brake adjustment is indicated if the service brake operates with sufficient pedal reserve, but the parking brake pedal travel is less than 9 ratchet clicks or more than 16 ratchet clicks.

1. Depress parking brake pedal three ratchet clicks, then raise and support rear of vehicle.
2. Check to ensure that equalizer nut groove is sufficiently lubricated with grease, then tighten adjusting nut until right rear wheel can just be rotated rearward, but is locked when forward rotation is attempted.
3. Release parking brake lever. Both wheels should rotate freely in either direction with no brake drag.

MODELS W/REAR DISC BRAKES

1. Apply service brake pedal three times, then apply and release parking brake lever three times.
2. Raise and support vehicle, then place alignment mark on wheel and axle flange.
3. Check parking brake hand lever for full release as follows:
   a. Turn ignition switch to On position and ensure "Brake" warning lamp is Off.
   b. If "Brake" warning lamp is still On, with hand lever fully released, pull front parking brake cable downward to remove slack from pedal assembly.
4. Remove rear wheels, then install two lug nuts to secure rotor.
5. Ensure parking brake levers on both calipers are against lever stops on caliper housings. If levers are not against stops, check for binding in rear cables, then loosen cable adjuster unit levers are properly positioned.
6. Tighten parking brake cable at adjuster until either left or right lever begins to move off the stop, then loosen adjuster until lever moves back barely touching stop.
7. Operate parking brake lever several times to ensure proper adjustment. Hand lever should not travel more than 8 ratchet clicks and rear wheels should not rotate forward when hand lever is applied 5 to 8 ratchet clicks.
8. Install rear wheels, aligning marks on wheel and axle flange.

MASTER CYLINDER

REPLACE

1. Disconnect master cylinder push rod from brake pedal.
2. Disconnect wire connector at brake warning pressure switch.
3. Disconnect brake lines from master cylinder, then remove two master cylinder mounting nuts and remove master cylinder.
4. Reverse procedure to install, then bleed brake system.

POWER BRAKE UNIT

REPLACE

1. Disconnect brake unit push rod from brake pedal.
2. Remove two master cylinder to power brake unit mounting nuts, then position master cylinder away from brake unit with brake lines attached. **Use care not to bend or kink brake lines.**
3. Disconnect vacuum hose from vacuum check valve. Plug vacuum hose to prevent entry of dirt.
4. Remove power brake unit to dash panel attaching nuts, then remove brake unit.
5. Reverse procedures to install.

Front Suspension & Steering Section

INDEX

DESCRIPTION

The front suspension, **Fig. 1**, on these vehicles is a MacPherson strut design. The lower control arms pivot from the engine cradle. This engine cradle has isolation mounts to the body and conventional rubber bushings are used for the lower control arm pivots. The upper end of the strut is isolated by a rubber mount incorporating a bearing for wheel turning. The lower end of the steering knuckle pivots on a ball stud which is retained in the lower control arm with rivets and is clamped to the steering knuckle. Sealed wheel bearings are used and are bolted to the steering knuckle.

WHEEL BEARING

REPLACE

REMOVAL

1. Loosen hub nut with vehicle on ground.
2. Raise and support vehicle and re-

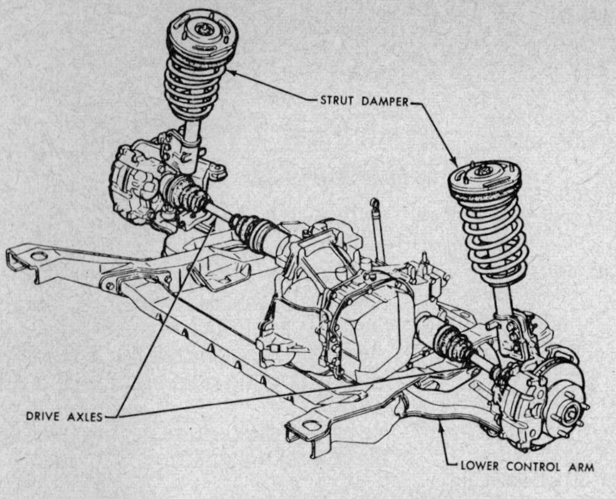

Fig. 1 Front suspension

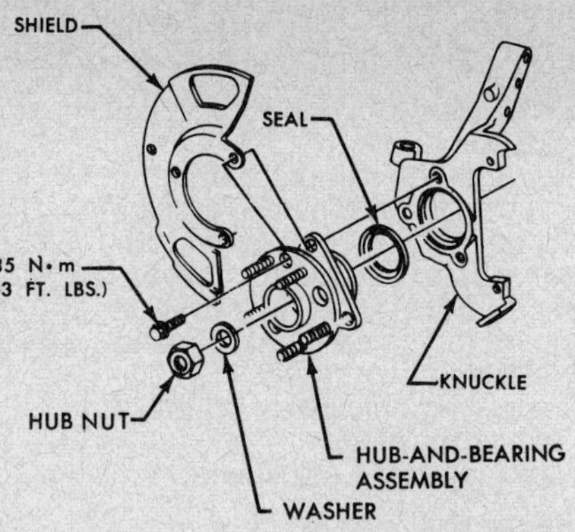

Fig. 2 Front wheel bearing assembly & seal

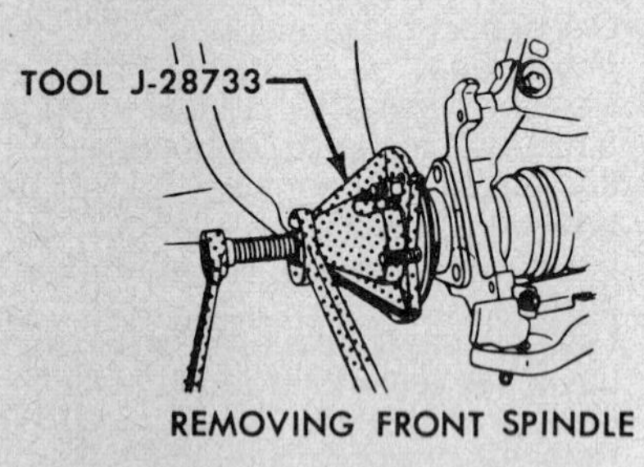

Fig. 3 Removing front wheel bearing & hub assembly

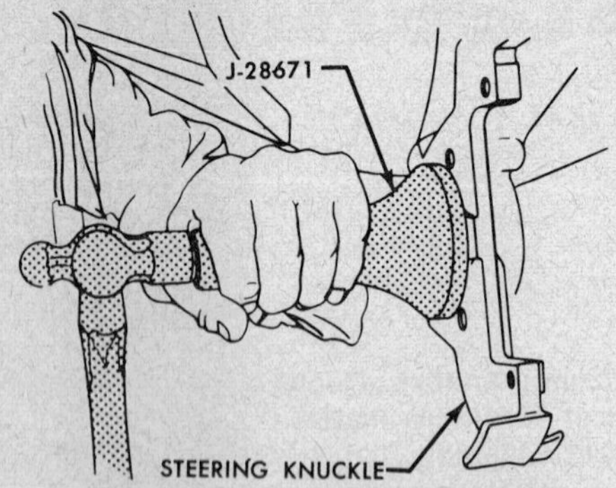

Fig. 4 Installing front wheel bearing seal

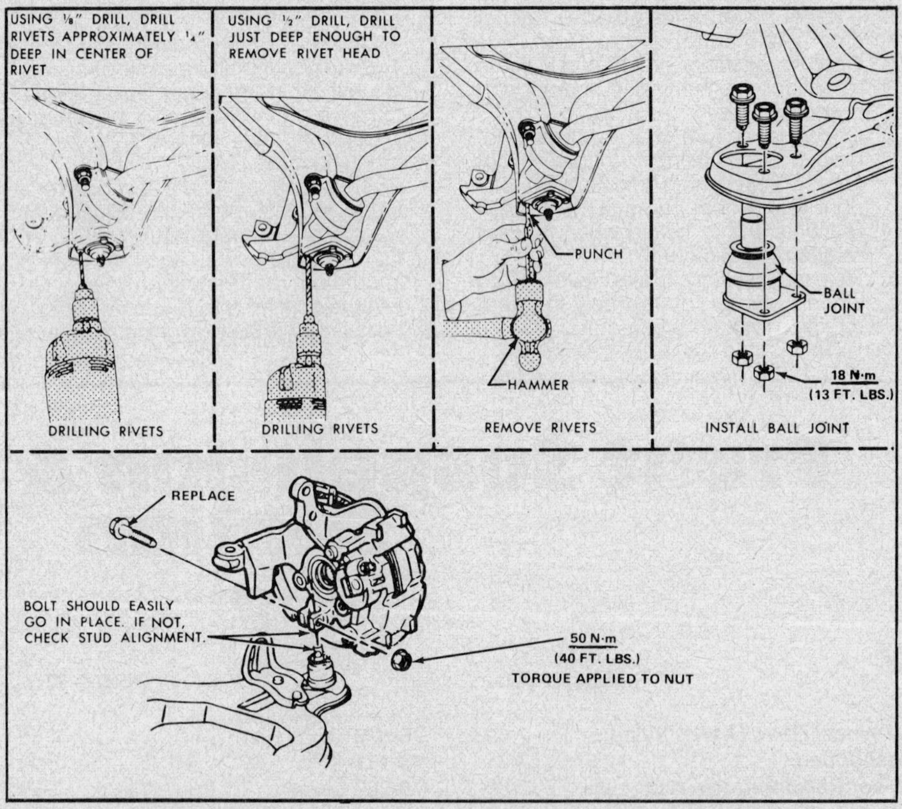

Fig. 5 Lower ball joint removal & installation

move front wheel.
3. Install drive axle boot cover, tool J-28712.
4. Remove and discard hub nut.
5. Remove brake caliper from support and suspend caliper from frame with a length of wire. Do not suspend caliper by the brake hose.
6. Remove three hub and bearing attaching bolts. If the old bearing is being reinstalled, mark attaching bolts and holes for reinstallation, **Fig. 2.**
7. Using tool J-28733 or equivalent, remove bearing, **Fig. 3. If excessive corrosion is present, ensure that the bearing is loose in the knuckle before using puller tool.**
8. If installing new bearing, replace steering knuckle seal.

INSTALLATION

1. Clean and inspect bearing mating surfaces and steering knuckle bore for dirt, nicks and burrs.
2. If installing steering knuckle seal, use tool J-28671 or equivalent to install seal, **Fig. 4.** Apply grease to seal and knuckle bore.
3. Push bearing onto axle shaft.
4. Tighten hub nut to fully seat bearing.
5. Install bearing attaching bolts and torque to 63 ft. lbs., **Fig. 2.**
6. Install caliper assembly and the wheel.
7. Lower vehicle and torque hub nut to

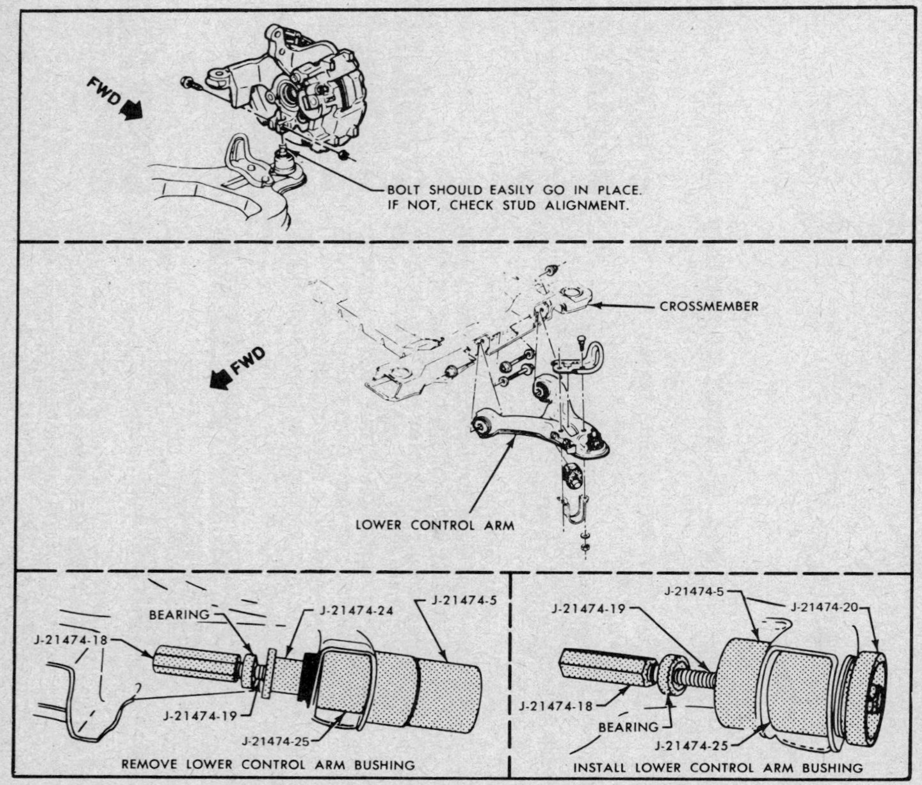
FWD
BOLT SHOULD EASILY GO IN PLACE.
IF NOT, CHECK STUD ALIGNMENT.
CROSSMEMBER
FWD
LOWER CONTROL ARM
BEARING
J-21474-24
J-21474-5
J-21474-18
J-21474-19
J-21474-25
REMOVE LOWER CONTROL ARM BUSHING
J-21474-5
J-21474-19
J-21474-20
J-21474-18
BEARING
J-21474-25
INSTALL LOWER CONTROL ARM BUSHING

Fig. 6 Lower control arm & bushing removal & installation

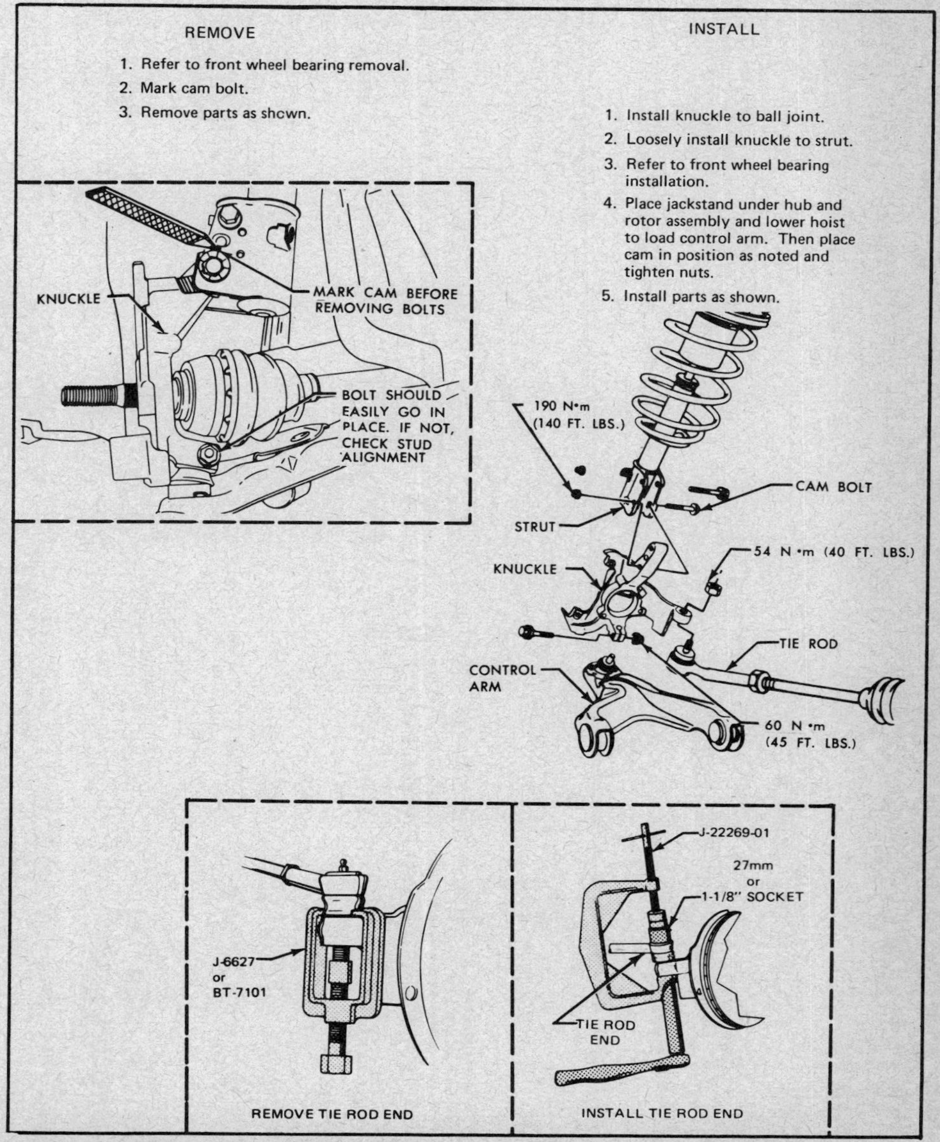
REMOVE
1. Refer to front wheel bearing removal.
2. Mark cam bolt.
3. Remove parts as shown.
INSTALL
1. Install knuckle to ball joint.
2. Loosely install knuckle to strut.
3. Refer to front wheel bearing installation.
4. Place jackstand under hub and rotor assembly and lower hoist to load control arm. Then place cam in position as noted and tighten nuts.
5. Install parts as shown.
KNUCKLE
MARK CAM BEFORE REMOVING BOLTS
BOLT SHOULD EASILY GO IN PLACE. IF NOT, CHECK STUD ALIGNMENT
190 N•m (140 FT. LBS.)
CAM BOLT
STRUT
54 N•m (40 FT. LBS.)
KNUCKLE
TIE ROD
CONTROL ARM
60 N•m (45 FT. LBS.)
J-6627 or BT-7101
REMOVE TIE ROD END
J-22269-01
27mm or 1-1/8" SOCKET
TIE ROD END
INSTALL TIE ROD END

Fig. 7 Steering knuckle removal & installation

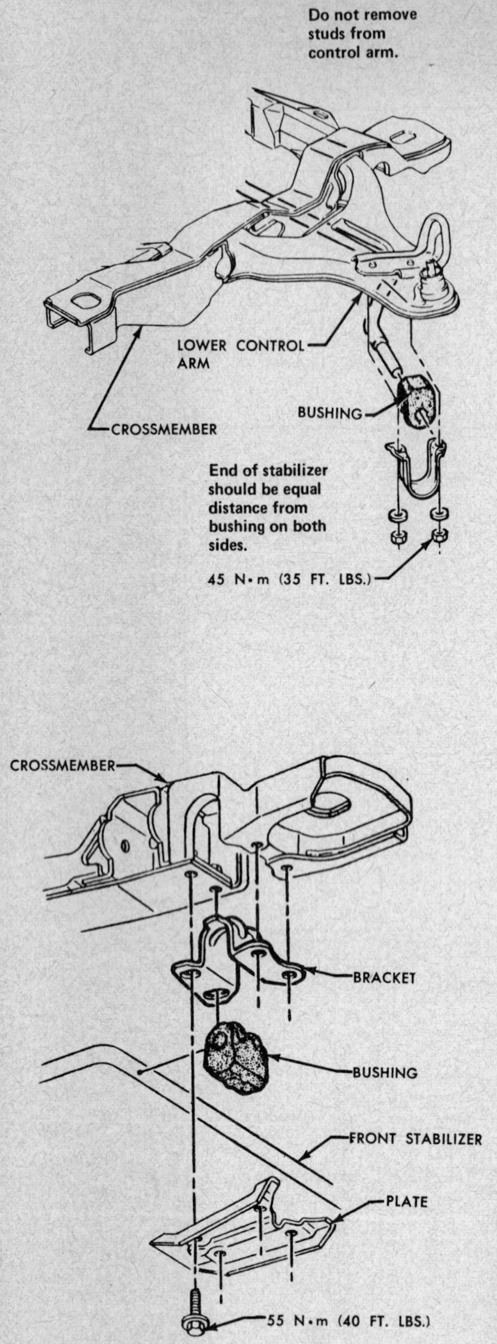

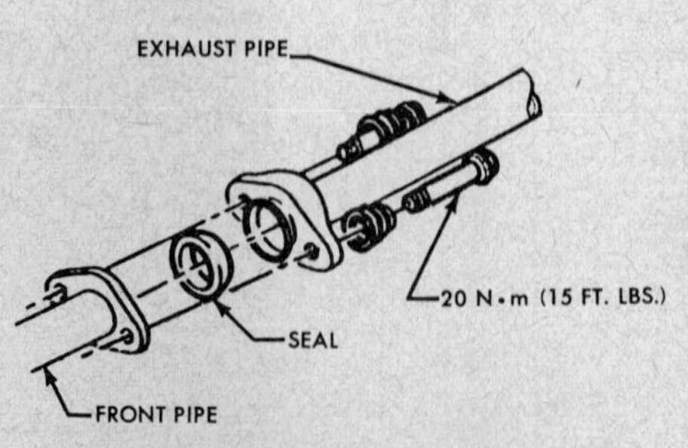

Fig. 8 Stabilizer bar & bushing removal & installation

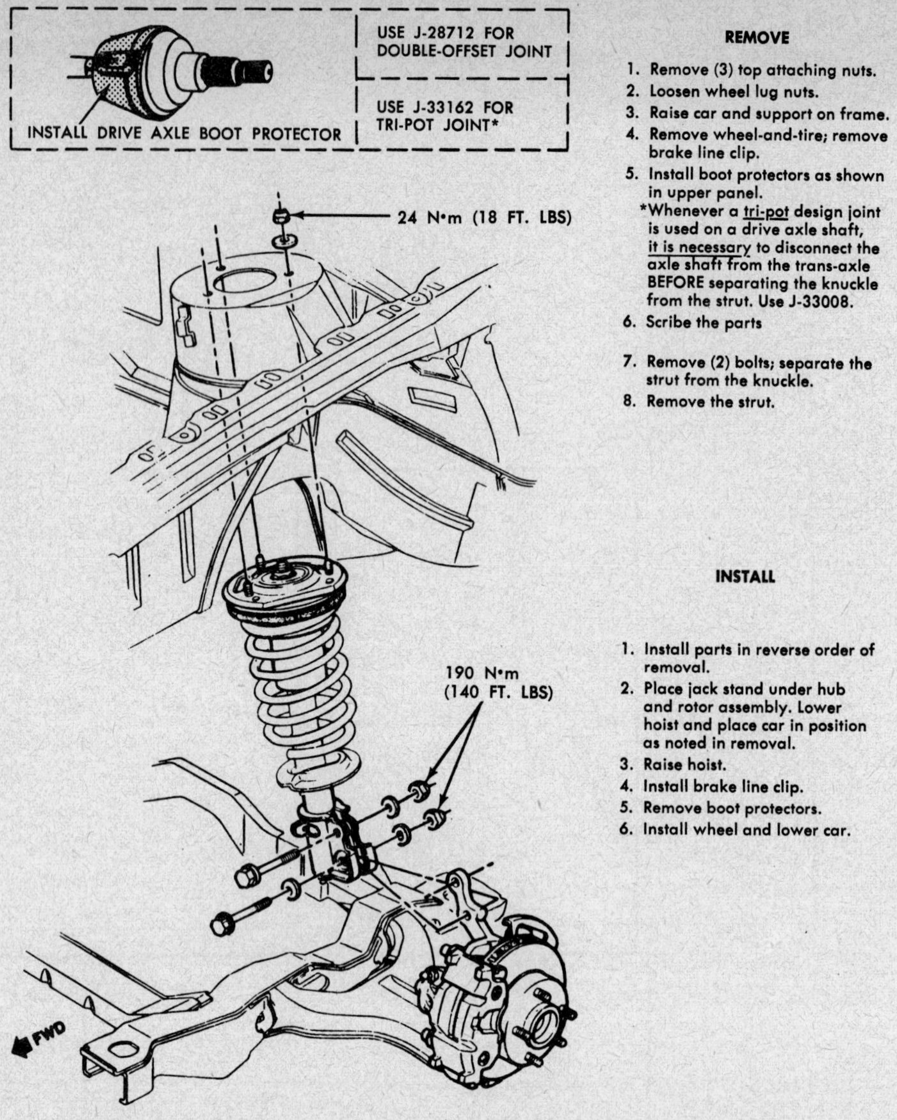

INSTALL DRIVE AXLE BOOT PROTECTOR
USE J-28712 FOR
DOUBLE-OFFSET JOINT
USE J-33162 FOR
TRI-POT JOINT*
24 N•m (18 FT. LBS)
190 N•m
(140 FT. LBS)
FWD
REMOVE
1. Remove (3) top attaching nuts.
2. Loosen wheel lug nuts.
3. Raise car and support on frame.
4. Remove wheel-and-tire; remove brake line clip.
5. Install boot protectors as shown in upper panel.
*Whenever a tri-pot design joint is used on a drive axle shaft, it is necessary to disconnect the axle shaft from the trans-axle BEFORE separating the knuckle from the strut. Use J-33008.
6. Scribe the parts
7. Remove (2) bolts; separate the strut from the knuckle.
8. Remove the strut.
INSTALL
1. Install parts in reverse order of removal.
2. Place jack stand under hub and rotor assembly. Lower hoist and place car in position as noted in removal.
3. Raise hoist.
4. Install brake line clip.
5. Remove boot protectors.
6. Install wheel and lower car.

Fig. 9 Strut assembly removal & installation

225 ft. lbs. on 1982 models, 185-192 ft. lbs. on 1983-88.

LOWER BALL JOINT
REPLACE

When servicing lower ball joint, be sure to align broached notch in ball joint stud with clamp bolt hole during reassembly. This prevents interference between stud and clamp bolt. To ensure proper bolt torque, replace clamp bolt and nut each time ball joint stud is separated from steering knuckle.

For removal and installation procedures, refer to **Fig. 5**.

LOWER CONTROL ARM & BUSHINGS
REPLACE

For removal and installation procedures, refer to **Fig. 6**. Torque ball joint clamping bolt to 40 ft. lbs. and control arm attaching bolts to66 ft.lbs.

STEERING KNUCKLE
REPLACE

For removal and installation procedures, refer to **Fig. 7**.

STABILIZER BAR & BUSHINGS
REPLACE

For removal and installation procedures, refer to **Fig. 8**.

STRUT ASSEMBLY
REPLACE

For removal and installation procedures, refer to **Fig. 9**.

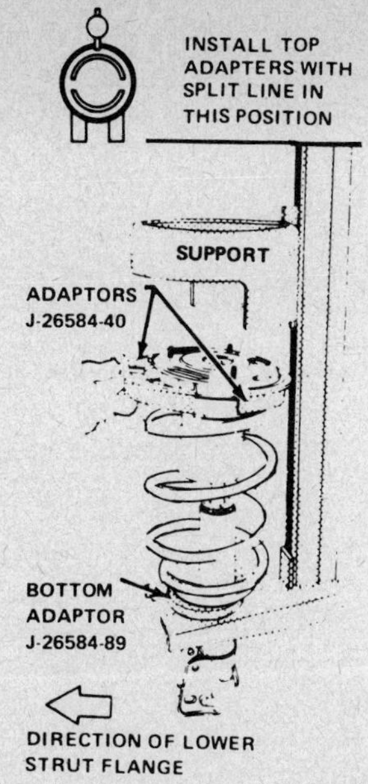

Fig. 10 Strut disassembly. 1982–83, 1984–88 similar

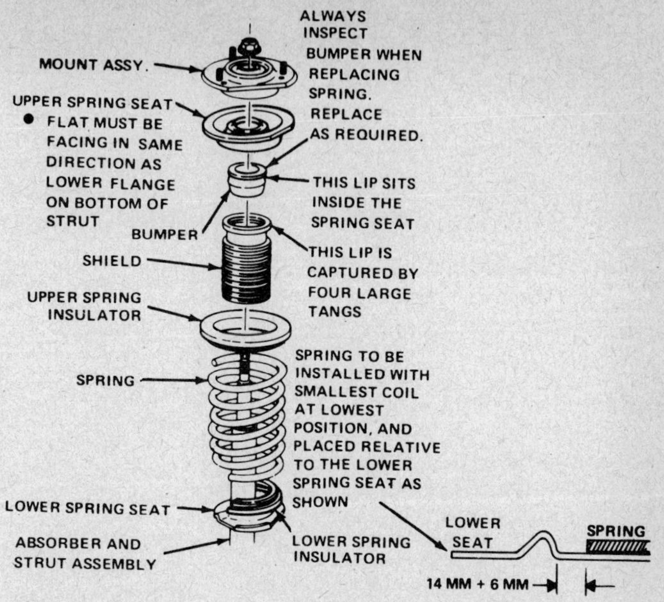

Fig. 11 Strut assembly exploded view. 1982–88

STRUT ASSEMBLY SERVICE

DISASSEMBLY

1. Mount compressor J-26584 in suitable vise.
2. Mount strut in compressor using bottom adapter J-26584-400 or equivalent.
3. Ensure that strut is fully contained by bottom adapter and that locating pins are fully engaged.
4. Rotate strut to align lip of top mount with notch in compressor support.
5. On 1982-83 models, install both J-26584-40 top adapters ensuring that split lines are at 9 o'clock and 3 o'clock positions, **Fig. 10.**
6. On 1984-88, install top adapter J-26584-430, aligning studs with properly marked holes on adapter.
7. Rotate compressor screw clockwise until top support contacts strut/adapter assembly, then keep turning screw until spring is compressed to approximately 1/2 of its height on 1984-88 models or 4 turns on 1982-83 models.
8. Remove nut from damper shaft and install suitable alignment rod.
9. Gradually release spring tension, then remove and disassemble strut noting position of components for reassembly, **Fig. 11.**

ASSEMBLY

1. Perform steps 1 through 3 as outlined in the "Disassembly" procedure.
2. Rotate strut assembly until mounting flange is facing outward opposite compressor forcing screw.
3. Install spring and related components on strut. Ensure spring is properly seated on bottom spring plate.

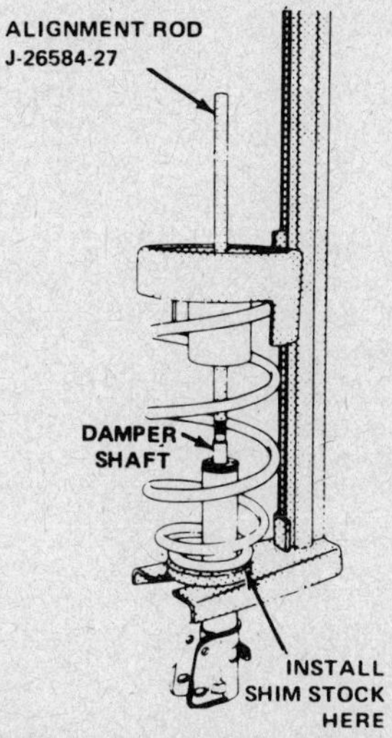

Fig. 12 Strut alignment rod installation (Typical)

4. Install strut spring seat assembly on top of spring. Ensure flat faces in same direction as lower flange.
5. Position top adapters over spring seat assembly.
6. Rotate compressor forcing screw until compressor top support makes contact with top adapters. Do not compress spring at this time.
7. Install suitable strut alignment rod through top spring seat. Thread rod onto damper shaft hand tight, **Fig. 12. Install shims between lower spring seat and bottom adapter to keep alignment rod centered in upper spring seat opening.**
8. Compress spring by slowly rotating forcing screw. While rotating screw, observe position of damper shaft, as it must pass directly through center of opening in upper spring seat to provide proper operation. If spring is off-center, back off screw and proceed as follows:
   a. Reposition both top adapters in support fixture to provide proper spring seat-to-damper position.
   b. Install thin shim stock between lower spring seat and bottom adapter to tilt strut assembly into proper position.
   c. When damper shaft can be held in proper position, rotate screw until approximately 1 1/2 inch of shaft can be pulled through upper spring seat. Do not compress spring beyond this point.
9. Remove alignment rod, place strut mounting assembly over damper shaft and install nut. Torque nut to 65 ft. lbs.
10. Rotate forcing screw counterclockwise and remove strut assembly from compressor.

STEERING GEAR REPLACE

REMOVAL

1. On models equipped with power steering, remove air cleaner, then disconnect and cap hydraulic lines from steering gear.
2. Pull intermediate shaft seal upward, then remove intermediate shaft to steering gear stub shaft pinch bolt, **Fig. 13.**
3. Raise and support vehicle, then remove both front wheel and tire assemblies.
4. Using tool J6627 or equivalent, disconnect tie rod ends from steering knuckles.
5. Remove AIR pipe bracket to crossmember attaching bolt, if equipped.
6. Remove two rear frame cradle mount-

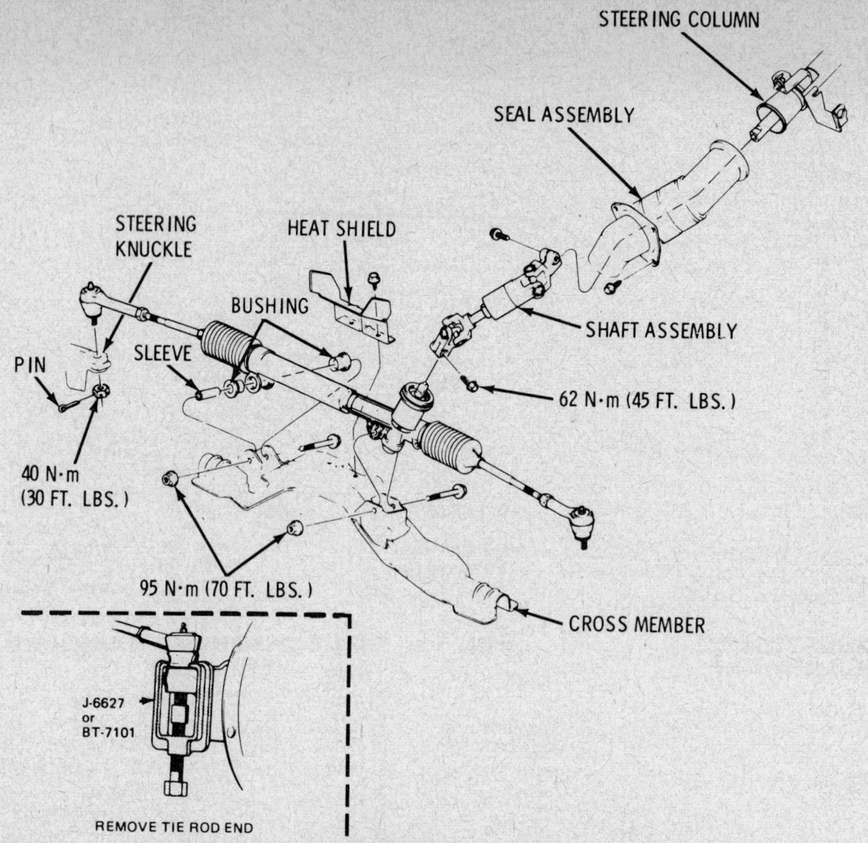

Fig. 13 Steering gear replacement

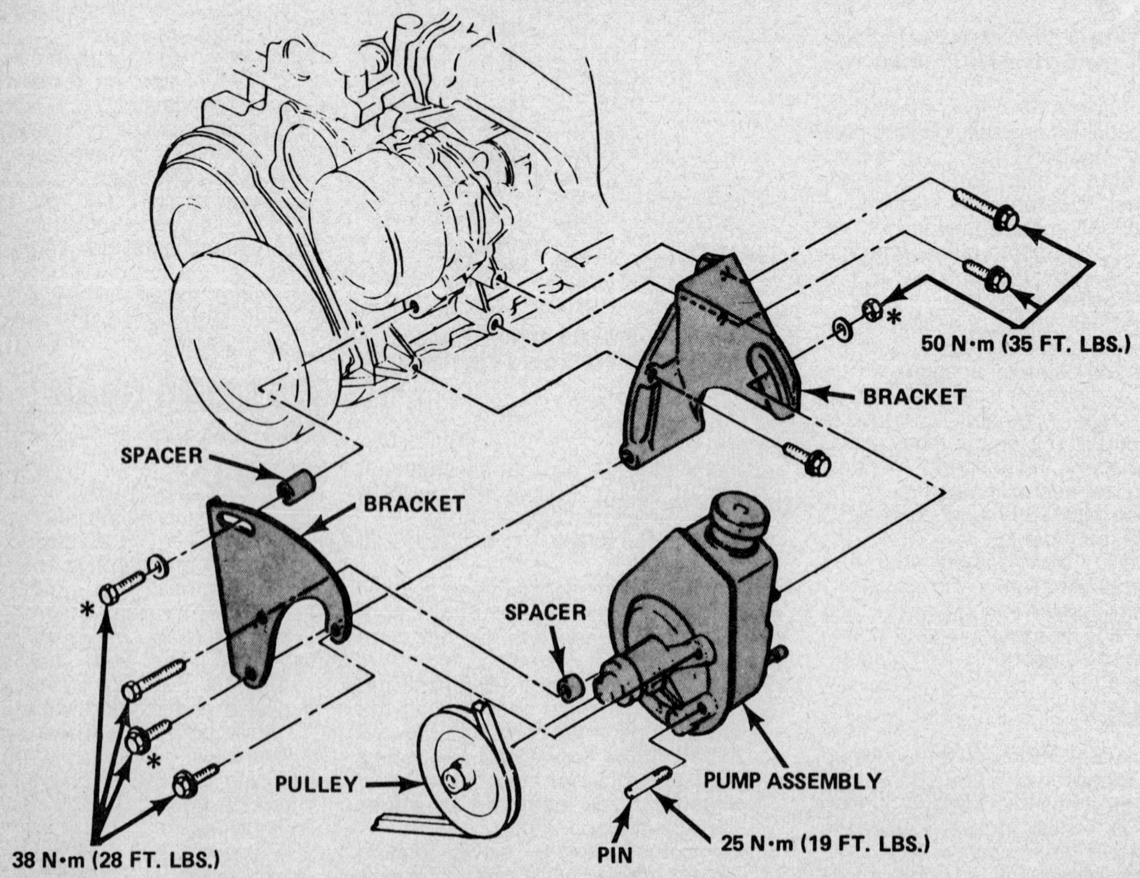

Fig. 14 Power steering pump replacement. 4-151

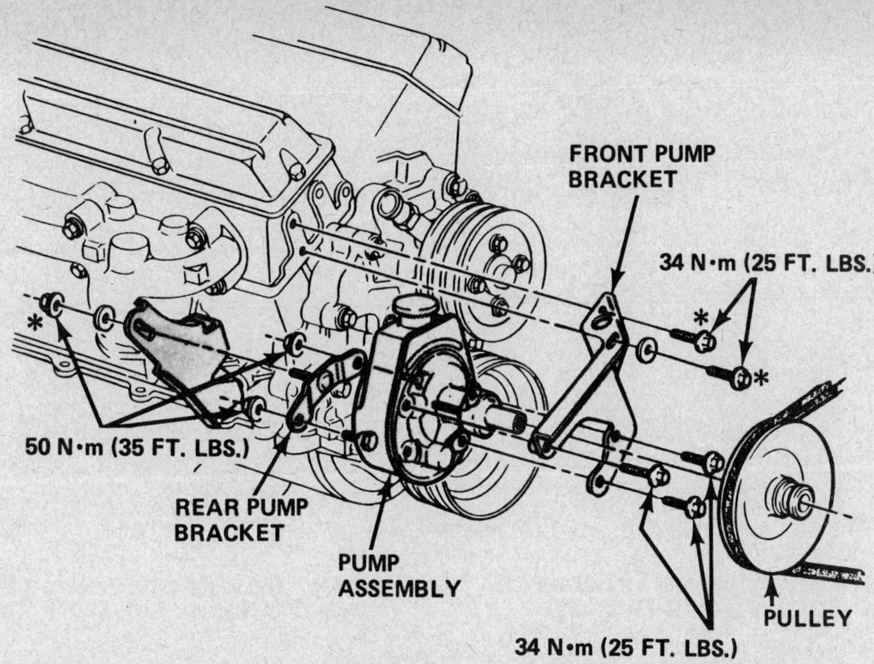

Fig. 15 Power steering pump replacement. V6-173

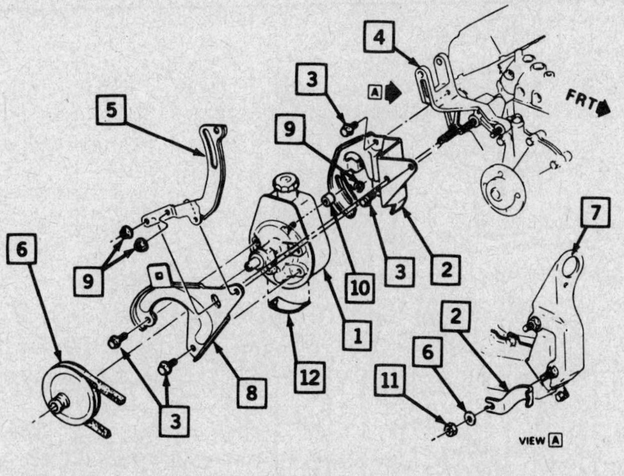

1. POWER STEERING PUMP
2. REAR ADJ. BRACKET
3. BOLT – 50 N•m (38 LBS. FT.)
4. GENERATOR MOUNTING BRACKET
5. GENERATOR ADJUSTING BRACKET
6. PULLEY
7. ENG. LIFT BRACKET AND SHIELD
8. FRONT ADJ. BRACKET
9. NUT – 50 N•m (38 LBS. FT.)
10. REAR BRACKET SPACER
11. NUT – 27 N•m (20 LBS. FT.)
12. PROTECTOR

Fig. 16 Power steering pump replacement. V6-181, 231

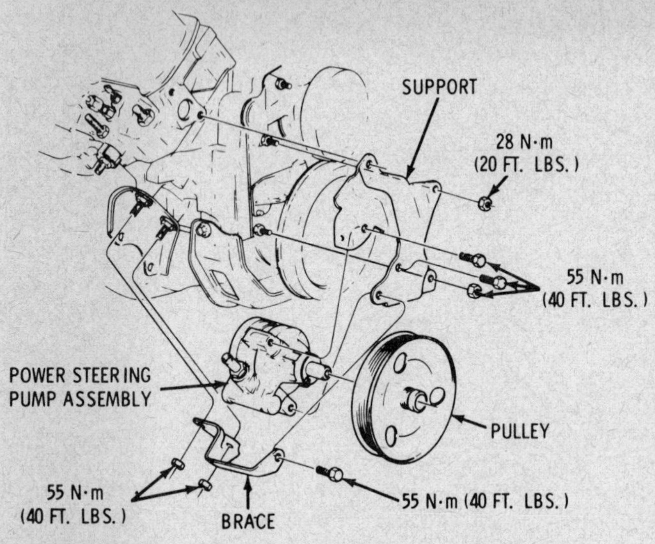

Fig. 17 Power steering pump removal & installation. 1982 V6-262 Diesel

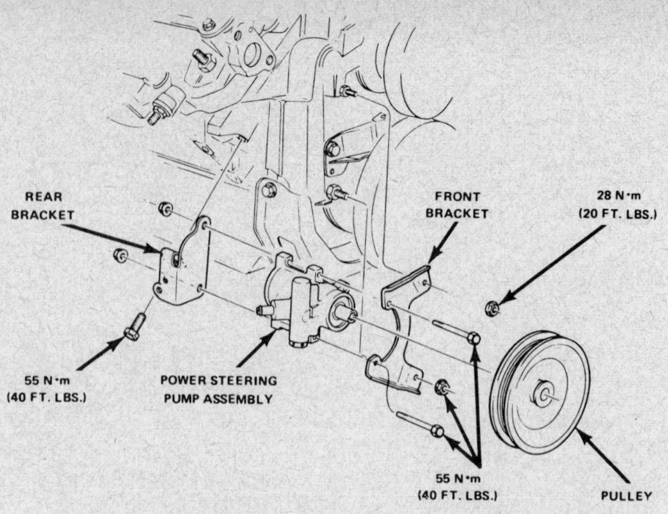

Fig. 18 Power steering pump removal & installation. 1983–84 V6-262 Diesel

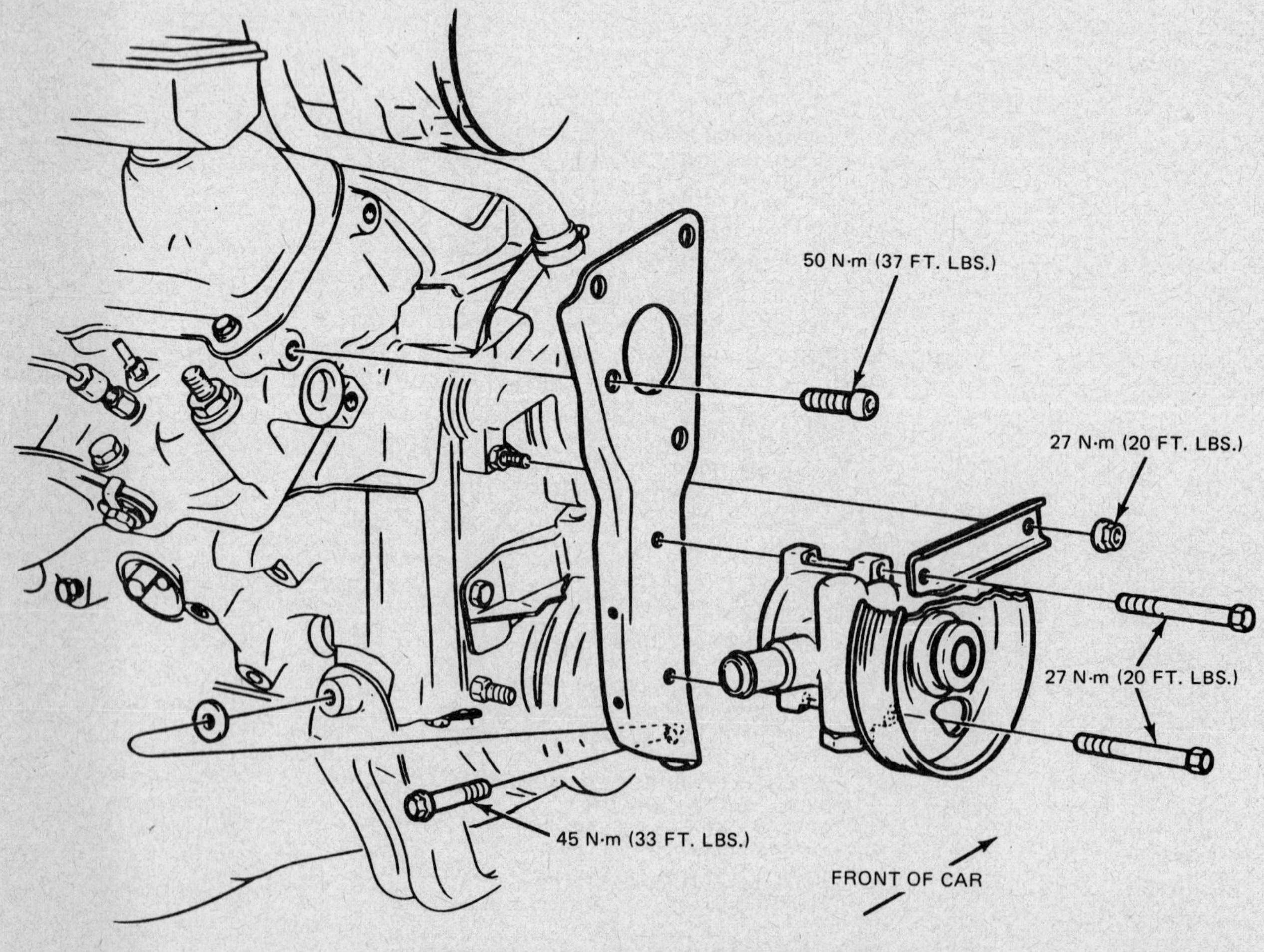

Fig. 19 Power steering pump removal & installation. 1985 V6-262 Diesel

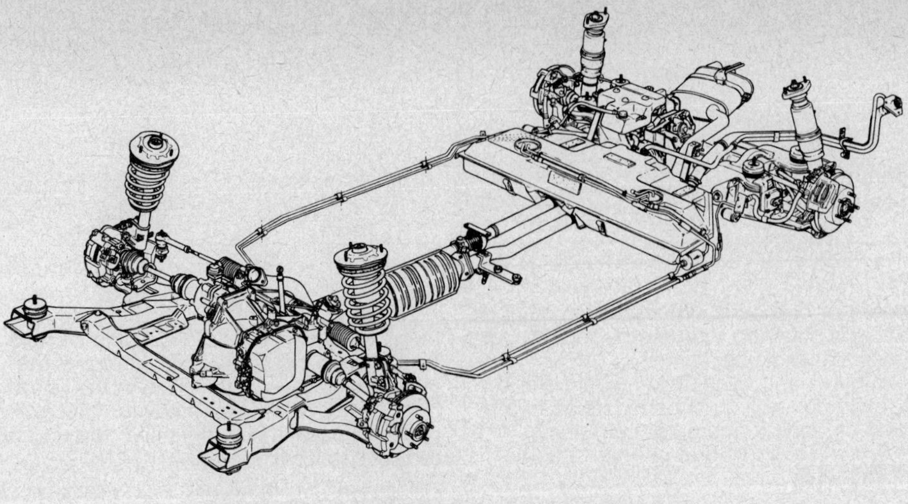

Fig. 20 All Wheel Drive System

ing bolts and lower rear of cradle 4 to 5 inches. **Do not lower cradle more than specified, as damage to engine components may result.**
7. Remove steering gear heat shield from crossmember.
8. Remove steering gear assembly mounting bolts, then the steering gear assembly through the left wheel opening.

INSTALLATION

1. Place steering gear assembly into mounts on crossmember, then install and torque mounting bolts to 70 ft. lbs.
2. Install heat shield.
3. Raise frame cradle and install mounting bolts. Torque bolts to 75 ft. lbs.
4. Install AIR pipe bracket to crossmember, then connect tie rod ends to steering knuckles. Torque ball studs to 30 ft. lbs.
5. Install wheel and tire assemblies and lower vehicle.
6. Connect intermediate shaft to steering gear stub shaft, install pinch bolt and torque to 45 ft. lbs.
7. Check and adjust toe-in as required.

POWER STEERING PUMP REPLACE

4-151

1. Raise and support vehicle, then remove radiator hose clamp bolt.
2. Disconnect and cap hydraulic lines at power steering pump.
3. Remove power steering pump to rear bracket attaching nut.
4. Remove front pump bracket to engine and front pump bracket to rear pump bracket attaching bolts, **Fig. 14.**
5. Remove pump and bracket assembly from vehicle.
6. Reverse procedure to install.

V6-173

1. Disconnect battery ground cable.
2. Disconnect electrical connector at blower motor, then remove blower motor from vehicle.
3. Disconnect heater hose from water pump and hydraulic lines from power steering pump. Cap lines to avoid fluid leakage.
4. Remove rear pump bracket to engine bracket attaching nut and front pump bracket to cylinder head attaching bolts, **Fig. 15.**
5. Remove pump and bracket assembly from vehicle.
6. Reverse procedure to install.

V6-181, 231

1. Disconnect battery ground cable, then remove air cleaner.
2. Remove alternator drive belt and alternator, then raise and support vehicle.
3. Remove rear adjustment bracket to pump retaining nut, **Fig. 16.**
4. Remove alternator adjustment bracket and power steering pump drive belt.
5. Remove double nut and two studs, then the alternator mounting bracket.
6. Remove rear pump adjustment bracket, then disconnect hydraulic lines from power steering pump. Cap lines to prevent spillage of fluid.
7. Remove pump and bracket assembly from vehicle.
8. Reverse procedure to install.

V6-262 DIESEL

1982

1. Remove drive belt, then drain power steering fluid from power steering pump reservoir.
2. Raise and support vehicle and disconnect pressure and return lines from power steering pump.
3. Working through access holes in pump pulley, remove three bolts from front of pump.
4. Remove two nuts holding lower brace to engine and remove bracket.
5. Remove pump and pulley assembly from vehicle.
6. Reverse procedure to install, **Fig. 17.**

1983–84

1. Remove drive belt, then drain power steering fluid from power steering pump reservoir.
2. Disconnect pressure and return lines from power steering pump.
3. Remove pulley using puller J-25034 or equivalent.
4. Remove two pump attaching bolts, then pump from vehicle.
5. Reverse procedure to install, **Fig. 18.**

1985

1. Rotate drive belt tensioner counterclockwise, remove serpentine drive belt, then slowly release tensioner.
2. Raise and support vehicle and remove right front wheel.
3. Place suitable drain pan under pump assembly, disconnect lines from pump, then plug lines and open ports.
4. Remove bolts and nut securing pump and the pump, **Fig. 19.**
5. Remove pulley using J-25034 or equivalent.
6. Install pulley on replacement pump using J-25033 or equivalent, then reverse remaining procedure to complete installation.

ALL WHEEL DRIVE (AWD) SYSTEM

The full time All Wheel Drive (AWD) system provides better directional control and improves traction and handling under most driving conditions, **Fig. 20.** This vehicle is powered by a V6-189/3.1L MFI engine which is directed through a THM-125C 3-speed automatic transaxle. The transaxle case has been modified to accept the AWD transfer case and also allows use of equal length half shafts. A redesigned cross member has been installed to allow for the additional space required for tailshaft and power steering rack.

With the exception of outer steering links and revised stabilizer bar, the front suspension components are the same as standard front wheel drive models.

Wheel Alignment Section

INDEX

Camber and toe-in are the only adjustments that can be performed on these vehicles.

CAMBER

The camber angle is adjusted by loosening the strut cam bolt and the through bolt and rotating the cam bolt to move the upper portion of the steering knuckle inboard or outboard. When correct camber angle is obtained, torque cam and through bolts to 140 ft. lbs.

When performing this adjustment, the top through bolt must be loosened to prevent damage to the outer cam guide.

TOE-IN

Toe-in is controlled by tie rod position. Adjustment is made by loosening the nuts at the steering knuckle end of the tie rods and rotating the rods to obtain proper toe-in setting. When adjusting toe-in, the tie rod boot clamps must be removed. After correct toe-in setting is obtained, torque tie rod nuts to 45 ft. lbs.

FRONT WHEEL DRIVE BUICK ELECTRA, LESABRE & PARK AVE., CADILLAC DEVILLE & FLEETWOOD, OLDSMOBILE EIGHTY EIGHT & NINETY EIGHT, PONTIAC BONNEVILLE

NOTE: Refer to the rear of this manual for vehicle manufacturer's special service tool suppliers.

INDEX OF SERVICE OPERATIONS

Specifications

GENERAL ENGINE SPECIFICATIONS

Year	Engine CID(1)/Liter	Engine VIN Code (2)	Carburetor	Bore and Stroke	Compression Ratio	Net H.P. @ RPM(3)	Maximum Torque Ft. Lbs. @ RPM	Normal Oil Pressure Pounds
1985	V6-181, 3.0L	E	E2ME, 2 Bbl.(5)	3.80 x 2.666	8.4	110 @ 4800	145 @ 2600	37
	V6-231 MFI, 3.8L	3	Fuel Injection	3.80 x 3.40	8	125 @ 4400	195 @ 2000	37
	V6-262, 4.3L(4)	T	Fuel Injection	4.057 x 3.385	22.5	85 @ 3600	165 @ 1600	30-45
	V8-250, 4.1L	8	Fuel Injection	3.465 x 3.307	9	125 @ 4200	190 @ 2200	30
1986	V6-181, 3.0L	L	Fuel Injection	3.80 x 2.66	8.45	125 @ 4900	150 @ 2400	37
	V6-231, 3.8L	B	Fuel Injection	3.80 x 3.40	8.5	150 @ 4400	200 @ 2000	37
	V6-231, 3.8L	3	Fuel Injection	3.80 x 3.40	8.5	140 @ 4400	200 @ 2000	37
	V8-250, 4.1L	8	Fuel Injection	3.465 x 3.307	9.0	130 @ 4200	200 @ 2200	30
1987	V6-231, 3.8L	3	Fuel Injection	3.80 x 3.40	8.50	150 @ 4400	200 @ 2000	37
	V8-250, 4.1L	8	Fuel Injection	3.46 x 3.31	9.0	130 @ 4200	200 @ 2200	30
1988	V6-231, 3.8L	—	Fuel Injection	3.80 x 3.40	8.50	150 @ 4400	200 @ 2000	37
	V6-231, 3.8L	—	Fuel Injection	3.80 x 3.40	8.50	165 @ 5200	210 @ 2000	37
	V8-273, 4.5L	—	Fuel Injection	3. 62 x 3.31	9.0	155 @ 4000	240 @ 2600	30

(1)—CID-Cubic inch displacement.
(2)—The eighth digit denotes engine code.
(3)—Ratings are net-as installed in vehicle.
(4)—Diesel engine.
(5)—Rochester.

ENGINE TIGHTENING SPECIFICATIONS*

*Torque specifications are for clean and lightly lubricated threads only. Dry or dirty threads produce increased friction which prevents accurate measurement of tightness.

Year	Engine Model/VIN	Spark Plugs Ft. Lbs.	Cylinder Head Bolts Ft. Lbs.	Intake Manifold Ft. Lbs.	Exhaust Manifold Ft. Lbs.	Rocker Arm Stud Ft. Lbs.	Rocker Arm Cover Ft. Lbs.	Connecting Rod Cap Bolts Ft. Lbs.	Main Bearing Cap Bolts Ft. Lbs.	Flywheel to Crankshaft Ft. Lbs.	Vibration Damper or Pulley Ft. Lbs.
1985	V6-181/E	15	72	47	25	25(2)	6	40	100	60	200
	V6-231/3	15	72	47	25	25(2)	6	40	100	60	200
	V6-262/T(1)	—	(3)(4)	41	31	(5)	(6)	42	89	76	203-350
	V8-250/8	11	(7)	(4)	18	22(8)	50(9)	22	85	63	18
1986	V6-181/L	20	(4)	32	37	45	7	40	100	60	200
	V6-231/B, 3	20	(4)	32	37	45	7	40	100	60	200
	V8-250/8	11	(7)	(4)	18	(8)	(10)	22	85	70	20
1987	V6-231/3	20	(4)	156(9)	37	43	88(9)	40	100	60	219
	V8-250/8	11	(7)	(4)	18	(8)	10	22	85	37	18
1988	V6-231/	—	—	—	—	—	—	—	—	—	—
	V8-273	—	—	—	—	—	—	—	—	—	—

(1)—Diesel engine.
(2)—Rocker arm shaft.
(3)—Clean & dip entire bolt in engine oil before tightening to obtain correct torque reading.
(4)—Refer to text for proper torque and sequence procedure.
(5)—Rocker arm pivot studs, 11 ft. lbs.; rocker arm nuts, 28 ft. lbs.
(6)—Fully driven, seated & not stripped.
(7)—Torque bolts in 3 steps: First-torque all bolts to 38 ft. lbs. Second-torque all bolts to 74 ft. lbs. Third-torque bolts 1, 3 and 4 to 90 ft. lbs. Refer to text for tightening sequence.
(8)—Rocker arm to support bolts, 22 ft. lbs.; support to cylinder head nuts, 37 ft. lbs.
(9)—Inch lbs.
(10)—Early models, 35 inch lbs.; Late models, 8 ft. lbs.

FRONT WHEEL ALIGNMENT SPECIFICATIONS

Year	Model	Caster Angle, Degrees		Camber Angle, Degrees				Toe-In Inch
				Limits		Desired		
		Limits	Desired	Left	Right	Left	Right	
1985	DeVille & Fleetwood	—	—	–.1 to +1.1	–.1 to +1.1	+.6	+.6	②
	Electra & Park Ave.	+1.8 to +2.8	+2.3	0 to 1①	0 to 1①	+.5①	+.5①	③
	98	+1.8 to +2.8	+2.3	+.25 to +.75	+.25 to +.75	+.5	+.5	②
1986	DeVille & Fleetwood	+1.5 to +3.5	+2.5	–1 to 0	0 to +1	–.5	+.5	④
	Electra & LeSabre	+1.8 to +2.8	+2.3	–1 to 0	0 to +1	–.5	+.5	④
	88 & 98	+1.8 to +2.8	+2.3	–1 to 0	0 to +1	–.5	+.5	④
1987	Bonneville	+1.5 to +3.0	+2.5	–.30 to +.70	–.30 to +.70	+.20	+.20	④
	DeVille & Fleetwood	+1.5 to +3.5	+2.5	–1 to 0	0 to +1	–.5	+.5	④
	Electra & LeSabre	+1.8 to +2.8	+2.3	–1 to 0	0 to +1	–.5	+.5	④
	88 & 98	+1.33 to +3.0	+2.5	–.3 to +.70	–.3 to +.70	+.2	+.2	④
1988	Bonneville	—	—	—	—	—	—	—
	DeVille & Fleetwood	—	—	—	—	—	—	—
	Electra & LeSabre	—	—	—	—	—	—	—
	88 & 98	—	—	—	—	—	—	—

①—Left and right side should be equal with 0.5°.
②—.125° toe-in.
③—.2° toe-out to .2° toe-in.
④—Toe-in 0° per wheel.

REAR WHEEL ALIGNMENT SPECIFICATIONS

Year	Model	Camber Angle, Degrees		Toe-In, Inches
		Limits	Desired	
1985	DeVille & Fleetwood	–.1 to +1.1	+.6	①
	Electra & Park Ave.	–.8 to +.2	–.3	②
	98	–.55 to –.05	–.3	②
1986	DeVille & Fleetwood	–.8 to +2	–.3	③
	Electra & LeSabre	–.8 to +.2	–.3	③
	88 & 98	–.8 to +.2	–.3	③
1987	Bonneville	③ –.8	to +.2	–.3
	DeVille & Fleetwood	–.8 to +.2	–.3	③
	Electra & LeSabre	–.8 to +.2	–.3	③
	88 & 98	–.8 to +.2	–.3	③
1988	Bonneville	—	—	—
	DeVille & Fleetwood	—	—	—
	Electra & LeSabre	—	—	—
	88 & 98	–.8 to +.2	–.3	③

①—0 to .4° toe-in.
②—0 to .2° toe-in.
③—Toe-in. 1° per wheel.

ALTERNATOR SPECIFICATIONS

Year	Model	Rated Hot Output Amps.
1985	01100278	108
	01105086	108
	01105200	85
	01105428	94
	01105553	97
1986	1101225	108
	1105615	108
	1105616	120
	1105625	108
	1105626	120
1987	1101250	108
	1101182	105
1988	—	—

STARTING MOTOR APPLICATIONS

Year	Engine/VIN	Starter Ident. No.
1985	V6-181/E	1998448
	V6-231 MFI/3	1998445
	V6-262 Diesel/T	22523207
	V8-250/8	1998476
1986	V6-181/L	1998521
	V6-231/B,3	1998521
	V6-231/B,3	1998544
	V8-250/8	—
1987	V6-231/3	1998544
	V8-250/	—
1988	V6-231/	—
	V8-273/	—

COOLING SYSTEM & CAPACITY DATA

Year	Model or Engine/VIN	Cooling Capacity, Qts.	Radiator Cap Relief Pressure, Lbs.	Thermo. Opening Temp.	Fuel Tank Gals.	Engine Oil Refill Qts.	Auto. Transaxle Qts. ①
1985	V6-181/E	13.3	15	195	18	4⑤	②
	V6-231/3	13.1	15	195	18	4⑤	②
	V8-250/8	13.2	15	195	18	5③	②
	V6-262/Diesel/T	13.4	17	195	18	6④	②
1986	V6-181/L, 88	12.8	15	195	18	4⑤	②
	V6-181/L, LeSabre	12.9	15	195	18	4⑤	②
	V6-231/B, 3, 88 & LeSabre	13.2	15	195	18	4⑤	②
	V6-231/B, Electra & 98	12.4	15	195	18	4⑤	②
	V8-250/8	13.2	15	195	18	5③	②
1987	V6-231/3, 88 & LeSabre	13.2	15	195	18	4⑤	②
	V6-231/3, Electra & 98	12.4	15	195	18	4⑤	②
	V8-250/8	13.2	15	195	18	4⑤	②
1988	V6-231	11.7	15	195	18	4⑤	②
	V8-273	—	15	195	18	4⑤	②

①—Approximate, make final check with dipstick.
②—Oil pan capacity, 6 qts.; total capacity, 10 qts.
③—With or without filter change.
④—Use recommended diesel engine oil, designate SF/CD or SF/CC.
⑤—Additional oil may be required to bring oil level to full mark when changing oil filter.

Electrical Section

INDEX

STARTER
REPLACE

When removing starter, note if any shims are used between the starter and mounting surface. If shims are found, reinstall in original locations.

If starter is noisy during cranking, remove one .015 inch double shim or add one .015 inch single shim to the outer bolt. If starter makes a high pitched whine after engine start, add .015 inch double shims until noise ceases.

EXC. V6-262 DIESEL

1. Disconnect battery ground cable and raise and support vehicle.
2. Remove starter braces, shields or other components that may hinder starter removal.
3. Support starter and remove mounting bolts.
4. Lower starter and disconnect solenoid wires and battery cable.
5. Remove starter from vehicle.
6. Reverse procedure to install. Refer to previous note.

V6-262 DIESEL

1. Disconnect battery ground cable. On vehicles with heavy duty option there are two batteries.
2. Install suitable engine lifting equipment.
3. Raise and support vehicle.
4. Remove left and center engine mount stud nuts, then the two front cradle mounting bolts and lower the cradle.
5. Remove flywheel cover.
6. Remove starter lower shield nut and starter flex shield.
7. Disconnect solenoid wires and battery cable from starter.
8. Remove starter mounting bolts and the starter from vehicle.
9. Reverse procedure to install.

STEERING WHEEL
REPLACE
STANDARD & TILT WHEEL

1. Disconnect battery ground cable.
2. Remove two steering wheel pad retaining screws.
3. Disconnect horn wire from cam tower.
4. Remove steering wheel nut retainer.

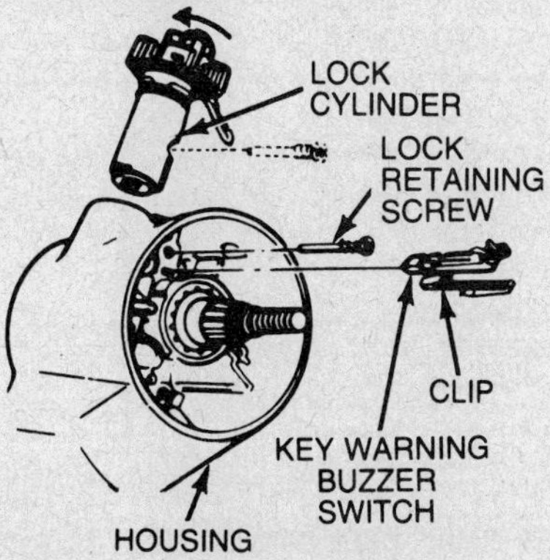

Fig. 1 Lock cylinder removal

5. Remove steering wheel retaining nut.
6. Using a suitable puller, remove steering wheel.
7. Reverse procedure to install.

TELESCOPING WHEEL
Exc. Cadillac

1. Disconnect battery ground cable.
2. Remove two steering wheel pad retaining screws.
3. Disconnect horn wire from steering wheel pad.
4. Remove steering shaft lock knob bolt positioning screws, then the lock knob bolt from steering shaft.
5. Remove steering wheel nut retainer and the steering wheel nut. Using a suitable puller, remove steering wheel.
6. Reverse procedure to install.

Cadillac

1. Disconnect battery ground cable.
2. Remove two steering wheel pad retaining screws.
3. Disconnect horn wire from steering wheel pad.
4. Remove three screws from telescoping adjusting lever.
5. Remove steering shaft lock knob from steering shaft.
6. Remove steering wheel nut.
7. Using a suitable puller, remove steering wheel.
8. Reverse procedure to install.

IGNITION LOCK
REPLACE

1. Remove steering wheel as outlined under "Steering Wheel, Replace" procedure.
2. Remove turn signal switch as outlined under "Turn Signal Switch, Replace" procedure.
3. Remove buzzer switch.
4. Turn lock cylinder to "Run" position, then remove lock cylinder retaining screw and the lock cylinder, **Fig. 1.**
5. To install, rotate lock cylinder to the stop while holding housing. Align cylinder key with keyway in housing, then push lock cylinder into housing until fully seated.
6. Install lock cylinder retaining screw.
7. Install buzzer switch, turn signal switch and steering wheel.

IGNITION & DIMMER SWITCHES
REPLACE

1. Remove turn signal switch as outlined under "Turn Signal Switch, Replace" procedure.
2. Refer to **Figs. 2 and 3** to remove ignition and dimmer switches.
3. When installing dimmer switch, depress switch slightly to install a 3/32 inch twist drill. Force switch upward to remove lash and tighten retaining screw.

TURN SIGNAL SWITCH
REPLACE

1. Disconnect battery ground cable.
2. Remove steering wheel as outlined previously.
3. Using a suitable screwdriver, pry cover from housing.
4. Using lock plate compressing tool J-23653, compress lock plate and pry snap ring from shaft groove, **Fig. 4.** Slowly release lock plate compressor and remove tool and lock plate from shaft end.
5. Slide cancelling cam and upper bearing preload spring from end of shaft.
6. Remove turn signal switch lever.

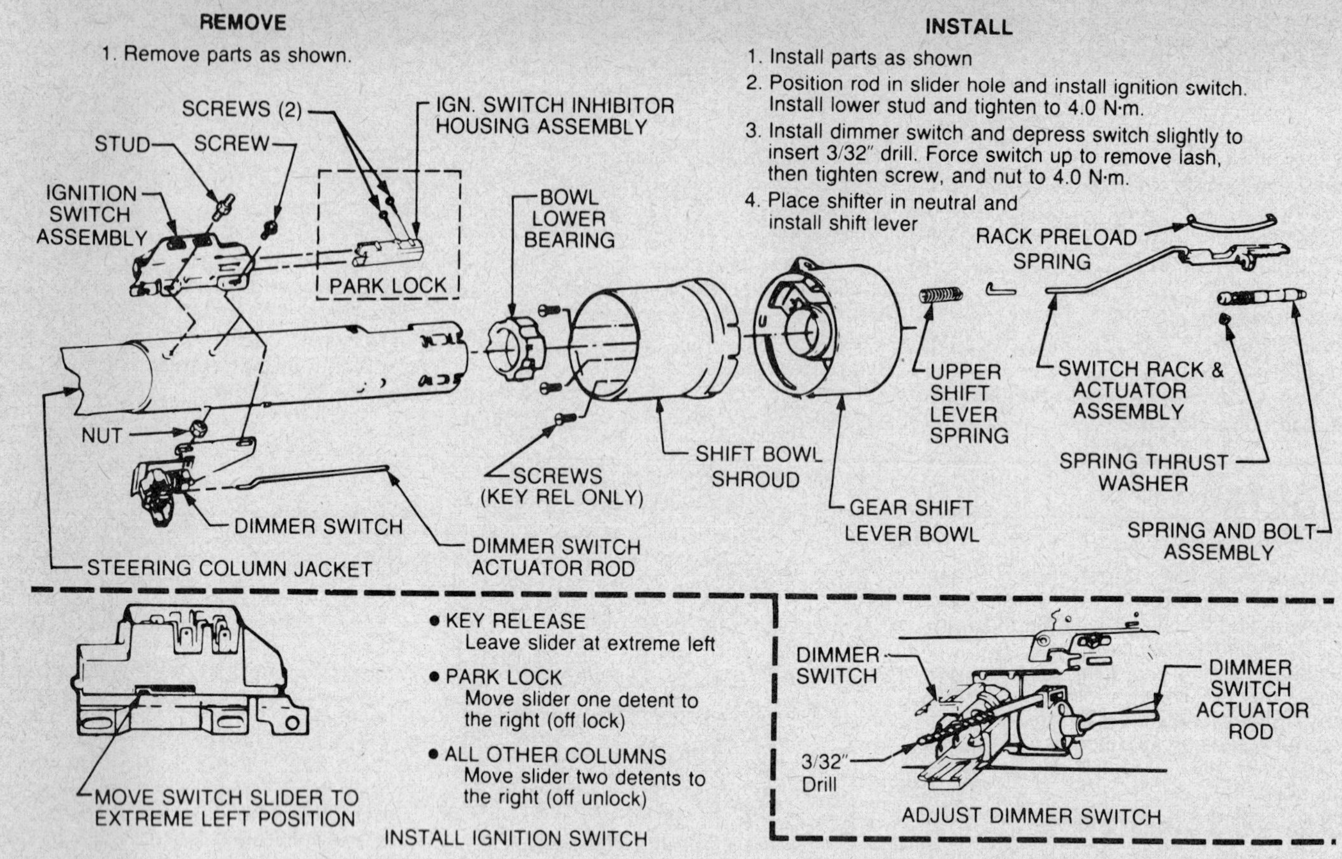
REMOVE
1. Remove parts as shown.
SCREWS (2)
STUD
SCREW
IGN. SWITCH INHIBITOR HOUSING ASSEMBLY
IGNITION SWITCH ASSEMBLY
PARK LOCK
BOWL LOWER BEARING
NUT
SCREWS (KEY REL ONLY)
SHIFT BOWL SHROUD
DIMMER SWITCH
STEERING COLUMN JACKET
DIMMER SWITCH ACTUATOR ROD
INSTALL
1. Install parts as shown
2. Position rod in slider hole and install ignition switch. Install lower stud and tighten to 4.0 N·m.
3. Install dimmer switch and depress switch slightly to insert 3/32" drill. Force switch up to remove lash, then tighten screw, and nut to 4.0 N·m.
4. Place shifter in neutral and install shift lever
RACK PRELOAD SPRING
UPPER SHIFT LEVER SPRING
SWITCH RACK & ACTUATOR ASSEMBLY
SPRING THRUST WASHER
GEAR SHIFT LEVER BOWL
SPRING AND BOLT ASSEMBLY
MOVE SWITCH SLIDER TO EXTREME LEFT POSITION
• KEY RELEASE
Leave slider at extreme left
• PARK LOCK
Move slider one detent to the right (off lock)
• ALL OTHER COLUMNS
Move slider two detents to the right (off unlock)
INSTALL IGNITION SWITCH
DIMMER SWITCH
3/32" Drill
DIMMER SWITCH ACTUATOR ROD
ADJUST DIMMER SWITCH

Fig. 2 Ignition & dimmer switch removal & installation. Except tilt column

7. Remove hazard warning knob retaining screw, button, spring and knob.
8. Remove pivot arm.
9. Wrap upper portion of electrical connector with tape to prevent snagging of wires during switch removal.
10. Remove switch retaining screws and pull switch up from column, guiding wiring harness through column.
11. Reverse procedure to install.

WIPER SWITCH
REPLACE

1. Remove turn signal switch as outlined under "Turn Signal Switch, Replace" procedure.
2. Refer to **Figs. 5 and 6** for wiper switch replacement.

MECHANICAL NEUTRAL START SYSTEM

Actuation of the ignition switch is prevented by a mechanical lockout system, **Fig. 7.** This prevents the lock cylinder from rotating when the transmission is out of the Park or Neutral position. When the selector lever is in the Park or Neutral position, the slots in the bowl plate and the finger on the actuator rod align, allowing the finger to pass through the bowl plate in turn actuating the ignition switch. If the transmission shift lever is in any other position, the finger contacts the bowl plate when the lock cylinder is rotated.

PARK/NEUTRAL & BACK-UP LAMP SWITCH
REPLACE

This switch is mounted on the transaxle.

1. Disconnect battery ground cable.
2. Disconnect shift cable from transaxle.
3. Disconnect electrical connector from switch.
4. Remove two switch mounting bolts and the switch.
5. Align flats on switch with flats on transaxle shaft and push switch over shaft and fully seat on transaxle.
6. Install and torque switch mounting bolts to 20 ft. lbs. **If switch was rotated and the pin broken, the switch will be automatically reset to the neutral position as follows:**
   a. Place transaxle shaft in neutral position.
   b. Install switch on transaxle as outlined previously and loosely install mounting bolts.
   c. Insert a 3/32 inch gauge pin into service adjustment hole of switch.
   d. Rotate switch until pin drops in detent.
   e. Torque mounting bolts to 20 ft. lbs.

HEADLAMP SWITCH
REPLACE
BUICK

Refer to **Fig. 8** for switch replacement.

CADILLAC

Refer to **Fig. 9** for switch replacement.

OLDSMOBILE

Refer to **Fig. 10** for switch replacement.

PONTIAC

Refer to **Fig. 11** for switch replacement.

INSTRUMENT CLUSTER
REPLACE
BUICK

Refer to **Figs. 12, 13 and 14** for instrument cluster replacement.

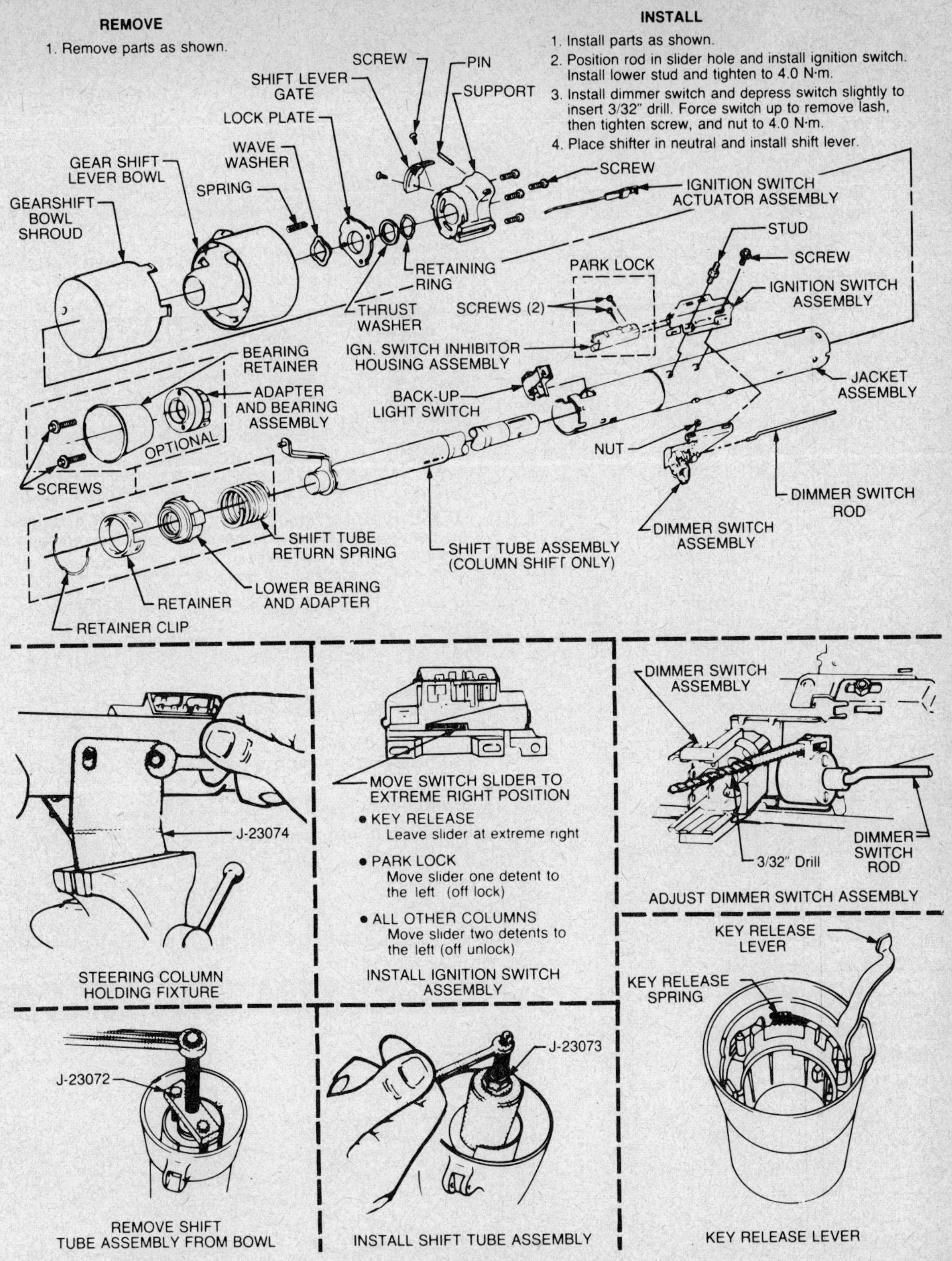

Fig. 3 Ignition & dimmer switch removal & installation. Tilt column

CADILLAC

1. Disconnect battery ground cable.
2. Remove upper trim pad as follows:
   a. Remove A/C outlets from upper trim pad.
   b. Remove screws locations 2 and 3 from both side of pad, **Fig. 15.**
   c. Remove upper trim pad.
3. Remove screw (88) and plate (87), **Fig. 16.**
4. Remove cluster attaching screws.
5. Disconnect wiring from rear of cluster and remove cluster from vehicle.
6. Reverse procedure to install.

OLDSMOBILE

Refer to **Figs. 17, 18 and 19** for switch replacement.

PONTIAC

1. Disconnect battery ground cable.
2. On models w/tilt wheel, place wheel in lowest position.
3. On all models, place selector lever in position "1."
4. lightly pry around perimeter of trimplate, then remove trimplate.
5. Remove IP trimplate, then the speaker, side defogger and defroster grilles.
6. Remove speaker attaching screws and electrical connectors.
7. Remove I/P pad.
8. Remove 5 attaching screws, **Fig. 20,** then disconnect PRNDL cable from steering column bowl.
9. Remove instrument cluster.
10. Reverse procedure to install.

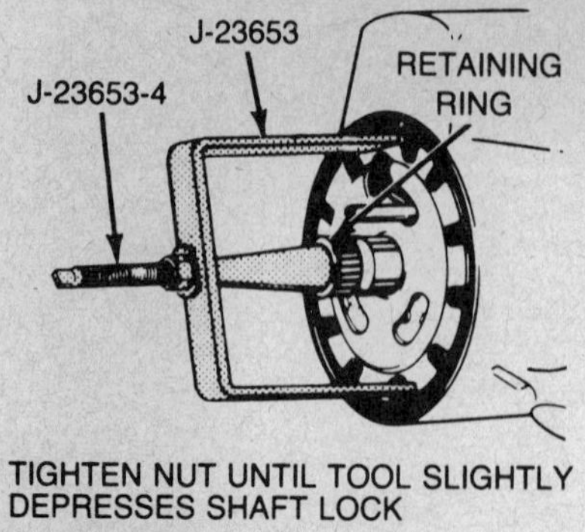
J-23653
J-23653-4
RETAINING RING
TIGHTEN NUT UNTIL TOOL SLIGHTLY DEPRESSES SHAFT LOCK

Fig. 4 Compressing lock plate

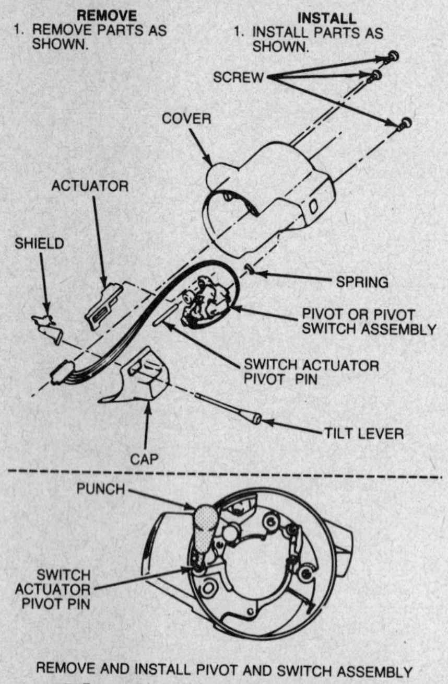
REMOVE
1. REMOVE PARTS AS SHOWN.
INSTALL
1. INSTALL PARTS AS SHOWN.
SCREW
COVER
ACTUATOR
SHIELD
SPRING
PIVOT OR PIVOT SWITCH ASSEMBLY
SWITCH ACTUATOR PIVOT PIN
TILT LEVER
CAP
PUNCH
SWITCH ACTUATOR PIVOT PIN
REMOVE AND INSTALL PIVOT AND SWITCH ASSEMBLY

Fig. 6 Cover & wiper switch removal & installation. Tilt steering column

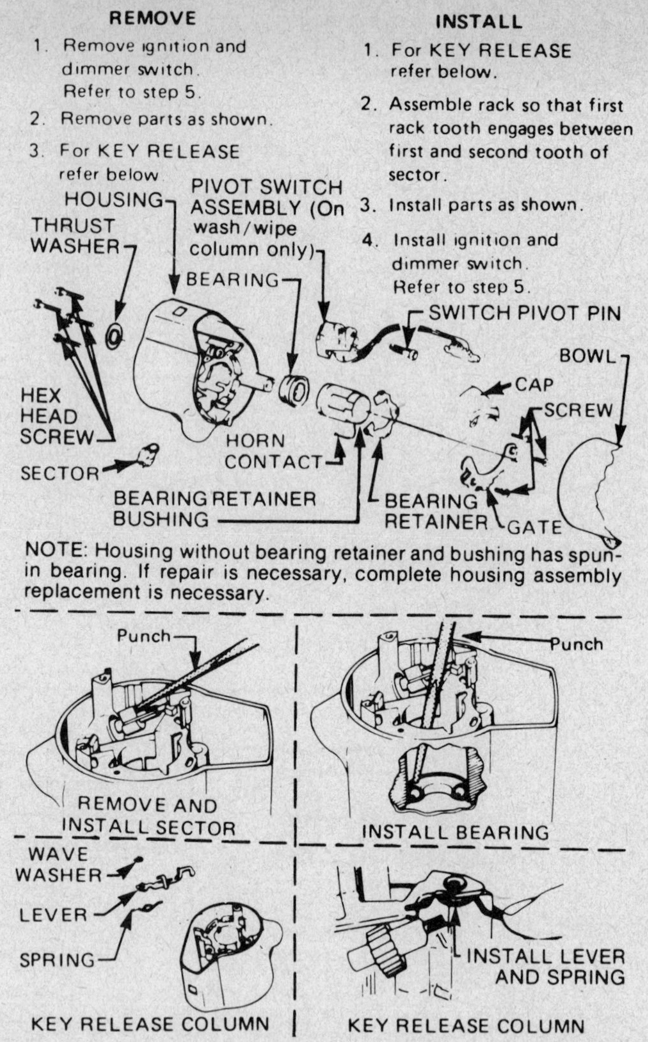
REMOVE
1. Remove ignition and dimmer switch. Refer to step 5.
2. Remove parts as shown.
3. For KEY RELEASE refer below.
INSTALL
1. For KEY RELEASE refer below.
2. Assemble rack so that first rack tooth engages between first and second tooth of sector.
3. Install parts as shown.
4. Install ignition and dimmer switch. Refer to step 5.
HOUSING
PIVOT SWITCH ASSEMBLY (On wash/wipe column only)
THRUST WASHER
BEARING
SWITCH PIVOT PIN
BOWL
CAP
SCREW
HEX HEAD SCREW
HORN CONTACT
SECTOR
BEARING RETAINER BUSHING
BEARING RETAINER
GATE
NOTE: Housing without bearing retainer and bushing has spun-in bearing. If repair is necessary, complete housing assembly replacement is necessary.
Punch
Punch
REMOVE AND INSTALL SECTOR
INSTALL BEARING
WAVE WASHER
LEVER
SPRING
INSTALL LEVER AND SPRING
KEY RELEASE COLUMN
KEY RELEASE COLUMN

Fig. 5 Housing & wiper switch removal & installation. Standard steering column

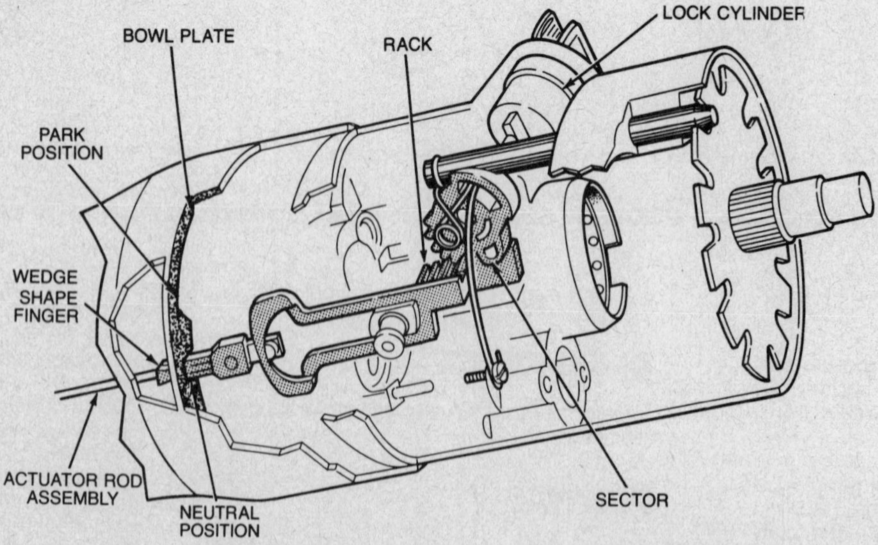
BOWL PLATE
RACK
LOCK CYLINDER
PARK POSITION
WEDGE SHAPE FINGER
ACTUATOR ROD ASSEMBLY
NEUTRAL POSITION
SECTOR

Fig. 7 Mechanical neutral start system

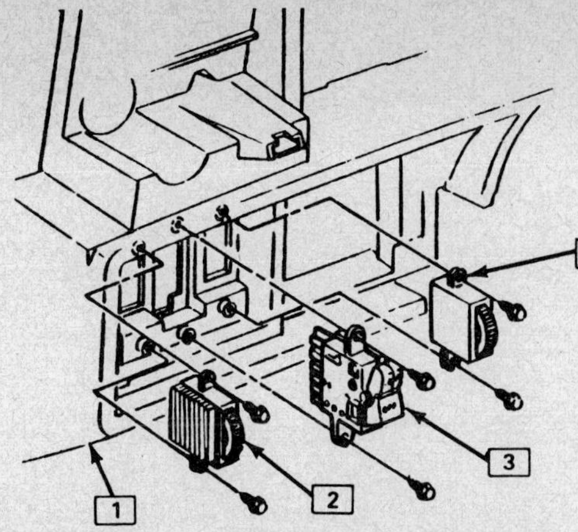

1 I/P CARRIER
2 INTERIOR LIGHT DIMMER
3 HEADLAMP SWITCH
4 TWILIGHT SENTINEL SWITCH

Fig. 8 Headlamp switch removal. Electra, LeSabre & Park Avenue

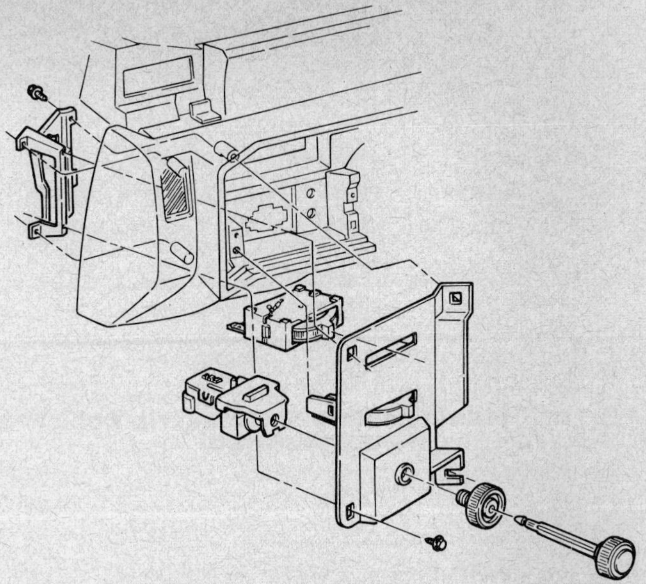

Fig. 9 Headlamp switch removal. DeVille & Fleetwood

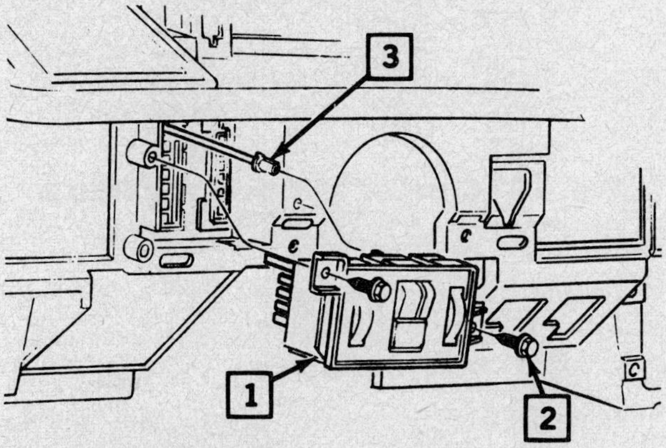

1. HEADLAMP SWITCH
2. FULLY DRIVEN, SEATED AND NOT STRIPPED
3. PLUG FIBER OPTIC INTO REAR OF SWITCH ASM.

Fig. 10 Headlamp switch removal. 88 & 98

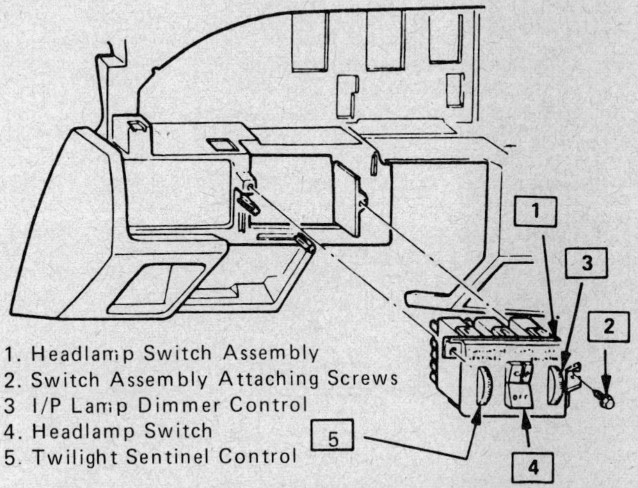

1. Headlamp Switch Assembly
2. Switch Assembly Attaching Screws
3 I/P Lamp Dimmer Control
4. Headlamp Switch
5. Twilight Sentinel Control

Fig. 11 Headlamp switch removal. Bonneville

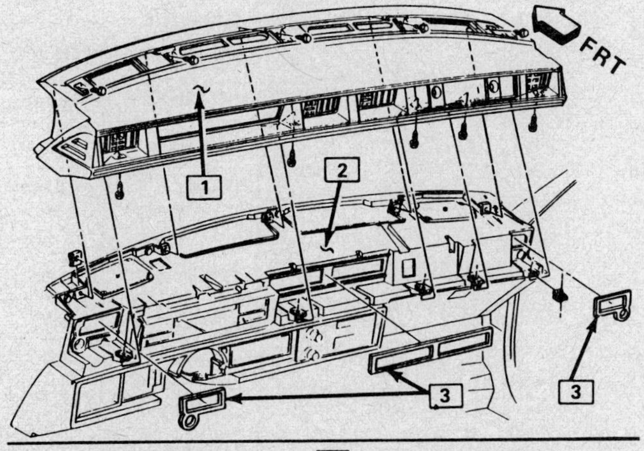

1 I/P TOP COVER (PAD)
2 I/P CARRIER
3 A/C OUTLET SEALS

Fig. 12 Removing instrument panel top cover pad. Electra, LeSabre & Park Avenue

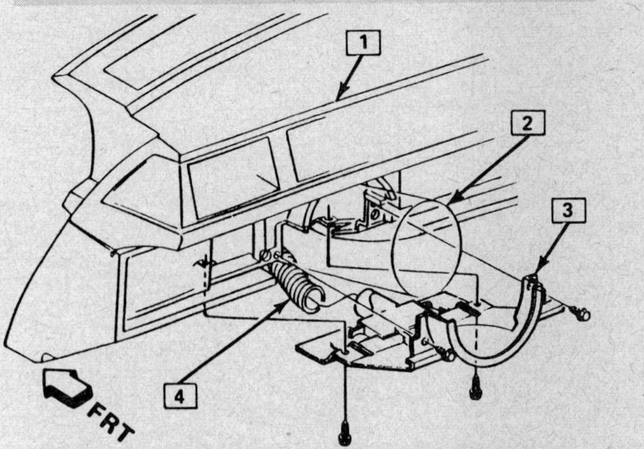

1 INSTRUMENT PANEL
2 STEERING COLUMN
3 TRIM COVER
4 A/C OUTLET HOSE

Fig. 13 Removing steering column cover to disconnect shift cable. Electra, LeSabre & Park Avenue w/quartz cluster

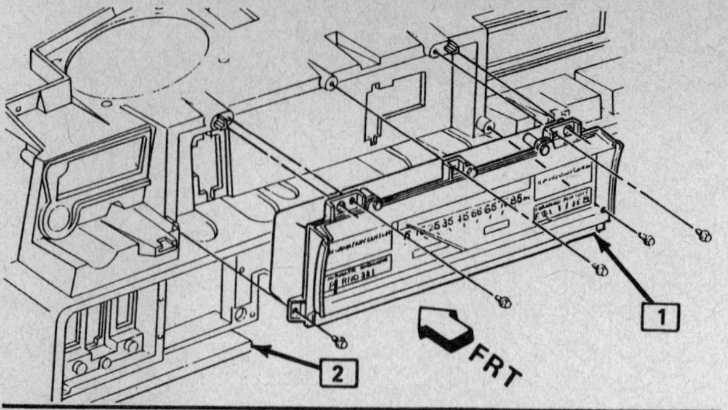

[1] CLUSTER HOUSING ASM. [2] I/P CARRIER

Fig. 14 Cluster removal. Electra, LeSabre & Park Avenue

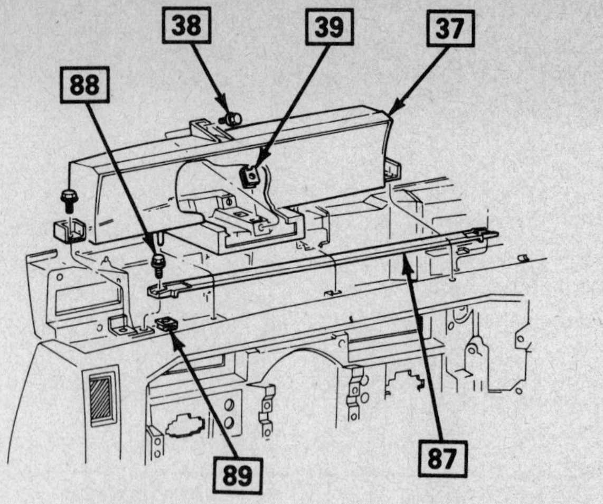

[37] CLUSTER ASSEMBLY
[38] SCREW
[39] NUT
[87] PLATE
[88] SCREW
[89] NUT

Fig. 16 Cluster removal. DeVille & Fleetwood

RADIO

REPLACE

BUICK

Refer to **Fig. 21** for radio replacement.

CADILLAC

1. Disconnect battery ground cable.
2. Remove radio trim plate, **Fig. 22.**
3. Remove screws from rear support bracket and front of radio. The ashtray must be opened for access.
4. Remove light bulb and socket.
5. Disconnect electrical connectors from radio.
6. Disconnect antenna lead from radio.
7. Remove radio from vehicle.
8. Reverse procedure to install.

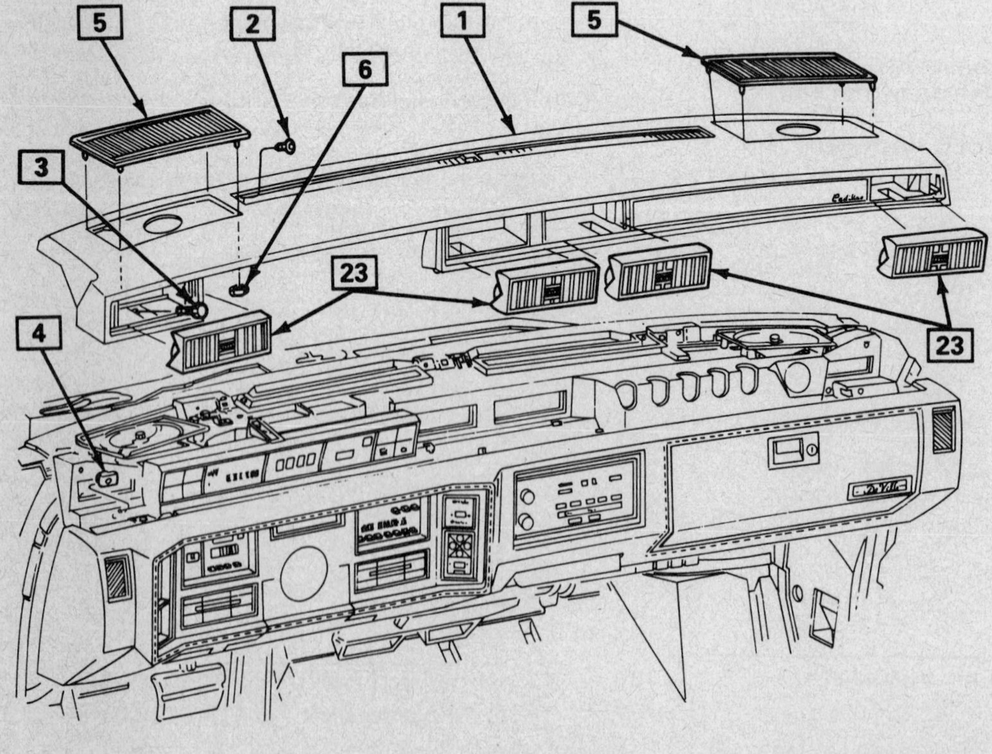

[1] CHART – PAD ASSEMBLY
[2] SCREW
[3] SCREW
[4] NUT
[5] GRILLE
[6] NUT
[23] OUTLET

Fig. 15 Upper trim pad assembly. DeVille & Fleetwood

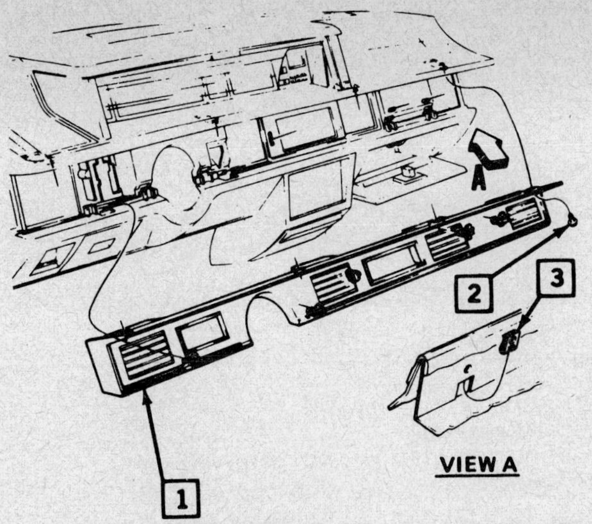

1. CENTER TRIM PLATE
2. FULLY DRIVEN, SEATED AND NOT STRIPPED
3. NUT

Fig. 17 Center instrument panel trim plate. 88 & 98

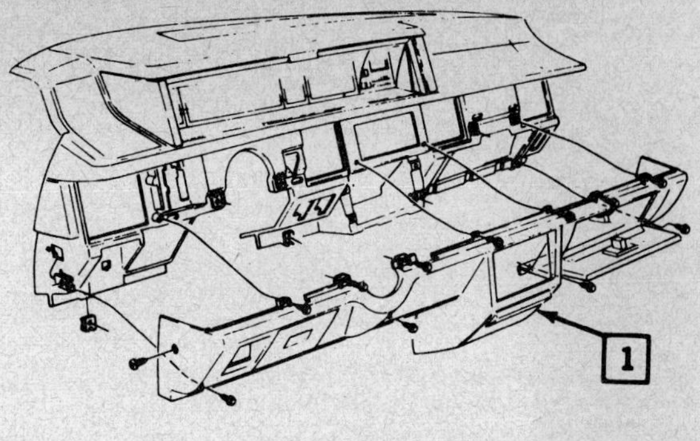

1. I.P. LOWER TRIM

TIGHTEN FASTENERS UNTIL THEY ARE FULLY DRIVEN, SEATED AND NOT STRIPPED – 1.8 N•m (16 LBS. IN.) MAXIMUM

Fig. 18 Lower instrument panel trim plate. 88 & 98

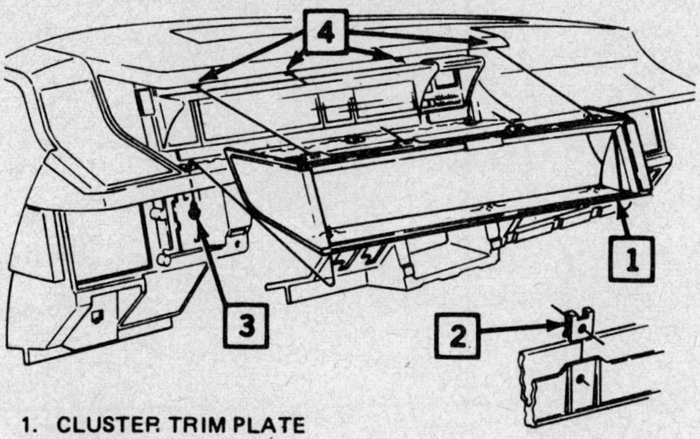

1. CLUSTER TRIM PLATE
2. NUT (3)
3. FULLY DRIVEN, SEATED AND NOT STRIPPED
4. WEDGE TRIM PLATE EXISTING CLIPS AND I.P. PAD ASSEMBLY

Fig. 19 Cluster removal. 88 & 98

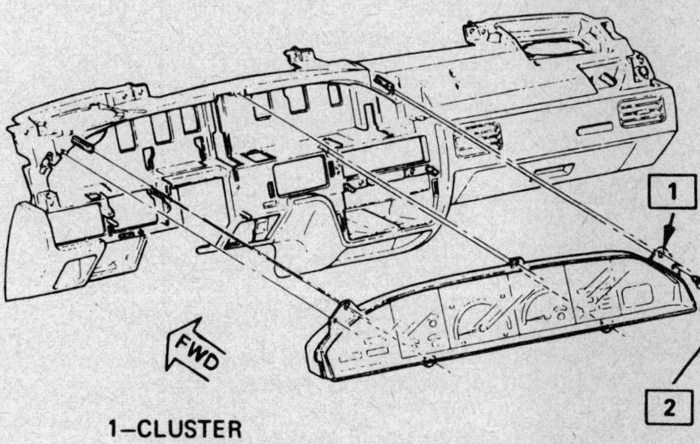

1–CLUSTER

2–FULLY DRIVEN, SEATED, NOT STRIPPED

Fig. 20 Cluster removal. Bonneville

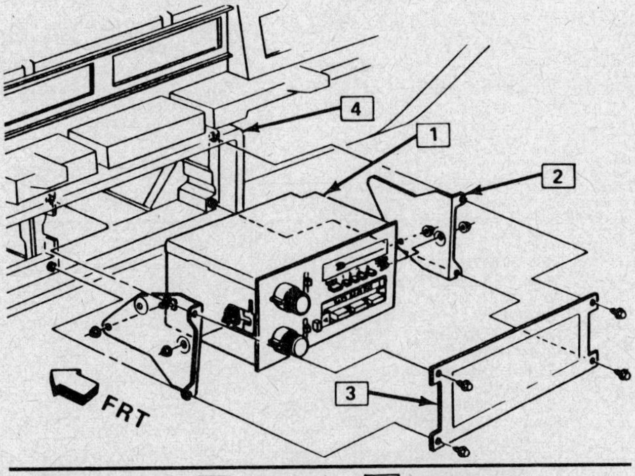

1 RADIO
2 BRACKET
3 COVER IF NO RADIO
4 I/P CARRIER

Fig. 21 Radio installation. Electra, LeSabre & Park Avenue

1 RADIO ASSEMBLY
2 TRIM PLATE
3 SCREW

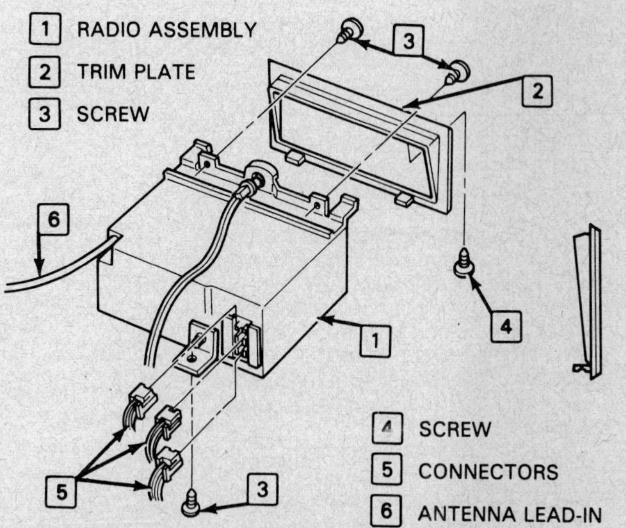

4 SCREW
5 CONNECTORS
6 ANTENNA LEAD-IN

Fig. 22 Radio installation. DeVille & Fleetwood

OLDSMOBILE

Refer to **Fig. 23** for radio replacement.

PONTIAC

Refer to **Fig. 24** for radio replacement.

BLOWER MOTOR REPLACE

1. Disconnect battery ground cable.
2. Disconnect blower motor electrical connector.
3. Remove blower motor attaching screws and the blower motor.
4. Reverse procedure to install.

HEATER CORE REPLACE

EXC. CADILLAC

1. Disconnect battery ground cable.
2. Drain cooling system.
3. Remove lower sound insulator.
4. Remove center and lower instrument panel trim plates.
5. Remove speaker grille and speaker for access to programmer attaching bolt.
6. Disconnect wiring and hoses from programmer.
7. Remove programmer linkage cover and disconnect linkage.
8. Remove programmer attaching bolt and the programmer.
9. Remove heater core cover and the splash cover for access to heater core.
10. Disconnect heater hoses from heater core.
11. Remove heater core from case.
12. Reverse procedure to install.

CADILLAC

1. Disconnect battery ground cable.
2. Remove glove box attaching screws, then the glove box.
3. Remove lower sound insulator attaching screws and nuts, then the lower sound insulator.
4. Remove programmer as follows:
   a. Remove programmer shield attaching screws, then the programmer shield.
   b. Disconnect threaded rod from programmer.
   c. Disconnect programmer electrical and vacuum connector, then remove programmer.
5. Disconnect body control module electrical connector, then remove module attaching screws and module.
6. Remove relay panel from module assembly, then the module assembly heater core cover.
7. Disconnect heater hoses from heater core.
8. Remove two heater core attaching screws, then the heater core.
9. Reverse procedure to install.

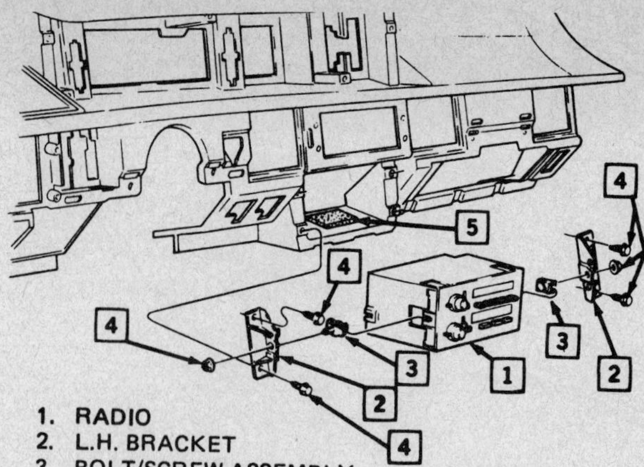

1. RADIO
2. L.H. BRACKET
3. BOLT/SCREW ASSEMBLY
4. FULLY DRIVEN, SEATED AND NOT STRIPPED
5. INSULATOR

Fig. 23 Radio replace. 88 & 98

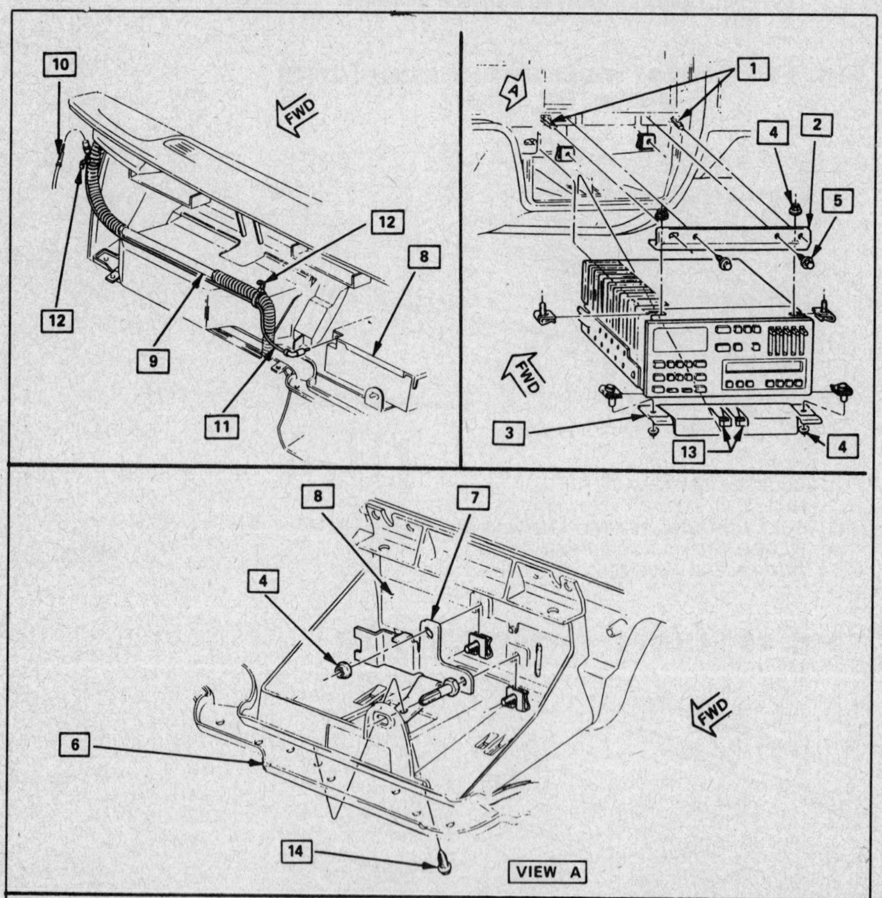

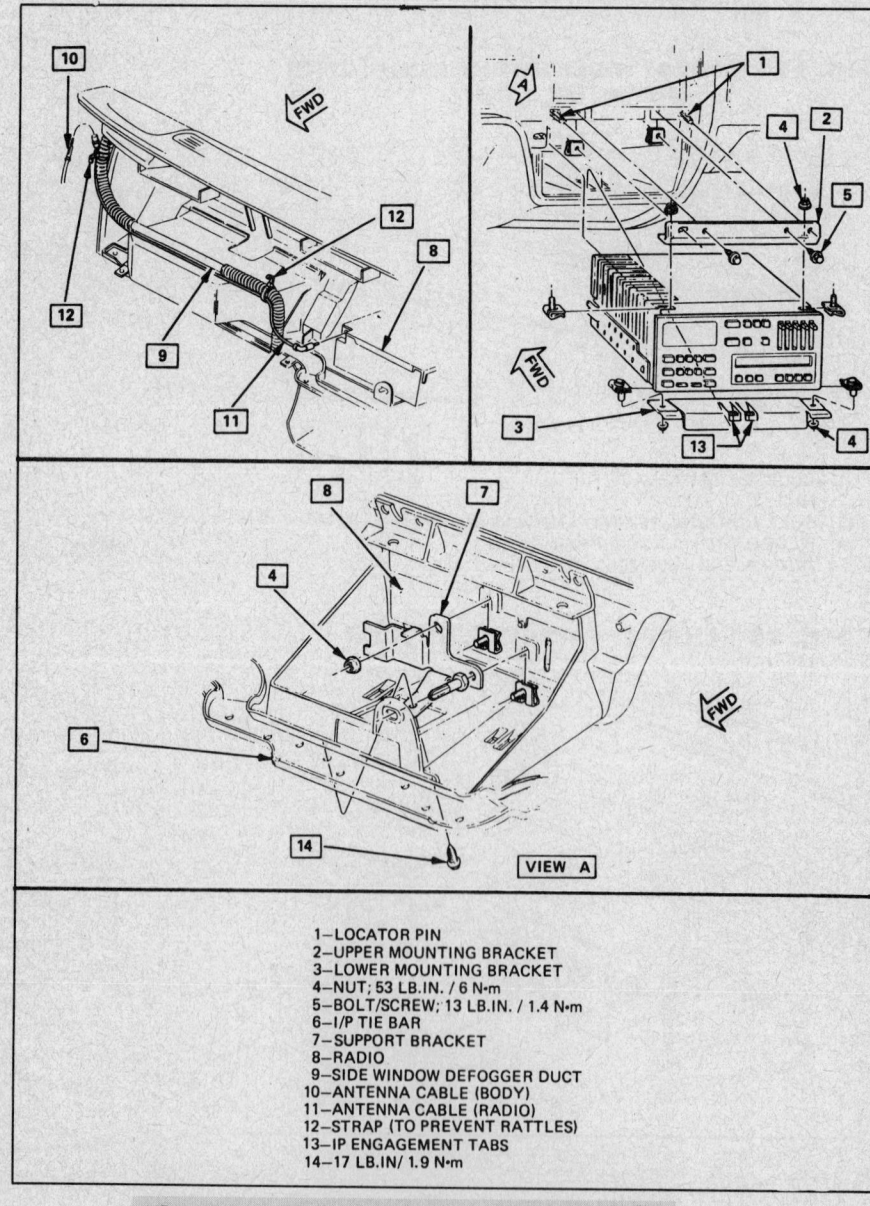

1–LOCATOR PIN
2–UPPER MOUNTING BRACKET
3–LOWER MOUNTING BRACKET
4–NUT; 53 LB.IN. / 6 N•m
5–BOLT/SCREW; 13 LB.IN. / 1.4 N•m
6–I/P TIE BAR
7–SUPPORT BRACKET
8–RADIO
9–SIDE WINDOW DEFOGGER DUCT
10–ANTENNA CABLE (BODY)
11–ANTENNA CABLE (RADIO)
12–STRAP (TO PREVENT RATTLES)
13–IP ENGAGEMENT TABS
14–17 LB.IN/ 1.9 N•m

Fig. 24 Radio replace. Bonneville

V6-181 (3.0L) & V6-231 (3.8L) Gasoline Engine Section

INDEX

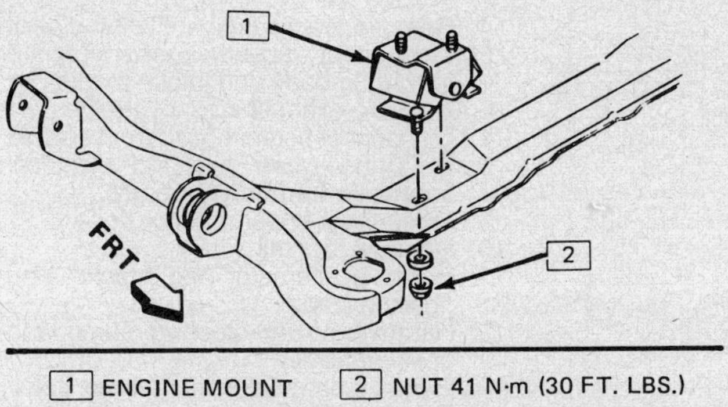

Fig. 1 Engine mount, right side

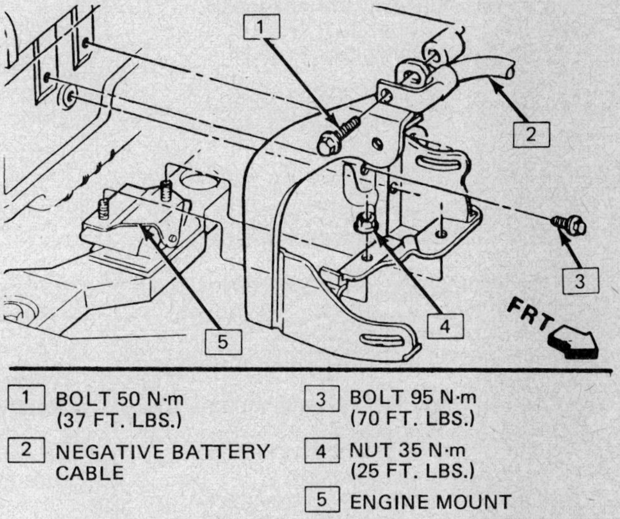

Fig. 2 Engine mount, left side

ENGINE MOUNTS
REPLACE

1. Raise and support front of vehicle.
2. Attach suitable engine lifting equipment to engine.
3. Remove mount to engine bracket nuts. Raise engine slightly and remove mount to frame nuts.
4. Remove engine mount, **Figs. 1 and 2.**
5. Reverse procedure to install.

ENGINE
REPLACE

1. Disconnect battery cables.
2. Disconnect mass airflow sensor electrical connector.
3. Remove air intake duct.
4. Drain cooling system.
5. Raise and support vehicle.
6. Disconnect exhaust pipe from exhaust manifolds.
7. Remove engine mount bolts.
8. Remove driveline vibration absorber, **Fig. 3.**
9. Remove starter motor.
10. Remove A/C compressor from bracket and position aside.
11. Disconnect power steering hoses from steering gear.
12. Remove lower transaxle to engine bolts. **One bolt is located between the transaxle case and the engine block and is installed in the opposite direction.**
13. Remove flexplate cover, then the flexplate to torque converter bolts.
14. Remove engine support bracket from transaxle.
15. Lower vehicle.
16. Disconnect radiator and heater hoses from engine.
17. Remove alternator from bracket and position aside.
18. Disconnect engine wiring harness.
19. Remove remaining transaxle to engine bolts.
20. Remove engine from vehicle.
21. Reverse procedure to install.

INTAKE MANIFOLD
REPLACE
1985

1. Disconnect battery ground cable.
2. Drain cooling system.
3. Remove mass airflow sensor and air intake duct.
4. Disconnect accelerator, cruise control and throttle valve cables from throttle body.
5. Remove crankcase ventilation pipe.
6. Disconnect vacuum line from throttle body.
7. Disconnect upper radiator and heater hoses from engine.
8. Disconnect fuel line.
9. Disconnect the following electrical connectors: TPS switch, IAC connector at throttle body, water temperature switch, coolant temperature switch and fan control switch.
10. Remove fuel rail.
11. Remove alternator and bracket and position aside.

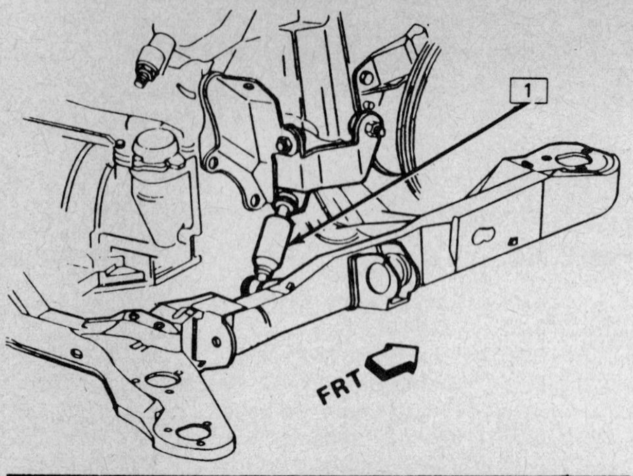

1 DRIVELINE VIBRATION ABSORBER

Fig. 3 Typical drive line vibration absorber

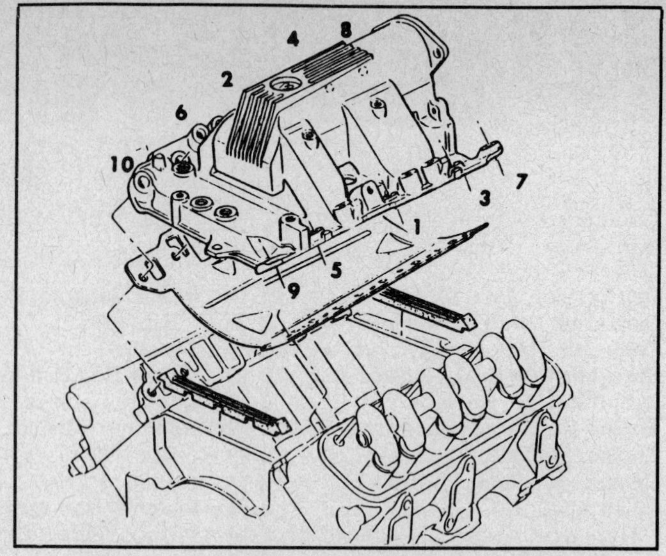

Fig. 4 Intake manifold bolt torque sequence. 1985

12. Remove distributor cap and rotor. This is for access to the torx head bolt.
13. Remove intake manifold bolts and the intake manifold.
14. Reverse procedure to install. Torque manifold bolts in sequence, **Fig. 4,** to 47 ft. lbs.

EXC. 1985

1. Disconnect battery ground cable.
2. Remove mass air flow sensor and air intake duct.
3. Remove serpentine accessory drive belt, generator and bracket.
4. Disconnect C3 ignition module electrical connector, then remove C3 ignition module.
5. Disconnect vacuum lines and wiring connectors as necessary.
6. Disconnect cruise control, throttle and T.V. cables from throttle body.
7. Drain cooling system, then disconnect heater hoses from throttle body.
8. Disconnect upper radiator hose, then the fuel lines, fuel rail and injectors.
9. Remove intake manifold attaching bolts, then the manifold and gasket.
10. Reverse procedure to install. Torque manifold bolts in sequence shown in **Fig. 5.**

EXHAUST MANIFOLD REPLACE

LEFT SIDE

1. Disconnect battery ground cable.
2. Remove mass airflow sensor, air intake duct and crankcase ventilation pipe.
3. Remove two bolts attaching exhaust crossover pipe to manifold.
4. Disconnect spark plug wires from spark plugs.
5. Remove exhaust manifold attaching bolts and the exhaust manifold. **The dipstick and tube may be removed to provide additional clearance.**
6. Reverse procedure to install.

RIGHT SIDE

1. Disconnect battery ground cable.

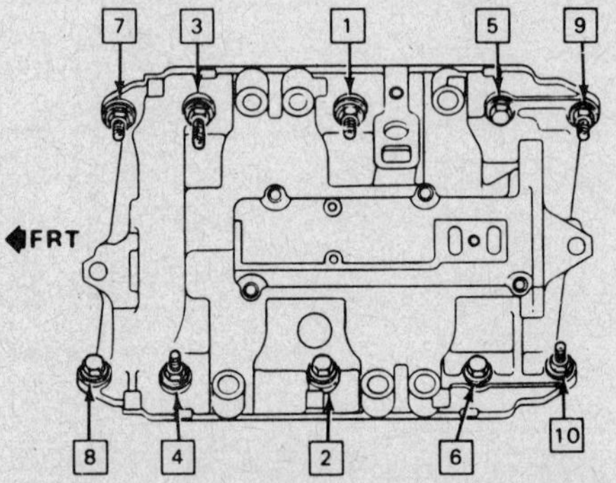

Fig. 5 Intake manifold bolt torque sequence. Exc. 1985

2. Remove mass airflow sensor, air intake duct and crankcase ventilation pipe.
3. Disconnect IAC wiring connector from throttle body.
4. Remove two bolts attaching exhaust crossover pipe to manifold.
5. Disconnect spark plug wires from spark plugs.
6. Disconnect oxygen sensor electrical lead.
7. Remove heater inlet pipe from manifold studs.
8. Remove alternator support bracket.
9. Remove exhaust manifold bolts.
10. Raise and support vehicle.
11. Remove exhaust pipe to manifold bolts.
12. Remove front exhaust pipe.
13. Remove exhaust manifold.
14. Reverse procedure to install.

CYLINDER HEAD REPLACE

1. Disconnect battery ground cable and drain cooling system.
2. Remove mass airflow sensor and air intake duct.
3. Disconnect accelerator, cruise control and throttle valve cables from throttle body.
4. Remove crankcase ventilation pipe.
5. Disconnect vacuum hoses attached to throttle body and intake manifold.
6. Remove exhaust crossover pipe.
7. Disconnect heater hoses from engine.
8. Disconnect fuel line and electrical connector from throttle body.
9. Disconnect upper radiator hose.
10. Remove fuel rail.
11. Remove alternator and bracket and position aside.
12. Remove power steering pump and position aside.
13. Remove right side exhaust manifold.
14. Remove distributor cap and rotor, if necessary.
15. Remove A/C compressor bracket bolt.
16. Remove left side exhaust manifold.
17. Remove valve covers.
18. Remove intake manifold.
19. Remove rocker arm shaft assemblies and push rods. All valve train parts must be installed in original locations.
20. Remove cylinder head bolts and the cylinder head.
21. Reverse procedure to install.
22. On 1985 engines, refer to tightening sequence, **Fig. 6,** and torque bolts in three steps until a final torque of 72 ft. lbs. is reached. After 15 minutes, retorque bolts to 72 ft. lbs.
23. On engines exc. 1985, refer to tightening sequence, **Fig. 6,** and tighten cylinder head bolts in 3 steps as follows:
    a. Torque all bolts to 25 ft. lbs.
    b. Tighten each bolt an additional 90°, in sequence, noting torque value as bolt is tightened. **Should torque on bolt being tightening reached 60 ft. lbs. at any time, stop at this point and do not complete 90° rotation. Uneven tightening of bolts may distort cylinder bores, causing loss of compression and increased oil consumption.**
    c. Tighten each bolt an additional 90°, in sequence, noting torque value as bolt is tightened.

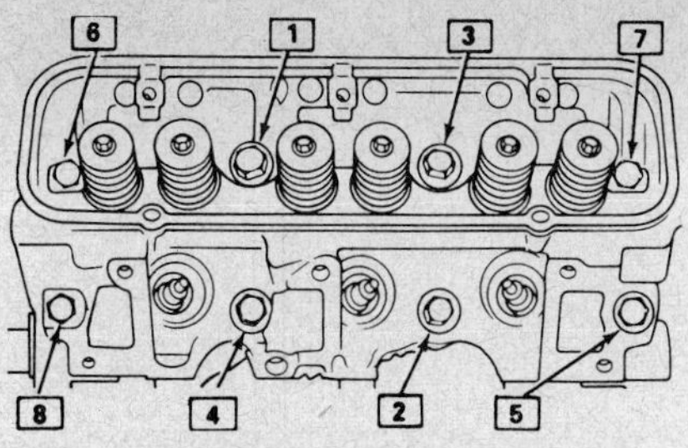

Fig. 6 Cylinder head bolt torque sequence

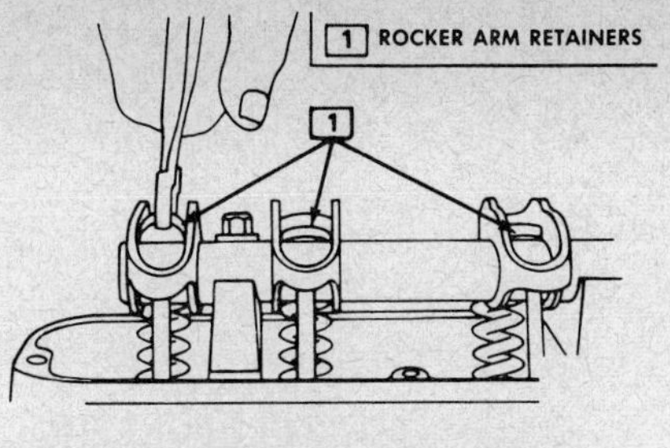

Fig. 7 Removing nylon retainer. 1985

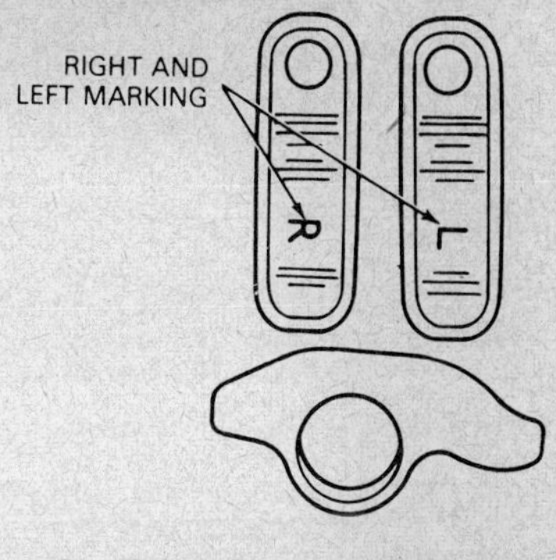

Fig. 8 Service rocker arm identification. 1985

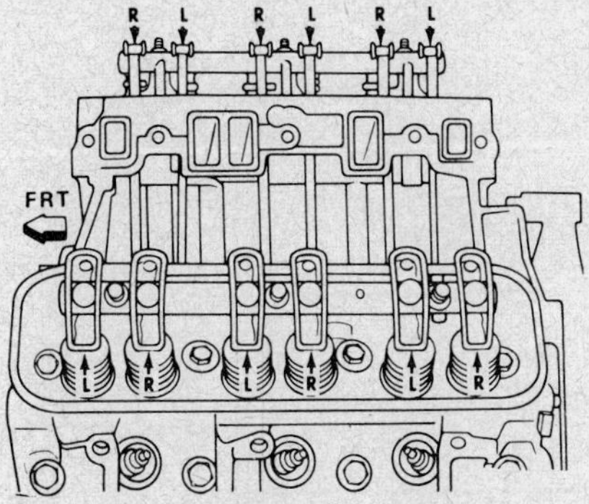

Fig. 9 Service rocker arm installation. 1985

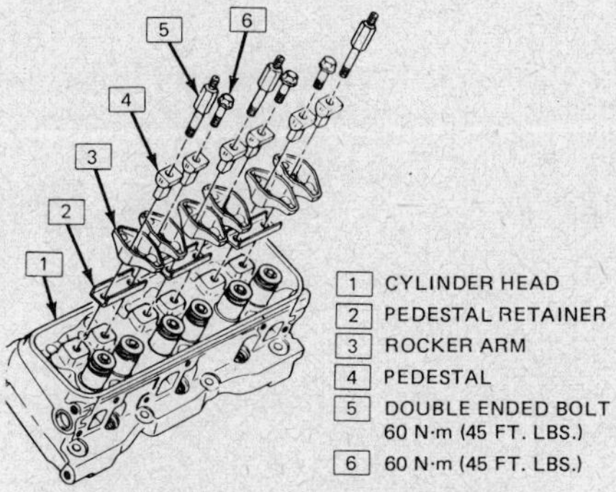

Fig. 10 Rocker arm installation. Exc. 1985

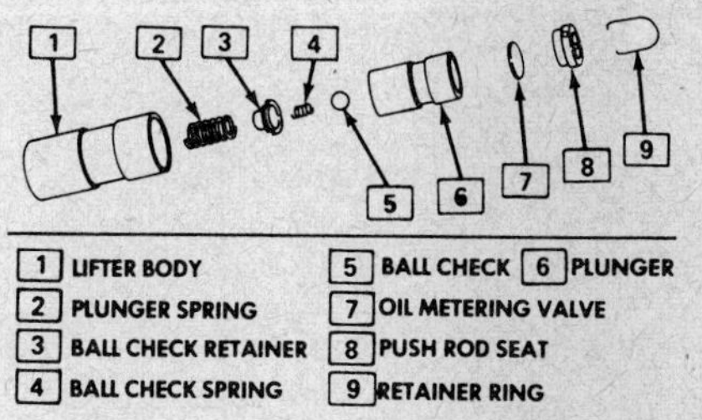

Fig. 11 Flat type hydraulic valve lifter exploded view

ROCKER ARMS

1985 MODELS

A nylon retainer is used to retain the rocker arm. Break them below their heads with a chisel or pry out with channel lock pliers, **Fig. 7.** Production rocker arms can be installed in any sequence since the rocker arms are identical.

Replacement rocker arms are identified with a stamping indicating right (R) or left (L), **Fig. 8**, and must be installed as shown in **Fig. 9.** To install, position rocker arm on shaft and center over 1/4 inch hole in shaft. Install new rocker arm retainers using a 1/2 inch drift. Torque rocker shaft bolts to 25 ft. lbs.

EXC. 1985 MODELS

Rocker arms are pedestal mounted, over support plates, **Fig. 10.** To replace rocker arms, remove valve cover, pedestal retaining bolt(s), pedestal and the rocker arm, noting position of double ended bolts for assembly. Replace rocker arms and pedestals as an assembly if they are damaged or excessively worn. If rocker arms are to be reused, they should be installed in original position.

VALVE ARRANGEMENT

FRONT TO REAR

V6-181, 231 . . . . E-I-I-E-I-E

CAM LOBE LIFT SPECIFICATIONS

Engine	Year	Int.	Exh.
V6-181	1985-87	—	—
V6-231	1985-87	.397	.397
V6-231	1988	—	—

VALVE GUIDES

The valve guides are an integral part of the cylinder head and cannot be replaced. If excessive valve stem clearance is noted, the valve guide must be reamed and an oversize valve guide installed. Valves are available in an oversize of .010 inch.

VALVE LIFTERS

On 1985 models and some 1986 models, flat type lifters are used, **Fig. 11.** These valve lifters can be removed after removal of rocker arms, pushrods and intake manifold. On all other models, roller type hydraulic valve lifters are used, **Fig. 12.** To remove lifters on these models, the retainer and support plates must also be removed, **Fig. 13.** Pliers with taped jaws can be used to remove lifters that are stuck due to carbon varnish, etc. Disassemble only one lifter at a time, **Fig. 11 and 12,** keeping components for each lifter separate. Replace lifters as an assembly if housing plunger or valve seat is damaged or excessively worn.

TIMING CASE COVER

REPLACE

1. Disconnect battery ground cable and drain cooling system.
2. Disconnect all hoses from water pump.
3. Remove water pump pulley and drive belts. **It may be necessary to remove two nuts from front engine mount at frame and raise engine to facilitate water pump pulley removal.**
4. Remove alternator and bracket and position aside.
5. Remove distributor. if necessary.
6. Remove crankshaft damper bolt and washer, then the damper.
7. Remove timing case cover to cylinder block attaching bolts.
8. Remove timing case cover to oil pan attaching bolts, then the timing case cover, **Fig. 14.**
9. Reverse procedure to install. **Before installing the case cover, remove oil pump cover and pack oil pump with petroleum jelly. Failure to pack oil pump may result in the pump losing its "Prime" when the engine is started. Also, apply suitable sealer to case cover bolts.**

TIMING CHAIN

REPLACE

1. Remove timing case cove as outlined under "Timing Case Cover, Replace" procedure.

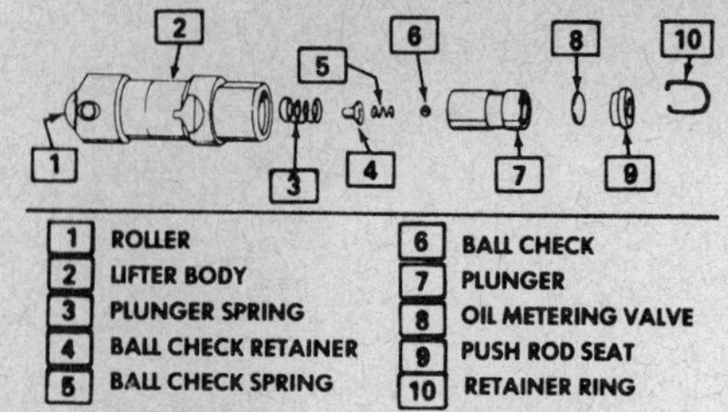

Fig. 12 Roller type hydraulic valve lifter exploded view

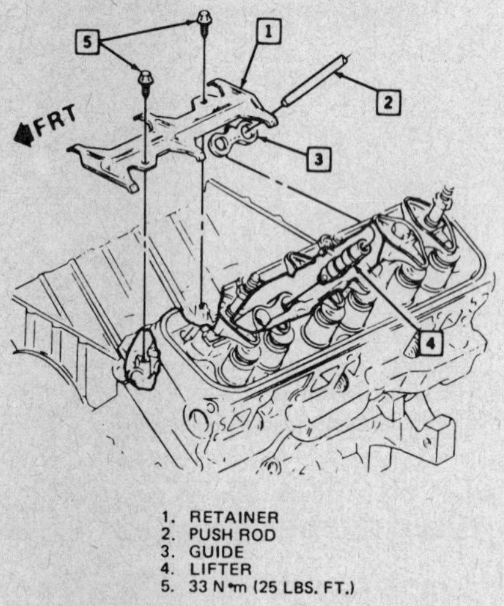

Fig. 13 Hydraulic roller lifter installation

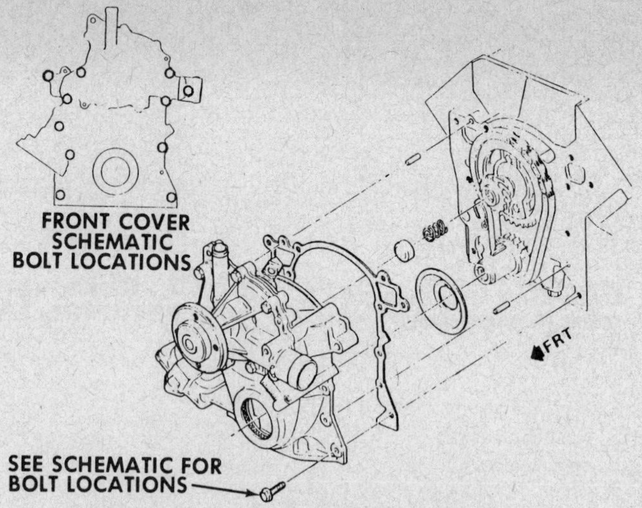

Fig. 14 Timing case cover removal & installation

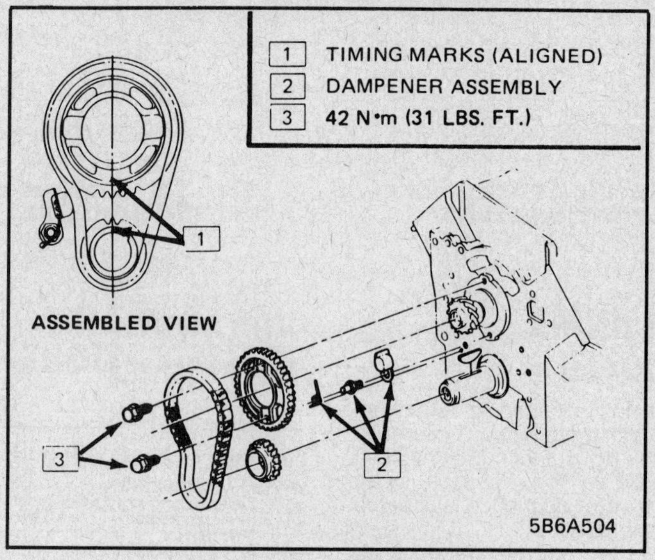

Fig. 15 Timing chain & sprocket (Typical)

2. Reinstall damper bolt and rotate crankshaft until the valve timing marks on camshaft sprocket and crankshaft sprocket are as close together as possible. Remove damper bolt without changing position of valve timing marks.
3. Remove crankshaft oil slinger if equipped, then the camshaft sprocket bolt.
4. Remove cam sensor magnet on V6-231 models, if equipped.
5. Pry off the two sprockets and timing chain assembly.
6. Assemble new chain on sprockets with timing marks aligned and slide assembly onto shafts. Be sure that marks are aligned, **Fig. 15.**
7. Install cam sensor magnet on V6-231 models, if equipped.
8. Install camshaft sprocket bolt and torque to 29-31 ft. lbs.
9. Install crankshaft oil slinger if equipped and the timing case cover.

CAMSHAFT

REPLACE

1. Remove engine as outlined under "Engine, Replace" procedure.
2. Remove intake manifold, rocker arms, valve lifters, timing case cover and timing chain.
3. Slide camshaft out from engine with care not to damage bearings.
4. Reverse procedure to install.

PISTON & ROD ASSEMBLE

Pistons should be assembled to rods as shown in **Fig. 16.**

After piston and rod installation, measure connecting rod side clearance. Side clearance should be .003-.015 inch.

PISTONS, PINS & RINGS

Pistons and ring are available in standard sizes and oversizes of .010 and .030. Piston pins are supplied with the piston and are available in standard size only.

To check piston fit in bore, measure bore diameter using suitable telescoping gauges and record reading. Measure piston across skirt at a point 3/4 inch below piston pin center line and record reading. Subtract piston diameter from bore diameter and compare to specified clearance.

MAIN & ROD BEARINGS

Main bearings are available in standard sizes and undersizes of .001 and .002 inch. Rod bearings are available in standard size and an undersize of .008 inch.

OIL PAN

REPLACE

1. Disconnect battery ground cable and raise and support vehicle.
2. Drain oil pan and remove flexplate cover.
3. Remove oil pan bolts, oil pan and gasket, as equipped. **Production engines with 14 bolt oil pan are produced using RTV sealer to seal pan, while models with 20 bolt pan use a formed rubber gasket. If oil pan must be removed for service, use replacement composition gas-**

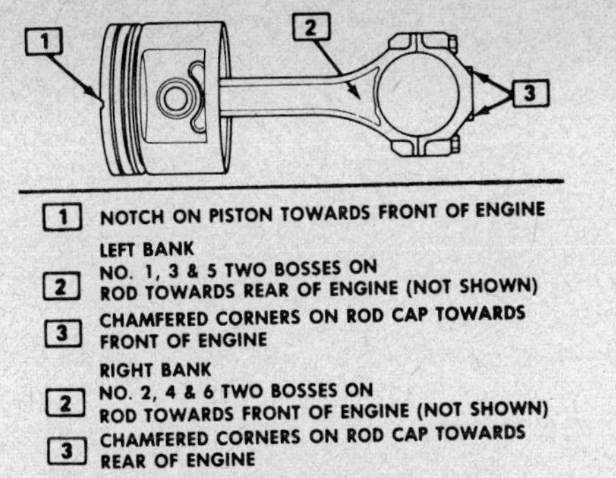

Fig. 16 Piston & rod assembly

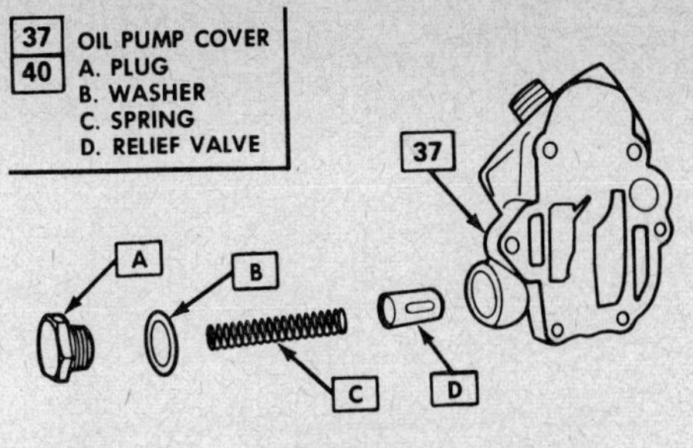

Fig. 17 Oil pump cover. 1985

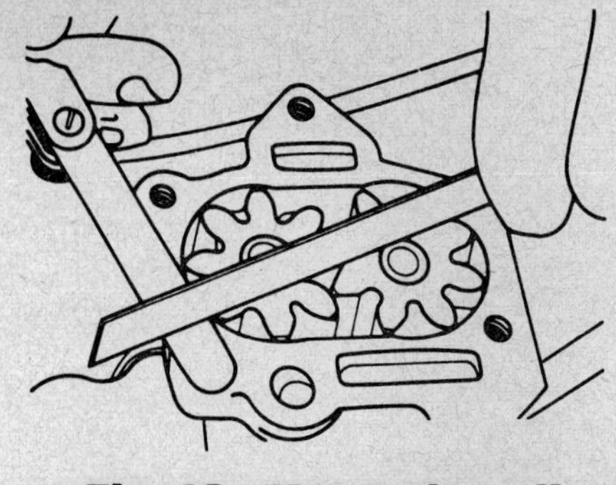

Fig. 18 Measuring oil pump gear end clearance. 1985

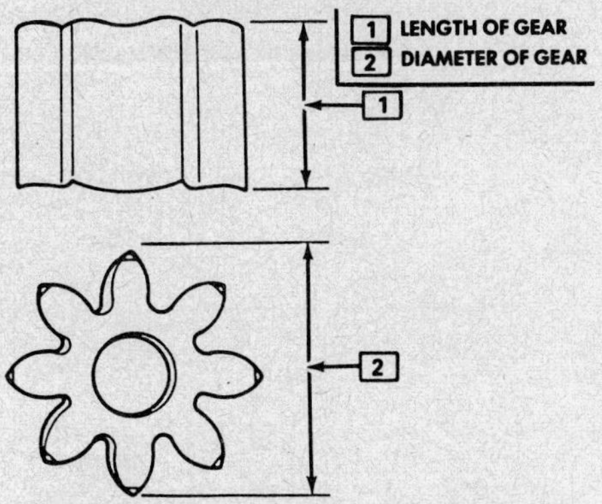

Fig. 19 Measuring length & diameter of pump gear. 1985

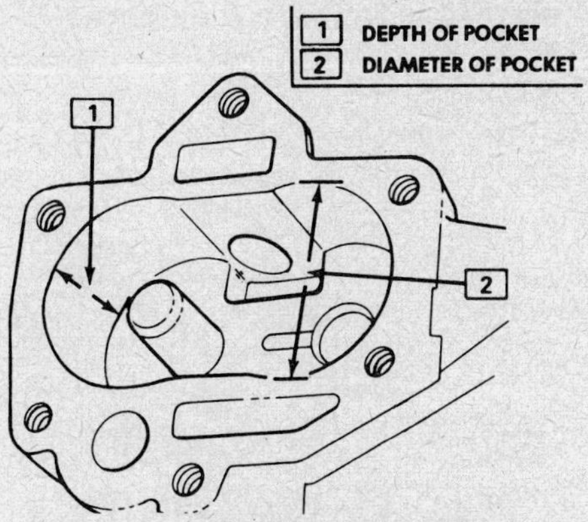

Fig. 20 Measuring depth & diameter of pump gear pocket. 1985

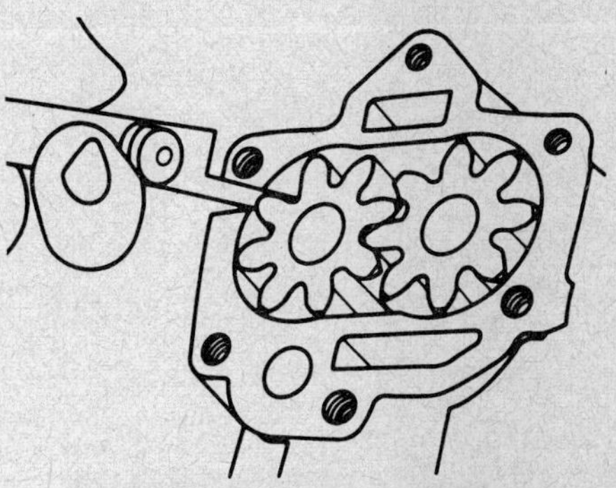

Fig. 21 Measuring oil pump gear side clearance. 1985

ket for models with 14 bolt pan and new formed rubber gasket for models with 20 bolt pan.

4. Position replacement gasket on pan, insert 2 bolts to maintain position, then install pan and gasket assembly.
5. Install remaining bolts, then evenly torque bolts on 20 bolt pan to 88 inch lbs., or bolts on 11 bolt pan to 13 ft. lbs. **Do not over tighten oil pan retaining bolts as pan may be damaged, resulting in oil leaks.**
6. Reverse remaining procedure to complete installation.

OIL PUMP SERVICE

1985

Removal & Inspection

1. Remove oil filter.
2. Remove oil pump cover attaching screws and the cover.
3. Slide oil pump gears from pump.
4. Inspect gears for wear and damage. Replace if necessary.
5. Remove oil pressure relief valve cap, spring and valve, **Fig. 17.** Oil filter bypass valve and spring is staked in place and should not be removed.
6. Inspect relief valve and spring. Replace if necessary.
7. Check fit of relief valve in cover bore. The clearance should be an easy slip fit. If excessive clearance is noted, replace valve and/or cover.
8. Check bypass valve for cracks and warping. Replace if necessary.

Assembly & Installation

1. Lubricate and install pressure relief valve and spring in cover bore, **Fig. 17.**
2. Install and torque cap to 35 ft. lbs.
3. Install pump gears and shaft in housing.
4. Check gear end clearance by placing a straightedge over gears and with a feeler gauge, measure clearance between straightedge and gears, **Fig. 18.** Clearance should be .002-inch, measure gears and pocket to determine which is out of specification, **Figs. 19 and 20.**
5. Check gear side clearance, **Fig. 21.** Clearance should be .002-.005 inch. If clearance is excessive, measure gears and pocket to determine which is out of specification, **Figs. 19 and 20.**
6. Check pump cover for flatness with a straightedge and feeler gauge. If clearance is greater than .001 inch, replace pump cover.
7. Remove gears and pack gear pocket with petroleum jelly and reinstall gears. The pump must be filled with petroleum jelly to prime the pump.
8. Place new gasket and cover on pump. Install and torque cover screws to 97 inch lbs.
9. Install new oil filter.

EXC. 1985

Removal & Inspection

1. Remove timing case cover, refer to "Timing Case Cover, Replace" procedure.
2. Remove oil filter adapter, pressure regulator valve and spring.
3. Remove oil pump cover attaching screws, then the cover and gears, **Fig. 22.**
4. Check pump cover and housing for cracks, scoring, porous or damaged casting, damaged threads or excessive wear or galling. Replace as required.
5. Check pressure regulator valve for scoring, burrs or sticking in valve bore. Replace as required.
6. Check pressure regulator valve spring for tension loss or bending. Replace spring as required.
7. Check gears for chipping galling or excessive wear. Replace as required.

Assembly & Installation

1. Measure oil pump inner gear tip clearance, **Fig. 23.** Maximum clearance should be .006 inch.
2. Measure oil pump outer gear diameter clearance, **Fig. 24.** Clearance should be .008-.015 inch.
3. Measure oil pump gear end clearance with gear dropped in housing, **Fig. 25.** Clearance should be .0010-.0035 inch.

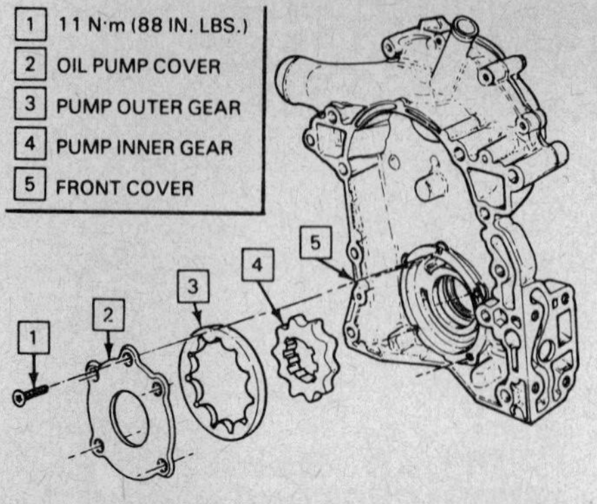

Fig. 22 Oil pump. Exc. 1985

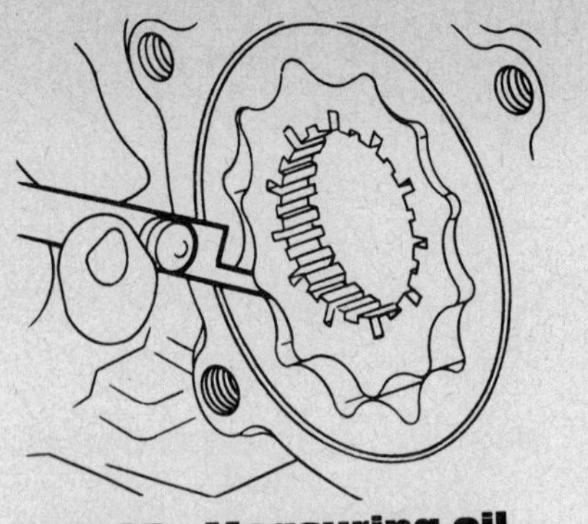

Fig. 23 Measuring oil pump inner gear tip clearance. Exc. 1985

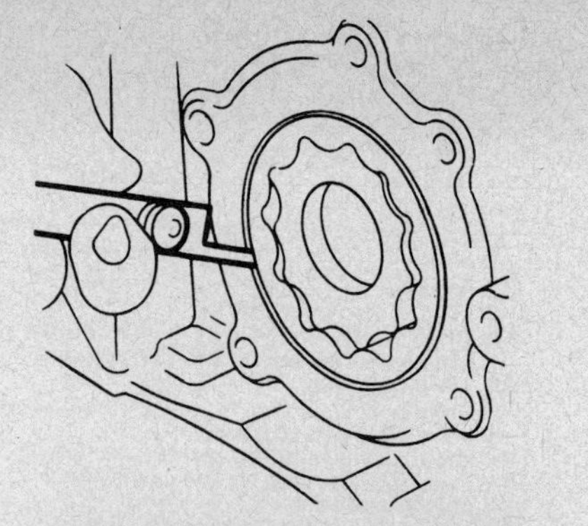

Fig. 24 Measuring oil pump outer gear diameter clearance. Exc. 1985

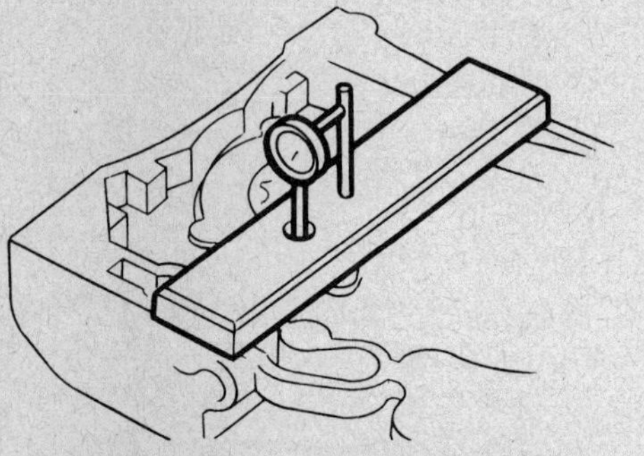

Fig. 25 Measuring oil pump gear end clearance. Exc. 1985

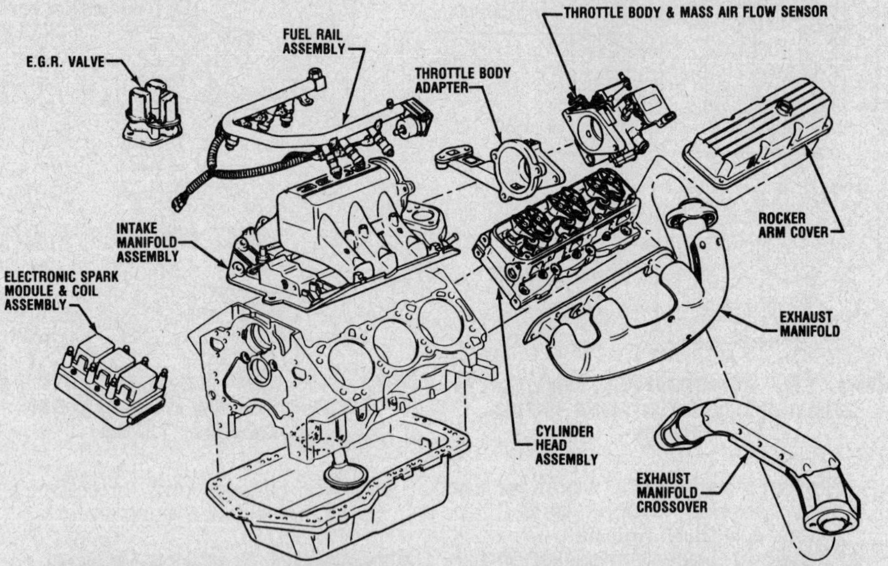

Fig. 26 Exploded view of V6-231 (3.8L) engine (Part 1 of 2). 1988 models

4. Lubricate all gears with clean motor oil, then install gears in housing.
5. Pack pump cavity with suitable petroleum jelly.
6. Install pump cover and cover attaching screws. Torque cover attaching screws to 97 inch lbs.
7. Install pressure regulator valve and spring.
8. Install oil filter adapter using a new gasket. Torque oil filter adapter attaching bolts to 30 ft. lbs.
9. Install timing chain cover on engine. **During front cover installation, ensure inner pump gear is properly engaged on crankshaft sprocket.**

CRANKSHAFT OIL SEAL
REPLACE

1. Remove oil pan and oil pump.
2. Remove rear main bearing cap.
3. Using tool J-21526-2, drive upper seal into groove approximately 1/4 inch.
4. Repeat step 3 for other end of seal.
5. Measure the amount that was driven in on one side and add 1/16 inch. Cut this length from lower seal removed from lower cap.
6. Repeat step 5 for other end of seal.
7. Place piece of cut seal into groove of seal installer tool J-21526-1 and install tool guide onto block.
8. Using seal packing tool J-21526-2, drive piece of seal into place. Drive seal in until tool contacts machined stop.
9. Remove tool guide and repeat steps 7 and 8 for other end of seal.
10. Install replacement seal in bearing cap as follows:
    a. Ensure that cap mating surfaces, seal grooves and side seal channels are clean and free from old seal material.
    b. Soak sealing strips in kerosene or light oil for 5 minutes and apply GM sealer 1052621, Loctite 414 or equivalent to seal groove in cap.
    c. Within 1 minute after applying sealer, roll seal into groove using installer J-28693, pressing seal into groove until seal projects no more than 1/16 inch above each mating surface of cap.
    d. Holding seal in place, cut seal flush with mating surfaces of cap using tool sharp enough to produce clean cut.
    e. Apply thin film of chassis grease to seal surface and thin film of suitable sealer to cap mating surfaces. **Do not allow sealer to contact journal or bearing surfaces.**
11. Install side seals in cap, position bearing cap in block ensuring that cap is properly seated, then torque cap bolts to specifications.
12. Reverse remaining procedure to complete installation.

FUEL PUMP
REPLACE

1. Disconnect battery ground cable.
2. Drain fuel tank and disconnect tank unit wire from connector in rear compartment.
3. Remove ground wire retaining screw from underbody.
4. Disconnect hoses from tank unit.
5. Support fuel tank and release the two retaining straps. Lower tank from vehicle.

BELT TENSION DATA

Belt	New Lbs.	Used Lbs.
1985–87		
Air Cond.	165	90
Alternator	145	70
Power Steer.	165	90
AIR or Vacuum Pump	75	45

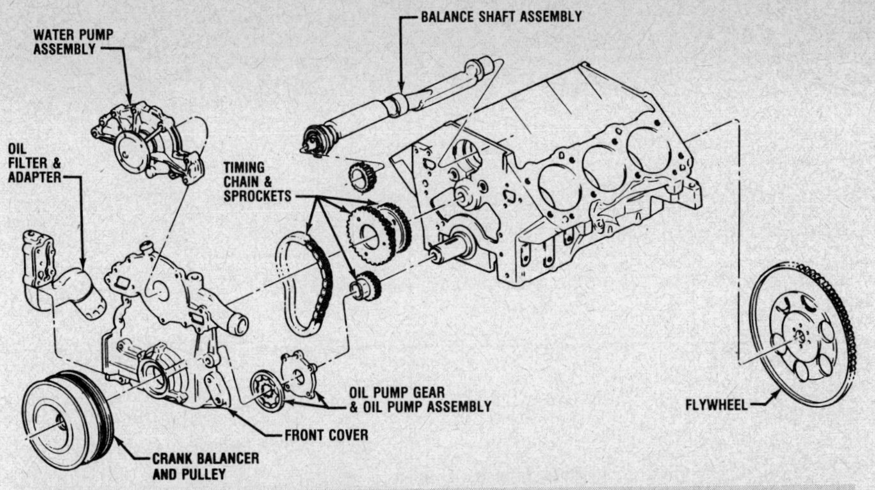

Fig. 27 Exploded view of V6-231 (3.8L) engine (Part 2 of 2). 1988 models

6. Using tool J-24187 or equivalent, release retaining cam and remove sending unit and pump assembly from tank.
7. Remove pump from sending unit.
8. Reverse procedure to install.

WATER PUMP

REPLACE

1. Disconnect battery ground cable and drain cooling system.
2. Remove drive belts and disconnect radiator hoses and heater hoses from pump.
3. Remove water pump pulley attaching bolts. The long bolt is accessed through hole in body side rail. Remove pump pulley.
4. Remove water pump attaching bolts and the water pump.
5. Reverse procedure to install.

1988 V6 3800 ENGINE

The 1988 V6-231/3.8L 3800 (90° arrangement) series engine, **Figs. 26 and 27,** is a modified version of previous models. This engine incorporates Sequential Port Fuel Injection with Electronic Mass Air Flow measurement. The cylinder block has been lengthened, allowing the connecting rods to be positioned in the center line of the bore and on the center line of the pistons. This improvement allows the use of new low tension compression rings, which results in improved fuel economy.

The V6 3800 incorporates a balance shaft which is gear driven from the camshaft sprocket and counter-rotates at engine speed to eliminate first order primary imbalance.

V8-250 (4.1L) & V8-273 (4.5L) Gasoline Engine Section

INDEX

ENGINE MOUNTS

REPLACE

RIGHT SIDE

1. Remove brace from engine bracket to engine, **Fig. 1.**
2. Remove two nuts securing engine bracket to mount.
3. Raise and support vehicle.
4. Remove two nuts securing engine mount to frame.
5. Remove two nuts securing transaxle bracket to frame.
6. Remove two nuts securing transaxle mount to frame bracket.
7. Attach suitable engine lifting equipment to engine and raise engine until bracket is free from engine mount and transaxle mount.
8. Remove stud and two bolts securing bracket to block.
9. Remove mount and bracket by pulling forward.
10. Remove transaxle mount bracket from transaxle.
11. Remove engine mount assembly.
12. Reverse procedure to install.

LEFT SIDE

1. Raise and support vehicle.
2. Remove one nut securing mount to transaxle bracket and two nuts securing mount to frame, **Fig. 2.**
3. Attach suitable engine lifting equipment to engine.
4. Remove three bolts securing bracket to transaxle.
5. Raise engine until brackets are free from mounts.
6. Remove mount and bracket by pulling upward.
7. Reverse procedure to install.

ENGINE

REPLACE

1. Disconnect battery ground cable.
2. Drain cooling system.
3. Remove air cleaner and hood.
4. Disconnect A/C hose strap from right side strut tower.
5. Remove A/C accumulator from bracket and position aside.
6. Remove canister hoses from A/C accumulator bracket.
7. Disconnect ground wire from A/C accumulator bracket.

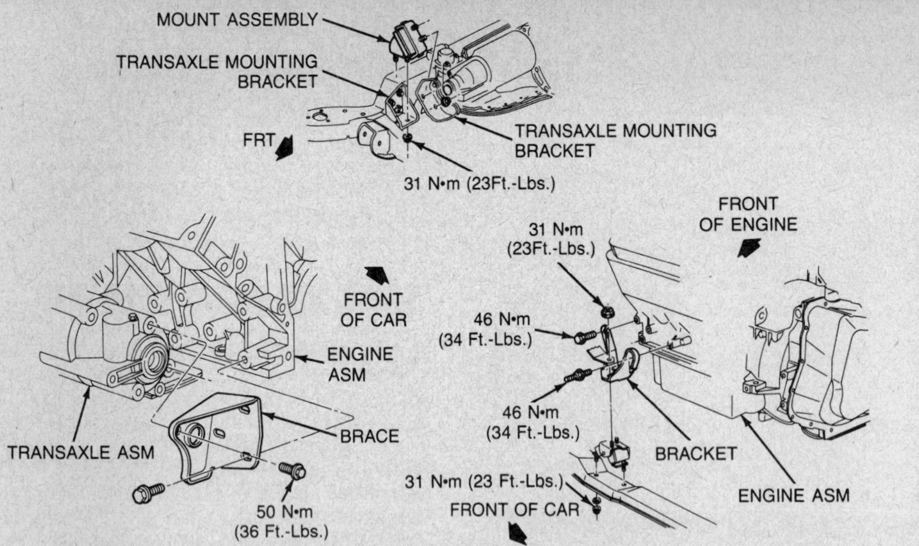

Fig. 1 Right side engine, brace & transaxle mount

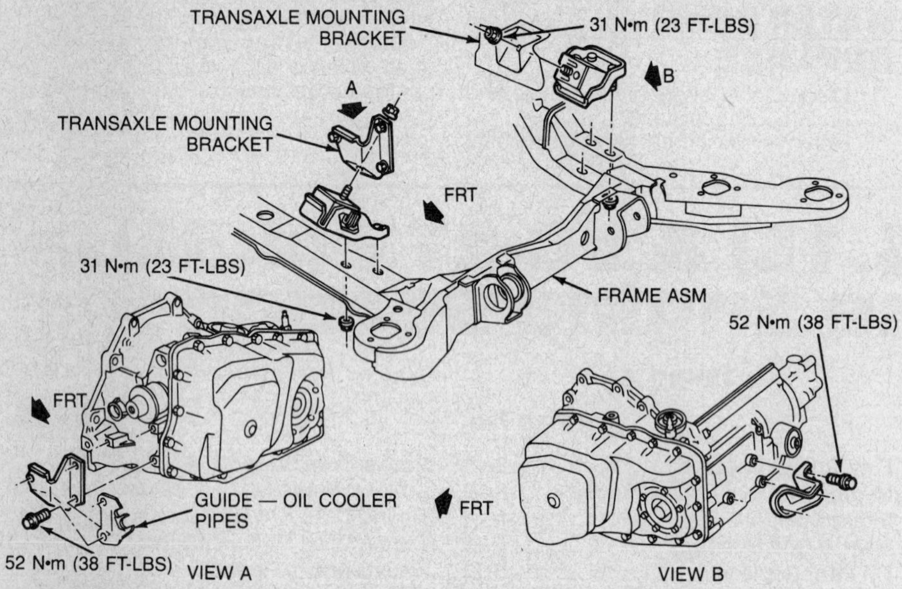

Fig. 2 Left side engine & transaxle assembly mounts

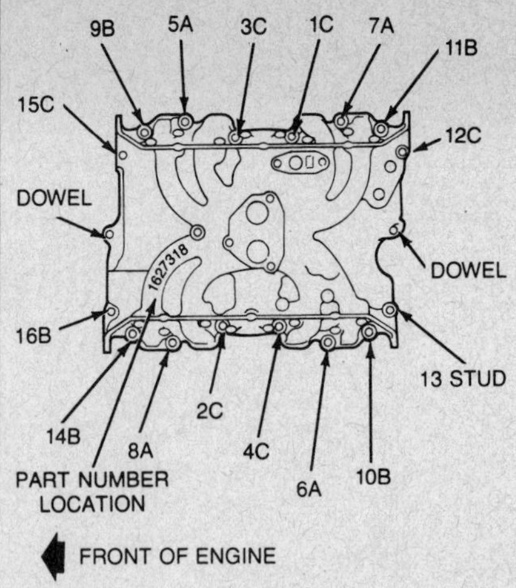

BOLT TIGHTENING SEQUENCE

1. TIGHTEN BOLTS 1, 2, 3, & 4 IN SEQUENCE TO 20.0 N•m (15 FT-LBS).
2. TIGHTEN BOLTS 5 THRU 16 IN SEQUENCE TO 30.0 N•m (22 FT-LBS).
3. RETIGHTEN ALL BOLTS IN SEQUENCE TO 30.0 N•m (22 FT-LBS).
4. REPEAT STEP 3.

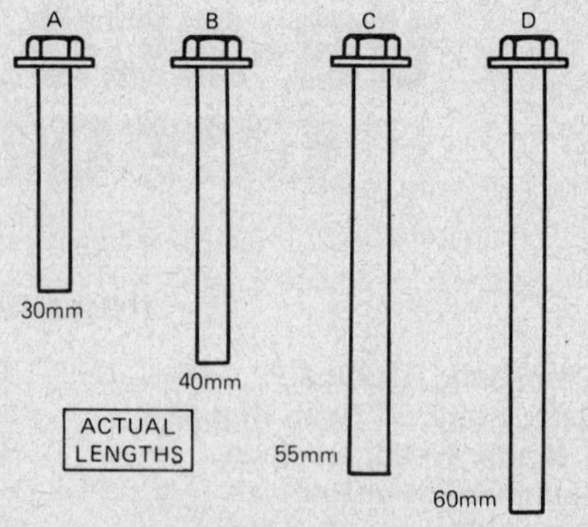

Fig. 3 Intake manifold bolt size & bolt torque sequence

8. Remove A/C accumulator bracket from wheel house.
9. Remove cooling fans.
10. Remove drive belts and disconnect heater hoses.
11. Disconnect electrical connectors from: oil pressure switch, coolant temperature sensor, distributor, EGR solenoid and engine temperature switch.
12. Disconnect cables from: accelerator, cruise control and transaxle throttle valve.
13. Remove cruise control diaphragm and position aside.
14. Disconnect vacuum supply hose.
15. Remove exhaust crossover pipe.
16. Disconnect oil cooler lines from oil filter adapter.
17. Remove oil cooler line bracket from transaxle and position aside.
18. Remove air cleaner mounting bracket.
19. Disconnect fuel lines from throttle body. **Carefully bleed fuel pressure at fuel line schraeder valve using a suitable tool. Use a container or rag to catch fuel.**
20. Remove fuel line bracket from transaxle and position fuel lines aside.
21. Disconnect small vacuum line from brake booster.
22. Disconnect AIR solenoid electrical and hose connections.
23. Remove AIR valves with bracket.
24. Disconnect electrical connectors from: ISC, TPS, fuel injectors, MAT sensor, oxygen sensor, throttle body base warmer and ground wires from alternator bracket.
25. Remove idler pulley.
26. Remove power steering hose strap from stud-headed bolt in front of right side cylinder head, then the stud-headed bolt.
27. Disconnect AIR pipe clip near number 2 spark plug.
28. Remove power steering pump with bracket and position aside.
29. Raise and support vehicle.
30. Disconnect electrical connectors from starter motor and ground wires from cylinder block.
31. Remove two flexplate covers and the starter motor.
32. Remove three flexplate to torque converter bolts.
33. Remove A/C compressor lower dust shield.
34. Remove right front wheel assembly.
35. Remove outer wheelhouse plastic shield.
36. Remove A/C compressor mounting bolts and position compressor aside.
37. Remove lower radiator hose.
38. Remove driveline dampener with brackets from lower right front of engine and cradle.
39. Remove three right front engine to transaxle bracket bolts.
40. Pull alternator wire with plastic cover down out of way.
41. Remove two exhaust pipe to manifold bolts and springs.

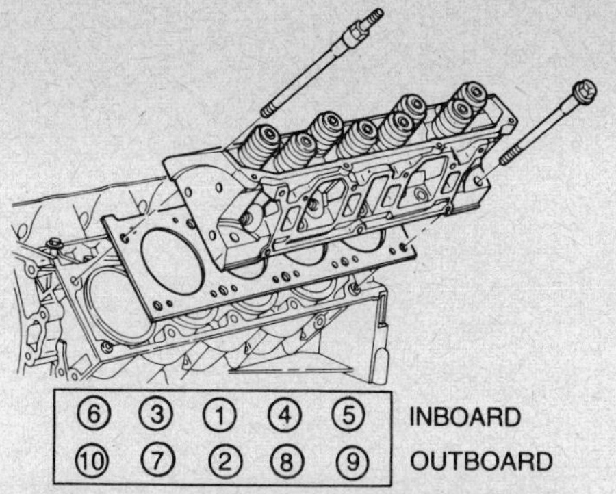

Fig. 4 Cylinder head bolt torque sequence

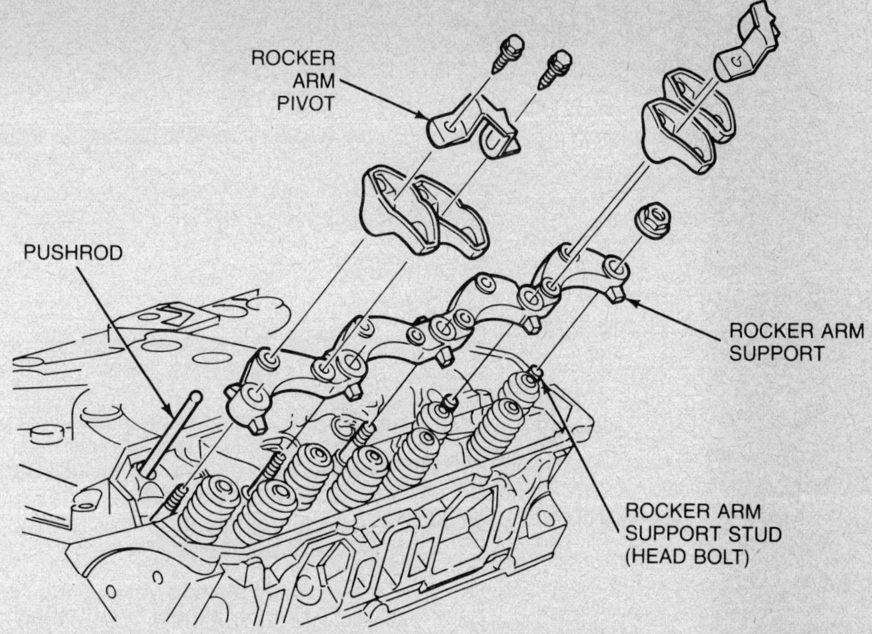

Fig. 5 Typical rocker arm support, rocker arms & pivots

42. Disconnect AIR pipe to converter bracket from exhaust manifold stud.
43. Remove lower right hand transaxle bellhousing to engine bolt.
44. Attach suitable engine lifting equipment to engine and support engine.
45. Remove five upper transaxle bellhousing to engine bolts.
46. Remove three left front engine mount bracket to engine bolts.
47. Remove engine from vehicle.
48. Reverse procedure to install.

INTAKE MANIFOLD REPLACE

1. Disconnect battery ground cable.
2. Drain cooling system.
3. Remove air cleaner.
4. Remove drive belts.
5. Disconnect spark plug wires from spark plugs.
6. Remove two upper power steering pump bracket bolts and loosen lower nuts.
7. Remove distributor cap, wires and conduit.
8. Disconnect heater hose from thermostat housing.
9. Disconnect electrical connectors from: distributor, oil pressure switch, coolant sensor and EGR solenoid.
10. Remove distributor.
11. Disconnect cables from: accelerator, cruise control and transaxle throttle valve.
12. Disconnect fuel lines from throttle body. **Carefully bleed fuel pressure at fuel line schraeder valve using a suitable tool. Use a container or rag to catch fuel.**
13. Disconnect upper radiator hose from thermostat housing.
14. Remove fuel line brackets from transaxle and position fuel lines aside.
15. Remove cruise control servo bracket from intake manifold.
16. Remove vacuum line bracket from engine lift brackets.
17. Disconnect vacuum supply line from throttle body.
18. Disconnect transaxle modulator vacuum line.
19. Remove belt tensioner and power steering pump and bracket assembly and position aside.
20. Disconnect alternator electrical connectors and remove alternator.
21. Disconnect AIR management solenoid electrical connectors.
22. Remove AIR management valves and bracket assembly.
23. Disconnect electrical connectors from: ISC, TPS, fuel injectors, MAT sensor, oxygen sensor and throttle body base warmer.
24. Disconnect MAP hose.
25. Remove EGR solenoid and bracket assembly.
26. Remove rocker arm covers.
27. Remove rocker arm support assemblies.
28. Remove triangular seals.
29. Remove pushrods. **Pushrods must be installed in original locations.**
30. Remove idler pulley.
31. Remove power steering pipe and AIR pipe brackets from right side cylinder head.
32. Remove alternator mounting bracket.
33. Remove right front engine lift bracket bolt and position bracket aside.
34. Remove oil filter.
35. Remove right rear engine lift bracket.
36. Remove intake manifold bolts, noting position for installation.
37. Remove intake manifold from vehicle.
38. Reverse procedure to install. Install and torque manifold bolts to specifications in sequence shown in **Fig. 3.**

EXHAUST MANIFOLD REPLACE

RIGHT SIDE

1. Disconnect battery ground cable.
2. Remove air cleaner and exhaust crossover pipe.
3. Disconnect oxygen sensor and coolant temperature sensor electrical connectors.
4. Remove catalytic converter air pipe to AIR pipe clip bolt.
5. Remove two forward, upper exhaust manifold to cylinder head bolts.
6. Raise and support vehicle.
7. Remove converter air pipe bracket from stud.
8. Remove manifold to converter exhaust pipe.
9. Remove five remaining exhaust manifold to cylinder head attaching bolts.
10. Disconnect AIR pipe from manifold.
11. Remove exhaust manifold from vehicle.
12. Reverse procedure to install.

LEFT SIDE

1. Disconnect ground cable.
2. Remove cooling fans.
3. Remove exhaust crossover pipe.
4. Remove drive belts.
5. Remove AIR pump pivot bolt.
6. Remove belt tensioner and power steering pump brace.
7. Disconnect AIR pipe from manifold.
8. Remove exhaust manifold from vehicle.
9. Reverse procedure to install.

CYLINDER HEAD REPLACE

1. Disconnect battery ground cable.
2. Drain cooling system.
3. Remove intake manifold as outlined under "Intake Manifold, Replace" procedure.
4. If removing left side cylinder head, remove the two cooling fans.
5. Remove appropriate exhaust manifold as outlined under "Exhaust Manifold, Replace," procedure.
6. Remove ten cylinder head bolts.
7. Reverse procedure to install, referring to **Fig. 4** for bolt tightening sequence. Torque cylinder head bolts in 3 steps as follows:
   a. Torque all bolts to 38 ft. lbs. in specified sequence.

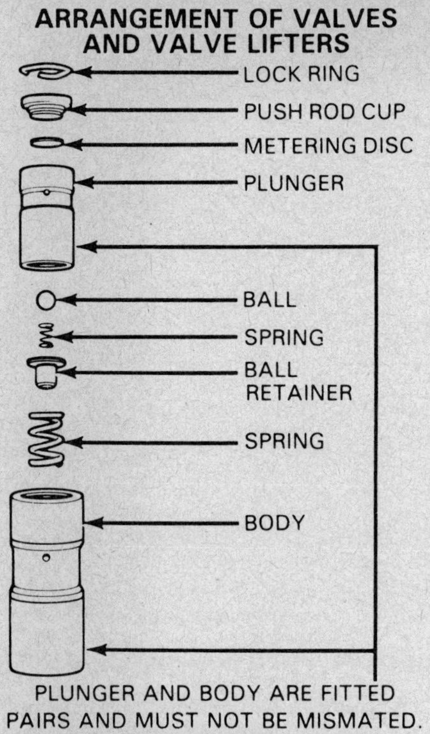

Fig. 6 Hydraulic valve lifter

b. Torque all bolts to 74 ft. lbs. in specified sequence.
c. Torque bolts 1, 3 and 4 to 90 ft. lbs.

VALVE ARRANGEMENTS

FRONT TO REAR

V8-250 . . . . I-E-I-E-E-I-E-I

VALVE LIFT SPECIFICATIONSS

Engine	Year	Int.	Exh.
V8-250	1985-87	.384	.396

VALVE TIMING

INTAKE OPENS BEFORE TDC

Engine	Year	Degrees
V8-250	1985	37
V8-250	1986—87	20

ROCKER ARM SUPPORT, ROCKER ARM & PIVOT

REPLACE

1. Remove rocker arm covers.
2. Remove rocker arm support retaining nuts from stud headed cylinder head bolts, **Fig. 5. Removing the rocker arm support with the rocker arms and pivots attached is recommended since the pivot assemblies may be damaged if pivot bolt torque is not removed evenly against valve spring pressure.**

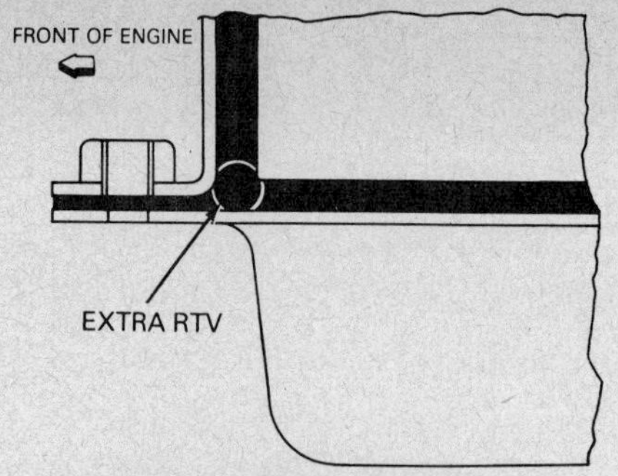

Fig. 7 RTV sealant application

3. Secure support in a suitable vise and remove rocker arms and pivots.
4. Reverse procedure to install. Torque pivot bolts to 22 ft. lbs.

VALVE GUIDES

Check valve stem to valve guide clearance. Clearance should be .005 inch or less. Service valves are available in standard size (.343 inch) or oversizes of .003 and .006 inch. If clearance is excessive, ream valve guide to accommodate next oversize valve. Some engines are factory fitted with .003 inch oversize valve guides and valves and are identified by a "3" stamped on the cylinder head gasket surface inline with the oversize valve.

HYDRAULIC VALVE LIFTERS

REPLACE

Valve lifters may be removed from their bores after the intake manifold, rocker arms and pushrods are removed. Adjustable pliers with taped jaws may be used to remove lifters that are stuck due to varnish, carbon, etc. **Fig. 6** illustrates the type of lifter used.

TIMING CASE COVER

REPLACE

1. Disconnect battery ground cable.
2. Drain cooling system.
3. Remove air cleaner.
4. Remove drive belt.
5. Remove alternator and position aside.
6. Remove A/C accumulator from bracket and position aside.
7. Remove idler pulley, water pump pulley and water pump.
8. Raise and support vehicle.
9. Remove crankshaft puller and hub.
10. Remove cover attaching bolts and the cover.
11. Reverse procedure to install. When installing, place a bead of RTV sealer on the front cover lip on the oil pan sealing surface and a 1/4 inch bead of RTV sealer on the oil pan where the oil pan, cylinder block and cover join together, **Fig. 7.** The 1/4 inch bead is needed because the cover has a rounded corner instead of a square corner. If the extra RTV is not applied an oil leak may occur.

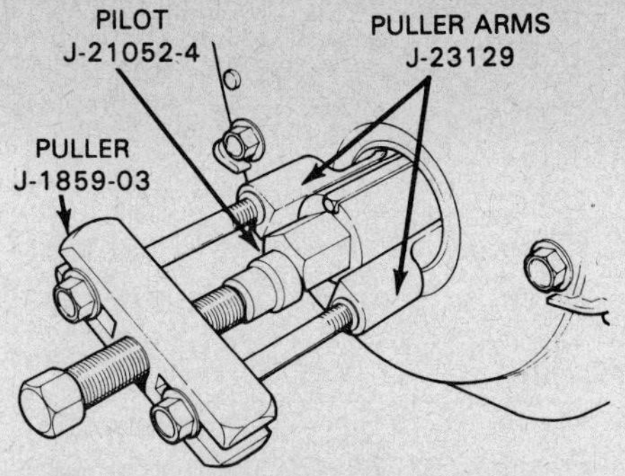

Fig. 8 Timing case oil seal removal

TIMING CASE OIL SEAL

REPLACE

1. Remove crankshaft pulley and vibration damper.
2. Remove oil seal with tools J-1859-03 and J-23129 or equivalents, **Fig. 8.**
3. Lubricate new oil seal with engine oil and install with tool J-29662 or equivalent.
4. Install crankshaft puller and vibration damper.

TIMING CHAIN

REPLACE

1. Remove timing case cover as outlined under "Timing Case Cover, Replace" procedure.
2. Remove oil slinger from crankshaft.
3. Rotate crankshaft to align camshaft and crankshaft sprocket timing marks, **Fig. 9.**
4. Remove screw attaching camshaft sprocket to camshaft, then the camshaft and crankshaft sprockets with the timing chain attached.
5. Reverse procedure to install. Ensure that timing marks are aligned, **Fig. 9.**

CAMSHAFT

REPLACE

1. Remove engine as outlined under "Engine, Replace" procedure.
2. Remove timing case cover and timing chain.
3. Remove intake manifold and valve lifters.
4. Slide camshaft forward carefully from engine.
5. Reverse procedure to install.

PISTON & RODS

ASSEMBLE

Assemble pistons to rods as shown in **Fig. 10.** Measure connecting rod side clearance with a suitable feeler gauge after installation. Clearance should be .008 to .020 inch.

PISTONS

When measuring piston diameter, place micrometer 3/16 inch below cross slot or 3/8

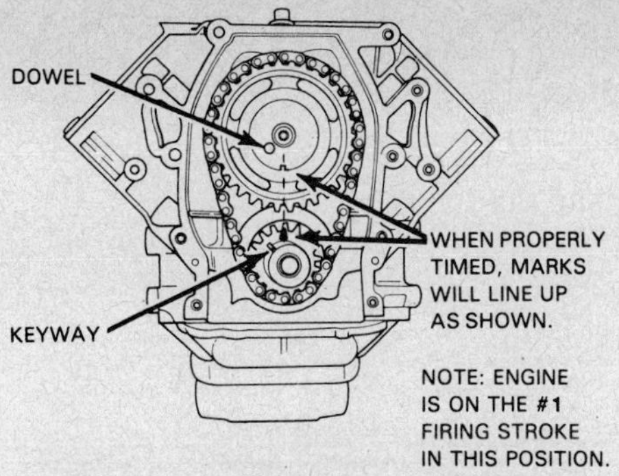
DOWEL
WHEN PROPERLY TIMED, MARKS WILL LINE UP AS SHOWN.
KEYWAY
NOTE: ENGINE IS ON THE #1 FIRING STROKE IN THIS POSITION.

Fig. 9 Camshaft timing marks

NOTCH TOWARD FRONT OF ENGINE

Fig. 10 Piston & rod assembly

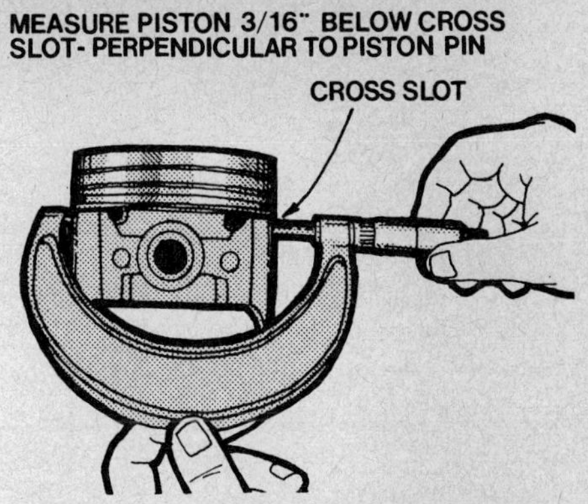
MEASURE PISTON 3/16" BELOW CROSS SLOT- PERPENDICULAR TO PISTON PIN
CROSS SLOT

Fig. 11 Measuring piston diameter

inch below oil ring groove, **Fig. 11.** Cylinder liner diameter is measured two inches down from top of liner and perpendicular to the cylinder center line. The difference between the two readings should be .0010-.0018 inch. Cylinder bore out-of-round should not exceed .0005-.002 inch on 1985 models or .0008 inch on 1986-87 models. If any reading is not within specifications, the piston and cylinder liner must be replaced. No attempt should be made to rebore or hone the cylinder liner. Refer to "Cylinder Liner, Replace" procedure.

PISTON RINGS

On these engines, replacement rings are available in standard size only. If piston ring clearance is excessive, the piston and cylinder liner must be replaced. Refer to "Cylinder Liner, Replace" procedure.

PISTON PINS

Piston pins are a matched fit with the piston and are not available for separate replacement. Piston pins are pressed into the connecting rods and will not become loose enough to cause a knock or tapping until after very high mileage.

CYLINDER LINER

REPLACE

The cylinder heads, pistons and connecting rods must be removed before replacing cylinder liner. After removing cylinder heads, install tool J-29775 to retain the cylinder liners not being replaced.

1. If original liners are to be reinstalled, mark position of cylinder liner in cylinder block and keep piston with original liner for reference during installation.
2. Pull cylinder liner from cylinder block. Discard O-ring from base of liner.
3. Check cylinder liner and cylinder block mating surfaces.
4. If original cylinder liner is to be installed and engine has not experienced overheating, install new O-ring onto bottom of liner. Align reference marks made during removal and install liner into cylinder block.
5. If new liner is being installed or if original liner is being installed and the engine has experienced overheating, then cylinder liner height must be measured as follows:
   a. Place liner in cylinder block without O-ring.
   b. Place gauge J-29776 or equivalent on cylinder liner. Check that spring-loaded guide pins fit into liner with machined pads resting on edge of liner and dial indicator plunger contacting block deck face. Apply moderate pressure to gauge until dial indicator stops moving. Record this reading. If reading is on the + side of dial indicator, cylinder liner is higher than block face. If reading is on the − side, the liner is lower than the block face.
   c. Repeat step b at two other locations on the liner. Use average of the three readings as actual liner height.
   d. Cylinder liner height should be .0004 liner.
   e. Check liner-to-liner height with tool J-29766 or equivalent. Install adjacent liners with O-ring. Liner-to-liner height should be −.002 to +.002 inch. Mark liners in measured positions.
6. When installing liners into block, check alignment marks. Be sure to install O-ring onto liner.

MAIN & ROD BEARINGS

Main and rod bearings are supplied in standard sizes only.

CRANKSHAFT OIL SEAL

REPLACE

Before replacing the crankshaft oil seal, be sure that the apparent oil seal leak is not actually a leak between the sides of the rear main cap and crankcase.

1. Remove transaxle, then the flex plate from crankshaft.
2. Remove old seal with tool J-26868 or equivalent.
3. Lubricate new seal lip with wheel bearing grease and place on crankshaft with spring facing inside of engine.
4. Press seal into position with tool J-34604 or equivalent. Seal is fully installed when flush with block or slightly below. The use of the tool is recommended since the seal must fit squarely on the crankshaft, otherwise an oil leak could result.

OIL PAN

REPLACE

1. Disconnect battery ground cable.
2. Raise and support vehicle.
3. Remove two flexplate covers.
4. Drain oil pan.
5. Remove oil pan attaching bolts and the two nuts from studs.
6. Remove oil pan, **Fig. 12.**
7. Reverse procedure to install. RTV sealer is used to seal the oil pan. Torque oil pan bolts and nuts to 22 ft. lbs.

OIL PUMP

REPLACE

1. Remove oil pan as outlined under "Oil Pan, Replace" procedure.
2. Remove bolts securing oil pump to engine, **Fig. 13.**
3. Remove oil pump.
4. Reverse procedure to install.

OIL PUMP SERVICE

1. Remove screws securing pump cover to housing, **Fig. 13.**
2. Remove driveshaft, drive gear and driven gear from housing.
3. Remove oil pressure regulator valve and spring from bore in housing. Inspect regulator for nicks and burrs.
4. Check regulator spring free length. Length should be 2.57 inches. Spring compressed length should be 1.46 inches under 9.3-10.5 pound load.
5. Check pump housing for wear and gears for nicks and burrs.
6. Install drive gear over driveshaft so that retaining ring is inside gear. Place drive gear over pump housing shaft closest to pressure regulator bore.
7. Place driven gear over remaining shaft in pump housing, meshing driven gear with drive gear.
8. Install pressure regulator spring and valve in housing bore.
9. Install pump cover over driveshaft. Install and torque retaining screws to 5 ft. lbs.

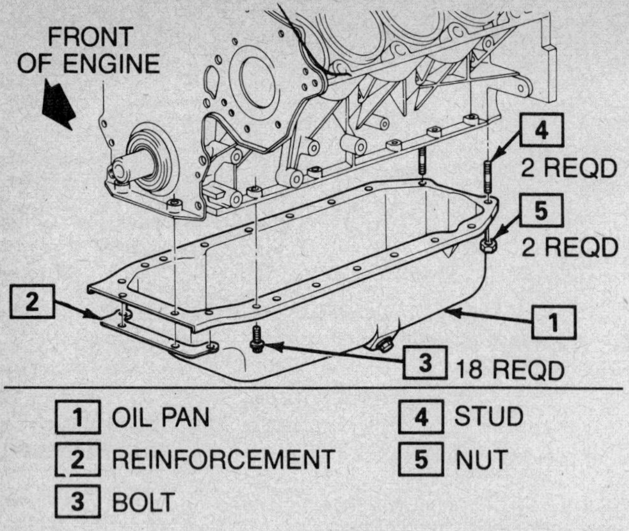

Fig. 12 Oil pan removal & installation

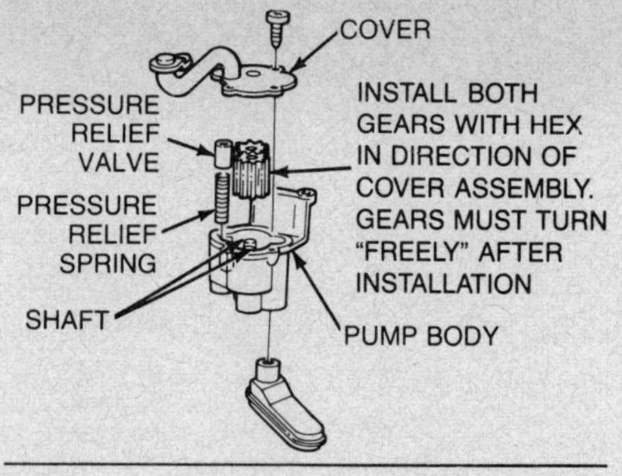

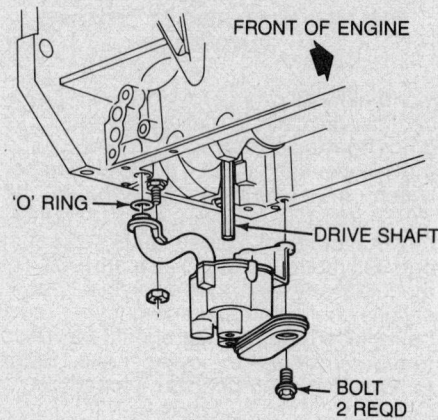

Fig. 13 Oil pump assembly

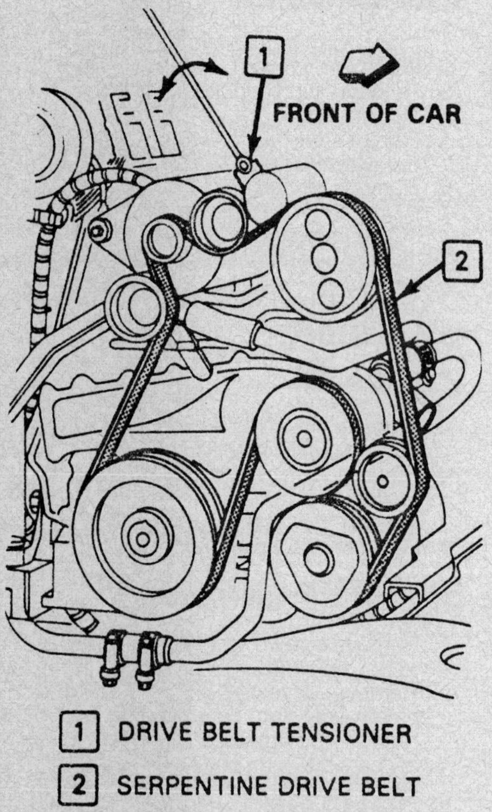

Fig. 14 Drive belt removal

WATER PUMP REPLACE

1. Disconnect battery ground cable and drain cooling system.
2. Remove A/C accumulator from bracket and position aside.
3. Remove A/C accumulator bracket from wheel house.
4. Remove righthand cross-car brace.
5. Remove drive belt. **These engines use a serpentine drive belt, Fig. 14.**
6. Remove drive belt idler puller and bracket.
7. Remove water pump pulley.
8. Remove water pump attaching bolts and the water pump.
9. Reverse procedure to install.

FUEL PUMP REPLACE

1. Remove fuel tank.
2. Remove cam lock with tool J-24187 or equivalent.
3. Remove fuel sending unit and fuel pump assembly from tank.
4. Remove fuel pump from sending unit.
5. Reverse procedure to install.

1988 V8-273/4.5L ENGINE

The V8-273/4.5L engine is new for 1988. The intake manifold is of the dual plane design, with runners arranged in two groups of four. Within each group, a cylinder draws an intake charge every 180° of crankshaft rotation. This regular interval between intake events allows the runner shape, length and area to be tuned for maximum volumetric efficiency. This increased efficiency has allowed the elimination of the grid heater located between the throttle body and intake manifold on 4.1L engines. The throttle body bores have been enlarged, and provide over 50 percent more flow area than the 4.1L engine.

To aid in decreasing engine friction, the 4.5L incorporates roller lifters in the valve train. Friction is reduced by eliminating the sliding motion between the bottom surface of the lifter and the cam lobe.

V6-262 (4.3L) Diesel Engine Section

NOTE: Refer to section 7 for service procedures not found in this section.

INDEX

Page No.

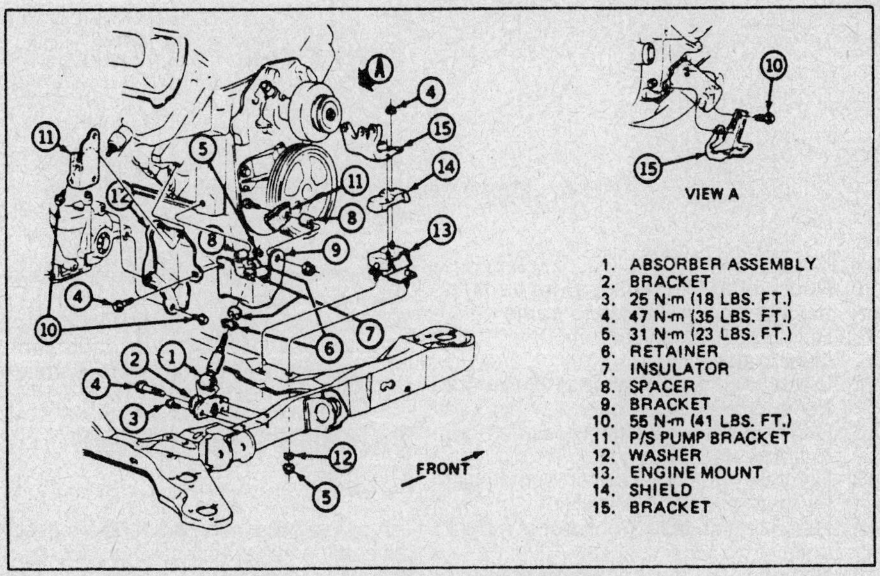

Fig. 1 Engine mounting

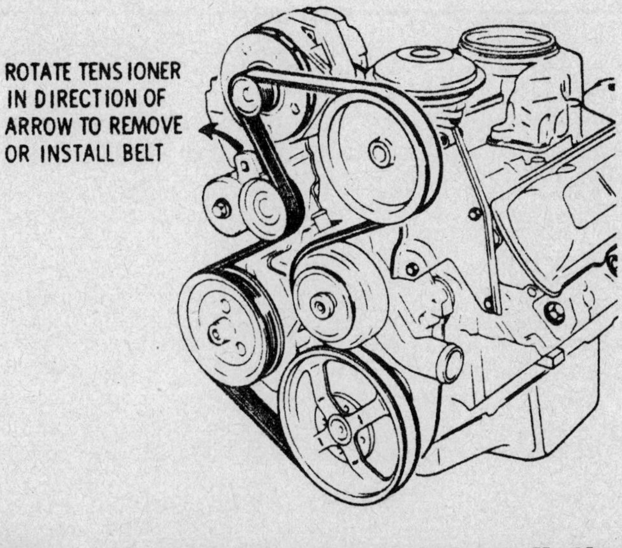

Fig. 2 Serpentine drive belt installation

ENGINE MOUNT
REPLACE

Refer to **Fig. 1** for engine mount replacement.

ENGINE
REPLACE

1. Remove hood. Scribe locations of hinges for reassembly.
2. Disconnect battery cables and drain cooling system.
3. Remove serpentine drive belt and vacuum pump drive belt.
4. Remove air cleaner and install cover J-26996-1.
5. Disconnect ground wires at inner fender panel.
6. Disconnect engine ground strap.
7. Raise and support vehicle.
8. Remove engine to transaxle brace.
9. Remove flexplate cover and the flexplate to torque converter bolts.
10. Disconnect exhaust pipe from right side exhaust manifold.
11. Remove engine mount to cradle retaining nuts and washers.
12. Remove engine absorber assembly from frame bracket.
13. Disconnect wiring from starter motor.
14. Disconnect No. 2 cylinder glow plug wire.
15. Disconnect lower oil cooler hose and plug opening.
16. Remove accessible power steering pump bracket bolts.
17. Lower vehicle.
18. Remove remaining power steering pump bracket bolts and position assembly aside.
19. Disconnect radiator hoses and heater hoses from engine.
20. Disconnect remaining glow plug wires.
21. Disconnect all other electrical leads from engine and the engine harness connector at cowl connector and body mounted relays.
22. Remove A/C compressor bracket bolts and position assembly aside.
23. Disconnect fuel and vacuum hoses.
24. Disconnect accelerator and throttle valve cables from fuel injection pump.
25. Disconnect and plug upper oil cooler hose.

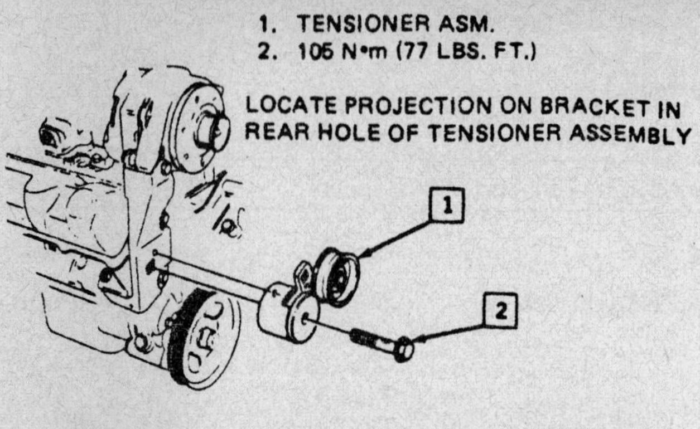

Fig. 3 Belt tensioner installation

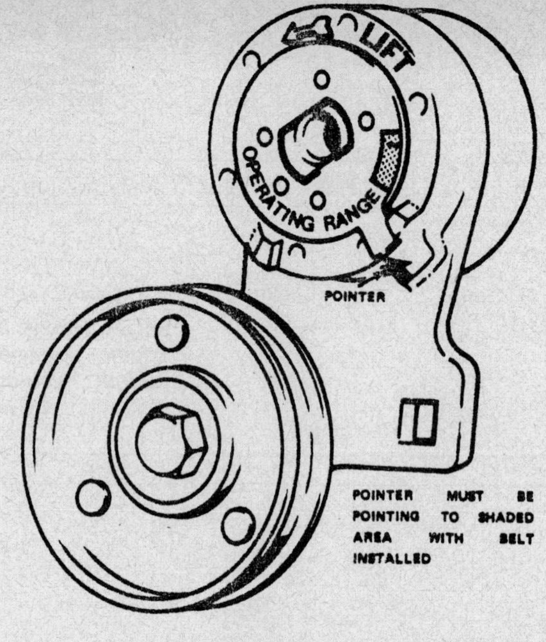

Fig. 4 Belt tensioner operating range indicator

26. Remove exhaust crossover pipe heat shield.
27. Remove transaxle filler tube.
28. Install suitable engine lifting equipment to engine.
29. Place a suitable support under transaxle rear extension.
30. Remove engine to transaxle bolts and carefully lift engine from vehicle.
31. Reverse procedure to install.

OIL PAN REPLACE

1. Disconnect battery ground cable.
2. Install engine support fixture J-28467 or equivalent. **The engine must be properly supported, otherwise, personal injury could result.**
3. Raise and support vehicle.
4. Support front of vehicle body at forward lift points.
5. Remove left front wheel assembly.
6. Drain oil pan.
7. Remove left side lower control arm to frame bolts and the left side stabilizer bar link. Position control arm out of way.
8. Remove engine splash shield.
9. Remove engine mount to frame nuts and the front transaxle to frame nuts.
10. Raise transaxle until mount studs clear cradle.
11. Disconnect wiring harness from front frame crossmember.
12. Remove left side rear crossmember to frame attaching bolts.
13. Remove right side front crossmember to frame attaching bolts.
14. Remove left side front body mount bolts.
15. Remove left and front crossmember assembly.
16. Remove flexplate cover and starter motor.
17. Remove engine mount bracket.
18. Remove engine absorber assembly.
19. Remove oil pan attaching bolts and the oil pan.
20. Reverse procedure to install. Apply sealer No. 1050026 or equivalent to both sides of pan gaskets. Torque oil pan attaching bolts to 10 ft. lbs.

SERPENTINE DRIVE BELT

A single serpentine drive belt is used to drive all engine accessories except the vacuum pump, **Fig. 2.** Tension is maintained by a spring loaded tensioner. To replace belt, refer to **Fig. 3.** The tensioner has provisions for a visual check to verify belt tension is in the operating range, **Fig. 4.**

Rear Suspension & Brake Section

INDEX

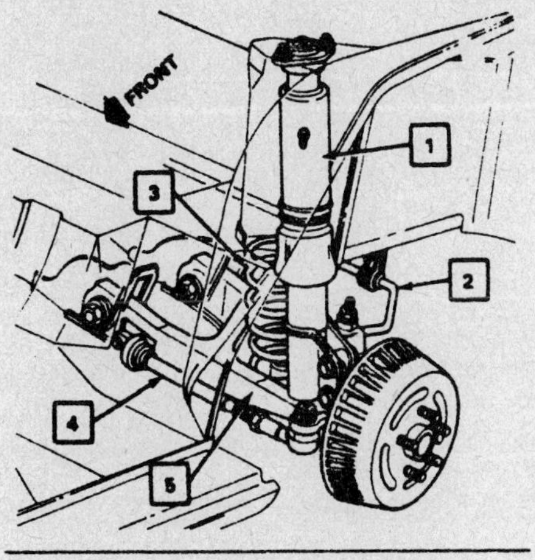

1 SUPERLIFT® STRUT
2 STABILIZER BAR
3 COIL SPRING
4 SUSPENSION ADJUSTMENT LINK
5 LOWER CONTROL ARM

Fig. 1 Rear suspension

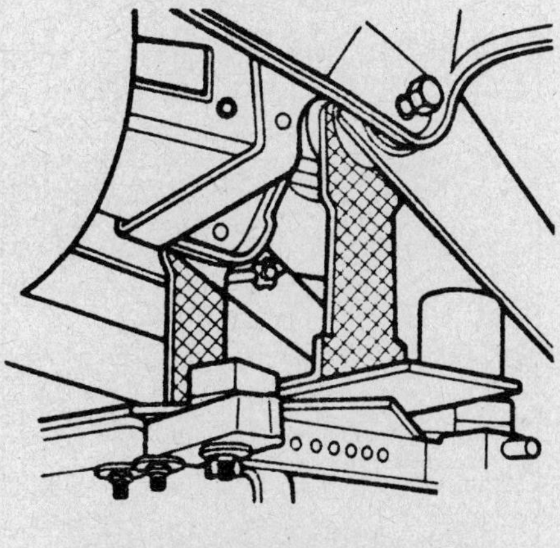

Fig. 3 Installing tool J-23028-01

DESCRIPTION

These vehicles use an independent rear suspension consisting of lower control arms, coil springs, toe links, suspension knuckles, superlift struts and stabilizer bar, **Fig. 1.** The hub and wheel bearing is an assembly and does not require periodic lubrication.

HUB & BEARING ASSEMBLY
REPLACE

1. Raise and support rear of vehicle. Remove wheel assembly and brake drum. **Do not hammer on drum since damage to bearing may occur.**
2. Remove four hub and bearing assembly to axle attaching bolts and the assembly from axle, **Fig. 2.**
3. Reverse procedure to install. Torque attaching bolts to 51 ft. lbs.

COIL SPRING
REPLACE

1. Support vehicle so the rear wheel and control arm hang free. Remove rear wheel.
2. Disconnect rear stabilizer bar from knuckle bracket.
3. Disconnect electronic level control height sensor link if removing right control arm.
4. Disconnect parking brake cable clip from frame if removing left control arm.
5. Place tool J-23028-01 in position to cradle control arm bushings, **Fig. 3. Tool J-23028-01 should be secured to a suitable jack, otherwise, personal injury could result.**
6. Raise jack to relieve tension from control arm pivot bolts.
7. Place a chain around spring and control for safety.
8. Remove rear control arm pivot bolt and nut, **Fig. 4.**
9. Slowly lower jack until front bolt and nut can be removed.
10. Remove coil spring. **Do not apply force on lower arm and ball joint to remove spring. Maneuver spring to remove.**
11. Reverse procedure to install, noting the following:
    a. Replace spring insulators that are damaged or if vehicle has been in service for more than 50,000 miles.
    b. Install springs so that upper pigtail end of left spring faces rear of vehicle, or upper pigtail end of right spring faces front of vehicle when vehicle is at normal ride height.

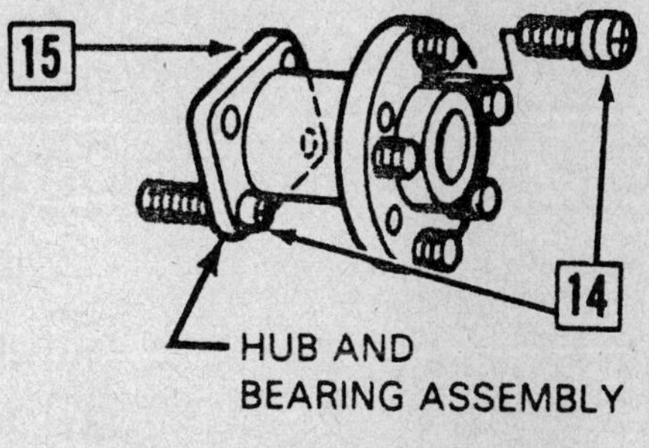

Fig. 2 Hub & bearing assembly

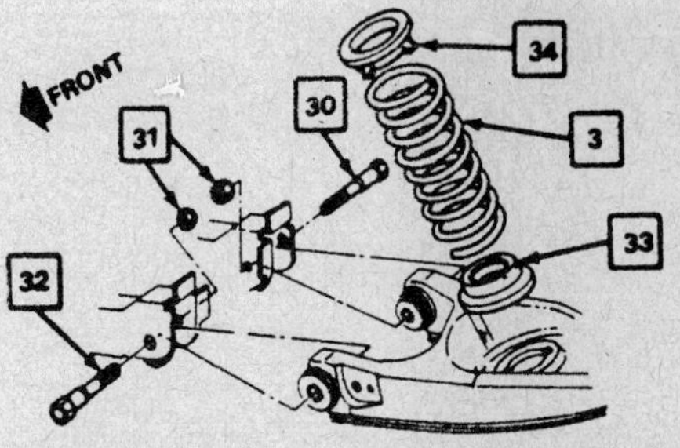

3 COIL SPRING
30 CONTROL ARM PIVOT BOLT-REAR (170 N·m/125 FT. LB.)
31 CONTROL ARM PIVOT NUTS (115 N·m/85 FT. LB.)
32 CONTROL ARM PIVOT BOLT-FRONT (170 N·m/125 FT. LB.)
33 LOWER COIL SPRING INSULATOR
34 UPPER COIL SPRING INSULATOR

Fig. 4 Coil spring replacement

c. Tighten suspension fasteners sufficiently to retain position of components, lower vehicle so that it rests on the wheels at normal ride height, then torque fasteners as follows: 1-Torque control arm pivot nuts to 85 ft. lbs. 2-Torque control arm pivot bolts to 125 ft. lbs. 2-Torque stabilizer support bolt to 160 inch lbs. **Failure to torque fasteners to specifications in listed sequence may adversely affect ride and handling.**

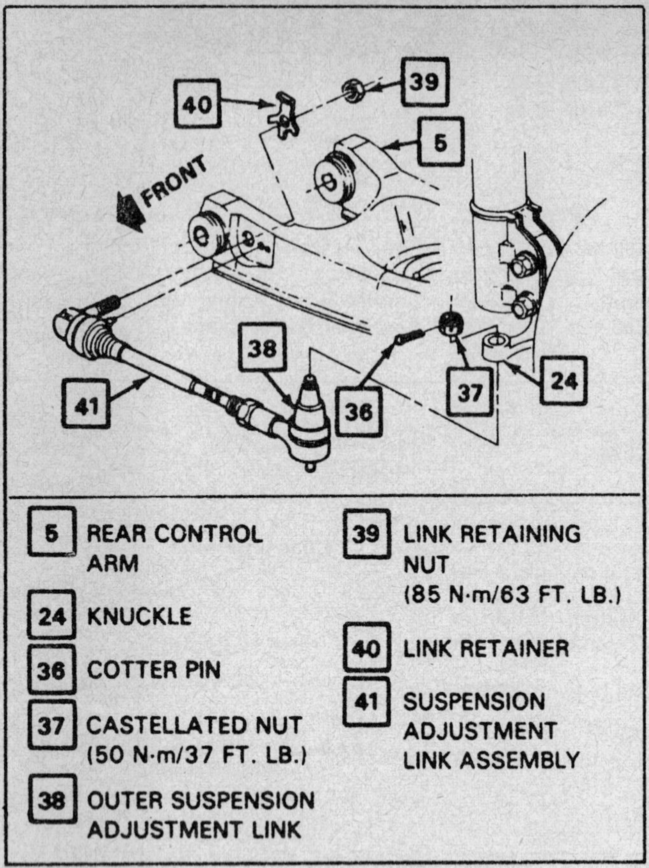

Fig. 5 Tie rod/adjustment link installation

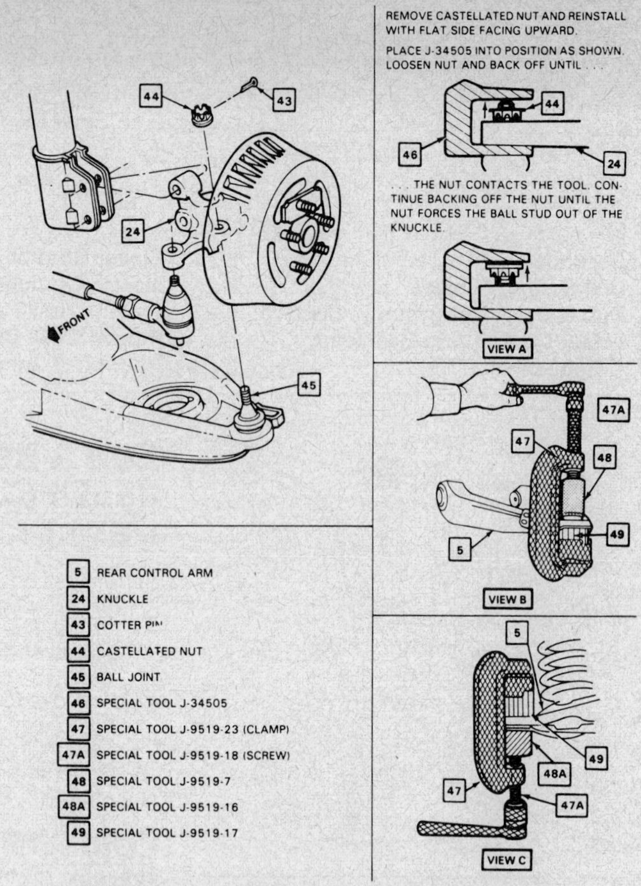

Fig. 6 Ball joint replacement

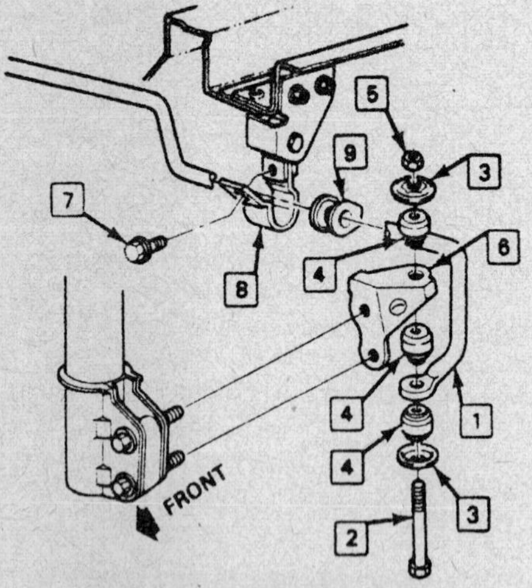

Fig. 7 Stabilizer bar & bushing

REAR TIE ROD/ADJUSTMENT LINK
REPLACE

1. Raise and support vehicle.
2. Remove wheel assembly, cotter key and castle nut, **Fig. 5.**
3. Using tool J-24319-01, disconnect outer tie rod/adjustment from knuckle. **When disconnecting the tie rod/adjustment from knuckle, do not use a wedge since seal damage will occur.**
4. Remove rod/link assembly retaining nut and retainer.
5. Remove rod/link assembly from lower control arm.
6. Reverse procedure to install. Torque link retaining nut to 63 ft. lbs. and castellated nut securing ball stud to 37 ft. lbs. Install cotter pin retaining castellated nut, tightening nut as needed to insert pin through hole in stud. Do not loosen nut to align slots with hole.

LOWER CONTROL ARM BALL JOINT
REPLACE

1. Raise and support vehicle.
2. Remove wheel assembly, cotter key and castle nut.
3. Disconnect outer tie rod/adjustment link from knuckle as outlined previously.
4. Disconnect electronic level control height sensor link from right side control arm.
5. Support control arm with a suitable jack.
6. Remove ball joint cotter pin and nut.
7. Using tool J-29330, disconnect ball joint from knuckle, **Fig. 6.**
8. Using tool J-9519-7, remove ball joint from control arm.
9. Reverse procedure to install.

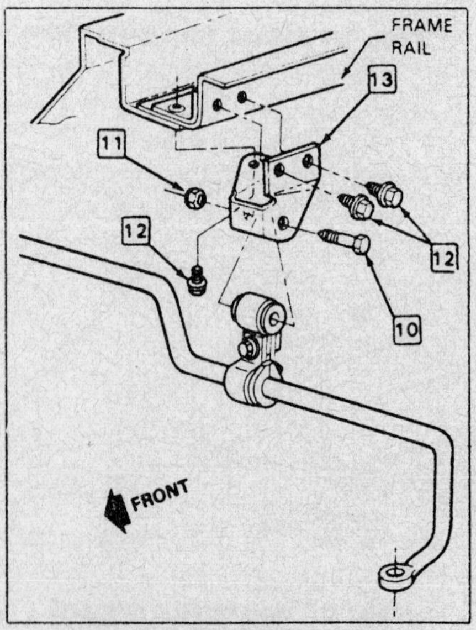

Fig. 8 Stabilizer bar mounting bracket

STABILIZER BAR
REPLACE

Refer to **Figs. 7 and 8** for replacement.

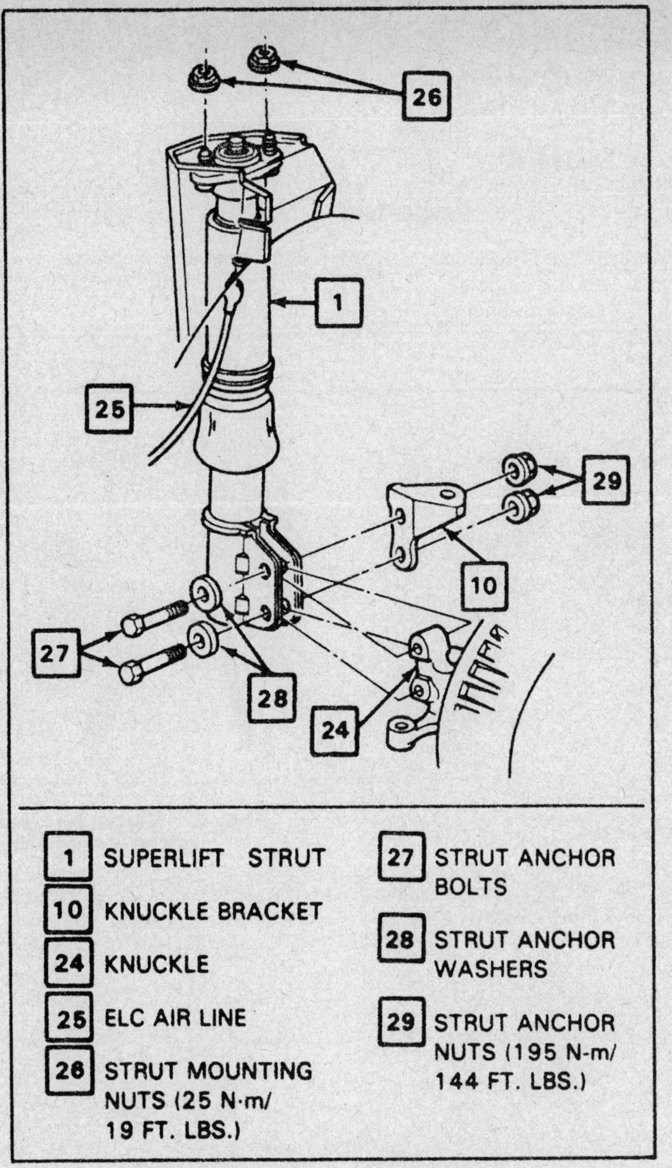

Fig. 9 Strut assembly

LOWER CONTROL ARM REPLACE

1. Remove coil spring as outlined under "Coil Spring, Replace" procedure.
2. Remove control arm front pivot bolt.
3. Remove control arm from vehicle.
4. Reverse procedure to install.

REAR STRUT REPLACE

1. Raise and support vehicle.
2. Remove trunk side cover.
3. Remove wheel assembly.
4. Disconnect air tube from superlift strut, **Fig. 9.**
5. Remove two strut tower mount nuts.
6. Remove two strut anchor bolts, washers and nuts from knuckle, then the knuckle bracket.
7. Remove strut from vehicle.
8. Reverse procedure to install.

SERVICE BRAKE ADJUSTMENT

The rear brakes are self-adjusting and require no periodic adjustment. Self-adjustment is made when the vehicle stops in reverse.

PARKING BRAKE ADJUSTMENT

1. Depress parking brake pedal 1.33 inches.
2. Raise and support vehicle.
3. Tighten adjusting nut until left rear wheel can just be rotated in reverse direction by hand and is locked when forward rotation is attempted.
4. Release parking brake. Both rear wheel should be able to rotate freely with no brake drag.

MASTER CYLINDER REPLACE

1. Disconnect master cylinder push rod from brake pedal.
2. Disconnect electrical connector from brake warning pressure switch.
3. Disconnect brake lines from master cylinder.
4. Remove master cylinder attaching nuts and the master cylinder.
5. Reverse procedure to install. Bleed master cylinder and brake system.

POWER BRAKE UNIT REPLACE

1. Remove master cylinder as outlined previously with brake lines attached and position aside. **Use care not to kink or bend brake lines.**
2. Disconnect vacuum hose from check valve and plug hose to prevent entry of dirt.
3. Remove power brake unit attaching nuts and the power brake unit.
4. Reverse procedure to install.

Front Suspension & Steering Section

INDEX

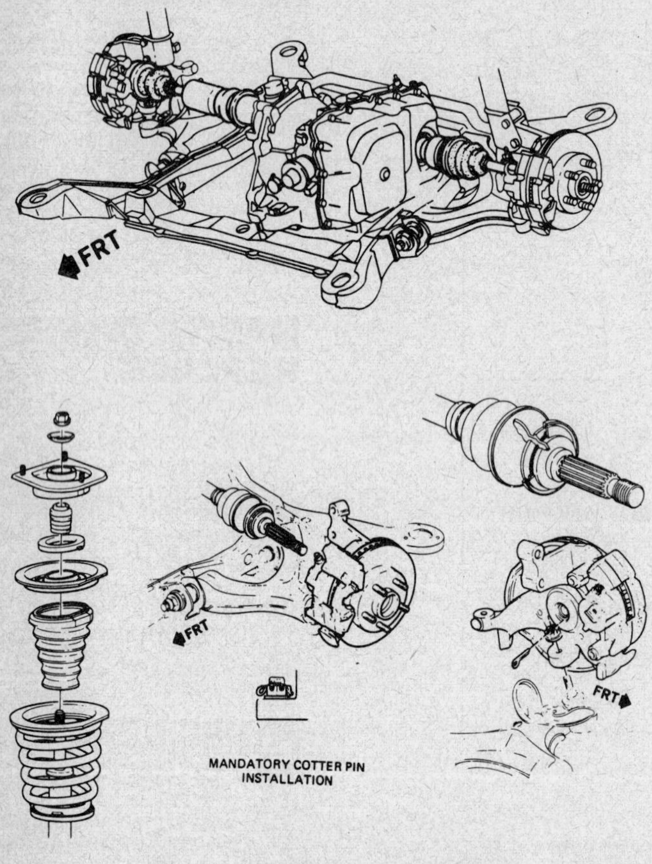

Fig. 1 Front suspension

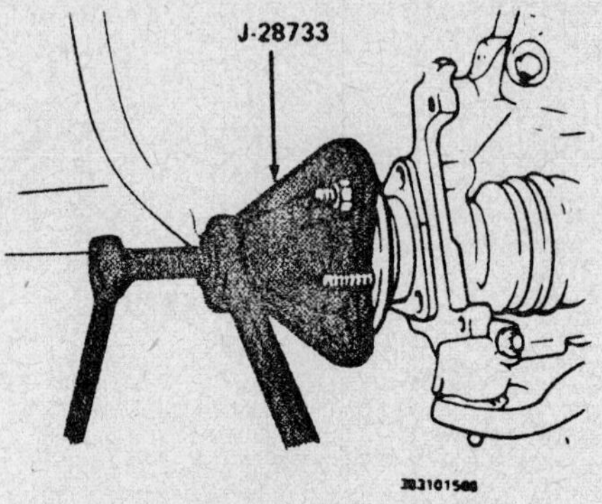

Fig. 2 Separating drive axle from hub

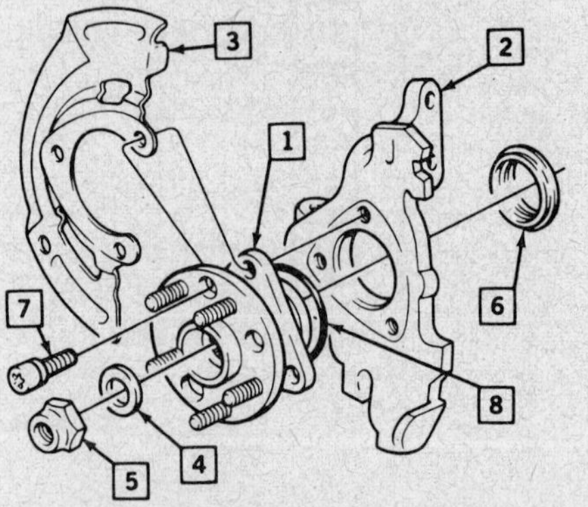

1. HUB AND BEARING ASSEMBLY
2. STEERING KNUCKLE
3. SHIELD
4. WASHER
5. HUB NUT 245 N•m (180 LBS. FT.)
6. SEAL
7. HUB AND BEARING RETAINING BOLT (55 TORX) 95 N•m (70 LBS. FT.)
8. "O" RING

Fig. 3 Hub & bearing assembly

DESCRIPTION

The front suspension is of the MacPherson design, **Fig. 1.** The control arm pivots from the cradle and is mounted in rubber bushings. The upper end of the strut is isolated by a rubber mount and contains a non-serviceable bearing to allow for rotation. The lower end of the steering knuckle pivots on a ball joint riveted to the control arm. The ball joint is fastened to the steering knuckle with a castle nut and cotter pin.

HUB & BEARING
REPLACE

1. Raise and support vehicle and remove wheel assembly.
2. Install drive axle boot protector tool J-28712 on outer joints and J-34754 on inner joints.
3. Insert a suitable drift through opening in caliper into rotor cooling fins to prevent assembly from rotating, then remove hub nut and washer.
4. Remove caliper bracket mounting bolts and the caliper and bracket assembly, then secure assembly aside taking care not to stretch brake hose. Use care not to damage brake hose.
5. Remove rotor, then press drive axle from hub using J-28733 or equivalent, **Fig. 2.**
6. Remove hub assembly retaining bolts, shield, hub and bearing assembly, and O-ring, **Fig. 3**
7. Reverse procedure to install. Torque hub attaching bolts to 70 ft. lbs., caliper bolts to 38 ft. lbs. and hub nut to 180-185 ft. lbs.

BALL JOINT
REPLACE

1. Raise and support vehicle and place jack stands under cradle. Vehicle weight should not be placed on the control arms.
2. Remove wheel assembly.

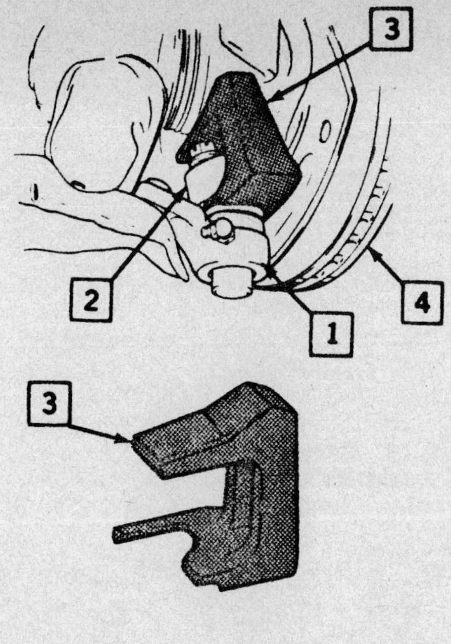

1. BALL JOINT
2. STEERING KNUCKLE
3. BALL JOINT SEPERATOR J-34505
4. ROTOR

Fig. 4 Separating ball joint from steering knuckle

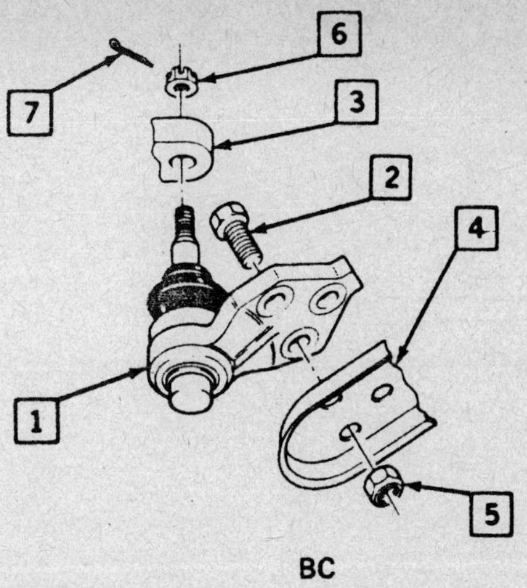

1. SERVICE BALL JOINT
2. BALL JOINT MOUNTING BOLTS MUST FACE DOWN
3. STEERING KNUCKLE
4. CONTROL ARM
5. BALL JOINT MOUNTING NUTS 68 N·m (50 LBS. FT.)
6. BALL JOINT TO STEERING KNUCKLE NUT 110 N·m (81 LBS. FT.) BEFORE COTTER PIN INSTALLATION
7. COTTER PIN

Fig. 5 Service ball joint attachment

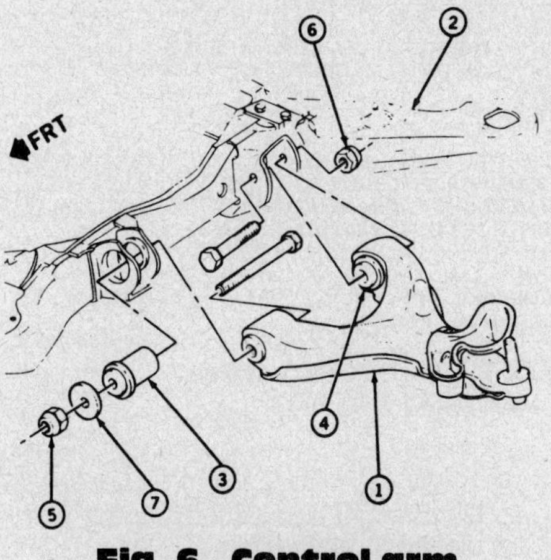

Fig. 6 Control arm assembly

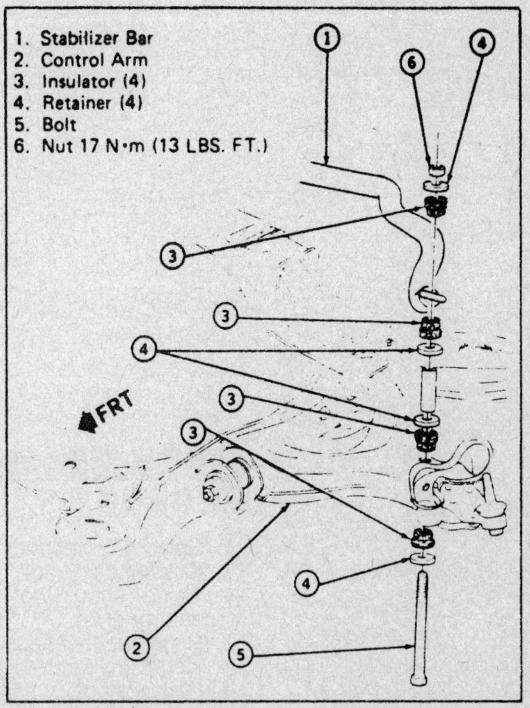

Fig. 7 Stabilizer bar bushing assembly

3. Install drive axle boot protectors.
4. Remove cotter key from ball joint nut and, using tool J-34505, separate ball joint from steering knuckle, **Fig. 4.**
5. Drill out ball joint retaining rivets.
6. Remove stabilizer bar bushing to control arm bolt.
7. Pull control arm downward and remove ball joint from steering knuckle and control arm.
8. Reverse procedure to install. Torque new ball joint attaching nuts to 50 ft. lbs., **Fig. 5,** and ball joint castle nut to 81 ft. lbs.

CONTROL ARM REPLACE

1. Raise and support vehicle and place jackstands under cradle. Vehicle weight should not be placed on the control arms.
2. Remove wheel assembly.
3. Install drive axle boot protectors.
4. Remove cotter key from ball joint nut and, using tool J-34505, separate ball joint from steering knuckle.
5. Remove stabilizer bar bushing to control arm bolt.
6. Remove control arm mounting bolts and the control arm, **Fig. 6.**
7. Reverse procedure to install. When installing control arms, install but do not torque control arm mounting bolts. Sufficiently tighten bolts to assure security but final torque is applied when vehicle weight is supported by control arms. Torque rear arm bolt to 90 ft. lbs. and front bolt to 140 ft. lbs.

1. Stabilizer Bar
2. Stabilizer Bar Mounting Bracket
3. Stabilizer Bar Mounting Bushing
4. 50 N·m (37 LBS. FT.)
5. Frame Welded Nuts
6. Cradle

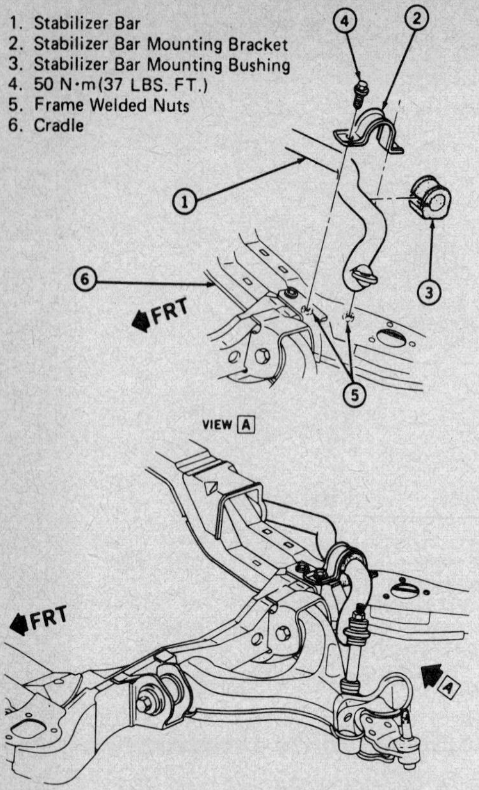

Fig. 8 Stabilizer bar mounting

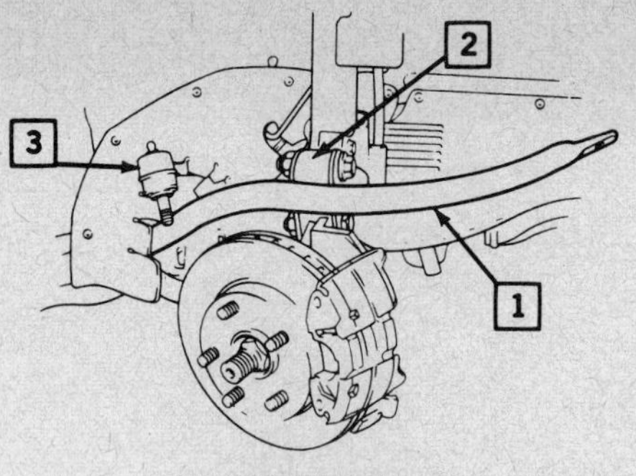

1. STABILIZER BAR
2. STEERING KNUCKLE
3. TIE ROD

Fig. 9 Stabilizer bar replacement

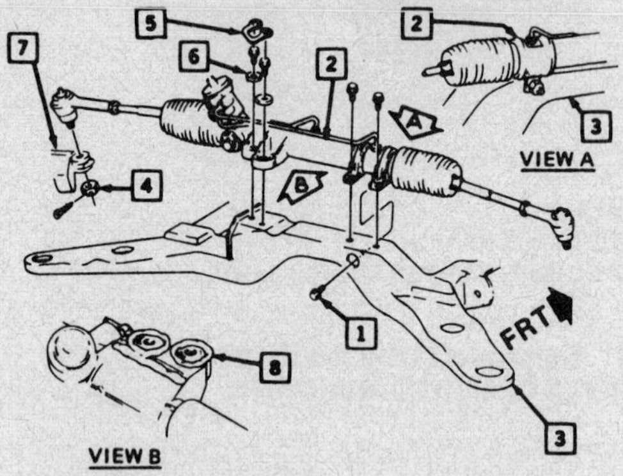

1. BOLT 68 N·m (50 LBS. FT.) AFTER SECOND REUSE OF BOLT, LOCKTITE THREAD LOCKING KIT NO. 1052624 MUST BE USED.
2. STEERING GEAR
3. FRAME
4. 40 N·m (30 LBS. FT.), 70 N·m (52 LBS. FT.) MAXIMUM PERMISSIBLE TORQUE TO ALIGN COTTER PIN SLOT. (1/6 TURN MAXIMUM) DO NOT BACK OFF FOR COTTER PIN INSERTION.
5. RETAINER
6. WASHER
7. STEERING KNUCKLE
8. RTV SEALER AROUND INSERTS

Fig. 11 Steering gear replacement

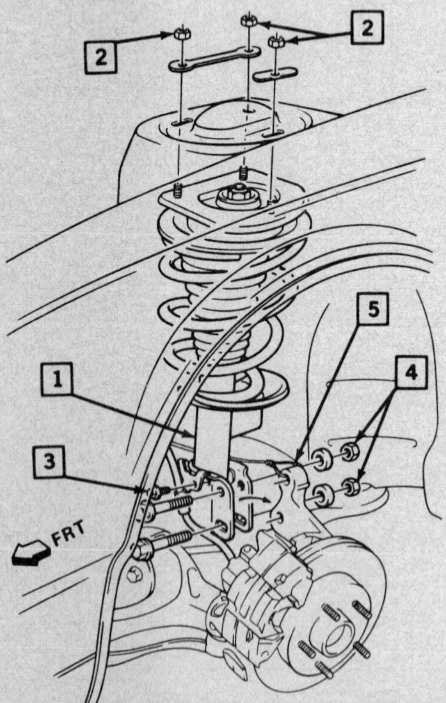

1. STRUT ASSEMBLY
2. STRUT TO BODY NUTS 24 N·m (18 LBS.FT.)
3. BRAKE LINE BRACKET BOLT 17 N·m (13 LBS. FT.)
4. STRUT TO STEERING KNUCKLE NUTS 195 N·m (144 LBS. FT.)
5. RETAIN STEERING KNUCKLE WITH WIRE ONCE STRUT ASSEMBLY IS REMOVED

Fig. 10 Strut assembly

STABILIZER BAR REPLACE

1. Raise and support vehicle and place jackstands under cradle. Vehicle weight should not be placed on the control arms.
2. Remove wheel assembly.
3. Install drive axle boot protectors.
4. Remove nuts, washers, bushings and bolt securing stabilizer shaft to each control arm, **Fig. 7.**
5. Remove stabilizer bar mounting bolts, two bolts from each side, **Fig. 8.**
6. Disconnect tie rods from steering knuckles.
7. Remove exhaust pipe between exhaust manifold and catalytic converter. Remove intermediate pipe on diesel models.
8. On vehicles with V6-181 and V8-250 engines, remove air pipe to exhaust pipe bolt, if equipped.
9. Rotate right side strut assembly completely to the right.
10. Slide stabilizer bar to the right over the steering knuckle and pull downward on left side until stabilizer bar clears the cradle, **Fig. 9.**
11. Reverse procedure to install.

STRUT ASSEMBLY REPLACE

1. Remove three nuts attaching top of strut to body, **Fig. 10.**
2. Raise and support vehicle and place jackstands under cradle. Vehicle weight should not be placed on the control arms.
3. Remove wheel assembly.
4. Install drive axle boot protectors.
5. Remove brake line bracket bolt from strut assembly.
6. Remove strut to steering knuckle attaching bolts.

7. Remove strut assembly from vehicle.
8. Reverse procedure to install. Torque strut mounting bolts to 144 ft. lbs.

STRUT SERVICE

1. Remove strut as outlined under "Strut Assembly, Replace" procedure.
2. Mount strut in compressor tool J-34013 and holding fixture J-3289-20.
3. Rotate compressor forcing screw until spring compresses slightly.
4. Hold damper shaft from rotating and remove nut from top of strut assembly.
5. Use tool J-34013-30 to guide damper shaft from assembly.
6. Loosen compressor forcing screw while guiding damper shaft from assembly. Continue to loosen nut until strut damper and spring can be removed.
7. Reverse procedure to assemble. When assembling spring, the flat on upper spring seat must face outward 90 degrees from center line of vehicle or when mounted in the strut compressor, the seat faces in the same direction as the steering knuckle mounting flange.

POWER STEERING GEAR REPLACE

1. Raise and support vehicle with weight resting on suspension.
2. Remove front wheel assemblies.
3. Disconnect intermediate shaft from steering gear stub shaft.
4. Disconnect both tie rod ends from steering knuckles.
5. Remove line retainers and disconnect hydraulic lines from steering gear.
6. Remove five steering gear attaching bolts, **Fig. 11.**
7. Remove steering gear from vehicle by sliding out to the side.
8. Reverse procedure to install. Torque steering gear attaching bolts to 50 ft. lbs.

POWER STEERING PUMP REPLACE

V6-181, 231 GASOLINE ENGINES

1. Disconnect battery ground cable.
2. Remove air cleaner on V6-181 engine, if necessary.
3. Remove alternator drive belt and alternator.
4. Raise and support vehicle.
5. Disconnect hydraulic lines from pump.
6. Remove rear pump adjustment bracket to pump nut.
7. Remove pump drive belt.
8. Lower vehicle.
9. Remove pump rear adjustment bracket.
10. Remove power steering pump from vehicle.
11. Reverse procedure to install.

V8-250 & 273 GASOLINE ENGINE

1. Disconnect battery ground cable.
2. Remove pump drive belt and the pulley.
3. Disconnect hydraulic lines from pump.
4. Remove two pump mounting bolts.
5. Remove power steering pump from vehicle.
6. Reverse procedure to install.

V6-262 DIESEL ENGINE

1. Disconnect battery ground cable.
2. Remove pump drive belt.
3. Raise and support vehicle.
4. Remove engine splash shield and crankshaft pulley.
5. Remove engine absorber.
6. Disconnect reservoir hose from pump and drain pump.
7. Remove high pressure support and disconnect high pressure hose from pump.
8. Remove two front bracket nuts.
9. Remove one rear bracket bolt.
10. Remove power steering pump with brackets attached.
11. Remove brackets from pump assembly.
12. Reverse procedure to install.

Wheel Alignment Section

INDEX

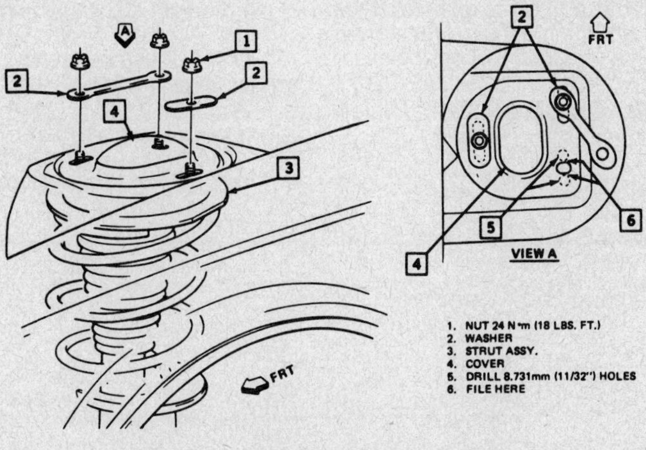

Fig. 1 Caster adjustment

FRONT WHEEL ALIGNMENT

Camber and toe are the only adjustments normally required. After checking settings, perform adjustments in the following order: caster, camber and toe-in.

CASTER, ADJUST

1. Loosen, but do not remove, two of the three top strut mounting nuts covering the slotted mounting holes, **Fig. 1.**
2. Remove the third nut over the oval strut mounting hole and move the washer away from the mounting hole.
3. Raise vehicle by the body to separate the strut from inner wheel house.
4. Drill 11/32 inch holes at front and rear of oval strut mounting hole and file excess metal, **Fig. 1.**
5. Lower body and insert strut into proper position.

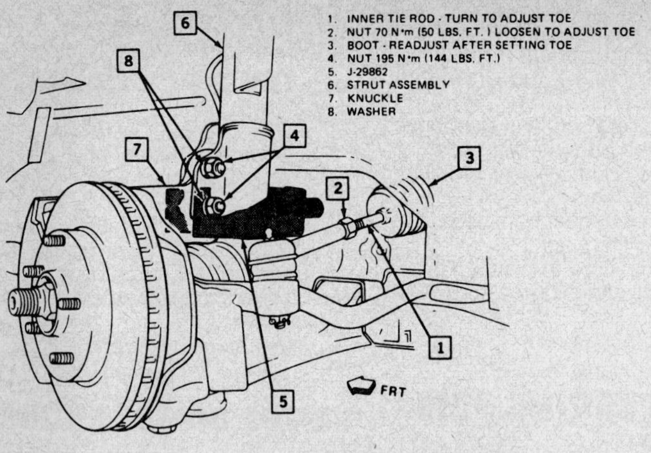

Fig. 2 Camber adjustment

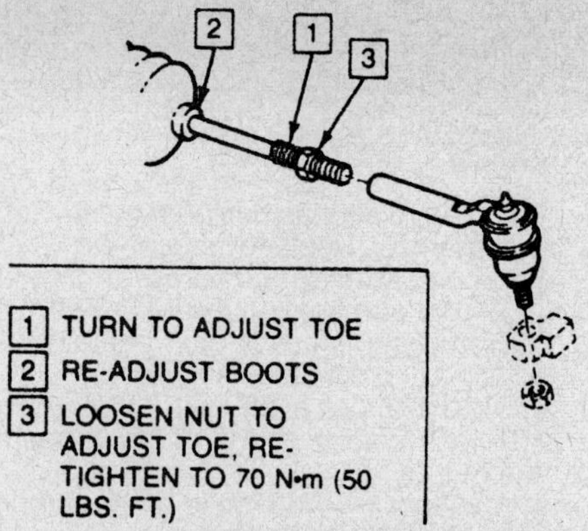

Fig. 3 Rear camber & toe adjustments

6. Set caster to specifications by moving top of strut forward or backward as needed.
7. Install mounting nut and washer. Torque all mounting nuts to 18 ft. lbs.
8. Recheck caster.

CAMBER, ADJUST

1. Loosen both strut to knuckle attaching nuts, **Fig. 2.**
2. Install camber adjusting tool J-29862.
3. Set camber to specifications.
4. Remove adjusting tool and torque strut to knuckle attaching nuts to 144 ft. lbs.
5. Recheck camber.

TOE, ADJUST

1. Loosen lock nuts on both inner tie rods, **Fig. 3.**
2. Adjust toe to specifications by rotating inner tie rod.
3. Torque lock nuts to 50 ft. lbs.
4. Recheck toe setting.

REAR WHEEL ALIGNMENT

When checking rear wheel alignment, the electronic leveling system must have the superlift struts inflated with residual pressure only.

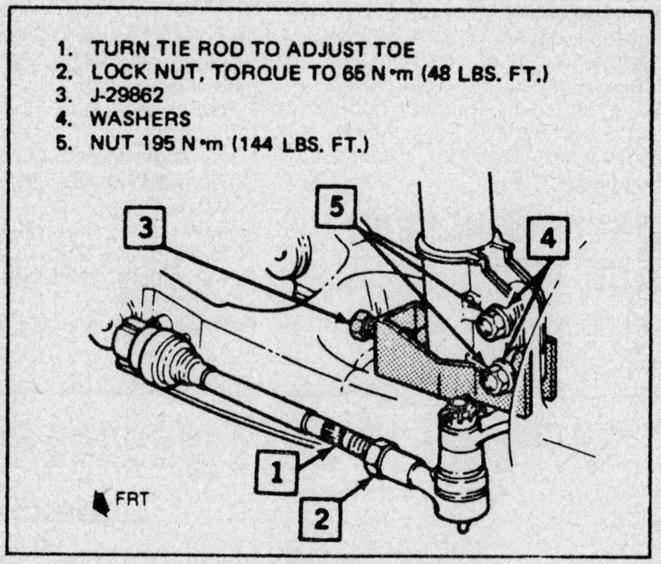

Fig. 4 Toe adjustment

Place a weight in trunk and turn ignition on and move transmission selector from Park to Reverse position and back. This will activate the compressor. Turn ignition off and remove weight from trunk. Wait 30 seconds for the system to exhaust. Roll vehicle forward one complete wheel rotation. Jounce vehicle before checking alignment.

CAMBER, ADJUST

1. Loosen strut to knuckle attaching nuts.
2. Install camber adjusting tool J-29862, **Fig. 4.**
3. Move strut to set camber to specifications.
4. Remove camber adjusting tool and torque strut to knuckle nuts to 144 ft. lbs.
5. Recheck camber setting.

TOE, ADJUST

Toe adjustment is made by loosening the lock nut at tie rod end and turning inner tie rod to set toe to specifications, **Fig. 4.**

1986-88 BUICK RIVIERA, CADILLAC ELDORADO & SEVILLE, OLDSMOBILE TORONADO

INDEX OF SERVICE OPERATIONS

NOTE: Refer to rear of this manual for vehicle manufacturer's special service tool suppliers.

Specifications

GENERAL ENGINE SPECIFICATIONS

Year	Engine CID①/Liter	Engine V.I.N. Code②	Fuel Injection System	Bore Stroke	Compression Ratio	Net H.P. @ R.P.M. ③	Maximum Torque Ft. Lbs @ R.P.M.	Normal Oil Pressure Pounds
1986	V6-231/3.8L	B	S.F.I.④	3.80 x 3.40	8.0	140 @ 4400	200 @ 2000	37
	V8-250/4.1L	8	D.F.I.⑤	3.465 x 3.307	9.0	130 @ 4200	200 @ 2200	30
1987	V6-231/3.8L	3	S.F.I.④	3.80 x 3.40	8.5	⑥	200 @ 2000	37
	V8-250/4.1L	8	D.F.I.⑤	3.465 x 3.307	9.0	130 @ 4200	200 @ 2200	30
1988	V6-231/3.8L	—	S.F.I.④	3.80 x 3.40	8.5	165 @ 5200	210 @ 2000	37
	V8-273/4.5L	—	D.F.I.⑤	3.62 x 3.31	9.0	155 @ 4000	240 @ 2600	—

①—CID-Cubic inch displacement.
②—The eighth digit denotes engine code.
③—Ratings are net-as installed in vehicle.
④—Sequential-port Fuel Injection.
⑤—Digital Fuel Injection.

ALTERNATOR SPECIFICATIONS

Year	Ident. No.	Rated Hot Output Amps.
1986	1105615	108
	1105616	120
	1105657	120
1987	1105615	108
	1105616	120

STARTING MOTOR APPLICATIONS

Year	Engine/V.I.N.	Starter Ident. No.
1986	V6-231/B	1998545
	V8-250/8	1998509
1987	V6-231/3	1998545
	V8-250/8	—
1988	V6-231/	—
	V8-273/	—

ENGINE TIGHTENING SPECIFICATIONS*

*Torque specifications are for clean and lightly lubricated threads only. Dry or dirty threads produce increased friction which prevents accurate measurement of tightness

Year	Engine/ V.I.N.	Spark Plugs Ft. Lbs.	Cylinder Head Bolts Ft. Lbs.	Intake Manifold Ft. Lbs.	Exhaust Manifold Ft. Lbs.	Rocker Arm to Cylinder Head Ft. Lbs.	Rocker Arm Cover Ft. Lbs.	Connecting Rod Cap Bolts Ft. Lbs.	Main Bearing Cap Bolts Ft. Lbs.	Flywheel to Crankshaft Ft. Lbs.	Vibration Damper or Pulley Ft. Lbs.
1986	V6-231/B	20	①	32	37	43	88②	45	100	60	200
	V8-250/8	11	①	①	18	③	8	22	85	37	—
1987	V6-231/3	20	①	32	37	43	115②	45	100	60	219
	V8-250/8	11	①	①	18	③	8	22	85	37	—
1988	V6-231/	—	—	—	—	—	—	—	—	—	—
	V8-273/	—	—	—	—	—	—	—	—	—	—

①—Refer to text for procedure.
②—Inch pounds.
③—Rocker arm pivot to support, 22 ft. lbs.; rocker arm pivot to head bolt nuts, 37 ft. lbs.; rocker arm support to head, 7 ft. lbs.

WHEEL ALIGNMENT SPECIFICATIONS

Year	Model	Caster Angle, Degrees		Camber Angle, Degrees				Toe-in Degree
				Limits		Desired		
		Limits	Desired	Left	Right	Left	Right	
1986	Eldorado, Seville①	+1.7° to +3.3°	+2.5°	−.5° to +.5°	−.5° to + .5°	0°	0°	−.1° to +.1°②
	Eldorado, Seville③	—	—	—	—	—	—	0 to +.2°②
	Riviera①	+1.5° to +3.5°	+2.5°	−.3° to +1.3°	−.3° to +1.3°	+.5°	+.5°	−.1° to +.1°
	Riviera③	—	—	−.8° to −.6°	−.8° to −.6°	−.7°	−.7°	0 to +.2°②
	Toronado①	+1.3° to +3.3°	+2.3°	−.8° to +8°	−.8° to +.8°	0°	0°	−.1° to + .1°②
	Toronado③	—	—	−.7° to −.1°	−.7° to −.1°	−.4°	−.4°	0° to .2°②
1987	Eldorado, Seville①	+1.3° to +3.3°	+2.3°	−.8° to +.8°	−.8° to +.8°	0	0	−.2° to +.2°
	Eldorado, Seville③	—	—	−.4° to +.2°	−.4° to +.2°	−.1°	−.1°	0 to +.4°
	Riviera①	+1.3° to +3.3°	+2.3°	−.8° to +.8°	−.8° to +.8°	0	0	−.2° to +.2°
	Riviera③	—	—	−.4° to −1°	−.4° to −1°	−.7°	−.7°	0 to +.4°
	Toronado①	+1.3° to +3.3°	+2.3°	−.8° to +.8°	−.8° to +.8°	0	0	−.2° to +.2°
	Toronado③	—	—	−.1° to −.7°	−.1° to −,.7°	−.4°−.4°0 to +.4°		
1988	Eldorado, Seville①	—	—	—	—	—	—	—
	Eldorado, Seville③	—	—	—	—	—	—	—
	Riviera①	+1.5° to +3.5°	+2.5°	−.8° to +.8°	−.8° to +.8°	0	0	−.1° to +.1°
	Riviera③	—	—	−.7° to −1.3°	−.7° to −1.3°	−1°	−1°	0 to +.2°
	Toronado①	+1.5° to +3.5°	+2.5°	−.8° to +.8°	−.8° to +.8°	0	0	−.1° to +.1°
	Toronado③	—	—	−.7° to −1.3°	−.7° to −1.3°	−1°	−1°	−.4° to −1°

①—Front.
②—Per wheel.
③—Rear.

COOLING SYSTEM & CAPACITY DATA

Year	Model or Engine/V.I.N.	Cooling Capacity, Qts.		Radiator Cap Relief Pressure, Lbs.	Thermo. Opening Temp.	Fuel Tank Gals	Engine Oil Refill Qts.	Auto Transaxle Qts.①
		Less A/C	With A/C					
1986	V6-231/B	12	12	15	195	18	4②	③
	V8-250/8	—	12.6	15	195	18	5	③
1987	V6-231/3	—	12	15	195	18	4②	③
	V8-250/8	—	12.6	15	195	18	5④	③
1988	V6-231/	—	12	—	—	18.8	4②	③
	V8-273/	—	—	—	—	—	—	—

①—Approximate make final check with dipstick.
②—Additional oil will be necessary when changing filter.
③—Drain & refill, 6.5 qts.; overhaul, 11 qts.
④—Add an additional .5 qt. when changing filter.

Electrical Section

INDEX

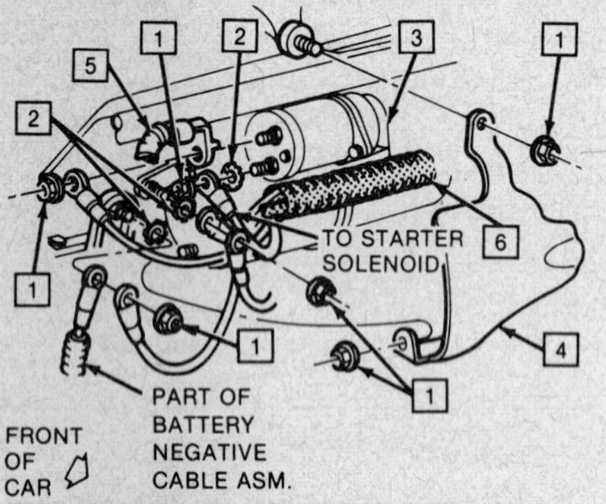

1 RETAINING NUT (6)
2 STAR WASHER (3)
3 STARTER MOTOR SOLENOID
4 SHIELD
5 POSITIVE BATTERY CABLE
6 ENGINE WIRING HARNESS ASM.

Fig. 1 Starter wiring. Eldorado & Seville

STARTER MOTOR

REPLACE

If shims are used between starter and engine block, they should be placed in original position during installation. If starter is noisy during cranking, remove double .015 inch shim or add .015 inch shim at outer bolt only. If high pitched whine is observed after engine starts, add double .015 inch shims (to maximum of .045 inch) until noise is corrected.

ELDORADO & SEVILLE

1. Disconnect battery ground cable, then raise and support vehicle.
2. Remove nuts securing starter shield and the shield.
3. Remove nuts securing solenoid wires and battery cable, then disconnect wiring, **Fig. 1.**

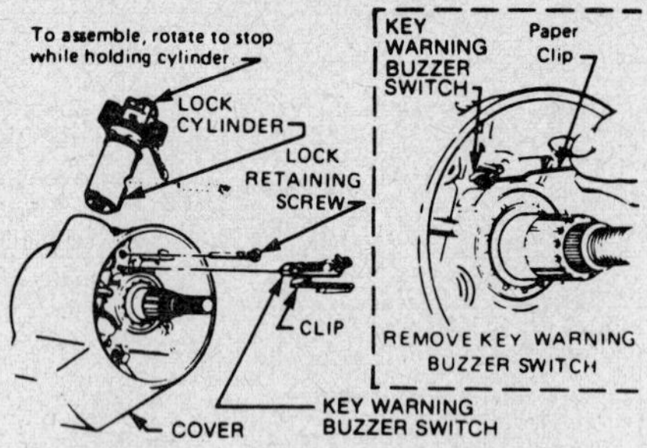

Fig. 2 Ignition lock cylinder & key warning switch

4. Remove starter brace, mounting bolts and the starter motor.
5. Reverse procedure to install.

RIVIERA & TORONADO

1. Disconnect battery ground cable, then raise and support vehicle.
2. Remove starter splash shield, if equipped.
3. Remove 2 bolts securing starter to engine block, then lower starter motor.
4. Remove retaining nuts and disconnect electrical connectors, noting position for installation.
5. Reverse procedure to install.

IGNITION LOCK

REPLACE

1. Disconnect battery ground cable and remove turn signal switch as outlined.
2. Rotate key to "Run" position, then remove key warning switch, **Fig. 2.**
3. Remove lock retaining screw, then withdraw lock cylinder assembly from column.
4. Reverse procedure to install. Torque lock retaining screw to 35 inch lbs.

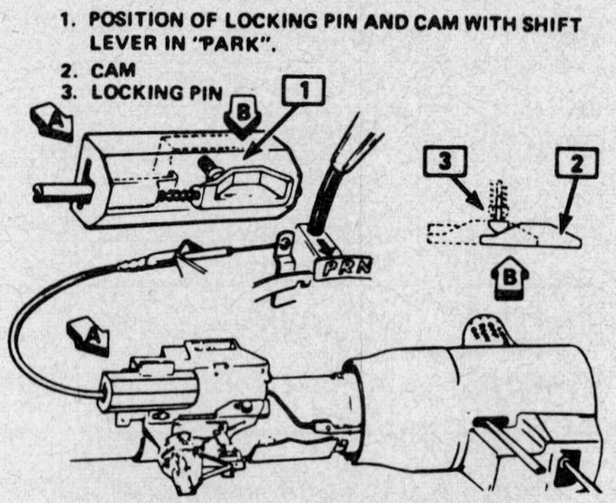

Fig. 3 Park-lock cable. Models w/floor shift

IGNITION & DIMMER SWITCH

REPLACE

REMOVAL

1. Disconnect battery ground cable.
2. On models with floor shift, place transmission selector in park and rotate ignition lock to "Run" position.
3. On all models, remove left hush panel, lower steering column cover, insulator at toe plate, and the lower steering column mounting screws.
4. Remove nuts securing upper steering column bracket to instrument panel, then carefully lower column. **Disconnect shift indicator cable and electrical connectors, as needed, prior to lowering column. Do not force column down as it may be damaged.**
5. Remove dimmer switch mounting nut, screw and the dimmer switch, then tape actuator rod to steering column.
6. On models with floor shift, insert screwdriver into slot in ignition switch inhibitor, depress park-lock cable latch and disconnect cable from inhibitor, **Fig. 3. Ignition switch must be in "Run" position. Do not attempt to disconnect park-lock cable with switch in any other position.**

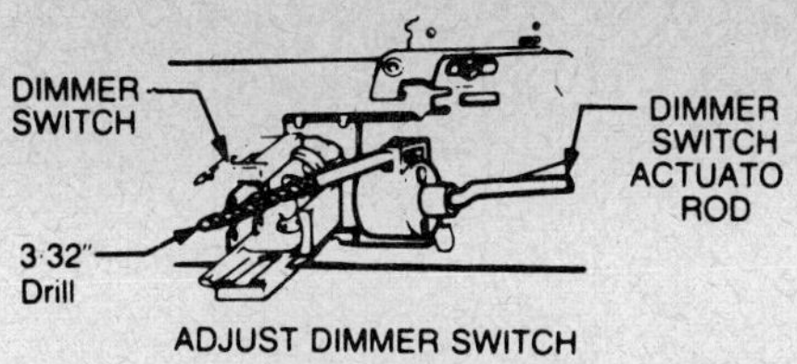

Fig. 4 Dimmer switch installation

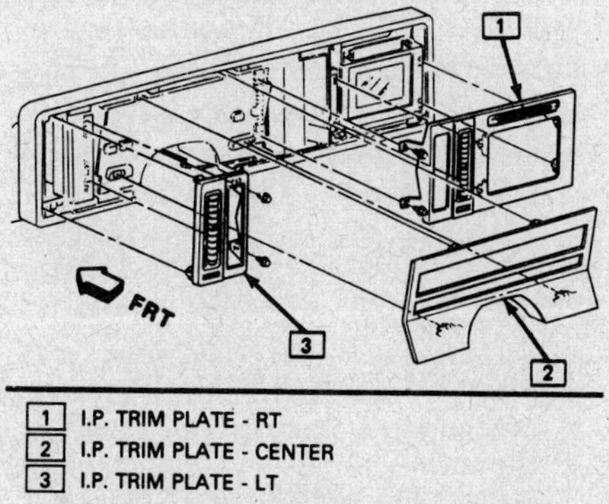

Fig. 6 Instrument cluster trim plate removal. Riviera

7. Rotate ignition key to "Off-Lock" position.
8. On all models, remove ignition switch stud bolt, disconnect electrical connector, then remove switch assembly.

INSTALLATION

1. Move ignition switch slider to extreme right, then one detent to the left to place switch in "Off-Lock" position.
2. Connect electrical connector to ignition switch, install switch assembly on column ensuring actuator is properly engaged, and torque stud bolt to 35 inch lbs.
3. Install dimmer switch assembly, depress switch against actuator and insert 3/32 inch drill into adjustment slot, **Fig. 4,** then torque nut and retaining screw to 35 inch lbs.
4. On models with floor shift, rotate ignition lock to "Run" position, then install shift-lock cable on inhibitor.
5. On all models, reverse remaining procedure to complete installation. Torque upper column bracket bolts to 20 ft. lbs and lower column bolts to 25 ft. lbs.

HORN SOUNDER & STEERING WHEEL
REPLACE
ELDORADO & SEVILLE

1. Remove 2 screws securing pad from rear of steering wheel.
2. Disconnect horn and cruise control electrical connectors, then remove pad.
3. Remove 3 telescope adjusting lever screws, unscrew telescope adjusting mechanism from steering shaft, then remove adjusting lever.
4. Scribe alignment mark between steering wheel and steering shaft, then remove steering wheel retaining nut.
5. Remove steering wheel using suitable puller.
6. Reverse procedure to install, noting the following:
   a. Align matching marks between steering wheel and shaft, and torque retaining nut to 35 ft. lbs.
   b. Fully extend steering shaft, mount telescope adjusting lever in 5 o'clock position, thread adjuster mechanism onto shaft and hand tighten, then install adjusting lever retaining screws.
   c. Ensure steering wheel moves in and out freely when lever is moved fully to the right, and that lever does not contact shroud in fully locked position.

RIVIERA & TORONADO

1. On models with standard wheel, remove 2 screws securing pad from rear of steering wheel. On models with sport wheel, carefully pry up center cap.
2. Disconnect horn lead from cam tower, and disconnect cruise control electrical connector, if equipped.
3. Scribe alignment mark between steering wheel and shaft, then remove retainer and nut.
4. Remove steering wheel using suitable puller.
5. Reverse procedure to install. Torque steering wheel nut to 35 ft. lbs.

TURN SIGNAL SWITCH
REPLACE

1. Disconnect battery ground cable and remove steering wheel.
2. Remove left hush panel and lower steering column trim cover.
3. Remove turn signal switch harness cover, then disconnect switch harness connector.
4. Pry off shaft lock cover, then mount suitable spring compressor on steering shaft, **Fig. 5.**
5. Remove lock plate retaining ring and telescoping wheel components, as equipped, then remove spring compressor.
6. Remove lock plate, canceling cam and shaft spring.
7. Remove turn signal lever, screw securing signal switch actuator arm and the arm, if equipped.
8. Remove turn signal switch retaining screws and the switch assembly.
9. Reverse procedure to install.

WINDSHIELD WIPER SWITCH
REPLACE
ELDORADO & SEVILLE

1. Remove A/C vent and radio trim plate from instrument cluster bezel.
2. Remove 7 screws securing instrument cluster bezel and the bezel.

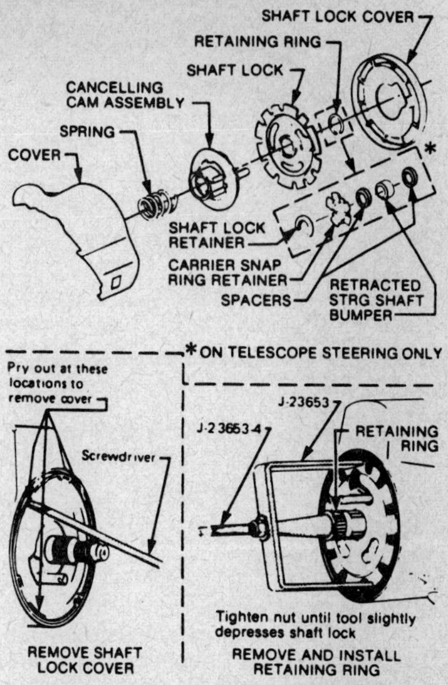

Fig. 5 Lock plate & cancelling cam removal

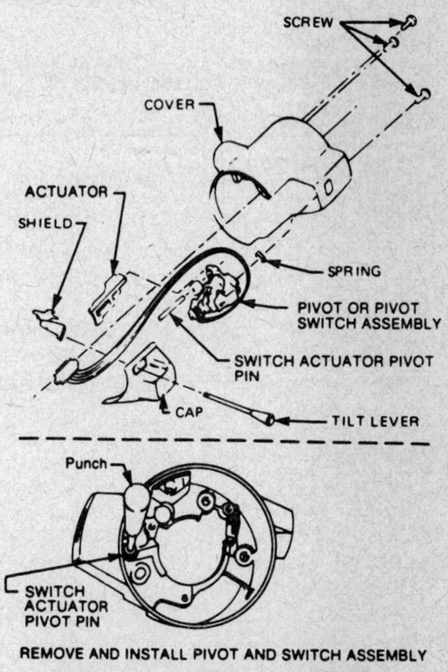

Fig. 7 Wiper switch removal. Toronado

3. Remove 2 screws securing right switch module and pull module from instrument panel socket.
4. Reverse procedure to install.

RIVIERA

1. Pull center instrument cluster trim plate straight out of instrument panel.
2. Remove screws securing right trim plate and the right trim plate and air outlet assembly, **Fig. 6.**
3. Remove screws securing right switch module and pull switch module out of instrument panel.
4. Disconnect electrical connector and remove switch.
5. Reverse procedure to install.

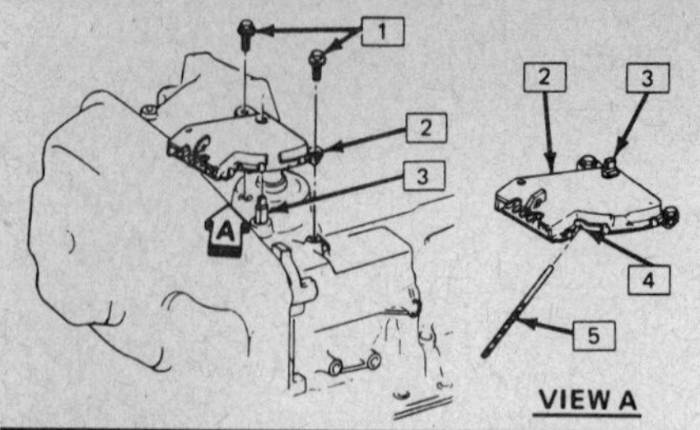

1 BOLT 30N·m (22 FT. LBS.)
2 SWITCH ASM.
3 TRANS. SHAFT
4 SERVICE ADJUSTMENT HOLE
5 3/32 INCH DRILL BIT OR 2.34 DIA. GAGE PIN

Fig. 8 Back up lamp/neutral safety switch installation

TORONADO

1. Remove steering wheel, turn signal switch and ignition lock as outlined.
2. Remove screws securing upper mast jacket cover and the cover assembly.
3. Remove switch and pivot from cover as shown in **Fig. 7.**
4. Reverse procedure to install.

BACK-UP LAMP/NEUTRAL SAFETY SWITCH

REPLACE

REMOVAL

1. Remove nut securing shift lever to transaxle and disconnect lever from shaft.
2. Release "T" latch and disconnect electrical connector from switch.
3. Remove switch mounting bolts and the switch, **Fig. 8.**

INSTALLATION

New Switch

New switch is pinned in position to provide correct adjustment. If pin is missing or has been broken by rotating switch, follow procedure for installation and adjustment of used switch.

1. Rotate shift shaft to neutral position.
2. Align flats on switch with flats on shaft, then install switch.
3. Install and tighten mounting bolts. **Do not rotate switch if bolts will not align with case mounting boss, ensure shift shaft is in neutral position. If shaft is properly positioned but bolts still do not line-up with mounting boss, refer to procedure for old switch.**
4. Install shift lever and reconnect electrical connector to switch.
5. Ensure engine will only start with selector in "Park" and "Neutral" positions and verify proper operation of back up lamps.

Used Switch

1. Rotate shift shaft to neutral position.
2. Align flats on switch with flats on shaft, then install switch.
3. Install mounting bolts, leaving switch free to rotate.
4. Insert 3/32 inch gauge pin into service adjustment hole, **Fig. 8.**
5. Rotate switch until gauge pin can be pressed into a depth of 15/32 inch on 1986 models, or 9/64 inch on 1987-88 models, then secure switch position by tightening switch mounting bolts.
6. Remove gauge pin, install shift lever and reconnect electrical connector to switch.
7. Ensure engine will only start with selector in "Park" and "Neutral" positions and verify proper operation of back up lamps.

ADJUSTMENT

1. Position transaxle shifter assembly in "neutral" notch in detent plate, then loosen switch attaching screws.
2. Rotate switch on shifter assembly until adjustment hole aligns with carrier tang hole.
3. Insert 3/32 inch gauge pin into adjustment hole to a depth of 5/8 inch on 1987-88 Riviera and Toronado, or 15/32 inch on all other models.
4. Tighten switch mounting bolts, then remove gauge pin.

LIGHT SWITCH

REPLACE

ELDORADO & SEVILLE

1. Disconnect battery ground cable.
2. Remove A/C vent and radio bezel from instrument cluster bezel.
3. Remove 7 screws securing instrument cluster bezel and the bezel.
4. Remove screws securing switch module and pull module from socket in instrument panel.
5. Reverse procedure to install.

RIVIERA

1. Disconnect battery ground cable and place tilt wheel in fully lowered position.
2. Pull center cluster trim panel straight out of dash and remove 2 screws securing left trim panel, **Fig. 6.**
3. Grasp both sides of left trim panel and pull panel straight out of dash.
4. Remove screws securing switch module, pull module from instrument panel and disconnect electrical connector.
5. Reverse procedure to install. Ensure trim panels are properly aligned, then press panels straight back into instrument panel.

TORONADO

1. Disconnect battery ground cable.
2. Remove screws securing instrument cluster bezel, then pull bezel away from instrument panel to disengage retaining clips.
3. Disconnect electrical connectors to bezel mounted switches.
4. Remove switch from cluster bezel.
5. Reverse procedure to install.

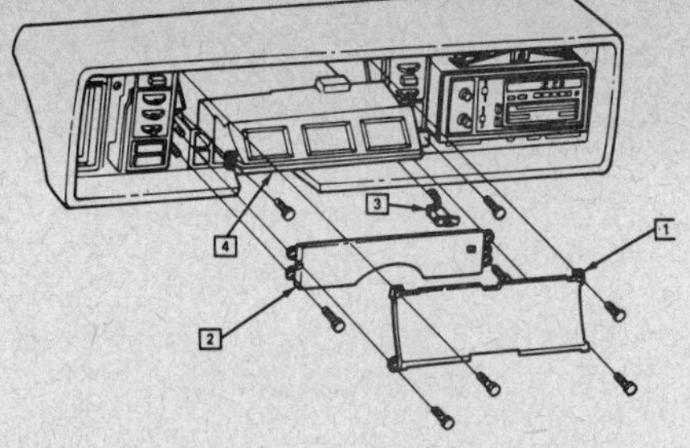

1 DIGITAL DISPLAY FILTER LENSE
2 WARNING LIGHT LENSE
3 TRIP ODOMETER RESET BUTTON
4 DIGITAL INSTRUMENT CLUSTER ASSEMBLY

Fig. 9 Instrument cluster removal. Eldorado & Seville

INSTRUMENT CLUSTER

REPLACE

ELDORADO & SEVILLE

1. Disconnect battery ground cable.
2. Remove A/C duct and radio trim plate from instrument cluster bezel.
3. Remove 7 screws securing instrument cluster bezel and the bezel.
4. Remove digital display and warning lamp lenses, and the trip odometer reset button, **Fig. 9.**
5. Remove two screws securing cluster, then pull cluster from instrument panel socket, using pliers to hold retaining tabs at each end of cluster.
6. Reverse procedure to install, ensuring electrical connector pins are properly aligned when cluster is pressed into instrument panel.

RIVIERA

1. Disconnect battery ground cable.
2. Pull instrument cluster center trim plate straight out of dash, then remove left and right trim plates, **Fig. 6.**
3. Remove 4 screws securing cluster, then pull cluster straight out of instrument panel.
4. Reverse procedure to install, ensuring electrical connector pins are properly aligned when cluster is pressed into instrument panel.

TORONADO

1. Remove body ignition fuse No. 14.
2. Remove left hush panel, lower steering column cover, insulator at toe plate, and the lower steering column mounting screws.
3. Remove nuts securing upper steering column bracket to instrument panel, then carefully lower column. **Disconnect shift indicator cable and electrical connectors, as needed, prior to lowering column. Do not force column down as it may be damaged.**
4. Remove screws securing instrument cluster bezel, then pull bezel away from instrument panel to disengage retaining clips.
5. Disconnect electrical connectors and remove cluster bezel.
6. Remove screws securing instrument cluster, then pull cluster straight out of

dash.

7. Reverse procedure to install, ensuring electrical connector pins are properly aligned when cluster is pressed into instrument panel.

RADIO

REPLACE

ELDORADO & SEVILLE

1. Disconnect battery ground cable.
2. Remove radio trim plate from instrument cluster bezel.
3. Remove 7 screws securing instrument cluster bezel and the bezel.
4. Loosen lower mounting nuts and pull radio away from instrument panel.
5. Disconnect electrical connectors and antenna lead, then remove radio assembly.
6. Reverse procedure to install.

RIVIERA

Radio

1. Disconnect battery ground cable.
2. Remove shifter handle and the shift indicator assembly.
3. Remove 4 screws securing top console trim plate.
4. Remove console left front floor panel.
5. Remove screws from top of bracket securing radio.
6. Disconnect bracket, electrical connectors and antenna lead, noting position for installation, then remove radio.
7. Reverse procedure to install.

Tape Player

1. Disconnect battery ground cable.
2. Pull upper console trim panel straight out of console.
3. Remove 4 screws securing tape player assembly and pull tape player from console.
4. Disconnect electrical connectors and remove tape player.
5. Reverse procedure to install.

TORONADO

Radio

1. Disconnect battery ground cable.
2. Remove screws securing instrument cluster bezel, then pull bezel away from instrument panel to disengage retaining clips.
3. Disconnect electrical connectors and remove cluster bezel.
4. Remove screws securing ECC panel and radio brackets to instrument panel and pull assembly away from panel.
5. Disconnect electrical connectors, noting position for installation, then remove ECC panel and radio assembly.
6. Remove nuts securing Radio to brackets, then the radio.
7. Reverse procedure to install.

Console Mounted Tape Player & Booster

1. Disconnect battery ground cable, then carefully pull trim plate from console.
2. Lift out shift indicator assembly and disconnect bulbs from indicator.
3. Remove screws securing console mounting plate.
4. Disconnect electrical connectors and remove mounting plate assembly.
5. Remove nuts securing tape player or booster to mounting plate and remove components as required.
6. Reverse procedure to install, pressing console trim plate into retaining clip until trim plate is secured.

BLOWER MOTOR

REPLACE

ELDORADO & SEVILLE

1. Disconnect battery ground cable and remove strut tower cross brace.
2. Remove wiring harness bracket, then disconnect electrical connector and cooling hose from blower motor.
3. Remove blower motor retaining screws, then tilt blower motor fin case to allow fan removal. **Fan must be removed prior to blower motor to prevent fan from being bent.**
4. Remove fan retainer and fan from blower motor, then remove motor.
5. Remove blower fan from case.
6. Reverse procedure to install.

RIVIERA

1. Disconnect battery ground cable.
2. Remove vacuum tank and wiring harness cover, as needed, to gain access.
3. Disconnect electrical connector and cooling tube from blower motor.
4. Remove blower motor mounting screws and the blower motor.
5. Reverse procedure to install.

TORONADO

1. Disconnect battery ground cable and remove front of cowl shield.
2. Remove bulkhead connector screw and disconnect bulkhead connector.
3. Disconnect electrical connector from Electronic Spark Control module, then remove bracket retaining screws and the module.
4. Remove power steering pump bracket support bolts and the support.
5. Remove coil bracket nuts, disconnect high tension leads and electrical connectors from coil, remove wiring conduits and plug wire guides, and position coil aside.
6. Remove shields from blower motor harness, then disconnect cooling tube and electrical connector from blower motor.
7. Remove blower motor mounting screws and the blower motor.
8. Reverse procedure to install.

HEATER CORE

REPLACE

ELDORADO & SEVILLE

1. Disconnect battery ground cable and drain cooling system.
2. Remove right hush panel, 4 screws securing glove box module and the glove box.
3. Disconnect air mix door link rod, and the electrical and vacuum connectors from programmer assembly, then remove mounting screws and programmer.
4. Remove electronic control module and bracket.
5. Remove module assembly and heater core cover.
6. Disconnect heater hoses from heater core.
7. Remove heater core retaining screws and the heater core.
8. Reverse procedure to install. Prior to installing glove box module, adjust air mix door link rod as follows:
   a. Set temperature control for 90°F. and allow 1-2 minutes for programmer arm to travel to maximum heat position.
   b. Disconnect air mix door link rod from programmer and ensure air mix door operated freely.
   c. Pre-load air mix door in maximum heat position by pulling rod to seat door against seal, then snap rod into connector on programmer arm, taking care not to disturb position of arm or air mix door.
   d. Set control for 60°F. and ensure programmer arm and air mix door travel to maximum cooling position.

RIVIERA

1. Disconnect battery ground cable and drain cooling system.
2. Remove right hush panel, and the center and lower instrument panel trim plates.
3. Disconnect electrical connector, then remove right speaker and grille to gain access to programmer.
4. Disconnect electrical and vacuum connectors from programmer.
5. Remove linkage cover and disconnect linkage, then remove programmer.
6. Remove heater core cover and splash cover access to heater hoses.
7. Disconnect heater hoses from heater core and remove heater core.
8. Reverse procedure to install.

TORONADO

1. Disconnect battery ground cable and drain cooling system.
2. Remove left and right hush panels and under dash courtesy lamps.
3. Remove lower steering column cover, insulator at toe plate, and the lower steering column mounting screws.
4. Remove nuts securing upper steering column bracket to instrument panel, then carefully lower column. **Disconnect shift indicator cable and electrical connectors, as needed, prior to lowering column. Do not force column down as it may be damaged.**
5. Remove windshield defroster grille and both deflector housings.
6. Remove 5 screws securing top of instrument panel and 2 bolts securing bottom of instrument panel.

7. Disconnect instrument panel bulkhead connector and pull instrument panel rearward.
8. Remove aspirator duct.
9. Disconnect fuel filler door and deck lid release electrical connectors and the antenna lead.
10. Disconnect fuse panel, then remove instrument panel from vehicle.
11. Disconnect heater hoses from heater core.
12. Remove A/C programmer screws, disconnect electrical and vacuum connectors and remove programmer.
13. Remove A/C power module retaining screws, disconnect electrical connectors and remove module.
14. Remove heater core cover and retaining strap.
15. Remove retaining screws and the heater core.
16. Reverse procedure to install.

Engine Section

NOTE: Refer to Section 8 for service procedures on V6-231/3.8L, V8-250/4.1L and V8-273/4.5L engines not found in this section.

INDEX

ENGINE MOUNTS REPLACE

ELDORADO & SEVILLE

Right Side Engine & Transaxle Mount

1. Open hood and remove brace between engine bracket and engine, **Fig. 1.**
2. Remove 2 nuts securing mount to engine bracket.
3. Raise vehicle on suitable hoist and support with stands at each front frame horn.
4. Remove 2 nuts securing engine mount to frame.
5. Remove 2 nuts securing transaxle bracket to mount.
6. Remove 2 nuts securing transaxle mount to frame bracket.
7. Raise engine using support J-28467 or equivalent, lifting engine until bracket is free from engine and transaxle mounts.
8. Remove stud and bolts securing bracket to block, then remove bracket and mount by pulling forward.
9. Remove transaxle mounting bracket from transaxle, then remove mount.
10. Position engine mount and bracket between block and frame, then torque bracket bolts and stud to specifications, **Fig. 1.**
11. Position transaxle mount and bracket between transaxle and frame, then torque bracket retaining bolts to specifications, **Fig. 1.**
12. Guide mounts into position while lowering engine and reverse remaining procedure to complete installation, torquing all fasteners to specifications shown in **Fig. 1.**

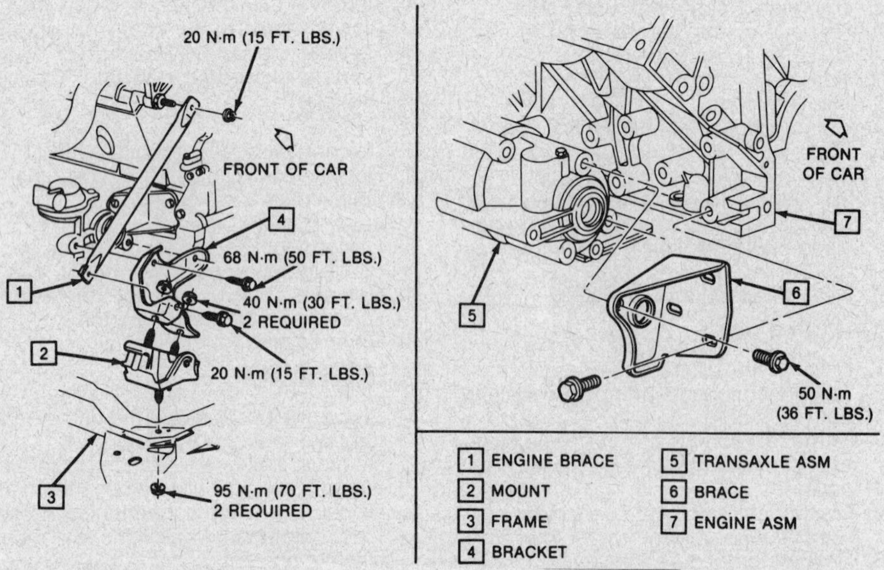

Fig. 1 Right engine & transaxle mount. Eldorado & Seville

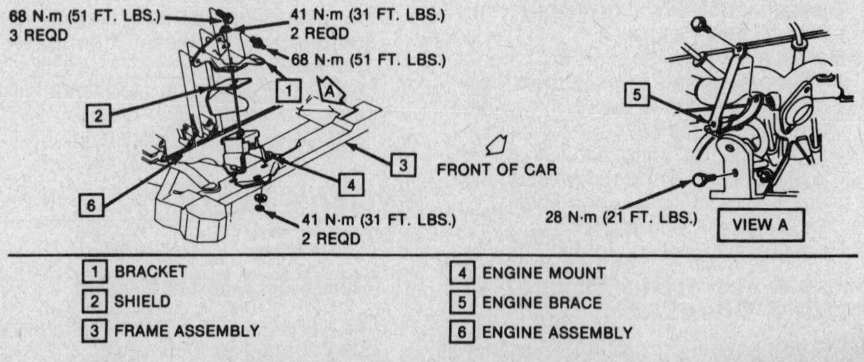

Fig. 2 Left engine mount. Eldorado & Seville

Left Engine Mount

1. Open hood, disconnect battery ground cable and remove air cleaner assembly.
2. Remove serpentine drive belt and discharge A/C system.

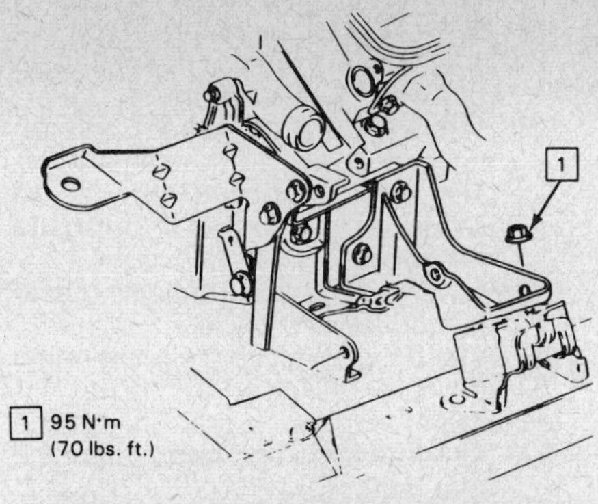

Fig. 3 Front engine mount. 1986 Riviera & Toronado

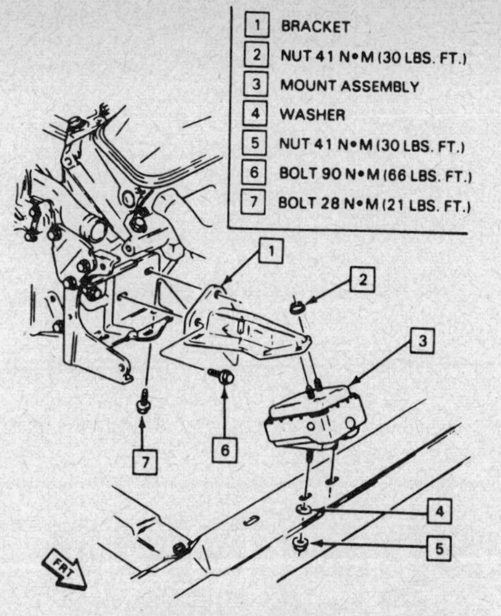

Fig. 4 Front engine mount. 1987–88 Riviera & Toronado

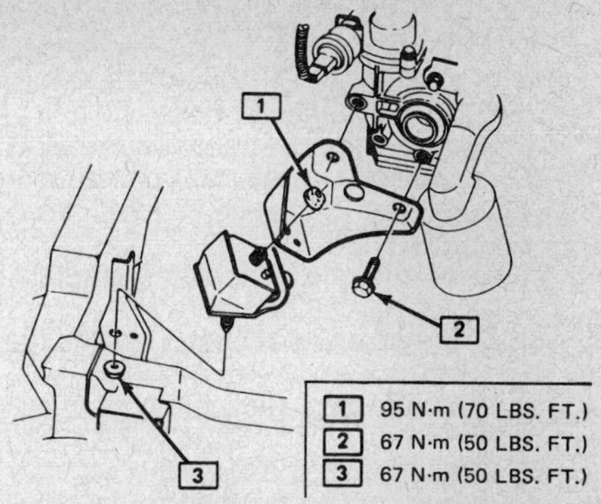

Fig. 5 Rear engine mount. Riviera & Toronado

3. Install engine support tool J-28467 or equivalent.
4. Remove lower center exhaust manifold nut and top nut from engine damper.
5. Raise and support vehicle, then remove right engine splash shield and A/C splash shield.
6. Remove engine damper.
7. Remove 2 A/C compressor brackets and the A/C compressor.
8. Remove water pipe bracket bolt.
9. Remove bolts securing engine mount bracket to block and cradle, **Fig. 2.**
10. Remove engine mount and bracket assembly through right wheel opening.
11. Remove engine mount from bracket.
12. Reverse procedure to install, torquing engine mount fasteners to specifications shown in **Fig. 2.**

RIVIERA & TORONADO

1. Support engine using tool J-28467 or equivalent.
2. Raise and support vehicle.
3. Remove nuts securing engine mount to bracket, **Figs. 3, 4 and 5,** then raise engine slightly.
4. Remove nuts securing mount to frame and the engine mount.
5. Reverse procedure to install. Torque mount fasteners to specifications as shown in **Figs. 3, 4 and 5.**

ENGINE REPLACE

ELDORADO & SEVILLE

1. Disconnect battery ground cable and drain cooling system.
2. Remove air cleaner assembly.
3. Mark position of hood hinges, disconnect necessary electrical connectors, then remove hood hinge bolts and the hood.
4. Remove engine cooling fan and serpentine drive belt.
5. Disconnect upper radiator and heater hoses from thermostat housing.
6. Disconnect electrical connectors from the following components: oil pressure switch, coolant temperature sensor, distributor, EGR solenoid, engine temperature switch, ISC motor, throttle position switch, injectors, MAT sensor, oxygen sensor, throttle body base warmer, alternator and ground wiring at alternator bracket.
7. Release engine harness from retainers and secure aside.
8. Disconnect accelerator, cruise control and transmission cables from throttle body.
9. Remove cruise control diaphragm brackets and secure assembly aside.
10. Disconnect oil and transmission cooler lines from radiator.
11. Disconnect remaining hoses and remove radiator.
12. Disconnect oil cooler lines at filter adapter and remove lines.
13. Remove oil cooler line bracket at transaxle and the air cleaner bracket.
14. Remove oil filter adapter housing.
15. Disconnect AIR tubes from diverter valve.
16. Remove front right and rear body cross braces.
17. Disconnect and remove right front heater hose and coolant reservoir.
18. Remove AIR filter box and bracket.
19. Remove idler pulley.
20. Disconnect power steering line bracket from right cylinder head, remove power steering pump and tensioner retaining bolts and secure assembly aside.
21. Discharge A/C system, disconnect A/C lines at accumulator and condenser, and plug lines and open fittings.
22. Connect suitable tool to fuel line Schraeder valve and slowly bleed fuel system pressure into suitable container.
23. Disconnect fuel lines at throttle body and fuel line bracket from transaxle, then position fuel lines aside.
24. Remove EGR lines and brackets.
25. Disconnect vacuum modulator line and fuel filter and position aside.
26. Raise and support vehicle, remove starter shield, and disconnect starter wiring and block ground straps.
27. Remove exhaust crossover pipe and the starter motor.
28. Remove both flexplate dust shields and bolts securing torque converter to flexplate.
29. Remove A/C compressor dust shield.
30. Remove right front tire and wheel, then the outer wheelhouse plastic shield.
31. Remove right rear engine to transaxle mounting bolt and the lower engine damper nut.
32. Remove front (left) engine mount nuts and right rear engine/transaxle mount bolts, **Figs. 1 and 2.**
33. Remove alternator and oxygen sensor wiring and the heater bypass bracket from right side of vehicle.
34. Remove right engine brace, then lower vehicle.
35. Remove 5 top engine to transaxle mounting bolts.
36. Install suitable lift equipment and support transaxle with suitable jack.
37. Raise engine and separate engine from transaxle, then remove engine from vehicle.
38. Reverse procedure to install.

RIVIERA & TORONADO

1. Relieve fuel system pressure as follows:
   a. Disconnect fuel pump electrical connector from fuel tank, then start engine.
   b. After engine stalls, continue to crank for three seconds to ensure relief of any residual pressure.
   c. Turn ignition off and reconnect fuel pump electrical connector.
2. Disconnect battery ground cable and drain cooling system.
3. Mark position of hood hinges, disconnect necessary electrical connectors, then remove hood hinge bolts and the hood.
4. Disconnect radiator and air inlet hoses.
5. Disconnect electrical connectors from the following components: fuel rail, C3I ignition, ground straps, oil pressure sender, EGR solenoid, coolant temperature sensor, throttle body, crankshaft and camshaft position sensors, and the alternator.
6. Release harness from clips and secure aside.

7. Remove serpentine drive belt, power steering pump and alternator.
8. Disconnect heater hoses.
9. Remove throttle cable bracket and disconnect accelerator, cruise control and transaxle cables from throttle body.
10. Disconnect fuel supply and return lines from throttle body.
11. Remove engine cooling fan and radiator.
12. Remove front (left) exhaust manifold.
13. Disconnect necessary vacuum hoses, noting position for installation.
14. Remove 3 top engine to transaxle retaining bolts.
15. Remove engine damper and bracket from engine.
16. Remove ground strap and engine harness retainer bolts.
17. Remove engine to transaxle bracket, then raise and support vehicle.
18. Remove A/C compressor and secure aside.
19. Remove exhaust pipe.
20. Disconnect electrical connectors from starter motor.
21. Remove engine mount nuts, **Figs. 3, 4 and 5.**
22. Remove torque converter dust shield, scribe alignment mark between converter and flexplate and remove converter bolts.
23. Remove left front wheel and remaining engine to transaxle bolts. **One bolt securing engine to transaxle is installed in opposite direction.**
24. Remove engine to transaxle bracket, then lower vehicle.
25. Attach suitable lifting equipment to engine and support transaxle.
26. Raise engine, separate engine from transaxle and remove engine from vehicle.
27. Reverse procedure to install.

Rear Suspension & Brake Section

INDEX

DESCRIPTION

All rear suspension components are mounted on a suspension support assembly, **Fig. 1,** which is attached to the body at four points. The transverse leaf spring is fully isolated from the crossmember and is held in position by left and right retainers and insulators. On their inboard end, the control arms pivot on the suspension support, allowing each end of the leaf spring to act directly on the control arm surface. A suspension knuckle pivots on the outboard end of each control arm, and each knuckle contains a sealed hub and wheel bearing assembly. Each knuckle is located at the top by an air adjustable strut assembly which is connected to the suspension support. On some models, a stabilizer shaft is used to further locate the knuckle assemblies an provide increased roll stiffness. Strut charging is controlled by an Electronic Level Control (ELC) system, which maintains a standard rear trim height under a variety of load conditions.

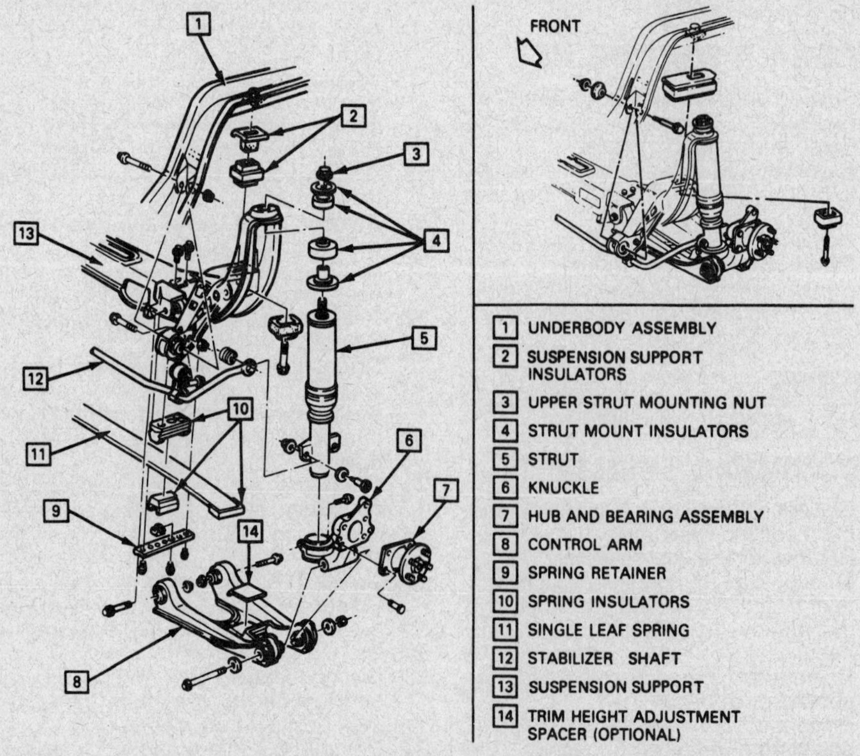

Fig. 1 Rear suspension exploded view. Left side shown

STRUT
REPLACE

1. Raise and support vehicle on frame contact type hoist, remove wheel and tire assembly and reinstall 2 wheel nuts to retain brake rotor.
2. If left strut is to be replaced, disconnect ELC height sensor link.
3. Remove stabilizer shaft mounting bolt at strut, if equipped.
4. Remove brake caliper as outlined, and secure aside leaving hoses connected.

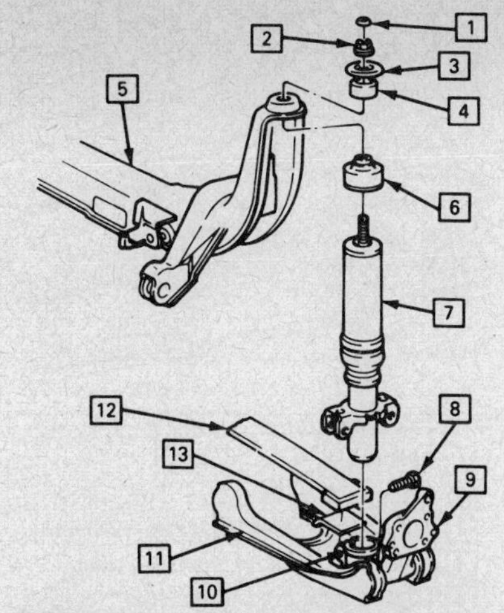

1 STRUT ROD CAP
2 NUT 88 N•m (65 LBS. FT.)
3 RETAINER
4 UPPER INSULATOR
5 SUSPENSION SUPPORT
6 LOWER INSULATOR
7 STRUT
8 LOWER PINCH BOLT 55 N•m (40 LBS. FT.)
9 KNUCKLE
10 LOCATING SLOT
11 CONTROL ARM
12 SPRING
13 TRIM HEIGHT ADJUSTMENT SPACER (OPTIONAL)

Fig. 2 Rear strut installation

5. Loosen but do not remove knuckle pivot bolt at outboard end of control arm.
6. Remove clip and disconnect air line from strut.
7. Remove upper strut rod cap, mounting nut and insulator, **Fig. 2.**
8. Compress strut by hand and remove lower insulator.
9. Rotate strut and knuckle assembly outward, remove pinch bolt, then separate strut from knuckle.
10. Reverse procedure to install, ensuring strut is fully seated with tang on strut bottomed in steering knuckle slot. When suspension is fully assembled, torque bolts to specifications as follows: pinch bolt, 40 ft. lbs.; upper strut nut, 65 ft. lbs.; knuckle pivot bolt, 59 ft. lbs; stabilizer bolt, 43 ft. lbs.

KNUCKLE
REPLACE

1. Raise and support vehicle on frame contact type hoist, remove wheel and tire assembly.
2. If left knuckle is to be replaced, disconnect ELC height sensor link.
3. Remove stabilizer shaft mounting bolt at strut, if equipped.
4. Remove brake caliper as outlined, and secure aside leaving hoses connected.
5. Remove brake rotor, hub retaining bolts and the hub and bearing assembly.
6. Loosen but do not remove knuckle pivot bolt at outboard end of control arm.

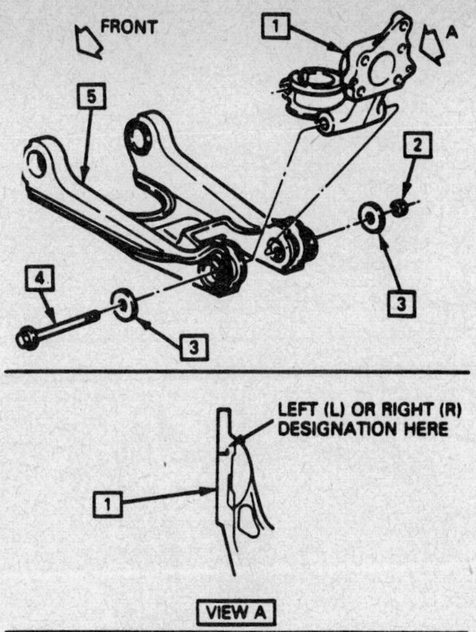

1 KNUCKLE
2 NUT (80 N•m/59 FT. LBS.)
3 RETAINER
4 PIVOT BOLT
5 CONTROL ARM

Fig. 3 Knuckle installation

7. Remove clip and disconnect air line from strut.
8. Remove upper strut rod cap, mounting nut and insulator, **Fig. 2.**
9. Compress strut by hand and remove lower insulator.
10. Rotate strut and knuckle assembly outward, remove pinch bolt, then separate strut from knuckle.
11. Remove knuckle pivot bolt and the knuckle, **Fig. 3.**
12. Reverse procedure to install, ensuring strut is fully seated with tang on strut bottomed in steering knuckle slot. When suspension is fully assembled, torque bolts to specifications as follows: pinch bolt, 40 ft. lbs.; upper strut nut, 65 ft. lbs.; knuckle pivot bolt, 59 ft. lbs.; hub mounting bolts, 52 ft. lbs.; stabilizer bolt to 43 ft. lbs.

LOWER CONTROL ARM
REPLACE

1. Raise and support vehicle on frame contact type hoist, remove wheel and tire assembly and reinstall 2 wheel nuts to retain brake rotor.
2. If left control arm is to be replaced, disconnect ELC height sensor link.
3. Remove stabilizer shaft mounting bolt at strut, if equipped.
4. Remove brake caliper as outlined, and secure aside leaving hoses connected.
5. Loosen but do not remove knuckle pivot bolt at outboard end of control arm.
6. Remove clip and disconnect air line from strut.
7. Remove upper strut rod cap, mounting nut and insulator, **Fig. 2.**

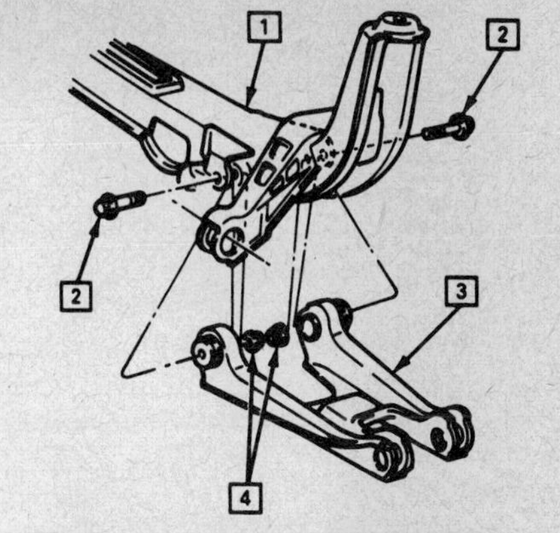

1 SUSPENSION CROSSMEMBER ASSEMBLY
2 INNER CONTROL ARM BOLTS
3 CONTROL ARM
4 NUTS (90 N•m/66 FT. LBS.)

Fig. 4 Lower control arm installation

8. Compress strut by hand and remove lower insulator.
9. Support knuckle assembly, remove knuckle pivot bolt, then remove strut and knuckle as an assembly.
10. Remove both inner control arm bolts and the control arm, **Fig. 4.**
11. Reverse procedure to install, ensuring strut is fully seated with tang on strut bottomed in steering knuckle slot. When suspension is fully assembled, torque bolts to specifications as follows: pinch bolt, 40 ft. lbs.; upper strut nut, 65 ft. lbs.; control arm bolts, 66 ft. lbs.; knuckle pivot bolt,stabilizer bolt, 43 ft. lbs.

LOWER CONTROL ARM BUSHINGS
REPLACE

Outer control arm bushings can be replaced without removing control arm from vehicle after performing steps 1-9 of "Control Arm, Replace" procedure. If inner control arm bolts are not loosened, or removed, alignment will not be disturbed and it will not be necessary to perform wheel alignment after outer bushing replacement.

Control arm must be removed from vehicle to replace inner control arm bushings. After replacing inner bushings, check wheel alignment as outlined.

When replacing lower control arm bushings, refer to **Fig. 5.**

SPRING
REPLACE

Removal of rear spring requires disassembly of either left or right side of suspension while leaving opposite side intact. Spring may be removed from either side of vehicle.

1. Remove lower control arm as outlined.
2. Place suitable support under end of spring as shown in **Fig. 6,** then lower

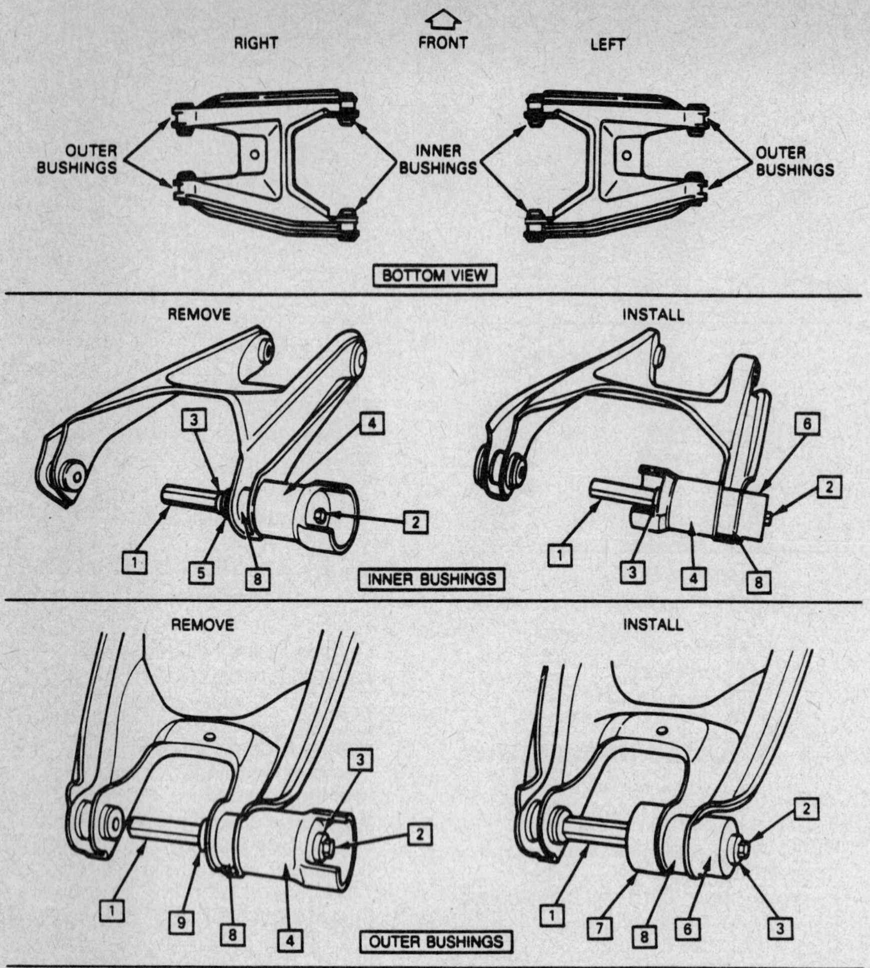

1 J-21474-18 NUT
2 J-21474-19 BOLT
3 BEARING (PART OF J-21474-19)
4 J-21474-5
5 J-21474-23
6 J-28576-1
7 J-35739-3
8 J-35739-1 SPACER — USE WIDER SIDE ON OUTER BUSHINGS, NARROW SIDE ON INNER BUSHINGS
9 J-35739-2

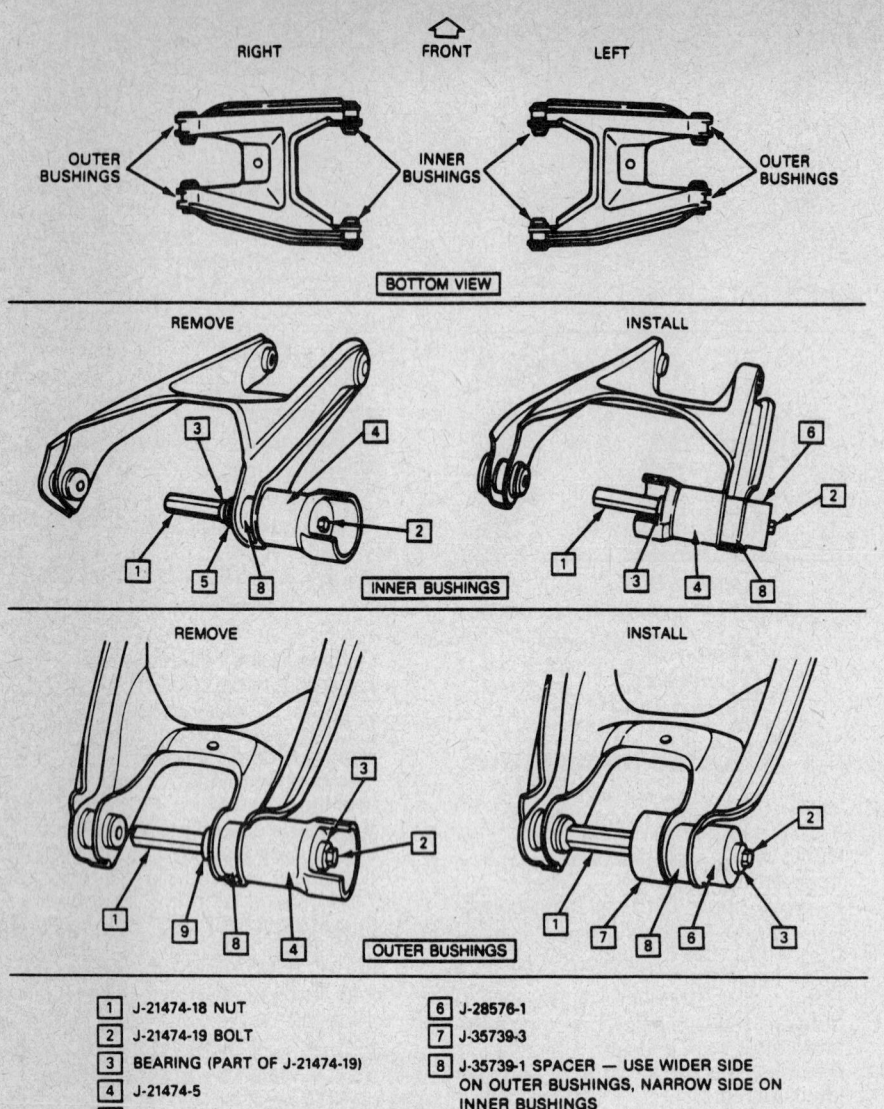

Fig. 5 Replacing lower control arm bushings

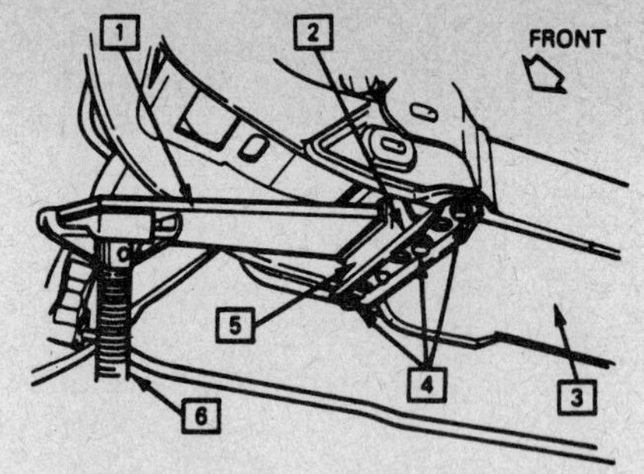

1 SPRING
2 SPRING RETAINER
3 SUSPENSION CROSSMEMBER ASSEMBLY
4 RETAINER BOLTS (28 N•m/21 FT. LBS.)
5 LOWER OUTBOARD INSULATOR
6 JACKSTAND

Fig. 6 Removing spring

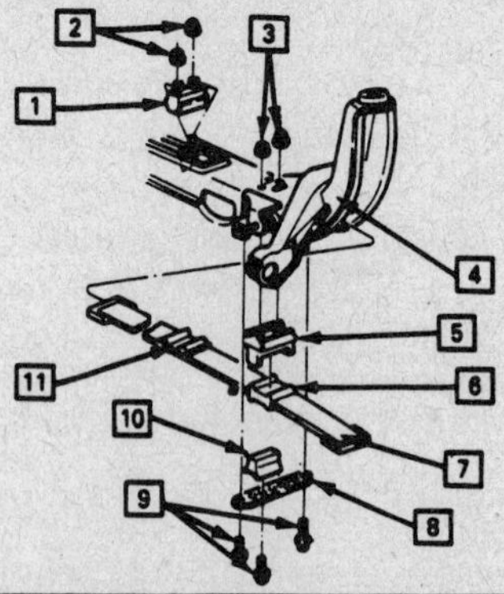

1 CENTER INSULATOR
2 CENTER INSULATOR NUTS (28 N•m/21 FT. LBS.)
3 OUTBOARD INSULATOR NUTS (28 N•m/21 FT. LBS.)
4 SUSPENSION CROSSMEMBER ASSEMBLY
5 UPPER OUTBOARD INSULATOR
6 OUTBOARD INSULATOR LOCATING BAND
7 SPRING
8 SPRING RETAINER
9 RETAINER BOLTS (28 N•m/21 FT. LBS.)
10 LOWER OUTBOARD INSULATOR
11 CENTER INSULATOR LOCATING BAND

Fig. 7 Exploded view of spring installation

vehicle so weight of vehicle compresses spring. **Ensure jack stand can support weight of vehicle and is properly positioned under spring.**

3. Remove 3 spring retainer bolts, retainer and lower insulator, **Fig. 7,** from end of spring nearest support stand.
4. Slowly raise vehicle, allowing spring to deflect downward until spring no longer exerts force on stand.
5. Remove retainer bolts, retainer and insulator from opposite end of spring, then withdraw spring from crossmember.
6. Remove upper spring insulators.
7. Inspect spring insulators and retainers and replace as needed.
8. Install center and upper outboard insulators in crossmember and torque bolts to 21 ft. lbs. **Ensure arrows on upper outboard insulators point toward centerline of vehicle.**
9. Position spring in crossmember, ensuring outboard and center insulator bands are centered on spring insulators.
10. Install lower insulator and retainer on side opposite disassembled portion of suspension, torque retaining bolts to 21 ft. lbs, then place suitable stand under free end of spring.
11. Lower vehicle, allowing weight to load spring and deflect free end of spring into position.
12. Install lower insulator and retainer, and torque bolts to 21 ft. lbs.
13. Raise vehicle and remove stand.
14. Reverse remaining procedure to complete installation.

REAR CALIPER REPLACE

REMOVAL

1. Siphon approximately 2/3 of brake fluid from master cylinder.
2. Raise and support vehicle, then remove wheel and tire assembly.
3. Loosen tension on parking brake cable at equalizer.
4. Remove retaining clip from parking brake lever, then disconnect cable and spring, **Fig. 8.**
5. Hold parking brake lever and loosen locknut, then remove nut, lever, seal and washer.
6. If caliper is to be overhauled or replaced, remove bolt securing fluid line union, then disconnect fluid line.
7. Remove caliper mounting bolts, then lift caliper assembly off rotor and mounting bracket.
8. If rotor is to be replaced, remove caliper bracket mounting bolts and the

bracket. **Prevailing torque bolts used to secure mounting bracket cannot be reused. If bolts become loose or are removed, bolts must be replaced.**

INSTALLATION

1. Install mounting bracket and torque bolts to 83 ft. lbs.
2. Position caliper over bracket and rotor, ensuring insulators are in place.
3. Coat caliper bolts with thin film of silicone grease and torque bolts to 55-70 ft. lbs.
4. Install fluid line union using new copper washers, and torque union bolt to 30 ft. lbs. on 1986 models, or 15 ft. lbs. on 1987-88 models.
5. Install friction washer, seal, lever and nut on parking brake shaft as shown in **Fig. 8**, then torque nut to 30-40 ft. lbs. while holding lever.
6. Rotate parking brake lever back against stop on caliper, then install spring, cable and retainer.
7. Tighten parking brake cable at equalizer until lever begins to move off stop, then loosen cable until lever returns to stop.
8. Bleed brakes as needed.

PARKING BRAKE
ADJUST

1. On 1986 models, apply service brake with force of approximately 150 lbs., then release.

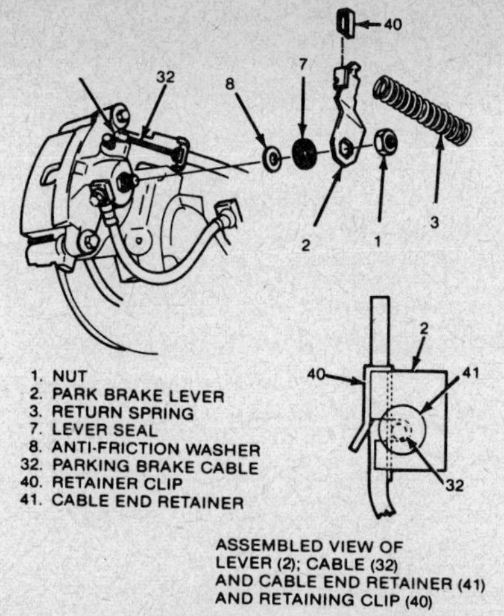

Fig. 8 Parking brake lever installation. Rear brake caliper removal

2. On 1987-88 models, apply and release service brake three times with a force of approximately 175 lbs.
3. On all models, fully apply parking brake (may require up to 4 pedal strokes) using approximately 125 lbs. force on last stroke, then release. Repeat procedure 2 more times.
4. Inspect parking brake pedal assembly for full release by observing brake warning lamp.
5. If lamp is on and parking brake appears to be fully released, operate manual pedal release lever and pull down on front cable to remove slack from pedal assembly.
6. Raise and support vehicle and inspect parking brake levers on rear calipers.
7. If levers are not against stops, inspect rear cables for binding and position levers against stops.
8. Tighten brake cable at equalizer until either lever begins to move off stop.
9. Loosen cable until lever returns to stop. Both levers must be resting on stops after adjustment.
10. Operate parking brake several times, ensuring that firm pedal can be obtained by pumping pedal less than 3½ strokes.
11. Release parking brake and ensure both caliper levers are against stops.

MASTER CYLINDER
REPLACE

1. Disconnect electrical connector from fluid level sensor switch.
2. Disconnect hydraulic lines at master cylinder, plugging lines and openings.
3. Remove master cylinder attaching nuts and the master cylinder.
4. Reverse procedure to install, torquing master cylinder attaching nuts to 26 ft. lbs and hydraulic lines to 150 inch lbs.

BRAKE BOOSTER
REPLACE

1. Remove master cylinder.
2. Remove booster attaching nuts.
3. Disengage booster pushrod at brake pedal and remove booster.
4. Reverse procedure to install, torquing booster attaching nuts to 28 ft. lbs.

Front Suspension & Steering Section

INDEX

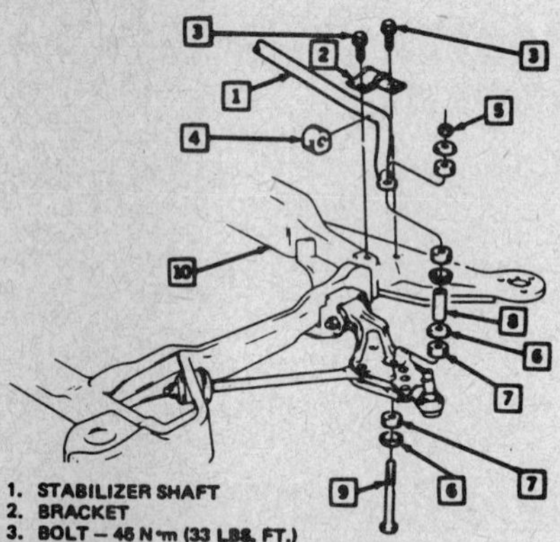

1. STABILIZER SHAFT
2. BRACKET
3. BOLT – 45 N·m (33 LBS. FT.)
4. INSULATOR – INSTALL WITH SLIT TO REAR OF CAR
5. NUT 17 N·m (13 LBS. FT.) OBTAIN TORQUE BY RUNNING NUT TO UNTHREADED PORTION OF BOLT
6. RETAINER
7. INSULATOR
8. SPACER
9. BOLT – INSTALL IN DIRECTION SHOWN
10. FRAME

Fig. 1 Stabilizer shaft installation

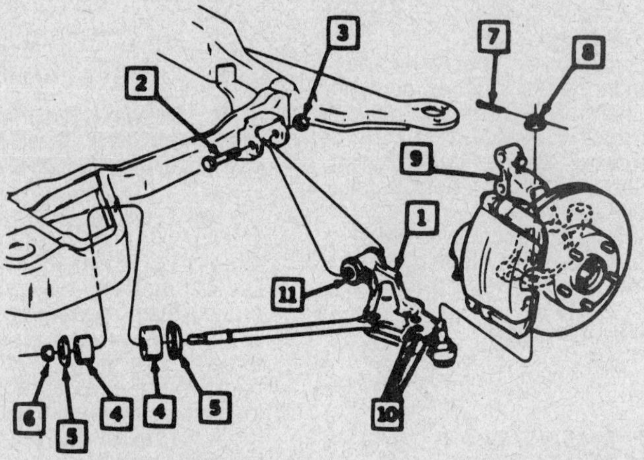

1. CONTROL ARM
2. BOLT – 140 N·m (100 LBS. FT.) TIGHTEN WITH CAR AT PROPER TRIM HEIGHT
3. NUT – 123 N·m (91 LBS. FT.) TIGHTEN WITH CAR AT PROPER TRIM HEIGHT
4. INSULATOR
5. RETAINER
6. NUT – 70 N·m (52 LBS. FT.)
7. PIN
8. NUT – TIGHTEN NUT TO 10 N·m (88 LBS. IN.). CONTINUE TIGHTENING BY ROTATING NUT AN ADDITIONAL 120°, DURING WHICH A MINIMUM TORQUE OF 50 N·m (37 LBS. FT.) MUST BE OBTAINED. INSTALL COTTER PIN
9. KNUCKLE
10. BALL JOINT ATTACHMENT RIVETS
11. BUSHING

Fig. 2 Lower control arm installation

STABILIZER SHAFT
REPLACE

1. Raise vehicle and support with weight of vehicle resting on frame, not the lower control arms.
2. Remove right front wheel and tire.
3. Remove left and right insulators, retainers, spacers and bolts, **Fig. 1.**
4. Remove left and right bracket bolts, brackets and insulators.
5. Disconnect exhaust pipe from rear manifold, raise pipe to gain clearance, then withdraw stabilizer shaft.
6. Reverse procedure to install.

BALL JOINT
REPLACE

Care must be taken not to overextend driveshaft Tri-Pot joints when replacing suspension components. Overextending joint could cause separation of internal joint components, resulting in failure of the joint.

1. Raise vehicle and support frame with suitable stands.
2. Remove wheel and tire assembly.
3. Remove insulator, retainers, spacer and bolt securing stabilizer shaft to control arm, **Fig. 1.**
4. Cut inner tabs from boot protector J-34754 and install protector over drive axle outer joint.
5. Remove nut and cotter pin securing ball joint to steering knuckle.
6. Separate ball joint from knuckle using separator J-35315 or equivalent.
7. Center punch rivets securing ball joint to control arm, then drill out rivets starting with 1/4 inch drill bit and finishing with 1/2 inch bit.
8. Install service replacement joint in control arm, Insert bolts from underside of arm, and torque to 50 ft. lbs.
9. Insert ball stud into steering knuckle and install nut.
10. Torque ball joint nut to 84 inch lbs. using 90° adapter J-35551 or equivalent.
11. Tighten nut an additional 180° on Eldorado and Seville models, or 120° on Riviera and Toronado models, noting torque reading, then tighten nut up to 60° additional to align holes and install cotter pin. **When tightening nut, minimum torque of 48 ft. lbs. on Eldorado and Seville models, or 37 ft. lbs. on Riviera and Toronado mod-**

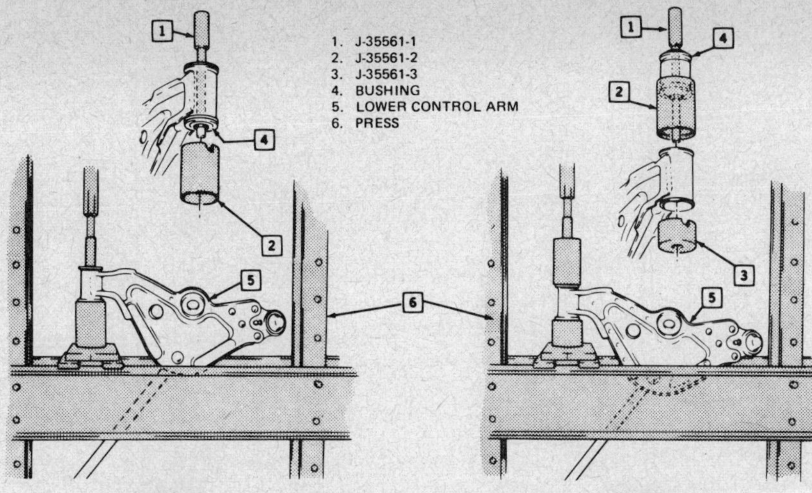

Fig. 3 Replacing lower control arm bushings

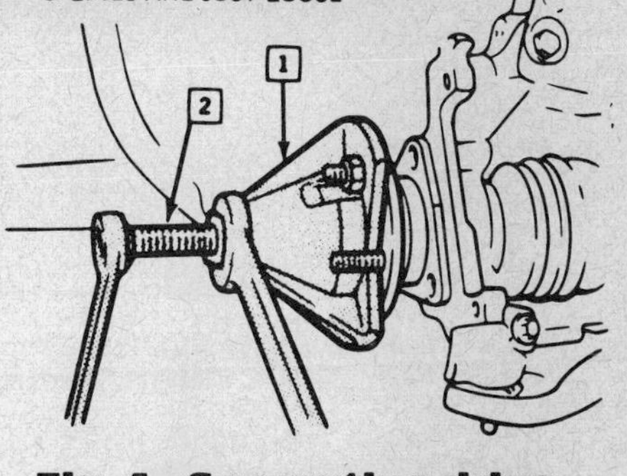

Fig. 4 Separating drive axle from hub

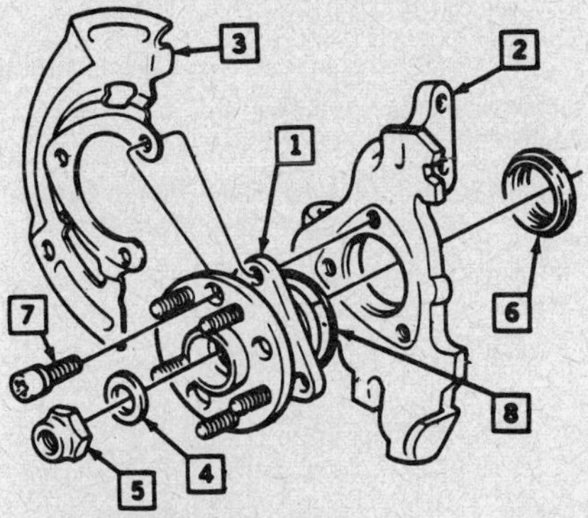

Fig. 5 Hub & bearing assembly installation

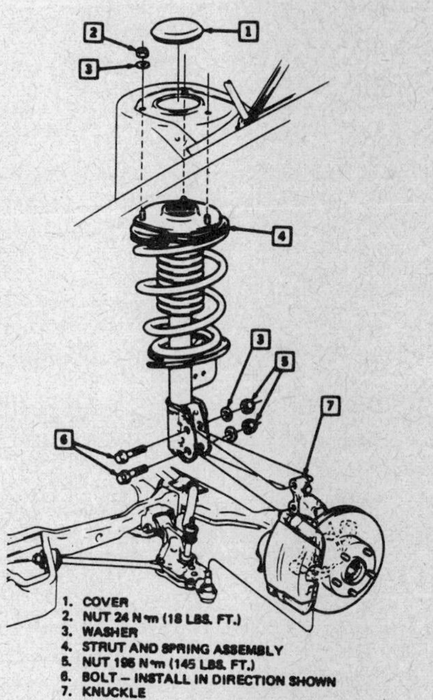

Fig. 6 Steering knuckle & strut installation

els must be obtained. If minimum torque cannot be obtained, check for stripped threads and repair as needed. If threads are satisfactory, replace ball joint and steering knuckle.

12. Reverse remaining procedure to complete installation.

CONTROL ARM
REPLACE

1. Remove ball joint from steering knuckle as outlined in steps 1-6 of "Ball Joint, Replace."
2. Remove control arm bushing bolt and front nut, retainer and insulator, **Fig. 2,** then the control arm.
3. Install control arm on frame.
4. Install control arm bushing bolt and nut, retainer and insulator but do not tighten bolt.
5. Install lower ball joint in steering knuckle as outlined.
6. Reverse remaining procedure to complete installation. Torque bolts to specifications shown in **Figs. 1 and 2.**

LOWER CONTROL ARM BUSHINGS
REPLACE

When replacing lower control arm bushings, refer to **Fig. 3.**

HUB & BEARING ASSEMBLY
REPLACE

1. Siphon 2/3 of the brake fluid from master cylinder, raise vehicle and support frame with suitable stands.
2. Remove wheel and tire assembly.
3. Insert suitable drift through rotor and remove hub nut and washer.
4. Remove caliper boots, lift caliper off rotor and bracket and secure caliper aside.
5. Remove bolts securing caliper bracket, bracket and the brake rotor. **Prevailing torque bolts used to secure mounting bracket cannot be reused. If bolts become loose or are removed, bolts must be replaced.**
6. Mount tool J-28733 or equivalent on hub , **Fig. 4,** and tighten screw just enough to separate drive axle from hub.
7. Remove hub retaining bolts and the hub and bearing assembly, **Fig. 5.**
8. If seal is being replaced, drive seal toward engine, then cut seal off drive axle.
9. Lubricate seal lip and install using suitable driver, install O-ring and fill cavity between seal and bearing with grease.
10. Install hub and bearing assembly over drive axle and torque bolts to 70 ft. lbs.
11. Install rotor and caliper mounting bracket and torque new bracket bolts to 83 ft. lbs.
12. Install caliper ensuring insulators are properly positioned, coat mounting bolt shafts with silicone grease and torque bolts to 63 ft. lbs.
13. Install hub nut and washer, insert drift through rotor and tighten nut securely.
14. Remove drift, install wheel and tire assembly and lower vehicle, then torque hub nut to 180 ft. lbs.

STEERING KNUCKLE
REPLACE

1. Remove hub assembly as outlined.
2. Remove nut securing tie rod, then separate tie rod from knuckle.
3. Cut inner tabs from boot protector J-34754 and install protector over drive axle outer joint.
4. Remove cotter pin and nut securing lower ball joint and separate ball stud from steering knuckle.
5. Remove bolts securing strut to steering knuckle, **Fig. 6,** and the steering knuckle.
6. Reverse procedure to install.

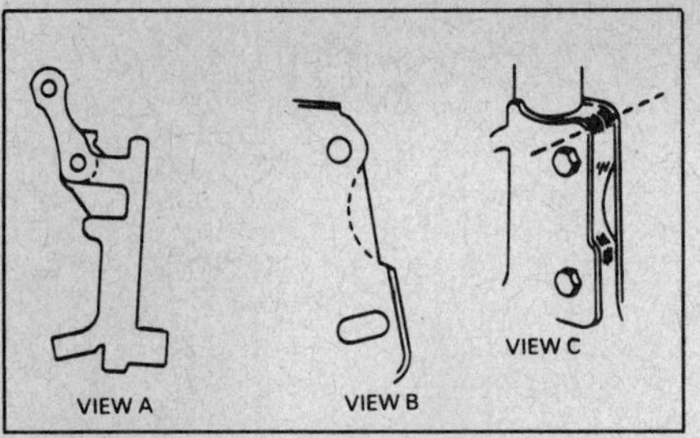

Fig. 7 Marking steering knuckle & strut alignment

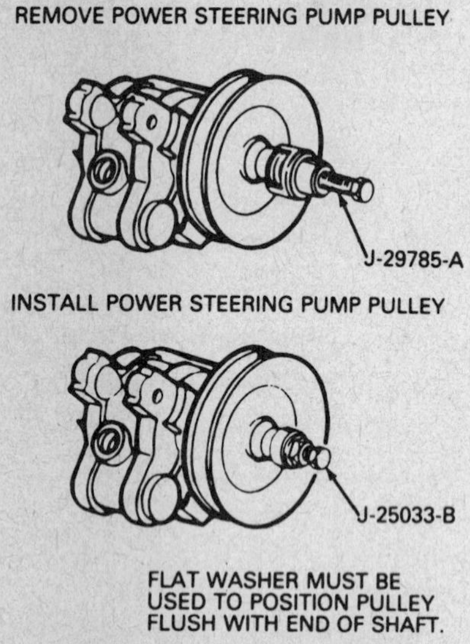

Fig. 10 Power steering pump pulley removal. Eldorado & Seville

STRUT ASSEMBLY
REPLACE

Care must be taken not to overextend driveshaft Tri-Pot joints when replacing suspension components. Overextending joint could cause separation of internal joint components, resulting in failure of the joint.

1. Remove nuts securing top of strut assembly to body, **Fig. 6.**
2. Raise vehicle and support frame with suitable stands, then remove wheel and tire.
3. Scribe reference marks between strut and steering knuckle as follows;
   a. Scribe strut along lower outboard strut radius (A), **Fig. 7.**
   b. Scribe strut flange on inboard side along curve of knuckle (B).
   c. Scribe mark along strut/knuckle interface (C).
4. Disconnect brake line bracket from strut.
5. Remove bolts securing strut to steering knuckle, support knuckle with wire and remove strut.
6. Reverse procedure to install, aligning with scribe marks made during disassembly. Torque top mounting nuts to 18 ft. lbs. and strut to knuckle bolts to 145 ft. lbs., then check alignment.

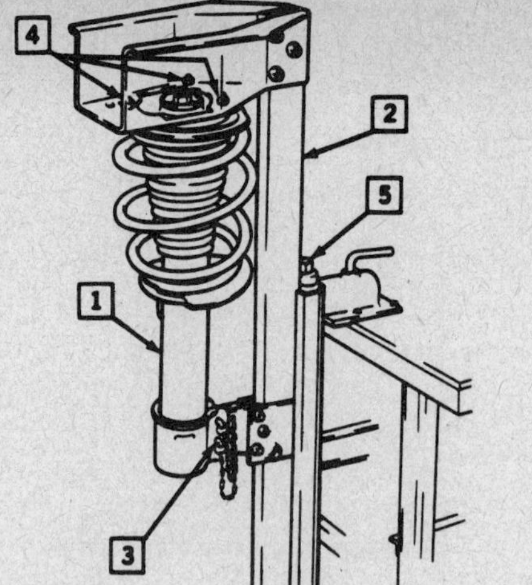

1. STRUT ASSEMBLY
2. STRUT COMPRESSOR J-34013
3. INSTALL LOCKING PINS THROUGH STRUT ASSEMBLY
4. TIGHTEN NUTS TILL FLUSH WITH STRUT COMPRESSOR
5. COMPRESSOR FORCING SCREW

Fig. 8 Installing strut assembly in strut compressor

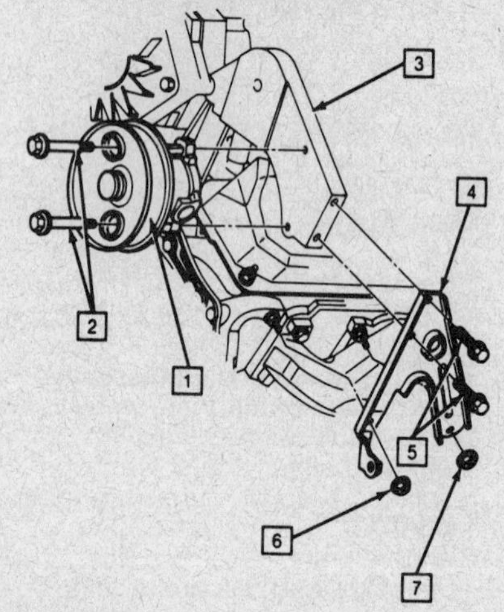

1. PUMP
2. PUMP MOUNTING BOLTS (25 N·m/18 FT. LBS.)
3. PUMP AND TENSIONER BRACKET
4. BRACE
5. BOLTS (45 N·m/33 FT. LBS.)
6. NUT (45 N·m/33 FT. LBS.)
7. NUT (25 N·m/18 FT. LBS.)

Fig. 11 Power steering pump installation. Eldorado & Seville

STRUT SERVICE

1. Place strut assembly in strut compressor J-34013, **Fig. 8.**
2. Turn compressor forcing screw until spring compresses slightly.
3. Keep dampener shaft from turning with socket and remove 24mm nut on top of dampener shaft.
4. Using tool J-34013-38 or equivalent, guide dampener shaft out of assembly.

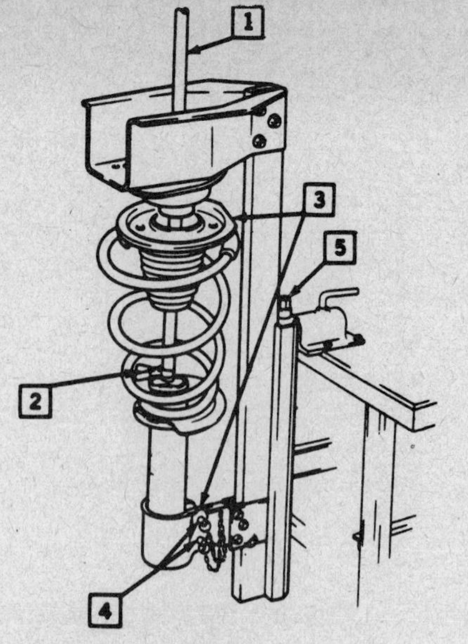

1. ROD J-34013-38 INSTALLED
2. CLAMP J-34013-20 INSTALLED
3. FLAT ON SPRING SEAT MUST FACE SAME DIRECTION AS STEERING KNUCKLE FLANGE
4. BOTH LOCKING PINS INSTALLED
5. COMPRESSOR FORCING SCREW

Fig. 9 Aligning flat on upper spring seat

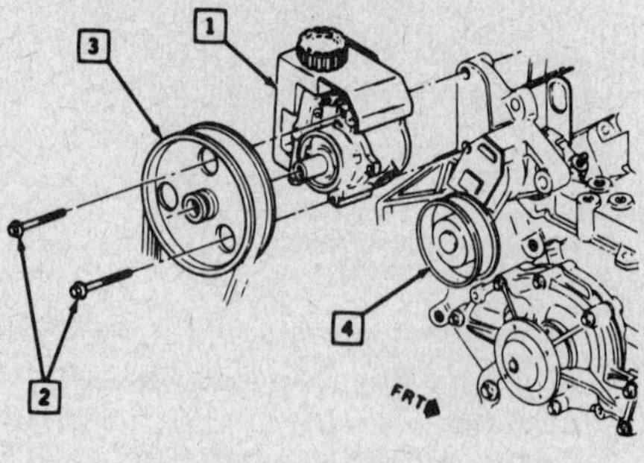

1. POWER STEERING PUMP
2. BOLT – 27 N·m (20 LBS. FT.)
3. PULLEY
4. BELT TENSIONER ASSEMBLY

Fig. 12 Power steering pump installation. Riviera & Toronado

5. Loosen compressor screw while guiding dampener shaft out of assembly, continually loosening compressor screw till strut dampener and spring can be removed. **Be careful to avoid chipping or cracking the spring coating when handling the front suspension coil spring.**
6. Install strut dampener in strut compressor J-34013 with clamp J-34013-20 clamped on dampener shaft.
7. Install spring over strut in correct position and move assembly upright in strut compressor and install upper locking pin. **Flat on upper spring seat must face out from centerline of vehicle, Fig. 9,** or when mounted in strut compressor spring seat faces same direction as steering knuckle mounting flange.

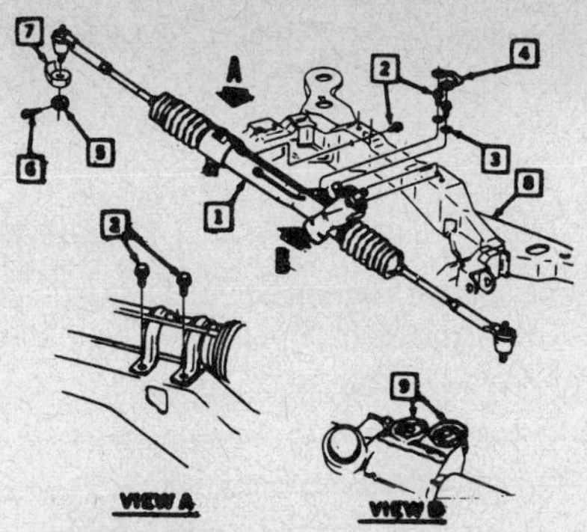

1. STEERING GEAR
2. BOLT – 68 N·m (50 LBS. FT.) AFTER SECOND REUSE OF BOLT, LOCKTITE THREAD LOCKING KIT NO. 1052624 MUST BE USED.
3. WASHER
4. RETAINER
5. NUT – TIGHTEN NUT TO 10 N·m (7 LBS. FT.) THEN TIGHTEN NUT AN ADDITIONAL 120 DEGREES (2 FLATS) DURING WHICH A MINIMUM TORQUE OF 45 N·m (33 LBS. FT.) IS TO BE OBTAINED. IF 45 N·m (33 LBS. FT.) IS NOT OBTAINED, INSPECT FOR STRIPPED THREADS. IF THREADS ARE SATISFACTORY, REPLACE KNUCKLE.
6. PIN
7. KNUCKLE
8. FRAME
9. RTV SEALER AROUND INSERTS

Fig. 13 Power steering gear installation. Riviera & Toronado

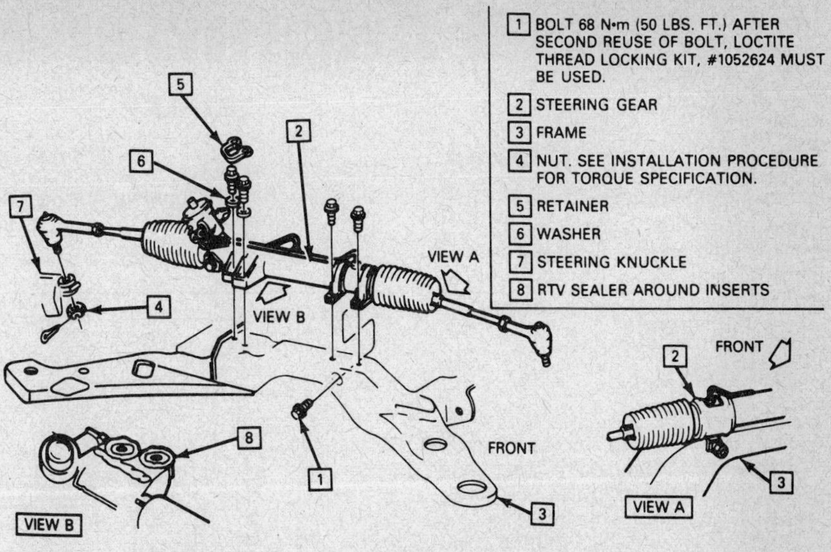

Fig. 14 Power steering gear installation. ldorado & Seville

8. Install rod J-34013-38 or equivalent into strut assembly to guide dampener shaft on reassembly of strut.
9. Start turning compressor screw clockwise on J-34013 while guiding J-34013-38 which will center dampener shaft in the assembly.
10. Continue turning compressor screw until dampener shaft threads are visible through top of strut assembly.
11. Install washer and nut, then remove J-34013-20 from dampener shaft.
12. Hold dampener shaft with socket and, torque dampener shaft nut to 44 ft. lbs using 24mm flare nut crowsfoot.
13. Remove three nuts securing strut assembly to strut compressor, the two locking pins at bottom of strut compressor and the strut assembly.

POWER STEERING PUMP REPLACE

ELDORADO & SEVILLE

1. Remove serpentine drive belt.
2. Remove pump pulley using suitable puller, **Fig. 10.**
3. Disconnect pressure and return lines from pump, noting position for installation.
4. Remove 2 pump mounting bolts, **Fig. 11,** and the pump.
5. Reverse procedure to install.

RIVIERA & TORONADO

1. Remove drive belt.
2. Disconnect pressure and return lines from pump.
3. Remove pump mounting bolts, **Fig. 12,** and the pump.
4. Reverse procedure to install.

POWER STEERING GEAR REPLACE

1. Raise vehicle and support vehicle on frame contact hoist, then remove front wheels.
2. Remove pinch bolt and disconnect intermediate shaft from steering gear.
3. Disconnect tie rods from steering knuckles.
4. Remove power steering line retainer, then disconnect pressure and return lines from steering gear.
5. Remove steering gear mounting bolts, **Figs. 13 and 14,** then withdraw gear through wheel opening.
6. Reverse procedure to install. Tighten tie rod nuts to 7.5 ft. lbs, then tighten nut an additional 1/3 turn, ensuring torque obtained is at least 33 ft. lbs. After tightening nut as specified, continue tightening nut to align cotter pin holes, then install new cotter pins.

Wheel Alignment Section

INDEX

FRONT WHEEL ALIGNMENT

Steering and vibration complaints are not always the result of improper alignment. Another possibility is tire "lead" due to worn or improperly manufactured tires. "Lead" is the vehicles's deviation from a straight path on a level road without pressure on the steering wheel.

Before making any adjustment affecting wheel alignment, make the following checks to ensure correct alignment readings and alignment adjustments.

1. Check all tires for proper inflation pressures and ensure that all tires have approximately equal tread wear.
2. Check hub and bearing assemblies for excessive wear, correcting as necessary.
3. Check ball joints and tie rod ends. If they are excessively loose, correct before making adjustment.
4. Check run out of wheels and tires.
5. Check vehicle trim height, correcting as necessary before adjusting alignment.
6. Check strut dampers for proper operation.
7. Check control arms for loose bushings.
8. Check stabilizer bar for loose or missing parts.

Consideration must also be given to excess loads, such as tool boxes or sample cases. If these items are normally carried in the vehicle, they should remain in the vehicle during alignment adjustments. Consideration should be given to condition of equipment being used to adjust alignment. Be sure to follow equipment manufacturer's instructions. Regardless of equipment being used, vehicle must be on level surface, both fore and aft and sideways.

MEASURING FRONT ALIGNMENT ANGLES

Install alignment equipment following equipment manufacturer's instructions. Measure alignment angles, **Fig. 1,** and record the readings. If adjustments are necessary, they must be made in order; caster first, camber second and toe third. Jounce front and rear bumpers 3 times to normalize suspension prior to measuring angles.

CASTER ADJUSTMENT

1. Loosen but do not remove, 2 of 3 top strut attaching nuts covering slotted mounting holes, **Fig. 2,** then remove nut over remaining oval strut mounting hole.

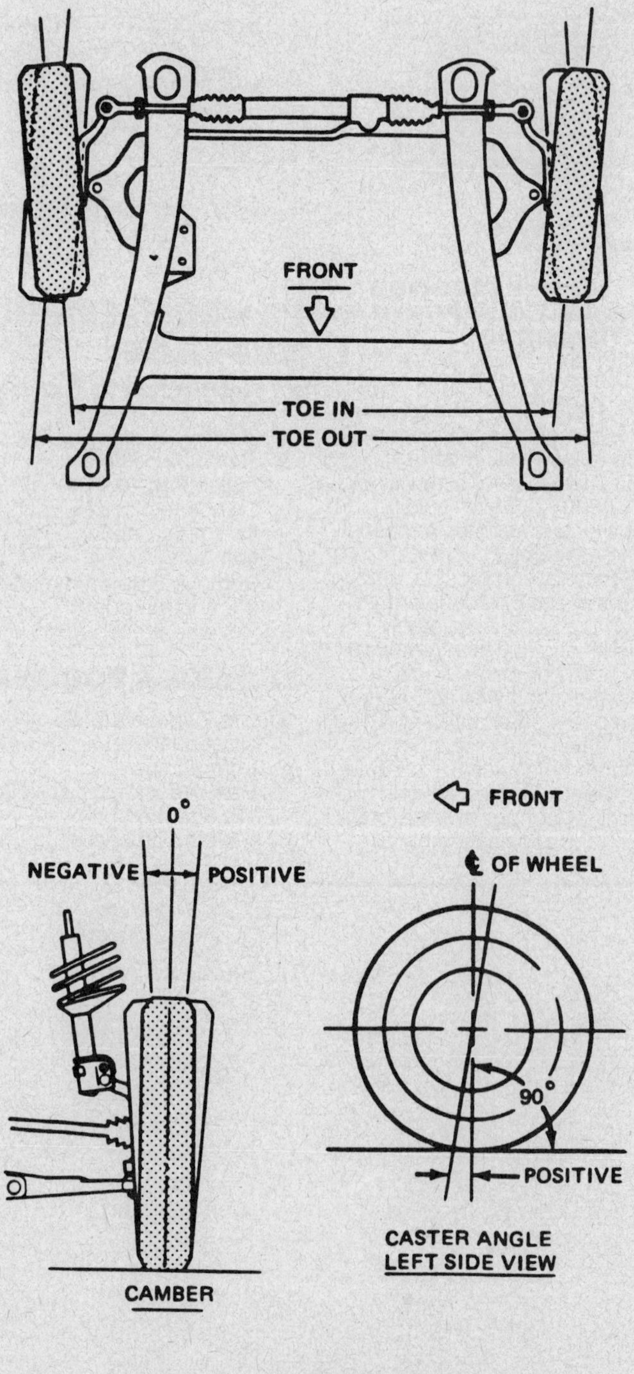

Fig. 1 Front end alignment angles

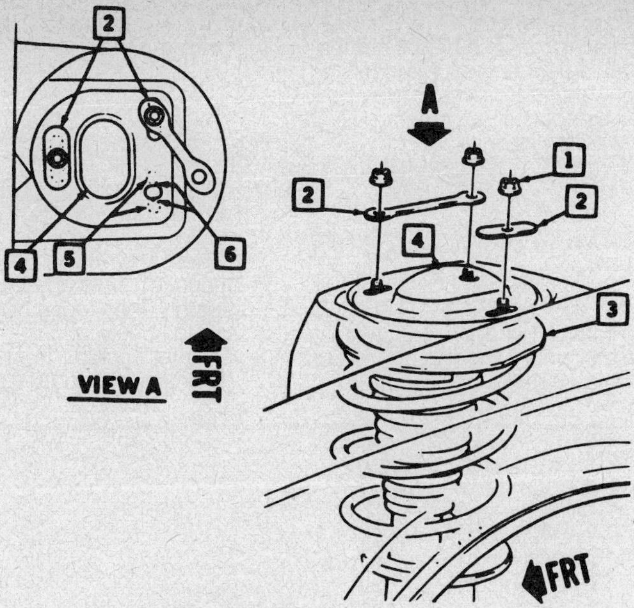

1. NUT 24 N·m (18 LBS. FT.)
2. WASHER
3. STRUT ASSY.
4. COVER
5. DRILL 8.731mm (11/32") HOLES
6. FILE HERE THEN PAINT WITH PRIMER

Fig. 2 Adjusting front wheel caster

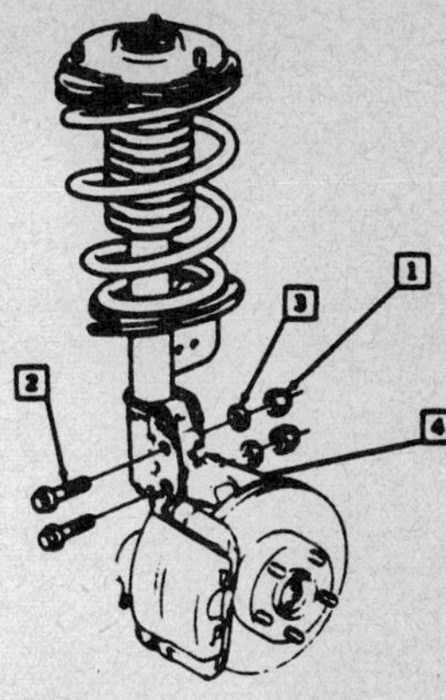

1. NUT 185 N·m (145 LBS. FT.)
2. BOLT
3. WASHER
4. CAMBER ADJUSTMENT BOLT

Fig. 3 Adjusting front wheel camber

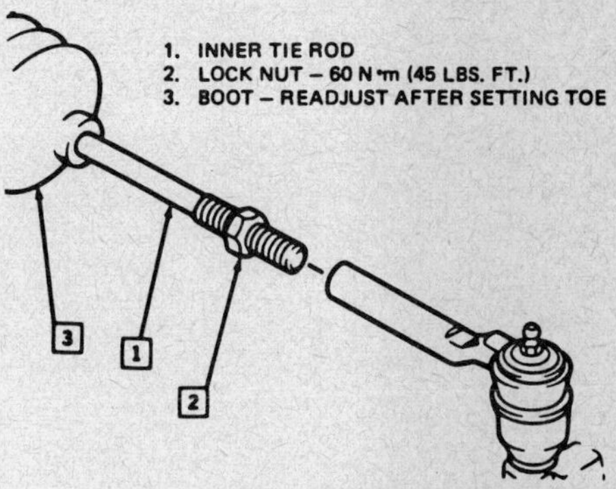

1. INNER TIE ROD
2. LOCK NUT – 60 N·m (45 LBS. FT.)
3. BOOT – READJUST AFTER SETTING TOE

Fig. 4 Adjusting front wheel toe

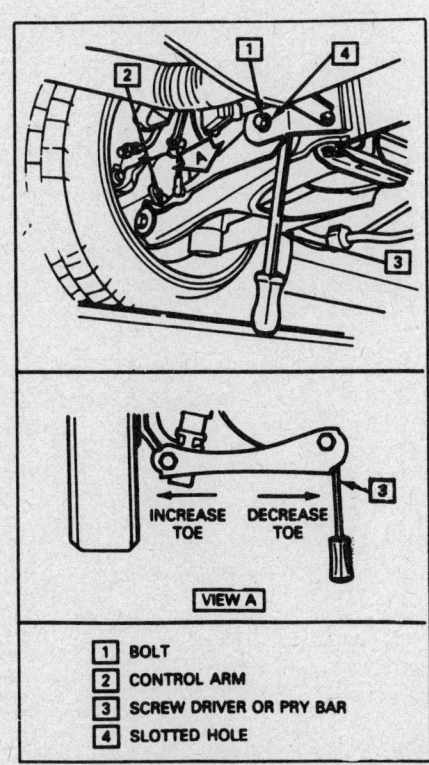

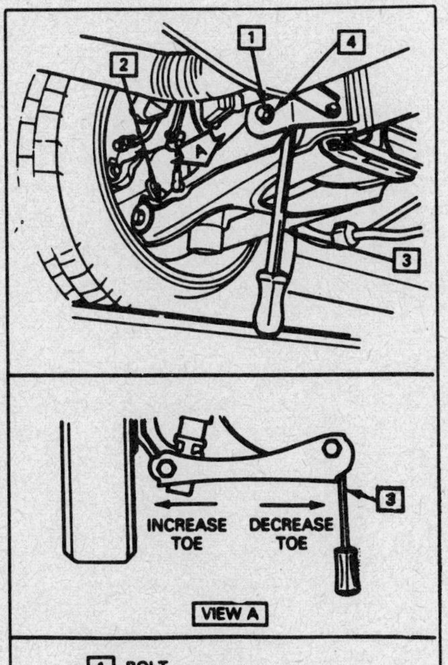

1. BOLT
2. CONTROL ARM
3. SCREW DRIVER OR PRY BAR
4. SLOTTED HOLE

Fig. 5 Adjusting rear toe

2. Move washer away from oval strut mounting hole.
3. Lift front of vehicle by body to separate strut from inner wheel house.
4. Drill two 11/32 inch holes at front and rear of oval strut mounting hole, then file away excess metal.
5. Lower front of vehicle and install washer and nut.
6. Adjust caster by moving top of strut forward or rearward.
7. Torque top strut attaching nuts to 18 ft. lbs.

CAMBER ADJUSTMENT

1. Loosen both strut to knuckle bolts just enough to allow movement.
2. Adjust camber by turning camber adjustment bolt, **Fig. 3.**
3. Torque strut to knuckle nuts to 140 ft. lbs.

4. Torque camber adjustment bolt to 7 ft. lbs.

TOE ADJUSTMENT

1. Loosen locknut on inner tie rods, **Fig. 4.**
2. Adjust toe by turning inner tie rods.
3. Adjust boots so that they are not twisted.
4. Torque locknuts to 45 ft. lbs.

REAR WHEEL ALIGNMENT

Rear wheel toe is the only adjustable angle. If camber is not within specifications, inspect for worn or damaged rear suspension components.

Before checking rear trim height or measuring rear alignment angles, the following procedure should be performed to ensure that the rear air-adjustable struts are filled with residual pressure only.

1. Place a weight of at least 300 lbs. in vehicle trunk.
2. Turn ignition on.
3. Turn ignition off and remove weight from trunk.
4. Wait 30 seconds for ELC system to exhaust.
5. Roll car forward or backward at least 25 ft. to eliminate the effects of tire camber side thrust.
6. Jounce front and rear bumpers 3 times to normalize suspension prior to measuring angles.

TOE ADJUSTMENT

1. Loosen front and rear inside control arm mounting bolts, **Fig. 5.**
2. Insert a screwdriver or pry bar between the inside rear control arm mounting bolt and rear support assembly, then move control arm to set toe to specifications.
3. Torque inside front control arm mounting bolt to 66 ft. lbs.

CHEV. CAVALIER • BUICK SKYHAWK • CAD. CIMARRON • OLDS. FIRENZA • PONT. SUNBIRD & 2000

INDEX OF SERVICE OPERATIONS

NOTE: Refer to the rear of this manual for manufacturer's special service tool suppliers.

Specifications

GENERAL ENGINE SPECIFICATIONS

Year	Engine CID①/Liter	Engine VIN Code ②	Fuel System	Bore and Stroke	Compres sion Ratio	Net H.P. @ RPM ③	Maximum Torque Ft. Lbs @ RPM	Normal Oil Pressure Pounds
1982	4-112/1.8L⑤	G	E2SE, 2 Bbl.④	3.50 x 2.90	9.0	85 @ 5100	100 @ 2800	45
	4-110/1.8L⑥	O	E.F.I.⑦	3.34 x 3.12	9.0	84 @ 5200	102 @ 2800	65
	4-121/2.0L	B	E2SE, 2 Bbl.④	3.50 x 3.14	9.0	90 @ 5100	111 @ 2700	45
1983	4-110/1.8L⑥	O	E.F.I.⑦	3.34 x 3.12	9.0	84 @ 5200	102 @ 2800	45
	4-121/2.0L	P	E.F.I.⑦	3.50 x 3.15	9.3	86 @ 4900	110 @ 3000	63-77
1984	4-110/1.8L⑥	O	E.F.I.⑦	3.34 x 3.12	9.0	84 @ 5200	102 @ 2800	65
	4-110/1.8L⑥⑧	J	E.F.I.⑦	3.34 x 3.12	8.0	150 @ 5600	150 @ 2800	65
	4-121/2.0L	P	E.F.I.⑦	3.50 x 3.15	9.3	86 @ 4900	110 @ 2400	63-77
1985	4-110/1.8L⑥	O	E.F.I.⑦	3.34 x 3.12	9.0	84 @ 5200	102 @ 2800	65
	4-110/1.8L⑥⑧	J	E.F.I.⑦	3.34 x 3.12	8.0	150 @ 5600	150 @ 2800	65
	4-121/2.0L	P	E.F.I.⑦	3.50 x 3.15	9.3	86 @ 4900	110 @ 2400	63-77
	V6-173/2.8L	W	E.F.I.⑦	3.50 x 2.99	8.9	130 @ 4800	160 @ 3600	50-55
1986	4-110.1.8L⑥	O	E.F.I.⑦	3.34 x 3.13	8.8	84 @ 5200	98 @ 2800	65
	4-110/1.8L⑥⑧	J	E.F.I.⑦	3.34 x 3.13	8.0	150 @ 5600	150 @ 2800	65
	4-121/2.0L	P	E.F.I.⑦	3.50 x 3.15	9.0	88 @ 4800	110 @ 2400	63-77
	V6-173/2.8L	W	E.F.I.⑦	3.50 x 2.99	8.5	120 @ 4800	155 @ 3600	50-55
1987	4-121/2.0L OHC⑥	K	E.F.I.⑦	3.39 x 3.39	8.8	⑨	⑩	45
	4-121/2.0L OHC Turbo⑥	M	E.F.I.⑦	3.39 x 3.39	8.0	165 @ 5600	175 @ 4000	—
	4-121/2.0L OHV⑤	1	E.F.I.⑦	3.50 x 3.15	9.0	90 @ 5600	108 @ 3200	63-77
	V6-173/2.8L	W	E.F.I.⑦	3.50 x 2.99	⑪	⑫	⑬	50-65
1988	4-121/2.0L OHC⑥	K	E.F.I.⑦	3.39 x 3.39	8.8	—	—	65
	4-121/2.0L OHC Turbo⑥	M	E.F.I.⑦	3.39 x 3.39	—	—	—	—
	4-121/2.0L OHV⑤	1	E.F.I.⑦	3.50 x 3.15	9.0	90 @ 5600	108 @ 3200	63-77
	V6-173/2.8L	W	E.F.I.⑦	3.50 x 2.99	8.9	125 @ 4500	160 @ 3600	50-65

①—CID-cubic inch displacement.
②—The eighth digit denotes engine code.
③—Ratings are net as installed in vehicle.
④—Rochester.
⑤—Overhead valve engine.
⑥—Overhead cam engine.
⑦—Electronic Fuel Injection.
⑧—Turbocharged engine.
⑨—102 @ 5200 on Firenza models; 96 @ 4800 on all others.
⑩—130 @ 2800 on Firenza models; 118 @ 3600 on all others.
⑪—8.5 on Cavalier; 8.9 on all others.
⑫—130 @ 4500 on Cavalier; 125 @ 4500 on all others.
⑬—165 @ 3600 on Cavalier; 160 @ 3600 on all others.

ENGINE TIGHTENING SPECIFICATIONS*

*Torque specifications are for clean and lightly lubricated threads only. Dry or dirty threads produce increased friction which prevents accurate measurement of tightness.

Year	Engine Model/VIN	Spark Plugs Ft. Lbs.	Cylinder Head Bolts Ft. Lbs.	Intake Manifold Ft. Lbs.	Exhaust Manifold Ft. Lbs.	Rocker Arm Stud Ft. Lbs.	Rocker Arm Cover Ft. Lbs.	Connecting Rod Cap Bolts Ft. Lbs.	Main Bearing Cap Bolts Ft. Lbs.	Flywheel to Crankshaft Ft. Lbs.	Vibration Damper or Pulley Ft. Lbs.
1982	4-112/G①	7-15	65-75	20-25	22-28	43-49	6-9	34-40	63-74	45-55	66-84
1982-83	4-110/O②	15	③	16	19	—	5	39	57	45	20
	4-121/B,P	7-15	65-75	20-25	22-28	43-49	6-9	34-40	63-74	45-55	66-84
1984	4-121/P	7-20	65-75	18-25	20-30	43-49	4-9	34-43	63-77	④	66-89
1984-85	4-110/J,O②	15	③	25	16	—	5	39	57	45	20
1985	4-121/P	7-20	73-85	18-25	34-44	43-49	4-9	34-43	63-77	④	66-89
	V6-173/W	17-33	65-90	13-25	19-31	—	7-15	34-45	63-83	—	67-85
1986	4-110/O	15	③	25	16	—	5	39	57	45	20
	4-110/J	15	③	25	16	—	5	39	57	45	20
	4-121/P	7-20	73-85	18-25	34-44	43-49	4-9	34-43	63-77	④	66-89
	V6-173/W	7-15	65-90	13-25	19-31	—	4-5.5	34-45	63-83	—	67-85
1987	4-121/K	15	③	16	16	—	6	26⑦	44⑧	48⑨	20
	4-121/M	15	③	16	16	—	6	26⑦	44⑧	48⑨	20
	4-121/1	7-20	⑤	15-22	6-13	33-40	4-9	34-43	63-73	④	67-85
	V6-173/W	10-25	⑥	25	15-23	—	6-9	34-45	63-83	—	67-85
1988	4-121/K	—	—	—	—	—	—	—	—	—	
	4-121/M	—	—	—	—	—	—	—	—	—	
	4-121/1	—	—	—	—	—	—	—	—	—	
	V6-173/W	—	—	—	—	—	—	—	—	—	

①—Overhead valve engine.
②—Overhead cam engine.
③—Torque cylinder head & camshaft carrier bolts to 18 ft. lbs., then tighten bolts an additional 180° in 60° increments. Start engine & allow to reach operating temperature, then tighten bolts an additional 30° to 50°.
④—Auto. trans., 45 to 59 ft. lbs.; man. trans., 45-63 ft. lbs.
⑤—Long bolts, 73-83 ft. lbs.; short bolts, 62-70 ft. lbs.
⑥—Coat bolt threads with sealer, then install and torque to 33 ft. lbs.
⑦—Plus an additional 40 to 45 degrees.
⑧—Plus an additional 40 to 50 degrees.
⑨—Plus an additional 30 degrees.

ALTERNATOR SPECIFICATIONS

Year	Model	Rated Hot Output Amps.
1982	1100169①	63
	1100220①	63
	1101438②	70
1983	1105249②	85
	1105331②	85
	1105335③	63
1983-85	1100288③	78
	1100289③	78
	1100290③	56
	1100291③	56
	1105091③	66
	1105092③	66
	1105446	94
	1105447	94
	1105508	78
	1105541	94
1983-86	1100258③	78
	1105329	85
	1105354①	42
	1105439③	78
	1105440③	66
	1105441	94
	1105599③	56
	1105602③	94
	1105610③	78
	1105611③	66
1987	1101144	85
	1101145	100
	1101190	105
	1101191	100
	1105694	100
	1105697	74
	1105698	85
	1105701	85

①—10 SI.
②—15 SI.
③—12 SI.

WHEEL ALIGNMENT SPECIFICATIONS

Year	Model	Caster Angle, Degrees		Camber Angle, Degrees				Toe-Out Inch		
				Limits		Desired				
		Limits	Desired	Left	Right	Left	Right			
1982	All	—	—	+.1 to +1.1	+.1 to +1.1	+.6	+.6	①		
1983-86	③	+.7 to +2.7	+1.7	+.2 to +1.2	+.2 to +1.2	+.7	+.7	②		
1984-86	Cavalier	+.7 to +2.7	+1.7	+.2 to +1.5	+.2 to +1.2	+.85	+.85	②		
1987	All	+.7 to +2.7	+1.7	+.2 to +1.4	+.2 to +1.4	+.8	+.8	④		
1988	All	−.8 to +4.2	+1.7	−.2 to +1.8	−.2 to +1.8	+.8	+.8	0°		

①—.25° toe-out.
②—.13° toe-out.
③—Exc. 1984-86 Cavalier.
④— −.12° toe-out on Cavalier Z-24 & Sunbird W/60 series tires; 0° toe-out on all others.

COOLING SYSTEM & CAPACITY DATA

Year	Model or Engine/VIN	Cooling Capacity, Qts.		Radiator Cap Relief Pressure, Lbs.	Thermo. Opening Temp.	Fuel Tank Gals.	Engine Oil Refill Qts.	Transaxle Oil	
		Less A/C	With A/C					Manual Transaxle Pts.	Auto. Transaxle Qts.①
1982	Cavalier 4-112/G	9.0	9.3⑥	15	195	14	4②	6	③
	Cimarron 4-112/G	—	8.28	15	195	14	4②	6	③
	Firenza 4-112/G	8.0	8.0	15	195	14	4②	6	③
	J2000 4-112/G	8.3	8.3	15	195	14	4②	6	③
	Skyhawk 4-112/G	8.0	8.0	15	195	14	4②	6	③
	All 4-110/O	7.8	7.9	15	195	14	3②	6	③
	All 4-110/B	8.0	8.0	15	195	14	4②	6	③
1983	Cavalier 4-110/O	9.6	9.6⑥	15	195	13.6	3②	5.4	③
	Firenza 4-110/O	8.0	8.0	15	195	13.6	3②	5.4	③
	2000 4-110/O	7.8	7.9	15	195	13.6	3②	⑤	③
	Skyhawk 4-110/O	7.8	7.8	15	195	13.6	3②	5.4	③
	Cavalier 4-121/P	9.6⑥	9.6⑥	15	195	13.6	4②	5.4	③
	Cimarron 4-121/P	④	④	15	195	13.6	4②	5.4	③
	Firenza 4-121/P	8.0	8.0	15	195	13.6	4②	5.4	③
	2000 4-121/P	7.8	7.9	15	195	13.6	4②	⑤	③
	Skyhawk 4-121/P	9.7	9.75	15	195	13.6	4②	5.4	③
1984	Cavalier 4-121/P	9.6⑥	9.6⑥	15	195	13.6	4②	6	③
	Cimarron 4-121/P	④	④	15	195	13.6	4②	6	③
	Firenza 4-110/O	8.0	8.0	15	195	13.6	3②	6	③
	Firenza 4-121/P	9.5	9.75	15	195	13.6	4②	6	③
	Skyhawk 4-110/O	7.8	7.8	15	195	13.6	3②	6	③
	Skyhawk 4-110 Turbo/J	7.8	7.8	15	195	13.6	4②⑦	6	③
	Skyhawk 4-121/P	9.5	9.75	15	195	13.6	4②	6	③
	Sunbird 4-110/O	7.8	7.9	15	195	13.6	3②	⑤	③
	Sunbird 4-110 Turbo/J	7.8	7.9	15	195	13.6	4②⑦	⑤	③
	Sunbird 4-121/P	7.8	7.9	15	195	13.6	4②	⑤	③

Continued

COOLING SYSTEM & CAPACITY DATA—Continued

Year	Model or Engine/VIN	Cooling Capacity, Qts.		Radiator Cap Relief Pressure, Lbs.	Thermo. Opening Temp.	Fuel Tank Gals.	Engine Oil Refill Qts.	Transaxle Oil	
		Less A/C	With A/C					Manual Transaxle Pts.	Auto. Transaxle Qts. ①
1985	Cavalier 4-121/P	9.6	9.8	15	195	14	4②	6	③
	Cavalier V6-173/W	11	11.1	15	195	14	4②	6	③
	Cimarron 4-121/P	9.6	9.8	15	195	14	4②	6	③
	Cimarron V6-173/W	11	11.1	15	195	14	4②	6	③
	Firenza 4-110/O	8	8	15	195	13.6	4②	6	③
	Firenza 4-121/P	9.5	9.7	15	195	13.6	4②	6	③
	Fiernza V6-173/W	10.7	11.1	15	195	13.6	4②	6	③
	Skyhawk 4-110/O	7.8	7.8	15	195	13.6	4②	6	③
	Skyhawk 4-110 Turbo/J	7.8	7.8	15	195	13.6	4②⑦	6	③
	Skyhawk 4-121/P	9.5	9.7	15	195	13.6	4②	6	③
	Sunbird 4-110/O	7.9	7.9	15	195	13.6	4②	6	③
	Sunbird 4-110 Turbo/J	7.9	7.9	15	195	13.6	4②⑦	6	③
1986	Cavalier 4-121	8.8	8.8	15	195	13.6	4②	6	③
	Cavalier V6-173	11.3	11.3	15	195	13.6	4②	6	③
	Cimarron 4-121	9.6	9.8	15	195	13.6	4②	6	③
	Cimarron V6-173	11.0	11.1	15	195	13.6	4②	6	③
	Firenza 4-110	7.8	7.9	15	195	13.6	4②	6	③
	Firenza 4-121	7.8	7.9	15	195	13.6	4②	6	③
	Firenza V6-173	10.7	11.1	15	195	13.6	4②	6	③
	Skyhawk 4-110	7.8	7.8	15	195	13.6	4②	6	③
	Skyhawk 4-110 Turbo	7.8	7.8	15	195	13.6	4②⑦	6	③
	Skyhawk 4-121	9.5	9.7	15	195	13.6	4②	6	③
	Sunbird 4-110	7.9	7.9	15	195	13.6	4②	6	③
	Sunbird 4-110 Turbo	7.9	7.9	15	195	13.6	4②⑦	6	③
1987	Cavalier 4-121/1	9.6	9.6	15	195	14	4②	⑧	③
	Cavalier V6-173/W	11	11.1	15	195	14	4②	⑧	③
	Cimarron V6-173/W	11.1	11.1	15	195	14	4②	⑧	③
	Firenza 4-121/K	8	8	15	195	13.6	4②	⑧	③
	Firenza 4-121/1	11.2	12	15	195	13.6	4②	⑧	③
	Firenza V6-173/W	12	12	15	195	13.6	4②	⑧	③
	Skyhawk 4-121/K	8	8	15	195	13.6	4②	⑧	③
	Skyhawk 4-121 Turbo/M	8	8	15	195	13.6	4②	⑧	③
	Skyhawk 4-121/1	9.5	9.75	15	195	13.6	4②	⑧	③
	Sunbird 4-121/K	8	8	15	195	13.6	4②	⑧	③
	Sunbird 4-121 Turbo/M	8	8	15	195	13.6	4②	⑧	③
1988	Cavalier 4-121/1	7.8	7.9	15	195	13.6	4②	⑧	③
	Cavalier V6-173/W	11	11.1	15	195	13.6	4②	⑧	③
	Cimarron V6-173/W	—	—	—	—	—	—	—	—
	Firenza 4-121/K	7.8	7.9	15	195	13.6	3.7	⑧	③
	Firenza 4-121/1	7.8	7.9	15	195	13.6	4②	⑧	③
	Skyhawk	—	—	15	195	13.6	—	—	—
	Sunbird	—	—	15	195	13.6	—	—	—

①—Approximate, make final check with dipstick.
②—With or without filter change.
③—Oil pan only, 4 qts. After overhaul, less torque converter drain, 6 qts.; with torque converter drain, 9 qts.
④—Man. trans., 8.7 qts.; auto. trans., 9.3 qts.
⑤—4 spd., 5.9 pts.; 5 spd., 5.3 pts.
⑥—With heavy duty cooling system, 9.8 qts.
⑦—Before allowing engine to start after oil change, crank engine over until a steady oil pressure reading is obtained to prime engine and turbocharger lubrication system.
⑧—4 spd., 6 pts.; 5 spd. Isuzu, 5.4 pts.; 5 spd. Muncie, 5 pts.

Electrical Section

INDEX

STARTER

REPLACE

4-112 & 4-121 OVERHEAD VALVE ENGINES

1. Disconnect battery ground cable.
2. Raise and support front of vehicle.
3. Disconnect solenoid wires and battery cable at starter.
4. Remove rear engine mount support bracket, then the A/C compressor support rod (if equipped).
5. Remove starter to engine mounting bolts and lower starter. Note position of shims if used.
6. Reverse procedure to install.

1982–84 4-110 OVERHEAD CAM ENGINE EXC. TURBOCHARGED

Models W/Manual Transaxle

1. Disconnect battery ground cable.
2. Remove upper starter to engine block bolt.
3. Raise and support front of vehicle.
4. Remove rear starter brace attaching bolt from engine block and nut from starter, then the brace.
5. Remove lower starter to engine mounting bolt.
6. Disconnect battery positive cable and solenoid leads from starter motor, then lower starter from engine.
7. Reverse procedure to install.

Models W/Automatic Transaxle

1. Disconnect battery ground cable.
2. Remove air cleaner from engine.
3. Remove lower starter to engine block bolt.
4. Remove rear starter brace attaching bolt from engine block and nut from starter, then the brace.
5. Disconnect battery positive cable and solenoid leads from starter motor.
6. Remove starter to engine block bolt, then raise and support front of vehicle.
7. Disconnect speedometer cable.
8. While pushing upward on shift cable, lower armature end of starter motor down between stabilizer bar and engine, then remove starter motor from engine. **It may be necessary to pry engine block forward to provide clearance for starter motor removal.**
9. Reverse procedure to install.

1985–86 4-110 & 1987–88 4-122 OVERHEAD CAM ENGINE EXC. TURBOCHARGED

1. Disconnect battery ground cable, then remove wiring harness clamp at motor mount.
2. Remove upper starter-to-engine block bolt.
3. Raise and support vehicle.
4. On automatic transaxle equipped models, disconnect speedometer cable, then remove rear transaxle strut.
5. On all models, remove throttle cable bracket, rear starter brace bolts and brace.
6. Remove lower starter-to-engine block bolt, then disconnect starter wiring.
7. Position starter nose down between transaxle and sway bar and attempt to remove. If necessary, pry engine forward or detach sway bar.
8. Reverse procedure to install.

1982–86 4-110 OVERHEAD CAM TURBOCHARGED ENGINE

1. Disconnect battery ground cable.
2. Remove intake manifold support brace.
3. On 1982-84 models, disconnect lead at coil and MAT electrical connector at intake manifold.
4. Remove upper starter to engine block bolt.
5. Remove engine harness bracket to intake manifold bolt.
6. Raise and support front of vehicle, then remove transmission strut.
7. Remove fuel line to support bracket bolt, then loosen fuel lines 1/2 turn to gain access to the starter motor.
8. Remove fuel line support bracket.
9. Remove rear starter support bracket. Do not bend turbocharger oil supply line.
10. Disconnect battery positive cable and solenoid leads from starter motor.
11. Remove lower starter bolt, then starter from engine.
12. Reverse procedure to install.

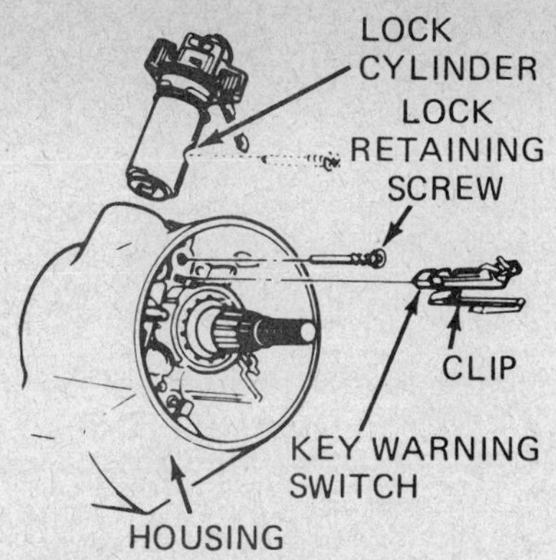

Fig. 1 Lock cylinder removal

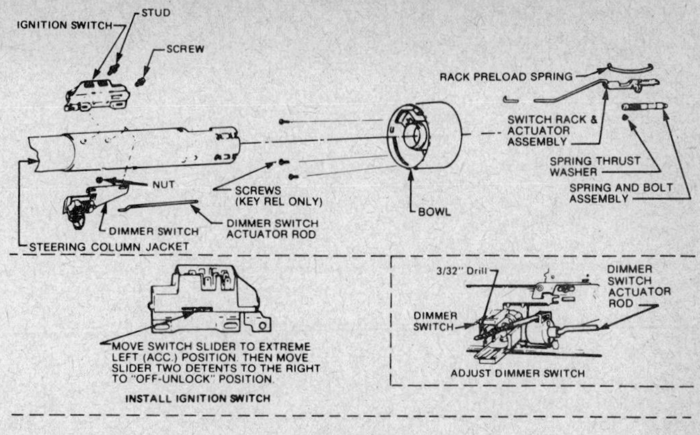

Fig. 2 Ignition & dimmer switch removal. Models less tilt column

1987–88 4-121 OVERHEAD CAM TURBOCHARGED ENGINE

1. Disconnect battery ground cable.
2. Remove intake manifold support brace.
3. Disconnect wire harness clamp at motor mount, then the upper starter to engine block attaching bolt.
4. Raise and support vehicle.
5. On models equipped with automatic transaxle, remove transaxle rear strut.
6. On all models, remove fuel line to support bracket attaching bolt, then loosen fuel lines 1/2 turn to gain access to starter.
7. Remove rear starter brace attaching bolts, then the rear starter brace.
8. Remove lower starter to engine block attaching bolt.
9. Disconnect starter motor electrical connectors, then remove starter motor.
10. Reverse procedure to install.

V6-173 ENGINES

1. Disconnect battery ground cable, then raise and support vehicle.
2. Remove nuts and washers securing electrical connectors to starter solenoid, then disconnect connectors noting position for installation.
3. Remove starter mounting bolts, then the starter motor, noting installation position of starter shims if equipped.
4. Reverse procedure to install.

IGNITION LOCK

REPLACE

1. Remove steering wheel as outlined under "Steering Wheel, Replace" procedure.
2. Remove turn signal switch as outlined under "Turn Signal Switch, Replace" procedure.
3. Remove buzzer switch.
4. Turn lock cylinder to "Run" position, then remove the lock cylinder retaining screw and lock cylinder, **Fig. 1.**
5. To install, rotate lock cylinder to stop while holding housing. Align cylinder key with keyway in housing, then push cylinder into housing until fully seated.
6. Install lock cylinder retaining screw.
7. Install buzzer switch, turn signal switch and steering wheel.

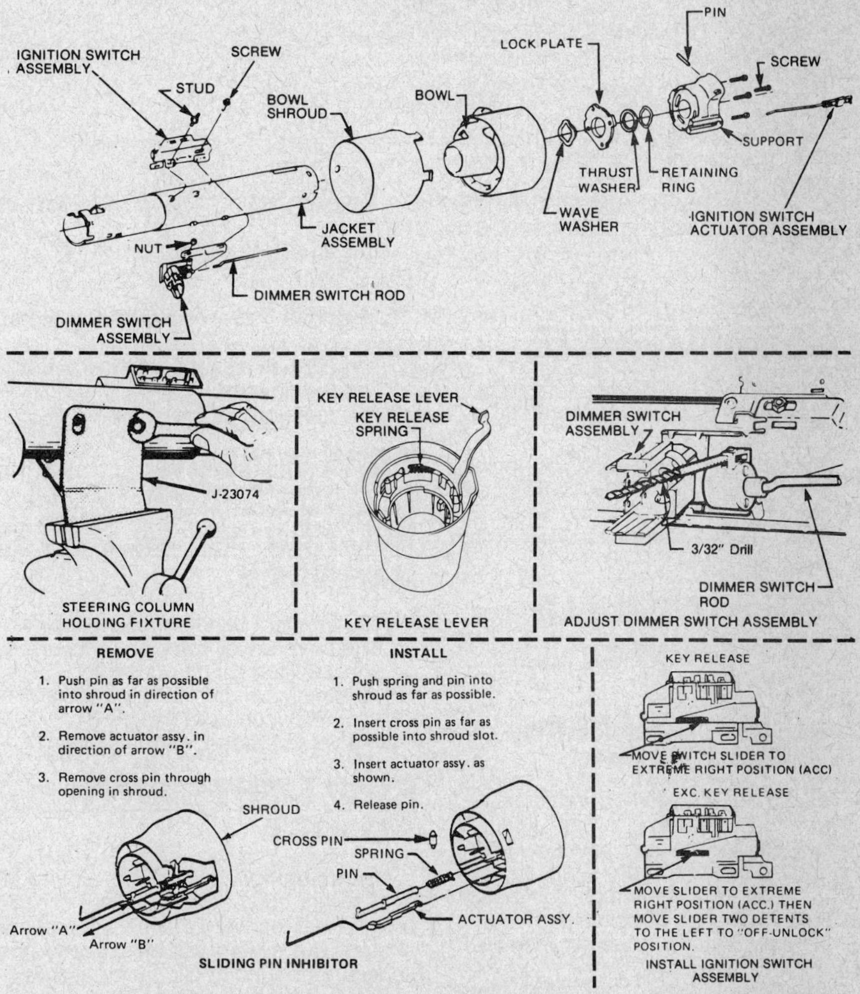

Fig. 3 Ignition & dimmer switch removal. Models with tilt column

IGNITION & DIMMER SWITCHES

REPLACE

1. Remove steering wheel as outlined under "Steering Wheel, Replace" procedure, then the turn signal switch and lock cylinder as previously described.
2. Refer to **Figs. 2 and 3** to remove ignition and dimmer switches.
3. When installing dimmer switch, depress switch slightly and install a 3/32 drill into switch. Force switch upward to remove lash and tighten retaining screw.

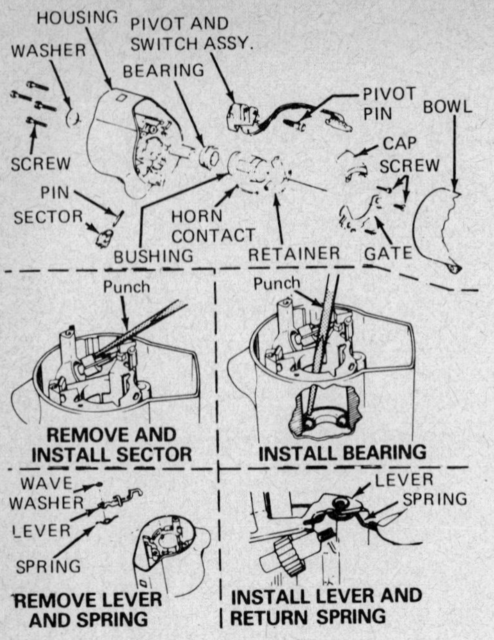

Fig. 4 Windshield wiper switch removal. Models less tilt column

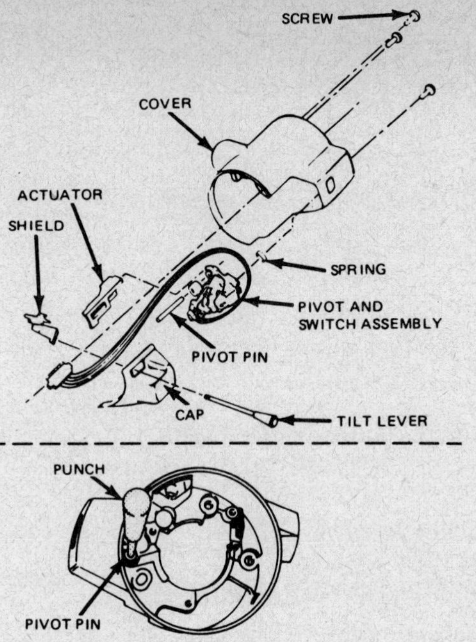

Fig. 5 Windshield wiper switch removal. Models with tilt column

WINDSHIELD WIPER SWITCH

REPLACE

1. Remove turn signal switch as outlined under "Turn Signal Switch, Replace" procedure.
2. Refer to **Figs. 4 and 5** for wiper switch replacement.

PULSE WINDSHIELD WIPER MODULE

REPLACE

CAVALIER, CIMARRON, SUNBIRD & 2000

1. Disconnect battery ground cable.
2. Remove headlamp switch knob by depressing retaining clip behind knob and pulling knob from shaft.
3. Remove lefthand trimplate attaching screws and the trimplate.
4. Remove screws retaining module to adapter assembly.
5. Disconnect wire connectors from module.
6. Remove module from instrument panel.
7. Reverse procedure to install.

FIRENZA & SKYHAWK

1. Disconnect battery ground cable.
2. Remove six screws attaching steering column trim cover to instrument panel and two screws attaching cover to lefthand instrument panel insulator, then remove trim cover.
3. Disengage retaining clip and remove pulse wiper module from cover.
4. Remove screw attaching module ground wire to instrument panel lower brace, then disconnect wire connector and remove module.
5. Reverse procedure to install.

REAR WINDOW DEFROSTER OR WASHER/WIPER SWITCH

REPLACE

1. Disconnect battery ground cable.
2. Remove lower trimplate and disconnect switch wiring connector.
3. Depress switch retaining tabs and remove switch from dash.
4. Reverse procedure to install.

STOP LIGHT SWITCH

ADJUST

Insert stop light switch into tubular clip until switch body seats fully into clip. Pull brake pedal rearward against internal pedal stop. The switch will be properly positioned in the tubular clip automatically.

Rotate switch $1/2$ turn counterclockwise to besure that switch does not hold brake pedal down after adjustment.

BACK-UP LIGHT/NEUTRAL START SWITCH

REPLACE

On vehicles equipped with automatic transmission, the neutral start and back-up light switches are combined into oneunit and must be replaced as an assembly.

MAN. TRANS.

1. Disconnect battery ground cable.
2. Apply parking brake and block wheels, then place gear shift lever in Neutral position.
3. Remove front ashtray, then remove two console attaching screws through ashtray opening.
4. Remove retaining screw, then remove gear shift knob.
5. On Cavalier, Cimarron, Sunbird and 2000 proceed as follows:
   a. Remove console attaching screw located under parking brake handle.
   b. Toward rear of console, remove one screw from each side, retaining console to rear bracket.
6. On Firenza and Skyhawk, proceed as follows:
   a. Pull upward on front of console trim cover, then lift cover from console and disconnect wire connector.
   b. Remove three screws attaching console to front mounting bracket.
   c. Remove rear ashtray, then remove screw attaching console to rear mounting bracket.
7. On all models, remove console assembly. **On models equipped with arm rest, it may be necessary to remove arm rest assembly to provide clearance for console removal.**
8. Disconnect wire connector from back-up light switch.
9. Remove retaining clip, then remove back-up light switch from side of shifter.
10. Reverse procedure to install.

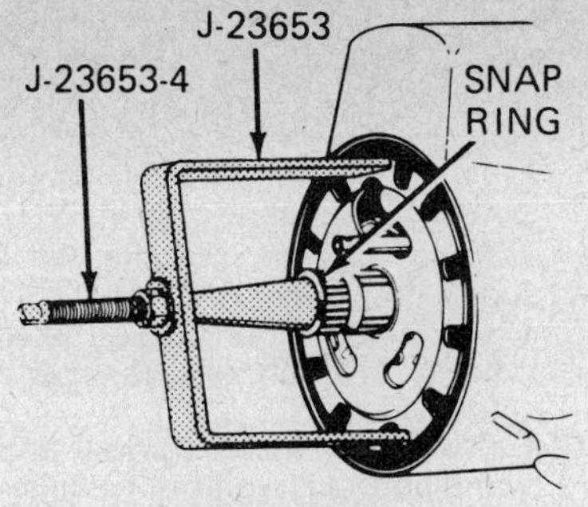

Fig. 6 Compressing lock plate

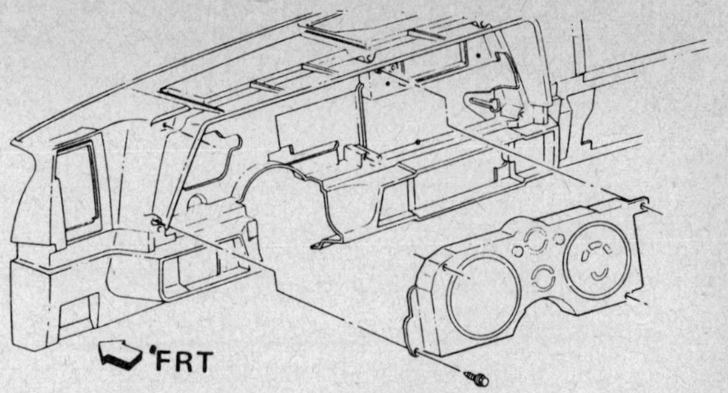

Fig. 7 Instrument cluster. Cavalier, Cimarron, Sunbird & 2000

AUTO. TRANS.

1. Disconnect battery ground cable.
2. Apply parking brake and block wheels, then place gear shift lever in Neutral position.
3. Remove front ashtray, then remove two console attaching screws through ashtray opening.
4. Carefully pry button from center of shift lever knob, then remove snap ring retaining knob.
5. Pull front of console trim cover upward, then lift trim cover from console and disconnect wire connector.
6. Remove three screws attaching front of console to mounting bracket.
7. Remove rear ashtray, then remove screw attaching console to rear support.
8. Remove console assembly. **On models equipped with arm rest, it may be necessary to remove arm rest assembly to provide clearance for console removal.**
9. Disconnect wire connector from Neutral Safety/Back-up light switch.
10. Remove screws attaching switch to shifter lever, then remove switch.
11. If the same switch is to be reinstalled, proceed as follows:
    a. Place shift lever in Neutral position.
    b. Position switch to shift lever and loosely install attaching screws.
    c. Rotate switch on shifter to align adjustment hole with carrier tang, then insert a 2.34 mm diameter pin into hole to a depth of 5 mm.
    d. Torque switch attaching screws to 20 inch lbs., then remove gauge pin.
12. If a new replacement switch is to be installed, proceed as follows:
    a. Position shift lever in the Neutral position.
    b. Insert switch carrier tang into hole on shift lever, then install switch and torque attaching screws to 20 inch lbs. **Replacement switches are held in the Neutral position by an internal plastic pin.**
    c. Move shift lever out of Neutral position to shear switch internal plastic pin.
13. Install console and connect battery ground cable.
14. Check to ensure that vehicle will not start in any shift lever position except Neutral and Park.

CLUTCH START SWITCH REPLACE

1. Remove lower left hush panel.
2. Disconnect wiring connector from switch.
3. Disconnect switch link from pedal, then remove switch retaining screw and switch.
4. Reverse procedure to install.

TURN SIGNAL SWITCH REPLACE

1. Disconnect battery ground cable.
2. Remove steering wheel as outlined under "Steering Wheel, Replace" procedure.
3. Using a suitable screwdriver, pry cover from housing.
4. Using lock plate compressing tool J-23653-4, compress lock plate and pry snap ring from groove on steering shaft, **Fig. 6.** Slowly release compressing tool, then remove tool and lock plate from shaft.
5. Slide canceling cam and bearing preload spring from steering shaft.
6. Remove turn signal (multi-function) lever.
7. Remove hazard warning knob retaining screw, button, spring and knob.
8. Remove actuator arm screw and actuator arm.
9. Remove switch retaining screws and pull switch upward from column, guiding wire harness through column.
10. Reverse procedure to install.

STEERING WHEEL REPLACE

1. Disconnect battery ground cable.
2. Remove steering wheel center pad.
3. Remove steering wheel retaining nut and retainer.
4. Scribe alignment marks on steering wheel and shaft to aid installation.
5. Using tool J-1859-03 or equivalent, remove steering wheel from shaft.
6. Reverse procedure to install.

INSTRUMENT CLUSTER REPLACE

CAVALIER, CIMARRON, SUNBIRD & 2000

1. Disconnect battery ground cable.
2. Remove six screws attaching instrument panel trimplate to instrument panel.
3. Pull top of trimplate outward and remove trimplate from instrument panel.
4. Remove four screws securing instrument cluster to instrument panel, **Fig. 7.**
5. Remove screws attaching steering column cover to instrument panel, then the lower column cover.
6. Remove two steering column retaining bolts and lower steering column to floor.
7. Pull instrument cluster out slightly and disconnect speedometer cable.
8. On automatic transmission equipped vehicles, disconnect vehicle speed sensor (VSS) connector from rear of cluster.
9. Remove cluster and disconnect instrument panel harness connector from printed circuit located at rear of cluster.
10. Reverse procedure to install.

FIRENZA & SKYHAWK

1. Disconnect battery ground cable.
2. Remove six screws attaching steering column trim cover to instrument panel and two screws attaching trim cover to lefthand instrument panel trim cover, then remove trim cover.
3. Remove screw attaching right end of lefthand trim cover to instrument panel, then pull trim cover rearward to disengage retaining clips and remove cover.
4. Remove screw attaching left end of righthand trim cover to instrument panel, then remove two screws from under center trim cover and four screws from front of glove compartment. Pull righthand trim cover rearward to disengage retaining clips, then disconnect wire connectors and remove trim cover.
5. Remove seven screws attaching cluster trim cover to instrument cluster pad, then remove trim cover.

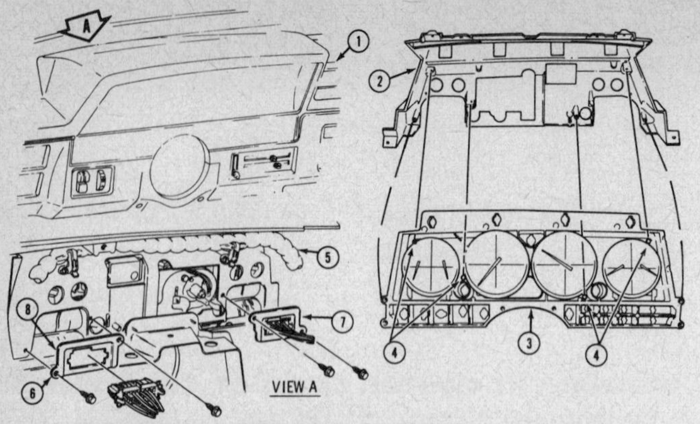

Fig. 8 Instrument cluster. Firenza & Skyhawk

6. Remove five screws attaching bezel and lens to instrument cluster carrier, then remove bezel and lens.
7. Loosen two upper steering column mounting bolts, then lower steering column slightly to provide clearance for cluster removal.
8. Remove four screws attaching cluster housing to cluster carrier, then pull housing slightly outward and disconnect speedometer cable and remove cluster housing, **Fig. 8.**
9. Reverse procedure to install.

HEADLIGHT SWITCH

REPLACE

CAVALIER, CIMARRON, SUNBIRD & 2000

1. Disconnect battery ground cable.
2. Remove headlight switch knob by pulling knob to full "On" position, depressing retaining clip behind knob and pulling knob from shaft.
3. Gently pry lefthand side trimplate out of instrument panel.
4. Remove switch retaining nut, rotate and tilt switch forward and pull switch from instrument panel.
5. Disconnect wiring connector and remove switch.
6. Reverse procedure to install.

FIRENZA & SKYHAWK

1. Disconnect battery ground cable.
2. Remove six screws attaching steering column lower cover to instrument panel, then remove lower cover.
3. Remove one screw attaching right end of left hand trim cover to instrument panel, then pull cover rearward to detach retaining clips.
4. Remove four screws attaching headlamp switch to instrument panel, then pull switch rearward and disconnect wire connector.
5. Reverse procedure to install.

RADIO

REPLACE

CAVALIER, CIMARRON, SUNBIRD & 2000

1. Disconnect battery ground cable.
2. Loosen six instrument panel trimplate to instrument panel attaching screws and remove trimplate. **Determine whether right side of radio is retained with nut or rubber stud.**
3. On vehicles equipped with radio side retainer nut:
   a. Without A/C, remove right lower hush panel then loosen side retainer nut. Disconnect wire and antenna connections and remove radio from instrument panel.
   b. With A/C, remove right lower hush panel, A/C duct and A/C control head, then loosen side retainer nut. Disconnect wiring and antenna connections and remove radio from instrument panel.
4. On vehicles equipped with radio side retainer rubber stud, remove two radio bracket to instrument panel attaching screws, then pull radio forward and disconnect wiring and antenna connections. Remove radio from instrument panel.
5. Reverse procedures to install.

FIRENZA & SKYHAWK

1. Disconnect battery ground cable.
2. Remove six screws attaching steering column trim cover to instrument panel, then lower trim cover.
3. Remove screw attaching left end of right hand trim cover to instrument panel.
4. Remove two screws from under center trim cover and four screws from front of glove compartment, then pull trim cover rearward to disengage retaining clips and disconnect wire connectors.
5. Remove four screws attaching upper and lower radio mounting brackets to instrument panel.
6. Pull radio out just enough to disconnect wire connector and antenna lead, then remove radio.
7. Reverse procedure to install.

WINDSHIELD WIPER MOTOR

REPLACE

1. Disconnect battery ground cable.
2. Remove wiper arms from transmission spindle shafts.
3. Remove shroud top vent grille panel and screen.
4. Loosen, but do not remove, transmission drive link to motor crank arm attaching nuts, then pull drive link out of motor crank arm.
5. Disconnect wiper motor electrical connections and remove wiper motor attaching bolts.
6. Rotate wiper motor upward and outward, and remove from vehicle.
7. Reverse procedure to install.

WINDSHIELD WIPER TRANSMISSION ASSEMBLY

REPLACE

1. Remove wiper arms from transmission spindle shafts.
2. Remove shroud top vent grille panel and screen.
3. Loosen, but do not remove, transmission drive link to motor crank arm attaching nuts then pull drive link from motor crankarm.
4. Remove transmission to cowl panel attaching screws and the transmission assembly.
5. Reverse procedure to install.

BLOWER MOTOR

REPLACE

1. Disconnect battery ground cable.
2. Disconnect blower motor electrical connections.
3. Remove plastic water shield from right side of cowl.
4. Remove blower motor retaining screws and blower motor.
5. Reverse procedure to install.

HEATER CORE

REPLACE

LESS AIR CONDITIONING

1. Disconnect battery ground cable and drain cooling system.
2. Disconnect heater hoses from heater core.
3. Remove heater outlet deflector.
4. Remove heater core module cover retaining screws and module cover, **Fig. 9.**
5. Remove heater core retaining straps and heater core.
6. Reverse procedure to install.

WITH AIR CONDITIONING

1. Disconnect battery ground cable and drain cooling system.
2. Raise and support vehicle and disconnect drain tube from heater and evaporator assembly.
3. Lower vehicle and remove right and left hush panels, steering column trim cover and glovebox.
4. Remove heater duct retaining screw and heater duct.
5. Remove heater core cover attaching

screws, then gently pull cover rearward and out of vehicle, **Fig. 10. When removing heater core assembly, pull assembly straight toward interior of vehicle until plastic drain tube clears cowl. If assembly is tilted in any direction before tube clears cowl, the drain tube may break.**

6. Remove heater core retaining clamps and heater core from case.
7. Reverse procedure to install.

CRUISE CONTROL

RELEASE SWITCHES

Automatic Transmission

Both the electrical and vacuum release switches are located at the brake pedal. To adjust, depress brake pedal and insert switch fully into tubular clip. Pull pedal rearward until clicking sounds are no longer audible. The switch is now automatically adjusted.

Manual Transmission

On manual transmission equipped vehicles, the electrical release switch is located at the clutch pedal, while the vacuum release switch is found at the brake pedal. Adjustment procedures for these switches are the same as for those under automatic transmission equipped vehicles.

SERVO, ADJUST

With engine off and carburetor in slow idle position, connect cable swivel to third ball on servo chain. Adjust cable nuts until chain has a slight amount of slack, then tighten locknut securely.

CRUISE SPEED, ADJUST

1982–83

The cruise speed adjustment can be set as follows:

1. If cruise speed is lower than engagement speed, loosen orifice tube locknut and turn orifice tube counterclockwise.
2. If cruise speed is higher than engagement speed, loosen orifice tube locknut and turn orifice tube clockwise. **Each 1/4 turn of orifice tube will change cruise speed approximately one mile per hour. Tighten locknut after adjustment is completed.**

1984–88

On these models, the cruise speed cannot be adjusted. If cruise speed is lower or higher than engagement speed, the cruise control module should be replaced.

ASPIRATOR ASSISTED VACUUM SYSTEM

The aspirator assisted vacuum system supplements engine vacuum when engine vacuum is low. The system, **Fig. 11,** consists of an aspirator, 3-port check valve, 2-port check valve and related components such as the air pump and air management valve. The air for the aspirator is tapped off the air line that connects the air pump to

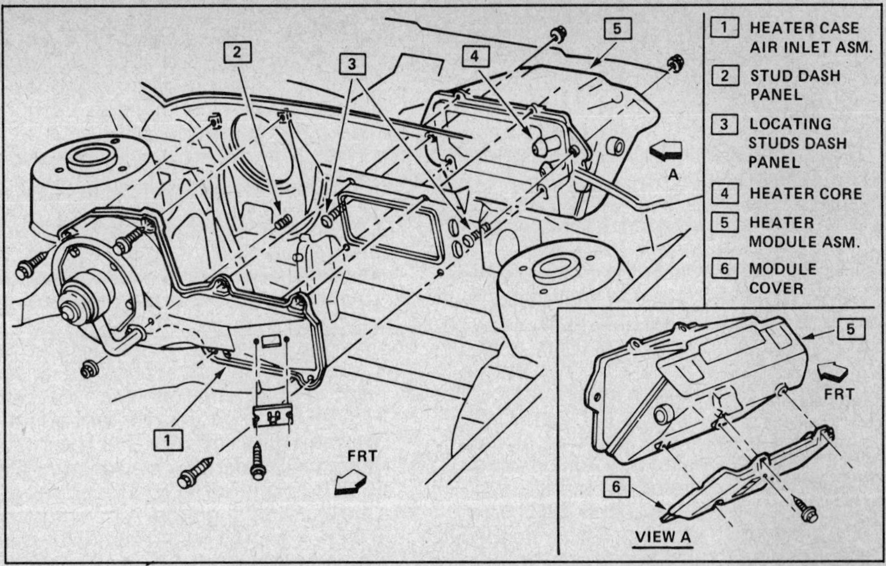

Fig. 9 Heater core & blower motor. (Typical) Models less A/C

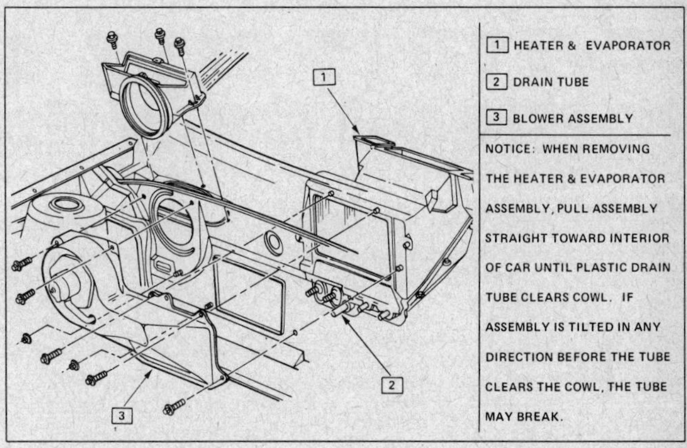

Fig. 10 Heater core & blower motor. (Typical) Models with A/C

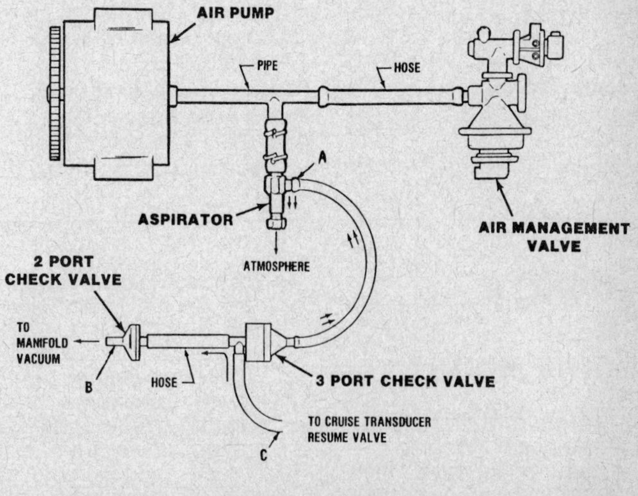

Fig. 11 Aspirated assisted vacuum system schematic

the air management valve. Aspirator vacuum and manifold vacuum (after passing through the 2-port check valve) supply the two upper ports of the 3-port check valve. The lower of the 3-port check valve supplies air to the cruise control transducer. The aspirator assisted vacuum system operates as follows:

1. Under normal vacuum conditions, air is bled into the system from the transducer resume valve to the lower "T" of the 3-port check valve, then to the 2-port check valve and finally into the intake manifold, **Fig. 11.**
2. Also during normal operation, as the air pump is pumping air into the air management valve, a small amount of air is diverted through the aspirator to the atmosphere. As air passes through the aspirator, a venturi action inside the aspirator assembly develops a vacuum. This vacuum is used to provide the vacuum assist needed under high cruise conditions.
3. Should manifold vacuum fall below aspirator vacuum, the 2-port check valve is designed to close while the 3-port check valve is designed to open. Opening of the 3-port check valve exposes the higher vacuum at the aspirator, providing the needed vacuum for proper cruise operation.

To check the aspirator system for correct operation, note the following information:

1. Ensure all hoses and connections are secure and check valves are correctly installed. **The check valves are arrowhead shaped in the direction of air flow.**
2. Connect a suitable vacuum gauge to the aspirator output at point A, **Fig. 11.**
3. Start and operate engine at 2500 RPM. **Engine should be thoroughly warmed up to ensure that the computer command control system (CCC) is operating in closed loop.**
4. Check vacuum gauge. A minimum of 6 inches should be indicated. If vacuum reading is not within specified amount, clean aspirator using a suitable solvent and recheck. Also check air pump for air output. If there is no air output from the air pump, check air pump for damage. If air pump is not damaged, proceed to step a.
   a. Disconnect vacuum gauge at port A, **Fig. 11.** Disconnect and plug 2-port check valve at port B. Blow air into the resume valve hose at port C. Air should flow through and exit at port A.
   b. Remove plug from 2-port check valve at port B and plug hose at port A. Blow air into cruise resume valve at port C. Air should flow and exit at port B. **Steps a & b determine if the hoses and check valves are operating in one direction. To check for operation in the opposite direction, proceed to step c.**
   c. Blow air into hose at port A while port B is plugged, then into port B while hose at port A is plugged. **No air should exist at port C in either case.**

4-110 (1.8L) & 4-121 (2.0L) Overhead Cam Engine Section

INDEX

ENGINE MOUNTS REPLACE

FRONT ENGINE MOUNT

1982–84

1. Disconnect battery ground cable.
2. Remove engine mount nuts, then raise and support vehicle.
3. Remove inner fender shield attaching bolts, then the shield.
4. Support engine and remove and discard engine mount attaching bolts, **Figs. 1 and 2.**
5. Remove engine mount from vehicle. **Whenever engine mount is removed, alignment bolt M6X1X65 must be used during installation to prevent power train misalignment.**
6. Reverse procedure to install, using new engine mount bolts. Remove alignment bolt. **If excessive effort is required to remove alignment bolt, loosen transaxle adjusting bolts to align power train components.**

1985–88

1. Disconnect battery ground cable.
2. Support engine, then remove two mount to bracket attaching bolts, **Fig. 3.**
3. Remove two top mount attaching bolts, then raise and support vehicle.
4. Remove lower mount attaching bolt, then the engine mount.
5. Reverse procedure to install.

REAR ENGINE MOUNT

1982–84

1. Disconnect battery ground cable.
2. Raise and support vehicle.
3. If equipped with manual transaxle, remove oil filter.
4. Support engine and remove engine mount nuts, **Fig. 4.**
5. Remove and discard engine mount to engine attaching bolts.
6. Remove engine mount from vehicle.
7. Reverse procedure to install.

1985–88

1. Disconnect battery ground cable.
2. Support engine, then remove two mount to bracket attaching bolts, **Fig. 5.**
3. Raise and support vehicle.
4. Remove two lower mount attaching nuts and reinforcement, then the engine mount.
5. Reverse procedure to install.

ENGINE
REPLACE

1. Disconnect battery ground cable, then drain cooling system.
2. Remove air cleaner, then disconnect engine electrical harness connector at bulkhead and electrical connector at brake cylinder.
3. Disconnect throttle cable from bracket and throttle body assembly.
4. Disconnect vacuum hoses from throttle body assembly, then disconnect power steering high pressure hose at cut-off switch.
5. Disconnect vacuum hoses at map sensor and canister, then disconnect air conditioning relay cluster switches.
6. Disconnect power steering return hose at power steering pump.
7. Disconnect ECM electrical connectors, then pull harness through bulkhead and position harness over engine.
8. Disconnect upper and lower radiator hoses from engine, then disconnect wire connector at temperature switch on thermostat housing.
9. Disconnect transmission shift cable at transmission, then raise and support vehicle.
10. Disconnect speedometer cable at transmission and bracket.
11. Disconnect exhaust pipe at exhaust manifold and remove exhaust pipe from converter.
12. Remove heater hoses from heater core, fuel lines at flex hoses and transmission cooler lines at flex hoses.
13. Remove front wheels, righthand spoiler section and splash shield.
14. Remove and support right and left brake calipers.
15. Using tool No. J-24319-1 or equivalent, remove rightand left tie rod ends.
16. Disconnect electrical connectors at A/C compressor, then remove A/C compressor and mounting brackets. Using a piece of wire, support compressor in wheel opening.

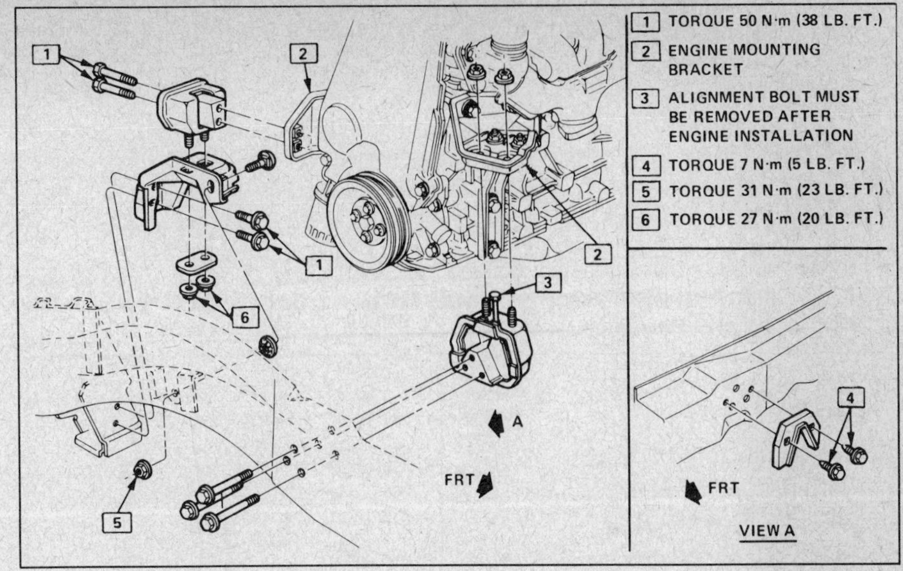

Fig. 1 Front engine mounts. 1982–84

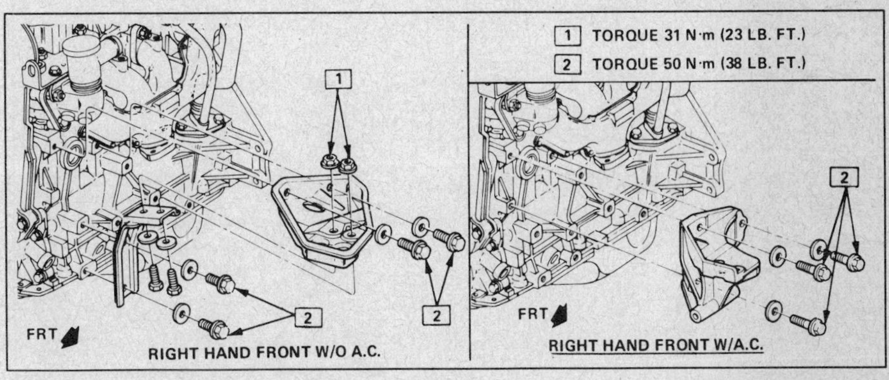

Fig. 2 Righthand front engine mount brackets. 1982–84

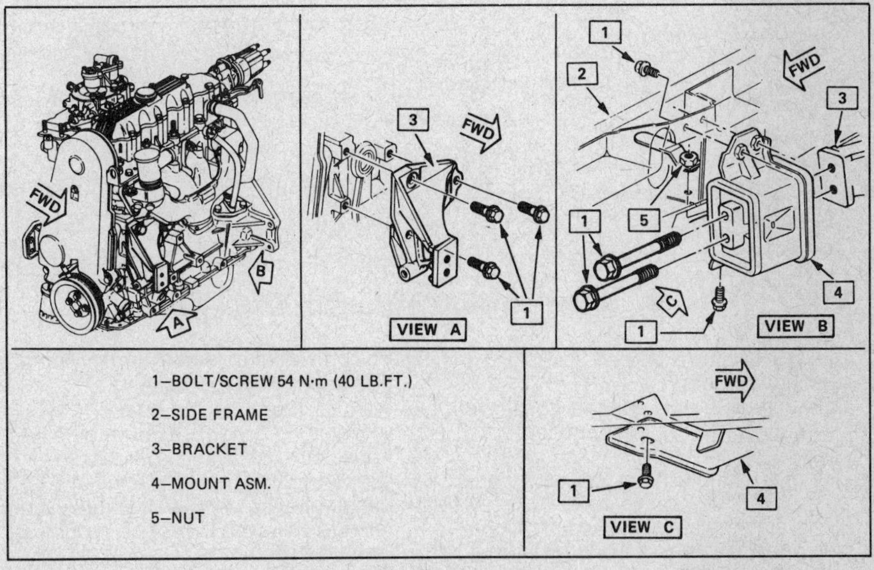

Fig. 3 Front engine mounts. 1985–88

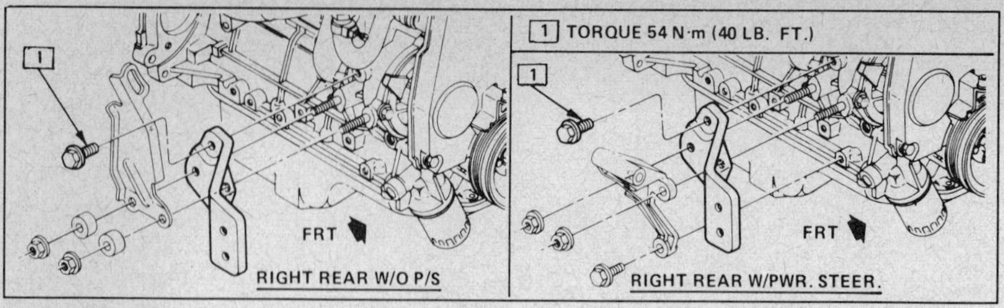

Fig. 4 Righthand rear engine mount brackets. 1982–84

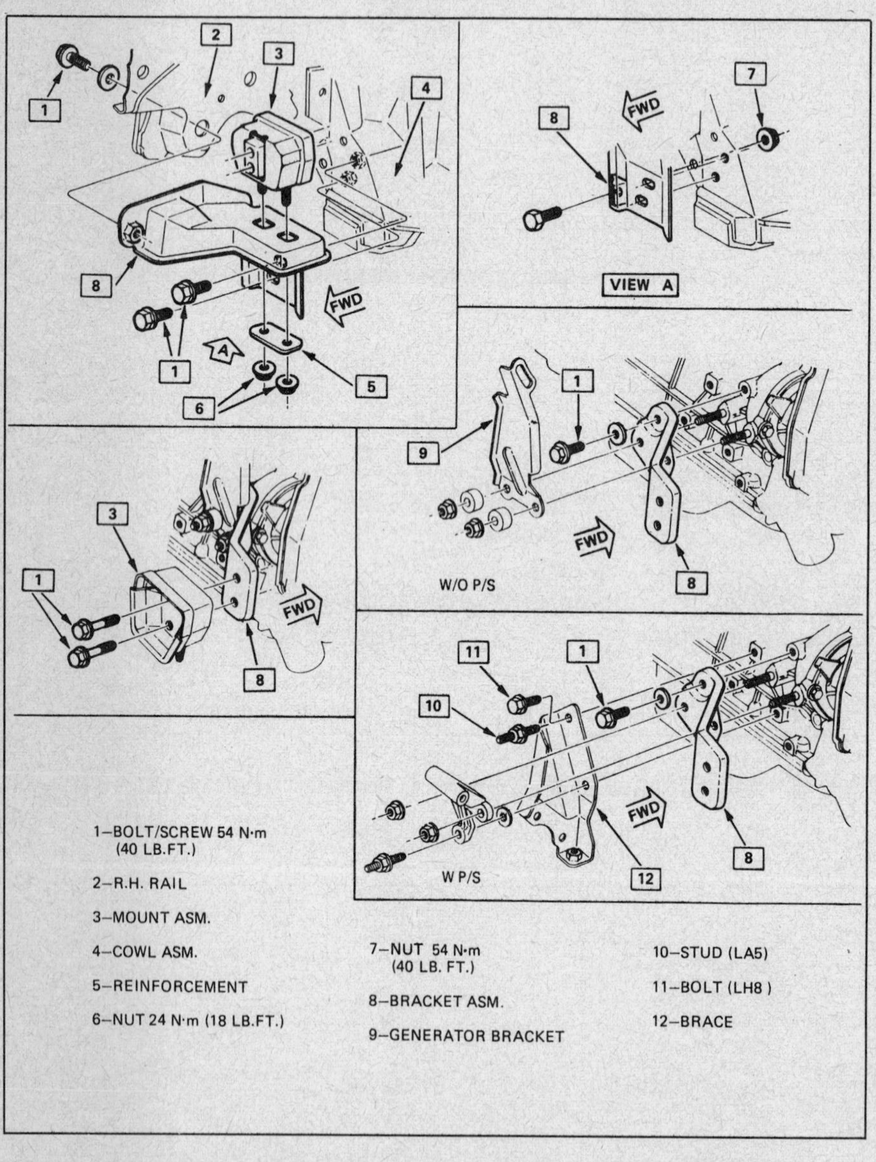

Fig. 5 Rear engine mounts. 1985–88

17. Remove six front suspension support attachment bolts.
18. Lower vehicle and support front end by placing jack stands under core support.
19. Using a suitable hoist, position front post of hoist to rear of cowl.
20. Using a suitable piece of wood (4 inch x 4 inch x 6 inch), position onto front post of hoist.
21. Raise vehicle slightly and remove jack stands from front end.
22. Position a suitable dolly under engine and transaxle assembly.
23. Position three pieces of wood (4 inch x 4 inch x 12 inch) under engine and transaxle assembly only, allowing support rails to hang free.
24. Slightly lower vehicle onto dolly and remove two rear transaxle mount attaching bolts.
25. Remove three left front engine mount attaching bolts and two engine support to body attaching bolts behind righthand inner axle U-joint.
26. Remove one bolt and nut from righthand chassis side rail to engine mount bracket.
27. Remove six strut attaching nuts, then raise vehicle, allowing engine, transaxle and suspension assemblies to rest onto dolly.
28. Remove engine and transaxle as an assembly.
29. Position engine and transaxle assembly into vehicle.
30. Loosely install transaxle and left front mounts to side rail bolts.
31. To prevent power train misalignment, install bolt No. M6X1X65 into left front mount, on 1982-84 models.
32. Torque transaxle mount bolts to 40 ft. lbs. and left front mount bolts to 18 ft. lbs. on 1982-84 models or 40 ft. lbs. on all other models.
33. Install right rear mount to body bolts and torque to approximately 38 ft. lbs.
34. Position a suitable jack under control arms and raise struts into position, then install retaining nuts.
35. Raise vehicle, then using suitable lifting equipment, raise control arms and install tie rod ends.
36. Reverse procedure to complete installation.

CYLINDER HEAD REPLACE

4-110 ENGINE

1. Disconnect battery ground cable, remove air cleaner and drain cooling system.
2. Remove alternator and pivot bracket from camshaft carrier housing.
3. Remove power steering pump and bracket and position aside.
4. Disconnect ignition coil electrical connectors, then remove coil.
5. Disconnect spark plug wires from distributor cap.
6. Remove throttle cable from bracket on intake manifold.
7. Disconnect accelerator cable, downshift cable and throttle valve cable from throttle body assembly.
8. Disconnect ECM connectors from throttle body assembly.
9. Disconnect vacuum brake hose from filter, then disconnect inlet and return fuel lines from flex joints.
10. Remove water pump bypass hose from intake manifold and water pump.
11. Disconnect ECM harness connectors and heater hose from intake manifold.
12. Disconnect exhaust pipe from exhaust manifold and breather hose from camshaft carrier.
13. Disconnect upper radiator hose, then disconnect engine electrical harness and wires from thermostat housing.
14. Remove timing cover and timing probe holder.
15. Loosen water pump bolts and remove timing belt.
16. Loosen camshaft carrier and cylinder head bolts a little at a time in sequence shown in **Fig. 6. Camshaft carrier and cylinder head bolts should only be removed when en-**

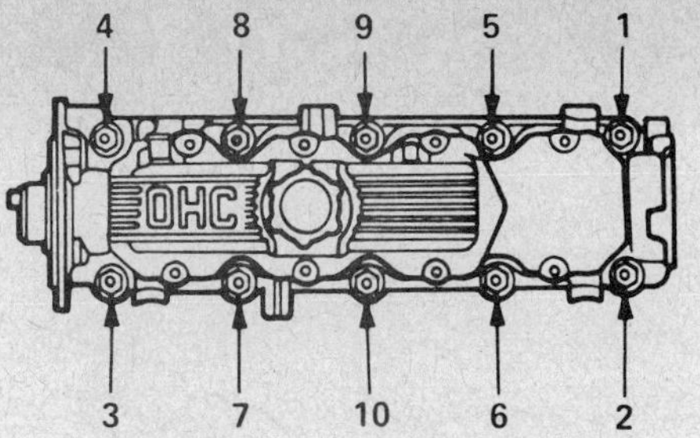

Fig. 6 Cylinder head & camshaft carrier bolt loosening sequence

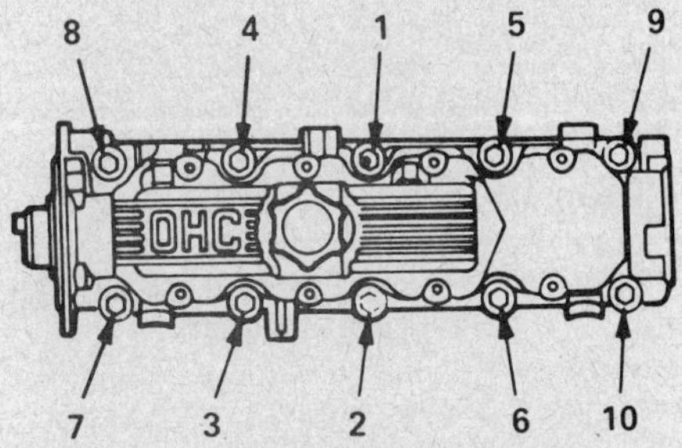

Fig. 7 Cylinder head & camshaft carrier bolt tightening sequence

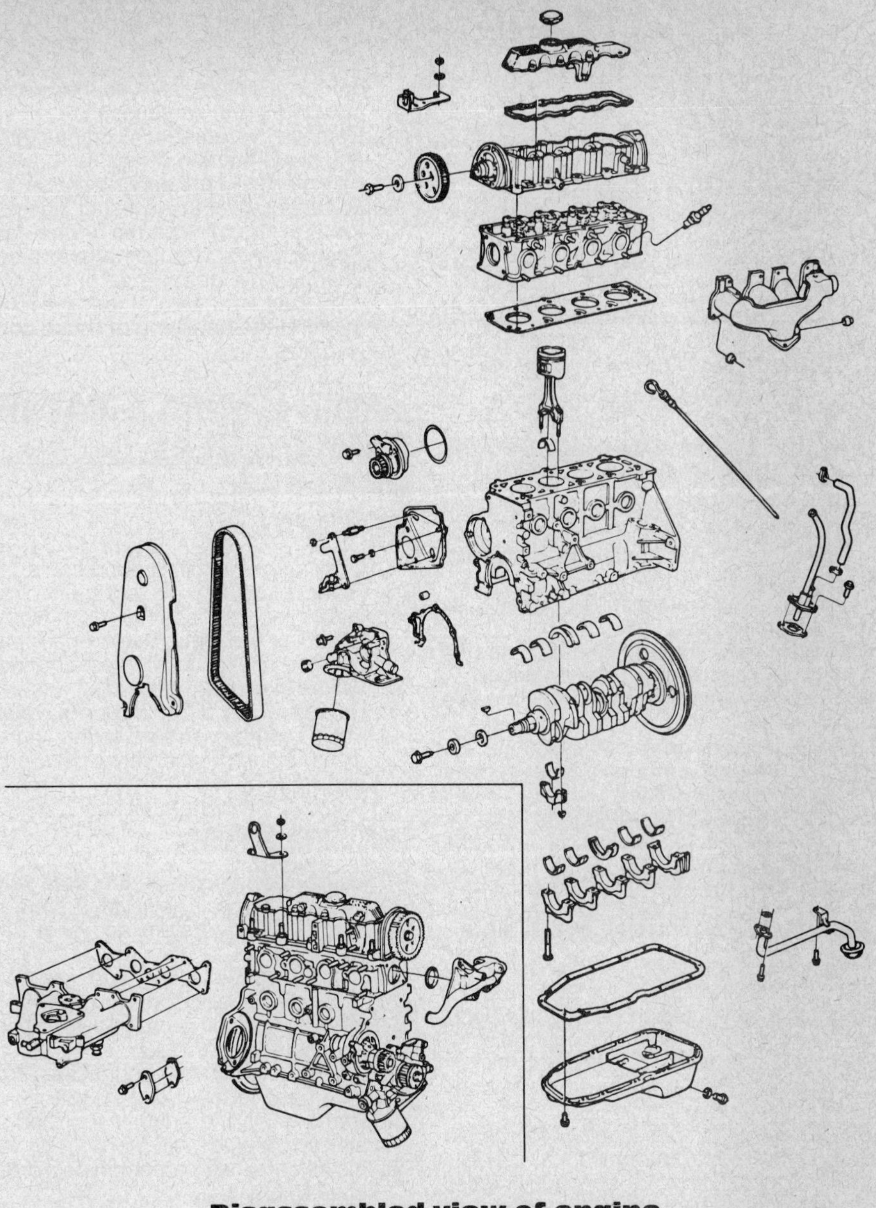

Disassembled view of engine

gine is cold.

17. Remove camshaft carrier assembly.
18. Remove cylinder head, intake manifold and exhaust manifold as an assembly.
19. Remove all carbon deposits from combustion chambers and valve ports. Check cylinder head for cracks in the exhaust ports and combustion chambers. Remove water jacket plugs and clean, if necessary.
20. Reverse procedure to install. Torque cylinder head bolts a little at a time in sequence shown in **Fig. 7** to 18 ft. lbs. Tighten each bolt in the proper sequence an additional 180° in 60° increments.
21. After installation is completed (with the exception of brackets that install onto carrier), start engine and let engine idle until thermostat opens. Turn engine off and torque all bolts an additional 30 to 50° in the proper sequence.

4-121 ENGINE

Cylinder head bolts should only be loosened when engine is cold. Do not reuse cylinder head bolts.

1. Disconnect battery ground cable.
2. Remove air cleaner on models equipped with non-turbocharged engines or induction tube on models equipped with turbocharged engines.
3. Remove generator and bracket from carrier, then the ignition coil.
4. Remove distributor assembly.
5. Remove cables from intake manifold bracket, TBI or throttle body.
6. Remove downshift cable, then the ECM electrical connectors from TBI or throttle body and intake manifold.
7. Remove vacuum brake hose, then the fuel inlet and return lines. **Relieve fuel pressure before removing fuel lines on models equipped with turbocharged engine.**
8. Remove coolant and heater hoses.
9. Remove exhaust pipe at manifold on models equipped with non-turbocharged engine or exhaust manifold to turbo connection on models equipped with turbocharged engine.
10. Remove oxygen sensor and thermostat housing electrical connector, if equipped.
11. Remove engine harness, then the timing belt.
12. With engine cold, loosen cam carrier/cylinder head attaching bolts as shown in **Fig. 6.**
13. Remove camshaft carrier, rocker arms and valve lash compensators.
14. Remove cylinder head with intake manifold and exhaust manifold as an assembly.
15. Reverse procedure to install. Torque cylinder head bolts a little at a time in sequence shown in **Fig. 7** to 18 ft. lbs. Tighten each bolt in the proper sequence an additional 180° in 60° increments.
16. After installation is completed (with the exception of brackets that install onto carrier), start engine and let engine idle until thermostat opens. Turn engine off and torque all bolts an additional 30 to 50° in the proper sequence.

INTAKE MANIFOLD REPLACE

NON-TURBOCHARGED MODELS

1. Disconnect battery ground cable.
2. Remove air cleaner, then drain cooling system.

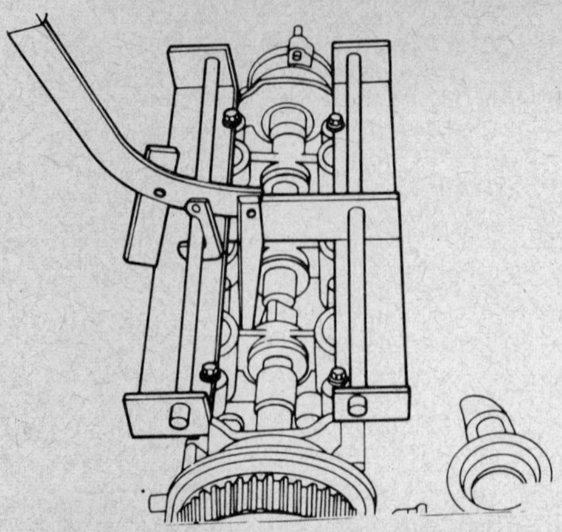

Fig. 8 Using tool No. 33302 to compress valve spring

3. Remove generator and bracket at camshaft carrier.
4. Disconnect power steering pump and position aside.
5. Remove power steering bracket at intake manifold.
6. Remove ignition coil, then the throttle cable from intake manifold bracket.
7. Remove throttle cable and TV cable from TBI unit.
8. Remove TBI unit electrical connector.
9. Remove vacuum brake hose, coolant hoses and fuel lines.
10. Remove ECM harness, then the intake manifold attaching nuts and manifold.
11. Reverse procedure to install.

TURBOCHARGED MODELS

1. Disconnect battery ground cable.
2. Remove induction tube and hoses.
3. Disconnect ignition coil, throttle body, M.A.P. sensor and wastegate electrical connectors.
4. Remove PCV hose and throttle body vacuum hose.
5. Remove throttle cable and cruise control cable, as required.
6. Remove manifold support bracket, then disconnect fuel injector electrical connectors.
7. Remove rear alternator bracket attaching bolt, then the power steering adjusting bracket.
8. Remove alternator front adjusting bracket, then the fuel lines.
9. Remove intake manifold attaching bolts, then the intake manifold.
10. Reverse procedure to install.

VALVE CLEARANCE SPECIFICATIONS

Valve lash is obtained through the use of hydraulic valve lash compensators. No provision for adjustment is provided.

ROCKER ARM & HYDRAULIC VALVE LASH COMPENSATORS

REPLACE

1. Disconnect battery ground cable.
2. Remove camshaft carrier cover.
3. Using tool No. J-33302 or equivalent, **Fig. 8**, compress valve springs and remove rocker arms. Place rocker arms in a suitable rack so they can be installed in the same location.
4. Remove hydraulic lash compensators and place them in a rack so they can be installed in the same location.
5. Reverse procedure to install. **The preload of the hydraulic valve lash compensator is automatic and servicing of the compensator requires only care and cleanliness be exercised in the handling of these components.**

VALVE SPRING & VALVE STEM OIL SEAL

REPLACE

REMOVAL

1. Disconnect battery ground cable.
2. Remove rocker arms and spark plugs.
3. Install air line adapter tool No. J-23590 or equivalent, into spark plug port and apply compressed air to hold valves in place.
4. Using tool No. J-33302 or equivalent, **Fig. 8**, compress valve spring and remove rocker guides, valve locks, caps and valve spring.
5. Remove valve stem oil seal.

INSTALLATION

1. Using clean engine oil, lubricate valve stem and install new valve stem oil seal over valve stem and seat onto valve guide.
2. Position valve spring and cap over valve stem. Using tool No. J-33302 or equivalent, compress valve spring and install valve locks.
3. Install rocker guides and rocker arms, then remove tool No. J-33302.
4. Remove air line adapter tool and install spark plugs.
5. Install camshaft carrier cover. Torque bolts to 5 ft. lbs.

VALVE SEAT SERVICE

Using a suitable dial indicator measure valve seat concentricity. Valve seat should be concentric to within .002 inch of total indicator reading. Ensure valve guide bores are free from carbon or dirt to allow proper seating of the pilot in the valve guide. When reconditioning the valve seats, use a 45° stone to rough the valve seat and another stone with the same angle to finish the valve seat. Narrow down the valve seats to the proper width, .051-.055 inch for intake valves and .067-.071 for exhaust valves.

VALVE GUIDES

Valve guides are an integral part of the cylinder head. If valve stem to guide clearance is excessive, the guide should be reamed to the next oversize and the appropriate oversize valve installed. Valves are available in standard size and oversize of .010 inch (.25 mm).

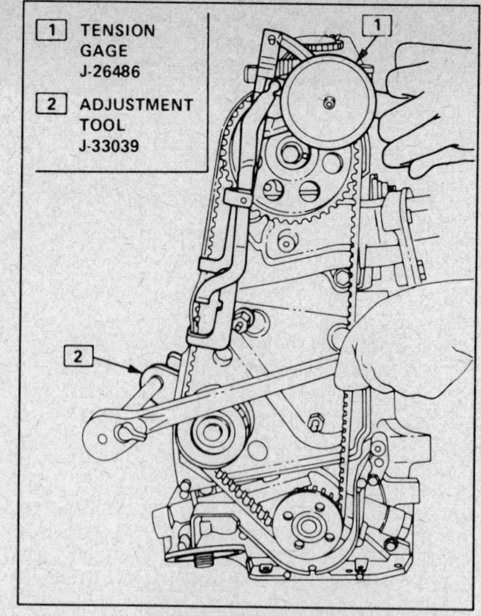

Fig. 9 Timing belt tension adjustment

CRANKSHAFT PULLEY

REMOVAL

1. Disconnect battery ground cable.
2. Loosen alternator and power steering bracket bolt, then remove drive belt.
3. Remove inner fender splash shield, then remove crankshaft pulley bolts and pulley.

INSTALLATION

1. Position pulley onto crankshaft sprocket. Using a suitable sealer, coat threads of pulley bolts and install onto pulley. Torque bolts to 15 ft. lbs.
2. Install splash shield.
3. Install alternator and power steering belt, then connect battery ground cable.

TIMING BELT

REPLACE

1. Disconnect battery ground cable.
2. Remove timing belt front cover, then rotate crankshaft until timing mark on crankshaft pulley aligns with 10° BTDC mark on indicator tab. The mark on the camshaft sprocket must align with mark on camshaft carrier.
3. Remove crankshaft pulley as previously described.
4. Remove timing probe holder.
5. Loosen water pump bolts, then rotate water pump to loosen and remove timing belt.
6. Reverse procedure to install. Note the following information:
   a. Ensure mark on camshaft sprocket aligns with mark on camshaft carrier. The timing mark on the crankshaft pulley should align with the 10° BTDC mark on the indicator tab.
   b. Using tool No. J-33039 or equivalent, **Fig. 9**, rotate water pump

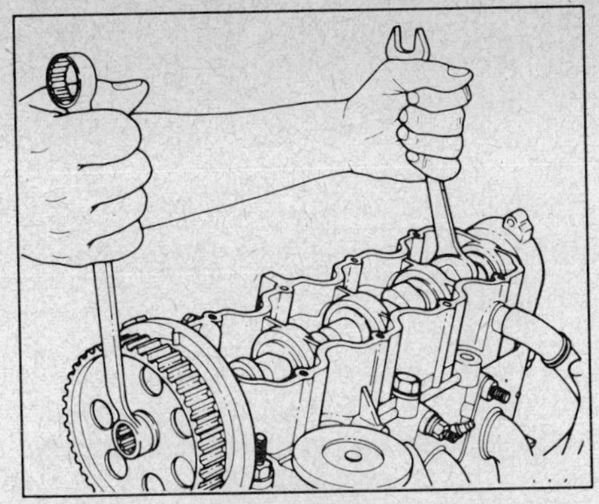

Fig. 10 Camshaft sprocket removal

clockwise until all slack is removed from timing belt. Install tool No. J-26486 or equivalent, **Fig. 9**, between water pump and camshaft sprockets so pointer is midway between sprockets.

7. To adjust timing belt tension, refer to **Fig. 9** and note the following information:

Belt Size 748inch

Initial Adjustment

New Belt.................. 74ft.lbs.

Used Belt.................. 59ft.lbs.

Checking Value

New Belt............... 59-88ft.lbs.

Used Belt............... 44-74ft.lbs.

These values are for a cold engine.

a. If timing belt tension is incorrect, loosen and using tool No. J-33039 or equivalent, rotate water pump until proper tension is obtained.
b. Torque water pump bolts to 19 ft. lbs. Ensure water pump does not shift when torquing bolts.

TIMING BELT REAR COVER

REPLACE

1. Disconnect battery ground cable.
2. Remove timing belt as described under "Timing Belt, Replace."
3. Remove timing belt rear cover bolts and cover.
4. Reverse procedure to install. Torque cover bolts to 19 ft. lbs.

CAMSHAFT CARRIER COVER

REPLACE

1. Remove air cleaner and disconnect breather hoses.
2. Remove cover bolts and cover.
3. Reverse procedure to install. Torque camshaft carrier cover bolts to 5 ft. lbs.

CAMSHAFT SPROCKET

REPLACE

1. Disconnect battery ground cable.

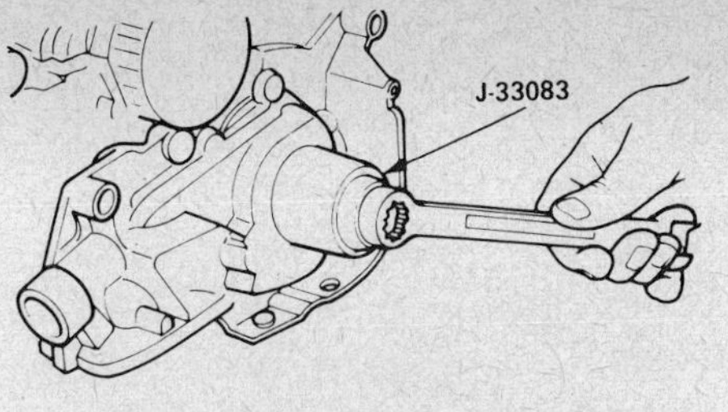

Fig. 11 Crankshaft front oil seal installation

2. Remove timing belt front cover and align mark on camshaft sprocket with mark on camshaft carrier cover.
3. Remove timing probe holder.
4. Loosen water pump bolts and remove timing belt from camshaft sprocket.
5. Remove camshaft carrier cover.
6. Using a suitable tool, secure camshaft and remove camshaft sprocket bolt, washer and sprocket, **Fig. 10.**
7. Reverse procedure to install. Torque camshaft sprocket bolt to 34 ft. lbs, timing probe holder to 19 ft. lbs. and camshaft carrier cover bolts to 5 ft. lbs.

CAMSHAFT

REMOVAL

1. Disconnect battery ground cable.
2. Remove camshaft carrier cover.
3. Using tool No. J-33302 or equivalent, **Fig. 8**, compress valve springs and remove rocker arms.
4. Remove timing belt front cover and timing belt as described under "Timing Belt, Replace."
5. Remove camshaft sprocket as described under "Camshaft Sprocket, Replace."
6. Disconnect spark plug wires from spark plugs, then remove distributor from engine.
7. Remove camshaft thrust plate from rear of camshaft carrier.
8. Slide camshaft rearward and remove camshaft from carrier.

INSTALLATION

1. Using tool No. J-33085 or equivalent, install new front oil seal onto camshaft carrier.
2. Position camshaft into carrier. **Ensure not to damage front oil seal when installing camshaft.**
3. Install camshaft thrust plate and bolts. Torque bolts to 70 inch lbs.
4. Check camshaft endplay. Endplay should be within .016 to .064 inch.
5. Install distributor, camshaft sprocket, timing belt and timing belt front cover.
6. Using tool No. J-33302 or equivalent, **Fig. 8**, compress valve springs and install rocker arms.
7. Install camshaft carrier cover. Torque bolts to 5 ft. lbs.

CRANKSHAFT SPROCKET

REPLACE

1. Disconnect battery ground cable.

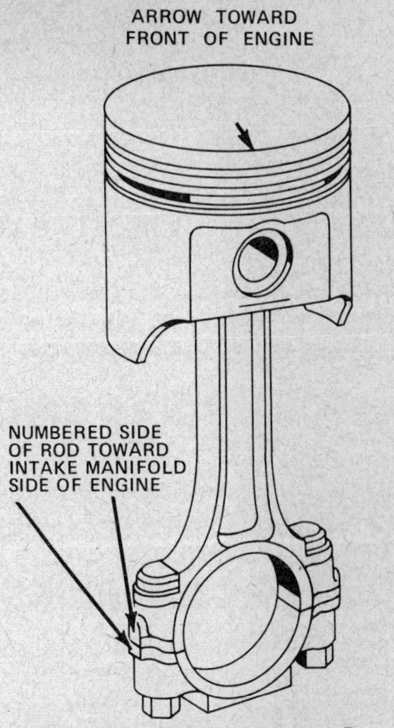

Fig. 12 Piston & rod assembly

2. Remove timing belt as described under "Timing Belt, Replace."
3. Remove crankshaft sprocket bolt, washer and sprocket.
4. Reverse procedure to install. Refer to step 7 under "Timing Belt, Replace" and adjust belt tension. Torque crankshaft sprocket bolt to 115 ft. lbs. on 1982-84 models or 107 ft. lbs. on 1985-88 models.

CRANKSHAFT FRONT OIL SEAL

REPLACE

1. Disconnect battery ground cable.
2. Remove crankshaft sprocket as described under "Crankshaft Sprocket, Replace."
3. Remove key and rear thrust washer from end of crankshaft.
4. Using a suitable tool, remove crankshaft front oil seal.
5. During installation of crankshaft front oil seal, position tool No. J-33083 or equivalent, **Fig. 11**, onto crankshaft. Lubricate front oil seal lip and install onto crankshaft.
6. Reverse procedure to complete installation.

PISTON & ROD ASSEMBLE

Assemble piston to rod, with arrow on piston facing toward front of engine and numbered side toward intake manifold side of engine, **Fig. 12.** Upon installation, measure connecting rod side clearance using a suitable feeler gauge. Side clearance should be .0027 to .0095 inch.

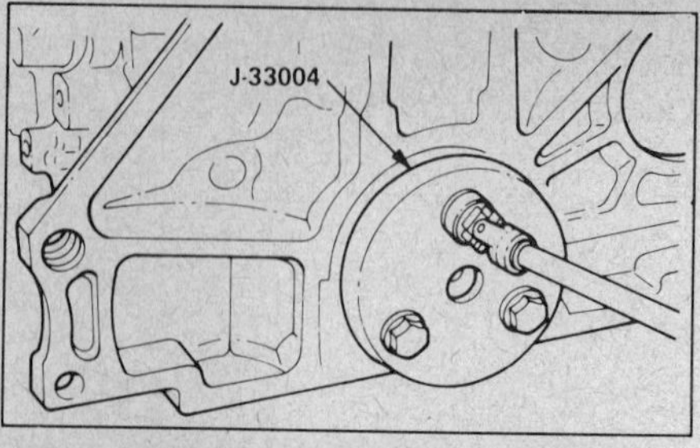

Fig. 13 Rear main bearing oil seal installation

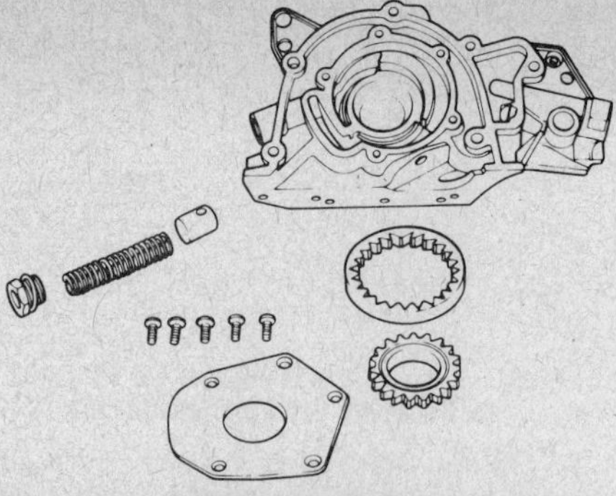

Fig. 14 Disassembled view of oil pump

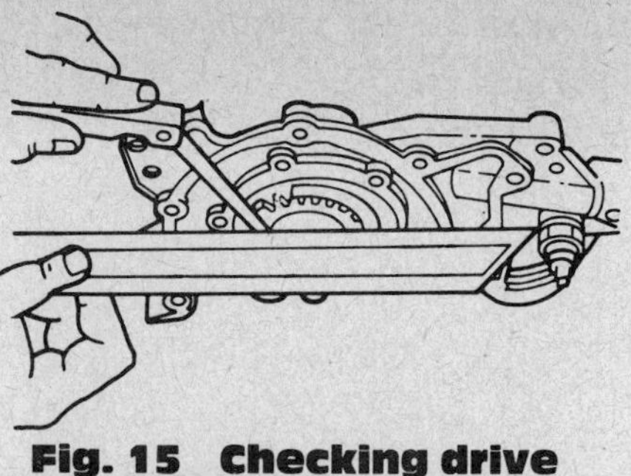

Fig. 15 Checking drive gear to oil pump housing clearance

PISTONS, PINS & RINGS

Pistons and rings are available in standard size and oversize of .020 inch (.5 mm). Piston pins are available in standard size only.

MAIN & ROD BEARINGS

Main and rod bearings are available in standard sizes and undersizes of .010 inch (.25 mm) and .020 inch (.5 mm).

REAR MAIN BEARING OIL SEAL

REPLACE

1. Remove engine from vehicle as described under "Engine, Replace."
2. On vehicles equipped with automatic transaxle, remove flywheel dust cover and flex plate to torque converter bolts.
3. Remove bellhousing bolts and separate engine from transaxle assembly.
4. On vehicles equipped with automatic transaxle, remove flex plate.
5. On vehicles equipped with manual transaxle, remove pressure plate, clutch disc and flywheel.
6. Using a suitable tool, remove rear main bearing oil seal.
7. Reverse procedure to install. During installation of seal, position seal over seal pilot tool No. J-33004 or equivalent, **Fig. 13.** Using clean engine oil, lubricate new rear oil seal and position onto crankshaft by turning starter bolts on tool No. J-33004 in rotational sequence until rear oil seal bottoms in engine block.

OIL PAN

REPLACE

1. Disconnect battery ground cable.
2. Raise and support vehicle.
3. Remove right front wheel and right-hand splash shield.
4. Remove lower A/C bracket strut rod bolt and swing aside.
5. Remove flywheel dust cover.
6. Disconnect exhaust pipe from exhaust manifold or waste gate, as required.
7. Drain engine oil, remove oil pan bolts and oil pan.
8. Reverse procedure to install. Using a suitable sealer, coat threads of oil pan bolts. Torque bolts to 4 ft. lbs.

OIL PUMP SCREEN & PICKUP TUBE

REPLACE

1. Disconnect battery ground cable.
2. Remove oil pan as described under "Oil Pan, Replace."
3. Remove pickup tube support bolts, pickup tube to oil pump bolts, pickup tube and O-ring.
4. Reverse procedure to install. Torque pickup tube to oil pump bolts to 5 ft. lbs. Torque pickup tube support bolts to 5 ft. lbs.

OIL PUMP

REMOVAL

1. Disconnect battery ground cable.
2. Remove crankshaft sprocket and timing belt rear cover.
3. Disconnect engine oil pressure switch electrical connector from the switch.
4. Remove oil pan and oil filter.
5. Remove pickup tube to engine block bolts, pickup tube and oil pump.

DISASSEMBLE

1. Remove five screws and rear cover from oil pump, **Fig. 14.**
2. Remove gears, plug, pressure regulator valve plunger and spring.
3. If necessary, remove pickup tube and O-ring from oil pump body.

INSPECTION

After disassembling the oil pump, thoroughly clean all oil pump components and check them for excessive wear and damage.

1. Using a suitable straightedge and feeler gauge, **Fig. 15,** check oil pump clearances.
2. Check clearances for the following oil pump components:
   a. Clearance between idler gear and oil pump body should be .004-.007 inch.
   b. Clearance between drive gear and oil pump body should be .014-.018 inch.
   c. Clearance between gears and oil pump cover should be .002-.004 inch.
3. If clearances obtained are not within specified limits, replace worn or damaged oil pump components.

ASSEMBLE

1. Install valve plunger and spring.
2. Using a suitable sealer, coat threads of pressure regulator valve plunger plug and install. Torque plug to 15 ft. lbs.
3. Install oil pump gears into oil pump body.

INSTALLATION

1. Install gasket and oil pump onto engine. Torque oil pump bolts to 5 ft. lbs.
2. Install pickup tube and bolts. Torque bolts to 5 ft. lbs.
3. Install oil pan and oil filter.
4. Connect engine oil pressure switch electrical connector to switch.
5. Install timing belt rear covers and crankshaft sprocket.

WATER PUMP

REPLACE

1. Drain cooling system, then remove timing belt. Refer to "Timing Belt, Replace" for procedure.
2. Remove timing belt rear protective covers, as required.
3. Remove lower radiator hose from water pump.
4. Remove water pump attaching bolts then the water pump and sealing ring.
5. Clean engine block and water pump sealing surfaces, then apply a 3/32 inch of RTV sealant to sealing surfaces. While RTV sealant is still wet, install water pump. Tighten attaching bolts finger tight.
6. Install lower radiator hose on water pump, then timing belt rear protective covers.
7. Install timing belt. Refer to "Timing Belt, Replace" for procedure.

ELECTRIC FUEL PUMP

REPLACE

1. Depressurize fuel system as follows:
   a. Remove fuel pump fuse from fuse panel.
   b. Start engine and operate until fuel supply remaining in fuel lines is consumed. Engage starter for approximately 3 seconds to ensure fuel pressure has been relieved.
   c. With ignition switch in the "Off" position, install fuel pump fuse. **Unless this procedure is followed before servicing fuel system, fuel spray could occur.**

2. Disconnect battery ground cable.
3. Raise and support vehicle.
4. Remove fuel tank.
5. Remove fuel meter pump assembly by turning cam lock ring counterclockwise.
6. Remove fuel meter pump assembly from fuel tank and fuel pump from fuel meter.
7. Pull fuel pump upward into fuel hose while pulling outward away from bottom support. **Do not damage rubber insulator and strainer during fuel pump removal.**
8. After fuel pump assembly is clear of bottom support, pull pump assembly out of rubber connector and from vehicle.
9. Reverse procedure to install.

TURBOCHARGER

The turbocharger is used to increase power on a demand basis. As engine load increases and the throttle is opened, more air/fuel mixture is drawn into the combustion chambers. As this increased volume is burned, a larger volume of high energy exhaust gasses enters the engine exhaust system and is directed through the turbocharger turbine housing. Some of the exhaust gas energy is used to increase the speed of the turbine wheel which is connected to the compressor wheel. The increased speed of the compressor wheel compresses the air/fuel mixture and delivers it to the intake manifold. The high pressure in the intake manifold allows a denser charge to enter the combustion chambers, in turn developing more engine power during the combustion cycle. The intake manifold pressure (boost) is controlled to a maximum value by an exhaust gas bypass valve (wastegate). The wastegate allows a portion of the exhaust gas to bypass the turbine wheel, thereby not increasing turbine speed. The wastegate is operated by a spring-loaded diaphragm device sensing the pressure differential across the compressor. When intake manifold pressure reaches a predetermined value above ambient pressure, the wastegate begins to bypass the exhaust gas.

4-112 (1.8L) & 4-121 (2.0L) Overhead Valve Engine Section

INDEX

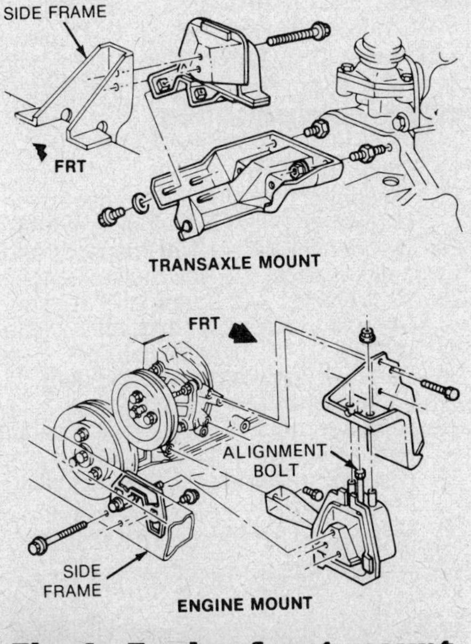

Fig. 1 Engine front mount. 1982–84

ENGINE MOUNTS REPLACE

FRONT ENGINE MOUNT

1982–84

1. Disconnect battery ground cable.
2. Remove engine mount nuts, then raise and support vehicle.
3. Remove inner fender shield attaching bolts, then the shield.
4. Support engine and remove and discard engine mount attaching bolts, **Fig. 1.**
5. Remove engine mount from vehicle. **Whenever engine mount is removed, alignment bolt M6.0 x 1 x 65 must be used during installation to prevent power train misalignment.**
6. Reverse procedure to install, using new engine mount bolts. Remove alignment bolt and torque engine mount to side frame bolts to 35-45 ft. lbs. Torque all other nuts and bolts to

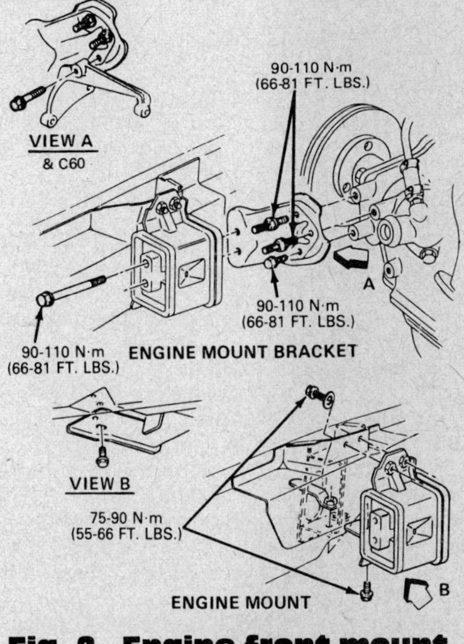

Fig. 2 Engine front mount. 1985–88

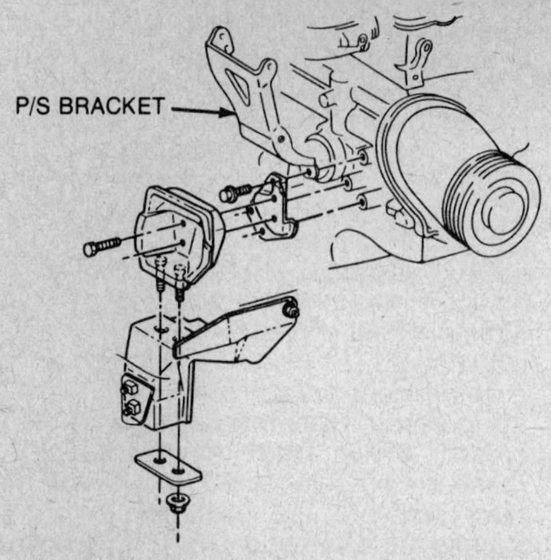

Fig. 3 Engine rear mount

25-35 ft. lbs. **If excessive effort is required to remove alignment bolt, loosen transaxle adjusting bolts to align power train components.**

1985–88

1. Disconnect battery ground cable.
2. Remove upper engine mount to body bracket attaching bolts, then the upper engine mount to engine bracket attaching bolt, **Fig. 2.**
3. Raise vehicle and support engine, then remove inner fender shield.
4. Remove lower engine mount to body bracket attaching bolt.
5. Remove lower engine mount to engine bracket attaching bolt.
6. Remove engine mount.
7. Reverse procedure to install. Apply suitable locking compound to bolt threads before installation.

REAR ENGINE MOUNT

1. Disconnect battery ground cable.
2. Raise and support vehicle.
3. If equipped with manual transaxle, remove oil filter.
4. Support engine and remove engine mount nuts, **Fig. 3.**
5. Remove and discard engine mount to engine attaching bolts.
6. Remove engine mount from vehicle.
7. Reverse procedure to install. Check oil level and torque nuts to 15-20 ft. lbs. and bolts to 25-35 ft. lbs.

ENGINE REPLACE

1. Disconnect battery and drain cooling system.
2. Remove air cleaner.
3. Disconnect accelerator and, if so equipped, TV cables.
4. Disconnect ECM wiring on engine.
5. Disconnect any vacuum hoses interfering with engine removal.
6. Disconnect radiator and heater hoses at engine.
7. Remove exhaust heat shield, if equipped.
8. On vehicles equipped with A/C, remove adjustment bolt at engine mount.

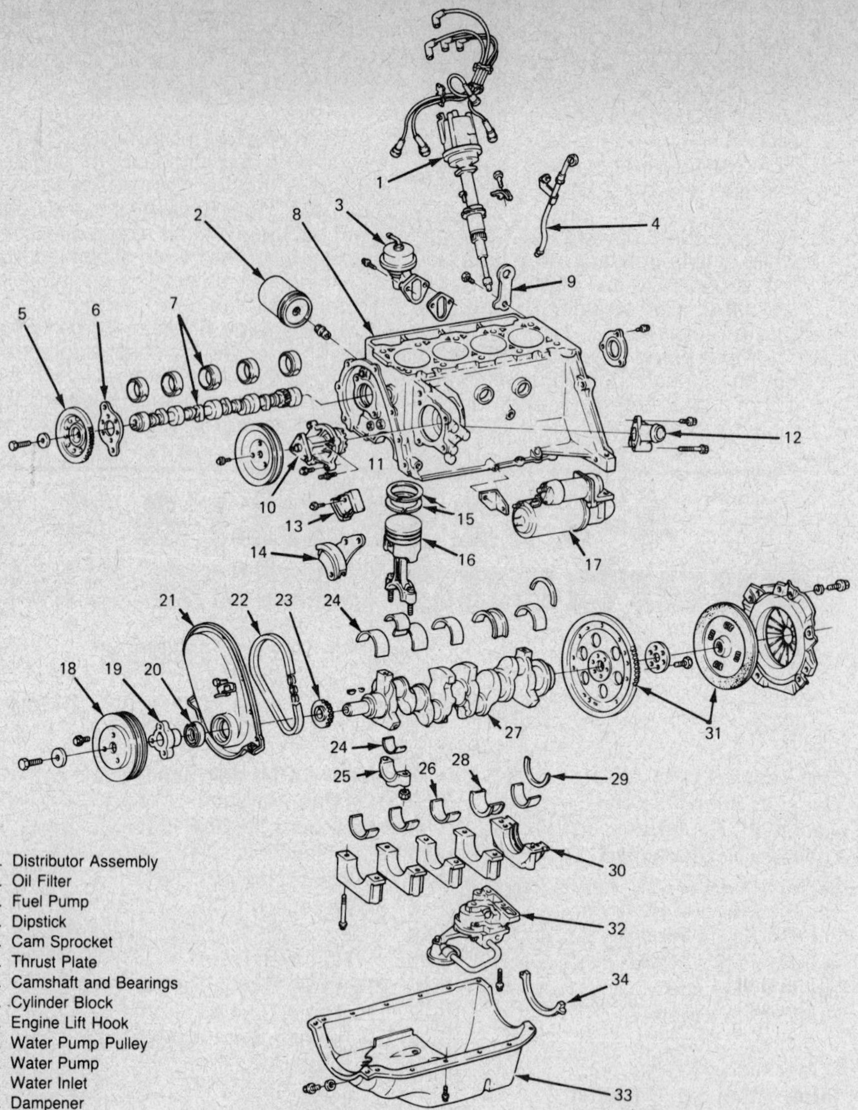

1. Distributor Assembly
2. Oil Filter
3. Fuel Pump
4. Dipstick
5. Cam Sprocket
6. Thrust Plate
7. Camshaft and Bearings
8. Cylinder Block
9. Engine Lift Hook
10. Water Pump Pulley
11. Water Pump
12. Water Inlet
13. Dampener
14. Tensioner
15. Piston Rings
16. Piston
17. Starter
18. Accessory Drive Pulley
19. Hub
20. Seal
21. Front Cover
22. Timing Chain
23. Cranksprocket
24. Connecting Rod Bearings
25. Connecting Rod Bearing Cap
26. Main Bearings
27. Crankshaft
28. Main Thrust Bearing
29. Rope Seal
30. Main Bearing Caps
31. Flywheel and Flex Plate
32. Oil Pump
33. Oil Pan
34. Seal

Typical block assembly & components

9. On all vehicles, disconnect engine wiring harness at firewall.
10. Remove windshield washer reservoir.
11. Remove alternator drive belt.
12. Remove power steering belt.
13. Disconnect fuel lines.
14. Raise and support vehicle.
15. On vehicles equipped with A/C, remove A/C brace.
16. On all vehicles, remove inner fender splash shield.
17. On vehicles equipped with A/C, remove A/C compressor.
18. Remove flywheel splash shield and disconnect starter wiring.
19. Disconnect front starter brace and remove starter.
20. On vehicles with automatic transaxles, remove torque converter bolts.
21. Remove crankshaft pulley using tool J-24420 or equivalent.
22. Remove oil filter.
23. Disconnect engine to transmission bracket and right rear engine mount.
24. Disconnect exhaust at manifold and center hanger. Loosen muffler hanger.
25. On vehicles with automatic transaxles, disconnect TV and shift cable bracket.
26. Remove 2 lower bellhousing bolts.
27. Lower vehicle.
28. Remove right front engine mount nuts.
29. Remove alternator and adjusting bracket.
30. Disconnect master cylinder and position aside.
31. Attach suitable lifting device to engine.
32. Remove right front engine mount bracket.
33. Remove upper bellhousing bolts

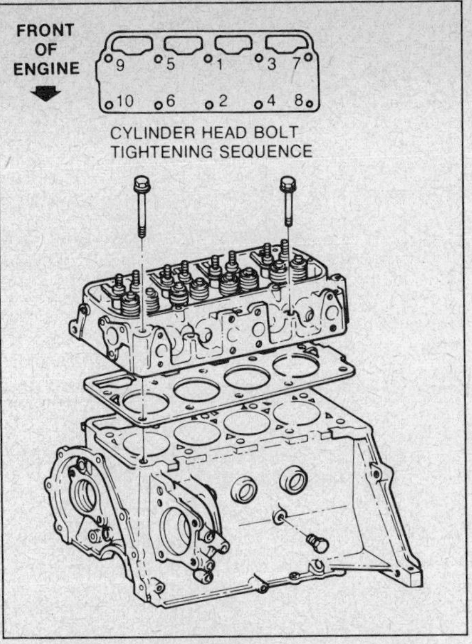

Fig. 4 Cylinder head bolt tightening sequence. 1982–86

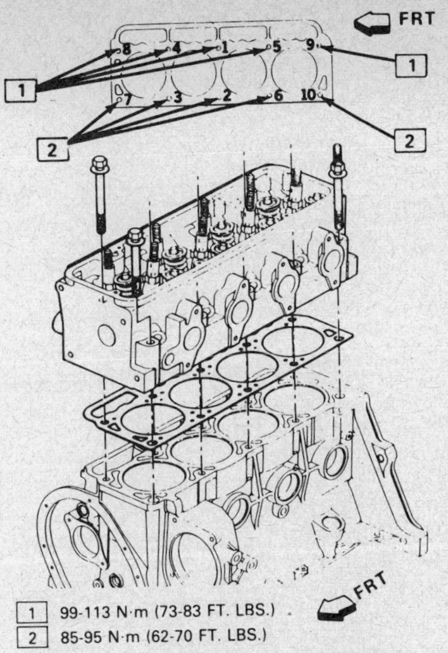

Fig. 5 Cylinder head bolt tightening sequence. 1987–88

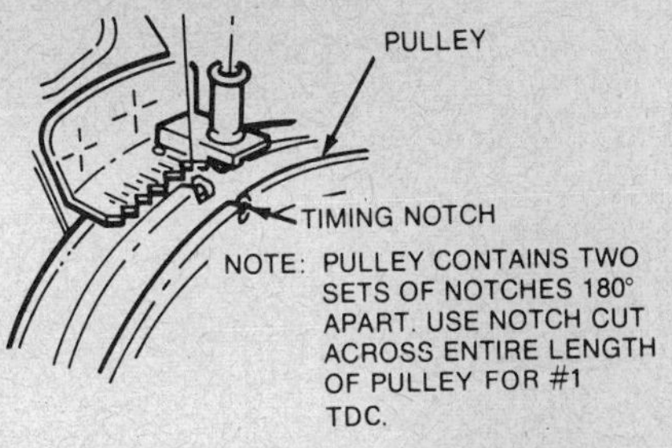

Fig. 6 Aligning crankshaft pulley timing marks

34. Lift engine and remove power steering pump, if so equipped.
35. Remove engine.
36. Install engine mount alignment bolt M6.0 x 1 x 65, **Fig. 1**, to ensure proper power train alignment.
37. Lower engine into vehicle.
38. Install upper bellhousing bolts and left front engine mount nuts.
39. Reverse removal procedure to install. On 1982-83 models, once engine is installed, check alignment bolt. If excessive effort is required to remove bolt, loosen transaxle mount adjusting bolts and realign power train.

CYLINDER HEAD

REPLACE

The cylinder head, carburetor or TBI (Throttle Body Injection) unit and the intake and exhaust manifolds are removed as an assembly.

1. Disconnect battery ground cable, then drain cooling system and remove air cleaner or TBI cover.
2. Raise and support vehicle, then remove exhaust manifold shield, if equipped.
3. Disconnect exhaust pipe at exhaust manifold and heater hose at intake manifold.
4. Lower vehicle, then remove engine lift bracket and distributor.
5. Disconnect vacuum manifold from alternator bracket.
6. Disconnect and tag all vacuum lines that will interfere with cylinder head removal, then disconnect AIR pipe at exhaust check valve.
7. Disconnect accelerator linkage at carburetor or TBI unit, then remove accelerator linkage bracket bolt and the bracket.
8. Disconnect all electrical wires that will interfere with cylinder head removal, then remove upper radiator hose from cylinder head.
9. Remove dipstick tube bracket bolt and the hot water tube bracket.
10. Remove idler pulley assembly and AIR/power steering belt, if equipped.
11. Remove power steering pump, if equipped, and position aside.
12. Remove AIR bracket to intake manifold bolt, if equipped.
13. On power steering equipped vehicles, remove AIR pump pulley, AIR pump through bolt and power steering pump adjusting bracket.
14. Loosen AIR bracket lower bolt and rotate bracket aside, if equipped.
15. Disconnect fuel line from carburetor or TBI unit.
16. Remove alternator and position aside. Do not remove wires.
17. Remove alternator upper support bracket and brace.
18. Remove rocker arm cover and rocker arms, then the pushrods.
19. Remove cylinder head bolts and the cylinder head assembly.
20. Reverse procedure to install. Coat cylinder head and cylinder head bolts with sealer and install bolts finger tight. Torque cylinder head bolts to specification in sequence shown in **Figs. 4 and 5.**

INTAKE MANIFOLD

REPLACE

1982–86

1. Disconnect battery ground cable.
2. Remove air cleaner, then drain engine coolant.
3. Disconnect vacuum lines and electrical connectors, as required.
4. Remove idler pulley.
5. Remove power steering belt and power steering pump, as required.
6. Disconnect fuel lines, then the TBI linkage.
7. Remove TBI assembly, then the distributor.
8. Remove intake manifold attaching nuts and bolts, then the intake manifold.
9. Disconnect heater hose and condenser from bottom of intake manifold.
10. Reverse procedure to install.

1987–88

1. Disconnect battery ground cable.
2. Remove TBI cover, then drain engine coolant.
3. Disconnect vacuum lines and electrical connectors, as required.
4. Disconnect fuel lines, then the TBI linkage.
5. Remove TBI assembly.
6. Remove power steering pump and position aside.
7. Raise and support vehicle.
8. Remove accelerator and TV cables and bracket.
9. Remove hose at bottom of intake manifold, then lower vehicle.
10. Remove intake manifold attaching nuts and bolts, then the intake manifold.
11. Reverse procedure to install.

ROCKER ARM STUDS

Rocker arm studs that have stress cracks or damaged threads can be replaced. If threads in cylinder head are damaged or stripped, the head can be retapped and a helical type insert added. When installing a new rocker arm stud, torque stud to 43-49 ft. lbs.

VALVE CLEARANCE SPECIFICATIONS

Refer to "Valves, Adjust" procedure.

VALVES

ADJUST

1. Crank engine until mark on crankshaft pulley is aligned with TDC mark on timing tab. Check to ensure engine is in the No. 1 cylinder firing position by placing fingers on No. 1 cylinder rocker arms as mark on pulley comes near TDC mark on timing tab. If valves are not moving, the engine is in the No. 1 firing position. If valves move as pulley

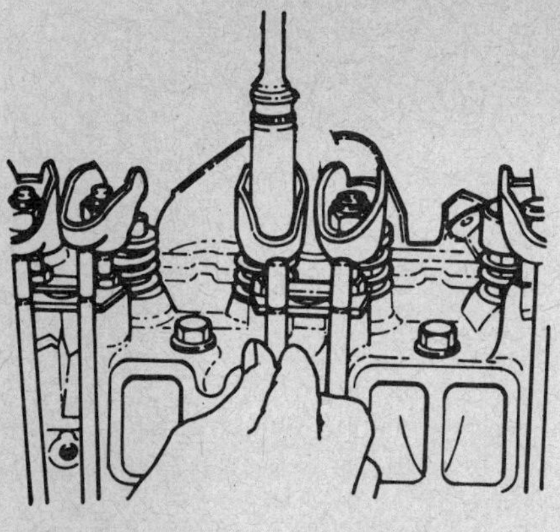

Fig. 7 Valve adjustment

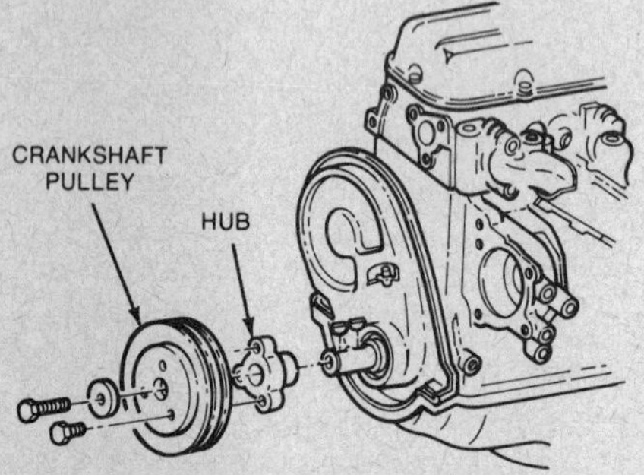

Fig. 10 Removing crankshaft pulley & hub

nears TDC mark on timing tab, engine is in No. 4 cylinder firing position and should be rotated one revolution to reach the No. 1 cylinder firing position. **The crankshaft pulley contains two sets of marks 180° apart. Use those marks which cut across entire length of pulley to find No. 1 cylinder firing position, Fig. 6.**

2. With engine in No. 1 cylinder firing position, adjust the following valves: Exhaust: 1, 3; Intake: 1, 2. To adjust valves, back off adjusting nut until lash is felt at pushrod, then tighten adjusting nut until all lash is removed, **Fig. 7.** This can be determined by rotating the pushrod while tightening the adjusting nut. When all lash has been eliminated, the pushrod will no longer rotate, **Fig. 8.** After all lash is eliminated, tighten adjusting nut an additional 1 1/2 turns.
3. Crank engine one full revolution until mark on crankshaft pulley and TDC mark are again aligned. This is the No. 4 cylinder firing position. With engine in this position, the following valves can be adjusted: Exhaust 2, 4; Intake 3, 4.
4. Install rocker arm cover, then start engine and check timing and idle speed.

VALVE ARRANGEMENT

FRONT TO REAR

4-112 & 4-121 . . . . E-I-I-E-E-I-I-E

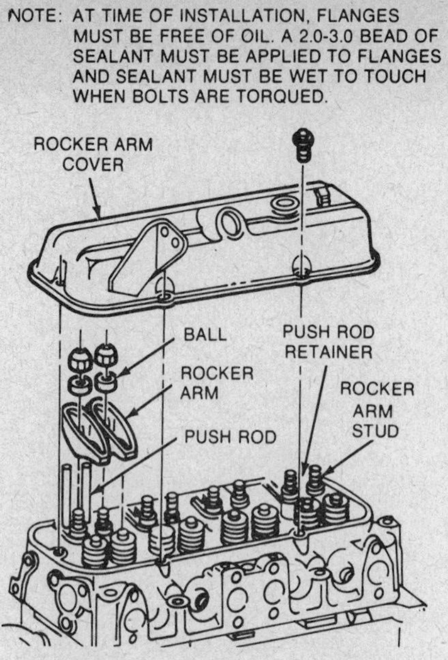

Fig. 8 Rocker arms & rocker arm cover

CAM LIFT SPECIFICATIONS

Engine	Year	Int.	Exh.
4-112 & 4-121	1982	.260	.260
4-121	1983-88	.260	.260

VALVE TIMING

INTAKE OPENS BEFORE TDC

Year	Engine	Degrees
1982	4-112 & 4-121	32

VALVE GUIDES

Valve guides are an integral part of the cylinder head and are not removable. If valve stem clearance becomes excessive, the valve guide should be reamed to the next oversize and the appropriate oversize valves installed. Valves are available in .003, .006, and .012 inch oversizes.

VALVE LIFTERS

REPLACE

Some 4-121 engines have been manufactured with 0.26 mm oversize lifter bores. An oversize lifter bore can be identified by a vertical stripe of white paint on both sides of the lifter bore inside the lifter cavity. In addition, these engines can also be identified buy a .26 OS stamp on the top right front cylinder block machining pad.

1. Remove rocker arm cover attaching bolts and rocker arm cover, **Fig. 8.**
2. Loosen rocker arm stud nut and rotate rocker arm so that pushrod can be removed. Remove pushrod.

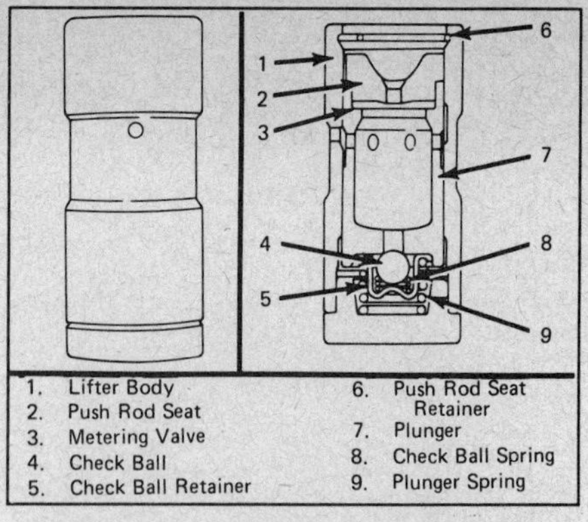

Fig. 9 Sectional view of hydraulic valve lifter

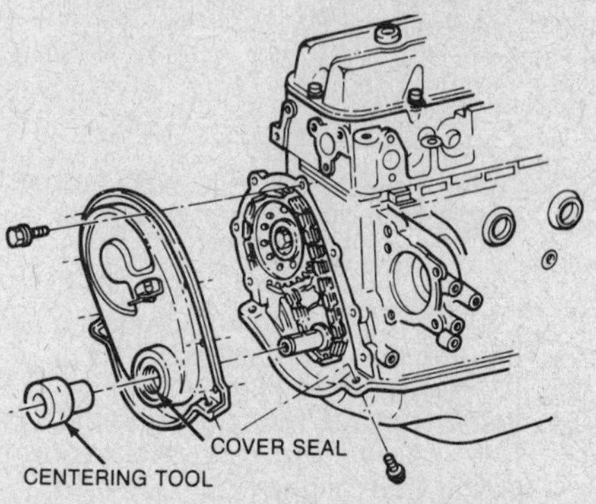

Fig. 11 Installing front cover

3. Using tool J-29834, remove valve lifter from lifter bore.
4. Coat base of new lifter, **Fig. 9,** with Molykote, or equivalent, and install lifter into lifter bore.
5. Reverse procedure to install and adjust valves as outlined under "Valves, Adjust" procedure.

ENGINE FRONT COVER

REPLACE

1. Disconnect battery ground cable.
2. Remove accessory drive belts, then raise and support vehicle.
3. Remove right front wheel and tire.
4. Remove right inner fender splash shield attaching bolts and the shield.
5. Remove A/C drive belt, if equipped.
6. Remove crankshaft pulley retaining bolts and crankshaft pulley, **Fig. 10.**
7. Using tool J-24420, remove crankshaft hub from crankshaft.
8. Remove engine front cover retaining bolts and front cover.
9. Clean sealing surface of front cover and engine block. Apply a 2 mm bead of RTV sealant to front cover sealing surface.
10. Position front cover to engine block. Using centering tool J-23042, install front retaining bolts and torque bolts to 6-9 ft. lbs. Remove centering tool, **Fig. 11.**
11. Reverse procedure to install.

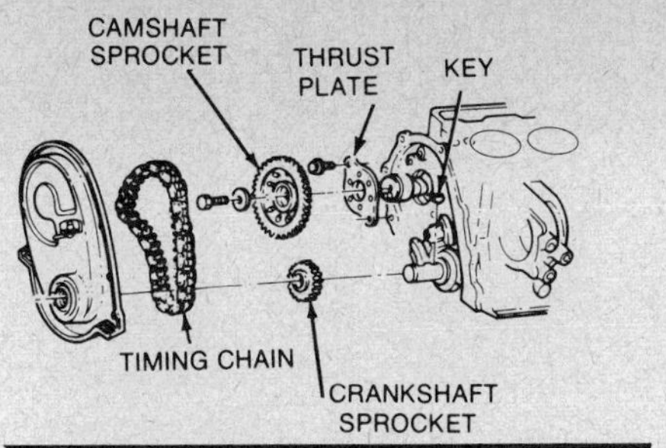

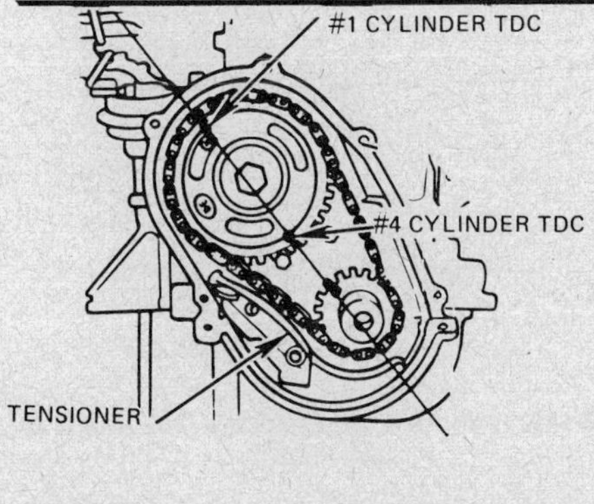

Fig. 12 Valve timing marks

TIMING CHAIN REPLACE

1. Remove engine front cover as previously described.
2. Place No. 1 cylinder at TDC and align timing marks on crankshaft and camshaft sprockets, **Fig. 12.**
3. On 1982 models, remove timing chain upper attaching bolts, then loosen nut as far as possible without removing. On 1983-88 models, remove timing chain tensioner as described under "Timing Chain Tensioner, Replace."
4. Remove camshaft sprocket retaining bolt. Tap lower edge of sprocket with plastic mallet and remove sprocket and timing chain.
5. If crankshaft sprocket is to be replaced, remove sprocket using a suitable puller.
6. To install crankshaft sprocket, align keyway on sprocket with key on crankshaft.
7. Align timing marks, **Fig. 12,** and install timing chain on sprockets.
8. Align dowel on camshaft with dowel hole on camshaft sprocket, then install sprocket to camshaft, using retaining bolt to draw sprocket fully to camshaft. Torque bolt to 66-85 ft. lbs.
9. Lubricate timing chain with engine oil, then install timing chain tensioner.
10. Install engine front cover as outlined previously.

TIMING CHAIN TENSIONER REPLACE

1982 4-112 & 4-121

1. Remove engine front cover as described under "Engine Front Cover, Replace."

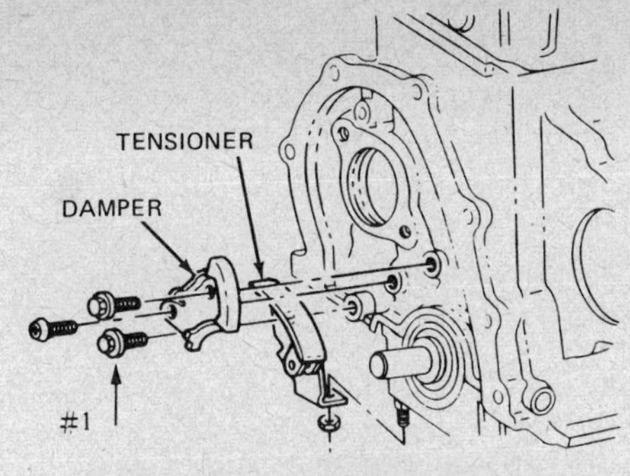

Fig. 13 Timing chain tensioner. 1982 4-112 & 4-121

2. Remove attaching bolt (1), **Fig. 13,** and lower nut. **Use a suitable tool, such as a loop of wire, to prevent nut from falling into oil pan.**
3. Remove timing chain tensioner.
4. Position timing chain tensioner to engine.
5. Using a suitable tool, such as a wire loop around nut, position nut on stud.
6. Install bolt (1), **Fig. 13,** finger tight.
7. Torque nut to 15 to 22 ft. lbs. and bolt to 13 to 18 ft. lbs.

1983–84 4-121

1. Remove engine front cover as described under "Engine Front Cover, Replace."
2. Remove tensioner attaching bolts, then remove tensioner.
3. Position tangs of tool No. J33875 under tensioner sliding blocks, then pull tool to compress tensioner spring.
4. While compressing tensioner spring, insert a cotter pin or other suitable tool into hole (A), **Fig. 14,** to hold spring in the compressed position, then remove tool No. J33875.
5. Position tensioner to engine, then install attaching bolts and remove cotter pin holding tensioner spring in the compressed position.

1985–88 4-121

1. Remove front cover as described previously.
2. Remove attaching bolts.
3. Remove tensioner and damper.
4. Compress spring in direction of arrow, **Fig. 15.**
5. While compressing spring, use a cotter pin and insert into hole A shown.
6. Install chain tensioner.
7. Remove cotter pin from tensioner.

CAMSHAFT REPLACE

1. Remove engine from vehicle as previously described.
2. Remove valve lifters and engine front cover as described previously.
3. Mark position of rotor to distributor body, then remove distributor from engine.
4. Remove fuel pump and fuel pump pushrod from engine block.
5. Remove timing chain and camshaft sprocket as previously described.

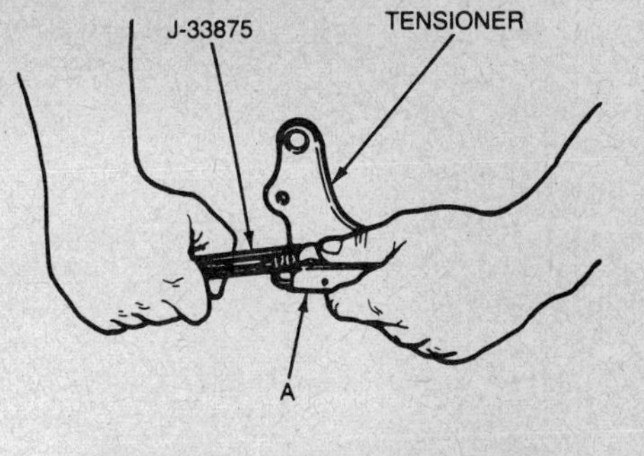

Fig. 14 Compressing timing chain tensioner spring. 1983–84 4-121

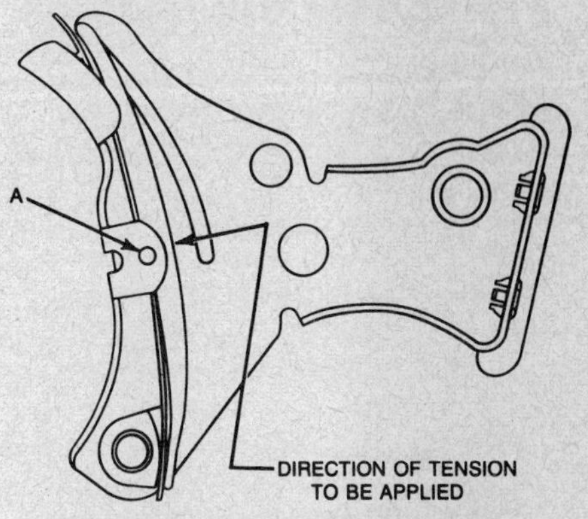

Fig. 15 Compressing timing chain tensioner spring. 1985–88 4-121

6. Remove camshaft thrust plate to engine block retaining bolts and the thrust plate, **Fig. 12.**
7. Remove camshaft from engine block.
8. Reverse removal procedure to install. When installing camshaft, align crankshaft and camshaft sprocket timing marks, **Fig. 12.**

PISTON & ROD ASSEMBLE

Install piston to rod with notch or arrow and hole on piston facing toward front of engine and rod bearing tang slot opposite camshaft, **Figs. 16 and 17.** Upon installation, measure the connecting rod side clearance using a suitable feeler gauge. Measurement taken should be as follows:

Engine	Year	Clearance In Inch
4-112	1982	.004-.024
4-121	1982-88	.004-.024

PISTONS, PINS, & RINGS

Pistons and rings are available in standard and oversizes of .020 and .040 inch. Oversize piston pins are not available due to the press fit design.

MAIN & ROD BEARINGS

When removing No. 1 main bearing cap, it will be necessary to remove the timing

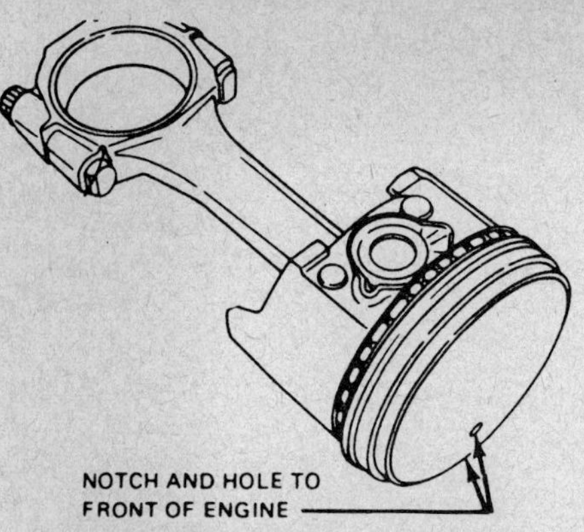

Fig. 16 Piston & rod assembly. Exc. 1985–86

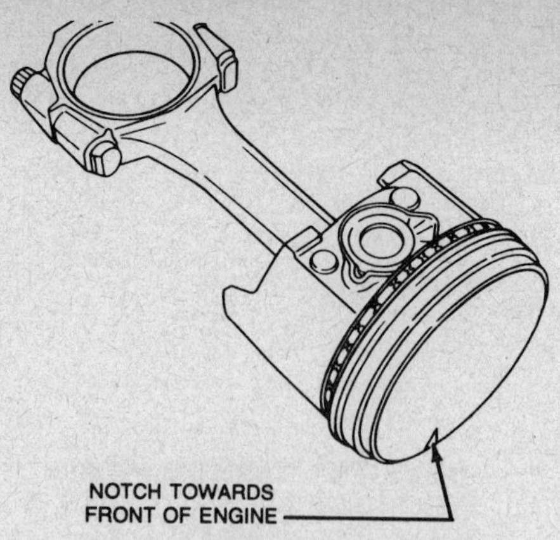

Fig. 17 Piston & rod assembly. 1985–88

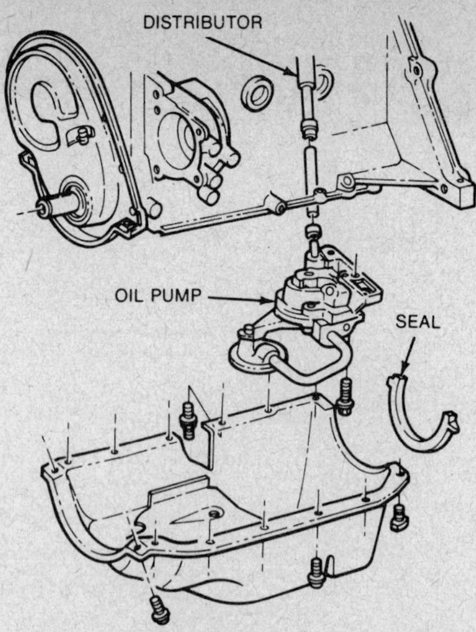

Fig. 18 Removing oil pan & pump

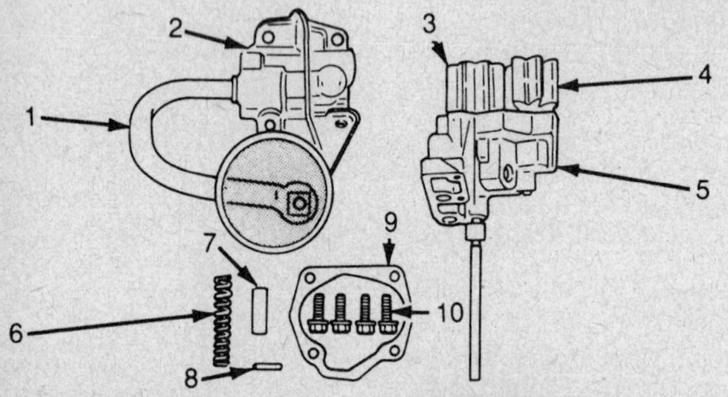

1. PICK UP TUBE AND SCREEN.
2. PUMP COVER.
3. DRIVE GEAR AND SHAFT.
4. IDLER GEAR.
5. PUMP BODY.
6. PRESSURE REGULATOR SPRING.
7. PRESSURE REGULATOR VALVE.
8. RETAINING PIN.
9. GASKET.
10. ATTACHING BOLTS.

Fig. 19 Sectional view of oil pump assembly

chain tensioner, refer to Timing Chain Tensioner, Replace.

Main bearings are available in standard size and undersizes of .0013 inch, and connecting rod bearings are available in standard size and undersizes of .0010 inch.

OIL PAN

REPLACE

1. Disconnect battery ground cable, then remove exhaust pipe shield.
2. Raise and support front of vehicle, then drain crankcase.
3. Disconnect exhaust pipe at exhaust manifold.
4. Detach A/C compressor brace at starter motor and A/C compressor bracket, as required.
5. Remove flywheel cover and starter motor bracket, then remove starter motor and position aside.
6. Remove A/C compressor mounting bracket, as required.
7. Remove four righthand suspension support bolts, then lower suspension support slightly to provide clearance for oil pan removal.
8. On models equipped with auto. transaxle, remove oil filter adapter.
9. Remove oil pan attaching bolts and oil pan.
10. Reverse procedure to install. Before installing oil pan, apply a thin coat of RTV sealer to both ends of oil pan rear seal, then seat seal firmly into rear main bearing cap. Do not allow sealer to extend beyond oil pan rear seal tabs. Apply a continuous 2 mm bead of RTV sealer along oil pan side rails in line with bolt holes, circling inward around each bolt hole location. Also apply RTV sealer to oil pan surface which contacts engine front cover. This bead of sealer must meet the bead at each oil pan side rail. Do not apply any RTV sealer to oil pan rear seal mating surface. Carefully install oil pan and torque attaching bolts alternately and evenly to 6 to 9 ft. lbs., then to a final torque of 13 to 18 ft. lbs. Torque attaching bolts while RTV sealer is still wet to touch.

OIL PUMP SERVICE

REMOVAL

1. Drain crankcase, then remove oil pan as previously described.
2. Remove pump to rear main bearing attaching bolt, then remove pump, extension shaft and retainer, **Fig. 18.**

DISASSEMBLE

1. Remove four pump cover to body attaching bolts, then remove cover, idler and drive gears and shaft, **Fig. 19. Place align mark on oil pump drive and idler gear teeth so they can be installed in the same position.**
2. Remove pressure regulator valve retaining pin, spring and the valve from pump body.

INSPECTION

Inspect pump components and should any of the following conditions exist, the oil pump assembly should be replaced.

1. Inspect pump body, gears and cover for cracks or excessive wear.
2. Check drive gear shaft for looseness in housing.
3. Check inside of pump cover for wear that would allow oil to leak past ends of gears.
4. Check oil pickup screen assembly for damage to screen or pickup tube.
5. Check pressure regulator valve for fit in pump body.

ASSEMBLE

1. Install a replacement pickup screen and tube assembly, if removed. Position pump in a soft jawed vise, then apply sealer to end of tube and tap into position using tool No. J8369 and a plastic hammer. Use care not to damage inlet screen and tube assembly when installing on pump housing.
2. Place pressure regulator valve, spring and retaining pin into pump body, then install drive gear and shaft.

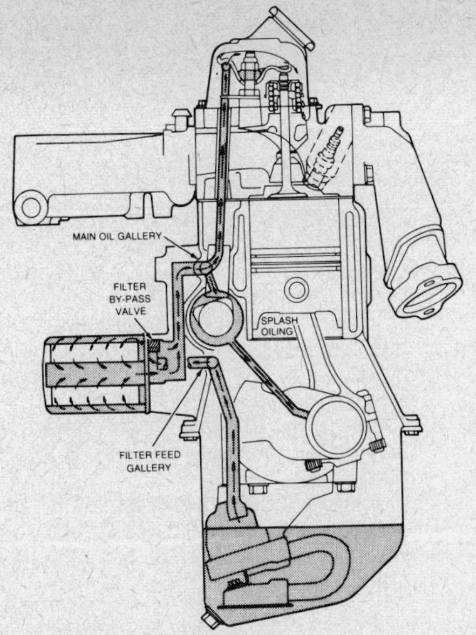

Typical engine oiling system

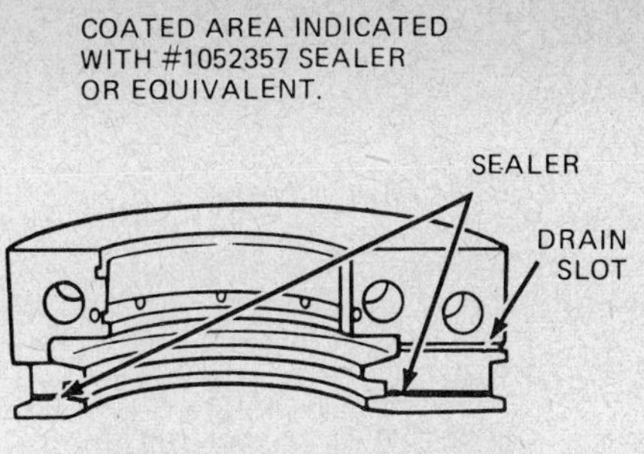

Fig. 20 Replacing crankshaft rear main bearing oil seal

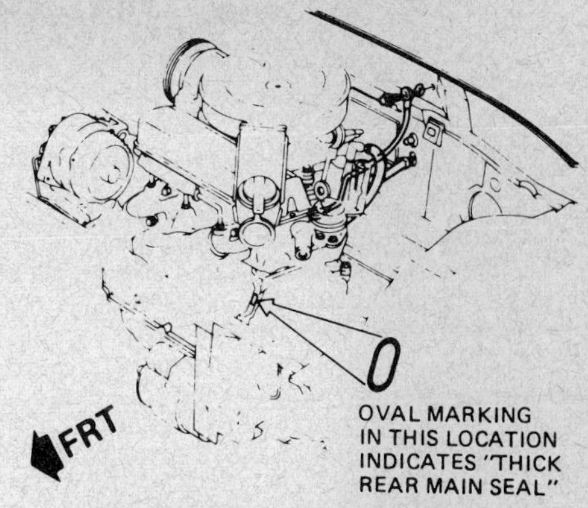

Fig. 21 Thick seal identification mark location. 1984 4-121

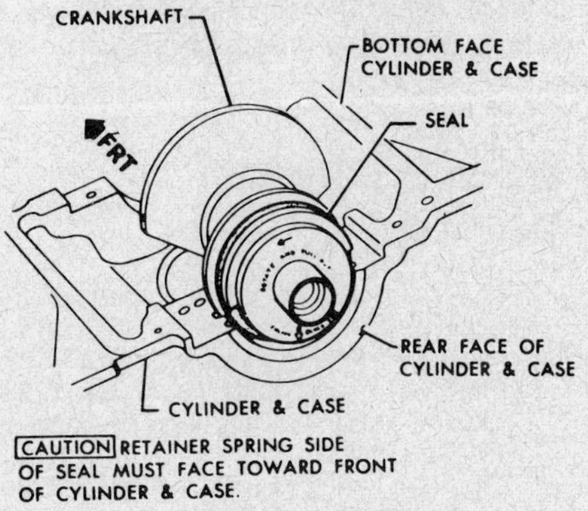

Fig. 22 Installing thin seal. 4-121

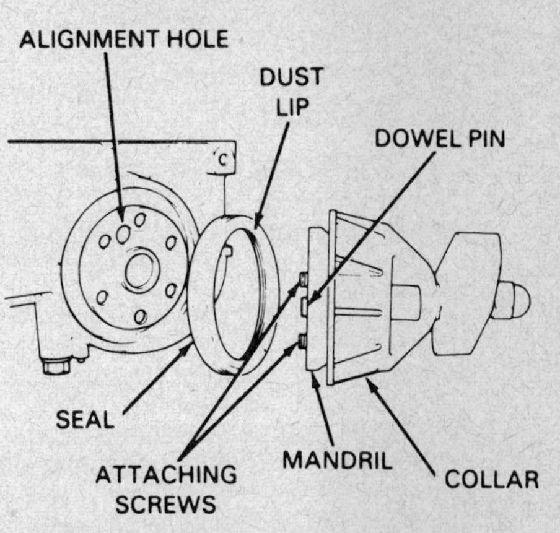

Fig. 23 Installing thick seal. 4-121

3. Install idler gear into pump body, then the pump cover gasket. **Fig. 19.**
4. Install pump cover and cover retaining bolts, then torque bolts to 6-9 ft. lbs.

INSTALLATION

1. Align oil pump extension shaft to distributor drive gear socket and pump housing with dowels on cap, then install shaft retainer and pump assembly.
2. Install oil pump assembly retaining bolt to rear main bearing cap and torque bolt to 26-35 ft. lbs.
3. Install oil pan as previously described.

REAR MAIN BEARING OIL SEAL

REPLACE

4-112

4-112 engines use a rope type rear main bearing oil seal. When service replacement of seal is indicated, a new rubber split seal, Part No. 14069889, should be used. Refer to procedure below when replacing rope type seal with rubber split design.

1. Remove oil pan and oil pump as described previously.
2. Remove rear main bearing cap.
3. Remove upper and lower seal, then clean seal channel of oil. **Loosening No. 2, 3 & 4 main bearing caps may be helpful when removing and replacing upper seal.**
4. Apply a thin coat of sealing compound 1050026, or equivalent, to outer diameter of upper seal. Roll seal into position in block, turning crankshaft to ease installation.
5. Apply sealer to lower seal as described above, and position into main bearing cap.
6. Position a piece of Plastigage onto main journal or bearing, install main bearing cap and torque to specifications.
7. Remove bearing cap and measure Plastigage for proper bearing clearance. If clearance is not within specifications, correct as necessary.
8. Clean Plastigage from journal and bearing, then lubricate bearing lightly.
9. Apply a 1 mm bead of sealant 1052357 or equivalent to the bearing cap between the rear main seal end and the oil pan rear seal groove as shown, **Fig. 20.** Keep sealant off main seal and out of drain slot in bearing cap.
10. Apply light coat of engine oil to crankshaft to seal contact surface.
11. Install rear main bearing cap, then torque all bolts to specifications.
12. Install oil pump and oil pan, then start engine and check for leaks.

A new 1-piece rear crankshaft oil seal is available to replace the 2-piece seal previously used on 1983 and some 1984 engines. Some 1984 and all 1985-88 engines are assembled with the 1-piece seal. The new seal should be used on early models if replacement is necessary. Before replacing a rear oil seal, make absolutely sure it is the exact source of leakage. On 1984 models, once it has been determined that the seal must be replaced, it is necessary to determine the type of seal (thin or thick) installed in the engine, Fig. 21. Refer to the appropriate following procedures.

THIN SEAL

1. Drain coolant and oil from engine.
2. Remove engine and mount on engine stand in inverted position. Remove oil pan and pump.
3. Remove timing chain cover, then lock chain tensioner with pin.
4. Rotate crankshaft so crankshaft and camshaft sprocket timing marks line up.
5. Remove camshaft sprocket and timing chain.
6. Rotate crankshaft to horizontal position.
7. Remove connecting rod caps and bearings, taking care not to mix caps and bearings.
8. Remove main bearing caps and bearings, taking care not to mix caps and bearings.
9. Remove crankshaft.
10. Remove old oil seal and clean sealant from grooves in block and cap.
11. Using solvent, clean crankshaft seal area to remove excess solvent, taking care not to damage surface.
12. Inspect sealing and mating surfaces and crankshaft journal, checking for nicks, scratches, or machining defects.
13. Apply a 1 mm bead of anaerobic sealant 1052357 or equivalent to outside circumference of seal.

14. Place seal and tool assembly on rear of crankshaft.
15. Position seal tool so arrow points toward engine block, **Fig. 22.**
16. Position crankshaft in engine block with seal tool in place.
17. Remove seal tool and discard.
18. Lightly oil crankshaft journals.
19. Apply sealant 1052357 or equivalent to rear journal mating surfaces and install main bearing and cap.
20. Install remaining bearings and caps. Torque cap bolts to 63-75 ft. lbs.
21. Install connecting rod bearings and caps. Torque cap bolts to 34-40 ft. lbs.
22. Install oil pump, making sure that mating surface is clean. Torque oil pump to 26-35 ft. lbs.
23. Align crankshaft sprocket timing mark and install camshaft sprocket and timing chain. Torque sprocket bolt to 66-84 ft. lbs.
24. Clean, seal and install oil pan.

THICK SEAL

Some 1984 and all 1985-88 models use the thick seal.

1. Support engine and remove transaxle.
2. Remove flywheel and check that rear seal is leaking.
3. Remove seal by carefully inserting screwdriver in through dust lip and prying towards end of crankshaft pilot. Repeat as necessary around circumference of seal until seal is removed, taking care not to damage crankshaft circumference.
4. Check inside of seal bore for nicks or burrs and correct as necessary. Inspect crankshaft for burrs or nicks on seal contact surface. Repair or replace crankshaft as necessary.
5. Install new seal using tool J-34686.
6. Place seal on mandrel, making sure that dust lip on seal bottoms squarely against collar of tool, **Fig. 23.**
7. After aligning dowel pin with dowel pin hole in crankshaft, attach tool to crankshaft and torque screws to 2-5 ft. lbs.
8. Turn T-handle of tool until collar is tight against engine block to ensure that seal is seated properly in block.
9. Loosen T-handle of tool until it comes to a stop. Remove attaching screws.
10. Check that seal is seated squarely in bore.
11. Install flywheel and engine.
12. Start engine and check for leaks.

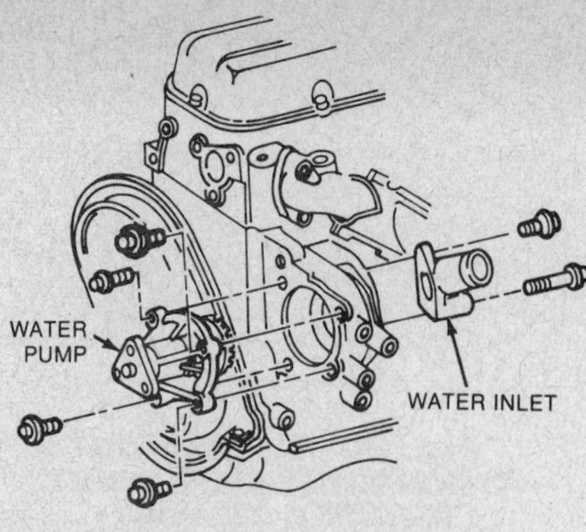

Fig. 24 Replacing water pump assembly

WATER PUMP REPLACE

1. Disconnect battery ground cable and drain cooling system.
2. Remove accessory drive belts.
3. Remove alternator to alternator bracket retaining bolts and position alternator aside.
4. Remove water pump pulley to water pump attaching bolts, then the pulley from water pump.
5. Remove four water pump to block attaching bolts and the water pump, **Fig. 24.**
6. Clean sealing surfaces of pump and engine block and place a 1/8 inch bead of sealant 1052289, or equivalent, to sealing surfaces. Install pump. Coat threaded area of pump bolts with sealant 1052080, install torque bolts to 13-18 ft. lbs.
7. Reverse removal procedures to complete installation.

BELT TENSION DATA

Belt	New Lbs.	Used Lbs.
Air Cond.	168②	90①
Alternator	145②	70①
Power Steer.	145②	70①
Air Pump	145②	70①

①—Minimum.
②—Maximum.

FUEL PUMP REPLACE

MECHANICAL PUMP

1. Disconnect battery ground cable.
2. Raise and support vehicle.
3. Disconnect inlet hose and outlet pipe from fuel pump.
4. Remove two fuel pump retaining nuts and rotate pump upward to clear studs in block. Remove fuel pump from vehicle.
5. Clean block to pump mating surface and install new gasket over studs in block.
6. Install pump and pump retaining nuts and torque nuts to 15-22 ft. lbs.
7. Reverse procedure to complete installation.

ELECTRIC PUMP

1. Relieve system fuel pressure as follows:
   a. Remove fuel pump fuse from fuse block.
   b. Start engine and allow to run until fuel supply remaining in pipes is consumed, then crank starter an additional 3 seconds to relieve remaining pressure.
   c. With ignition switch in Off position, install fuse.
2. Disconnect battery ground cable, then raise and support vehicle.
3. Drain tank, then disconnect sending unit electrical connector and ground strap.
4. Disconnect all hoses and vent pipes at fuel tank.
5. Support fuel tank using a suitable jack, then remove tank retaining straps.
6. Lower fuel tank from vehicle.
7. Remove fuel tank sending unit and pump assembly by turning cam lock ring counterclockwise.
8. Lift assembly from tank, then disconnect pump from sending unit.
9. Reverse procedure to install.

V6-173 (2.8L) Engine Section

INDEX

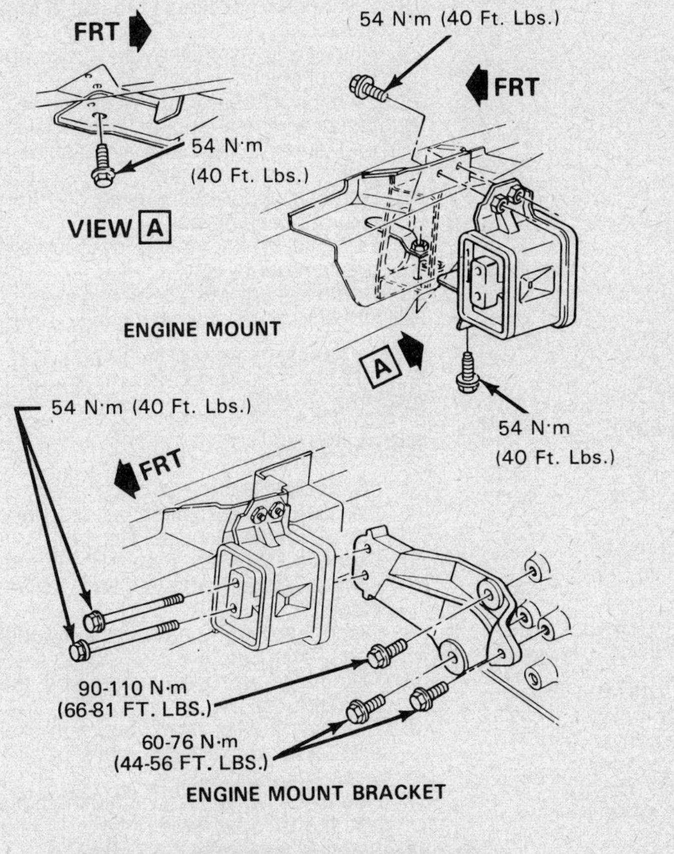

Fig. 1 Front engine mount

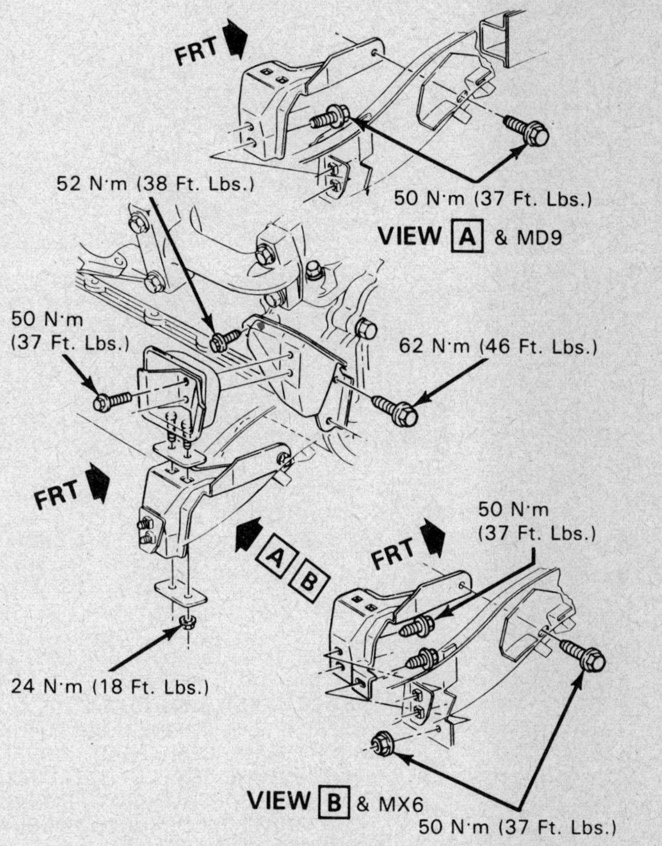

Fig. 2 Rear engine mount

ENGINE MOUNTS REPLACE

FRONT MOUNT

1. Disconnect battery ground cable.
2. Remove engine mount nuts, then raise and support vehicle.
3. Support engine with suitable jack.
4. Remove inner fender shield.
5. Remove and discard engine mount bolts, **Fig. 1.**
6. Remove engine mount from vehicle.
7. Reverse procedure to install, using new engine mount bolts. Remove alignment bolt. **If excessive force is required to remove alignment bolt, loosen transaxle adjusting bolts to align power train components.**

REAR MOUNT

1. Disconnect battery ground cable, then raise and support vehicle.
2. Support engine with suitable jack.
3. Remove motor mount nuts and attaching bolts, **Fig. 2.**
4. Reverse procedure to install.

ENGINE REPLACE

1. Disconnect battery ground cable and drain cooling system.
2. Remove air cleaner and the mass air flow meter.
3. Remove exhaust crossover heat shield and the exhaust crcssover pipe.
4. Remove accessory drive belt and the tensioner.
5. Remove power steering pump mount-

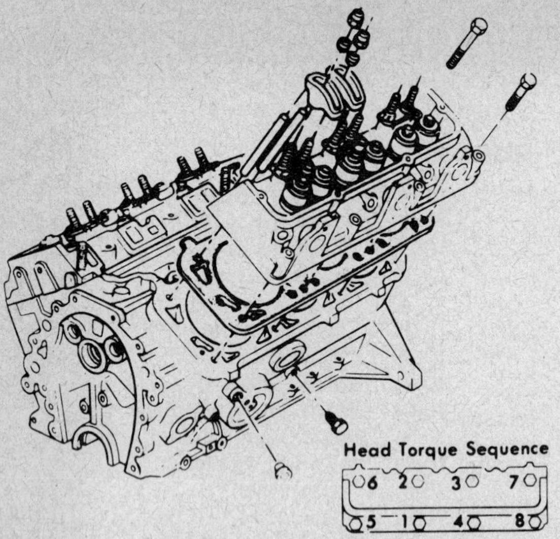

Fig. 3 Installing cylinder head

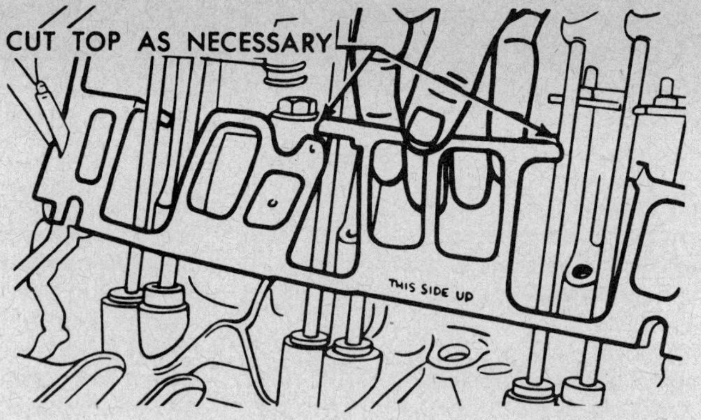

Fig. 4 Installing intake manifold gasket

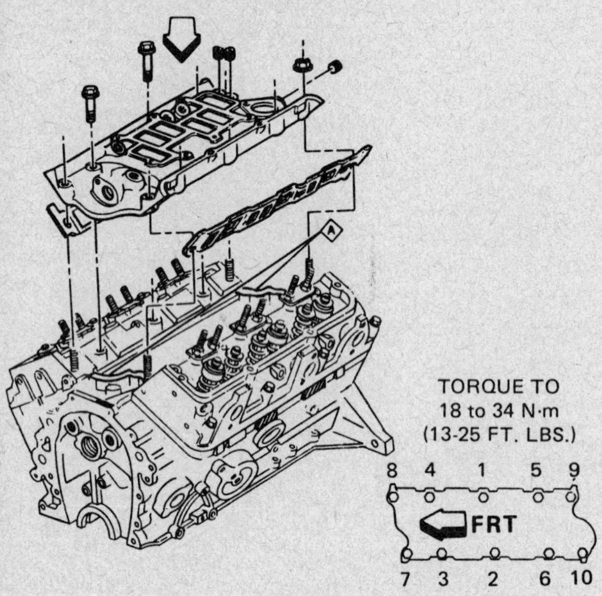

INLET MANIFOLD BOLT/SCREW & NUT TIGHTENING SEQUENCE

(A) NOTE APPLY A SMOOTH CONTINUOUS BEAD APPROX. 2.0-3.0 WIDE AND 3.0-5.0 THICK ON BOTH SURFACES. BEAD CONFIGURATION MUST INSURE COMPLETE SEALING OF WATER AND OIL. SURFACE MUST BE FREE OF OIL AND DIRT TO INSURE ADEQUATE SEAL.

Fig. 5 Installing intake manifold

ing bracket and disconnect heater pipe at power steering pump mounting bracket.
6. Disconnect radiator hose at engine.
7. Disconnect accelerator and T.V. cables at throttle valve.
8. Remove alternator and disconnect wiring harness at engine.
9. Disconnect fuel hoses and the coolant bypass and overflow hoses at engine.
10. Disconnect canister purge hose at canister and remove vacuum hoses as necessary.
11. Raise and support vehicle, then remove right inner fender splash shield.
12. Remove harmonic balance and the flywheel cover.
13. Remove starter attaching bolts, disconnect electrical connectors at starter and remove starter.
14. Disconnect electrical connector at oil sending unit.
15. Remove A/C compressor and its mounting bracket(s).
16. Disconnect exhaust pipe at rear of manifold.
17. Remove flex plate to torque converter attaching bolts and the transaxle to engine brace bolts.
18. Remove engine rear mount to frame nuts.
19. Disconnect shift cable bracket at transaxle.
20. Remove lower bellhousing bolts and lower vehicle.
21. Disconnect heater hoses at engine.
22. Install suitable engine lifting device and support transaxle with suitable jack.
23. Remove upper bellhousing and front mount attaching bolts.
24. Remove brake master cylinder and position out of way.
25. Remove engine from vehicle.
26. Reverse procedure to install.

CYLINDER HEAD REPLACE

REMOVAL

1. Disconnect battery ground cable.
2. Remove intake manifold as described under "Intake Manifold, Replace."
3. Remove exhaust manifold as described under "Exhaust Manifold, Replace."
4. Disconnect wiring harness at cylinder head.
5. Remove spark plug wires and the spark plugs.
6. Remove rocker arm covers, rocker arm nuts, rocker arm balls, rocker arms and pushrods.
7. Remove cylinder head attaching bolts and the cylinder head.

INSTALLATION

Gasket surfaces on cylinder head and case must be clean and free of nicks or heavy scratches. Cylinder bolt threads in case and threads on cylinder head bolts must be clean to obtain true torque.

1. Place gasket in position over dowel pins with note "This Side Up" showing and install cylinder head.
2. Coat cylinder head bolt threads with suitable sealant and install bolts.
3. Torque bolts in proper sequence, **Fig. 3.**
4. Install pushrods and loosely retain with rocker arms, ensuring lower ends of pushrods are in lifter seats.

5. Install spark plugs and wires.
6. Install intake and exhaust manifolds, then adjust valves as necessary.

INTAKE MANIFOLD
REPLACE

1. Disconnect battery ground cable.
2. Disconnect accelerator and T.V. cable bracket at plenum.
3. Disconnect throttle body at plenum.
4. Disconnect E.G.R. pipe at E.G.R. valve, then remove plenum.
5. Disconnect fuel inlet and return pipes at fuel rail.
6. Disconnect serpentine belt, then remove power steering pump mounting bracket.
7. Disconnect heater pipe at power steering pump bracket.
8. Disconnect electrical connectors at alternator and remove alternator.
9. Disconnect electrical connector at cold start injector and remove injector.
10. Disconnect idle air vacuum hose at throttle body and the electrical connectors at injectors.
11. Remove fuel rail, breather tube and the runners.
12. Disconnect coil wires at bracket.
13. Remove both rocker arm covers and drain cooling system.
14. Disconnect radiator hose at thermostat outlet and the heater pipe at thermostat housing.
15. Disconnect electrical connectors at thermostat housing.
16. Remove distributor, thermostat housing, intake manifold attaching bolts and the intake manifold.
17. Reverse procedure to install, noting the following:
    a. When installing gaskets, install only on right or left side as marked.
    b. Clean cylinder case sealing surface front and rear ridges and apply a 3/16 inch bead of suitable sealant on each ridge.
    c. Install new intake gaskets on cylinder heads, holding in place by extending ridge sealant bead up 6 mm onto onto gasket ends. On 1982-86 models new intake gaskets will have to be cut where indicated, **Fig. 4,** to install behind push rods. Cut only those areas that are necessary.
    d. When installing intake manifold, ensure areas between case ridges and manifold are completely sealed.
    e. On 1982-86 models, install manifold retaining bolts and nuts, torquing in proper sequence, **Fig. 5.** On 1987-88 models, torque manifold retaining bolts and nuts to specifications.
    f. After completing installation, start engine and set initial timing, torque distributor hold-down clamp bolt to 25 ft. lbs. and recheck timing.

EXHAUST MANIFOLD
REPLACE
LEFT SIDE

1. Disconnect battery ground cable and remove air cleaner.
2. Remove mass air flow sensor and the heat shield.
3. Disconnect crossover pipe at manifold, then remove manifold attaching bolts and the manifold.
4. Reverse procedure to install, torquing bolts to 25 ft. lbs.

RIGHT SIDE

1. Disconnect battery ground cable and remove air cleaner.
2. Remove mass air flow sensor and the heat shield.
3. Disconnect crossover pipe at manifold.
4. Disconnect accelerator and T.V. cable at throttle lever.
5. Remove accelerator and T.V. cable bracket at plenum and position out of way.
6. Disconnect power steering line at pump.
7. Remove E.G.R. valve and related parts.
8. Raise and support vehicle.
9. Disconnect exhaust pipe at exhaust manifold, then lower vehicle.
10. Remove manifold attaching bolts and the manifold.
11. Reverse procedure to install.

VALVE CLEARANCE SPECIFICATIONS

Refer to "Valves, Adjust" procedure.

VALVES
ADJUST

1. Remove rocker arm covers.
2. Crank engine until mark on torsional damper lines up with O mark on timing tab. The engine should also be in the No. 1 firing position. This can be determined by placing fingers on No. 1 rocker arms as mark on damper approaches O mark.
3. If valves are not moving, engine is in No. 1 firing position. If valves move as the mark comes up to the timing tab, engine is in No. 4 firing position and should be rotated one revolution to reach No. 1 position.
4. With engine in No. 1 firing position, adjust exhaust valves 1, 2 and 3 and intake valves 1, 5 and 6, as follows:
    a. Back out adjusting nut until lash is felt at pushrod, then turn in adjusting nut until all lash is removed.
    b. When lash has been removed, turn adjusting nut in additional 1 1/2 turns to center lifter plunger.
5. Crank engine one revolution until timing tab O mark and torsional damper mark are again in alignment.
6. With the engine in this, the No. 4 firing position. adjust exhaust valves 4, 5 and 6 and intake valves 2, 3 and 4 as previously described.
7. Install rocker arm covers, then start engine and check timing and idle speed.

VALVE ARRANGEMENT
FRONT TO REAR

Right .... E-I-E-I-I-E
Left.......................... E-I-I-E-I-E

CAM LIFT SPECIFICATIONS

Engine	Int.	Exh.
V6-173	.262	.273

VALVE STEM OIL SEAL & VALVE SPRING
REPLACE
REMOVAL

1. Remove rocker arm cover, then the spark plug, rocker arm and pushrod on cylinder(s) being serviced.
2. Install air line adapter tool J-23590 or equivalent to spark plug port and apply compressed air to hold valves in place.
3. Using tool J-5892 or equivalent to compress valve spring, remove valve locks, valve caps, oil shedder and valve spring and damper.
4. Remove valve stem oil seal.

INSTALLATION

1. Set valve spring and damper around valve guide boss.
2. Install a valve stem seal over the valve stem and valve guide base-inlet only.
3. Drop an oil shedder and valve rotator over the exhaust, and a valve spring cap over the valve spring.
4. Compress spring with tool J-5892 and install oil seal in lower groove of stem, ensuring seal is flat and not twisted.
5. Install valve locks and release compressor tool, ensuring locks seat properly in upper groove of valve stem. Use suitable grease as necessary to hold locks in place while releasing compressor tool.
6. Using tool J-23994 or equivalent, apply vacuum to valve cap to ensure no air leaks past seal.
7. Install spark plug, torquing to 11 ft. lbs.
8. Install and adjust valve mechanism.

VALVE GUIDES

Valve guides are an integral part of the cylinder head and are not removable. If valve stem clearance becomes excessive, the valve guide should be reamed to the next oversize and the appropriate oversize valves installed. Valves are available in .003, .015 and .030 inch oversizes.

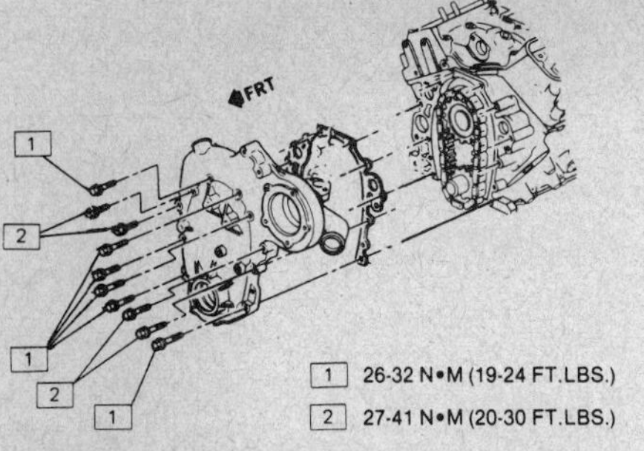

Fig. 6 Installing front cover

VALVE LIFTERS
REPLACE

1. Remove intake manifold as previously described.
2. Remove valve mechanism, then the valve lifters.
3. Install valve lifters. When installing new lifters, coat foot of valve lifters with Molykote or equivalent, ensuring lifter foot is convex.
4. Install intake manifold as previously described.
5. Install and adjust valve mechanism.

FRONT COVER
REPLACE

1. Disconnect battery ground cable and drain cooling system.
2. Disconnect M.A.P. sensor and E.G.R. solenoid.
3. Remove coolant recovery tank and the serpentine belt adjusting pulley.
4. Remove alternator and disconnect electrical connectors.
5. Remove power steering pump bracket and disconnect heater pipe at bracket.
6. Raise and support vehicle, then remove inner splash shield.
7. Remove A/C compressor belt and the flywheel cover at transaxle.
8. Using tool J-23523-1 or equivalent, remove harmonic balance.
9. Remove serpentine belt idler pulley.
10. Remove pan to front cover attaching bolts and the lower attaching bolts.
11. Lower vehicle, then disconnect radiator hose at water pump.
12. Remove heater pipe at goose neck.
13. Disconnect bypass and overflow hoses.
14. Disconnect canister purge hose.
15. Remove upper front cover attaching bolts and the front cover.
16. Reverse procedure to install, noting the following:
    a. With a clean sealing surface on both the front cover and oil pan, apply a continuous 3 mm bead of suitable sealant to oil pan surface of front cover.
    b. Torque bolts to specifications, **Fig. 6.**

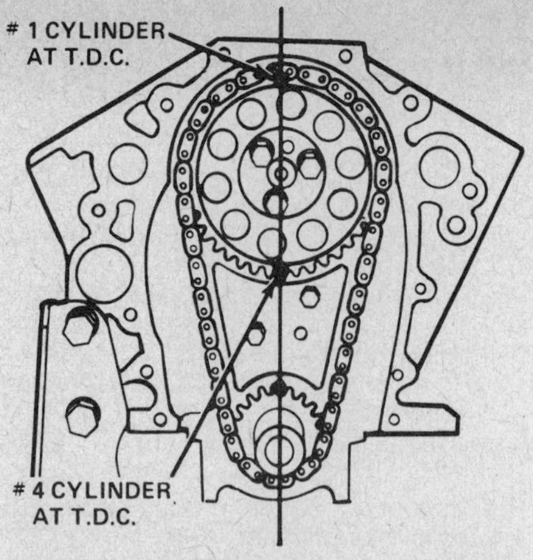

Fig. 7 Valve timing marks

FRONT COVER OIL SEAL
REPLACE

1. Remove inner splash shield and torsional damper, then pry seal from cover using a suitable screwdriver. **Use caution not to damage crankshaft surface during seal removal.**
2. Install new seal so open end faces toward inside of cover, then drive seal into position using suitable tool.

TIMING CHAIN & SPROCKET
REPLACE

1. Remove crankcase front cover, refer to "Front Cover, Replace" procedure.
2. Place No. 1 cylinder at TDC and align timing marks on crankshaft and camshaft sprockets, **Fig. 7.**
3. Remove camshaft sprocket attaching bolts. Tap lower edge of sprocket with plastic mallet and remove sprocket and timing chain.
4. Align timing marks, **Fig. 7**, and install timing chain on sprockets.
5. Align dowel on camshaft with dowel hole on camshaft sprocket, then install sprocket to camshaft, using attaching bolts to to draw sprocket fully to camshaft. Torque attaching bolts to 15-20 ft. lbs.
6. Lubricate timing chain with engine oil, then install front cover.

CAMSHAFT
REPLACE

1. Remove engine from vehicle, refer to "Engine, Replace" procedure.
2. Remove valve lifters, refer to "Valve Lifter, Replace" procedure.
3. Remove crankcase front cover, refer to "Front Cover, Replace" procedure.
4. Remove fuel pump and pushrod, then the timing chain and sprocket. Refer to "Timing Chain & Sprocket, Replace" procedure.

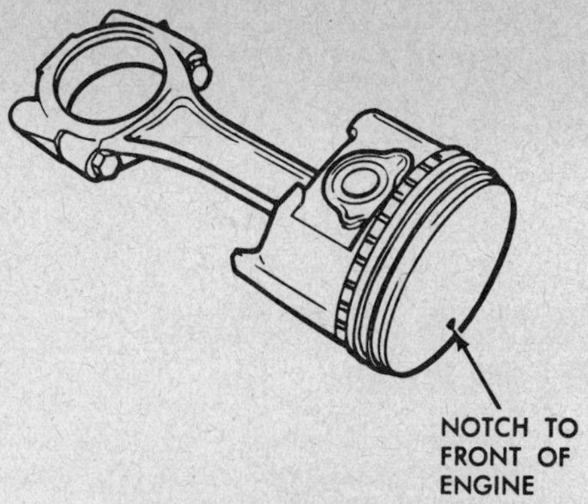

Fig. 8 Piston & rod assembly

5. Remove camshaft. **Use caution not to damage bearings during camshaft removal.**
6. Reverse procedure to install. Coat camshaft lobes with suitable grease before installation.

PISTON & ROD ASSEMBLE

There is a machined hole or cast notch in the top of all pistons. The piston assemblies should always be installed with the hole or notch toward front of engine, **Fig. 8.**

PISTONS, PINS & RINGS

Pistons and rings are available in standard and oversize. Piston pins are available in standard size only.

MAIN & ROD BEARINGS

Main and rod bearing are available in standard sizes and undersizes.

REAR MAIN BEARING OIL SEAL
REPLACE

1. Support engine, then remove transaxle assembly.
2. Remove flywheel assembly.
3. Remove oil seal as shown in **Fig. 9.** Use caution not to damage crankshaft surface with removal tool.
4. Check inside diameter of bore and crankshaft for nicks or burrs. Repair as required.
5. Apply oil to inside diameter of new seal, then install seal on mandrel of tool No. J-34686 until back of seal bottoms squarely against collar of tool, **Fig. 10.**
6. Align dowel pin of tool with dowel pin of crankshaft, then attach tool to crankshaft. Torque attaching screws to 2-5 ft. lbs.
7. Turn "T" handle of tool so collar pushes seal into bore. Ensure seal is properly seated.
8. Loosen "T" handle of tool until it comes to a stop, then remove tool attaching screws. Ensure seal is seated squarely in bore.
9. Install flywheel and transaxle assembly.

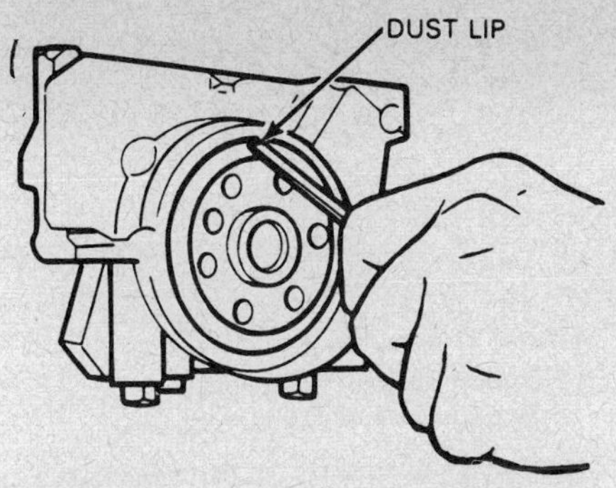

Fig. 9 Removing oil seal

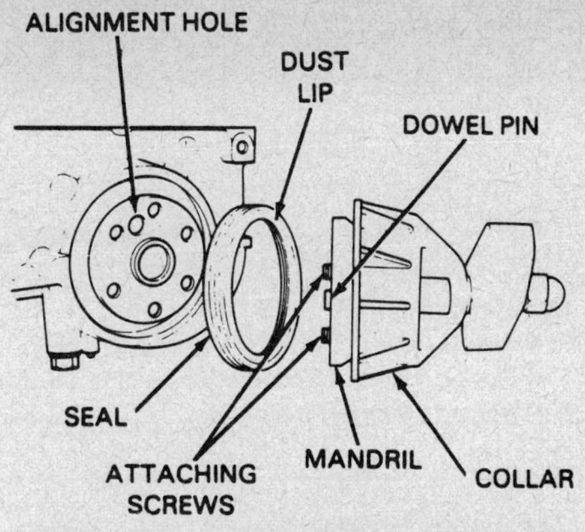

Fig. 10 Installing oil seal

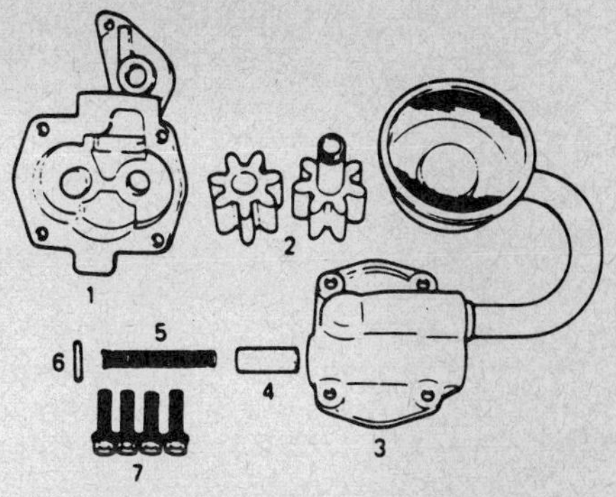

Fig. 11 Oil pump assembly

OIL PAN

REPLACE

1. Disconnect battery ground cable.
2. Raise and support vehicle, then drain crankcase.
3. Remove flywheel dust cover, then the starter motor.
4. Remove oil pan attaching bolts, then the oil pan.
5. Reverse procedure to install. Apply suitable sealer to oil pan mating surfaces, then torque 6 mm bolts to 6-15 ft. lbs. and 8 mm bolts to 15-30 ft. lbs.

OIL PUMP

REMOVAL

1. Remove oil pan, refer to "Oil Pan, Replace" procedure.
2. Remove pump to rear main bearing attaching bolt, then the pump and extension shaft.

DISASSEMBLY

1. Remove pump cover attaching bolts (7), **Fig. 11,** and pump cover (3). **Mark gear teeth to ensure correct position during assembly.**
2. Remove idler gear and drive gear (2), then the shaft from pump body (1).
3. Remove pressure regulator valve retaining pin (6), pressure regulator spring (5) and valve (4).
4. If pickup screen and pipe assembly need to be replaced, mount pump in a suitable vise, then remove pipe from pump cover. **Do not remove pickup screen from pipe. This is serviced as an assembly.**

CLEANING & INSPECTION

1. Wash all parts in suitable cleaning solvent, then dry with compressed air.
2. Inspect pump body and cover for cracks or excessive wear.
3. Inspect pump gears for damage or excessive wear. Pump gears and body are not serviced separately. If pump gears are defective, replace entire oil pump assembly.
4. Check drive gear shaft for looseness in the pump body.
5. Inspect inside of pump cover for wear that would permit oil to leak past ends of gears.
6. Inspect pickup screen and pipe assembly for looseness or damage.
7. Check pressure regulator valve for damage and proper fit.

ASSEMBLY

1. If pickup screen and pipe assembly was removed, it should be replaced with a new part. Mount pump in suitable vise and apply suitable sealer to outside diameter of swaged end of pipe, then tap pipe in place using a suitable tool. **Loss of press fit condition could result in an air leak and loss of oil pressure. Also use caution not to twist, shear or collapse pipe during installation.**
2. Install pressure regulator valve assembly.
3. Install drive gear and shaft in pump body.
4. Align idler gear installation marks, then install gear in pump body.
5. Install cover gasket, then the pump cover and attaching bolts.
6. Turn drive shaft by hand to ensure smooth operation.

INSTALLATION

1. Install pump and extension shaft with retainer to rear main bearing cap, aligning top end of hexagon extension shaft with hexagon socket of distributor drive gear.
2. Install pump to rear bearing cap bolt and tighten securely.
3. Install oil pan, refer to "Oil Pan, Replace" procedure.

WATER PUMP

REPLACE

1. Disconnect battery ground cable, then drain cooling system.
2. Disconnect serpentine belt at the water pump pulley.
3. Disconnect A/C pressure cycling switch electrical connectors, then remove pressure cycling switch.
4. Remove water pump pulley, then the water pump.
5. Reverse procedure to install.

BELT TENSION DATA

Belt	New Lbs.	Used Lbs.
Air Cond.	160	100
Alternator	①	①
Power Steer.	①	①

①—Serpentine belt.

FUEL PUMP

REPLACE

1. Relieve fuel system pressure, then disconnect battery ground cable.
2. Raise and support vehicle, then remove fuel tank.
3. Remove fuel lever sending unit and pump assembly by turning cam lock ring counterclockwise. Lift assembly from fuel tank, then remove fuel pump from fuel lever sending unit.
4. Pull fuel pump up to attaching hose or pulsator while pulling outward away from bottom support. After pump assembly is clear of bottom support, remove assembly from rubber connector or pulsator. **Use caution not to damage rubber insulator and strainer during removal.**
5. Reverse procedure to install.

Clutch & Transaxle Section

INDEX

CLUTCH PEDAL

ADJUST

1982–84 MODELS

The clutch is automatically adjusted by a self-adjusting mechanism, **Fig. 1**, mounted to the clutch pedal and bracket assembly. The clutch cable is a fixed length and cannot be shortened or lengthened, however, the position of the cable can be changed by adjusting the position of the detent in relation to the clutch pedal. This is accomplished by pulling the clutch pedal upward to the rubber bumper. This action forces the pawl against the stop and causes the pawl to be out of mesh with the detent teeth, allowing the cable to play out until the detent spring load is balanced against the load applied by the release bearing.

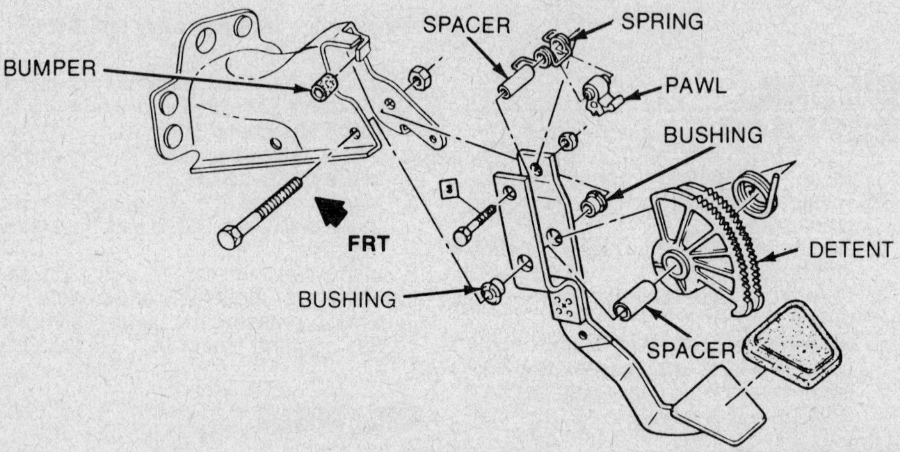

Fig. 1 Clutch self-adjusting mechanism. 1982–84 Models

Inspection

1. With engine running and parking brake applied, depress clutch pedal to approximately 1/2 inch from floor mat.
2. Move shift lever between "First" and "Reverse" gears several times. If no gear clashing occurs when shifting into "Reverse," the clutch is releasing fully.
3. If the shifting in Step 2 is not smooth, the clutch is not releasing fully and the linkage should be inspected.
4. Check clutch pedal bushings for sticking or excessive wear.
5. Have an assistant depress the clutch pedal to the floor and observe clutch fork lever travel at transaxle. The end of the clutch fork lever should have a total travel of approximately 1.5 to 1.7 inches.
6. To check the self-adjusting mechanism, depress the clutch pedal and observe if the pawl firmly engages the teeth of the detent.

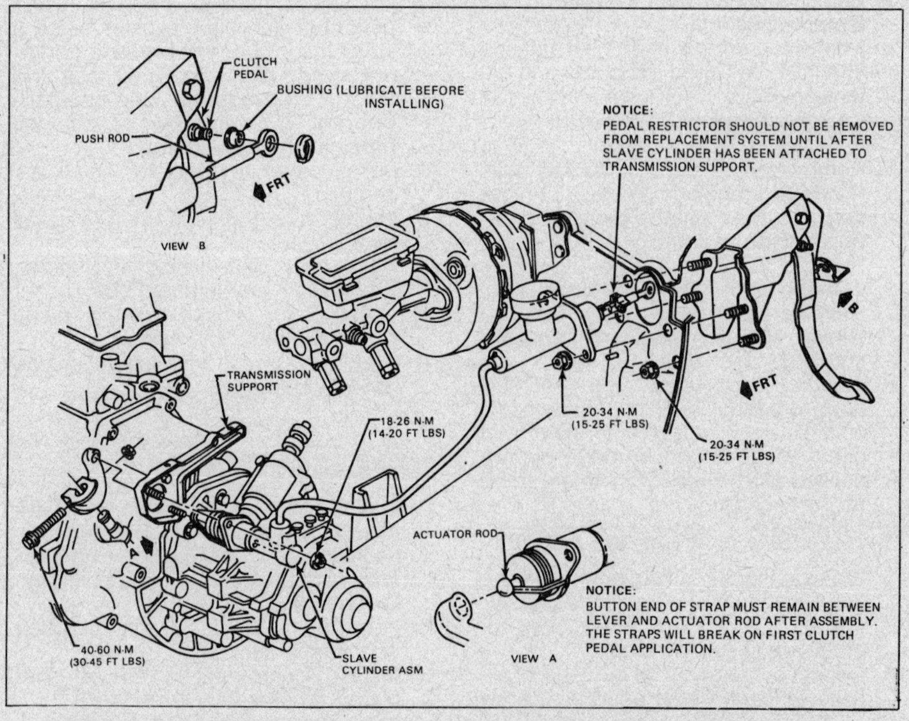

Fig. 2 Hydraulic clutch assembly. 1985–88 Models

1985–88 MODELS

On these models, a hydraulic clutch system is used, **Fig. 2.** The system consists of a dash mounted master cylinder with integral reservoir, a transmission mounted slave cylinder and high pressure tubing to connect the two components.

The hydraulic clutch system provides automatic clutch adjustment, therefore, there is no provision for adjustment.

Inspection

1. While observing clutch slave cylinder pushrod travel, have an assistant depress clutch pedal.
2. If slave cylinder pushrod moves .433 inch or more, hydraulic system is operating properly.
3. If slave cylinder pushrod did not move .433 inch, proceed as follows:
   a. Check clutch master cylinder fluid level. The clutch slave cylinder must be installed during this oper-

ation. Refill as necessary.

b. If master cylinder requires fluid, check hydraulic system components for leakage. Remove rubber boots from cylinders and check for leakage past pistons. A slight wetting of piston and wall surfaces is acceptable.

c. If excessive leakage is indicated, entire hydraulic system must be replaced.

CLUTCH

REPLACE

1. Disconnect battery ground cable.
2. Remove hush panel from driver's footwell, as required, then disconnect clutch master cylinder pushrod from clutch pedal.
3. Remove transaxle as outlined under "Manual Transaxle, Replace" procedure.
4. Mark position of pressure plate to flywheel to aid reassembly.
5. Gradually loosen pressure plate to flywheel attaching bolts until spring tension is relieved.
6. Support pressure plate and remove attaching bolts, pressure plate and driven disc, **Fig. 3.**
7. Clean pressure plate and flywheel mounting surfaces. Inspect bearing retainer outer surface of the transaxle.
8. Place pressure plate and driven disc in position and support with tool No. J-29074, **Fig. 4. The driven disc is installed with the damper springs offset toward the transaxle. Stamped letters found on the driven disc identify the "Flywheel Side."**
9. Install and gradually torque the pressure plate to flywheel attaching bolts to 15 ft. lbs. Remove support tool.
10. Lubricate the release bearing outside diameter groove and inside diameter recess.
11. Install transaxle.

MANUAL TRANSAXLE SHIFT CABLE

ADJUST

4 SPEED MANUAL TRANSAXLE

Shift Cable Adjustment

1. Disconnect battery ground cable.
2. Place shift lever into first gear position, then loosen shift cable nuts (E) at levers (D) and (F), **Fig. 5.**
3. Remove console trim plate, then slide shift lever boot upward on shift lever.
4. Remove console assembly.
5. With shift lever in the first gear position and held against stop, insert a suitable yoke type clip to hold lever in position, **Fig. 5.**
6. Insert a 5/32 inch drill bit into alignment hole on side of shifter assembly, **Fig. 5.**
7. Rotate lever (D), **Fig. 5,** in direction of arrow while tightening cable retaining nut.

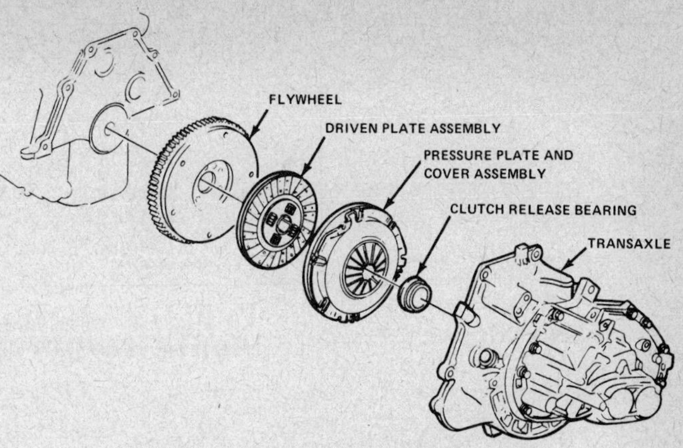

Fig. 3 Clutch assembly

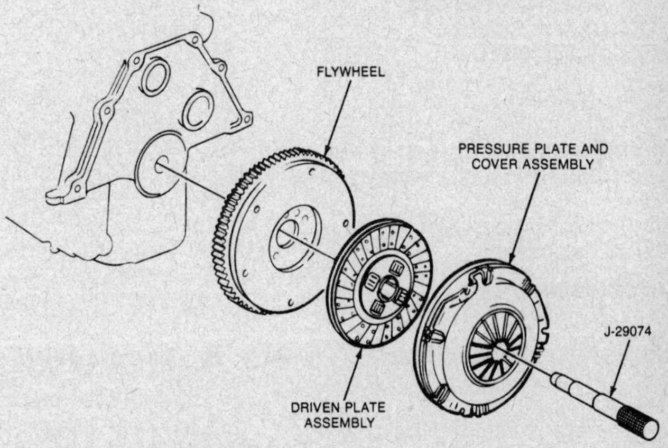

Fig. 4 Aligning clutch disc & pressure plate

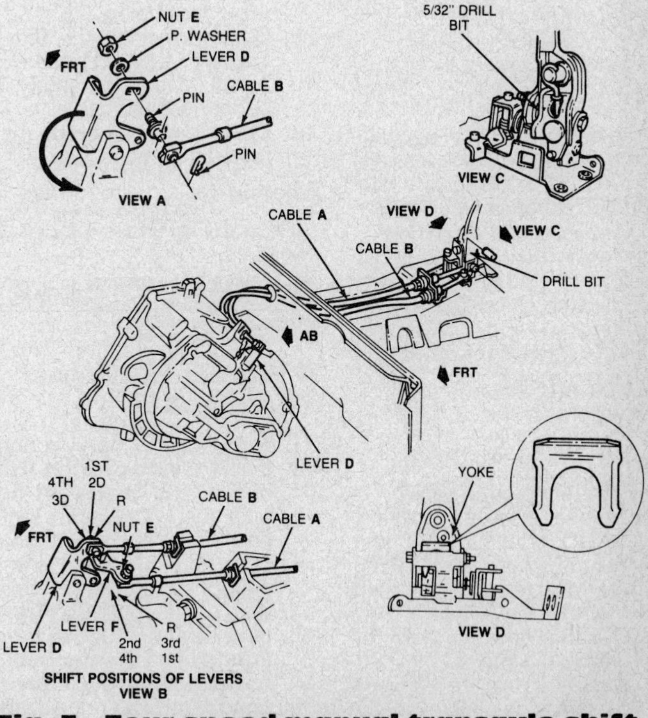

Fig. 5 Four speed manual transaxle shift cable adjustment

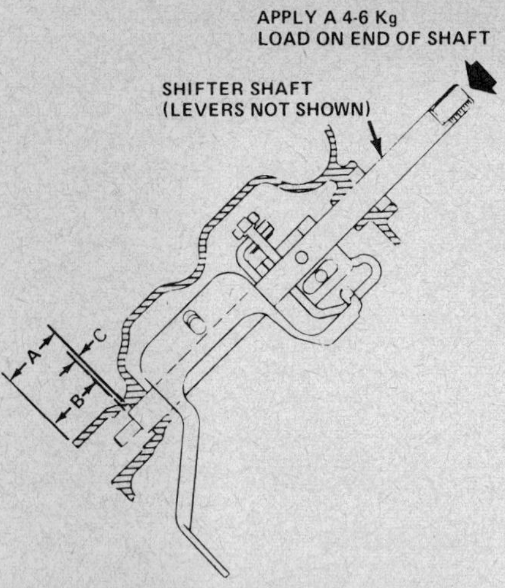

Fig. 6 Four speed manual transaxle shifter shaft selective washer measurement

Dimension "C" Fig. 6 Inch (mm)	Ident. Color & No. of Stripes	Shim Part No.
.0708 (1.8)	3 White	14008235
.0827 (2.1)	1 Orange	476709
.0945 (2.4)	2 Orange	476710
.1063 (2.7)	3 Orange	476711
.1181 (3.0)	1 Blue	476712
.1299 (3.3)	2 Blue	476713
.1417 (3.6)	3 Blue	476714
.1535 (3.9)	1 White	476715
.1654	2 White	476716

Fig. 7 Shifter shaft selective thrust washer identification chart. Four speed manual transaxle

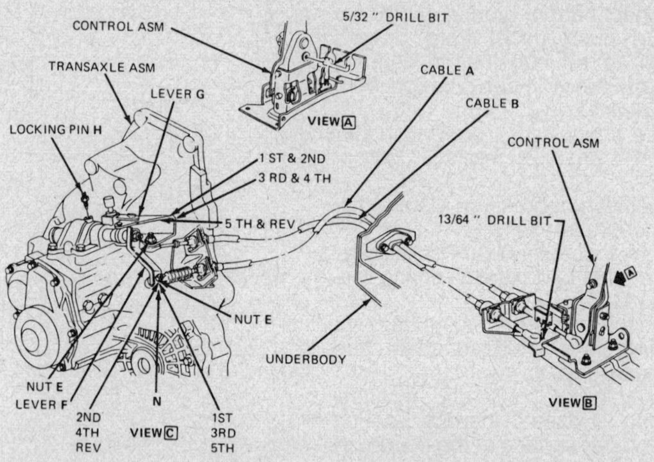

Fig. 8 Isuzu five speed manual transaxle shift cable adjustment

8. Tighten cable retaining nut at lever (F), **Fig. 5.**
9. Remove drill bit and yoke clip, then install console and connect battery ground cable.
10. Check shift lever for proper operation and readjust as necessary.

Shifter Shaft Washer Selection

When shift cables are properly adjusted, but improper first and second gear shifts are encountered, it may be necessary to check the shifter shaft selective thrust washer. This washer helps position the shifter shaft for proper shifter operation. Proceed as follows to determine the correct selective thrust washer thickness:

1. Remove reverse inhibitor fitting, spring and washer from end housing, then position shifter shaft into second gear.
2. Measure distance from end of housing to shifter shaft shoulder, dimension A, **Fig. 6.**
3. Apply a load of 9 to 13 lbs. to opposite end of shifter shaft, then measure distance from end of housing to shifter shaft shoulder, dimension B, **Fig. 6.**
4. Subtract measurement obtained in step 2 from measurement obtained in step 3, which will equal the thickness of the selective thrust washer to be installed, dimension C, **Fig. 6.** When selecting a thrust washer, refer to **Fig. 7.**

5 SPEED MANUAL TRANSAXLE

Isuzu

1. Disconnect battery ground cable.
2. Place shift lever in third gear position, then remove lock pin (H), **Fig. 8,** and reinstall with tapered end of pin facing downward to lock transaxle in third gear.
3. Loosen shift cable retaining nuts (E) at levers (G) and (F), **Fig. 8.**
4. Remove console trim plate and pull shifter boot upward on shift lever.
5. Remove console assembly from vehicle.
6. Insert a 5/32 inch drill bit into align hole on side of shifter assembly, **Fig. 8.**
7. Align shifter lever slot with slot in shifter plate, then insert a 13/16 inch drill bit.
8. Tighten nuts (E) at levers (G) and (F), **Fig. 8,** then remove drill bits from alignment holes.
9. Remove lock pin (H), **Fig. 8,** and reinstall with tapered end facing upward.
10. Install console assembly and connect battery ground cable.
11. Check shifter for proper operation and readjust as necessary.

Munci

Refer to **Fig. 9** for exploded view of shifter cables.

MANUAL TRANSAXLE REPLACE

4 SPEED MANUAL TRANSAXLE

1. Disconnect battery ground cable.
2. Install engine support fixture so that one end is supported on cowl tray over the wiper motor and the other end rests on the radiator support. Connect fixture hook to engine lift ring and raise engine to relieve weight from engine mounts, **Fig. 10. The engine support fixture must be positioned in the center of the cowl and the attaching parts properly tightened before supporting engine. This fixture is not intended to support entire weight of engine and transaxle. Personal injury may result from improper use of support fixture.**
3. Remove heater hose clamp at transaxle mount bracket, then disconnect horn wires and remove horn assembly. **Whenever the transaxle mount is removed, alignment bolt M6.0 x 1 x 65 must be installed in right front engine mount to prevent power train misalignment.**
4. Remove transaxle mount attaching bolts. Discard mount to side frame attaching bolts.
5. On 1985-88 models, remove clutch slave cylinder from support assembly. On 1982-84 models, disconnect clutch cabl e at clutch release lever, then remove transaxle mount bracket attaching bolts and nuts.
6. Disconnect shift cables and remove retaining clips at transaxle.
7. Disconnect ground cable at transaxle mounting stud, then remove air management valve attaching bolts (if equipped) to provide clearance for removal of upper righthand transaxle to engine attaching bolt. Remove four upper transaxle to engine mounting bolts.
8. Raise and support vehicle, then remove left front wheel.
9. Remove left front inner splash shield retaining screws and the splash shield.
10. Remove transaxle strut to transaxle bracket and crossmember attaching bolts and remove strut from vehicle.

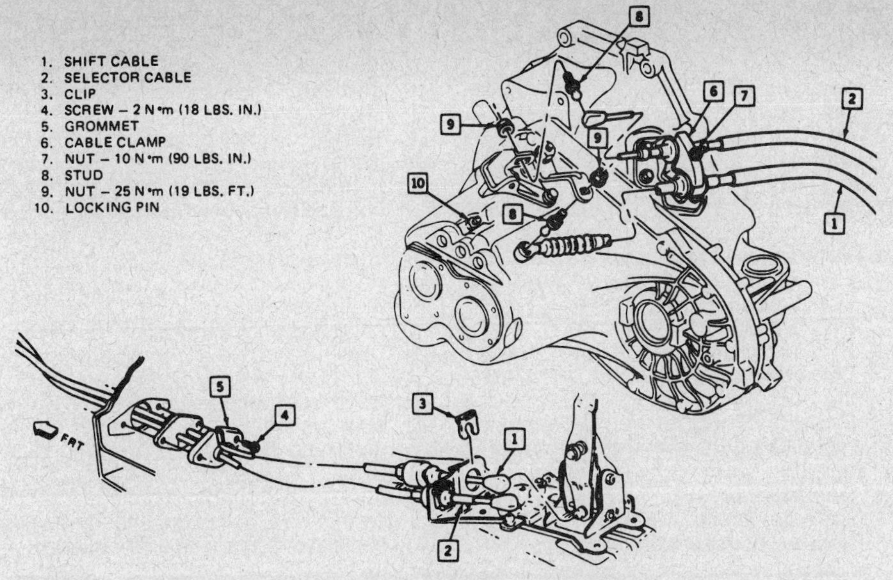

Fig. 9 Munci five speed manual transaxle shift cable assembly

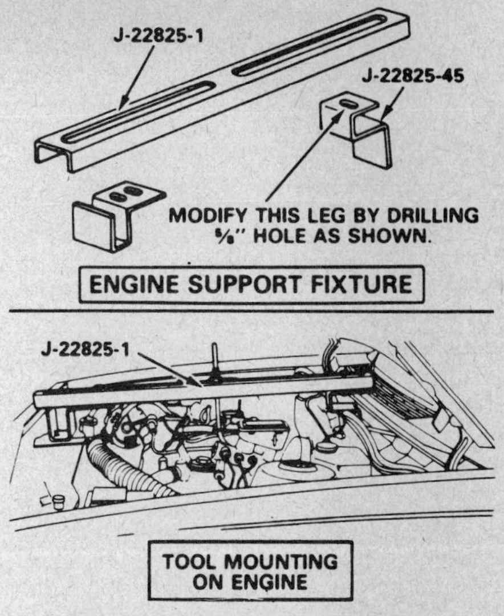

Fig. 10 Engine support fixture installation

11. Remove transaxle strut bracket attaching bolts and the strut bracket.
12. Remove clutch housing cover attaching bolts, then disconnect speedometer cable at transaxle.
13. Disconnect stabilizer bar at the left suspension support and control arm.
14. Using tool J-29330, separate left ball joint from steering knuckle.
15. Remove left suspension support to chassis attaching bolts, then remove the support and lower control arm as an assembly.
16. Install boot protectors at drive axles, then disengage both drive axles at transaxle. Remove left drive axle from transaxle housing bore.
17. Attach the transaxle case to a suitable jack, then remove two lower transaxle to engine mounting bolts.
18. Slide transaxle away from engine, lower jack and guide right drive axle from transaxle housing bore. Remove transaxle from vehicle.
19. Reverse removal procedure to install. **When installing transaxle, guide the right drive axle into transaxle bore as transaxle is being raised. The right drive axle cannot be installed after the transaxle is connected to engine.**

5 SPEED MANUAL TRANSAXLE

Exc. 1987–88

1. Disconnect battery ground cable.
2. Support engine using suitable engine holding fixture. Position holding fixture so that one end is supported by the cowl tray and the other end is resting on the radiator support, **Fig. 10.** Attach holding fixture hook to engine lifting bracket and raise engine just enough to relieve weight from engine mounts. **The engine holding fixture must be located in center of cowl and fixture attachments properly tightened before supporting engine. This support is not designed to support the entire weight of the engine and transaxle assembly.**
3. Remove transaxle mount attaching bolts. **When removing transaxle mount, alignment bolt M6.0 x 1 x 65 must be installed in right front engine mount to ensure proper power train alignment.**
4. On 1985-86 models, remove clutch slave cylinder from support assembly. On1982-84 models, disconnect clutch cable at clutch fork, then remove transaxle mount bracket retaining bolts and nuts.
5. Disconnect shift cables and remove retaining clips at transaxle.
6. Disconnect ground cables at transaxle mounting stud, then remove air management valve attaching bolts to provide clearance for upper right hand transaxle to engine attaching bolt.
7. Raise and support front of vehicle, then drain transaxle fluid.
8. Remove lefthand front wheel and tire assembly, then remove front inner splash shield.
9. Remove transaxle strut and strut bracket.
10. Remove clutch cover attaching bolts, then disconnect speedometer cable at transaxle.
11. Disconnect stabilizer bar at lefthand suspension support and control arm.
12. Detach ball joint from steering knuckle.
13. Remove lefthand front suspension support attaching bolts, then remove support and control arm as an assembly.
14. Install boot protectors, then disengage drive axle shafts at transaxle using tool Nos. J28468, J29794 and a suitable screwdriver. Remove lefthand drive axle shaft from transaxle.
15. Secure transaxle to a suitable transaxle jack, then remove transaxle to engine attaching bolts.
16. Remove transaxle by sliding toward drivers side of vehicle (away from engine), then carefully lower jack while guiding righthand drive axle shaft out of transaxle.
17. Reverse procedure to install. When installing transaxle, carefully guide righthand drive axle shaft into transaxle bore as transaxle is being raised. The righthand drive axle shaft cannot be installed once the transaxle has been connected to the engine.

1987–88 Isuzu

1. Disconnect battery ground cable.
2. Install engine support fixture J-28467 or equivalent, then raise engine enough to take pressure off motor mounts.
3. Remove left sound insulator.
4. Remove clutch master cylinder pushrod from clutch pedal.
5. Remove wire harness at mount bracket.
6. Remove clutch slave cylinder from transaxle support bracket and position aside.
7. Remove transaxle mount and mount bracket attaching bolts.
8. Remove shift cables and retaining clamp at transaxle.
9. Remove ground cable at transaxle attaching bolts, then disconnect shift indicator electrical connector.
10. Raise and support vehicle, then drain transaxle fluid.
11. Remove left front wheel and inner splash shield.
12. Remove transaxle front strut and front strut bracket.
13. Remove clutch housing cover attaching bolts, then the speedometer sensor at transaxle.
14. Remove stabilizer shaft at left suspension support and control arm.
15. Remove left suspension support attaching bolts and swing aside.
16. Remove drive axles and left shaft at transaxle.

17. Position suitable jack under transaxle, then remove transaxle to engine attaching bolts.
18. Slide transaxle towards drivers side, away from engine, then lower transaxle from vehicle while guiding right drive axle out of transaxle.
19. Reverse procedure to install. When installing transaxle, carefully guide righthand drive axle shaft into transaxle bore as transaxle is being raised. The righthand drive axle shaft cannot be installed once the transaxle has been connected to the engine.

1987–88 Muncie

1. Disconnect battery ground cable.
2. Install engine support fixture J-28467 or equivalent, then raise engine enough to take pressure off motor mounts.
3. Remove left sound insulator.
4. Remove clutch master cylinder push rod from clutch pedal.
5. Remove air cleaner and air intake duct assembly.
6. Remove clutch slave cylinder from transaxle support bracket and position aside.
7. Remove transaxle mount through bolt, then raise and support vehicle.
8. Remove exhaust crossover bolts at RH manifold, then lower vehicle.
9. Remove LH exhaust manifold, then the transaxle mount bracket.
10. Remove transaxle shift cables, then the upper transaxle to engine attaching bolts.
11. Raise and support vehicle, then remove left front tire and inner splash shield.
12. Remove transaxle strut and bracket.
13. Drain transaxle, then remove clutch housing cover attaching bolts.
14. Remove speedometer cable, then the stabilizer shaft at left suspension support and control arm.
15. Remove LH suspension support attaching bolts and swing aside.
16. Remove LH drive axle from transaxle.
17. Remove intermediate shaft housing to transaxle attaching bolts, then slide housing away from transaxle. Using a suitable tool, disconnect intermediate shaft from transaxle.
18. Position suitable jack under transaxle, then remove remaining transaxle to engine attaching bolts.
19. Lower transaxle assembly from vehicle.
20. Reverse procedure to install. When installing transaxle, carefully guide righthand drive axle shaft into transaxle bore as transaxle is being raised. The righthand drive axle shaft cannot be installed once the transaxle has been connected to the engine.

Rear Axle, Rear Suspension & Brakes Section

INDEX

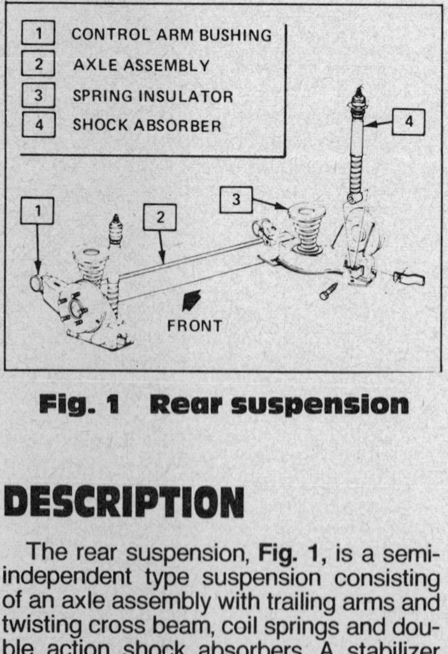

Fig. 1 Rear suspension

DESCRIPTION

The rear suspension, **Fig. 1,** is a semi-independent type suspension consisting of an axle assembly with trailing arms and twisting cross beam, coil springs and double action shock absorbers. A stabilizer bar is available and is attached to the inside of the axle beam and to the lower end of the control arms. A single unit hub and bearing assembly is bolted to each end of the axle assembly. The hub and bearing assembly is a sealed, non-serviceable unit and must be replaced as an assembly.

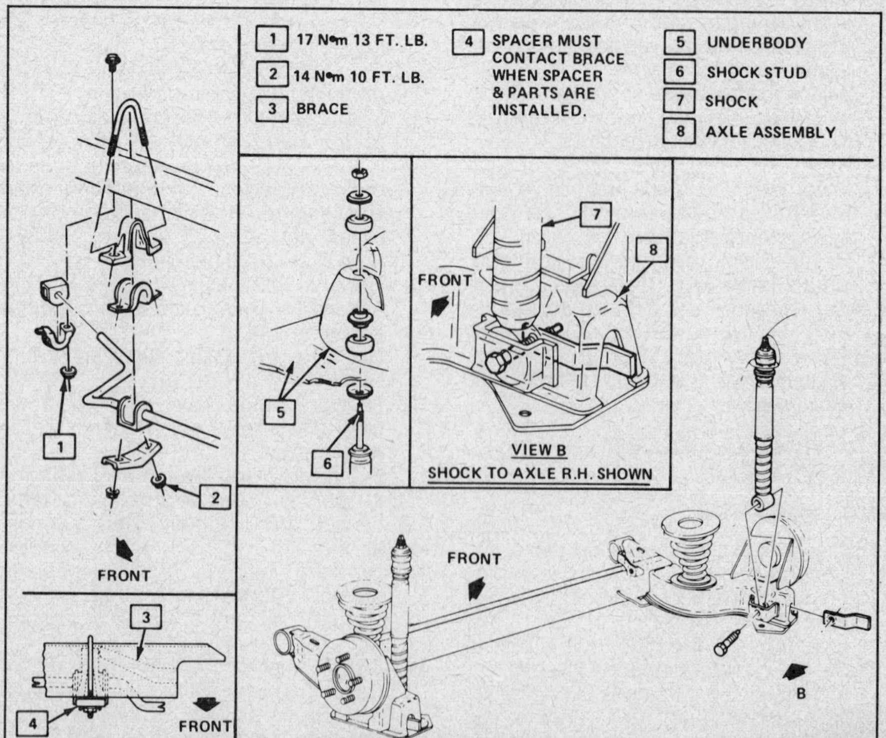

Fig. 2 Rear shock absorber upper attachment components

REAR AXLE
REPLACE

1. Raise vehicle and support vehicle. Support rear suspension with suitable jack.
2. Disconnect stabilizer bar at axle assembly, if equipped, **Fig. 2.**
3. Remove rear wheel assembly and brake drum. Do not hammer on brake drum since damage to bearings may result.
4. Remove shock absorber to lower mounting bracket attaching bolts, then disconnect shock absorbers from axle assembly, **Figs. 2 and 3.**
5. Disconnect parking brake cable and brake lines at axle brackets.
6. Carefully lower rear axle assembly and remove coil springs and insulators.
7. Remove control arm to underbody bracket bolts, then lower the axle assembly and remove from vehicle.
8. Remove hub to rear axle attaching bolts, then the hubs, bearings and backing plates from rear axle assembly.
9. Reverse procedure to install and bleed brake system.

HUB & BEARING ASSEMBLY
REPLACE

1. Raise and support vehicle, then remove wheel and tire assembly and brake drum. **Do not hammer brake drum since damage to bearing may result.**
2. Remove four hub/bearing assembly to rear axle attaching bolts, then the hub/bearing assembly from axle. **The upper rear hub attaching bolt may not clear brake shoe when removing hub and bearing assembly. Partially remove hub and bearing assembly prior to removing this bolt.**
3. Reverse procedure to install. Torque hub to axle attaching bolts to 37 ft. lbs. **Use care not to drop hub/bearing assembly since damage to bearing may result.**

SHOCK ABSORBER
REPLACE

1. Open deck lid, then remove trim cover and shock absorber upper retaining nut.
2. Raise rear of vehicle and support rear axle using a suitable jack.
3. Remove shock absorber lower attaching bolt, then disconnect shock absorber from mounting bracket, **Fig. 2.** Remove shock absorber from vehicle.
4. Reverse procedure to install. Torque lower attaching bolt to 41 ft. lbs. and upper attaching nut to 13 ft. lbs. **When installing upper shock absorber attachment components, refer to Fig. 3,** for proper installation order.

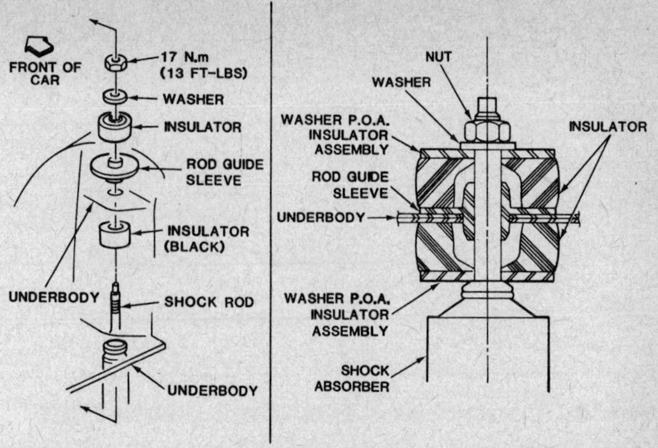

Fig. 3 Stabilizer bar & shock absorber removal

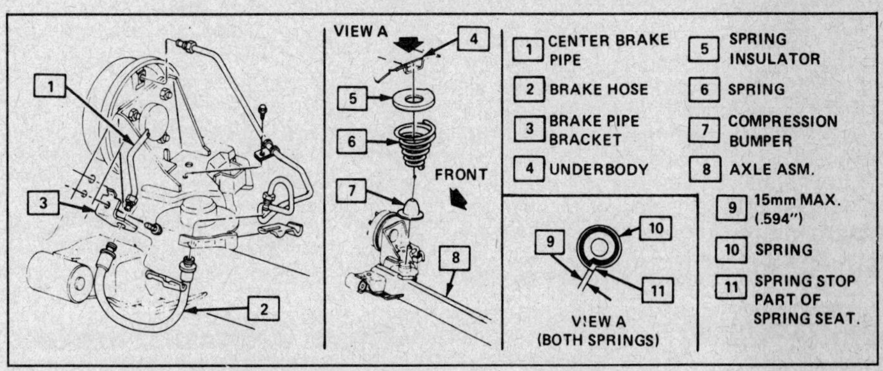

Fig. 4 Coil spring installation

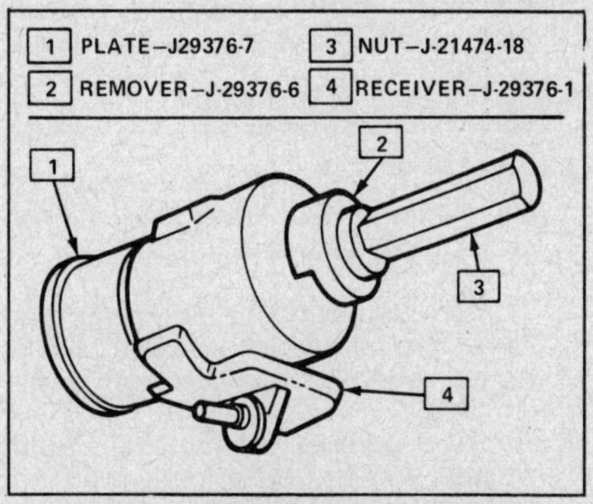

Fig. 5 Control bushing removal

COIL SPRING
REPLACE

1. Raise and support rear of vehicle. Support rear axle using a suitable jack.
2. Remove wheel and tire assemblies.
3. Remove brake line bracket attaching bolts from frame, **Fig. 2,** and allow brake lines to hang freely.
4. Remove shock absorber to lower mounting bracket bolts, then disconnect shock absorbers from axle assembly. **Do not suspend rear axle by brake hoses since damage to hoses may result.**
5. Carefully lower rear axle assembly and remove springs and insulators.
6. Reverse procedure to install. Position ends of upper coil in seat of body and within limits shown in **Fig. 4.**

CONTROL ARM BUSHING
REPLACE

1. Raise rear of vehicle and support rear axle under front side of spring seat using a suitable jack.
2. Remove wheel and tire assembly.
3. If righthand side bushing is to be replaced, disconnect brake line bracket from body. If lefthand side bushing is to be replaced, disconnect brake line bracket from frame and parking brake cable at hook guide.
4. Remove control arm to mounting bracket attaching nut, bolt and washer, then allow control arm to rotate downward.
5. The bushing can now be replaced using tools shown in **Figs. 5 and 6.** When installing bushing, the arrow on the installer must align with arrow on the receiver, **Fig. 5.**
6. Reverse procedure to complete installation. **The control arm attaching bolt must be torqued after vehicle is lowered to floor and is in its standing height position. Torque attaching bolt to 67 ft. lbs.**

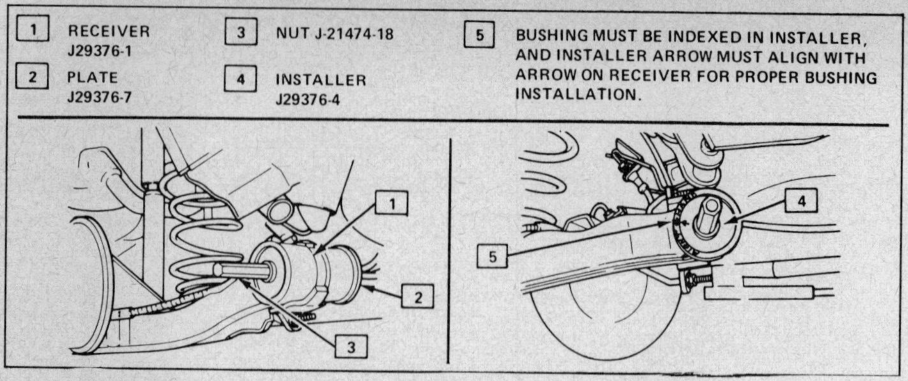

Fig. 6 Control arm bushing installation

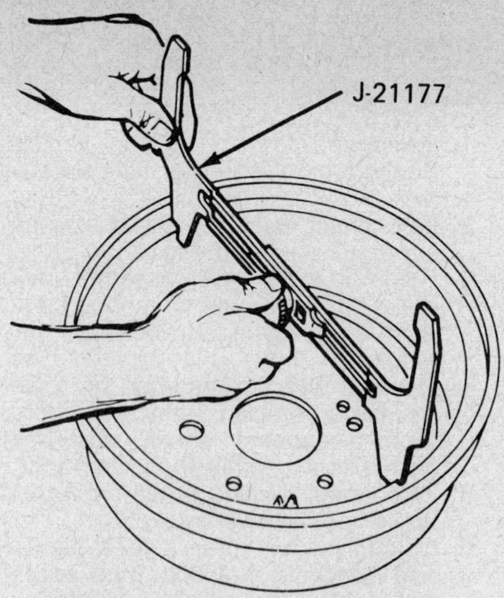

Fig. 7 Measuring brake drum inside diameter

DRUM BRAKE ADJUSTMENTS

The rear drum brakes, have self-adjusting shoe mechanisms that assure correct lining-to-drum clearances at all times. The automatic adjusters operate only when the brakes are applied as the vehicle is moving rearward.

Although the brakes are self-adjusting, an initial adjustment is necessary after the brake shoes have been replaced, or when the length of the star wheel adjuster has been changed during some other service operation.

ADJUSTMENT

1. Raise and support vehicle, then remove rear wheels and brake drums.
2. Check to make sure that parking brake cable linkage and levers on secondary brake shoe are in "free" position.
3. Using tool J-21177, measure brake drum inside diameter, **Fig. 7.**
4. Turn brake adjusting screw to expand shoes to diameter obtained on outside caliper portion of tool J-21177, **Fig. 8.**
5. Adjust parking brake. **Whenever rear drum brakes are serviced, the parking brake linkage cable at the equalizer must always be readjusted to prevent possible damage to brake shoes.**
6. Install brake drums, wheels and tires and lower vehicle to floor.

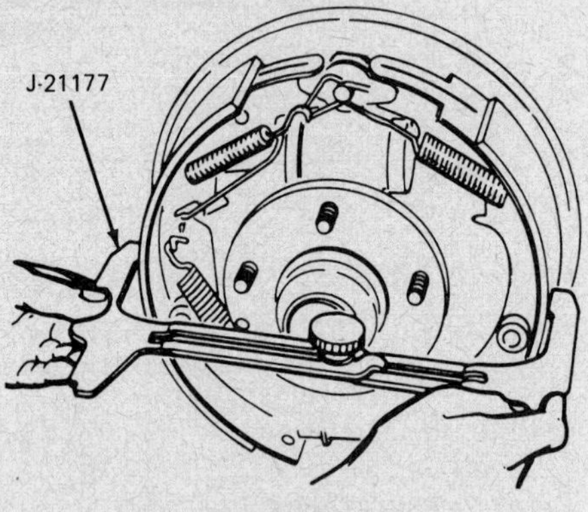

Fig. 8 Adjusting brake shoe clearance

7. Drive vehicle alternately forward and backward, applying brakes moderately, to obtain satisfactory pedal height.

PARKING BRAKE
ADJUST

1. Lift parking brake lever five ratchet clicks, then raise and support rear of vehicle.
2. Tighten adjusting nut until right rear wheel can be rotated backward, but is locked when forward rotation is attempted.
3. Release parking brake lever. Both wheels should rotate freely with no brake drag.

MASTER CYLINDER
REPLACE

1. Disconnect electrical connector and four brake lines at master cylinder.
2. Remove two master cylinder to brake booster attaching nuts, then the master cylinder from vehicle.
3. Reverse procedure to install. Bleed brake system.

POWER BRAKE UNIT
REPLACE

1. Remove master cylinder as previously described.
2. Disconnect power brake unit pushrod at brake pedal.
3. Disconnect vacuum hose from vacuum check valve. Plug vacuum hose to prevent entry of dirt.
4. Remove four power brake unit to dash panel attaching nuts, then the power brake unit from vehicle.
5. Reverse procedure to install. Torque attaching bolts to 22-33 ft. lbs.

Front Suspension & Steering Section

INDEX

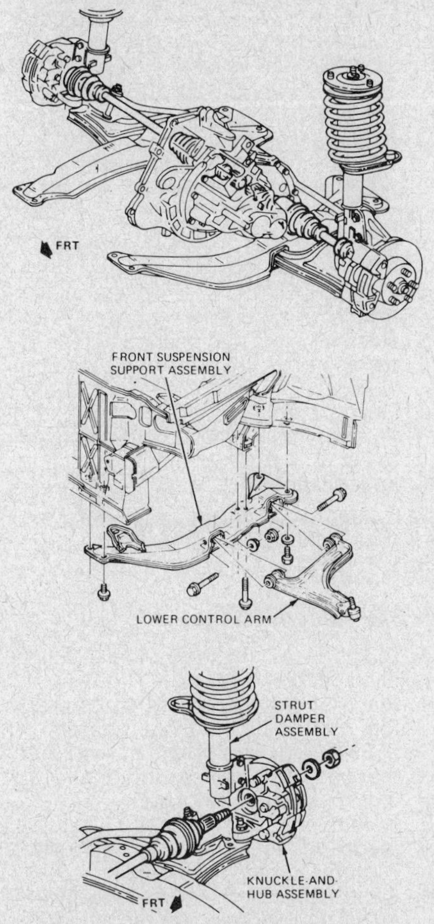

Fig. 1 Front suspension

DESCRIPTION

The front suspension, **Fig. 1**, on these vehicles is of the MacPherson strut design. The lower control arms pivot from the lower side rails through rubber bushings. The upper end of the strut is isolated by a rubber mount incorporating a nonserviceable bearing for wheel turning. The tie rods connect to the steering arm on the strut, below the spring seat. The lower end of the steering knuckle pivots on a ball stud which is retained to the lower control arm by rivets and is secured to the steering knuckle with a nut and cotter pin. The sealed wheel bearings are integral with the hub and are serviced as an assembly.

WHEEL BEARING REPLACE

REMOVAL

1. Loosen hub nut with vehicle on ground.
2. Raise and support vehicle, then remove front wheel.
3. Install drive axle protective boot cover J-28712.
4. Remove hub nut.
5. Remove brake caliper from support and suspend caliper from flame with a length of wire. Do not suspend caliper by brake hose.
6. Remove three hub and bearing attaching bolts. If the old bearing is being reinstalled, mark attaching bolts and corresponding holes for reinstallation, **Fig. 2.**
7. Using tool J-28733 or equivalent, remove bearing from steering knuckle, **Fig. 3. If excessive corrosion is present, ensure that bearing is loose in the knuckle before using puller tool.**
8. If installing new bearing, replace steering knuckle seal. **Do not move drive axle until hub nut is installed and torqued to specifications.**

INSTALLATION

1. Clean and inspect bearing mating surfaces and steering knuckle bore for dirt, nicks and burrs.
2. If installing new steering knuckle seal, apply grease to seal and knuckle bore, then press seal into steering knuckle.
3. Push bearing onto axle shaft and install two hub to steering knuckle attaching bolts. Install a longer bolt into third mounting hole and through hub cutout. Install hub to axle retaining nut and torque to 70 ft. lbs., **Fig. 4.**
4. Remove long bolt and replace with original bolt. Torque hub to steering knuckle attaching bolts to 63 ft. lbs. on 1982-83 models, or 40 ft. lbs. on 1984-88 models.
5. Install brake caliper and wheel assembly.
6. Lower vehicle and torque hub to axle nut to 185 ft. lbs.

LOWER BALL JOINT REPLACE

1. Raise and support vehicle, then remove wheel and tire.
2. Locate center of rivet body and mark with a center punch.
3. Using a 1/8 inch drill, drill pilot holes completely through the rivets. Using a 1/2 inch drill, drill final holes through rivets to ensure fitting of new ball joint.
4. Remove ball joint stud retaining nut, then, using tool J-29330, separate ball joint from steering knuckle. Remove ball joint from lower control arm.
5. Assemble new ball joint to lower control arm with bolts provided in service package, **Fig. 5.** Torque bolts to 50 ft. lbs.
6. Insert ball joint stud into steering knuckle and torque nut to 55 ft. lbs.
7. Install wheel and tire, check toe setting and adjust as required.

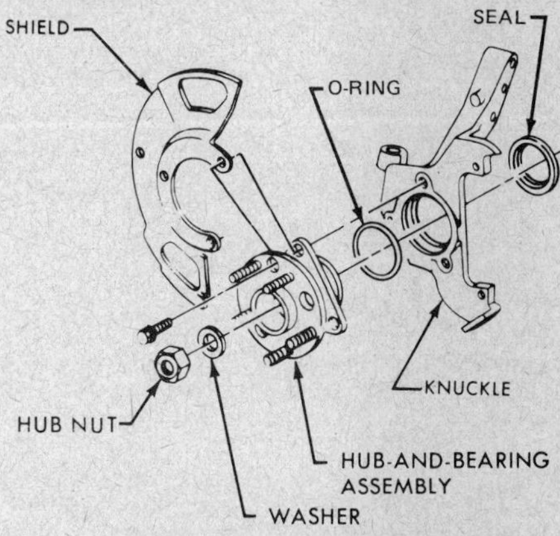

Fig. 2 Front hub & wheel bearing assembly

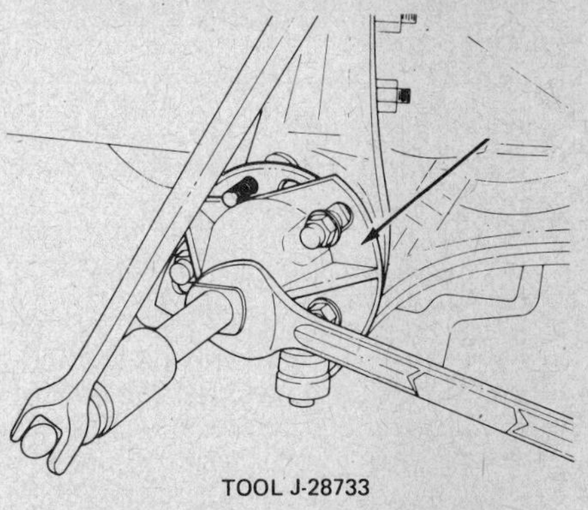

Fig. 3 Front hub & bearing assembly removal

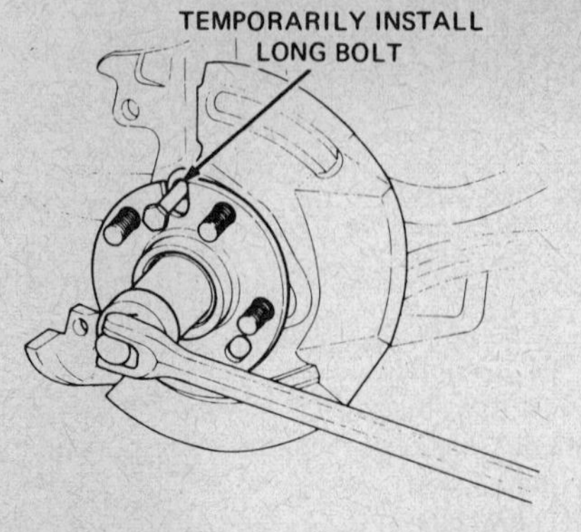

Fig. 4 Hub nut installation

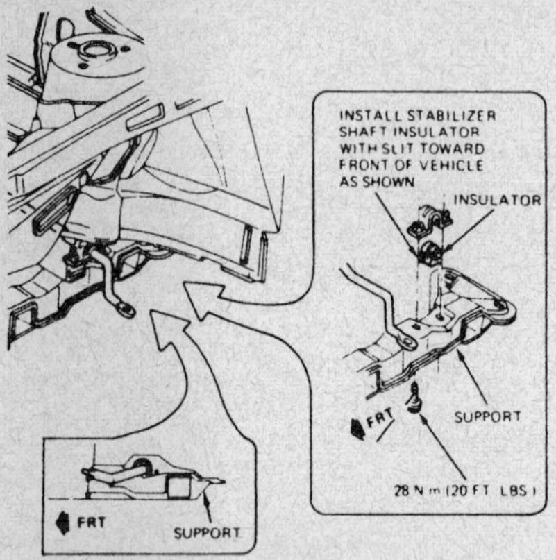

Fig. 7 Stabilizer bar installation

LOWER CONTROL ARM & BUSHING

REPLACE

1. Raise and support vehicle, then remove wheel and tire.
2. Disconnect stabilizer bar at lower control arm and control arm support.
3. Using tool J-29330, separate ball joint from steering knuckle.
4. Remove control arm support to chassis retaining bolts and remove control arm support and control arm as an assembly.
5. Separate control arm from support, then using tools J29792-1 and J29792-2 or equivalent, remove bushings from control arm.
6. Lubricate new bushings and install into control arm using tools J29792-1, J29792-2 and J29792-3 or equivalent.
7. Attach lower control arm to control arm support and torque pivot bolts to 67 ft. lbs.
8. Install control arm support to chassis, using attaching bolt tightening sequence shown in **Fig. 6.** Torque bolts to 63 ft. lbs.
9. Reverse procedure to complete installation. Check toe setting and adjust as required.

STEERING KNUCKLE

REPLACE

1. Raise and support vehicle, then remove wheel and tire.

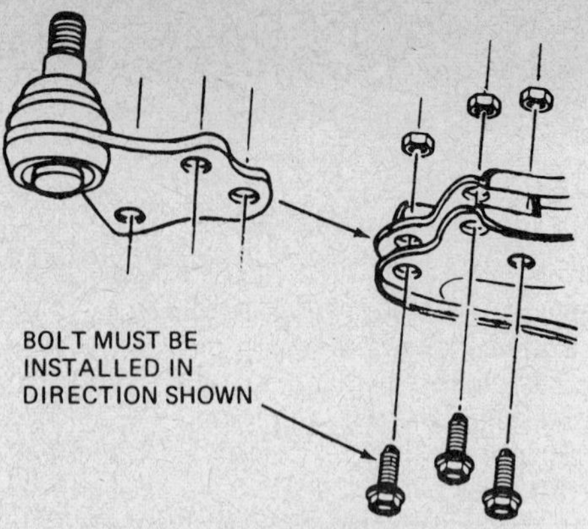

Fig. 5 Assembling lower ball joint to lower control arm

2. Remove front hub and bearing as outlined under "Wheel Bearing, Replace" procedure.
3. Using tool J-29330, separate ball joint from steering knuckle.
4. Remove strut to steering knuckle attaching bolts, then disconnect strut from steering knuckle.
5. Assemble strut to new steering knuckle and install attaching bolts finger tight.
6. Insert ball joint stud into steering knuckle and torque stud nut to 55 ft. lbs.
7. Torque strut to steering knuckle attaching bolts to 140 ft. lbs.
8. Reverse removal procedure to complete installation.

STABILIZER BAR & BUSHINGS

REPLACE

1. Raise and support vehicle, allowing control arms to hang freely.
2. Remove left front wheel and tire.
3. Disconnect stabilizer bar at control arms and control arm supports.
4. Remove rear and center control arm support bolts, lower support assembly and remove stabilizer bar through left side of vehicle.
5. Install stabilizer bar bushing with slit facing toward front of vehicle, **Fig. 8.**
6. Holding stabilizer bar approximately 2 1/4 inches above support assembly, torque stabilizer bar to control arm support attaching bolts to 20 ft. lbs., **Fig. 7.**
7. Install stabilizer bar to lower control arm and torque attaching bolts to 15 ft. lbs., **Fig. 7.**

STRUT ASSEMBLY

REPLACE

1. Raise hood and remove strut protective cap and three strut to body attaching nuts.
2. Raise and support vehicle, allowing suspension to hang freely.
3. Remove wheel and tire, then install drive axle protective cover, J-28712.
4. Using tool J-24319, disconnect tie rod

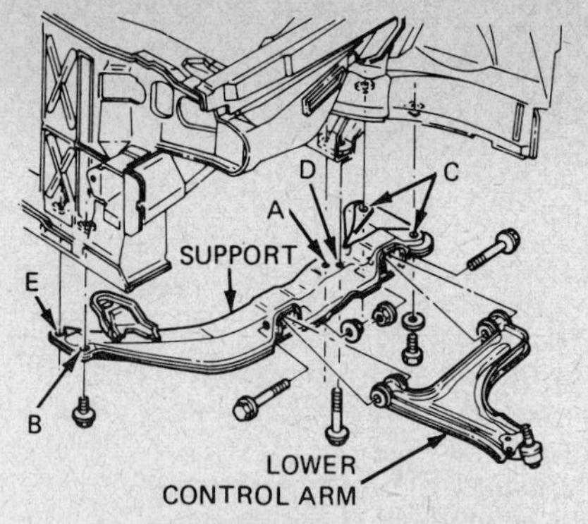

1. LOOSELY INSTALL CENTER BOLT INTO HOLE (A).
2. LOOSELY INSTALL TIE BAR BOLT INTO OUTBOARD HOLE (B).
3. INSTALL BOTH REAR BOLTS INTO HOLES (C) TORQUE REAR BOLTS.
4. INSTALL BOLT INTO CENTER HOLE(D), THEN TORQUE.
5. TORQUE BOLT IN HOLE (A).
6. INSTALL BOLT INTO FRONT HOLE (E), THEN TORQUE.
7. TORQUE BOLT IN HOLE (B).

Fig. 6 Replacing lower control arm

from strut assembly.

5. Remove strut to steering knuckle attaching bolts, then remove strut from vehicle.
6. Reverse procedure to install. Position flats of strut mounting bolts as shown in **Fig. 8.** Torque all nuts and bolts to specifications.

STRUT ASSEMBLY SERVICE

DISASSEMBLY

1. Clamp strut compressor tool J-26584 in a suitable vise.
2. Place strut assembly in compressor tool and install bottom adapter J-26584-86 or equivalent, making sure that adapter captures strut and locating pins are fully engaged.
3. Rotate strut assembly to align top mounting asse mbly lip with strut compressor support notch.
4. Insert J-26584-88 or equivalent top adapt ers between top mounting assembly and top spring seat. Position top adapters so that split line is perpendicular to spring compressor.
5. Rotate compressor forcing screw clockwise until top support flange contacts top adapters. Continue rotating forcing screws until strut spring is compressed approximately 1/2 inch. **Do not bottom the spring or strut damper rod.**
6. Remove damper top nut, then remove strut mounting assembly from damper shaft.
7. Rotate forcing screw counterclockwise to relieve spring tension, then remove spring from strut assembly.

STRUT CARTRIDGE REPLACEMENT

1. Clamp strut assembly firmly in a suitable vise. Do not overtighten.

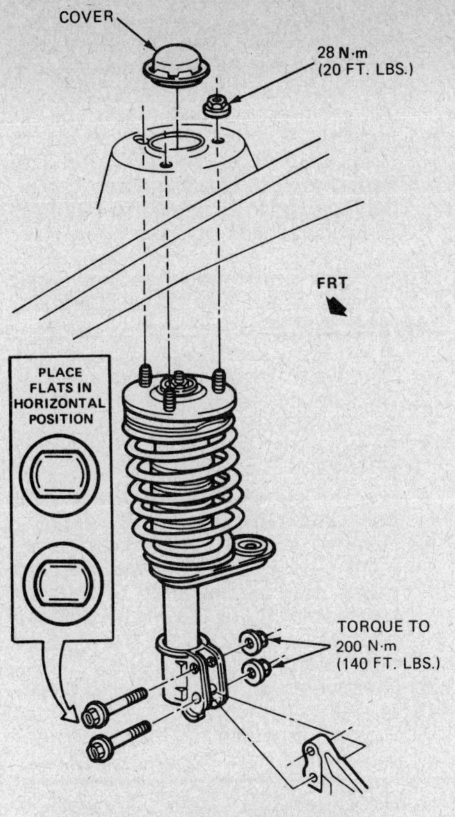

Fig. 8 Installing strut assembly

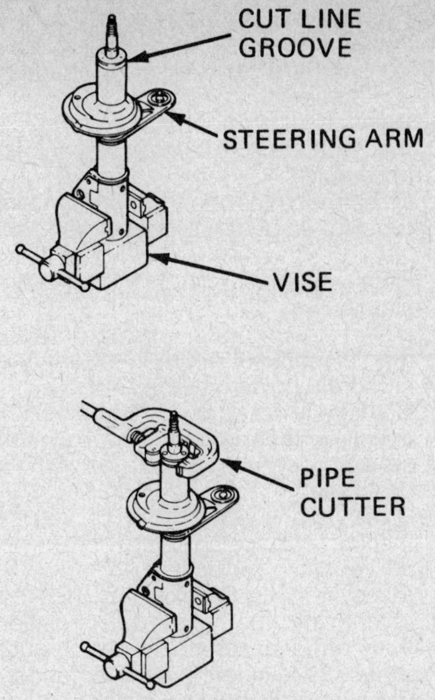

Fig. 9 Strut reservoir tube removal

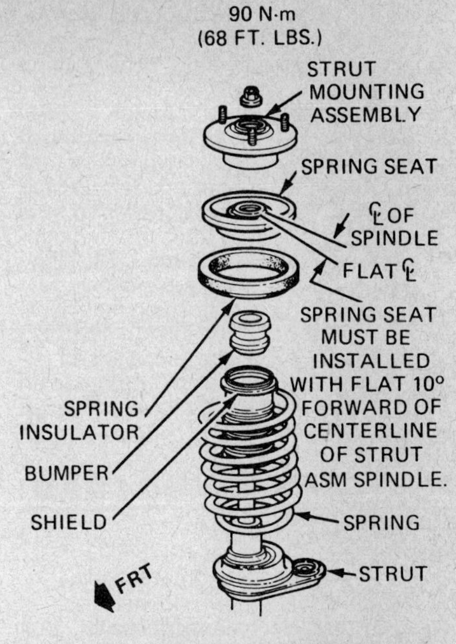

Fig. 10 Strut coil spring & upper mounting installation

2. Install pipe cutter at cut line groove located at top of strut damper. Cut around groove until reservoir tube is cut completely through, **Fig. 9.**
3. Remove and discard end cap, cylinder and piston rod assembly.
4. Place flaring cup tool, provided in service package, onto open end of reservoir tube and strike with hammer until cup flat outer surface rests on reservoir tube.
5. Install strut carriage into reservoir tube and align grooves on cartridge base with pads at bottom of reservoir tube.
6. Using tool J-29778 or equivalent, torque cartridge retaining hex nut to 140-170 ft. lbs.

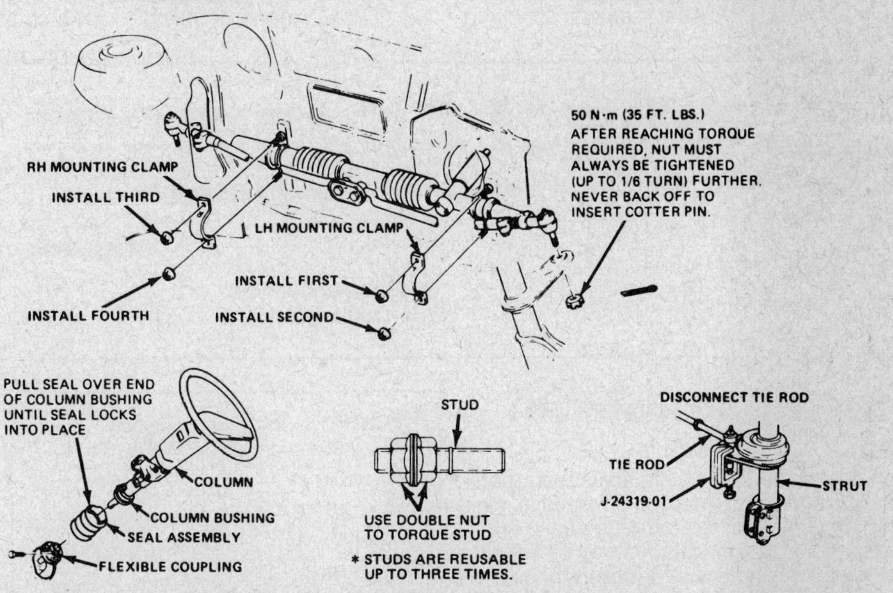

Fig. 11 Power rack & pinion steering gear removal

ASSEMBLY

1. Perform Steps 1 & 2 as outlined in the "Disassembly" procedure.
2. Rotate strut assembly until mounting flange is facing outward, opposite compressor forcing screw.
3. Position spring on strut, making sure spring is properly seated on bottom spring plate, **Fig. 10.**
4. Install strut spring seat assembly and J26584-88 top adapters over strut spring.
5. Turn compressor forcing screw until compressor top support contacts top adapters.
6. Install a long extension and socket onto hex on damper shaft to align components during installation.
7. Compress spring until approximately 1½ inch of damper shaft extends through spring plate.
8. Remove extension and socket, then position top mounting assembly over damper shaft and install retaining nut. Torque retaining nut to 68 ft. lbs.
9. Turn forcing screw counterclockwise and remove strut assembly from compressor.

MANUAL STEERING GEAR

REPLACE

1. Disconnect battery ground cable.
2. Remove lefthand sound insulator.
3. From under instrument panel, pull downward on steering column seal, then remove upper pinch bolt from flexible coupling.
4. Remove air cleaner, then remove windshield washer reservoir attaching screws and position reservoir aside.
5. Raise and support front of vehicle, then remove both front wheel and tire assemblies.
6. Disconnect tie rods from struts using tool No. J24319-01, then lower vehicle.
7. Remove steering gear mounting clamps, **Fig. 11.**
8. Move steering gear assembly slightly forward, then remove lower pinch bolt from flexible coupling and detach coupling from steering gear stub shaft.
9. Remove dash panel seal from steering gear.
10. Raise and support front of vehicle, then remove splash shield from left inner fender.

11. Place lefthand knuckle and hub assembly in the full left turn position, then remove steering gear through access hole in lefthand inner fender.
12. Reverse procedure to install. If steering gear mounting clamp studs have backed out during removal, install double nuts on stud and torque stud to 15 ft. lbs. Torque coupling to stub shaft pinch bolt to 29 ft. lbs. and coupling to steering column shaft pinch bolt to 30 ft. lbs. Torque steering gear mount ing clamp attaching nuts to 28 ft. lbs. Torque tie rod to strut attaching nuts to 35 ft. lbs. The tie rod to strut attaching nuts can be tightened up to an additional 1/6 turn to allow installation of cotter pin.

POWER STEERING GEAR REPLACE

1. Disconnect battery ground cable.
2. Remove lefthand sound insulator.
3. From under instrument panel, pull downward on steering column seal, then remove upper pinch bolt from flexible coupling.
4. Remove air cleaner, then remove windshield washer reservoir attaching screws and position reservoir aside.
5. Disconnect pressure line from steering gear and remove screw attaching line bracket to cowl.
6. Raise and support front of vehicle, then remove both front wheel and tire assemblies.
7. Disconnect tie rods from struts using tool No. J24319-01, then lower vehicle.
8. Remove steering gear mounting clamps, **Fig. 11.**
9. Move steering gear slightly forward, then disconnect return line from gear and drain power steering fluid.
10. Remove lower pinch bolt from flexible coupling, then detach coupling from steering gear stub shaft and remove dash seal.
11. Raise and support front of vehicle, then remove splash shield from left inner fender.
12. Place steering knuckle and hub assembly into the full left turn position, then remove steering gear through access hole in lefthand inner fender.
13. Reverse procedure to install. If steering gear mounting clamps have backed out during removal, install double nuts on stud and torque to 15 ft. lbs. Torque coupling to stub shaft pinch bolt to 37 ft. lbs. and coupling to steering column shaft pinch bolts to 30 ft. lbs. Torque steering gear mounting clamp attaching nuts to 28 ft. lbs. Torque pressure and return line fittings to 20 ft. lbs. Torque tie rod to strut attaching nuts to 35 ft. lbs. The tie rod to strut attaching nuts can be tightened up to an additional 1/6 turn to allow installation of cotter pin.

POWER STEERING PUMP REPLACE

1. Remove air cleaner assembly.
2. Disconnect reservoir to pump hose and pressure line from pump.
3. Remove clip attaching pressure line to pump.
4. Loosen pump pivot and adjusting bolts, then remove pump drive belt.
5. Remove three pump to bracket attaching bolts. **On some models, the pump may be attached to bracket by special bolts. To remove these special bolts, use tool No. T-45 or equivalent.**
6. Remove pump from mounting bracket.
7. Reverse procedure to install.

Wheel Alignment Section

INDEX

CAMBER ADJUSTMENT

Toe setting is the only adjustment normally required. However, in special circumstances, such as damage due to road hazard or collision, camber may be adjusted by modifying the strut assembly.

1. Secure bottom of strut assembly in a suitable vise.
2. Enlarge bottom holes in outer flanges with a round file until holes in outer flanges match slots in inner flanges, **Fig. 1.**
3. Connect strut to steering knuckle and install bolts finger tight.

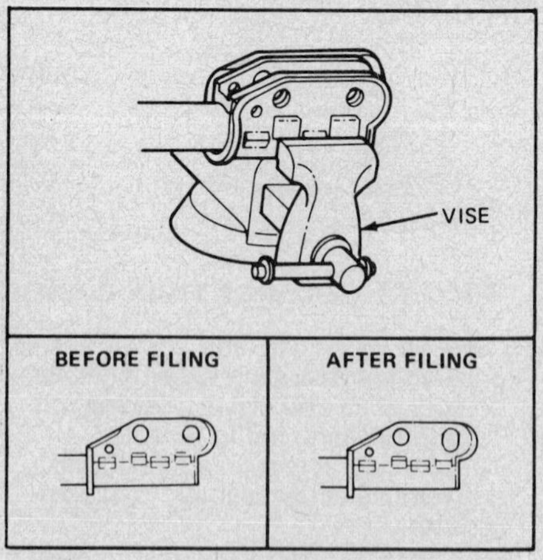

Fig. 1 Modifying strut bracket to adjust camber

4. Grasp top of tire firmly, then move tire inboard or outboard until correct camber reading is obtained. Tighten retaining bolts enough to secure camber setting.
5. Remove wheel and tire and torque strut to steering knuckle retaining bolts to 140 ft. lbs.

TOE-OUT ADJUSTMENT

Toe-out is controlled by tie rod position. Adjustment is made by loosening the clamp bolts at the steering knuckle end of the tie rods and rotating the rods to obtain proper toe setting. After correct toe setting is obtained, torque clamp bolts to 14 ft. lbs.

CHEVROLET BERETTA & CORSICA

INDEX OF SERVICE OPERATIONS

NOTE: Refer to the rear of this manual for vehicle manufacturer's special special service tool suppliers.

Specifications

GENERAL ENGINE SPECIFICATIONS

Year	Engine		Fuel System	Bore & Stroke	Compression Ratio	Net H.P. @ RPM	Maximum Torque Ft. Lbs. @ RPM	Normal Oil Pressure Pounds
	CID①/Liter	VIN Code ②						
1987-88	4-121/2.0L	1	Fuel Injection	3.5 x 3.15	9.0	90 @ 5600	108 @ 3200	63-77③
	V6-173/2.8L	W	Fuel Injection	3.5 x 2.99	8.9	125 @ 4500	160 @ 3600	50-65③

①—CID-cubic inch displacement.
②—The eighth digit denotes engine code.
③—At 1200 RPM.

ENGINE TIGHTENING SPECIFICATIONS

*Torque specifications are for clean and lightly lubricated threads only. Dry or dirty threads produce increased friction which prevents accurate measurement of tightness.

Year	Engine Model/VIN	Spark Plugs Ft. Lbs.	Cylinder Head Bolts Ft. Lbs.	Intake Manifold Ft. Lbs.	Exhaust Manifold Ft. Lbs.	Rocker Arm Stud Ft. Lbs.	Rocker Arm Cover Ft. Lbs.	Connecting Rod Cap Bolts Ft. Lbs.	Main Bearing Cap Bolts Ft. Lbs.	Flywheel to Crankshaft Ft. Lbs.	Vibration Damper or Pulley Ft. Lbs.
1987-88	4-121/1	7-20	①	15-22	6-13	②	4-9	34-43	63-77	③	66-89
	V6-173/W	10-25	④	18	15-23	15-20⑤	6-9	34-44	63-83	—	67-85

①—Long bolts, 73-83 ft. lbs.; short bolts, 62-70 ft. lbs.
②—Rocker arm stud, 33-40 ft. lbs.; rocker arm stud nut, 11-18 ft. lbs.
③—Auto. trans. models, 45-49 ft. lbs.; man. trans. models, 47-63 ft. lbs.
④—Torque to 33 ft. lbs., then tighten an additional 90°.
⑤—Rocker arm nuts.

ALTERNATOR SPECIFICATIONS

Year	Model	Rated Hot Output Amps.
1987-88	1105697	74
	1105694	100
	1105698	85
	1105701	85

STARTING MOTOR APPLICATIONS

Year	Engine/VIN	Starter Ident. No.
1987-88	V6-173/W	1109564
	V6-173/W	1998511

FRONT WHEEL ALIGNMENT SPECIFICATIONS

Year	Model	Caster Angle, Degrees		Camber Angle, Degrees				Toe Degrees
				Limits		Desired		
		Limits	Desired	Left	Right	Left	Right	
1987-88	All	+.7 to +2.7	+1.7	+.2 to +1.4	+.2 to +1.4	+.8	+.8	0

REAR WHEEL ALIGNMENT SPECIFICATIONS

Year	Model	Camber Angle, Degrees				Toe Degrees
		Limits		Desired		
		Left	Right	Left	Right	
1987-88	All	①	①	②	②	② ③

①—Beretta, −.10 to −.40; Corsica, −.17 to −.33.
②—Not adjustable.
③—Beretta, 0 to .30; Corsica, .117 to .133

COOLING SYSTEM & CAPACITY DATA

Year	Model or Engine/VIN	Cooling Capacity, Qts.		Radiator Cap Relief Pressure, Lbs.	Thermo. Opening Temp. °F	Fuel Tank Gals.	Engine Oil Refill Qts.	Transaxle Oil	
		Less A/C	With A/C					Manual Transaxle Pts.	Auto. Transaxle Qts. ①
1987-88	4-121/1	③	14.1	15	195	13.6	4②	5.3	⑥
	V6-173/W	④	⑤	15	195	13.6	4②	4.5	⑥

①—Approximate, make final check with dipstick.
②—With or without filter change.
③—W/auto. trans., 13.2 qts.; w/man. trans., 13.3 qts.
④—W/auto. trans., 16.7 qts.; w/man. trans., 16.2 qts.
⑤—W/auto. trans., 16.6 qts.; w/man. trans., 16.1 qts.
⑥—Oil pan only, 4 qts.; after disassembly, 6 qts.

Electrical Section

INDEX

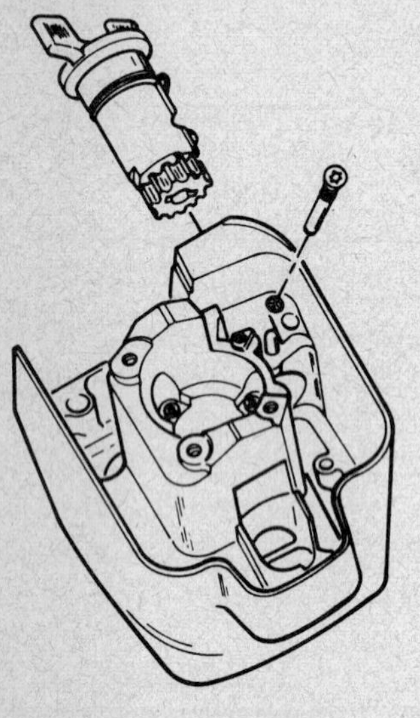

Fig. 1 Lock cylinder set removal

STARTER REPLACE

4-121 ENGINE

1. Disconnect battery ground cable.
2. Raise and support front of vehicle.
3. Disconnect solenoid wires and battery cable at starter motor.
4. Remove rear engine mount support bracket, then the A/C compressor support rod (if equipped).
5. Remove starter attaching bolts, then carefully lower starter. Note position of shims, if used.
6. Reverse procedure to install.

V6-173 ENGINE

1. Disconnect battery ground cable.
2. Raise and support front of vehicle.
3. Disconnect solenoid wires and battery cable at starter motor.
4. Remove starter attaching bolts, then carefully lower starter. Note position of shims, if used.
5. Reverse procedure to install.

IGNITION LOCK REPLACE

1. Remove steering wheel as outlined under Steering Wheel, Replace procedure.
2. Remove turn signal switch as outlined under Turn Signal Switch, Replace procedure.
3. Position lock cylinder in Run position, then remove turn signal switch housing attaching screws. Remove turn signal switch housing and steering shaft as an assembly.
4. Pry buzzer switch tab with suitable screwdriver, then gently pull on wires to remove buzzer switch.
5. Position lock cylinder in Accessory position, then remove lock retaining screw and the lock cylinder, **Fig. 1.**
6. Reverse procedure to install, noting the following:
   a. Torque lock cylinder retaining screw to 22 inch lbs.
   b. Torque turn signal switch housing attaching screws to 88 inch lbs.

IGNITION & DIMMER SWITCHES REPLACE

1. Disconnect battery ground cable.
2. Position lock cylinder in Accessory position.
3. Remove steering column to instrument panel attaching bolts, then gently lower steering column to drivers seat.
4. Remove dimmer and ignition switch mounting stud nut, then the dimmer switch attaching screw and dimmer switch.
5. Remove dimmer switch actuator rod.

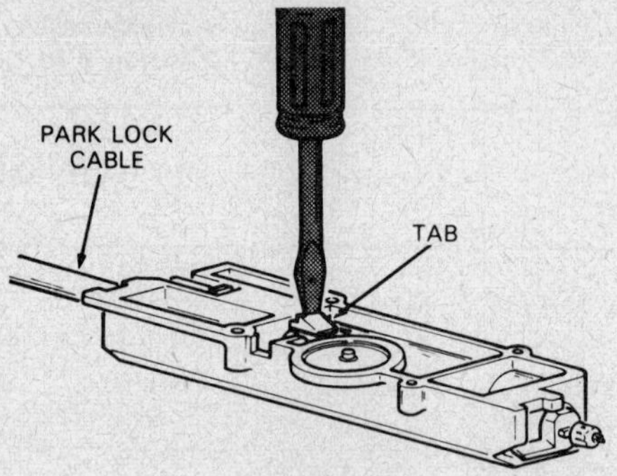

Fig. 2 Park lock cable removal

6. Remove dimmer and ignition switch mounting stud.
7. Remove ignition switch assembly from ignition switch actuator.
8. Remove inhibitor switch housing to ignition switch assembly attaching screws, then the inhibitor switch housing.
9. On models equipped with park lock steering column, use suitable screwdriver to remove park lock cable from switch inhibitor, **Fig. 2.**
10. Install inhibitor switch housing on ignition switch, then install attaching screws and torque to 9 inch lbs.
11. On models equipped with park lock steering column, insert park lock cable into switch inhibitor housing, then push in until locking tabs engage.
12. Ensure lock cylinder is positioned in Accessory position, then place ignition switch slider in far left (accessory) position and install ignition switch over switch actuator.
13. Position ignition switch on steering column, then install dimmer and ignition switch mounting stud. Torque stud to 35 inch lbs.
14. Position dimmer switch actuator rod into dimmer switch rod cap hole, then install actuator rod.

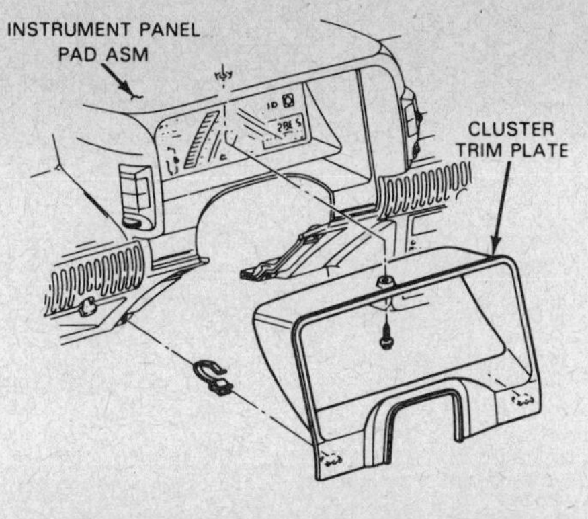

Fig. 3 Instrument cluster removal. Beretta models

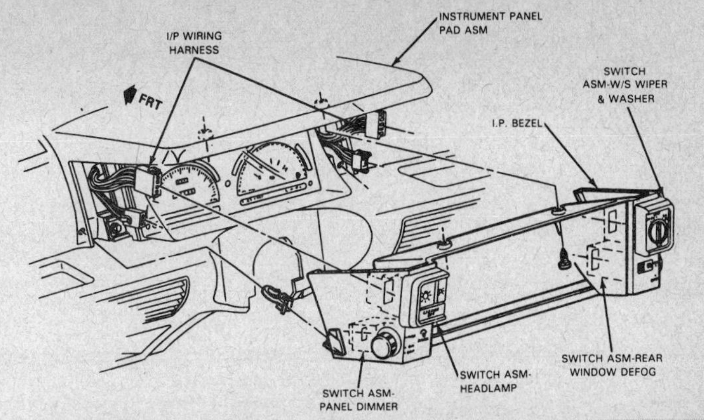

Fig. 4 Instrument cluster removal. Corsica models

15. Install dimmer switch on dimmer and ignition switch mounting stud. Install dimmer switch mounting nut and screw. Do not tighten at this time.
16. Position dimmmer switch in such a way so click is heard whenever the turn signal lever is pulled back, then torque attaching nut and screw to 35 inch lbs.
17. Install steering column. Torque attaching bolts to 29 ft. lbs.

HEADLIGHT, REAR WINDOW DEFOGGER OR WINDSHIELD WIPER/WASHER SWITCH

REPLACE

1. Disconnect battery ground cable.
2. Using suitable tool, pry switch from instrument panel.
3. Disconnect switch wiring, then remove switch.
4. Reverse procedure to install.

PULSE WINDSHIELD WIPER MODULE

REPLACE

The windshield wiper pulse module circuitry is an integral part of the windshield wiper motor cover.

STOP LIGHT SWITCH

ADJUST

Insert stop light switch into tubular clip above brake pedal until switch body seats fully into clip. Pull brake pedal rearward against internal pedal stop. The switch will be properly positioned in the tubular clip automatically. **Rotate switch 1/2 turn counterclockwise to ensure that switch does not hold brake pedal down after adjustment.**

BACK-UP LIGHT/NEUTRAL START SWITCH

REPLACE

MODELS EQUIPPED W/AUTO. TRANS.

1. Disconnect battery ground cable.
2. Disconnect shift linkage from transaxle.
3. Disconnect electrical connector from back-up light/neutral start switch.
4. Remove back-up light/neutral start switch attaching screws, then the switch.
5. Ensure transaxle shift shaft is in Neutral position.
6. If installing new switch, align new back-up light/neutral start switch flats with flats of shift shaft, then install switch. Torque attaching bolts to 22 ft. lbs.
7. If used switch is being installed, proceed as follows:
   a. Align back-up light/neutral start switch flats with flats of shift shaft, then install switch. Loosely install attaching bolts.
   b. Insert 3/32 inch drill in service adjustment hole, then rotate switch until drill drops to a depth of 9/64 inch.
   c. Torque attaching bolts to 22 ft. lbs.
8. With either new or used switch, ensure engine will only start in Neutral and Start positions.

CLUTCH START SWITCH

REPLACE

1. Disconnect battery ground cable.
2. Disconnect wiring connector from switch located on clutch pedal support above clutch pedal.
3. Disconnect switch link from pedal, then remove switch retaining link and switch.
4. Reverse procedure to install.

TURN SIGNAL SWITCH

REPLACE

1. Remove steering wheel, then the turn signal cancel cam assembly.
2. Remove hazard warning knob attaching screw, then the hazard warning knob.
3. Position turn signal switch in such a way so column cover attaching screw and turn signal attaching screws are accessible.
4. Remove column cover attaching screw, then the column cover.
5. Remove dimmer switch actuator upper attaching screw, then the dimmer switch actuator.
6. Remove turn signal lever attaching screw from dimmer switch actuator, then remove lever. **On models equipped with cruise control, disconnect wire connector.**
7. Remove turn signal switch attaching screws.
8. Remove buzzer switch wires (light green and tan/black wires) from turn signal switch wiring connector using tool J-35689-A.
9. Remove turn signal switch.
10. Reverse procedure to install, noting the following:
    a. Torque turn signal switch attaching screws to 35 inch lbs.
    b. Attach light green buzzer switch wire to terminal F of turn signal switch wiring connector.
    c. Attach tan/black buzzer switch wire to terminal G of turn signal switch wiring connector.
    d. Torque turn signal lever attaching screw to 18 inch lbs.
    e. Torque dimmer switch actuator attaching screw to 20 inch lbs.
    f. Torque column cover attaching screw to 35 inch lbs.
    g. Torque hazard warning switch attaching screw to 7 inch lbs.
    h. Torque steering wheel attaching nut to 30 ft. lbs.

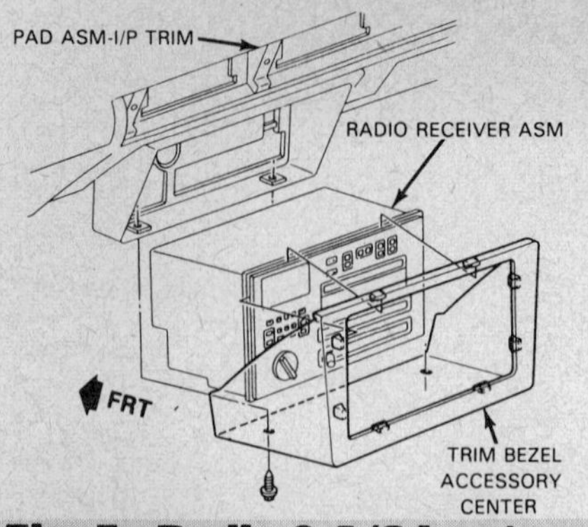

Fig. 5 Radio & A/C-heater control head removal. Beretta models

STEERING WHEEL
REPLACE

1. Disconnect battery ground cable.
2. Remove horn pad attaching screws from behind steering wheel spokes, then pull horn pad away from steering wheel, disconnect horn wire and remove pad.
3. If necessary, remove horn pad damper.
4. Remove retainer from end of steering column, then remove steering wheel retaining nut.
5. Scribe reference marks on steering wheel hub and steering shaft, then using puller, tool No. J-1859-03, remove steering wheel.
6. Reverse procedure to install. Torque steering wheel retaining nut to 30 ft. lbs.

INSTRUMENT CLUSTER
REPLACE

Refer to **Figs. 3 and 4,** for instrument cluster replacement procedures.

RADIO
REPLACE

The radio is removed as an assembly with the A/C and heater control head, **Figs. 5 and 6.**

WINDSHIELD WIPER MOTOR
REPLACE

1. Disconnect battery ground cable.
2. Remove left side wiper arm using following procedure:
   a. Remove plastic cap from end of wiper arm shaft.
   b. Remove nut from end of wiper arm shaft.
   c. Using suitable tool, pry wiper arm from wiper arm shaft.
3. Remove wiper drive link from crank arm.
4. Disconnect electrical connectors and washer hoses from wiper motor.
5. Remove wiper motor attaching bolts, then remove wiper motor, guiding crank arm through drive hole.
6. Reverse procedure to install.

WINDSHIELD WIPER TRANSMISSION
REPLACE

1. Disconnect battery ground cable.
2. Remove left and right side wiper arms using following procedure:
   a. Remove plastic cap from end of wiper arm shaft.
   b. Remove nut from end of wiper arm shaft.
   c. Using suitable tool, pry wiper arm from wiper arm shaft.
3. Loosen, but do not remove, transmission drive link(s) to wiper motor crank arm attaching screws.
4. Remove air inlet screen.
5. Disconnect transmission drive link(s) from wiper motor crank arm.
6. Remove wiper transmission to body attaching bolts.
7. Remove wiper transmission by guiding it through shroud upper panel access hole.
8. Reverse procedure to install.

BLOWER MOTOR
REPLACE
LESS A/C

1. Disconnect battery ground cable.
2. Disconnect blower motor and blower motor resistor electrical connections.
3. Remove plastic water shield from right side of cowl.
4. Remove blower motor attaching screws, then the blower motor.
5. Remove blower motor cage attaching nut, then the cage.
6. Reverse procedure to install.

WITH A/C

1. Disconnect battery ground cable.
2. Disconnect blower motor electrical connections.
3. Disconnect blower motor attaching screws, then pull blower motor and cage out.
4. Remove plastic water shield from right side of cowl.
5. Remove blower motor.
6. Remove blower cage attaching nut, then the blower cage.
7. Reverse procedure to install.

HEATER CORE
REPLACE
LESS A/C

1. Disconnect battery ground cable.
2. Drain cooling system into suitable container.
3. Disconnect coolant inlet and outlet hoses from heater core.
4. Remove heater outlet deflector from heater assembly.
5. Remove heater core cover from heater assembly.
6. Remove heater core and retaining straps.
7. Reverse procedure to install.

WITH A/C

1. Disconnect battery ground cable.
2. Drain cooling system into suitable container.
3. Raise and support vehicle.
4. Disconnect drain tube from heater case, then disconnect coolant inlet and outlet hoses from heater core.
5. Lower vehicle, then remove right and left side hush panels and steering column trim covers from under dash.
6. Remove heater outlet duct, then the glove compartment.
7. Pull heater core cover straight back, ensuring not to break drain tube.
8. Remove heater core clamps, then the heater core.
9. Reverse procedure to install.

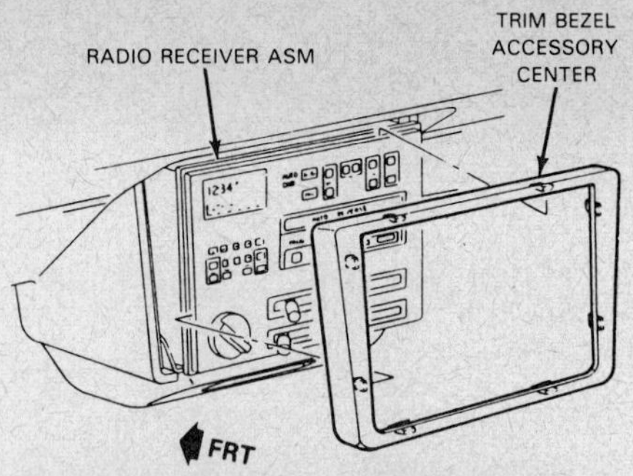

Fig. 6 Radio & A/C-heater control head removal. Corsica models

CRUISE CONTROL
RELEASE SWITCHES
Automatic Transmission

Both the electrical and vacuum release switches are located at the brake pedal. To adjust, depress brake pedal and insert switch fully into tubular clip. Pull pedal rearward until clicking sounds are no longer audible. The switch is now automatically adjusted.

Manual Transmission

On manual transmission equipped vehicles, the electrical release switch is located at the clutch pedal, while the vacuum release switch is found at the brake pedal. Adjustment procedures for these switches are the same as for those under automatic transmission equipped vehicles.

SERVO, ADJUST

With engine off and throttle valve in slow idle position, insert cable end pin in closest hole in servo tab assembly without tensioning cable. If no holes line up, move cable away from servo assembly until next closest hole ligns up. After installing cable end pin in servo tab, install pin retainer.

CRUISE SPEED, ADJUST

The cruise speed cannot be adjusted. If cruise speed is lower or higher than engagement speed, the cruise control module should be replaced.

4-121 (2.0L) Overhead Valve Engine Section

INDEX

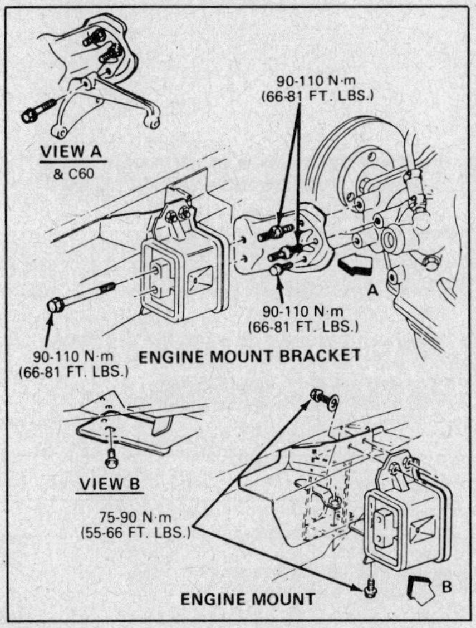

Fig. 1 Engine front mount

ENGINE MOUNTS REPLACE

FRONT ENGINE MOUNT

1. Disconnect battery ground cable.
2. Remove two upper front engine mount to body bracket attaching bolts.
3. Remove upper front engine mount to engine bracket attaching bolt.
4. Raise and support vehicle, then support engine assembly.
5. Remove inner fender shield.
6. Remove lower front engine mount to body bracket attaching bolt.
7. Remove lower front engine mount to engine bracket attaching bolt.
8. Remove front engine mount.
9. Reverse procedure to install. Refer to Fig. 1, for torque specifications.

Prior to installing mount attaching bolts, clean all bolts in suitable cleaning solvent and apply Loctite to threads.

REAR ENGINE MOUNT

1. Disconnect battery ground cable.
2. Raise and support vehicle, then support engine assembly.
3. Remove rear engine mount attaching nuts.
4. Remove rear engine mount attaching bolt.
5. Remove rear engine mount.
6. If rear engine mount bracket is removed, use the following procedure to ensure proper rear engine mount bracket positioning:
   a. Loosely install engine mount bracket.
   b. Raise engine and transaxle assembly.
   c. Tighten engine mount attaching nuts and bolt.
7. Reverse procedure to install. Refer to Fig. 2, for torque specifications.

Prior to installing mount attaching bolts, clean all bolts in suitable cleaning solvent and apply Loctite to threads.

ENGINE REPLACE

1. Disconnect battery ground cable, then the positive battery cable.
2. Drain cooling system into suitable container, then remove air intake hose from between air cleaner cover and Throttle Body Injection (TBI) unit.
3. Remove accessory drive belt.
4. Remove air cleaner retainer, then disconnect upper and lower radiator hoses.
5. Remove power steering pump front bolts.
6. Disconnect fuel lines and necessary vacuum hoses.

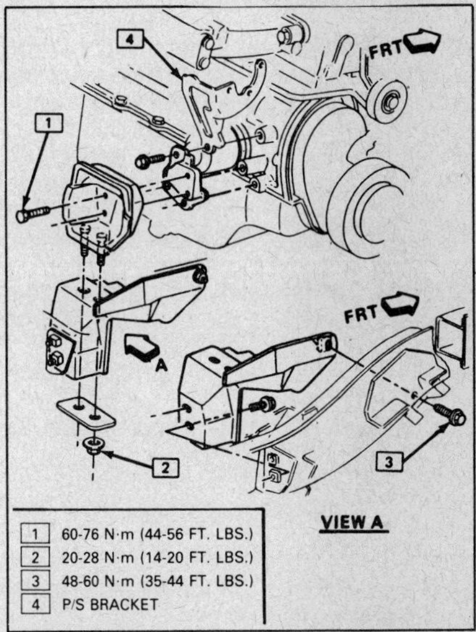

Fig. 2 Engine rear mount

7. Disconnect shift cables from transaxle, then the throttle cable(s) from TBI unit.
8. Remove wiring shield at bulkhead, then disconnect engine harness at bulkhead.
9. Disconnect wires at Electronic Control Module (ECM), then pull wires through bulkhead.
10. Remove any wires interfering with engine removal.
11. Remove relay bracket from bulhead.
12. Raise and support vehicle, then disconnect exhaust system at exhaust manifold and position aside.
13. Disconnect coolant inlet and outlet hoses from heater core.
14. Remove rear power steering pump bolt.
15. Disconnect stabilizer bar at left side lower control arm and support.
16. Remove transaxle strut from lefthand support.

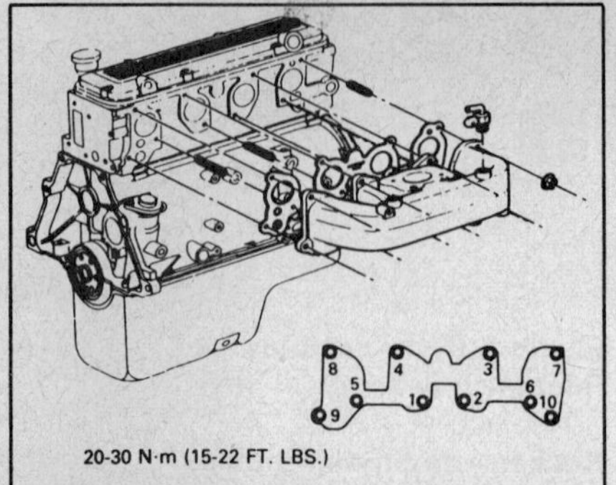

Fig. 3 Intake manifold installation

17. Drain transaxle lubricant, then remove front wheels.
18. Disengage drive axles from transaxle.
19. Remove support to body attaching bolts, then swing supports aside.
20. Disconnect A/C compressor mounting bolts (if equipped) and position aside.
21. Remove clutch slave cylinder from transaxle and position aside with hydraulic line connected.
22. Position engine support table J-36295 or equivalent under engine/transaxle assembly, then lower vehicle until engine/transaxle assembly is resting on table. Secure engine/transaxle to table.
23. Remove transaxle through bolt, then remove power steering pump from bracket and position aside.
24. Remove front mount to engine attaching bolts.
25. Remove rear mount and bracket assembly.
26. Slowly raise vehicle ensuring engine/transaxle assembly clears components.
27. Reverse procedure to install. Refer to **Figs. 1 and 2,** for engine mount torque specifications.

INTAKE MANIFOLD
REPLACE

1. Disconnect battery ground cable.
2. Remove air inlet duct from Throttle Body Injection (TBI) unit.
3. Drain engine coolant into suitable container.
4. Disconnect necessary vacuum hoses and electrical wiring.
5. Disconnect fuel line, then TBI linkage.
6. Remove power steering pump and position aside.
7. Raise and support front of vehicle.
8. Remove accelerator and T.V. cable bracket.
9. Disconnect heater hose from intake manifold.
10. Lower vehicle.
11. Remove intake manifold attaching nuts and bolts.
12. Remove intake manifold.
13. Reverse procedure to install. Torque intake manifold attaching nuts and bolts to specifications, following sequence given in **Fig. 3.**

EXHAUST MANIFOLD
REPLACE

1. Disconnect battery ground cable.
2. Disconnect oxygen sensor lead.
3. Remove accessory drive belt.
4. Remove alternator and position aside.
5. Raise and support vehicle.
6. Disconnect exhaust pipe from exhaust manifold.
7. Lower vehicle.
8. Remove exhaust manifold attaching nuts, then the manifold.
9. Reverse procedure to install.

CYLINDER HEAD
REPLACE

1. Disconnect battery ground cable.
2. Drain engine coolant into suitable container.
3. Remove air inlet duct from Throttle Body Injection (TBI) unit.
4. Raise and support vehicle.
5. Disconnect exhaust pipe at exhaust manifold, then the heater hose from intake manifold.
6. Remove accelerator and T.V. cable bracket.
7. Lower vehicle.
8. Disconnect any vacuum lines interfering with cylinder head removal from intake manifold and thermostat housing.
9. Disconnect linkage at TBI unit.
10. Disconnect necessary wiring.
11. Disconnect upper radiator from thermostat housing.
12. Remove accessory drive belt.
13. Remove power steering pump and position aside.
14. Disconnect fuel lines.
15. Remove alternator and alternator rear brace, leaving wires attached and position aside.
16. Remove rocker arm cover, then the rocker arms and pushrods. **Keep rocker arms and pushrods in order so they can be reinstalled in position they were removed from.**
17. Remove cylinder head attaching bolts, then the cylinder head, intake and exhaust manifolds as an assembly.
18. Reverse procedure to install. Refer to **Fig. 4,** for bolt tightening sequence and torque values.

ROCKER ARM STUDS
REPLACE

Rocker arm studs that have stress cracks or damaged threads can be replaced. If threads in cylinder head are damaged or stripped, then head can retapped and a helical type insert installed. When installing a new rocker arm stud, torque to 33-40 ft. lbs.

VALVES
ADJUST

These engines use hydraulic valve lifters. No provision for adjustment is provided.

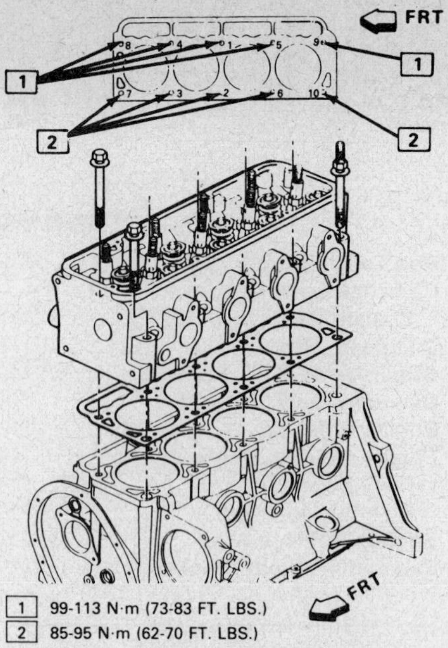

Fig. 4 Cylinder head installation

VALVE ARRANGEMENT
FRONT TO REAR

4-121 .... I-E-I-E-I-E-I-E

CAMSHAFT LOBE LIFT SPECIFICATIONS

Engine	Year	Int.	Exh.
4-121	1987-88	.260	.260

VALVE GUIDES

Valve guides are an integral part of the cylinder head and are not removable. If valve stem clearance becomes excessive, the valve guide should be reamed to the next oversize and the appropriate oversize valves installed. Valves are available in .003, .015, and .030 inch oversizes.

VALVE LIFTERS
REPLACE

1. Remove rocker arm cover attaching bolts, then the rocker arm cover.
2. Loosen rocker arm stud nut and rotate rocker arm so that pushrod can be removed. Remove pushrod. **Keep removed parts in order so they can be reinstalled in position removed from.**
3. Using tool J-29834, remove valve lifter from lifter bore.
4. Coat base of replacement with "Molykote," or equivalent, and install lifter into lifter bore.
5. Reverse procedure to install.

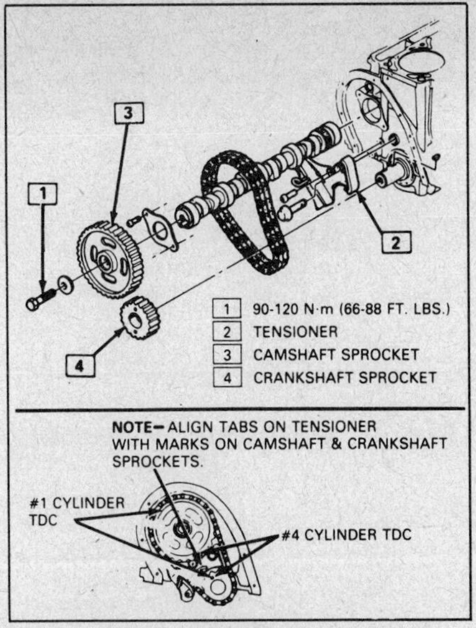

Fig. 5 Timing chain installation

CRANKSHAFT PULLEY REPLACE

1. Disconnect battery ground cable.
2. Remove accessory drive belt.
3. Raise and support vehicle, then remove right side tire and wheel assembly.
4. Remove right side inner fender shield, then the crankshaft pulley attaching bolt.
5. Using puller tool J-24420-B or equivalent, remove pulley.
6. Reverse procedure to install. Prior to installing pulley, coat front cover oil seal contact area with engine oil and apply suitable RTV sealer to pulley keyway.

ENGINE FRONT COVER REPLACE

1. Disconnect battery ground cable.
2. Remove crankshaft pulley as described previously.
2. Raise and support vehicle, then remove oil pan.
3. Lower vehicle, then remove accessory drive belt tensioner.
4. Remove front cover attaching bolts, then the front cover. **If front cover is difficult to remove, loosen with soft faced mallet.**

TIMING CHAIN REPLACE

1. Remove engine front cover as previously described.
2. Place No. 1 cylinder at TDC and align timing marks on crankshaft and camshaft sprockets, **Fig. 5.**
3. Remove timing chain tensioner upper attaching bolt, then loosen timing chain tensioner attaching nut as much as possible without removing it.
4. Remove camshaft sprocket attaching bolt, then the sprocket and timing chain.
5. If crankshaft sprocket is to be replaced, remove sprocket using puller J-5590 or equivalent.
6. To install crankshaft sprocket, align keyway on sprocket with key on crankshaft.
7. Align timing marks, **Fig. 5,** and install timing chain on sprockets.
8. Align dowel on camshaft with dowel hole on camshaft sprocket, then install sprocket to camshaft, using retaining bolt to draw sprocket fully to camshaft. Torque bolt to 66-88 ft. lbs.
9. Lubricate timing chain with engine oil, then install timing chain tensioner.
10. Install engine front cover as outlined previously.

TIMING CHAIN TENSIONER REPLACE

1. Remove front cover as described previously.
2. Remove attaching bolts.
3. Remove tensioner and damper.
4. Compress spring in direction of arrow, **Fig. 6.**
5. While compressing spring, use a cotter pin and insert into hole A shown.
6. Install chain tensioner.
7. Remove cotter pin from tensioner.

CAMSHAFT REPLACE

1. Remove engine from vehicle as previously described.
2. Drain engine oil, then remove oil filter.
3. Remove valve lifters and engine front cover as described previously.
4. Remove oil pump drive.
5. Remove timing chain and camshaft sprocket as previously described.
6. Remove camshaft thrust plate to engine block retaining bolts and the thrust plate, **Fig. 5.**
7. Remove camshaft from engine block. **Use caution when removing camshaft not to damage bearings.**
8. Reverse removal procedure to install. Prior to installing camshaft, lubricate camshaft bearings with engine oil and camshaft lobes with GM E.O.S. 1051396 lubricant or equivalent. When installing camshaft, align crankshaft and camshaft sprocket timing marks, **Fig. 5.**

PISTON & ROD ASSEMBLY

Install piston to rod with notch or arrow on piston facing toward front of engine and rod bearing tang slot opposite camshaft, **Fig. 7.** Upon installation, measure the connecting rod side clearance using a suitable feeler gauge. Measurement taken should be as follows:

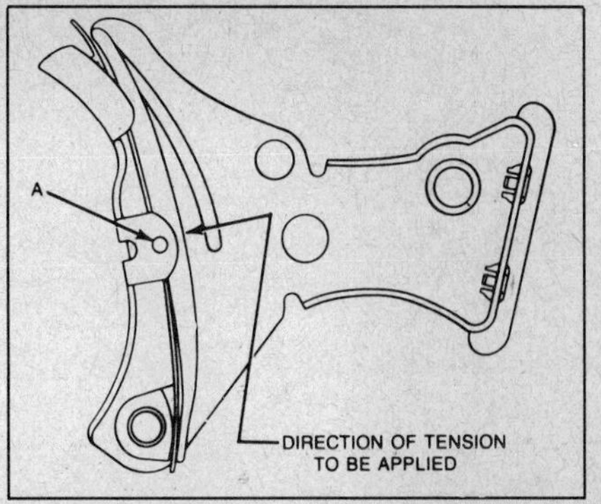

Fig. 6 Compressing timing chain tensioner spring

Engine	Year	Clearance In Inch
4-121	1987-88	.004-.015

PISTONS, PINS & RINGS

Pistons and rings are available in standard and oversize. Oversize piston pins are not available.

MAIN & ROD BEARINGS

Main and connecting rod bearings are available in standard and various undersizes.

OIL PAN REPLACE

1. Disconnect battery ground cable, then remove exhaust pipe shield.
2. Raise and support front of vehicle, then drain crankcase.
3. Disconnect exhaust pipe at exhaust manifold.
4. Detach A/C compressor brace at starter motor and A/C compressor bracket.
5. Remove flywheel cover and starter motor bracket, then remove starter motor and position aside.
6. Remove A/C compressor mounting brace.
7. Remove four righthand suspension support bolts, then lower suspension support slightly to provide clearance for oil pan removal.
8. On models equipped with auto. transaxle, remove oil filter adapter and extension.
9. Remove oil pan attaching bolts and oil pan.
10. Reverse procedure to install. Before installing oil pan, apply a thin coat of RTV sealer to both ends of oil pan rear seal, then seat seal firmly into rear main bearing cap. Do not allow sealer to extend beyond oil pan rear seal tabs. Apply a continuous 2 mm bead of RTV sealer along oil pan side rails in line with bolt holes, circling inward around each bolt hole location. Also apply RTV sealer to oil pan surface which contacts engine front cover. This bead of sealer must meet the bead at each oil pan side rail. Do not

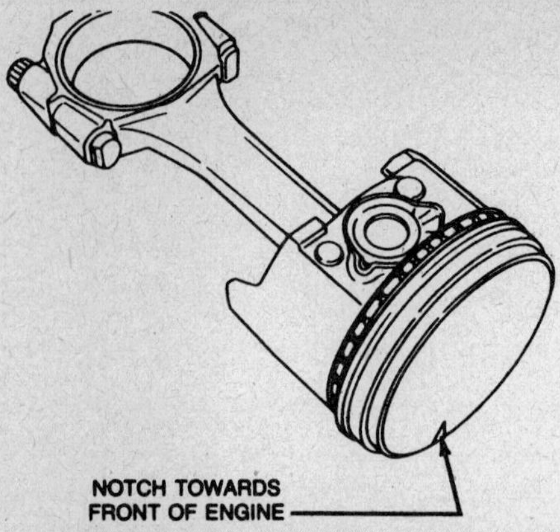

Fig. 7 Piston & rod assembly

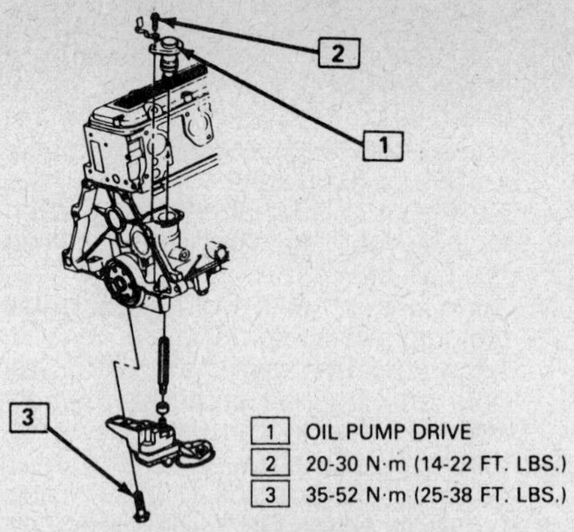

Fig. 8 Oil pump installation

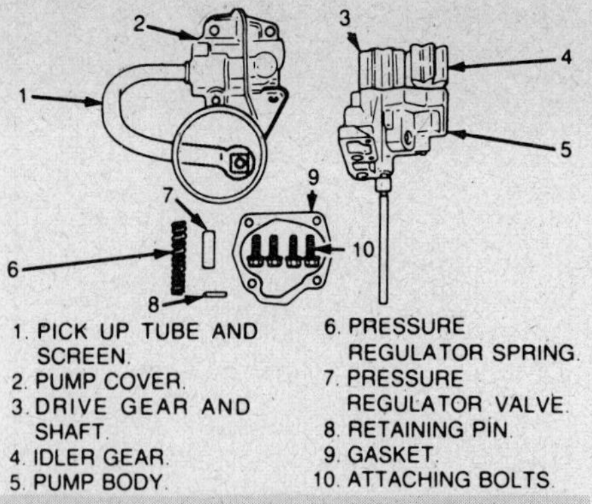

Fig. 9 Oil pump assembly

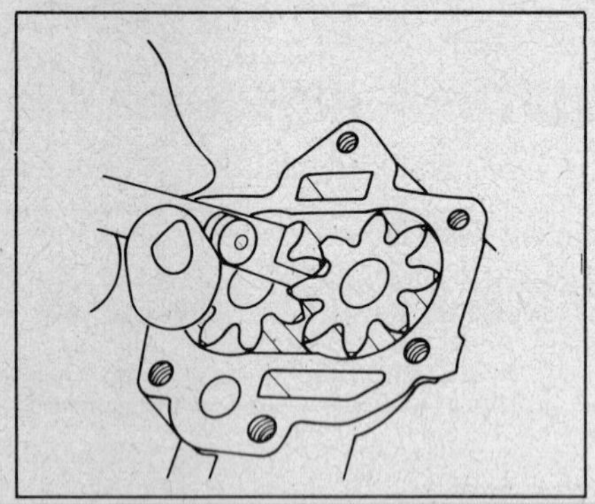

Fig. 10 Measuring oil pump gear lash

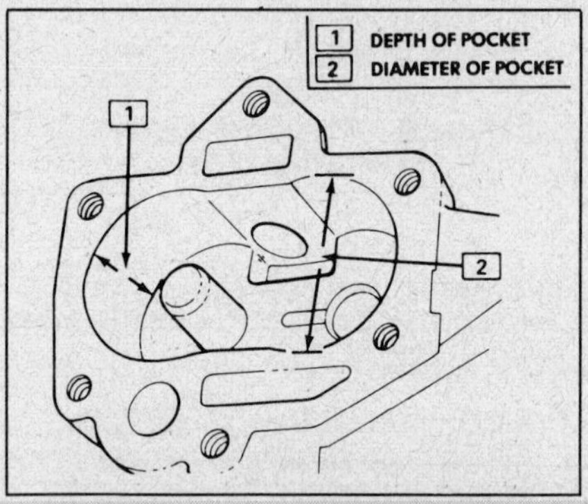

Fig. 11 Measuring oil pump housing pocket

apply any RTV sealer to oil pan rear seal mating surface. Carefully install oil pan and torque attaching bolts alternately and evenly to a minimum of 6 ft. lbs. Torque attaching bolts while RTV sealer is still wet to touch.

OIL PUMP SERVICE

REMOVAL

1. Drain crankcase, then remove oil pan as previously described.
2. Remove pump to rear main bearing attaching bolt, then remove pump and extension shaft, **Fig. 8.**

DISASSEMBLY

1. Drain oil from pump, then remove driveshaft and driveshaft extension.
2. Remove pick up tube and screen.
3. Remove four pump cover to body attaching bolts, then remove cover, idler and drive gears, **Fig. 9. Place alignment mark on oil pump drive and idler gear teeth so they can be installed in the same position.**
4. Remove pressure regulator valve retaining pin, spring and the valve from pump body.

INSPECTION

1. Inspect pump components and should any of the following conditions exist, the oil pump assembly should be replaced.
   a. Inspect pump body, gears and cover for cracks or excessive wear.
   b. Check drive gear shaft for looseness in housing.
   c. Check inside of pump cover for wear that would allow oil to leak past ends of gears.
   d. Check oil pickup screen assembly for damage to screen or pickup tube.
   e. Check pressure regulator valve for fit in pump body.
2. Install pump gears, then using suitable feeler gauge, measure oil pump gear lash at several locations, **Fig. 10.** Clearance should be .009-.015 inch.
3. Remove pump gears, then measure depth of oil pump housing pocket, **Fig. 11.** Depth should be 1.195-1.198 inch.
4. Measure pump gear length. Length should be 1.199-1.2 inches.
5. Measure pump gear diameters. Diameters should be 1.498-1.5 inch.
6. Install pump gears, then measure side clearance between pump gears and oil pump housing. Side clearance should be .003-.004 inch.
7. If oil pump components are not within specifications, it should be replaced.

ASSEMBLY

Lubricate internal pars with engine oil during assembly.

1. Install replacement pickup screen and tube assembly, if removed. Position pump in a soft jawed vise, then apply sealer to end of tube and tap into position using tool No. J-8369 and a plastic hammer. Use care not to damage inlet screen and tube assembly when installing into pump housing.
2. Place pressure regulator valve, spring and retaining pin into pump body, then install drive gear and shaft.
3. Install idler gear into pump body, then the pump cover gasket. **Fig. 9.**
4. Install pump cover and cover retaining bolts, then torque bolts to 8 ft. lbs.

INSTALLATION

1. Align oil pump extension shaft drive gear socket and pump housing, then install pump assembly.
2. Install oil pump assembly retaining bolt to rear main bearing cap and torque bolt to 25-38 ft. lbs.
3. Install oil pan as previously described.

REAR MAIN BEARING OIL SEAL

REPLACE

1. Support engine and remove transaxle.
2. Remove flywheel and ensure rear seal is leaking.
3. Remove seal by carefully inserting screwdriver in through dust lip and prying towards end of crankshaft. Repeat as necessary around circumference of seal until seal is removed, taking care not to damage crankshaft circumference.
4. Check inside of seal bore for nicks or burrs and correct as necessary. Inspect crankshaft for burrs or nicks on seal contact surface. Repair or replace crankshaft as necessary.
5. Install new seal using tool J-34686.
6. Place seal on mandrel, making sure that dust lip on seal bottoms squarely against collar of tool, **Fig. 12.**

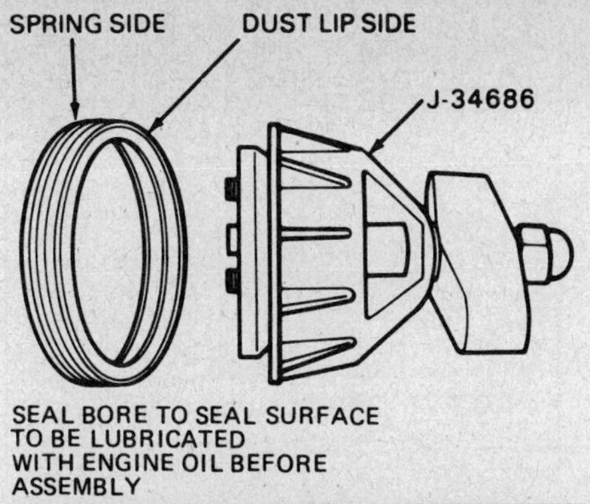

Fig. 12 Rear main oil seal installation

7. After aligning dowel pin with dowel pin hole in crankshaft, attach tool to crankshaft and torque screws to 2-5 ft. lbs.
8. Turn T-handle of tool until collar is tight against engine block to ensure that seal is seated properly in block.
9. Loosen T-handle of tool until it comes to a stop. Remove attaching screws.
10. Check that seal is seated squarely in bore.
11. Install flywheel and transaxle.
12. Start engine and check for leaks.

WATER PUMP REPLACE

1. Disconnect battery ground cable, then drain cooling system.
2. Remove accessory drive belt.
3. Remove alternator and alternator bracket.

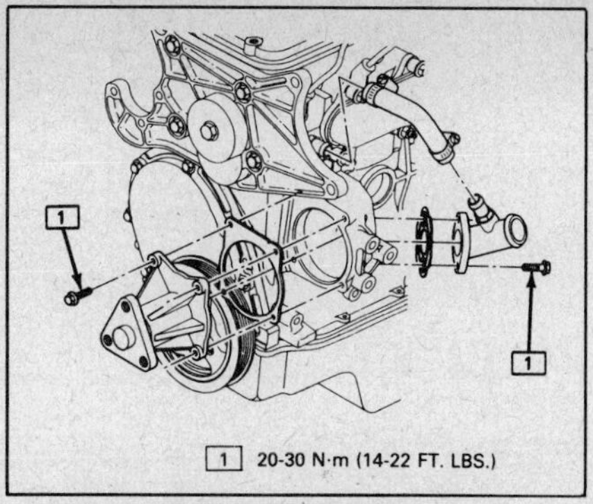

Fig. 13 Water pump installation

4. Remove water pump pulley to water pump attaching bolts, then the pulley from water pump.
5. Remove four water pump to block attaching bolts, then the water pump, **Fig. 13.**
6. Clean sealing surfaces of pump and engine block. Install new gasket and pump, then bolts and torque to 15-22 ft. lbs.
7. Reverse removal procedures to complete installation.

BELT TENSION DATA

Belt tension is maintained by a spring loaded belt tensioner. To remove or install drive belt, rotate tensioner with with a 15 mm socket. If belt tension is not satisfactory, ensure belt tensioner is within operating limits, **Fig. 14.** If belt tensioner is allowed to operate outside its operating limits, damage to belt tensioner may result.

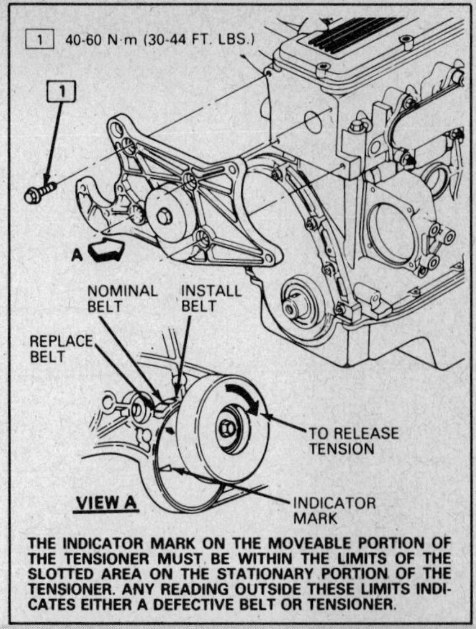

Fig. 14 Belt tensioner operating range

FUEL PUMP REPLACE

1. Disconnect battery ground cable.
2. Raise and support vehicle.
3. Drain, then remove fuel tank.
4. Rotate fuel sender/pump assembly cam lock ring, then lift out fuel sender/pump assembly.
5. Remove fuel pump from fuel sender by pulling fuel pump up into attaching hose while pulling outwards from lower support.
6. Reverse procedure to install. Install new fuel sender/pump assembly O-ring onto fuel tank before installation.

V6-173 (2.8L) Engine Section

INDEX

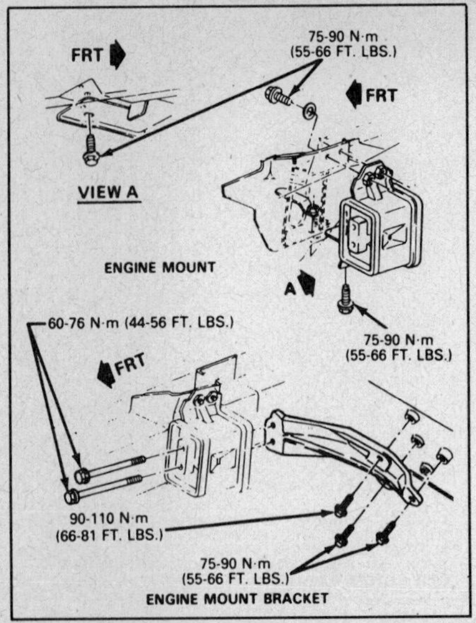

Fig. 1 Engine front mount

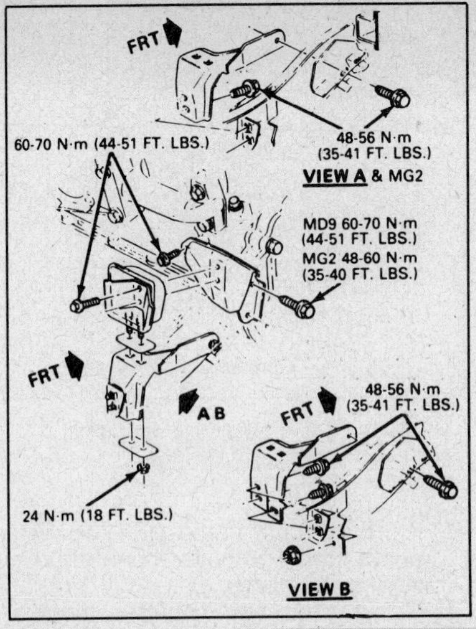

Fig. 2 Engine rear mount

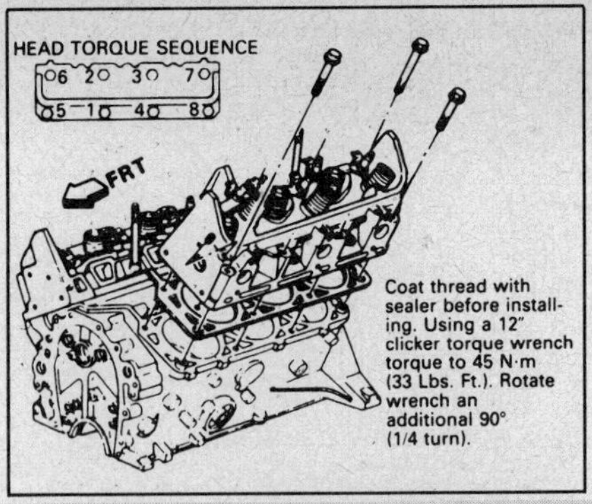

Fig. 3 Cylinder head installation

ENGINE MOUNTS

REPLACE

FRONT MOUNT

1. Disconnect battery ground cable.
2. Remove two engine mount to body bracket bolts, then the upper engine mount to engine bracket bolt. Raise and support vehicle.
3. Support engine with suitable jack.
4. Remove inner fender shield.
5. Remove lower engine mount to body bracket bolt, **Fig. 1.**
6. Remove lower engine mount to engine bracket bolt, then remove mount.
7. Reverse procedure to install. Clean all bolts with suitable solvent and apply suitable locking compound to threads prior to installation. Torque bolts to specifications given in **Fig. 1.**

REAR MOUNT

1. Disconnect battery ground cable, then raise and support vehicle.
2. Support engine with suitable jack.
3. Remove motor mount nuts and attaching bolts, **Fig. 2.**
4. Reverse procedure to install.

ENGINE

REPLACE

1. Disconnect battery ground cable and drain cooling system.
2. Remove air cleaner and the mass air flow meter.
3. Remove exhaust manifold/crossover assembly.
4. Remove accessory drive belt and the tensioner.
5. Remove power steering pump and position aside, then remove idler (if equipped).
6. Disconnect radiator hose at engine.
7. Disconnect accelerator and T.V. cables at throttle valve bracket.
8. Remove alternator and position aside, then disconnect engine wiring harness.
9. Disconnect fuel hoses and the coolant bypass and overflow hoses at engine.
10. Disconnect canister purge hose at canister and remove vacuum hoses as necessary. Support engine with engine holding fixture J-28467.
11. Raise and support vehicle, then remove right inner fender splash shield.
12. Remove harmonic balance and the flywheel cover.
13. Remove starter attaching bolts, disconnect electrical connectors at starter and remove starter.
14. Disconnect electrical connector at oil sending unit.
15. Remove A/C compressor and its mounting bracket(s).
16. Disconnect exhaust pipe at rear of manifold.
17. Remove flex plate to torque converter attaching bolts.
18. Remove front and rear motor mount bolts and brackets, then the intermediate shaft bracket from engine.
19. Disconnect shift cable bracket at transaxle.
20. Remove lower bellhousing bolts and lower vehicle.
21. Disconnect heater hoses at engine.
22. Install suitable engine lifting device and support transaxle with suitable jack. Remove engine support tool.
23. Remove upper bellhousing and front mount attaching bolts.
24. Remove transaxle mount bracket, then the engine.
25. Reverse procedure to install.

CYLINDER HEAD

REPLACE

LEFT SIDE

1. Disconnect battery ground cable.
2. Drain engine coolant into suitable container, then remove rocker arm cover.
3. Remove intake manifold. Refer to Intake Manifold, Replace for procedure.
4. Remove exhaust crossover at right side exhaust manifold.
5. Remove oil dipstick tube bracket.
6. Loosen rocker arm nuts until pushrods can be removed. **Keep pushrods in order they are removed so they can be installed in their original position.**
7. Remove cylinder head attaching bolts, then the cylinder head.
8. Reverse procedure to install, noting the following:
   a. Clean cylinder head bolts and cylinder head bolt holes with suitable solvent.
   b. Apply GM 1052080 sealer or equivalent to cylinder head bolt threads prior to installation.
   c. Position new head gasket on deck surface over dowel pins with "This Side Up" facing up, then install cylinder head.
   d. Torque bolts in sequence shown to specifications, **Fig. 3.**

RIGHT SIDE

1. Raise and support vehicle, then remove right side exhaust manifold.
2. Lower vehicle, then remove rocker arm cover.
3. Remove intake manifold. Refer to Intake Manifold, Replace for procedure.
4. Loosen rocker arm nuts until pushrods can be removed. **Keep pushrods in order they are removed so they can be installed in their original position.**
5. Remove cylinder head attaching bolts, then the cylinder head.
6. Reverse procedure to install, noting the following:
   a. Clean cylinder head bolts and cylinder head bolt holes with suitable solvent.
   b. Apply GM 1052080 sealer or equivalent to cylinder head bolt threads prior to installation.
   c. Position new head gasket on deck surface over dowel pins with "This Side Up" facing up, then install cylinder head.
   d. Torque bolts in sequence shown to specifications, **Fig. 3.**

INTAKE MANIFOLD
REPLACE

1. Disconnect battery ground cable.
2. Disconnect accelerator and T. V. cable bracket at plenum.
3. Disconnect throttle body at plenum.
4. Disconnect E.G.R. pipe at E.G.R. valve, then remove plenum.
5. Disconnect fuel inlet and return pipes at fuel rail.
6. Remove auxiliary drive belt.
7. Remove power steering pump and position aside.
8. Remove alternator with wiring attached and position aside.
9. Loosen alternator bracket.
10. Disconnect idle air vacuum hose at throttle body and the electrical connectors at injectors.
11. Remove fuel rail, breather tube and the runners.
12. Remove both rocker arm covers.
13. Drain cooling system into suitable container.
14. Disconnect radiator hose at thermostat outlet.
15. Disconnect coolant sensor and oil sender switch electrical connectors.
16. Remove coolant sensor, then disconnect cooling system bypass hose and heater inlet pipe at manifold.
17. Remove intake manifold attaching bolts, then the intake manifold.
18. Loosen rocker arm nuts until pushrods can be removed. **Keep pushrods in order they are removed so they can be installed in their original position.**
19. Reverse procedure to install, noting the following:
    a. When installing gaskets, install only on right or left side as marked.
    b. Clean cylinder case sealing surface front and rear ridges and apply a 3/16 inch bead of suitable RTV sealant on each cylinder block ridge.
    c. Install new intake gaskets on cylinder heads, then install pushrods. Torque rocker arm attaching nuts to specifications.
    d. When installing intake manifold, ensure areas between case ridges and manifold are completely sealed.
    e. Install manifold retaining bolts and nuts, torquing to specifications.

EXHAUST MANIFOLD
REPLACE

1. Disconnect battery ground cable, then drain engine coolant into suitable container.
2. Remove air cleaner, inlet hose/mass air flow sensor, coolant bypass hose and the heat shield.
3. Disconnect crossover pipe at right side manifold, then remove manifold attaching bolts and the manifolds.
4. Reverse procedure to install, torquing bolts to 19 ft. lbs.

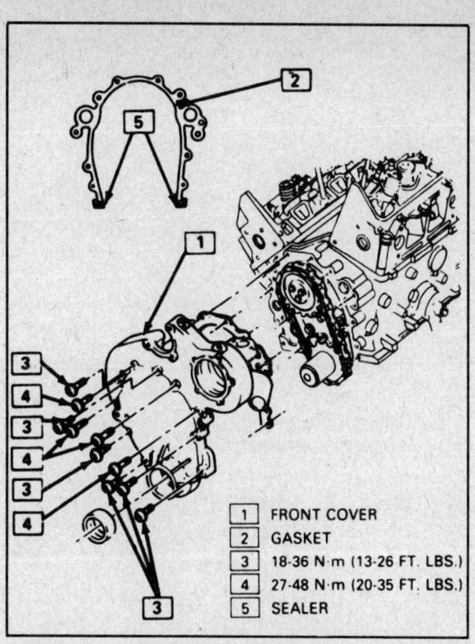

Fig. 4 Engine front cover installation

VALVES
ADJUST

1. Remove rocker arm covers.
2. Crank engine until assembly alignment mark on front face of torsional damper lines up with the arrow on the front cover. The engine should also be in the No. 1 firing position. This can be determined by placing fingers on No. 1 rocker arms as mark on torsional damper approaches arrow on front cover.
3. If valves are not moving, engine is in No. 1 firing position. If valves move as the mark comes up to the arrow on front cover, engine is in No. 4 firing position and should be rotated one revolution to reach No. 1 position.
4. With engine in No. 1 firing position, adjust exhaust valves 1, 2 and 3 and intake valves 1, 5 and 6, as follows:
    a. Back out adjusting nut until lash is felt at pushrod, then turn in adjusting nut until all lash is removed.
    b. When lash has been removed, turn adjusting nut in additional 1 1/2 turns to center lifter plunger.
5. Crank engine one revolution until arrow on front cover and torsional damper mark are again in alignment.
6. With the engine in this, the No. 4 firing position. adjust exhaust valves 4, 5 and 6 and intake valves 2, 3 and 4 as previously described.
7. Install rocker arm covers.

VALVE ARRANGEMENT
FRONT TO REAR

Right .... E-I-E-I-I-E
Left.......................... E-I-I-E-I-E

CAMSHAFT LOBE LIFT SPECIFICATIONS

Engine	Int.	Exh.
V6-173	.2626	.2732

VALVE STEM OIL SEAL & VALVE SPRING
REPLACE

1. Remove rocker arm cover, then the spark plug, rocker arm and pushrod on cylinder(s) being serviced. **Keep valve train parts in order they are removed so they can be installed in their original position.**
2. Install air line adapter tool J-23590 or equivalent to spark plug port and apply compressed air to hold valves in place.
3. Using tool J-5892 or equivalent to compress valve spring, remove valve locks, valve caps, valve spring and seat.
4. Remove valve stem oil seal.
5. Reverse procedure to install.

VALVE GUIDES

Valve guides are an integral part of the cylinder head and are not removable. If valve stem clearance becomes excessive, the valve guide should be reamed to the next oversize and the appropriate oversize valves installed. Valves are available in .003, .015 and .030 inch oversizes.

VALVE LIFTERS
REPLACE

1. Remove intake manifold as previously decribed.
2. Remove valve mechanism, then the valve lifters.
3. Install valve lifters. When installing new lifters, coat foot of valve lifters with "Molykote" or equivalent, ensuring lifter foot is convex.
4. Install intake manifold as previously described.
5. Install and adjust valve mechanism.

ENGINE FRONT COVER
REPLACE

1. Disconnect battery ground cable, then drain cooling system.
2. Remove auxiliary drive belt and tensioner.
3. Remove alternator with wiring connected and position aside.
4. Loosen alternator bracket.
5. Remove power steering pump and position aside.
6. Remove idler (if equipped).
7. Raise and support vehicle, then remove inner splash shield.
8. Remove flywheel cover from transaxle, then using tool J-24420, remove damper.
9. Remove starter, then the oil pan.

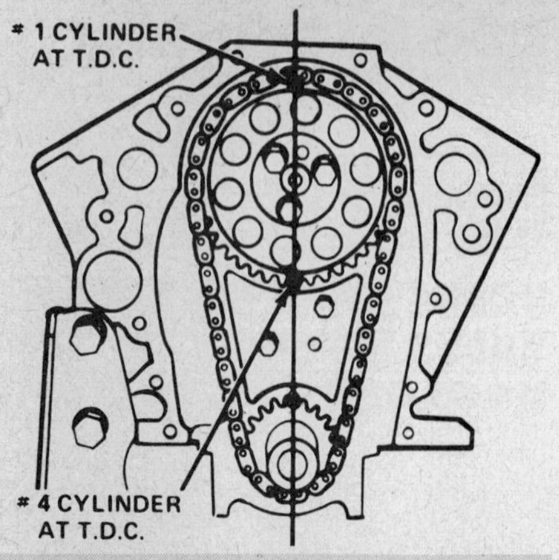

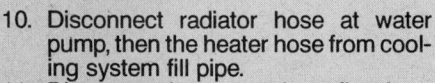

Fig. 5 Timing gear mark alignment

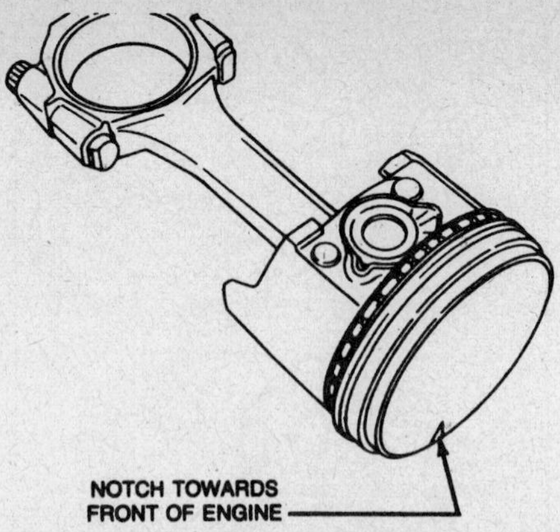

Fig. 6 Piston & rod assembly

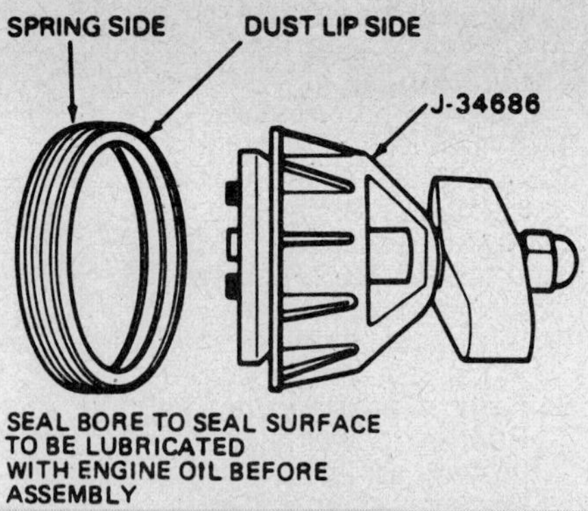

Fig. 7 Rear main oil seal installation

10. Disconnect radiator hose at water pump, then the heater hose from cooling system fill pipe.
11. Disconnect bypass and overflow hoses.
12. Remove water pump pulley.
13. Remove plug wire shield at water pump.
14. Remove canister purge hose.
15. Remove front cover attaching bolts, then the front cover.
16. Reverse procedure to install, noting the following:
    a. Clean all parts in suitable solvent.
    b. Apply sealer, GM 1052080 or equivalent to bolts as shown, **Fig. 4.**

ENGINE FRONT COVER OIL SEAL

REPLACE

1. Remove inner splash shield and torsional damper, then pry seal from cover using a suitable screwdriver. **Use caution not to damage crankshaft surface during seal removal.**
2. Install new seal so open end faces toward inside of cover, then drive seal into position using suitable tool.

TIMING CHAIN & SPROCKET

REPLACE

1. Remove crankcase front cover, refer to Front Cover, Replace for procedure.
2. Place No. 1 cylinder at TDC and align timing marks on crankshaft and camshaft sprockets, **Fig. 5.**
3. Remove camshaft sprocket attaching bolts. Tap lower edge of sprocket with plastic mallet and remove sprocket and timing chain.
4. If necessary, replace crankshaft sprocket.
5. Apply Molykote or equivalent to sprocket thrust surface.
6. Align timing marks, **Fig. 5,** and install timing chain on sprockets.
7. Align dowel on camshaft with dowel hole on camshaft sprocket, then install sprocket to camshaft, using attaching bolts to to draw sprocket fully to camshaft. Torque attaching bolts to 15-20 ft. lbs.
8. Lubricate timing chain with engine oil, then install front cover.

CAMSHAFT

REPLACE

1. Remove engine from vehicle, refer to Engine, Replace for procedure.
2. Remove valve lifters, refer to Valve Lifter, Replace for procedure.
3. Remove engine front cover, refer to Front Cover, Replace procedure.
4. Remove timing chain and sprocket. Refer to Timing Chain & Sprocket, Replace for procedure.
5. Remove camshaft. **Use caution not to damage bearings during camshaft removal.**
6. Reverse procedure to install. Coat camshaft lobes with GM E.O.S. 1052367 or equivalent prior to installation.

PISTON & ROD ASSEMBLY

There is a machined hole or cast notch in the top of all pistons. The piston assemblies should always be installed with the hole or notch toward front of engine, **Fig. 6.**

PISTONS, PINS & RINGS

Pistons and rings are available in standard and oversize. Piston pins are available in standard size only.

MAIN & ROD BEARINGS

Main and rod bearing are available in standard sizes and undersizes.

REAR MAIN BEARING OIL SEAL

REPLACE

1. Support engine and remove transaxle.
2. Remove flywheel.
3. Remove seal by carefully inserting screwdriver in through dust lip and prying towards end of crankshaft. Repeat as necessary around circumference of seal until seal is removed, taking care not to damage crankshaft circumference.
4. Check inside of seal bore for nicks or burrs and correct as necessary. Inspect crankshaft for burrs or nicks on seal contact surface. Repair or replace crankshaft as necessary.
5. Install new seal using tool J-34686.
6. Place seal on mandrel, making sure that dust lip on seal bottoms squarely against collar of tool, **Fig. 7.**
7. After aligning dowel pin with dowel pin hole in crankshaft, attach tool to crankshaft and torque screws to 2-5 ft. lbs.
8. Turn T-handle of tool until collar is tight against engine block to ensure that seal is seated properly in block.
9. Loosen T-handle of tool until it comes to a stop. Remove attaching screws.
10. Check that seal is seated squarely in bore.
11. Install flywheel and transaxle.
12. Start engine and check for leaks.

OIL PAN

REPLACE

1. Disconnect battery ground cable.
2. Raise and support vehicle, then drain crankcase.
3. Remove flywheel dust cover, then the starter motor.
4. Remove oil pan attaching bolts, then the oil pan.
5. Reverse procedure to install. Apply suitable sealer to oil pan mating surfaces, then torque 6 mm bolts to 6-9 ft. lbs. and 8 mm bolts to 15-23 ft. lbs.

OIL PUMP SERVICE

REMOVAL

1. Drain crankcase, then remove oil pan as previously described.
2. Remove pump to rear main bearing attaching bolt, then remove pump, **Fig. 8.**

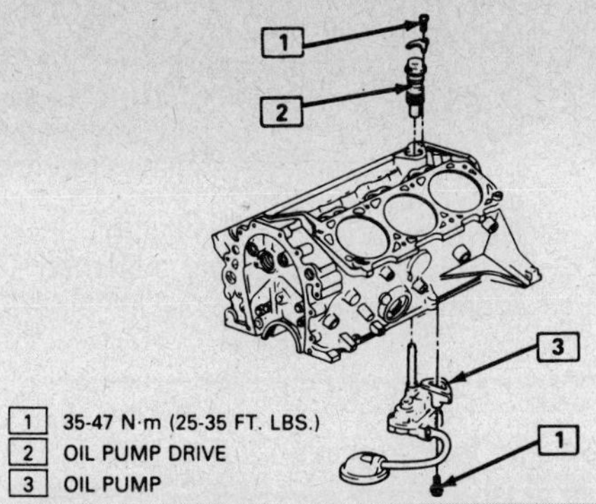

Fig. 8 Oil pump removal

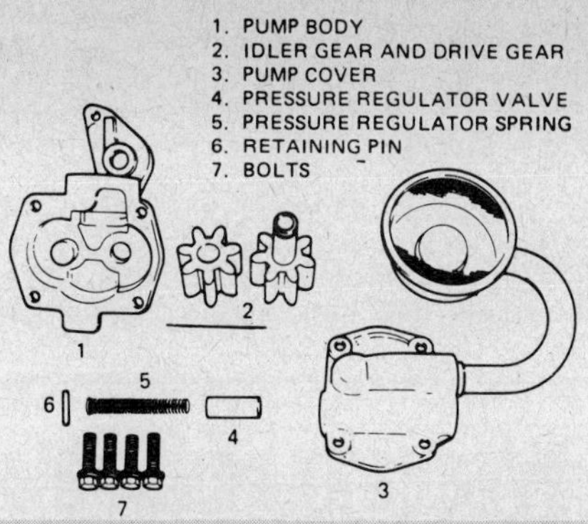

Fig. 9 Oil pump assembly

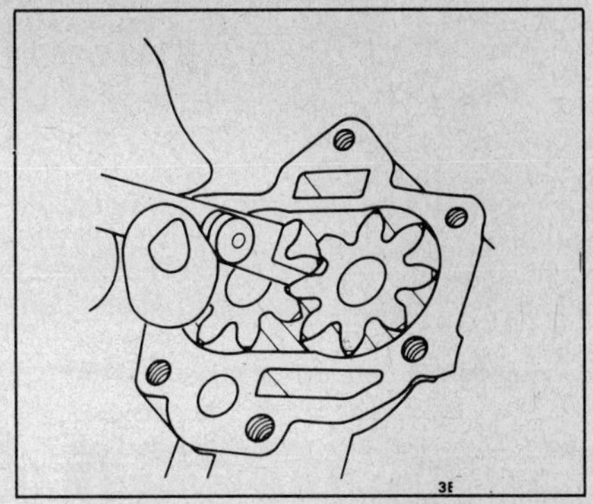

Fig. 10 Measuring oil pump gear lash

DISASSEMBLY

1. Drain oil from pump, then remove driveshaft and driveshaft extension.
2. Remove pickup tube and screen.
3. Remove four pump cover to body attaching bolts, then remove cover, idler and drive gears, **Fig. 9. Place alignment mark on oil pump drive and idler gear teeth so they can be installed in the same position.**
4. Remove pressure regulator valve retaining pin, spring and the valve from pump body.

INSPECTION

1. Inspect pump components and should any of the following conditions exist, the oil pump assembly should be replaced.
   a. Inspect pump body, gears and cover for cracks or excessive wear.
   b. Check drive gear shaft for looseness in housing.
   c. Check inside of pump cover for wear that would allow oil to leak past ends of gears.
   d. Check oil pickup screen assembly for damage to screen or pickup tube.
   e. Check pressure regulator valve for fit in pump body.
2. Install pump gears, then using suitable feeler gauge, measure oil pump gear lash at several locations, **Fig. 10.** Clearance should be .009-.015 inch.

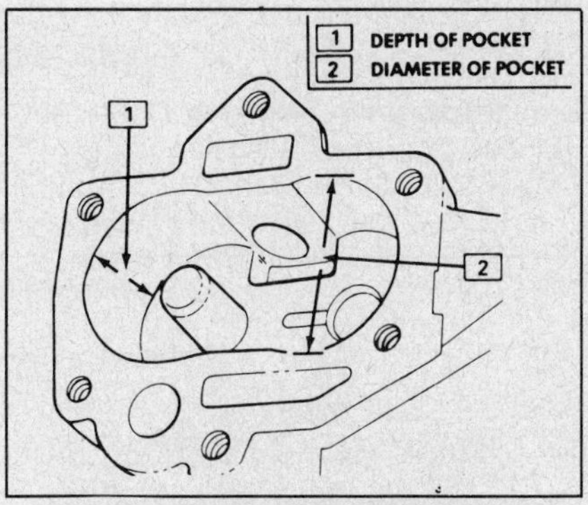

Fig. 11 Measuring oil pump housing pocket

3. Remove pump gears, then measure depth of oil pump housing pocket, **Fig. 11.** Depth should be 1.195-1.198 inch.
4. Measure pump gear length. Length should be 1.199-1.2 inches.
5. Measure pump gear diameters. Diameters should be 1.498-1.5 inch.
6. Install pump gears, then measure side clearance between pump gears and oil pump housing. Side clearance should be .003-.004 inch.
7. If oil pump components are not within specifications, it should be replaced.

ASSEMBLY

Lubricate internal parts with engine oil during assembly.

1. Install replacement pickup screen and tube assembly, if removed. Position pump in a soft jawed vise, then apply sealer to end of tube and tap into position using tool No. J-8369 and a plastic hammer. Use care not to damage inlet screen and tube assembly when installing into pump housing.
2. Place pressure regulator valve, spring and retaining pin into pump body, then install drive gear and shaft.
3. Install idler gear into pump body, then the pump cover gasket. **Fig. 9.**
4. Install pump cover and cover retaining bolts, then torque bolts to 8 ft. lbs.

INSTALLATION

1. Align oil pump extension shaft drive gear socket and pump housing, then install pump assembly.
2. Install oil pump assembly retaining bolt to rear main bearing cap and torque bolt to 25-38 ft. lbs.
3. Install oil pan as previously described.

WATER PUMP

REPLACE

1. Disconnect battery ground cable, then drain cooling system.
2. Remove accessory drive belt.
3. Remove water pump pulley, then the water pump, **Fig. 12.**
5. Reverse procedure to install.

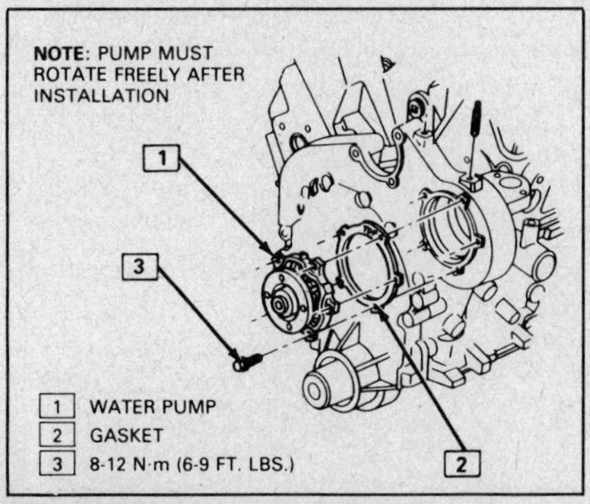

Fig. 12 Water pump installation

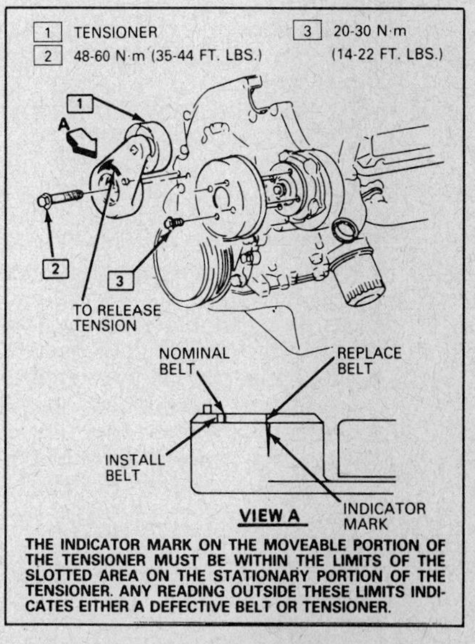

Fig. 13 Belt tensioner operating range

BELT TENSION DATA

Belt tension is maintained by a spring loaded belt tensioner. To remove or install drive belt, rotate tensioner with with a 3/4 inch socket. If belt tension is not satisfactory, ensure belt tensioner is within operating limits, **Fig. 13.** If belt tensioner is allowed to operate outside its operating limits, damage to belt tensioner may result.

FUEL PUMP
REPLACE

1. Disconnect battery ground cable.
2. Raise and support vehicle.
3. Drain, then remove fuel tank.
4. Rotate fuel sender/pump assembly cam lock ring, then lift out fuel sender/pump assembly.
5. Remove fuel pump from fuel sender by pulling fuel pump up into attaching hose while pulling outwards from lower support.
6. Reverse procedure to install. Install new fuel sender/pump assembly O-ring onto fuel tank before installation.

Clutch & Manual Transaxle Section

INDEX

CLUTCH
ADJUST

On these models, a hydraulic clutch system is used, **Fig. 1.** The system consists of a dash mounted master cylinder with integral reservoir, a transmission mounted slave cylinder and high pressure tubing to connect the two components.

The hydraulic clutch system provides automatic clutch adjustment, therefore, there is no provision for adjustment.

INSPECTION

1. While observing clutch slave cylinder pushrod travel, have an assistant depress clutch pedal. Brake pedal should travel approximately 7.4 inches.
2. If slave cylinder pushrod moves .433 inch or more, hydraulic system is operating properly.
3. If slave cylinder pushrod did not move .433 inch, proceed as follows:
   a. Check clutch master cylinder fluid level. The clutch slave cylinder must be installed during this operation. Refill as necessary.
   b. If master cylinder requires fluid, check hydraulic system components for leakage. Remove rubber boots from cylinders and check for leakage past pistons. A slight wetting of piston and wall surfaces is acceptable.
   c. If excessive leakage is indicated, entire hydraulic system must be replaced.

CLUTCH
REPLACE

1. Disconnect battery ground cable.
2. Remove hush panel from driver's footwell, then disconnect clutch mas-

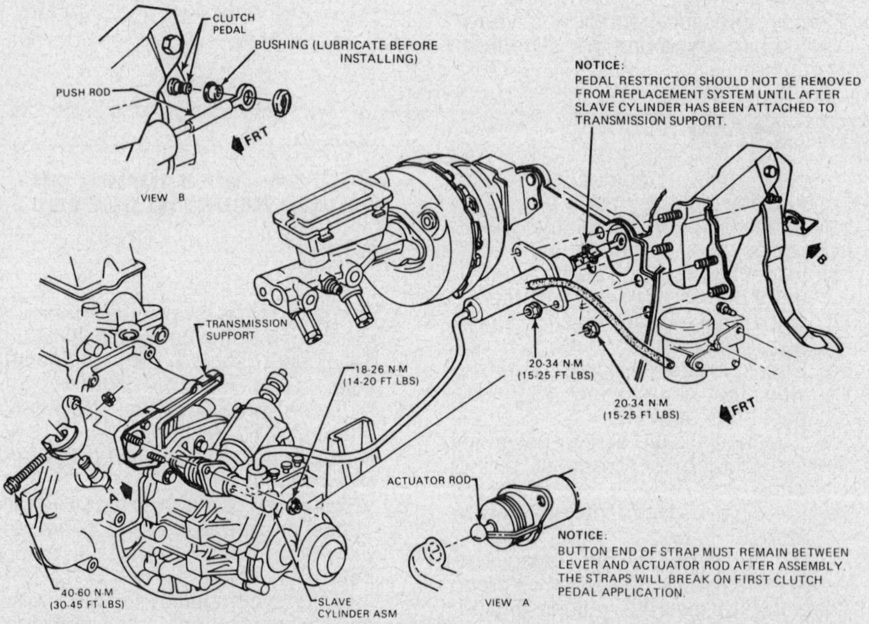

Fig. 1 Hydraulic clutch assembly. 1987–88 Models

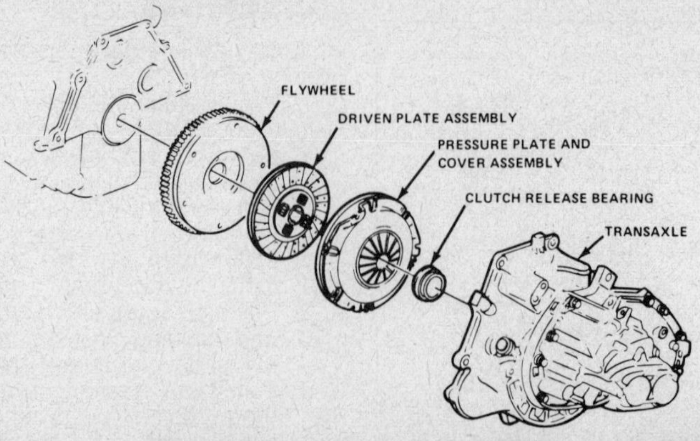

Fig. 2 Clutch assembly

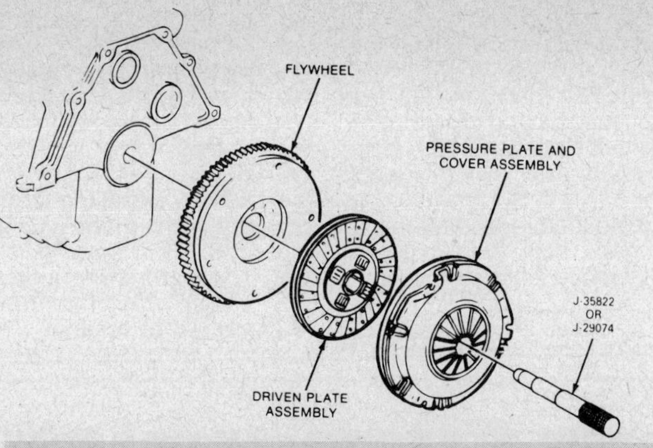

Fig. 3 Aligning clutch disc & pressure plate

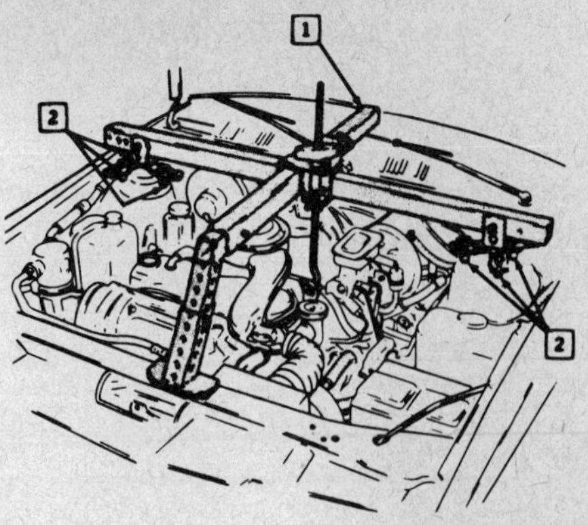

1. TOOL J-28467
2. THREAD ONTO STRUT ATTACHING BOLTS, ABOVE NUTS – 3 PER SIDE

Fig. 4 Engine support fixture installation

ter cylinder pushrod from clutch pedal.

3. Remove transaxle as outlined under Manual Transaxle, Replace procedure.
4. Mark position of pressure plate to flywheel to aid reassembly.
5. Gradually loosen pressure plate to flywheel attaching bolts until spring tension is relieved.
6. Support pressure plate and remove attaching bolts, pressure plate and driven disc, **Fig. 2.**
7. Clean pressure plate and flywheel mounting surfaces. Inspect bearing retainer outer surface of the transaxle.
8. Place pressure plate and driven disc in position and support with tool No. J-29074, **Fig. 3. The driven disc is installed with the damper springs offset toward the transaxle. Stamped letters found on the driven disc identify the "Flywheel Side."**
9. Install and gradually torque the pressure plate to flywheel attaching bolts to 15 ft. lbs. Remove support tool.
10. Lubricate the clutch throwout fork where it contacts the release bearing and pack the release bearing inside diameter recess with suitable grease.
11. Install transaxle and hush panel, then connect battery ground cable.

MANUAL TRANSAXLE SHIFT CABLES

REPLACE

1. Disconnect battery ground cable.
2. Remove clamp and nut from each transaxle shift lever.
3. Remove shift knob, console and shift boot.
4. Remove shift cables from shifter control assembly by twisting between cable socket and control lever with suitable screwdriver.
5. Remove spring clips retaining cables to control assembly.
6. Remove right front sill plate, then pull back carpet to gain access to shift cables.
7. Remove shift cable grommet cover attaching screws, then remove cable cover at floor pan and remove shift cables.
8. Reverse procedure to install.

SHIFT CONTROL ASSEMBLY

REPLACE

1. Disconnect battery ground cable.
2. Remove shift knob, console and shift boot.
3. Remove shift cables from shifter control assembly by twisting between cable socket and control lever with suitable screwdriver.
4. Remove spring clips retaining cables to control assembly.
5. Remove shift control assembly.
6. Reverse procedure to install.

MANUAL TRANSAXLE

REPLACE

MODELS W/ISUZU TRANSAXLE

1. Disconnect battery ground cable.
2. Install engine support fixture, **Fig. 4.** Connect fixture hook to engine lift ring and raise engine enough to relieve weight from engine mounts. The engine support fixture must be positioned in the center of the cowl and the attaching parts properly tightened before supporting engine.
3. Remove left sound insulator from under instrument panel, then disconnect clutch master cylinder pushrod from clutch pedal.
4. Remove clutch slave cylinder from transaxle support and position aside.
5. Remove transaxle mount attaching bolts.
5. Remove transaxle mount bracket attaching bolts and nuts.
6. Disconnect shift cables and remove retaining clips at transaxle.
7. Disconnect ground cable at transaxle mounting stud, then the shift light wiring.
8. Raise and support vehicle, then remove left front wheel.
9. Remove left front inner splash shield retaining screws and the splash shield.
10. Remove transaxle front strut and front strut bracket.
11. Remove clutch housing cover attaching bolts, then disconnect speedometer cable at transaxle.
12. Disconnect stabilizer bar at the left suspension support and control arm.
13. Remove left side support attaching bolts, then swing support aside.
16. Install boot protectors at drive axles, then disengage both drive axles at transaxle. Remove left drive axle from transaxle housing bore.
17. Attach the transaxle case to a suitable jack, then remove transaxle to engine mounting bolts.
18. Slide transaxle away from engine, lower jack and guide right drive axle from transaxle housing bore. Remove transaxle from vehicle.
19. Reverse removal procedure to install. **When installing transaxle, guide the right drive axle into transaxle bore as transaxle is being raised. The right drive axle cannot be installed after the transaxle is connected to engine.**

MODELS W/MUNCIE TRANSAXLE

1. Disconnect battery ground cable.
2. Install engine support fixture, **Fig. 4.** Connect fixture hook to engine lift ring and raise engine enough to relieve weight from engine mounts. The engine support fixture must be positioned in the center of the cowl and the attaching parts properly tightened before supporting engine.
3. Remove left sound insulator from under instrument panel, then disconnect clutch master cylinder pushrod from clutch pedal.
4. Remove air cleaner and air intake duct assembly.
5. Remove clutch slave cylinder from transaxle brace and position aside.
6. Remove transaxle mount through bolt.

7. Raise and support vehicle, then remove two exhaust crossover bolts from right side manifold.
8. Lower vehicle, then remove left side exhaust manifold.
9. Remove shift cables, then upper transaxle to engine attaching bolts.
10. Raise and support vehicle, then remove left tire and wheel assembly.
11. Remove left front inner splash shield, then the transaxle strut and bracket.
12. Drain transaxle into suitable container, then remove clutch housing cover bolts.
13. Disconnect speedometer wire connector.
14. Remove stabilizer bar from left side suspension support and control arm.
15. Remove left side suspension support attaching bolts, then swing support aside.
16. Install boot protectors at drive axles, then disengage both drive axles at transaxle. Remove left drive axle from transaxle housing bore.
17. Attach the transaxle case to a suitable jack, then remove transaxle to engine mounting bolts.
18. Slide transaxle away from engine, lower jack and guide right drive axle from transaxle housing bore. Remove transaxle from vehicle.
19. Reverse removal procedure to install. **When installing transaxle, guide the right drive axle into transaxle bore as transaxle is being raised. The right drive axle cannot be installed after the transaxle is connected to engine.**

Rear Axle, Rear Suspension & Brakes Section

INDEX

DESCRIPTION

This rear suspension is a semi-independent type suspension consisting of an axle assembly with trailing arms and twisting cross beam, coil springs and double action shock absorbers. A stabilizer bar is available and is attached to the inside of the axle beam and to the lower end of the control arms. A single unit hub and bearing assembly is bolted to each end of the axle assembly. The hub and bearing assembly is a sealed, nonserviceable unit and must be replaced as an assembly.

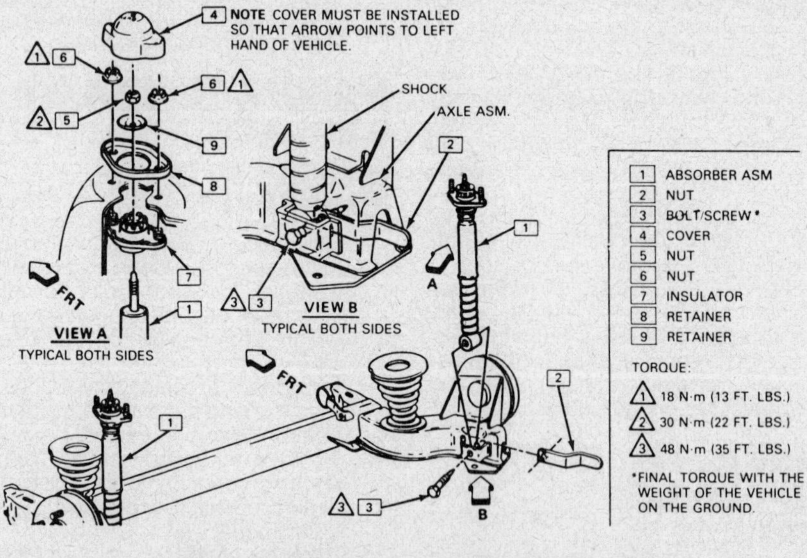

Fig. 1 Rear suspension. Corsica

REAR AXLE
REPLACE

1. Raise vehicle and support vehicle. Support rear suspension with suitable jack.
2. Disconnect stabilizer bar at axle assembly, if equipped.
3. Remove rear wheel assembly and brake drum. **Do not hammer on brake drum since damage to bearings may result.**
4. Remove shock absorber to lower mounting bracket attaching bolts, then disconnect shock absorbers from axle assembly, **Figs. 1 and 2.**
5. Disconnect parking brake cable and brake lines at axle brackets.
6. Carefully lower rear axle assembly and remove coil springs and insulators.
7. Remove control arm to underbody bracket bolts, then lower the axle assembly and remove from vehicle.
8. Remove hub to rear axle attaching bolts, then the hubs, bearings and backing plates from rear axle assembly.
9. Reverse procedure to install and bleed brake system.

HUB & BEARING ASSEMBLY
REPLACE

1. Raise and support vehicle, then remove wheel and tire assembly and brake drum. **Do not hammer brake drum since damage to bearing may result.**
2. Remove four hub/bearing assembly to rear axle attaching bolts, then the hub/bearing assembly from axle. **The upper rear hub attaching bolt may not clear brake shoe when removing hub and bearing assembly. Partially remove hub and bearing assembly prior to removing this bolt.**
3. Reverse procedure to install. Torque hub to axle attaching bolts to 38 ft. lbs. **Use care not to drop hub/bearing assembly since damage to bearing may result.**

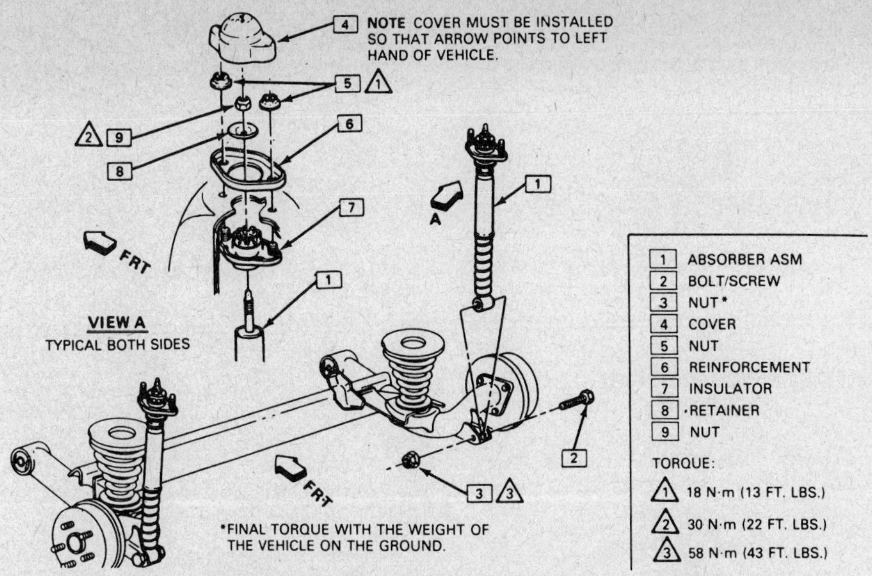

Fig. 2 Rear suspension. Beretta

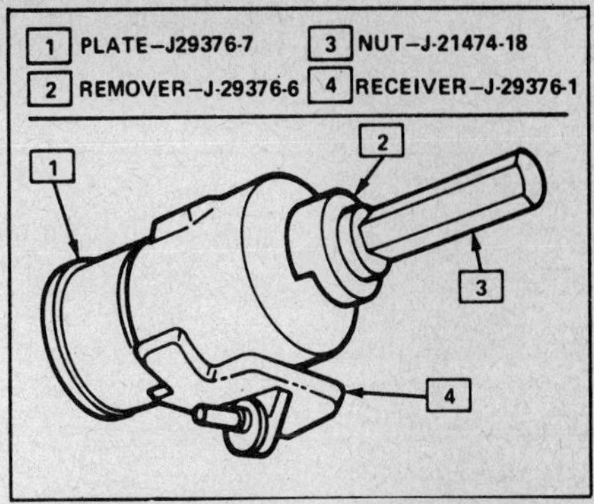

Fig. 4 Control bushing removal

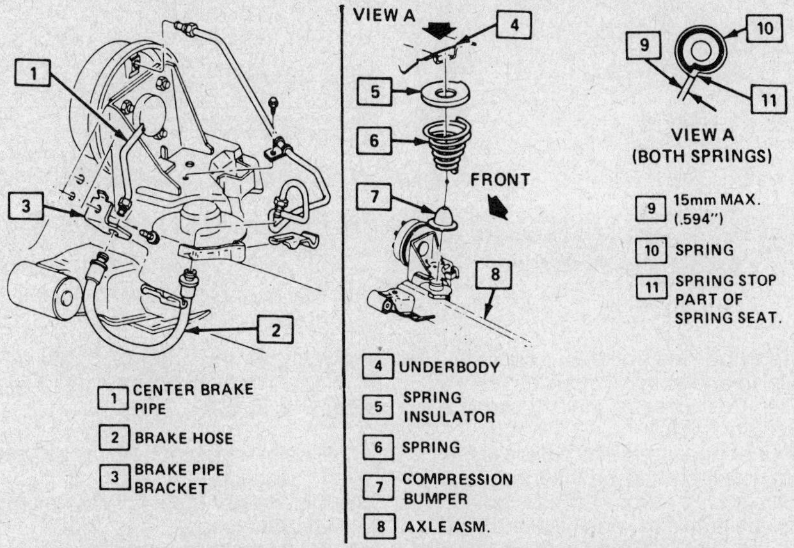

Fig. 3 Coil spring and brake line installation

SHOCK ABSORBER
REPLACE

1. Open deck lid, then remove trim cover (if equipped) and shock absorber upper retaining nut.
2. Raise rear of vehicle and support rear axle using a suitable jack.
3. Remove shock absorber lower attaching bolt, then disconnect shock absorber from mounting bracket, **Figs. 1 and 2.** Remove shock absorber from vehicle.
4. Reverse procedure to install. Torque attaching bolts to specifications given in **Figs. 1 and 2.**

COIL SPRING
REPLACE

1. Raise and support rear of vehicle. Support rear axle using a suitable jack.
2. Remove wheel and tire assemblies.
3. Remove brake line bracket attaching bolts, **Fig. 3,** from frame and allow brake lines to hang freely.
4. Remove shock absorber to lower mounting bracket bolts, then disconnect shock absorbers from axle assembly. **Do not suspend rear axle by brake hoses since damage to hoses may result.**
5. Carefully lower rear axle assembly and remove springs and insulators.
6. Reverse procedure to install. Position ends of upper coil in seat of body and within limits shown in **Fig. 3.**

CONTROL ARM BUSHING
REPLACE

1. Raise and support rear of vehicle.
2. Remove wheel and tire assembly, then support body with suitable jack stands.
3. Remove brake line bracket to body attaching screws from both sides.
4. Remove control arm to mounting bracket attaching nut, bolt and washer, then allow control arm to rotate downward.
5. The bushing can now be replaced using tools shown in **Figs. 4 and 5.** When installing bushing, the arrow on the installer must align with arrow on the receiver, **Fig. 4.**
6. Reverse procedure to complete installation. **The control arm attaching bolt must be torqued after vehicle is lowered to floor and is in its standing height position. Torque attaching bolt to 66 ft. lbs.**

DRUM BRAKE ADJUSTMENTS

The rear drum brakes, have self-adjusting shoe mechanisms that assure correct lining-to-drum clearances at all times. The automatic adjusters operate only when the brakes are applied as the vehicle is moving rearward on Corsica models. On Beretta models, the automatic adjusters operate whenever the service brakes are applied.

Although the brakes are self-adjusting, an initial adjustment is necessary after the brake shoes have been replaced, or when the length of the star wheel adjuster has been changed during some other service operation.

ADJUSTMENT

1. Raise and support vehicle, then remove rear wheels and brake drums.
2. Check to make sure that parking brake cable linkage and levers on secondary brake shoe are in "free" position.
3. Using tool J-21177, measure brake drum inside diameter, **Fig. 6.**
4. Turn brake adjusting screw to expand shoes to .050 inch less than diameter obtained on outside caliper portion of tool J-21177, **Fig. 7.**
5. Adjust parking brake. **Whenever rear drum brakes are serviced, the parking brake linkage cable at the equalizer must always be readjusted to prevent possible damage to brake shoes.**

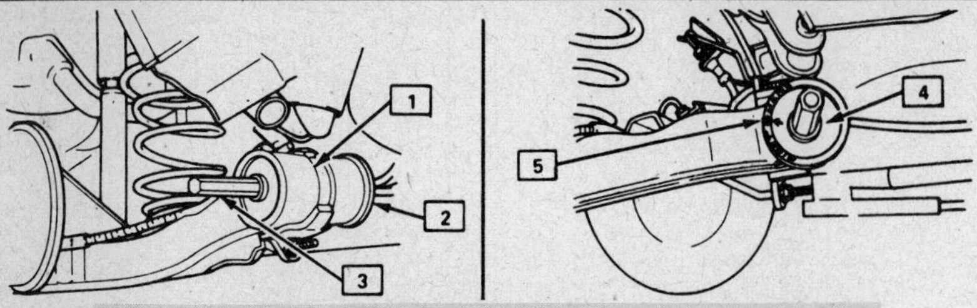

Fig. 5 Control arm bushing installation

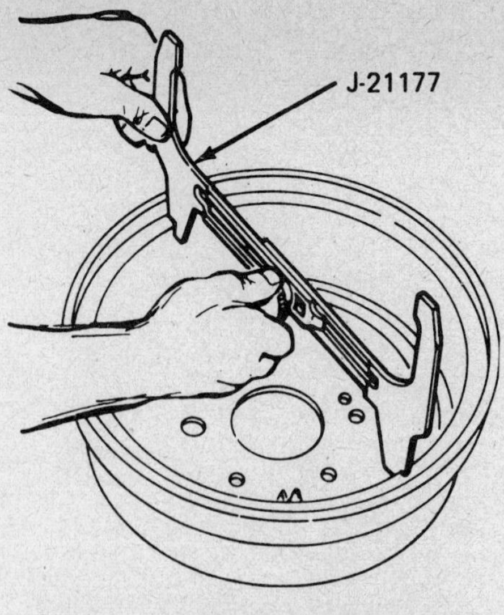

Fig. 6 Measuring brake drum inside diameter

6. Install brake drums, wheels and tires and lower vehicle to floor.
7. On Corsica models, drive vehicle alternately forward and backward, applying brakes moderately, to obtain satisfactory pedal height. On Beretta models, drive vehicle and apply and release service brake 30-35 times with normal pedal force. Allow about one second between brake applications until satisfactory pedal height is obtained.

PARKING BRAKE

ADJUST

CORSICA

1. Adjust service brakes.
2. Lift parking brake lever five ratchet clicks, then raise and support rear of vehicle.
3. Ensure equalizer nut groove is lubricated with grease, then tighten adjusting nut until rear wheel can be rotated backward, but is locked when forward rotation is attempted.
4. Release parking brake lever. Both wheels should rotate freely with no brake drag.

BERETTA

1. Adjust service brakes.
2. Apply and release parking brake approximately 8 times, then release.
3. Ensure parking brake is fully released by turning ignition On. Brake warning lamp should be off. If brake warning lamp is lit, determine reason and repair as necessary.

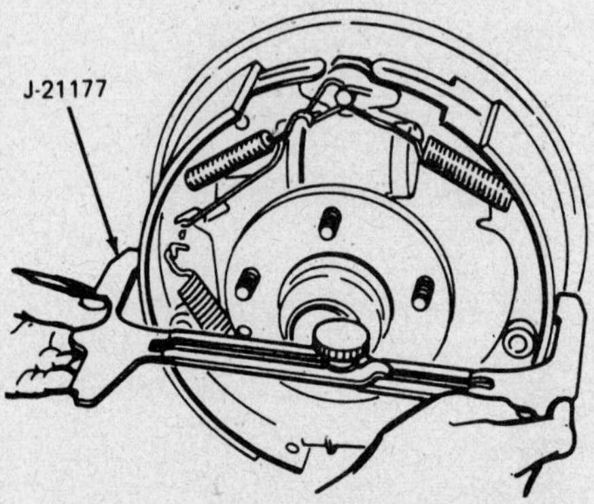

Fig. 7 Adjusting brake shoe clearance

4. Apply parking brake four clicks.
5. Raise and support vehicle.
6. Remove access hole cover from backing plate.
7. Adjust parking brake cable until a 1/8 inch drill bit can be inserted perpendicularly through access hole into space between shoe web and parking brake lever. Adjustment is correct when the 1/8 inch drill can be inserted, but a 1/4 inch drill cannot.
8. Release parking brake, then ensure rear wheels rotate freely. Repeat adjustment if necessary.
9. Install access hole cover, then lower vehicle.

MASTER CYLINDER

REPLACE

1. Disconnect electrical connector and four brake lines at master cylinder.
2. Remove two master cylinder to brake booster attaching nuts, then the master cylinder from vehicle.
3. Reverse procedure to install. Bleed brake system.

POWER BRAKE UNIT

REPLACE

1. Remove master cylinder as previously described.
2. Disconnect power brake unit pushrod at brake pedal.
3. Disconnect vacuum hose from vacuum check valve. Plug vacuum hose to prevent entry of dirt.
4. Remove four power brake unit to dash panel attaching nuts, then the power brake unit from vehicle.
5. Reverse procedure to install. Torque attaching bolts to 20 ft. lbs.

Front Suspension & Steering Section

INDEX

DESCRIPTION

The front suspension, **Fig. 1**, on these vehicles is of the MacPherson strut design. The lower control arms pivot from the lower side rails through rubber bushings. The upper end of the strut is isolated by a rubber mount incorporating a nonserviceable bearing for wheel turning. The tie rods connect to the steering arm on the strut, below the spring seat. The lower end of the steering knuckle pivots on a ball stud which is retained to the lower control arm by rivets and is secured to the steering knuckle with a nut and cotter pin. The sealed wheel bearings are integral with the hub and are serviced as an assembly.

WHEEL BEARING REPLACE

REMOVAL

1. Loosen hub nut with vehicle on ground.
2. Raise and support vehicle, then remove front wheel.
3. Install drive axle protective boot cover J-28712.
4. Remove hub nut.
5. Remove brake caliper from support and suspend caliper from flame with a length of wire. Do not suspend caliper by brake hose.
6. Remove brake rotor.
7. Remove three hub and bearing attaching bolts, then the splash shield. If the old bearing is being reinstalled, mark attaching bolts and corresponding holes for reinstallation, **Fig. 2.**
8. Using tool J-28733 or equivalent, remove bearing from steering knuckle, **Fig. 3. If excessive corrosion is present, ensure that bearing is loose in the knuckle before using puller tool.**
9. If installing new bearing, replace steering knuckle seal. **Do not move drive axle until hub nut is installed and torqued to specifications.**

INSTALLATION

1. Clean and inspect bearing mating surfaces and steering knuckle bore for dirt, nicks and burrs.
2. If installing new steering knuckle seal, apply grease to seal and knuckle bore, then press seal into steering knuckle.

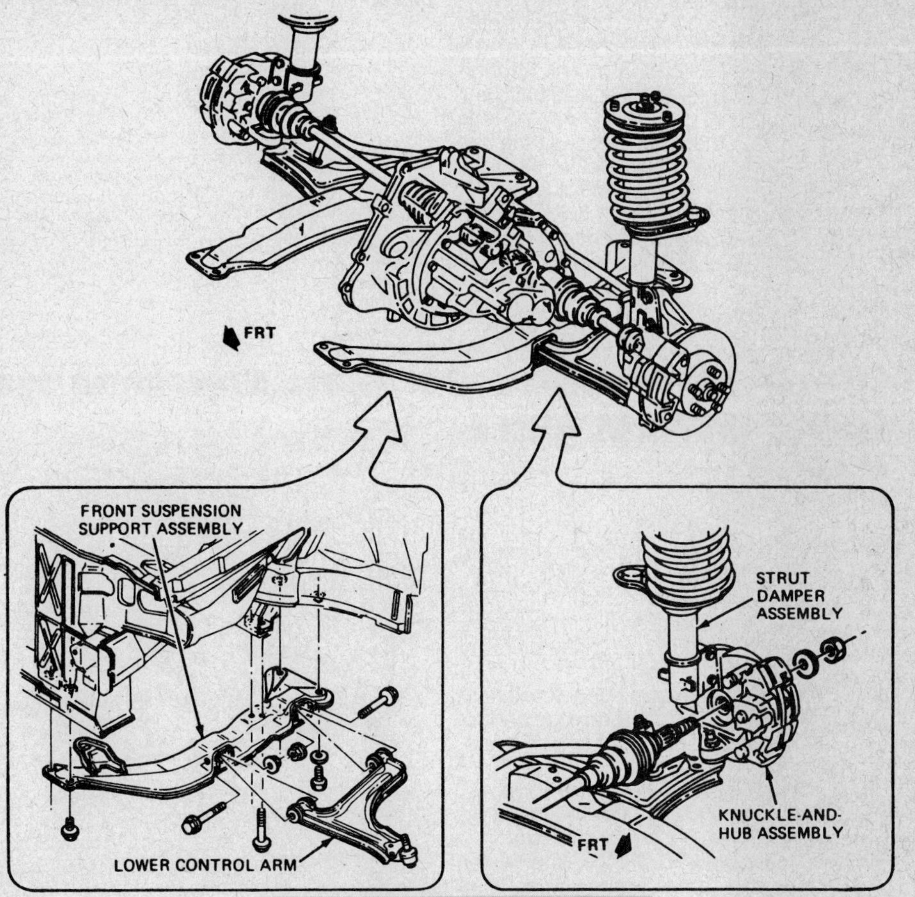

Fig. 1 Front suspension

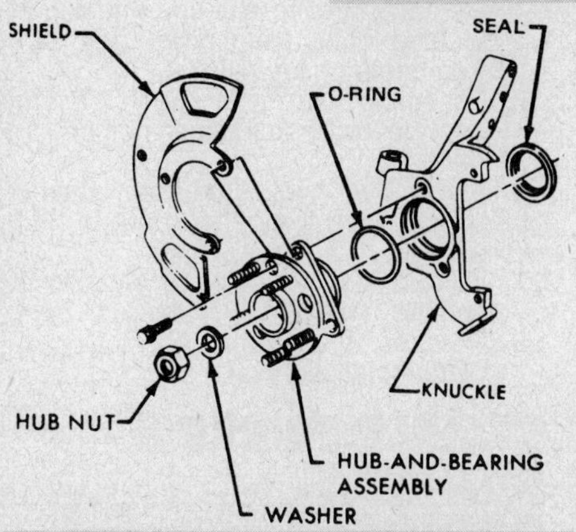

Fig. 2 Front hub & wheel bearing assembly

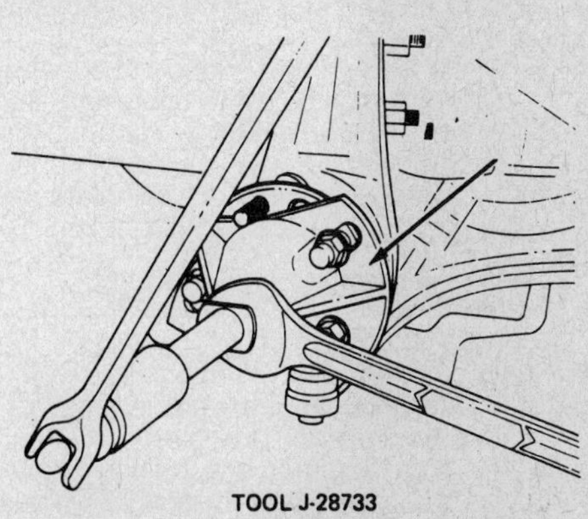

Fig. 3 Front hub & bearing assembly removal

3. Push bearing onto axle shaft, then install splash shield and hub to steering knuckle attaching bolts. Torque attaching bolts to 70 ft. lbs. Install hub to axle retaining nut and torque to 75 ft. lbs., **Fig. 4.**
4. Install rotor, brake caliper and wheel assembly.
6. Lower vehicle and torque hub to axle nut to 191 ft. lbs.

LOWER BALL JOINT
REPLACE

1. Raise and support vehicle, then remove wheel and tire.
2. Locate center of rivet body and mark with a center punch.
3. Using a 1/8 inch drill, drill pilot holes completely through the rivets. Using a 1/2 inch drill, drill final holes through rivets to ensure fitting of new ball joint.
4. Remove ball joint stud retaining nut, then, using tool J-29330, separate ball joint from steering knuckle. Remove ball joint from lower control arm.
5. Assemble new ball joint to lower control arm with bolts provided in service package, **Fig. 5.** Torque bolts to 50 ft. lbs.
6. Insert ball joint stud into steering knuckle and torque nut to 55 ft. lbs.
7. Install wheel and tire, check toe setting and adjust as required.

LOWER CONTROL ARM & BUSHING
REPLACE

1. Raise and support vehicle, then remove wheel and tire.
2. Disconnect stabilizer bar at lower control arm and control arm support.
3. Using tool J-29330, separate ball joint from steering knuckle.
4. Remove control arm support to chassis retaining bolts and remove control arm support and control arm as an assembly.
5. Separate control arm from support, then using tools shown in **Fig. 6**, remove bushings from control arm.
6. Lubricate new bushings and install into control arm using tools shown in **Fig. 6.**
7. Attach lower control arm to control arm support and torque pivot bolts to 63 ft. lbs.
8. Install control arm support to chassis, using attaching bolt tightening sequence shown in **Fig. 7.** Torque bolts to 66 ft. lbs.
9. Reverse procedure to complete installation. Check wheel alignment.

STEERING KNUCKLE
REPLACE

1. Raise and support vehicle, then remove wheel and tire.
2. Remove front hub and bearing as outlined under Wheel Bearing, Replace procedure.
3. Using tool J-29330, separate ball joint from steering knuckle.

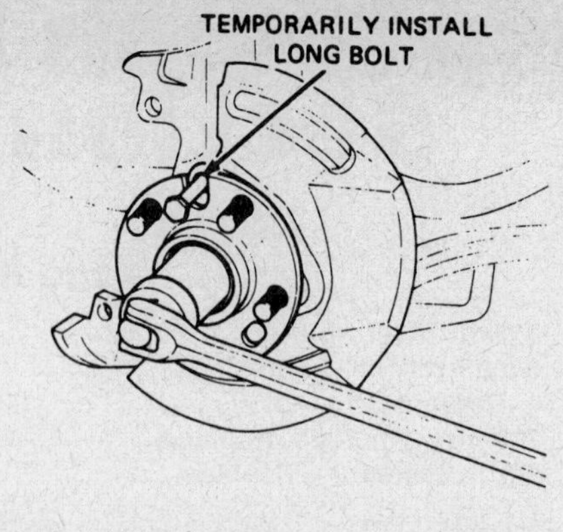
TEMPORARILY INSTALL
LONG BOLT

Fig. 4 Hub nut installation

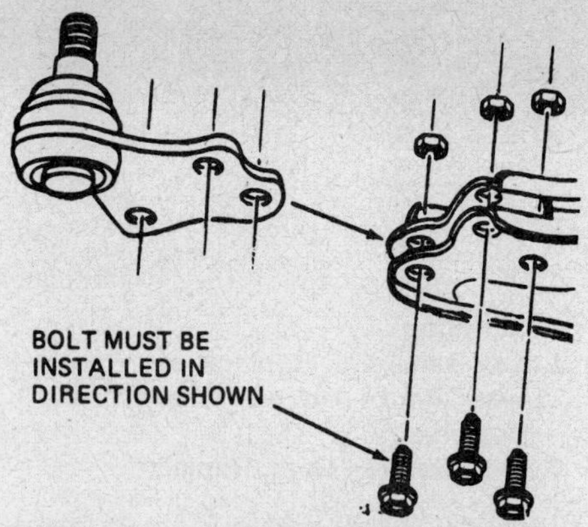
BOLT MUST BE
INSTALLED IN
DIRECTION SHOWN

Fig. 5 Assembling lower ball joint to lower control arm

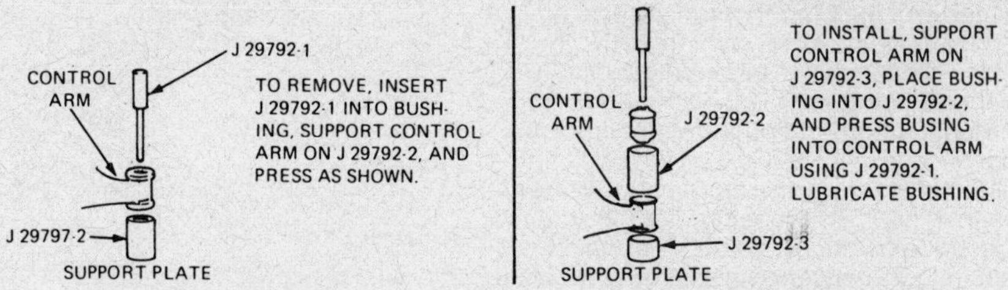
CONTROL
ARM
J 29792-1
TO REMOVE, INSERT J 29792-1 INTO BUSHING, SUPPORT CONTROL ARM ON J 29792-2, AND PRESS AS SHOWN.
J 29797-2
SUPPORT PLATE
CONTROL
ARM
J 29792-2
TO INSTALL, SUPPORT CONTROL ARM ON J 29792-3, PLACE BUSHING INTO J 29792-2, AND PRESS BUSING INTO CONTROL ARM USING J 29792-1. LUBRICATE BUSHING.
J 29792-3
SUPPORT PLATE

Fig. 6 Replacing lower control arm bushing

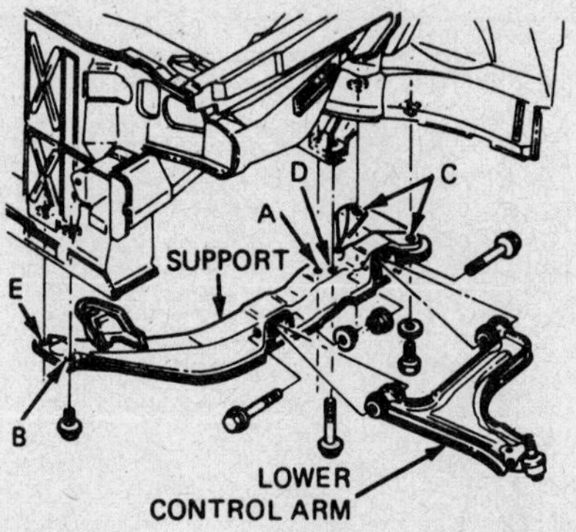
D
C
A
SUPPORT
E
B
LOWER
CONTROL ARM
1. LOOSELY INSTALL CENTER BOLT INTO HOLE (A).
2. LOOSELY INSTALL TIE BAR BOLT INTO OUTBOARD HOLE (B).
3. INSTALL BOTH REAR BOLTS INTO HOLES (C) TORQUE REAR BOLTS.
4. INSTALL BOLT INTO CENTER HOLE(D), THEN TORQUE.
5. TORQUE BOLT IN HOLE (A).
6. INSTALL BOLT INTO FRONT HOLE (E), THEN TORQUE.
7. TORQUE BOLT IN HOLE (B).

Fig. 7 Replacing lower control arm

4. Remove strut to steering knuckle attaching bolts, then disconnect strut from steering knuckle.
5. Assemble strut to new steering knuckle and install attaching bolts finger tight.
6. Insert ball joint stud into steering knuckle and torque stud nut to 55 ft. lbs.
7. Torque strut to steering knuckle attaching bolts to 129 ft. lbs.
8. Reverse removal procedure to complete installation.

STABILIZER BAR & BUSHINGS
REPLACE

1. Disconnect battery ground cable.
2. Install engine support tool J-28467 or equivalent.
3. Raise and support vehicle, allowing control arms to hang free.
4. Remove left front tire and wheel assembly.
5. Disconnect stabilizer bar from arms, then from support assemblies.
6. Loosen front support attaching bolts, then remove rear and center support bolts. Allow supports to drop down enough to remove stabilizer bar, **Fig. 8.**
7. Reverse procedure to install. Before tightening any attaching bolts, ensure stabilizer bar is centered in chassis. Refer to **Fig. 8**, for torque specifications.

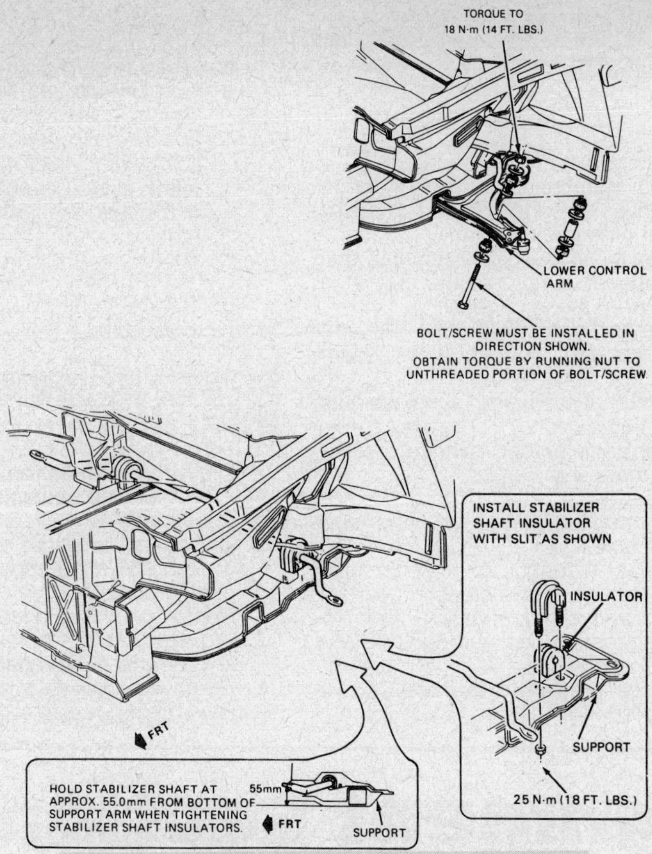

Fig. 8 Stabilizer bar installation

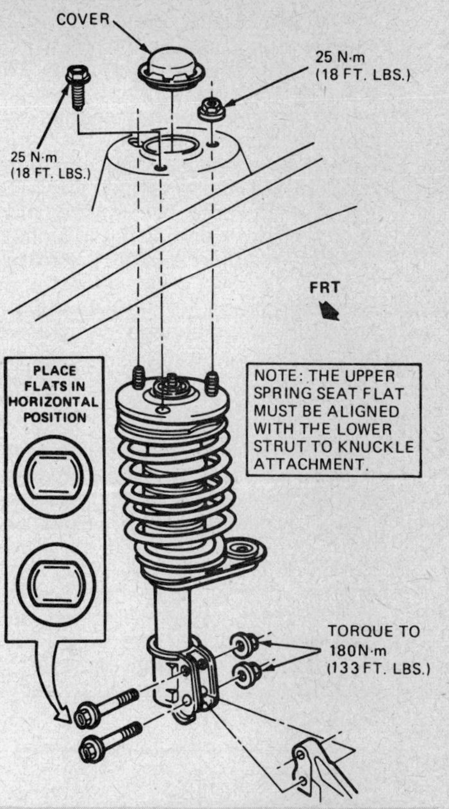

Fig. 9 Installing strut assembly

STRUT ASSEMBLY REPLACE

1. Raise hood and remove strut protective cap and three strut to body attaching nuts.
2. Raise and support vehicle, allowing suspension to hang freely.
3. Remove wheel and tire, then install drive axle protective cover, J-28712.
4. Using tool J-24319, disconnect tie rod from strut assembly.
5. Remove strut to steering knuckle attaching bolts, then remove strut from vehicle.
6. Reverse procedure to install. Position flats of strut mounting bolts as shown in **Fig. 9.** Torque all nuts and bolts to specifications.

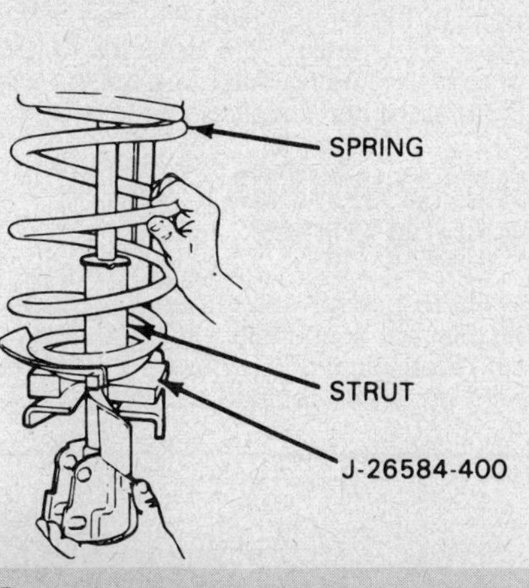

Fig. 10 Removing damper & coil spring from strut

STRUT ASSEMBLY SERVICE

DISASSEMBLY

Care must be taken not to damage special coating on coil springs. If special coating is damaged, coil spring damage could occur.

1. Clamp strut compressor tool J-26584 in a suitable vise.
2. Place strut assembly in compressor tool and install bottom adapter J-26584-400, making sure that adapter captures strut and locating pins are fully engaged, **Fig. 10.**
3. Position top adapter J-26584-430 on strut cap, aligning mounting holes as necessary.
4. Rotate compressor forcing screw clockwise until top support flange contacts top adapter. Continue rotating forcing screws until strut spring is compressed to approximately 1/2 its height. **Do not bottom the spring or strut damper rod.**
6. Remove damper top nut, then place alignment rod on strut shaft. Use alignment rod to guide shock shaft through spring cap during removal.
7. Remove strut components, then relieve compressor tension.

ASSEMBLY

1. Perform Steps 1 & 2 as outlined in the Disassembly procedure.
2. Position spring on strut, making sure spring is properly seated on bottom spring plate.

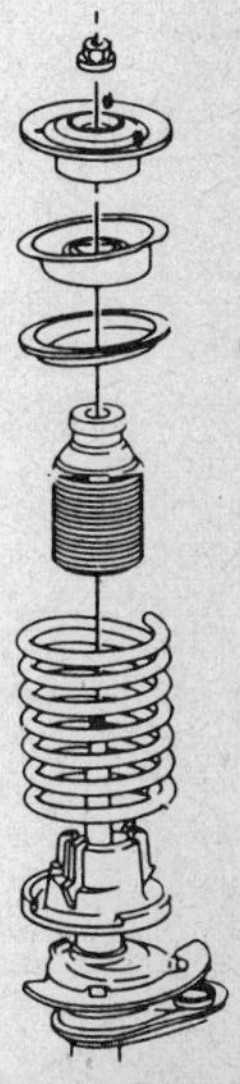

Fig. 11 Strut coil spring & upper mounting installation

3. Install shields, bumpers and insulators on spring seat, then install coil spring seat on top of spring, **Fig. 11.**
4. Install bearing cap on spring seat, ensuring they are centered together and properly aligned.
5. Rotate spring as necessary to have upper end of spring located within 10 mm from end of groove in upper insulator and lower end of spring located 10-15 mm from end of groove in lower insulator.
6. Position top adapter J-26584-430 on strut cap, then engage compressor slightly. Pull up strut rod to its full extension and clamp in place with tool No. J-34013-20
7. Insert alignment rod J-34013-27 through bearing and spring cap and position on top of strut rod. Compress spring slowly while guiding strut rod through bearing cap with alignment rod.
8. Continue compressing spring until one inch of strut rod is above bearing cap. Install strut attaching nut and torque to 60 ft. lbs.
9. Remove strut rod clamp, then release tension on coil spring and remove compressor.

POWER STEERING GEAR REPLACE

1. Disconnect battery ground cable.
2. Remove lefthand sound insulator.
3. Remove steering column coupling upper pinch bolt.
4. Remove hydraulic line retainer, then disconnect pump pressure and return lines from steering gear.
5. Raise and support vehicle.
6. Remove front wheel and tire assemblies.
7. Disconnect tie rods from steering knuckles.
8. Lower vehicle, then remove steering gear mounting clamps.
9. Move steering gear forward, then remove steering column coupling lower pinch bolt.
10. Remove steering column coupling and dash seal from steering gear.
11. Raise and support vehicle, then remove steering gear through left front wheel opening.
12. Reverse procedure to install, noting the following:
    a. Torque lower coupling pinch bolt to 37 ft. lbs.
    b. When installing steering gear, attach clamps and finger tighten all attaching nuts prior to tightening. Ensure dash seal is indexed and flush with steering gear. Torque lefthand side attaching nuts to 28 ft. lbs. then the right side attaching nuts.
    c. Torque tie rod end attaching nuts to 44 ft. lbs.
    d. Torque lower coupling pinch bolt to 29 ft. lbs.

POWER STEERING PUMP REPLACE

1. Disconnect battery ground cable.
2. Place suitable container under pump to catch fluid.
3. Disconnect pressure and return lines at pump, then plug open ends at hoses and pump.
4. Remove auxiliary drive belt.
5. Working through holes in pump pulley, remove pump attaching bolts.
6. Remove power steering pump.
7. Reverse procedure to install.

Wheel Alignment Section

INDEX

FRONT WHEEL ALIGNMENT

Toe setting is the only adjustment normally required. However, in special circumstances, such as damage due to road hazard or collision, camber may be adjusted by modifying the strut assembly. Caster is not adjustable.

CAMBER ADJUSTMENT

1. Secure bottom of strut assembly in a suitable vise.
2. Enlarge bottom holes in outer flanges with a round file until holes in outer flanges match slots in inner flanges, **Fig. 1.**
3. Connect strut to steering knuckle and install bolts finger tight.
4. Grasp top of tire firmly, then move tire inboard or outboard until correct camber reading is obtained. Tighten retaining bolts enough to secure camber setting.
5. Remove wheel and tire and torque strut to steering knuckle retaining bolts to 133 ft. lbs.

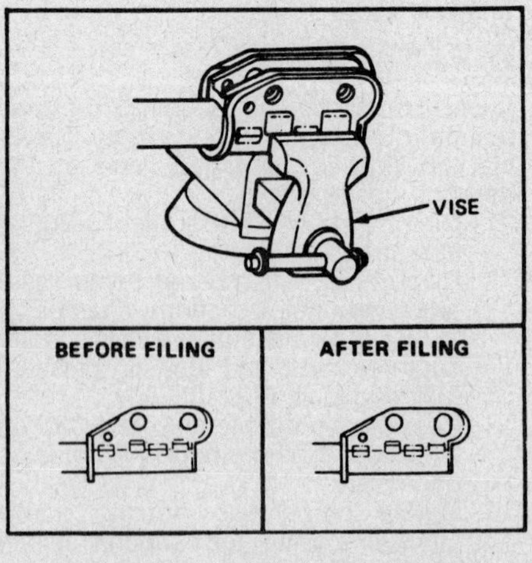

Fig. 1 Modifying strut bracket to adjust camber

TOE ADJUSTMENT

Toe is controlled by tie rod position. Adjustment is made by loosening the clamp bolts at the steering knuckle end of the tie rods and rotating the adjuster to obtain proper toe setting. After correct toe setting is obtained, torque clamp bolts to 35 ft. lbs.

REAR WHEEL ALIGNMENT

There are no adjustments to be made on this rear suspension. If alignment is outside specifications, check for broken or bent parts and replace as necessary.

BUICK SOMERSET & 1986–88 SKYLARK•OLDSMOBILE CALAIS & CUTLASS CALAIS•PONTIAC GRAND AM

INDEX OF SERVICE OPERATIONS

NOTE: Refer to rear of this manual for vehicle manufacturer's special service tool suppliers.

SPECIFICATIONS

GENERAL ENGINE SPECIFICATIONS

Year	Engine CID①/Liter	Engine VIN Code②	Fuel Injection System	Bore and Stroke	Compression Ratio	Net H.P. @ RPM③	Maximum Torque Ft. Lbs. @ RPM	Normal Oil Pressure Pounds
1985-86	4-151/2.5L	U	M.F.I.⑤	4.00 x 3.00	9	92 @ 4400	132 @ 2800	37
	V6-181/3.0L	L	E.F.I.④	3.80 x 2.70	9	125 @ 4900	150 @ 2400	37
1987	4-121/2.0L	M	M.F.I.⑤	3.39 x 3.39	8.0	165 @ 5600	175 @ 4000	—
	4-151/2.5L	U	E.F.I.④	4.00 x 3.00	9.0	98 @ 4000	132 @ 2800	37.5
	V6-181/3.0L	L	M.F.I.⑤	3.80 x 2.70	9.0	125 @ 4900	150 @ 2400	37
1988	4-138/2.3L	—	M.F.I.⑤	3.62 x 3.35	9.5	150 @ 5200	160 @ 4000	30
	4-151/2.5L	U	E.F.I.④	4.00 x 3.00	9.0	98 @ 4800	135 @ 3200	37.5
	V6-181/3.0L	L	M.F.I.⑤	3.80 x 2.70	9.0	125 @ 4900	150 @ 2400	45

①—CID-Cubic inch displacement.
②—The eighth digit denotes engine code.
③—Ratings are net-as installed in vehicle.
④—Electronic Fuel Injection.
⑤—Multi-Point Fuel Injection.

ALTERNATOR SPECIFICATIONS

Year	Model	Rated Hot Output Amps.
1985	1100257	78
	1105494	78
	1105495	94
	1105496	94
	1105497	108
1986	1105669	85
	1105670	100
	1105671	85
	1105672	100
1987	1101123	85
	1101124	100
	1101125	85
	1101126	100
	1101144	85
	1101145	100
	1101184	105
1988	1101123	85
	1101125	85
	1101126	100
	1101277	85
	1101278	100
	1101320	74

STARTING MOTOR APPLICATIONS

Year	Engine/VIN	Starter Ident. No.
1985	4-151/U	1998447
	V6-181/L	1998445
1986	4-151/U	1998531
	V6-181/L	1998526
	V6-181/L	1998546
1987	4-121/M	1998529
	4-151/U	1998531
	V6-181/L	1998544
	V6-181/L	1998546
1988	4-138/	—
	4-151/U	1998531
	V6-181/L	1998546

ENGINE TIGHTENING SPECIFICATIONS*

*Torque specifications are for clean and lightly lubricated threads only. Dry or dirty threads produce increased friction which prevents accurate measurement of tightness.

Year	Engine Model/V.I.N.	Spark Plugs Ft. Lbs.	Cylinder Head Bolts Ft. Lbs.	Intake Manifold Ft. Lbs.	Exhaust Manifold Ft. Lbs.	Rocker Arm Stud Ft. Lbs.	Rocker Arm Cover Ft. Lbs.	Connecting Rod Cap Bolts Ft. Lbs.	Main Bearing Cap Bolts Ft. Lbs.	Flywheel to Crankshaft Ft. Lbs.	Vibration Damper or Pulley Ft. Lbs.
1985	4-151/U	20	92①	29	44	20	4	32	70	44	200
	V6-181/L	15	②	45	25	45	7	40	100	60	200
1986	4-151/U	20	②	②	②	24	4	32	70	55	162
	V6-181/L	20	②	32	37	43	7	45	100	60	200
1987	4-121/M	15	②	16	16	—	6	26⑤	44④	48⑥	20
	4-151/U	20	②	②	②	24	4	32	70	③	—
	V6-181/L	20	②	32	37	43	7	40	100	60	229
1988	4-138/	—	—	—	—	—	—	—	—	—	—
	4-151/U	—	—	—	—	—	—	—	—	—	—
	V6-181/L	20	②	32	37	43	7	40	100	60	229

①—Requires thread sealer on bolt head and threads.
②—See text.
③—Auto. trans., 55 ft. lbs.; manual trans., 69 ft. lbs.
④—Plus an additional 40-50°.
⑤—Plus an additional 40-45°.
⑥—Plus an additional 30°.

COOLING SYSTEM & CAPACITY DATA

Year	Model or Engine/VIN	Cooling Capacity, Qts.		Radiator Cap Relief Pressure, Lbs.	Thermo. Opening Temp.	Fuel Tank Gals.	Engine Oil Refill Qts.	Transaxle Oil	
		Less A/C	With A/C					Manual Transaxle Pts.	Auto. Transaxle Qts.①
1985	4-151/U	9.5	9.75②	15	195	13.5	3③	6	④
	V6-181/L	12.75	12.25②	15	195	13.5	4③	6	④
1986	4-151/U	8	8	15	195	13.5	3③	6	④
	V6-181/L	10.3⑤	11⑤	15	195	13.5	4③	6	④
1987	4-121/M	8	8	15	195	13.6	4	⑦	④
	4-151/U	8	8	15	195	13.6	⑥	⑦	④
	V6-181/L	10⑤	10.3⑤	15	195	13.6	4③	⑦	④
1988	4-138/	7.6	7.6	15	192	13.6	4③	4	④
	4-151/U	7.8	7.8	15	195	13.6	4③	—	④
	V6-181/L	10	10.3	15	195	13.6	4③	—	④

①—Approximate; make final check with dipstick.
②—With heavy duty cooling, 10 qts.
③—Additional oil may be required.
④—Oil pan capacity, 4 qts; total capacity, 6 qts.
⑤—Grand Am, 7.8 qts.
⑥—Auto. trans., 3 qts.; manual trans., 4 qts.
⑦—Isuzu trans., 5.3 pts.; Muncie trans., 4.1 pts.

WHEEL ALIGNMENT SPECIFICATIONS

Year	Model	Caster Angle, Degrees		Camber Angle, Degrees				Toe-In Inch
				Limits		Desired		
		Limits	Desired	Left	Right	Left	Right	
1985	All	+.7 to +2.7	+1.7	+.25 to +1.5	+.25 to +1.5	+.85	+.85	①
1986	All	+.7 to +2.7	+1.7	+.2 to +1.4	+.2 to +1.4	+.8	+.8	②
1987	All	+.7 to +2.7	+1.7	+.2 to +1.4	+.2 to +1.4	+.8	+.8	③
1988	All	−.8 to +4.2	+1.7	−.2 to +1.8	−.2 to +1.8	+.8	+.8	④

①—Toe-out, −.13° per wheel.
②—Toe-out, −.06° per wheel.
③—Total toe, −.2° to +.2°.
④—Total toe, −.3° to +.3°.

Electrical Section

INDEX

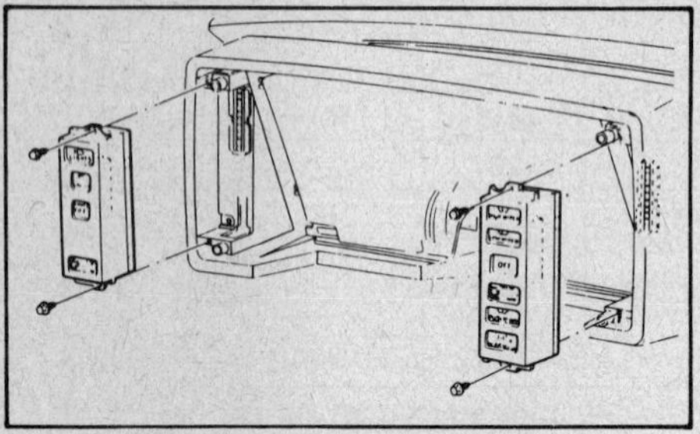

Fig. 1 Satellite switch removal. Skylark & Somerset

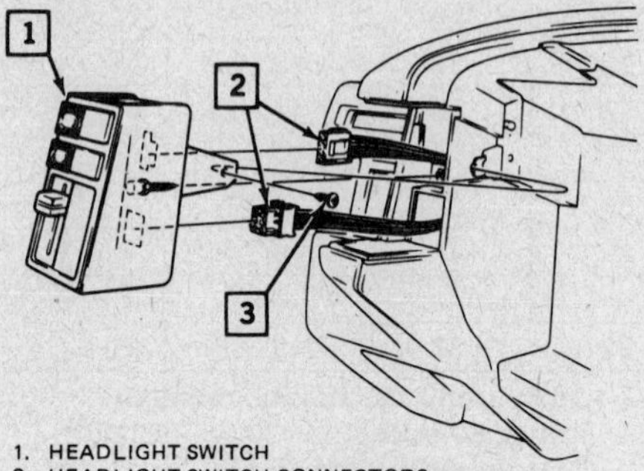

1. HEADLIGHT SWITCH
2. HEADLIGHT SWITCH CONNECTORS
3. FULLY DRIVEN, SEATED AND NOT STRIPPED

Fig. 2 Typical satellite switch removal. Calais, Cutlass Calais & Grand Am

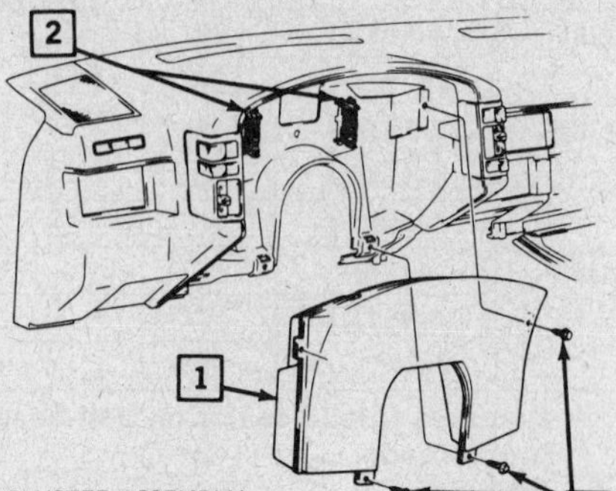

1. CLUSTER ASSEMBLY
2. CLUSTER CONNECTORS
3. FULLY DRIVEN, SEATED AND NOT STRIPPED

Fig. 3 Instrument cluster removal. Calais & Cutlass Calais

NOTE: Refer to section 10 "Electrical Section" for service procedures not covered in this section.

STARTER
REPLACE

1. Disconnect battery ground cable.
2. Raise and support vehicle, if necessary.
3. Remove rear starter motor support bracket bolts, then the bracket.
4. Remove A/C compressor support rod, if equipped.
5. Remove starter motor mounting bolts, then the starter motor.
6. Reverse procedure to install.

SATELLITE SWITCHES
REPLACE

The headlamp, hazard flasher, rear defogger and windshield wiper/washer controls are incorporated into switch modules mounted on either side of the instrument cluster.

1. Disconnect battery ground cable.
2. Remove steering column collar, if equipped, then the steering column filler plate screws and filler plate or lap duct assembly.
3. Remove instrument cluster trim plate attaching screws, then the trim plate.
4. On Somerset and Skylark models, remove switch bezel retaining screws and the bezels.
5. On all models, remove switch retaining screws, pull switch assembly away from instrument panel, **Figs. 1 and 2,** and disconnect electrical connectors as needed to complete removal.
6. Reverse procedure to install.

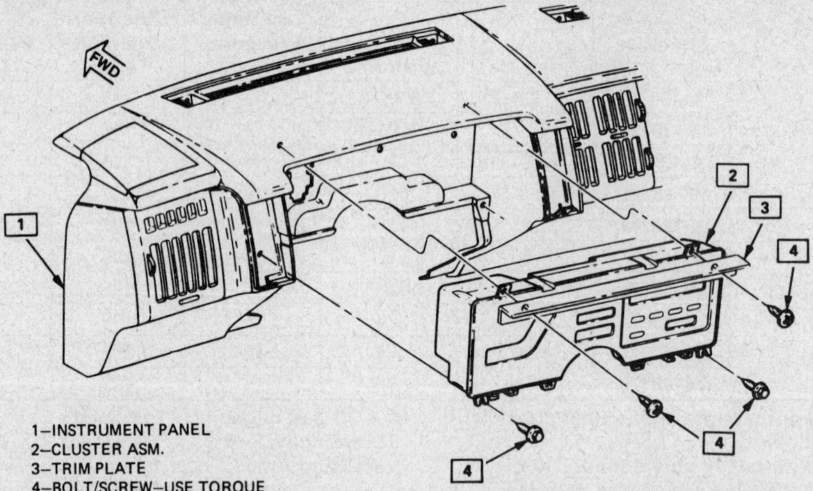

1—INSTRUMENT PANEL
2—CLUSTER ASM.
3—TRIM PLATE
4—BOLT/SCREW—USE TORQUE CONTROL TOOL 800 RPM MAX.

Fig. 4 Instrument cluster installation. Grand Am

INSTRUMENT CLUSTER
REPLACE

1. Disconnect battery ground cable.
2. Remove steering column collar, if equipped and the steering column opening filler plate or lap duct assembly.
3. Remove instrument cluster trim plate attaching screws, then the trim plate.
4. Remove screws attaching steering column support to lower steering column assembly.
5. Remove instrument cluster to instrument panel attaching screws, then pull cluster assembly rearward, **Figs. 3, 4 and 5. On models with electronic instrument cluster, note warning printed on front of cluster and do not touch electronic components as static electricity may damage components. Transfer NVM chip from rear of cluster, Fig. 6, and the odometer to replacement cluster.**
6. Reverse procedure to install.

REAR WINDOW DEFROSTER RELAY
REPLACE

1. Disconnect battery ground cable.
2. Remove glove compartment door and door stop strap.

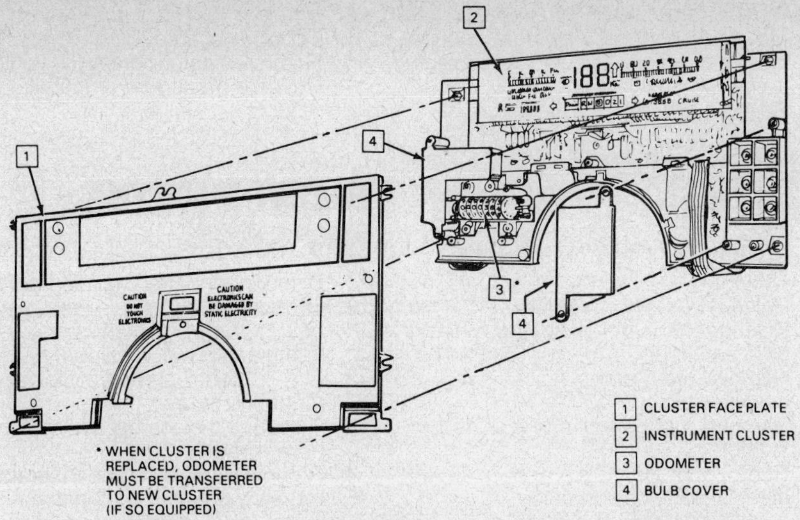

Fig. 5 Instrument cluster installation. Skylark & Somerset

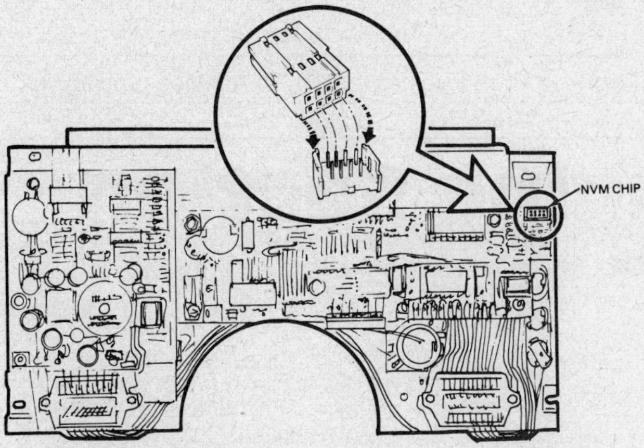

Fig. 6 NVM chip installation. Models w/electronic instrument cluster

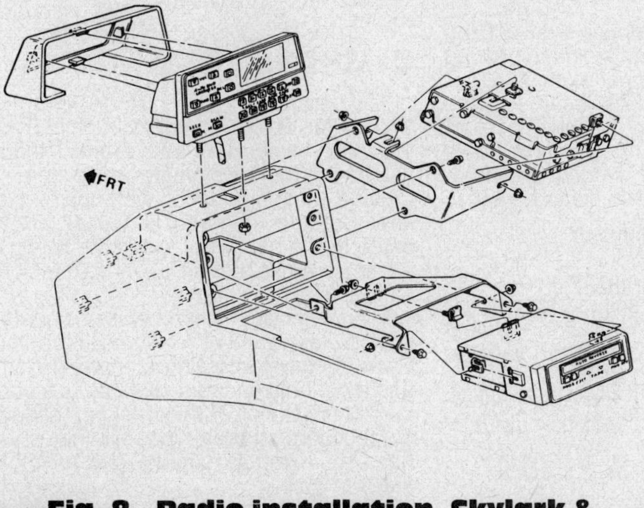

Fig. 8 Radio installation. Skylark & Somerset

3. Disconnect electrical connector from relay assembly.
4. Remove relay mounting screw, then the rear window defroster relay.
5. Reverse procedure to install.

RADIO

REPLACE

CALAIS & CUTLASS CALAIS

Models w/Auto Calculator

1. Disconnect battery ground cable.
2. Remove radio trim plate attaching screws, then the trim plate.
3. Remove radio mounting bracket attaching screws, then disconnect antenna lead and electrical connector(s) from radio.
4. Remove radio.
5. Reverse procedure to install.

Models Less Auto Calculator

1. Disconnect battery ground cable, then open ashtray and remove insert.
2. Depress tab on each ashtray locking tang, pull ashtray out to second stop, depress tabs again and remove ashtray. **There is a locking tang on each side of ashtray and each tang has a tab on the right side, Fig. 7.**
3. Remove 2 screws securing upper ashtray bracket and the bracket and trim plate assembly.

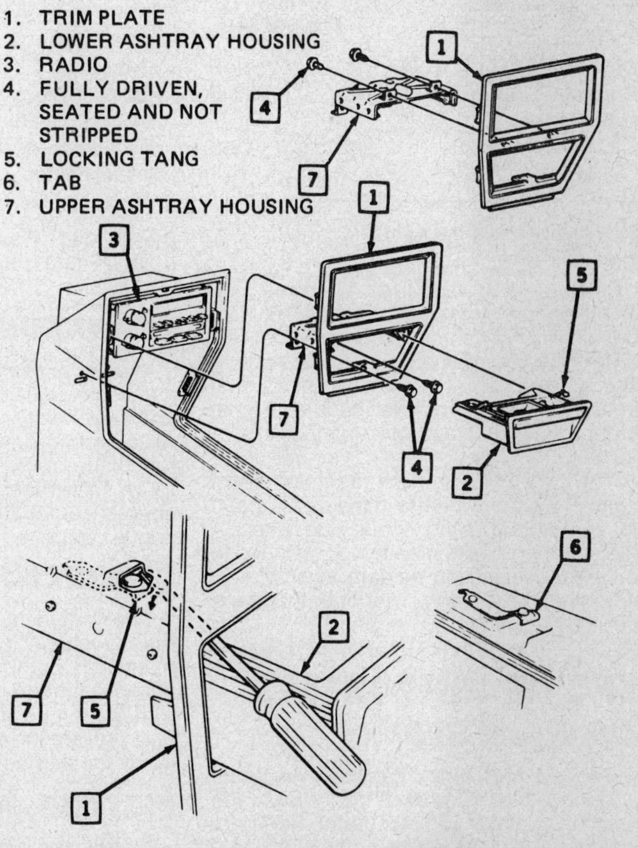

Fig. 7 Radio Installation. Calais & Cutlass Calais

4. Remove radio mounting screws and withdraw radio.
5. Disconnect antenna lead and electrical connectors, then remove radio.
6. Reverse procedure to install.

GRAND AM

1. Disconnect battery ground cable.
2. Remove right console extension panel and rear main plate.
3. Remove radio mounting screws.
4. Disconnect antenna lead and electrical connectors, then remove radio.
5. Reverse procedure to install.

SKYLARK & SOMERSET

1. Disconnect battery ground cable.
2. Remove console extensions, lower instrument panel trim and face plates, as needed, to gain access to components and mounting hardware.
3. Remove necessary screws and nuts, **Fig. 8**, disconnect electrical connectors and antenna lead if necessary, then remove components.
4. Reverse procedure to install.

HEATER CORE REPLACE

1. Disconnect battery ground cable.
2. Drain cooling system.
3. Raise and support vehicle.
4. Disconnect heater hoses from heater core assembly.
5. Remove drain tube.
6. Lower vehicle.
7. Remove instrument panel sound insulator.
8. Remove heater duct and hose assembly and position aside.
9. Remove 2 heater core cover attaching screws, then the covers.
10. Remove heater core from vehicle.
11. Reverse procedure to install.

BLOWER MOTOR REPLACE

1. Disconnect battery ground cable.
2. On 1986-88 models, remove drive belt(s), then unfasten power steering pump and position aside, if necessary.
3. On all models, remove blower motor mounting screws.
3. Disconnect electrical connectors from blower motor.
4. Remove blower motor assembly.
5. Reverse procedure to install.

4-121 (2.0L) Engine Section

NOTE: Refer to section 10, "4-110 (1.8L) & 4-121 (2.0L) Overhead Cam Engine Section" for service procedures.

4-138 (2.3L) Engine Section

INDEX

DESCRIPTION

The 4-138 (2.3L) "Quad 4" engine, **Fig. 1,** is a double overhead camshaft, 16 valve design. The valve train is comprised of two chain-driven camshafts with direct-acting lifters. The cylinder block is made of cast iron, whereas the cylinder head and most other engine components are made of aluminum.

The engine features an integrated direct ignition system which eliminates the need for a distributor and spark plug wires. A highly-tuned intake manifold is matched to a port fuel injection system to provide a combination of high power output and excellent fuel economy.

ENGINE COMPONENTS

CYLINDER BLOCK

The cylinder block casting is a semi-open deck construction that allows the casting to be made accurately for bore wall variation with no core plugs. A deep-skirt design is used for improved engine-transaxle stiffness as well as more precise machining and a flat sealing surface for the oil pan. The main bearing caps are press-fit into the cylinder block and retained with 11 mm bolts.

CRANKSHAFT

In order to minimize friction, the cast iron crankshaft uses cross-drilled main bearing journals and grooved upper main bearings. An oil pump drive gear is located at the rear of the crankshaft and an ignition reluctor wheel is machined into the number five counterweight. Crankshaft torsional vibration is controlled by a harmonic balancer.

CONNECTING RODS

The forged steel connecting rods use bronze piston pin bushings to provide maximum durability. An oil cooling hole drilled in the rod aligns once per revolution with the connecting rod feed oil hole, **Fig. 2,** to provide the piston cooling necessitated by the engine's high specific output.

PISTONS, PINS & RINGS

Cast-aluminum pistons are used together with light-weight piston pins to provide optimum durability with minimum mass. The piston rings are designed for function including friction, oil consumption and durability. The rings offer excellent sealing, blow-by and oil consumption characteristics as well as low engine friction due to the low tension values.

CYLINDER HEAD

The cast-aluminum cylinder head, **Fig. 3,** consists of four cylinders, each containing four valves. Both intake and exhaust valves use narrow diameter valve stems to provide minimum friction with optimum air flow. Rotators, used on all valves, are located at the bottom of the valve spring to eliminate any effect on valve train reciprocating mass.

The combustion chamber is designed to provide fast burn at high specific output. Each chamber contains a sumped piston and a centrally-located spark plug. A combustion chamber of this design maintains combustion stability and eliminates the need for external exhaust gas recirculation.

Both intake and exhaust valve ports are a Siamese design. Fuel injectors are positioned in the intake port to obtain optimum targeting.

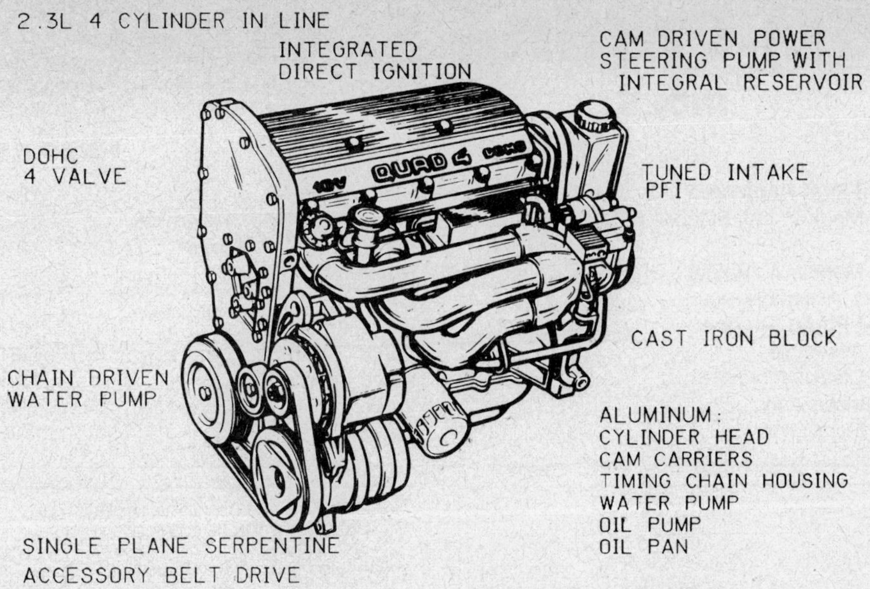

Fig. 1 4-138 (2.3L) "Quad 4" engine

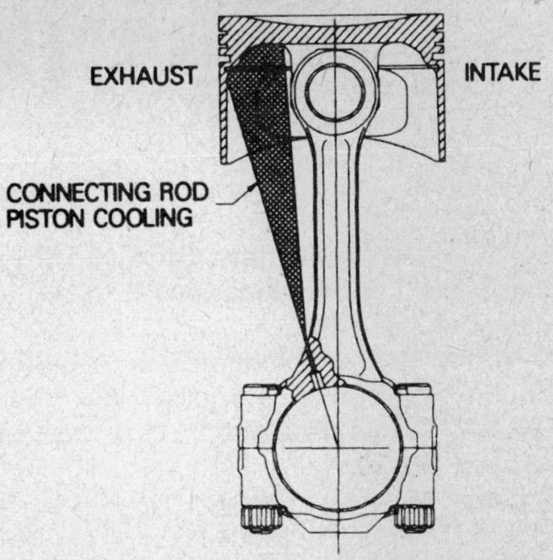

Fig. 2 Piston & connecting rod assembly

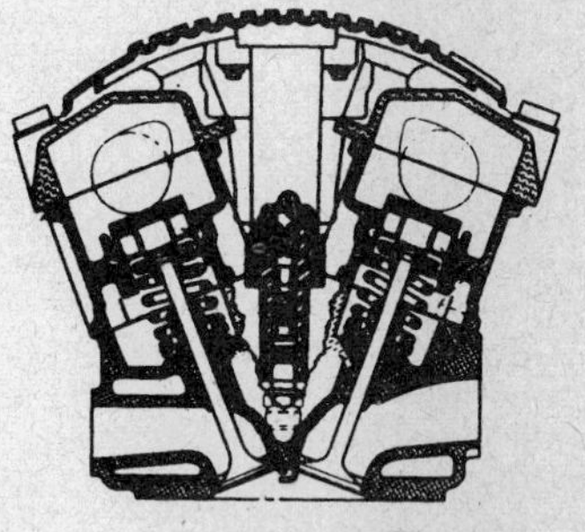

Fig. 3 Cylinder head assembly

VALVE LIFTERS

Direct-acting hydraulic valve lifters are used to eliminate the need for regular servicing and reduce valve train noise.

CAMSHAFTS

The cast iron camshafts are used in conjunction with iron lifter contact feet to provide maximum wear resistance. Lifter rotation is ensured under all conditions by the camshaft lobe taper, lifter offset and spherical surface of the lifter contact area.

The camshafts are driven by a double-row roller chain. Chain motion is controlled by a hydraulic tensioner and three dampers. In order to reduce camshaft drive noise, rubber isolated dampers, modified tooth profiles, a front cover mass damper and modified tensioner load and damping are employed.

The camshaft carriers are separate components from the cylinder head. Camshafts are run directly on the carrier and cover without bearing inserts. The carrier and cover are split at the bearing center line to allow for the use of small diameter bearings.

TIMING CHAIN HOUSING & COVER

The cast-aluminum timing chain housing is attached to the block and camshaft carriers. The housing includes the idler sprocket and bearing which drives the water pump.

The stamped-steel front cover houses the front crankshaft seal and the camshaft mass damper, used to reduce camshaft drive noise.

OIL PAN & OIL PUMP

The cast-aluminum oil pan is designed to ensure oil supply under the most severe vehicle maneuvers. The deep-skirt design of the block provides a flat surface on the pan sealing rail, enabling simplified gasket construction.

The oil pump is a gerotor type driven by the crankshaft. The gear cover and oil pump body are cast aluminum, whereas the gerotor cover is cast iron. A phenolic driven gear is used to minimize gear noise. A windage tray is used to maintain oil pressure and low friction at high engine speeds.

INTAKE SYSTEM

The intake system consists of an aluminum intake manifold, air cleaner, air cleaner snorkle and "zip tube" (the connector between the plenums). The system uses the air cleaner inlet as a clean air source and for acoustical tuning. In addition, the system uses the air cleaner as a filter housing as well as a secondary tuning plenum.

EXHAUST SYSTEM

The exhaust system is a 4-into-2-into-1 design. A dual-bed monolithic catalytic converter is used to keep back pressure as low as possible. The oxygen sensor is mounted in a cross tube at the 4-into-2 junction. The cross tube feed holes are calibrated to obtain oxygen sensor response without affecting system operation.

The stainless steel exhaust manifold incorporates a ceramic blanket insulator fastened to the top of the manifold to provide acceptable underhood temperatures under all operating conditions.

4-151 (2.5L) Engine Section

INDEX

ENGINE MOUNTS
REPLACE

1. Support engine using fixture No. J-28467 or equivalent.
2. Raise and support vehicle.
3. Remove engine mount-to-chassis attaching bolts from front mount, **Fig. 1,** and engine mount-to-bracket nuts from rear mount, **Fig. 2.**
4. Remove engine mount-to-bracket nuts from front mount and engine mount-to-chassis attaching bolts from rear mount.
5. Remove engine mounts.
6. Reverse procedure to install.

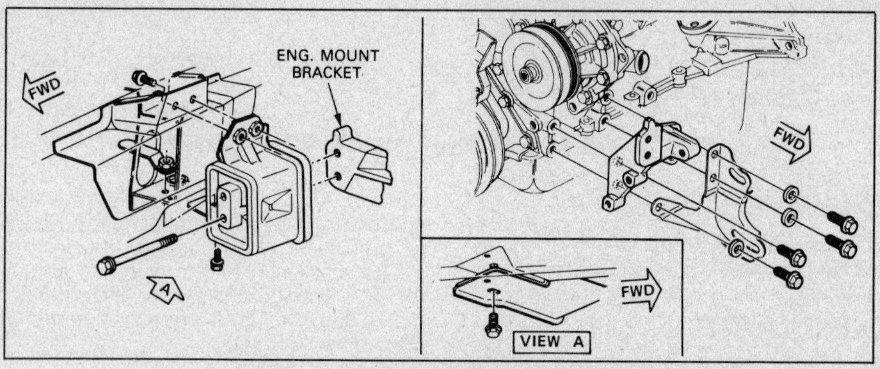

Fig. 1 Front engine mount

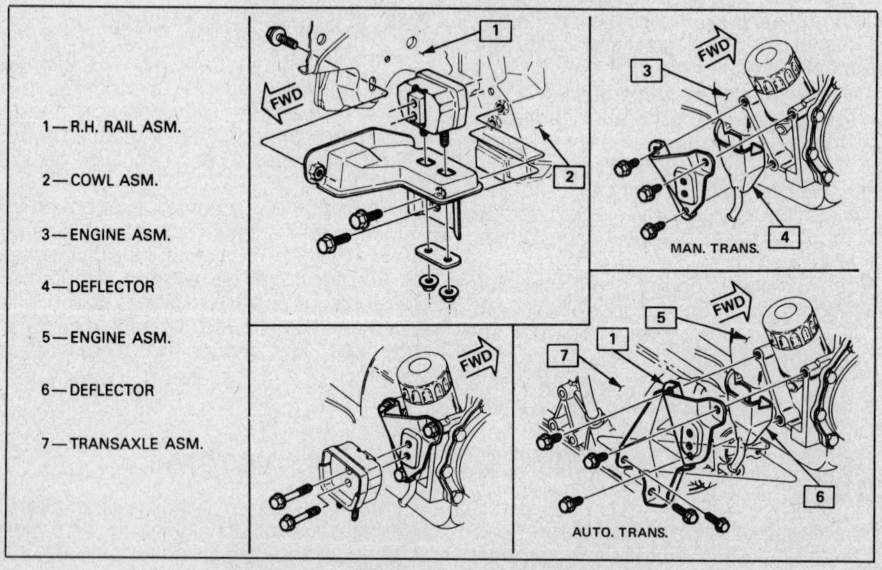

Fig. 2 Rear engine mount

ENGINE
REPLACE

1. Disconnect battery cables, then drain cooling system and remove air cleaner assembly.
2. Disconnect ECM electrical connectors. Route electrical harness through bulkhead and position aside.
3. Disconnect engine wiring harness and position aside.
4. Disconnect all vacuum and coolant hoses necessary for engine removal.
5. On models equipped with A/C, unfasten A/C compressor and position aside, leaving refrigerant lines attached.
6. On models equipped with power steering, unfasten power steering pump and position aside, leaving hoses attached.
7. On all models, remove front transaxle strut and on 1986-88 models with automatic transaxle, the rear transaxle strut.
8. Disconnect fuel lines from injection pump.
9. On models equipped with automatic transaxle, disconnect transaxle cooler lines, then the transaxle shift linkage and downshift cable.
10. On all models, disconnect throttle cable from injection pump.
11. Disconnect redundant ground wire, then remove multi-relay bracket.
12. Raise and support vehicle.
13. On models equipped with power steering, remove power steering line bracket from engine.
14. On all models, remove front wheels.
15. Remove brake calipers and rotors.
16. Remove 2 steering knuckle-to-strut attaching bolts from each side.
17. Disconnect exhaust pipe from exhaust manifold and position aside.
18. Remove 2 body-to-cradle attaching bolts from lower control arm on each side.
19. Loosen 8 remaining body-to-cradle attaching bolts.
20. Remove one bolt from each end of cradle side, leaving one bolt per corner.
21. Position suitable jack stands under front of body, then move hoist back to body pan with a 4 x 4 inch block of wood between hoist and vehicle.
22. Raise hoist and remove jack stands, then place dolly under engine with wooden blocks to maintain position on dolly.
23. Lower vehicle, allowing engine to rest on dolly, then remove engine mount bolts and right front bracket.
24. Remove 4 remaining cradle-to-body bolts, then slide engine/transaxle assembly out from under vehicle.

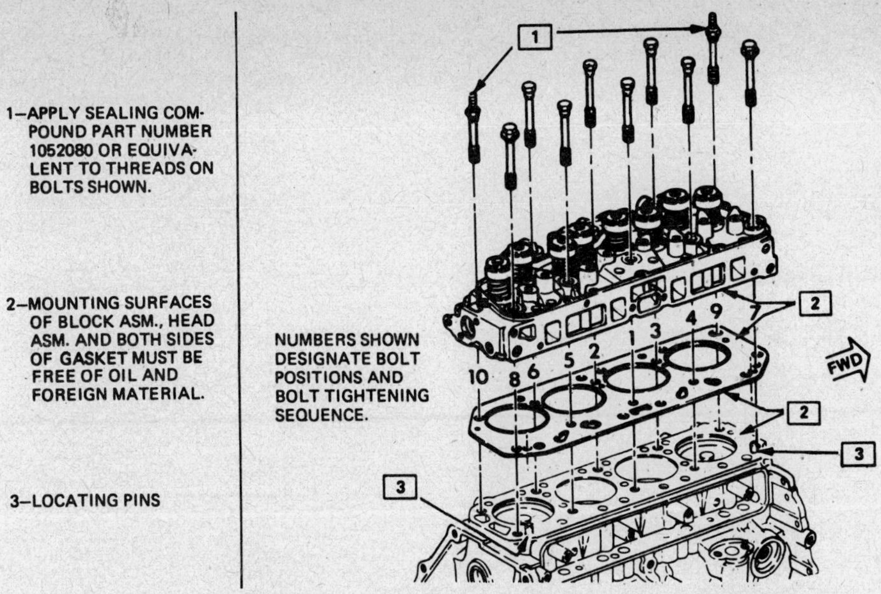
1—APPLY SEALING COMPOUND PART NUMBER 1052080 OR EQUIVALENT TO THREADS ON BOLTS SHOWN.
2—MOUNTING SURFACES OF BLOCK ASM., HEAD ASM. AND BOTH SIDES OF GASKET MUST BE FREE OF OIL AND FOREIGN MATERIAL.
3—LOCATING PINS
NUMBERS SHOWN DESIGNATE BOLT POSITIONS AND BOLT TIGHTENING SEQUENCE.
FWD

Fig. 3 Cylinder head bolt tightening sequence

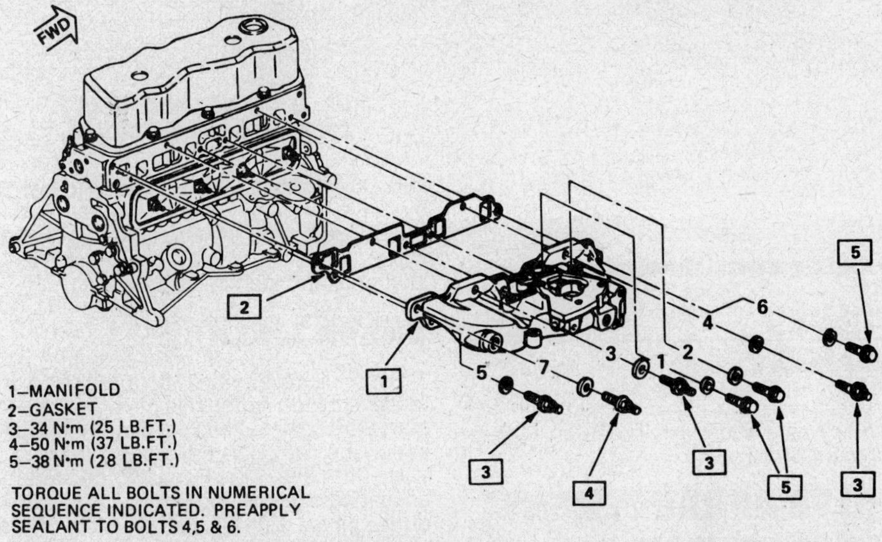

Fig. 4 Intake manifold bolt tightening sequence. 1985

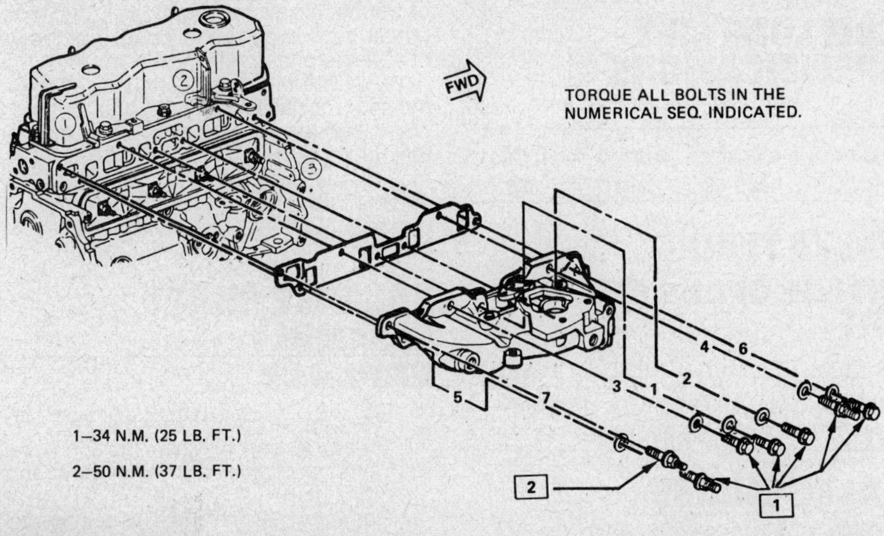

Fig. 5 Intake manifold bolt tightening sequence. 1986

25. Separate engine from transaxle.
26. Reverse procedure to install.

CYLINDER HEAD REPLACE

1. Disconnect battery ground cable, then drain cooling system.
2. Raise and support vehicle.
3. Disconnect exhaust pipe from exhaust manifold, then lower vehicle.
4. Remove oil level indicator tube, then the air cleaner assembly.
5. Disconnect electrical connectors, throttle linkage and fuel lines from throttle body unit. Disconnect heater hose from intake manifold.
6. On 1985-86 models, remove ignition coil.
7. On all models, disconnect all remaining electrical connectors from intake manifold and cylinder head.
8. Disconnect all vacuum lines from cylinder head.
9. On models equipped with A/C, unfasten A/C compressor and position aside, leaving refrigerant lines attached.
10. On all models, position alternator brackets aside, then remove upper power steering pump bracket.
11. Remove rocker arm cover, then the rocker arms and pushrods.
12. Remove cylinder head attaching bolts and the cylinder head.
13. Reverse procedure to install. Coat cylinder head bolts with sealer. Torque cylinder head attaching bolts in the following sequence:
    a. Torque all bolts in sequence, **Fig. 3,** to 18 ft. lbs.
    b. Tighten bolt No. 9 to 29 ft. lbs. and all other bolts to 22 ft. lbs.
    c. Tighten bolt No. 9 an additional 90° and all other bolts an additional 120°.

INTAKE MANIFOLD REPLACE

1. Disconnect battery ground cable.
2. Remove air cleaner and heat stove pipe.
3. Disconnect PCV valve and hose from throttle body unit.
4. Drain engine coolant, then disconnect fuel lines from manifold.
5. Disconnect electrical connectors and throttle linkage from throttle body unit.
6. Disconnect transaxle downshift cable and cruise control linkage, if equipped.
7. Unfasten throttle linkage and bellcrank and position aside.
8. Disconnect heater hose from manifold.
9. On 1985-86 models, remove alternator bracket or upper power steering pump bracket, then the ignition coil.
10. On all models, remove intake manifold attaching bolts and the manifold.
11. Reverse procedure to install. Torque attaching bolts to specifications in sequence shown in **Figs. 4 and 5. On 1987-88 models, torque all attaching bolts to 25 ft. lbs.**

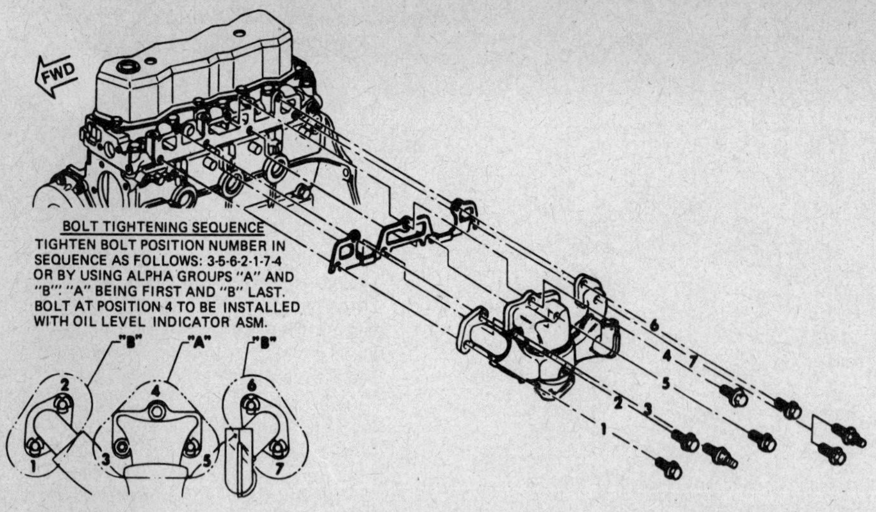

Fig. 6 Exhaust manifold bolt tightening sequence

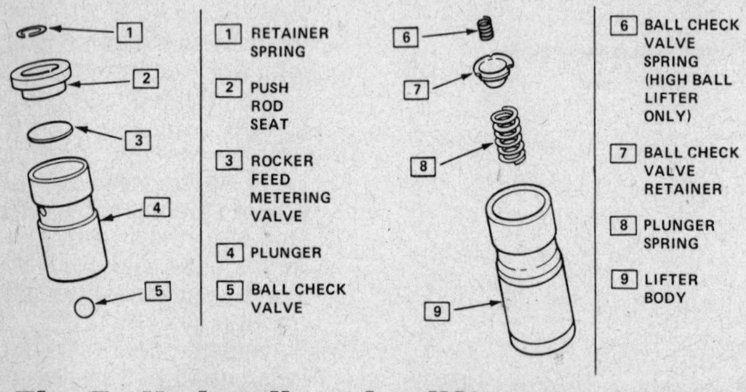

Fig. 7 Hydraulic valve lifter components

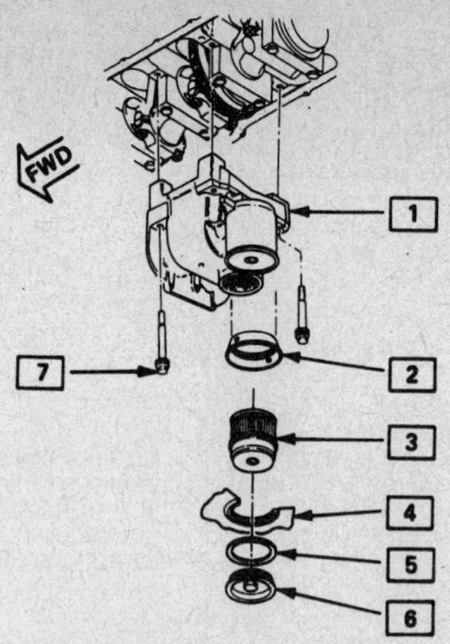

1 – BALANCER ASSEMBLY
2 – RESTRICTOR
3 – FILTER
4 – OIL PAN
5 – GASKET
6 – PLUG
7 – BOLT

Fig. 8 Balance shaft assembly removal

EXHAUST MANIFOLD
REPLACE

1. Disconnect battery ground cable.
2. Remove air cleaner assembly and heat stove tube.
3. Unfasten alternator upper mounting brackets and position aside.
4. Disconnect oxygen sensor electrical connector.
5. Raise and support vehicle.
6. Disconnect exhaust pipe from exhaust manifold, then lower vehicle.
7. Remove exhaust manifold attaching bolts, then the manifold and gasket.
8. Reverse procedure to install. Torque attaching bolts in sequence, **Fig. 6. On 1985 models, torque all exhaust manifold attaching bolts to 44 ft. lbs. On 1986-88 models, torque bolts 1, 2, 6 and 7 to 32 ft. lbs. and bolts 3, 4 and 5 to 37 ft. lbs.**

ROCKER ARM STUDS

Rocker arm studs that are cracked or have damaged threads can be removed from the cylinder head using a deep well socket. Install and torque new rocker arm stud to 75 ft. lbs.

VALVES
ADJUST

These engines are equipped with hydraulic valve lifters. No provision for adjustment is provided.

VALVE ARRANGEMENT
FRONT TO REAR

4-151 .... I-E-I-E-E-I-E-I

CAM LOBE LIFT SPECIFICATIONS

Engine	Year	Int.	Exh.
4-151	1985-88	.398	.398

VALVE TIMING
INTAKE OPENS BEFORE TDC

Engine	Year	Degrees
4-151	1985-88	33

VALVE GUIDES

Valve guides are an integral part of the cylinder head and are not removable. If valve stem clearance becomes excessive, the valve guide should be reamed to the next oversize and the appropriate oversize valves installed. Valves are available in .003 and .005 inch oversizes.

VALVE LIFTERS

Hydraulic roller valve lifters are used on these engines. Lifter retainers and guide plates are used to keep the lifter from rotating on the camshaft. Failure of a hydraulic valve lifter, **Fig. 7,** is generally caused by an inadequate oil supply or dirt. An air leak at the intake side of the oil pump or too much oil in the engine will cause air bubbles in the oil supply to the lifters causing them to collapse. This is a probable cause of trouble if several lifters fail to function, but air in oil is an unlikely cause of failure of a single unit.

Valve lifters can be removed after removing rocker arm cover and pushrod cover. Loosen rocker arm stud nut and rotate rocker arm so that pushrod can be removed, then remove lifter guide, retainer and the valve lifter. It may be necessary to use tool No. J-3049 to facilitate lifter removal.

BALANCE SHAFT ASSEMBLY
REPLACE

1. Remove engine assembly as described under "Engine, Replace."
2. Remove oil pan attaching bolts and the oil pan.
3. Remove balance shaft assembly attaching bolts and the balance shaft assembly, **Figs. 8 and 9.**

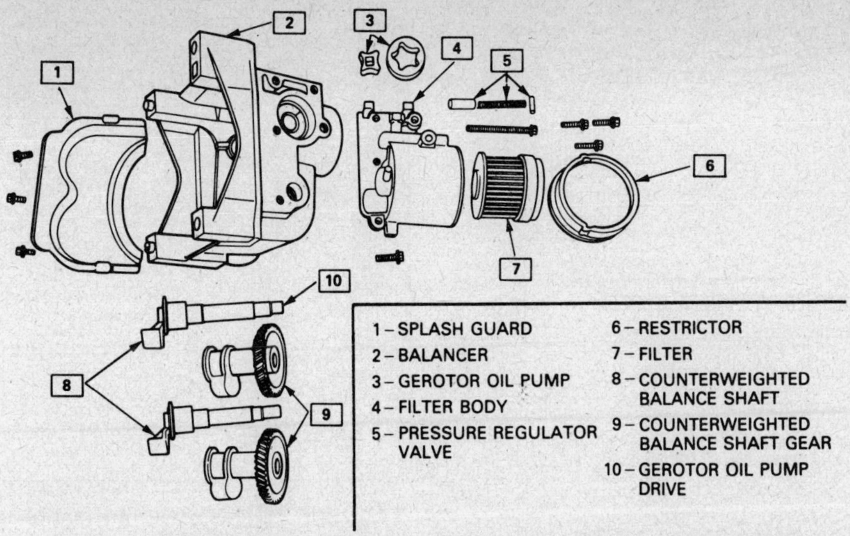

Fig. 9 Exploded view of balance shaft assembly

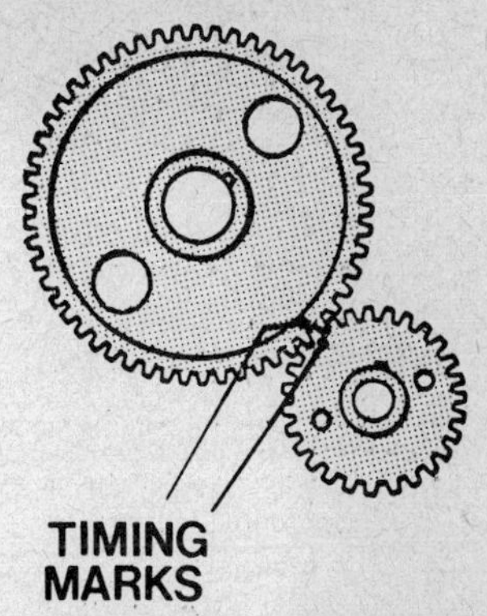

Fig. 10 Valve timing marks

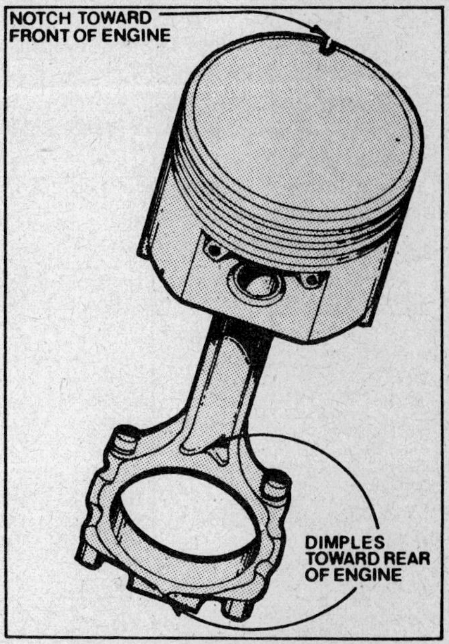

Fig. 11 Piston & rod assembly

4. Reverse procedure to install. Torque short attaching bolts to 9 ft. lbs. plus an additional 75° turn and long attaching bolts to 9 ft. lbs. plus an additional 90° turn.

ENGINE FRONT COVER
REPLACE

1. Remove drive belts, then the inner fender splash shield.
2. Remove crankshaft pulley attaching bolts, then slide pulley and hub from shaft.
3. Remove front cover attaching bolts and the front cover.
4. Clean gasket surfaces on cylinder block and front cover.
5. Install oil pan front seal in front cover, then apply a 3/8 inch bead of RTV sealant (3/16 inch thick) to joint at oil pan and front cover.
6. Apply a 1/4 inch bead of RTV sealant (1/8 inch thick) to front cover and cylinder block mating surfaces.
7. Install centering tool No. J-34995 or equivalent in front cover oil seal bore.
8. Install and partially tighten 2 opposing front cover screws with centering tool in place.
9. Install remaining cover-to-block screws and torque to 90 inch lbs.
10. Install hub, pulley and splash shield.

TIMING GEARS

When necessary to install a new camshaft gear, the camshaft will have to be removed as the gear is a pressed fit on the camshaft. The camshaft is held in place by a thrust plate which is retained to the engine by two capscrews which are accessible through the two holes in the gear web.

To remove gear, use an arbor press and a suitable sleeve to properly support gear on its steel hub.

Before installing gear, assemble thrust plate and gear spacer ring, then press gear onto shaft until it bottoms against spacer ring. The thrust plate end clearance should be .0015-.0050 inch. If clearance is less than .0015 inch, the spacer ring should be replaced. If clearance is greater than .0050 inch, the thrust plate should be replaced.

The crankshaft gear can be removed using a puller and two bolts in the tapped holes of the gear.

When installing timing gears, make sure that the marks on the gears are properly aligned, **Fig. 10.** The valve timing marks, **Fig. 10**, do not indicate TDC, compression stroke for No. 1 cylinder for use during distributor installation. When installing the distributor, rotate engine until No. 1 cylinder is on compression stroke and the camshaft timing mark is 180° from the valve timing position shown in **Fig. 10.**

CAMSHAFT
REPLACE

1. Remove engine from vehicle as described under "Engine, Replace."
2. Remove rocker arm cover, pushrods, pushrod cover and valve lifters.
3. Remove distributor, then the oil pump driveshaft.
4. Remove front cover as described under "Engine Front Cover, Replace."
5. Remove camshaft thrust plate screws, then slide camshaft and gear out through front of block. Use care not to damage camshaft bearings.
6. Reverse procedure to install. When installing camshaft, align crankshaft and camshaft valve timing marks on gear teeth, **Fig. 10.**

PISTONS & RODS
ASSEMBLE

Assemble piston to rod with notch on piston facing toward front of engine and the raised notch side of rod at bearing end facing toward rear of engine, **Fig. 11.**

Upon installation, measure the connecting rod side clearance using a suitable feeler gauge. Clearance should be .006 to .022 inch.

PISTONS, PINS & RINGS

Pistons and rings are available in standard and oversizes of .010, .020 and .030 inch. Piston pins are available in oversizes of .001 and .003 inch.

MAIN & ROD BEARINGS

Main and rod bearings are available in standard size and undersizes of .001, .002 and .010 inch.

OIL PAN
REPLACE

MODELS LESS BALANCE SHAFT ASSEMBLY

1. Disconnect battery ground cable.
2. Raise and support vehicle.
3. Drain engine oil, then disconnect exhaust pipe from exhaust manifold.
4. Remove starter and flywheel inspection cover, then the starter motor.
5. Remove oil pan attaching bolts and the oil pan.
6. Reverse procedure to install. Apply RTV sealant to locations shown in **Figs. 12 and 13.**

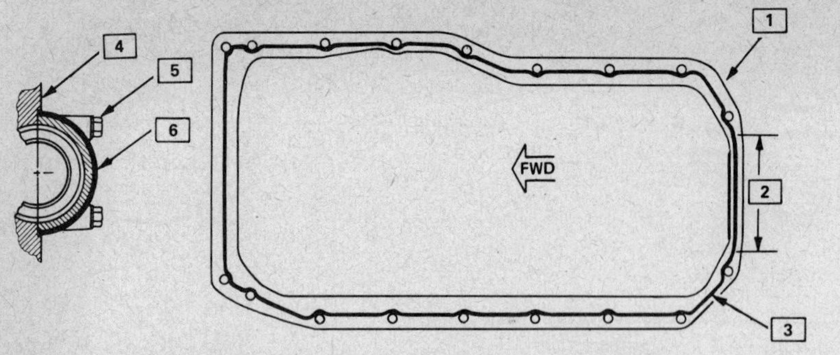

Fig. 12 Oil pan sealant application. 1985

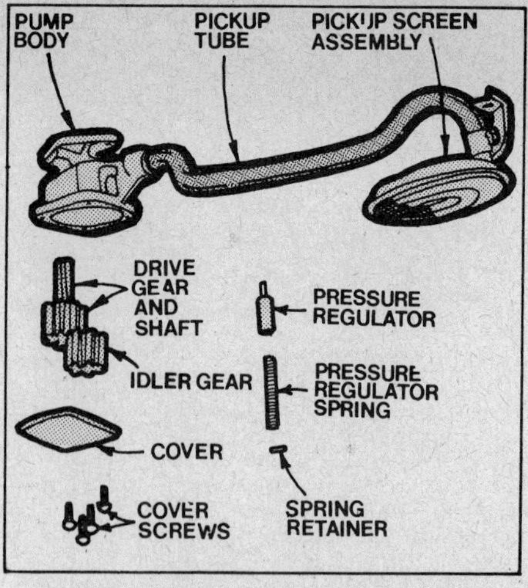

Fig. 14 Oil pump exploded view

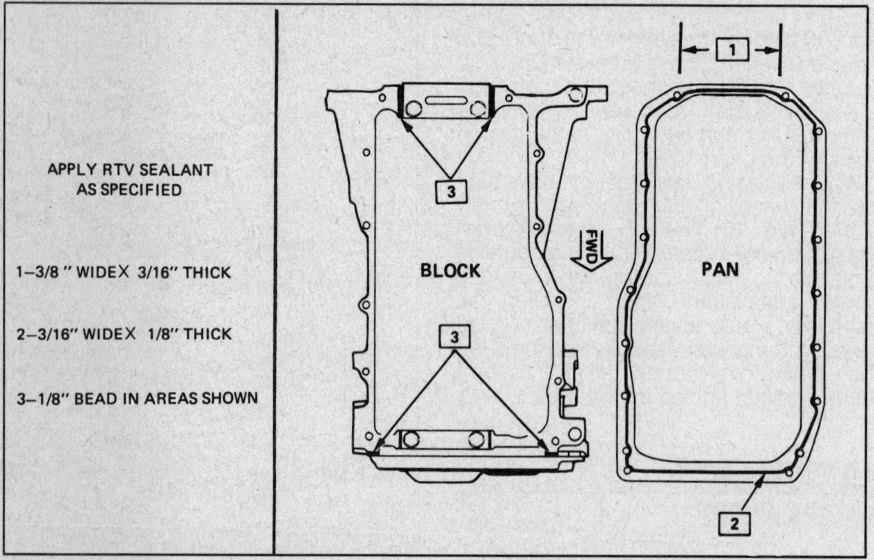

Fig. 13 Oil pan sealant application. 1986–88

MODELS w/BALANCE SHAFT ASSEMBLY

1. Remove engine assembly as described under "Engine, Replace."
2. Remove oil pan attaching bolts and the oil pan.
3. Reverse procedure to install.

OIL PUMP SERVICE

REMOVAL

1. Drain crankcase, then remove oil pan as described under "Oil Pan, Replace."
2. Remove balance shaft assembly attaching bolts and the balance shaft assembly, if equipped.
3. Remove two oil pump mounting bolts and nuts from main cap bolt and remove oil pump and screen as an assembly.

DISASSEMBLE

1. Remove four pump cover to body attaching screws, then remove cover, idler and drive gears and shaft, **Fig. 14.**
2. Remove pin, retainer, spring and pressure regular valve.

INSPECTION

Inspect pump components and should any of the following conditions be found, the oil pump assembly should be replaced.

1. Inspect pump body for cracks and excessive wear.
2. Inspect oil pump gears for damage, cracks or excessive wear.
3. Check shaft for looseness in housing.
4. Check cover for wear that would allow oil to leak past ends of gears.
5. Check oil pick screen for damage to screen or relief grommet. Also remove any debris from screen surface.
6. Check pressure regulator valve for fit in body.

ASSEMBLE

1. Place drive gear and shaft in pump body, then install idler gear with smooth side of gear facing pump cover, **Fig. 14.**
2. Install and torque pump cover attaching screws to 105 inch lbs. Check to ensure that pump rotates freely.
3. Install pressure regulator valve, spring, retainer and pin.

INSTALLATION

1. Align oil pump shaft with tang on oil pump driveshaft, then install pump on block, positioning pump flange over oil pump driveshaft lower bushing.
2. Install oil pump mounting bolts and torque bolts to 20 ft. lbs., then install oil pan as described under "Oil Pan, Replace."

V6-181 (3.0L) Engine Section

INDEX

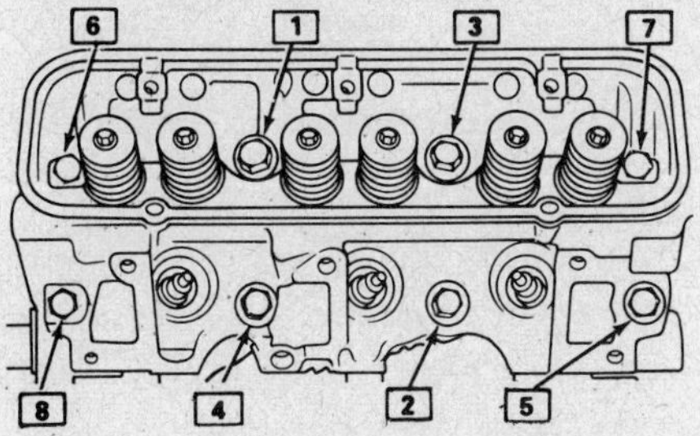

Fig. 1 Cylinder head bolt tightening sequence

ENGINE MOUNTS REPLACE

1. Support engine using fixture No. J-28467 or equivalent.
2. Raise and support vehicle.
3. Remove engine mount-to-bracket attaching nuts.
4. Raise engine slightly, then remove engine mount-to-frame attaching nuts and the mount.
5. Reverse procedure to install.

ENGINE REPLACE

1. Disconnect battery ground cable.
2. Scribe hood hinge locations and remove hood.
3. Raise and support vehicle.
4. Disconnect electrical connectors from starter motor and remove starter.
5. Remove flexplate cover, then mark relationship between flexplate and torque converter and remove 3 torque converter bolts.
6. On models equipped with A/C, unfasten A/C compressor and position aside.
7. On all models, drain cooling system, then disconnect lower radiator hose.
8. Remove right front engine mount attaching bolts.
9. Remove right inner fender splash shield.
10. Remove transaxle-to-engine mount attaching bolt located between cylinder block and transaxle.
11. Remove right rear engine mount attaching nuts.
12. Disconnect exhaust pipe from exhaust manifold.
13. Disconnect heater hoses from engine, then lower vehicle.
14. Remove serpentine drive belt.
15. Remove alternator.
16. On models equipped with power steering, unfasten power steering pump and position aside.
17. On all models, remove mass air flow sensor and air intake duct.
18. Disconnect electrical connector from cooling fan and remove the fan.
19. Disconnect upper radiator hose and remove the radiator.
20. Attach suitable lifting equipment to engine, then remove left upper transaxle mount.
21. Remove master cylinder, then disconnect fuel lines from fuel rail.
22. Disconnect throttle, throttle valve and cruise control (if equipped) cables from throttle body.
23. Remove remaining engine-to-transaxle attaching bolts, then lift engine from vehicle.
24. Reverse procedure to install.

CYLINDER HEAD REPLACE

1. Disconnect battery ground cable.
2. Remove mass air flow sensor and air intake duct.
3. Remove serpentine drive belt.
4. Remove alternator.
5. Remove ignition module complete with wiring.
6. Disconnect vacuum lines and electrical connectors necessary for cylinder head removal.
7. Disconnect throttle, throttle valve and cruise control (if equipped) cables from throttle body.
8. Remove fuel lines and fuel rail.
9. Disconnect throttle body and intake manifold heater and radiator hoses and drain coolant.
10. Disconnect ignition wires from spark plugs, then remove intake manifold and valve covers.
11. Remove radiator and cooling fan.
12. Remove left exhaust manifold, then the rocker arms, pedestals and push-rods.
13. On models equipped with power steering, remove power steering pump.
14. On all models, remove engine oil level indicator and tube.
15. Remove left cylinder head attaching bolts and the cylinder head.

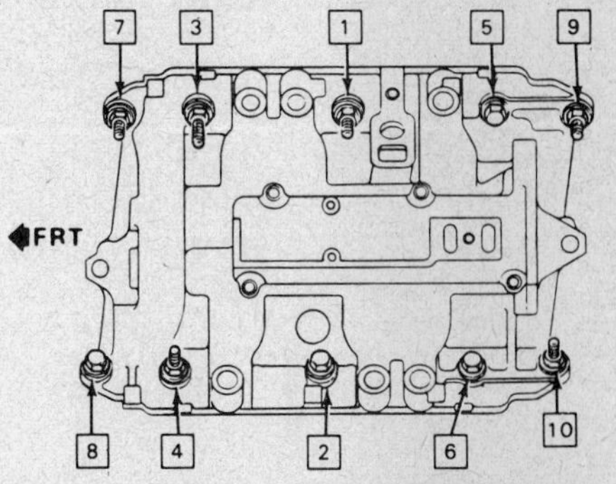

Fig. 2 Intake manifold bolt tightening sequence

16. Raise and support vehicle.
17. Disconnect exhaust pipe from exhaust manifold, then lower vehicle.
18. Remove right cylinder head attaching bolts and the cylinder head.
19. Install cylinder head(s) noting the following:
    a. If steel replacement gasket is used, coat both sides of gasket with suitable sealer.
    b. Use new head bolts when installing cylinder head.
    c. Torque bolts to specifications in sequence shown in **Fig. 1:** First, torque bolts to 25 ft. lbs. Second, tighten each bolt 90 degrees in sequence shown. Third, tighten each bolt an additional 90 degrees in sequence shown.
20. Reverse remaining procedure to complete installation, torquing intake manifold bolts to specifications in sequence shown in **Fig. 2.**

INTAKE MANIFOLD REPLACE

1. Disconnect battery ground cable.
2. Remove mass air flow sensor and air intake duct.
3. Remove serpentine drive belt, then the alternator and bracket assembly.
4. Remove ignition module complete with wiring.
5. Disconnect all vacuum hoses and electrical connectors necessary for intake manifold removal.
6. Disconnect throttle, throttle valve and cruise control (if equipped) cables from throttle body.

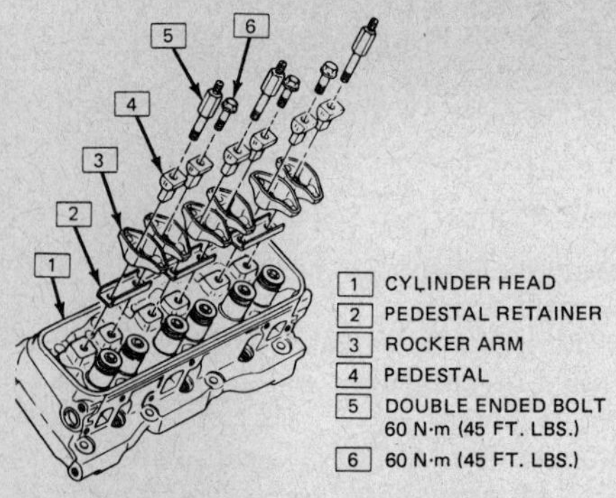

Fig. 3 Rocker arm installation

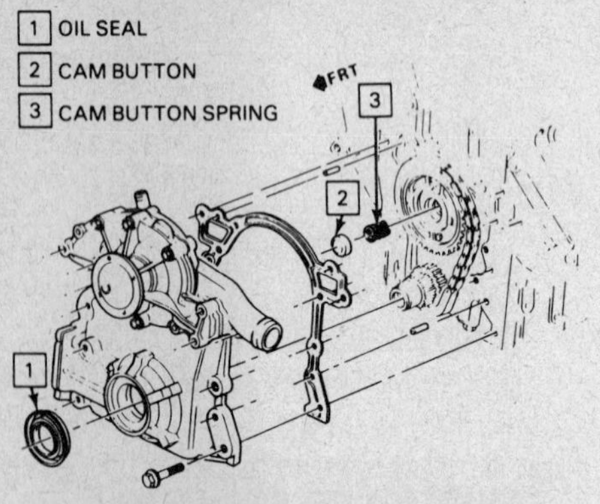

Fig. 5 Engine front cover replacement

7. Drain cooling system, then disconnect upper radiator hose and the heater hoses from throttle body.
8. Disconnect fuel lines, then remove fuel rail and injector assembly.
9. Disconnect spark plug wires, then remove intake manifold attaching bolts and the intake manifold.
10. Reverse procedure to install, noting the following:
    a. If steel replacement gasket is used, coat both sides of gasket with suitable sealer.
    b. Apply suitable lubricating sealer to pipe thread fittings.
    c. Torque intake manifold attaching bolts to specifications in sequence shown in **Fig. 2.**

EXHAUST MANIFOLD
REPLACE

FRONT

1. Disconnect battery ground cable.
2. Disconnect spark plug wires, then remove manifold-to-crossover pipe attaching bolts.
3. Remove air cleaner attaching bolts, then the engine cooling fan.
4. Remove exhaust manifold-to-cylinder head attaching bolts.
5. Remove oil level indicator tube and indicator, then the exhaust manifold.
6. Reverse procedure to install.

REAR

1. Disconnect battery ground cable.
2. Raise and support vehicle.
3. Remove exhaust pipe-to-manifold attaching bolts, then lower vehicle.
4. Disconnect oxygen sensor electrical connector and spark plug wires.
5. Remove manifold-to-crossover pipe retaining nuts.
6. Remove serpentine drive belt, then the power steering pump.
7. Disconnect heater hose from tube, then remove manifold heat shield.
8. Remove ignition module bracket attaching nuts.
9. Remove exhaust manifold attaching bolts and the manifold.
10. Reverse procedure to install. Transfer oxygen sensor and exhaust pipe seal to replacement manifold.

ROCKER ARMS

1. Remove valve cover.
2. Remove rocker arm pedestal retaining bolt, noting position of double ended bolts for assembly.
3. Remove rocker arm and pedestal, and the pedestal support plates, **Fig. 3. Keep rocker arms and pedestals together and note installation position. Components that are to be reused should be installed in original position.**
4. Reverse procedure to install, torquing pedestal retaining bolts to 45 ft. lbs.

VALVES
ADJUST

These engines are equipped with hydraulic valve lifters. No provision for adjustment is provided.

VALVE ARRANGEMENT
FRONT TO REAR

V6-181. . . . . E-I-I-E-I-E

VALVE GUIDES

The valve guides are an integral part of the cylinder head and cannot be replaced.

If the valve stem clearance is excessive, the valve guide must be reamed and an oversize valve installed. Valves are available in oversize of .010 inch.

VALVE LIFTERS

Failure of an hydraulic valve lifter, **Fig. 4**, is generally caused by dirt or an inadequate oil supply. An air leak at the intake side of the oil pump or too much oil in the engine will cause air bubbles in the oil supply to the lifters, causing them to collapse. This is a probable cause of trouble if several lifters fail to function, but air in the oil is an unlikely cause of failure of a single unit.

The valve lifters may be lifted out of their bores after removing the rocker arms, pushrods and intake manifold. Adjustable pliers with taped jaws may be used to remove lifters that are stuck due to varnish, carbon, etc.

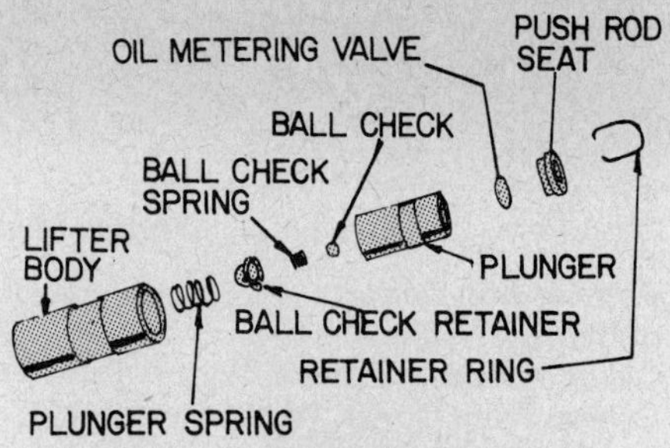

Fig. 4 Hydraulic valve lifter exploded view

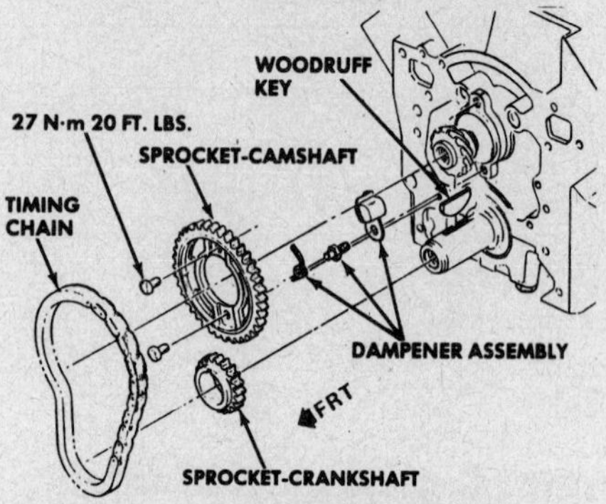

Fig. 6 Timing chain replacement

ENGINE FRONT COVER
REPLACE

1. Disconnect battery ground cable.
2. Loosen, but do not remove, water pump pulley attaching bolts.
3. Remove serpentine accessory drive belt.
4. Remove water pump pulley attaching bolts and the pulley.
5. Raise and support vehicle.
6. Remove right side wheel and tire assembly and inner fender splash shield.
7. Drain cooling system, then remove crankshaft balancer.
8. Drain engine oil, then remove oil filter.
9. Disconnect radiator and heater hoses, then remove crankshaft sensor.
10. Remove oil pan and gasket, then the water pump.
11. Remove front cover attaching bolts, then the front cover and gasket, **Fig. 5.**
12. Reverse procedure to install.

TIMING CHAIN
REPLACE

1. Remove engine front cover as described under "Engine Front Cover, Replace."
2. Align timing marks on sprockets so they are as close together as possible.
3. Remove camshaft sprocket attaching bolts, then the camshaft sprocket, chain and crankshaft sprocket, **Fig. 6.**
4. Reverse procedure to install. Install chain with No. 1 piston at TDC, timing mark on camshaft sprocket facing straight down and timing marks on sprockets as close together as possible.

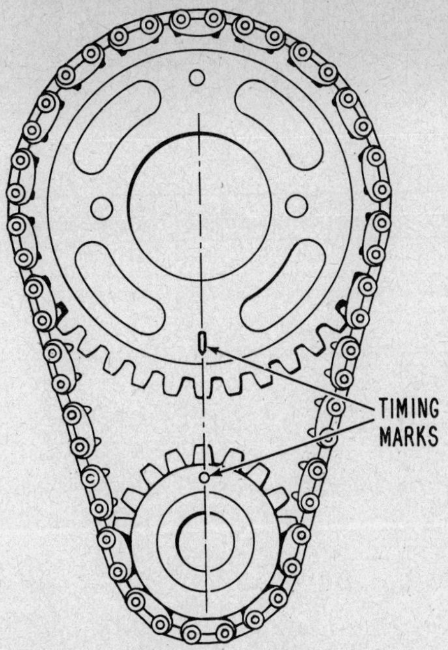

Fig. 7 Valve timing marks

CAMSHAFT
REPLACE

1. Remove engine as outlined in "Engine, Replace."
2. Remove intake manifold.
3. Remove rocker arm covers.
4. Remove rocker arm and shaft assemblies, pushrods and valve lifters.
5. Remove timing chain cover.
6. Align timing marks of camshaft and crankshaft sprocket. This avoids burring of camshaft journals by crankshaft during removal. Remove timing chain and sprocket.
7. Slide camshaft forward out of bearing bores, using care so as not to damage bearing surfaces.
8. Reverse procedure to install. When installing camshaft, align crankshaft and camshaft timing marks as shown in **Fig. 7.**

PISTONS & RODS
ASSEMBLE

Rods and pistons should be assembled and installed as shown in **Fig. 8.**

Measure connecting rod side clearance using a suitable feeler gauge. Clearance should be .0005-.0026 inch.

PISTONS, PINS & RINGS

Pistons are available in standard sizes and oversizes of .010 and .030 inch. Rings are available in standard sizes and oversizes of .010 and .030 inch. Piston pins are supplied with piston and available only in standard sizes.

MAIN & ROD BEARINGS

Main bearings are available in standard sizes and undersizes of .001 and .002 inch. Rod bearings are available in standard sizes and in undersize of .008.

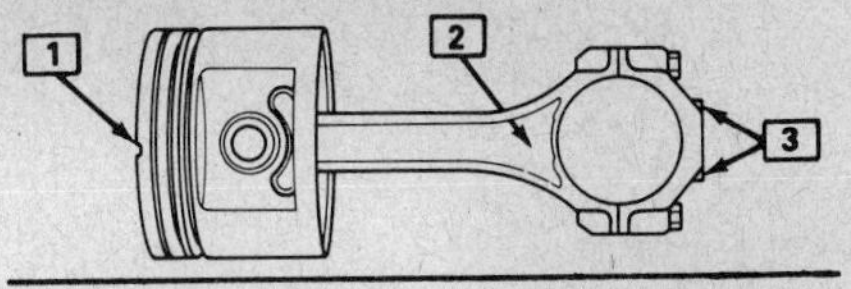

1 NOTCH ON PISTON TOWARDS FRONT OF ENGINE

LEFT BANK

2 NO. 1, 3 & 5 TWO BOSSES ON ROD TOWARDS REAR OF ENGINE (NOT SHOWN)

3 CHAMFERED CORNERS ON ROD CAP TOWARDS FRONT OF ENGINE

RIGHT BANK

2 NO. 2, 4 & 6 TWO BOSSES ON ROD TOWARDS FRONT OF ENGINE (NOT SHOWN)

3 CHAMFERED CORNERS ON ROD CAP TOWARDS REAR OF ENGINE

Fig. 8 Piston & rod assembly

OIL PAN
REPLACE

1. Disconnect battery ground cable.
2. Raise and support vehicle.
3. Drain oil and remove flywheel cover.
4. Remove oil pan.
5. Reverse procedure to install. Apply RTV sealer to oil pan flange and torque oil pan bolts to 8 ft. lbs.

BELT TENSION DATA

A self-adjusting serpentine drive belt is used to drive accessories in place of the usual v-type belt arrangement.

Clutch & Manual Transaxle Section

NOTE: Refer to Section 10, "Clutch & Transaxle Section" for service procedures.

Rear Axle, Rear Suspension & Brakes Section

NOTE: Refer to Section 10, "Rear Suspension & Brakes Section" for service procedures.

Front Suspension & Steering Section

NOTE: Refer to Section 10, "Front Suspension & Steering Section" for service procedures not covered in this section.

POWER STEERING PUMP, REPLACE

Refer to **Figs. 1, 2 and 3** when replacing the power steering pump.

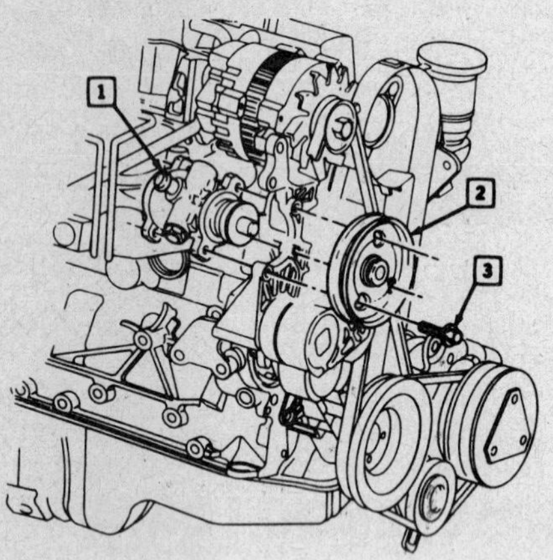

1. POWER STEERING PUMP
2. PULLEY
3. BOLT – 27 N·m (20 LBS. FT.)

Fig. 1 Power steering pump replacement. 4-121 engine

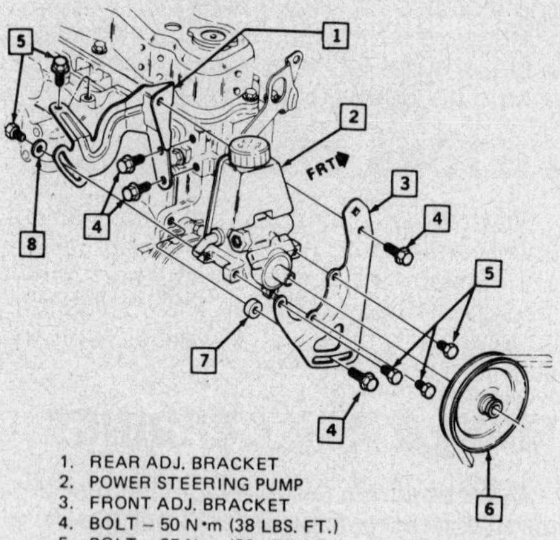

1. REAR ADJ. BRACKET
2. POWER STEERING PUMP
3. FRONT ADJ. BRACKET
4. BOLT – 50 N·m (38 LBS. FT.)
5. BOLT – 27 N·m (20 LBS. FT.)
6. PULLEY
7. SPACER
8. WASHER

Fig. 2 Power steering pump replacement. 4-151 engine

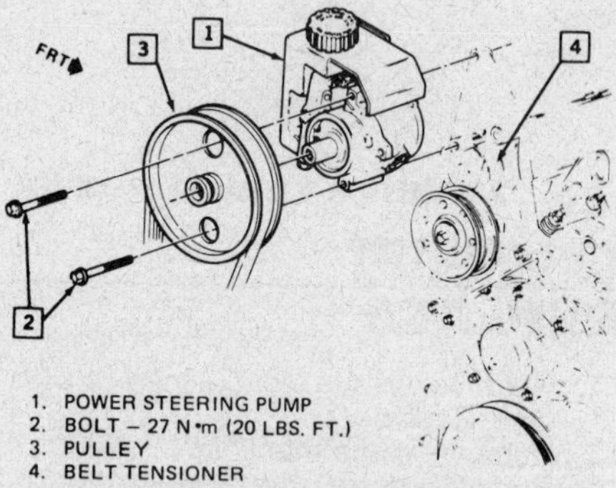

1. POWER STEERING PUMP
2. BOLT – 27 N·m (20 LBS. FT.)
3. PULLEY
4. BELT TENSIONER

Fig. 3 Power steering pump replacement. V6-181 engine

Wheel Alignment Section

NOTE: Refer to Section 10, "Wheel Alignment Section" for service procedures.

BUICK SKYLARK (1982–85) CHEVROLET CITATION OLDSMOBILE OMEGA PONTIAC PHOENIX

INDEX OF SERVICE OPERATIONS

NOTE: Refer to the rear of this manual for vehicle manufacturer's special service tool suppliers.

Specifications

GENERAL ENGINE SPECIFICATIONS

Year	Engine CID①/Liter	Engine VIN Code ②	Carburetor	Bore & Stroke	Compression Ratio	Net H.P. @ RPM③	Maximum Torque Ft. Lbs. @ RPM	Normal Oil Pressure Pounds
1982	4-151, 2.5L	R	T.B.I.⑥	4.0 x 3.0	8.2	90 @ 4000	134 @ 2400	37.5
	V6-173, 2.8L	X	E2SE, 2 Bbl.④	3.5 x 3.0	8.5	112 @ 5100	148 @ 2400	50-65
	V6-173, 2.8L H.O.	Z	E2SE, 2 Bbl.④	3.5 x 3.0	8.9	135 @ 5400	142 @ 2400	50-65
1983	4-151, 2.5L	R	T.B.I.⑥	4.0 x 3.0	8.2	90 @ 4000	134 @ 2800	37.5
	V6-173, 2.8L	X	E2SE, 2 Bbl.④	3.5 x 3.0	8.5	112 @ 4800	145 @ 2100	50-65
	V6-173, 2.8L H.O.	Z	E2SE, 2 Bbl.④	3.5 x 3.0	8.9	130 @ 5400	145 @ 2400	50-65
1984	4-151, 2.5L	R	T.B.I.⑥	4.0 x 3.0	8.2	92 @ 4400	132 @ 2800	37.5
	V6-173, 2.8L	X	E2SE, 2 Bbl.④	3.5 x 3.0	8.5	112 @ 4800	145 @ 2100	50-65
	V6-173, 2.8L H.O.	Z	E2SE, 2 Bbl.④	3.5 x 3.0	8.9	130 @ 5400	145 @ 2400	50-65
1985	4-151, 2.5L	R	T.B.I.⑥	4.0 x 3.0	9.0	92 @ 4400	134 @ 2800	37.5
	V6-173, 2.8L	W	M.F.I.⑤	3.5 x 3.0	8.9	130 @ 4800	160 @ 3600	50-65
	V6-173, 2.8L	X	E2SE, 2 Bbl.④	3.5 x 3.0	8.5	112 @ 4800	145 @ 2100	30-45

①—CID-cubic inch displacement.
②—On these vehicles the eighth digit denotes engine code.
③—Ratings are net-as installed in vehicle.
④—Rochester.
⑤—Multi-point Fuel Injection.
⑥—Throttle body injection.

ENGINE TIGHTENING SPECIFICATIONS*

*Torque specifications are for clean and lightly lubricated threads only. Dry or dirty threads produce increased friction which prevents accurate measurement of tightness.

Year	Engine Model/VIN	Spark Plugs Ft. Lbs.	Cylinder Head Bolts Ft. Lbs.	Intake Manifold Ft. Lbs.	Exhaust Manifold Ft. Lbs.	Rocker Arm Stud Ft. Lbs.	Rocker Arm Cover Ft. Lbs.	Connecting Rod Cap Bolts Ft. Lbs.	Main Bearing Cap Bolts Ft. Lbs.	Flywheel to Crankshaft Ft. Lbs.	Vibration Damper or Pulley Ft. Lbs.
1982-83	4-151/R	7-15	85②	29	44	20①	6	32	70	44	200
	V6-173/X, Z	7-15	65-75	20-25	22-28	43-49	6-9	34-40	63-74	③	66-84
1984	4-151/R	7-15	92②	29	44	20①	6	32	70	44	200
	V6-173/X, Z	7-15	65-75	20-25	22-28	43-49	6-9	34-40	63-74	③	66-84
1985	4-151/R	7-15	92②	29	44	20①	6	32	70	44	200
	V6-173/W, X	7-15	65-75	20-25	22-28	43-49	6-9	34-40	63-74	③	66-84

①—Rocker arm bolt.
②—Requires thread sealer on bolt head & threads.
③—Auto. trans., 25-35 ft. lbs.; manual trans., 45-55 ft. lbs.

ALTERNATOR SPECIFICATIONS

Year	Model	Rated Hot Output Amps.
1982	11100115	42
	1103187	42
	1103197	63
	1101067	70
1983	1100231	42
	1100233	42
	1100235	42
	1100208	63
	1100252	63
	1100254	63
	1100217	78
	1100260	78
	1100272	78
	1105199	85
1984	1100231	42
	1100233	42
	1100235	42

Year	Model	Rated Hot Output Amps.
	1100208	66
	1100252	66
	1100254	66
	1100217	78
	1100268	78
	1100272	78
	1105441	94
	1105443	94
	1105542	94
1985	1100200	78
	1100206	56
	1100208	66
	1100217	78
	1100231	42
	1100247	66
	1100257	78

Year	Model	Rated Hot Output Amps.
	1100260	78
	1105028	78
	1105441	94
	1105443	94
	1105444	94
	1105446	94
	1105447	94
	1105493	94
	1105494	78
	1105562	66
	1105588	78
	1105590	56
	1105592	94
	1105600	66
	1105607	42
	1105617	94

STARTING MOTOR APPLICATIONS

Year	Engine/VIN	Starter Ident. No.
1982	4-151/R, V6-173/X,Z	1109530
1983	4-151/R	1109556
	4-151/R	1998556
	V6-173/X,Z	1109533

Year	Engine/VIN	Starter Ident. No.
	V6-173/X, Z	1109564
1984	4-151/R	1998450
	V6-173/X, Z	1109564
1985	4-151/R	1998450
	V6-173/W, X	1109564

WHEEL ALIGNMENT SPECIFICATIONS

Year	Model	Caster Angle, Degrees		Camber Angle, Degrees				Toe-In Inch
				Limits		Desired		
		Limits	Desired	Left	Right	Left	Right	
1982-85	All	—	—	$-1/2°$ to $+1/2°$	$-1/2°$ to $+1/2°$	Zero	Zero	Zero

COOLING SYSTEM & CAPACITY DATA

Year	Model or Engine/VIN	Cooling Capacity, Qts.		Radiator Cap Relief Pressure, Lbs.	Thermo. Opening Temp.	Fuel Tank Gals.	Engine Oil Refill Qts.	Transaxle Oil	
		Less A/C	With A/C					Manual Transaxle Pts.	Auto. Transaxle Qts.①
1982	Citation 4-151/R	9.5	9.75	15	195	14	3②	5.9	⑪
	Omega 4-151/R	9.5	9.75	15	195	14	3②	5.9	⑪
	Phoenix 4-151/R	8.3④	8.6④	15	195	14	3②	5.9	⑪
	Skylark 4-151/R	9.4⑬	9.8⑬	15	195	14	3②	5.9	⑪
	Citation V6-173/X, Z	11.5	11.75	15	195	14	4②	5.9	⑪
	Omega V6-173/X, Z	11.5	11.75	15	195	14	4②	5.9	⑪
	Phoenix V6-173/X, Z⑦	10.2⑧	10.6⑧	15	195	14	4②	5.9	⑪
	Phoenix V6-173/X, Z⑨	10.5⑧	10.8	15	195	14	4②	5.9	⑪
	Skylark V6-173/X, Z	11.4	11.8	15	195	14	4②	5.9	⑪
1983	Citation 4-151/R	8.5	9	15	195	14.6	3②	5.9	⑪
	Omega 4-151/R	9.5⑬	9.75⑬	15	195	14.6	3②	5.9	⑪
	Phoenix 4-151/R	9.5⑩	9.8⑩	15	195	14.6	3②	5.9	⑪
	Skylark 4-151/R	9.5	9.7	15	195	14.6	3②	5.9	⑪
	Citation V6-173/X, Z	10.5	11	15	195	15.1	4②	5.9	⑪
	Omega V6-173/X, Z	10.25⑧	10.5⑧	15	195	15.1	4②	5.9	⑪
	Phoenix V6-173/X, Z	11.4⑫	11.8⑫	15	195	15.1	4②	5.9	⑪
	Skylark V6-173/X, Z	11.4⑫	11.8⑫	15	195	15.1	4②	5.9	⑪
1984	Citation 4-151/R	8.7⑤	9	15	195	14.6	3②	5.9	⑪
	Omega 4-151/R	9.3⑬	9.6⑬	15	195	14.2	3②	5.9	⑪
	Phoenix 4-151/R	9.5	10.4	15	195	14.6	3②	5.9	⑪
	Skylark 4-151/R	9.5⑫	9.7⑫	15	195	14.6	3②	5.9	⑪
	Citation V6-173/X, Z	10.7⑥	11	15	195	15.1	4②	5.9	⑪
	Omega V6-173/X, Z	③⑧	10.5⑧	15	195	15.1	4②	5.9	⑪
	Phoenix V6-173/X, Z	11.1	11.8	15	195	15.1	4②	5.9	⑪
	Skylark V6-173/X, Z	11.4	11.8	15	195	15.1	4②	5.9	⑪
1985	Citation 4-151/R	8.75	9.0	15	195	14.6	3②	5.9	⑪
	Citation V6-173/W	10.5	11.0	15	195	14.6	4②	5.9	⑪
	Citation V6-173/X	10.5	11.0	15	195	15.1	4②	5.9	⑪
	Skylark 4-151/R	9.5	9.7	15	195	14.6	3②	5.9	⑪
	Skylark V6-173/W	11.4	11.8	15	195	14.6	4②	5.9	⑪
	Skylark V6-173/X	11.4	11.8	15	195	15.1	4②	5.9	⑪

①—Approximate make final check with dipstick.
②—Additional oil may be required when changing filter.
③—Auto. trans., 9.9 qts.; man. trans., 10.5 qts.
④—With heavy duty cooling system, man. trans. 8.7 qts., auto. trans., 9.3 qts.
⑤—Heavy duty cooling system, 9 qts.
⑥—With heavy duty cooling system, 11 qts.
⑦—Exc. Calif.
⑧—Heavy duty cooling system, 10.8 qts.
⑨—California.
⑩—Heavy duty cooling system, 10.4 qts.
⑪—Oil pan capacity, 4 qts.; total capacity, 6 qts.
⑫—Heavy duty cooling system, 12 qts.
⑬—Heavy duty cooling system, 10 qts.

Electrical Section

INDEX

STARTER

REPLACE

EXC. 1983–84 PHOENIX

1. Disconnect battery ground cable.
2. Raise and support vehicle.
3. Remove the starter to engine brace, if equipped.
4. Remove starter mounting bolts and lower starter. Note position of shims, if used.
5. Disconnect solenoid wires and the battery cable.
6. Remove starter from vehicle.
7. Reverse procedure to install.

1983–84 PHOENIX

1. Disconnect battery ground cable.
2. Raise and support vehicle.
3. Remove three dust cover attaching bolts.
4. Pull dust cover back to gain access to front starter attaching bolt, then remove bolt.
5. Pull rear of dust cover backward and remove rear starter attaching bolt.
6. Push dust cover back into position, then pull starter back and out.
7. Disconnect solenoid wires and battery cable, then remove starter from vehicle.
8. Reverse procedure to install. Replace any shims that were removed.

IGNITION LOCK

REPLACE

1. Remove steering wheel as outlined under "Steering Wheel, Replace" procedure.

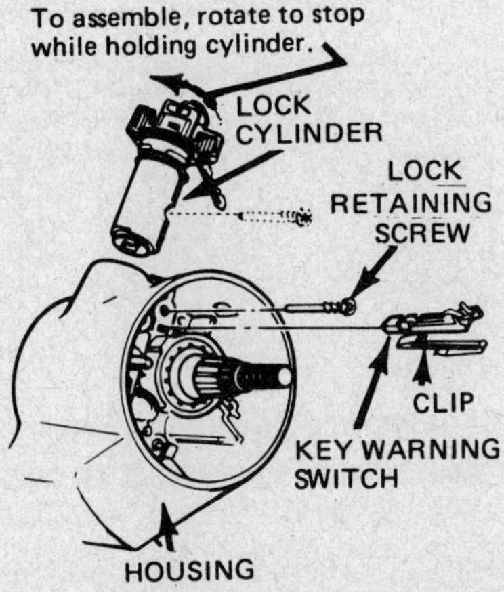

Fig. 1 Lock cylinder removal

2. Remove turn signal switch as outlined under "Turn Signal Switch, Replace" procedure.
3. Remove the buzzer switch and spring clip.
4. Turn lock cylinder to "Run" position, then remove the lock cylinder retaining screw and the lock cylinder, **Fig. 1.**
5. To install, rotate lock cylinder to the stop while holding housing. Align cylinder key with keyway in housing, then push lock cylinder into housing until fully seated.
6. Install lock cylinder retaining screw.
7. Install buzzer switch, turn signal switch and steering wheel.

IGNITION & DIMMER SWITCHES

REPLACE

1. Remove turn signal switch as outlined under "Turn Signal Switch, Replace" procedure.
2. Refer to **Figs. 2 and 3** to remove ignition and dimmer switches.
3. When installing dimmer switch, depress switch slightly to install a 3/32 inch twist drill. Force switch upward to remove lash and tighten retaining screw.

WINDSHIELD WIPER SWITCH

REPLACE

1. Disconnect battery ground cable.
2. Remove turn signal switch and ignition lock as outlined.
3. Remove lower steering column trim covers and bolts securing steering column bracket, then lower column and disconnect electrical connector to wiper switch.
4. Remove steering column housing screws and the housing, **Figs. 4 and 5.**
5. Remove housing cover screw and the cover.
6. Remove wiper switch pivot and the switch.
7. Reverse procedure to install.

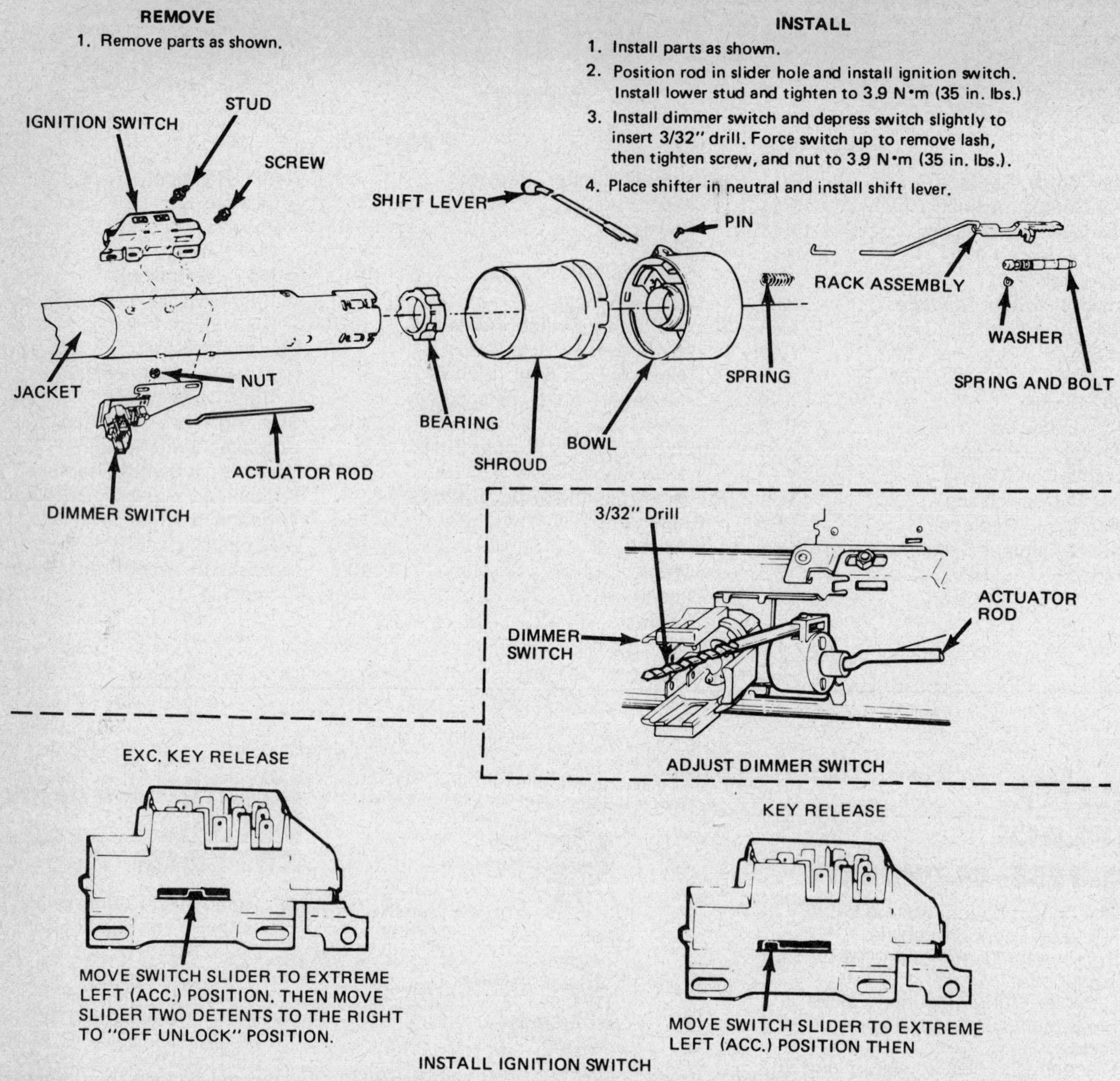
REMOVE
1. Remove parts as shown.
INSTALL
1. Install parts as shown.
2. Position rod in slider hole and install ignition switch. Install lower stud and tighten to 3.9 N•m (35 in. lbs.)
3. Install dimmer switch and depress switch slightly to insert 3/32" drill. Force switch up to remove lash, then tighten screw, and nut to 3.9 N•m (35 in. lbs.).
4. Place shifter in neutral and install shift lever.
STUD
IGNITION SWITCH
SCREW
SHIFT LEVER
PIN
RACK ASSEMBLY
WASHER
SPRING AND BOLT
SPRING
JACKET
NUT
BEARING
BOWL
SHROUD
ACTUATOR ROD
DIMMER SWITCH
3/32" Drill
DIMMER SWITCH
ACTUATOR ROD
ADJUST DIMMER SWITCH
EXC. KEY RELEASE
KEY RELEASE
MOVE SWITCH SLIDER TO EXTREME LEFT (ACC.) POSITION. THEN MOVE SLIDER TWO DETENTS TO THE RIGHT TO "OFF UNLOCK" POSITION.
MOVE SWITCH SLIDER TO EXTREME LEFT (ACC.) POSITION THEN
INSTALL IGNITION SWITCH

Fig. 2 Ignition & dimmer switch removal & installation. Except tilt column

PULSE WINDSHIELD WIPER SWITCH

REPLACE

On models where pulse wipers are controlled at turn signal lever, a malfunction may be caused by a faulty pulse wiper module. The module is located behind left-hand side of instrument panel.

CITATION

1. Disconnect battery ground cable.
2. Remove radio knobs and nuts and the clock knob.
3. Remove instrument cluster bezel to instrument panel carrier retaining screws and pull bezel rearward.
4. Depress headlamp switch shaft retaining button and pull knob and shaft assembly from switch.
5. Disconnect accessory switch wiring connectors.
6. Remove controller knob and ferrule nut attaching controller to bezel.
7. Disconnect wiring connector at steering column.
8. Remove switch from vehicle.
9. Reverse procedure to install.

OMEGA

Refer to "Windshield Wiper Switch, Replace" for pulse wiper switch replacement procedure on these models.

PHOENIX

Refer to "Windshield Wiper Switch, Replace" for pulse wiper switch replacement procedure on these models.

SKYLARK

Refer to "Windshield Wiper Switch, Replace" for pulse wiper switch replacement procedure on these models.

STOPLAMP SWITCH

ADJUST

Insert switch into tubular clip until the switch body seats on the tube clip. Pull the brake pedal rearward against internal pedal stop. The switch will be properly positioned in the tubular clip.

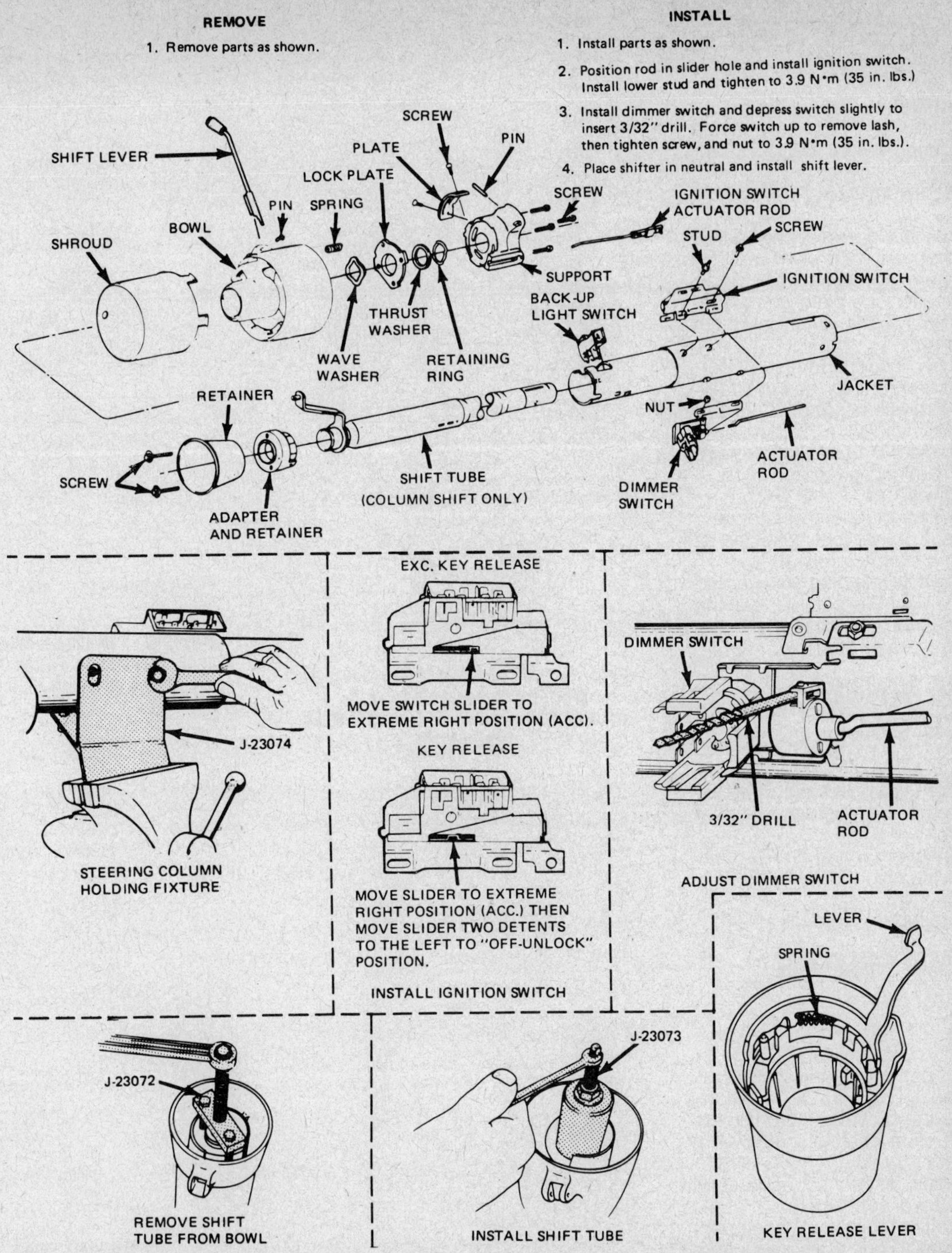

Fig. 3 Ignition & dimmer switch removal & installation. Tilt column

NEUTRAL SAFETY SWITCH

REPLACE

1982 MODELS W/ AUTO. TRANS. & CONSOLE SHIFT & ALL 1983–85 MODELS W/AUTO. TRANS. & KEY RELEASE

1. Disconnect battery ground cable.
2. Place gear selector in Neutral.
3. Gently rock switch out of steering column, **Fig. 6.**
4. Disconnect electrical connectors, then remove switch from vehicle.
5. Connect electrical connectors to new switch.
6. Align switch actuator with hole in shift tube.
7. Position connector side of switch into lower jacket cutout.
8. Push down front of switch, ensuring switch tangs snap into holes in steering column jacket.
9. Adjust switch by replacing gear selector in Park position. The switch main housing and housing back should ratchet, providing proper adjustment.
10. If readjustment is needed, move housing as far as possible toward Low gear position, then repeat step 9.

1982–85 MODELS W/AUTO. TRANS. LESS KEY RELEASE

These vehicles do not use a neutral safety switch. A mechanical block on the transmission gear selector, **Fig. 7,** prevents starting the engine when the transmission is in any gear other than Park or Neutral.

TURN SIGNAL SWITCH
REPLACE

1. Disconnect battery ground cable.
2. Remove steering wheel as outlined under "Steering Wheel, Replace" procedure.
3. Using a screwdriver, pry cover from housing.
4. Using lock plate compressing tool J-23653, compress lock plate and pry snap ring from groove on shaft, **Fig. 8.** Slowly release lock plate compressing tool, remove tool and lock plate from shaft end.
5. Slide canceling cam and upper bearing preload spring from end of shaft.
6. Remove turn signal (multi-function) lever.
7. Remove hazard warning knob retaining screw, button, spring and knob.
8. Remove pivot arm.
9. Wrap upper part of electrical connector with tape to prevent snagging of wires during switch removal.
10. Remove switch retaining screws and pull switch up from column, guiding wire harness through column.
11. Reverse procedure to install.

STEERING WHEEL
REPLACE

1. Disconnect battery ground cable.
2. Remove horn button or pad.
3. Remove retainer and steering wheel retaining nut.
4. Remove steering wheel with a suitable puller (tool No. J-1859-03 or BT-61-9).
5. Reverse procedure to install.

HEADLAMP SWITCH
REPLACE
CITATION

1. Disconnect battery ground cable.
2. Pull switch knob to full "On" position.
3. Remove spring clip retainer from knob shaft, then slide shaft out of switch housing.
4. On all models, disconnect accessory switch electrical connectors.
5. Remove switch ferrule nut, then push switch forward out from mounting hole.
6. Lift switch up and out through opening above switch mounting, then disconnect electrical connector.
7. Remove switch from instrument panel.
8. Reverse procedure to install.

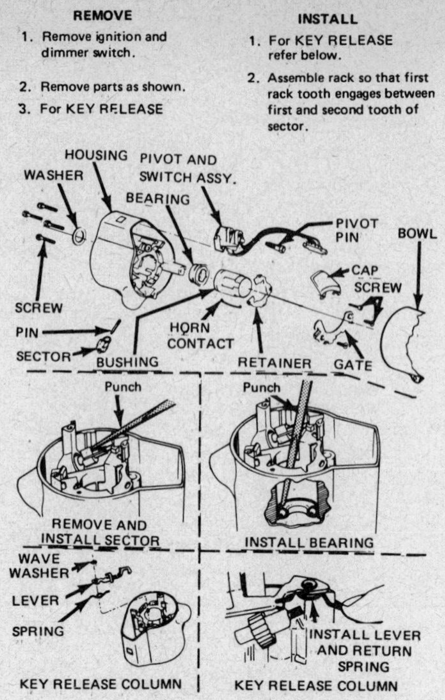

Fig. 4 Windshield wiper switch removal & installation. Except tilt column

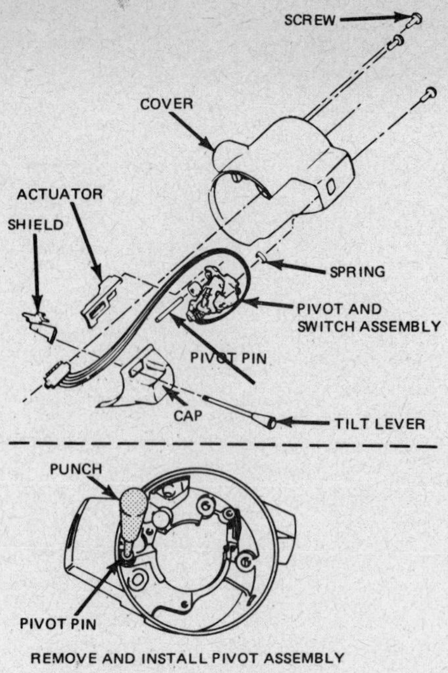

Fig. 5 Windshield wiper switch removal & installation. Tilt column

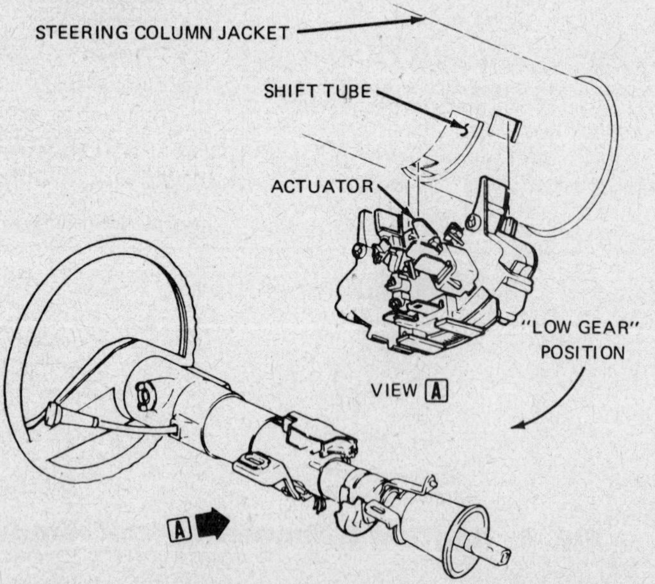

Fig. 6 Neutral safety switch removal. 1982 models with auto. trans. & console shift & all 1983–85 models with auto. trans. & key release

OMEGA

1. Disconnect battery ground cable.
2. Remove headlamp switch knob by depressing retaining clip behind knob and pulling knob from shaft.
3. Remove lefthand trim cover attaching screws and the trim cover.
4. Remove switch attaching screws and pull switch from panel. **The switch plugs directly into a terminal plug in the switch mounting cavity.**
5. Reverse procedure to install.

PHOENIX

1. Disconnect battery ground cable.
2. Remove steering column trim cover attaching screws and the trim cover.
3. Pull headlamp switch to full "On" position, depress knob release button on switch and remove rod and knob assembly.
4. Remove lefthand trim plate attaching screws and the trim plate.
5. Remove switch escutcheon, disconnect electrical connector from switch and remove switch from instrument panel.
6. Reverse procedure to install.

1983–85 SKYLARK

1. Disconnect battery ground cable.

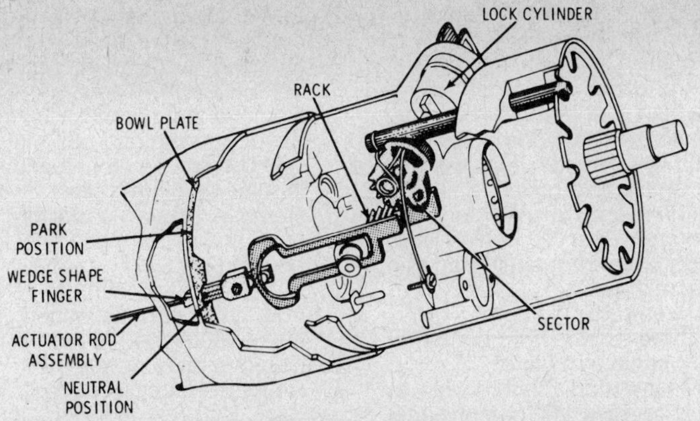

Fig. 7 Mechanical neutral start system. 1982–85 models with auto. trans. less key release

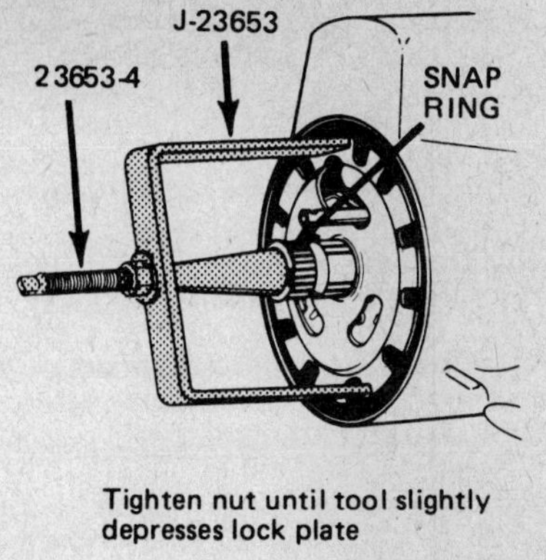

Fig. 8 Compressing lock plate

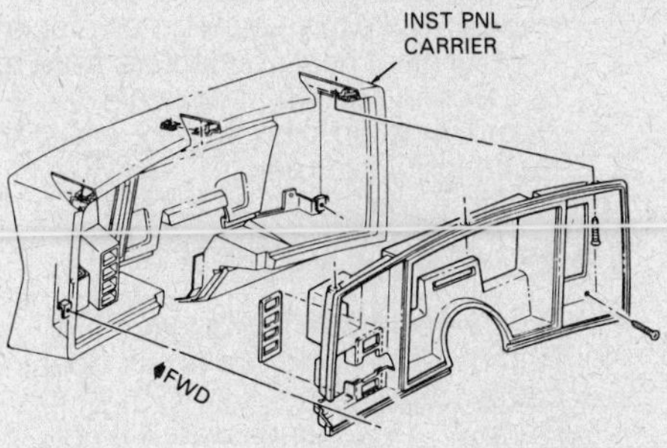

Fig. 9 Instrument cluster trim cover. Citation

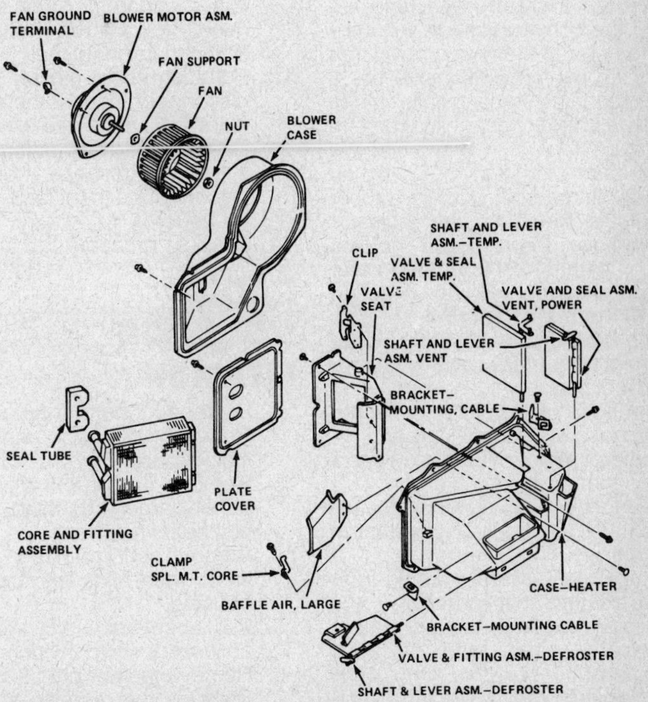

Fig. 10 Heater core & blower motor, less A/C

2. Remove headlamp switch knob by using a small screwdriver through slot to depress retainer while pulling knob out.
3. Remove switch bezel.
4. Remove rear window defogger switch knob, if equipped, by pulling straight off.
5. Remove 3 attaching screws from lower edge of lefthand trim panel.
6. Pull lefthand trim panel straight forward and remove from vehicle.
7. Remove 2 headlamp switch attaching screws and the switch. **Pulling switch straight out of dash will also disconnect the electrical connector.**
8. Reverse procedure to install.

1982 SKYLARK

1. Disconnect battery ground cable.
2. Remove headlamp switch knob by depressing retaining clip behind knob and pulling knob from shaft.
3. Remove escutcheon from switch and shaft.
4. Remove the knobs from the following: windshield wiper switch, rear window defogger switch and radio.
5. Remove radio retaining nuts.
6. Remove three screws from bottom of instrument panel trim plate.
7. Place transmission shift lever in "Low," then remove instrument panel trim plate.
8. Remove headlamp switch retaining screws and pull switch from panel. **The switch plugs directly into a terminal plug in the switch mounting cavity.**
9. Reverse procedure to install.

INSTRUMENT CLUSTER REPLACE

CITATION

1. Disconnect battery ground cable.
2. Remove radio knobs and nuts and the clock knob.
3. Remove instrument cluster bezel to panel carrier attaching screws, then pull bezel rearward for access, **Fig. 9.**
4. Remove spring clip retainer from knob shaft, then slide shaft out of switch housing.
5. Pull bezel rearward and disconnect accessory switch electrical connectors.
6. Remove instrument cluster bezel.
7. Remove four screws securing cluster assembly to instrument panel pad.
8. Disconnect shift indicator cable from steering column shift bowl.
9. Pull cluster rearward and disconnect speedometer cable and electrical connectors.
10. Remove instrument cluster from vehicle.
11. Reverse procedure to install.

1983–84 OMEGA

1. Disconnect battery ground cable.

2. Remove 4 steering column lower trim pad attaching screws and the pad.
3. Remove 6 center instrument panel trim cover attaching screws and the cover.
4. Disconnect shift indicator from steering column shift bowl.
5. Remove 4 instrument cluster-to-instrument panel attaching screws.
6. Disconnect speedometer cable from transaxle, or from transducer on models equipped with cruise control.
7. Pull cluster rearward and disconnect speedometer cable.
8. Remove vehicle speed sensor LED/photo cell attaching screw from rear of speedometer head.
9. Remove instrument cluster from vehicle.
10. Reverse procedure to install.

1982 OMEGA

1. Disconnect battery ground cable.
2. Remove the 2 screws attaching assembly line communication link connector bracket to steering column trim cover if so equipped. Remove the 2 screws attaching steering column trim cover to instrument panel and remove trim cover.
3. Mark location of shift indicator clip on steering column shift bowl for proper reassembly. Remove shift indicator clip. Remove the 2 bolts holding steering column to support and lower steering column, resting steering wheel on front seat.
4. Remove four screws attaching center instrument panel trim cover to instrument panel pad.
5. Pull trim cover rearward and disconnect accessory switch wiring and remote control mirror cable, if equipped. Remove trim cover.
6. Remove four screws attaching instrument cluster assembly to instrument panel pad.
7. Disconnect shift indicator cable from steering column shift bowl.
8. Pull cluster rearward and disconnect speedometer cable and electrical connections.
9. Remove instrument cluster from vehicle.
10. Reverse procedure to install.

PHOENIX

1. Disconnect battery ground cable.
2. Remove four speedometer cluster trim plate attaching screws and the trim plate.
3. Remove steering column trim cover attaching screws and the trim cover.
4. Remove speedometer cluster attaching screws.
5. Disconnect shift indicator detent cable, marking the cable location on steering column shift bowl.
6. Disconnect speedometer cable and pull cluster from panel.
7. Disconnect wiring harness from cluster and remove cluster from vehicle.
8. Reverse procedure to install.

SKYLARK

1. Disconnect battery ground cable.
2. Disconnect speedometer cable at cruise control transducer, if equipped, or at upper and lower cable connections.
3. Remove trip meter reset knob retaining screw and pull knob from meter.
4. Remove knobs from the following: windshield wiper switch, rear window defogger switch and radio.
5. Remove headlamp switch knob by depressing retaining clip behind knob and pulling knob from shaft. Remove switch escutcheon.
6. Remove radio retaining nuts.
7. Remove three screws from bottom of instrument panel trim plate.
8. Place transmission shift lever in "Low" and remove instrument panel trim plate.
9. Remove four instrument cluster lens plate screws and the lens plate.
10. Remove four instrument cluster cover plate screws and the cover plate.
11. Disconnect shift indicator spring below speedometer and slide indicator needle toward the right side and out from cluster housing.
12. Pull instrument cluster rearward and disconnect speedometer cable and electrical connections.
13. Remove screw securing vehicle speed sensor head, if equipped, then disconnect sensor and remove cluster housing.
14. Reverse procedure to install.

RADIO

REPLACE

CITATION

1. Disconnect battery ground cable.
2. Remove radio knob and nuts and the clock knob.
3. Remove instrument cluster bezel to panel carrier attaching screws, then pull bezel rearward.
4. Remove spring clip retainer from knob shaft, then slide shaft out of switch housing.
5. Pull bezel rearward and disconnect accessory switch wiring connectors.
6. Remove instrument cluster bezel.
7. Remove two screws securing radio bracket to instrument panel.
8. Pull radio rearward while twisting slightly toward left side and disconnect electrical connections. Remove lamp socket.
9. Remove radio from instrument panel.
10. Reverse procedure to install.

1983–84 OMEGA

1. Disconnect battery ground cable.
2. Remove 4 steering column lower trim pad attaching screws and the pad.
3. Remove 6 center instrument panel attaching screws and the cover.
4. Remove 4 radio-to-instrument panel attaching screws.
5. Pull radio rearward, then disconnect all electrical connections from radio.
6. Remove radio from vehicle.
7. Reverse procedure to install.

1982 OMEGA

1. Disconnect battery ground cable.
2. Remove radio knobs.
3. Pull out glove box switches and disconnect the wiring connectors.
4. Remove two screws securing glove box stop arm to door.
5. Remove two screws from instrument panel molding and pull molding rearward to remove. Note that the molding is retained by five clips.
6. Remove ashtray assembly, then the lamp and socket assembly from lamp housing.
7. Pull radio and ashtray retainer out from panel and disconnect all electrical connections.
8. Remove radio from panel.
9. Reverse procedure to install.

PHOENIX

1. Disconnect battery ground cable.
2. Remove eight screws attaching center instrument panel trim plate and the trim plate.
3. Removetwo radio attaching screws and pull radio from panel, then disconnect all elect rical connectors from radio. Remove radio from panel.
4. Remove radio knobs and separate face plate from radio.
5. Reverse procedure to install.

1983–85 SKYLARK

1. Disconnect battery ground cable.
2. Remove steering column opening cover plate.
3. Remove headlamp switch knob by using a small screwdriver through slot to depress retainer while pulling knob out.
4. Remove headlamp switch bezel.
5. Remove rear window defogger switch knob, if equipped, by pulling straight off.
6. Remove 3 attaching screws from lower edge of lefthand trim panel.
7. Pull lefthand trim straight forward and remove from vehicle.
8. Remove 2 attaching screws from left side of radio and 1 nut from lower right side of radio.
9. Pull radio out through instrument panel opening and disconnect all electrical connectors.
10. Remove radio from vehicle.
11. Reverse procedure to install.

1982 SKYLARK

1. Disconnect battery ground cable.
2. Remove knobs from the following: windshield wiper switch, rear window defogger switch and radio.
3. Remove headlamp switch knob by depressing retaining clip behind knob and pulling knob from shaft. Remove the switch escutcheon.
4. Remove radio retaining nuts.
5. Remove three screws at bottom of instrument panel trim plate.
6. Place transmission shift lever in "Low" and remove instrument panel trim plate.
7. Remove radio mounting plate screws.
8. Disconnect all electrical connection from radio.
9. Pull radio out through instrument panel opening.
10. Reverse procedure to install.

WINDSHIELD WIPER MOTOR

REPLACE

1. Remove wiper arms as outlined previously.
2. Remove the lower windshield reveal molding, front cowl panel and cowl screen. Disconnect washer hose. **Prior to removing the front cowl screen, mask the corners of the hood to prevent damage to paint.**
3. Loosen but do not remove transmission drive link to motor crank arm attaching nuts. Then, disconnect drive link from motor crank arm.
4. Disconnect wiper motor electrical leads.
5. Remove wiper motor attaching bolts.
6. On models equipped with A/C, support motor assembly and remove motor crank arm. Use a suitable pair of locking pliers and wrench, remove crank arm nut and the crank arm.
7. On all models, rotate motor assembly upward and outward to remove.
8. Reverse procedure to install.

WINDSHIELD WIPER TRANSMISSION

REPLACE

1. Remove lower windshield reveal molding, wiper arms and front cowl panel.
2. Loosen but do not remove drive link to motor crank arm attaching nuts.
3. Remove transmission to cowl panel attaching screws and the transmission.
4. Reverse procedure to install.

BLOWER MOTOR

REPLACE

1. Disconnect battery ground cable.
2. Disconnect blower motor electrical connections.
3. Remove blower motor attaching screws and the blower motor, **Fig. 10.**
4. Reverse procedure to install.

HEATER CORE

REPLACE

LESS AIR CONDITIONING

1. Disconnect battery ground cable and drain cooling system.
2. Disconnect the heater hoses from heater core.
3. Remove radio noise supression strap.
4. Remove heater core cover retaining screws and the cover, **Fig. 10.**
5. Remove heater core from vehicle.
6. Reverse procedure to install.

WITH AIR CONDITIONING

1. Disconnect battery ground cable and drain cooling system.
2. Disconnect heater hoses from heater core.
3. Remove right side hush panel and open the glove box.
4. Remove heater duct retaining screw and the duct.
5. Remove instrument panel support bracket.
6. Remove heater case side cover retainers and the cover.
7. Remove heater core retaining clamps and the inlet and outlet tube support clamps.
8. Remove heater core from case.
9. Reverse procedure to install.

CRUISE CONTROL

ADJUST

BRAKE RELEASE SWITCHES

Electrical & Vacuum Switches

Push the switch fully into the retaining clip, then pull the brake pedal upward to adjust switch position. The electrical switch should break the electrical circuit when the brake pedal is depressed approximately .23-.51 inch.

SERVO, ADJUST

Models With Rod

Install the pin retainer to provide minimum slack with carburetor in slow idle position.

Models With Bead Chain

Assemble the chain into swivel and install retainer so that slack in the chain is not greater than one-half the diameter of the ball stud with the engine at operating temperature and the idle solenoid deenergized.

Models With Cable

1. With cable installed in cable and servo brackets, rotate throttle lever so that stud aligns with hole in end of cable.
2. Engage cable with throttle lever stud, then release throttle lever.
3. Hold throttle lever position and pull cable taut from servo end.
4. Connect servo end of cable to servo actuator with pin, using hole which most closely aligns with cable end. **Do not stretch cable or open throttle to align cable, as this will not allow engine to return to idle.**

CRUISE SPEED, ADJUST

On 1984-85 vehicles, cruise speed is controlled by the electronic controller and is not adjustable.

1982–83

The cruise speed adjustment can be set as follows:

1. If car cruises below engagement speed, screw orifice tube on transducer outward.
2. If car cruises above engagement speed, screw orifice tube inward. **Each 1/4 turn of the orifice tube will change cruise speed about one mile per hour. Snug up locknut after each adjustment.**

4-151 (2.5L) & V6-173 (2.8L) Engine Section

NOTE: Refer to 4-151 (2.5L) & V6-173 (2.8L) Engine Section in Chapter 7 for service procedures not covered in this section.

INDEX

ENGINE MOUNTS REPLACE

4-151

1. Raise and support front of vehicle, then remove chassis to mount attaching nuts, **Fig. 1.**
2. On models equipped with A/C, remove forward torque rod attaching bolts at radiator support panel.
3. Raise engine slightly using a suitable engine lifting device. Raise engine only enough to provide clearance for mount removal.
4. Remove two upper mount to engine support bracket attaching nuts and remove engine mount.
5. Reverse procedure to install.

V6-173

1. Remove mount retaining nuts from below cradle mounting bracket.
2. Raise engine and remove mount to engine attaching nuts, then remove mount, **Figs. 2 and 3.** Raise engine only enough to provide clearance for mount removal.
3. Reverse procedure to install, then lower engine into position. Install retaining nuts and torque to 35 ft. lbs. **After engine mount is properly installed, check both transaxle mounts for proper alignment. If window "A" is not properly located, Fig. 4, loosen mount to cradle retaining nuts and allow mount to reposition itself. If transaxle mount is allowed to remain out of position, damage to drive train components may result. Torque retaining nuts to 18 ft. lbs.**

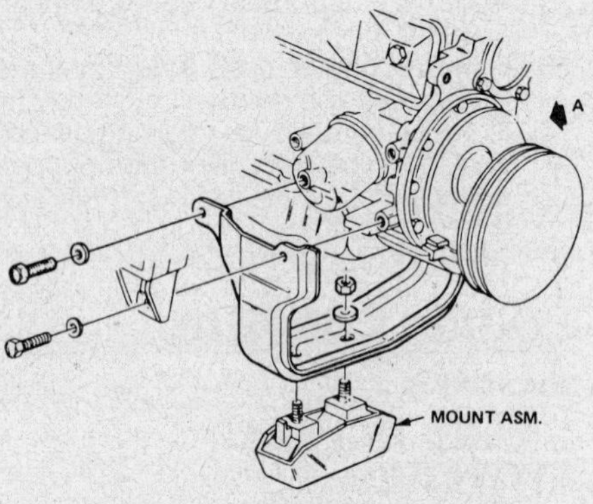

Fig. 1 Engine mounts. 4-151

ENGINE REPLACE

4-151

Manual Transaxle

1. Disconnect cables from battery.
2. Raise and support vehicle.
3. Remove front engine mount-to-cradle attaching nuts.
4. Remove front exhaust pipe, then disconnect starter motor and position aside.
5. Remove flywheel inspection cover, then lower vehicle.
6. Remove air cleaner assembly.
7. Remove all bellhousing attaching bolts.
8. Remove front torque reaction rod from engine and core support.
9. On models equipped with A/C, remove compressor drive belt, then disconnect compressor and position aside. Do not disconnect refrigerant lines from compressor.
10. Disconnect vacuum hoses from vapor canister.
11. On models equipped with power steering, disconnect power steering hose.
12. Disconnect all vacuum hoses and electrical connections needed for engine removal.
13. Remove heater blower motor as described under "Blower Motor, Replace" in the electrical section of this chapter.
14. Disconnect throttle cable.
15. Drain cooling system.
16. Disconnect heater hoses from engine and radiator hoses from radiator.
17. Disconnect engine electrical harness at bulkhead connector.
18. Install suitable engine lifting equipment and raise engine. Disconnect fuel line and the heater hose from intake manifold, then remove engine from vehicle.
19. Reverse procedure to install.

Automatic Transaxle

1. Disconnect cables from battery, then drain cooling system.
2. Remove air cleaner assembly and pre-heat tube.
3. Disconnect engine electrical harness connector.
4. Disconnect all external vacuum hose connections.
5. Remove throttle and transaxle linkages at the throttle body assembly and intake manifold.
6. On models equipped with A/C, disconnect compressor and position aside. Do not disconnect refrigerant lines from compressor.
7. Remove upper radiator hose and front engine strut assembly.
8. Disconnect heater hose from intake manifold.
9. Remove all transaxle-to-engine attaching bolts except the top two bolts.
10. Remove front engine mount-to-cradle nuts.
11. Remove front exhaust pipe, then the flywheel inspection cover.

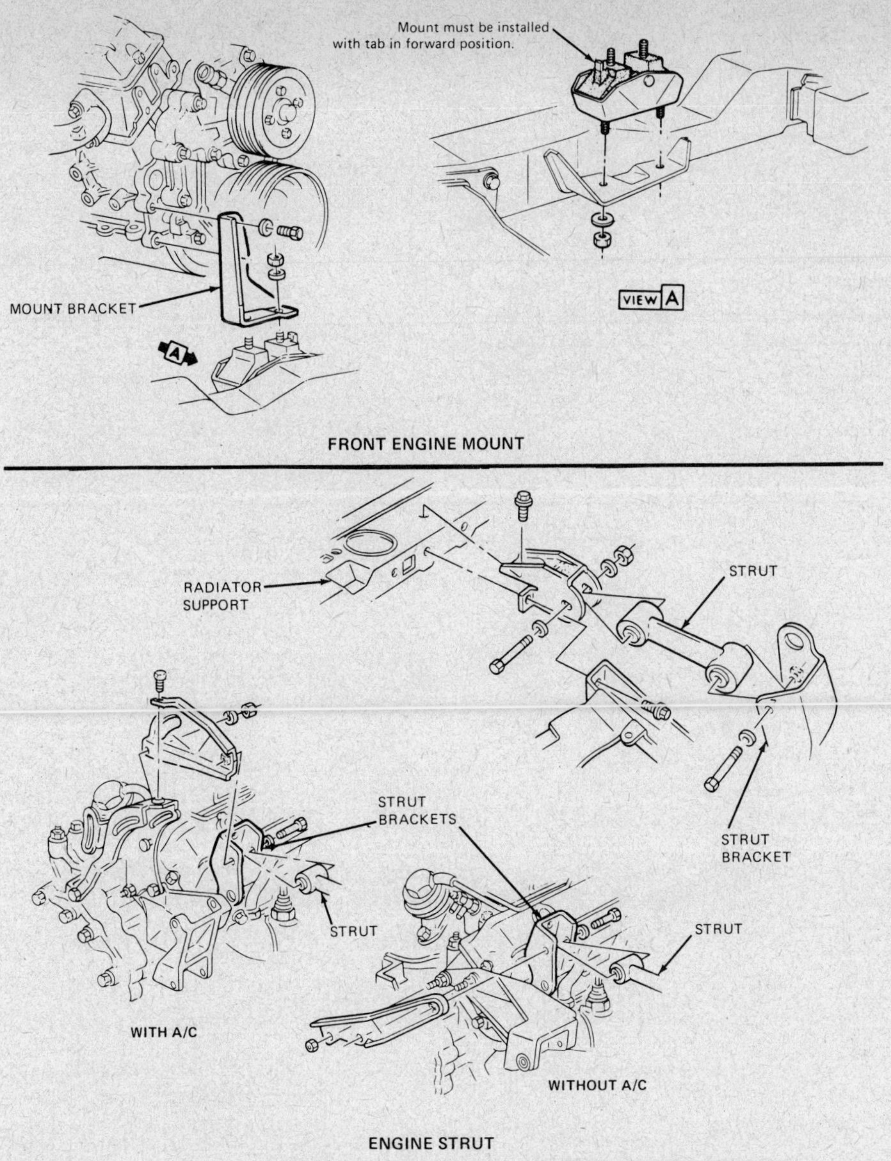

Fig. 2 Engine mounts. 1982–84 V6-173

12. Remove starter motor.
13. Remove torque converter-to-flywheel attaching bolts.
14. On models equipped with power steering, remove power steering pump and bracket and position aside.
15. Disconnect heater hose and lower radiator hose.
16. Remove 2 rear transaxle support bracket bolts.
17. Disconnect fuel feed line at fuel filter.
18. Using a suitable jack and a block of wood placed under transaxle, raise engine and transaxle until engine front mount studs clear cradle bracket.
19. Attaching suitable lifting equipment to engine. Put tension on engine and remove 2 remaining transaxle-to-engine attaching bolts.
20. Slide engine assembly forward and lift from vehicle.
21. Reverse procedure to install.

V6-173

1. Disconnect battery cables from battery and remove air cleaner.
2. Drain cooling system.
3. Remove engine strut bracket from radiator support and swing rearward.
4. Remove AIR pump and bracket, then remove A/C compressor from mounting bracket and place aside, if so equipped.
5. Disconnect vacuum hosing to all non-engine mounted components.
6. Disconnect accelerator cable and detent cable if so equipped.
7. Disconnect engine harness from ECM and pull connector through front of dash.
8. Disconnect engine harness from junction block at left side of dash panel.
9. Disconnect radiator and heater hoses from engine.
10. Remove power steering pump and bracket assembly from engine, if so equipped.
11. Disconnect fuel lines rubber hose connections at left side of engine compartment.
12. Raise vehicle, remove engine front mount-to-cradle and mount-to-engine bracket retaining nuts at right side of vehicle.
13. Disconnect battery cables from starter motor and transaxle case and remove starter.
14. Remove transaxle inspection cover and on automatic transaxle models, disconnect torque converter flex plate.
15. Remove crankshaft lower pulley and all belts.
16. Disconnect exhaust pipe.
17. Remove lower transaxle-to-engine bolt, located at back side of engine.
18. Disconnect power steering cut-off switch, if so equipped.
19. Remove exhaust crossover pipe, then lower vehicle.
20. Remove remaining transaxle-to-engine bolts. Make note of ground stud location.
21. Place a support under transaxle rear extension. Install suitable lifting device and remove engine.
22. Reverse procedure to install.

VALVE CLEARANCE SPECIFICATIONS

Engine	Year	Int.	Exh.
4-151	1982–85	①	①
V6-173	1982–85	②	②

①—No Adjustment provision.
②—1½ additional turns from zero lash position.

VALVES

ADJUST

4-151

These engines are equipped with hydraulic valve lifters, which automatically provide zero lash clearance. No provision for adjustment is available.

V6-173

1. Crank engine until mark on torsional damper is aligned with TDC mark on timing tab. Check to ensure engine is in the No. 1 cylinder firing position by placing fingers on No. 1 cylinder rocker arms as mark on damper comes near TDC mark on timing tab. If valves are not moving, the engine is in the No. 1 firing position. If valves move as damper mark nears TDC mark on timing tab, engine is in the No. 4 cylinder firing position and should be rotated one revolution to reach the No. 1 cylinder firing position.

2. With engine in the No. 1 cylinder firing position, adjust the following valves: Exhaust-1, 2, 3; Intake-1, 5, 6. To adjust valves, back off adjusting nut until lash is felt at pushrod, then tighten adjusting nut until all lash is removed. This can be determined by rotating the pushrod while tightening the adjusting nut. When all lash has been eliminated, turn adjusting nut an additional 1 1/2 turns.
3. Crank engine one revolution until mark on torsional damper and TDC mark are again aligned. This is the No. 4 cylinder firing position. With engine in this position, the following valves can be adjusted: Exhaust-4, 5 & 6; Intake-2, 3 & 4.
4. Install rocker arm covers, then start engine and check timing and idle speed.

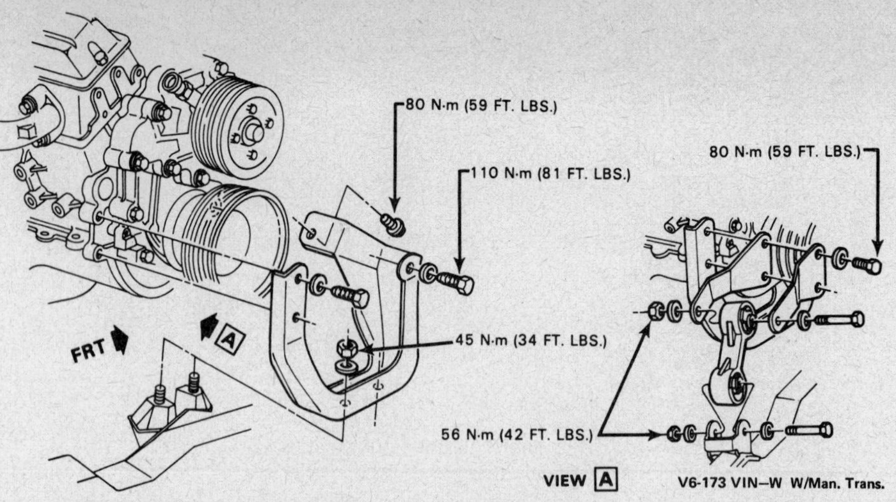

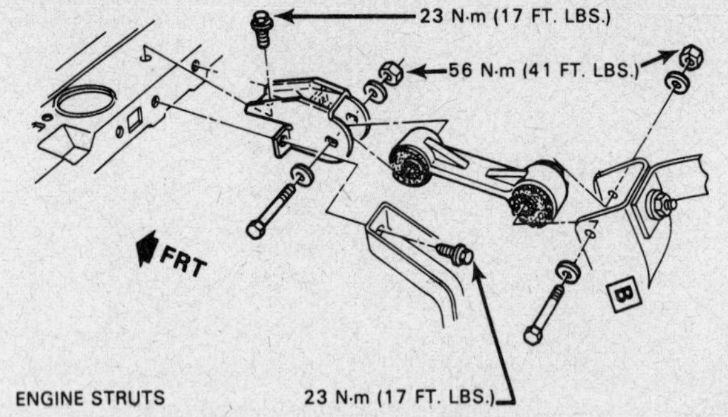

Fig. 3 Engine mounts. 1985 V6-173

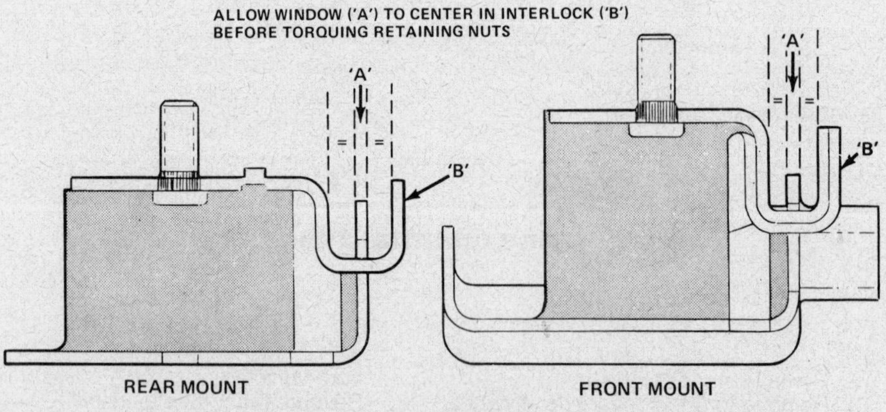

Fig. 4 Transaxle mount alignment. V6-173

VALVE ARRANGEMENT

FRONT TO REAR

4-151	I-E-I-E-E-I-E-I
V6-173 Right	E-I-E-I-I-E
V6-173 Left	E-I-I-E-I-E

VALVE LIFT SPECIFICATIONS

Engine	Year	Int.	Exh.
4-151	1982-85	.406	.406
V6-173	1982-85	.347	.394
V6-173 MFI	1985	.393	.410

VALVE TIMING

INTAKE OPENS BEFORE TDC

Engine	Year	Degrees
4-151	1982-85	33
V6-173	1982-85	25
V6-173 MFI	1985	31

OIL PAN

REPLACE

4-151

1. Raise vehicle and drain crankcase.
2. Remove engine front mount to cradle attaching nuts.
3. Disconnect exhaust pipe at manifold and rear transaxle mount.
4. Remove starter motor and flywheel housing cover.
5. Remove alternator upper mounting bracket.
6. Install a suitable engine lifting device and raise engine.
7. Remove lower alternator mounting bracket and engine support bracket.
8. Remove oil pan attaching bolts and oil pan.
9. Clean engine block and oil pan gasket surfaces.
10. Reverse procedure to install. Apply a 1/8 in. by 1/4 in. long bead of RTV sealer at split lines of front and side oil pan gaskets. Also apply a small amount of RTV sealer in depressions where rear oil pan gasket engages engine block. **When installing oil pan attaching bolts, the bolts attaching the oil pan to the front cover should be installed last. These bolts are installed at an angle and the bolt holes will only be aligned after the other oil pan bolts have been installed.**

V6-173

1. Disconnect battery ground cable.
2. Raise and support vehicle.
3. Drain engine oil from crankcase.
4. Remove flywheel housing shield or clutch housing cover as applicable.
5. Remove starter motor.
6. Attach suitable lifting equipment to engine. Remove engine mount bracket-to-engine attaching bolts and raise engine slightly.
7. Remove oil pan attaching bolts and

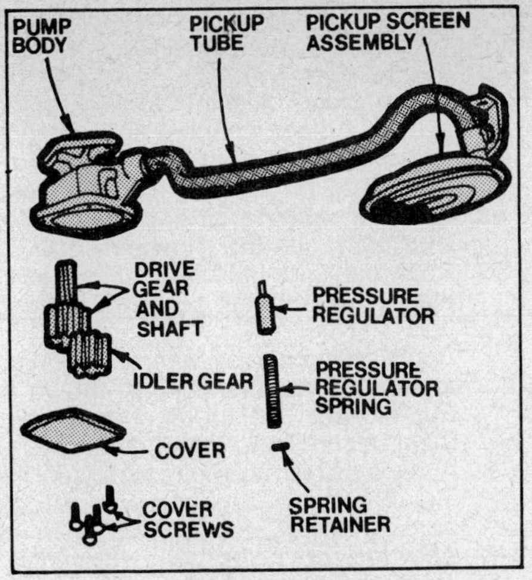

Fig. 5 Oil pump exploded view. 4-151

the oil pan.

8. Reverse procedure to install. Apply a 1/8 inch bead of RTV sealer to oil pan sealing flange.

OIL PUMP SERVICE

4-151

Removal

1. Drain crankcase, then remove oil pan as described under "Oil Pan, Replace."
2. Remove two oil pump mounting bolts and nuts from main cap bolt and remove oil pump and screen as an assembly.

Disassemble

1. Remove four pump cover to body attaching screws, then remove cover, idler and drive gears and shaft, **Fig. 5.**
2. Remove pin, retainer, spring and pressure regulator valve.

Inspection

Inspect pump components and should any of the following conditions be found, the oil pump assembly should be replaced.

a. Inspect pump body for cracks and excessive wear.
b. Inspect oil pump gears for damage, cracks or excessive wear.
c. Check shaft for looseness in housing.
d. Check cover for wear that would allow oil to leak past ends of gears.
e. Check oil pick screen for damage to screen or relief grommet. Also remove any debris from screen surface.
f. Check pressure regulator valve for fit in body.

Assemble

1. Place drive gear and shaft in pump body, then install idler gear with smooth side of gear facing pump cover, **Fig. 5.**

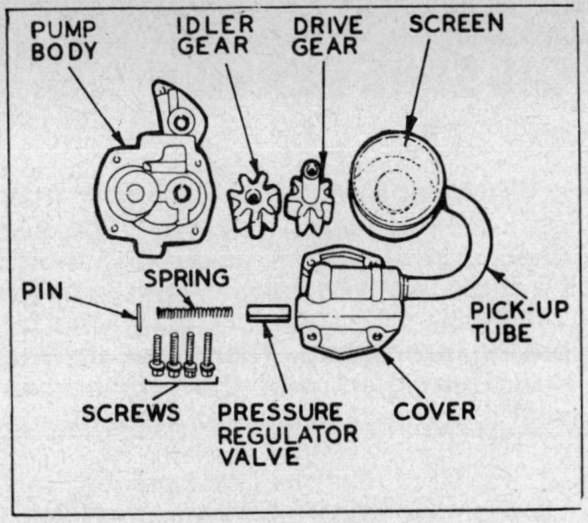

Fig. 6 Oil pump exploded view. V6-173

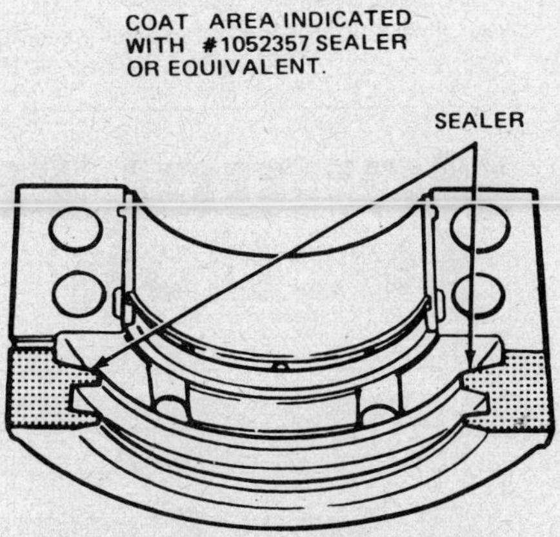

Fig. 8 Rear main bearing cap sealing areas. V6-173

2. Install and torque pump cover attaching screws to 105 inch lbs. Check to ensure that pump rotates freely.
3. Install pressure regulator valve, spring, retainer and pin.

Installation

1. Align oil pump shaft with tang on oil pump drive shaft, then install pump on block, positioning pump flange over oil pump drive shaft lower bushing.
2. Install oil pump mounting bolts and torque bolts to 20 ft. lbs., then install oil pan as described under "Oil Pan, Replace."

V6-173

Removal

1. Remove oil pan as described under "Oil Pan, Replace."
2. Remove pump to rear main bearing cap bolt and remove pump and extension shaft.

Disassembly

1. Remove pump cover attaching bolts and pump cover, **Fig. 6.**
2. Mark drive and idler gear teeth so they can be installed in the same position, then remove idler and drive gear and shaft from pump body.

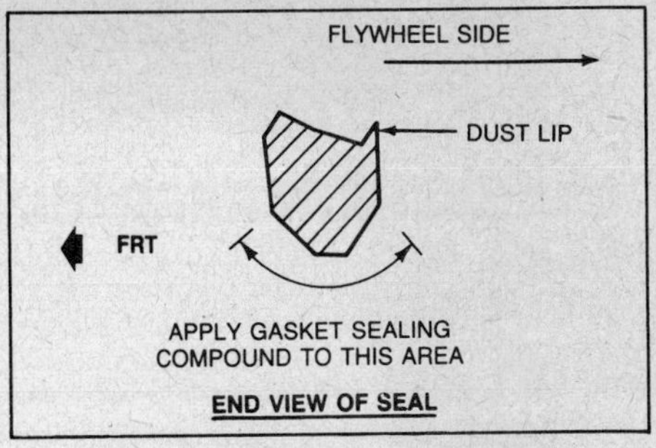

Fig. 7 Rear main seal installation. V6-173

3. Remove pin, spring and pressure regulator valve from pump cover.
4. If pickup tube and screen assembly are to be replaced, mount pump cover in a soft jawed vise and remove pickup tube from cover. Do not remove screen from pickup tube. These components are serviced as an assembly.

Inspection

1. Inspect pump body and cover for excessive wear and cracks.
2. Inspect pump gear for damage or excessive wear. If pump gears are damaged or worn, the entire pump assembly must be replaced.
3. Check drive gear shaft for looseness in pump body.
4. Inspect pump cover for wear that would allow oil to leak past gear teeth.
5. Inspect pickup tube and screen assembly for damage.
6. Check pressure regulator valve for fit in pump cover.

Assembly

1. If pickup tube and screen were removed, apply sealer to end of pickup tube, then mount pump cover in a soft jawed vise and using tool No. J-8369, tap pickup tube into position using a plastic mallet. **Whenever the pickup tube and screen assembly has been removed, a new pickup tube and screen assembly should be installed. Use care when installing pickup tube and screen assembly so that tube does not twist, shear or collapse. Loss of a press fit condition could result in an air leak and a loss of oil pressure.**
2. Install pressure regulator valve, spring and pin, **Fig. 6.**
3. Install drive gear and shaft in pump body.
4. Align marks made during disassembly, then install idler gear.
5. Install pump cover gasket, cover and attaching bolts. Torque bolts to 6 to 9 ft. lbs.
6. Rotate pump drive shaft by hand and check pump for smooth operation.

Installation

1. Assemble pump and extension shaft with retainer to rear main bearing cap, aligning top end of hexagon extension shaft with hexagon socket on lower end of distributor shaft.

2. Install pump to rear main bearing cap bolt.
3. Install oil pan as described under Oil Pan, Replace.

CRANKSHAFT REAR OIL SEAL

REPLACE

4-151

The rear main oil seal is a one piece unit and is replaced without removing the oil pan or crankshaft.

1. Remove transaxle and flywheel.
2. Using a suitable screwdriver, remove rear main bearing oil seal. Use care not to scratch crankshaft.
3. Lubricate inside and outside diameters of replacement seal with engine oil. Install seal by hand onto rear crankshaft flange with helical lip side facing toward engine. Ensure seal is firmly and evenly seated.
4. Install flywheel and transaxle.

REAR MAIN BEARING OIL SEAL SERVICE

V6-173

When replacement of the rear main seal is necessary, the rope type seal used during engine assembly should be replaced with rubber split seal No. 14069889, or equivalent using the following procedure. Disregard instructions furnished with the replacement seal that refer to Cavalier models.

1. Remove oil pan and oil pump.
2. Remove rear main bearing cap.
3. Remove upper and lower rope seals, taking care not to damage crankshaft, then clean seal remnants and oil from seal channels. **It may be necessary to loosen No. 2 and 4 bearing cap bolts to allow removal of the rope type seal and installation of the upper split seal.**
4. Apply a thin coating of gasket sealing compound 1050026 or equivalent to outer circumference of replacement seal, **Fig. 7**, keeping sealer off seal lips.
5. Use a piece of shim stock to guide seal into block channel and roll seal into block by turning crankshaft. **Ensure that large seal lip is toward front of engine and that smaller dust lip faces the flywheel.**
6. Apply sealer to lower half of seal as in step 4, then install seal into bearing cap.
7. Apply a thin bead of anaerobic sealant to bearing cap surface as shown in **Fig. 8.** Keep sealant off ends of seal, main bearing, and out of drain slot.
8. Apply a thin film of motor oil to seal lip, install bearing cap and torque cap bolts to specifications. **If other main bearing cap bolts were loosened, retorque as needed.**
9. Reinstall oil pump and pan as outlined.
10. Fill crankcase, start engine and check for leaks.

Clutch & Manual Transaxle Section

NOTE: Refer to "Clutch & Manual Transaxle Section" in Chapter 7, for service procedures.

Rear Axle, Rear Suspension & Brakes

NOTE: Refer to "Rear Axle, Rear Suspension & Brakes Section" in Chapter 7, for service procedures.

Front Suspension & Steering Section

NOTE: Refer to "Front Suspension & Steering Section" in Chapter 7, for service procedures.

Wheel Alignment Section

NOTE: Refer to "Wheel Alignment Section" in Chapter 7, for service procedures.

CHEVROLET CHEVETTE
PONTIAC 1000

INDEX OF SERVICE OPERATIONS

NOTE: Refer to the rear of this manual for vehicle manufacturer's special service tool suppliers.

Specifications

GENERAL ENGINE SPECIFICATIONS

Year	Engine CID①/Liter	Engine VIN	Fuel System	Bore & Stroke	Compression Ratio	Net H.P. @ RPM②	Maximum Torque Lbs. Ft. @ RPM	Normal Oil Pressure Pounds
1982-84	4-97, 1.6 Liter④	C⑥	6510C, 2 Bbl.⑤	3.228 x 2.980 82.0 x 75.7 mm	9.2	65 @ 5200	80 @ 3200	55
	4-110, 1.8 Liter③	D⑥	Fuel Injection	3.310 x 3.230 84.0 x 82.0 mm	22.0	51 @ 5000	72 @ 2000	64
1985-86	4-97, 1.6 Liter④	C⑥	6510C, 2 Bbl.⑤	3.228 x 2.980 82.0 x 75.7 mm	9.0	65 @ 5200	80 @ 3200	55
	4-110, 1.8 Liter③	D⑥	Fuel Injection	3.310 x 3.230 84.0 x 82.0 mm	22.0	51 @ 5000	72 @ 2000	64
1987	4-97, 1.6 Liter④	C⑥	6510C, 2 Bbl.⑤	3.228 x 2.980 82.0 x 75.7mm	9.0	65 @ 5200	80 @ 3200	55

①—CID-Cubic inch displacement.
②—Ratings are net as installed in vehicle.
③—Diesel engine.
④—1600 cc engine.
⑤—Holley.
⑥—Eighth digit in the VIN denotes engine code.

ENGINE TIGHTENING SPECIFICATIONS*

*Torque specifications are for clean and lightly lubricated threads only. Dry or dirty threads produce increased friction which prevents accurate measurement of tightness.

Year	Engine/VIN	Spark Plugs Ft. Lbs.	Camshaft Carrier Bolts Ft. Lbs.	Intake Manifold Ft. Lbs.	Exhaust Manifold Ft. Lbs.	Camshaft Sprocket Bolt Ft. Lbs.	Cam Cover In. Lbs.	Connecting Rod Cap Bolts Ft. Lbs.	Main Bearing Cap Bolts Ft. Lbs.	Flywheel to Crankshaft Ft. Lbs.	Vibration Damper or Pulley Ft. Lbs.
1982	4-97④	18	75	15	①	75	14	40	50	50	75
1982	4-110/D②	③	⑦	30	—	45	⑤	65	65-72	40⑥	110
1983-86	4-97④	18	75	18	25	75	14	40	50	50	100
	4-110②	③	⑦	30	—	55	⑤	65	65-72	40⑥	110
1987	4-97④	18	75	18	25	75	14	40	50	50	100

①—Center bolts, 15 ft. lbs.; end legs, 22 ft. lbs.
②—Diesel engine.
③—Glow Plugs-54 ft. lbs., 73 Nm.
④—For VIN code, refer to the General Engine Specifications at the beginning of the chapter.
⑤—Rocker arm cover-7 ft. lbs., 10 Nm.
⑥—Apply loctite to threads, do not lubricate bolts.
⑦—Cylinder head bolts; new, 83-98 ft. lbs.; used, 90-105 ft. lbs.

STARTING MOTOR APPLICATIONS

Year	Model	Starter Number
1982-83	4-97/C	1109532
1982-85	4-110 Diesel/D	9438758
1984	4-97/C	1998428
1985	4-97/C	1998525

ALTERNATOR SPECIFICATIONS

Year	Alternator		
	Model	Rated Hot Output Amps.	Field Current 12 Volts @ 80° F
1982	1100138 ②	42	4-5
	LR155-12B ①	55	—
1983-87	1100234 ②	38	4-5
	1100253 ②	70	4.5-5.0
	1100261 ②	81	4.5-5.0
	94234987 ①	55	—

①—Diesel engine.
②—Exc. diesel engine.

WHEEL ALIGNMENT SPECIFICATIONS

Year	Model	Caster Angle, Degrees		Camber Angle, Degrees				Toe-In Inch.
				Limits		Desired		
		Limits	Desired	Left	Right	Left	Right	
1982-86	All	+4° to +6°	+5°	−.2° to +.6°	−.2° to +.6°	+.2°	+.2°	①
1987	All	2.7° to 6.7°	4.7°	−.5° to +.9°	−.5° to +.9°	+.2°	+.2°	②

①—+.06° ± .04°.
②—+.06° ± .08°.

REAR AXLE SPECIFICATIONS

Year	Model	Carrier Type	Ring Gear & Pinion Backlash		Pinion Bearing Preload			Differential Bearing Preload		
			Method	Adjustment	Method	New Bearings Inch Lbs.	Used Bearings Inch Lbs.	Method	New Bearings Inch Lbs.	Used Bearings Inch Lbs.
1982-86	All	Integral	Shims	.005-.008	Spacer	①	5-10	Shims	②	②

①—With NDH bearings, 10-20 inch lbs; with Timken bearings, 5-15 inch lbs.
②—Slip fit plus .004 preload on each side.

COOLING SYSTEM & CAPACITY DATA

Year	Model or Engine/VIN	Cooling Capacity, Qts.		Radiator Cap Relief Pressure, Lbs.	Thermo. Opening Temp.	Fuel Tank Gals.	Engine Oil Refill Qts.	Transmission Oil			Rear Axle Oils Pints
		Less A/C	With A/C					4 Speed Pints	5 Speed Pints	Auto. Trans. Qts. ①	
1982	4-110/D ④	9	—	15	180	12.5	6 ⑤	3.25	4	⑥	1.75
	4-97/C	9	9.25	15	190	12.5	4 ⑤	3.5	4	②	1.75
1983-85	4-97/C	9	9.25	15	190	12.5	4 ⑤	3.4	4	⑥	1.75
	4-110/D ④	9	—	15	180	12.5	6 ⑤	3.3	4	⑥	1.75
1986	4-97/C	9	9.26	15	190	12.2	4 ⑦	3.4	4.5	③	1.75
	4-110/D ④	9	—	15	180	12.2	5 ⑦	—	3.3	—	1.75
1987	4-97/C	9	9.26	15	190	12.2	4 ⑦	3.4	4.5	③	1.75

①—Approximate. Make final check with dipstick.
②—After overhaul, 4.9 qts.; oil pan only, 3 qts.
③—Drain and refill, 2.43 qts.
④—Diesel engine.
⑤—Includes filter.
⑥—After overhaul, 5 qts., oil pan only, 3.5 qts.
⑦—Less filter.

Electrical Section

INDEX

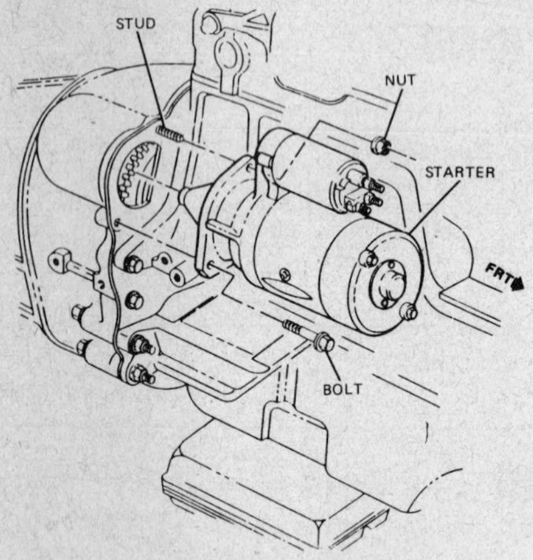

Fig. 1 Starter removal & installation

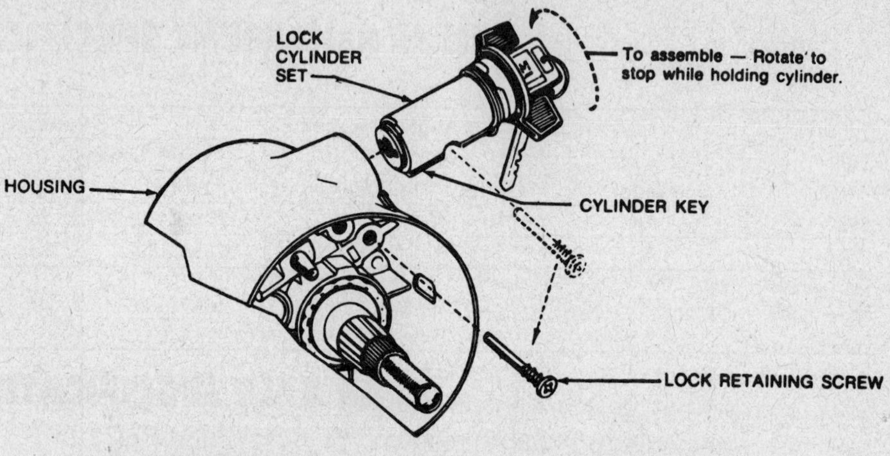

Fig. 2 Ignition lock removal & installation

STARTER REPLACE

DIESEL ENGINE

Refer to **Fig. 1** for starter removal and installation.

GASOLINE ENGINE

Less Power Brakes

1. Disconnect battery ground cable, then remove air cleaner.
2. Disconnect fuel line at carburetor and position aside.
3. Disconnect vacuum hoses at carburetor.
4. Remove splash shield from distributor coil and position aside.
5. Remove upper and lower starter retaining bolts.
6. Disconnect electrical leads from starter and position starter aside for access.
7. Remove master cylinder mounting nuts to gain access for removing starter. It will be necessary to move the master cylinder aside to remove the starter.
8. Remove starter.
9. Reverse procedure to install.

With Power Brakes

1. Disconnect battery ground cable, then remove air cleaner.
2. Disconnect fuel line at carburetor and position aside.
3. Remove splash shield from distributor coil and position aside.
4. Remove upper starter retaining bolt. **To remove the upper starter retaining bolt on models equipped with A/C, use a 15 mm short socket with short extension, universal 12 inch extension and a ratchet or speed handle. Access to the bolt is gained through the intake manifold 3rd and 4th runners. After completely loosening the bolt, remove it with a magnet.**
5. Remove steering column cover screws and cover.
6. Remove steering column upper mounting nuts and toe pan screw.
7. Raise and support front of vehicle.
8. Remove steering shaft from steering coupling. Lower vehicle and move steering column from inside vehicle for access to starter.
9. Disconnect electrical leads from starter.
10. Remove lower starter retaining bolt and remove starter.
11. Reverse procedure to install.

IGNITION LOCK REPLACE

1. Remove steering wheel as described under Horn Sounder and Steering Wheel.
2. Remove turn signal switch as described under Turn Signal Switch, Replace, then remove buzzer switch.
3. Place ignition switch in Run position, then remove lock cylinder retaining screw and lock cylinder.
4. To install, rotate lock cylinder to stop while holding housing, **Fig. 2.** Align cylinder key with keyway in housing, then push lock cylinder assembly into housing until fully seated.
5. Install lock cylinder retaining screw. Torque screw to 40 in. lbs. for standard columns. On adjustable columns, torque retaining screw to 22 in. lbs.
6. Install buzzer switch, turn signal switch and steering wheel.

LIGHT SWITCH REPLACE

1. Disconnect battery ground cable.
2. Pull headlamp switch knob to "On" position, **Fig. 3.**
3. Reach under instrument panel and depress switch shaft retainer button while pulling on the switch control shaft knob.
4. With a large bladed screwdriver, remove the light switch ferrule nut from front of instrument panel.

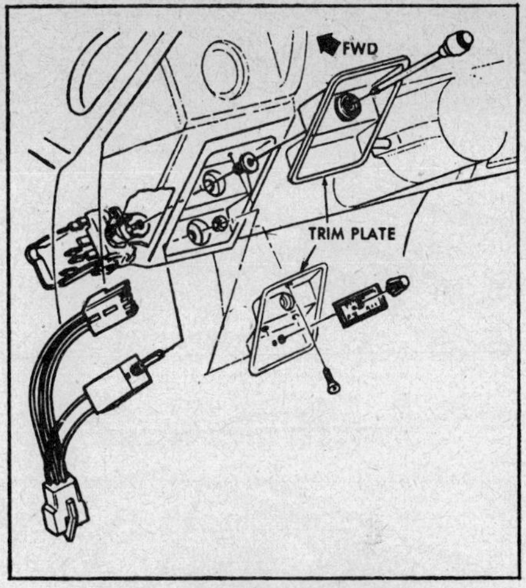

Fig. 3 Light switch replacement

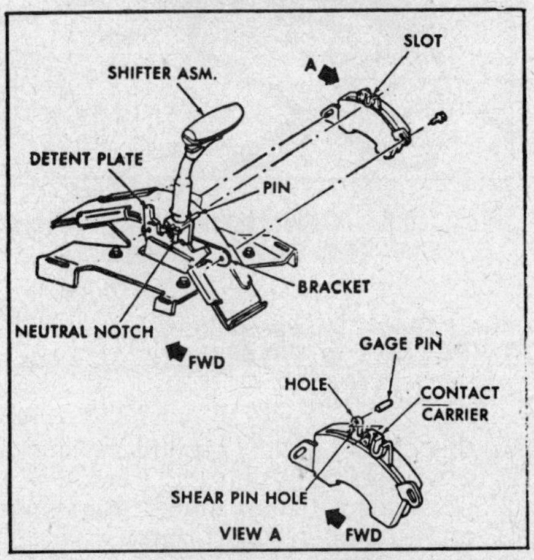

Fig. 5 Neutral start switch replacement

5. Disconnect the multi-contact connector from side of switch and remove switch.
6. Reverse procedure to install.

STOP LIGHT SWITCH

REPLACE

1. Reach under right side of instrument panel at brake pedal support and release wiring harness connector at switch.
2. Pull switch from mounting bracket.
3. When installing switch, adjust by bringing brake pedal to normal position. Electrical contact should be made when pedal is depressed .53 inch (13.5 mm). To adjust, the switch may be rotated or pulled in the clip.

CLUTCH START SWITCH

REPLACE

The clutch pedal must be fully depressed and the ignition switch in START position for the vehicle to start.

The clutch switch assembly mounts with two tangs to the clutch pedal brace switch pivot bracket and the clutch pedal arm, **Fig. 4.**

1. Working from underneath instrument panel, remove multi-contact connector from switch on clutch pedal support.
2. Compress switch assembly actuating shaft barb retainer and push out of clutch pedal.
3. Compress switch assembly pivot bracket barb and lift off switch.
4. When installing new switch, no adjustments are necessary as the switch is self aligning.

NEUTRAL SAFETY SWITCH

REPLACE

1. Remove floor console cover.
2. Disconnect electrical plugs on back-up contacts, seat belt warning contacts and neutral start contacts of switch assembly, **Fig. 5.**
3. Place shift lever in Neutral.
4. Remove two screws securing switch to lever assembly.
5. When installing switch, make sure it is in Neutral position. When switch is installed, shifting out of Neutral will shear the switch plastic locating pin.

A/C COMPRESSOR CUT-OUT SWITCH

Vehicles equipped with automatic transmission and air conditioning utilize a full throttle A/C compressor cut-out switch, **Fig. 6**, which de-energizes the A/C compressor clutch during full throttle acceleration. A pressure sensitive switch, located in the transmission, overrides the cut-out switch when the transmission is in third gear during full throttle acceleration.

TURN SIGNAL SWITCH

REPLACE

1. Remove steering wheel as described under "Horn Sounder & Steering Wheel" procedure.
2. Using a screw driver pry up and out to free cover from lock plate.
3. Position lock plate compressing tool No. J-23653 on end of steering shaft and compress lock plate, **Fig. 7.**
4. Pry snap ring out of groove and discard, then remove tool J-23653 and lift lock plate off end of shaft.
5. Slide canceling cam, upper bearing preload spring and thrust washer off end of shaft.
6. Rotate multi-function lever to off position, then pull lever straight out to disengage.
7. Depress hazard warning knob and unscrew knob.
8. Remove two screws, pivot arm and spacer, **Fig. 8.**
9. Wrap upper part of connector with tape to prevent snagging of wires during switch removal, **Fig. 9.**
10. Remove three switch attaching screws and pull switch straight up guiding wires through column housing.

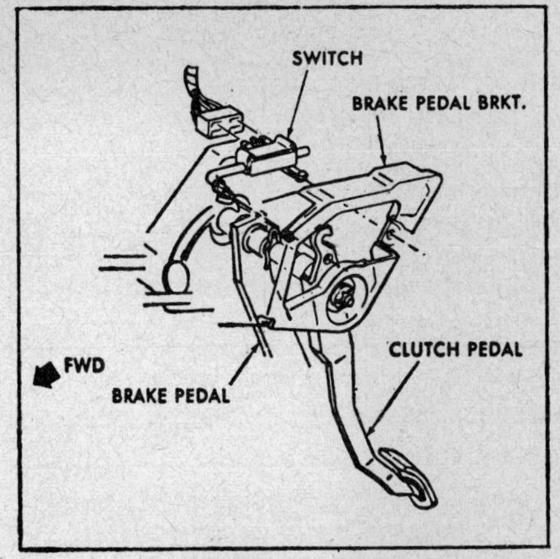

Fig. 4 Clutch start switch replacement

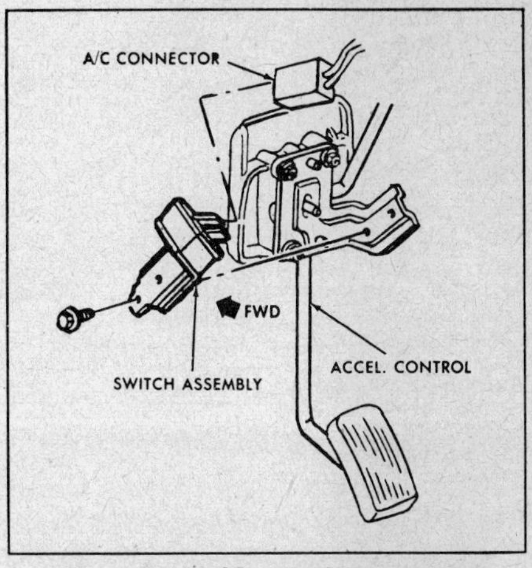

Fig. 6 A/C compressor cut-out switch

HORN SOUNDER & STEERING WHEEL

REPLACE

1. Disconnect battery ground cable.
2. Pry off horn button cap and retainer.
3. Remove steering wheel nut retainer and nut. **Do not over expand retainer.**
4. Using a suitable puller remove steering wheel.

WINDSHIELD WIPER, DIMMER OR IGNITION SWITCH

REMOVAL

1. Disconnect battery ground cable.
2. Remove steering column mounting bracket and unsnap switch connector from jacket.
3. Remove steering wheel.
4. Remove lock plate cover with a suitable screwdriver.
5. Remove ring and lock plate. Use caution to prevent shaft from sliding out bottom of column. Slide upper bearing preload spring and turn signal canceling cam off upper steering shaft, then the thrust washer off shaft.

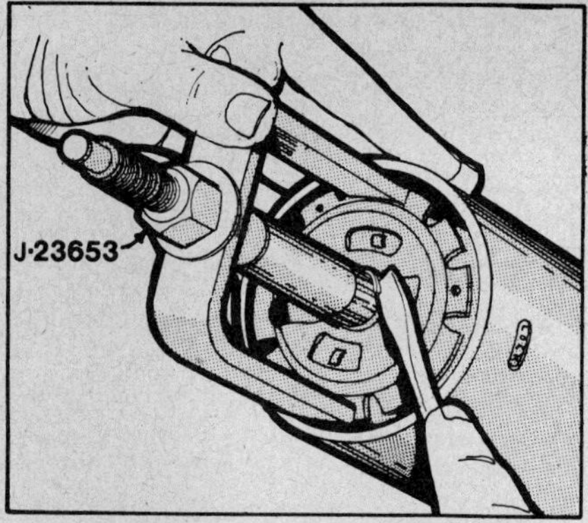

Fig. 7 Compressing lock plate and removing retaining ring

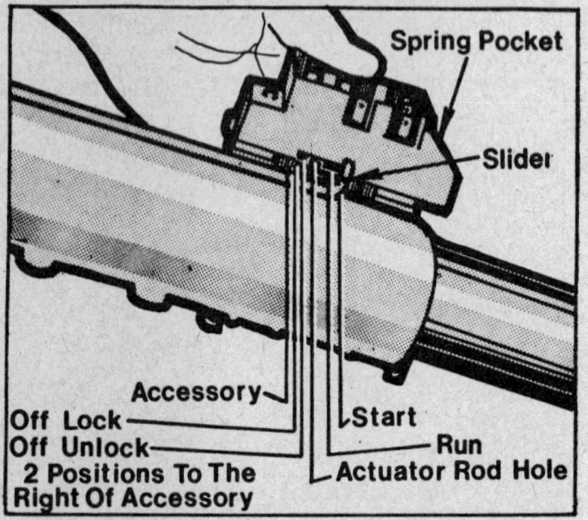

Fig. 10 Ignition switch

6. Rotate turn signal lever-W/S switch assembly counterclockwise to stop (off position) and pull straight out to disengage.
7. Remove two screws, pivot arm and spacer, **Fig. 8.** Note that pivot arm retains spacer.
8. Lower steering column, then remove turn signal switch mounting screws and the switch.
9. Pull actuator rod to the stop to place ignition switch in "Off-Unlock." Remove upper attaching screw, releasing dimmer switch and actuator. The switches may now be removed, **Figs. 10 and 11.**
10. Remove remaining ignition switch retaining screw and the ignition switch.

INSTALLATION

1. Assemble windshield wiper switch and pivot assembly onto housing.
2. Assemble buzzer switch and lock cylinder, then turn lock cylinder clockwise to stop and then counterclockwise to other stop (OFF-UNLOCK) position. Position ignition switch, **Fig. 10,** then move slider to extreme left (ACC) and slide back two positions to the right to OFF-UNLOCK position. Install actuator rod into slider and install the bottom screw only, to retain the ignition switch. Do not move switch out of detent.
3. Install washer, spring and cancelling cam on steering shaft. Position cancelling cam lobes in relation to signal switch springs and assemble shaft

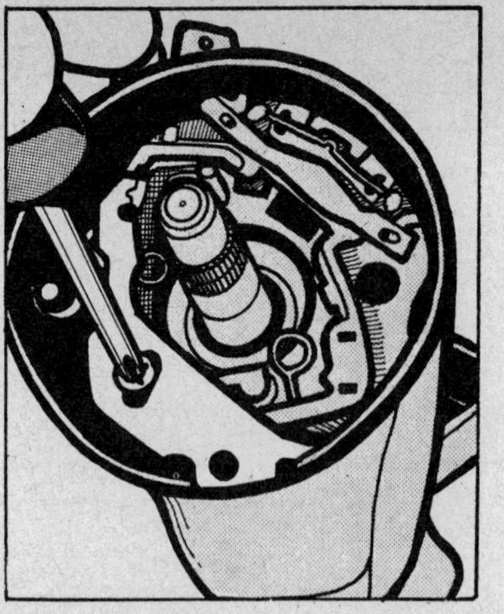

Fig. 8 Removing pivot arm

lock and install new retaining ring.
4. Install cover and snap ring, then install multi-function switch lever. Align lever pin with switch slot and push lever until it seats.
5. Install pinched end of dimmer switch actuator rod into dimmer switch, then install other end of rod into pivot switch. Install but do not tighten upper ignition switch screw. Depress dimmer switch and insert a 3/32 inch drill to lock switch body, **Fig. 12.**
6. Move dimmer switch up, removing lash between both switches and rod, then install and tighten upper ignition switch screw. Remove drill and check dimmer switch for proper operation.
7. Snap electrical connector into place and raise steering column, then install mounting nuts and torque to 22 ft. lbs. (30 Nm) and install steering wheel.

INSTRUMENT CLUSTER REPLACE

1. Disconnect battery ground cable.
2. Remove clock stem knob.
3. Remove cluster bezel and lens retaining screws, then the bezel and lens, **Fig. 13.**
4. Remove instrument cluster to instrument panel retaining nuts and pull cluster toward vehicle rear.
5. Disconnect all electrical connectors and speedometer cable from cluster, then remove cluster.
6. Reverse procedure to install.

RADIO REPLACE

1. Disconnect battery ground cable.
2. Remove mounting stud nut from bottom of radio, and the control knobs from shafts.
3. Remove screws from center trim panel and pull panel and radio toward the rear of the vehicle.
4. Disconnect all electrical connectors from radio.
5. Remove radio retaining nuts from radio control shafts.
6. Remove radio from vehicle.
7. Reverse procedure to install.

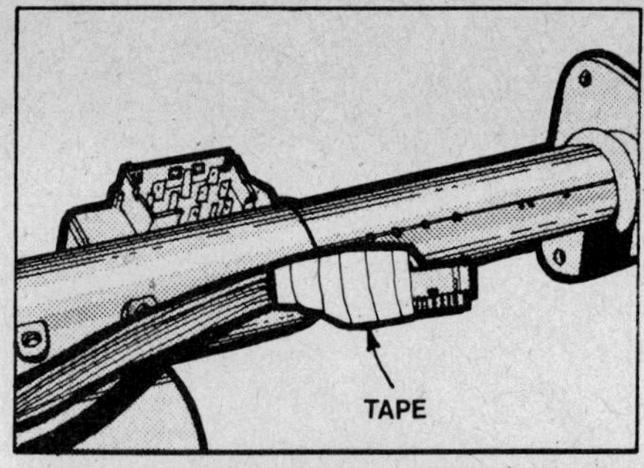

Fig. 9 Taping turn signal switch and wires

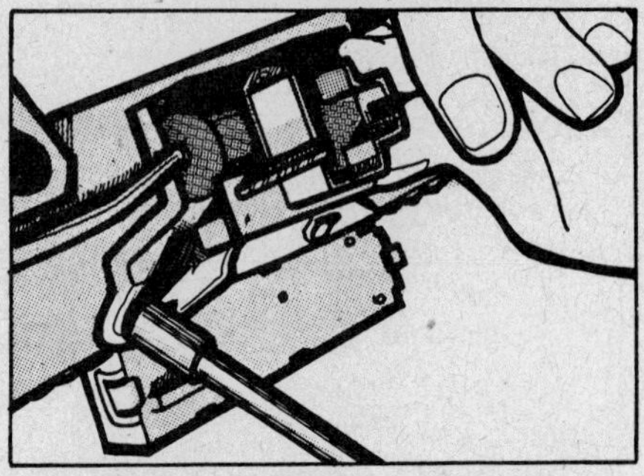

Fig. 11 Dimmer & ignition switch replacement

HEATER CORE REPLACE

1. Disconnect battery ground cable and drain cooling system.
2. Disconnect heater hoses from core and plug openings in core.
3. Remove heater core housing to dash panel attaching screws, then the housing.
4. Remove core from housing.

BLOWER MOTOR REPLACE

1. Disconnect battery ground cable.
2. Disconnect blower lead wire.
3. Remove blower motor to case attaching screws then the blower and wheel as an assembly. **Scribe mark on blower motor and case so motor is installed in original position.**
4. Remove nut and separate motor from wheel.
5. Reverse procedure to install. **At assembly position open end of blower wheel away from blower motor. Replace sealer at blower motor flange if necessary.**

WINDSHIELD WIPER MOTOR, REPLACE

1. Reach under instrument panel above steering column and loosen transmission drive link to motor crank arm attaching nuts.
2. Disengage transmission drive link from motor crank arm.
3. Raise hood and disconnect electrical connectors.

Fig. 12 Dimmer switch alignment

4. Remove motor attaching bolts.
5. Remove motor while guiding crank arm through hole.
6. To install, align sealing gasket to base of motor assembly and reverse remaining removal procedure. **If the wiper motor to dash panel sealing gasket is damaged during removal, it should be replaced to prevent possible water leaks.**

WINDSHIELD WIPER TRANSMISSION
REPLACE

1. Remove instrument panel pad and cluster housing.
2. On models with A/C, remove left A/C duct attaching screws and position duct aside.
3. On all models, remove left side air duct.
4. Remove speedometer cable shield and left side instrument brace.
5. From under instrument panel, loosen transmission drive link to motor crank arm attaching nuts and disengage drive link.
6. Remove wiper arms and blades, then remove transmission to dash panel attaching bolts.

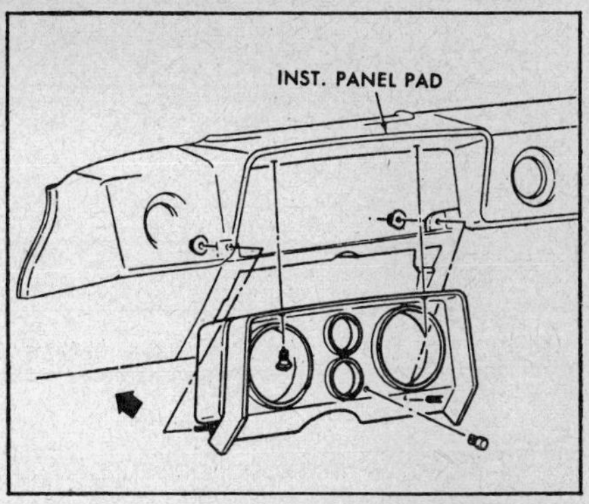

Fig. 13 Instrument cluster

7. Move transmission assembly to left, then while rotating assembly, work out through instrument panel access hole at right upper center of instrument panel. **When installing, ensure motor is in park position.**

4-97 (1.6L) Gasoline Engine

INDEX

ENGINE MOUNTS
REPLACE

FRONT

1. Remove heater assembly and position on top of engine.
2. Remove radiator upper support.
3. Remove engine mount nuts and the restraint cable.
4. Raise vehicle, install engine lifting device and raise engine to relieve weight from mounts.
5. Remove mount to engine bracket, then using tool J-25510, remove mount.

REAR

1. Raise vehicle and remove crossmember to mount bolts.
2. Raise transmission at extension housing to relieve weight from mount.
3. Remove mount to transmission bolts and the mount.

ENGINE
REPLACE

1. Remove hood.
2. Disconnect battery cables and remove clips securing battery cable to right side frame rail.
3. Drain cooling system and disconnect radiator and heater hoses.
4. Disconnect engine wiring harness.
5. Remove radiator upper support, radiator and fan.
6. Remove air cleaner.
7. Disconnect fuel line at rubber hose located along left side frame rail.
8. Disconnect accelerator and automatic transmission throttle valve linkage, if equipped.
9. Remove A/C compressor from mounting bracket and position aside, if equipped.
10. Raise vehicle and disconnect exhaust pipe at manifold.
11. Remove flywheel dust cover.
12. On models with automatic transmission, remove converter to flywheel bolts.
13. Remove converter housing to engine bolts on automatic transmission models or flywheel housing to engine bolt on manual transmission models, then lower vehicle.
14. Support transmission using a suitable jack.
15. Remove safety straps from engine mounts, then remove engine mount bolts.
16. Install engine lifting device, raise engine slowly, pull engine forward to clear transmission and remove engine from vehicle.

INTAKE MANIFOLD
REPLACE

1. Disconnect battery ground cable and drain cooling system.
2. Remove air cleaner and disconnect upper radiator hose and heater hoses from intake manifold.
3. Remove EGR valve.
4. Disconnect fuel line, wiring, vacuum hoses and linkage from carburetor.
5. If equipped with A/C, perform the following:

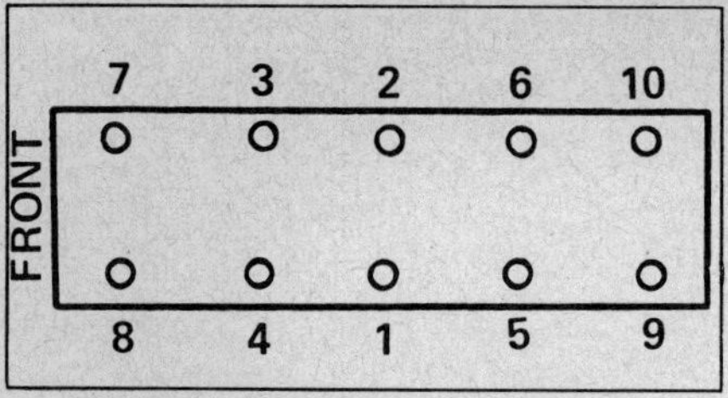

Fig. 1 Cylinder head bolt tightening sequence

a. Remove radiator upper support, alternator and A/C drive belts.
b. Remove fan, pulley and timing belt cover.
c. Position A/C compressor aside.
d. Raise vehicle and remove the lower A/C compressor bracket.
e. Lower vehicle and remove the upper A/C compressor bracket.

6. On all models, remove ignition coil and position aside.
7. Remove intake manifold attaching bolts and the intake manifold.
8. Reverse procedure to install.

CYLINDER HEAD
REPLACE

1. Remove timing belt.
2. Drain cooling system, remove upper radiator hose and heater hose at intake manifold.
3. Remove air cleaner, then remove accelerator support bracket and A/C compressor, if equipped.
4. Disconnect spark plug wires.
5. Disconnect wiring harnesses at idle solenoid, choke, temperature sending switch and alternator.
6. Raise vehicle and disconnect exhaust pipe at manifold.
7. Lower vehicle and remove bolt retaining dipstick bracket to manifold.
8. Disconnect fuel line at carburetor.
9. Remove coil bracket bolts and position coil aside.
10. Remove camshaft covers, then remove camshaft cover to housing attaching studs.
11. Remove rocker arms, guides and lash adjusters. **Rocker arms, guides and lash adjusters must be installed in original location during assembly.**
12. Remove camshaft carrier from cylinder head. **It may be necessary to use a wedge to separate camshaft carrier from cylinder head.**
13. Remove cylinder head and manifold as an assembly.
14. Reverse procedure to install, tighten cylinder head bolts in sequence shown, **Fig. 1.**

HYDRAULIC VALVE LASH ADJUSTERS

Failure of an hydraulic valve lash adjuster is generally caused by an inadequate oil supply or dirt. An air leak at the intake side of the oil pump or too much oil in the engine will cause air bubbles in the oil supply to the lash adjusters, causing them to collapse. This is a probable cause of trouble if several lash adjusters fail to function, but air in the oil is an unlikely cause of failure of a single unit.

Fig. 2 Depressing valve spring

VALVES
ADJUST

These engines are equipped with hydraulic valve lash adjusters which automatically allow for zero lash clearance. No provision for adjustment is provided.

ROCKER ARMS
REPLACE

1. Remove camshaft covers.
2. Remove carburetor.
3. Using tool J-25477, depress valve spring and remove rocker arm, guide and lash adjuster, **Fig. 2. Rocker arms, guides and lash adjusters must be installed in the same location during assembly.**

VALVE GUIDES

Valve guides are an integral part of the cylinder head. If stem to guide clearance is excessive, the guide should be reamed to the next oversize and the appropriate oversize valve installed. Valves are available in standard size and oversizes of .003 in. (.075 mm), .006 in. (.150 mm), and .012 in. (.300 mm).

CAMSHAFT COVER
REPLACE

1. Raise hood to fully open position.
2. Disconnect battery ground cable.
3. Remove air cleaner, PCV valve, air cleaner snorkle and heat tube assembly.
4. Remove spark plug wires from retainer on camshaft cover.
5. Remove accelerator cable support and position aside.
6. Remove retaining bolts and gasket, then the camshaft cover.

CAMSHAFT SPROCKET
REPLACE

1. Remove drive belts, then the fan and pulley.

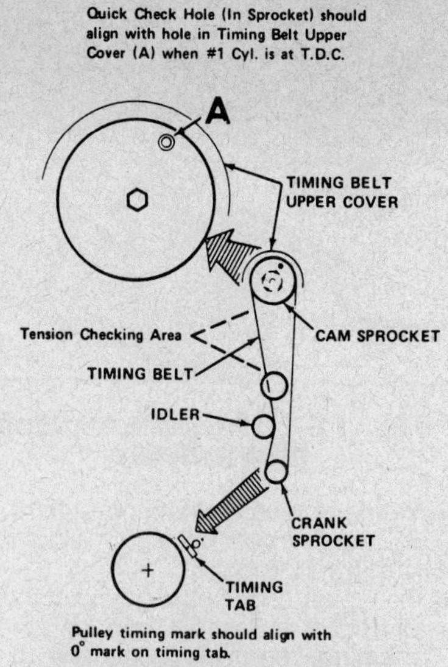

Fig. 3 Camshaft & crankshaft sprocket alignment marks

2. Remove timing belt front cover.
3. Loosen idler pulley and remove timing belt from camshaft sprocket.
4. Remove camshaft sprocket bolt and washer, then the camshaft sprocket.

CAMSHAFT
REPLACE

1. Remove camshaft sprocket as described previously.
2. Remove rocker arms.
3. Remove heater assembly and position aside.
4. Remove camshaft carrier rear cover.
5. Remove camshaft thrust plate bolts, slide camshaft rearward and remove thrust plate.
6. Raise engine, then carefully slide camshaft from carrier.

CAM LOBE LIFT SPECIFICATIONS

Year	Intake	Exhaust
1982-87	.2407	.2407

VALVE TIMING
INTAKE OPEN BEFORE TDC

Engine	Year	Degrees
Hi Output	1982-87	28

VALVE ARRANGEMENT
FRONT TO REAR

4-97 .... I-E-I-E-I-E-I-E

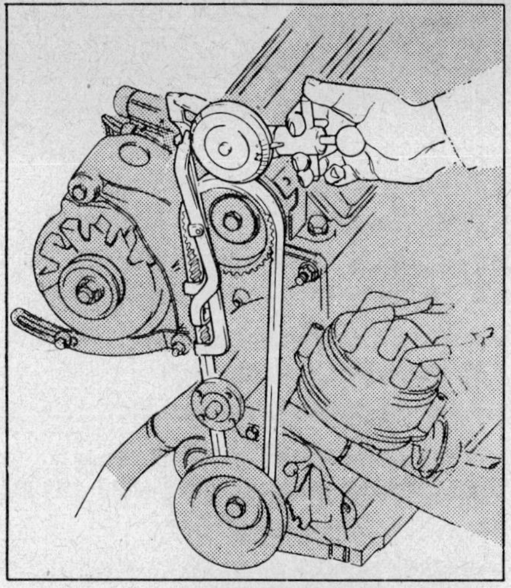

Fig. 4 Adjusting timing belt tension

TIMING BELT FRONT COVER
REPLACE
UPPER COVER

1. Raise hood and disconnect battery ground cable.
2. Remove fan.
3. Remove upper cover retaining screw and the upper cover.

LOWER COVER

1. Remove crankshaft pulley.
2. Remove upper front cover.
3. Remove lower cover attaching nut and the lower cover.

UPPER REAR TIMING BELT COVER
REPLACE

1. Remove timing belt front cover, timing belt and camshaft sprocket.
2. Remove three upper rear timing belt cover to camshaft carrier attaching screws.
3. Inspect camshaft seal and replace, if necessary.

TIMING BELT
REPLACE

To verify camshaft timing, position crankshaft so that No. 1 cylinder is at top dead center compression stroke. With No. 1 cylinder at top dead center compression stroke, a 1/8 inch drill bit can be inserted through a hole in upper rear cover and hole in camshaft sprocket, if timing is correct, **Fig. 3.**

1. Remove timing belt front upper and lower covers and crankshaft pulley.
2. Loosen idler pulley bolt and remove timing belt from camshaft and crankshaft sprockets.
3. Position timing belt over crankshaft sprocket, then install crankshaft pulley.
4. Position crankshaft at TDC number 1 cylinder.
5. Align timing mark on camshaft sprocket with hole in upper rear cover, **Fig. 3.**
6. Install timing belt on crankshaft and camshaft sprockets, then adjust belt tension.

TIMING BELT TENSION
ADJUST

1. Remove fan, drive belt, pulley and upper timing belt cover.
2. Rotate crankshaft at least one revolution and position No. 1 piston at top dead center.
3. Install belt tension gauge, Tool J-26486, **Fig. 4,** on timing belt midway between the cam sprocket and idler pulley. Ensure the gauge center finger engages in a notch on the belt.
4. Correct belt tension is 70 ft. lbs. To adjust, loosen idler pulley attaching bolt, **Fig. 5.** Then, using a 1/4 inch Allen wrench, rotate the pulley counterclockwise on the attaching bolt until correct belt tension is obtained and torque attaching bolt to 13-18 ft. lbs. (18-24 Nm).
5. Remove gauge and install upper timing belt cover, pulley, drive belt and fan.

CRANKSHAFT SPROCKET
REPLACE

1. Drain cooling system and remove radiator.
2. Remove timing belt front cover, crankshaft pulley and timing belt.
3. Remove crankshaft sprocket.

PISTON & ROD ASSEMBLE

Assemble pistons and rods as indicated in **Fig. 6.** Measure connecting rod side clearance with a feeler gauge. Side clearance should be .004-.012 inch.

PISTONS & RINGS

Pistons and rings are available in standard size, .001 and .030 in. (.750 mm) oversize.

MAIN & ROD BEARINGS

Main bearings are available in standard size and undersizes of .001 in. (.026 mm), .002 in. (.050 mm), .010 in. (.250 mm) and .020 in. (.500 mm).

Rod bearings are available in standard size and undersizes of .001 in. (.026 mm), .010 in. (.250 mm) and .020 in. (.500 mm).

OIL PAN
REPLACE
WITH MAN. TRANS. OR TURBO HYDRA-MATIC 180C TRANS.

1. Disconnect battery ground cable, then

Fig. 5 Timing belt idler arm and pulley

drain cooling system.
2. Remove upper radiator support. On models equipped with A/C, remove upper half of fan shroud.
3. On models equipped with automatic transmission, disconnect transmission oil cooler lines from radiator.
4. Disconnect radiator hoses, then remove radiator from vehicle.
5. If equipped with A/C, remove condenser to radiator support attaching nuts and position on top of engine.
6. Remove heater core housing and position on top of engine.
7. Remove engine mount retaining nuts and clips.
8. Raise and support front of vehicle, then drain crankcase.
9. Disconnect exhaust pipe at exhaust manifold, then remove body to crossmember braces.
10. Remove rack and pinion steering gear unit from crossmember and steering shaft, then pull unit down and out of way.
11. Remove stabilizer bar from body.
12. Install a suitable engine lifting device and raise engine sufficiently to permit oil pan removal.
13. Remove oil pan attaching screws, then pull pan down and remove oil pump pickup tube and screen assembly.
14. Remove oil pan through front of vehicle.
15. Reverse procedure to install. When installing oil pump pickup tube and screen assembly, use a new seal. Torque oil pan attaching screws to 55 inch lbs.

WITH TURBO HYDRA-MATIC 200C AUTO. TRANS.

1. Disconnect battery ground cable, then remove air cleaner.
2. Remove heater housing assembly from front of dash panel and position on top of engine.
3. Pull back on motor mount wire restraints and remove mount nuts.
4. Remove radiator upper support or fan shroud, as necessary.

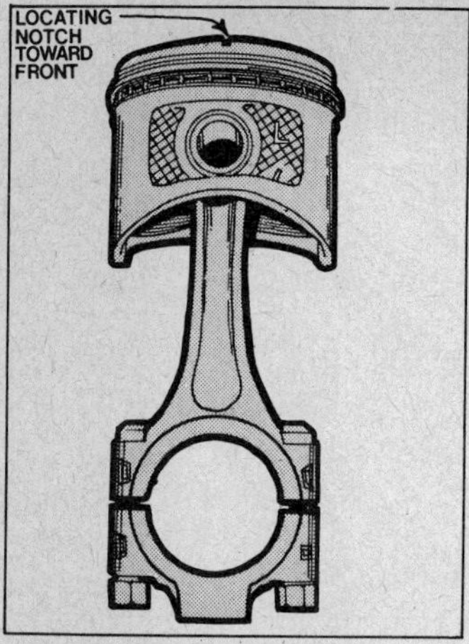

Fig. 6 Piston and rod assembly

5. Raise and support front of vehicle, then drain crankcase.
6. Remove converter housing splash shield.
7. Remove rack and pinion steering gear unit from front crossmember.
8. Loosen catalytic converter to rear exhaust pipe clamp bolts.
9. Install a suitable engine lifting device and raise engine sufficiently to permit oil pan removal.
10. Remove oil pan attaching screws, then remove oil pan.
11. Reverse procedure to install. Torque oil pan attaching screws to 55 inch lbs.

OIL PUMP

REPLACE

1. Remove coil bracket attaching bolts and position coil aside.
2. Remove fuel pump and pushrod.
3. Remove distributor.
4. Remove oil pan.
5. Remove oil pump screen and pipe assembly.
6. Remove oil pump.
7. Reverse procedure to install.

CRANKSHAFT REAR OIL SEAL

REPLACE

1. Disconnect battery ground cable.
2. Remove transmission.
3. Remove flywheel.
4. Remove rack and pinion bracket bolts.
5. Remove left side strut assembly.
6. Disconnect flex coupling and pull steering gear down.
7. Drain engine oil, then remove oil pan mounting bolts.
8. With oil pan pulled down away from engine block, remove oil pump suction pipe and screen.
9. With engine mounts attached, raise engine slightly with suitable jack and block of wood and remove oil pan from vehicle.
10. Remove rear main bearing cap and oil seal.
11. Clean bearing cap, case and crankshaft seal surface, then inspect crankshaft seal surface for excessive wear and nicks. If excessive wear or nicks exist, replace crankshaft.
12. Install new seal in case, then install bearing cap, but do not tighten bolts. **When installing seal in case, ensure seal is seated against rear main bearing bulkhead.**
13. Torque main bearing cap bolts to 11 ft. lbs., then using suitable soft-faced hammer, tap end of crankshaft rearward, then forward. Retorque main bearing cap to specifications.
14. Using 2 part RTV sealer or equivalent, pack sealer into vertical grooves until excess flows from slots adjacent to rear seal. Clean excess sealer.
15. Reverse steps 1 through 9 to install.

CRANKCASE FRONT COVER

REPLACE

1. Remove timing belt upper and lower front covers, crankshaft pulley, timing belt and crankshaft sprocket.
2. Remove three crankcase front cover to oil pan attaching bolts, then the crankcase cover to engine attaching bolts.
3. Remove crankcase front cover, cover gasket and front portion of oil pan gasket. **To fabricate a replacement crankcase front cover to oil pan gasket, position crankcase cover over a new oil pan gasket as shown in Fig. 7.** When installing gasket apply sealer to cut off portion of gasket.
4. Inspect crankshaft oil seal, replace if necessary.
5. Install crankcase front cover using alignment tool J-26434 or equivalent. **Failure to use above mentioned tool may result in subsequent oil leakage.**

BELT TENSION DATA

Belt	New Lbs.	Used Lbs.
1982-87		
A/C Comp.	**168**	**90**
All other belts	**146**	**70**

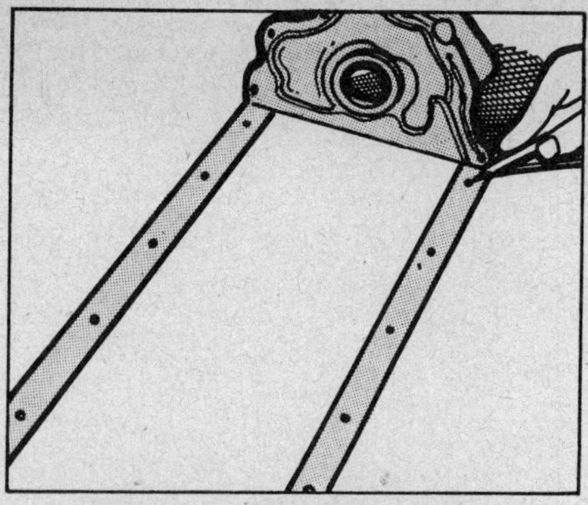

Fig. 7 Fabricating crankcase front cover to oil pan seal

FUEL PUMP

REPLACE

1. Disconnect battery ground cable.
2. Remove distributor cap and power steering pump, if equipped.
3. Remove spark plug wire retaining clips.
4. Remove coil wire and coil assembly.
5. Remove air cleaner assembly.
6. Disconnect fuel pump inlet and outlet hoses.
7. Remove fuel pump and gasket.
8. Reverse procedure to install.

WATER PUMP

REPLACE

1. Position No. 1 cylinder at top dead center. **When No. 1 cylinder is at top dead center, a 1/8 inch drill rod may be inserted through the hole in the upper rear timing belt cover into the hole located on camshaft sprocket.**
2. Disconnect battery ground cable, then drain cooling system.
3. Loosen alternator and A/C drive belts, then remove crankshaft pulley.
4. On models equipped with A/C, remove upper portion of fan shroud, if equipped.
5. On models less A/C, remove radiator upper mounting panel, if equipped.
6. On all models, remove engine fan.
7. Remove timing belt cover attaching bolts and nuts, then remove timing belt cover.
8. Loosen idler pulley mounting bolts and allow pulley to rotate clockwise.
9. Remove timing belt from camshaft and crankshaft pulleys.
10. Disconnect lower radiator hose and heater hose from water pump.
11. Remove water pump to cylinder block attaching bolts, then remove water pump.
12. Reverse procedure to install. Before installing timing belt cover, adjust timing belt tension as described under "Timing Belt Tension, Adjust."

4-110 (1.8L) Diesel Engine

INDEX

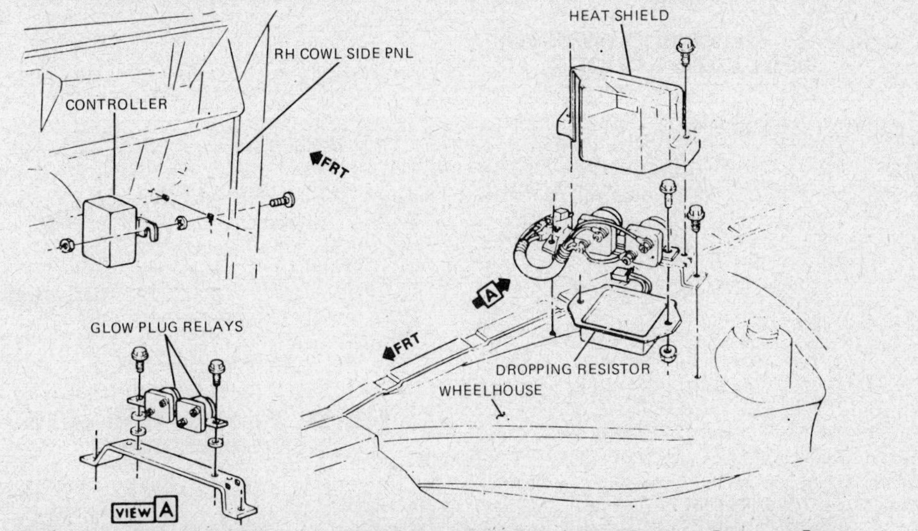

Fig. 1 Controller, dropping resistor & glow plug relay locations

ENGINE TROUBLESHOOTING

HARD STARTING

1. Check fuel level, replenish if necessary.
2. Check notched line on injection pump flange, reset timing as necessary.
3. Check to ensure fuel is reaching injection nozzles. If fuel is reaching injectors:
   a. Check connections of fuse, glow plugs, Q.S.S.I. controller and glow plug relays.
   b. Check fuel spray pattern, and ensure injection starting pressure is approximately 1707 psi.
   c. Check to ensure valve clearances are satisfactory. Refer to specifications.
   d. Check compression pressure in each cylinder. Standard value should be 441 psi.
   e. Check to ensure proper installation of timing belt and camshaft.
4. If fuel is not reaching injectors:
   a. Check for air in fuel filter.
   b. Check if air is being drawn into fuel line through leakage in the pipe joints.
   c. Check operation of fuel cut out solenoid.
   d. Check fuel filter for restrictions.
   e. Check fuel pipes for restrictions.
   f. Check delivery valve for possible sticking.
5. Replace or readjust setting of injection pump.

ENGINE IDLING ROUGH

1. Check if idle speed is within specifications.
2. Check to ensure accelerator control cable is not binding or twisting.
3. Check accelerator lever setting for looseness.
4. Check for air or water in fuel filter.
5. Check for proper alignment on injection pump flange.
6. Check engine mounting for cracks or looseness.
7. Check fuel spray pattern, and ensure injection starting pressure is 1707 psi.
8. Check to ensure intake clearances are satisfactory. Refer to specifications.
9. Check compression pressure in each cylinder. Standard value should be 441 psi.
10. Check to ensure proper installation of timing belt and camshaft.
11. Check delivery valve for sticking.
12. Replace or readjust setting of injection pump.

ENGINE LACKS POWER

1. Check air cleaner for restrictions.
2. Check to ensure accelerator control cable is not binding or twisting.
3. Check seals on full load adjustment bolt and maximum speed stop bolt.
4. Check to ensure accelerator control lever is in full contact with maximum speed stop bolt.
5. Check exhaust system for restrictions.
6. Check for air in fuel filter.
7. Check notched line on injection pump flange, repair as necessary.
8. Check engine mounting for cracks or looseness.
9. Check fuel spray pattern, and ensure injection starting pressure is 1707 psi.
10. Check to ensure valve clearances are satisfactory. Refer to specifications.
11. Check compression pressure in each cylinder. Standard value should be 441 psi.
12. Check to ensure proper installation of

timing belt and camshaft.
13. Check delivery valve for sticking.
14. Replace or readjust setting of injection pump.

ENGINE OVERHEATING

1. Check coolant level in radiator.
2. Check condition of coolant for contamination, ratio of anti-freeze to water, and leakage of oil into coolant.
3. Check for leakage in hoses, and clamps.
4. Check water pump and thermostat housing for leakage.
5. Check for damaged cylinder head gasket.
6. Check fan belt tension. Deflection of fan belt should be no more than .4 inch.
7. Check operation of fan clutch.
8. Check for proper operation of radiator cap.
9. Check thermostat operation. Thermostat opening temperature is 180° F.
10. Check injection timing.
11. Check condition of water pump impeller.
12. Check to ensure proper level of engine oil.
13. Replace or readjust setting of injection pump.

ENGINE KNOCKING

1. Check if engine has been thoroughly warmed up.
2. Check injection timing.
3. Check fuel spray pattern, and ensure injection starting pressure is 1707 psi.
4. Check compression pressure in each cylinder. Standard value should be 441 psi.
5. Check to ensure proper quality of fuel.
6. Replace or readjust setting of injection pump.

NOISE INDICATING ABNORMAL LEAKAGE

1. Check exhaust system for loose connections or leakage.
2. Check to ensure proper installation of nozzles and glow plugs.
3. Check for damaged cylinder head gasket.
4. Check to ensure valve clearances are satisfactory. Refer to specifications.
5. Check compression pressure in each cylinder. Standard value should be 441 psi.

CONTINUOUS NOISE

1. Check fan belt tension. Deflection of fan belt should be no more than .4 inch.
2. Check to ensure cooling fan is secure.
3. Check water pump bearing for wear and damage.
4. Check operation of generator and vacuum pump.
5. Check to ensure valve clearances are satisfactory. Refer to specifications.

SLAPPING NOISE

1. Check valve retainers for damage.
2. Check to ensure valve clearances are satisfactory. Refer to specifications.
3. Check rocker arms for damage.
4. Check camshaft for seizure.

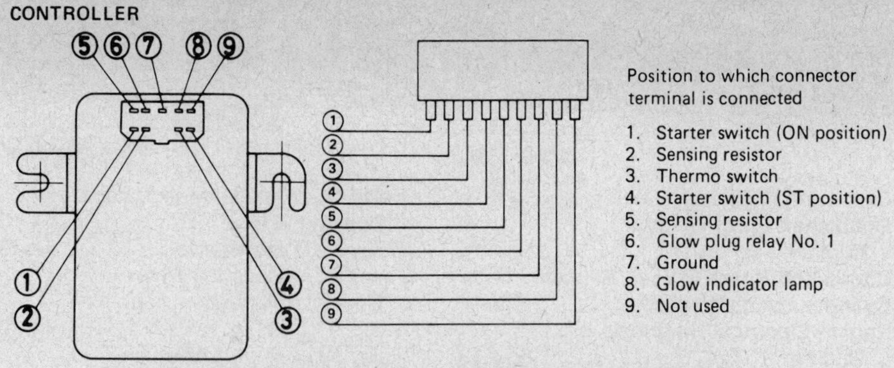

Fig. 2 Controller wiring connections

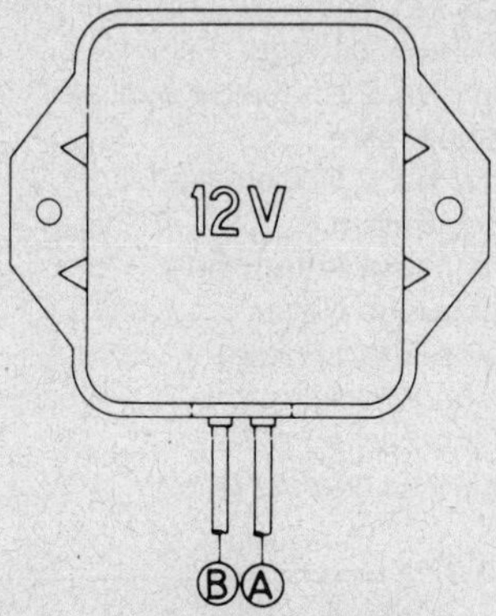

Fig. 3 Dropping resistor test connections

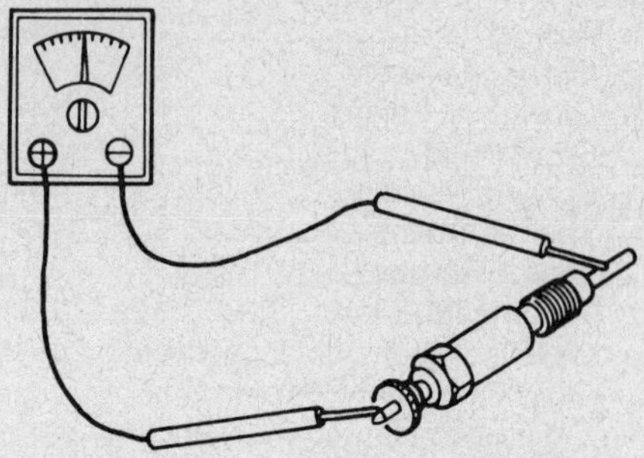

Fig. 4 Testing glow plug

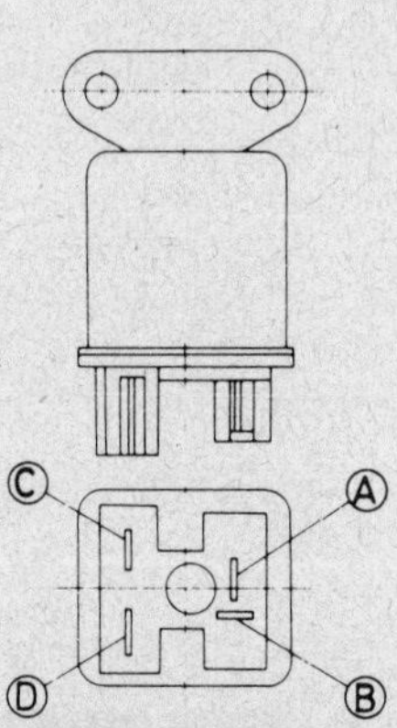

Fig. 5 Glow plug relay test connections

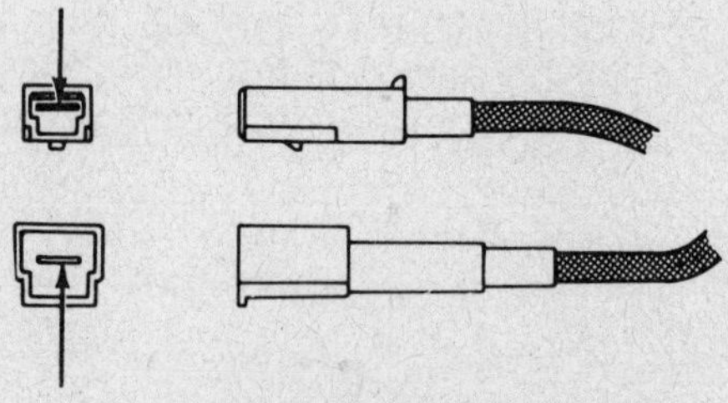

Fig. 6 Fusible link test connections

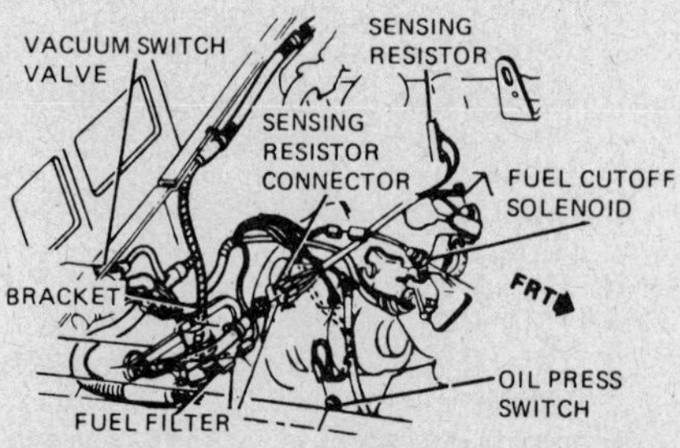

Fig. 7 Sensing resistor location

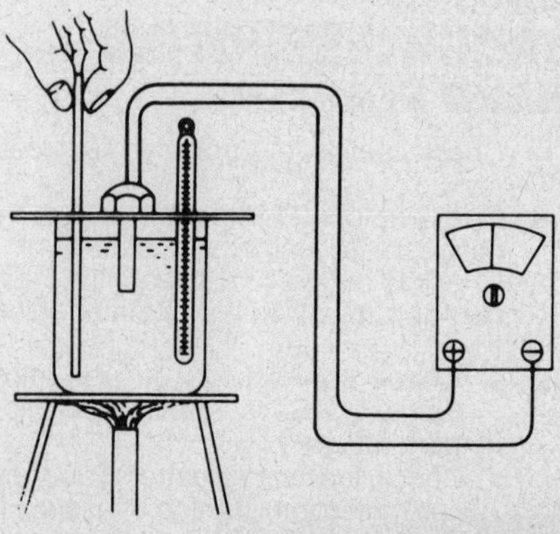

Fig. 8 Testing thermo switch

5. Check to ensure flywheel bolts are secure.
6. Check crankshaft and thrust bearing for wear and damage.
7. Check main bearing oil clearances.
8. Check connecting rod bearing and bushing oil clearances.
9. Check to ensure clearance between pistons and cylinder walls is satisfactory. Refer to specifications.

EXCESSIVE OIL CONSUMPTION

1. If oil is leaking:
   a. Check engine oil level.
   b. Check to ensure drain plug is secure.
   c. Check oil pipes for leakage.
   d. Check cooler seat gasket, oil filter and oil seal retainer for leakage.
   e. Check cylinder head cover, oil pan and oil pump gaskets for leakage.
   f. Check cylinder head gasket for leakage.
   g. Check oil seals for leakage.
   h. Check function of P.C.V.
   i. Check to ensure flywheel bolts are secure.
2. If oil is burning:
   a. Check to ensure quality of oil.
   b. Check valve stem oil seals.
   c. Check valve guides and valve stems for wear and damage.
   d. Check for damaged cylinder head gasket.
   e. Check to ensure proper setting of piston rings.
   f. Check piston rings for wear and damage.
   g. Check cylinder walls for wear and damage.

EXCESSIVE FUEL CONSUMPTION

1. Check air cleaner for restrictions.
2. Check fuel lead adjustment bolt seal for leakage.
3. Check fuel pipes for leakage.
4. Check exhaust system for restrictions.
5. Check if idle speed is within specifications.
6. Check to ensure proper quality of fuel.
7. Check injection timing.
8. Check fuel spray pattern, and ensure injection starting pressure is 1707 psi.
9. Check to ensure valve clearances are satisfactory. Refer to specifications.
10. Check compression pressure in each cylinder. Standard valve should be 441 psi.
11. Check delivery valve for sticking.
12. Replace or readjust setting of injection pump.

ENGINE ELECTRICAL TROUBLESHOOTING

In a normally operating quick start system, when coolant temperature is below 122° F and the key is in the "On" position, the glow plug indicator turns on for about 3.5 seconds and the No. 1 Relay turns on for a few seconds.

RELAY NO. 1 AND GLOW INDICATOR ARE BOTH INOPERATIVE

1. Starter circuit fuse is burnt out or fusible link wire is open.
2. Starter wire circuit is open or not properly connected.
3. Controller defective or not properly connected.
4. Starter switch is inoperative.

RELAY NO. 1 INOPERATIVE

1. Relay No. 1 is open.
2. Relay coil in relay No. 1 is open.
3. Controller to No. 1 relay circuitry is open or not properly connected.
4. Grounding circuit for No. 1 relay is open or not properly connected.
5. Controller is inoperative.
6. Circuit from controller to signal feed wire of sensing resistor is open or not properly connected.
7. Terminals of sensing resistor are not connected.
8. Main terminal of No. 1 relay not connected.
9. Main contact open in No. 1 relay.
10. Terminals in quick preheat circuit not connected.
11. Engine harness ground not properly connected.
12. Quick preheating wiring not properly connected or circuit open.

GLOW INDICATOR LIGHT INOPERATIVE

1. Controller damaged.
2. Indicator circuit not properly connected or open.
3. Light bulb burnt out.

RELAY NO. 1 TURNS OFF WITHIN 2 SECONDS

1. Controller damaged.
2. One or more glow plugs defective.
3. Wiring at connector poorly connected.

RELAY NO. 1 WILL NOT TURN OFF AFTER A FEW SECONDS

1. Controller damaged.

RELAY NO. 1 OPERATES WHEN COOLANT TEMPERATURE IS ABOVE 122° F

1. Thermostat switch is inoperative.
2. Short in circuit. **In a normally operating quick start system, when coolant temperature is below 122° F and, the key held in the "Start" position, the glow plug indicator and the No. 2 relay will remain on until key is moved to "On" position.**

RELAY NO. 2 AND GLOW INDICATOR INOPERATIVE

1. Starter switch "R" circuit not properly connected or open.

RELAY NO. 2 INOPERATIVE

1. Relay No. 2 terminals not connected.
2. Circuit between R terminal and No. 2 relay not properly connected or open.
3. No. 2 relay coil is open.

GLOW PLUG LIGHT REMAINS ON FOR 3.5 SECONDS AND CAUSES RELAY NO. 1 TO TURN ON

1. Thermo-switch circuit not properly connected or open.
2. Thermostat switch is inoperative.

ENGINE ELECTRICAL DIAGNOSIS & TESTING

CONTROLLER

The controller in this system has four functions. As engine coolant temperature changes, it controls the glow plug relay. For determining glow plug heating requirements, it monitors differences between sensing resistance and glow plug resistance. It controls rapid preheat circuit to 1652° F of glow plug temperature and, during pre-heat cycle, it controls the glow plug pre-heat indicator lamp (3.5 sec.). Refer to **Figs. 1 and 2** for wiring connections.

DROPPING RESISTOR

During stabilized heating, this fixed value resistor is used to lower voltage of glow plugs. Check dropping resistor by performing continuity check across the terminals. Replace resistor if no continuity is found. Refer to **Figs. 1 and 3.**

GLOW PLUGS

The glow plugs used in this system are the fast warm up type. Check glow plugs by performing continuity test across plug terminals and body. If no continuity is found, heater wire is damaged and glow plug should be replaced. Refer to **Fig. 4.**

GLOW PLUG RELAY

This relay is main relay for stabilized heating circuit and rapid pre-heat cycle. Check glow relay by performing continuity test across terminals C and D while battery voltage is applied to terminals A and B. If no continuity is found, replace glow plug relay. Refer to **Fig. 5.**

GLOW PLUG RELAY 2

During starting, this relay is used to provide stabilized heating. To check this relay, use same procedure as for glow plug relay 1.

FUSIBLE LINKS

These two inline fusible links are used to protect the glow plug electrical wiring. To check fusible links, perform continuity check across terminals. If no continuity is found, fusible link should be replaced. Refer to **Fig. 6.**

SENSING RESISTOR

Used in series with the glow plugs, this shunt type sensing resistor causes a small voltage drop which is monitored by the controller, **Fig. 7.**

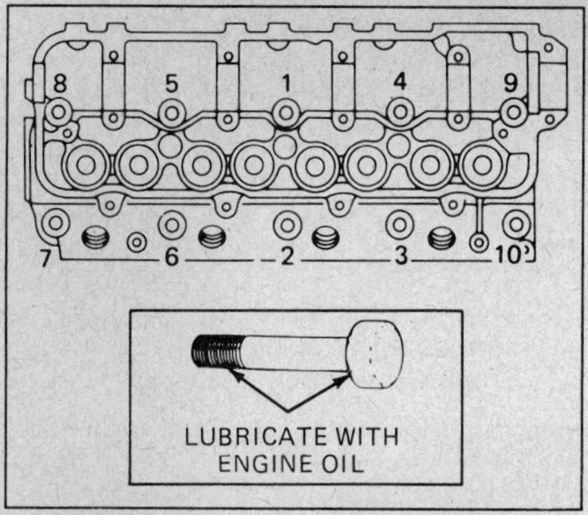

Fig. 9 Cylinder head bolt tightening sequence

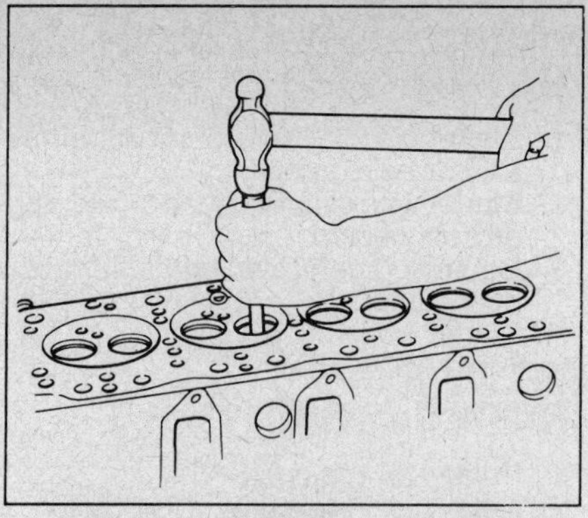

Fig. 10 Removing valve guides

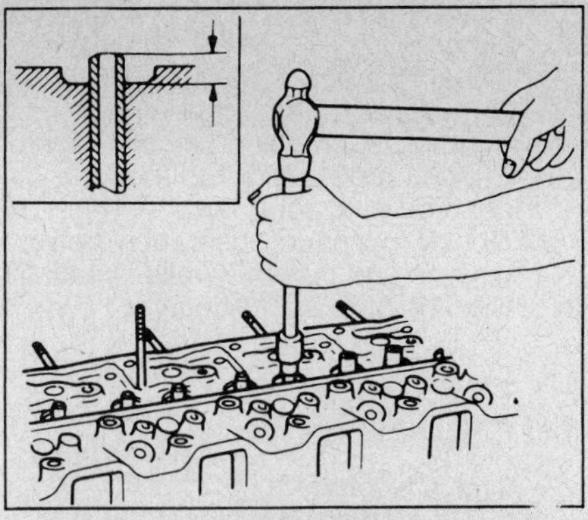

Fig. 11 Installing valve guides

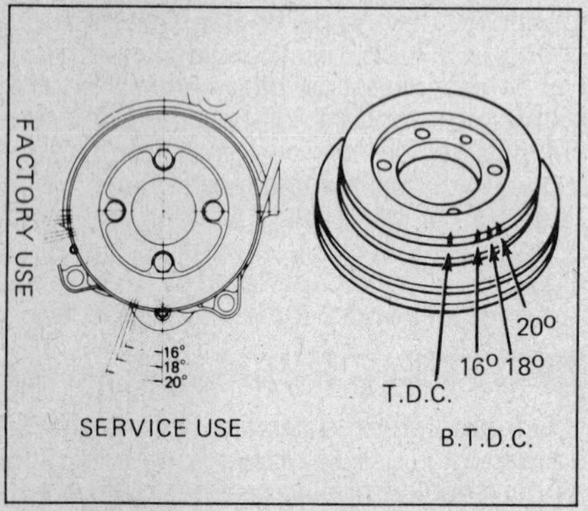

Fig. 12 Timing mark locations on damper pulley

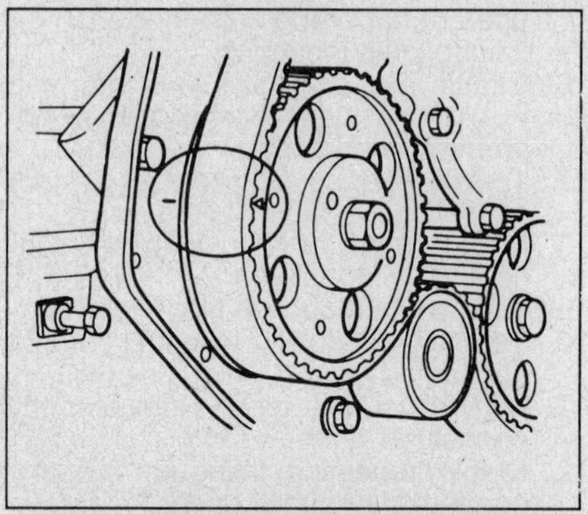

Fig. 13 Injection pump pulley alignment

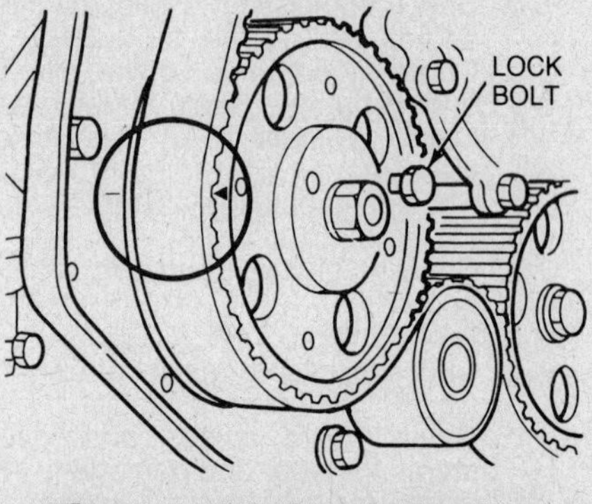

Fig. 14 Fixing injection pump pulley with lock bolt

THERMO SWITCH

This switch is used to provide a ground circuit to controller circuitry when engine temperature is above 122° F. To check thermo switch, perform continuity check across terminal and body while end of thermal switch is submerged in water. Gradually bring temperature of water to 122° F. Replace thermal switch if continuity is not found at this temperature. Refer to **Fig. 8.**

ENGINE

REPLACE

1. Remove hood.
2. Disconnect battery ground cable and drain cooling system.
3. Disconnect radiator hoses and remove radiator.
4. Disconnect engine wiring harnesses.
5. Remove air cleaner.
6. Disconnect accelerator and automatic transmission throttle valve linkage, if equipped.
7. Disconnect fuel lines and heater hoses.
8. Remove A/C compressor from mounting bracket and position aside, if equipped.
9. Remove power steering pump and bracket and position aside, if equipped.
10. Disconnect vacuum hose to master cylinder.
11. Remove engine mount nuts.
12. Raise vehicle and disconnect exhaust pipe at manifold.
13. Remove engine strut (shock type).
14. Remove flywheel dust cover.
15. On models with automatic transmission, remove converter to flywheel bolts.
16. Remove transmission rear crossmember to body bolts and bellhousing bolts.
17. Reinstall crossmember bolts.
18. Lower vehicle.
19. Remove oil filter.
20. Install engine lifting device, raise and remove engine.
21. Reverse procedure to install.

CYLINDER HEAD

REPLACE

1. Disconnect battery ground cable and drain cooling system.
2. Remove cam cover.
3. Remove timing belt. It will not be necessary to remove lower cover and damper.
4. Remove camshaft.
5. Remove glow plug resistor wires and injector lines.
6. Remove fuel return line hose.
7. Raise vehicle and disconnect exhaust pipe at manifold.
8. Lower vehicle and remove oil feed pipe at rear of cylinder head.
9. Disconnect upper radiator hose.
10. Remove cylinder head bolts. Remove cylinder head and gasket.
11. Reverse procedure to install, tighten cylinder head bolts in sequence shown in **Fig. 9.**

VALVE TIMING

INTAKE OPENS BEFORE TDC

Engine	Year	Degrees
4-110	1982-86	32°

VALVE CLEARANCE SPECIFICATIONS

Engine	Year	Int.	Exh.
4-110	1982-86	.010①	.014①

①—Engine cold.

VALVES

ADJUST

Refer to "Valve Clearance Specifications" for specified intake and exhaust valve clearances.

1. Remove cam cover.
2. Inspect the rocker arm shaft bracket bolts for looseness and retorque as necessary.
3. Bring No. 1 cylinder to TDC on compression stroke.

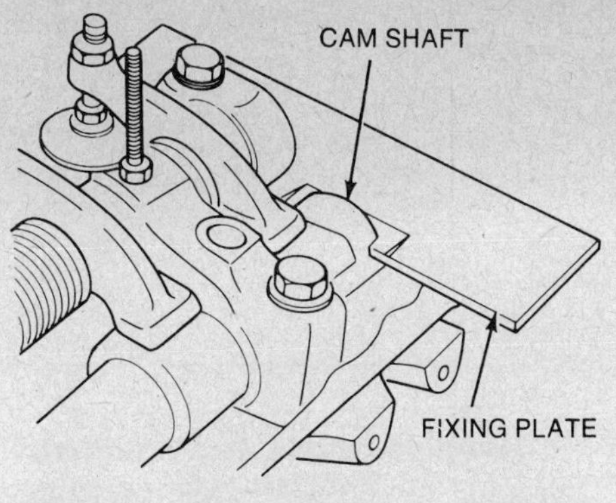

Fig. 15 Fixing camshaft in place with tool No. J-29761

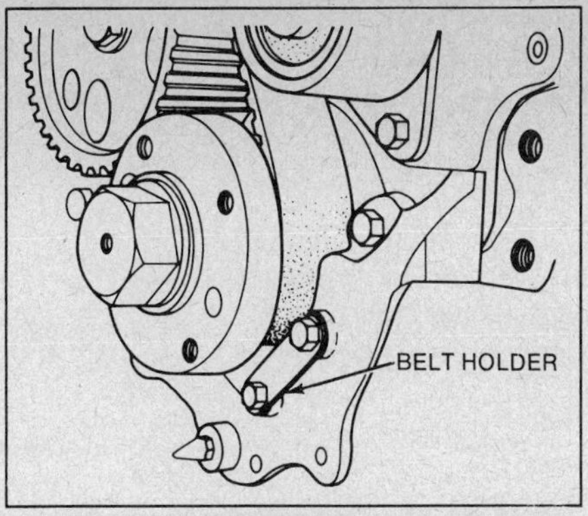

Fig. 16 Timing belt holder

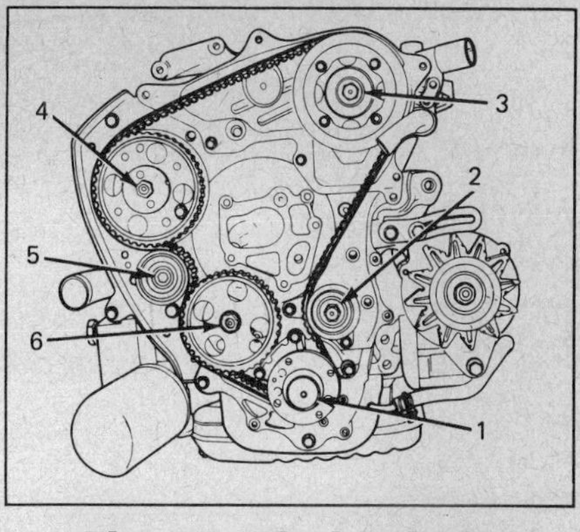

Fig. 17 Timing belt installation sequence

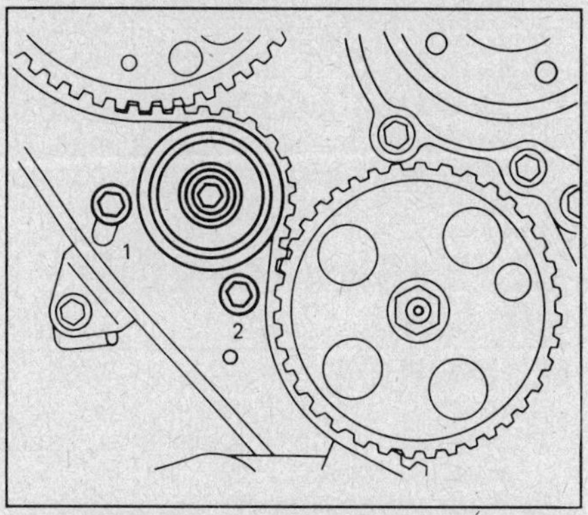

Fig. 18 Semi-tightening sequence of tension pulley

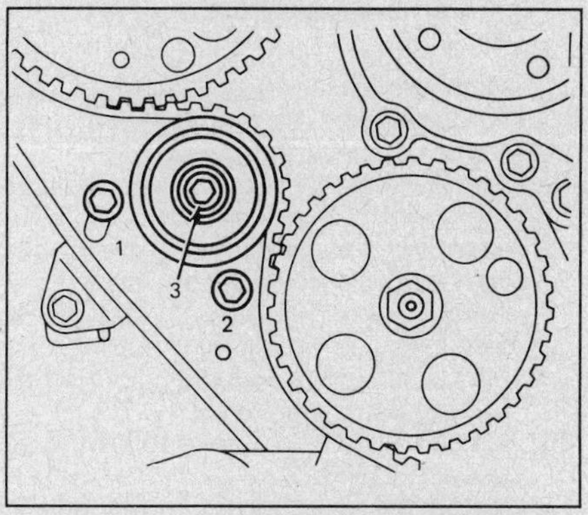

Fig. 19 Torquing tension pulley bolt sequence

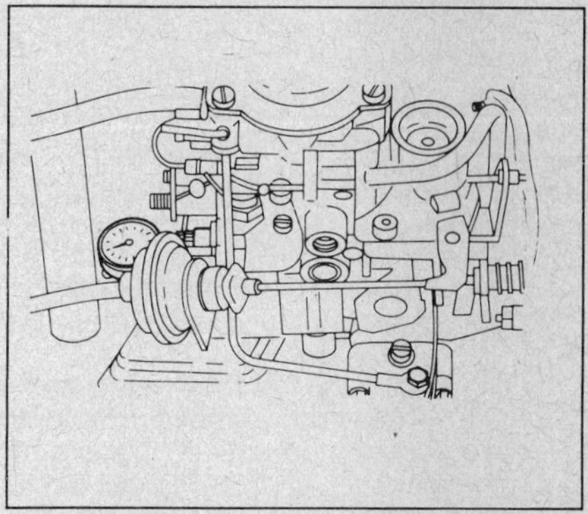

Fig. 20 Static timing gauge, J-29763 installed

4. Adjust valve clearances of cylinder No. 1, intake valve of No. 2 and exhaust valve of No. 3. Turn crankshaft one full revolution to bring cylinder No. 4 to TDC on compression stroke. Adjust clearances of cylinder No. 4, exhaust valve of No. 2 and intake valve of No. 3.
5. Reinstall cam cover.

VALVE GUIDE
REPLACE

1. Using tool No. J-26512 drive out the valve guide from the lower face of the cylinder head, **Fig. 10.**
2. Apply engine oil to outer circumference of valve guide, then using tool No. J-26512, drive the guide into position from the upper face of the cylinder head, **Fig. 11. Always replace valve guide and valve as a set.**

TIMING BELT
REPLACE

1. Disconnect battery ground cable.
2. Remove undercover and drain coolant.
3. Remove fan shroud, alternator belt, cooling fan and water pump pulley.
4. Remove ten bolts securing upper dust cover, remove dust cover.
5. Remove bypass hose.
6. Bring cylinder No. 1 to TDC, **Fig. 12,** ensure that setting mark on injection pump pulley is in alignment with front plate, then fix the pulley with 8 mm 1.25 pitch bolt, **Fig. 13 and Fig. 14.**
7. Remove cam cover and loosen valve adjustment screws so rocker arms are in a free state. Fix camshaft by installing fixing plate, tool No. J-29761, into the slit in rear end of the camshaft, **Fig. 15.**
8. Remove crankshaft damper pulley, lower dust cover and timing belt holder, **Fig. 16. Under no circumstances should the crankshaft be disturbed from TDC.**
9. Remove tension pulley spring then loosen tension pulley and plate bolts, remove timing belt.
10. Remove camshaft pulley bolt, using a suitable puller remove camshaft pulley, then reinstall pulley and bolt. Tighten bolt just enough to allow the pulley to be turned smoothly by hand.
11. Install new timing belt using sequence shown in **Fig. 17.** Ensure that belt cogs are properly installed in pulleys. Do not disturb crankshaft setting.
12. Concentrate belt looseness on tension pulley, depress tension pulley with finger and install tension spring. Semi-tighten bolts in numerical sequence 1 and 2 to prevent movement of tension pulley, **Fig. 18.**
13. Tighten camshaft pulley bolt.
14. Remove injection pump pulley lock bolt and camshaft fixing plate.
15. Install crankshaft damper pulley, ensure No. 1 cylinder is at TDC.
16. Ensure injection pump pulley mark is in alignment with mark on plate and fixing plate should fit smoothly into the rear slit of the camshaft. Remove plate.
17. Loosen tensioner plate bolts and pulley. Concentrate looseness of belt on tensioner, then tighten the bolts in numerical sequence 1, 2, and 3. **Fig. 19.** Torque bolts 1 and 2 to 11 to 18 ft. lbs. and bolt 3 to 47 to 61 ft. lbs.
18. Using a belt tension gauge, check tension between camshaft pulley and injection pump pulley. Tension should be 47 to 64 lbs.
19. Remove crankshaft damper and install timing belt holder.
20. Adjust valves. Refer to "Valves, Adjust" for procedure.
21. Reverse steps 1 through 8 to reassemble.

INJECTION TIMING
ADJUST

1. Check that alignment mark on injection pump flange is aligned with alignment mark on front plate.
2. Bring cylinder No. 1 to TDC on compression stroke by turning crankshaft until timing mark on pulley aligns with pointer, **Fig. 12. The damper pulley has eleven notched lines as shown in Fig. 12. Four lines on one side, seven elsewhere. The four lines are intended for service use while the**

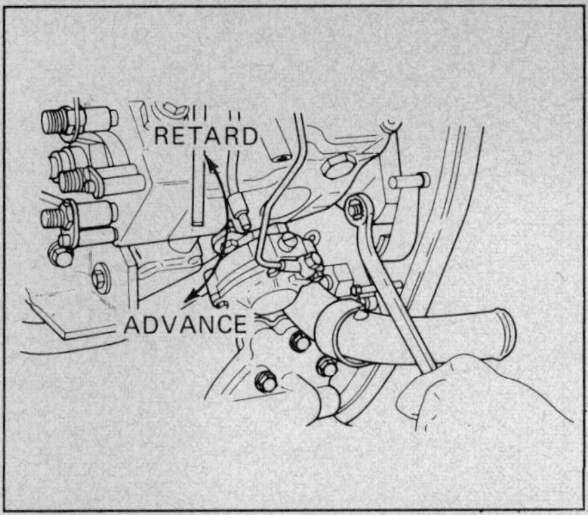

Fig. 21 Injection pump flange nuts

other seven are for factory use only.

3. Remove upper dust cover, ensure the injection pump belt is properly tensioned and the timing marks are aligned. See "Timing Belt, Replace."
4. Remove the cam cover and rear plug, ensure that the fixing plate fits smoothly into the camshaft rear slit, then remove the fixing plate. See "Timing Belt, Replace."
5. Disconnect the injection pipe from the injection pump, remove distributor head screw and gasket, install static timing gauge J-29763, **Fig. 20.** Set the lift approximately .040 inch (1 mm) from the plunger.
6. Bring No. 1 piston to a point 45-60 degrees BTDC by turning the crankshaft, then set dial indicator to zero. Turn crankshaft slightly in both directions, ensuring gauge indication is stable.
7. Turn crankshaft in normal direction of rotation until the 18 degree mark on the damper is aligned with the timing pointer, **Fig. 12.** Note reading of dial indicator, if reading is not .020 inch (.5 mm), hold crankshaft at 18 degrees and loosen the two nuts on injection pump flange, **Fig. 21.** Move pump until reading on dial indicator is .020 inch (.5 mm), then tighten nuts.

INJECTION PUMP
REPLACE

1. Remove timing belt. See "Timing Belt, Replace."
2. To prevent rotation of injection pump pulley during disassembly, thread a 8 mm 1.25 pitch bolt through the pulley into the housing, **Fig. 14.**
3. Remove injection pump pulley bolt.
4. Remove bolt installed in step two, then using a suitable puller remove injection pump pulley.
5. Disconnect fuel cut solenoid valve switch wiring and tachometer pickup sensor wiring at connector.
6. Disconnect accelerator cable from pump lever. If equipped with automatic transmission, remove throttle valve control cable.
7. Disconnect vacuum hose from fast idle actuator.
8. Disconnect fuel hoses from injection pump.

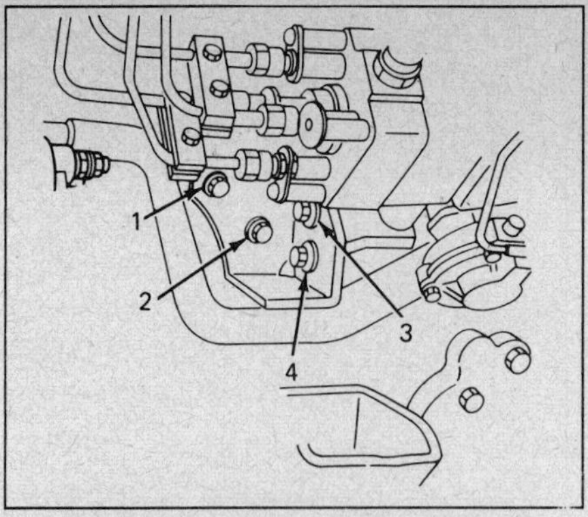

Fig. 22 Injection pump rear bracket tightening sequence

9. Remove six screws attaching injection pipe clips and remove.
10. Remove injection pipes.
11. Remove injection pump rear bracket then control lever spring.
12. Remove attaching nuts and pump with fast idle device installed.
13. Install injection pump with fast idle device installed by aligning notched line on pump flange with the line on the front plate.
14. Install rear bracket bolts following sequence in **Fig. 22.**
15. Install the injection pump pulley by aligning it with key groove, torque nut to 43 to 50 ft. lbs. Hold pulley from rotating by installing a bolt as described in step 2.
16. Refer to "Timing Belt, Replace" for reassembly procedures.

ROCKER ARM SHAFT ASSEMBLY
REPLACE

1. Remove cam cover.
2. Remove rocker arm shaft bracket bolts and nuts, then remove rocker arm shaft and rocker arm assembly.
3. Prior to installation, apply a generous amount of engine oil to the rocker arm shaft, rocker arms and valve stem end caps.
4. Install rocker arm shaft assembly and tighten bolts in sequence as shown in **Fig. 23.**
5. Adjust valves. Refer to "Valves, Adjust" for procedure.

CAMSHAFT
REPLACE

1. Remove cam cover.
2. Remove timing belt as described in "Timing Belt, Replace."
3. Remove camshaft gear as described in "Timing Belt, Replace."
4. Remove rocker arm shaft assembly as described in "Rocker Arm Shaft Assembly, Replace."
5. Remove bolts attaching front head plate and remove.
6. Remove the camshaft bearing cap bolts, then remove bearing caps with cap side bearing.

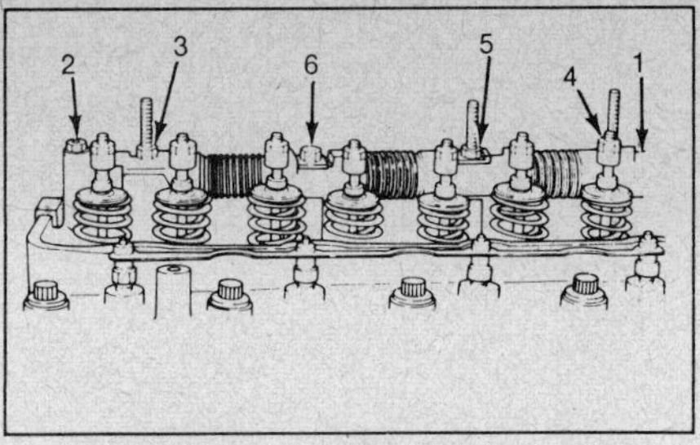

Fig. 23 Rocker arm bracket bolt tightening sequence

7. Remove camshaft oil seal followed by the camshaft.
8. Install camshaft oil seal, camshaft and rocker arm shaft assembly. Loosen rocker arm adjustment screws so the rocker arms are in a free state. Reverse procedure from step five to reinstall.

CRANKSHAFT FRONT OIL SEAL
REPLACE

1. Remove timing belt. Refer to "Timing Belt, Replace."
2. Remove crankshaft hub center bolt and washer.
3. Using a suitable puller, remove hub from crankshaft.
4. Using puller No. J-29752, remove crankshaft timing belt pulley.
5. Pry out front oil seal using a suitable screwdriver.
6. Apply clean engine oil to inner and outer surfaces of new seal, using a suitable seal installer, install the oil seal.
7. Position crankshaft timing belt pulley flange into seal, align pulley groove with crankshaft key. Drive pulley onto crankshaft using installer tool No. J-26587.
8. Align crankshaft hub keyway with crankshaft key, install center bolt. Torque to 98 to 119 ft. lbs.
9. Reinstall timing belt. Refer to "Timing Belt, Replace."

CRANKSHAFT REAR OIL SEAL
REPLACE

1. Remove the clutch pressure plate assembly.
2. Remove the six flywheel attaching bolts, then the flywheel.
3. Using a suitable screwdriver, pry out the rear seal.
4. Apply clean engine oil to all sides of new seal.
5. Install the oil seal in the oil seal retainer using tool No. J-29818.
6. Position flywheel on crankshaft hub. Using new bolts, apply Loctite to threads and install flywheel. Torque bolts 36 to 43 ft. lbs.
7. Reverse procedure to install remaining parts.

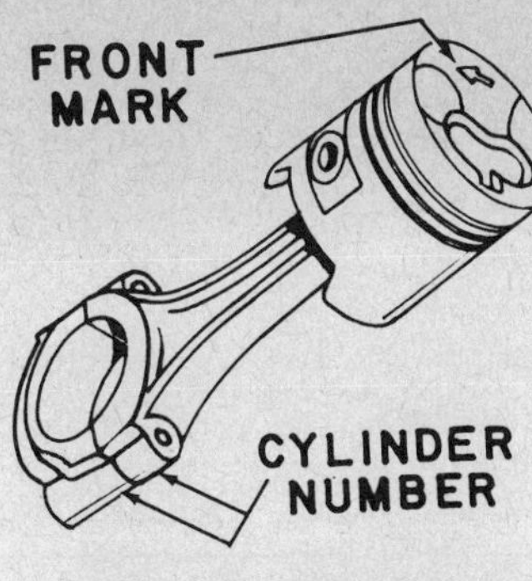

Fig. 24 Piston & connecting rod assembly

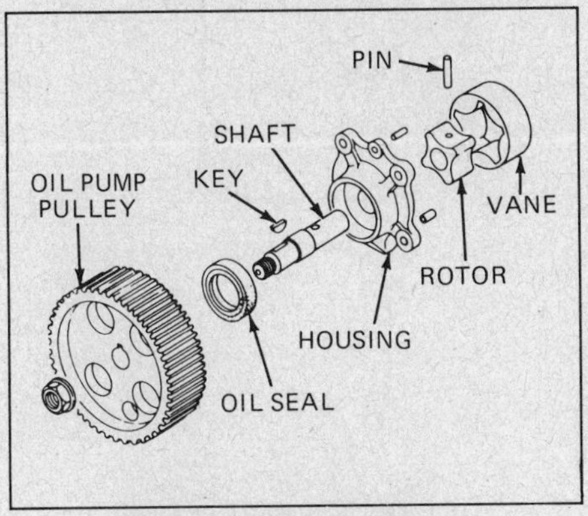

Fig. 26 Oil pump, disassembled

PISTON & CONNECTING ROD

Install the piston on the connecting rod, so that the combustion chamber on piston head is on the same side with the cylinder mark side (side with bearing stopper) of the connecting rod big end. The front of the piston should be on same side as the "Isuzu" mark on the connecting rod, **Fig. 24.** Pistons are available in oversizes of .010 and .030 in.

Check connecting rod side clearance with a feeler gauge. Clearance should be .003-.024 inch.

OIL PAN

REPLACE

1. Remove engine assembly. Refer to "Engine, Replace" for procedure.
2. Remove fourteen bolts and four nuts attaching oil pan and remove.
3. Discard old gasket, clean mounting surfaces. Install new gasket using a suitable sealing compound on oil pan, and install.
4. Torque bolts 4-6 ft. lbs.

OIL PUMP

REPLACE

1. Remove timing belt. Refer to "Timing Belt, Replace."
2. Remove four Allen bolts securing oil pump, remove oil pump and pulley as an assembly, see **Fig. 25.**
3. Refer to "Oil Pump, Inspection & Service."
4. Prior to installation apply a generous amount of clean engine oil to vane, install with taper side towards the cylinder body.
5. Install new pump O-ring, lubricate with motor oil and install in the housing groove. Lubricate oil pump rotor and install pump body together with pulley.
6. Reverse procedure to install.

OIL PUMP INSPECTION & SERVICE

1. Inspect all parts for any signs of abnormal wear, or damage, **Fig. 26.**
2. Measure outside diameter of pulley flange. Diameter should be 1.1-1.1035 inch (27.94-28.03 mm).
3. Using a straightedge and feeler gauge, check clearance between vane and cylinder body in direction of thrust. Clearance should be .0011-.0027 inch (.03-.07 mm).
4. Check clearance between vane and cylinder body. Clearance should be .0094-.0141 inch (.24-.36 mm).
5. Check clearance between vane and rotor. Clearance should be .0051-.0059 (.13-.15).
6. Reassemble as shown in **Fig. 26.**

OIL COOLER

REPLACE

1. Disconnect battery ground cable.
2. Remove oil cooler drain plug, allow cooler to drain.
3. Remove rubber hoses.
4. Remove two joint bolts securing cooler, **Fig. 27.** Remove cooler.

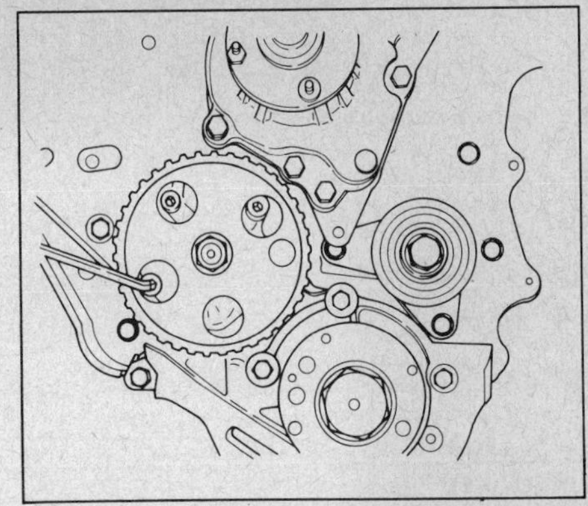

Fig. 25 Removing oil pump

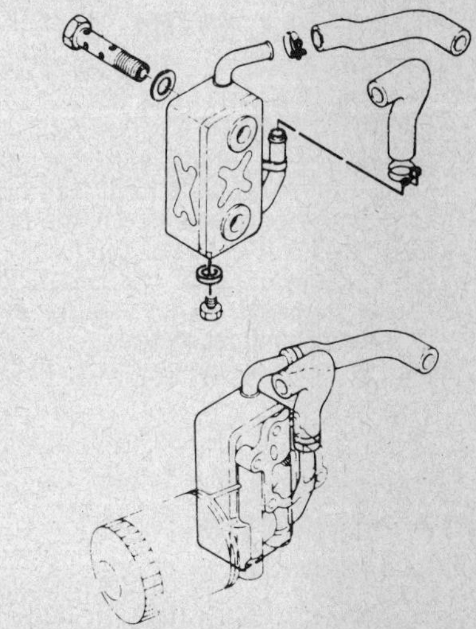

Fig. 27 Oil cooler assembly

5. Install new joint bolt gaskets and install cooler.
6. Reverse steps 1 to 3 to install.

WATER PUMP

REPLACE

1. Disconnect battery ground cable.
2. Drain cooling system.
3. Remove four nuts securing cooling fan and pulley assembly and remove. Remove fan belt.
4. Remove crankshaft damper pulley.
5. Remove front engine dust covers.
6. Remove bypass hose.
7. Remove five water pump attaching bolts and remove pump.
8. Reverse procedure to install.

Clutch & Manual Transmission Section

INDEX

CLUTCH

ADJUST

INITIAL BALL STUD ADJUSTMENT

4 Speed Units

1. Place gauge J-28449 with flat end against clutch housing front face and the hooked end positioned in the bottom depression of the clutch fork.
2. Turn ball inward until clutch release bearing contacts clutch spring and fork is snug against gauge.
3. Install and torque locknut to 25 ft. lbs.
4. Remove gauge.

CLUTCH CABLE ATTACHMENT & ADJUSTMENT

1. Install clutch cable through hole in clutch fork and seat, then install return spring.
2. From engine compartment, pull cable until clutch pedal is firmly against pedal stop and hold in position, **Fig. 1.**
3. Install snap ring in first fully visible groove in cable from sleeve, then release cable.
4. Clutch pedal lash should be .58-1.08 inch. If not, adjust clutch pedal as described under "Clutch Pedal Adjustment."

CLUTCH PEDAL ADJUSTMENT

1. If clutch pedal lash is insufficient, remove snap ring from cable and allow cable to move into dash by one cable notch, then reinstall snap ring, **Fig. 1.**
2. If clutch pedal lash is excessive, remove snap ring from cable, and pull cable out of dash by one cable notch, then reinstall snap ring, **Fig. 1.**
3. Check to ensure clutch pedal lash is .58-1.08 inch.

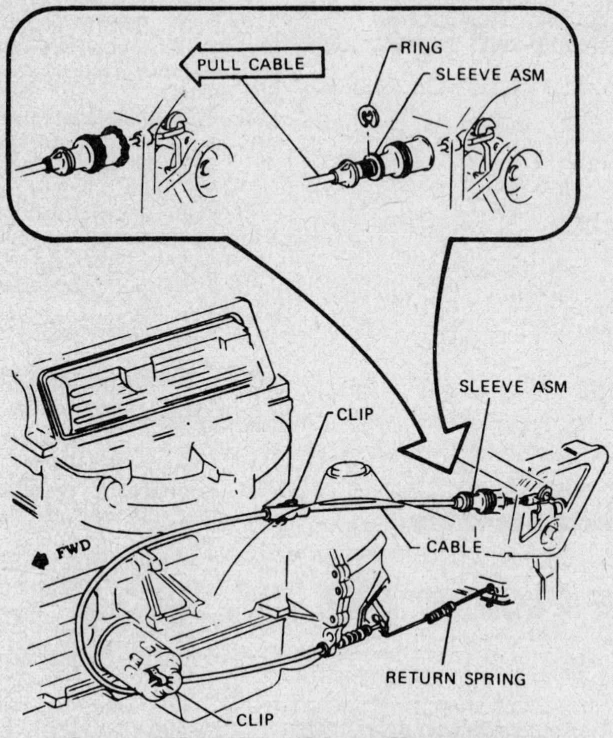

Fig. 1 Clutch cable adjustment

CLUTCH

REPLACE

1. Raise vehicle and remove transmission as outlined under "Transmission, Replace" procedure.
2. Remove release bearing from the clutch fork and sleeve by sliding lever off ball stud and against spring force. If ball stud is to be replaced, remove cap, locknut and stud from housing.
3. Make sure alignment marks on clutch assembly and flywheel are distinguishable.
4. Loosen clutch cover to flywheel bolts one turn at a time until spring pressure is released, to avoid bending the clutch cover flange.
5. Support the pressure plate and cover assembly while removing bolts and clutch assembly. **Do not disassemble the clutch cover, spring and pressure plate for repairs. If defective replace complete assembly.**
6. Reverse procedure to install making sure to index alignment marks. **Check position of engine in front mounts and realign as necessary.**

TRANSMISSION

REPLACE

1. Remove shifter assembly.
2. Raise vehicle and drain transmission lubricant.
3. Remove propeller shaft.
4. Disconnect speedometer cable, then the back-up lamp switch connector.
5. Disconnect return spring and clutch cable from clutch fork.
6. Remove transmission to crossmember bolts.
7. Remove exhaust manifold nuts and the catalytic converter to transmission bracket bolts.
8. Remove converter and converter hanger, if necessary.
9. Remove crossmember to frame bolts, then the crossmember from vehicle.
10. Remove dust cover.
11. Remove clutch housing to engine retaining bolts, slide transmission rearward and remove from vehicle.
12. Reverse procedure to install.

Rear Axle, Propeller Shaft & Brakes

INDEX

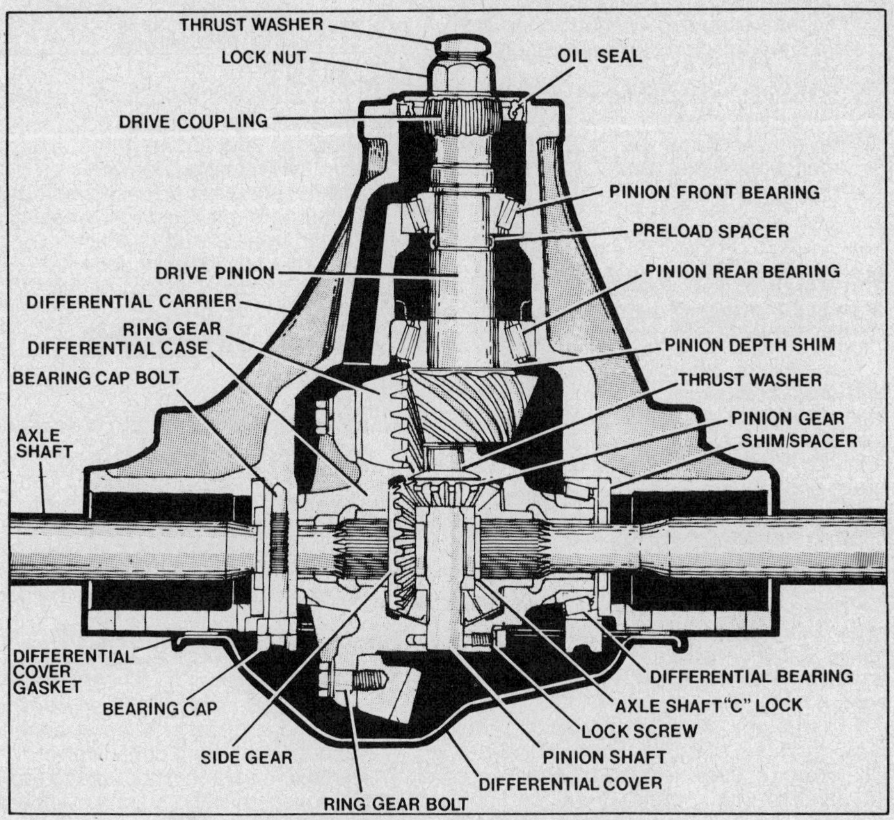

Fig. 1 Rear axle cross section

REAR AXLE

DESCRIPTION

The rear axle, **Fig. 1,** is a semi-floating type consisting of a cast carrier and large bosses on each end into which two welded steel tubes are fitted. The carrier contains an overhung hypoid pinion and ring gear. The differential is a two pinion arrangement.

The overhung hypoid drive pinion, is supported by two pre-loaded tapered roller bearings. The pinion shaft is sealed by means of a molded, spring loaded, rubber seal. The seal is mounted on the pinion shaft flange which is splined and bolts to the hypoid pinion shaft.

The ring gear is bolted to a one piece differential case and is supported by two pre-loaded tapered roller bearings.

A rear axle extension housing is bolted to the axle housing and is attached to the underbody by a center bearing support. An extension shaft inside the housing is splined to the drive pinion at the rear end and to the companion flange at the forward end.

REPLACEMENT

1. Raise vehicle on a hoist.
2. Place adjustable lifting device under axle.
3. Disconnect rear shock absorbers from axle and remove propeller shaft and extension housing, **Fig. 2.**
4. Remove both rear wheels.
5. Retract shoes and remove right and left brake drums.
6. Disconnect brake lines from clips on axle tubes.
7. Disconnect track and stabilizer bars from axle tube.
8. Remove differential cover and drain lubricant.
9. Unscrew differential lock screw, remove pinion shaft and axle shaft "C" locks. Reinstall pinion shaft and tighten lock screw to retain differential gears.
10. Remove both axle shafts.
11. Remove brake backing plate retaining nuts and remove backing plates, with shoes and brake lines attached, and wire to frame.
12. Remove right and left lower control arm pivot bolts at axle.
13. Lower axle assembly slowly until coil spring tension is released, then remove axle.
14. Reverse procedure to install.

AXLE SHAFT

REPLACE

1. Raise vehicle on a hoist and remove wheel and tire assembly and brake drum.
2. Drain lubricant from axle by removing carrier cover.
3. Unscrew pinion shaft lock screw and remove pinion shaft.
4. Push flanged end of axle shaft toward center of car and remove "C" lock from button end of shaft.
5. Remove axle shaft from housing being careful not to damage seal.

OIL SEAL AND/OR BEARING REPLACEMENT

1. If replacing seal only, remove the seal by using the button end of axle shaft. Insert the button end of shaft behind the steel case of the seal and pry seal out of bore being careful not to damage housing.
2. If replacing bearings, insert tool J-25593 into bore so tool head grasps behind bearing. Slide washer against seal, or bearing, and turn nut against washer. Attach slide hammer J-2619 and remove bearing.
3. Lubricate bearing with rear axle lubricant, then install bearing into housing bore with tool J-25594 and slide hammer J-8092. Make sure tool contacts end of axle housing to insure proper bearing depth.
4. Pack cavity between seal lips with a high melting point wheel bearing lubricant. Position seal on tool J-22922 and position seal in axle housing bore, tap seal in bore until flush with end of axle housing.

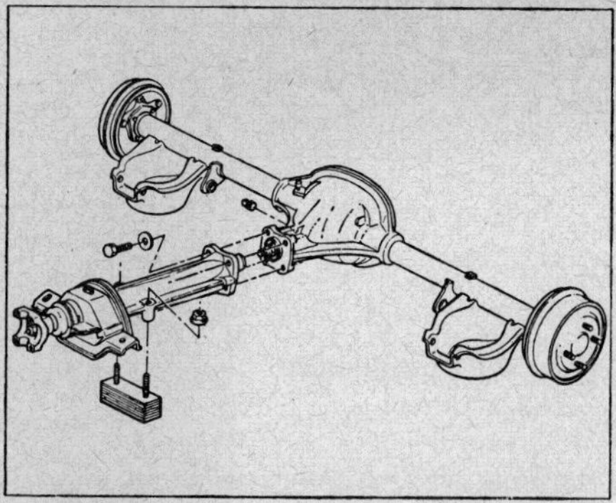

Fig. 2 Rear axle assembly

REAR AXLE EXTENSION

REPLACEMENT

1. Raise vehicle and support rear axle.
2. Disconnect propeller shaft from the rear yoke and remove from transmission, **Fig. 2.**
3. Support front end of rear axle carrier housing. Ensure the rear axle extension is also supported.
4. Disconnect center support bracket from underbody and the extension housing flange from axle housing.
5. Remove axle extension housing from vehicle. Pry extension housing from axle housing with a suitable screwdriver, if necessary.
6. Reverse procedure to install.

SERVICE

1. Remove bolts securing extension housing to center support bracket.
2. Mount companion flange in a vise and loosen locknut.
3. Drive splined companion flange off shaft by tapping on locknut end of shaft.
4. Remove locknut, companion flange and thrust washer, then pull shaft from housing. If centering bearing, located in the rubber cushion, remains on extension shaft, drive off shaft with a suitable drift.
5. Note position of bearing in rubber cushion and the cushion in center support. Then, using a suitable screwdriver, separate rubber cushion from center support bracket and remove bearing from cushion.
6. Clean, inspect and replace components, if necessary.
7. Install rubber cushion into center support bracket and place center support assembly over extension housing.
8. Press bearing onto extension shaft and insert shaft into housing through rubber cushion. Install thrust washer with circular cavity facing toward bearing, then the companion flange, using the locknut to press flange onto shaft splines.
9. Install bolts retaining bracket to housing.

PROPELLER SHAFT

REPLACE

1. Raise vehicle on a hoist. Mark relationship of shaft to companion flange and disconnect the rear universal joint by removing trunnion bearing U-bolts. Tape bearing cups to trunnion to prevent dropping and loss of bearing rollers.
2. Withdraw propeller shaft front yoke from transmission.
3. When installing, be sure to align marks made in removal to prevent driveline vibration.

SERVICE BRAKE ADJUSTMENTS

Disc brakes are used on front wheels and drum brakes are use on rear wheels. Rear brake adjustment is automatic. Adjustment takes place whenever brakes are applied. An adjuster is attached to each brake shoe by means of a pin, **Fig. 3.** This pin is smaller than the slot in the brake shoe. When brakes are applied and brake shoes move outward, the automatic adjuster follows. When brakes are released the brake shoe moves inward until it contacts the automatic adjuster pin. The space between adjuster pin and slot in brake shoe provides shoe to drum clearance.

If rear shoes have been replaced, perform initial brake adjustment as follows:

1. Using a suitable punch, knock out lanced area in brake drum. On vehicles where no lanced area is provided, it will be necessary to drill hole in backing plate to gain access to adjusting screw.
2. Turn adjusting screw and expand brake shoes against drum using suitable tool. Adjust screw until each wheel can just be turned by hand. Drag should be equal at both wheels.
3. Back off adjusting screw until no drag is felt at drum, then continue to back off screw an additional four notches.
4. Install rubber cover onto brake drum or backing plate, then check parking brake adjustment.

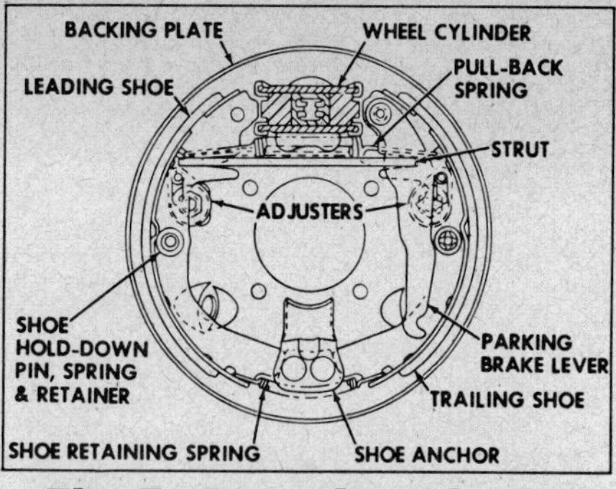

Fig. 3 Rear drum brake

PARKING BRAKE

ADJUST

1. Raise vehicle.
2. Apply parking brake three notches from fully released position.
3. Tighten equalizer adjusting nut until a light drag is felt when rear wheels are rotated in a forward direction.
4. Release parking brake and rotate rear wheels. No drag should be felt.

MASTER CYLINDER

REPLACE

1. Disconnect pushrod from brake pedal and remove pushrod boot.
2. Remove air cleaner.
3. Disconnect brake lines from master cylinder. Cap ends of lines to prevent entry of dirt.
4. Remove master cylinder to dash attaching nuts and the master cylinder.

POWER BRAKE UNIT

REPLACE

1. Remove air cleaner, then disconnect vacuum hose from check valve.
2. Remove master cylinder brace rod.
3. Remove remaining master cylinder to brake unit attaching nuts, then pull master forward until it clears brake unit mounting studs. Carefully move master cylinder aside with brake lines attached. **Support master cylinder to avoid stress on brake lines. Move master cylinder only enough to provide clearance for brake unit removal.**
4. Remove nuts attaching brake unit to dash panel.
5. Remove pushrod to pedal retainer and slide pushrod off pedal pin.
6. Remove power brake unit from vehicle.

Rear Suspension Section

INDEX

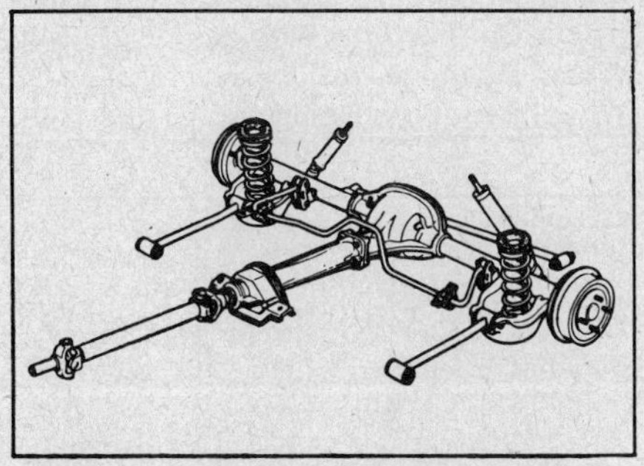

Fig. 1 Rear suspension

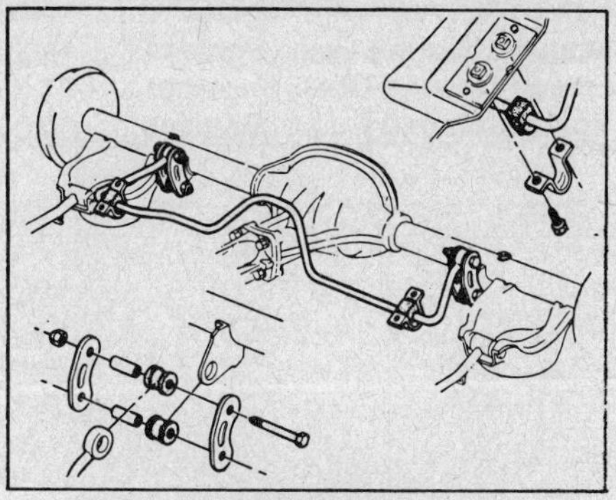

Fig. 2 Stabilizer bar installation

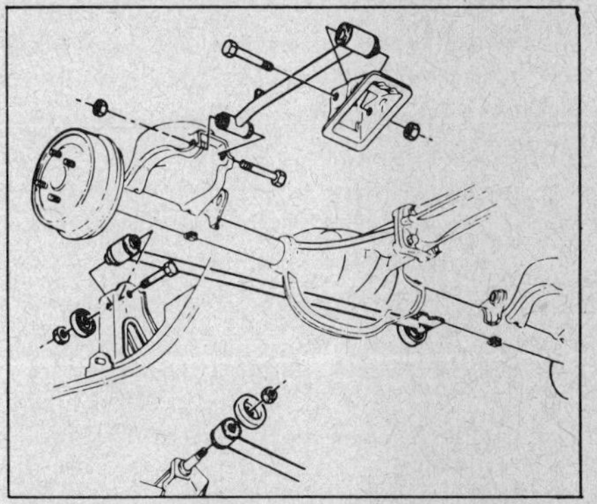

Fig. 3 Track rod and lower control arm

DESCRIPTION

This suspension system, **Fig. 1**, incorporates two tubular lower control arms, a straight track rod, two shock absorbers, two coil springs and a stabilizer bar.

SHOCK ABSORBER
REPLACE

1. Raise vehicle and support rear axle with a suitable jack.
2. Disconnect shock absorber from upper and lower mounting.
3. Reverse procedure to install.

COIL SPRING
REPLACE

1. Raise vehicle and support rear axle with a suitable jack.
2. Disconnect both shock absorbers from lower brackets.
3. Disconnect rear axle extension bracket. **Ensure axle is properly supported before disconnecting extension bracket.**
4. Slowly lower axle until springs and insulators can be removed. **When lowering axle ensure that brake hoses do not stretch or become damaged.**
5. Reverse procedure to install.

TRACK ROD
REPLACE

1. Raise vehicle and support rear axle with a suitable jack.
2. Disconnect stabilizer bar, if equipped, **Fig. 2.**
3. Remove control arm front and rear attaching bolts and control arm, **Fig. 3.**
4. Remove attaching bolts and track rod.
5. Reverse procedure to install. **Vehicle must be at curb height when tightening pivot bolts.**

LOWER CONTROL ARMS
REPLACE

1. Raise vehicle and support rear axle.
2. Disconnect stabilizer bar, if equipped, **Fig. 2.**
3. Disconnect the front and rear control arm attaching bolts and remove control arm from vehicle, **Fig. 3. Replace one control arm at a time to prevent axle from rolling or slipping sideways.**
4. Reverse procedure to install.

STABILIZER BAR
REPLACE

1. Raise vehicle and support rear axle.
2. Disconnect stabilizer bar from underbody and axle tube connections, **Fig. 2,** then remove stabilizer bar from vehicle.
3. Reverse procedure to install.

Front Suspension & Steering Section

INDEX

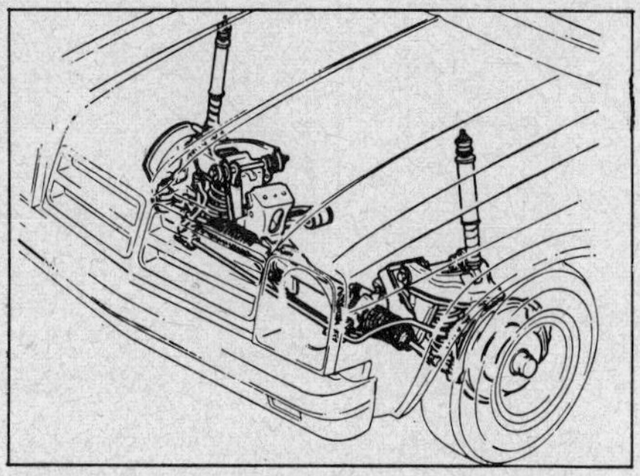

Fig. 1 Front suspension

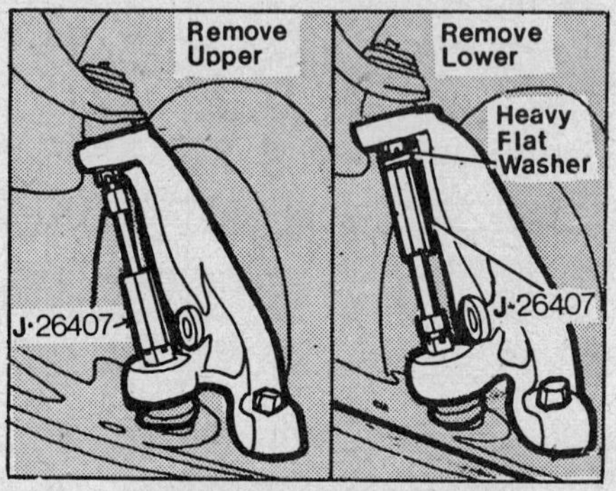

Fig. 2 Separating ball joint studs from steering knuckle

DESCRIPTION

The front suspension system, **Fig. 1**, uses long and short control arms with coil springs mounted between the lower control arms and front suspension crossmember.

WHEEL BEARINGS
ADJUST

1. While rotating wheel in the forward direction, torque spindle nut to 12 ft. lbs.
2. Back spindle nut off to the just loose position.
3. Hand tighten spindle nut, then loosen until cotter holes are aligned and install cotter pin. **Do not loosen nut more than 1/2 flat to align cotter pin holes.**
4. With bearings properly adjusted, endplay must be .001-.005 inch.

WHEEL BEARINGS
REPLACE

1. Raise vehicle, remove wheel and tire assembly.
2. Remove two caliper mounting bracket to steering knuckle attaching bolts, then the caliper.
3. Remove hub dust cap, cotter pin, spindle nut, washer, outer wheel bearing and hub.
4. Pry out grease seal, then remove inner bearing from hub.

SHOCK ABSORBER
REPLACE

1. Hold upper stem of shock absorber, and remove nut, retainer and grommet.
2. Raise vehicle and remove lower shock absorber retaining bolts.
3. Lower shock absorber from vehicle.
4. Reverse procedure to install. Torque shock absorber lower retaining bolts to 35-50 ft. lbs. on 1982-84 models or 29 ft. lbs. on 1985-87 models; and the upper retaining nut to 60-120 in. lbs. on 1982-84 models or 13 ft. lbs. on 1985-87 models.

BALL JOINTS
REPLACE

UPPER BALL JOINT

1. Raise vehicle and remove wheel and tire assembly.
2. Support lower control arm using a suitable jack.
3. Loosen upper ball joint stud nut, however, do not remove nut.
4. Position tool J-26407 or equivalent with cupped end over lower ball joint stud and turn threaded end of tool until upper ball joint stud is free of steering knuckle, **Fig. 2.**
5. Remove tool, then the upper stud nut. **Discard the stud nut. The stud nut is of special design and must be replaced whenever removed or loosened.**
6. Remove two nuts securing ball joint to upper control arm and the ball joint. **Inspect tapered hole in steering knuckle. If out of round or damaged, the knuckle must be replaced.**
7. Install ball joint on upper control arm and torque bolts to 29 ft. lbs.
8. Position upper ball joint stud on steering knuckle, then install a standard nut to draw ball joint into position on knuckle. Torque standard nut to 35 ft. lbs., then remove standard nut. Install special nut for final assembly and torque to 36 ft. lbs.
9. Install wheel and tire assembly and lower vehicle.

LOWER BALL JOINT

1. Raise vehicle and remove wheel and tire assembly.
2. Support lower control arm using a suitable jack.
3. Loosen lower ball joint stud nut, however, do not remove nut.
4. Position tool J-26407 or equivalent with cupped end of tool over upper ball joint stud and turn threaded end of tool until lower ball joint stud is free of steering knuckle, **Fig. 2.**
5. Remove tool, then the lower ball joint stud nut. **Discard the stud nut. The stud nut is of special design and must be replaced whenever removed or loosened.**
6. Remove ball joint from lower control arm. **Inspect tapered hole in steering knuckle. If out of round or dam-**

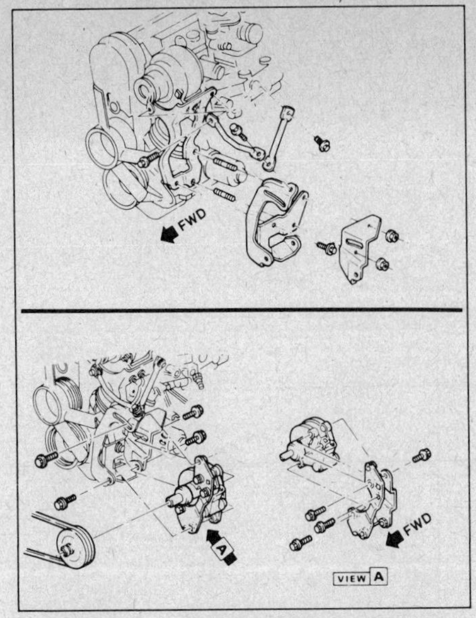

Fig. 3 Power steering pump installation (Typical)

aged, the knuckle must be replaced.

7. Insert ball joint through lower control arm and into steering knuckle.
8. Install a standard nut to draw ball joint into position on knuckle. Torque standard nut to 35 ft. lbs., then remove standard nut. Install special nut for final assembly and torque to 41-54 ft. lbs.
9. Install wheel and tire assembly and lower vehicle.

COIL SPRING
REPLACE

1. Support vehicle by frame, remove wheel and tire assembly.
2. Disconnect stabilizer bar from lower control arm and tie rod from steering knuckle.
3. Support lower control arm using a suitable jack.
4. Loosen lower ball joint stud nut, then use tool J-26407 or equivalent to free stud from steering knuckle. Position knuckle and hub out of way and remove stud nut. **Discard stud nut. The stud nut is of special design and must be replaced whenever removed or loosened.**
5. Loosen lower control arm pivot bolts.
6. Install a safety chain around spring and through lower control arm.
7. Slowly lower control arm until spring is extended as far as possible, then use pry bar to carefully lift spring over lower control arm spring seat.

LOWER CONTROL ARM
REPLACE

1. Remove coil spring as described in "Coil Spring, Replace."
2. Remove control arm pivot bolts, then the control arm.
3. Reverse procedure to install. Torque lower control arm pivot bolts to 49 ft. lbs.

UPPER CONTROL ARM
REPLACE

1. Support vehicle by frame, remove tire and wheel assembly.
2. Position jack to support lower control arm.
3. Disconnect upper ball joint as described in "Ball Joints, Replace."
4. Remove upper control arm pivot bolts, then remove control arm from vehicle.
5. Reverse procedure to install. Torque upper control arm pivot bolts to 47 ft. lbs.

MANUAL STEERING GEAR
REPLACE

1. Raise vehicle and remove bolts and shield.
2. Remove tie rod cotter pins and nuts from tie rod ends and separate tie rods from steering knuckles.
3. Remove flexible coupling pinch bolt.
4. Remove steering gear clamp bolts, then the steering gear assembly from vehicle.
5. Reverse procedure to install. Torque steering knuckle to tie rod nut to 30 ft. lbs., flex coupling pinch bolt to 30 ft. lbs. and steering gear clamp bolt to 14 ft. lbs.

POWER STEERING GEAR
REPLACE

The procedure for power steering gear replacement is identical to manual type gears. In addition, it is necessary to disconnect and connect the two hydraulic lines at the steering gear.

POWER STEERING PUMP
REPLACE

1. Remove pump adjusting bolt.
2. Remove lower brace to pump bracket attaching bolt, **Fig. 3.**
3. Remove crossmember to frame support brace, then disconnect hydraulic lines at pump.
4. Remove rear pump adjusting bracket, then the front pivot bolt.
5. Remove front pump bracket to engine attaching bolt, then the pump and bracket.
6. Reverse procedure to install.

Wheel Alignment Section

INDEX

FRONT WHEEL ALIGNMENT

CASTER

Caster angle is adjusted by rearranging washers located at both ends of the upper control arm, **Fig. 1.** A kit consisting of two washers, one of 3 mm thickness and one of 9 mm thickness, must be used when adjusting caster angle.

CAMBER

Camber is adjusted by removing the upper ball joint, rotating it 1/2 turn and reinstalling it with flat of upper flange on inboard side of control arm, **Fig. 2.** This will increase positive camber by approximately 1°.

TOE-IN

To adjust toe-in, loosen tie rod jam nuts at tie rod ends and loosen clamp at rubber bellows. Turn each tie rod to increase or decrease its length until proper toe-in is obtained. Torque jam nut to 50 ft. lbs.

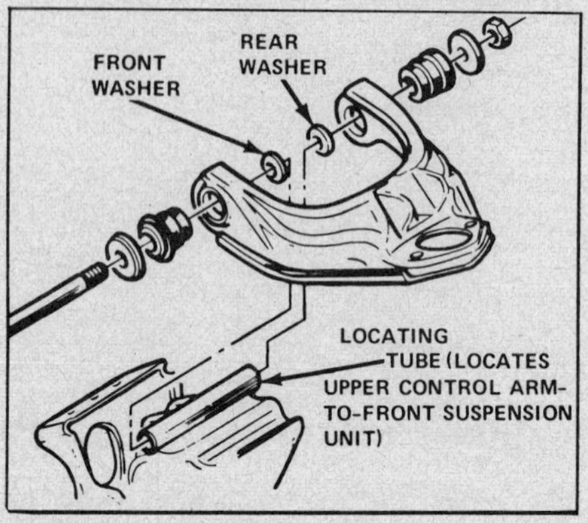

REAR WASHER
FRONT WASHER
LOCATING TUBE (LOCATES UPPER CONTROL ARM-TO-FRONT SUSPENSION UNIT)

Fig. 1 Caster adjustment

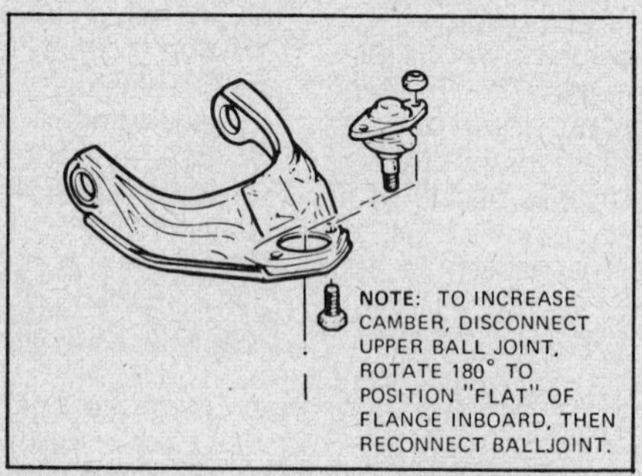

NOTE: TO INCREASE CAMBER, DISCONNECT UPPER BALL JOINT, ROTATE 180° TO POSITION "FLAT" OF FLANGE INBOARD, THEN RECONNECT BALLJOINT.

Fig. 2 Camber adjustment

CHEVROLET NOVA

INDEX OF SERVICE OPERATIONS

NOTE: Refer to rear of this manual for vehicle manufacturer's special service tool suppliers.

Specifications

GENERAL ENGINE SPECIFICATIONS

Year	Engine CID①/Liter	Engine VIN Code②	Fuel System	Bore & Stroke	Compression Ratio	Net H.P. @ RPM③	Maximum Torque Ft. Lbs. @ RPM	Normal Oil Pressure Pounds
1985	4-97/1.6L	4	2 Bbl.④	3.19 x 3.08	9.0	70 @ 4800	85 @ 2800	34
1986	4-97/1.6L	4	2 Bbl.④	3.19 x 3.08	9.0	74 @ 5200	86 @ 2800	34
1987	4-97/1.6L	4	2 Bbl.④	3.19 x 3.08	9.0	74 @ 5200	86 @ 2800	34
1988	4-97/1.6L	—	Fuel Injection	3.19 x 3.08	9.4	⑤	97 @ 4800	⑥

①—CID-Cubic inch displacement.
②—The eighth digit of the VIN denotes engine code.
③—Ratings are net-as installed in vehicle.
④—Aisan carburetor.
⑤—Exc. 16 valve engine, 112 @ 6600; 16 valve engine, 108 @ 6600.
⑥—Exc. 16 valve engine, 34; 16 valve engine, 57.

ENGINE TIGHTENING SPECIFICATIONS*

*Torque specifications are for clean and lightly lubricated threads only. Dry or dirty threads produce increased friction which prevents accurate measurement of tightness.

Year	Engine/VIN	Spark Plugs Ft. Lbs.	Cylinder Head Bolts Ft. Lbs.	Intake Manifold Ft. Lbs.	Exhaust Manifold Ft. Lbs.	Rocker Arm Support Bolts Ft. Lbs.	Rocker Arm Cover Ft. Lbs.	Connecting Rod Cap Bolts Ft. Lbs.	Main Bearing Cap Bolts Ft. Lbs.	Flywheel to Crankshaft Ft. Lbs.	Vibration Damper or Pulley Ft. Lbs.
1985-87	4-97/4	13	43①	18	18	18	—	②	43	58	87
1988	4-97/	13	43①	16	—	—	—	36	44	54	105

①—See text for procedure.
②—1985, 29 ft. lbs.; 1986–87, 36 ft. lbs.

ALTERNATOR SPECIFICATIONS

Year	Model	Rated Hot Output Amps.	Field Current 12 Volts @ 80°F
1985-88	—	60	—

STARTING MOTOR APPLICATIONS

Year	Engine/VIN	Starter Number
1985-88	4-97/4	—

WHEEL ALIGNMENT SPECIFICATIONS

Year	Location	Caster Angle, Degrees		Camber Angle, Degrees				Toe-In Inch
				Limits		Desired		
		Limits	Desired	Left	Right	Left	Right	
1985-87	Front	+2/15° to +1 19/30°	+53/60 °	+3/4° to +1/4°	−3/4° to +1/4°	−1/2°	−1/2°	0
	Rear	—	—	−1 8/30° +7/30°	−1 8/30 to +7/30°	−31/60°	−31/60°	.07
1988	Front	+2/15° to +1 19/32°	+53/60°	−3/4° to +3/3° −1/4°	−1/4°	1		
	Rear	—	—	−1 8/30° to +7/30°	−8/30° to +7/30°	−31/60°	−31/60°	.15

COOLING SYSTEM & CAPACITY DATA

Year	Model or Engine/VIN	Cooling Capacity, Qts.		Radiator Cap Relief Pressure, Lbs.	Thermo. Opening Temp.	Fuel Tank Gals.	Engine Oil Refill Qts.	Transaxle Oil	
		Less A/C	With A/C					Manual Transaxle Pts.	Auto. Transaxle Qts. ①
1985-87	4-97 (1.6L)/4	6.3	6.3	10.7-14.9	180	13.2	3.2②	5.4	5.8
1988	4-97 (1.6L)	6.3	6.3	12.8	180	13.2②	③	5.4	④

①—Approximate make final check with dipstick.
②—With filter change add .3 qt.
③—Exc. 16 valve engine, 3.17; 16 valve engine, 3.6 less filter, 3.9 with filter.
④—A131L models, 5.8; A240E models, 8.3.

Electrical Section

INDEX

IGNITION LOCK
REPLACE

1. Remove steering wheel assembly.
2. Remove instrument lower finish panel, air duct and column lower cover.
3. Disconnect ignition and turn signal switch electrical connector.
4. Remove switch assembly from column upper cover.
5. Remove three screws and retainer from upper bracket.
6. Remove snap ring, insert key into ignition and release steering lock.
7. Tap out tapered head bolt.
8. Remove lock cylinder and retaining screw.
9. Reverse procedure to install.

STARTER
REPLACE

1. Disconnect battery ground cable.
2. Disconnect electrical connectors from starter motor.
3. Remove transmission cable and bracket at transmission.
4. Remove starter motor attaching bolts.
5. Remove starter motor.
6. Reverse procedure to install.

COMBINATION SWITCH
REPLACE

1. Disconnect battery ground cable.
2. Remove steering wheel cover and steering wheel.
3. Remove instrument lower finish panel, air duct and column lower cover.
4. Disconnect electrical connector from ignition/turn signal switch.
5. Remove combination switch assembly with steering column upper cover.
6. Reverse procedure to install.

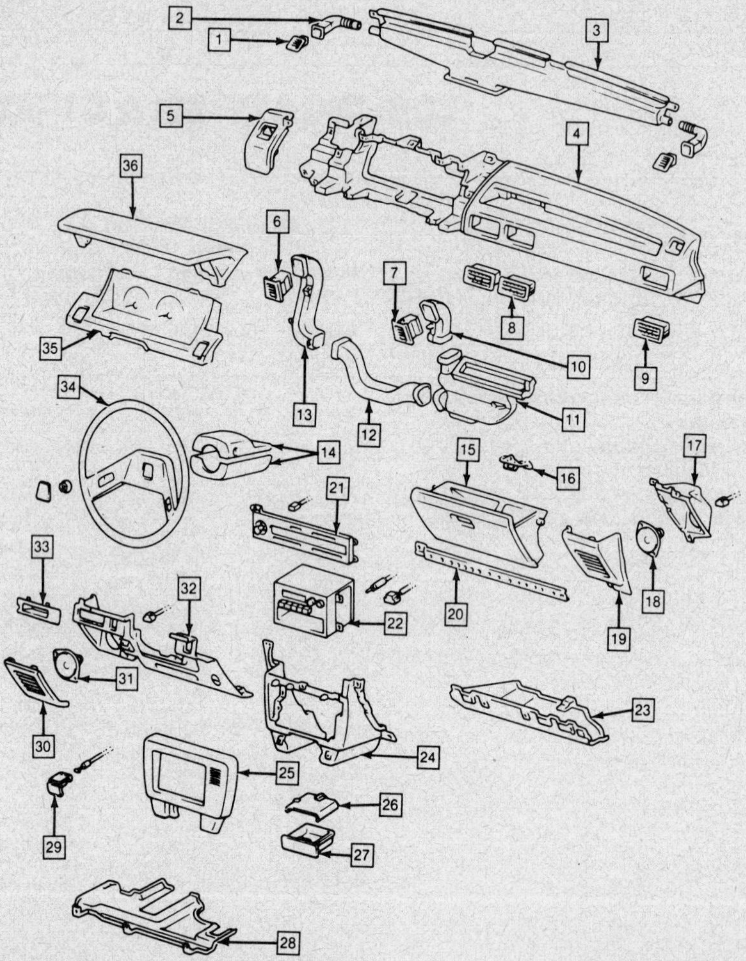

1. SIDE DEFROSTER NOZZLE
2. SIDE DEFROSTER DUCT
3. DEFROSTER NOZZLE
4. SAFETY PAD
5. END FINISH PANEL
6. NO. 1 REGISTER
7. NO. 2 REGISTER
8. CENTER REGISTER
9. SIDE REGISTER
10. NO. 3 HEATER DUCT
11. DUCT
12. NO. 2 HEATER DUCT
13. NO. 1 HEATER DUCT
14. COLUMN HOUSING
15. GLOVE COMPARTMENT DOOR
16. DOOR LOCK STRIKER
17. SPEAKER BRACKET
18. SPEAKER
19. NO. 2 SPEAKER PANEL
20. HINGE
21. HEATER CONTROL PANEL
22. RADIO
23. NO. 2 PANEL UNDER COVER
24. LOWER CENTER CLUSTER FINISH PANEL
25. CENTER CLUSTER FINISH PANEL
26. RETAINER
27. ASH RECEPTACLE
28. NO. 1 PANEL UNDER COVER
29. ENGINE HOOD RELEASE LEVER
30. NO. 1 SPEAKER PANEL
31. SPEAKER
32. LOWER FINISH PANEL
33. FINISH PANEL
34. STEERING WHEEL
35. COMBINATION METER
36. METER HOOD

Fig. 1 Instrument panel & related components

RADIO
REPLACE

Refer to "Instrument Panel Pad/Cluster, Replace" for radio removal procedure.

BLOWER ASSEMBLY
REPLACE

1. Disconnect battery ground cable.
2. Remove evaporator assembly, if equipped.
3. Disconnect electrical connector from blower motor.
4. Disconnect air source selector control cable from blower assembly side.
5. Loosen nuts and bolts, then remove blower assembly.
6. Reverse procedure to install.

INSTRUMENT PANEL PAD/CLUSTER
REPLACE

1. Disconnect battery ground cable.

2. Remove steering wheel assembly.
3. Remove left speaker grille.
4. Remove steering column lower trim cover.
5. Remove hood release lever.
6. Remove heater duct.
7. Remove meter hood, A/C registers and hood, **Fig. 1.**
8. Remove combination meter, disconnect speedometer cable and electrical connectors. Remove meter from instrument panel.
9. Remove end finish panel.
10. Remove panel under cover.
11. Remove right side speaker grille.
12. Remove speaker bracket and speaker.
13. Remove glove compartment door and hinge.
14. Remove glove compartment door lock striker.
15. Remove center cluster finish panel.
16. Remove radio equipment assembly.
17. Remove lower center cluster finish panel.
18. Disconnect vacuum lines and electrical connectors, then remove heater control panel.
19. Remove side defroster nozzle.
20. Remove instrument panel pad assembly.
21. Reverse procedure to install.

4-97 (1.6L) Engine Section

INDEX

ENGINE MOUNT REPLACE

1. Disconnect battery ground cable.
2. Raise and support vehicle.
3. Loosen center engine mount.
4. Lower vehicle.
5. Support engine assembly.
6. Disconnect engine mount at engine assembly.
7. Raise engine assembly.
8. Remove engine mount.
9. Reverse procedure to install.

ENGINE REPLACE

EXC. 16 VALVE ENGINE

1. Disconnect battery ground cable.
2. Drain coolant and engine oil.
3. Drain transmission fluid.
4. Mark hood hinges, then remove hood.
5. Remove air cleaner assembly.
6. Disconnect upper radiator hose at outlet and overflow hose.
7. Disconnect coolant hose at cylinder head rear coolant pipe.
8. Disconnect coolant hose at thermostat housing.
9. Disconnect fuel lines from fuel pump.
10. Mark, then disconnect all vacuum lines and electrical connectors from engine assembly.
11. Remove drive belts.
12. Disconnect speedometer cable from transaxle assembly.
13. Raise and support vehicle.
14. Disconnect exhaust pipe from exhaust manifold.
15. Disconnect air hose from converter pipe, if applicable.
16. Disconnect transaxle cooler lines from radiator.
17. Remove left and righthand under covers.
18. Remove power steering pump and A/C compressor, if equipped and position aside.
19. Disconnect cable and bracket from transaxle.
20. Disconnect steering knuckles from lower control arms.
21. Disconnect driveshafts from transaxle.
22. Remove flywheel cover.
23. Remove flex plate to torque converter attaching bolts.
24. Disconnect front and rear mounting from center crossmember.
25. Disconnect cable and remove center member.
26. Lower vehicle.
27. Remove radiator and fan assembly.
28. Install suitable engine lifting equipment onto engine lifting eyes.
29. Remove righthand motor mount through bolt.
30. Remove lefthand transaxle mount bolt and mount.
31. Remove engine and transaxle as an assembly.
32. Reverse procedure to install.

16 VALVE ENGINE

1. Disconnect battery ground and positive cables, then remove battery and engine compartment hood.
2. Remove right and left side engine under covers.
3. Drain engine oil into suitable container.
4. Drain coolant from radiator and engine block into suitable container.
5. On models equipped with man. trans., drain transaxle fluid into suitable container.
6. Remove air cleaner assembly and coolant reservoir tank.
7. Remove radiator and coolant fan as an assembly.
8. Disconnect heater hoses from coolant inlet housing.
9. Disconnect fuel pressure hose from fuel filter, then the heater and air hoses from air valve.
10. Disconnect fuel return hose from fuel pressure regulator.
11. On models equipped with man. trans., remove clutch slave cylinder without disconnecting hydraulic line and position aside.

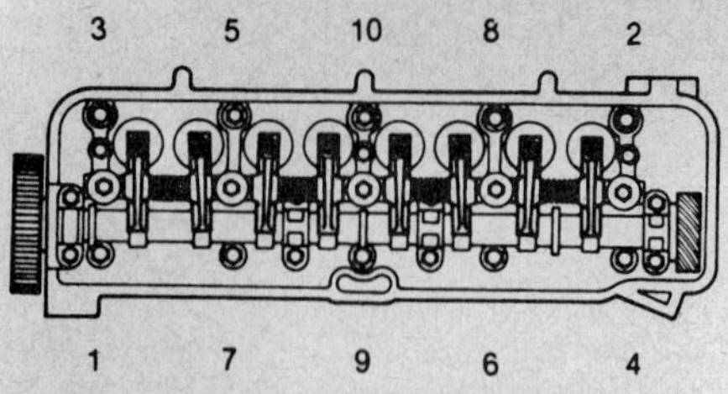

Fig. 1 Cylinder head bolt loosening sequence. Exc. 16 valve engine

12. On all models, disconnect vacuum hose from charcoal canister.
13. Disconnect transaxle shift control cables from transaxle.
14. Disconnect speedometer cable, then the cruise control cable (if equipped), accelerator cable and accelerator link.
15. On models equipped with cruise control, remove cruise control actuator.
16. On all models, disconnect ignition coil wiring, then remove coil.
17. Remove righthand side interior cowl panel, then disconnect No. 4 junction block connectors.
18. Remove Electronic Control Unit (ECU) cover, then disconnect ECU connectors.
19. Pull engine main wire harness into engine compartment, then disconnect the following:
    a. No. 2 junction block connectors (located in engine compartment).
    b. Starter cable from battery positive.
    c. Ground strap terminals.
    d. Washer change valve connector.
    e. Cruise control vacuum pump and vacuum switch connectors (if equipped).
    f. Solenoid resistor connector.
20. Disconnect brake booster hose from intake manifold.
21. Remove A/C compressor and power steering pump (if equipped) with lines attached and position aside.
22. Disconnect oxygen sensor electrical connector, then remove oxygen sensor.
23. Disconnect oil cooler hoses from oil cooler.
24. Raise and support vehicle, then disconnect catalytic converter clamp, engine pipe clamp and engine pipe from exhaust manifold.
25. Disconnect front and rear engine mounts-to-center member attaching bolts, then remove front mount through bolt and mount.
26. Remove center member-to-frame attaching bolts, then the center member.
27. Remove axle-to-side gear shaft attaching bolts, then disconnect right side lower arm from steering knuckle and separate. Remove axle shafts from side gear shafts and position aside with suitable wire.
28. Lower vehicle to ground level.
29. Attach suitable lifting equipment to engine/transaxle assembly, then remove right and left side mounts.
30. Carefully lift engine/transaxle assembly from vehicle and place on suitable stand.

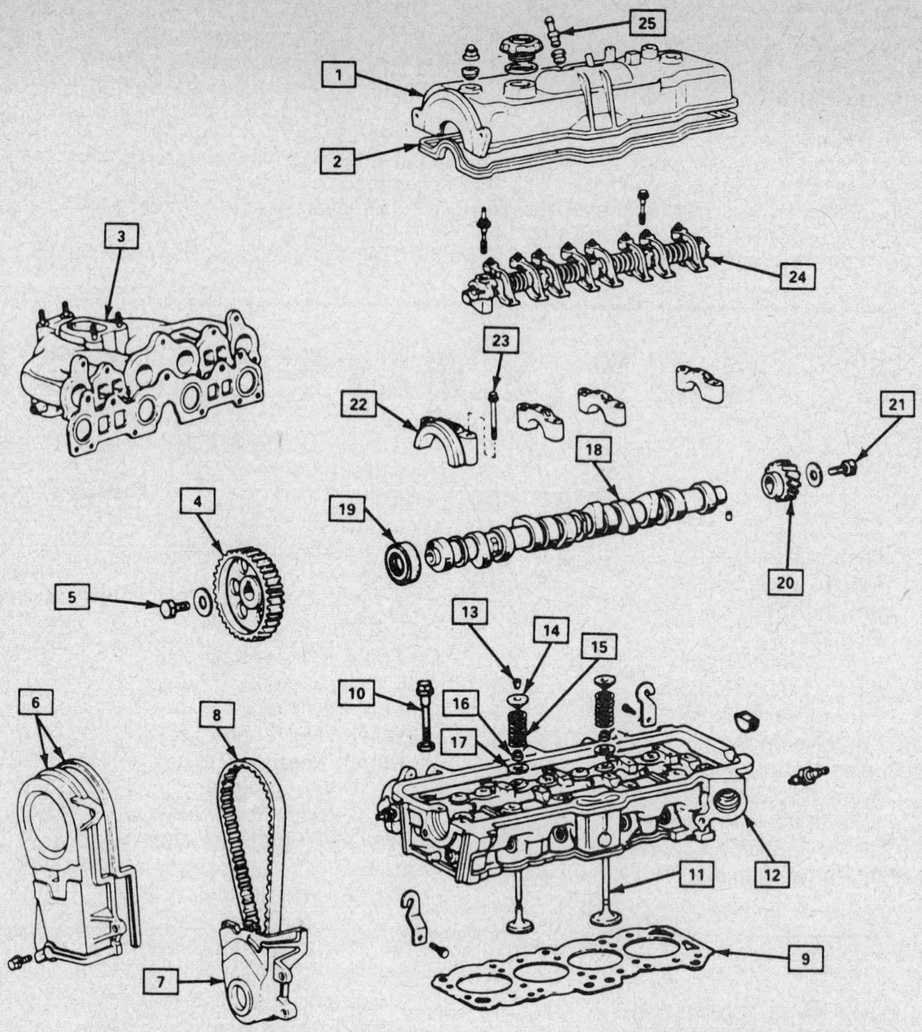

1. CYLINDER HEAD COVER
2. CYLINDER HEAD COVER GASKET
3. EXHAUST MANIFOLD
4. CAMSHAFT TIMING PULLEY
5. 47 N·m (34 FT.LBS)
6. TIMING BELT UPPER COVER AND GASKET
7. TIMING BELT LOWER COVER
8. TIMING BELT
9. HEAD GASKET
10. 59 N·m (43 FT.LBS)
11. VALVE
12. CYLINDER HEAD
13. VALVE KEEPER
14. VALVE SPRING RETAINER
15. VALVE SPRING
16. VALVE STEM OIL SEAL
17. VALVE SPRING SEAT
18. CAMSHAFT
19. CAMSHAFT OIL SEAL
20. DRIVE GEAR
21. 29 N·m (22 FT.LBS)
22. CAMSHAFT BEARING CAP
23. 13 N·m (9 FT.LBS)
24. ROCKER ARM ASSEMBLY
25. PCV VALVE

Cylinder head & related components. Exc. 16 valve engine

31. Remove radiator fan temperature switch connector and cold start injector time switch connector.
32. Disconnect vacuum hoses from Bi-Metal Vacuum Switching Valves (BVSV), then remove coolant inlet housing attaching bolts and nut.
33. Disconnect hoses from coolant by-pass tubes, then remove coolant inlet housing.
34. Disconnect back-up lamp switch connector, water temperature sensor connector and water temperature switch connector.
35. On models equipped with auto. trans., neutral start switch connectors and transaxle solenoid connector.
36. On models equipped with auto. trans., rotate crankshaft as necessary to gain access to and remove six torque converter attaching bolts.
37. Remove starter assembly, then separate transaxle from engine.
38. Reverse procedure to install.

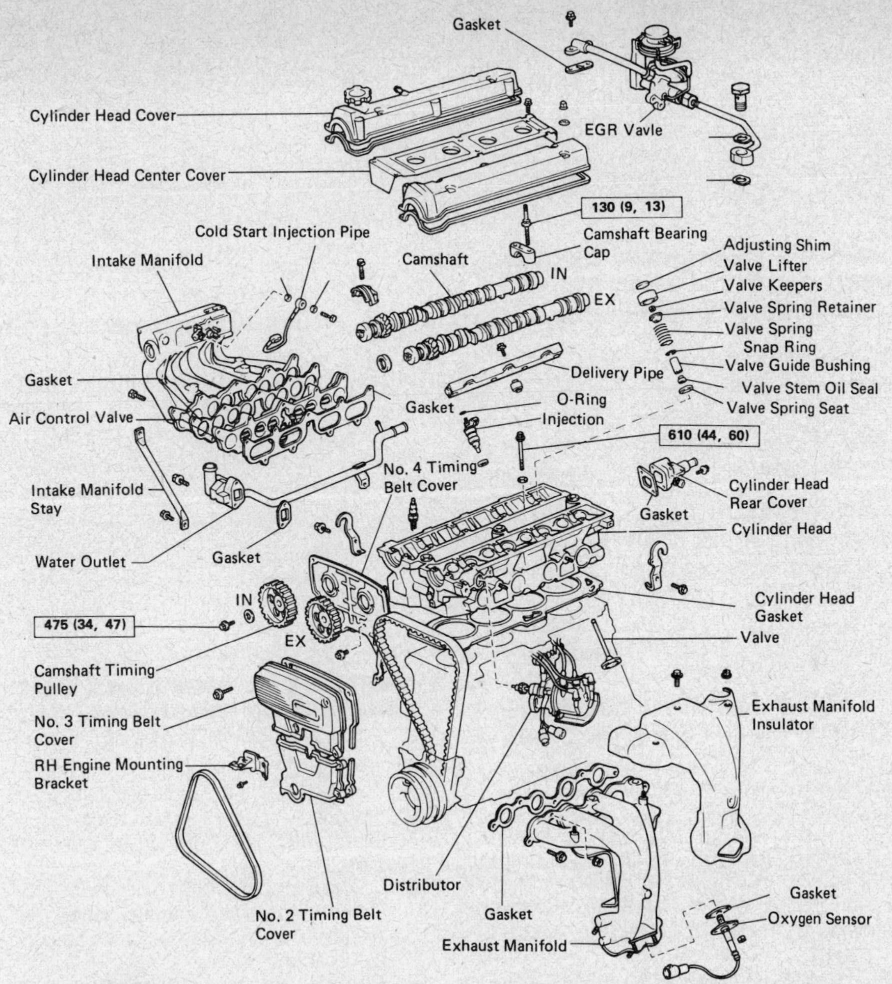

Cylinder head & related components. 16 valve engine

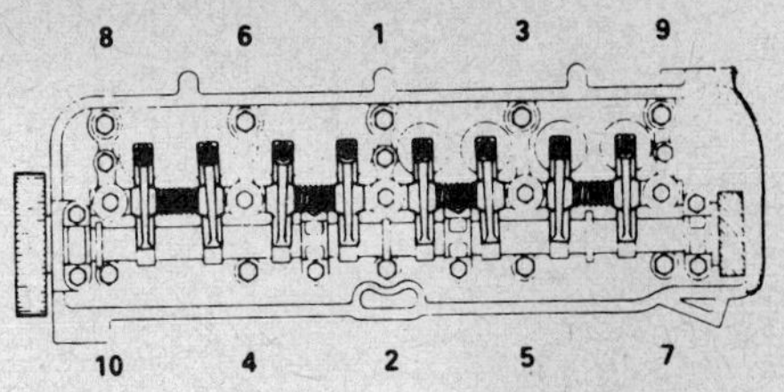

Fig. 2 Cylinder head bolt tightening sequence. Exc. 16 valve engine

CYLINDER HEAD REPLACE

EXC. 16 VALVE ENGINE

1. Disconnect battery ground cable.
2. Drain cooling system.
3. Remove air cleaner assembly.
4. Raise and support vehicle.
5. Drain engine oil.
6. Disconnect exhaust pipe from exhaust manifold and exhaust bracket from engine.
7. Disconnect air hose from converter pipe.
8. Loosen power steering pivot bolt, if equipped.
9. Lower vehicle.
10. Disconnect accelerator and throttle cable from carburetor and bracket.
11. Mark, then disconnect all vacuum lines and electrical connectors from cylinder head assembly.
12. Disconnect fuel lines from fuel pump.
13. Disconnect upper radiator hose, water outlet and heater hose.
14. Remove power steering bracket, if equipped.
15. Place No. 1 cylinder at TDC of compression stroke, then disconnect spark plug wires and remove distributor assembly.
16. Remove PCV valve and wiring harness.
17. Remove No. 1 (upper) timing belt cover bolts.
18. Remove cylinder head cover and gasket.
19. Remove alternator drive belt and water pump pulley bolts.
20. Remove No. 1 (upper) timing cover and gasket.
21. Mark camshaft timing pulley position and timing belt rotational direction.
22. Loosen idler pulley and move aside slightly to release timing belt tension, then snug down pulley bolt.
23. Pull timing belt away from camshaft timing pulley.
24. Loosen and remove cylinder head bolts gradually in three steps and in sequence shown in **Fig. 1.**
25. Remove cylinder head with intake and exhaust manifolds attached.
26. Reverse procedure to install, noting the following:
    a. Install cylinder head, then gradually tighten cylinder head bolts in three steps and in sequence shown in **Fig. 2,** to 43 ft. lbs.
    b. Install camshaft timing pulley and timing belt in original (marked) position as removed.

16 VALVE ENGINE

1. Disconnect battery ground cable.
2. Remove engine under cover, then drain coolant into suitable container.
3. Remove air cleaner assembly, then disconnect cruise control cable (if equipped) and accelerator cable and link.
4. Disconnect heater hose from rear cylinder head cover.
5. Identify, then disconnect vacuum hoses from throttle body.
6. Remove cruise control actuator (if equipped), ignition coil and coolant outlet hose.
7. Remove brake booster vacuum hose, then the PCV hose.
8. Remove EGR valve and tubes, then the cold start injector pressure hose.
9. Remove fuel system pulsation damper and pressure regulator.
10. Disconnect heater bypass hoses from auxiliary air valve.
11. Disconnect water temperature sensor connector and water temperature switch connector (if equipped), then identify and remove vacuum hoses from vacuum tubes. Remove vacuum tubes attaching bolts, then the vacuum tubes, cylinder head rear cover and wire clamp.
12. Disconnect all wires necessary for cylinder head removal, then lay wire harness aside.
13. Remove distributor, then the front exhaust pipe.
14. Remove exhaust manifold insulator, oxygen sensor and the manifold support bracket.
15. Remove exhaust manifold, then the oxygen sensor gasket.
16. Remove fuel delivery pipe and fuel injectors.
17. Remove intake manifold and intake air control valve.
18. Remove power steering drive belt and alternator drive belt.
19. Remove cylinder head center cover, then the valve covers.
20. Remove coolant outlet, coolant bypass pipe and drive belt adjusting bar and gasket.

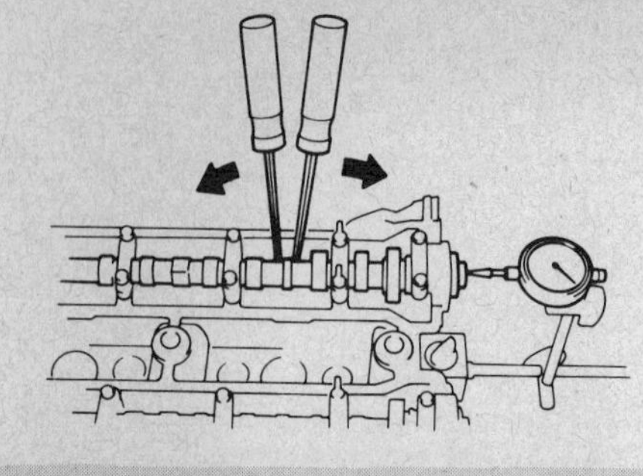

Fig. 3 Measuring camshaft thrust clearance. 16 valve engines

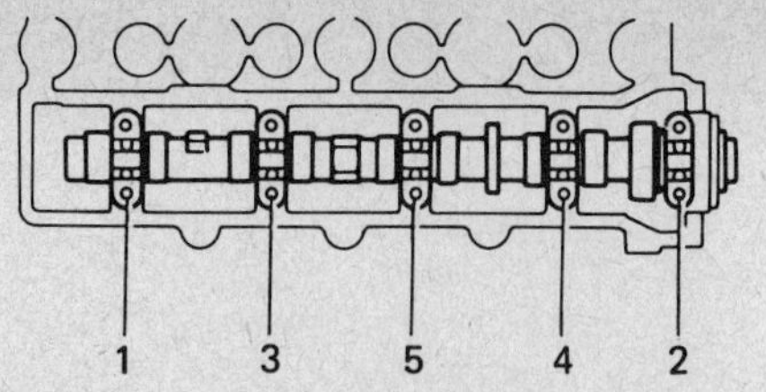

Fig. 4 Camshaft bearing cap removal sequence. 16 valve engines

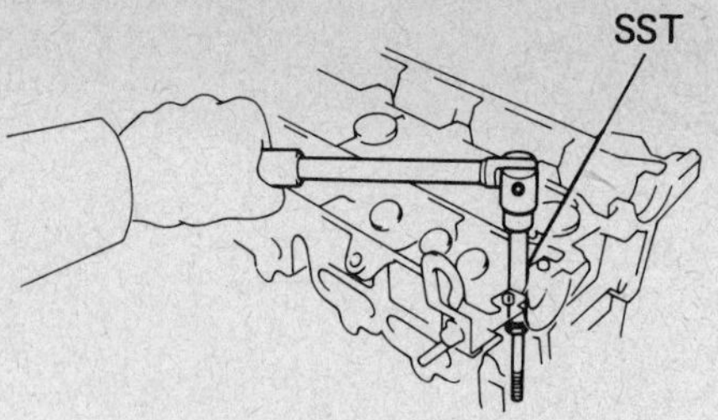

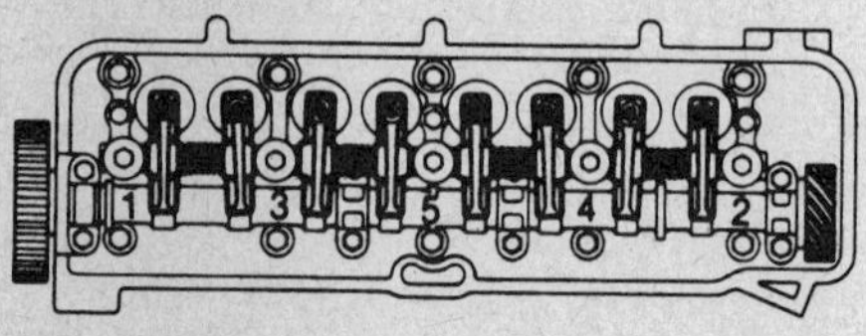

Fig. 6 Rocker arm support loosening sequence. Exc. 16 valve engine

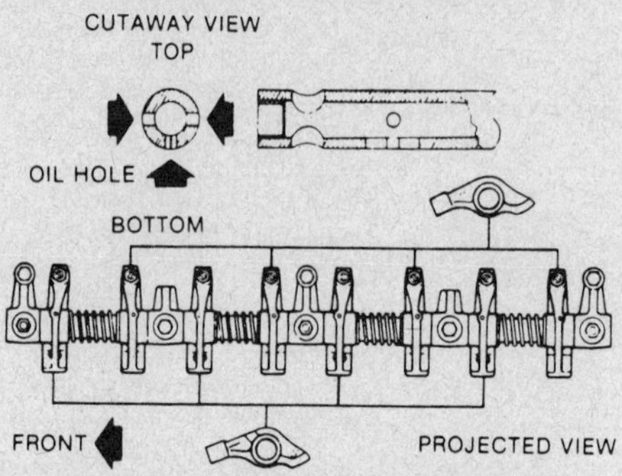

Fig. 7 Rocker shaft oil holes. Exc. 16 valve engine

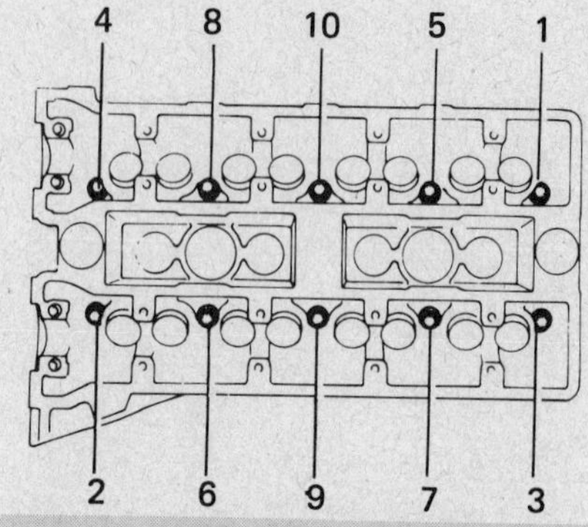

Fig. 5 Cylinder head bolt loosening sequence. 16 valve engines

21. Remove spark plugs, then set crankshaft pulley at TDC compression stroke. **Ensure valve lifters for No. 1 cylinder are loose. If not, rotate crankshaft pulley an additional 360° to set engine at TDC compression.**
22. Position suitable jack and wooden block under engine and raise slightly, then remove right side engine mount through bolt and mount.
23. Remove water pump pulley, then on models equipped with A/C, the A/C compressor idler pulley. On all models, remove No. 2 and 3 timing belt covers.
24. If timing belt is to be replaced, refer to "Timing Belt, Replace" for procedure. If timing belt is to be reused, proceed as follows:
    a. Place alignment marks on the camshaft timing pulleys and belt.
    b. Loosen idler pulley bolt, then push idler pulley as far left as possible and temporarily tighten it.
    c. Remove timing belt from camshaft timing pulleys. **Support timing belt so meshing of crankshaft timing pulley and timing belt does not shift.**
    d. Remove camshaft timing pulleys, right mounting bracket attaching bolts and mount and No. 4 timing belt cover.
25. Measure camshaft thrust clearance, **Fig. 3.** If clearance is greater than .0118 inch, replace camshaft and/or cylinder head.
26. Loosen and remove camshaft bearing cap attaching bolts gradually in sequence shown in **Fig. 4.**
27. Remove camshaft bearing caps, oil seal and camshaft.
28. Loosen and remove cylinder head attaching bolts gradually in sequence shown in **Fig. 5. Head warpage or cracking could result from removing cylinder head in incorrect order.**
29. Reverse procedure to install. Torque cylinder head attaching bolts gradually in three steps in reverse sequence as disassembly, **Fig. 4,** to 44 ft. lbs. Torque bearing cap attaching bolts gradually in three steps in reverse sequence as disassembly, **Fig. 5,** to 9 ft. lbs.

INTAKE & EXHAUST MANIFOLDS

REPLACE

EXC. 16 VALVE ENGINE

1. Disconnect battery ground cable.
2. Remove air cleaner assembly.
3. Disconnect vacuum lines.
4. Disconnect throttle valve cable.
5. Disconnect accelerator cable.
6. Disconnect electrical connector from carburetor.
7. Disconnect fuel line from fuel pump.
8. Disconnect all necessary vacuum lines and remove carburetor assembly.
9. Remove early fuel evaporation (EFE) gasket.
10. Disconnect vacuum line, then remove dashpot bracket.
11. Remove heat shield.
12. Raise and support vehicle.
13. Disconnect exhaust pipe from exhaust manifold.
14. Remove exhaust bracket from engine.
15. Disconnect air hose from converter pipe.
16. Lower vehicle.
17. Disconnect brake vacuum hose.
18. Remove accelerator and throttle cable bracket.
19. Remove intake and exhaust manifolds and gaskets.
20. Reverse procedure to install.

ROCKER ARM SHAFT & ROCKER ARMS

REPLACE

EXC. 16 VALVE ENGINE

1. Remove cylinder head cover attaching bolts, then the cylinder head cover.
2. Loosen each rocker support bolt a little at a time and in sequence shown ir **Fig. 6.**
3. During installation, proceed as follows:
    a. Loosen adjusting screw locknuts.
    b. Assemble rocker arm assembly and face the oil holes of the rocker shaft to the right, left and bottom as shown in **Fig. 7.**
    c. Install and tighten rocker support bolts gradually in three steps in sequence shown in **Fig. 8.**

VALVE CLEARANCE SPECIFICATIONS

Refer to "Valves, Adjust" procedure for specifications.

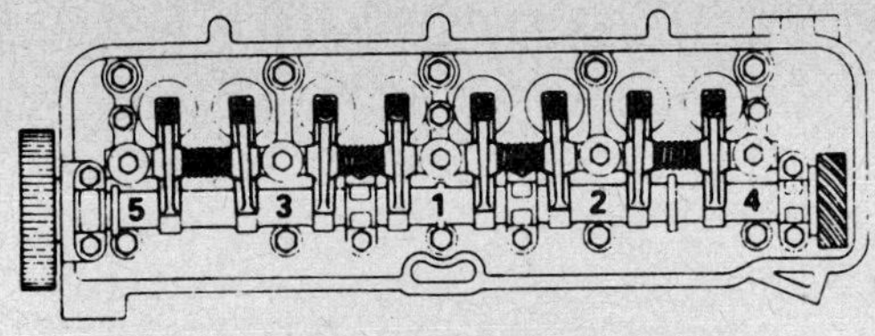

Fig. 8 Rocker arm torque sequence. Exc. 16 valve engine

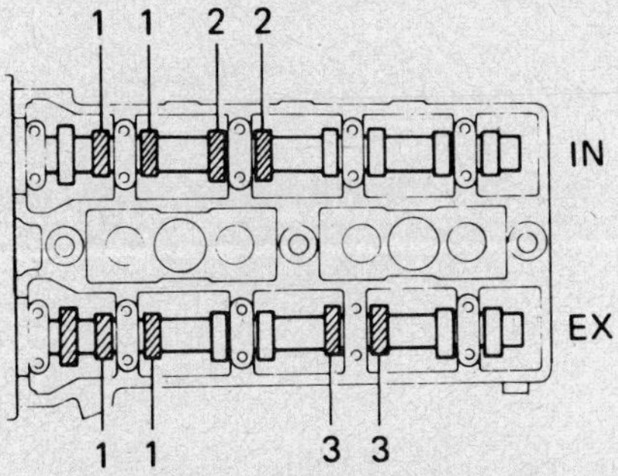

Fig. 11 First valve clearance adjustment. 16 valve engine

VALVES ADJUST

EXC. 16 VALVE ENGINE

Perform valve adjustment with engine at normal operating temperature. Adjust intake valve clearances to .008 inch, and exhaust valve clearances to .012 inch.

1. Position No. 1 cylinder to TDC of compression stroke.
2. Turn crankshaft in normal direction of rotation to align timing marks at TDC, then set groove on pulley to the "0" position.
3. Ensure rocker arms on No. 1 cylinder are loose and rockers on No. 4 are tight. If not, turn crankshaft one complete revolution and align marks.
4. Adjust valve clearances of the valves shown in **Fig. 9,** to specification.
5. Turn crankshaft one revolution and align the timing marks.
6. Adjust remaining valves as shown in **Fig. 10,** to specification.

16 VALVE ENGINE

Perform valve adjustment with engine at normal operating temperature. Adjust intake valve clearances to .008-.012 inch, and exhaust valve clearances to .010-.014 inch.

1. Position No. 1 cylinder to TDC of compression stroke.
2. Rotate crankshaft in normal direction of rotation to align timing marks at TDC, then set groove on pulley to the "0" position.

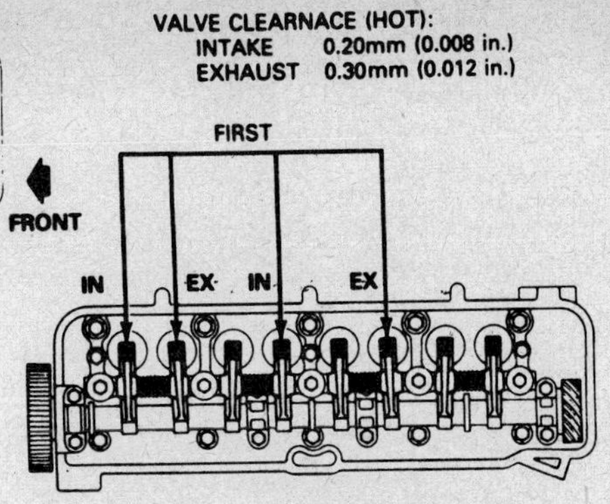

Fig. 9 First valve clearance adjustment. Exc. 16 valve engine

3. Check that valve lifters on No. 1 cylinder are loose, and that valve lifters on No. 4 cylinder are tight.
4. Adjust valve clearances of the valves shown in **Fig. 11,** to specification.
5. Rotate crankshaft pulley one revolution and align the timing marks.
6. Adjust remaining valves as shown in **Fig. 12,** to specification.

TIMING BELT COVER REPLACE

EXC. 16 VALVE ENGINE

No. 1 (Upper) Timing Belt Cover, Replace

1. Disconnect battery ground cable.
2. Loosen water pump pulley bolts.
3. Remove alternator drive belt.
4. Remove power steering pump drive belt, if equipped.
5. Remove water pump pulley.
6. Drain cooling system.
7. Disconnect upper radiator hose at outlet.
8. Disconnect all necessary vacuum lines.
9. Remove upper No. 1 timing cover attaching bolts.
10. Raise and support vehicle.
11. Remove lower cover attaching bolts.
12. Lower vehicle, then remove No. 1 timing cover.
13. Reverse procedure to install.

No. 2 (Lower) Timing Belt Cover, Replace

1. Disconnect battery ground cable.
2. Remove alternator belt.
3. Remove A/C drive belt, if equipped.
4. Raise and support vehicle.
5. Remove righthand under cover.
6. Remove flywheel cover.
7. Remove crankshaft pulley.
8. Remove No. 2 timing cover and gasket.
9. Reverse procedure to install.

No. 3 (Middle) Timing Belt Cover, Replace

1. Remove No. 1 timing belt cover as described previously.
2. Loosen A/C idler pulley mount nut and adjusting bolt, then remove A/C

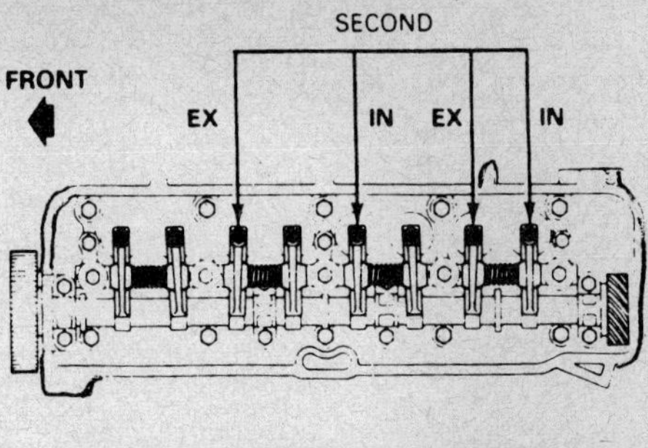

Fig. 10 Second valve clearance adjustment. Exc. 16 valve engine

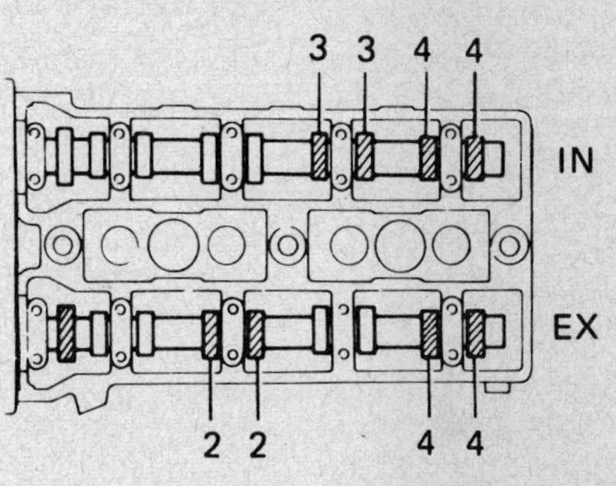

Fig. 12 Second valve clearance adjustment. 16 valve engine

belt, if equipped.
3. Remove A/C idler pulley and adjusting bolt, if equipped.
4. Remove alternator and position aside.
5. Remove No. 3 timing belt cover and gasket.
6. Reverse procedure to install.

TIMING BELT & CAMSHAFT TIMING PULLEY REPLACE

EXC. 16 VALVE ENGINE

1. Disconnect battery ground cable.
2. Drain cooling system.
3. Loosen water pump pulley bolts.
4. Remove alternator drive belt.
5. Remove power steering pump belt, if equipped.
6. Remove water pump pulley.
7. Loosen A/C idler pulley mount nut and adjusting bolt, then remove drive belt, if applicable.
8. Remove A/C idler pulley and adjusting bolt, if applicable.
9. Raise and support vehicle.
10. Remove righthand under cover.
11. Remove flywheel cover and crankshaft pulley.
12. Remove No. 2 timing belt cover with gasket.
13. Disconnect engine mounting center member.
14. Lower vehicle.

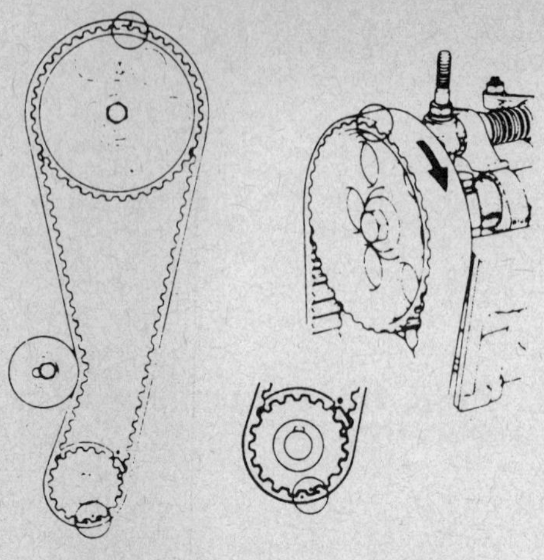

Fig. 13 Belt & pulley alignment. Exc. 16 valve engine

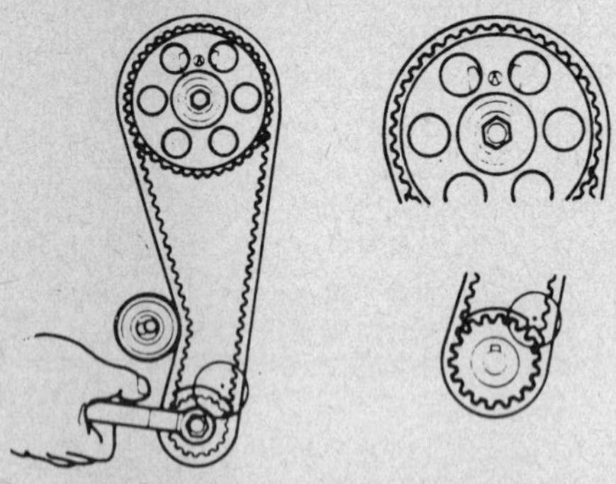

Fig. 16 Timing mark alignment. Exc. 16 valve engine

15. Disconnect upper radiator hose at outlet.
16. Disconnect all necessary vacuum hoses.
17. Remove No. 1 timing belt cover and gasket.
18. Remove alternator and position aside.
19. Remove No. 3 timing belt cover.
20. Support engine with a suitable jack.
21. Position No. 1 cylinder at TDC of compression stroke by turning crankshaft until the timing mark is aligned with the TDC mark. The rocker arms on the No. 1 cylinder should be loose. If not, turn crankshaft one complete turn.
22. Disconnect righthand engine mount.
23. Loosen idler pulley to relieve belt tension.
24. Lower engine and remove timing belt. **If reusing the timing belt, draw a direction arrow on the belt (in direction of engine rotation) and place alignment marks on the pulleys and belt as shown in Fig. 13.**
25. Remove idler pulley bolt, pulley and return spring.
26. Remove camshaft timing pulley.
27. During installation of belt and timing pulley, proceed as follows:
    a. Align camshaft knock pin and camshaft timing pulley. Torque bolt to 34 ft. lbs.

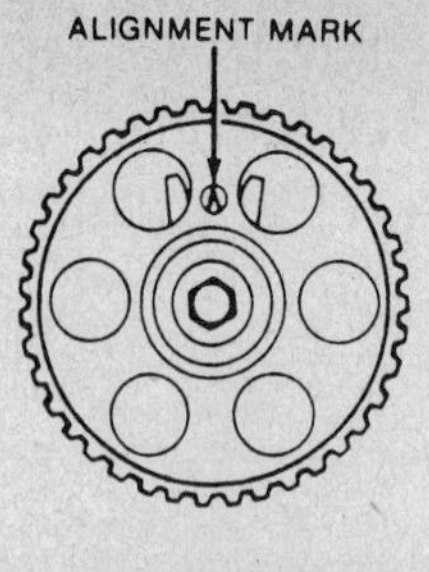

Fig. 14 Camshaft timing pulley alignment. Exc. 16 valve engine

    b. Align bearing cap mark and the center of the small hole on the camshaft timing pulley as shown in **Fig. 14.**
    c. Align TDC marks on the oil pump body and crankshaft timing pulley as shown in **Fig. 15.**
    d. Remove any oil or water on the crankshaft timing pulley and keep it clean.
    e. Install timing belt idler pulley and tension spring. Pry timing belt idler pulley toward the left as far as it will go and temporarily tighten it.
    f. Install timing belt. If reusing the original timing belt, align the points marked during removal and install the belt with the arrow pointing in the direction of engine rotation.
    g. Raise engine slightly, then loosen timing belt idler pulley mounting bolt. Temporarily install the crank pulley bolt and turn the crankshaft two revolutions clockwise from TDC to TDC.
    h. Check valve timing. Ensure each pulley aligns with the marks as shown in **Fig. 16.**
    i. Reverse remaining removal procedure to complete installation procedure.

16 VALVE ENGINE

Removal

1. Disconnect battery ground cable, then remove right front wheel and engine under cover.
2. Drain radiator coolant, then disconnect cruise control cable (if equipped), accelerator cable and link.
3. Remove cruise control actuator (if equipped), then the ignition coil and coolant outlet hose.
4. Remove accessory drive belts, then the spark plugs.
5. Turn crankshaft pulley and align groove with "0" mark on the No. 1 timing belt cover, then remove oil filler cap and ensure cavity in camshaft is visible indicating TDC compression. If camshaft cavity is not visible, rotate crankshaft an additional 360° to set engine at TDC compression.
6. Raise engine with suitable jack, then remove right side engine mount through bolt and the mount. **Insert suitable piece of wood between jack and engine to prevent damage.**

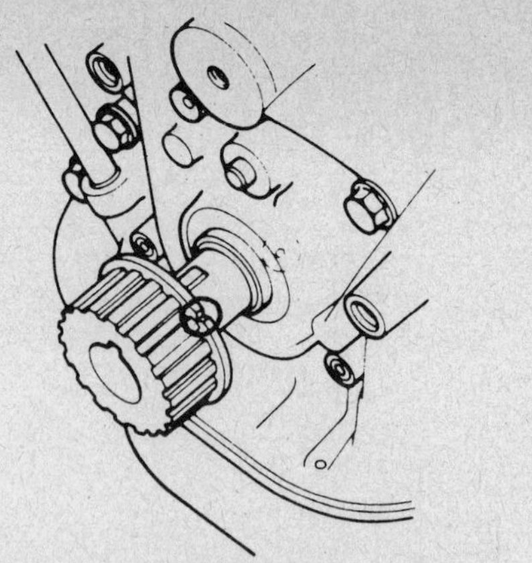

Fig. 15 Crankshaft timing pulley alignment. Exc. 16 valve engine

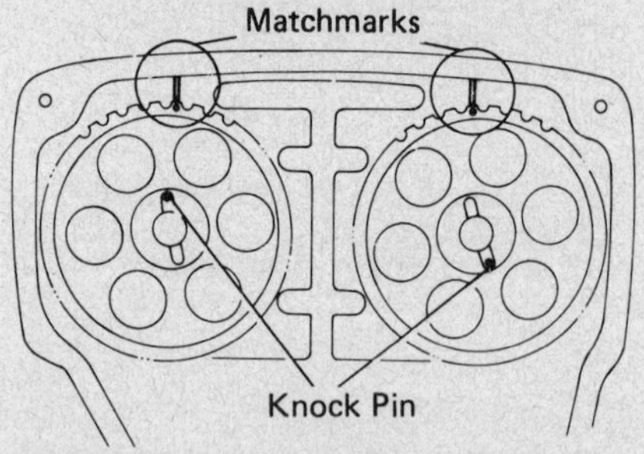

Fig. 17 Camshaft timing pulley alignment. 16 valve engine

7. Remove crankshaft pulley using suitable tools.
8. Remove timing belt covers and gaskets, then the timing belt guide from crankshaft sprocket.
8. Loosen idler pulley bolt, then push idler pulley as far left as possible and temporarily tighten idler pulley bolt.
9. Remove timing belt, idler pulley bolt, pulley and tension spring. **If timing belt is to reused, mark direction and belt-to-sprocket reference marks to ensure correct position during installation.**
10. Remove cylinder head covers, then using suitable wrench positioned on camshaft flats, remove camshaft sprocket attaching bolts and sprockets.

Installation

1. Install camshaft sprockets, aligning marks as shown in **Fig. 17.** Install sprocket attaching bolts and torque to 34 ft. lbs.
2. Install cylinder head covers, then the crankshaft sprocket, idler pulley and tension spring. Pry idler pulley towards the left as far as possible and temporarily tighten attaching bolt.
3. Install timing belt. **If belt is being reused, ensure it is installed in the same position as removed.**

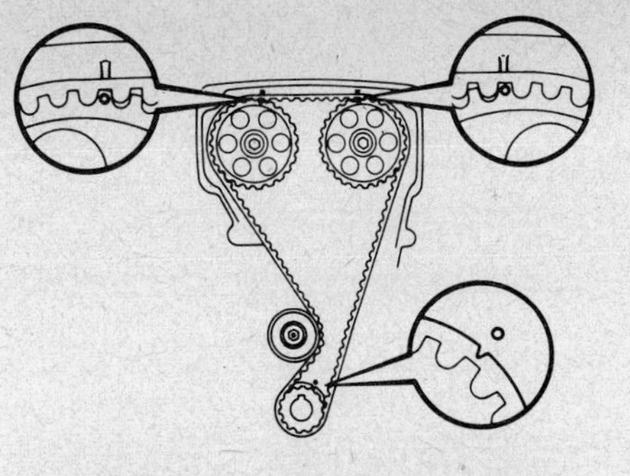

Fig. 18 Belt & pulley alignment. 16 valve engine

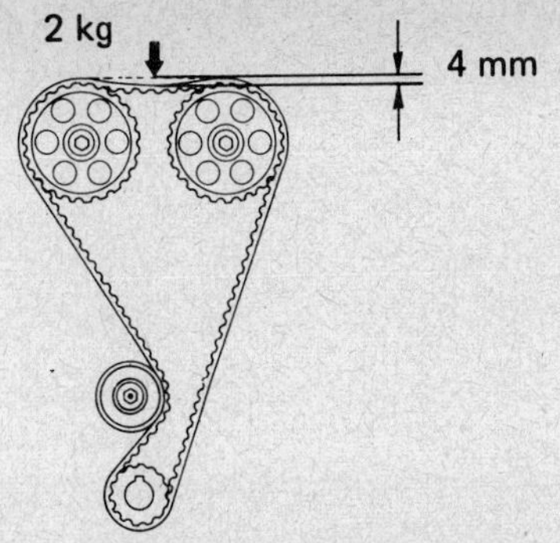

Fig. 19 Measuring belt deflection. 16 valve engine

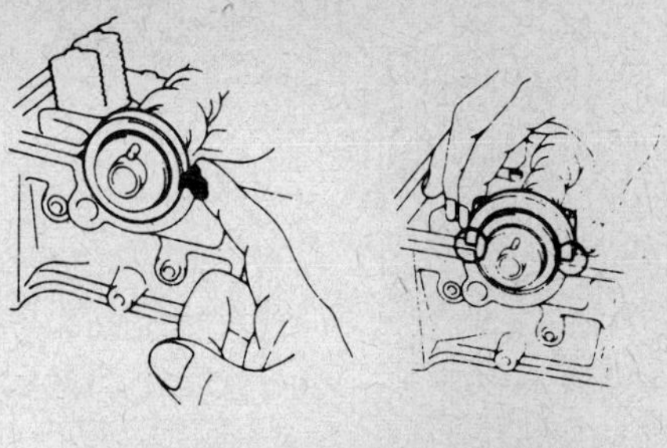

Fig. 20 Applying RTV sealant to oil seal. Exc. 16 valve engine

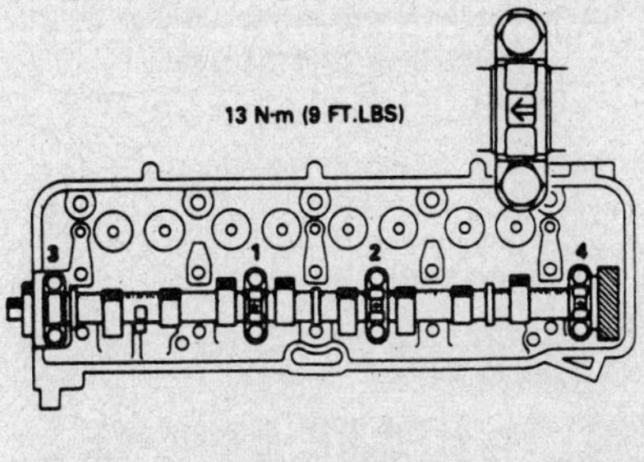

Fig. 21 Camshaft bearing cap torque specifications and sequence. Exc. 16 valve engine

4. Slowly loosen timing belt idler bolt, then temporarily install crankshaft pulley bolt.
5. Turn crankshaft two complete revolutions clockwise from TDC of compression stroke to TDC of compression stroke.
6. Check valve timing. Ensure each sprocket is aligned as shown in **Fig. 18.**
7. Tighten timing belt idler pulley bolt to 27 ft. lbs.
8. Measure timing belt deflection as shown in **Fig. 19.** If deflection is not .16 inch with 4.4 lbs. of pressure, readjust as necessary with idler pulley.
9. Remove crankshaft pulley bolt, then install timing belt guide. Ensure guide cup side is facing outward.
10. Install timing belt covers and gaskets.
11. Reverse steps 1 through 5 of removal procedure to complete installation. When installing crankshaft pulley torque pulley bolt to 105 ft. lbs.

CAMSHAFT

REPLACE

EXC. 16 VALVE ENGINE

1. Disconnect battery ground cable.
2. Remove cylinder head cover.
3. Drain cooling system.
4. Loosen water pump pulley bolts and remove alternator drive belt.
5. Raise and support vehicle.
6. Remove power steering pivot bolt, if equipped.
7. Remove bolt that goes through both the No. 1 and No. 2 timing covers.
8. Lower vehicle.
9. Remove power steering drive belt, if equipped.
10. Remove water pump pulley.
11. Disconnect upper radiator hose at outlet.
12. Disconnect all necessary vacuum lines.
13. Remove No. 1 timing belt cover and gasket.
14. Disconnect spark plug wires and electrical connectors.
15. Remove distributor.
16. Disconnect fuel lines, then remove fuel pump.
17. Remove distributor gear bolt.
18. Remove rocker arm assembly.
19. Turn crankshaft clockwise and position No. 1 cylinder to TDC of compression stroke.
20. Place alignment marks on the camshaft timing pulley and belt.
21. Loosen idler pulley mount bolt and push idler pulley toward the left as far as it will go and temporarily tighten it. Remove belt.
22. Support belt so that the meshing of the crankshaft timing pulley and timing belt does not shift.
23. Do not allow belt to contact oil, water or dust.
24. Remove camshaft bearing caps and camshaft.
25. Reverse procedure to install, noting the following:
    a. Install camshaft bearing caps with the arrows on caps facing toward the front.
    b. When installing No. 1 bearing cap and oil seal, apply suitable liquid sealer to seal outer circumference, then coat mating areas shown in **Fig. 20** with RTV sealant.
    c. Ensure timing belt and timing pulley alignment marks align properly.
    d. Torque bearing caps to specifications and in sequence shown in **Fig. 21.**

PISTONS & RODS ASSEMBLE

Assemble pistons to connecting rods as shown in **Fig. 22.**

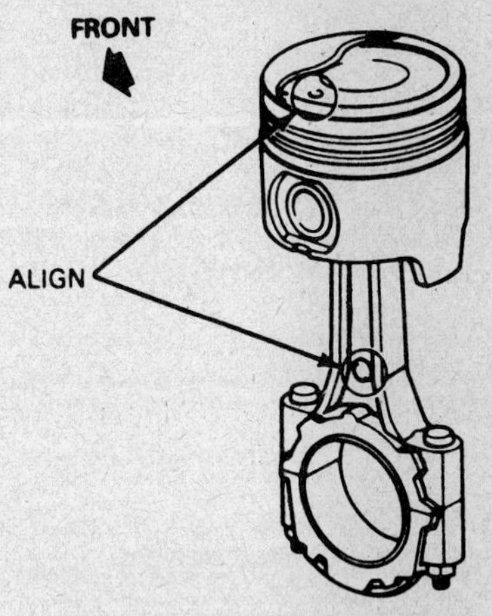

Fig. 22 Piston & rod assembly

MAIN & ROD BEARINGS

On engines except 16 valve models, connecting rod service bearings are available in 3 standard sizes, marked either 1, 2 or 3. Replace the bearing with one having the same mark on the bearing cap. Main bearings are available in 3 standard sizes marked 1, 2 or 3. If replacing the bearing, replace with one having the same number as marked on the cylinder block.

On 16 valve engines, main and connecting rod bearings are available in standard and undersizes of .010 inch (.25 mm).

CRANKSHAFT REAR OIL SEAL

REPLACE

EXC. 16 VALVE ENGINE

1. Remove transaxle and flywheel assembly.
2. Remove rear end plate.
3. Carefully pry oil seal from groove.
4. Replace old oil seal with a new one, then apply a suitable lubricant.
5. Assemble rear end plate onto engine, then insert and securely tighten attaching bolts.
6. Assemble flywheel assembly to engine, then install transaxle.

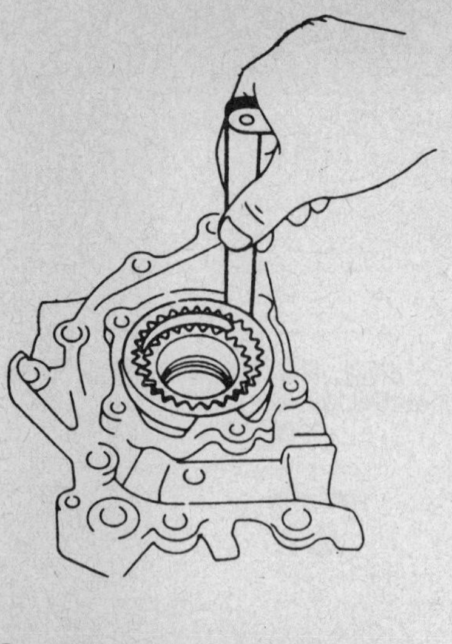

Fig. 23 Oil pump body clearance check. Exc. 16 valve engine

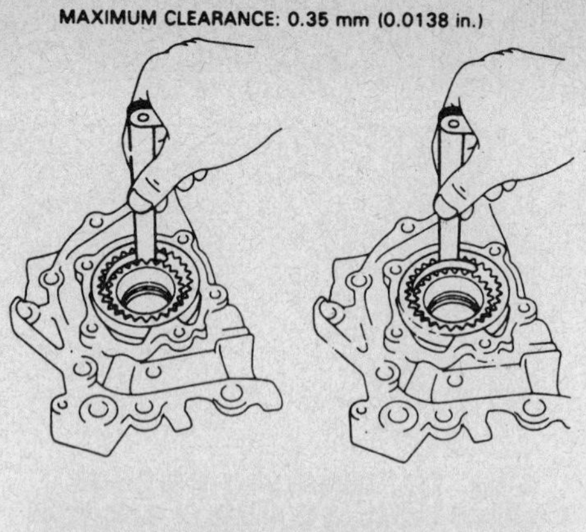

Fig. 24 Oil pump gear tip clearance check. Exc. 16 valve engine

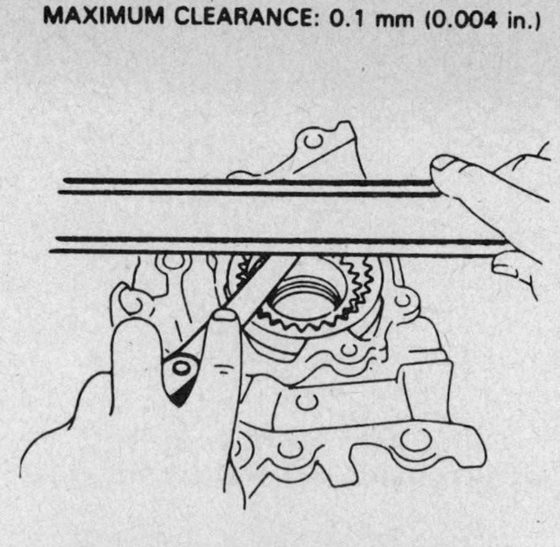

Fig. 25 Oil pump side clearance check. Exc. 16 valve engine

OIL PAN

REPLACE

EXC. 16 VALVE ENGINE

1. Disconnect battery ground cable.
2. Raise and support vehicle.
3. Drain engine oil.
4. Remove righthand under cover.
5. Remove oil pan bolts.
6. Remove oil pan.
7. Reverse procedure to install.

OIL PUMP

REPLACE

EXC. 16 VALVE ENGINE

1. Remove Nos. 1, 2 and 3 timing belt covers as described previously.
2. Remove oil pan attaching bolts, then the oil pan.
3. Remove righthand under cover.
4. Remove flywheel cover and crankshaft pulley.
5. Mark position of camshaft and crankshaft timing pulleys and timing belt rotational direction.
6. Loosen idler pulley bolt, move pulley over to relieve belt tension and tighten bolt.
7. Pull timing belt off of crankshaft timing pulley.
8. Remove dipstick tube.
9. Remove timing belt idler pulley.
10. Remove oil pump bolts and oil pump.
11. Reverse procedure to install, noting the following:
    a. Using a feeler gauge, measure clearance between the driven gear and body, **Fig. 23.**
    b. If clearance is greater than .008 inch, replace gear and/or body.
    c. Using a feeler gauge, measure clearance between both gear tips and crescent as shown in **Fig. 24.**
    d. If clearance is greater than .0138 inch, replace gear and/or body.
    e. Using a feeler gauge and flat block, measure side clearance as shown in **Fig. 25.**
    f. If clearance is greater than .004 inch, replace gear and/or body.

OIL PAN & PUMP

REPLACE

16 VALVE ENGINE

1. Disconnect battery ground cable, then make reference marks in hood hinge area and remove hood.
2. Raise and support vehicle, then drain engine oil into suitable container and remove engine under cover.
3. Remove oil pan attaching nuts and bolts, then the oil pan.
4. Remove oil strainer attaching bolts and nuts, then remove strainer and gasket.
5. Remove timing belt and crankshaft sprocket. Refer to "Timing Belt, Replace" for procedure.
6. Remove baffle plate from cylinder block, then the dipstick and tube.
7. Remove seven oil pump attaching bolts, then the oil pump.
8. Reverse procedure to install.

WATER PUMP

REPLACE

EXC. 16 VALVE ENGINE

1. Disconnect battery ground cable.
2. Remove No. 1 timing belt cover.
3. Remove inlet pipe mount bolt, nuts and inlet pipe.
4. Remove inlet pipe from water inlet housing.
5. Remove inlet pipe from water pump.
6. Remove oil level gauge guide.
7. Remove right hand under cover.
8. Remove power steering adjusting bracket, if equipped.
9. Remove water pump attaching bolts, then the water pump.
10. Reverse procedure to install.

16 VALVE ENGINE

1. Drain engine coolant.
2. Remove power steering drive belt, then the alternator drive belt.
3. Remove water pump pulley, then the coolant inlet pipe.
4. Remove oil dipstick and tube.
5. Remove timing belt cover, then the water pump.
6. Reverse procedure to install.

FUEL PUMP

REPLACE

1. Disconnect battery ground cable.
2. Disconnect fuel hoses from fuel pump.
3. Remove mounting bolts.
4. Remove fuel pump and heat insulator assembly.
5. Remove fuel pump.
6. Reverse procedure to install.

Clutch & Manual Transmission Section

INDEX

Page No.

CLUTCH PEDAL
ADJUST

1. Check height as shown in **Fig. 1.**
2. If it is necessary to adjust pedal height, remove instrument lower finish panel and air duct.
3. Loosen locknut and turn stopper bolt until the height is correct, then tighten lock nut.
4. Push in on clutch pedal until resistance is felt, then check pushrod and pedal freeplay. Pushrod play should be .039-.197 inch, while freeplay should be .51-.91 inch for 1985 vehicles, or .20-.59 inch for 1986-88 vehicles.
5. To adjust, loosen locknut and turn pushrod until freeplay and pushrod play are within specification, then tighten locknut.
6. Recheck pedal height and adjust as necessary.
7. Reinstall air duct and lower finish panel.

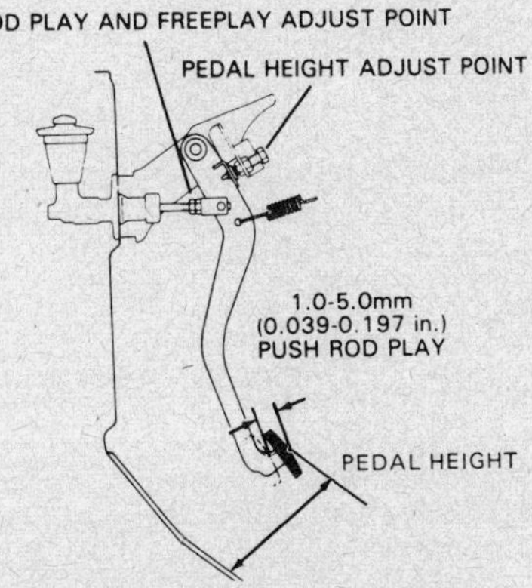

Fig. 1 Clutch pedal adjustment

CLUTCH
REPLACE

1. Remove transaxle assembly from vehicle.
2. Loosen each set bolt one turn at a time until spring tension is released.
3. Remove attaching bolts and pull off clutch assembly.
4. Remove release bearing fork and boot from the transaxle.
5. Reverse procedure to install. Torque set bolts to 14 ft. lbs.

MANUAL TRANSAXLE
REPLACE

Refer to "4-97 (1.6L) Engine Section" under "Engine, Replace" for transaxle replace procedure. The engine and transaxle assembly is removed as an assembly.

SHIFT LEVER FREEPLAY
ADJUST
1985

1. Remove shift lever cover.
2. Using a feeler gauge measure clearance between shim and shift lever retainer through slot provided at side of shift lever cap.
3. Select a shim that will allow a 0-.004 inch clearance between adjusting shim and retainer.
4. Shims are available in .020, .024, .028, .031, .035, .039, .043 and .047 inch thicknesses.

1986–88

1. Remove shift lever cover.
2. Using a suitable spring scale attached to top of lever, select a shim that will allow a preload of .1-.2 lbs.
3. Shims are available in .031, .035, .039, .043 and .047 inch thicknesses.

Rear Axle, Rear Suspension & Brakes

INDEX

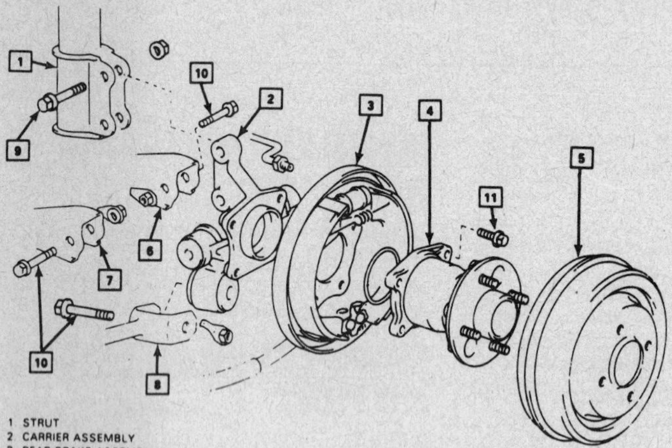

1 STRUT
2 CARRIER ASSEMBLY
3 REAR BRAKE ASSEMBLY
4 REAR AXLE HUB ASSEMBLY
5 BRAKE DRUM
6 REAR SUSPENSION ARM
7 FRONT SUSPENSION ARM
8 STRUT ROD
9 BOLT 142 N·M (105 FT. LBS.)
10 87 N·M (64 FT. LBS.)
11 80 N·M (50 FT. LBS.)

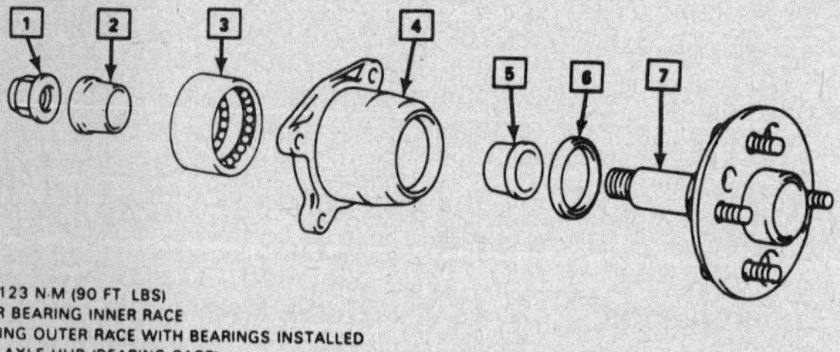

1 NUT 123 N·M (90 FT. LBS.)
2 INNER BEARING INNER RACE
3 BEARING OUTER RACE WITH BEARINGS INSTALLED
4 REAR AXLE HUB (BEARING CASE)
5 OUTER BEARING INNER RACE
6 AXLE SEAL
7 AXLE

Fig. 1 Rear hub assembly

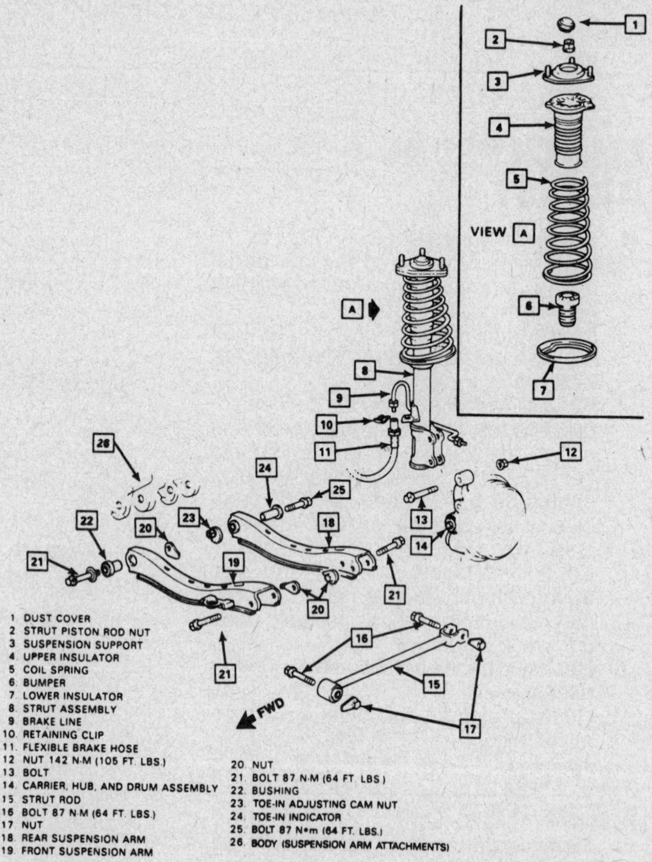

1 DUST COVER
2 STRUT PISTON ROD NUT
3 SUSPENSION SUPPORT
4 UPPER INSULATOR
5 COIL SPRING
6 BUMPER
7 LOWER INSULATOR
8 STRUT ASSEMBLY
9 BRAKE LINE
10 RETAINING CLIP
11 FLEXIBLE BRAKE HOSE
12 NUT 142 N·M (105 FT. LBS.)
13 BOLT
14 CARRIER, HUB, AND DRUM ASSEMBLY
15 STRUT ROD
16 BOLT 87 N·M (64 FT. LBS.)
17 NUT
18 REAR SUSPENSION ARM
19 FRONT SUSPENSION ARM
20 NUT
21 BOLT 87 N·M (64 FT. LBS.)
22 BUSHING
23 TOE-IN ADJUSTING CAM NUT
24 TOE-IN INDICATOR
25 BOLT 87 N•m (64 FT. LBS.)
26 BODY (SUSPENSION ARM ATTACHMENTS)

Fig. 2 Rear suspension assembly

REAR AXLE
REPLACE

1. Remove rear axle hub.
2. Disconnect brake line from wheel cylinder.
3. Remove bolt and nut holding axle carrier to strut rod.
4. Remove bolt and nut holding axle carrier to the front suspension arm.
5. Remove bolt and nut holding axle carrier to the rear suspension arm.
6. Remove bolts and nuts holding axle carrier to the strut, then remove axle carrier assembly.
7. Reverse procedure to install.

REAR AXLE HUB
REPLACE

1. Raise and support vehicle.
2. Remove wheel and tire assembly.
3. Remove brake drum, **Fig. 1.**
4. Remove four bolts attaching axle hub and rear brake assembly.
5. Remove hub, brake assembly and O-ring.
6. Reverse procedure to install.

STRUT/COIL SPRING ASSEMBLY
REPLACE

Do not attempt to disassemble strut, since cylinder is filled with high pres-

sure gas. When discarding strut, drill a .090 inch hole in bottom of strut to relieve all gas pressure.

1. Remove quarter window garnish molding and back window panel.
2. Raise and support vehicle, then remove tire and wheel assembly.
3. Remove brake line at flex hose on strut, **Fig. 2.**
4. Disconnect flexible hose from shock absorber.
5. Remove bolts attaching strut to axle carrier.
6. Reverse procedure to install.

REAR SUSPENSION ARM
REPLACE

1. Raise and support vehicle.
2. Remove bolt and nut attaching rear suspension arm to axle carrier.
3. Remove cam and bolt attaching rear suspension arm to body, then the rear suspension arm.
4. Note location of cam plate mark before removing bolt and cam.
5. Reverse procedure to install.

FRONT SUSPENSION ARM
REPLACE

1. Raise and support vehicle.
2. Remove bolt and nut attaching front suspension arm to axle carrier.
3. Remove bolt and nut attaching front suspension arm to the body, then the front suspension arm.
4. Reverse procedure to install.

STRUT ROD
REPLACE

1. Raise and support vehicle.
2. Remove bolt and nut attaching strut rod to axle carrier.
3. Remove bolt and nut attaching strut rod to body, then the strut rod assembly from the vehicle.
4. Reverse procedure to install.

PARKING BRAKE
ADJUST

1. Check that parking brake lever travel is correct by pulling parking brake lever all the way up and counting the number of clicks.
2. Parking brake lever travel should be 4-7 clicks. If not, remove console, loosen locknut and turn adjusting nut until travel is correct.

MASTER CYLINDER
REPLACE

1. Clean area around reservoir and brake pipes at master cylinder.
2. Disconnect level warning switch electrical connector.
3. Remove brake fluid from master cylinder.
4. Disconnect, then cap brake lines.
5. Remove two attaching nuts.
6. Remove master cylinder and gasket from booster.
7. Reverse procedure to install. Ensure that zero clearance exists between brake booster pushrod and master cylinder.

Front Suspension & Steering Section

INDEX

DESCRIPTION

The front suspension, **Fig. 1**, on this vehicle is a MacPherson strut design. The upper end of the strut is anchored to the body by a strut support. The strut and strut support are isolated by a rubber mount. The lower end of the strut is connected to the upper end of the steering knuckle. The lower end of the knuckle is attached to the ball joint, which is attached to the suspension control arm assembly. Movement of the steering wheel is transmitted to the tie-rod end and then to the knuckle, turning the wheel and tire assembly.

STRUT
REPLACE

1. Open hood, then remove strut to body attaching nuts.
2. Loosen wheel lug nuts. Loosen axle shaft nut if knuckle will be removed.
3. Raise and support vehicle until wheels are clear from ground.
4. Remove tire and wheel assembly.
5. Disconnect brake flex hose clip at strut bracket.
6. Disconnect brake flex hose to brake pipe connection. Remove brake hose clip.
7. Pull brake hose back through strut bracket opening, then tape or cap brake hose and caliper.
8. Remove two brake caliper mounting bracket bolts, then the caliper.
9. Mark adjusting cam, then remove both strut to knuckle attaching nuts and bolts.
10. Remove strut assembly and camber adjusting cam from knuckle.
11. Reverse procedure to install. Torque strut to knuckle attaching nuts and bolts to 105 ft. lbs., upper mount bolts to 13 ft. lbs., and wheel nuts to 76 ft. lbs.

LOWER CONTROL ARM
REPLACE

1. Raise and support vehicle.
2. Remove lower control arm attaching nuts and bolts.
3. Remove control arm from vehicle.
4. Reverse procedure to install. Torque control arm to body front nuts and bolts to 83 ft. lbs., and rear nuts and bolts to 64 ft. lbs.

LOWER CONTROL ARM BUSHING
REPLACE

1. Remove control arm.
2. Using a suitable tool, remove lower control arm bushing from lower control arm.
3. Reverse procedure to install. Torque bushing nut to 76 ft. lbs.

LOWER BALL JOINT
REPLACE

1. Loosen wheel lug nuts.
2. Raise and support vehicle.
3. Remove tire and wheel assembly.
4. Using tool J-35413 or equivalent, separate ball joint from knuckle assembly.
5. Remove two nuts and bolts attaching ball joint and control arm.
6. Remove ball joint.
7. Reverse procedure to install. Torque knuckle to ball joint nut to 82 ft. lbs.

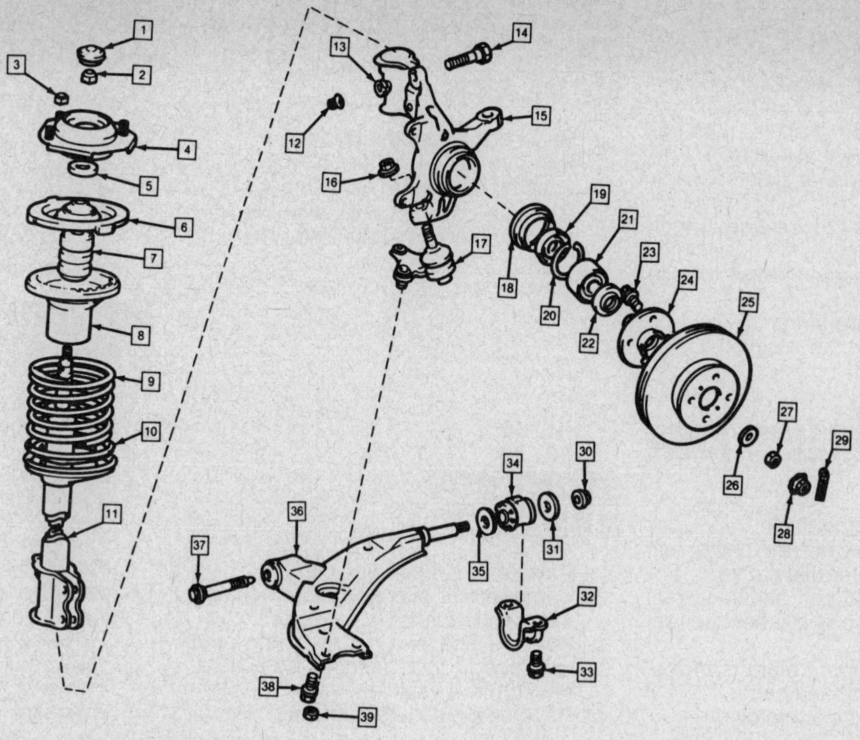

1. COVER, DUST
2. NUT, ABSORBER SHAFT
3. NUT, STRUT SUPPORT
4. SUPPORT, STRUT
5. SEAL, SUPPORT
6. SEAT, SPRING
7. BUMPER, SPRING
8. INSULATOR, UPPER
9. SPRING, COIL
10. INSULATOR, LOWER
11. ABSORBER, SHOCK/STRUT
12. NUT, STRUT TO KNUCKLE
13. CAM, CAMBER ADJUST
14. BOLT, STRUT TO KNUCKLE
15. KNUCKLE, STEERING
16. NUT, BALL JOINT TO KNUCKLE
17. JOINT, LOWER BALL
18. DEFLECTOR, DUST
19. SEAL, INNER HUB
20. RING, SNAP
21. BEARING, FRONT AXLE HUB
22. SEAL OUTER HUB
23. STUD, WHEEL
24. HUB, FRONT AXLE
25. DISC, FRONT BRAKE
26. WASHER, FRONT HUB
27. NUT, FRONT HUB
28. CAP, FRONT HUB
29. PIN, COTTER
30. NUT, CONTROL ARM
31. RETAINER, BUSHING
32. BRACKET, BUSHING
33. BOLT, BUSHING BRACKET
34. BUSHING, CONTROL ARM
35. RETAINER, BUSHING
36. ARM, LOWER CONTROL
37. BOLT, CONTROL ARM
38. BOLT, BALL JOINT
39. NUT, BALL JOINT

Fig. 1 Disassembled view of front suspension

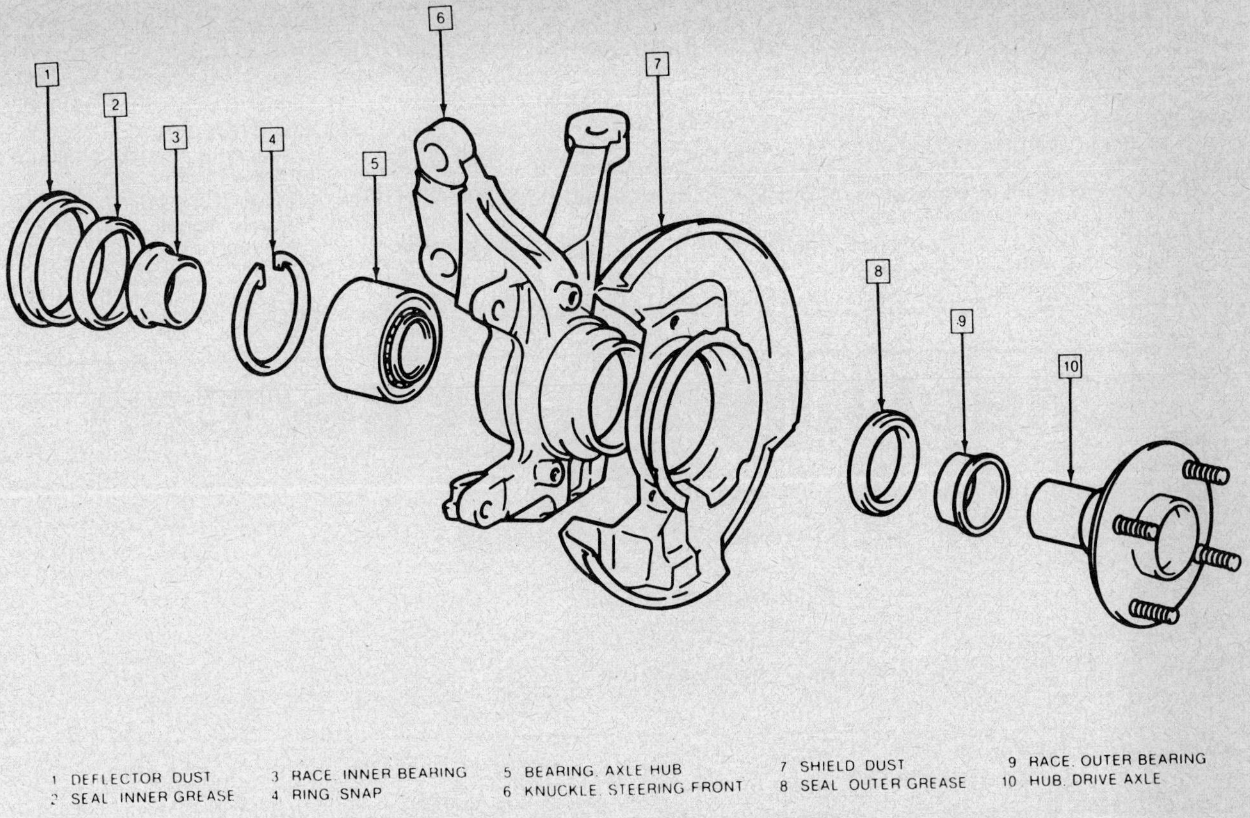

Fig. 2 Disassembled view of hub & bearing assembly

and control arm attaching nuts to 47 ft. lbs. During installation, always replace a self-locking nut with a new one.

STEERING KNUCKLE
REPLACE

1. Loosen wheel and hub nuts.
2. Raise and support vehicle.
3. Remove tire and wheel assembly.
4. Remove brake hose retaining clip at strut.
5. Disconnect flex hose from brake line.
6. Remove caliper bracket to knuckle mounting bolts, then support caliper.
7. Remove disc assembly.
8. Remove drive axle unit. Use tool J-25287 or equivalent, to push out drive axle assembly.
9. Remove cotter pin and tie rod to knuckle attaching nut. Use tool J-24319-01 or equivalent to separate the tierod assembly.
10. Remove ball joint to control arm attaching nuts and bolt.
11. Mark camber relationship for installation, then remove two strut to knuckle attaching nuts and bolts, then the knuckle.
12. Reverse procedure to install. Torque control arm nuts and bolts to 47 ft. lbs, ball joint to knuckle, 14 ft. lbs., strut to lower bracket bolts to 105 ft. lbs., tie rod to knuckle 38ft. lbs. and brake caliper bracket to knuckle attaching bolts to 65 ft. lbs.

HUB
REPLACE

1. Remove knuckle from vehicle and mount into a suitable vise.
2. Using a suitable screwdriver, remove dust deflector.
3. Using tool J-26941 or equivalent, remove inner grease seal from knuckle, **Fig. 2.**
4. Remove inner bearing snap ring and disc brake dust shield.
5. Push out hub using tool J-25287 and J-35378 or equivalents.
6. Using tools mentioned in step 5, remove outer bearing race from hub.
7. Using tool J-26941 or equivalent, remove outer grease seal.
8. Using tools J35399 and J-35379 or equivalents, remove bearing assembly.
9. Reverse procedure to install. Use tool J-8092 and J-35411 to install hub bearing assembly. Use tool J-35737 to install outer grease seal. Install hub using tools J-8092 and J-35399. Use tool J-35737 to install inner grease seal. Use tool J-35379 to install dust deflector ring. Ensure dust deflector ring faces down (open end down).

MANUAL STEERING GEAR
REPLACE

1. Disconnect battery ground cable.
2. Remove intermediate shaft cover.
3. Loosen upper pinch bolt. Remove lower pinch bolt from pinion shaft.
4. Loosen wheel lug nuts.
5. Raise and support vehicle.
6. Remove both front wheel and tire assemblies.
7. Remove cotter pins from tierod ends.
8. Disconnect both tie rod ends from steering knuckles. Use tool J-24319-01, or equivalent only, to separate tierod joints.
9. Remove steering gear to body mounting nuts and bolts.
10. Remove steering assembly from vehicle.
11. Reverse procedure to install. Torque intermediate shaft pinch bolts to 26 ft. lbs., torque tie rod to knuckle nuts to 36 ft. lbs., gear housing to mounting nuts and bolts to 43 ft. lbs., tie rod end locking nut to 35 ft.lbs., inner tie rod to rack nuts to 61 Ft. lbs., and wheel nuts to 76 ft. lbs.

POWER STEERING GEAR
REPLACE

1. Remove intermediate steering shaft protector.

2. Loosen upper, and remove lower intermediate shaft pinch bolts.
3. Open hood and place drain pan under gear assembly.
4. Loosen wheel lug nuts.
5. Raise and support vehicle.
6. Remove both front wheel and tire assemblies.
7. Using tool J-24319-01 or equivalent, remove both tie rod ends from knuckles.
8. Support transaxle with a suitable jack.
9. Remove rear center engine mounting member to body mounting bolts.
10. Remove rear engine mount to mount bracket attaching nut and bolt. Raise and lower rear of transaxle to gain access to steering gear to body attaching nuts and bolts.
11. Disconnect pressure and return lines at steering gear.
12. Remove four gear to body mounting nuts and bolts.
13. Remove gear through access opening.
14. Reverse procedure to install.

POWER STEERING PUMP REPLACE

1. Remove air cleaner assembly.
2. Remove return hose clamp.
3. Disconnect and cap pressure and return lines from pump.
4. Loosen pump pulley.
5. Remove adjusting bolt, pivot bolt and drive belt.
6. Remove pump assembly.
7. Reverse procedure to install.

Wheel Alignment Section

INDEX

FRONT WHEEL ALIGNMENT

CASTER & CAMBER

Camber is adjusted by first loosening the upper and lower strut to knuckle nuts and bolts, then rotating cam to obtain correct specification.

Caster cannot be adjusted. Should caster be found out of specification, locate cause first. If components are damaged, bent, loose, dented or worn, they should be replaced. To prevent an incorrect reading of camber or caster, jounce the bumper three times before checking.

After adjustment, tighten nuts to specification.

TOE-IN

Toe-in is adjusted by changing tierod length. Loosen boot clamps and slide from the boot assembly. Loosen right and left tierod end locknuts, then turn right and left tierods to align toe-in to specification. Right and left tie rods must be equal in length.

After adjustment, install boot clamps, tighten nuts to specification and ensure rack boots are not twisted.

Torque strut-to-knuckle nut to 105 ft. lbs., and tie rod locking nut to 35 ft. lbs.

REAR WHEEL ALIGNMENT

For rear wheel alignment specifications, refer to chart at beginning of chapter. No provision to adjust rear wheel alignment to specifications is provided.

PONTIAC FIERO

INDEX OF SERVICE OPERATIONS

NOTE: Refer to the rear of this manual for vehicle manufacturer's special service tool suppliers.

Specifications

GENERAL ENGINE SPECIFICATIONS

Year	Engine CID①/Liter	Engine VIN Code	Fuel System	Bore & Stroke	Compression Ratio	Net H.P. @ RPM②	Maximum Torque Ft. Lbs. @ RPM	Normal Oil Pressure Pounds
1984	4-151, 2.5L	R	E.F.I.③	4.00 x 3.00	9.0	92 @ 4000	134 @ 2800	36-41
1985	4-151, 2.5L	9	E.F.I.③	4.00 x 3.00	9.0	92 @ 4400	134 @ 2800	36-41
	V6-173, 2.8L	9	MPFI④	3.50 x 2.99	8.5	140 @ 5200	170 @ 3600	30-45
1986	4-151, 2.5L	R	E.F.I.③	4.00 x 3.00	9.0	92 @ 4400	134 @ 2800	36-41
	V6-173, 2.8L	9	MPFI④	3.50 x 2.99	8.5	140 @ 5200	170 @ 3600	30-45
1987	4-151, 2.5L	R	E.F.I.③	4.00 x 3.00	9.0	98 @ 4800	135 @ 3200	36-41
	V6-173, 2.8L	9	MPFI④	3.50 x 2.99	8.5	135 @ 4500	165 @ 3600	30-45
1988	4-151, 2.5L	R	E.F.I.③	4.00 x 3.00	9.0	98 @ 4800	135 @ 3200	—
	V6-173, 2.8L	9	MPFI④	3.50 x 2.99	8.5	135 @ 4500	165 @ 3600	—

①—CID-Cubic inch displacement.
②—Ratings are net as installed in vehicle.
③—Electronic fuel injection.
④—Multi-point fuel injection.

ALTERNATOR SPECIFICATIONS

Year	Model	Rated Hot Output Amps.
1984-85	—	66①
1986	Less A/C	66
	With A/C	94
1987	1101148	85
	1101149	100
	1105604	103
	1105620	70
1988	—	—

STARTING MOTOR APPLICATIONS

Year	Model	Starter Number
1984	All	1109564
	All	1998429
1985-86	All	1998503
1987	All	1998533
1988	—	—

ENGINE TIGHTENING SPECIFICATIONS*

*Torque specifications are for clean and lightly lubricated threads only. Dry or dirty threads produce increased friction which prevents accurate measurement of tightness.

Year	Engine Model/VIN	Spark Plugs Ft. Lbs.	Cylinder Head Bolts Ft. Lbs.	Intake Manifold Ft. Lbs.	Exhaust Manifold Ft. Lbs.	Rocker Arm Stud Ft. Lbs.	Rocker Arm Cover Ft. Lbs.	Connecting Rod Cap Bolts Ft. Lbs.	Main Bearing Cap Bolts Ft. Lbs.	Flywheel to Crankshaft Ft. Lbs.	Vibration Damper or Pulley Ft. Lbs.
1984	4-151/R	7-15	①	①	44	20②	6	32	70	44	200
1985	4-151/R	7-15	①	①	44	20②	45③	32	70	44	200
	V6-173/9	7-15	65-75	20-25	22-28	43-49	6-9	34-40	63-74	45-55	66-84
1986	4-151/R	7-15	①	①	44	24②	45③	32	70	44	160
	V6-173/9	7-15	65-75	20-25	22-28	43-49	6-9	34-40	63-74	45-55	66-84
1987	4-151/R	7-15	①	①	①	24②	45③	32	70	④	162
	V6-173/9	7-15	65-90	20-25	22-28	43-49	6-9	34-40	63-74	45-55	66-84
1988	4-151/R	—	—	—	—	—	—	—	—	—	—
	V6-173/9	—	—	—	—	—	—	—	—	—	—

①—Refer to text for procedure.
②—Rocker arm bolt.
③—Inch lbs.
④—Auto. trans., 55 ft. lbs.; manual trans., 69 ft. lbs.

WHEEL ALIGNMENT SPECIFICATIONS

Year	Model	Caster Angle, Degrees		Camber Angle, Degrees				Toe-In mm
				Limits		Desired		
		Limits	Desired	Left	Right	Left	Right	
1984-86	All ①	+3° to +7° ②	+5°	−.3° to +1.3°	−.3° to +1.3°	+.5°	+.5°	1.6
	All ③	—	—	−1.5° to −.5°	−1.5° to −.5°	−1°	−1°	1.6
1987	All ①	+3° to +7° ②	+5°	−.3° to +1.3°	−.3° to +1.3°	+.5°	+.5°	④
	All ③	—	—	−.6° to +.4°	−.6° to +.4°	−.1°	−.1°	④
1988	—	—	—	—	—	—	—	—

①—Front wheel alignment.
②—Left & right side should be equal within 2°.
③—Rear wheel alignment.
④—Total toe, −.2° to +.2°.

COOLING SYSTEM & CAPACITY DATA

Year	Model or Engine/VIN	Cooling Capacity, Qts.		Radiator Cap Relief Pressure Lbs.	Thermo. Opening Temp.	Fuel Tank Gals.	Engine Oil Refill Qts.	Transaxle Oil	
		Less A/C	With A/C					Manual Transaxle Pts.	Auto. Transaxle Qts. ①
1984	4-151/R	13.0	13.4	15 ③	195	10.5	3 ②	5.9	③
1985	4-151/R	13.8	⑥	15	195	10.3	3 ②	④	⑤
	V6-173/9	13.8	13.8	15	195	10.3	4 ②	④	⑤
1986	4-151/R	13.8	⑥	15	195	10.3	3 ②	④	⑤
	V6-173/9	13.8	13.8	15	195	10.3	4 ②	④	⑤
1987	4-151/R	13.8	⑥	15	195	11.9	3 ②	⑦	⑤
	V6-173/9	13.8	13.8	15	195	11.9	4 ②	⑦	⑤
1988	4-151/R	—	—	—	—	—	—	—	—
	V6-173/9	—	—	—	—	—	—	—	—

①—Approximate; make final check with dipstick.
②—With or without filter change.
③—Oil pan capacity, 4 qts.; total capacity, 6 qts.
④—4 speed, 5.9 pts.; 5 speed, 5.3 pts.
⑤—Oil pan capacity, 4 qts.; total capacity, 5 qts.
⑥—Auto. trans., 13.8 qts.; man. trans., 14.1 qts.
⑦—Isuzu 5 speed, 5.3 pts.; Muncie 5 speed, 4.1 pts.

Electrical Section

INDEX

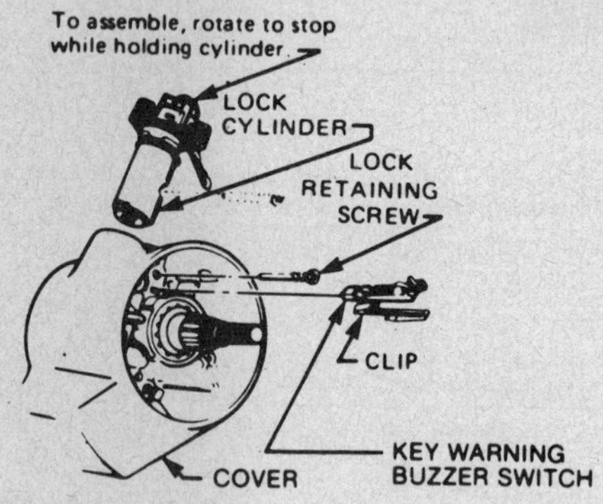

To assemble, rotate to stop while holding cylinder
LOCK CYLINDER
LOCK RETAINING SCREW
CLIP
COVER
KEY WARNING BUZZER SWITCH

Fig. 1 Lock cylinder replacement

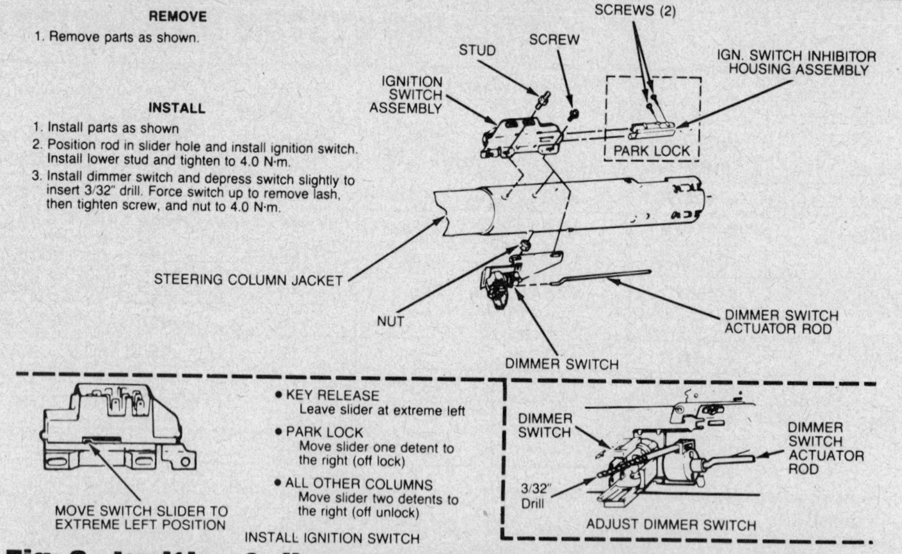

REMOVE
1. Remove parts as shown.
INSTALL
1. Install parts as shown
2. Position rod in slider hole and install ignition switch. Install lower stud and tighten to 4.0 N·m.
3. Install dimmer switch and depress switch slightly to insert 3/32" drill. Force switch up to remove lash, then tighten screw, and nut to 4.0 N·m.
SCREWS (2)
SCREW
STUD
IGN. SWITCH INHIBITOR HOUSING ASSEMBLY
IGNITION SWITCH ASSEMBLY
PARK LOCK
STEERING COLUMN JACKET
NUT
DIMMER SWITCH ACTUATOR ROD
DIMMER SWITCH
MOVE SWITCH SLIDER TO EXTREME LEFT POSITION
• KEY RELEASE Leave slider at extreme left
• PARK LOCK Move slider one detent to the right (off lock)
• ALL OTHER COLUMNS Move slider two detents to the right (off unlock)
INSTALL IGNITION SWITCH
DIMMER SWITCH
3/32" Drill
DIMMER SWITCH ACTUATOR ROD
ADJUST DIMMER SWITCH

Fig. 2 Ignition & dimmer switch replacement. Except tilt column

STARTER
REPLACE

1. Disconnect battery ground cable.
2. Disconnect solenoid wires from starter motor.
3. Raise and support vehicle.
4. Remove heat shield, if equipped.
5. On models with 4-151 engine, remove rear starter bracket attaching bolts.
6. On all models, remove the 2 starter motor motor-to-engine bolts.
7. Remove starter motor through front of converter toward front of engine.
8. Reverse procedure to install.

IGNITION LOCK
REPLACE

1. Remove turn signal switch as described under "Turn Signal Switch, Replace."
2. Remove key warning buzzer switch.
3. Turn lock cylinder to Run position, then remove retaining screw and the lock cylinder, **Fig. 1.**
4. Reverse procedure to install. Turn lock cylinder to Run position before installing key warning buzzer switch.

IGNITION & DIMMER SWITCHES
REPLACE

1. Remove turn signal switch as described under "Turn Signal Switch, Replace."
2. Refer to **Figs. 2 and 3** to replace ignition and dimmer switches.

TURN SIGNAL SWITCH
REPLACE

1. Disconnect battery ground cable.
2. Remove steering wheel as described under "Steering Wheel, Replace."
3. Refer to **Fig. 4** to replace turn signal switch.

STEERING WHEEL
REPLACE

1. Disconnect battery ground cable.
2. Remove horn button.
3. Remove retainer and steering wheel retaining nut.
4. Remove steering wheel using puller J-1859-03 or equivalent.
5. Reverse procedure to install.

WINDSHIELD WIPER SWITCH
REPLACE

1. Remove ignition lock as described under "Ignition Lock, Replace."
2. Refer to **Figs. 5 and 6** to replace wiper switch.

WINDSHIELD WIPER PULSE MODULE
REPLACE

The pulse module is located under the instrument panel on the righthand steering column support bracket.

1. Disconnect battery ground cable.
2. Remove instrument panel steering column cover.
3. Disconnect electrical connectors from module.
4. Disconnect module ground wire.
5. Remove module attaching bolt and the module.
6. Reverse procedure to install.

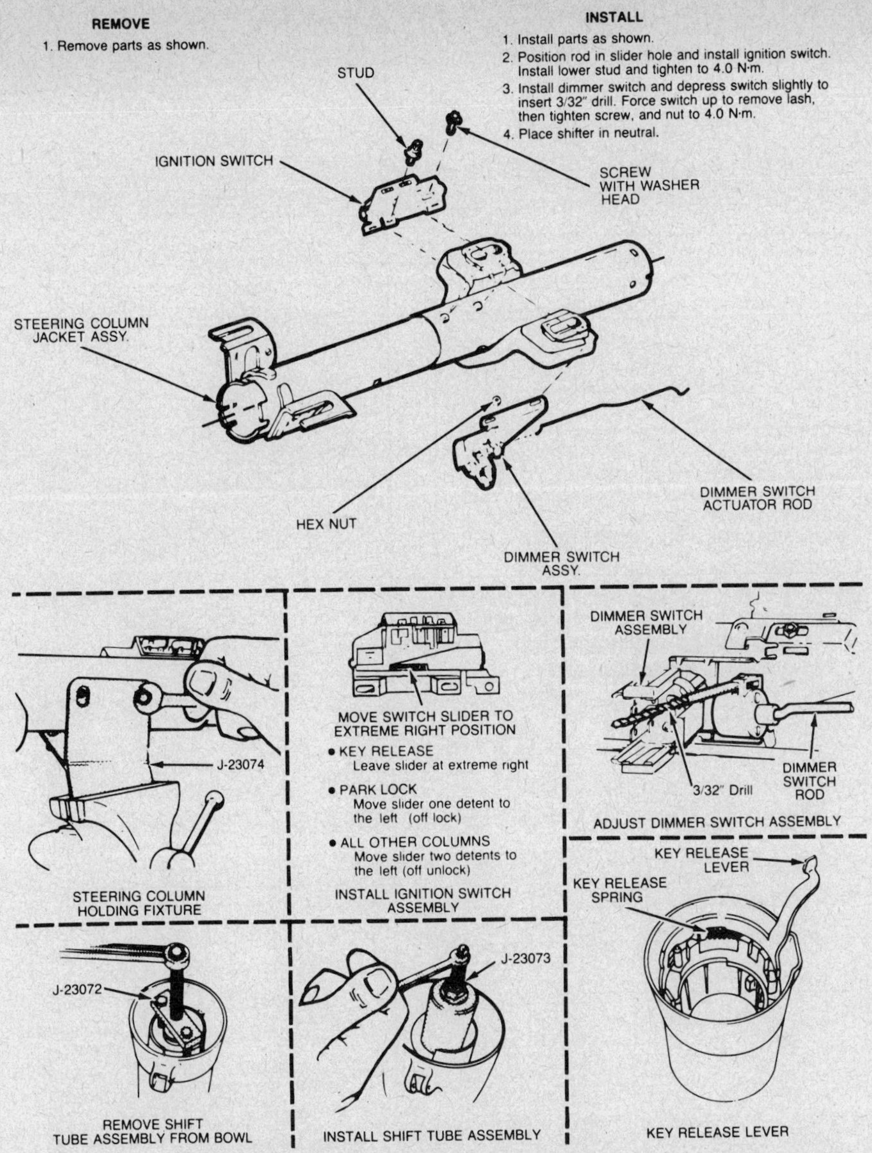
REMOVE
1. Remove parts as shown.
INSTALL
1. Install parts as shown.
2. Position rod in slider hole and install ignition switch. Install lower stud and tighten to 4.0 N·m.
3. Install dimmer switch and depress switch slightly to insert 3/32" drill. Force switch up to remove lash, then tighten screw, and nut to 4.0 N·m.
4. Place shifter in neutral.
STUD
IGNITION SWITCH
SCREW WITH WASHER HEAD
STEERING COLUMN JACKET ASSY.
DIMMER SWITCH ACTUATOR ROD
HEX NUT
DIMMER SWITCH ASSY.
J-23074
STEERING COLUMN HOLDING FIXTURE
MOVE SWITCH SLIDER TO EXTREME RIGHT POSITION
• KEY RELEASE
Leave slider at extreme right
• PARK LOCK
Move slider one detent to the left (off lock)
• ALL OTHER COLUMNS
Move slider two detents to the left (off unlock)
INSTALL IGNITION SWITCH ASSEMBLY
DIMMER SWITCH ASSEMBLY
3/32" Drill
DIMMER SWITCH ROD
ADJUST DIMMER SWITCH ASSEMBLY
J-23072
REMOVE SHIFT TUBE ASSEMBLY FROM BOWL
J-23073
INSTALL SHIFT TUBE ASSEMBLY
KEY RELEASE SPRING
KEY RELEASE LEVER
KEY RELEASE LEVER

Fig. 3 Ignition & dimmer switch replacement. Tilt column

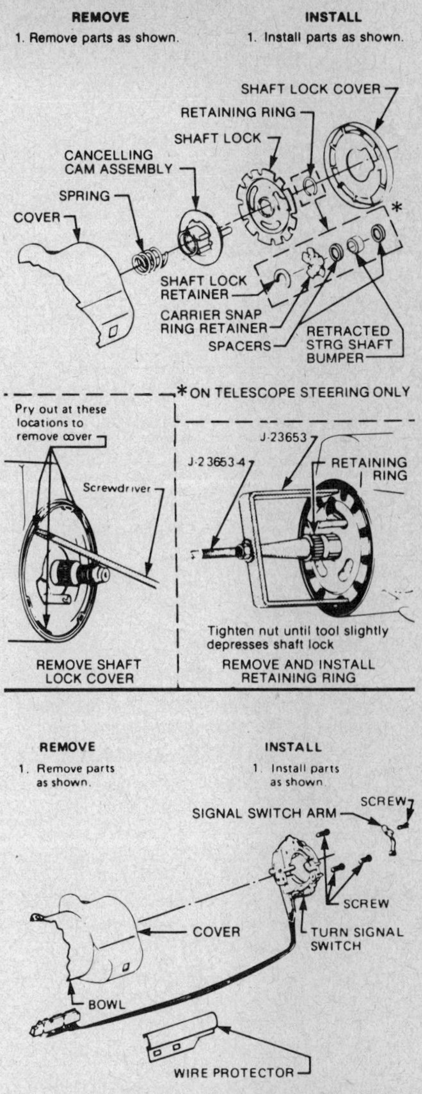
REMOVE
1. Remove parts as shown.
INSTALL
1. Install parts as shown.
SHAFT LOCK COVER
RETAINING RING
SHAFT LOCK
CANCELLING CAM ASSEMBLY
SPRING
COVER
SHAFT LOCK RETAINER
CARRIER SNAP RING RETAINER
SPACERS
RETRACTED STRG SHAFT BUMPER
*ON TELESCOPE STEERING ONLY
Pry out at these locations to remove cover
Screwdriver
REMOVE SHAFT LOCK COVER
J-23653
J-23653-4
RETAINING RING
Tighten nut until tool slightly depresses shaft lock
REMOVE AND INSTALL RETAINING RING
REMOVE
1. Remove parts as shown.
INSTALL
1. Install parts as shown.
SCREW
SIGNAL SWITCH ARM
SCREW
COVER
TURN SIGNAL SWITCH
BOWL
WIRE PROTECTOR

Fig. 4 Turn signal switch replacement

STOP LAMP SWITCH

ADJUST

Insert switch into retainer until switch body seats on retainer. Pull brake pedal rearward until clicks are no longer audible.

BACK-UP LIGHT/NEUTRAL START SWITCH

REPLACE

On vehicles equipped with automatic transmission, the neutral start and back-up light switches are combined into one unit and must be replaced as an assembly.

MANUAL TRANSMISSION

1. Disconnect battery ground cable.
2. Remove shift trim plate cover.
3. Disconnect electrical connector from switch, **Figs. 7 and 8.**
4. Remove switch retainer and the switch.
5. Reverse procedure to install.

AUTOMATIC TRANSMISSION

1. Disconnect battery ground cable.
2. Open deck lid, then open retaining clip and disconnect electrical connector from switch.
3. Pry cable from pivot pin at bottom of shift lever, then remove lever-to-transmission shaft attaching nut.
4. Remove 2 switch-to-transaxle attaching bolts and the switch, **Fig. 9.**
5. Reverse procedure to install, noting the following:
   a. Transmission must be in Neutral when installing switch.
   b. Torque switch attaching bolts to 20 ft. lbs.
   c. Torque lever attaching nut to 20 ft. lbs. while holding lever out of Park.

BACK-UP LIGHT/NEUTRAL START SWITCH

ADJUST

AUTOMATIC TRANSMISSION

1. Shift transmission into Neutral.
2. Align flats in switch insert with flats on transmission shaft, and slide switch over shaft.
3. Install attaching bolts hand tight.
4. Insert a 2.34 inch diameter gauge pin into adjustment hole, then rotate switch until pin drops to .354 inch.
5. Torque attaching bolts to 20 ft. lbs. and remove gauge pin.

CLUTCH START SWITCH

REPLACE

1. Disconnect battery ground cable.
2. Disconnect electrical connector from switch.

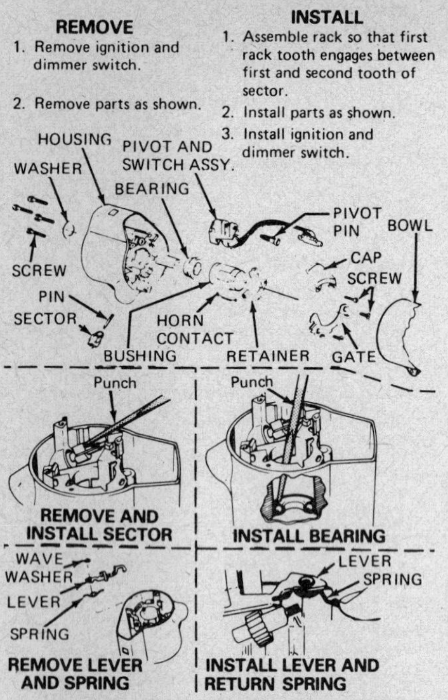

Fig. 5 Windshield wiper switch replacement. Except tilt column

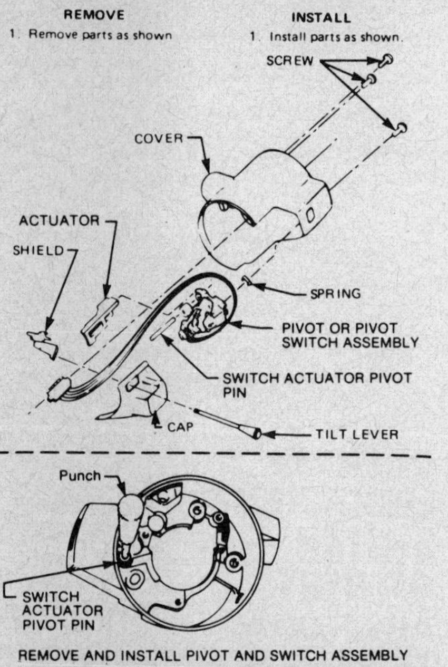

Fig. 6 Windshield wiper switch replacement. Tilt column

3. Remove switch attaching bolt. Rotate switch to disconnect shaft from clutch pedal hole, then remove switch from vehicle, **Fig. 10.**
4. Reverse procedure to install.

HEADLAMP SWITCH
REPLACE

1. Disconnect battery ground cable.
2. Remove 4 switch attaching screws.
3. Pull switch out of panel and disconnect electrical connectors, then remove switch from vehicle.

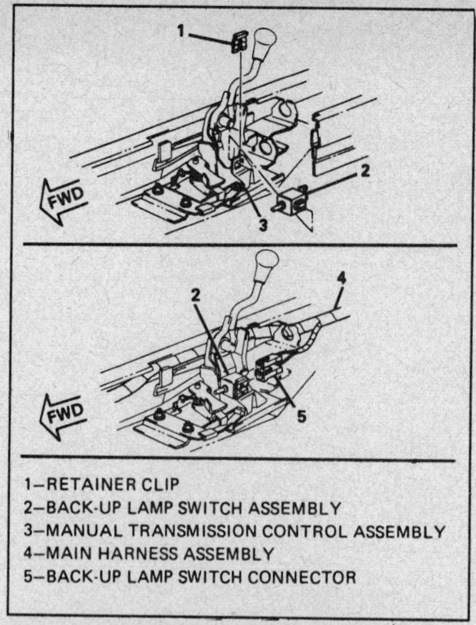

Fig. 7 Back-up light switch replacement. 1984–86 models w/manual transmission

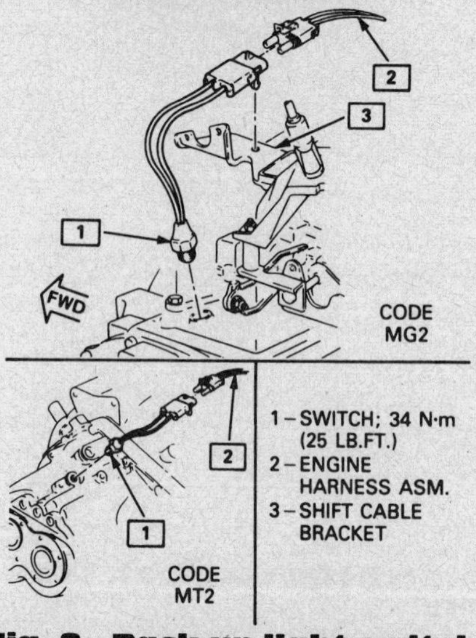

Fig. 8 Back-up light switch replacement. 1987–88 models w/manual transmission

4. Reverse procedure to install. **When replacing switch, install lower attaching screws first.**

INSTRUMENT CLUSTER
REPLACE

1. Disconnect battery ground cable.
2. Remove rear cluster cover, front trim plate and steering column cover.
3. Remove instrument cluster attaching screws.
4. Pull cluster rearward and disconnect all electrical connectors, then remove cluster from vehicle, **Figs. 11 and 12.**
5. Reverse procedure to install.

RADIO
REPLACE

1. Disconnect battery ground cable.
2. Remove shift knob and both ashtrays.

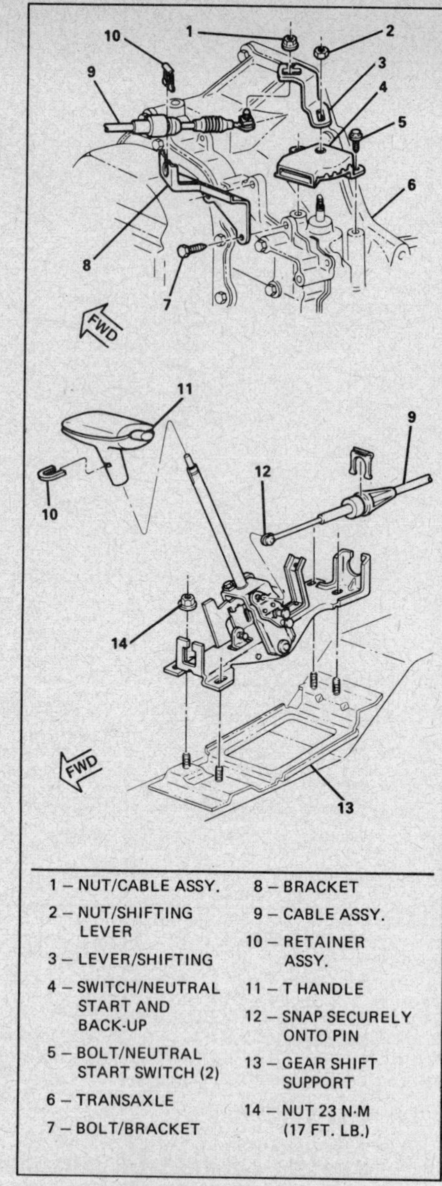

Fig. 9 Back-up light/neutral start switch replacement. Automatic transmission

3. Remove 4 shift plate attaching bolts and the plate.
4. Remove front trim plate, then the front pad attaching screws and front pad.
5. Remove radio attaching screws.
6. Pull radio rearward and disconnect all electrical connectors, then remove radio from vehicle.
7. Reverse procedure to install.

WINDSHIELD WIPER MOTOR
REPLACE
1984

1. Disconnect battery ground cable.
2. Remove both wiper arms using tool No. J-8966 or equivalent.
3. Remove cowl top vent screen.
4. Remove drive link from crank arm.

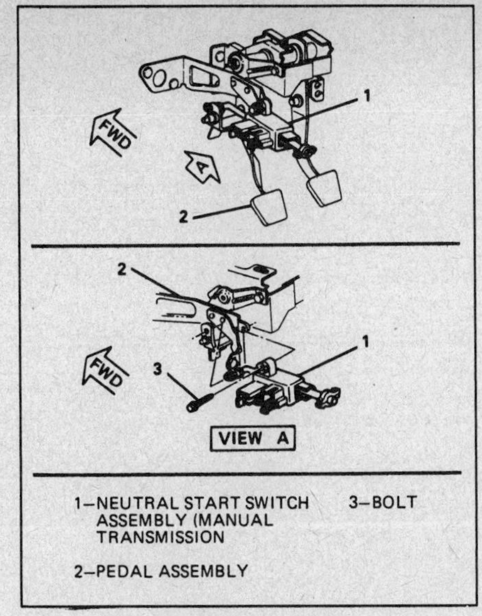

Fig. 10 Clutch start switch replacement

5. Disconnect electrical connectors from wiper motor.
6. Remove wiper motor attaching screws and the motor.
7. Reverse procedure to install. Torque motor attaching screws to 40-58 inch lbs. and drive link attaching nuts to 49-80 inch lbs.

1985–88

1. Disconnect battery ground cable.
2. Loosen transmission drive link-to-motor attaching nuts, then disconnect drive link from motor crank arm.
3. Disconnect electrical connectors from wiper motor.
4. Rotate motor up and remove from vehicle.
5. Reverse procedure to install.

WINDSHIELD WIPER TRANSMISSION REPLACE

1984

1. Remove both wiper arms using tool No. J-8966 or equivalent.
2. Remove cowl top vent screen.
3. Remove drive link from crank arm.
4. Remove 6 cowl panel attaching screws and the cowl panel.
5. Remove transmission assembly from vehicle.
6. Reverse procedure to install. Torque cowl attaching screws and drive link attaching nuts to 49-80 inch lbs.

1985–88

1. Remove cowl top vent screen, then both wiper arms using tool No. J-8966 or equivalent.
2. Loosen drive link-to-crank arm attaching nuts, then disengage drive link from crank arm.
3. Remove transmission-to-cowl panel attaching screws and the transmission.

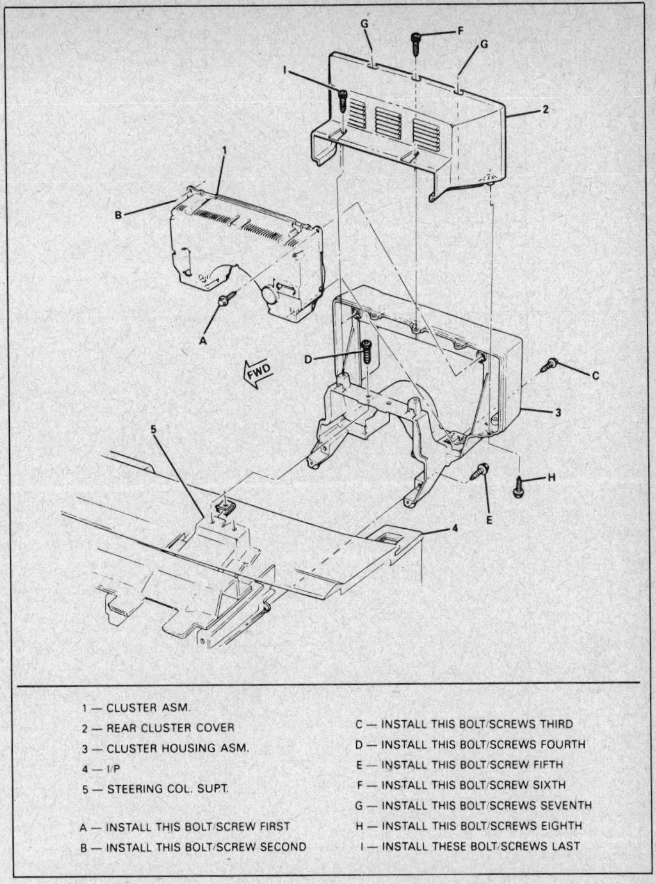

Fig. 11 Instrument cluster. 1984–86

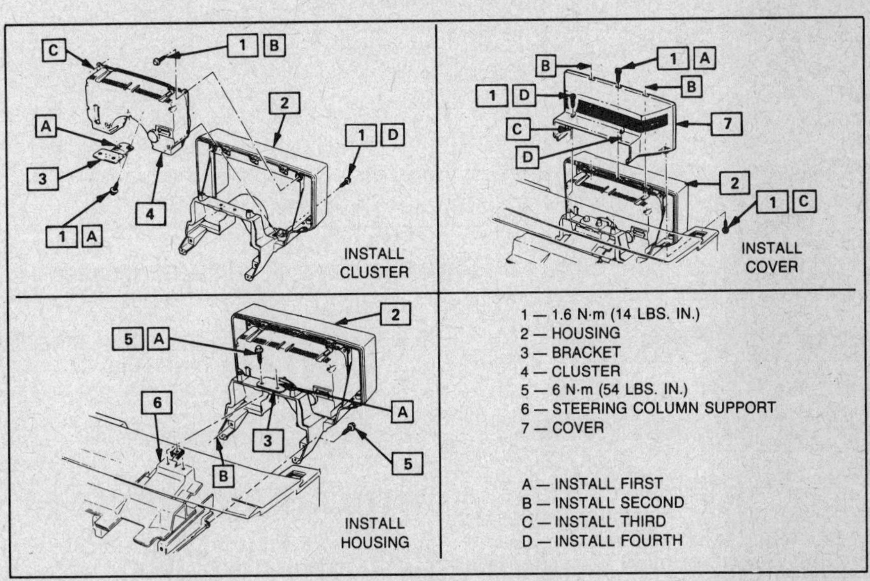

Fig. 12 Instrument cluster. 1987–88

4. Reverse procedure to install. Torque attaching screws and nuts to 64 inch lbs.

BLOWER MOTOR REPLACE

1. Disconnect battery ground cable.
2. Remove cooling tube from blower motor.
3. Disconnect blower motor electrical connections.
4. Remove 5 blower motor attaching screws and the blower motor assembly, **Fig. 13.**
5. Remove fan cage attaching screw and slide cage off motor shaft.
6. Reverse procedure to install.

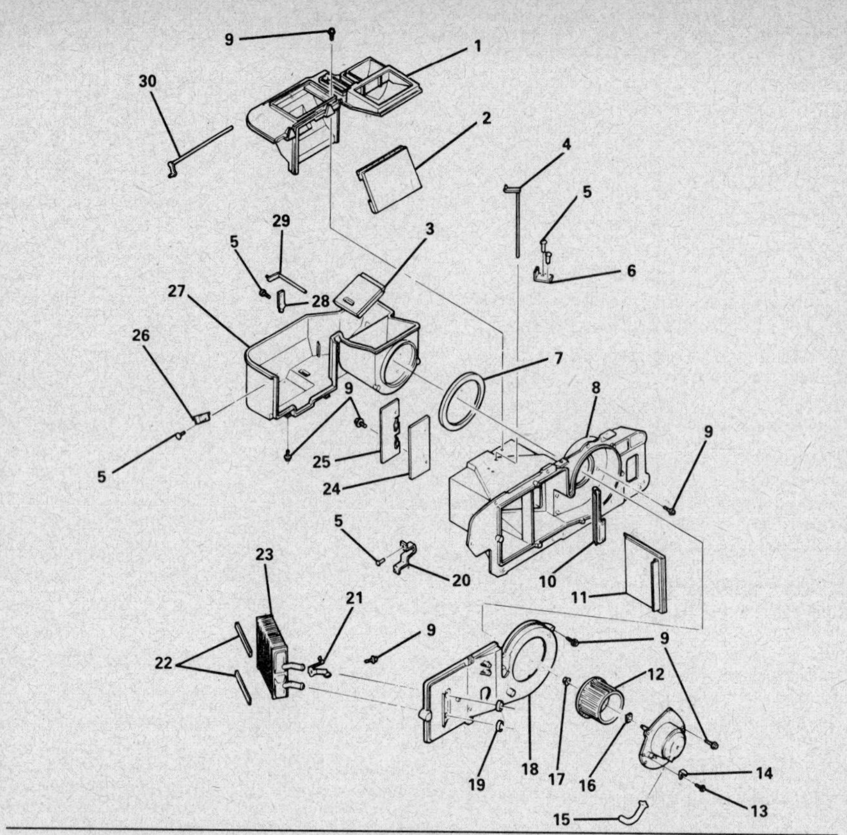

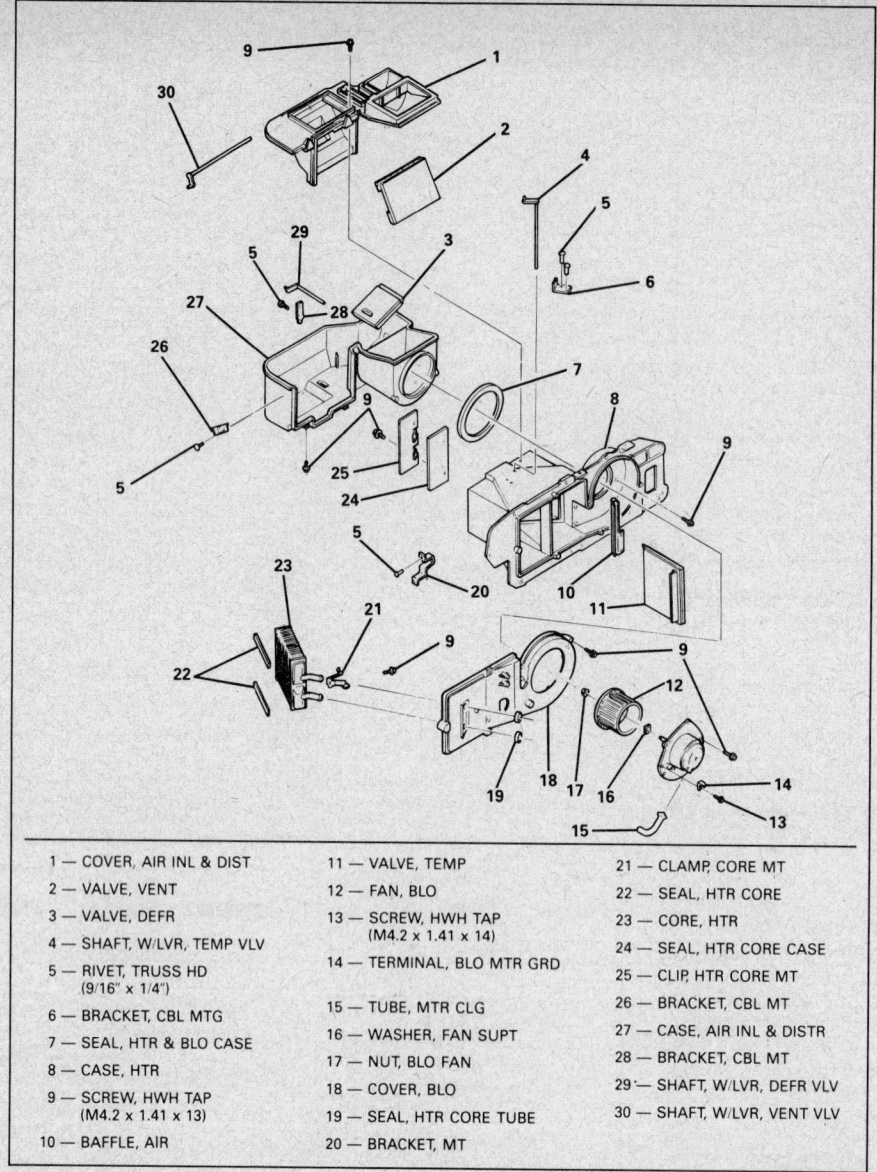

1 — COVER, AIR INL & DIST
2 — VALVE, VENT
3 — VALVE, DEFR
4 — SHAFT, W/LVR, TEMP VLV
5 — RIVET, TRUSS HD (9/16" x 1/4")
6 — BRACKET, CBL MTG
7 — SEAL, HTR & BLO CASE
8 — CASE, HTR
9 — SCREW, HWH TAP (M4.2 x 1.41 x 13)
10 — BAFFLE, AIR
11 — VALVE, TEMP
12 — FAN, BLO
13 — SCREW, HWH TAP (M4.2 x 1.41 x 14)
14 — TERMINAL, BLO MTR GRD
15 — TUBE, MTR CLG
16 — WASHER, FAN SUPT
17 — NUT, BLO FAN
18 — COVER, BLO
19 — SEAL, HTR CORE TUBE
20 — BRACKET, MT
21 — CLAMP, CORE MT
22 — SEAL, HTR CORE
23 — CORE, HTR
24 — SEAL, HTR CORE CASE
25 — CLIP, HTR CORE MT
26 — BRACKET, CBL MT
27 — CASE, AIR INL & DISTR
28 — BRACKET, CBL MT
29 — SHAFT, W/LVR, DEFR VLV
30 — SHAFT, W/LVR, VENT VLV

Fig. 13 Heater core & blower motor. Models less A/C

HEATER CORE REPLACE

LESS AIR CONDITIONING

1. Disconnect battery ground cable.
2. Disconnect all electrical connectors from rear of heater case.
3. Disconnect electrical connector from courtesy lamp bulb socket, if equipped.
4. Remove windshield washer fluid tank.
5. Disconnect heater hoses from heater core, then remove heater core grommets. Plug hoses to prevent spillage.
6. Remove heater case cover attaching screws and the cover, **Fig. 13.**
7. Remove heater core retainer and the heater core.
8. Reverse procedure to install.

WITH AIR CONDITIONING

1. Disconnect battery ground cable.
2. Disconnect heater hoses from heater core. Plug hoses to prevent spillage.
3. Remove speaker grille and the speaker.
4. Remove heater core cover, then the heater core retainers and heater core.
5. Reverse procedure to install.

CRUISE CONTROL ADJUST

SERVO CABLE, ADJUST

1. Install cable assembly end onto throttle body unit lever stud, with cable installed in bracket, and secure with retainer.
2. Pull servo end of cable toward servo without moving injector lever.
3. Connect pin to tab with retainer. **If a tab hole does not line up with pin, move cable away from servo until the next closest hole aligns, then connect pin to tab.**

4-151 (2.5L) Engine Section

INDEX

ENGINE MOUNTS
REPLACE

1. Raise and support vehicle.
2. Remove engine mount-to-chassis attaching nuts, **Fig. 1.**
3. On 1984 models equipped with A/C, and all 1985-88 models, remove forward torque reaction rod attaching bolts.
4. On all models, raise engine slightly using a suitable engine lifting device. Raise engine only enough to provide clearance for mount removal.
5. Removal 2 upper mount-to-engine support bracket attaching nuts and the engine mount.
6. Reverse procedure to install.

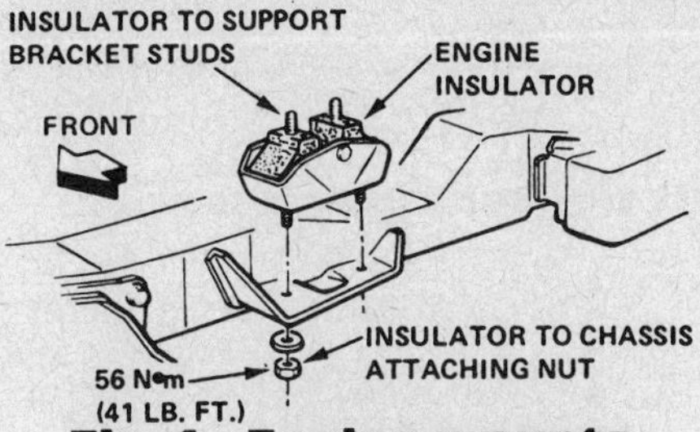

Fig. 1 Engine mounts

ENGINE
REPLACE

1. Disconnect battery cables, then drain cooling system.
2. Remove rear compartment lid. **Do not remove torsion rod retaining bolts.**
3. Remove air cleaner, then disconnect throttle and transaxle cables.
4. Disconnect all necessary vacuum hoses from non-engine components.
5. Disconnect heater hose from intake manifold.
6. Disconnect fuel lines and remove fuel filter.
7. Disconnect fuel pump relay and oxygen sensor electrical connectors.
8. On models equipped with automatic transaxle, disconnect transaxle cooler lines.
9. On models equipped with manual transaxle, remove slave cylinder.
10. On all models, disconnect engine ground strap.
11. Disconnect radiator and heater hoses.
12. Disconnect engine harness connector from bulkhead.
13. On models equipped with A/C, discharge refrigerant from system, then disconnect and cap lines from A/C compressor.
14. Remove rear console.
15. Disconnect electronic control module (ECM) electrical connector through bulkhead panel.
16. Install engine support fixture, tool No. J-28467 or equivalent to engine.
17. Mark the engine strut bracket and attaching bolt for assembly reference, then remove bolt and bracket.
18. Raise and support vehicle.
19. Remove rear wheels.
20. On models equipped with automatic transaxle, remove torque converter attaching bolts.
21. Disconnect parking brake cable.
22. Remove brake calipers and suspend from frame with a piece of wire. Do not suspend calipers by brake hoses.
23. Mark struts for proper realignment as described under "Strut Assembly, Replace" in the "Rear Axle, Rear Suspension & Brakes" section, then remove strut attaching bolts.
24. Disconnect any remaining electrical connectors interfering with engine removal.
25. Remove engine cradle attaching bolts.
26. Release parking brake cables from cradle using tool No. J-34065 or equivalent.
27. Support engine, transaxle and cradle assembly with a suitably dolly, then lower vehicle and remove engine support fixture. **When lowering vehicle, ensure outboard ends of lower control arms are properly supported.**
28. Raise vehicle and slide engine, transaxle and cradle assembly out from under vehicle.
29. Separate engine from transaxle.
30. Reverse procedure to install.

CYLINDER HEAD
REPLACE

1. Disconnect battery ground cable.
2. Drain cooling system.
3. Raise and support vehicle.
4. Disconnect exhaust pipe from exhaust manifold, then lower vehicle.
5. Remove oil dipstick tube and air cleaner.
6. On 1984 models, disconnect throttle body injection unit electrical connectors and vacuum hoses.
7. On 1985-88 models, disconnect electrical connectors and throttle linkage from throttle body injection unit.
8. On 1984 models, remove EGR base plate, then disconnect heater hose from intake manifold. Remove ignition coil lower attaching bolt, then disconnect wiring from coil.
9. On 1985-88 models, disconnect heater hose from intake manifold, then remove ignition coil.
10. On all models, disconnect all electrical connectors from cylinder head and intake manifold.
11. Remove engine strut attaching bolt from upper engine support.
12. On 1984 models, remove alternator drive belt, then disconnect throttle and throttle valve cables from intake manifold.
13. On 1985-88 models, remove or reposition accessory brackets as necessary.
14. On all models, disconnect upper radiator hose from cylinder head.
15. Remove rocker arm cover, then the rocker arms and pushrods.
16. Remove cylinder head attaching bolts, then lift cylinder head and intake and exhaust manifolds as an assembly from cylinder block.
17. Install new head gasket, then the cylinder head assembly, ensuring gasket and head are seated over dowel pins.
18. Coat threads of bolts 9 and 10, **Fig. 2,** with sealer, apply oil to remaining bolts and install all bolts finger tight.
19. Tighten bolts in 3 steps following sequence shown in **Fig. 2.** First torque all bolts to 18 ft. lbs. Second, torque all bolts except bolt No. 9 to 22 ft. lbs. Torque bolt No. 9 to 29 ft. lbs. Third, tighten all bolts except No. 9 an additional 120° (2 flats). Tighten bolt No. 9 an additional 90° (1/4 turn).
20. Reverse remaining procedure to complete installation.

INTAKE MANIFOLD
REPLACE

1. Disconnect battery ground cable and drain cooling system.

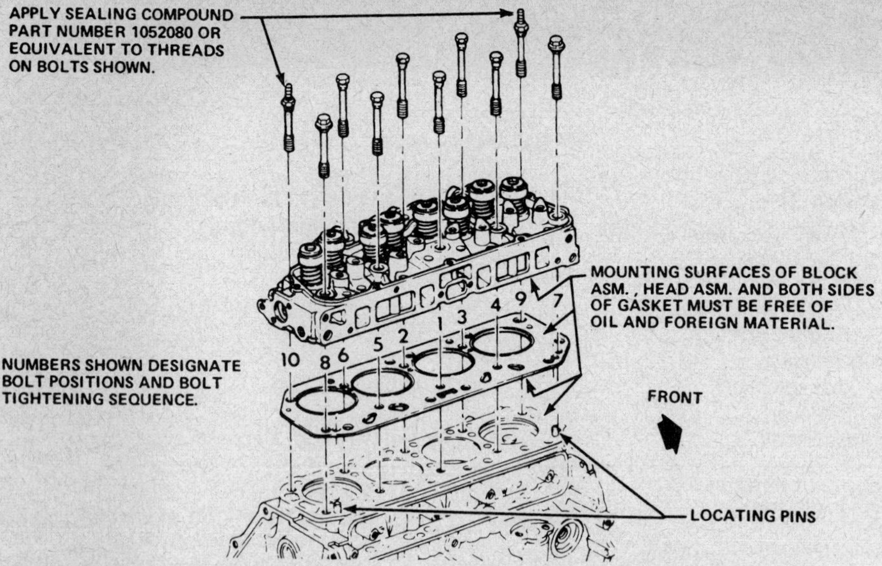

Fig. 2 Cylinder head bolt tightening sequence

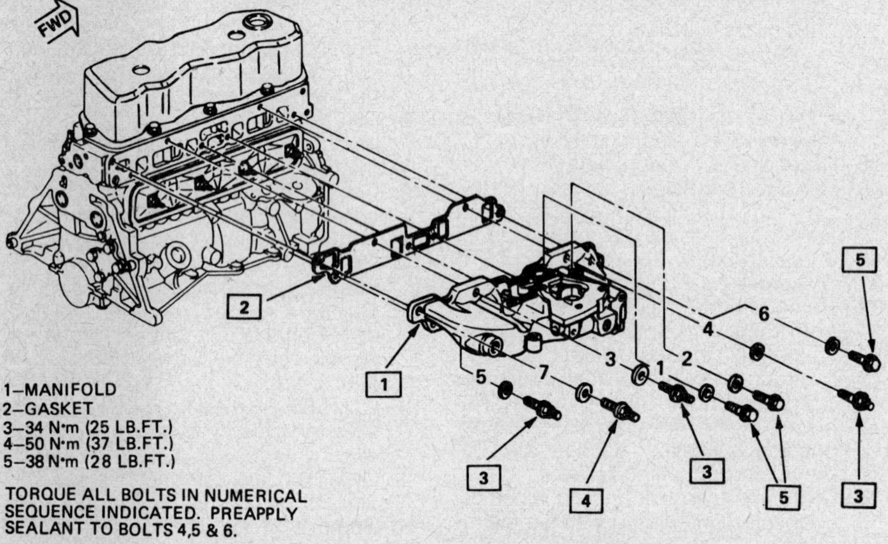

Fig. 3 Intake manifold installation

2. Remove air cleaner and heat stove pipe.
3. Disconnect PCV valve and hose, fuel lines and necessary vacuum hoses, noting position for installation.
4. Disconnect electrical connectors and throttle linkage from TBI unit.
5. Disconnect transaxle kickdown and cruise control linkages, as equipped.
6. Remove throttle linkage and bellcrank from manifold and position aside.
7. Disconnect heater hose and generator brace from manifold, and remove ignition coil.
8. Remove manifold bolts and manifold.
9. Reverse procedure to install. Torque manifold bolts to specifications as shown in **Fig. 3.** On 1987-88 models, torque all attaching bolts to 25 ft. lbs.

ROCKER ARM STUDS

Rocker arm studs which are cracked or have damaged threads can be removed from the cylinder head using a deep well socket. Install and torque new rocker arm stud to 75 ft. lbs.

VALVES

ADJUST

These engines are equipped with hydraulic valve lifters. No provision for adjustment is provided.

VALVE ARRANGEMENT

FRONT TO REAR

All........................ I-E-I-E-E-I-E-I

CAM LOBE LIFT SPECIFICATIONS

Year	Intake	Exhaust
1984-88	.398	.398

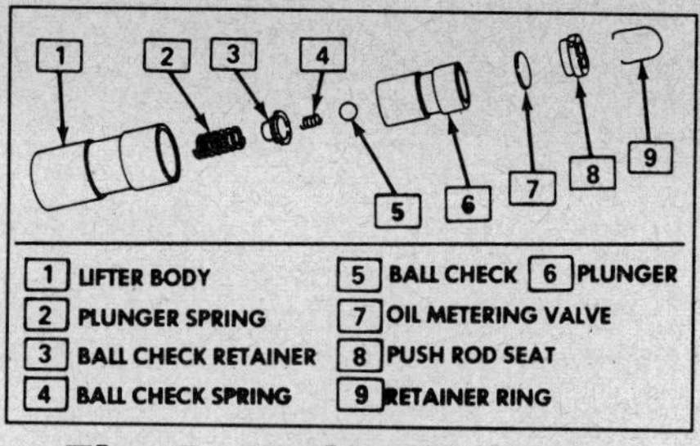

Fig. 4 Hydraulic valve lifter

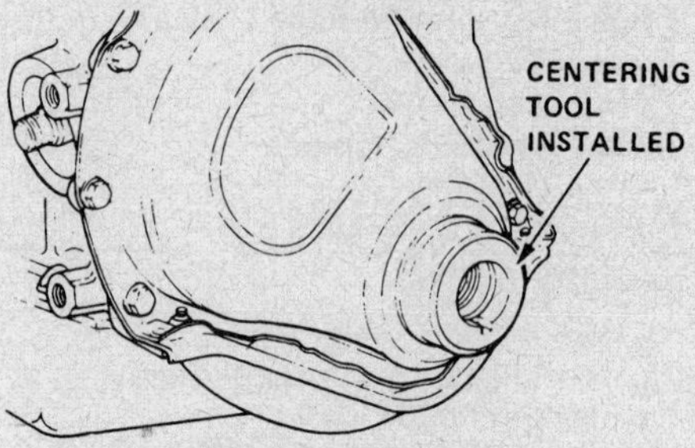

Fig. 5 Engine front cover installation

VALVE TIMING

INTAKE OPENS BEFORE TDC

Year	Degrees
1984-88	33

VALVE GUIDES

Valve guides are an integral part of the cylinder head and are not removable. If valve stem clearance becomes excessive, the valve guide should be reamed to the next oversize and the appropriate oversize valves installed. Valves are available in oversizes of .003 and .005 inch.

VALVE LIFTERS

Failure of a hydraulic valve lifter, **Fig. 4**, is generally caused by an inadequate oil supply or dirt. An air leak at the intake side of the oil pump or excessive oil in the engine will produce air bubbles in the oil supply to the lifters, causing them to collapse. This is a probable cause of trouble when several lifters fail to function, but air in oil is not likely to cause failure of a single unit.

Valve lifters can be removed after removing rocker arm cover, intake manifold and pushrod cover. Loosen rocker arm stud nut and rotate rocker arm so pushrod can be removed, then remove valve lifter. It may be necessary to use tool No. J-3049 to facilitate lifter removal.

ENGINE FRONT COVER

REPLACE

1. Remove drive belts, then the right rear inner splash shield.
2. Remove pulley attaching bolt, then the pulley and hub from shaft.

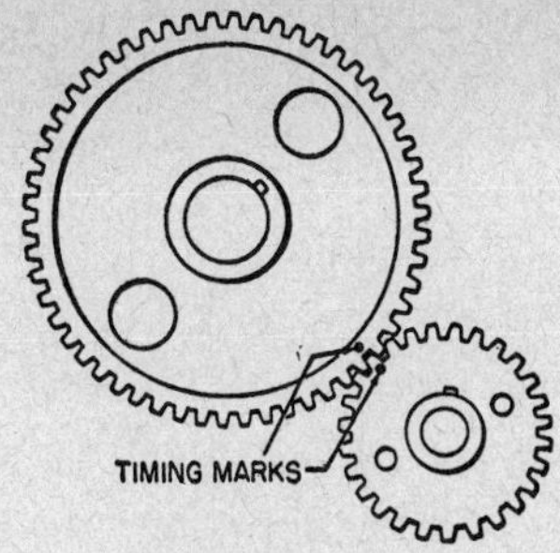

Fig. 6 Valve timing marks

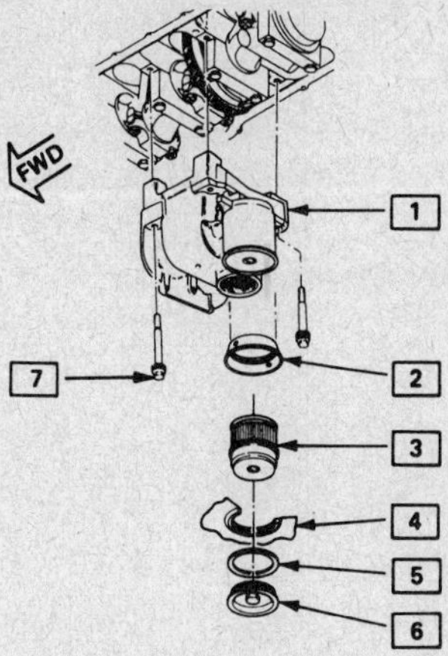

1 - BALANCER ASSEMBLY
2 - RESTRICTOR
3 - FILTER
4 - OIL PAN
5 - GASKET
6 - PLUG
7 - BOLT

Fig. 7 Balance shaft assembly removal

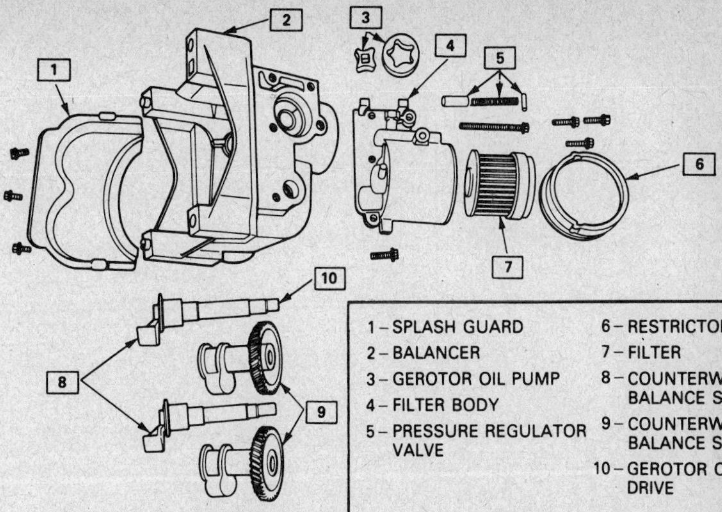

1 - SPLASH GUARD
2 - BALANCER
3 - GEROTOR OIL PUMP
4 - FILTER BODY
5 - PRESSURE REGULATOR VALVE
6 - RESTRICTOR
7 - FILTER
8 - COUNTERWEIGHTED BALANCE SHAFT
9 - COUNTERWEIGHTED BALANCE SHAFT GEAR
10 - GEROTOR OIL PUMP DRIVE

Fig. 8 Exploded view of balance shaft assembly

3. On 1984 models, remove oil pan-to-front cover attaching screws and the front cover.
4. On 1985-88 models, support engine using fixture No. J-28467, then remove engine mount and bracket as an assembly. Remove front cover attaching screws and the front cover.
5. Clean cylinder block and front cover sealing surfaces, then position oil pan front seal on front cover.
6. Apply a 3/8 inch wide by 3/16 inch thick bead of RTV sealer to joint formed at oil pan and front cover.
7. Apply a 1/4 inch wide by 1/8 inch thick bead of RTV sealer on front cover to block mating surface.
8. Install centering tool No. J-23042 in front cover seal, **Fig. 5.**
9. Install front cover. Install 2 attaching screws finger tight, then install remaining screws and torque all screws to 90 inch lbs.
10. Remove centering tool and install pulley, hub, splash shield and drive belts.

TIMING GEARS

When necessary to install a new camshaft gear, the camshaft will have to be removed as the gear is a pressed fit on the camshaft. The camshaft is held in place by a thrust plate retained to the engine by two capscrews which are accessible through the two holes in the gear web.

To remove gear, use an arbor press and a suitable sleeve to properly support gear on its steel hub.

Before installing gear, assemble thrust plate and gear spacer ring, then press gear onto shaft until it bottoms against spacer ring. The thrust plate end clearance should be .0015-.0050 inch. If clearance is less than .0015 inch, the spacer ring should be replaced. If clearance is greater than .0050 inch, the thrust plate should be replaced.

The crankshaft gear can be replaced using a puller and two bolts in the tapped holes of the gear.

When installing timing gears, ensure marks on gears are properly aligned, **Fig. 6.**

The valve timing marks, **Fig. 6,** do not indicate TDC compression for No. 1 cylinder for use during distributor installation. When installing the distributor, rotate engine until No. 1 cylinder is on compression stroke and the camshaft timing mark is 180° from the valve timing position shown in **Fig. 6.**

CAMSHAFT
REPLACE

1. Remove engine as described under "Engine, Replace." Do not separate engine from transaxle.
2. Remove rocker arm cover, then loosen rocker arm stud nuts. Pivot rocker arms clear of pushrods and remove the rods.
3. Remove distributor, then, on 1984 models, the alternator and mounting brackets.
4. Remove front engine mount and bracket assembly.
5. Remove oil pump driveshaft.
6. Remove front cover as described under "Engine Front Cover, Replace."
7. Remove camshaft thrust plate attaching screws.
8. Carefully remove camshaft and gear through front of block.
9. Reverse procedure to install. When installing camshaft, align crankshaft and camshaft timing marks on gear teeth, **Fig. 6.**

BALANCE SHAFT ASSEMBLY
REPLACE

1. Remove engine assembly as described under "Engine, Replace."
2. Remove oil pan attaching bolts and the oil pan.
3. Remove balance shaft assembly attaching bolts and the balance shaft assembly, **Figs. 7 and 8.**
4. Reverse procedure to install. Torque short attaching bolts to 9 ft. lbs. plus an additional 75° turn and long attaching bolts to 9 ft. lbs. plus an additional 90° turn.

PISTONS & RODS ASSEMBLE

Assemble piston to rod with notch on piston facing toward front of engine and the raised notch side of rod at bearing end facing toward rear of engine, **Fig. 9.**

Upon installation, measure connecting rod side clearance using a suitable feeler gauge. Clearance should be .006-.022 inch.

PISTONS, PINS & RINGS

Pistons and rings are available in standard size and oversizes of .010, .020 and .030 inch. Piston pins are available in oversizes of .001 and .003 inch.

MAIN & ROD BEARINGS

Main and rod bearings are available in standard size and oversizes of .001, .002 and .010 inch.

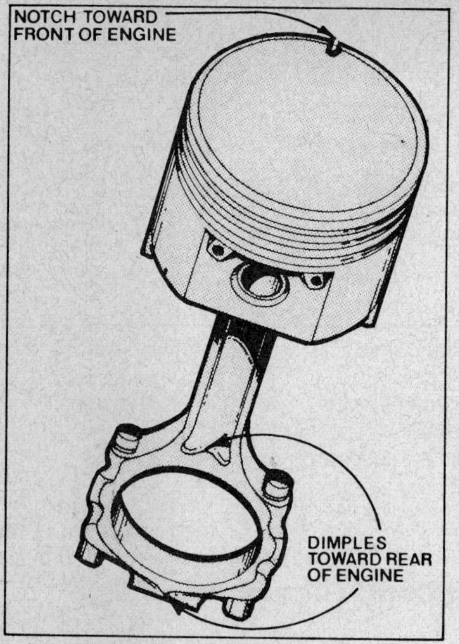

Fig. 9 Piston & rod assembly

OIL PAN

REPLACE

MODELS LESS BALANCE SHAFT ASSEMBLY

1984

1. Install engine support fixture, tool No. J-28467 or equivalent, and raise engine slightly to relieve tension from cradle mounts, **Fig. 10.**
2. Raise and support vehicle.
3. Disconnect exhaust pipe from exhaust manifold, then remove rear wheels.
4. Disconnect both lower control arms and toe link rods from knuckle.
5. Disconnect parking brake cable from cradle.
6. Remove engine and transmission attaching bolts.
7. Remove cradle attaching bolts and the cradle.
8. Drain engine oil, then remove front engine mount-to-support bracket attaching nuts.
9. Disconnect exhaust pipe from rear transaxle mount.
10. Remove starter and flywheel cover, then the upper alternator bracket.
11. Remove lower alternator and engine support brackets.
12. Remove oil pan retaining bolts and the oil pan.
13. Reverse procedure to install, noting the following:
    a. Apply RTV sealer as shown in **Fig. 11.**
    b. Install 2 bolts in front cover after all other pan attaching bolts have been torqued to 75 inch lbs. Torque front cover bolts to 90 inch lbs.
    c. When installing cradle, first install front cradle attaching bolts and nuts finger tight, then note the following torques: rear cradle bolts,

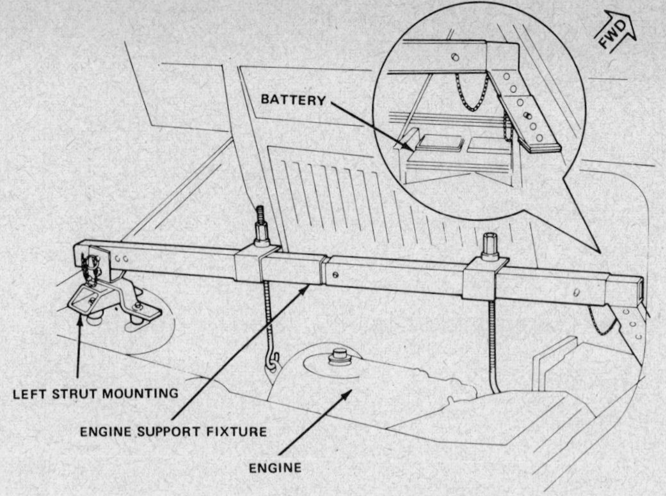

Fig. 10 Engine support fixture

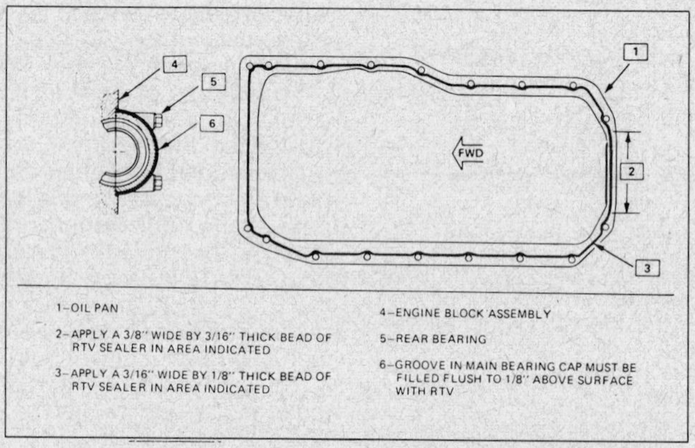

Fig. 11 Oil pan installation. 1984–85

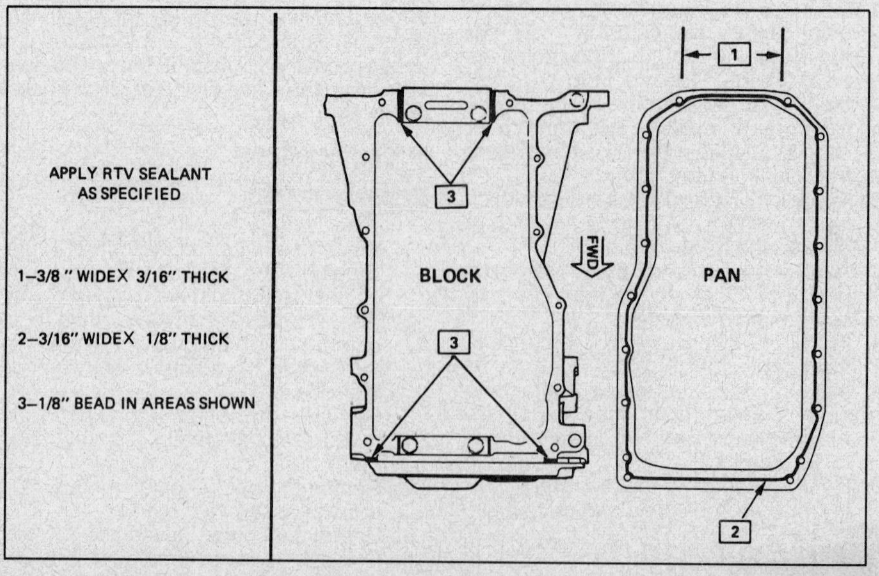

Fig. 12 Oil pan installation. 1986–88

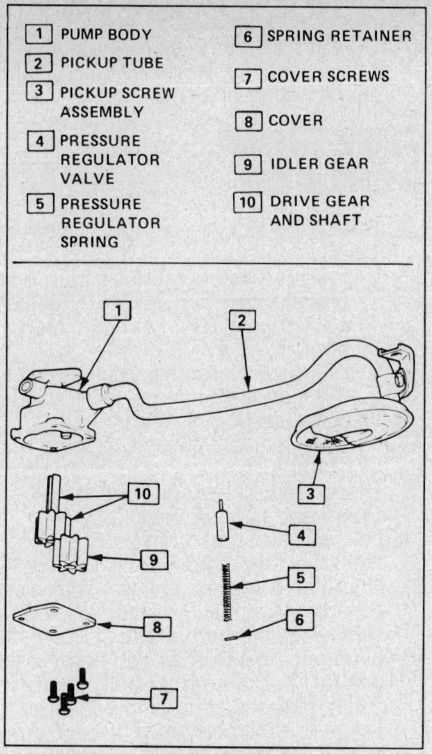

Fig. 13 Exploded view of oil pump

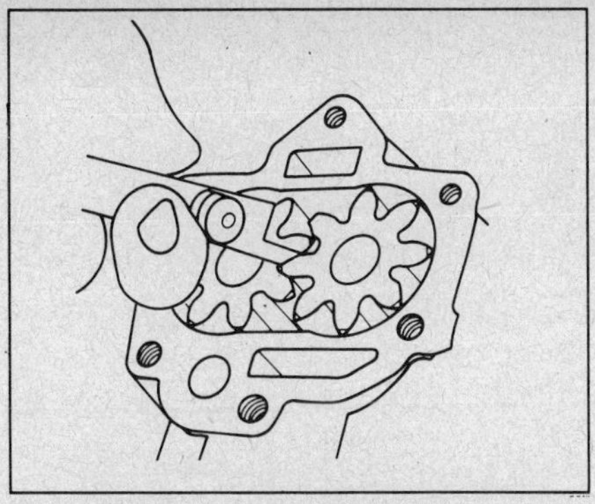

Fig. 14 Measuring oil pump gear backlash

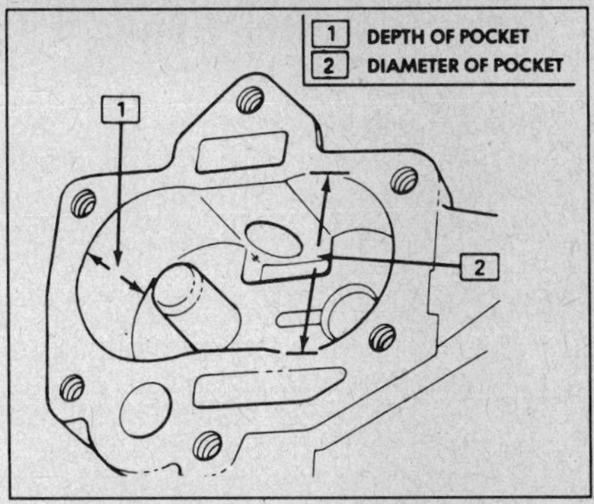

Fig. 15 Measuring oil pump gear pocket

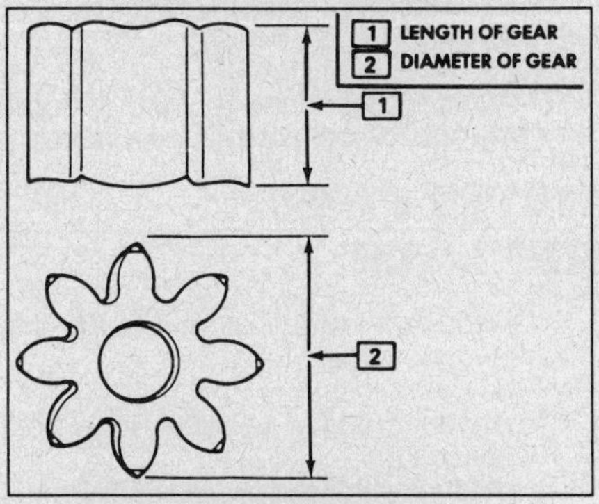

Fig. 16 Measuring oil pump gears

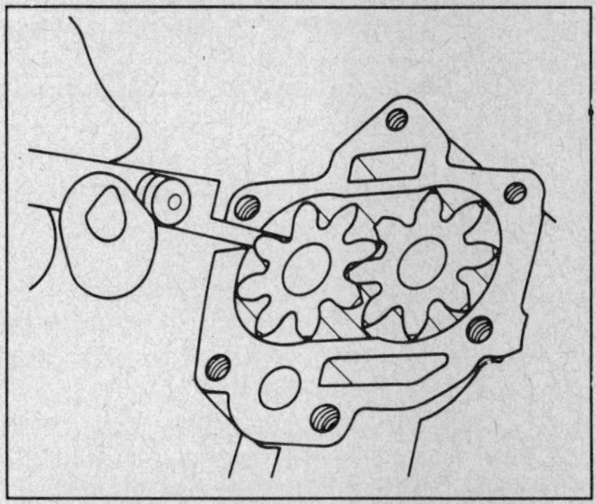

Fig. 17 Measuring oil pump gear side clearance

76 ft. lbs.; front cradle nut, 67 ft. lbs.; engine mount bolts, 42 ft. lbs.; rear mount bolts, 18 ft. lbs.; front mount bolts, 36 ft. lbs.; lower control arm-to-knuckle bolts, 33 ft. lbs.; lower control arm-to-cradle bolts, 69 ft. lbs.; tow rod-to-knuckle bolts, 35 ft. lbs.; exhaust pipe-to-manifold bolts, 25 ft. lbs.

1985–88

1. Disconnect battery cables.
2. Remove engine compartment lid and side panels.
3. Raise and support vehicle.
4. Drain engine oil, then remove front engine mount-to-cradle nuts.
5. Remove flywheel cover, then the starter motor, splash shield and alternator.
6. Lower vehicle, then remove engine strut.
7. Install engine support fixture tool No. J-28467 or equivalent.
8. Raise and support vehicle.
9. Remove engine front support brackets.
10. Remove oil pan attaching bolts and the oil pan.
11. Reverse procedure to install, noting the following:
    a. Apply RTV sealant as as shown in **Figs. 11 and 12.**
    b. On 1985 models, install 2 bolts in front cover after all other pan attaching bolts have been torqued to 54 inch lbs.
    c. Torque all attaching bolts to 90 inch lbs. on 1986 models, or 20 ft. lbs. on 1987-88 models.

MODELS W/BALANCE SHAFT ASSEMBLY

1. Remove engine assembly as described under "Engine, Replace."
2. Remove oil pan attaching bolts and the oil pan.
3. Reverse procedure to install.

OIL PUMP SERVICE

REMOVAL

1. Remove oil pan as described under "Oil Pan, Replace."
2. Remove oil pump attaching bolts and nuts, then the oil pump and screen as an assembly.

DISASSEMBLY

1. Drain residual oil from pump.
2. Remove suction pipe and screen assembly from pump.
3. Remove pump cover attaching screws, then the pump cover and gears, **Fig. 13.**
4. Remove pump regulator valve. Remove plug, spring and ball from valve.

INSPECTION

1. Inspect pump housing and cover for wear or damage, and replace if necessary.
2. Inspect pressure regulator valve for scoring or sticking. Burrs may be removed with a fine oil stone, however more extensive damage requires replacement of valve.
3. Inspect idler gear shaft for wear or damage, and replace if necessary.
4. Inspect pressure regulator spring for lack of tension or distortion, and replace if necessary.
5. Inspect suction pipe and screen, and clean or replace as necessary. **If suction pipe is permanently pressed into the pump body, and if it is loose or has been removed, a new pipe must be installed.**
6. Inspect gears and driveshaft for wear or damage and replace as necessary.
7. Install gears into housing and measure gear backlash, **Fig. 14.** Backlash should measure .009-.015 inch.
8. Measure pump housing gear pocket depth and diameter, **Fig. 15.** Depth should measure .995-.998 inch and diameter 1.503-1.506 inches.
9. Measure length and diameter of gears, **Fig. 16.** Length of both gears should be .999-1.002 inch and diameter should be 1.496-1.500 inches.
10. Measure gear side clearance, **Fig. 17.** Side clearance should measure no more than .004 inch.
11. Measure gear end clearance, **Fig. 18.** End clearance should be .002-.005 inch.
12. If any measurements taken in steps 7 through 11 are not within specifications, replace oil pump components as necessary.

ASSEMBLY

1. Lubricate all internal components with clean engine oil and pack all pump cavities with petroleum jelly.
2. Install pump gears into housing.
3. Install pump cover, pressure regulator valve and spring. Torque cover at-

taching bolts to 10 ft. lbs. and the pressure regulator valve plug to 15 ft. lbs.
4. Apply suitable sealer to new pipe, then tap pipe into position using a plastic hammer and tool No. J-8369.

INSTALLATION

1. Align oil pump shaft with tang on oil pump driveshaft, then install pump on block, positioning pump flange over oil pump driveshaft lower bushing.
2. Install pump attaching bolts and torque to 20 ft. lbs.
3. Install oil pan.

CRANKSHAFT REAR OIL SEAL

REPLACE

The rear main oil seal is a one-piece seal which can be replaced without removing the oil pan or crankshaft.

1. Remove transaxle and flywheel.
2. On models equipped with manual transaxle, remove pressure plate and disc.
3. On all models, remove rear main bearing oil seal using a suitable screwdriver. Use care not to scratch crankshaft.

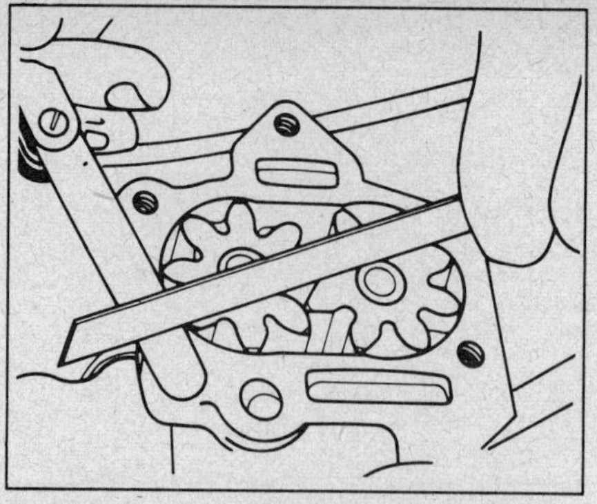

Fig. 18 Measuring oil pump gear end clearance

4. Reverse procedure to install. Lubricate outside of seal to ease assembly.

WATER PUMP

REPLACE

1. Disconnect battery ground cable and drain cooling system.
2. Remove accessory drive belts.
3. Disconnect lower radiator hose from water pump.
4. Remove water pump attaching bolts and the pump.
5. Reverse procedure to install. Apply a 1/8 inch bead of suitable sealer to pump sealing surface, and install pump before sealer dries.

FUEL PUMP

REPLACE

1. Release pressure from fuel system as follows:
   a. Remove fuel pump fuse from fuse block, then start and run engine until engine stalls from fuel starvation.
   b. Energize starter for approximately 3 seconds to release any residual pressure from system.
   c. Turn ignition off and replace fuel pump fuse.
2. Disconnect battery ground cable.
3. Raise and support vehicle.
4. Remove fuel tank from vehicle.
5. Remove fuel meter/pump assembly. Turn cam lock ring counterclockwise, then lift assembly from fuel tank and remove pump from meter.
6. Lift pump up into attaching hose while pulling away from bottom support. When pump is clear of lower support, remove assembly from rubber connector. **Use care to avoid damage to rubber insulator and strainer during removal.**
7. Reverse procedure to install.

V6-173 (2.8L) Engine Section

INDEX

ENGINE MOUNTS

REPLACE

ENGINE MOUNT

1. Disconnect battery ground cable.
2. Remove engine compartment lid and side cover panels.
3. Support engine with tools J-28467 and J-35563.
4. Remove torque reaction rod bolt.
5. Raise and support vehicle.
6. Remove engine mount to chassis attaching nuts, **Fig. 1.**
7. Remove engine mount to support bracket upper nuts.
8. Remove engine mount from vehicle.
9. Reverse procedure to install.

TRANSAXLE MOUNTS

1. Disconnect battery ground cable.
2. Remove engine compartment lid and side cover panels. Do not remove torsion rod retaining bolts.
3. Support engine and transaxle with tools J-28467 and J-35563.
4. Remove mount to cradle and support bracket attaching nuts, **Fig. 2.**
5. Remove transaxle mount and shield, if equipped.
6. Reverse procedure to install.

ENGINE

REPLACE

1. Disconnect battery ground cable and drain cooling system.
2. Remove engine compartment lid and side cover panels. **Do not remove torsion rod retaining bolts.**
3. Remove intake flex duct.
4. Disconnect throttle and shift cable.
5. Disconnect heater hoses from engine.
6. Disconnect vacuum hoses to components not engine mounted.
7. Disconnect fuel lines from engine and remove fuel pump relay.

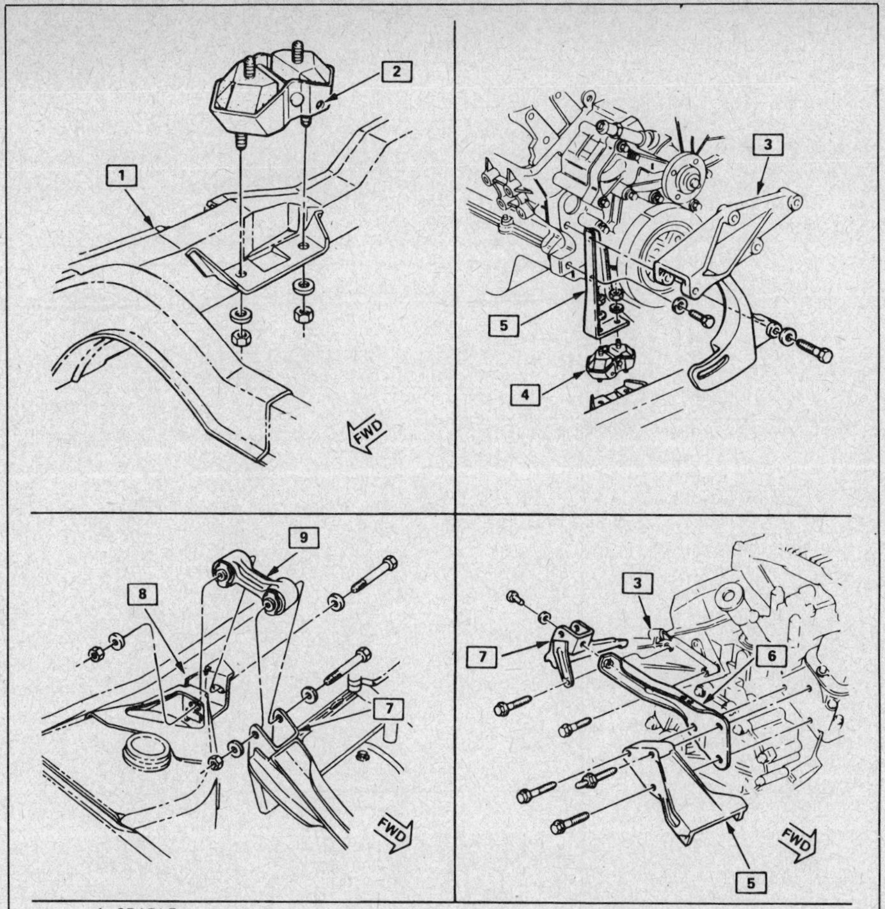

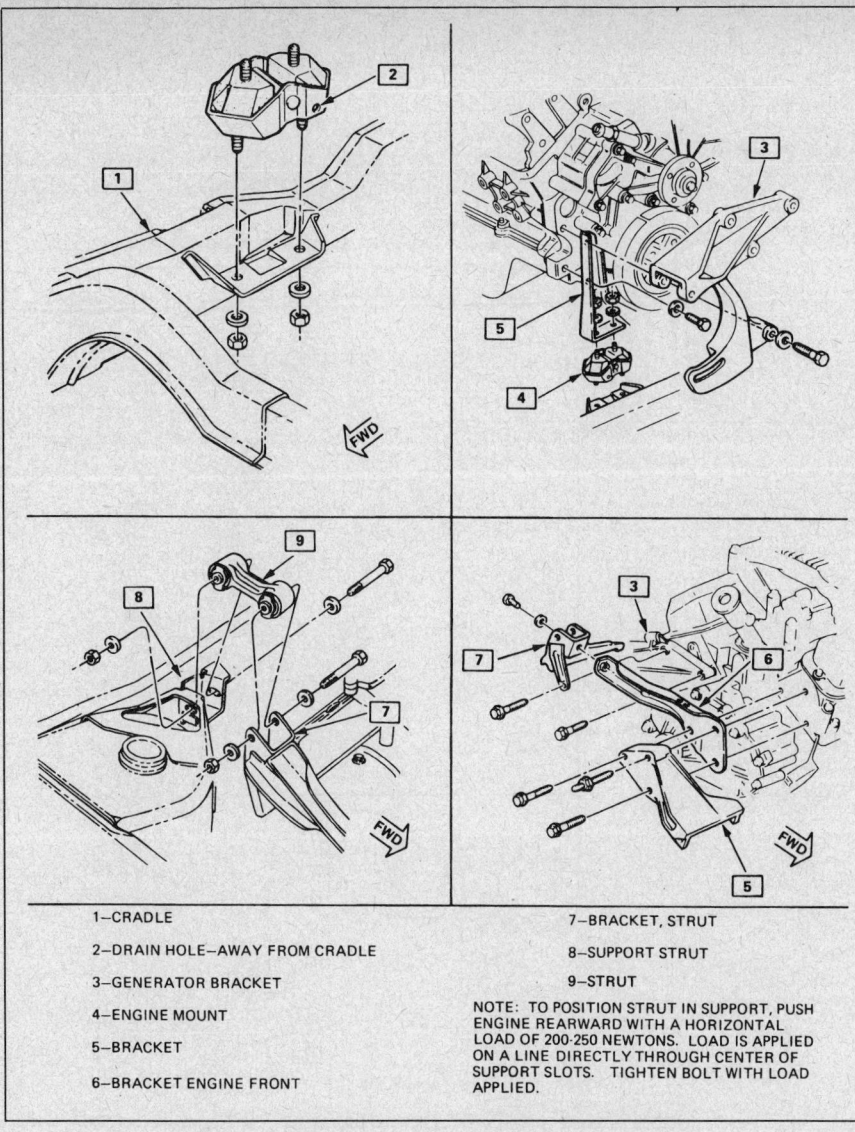

1—CRADLE
2—DRAIN HOLE—AWAY FROM CRADLE
3—GENERATOR BRACKET
4—ENGINE MOUNT
5—BRACKET
6—BRACKET ENGINE FRONT
7—BRACKET, STRUT
8—SUPPORT STRUT
9—STRUT

NOTE: TO POSITION STRUT IN SUPPORT, PUSH ENGINE REARWARD WITH A HORIZONTAL LOAD OF 200-250 NEWTONS. LOAD IS APPLIED ON A LINE DIRECTLY THROUGH CENTER OF SUPPORT SLOTS. TIGHTEN BOLT WITH LOAD APPLIED.

Fig. 1 Engine mount installation

8. On automatic transaxle models, disconnect transaxle cooler lines.
9. On manual transaxle models, remove slave cylinder and shield from transaxle.
10. Disconnect ground strap from engine.
11. Remove radiator hoses.
12. Disconnect engine harness at junction block.
13. Remove rear heat shield.
14. If equipped, discharge air conditioning system. Disconnect A/C lines and wiring from compressor. Plug A/C lines.
15. Remove rear console.
16. Disconnect ECM harness through bulkhead panel.
17. Remove engine strut front bolt.
18. Install engine support fixture and bracket.
19. Raise and support vehicle.
20. Remove rear wheels.
21. Remove brake calipers and position aside. **Do not disconnect brake hoses.**
22. Remove two strut bolts on each side. **Scribe alignment marks on bolts to retain camber setting.**
23. Loosen four cradle bolts.
24. Lower vehicle.
25. Support engine and transaxle assembly on a suitable dolly.
26. Remove four cradle bolts.
27. Raise vehicle, leaving engine and transaxle assembly on dolly.
28. Reverse procedure to install. Torque rear cradle bolts to 76 ft. lbs. and front cradle bolts to 66 ft. lbs.

INTAKE MANIFOLD
REPLACE

1. Disconnect battery ground cable. Drain cooling system.
2. Remove rocker arm covers.
3. Remove intake duct.
4. Remove distributor. Mark location of distributor on engine and rotor on distributor body.
5. Disconnect throttle body from upper plenum.
6. Remove radiator hose and radiator fill inlet.
7. Disconnect heater hoses and the pipe to throttle body.
8. Disconnect wiring harness.
9. Remove heater hoses and disconnect vacuum hoses.
10. Remove brake booster pipe and bracket.
11. Disconnect EGR pipe.
12. Remove upper manifold plenum and gaskets, **Fig. 3.**
13. Remove intermediate intake manifold and gasket.
14. Remove lower intake manifold and gaskets.
15. Reverse procedure to install. Refer to **Fig. 3** for torque sequence. Torque lower intake manifold bolts to 19 ft. lbs. Torque intermediate intake manifold bolts to 15 ft. lbs. Torque upper manifold plenum bolts to 19 ft. lbs.

EXHAUST MANIFOLD
REPLACE
FRONT

1. Disconnect battery ground cable.
2. Remove engine compartment lid. **Do not remove torsion rod retaining bolts.**
3. Disconnect brake vacuum hose.
4. Remove manifold heat shield.
5. Remove front crossover bolts, **Fig. 4.**
6. Raise and support vehicle.
7. Remove front converter heat shield.
8. Remove lower manifold bolts.
9. Lower vehicle.
10. Remove upper manifold bolts and the manifold.
11. Reverse procedure to install. Torque manifold bolts to 18 ft. lbs. Torque crossover bolts to 22 ft. lbs.

REAR

1. Remove manifold to crossover bolts, **Fig. 4.**
2. Remove manifold bolts and the manifold.
3. Reverse procedure to install. Torque manifold bolts to 18 ft. lbs. Torque crossover bolts to 22 ft. lbs.

CYLINDER HEAD
REPLACE
LEFT SIDE

1. Disconnect battery ground cable and drain cooling system.
2. Remove intake manifold and exhaust crossover pipe.
3. Remove alternator bracket and oil dipstick tube.
4. Remove rocker arm cover, rocker arms and pushrods.
5. Remove cylinder head bolts and cylinder head.
6. Reverse procedure to install. Torque cylinder head bolts in sequence, **Fig. 5,** to 66 ft. lbs.

RIGHT SIDE

1. Disconnect battery ground cable and drain cooling system.
2. Raise and support vehicle.
3. Disconnect exhaust pipe from manifold.
4. Remove cruise control servo bracket.
5. Remove intake manifold and exhaust crossover pipe.
6. Remove rocker arm cover, rocker arms and pushrods.
7. Remove cylinder head bolts and cylinder head.
8. Reverse procedure to install. Torque cylinder head bolts in sequence, **Fig. 5,** to 66 ft. lbs.

ROCKER ARM COVER

REPLACE

FRONT

1. Disconnect battery ground cable.
2. Remove engine compartment lid. **Do not remove torsion rod retaining bolts.**
3. Remove vacuum boost line and tube.
4. Disconnect throttle and downshift cables and remove bracket.
5. Disconnect cruise control cable, if equipped.
6. Remove ground cable.
7. Remove PCV valve from rocker arm cover.
8. Remove oil dipstick tube.
9. Disconnect spark plug wires and remove bracket.
10. Remove engine lift hook.
11. Remove rocker arm cover bolts and the cover. **If cover adheres to cylinder head, shear the adhesion by tapping the end of the cover with a rubber mallet. If cover will not release, pry carefully until loose. Do not distort the sealing flange.**
12. Reverse procedure to install. Torque cover bolts to 90 inch lbs.

REAR

1. Disconnect battery ground cable.
2. Remove torque reaction rod attaching bolt from cylinder head.
3. Pivot torque reaction rod upward and remove cylinder head bracket attaching bolt from bracket at front of engine.
4. Loosen lower torque reaction rod bracket attaching bolt at front of engine.
5. Remove upper two torque reaction rod bracket attaching bolts from front of engine.
6. Remove torque reaction rod bracket attaching bolts from cylinder head-to-exhaust manifold connection.
7. Disconnect wiring harness between rocker arm cover and lower plenum.
8. Remove rocker arm cover attaching bolts and the cover. **If cover adheres to cylinder head, shear the adhesion by tapping the end of the cover with a rubber mallet. If cover will not release, pry carefully until loose. Do not distort the sealing flange.**
9. Reverse procedure to install. Torque cover attaching bolts to 90 inch lbs.

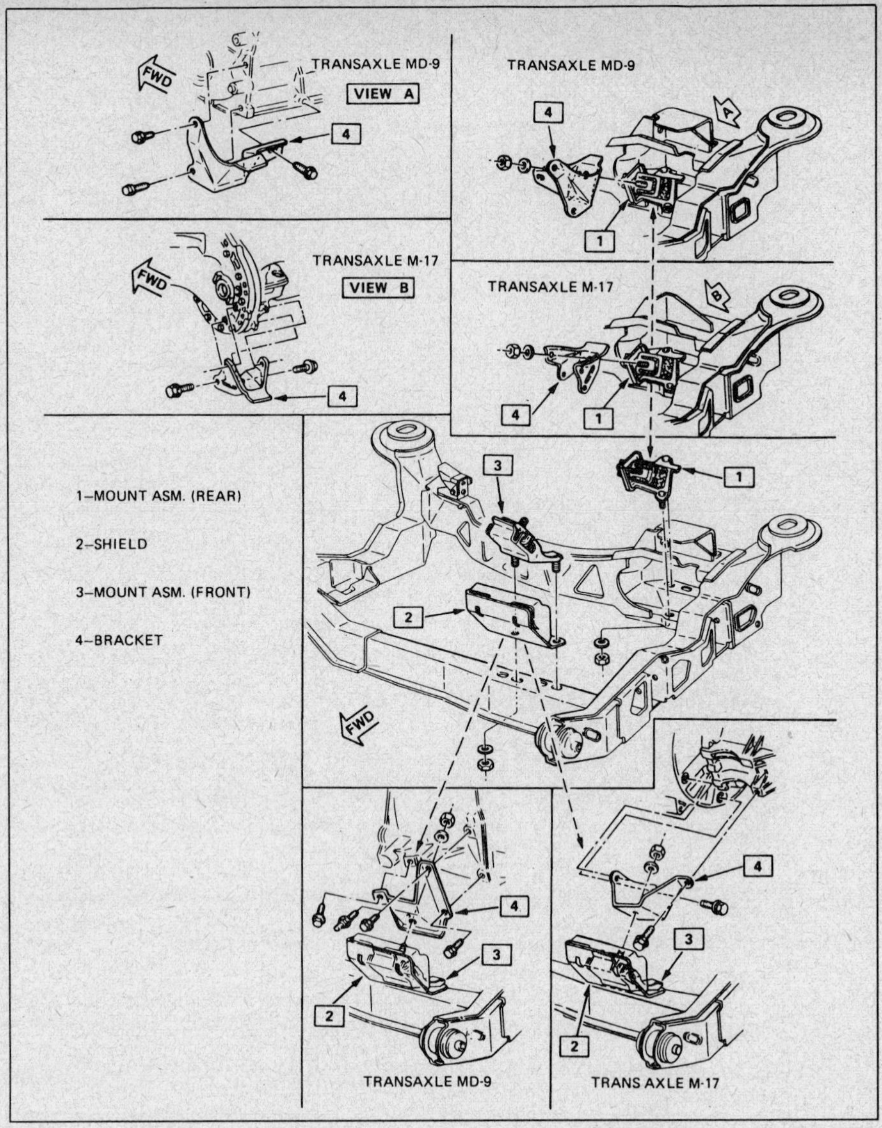

Fig. 2 Transaxle mount installation

VALVE ARRANGEMENT

FRONT TO REAR

Right .... E-I-E-I-I-E
Left.......................... E-I-I-E-I-E

CAM LOBE LIFT SPECIFICATIONS

Engine	Year	Int.	Exh.
V6-173	1985–88	.267	.268

VALVE TIMING

INTAKE OPENS BEFORE TDC

Engine	Year	Degrees
V6-173	1985-88	31

ROCKER ARM STUDS

Rocker arm studs that are cracked or have damaged threads can be replaced. If threads in cylinder head are damaged or stripped, the head can be re-tapped and a helical type insert added. When installing a new rocker arm stud, torque to 43-49 ft. lbs.

VALVE CLEARANCE SPECIFICATIONS

Refer to "Valves, Adjust" procedure.

VALVES

ADJUST

1. Crank engine until mark on torsional damper is aligned with TDC mark on timing tab. Check to ensure engine is in the No. 1 cylinder firing position by

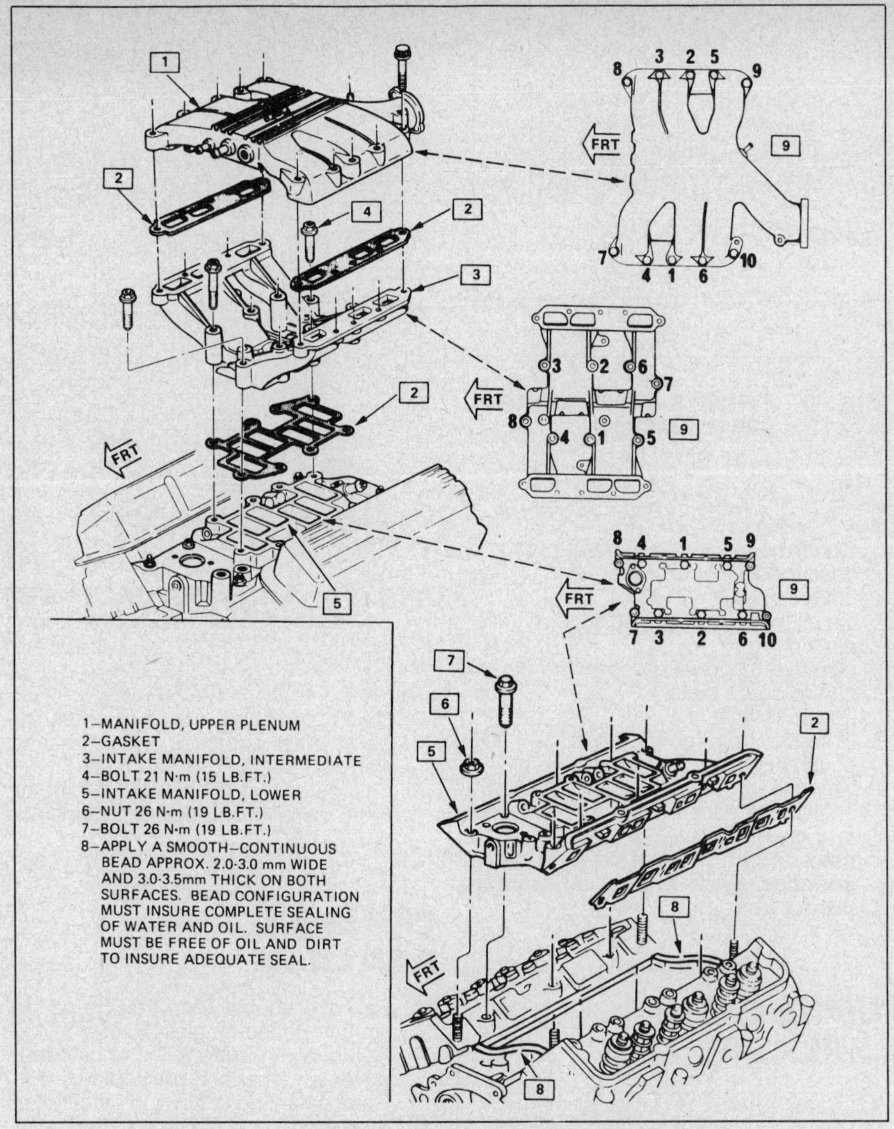

Fig. 3 Intake manifold installation

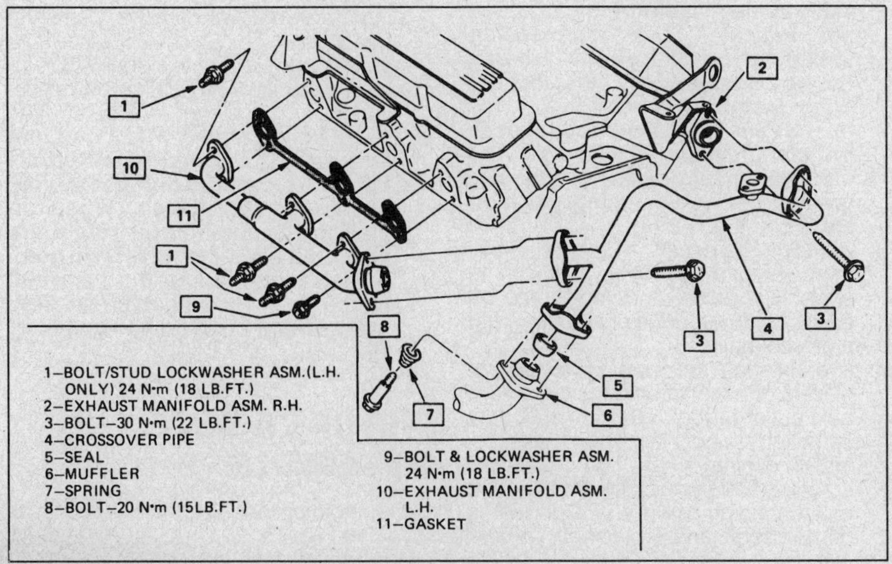

Fig. 4 Exhaust manifold installation

Head Torque Sequence

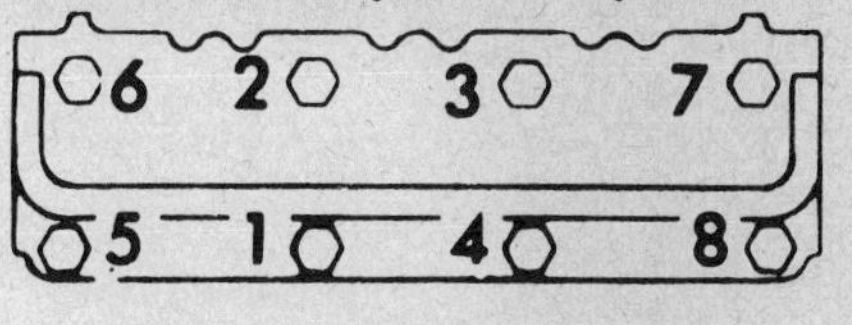

Fig. 5 Cylinder head installation & torque sequence

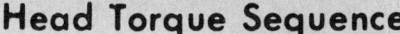

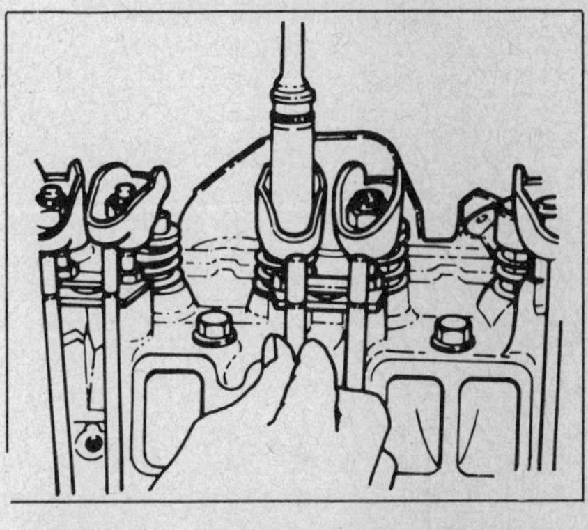

Fig. 6 Adjusting valves

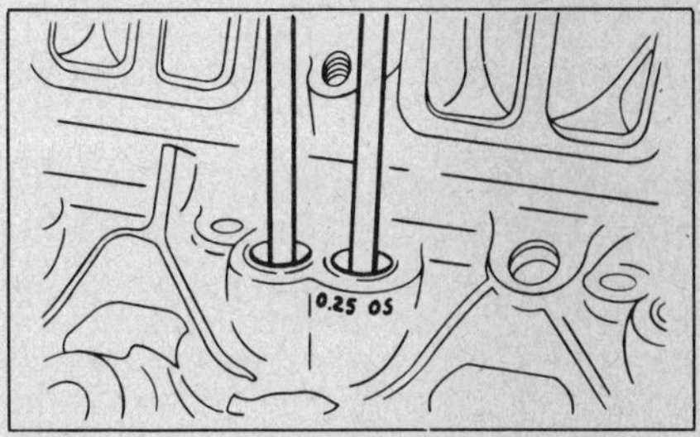

Fig. 7 Oversize valve lifter marking

placing fingers on No. 1 cylinder rocker arms as mark on damper comes near TDC mark on timing tab. If valves are not moving, the engine is in the No. 1 firing position. If valves move as damper mark nears TDC inch mark on timing tab, engine is in the No. 4 cylinder firing position and should be rotated one revolution to reach the No. 1 cylinder firing position.

2. With engine in the No. 1 cylinder firing position, adjust the following valves: Exhaust- 1, 2, 3; Intake- 1, 5, 6. To adjust valves, back off adjusting nut until lash is felt at pushrod, then tighten adjusting nut until all lash is removed, **Fig. 6.** This can be determined by rotating the pushrod while tightening the adjusting nut. When all lash has been eliminated, turn adjusting nut an additional 1½ turns.
3. Crank engine one revolution until mark on torsional damper and TDC mark are again aligned. This is the No. 4 cylinder firing position. With engine in this position, the following valves can be adjusted: Exhaust- 4, 5 & 6; Intake- 2, 3 & 4.
4. Install rocker arm covers, then start engine and check timing and idle speed.

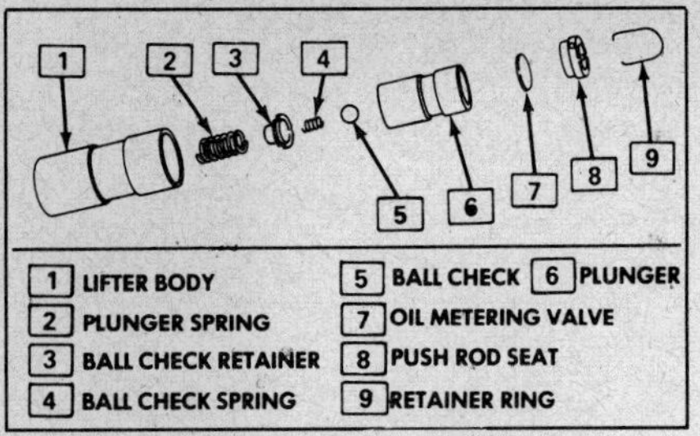

Fig. 8 Valve lifter. Exploded view

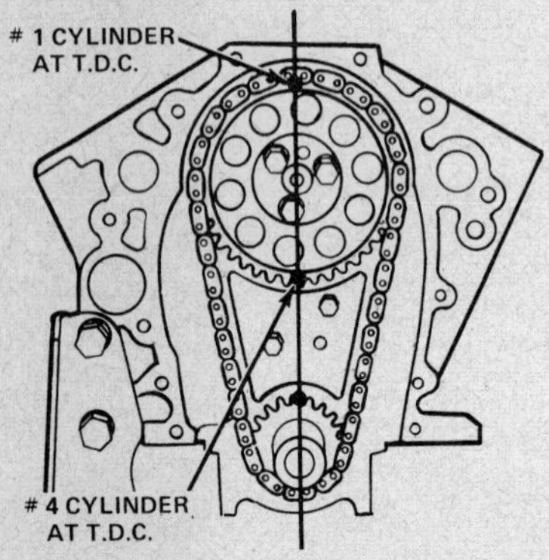

Fig. 11 Valve timing marks

VALVE GUIDES

Valve guides are an integral part of the cylinder head and are not removable. If valve stem clearance becomes excessive, the valve guide should be reamed to the next oversize and the appropriate oversize valves installed. Valves are available in of oversizes .0035, .0155 and .0305 inch.

VALVE LIFTERS

Some engines will be equipped with both standard and .25 mm oversize valve lifters. The cylinder case will be marked where the oversize valve lifters are installed with a dab of white paint and .25 mm O.S. will be stamped on the valve lifter boss, **Fig. 7.**

Failure of a hydraulic valve lifter, **Fig. 8,** is generally caused by an inadequate oil supply or dirt. An air leak at the intake side of the oil pump or too much oil in the engine will cause air bubbles in the oil supply to the lifters causing them to collapse. This is a probable cause of trouble if several lifters fail to function, but air in oil is an unlikely cause of failure of a single unit.

Valve lifters can be removed after removing rocker arm covers, intake manifold, rocker stud nuts, rocker arm balls, rocker arms and pushrods.

ENGINE FRONT COVER

REPLACE

1. Disconnect battery ground cable.
2. Remove accessory drive belts.
3. On models equipped with air conditioning, remove A/C compressor and bracket.

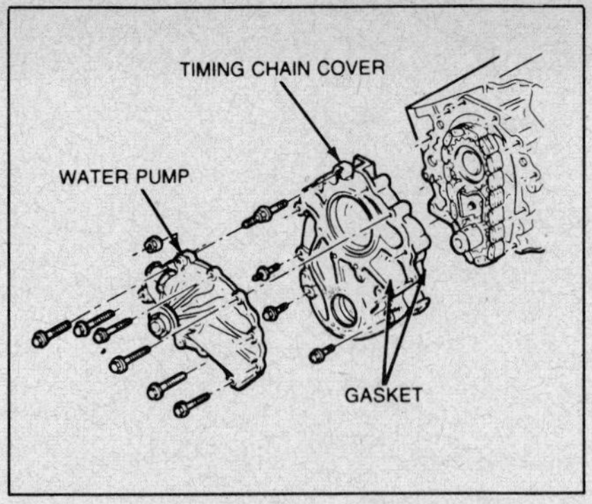

Fig. 9 Engine front cover installation

4. On all models, remove water pump as described under "Water Pump, Replace."
5. On all models, raise and support vehicle.
6. Remove torsional damper and the oil pan to cover bolts.
7. Lower vehicle.
8. Remove front cover bolts and the cover, **Fig. 9.**
9. Reverse procedure to install. Apply sealant to mating surfaces as shown in **Fig. 10. It is only necessary to coat oil pan to front cover sealing surfaces since gasket is used in production.**

TIMING CHAIN

REPLACE

1. Remove front cover as described under "Engine Front Cover, Replace."
2. Place No. 1 piston at top dead center with marks on camshaft and crankshaft sprockets aligned, **Fig. 11. The valve timing marks, Fig. 11, does not indicate TDC compression stroke for No. 1 cylinder for use during distributor installation. When installing the distributor, rotate engine until No. 1 cylinder is on compression stroke and the camshaft timing mark is 180 degrees from valve timing position shown in Fig. 11.**
3. Remove camshaft sprocket bolts, then remove sprocket and timing chain. If sprocket does not come off easily, tap lower edge of sprocket with a plastic mallet.
4. If crankshaft sprocket is to be replaced, remove sprocket using a suitable puller or tool J-5825. Install new sprocket, aligning key and keyway.
5. Install timing chain on camshaft sprocket. Hold sprocket vertically with chain hanging down and align marks on camshaft and crankshaft sprockets.
6. Align dowel pin hole in sprocket with dowel pin on camshaft, then install sprocket on camshaft.

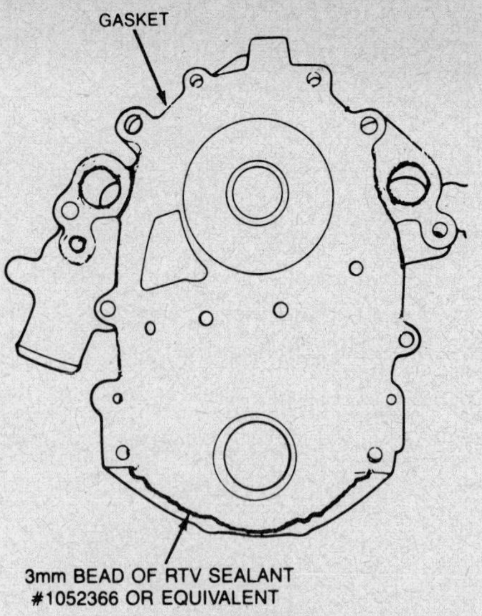

Fig. 10 Engine front cover sealant location

7. Using camshaft sprocket attaching bolts, draw sprocket onto camshaft. Torque bolts to 15 to 20 ft. lbs.
8. Lubricate timing chain with engine oil, then install front cover as outlined previously.

CAMSHAFT

REPLACE

1. Remove engine from vehicle as described under "Engine, Replace."
2. Remove valve lifters and engine front cover as described previously.
3. Remove timing chain and sprocket as described under "Timing Chain, Replace."
4. Remove camshaft rear cover, **Fig. 12.**
5. Withdraw camshaft from engine, using care not to damage camshaft bearings.
6. Reverse procedure to install. When installing timing chain, align valve timing marks as shown in **Fig. 11. The valve timing marks, Fig. 11, do not indicate TDC compression stroke for No. 1 cylinder for use during distributor installation. When installing the distributor, rotate engine until No. 1 cylinder is on compression stroke and the camshaft timing mark is 180 degrees from valve timing position shown in Fig. 11.**

PISTONS & RODS

ASSEMBLE

Assemble pistons to connecting rods as shown in **Fig. 13.**

Upon installation, measure the connecting rod side clearance using a suitable feeler gauge. Clearance should be .006 to .017 inch.

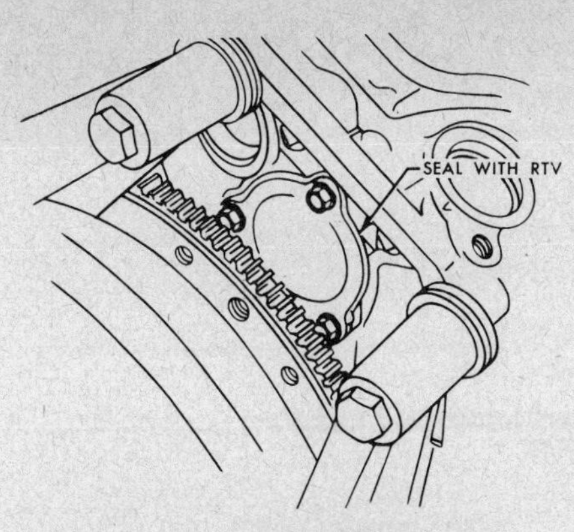

Fig. 12 Camshaft rear cover installation

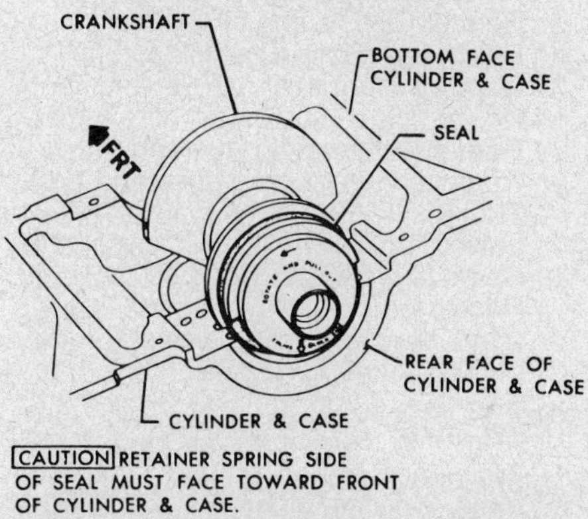

Fig. 15 Rear main bearing oil seal installation. Thin seal

PISTONS, PINS & RINGS

Pistons and rings are available in standard size and oversizes of .05 and 1 mm.

MAIN & ROD BEARINGS

Main bearings are available in standard size and undersizes of .013 and .026 mm and connecting rod bearings are available in standard size and undersizes of .016 and .032 mm.

OIL PAN

REPLACE

1. Disconnect battery ground cable.
2. Raise and support vehicle.
3. Drain engine oil from crankcase.
4. Remove flywheel housing shield or clutch housing cover as applicable.
5. Remove starter motor.
6. Remove oil pan attaching bolts and the oil pan.
7. Reverse procedure to install. Apply a 1/8 inch bead of RTV sealer to oil pan sealing flange.

OIL PUMP SERVICE

REMOVAL

1. Remove oil pan as described under "Oil Pan, Replace."

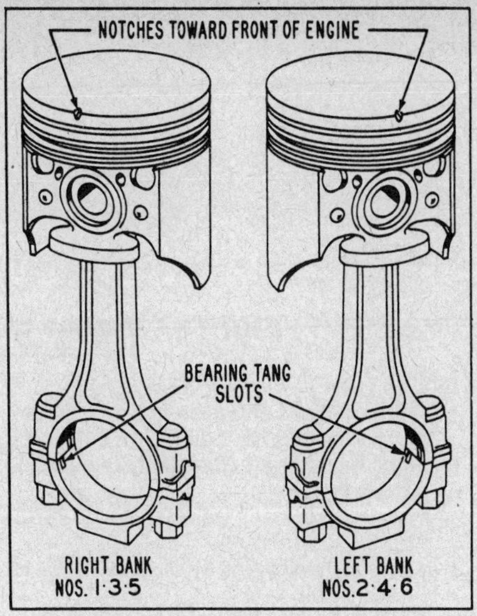

Fig. 13 Piston & rod assembly

2. Remove pump to rear main bearing cap bolt and remove pump and extension shaft.

DISASSEMBLY

1. Remove pump cover attaching bolts and pump cover, **Fig. 14.**
2. Mark drive and idler gear teeth so they can be installed in the same position, then remove idler and drive gear and shaft from pump body.
3. Remove pin, spring and pressure regulator valve from pump cover.
4. If pickup tube and screen assembly are to be replaced, mount pump cover in a soft jawed vise and remove pickup tube from cover. Do not remove screen from pickup tube, these components are serviced as an assembly.

INSPECTION

1. Inspect pump body and cover for excessive wear and cracks.
2. Inspect pump gear for damage or excessive wear. If pump gears are damaged or worn, the entire pump assembly must be replaced.
3. Check drive gear shaft for looseness in pump body.
4. Inspect pump cover for wear that would allow oil to leak past gear teeth.
5. Inspect pickup tube and screen assembly for damage.
6. Check pressure regulator valve for fit in pump cover.

ASSEMBLY

1. If pickup tube and screen were removed, apply sealer to end of pickup tube, then mount pump cover in a soft jawed vise and using tool No. J-8369, tap pickup tube into position using a plastic mallet. **Whenever the pickup tube and screen assembly has been removed, a new pickup tube and screen assembly should be installed. Use care when installing pickup tube and screen assembly**

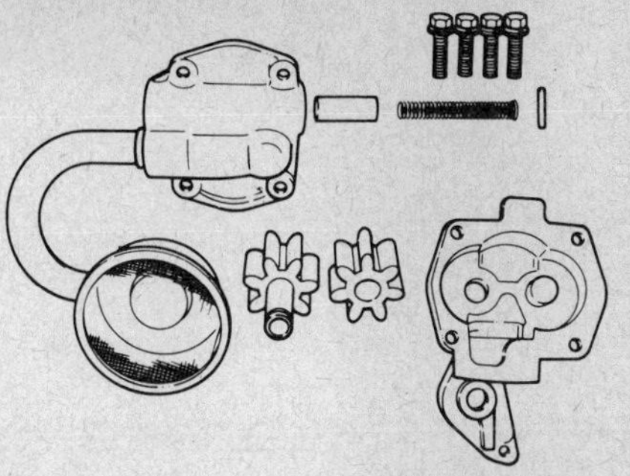

Fig. 14 Oil pump. Exploded view

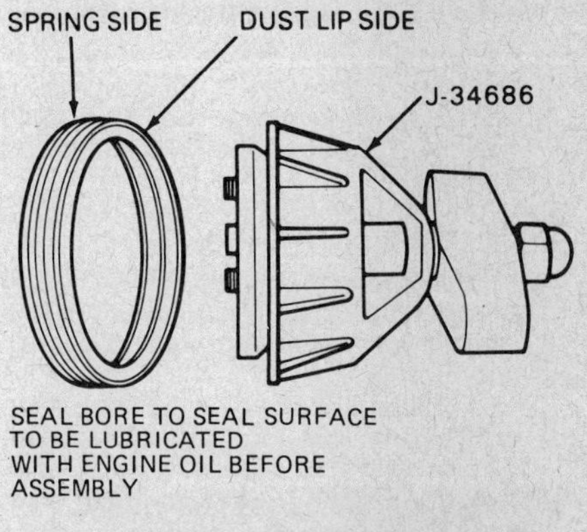

Fig. 16 Rear main bearing oil seal installation. Thick seal

so that tube does not twist, shear or collapse. Loss of a press fit condition could result in an air leak and a loss of oil pressure.

2. Install pressure regulator valve, spring and pin, **Fig. 14.**
3. Install drive gear and shaft in pump body.
4. Align marks made during disassembly, then install idler gear.
5. Install pump cover gasket, cover and attaching bolts. Torque bolts to 6 to 9 ft. lbs.
6. Rotate pump driveshaft by hand and check pump for smooth operation.

INSTALLATION

1. Assemble pump and extension shaft with retainer to rear main bearing cap, aligning top end of hexagon extension shaft with hexagon socket on lower end of distributor shaft.
2. Install pump to rear main bearing cap bolt.
3. Install oil pan as described under Oil Pan, Replace.

REAR MAIN BEARING OIL SEAL REPAIR

THIN SEAL

1. Remove engine as outlined under "Engine, Replace" procedure.
2. Remove oil pan and oil pump assembly.
3. Remove water pump and timing chain.

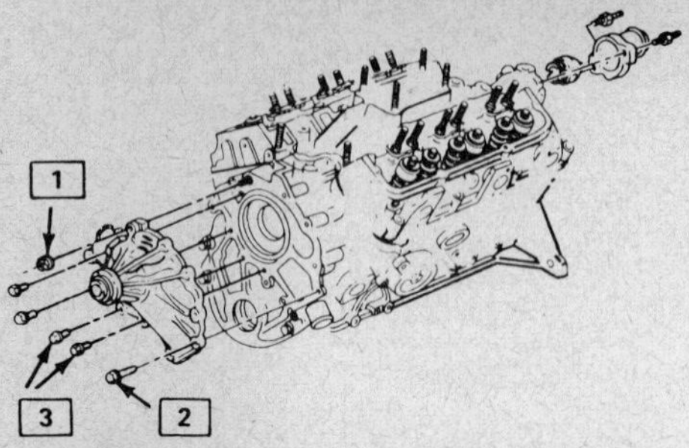

1— 30 N•m (22 FT-LBS) 2— 30 N•m (22 FT-LBS) 3— 10 N•m (7 FT-LBS)

Fig. 17 Water pump installation. 1985–86

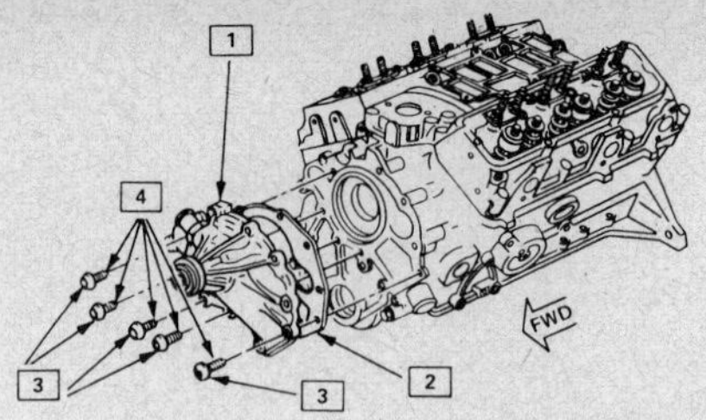

1—WATER PUMP
2—GASKET
3—BOLT · 10 N•m (7 LB. FT.)
4—SEALER

Fig. 18 Water pump installation. 1987–88

4. Remove connecting rod and main bearing caps, then the crankshaft and oil seal.
5. Coat outer diameter of new seal with sealant 1052756 or equivalent.
6. Position seal/tool assembly on rear of crankshaft, ensuring arrows on tool face toward cylinder and case assembly, **Fig. 15.**
7. Install crankshaft, discard tool, then coat crankshaft journals with engine oil.
8. Apply a 1 mm bead of anaerobic sealant to bearing cap surface.
9. Reinstall rear main cap, main bearing caps and connecting rod caps and torque to specifications.
10. Reverse removal procedure to complete installation.

THICK SEAL

1. Remove transaxle and flexplate.
2. Using a screwdriver or similar tool, pry out old seal. Use care to avoid damaging crankshaft. File all burrs or nicks as required.
3. Install new seal using tool J34686, **Fig. 16,** as follows:
   a. Apply a light coat of engine oil to I.D. of oil seal.
   b. Slide seal over tool mandrel until dust lip bottoms squarely against collar of tool.
   c. Align dowel pin of tool with dowel pin hole in crankshaft, **Fig. 16,** then attach tool to crankshaft with screw provided.
   d. Turn handle of tool until seal is pushed into bore and collar is positioned firmly against case. Remove tool.
4. Install flywheel and transmission, then start engine and check for leaks.

WATER PUMP REPLACE

1985–86

1. Disconnect battery ground cable, then drain cooling system.
2. Remove right hand louvered outer cover.
3. Remove plastic battery cover.
4. Disconnect wires from junction block.
5. Remove EVRV and bracket.
6. Raise and support vehicle.
7. Remove right rear wheel and inner fender splash shield.
8. Remove alternator drive belt.
9. Remove water pump attaching bolts, **Fig. 17.**
10. Lower vehicle.
11. Remove water pump.
12. Reverse procedure to install. Apply a 2 mm bead of suitable sealer to water pump sealing surface.

1987–88

1. Disconnect battery ground cable, then drain cooling system.
2. Remove accessory drive belts, then the radiator and heater hose.
3. REmove water pump attaching bolts and the water pump, **Fig. 18.**
4. Reverse procedure to install. Apply a 2 mm bead of suitable sealer to water pump sealing surface.

Clutch & Transaxle Section

INDEX

HYDRAULIC CLUTCH BLEED

Extreme cleanliness must be maintained while bleeding the clutch system. Do not use linty rags, and ensure no dirt enters the system, particularly at the supply tank. Never add previously used fluid to the supply tank as it may be contaminated or have an excessive moisture content.

1. Fill supply tank with suitable brake fluid.
2. Remove floormat or any other object which may impede full travel of clutch pedal.
3. Back out bleed screw on slave cylinder until fluid can be pumped out (approximately 1/2 turn).
4. Depress clutch pedal fully, then apply three short, rapid strokes.
5. Release pressure to allow clutch pedal to return quickly to its stop.
6. Repeat steps 2 and 3 until all air has been released from bleed screw.
7. Close bleed screw immediately following last downward stroke of pedal when air bubbles no longer appear.

CLUTCH REPLACE

1. Remove transaxle as described under "Manual Transaxle, Replace."
2. Mark position of pressure plate to flywheel for assembly reference.
3. Gradually loosen pressure plate attaching bolts until spring pressure is relieved.
4. Support pressure plate and remove mounting bolts, pressure plate and driven disc, **Fig. 1.**

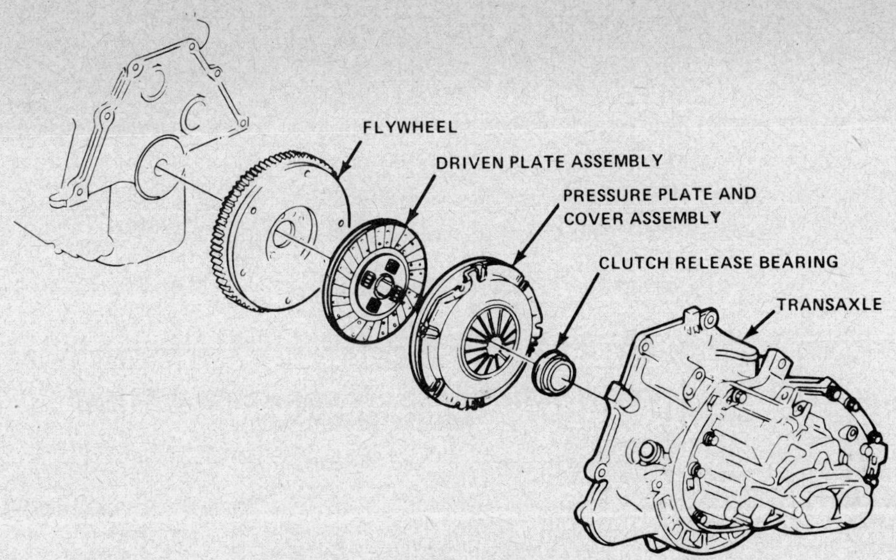

Fig. 1 Clutch assembly

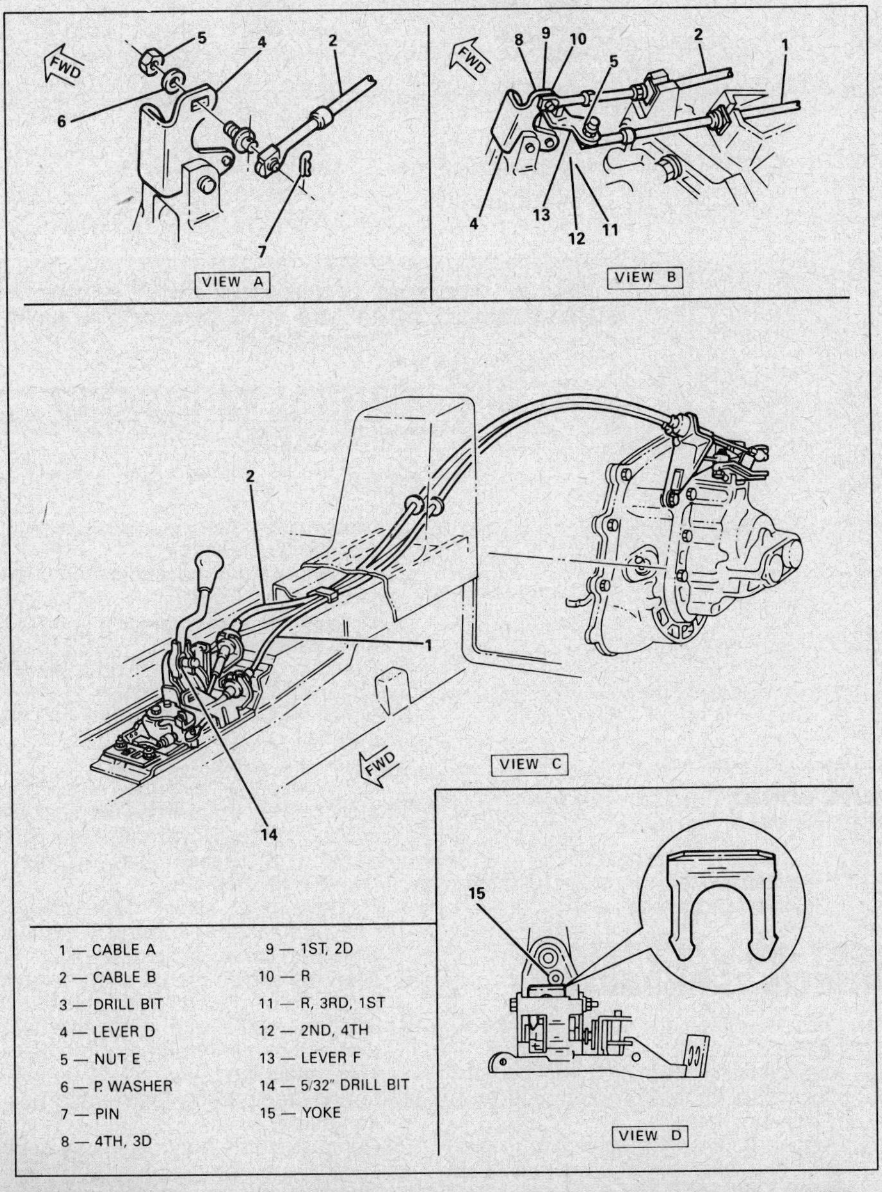

Fig. 2 Manual transaxle shift cable adjustment. 1984

5. Reverse procedure to install. Evenly tighten pressure plate retaining bolts in crossing pattern until pressure plate is seated on flywheel, then torque bolts to 15 ft. lbs.

MANUAL TRANSAXLE SHIFT CABLE

ADJUST

1984

1. Disconnect battery ground cable.
2. Shift transaxle into first gear.
3. Loosen shift cable attaching nuts "E" on transaxle levers "D" and "F," **Fig. 2.**
4. Remove console and trim plates to provide access to shifter.
5. With transaxle in first gear, insert a yoke clip to retain lever, **Fig. 2,** view "D."
6. Insert a No. 22 or 5/32 inch drill bit into alignment hole at side of shifter assembly, **Fig. 2,** view "C."
7. Remove backlash from transaxle by rotating lever "D" in direction of arrow while torquing nut "E" on lever "F" to 20 ft. lbs., **Fig. 2.**
8. Remove drill bit and yoke from shifter.
9. Install console and trim pads.
10. Connect battery ground cable, then road test vehicle and check shifter for proper operation. If "hang-up" is encountered when shifting in the 1-2 gear range, and the shift cables are properly adjusted, it may be necessary to change the shifter shaft selective washer. Perform the following procedure to determine correct washer thickness:
    a. Remove reverse inhibitor fitting spring and washer from end of housing, then place shifter shaft in second gear.
    b. Measure dimension "A," **Fig. 3,** which is the distance between end of housing and shoulder just behind end of shaft.
    c. Apply a 9-13 lb. load on opposite end of shaft, then measure dimension "B," **Fig. 3,** which is distance between end of housing and end of shifter shaft major diameter.
    d. Subtract dimension "B" from dimension "A" to obtain dimension "C."
    e. Refer to chart, **Fig. 4,** to determine correct thickness shim.

1985–86 & 1987–88 w/5 SPEED ISUZU TRANSAXLE

1. Disconnect battery ground cable.
2. Shift transaxle into first gear.
3. Loosen shift cable attaching nuts "E" on transaxle levers "D" and "F," **Fig. 5.**
4. Remove console and trim plates to provide access to shifter.
5. With transaxle in first gear, insert alignment pins "F" and "G," view "C," **Fig. 5.**
6. Remove backlash from transaxle by rotating lever "D" in direction of arrow while tightening nut "A" to 20 ft. lbs. Repeat procedure for nut "E" on lever

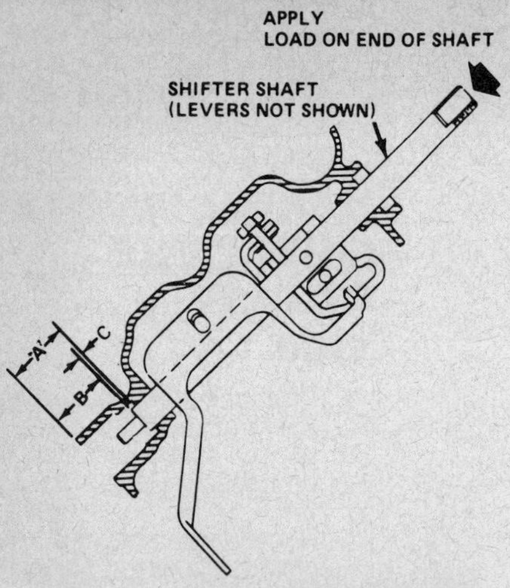

Fig. 3 Manual transaxle shifter shaft selective washer measurement

Dimension "C" Inch (mm)	Ident. Color & No.of Stripes	Shim Part No.
.0708 (1.8)	3 White	14008235
.0827 (2.1)	1 Orange	476709
.0945 (2.4)	2 Orange	476710
.1063 (2.7)	3 Orange	476711
.1181 (3.0)	1 Blue	476712
.1299 (3.3)	2 Blue	476713
.1417 (3.6)	3 Blue	476714
.1535 (3.9)	1 White	476715
.1654 (4.2)	2 White	476716

Fig. 4 Shifter shaft selective washer identification

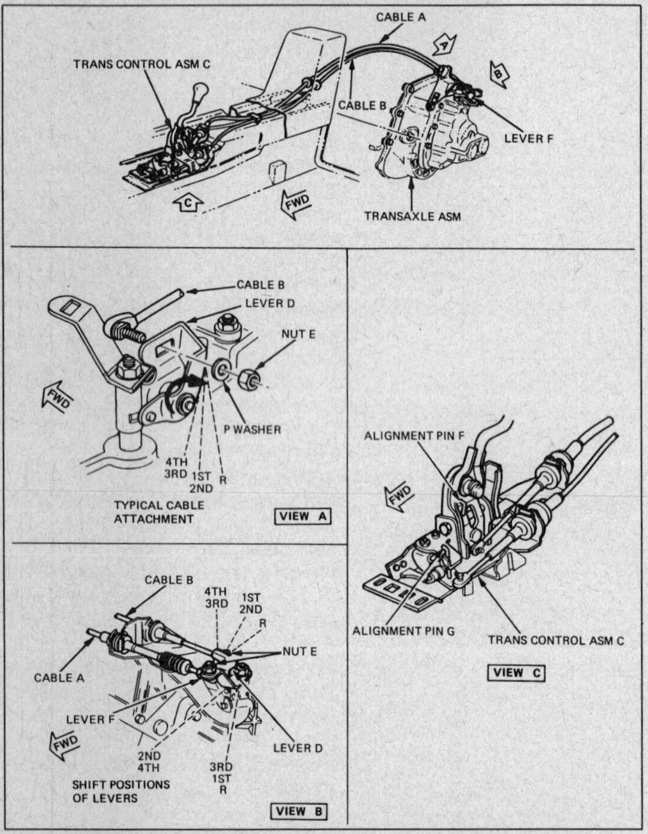

Fig. 5 Manual transaxle shift cable adjustment. 1985–86 & 1987–88 w/5 Speed Isuzu Transaxle

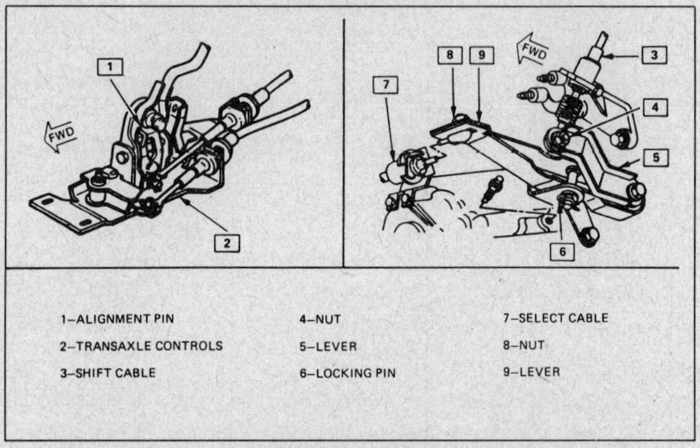

Fig. 6 Manual transaxle shift cable adjustment. 1987–88 w/5 Speed Muncie Transaxle

"F." **Levers "D" and "F" must remain stationary while tightening nuts.**

7. Ensure reverse inhibit cam is against roller and align if necessary.
8. Remove alignment pins from shifter assembly.
9. Install console trim plate and reconnect battery ground cable.
10. Road test vehicle and check shifter for proper operation. If "hang-up" is encountered when shifting in the 1-2 gear range and the shift cables are properly adjusted, it may be necessary to replace the shifter shaft selective washer. Refer to step 10 under "1984" for procedure.

1987–88 W/5 SPEED MUNCIE TRANSAXLE

1. Loosen nut on transaxle shift lever ball stud on shift cable only, **Fig. 6.**
2. Position transaxle in 3rd gear, then remove shift knob, front trimplate and shifter trimplate.
3. Engage floor shift mechanism in 3rd gear, then torque shift cable ball stud nut to 18 ft. lbs.
4. Reinstall trim plates and shift knob.

MANUAL TRANSAXLE REPLACE

1984

1. Disconnect battery ground cable, then remove air cleaner.
2. Disconnect ground cable from transaxle.
3. Disconnect shift and select cables from transaxle.
4. Remove upper transaxle-to-engine attaching bolts.
5. Install engine support fixture, tool No. J-28467 or equivalent, **Fig. 7.**
6. Raise and support vehicle.
7. Remove rear wheels, then disconnect axle shafts from transaxle as described in the "Drive Axle, Rear Suspension & Brakes" section under "Drive Axle, Replace."
8. Remove heat shield from catalytic converter, then disconnect exhaust pipe from exhaust manifold.
9. Remove engine mount and transaxle mount-to-cradle attaching nuts.
10. Support cradle with a suitable jack, then remove front and rear cradle-to-body attaching bolts.
11. Lower cradle from vehicle and position aside.
12. Remove starter and inspection cover shields, then the starter motor.
13. Remove flywheel-to-converter attaching bolts.

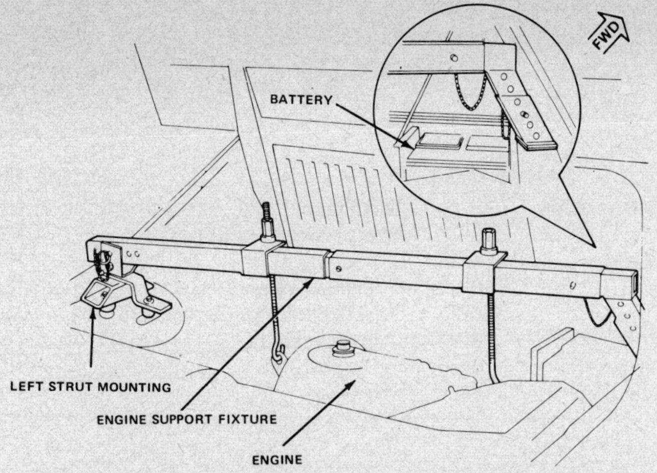

Fig. 7 Engine support fixture. 1984–86 & 1987–88 w/5 Speed Isuzu Transaxle

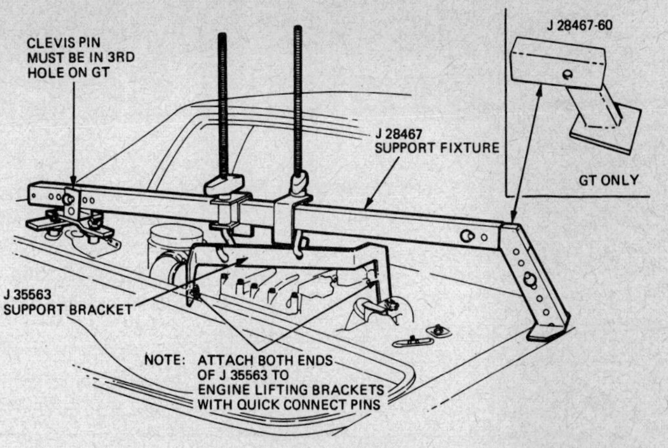

Fig. 8 Engine support fixture. 1987–88 w/5 Speed Muncie Transaxle

14. Support transaxle with a suitable jack, then remove lower transaxle-to-engine attaching bolts and lower transaxle assembly from vehicle.
15. Reverse procedure to install. **When installing cradle, work into position on rear mounts, then raise front into position.**

1985–86 & 1987–88 W/5 SPEED ISUZU TRANSAXLE

1. Disconnect battery ground cable.
2. Remove deck lid and louvered panels.
3. Remove upper rear engine support bolt.
4. Install engine support fixture tool No. J-28467 or equivalent, **Fig. 7.**
5. Raise and support vehicle.
6. Unfasten slave cylinder from clutch, leaving hydraulic line connected.
7. Disconnect shift cables from transaxle.
8. Disconnect EGR valve output pipe from exhaust manifold.
9. Remove both wheel and tire assemblies.
10. Disconnect parking brake cable from brake calipers and body brackets.
11. Remove lower ball joints, then disconnect tie rods.
12. Remove axle shafts from transaxle.
13. Remove rubber boots from splash shield cradle retainers.
14. Remove rear transaxle bracket mount attaching bolts.
15. Remove motor mount nuts from cradle and from engine mount shock.
16. Remove crossover pipe-to-converter attaching bolts.
17. Support cradle with a suitable jack, then remove cradle attaching bolts and lower cradle from vehicle.
18. Disconnect electrical connector from oxygen sensor.
19. Remove crossover pipe heat shields, then the exhaust crossover pipe.
20. Support transaxle with a suitable jack.
21. Remove upper transaxle-to-engine attaching bolts, then the clutch inspection plate cover.
22. Remove lower engine blot studs, then the coolant pipe from stud and nut.
23. Lower transaxle assembly from vehicle.
24. Reverse procedure to install.

1987–88 W/5 SPEED MUNCIE TRANSAXLE

1. Disconnect battery ground cable.
2. Remove drain plug and drain transaxle fluid into a suitable container.
3. Disconnect select and shift cables from transaxle brackets.
4. Disconnect back-up light switch electrical connector and remove the switch.
5. Remove shift cables and stud nut securing bracket to transaxle.
6. Remove two select cable mount attaching bolts.
7. Remove two clutch slave cylinder bracket attaching bolts.
8. Remove exhaust crossover pipe.
9. Remove nut, clip and wire from center stud, then the three upper bolts and one stud securing transaxle to engine.
10. Install engine support fixtures as shown in **Fig. 8.**
11. Attach lifting hook to engine lifting ring and raise engine just enough to relieve pressure from mounts.
12. Remove front and rear transaxle mounts.
13. Raise and support vehicle.
14. Remove inspection plate attaching bolts and the inspection plate.
15. Lower frame and tilt, then remove both axle shafts.
16. Support transaxle with a suitable jack.
17. Remove two nuts securing wiring harness to two lower studs.
18. Remove two studs, then carefully lower transaxle from vehicle. **Tilt engine as necessary to provide clearance for transaxle removal.**
19. Reverse procedure to install.

Drive Axle, Rear Suspension & Brakes Section, 1984–87

INDEX

DESCRIPTION

The drive axles are completely flexible assemblies which consist of an inner and outer constant velocity joint connected by an axle shaft. The inner constant velocity joint has the capability of moving in and out, whereas the outer joint does not.

The rear suspension, **Fig. 1,** is a MacPherson strut design. The lower control arms pivot from the engine cradle. The cradle uses isolation mounts to the body and conventional rubber bushings at the lower control arm pivots. A rubber mount isolates the upper end of the strut.

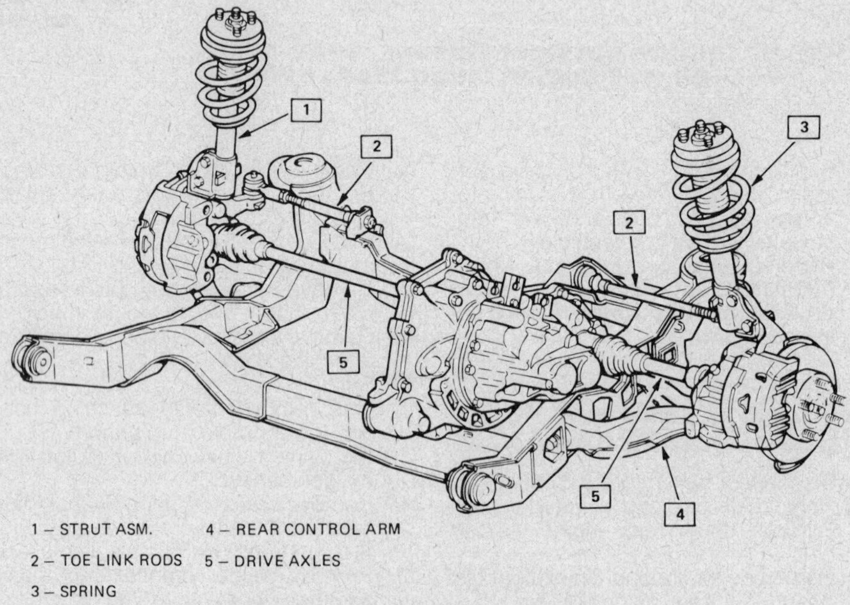

Fig. 1 Rear suspension

DRIVE AXLE
REPLACE

It is important that the axle not be over-extended. When one or both ends of the shaft are disconnected, over-extending the joint may cause separation of internal components, which could lead to failure of the joint.

1984

1. Remove and discard hub nut.
2. Raise and support vehicle.
3. Remove wheel and tire assembly.
4. Install axle shaft boot seal protector J-27812 on outer seal and J-33162 on inner seal, **Fig. 2.**
5. Disconnect toe link rod from knuckle assembly.
6. Disconnect parking brake cables from engine cradle.
7. Remove brake line bracket from underbody in inner wheel house opening.
8. Remove axle shaft from hub and bearing assembly using tool No. J-28733 or equivalent.
9. Support axle shaft and remove clamp bolt from lower control arm ball stud.
10. Separate knuckle from lower control arm.
11. Move strut, knuckle and caliper assembly away from body, and secure in this position.
12. Disengage snap rings retaining drive axle using tools J-33008 and J-2619-01, then carefully pry drive axles from transaxle.
13. Reverse procedure to install. Torque hub nut to 70 ft. lbs., toe link rod nut to 15 ft. lbs. and lower control arm ball stud nut to 33 ft. lbs.

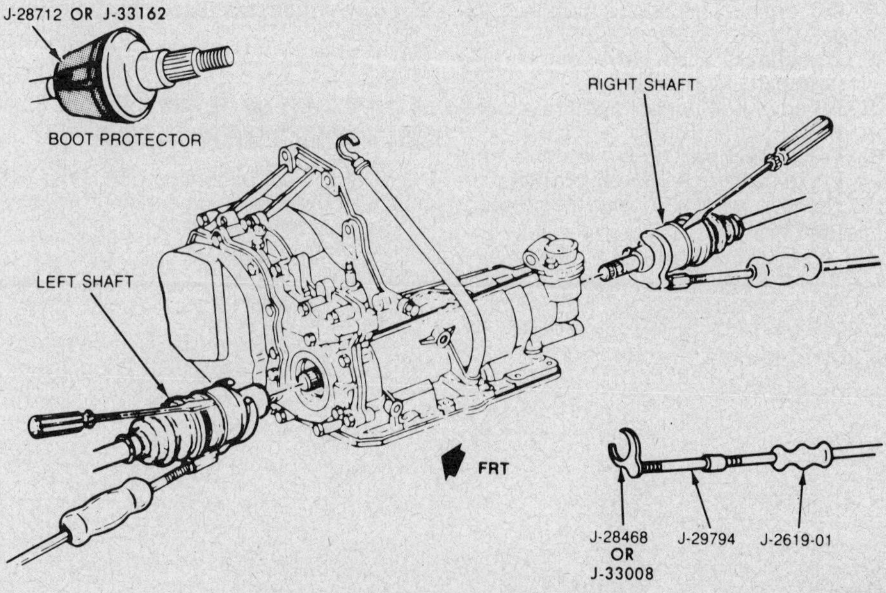

Fig. 2 Drive axle removal

Key No. Part Name
1 – RACE, C.V. JOINT OUTER
2 – CAGE, C.V. JOINT
3 – RACE, C.V. JOINT INNER
4 – RING, SHAFT RETAINING
5 – BALL (6)
6 –
7 – SEAL, C.V. JOINT
8 – CLAMP, SEAL RETAINING
9 – SHAFT, AXLE (LH)
10 – SEAL, TRI-POT JOINT
11 – SPIDER, TRI-POT JOINT
12 – ROLLER, NEEDLE
13 – BALL, TRI-POT JOINT (3)
14 – RETAINER, BALL & NEEDLE (3)
15 – HOUSING ASM, TRI-POT
16 – HOUSING ASM, DAMPER & TRI-POT (RH)
17 – SHAFT, AXLE (RH)
18 – RING, SPACER
19 – RING, RACE RETAINING
20 – CLAMP, SEAL RETAINING
21 – RETAINER, NEEDLE
22 – RING, NEEDLE RETAINER
23 – RING, JOINT RETAINING
24 – HOUSING, TRI-POT (RH)
25 – SHAFT ASM, DAMPER &
26 – RING, DEFLECTOR
27 – BUSHING, TRILOBAL TRI-POT

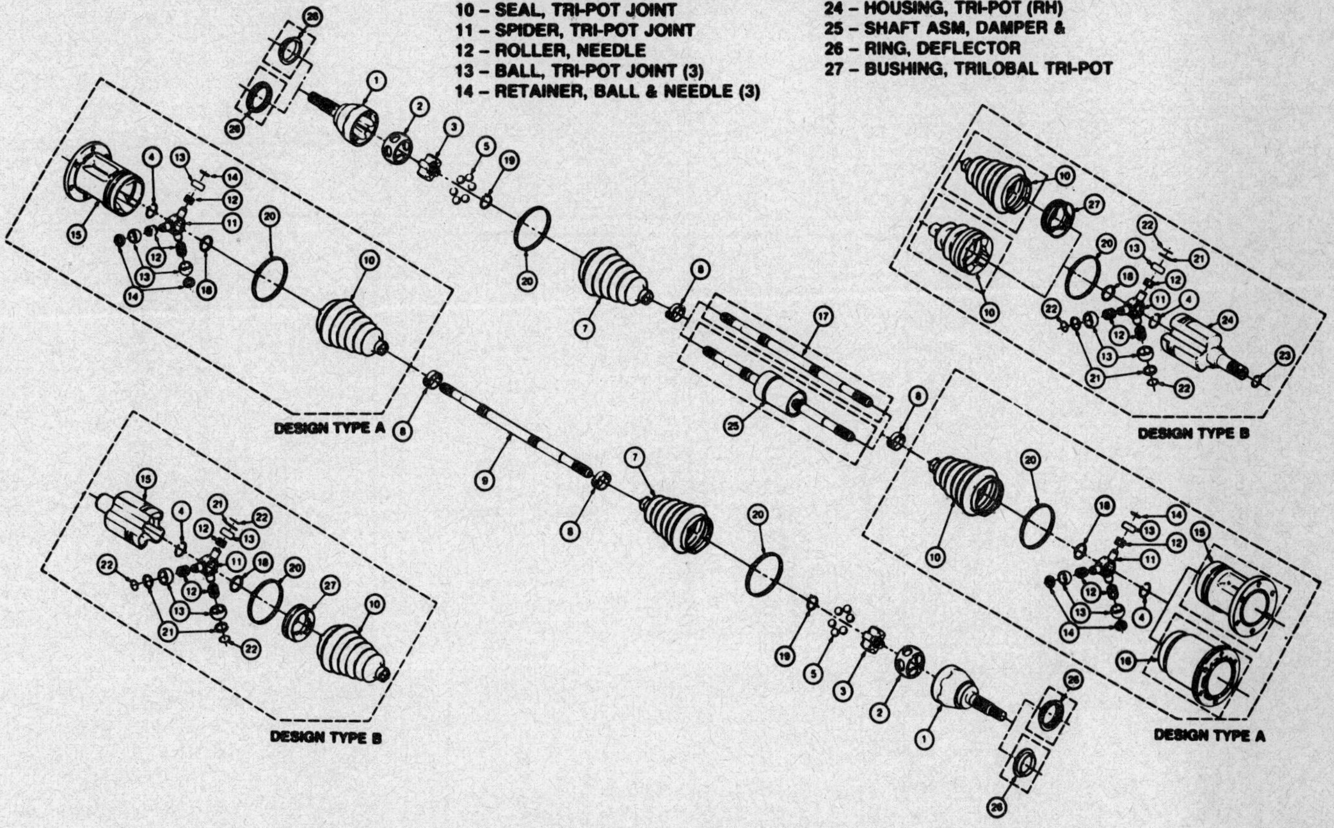

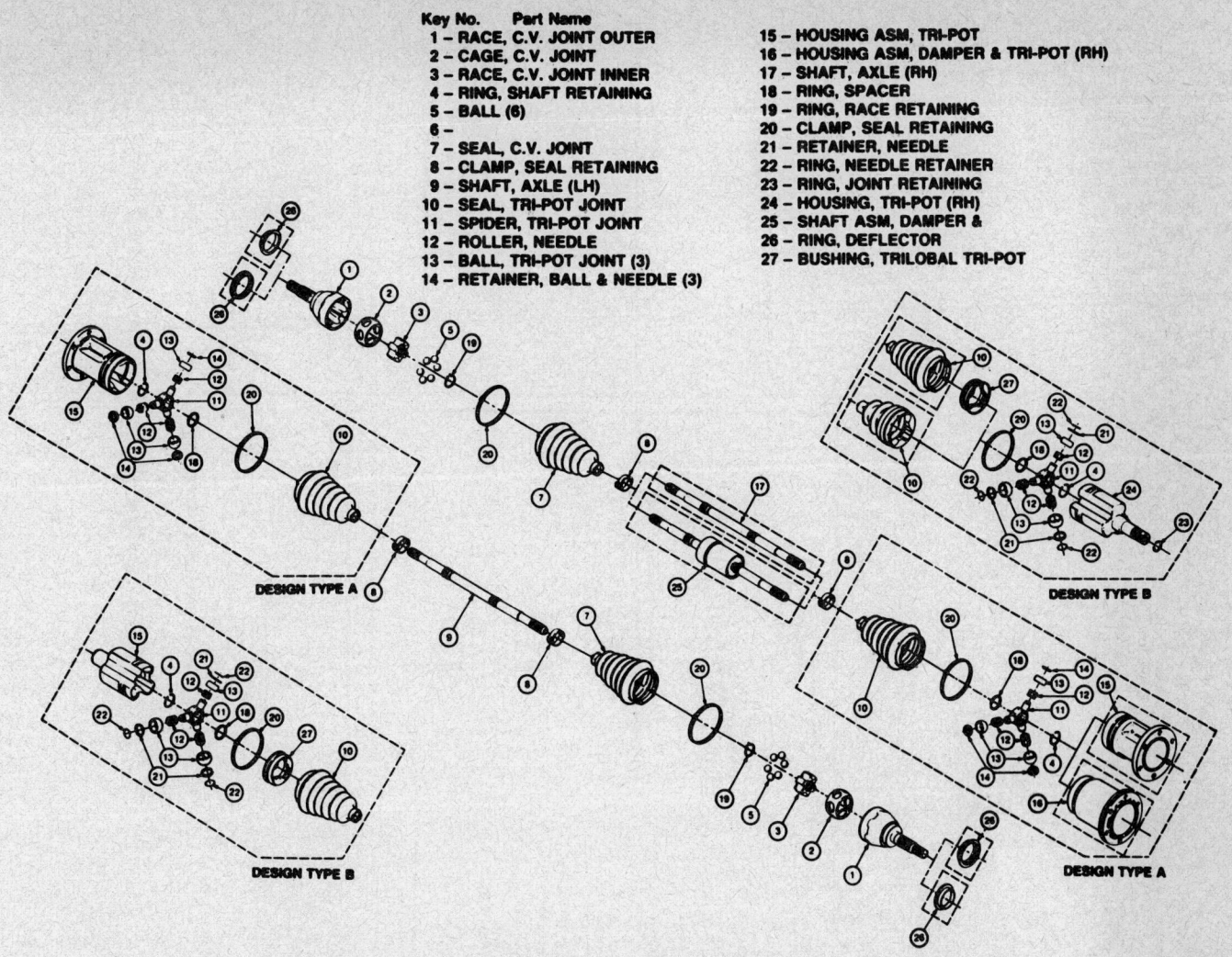

Fig. 3 Exploded view of drive axle

1985–87

1. Shift transaxle to Neutral position.
2. Raise and support vehicle.
3. Remove wheel and tire assembly.
4. Remove lower ball joint bolt, then loosen tie rod end nut.
5. Position suitable punch through rotor and remove hub nut and washer. **A new nut must be used during installation.**
6. Separate tie rod shaft from tie rod end, then remove brake caliper and rotor assembly.
7. Depress lower control arm and separate strut from drive axle.
8. Remove drive axle from hub.
9. Remove drive axle from transaxle using tool No. J-28468 or J-33008 with J-29794 and J-2619-01 or equivalents.
10. Reverse procedure to install, noting the following:
    a. Install boot protectors (tool No. J-33162 or equivalent) prior to axle installation, **Fig. 2.**
    b. Torque lower ball joint bolt to 30-36 ft. lbs.
    c. Torque hub nut to 183-208 ft. lbs.

DRIVE AXLE SERVICE

Refer to **Figs. 3 and 4** for service procedures on drive axle assembly.

WHEEL BEARING REPLACE

REMOVAL

1. On vehicles equipped with steel wheels, remove hub cap and loosen hub nut, then raise and support vehicle and remove wheel and tire assembly.
2. On vehicles equipped with 14 inch aluminum wheels, set parking brake, then raise and support vehicle and remove wheel and tire assembly.
3. On all models, install drive axle boot protector J-33162.
4. Remove and discard hub nut.
5. Remove brake caliper and rotor. Suspend caliper from frame with a piece of wire.
6. Remove hub and bearing attaching bolts. **If the old bearing is being reinstalled, mark attaching bolts and corresponding holes for installation reference, Fig. 5.**
7. Remove hub and bearing assembly using tool No. J-28671 or equivalent, **Fig. 6. If assembly is heavily corroded, ensure hub and bearing are loose in knuckle before using puller tool.**
8. Replace knuckle seal if installing new bearing. **Do not move drive axle until hub nut is installed and torqued to specifications.**

INSTALLATION

1. Clean and inspect knuckle bore and bearing mating surfaces for dirt, nicks and burrs.
2. If installing new knuckle seal, apply suitable grease to seal and knuckle bore, then press seal into knuckle using tool No. J-28671 or equivalent.
3. Install hub and bearing assembly onto axle shaft. Torque attaching bolts to 55-70 ft. lbs.
4. Install hub nut and torque to 74 ft. lbs.
5. Install brake rotor and caliper.
6. Install wheel and tire assembly, then lower vehicle and torque hub nut to 200 ft. lbs.

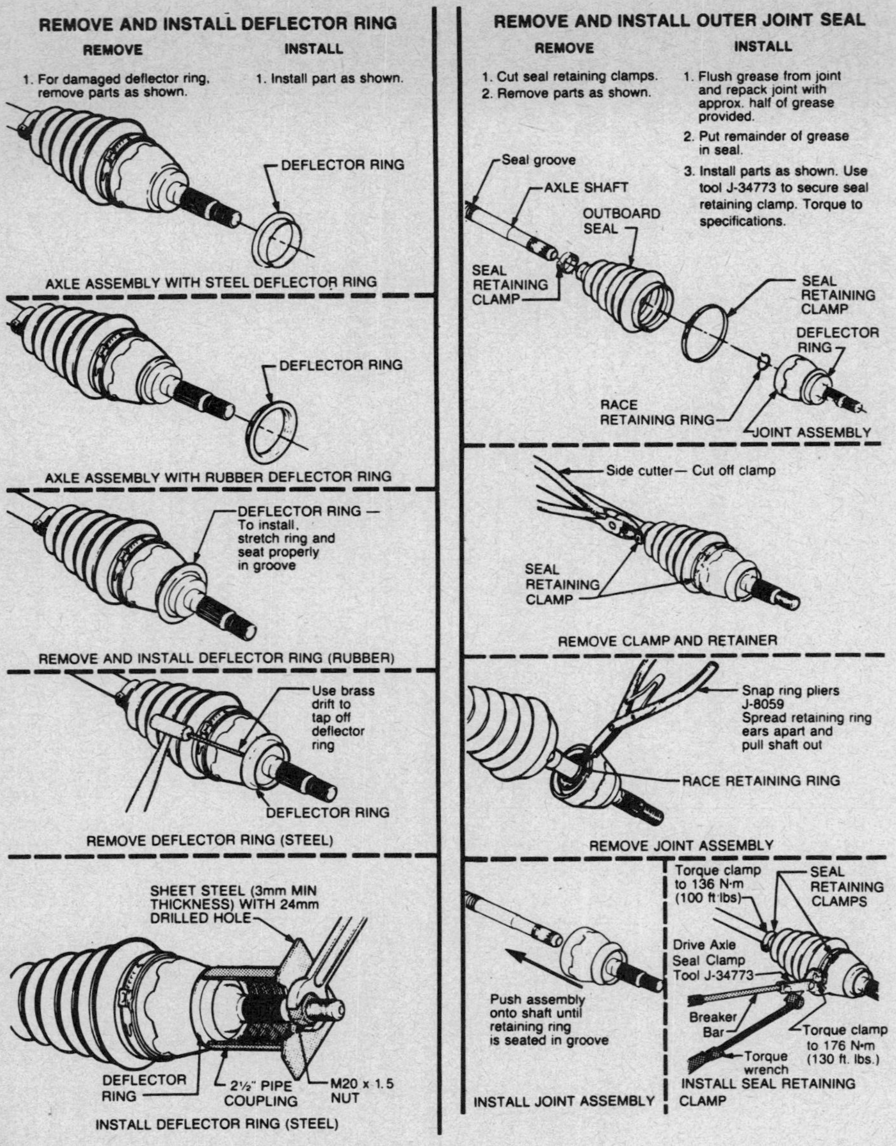

REMOVE AND INSTALL DEFLECTOR RING
REMOVE
1. For damaged deflector ring, remove parts as shown.
INSTALL
1. Install part as shown.
DEFLECTOR RING
AXLE ASSEMBLY WITH STEEL DEFLECTOR RING
DEFLECTOR RING
AXLE ASSEMBLY WITH RUBBER DEFLECTOR RING
DEFLECTOR RING — To install, stretch ring and seat properly in groove
REMOVE AND INSTALL DEFLECTOR RING (RUBBER)
Use brass drift to tap off deflector ring
DEFLECTOR RING
REMOVE DEFLECTOR RING (STEEL)
SHEET STEEL (3mm MIN THICKNESS) WITH 24mm DRILLED HOLE
DEFLECTOR RING
2½" PIPE COUPLING
M20 x 1.5 NUT
INSTALL DEFLECTOR RING (STEEL)
REMOVE AND INSTALL OUTER JOINT SEAL
REMOVE
1. Cut seal retaining clamps.
2. Remove parts as shown.
INSTALL
1. Flush grease from joint and repack joint with approx. half of grease provided.
2. Put remainder of grease in seal.
3. Install parts as shown. Use tool J-34773 to secure seal retaining clamp. Torque to specifications.
Seal groove
AXLE SHAFT
OUTBOARD SEAL
SEAL RETAINING CLAMP
SEAL RETAINING CLAMP
DEFLECTOR RING
RACE RETAINING RING
JOINT ASSEMBLY
Side cutter— Cut off clamp
SEAL RETAINING CLAMP
REMOVE CLAMP AND RETAINER
Snap ring pliers J-8059 Spread retaining ring ears apart and pull shaft out
RACE RETAINING RING
REMOVE JOINT ASSEMBLY
Push assembly onto shaft until retaining ring is seated in groove
INSTALL JOINT ASSEMBLY
Torque clamp to 136 N·m (100 ft lbs)
SEAL RETAINING CLAMPS
Drive Axle Seal Clamp Tool J-34773
Breaker Bar
Torque wrench
Torque clamp to 176 N·m (130 ft. lbs.)
INSTALL SEAL RETAINING CLAMP

Fig. 4 Drive axle service (Part 1 of 2)

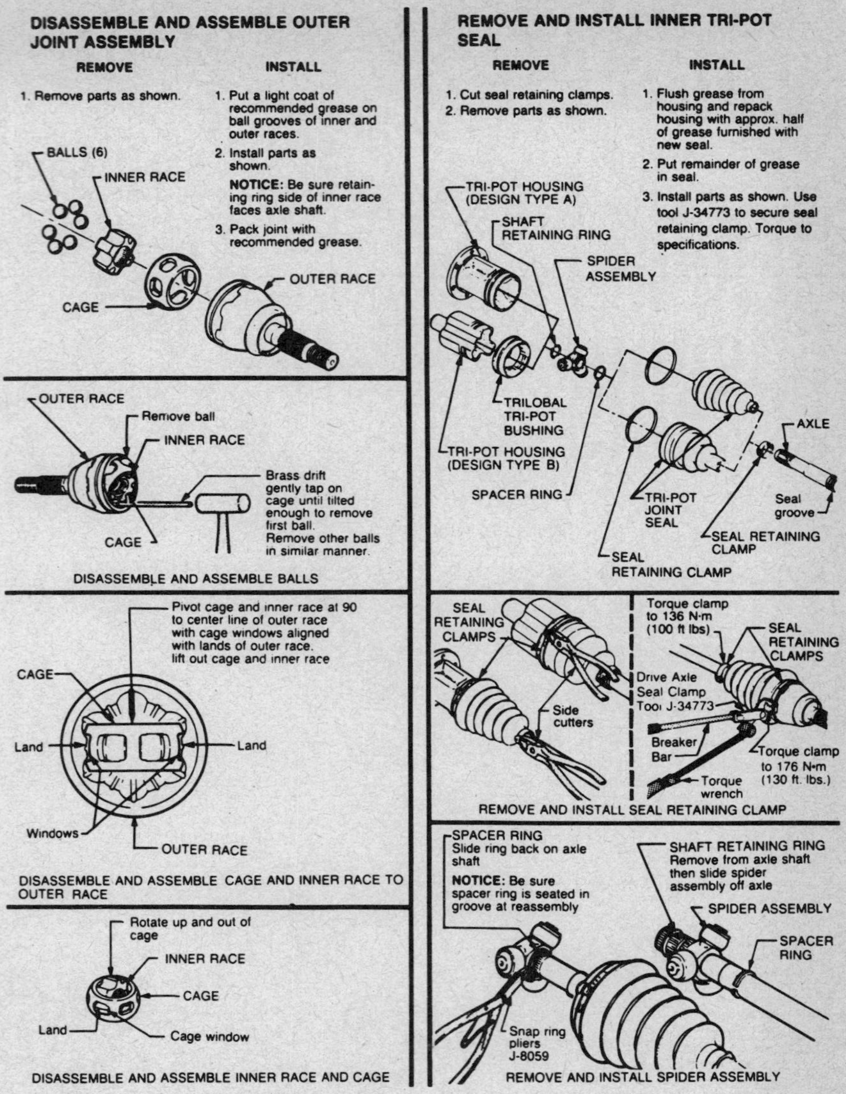

DISASSEMBLE AND ASSEMBLE OUTER JOINT ASSEMBLY
REMOVE
1. Remove parts as shown.
INSTALL
1. Put a light coat of recommended grease on ball grooves of inner and outer races.
2. Install parts as shown.
NOTICE: Be sure retaining ring side of inner race faces axle shaft.
3. Pack joint with recommended grease.
BALLS (6)
INNER RACE
CAGE
OUTER RACE
OUTER RACE
Remove ball
INNER RACE
CAGE
Brass drift gently tap on cage until tilted enough to remove first ball. Remove other balls in similar manner.
DISASSEMBLE AND ASSEMBLE BALLS
Pivot cage and inner race at 90 to center line of outer race with cage windows aligned with lands of outer race. lift out cage and inner race
CAGE
Land
Land
Windows
OUTER RACE
DISASSEMBLE AND ASSEMBLE CAGE AND INNER RACE TO OUTER RACE
Rotate up and out of cage
INNER RACE
CAGE
Land
Cage window
DISASSEMBLE AND ASSEMBLE INNER RACE AND CAGE
REMOVE AND INSTALL INNER TRI-POT SEAL
REMOVE
1. Cut seal retaining clamps.
2. Remove parts as shown.
INSTALL
1. Flush grease from housing and repack housing with approx. half of grease furnished with new seal.
2. Put remainder of grease in seal.
3. Install parts as shown. Use tool J-34773 to secure seal retaining clamp. Torque to specifications.
TRI-POT HOUSING (DESIGN TYPE A)
SHAFT RETAINING RING
SPIDER ASSEMBLY
TRILOBAL TRI-POT BUSHING
TRI-POT HOUSING (DESIGN TYPE B)
SPACER RING
AXLE
TRI-POT JOINT SEAL
Seal groove
SEAL RETAINING CLAMP
SEAL RETAINING CLAMP
SEAL RETAINING CLAMPS
Side cutters
Torque clamp to 136 N·m (100 ft lbs)
SEAL RETAINING CLAMPS
Drive Axle Seal Clamp Tool J-34773
Breaker Bar
Torque wrench
Torque clamp to 176 N·m (130 ft. lbs.)
REMOVE AND INSTALL SEAL RETAINING CLAMP
SPACER RING Slide ring back on axle shaft
NOTICE: Be sure spacer ring is seated in groove at reassembly
SHAFT RETAINING RING Remove from axle shaft then slide spider assembly off axle
SPIDER ASSEMBLY
SPACER RING
Snap ring pliers J-8059
REMOVE AND INSTALL SPIDER ASSEMBLY

Fig. 4 Drive axle service (Part 2 of 2)

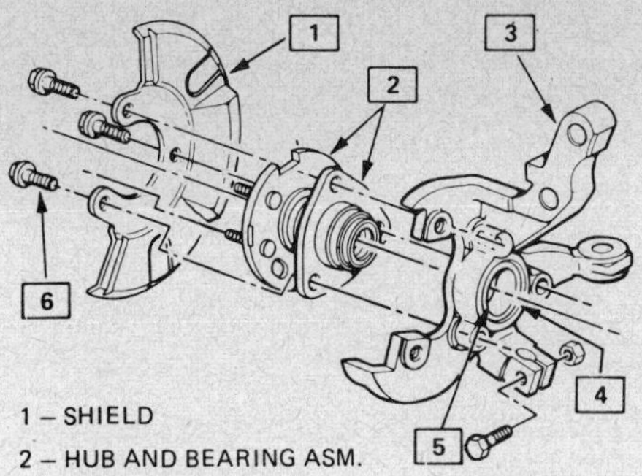

1 – SHIELD
2 – HUB AND BEARING ASM.
3 – KNUCKLE
4 – KNUCKLE SEAL ASM.
5 – FILL HUB BEARING CAVITY BETWEEN SEALING LIPS WITH .8 GRAMS OF CHASSIS LUBRICANT.
6 – BOLT 75-95 N·m (55-70 FT. LB.)

Fig. 5 Rear wheel hub & bearing assembly

LOWER BALL JOINT
REPLACE

1. Raise and support vehicle.
2. Remove wheel and tire assembly, then the ball stud clamp bolt.
3. Disconnect ball joint from knuckle by tapping with a mallet.
4. Replace ball joint as shown in **Fig. 7.**

LOWER CONTROL ARM & BUSHINGS
REPLACE

1. Raise and support vehicle.
2. Remove wheel and tire assembly, then the ball joint clamp bolt.
3. Disconnect ball joint from knuckle by tapping with a mallet.
4. Remove lower control arm pivot bolts from frame.
5. Replace lower control arm and bushings as shown in **Fig. 8.**

REAR KNUCKLE
REPLACE

Refer to **Fig. 9** for removal and installation procedures.

STRUT ASSEMBLY
REPLACE

1. Remove engine compartment cover.
2. Remove three upper strut nuts and washers, **Fig. 10.**
3. Loosen wheel lug nuts, then raise vehicle and support at rear control arm.
4. Remove wheel and tire assembly, then the brake line retaining clip.
5. Scribe strut and knuckle, **Fig. 11,** for assembly reference. When servicing the jounce bumper, strut mount, strut shield, spring seal or spring insulator, the strut and knuckle must be scribed as shown in **Fig. 11** to maintain the original camber setting. However, it will be necessary to check toe-in setting and adjust as necessary. When servicing the strut damper, knuckle or rear ride spring, the scribe marks should not be made. However, it will be necessary to check both toe-in and camber settings and correct as necessary.
6. Remove strut attaching nuts and bolts, then the strut assembly and spacer plate.
7. Reverse procedure to install. Torque knuckle attaching nuts to 140 ft. lbs., and upper strut attaching nuts to 18 ft. lbs.

STRUT ASSEMBLY SERVICE
DISASSEMBLY

1. Clamp strut compressor, tool No. J-26854, in a suitable vise.
2. Install strut assembly into bottom adapter of compressor and install bottom adapter, **Fig. 12.** Ensure strut and locating pins are fully engaged.
3. Rotate strut assembly until top mounting assembly lip is aligned with compressor support notch.
4. Install upper adapter onto top spring seal, **Fig. 12,** so long stud is at high location to strut flange.
5. Rotate compressor forcing screw clockwise until top support flange contacts top adapter, and continue turning screw to compress strut spring.
6. Install second upper adapter over spring seat assembly, then rotate forcing screw counterclockwise until strut spring tension is relieved.
7. Remove top adapters, bottom adapter and strut.

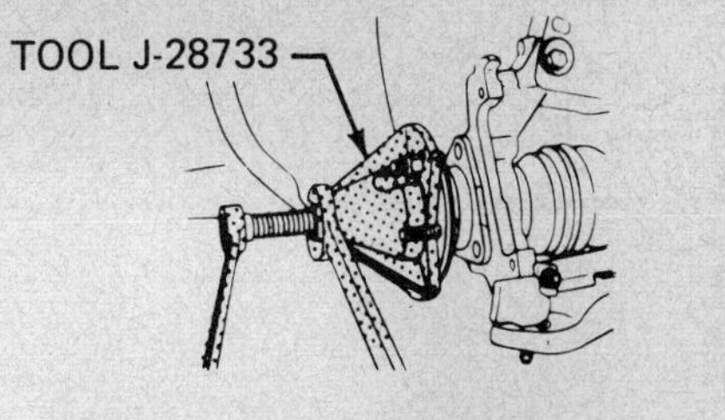

Fig. 6 Hub & bearing assembly removal

ASSEMBLY

1. Perform steps 1 and 2 as outlined in the "Disassembly" procedure.
2. Rotate strut assembly until mounting flange is facing outward, opposite compressor forcing screw.

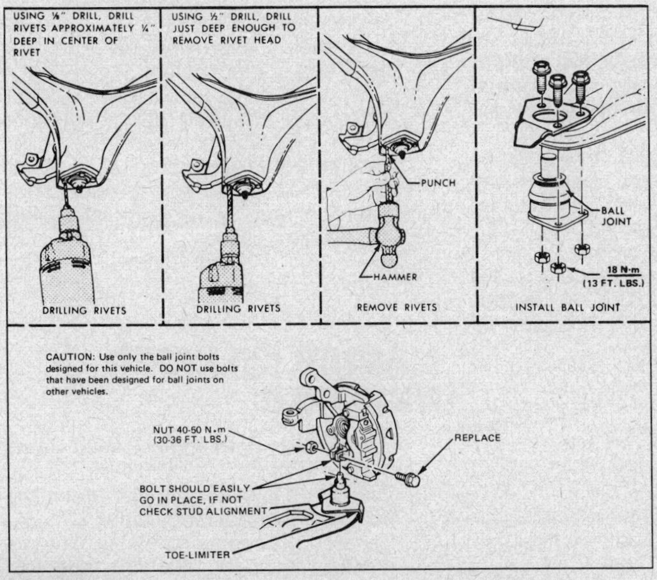

Fig. 7 Lower ball joint replacement

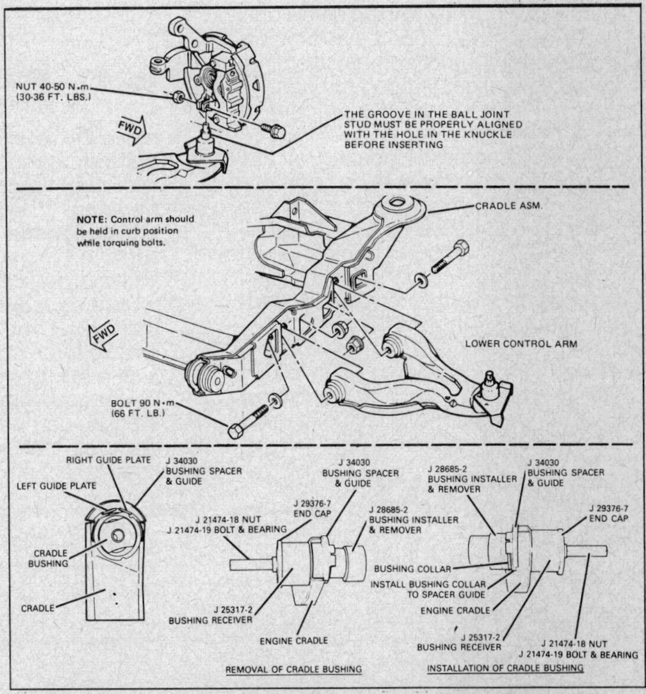

Fig. 8 Lower control arm & bushing replacement

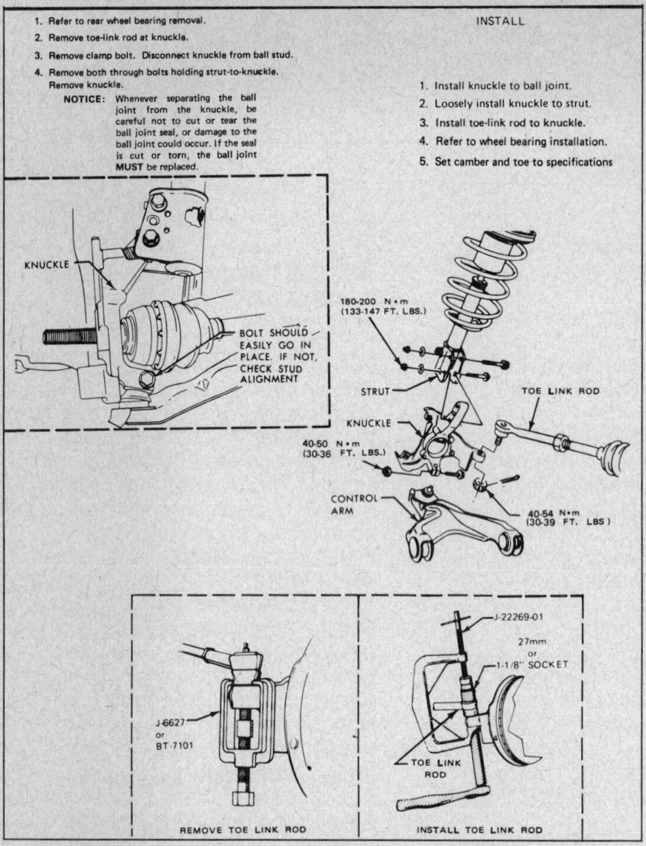
1. Refer to rear wheel bearing removal.
2. Remove toe-link rod at knuckle.
3. Remove clamp bolt. Disconnect knuckle from ball stud.
4. Remove both through bolts holding strut-to-knuckle. Remove knuckle.
NOTICE: Whenever separating the ball joint from the knuckle, be careful not to cut or tear the ball joint seal, or damage to the ball joint could occur. If the seal is cut or torn, the ball joint MUST be replaced.
INSTALL
1. Install knuckle to ball joint.
2. Loosely install knuckle to strut.
3. Install toe-link rod to knuckle.
4. Refer to wheel bearing installation.
5. Set camber and toe to specifications
KNUCKLE
BOLT SHOULD EASILY GO IN PLACE. IF NOT, CHECK STUD ALIGNMENT
180-200 N•m (133-147 FT. LBS.)
STRUT
TOE LINK ROD
KNUCKLE
40-50 N•m (30-36 FT. LBS.)
CONTROL ARM
40-54 N•m (30-39 FT. LBS)
J-6627 or BT-7101
REMOVE TOE LINK ROD
J-22269-01
27mm or 1-1/8" SOCKET
TOE LINK ROD
INSTALL TOE LINK ROD

Fig. 9 Rear knuckle replacement

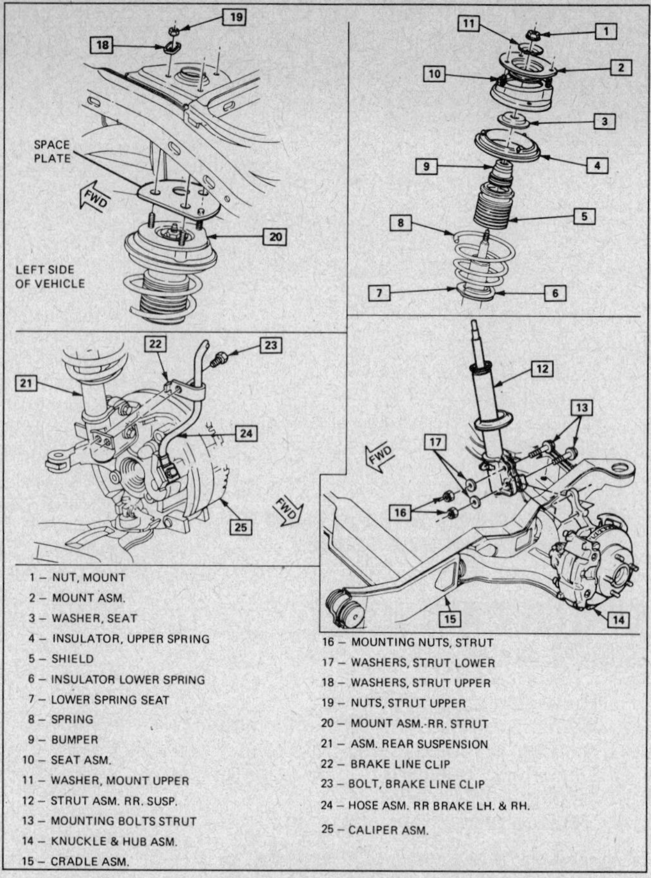
SPACE PLATE
FWD
LEFT SIDE OF VEHICLE
1 – NUT, MOUNT
2 – MOUNT ASM.
3 – WASHER, SEAT
4 – INSULATOR, UPPER SPRING
5 – SHIELD
6 – INSULATOR LOWER SPRING
7 – LOWER SPRING SEAT
8 – SPRING
9 – BUMPER
10 – SEAT ASM.
11 – WASHER, MOUNT UPPER
12 – STRUT ASM. RR. SUSP.
13 – MOUNTING BOLTS STRUT
14 – KNUCKLE & HUB ASM.
15 – CRADLE ASM.
16 – MOUNTING NUTS, STRUT
17 – WASHERS, STRUT LOWER
18 – WASHERS, STRUT UPPER
19 – NUTS, STRUT UPPER
20 – MOUNT ASM.-RR. STRUT
21 – ASM. REAR SUSPENSION
22 – BRAKE LINE CLIP
23 – BOLT, BRAKE LINE CLIP
24 – HOSE ASM. RR BRAKE LH. & RH.
25 – CALIPER ASM.

Fig. 10 Strut assembly replacement

3. Install strut components, **Fig. 13.** Ensure spring is properly seated on bottom spring plate.
4. Install strut spring seat assembly on top of spring with long stud positioned 180° from strut mounting flange.
5. Install top adapter over spring seat assembly.
6. Rotate compressor forcing screw until compressor top support just contacts top adapter. Do not compress spring.
7. Install strut alignment rod through top spring seat and thread onto damper shaft hand tight, **Fig. 13.**
8. Rotate compressor forcing screw clockwise to compress spring until damper shaft is exposed enough so nut can be threaded securely, then install the nut. Ensure damper shaft comes through center of spring seat opening to prevent damage. **Do not compress spring until bottomed.**
9. Remove alignment rod, then install mount and torque nut to 65 ft. lbs.
10. Rotate compressor forcing screw counterclockwise and remove strut assembly from compressor.

PARKING BRAKE

ADJUST

1984–86

1. Jack up both rear wheels with parking brake fully released.
2. Apply suitable lubricant to groove in equalizer nut.
3. Remove slack from cable by tightening equalizer nut while preventing brake cable stud from turning. **After tightening nut, ensure caliper levers are against stops on caliper housing. If levers are not against stops, loosen cable until they return.**
4. Activate parking brake several times to check adjustment. The parking brake lever should move 5-8 notches when a force is applied perpendicularly at a midway point on handle grip.
5. Lower rear wheels and ensure levers are on caliper stops. If necessary, back off parking brake adjuster to keep levers on stops.

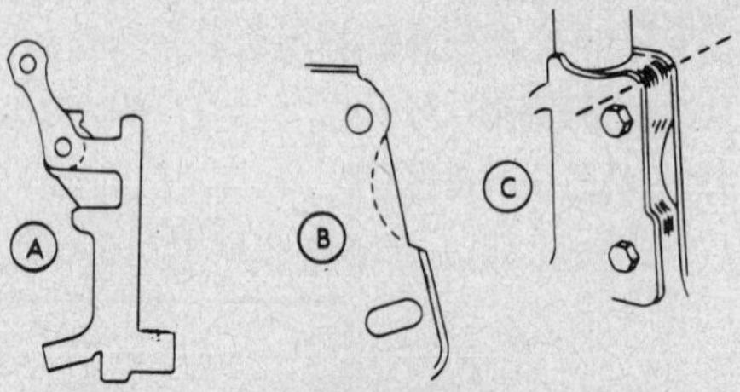
A
B
C

Fig. 11 Scribing strut & knuckle

1987

1. Apply service brake pedal three times with a force of approximately 175 lbs.
2. Apply and release parking brake three times.
3. Raise and support vehicle.
4. Mark relationship between wheel and axle flange.
5. Ensure parking brake lever is fully released, then turn ignition switch on and note brake warning lamp. If warning lamp is lit, pull down on front parking brake cable to remove slack from pedal.
6. Remove rear wheel and tire assemblies. Retain rotors with two lug nuts.
7. Ensure parking brake levers on both calipers are in contact with lever stops on caliper housings. If not, check for binding in rear cables and/or loosen cables as necessary.
8. Tighten parking brake cable at adjuster until either lever begins to move off stop, then loosen until lever moves back and contacts stop.
9. Operate parking brake lever several times and ensure proper operation. When properly adjusted, the lever should not travel more than eight clicks and the rear wheels should not rotate forward when lever is applied five to eight clicks.

MASTER CYLINDER

REPLACE

1. Disconnect both brake lines from master cylinder.
2. Remove 2 master cylinder attaching nuts and the master cylinder.
3. Reverse procedure to install. Torque master cylinder attaching nuts to 22-30 ft. lbs., and brake line nuts to 120-180 inch lbs.

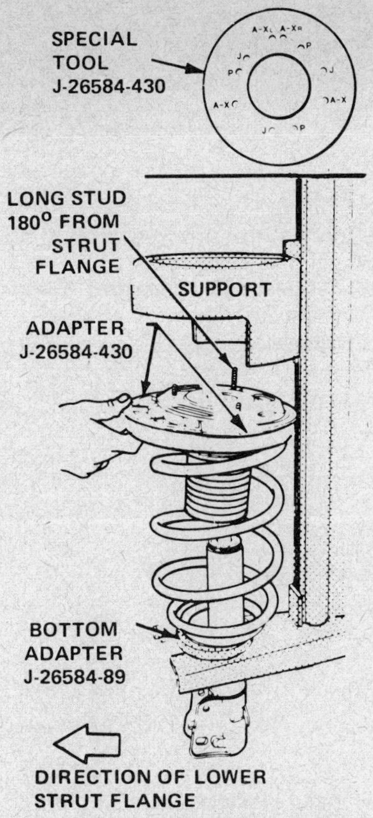

Fig. 12 Removing damper & coil spring from strut

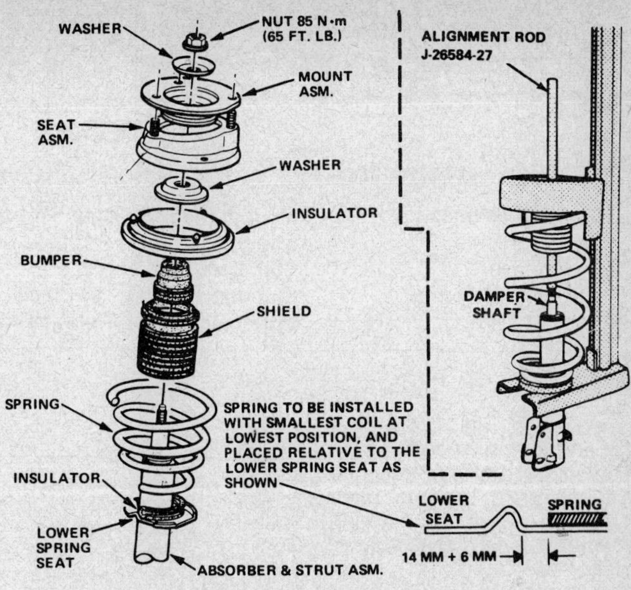

Fig. 13 Strut assembly alignment & components

POWER BRAKE UNIT REPLACE

1. Remove 2 master cylinder-to-power brake unit attaching nuts, and position master cylinder aside with brake lines attached.
2. Disconnect power brake unit pushrod from brake pedal.
3. Remove power brake unit attaching nuts and the power brake unit.
4. Reverse procedure to install. Torque attaching nuts to 22-30 ft. lbs.

Drive Axle, Rear Suspension & Brakes Section, 1988

INDEX

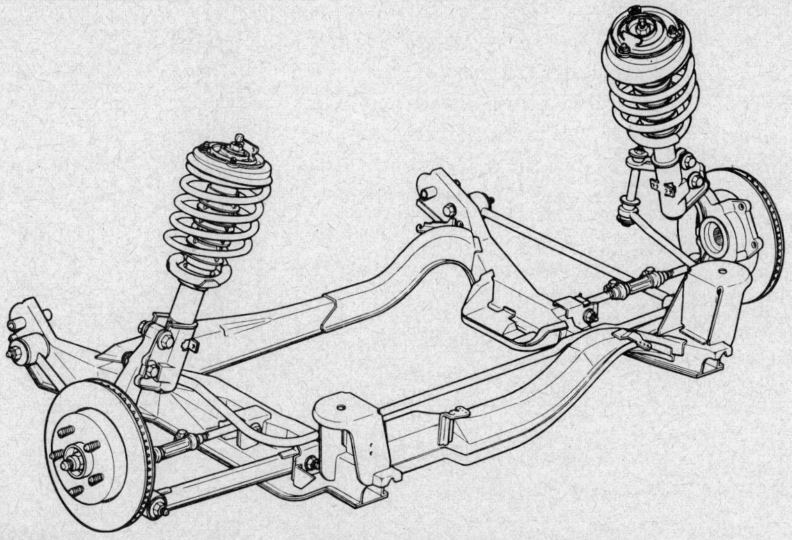

Fig. 1 Rear suspension

DESCRIPTION

The rear suspension, **Fig. 1,** used on 1988 models features several improvements over the design used on earlier models. Major changes include the use of a "tri-link" design which allows for specific tuning of each component. In addition, a stabilizer bar is available on some models and the chassis cradle has been revised for suspension attachments.

Front Suspension & Steering Section, 1984–87

INDEX

DESCRIPTION

The front suspension, **Fig. 1** is a conventional short and long arm design with coil springs. The control arms are attached with bolts and bushings at the inner pivot points, and are attached to the steering knuckle/front wheel spindle assembly at the outer pivot points.

WHEEL BEARINGS

ADJUST

1. Raise and support vehicle.
2. Remove wheel and tire assembly.
3. Remove dust cap from hub, then the cotter pin from spindle and spindle nut.
4. Torque spindle nut to 12 ft. lbs. while rotating wheel forward by hand.
5. Back off spindle nut until just loose, then hand tighten nut and back off again until either hole in spindle lines up with hole in nut. **Do not back off nut more than 1/2 flat.**
6. Install new cotter pin, then measure hub endplay. With bearing properly adjusted, endplay should measure .001-.005 inch.

WHEEL BEARINGS

REPLACE

REMOVAL

1. Raise and support vehicle.
2. Remove wheel and tire assembly, then disconnect brake caliper from steering knuckle and suspend from frame with a piece of wire. Do not let brake lines support weight of caliper.
3. Remove hub dust cap, cotter pin, spindle nut and washer.
4. Remove hub and bearing from spindle.
5. Remove outer bearing from hub, then pry out grease seal and remove inner bearing. Discard seal.

INSTALLATION

1. Clean all grease from hub, spindle and bearing.
2. Apply a thin film of suitable grease to spindle at outer bearing seat and the inner bearing seat, shoulder and seal seat.
3. Apply grease inboard of each bearing race in hub.
4. Completely fill bearing cone and roller assemblies with grease.

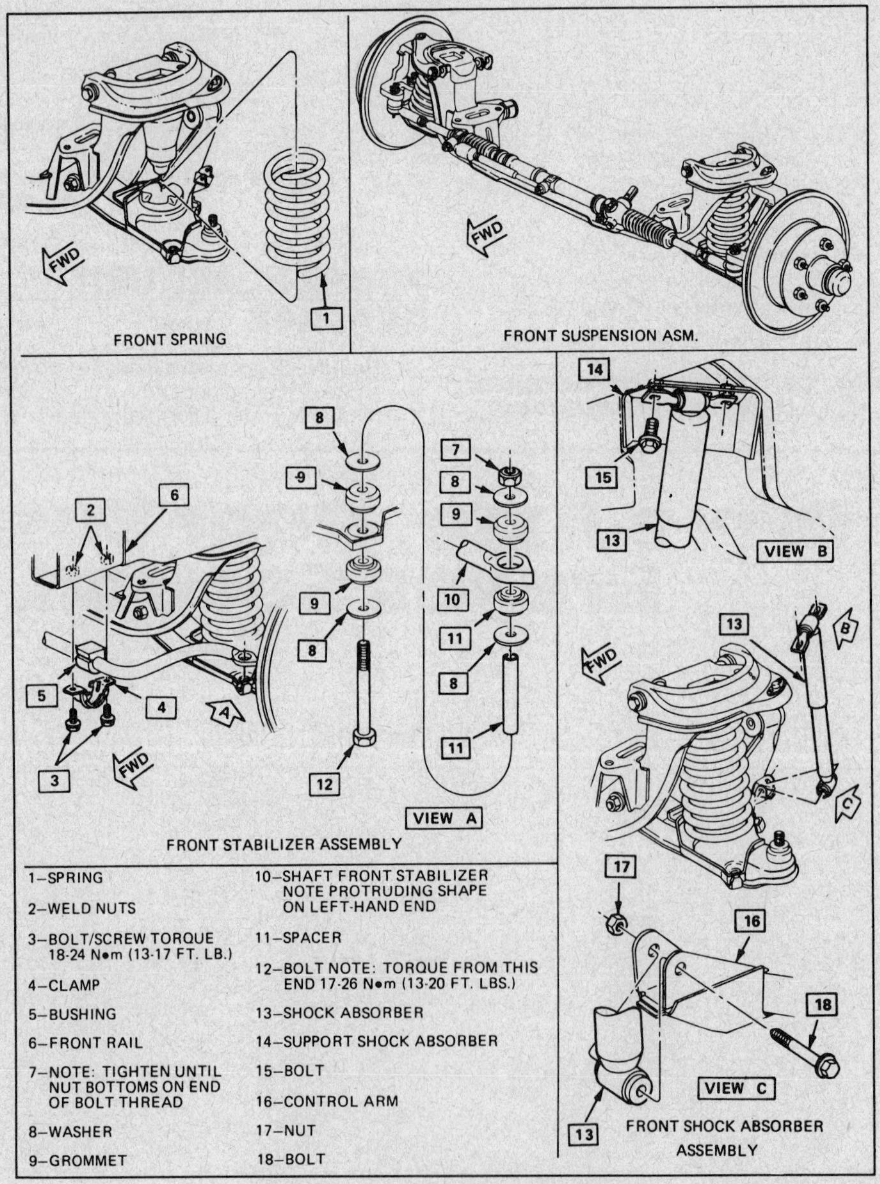

Fig. 1 Front suspension

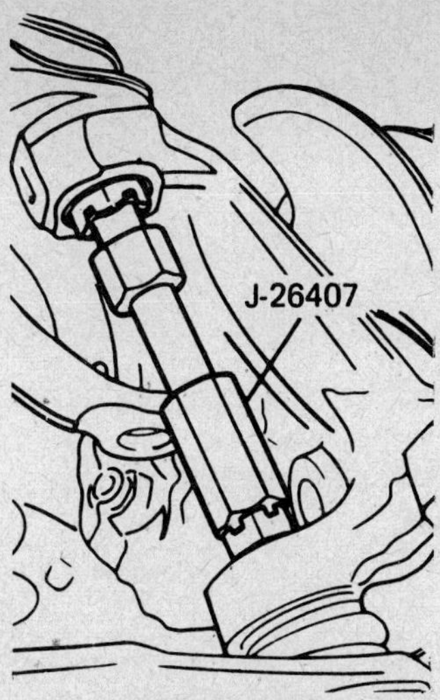

Fig. 2 Upper ball joint removal

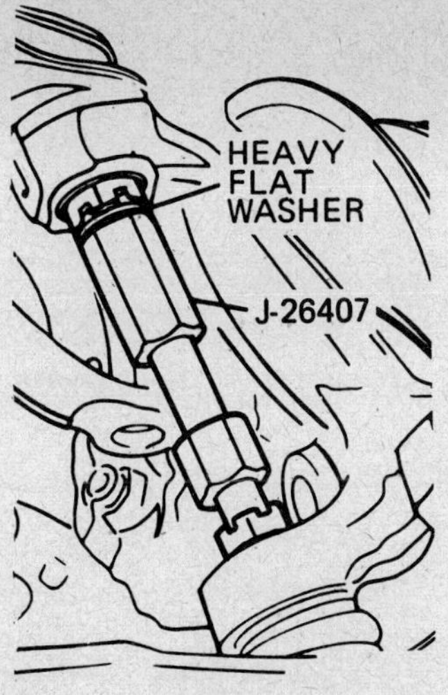

Fig. 3 Lower ball joint removal

5. Install inner bearing into hub and apply additional grease outboard of bearing.
6. Install new grease seal flush with hub and lubricate seal lip with a thin coating of grease.
7. Install hub and rotor assembly onto spindle, then position outer bearing in race.
8. Install washer and nut, then adjust bearing as previously described.
9. Install brake caliper, then the wheel and tire assembly.

UPPER BALL JOINT

REPLACE

1. Raise and support vehicle.
2. Remove wheel and tire assembly, then support lower control arm with a suitable jack.
3. Remove upper ball joint stud nut, then reinstall nut finger tight.
4. Install tool No. J-26407 with cup end over lower ball joint stud nut. Rotate threaded end of tool until upper stud is free of steering knuckle, then remove tool and nut from stud, **Fig. 2.**
5. Remove 2 ball joint-to-upper control arm attaching bolts and nuts.
6. Note position of flat on ball joint for proper installation, then remove ball joint from vehicle.
7. Reverse procedure to install. Torque ball joint-to-upper control arm attaching bolts to 28 ft. lbs. Torque stud nut to 35 ft. lbs., then tighten nut up to an additional 1/6 turn to align cotter pin hole.

LOWER BALL JOINT

REPLACE

The lower ball joint is permanently attached to the lower control arm and cannot be serviced separately. If the lower ball joint requires replacement, the entire lower control arm must be replaced.

SHOCK ABSORBER

REPLACE

1. Raise and support vehicle.
2. Remove wheel and tire assembly, then the 2 shock absorber upper attaching bolts.
3. Remove shock absorber lower attaching bolts and nut, **Fig. 3**
4. Remove shock absorber from vehicle.
5. Reverse procedure to install. Torque upper attaching bolts to 20 ft. lbs., and lower attaching bolt to 35 ft. lbs.

STABILIZER BAR

REPLACE

1. Raise and support vehicle.
2. Remove stabilizer bar attaching bolt and nut and associated components from lower control arms, **Fig. 1**
3. Remove stabilizer bar clamp and the stabilizer bar from vehicle.
4. Reverse procedure to install. Torque clamp attaching bolts to 15 ft. lbs., and stabilizer bar attaching bolt to 16 ft. lbs.

LOWER CONTROL ARM & COIL SPRING

REPLACE

1. Raise vehicle and support at frame crossmember.
2. Remove wheel and tire assembly, then disconnect stabilizer bar from lower control arm.
3. Disconnect tie rod from steering knuckle, then the shock absorber from lower control arm.
4. Support lower control arm with a suitable jack, then remove lower ball joint stud nut and press ball joint out of steering knuckle, using tool No. J-26407, **Fig. 3.** Position steering knuckle and hub aside.
5. Loosen lower control arm pivot bolts.
6. Install a safety chain through coil spring, then slowly lower jack and remove spring, **Fig. 1.**
7. Remove lower control arm attaching bolts and the lower control arm. **It may be necessary to loosen or remove steering gear attaching bolts to gain access to the control arm attaching bolt at the crossmember.**
8. Reverse procedure to install, noting the following:
   a. Install control arm attaching bolts finger tight. Do not torque bolts until all other components have been assembled and torqued to specifications.
   b. Torque ball joint stud nut to 55 ft. lbs.
   c. Torque stabilizer bar attaching bolt to 16 ft. lbs.
   d. Torque tie rod attaching nut to 29 ft. lbs.
   e. Torque shock absorber lower attaching bolt to 35 ft. lbs.
   f. If steering gear attaching bolts have been loosened or removed, install new bolts and torque to 21 ft. lbs.
   g. Torque control arm-to-body attaching bolt to 62 ft. lbs. and control arm-to-crossmember nut to 52 ft. lbs.

UPPER CONTROL ARM

REPLACE

1. Raise and support vehicle.
2. Remove wheel and tire assembly, then the rivet securing brake line clip to upper control arm.
3. Support lower control arm with a suitable jack, then remove upper ball joint as described under "Upper Ball Joint, Replace."
4. Remove control arm attaching bolt and the control arm from vehicle.
5. Reverse procedure to install. Torque control arm attaching bolt to 66 ft. lbs. **Washers and shims must be installed in their original positions unless a change in caster angle is desired.**

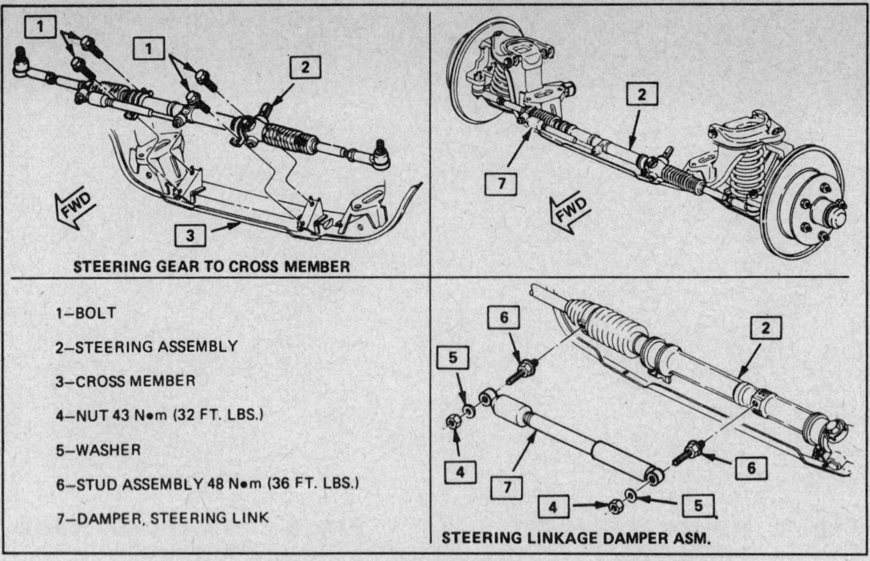

Fig. 4 Steering gear replacement

CROSSMEMBER BUMPER
REPLACE

1. Remove coil spring as described under "Lower Control Arm & Coil Spring, Replace."
2. Remove crossmember bumper from vehicle.
3. Reverse procedure to install.

STEERING KNUCKLE
REPLACE

1. Raise and support vehicle. Support lower control arm with a suitable jack.
2. Remove wheel and tire assembly, then disconnect brake caliper from steering knuckle and suspend from frame with a piece of wire. Do not let brake lines support weight of caliper. **Install a block of wood between brake shoes to hold piston in caliper bore.**
3. Remove hub, disc and splash shield.
4. Remove both ball joint studs as previously described.
5. Disconnect tie rod end from steering knuckle.
6. Press both ball joint studs from steering knuckle using tool No. J-26407 or equivalent.
7. Remove ball joint stud nuts, then the steering knuckle.
8. Reverse procedure to install, noting the following torques: lower ball joint stud nut, 55 ft. lbs.; upper ball joint stud nut, 35 ft. lbs.; splash shield bolts, 7 ft. lbs.; tie rod nut, 29 ft. lbs.

MANUAL STEERING GEAR
REPLACE

1. Raise and support vehicle.
2. Remove both front crossmember braces.
3. Remove flex coupling pinch bolt from shaft.
4. Remove outer tie rod cotter pins and nuts on both sides, and disconnect tie rods from steering knuckles.
5. Remove 4 steering gear attaching bolts and the steering gear, **Fig. 4.**
6. Reverse procedure to install, noting the following torques: flex coupling bolt, 46 ft. lbs.; steering gear bolts, 21 ft. lbs.; tie rod nuts, 29 ft. lbs., plus up to an additional 1/6 turn to align cotter pin hole; front crossmember brace bolts, 20 ft. lbs.

Front Suspension & Steering Section, 1988

INDEX

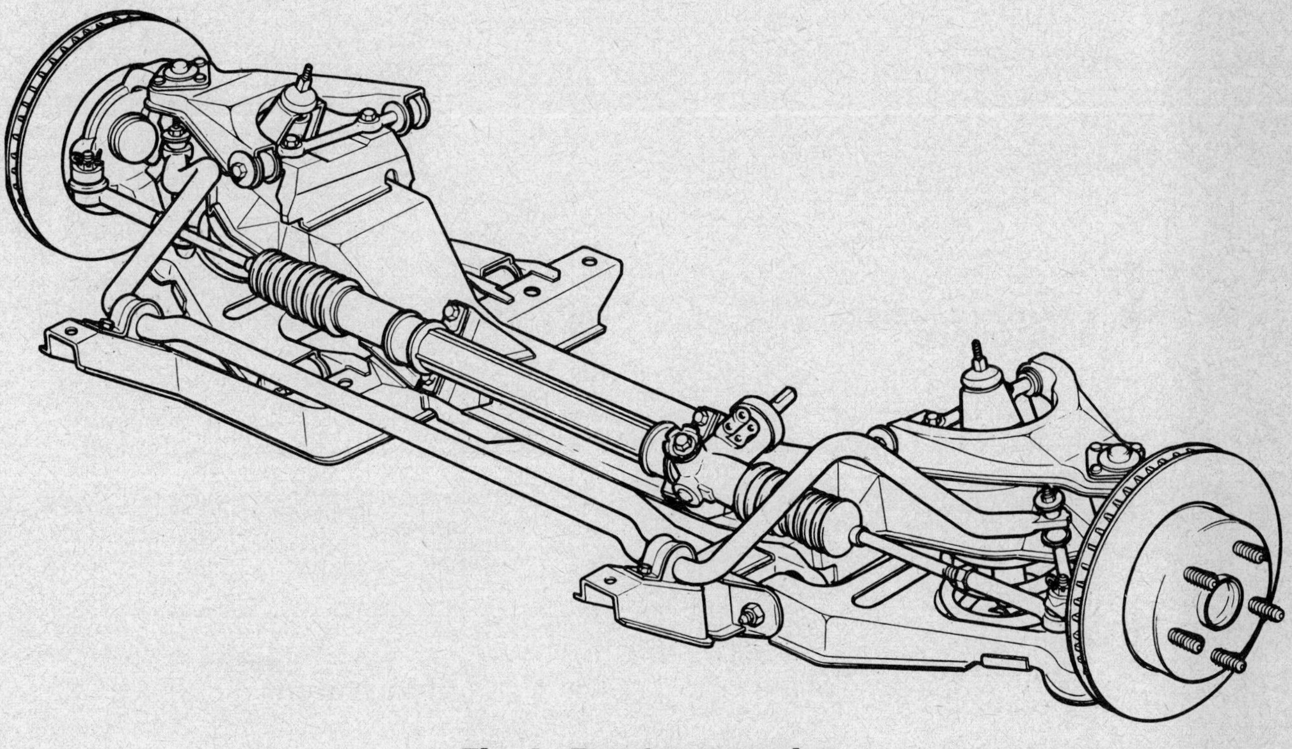

Fig. 1 Front suspension

DESCRIPTION

The front suspension, **Fig. 1,** used on 1988 models features several improvements over the design used on earlier models. In conjunction with the elimination of the steering damper assembly, a larger stabilizer bar is used. Additionally, both the king pin angle and scrub radius have been reduced. Other notable changes include the use of a shorter spindle and an increase in both upper and lower control arm lengths. Besides producing lighter steering effort and a smoother ride, the redesigned suspension also results in a shorter turning radius.

Wheel Alignment Section

INDEX

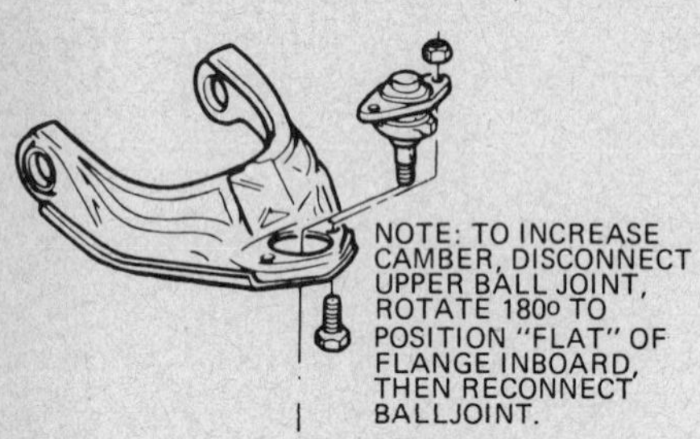

NOTE: TO INCREASE CAMBER, DISCONNECT UPPER BALL JOINT, ROTATE 180° TO POSITION "FLAT" OF FLANGE INBOARD, THEN RECONNECT BALLJOINT.

Fig. 1 Front camber adjustment

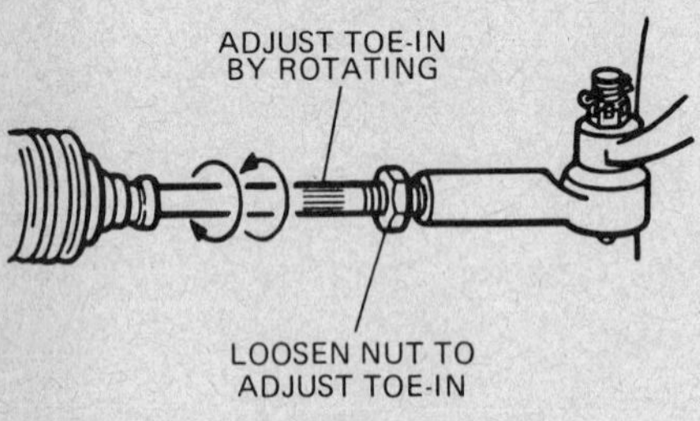

Fig. 3 Toe-in adjustment

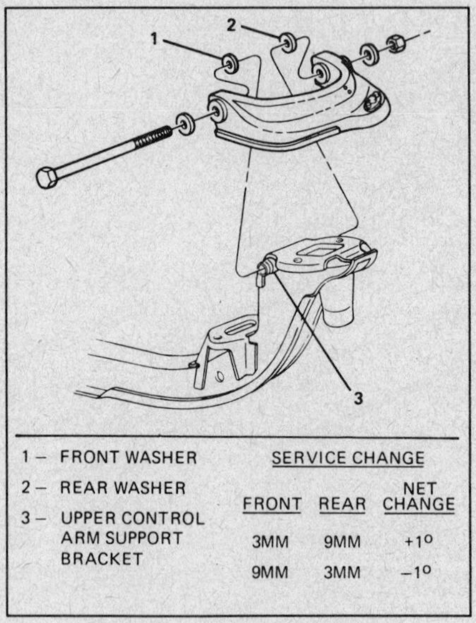

Fig. 2 Front caster adjustment

FRONT WHEEL ALIGNMENT

CAMBER ADJUSTMENT

1. Remove upper ball joint as described in the "Front Suspension & Steering Section, 1984-87."
2. Camber may be increased approximately 1° by rotating 1/2 turn and reinstalling with flat of upper flange on inboard side of control arm, **Fig. 1.**

CASTER ADJUSTMENT

1. Remove upper control arm as described in the "Front Suspension & Steering Section, 1984-87."
2. Adjust caster by installing washers between legs of upper control arm, **Fig. 2. When caster is adjusted, two washers totalling .472 inch (12 mm) must be installed, with one at each end of locating tube.**

TOE-IN ADJUSTMENT

1. Loosen jam nuts on toe link rod, then rotate rods until toe-in is within specifications, **Fig. 3.**
2. Torque jam nuts to 47 ft. lbs. **Use care not to twist or damage rubber boots.**

REAR WHEEL ALIGNMENT

CAMBER ADJUSTMENT

1. Loosen both strut-to-knuckle attaching bolts sufficiently to allow movement between strut and knuckle.
2. Move top of tire inboard or outboard until camber is within specifications, then torque both strut-to-knuckle bolts to 140 ft. lbs. **If complete torque cannot be applied to bolts due to inaccessibility, tighten bolts just enough to hold camber position, then remove wheel and wire and apply final torque.**

TOE-IN ADJUSTMENT

1. Loosen jam nuts on toe link rod, then rotate rods until toe-in is within specifications, **Fig. 3.**
2. Torque jam nuts to 47 ft. lbs. **Use care not to twist or damage rubber boots.**

1988 BUICK REGAL • OLDSMOBILE CUTLASS SUPREME (FWD) • PONTIAC GRAND PRIX

INDEX OF SERVICE OPERATIONS

NOTE: Refer to rear of this manual for vehicle manufacturer's special service tool suppliers.

Specifications

GENERAL ENGINE SPECIFICATIONS

Year	Engine CID ①/Liter	Engine VIN Code ②	Carburetor	Bore and Stroke	Compression Ratio	Net H.P. @ RPM ③	Maximum Torque Ft. Lbs. @ RPM	Normal Oil Pressure Pounds
1988	V6-173, 2.8L	—	Fuel Injection	3.50 x 2.99	8.90	125 @ 4500	160 @ 3600	50-65

ENGINE TIGHTENING SPECIFICATIONS*

*Torque specifications are for clean and lightly lubricated threads only. Dry or dirty threads produce increased friction which prevents accurate measurement of tightness.

Year	Engine Model/VIN	Spark Plugs Ft. Lbs.	Cylinder Head Bolts Ft. Lbs.	Intake Manifold Ft. Lbs.	Exhaust Manifold Ft. Lbs.	Rocker Arm Stud Ft. Lbs.	Rocker Arm Cover Ft. Lbs.	Connecting Rod Cap Bolts Ft. Lbs.	Main Bearing Cap Bolts Ft. Lbs.	Flywheel to Crankshaft Ft. Lbs.	Vibration Damper or Pulley Ft. Lbs.
1988	V6-173	7-15	65-75	20-25	22-28	43-49	6-9	34-40	63-74	45-55	66-84

ALTERNATOR SPECIFICATIONS

Year	Model	Rated Hot Output Amps.
1988	—	42

STARTING MOTOR APPLICATIONS

Year	Engine/VIN	Starter Ident. No.
1988	V6-173	—

FRONT WHEEL ALIGNMENT SPECIFICATIONS

Year	Model	Caster Angle, Degrees		Camber Angle, Degrees				Toe-In Inch
				Limits		Desired		
		Limits	Desired	Left	Right	Left	Right	
1988	Cutlass Supreme	+1.5 to +2.5	+2.0	−.2 to +.12	−.2 to +.12	+.7	+.7	①
	Grand Prix	+1.5 to +2.5	+2.0	−.2 to +.12	−.2 to +.12	+.7	+.7	①
	Regal	+1.5 to +2.5	+2.0	−.2 to +.12	−.2 to +.12	+.7	+.7	①

①—Toe-in 0° per wheel.

COOLING SYSTEM & CAPACITY DATA

Year	Model or Engine/VIN	Cooling Capacity, Qts.	Radiator Cap Relief Pressure, Lbs.	Thermo. Opening Temp.	Fuel Tank Gals.	Engine Oil Refill Qts.	Transaxle Oil Manual Transaxle Pts.	Transaxle Oil Auto. Transaxle Qts. ①
1988	V6-173	11.3	15	195	16.6	4①	5.4	8.5

①—Additional oil may be required to bring oil level to full mark when changing oil filter.

Electrical Section

INDEX

STARTER REPLACE

1. Disconnect battery ground cable.
2. Raise and support vehicle.
3. Remove solenoid wires and battery cables.
4. Remove rear motor support bracket, then the a/c compressor support rod, if equipped.
5. Remove two starter motor to engine attaching bolts, then remove starter.
6. Reverse procedure to install. When removing starter, note if any shims are used between starter and mounting surface. If shims are found, reinstall in original location.

STEERING WHEEL REPLACE

STANDARD & TILT

1. Disconnect battery ground cable.
2. Remove two steering wheel pad retaining screws.
3. Disconnect horn wire from cam tower.
4. Remove steering wheel nut retainer.
5. Remove steering wheel retaining nut.
6. Using a suitable puller, remove steering wheel.
7. Reverse procedure to install.

V6-173 (2.8L) Engine Section

INDEX

ENGINE REPLACE

1. Disconnect battery ground cable.
2. Remove air cleaner, inlet hose and mass air flow sensor.
3. Drain cooling system, then remove exhaust manifold/crossover assembly, if equipped.
4. Remove serpentine, belt tensioner and belt.
5. Loosen power steering pump attaching bolts, then position pump aside.
6. Remove idler, if equipped, then disconnect radiator hose at engine.
7. Disconnect accelerator and throttle valve cables at throttle valve bracket.
8. Remove alternator attaching bolts, then position aside.
9. Remove engine wiring harness, then disconnect fuel hoses.
10. Remove coolant bypass and overflow hoses at engine, then disconnect necessary vacuum hoses.
11. Support engine using a suitable holding fixture, then raise and support vehicle.
12. Remove right inner fender splash shield, then the harmonic dampener.
13. Remove flywheel cover, then the starter attaching bolts.
14. Disconnect electrical wires at starter, then remove starter.
15. Disconnect wires at oil sending unit, then remove a/c compressor and attaching bracket.
16. Remove exhaust pipe at rear of manifold, then the flywheel to torque converter attaching bolts.
17. Remove front and rear motor mount attaching bolts, then the front and rear mount brackets.
18. Remove intermediate shaft bracket at engine, then disconnect shift cable bracket at transaxle.
19. Remove lower bell housing attaching bolts, then lower vehicle.
20. Remove heater hoses at engine, then attach a suitable engine lifting device to engine.
21. Remove engine holding fixture, then support transaxle with a suitable jack.
22. Remove upper bellhousing attaching bolts, then remove front mount bolts.
23. Remove transaxle mount bracket.
24. Remove engine and transaxle as an assembly.

Rear Suspension & Brake Section

INDEX

DESCRIPTION

These vehicles use a tri-link independent rear suspension system with a transverse leaf spring and tubular struts with large lateral links attached to the body crossmember, **Figs. 1 and 2.** The three mounting points are the crossmember, strut tower and trailing arm. The cross member is stamped steel and the composite fiberglass mono leaf spring is transversely mounted to the under side of the crossmember, with its padded ends free riding on the cast knuckle assembly.

BRAKE SYSTEM

DESCRIPTION

The brake system used on these vehicles is a vacuum powered hydraulically actuated four wheel disc system with a proportioning valve. Braking performance is achieved through the power assisted four wheel disc system by incorporating composite material rotors. The front rotors are of the vented design with twin piston calipers. The rear discs incorporate solid rotors and single bore calipers.

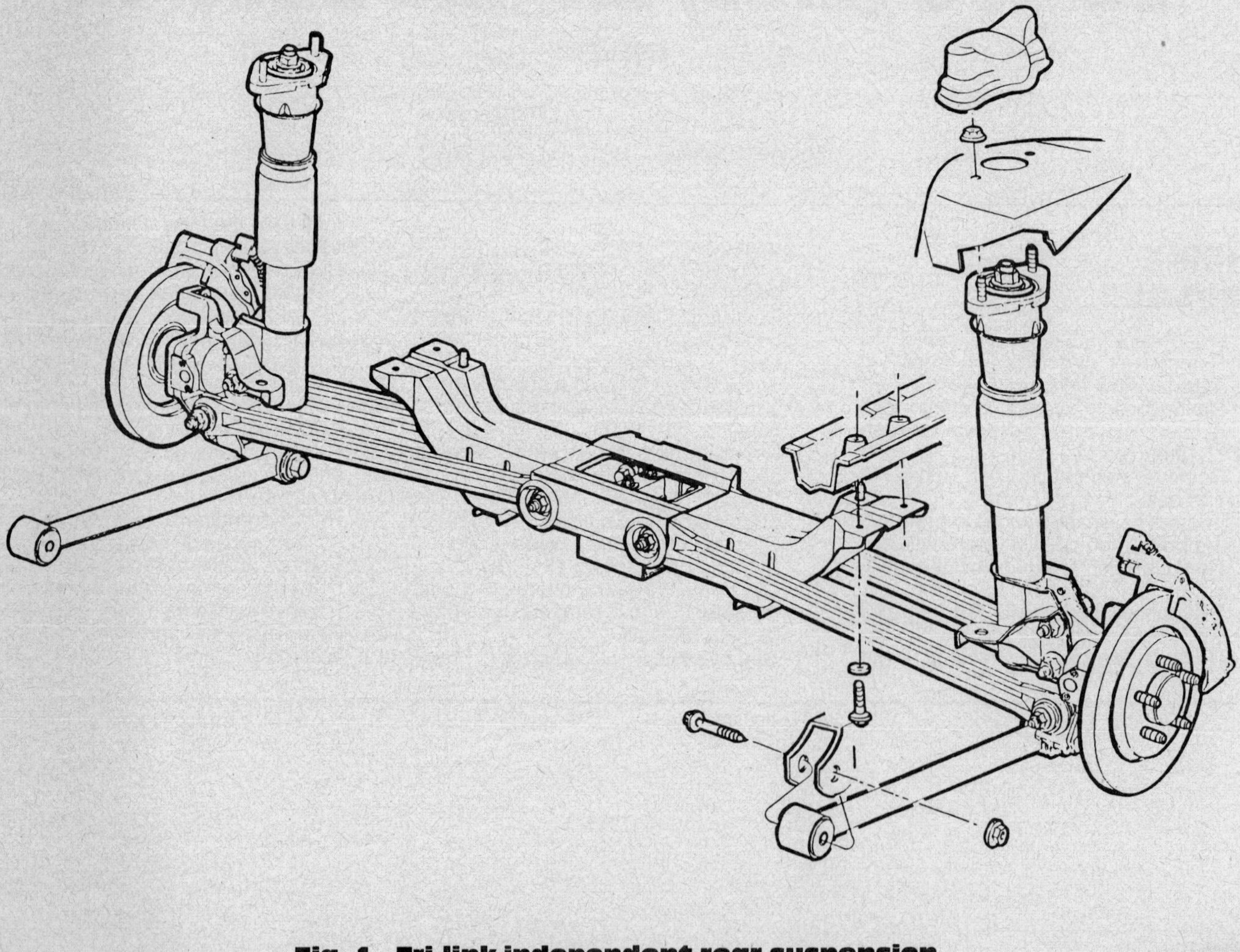

Fig. 1 Tri-link independent rear suspension

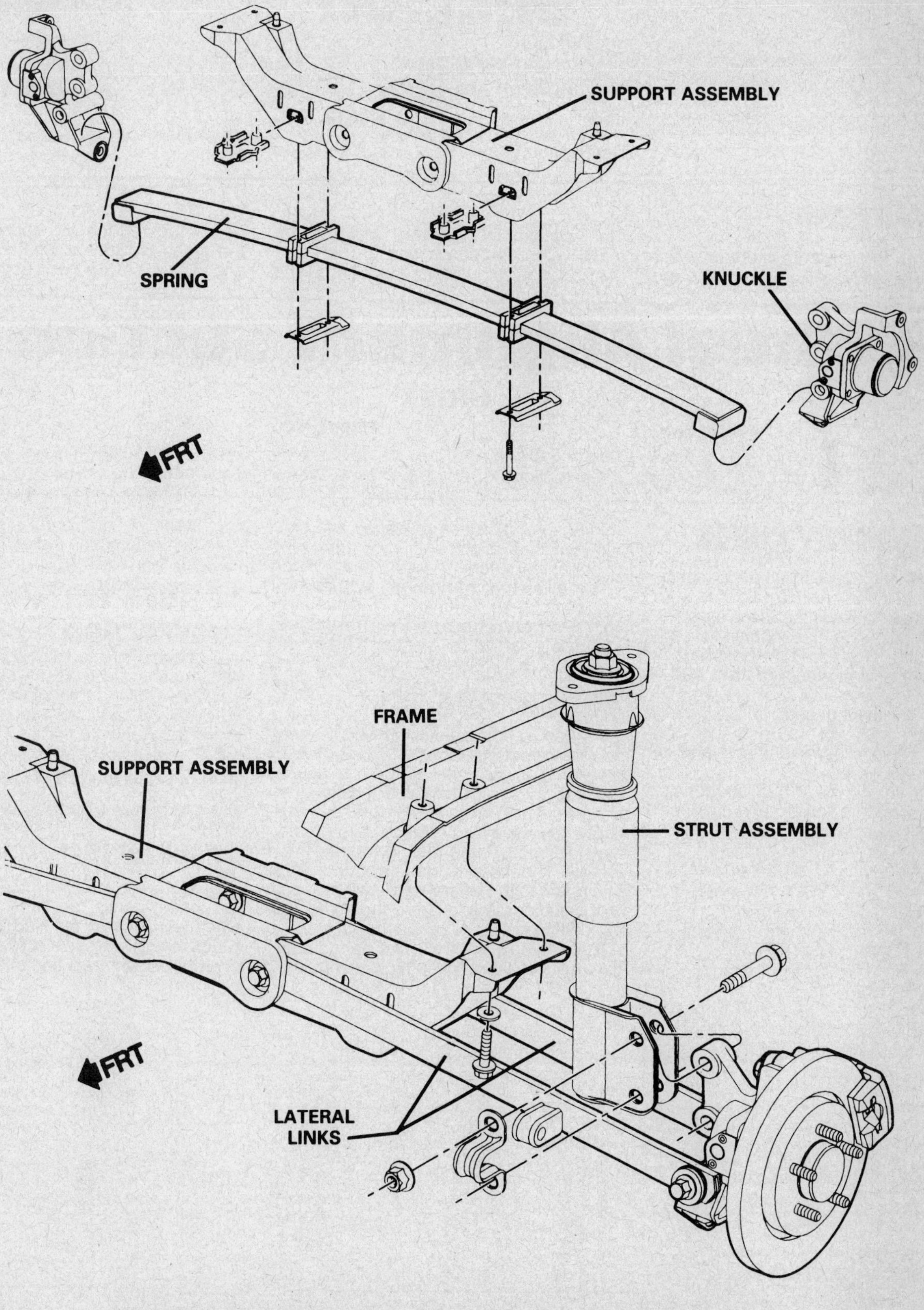

Fig. 2 Exploded view of rear suspension assembly

Front Suspension & Steering Section

INDEX

DESCRIPTION

The front suspension system on these vehicles is of the MacPherson strut design. This design incorporates MacPherson struts with coil springs and a one piece configuration with lower control arms. The use of tapered top coil springs on top of the struts provides a well controlled ride and allows a lower hood profile.

Wheel Alignment Section

INDEX

PRELIMINARY CHECK

1. Ensure tires are inflated to correct pressure, and check for uneven wear.
2. Check front wheel bearings and related suspension components for damage and replace as necessary, to eliminate improper alignment due to faulty components.
3. Check steering gear and adjust as necessary.
4. Check shocks for damage and replace as necessary.
5. Rock vehicle backward and forward and bounce it upward and downward to settle vehicle prior to alignment.
6. Ensure vehicle is unloaded and on a suitable alignment rack following manufacturers' instructions. **When measuring equipment is attached directly to outer end of driveshaft and front wheels are on turntables, apply brake to prevent improper vehicle movement.**

TOE SETTING

As viewed from above, the wheels must be set so that distances A and B, **Fig. 1**, measured at wheel rims and at axle height, are different at a given value. If distance A is smaller than distance B, the setting is known as toe-in. If Distance A is greater than distance B, the setting is known as toe-out. The toe setting is given in inches and refers to the difference between A and B. If distances A and B are the same, the toe setting is 0.

Toe setting is controlled by tie rod position. Adjustment is made by loosening the nuts at the steering knuckle end of the tie rods, and rotating the rod ends until proper toe setting is obtained.

CAMBER SETTING

DESCRIPTION

Camber refers to the angle at which a wheel leans in or out as shown, **Fig. 2.** Positive camber is when the wheel leans outward and negative camber is when the wheel leans inward.

For setting angles, refer to specifications chart at beginning of this chapter.

CASTER SETTING

DESCRIPTION

Caster angle refers to the angle at which the wheel center deviates from vertical when viewed from the side, **Fig. 3.**

For setting angles, refer to specifications chart at beginning of this chapter.

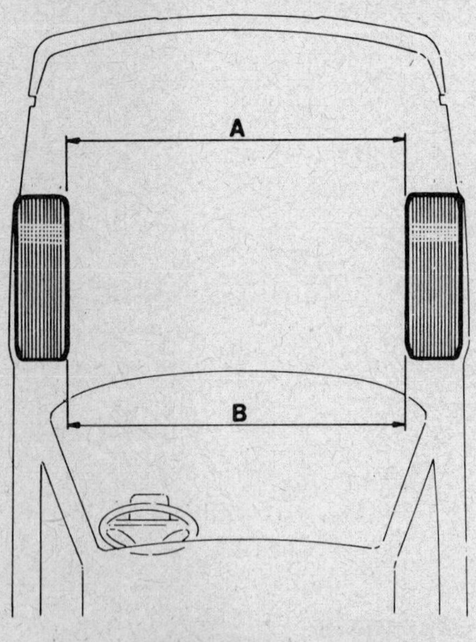

Fig. 1 Measuring wheel alignment angles

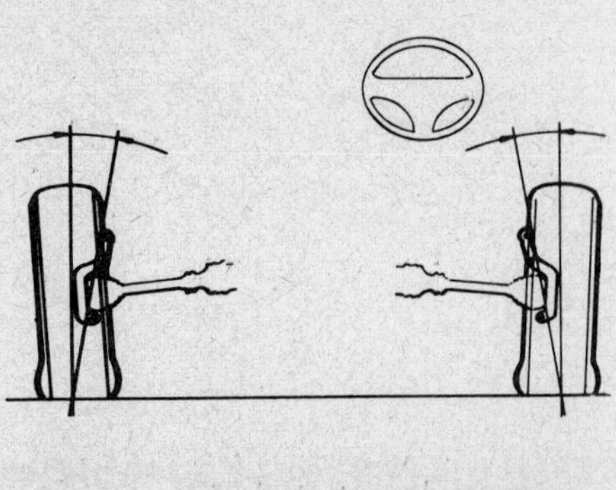

Fig. 2 Measuring camber

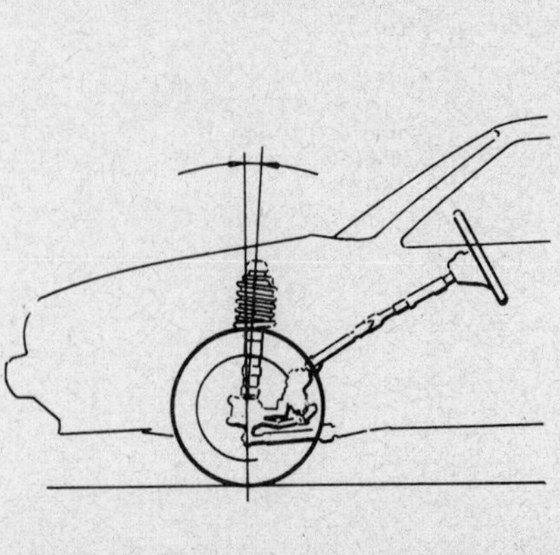

Fig. 3 Measuring caster

AIR CONDITIONING

TABLE OF CONTENTS

System Testing

INDEX

GENERAL PRECAUTIONS

The Freon refrigerant used is also known as R-12 or F-12. It is colorless and odorless both as a gas and a liquid. Since it boils (vaporizes) at −21.7°F, it will usually be in a vapor state when being handled in a repair shop. But if a portion of the liquid coolant should come in contact with the hands or face, note that its temperature momentarily will be at least 22° below zero.

Protective goggles should be worn when opening any refrigerant lines. If liquid coolant does touch the eyes, bathe the eyes quickly in cold water, then apply a bland disinfectant oil to the eyes. See an eye doctor.

When checking a system for leaks with a torch type leak detector, do not breathe the vapors coming from the flame. Do not discharge refrigerant in the area of a live flame. A poisonous phosgene gas is produced when R-12 or F-12 is burned. While the small amount of gas produced by a leak detector is not harmful unless inhaled directly at the flame, the quantity of refrigerant released into the air when a system is purged can be extremely dangerous if allowed to come into contact with an open flame. Thus, when purging a system, be sure that the discharge hose is routed to a well ventilated area where no flame is present. Under these conditions the refrigerant will be quickly dissipated into the surrounding air.

Never allow the temperature of refrigerant drums to exceed 125°F. The resultant increase in temperature will cause a corresponding increase in pressure which may cause the safety plug to release or the drum to burst.

If it is necessary to heat a drum of refrigerant when charging a system, the drum should be placed in water no hotter than 125°F. Never use a blow torch or other open flame. If possible, a pressure release mechanism should be attached before the drum is heated.

When connecting and disconnecting service gauges on an A/C system, ensure that gauge hand valves are fully closed and that compressor service valves, if equipped, are in the back-seated (fully counterclockwise) position. Do not disconnect gauge hoses from service port adapters, if used, while gauges are connected to A/C system. To disconnect hoses, always remove adapter from service port. Do not disconnect hoses from gauge manifold while connected to A/C system, as refrigerant will be rapidly discharged.

After disconnecting gauge lines, check the valve areas to be sure service valves are correctly seated and Schraeder valves, if used, are not leaking.

EXERCISE SYSTEM

An important fact most owners ignore is that A/C units must be used periodically. Manufacturers caution that when the air conditioner is not used regularly, particularly during the cold months, it should be turned on for a few minutes once every two or three weeks while the engine is running. This keeps the system in good operating condition.

Checking out the system for the effects of disuse before the onset of summer is one of the most important aspects of A/C servicing.

First clean out the condenser core, mounted in all cases at the front of the radiator. All obstructions, such as leaves, bugs or dirt, must be removed, as they will reduce heat transfer and impair the efficiency of the system. Make sure the space between the condenser and the radiator also is free of foreign matter.

Make certain the evaporator water drain is open. The evaporator cools and dehumidifies the air before it enters the passenger compartment; there, the refrigerant is changed from a liquid to a vapor. As the core cools the air, moisture condenses on it but is prevented from collecting in the evaporator by the water drain.

PERFORMANCE TEST

The system should be operated for at least 15 minutes to allow sufficient time for all parts to become completely stabilized. Determine if the system is fully charged by the use of test gauges and sight glass if one is installed on system. Head pressure will read from 180 psi to 220 psi or higher, depending upon ambient temperature and the type unit being tested. The sight glass should be free of bubbles if a glass is used in the system. Low side pressures should read approximately 15 psi to 30 psi, again depending on the ambient temperature and the unit being tested. It is not feasible to give a definite reading for all types of systems used, as the type control and component installation used on a particular system will directly influence the pressure readings on the high and low sides, **Fig. 1.**

The high side pressure will definitely be affected by the ambient or outside air temperature. A system that is operating normally will indicate a high side gauge reading between 150-170 psi with an 80°F ambient temperature. The same system will register 210-230 psi with an ambient temperature of 100°F. No two systems will register exactly the same, which requires that allowance for variations in head pressures must be considered. Following are the most important normal readings likely to be encountered during the season.

Ambient Temp.	High Side Pressure
80	150-170
90	175-195
95	185-205
100	210-230
105	230-250
110	250-270

RELATIVE TEMPERATURE OF HIGH AND LOW SIDES

The high side of the system should be uniformly hot to the touch throughout. A difference in temperature will indicate a partial blockage of liquid or gas at this point.

The low side of the system should be uniformly cool to the touch with no excessive sweating of the suction line or low side service valve. Excessive sweating or frosting of the low side service valve usually indicates an expansion valve is allowing an excessive amount of refrigerant into the evaporator.

EVAPORATOR OUTPUT

At this point, provided all other inspection tests have been performed, and components have been found to operate as they should, a rapid cooling down of the interior of the vehicle should result. The use of a thermometer is not necessary to determine evaporator output. Bringing all units to the correct operating specifications will insure that the evaporator performs as intended.

Evaporator Pressure Gauge Reading	Evaporator Temperature F°	High Pressure Gauge Reading	Ambient Temperature
0	-21°	45	20°
0.6	-20°	55	30°
2.4	-15°	72	40°
4.5	-10°	86	50°
6.8	- 5°	105	60°
9.2	0°	126	70°
11.8	5°	140	75°
14.7	10°	160	80°
17.1	15°	185	90°
21.1	20°	195	95°
22.5	22°	220	100°
23.9	24°	240	105°
25.4	26°	260	110°
26.9	28°	275	115°
28.5	30°	290	120°
37.0	40°	305	125°
46.7	50°	325	130°
57.7	60°		
70.1	70°		
84.1	80°		
99.6	90°		
116.9	100°		
136.0	110°		
157.1	120°		
179.0	130°		

Fig. 1 Pressure-temperature relationship (Typical). Conditions equivalent to 30 mph or 1750 engine RPM

DISCHARGING & EVACUATING SYSTEM

DISCHARGING SYSTEM

1. Connect gauges into system, **Fig. 2**, and adjust controls for maximum cooling. This is necessary when the system has not been operating to return excess oil to the compressor.
2. Operate engine for 10 to 15 minutes to stabilize the system at 1500-1750 rpm.
3. Adjust engine speed to slow idle, then shut off engine and controls.
4. Open low side hand manifold valve slightly, using a container to catch oil and refrigerant. Do not discharge the refrigerant near an open flame as a toxic gas (phosgene) can result.
5. Allow all refrigerant to discharge through the low side fitting only. **Open hand valve(s) only enough to bleed refrigerant from system. Too rapid purging will draw excessive oil from compressor and system.**
6. When refrigerant ceases to bleed from the discharge hose on the low side, crack open the high side hand valve to check for any remaining pressure. If pressure does exist, allow high side to discharge slowly. This condition indicates a high side restriction, and it must be diagnosed and corrected before evacuating and charging the system.

EVACUATE SYSTEM WITH VACUUM PUMP

Vacuum pumps suitable for removing air and moisture from A/C systems are commercially available. A specification for system pump-down used here is 28 to 29$^{1}/_{2}$ inches vacuum. This reading can be attained at or near sea level only. For each 1000 feet of altitude this operation is being performed, the reading will be 1 inch vacuum lower. As an example, at 5000 feet elevation, only 23-24$^{1}/_{2}$ inch of vacuum can be obtained. **The system must be completely discharged before it can be evacuated. Damage to vacuum pump may result if pressurized refrigerant is allowed to enter.**

1. With hand gauges connected into system, remove cap from vacuum hose connector. Install hand gauge manifold center hose to vacuum pump connector. Open low side gauge manifold hand valve only.
2. Ensure low side gauge is calibrated correctly. It should be reading zero. If

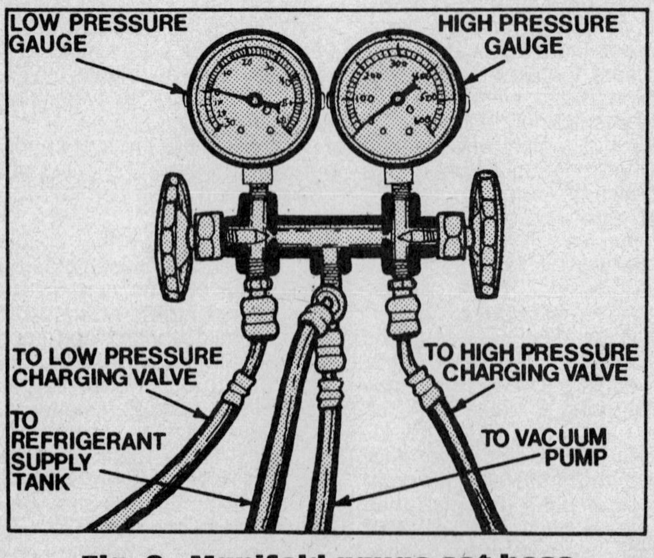

Fig. 2 Manifold gauge set hose connections (Typical)

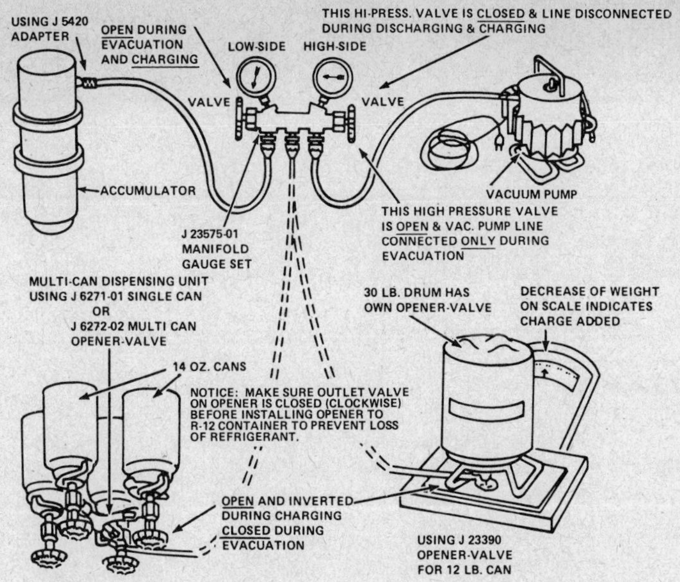

Fig. 3 Charging C.C.O.T. A/C system

not, adjust calibration.

3. Evacuate system with the vacuum pump until the low pressure gauge reads at least 28 inches of vacuum. Continue evacuating system for an additional 15 minutes for routine system servicing or 20 to 30 minutes, if any parts have been replaced.
4. When system evacuation is complete, close low side gauge manifold hand valve, then turn vacuum pump off.
5. Check ability of system to hold vacuum. Watch low side gauge to see that gauge does not rise at a faster rate than 1 inch vacuum every 4 to 5 minutes. If low side gauge rises at too rapid a rate, install partial charge and leak test. Evacuate system again.
6. If system holds vacuum, charge system with refrigerant.

EVACUATE SYSTEM USING CHARGING STATION

A vacuum pump is built into the charging station and is constructed to withstand repeated and prolonged use without damage. Complete moisture removal from the system is possible only with a vacuum pump constructed for the purpose.

The system must be completely discharged before it can be evacuated. Damage to the vacuum pump may result if pressurized refrigerant is allowed to enter.

1. Connect hose to vacuum pump, if system was discharged through charging station.
2. Open low side gauge hand valve of charging station.
3. Connect station into 110 volt current.
4. Turn vacuum pump on according to instructions for specific station being used.
5. Evacuate system with the vacuum pump until the low pressure gauge reads at least 28 inches of vacuum. Continue evacuating system for an additional 15 minutes for routine system servicing or 20 to 30 minutes, if any parts have been replaced.
6. Close low side gauge hand valve, then turn vacuum pump off.
7. Check ability of system to hold vacuum. Watch low side gauge to see that gauge does not rise at a faster rate than 1 inch vacuum every 4 to 5 minutes. If low side gauge rises at too rapid a rate, install partial charge and leak test. Then evacuate system again.
8. If system holds vacuum, charge system with refrigerant.

CHARGING THE SYSTEM

USING CHARGING STATION J-23500-01

Use instructions provided with charging station with the following exceptions:

1. Do not connect high pressure line to A/C system.
2. Always keep high pressure valve closed on charging station.
3. Perform all evacuation and charging through accumulator low-side pressure service fitting.

Use of these procedures will prevent charging station from being accidentally exposed to high-side vehicle system pressure.

USING DISPOSABLE CANS OR REFRIGERANT DRUM

Never use these cans to charge into the high pressure side of the system (compressor discharge port) or into a system that is at high temperature, because the high system pressures could be transferred into the charging can causing it to explode.

If R-12 drum is used, place on scale and note total weight before charging. During charging, watch scale to determine amount of R-12 used.

If 14 ounce R-12 cans are used, close tapping valve, then attach cans following instructions included with manifold adaptor.

Charging Of System

1. Start engine and allow to warm up (choke off, normal idle). Set A/C control lever to OFF.
2. With R-12 drum or cans inverted, open R-12 supply valve and allow 1 lb. of liquid R-12 to flow into system through low-side service fitting on accumulator, **Fig. 3.**
3. When 1 lb. of refrigerant has entered system, engage compressor by setting A/C lever to NORM and blower switch to HI to draw in remainder of charge. Cooling condenser with a large fan will speed up charging procedure by maintaining condenser temperature below charging cylinder temperature.
4. Close refrigerant supply valve and run engine for 30 seconds to clear lines and gauges.
5. With engine running, remove charging low side hose adapter from accumulator service fitting. Unscrew rapidly to avoid excessive refrigerant loss. **Do not remove a gauge line from its adapter when line is connected to A/C system. To disconnect line, always remove line adapter from service fitting. Do not remove charging hose at gauge set while attached to accumulator, as system will be discharged due to depressed Schraeder valve.**
6. Replace protective cap on accumulator fitting and turn engine off.
7. Check system for leaks.
8. Start engine and check for proper system pressures.

LEAK TEST SYSTEM

The propane torch Halide Leak Detector is the most widely used of the detection devices. Therefore, only the procedure for this device will be given. The procedure is the same for any electronic detector, except that the pickup device registers the presence of refrigerant by a flashing light or high pitched squeal instead of changing the color of the flame. All other steps in preparing the system and leak testing are the same and can be followed as outlined below:

1. Stabilize system at 1500-1750 RPM. If system is empty of refrigerant, it will be necessary to install a partial charge before continuing. With gauges connected into system, adjust A/C controls for maximum cooling. Operate for 10 to 15 minutes, then shut off car engine.
2. Light leak detector. Open valve to a low flame that will not blow itself out. Warm up until copper element turns cherry red. Lower flame until flame tip is even with or slightly below center of element. For electronic tester, follow preparation procedure as given in operating instructions.
3. Move leak detector pickup under hoses, joints, seals, and any possible place for a leak to occur. **R-12 refrigerant is heavier than air and will move downward. If concentration of refrigerant is located, move**

pickup upward to locate leak. Do not inhale fumes produced by burning refrigerant.

4. Watch for color change of flame: Pale blue, no refrigerant; yellow, small amount of refrigerant; purplish-blue, large amount of refrigerant. Repair system as necessary if leaks are located.
5. Check sensitivity of reaction plate: Pass pickup hose over empty can or crack open refrigerant container; flame should show violent reaction. If no color change, replace reaction plate, following instructions accompanying leak detector. Too high a flame will shorten life of reaction plate, and poor reaction and will soon burn out element.
6. Charge system if repairs were necessary.

System Service

INDEX

OIL CHARGE

COMPRESSOR MODELS WITH CYCLING CLUTCH

Oil Charge—Component Replacement

If there are no signs of excessive leakage, add the following amount of oil depending on component to be replaced.

Evaporator .... 3 ounces
Condenser .... ounce

If accumulator or compressor are to be replaced, drain oil from component to be replaced and measure, then add same amount of new oil to replacement component plus one additional ounce.

R-4 and DA-6 compressors do not have an oil sump. On all compressor models, if accumulator is being replaced, two additional ounces on 1981-82 models, or three additional ounces on 1983-86 models must be added to replace amount captured by desiccant in old accumulator.

Oil Charge-Leak Condition

On models with A-6 or DA-V5 compressor, both accumulator and compressor must be removed and oil drained and measured in cases of excessive oil leakage. If oil recovered is 4 ounces or more, add same amount of new refrigerant oil to system. If amount of oil recovered is less than 4 ounces, add 6 ounces of new refrigerant oil to system.

On models with radial R-4 or DA-6 compressor, it will only be necessary to remove, drain and measure oil from accumulator assembly in cases of excessive oil leakage. These compressors do not have an oil sump, therefore it is not necessary to remove compressor in cases of oil leakage. If amount of oil recovered is 3 ounces or more, add the same amount of new refrigerant oil to system. If amount recovered is less than 3 ounces, add 3 ounces of new refrigerant oil to system.

If accumulator is replaced, two additional ounces of oil on R-4 compressors, or 3 additional ounces of oil on DA-6 compressor must be added to replace amount captured by desiccant in old accumulator.

MODELS LESS CYCLING CLUTCH

RADIAL 4 CYLINDER COMPRESSOR

Component Replacement

When replacing a system component, oil should be added to the system as follows. If compressor is operating, idle engine for 10 minutes with A/C controls set for maximum cooling and high blower prior to discharging system.

Add additional oil as specified if any of components are replaced.

Condenser .... 1 ounce
Evaporator .... 1 ounce
VIR .... 3 ounces
Accumulator .... 1 ounce

Compressor Replacement

1. Discharge system and remove compressor from vehicle.
2. Position compressor with shaft end up and allow oil to drain from suction and discharge ports into a container calibrated in ounces.
3. Drain oil from new compressor, then add same amount of new refrigerant oil to new compressor as was drained from original compressor. **If system was flushed the total oil capacity must be added to the compressor as specified in the A/C Data Table.**
4. Install new compressor and charge system.

Component Rupture, Fast Discharge

1. Repair leak and flush system.
2. Remove compressor and drain oil.
3. Add total capacity as specified in A/C Data Table of new refrigerant oil to suction port of compressor.
4. Install compressor, charge system and perform leak check.

Slow Leak

1. If refrigerant loss has occurred over an extended period of time, add 3 ounces of refrigerant oil to system.
2. Recharge system.

System Performance Evaluation

When system performance, efficiency and proper oil charge are in doubt, the system should be flushed and the total capacity, as specified in the A/C Data Table, of new refrigerant oil be added to the compressor prior to any further checks of the system.

AXIAL 6 CYLINDER COMPRESSOR

Oil Charge

1. Idle engine for 10 minutes at 1250 RPM with system controls set for maximum cooling and high blower speed.
2. Stop engine, discharge system and remove compressor.
3. With compressor in a horizontal position and drain plug down, remove plug and drain oil into a measured container.
4. If 4 ounces or more of oil was drained, add the same amount to the compressor. If less than 4 ounces of oil was drained, add 6 ounces of oil to compressor.

Compressor Replacement

1. Idle engine for 10 minutes at approximately 1250 RPM at maximum cooling and high blower speed to distribute oil in system.
2. Remove compressor from vehicle.
3. Remove plug and allow oil to drain from compressor into a container calibrated in ounces.
4. Drain oil from new compressor.
5. If amount drained from original compressor is more than four ounces, add the same amount of new refrigerant oil to the new compressor plus amount lost during discharge.
6. If amount of oil drained from original compressor is less than 4 ounces, add 6 ounces of new refrigerant oil to the new compressor plus amount lost during discharge.

Component Replacement

Whenever a component of the A/C system is replaced, and the component is not pre-charged at the factory, measured quantities of refrigeration oil should be added to the component to assure that the total oil charge in the system is correct before the system is placed into operation.

The oil is poured directly into the replacement component. If an evaporator is installed, pour oil into the inlet pipe with the pipe held vertically so the oil will drain into the evaporator core. No additional oil is required if valves and hoses are replaced.

Add additional oil as specified if any of the following components are replaced.

Evaporator .... 3 ounces
Condenser .... 1 ounce
VIR .... 1 ounce
Accumulator .... 1 ounce
Receiver .... 1 ounce

If the system is flushed with a sufficient amount of a flushing agent that would remove oil from the system, install the full amount specified in the A/C Data Table. On a newly installed system, install the full capacity of oil prior to operation. On systems containing metal particles in the oil, flush the system, replace or overhaul the compressor, replace receiver-dehydrator or VIR dessicant, and install a high capacity, low pressure drop filter in the liquid line to protect the expansion valve and new compressor from damage due to foreign particles.

CHARGING VALVE LOCATION

On all models except the Chevrolet Nova the high pressure charging valve is located either on the high pressure vapor line or the muffler, and the low pressure charging valve is on the accumulator. On Chevrolet Nova the high pressure charging valve is on the liquid line ahead of the strut tower, and the low pressure charging valve is on the suction line ahead of the strut tower.

A/C DATA TABLE

Year	Model	Refrigerant Capacity, Lbs.	Refrigeration Oil: Viscosity	Refrigeration Oil: Total System Capacity, Ounces	Refrigeration Oil: Compressor Oil Level Check, Inches	Compressor Clutch Air Gap Inch
BUICK: REAR WHEEL DRIVE MODELS & 1982-85 RIVIERA						
1982-85	Regal & Riviera	3¼	525	6	①	.020-.040
	Electra & Sabre	3½	525	6	①	.020-.040
1986-87	Estate Wagon	3½	525	6	①	.020-.040
	Regal	3¼	525	6	①	.020-.040
CHEV. CELEBRITY, BUICK CENTURY, OLDS CUTLASS CIERA & PONT. 6000; 1984-87 OLDS. CUTLASS CRUISER						
1982	All	2¾	525	6	①	.020-.040
1983-87	All	⑧	525	④	①	⑤
FRONT WHEEL DRIVE BUICK ELECTRA, LESABRE & PARK AVE.; CADILLAC DEVILLE & FLEETWOOD; OLDS 88 & 98; PONT. BONNEVILLE						
1985	All	2¾	525	④	①	⑤
1986	All	⑦	525	8	①	.015-.025
1987	Deville, Fleetwood & Electra	2⅞	525	8	①	.015-.025
	LeSabre, 88 & 98	2.40	525	8	①	.015-.025
1986-87 BUICK RIVIERA, CADILLAC ELDORADO & SEVILLE & OLDS. TORONADO						
1986-87	All	2¾	525	8	①	.015-.025
BUICK SKYLARK (1982-85), CHEVROLET CITATION, OLDS. OMEGA & PONTIAC PHOENIX						
1982-86	All	2¾	525	④	①	⑤
BUICK SOMERSET REGAL, OLDS. CALAIS & PONTIAC GRAND AM; 1986-87 BUICK SKYLARK						
1985-87	All	2¼	525	8	①	.015-.025
CHEV. CAVALIER, BUICK SKYHAWK, CAD. CIMARRON, OLDS. FIRENZA & PONT. SUNBIRD/2000						
1982-83	All	2¾	525	6	①	.020-.040
1984-85	All	2¾	525	④	①	⑤
1986-87	All	⑥	525	8	①	.015-.025
CADILLAC: REAR WHEEL DRIVE MODELS & 1982-85 ELDORADO & SEVILLE						
1982	All	3¼	525	6	①	.020-.040
1983	All	3½	525	6	①	.020-.040
1984-86	All	3½	525	④	①	⑤
1987	Fleetwood Brougham	3½	525	6	①	.020-.040

—Continued

A/C DATA TABLE—Continued

Year	Model	Refrigerant Capacity, Lbs.	Refrigeration Oil: Viscosity	Refrigeration Oil: Total System Capacity, Ounces	Refrigeration Oil: Compressor Oil Level Check, Inches	Compressor Clutch Air Gap Inch
CHEVROLET: CAMARO, CHEVROLET, MALIBU & MONTE CARLO						
1982	Caprice & Impala	3½	525	②	①	③
	Malibu & Monte Carlo	3¼	525	②	①	③
1982-83	Camaro	3	525	6	①	.020-.040
1983-86	Caprice & Impala	3½	525	6	①	.020-.040
	Malibu & Monte Carlo	3¼	525	6	①	.020-.040
1984-87	Camaro	3	525	④	①	⑤
1987	Caprice	3½	525	6	①	.020-.040
CHEROLET CORVETTE						
1982	All	3	525	6	①	.020-.040
1984-87	All	2¾	525	6	①	.020-.040
CHEVROLET CHEVETTE & PONTIAC 1000						
1982-87	All	2¼	525	6	①	.020-.040
CHEVROLET NOVA						
1985-87	All	1½	500	2-3⅖	①	.016-.028
OLDS.: REAR WHEEL DRIVE & 1982-85 TORONADO						
1982-85	Cutlass	3¼	525	6	①	.020-.040
1982-86	All exc. Cutlass	3½	525	6	①	.020-.040
1986	Cutlass	3	525	6	①	.020-.040
1987	Custom Cruiser	3.30	525	6	①	.020-.040
	Cutlass	2.85	525	6	①	.020-.040
PONTIAC: EXC. FIERO, 1000 & FRONT WHEEL DRIVE						
1982-86	All Exc. Firebird & Parisienne	3¼	525	6	①	.020-.040
1982-87	Firebird	3	525	④	①	⑤
1983-86	Parisienne	3½	525	6	①	.020-.040
1987	Safari	3½	525	6	①	.020-.040
PONTIAC FIERO						
1984-87	All	2½	525	8	①	.015-.025

①—Note that "Oil level inches" cannot be checked. Refer to total capacity in ounces. See text for procedure.
②—Axial compressor, 10 ounces; radial compressor, 6 ounces.
③—R-4 compressor, .020-.040 inch; A-6 compressor, .022-.057 inch.
④—Axial compressor, 8 ounces; radial compressor, 5 ounces.
⑤—Axial compressor, .015-.025 inch; radial compressor, .020-.040 inch.
⑥—Exc. Skyhawk Turbo, 2¼ lbs.; Skyhawk Turbo, 2¾ lbs.
⑦—Exc. 88 with V6-181 engine and LeSabre, 2⅞ lbs.; 88 with V6-181 engine & LeSabre, 2⅖ lbs.
⑧—Exc. 1986-87 6000 STE, 2¾ lbs.; 1986-87 6000 STE, 2½ lbs.

ENGINE COOLING FANS

TABLE OF CONTENTS

Variable Speed Fans

INDEX

Fig. 1 Typical variable-speed fan installed

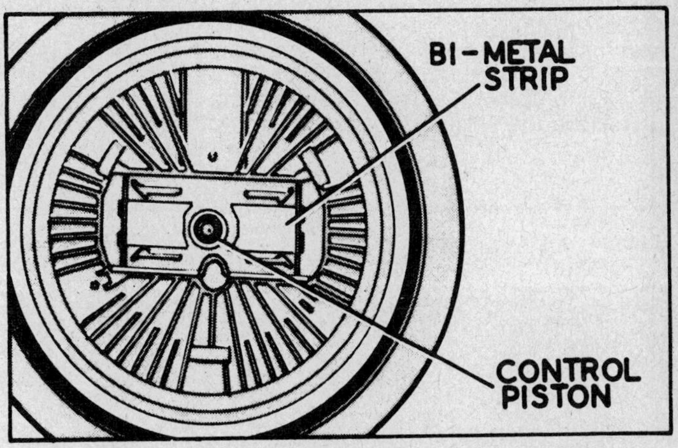

Fig. 2 Variable-speed fan with flat bi-metal thermostatic spring

DESCRIPTION

The fan drive clutch, **Fig. 1,** is a fluid coupling containing silicone oil. Fan speed is regulated by the torque-carrying capacity of the silicone oil. The more silicone oil in the coupling the greater the fan speed, and the less silicone oil the slower the fan speed.

Two types of fan drive clutches are in use. On one, **Fig. 2,** a bi-metallic strip and control piston on the front of the fluid coupling regulates the amount of silicone oil entering the coupling. The bi-metallic strip bows outward with an increase in surrounding temperature and allows a piston to move outward. The piston opens a valve regulating the flow of silicone oil into the coupling from a reserve chamber. The silicone oil is returned to the reserve chamber through a bleed hole when the valve is closed.

On the other type of fan drive clutch, **Fig. 3,** a heat-sensitive, bi-metal spring connected to an opening plate brings about a similar result. Both units cause the fan speed to increase with a rise in temperature and to decrease as the temperature goes down.

In some cases a Flex-Fan is used instead of a Fan Drive Clutch. Flexible blades vary the volume of air being drawn through the radiator, automatically increasing the pitch at low engine speeds.

FAN DRIVE CLUTCH TEST

Do not operate the engine until the fan has been first checked for possible cracks and separations.

Run the engine at a fast idle speed (1000 RPM) until normal operating temperature is reached. This process can be speeded up by blocking off the front of the radiator with cardboard. Regardless of temperatures, the unit must be operated for at least five minutes immediately before being tested.

Stop the engine and, using a glove or a cloth to protect the hand, immediately check the effort required to turn the fan. If considerable effort is required, it can be assumed that the coupling is operating satisfactorily. If very little effort is required to turn the fan, it is an indication that the coupling is not operating properly and should be replaced.

If the clutch fan is the coiled bi-metal spring type, it may be tested while the vehicle is being driven. To check, disconnect the bi-metal spring, **Fig. 4,** and rotate 90 degrees counterclockwise. This disables the temperature-controlled free-wheeling feature and the clutch performs like a conventional fan. If this cures the overheating condition, replace the clutch fan.

SERVICE PROCEDURE

To prevent silicone fluid from draining into fan drive bearing, do not store or place drive unit on bench with rear of shaft pointing downward.

The removal procedure for either type of fan clutch assembly is generally the same for all cars. Merely unfasten the unit from the water pump and remove the assembly from the car.

The type of unit shown in **Fig. 2** may be partially disassembled for inspection and cleaning. Take off the capscrews that hold the assembly together and separate the fan from the drive clutch. Next remove the metal strip on the front by pushing one end of it toward the fan clutch body so it clears the retaining bracket. Then push the strip to the side so that its opposite end will

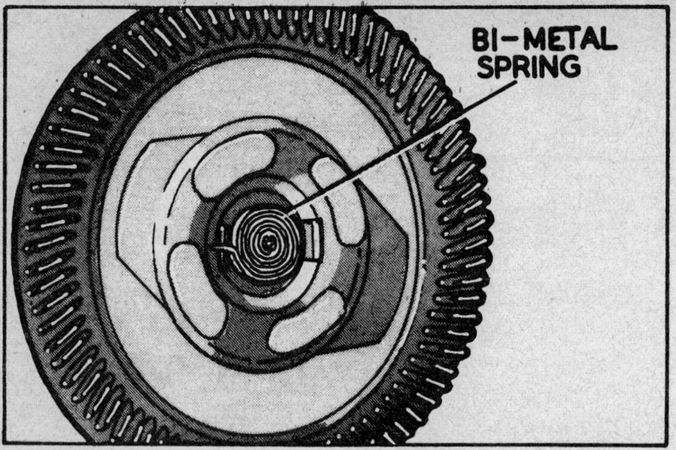

Fig. 3 Variable-speed fan with coiled bi-metal thermostatic spring

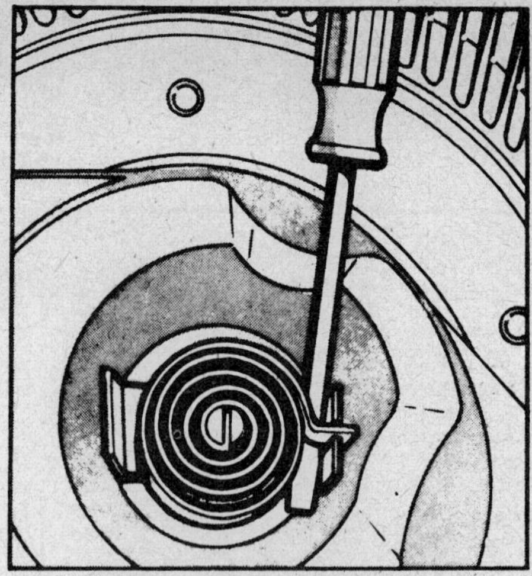

Fig. 4 Disconnecting bi-metal spring

spring out of place. Now remove the small control piston underneath it.

Check the piston for free movement of the coupling device. If the piston sticks, clean it with emery cloth. If the bi-metal strip is damaged, replace the entire unit. These strips are not interchangeable.

When reassembling, install the control piston so that the projection on the end of it will contact the metal strip. Then install the metal strip. After reassembly, clean the clutch drive with a cloth soaked in solvent. Avoid dipping the clutch assembly in any type of liquid. Install the assembly in the reverse order of removal.

The coil spring type of fan clutch cannot be disassembled, serviced or repaired. If it does not function properly it must be replaced with a new unit.

Electric Cooling Fans

INDEX

On models equipped with electric engine cooling fans, the battery ground cable should be disconnected whenever underhood service is performed.

1982 CORVETTE AUXILIARY FAN

DESCRIPTION

Current is supplied to the auxiliary fan motor through a 30 amp. circuit breaker located in the fuse panel. The fan motor is controlled by an engine temperature switch located at the rear of the right hand cylinder head. When engine temperature reaches approximately 238 degrees F, the engine temperature switch will close and the fan motor will operate to provide supplementary air flow in addition to that supplied by the engine cooling fan. When engine temperature decreases to approximately 201 degrees F, the engine temperature switch will open and current will no longer be supplied to the fan motor. The fan motor will only operate when the ignition switch is in the "Run" position.

FAN MOTOR, REPLACE

1. Disconnect battery ground cable, then remove fresh air scoop.
2. Remove engine cooling fan, then disconnect fan motor wire connector from vehicle wire connector. Remove retainer securing fan motor wiring to chassis, if equipped.
3. Remove upper fan shroud mounting bolts, then remove fan shroud and auxiliary fan motor as an assembly.
4. Remove nuts attaching auxiliary fan motor to fan shroud, then disconnect wiring from fan motor and remove motor.
5. Reverse procedure to install.

1984 CORVETTE

DESCRIPTION

Current is supplied to the engine cooling fan relay through an ignition switch controlled 3 amp fuse. When engine tempera-

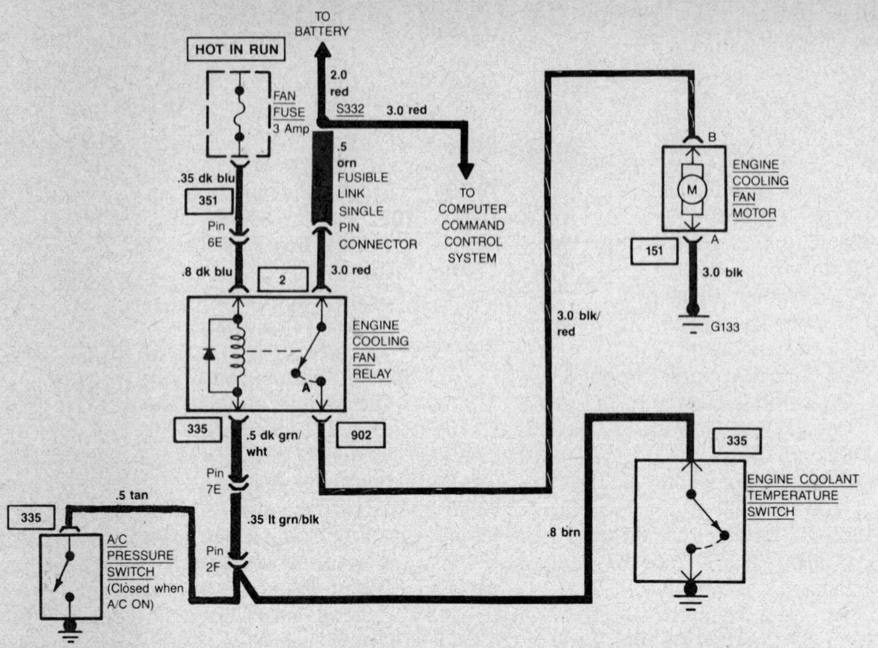

Fig. 1 Electric engine cooling fan wiring diagram. Corvette

ture reaches approximately 238 degrees F, the engine coolant temperature switch closes, which completes the fan motor circuit to ground. The fan motor frame serves as the fan motor ground and is insulated from the engine ground by plastic shroud surrounding it. When engine temperature decreases to approximately 201 degrees F, the engine coolant temperature switch opens the fan ground circuit, shutting off the fan. The fan motor will only operate when the ignition switch is in the "Run" position.

TROUBLESHOOTING

1. Check fan fuse. If fuse is satisfactory, proceed to step 2. If fuse is not satisfactory, replace fuse and retest.
2. Check voltage to relay, **Fig. 1.** If voltage is satisfactory, proceed to step 3. If voltage is not satisfactory, repair wiring as necessary.
3. Check relay operation. If satisfactory, proceed to step 4. If unsatisfactory, replace relay.
4. Check coolant temperature switch. If satisfactory, proceed to step 5. If not satisfactory, replace switch.
5. With ignition switch in the "Run" position, ground circuit 335 (dark green wire), **Fig. 1**, at relay. If coolant fan motor does not operate, check circuit 2, **Fig. 1**, for power at relay. Repair as required.

1984 FIERO

DESCRIPTION

A single speed electric cooling fan is used on models less air conditioning, while air conditioned models use a two speed electric cooling fan. On all models, a single relay is used to control the electric fan, **Figs. 2 and 3.** On single speed models, when coolant temperature exceeds 235 degrees F, the coolant temperature switch closes. On two speed models, when coolant temperature exceeds 221 degrees F, the low speed coolant temperature switch closes, and at 246 degrees F, the high speed coolant temperature switch closes. When the coolant temperature switch closes, it allows current to pass through the choke heater fuse and coolant fan relay to ground, thus closing the relay contacts. When the contacts are closed, current flows through a fusible link and into the fan motor.

TROUBLESHOOTING

1. If coolant fan motor does not operate, check the following:
   a. Check for blown fuse.
   b. Check fusible link.
   c. Disconnect wire connector from engine coolant temperature switch. With ignition "On," ground end of wire. Fan motor should operate.
2. If cooling fan operates whenever the ignition switch is in the Run position, check the following:
   a. Check cooling fan temperature switch, compressor pressure switch, if equipped and other related mechanical components.
   b. Check cooling fan relay.

FAN MOTOR, REPLACE

1. Disconnect battery ground cable.
2. Disconnect wiring harness from fan motor and frame.
3. Remove fan frame to radiator support attaching bolts.
4. Remove fan motor and frame assembly.
5. Reverse procedure to install. Torque fan frame to radiator support attaching bolts to 85 inch lbs.

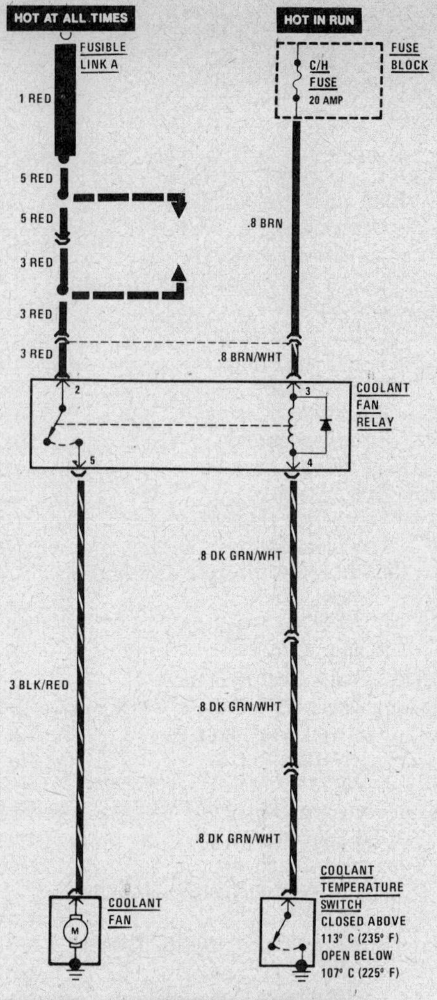

Fig. 2 Electric engine cooling fan wiring diagram. Fiero less A/C

1982–84 GM FRONT WHEEL DRIVE MODELS EQUIPPED WITH TRANSVERSE MOUNTED ENGINES

DESCRIPTION

The single speed electric cooling fan is used on all models except those equipped with V6 gasoline engines with heavy duty cooling systems and all diesel engines, which use a two-speed electric motor. The fan motor is operated by the cooling fan relay on single speed models or cooling fan relay and cooling fan speed control on two speed models. On single speed models, when coolant temperature exceeds 230 degrees F, the cooling fan temperature switch closes. On two-speed models, when the coolant temperature reaches approximately 226 (diesel 223) degrees F, the low speed cooling fan temperature switch closes, and at approximately 239 (diesel 246) degrees F, the high speed cooling fan temperature switch closes. On all models, when the cooling fan temperature switch closes on single speed models, or the low speed cooling fan temperature

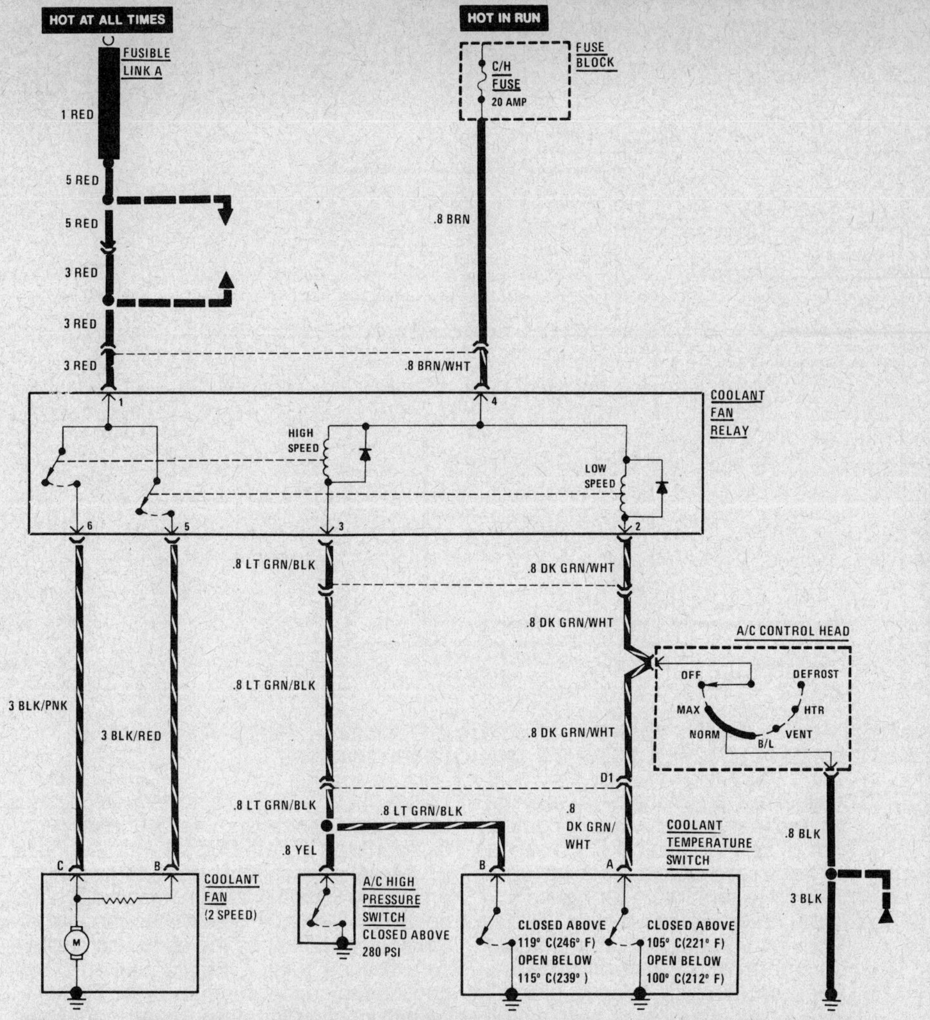

Fig. 3 Electric engine cooling fan wiring diagram. Fiero with A/C

switch closes on two speed models, it allows current to pass through the fuse and cooling fan relay coil to ground, thus closing the relay contacts. On single speed models, when the relay contacts are closed, current flows through a fusible link to the fan motor. On two speed models when the relay contacts are closed, current flows through a fusible link, then cooling fan speed control low speed contacts, and into the fan motor. On two speed models, when the high speed cooling fan temperature switch closes, the solid state circuitry of the cooling fan speed control is grounded, causing cooling fan speed control high speed contacts to close and cooling fan motor to operate at high speed. On single speed models, when coolant temperature falls below a predetermined level, the cooling fan temperature switch opens and current is no longer supplied to the fan motor. On two speed models, when coolant temperature falls below the high speed cooling fan temperature switch predetermined level, the contacts open, opening the ground circuit to the cooling fan speed control and causing the fan motor to operate at low speed. When the coolant temperature falls below the low speed cooling fan temperature switch predetermined level, the contacts open, causing the cooling fan relay to open and shut off current to the cooling fan speed control and the cooling fan motor. On 1982-85 diesel engine models with A/C, a second switch (diesel engine models use two switches) which senses compressor head pressure to the condenser, is used to activate the fan motor when the A/C compressor is operating. On all other models equipped with A/C, the cooling fan relay is grounded whenever the A/C selector switch is in the Max., Normal or Bi-Level position, causing the cooling fan to operate. On some automatic transmission models with gasoline V6 engines, the electric engine cooling fan operates when the torque converter clutch is engaged.

TROUBLESHOOTING

1. If coolant fan motor does not operate, check the following:
   a. Check for blown fuse.
   b. Check fusible link.
   c. Disconnect wire connector from engine coolant temperature switch. With ignition "On," ground end of wire. Fan motor should operate.
2. If cooling fan operates whenever the ignition switch is in the Run position, check the following:
   a. Check cooling fan temperature switch, compressor pressure switch, if equipped and other related mechanical components.
   b. Check cooling fan relay.

FAN MOTOR, REPLACE

1. Disconnect battery ground cable, then disconnect wire connector from fan motor.
2. Detach front lamp wiring harness from fan motor, then remove harness from fan motor frame.
3. Remove fan motor frame to radiator support attaching bolts, then remove fan motor.
4. Reverse procedure to install. Torque fan to radiator support attaching bolts to 85 inch lbs.

1985 BUICK ELECTRA, PARK AVENUE & OLDSMOBILE NINETY-EIGHT

DESCRIPTION

On gasoline engine equipped models less heavy duty cooling, a single two speed fan is used for cooling purposes. On gasoline engine models equipped with heavy duty cooling and all diesel engine models, dual cooling fans are used.

On models equipped with dual cooling fans, the left side fan has two speeds while the right side has one speed and only operates when the left side is running in the high speed mode.

The on and off operation of the cooling fan(s) is controlled by the Electronic control Module (ECM), while the fan speed and mode of operation are controlled by vehicle speed, engine temperature, A/C head pressure and transmission converter clutch operation.

TROUBLESHOOTING

Gasoline Engines

1. Check fuse No. 21. If satisfactory, proceed to step 2. If not satisfactory, replace fuse and retest.
2. Check all system grounds, **Figs. 4 and 6.** If satisfactory, proceed to step 3. If not satisfactory, repair grounds as necessary.
3. Check fusible link. If satisfactory, proceed to step 4. If not satisfactory, repair fusible link, then inspect electrical system for short circuits.
4. Check red wire between fusible link and relay(s) for opens. If satisfactory, proceed to step 5. If not satisfactory, repair opens.
5. If large cooling fan (if equipped) does not run, proceed as follows:
   a. Disconnect coolant temperature switch connector, then connect to a suitable ground.
   b. Using a suitable test light, check for battery voltage at the B terminal (white wire) of the high speed cooling fan relay, **Figs. 4 and 5.** If voltage is present, proceed to step c. If voltage is not present, check the high speed relay and replace as necessary.

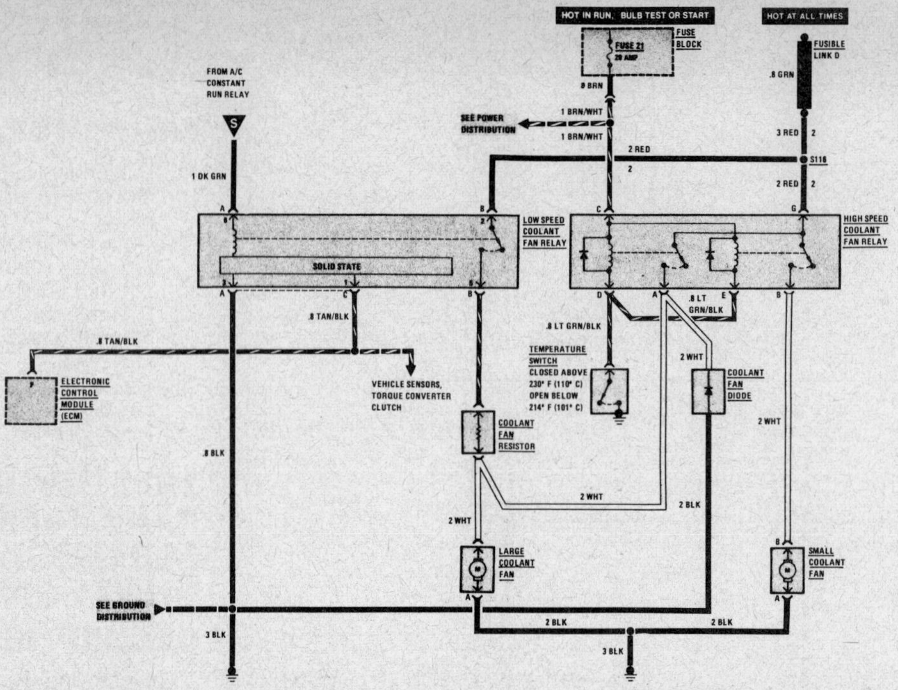

Fig. 4 Electric engine cooling fan wiring diagram. Buick Electra, Park Avenue & Oldsmobile Ninety-Eight with V6-181 gasoline engine

c. If voltage is present, check for an open in the white wire between high speed cooling fan relay and large cooling fan and repair as necessary. If cooling fan still does not run, check common ground between large and small fans and repair as necessary.

6. If small cooling fan does not run at high speed, proceed as follows:
   a. Disconnect coolant temperature switch connector, then connect to a suitable ground.
   b. Using a suitable test light, check for battery voltage at the A terminal (2 white wires) of the high speed cooling fan relay, **Figs. 4 and 5.** If voltage is present, proceed to step c. If voltage is not present, check the high speed relay and replace as necessary.
   c. If voltage is present, check for an open in the white wire between high speed cooling fan relay and small cooling fan and repair as necessary. If cooling fan still does not run, check fan motor ground and repair as necessary.
7. If small cooling fan does not run at low speed, proceed as follows:
   a. Start engine, then place A/C selector switch in "Norm" position.
   b. Connect a suitable jumper wire across the coolant fan resistor. If cooling fan runs, replace coolant fan resistor.
   c. With engine still running and A/C operating, use a suitable test light to test for voltage at terminal B (red wire) of low speed cooling fan relay, **Figs. 4 and 5.** If voltage is not present, check for opens in red wire between fusible link and low speed cooling fan relay.
   d. Using test light, check for voltage at terminal A of low speed cooling fan relay, **Figs. 4 and 5.** If voltage is not present, check wiring connected to terminal A for opens.
   e. On models equipped with V6-181 engine, connect suitable jumper wire from black wire terminal of low speed cooling fan relay to ground. If relay operates, repair open circuit in black wire between relay and ground. If relay does not operate, check relay.
   f. On models equipped with V6-231 engine, disconnect A/C pressure switch connector, then connect a jumper wire from dark green wire of connector to ground. If cooling fan runs, check connector ground wire for opens. If satisfactory, replace A/C pressure switch.

Diesel Engine Models

1. If coolant fan motor does not operate, check the following:
   a. Check for blown fuse, **Fig. 6.**
   b. Check for blown fusible link.
   c. Connect jumper wire from one of the cooling fan relay coils to ground. Cooling fan should run.
2. If fan motor operates whenever the ignition switch is in the Run, Bulb Test or Start position, check the following:
   a. Dual temperature switch and A/C high pressure switch to see if any contacts are closed at all times.
   b. Coolant fan relay for stuck contacts.

1985–87 CADILLAC DEVILLE & FLEETWOOD

DESCRIPTION

The radiator cooling system is comprised of two electric motor driven cooling fans. The electric motors are controlled electronically by the Body Control Module (BCM) which monitors engine temperature and the A/C high pressure refrigerant temperature. The BCM determines the proper fan speed and varies the speed as necessary through pulse width modulation to the cooling fan control module, **Figs. 7 and 8.**

Both cooling fans are turned on at half power when engine coolant temperature or A/C high pressure refrigerant temperature reaches a predetermined level. As engine coolant temperature or A/C high pressure refrigerant temperature increases, fan power also increases until full power is reached. On then Off operation of the fans is eliminated due to utilizing turn off temperatures lower than turn on temperatures.

1985 BUICK SKYLARK & CHEVROLET CITATION

SYSTEM DESCRIPTION

The cooling fan located between radiator and condenser cools both engine coolant and A/C refrigerant. The fan is controlled by the cooling fan relay (located on LH side of engine compartment) which in turn is controlled by the coolant temperature fan switch (located on front of engine left of exhaust manifold on 4-151 engines; top of engine left of carburetor on V6-173 VIN X engines). The coolant switch closes at temperatures above 230 degrees F.

On vehicles equipped with air conditioning, the relay is energized when the A/C is operating in certain modes. The relay is also energized under certain conditions when the A/C high pressure switch (located on compressor) closes at pressures above 280 psi. The switch then reopens when pressure drops below 180 psi.

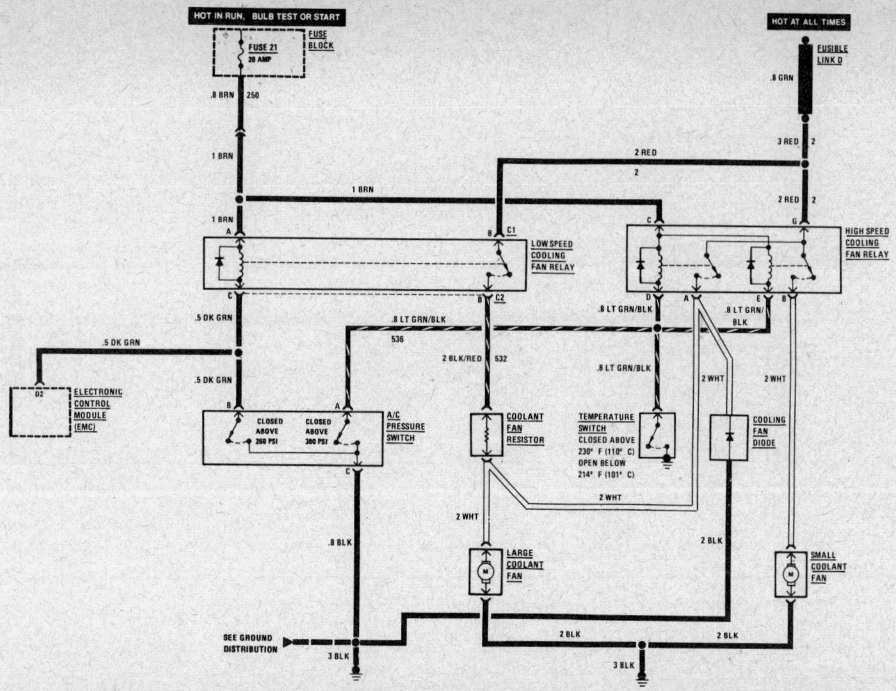

Fig. 5 Electric engine cooling fan wiring diagram. Buick Electra, Park Avenue & Oldsmobile Ninety-Eight with V6-231 gasoline engine

Models Less A/C

With ignition switch in RUN position voltage is applied through C-H fuse to cooling fan relay coil. Voltage is applied at all times through fusible link C (located at front of engine at starter solenoid) to cooling fan relay contacts.

When coolant temperature fan switch is closed, circuit through C-H fuse, relay coil, and switch is completed to ground. This causes relay contacts to close, thus completing circuit through fusible link C, relay contacts, and cooling fan motor to ground, causing fan to run.

Models W/4-151 & A/C

When vehicle speed is below 35 mph, the ECM (Electronic Control Module, located behind RH side of instrument panel) grounds fan relay circuit. Current can flow in this circuit under either 1 of 2 conditions:

1. When high refrigerant pressure causes the A/C high pressure switch to close, the circuit is completed through C-H fuse, relay coil, A/C high pressure switch, and ECM to ground. This causes relay contacts to close and fan to run.
2. When A/C selector lever is set to MAX, NORM, or BI-LEVEL, circuit is completed through C-H fuse, relay coil, dark green/white wire, A/C selector switch, and ECM to ground. This causes relay contacts to close and fan to run.

Models W/V6-173 VIN X & A/C

With ignition switch in RUN, voltage is applied through C-H fuse to cooling fan relay coil. Voltage is always applied through fusible link C (located at front of engine, at starter solenoid) to cooling fan relay (located at front side of LH strut tower) contacts. Current can flow in this circuit under 2 conditions:

1. When coolant temperature fan switch closes, it completes circuit through C-H fuse, cooling fan relay coil, and coolant temperature fan switch to ground. This causes relay contacts to close and fan to run.
2. When A/C high pressure switch closes at pressures above 280 psi, circuit is completed through C-H fuse, relay coil, dark green/white wire, and A/C high pressure switch to ground. This causes relay contacts to close and fan to run. When refrigerant pressure drops below 180 psi, switch reopens and relay de-energizes.

Models W/V6-173 VIN W & A/C

With ignition switch in RUN position, voltage is applied through C-H fuse to cooling fan relay coil. Voltage is always applied from battery junction block to cooling fan relay contacts.

Cooling fan relay is switched on by ECM which provides a ground path for relay coil to energize relay and close relay contacts.

When refrigerant pressure exceeds 240 psi, cooling fan pressure switch grounds ECM input causing ECM to switch on cooling fan.

TROUBLESHOOTING

Cooling Fan Does Not Operate

1. Check C-H fuse.
2. Check fusible link C, located at front of engine at starter solenoid.
3. Connect wire from cooling fan relay coil (dark green/white wire) to ground-cooling fan should run.

Cooling Fan Runs Whenever Ignition Is In RUN Position

1. Check temperature switch, pressure switch, and related mechanical systems.
2. Check cooling fan relay.

COOLING FAN, REPLACE

1. Disconnect battery ground cable.
2. Disconnect wiring from fan motor and frame.
3. Remove fan assembly from radiator support.
4. Reverse procedure to install.

1985 BUICK SOMERSET REGAL & OLDSMOBILE CALAIS

SYSTEM DESCRIPTION

4-151 Engines

A cooling fan relay is used to control the cooling fan. When coolant temperature is high, the cooling fan temperature switch closes and provides a path to ground for the relay coil. The contacts close applying battery voltage to the fan.

On vehicles equipped with A/C, the cooling fan runs when the compressor is on. The coil of a separate A/C cooling fan relay receives battery voltage through the A/C mode selector and the pressure cycling switch and is grounded through the ECM. When the compressor clutch is on, the ECM grounds the coil of the separate A/C cooling fan relay whose contacts close to ground the cooling fan relay coil. The cooling fan relay is energized and battery voltage is applied to the cooling fan causing it to run. A diode is connected across the cooling fan relay coil to absorb voltage spikes.

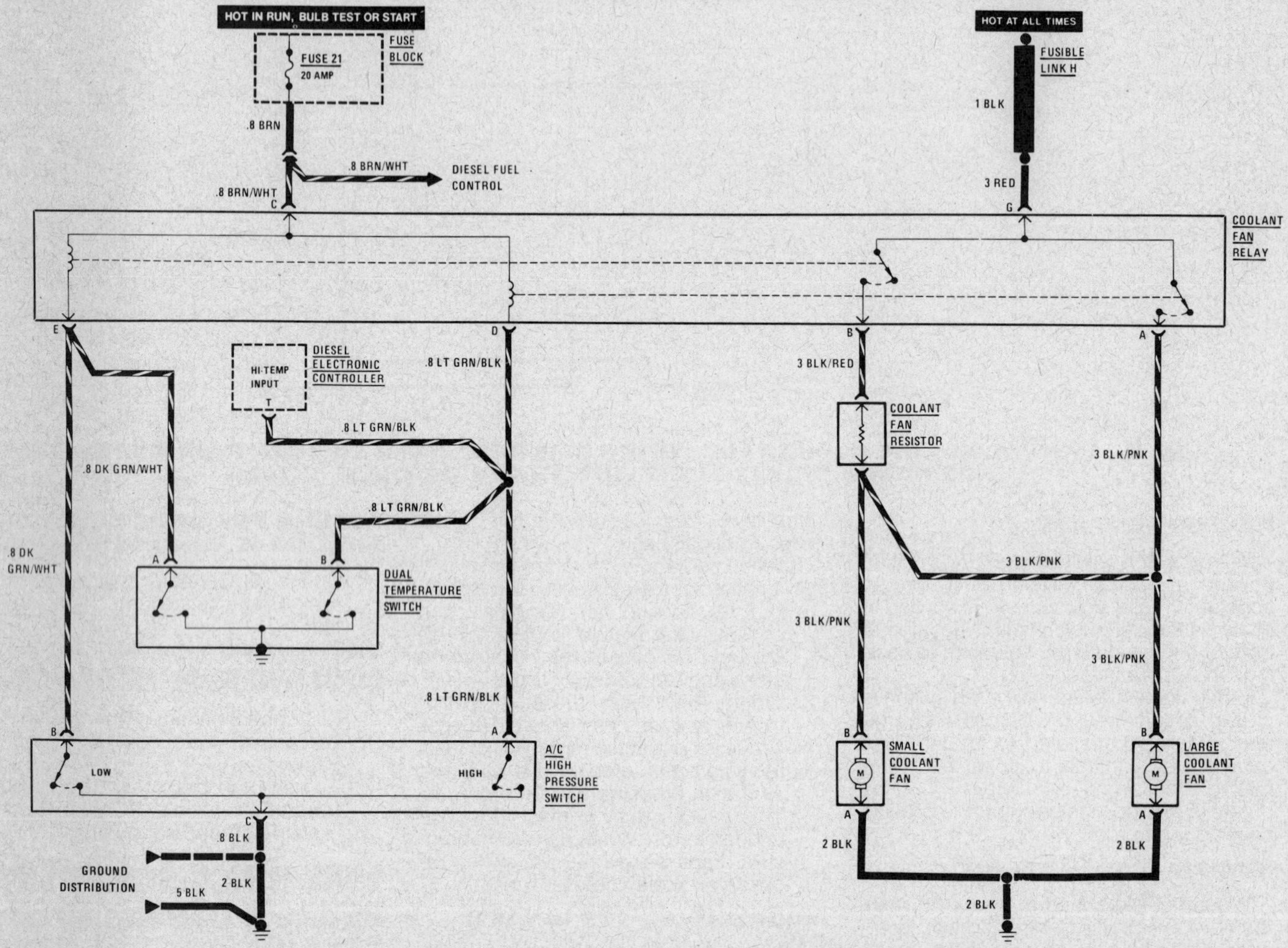

Fig. 6 Electric engine cooling fan wiring diagram. Buick Electra, Park Avenue & Oldsmobile Ninety-Eight with V6-260 diesel engine

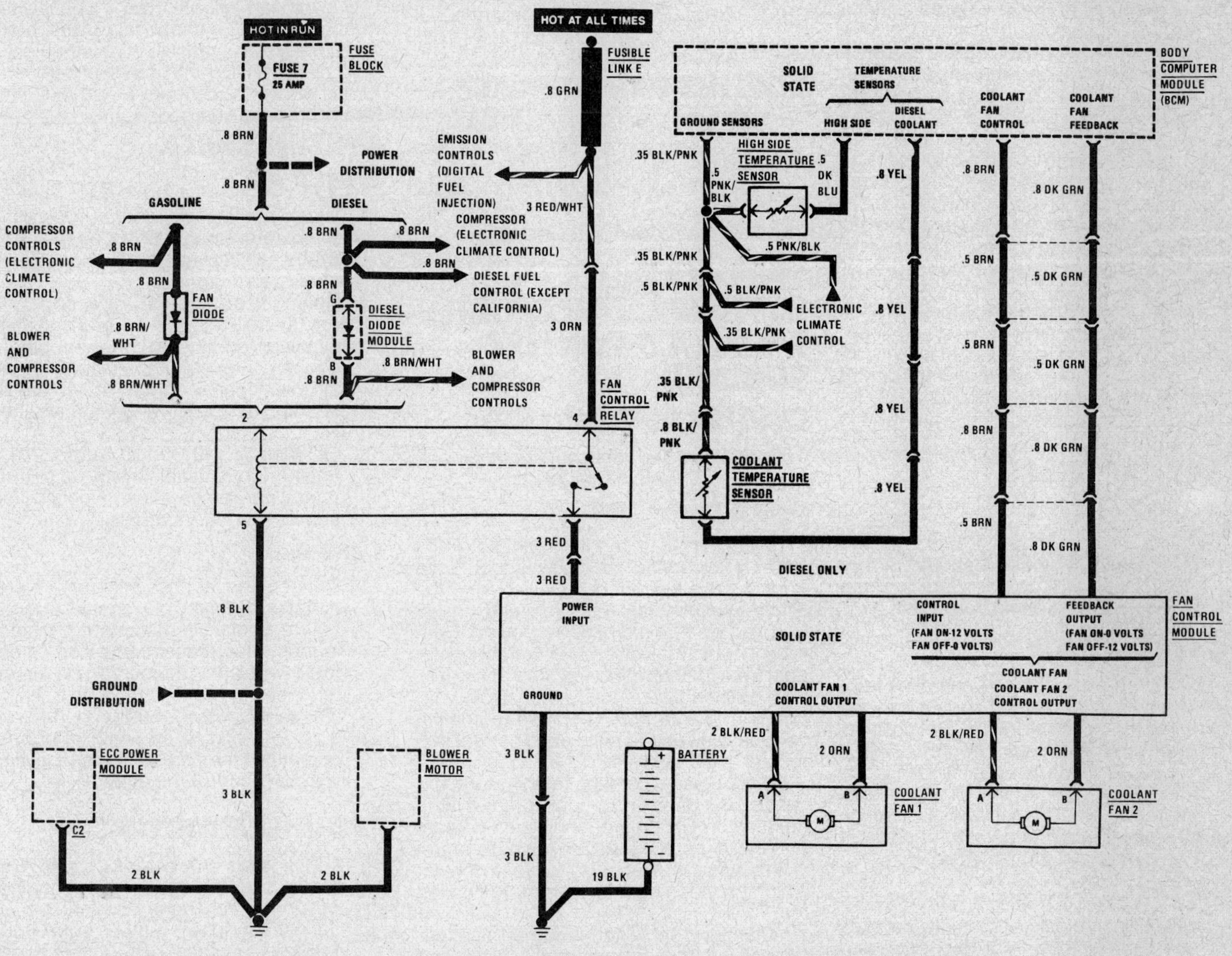

Fig. 7 Electric engine cooling fan wiring diagram. Cadillac DeVille & Fleetwood

V6-183 Engines

These vehicles use a 2-speed heavy duty cooling fan which is controlled by a cooling fan relay having 2 coils and 2 independent sets of contacts.

During low speed cooling fan operation, the low speed relay is grounded through either the ECM or the low speed contacts of the A/C high pressure switch. The ECM grounds the coil when vehicle speed is less than 45 mph and the engine coolant is at normal operating temperature. The low speed contacts of the A/C high pressure switch close when high refrigerant pressure is present at the compressor.

With the low speed relay coil grounded, the appropriate contacts close thus applying voltage through the cooling fan resistor to the cooling fan motor. The resistor drops part of the battery voltage so the fan runs at low speed.

During high speed cooling fan operation, the high speed relay coil is grounded through the high speed contacts in the A/C high pressure switch or through the cooling fan temperature switch. The fan the runs at high speed.

SYSTEM CHECK

4-151 Less A/C

1. Run engine at fast idle for several minutes. Cooling fan should turn on before coolant temperature indicator on instrument panel comes on.

4-151 With A/C

1. With engine at normal operating temperature and running at slow idle, set A/C mode selector to NORM position. Cooling fan should turn on.
2. Set A/C mode selector to OFF position. Run engine at fast idle for several minutes. Cooling fan should turn on before coolant temperature indicator on instrument panel comes on.

V6-183

1. With engine cold and at idle, set A/C mode selector to NORM position and blower to HI position. Set temperature selector to COLD position. Leave vehicle doors open. Cooling fan should run first at low speed, then at high speed.
2. Set A/C mode selector to OFF position, and run engine at fast idle. After a few minutes, cooling fan should run at low speed. Cooling fan should run at high speed before coolant temperature indicator on instrument panel comes on.

TROUBLESHOOTING

1. On models with 4-151 engine, operate A/C blower to check fuse 22 on Calais; HTR-A/C fuse on Somerset.
2. On all models, visually check fuse 21 on Calais; ENG/FAN fuse on Somerset.
3. If cooling fan operates only with compressor on and not for hot engine, install new cooling fan temperature switch.
4. Connect a fused jumper wire from battery to cooling fan terminal B, blue/black wire on Calais; red/black wire on Somerset.
   a. If fan runs, ECM diagnosis must be performed.
   b. If fan does not run, check that black wire terminal E on Calais; terminal A on Somerset, is grounded. If ground is good, cooling fan is defective.

COOLING FAN, REPLACE

1. Disconnect battery ground cable.
2. Disconnect wiring from fan motor and frame.
3. Remove fan assembly from radiator support.
4. Reverse procedure to install.

1985–87 BUICK SKYHAWK, OLDSMOBILE FIRENZA & PONTIAC SUNBIRD

SYSTEM DESCRIPTION

The cooling fan cools both engine coolant and A/C system refrigerant.

4-110 Turbo VIN J

The cooling fan can be switched on by either the cooling fan relay (located on front of dash, left of master cylinder) or the 5 minute turbo fan relay (located on LH front fender, forward of shock tower). Both relay contacts always have voltage available from fusible link C (located at starter). With ignition switch in RUN position, voltage is available from C-H fuse to cooling fan relay coil and to solid state control in 5 minute turbo fan relay.

When engine coolant temperature exceeds 238 degrees F, cooling fan switch (located on RH front of engine, on coolant outlet) closes, signalling solid state control in 5 minute turbo fan relay to close contact which provides path for current to cooling fan.

When ignition switch is turned off, contacts in 5 minute turbo fan relay close and set 5 minute timer, allowing cooling fan to run for 5 minutes.

4-110 VIN O

When coolant temperature exceeds 238 degrees, cooling fan switch (located on front RH side of engine, bottom of thermostat housing) provides ground for cooling fan relay (located on front of dash, left of master cylinder). The relay energizes and current flows from fusible link C to cooling fan.

When A/C mode selector lever is in MAX, NORM, or BI-LEVEL position, and vehicle speed is below 35 mph, ECM will provide path to ground for cooling fan relay so A/C refrigerant can be cooled. At speeds above 35 mph, ECM shuts off cooling fan.

At high refrigerant pressures, A/C high pressure fan switch (located on RH front of engine, near LH end of compressor) sends voltage to ECM, which then switches on fan.

4-121 VIN P

Cooling fan relay is activated by ECM when engine coolant sensed by coolant temperature sensor is above 238 degrees F and vehicle speed is below 35 mph. ECM also activates cooling fan relay when A/C mode selector sends voltage to ECM.

Cooling fan will also run if cooling fan switch and A/C high pressure switch are closed, such as when A/C mode selector is in DEF position and ambient temperature is above 32 degrees F and A/C system is properly charged.

SYSTEM CHECK

With A/C

1. When engine at normal operating temperature and idle speed, set A/C mode selector to NORM. Cooling fan should turn on.
2. Set mode selector off. Allow engine to run at fast idle for several minutes. Cooling fan should turn on before coolant temperature indicator in instrument panel comes on or before coolant temperature gauge reaches H.
3. On models with 4-110 Turbo VIN J engine, turn engine off when at normal operating temperature. Cooling fan should run for 5 minutes.

Less A/C

1. Run engine at fast idle for several minutes. Coolant fan should turn on before coolant temperature indicator in instrument panel comes on or before coolant temperature gauge reaches H.
2. On models with 4-110 Turbo Vin J engine, turn engine off when at normal operating temperature. Cooling fan should run for 5 minutes.

TROUBLESHOOTING

1. If cooling fan only comes on with A/C compressor and not for a hot engine, install new cooling fan switch.
2. Connect a fused jumper wire from positive terminal of battery to terminal B (black/red) on all Buick Skyhawk engines and on Oldsmobile Firenza and Pontiac Sunbird with 4-121 VIN P engine; to terminal B (red/white) on Pontiac Sunbird with 4-110 Turbo VIN J engine; to terminal A (red/white) on Oldsmobile Firenza and Pontiac Sunbird with 4-110 VIN O engine.
   a. If fan runs, ECM diagnosis must be performed since circuit is controlled by ECM.
   b. If fan does not run, check continuity to ground at terminal B on Oldsmobile Firenza and Pontiac Sunbird with 4-110 VIN O engine; terminal A on models exc. Oldsmobile Firenza and Pontiac Sunbird with 4-110 VIN O engine.
3. If a cooling fan relay has failed, test cooling fan switch for intermittent operation as follows:
   a. Warm up engine until cooling fan comes on.
   b. Remove connector from cooling fan switch.

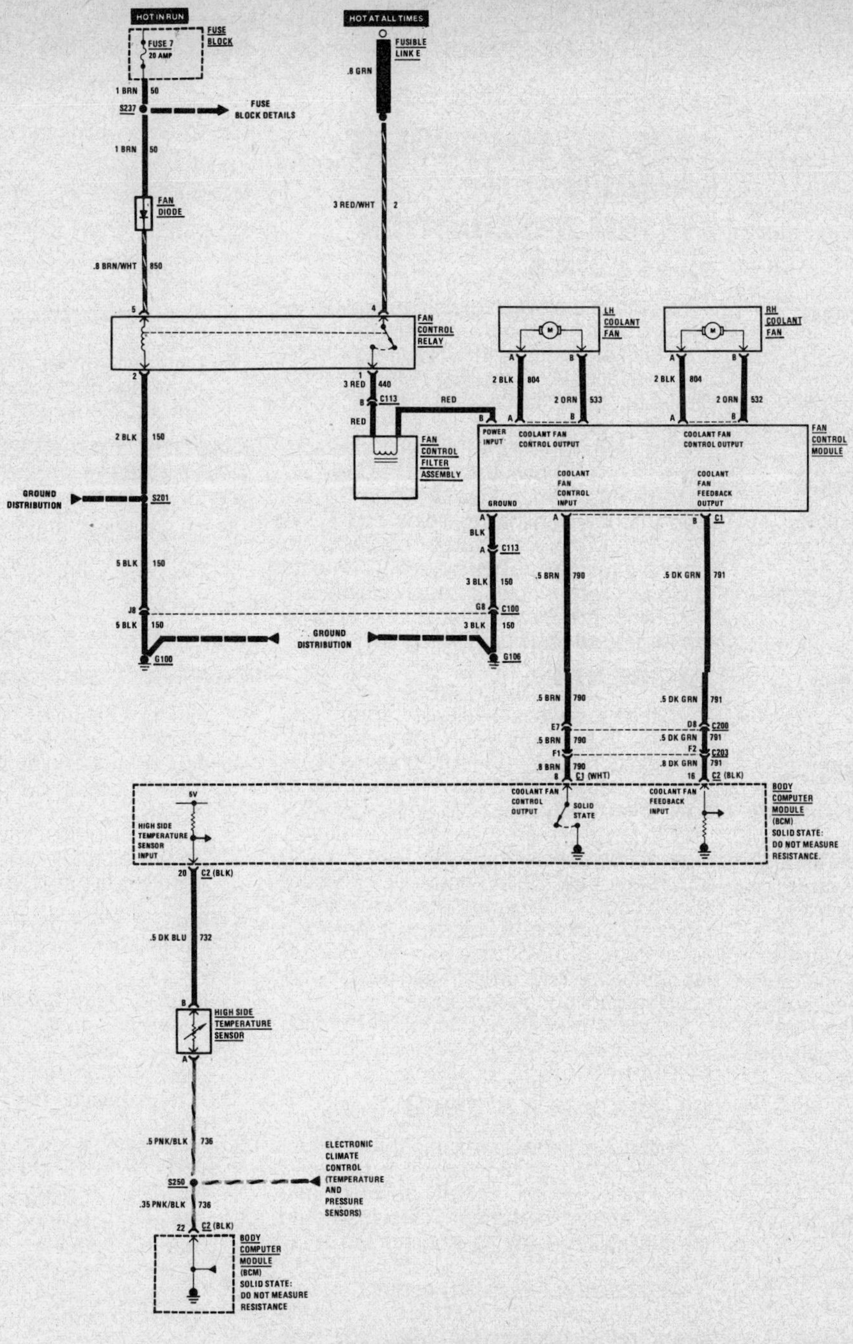

Fig. 8 Electric engine cooling fan wiring diagram. Cadillac DeVille & Fleetwood

c. Connect self-powered test lamp to switch and to ground. Test lamp should light steadily. If test lamp flickers, install new cooling fan switch.
d. Test both high speed and low speed switches if vehicle is so equipped.

COOLING FAN, REPLACE

1. Disconnect battery ground cable.
2. Disconnect wiring from fan motor and frame.
3. Remove fan assembly from radiator support.
4. Reverse procedure to install.

1985–87 CADILLAC CIMARRON

SYSTEM DESCRIPTION

The cooling fan is controlled by the cooling fan relay whose contacts have voltage available at all times. The relay coil has voltage through the C-H fuse when ignition switch is in RUN position.

The cooling fan relay is activated by any of the following conditions:

a. When engine coolant temperature exceeds 234 degrees F, coolant temperature sender signals ECM. The ECM in turn activates cooling fan relay which receives voltage through C-H fuse. The cooling fan relay contacts close, allowing current to flow through fusible link C and operate cooling fan.
b. On 4-121 VIN P engine, ECM will activate cooling fan relay when A/C is on and vehicle speed is below 40 mph. With vehicle speed above 40 mph, engine temperature determines operation of cooling fan relay. When A/C is off, and vehicle speed is above 40 mph, ECM will deactivate cooling fan relay at 225 degrees F.
c. On V6-173 VIN W engine, ECM ac-

tivates cooling fan relay when A/C high side pressure exceeds 240 psi.

TROUBLESHOOTING

Cooling Fan Does Not Run

1. Check C-H fuse.
2. Check fusible link C.
3. Check cooling fan relay by listening for click when grounding dark green/white wire at cooling fan relay.

Cooling Fan Runs Constantly With Ignition Switch In RUN

1. Check cooling fan relay.
2. Disconnect dark green/white wire at cooling fan relay. If fan stops, check ECM.

COOLING FAN, REPLACE

1. Disconnect battery ground cable.
2. Disconnect wiring from fan motor and frame.
3. Remove fan assembly from radiator support.
4. Reverse procedure to install.

1985–87 CHEVROLET CAVALIER

SYSTEM DESCRIPTION

The cooling fan is operated by a cooling fan relay. The relay contacts have voltage at all times, while coil has voltage through C-H fuse on 4 door models; or fuse 17 on 2 door models when ignition switch is in RUN position.

When engine coolant temperature exceeds 238 degrees F, coolant temperature sensor sends a signal to ECM which controls cooling fan relay. By acting as a ground, ECM allows cooling fan relay coil to energize, causing relay contacts to close, allowing current to flow through fusible link C to operate cooling fan.

When coolant temperature decreases to below 214 degrees F, ECM no longer acts as ground, de-energizing cooling fan relay. The cooling fan relay contacts open and cooling fan stops.

TROUBLESHOOTING

Cooling Fan Runs Constantly With Ignition Switch In RUN

1. Check dark green/white wire for short to ground.
2. Check cooling fan relay.

Cooling Fan Does Not Run At All

1. Check dark green/white wire for open.
2. Check black wire for continuity to ground.
3. Check black/red wire for continuity.
4. Check cooling fan relay.
5. With ignition switch in RUN position, check cooling fan relay for 12 volts at red wire and at brown/white wire.

COOLING FAN, REPLACE

1. Disconnect battery ground cable.
2. Disconnect wiring from fan motor and frame.
3. Remove fan assembly from radiator support.
4. Reverse procedure to install.

1985–86 CHEVROLET CAMARO

SYSTEM DESCRIPTION

V6-173 VIN S

Voltage is always available through fusible link E to cooling fan relay contacts. With ignition switch in RUN position, voltage is available through C-H fan fuse on Berlinetta; or FP fan fuse on Sport Coupe to cooling fan relay coil.

With fan pressure switch contacts closed, current flows through C-H fan fuse on Berlinetta; FP fan fuse on Sport Coupe, then through cooling fan relay coil, ECM, and fan pressure switch contacts to ground causing cooling fan relay contacts to close. Current flows through fusible link E, cooling fan relay contacts, and cooling fan to ground causing cooling fan to run.

V8-305 VIN F

Voltage is always available through fusible link D to cooling fan relay contacts. With ignition switch in RUN position, voltage is available through FP fan fuse to cooling fan relay coil.

With fan pressure switch contact closed, current flows through FP fan fuse, cooling fan relay coil, ECM, and fan pressure switch contacts to ground, causing cooling fan relay contacts to close. Current then flows through fusible link E, cooling fan relay contacts, and cooling fan to ground, causing cooling fan to operate.

On vehicles with A/C, cooling fan also runs when A/C mode selector is in MAX, NORM, or BI-LEVEL positions.

V8-305 VIN G & VIN H

Voltage is always available through fusible link B to cooling fan relay contacts. With ignition switch in RUN position, voltage is available through C-H fuse, and throttle kicker relay to cooling fan relay coil.

With cooling fan switch contact closed, current flows through C-H fan fuse, throttle kicker relay, cooling fan relay coil, and cooling fan switch contact to ground, causing cooling fan relay contacts to close. Current flows through fusible link B, cooling fan relay contacts, and cooling fan to ground, causing cooling fan to operate.

TROUBLESHOOTING

V6-173 VIN S

Cooling Fan Does Not Run

1. Check C-H fan fuse on Berlinetta; FP fuse on Sport Coupe.
2. Check fusible link E located at junction block.
3. Check that grounds are clean and tight.
4. Connect jumper wire from cooling fan relay coil (dark green/white wire) to ground. Cooling fan should run.

Cooling Fan Runs Constantly With Ignition Switch In RUN

1. Check that fan pressure switch is closed at all times.
2. Check cooling fan relay for stuck contacts.

V8-305 VIN F

Cooling Fan Does Not Run

1. Check FP fan fuse.
2. Check fusible link D located at battery.
3. Check that grounds are clean and tight.
4. Connect jumper wire from cooling fan relay coil (dark green/white wire) to ground. Cooling fan should run.

Cooling Fan Runs Constantly With Ignition Switch In RUN

1. Check that fan pressure switch is closed at all times.
2. Check cooling fan relay for stuck contacts.

V8-305 VIN G & VIN H

Cooling Fan Does Not Run

1. Check C-H fuse.
2. Check fusible link B located at lower RH side of engine, near starter.
3. Check that grounds are clean and tight.
4. Connect jumper wire from cooling fan relay coil (dark green wire) to ground. Cooling fan should run.

Cooling Fan Runs Constantly With Ignition In RUN

1. Check that cooling fan switch is closed.
2. Check that A/C control head is grounded at all times.
3. Check cooling fan relay for stuck contacts.

COOLING FAN, REPLACE

1. Disconnect battery ground cable.
2. Disconnect wiring from fan motor and frame.
3. Remove fan assembly from radiator support.
4. Reverse procedure to install.

1985–87 PONTIAC FIREBIRD

SYSTEM DESCRIPTION

V6-173 VIN S & V8-305 VIN F

The cooling fan is controlled by a cooling fan relay whose coil is controlled by the redundant cooling fan switch and by the ECM which closes when coolant temperature exceeds 228 degrees F. The relay is then energized and its contacts close to supply battery voltage to cooling fan.

V8-305 VIN G & VIN H

The cooling fan is controlled by a cooling fan relay whose coil is grounded by the cooling fan switch (which closes when coolant temperature is above 228 degrees

F) and also through the A/C control head. The relay is then energized and its contacts close to supply battery voltage to cooling fan.

TROUBLESHOOTING

V6-173 VIN S & V8-305 VIN F

If cooling fan relay has failed, test redundant cooling fan switch for intermittent operation as follows:

1. Warm up engine until cooling fan comes on.
2. Disconnect connector from redundant cooling fan switch.
3. Connect self-powered test lamp to switch and to ground. Test lamp should light steadily.
4. If test lamp flickers at all, install new redundant cooling fan switch.

V8-305 VIN G & VIN H

If cooling fan relay has failed, test cooling fan switch for intermittent operation as follows:

1. Warm up engine until cooling fan comes on.
2. Disconnect connector from cooling fan switch.
3. Connect self-powered test lamp to switch and to ground. Test lamp should light steadily.
4. If test lamp flickers at all, install new cooling fan switch.

SYSTEM DIAGNOSIS

V6-173 VIN S & V8-305 VIN F

Fan Runs When Jumped; Does Not Operate In Normal Use

1. Disconnect connectors from cooling fan relay (located at upper LH side of front of dash, V6-173 VIN S; RH side of radiator support, V8-305 VIN F) and check voltage to ground at connectors with ignition switch in RUN. Battery voltage should be at terminal E, red wire, V6-173 VIN S; orange wire V8-305 VIN F, and at terminal, C brown wire.
2. If battery voltage is not available at terminals, check circuit that supplies terminal. If voltage is available, proceed to step 3.
3. Reconnect connector to cooling fan relay. Disconnect dark green/white wire from redundant cooling fan switch (located rear of engine, near distributor, V6-173 VIN S; lower RH rear of engine, V8-305 VIN F). Connect fused jumper from wire to ground.
4. With ignition switch in RUN, check that fan runs.
5. If fan runs, relay and wiring are OK. Install new redundant cooling fan switch.
6. If cooling fan does not run, check dark green/white wire to relay and black/red wire to fan. If wiring is OK, install new cooling fan relay.

V8-305 VIN G & VIN H

Fan Runs When Jumped; Does Not Run In Normal Use.

1. Disconnect connectors from cooling fan relay (located on engine harness, LH front of dash) and measure voltage to ground at connectors with ignition switch in RUN. Battery voltage should be available at terminal D, red wire, and terminal C, brown/white wire.
2. If battery voltage is not available at terminal, check circuit that supplies terminal. If voltage is correct, proceed to step 3.
3. Reconnect connector to cooling fan relay. Disconnect dark green wire from cooling fan switch (located at RH side of engine, above rear of starter solenoid).
4. Connect fused jumper wire from dark green wire to ground. With ignition switch in RUN, cooling fan should run and battery voltage should be available at terminal D, red wire.
5. If cooling fan runs, relay and wiring are OK. Cooling fan switch should be replaced.
6. If cooling fan does not run, check dark green wire to relay and black/red wire to fan. If OK, install new cooling fan relay.

COOLING FAN, REPLACE

1. Disconnect battery ground cable.
2. Disconnect wiring from fan motor and frame.
3. Remove fan assembly from radiator support.
4. Reverse procedure to install.

1985–87 PONTIAC FIERO

SYSTEM DESCRIPTION

Single Speed Fan

A cooling fan relay controls operation of the cooling fan. Voltage is always available to relay contacts through fusible link A (located at RH front of engine compartment, at battery junction block). With ignition switch in RUN position, voltage is available through C-H fuse on 1985 models or E fuse on 1986 models, to relay coil.

At coolant temperatures above 235 degrees F, coolant temperature switch closes. Current flows through the fuse, the cooling fan relay coil, then the closed coolant temperature switch to ground, causing relay contacts to close. Current then flows through fusible link A, through closed relay contacts, through cooling fan to ground, causing cooling fan to run.

On vehicles equipped with A/C, cooling fan relay is also operated by A/C high pressure switch when closed, or by A/C mode selector when in MAX, NORM, or BI-LEVEL positions.

Two Speed Fan

Voltage is always available through fusible link A (located at RH front of engine compartment, at battery junction block), to low and high speed contacts of cooling fan relay. With ignition switch in RUN position, voltage is available through the fuse to low and high speed coils of cooling fan relay.

With A/C mode selector in MAX, NORM, or BI-LEVEL position and with either A/C high pressure switch closed or low temperature side of coolant temperature switch closed, current flows through the fuse, through low speed relay coil to ground.

The low speed contacts then close. Current then flows through fusible link A, through low speed relay contact to terminal C of cooling fan, through an internal resistor, through fan motor and to ground. Cooling fan then operates at low speed.

With high temperature side of coolant temperature switch closed, current flows through the fuse and high speed relay coil to ground, causing high speed contacts of cooling fan relay to close. Current then flows through fusible link A and the high speed cooling fan contacts to terminal B of cooling fan. Current then flows directly through fan motor to ground, causing cooling fan to operate at high speed.

TROUBLESHOOTING

Cooling Fan Does Not Run

1. Check C-H on 1985 models or E fuse on 1986-87 models.
2. Check fusible link A.
3. On vehicles with single speed fan, connect jumper wire from Low Speed cooling fan relay coil (dark green/white wire) to ground. Cooling fan should run.
4. Vehicles with two speed fan:
   a. Connect jumper wire from low speed cooling fan relay coil (dark green/white wire) to ground. Cooling fan should run at low speed.
   b. Connect jumper wire from high speed cooling fan relay coil (lt green/white wire) to ground. Cooling fan should run at high speed.

Cooling Fan Runs Constantly With Ignition In RUN

1. Check that coolant temperature switch contacts are open with engine cold.
2. Check that cooling fan relay contacts are open with ignition off.
3. On 1986-87 models, ensure A/C coolant fan relay contacts are open with ignition switch in RUN and A/C "Off."

1985 CHEVROLET CORVETTE

SYSTEM DESCRIPTION

SINGLE FAN

With ignition switch in RUN, voltage is applied through cooling fan fuse, through cooling fan relay, and then through cooling fan temperature switch which closes when coolant temperature exceeds 238 degrees F.

This energizes cooling fan relay and completes circuit to cooling fan motor.

Voltage from fusible link D (located near LH rear of engine compartment, near battery) is applied through cooling fan relay to operate cooling fan motor.

The ECM also controls the cooling fan motor by grounding the cooling fan relay coil.

DUAL FANS

With ignition switch in RUN, voltage is applied through cooling fan fuse, through either cooling fan relay or auxiliary cooling fan relay.

When coolant temperature exceeds 238 degrees F, auxiliary cooling fan temperature switch closes, thus energizing relay which closes switch to auxiliary cooling fan motor. Current flows through fusible link E (located at LH rear of engine compartment, near battery) through auxiliary cooling fan relay to auxiliary cooling fan motor.

The cooling fan motor is operated by the ECM.

TROUBLESHOOTING

Single Fan

1. Check cooling fan fuse.
2. Disconnect connector from cooling fan relay and connect a fused jumper wire from terminal A to D. Cooling fan should run.
3. If cooling fan does not run, check fusible link D and wiring to cooling fan motor. Check that ground G117 (located at LH side of engine compartment) is clean and tight. If wiring and fusible link D are OK, replace cooling fan motor.
4. If cooling fan runs, ECM diagnosis must be performed.

Dual Fan

1. Check cooling fan fuse.
2. If auxiliary cooling fan does not run with hot engine, check temperature switch as follows:
   a. Disconnect connector from auxiliary cooling fan temperature switch. Using fused jumper wire, ground dark green wire. Auxiliary cooling fan should run.
   b. If fan runs, replace temperature switch.
   c. If fan does not run, disconnect connector at auxiliary cooling fan relay and measure voltage at relay connector. Battery voltage should be available at terminal C (dark blue wire) and terminal D (red wire).
   d. If either terminal does not have battery voltage, check circuit supplying that terminal.
   e. If battery voltage is available at both terminals, connect a fused jumper wire between terminals A and D.
   f. If fan does not run, check ground and black/red wire to fan. If OK, install new auxiliary cooling fan motor.
   g. If fan runs with jumper wire, relay may be defective. Check dark green/white wire to temperature switch for an open. If wire is OK, install new auxiliary cooling fan relay.
3. If cooling fan does not run, check if motor is OK as follows:
   a. Connect fused jumper wire from battery positive terminal to terminal B of cooling fan motor (black/red wire).
   b. If cooling fan motor does nut run, check ground at terminal A. If ground is OK, replace cooling fan motor.
   c. If motor does run with jumper, ECM diagnosis must be performed.

COOLING FAN, REPLACE

1. Disconnect battery ground cable.
2. Disconnect wiring from fan motor and frame.
3. Remove fan assembly from radiator support.
4. Reverse procedure to install.

1985 BUICK CENTURY & OLDSMOBILE CUTLASS CIERA

System Description

The cooling fan is controlled by a cooling fan relay whose coil is grounded by the cooling fan switch when coolant temperature exceeds 228 degrees F. The cooling fan relay is energized and its contacts close to supply battery voltage to cooling fan.

The cooling fan delay relay operates cooling fan for short time after engine is turned off. A solid state timer removes ground from cooling fan delay relay coil to switch off cooling fan.

4-151 VIN R

The cooling fan is controlled by the following:

1. Coolant temperature fan switch.
2. ECM and A/C mode selector switch.
3. ECM and A/C high pressure switch.

These switch combinations complete circuit to ground through cooling fan relay coil. With coil energized and relay contacts closed, battery voltage is applied to cooling fan.

On vehicles equipped with A/C, cooling fan also runs when compressor is on. With A/C mode selector is in MAX, NORM, or BI-LEVEL position, a path to ground exists through mode selector switch and ECM.

A suppression resistor is connected across cooling fan relay coil to absorb voltage spikes. An A/C high pressure switch is included in A/C relay grounding circuit to ensure grounding of cooling fan relay coil and cooling fan operation when mode selector is in DEF position and ambient temperature is above 32 degrees F.

V6-183 VIN E

Three types of cooling fans are used with V6-183 VIN E engines:

a. Single speed.
b. Two speed (internal resistor).
c. Heavy Duty Two Speed (external resistor).

On vehicles with single speed fan, cooling fan relay coil is grounded through cooling fan switch, which closes when coolant temperature exceeds 228 degrees F. With relay coil grounded, cooling fan relay contacts close and battery voltage is applied to cooling fan causing it to run.

On vehicles with 2 speed cooling fan, the fan is controlled by low speed and high speed cooling fan relays. A resistor is connected in series with the cooling fan for low speed operation.

On vehicles less A/C, two separate cooling fan switches are combined in a single unit. During low speed operation low speed cooling fan relay coil is grounded through low speed contacts of cooling fan switch.

On vehicles with A/C, low speed cooling fan relay coil is grounded through solid state relay and A/C mode selector. The circuit to ground is completed when A/C mode selector in MAX, NORM, or BI-LEVEL position. When vehicle speed exceeds 35 mph and torque converter clutch is energized, ECM breaks connection to ground causing fan to stop. When vehicle speed is above 35 mph, ECM applies a ground to low speed cooling fan relay to energize solid state relay coil. (Same ground is applied to torque converter clutch and assembly line communications link connector.) The solid state relay contacts open to interrupt current flow through a second relay coil, whose contacts open to switch off low speed fan operation.

When coolant temperature is above 228 degrees F, cooling fan switch closes to energize high speed cooling fan relay whose contacts close to apply battery voltage directly to cooling fan causing it to run at high speed.

V6-231 VIN 3

Three types of cooling fans are used with V6-231 VIN 3 engines:

a. Single speed.
b. Two speed (internal resistor).
c. Heavy Duty Two Speed (external resistor).

On vehicles with single speed cooling fans, cooling fan relay coil is grounded through cooling fan switch. At coolant temperatures exceeding 228 degrees F, switch contacts close and ground relay coil causing relay contacts to close, thus applying battery voltage to cooling fan.

On vehicles with two speed cooling fans, low speed cooling fan relay coil is grounded through low speed contacts of A/C high pressure switch (with A/C on) or through ground provided by ECM. On vehicles with Heavy Duty Two Speed cooling fan less A/C, ground is only provided by ECM with vehicle speed below 35 mph.

With low speed cooling fan relay coil grounded, relay contacts close, applying battery voltage through cooling fan resistor to heavy duty fan or directly to two speed fan. The resistor which is external with heavy duty cooling fan; internal with two speed fan, drops part of voltage so fan runs at low speed.

During high speed operation, high speed cooling fan relay coil is grounded through high speed contacts of A/C high pressure switch (with A/C on) or cooling fan switch.

With high speed cooling fan relay coil grounded, relay contacts close. Battery voltage is applied directly to cooling fan causing it to run at high speed.

V6-262 DIESEL VIN T

Two types of cooling fans are used: a single speed or a two speed cooling fan.

The two speed cooling fan is controlled by a cooling fan relay that has two coils and two independent sets of contacts.

During low speed operation, either low speed switch in cooling fan switch closes to ground or low speed switch in A/C high pressure switch closes to ground. The low speed coil of cooling fan relay is energized, causing contacts to apply battery voltage to resistor in two speed fan so fan runs at low speed.

During high speed operation, either high speed cooling fan switch or high speed A/C high pressure switch closes. Circuit is then completed through high speed coil of cooling fan relay, causing battery voltage to be applied directly to cooling fan so it runs at high speed.

The single speed cooling fan uses same relay and switch circuits without a resistor. It runs only at high speed controlled by low speed relay contacts (black/red wire), while high speed relay contacts (black/pink wire) are unused.

System Check

BUICK CENTURY

Less A/C

1. Run engine at fast idle for several minutes.
2. Cooling fan should turn on before coolant temperature indicator in instrument panel comes on.

With A/C

1. With engine at normal operating temperature, and running at curb idle, set A/C mode selector to NORM position. Cooling fan should turn on.
2. Set A/C mode selector to OFF. Run engine at fast idle for several minutes. Cooling fan should come on before coolant temperature indicator on instrument panel comes on.

OLDSMOBILE CUTLASS CIERA

4-151 VIN R Less A/C

1. Run engine at fast idle for several minutes. Cooling fan should turn on before coolant temperature indicator comes on.

4-151 VIN R With A/C

1. With engine at normal operating temperature and running at curb idle, move A/C selector switch to NORM position. Cooling fan should go on.
2. Move A/C selector switch to OFF position. Allow engine to run at fast idle for several minutes. Cooling fan should turn on before coolant temperature indicator goes on.

Troubleshooting

BUICK CENTURY

If cooling fan relay has failed, replace it and check cooling fan switch for intermittent operation as flows:

1. Warm up engine until cooling fan turns on.
2. Disconnect connector from cooling fan switch.
3. Connect self-powered test lamp to switch and to ground. Test lamp should light steadily.
4. If test lamp flickers, replace cooling fan switch.
5. Perform test on both high and low speed switches, if equipped.

Cooling Fan Does Not Operate

1. Check applicable A/C or heater fuse. On V6-231 VIN 3, check ECM/ERLS fuse.
2. On all models, check for loose connections on fan and relays.
3. If OK, connect fused jumper wire from positive battery terminal to cooling fan black/red and/or pink/black wires.
4. If fan does not run, check that black wire is grounded and that fan mounting bolts are clean and tight. If fan is properly grounded and does not run, replace cooling fan.
5. If cooling fan runs in step 3, problem is in control switches or wiring:
   a. On vehicles with 4-151 VIN R, V6-183 VIN E with A/C, V6-231 VIN 3, perform ECM diagnosis.
   b. On vehicles with V6-183 VIN E less A/C, or V6-262 Diesel VIN T, refer to "System Diagnosis."

OLDSMOBILE CUTLASS CIERA W/4-151 VIN R

1. If cooling fan comes on only with A/C compressor and not for hot engine, install new cooling fan switch.
2. If cooling fan does not come on with A/C compressor, check for continuity to ground at terminal A (dark green/yellow wire) of A/C selector switch. If ground is good, check for continuity between terminal B of A/C selector switch and terminal B of coolant fan relay (dark green/white wire) with relay disconnected. If good, replace A/C selector switch.

System Diagnosis

BUICK CENTURY W/V6-231 VIN E LESS A/C

SINGLE SPEED FAN

Fan Runs When Jumped; Does Not Run In Normal Use

1. Disconnect connectors from cooling fan relay. With ignition switch in RUN position, check for battery voltage at terminal A (brown wire), and at terminal B (red wire).
2. If battery voltage is not available at a terminal, check circuit that supplies terminal. If voltages are correct, proceed to step 3.
3. Connect connector to cooling fan relay.
4. Disconnect dark green/yellow wire from cooling fan switch. Connect fused jumper wire from connector on dark green/yellow wire to ground.
5. With ignition switch in RUN, fan should run.
6. If fan runs, relay and wiring are good, install new cooling fan switch.
7. If fan does not run in step 5, check dark green/yellow wire to relay and black/red wire to fan. If OK, install new cooling fan relay.

TWO SPEED FAN

Fan Runs At Both Speeds When Jumped; Does Not Run In Normal Use

1. Disconnect connector from high speed cooling fan relay.
2. With ignition in RUN position, measure voltage to ground at connector. Battery voltage should be available at terminal 1 (red wire) and at terminal 5 (brown wire).
3. If any terminal does not have battery voltage, check circuit supplying terminal.
4. If voltages are correct, re-connect connector to high speed cooling fan relay.
5. Disconnect connector form cooling fan switch. Connect fused jumper from connector to ground.
6. With ignition switch in RUN, fan should run at high speed.
7. If fan runs, relay and wiring are OK. Install new high speed cooling fan relay.
8. Disconnect connectors from low speed cooling fan relay. With ignition switch in RUN, check voltage to ground.
9. Battery voltage should be available at terminal A (brown wire) and at terminal C (dark green/yellow wire).
10. If any terminal does not have battery voltage, check circuit supplying terminal.
11. If voltages in step 9 are OK, reconnect connector to low speed cooling fan relay.
12. Disconnect connector from cooling fan switch.
13. Connect a fused jumper from terminal A to ground. With ignition switch in RUN, cooling fan should run at low speed.
14. If cooling fan runs at low speed, relay, cooling fan resistor, and wiring are good. Install new cooling fan switch.
15. If cooling fan does not run, check dark green/yellow wire to relay. Check black/red and black/pink wires and cooling fan resistor. If OK, install new low speed cooling fan relay.

BUICK CENTURY V6-262 DIESEL VIN T

Fan Runs At Both Speeds When Jumped; Does Not Run In Normal Use

1. Disconnect connector from cooling fan relay. With ignition in RUN, measure voltage to ground at connector. Battery voltage should be available at terminal C (brown/white wire) and terminal G (red wire).
2. If any terminal does not have battery voltage, check circuit supplying terminal. If voltages are correct, proceed to

step 3.

3. Re-connect connector to cooling fan relay. Disconnect connector from cooling fan switch and connect fused jumper from connector to ground.
4. With ignition switch in RUN, check that cooling fan runs at low speed when grounding dark green/white wire. Check that fan runs at high speed when grounding lt green/black wire.
5. If an does not run at one speed or both, check wires to fan motor and to cooling fan switch from relay. If wiring is OK, install new cooling fan relay.
6. With connector still disconnected from cooling fan switch, start engine. Turn A/C mode selector switch to NORM, and blower to HI, and leave vehicle doors open. Cooling fan should run at low speed, then at high speed. If not, install new A/C high pressure switch.
7. Re-connect connector to cooling fan switch and disconnect connector from A/C high pressure switch.
8. Turn A/C mode selector to OFF. Run engine at fast idle. Cooling fan should run at low speed and then at high speed, before temperature indicator comes on. Install new cooling fan switch if fan does not run at both speeds. **If engine temperature is high enough that cooling fan is running at high speed, turn engine off. The cooling fan will switch to low speed as engine cools down.**

OLDSMOBILE CUTLASS CIERA

4-151 VIN R

Cooling Fan Does Not Run

1. Check that cooling fan case ground is clean and tight.
2. Check F-P fuse.
3. Turn ignition switch to RUN without starting engine. Disconnect cooling fan switch connector (dark green/white wire). Connect jumper wire from dark green/white wire to ground and leave connected for duration of test.
4. If fan runs, replace cooling fan switch.
5. If fan does not run in step 3, connect test lamp to ground and check for voltage at terminal C (brown/white wire) of coolant fan relay.
6. If test lamp does not light, repair open in brown/white or brown wire between relay and fuse block.
7. If test lamp lights in step 5, check for voltage at terminal D (red wire).
8. If test lamp does not light, check and, if necessary, repair red wire between relay and fusible link C. Check and, if necessary, repair fusible link C.
9. If test lamp lights in step 7, check for voltage at terminal B (dark green/white wire) of relay.
10. If test lamp lights, repair open in dark green/white wire between relay and cooling fan switch.
11. If test lamp does not light, check for voltage at terminal A (black/red wire) of relay.
12. If test lamp does not light, replace cooling fan relay.
13. If test lamp lights in step 11, check for voltage at cooling fan connector (black/red wire).
14. If test lamp does not light, repair open in black/red wire between relay and cooling fan.
15. If test lamp lights in step 13, repair or replace cooling fan.

V6-183 VIN E WITH SINGLE SPEED FAN LESS A/C

Cooling Fan Does Not Run

1. Check applicable A/C or heater fuses.
2. Check that cooling fan housing ground is clean and tight.
3. Turn ignition to RUN without starting engine.
4. Disconnect cooling fan switch connector (single dark green/yellow wire). Connect jumper wire from dark green/yellow wire to ground and leave connected for duration of test.
5. If fan operates, replace cooling fan switch.
6. If fan does not run in step 4, connect test lamp to ground and check for voltage at terminal B (red wire) of connector C2 on cooling fan relay.
7. If test lamp does not light, check, and if necessary, repair open in red wire between relay and fusible link C. Check, and if necessary, repair open in fusible link C.
8. If test lamp lights in step 6, connect test lamp to ground and check for voltage at terminal A (brown wire) of connector C1 on relay.
9. If test lamp does not light, repair open in brown wire between relay and fuse block.
10. If test lamp lights in step 8, check for voltage at terminal C (dark green/yellow wire) of connector C1 on relay.
11. If test lamp lights, repair open in dark green/yellow wire between relay and cooling fan switch.
12. If test lamp does not light in step 10, check for voltage at terminal B (black/red wire) of connector C1 on relay.
13. If test lamp does not light, replace cooling fan relay.
14. If test lamp lights in step 12, check for voltage at cooling fan connector (single black/red wire).
15. If test lamp does not light, repair open in black/red wire between relay and cooling fan.
16. If test lamp lights in step 14, repair or replace cooling fan.

V6-183 VIN E WITH 2 SPEED FAN LESS A/C

Cooling Fan Does Not Run At Any Speed

1. Check applicable A/C or Heater fuses.
2. Turn ignition switch to RUN without starting engine.
3. Connect test lamp to ground and check for voltage at terminal E (brown wire) of high speed cooling fan relay.
4. If test lamp does not light, repair open between splice S129 (engine harness, front of LH shock tower) and fuse block.
5. If test lamp lights in step 3, check for voltage at terminal A (red wire) of high speed relay.
6. If test lamp does not light, check, and if necessary, repair red wire. Check, and if necessary, repair fusible link C (located at starter solenoid).
7. If test lamp lights in step 5, disconnect cooling fan connector and check for voltage at terminal B (black/pink wire) of cooling fan.
8. If test lamp does not light, repair open in black/pink wire between cooling fan harness connector and splice S154 (located in engine harness, LH front of engine).
9. If test lamp lights in step 7, re-connect cooling fan connector and check for voltage at terminal A (black wire) or cooling fan.
10. If test lamp does not light, repair or replace cooling fan.
11. If test lamp lights in step 9, repair open in black wire between cooling fan and ground G104 (located on top LH side of engine).

V6-183 VIN E WITH A/C

Cooling Fan Does Not Run At Any Speed

1. Check applicable A/C or Heater fuses.
2. Turn A/C mode selector to Norm.
3. Set ignition switch to RUN without starting engine.
4. Connect test lamp to ground and check for voltage at terminal E (brown wire) of high speed cooling fan relay.
5. If test lamp does not light, repair open in brown wire between splice S129 (located in engine harness, front of LH shock tower) and fuse block.
6. If test lamp lights in step 4, check for voltage at terminal A (red wire) of high speed relay.
7. If test lamp does not light, check and, if necessary, repair red wire. Also, check and, if necessary, repair fusible link C.
8. If test lamp lights in step 6, disconnect cooling fan connector and check for voltage at terminal B (black/pink wire) of cooling fan.
9. If test lamp does not light, repair open in black/pink wire between cooling fan harness connector and terminal D of high speed relay.
10. If test lamp lights in step 8, re-connect cooling fan connector. Check for voltage at terminal A (black wire) of heavy duty cooling fan or terminal C (black wire) of two speed cooling fan.
11. If test lamp does not light, repair or replace cooling fan.
12. If test lamp lights in step 10, repair open in black wire between cooling fan and ground G104 (located top LH side of engine).

Two Speed Cooling Fan Does Not Run At Low Speed

1. Turn ignition switch to RUN without starting engine.
2. Turn A/C mode selector to NORM position.

3. Connect test lamp to ground and check for voltage at terminal A of connector C1 (brown wire) on low speed cooling fan relay.
4. If test lamp does not light, repair open in brown wire between low speed relay and splice S129.
5. If test lamp lights in step 3, check for voltage at terminal B of connector C2 (red wire) on low speed relay.
6. If test lamp does not light, repair open in red wire between fusible link C and low speed relay.
7. If test lamp lights in step 5, check for voltage at terminal B of connector C1 (black/red wire) on low speed relay.
8. If test lamp lights, check for voltage at terminal A (black/red wire) of cooling fan connector.
   a. If test lamp lights, replace cooling fan.
   b. If test lamp does not light, repair open in black/red wire between relay and of cooling fan connector.
9. If test lamp does not light in step 7, check for voltage at terminal B of connector C2 (red wire) on low speed relay.
10. If test lamp does not light, disconnect connector C2 from relay. Remove terminal C from connector C2 and reconnect C2 to relay.
    a. If fan runs, check for short to ground in tan/black wires. If no short is found, ECM diagnosis must be performed.
    b. If fan does not run, replace low speed relay.
11. If test lamp lights in step 9, connect jumper wire from terminal A of C2 (lt green wire) to ground.
    a. If fan does not run, replace low speed relay.
    b. If fan runs, check for open in lt green or dark green/white wire between low speed relay and A/C mode selector. Also check for open in A/C mode selector and in black wire between A/C mode selector and ground G104.

Heavy Duty Fan Does Not Run At Low Speed

1. Turn ignition switch to RUN position without starting engine.
2. Set A/C mode selector to NORM.
3. Connect test lamp to ground and check for voltage at terminal A of connector C1 (brown wire) on low speed coolant fan relay.
4. If test lamp does not light, repair open in brown wire between low speed relay and splice S129.
5. If test lamp lights in step 3, check for voltage at terminal B of connector C2 (red wire).
6. If test lamp does not light, repair open in red wire between fusible link C and low speed relay.
7. If test lamp lights in step 5, check for voltage at terminal B of connector C1 (black/red wire) on low speed relay.
8. If test lamp lights, disconnect cooling fan resistor connector. Connect jumper wire in place of resistor.
   a. If fan runs, replace cooling fan resistor.
   b. If fan does not run, check for open in black/red wire between relay and connector C141 (LH front of engine). Also check for open in black/pink wire between connector C141 and splice S154 (engine harness, LH front of engine).
9. If test lamp does not light in step 7, check for voltage at terminal B of connector C2 (red wire) on low speed relay.
10. If test lamp does not light, disconnect connector C2 from relay. Remove terminal C from C2 and reconnect C2 to relay.
    a. If fan runs, check for short to ground in tan/black wires. If not short is found, refer to ECM diagnosis.
    b. If fan does not run, replace low speed relay.
11. If test lamp lights in step 9, connect jumper wire from terminal A of C2 (lt green wire) to ground.
    a. If fan does not run, replace low speed relay.
    b. If fan runs, check for open in lt green or dark green/white wire between low speed relay and A/C mode selector. Also check for open in A/C mode selector and in black wire between A/C mode selector and ground G104 located on top LH side of engine.

Cooling Fan Does Not Run At High Speed

1. Turn ignition switch to RUN without starting engine.
2. Disconnect cooling fan switch connector (single dark green/yellow wire) and connect jumper wire from dark green/yellow wire to ground and leave connected for duration of test.
3. If fan runs, replace cooling fan switch.
4. If cooling fan does not run in step 2, connect test lamp to ground and check for voltage at terminal E (brown wire) of high speed cooling fan relay.
5. Connect test lamp to ground and check for voltage at terminal E (brown wire) of high speed cooling fan relay.
6. If test lamp does not light, repair open in brown wire between high speed cooling fan relay and splice S129.
7. If test lamp lights in step 5, check for voltage at terminal A (red wire) of high speed cooling fan relay.
8. If test lamp does not light, repair open in red wire between fusible link C and high speed relay.
9. If test lamp lights in step 7, check for voltage at terminal D (black wire) of high speed relay.
10. If test lamp does not light, replace high speed relay.
11. If test lamp lights in step 9, repair open in black/pink wire between high speed relay and cooling fan.

V6-231 VIN 3 WITH SINGLE SPEED FAN

Cooling Fan Does Not Run

1. Check crank/fan fuse.
2. Check that cooling fan case ground is clean and tight.
3. Turn ignition switch to RUN without starting engine.
4. Disconnect cooling fan switch connector (single dark green/yellow wire) and connect a jumper wire from dark green/yellow wire to ground and leave connected for duration of test.
5. If fan runs in step 4, replace cooling fan switch.
6. If cooling fan does not run in step 4, connect test lamp to ground and check for voltage at terminal A (red wire) of connector on cooling fan relay.
7. If test lamp does not light, check, and if necessary, repair open in red wire between relay and fusible link C. Check, and if necessary, repair open in fusible link C (at starter solenoid).
8. If test lamp lights in step 6, check for voltage at terminal E (brown wire) of connector on relay.
9. If test lamp does not light, repair open in brown wire between relay and fuse block.
10. If test lamp lights in step 8, check for voltage at terminal B (dark green/yellow wire) of connector on relay.
11. If test lamp lights, repair open in dark green/yellow wire between relay and cooling fan switch.
12. If test lamp does not light in step 10, check for voltage at terminal D (black/red wire) of connector on relay.
13. If test lamp does not light, replace cooling fan relay.
14. If test lamp lights in step 12, check for voltage at cooling fan connector (single black/red wire).
15. If test lamp does not light, repair open in black/red wire between relay and cooling fan.
16. If test lamp lights, repair or replace cooling fan.

Cooling Fan Does Not Run For Delay Period After Engine Is Shut Off With Coolant Hot

1. Check ECM/ERLS fuse.
2. Connect test lamp to ground and check for voltage at terminal A (red wire) of connector C1 on cooling fan delay relay.
3. If test lamp lights, check, and if necessary, repair open in red wire between coolant fan delay relay and fusible link C.
4. If test lamp lights, check for voltage at terminal A (red wire) of connector C2 on cooling fan delay relay.
5. If test lamp does not light, check, and if necessary, repair red wire between delay relay and fusible link F.
6. If test lamp lights in step 4, check for voltage at terminal C (black/pink wire) of connector C1 on delay relay.
7. If test lamp lights, repair open in black/pink wire between delay relay and splice S181 (engine harness, front of LH shock tower).
8. If test lamp does not light, disconnect cooling fan switch connector (single dark green/yellow wire) and connect a jumper from dark green/yellow wire

to ground. Turn ignition switch to RUN then off.
9. If fan operates, replace cooling fan switch.
10. If fan does not operate in step 8, check for voltage at terminal B (dark green/yellow wire) of connector C1 on delay relay.
11. If test lamp does not light, replace cooling fan delay relay.
12. If test lamp lights, repair open in dark green/yellow wire between delay relay and splice S182 (engine harness, top RH end of engine).

V6-231 VIN 3 WITH 2 SPEED FAN

Coolant Fan Does Not Run At Any Speed

1. Check crank/fan fuse.
2. Connect test lamp to ground and check for voltage at terminal E (brown wire) of high speed cooling fan relay.
3. If test lamp does not light, repair open in brown wire between high speed cooling fan relay (LH side of radiator on bracket) and fuse block.
4. If test lamp lights, check for voltage at terminal E (brown wire) of low speed cooling fan relay.
5. If test lamp does not light, check, and if necessary, repair brown wire between low speed cooling fan relay (LH side of radiator on bracket) and high speed cooling fan relay.
6. If test lamp does not light in step 4, check for voltage at terminal A (red wire) of high speed cooling fan relay.
7. If test lamp does not light, check, and if necessary, repair red wire between high speed cooling fan relay and fusible link C. Check, and if necessary, repair fusible link C.
8. If test lamp lights, check for voltage at terminal A (red wire) of low speed cooling fan relay.
9. If test lamp does not light, check, and if necessary, repair red wire between low speed cooling fan relay and high speed cooling fan relay.
10. If test lamp lights in step 8, disconnect cooling fan switch connector (single dark green/yellow wire) and connect jumper wire from dark green/yellow wire to ground. Check for voltage at terminal D (black/pink wire) of high speed cooling fan relay.
11. If test lamp does not light, replace high speed cooling fan relay.
12. If test lamp lights in step 10, check for voltage at terminal B (black/pink wire) of cooling fan.
13. If test lamp does not light, repair open in black/pink wire between cooling fan and high speed cooling fan relay.
14. If test lamp lights, replace cooling fan.

Cooling Fan Does Not Run At Low Speed

1. Turn ignition switch to RUN without starting engine.
2. Connect test lamp to ground and check for voltage at terminal D (black/red wire) on low speed cooling fan.
3. If test lamp does not light, check for voltage at terminal B (dark green wire) of low speed cooling fan relay.
   a. If lamp does not light, replace low speed cooling fan relay.
   b. If test lamp lights, check, and repair, if necessary, open dark green wire between relay and splice S175. Also check, and if necessary, repair open in black/white wire between splice S166 and ground G104.
4. If test lamp lights in step 2, proceed as follows:
   a. On vehicles with internal cooling fan resistor, check for voltage at terminal A of cooling fan. If test lamp lights, replace cooling fan. If test lamp does not light, repair open in black/red wire between low speed cooling fan relay and cooling fan.
   b. On vehicles with external cooling fan resistor (heavy duty fan), disconnect cooling fan resistor connector and connect jumper wire in place of cooling fan resistor. If fan operates, replace cooling fan resistor. If fan does not operate, repair open in black/red wire between low speed relay and connector C141 (LH front of engine) or in black/pink wire between connector C141 and splice S154.

Cooling Fan Does Not Run At High Speed

1. Turn ignition switch to RUN without starting engine.
2. Disconnect cooling fan switch connector (single dark green/yellow wire) and connect a jumper wire from dark green/yellow wire to ground.
3. If cooling fan operates, replace cooling fan switch.
4. If cooling fan does not operate in step 2, leave jumper connected. Connect test lamp to ground and check for voltage at terminal D (black/pink wire) of high speed cooling fan relay.
5. If test lamp lights, repair open in black/pink wire between relay and splice S154.
6. If test lamp does not light, check for voltage at terminal B (dark green/yellow wire) of high speed cooling fan relay.
7. If test lamp lights, reconnect cooling fan switch connector. Repair dark green/yellow wire between high speed relay and splice S155 (engine harness, top RH end of engine.
8. If test lamp does not light, reconnect cooling fan switch connector and replace high speed cooling fan relay.

Cooling Fan Does Not Run At Low And/Or High Speed With A/C On

1. Start engine and set A/C mode selector to NORM and blower to HI.
2. Disconnect cooling fan switch connector (single dark green/yellow wire) and connect test lamp to ground. Check voltage at terminal B (dark green wire) on A/C high pressure switch connector.
3. If test lamp does not light, repair open in dark green wire between pressure switch connector and splice S175 (engine harness, front of LH shock tower).
4. If test lamp lights in step 2, check for voltage at terminal C (black/white wire) of A/C high pressure switch.
5. If test lamp does not light, replace A/C high pressure switch.
6. If test lamp lights in step 4, repair open in black/white wire between pressure switch connector and splice S166 (EFI harness, behind I/P near grommet). Operate engine at fast idle with A/C on and check for voltage at terminal A (dark green/yellow wire) of A/C high pressure switch.
7. If test lamp lights, replace A/C high pressure switch.
8. If test lamp does not light in step 6, repair open in dark green/yellow wire between pressure switch connector and splice S155.

Cooling Fan Does Not Run For Delay Period After Engine Is Shut Off With Coolant Hot

1. Check ECM/ERLS fuse.
2. Connect test lamp to ground and check for voltage at terminal A (red wire) of connector C1 on cooling fan delay relay.
3. If test lamp does not light, check/repair open in red wire between cooling fan delay relay and fusible link C (at starter solenoid).
4. If test lamp lights in step 2, check for voltage at terminal A (red wire) of connector C2 on cooling fan delay relay.
5. If test lamp does not light, check/repair open in red wire between delay relay and fusible link F.
6. If test lamp lights in step 4, check for voltage at terminal C (black/pink wire) of connector C1 on delay relay.
7. If test lamp lights, repair open in black/pink wire between delay relay and splice S154.
8. If test lamp lights in step 6, disconnect cooling fan switch connector (single dark green/yellow wire). Connect jumper wire from dark green/yellow wire to ground. Turn ignition switch to RUN, then turn switch off.
9. If cooling fan operates, replace cooling fan switch.
10. If cooling fan does not run in step 8, check for voltage at terminal B (dark green/yellow wire) of connector C1 on delay relay.
11. If test lamp lights, replace cooling fan delay relay.
12. If test lamp lights in step 10, repair open in dark green/yellow wire between delay relay and splice S155 (engine harness, top of RH end of engine).

V6-262 DIESEL VIN T

Cooling Fan Does Not Run At Any Speed

1. Check that cooling fan case ground is clean and tight.
2. Check applicable A/C or heater fuses.
3. Turn ignition switch to RUN without starting engine.

4. Disconnect cooling fan switch connector and connect a jumper wire from either terminal on cooling fan switch to ground and leave connected for duration of test.
5. If fan operates, replace cooling fan switch.
6. If fan does not operate in step 4, connect teat lamp to ground and check for voltage at terminal C (brown/white wire) of cooling fan relay.
7. If test lamp does not light, repair open in brown/white or brown wire between fuse block and relay.
8. If test lamp lights in step 6, check voltage at terminal G (red wire) of relay.
9. If test lamp does not light, check/repair open in red wire between relay and fusible link C. Check/repair fusible link C.
10. If test lamp lights in step 8, check voltage at terminal A (black/pink wire) of relay or terminal B (black/red wire) of relay.
11. If test lamp does not light on either terminal, replace cooling fan relay.
12. If test lamp lights on either terminal in step 10, check voltage at terminal B of cooling fan or terminal C of connector C108.
13. If test lamp does not light, repair open in black/pink wire or black/red wire between relay and cooling fan.
14. If test lamp lights in step 12, repair or replace cooling fan.

Cooling Fan Does Not Run At Low Speed

1. Turn ignition switch to RUN without starting engine.
2. Disconnect cooling fan switch connector and connect jumper from terminal A (dark green/white wire) to ground and leave connected for duration of test.
3. If cooling fan operates, replace cooling fan switch.
4. If cooling fan does not operate in step 2, connect test lamp to ground and check for voltage at terminal B (black/red wire) of cooling fan relay.
5. If test lamp does not light, replace cooling fan relay.
6. If test lamp lights in step 4, check for voltage at terminal C (black/red wire) of cooling fan.
7. If test lamp does not light, repair open in black/red wire between relay and cooling fan.
8. If test lamp lights in step 6, replace cooling fan.

Cooling Fan Does Not Run At High Speed

1. Turn ignition switch to RUN without starting engine.
2. Disconnect cooling fan switch connector and connect a jumper wire from terminal B (lt green/black wire) to ground and leave connected for duration of test.
3. If fan operates, replace cooling fan switch.
4. If cooling fan does not operate in step 2, connect test lamp to ground and check for voltage at terminal A (black/pink wire) of cooling fan relay. If test lamp does not light, replace cooling fan relay.
5. If test lamp does not light, check for voltage at terminal B (black/pink wire) of cooling fan.
6. If test lamp lights, replace cooling fan.
7. If test lamp does not light in step 5, repair open in black/pink wire between cooling fan and relay.

Cooling Fan, Replace

1. Disconnect battery ground cable.
2. Disconnect wiring from fan motor and frame.
3. Remove fan assembly from radiator support.
4. Reverse procedure to install.

1985–87 CHEVROLET CELEBRITY

SYSTEM DESCRIPTION

4-151 VIN R & V6-173 VIN X

Less A/C

Voltage is always available through fusible link C (located at front of engine, near starter) to cooling fan relay contacts. With ignition switch in RUN, voltage is available through C-H fuse to cooling fan relay coil.

When high coolant temperatures close cooling fan switch contacts, current flows through C-H fuse, cooling fan relay coil, and cooling fan switch contact to ground. This causes cooling fan relay contacts to close, which allows current to flow through fusible link C, cooling fan relay contacts, and cooling fan to ground.

With A/C

Voltage is always available through fusible link C to cooling fan relay contacts. With ignition switch in RUN, voltage is available through C-H fuse to cooling fan relay coil.

With cooling fan switch contacts closed at high temperatures, current flows through C-H fuse, cooling fan relay coil, and cooling fan switch contacts to ground. The cooling fan relay contacts then close, allowing current to flow through fusible link C, cooling fan relay contacts, and cooling fan to ground.

To ensure adequate air flow over condenser, cooling fan operates with A/C compressor.

In vehicles with 4-151 VIN R, cooling fan operates when A/C mode selector is in MAX, NORM, or BI-LEVEL positions, or when A/C high pressure switch closes and ECM completes current path to ground.

In vehicles with V6-173 VIN X, cooling fan also operates when A/C high pressure switch closes.

V6-173 VIN W

Voltage is always available through battery junction block to cooling fan relay contacts. With ignition switch in RUN, voltage is available through C-H fuse to cooling fan relay coil.

When ECM receives signal from coolant temperature sensor, it provides a ground for cooling fan relay between ECM's cooling fan control terminal and ground terminal. Current then flows through C-H fuse, cooling fan relay coil, and ECM to ground, causing cooling fan relay contacts to close. Current then flows through battery junction block, cooling fan relay contacts, and cooling fan to ground, causing cooling fan to operate.

To ensure adequate air flow over A/C condenser, cooling fan operates with A/C compressor on.

The cooling fan operates when A/C high pressure switch closes and ECM provides ground.

V6-262 DIESEL VIN T

This circuit provides automatic 2 speed operation of cooling fan.

Voltage is always available through fusible link C (located behind LH battery, near bracket) to cooling fan relay contacts. With ignition switch in RUN position, voltage is available through C-H fuse to cooling fan relay coils.

With cooling fan switch low speed contacts closed, current flows through C-H fuse, cooling fan relay low speed coil, and cooling fan switch low speed contact to ground. This causes cooling fan low speed contacts to close. Current then flows through fusible link C, cooling fan relay contacts, and cooling fan to ground, causing cooling fan to operate at low speed. Operation of the high speed circuit is similar.

On vehicles equipped with A/C, cooling fan operates when contacts of either A/C high pressure switch are closed to ensure adequate air flow over A/C condenser.

TROUBLESHOOTING

Cooling Fan Does Not Run

1. Check C-H fuse.
2. Check fusible link C.
3. Connect jumper from cooling fan relay coil to ground. Cooling fan should operate.

Cooling Fan Runs Constantly With Ignition On

1. Check if cooling fan switch contacts are closed at all times.
2. Check cooling fan relay for stuck contacts.
3. On vehicles with A/C, check if A/C high pressure switch contacts are constantly closed.
4. On vehicles with 4-151 VIN R, check if A/C mode selector is grounded at all times.

COOLING FAN, REPLACE

1. Disconnect battery ground cable.
2. Disconnect wiring from fan motor and frame.
3. Remove fan assembly from radiator support.
4. Reverse procedure to install.

1985 PONTIAC 6000

SYSTEM DESCRIPTION

The cooling fan is controlled by a cooling fan relay whose coil is grounded by cooling fan switch which closes when coolant temperature exceeds 228 degrees F. The relay is then energized, causing its contacts to close to supply battery voltage to fan.

Exc. Diesel Engine

On vehicles equipped with 4-151 VIN R engine with A/C, cooling fan is controlled by the following:

a. Coolant temperature fan switch.
b. ECM and A/C mode selector.
c. ECM and A/C high pressure switch.

On vehicles equipped with V6-173 VIN X engine with A/C, cooling fan is controlled by the following:

a. Coolant temperature switch.
b. A/C mode selector.
c. A/C high pressure switch.

Any of these switch combinations will complete circuit to ground through coil of cooling fan relay. The relay then energizes causing contacts to close and to apply battery voltage to cooling fan.

On vehicles equipped with V6-VIN W, the cooling fan is also controlled by the ECM. The ECM provides a ground path for relay coil to energize relay and close relay contacts. The A/C high pressure switch closes when refrigerant pressure exceeds 280 psi. This grounds an ECM input, causing ECM to turn on cooling fan.

V6-262 Diesel VIN T

Two types of cooling fans are used: a single speed or a two speed cooling fan.

The two speed cooling fan is controlled by a cooling fan relay that has two coils and two independent sets of contacts.

During low speed operation, either low speed switch in cooling fan switch closes to ground or low speed switch in A/C high pressure switch closes to ground. The low speed coil of cooling fan relay is energized, causing contacts to apply battery voltage to resistor in two speed fan so fan operates at low speed.

During high speed operation, either high speed cooling fan switch or high speed A/C high pressure switch closes. Circuit is then completed through high speed coil of cooling fan relay, causing battery voltage to be applied directly to cooling fan so it operates at high speed.

The single speed cooling fan uses same relay and switch circuits without a resistor. It operates only at high speed controlled by low speed relay contacts (black/red wire), while high speed relay contacts (black/pink wire) are unused.

TROUBLESHOOTING

EXC. V6-162 DIESEL VIN T

Cooling Fan Does Not Operate

1. Check C-H or Fan/Elec fuse.
2. Check for loose connectors on fan and relays.
3. If fuses and connectors are OK, connect fused jumper wire from positive battery terminal to cooling fan black/red and/or pink/black wires.
4. If fan does not operate, check that black wire is grounded and that mounting bolts are clean and tight. If fan is grounded and does not operate, install new cooling fan.
5. If fan does not operate in step 3, problem is in control switches or wiring. Proceed as follows:
   a. Vehicles with 4-151 VIN R less A/C or V6-173 VIN X, perform system diagnosis.
   b. Vehicles with 4-151 VIN R with A/C or V6-173 VIN W, perform ECM diagnosis.

SYSTEM CHECK

V6-262 DIESEL VIN T LESS A/C

1. Operate engine at fast idle for several minutes. Cooling fan should turn on before coolant temperature indicator on instrument panel comes on.

V6-262 Diesel VIN T with A/C

1. With engine idling, set A/C mode selector to NORM and blower to HI. Set temperature selector to COLD. Cooling fan should turn on and operate at low speed, before coolant temperature indicator comes on. Fan will operate at low speed as long as coolant temperature remains below 246 degrees F.
2. Increase engine speed from idle. Operate engine for several minutes. Cooling fan should switch to high speed before coolant temperature indicator comes on.

SYSTEM DIAGNOSIS

4-151 VIN R & V6-173 VIN X LESS A/C

Fan Runs When Jumped, Does Not Run In Normal Use

1. Disconnect connector from cooling fan relay. With ignition is RUN position, check for battery voltage at terminal C (brown/white wire) and at terminal D (red wire) and terminal E (red wire).
2. If any terminal does not have battery voltage, check circuit that supplies terminal. If voltages are correct, proceed to step 3.
3. Reconnect connector to cooling fan relay. Disconnect dark green/white wire from cooling fan switch. Connect fused jumper from wire to ground. Turn ignition switch to RUN.
4. If fan operates, relay and wiring are OK. Install new cooling fan switch.
5. If fan does not operate, check dark green/white wire to relay and black/red wire to fan. If OK, install new cooling fan relay.
6. If cooling fan relay has failed, cooling fan switch should be checked for intermittent operation as follows:
   a. Warm up engine until cooling fan operates.
   b. Disconnect connector from cooling fan switch.
   c. Connect self-powered test lamp to switch and ground. Test lamp should light steadily.
   d. If test lamp flickers at all, install new cooling fan switch.
   e. Test both high speed and low speed switches, if so equipped.
7. On vehicles with V6-173 VIN X with A/C, check operation of A/C high pressure switch and A/C mode selector as follows:
   a. Disconnect connector from A/C high pressure switch. With engine idling, turn mode selector to NORM. A/C compressor will operate and cooling fan come on.
   b. If cooling fan does not operate, connect jumper wire from dark green/white wire at terminal B on mode selector to ground.
   c. If fan operates, check that black wire at A is grounded. If ground is OK, install new A/C mode selector.
   d. With A/C compressor running, and connector disconnected from A/C high pressure switch, test switch terminals for continuity to ground using self-powered test lamp. If both terminals are not grounded, install new A/C high pressure switch.

V6-262 DIESEL VIN T

Fan Runs At Both Speeds When Jumped, But Does Not Run In Normal Service

1. Disconnect connector from cooling fan relay and measure voltage to ground at connector. With ignition switch in RUN position, battery voltage should be available at terminal C (brown/white wire) and at terminal G (red wire).
2. If any terminal does not have battery voltage, check circuit supplying terminal. If voltages are correct, proceed to next step.
3. Reconnect connector to cooling fan relay. Disconnect connector from cooling fan switch and connect fused jumper wire from connector to ground. With ignition switch in RUN position, cooling fan should operate at low speed when dark green/white wire is grounded; high speed when lt green/white wire is grounded.
4. If fan does not operate at one or both speeds, check wires to motor and to cooling fan switch from relay. If wiring is OK, install new cooling fan relay.
5. With connector still disconnected from cooling fan switch, start engine. Turn A/C mode selector to NORM and blower to HI, and leave vehicle doors open. Cooling fan should operate at low speed, then at high speed. Install new A/C high pressure switch if not.
6. Reconnect connector to cooling fan switch and remove connector from A/C high pressure switch. Turn A/C mode selector off. Operate engine at fast idle. Cooling fan should operate at low speed, then at high speed, before temperature indicator comes on. Install new cooling fan switch if fan does not operate at both speeds. Note that if engine has warmed up enough for fan to operate at high speed, turn engine off. As engine cools off, fan will switch to low speed.

COOLING FAN, REPLACE

1. Disconnect battery ground cable.

2. Disconnect wiring from fan motor and frame.
3. Remove fan assembly from radiator support.
4. Reverse procedure to install.

1986–87 BUICK ELECTRA, PARK AVENUE, & LESABRE & OLDSMOBILE 88 & 98

DESCRIPTION

The coolant fan is turned on and off by the low and high speed coolant fan relays. The low speed relay coil is grounded through the ECM or the low speed contacts of the A/C pressure switch. The ECM grounds the coil when vehicle speed is less than 45 mph and engine coolant is at operating temperatures. The high speed relay coil is grounded through the Hi speed contacts in the A/C pressure switch or the temperature switch. The temperature switch closes when coolant temperature is too high. With the high speed relay coil grounded, the related contacts close, battery voltage is applied to the coolant fan and fan operation begins.

TROUBLESHOOTING

1. If coolant fan does not operate at low and/or high speed, proceed as follows:
   a. Check fuse 6. Turn ignition switch "On," then ground diagnostic terminal B at ALCL connector. If coolant fan does not operate and the dark green (535) wire and coolant fan diode are satisfactory, proceed to step b. If coolant fan operates, an ECM malfunction is indicated. **Perform steps b, c and d for the low speed coolant fan relay, then repeat steps for high speed coolant fan relay.**
   b. Remove connector from coolant fan relays, then connect a suitable test lamp between terminals 2 and ground. Turn ignition switch "On." If test lamp lights, proceed to step c. If test lamp does not light, an open circuit in brown (250) wires are indicated.
   c. Move test lamp lead from terminal 2 to terminal 1 on relay connector. If test lamp lights, proceed to step d. If test lamp does not light, check red wires (2) and fusible link D for opens.
   d. Connect a fused jumper between terminals 1 and 4 of relay connector. If coolant fan does not operate, proceed to step e. If coolant fan operates with low speed coolant fan relay connector jumped, replace relay. If coolant fan operates with high speed coolant fan relay connector jumped, proceed to step g.
   e. With jumpers in place, remove connector from coolant fan, then connect a suitable test lamp between terminals B and ground. If test lamp lights, proceed to step f. If test lamp does not light, an open is indicated in black/red (532) and white (533) wires. Repair as necessary.
   f. Move test lamp ground lead to terminal A of the coolant fan connector. If test lamp does not light, an open is indicated in black (150) wires. If test lamp lights, replace coolant fan.
   g. Reconnect high speed coolant fan relay, then turn ignition switch "On." Disconnect temperature switch, then ground light green/black wire (536). If coolant fan operates, replace temperature switch. If coolant fan does not operate, check light green/black (536) wires for opens and repair as necessary. If wires are satisfactory, replace high speed coolant fan relay.
2. If heavy duty coolant fan does not operate, proceed as follows:
   a. Remove connector from heavy duty coolant fan relay, then connect a suitable test lamp between terminals 2 and ground. Turn ignition switch "On." If test lamp lights, proceed to step b. If test lamp does not light, an open is indicated in brown (250) wire.
   b. Move test lamp from terminal 2 to terminal 1 of relay connector. If test lamp lights, proceed to step c. If test lamp does not light, an open is indicated in red (2) wires.
   c. Connect a fused jumper between terminals 1 and 4 of relay connector. If heavy duty coolant fan does not operate, proceed to step d. If coolant fan operates, proceed to step f.
   d. With fused jumpers in place, remove connector from fan and connect a suitable test lamp between terminal B and ground. If test lamp lights, proceed to step e.
   e. If test lamp does not light, an open is indicated in white (533) wire. Repair as necessary.
   f. Move test lamp ground lead to terminal A. If test lamp does not light, an open is indicated in black (150) wire. If test lamp lights, replace heavy duty coolant fan.
   g. Reconnect heavy duty coolant fan relay connector, then turn ignition switch "On." Disconnect temperature switch, then ground light green/black wire. If coolant fan operates, replace temperature switch. If coolant fan does not operate, an open is indicated in light green (536) wire. If wire is satisfactory, replace heavy duty coolant fan relay.
3. If coolant fan operates continuously with ignition switch "On," proceed as follows:
   a. Start and operate engine, until coolant is at normal operating temperature. Check for diagnostic code 14 or 15. If no code is present, proceed to step b. If code is present, an ECM malfunction is indicated.
   b. Disconnect low speed coolant fan relay connector, then turn ignition switch "On." If coolant fan operates, proceed to step e. If coolant fan does not operate, proceed to step c.
   c. Connect a suitable test lamp between terminals 2 and 5 of low speed coolant fan relay connector, then turn ignition switch "On." If test lamp lights, proceed to step d. If test lamp does not light, replace low speed coolant fan relay.
   d. Reconnect low speed coolant fan relay connector, then disconnect A/C pressure switch connector. Turn ignition switch "On." If coolant fan operates, a short is indicated in dark green (535) wire. If coolant fan does not operate, replace A/C pressure switch.
   e. Disconnect temperature switch connector, then turn ignition switch "On." If coolant fan operates, proceed to step f. If coolant fan does not operate, replace temperature switch.
   f. Disconnect A/C pressure switch connector, then turn ignition switch "On." If coolant fan operates, proceed to step g. If coolant fan does not operate, replace A/C pressure switch.
   g. Disconnect high speed coolant fan relay connector, then connect a suitable test lamp between terminals 2 and 5 and turn ignition switch "On." If test lamp lights, a short is indicated light green/black wires. If test lamp does not light, replace high speed coolant fan relay.
4. On 98 and Electra Park Avenue models, if coolant fan operates continuously at low speed, with ignition switch "Off," proceed as follows:
   a. Check black/red (532) wire for short to battery voltage. If short is present, repair as necessary. If wire is satisfactory, replace low speed coolant fan relay.
5. On 98 and Electra Park Avenue models, if coolant fan operates continuously at high speed, with ignition switch "Off," check white (533) wire and/or brown (250) wires for short. If short is present, repair as necessary. If wire is satisfactory but coolant fan continues to operate, replace high speed coolant fan relay. If wire is satisfactory, but heavy duty coolant fan still operates, replace heavy duty coolant fan relay.

COOLING FAN, REPLACE

1. Disconnect battery ground cable.
2. Disconnect wiring from fan motor and frame.
3. Remove fan assembly from radiator support.
4. Reverse procedure to install.

1986–87 BUICK SOMERSET REGAL & SKYLARK

DESCRIPTION

On 4 cylinder models, the coolant fan is controlled by the coolant fan relay. The coolant fan temperature switch closes when coolant temperature is high, providing a path to ground for the relay coil. The relay contacts close to apply battery voltage to the fan. On vehicles equipped with A/C, the coolant fan also operates when the compressor fan is on. The A/C relay, controlled by the ECM, supplies battery voltage through the A/C function selector and pressure cycling switch. When the A/C compressor clutch is on, the ECM turns on the A/C coolant fan relay, then its contacts close to ground the coolant fan relay coil. The coolant fan relay is energized, and its contacts apply battery voltage to the fan.

On 6 cylinder models, a two speed puller coolant fan and single speed pusher fan are used. The fans are turned operated by coolant fan relays which have two coils and two independent sets of contacts. For low speed operation, the Lo speed relay coil is grounded through the ECM or the low speed contacts of the A/C high pressure switch. The ECM grounds the coil when vehicle speed is less than 45 mph and engine coolant is warm. For high speed operation, the Hi speed relay coil is grounded through the Hi speed contacts in the A/C high pressure switch or the coolant fan temperature switch. The pressure switch Hi speed contacts close at a refrigerant pressure higher than the pressure that closed the Lo speed contacts. The coolant fan temperature switch closes when coolant temperature is high. With the Hi speed relay coil grounded, the associated contacts close and battery voltage is applied to the heavy duty coolant fan that operates at high speed.

TROUBLESHOOTING

4 Cylinder Models

1. Check coolant fan related fuses, then on models less A/C, proceed as follows:
   a. If coolant fan does not operate, connect a suitable test lamp between terminals E and ground and terminals C and ground. If test lamp does not light, repair or replace fusible link F, engine fan fuse or related wiring. If test lamp lights, proceed to step b.
   b. Connect test lamp to terminal A. When engine coolant temperature is above 230 degrees F and test lamp does not light, disconnect coolant fan temperature switch connector. Connector a suitable jumper from dark green/white wire to ground. If test lamp lights, replace temperature switch. If temperature switch is satisfactory and test lamp lights on terminal A, repair or replace coolant fan. If temperature switch is satisfactory and test lamp does not light on terminal A, replace coolant fan relay.
2. Check coolant fan related fuses, then on models with A/C, proceed as follows:
   a. If coolant fan does not operate when A/C is turned on, connect a suitable test lamp between pins A and C of the A/C coolant fan relay. If test lamp does not light and fuse is satisfactory, replace A/C coolant fan relay. If test lamp lights, a short is indicated in light blue/black (409) wire. If no short is present, an ECM malfunction is indicated.

6 Cylinder Models

1. Check coolant fan related fuses, then on models less A/C, proceed as follows:
   a. If pusher coolant fan does not operate, connect a suitable test lamp between terminals 1 and ground and terminals 5 and ground. If test lamp does not light, repair or replace fusible link F, engine fan fuse or related wiring. If test lamp lights, proceed to step b.
   b. Connect the test lamp to terminal 4. When engine temperature is above 230 degrees F, and test lamp does not light, disconnect coolant fan temperature switch connector. Connect a suitable jumper from light green (536) wire to ground. If test lamp lights, replace temperature switch. If temperature switch is satisfactory and test lamp lights on terminal 4, replace pusher coolant fan. If temperature switch is satisfactory and test lamp does not light on terminal 4, replace pusher coolant fan relay.
   c. If puller coolant fan does not operate, check fusible link F and engine fan for open and repair as necessary. If both are satisfactory, proceed to step d.
   d. If puller coolant fan does not operate at low speed, connect a suitable test lamp to terminals A and B of connector C108. If test lamp lights on terminal B but not A, replace coolant fan resistor.
   e. If puller coolant fan does not operate in high, check for pusher coolant fan operation. If pusher coolant fan is operating, check black/pink (533) wire for open and repair as necessary.
2. Check coolant fan related fuses, then on models with A/C, proceed as follows:
   a. If coolant fan temperature switch is satisfactory, both the pusher coolant fan and puller coolant fan will operate on high when A/C switch is turned on. Disconnect A/C high pressure switch connector and connect a suitable jumper wire from light green/black wire to ground. If both fans operate, replace A/C high pressure switch or repair open in black/white wire (450).

COOLING FAN, REPLACE

1. Disconnect battery ground cable.
2. Disconnect wiring from fan motor and frame.
3. Remove fan assembly from radiator support.
4. Reverse procedure to install.

1986–87 CHEVROLET CORVETTE

DESCRIPTION

The coolant fan operates to cool engine coolant at a certain temperature and also to cool A/C refrigerant under certain conditions when the A/C compressor is operating. The coolant fan relay is activated by the Electronic Control Module (ECM) when engine coolant is above 218 degrees F and when A/C head pressure exceeds 233 psi and vehicle speed is less than 40 mph.

TROUBLESHOOTING

1. With engine coolant at normal operating temperature, operate engine at fast idle for several minutes. Coolant fan should turn on before coolant temperature indicator lamp lights or coolant gauge reads 218 degrees F. If equipped with A/C, allow engine to operate at low idle, then move A/C function switch to NORM. Coolant fan should operate.
2. If coolant fan does not operate, check applicable A/C or heater fuses, then turn ignition switch "On," and ground diagnostic terminal B at ALCL. If coolant fan operates, an ECM malfunction is indicated. If coolant fan does not operate, and dark green/white wire is satisfactory, proceed to step 3.
3. Remove connector from coolant fan relay, then connect a suitable test lamp between connector terminal C and ground. Turn ignition switch "On." If test lamp does not light, check dark blue (351) wire for open and repair as necessary. If test lamp lights, proceed to step 4.
4. Move test lamp from terminal C to terminal E. If test lamp does not light, check for open in red (2) wire and fusible link D and repair as necessary. Repair as necessary. If test lamp lights, proceed to step 5.
5. Connect a fused jumper between terminals E and A of coolant fan relay connector. If coolant fan operates, replace relay. If coolant fan does not operate, proceed to step 6.
6. With fused jumper in place, remove coolant fan connector, and connect a suitable test lamp between terminal A and ground. If test lamp does not light, check black/red (902) wire for open and repair as necessary. If test lamp lights, proceed to step 7.
7. Move test lamp ground lead to terminal A of coolant fan connector. If test lamp does not light, check black (151) wire for open and repair as necessary. If test lamp lights, replace coolant fan.
8. If coolant fan operates continuously with ignition switch "On," check for diagnostic code 14 or 15. If code is present, an ECM malfunction is indicated. If no code is present, check dark green/white wire (935) for short and repair as necessary. If wire is satisfactory, replace coolant fan relay.
9. If coolant fan operates continuously with ignition switch "Off," remove coolant fan relay connector. If coolant fan stops, replace relay. If coolant fan continues to operate, check black/red (902) wire for short and repair as necessary.

COOLING FAN, REPLACE

1. Disconnect battery ground cable.

2. Disconnect wiring from fan motor and frame.
3. Remove fan assembly from radiator support.
4. Reverse procedure to install.

1986-87 BUICK CENTURY & OLDSMOBILE CUTLASS CIERA

SYSTEM DESCRIPTION

The cooling fan is controlled by a cooling fan relay whose coil is grounded by the cooling fan switch when coolant temperature exceeds 228 degrees F. The cooling fan relay is energized and its contacts close to supply battery voltage to cooling fan.

The cooling fan delay relay operates cooling fan for short time after engine is turned off. A solid state timer removes ground from cooling fan delay relay coil to switch off cooling fan.

4 Cylinder Models

The cooling fan is controlled by the following:

1. Coolant temperature fan switch.
2. ECM and A/C mode selector switch.
3. ECM and A/C low pressure cut-off switch.

These switch combinations complete circuit to ground through cooling fan relay coil. With coil energized and relay contacts closed, battery voltage is applied to cooling fan.

On vehicles equipped with A/C, cooling fan also operates when compressor is on. With A/C mode selector is in MAX, NORM, or BI-LEVEL position, a path to ground exists through mode selector switch and ECM.

A suppression resistor is connected across cooling fan relay coil to absorb voltage spikes. An A/C high pressure switch is included in A/C relay grounding circuit to ensure grounding of cooling fan relay coil and cooling fan operation when mode selector is in DEF position and ambient temperature is above 32 degrees F.

6 Cylinder Models

On V6-173 VIN X, the coolant fan is controlled by the coolant fan switch and the A/C high pressure switch. The A/C high pressure switch closes when the compressor is operating and there is an adequate refrigerant charge.

On V6-173 VIN W, the coolant fan is controlled by the coolant fan switch and the Electronic Control Module (ECM). The ECM will only turn on the coolant fan when it senses high engine coolant temperature or high A/C pressure. The coolant fan switch or ECM can provide a ground path for the coolant fan relay and energize it. When energized, the coolant fan relay contacts close and battery voltage is applied to the coolant fan.

On V6-231 VIN B, two types of fan are used. These fans are controlled by either the coolant fan relay, the coolant fan delay relay, the pusher coolant fan relay, the puller coolant fan relay or the A/C high pressure switch, depending on specific application or engine requirement.

On vehicles less A/C, the coolant fan relay is controlled by the coolant fan switch or ECM. For operation with A/C, the coolant fan relay is controlled by the coolant fan switch, the A/C high pressure switch and the ECM. When one of these components grounds the coil of the coolant fan relay, the contacts close and the fan comes on.

SYSTEM OPERATION

1. If equipped with A/C, allow engine to operate at low idle, then move A/C selector lever to NORM. Coolant fan should operate.
2. With engine coolant at normal operating temperature, operate engine at fast idle for several minutes. Coolant fan should begin operation before coolant temperature gauge needle reaches H.
3. If equipped with heavy duty coolant fans, fans will operate for short periods after engine is turned off and coolant is hot.

TROUBLESHOOTING

4-151 VIN R

1. Check applicable A/C or heater fuse using a suitable fuse tester.
2. If coolant fan does not operate when engine is hot, but does operate when A/C is "On," proceed as follows:
   a. Remove connector from coolant fan switch, then ground dark green/white wire. If coolant fan operates, replace coolant fan switch. If coolant fan does not operate, check dark green/white wire for open, then repair as necessary and proceed to step 3.
3. If coolant fan does not operate at all, proceed as follows:
   a. Disconnect coolant fan relay, then connect a suitable test lamp between terminals C and ground. If test lamp does not light, check brown/white wire for open and repair as necessary. If test lamp lights, proceed to step b.
   b. Move test lamp lead from terminal C to terminal E. If test lamp does not light, check red wire and fusible link C for open and repair as necessary. If test lamp lights, proceed to step c.
   c. Disconnect dark green white wire from coolant fan switch, then jumper terminal of this wire to ground. With ignition switch "On," connect a suitable test lamp between terminals C and B of coolant fan relay. If test lamp lights, proceed to step d. If test lamp does not light, check dark green/white wire for open and repair as necessary.
   d. Disconnect coolant fan relay, then connect a fused jumper between terminals E and A of connector. If test lamp does not light, check black wire for open and repair as necessary. If test lamp lights, replace coolant fan.
4. If coolant fan does not operate with A/C and ignition switch "On," and A/C operation is satisfactory, proceed as follows:
   a. Remove A/C coolant fan relay, then connect a suitable test lamp between terminals A and C of connector. Ground diagnostic terminal. If test lamp does not light, check light blue/black wire for open and repair as necessary. If wires are satisfactory, an ECM malfunction is indicated. If test lamp lights, proceed to step b.
   b. Jumper terminal B to terminal D using a suitable fused jumper. If coolant fan operates, replace A/C coolant fan relay. If coolant fan does not operate, check dark green/white wire and black wire for open and repair as necessary.
5. If coolant fan operates continuously with ignition switch "On" the A/C "Off" but operating satisfactorily, proceed as follows:
   a. Disconnect coolant fan switch. If coolant fan stops, replace switch. If coolant fan operation does not stop, check wire 335 for short to ground, then proceed to step b.
   b. Disconnect A/C coolant fan relay. If coolant fan stops, replace A/C coolant fan relay. If coolant fan does not stop, check black/red wire for short to battery voltage.
6. If coolant fan operates continuously with ignition switch "Off," proceed as follows:
   a. Disconnect coolant fan relay. If coolant fan stops, replace relay. If coolant fan does not stop, check black red wire for short to battery voltage.

V6 VIN X

1. Check applicable A/C or heater fuse, using a suitable fuse tester.
2. If coolant fan does not operate when engine is warm or when A/C is "On," proceed as follows:
   a. Disconnect coolant fan switch connector, then jumper connector to ground, using a suitable fused jumper. Turn ignition switch "On." If coolant fan operates, replace coolant fan switch. If coolant fan does not operate, check dark green/white wire for open, then repair as necessary and proceed to step 4.
3. If coolant fan does not operate when A/C is on but operates when engine is warm and A/C compressor is satisfactory, proceed as follows:
   a. Disconnect A/C high pressure switch. Connect a suitable test lamp between battery voltage and connector black wire. If test lamp lights, proceed to step b. If test lamp does not operate, check black wire for open and repair as necessary.
   b. Ground dark green/white wire at A/C high pressure switch, then turn ignition switch "On." If coolant fan operates, replace A/C high

pressure switch. If coolant fan does not operate, check dark green/white wire for open, then repair as necessary and proceed to step 4.

4. If coolant fan does not operate at all, proceed as follows:
   a. Remove connector from coolant fan relay, then connect a suitable test lamp between terminal C and ground. Turn ignition switch "On." If test lamp does not light, check brown/white wire for open and repair as necessary. If test lamp lights, proceed to step b.
   b. With coolant temperature switch connector jumped to ground, connect a test lamp from terminal C to terminal B of the coolant relay connector. If test lamp lights, proceed to step c. If test lamp does not light, check dark green/white wire for open and repair as necessary.
   c. Move test lamp from terminal C to terminal D of coolant fan relay connector. If test lamp does not light, check red wire and fusible link C for open and repair as necessary. If test lamp lights, proceed to step d.
   d. Connect a fused jumper between terminals D and A of coolant fan relay connector. If coolant fan operates, replace coolant fan relay. If coolant fan does not operate, proceed to step e.
   e. With fused jumper in place, remove coolant fan connector, then connect a suitable test lamp from terminal B to ground. If test lamp does not light, check black/red wire for open and repair as necessary. If test lamp lights, proceed to step f.
   f. Move test lamp ground lead to terminal A of coolant fan connector. If test lamp does not light, check black wire for open and repair as necessary. If test lamp lights, replace coolant fan.
5. If coolant fan operates continuously with ignition switch "On," proceed as follows:
   a. Disconnect A/C high pressure switch, if equipped. If coolant fan stops, replace A/C high pressure switch. If coolant fan does not stop, or if vehicle is not equipped with A/C, proceed to step b.
   b. Remove coolant temperature switch connector, then turn ignition switch "On." If coolant fan stops, replace coolant temperature switch. If coolant fan operates, replace coolant fan relay.
6. If coolant fan operates continuously with ignition switch "Off," proceed as follows:
   a. Remove coolant fan relay connector. If coolant fan stops, replace relay. If coolant fan continues, check black/red wire for short to battery voltage.

V6 VIN W

1. Check applicable A/C or heater fuse, using a suitable fuse tester.
2. If coolant fan does not operate, proceed as follows:
   a. Turn ignition switch "On," then ground diagnostic terminal B at ALCL. If coolant fan operates, a malfunction is indicated. If coolant fan does not operate, proceed to step b.
   b. Remove connector from coolant fan switch and ground dark green/white wire. If coolant fan operates, an ECM malfunction is indicated. If coolant fan does not operate, proceed to step c.
   c. Remove connector from coolant fan relay, then connect a suitable test lamp between terminal C of connector and ground and turn ignition switch "On." If test lamp does not light, check brown wire for open and repair as necessary. If test lamp lights, proceed to step d.
   d. Move test lamp from terminal C to terminal E of coolant fan relay connector. If test lamp does not light, check red wire and fusible link F for open and repair as necessary. If test lamp lights, proceed to step e.
   e. With coolant fan switch grounded, connect test lamp from terminal C to terminal B of coolant fan relay. If test lamp lights, proceed to step f. If test lamp does not light, check dark green/white wire for open and repair as necessary.
   f. Connect a fused jumper between terminals E and A of the coolant fan relay connector. If coolant fan operates, replace coolant fan relay. If coolant fan does not operate, proceed to step g.
   g. With fused jumper in place, remove coolant fan connector, then connect a suitable test lamp between terminal B and ground. If test lamp does not light, check yellow wire for open and repair as necessary. If test lamp lights, proceed to step h.
   h. Move test lamp ground lead to terminal A of coolant fan connector. If test lamp does not light, check black wire for open and repair as necessary. If test lamp lights, replace coolant fan.
3. If coolant fan operates continuously with ignition switch "On," proceed as follows:
   a. Check for diagnostic codes 14 or 15. If code is present, an ECM malfunction is indicated. If no code is present, proceed to step b.
   b. Check dark green/white wire short to ground. If short is present, repair as necessary. If wire is satisfactory, proceed to step c.
   c. Remove connector from coolant fan switch, then turn ignition switch "On." If coolant fan operates, replace coolant fan relay. If coolant fan does not operate, replace coolant fan switch.
4. If coolant fan operates continuously with ignition switch "Off," proceed as follows:
   a. Remove connector from coolant fan relay. If coolant fan stops, check brown wire for short to battery voltage. If wire is satisfactory, replace coolant fan. If coolant fan operates, check yellow wire for short to battery voltage and repair as necessary.

V6 VIN B Less A/C

1. Check applicable A/C or heater fuse, using a suitable fuse tester.
2. If coolant fan does not operate, proceed as follows:
   a. Turn ignition switch "On," then ground diagnostic terminal B at ALCL. If coolant fan operates, an ECM malfunction is indicated. If coolant fan does not operate and dark green wires are satisfactory, proceed to step b.
   b. Remove connector from coolant fan relay, then connect a suitable test lamp between terminal 5 and ground and turn ignition switch "On." If test lamp does not light, check brown wire for open and repair as necessary. If test lamp lights, proceed to step c.
   c. Move test lamp from terminal 5 to terminal 1 of coolant fan relay connector. If test lamp does not light, check red wire and fusible link C for open and repair as necessary. If test lamp lights, proceed to step d.
   d. Remove connector from coolant fan switch and ground dark green/yellow wire. If coolant fan operates, proceed to step e. If coolant fan does not operate, check dark green yellow wire for open and repair as necessary.
   e. Connect a fused jumper between terminals 1 and 4 of coolant fan relay connector. If coolant fan operates, replace coolant fan relay. If coolant fan does not operate, proceed to step f.
   f. With fused jumper in place, remove coolant fan connector, then connect a suitable test lamp between terminal B and ground. If test lamp does not light, check black/red wires for open and repair as necessary. If test lamp lights, proceed to step g.
   g. Move test lamp ground lead to terminal A of coolant fan connector. If test lamp does not light, check black wire for open and repair as necessary. If test lamp lights, replace coolant fan.
3. If coolant fan operates continuously with ignition switch "On," and engine is cool, allow sufficient time for time delay relay to de-energize, then proceed as follows:
   a. Check for diagnostic codes 14 or 15. If codes are present, an ECM malfunction is indicated. If codes are not present, proceed to step b.
   b. Remove connector from coolant fan switch. If coolant fan stops, replace coolant fan switch. If coolant fan does not stop, check circuits 535 and 335 for grounds, then proceed to step c.
   c. Remove connector from the coolant fan relay. If coolant fan stops, replace relay. If coolant fan does not stop, proceed to step d.
   d. Remove connector from coolant fan delay relay. If coolant fan stops, replace delay relay, allowing sufficient time to de-energize before removing.
4. If coolant fan does not operate for delay period after engine is turned "Off"

and coolant is hot, proceed as follows:
a. Disconnect coolant fan delay relay, then connect a suitable test lamp between terminals C of C2 connector and ground with ignition switch "On." If test lamp does not light, check pink/black and dark green/white wires for open and repair as necessary. If test lamp lights, proceed to step b.
b. Move lead of test lamp from terminal C of C2 to terminal A of C2. If test lamp does not light, check red wire (440) and fusible link G for open and repair as necessary. If test lamp lights, proceed to step c.
c. Move lead of test lamp from terminal A of C2 to terminal to A of C1. If test lamp does not light, check red wire (2) for open and repair as necessary. If test lamp lights, proceed to step d.
d. Move test lamp lead from ground to terminal B of C2. If test lamp does not light, check black/white wire for open and repair as necessary. If test lamp lights, proceed to step e.
e. Move test lamp lead from terminal B of C2 to terminal B of C1. Remove, then ground connector for coolant fan switch. If test lamp does not light, check dark green/yellow wire for open and repair as necessary. If test lamp lights, replace coolant fan delay relay.

V6 VIN B With A/C L/Heavy Duty Cooling System

1. Check applicable A/C or heater fuse, using a suitable fuse tester.
2. If coolant fan does not operate, proceed as follows:
a. Turn ignition switch "On," then ground diagnostic terminal B at ALCL. If coolant fan operates, an ECM malfunction is indicated. If coolant fan does not operate and dark green wires are satisfactory, proceed to step b.
b. Remove connector from coolant fan relay, then connect a suitable test lamp between terminal 5 and ground and turn ignition switch "On." If test lamp does not light, check brown wire for open and repair as necessary. If test lamp lights, proceed to step c.
c. Move test lamp from terminal 5 to terminal 1 of coolant fan relay connector. If test lamp does not light, check red wire and fusible link C for open and repair as necessary. If test lamp lights, proceed to step d.
d. Remove connector from coolant fan switch, then ground terminal. Connect a suitable test lamp from terminal 5 to terminal 2. If test lamp lights, proceed to step e. If test lamp does not light, check circuits 335 and 535 for opens, check coolant fan diode and repair as necessary.
e. Connect a suitable fused jumper between terminals 1 and 4 of coolant fan relay connector. If coolant fan operates, replace relay. If coolant fan does not operate, proceed to step f.
f. With fused jumper in place, remove coolant fan connector, then connect a suitable test lamp between terminal B and ground. If test lamp does not light, check black/red wires for open and repair as necessary. If test lamp lights, proceed to step g.
g. Move test lamp ground lead to terminal A of coolant fan connector. If test lamp does not light, check black wire for open and repair as necessary. If test lamp lights, replace coolant fan.
3. If coolant fan operates continuously with ignition switch "On," the A/C operating satisfactorily and "Off" and coolant is cool, proceed as follows:
a. Check for diagnostic codes 14 and 15. If codes are present, an ECM malfunction is indicated. If no codes are present, proceed to step b.
b. Check dark green and dark green/yellow wires for short to ground. If wires are shorted, repair as necessary. If wires are satisfactory, proceed to step c.
c. Remove A/C high pressure switch connector, then turn ignition switch "On." If coolant fan stops, replace A/C high pressure switch. If coolant fan does not stop, proceed to step d.
d. Remove connector from coolant fan switch. If coolant fan stops, replace coolant fan switch. If coolant fan does not stop, proceed to step 4.
4. If coolant fan continues to operate after minimum delay shut-off period, proceed as follows:
a. Remove connector C1 from coolant fan delay relay. If coolant fan stops, replace coolant fan delay relay, allowing sufficient time for delay relay to de-energize. If coolant fan does not stop, proceed to step b.
b. Remove coolant fan relay. If coolant fan stops, replace coolant fan relay. If coolant fan does not stop, check terminal B wiring for shorts and repair as necessary.
5. If coolant fan does not operate for delay period after engine is turned "Off" with coolant hot, proceed as follows:
a. Disconnect coolant fan delay relay, then connect a suitable test lamp between terminal C of connector C2 and ground with ignition switch "On." If test lamp does not light, check pink/black and dark green/white wires for open and repair as necessary. If test lamp lights, proceed to step b.
b. Move test lamp lead from terminal C of C2 to A of C2. If test lamp does not light, check red wire and fusible link G for open and repair as necessary. If test lamp lights, proceed to step c.
c. Move test lamp lead from A of C2 to A of C1. If test lamp does not light, check red wire for open and repair as necessary. If test lamp lights, proceed to step d.
d. Move test lamp lead from ground to terminal B of C2. If test lamp does not light, check black/white wire for open and repair as necessary. If test lamp lights, proceed to step e.
e. Move test lamp lead from terminal B of C2 to terminal B of C1. Remove connector from coolant fan switch and jumper to ground. If test lamp does not light, check dark green/yellow wire for open and repair as necessary. If test lamp lights, replace coolant fan delay relay.

V6 VIN B With A/C & Heavy Duty Cooling System

1. Check applicable A/C or heater fuse, using a suitable fuse tester.
2. If coolant fan does not operate, proceed as follows:
a. Turn ignition switch "On," then ground diagnostic terminal B at ALCL. If coolant fan operates, an ECM malfunction is indicated. If coolant fan does not operate and dark green wires are satisfactory, proceed to step b.
b. Remove connector from puller coolant fan relay, then connect a suitable test lamp between terminal 5 and ground and turn ignition switch "On." If test lamp does not light, check brown wire for open and repair as necessary. If test lamp lights, proceed to step c.
c. Move test lamp from terminal 5 to terminal 1 of puller coolant fan relay connector. If test lamp does not light, check red wire and fusible link C for open and repair as necessary. If test lamp lights, proceed to step d.
d. Remove connector from A/C high pressure switch, then jumper dark green wire to ground. Connect a suitable test lamp from terminal 5 to terminal 2 of puller coolant fan relay connector. If test lamp lights, proceed to step e. If test lamp does not light, check dark green wire for open and repair as necessary.
e. Connect a fused jumper between terminals 1 and 4 of puller coolant fan relay connector. If puller fan operates, replace puller coolant fan relay. If puller fan does not operate, proceed to step f.
f. With fused jumper in place, remove puller coolant fan connector, then connect test lamp between terminal B and ground. If test lamp does not light, check brown wire for open and repair as necessary. If test lamp lights, proceed to step g.
g. Move test lamp lead to terminal A of puller coolant fan connector. If test lamp does not light, check black wire for open and repair as necessary. If test lamp lights, replace puller coolant fan.
3. If pusher coolant fan does not operate, proceed as follows:
a. Remove connector from pusher coolant fan relay, then connect a suitable test lamp between terminal 5 and ground and turn ignition switch "On." If test lamp does not light, check brown wire for open and repair as necessary. If test lamp lights, proceed to step b.

b. Move test lamp from terminal 5 to terminal 1 of pusher coolant fan relay connector. If test lamp does not light, check red wire and fusible link C for open and repair as necessary. If test lamp lights, proceed to step c.

c. Remove connector from A/C high pressure switch, then jumper dark green/yellow wire to ground. Connect a suitable test lamp from terminal 5 to terminal 2 of pusher coolant fan relay connector. If test lamp lights, proceed to step d. If test lamp does not light, check dark green/yellow wire for open and repair as necessary.

d. Connect a fused jumper between between terminals 1 and 4 of pusher coolant fan relay connector. If pusher fan operates, replace pusher coolant fan relay. If pusher fan does not operate, proceed to step e.

e. With fused jumper in place, remove pusher coolant fan connector, then connect test lamp between terminal B and ground. If test lamp does not light, check brown wire for open and repair as necessary. If test lamp lights, proceed to step f.

f. Move test lamp lead to terminal A of pusher coolant fan connector. If test lamp does not light, check black wire for open and repair as necessary. If test lamp lights, replace pusher coolant fan.

4. If pusher and puller coolant fans operate continuously with ignition switch "On," the A/C operating satisfactorily and "Off" and coolant is cool, proceed as follows:
   a. Disconnect coolant fan switch. If coolant fans stop, replace coolant fan switch. If coolant fan does not stop, proceed to step b.
   b. Disconnect A/C high pressure switch. If coolant fans stop, replace A/C high pressure switch. If coolant fans operate, check circuits 335 and 535 for grounds and repair as necessary.
5. If puller coolant fan operates continuously with ignition switch "On," the A/C operating satisfactorily and "Off" and coolant is cool, proceed as follows:
   a. Check for diagnostic codes 14 and 15. If codes are present, an ECM malfunction is indicated. If no codes are present, proceed to step b.
   b. Remove A/C high pressure switch connector, then turn ignition switch "On." If puller coolant fan stops, replace A/C high pressure switch. If coolant fan does not stop, check dark green and dark green/yellow wires for shorts to ground and repair as necessary.
6. If pusher coolant fan operates continuously with ignition switch "On," the A/C operating satisfactorily and "Off" and coolant is cool, proceed as follows:
   a. Remove connector from A/C high pressure switch. If pusher coolant fan stops, replace A/C high pressure switch. If coolant fan does not stop, check dark green/yellow wire for short to ground and repair as necessary.
7. If puller fan continues to operate after minimum delay shut-off period with ignition "Off," proceed as follows:
   a. Remove connector C1 from coolant fan delay relay. If puller coolant fan stops, replace coolant fan delay relay. If puller coolant fan does not stop, proceed to step b.
   b. Remove puller coolant fan relay. If puller coolant fan stops, replace puller coolant fan relay. If puller coolant fan does not stop, check wires at terminal B of puller coolant fan for short to battery voltage and repair as necessary.
8. If pusher fan continues to operate with ignition "Off," remove pusher coolant fan relay. If pusher coolant fan stops, replace pusher coolant fan relay.
9. If puller coolant fan does not operate for delay period after engine is turned "Off" and coolant is hot, proceed as follows:
   a. Disconnect coolant fan delay relay, then connect a suitable test lamp between terminals C of C2 and ground with ignition switch "On." If test lamp does not light, check pink/black and dark green/white wire for opens and repair as necessary. If test lamp lights, proceed to step b.
   b. Move test lamp lead from terminal C to terminal A. If test lamp does not light, check red wire and fusible link G for open and repair as necessary. If test lamp lights, proceed to step c.
   c. Move test lamp lead from A of C2 to A of C1. If test lamp does not light, check red wire for open and repair as necessary. If test lamp lights, proceed to step d.
   d. Move test lamp lead from ground to terminal B of C2. If test lamp does not light, check black/white wire for open and repair as necessary. If test lamp lights, proceed to step e.
   e. Move test lamp lead from terminal B of C1, then ground coolant fan switch connector. If test lamp does not light, check dark green/yellow wire for open and repair as necessary. If test lamp lights, replace coolant fan delay relay.

COOLING FAN, REPLACE

1. Disconnect battery ground cable.
2. Disconnect wiring from fan motor and frame.
3. Remove fan assembly from radiator support.
4. Reverse procedure to install.

1986–87 PONTIAC 6000

SYSTEM DESCRIPTION

The coolant fan is electrically operated and is activated when engine temperature is high enough to require cooling. The coolant fan is controlled by a coolant fan relay which is grounded through the coolant temperature switch that closes when coolant temperature is above 230 degrees F. The relay is energized and its contacts close to supply battery voltage to the coolant fan.

On 4 cylinder models, the coolant fan is controlled by the Coolant Temperature Switch, the Electronic Control Module (ECM), the A/C Function Selector, the A/C Coolant Fan Relay and the A/C Low Pressure Cut-Out Switch. Any of these switch combinations will complete the circuit to ground through the Coolant Fan Relay coil.

On V6 models VIN X models, the coolant fan is operated by the Coolant Temperature switch, the Electronic Control Module (ECM) and the A/C High Pressure Switch. The A/C High Pressure Switch closes when the compressor is operating and an adequate refrigerant charge is available.

On V6 VIN W models, the coolant fan is controlled by the Coolant Temperature Switch and the ECM. The ECM will only be activated when the coolant fan senses high engine coolant temperature or high A/C pressure. The coolant temperature switch or ECM can provide a ground path for the coolant fan relay and energize it. When energized, the coolant fan relay contacts close and battery voltage is applied to the coolant fan.

SYSTEM CHECK

1. With engine at normal operating temperature, operate at fast idle for several minutes. Coolant fan should operate on or before temperature indicator lights or gauge needle indicates H.
2. If equipped with A/C, allow engine to operate at low idle, then move A/C function selector to NORM. Coolant fan should operate.

TROUBLESHOOTING

4 Cylinder Models With A/C

1. Check applicable A/C or heater fuse, using a suitable fuse tester.
2. If coolant fan does not operate, proceed as follows:
   a. Disconnect coolant fan relay, then connect a suitable test lamp between terminal C of connector and ground. If test lamp does not light, check brown/white wire for open and repair as necessary. If test lamp lights, proceed to step b.
   b. Move test lamp lead from terminal C to terminal E. If test lamp does not light, check red wire and fusible link C for open and repair as necessary. If test lamp lights, proceed to step c.
   c. Reconnect coolant fan relay, then disconnect dark green/white wire from coolant temperature switch. Jumper terminal on this wire to ground then turn ignition switch "On." If coolant fan operates, check dark green/white wires for open and repair as necessary. If wires are satisfactory, and coolant fan does not operate, proceed to step d.

d. Disconnect coolant fan relay, then connect a fused jumper between terminals E and A of connector. If coolant fan operates, replace coolant fan relay. If coolant fan does not operate, proceed to step e.
e. With fused jumper in place, remove coolant fan connector, then connect a suitable test lamp between black/red wire terminal and ground. If test lamp does not light, check black/red wire for open and repair as necessary. If test lamp lights, proceed to step f.
f. Move test lamp lead to black wire terminal of coolant fan connector. If test lamp does not light, check black wire for open and repair as necessary. If test lamp lights, replace coolant fan.

3. If coolant fan does not operate with the A/C and ignition switch "On" and the A/C is operating satisfactorily, proceed as follows:
   a. Turn ignition switch' 'On," then ground diagnostic terminal B at ALCL. If coolant fan operates, an ECM malfunction is indicated. If coolant fan does not operate proceed to step b.
   b. Remove A/C coolant fan relay, then connect a suitable test lamp between terminals A and C. If test lamp does not light, check light blue/black wires for open and repair as necessary. If wires are satisfactory, an ECM malfunction is indicated. If test lamp lights, proceed to step c.
   c. Jumper terminal B to terminal D of connector using a suitable fused jumper. If coolant fan operates, replace A/C coolant fan relay. If coolant fan does not operate, check dark green/white wire and black wire for opens and repair as necessary.
4. If coolant fan operates continuously with ignition "On" and A/C "Off" but functioning properly, proceed as follows:
   a. Disconnect the coolant temperature switch. If coolant fan stops, replace coolant temperature switch. If coolant fan does not stop, proceed to step b.
   b. Disconnect A/C coolant fan relay. If coolant fan stops, replace A/C coolant fan relay. If coolant fan does not stop, check dark green/white wires for short and repair as necessary. If wires are satisfactory, proceed to step c.
   c. Disconnect coolant fan relay. If coolant fan stops, replace coolant fan relay. If coolant fan does not stop, check black/red wire for short to battery voltage.
5. If coolant fan operates continuously with ignition switch "Off," disconnect coolant fan relay. If coolant fan stops, check brown/white wire for short to battery voltage and repair as necessary. If wires are satisfactory, replace coolant fan relay. If coolant fan does not stop, check black red wire for short to battery voltage.

4 Cylinder (VIN R) Less A/C & V6 (VIN X)

1. If coolant fan does not operate, proceed as follows:
   a. Disconnect and ground coolant temperature switch connector, using a suitable jumper, then turn ignition switch "On." If coolant fan operates, replace coolant temperature switch. If coolant fan does not operate, proceed to step b. relay.
   b. Remove coolant fan relay connector, then connect a suitable test lamp between terminal C and ground and turn ignition switch "On." If test lamp does not light, check brown/white wire for open and repair as necessary. If test lamp lights, proceed to step c.
   c. Move test lamp lead from terminal C to terminal E on 4 cylinder models or terminal D on V6 models. if test lamp does not light, check red wire and fusible link C and repair as necessary. If test lamp lights, proceed to step d.
   d. Connect a fused jumper between terminals E on 4 cylinder models or terminal D on V6 models and terminal A of coolant fan relay connector. If coolant fan operates, replace coolant fan relay. If coolant fan does not operate, proceed to step e.
   e. With fused jumper in place, remove coolant fan connector, then connect a suitable test lamp between black/red wire terminal and ground. If test lamp does not light, check black/red wire for open and repair as necessary. If test lamp lights, proceed to step f.
   f. Move test lamp ground lead to black wire terminal of coolant fan connector. If test lamp does not light, check black wire for open and repair as necessary. If test lamp lights, replace coolant fan.
2. If coolant fan operates continuously with ignition switch "On," proceed as follows:
   a. Check dark green/white wire for short to ground and repair as necessary. If wires are satisfactory, proceed to step b, on 4 and 6 cylinder models less A/C or step c on V6 with A/C.
   b. Remove connector from coolant temperature switch, then turn ignition switch "On." If coolant fan operates, replace coolant fan relay. If coolant fan does not operate, replace coolant fan temperature switch.
   c. Disconnect A/C high pressure switch. If coolant fan stops, replace A/C high pressure switch. If coolant fan does not stop, replace coolant fan relay.
3. If coolant fan operates continuously with ignition switch "Off," proceed as follows:
   a. Check brown/white wire for short to battery voltage and repair as necessary. If wires are satisfactory, proceed to step b.
   b. Remove connector from coolant fan relay. If coolant fan stops, replace relay. If coolant fan does not stop, check black/red wire for short to battery voltage.

V6 VIN W

1. If coolant fan does not operate, proceed as follows:
   a. Turn ignition switch "On," then ground diagnostic terminal B at ALCL. If coolant fan operates, an ECM malfunction is indicated. If coolant fan does not operate and dark green wires are satisfactory, proceed to step b.
   b. Remove connector from coolant fan relay, then connect a suitable test lamp between terminal C and ground and turn ignition switch "On." If test lamp does not light, check brown/white wire for open and repair as necessary. If test lamp lights, proceed to step c.
   c. Move test lamp from terminal C to terminal E of coolant fan relay connector. If test lamp does not light, check red wire and fusible link A for open and repair as necessary. If test lamp lights, proceed to step d.
   d. Connect a fused jumper between terminals E and A. If test lamp operates, replace coolant fan relay. If coolant fan does not operate, proceed to step e.
   e. With fused jumper in place, remove coolant fan connector, then connect a suitable test lamp between yellow wire terminal and ground. If test lamp does not light, check yellow wire for open and repair as necessary. If test lamp lights, proceed to step f.
   f. Move test lamp ground lead to black wire terminal. If test lamp does not light, check black wire for open and repair as necessary. If test lamp lights, replace coolant fan.
2. If coolant fan operates continuously with ignition switch "On," proceed as follows:
   a. Check for diagnostic codes 14 or 15. If codes are present, an ECM malfunction is indicated. If no codes are present, proceed to step b.
   b. Check dark green and dark green/white wires for short to ground. If wires are shorted, repair as necessary. If wires are satisfactory, proceed to step c.
   c. Remove connector from coolant temperature switch, then turn ignition switch "On." If coolant fan operates, replace coolant fan relay. If coolant fan does not operate, replace coolant temperature switch.
3. If coolant fan operates continuously with ignition switch "Off," remove coolant fan relay connector. If coolant fan stops, check brown/white wire for short to battery voltage. If wire is satisfactory, replace coolant fan relay. If coolant fan operates, check yellow wire for short to battery voltage and repair as necessary.

COOLANT FAN, REPLACE

1. Disconnect battery ground cable.
2. Disconnect wiring from fan motor and frame.
3. Remove fan assembly from radiator support.
4. Reverse procedure to install.

1986–87 OLDSMOBILE CALAIS & PONTIAC GRAND AM

SYSTEM DESCRIPTION

On 4 Cylinder models, the coolant fan is controlled by the Coolant Fan Relay. The Coolant Fan Temperature Switch closes when coolant temperature is high, providing a path to ground through the relay coil. The relay contacts close to apply battery voltage to the fan.

On models with A/C, the coolant fan also operates when the compressor is "On." The A/C Coolant Fan Relay is controlled by the Electronic Control Module (ECM). The ECM coil is supplied battery voltage through the A/C Mode Selector and the A/C Low Pressure Switch. The circuit is grounded through the ECM to the A/C coolant fan relay when the vehicle is traveling less than 35 mph. Its contacts close to ground the coolant fan relay coil. The fan is energized and its contacts apply battery voltage to the fan.

On V6 models, a two speed heavy duty cooling fan is used which is controlled by cooling fan relays.

During low speed operation, the low speed relay coil is grounded through the ECM or the low speed contacts of the A/C high pressure switch. The ECM grounds the coil when vehicle speed is less than 45 mph and engine coolant temperature exceeds 208 degrees F. The low speed contacts ground the coil of the coolant fan relay when there is high compressor pressure. With the low speed relay coil grounded, the associated contacts close and voltage is applied through the coolant fan resistor to the heavy duty coolant fan. The resistor drops part of the battery voltage and the fan operates at low speed.

During high speed operation, the high speed relay coil is grounded through the high speed contacts in the A/C high pressure switch or the coolant fan temperature switch. The pressure switch high speed contacts close at refrigerant pressure higher than the pressure that closed the low speed contacts. The coolant fan temperature switch closes when coolant temperature reaches 228 degrees F.

SYSTEM CHECK

4 Cylinder Models

1. On models with A/C, start engine, then place A/C control selector in NORM position. Coolant fan should operate.
2. Return A/C control selector to OFF before engine warning lamp lights. Coolant fan should go "Off."
3. On all models, operate engine at fast idle for approximately ten minutes. Coolant fan should turn on before coolant temperature indicator comes on or gauge needle reaches H.

V6 Models

1. On models with A/C, start engine, then place A/C control selector in NORM position. Coolant fan should operate at low speed after compressor has operated for a short period of time. Coolant fan should switch to high speed operation if refrigerant pressure rises above 300 psi.
2. Return A/C control selector to OFF before engine warning lamp lights. Coolant fan should go "Off."
3. On all models, operate engine at fast idle for approximately ten minutes. Coolant fan should operate at low speed as engine begins to warm up. Coolant fan should switch to high speed operation before coolant temperature indicator comes on or gauge needle reaches H.

TROUBLESHOOTING

4 Cylinder Models

1. Check applicable A/C or heater fuse, using a suitable fuse tester. Check fusible link F on Calais models.
2. If coolant fan does not operate at all, proceed as follows:
   a. Remove coolant fan temperature switch, then connect a suitable jumper between dark green/white wire and ground and turn ignition switch "On." If coolant fan does not operate, proceed to step b. If coolant fan operates and connections are satisfactory, replace coolant fan temperature switch.
   b. With jumper in place, connect a suitable test lamp between red wire E and ground. Test lamp should light. Red wire E and dark green/white wire. Test lamp should light. Brown/white wire to dark green/white wire. Test lamp should light. If lamp lights in all cases, proceed to step c. If lamp does not light from E to ground, check fusible link F and red wire for open and repair as necessary. If lamp does not light from E to B, check dark green/white wire for open and repair as necessary. If lamp does not light from C to B, check brown/white wire, brown wire and connector C100 and repair as necessary.
   c. Reconnect coolant fan temperature switch.
   d. Move jumper between terminals E and A of coolant fan relay connector. If coolant fan operates, replace coolant fan relay. If coolant fan does not operate, proceed to step e.
   e. With ignition switch "Off" and jumper installed, connect a suitable test lamp between black/red (B) wire and ground. Test lamp should light. Connect test lamp between black/red (B) wire and black (A) wire. Test lamp should light. If test lamp lights in both checks, replace coolant fan motor. If lamp does not light from B to ground, check black/red wire for open and repair as necessary. If lamp does not light from B to A, check black wire for open and repair as necessary.
   f. Reconnect coolant fan relay and coolant fan connectors.
3. If coolant fan does not operate when A/C is selected, but operates when engine is hot, proceed as follows:
   a. Start and idle engine, position A/C selector lever in NORM and if necessary, provide auxiliary floor fan, then connect test lamp between light blue/black wire (A) and ground. Test lamp should light. Connect test lamp between light blue/black wire (A) and light blue/black wire (C). Test lamp should light. Connect test lamp between light blue/black wire (A) and black wire (D). Test lamp should light. If all checks are satisfactory, proceed to step b. If test lamp does not light from A to ground, check light blue/black wire for open and repair as necessary. If lamp does not light from A to C, check light blue/black wire for open, repair as necessary, then check ECM for malfunction. If test lamp does not light from A to D, check black wire for open and repair as necessary.
   b. Connect a fused jumper between terminals B and D of A/C coolant fan relay connector. If coolant fan operates, check connector or replace coolant fan relay. If coolant fan does not operate, check dark green/white wire at S130.
   c. Reconnect A/C coolant fan relay.
4. If coolant fan operates at all times with ignition "On" with engine cool and A/C "Off," if equipped, proceed as follows:
   a. Remove coolant fan temperature switch connector (dark green/white wire). If coolant fan stops, replace coolant fan temperature switch. If coolant fan does not stop, proceed to step b.
   b. Remove coolant fan relay connector, then connect a suitable test lamp between terminal C (brown/white) to terminal B (dark green/white). If test lamp lights, check terminal B for ground. If test lamp does not light, replace coolant fan relay.

6 Cylinder Models

1. If coolant fan does not operate at all, proceed as follows:
   a. Remove high speed coolant fan relay connector, then with ignition switch "Off," connect a suitable test lamp between red wire and ground. If test lamp lights, proceed to step b. If test lamp does not light, check red wire for open and repair as necessary.
   b. With ignition "Off," connect fused jumper between terminals 1 (red) and 4 (black/pink) of high speed coolant fan relay connector (disconnected). Connect a suitable

test lamp between black/pink wire and ground. Test lamp should light. Connect test lamp leads between black/pink wire and black wire. Test lamp should light. If test lamp lights in both checks, proceed to step c. If test lamp does not light between black/pink and ground, check black/pink wire for open and repair as necessary. If test lamp does not light between black/pink wire and black wire, check black wire for open and repair as necessary.

c. Reconnect high speed coolant relay and coolant fan.

2. If coolant fan does not operate at low speed, proceed as follows:
   a. Remove low speed coolant fan relay connector, then with ignition switch "On" and ECM ALCL diagnostic terminal grounded, connect a test lamp between brown/white wire and ground. Test lamp should light. Connect test lamp between brown/white wire and dark green wire. Test lamp should light. Connect test lamp between red wire and dark green wire. Test lamp should light. If test lamp lights in all checks, proceed to step b. If test lamp does not light between brown/white wire and ground, check brown/white wire for open and repair as necessary. If test lamp does not light between brown/white wire and dark green wire, check dark green wire for open and repair as necessary. If test lamp does not light between red wire and dark green wire, check red wire for open and repair as necessary.
   b. Connect a fused jumper between terminals 1 (red) and terminal 4 (black/red) of low speed coolant fan relay connector. If coolant fan does not operate, proceed to step c. If coolant fan operates, replace low speed coolant fan relay.
   c. With jumper in place, remove connector from coolant fan resistor. Connect a fused jumper between black/pink and black/red wires of coolant fan resistor connector. If coolant fan does not operate, check black/red wire and pink/black wire. If coolant fan operates, replace coolant fan resistor.
   d. Remove jumper, then reconnect relay and resistor. If coolant fan does not operate at low speed with A/C off (or vehicle is not equipped), an ECM malfunction is indicated.
   e. If coolant fan operates at low speed when ALCL is grounded, but not when engine is cool, ALCL is not grounded and A/C is on (if equipped), connect a suitable test lamp between battery voltage and terminal C (black/white) of A/C high pressure switch connector (disconnected). If test lamp lights, proceed to step f. If test lamp does not light, check black/white wire for open and repair as necessary.
   f. Connect a jumper between terminals B (dark green) and C (black/white) of A/C high pressure switch with ignition switch "On." If coolant fan operates, check refrigerant system for proper operating pressures. If coolant fan does not operate, check dark green wire from A/C high pressure switch to S140 and repair as necessary.
3. If coolant fan does not operate at high speed, proceed as follows:
   a. Remove coolant fan temperature switch connector, then connect light green/black wire to ground, using a suitable jumper, then with ignition switch "On," connect test lamp between brown/white wire and ground. Test lamp should light. Connect test lamp between brown/white wire and light green/black wire. Test lamp should light. Connect test lamp between red wire and light green/black wire. Test lamp should light. If lamp lights in all checks, proceed to step b. If lamp does not light between brown/white wire and ground, check white wire, check brown white wire and repair as necessary. If lamp does not light between brown/white wire and light green/black wire, check light green/black wire and repair as necessary, then proceed to step b or c. If lamp does not light between red wire and light green/black wire, check red wire and repair as necessary.
   b. If coolant fan does not operate at high speed when A/C is off (or vehicle is not equipped), turn ignition switch "On," and jumper light green/black wire of coolant fan temperature switch connector to ground. Connect a suitable test lamp between battery voltage and light green/black wire. Test lamp should light. If lamp lights, replace coolant temperature switch. If test lamp does not light, check light green/black wire for open and repair as necessary.
   c. If coolant fan does not operate at high speed when engine is not at operating temperature but A/C load is high, connect a suitable test lamp from terminal C (black/white) of A/C high pressure switch (disconnected) to battery voltage. If test lamp lights, proceed to step d. If test lamp does not light, check black/white wire for open and repair as necessary.
   d. Connect jumper between terminals A (light green/black) and C (black/white) of A/C high pressure switch with ignition "On." If coolant fan operates, check refrigerant system for sufficient charge. If coolant fan does not operate, check light green/black wire for open at S120 and repair as necessary.
   e. Connect a fused jumper between terminals 1 (red) and 4 (black/pink) of high speed coolant fan relay connector. If coolant fan operates, replace high speed coolant fan relay. If coolant fan does not operate, check black/pink wire for open and repair as necessary.
4. If coolant fan operates continuously (high speed) with ignition switch "On," proceed as follows:
   a. Remove connector (light green/black) from coolant fan temperature switch. If coolant fan stops, replace coolant fan temperature switch. If coolant fan does not stop, proceed to step b.
   b. Remove A/C high pressure switch connector from switch. If coolant fan stops, replace A/C high pressure switch. If coolant fan does not stop, proceed to step c.
   c. Remove connector from high speed coolant fan relay, then connect a suitable test lamp, between terminals 5 (brown/white) and 2 (light green/black). If test lamp lights, check light green/black wire for ground and repair as necessary. If lamp does not light, replace high speed coolant fan relay.
5. If coolant fan operates continuously (low speed) with ignition switch "On," proceed as follows:
   a. Remove connector from A/C high pressure switch. If coolant fan stops, replace A/C high pressure switch. If coolant fan does not stop, proceed to step b.
   b. Remove connector from low speed coolant fan relay, then connect a suitable test lamp, between terminals 5 (brown/white) and 2 (dark green). If test lamp lights, check dark green wire for ground and repair as necessary (check for ECM malfunction). If lamp does not light, replace low speed coolant fan relay.

COOLANT FAN, REPLACE

1. Disconnect battery ground cable.
2. Disconnect wiring from fan motor and frame.
3. Remove fan assembly from radiator support.
4. Reverse procedure to install.

1987 CHEVROLET CORSICA & BERETTA

TROUBLESHOOTING

4-121

1. Turn ignition switch to ON position, engine not operating.
2. Ensure coolant temperature is less than approximately 230°F.
3. Ensure A/C, if equipped, is OFF.
4. Check fan operation. If fan operates, proceed as follows:
   a. Check wire (circuit) 335 for short to ground.
   b. Check for faulty relay.
5. If fan does not operate, proceed as follows:
   a. Ground diagnostic terminal and note fan operation.

b. If fan does not operate, check fuse.
c. If fuse is blown, check for short to ground in wire (circuit) 39. If wire is satisfactory, check for a faulty relay.
d. If fuse is satisfactory, disconnect relay electrical connector. Connect a suitable test lamp between harness connector terminals wires (circuits) 39 and 335. If test lamp lights, connect test lamp between harness connector terminal wires (circuits) 2 and ground. If test lamp lights, jump harness connector terminals (circuits) 2 and 702. Check fan operation. If fan operates, replace relay. If fan does not operate check for an open circuit 702, open ground circuit 150 or a defective fan motor.
e. If test lamp does not light, connect a test lamp between harness connector terminal wire (circuit) 39 and chassis ground.
f. If test lamp lights, check for an open wire (circuit) 335. If circuit is satisfactory, check ECM terminal E8 or ECM. If test lamp does not light, repair open circuit 39.

V6-173

1. Turn ignition switch to ON (engine not operating) and A/C, if equipped, OFF.
2. Ensure coolant temperature is below 212°F.
3. Coolant fan should not be operating. If coolant fan is operating, disconnect fan relay. Fan should stop. If fan stops, connect a suitable test lamp to wire (circuit) 335 and to battery (12 volts). If test lamp lights, circuit 335 is shorted to ground or the ECM is defective. If test lamp does not light, replace relay assembly.
4. If coolant fan does not operate, ground diagnostic terminal. Fan should operate. If coolant fan does not operate, proceed to step 5. If coolant fan operates, remove ground from diagnostic terminal. Start and operate engine at idle. Ensure A/C, if equipped is off. Fan should be OFF (while coolant temperature is below 212°F). If coolant fan operates, replace ECM. If coolant fan does not operate, check A/C system, fan control switch, circuits 935 (for short) and A/C pressure fan control switch.
5. If fan is not operating, disconnect fan control relay. Turn ignition switch to ON (engine not operating). Probe harness terminals A and D with a suitable test lamp connected to ground. If no light ON (one or both), repair open of shot to ground in wire (circuit) that did not light (test lamp light). If test lamp lights for both, ground diagnostic terminal and probe wire (circuit) 335 with a test lamp connected to battery (12 volts). If test lamp is OFF, repair open or short in wire (circuit) 335 or faulty connection at ECM or defective ECM. If test lamp lights, jump harness terminals A and E together using a fused jumper wire. Fan should operate. If fan operates, replace relay. If does not operate, connect a test lamp across cooling fan motor harness connector terminals (with A and E terminals still jumped). If test lamp lights, replace motor. If test lamp is OFF, probe each terminal with a test lamp connected to ground. If light comes on (one), repair open in ground wire (circuit 150). If test lamp is OFF, repair open in circuit between relay and cooling fan motor.

COOLING FAN, REPLACE

1. Disconnect battery ground cable.
2. Disconnect electrical connectors from motor and fan frame.
3. Remove fan assembly from radiator.
4. Reverse procedure to install. Torque attaching bolts to 7 ft. lbs.

DASH GAUGES

INDEX

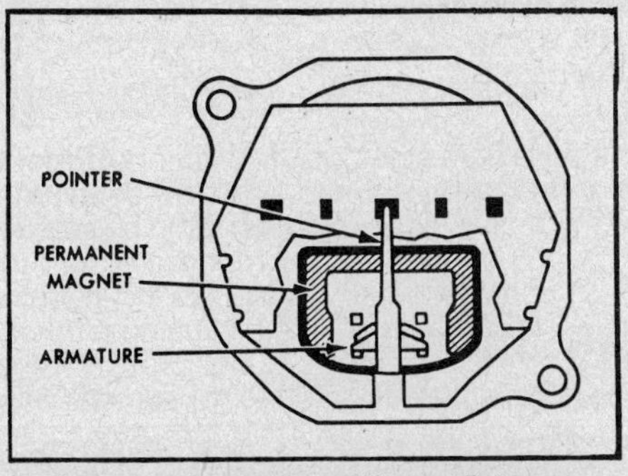

Fig. 1 Conventional type ammeter (typical)

GENERAL TESTING

Gauge failures are often caused by defective wiring or grounds. The first step in locating trouble should be a thorough inspection of all wiring, terminals and printed circuits. If wiring is secured by clamps, check to see whether the insulation has been severed thereby grounding the wire. In the case of a fuel gauge installation, rust may cause failure by corrosion at the ground connection of the tank unit.

VARIABLE VOLTAGE GAUGES

The variable voltage type dash gauge consists of two magnetic coils to which battery voltage is applied. The coils act on the gauge pointer and pull in opposite directions. One coil is grounded directly to the chassis, while the other coil is grounded through a variable resistor within the sending unit. Resistance through the sending unit determines current flow through its coil, and therefore pointer position.

When resistance is high in the sending unit, less current is allowed to flow through its coil, causing the gauge pointer to move toward the directly grounded coil. When resistance in the sending unit decreases, more current is allowed to pass through its coil, increasing the magnetic field. The gauge pointer is then attracted toward the coil which is grounded through the sending unit.

A special tester is required to diagnose this type gauge. Follow instructions included with the tester.

AMMETERS

The ammeter is an instrument used to indicate current flow into and out of the battery. When electrical accessories in the vehicle draw more current than the alternator can supply, current flows from the battery and the ammeter indicates a discharge (−) condition. When electrical loads of the vehicle are less than alternator output, current is available to charge the battery, and the ammeter indicates a charge (+) condition. If battery is fully charged, the voltage regulator reduces alternator output to meet only immediate vehicle electrical loads. When this happens, ammeter reads zero.

A conventional ammeter must be connected between the battery and alternator in order to indicate current flow. This type ammeter, **Fig. 1,** consists of a frame to which a permanent magnet is attached. The frame also supports an armature and pointer assembly. Current in this system flows from the alternator through the ammeter, then to the battery or from the battery through the ammeter into the vehicle electrical system, depending on vehicle operating conditions.

When no current flows through the ammeter, the magnet holds the pointer armature so that the pointer stands at the center of the dial. When current passes in either direction through the ammeter, the resulting magnetic field attracts the armature away from the effect of the permanent magnet, thus giving a reading proportional to the strength of the current flowing.

TROUBLESHOOTING

When the ammeter apparently fails to register correctly, there may be trouble in the wiring which connects the ammeter to the alternator and battery or in the alternator or battery itself.

To check the connections, first tighten the two terminal posts on the back of the ammeter. Then, following each wire from the ammeter, tighten all connections on the ignition switch, battery and alternator. Chafed, burned or broken insulation can be found by following each ammeter wire from end to end.

All wires with chafed, burned or broken insulation should be repaired or replaced. After this is done, and all connections are tightened, connect the battery cable and turn on the ignition switch. The needle should point slightly to the discharge (−) side.

Start the engine and speed it up a little above idling speed. The needle should then move to the charge side (+), and its movement should be smooth.

If the pointer does not behave correctly, the ammeter itself is out of order and a new one should be installed.

ALTERNATOR INDICATOR LAMP

DELCOTRON SI INTEGRAL CHARGING SYSTEM

This system features an integral solid state regulator mounted inside the alternator slip ring end frame. The alternator indicator lamp is installed in the field wire circuit connected between the ignition "Ign." terminal and alternator No. 1 terminal, **Fig. 2.** The resistance provided by the alternator warning light circuit is needed to protect the diode trio. The alternator indicator lamp should light when the ignition switch is turned on before engine is started. If lamp does not light, either lamp is burned out or indicator lamp wiring has an open circuit. After engine is started, the indicator

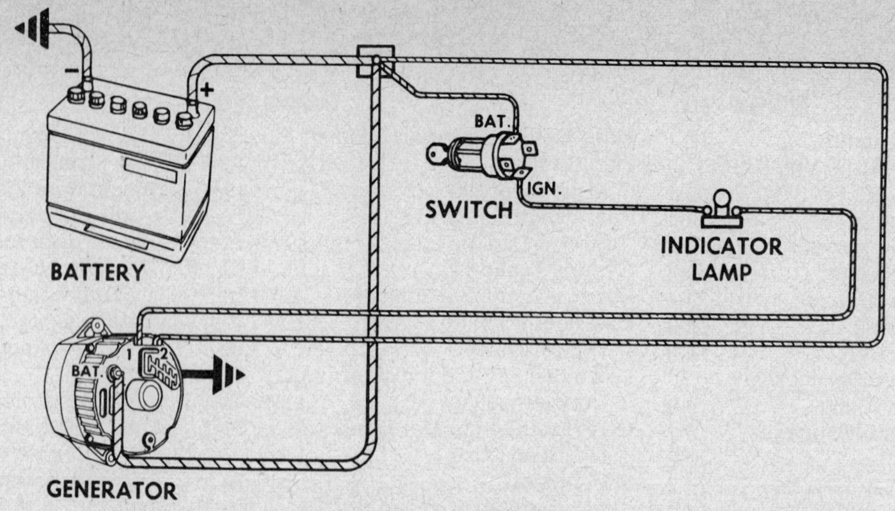

Fig. 2 Typical charge indicator lamp wiring. Delco SI type charging system

lamp should be out at all times. If indicator lamp comes on, alternator belt may be loose, alternator or regulator may be defective, charging circuit may be defective or fuse may be blown.

Troubleshooting

1. Switch Off, Lamp On:
   a. Disconnect electrical connector from alternator terminals 1 and 2.
   b. If indicator light remains lit, repair short circuit between leads.
   c. If indicator light goes out, replace alternator rectifier bridge.
2. Switch On, lamp Off, engine not running:
   a. Perform tests described in step 1.
   b. If problem still exists, there may be an open circuit.
   c. To locate open circuit, check for blown fuse or fusible link, burned out bulb, defective bulb socket or an open in No. 1 lead circuit between alternator and ignition switch.
   d. If no faults are found, check charging system for proper operation.
3. Switch On, lamp On, engine running:
   a. On models so equipped, check condition of fuse between indicator light and ignition switch and fuse in A/C circuit.
   b. Check charging system for proper operation.

VOLTMETER

The voltmeter is a gauge which measures the electrical flow from the battery to indicate whether the battery output is within tolerances. The voltmeter reading can range from 13.5-14.0 volts under normal operating conditions. If an undercharge or overcharge condition is indicated for an extended period, the battery and charging system should be checked.

TROUBLESHOOTING

To check voltmeter, turn key and headlights on with engine off. Pointer should move to 12.5 volts. If no needle movement is observed, check connections from battery to circuit breaker. If connections are tight and meter shows no movement, check wire continuity. If wire continuity is satisfactory, the meter is inoperative and must be replaced.

ELECTRICAL TEMPERATURE GAUGES

This temperature indicating system consists of a sending unit, located on the cylinder head, electrical temperature gauge and an instrument voltage regulator. As engine temperature increases or decreases, the resistance of the sending unit changes, in turn controlling current flow through the gauge. When engine temperature is low sending unit resistance is high, current flow through the gauge is restricted, and the gauge pointer remains against the stop or moves very little. As engine temperature increases sending unit resistance decreases and current flow through the gauge increases, resulting in increased pointer movement.

TROUBLESHOOTING

Troubleshooting for the electrical temperature indicating system is the same as for the electrical oil pressure indicating system.

ELECTRICAL OIL PRESSURE GAUGES

This oil pressure indicating system incorporates an instrument voltage regulator, electrical oil pressure gauge and a sending unit which are connected in series. The sending unit consists of a diaphragm, contact and a variable resistor. As oil pressure increases or decreases, the diaphragm actuated the contact on the variable resistor, in turn controlling current flow through the gauge. When oil pressure is low, the resistance of the variable resistor is high, restricting current flow to the gauge, in turn indicating low oil pressure. As oil pressure increases, the resistance of the variable resistor is lowered, permitting an increased current flow to the gauge, resulting in an increased gauge reading.

TROUBLESHOOTING

Disconnect the oil pressure gauge lead from the sending unit, connect a 12 volt test lamp between the gauge lead and the ground and turn ignition ON. If test lamp flashes, the instrument voltage regulator is functioning properly and the gauge circuit is not broken. If the test lamp remains lit, the instrument voltage regulator is defective and must be replaced. If the test lamp does not light, check the instrument voltage regulator for proper ground or an open circuit. Also, check for an open in the instrument voltage regulator to oil pressure gauge wire or in the gauge itself. **If test lamp flashes and gauge is not accurate, the gauge may be out of calibration, requiring replacement.**

OIL PRESSURE INDICATOR LAMP

Many cars utilize a warning light on the instrument panel in place of the conventional dash indicating gauge to warn the driver when the oil pressure is dangerously low. The warning light is wired in series with the ignition switch and the engine unit—which is an oil pressure switch.

The oil pressure switch contains a diaphragm and a set of contacts. When the ignition switch is turned on, the warning light circuit is energized and the circuit is completed through the closed contacts in the pressure switch. When the engine is started, build-up of oil pressure compresses the diaphragm, opening the contacts, thereby breaking the circuit and putting out the light.

TROUBLESHOOTING

On some models, the oil pressure indicator light also serves as the electric choke defect indicator. If Oil or Eng. indicator light does not light, check to ensure electric choke is not disconnected at carburetor. Also check for defect in electric choke heater, blown gauge fuse or defect in lamp or wiring circuit. If indicator light stays on with engine running possible causes are: oil pressure is low, switch to indicator light wiring has an open circuit, oil pressure switch wire connector has disconnected or on some models, gauge or radio fuse has blown.

The oil pressure warning light should go on when the ignition is turned on. If it does not light, disconnect the wire from the engine unit and ground the wire to the frame or cylinder block. Then if the warning light still does not go on with the ignition switch on, replace the bulb.

If the warning light goes on when the wire is grounded to the frame or cylinder block, the engine unit should be checked for being loose or poorly grounded. If the unit is found to be tight and properly grounded, it should be removed and a new one installed. (The presence of sealing compound on the threads of the engine unit will cause a poor ground).

If the warning light remains lit when it normally should be out, replace the engine unit before proceeding further to determine the cause for a low pressure indication.

The warning light sometimes will light up or will flicker when the engine is idling, even though the oil pressure is adequate. However, the light should go out when the engine is speeded up. There is no cause for alarm in such cases; it simply means that the pressure switch is not calibrated precisely correct.

TEMPERATURE INDICATOR LAMP

TROUBLESHOOTING

If the red light is not lit when the engine is being cranked, check for a burned out bulb, an open in the light circuit, or a defective ignition switch.

If the red light is lit when the engine is running, check the wiring between light and switch for a ground, temperature switch defective, or overheated cooling system. **As a test circuit to check whether the red bulb is functioning properly, a wire which is connected to the ground terminal of the ignition switch is tapped into its circuit. When the ignition is in the start (engine cranking) position, the ground terminal is grounded inside the switch and the red bulb will be lit. When the engine is started and the ignition switch is in the on position, the test circuit is opened and the bulb is then controlled by the temperature switch.**

SPEEDOMETERS

The following material covers only that service on speedometers which can be performed by the average service man. Repairs on the units themselves are not included as they require special tools and extreme care when making repairs and adjustments and only an experienced speedometer mechanic should attempt such servicing.

The speedometer has two main parts: the indicator head and the speedometer drive cable. When the speedometer fails to indicate speed or mileage, the cable or housing is probably broken.

SPEEDOMETER CABLE

Most cables are broken due to lack of lubrication or a sharp bend or kink in the housing.

A cable might break because the speedometer head mechanism binds. If such is the case, the speedometer head should be repaired or replaced before a new cable or housing is installed.

A jumpy pointer condition, together with a sort of scraping noise, is due, in most instances, to a dry or kinked speedometer cable. The kinked cable rubs on the housing and winds up, slowing down the pointer. The cable then unwinds and the pointer jumps.

To check for kinks, remove the cable, lay it on a flat surface and twist one end with the fingers. If it turns over smoothly the cable is not kinked. But if part of the cable flops over as it is twisted, the cable is kinked and should be replaced.

LUBRICATION

The speedometer cable should be lubricated with special cable lubricant every 10,000 miles.

Fill the ferrule on the upper end of the housing with the cable lubricant. Insert the cable in the housing, starting at the upper end. Turn the cable around carefully while feeding it into the housing. Repeat filling the ferrule except for the last six inches of cable. Too much lubricant at this point may cause the lubricant to work into the indicating hand.

INSTALLING CABLE

During installation, if the cable sticks when inserted in the housing and will not go through, the housing is damaged inside or kinked. Be sure to check the housing from one end to the other. Straighten any sharp bends by relocating clamps or elbows. Replace housing if it is badly kinked or broken. Position the cable and housing so that they lead into the head as straight as possible.

Check the new cable for kinks before installing it. Use wide, sweeping, gradual curves when the cable comes out of the transmission and connects to the head so the cable will not be damaged during its installation.

If inspection indicates that the cable and housing are in good condition, yet pointer action is erratic, check the speedometer head for possible binding.

The speedometer drive pinion should also be checked. If the pinion is dry or its teeth are stripped, the speedometer may not register properly.

The transmission mainshaft nut must be tight or the speedometer drive gear may slip on the mainshaft and cause slow speed readings.

ELECTRIC CLOCKS

Regulation of electric clocks used on automobiles is accomplished automatically by merely resetting the time. If the clock is running fast, the action of turning the hands back to correct the time will automatically cause the clock to run slightly slower. If the clock is running slow, the action of turning the hands forward to correct the time will automatically cause the clock to run slightly faster (10 to 15 seconds day).

A lock-out feature prevents the clock regulator mechanism from being reset more than once per wind cycle, regardless of the number of times the time is reset. After the clock rewinds, if the time is then reset, automatic regulation will take place. If a clock varies over 10 minutes per day, it will never adjust sufficiently, and must be repaired or replaced.

WINDING CLOCK WHEN CONNECTING BATTERY OR CLOCK WIRING

The clock requires special attention when reconnecting a battery that has been disconnected for any reason, a clock that has been disconnected, or when replacing a blown clock fuse. It is very important that the initial wind be fully made. The procedure is as follows:

1. Make sure that all other instruments and lights are turned off.
2. Connect positive cable to battery.
3. Before connecting the negative cable, press the terminal to its post on the battery. Immediately afterward strike the terminal against the battery post to see if there is a spark. If there is a spark, allow the clock to run down until it stops ticking, and repeat as above until there is no spark. Then immediately make the permanent connection before the clock can again run down. The clock will run down in approximately two minutes.
4. Reset clock after all connections have been made. The foregoing procedure should also be followed when reconnecting the clock after it has been disconnected, or if it has stopped because of a blown fuse. Be sure to disconnect battery before installing a new fuse.

TROUBLESHOOTING

If clock does not run, check for blown clock fuse. If fuse is blown check for short in wiring. If fuse is not blown check for open circuit. With an electric clock, the most frequent cause of clock fuse blowing is voltage at the clock which will prevent a complete wind and allow clock contacts to remain closed. This may be caused by any of the following: discharged battery, corrosion on contact surface of battery terminals, loose connections at battery terminals, at junction block, at fuse clips, or at terminal connection of clock. Therefore, if in reconnecting battery or clock it is noted that the clock is not ticking, always check for blown fuse, or examine the circuits at the points indicated above to determine and correct the cause.

FIBER OPTIC MONITORING SYSTEM

Fiber optics are non-electric light conductors made up of coated strands which, when exposed to a light source at one end, will reflect the light through their entire length, thereby illuminating a monitoring lens on the instrument panel or fender without the use of a bulb when the exterior lights are turned on.

FUEL GAUGES

The fuel gauge system consists of a sending unit, instrument voltage regulator and an electric fuel gauge. The sending unit is a variable resistor that is controlled by a float, and the float rises and falls in response to fuel level. When the ignition is on voltage is applied to the gauge through the voltage regulator, and the gauge ground circuit is completed through the sending unit.

When the tank is full and the float is raised, maximum resistance (approximately 90 ohms) is produced by the sending unit, current flow through the gauge is decreased, and the gauge pointer moves very little. As the tank empties and the float drops resistance in the sending unit decreases, current flow through the gauge increases and the gauge pointer moves toward empty.

Most analog fuel gauges are of the free floating type, which means that the gauge pointer does not remain against the full stop when the ignition is off. Rather, the pointer floats to a mid-position when no voltage is applied to the gauge.

TROUBLESHOOTING

Gauge Reads Empty When Tank Is Full

This condition is generally caused by a short in the tank unit circuit.

1. Disconnect electrical connector to sending unit, then turn on ignition.
2. If gauge reads past full, test gauge with tester BT-6508 or equivalent. If gauge still reads empty, disconnect main body harness connector (near fuse block).
3. If gauge still shows empty, check for short in printed circuit or defective gauge. If gauge reads beyond full, reconnect front body harness connector and disconnect rear body harness connector (in left wheel house).
4. If gauge shows empty, locate and repair grounded wire in harness between front and rear body harness connectors. If gauge reads beyond full, check for short between rear body harness connector, damaged float or defective sending unit.

Gauge Reads Full Or Beyond At All Times

This condition is generally caused by an open in the tank unit circuit.

1. Check tank unit ground for proper contact with body or chassis and repair as needed.
2. If tank unit ground is satisfactory, disconnect electrical connector to tank unit and connect harness side of connector to suitable ground with jumper wire, then turn on ignition.
3. If gauge reads empty, remove fuel tank and inspect wiring to sending unit. If wiring and connections are satisfactory, replace tank unit.
4. If gauge still shows full, disconnect front body harness connector and ground fuel gauge wire terminal in instrument panel side of connector.
5. If gauge still reads full, check for loose connection in cluster, open (crack) in printed circuit or defective gauge. If gauge reads empty, locate and repair open or poor connection between front body connector and tank unit connector.

Fuel Gauge Inaccurate

Tester BT-6508 or equivalent must be used to diagnose dash gauge malfunction

1. Ensure battery is fully charged, disconnect electrical connector to tank unit and connect tester to between harness connector and suitable ground following manufacturer's instructions.
2. Set tester on empty then turn on ignition. Gauge should read empty or below.
3. Set tester on full. Gauge should read full or above.
4. If gauge does not respond to tester input, replace dash gauge. If gauge responds correctly, check for poor connections at tank unit, poor tank unit ground or defective tank unit.

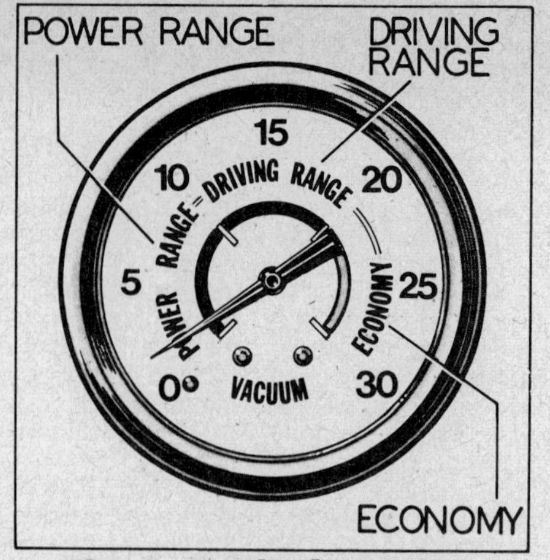

Fig. 3 Typical vacuum gauge

LOW FUEL WARNING SYSTEM

The switch type consists of an indicator light and a low fuel warning switch located on the instrument panel.

The warning switch contacts are closed by the difference in voltage potential between the fuel gauge terminals. This voltage differential will activate the warning switch when the fuel tank is less than 1/4 full and, in turn, cause the indicator to light.

TROUBLESHOOTING

This system incorporates an indicator light. With ignition switch turned to on, the indicator should light. If not, check bulb and all electrical connections. Replace warning switch if bulb and connections prove satisfactory.

LOW WASHER FLUID INDICATOR

There are two types of low washer fluid indicating systems. They are the mechanical type and electrically controlled type. The mechanical type consists of a float and rod assembly, sending unit and a fiber optic. The electrically controlled type consists of a float, magnet, contact points and a resistor.

On the mechanical type, the upper end of the rod extends into the sending unit and has colored red and green portions. When the windshield wipers are activated, a lamp bulb in the sending unit lights either the red or green sections of the rod. The colored light is then picked up by the fiber optic and is transmitted through it to the telltale lens. The lens will show red or green depending upon washer fluid level.

The electrically controlled indicator is activated when the windshield wipers are engaged. A slight amount of current flows from the wiper motor to the washer bottle float unit. This current will either pass through the contact points or the resistor which is in parallel with the points. When the washer fluid level is high, the magnet holds the contact points open. The current will now flow through the resistor where it is reduced so the indicator will not light. When the washer fluid level is low, the float drops and the magnet will separate from the cap assembly allowing the current to pass through the contact points and activate the indicator light.

TROUBLESHOOTING

On the mechanical indicating system, if the telltale lens fails to glow when the windshield wipers are activated, check lamp bulb in sending unit and see that fiber optic is not broken.

On the electrically controlled system, the first item to check is the indicator bulb. With the windshield wipers "On", connect a jumper wire between the two terminals on the washer bottle cap. The indicator should then light. If not, replace bulb. If the bulb is found to be satisfactory, remove cap and float assembly from washer bottle. Float should be able to move to the bot-

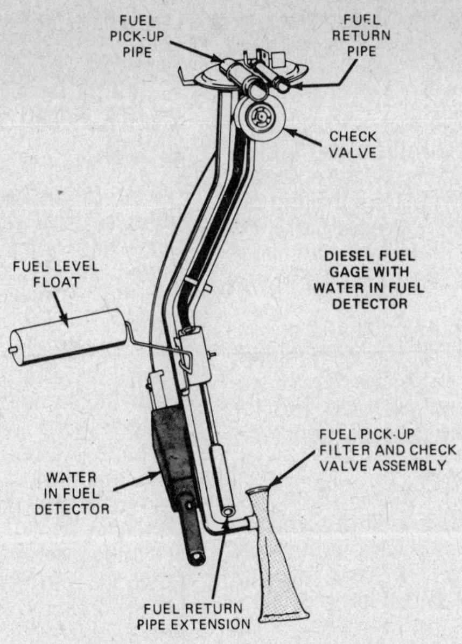

FUEL TANK PURGE PROCEDURE

Cars which have a "Water in Fuel" light may have the water removed from the fuel tank with a pump or by siphoning. The pump or siphon hose should be hooked up to the 1/4 inch fuel return hose (smaller of the two fuel hoses) above the rear axle or under the hood near the fuel pump. Siphoning should continue until all water is removed from the fuel tank. Use a clear plastic line or observe filter bowl on draining equipment to determine when clear fuel begins to flow. Be sure to remove the cap on fuel tank while using this purge procedure. Replace the cap when finished. The same precautions for handling gasoline should be observed when purging diesel fuel tanks.

Fig. 4 Water in fuel indicator & tank purge procedure. 1982–84 GM with diesel engine

tom of the stem and the magnet should separate from the cap. If not, replace float and cap assembly.

VACUUM GAUGE

This gauge, **Fig. 3,** measures intake manifold vacuum. The intake manifold vacuum varies with engine operating conditions, carburetor adjustments, valve timing, ignition timing and general engine condition.

Since the optimum fuel economy is directly proportional to a properly functioning engine, a high vacuum reading on the gauge relates to fuel economy. For this reason some manufacturers call the vacuum gauge a "Fuel Economy Indicator." Most gauges have colored sectors the green sector being the "Economy" range and red the "Power" range. Therefore, the vehicle should be operated with gauge registering in the green sector or a high numerical number, **Fig. 3,** for maximum economy.

LOW COOLANT LEVEL INDICATOR

Some vehicles use a buzzer or indicator lamp to indicate a low coolant level condition. The buzzer or lamp is activated by a sensor, located in the radiator, when the coolant level becomes one quart or more low.

FUEL USAGE GAUGE

BUICK & CADILLAC

Operation

This system consists of green and amber indicator lights located on the fuel gauge or telltale lamp cluster, a switch mounted on the instrument panel behind the gauges and an interconnecting vacuum hose and tee. The system operates on engine vacuum through a dual contact vacuum sensing switch. When the accelerator is operated slowly and smoothly, engine vacuum remains high and the switch passes current to the green indicator light which indicates economical fuel consumption. When the accelerator pedal is depressed rapidly, vacuum decreases and the switch passes current to the amber indicator light, which indicates high fuel consumption. The amber indicator light will glow when the ignition switch is in the "On" position with the engine stopped.

Functional Test

1. With ignition switch in the On position, ground each terminal at the economy switch. Both green and amber indicator lights should glow. If not check for burned out bulbs.
2. With ignition switch in on position, amber indicator light should glow. If not, check for loose or disconnected wires at fuel economy switch or for poor ground. If amber indicator light still does not glow replace switch.
3. Start engine and allow to idle, the green indicator light should glow. If not, check for leaking, plugged or kinked vacuum hose between vacuum source and fuel economy switch. Check for loose or disconnected wires at economy switch or poor ground. If green indicator lamp still does not glow, replace switch.

TURBO-POWER INDICATOR

BUICK W/V6-231 (3.8L) TURBOCHARGED ENGINE

Century, Regal and Riviera models utilize two lights located in the lower right hand gauge area. The yellow light indicates moderate acceleration and the orange light indicates power or heavy acceleration. When neither light is illuminated, the indication visible is a green paint band signifying economy. LeSabre models utilize three lights located at the bottom of the fuel gauge. On light acceleration or cruising, a green light indicates economy. Moderate acceleration activates a yellow indicator light. The orange light is activated during heavy acceleration.

WATER IN FUEL INDICATOR

DESCRIPTION & OPERATION

1982–84 Models W/Diesel Engine

The Water In Fuel warning system employs an electronic water detector, mounted inside the fuel tank, on the fuel gauge sending unit. The detector provides a warning when a predetermined amount of water is present in the fuel tank by lighting a warning lamp on the instrument panel. The sending unit assembly also contains a provision for siphoning-off water in the tank through the fuel return line, **Fig. 4.**

The water in fuel lamp will come on for 2-5 seconds each time ignition is switched to RUN position to insure that the lamp is operating. If there is water in the fuel, the warning lamp will come back on after a 15-20 second delay and remain on.

1985 Models W/Diesel Engine, Exc. Chevette & 1000

The Water In Fuel warning system employs a fuel detector integral with the fuel filter and fuel heater, and mounted on the engine. When more than 2.2 ounces of water has been collected in the filter, the Water In Fuel lamp on the instrument panel will light. After the light comes on, the filter should be drained as soon as possible to prevent fuel injection system failure or damage.

Chevette & 1000

The water in fuel system incorporates an electronic water detector mounted inside the fuel tank on the fuel gauge sender.

The detector will warn the driver when 1-2½ gallons of water are present in the fuel tank by illuminating the "Water In Fuel" indicator on the instrument panel. The lamp will also light for 2-5 seconds each time the ignition switch is turned "On" to ensure lamp is operable. If water is present in the fuel, the lamp will illuminate after a 3-6 second delay and remain on.

TROUBLESHOOTING

1982–84

If warning indicator fails to light during bulb check, disconnect wiring harness connector at fuel gauge sending unit, containing a yellow/black stripe wire. With ignition switch in RUN position, connect yellow/black stripe wire to ground, using a suitable jumper wire. If lamp lights, problem is in water detector. If lamp fails to light, check for open circuit between sender and warning lamp, a burned out bulb, or a blown fuse.

If warning lamp remains on at all times, disconnect wiring harness connector at fuel tank sending unit with ignition switch in RUN position. If warning lamp remains on, check for short circuit to ground between sender and warning lamp. If warning lamp goes out when harness is disconnected, first purge water in fuel tank, **Fig. 4,** then recheck circuit. If lamp remains on with harness connected to sending unit, water detector is defective.

1985 Exc. Chevette & 1000

1. If warning lamp lights intermittently, drain water in fuel filter.
2. If warning lamp remains light lit with engine running and ambient temperature above 32° F, drain fuel filter immediately. If lamp remains light, replace filter.
3. If warning lamp remains lit with engine running and ambient temperature 32° F or below, drain fuel filter immediately. If water is frozen and cannot be drained, open air bleed to check for fuel pressure. If no fuel pressure is present, replace filter.
4. If warning lamp lights at high speed or under heavy acceleration, the fuel filter is plugged and must be replaced.
5. If warning lamp remains light and engine stalls and will not restart after initial start-up, then fuel filter or fuel lines may be plugged. Repair or replace as required.
6. If warning lamp remains lit and engine stalls and will not restart immediately after refueling, a large quantity of water has likely been pumped into the fuel tank and should be purged.

Chevette & 1000

1. If Water In Fuel lamp is lit at all times, disconnect the two wire connector (yellow/black-pink) at rear of fuel tank, then check lamp. If lamp is lit, locate and repair short in yellow/black wire from 2 wire connector to instrument panel lamp. If lamp goes out, drain fuel tank in accordance with draining instructions, then reconnect electrical connector. If lamp lights, remove tank unit, then check wires for shorts. If no shorts exist, replace detector.
2. If Water In Fuel lamp does not light when ignition switch is turned on, disconnect 2 wire connector (yellow/black-pink) wire at rear of fuel tank, then ground yellow black wire in body harness. With ignition switch on, check Water In Fuel Lamp. If lamp is lit, remove fuel gauge tank unit, then check yellow/black wire for opens. Check connections to indicator, and mounting screw for tightness. If no fault is found, replace detector. If lamp is off, check bulb. If bulb is satisfactory, check for open circuit in yellow/black wire from 2 wire connector to indicator socket.

DRIVER REMINDER PACKAGE

CUTLASS, TORONADO, 88 & 98

The driver reminder package incorporates several warning and reminder features into one system. The system uses three distinct sounds, and warning and reminder lights on the center instrument cluster.

If engine coolant level is 3 quarts or more low, a red LOW COOLANT warning light will illuminate and a fast-pulsed tone will be heard. The light will remain lit and the tone will be heard until coolant is added to the cooling system. The light will also illuminate during engine starting as a bulb check.

When the headlight switch is in the ON position and the ignition is off, a red LIGHTS ON warning light will illuminate and a fast-pulsed tone will be heard. Turning the headlight switch to the right will dim the instrument panel lights and shut off the tone.

When there is less than approximately 3 gallons of fuel in the tank, an amber LOW FUEL warning light will illuminate and a steady 5 second tone will be heard, however the lamp may not light until fuel level is diminished to as low as ½ gallon. The light will remain lit until fuel is added to the tank. This warning light will also illuminate during engine starting as a bulb check.

The amber LOW WASH FLUID reminder light will illuminate while the windshield wipers are operated if the washer fluid reservoir is less than approximately ⅓ full. This light will remain lit during wiper operation until fluid is added.

Additional tones used to warn operator of potential problems are: engine overheating, fast-pulsed tone; malfunction in the charging system, fast-pulsed tone; seat belt reminder, slow-pulsed tone; key reminder, steady tone.

STARTER MOTORS & SWITCHES

TABLE OF CONTENTS

General Information

INDEX

STARTER TROUBLE CHECK-OUT

When trouble develops in the starting motor circuit, and the starter cranks the engine slowly or not at all, several preliminary checks can be made to determine whether the trouble lies in the battery, in the starter, in the wiring between them, or elsewhere. Many conditions besides defects in the starter itself can result in poor cranking performance.

To make a quick check of the starter system, turn on the headlights. They should burn with normal brilliance. If they do not, the battery may be run down.

If the battery is in a charged condition so that lights burn brightly, operate the starting motor. Any one of three things will happen to the lights: (1) They will go out, (2) dim considerably or (3) stay bright without any cranking action taking place.

IF LIGHTS GO OUT

If the lights go out as the starter switch is closed, it indicates that there is a poor connection between the battery and starting motor. This poor connection will most often be found at the battery terminals. Correction is made by removing the cable clamps from the terminals, cleaning the terminals and clamps, replacing the clamps and tightening them securely. A coating of corrosion inhibitor (petroleum jelly will do) may be applied to the clamps and terminals to retard the formation of corrosion.

IF LIGHTS DIM

If the lights dim considerably as the starter switch is closed and the starter operates slowly or not at all, the battery may be run down, or there may be some mechanical condition in the engine or starting motor that is throwing a heavy burden on the starting motor. This imposes a high discharge rate on the battery which causes noticeable dimming of the lights.

Check the battery state of charge. If it is charged, the trouble probably lies in either the engine or starting motor itself. In the engine, tight bearings or pistons or heavy oil place an added burden on the starting motor. Low temperatures also hamper starting motor performance since it thickens engine oil and makes the engine considerably harder to crank and start. Also, a battery is less efficient at low temperatures.

In the starting motor, a bent armature, loose pole shoe screws or worn bearings, any of which may allow the armature to drag, will reduce cranking performance and increase current draw.

In addition, more serious internal damage is sometimes found. Thrown armature windings or commutator bars, which sometimes occur on over-running clutch drive starting motors, are usually caused by excessive overrunning after starting. This is the result of such conditions as the driver keeping the starting switch closed too long after the engine has started, the driver opening the throttle too wide in starting, or improper carburetor fast idle adjustment. Any of these subject the overrunning clutch to extra strain so it tends to seize, spinning the armature at high speed with resulting armature damage.

Another cause may be engine backfire during cranking which may result, among other things, from ignition timing being too far advanced.

To avoid such failures, the driver should pause a few seconds after a false start to make sure the engine has come completely to rest before another start is attempted. In addition, the ignition timing should be checked if engine backfiring has caused the trouble.

LIGHTS STAY BRIGHT; NO CRANKING ACTION

This condition indicates an open circuit at some point, either in the starter itself, the starter switch or control circuit. The solenoid control circuit can be eliminated momentarily by placing a heavy jumper lead across the solenoid main terminals to see if the starter will operate. This connects the starter directly to the battery and, if it operates, it indicates that the control circuit is not functioning normally. The wiring and control units must be checked to locate the trouble.

If the starter does not operate with the jumper attached, it will probably have to be removed from the engine so it can be examined in detail.

CHECKING CIRCUIT WITH VOLTMETER

Excessive resistance in the circuit between the battery and starter will reduce cranking performance. The resistance can be checked by using a voltmeter to measure voltage drop in the circuits while the starter is operated. There are three checks to be made:

1. Voltage drop between car frame and grounded battery terminal post (not cable clamp).
2. Voltage drop between car frame and starting motor field frame.
3. Voltage drop between insulated battery terminal post and starting motor terminal stud (or the battery terminal stud of the solenoid).

Each of these should show no more than one-tenth (0.1) volt drop when the starting motor is cranking the engine. Do not use the starter for more than 30 seconds at a time to avoid overheating it.

If excessive voltage drop is found in any of these circuits, make correction by disconnecting the cables, cleaning the connections carefully, and then reconnecting the cables firmly in place. A coating of petroleum jelly on the battery cables and terminal clamps will retard corrosion.

On some cars, extra long battery cables may be required due to the location of the battery and starter. This may result in somewhat higher voltage drop than the above recommended 0.1 volt. The only means of determining the normal voltage drop in such cases is to check several of these vehicles. Then when the voltage drop is well above the normal figure for all cars checked, abnormal resistance will be indicated and correction can be made as already explained.

SOLENOID SWITCHES

The solenoid switch on a cranking motor not only closes the circuit between the battery and the cranking motor but also shifts the drive pinion into mesh with the engine flywheel ring gear. This is done by means of a linkage between the solenoid switch plunger and the shift lever on the cranking motor.

There are two windings in the solenoid; a pull-in winding and a hold-in winding. Both windings are energized when the external control switch is closed. They produce a magnetic field which pulls the plunger in so that the drive pinion is shifted into mesh, and the main contacts in the solenoid switch are closed to connect the battery directly to the cranking motor. Closing the main switch contacts shorts out the pull-in winding since this winding is connected across the main contacts. The magnetism produced by the hold-in winding is sufficient to hold the plunger in, and shorting out the pull-in winding reduces drain on the battery. When the control switch is opened, it disconnects the hold-in winding from the battery. When the hold-in winding is disconnected from the battery, the shift lever spring withdraws the plunger from the solenoid, opening the solenoid switch contacts and at the same time withdrawing the drive pinion from mesh. Proper operation of the switch depends on maintaining a definite balance between the magnetic strength of the pull-in and hold-in windings.

This balance is established in the design by the size of the wire and the number of turns specified. An open circuit in the hold-in winding or attempts to crank with a discharged battery will cause the switch to chatter.

STARTING MOTOR SERVICE

To obtain full performance data on a starting motor or to determine the cause of abnormal operation, the starting motor should be submitted to a no-load and torque test. These tests are best performed on a starter bench tester with the starter mounted on it.

From a practical standpoint, however, a simple torque test may be made quickly with the starter in the car. Make sure the battery is fully charged and that the starter circuit wires and terminals are in good condition. Then operate the starter to see if the engine turns over normally. If it does not, the torque developed is below standard and the starter should be removed for further checking.

STARTER DRIVE TROUBLES

Starter drive troubles are easy to diagnose and they usually cannot be confused with ordinary starter difficulties. If the starter does not turn over at all or if it drags, look for trouble in the starter or electrical supply system. Concentrate on the starter drive or ring gear if the starter is noisy, if it turns but does not engage the engine, or if the starter won't disengage after the engine is started. After the starter is removed, the trouble can usually be located quickly.

Worn or chipped ring gear or starter pinion are the usual causes of noisy operation. Before replacing either or both of these parts try to find out what caused the damage. With the Bendix type drive, incomplete engagement of the pinion with the ring gear is a common cause of tooth damage. The wrong pinion clearance on starter drives of the over-running clutch type leads to poor meshing of the pinion and ring gear and too rapid tooth wear.

A less common cause of noise with either type of drive is a bent starter armature shaft. When this shaft is bent, the pinion gear alternately binds and then only partly meshes with the ring gear. Most manufacturers specify a maximum of .003 inch radial runout on the armature shaft.

DRIVE CLUTCH FAILURE

The over-running clutch type drive seldom becomes so worn that it fails to engage since it is directly activated by a fork and lever. The only thing that is likely to happen is that, once engaged, it will not turn the engine because the clutch itself is worn out. A much more frequent difficulty and one that rapidly wears ring gear and teeth is partial engagement. Proper meshing of the pinion is controlled by the end clearance between the pinion gear and the starter housing or pinion stop, if used.

On some starters, the solenoids are completely enclosed in the starter housing and the pinion clearance is not adjustable. If the clearance is not correct, the starter must be disassembled and checked for excessive wear of solenoid linkage, shift lever mechanism, or improper assembly of parts.

Failure of the over-running clutch drive to disengage is usually caused by binding between the armature shaft and the drive. If the drive, particularly the clutch, shows signs of overheating it indicates that it is not disengaging immediately after the engine starts. If the clutch is forced to overrun too long, it overheats and turns a bluish color. For the cause of the binding, look for rust or gum between the armature shaft and the drive, or for burred splines. Excess oil on the drive will lead to gumming, and inadequate air circulation in the flywheel housing will cause rust.

Over-running clutch drives cannot be overhauled in the field so they must be replaced. In cleaning, never soak them in a solvent because the solvent may enter the clutch and dissolve the sealed-in lubricant. Wipe them off lightly with kerosene and lubricate them sparingly with SAE 10 or 10W oil.

BENDIX DRIVE FAILURE

When a Bendix type drive doesn't engage the cause usually is one of three things: either the drive spring is broken, one of the drive spring bolts has sheared off, or the screw shaft threads won't allow the pinion to travel toward the flywheel. In the first two cases, remove the drive by unscrewing the setscrew under the last coil of the drive spring and replace the broken parts. Gummed or rusty screw shaft threads are fairly common causes of Bendix drive failure and are easily cleaned with a little kerosene or steel wool, depending on the trouble. Here again, as in the case of over-running clutch drives, use light oil sparingly, and be sure the flywheel housing has adequate ventilation. There is usually a breather hole in the bottom of the flywheel housing which should be open.

The failure of a Bendix drive to disengage or to mesh properly is most often caused by gummed or rusty screw shaft threads. When this is not true, look for mechanical failure within the drive itself.

Starting Motor Specifications

Starter Make	Starter Model Number	Brush Spring Tension, Ounces	Free Speed Test			Solenoid	
			Amps	Volts	RPM	Hold-In Windings	Pull-In Windings
Delco-Remy	1100214	—	—	—	—	—	—
	1100215	—	—	—	—	—	—
	1100534	35(1)	45-70(2)	10	7000-11900	—	—
	1100941	—	—	—	—	—	—
	1102844	35(1)	60-85(2)	9	6800-10300	—	—
	1103519	—	—	—	—	—	—
	1108415	35(1)	35-75(2)	9	6000-9000	—	—
	1108758	35(1)	55-80(2)	9	3500-6000	14.5-16.5	13-15.5
	1108759	35(1)	65-95(2)	9	7500-10500	—	—
	1108762	35(1)	55-80(2)	9	3500-6000	14.5-16.5	13-15.5
	1108764	35(1)	65-95(2)	9	7500-10000	—	—
	1108765	35(1)	55-80(2)	9	3500-6000	14.5-16.5	13-15.5
	1108771	35(1)	50-75(2)	9	6500-10000	—	—
	1108772	35(1)	50-75(2)	9	6500-10000	—	—
	1108774	35(1)	60-88(2)	9	6500-10100	—	—
	1108779	35(1)	50-80(2)	9	5500-10000	—	—
	1108790	35(1)	55-80(2)	9	3500-6000	—	—
	1108794	35(1)	65-95(2)	9	7500-10000	14.5-16.5	13-16.5
	1108795	35(1)	65-95(2)	9	7500-10000	—	—
	1108796	35(1)	65-95(2)	9	7500-10000	—	—
	1108797	35(1)	55-80(2)	9	5500-10000	14.5-16.5	13-15.5
	1108799	35(1)	50-80(2)	9	5500-10500	14.5-16.5	13-15.5
	1109038	35(1)	65-95(2)	9	7000-10500	—	—
	1109039	35(1)	65-95(2)	9	7000-10500	—	—
	1109052	35(1)	65-95(2)	9	7500-10500	14.5-16.5	13-16.5
	1109056	35(1)	50-80(2)	9	5500-10500	14.5-16.5	13-15.5
	1109059	35(1)	65-95(2)	9	7500-10500	—	—
	1109061	35(1)	65-85(2)	9	6800-10300	17-19	24-27
	1109062	35(1)	65-95(2)	9	7500-10500	17-19	24-27
	1109063	—	70-110(2)	10	6500-10700	—	—
	1109064	35(1)	60-85(2)	9	6800-10300	17-19	24-27
	1109065	35(1)	65-95(2)	9	7500-10500	17-19	24-27
	1109067	35(1)	65-95(2)	9	7500-10500	—	—
	1109070	35(1)	65-95(2)	9	7500-10500	—	—
	1109072	35(1)	65-95(2)	9	7500-10500	17-19	24-27
	1109074	35(1)	60-85(2)	9	6800-10300	15-20	20-30
	1109213	35(1)	40-140(2)	9	8000-13000	—	—
	1109214	35(1)	40-140(2)	9	8000-13000	—	—
	1109215	35(1)	40-140(2)	9	8000-13000	—	—
	1109216	35(1)	120-210(2)	10.6	9000-13400	15-20	20-30
	1109218	35(1)	120-210(2)	10.6	9000-13400	—	—
	1109412	35(1)	50-75(2)	9	6500-10500	—	—
	1109414	35(1)	50-75(2)	9	6500	—	—
	1109495	35(1)	120-210(2)	11	9000-13400	—	—
	1109521	35(1)	45-75(2)	9	6500-9700	—	—
	1109522	—	55-85(2)	10	6000-12000	—	—
	1109523	35(1)	45-70(2)	9	7000-11900	17-23	16-18
	1109524	35(1)	45-70(2)	9	7000-11900	17-23	16-18
	1109526	35(1)	45-70(2)	9	7000-11900	15-20	20-30
	1109530	35(1)	85(4)	9	6800-10300	15-20	20-30
	1109531	—	50-75(2)	10	6000-11900	—	—

STARTING MOTOR SPECIFICATIONS—Continued

Starter Make	Starter Model Number	Brush Spring Tension, Ounces	Free Speed Test			Solenoid	
			Amps	Volts	RPM	Hold-In Windings	Pull-In Windings
	1109532	35①	55-85②	10	6000-12000	—	—
	1109533	35①	45-70②	9	7000-11900	13-19	23-30
	1109534	35①	45-70②	9	7000-11900	—	—
	1109535	35①	45-70②	9	7000-11900	13-19	26-38
	1109537	35①	45-75②	9	7000-11900	13-19	46-60
	1109544⑥	35①	45-70②	9	7000-11900	—	—
	1109544	—	50-75②	10	6000-11900	—	—
	1109551	35①	55-85②	10	6000-12000	13-19	23-30
	1109556⑦	35①	55-85②	10	6000-12000	—	—
	1105556⑧	35①	60-90②	10	6500-10500	—	—
	1109560	35①	50-75②	10	6000-11900	—	—
	1109562	35①	45-70②	9	7000-11900	13-19	23-30
	1109564	35①	50-74②	10	6000-11900	—	—
	1998204	35①	60-85②	9	6800-10300	17-19	24-27
	1998205	35①	65-95②	9	7500-10500	17-19	24-27
	1998217	—	70-110②	10	6500-10700	—	—
	1998227	35①	65-95②	9	7500-10500	—	—
	1998233	—	60-90②	10	6500-10500	—	—
	1998234	35①	65-95②	9	7500-10500	—	—
	1998236⑥	35①	60-85②	9	6800-10300	—	—
	1998236	—	60-90	10	6500-10500	—	—
	1998237⑥	35①	65-95②	9	7500-10500	—	—
	1998237⑤	—	7—110②	10	6500-10700	—	—
	1998240	35①	60-85②	9	6800-10300	—	—
	1998241	35①	70-110②	9	6500-10700	—	—
	1998400	—	70-110②	10.6	6500-10700	—	—
	1998427	—	52-76②	10	6000-11500	—	—
	1998428	—	55-85②	10	6000-12000	—	—
	1998429	—	50-75②	10	6000-11900	—	—
	1998430	—	50-75②	10	6000-11900	—	—
	1998435	—	70-110②	10.6	6500-10700	—	—
	1998435	—	50-705②	10	6000-11900	—	—
	1998436	—	70-110②	10	6500-10700	—	—
	1998445	—	52-76②	10	6000-12000	—	—
	1998437	—	55-85②	10	6000-12000	—	—
	1998448	—	50-75②	10	6000-11900	—	—
	1998450	—	50-75②	10	6000-11900	—	—
	1998452	—	50-75②	10	6000-11900	—	—
	1998466	—	52-76②	10	6000-12000	—	—
	1998477	—	55-85②	10	6000-12000	—	—
	1998511	—	50-75②	10	6000-11900	—	—
	1998516	—	60-100②	10	5500-10500	—	—
	1998521	—	48-75②	10	9000-13000	—	—
	1998523	—	52-76②	10	6000-11500	13-19	23-30
	1998527	—	70-110②	10.6	6500-10700	—	—
	1998528	—	50-75②	10	6000-12000	—	—
	1998529	—	55-85②	10	6000-12000	13-19	23-30
	1998530	—	52-76②	10	6000-11500	—	—
	1998531	—	55-85②	10	6000-12000	13-19	23-30
	1998533	—	50-75②	10	6000-11900	13-19	23-30
	1998536	—	50-75②	10	6000-11900	—	—
	1998544	—	45-74②	10	8600-12900	13-19	23-30

STARTING MOTOR SPECIFICATIONS—Continued

Starter Make	Starter Model Number	Brush Spring Tension, Ounces	Free Speed Test			Solenoid	
			Amps	Volts	RPM	Hold-In Windings	Pull-In Windings
	1998545	—	65-90 (2)	10	3500-5500	—	—
	1998546	—	52-76	10	6000-12000	13-19	23-30
	1998552	35 (1)	160-220 (2)	9	4000-5500	—	—
	1998553 (6)	35 (1)	160-220 (2)	9	4000-5500	15-20	30-40
	1998553 (5)	—	160-220 (2)	10	4400-6300 (3)	—	—
	1998554	35 (1)	160-240 (2)	10	4400-6300 (3)	—	—
	1998556 (6)	35 (1)	55-85 (2)	9	6000-12000	13-19	23-30
	1998556 (5)	—	160-240 (2)	10	4400-6300 (3)	—	—
	1998557	—	70-110 (2)	10	6500-10700	13-19	23-30
	1998558	—	70-120 (2)	10	5500-10700	—	—
	1998564	—	70-120 (2)	10	5500-10700	—	—
	3236659	—	45-70 (2)	9	7000-11900	—	—
Hitachi	94238754	—	—	—	—	—	—
	94238758	—	—	—	—	—	—
Mitsubishi	1998518	—	90 (4)	10	3500	—	—
	22511854	—	125-170	10	3200-4100 (3)	—	—
	22515863	—	125-170	10	3200-4100 (3)	—	—
	22523207	—	125-170	10	3200-4100 (3)	—	—
Nippondenso	(9)	—	63-85	90 (4)	11.5	—	—

(1)—Minimum.
(2)—Includes solenoid.
(3)—Pinion speed.
(4)—Maximum.
(5)—1984-85 models.
(6)—Except 1984-85 models.
(7)—Except 1985 models.
(8)—1985 models.
(9)—Nova models.

Delco-Remy Starters

INDEX

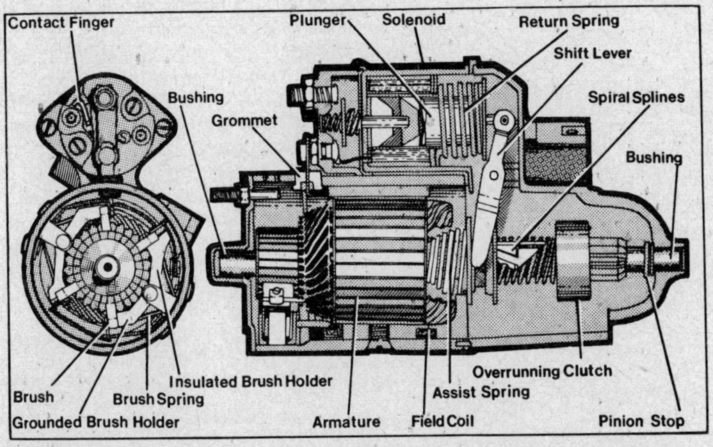

Fig. 1 Typical Delco-Remy starter motor

DESCRIPTION

The Delco-Remy starter, **Fig. 1,** has the solenoid shift lever mechanism and the solenoid plunger enclosed in the drive housing to protect them from exposure to road dirt, icing conditions and splash. They have an extruded field frame and an overrunning clutch type drive. The overrunning clutch is operated by a solenoid switch mounted to a flange on the drive housing. The diesel engine starters have a center bearing.

The solenoid is attached to the drive end housing by two screws. The cover can be removed to inspect the contacts and contact disc, but the switch is serviced as assembly only.

Most motors of this type have graphite and oil impregnated bronze bearings which ordinarily require no added lubrication except at time of overhaul when a few drops of light engine oil should be placed on each bearing before reassembly.

DIAGNOSIS

When diagnosing Delco-Remy starters, refer to **Fig. 2.**

IN-VEHICLE TESTING

FREE SPEED TEST

With the circuit connected as shown in **Fig. 3,** use a tachometer to measure armature revolutions per minute. Failure of the motor to perform to specifications may be due to tight or dry bearings, or high resistance connections.

PINION CLEARANCE

There is no provision for adjusting pinion clearance on this type motor. When the shift lever mechanism is correctly assembled, the pinion clearance should fall with-

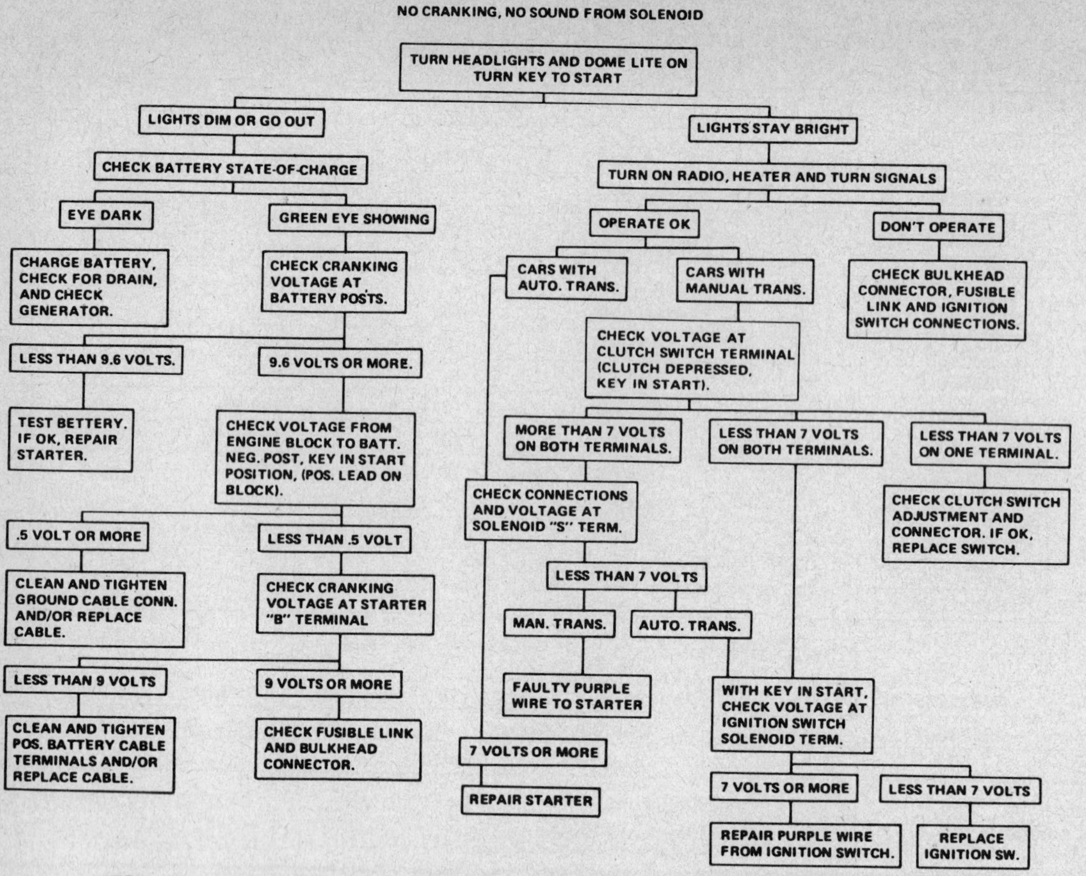

Fig. 2 Delco-Remy starter motor diagnosis (Part 1 of 2)

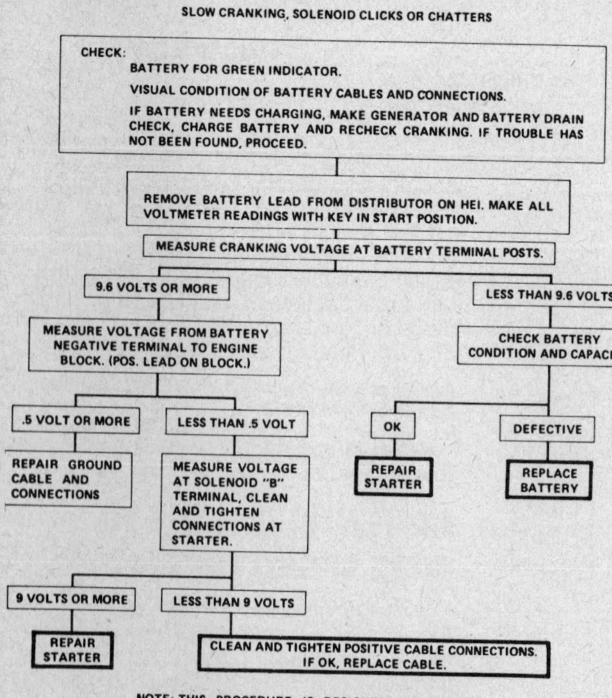

NOTE: THIS PROCEDURE IS DESIGNED FOR USE ON ENGINES AND BATTERIES AT ROOM OR NORMAL OPERATING TEMPERATURES. IT ALSO ASSUMES THERE ARE NO ENGINE DEFECTS WHICH WOULD CAUSE CRANKING PROBLEMS. TO USE IT UNDER OTHER CONDITIONS MIGHT RESULT IN MISDIAGNOSIS.

Fig. 2 Delco-Remy starter motor diagnosis (Part 2 of 2)

in the limits of .010 to .140 inch. When the clearance is not within these limits, it may indicate excessive wear of the solenoid linkage or shift lever yoke buttons.

Pinion clearance should be checked after the motor has been disassembled and reassembled. To check, disconnect motor field coil connector from solenoid terminal and insulate end. Connect one battery lead to solenoid switch terminal and the other lead to the solenoid frame, **Fig. 4.** Using a jumper lead connected to the solenoid motor terminal, momentarily flash the lead to the solenoid frame. This will shift the pinion into the cranking position until the battery is disconnected.

After energizing the solenoid with the clutch shifted toward the pinion stop retainer, push the pinion back toward the commutator end as far as possible to take up any slack movement; then check the clearance with feeler gauge, **Fig. 5.**

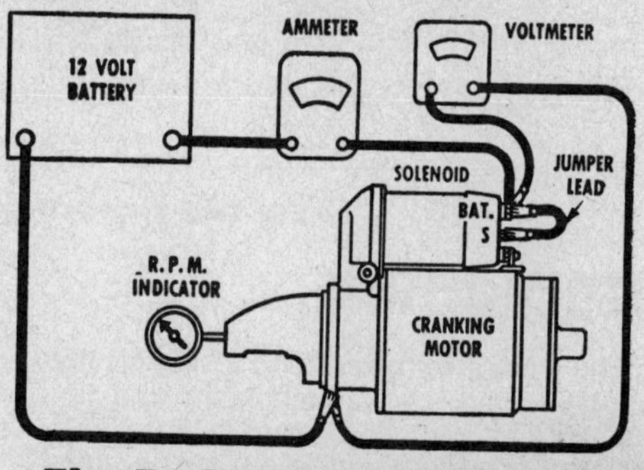

Fig. 3 Starter free speed test connections

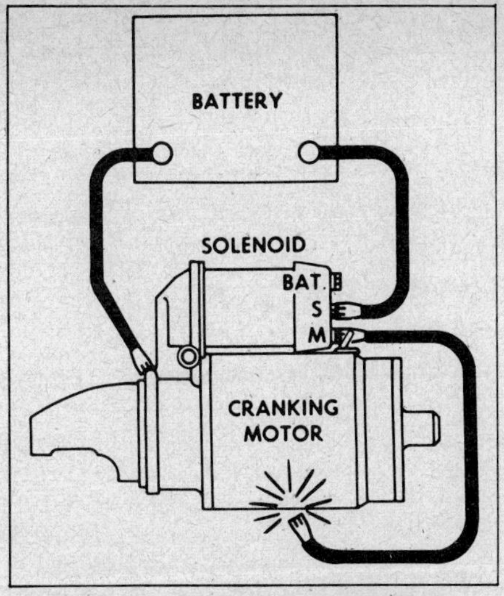

Fig. 4 Starter pinion clearance test connections

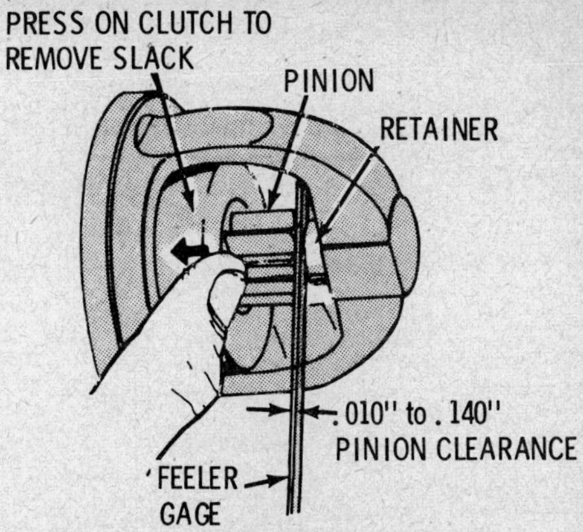

Fig. 5 Checking pinion clearance

Hitachi Starter

INDEX

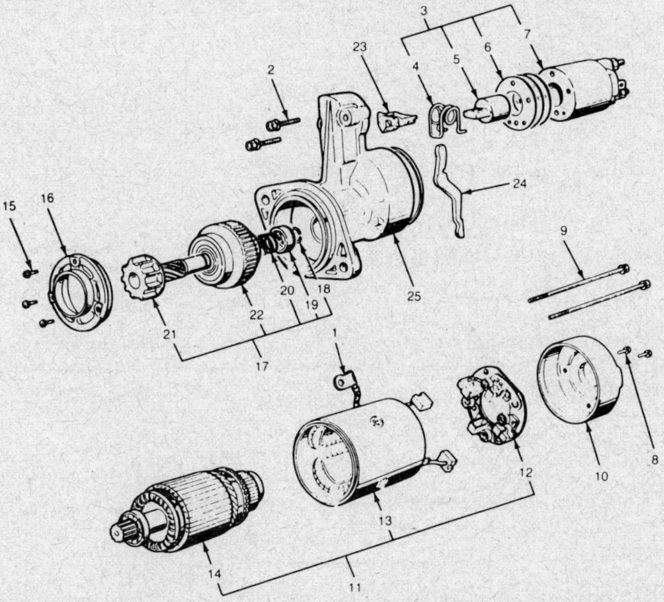

DISASSEMBLY ORDER

1. Lead wire
2. Bolt
3. Solenoid assembly
4. Torsion spring
5. Plunger
6. Adjusting plates
7. Solenoid
8. Screw
9. Through bolt
10. Rear cover
11. Motor assembly
12. Brush holder
13. Yoke
14. Armature
15. Screw
16. Bearing retainer
17. Pinion assembly
18. Pinion stop retainer
19. Pinion stop retainer clip
20. Return spring
21. Pinion shaft
22. Clutch
23. Dust cover
24. Shift lever
25. Gear case

Fig. 1 Hitachi S13-62A starter

DESCRIPTION

In this starter, **Fig. 1,** the solenoid windings are energized when the switch is closed. The resulting plunger and shift lever movement causes the pinion to engage the engine flywheel ring gear and the solenoid main contacts to close, and cranking takes place. When the engine starts, pinion overrun protects the armature from excessive speed until the switch is opened, at which time the return spring causes the pinion to disengage. To prevent excessive overrun, the switch should be opened immediately when the engine starts.

DIAGNOSIS

When diagnosing this starter, refer to **Fig. 2.**

Complaint	Faulty parts	Cause	Correction
Pinion does not jump out when starter switch is turned on	Wiring	Circuit open, battery or switch terminals loosened, or poor connections at connector	Correct and retighten
	Starter switch	Current not flowing due to poor contact	Correct or replace
	Starter	1. Helical splines on pinion shaft damaged preventing smooth movement of pinion	Correct or replace
		2. Torsion spring or shift lever broken	Replace
	Solenoid	Plunger operation sluggish, coil open or shorted	Correct or replace
	Battery	Under-charged	Recharge
Pinion engages ring gear but starter does not turn over	Wiring	1. Cable connecting solenoid to battery broken	Correct, retighten or replace
		2. Lead wire between solenoid and motor poorly connected.	
	Starter	1. Incorrectly installed.	Remove and reinstall correctly
		2. Brushes worn beyond limit	Replace
		3. Commutator face fouled	Correct
		4. Armature or field coil(s) shorted	Replace
		5. Brushes not properly connected to field coils	Correct
		6. Ball bearing locked	Replace
	Solenoid	Contact points defective	Replace
Motor operates before pinion engages ring gear	Starter	1. Torsion spring weakened or shift lever distorted	Replace
		2. Pinion shaft sticking or binding	Replace
		3. Pinion gear teeth worn	Correct
		4. Pinion setting incorrect	Replace
	Engine	Ring gear worn	Replace
Pinion engages ring gear and motor operates but power is not carried to engine	Starter	1. Clutch defective	Replace
		2. Reduction gear broken	Replace
Motor continues to spin even when starter switch is turned off after engine starting.	Starter switch	Contact point returning action poor	Replace
	Solenoid	Contact point returning action poor	Replace

Fig. 2 Diagnosis chart

Mitsubishi Starter

INDEX

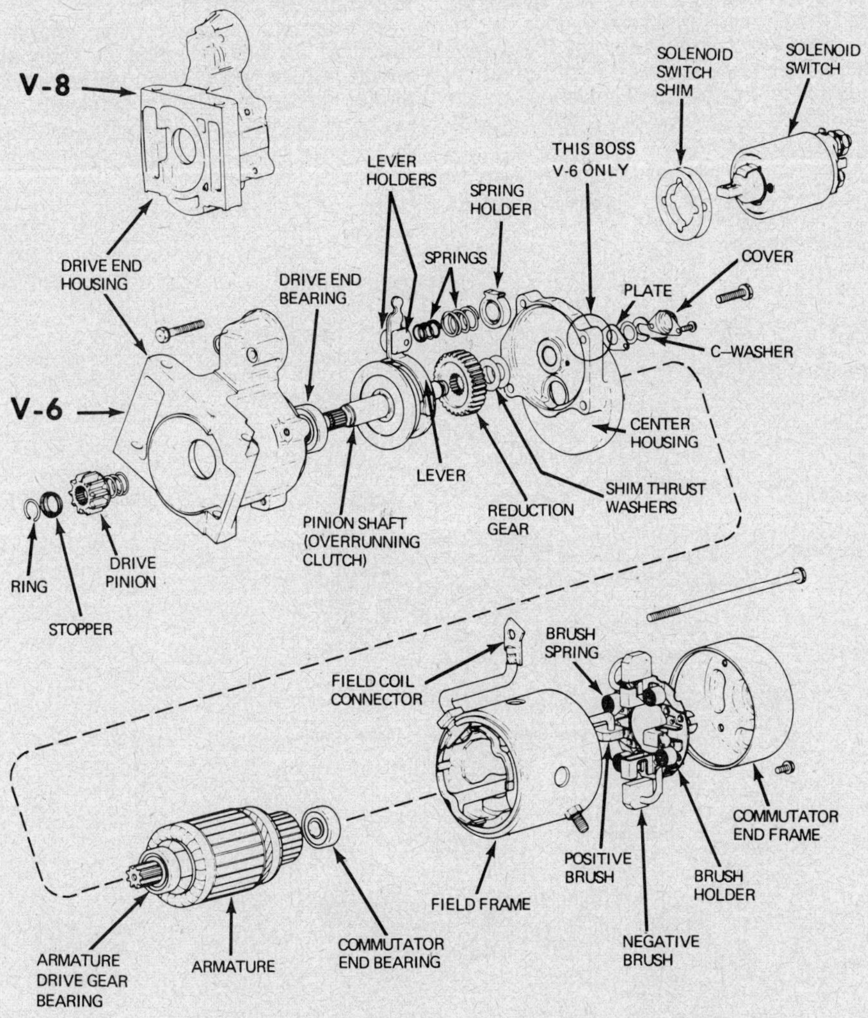

Fig. 1 Disassembled view of Mitsubishi starter

DESCRIPTION

The Mitsubishi starter, **Fig. 1,** is a gear reduction starter that has the solenoid shift lever mechanism enclosed in the drive end housing to protect them from exposure to road dirt, icing conditions and splash They also have an an overrunning clutch type drive. The overrunning clutch is operated by a solenoid switch mounted to a flange on the drive end housing.

The solenoid is attached to the drive end housing by two screws and is serviced as an assembly only.

These motors use sealed bearings at either end of the armature shaft and on the pinion shaft.

IN-VEHICLE TESTING

FREE SPEED TEST

Refer to "Delco-Remy Starters" for Free Speed Test.

PINION CLEARANCE CHECK

1. Disconnect field coil connector from solenoid terminal and insulate carefully.
2. Connect one 12 volt battery lead to solenoid switch terminal and other lead to starter motor frame.
3. Flash a jumper lead momentarily from solenoid motor terminal to starter motor frame. This will shift pinion into cranking position until battery is disconnected.
4. Push pinion back as far as possible to take up any movement, then check pinion clearance using a feeler gauge. Pinion clearance should be .020-.080 inch. If clearance is not within limits, check for improper installation or worn parts and replace as necessary. **Clearance may be adjusted by adding or removing shims located between the switch and front bracket. Adding shims decreases amount of movement. Shims are available in thicknesses of .010 and .020 inch.**

Nippondenso Starter

INDEX

DESCRIPTION

The Nippondenso starter, **Fig. 1**, is a gear reduction starter with the solenoid switch mounted on the underside of the starter motor.

The 1.0 Kw starter gear reduction mechanism consists of a drive gear machined onto the armature shaft which drives a pinion gear, which in turn rotates the starter clutch assembly. The 1.4 Kw starter armature drives a pinion gear, which drives an idler gear, which drives the starter clutch assembly.

The armature used on this starter is mounted on ball bearings at each end which require lubrication only when the starter is disassembled for service.

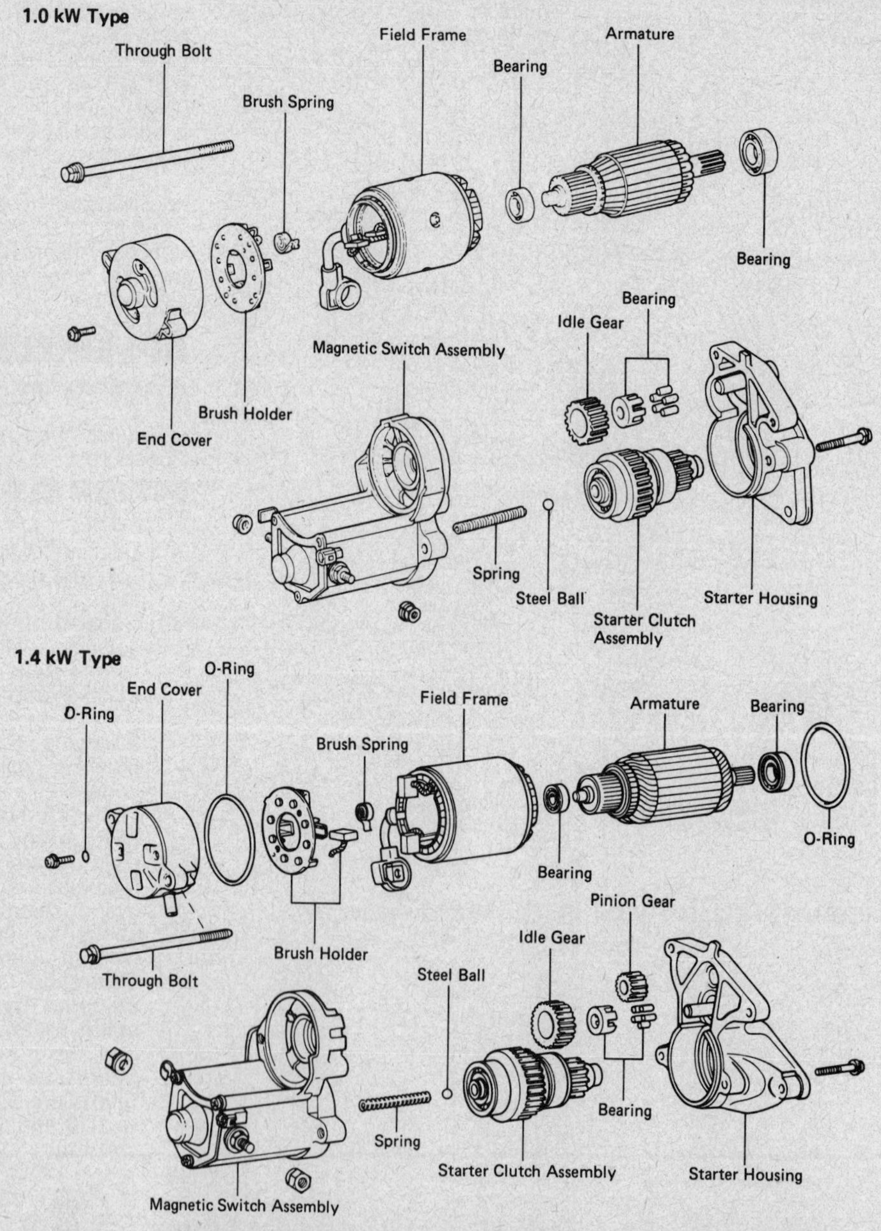

Fig. 1 Nippondenso starter motor exploded view

ALTERNATOR SYSTEMS

TABLE OF CONTENTS

General Information

INDEX

INTRODUCTION

Alternators are composed of the same functional parts as the conventional D.C. generator but they operate differently: The field is called a rotor and is the turning portion of the unit. A generating part, called a stator, is the stationary member, comparable to the armature in a D.C. generator. The regulator, similar to those used in a D.C. system, regulates the output of the alternator-rectifier system.

The power source of the system is the alternator. Current is transmitted from the field terminal of the regulator through a slip ring to the field coil and back to ground through another slip ring. The strength of the field regulates the output of the alternating current. This alternating current is then transmitted from the alternator to the rectifier where it is converted to direct current.

These alternators employ a three-phase stator winding in which the phase windings are electrically 120 degrees apart. The rotor consists of a field coil encased between interleaved sections producing. When the rotor is energized, a magnetic field with alternate north and south poles is created. By rotating the rotor inside the stator the alternating current is induced in the stator windings. This alternating current is rectified (changed to D.C.) by silicon diodes and brought out to the output terminal of the alternator.

DIODE RECTIFIERS

Six silicon diode rectifiers are used and act as electrical one-way valves. Three of the diodes have ground polarity and are pressed or screwed into a heat sink which is grounded. The other three diodes (ungrounded) are pressed or screwed into and insulated from the end head; these diodes are connected to the alternator output terminal.

Since the diodes have a high resistance to the flow of current in one direction and a low resistance in the opposite direction, they may be connected in a manner which allows current to flow from the alternator to the battery in the low resistance direction. The high resistance in the opposite direction prevents the flow of current from the battery to the alternator. Because of this feature no circuit breaker is required between the alternator and battery.

SERVICE PRECAUTIONS

1. Be certain that battery polarity is correct when servicing units. Reversed battery polarity will damage rectifiers and regulators.
2. If booster battery is used for starting, be sure to use correct polarity in hook up.
3. When a fast charger is used to charge a vehicle battery, the vehicle battery cables should be disconnected unless the fast charger is equipped with a special Alternator Protector, in which case the vehicle battery cables need not be disconnected. Also the fast charger should never be used to start a vehicle as damage to rectifiers will result.
4. Unless the system includes a load relay or field relay, grounding the alternator output terminal will damage the alternator and/or circuits. This is true even when the system is not in operation since no circuit breaker is used and the battery is applied to the alternator output terminal at all times. The field or load relay acts as a circuit breaker in that it is controlled by the ignition switch.
5. When adjusting the voltage regulator, do not short the adjusting tool to the regulator base as the regulator may be damaged. The tool should be insulated by taping or by installing a plastic sleeve.
6. Before making any on vehicle tests of the alternator or regulator, the battery should be checked and the circuit inspected for faulty wiring or insulation. loose or corroded connections and poor ground circuits.
7. Check alternator belt tension to be sure the belt is tight enough to prevent slipping under load.
8. The ignition switch should be off and the battery ground cable disconnected before making any test connections to prevent damage to the system.
9. The vehicle battery must be fully charged or a fully charged battery may be installed for test purposes.

Delcotron Type SI Integral Charging System

INDEX

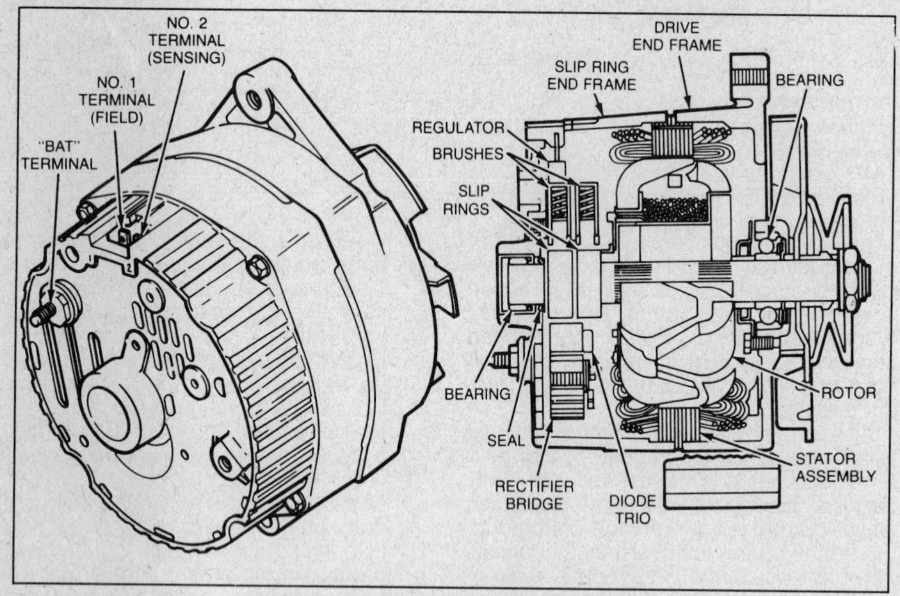

Fig. 1 Typical Delcotron type SI alternator

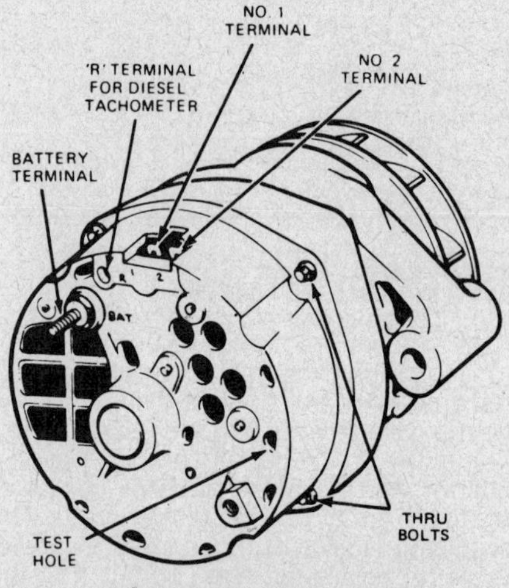

Fig. 3 Delcotron type 12 SI alternator. Typical of models used on diesel engines

DESCRIPTION

These units, **Figs. 1 and 2,** feature a solid state regulator mounted inside the alternator slip ring end frame, along with the brush holder assembly. All regulator components are enclosed in a solid mold with no need or provision for adjustment of the regulator. A rectifier bridge, containing six diodes and connected to the stator windings, changes A.C. voltage to D.C. voltage which is available at the output terminal. Generator field current is supplied through a diode trio which is also connected to the stator windings. The diodes and rectifiers are protected by a capacitor which is also mounted in the end frame.

General Motors units incorporate a resistor in the warning indicator circuit. **Fig. 3.**

Some alternators used on diesel engines are equipped with an R terminal for the tachometer, **Fig. 2.** On these units, if the alternator pulley is to be replaced, a pulley of the same diameter as the one removed must be installed, otherwise tachometer may provide inaccurate readings.

No maintenance or adjustments of any kind are required on this unit.

TROUBLESHOOTING

If a condition of a dimly lit No Charge indicator lamp occurs under heavy electrical load on 1982 and some 1983 Cadillac Brougham and Deville models with Digital Fuel Injection, it may be caused by insufficient filtering of the No Charge indicator bulb.

This condition is not caused by a low charging rate but, by the alternator charging at near maximum capacity, with alternator voltage output in excess of battery voltage. This causes a voltage potential difference across the indicator lamp terminals, resulting in a dim bulb glow.

This condition can be checked by thoroughly testing the charging system. If all systems are satisfactory, the indicator lamp should be removed and a filter (GM part No. 25076102) installed over the bulb. The bulb should then be reinstalled.

UNDERCHARGED BATTERY

1. Disconnect battery ground cable.
2. Disconnect wire at BAT terminal of alternator, connect ammeter, positive lead to BAT terminal and negative lead to wire.
3. Connect battery ground cable.
4. Turn on all accessories, then connect a carbon pile regulator across battery.
5. Operate engine at moderate speed, adjust carbon pile regulator to obtain maximum current output.
6. If ammeter reading is within 10 amps of rated output, alternator is not at fault. **Alternator rated output is stamped on alternator frame.**
7. If ammeter reading is not within 10 amps of rated output, ground field winding by inserting screwdriver in end frame hole, contacting tab, **Fig. 4. Do not insert screwdriver deeper than one inch since tab is usually located within 3/4 inch of casing surface.**
8. If reading is within 10 amps of rated output, regulator must be replaced. If reading is not within limits, check field winding, diode trio, rectifier bridge and stator.
9. Turn off all accessories and disconnect ammeter and carbon pile regulator.

IN-VEHICLE VOLTAGE REGULATOR TEST

1. Connect voltmeter and fast charger to 12 volt battery as shown in **Fig. 5.**
2. Connect regulator and test light as shown, observing battery polarity.
3. Test light should be on.

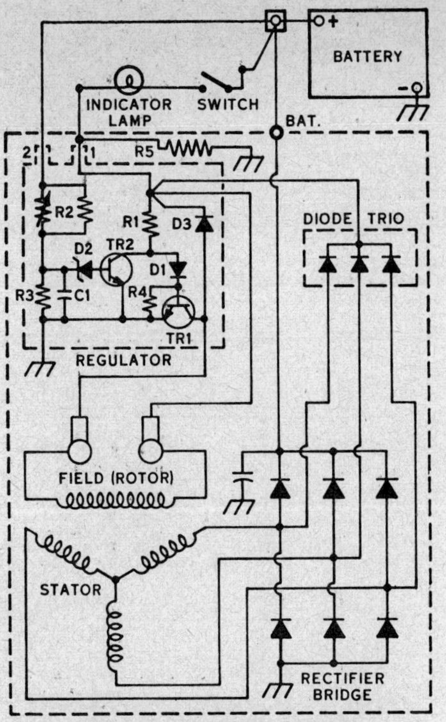

Fig. 3 Typical wiring diagram of charging circuit

4. Turn on fast charger and slowly increase charge rate. Observe voltmeter, light should go out at a voltage regulator setting of 13.5-16.0 volts.

The test light is connected into the circuit, exactly as the rotor is when the regulator is inside the generator. The regulator shuts off the current to the test light when the regulator setting is reached. This voltage will vary with changes in temperature.

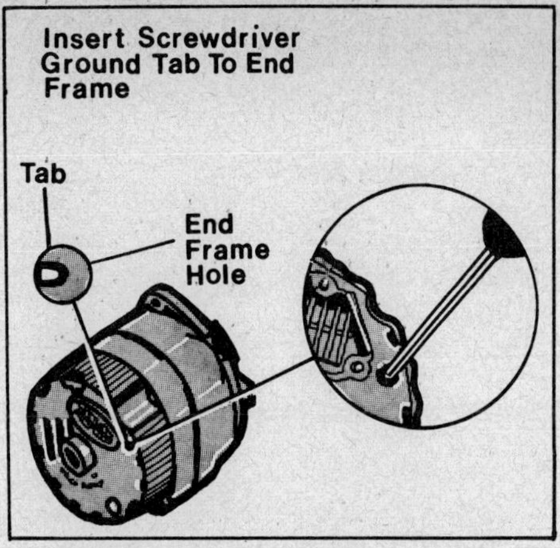

Fig. 4 Grounding field windings

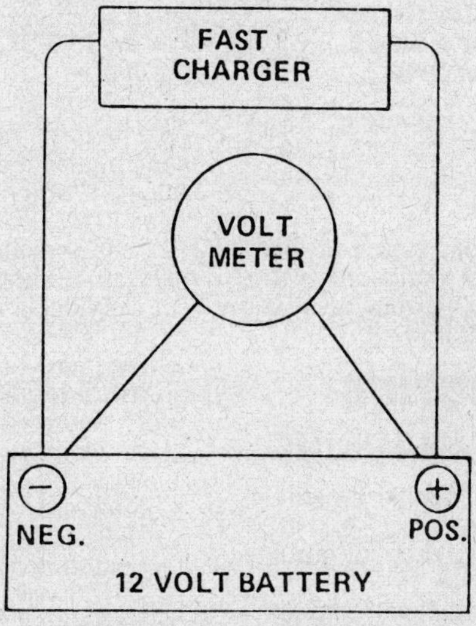

Fig. 5 Testing voltage regulator

Hitachi LR155-12B Alternator

INDEX

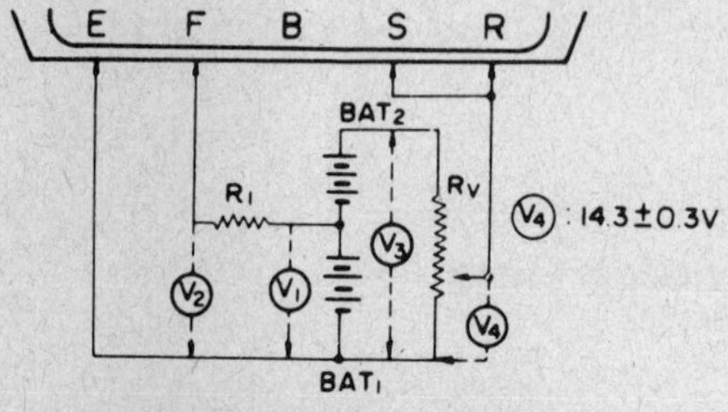

Fig. 1 IC regulator preliminary test connections

DESCRIPTION

This alternator is a solid state unit which incorporates an integral regulator. A vacuum pump is attached to the rear cover and is driven off the alternator shaft.

TROUBLESHOOTING

BATTERY NOT CHARGING

1. Cable between terminals broken or connector defective.
2. Charging system not properly grounded.
3. Brushes not in contact with slip ring.
4. Stator coils open or burned. Measure resistance across terminals at connectors between diode cover and stator coil leads.
5. Rotor coil open or burned. Measure resistance across F and E with connector at alternator disconnected.
6. Diodes defective. Make continuity test across B-N, B-E and N-E.
7. IC regulator defective.

BATTERY UNDER CHARGING

1. Wires between terminals poorly connected.
2. Drive belt slipping.
3. Brushes in poor contact with slip ring.
4. Rotor coil layers shorted.
5. Stator coils open or shorted.
6. Diodes defective.
7. Regulated voltage adjusted too low.
8. Electrical load excessive.

BATTERY OVER CHARGING

1. Short circuit between B terminal and F terminal.
2. IC regulated voltage too high.

VOLTAGE REGULATOR TEST

To perform regulator tests, the following measuring instruments will be needed: resistor (10 ohms, 3 watts) R1, variable resistor (0-300 ohms, 3 watts) Rv, battery (12 volts, 2 pieces). BAT1, BAT2, DC voltmeter (0-30 volts).

1. Connect instruments as shown in **Fig. 1.**
2. Measure voltage at BAT1 (V1). Voltmeter reading should be 10-13 volts.
3. Measure voltage between terminals F and E (V2). Voltmeter reading should be approximately 2 volts.
4. Measure voltage between BAT1 and BAT2 (V3) with terminal S disconnected. Voltmeter reading should be 20-26 volts.
5. Measure voltage between terminals E and F while varying resistance gradually with variable resistor. Voltage should increase from 2 volts to 10-13 volts without any interruption. If voltage increase is interrupted, replace regulator.
6. Measure voltage between intermediate tap on variable resistor and terminal E (V4) without actuating variable resistor. Voltmeter should read 14.0-14.6 volts, or regulator must be replaced.
7. Connect instruments as shown in **Fig. 2.**
8. Measure voltage between terminals B and E while gradually increasing voltage with variable resistor. Voltage should increase from approximately 2 volts to 10-13 volts. If voltage does not vary, replace regulator.
9. Check voltage between intermediate tap of variable resistor and terminal E without actuating variable resistor. Voltmeter should read 14.5-16.6 volts, or regulator must be replaced.

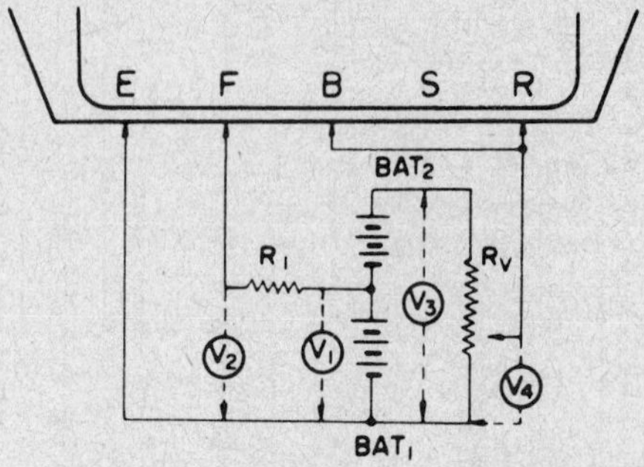

Fig. 2 IC regulator final test connections

VACUUM PUMP INSPECTION

1. Measure length of vanes. Vanes should measure .511-.531 inch, or must be replaced.
2. Measure inside diameter of pump housing. Diameter should be 2.2440-2.2441 inches.
3. Apply light pressure to check valve with a screwdriver and ensure smooth operation of valve.
4. Inspect inner face of rear cover for signs of oil leakage and inspect oil seal for excessive wear or damage.
5. If rear seal requires replacement, remove old seal from rear cover side with a screwdriver and install new seal with seal installer.

Nippondenso Alternator

INDEX

DESCRIPTION

This alternator has an IC integral solid state regulator. All regulator components are enclosed into a solid mold and are attached to the slip ring end frame along with the brush holder assembly. The alternator voltage setting cannot be adjusted.

The alternator rotor bearing contain enough grease to eliminate the need for periodic lubrication. Two brushes carry current through the two slip rings to the field coil mounted on the rotor.

The stator windings are assembled on the inside of a laminated core that form part of the alternator frame. The rectifier bridge contains six diodes which electrically change stator A.C. voltage into D.C. voltage. The neutral diodes serve to convert the voltage fluctuation at the neutral point to direct current for increasing generator output.

IN-VEHICLE TESTING

1. Connect suitable ammeter and voltmeter as follows:
   a. Disconnect wire from B terminal of alternator, then connect ammeter negative probe to the wire.
   b. Connect ammeter positive probe to B terminal of alternator.
   c. Connect voltmeter positive probe to B terminal of alternator and the negative probe to ground.
2. Start engine and allow to run at 2,000 RPM, then check reading of ammeter and voltmeter. Ammeter should read less than 10 amps. Voltmeter should read 13.9-15.1 volts at 77° F.
3. If voltage reading is greater than specified voltage, replace IC regulator. If voltage reading is less than specified voltage, check the IC regulator and alternator as follows:
   a. With engine running and F terminal grounded, check voltage reading at B terminal.
   b. If voltage reading is greater than specified voltage, replace IC regulator. If voltage reading is less than specified voltage, check alternator.
4. With engine running at 2,000 RPM, turn on high beam headlights and place heater fan control switch in the HI position.
5. Check ammeter reading. If reading is less than 30 amps, repair alternator.

Delcotron Type CS Charging System

INDEX

DESCRIPTION

The CS alternator is available in three sizes: CS121, CS130 and CS144. The numerals denote the outer diameter of the stator lamenations and the letters CS stand for charging system.

CS alternators use a new type regulator and a diode trio is not used. A delta stator, rectifier bridge, and rotor with slip rings and brushes are electrically similar to earlier alternators. A conventional pulley and fan is used and, on CS-130, an internal fan cools the slip ring end frame, rectifier bridge and regulator.

CS130 and CS144 alternators may be used with only two connections **Fig. 1, battery positive and an L terminal to charge the indicator bulb. Use of P, F and S terminals is optional. The P terminal is connected to the stator, and may be connected to a tachometer or other device. The F terminal is connected internally to field positive, and may be used as a fault indicator. The S terminal may be connected externally to a voltage, such as battery voltage, to sense voltage to be controlled.**

The regulator voltage setting varies with temperature, and limits system voltage by controlling rotor field current.

IN-VEHICLE TESTING

1. Visually check belt and wiring and make any necessary repairs.
2. On models without charge indicator light, proceed to step 5.
3. On all models, with ignition switch on and engine stopped, lamp should be on. If not, disconnect harness from alternator, and ground L terminal.
   a. If lamp lights, repair or replace alternator.
   b. If lamp does not light, locate open circuit between grounding lead and ignition switch.
4. With ignition switch on and engine stopped, lamp should be off. If not, disconnect wiring harness from alternator.
   a. If lamp goes off, replace or repair alternator.
   b. If lamp stays on, check for grounded L terminal in wiring harness.
5. Battery undercharged or overcharged.
   a. Detach wiring harness connector from alternator.
   b. With ignition switch on and engine not running, connect voltmeter from ground to L terminal.
   c. Zero reading indicates open circuit between terminal and battery. Correct as required.
   d. Reconnect harness connector to alternator.
   e. Measure voltage across battery terminals with engine running at approximately 2000 RPM. If voltage is above 16 volts, replace or repair alternator.
   f. Turn on accessories and load battery with carbon pile to obtain maximum amperage. Maintain voltage at 13 volts or less. If alternator is within 15 amps of rated output, it is acceptable.

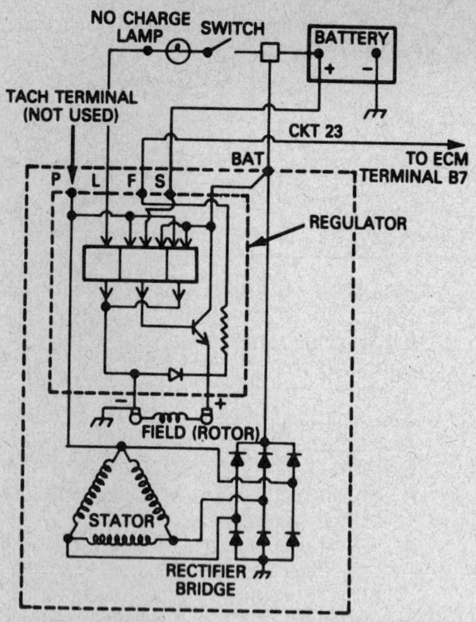

Fig. 1 CS charging system wiring diagram

BENCH TEST

1. Make connections as shown in **Fig. 2, however leave the carbon pile disconnected. The ground polarity of the alternator and battery must be the same. The battery must be fully charged. Use a 30-500 ohm resistor between battery and L terminal.**
2. Slowly increase alternator speed and observe voltage.
3. If voltage is uncontrolled and increases above 16 volts, the rotor field is shorted, the regulator is defective or both. A shorted rotor field can cause the regulator to become defective. **Battery must be fully charged when making this test.**
4. If voltage is below 16 volts, increase speed and adjust carbon pile obtain maximum amperage output. Maintain voltage above 13 volts.
5. If output is within 15 amps of rated output, alternator is satisfactory.
6. If output is not within 15 amps of rated output, alternator is defective and requires repair.

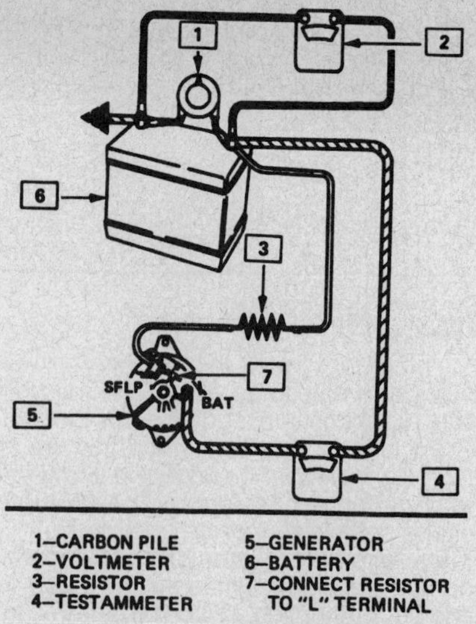

Fig. 2 CS alternator bench check

DISC BRAKES

NOTE: Refer to "Applications" to determine which type brakes are used on vehicle being serviced.

TABLE OF CONTENTS

Applications

Page No.

DELCO-MORAINE Opposed Piston 22-6

Chevrolet Corvette (4 Wheel Disc Brakes), 1982

DELCO-MORAINE Single Piston W/Single Mounting Bolt 22-4

Chevrolet Chevette, 1982
Pontiac 1000, 1982

DELCO-MORAINE Single Piston W/Dual Mounting Bolt:

TYPE 1 22-8
- Buick Electra, 1982-84
- Buick Estate Wagon, 1982-87
- Buick LeSabre, 1982-85
- Buick Regal, 1982-87
- Buick Riviera, 1982-85
- Cadillac Brougham, 1982-87
- Cadillac Deville, 1982-84
- Cadillac Eldorado, 1982-85
- Cadillac Seville, 1982-85
- Chevrolet Camaro (Front), 1982-87
- Chevrolet Caprice, 1982-87
- Chevrolet Impala, 1982-85
- Chevrolet Malibu, 1982-83
- Chevrolet Monte Carlo, 1987-87
- Oldsmobile Custom Cruiser, 1982-87
- Oldsmobile Cutlass Exc. Ciera, 1982-87
- Oldsmobile Toronado, 1982-85
- Oldsmobile 88, 1982-85
- Oldsmobile 98, 1982-84
- Pontiac Bonneville, 1982-86
- Pontiac Firebird, 1982-87 (Front)
- Pontiac Grand Prix, 1982-87
- Pontiac Parisienne, 1983-86
- Pontiac Safari, 1987

TYPE 2 22-10
- Buick Century, 1982-87
- Buick Electra, 1985-87
- Buick LeSabre, 1986-87
- Buick Skyhawk, 1982-87
- Buick Skylark, 1982-87
- Buick Somerset, Somerset Regal, 1985-87
- Cadillac Cimarron, 1982-87
- Cadillac Deville, 1985-87
- Cadillac Fleetwood, 1985-87
- Chevrolet Beretta, 1987
- Chevrolet Cavalier, 1982-87
- Chevrolet Celebrity, 1982-87
- Chevrolet Chevette, 1983-87
- Chevrolet Citation, 1982-85
- Chevrolet Corsica, 1987
- Oldsmobile Calais, 1985-87
- Oldsmobile Cutlass Ciera, 1982-87
- Oldsmobile Firenza, 1982-87
- Oldsmobile Omega, 1982-84
- Oldsmobile 88, 1986-87
- Oldsmobile 98, 1985-87
- Pontiac Bonneville, 1987
- Pontiac Phoenix, 1982-84
- Pontiac 1000, 1983-87
- Pontiac 2000/Sunbird, 1982-87
- Pontiac 6000 STE (Front), 1982-87

TYPE 3 22-13
- Pontiac Fiero (4 Wheel Disc Brakes), 1984-87
- Pontiac 6000 STE (Rear), 1984-87

TYPE 4 22-16
- Buick Riviera, 1986-87
- Cadillac Eldorado, 1986-87
- Cadillac Seville, 1986-87
- Oldsmobile Toronado, 1986-87

DELCO-MORAINE Single Piston Rear Wheel Disc Brake 22-18

Buick Riviera, 1982-85
DELCO-MORAINE Single Piston Rear Wheel Disc Brake................ 22-18
Buick Riviera, 1982-85
Cadillac Eldorado, 1982-85
Cadillac Seville, 1982-85
Chevrolet Camaro, 1982-87
Oldsmobile Toronado, 1982-85
Pontiac Firebird, 1982-87

GIRLOCK Single Piston Caliper 22-20

GIRLOCK Single Piston Caliper...... 22-20
Corvette (4 Wheel Disc Brakes), 1984-87

TOYOTA/GM Single Piston Caliper 22-23

TOYOTA/GM Single Piston Caliper.. 22-23
Chevrolet Nova, 1985-87

General Information

INDEX

Fig. 1 Checking rotor for lateral runout

BRAKE SHOES, LININGS & CALIPERS

Remove wheels and inspect brake disc, caliper and linings. The wheel bearings should be inspected at this time and repacked if necessary. Do not get any grease on the linings.

On all models except Chevrolet Corvette, the brake shoe and lining assemblies should be replaced if the lining is worn to within 1/32 inch of rivet heads (riveted linings) or brake shoe (bonded linings). On Chevrolet Corvette, the brake shoe and lining assemblies should be replaced when the lining is the approximate thickness of the brake shoe. On Pontiac Fiero rear brake shoes, note that a 1/10 inch thick thermal insulation is included between the brake pad friction material and shoe, and that this thickness should not be considered as usable lining material. It is recommended that brake linings always be replaced as axle sets. Do not replace individual pads or replace pads on one wheel of an axle set alone, as braking performance will be adversely affected.

If a visual inspection does not adequately determine the condition of the linings, the brake shoe and lining assemblies should be removed and inspected. If shoes do not require replacement, reinstall them in their original positions. Brake shoes and linings should also be replaced if cracked or damaged.

If the caliper is cracked or fluid leakage through the casting is evident, it must be replaced as a unit.

BRAKE ROUGHNESS

The most common cause of brake chatter on disc brakes is a variation in thickness of the disc. If roughness or vibration is encountered during highway operation or if pedal pumping is experienced at low speeds, the disc may have excessive thickness variation. To check for this condition, measure the disc at 12 points with a micrometer at a radius approximately one inch from edge of disc. If thickness measurements vary by more than .0005 inch, the disc should be replaced with a new one.

Excessive lateral runout of braking disc may cause a "knocking back" of the pistons, possibly creating increased pedal travel and vibration when brakes are applied.

Before checking the runout, wheel bearings should be adjusted. The readjustment is very important and will be required at the completion of the test to prevent bearing failure. Be sure to make the adjustment according to the recommendations given under "Front Wheel Bearings, Adjust" in the car chapters.

BRAKE DISC SERVICE

Servicing of disc brakes is extremely critical due to the close tolerances required in machining the brake disc to insure proper brake operation.

The maintenance of these close controls of the shape of the rubbing surfaces is necessary to prevent brake roughness. In addition, the surface finish must be non-directional and maintained at a micro inch finish. This close control of the rubbing surface finish is necessary to avoid pulls and erratic performance, and to promote long lining life and equal lining wear of both left and right brakes.

In light of the foregoing remarks, refinishing of the rubbing surfaces should not be attempted unless precision equipment, capable of measuring in micro inches (millionths of an inch) is available.

To check lateral runout of a disc, mount a dial indicator on a convenient part (steering knuckle, tie rod, disc brake caliper housing) so that the plunger of the dial indicator contacts the disc at a point one inch from the outer edge, **Fig. 1.** If the total indicated runout exceeds specifications, install a new disc.

Fig. 2 Checking rotor parallelism (thickness variation)

To check parallelism (thickness variation), mount dial indicators, **Fig. 2,** so the plunger contacts rotor approximately 1 inch from outer edge. If parallelism exceeds specifications, replace rotor.

GENERAL PRECAUTIONS

1. Grease or any other foreign material must be kept off the brake linings, caliper, surfaces of the disc and external surfaces of the hub, during service procedures. Handling the brake disc and caliper should be done in a way to avoid deformation of the disc and nicking or scratching brake linings.
2. If inspection reveals rubber piston seals are worn or damaged, they should be replaced immediately.
3. During removal and installation of a wheel assembly, exercise care so as not to interfere with or damage the caliper splash shield, or bleeder screw.
4. Front wheel bearings should be adjusted to specifications.
5. Be sure vehicle is centered on hoist before servicing any of the front end components to avoid bending or damaging the disc splash shield on full right or left wheel turns.
6. Before the vehicle is moved after any brake service work, be sure to obtain

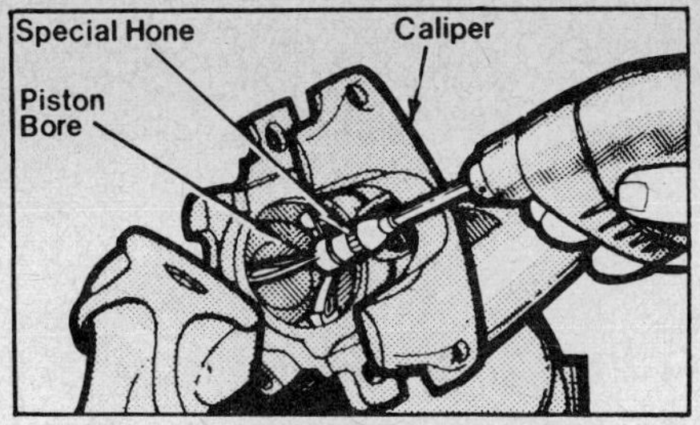

Fig. 3 Honing caliper piston bore

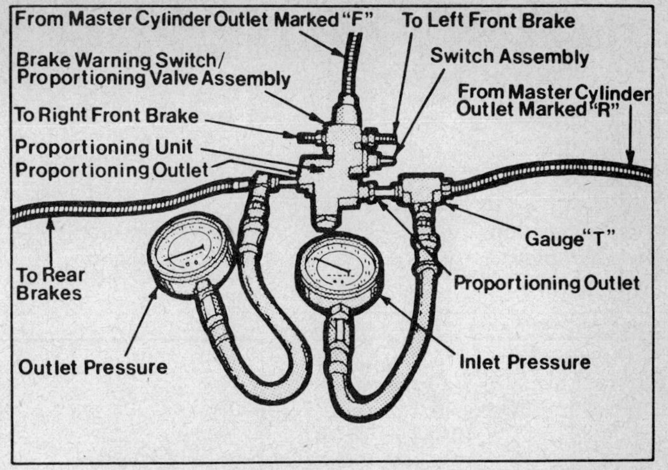

Fig. 4 Gauge hook-up for testing proportioning valve (typical)

a firm brake pedal.

7. The assembly bolts of two piece caliper housings should not be disturbed unless the caliper requires service.

INSPECTION OF CALIPER

Should it become necessary to remove the caliper for installation of new parts, clean all parts in alcohol, wipe dry using lint free cloths, using an air hose to blow out drilled passages and bores. Check dust boots for punctures or tears. If punctures or tears are evident, new boots should be installed upon reassembly.

Inspect piston bores in both housings for scoring or pitting. Bores that show light scratches or corrosion can usually be cleaned with crocus cloth. However, bores that have deep scratches or scoring may be honed, provided the diameter of the bore is not increased more than .002 inches. If the bore does not clean up within this specification, a new caliper housing should be installed (black stains on the bore walls are caused by piston seals and will do no harm).

When using a hone, **Fig. 3,** be sure to install the hone baffle before honing bore. The baffle is used to protect the hone stones from damage. Use extreme care in cleaning the caliper after honing. Remove all dust and grit by flushing the caliper with alcohol. Wipe dry with clean lint free cloth and then clean a second time in the same manner.

BLEEDING DISC BRAKES

Pressure bleeding is recommended for all hydraulic disc brake systems.

The disc brake hydraulic system can be bled manually or with pressure bleeding equipment. On vehicles with disc brakes the brake pedal will require more pumping and frequent checking of fluid level in master cylinder during bleeding operation.

Never use brake fluid that has been drained from hydraulic system when bleeding the brakes. Be sure the disc brake pistons are returned to their normal positions and that the shoe and lining assemblies are properly seated. Before driving the vehicle, check brake operation to be sure that a firm pedal has been obtained.

PROPORTIONING VALVE

The proportioning valve (when used), **Fig. 4,** provides balanced braking action between front and rear brakes under a wide range of braking conditions. The valve regulates the hydraulic pressure applied to the rear wheel cylinders, thus limiting rear braking action when high pressures are required at the front brakes. In this manner, premature rear wheel skid is prevented.

TESTING PROPORTIONING VALVE

When a premature rear wheel slide is obtained on a brake application, it usually is an indication that the fluid pressure to the rear wheels is above the 50% reduction ratio for the rear line pressure and that malfunction has occurred within the proportioning valve.

To test the valve, install gauge set shown in **Fig. 4** in brake line between master cylinder and proportioning valve, and at output end of proportioning valve and brake line as shown. Be sure all joints are fluid tight.

Have a helper exert pressure on brake pedal (holding pressure). Obtain a reading on master cylinder output of approximately 700 psi. While pressure is being held as above, reading on valve outlet should be 550-610 psi. If the pressure readings do not meet these specifications, the valve should be removed and a new valve installed.

Delco-Moraine Single Piston W/Single Mounting Bolt

INDEX

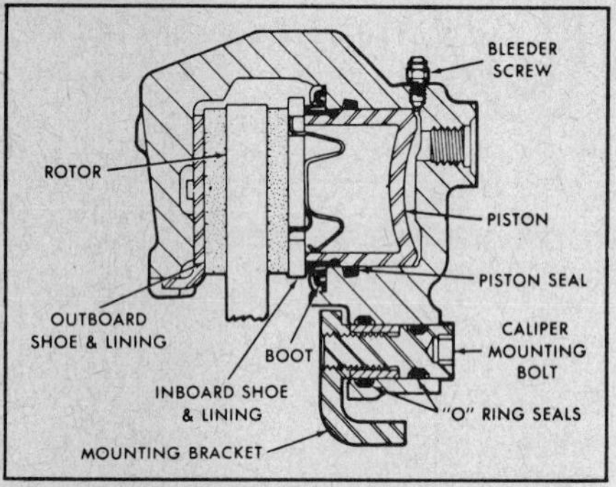

Fig. 1 Single piston disc brake assembly cross sectional view

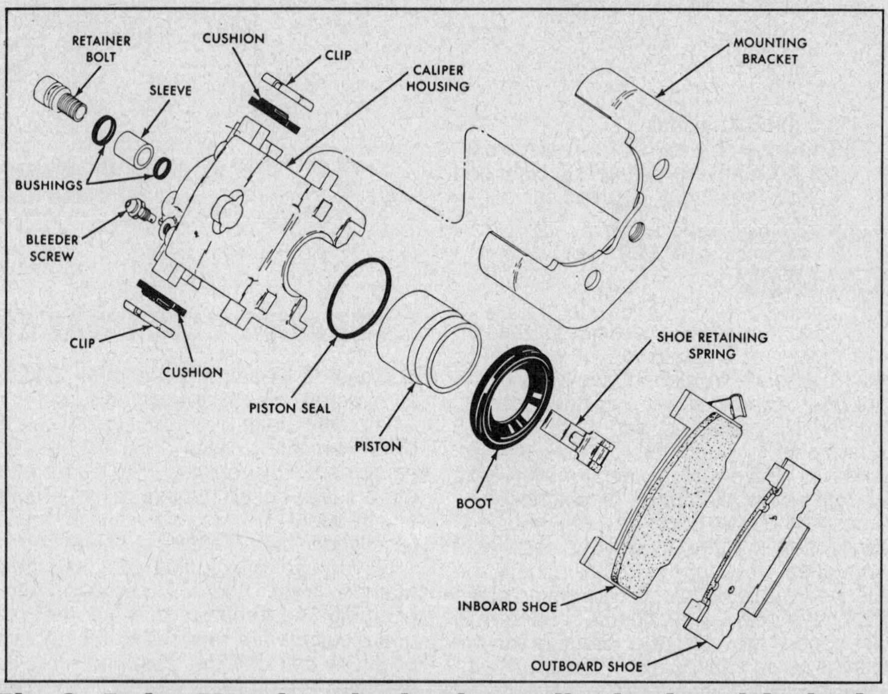

Fig. 2 Delco-Moraine single piston disc brake with single mounting bolt

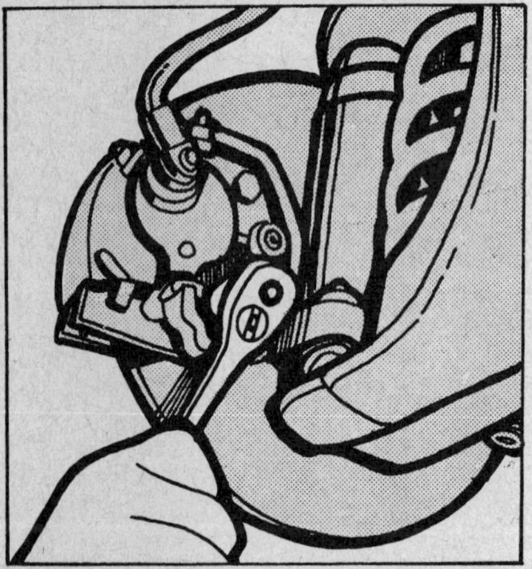

Fig. 3 Removing mounting bracket from steering knuckle

DESCRIPTION

This single piston sliding caliper assembly, **Figs. 1 and 2,** incorporates a one piece housing with the inboard side of the housing bored for the piston. A seal within the housing bore provides a hydraulic seal between the piston and housing wall.

A spring steel scraper (wear sensor) is incorporated on each inboard shoe. When shoe lining has worn to within .030 inch of the shoe, the sensor scrapes the rotor and emits an audible high frequency sound indicating that the linings should be replaced.

The caliper assembly slides on a mounting sleeve which is secured by a mounting bolt. Upon brake application fluid pressure against the piston forces the inboard shoe against the inboard side of the rotor. This action causes the caliper to slide until the outboard shoe comes in contact with the rotor.

CALIPER REMOVAL

1. Siphon brake fluid from master cylinder to bring level to 1/3 full, discard brake fluid removed.
2. Raise vehicle and remove wheel and tire assembly.
3. Install a 7 inch C-clamp on caliper with solid end of clamp on caliper housing and screw end on metal portion of outboard brake shoe. Tighten clamp until piston bottoms in caliper bore, then remove clamp.
4. Disconnect brake hose from caliper and remove copper gaskets, cap end of brake hose. **If only brake shoes are to be replaced do not disconnect brake hose.**
5. Remove the two mounting brackets to steering knuckle bolts, **Fig. 3. Do not remove socket head retaining bolt. Support caliper when removing second bolt to prevent caliper from falling.**
6. Slide caliper from rotor. **If only brake shoes are to be replaced support caliper from suspension using wire. Do not stretch or kink brake hose.**

BRAKE SHOE REMOVAL

1. Remove caliper as described under "Caliper Removal."
2. Remove brake shoes, if retaining spring does not come off with inboard shoe remove it from piston.

CALIPER DISASSEMBLY

1. Using clean brake fluid clean exterior of caliper.
2. Drain brake fluid from caliper.
3. Remove caliper mounting bracket bolt and slide bracket from caliper, **Fig. 4,** then remove sleeve and bushing from bolt and bushing from caliper mounting hole, **Fig. 2.**
4. Remove clips if still in place, then remove cushions, **Fig. 5.**
5. Pad interior of caliper with clean shop towels, then direct compressed air through caliper inlet hole to remove piston. **Use only enough air pressure to ease piston out of bore. Do not place fingers in front of piston for any reason when applying compressed air. This could result in serious personal injury.**

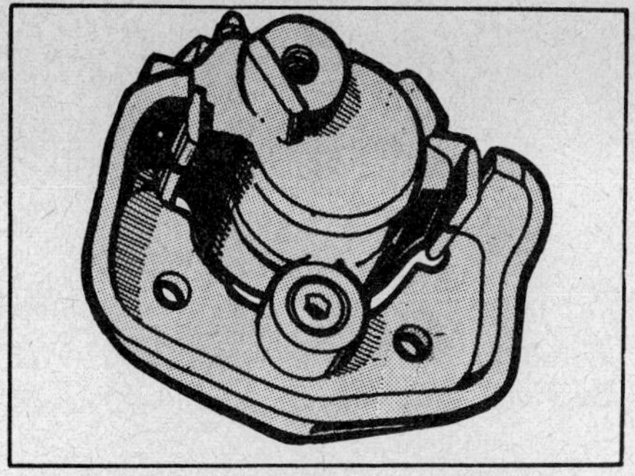

Fig. 4 Bracket assembly installed on caliper

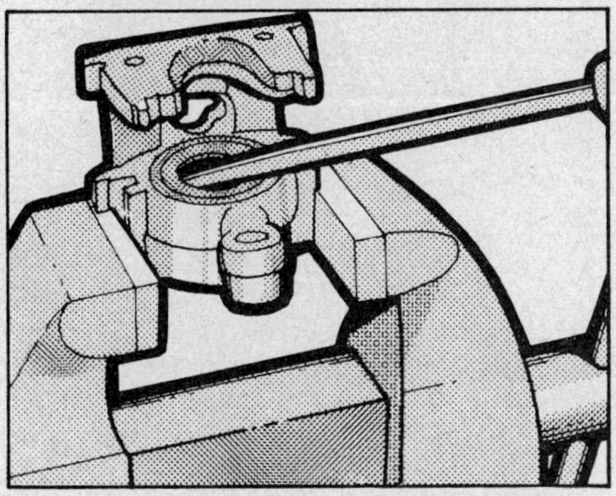

Fig. 6 Removing piston boot

6. Using a screwdriver carefully pry boot from caliper, **Fig. 6.**
7. Remove piston seal from caliper bore using a piece of wood or plastic. **Do not use metal tool to remove piston seal as it may damage caliper bore.**
8. Remove bleeder valve boot.

CALIPER ASSEMBLY

1. Lubricate caliper bore and piston seal with clean brake fluid, then position seal in caliper bore groove.
2. Lubricate piston with clean brake fluid and install boot into piston groove with fold facing the open end of piston, **Fig. 2.**
3. Insert piston into caliper, then using care to avoid unseating seal, force piston into caliper. **To force piston into caliper a force of 50-100 pounds will be required.**
4. Position outside diameter of boot into caliper counterbore and seat with suitable boot installer. **Fig. 7. Ensure that retaining ring molded into boot is not bent and that boot is installed fully and evenly below and around the caliper, as dirt and moisture may enter caliper and cause damage and corrosion.**
5. Install bleeder screw.
6. Position and stretch cushions over caliper lugs, fitting the heavy section in the lug recess and saw-tooth edges of cushions facing out, **Fig. 5.**
7. Using silicone lubricant, liberally lubricate sleeve and bushings and the unthreaded portion of the retainer bolt. Install the larger bushing in the caliper hole groove and install the sleeve. Install the smaller bushing in the retainer bolt groove.
8. With caliper clamped in a vise, position clips over cushions and squeeze mounting bracket over clips, aligning the bolt hole. Move bracket against retainer boss on caliper and install retainer bolt. Torque bolt to 28 ft. lbs., (38 Nm). **Considerable force may be required to squeeze bracket over cushions and clips on caliper. Start open end of bracket over ends of clips near the boot and move the bracket toward the closed end of caliper.**

BRAKE SHOE INSTALLATION

1. Position retaining spring on inboard shoe, place single leg in brake shoe hole, then snap two other legs over notch in shoe. **Some inboard replacement brake pads incorporate wear sensors and have a specific left and righthand assembly. Properly installed, the wear sensor will face toward the rear of caliper.**
2. Install shoe in caliper.
3. Position caliper over rotor, align mounting holes, install and torque bolts to 70 ft. lbs., (95 Nm).
4. Using suitable pliers clinch outboard shoe to caliper, place lower jaw of pliers on bottom edge of shoe, place upper jaw of pliers on shoe tab, squeeze pliers and bend tab. Clinch other end of shoe in same manner. Outboard end play should be zero to .005 inch., (zero to 0.127 mm).
5. Install wheel and tire assembly and lower vehicle.
6. Add brake fluid to within 1/4 inch from top of master cylinder. **Pump brake pedal several times to ensure it is firm before moving vehicle.**

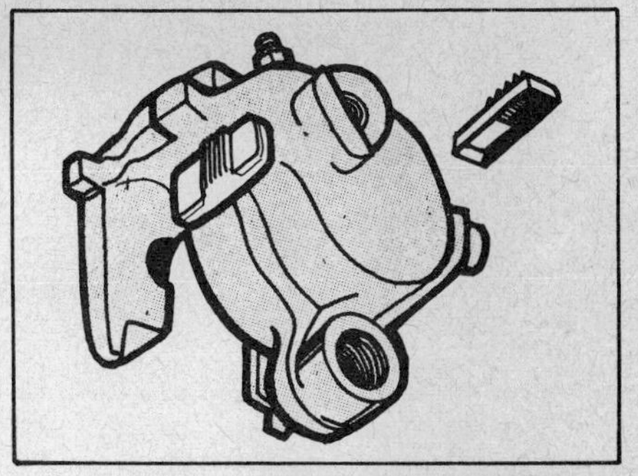

Fig. 5 Removing and installing cushions

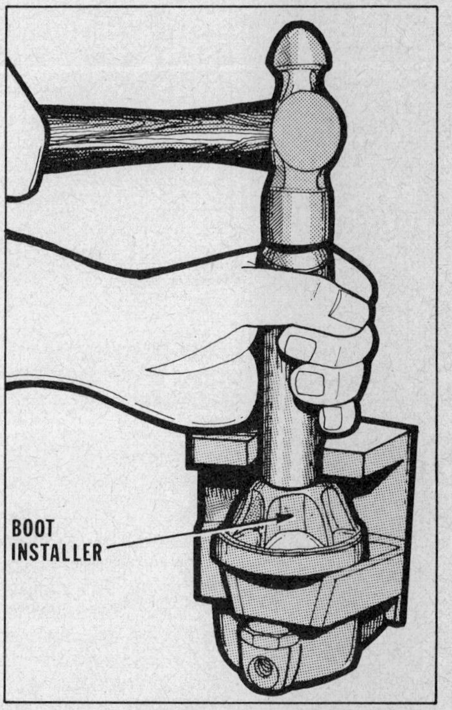

Fig. 7 Installing boot on caliper

CALIPER INSTALLATION

1. Install caliper as described under "Brake Shoe Installation", then install brake hose with new copper gaskets, torque fitting to 21 ft. lbs., (29 Nm), if removed, bleed brake system. **Brake hose fitting must be against machined surface on caliper to ensure proper hose positioning.**

Delco-Moraine W/Opposed Pistons

INDEX

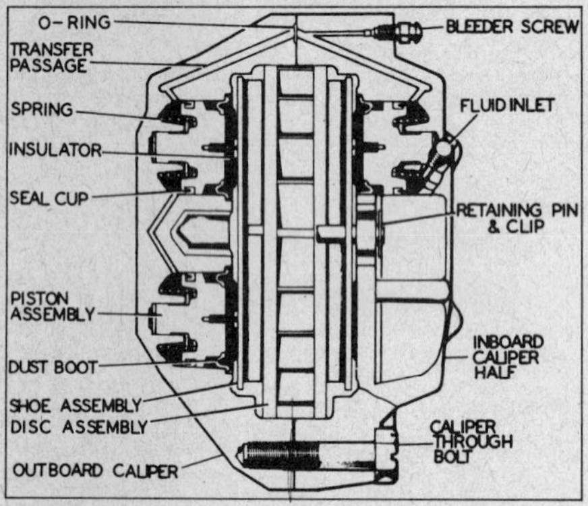

Fig. 1 Delco-Moraine opposed piston disc brake assembly

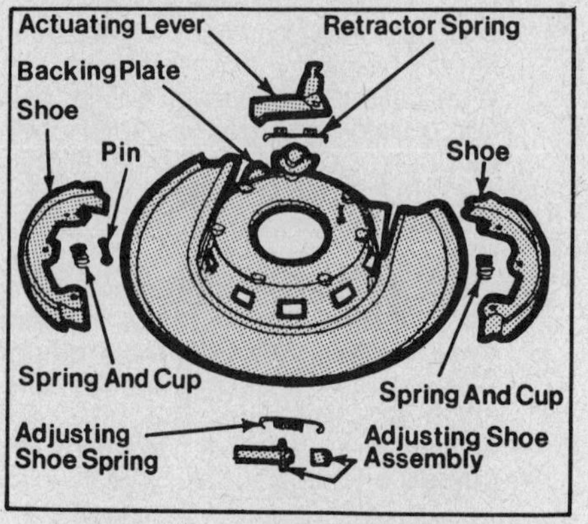

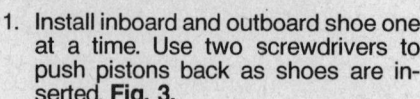

Fig. 2 Delco-Moraine parking brake components

Fig. 3 Installing Delco-Moraine disc brake shoes

DESCRIPTION

These brakes are used on all four wheels. The components of the disc brake system are shown in **Fig. 1.** The caliper assemblies replace the conventional wheel cylinder, brake shoes and linings, and the disc replaces the brake drum.

The caliper assembly contains four pistons, two acting on each shoe with one shoe on each side of the disc.

The brake disc is riveted to the hub flange at the front wheel and to the spindle flange at the rear wheel. The disc rotates through the caliper assembly, which is bolted to a support that is attached to the steering knuckle at the front wheel and the spindle support bolts at the rear wheel. The disc has cooling fins between the two shoe reacting surfaces. When a disc must be replaced, the rivets can be drilled out and then the wheel studs will be used for disc retention purposes.

A miniature set of brake shoes, mounted on a flange plate and shield assembly attached to the rear wheel spindle support bolts, are used for vehicle parking, **Fig. 2.**

REMOVING LINING

1. To prevent overflow, remove two thirds of brake fluid from master cylinder.
2. Support vehicle on hoist and remove wheel.
3. Remove cotter pin from inboard end of retaining pin.
4. Remove inboard and outboard shoe by pulling up.

INSTALLING LINING

1. Install inboard and outboard shoe one at a time. Use two screwdrivers to push pistons back as shoes are inserted, **Fig. 3.**
2. Install retaining pin through outboard caliper half, outboard shoe, inboard shoe and inboard caliper half. Insert a new 3/32 x 5/8 inch plated cotter pin through retaining pin.
3. Repeat above procedure at each wheel where shoes are to be replaced.
4. Refill master cylinder, then install wheel and lower vehicle. **Do not move vehicle until a firm brake pedal has been obtained.**

CALIPERS

The caliper assembly, **Fig. 4,** incorporates two halves retained by bolts at the flange end. The two halves contain fluid crossover passages from one to the other, sealed with O-rings.

The bleeder screw is threaded into a passage drilled to intersect the fluid crossover passage. The bleeder screws are located at the front of each caliper. There are two bleeder screws, one inboard, one outboard at the rear wheels, and one bleeder screw at the inboard side at the front wheel. It is necessary, therefore, to remove the rear wheel when bleeding the rear caliper.

REMOVING CALIPER

1. Support vehicle on hoist and remove wheel.
2. On front caliper, disconnect brake hose from support bracket. On rear caliper, disconnect tubing from inboard caliper. Tape open tube or line end to prevent entry of dirt.
3. Remove caliper mounting bolts and remove caliper.

DISASSEMBLING CALIPER

1. Remove brake hose from front caliper.
2. Remove cotter pin from retaining pin, then remove pin and shoe assembly from caliper.
3. Remove caliper retaining bolts and separate caliper halves, then remove the two O-rings from fluid transfer cavities in ends of caliper halves.
4. Push piston into caliper as far as it will move, then insert a screwdriver under inner edge of steel ring in boot and using piston as a fulcrum, pry piston boot from its seat in caliper half. **Use care not to puncture seal when removing pistons from caliper.**
5. Remove pistons and springs from caliper half, then remove boot and seal from piston.

CLEANING & INSPECTION

1. Clean all metal parts using clean brake fluid, removing all traces of dirt and grease. **Never use mineral base cleaning solvents as they can cause deterioration of rubber parts or make them soft and swollen.**
2. Using air pressure, blow out all fluid passages in caliper halves, making sure that these passages are not obstructed.
3. Discard all rubber parts and replace with new service kit parts.

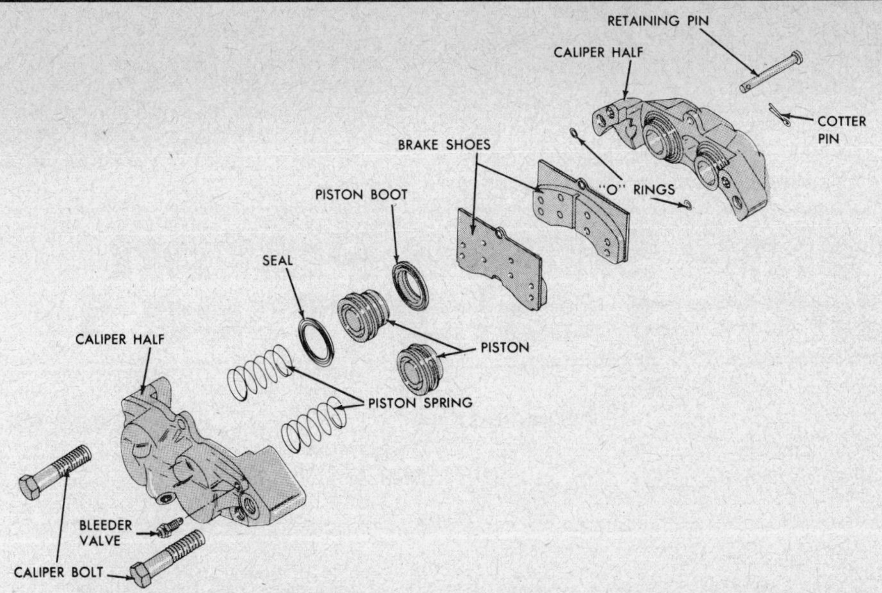

Fig. 4 Delco-Moraine disc brake caliper components

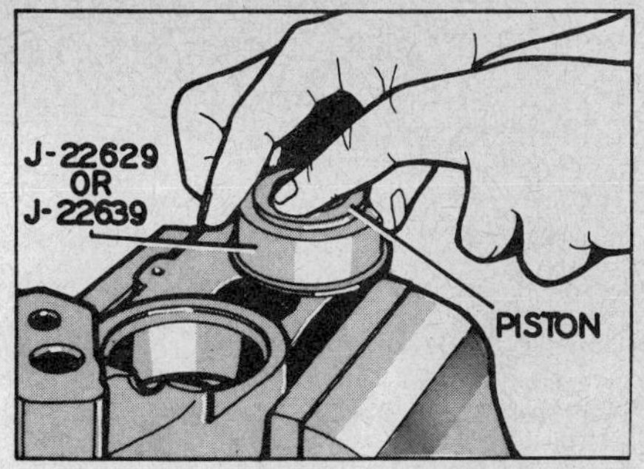

Fig. 5 Installing piston in caliper

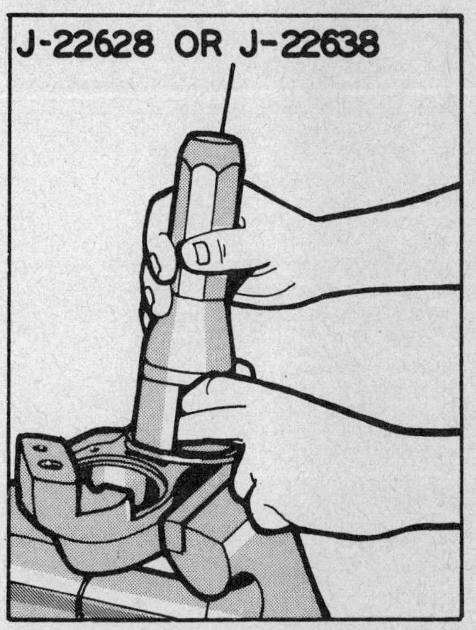

Fig. 6 Installing boot seal in caliper

4. Inspect piston bores. They must be free of scores and pits. A damaged bore will cause leaks and unsatisfactory brake operation. If either caliper half is damaged to the extent that polishing with fine crocus cloth will not restore to satisfactory condition, replace the caliper half.
5. Check fit of piston in bore using a feeler gauge. Clearance should be as follows: 7/8 inch bore, .0045-.010; 1 3/8 inch bore, .0035-.009. If bore is not damaged and clearance exceeds specifications, only a new piston will be required.

ASSEMBLING CALIPER

1. Install seal in piston groove which is closest to flat end of piston. The seal lip must face toward large end of piston. **Make certain seal lips are in piston groove and do not extend over step in end of groove.**
2. Place spring in piston bore, then lubricate seal with brake fluid.
3. Install piston assembly in bore using tool J-22591, 22629 or 22639, **Fig. 5.** Use care not to damage seal lip as piston is pressed past edge of bore.
4. Install piston boot in groove closest to concave end of piston with fold in boot facing toward end of piston with seal attached. **Apply a bead of suitable sealer (GM 1052366 or equivalent) into piston boot groove, then install boot into groove.**
5. Make certain that piston slides smoothly into bore until end of piston is flush with end of bore. If not, recheck piston assembly and position of piston spring and seal.
6. Using boot seal installer tool J-22592, J-22628 or J-22638, **Fig. 6,** over piston, seat steel boot retaining ring evenly into counterbore. **Boot retaining ring must be flush or below machined face of caliper. Any distortion or uneven seating could allow corrosive elements to enter bore. Push pistons into bore fully and hold in place. Apply a bead of suitable sealer (GM 1052366 or equivalent) onto outer edge of boot retaining ring to form a seal between retaining ring and caliper housing.**
7. Install O-rings in cavities around brake fluid transfer holes at both ends of outboard caliper halves. Lubricate caliper bolts with Delco Brake Lube 540032 (or equivalent) or clean brake fluid, then secure caliper halves together and torque front caliper housing bolts to 130 ft. lbs. and rear caliper housing bolts to 68 ft. lbs.

INSTALLING CALIPER

1. Mount caliper over disc, then using two screwdrivers, depress pistons so that caliper can be lowered into place. **Use care not to damage boots on edge of disc as caliper is installed.**
2. Install mounting bolts and torque to 70 ft. lbs. **If reusing old shoe assemblies, be sure to install shoes in same location from which removed.**
3. Install disc pads as outlined previously.
4. Place a new copper gasket on male end of front wheel brake hose and install brake hose in calipers. With wheels straight ahead, pass female end of hose through support bracket, then making certain that tube seat is clean, connect brake line tube nut to caliper and tighten securely.
5. Allowing hose to seek a normal position, without twist, insert hose fitting in support bracket and secure with U-shaped retainer, then while turning steering geometry from stop to stop, check that hose does not contact other parts at anytime. If contact does occur, remove U-shaped retainer and twist hose in a direction that will eliminate hose contact. Reinstall retainer and recheck for hose contact. If satisfactory, place steel tube connecter in hose fitting and tighten securely.
6. If rear caliper is being serviced, connect brake line to caliper.
7. Bleed brakes and install wheels. **Do not move vehicle until a firm pedal has been obtained.**

SERVICE SUMMARY

1. There is no brake shoe adjustment on the disc brakes.
2. The groove in the brake shoe is an indicator of brake wear. When the groove is just about gone it is time for shoe replacement.
3. When replacing shoes it is necessary to siphon fluid from master cylinder reservoir to make room for fluid to return to the reservoir when pushing the caliper pistons back into their bores to make room for the thickness of the new shoes.
4. The shoes have a directional arrow on the back of the shoe plate. This arrow points to the forward rotation of the disc, and the purpose is for aligning the grain of the lining material in relation to the disc.
5. When bleeding the calipers, the rear wheel must be removed to reach the outboard bleeder screw.
6. A retaining clip of thin metal is used to hold the pistons into the bores while installing the new brake shoes.

7. The caliper assembly is removable, after disconnecting the brake line, by removing the two mounting bolts and lifting the assembly off the disc.
8. The disc is riveted to the spindle flange in production. However, the rivets may be drilled out and the wheel studs and nuts are sufficient to hold the new disc in place when replacing the disc.
9. The rear wheel spindle must be removed to gain access to the parking brake shoes. It is necessary then to remove the caliper, the axle drive shaft, the spindle drive shaft yoke and remove the spindle and disc as an assembly from the wheel support. You now have access to the parking brake shoes the same as any other conventional bendix type brake shoe, **Fig. 2.**

Delco-Moraine Single Piston W/Dual Mounting Bolts (Type 1)

INDEX

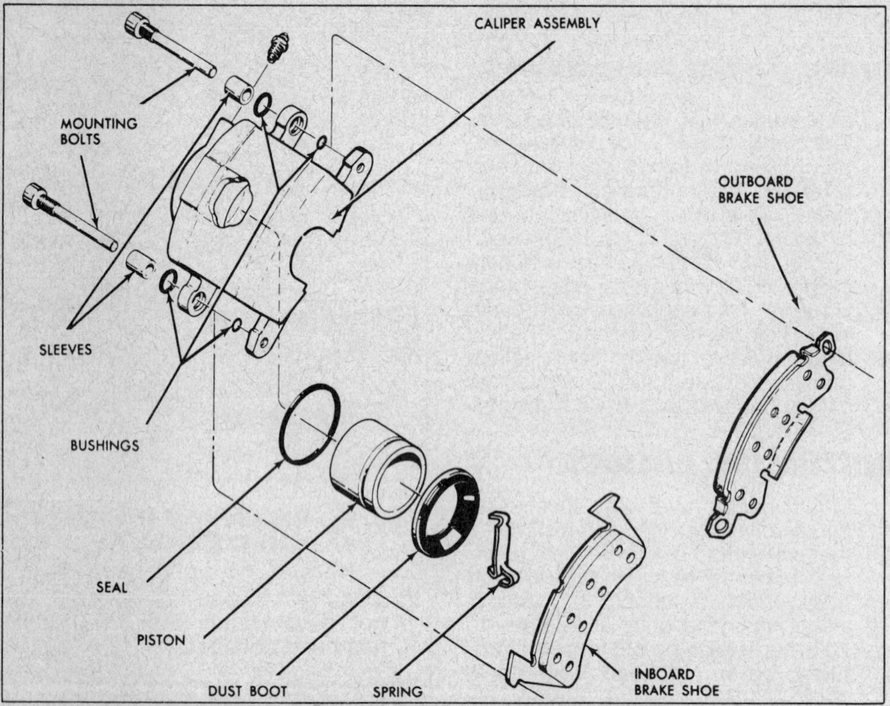

Fig. 1 Typical Delco-Moraine 3000/3075/3100 series caliper exploded view

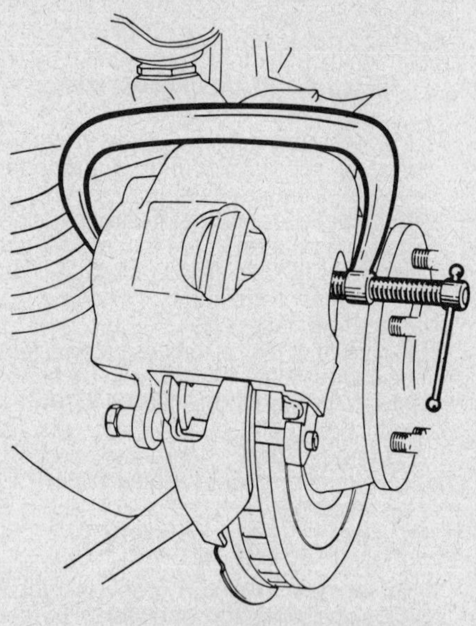

Fig. 2 Compressing piston and shoes with C-clamp

DESCRIPTION

This single piston sliding caliper assembly, **Fig. 1,** incorporates a one piece housing with the inboard side of the housing bored for the piston. A seal within the housing bore provides a hydraulic seal between the piston and housing wall.

A spring steel scraper (wear sensor) is incorporated on each inboard shoe. When the shoe lining has worn to within .030 inch of the shoe, the sensor scrapes the rotor and emits an audible high frequency sound indicating that the linings should be replaced.

The caliper assembly slides on the mounting bolts. Upon brake application, fluid pressure against the piston forces the inboard shoe and lining assembly against the inboard side of the disc. This action causes the caliper assembly to slide until the outboard lining comes into contact with the disc. As pressure builds up, the linings are pressed against the disc with increased force.

CALIPER REMOVAL

1. Siphon enough brake fluid out of the master cylinder to bring fluid level to 1/3 full to avoid fluid overflow when the caliper piston is pushed back into its bore.
2. Raise vehicle and remove front wheels.
3. Using a C-clamp, as illustrated in **Fig. 2,** push piston back into its bore.
4. Remove two mounting bolts, **Fig. 3,** and lift caliper away from disc.

BRAKE SHOE REMOVAL

1. Remove caliper assembly as outlined above.
2. Remove inboard shoe. Dislodge outboard shoe and position caliper on the front suspension so the brake hose will not support the weight of the caliper.
3. Remove shoe support spring from piston.
4. Remove two sleeves from inboard ears of the caliper.
5. Remove four rubber bushings from the grooves in each of the caliper ears.

BRAKE SHOE INSTALLATION

1. Lubricate new sleeves, rubber bushings, bushing grooves and mounting bolt ends with Delco Silicone Lube or its equivalent.
2. Install new bushings and sleeves in caliper ears. **Position the sleeve so that the end toward the shoe is flush with the machined surface of the ear.**
3. Install shoe support spring by positioning single tang end of spring into

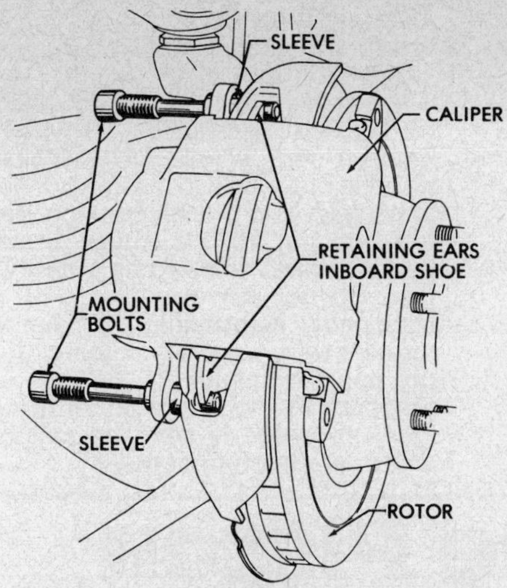

Fig. 3 Caliper & mounting bolts

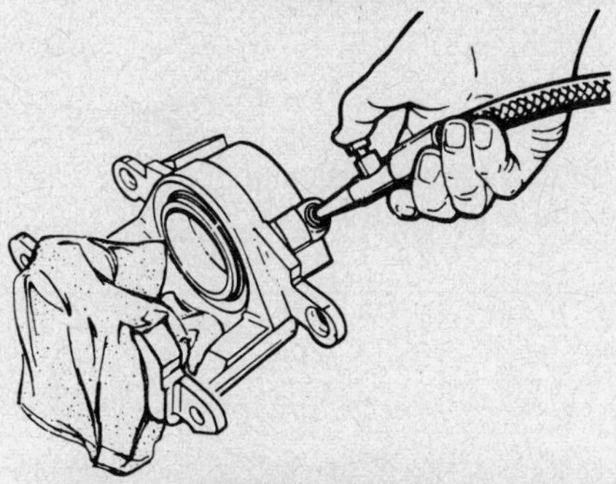

Fig. 6 Removing piston from caliper

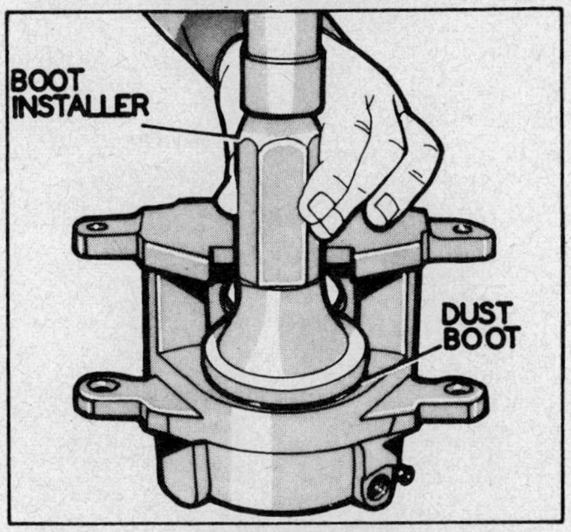

Fig. 8 Installing boot to caliper

notch cut at top of inboard shoe. Press remaining end of spring over bottom edge of shoe until shoe is engaged securely, **Fig. 4.**

4. Position inboard shoe with spring attached into caliper with ear end facing downward and bottom end facing upward with spring resting on inside diameter of piston. Press downward on both ends of shoe until shoe contacts piston and support spring contacts piston inside diameter. **Some inboard replacement brake pads incorporate wear sensors and have a specific left and righthand assembly. Properly installed, the wear**

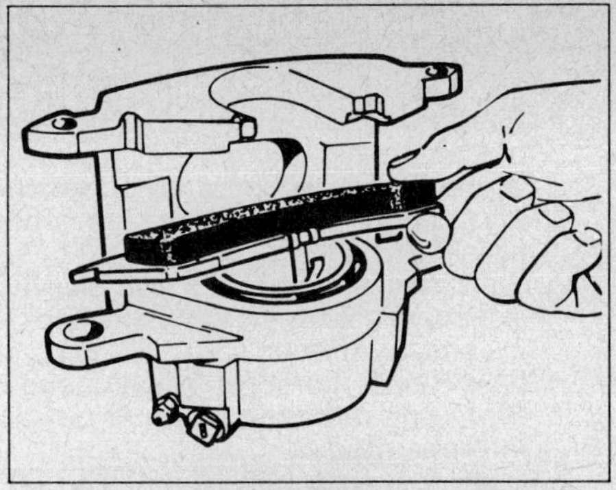

Fig. 4 Installing support spring

sensor will face toward the rear of caliper.

5. Position outboard shoe in caliper with shoe ears over caliper ears and tab at bottom of shoe engaged in caliper cutout.
6. With shoes installed, lift caliper and rest bottom edge of outboard lining on outer edge of brake disc to be sure there is no clearance between outboard shoe tab and caliper abutment.
7. Install caliper and torque mounting bolts to 28 ft. lbs.
8. Clinch upper ears of outboard shoe by positioning pliers with one jaw on top of upper ear and one jaw in notch on bottom shoe opposite ear, **Fig. 5.** Ears are to be flat against caliper housing with no radial clearance. If clearance exists, repeat clinching procedure. **Before moving vehicle, pump brake pedal several times to be sure it is firm. Do not move vehicle until a firm pedal is obtained. On some models with low drag calipers, apply approximately 175 pounds of pressure to the brake pedal three times to properly seat the caliper and related components.**

DISASSEMBLING CALIPER

1. Remove caliper as outlined above.
2. Disconnect hose from steel line, remove U-shaped retainer and withdraw hose from frame support bracket.
3. After cleaning outside of caliper, remove brake hose and discard copper gasket.
4. Drain brake fluid from caliper.
5. Pad caliper interior with clean shop towels and use compressed air to remove piston, **Fig. 6. Use just enough air pressure to ease piston out of bore. Do not blow piston out of bore. Do not place fingers in front of piston in an attempt to catch or protect it when applying compressed air. This could result in serious injury.**
6. Carefully pry dust boot out of bore.
7. Using a small piece of wood or plastic, remove piston seal from bore. **Do not use a metal tool of any kind to remove seal as it may damage bore.**
8. Remove bleeder valve.

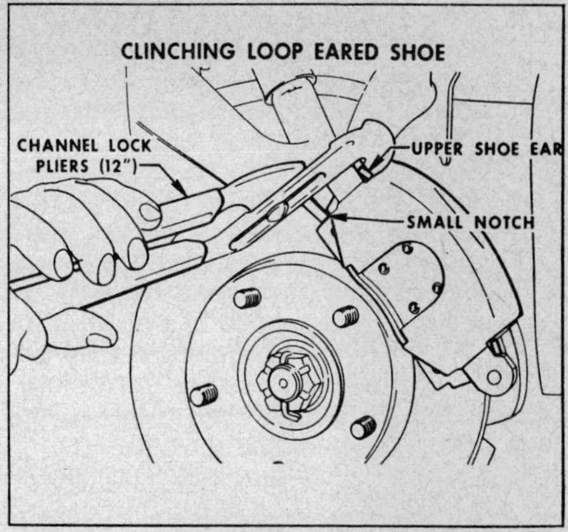

Fig. 5 Clinching loop eared brake shoe

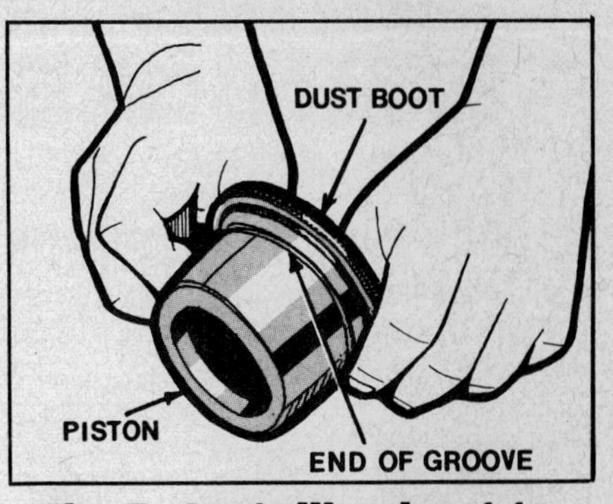

Fig. 7 Installing boot to piston

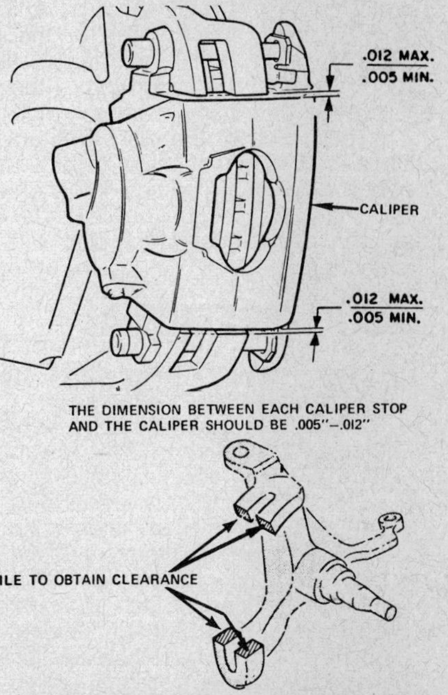

Fig. 9 Checking clearance between caliper & stops

ASSEMBLING CALIPER

1. Lubricate caliper piston bore and new piston seal with clean brake fluid. Position seal in bore groove.
2. Lubricate piston with clean brake fluid and assemble a new boot into the groove in the piston so the fold faces the open end of the piston, **Fig. 7.**

3. Using care not to unseat the seal, insert piston into bore and force the piston to the bottom of the bore.
4. Position dust boot in caliper counterbore and install, using suitable seal installer, **Fig. 8. Check the boot installation to be sure the retaining ring molded into the boot is not bent and that the boot is installed below the caliper face and evenly all around. If the boot is not fully installed, dirt and moisture may enter the bore and cause corrosion.**
5. Install the brake hose in the caliper using a new copper gasket.
6. Install shoes and re-install caliper assembly.

CALIPER INSTALLATION

1. Position caliper over disc, lining up holes in caliper with holes in mounting bracket. If brake hose was not disconnected during removal, be sure not to kink it during installation.
2. Start mounting bolts through sleeves in inboard caliper ears and the mounting bracket, making sure ends of bolts pass under ears on inboard shoe. **Right and left calipers must not be interchanged.**
3. Push mounting bolts through to engage holes in the outboard ears. Then thread mounting bolts into bracket.
4. Torque mounting bolts to 28 ft. lbs.
5. Check the dimensions between each caliper stop and caliper, **Fig. 9.**
6. If brake hose was removed, reconnect it and bleed the calipers.
7. Replace front wheels, lower vehicle and add brake fluid to master cylinder to bring level to 1/4 inch from top. **Before moving vehicle, pump brake pedal several times to be sure it is firm. Do not move vehicle until a firm pedal is obtained. On some models with low drag calipers, apply approximately 175 pounds of pressure to the brake pedal three times to properly seat the caliper and related components.**

Delco-Moraine Single Piston W/Dual Bolt Mounting (Type 2)

INDEX

DESCRIPTION

The caliper has a single piston and is mounted to the support bracket by two mounting bolts, **Figs. 1 through 4.** The caliper assembly slides on the two mounting bolts. Upon brake application, fluid pressure against the piston forces the inboard shoe and lining assembly against the inboard side of the disc. This action causes the caliper assembly to slide until the outboard lining comes into contact with the disc. As pressure builds up the linings are pressed against the disc with increased force.

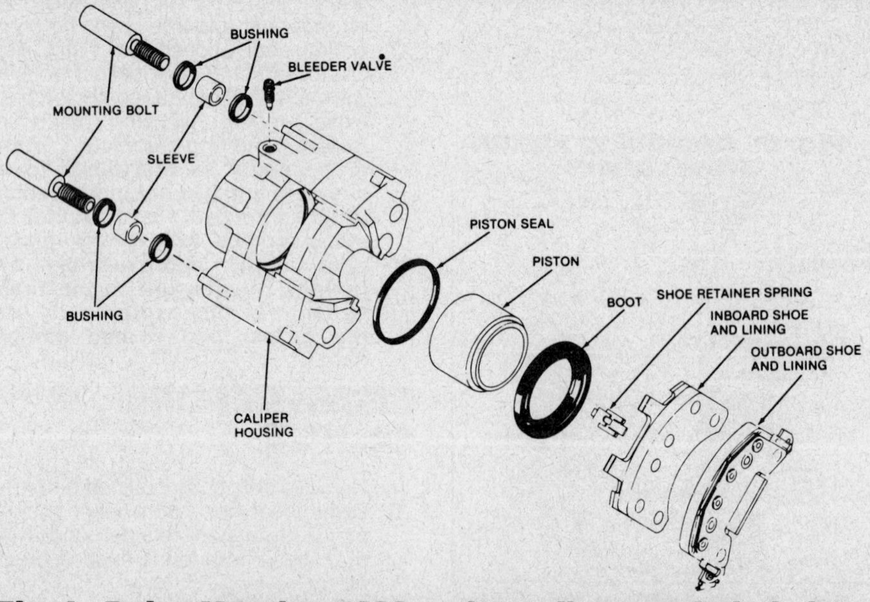

Fig. 1 Delco-Moraine 3200 series caliper exploded view. 1982–83 Exc. Chevette & 1000

CALIPER REMOVAL

1. Remove approximately 2/3 of brake fluid from master cylinder.
2. Raise and support front of vehicle, then remove wheel and tire assembly.
3. On 1982-83 models except Chevette, position C-clamp as shown in **Fig. 5,** tighten C-clamp until piston bottoms in piston bore, then remove C-clamp.
4. On 1983 Chevette and all 1984-87 models, position 12 inch slip joint pliers over inboard pad and housing as shown in **Fig. 6,** and squeeze pliers to compress caliper piston.
5. If caliper assembly is being removed for service, remove brake line fitting mounting bolt, **Fig. 6.** If only shoe and lining assemblies are to be replaced, do not disconnect brake line fitting from caliper.
6. Remove Allen head caliper mounting bolts, **Fig. 7.** If bolts show signs of corrosion, use new bolts when installing caliper assembly.
7. Remove caliper assembly from disc. If only shoe and lining assemblies are to be replaced, using a length of wire suspend caliper from spring coil. Never allow caliper to hang from brake hose.

SHOE & LINING REMOVAL

1. Remove caliper assembly as described under "Caliper Removal."
2. Remove shoe and lining assemblies from caliper, **Figs. 1 through 4,** noting the following:
   a. On models with tab mount outer shoe (all except series 3264), straighten bent over shoe tabs with suitable pliers.
   b. On models with spring mount outer shoe (series 3264), insert screwdriver between shoe and caliper and disengage buttons on shoe from holes in caliper.
3. Remove sleeves and bushings from grooves in caliper mounting bolt holes, **Figs. 1 through 4.**

CALIPER DISASSEMBLY

1. Use clean shop towels to pad interior of caliper assembly, then remove piston by directing compressed air into caliper brake line inlet hole, **Fig. 8. Use just enough air pressure to ease piston out of bore. Do not**

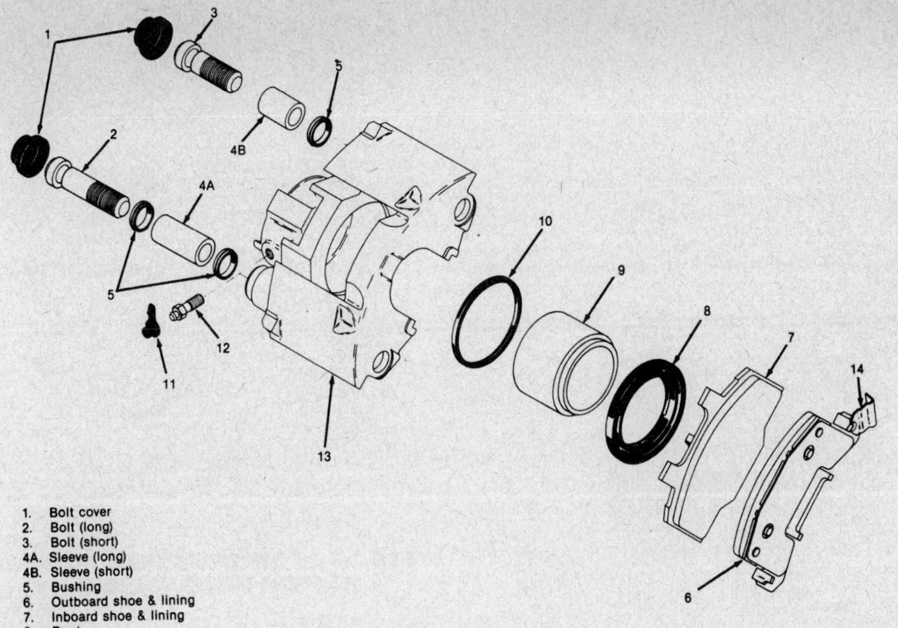

1. Bolt cover
2. Bolt (long)
3. Bolt (short)
4A. Sleeve (long)
4B. Sleeve (short)
5. Bushing
6. Outboard shoe & lining
7. Inboard shoe & lining
8. Boot
9. Piston
10. Piston seal
11. Port protector
12. Bleeder valve
13. Caliper housing
14. Wear sensor

Fig. 2 Delco-Moraine 3352 series caliper exploded view. 1983–87 Chevette & 1000

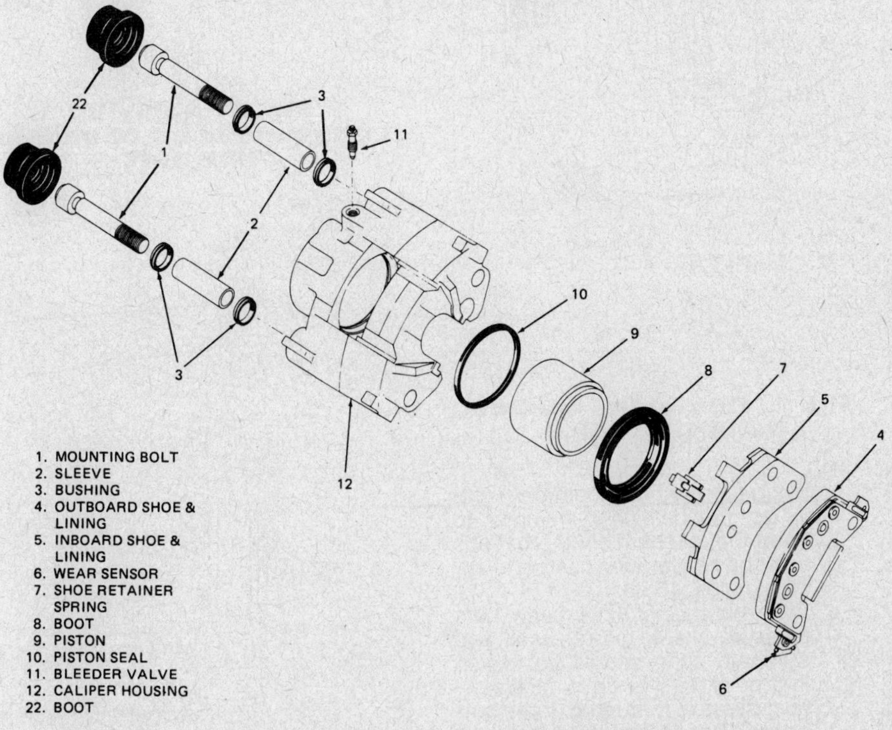

1. MOUNTING BOLT
2. SLEEVE
3. BUSHING
4. OUTBOARD SHOE & LINING
5. INBOARD SHOE & LINING
6. WEAR SENSOR
7. SHOE RETAINER SPRING
8. BOOT
9. PISTON
10. PISTON SEAL
11. BLEEDER VALVE
12. CALIPER HOUSING
22. BOOT

Fig. 3 Delco-Moraine 3257 series caliper exploded view. 1984–87 exc. Chevette & 1000

place fingers in front of piston for any reason when applying compressed air. This could result in serious personal injury.

2. Remove bleeder screw from caliper body.
3. Using a suitable screwdriver, remove dust boot from caliper bore, **Fig. 9.**
4. Using a piece of wood or plastic, remove piston seal from groove in caliper bore. **Do not use any type of metal tool to remove piston seal, since damage to caliper bore may result.**
5. Inspect piston for corrosion, scoring, nicks, wear and damage to chrome plating. If any of the above defects are found, replace piston.
6. Inspect caliper bore for corrosion, scoring, nicks, and wear. Light corrosion can be polished out using crocus cloth. If crocus cloth fails to remove corrosion, the caliper housing must be replaced.

CALIPER ASSEMBLY

1. Lubricate piston seal with clean brake fluid, then install piston seal into caliper bore groove. Check to ensure that piston seal is not twisted.
2. Lubricate caliper bore with clean brake fluid.
3. Insert piston into caliper bore, then force piston down until piston bottoms in bore.
4. Position outer diameter of dust boot in caliper housing counterbore, then seat boot as shown in **Fig. 10.**
5. Install bleeder screw on caliper housing.

SHOE & LINING INSTALLATION

1. Lubricate new bushings with suitable grease, install bushings in caliper grooves, then insert sleeves through bushings.
2. Install retaining spring onto inboard shoe and lining assembly, **Fig. 11,** if equipped, then install inboard shoe into caliper housing.
3. Install outboard shoe and lining assembly into caliper housing ensuring wear sensor is properly positioned. On models with spring mount shoe (series 3264), ensure buttons on shoe are properly engaged in holes in caliper.
4. Install caliper assembly as outlined.
5. On models with tab mount outer shoe (except series 3264), clinch outboard shoe to brake caliper as follows:
   a. Apply brakes several times to ensure caliper piston is extended and shoes are fully seated.
   b. Wedge a large flat blade screwdriver between outboard shoe flange and hat section of rotor, **Fig. 12.**
   c. Hold outer pad against caliper with suitable clamp or by applying moderate pressure on brake pedal.
   d. Position a ball peen hammer on outboard shoe tab, **Fig. 13,** then

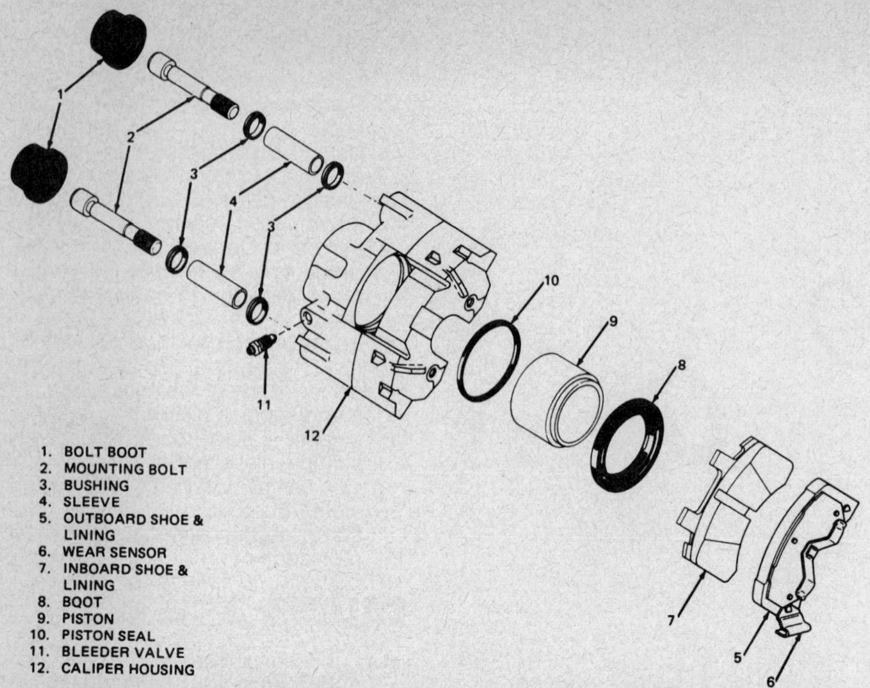

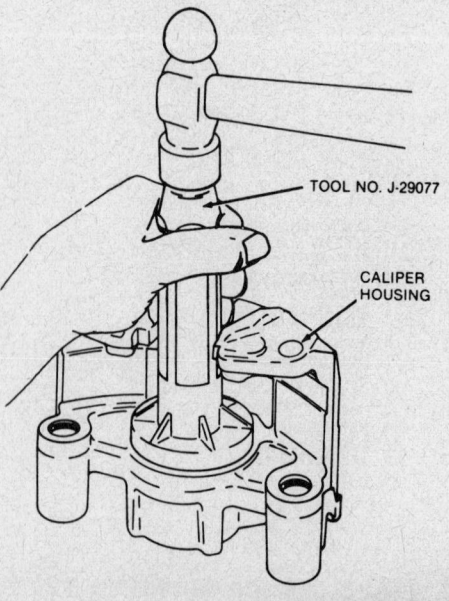

1. BOLT BOOT
2. MOUNTING BOLT
3. BUSHING
4. SLEEVE
5. OUTBOARD SHOE & LINING
6. WEAR SENSOR
7. INBOARD SHOE & LINING
8. BOOT
9. PISTON
10. PISTON SEAL
11. BLEEDER VALVE
12. CALIPER HOUSING

Fig. 4 Delco-Moraine 3264 series caliper exploded view. 1985–87 exc. Chevette & 1000

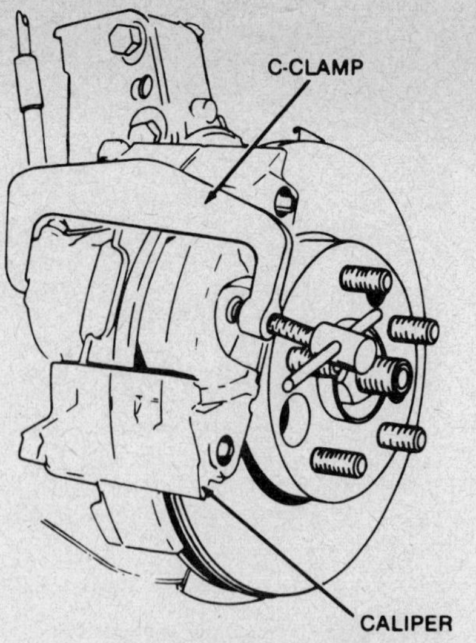

Fig. 5 Compressing caliper piston with C-clamp

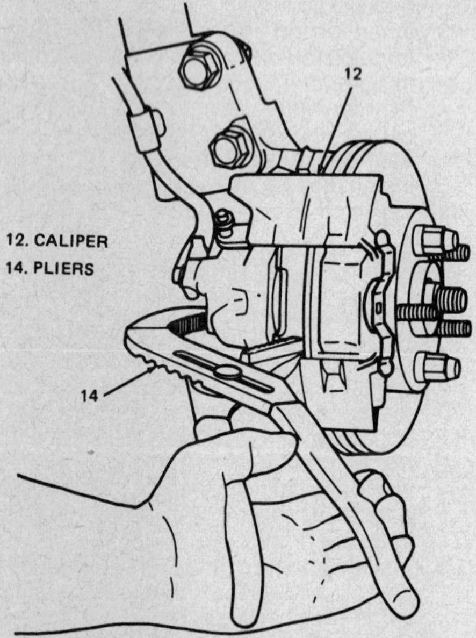

Fig. 6 Compressing caliper piston w/slip joint pliers

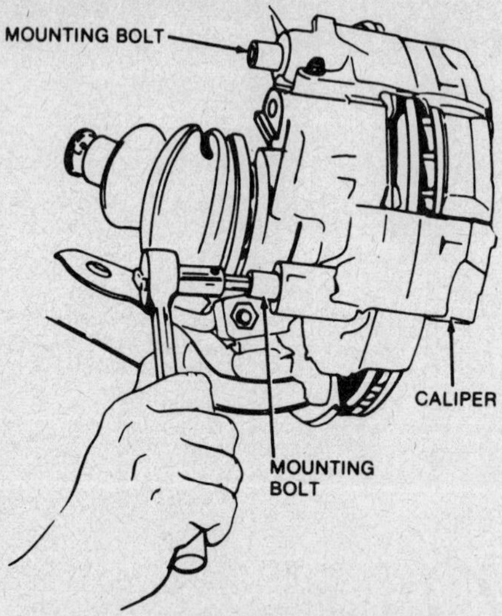

Fig. 7 Removing caliper mounting bolts

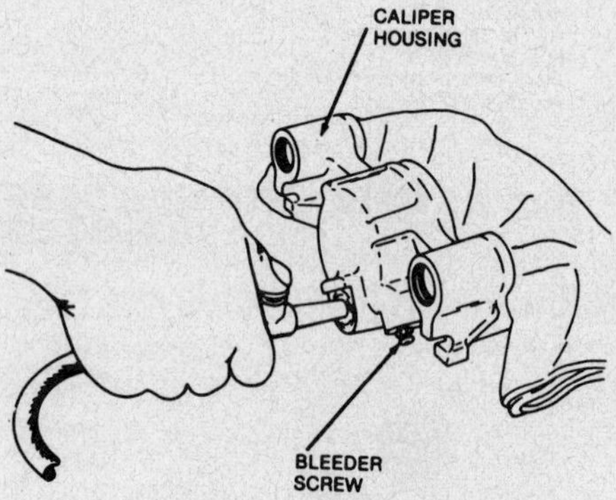

Fig. 8 Applying compressed air to caliper line port

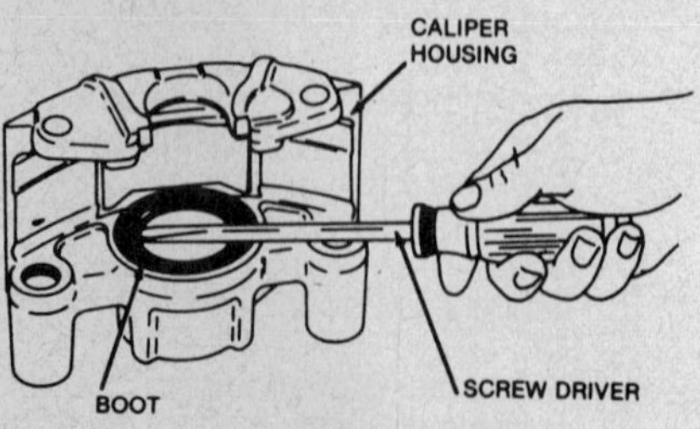

Fig. 9 Removing dust boot

using a larger brass hammer, lightly tap the ball peen hammer to bend the outboard shoe tab. Tabs must be bent around casting to approximately 45 degrees.

e. After both tabs have been bent pressure should be released and outboard shoe should be locked into position. If shoe is loose, repeat steps a. through d. **If an outboard shoe is removed from the caliper, or the tabs unclinched for any reason, then it will be necessary to replace the shoe and lining assemblies. Do not re-clinch outboard shoe locking tabs after having removed shoe from caliper.**

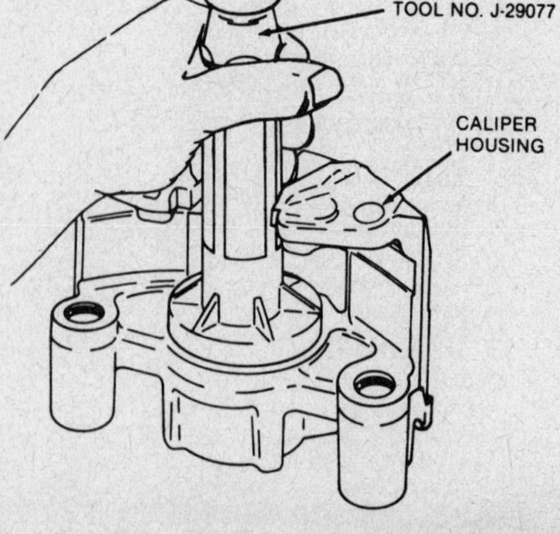

Fig. 10 Seating dust boot in caliper

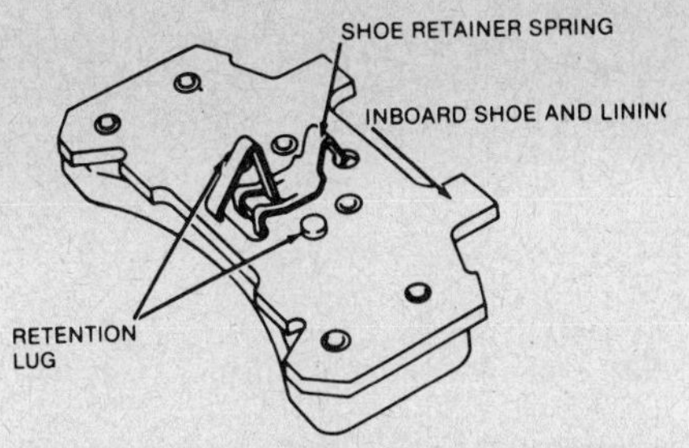

Fig. 11 Installing retainer spring on inboard shoe

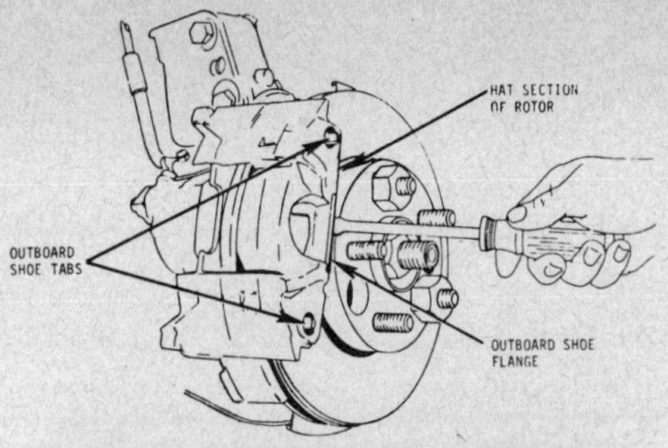

Fig. 12 Screwdriver in position between outboard shoe flange & hat section of rotor

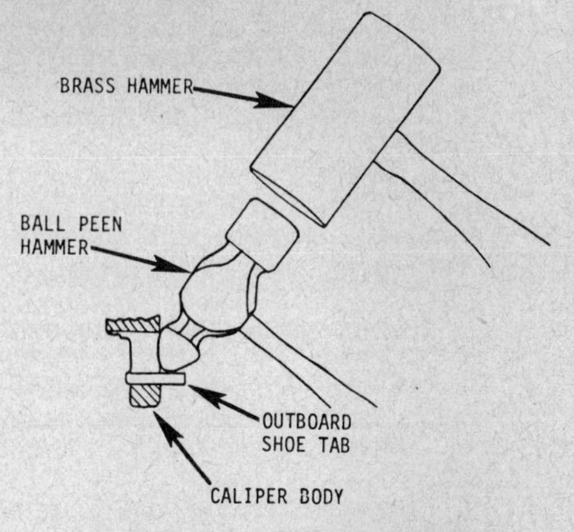

Fig. 13 Positioning hammer to clinch brake pad tabs

CALIPER INSTALLATION

1. Position caliper assembly over disc and align mounting bolt holes. If brake hoses were not disconnected during removal, use care not to kink hoses during installation.
2. Install mounting bolts and torque to 21 to 35 ft. lbs., **Fig. 7.**
3. If brake line fitting was disconnected during removal, install brake line fitting and torque retaining bolt to 18 to 30 ft. lbs.
4. Fill master cylinder. Bleed brake system if brake line was disconnected and recheck master cylinder fluid level.
5. Install wheel and tire assembly on vehicle, then lower vehicle and check brake system operation.

Delco-Moraine Single Piston W/Dual Mounting Bolts (Type 3)

INDEX

DESCRIPTION

This caliper, **Figs. 1 and 2,** has a single bore and is mounted to the support bracket with two mounting bolts. Hydraulic force, created by applying force to the brake pedal, is converted by the caliper into friction. The hydraulic force is applied equally against the piston and the bottom of the caliper bore moving the piston outward, resulting in a clamping action on the brake rotor.

FRONT BRAKE ASSEMBLY

CALIPER REMOVAL

1. Drain approximately 2/3 of brake fluid from master cylinder assembly.
2. Raise and support vehicle, then remove tire and wheel assembly.
3. If caliper is to be serviced or replaced, remove bolt securing inlet fitting, then disconnect brake hose and secure in raised position. **If only shoe and lining assemblies are being replaced, do not disconnect brake hose from caliper.**
4. Remove caliper retaining bolts and boots, **Fig. 1.**
5. Compress piston, placing suitable adjustable pliers over inboard surface of caliper housing and support bracket as shown in **Fig. 3.**
6. Remove caliper from disc. If shoe and lining assemblies are to be replaced, use a length of wire to suspend caliper. Do not allow caliper to hang from brake line.

SHOE & LINING REMOVAL

1. Remove caliper as described under "Caliper Removal."
2. To remove outboard shoe and lining assembly, use a suitable screwdriver to disengage shoe buttons from caliper holes.
3. Remove inboard shoe and lining assembly from caliper.
4. Remove sleeves from mounting bolt holes.
5. Remove bushings from mounting bolt hole grooves.

CALIPER DISASSEMBLY

1. Position a clean shop towel on inside of caliper, then using compressed air, remove piston from caliper.
2. Remove piston protector from piston.
3. Inspect piston for wear, corrosion or damage. Replace piston, if necessary.
4. Inspect caliper housing for corrosion. If corrosion exists, use a crocus cloth to remove light surface corrosion. If corrosion cannot be removed with crocus cloth, replace caliper.
5. Remove bleeder valve protector.

CALIPER ASSEMBLY

1. Clean all brake components in clean denatured alcohol. Use dry, filtered compressed air to dry components and blow out caliper housing passages.
2. Install bleeder valve onto caliper. Torque valve to 80-140 inch lbs.
3. Using clean brake fluid, lubricate caliper housing bore and bore seals.
4. Install piston seal into caliper bore groove. Ensure seal is not twisted in groove.
5. Install boot and piston protector onto piston.
6. Install piston into caliper bore and push piston completely to the bottom.
7. Using tool No. J-29077 or equivalent, install boot into caliper housing counterbore.

SHOE & LINING INSTALLATION

1. Lubricate, then install bushings into mounting bolt hole grooves.
2. Lubricate, then install sleeves into mounting bolt holes.

3. Install inboard shoe and lining onto caliper. **Ensure that tabs on inboard shoe are positioned so that they fit into corresponding holes in face of piston.**
4. Install outboard shoe and lining onto caliper. Ensure wear sensor is positioned at leading edge of brake shoe.

CALIPER INSTALLATION

1. Install caliper onto brake rotor mounting bracket.
2. Using silicone grease or equivalent, liberally coat shoulder and mounting bolt threads so caliper cavity will be filled.
3. Install caliper mounting bolts. Torque bolts to 21-35 ft. lbs.

REAR BRAKE ASSEMBLY

CALIPER REMOVAL

1. Drain approximately ²/₃ of brake fluid from master cylinder assembly.
2. Raise and support vehicle, then remove tire and wheel assembly.
3. Loosen tension on parking brake cable at equalizer, remove cable and spring from parking brake lever, **Fig. 4.**
4. While holding parking brake lever, remove locknut, parking brake lever, lever seal and anti-friction washer, **Fig. 4. Parking brake lever assembly must be removed to provide clearance for compressing caliper piston. Failure to remove lever will cause piston to be damaged when it is bottomed in bore.**
5. Remove brake line fittings from caliper if caliper is to be removed for ser-

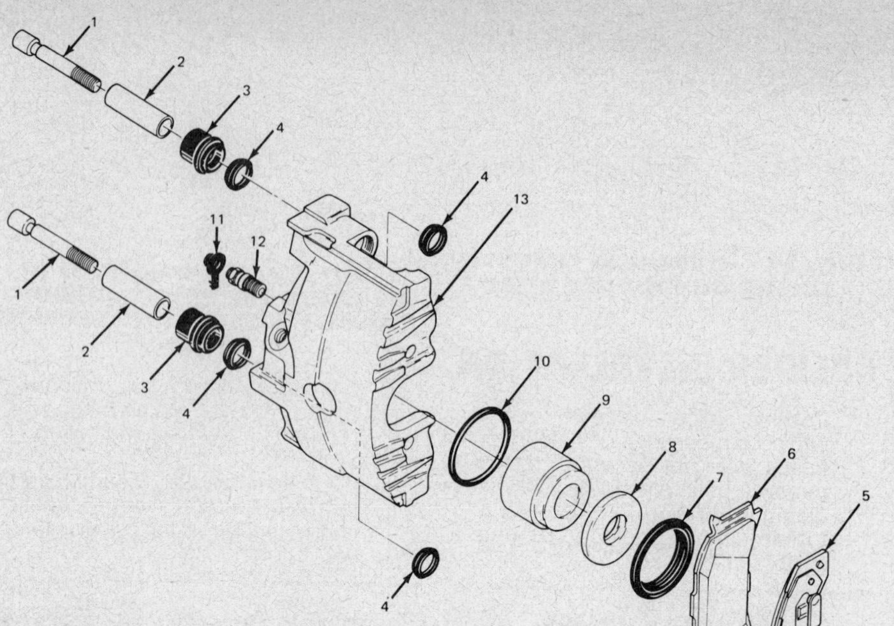

1. MOUNTING BOLT
2. SLEEVE
3. BOLT BOOT
4. BUSHING
5. OUTBOARD SHOE & LINING
6. INBOARD SHOE & LINING
7. CALIPER BOOT
8. PISTON PROTECTOR
9. PISTON
10. PISTON SEAL
11. PROTECTOR
12. BLEEDER VALVE
13. CALIPER HOUSING
18. WEAR SENSOR

Fig. 1 Delco-Moraine series 5349 front disc brake caliper exploded view

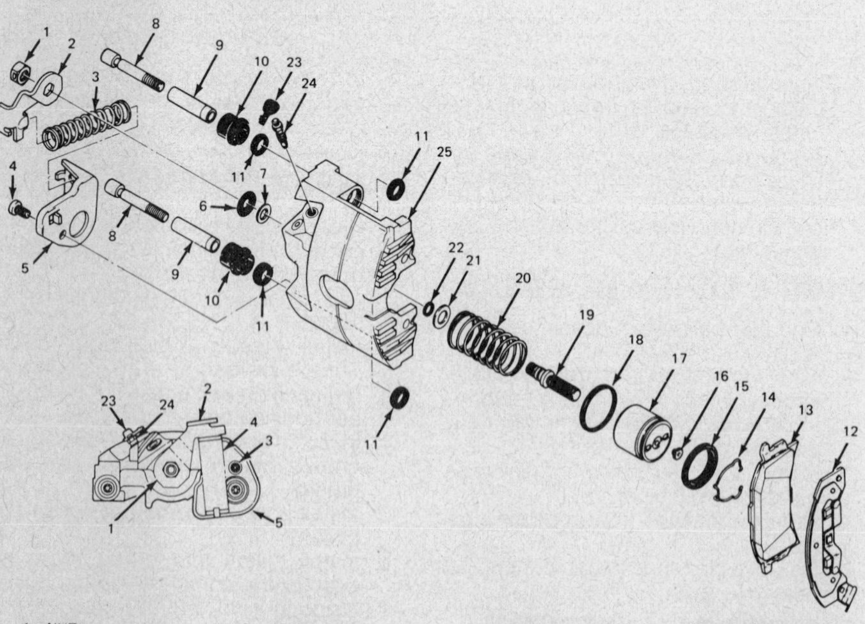

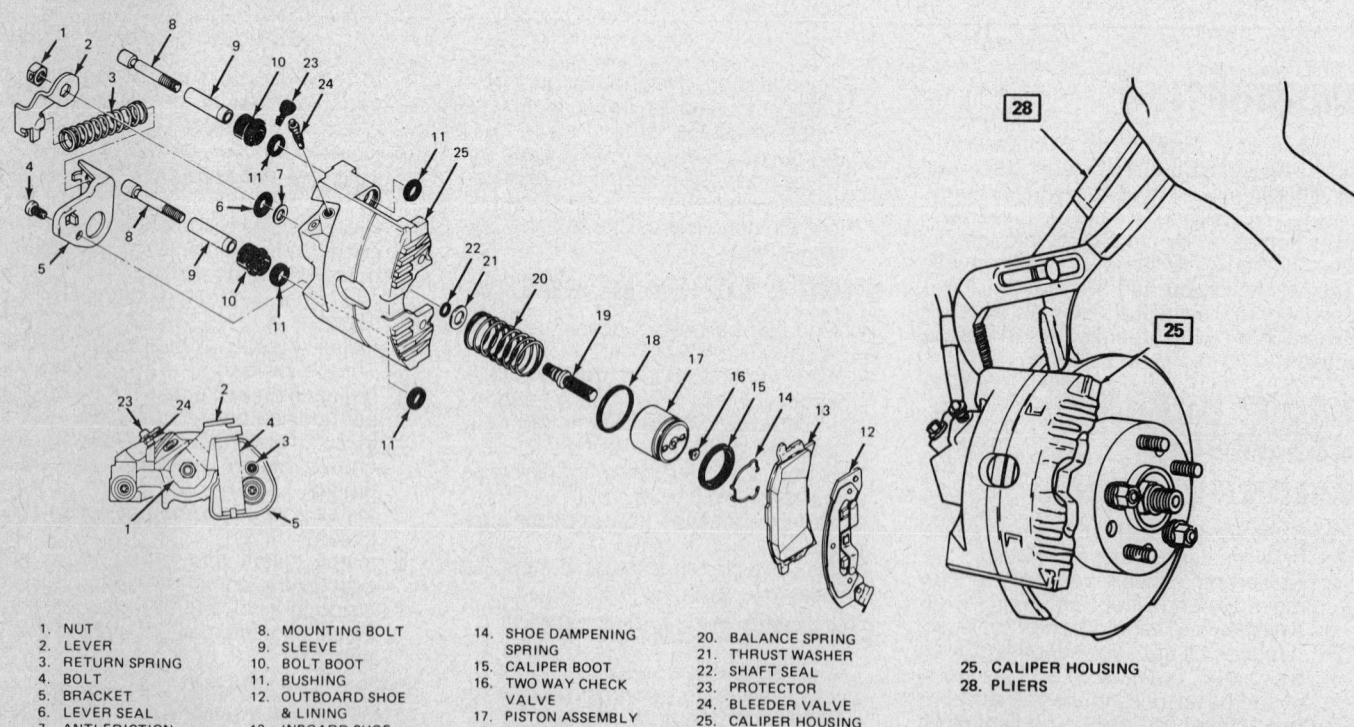

1. NUT
2. LEVER
3. RETURN SPRING
4. BOLT
5. BRACKET
6. LEVER SEAL
7. ANTI-FRICTION WASHER
8. MOUNTING BOLT
9. SLEEVE
10. BOLT BOOT
11. BUSHING
12. OUTBOARD SHOE & LINING
13. INBOARD SHOE & LINING
14. SHOE DAMPENING SPRING
15. CALIPER BOOT
16. TWO WAY CHECK VALVE
17. PISTON ASSEMBLY
18. PISTON SEAL
19. ACTUATOR SCREW
20. BALANCE SPRING
21. THRUST WASHER
22. SHAFT SEAL
23. PROTECTOR
24. BLEEDER VALVE
25. CALIPER HOUSING
26. WEAR SENSOR

Fig. 2 Delco-Moraine series 5748 rear disc brake caliper exploded view

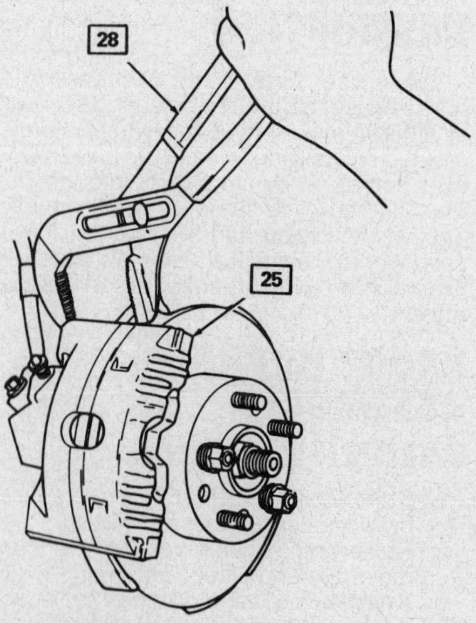

25. CALIPER HOUSING
28. PLIERS

Fig. 3 Compressing front caliper piston for caliper removal

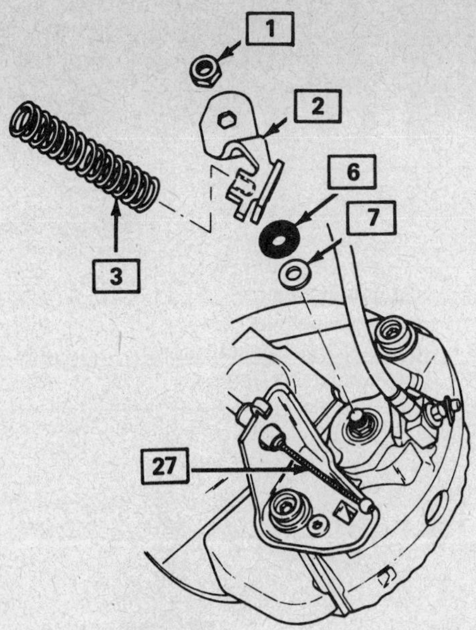

1. NUT
2. LEVER
3. RETURN SPRING
6. LEVER SEAL
7. ANTI-FRICTION WASHER
27. CABLE

Fig. 4 Parking brake lever assembly

vice or replacement. **If only the shoes and linings are to be replaced, do not disconnect brake hose from caliper.**

6. Remove caliper mounting bolts, then position C-clamp onto caliper as shown in **Fig. 5,** and tighten clamp until piston bottoms in piston bore.
7. Lift caliper off rotor and mounting bracket and support caliper, as needed, to prevent stretching brake hose.

SHOE & LINING REMOVAL

1. Remove caliper as described under "Caliper Removal."
2. Remove inboard shoe and lining assembly from caliper.
3. To remove outboard shoe and lining assembly, use a suitable screwdriver to disengage shoe buttons from caliper holes.
4. Remove sleeves from mounting bolt holes.
5. Remove bolt boots and bushings from caliper.
6. Using a suitable screwdriver, remove two-way check valve from piston end.

CALIPER DISASSEMBLY

1. Remove dampening spring from piston end, **Fig. 2.**
2. Remove nut and lever assembly.
3. Remove lever seal and anti-friction washer.
4. Place caliper into a soft jaw vise. Place a clean shop towel on inside of caliper, then using compressed air, remove piston from caliper.
5. Press on threaded end of actuator screw, then remove screw.
6. Remove shaft seal and thrust washer.
7. Remove boot from caliper housing bore. Do not use a sharp tool to remove boot from caliper.
8. Inspect piston for wear and damage. Replace caliper, if necessary.
9. If surface corrosion exists on caliper, use crocus cloth to remove corrosion from caliper.
10. Remove bleeder valve and protector.
11. Inspect caliper mounting bracket. If mounting bracket is damaged, replace as required.

CALIPER ASSEMBLY

1. Install bleeder valve. Torque valve to 80-140 inch lbs.
2. Install protector onto bleeder valve.
3. Install mounting bracket, if removed. Torque bracket bolt to 24-38 ft. lbs.
4. Using clean brake fluid, lubricate caliper housing bore seals.
5. Install piston seal into caliper bore groove.
6. Ensure caliper seal is not twisted in groove.
7. Install boot onto piston with inside lip of boot in piston groove and boot fold toward end of piston.
8. Install thrust washer onto actuator screw with bearing surface toward caliper housing.
9. Lubricate shaft seal with clean brake fluid, then install seal onto actuator screw.
10. Lubricate actuator screw, then install screw into piston.
11. Install balance spring into piston.
12. Lubricate piston with clean brake fluid, then install piston into caliper bore. Use tool No. J-23072 or equivalent to push piston completely down into bore.
13. Install anti-friction washer and lever seal onto actuator screw. ensure sealing bead on lever is against housing. Install lever onto actuator screw. Rotate lever away from stop slightly and hold while install nut. Torque nut to 30-40 ft. lbs. After nut is torqued, rotate lever back to the stop.
14. Install boot into caliper housing counterbore. Using tool No. J-28678, seat boot into counterbore.
15. Install dampening spring into groove end of piston. It may be necessary to move parking brake lever off the stop to extend piston and make spring groove accessible.

SHOE & LINING INSTALLATION

1. Lubricate, then install bushings into mounting bolt hole grooves.
2. Lubricate, then install bolt boots into mounting bolt holes.
3. Lubricate, then install sleeves into mounting bolt holes.
4. Install two-way check valve into piston end.
5. Install inboard shoe and lining into caliper. Note the following:

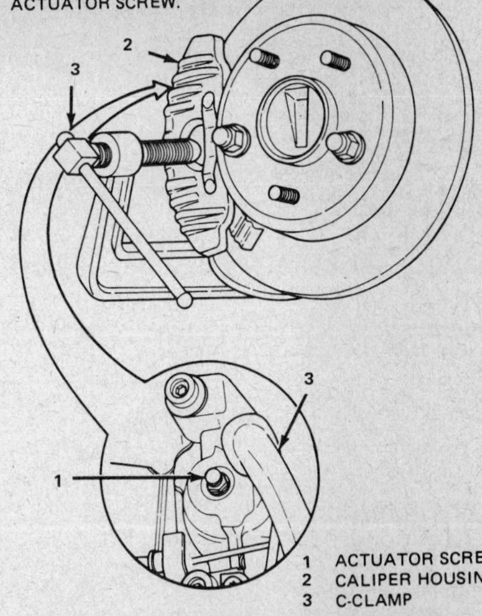

1 ACTUATOR SCREW
2 CALIPER HOUSING
3 C-CLAMP

Fig. 5 Positioning C-clamp to compress rear caliper piston

a. Ensure D-shaped tab on shoe engages D shaped notch in piston.
b. If tab and notch do not align, use tool J-7624 or equivalent to turn piston.
c. Brake wear sensor must be at leading edge of shoe during forward wheel rotation.
d. Slide edge of metal shoe under ends of dampening spring and snap shoe into position, flat against the piston.

6. Install outboard shoe and lining assembly into piston. Ensure spring ends on outboard shoe snap into piston recess.
7. After installation of caliper assembly, apply brakes slowly and firmly three times to seat linings.

CALIPER INSTALLATION

1. Install caliper onto brake rotor mounting bracket.
2. Torque caliper mounting bolts to 30-45 ft. lbs.
3. Install brake line fitting onto caliper. Torque fitting to 30 ft. lbs.
4. Install anti-friction washer.
5. Lubricate seal, then install into caliper housing. Ensure sealing bead on seal contacts housing.
6. Install lever onto actuator screw.
7. While holding lever, install nut. Torque nut to 30-40 ft. lbs.
8. Rotate lever back against caliper stop, then install spring.
9. Install parking brake cable. Tighten cable at equalizer until lever starts to move off caliper stop. Loosen adjustment until lever moves back against caliper stop.
10. Install tire and wheel assembly, then lower vehicle.
11. Fill master cylinder with brake fluid.
12. Bleed brake system, if necessary.

Delco-Moraine Single Piston W/Dual Bolt Mounting (Type 4)

INDEX

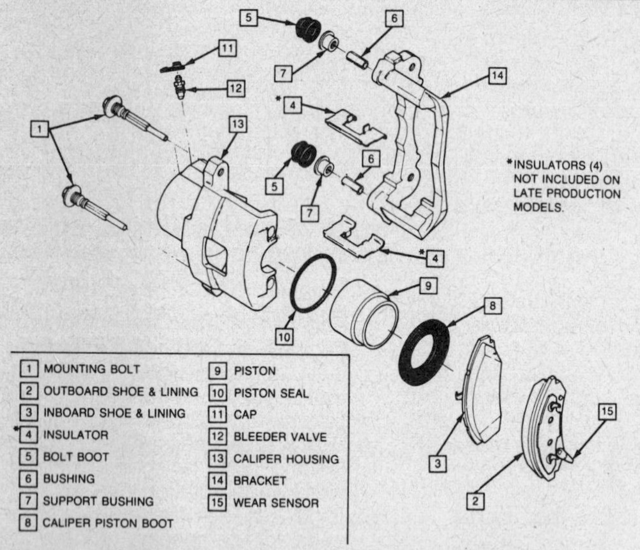

Fig. 1 Delco-Moraine series 3264M front disc brake caliper exploded view

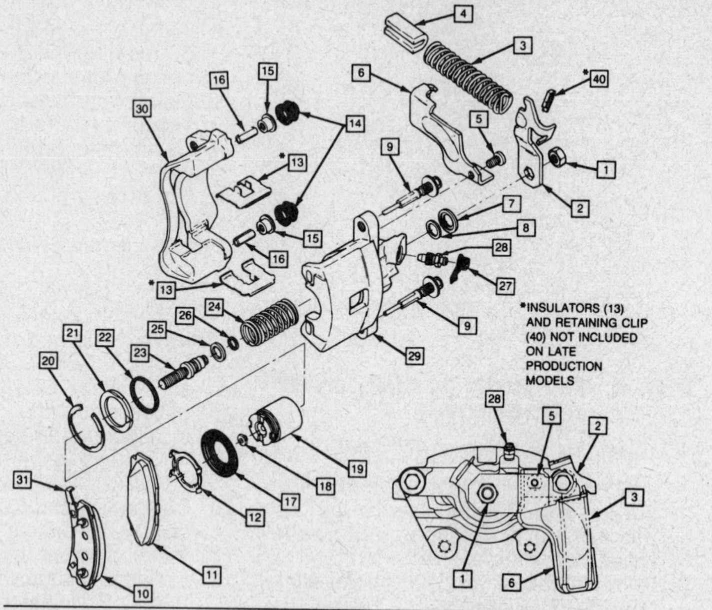

*INSULATORS (13) AND RETAINING CLIP (40) NOT INCLUDED ON LATE PRODUCTION MODELS

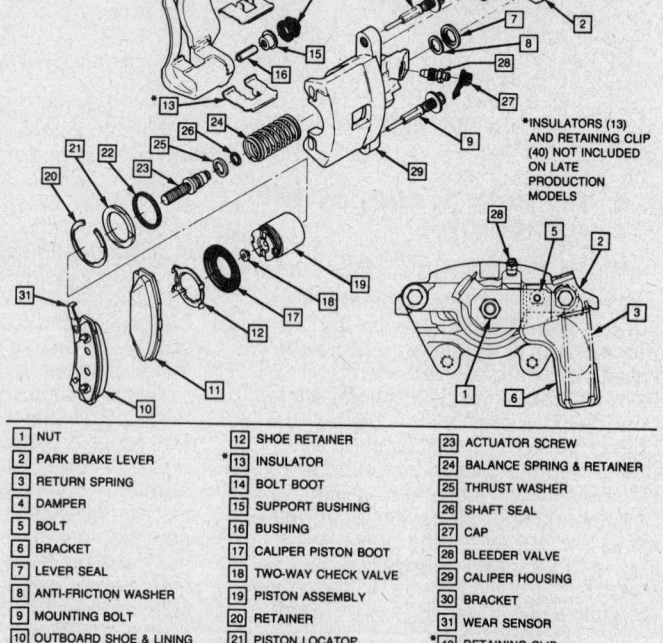

1 NUT
2 PARK BRAKE LEVER
3 RETURN SPRING
4 DAMPER
5 BOLT
6 BRACKET
7 LEVER SEAL
8 ANTI-FRICTION WASHER
9 MOUNTING BOLT
10 OUTBOARD SHOE & LINING
11 INBOARD SHOE & LINING
12 SHOE RETAINER
*13 INSULATOR
14 BOLT BOOT
15 SUPPORT BUSHING
16 BUSHING
17 CALIPER PISTON BOOT
18 TWO-WAY CHECK VALVE
19 PISTON ASSEMBLY
20 RETAINER
21 PISTON LOCATOP
22 PISTON SEAL
23 ACTUATOR SCREW
24 BALANCE SPRING & RETAINER
25 THRUST WASHER
26 SHAFT SEAL
27 CAP
28 BLEEDER VALVE
29 CALIPER HOUSING
30 BRACKET
31 WEAR SENSOR
*40 RETAINING CLIP

Fig. 2 Delco-Moraine series 3738M rear disc brake caliper exploded view

DESCRIPTION

This caliper, **Figs. 1 and 2**, has a single bore and is mounted to the support bracket with two mounting bolts. Hydraulic force, created by applying force to the brake pedal, is converted by the caliper into friction. The hydraulic force is applied equally against the piston and the bottom of the caliper bore moving the piston outward, resulting in a clamping action on the brake rotor.

Rear disc brake calipers include an integral parking brake mechanism. When the parking brake is applied, the lever turns an actuator screw which is threaded into a nut in the caliper piston. As the actuator screw turns, the piston is forced out, applying force on the rotor. The piston contains a self adjusting mechanism to keep the parking brake in proper adjustment and to ensure proper clearance when the parking brake is released.

FRONT BRAKE ASSEMBLY

CALIPER REMOVAL

1. Drain approximately 2/3 of brake fluid from master cylinder assembly.
2. Raise and support vehicle, then mark position of wheel and remove tire and wheel assembly.
3. If caliper is to be serviced or replaced, remove bolt securing inlet fitting, then disconnect brake hose and secure in raised position. **If only shoe and lining assemblies are being replaced, do not disconnect brake hose from caliper.**
4. Remove caliper to support mounting bolts, then lift caliper off support. If only shoe and lining assemblies are to be replaced, suspend caliper from chassis using suitable hanger. **Do not allow caliper to hang by brake hose.**
5. Remove insulators (4) from caliper support if equipped, **Fig. 1.**

SHOE & LINING REMOVAL

1. Remove caliper assembly as outlined.
2. Remove outboard shoe and lining assembly, using screwdriver to disengage shoe springs from holes in caliper housing.
3. Remove inboard shoe and lining assembly, unsnapping shoe retainer spring from caliper piston bore.
4. If new shoe and lining assemblies are to be installed, compress piston into housing with suitable clamp or pliers, taking care not to damage piston.
5. Remove bushings (6) from mounting bolt holes in bracket.

CALIPER DISASSEMBLY

1. Use clean shop towels to pad inside of caliper, then remove piston by applying compressed air to fluid inlet port. Use only enough air pressure to ease piston from bore. **Keep fingers away from piston to avoid injury as piston is forced out.**
2. Remove bleeder screw from caliper housing, **Fig. 1.**
3. Pry dust boot from caliper, then re-

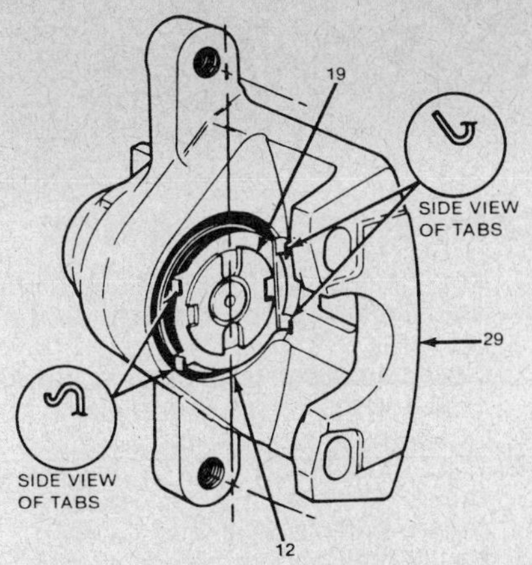

12. SHOE RETAINER
19. PISTON ASSEMBLY
29. CALIPER HOUSING

Fig. 3 Positioning caliper piston and pad retainer. Rear disc brake

move piston seal, taking care not to damage housing.
4. Clean components with suitable brake cleaner and wipe dry with lint free shop towels.
5. Inspect piston for scoring nicks, corrosion, wear and damage and replace as needed.
6. Inspect caliper housing and seal groove for damage, corrosion, nicks, scoring and excessive wear, and use crocus cloth to polish away corrosion from housing bore. Replace caliper housing if damaged or if corrosion in and around seal groove will not clean up with crocus cloth.

CALIPER ASSEMBLY

1. Lubricate piston seal, piston, caliper bore and dust boot with new brake fluid.
2. Roll piston seal into seal groove in caliper bore, ensuring seal is fully seated and not twisted.
3. Install dust boot over piston, ensuring lip of boot engages piston groove.
4. Install piston in caliper bore, press piston to bottom of bore, then seat boot in caliper counterbore with suitable driver.
5. Install bleeder screw and torque to 110 inch lbs.
6. Install new bushings and dust seals in caliper bracket, **Fig. 1,** and lubricate sliding surfaces on bracket with suitable brake grease.

SHOE & LINING INSTALLATION

A revised shoe and lining assembly is used on late production 1987 Cadillacs. The revised assembly includes a new lining material and extended shoes, eliminating the need for the stainless steel shoe abutment insulators (4), **Fig. 1.** This shoe and lining assembly can also be identified by the lining edge code: The original lining code is DM 121 FE, while the revised lining code is DM 128 FE. The revised shoe and lining assembly can be used on earlier models, however, the insulators must be removed and discarded.

1. Lubricate and install new bushings (6) in caliper mounting bracket, **Fig. 1.**
2. If new shoe and lining assemblies are being installed, compress piston into caliper bore, taking care not to damage piston.
3. Install inboard shoe, snapping shoe retainer spring into piston bore, and ensure shoe is flat against piston.
4. Install outboard shoe assembly, snapping shoe springs into holes in caliper, and ensure shoe is flat against caliper housing.

CALIPER INSTALLATION

1. If first design shoe and lining assemblies are being installed, mount insulators (4), **Fig. 1**, on caliper bracket.
2. Position caliper on mounting bracket, ensuring insulators and mounting bolt boots remain in place.
3. Apply thin coating of brake lubricant to caliper mounting bolts, install bolts and torque to 63 ft. lbs.
4. Install brake hose, if removed, and torque fitting bolt to 24 ft. lbs.
5. Install wheels and lower vehicle.
6. Fill master cylinder and bleed brakes as needed. **Do not attempt to move vehicle until brake pedal has been pumped several times and sufficient braking action has been restored.**

REAR BRAKE ASSEMBLY

CALIPER REMOVAL

1. Drain approximately $^{2}/_{3}$ of brake fluid from master cylinder assembly.
2. Raise and support vehicle, then remove tire and wheel assembly.
3. Loosen tension on parking brake cable at equalizer.
4. Remove cable clip from parking brake lever, disconnect cable, then remove spring, **Fig. 2.**
5. Hold parking brake lever, loosen nut, then remove nut, lever, seal and washer.
6. If caliper is to be serviced, remove fluid line bolt, then disconnect and plug fluid line. If only shoe and lining assemblies are to be replaced, do not disconnect brake line.
7. Remove caliper mounting bolts, then lift caliper from bracket. If only shoe and lining assemblies are being replaced, suspend caliper from chassis with suitable hanger. **Do not allow caliper to hang from brake hose.**
8. Remove insulators from caliper bracket, if equipped.

SHOE & LINING REMOVAL

1. Remove caliper assembly as outlined.
2. Remove outboard shoe assembly, unsnapping springs from holes in caliper.
3. Remove inboard shoe assembly, pressing in on edge of shoe from open side of caliper and tilting shoe outward to release it from retainer.
4. Remove bushings from caliper mounting bracket holes, **Fig. 2,** and remove two-way check valve from end of piston with screwdriver. **If leakage is noted from piston hole after removing check valve, caliper must be overhauled.**

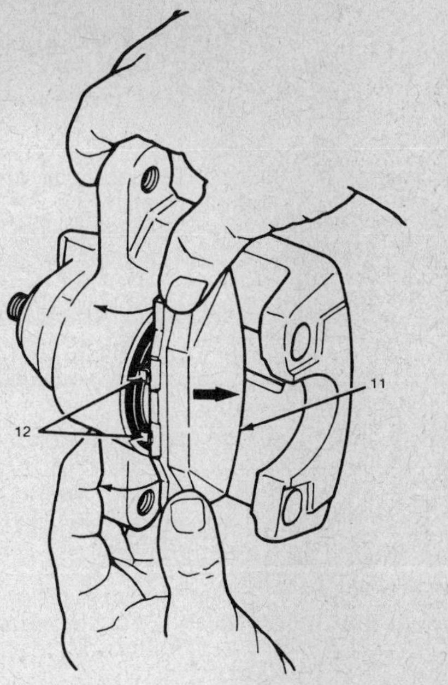

11. INBOARD SHOE & LINING
12. SHOE RETAINER

Fig. 4 Inboard shoe installation. Rear disc brake

CALIPER DISASSEMBLY

1. Remove parking brake lever from caliper, then remove caliper assembly as outlined.
2. Rotate shoe retainer until tabs are aligned with recesses in piston, then remove shoe retainer, **Fig. 2.**
3. Secure caliper assembly in vise and insulate interior of caliper with shop towels.
4. Remove piston by rotating actuator screw in parking brake apply direction to work piston from caliper bore.
5. Remove balance spring (24), then remove actuator screw by pressing on threaded end, **Fig. 2.**
6. Remove seal and thrust washer from actuator screw.
7. Pry dust boot from caliper taking care not to damage caliper.
8. Remove piston locator snap ring, then the locator.
9. Remove piston seal, taking care not to mar caliper bore, then remove bleeder screw.
10. Clean components with suitable brake cleaner and wipe dry with lint free shop towels.
11. Inspect piston for scoring nicks, corrosion, wear and damage and replace as needed.
12. Inspect caliper housing and seal groove for damage, corrosion, nicks, scoring and excessive wear, and use crocus cloth to polish away corrosion from housing bore. Replace caliper housing if damaged or if corrosion in and around seal groove will not clean up with crocus cloth.

CALIPER ASSEMBLY

1. Lubricate piston seal, piston, caliper bore and dust boot with new brake fluid.
2. Roll piston seal into seal groove in caliper bore, ensuring seal is fully seated and not twisted.
3. Lubricate piston locator with new brake fluid, then position locator on piston using J135588-1 and J135588-2, with grayish side facing caliper housing.
4. Install thrust washer and lubricated seal on actuator screw, then install screw in piston.
5. Install balance spring in piston recess in housing.
6. Install piston assembly, pressing piston in until locator is past snap ring groove, then install snap ring.
7. Install lubricated dust boot over piston with inside lip in groove in piston and fold toward end of piston that contacts brake shoe, then bottom piston in caliper bore.
8. Install anti-friction washer and seal over end of actuator screw, ensuring seal bead is against caliper housing.
9. Install parking brake lever over actuator screw, rotate lever away from stop, hold lever and torque retaining nut to 35 ft. lbs., then rotate lever back to stop.
10. Seat dust boot in caliper counterbore using suitable driver.
11. Install shoe retainer on end of piston, ensuring piston and retainer are positioned as shown in **Fig. 3.**
12. Install bleeder screw and torque to 110 inch lbs.

SHOE & LINING INSTALLATION

A revised shoe and lining assembly is used on late production 1987 Cadillacs. The revised assembly includes a new lining material and extended shoes, eliminating the need for the stainless steel shoe abutment insulators (13), **Fig. 2.** This shoe and lining assembly can also be identified by the lining edge code: The original lining code is DM 121 FE, while the revised lining code is DM 128 FE. The revised shoe and lining assembly can be used on earlier models, however, the insulators must be removed and discarded.

1. Install lubricated bushings into bolt holes in caliper bracket.
2. Bottom piston in caliper bore using suitable pliers, protecting piston to prevent damage. **Do not allow pliers to contact actuator screw.**
3. Lubricate new two-way check valve, then insert valve into piston.
4. Install inboard shoe assembly as follows:
   a. Engage inboard shoe edge in straight tabs of retainer, then press down and snap shoe under S-shaped tabs, **Fig. 4.**
   b. Ensure shoe lays flat against piston and that retainer and piston are properly aligned. Note that tabs on retainer are different, **Fig. 3**, and rotate retainer as needed.
   c. Ensure buttons on back of shoe engage D-shaped notches in piston. Rotate piston as needed with spanner J-7624 or equivalent. Piston is properly aligned when D-shaped notches are aligned with caliper mounting bolt holes, **Fig. 3.**
5. Install outboard shoe assembly, snap shoe springs into holes in caliper and ensure pad lays flat against caliper.

CALIPER INSTALLATION

1. Lubricate sliding surfaces and mount insulators on caliper bracket, as needed.
2. Position caliper on mounting bracket ensuring insulators and retaining bolt boots remain in position.
3. Coat mounting bolts with thin film of brake lubricant, install bolts and torque bolts to 63 ft. lbs.
4. Install brake hose using new sealing washers and torque fitting bolt to 15 ft. lbs.
5. Install parking brake lever as follows:
   a. Lubricate lever seal and anti-friction washer.
   b. Install washer, seal and parking brake lever.
   c. Move lever off stop, hold lever and torque retaining nut to 35 ft. lbs., then rotate lever against stop.
6. Install spring and damper, connect parking brake cable, then secure assembly with retaining clip, if used.
7. Tighten brake cable at equalizer until parking brake lever moves off stop, then loosen cable until lever just contacts stop.
8. Install wheels and lower vehicle, fill master cylinder, and bleed brakes as needed. **Do not attempt to move vehicle until brake pedal has been moved several times and full braking action is restored.**

Delco-Moraine Single Piston Rear Disc Brake

INDEX

OPERATION

Upon application of brake, **Figs. 1 & 2**, the cone and piston move out as one part. The nut remains stationary on the high lead screw and a gap develops between the cone and nut. When lining wear occurs, the cone and piston do not return to their original position, thereby leaving a small gap equal to the lining wear between the nut and cone. The adjusting spring causes the nut to rotate on the high lead screw to close the gap and adjust the caliper.

Upon application of parking brake, the lever rotation causes the high lead screw to turn and the nut to move down the screw, thereby loading through the cone and the cone-clutch interface of the piston, resulting in a clamp load on the linings. When the parking brake is released, the cone rotates on the clutch interface to adjust the caliper. The clutch interface prevents the cone from turning when the parking brake is applied.

CALIPER REMOVAL

Do not mix power steering fluid with brake fluid. If brake seals contact steering fluid or steering seals contact brake fluid, damage will result.

1. Remove two thirds of the total brake fluid capacity from the master cylinder front reservoir, to prevent overflow of brake fluid.
2. Support vehicle on a hoist and remove tire and wheel assembly.
3. Install one nut with flat side facing rotor to prevent rotor from falling out when caliper is removed.
4. Loosen parking brake cable tension at equalizer, then remove cable from parking brake lever and remove return spring, locknut, lever, lever seal and anti-friction washer. **Lever must be held in place while removing nut.**
5. Clean surface in area of lever seal, then using a 7 inch (or larger) C-clamp, with the solid end on lever stop and screw end on back of outboard lining, turn clamp until piston is bottomed in caliper. **Do not position C-clamp on actuator screw.**
6. Before removing clamp, lubricate housing surface under lever seal with silicone lubricant.
7. Install a new anti-friction washer, a new lever seal and lever. **Install lever on hex with arm pointing down-**

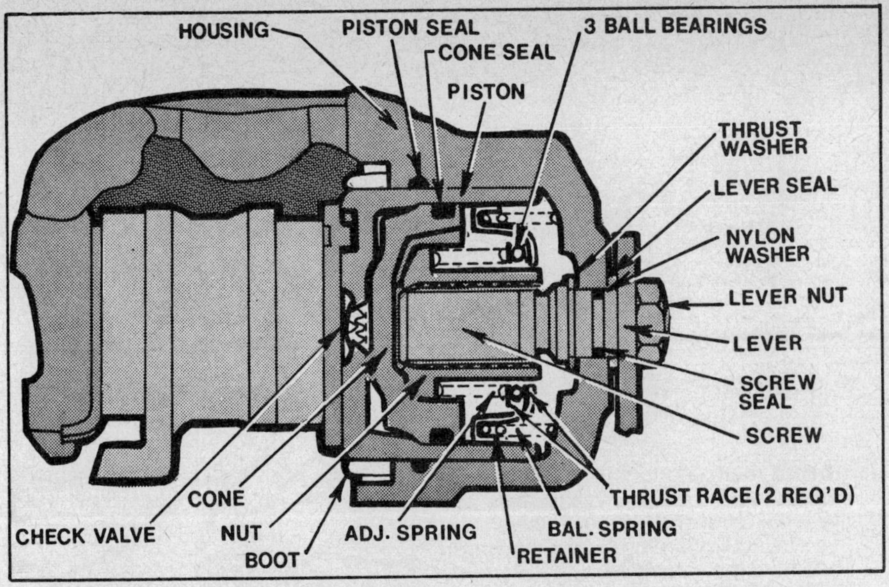

Fig. 1 Typical Delco-Moraine rear disc brake cross sectional view

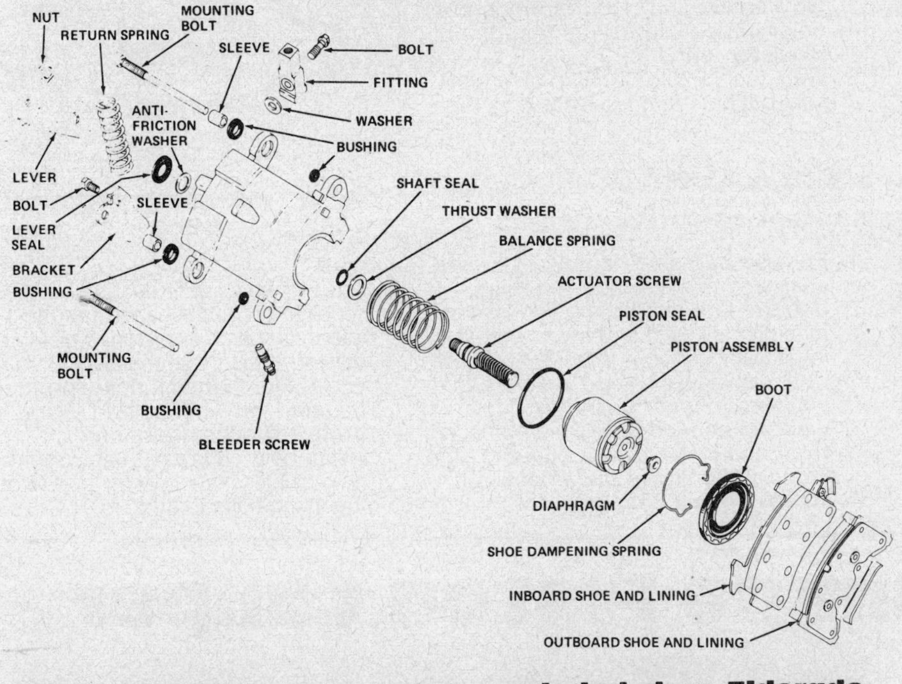

Fig. 2 Rear disc brake caliper exploded view. Eldorado, Firebird, Riviera, Seville, Toronado & 1982–86 Camaro

ward.

8. Rotate lever toward front of vehicle and while holding in this position, install nut and torque to 25 ft. lbs. and rotate lever back to stop.
9. Install lever return spring and remove C-clamp. **On Cadillac springs are color coded, red for the righthand caliper and black for the lefthand caliper.**
10. Disconnect brake line from caliper and plug openings to prevent loss of fluid and entry of dirt.
11. On all calipers except Eldorado and righthand Brougham remove the brass bolt from the block. **If brake line nut is seized, brass bolt and block can be removed with brake line attached by removing bolt. Plug openings to prevent loss of fluid and entry of dirt.**
12. Remove caliper mounting bolts and remove caliper.
13. Reverse procedure to install and torque caliper mounting bolts to 30 ft. lbs. **When installing brass bolt and block, use two new copper gaskets. Torque bolt or connector to 30 ft. lbs.**

INSPECTION

1. Clean corrosion and dirt from face of piston. Inspect piston and check valve area for fluid leakage, indicated by excessive moisture around boot area.

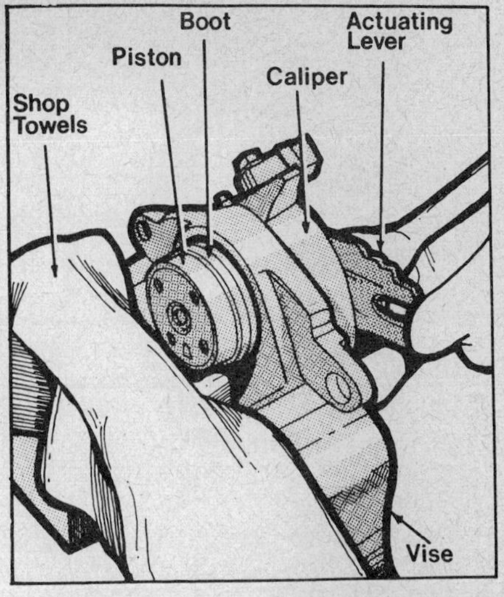

Fig. 3 Removing piston from bore

2. Inspect dust boot for cuts, cracks or other damage which may affect its sealing ability. If leaks are present, replace dust boot. **Do not use compressed air to clean caliper as it may unseat the dust boot.**
3. Inspect piston boot seal. Replace boot seal if leakage is indicated.
4. Inspect for leaks at threaded end of actuator screw. Replace seal if leakage is indicated. If bore is nicked or scratched, replace caliper.

CALIPER OVERHAUL

DISASSEMBLY

1. Clamp caliper in a vise and remove the two mounting sleeves and four bushings, **Fig. 2.**
2. Remove brake shoes and lever return spring.
3. Rotate parking brake lever back and forth to remove piston from housing, **Fig. 3.** If piston will not move from housing, remove locknut, lever and anti-friction washer. With a 9/16 inch wrench, rotate screw clockwise on right hand caliper or counterclockwise on lefthand caliper until the piston moves from housing. **Pad caliper with shop cloths when removing piston.**
4. Remove piston assembly and balance spring.
5. Remove lock nut, lever, lever seal and anti-friction washer if not removed previously.
6. Push screw from housing, then remove piston seal and boot.

ASSEMBLY

1. Install new piston seal.
2. Install new boot onto piston assembly with lip of boot located in piston groove.
3. Install new thrust washer and seal on actuator screw.
4. Install actuator screw into piston assembly. The piston assemblies are identified by a stamped letter on the adjuster nut end. "L" denote lefthand

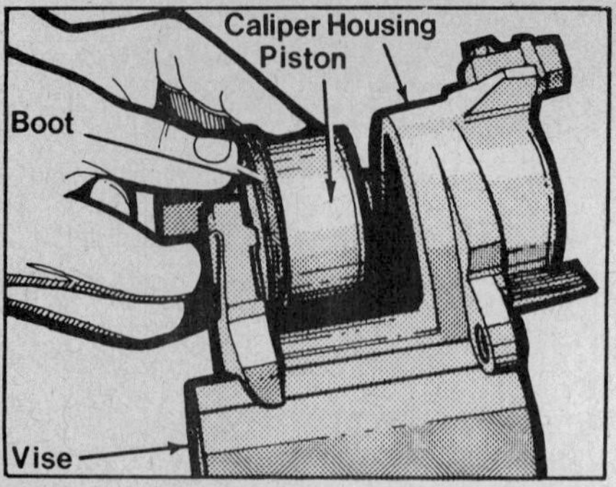

Fig. 4 Positioning piston in caliper

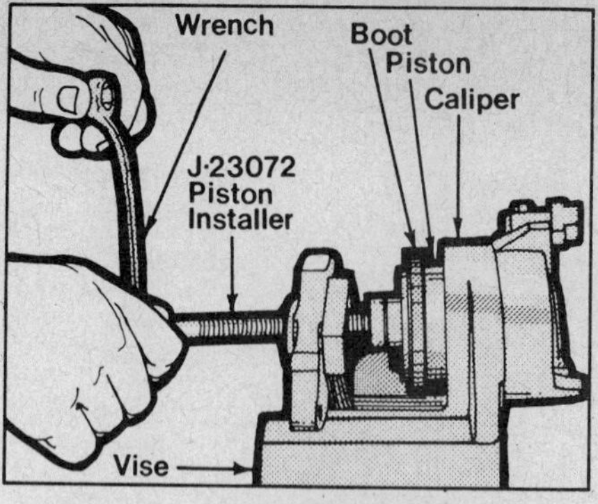

Fig. 5 Installing piston into caliper

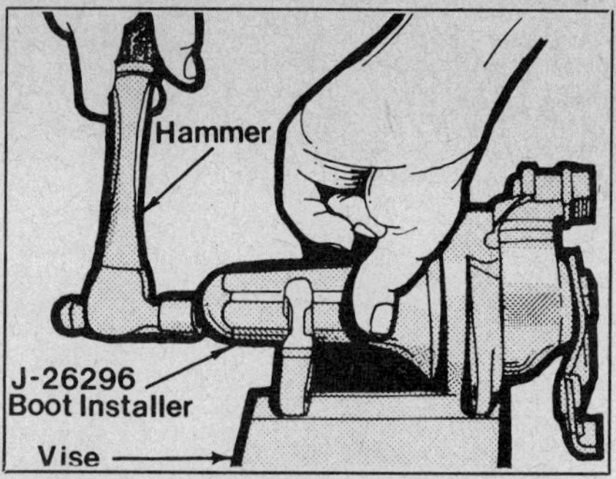

Fig. 6 Driving boot into caliper

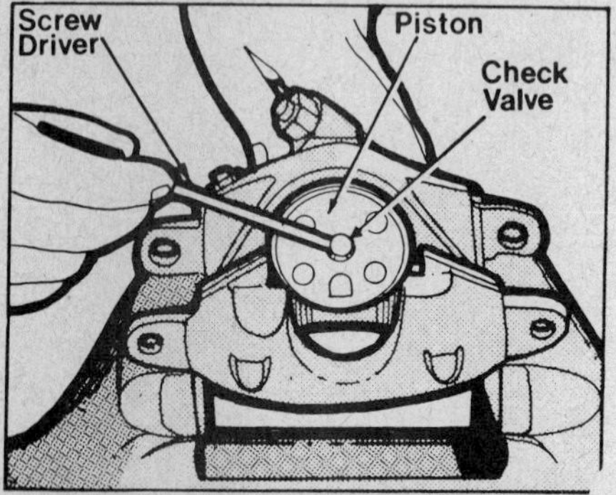

Fig. 7 Removing piston check valve

and "R" denotes righthand. The caliper housing is also marked with a letter. The parking brake will not function if the caliper and actuator screw are located on the wrong side of vehicle.

5. Coat piston seal with clean brake fluid. Install balance spring into piston and install assembly into caliper housing, **Fig. 4.**
6. With tool J-23072, push piston fully into caliper housing, **Fig. 5. The piston must be pushed straight into caliper to prevent damage to the actuator screw seal as it passes through hole in rear of piston bore.**
7. Before removing tool J-23072, install lubricated anti-friction washer, new lever seal, lever and locknut. Position lever away from stop, rotate forward and hold lever in position, then torque nut to 25 ft. lbs.
8. Remove tool J-23072, rotate lever back to stop and install return spring. **On Cadillac the return springs are color coded red for righthand and black for lefthand.**
9. With tool J-26296, drive boot until seal bottoms in caliper housing, **Fig. 6.**

SHOE & LINING REPLACEMENT

1. Remove caliper as described previously and remove shoe and lining.
2. Remove and discard the two caliper mounting sleeves and the four bushings. Using silicone lubricant, install new bushings and seals. **Sleeves are installed in inner bushings.**
3. Remove and discard piston check valve and install a new one, **Fig. 7. Front brake shoes must not be installed on rear calipers.**

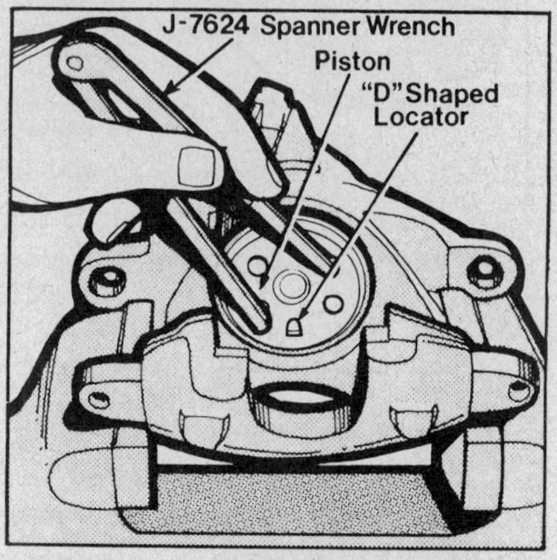

Fig. 8 Rotating piston in bore

4. Position new inboard shoe assembly on piston. The D-shaped tab must fit into indentation in piston. If piston requires rotation, use tool J-7642 to rotate it, **Fig. 8. Install new spring retainers on all exc. Eldorado outboard shoe assembly.**
5. Install new outboard shoe assembly onto caliper. Install caliper and torque mounting bolts to 30 ft. lbs.

Girlock Single Piston Caliper

INDEX

DESCRIPTION

This caliper, **Fig. 1,** has a single piston in an aluminum housing suspended in the mounting bracket on two slide pins. Hydraulic pressure, created by applying force to the brake pedal, acts equally against the piston and the bottom of the caliper bore to move the piston outward and to slide the caliper inward resulting in a clamping action on the brake rotor.

BRAKE SHOE & LINING REMOVAL

1. Drain approximately 2/3 of brake fluid from master cylinder.
2. Raise and support vehicle.
3. Mark relationship of wheel to axle assembly, then remove wheel(s).
4. Position a suitable C-clamp into caliper, with one end of clamp against inlet fitting bolt head and other end of clamp against outboard shoe.
5. Tighten clamp screw until caliper piston bottoms in piston bore.
6. Remove and discard upper caliper self locking bolt.
7. Rotate caliper until shoe and lining assemblies are exposed.
8. Remove shoe and lining assemblies.

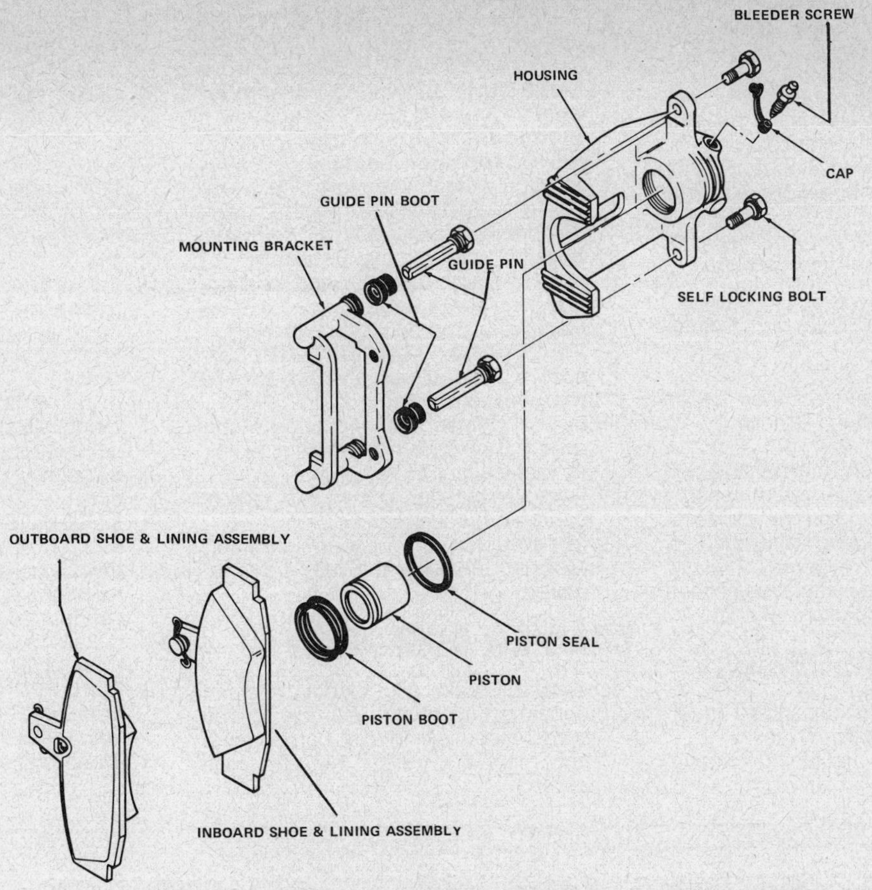

Fig. 1 Girlock single piston caliper exploded view

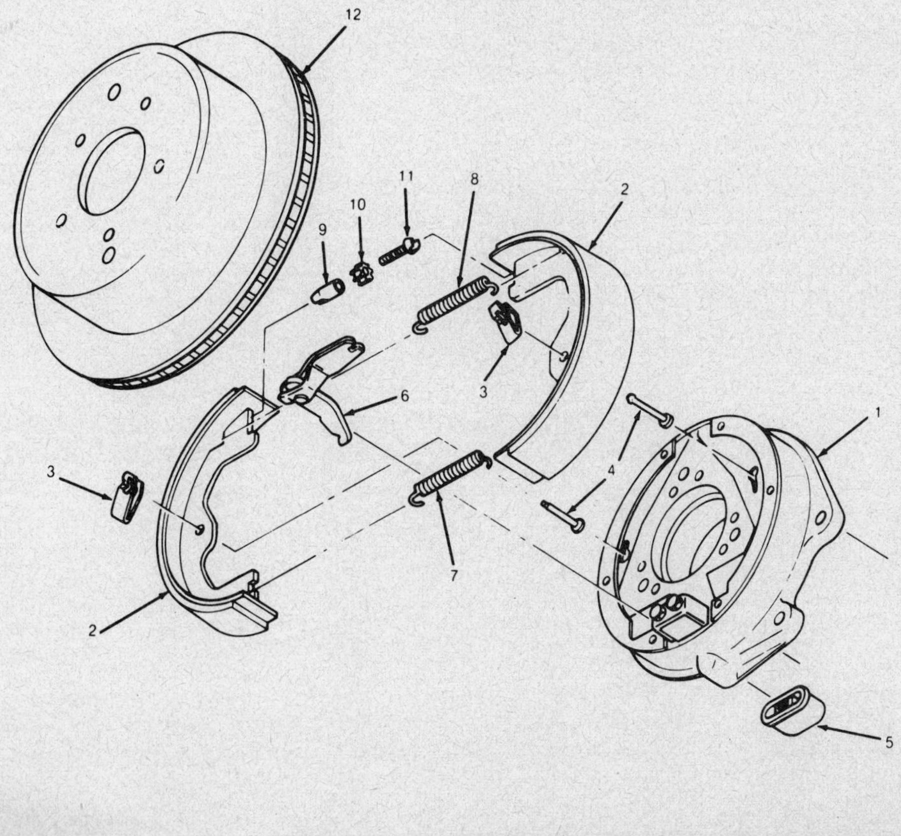

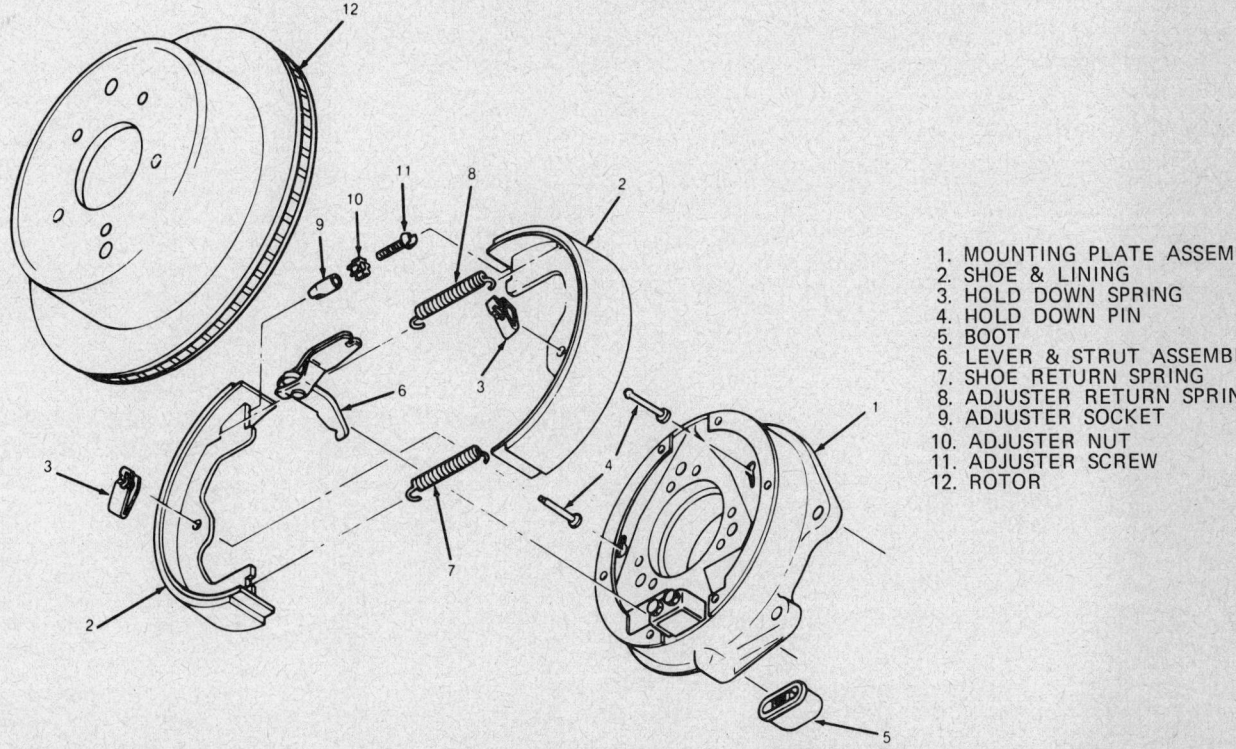

1. MOUNTING PLATE ASSEMBLY
2. SHOE & LINING
3. HOLD DOWN SPRING
4. HOLD DOWN PIN
5. BOOT
6. LEVER & STRUT ASSEMBLY
7. SHOE RETURN SPRING
8. ADJUSTER RETURN SPRING
9. ADJUSTER SOCKET
10. ADJUSTER NUT
11. ADJUSTER SCREW
12. ROTOR

Fig. 2 Parking brake assembly exploded view

BRAKE SHOE & LINING INSTALLATION

1. Install new shoe and lining assemblies onto mounting bracket.
2. Rotate caliper into position and install a new self locking bolt. Torque bolt to 22-25 ft. lbs.
3. Install wheel(s) and lower vehicle. Bleed brake system, if necessary.

PARKING BRAKE SHOES REPLACE

1. Remove caliper as described under "Brake Shoe & Lining Removal."
2. Remove rotor, **Fig. 2.**
3. Spread shoes, then remove adjuster assembly and adjuster return spring.
4. Remove hold-down springs and pins, then shoe return spring using suitable pliers.
5. Remove shoe and lining assemblies.
6. Reverse procedure to install.

CALIPER DISASSEMBLY

1. Remove caliper as described under "Brake Shoe & Lining Removal."
2. If caliper requires machining, remove inlet fitting.
3. Remove and discard self locking bolts.
4. Remove bracket bolts. **Remove brake shoe and lining assemblies only if they are to be replaced or if the mounting bracket is being removed for rotor machining.**
5. Position a clean shop towel on the inside of the caliper housing, then using compressed air, apply air to brake hose port and remove piston.
6. Inspect piston for wear and/or damage. Replace, if necessary.
7. Remove piston boot from housing.
8. Remove piston seal from caliper bore groove. **Do not use a sharp tool to remove piston seal.**
9. Inspect caliper bore for scoring or corrosion. If scoring or corrosion exists, replace caliper as required.
10. Remove bleeder screw and rubber cap from bleeder screw.
11. Inspect guide pins for corrosion. If corrosion exists, replace guide pins as required.

CALIPER ASSEMBLY

1. Clean all brake components in clean denatured alcohol. Use dry, filtered compressed air to dry components and blow out caliper housing passages.
2. Check piston to bore fit, by sliding piston in and out of piston bore. Piston should slide in and out smoothly.
3. Install rubber cap onto bleeder screw, then insert bleeder screw into caliper.
4. Using clean brake fluid, lubricate piston seal, then install seal into caliper bore groove. Ensure seal is not twisted in piston bore groove.
5. Using clean brake fluid, lubricate caliper bore and piston assembly.
6. Install boot over end of piston. Place piston into caliper bore. Push piston completely down into caliper bore. Ensure boot is properly seated into groove around piston and into groove in caliper bore.
7. Using silicone grease or equivalent, lubricate caliper guide pins.
8. Install new guide pin boots over guide pins.
9. Install guide pins into mounting bracket.
10. Install caliper over rotor and into mounting bracket. Ensure brake shoe springs are positioned properly.
11. Install new self locking bolts. Torque bolts to 26-40 ft. lbs.
12. Pump brake pedal firmly and slowly three times to bring pads into contact with brake rotor.
13. Bleed brake system, if necessary.

Toyota/GM Single Piston Caliper

INDEX

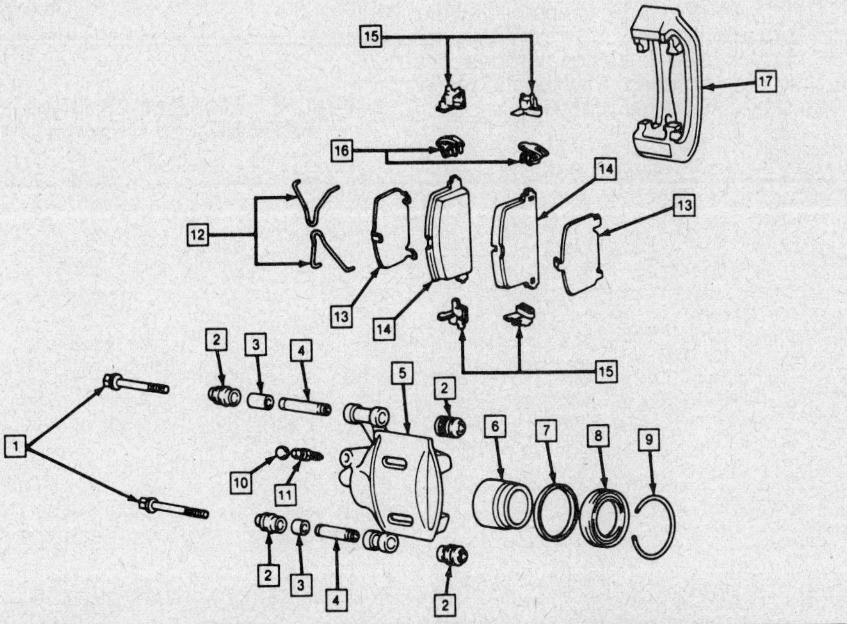

1. MOUNTING BOLT
2. DUST BOOT
3. COLLAR
4. SLIDE BUSHING
5. CALIPER HOUSING
6. PISTON
7. PISTON SEAL
8. BOOT
9. SET RING
10. CAP
11. BLEEDER SCREW
12. ANTI-RATTLE SPRING
13. ANTI-SQUEAL SHIM
14. PAD
15. PAD SUPPORT PLATE
16. PAD WEAR INDICATOR PLATE
17. MOUNTING BRACKET

Fig. 1 Toyota/GM front brake caliper exploded view

CALIPER REPLACE

REMOVAL

1. Siphon 2/3 of the brake fluid from master cylinder, raise and support vehicle, and remove wheels.
2. Reinstall 2 wheel nuts to retain rotor, then remove caliper mounting bolts, **Fig. 1.**
3. Remove union nut securing brake hose to caliper and drain fluid into suitable container. **If caliper is only being removed for brake pad replacement, do not disconnect brake hose.**
4. Compress piston as needed, then remove caliper. If brake hose remains connected, secure caliper aside to prevent hose from being stretched.

INSTALLATION

1. Seat piston in caliper bore, taking care not to damage piston.
2. Ensure that support plates, **Fig. 2,** and anti-rattle springs are properly positioned, then mount caliper over rotor onto mounting bracket.
3. Install caliper mounting bolts and torque bolts to 18 ft. lbs.
4. Install brake hose and mounting bolts, using new copper gaskets, then torque bolt to 17 ft. lbs.
5. Refill master cylinder and bleed brake system.

BRAKE PADS REPLACE

Replace brake pads on one wheel at a time to prevent opposite side caliper piston from being forced out of bore.

REMOVAL

1. Remove caliper as outlined, leaving brake hose connected, and secure caliper aside.
2. Remove 2 anti-rattle clips, then the brake brake pads, **Fig. 3.**
3. Remove pad wear indicator plates and anti-squeal shims.
4. Remove support plates.

INSTALLATION

1. Install new support plates on caliper mounting bracket, **Fig. 2.**

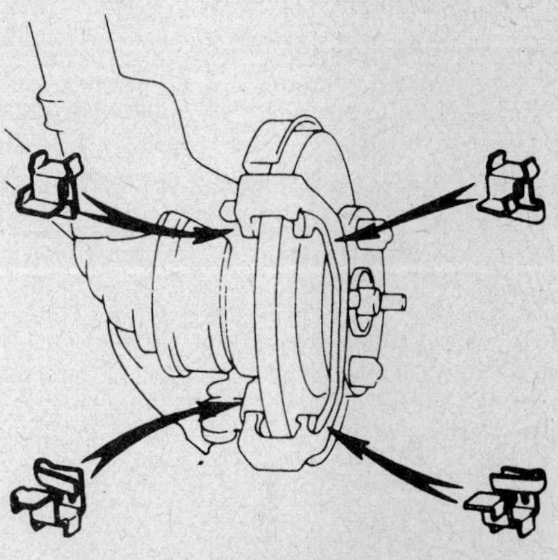

Fig. 2 Caliper support installation

2. Install new wear indicators and anti-squeal shims on each pad, **Fig. 3,** then position pads in caliper mounting bracket. **Ensure that arrow on wear indicator is pointing in rotating direction of rotor.**
3. Install anti-rattle springs.
4. Seat piston in caliper bore, then install caliper and mounting bolts, and torque bolts to 18. ft. lbs.
5. Refill master cylinder and bleed brakes as needed.

CALIPER OVERHAUL

DISASSEMBLY

1. Remove 2 caliper slide bushings, 4 dust boots and spacer collars, **Fig. 1.**
2. Pry out caliper dust boot retaining ring and remove dust boot.
3. Place clean shop towels in caliper web to protect piston, then apply compressed air to caliper fluid inlet to force piston from bore. **Keep fingers clear of caliper web when removing piston. Use only enough air pressure to ease piston out of bore, or piston may be damaged.**
4. Remove piston seal from caliper bore, taking care not to mar machined surface of caliper.
5. Remove bleeder valve.
6. Clean components with alcohol and wipe dry with clean, lint free shop towels. Blow out caliper body and fluid passages with clean, filtered compressed air.
7. Inspect caliper and piston for damage, distortion, excessive wear and pitting, and replace as needed.
8. Replace mounting bolts, collars and caliper slides if they are damaged or worn.

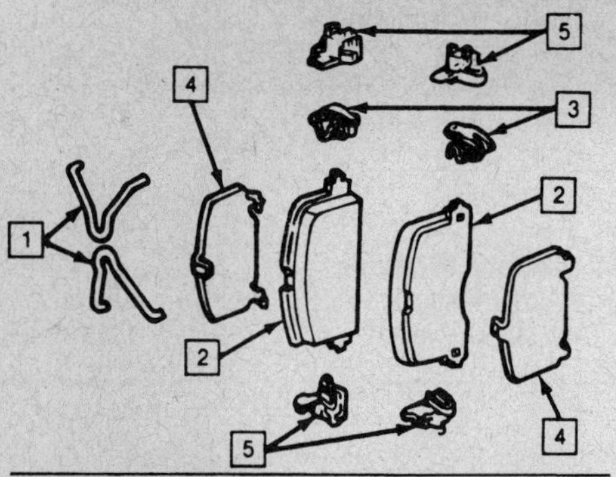

1. ANTI-RATTLE SPRINGS
2. BRAKE PADS
3. WEAR INDICATOR
4. ANTI-SQUEAL SHIMS
5. SUPPORT PLATES

Fig. 3 Brake pad assembly

ASSEMBLY

1. Apply lithium soap base glycol grease to components shown in **Fig. 4**.
2. Install piston seal in caliper, ensuring that seal is squarely seated in groove.
3. Press piston into bore, ensuring that piston enters bore straight.
4. Seat piston dust boot in caliper groove, then install retaining ring.
5. Install 2 collars and 4 slide bushing dust boots, **Fig. 1,** rotating boots as they are pressed in to ensure that they are fully seated.
6. Install slide bushings through dust boots, ensuring that boots remain seated in caliper grooves.

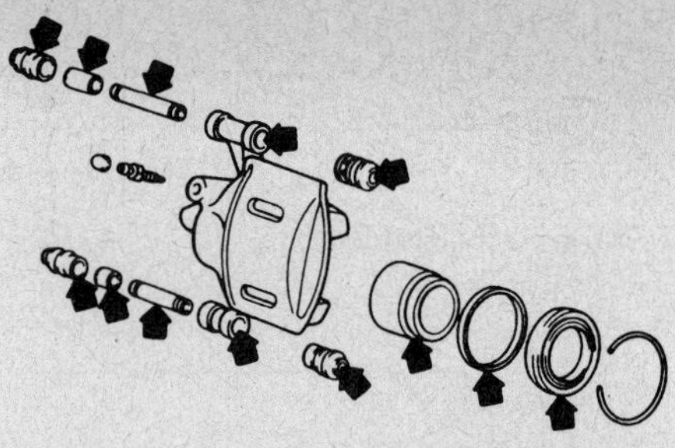

Fig. 4 Lubrication points for caliper assembly

Disc Brake Caliper Specifications

Year	Model	Caliper Bore Dia. In.
BUICK: REAR WHEEL DRIVE & 1982-85 RIVIERA		
1982-85	Riviera	2 1/2
	Exc. Century, Regal & Riviera	2 15/16
1982-87	Regal	2 1/2
1986–87	Estate Wagon	2 15/16
BUICK SOMERSET REGAL, OLDS. CALAIS, PONT. GRAND AM & 1986–87 BUICK SKYLARK		
1985-87	All	2.24
CADILLAC REAR WHEEL DRIVE & 1982–85 ELDORADO & SEVILLE		
1982-85	Eldorado & Seville	⑤
1982-87	Exc. Eldorado & Seville	2 15/16
1985-87 BUICK ELECTRA, CAD. DEVILLE, FLEETWOOD & OLDS. 98; 1986-87 BUICK LESABRE & OLDS. 98; 1987 PONT. BONNEVILLE		
1985-87	All	2.52
CHEVROLET (CAMARO, CHEVROLET, CORVETTE, MALIBU & MONTE CARLO)		
1982	Corvette	①
1982-83	Malibu	2 1/2
1982-87	Camaro	②
	Chevrolet	2 15/16
	Monte Carlo	2.5
1984-87	Corvette	③

Year	Model	Caliper Bore Dia. In.
CHEV. CAVALIER, BUICK SKYHAWK, CAD. CIMARRON, OLDS. FIRENZA, PONTIAC 2000/ SUNBIRD		
1982-87	All	2.24
CHEVROLET CHEVETTE • PONTIAC 1000		
1982	All	1 7/8
1983-87	All	2.05
CHEV. CITATION, OLDS. OMEGA, PONT. PHOENIX & 1982-85 BUICK SKYLARK		
1982-85	All	2.24
CHEV. CELEBRITY, BUICK CENTURY, OLDS. CUTLASS CIERA, PONT. 6000 & 1984-87 CUTLASS CRUISER		
1982-87	All	④
OLDSMOBILE: REAR WHEEL DRIVE & 1982-85 TORONADO		
1982-85	Exc. Cutlass & Toronado	2 15/16
	Cutlass & Toronado	2 1/2
1986-87	Cutlass	2 1/2
	Custom Cruiser	2 15/16
PONTIAC (EXC. 1000 & FRONT WHEEL DRIVE)		
1982-87	Exc. Firebird & Fiero	2.9375
	Firebird	②
1984-87	Fiero	2.52

①—Front, 1 7/8 inches; rear, 1 3/8 inches.
②—Front, 2.5 inches; rear, 1.89 inches.
③—Front, 2.1 inches; rear, 1.6 inches.
④—Exc. heavy duty, 2.24 inches; heavy duty, 2.50 inches.
⑤—Piston Diameter: Front, 2.5 inches; rear, 2.125 inches.

Disc Brake Rotor Specifications

Car	Year	Nominal Thickness	Minimum Refinish Thickness ①	Thickness Variation (Parallelism)	Lateral Runout (T.I.R.)	Finish (Microinch)
BUICK: REAR WHEEL DRIVE & 1982-85 RIVIERA						
Exc. Riviera	1982-83	1.040	.980	.0005	.004	30-80
Riviera ②	1982-83	1.040	.980	.0005	.005	19-80
Riviera ③	1982-83	.974	.921	.0005	.005	19-80
All	1984-87	1.043	.980	.0005	.005	—
1986–87 BUICK RIVIERA, CAD. ELDORADO & SEVILLE & OLDS. TORONADO						
All ②	1986	1.043	.971	.0005	.004	—
All ③	1986	.494	.444	.0005	.003	—
BUICK SOMERSET REGAL, OLDS. CALAIS, PONT. GRAND AM & 1986-87 BUICK SKYLARK						
All	1985-87	.885	.830	.0005	.004	—
1985-87 BUICK ELECTRA & PARK AVE., CAD. DEVILLE & FLEETWOOD & OLDS. 98; 1986-87 BUICK LESABRE & OLDS. 88; 1987 PONT. BONNEVILLE						
All	1985-87	1.043	.972	.0005	.004	—
CADILLAC: REAR WHEEL DRIVE & 1982-85 ELDORADO & SEVILLE						
All	1982-84	1.000	—	.0005	.004	—
Eldorado & Seville	1985	1.035	.965	.0005	.004	—
Brougham	1985-87	1.031	.972	.0005	.004	—
CHEVROLET (CAMARO, CHEVROLET, CORVETTE, MALIBU & MONTE CARLO)						
Camaro ②	1982-87	1.043	.980	.0005	.004	30-80
Camaro ③	1982-87	1.042	.986	.0005	.005	40-80
Corvette	1982	1.250	1.230	.0005	.005	20-60
	1984-87	.780	.724	.0005	.006	—
All Exc. Camaro & Corvette	1982-83	1.030	.980	.0005	.004	20-60
	1984-87	1.043	.980	.0005	.004	30-80
CHEV. CAVALIER. BUICK SKYHAWK, CAD. CIMARRON, OLDS. FIRENZA, PONT. 2000 • SUNBIRD						
All	1982-87	.885	.830	.0005	.002	—
CHEVROLET CHEVETTE, PONTIAC 1000						
All	1982-87	.4334 (11 mm)	.390 (9.9 mm)	.0005 (.013 mm)	.005 (.13 mm)	20-60 (.5-1.6 micro/m)
CHEV. CELEBRITY & CITATION; BUICK SKYLARK (1982-85) & CENTURY; OLDS. CUTLASS CRUISER (1984-86), CUTLASS CIERA & OMEGA; PONT. PHOENIX & 6000						
All	1982-87	.885	.830	.0005	.004	12-50
OLDSMOBILE: REAR WHEEL DRIVE & 1982-85 TORONADO						
Exc. Cutlass & Toronado	1982	1.020	.984	.0005	.004	—
	1984-87	1.035	1.020	.0005	.004	—
Cutlass	1982-87	1.020	.984	.0005	.004	—
Toronado	1982-85	1.020	.984	.0005	.004	19-80
PONTIAC (EXC. 1000 & FRONT WHEEL DRIVE)						
Bonneville	1982-84	1.043	.980	.0005	.005	20-60
Fiero ②	1984-87	.445	.386	.0005	.004	—
Fiero ③	1984-87	.500	.440	.0005	.004	—
Firebird ②	1982-87	1.043	.980	.0005	.004	30-80
Firebird ③	1982-87	1.042	.986	.0005	.005	40-80
Grand Prix	1982-86	1.043	.980	.0005	.005	30-80
Parisienne	1983-86	1.043	.980	.0005	.004	—
Safari	1987	1.043	.980	.0005	.004	40-80

①—All brake rotors have a discard dimension cast into them. This is a wear dimension, not a refinish dimension. Any rotor that does not meet specifications should be discarded.

②—Front.
③—Rear.

DRUM BRAKES

NOTE: Refer to "Applications" to determine which type brakes are used on vehicle being serviced.

TABLE OF CONTENTS

Applications

	Type No.
BUICK	
Century:	
1982-84	4
1985-87	5
Electra:	
1982-84	1
1985-87 Estate Wagon	1
1985-86 Exc. Estate Wagon	5
1987 Exc. Estate Wagon	6
LeSabre:	
1982-85	1
1986-87	6
Regal	3
Riviera:	
1982-84	2
1985	1
Skyhawk:	
1982-84	4
1985-87	5
Skylark:	
1982-84	4
1985-87	5
Somerset	5
CADILLAC	
Cimarron:	
1982-84	4
1985-87	5
Deville (FWD):	
1985-86	5
1987	6
Eldorado, 1982-85	1
Fleetwood (FWD):	
1985-86	5
1987	6
Rear Wheel Drive	1
Seville	1
CHEVROLET	
Camaro	3
Cavalier:	
1982-84	4
1985-87	5
Celebrity:	
1982-84	4
1985-87	5
Chevette:	
1982-84	4
1985-87	5
Citation:	
1982-84	4
1985	5
Full Size:	
1982-84	3
1985-87	1
Malibu	3
Monte Carlo	3
Nova	7
OLDSMOBILE	
Calais	5
Custom Cruiser	1
Cutlass Exc. Ciera	3
Cutlass Ciera:	
1982-84	4
1985-87	5
Cutlass Cruiser:	
1984	4
1985-87	5
Firenza:	
1982-84	4
1985-87	5
Omega	4
Toronado, 1982-83	2
88:	
1982-85	1
1986-87	6
98:	
1982-84	1
1985-86	5
1987	6
PONTIAC	
Bonneville:	
1982-86	3
1987	5
Firebird	3
Grand Am	5
Grand Prix	3
Parisienne	1
Safari	1
Sunbird/2000:	
1982-84	4
1985-87	5
1000:	
1982-85	4
1986-87	5
6000:	
1982-84	4
1985-87	5

General Information

INDEX

SERVICE PRECAUTIONS

When working on or around brake assemblies, care must be taken to prevent breathing asbestos dust, as many manufacturers incorporate asbestos fibers in the production of brake linings. During routine service operations the amount of asbestos dust from brake lining wear is at a low level due to a chemical breakdown during use, and a few precautions will minimize exposure.

1. Do not sand or grind brake linings unless suitable local exhaust ventilation equipment is used to prevent excessive asbestos exposure.
2. Wear a suitable respirator approved for asbestos dust use during all repair procedures.
3. When cleaning brake dust from brake parts, use a vacuum cleaner with a highly efficient filter system. If a suitable vacuum cleaner is not available, use a water soaked rag. **Do not use compressed air or dry brush to clean brake parts.**
4. Keep work area clean using same equipment as for cleaning brake parts.
5. Properly dispose of rags and vacuum cleaner bags by placing them in plastic bags.
6. Do not smoke or eat while working on brake systems. **Never use gasoline, kerosene, alcohol, motor oil, transmission fluid, or any fluid containing mineral oil to clean brake system components. These fluids will damage the rubber caps and seals. If system contamination is suspected, check brake fluid in the reservoir for dirt, discoloration, or separation (breakdown) of the brake fluid into distinct layers. Drain and flush the hydraulic system with clean brake fluid if contamination is suspected.**

GENERAL INSPECTION

BRAKE DRUMS

Any time the brake drums are removed for brake service, the braking surface diameter should be checked with a suitable brake drum micrometer at several points to determine if they are within the safe oversize limit stamped on the brake drum outer surface. If the braking surface diameter exceeds specifications, the drum must be replaced. If the braking surface diameter is within specifications, drums should be cleaned and inspected for cracks, scores, deep grooves, taper, out of round and heat spotting. If drums are cracked or heat spotted, they must be replaced. Minor scores should be removed with sandpaper. Grooves and large scores can only be removed by machining with special equipment, as long as the braking surface is within specifications stamped on brake drum outer surface. Any brake drum sufficiently out of round to cause vehicle vibration or noise while braking or showing taper should also be machined, removing only enough stock to true up the brake drum.

After a brake drum is machined, wipe the braking surface diameter with a denatured alcohol soaked cloth. If one brake drum is machined, the other should also be machined to the same diameter to maintain equal braking forces.

BRAKE LININGS & SPRINGS

Inspect brake linings for excessive wear, damage, oil, grease or brake fluid contamination. If any of the above conditions exists, brake linings should be replaced. Do not attempt to replace only one set of brake shoes; they should be replaced as an axle set only to maintain equal braking forces. Examine brake shoe webbing, hold-down and return springs for signs of overheating indicated by a slight blue color. If any component exhibits overheating signs, replace hold-down and return springs with new ones. Overheated springs lose their pull and could cause brake linings to wear out prematurely. Inspect all springs for sags, bends and external damage and replace as necessary.

Inspect hold-down retainers and pins for bends, rust and corrosion. If any of the above is found, replace as required.

BACKING PLATE

Inspect backing plate shoe contact surface for grooves that may restrict shoe movement and cannot be removed by lightly sanding with emery cloth or other suitable abrasive. If backing plate exhibits above condition, it should be replaced. Also inspect for signs of cracks, warpage and excessive rust, indicating need for replacement.

ADJUSTER MECHANISM

Inspect all components for rust, corrosion, bends and fatigue. Replace as necessary. On adjuster mechanism equipped with adjuster cable, inspect cable for kinks, fraying or elongation of eyelet and replace as necessary.

PARKING BRAKE CABLE

Inspect parking brake cable end for kinks, fraying and elongation and replace as necessary. Use a small hose clamp to compress clamp where it enters backing plate to remove.

Types 1, 2 & 3

INDEX

REMOVAL

1. Raise and support rear of vehicle, then remove tire and wheel assembly.
2. Remove brake drum. If brake lining is dragging on brake drum, back off brake adjustment by rotating adjustment screw. Refer to individual car chapter for procedure. **If brake drum is rusted or corroded to axle flange and cannot be removed, lightly tap axle flange to drum mounting surface with a suitable hammer.**
3. Using brake spring pliers or equivalent, unhook primary and secondary return springs, **Figs. 1, 2 and 3. Observe location of brake parts being removed to aid during installation.**
4. Remove brake hold-down springs with suitable tool.
5. Lift actuating lever, then unhook actuating link from anchor pin and remove.
6. Remove actuating lever(s) and return spring.
7. Spread shoes apart and remove parking brake strut and spring.
8. Disconnect parking brake cable from lever, then remove brake shoes from backing plate.
9. Separate brake shoes by removing adjusting screw and spring, then unhook parking brake lever from shoe

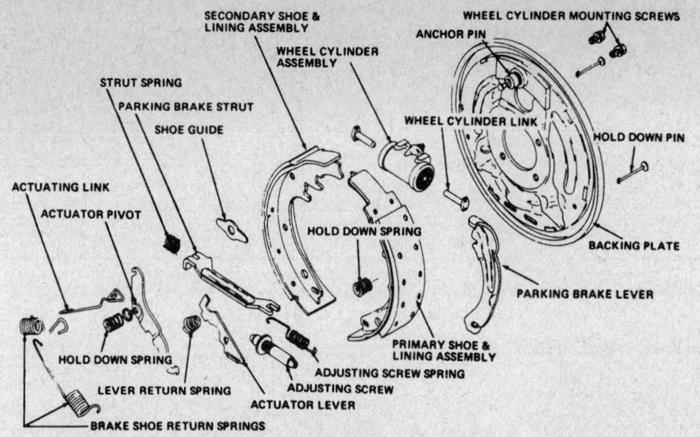

Fig. 1 Drum brake assembly. Type 1 typical

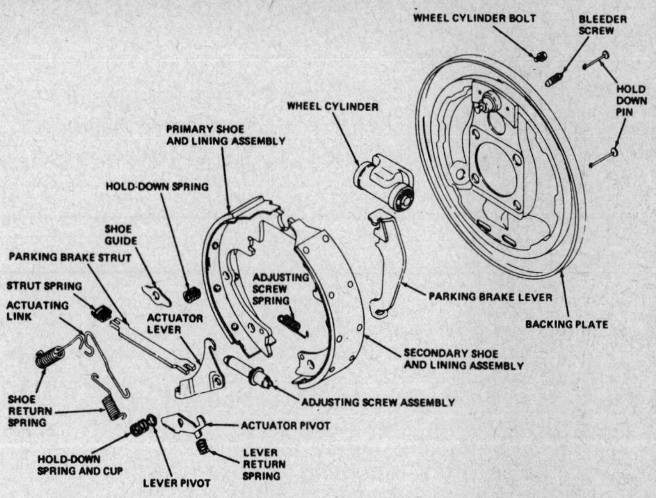

Fig. 2 Drum brake assembly. Type 2 typical

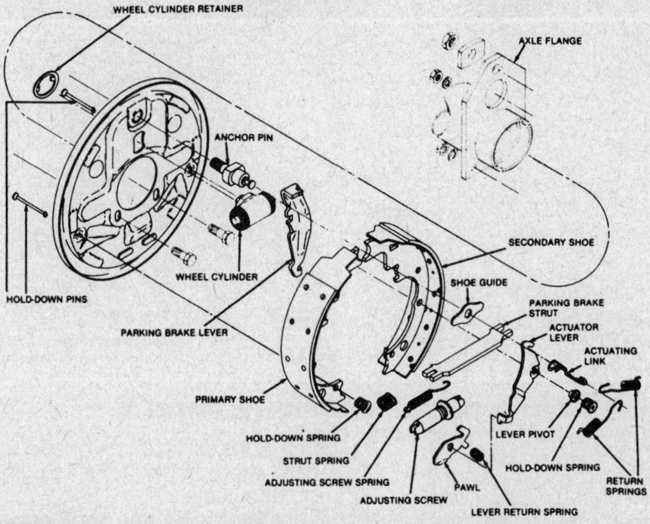

Fig. 3 Drum brake assembly. Type 3

assembly.

10. Clean dirt from brake drum, backing plate and all other components. **Do not use compressed air or dry brush to clean brake parts. Many brake parts contain asbestos fibers which, if inhaled, can cause serious injury. Clean brake parts with a water soaked rag or a suitable vacuum cleaner to minimize airborne dust.**

INSPECTION

1. Inspect components for damage and unusual wear. Replace as necessary.
2. Inspect wheel cylinders. Boots which are torn, cut or heat damaged indicate need for wheel cylinder replacement. On type 1 brakes, remove wheel cylinder links. Fluid spill from boot center hole indicates cup leakage and need for wheel cylinder replacement. On type 2 and 3 brakes, use a small screwdriver to pry center hole of boot away from piston. If fluid spills from center hole, cup leakage is indicated and wheel cylinder should be replaced. On all types, light fluid coatings on piston within cylinder is considered normal.
3. Inspect backing plate for evidence of axle seal leakage. If leakage exists, refer to individual car chapters for axle seal replacement procedures.
4. Inspect backing plate attaching bolts, and ensure they are tight.
5. Using fine emery cloth or other suitable abrasive, clean rust and dirt from shoe contact surface on backing plate.

INSTALLATION

1. Lubricate parking brake lever fulcrum with suitable brake lube, then attach lever to brake shoe. Ensure lever operates smoothly.
2. Connect brake shoes with adjusting screw spring, then position adjusting screw. **Ensure adjusting screw star wheel does not contact adjusting screw spring after installation and also ensure righthand thread adjusting screw is installed on left side of vehicle and lefthand thread adjusting screw is installed on right side of vehicle. When brake shoe installation is completed, ensure starwheel lines up with adjusting hole in backing plate.**
3. Lightly lubricate backing plate shoe contact surfaces with suitable brake lube, then the area where parking brake cable contacts backing plate.
4. Install brake shoes on backing plate while engaging wheel cylinder links (if equipped) with shoe webbing. Connect parking brake cable to parking brake lever. **The primary shoe (short lining) faces towards front of vehicle.**
5. Install actuating levers, actuating link and return spring, **Figs. 1, 2 and 3.**
6. Install hold-down springs with suitable tool.
7. Install primary and secondary shoe return springs using brake spring pliers or equivalent.
8. Using suitable brake drum to shoe gauge, measure brake drum inside diameter. Adjust brake shoes to dimension obtained on outside portion of gauge.
9. Install brake drum, wheel and tire assembly.
10. If any hydraulic connections have been opened, bleed brake system.
11. Adjust parking brake. Refer to individual car chapters for procedures.
12. Inspect all hydraulic lines and connections for leakage and repair as necessary.
13. Check master cylinder fluid level and replenish as necessary.
14. Check brake pedal for proper feel and return.
15. Lower vehicle and road test. **Do not severely apply brakes immediately after installation of new brake linings or permanent damage may occur to linings, and/or brake drums may become scored. Brakes must be used moderately during first several hundred miles of operation to ensure proper burnishing of linings.**

Type 4

INDEX

REMOVAL

1. Raise and support rear of vehicle, then remove tire and wheel assembly.
2. Remove brake drum. If brake lining is dragging on brake drum, back off brake adjustment by rotating adjustment screw. **If brake drum is rusted or corroded to axle flange and cannot be removed, lightly tap axle flange to drum mounting surface with a suitable hammer.**
3. Using brake spring pliers or equivalent, unhook primary and secondary return springs, **Fig. 1.**
4. Remove hold-down springs with suitable tool, then lift off lever pivot.
5. Remove hold-down pins, then lift actuator lever and remove actuator link.
6. Remove actuator lever, pivot and return spring.
7. Spread shoes apart and remove parking brake strut and spring.
8. With brake shoes spread, disconnect parking brake spring from lever, then lift brake shoes, adjusting screw and spring from backing plate.
9. Note position of adjusting screw and spring, then remove from shoe assemblies.
10. Remove parking brake lever from secondary shoe.
11. Clean dirt from brake drum, backing plate and all other components. **Do not use compressed air or dry brush to clean brake parts. Many brake parts contain asbestos fibers which, if inhaled, can cause serious injury. Clean brake parts with a water soaked rag or a suitable vacuum cleaner to minimize airborne dust.**

INSPECTION

1. Inspect components for damage or unusual wear. Replace as necessary.
2. On Chevette and 1000 models, inspect backing plate for evidence of axle seal leakage. If leakage exists, refer to individual car chapter for axle seal replacement procedure.
3. Inspect backing plate attaching bolts, and ensure they are tight.
4. Inspect wheel cylinders. Excessive fluid indicates cup leakage and need for wheel cylinder replacement. **A slight amount of fluid is always present and is considered normal, acting as a lubricant for the cylinder pistons.**
5. Check adjuster screw operation. If satisfactory, lightly lubricate adjusting screw and washer with suitable brake lube. If operation is unsatisfactory, replace.
6. Using fine emery cloth or other suitable abrasive, clean rust and dirt from shoe contact surfaces on backing plate, **Fig. 1.**

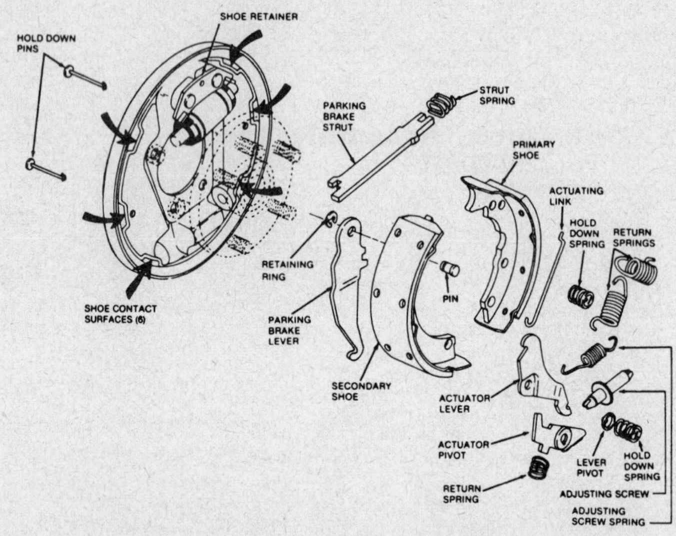

Fig. 1 Drum brake assembly. Type 4

INSTALLATION

1. Lightly lubricate backing plate shoe contact surfaces with suitable brake lube.
2. Install parking brake lever on secondary shoe.
3. Connect primary and secondary brake shoes with adjusting screw spring, then position adjusting screw in same position from which it was removed. **Ensure adjusting screw spring starwheel does not contact adjusting screw spring after installation, and also ensure righthand thread adjusting screw is installed on left side of vehicle and lefthand thread adjusting screw is installed on right side of vehicle.**
4. Spread brake shoes apart to clear axle flange, then install parking brake cable on lever. Position brake assembly on backing plate.
5. Spread brake shoes slightly, then install parking brake strut and spring. Spring end of strut engages the primary shoe, while the other end engages the parking brake lever and secondary shoe.
6. Install actuator lever, pivot and return spring, then hook actuating link in shoe retainer.
7. Lift actuator lever and hook actuating link to lever.
8. Install hold-down pins, lever pivot and hold-down springs.
9. Install primary and secondary return springs using suitable brake spring pliers.
10. Using suitable brake drum to shoe gauge, measure brake drum inside diameter. Adjust brake shoes to dimension obtained on outside portion of gauge.
11. Install brake drum, tire and wheel assembly.
12. If any hydraulic connections have been opened, bleed brake system.
13. Adjust parking brake. Refer to individual car chapters for procedures.
14. Inspect all hydraulic lines and connections for leakage, and repair as necessary.
15. Check master cylinder fluid level, and replenish as necessary.
16. Check brake pedal for proper feel and return.
17. Lower vehicle and road test. **Do not severely apply brakes immediately after installation of new brake linings or permanent damage may occur to linings, and/or brake drums may become scored. Brakes must be used moderately during first several hundred miles of operation to ensure proper burnishing of linings.**

Type 5

INDEX

Page No.

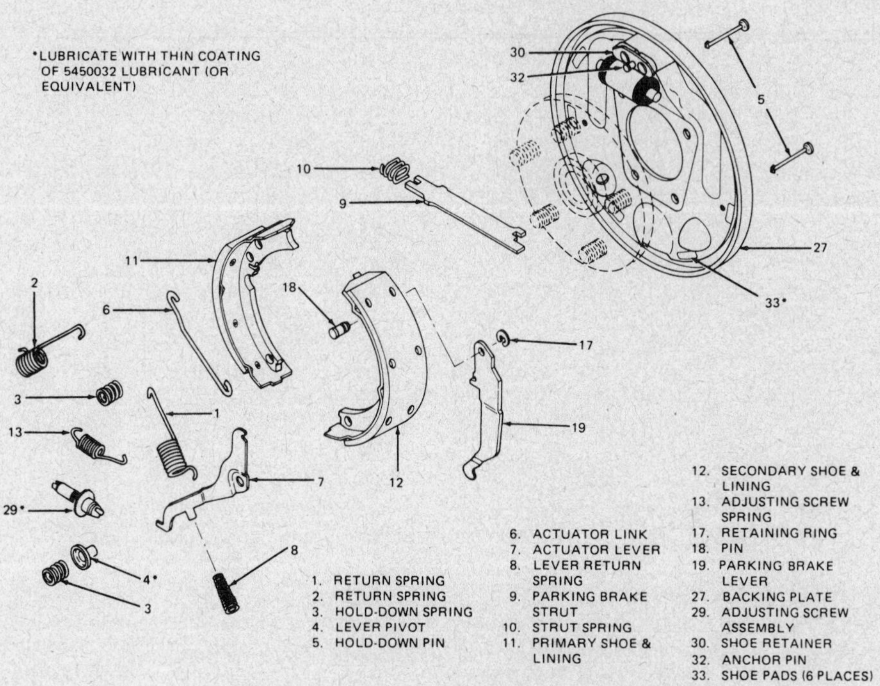

Fig. 1 Drum brake assembly. Type 5

REMOVAL

1. Raise and support rear of vehicle, then remove tire and wheel assembly.
2. Remove brake drum. If brake lining is dragging on brake drum, back off brake adjustment by rotating adjusting screw. Refer to individual car chapter for procedure. **If brake drum is rusted or corroded to axle flange and cannot be removed, lightly tap axle flange to drum mounting surface with a suitable hammer.**
3. Using tool No. J-8049 or equivalent, remove brake return springs, **Fig. 7.**
4. Using suitable pliers, remove hold-down springs and lever pivot.
5. While lifting up on actuator lever, disconnect actuating link.
6. Remove actuator lever and return spring.
7. Remove parking brake strut and spring.
8. Disconnect parking brake cable, then remove brake shoe and lining assembly.
9. Remove adjusting screw assembly and spring as follows:
   a. Note position of adjusting spring.
   b. Remove retaining ring, pin, and parking brake lever from secondary shoe.
   c. Remove adjusting screw and spring. **Do not interchange adjusting screws from right and left brake assemblies.**

INSPECTION

1. Inspect brake components for damage and/or wear. Replace as necessary.
2. Inspect wheel cylinders. Excessive fluid indicates cup leakage and need for wheel cylinder replacement.
3. Inspect backing plate for evidence of axle seal leakage.
4. Inspect backing plate attaching bolts. Ensure bolts are tight.
5. Check adjuster operation. If adjusters are worn, frozen or loose, replace adjuster and backing plate assembly as required.
6. Using fine emery cloth or other suitable abrasive, clean rust and/or dirt from shoe contact surface on backing plate.

INSTALLATION

1. Install parking brake lever, pin and retaining ring onto secondary shoe.
2. Apply silicone brake lubricant onto adjuster screw threads, inside diameter of socket and socket face. Adequate lubrication is achieved when a continuous bead of lubricant is at open end of pivot nut and socket when adjuster threads are completely engaged.
3. Install adjusting screw assembly and spring. **Spring coils must not overlap star wheel. Do not interchange right and lefthand springs.**
4. Connect parking brake cable, then install shoe and lining assembly.
5. Using a suitable tool, spread brake shoes apart, then install parking brake strut and spring. **Ensure parking brake strut is properly positioned. Ensure strut end without spring engages parking brake lever. Ensure strut end with spring engages primary brake shoe.**
6. Install actuator lever and return spring.
7. Install actuator link onto anchor pin.
8. While holding up on actuator lever, install link onto lever.
9. Install hold-down pins, lever pivot and hold-down springs.
10. Install shoe return springs.
11. Install brake drum, tire and wheel assembly.
12. If any hydraulic connections have been opened, bleed brake system.
13. Adjust brakes. Refer to individual car chapters for procedure.

Type 6

INDEX

REMOVAL

1. Raise and support vehicle.
2. Mark relationship of wheel to axle flange, then remove wheel and tire assembly.
3. Mark relationship of brake drum to axle flange, then remove drum. **If brake drum is difficult to remove, back off parking brake cable adjustment, remove inspection hole plug from backing plate, insert screwdriver through hole and press in to push parking brake lever off stop.**
4. Using suitable tool, remove upper return spring, **Fig. 1.**
5. Remove hold-down springs and pins.
6. Remove adjusting screw assembly.
7. Remove shoe and lining assembly together with lower return spring.
8. Remove retaining ring, pin, spring washer and parking brake lever from shoe and lining assembly.
9. Remove spring connecting link, adjuster actuator and actuator spring from adjusting shoe.
10. Press adjuster pin and spring washer from adjuster shoe.

INSPECTION

1. If any parts are of doubtful strength or quality due to heat discoloration, or are worn, replace them.
2. Inspect wheel cylinder dust boots for signs of excessive wear or damage.
3. Inspect adjusting screw for smooth operation over full length.
4. Clean adjusting screw components in denatured alcohol. **Ensure spring clip is installed in correct position, Fig. 1.**
5. Apply suitable lubricant to adjuster screw threads, inside diameter of socket and socket face. Adequate lubrication is achieved when a continuous bead of lubricant is at open end of adjuster nut and socket when threads are fully engaged.
6. Clean dirt and/or rust from brake drum, backing plate and all other components. **Do not use compressed air or dry brush to clean brake parts. Many brake parts contain asbestos fibers which, if inhaled, can cause serious injury. Clean brake parts with a water soaked rag or a suitable vacuum cleaner to minimize airborne dust.**
7. Ensure adjuster nut turns freely on adjuster screw.

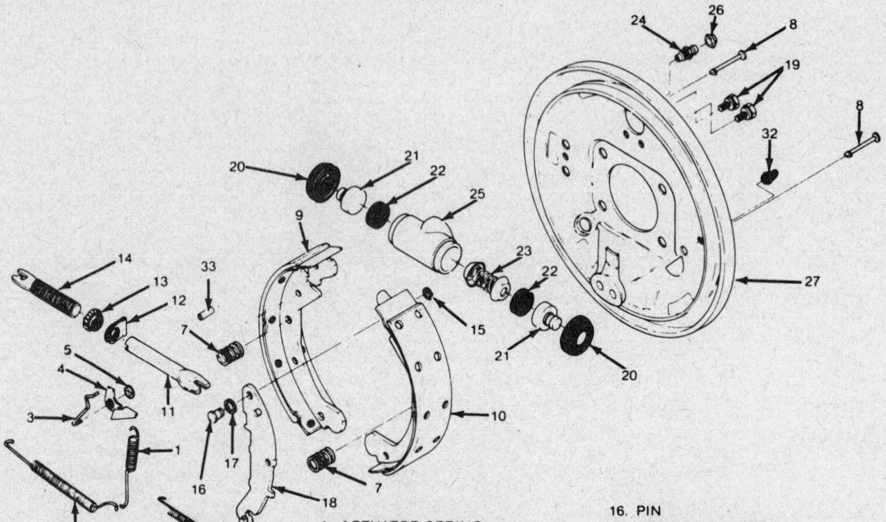

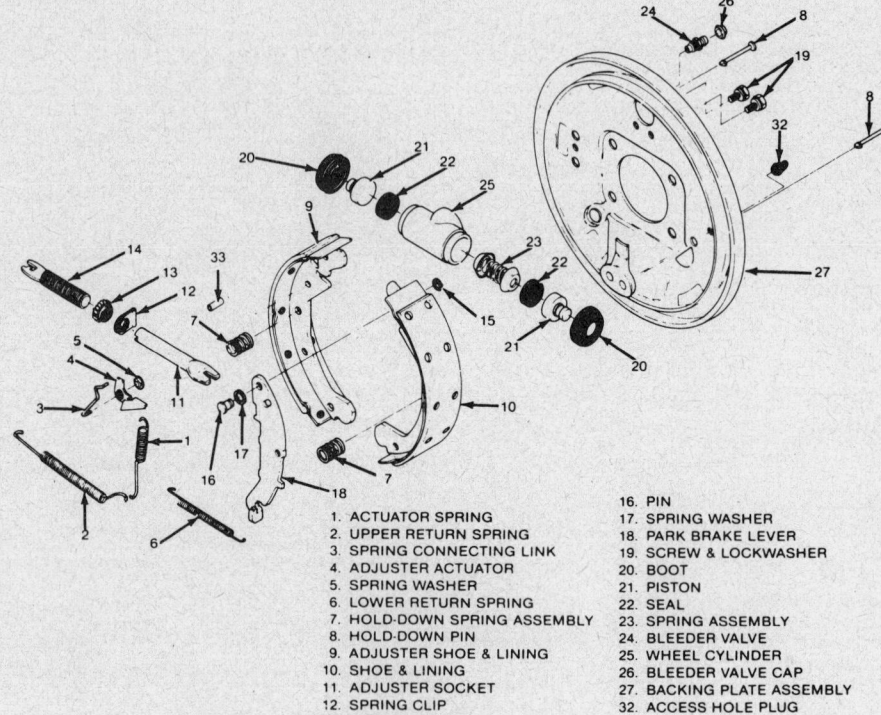

1. ACTUATOR SPRING
2. UPPER RETURN SPRING
3. SPRING CONNECTING LINK
4. ADJUSTER ACTUATOR
5. SPRING WASHER
6. LOWER RETURN SPRING
7. HOLD-DOWN SPRING ASSEMBLY
8. HOLD-DOWN PIN
9. ADJUSTER SHOE & LINING
10. SHOE & LINING
11. ADJUSTER SOCKET
12. SPRING CLIP
13. ADJUSTER NUT
14. ADJUSTER SCREW
15. RETAINING RING
16. PIN
17. SPRING WASHER
18. PARK BRAKE LEVER
19. SCREW & LOCKWASHER
20. BOOT
21. PISTON
22. SEAL
23. SPRING ASSEMBLY
24. BLEEDER VALVE
25. WHEEL CYLINDER
26. BLEEDER VALVE CAP
27. BACKING PLATE ASSEMBLY
32. ACCESS HOLE PLUG
33. ADJUSTER PIN

Fig. 1 Drum brake assembly. Type 6

INSTALLATION

1. Press adjuster pin and spring washer into shoe and lining so that pin projects .275-.283 inch from the side on which the adjuster actuator is installed.
2. Install adjuster shoe and lining, to front of vehicle on left side or to rear of vehicle on right side.
3. Install parking brake lever on shoe and lining with spring washer, pin and retaining ring. Install spring washer with concave side against parking brake lever.
4. Attach adjuster shoe and lining to remaining shoe with lower return spring.
5. Install both shoes on backing plate, securing with hold-down pins and springs.
6. Install adjuster actuator, spring connecting link and actuator spring onto adjuster shoe and lining.
7. Install adjusting screw assembly, ensuring adjuster screw engages notch in adjuster shoe. Ensure adjuster screw spring clip is properly positioned and the adjuster actuator is properly engaged in notch in adjuster screw. **Do not over extend upper return spring. The spring will be damaged if extended length exceeds 5.49 inches.**
8. Install upper return spring by inserting angled hook end of spring through parking brake lever and shoe lining, using suitable tool to pull spring straight across and then down to hook into crook in spring connecting link.
9. Back off parking brake adjustment until parking brake lever rests on brake shoe.
10. Install brake drum and tire and wheel assembly, then lower vehicle.
11. Apply and release service brake at least 25 times, then continue to pump brake pedal until clicking noise at drum brake self adjusters stops on both sides.
12. Adjust parking brake. Refer to individual car chapters for procedure.

Type 7

INDEX

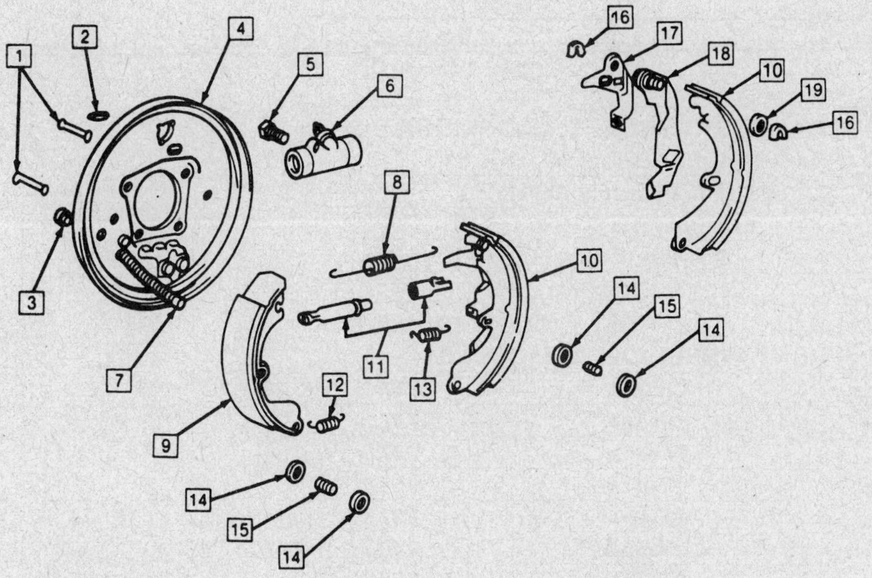

1. HOLD-DOWN PIN
2. PLUG
3. INSPECTION HOLE PLUG
4. BACKING PLATE
5. BOLT
6. WHEEL CYLINDER
7. PARKING BRAKE CABLE
8. RETURN SPRING
9. FRONT SHOE
10. REAR SHOE
11. STRUT
12. ANCHOR SPRING
13. ADJUSTING LEVER SPRING
14. RETAINER
15. HOLD-DOWN SPRING
16. C-WASHER
17. AUTOMATIC ADJUSTING LEVER
18. PARKING BRAKE LEVER
19. SHIM

Fig. 1 Drum brake assembly. Type 7

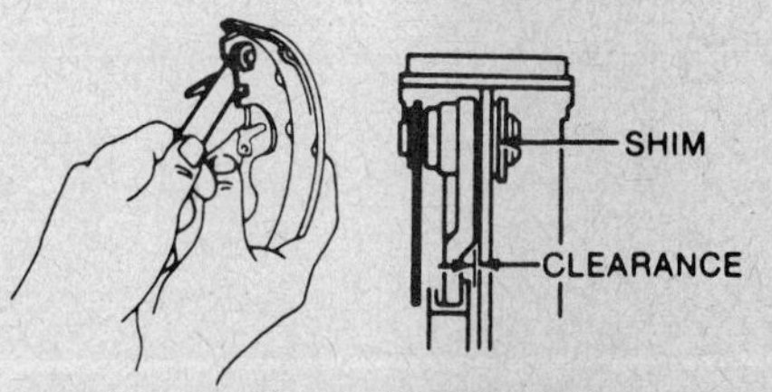

SHIM THICKNESS	
THICKNESS	THICKNESS
0.2 MM (0.008 IN.)	0.5 MM (0.020 IN.)
0.3 MM (0.012 IN.)	0.6 MM (0.024 IN.)
0.4 MM (0.016 IN.)	0.9 MM (0.035 IN.)

Fig. 2 Checking lever to shoe clearance

REMOVAL

1. Raise and support vehicle.
2. Mark relationship of wheel to axle, then remove wheel and tire assembly.
3. Remove brake drum. If drum is difficult to remove, insert screwdriver through hole in backing plate and hold automatic adjusting lever away from adjusting bolt, then, using a second screwdriver, reduce brake shoe adjustment.
4. Remove return spring, **Fig.1**
5. Remove hold-down spring, retainers and pin retaining front shoe.
6. Disconnect anchor spring from front shoe, then remove front shoe.
7. Remove anchor spring.
8. Remove hold-down spring, retainers and pin retaining rear shoe.
9. Using screwdriver, disconnect parking brake cable from anchor plate.
10. Using pliers, disconnect parking brake cable from lever and remove rear shoe together with strut.
11. Remove adjusting lever spring, then the strut together with return spring.
12. Remove parking brake lever and automatic adjusting lever from rear shoe by prying out "C" washer and removing shims and levers.
13. Clean dirt from brake drum, backing plate and all other components. **Do not use compressed air or dry brush to clean brake parts. Many brake parts contain asbestos fibers which, if inhaled, can cause serious injury. Clean brake parts with a water soaked rag or a suitable vacuum cleaner to minimize airborne dust.**

INSPECTION

1. Check brake drum, shoes, strut, auto adjuster lever, springs and backing plate for wear, distortion, cracks or other abnormal conditions.
2. If any parts are of doubtful strength or quality due to damage, heat discoloration, stress or wear, replace them.
3. Measure brake drum inside diameter and the brake shoe lining thickness.
4. Inspect lining and drum for proper contact.

INSTALLATION

1. Apply suitable lubricant to backing plate brake shoe contact points, anchor plate brake shoe contact points, strut and adjusting bolt contact points and the strut and brake shoe contact points.
2. Install parking brake lever and automatic adjusting lever to rear shoe as follows:
   a. Temporarily install levers and shim with a new "C" washer.
   b. Using feeler gage, measure clearance between shoe and lever, **Fig. 2.**
   c. If clearance is not 0-.0138 inch, adjust by installing replacement shim.
   d. Using pliers, stake "C" washer.
3. Set strut and return spring in place on rear shoe and install adjusting lever spring.
4. Install rear shoe as follows:
   a. Using pliers, connect parking brake cable to lever.
   b. Pass parking brake cable through notch in anchor plate.
   c. Set rear shoe in place with end of shoe inserted in wheel cylinder and other end in anchor plate.
   d. Install hold-down spring, retainers and pin.
5. Install front shoe as follows:
   a. Install anchor spring between front and rear shoes.
   b. Set front shoe in place with end of shoe inserted in wheel cylinder and the strut in place.
   c. Install hold-down spring, retainers and pin.
   d. Connect return spring.
6. Check operation of automatic adjuster mechanism as follows:
   a. Move parking brake lever of rear shoe back and forth and check whether adjusting bolt turns. If bolt does not turn, check brakes for incorrect installation.
   b. Adjust strut length to shortest possible distance.

c. Install brake drum.
d. Pull parking brake lever all the way up until a clicking sound can no longer be heard.

7. Check clearance between brake shoes and drum. Remove drum and measure brake drum inside diameter and diameter of brake shoes.
8. If clearance is not .024 inch, check parking brake system.
9. Install brake drum and the wheel and tire assembly.
10. Fill master cylinder as necessary and bleed brake system.
11. Check for fluid leakage.

Specifications

Year	Model	Brake Drum Inside Dia. Inch
BUICK, CADILLAC, CHEVROLET, OLDSMOBILE & PONTIAC (REAR WHEEL DRIVE MODELS)		
1982-84	Cadillac Brougham & DeVille	11
1982-86	Exc. Chevette & 1000	①
	Chevette & 1000	7.88
1985-87	Cadillac Brougham	11
BUICK, CADILLAC, CHEVROLET, OLDSMOBILE & PONTIAC (FRONT WHEEL DRIVE MODELS)		
1982-85	Citation	7.87
	Omega	7.87
	Phoenix	7.87
	Riviera	9.50
	Skylark	7.87
	Toronado	9.50
1982-87	Cavalier	7.87
	Celebrity	7.87
	Century	8.86
	Cimarron	7.87
	Cutlass Ciera	8.86
	Cutlass Cruiser	8.86
	Firenza	7.87
	Skyhawk	7.87
	Sunbird/2000	7.87
	6000	8.86
1985-87	Calais	7.87
	DeVille & Fleetwood	8.86
	Electra & Park Ave.	8.86
	Grand Am	7.87
	Ninety-Eight	8.86
	Nova	7.87
	Somerset & Somerset Regal	7.87
1986-87	LeSabre	8.86
	Eighty-Eight	8.86
	Skylark	7.87

①—With 4¾ inch bolt circle, 9.5 inches; with 5 inch bolt circle, 11 inches.

AUTOMATIC TRANSMISSIONS/TRANSAXLES

TABLE OF CONTENTS

Aisin Warner A131L Automatic Transaxle

INDEX

IDENTIFICATION

The transaxle identification number is stamped at top of transaxle rear cover at rear of transaxle.

DESCRIPTION

The A131L 3 speed automatic transaxle is used on 1985-87 Chevrolet Nova vehicles. The torque converter is equipped with an integral lock-up clutch. For higher performance, greater fuel economy and quietness, a high efficiency torque converter, wider gear ratio, compact high-precision valve body, high efficiency oil pump and a light weight durable integral transaxle case are used.

TROUBLESHOOTING

FLUID DISCOLORED OR SMELLS BURNT

1. Contaminated fluid.
2. Faulty torque converter.
3. Faulty transaxle.

VEHICLE DOES NOT MOVE IN ANY DRIVE GEAR

1. Improperly adjusted transaxle control cable.
2. Faulty valve body or primary regulator.
3. Faulty transaxle.

VEHICLE DOES NOT MOVE IN ANY RANGE

1. Faulty park lock pawl.
2. Faulty valve body or primary regulator.
3. Faulty torque converter.
4. Broken converter drive plate.
5. Blocked oil pump intake strainer.
6. Faulty transmission.

INCORRECT SHIFT LEVER POSITION

1. Improperly adjusted transaxle control cable.
2. Faulty manual valve and lever.
3. Faulty transaxle.

HARSH ENGAGEMENT INTO ANY DRIVE RANGE

1. Improperly adjusted transaxle control cable.
2. Faulty valve body or primary regulator.
3. Faulty accumulator pistons.
4. Faulty transaxle.

DELAYED UPSHIFTS & DOWNSHIFTS

1. Improperly adjusted throttle cable.
2. Faulty governors.
3. Faulty valve body.

SLIPS ON UPSHIFTS OR SHUDDERS ON TAKEOFF

1. Improperly adjusted transaxle control cable.
2. Improperly adjusted throttle cable.
3. Faulty valve body.
4. Faulty transaxle.

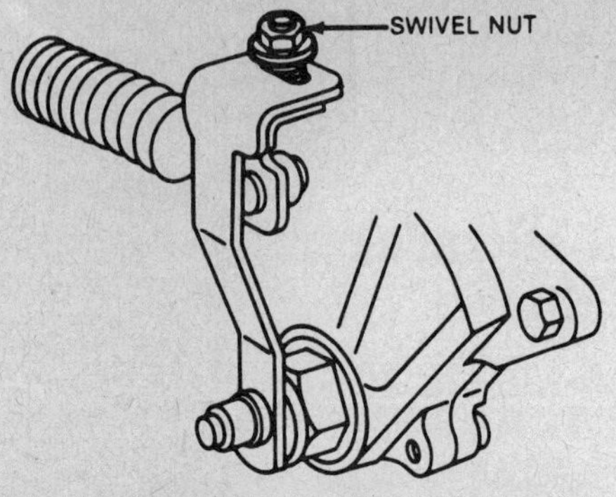

Fig. 1 Manual shift linkage adjustment

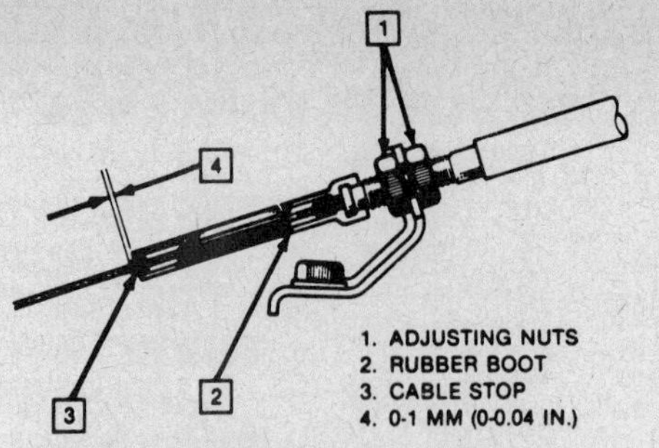

Fig. 2 Throttle cable adjustment

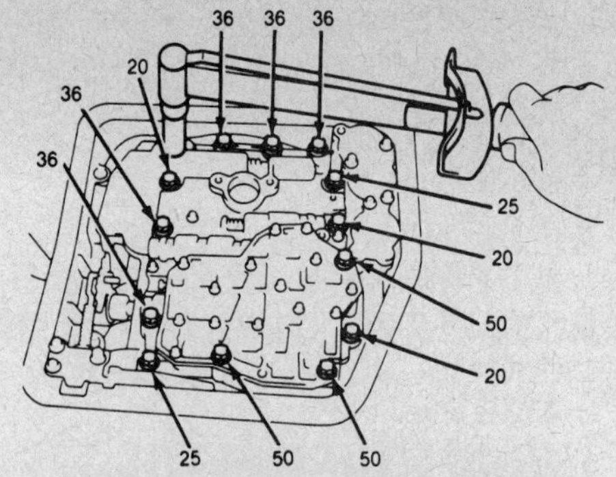

Fig. 3 Valve body bolt identification

DRAG OR BINDING ON UPSHIFT

1. Improperly adjusted transmission control cable.
2. Faulty valve body.
3. Faulty transaxle.

HARSH DOWNSHIFT

1. Improperly adjusted throttle cable.
2. Faulty accumulator pistons.
3. Faulty valve body.
4. Faulty transaxle.

NO DOWNSHIFT WHEN COASTING

1. Faulty governor.
2. Faulty valve body.

INCORRECT DOWNSHIFT

1. Improperly adjusted throttle cable.
2. Faulty governor.
3. Faulty valve body.
4. Faulty transaxle.

NO KICKDOWN

1. Improperly adjusted throttle cable.
2. Faulty governor.
3. Faulty valve body.

NO ENGINE BRAKING

1. Faulty valve body.
2. Faulty transaxle.

NO HOLD IN PARK

1. Improperly adjusted transaxle control cable.
2. Faulty parking lock pawl and rod.

MAINTENANCE

CHANGING FLUID

1. Raise and support vehicle, then place a suitable container under transaxle drain plug.
2. Remove drain plug and drain fluid, then reinstall and tighten drain plug.
3. With engine off, add 2.4 quarts of Dexron II type transmission fluid.
4. Start engine, then move selector lever through all ranges and end in "Park."
5. With engine idling, check fluid level, then if necessary, add fluid as necessary to bring fluid to "Cool" level on dipstick.

IN-VEHICLE ADJUSTMENTS

MANUAL SHIFT LINKAGE, ADJUST

1. Loosen swivel nut on lever, then push manual lever fully toward right side of vehicle, **Fig. 1.**
2. Return lever two notches to Neutral position, then place selector lever in Neutral position.
3. Manually hold lever lightly toward R range, then tighten swivel nut.

THROTTLE CABLE, ADJUST

1. Hold accelerator pedal in fully depressed position, then loosen cable adjusting nuts. **Fig. 2.**
2. Adjust cable to obtain .04 inch between end of boot and stopper on cable, then tighten adjusting nut.
3. Fully depress accelerator pedal and recheck adjustment, then road test vehicle.

NEUTRAL SAFETY SWITCH, ADJUST

1. Loosen neutral start switch attaching bolts, then place selector lever in Neutral position.
2. Disconnect electrical connector, then connect a suitable ohmmeter between terminals.
3. Rotate switch until meter indicates continuity, then torque switch retaining bolts to 48 inch lbs. to secure adjustment.
4. Reconnect electrical connector to switch then ensure engine starts with selector lever in Neutral and Park only.

IN-VEHICLE REPAIRS

VALVE BODY, REPLACE

Removal

1. Clean area around pan, then drain transmission fluid.
2. Remove oil pan and gasket, then the oil strainer.
3. Remove oil apply tube bracket attaching bolts, then the apply tube.
4. Remove oil tubes using a suitable screwdriver, then the manual detent spring.
5. Remove manual valve attaching bolts, then the manual valve assembly.
6. Remove valve body to cable bracket attaching bolt, then disconnect throttle cable.
7. Remove valve body attaching bolts, then valve body, governor, apply gasket and governor oil gasket.

Installation

1. Install governor oil gasket, then the governor and governor apply gasket.
2. Hold valve body in place, then manually retain cam in downward position and slip cable end into slot.
3. Position valve body into place, then insert and finger tighten 14 attaching bolts. Torque bolts to 7 ft. lbs. **Attaching bolt lengths (mm) are indicated in Fig. 3.**
4. Align manual valve with pin on manual valve lever, then install manual valve body.
5. Insert and finger tighten attaching bolts, then torque to 7 ft. lbs. **Attaching bolt lengths (mm) are indicated in Fig. 4.**
6. Install detent spring, then insert and finger tighten attaching bolts. Torque attaching bolts to 7 ft. lbs.
7. Ensure manual lever is in contact with center of roller at tip of detent spring, then install oil tubes.
8. Install apply tube bracket, then the oil strainer.
9. Insert magnet into pan, then install oil pan with new gasket.
10. Insert oil pan attaching bolts, then torque to 43 inch lbs.
11. Install drain plug with new gasket, then torque to 36 ft. lbs.
12. Fill transaxle to specifications, then ensure proper fluid level.

THROTTLE CABLE, REPLACE

Removal

1. Disconnect throttle cable from engine, then the transaxle control cable from manual shift lever.
2. Remove manual shift lever, then the neutral start switch.
3. Remove valve body as previously described, then the retaining plate bolt and retaining plate.
4. Pull cable from transaxle case.

Installation

1. Insert cable into transaxle case, then install retaining plate and bolt.

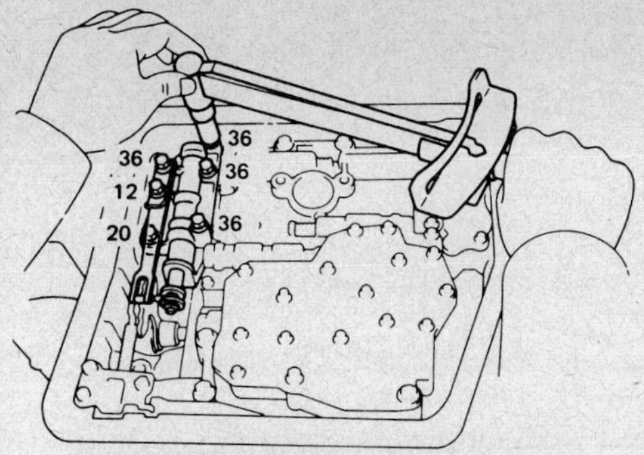

Fig. 4 Manual valve body bolt identification

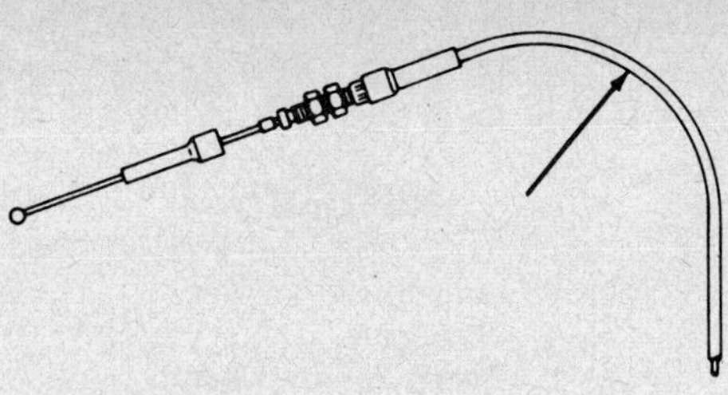

Fig. 5 Positioning throttle cable for stopper installation

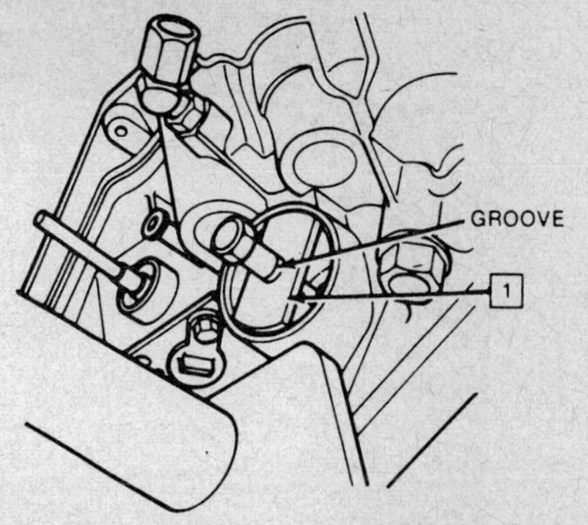

Fig. 6 Second brake servo plunger installation

2. Install valve body as previously described, then position cable stop for adjustment reference as follows. **Cable stop is not staked in place on replacement cable.**
   a. Bend cable to a radius of approximately 7.87 inches as shown, **Fig. 5.**
   b. Lightly pull inner cable from housing until a slight resistance is felt, then hold in position.
   c. Stake stopper onto inner cable so that .031-.059 inch clearance exists between stop and cable housing.
3. Connect throttle cable to throttle linkage, then adjust cable as previously described.
4. Install neutral safety switch, then the manual shift lever. Adjust switch as previously described.
5. Ensure transaxle fluid level is to specifications, then road test vehicle.

GOVERNOR VALVE, REPLACE

Removal

1. Remove transaxle cover, then the LH driveshaft.
2. Remove governor cover, then the O-ring.
3. Remove governor body with thrust washer.
4. Remove washer, then the governor body adapter.

Installation

1. Install governor body adapter, then the governor body with thrust washer.
2. Install governor cover with O-ring, then the LH driveshaft.

SECOND BRAKE SERVO ASSEMBLY, REPLACE

Removal

1. Raise and support vehicle, then remove shift cable bracket at transaxle.
2. Remove snap ring.
3. Remove cover.
4. Remove piston, then the outer spring.

Installation

1. Insert piston, less outer spring, then install snap ring.
2. Install tool No. J-35679, then observe groove on plunger of tool.
3. Push button on tool, **Fig. 6.** This allows tool to push brake apply rod into case. If groove is visible, piston stroke is correct (.059-.118 inch). If stroke is greater than specified, replace piston rod with 2.870 inch or 2.811 inch rod as needed.
4. Remove snap ring, then install piston and outer spring.
5. Install tool No. J-35549 to compress spring, then insert snap ring.
6. Install cover, then the shift cable bracket.
7. Lower vehicle.

TRANSAXLE REPLACE

1. Disconnect battery ground cable.
2. Remove air intake tube, then disconnect speedometer cable at transaxle.
3. Disconnect thermostat housing and ground cable at transaxle, then remove upper mount to bracket attaching bolt.
4. Disconnect transaxle electrical connectors, then the T.V. cable at carburetor.
5. Remove 2 upper bellhousing attaching bolts, then support engine using a suitable support tool.
6. Raise and support vehicle, then remove left wheel assembly.
7. Remove left and right splash shields, then the center splash shield.
8. Remove center beam, then disconnect shift cable at transaxle.
9. Remove shift cable bracket, then the cooler bracket.
10. Disconnect cooler lines at outlets, then remove inspection cover.
11. Remove torque converter attaching bolts, then the left control arm at ball joint.
12. Remove right and left axle shafts at transaxle, then the starter attaching bolts.
13. Remove 3 rear transaxle attaching bolts, then support transaxle, using a suitable jack.
14. Remove remaining transaxle attaching bolts, then the remaining bellhousing attaching bolts.
15. Remove transaxle from vehicle.
16. Reverse procedure to install, noting the following:
    a. Torque transaxle housing attaching bolts to 47 ft. lbs. for 12 mm bolts or 34 ft. lbs. for 10 mm bolts.
    b. Torque LH engine mount bolts to 38 ft. lbs.
    c. Install white torque converter bolt first, then the five yellow bolts. Torque bolts evenly to 13 ft. lbs.
    d. Torque engine mount center support bolts to 29 ft. lbs.
    e. Torque front and rear mount bolts to 29 ft. lbs.

3. Install transaxle dust cover, then ensure transaxle fluid level is to specifications.
4. Road test vehicle.

Turbo Hydra-Matic 125C Automatic Transaxle

INDEX

IDENTIFICATION

This transaxle may be identified by a model tag attached to the oil pan flange pad to the right of the oil dipstick at the rear of the transaxle.

DESCRIPTION

This automatic transaxle, **Fig. 1,** is designed for use as a transverse mounted front wheel drive unit. The unit consists primarily of a 3 element torque converter, **Fig. 2,** compound planetary gear set and dual sprockets, drive link assembly and a pressure plate and damper assembly. A differential and final drive gear set is also incorporated in the transaxle case. Three multiple disc clutches, a roller clutch and a band provide the friction elements required to obtain the desired functions of the planetary gear set. Hydraulic pressure required to operate the friction elements and automatic control is provided by a vane type pump.

TROUBLESHOOTING

NO DRIVE IN DRIVE RANGE: INTERMEDIATE, LOW & REVERSE OK

1. Low fluid level.
2. Forward clutch feed in input shaft restricted.
3. Leak between case cover and driven sprocket passages. Check gaskets.

1-2 SHIFT COMPLAINTS

Before diagnosing 1-2 shift problems, check and correct transmission fluid and set T.V. cable to specifications.

Slow, Early Or Drawn Out Shifts With End Bump

1. Disconnected or binding T.V. cable.
2. Low oil pressure. Check oil pressure in neutral at full T.V.
3. Intermediate servo piston oil seal missing or damaged.
4. Servo piston damaged.
5. Leak between servo apply pin and case.
6. Intermediate servo band apply pin binding in case.
7. T.V. plunger, T.V. shift valve or 1-2 accumulator valve binding.
8. 1-2 accumulator piston, seal, spring or bore damaged.
9. Incorrect or leaking spacer plate and/or gaskets.
10. Case porous in 2nd, servo apply and/or 1-2 accumulator passages.
11. Burned intermediate band.
12. Case cover improperly torqued.

Hunts 1-2-1 At Low Speed

1. Governor springs distorted and/or weights binding.

Firm, Harsh Or Delayed Shifts

1. Disconnected or binding T.V. cable.
2. High oil pressure. Check oil pressure in neutral at minimum T.V.
3. Compare 1-2 shift feel at part throttle in Drive range to 1-2 shift feel at part throttle in intermediate range. If intermediate range is firmer, follow steps 2 through 12 under "Slow, Early or Drawn Out Shifts With End Bump." If shift feels the same for both ranges, proceed to next step.
4. Intermediate servo piston, piston seal or piston bore damaged.
5. Missing servo orifice bleed cup plug.
6. Leak between servo apply pin and and case or wrong apply pin.
7. Incorrect T.V. link.
8. T.V. plunger, T.V. shift valve or 1-2 accumulator valve binding.
9. 1-2 accumulator piston piston, seal spring or bore damaged.
10. Incorrect or leaking spacer plate and/or gaskets.
11. Leaking 2nd oil passage in case or case cover.

2-3 SHIFT COMPLAINTS

Before diagnosing 2-3 shift problems, check transmission fluid level and adjust T.V. cable and manual linkage as required.

Delayed Harsh Upshift

1. High oil pressure.
2. Direct clutch accumulator exhaust hole plugged or not drilled.
3. Direct clutch exhaust valve check ball (1) missing, improperly located or leaking.
4. Valve body throttle valve and plunger binding.
5. T.V. shift valve binding.

Slow, Early Or Drawn Out Shifts With End Bump

1. Low oil pressure.
2. Intermediate servo piston to case seal ring missing or damaged.
3. Servo piston or bore (case) damaged.
4. Orifice plug missing from case servo bore area.
5. Accumulator exhaust check valve not seated.
6. Direct clutch feed orifice in spacer plate restricted.
7. Spacer plate or gaskets leaking or incorrectly installed.
8. Check ball 5 not seated.
9. Direct clutch case cover passages porous or incorrect cover gasket.
10. Driven sprocket support passages interconnected, leaking or restricted.
11. Driven sprocket support oil seal rings damaged or missing. Support inner sleeve loose or out of position.
12. Direct clutch check ball, check ball capsule or seals damaged or leaking.

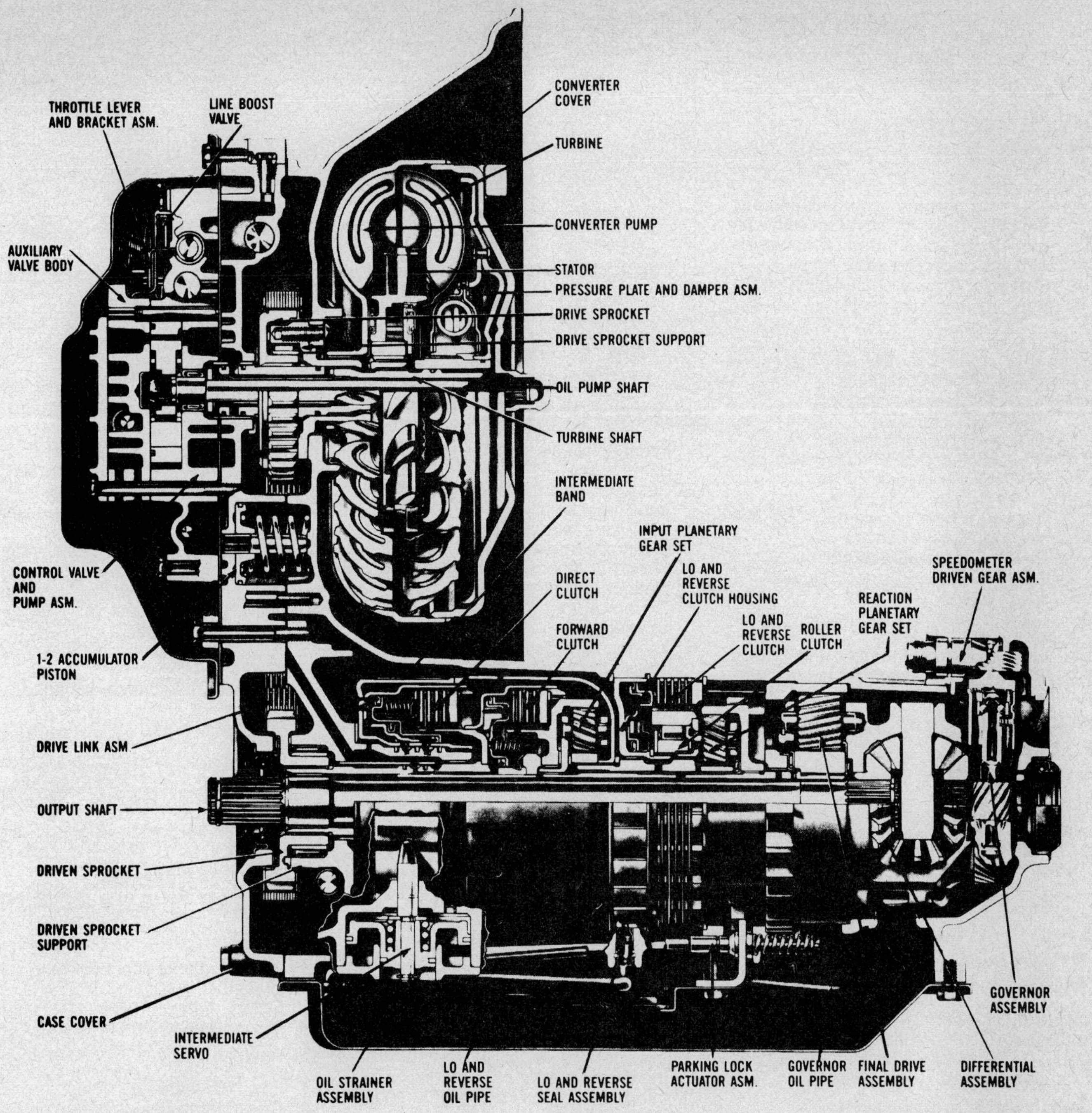

Fig. 1 Cross sectional view of Turbo Hydra-Matic 125C automatic transaxle

13. Direct clutch piston or housing cracked, apply ring missing or incorrect number of clutch plates.

FAILS TO SHIFT 2-3 OR DELAYED 2-3 SHIFT

Check transmission fluid level, set T.V. cable to specifications and check manual linkage before diagnosing shift problems.

1. Incorrect, broken, disconnected or binding T.V. cable.
2. Worn governor cover.
3. Governor thrust washer and seal worn or missing.
4. Governor spring unseated, weights binding or exhaust check balls missing.
5. Governor driven gear stripped or missing.
6. Intermediate servo piston, bore or seal ring damaged.
7. Intermediate servo orifice bleed cup in case missing or case porous in servo bore area.
8. Direct clutch accumulator cup plug or accumulator exhaust check valve leaking or missing.
9. Binding throttle lever and bracket assembly or wrong or disconnected T.V. link.
10. 2-3 shift valve, 2-3 T.V. valve or shift T.V. valve sticking or binding.
11. Governor feed to 2-3 T.V. valve or direct clutch feed orifice restricted.
12. Valve body spacer plate or gaskets leaking, damaged or incorrectly installed.
13. Missing or improperly located #5 check ball.
14. Governor shaft case sleeve or driven sprocket support oil seal damaged or missing.
15. Direct clutch piston, piston housing or seals damaged.
16. Direct clutch plates or check ball capsule damaged. Backing plate snap ring out of groove.
17. Leaking case center gasket or loose case cover bolts.
18. Leaking, interconnected or restricted driven sprocket support passages.

19. Driven sprocket support oil seal rings missing or damaged.
20. Driven sprocket support sleeve loose or out of position.

DELAY IN DRIVE & REVERSE

1. Low fluid level.
2. Low line pressures. **A 3-5 second delay in Drive or reverse with engine off for 60 minutes or longer indicates converter drain-back.**
3. Damaged turbine shaft Teflon seals. Replace with solid seals.

NO UPSHIFTS, DELAYED UPSHIFTS OR FULL THROTTLE UPSHIFTS

1. Improperly adjusted linkage
2. T.V. cable improperly adjusted, disconnected or broken.
3. Oil level low.
4. Governor cover worn or thrust washer missing.
5. Governor seal worn or cut.
6. Governor spring not seated or weights binding on pin.
7. Governor ball missing or driven gear stripped.
8. Intermediate servo apply pin sticking.
9. Intermediate servo seals cut or damaged, piston sticking or porosity in servo case bore.
10. Valves sticking in control valve assembly or spacer plate gaskets leaking.
11. Governor feed orifice to 1-2 and 2-3 shift valve clogged.
12. Valve body spacer drive to governor orifice clogged.
13. Intermediate band worn or burned.
14. Porosity in case cover, missing cup plugs or 2nd oil passage leaking.

2ND SPEED START, MISSES 1ST

1. Governor springs distorted or out of place. Governor weights binding.
2. 1-2 Shift or throttle valves stuck in upshift position.

SHIFTS 2-1 AT HIGH SPEEDS, PASSING GEAR

1. Damaged governor assembly.
2. Sticking intermediate servo.
3. Direct clutch orifice controlled by 2 check ball restricted.
4. 1-2 accumulator piston or seal missing or leaking.

SLIPS OR CHATTERS IN 1ST

1. Low fluid level.
2. Wrong or incorrectly adjusted T.V. cable.
3. Low oil pressure.
4. Restricted feed to forward clutch.
5. Burned forward clutch.
6. Rough machined surface on driven sprocket support.
7. Incorrect case cover gaskets.

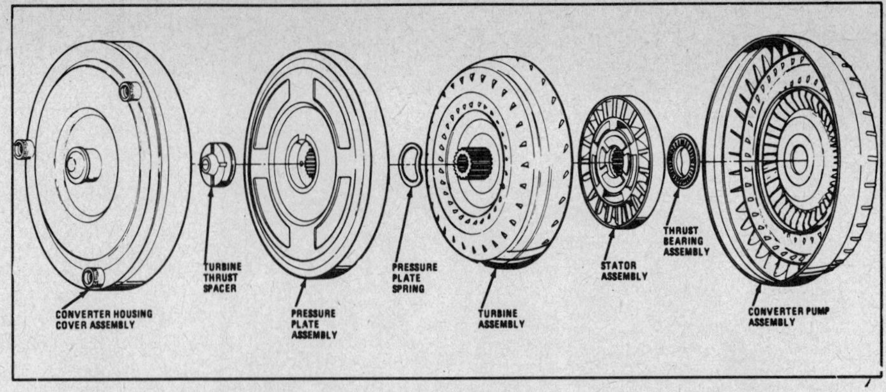

Fig. 2 Exploded view of torque converter clutch

SHIFTS 1-3 (MISSES 2ND)

1. Intermediate servo sticking, leaking or damaged.
2. Stuck or unseated accumulator exhaust check valve.
3. 1-2 valve sticking in control valve pump assembly.
4. Wrong or incorrectly installed spacer plate or gasket.
5. Governor feed passage to 1-2 valve blocked.
6. Intermediate band apply feed orifice blocked.
7. Case or case cover intermediate servo apply passage blocked.
8. Burned, improperly installed or broken intermediate band.

NO FULL THROTTLE 3-2 DOWNSHIFT

1. Wrong, improperly adjusted or binding T.V. cable or link.
2. Accelerator pedal and/or linkage will not open carburetor to wide open position.
3. Binding shift T.V. or throttle valve.
4. Spacer plate holes plugged and/or gaskets damaged or mispositioned.

NO INTERMEDIATE RANGE (2ND GEAR)

1. Intermediate servo oil seal ring missing or damaged.
2. Intermediate band broken, burned or mispositioned.
3. 1-2 accumulator piston or pin damaged or missing.

NO OVERRUN BRAKING IN LO, REVERSE OK

1. Manual linkage improperly adjusted.
2. Lo-reverse pipe or piston seals leaking.
3. Damaged low blow off valve assembly.

TRANSAXLE NOISY

1. Low fluid level.
2. Screen plugged or screen O-ring damaged.
3. Coolant in fluid.
4. Transaxle grounded to body.
5. Roller bearing damaged or worn.
6. If noisy in 3rd gear or on turns only, check differential and final drive unit.

HIGH OR LOW FLUID PRESSURE

1. Throttle valve cable improperly adjusted or binding.
2. Throttle lever and bracket assembly binding or damaged.
3. Throttle valve or plunger binding.
4. Shift throttle valve binding.
5. Line boost valve binding.
6. Throttle valve boost valve or reverse boost valve binding.
7. Pressure regulator valve and spring binding.
8. Pressure relief valve damaged.
9. Manual valve disconnected.
10. Pump damaged.

NO DRIVE IN FORWARD RANGE, REVERSE TIES UP

1. Driven sprocket support sleeve turned.

NO FORWARD OR REVERSE IN ANY RANGE

Ties Up

1. Internal mechanical damage.
2. Broken differential.
3. Object between link and sprocket locking link assembly.

Slippage

1. Low fluid level.
2. Converter to flex plate bolts missing.
3. Low line pressure in drive.
4. Manual linkage binding.
5. Input shaft to forward clutch drum broken loose.
6. Reaction carrier broken at low roller clutch cam.
7. Broken chain assembly.

NO DRIVE IN FORWARD RANGES, REVERSE OK

1. Low line pressure in Drive.
2. Binding manual linkage.
3. Driven sprocket support drive oil passage or case cover gasket restricted.
4. Drive oil passage leak in case cover.
5. Driven sprocket support sleeve loose or improperly located.
6. Burned forward clutch.
7. Leaking valve body pipe in control valve assembly.

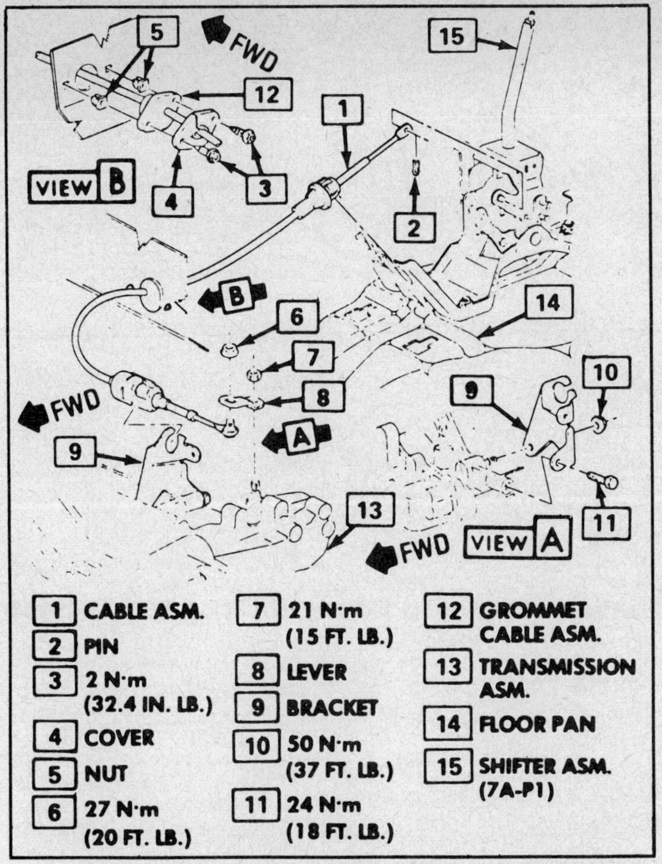

Fig. 3 Typical manual cable mounting. 1982–87 Cavalier, Cimarron, Firenza, Skyhawk, Sunbird & 2000; 1985–87 Calais, Grand Am & Somerset Regal; 1986–87 Skylark

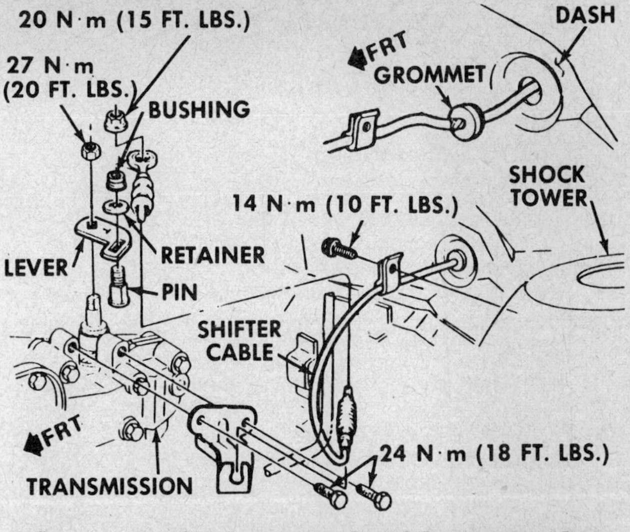

Fig. 4 Typical manual cable mounting. 1982–85 Citation, Omega, Phoenix & Skylark; 1982–87 Celebrity, Century, Cutlass Ciera & 6000

NO REVERSE, ALL FORWARD RANGES OK

Ties Up

1. Forward clutch not releasing due to burned clutch plates, piston seal ring missing or sticking exhaust check ball.

Slippage

1. Low Line Pressure in reverse.
2. Restricted case to low and reverse clutch housing cup plug assembly.
3. Low and reverse clutch piston or seal leakage.
4. Low and reverse pipe O-ring or washer damaged or missing.
5. Incorrect gasket for driven sprocket support height.
6. Low 1st orifice in spacer plate plugged or missing.
7. Burned direct clutch.
8. Burned low and reverse clutch.

MAINTENANCE

To check fluid, drive vehicle for at least 15 minutes to bring fluid to operating temperature (200° F). With vehicle on a level surface and engine idling in Park and parking brake applied, the level on the dipstick should be at the "Full" mark. To bring the fluid level from the ADD mark to the FULL mark requires one pint of fluid. If vehicle cannot be driven sufficiently to bring fluid to operating temperature, the level on the dipstick should be between the two dimples on the dipstick with fluid temperature at 70° F. Note that the two dimples are located above the FULL mark.

If additional fluid is required, use only Dexron II automatic transmission fluid.

An early change to a darker color from the usual red color and or a strong odor that is usually associated with overheated fluid is normal and should not be considered as a positive sign of required maintenance or unit failure.

When adding fluid, do not overfill, as foaming and loss of fluid through the vent may occur as the fluid heats up. Also, if fluid level is too low, complete loss of drive may occur especially when cold, which can cause transmission failure.

Every 100,000 miles, the oil should be drained, the oil pan removed, the screen cleaned and fresh fluid added. For vehicles subjected to more severe use such as heavy city traffic especially in hot weather, prolonged periods of idling or towing, this maintenance should be performed every 15,000 miles.

CHANGING FLUID

1. Raise and support vehicle, then position drain pan under oil pan.
2. Remove front and side oil pan attaching bolts, then loosen rear pan attaching bolts.
3. Carefully pry oil pan loose from transaxle case and allow fluid to drain.
4. Remove remaining attaching bolt, oil pan and gasket. Thoroughly clean pan before reinstalling.
5. Remove and discard screen and O-ring seal.
6. Install replacement screen and O-ring seal, locating screen against dipstick stop.
7. Install gasket on oil pan, then install pan and torque attaching bolts to 12 ft. lbs. on 1982-84 models, or 8 ft. lbs. on 1985-87 models.
8. Lower vehicle and add approximately 4 qts. of fluid.
9. With selector in park, parking brake applied and engine at idle speed and operating temperature, check fluid level and add fluid as necessary. **Do not race engine. Move shift lever through ranges, then back to "Park" position.**

IN-VEHICLE ADJUSTMENTS

MANUAL LINKAGE, ADJUST

Exc. Fiero

1. Place transaxle shift lever in "Neutral" position.
2. Place transaxle lever in "Neutral" position by moving transaxle lever clockwise to the "L" detent, then move lever counterclockwise through three detent positions to "Neutral."
3. Loosely assemble retainer, bushing and shift cable to pin, **Figs. 3 through 6,** then torque attaching nut to specifications.

Fiero

1. Place transaxle shift lever in "Neutral" position.
2. Place transaxle lever in "Neutral" position by rotating transaxle lever clockwise from "Park," through "Reverse" and into "Neutral."

3. Insert shift cable threaded pin through slotted hole in lever and hand start nut, **Fig. 7.**
4. Torque nut to 15-25 ft. lbs. while holding lever out of "Park" position.

DETENT/T.V. CABLE, ADJUST

On vehicles equipped with diesel engine, remove injection pump rod from throttle lever prior to adjusting cable.

1. Depress and hold metal lock tab, **Fig. 8.**
2. Move slider back through fitting in direction away from throttle idler lever until slider stops against fitting, then release lock tab.
3. Rotate throttle idler lever to full travel stop position to set automatic cable adjuster on cable to correct setting, then release throttle idler lever.

IN-VEHICLE, REPAIRS

VALVE BODY, REPLACE

1. Remove valve body cover and gasket.
2. Remove solenoid retaining bolt and the solenoid, then disconnect converter clutch wires from 3rd gear pressure switch.
3. Remove screws attaching throttle lever and bracket assembly, then remove throttle lever and bracket assembly with T.V. cable link.
4. Remove the auxiliary valve body screws except for the one screw shown in **Fig. 9.** Loosen, but do not remove, this screw.
5. Remove remaining valve body retaining screws, then the valve body and pump assembly.
6. Separate valve body from auxiliary valve body.
7. Reverse procedure to install. Torque all 6 mm bolts to 8 ft. lbs. and all 8 mm bolts to 18 ft. lbs.
8. Using new gasket, install valve body cover to transaxle and torque bolts to 12 ft. lbs. **Transaxle valve body covers and oil pans can have a raised rib, depressed rib or flat sealing flange. RTV sealant should be used on all oil pans and valve body covers that have a flat sealing flange. Gaskets should be used on all oil pans and valve body covers that have either depressed or raised rib sealing flanges.**

INTERMEDIATE SERVO, REPLACE

1. Remove oil pan and gasket, then remove screen and O-ring.
2. Remove reverse oil pipe retaining brackets, intermediate servo cover and gasket.
3. Remove intermediate servo assembly.
4. Reverse procedure to install. Torque intermediate servo cover screws to 8 ft. lbs.

GOVERNOR, REPLACE

1. Raise and support vehicle.
2. Remove engine-to-transaxle brace attaching bolts, then the heat shield, if equipped.
3. Remove speedometer cable or wire connector from transaxle.
4. Remove speedometer driven gear and sleeve assembly or speed sensor, as equipped.
5. Remove governor cover and O-ring.
6. Remove speedometer drive gear thrust washer and gear, then the governor assembly, **Fig. 10.**

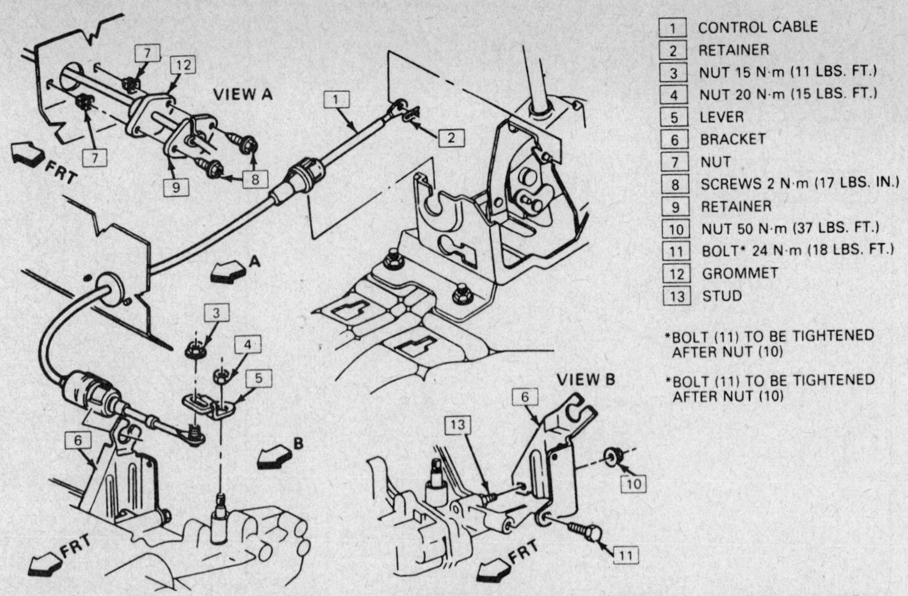

Fig. 5 Manual cable mounting (Floor shift). 1987 Corsica & Beretta

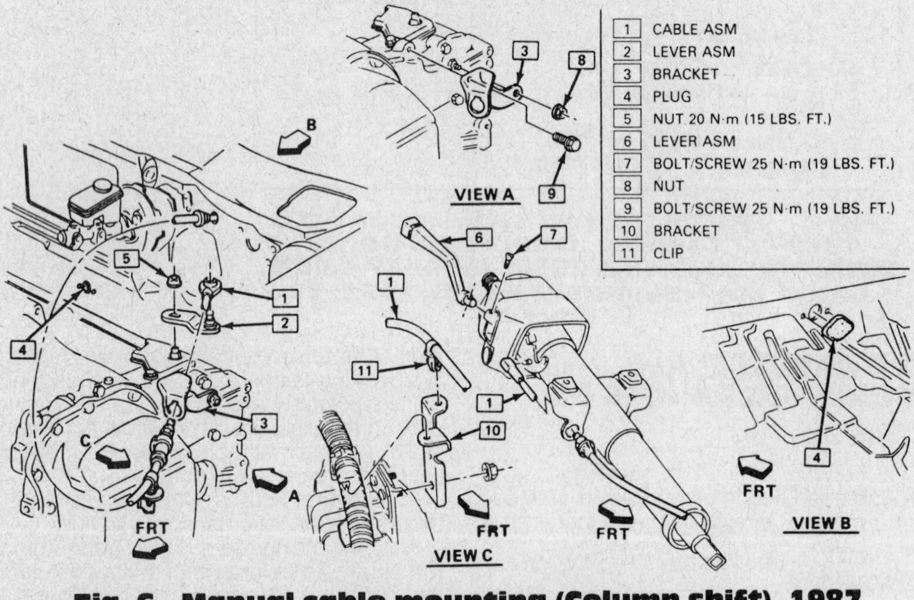

Fig. 6 Manual cable mounting (Column shift). 1987 Corsica & Beretta

TRANSAXLE

REPLACE

1982–85 CITATION, OMEGA, PHOENIX & SKYLARK; 1982–87 CELEBRITY, CENTURY, CUTLASS CIERA & 6000

1. Disconnect battery ground cable, then remove air cleaner.
2. Disconnect T.V. cable from transaxle and carburetor, then remove strut shock bracket bolts from transaxle.
3. Remove oil cooler lines from strut bracket.
4. Remove all transaxle to engine attaching bolts except the one nearest the starter. Loosen, but do not remove this bolt.
5. Disconnect speedometer cable at upper and lower couplings, then remove shift linkage retaining clip, washer and bracket bolts.
6. Disconnect oil cooler lines at transaxle.
7. Remove front and left sections of cradle as follows:
   a. Install engine support fixture J-22825-1 and J-22825-45 and torque fasteners to 30 ft. lbs.

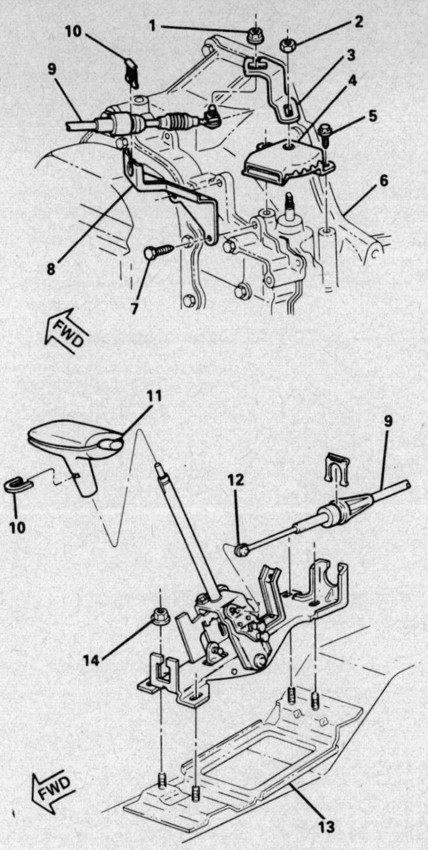

1 – NUT/CABLE ASSY.	8 – BRACKET
2 – NUT/SHIFTING LEVER	9 – CABLE ASSY.
3 – LEVER/SHIFTING	10 – RETAINER ASSY.
4 – SWITCH/NEUTRAL START AND BACK-UP	11 – T HANDLE
5 – BOLT/NEUTRAL START SWITCH (2)	12 – SNAP SECURELY ONTO PIN
6 – TRANSAXLE	13 – GEAR SHIFT SUPPORT
7 – BOLT/BRACKET	14 – NUT 23 N·M (17 FT. LB.)

Fig. 7 Manual cable mounting. 1984–87 Fiero

b. Position support hook into lifting bracket and tighten coupling nut only enough to remove slack from hook. **Engine support fixture must be located in center of cowl for 4 cylinder engines and on strut towers for 6 cylinder engines. Support fixture is not designed to support entire weight of engine and transaxle. Improper use may result in vehicle damage and/or personal injury.**
c. Remove intermediate shaft to steering gear stub shaft attaching bolt, then raise and support vehicle.
d. Support engine with suitable jack, then remove left front wheel/tire assembly.
e. Remove power steering line brackets and steering gear mounting bolts.
f. Disconnect drive line vibration absorber, if equipped.

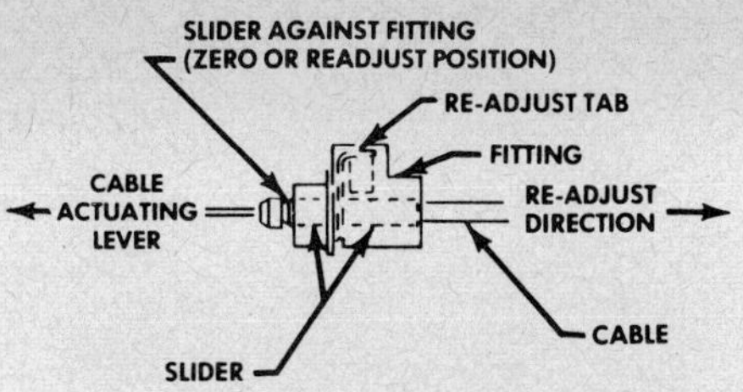

Fig. 8 Downshift cable adjustment

g. Disconnect left lower ball joint at steering knuckle, then remove both front stabilizer bar reinforcements and bushings.
h. Using a 1/2 inch drill bit, drill through spot weld located between rear holes of left stabilizer bar mounting, **Fig. 11.**
i. Disconnect engine and transaxle mounts from cradle, then remove side crossmember bolts.
j. Remove left side body mount bolts, then the left and front cradle assembly.

8. Install axle shaft boot protectors, then position axle shaft puller behind axle shaft cones and pull cones away from transaxle.
9. Remove left axle shaft and plug bore in transaxle to avoid fluid leakage.
10. Remove starter, then the converter shield.
11. Remove the three flywheel to converter attaching bolts.
12. Remove engine to transaxle bracket extension bolts, then the rear transaxle mount bracket assembly. Raise transaxle if necessary.
13. Remove the one remaining engine to transaxle bolt located near the starter.
14. Slide transaxle towards drivers side and remove from vehicle.
15. Reverse procedure to install. Note the following when installing transaxle:
    a. Position a 1/2 inch drill bit into drilled hole, **Fig. 11,** before tightening cradle bolts.
    b. Slide right axle shaft into case as transaxle is being installed.
    c. Check front suspension alignment after transaxle installation.
    d. Check and adjust T.V. cable if necessary.
    e. Torque transaxle mount bolts to 22 ft. lbs. (30 Nm).
    f. Torque transaxle-to-engine mount bolts to 55 ft. lbs. (75 Nm).

1982–84 CAVALIER, CIMARRON, FIRENZA, SKYHAWK, SUNBIRD & 2000; 1985–87 CIMARRON & 1985–86 CAVALIER W/4-121 ENGINE

1. Disconnect battery ground cable from transaxle.
2. Insert a 1/4 x 2 inch bolt into hole in right front motor mount to prevent improper location of mount during transaxle removal.
3. Remove air cleaner, then disconnect T.V. cable from carburetor.

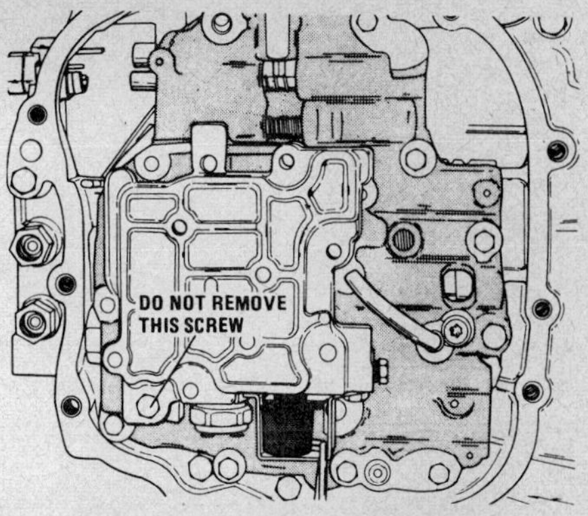

Fig. 9 Valve body & auxiliary valve body retaining screws

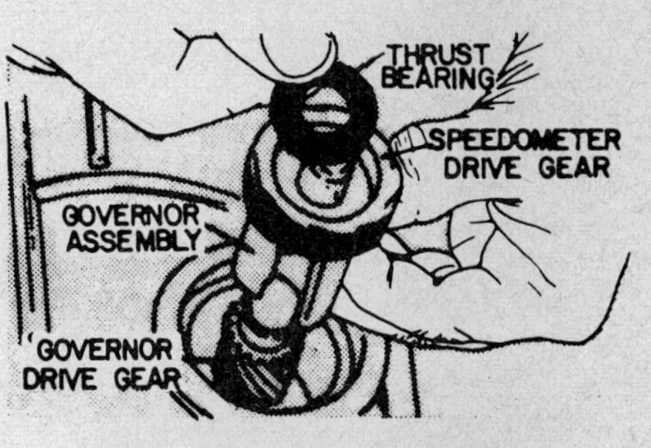

Fig. 10 Removing & installing governor assembly

4. Remove T.V. cable retaining bolt from transaxle, pull up cable cover and disconnect cable from transaxle rod.
5. Remove engine wire harness retaining bolt, disconnect air management hose, then position harness aside.
6. Raise and support engine with a suitable lifting device so that weight is taken off motor mounts.
7. Remove top transaxle mount and bracket assembly, then disconnect shift control linkage from transaxle.
8. Remove top engine to transaxle attaching bolts and loosen, but do not remove, the bolt nearest the starter.
9. Raise and support vehicle, unlock steering column and remove both front wheel/tire assemblies.
10. Remove cotter pin and ball joint retaining nut, then separate ball joint from control arm. Repeat procedure for other side.
11. Remove stabilizer bar to left lower control arm attaching bolt.
12. Remove the six left front suspension support to body attaching bolts, then position axle shaft removal tools J-28468 and J-23907 behind axle shaft cones and pull cones away from transaxle.
13. Remove axle shafts and plug transaxle bores to prevent fluid leakage.
14. Remove transaxle control cable bracket retaining nut, then the transaxle to engine attaching stud.
15. Disconnect speedometer cable and transaxle mounting strut.
16. Remove the four torque converter shield to transaxle attaching bolts, then the shield.

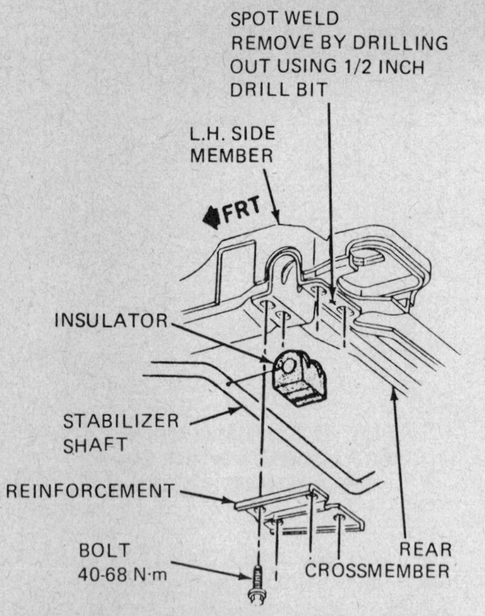

Fig. 11 Drilling cradle spot weld

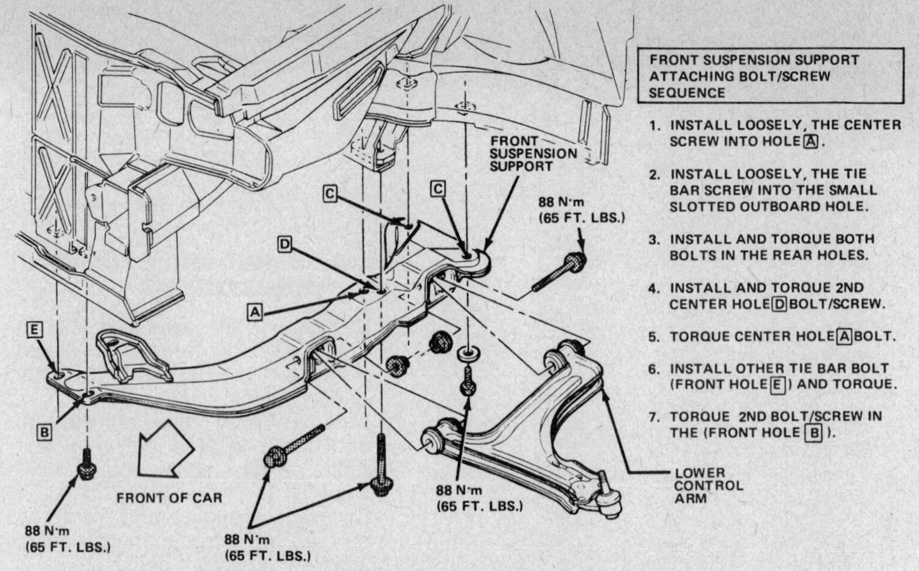

Fig. 12 Front suspension support attaching bolt sequence

17. Remove the torque converter to flex plate retaining bolts, then disconnect and plug the transaxle cooler lines.
18. Remove starter.
19. Remove brake and fuel line brackets from left side of underbody and position aside.
20. Remove the last engine to transaxle attaching bolt, separate transaxle from engine by sliding away from engine and remove transaxle from vehicle.
21. Reverse procedure to install, making sure:
    a. Axle shafts are installed after transaxle is in place.
    b. To follow the tightening sequence shown in **Fig. 12** when installing the front suspension support assembly.
    c. To readjust throttle valve (T.V.) cable.
    d. To check front suspension alignment.

1985–87 CIMARRON & CAVALIER W/V6-173 ENGINE

1. Disconnect battery ground cable.
2. Remove air intake duct from air cleaner, then the left fender brace.
3. Disconnect M.A.T. sensor electrical connector from air cleaner.
4. Disconnect mass air flow sensor electrical connector, then the PCV pipe clamp from air intake duct.
5. Remove air intake duct from throttle body, then the mass air flow sensor attaching bolt.
6. Remove air cleaner bracket attaching bolts from battery tray, then the air cleaner mass air flow sensor and air intake duct as an assembly.
7. Disconnect T.V. cable from throttle body.
8. Remove T.V. cable attaching bolt from transaxle, then pull up cable cover and disconnect cable from transaxle rod.
9. Disconnect heat shield from crossover pipe, then remove exhaust crossover pipe.
10. Install suitable engine support fixture, then remove transaxle mount and bracket assembly. **It may be necessary to raise engine to facilitate mount removal.**
11. Disconnect shift control linkage from transaxle.
12. Remove upper transaxle-to-engine attaching bolts, then loosen, but do not remove, the bolt nearest the starter.
13. Raise and support vehicle, then remove front wheels.
14. Remove ball joint cotter pin, then loosen castle nut until ball joint separates from control arm.
15. Remove stabilizer bar to LH lower control arm attaching bolt.
16. Remove six LH front suspension support assembly attaching bolts, then position axle shaft removing tools J-28468 and J-23907 behind axle shaft cones and pull cones away from transaxle.
17. Remove axle shafts and plug transaxle bore to prevent fluid leakage.
18. Remove transaxle control cable brackets-to-transaxle attaching nut, then the engine-to-transaxle stud.
19. Remove speedometer cable from transaxle, then the transaxle stabilizer from transaxle.
20. Remove torque converter shield, then the torque converter-to-flex plate attaching bolts.
21. Remove and plug transaxle cooler lines.
22. Remove starter, then loosen brake and fuel line brackets at LH side of underbody.
23. Remove remaining transaxle-to-engine attaching bolts, then lower transaxle from vehicle.
24. Reverse procedure to install, noting the following:
    a. Follow the tightening sequence shown in **Fig. 12** when installing the front suspension support assembly.
    b. Readjust T.V. cable.
    c. Check front suspension alignment.

1985–87 CALAIS, FIRENZA, GRAND AM, SKYHAWK, SOMERSET REGAL & SUNBIRD & 1986–87 SKYLARK

1. Disconnect battery ground cable.
2. On models except V6-181 engine, remove air cleaner assembly.
3. On models with V6-181 engine, remove mass air flow sensor and air intake duct.
4. On all models, disconnect T.V. cable from throttle lever and transaxle.
5. Remove fluid level indicator and fill tube.
6. Install suitable engine support fixture, then insert a 1/4 x 2 inch bolt in hole at right front motor mount to ensure proper driveline alignment.
7. Remove wiring harness-to-transaxle attaching nut, then disconnect the following electrical connectors:
    a. Speed sensor.
    b. TCC connector.
    c. Park/neutral and back-up lamp switch. **On Calais, Grand Am, Somerset Regal and 1986-87 Skylark, it may be easier to reach the park/neutral and back-up lamp switch when vehicle is raised.**
8. Remove shift linkage from transaxle, then the top two transaxle-to-engine attaching bolts and left upper transaxle mount and bracket assembly.
9. Remove transaxle-to-vent pipe rubber hose.
10. Remove remaining upper engine-to-transaxle attaching bolts, then raise and support vehicle.
11. Remove front wheels, then drain transaxle fluid.
12. Remove shift linkage and bracket from transaxle.

13. Install drive axle boot seal protector J-33162 or equivalent on inner seals. **Some vehicles may use a silicone (gray) boot on the inboard axle joint. Use protector J-33162 on these boots. All other boots are made from a thermo-plastic material (black) and do not require use of a boot seal protector.**
14. Separate ball joints from control arms, then remove both drive axles.
15. Remove transaxle mounting strut, then the left stabilizer bar link pin bolt.
16. Remove left stabilizer bar frame bushing clamp attaching nuts, then the left frame support assembly.
17. On models equipped with 4-110 engine, remove exhaust pipe from manifold.
18. On Firenza, Skyhawk and Sunbird, remove starter and speedometer cable.
19. On all models, remove transaxle converter cover.
20. Scribe alignment mark on flexplate and torque converter, then remove torque converter-to-flexplate attaching bolts.
21. Remove and plug transaxle cooler lines.
22. Remove transaxle-to-engine support bracket.
23. Position suitable jack under transaxle, then remove remaining engine-to-transaxle attaching bolts.
24. Lower transaxle from vehicle.
25. Reverse procedure to install, noting the following;
    a. Torque converter-to-flexplate attaching bolts to 46 ft. lbs.
    b. Readjust T.V. cable.
    c. Check front suspension alignment.

1984–87 FIERO

1. Disconnect battery ground cable.
2. Remove air cleaner assembly, then disconnect all electrical connectors from transaxle.
3. Disconnect shift cable and T.V. cable from transaxle.
4. Remove transaxle cooler line supports.
5. Remove upper transaxle-to-engine attaching bolts.
6. Install suitable engine support fixture (tool No. J-28467 or equivalent).
7. Raise and support vehicle.
8. Remove both rear wheels, then disconnect axle shafts from transaxle.
9. Remove heat shield from catalytic converter.
10. Disconnect exhaust pipe from exhaust manifold.
11. Remove engine mount-to-cradle nuts.
12. Support cradle with a suitable jack, then remove rear cradle-to-body attaching bolts.
13. Remove forward cradle-to-body through bolts, then lower cradle and position aside.
14. Remove shields from starter motor and inspection cover.
15. Remove starter motor.
16. Mark relationship of flywheel to converter, then remove flywheel attaching bolts.
17. Disconnect cooler lines from transaxle, then support transaxle with a suitable jack.
18. Remove right side transaxle support bracket bolts.
19. Remove lower transaxle-to-engine attaching bolts, then carefully lower transaxle from vehicle.
20. Reverse procedure to install.

1987 CORSICA & BERETTA
W/4-121 Engine

1. Disconnect battery ground cable, then remove air cleaner assembly and air intake duct.
2. Disconnect T.V. cable from throttle lever and transaxle.
3. Remove fluid lever indicator and fill tube.
4. Install engine support fixture J-28467 and adapter J-35953, or equivalent.
5. Remove wire harness-to-transaxle attaching nut, then disconnect electrical connectors from speed sensor, TCC connector, park/neutral and back-up lamp switch.
6. Disconnect shift linkage from transaxle, then remove the two top transaxle-to-engine attaching bolts, transaxle mount and bracket assembly.
7. Remove transaxle-to-vent pipe rubber hose, then the remaining upper engine-to-transaxle attaching bolts.
8. Raise and support vehicle, then remove both front wheels.
9. Remove shift linkage and bracket assembly from transaxle.
10. Install drive axle boot seal protectors J-34754 or equivalent on inner seals. **Failure to install seal protectors can result in seal damage and possible joint failure.**
11. Remove LH splash shield, then both drive axles.
12. Remove transaxle mounting strut, then left stabilizer bar link pin bolt.
13. Remove left stabilizer bar frame bushing clamp attaching nuts, then the left frame support assembly.
14. Disconnect speedometer connector from transaxle.
15. Remove transaxle converter cover.
16. Scribe alignment marks on flexplate and torque converter, then remove torque converter-to-flexplate attaching bolts.
17. Remove transaxle cooler lines. **Plug lines to prevent leakage or dirt from entering the system.**
18. Remove transaxle-to-engine support bracket, then position a suitable jack under transaxle.
19. Remove remaining engine-to-transaxle attaching bolts, then lower transaxle from vehicle.
20. Reverse procedure to install noting then following:
    a. Torque converter-to-flexplate attaching bolts to 46 ft. lbs. (62 Nm).
    b. Torque transaxle-to-engine mounting bolts to 55 ft. lbs. (75 Nm).
    c. Torque transaxle mount bolts to 40 ft. lbs. (54 Nm), transaxle mount nuts to 23 ft. lbs. (31 Nm) and transaxle mount through bolts to 82 ft. lbs. (110 Nm).
    d. Readjust T.V. cable and shift linkage.
    e. Check for proper oil level and leaks.
    f. Check front suspension alignment.

W/V6 Engine

1. Disconnect battery ground cable.
2. Remove air cleaner, mounting bracket, MAF sensor and air tube as an assembly.
3. Remove exhaust crossover bolts at RH manifold, then LH manifold bolts at cylinder head. **If necessary, raise and support manifold/crossover assembly.**
4. Disconnect T.V. cable from throttle lever and transaxle, then transaxle-to-vent pipe rubber hose.
5. Disconnect shift cable from transaxle.
6. Disconnect neutral start switch and T.C.C. electrical connectors.
7. Remove fluid level indicator and fill tube.
8. Install engine support fixture J-28467 and adapter J-35953 or equivalent.
9. Remove nut attaching wiring harness from transaxle.
10. Remove transaxle mount through bolt, then mount bracket and mount from transaxle.
11. Remove upper transaxle-to-engine attaching bolts, then raise and support vehicle.
12. Remove both front wheels, then LH splash shield.
13. Remove transaxle converter cover, then scribe alignment marks on flex plate and torque converter for reassembly.
14. Remove torque converter-to-flex plate attaching bolts.
15. Remove torsional strut and lateral strut from transaxle, then transaxle bracket bolts.
16. Disconnect speedometer connector from transaxle, then shift cable bracket.
17. Install drive axle boot seal protectors J-34754 or equivalent on inner seals. **Failure to install seal protectors can result in seal damage and possible joint failure.**
18. Remove both drive axles.
19. Remove left stabilizer bar link pin bolt, left stabilizer bar frame bushing attaching nuts, then the left frame support assembly.
20. Remove transaxle cooler lines. **Plug lines to prevent leakage or dirt from entering the system.**
21. Position a suitable jack under transaxle, then remove remaining transaxle-to-engine attaching bolts.
22. Remove transaxle assembly from vehicle.
23. Reverse procedure to install noting the following:
    a. Torque converter-to-flexplate attaching bolts to 46 ft. lbs. (62 Nm).
    b. Torque transaxle-to-engine mounting bolts to 55 ft. lbs. (75 Nm).
    c. Torque transaxle mount bolts to 40 ft. lbs. (54 Nm), transaxle mount nuts to 23 ft. lbs. (31 Nm) and transaxle mount through bolts to 82 ft. lbs (110 Nm).
    d. Readjust T.V. cable and shift linkage.

e. Check for proper oil level and leaks.
f. Check front suspension alignment.

1987 CAVALIER W/4-121 ENGINE

1. Disconnect battery ground cable.
2. Remove air cleaner assembly, then disconnect T.V. cable from throttle body. Pull up cable cover at transaxle until cable is visible. Disconnect cable from transaxle rod.
3. Remove bolt attaching engine wire harness to transaxle.
4. Disconnect hose from air management valve to allow the engine wire harness to be pulled up positioned aside.
5. Install engine support fixture J-28467 or equivalent, then raise engine slightly to remove pressure off mounts.
6. Remove transaxle top mount and bracket assembly. If necessary raise engine slightly to allow for removal.
7. Remove shift control linkage from transaxle.
8. Remove top transaxle-to-engine attaching bolts. Loosen bolt near starter but do not remove.
9. Unlock steering column, raise and support vehicle, then remove front wheels.
10. Assemble tools J-28468, J-33008 to J-29794 and J-2619-01, then position tool behind axle shaft cones to remove cones from transaxle.
11. Remove LH axle shaft. Plug transaxle bore to prevent fluid leakage and dirt.
12. Remove nut attaching transaxle control cable to bracket to transaxle, then engine to transaxle stud.
13. Disconnect speedometer cable from transaxle.
14. Disconnect transaxle stabilizer from front and rear of transaxle, then remove torque converter shield.
15. Remove three bolts attaching torque converter to flex plate.
16. Disconnect transaxle cooler lines. Plug openings to prevent leakage and dirt from entering system.
17. Loosen brake and fuel line brackets at LH side of underbody, bolts at RH transaxle brace, then remove transaxle dipstick filler tube.
18. Position a suitable jack under transaxle, then remove remaining transaxle-to-engine attaching bolt (near starter).
19. Remove transaxle from engine.
20. Reverse procedure to install.

Turbo Hydra-Matic 440-T4 Automatic Transaxle

INDEX

IDENTIFICATION

This transaxle may be identified by the following codes stamped into the horizontal cast rib on the right rear side of the transaxle housing.

DESCRIPTION

The 440-T4 transaxle is a fully automatic unit which provides four forward speeds including an overdrive top gear. The transmission unit includes a three element hydraulic torque converter and lock-up clutching element, four multiple disc clutch, two bands and a compound reaction planetary gear set, **Fig. 1.** Power transmitted to the drive wheels from the planetary gear through a final drive gear set and differential assembly.

The converter is designed to provide torque multiplication during acceleration and at slow vehicle speed, and lock-up during normal operation for increase operating economy. Operation of the converter lock-up is controlled automatically by the engine fuel system electronic control module. In addition, the converter drives the vane type oil pump by means of a shaft splined to the converter cover.

The torque converter hydraulically couples the engine to the planetary gears through a turbine and shaft assembly which drives the transmission output shaft by means of a drive link chain and sprockets.

TROUBLESHOOTING

OIL LEAK

1. Side cover distorted.
2. Oil pan attaching bolts loose.
3. Oil pan gaskets damaged.
4. T.V. cable, fill tube and/or electrical connector seal damaged.
5. Manual shaft seal assembly damaged.
6. Governor cover and/or servo covers O-rings damaged.
7. Cooler fittings and/or pressure taps insufficiently tightened, or threads stripped.
8. Converter seal damaged, or garter spring missing.
9. Axle seals damaged, or garter spring missing.
10. Modulator O-ring damaged.
11. Parking plunger guide O-ring damaged.
12. Speedometer O-ring damaged.

OIL FORCED OUT VENT OR FOAMING OIL

1. High fluid level.
2. Overheated or contaminated oil.
3. Damaged filter or filter seal.
4. Leaking accumulator cover pipe or drive socket support lubrication pipes.
5. Thermo element not closing properly.
6. Thermo element improperly installed or incorrect pin height.
7. Defective or improperly installed modulator port gasket.
8. Plugged drive sprocket support drain back holes.

OIL PRESSURE HIGH OR LOW

1. Incorrect fluid level.
2. Contaminated fluid or engine overheating.

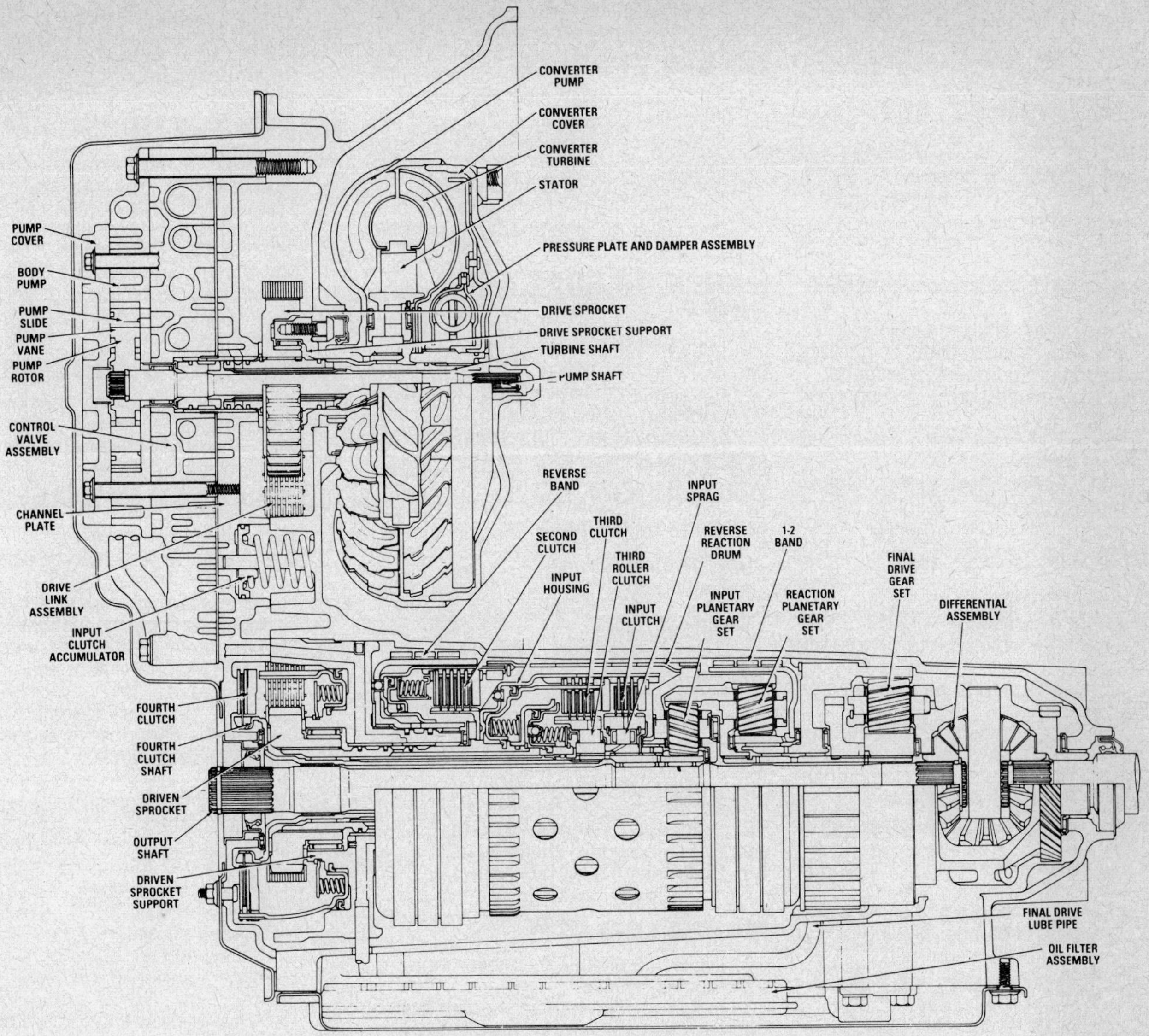

Fig. 1 Turbo Hydra-Matic 440-T4 automatic transaxle

3. Vacuum line leaking.
4. Modulator leaking or modulator diaphragm damaged.
5. Nicked, scored or stuck modulator valve.
6. Pressure regulator valve or spring damaged.
7. Pressure relief valve spring damaged or ball missing.
8. Oil pump damaged or restricted.
9. Aspirator "T" blocked or incorrectly installed.

DELAYED ENGAGEMENT

1. Low oil level.
2. Cooler check ball not seating.
3. Damaged or defective reverse servo seal.
4. Damaged or defective 1-2 servo seal.
5. Leaking 1-2 servo oil pipes.

NO DRIVE IN D RANGE

1. Low fluid level.
2. Low oil pressure.
3. Manual linkage improperly adjusted or disconnected.
4. Torque converter stator roller clutch sluggish or converter not properly attached to flex plate.
5. Drive axles disengaged.
6. Damaged or broken drive link chain, sprockets or bearings.
7. Damaged 1-2 servo or incorrect apply pin.
8. 1-2 servo oil pipes or pipe seals leaking.
9. Damaged oil pump or pump drive shaft.
10. Input clutch reverse check ball out of position.
11. Burned input clutch plates, damaged clutch seals or damaged piston.
12. Leaking input housing check ball.
13. Damaged input shaft seals or blocked input shaft passages.
14. Defective input sprag or improper sprag and input sun gear assembly. **When servicing transaxle for intermittent or complete loss of drive, the input sprag assembly should always be replaced. A sprag causing intermittent loss of drive may appear in satisfactory condition while still being susceptible to "pop-out" during operation.**
15. Third roller clutch burned due to lack of lubrication.
16. Damaged input carrier and/or reaction carrier.
17. Damaged or improperly installed output shaft.
18. Burned or improperly installed 1-2 band.
19. Damaged final drive assembly and/or final drive sun gear shaft.
20. Broken parking pawl spring.

SLIPS IN DRIVE

1. Incorrect oil level.
2. Cut or damaged vacuum line to modulator or defective modulator.
3. Low oil pressure.
4. Damaged 1-2 servo or servo piston seal.
5. Plugged filter screen.
6. Leaking servo oil pipes or pipe seals.
7. Defective converter stator clutch.

8. Defective input clutch accumulator or damaged input shaft seals.
9. Damaged or defective input clutch or leaks at ball capsule.

NO 1–2 UPSHIFT, 1ST SPEED ONLY

1. Governor weights binding.
2. Governor springs or gear damaged.
3. Leaking governor oil pipes.
4. Leaking governor retainer or blocked governor screen.
5. Leaking accumulator cover, retainer or oil pipes.
6. 1-2 shift valve sticking or binding.
7. Valve body spacer plate or gaskets damaged or improperly positioned.
8. Damaged driven sprocket support oil rings.
9. Damaged or improperly assembled second clutch.
10. Clutch housing check ball damaged.
11. Damaged reverse reaction drum splines or missing drum plate.

HARSH OR SOFT 1–2 SHIFT

1. Incorrect oil pressure.
2. Accumulator cover bolts improperly tightened.
3. Accumulator pistons, seals or springs damaged.
4. Control valve assembly accumulator valve binding.
5. Check ball No. 8 missing or improperly installed.

INCORRECT SHIFT SPEED

1. T.V. cable disconnected or improperly adjusted.
2. T.V. link, lever or bracket damaged.
3. T.V. valve and plunger binding.
4. Governor pressure incorrect.

NO 2–3 UPSHIFT, 1ST & 2ND SPEEDS ONLY

1. Governor damaged.
2. Accumulator cover oil hole blocked.
3. Leaking drive sprocket support oil pipe.
4. 2-3 shift valve binding or sticking.
5. Control valve assembly bolts improperly torqued.
6. Leaking or mispositioned check balls.
7. Sticking 2-3 accumulator valve.
8. Leaking 1-2 servo release oil pipe.
9. Improperly installed channel plate gasket.
10. Blocked oil passage to driven sprocket support.
11. Damaged input housing and shaft seals or blocked oil passages.
12. Damaged third clutch assembly.
13. Damaged third clutch piston check ball.
14. Damaged third roller clutch assembly.
15. Third roller clutch improperly assembled on input sun gear shaft.

HARSH OR SOFT 2–3 SHIFT

1. Incorrect oil pressure.
2. Leaking 1-2 servo check ball and capsule assembly.
3. Leaking 1-2 servo release oil pipe or pipe seals.
4. Mislocated 1-2 servo feed passage check ball.

NO 3–4 UPSHIFT

1. Incorrect throttle valve adjustment.
2. Defective governor.
3. Leaking governor feed or return oil pipes.
4. 3-4 shift valve binding or stuck.
5. Damaged fourth clutch shift spline.
6. Damaged or improperly assembled fourth clutch.

HARSH OR SOFT 3–4 SHIFT

1. Incorrect oil pressure.
2. Accumulator cover and pistons seal damaged or cover bolts improperly tightened.
3. Check ball No. 1 improperly located.

NO CONVERTER CLUTCH OPERATION

Models w/ECM

1. ECM malfunction.
2. Damaged, loose or corroded connectors.
3. Pinched wires.
4. Third clutch switch inoperative.
5. Inoperative solenoid.
6. Solenoid screen blocked.
7. Solenoid seal leaking.
8. Converter clutch shift valve and/or apply valve sticking.
9. Damaged or defective torque converter.
10. Damaged turbine shaft seals.
11. Damaged pump shaft seals.
12. Converter clutch blow-off check ball not properly seated in channel plate.

Models Less ECM

1. Damaged electrical connectors.
2. Pinched wires.
3. Inoperative governor pressure switch.
4. Inoperative third clutch switch.
5. Inoperative fourth clutch switch.
6. Inoperative solenoid valve.
7. Stuck converter clutch shift valve.
8. Stuck converter clutch apply valve.
9. Missing No. 10 check ball.
10. Improperly seated or damaged converter clutch blow-off check ball.
11. Damaged turbine shaft seals.
12. Damaged oil pump drive shaft seal.
13. Damaged TCC accumulator piston or seal.

CONVERTER CLUTCH DOES NOT RELEASE

1. No ECM signal to solenoid or defective solenoid, if equipped.
2. Sticking converter clutch apply piston.

ROUGH CONVERTER CLUTCH OPERATION

1. Sticking converter clutch regulator valve.
2. Turbine shaft seals damaged or missing.
3. Converter clutch blow-off valve check ball damaged.
4. Damaged converter clutch accumulator piston or seal.
5. Damaged or incorrect TCC blow-off spring.

HARSH 4–3 DOWNSHIFT

1. Control valve assembly check ball No. 1 missing.

HARSH 3–2 DOWNSHIFT

1. Improper vacuum signal or defective modulator.
2. Sticking 1-2 servo control valve.
3. No. 12 check ball missing.
4. Sticking 3-2 control valve.
5. No. 4 check ball missing.
6. Sticking 3-2 coast valve.
7. No. 2 check ball missing or improperly positioned.

HARSH 2–1 DOWNSHIFT

1. Control valve assembly check ball No. 8 missing.
2. No. 2 check ball missing or improperly positioned.

NO REVERSE IN R RANGE

1. Incorrect oil pressure.
2. Damaged reverse servo piston or seal.
3. Reverse servo improperly assembled or improper apply pin installed.
4. Damaged or defective oil pump.
5. Damaged input clutch accumulator piston seal.
6. Damaged drive link assembly.
7. Burned, damaged or improperly installed reverse band.
8. Damaged or defective input clutch.
9. Defective input sprag.
10. Reverse reaction drum splines, input carrier and/or reaction carrier damaged.

SLIPS IN REVERSE

1. Incorrect oil pressure.
2. Damaged reverse servo seal.
3. Damaged reverse reaction carrier splines.
4. Refer to "Slips In Drive" comments.

WILL NOT HOLD IN PARK

1. Damaged or disconnect manual linkage.
2. Damaged parking pawl spring, pawl and/or parking gear.
3. Damaged actuator assembly or actuator spring.

HARSH N–D OR D–N SHIFT

1. Improper vacuum signal to modulator or defective modulator.
2. Aspirator T-fitting improperly installed or plugged.
3. No. 9 check ball missing from control valve (harsh into reverse).
4. No. 12 check ball missing from control valve (harsh into drive).
5. Thermal element does not close when hot.

TAKES-OFF WHEN HOT

1. Excessive oil pressure.
2. Sticking 1-2 shift valve.

NO VISCOUS CLUTCH OPERATION

1. Improper operation of ECM.
2. Damaged ECM thermistor.
3. Damaged ECM temperature switch.

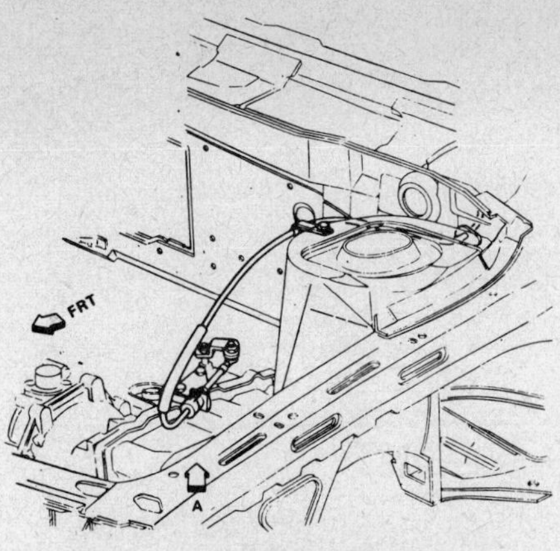

Fig. 2 Manual linkage adjustment

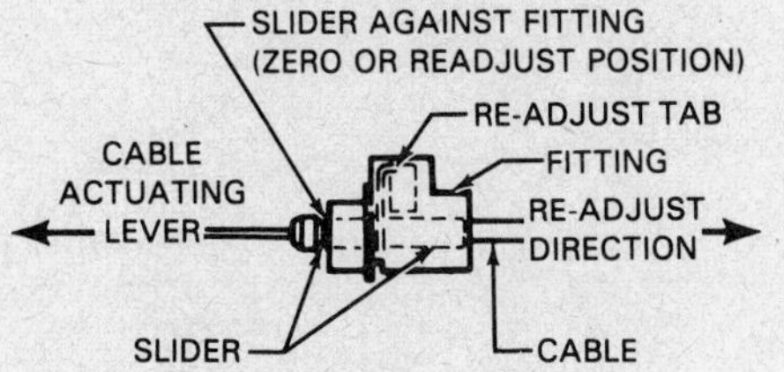

Fig. 3 T.V. cable adjustment

MAINTENANCE

To check fluid, drive vehicle for at least 15 minutes to bring fluid to operating temperature (200° F). With vehicle on a level surface and engine idling in Park and parking brake applied, the level on the dipstick should be at the FULL mark. To bring the fluid level from the ADD mark to the FULL mark requires one pint of fluid. If vehicle cannot be driven sufficiently to bring fluid to operating temperature, the level on the dipstick should be between the two dimples on the dipstick with fluid temperature at 70° F. Note that the two dimples are located above the FULL mark.

If additional fluid is required, use only Dexron II automatic transmission fluid.

An early change to a darker color from the usual red color and/or a strong odor that is usually associated with overheated fluid is normal and should not be considered as a positive sign of required maintenance or unit failure.

When adding fluid, do not overfill, as foaming and loss of fluid through the vent may occur as the fluid heats up. Also, if fluid level is too low, complete loss of drive may occur especially when cold, which can cause transmission failure.

Every 100,000 miles, the oil should be drained, the oil pan removed, the screen cleaned and fresh fluid added. For vehicles subjected to more severe use such as heavy city traffic especially in hot weather, prolonged periods of idling or towing, this maintenance should be performed every 15,000 miles.

CHANGING FLUID

1. Raise and support vehicle, then position drain pan under oil pan.

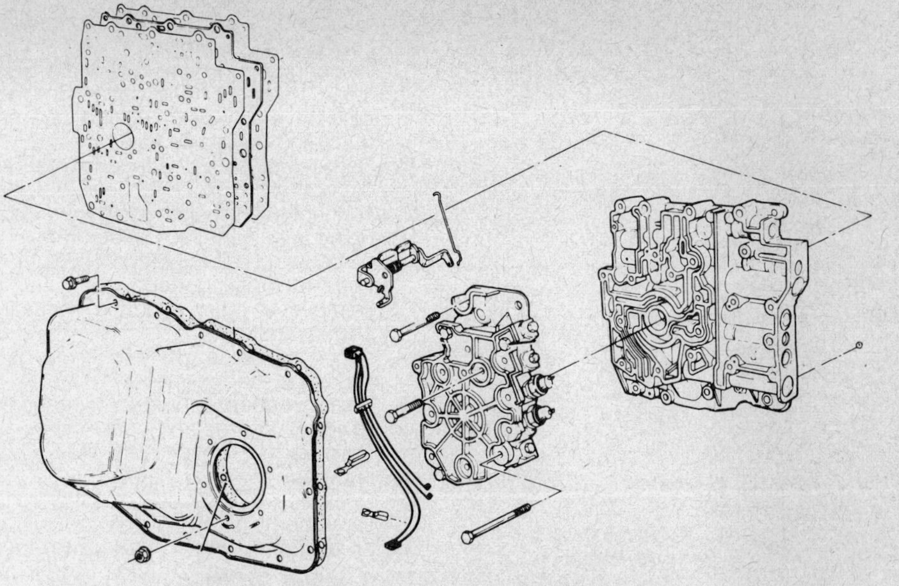

Fig. 4 Valve body replacement

2. Remove front and side oil pan attaching bolts, then loosen rear pan attaching bolts.
3. Carefully pry oil pan loose from transaxle case and allow fluid to drain.
4. Remove remaining attaching bolt, oil pan and gasket. Thoroughly clean pan before reinstalling.
5. Remove and discard screen and O-ring seal.
6. Install replacement screen and O-ring seal, locating screen against dipstick stop.
7. Install gasket on oil pan, then install pan and torque attaching bolts to 10 ft. lbs.
8. Lower vehicle and add approximately 6 qts. of fluid.
9. With selector in park, parking brake applied and engine at idle speed and operating temperature, check fluid level and add fluid as necessary. **Do not race engine or move shift lever through ranges.**

IN-VEHICLE ADJUSTMENTS

MANUAL LINKAGE, ADJUST

1. Place transaxle shift lever in Neutral position.
2. On column shift models, ensure transaxle control cable is properly assembled to pin, steering column shift lever pin and transaxle control cable bracket.
3. On console shift models, ensure transaxle control cable is properly assembled to shift control assembly and at transaxle control cable bracket.
4. On all models, loosen nut securing cable to pin on transaxle manual lever, **Fig. 2.**
5. Ensure transaxle manual lever is in Park position by rotating lever counterclockwise from Park position, through Reverse detent into Neutral.
6. Hold position on manual lever and torque retaining nut to 20 ft. lbs.

T.V. CABLE, ADJUST

1. Ensure ignition is in the Off position.
2. Depress and hold metal readjust tab at engine end of T.V. cable, **Fig. 3.**
3. Move slider until it contacts fitting, then release tab.
4. Check cable for sticking or binding and road test vehicle. **Recheck cable after engine has reached normal operating temperature, as cable may appear to operate properly with engine cold.**

IN-VEHICLE REPAIRS

VALVE BODY, REPLACE

Celebrity, Century, Cutlass Ciera & 6000

1. Disconnect battery ground cleaner and remove air cleaner assembly.
2. Install engine support assembly J-28467 or equivalent.
3. Rotate steering wheel until bolt securing intermediate shaft to steering gear is facing up. Remove bolt, then disconnect intermediate shaft from steering gear stub shaft.
4. Remove upper case side cover retaining bolts.
5. Raise and support vehicle. Position jack and block of wood under engine to act as support during cradle removal, then remove left front wheel.
6. Disconnect brake line support clip from underbody.
7. Remove power steering line brackets, steering gear brackets and driveline vibration damper as needed.
8. Remove pinch bolt from left steering knuckle and disconnect lower ball joint.
9. Disconnect stabilizer bar from left control arm, then remove both front stabilizer bar reinforcements and bushings from left and right side members.
10. Drill through spot weld located between rear holes of left front stabilizer bar mounting using a 1/2 inch bit.

Fig. 5 Governor replacement

11. Disconnect engine and transaxle mounts from cradle.
12. Remove side member-to-cross-member attaching bolts.
13. Remove bolts securing left side body mount.
14. Remove left side member and front crossmember assembly. **It may be necessary to pull or gently pry crossmember loose.**
15. Disconnect and remove AIR pipe.
16. Remove jack and lower vehicle, then lower transaxle by adjusting engine support fixture.
17. Remove remaining bolts securing transaxle side cover pan.
18. Disconnect drive axle and remove nuts surrounding flange at channel plate. **Do not pry against case side cover to remove axle. Insert pry bar behind axle and use suitable block of wood as fulcrum when removing axle.**
19. Remove case side cover pan and gaskets.
20. Remove valve body retaining bolts, valve body and oil pump as an assembly, **Fig. 4. Do not remove 3 pump cover-to-valve body attaching bolts.**
21. Reverse procedure to install.

Electra, LeSabre, Riviera, Toronado, 88 & 98

1. Disconnect battery ground cable.
2. Disconnect vacuum hoses from cruise control servo unit, if equipped.
3. Disconnect electrical connector from neutral/back-up lamp switch.
4. Raise and support vehicle, then remove left front wheel.
5. Remove inner splash shield.
6. Disconnect left tie rod from steering knuckle using suitable puller.
7. Disconnect stabilizer link from left control arm.
8. Install drive axle boot protectors, as needed. **Models using silicone (gray) boots on drive axle joints require the use of seal protectors J-33162 or equivalent. Models using thermoplastic boots (black) do not require the use of seal protectors.**
9. Disconnect ball joint from left steering knuckle.
10. Disconnect left drive axle from transaxle, using suitable puller, and secure drive axle aside, taking care not to extend drive axle joints.
11. Remove pinch bolt securing intermediate shaft to steering gear and disconnect intermediate shaft from gear.
12. Position suitable jack under transaxle oil pan and raise jack until weight of transaxle is supported.
13. Remove 3 bolts securing frame to body on left side.
14. Lower transaxle just enough to gain access to side cover pan bolts.
15. Disconnect cooler lines from transaxle and plug lines and open fittings.
16. Remove side cover bolts, side cover and gaskets.
17. Remove valve body retaining bolts, valve body, oil pump and gaskets as an assembly, **Fig. 4. Do not remove 3 pump cover-to-valve body attaching bolts.**
18. Reverse procedure to install.

DeVille & Fleetwood

1. Disconnect battery ground cable and remove air cleaner.
2. Install engine support fixture J-28467 or equivalent.
3. Remove upper side cover retaining bolts and the fuel pipe bracket.
4. Raise and support vehicle, then remove left front wheel.
5. Disconnect stabilizer shaft from left control arm, noting position of bushings and spacers.
6. Support control arm using suitable jack, then disconnect ball joint from left steering knuckle using suitable puller.
7. Remove left engine splash shield.
8. Remove vacuum pump mounting bolts and secure pump aside, leaving hoses connected.
9. Install drive boot seal protectors J-34754 or equivalent.
10. Disconnect left drive axle from transaxle and secure aside, using care to avoid extending drive axle joints.
11. Support transaxle using suitable jack and remove left front transaxle mount.
12. Remove right front engine mount as follows. **Vehicle should be supported at each front frame horn to prevent vehicle from tipping on hoist.**
    a. Disconnect brace between engine bracket and engine.
    b. Remove 2 nuts securing mount to frame.
    c. Remove 2 nuts securing transaxle bracket to mount.
    d. Remove 2 nuts securing transaxle mount to frame bracket.
    e. Raise engine using support fixture, then remove stud and 2 bolts securing mount bracket to block.
    f. Remove mount and bracket by pulling forward.
13. Loosen left and right rear transaxle mounts.
14. Remove left cradle mounts, then separate left cradle and remove from vehicle.

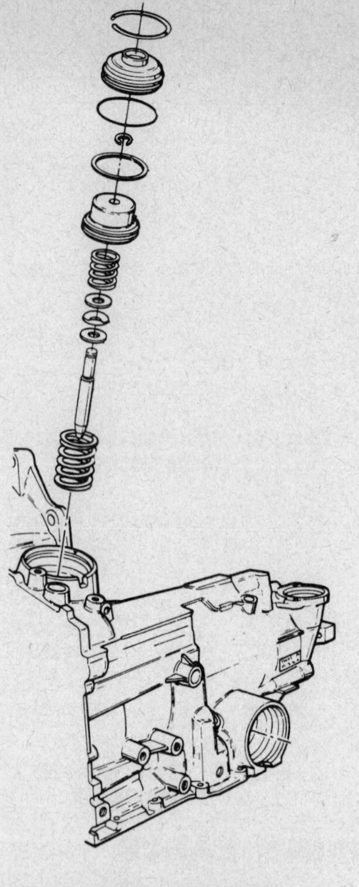

Fig. 6 Reverse servo replacement

15. Loosen, but do not remove, right cradle mounts.
16. Remove jacks, ensuring vehicle remains stable, then lower vehicle.
17. Note position of engine support fixture support rods and lower engine/transaxle assembly as follows. **In order to obtain maximum clearance for side cover removal it is necessary to tilt front of engine downward.**
    a. Move left rear support rod until it extends approximately 6 inches above "T" nut.
    b. Lower left front support rod until top is flush with top of "T" nut.
18. Raise and support vehicle.
19. Disconnect transaxle cooler lines from bracket and secure aside.
20. Remove remaining side cover retaining bolts and nuts securing axle opening cover.
21. Remove side cover pan and gaskets.
22. Remove wiring harness and VCC solenoid, disconnecting harness from pressure switches and case connector.
23. Remove T.V. lever, bracket and link assembly.
24. Remove oil pump retaining bolts and the pump assembly. **Do not remove 3 pump cover-to-valve body attaching bolts.**
25. Remove valve body retaining bolts and the valve body, noting position of 4 control valve-to-spacer plate check balls.

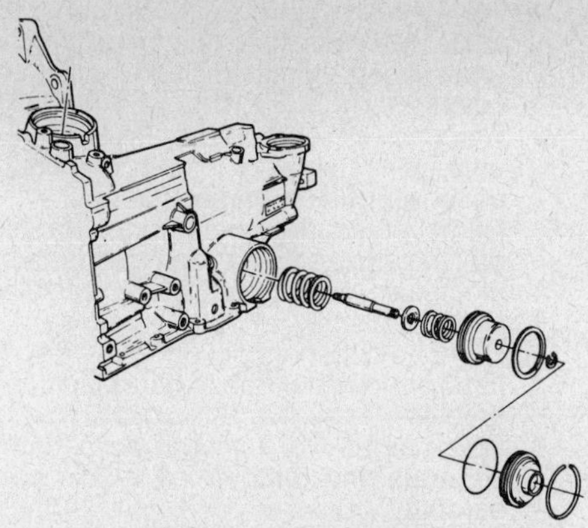

Fig. 7 1–2 servo replacement

26. Remove oil pump driveshaft.
27. Remove spacer plate and gaskets, noting position of 8 spacer-to-channel plate check balls.
28. Reverse procedure to install.

Eldorado & Seville

1. Disconnect battery ground cable and remove air cleaner assembly.
2. Remove inner engine cooling fan assembly.
3. Disconnect vacuum hoses from cruise control servo and vacuum modulator.
4. Disconnect electrical connectors from cruise control servo, distributor, oil pressure sending unit and transaxle.
5. Disconnect T.V. cable from throttle lever and bracket, and from transaxle.
6. Remove vacuum modulator.
7. Install engine support fixture J-28467 or equivalent and note position of left side support hooks.
8. Raise and support vehicle, then remove left front wheel.
9. Remove right and left wheel housing lower splash shields.
10. Remove left stabilizer bar link and support left control arm with suitable jack.
11. Remove left ball joint cotter pin and nut, then disconnect ball joint using suitable puller.
12. Remove 4 nuts securing transaxle to cradle and bracket.
13. Remove A/C compressor splash shield, No. 1 cradle mount insulator cover and the left side engine mount and damper fasteners.
14. Remove 6 right front cradle joining bolts.
15. Remove left stabilizer mount retaining bolts.
16. Remove 2 left rear cradle joining bolts.
17. Disconnect wire loom and vacuum hoses from retainers on cradle and transaxle.
18. Disconnect hoses from AIR pump and disconnect pipe retainer from rear of cradle.
19. Lower vehicle.
20. Raise engine/transaxle assembly 2 inches using support fixture hooks at flywheel end of engine.
21. Raise and support vehicle.
22. Remove No. 1 insulator bolt and separate right front corner of cradle assembly, then remove left cradle section.
23. Disconnect AIR valve from transaxle and position aside.
24. Remove stud bolts securing transaxle bracket to bellhousing, noting position of bolts for installation reference.
25. Lower vehicle, then lower engine/transaxle assembly to position noted in step 7.
26. Remove transaxle mount bracket upper stud bolts and the bracket, rotating bracket clockwise to aid removal.
27. Lower left side of transaxle to limit allowed by support hooks.
28. Raise vehicle and install suitable drive axle boot seal protectors.
29. Disconnect drive axle and secure toward rear of vehicle, using care to avoid overextending drive axle joints.
30. Remove case side cover pan bolt, pan and gaskets.
31. Remove wiring harness and VCC solenoid from pressure switches and case connector.
32. Remove T.V. lever, bracket and link assembly.
33. Remove oil pump retaining bolts and the pump assembly. **Do not remove 3 pump cover-to-valve body attaching bolts.**
34. Remove valve body retaining bolts and the valve body, noting position of 4 control valve-to-spacer plate check balls.
35. Remove oil pump driveshaft.
36. Remove spacer plate and gaskets, noting position of 8 spacer-to-channel plate check balls.
37. Reverse procedure to install.

GOVERNOR, REPLACE

1. Raise and support vehicle.
2. Remove speed sensor assembly.
3. Remove governor cover attaching bolts, then the cover and seal.
4. Remove governor complete with sleeve and speedometer drive gear, **Fig. 5.**
5. Reverse procedure to install.

ACCUMULATOR, REPLACE

1. Raise and support vehicle.
2. Drain transaxle fluid and remove oil pan.
3. Remove oil filter and seal, then the accumulator cover attaching bolts and cover.
4. Remove accumulator piston, oil seal and spring.
5. Reverse procedure to install.

REVERSE SERVO, REPLACE

1. Disconnect exhaust crossover pipe.
2. Depress servo cover, then remove snap ring and servo cover.
3. Remove servo piston, sealing ring, apply pin and servo spring, **Fig. 6.**
4. Reverse procedure to install.

1–2 SERVO, REPLACE

1. Depress servo cover, then remove snap ring and servo cover.

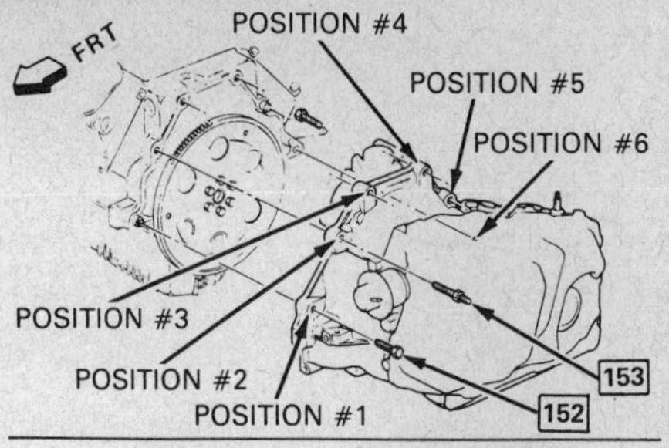

152 BOLT (75 N·m/55 FT. LBS.)
153 STUD (75 N·m/55 FT. LBS.)

Fig. 8 Transaxle bolt identification. DeVille, Eldorado, Fleetwood & Seville

2. Remove servo piston, sealing ring, apply pin and servo spring, **Fig. 7.**
3. Reverse procedure to install.

TRANSAXLE REPLACE

CELEBRITY, CENTURY, CUTLASS CIERA & 6000

1. Disconnect battery ground cable.
2. Remove air cleaner assembly, then disconnect T.V. cable at both ends.
3. Disconnect shift linkage from transaxle.
4. Install engine support fixture, then disconnect converter clutch electrical connector.
5. Remove 3 transaxle-to-engine attaching bolts.
6. Disconnect vacuum line from modulator.
7. Raise and support vehicle.
8. Remove left front wheel, then the lower ball joint pinch nut.
9. Remove brake line bracket from strut, then disconnect drive axles from transaxle.
10. Remove cradle-to-stabilizer attaching bolts.
11. Remove stabilizer-to-control arm attaching bolts, then the left front cradle assembly.
12. Disconnect speedometer cable from transaxle, then remove extension housing-to-engine block support bracket.
13. Disconnect cooler lines from transaxle, then remove right and left insulator attaching bolts.
14. Remove flywheel splash shield.
15. Mark relationship of flywheel to converter, then remove flywheel attaching bolts.
16. Remove all remaining transaxle-to-engine attaching bolts except one.
17. Support transaxle with a suitable jack, then remove remaining bolt and carefully lower transaxle from vehicle.
18. Reverse procedure to install.

BONNEVILLE, ELECTRA, LESABRE, 88 & 98

V6-181 & V6-231 Engines

1. Disconnect battery ground cable.
2. Disconnect electrical connector from mass air flow sensor.

3. Loosen two hose clamps at air intake duct, then remove intake duct and mass air flow sensor as an assembly.
4. Disconnect T.V. cable at both ends.
5. On models equipped with cruise control, disconnect cable from throttle body and the vacuum hoses from servo, then remove servo assembly.
6. On all models, disconnect shift control linkage from transaxle.
7. Disconnect electrical connectors from park/neutral switch, torque converter clutch and vehicle speed sensor.
8. Disconnect vacuum modulator hose from modulator.
9. Remove 3 upper transaxle-to-engine attaching bolts, then install suitable engine support fixture.
10. Turn steering wheel to the full left position, then remove both front wheels.
11. Remove right front ball joint nut and separate control arm from steering knuckle.
12. Remove right drive axle from case, using care to avoid damaging the seal.
13. Remove left drive axle, using a suitable pry bar with axle boot seal protectors installed.
14. Disconnect electrical connector from aspirator, then remove left front transaxle mount.
15. Remove right front transaxle mount attaching nuts.
16. Remove left rear transaxle mount-to-transaxle attaching bolts, then the right rear transaxle mount.
17. Remove engine support bracket-to-transaxle case attaching bolts.
18. Remove stabilizer link-to-control arm bolt.
19. Remove flywheel cover attaching bolts and the cover.
20. Mark relationship of flywheel to converter, then remove flywheel attaching bolts.
21. Remove rear cradle-to-front cradle attaching bolts.
22. Install suitable transaxle support fixture, then cradle assembly by swinging to one side and supporting with a suitable stand.
23. Disconnect cooler lines from transaxle, then remove remaining lower transaxle-to-engine attaching bolts.
24. Carefully lower transaxle from vehicle.
25. Reverse procedure to install.

V6-262 Diesel Engine

1. Disconnect battery ground cable.
2. Disconnect T.V. cable at both ends.
3. Remove crossover pipe shield, then disconnect shift control linkage from transaxle.
4. Disconnect electrical connectors from park/neutral switch, torque converter clutch and vehicle speed sensor.
5. Disconnect vacuum modulator hose from modulator.
6. Remove 3 upper transaxle-to-engine attaching bolts, then loosen transaxle-to-engine bolt at starter.
7. Install suitable engine support fixture, then turn steering wheel to the full left position.
8. Raise and support vehicle.
9. Remove both front wheels.
10. Remove right front ball joint from steering knuckle.
11. Remove right drive axle from transaxle.
12. Remove left front and rear transaxle-to-cradle mounts, then the transaxle brace and brackets.
13. Disconnect speedometer cable from transaxle, then remove right rear transaxle mount, left stabilizer link and flywheel cover.
14. Mark relationship of flywheel to converter, then remove flywheel attaching bolts.
15. Remove rear cradle-to-front cradle attaching bolts.
16. Remove one stabilizer brace and loosen the opposite brace.
17. Remove front cradle-to-body attaching bolt.
18. Remove right front motor mount, then unfasten wiring harness cover from cradle and position aside.
19. Install suitable transaxle support fixture, then shift cradle assembly to one side and support.
20. Disconnect cooler lines, exhaust connector pipe and rear exhaust manifold.
21. Remove remaining transaxle-to-engine attaching bolts, then carefully lower transaxle from vehicle.
22. Reverse procedure to install.

DEVILLE & FLEETWOOD

1. Disconnect battery ground cable and remove air cleaner assembly.
2. Remove T.V. cable and cable-to-cooler line bracket.
3. Remove exhaust crossover pipe.
4. Disconnect shift cable bracket and manual lever from transaxle, then secure cable, bracket and lever aside.
5. Disconnect electrical connectors from transaxle, cruise control servo and neutral/back-up lamp switch.
6. Remove upper bolts and studs securing bellhousing to engine block (positions 2, 3, 4 and 5), **Fig. 8.**
7. Disconnect vacuum line from modulator.
8. Install engine support fixture J-28467 or equivalent, noting the following:
   a. Ensure fixture is installed in extreme forward position across both strut towers.
   b. The two-piece, link-type hook should be used at passenger side rear engine hook, and both drivers side hooks should be positioned vertically.
   c. Hooks should be tightened to remove all looseness and slack, but it is not necessary to actually raise engine.
9. Raise and support vehicle, then remove front wheels.
10. Support lower control arms using suitable jacks, then disconnect both ball joints from steering knuckles using suitable puller.
11. Install suitable drive axle boot seal protectors, separate drive axles from transaxle, then secure drive axles aside. **Care must be taken not to overextend driveshaft pot joints, as joint will be damaged.**
12. Remove left stabilizer link and mounting clamp bolts, then clamp, bushings and spacers, noting position for installation.
13. Remove A/C compressor and left engine splash shields, left No. 1 mount cover and wiring harness cover.
14. Remove vacuum pump from left cradle and secure aside, then disconnect electrical connector from vehicle speed sensor.
15. Remove fasteners securing right and left front engine/transaxle mounts to cradle.
16. Remove left No. 1 mount bolts, then separate and remove left cradle assembly.
17. Disconnect and plug cooler lines, then unfasten cooler line bracket.
18. Remove transaxle-to-engine support bracket.
19. Remove right rear mount-to-transaxle bracket and fasteners securing left rear mount to transaxle.
20. Remove flexplate dust cover and colts securing flexplate to torque converter.
21. Support transaxle with suitable jack, then remove bellhousing-to-engine bolts at positions No. 1 and 6, **Fig. 8. To remove bolt No. 6, it is necessary to use a suitable extension and access bolt through right wheel house opening.**
22. Separate and remove transaxle assembly.
23. Reverse procedure to install.

ELDORADO & SEVILLE

1. Disconnect battery ground cable and remove air cleaner assembly.
2. Disconnect and remove T.V. cable.
3. Remove cruise control servo.
4. Disconnect electrical connectors from distributor, oil pressure sending unit and transaxle.
5. Remove engine oil cooler line bracket.
6. Disconnect shift cable bracket and manual lever from transaxle, then secure cable, bracket and lever aside.
7. Remove fuel line bracket and disconnect neutral safety switch electrical connector.
8. Remove vacuum modulator.
9. Remove T.V. cable support bracket and remaining engine oil cooler line bracket.
10. Remove bellhousing bolts No. 2, 3, 4 and 6, **Fig. 8.**
11. Disconnect AIR crossover pipe fitting and reposition pipe.
12. Remove radiator hose bracket and fasteners securing transaxle mount to bracket.
13. Install engine support bracket J-28467 or equivalent, and note position of support hooks.
14. Raise and support vehicle and remove front wheels.
15. Remove left and right stabilizer link bolts, ball joint cotter pins and ball joint retaining nuts.
16. Support control arms using suitable jacks, then disconnect left and right ball joints using suitable puller.
17. Remove A/C compressor splash shield and No. 1 cradle mount cover.

18. Disconnect AIR pipe end hose connections and rear mounting clip.
19. Disconnect vacuum hoses and wire loom from front of cradle.
20. Remove fasteners securing engine mount, damper and transaxle mount to cradle and wire loom to transaxle bracket.
21. Lower vehicle, then raise transaxle 2 inches from position noted in step 13 using left support hooks of engine support fixture.
22. Raise and support vehicle.
23. Remove left side stabilizer mounting bolts and bolts joining cradle at right front and left rear corners.
24. Remove No. 1 cradle mount bolts. Separate cradle at right front corner, then remove left cradle section.
25. Disconnect AIR management valve bracket from transaxle mounting bracket and secure valve and bracket assembly to transaxle stud bolt.
26. Lower vehicle, then lower engine/transaxle assembly to position noted in step 13.
27. Remove transaxle mounting bracket.
28. Raise and support vehicle.
29. Remove bracket from right transaxle mount to transaxle and bolts securing engine/transaxle brace to transaxle.
30. Disconnect electrical connector from vehicle speed sensor.
31. Remove flexplate dust covers and bolts securing flexplate to torque converter.
32. Support transaxle with suitable jack, then remove bellhousing bolts No. 1 and 6, **Fig. 8. To remove bolt No. 6, use suitable extension to gain access through right front wheel house opening.**
33. Disconnect cooler lines from transaxle, then plug lines and open fittings.
34. Install suitable drive axle boot seal protectors, separate drive axles from transaxle and secure axles aside. **Care must be taken not to overextend drive axle pot joints, as joint will be damaged.**
35. Separate and remove transaxle assembly.
36. Reverse procedure to install.

RIVIERA & TORONADO

1. Disconnect battery ground cable and install engine support fixture J-28467 or equivalent.
2. Disconnect vacuum hose from modulator and electrical connectors from transaxle.
3. Disconnect T.V. cable from throttle body and transaxle.
4. Remove cruise control servo, if equipped.
5. Disconnect selector cable bracket and manual selector lever from transaxle, then secure cable, bracket and lever assembly aside.
6. Remove neutral start/back-up lamp switch assembly.
7. Remove top 3 bellhousing bolts, bolts securing wiring harness and the driveline damper bracket.
8. Raise and support vehicle.
9. Disconnect cooler lines from transaxle, then plug lines and open fittings.
10. Remove flexplate dust cover and bolts securing flexplate to torque converter.
11. Remove engine mount nuts and left transaxle mounting bolts.
12. Remove sway bar links from lower control arms.
13. Ensure control arm is properly supported, then remove cotter pin and nut and disconnect left ball joint.
14. Disconnect left drive axle from transaxle, taking care not to overextend drive axle pot joints. **Use drive axle boot seal protector J-33162 or equivalent on models with silicone (gray) drive axle boots. Models with thermoplastic (black) boots do not require the use of protectors.**
15. Remove left side frame (cradle) as follows:
    a. Remove bolt securing lower control arm assembly to frame and the strut rod nut, then rotate control arm aside.
    b. Remove engine splash shield.
    c. Disconnect wiring harness from front crossmember.
    d. Remove lower nut securing driveline vibration damper and 2 nuts securing front engine mount to frame.
    e. Disconnect left transaxle mount from frame.
    f. Remove 3 bolts from rear left side of rail and 4 bolts from right end of front crossmember.
    g. Remove left front frame mount cover and mounting bolt.
    h. Separate and remove left frame section.
16. Support transaxle with suitable jack, then remove 2 remaining bellhousing bolts.
17. Remove engine-to-transaxle brace.
18. Disconnect right drive axle and secure aside, taking care not to overextend drive axle pot joints.
19. Separate and remove transaxle.
20. Reverse procedure to install.

Turbo Hydra-Matic 180C Automatic Transmission

INDEX

TRANSMISSION IDENTIFICATION

This transmission may be identified by the following codes located on the tag attached to the right side of the transmission.

GENERAL DESCRIPTION

This transmission is a fully automatic unit consisting of a four-element hydraulic torque converter on the 180C series, and a planetary gear set, **Fig. 1.** Three multiple disc clutches, a roller clutch and a band provide the friction elements required to obtain the desired function of the compound planetary gear set. The compound planetary gear set provides three forward speeds and reverse.

The torque converter couples the engine to the planetary gears through oil and provides torque multiplication. It consists of a pump or driving member, a turbine or driven member and a stator assembly. The stator is mounted on a one-way roller clutch which allows the stator to turn clockwise but not counterclockwise.

The torque converter housing is filled with oil and rotates at engine speed. The converter pump is an integral part of the converter housing, therefore the pump blades rotating at engine speed set the oil within the converter into motion and direct it to the turbine causing the turbine to rotate. As the oil passes through the turbine it travels in such a direction that if it were not redirected by the stator it would strike the rear of the converter pump blades and impede its pumping action. Therefore at low turbine speeds, the oil is redirected by the stator to the converter pump in such a manner that it actually assists the converter pump to deliver power or multiply engine torque. As turbine speed increases, the direction of the oil leaving the turbine changes and flows against the rear side of the stator vanes in a clockwise direction. Since the stator is now impeding the smooth flow of oil, its roller clutch releases and it revolves freely on its shaft. Once the stator becomes inactive, there is no further multiplication of torque within the converter. At this point the converter is acting as a fluid coupling since the converter pump and turbine are being driven at about the same speed, or at a one-to-one ratio.

The hydraulic system in this transmission is pressurized by a gear type pump to provide the working pressures required to operate the friction elements and automatic controls.

TROUBLESHOOTING

LOW FLUID LEVEL

1. Fluid coming out of filler tube.
2. External fluid leak.
3. Defective vacuum modulator.

FLUID COMING OUT OF FILLER TUBE

1. High fluid level.
2. Engine coolant in transmission fluid.
3. Clogged external vent.
4. Leak in pump suction circuit.

TORQUE CONVERTER HOUSING LEAK

1. Converter housing seal.
2. Converter to case seal.
3. Loose transmission attaching bolts.

TRANSMISSION CASE EXTERNAL LEAK

1. Shifter shaft seal.
2. Extension seal.
3. Oil pan gasket.
4. Extension to case gasket.
5. Vacuum modulator gasket.
6. Drain plug gasket.
7. Cooler line fittings.
8. Fluid tube seal ring.
9. Detent cable seal ring.
10. Pressure gauge fitting.
11. Electrical connector seal.

LOW FLUID PRESSURE

1. Low fluid level.
2. Clogged screen.
3. Leak in oil pump suction or pressure circuit.
4. Stuck priming valve.
5. Faulty pressure regulator valve.
6. Missing sealing ball in valve body.

HIGH FLUID PRESSURE

1. Modulator vacuum line leaking.
2. Defective vacuum modulator.
3. Leak in vacuum system.
4. Defective pressure regulator valve.

NO DRIVE

1. Low fluid level.
2. Clogged screen.
3. Manual valve linkage or inner transmission selector lever disconnected.
4. Broken input shaft.
5. Pressure regulator valve stuck in open position.
6. Defective oil pump.

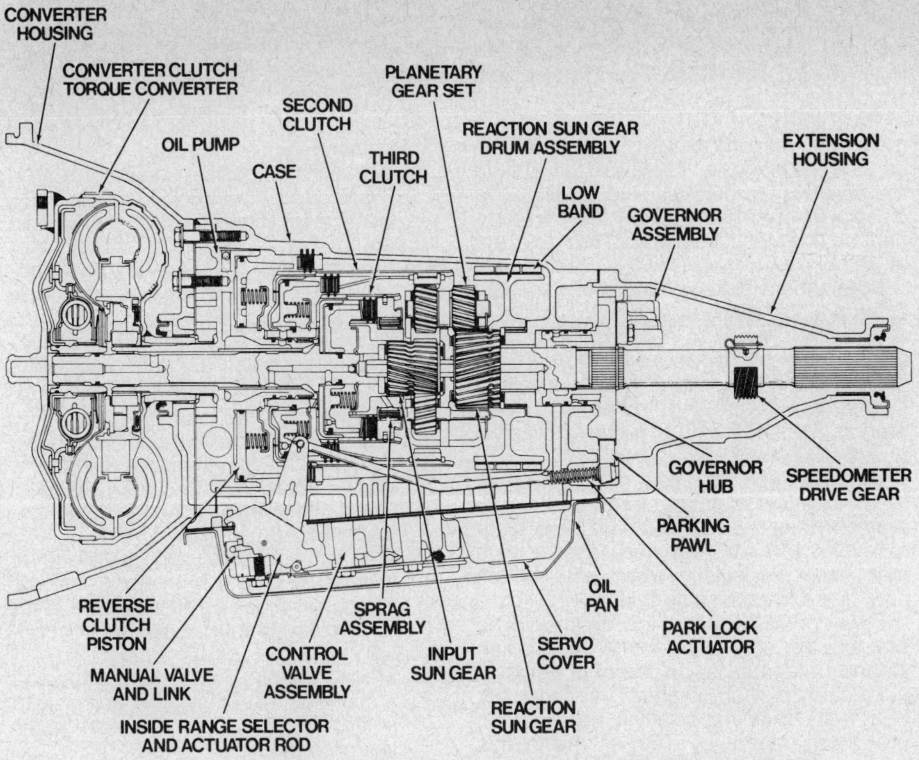

Fig. 1 Turbo Hydra-Matic 180C transmission

DELAYED ENGAGEMENT

1. Manual valve position does not coincide with valve body channels.
   a. Missing selector lever shaft retaining pin.
   b. Loose connecting rod to manual valve connection.
   c. Loose selector lever shaft nut.

NO DRIVE WHEN SHIFTING FROM P TO D, L2 OR L1

1. Parking pawl does not engage.

HARSH ENGAGEMENT

1. Band servo piston jamming.
2. Low fluid level.
3. Defective oil pump.
4. Missing screen.
5. Missing sealing ball in valve body.

SHUDDER ON ACCELERATION

1. Low fluid pressure.
2. Wrong modulator valve installed.
3. Stuck pressure regulator valve.
4. Missing sealing ball in valve body.

DRIVE IN L1 & R BUT NOT IN D OR L2

1. Input sprag installed backwards.
2. Failed input sprag.

DRIVE IN R BUT NOT IN D, L2 OR L1

1. Worn band, slipping.
2. Band servo piston jamming.
3. Excessive leak in band servo.
4. Parking pawl does not disengage.

DRIVE IN D, L2 & L1 BUT NOT IN R

1. Failed reverse clutch.

DRIVE IN NEUTRAL POSITION

1. Linkage improperly adjusted.
2. Broken planetary gear set.
3. Band improperly adjusted.

NO 1-2 UPSHIFT IN D & L2

1. Stuck governor valves.
2. 1-2 shift valve stuck in first gear position.
3. Leaking seal rings in oil pump hub.
4. Excessive leak in governor pressure circuit.
5. Clogged governor screen.

NO 2-3 UPSHIFT IN D

1. 2-3 shift valve stuck.
2. Excessive leak in governor pressure circuit.

UPSHIFTS IN D & L2 ONLY AT FULL THROTTLE

1. Faulty vacuum modulator.
2. Modulator vacuum line leaking.
3. Leak in vacuum system.
4. Stuck detent valve or cable.

UPSHIFTS IN D OR L2 ONLY AT PART THROTTLE NO DETENT UPSHIFT

1. Stuck detent regulator valve.
2. Detent cable broken or improperly adjusted.

DRIVE IN 1ST GEAR OF D OR L2

1. L1 and R control valve stuck in L1 or R position.

NO PART THROTTLE 3-2 DOWNSHIFT AT LOW SPEED

1. Stuck 3-2 downshift control valve.

NO FORCED DOWNSHIFTS

1. Detent cable broken or improperly adjusted.
2. Stuck detent pressure regulator valve.

IMMEDIATE DOWNSHIFT AFTER FULL THROTTLE UPSHIFT & RELEASING ACCELERATOR

1. Detent valve stuck in open position.
2. Detent cable stuck.
3. Clogged or leaking vacuum modulator line.

TRANSMISSION DOWNSHIFTS AT HIGH VEHICLE SPEEDS

1. Missing selector lever shaft retaining pin.
2. Loose selector lever linkage to manual valve connection.
3. Pressure leak at governor.

HARD DISENGAGEMENT FROM PARK POSITION

1. Missing steel guide bushing from parking pawl actuating rod.
2. Stuck manual valve selector lever.

SLIPPING 1-2 SHIFT

1. Low fluid pressure.
2. Missing sealing ball in valve body.
3. Leaking second clutch piston seals.
4. Second clutch piston centrifugal ball stuck open.
5. Second clutch piston cracked or broken.
6. Second clutch plates worn.
7. Leaking oil pump hub sealing rings.

SLIPPING 2-3 SHIFT

1. Low fluid pressure.
2. Improper band adjustment.
3. Third clutch piston seals leaking.
4. Third clutch piston centrifugal ball stuck open.
5. Third clutch piston cracked or broken.
6. Worn input shaft bushing.
7. Missing sealing ball in valve body.

HARSH 1-2 SHIFT

1. High fluid pressure.
2. 1-2 accumulator valve stuck.
3. Second clutch spring cushion broken.
4. Second gear ball valve missing.

HARSH 2-3 SHIFT

1. High fluid pressure.
2. Improper band adjustment.

HARSH 3-2 DETENT DOWNSHIFT AT HIGH VEHICLE SPEEDS

1. High speed downshift valve stuck open.
2. Improper band adjustment.

HARSH 3-2 COAST DOWNSHIFT

1. Low speed downshift timing valve stuck open.

ENGINE FLARE ON HIGH SPEED FORCED DOWNSHIFT

1. Low fluid pressure.
2. Loose band adjustment.

ENGINE FLARE ON LOW SPEED FORCED DOWNSHIFT

1. Low fluid pressure.
2. Loose band adjustment.
3. High speed downshift timing valve stuck in closed position.
4. Sprag race does not engage on 3-1 downshift.

NO ENGINE BRAKING IN L1

1. Selector level linkage improperly adjusted.
2. Stuck low manual control valve.

NO ENGINE BRAKING IN L2

1. Selector lever linkage improperly adjusted.

NO PARK

1. Selector lever linkage improperly adjusted.
2. Parking lock actuator spring broken.
3. Parking pawl.
4. Governor hub.

EXCESSIVE NOISES IN ALL DRIVE RANGES

1. Excessive backlash between sun gear and planetary gears.
2. Lock plate on planetary carrier loose.
3. Defective thrust bearing.
4. Worn bearing bushings.
5. Excessive transmission axial play.
6. Unhooked parking pawl spring contacting governor hub.
7. Converter balancing weights loose.
8. Converter housing attaching bolts loose and contacting converter.

SCREECHING NOISE ON ACCELERATION

1. Converter failure.

SHORT VIBRATING HISSING NOISE BEFORE 1-2 UPSHIFT

1. Reverse clutch dampening cushion wearing into transmission case.

MAINTENANCE

To check fluid, drive vehicle for at least 15 minutes to bring fluid to operating temperature (200° F). With vehicle on a level surface and engine idling in Park and parking brake applied, the level on the dipstick should be at the "F" mark. To bring the fluid level from the ADD mark to the FULL mark requires one pint of fluid. If vehicle cannot be driven sufficiently to bring fluid to operating temperature, the level on the dipstick should be between the two dimples on the dipstick with fluid temperature at 70° F.

If additional fluid is required, use only Dexron II automatic transmission fluid.

An early change to a darker color from the usual red color and or a strong odor that is usually associated with overheated fluid is normal and should not be considered as a positive sign of required maintenance or unit failure.

When adding fluid, do not overfill, as foaming and loss of fluid through the vent may occur as the fluid heats up. Also, if fluid level is too low, complete loss of drive may occur especially when cold, which can cause transmission failure.

Every 100,000 miles, the oil should be drained, the oil pan removed, the screen cleaned and fresh fluid added. For vehicles subjected to more severe use such as heavy city traffic especially in hot weather, prolonged periods of idling or towing, this maintenance should be performed every 15,000 miles.

DRAINING BOTTOM PAN

1. Raise vehicle, then remove drain plug and allow fluid to drain for at least 5 minutes.
2. If oil screen is to be serviced, remove oil pan bolts, oil pan and gasket.
3. Remove oil screen to valve body bolts, screen and gasket.
4. Thoroughly clean oil screen and oil pan with solvent.
5. Install oil screen using a new gasket and torque attaching bolts to 13-15 ft. lbs., then install oil pan using a new gasket and torque attaching bolts to 7-10 ft. lbs.
6. Add three quarts of fluid, then with engine idling and parking brake applied, move selector lever through each range and return selector lever to PARK.
7. Check fluid level and add fluid as required to bring level between the two dimples on the dipstick.

ADDING FLUID TO DRY TRANSMISSION

1. Add 4.9 quarts of fluid.
2. With transmission in PARK and parking brake applied, start engine and place carburetor on fast idle cam.
3. Move shifter lever through each range then with transmission in PARK, add additional fluid as required to bring the level between the two dimples on the dipstick.

IN-VEHICLE ADJUSTMENTS

MANUAL LINKAGE, ADJUST

The following procedures must be followed exactly, since any inaccuracies may result in premature failure of the transmission due to operation without control in full detent.

1982

1. Place shifter assembly (A) in Neutral position, **Fig. 2.**
2. With link (B) loosely assembled to rod (F) and rod (F) attached to lever (G), place lever (G) in Neutral position. To obtain Neutral position, move lever (G) clockwise to maximum detent position (Park), then counterclockwise two detents to Neutral position.
3. While holding lever (G) in Neutral position, adjust link (B) until hole aligns with shifter assembly pin (C), then install link onto pin.
4. Install shim (D) and retainer (E).

1983

1. Place shifter assembly (A) in Park position, **Fig. 3.**
2. With link (B) loosely attached to lever (G), place lever (G) in Park position. To obtain Park position, move lever (G) clockwise to maximum detent position (Park).
3. Maintain lever (G) in Park position and adjust link (B) until hole aligns with shifter assembly pin (C), then install link onto pin.
4. Install washer (D) and retainer (E).

1984

1. Snap cable (1) into bracket (2), **Fig. 4.**
2. Turn ignition switch to Lock position.
3. Snap end of cable (1) onto sliding pin (3).
4. Place shifter lever (4) in Park position.
5. Install cable (1) onto shifter lever pin (5).
6. Attach cable (1) to shifter mounting bracket (7) by pressing lock assembly against spring (9) and dropping cable through slot in bracket.
7. Depress lock button (10) to complete adjustment.

1985–87

1. Position shifter assembly (A), **Fig. 3,** into Neutral position of detent plate.
2. With link (B) loosely assembled to rod (F), and rod attached to lever, place lever (G) into Neutral position.
3. Obtain Neutral position by moving lever (G) clockwise to maximum detent position (Park), then counterclockwise two detents to Neutral.
4. Retain lever (G) in neutral, then adjust link until hole aligns with shifter assembly pin (C).
5. Install link onto pin, install washer (D), then insert clip (E).

T.V. OR DETENT CABLE, ADJUST

1. Depress readjust tab and move slider back through fitting away from throttle body until slider stops against fitting, **Fig. 5.**
2. Release readjust tab and open carburetor or pump lever to "full throttle stop" position to automatically adjust cable. Release carburetor or pump lever.

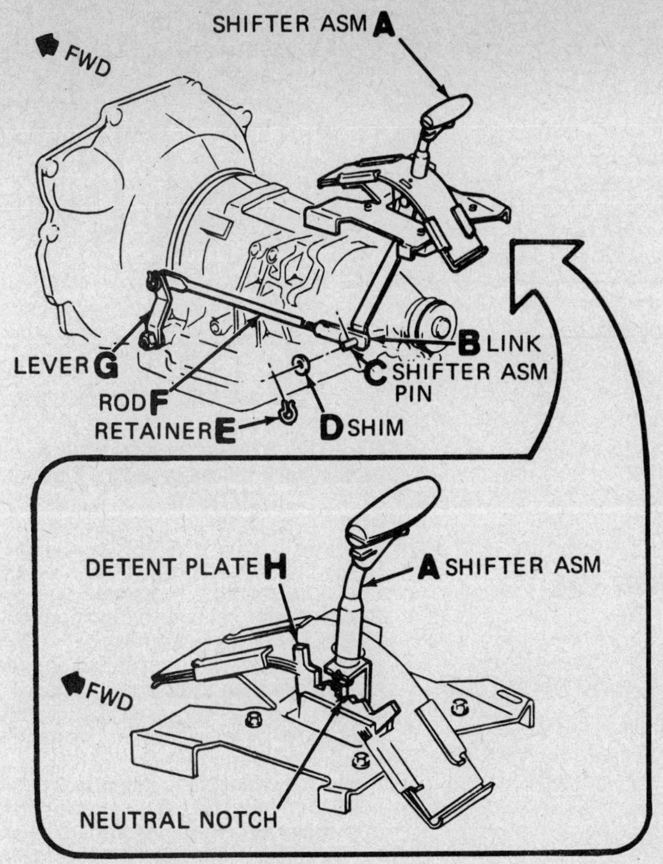

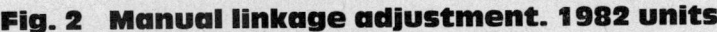

Fig. 2 Manual linkage adjustment. 1982 units

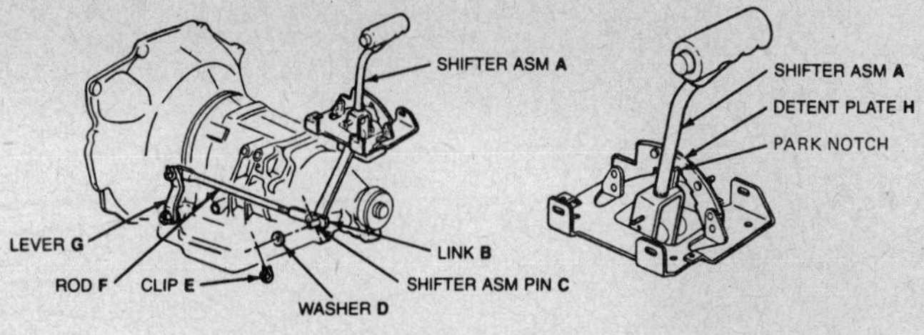

Fig. 3 Manual linkage adjustment. 1983 units & 1985-87 units

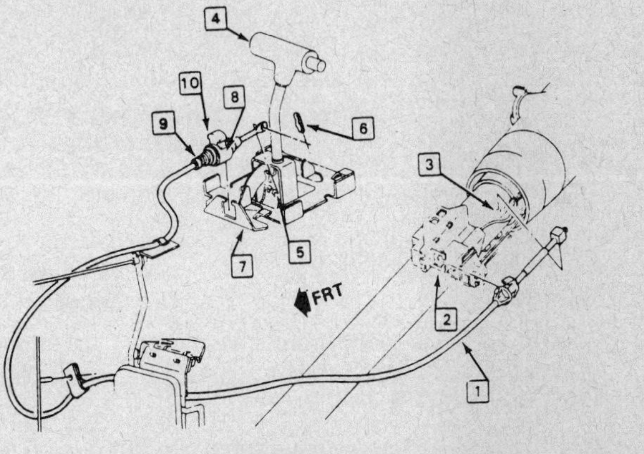

Fig. 4 Manual linkage adjustment. 1984 units

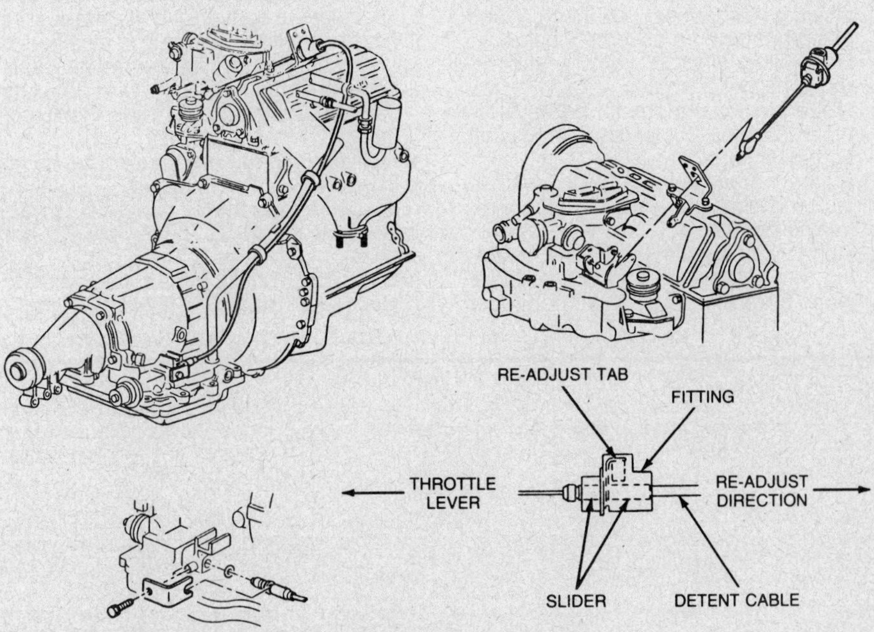

Fig. 5 Detent cable adjustment

3. Check cable for sticking or binding as shown in **Fig. 6**. If delayed or only full throttle shifts still occur, proceed as follows:
   a. Remove oil pan and inspect throttle lever and bracket assembly, **Fig. 7.**
   b. Check T.V. exhaust valve lifter rod for distortion or binding in control valve assembly or spacer plate.
   c. Check that the lifter spring holds lifter rod up against bottom of control valve assembly.
   d. Check that T.V. plunger is not binding, and inspect transmission for proper throttle lever to cable link.

IN-VEHICLE REPAIRS

VALVE BODY, REPLACE

1. Drain transmission and remove oil pan and screen.
2. Remove screw and retainer securing detent cable to transmission, then disconnect detent cable.
3. Remove throttle lever and bracket assembly. Use caution not to bend the throttle lever link.
4. Remove manual detent roller and spring assembly
5. Remove transfer plate reinforcement attaching bolts and the reinforcement.
6. Remove servo cover and gasket.
7. Remove valve body attaching bolts, then the valve body and transfer plate. **The two check balls in the case may fall out when removing the valve body.**
8. Remove transfer plate to valve body bolts, then the plate from valve body.
9. Reverse procedure to install.

1. CABLE ACTUATING LEVER
2. T.V. CABLE STUCK

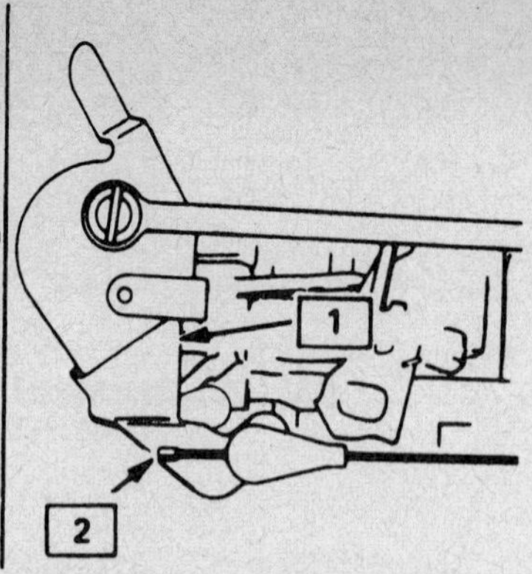

Fig. 6 Checking T.V. cable. 180C units

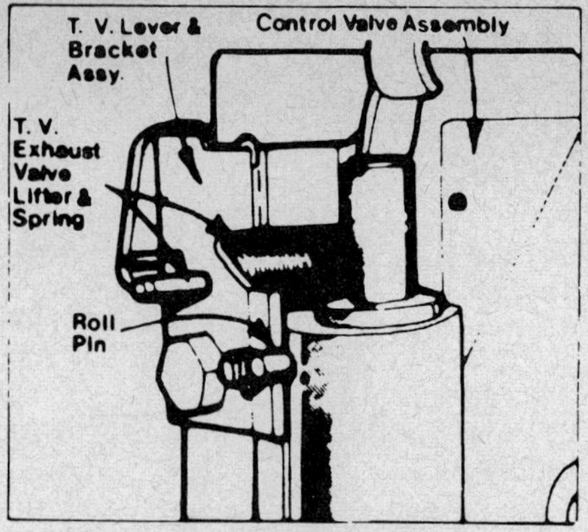

Fig. 7 Throttle lever & bracket assembly. 180 units

SERVO ASSEMBLY, REPLACE

1. Remove valve body from transmission as outlined previously.
2. Compress servo piston with tool J-23075.
3. With suitable pliers, remove servo piston snap ring and slowly loosen the tool. Remove tool, servo piston return spring and apply rod from transmission.
4. Install apply rod, return spring and piston into case.
5. Use tool J-23075 to compress spring and install snap ring. Remove tool.
6. With a 3/16 inch wrench on servo adjusting bolt, adjust apply rod by torquing bolt to 40 inch lbs, then back off bolt exactly 5 turns. Tighten locknut while holding apply rod in position.
7. Install valve body.

SPEEDOMETER DRIVEN GEAR, REPLACE

1. Remove bolt securing driven gear housing retainer, then the retainer.
2. Pull speedometer driven gear from housing.
3. Install speedometer driven gear into housing, then the retainer into slot of driven gear housing.
4. Install retainer attaching bolt

REAR EXTENSION OIL SEAL

1. Remove propeller shaft.
2. Remove oil seal with a screwdriver or suitable tool.
3. Lubricate new seal lip with transmission fluid and install seal into extension housing with tool J-21426.
4. Install propeller shaft.

TRANSMISSION REPLACE

1. Disconnect battery ground cable then disconnect detent downshift cable from bracket.
2. Remove air cleaner and dipstick, then on vehicles with air conditioning remove the 5 heater core retaining screws, disconnect connector and place heater core assembly aside.
3. Raise and support vehicle and remove propeller shaft.
4. Disconnect speedometer cable, electrical lead, oil cooler lines, and shift control linkage.
5. Support transmission with suitable jack and remove the crossmember retaining bolts.
6. Remove converter to bracket retaining nuts, then disconnect exhaust pipes from rear of catalytic converter and from exhaust manifolds and remove catalytic converter and converter bracket as an assembly.
7. Remove converter dust shield and remove converter to flywheel bolts.
8. Lower transmission until it is barely supported by jack and remove transmission to engine bolts.
9. Raise transmission to its normal position, then support engine with jack and lower and remove transmission from vehicle. **Use converter holding tool J-5384, or keep rear of transmission lower than the front to prevent the converter from sliding out.**
10. Before installing transmission, place two inch blocks between rack and pinion housing assembly and oil pan to permit correct alignment of engine and transmission. Before installing flexplate to converter bolts, make sure than converter pilot hub is installed in crankshaft and that welded brackets on converter are flush with flexplate and converter rotates freely in this position.
11. Reverse remaining procedure to install, noting the following:
    a. On 180 units, torque converter to flexplate bolts to 20-30 ft. lbs. (27-41 Nm).
    b. On 180C units, torque converter to flexplate bolts to 35 ft. lbs. (48 Nm).

Turbo Hydra-Matic 200C Automatic Transmission

INDEX

IDENTIFICATION

This transmission may be identified by the following codes located on the serial number plate attached to the right side of the transmission.

DESCRIPTION

The Turbo Hydra-Matic 200C transmission, **Fig. 1,** is fully automatic and consists of a three element torque converter and a compound planetary gear set. Three multiple disc clutches, a roller clutch and a band provide the required friction elements to obtain the desired function of the planetary gear set. In addition, the 200C transmission is equipped with a locking torque converter. The converter clutch assembly, **Fig. 2,** consists of a three element torque converter with a converter clutch. The converter clutch is splined to the turbine assembly and, when operated, applies against the converter cover, providing a mechanical direct drive coupling of the engine to the planetary gears. When the converter clutch is released the assembly operates as a normal torque converter.

TROUBLESHOOTING

NO DRIVE IN DRIVE RANGE

1. Low oil level.
2. Manual linkage improperly adjusted.
3. Low oil pressure due to:
   a. Restricted or plugged oil screen.
   b. Oil screen gasket improperly installed.
   c. Oil pump pressure regulator.
   d. Pump drive gear tangs damaged by converter.
   e. Case porosity in intake bore
4. Forward clutch malfunctioning due to:
   a. Forward clutch not applying due to cracked piston, damaged or missing seals, burned clutch plates, snap ring not in groove.
   b. Forward clutch seal rings damaged or missing on turbine shaft, leaking feed circuits due to damaged or mispositioned gasket.
   c. Clutch housing check ball stuck or missing.
   d. Cup plug leaking or missing from rear of turbine shaft in clutch apply passage.
   e. Incorrect forward clutch piston assembly or incorrect number of clutch plates.
5. Roller clutch malfunctioning due to missing rollers or springs or possibly galled rollers.

OIL PRESSURE HIGH OR LOW

1. Throttle valve cable improperly adjusted, binding, disconnected or broken.
2. Throttle lever and bracket improperly instal led, disconnected or binding.
3. Throttle valve shift valve, throttle valve or plunger binding.
4. Pressure regulator valve and spring malfunctioning due to:
   a. Binding valve.
   b. Incorrect spring.
   c. Oil pressure control orifice in pump cover plugged, causing high oil pressure.
   d. Pressure regulator bore plug leaking.
5. Manual valve disconnected.
6. Intermediate boost valve binding, causing oil pressures to be incorrect in 2nd and low ranges.
7. Orifice in spacer plate at end of intermediate boost valve plugged.
8. Reverse boost valve binding, causing pressure to be incorrect in reverse only.
9. Orifice in spacer plate at end of reverse boost valve plugged.
10. No. 1 check ball missing or leaking.

1-2 SHIFT AT FULL THROTTLE ONLY

1. Throttle valve cable improperly adjusted, binding, disconnected or broken.
2. Throttle lever and bracket assembly binding or disconnected.
3. Throttle valve exhaust ball lifter or number 5 check ball binding, mispositioned or disconnected. **If number 5 ball is fully seated, it will cause full throttle valve pressure regardless of throttle valve position.**
4. Throttle valve and plunger binding.
5. Valve body gaskets leaking, damaged or incorrectly installed.
6. Porous control valve assembly.

FIRST SPEED ONLY, NO 1-2 SHIFT

1. Due to governor and governor feed passages:
   a. Plugged governor oil feed orifice in spacer plate.
   b. Plugged orifice in spacer plate that feeds governor oil to the shift valves.
   c. Balls missing in governor assembly.
   d. Governor cover O-ring missing or leaking. If governor cover O-ring leaks, an external oil leak will be present and there will be no upshift.
   e. Governor shaft seal missing or damaged.
   f. Governor driven gear stripped.
   g. Governor weights binding.
   h. Governor assembly missing.
2. Control valve assembly 1-2 shift valve or 1-2 throttle valve stuck in downshift position.
3. Porosity in case channels or undrilled 2nd speed feed holes.
4. Excessive leakage between case bore and intermediate band apply ring.

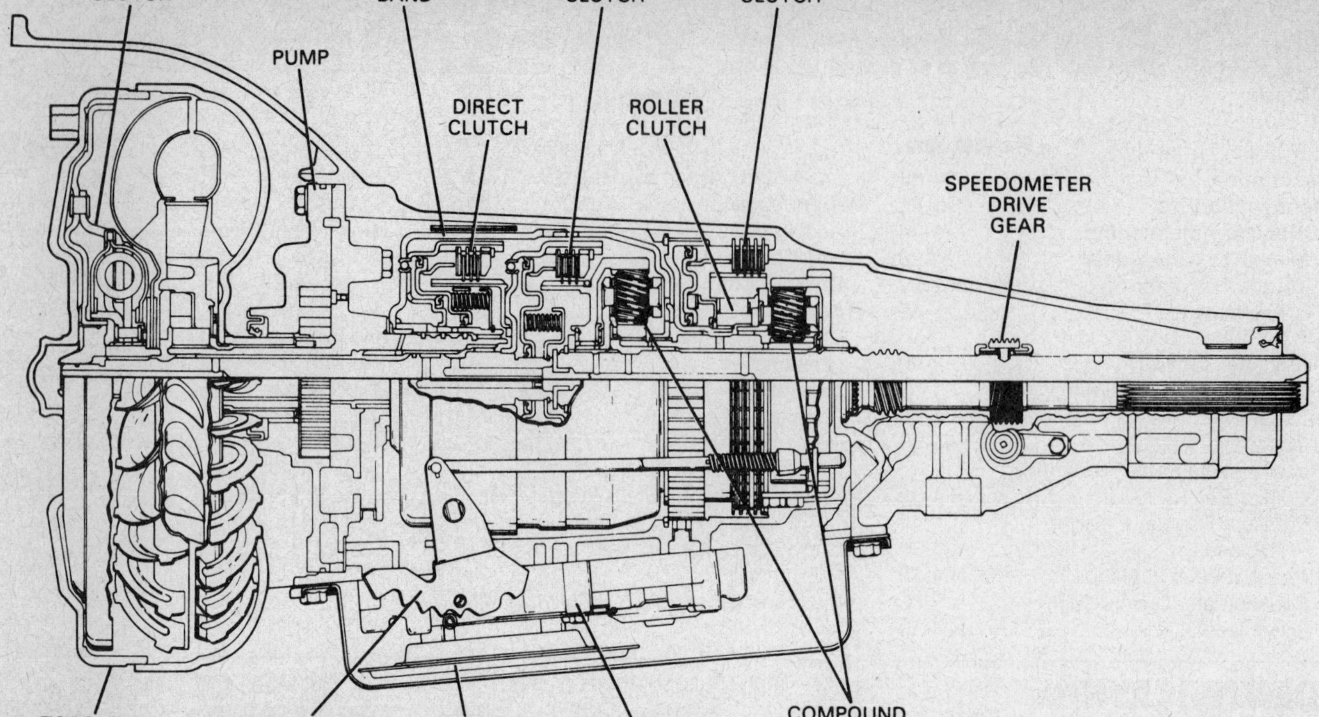

Fig. 1 Turbo Hydra-Matic 200C transmission

5. Intermediate band anchor pin missing or disconnected from band.
6. Missing or broken intermediate band.
7. Due to intermediate servo assembly:
   a. Servo to cover oil seal ring damaged or missing.
   b. Porous servo cover or piston.
   c. Incorrect intermediate band apply pin.
   d. Incorrect cover and piston.

1ST & 2ND ONLY, NO 2-3 SHIFT

1. 2-3 shift valve or 2-3 throttle valve stuck in downshift position.
2. Direct clutch feed orifice in spacer plate plugged.
3. Valve body gaskets leaking, damaged or incorrectly installed.
4. Porosity between case passages.
5. Pump passages plugged or leaking.
6. Pump gasket incorrectly installed.
7. Rear seal on pump cover leaking or missing.
8. Direct clutch oil seals missing or damaged.
9. Direct clutch piston or housing cracked.
10. Direct clutch plates damaged or missing.
11. Direct clutch backing plate snap ring out of groove.
12. Intermediate servo to case oil seal broken or missing on intermediate servo piston.
13. Intermediate servo exhaust hole in case between servo piston seals plugged or undrilled.

MOVES FORWARD IN NEUTRAL

1. Manual linkage improperly adjusted.
2. Forward clutch does not release.
3. Cross leakage between pump passages.
4. Cross leakage to forward clutch through clutch passages.

NO DRIVE IN REVERSE OR SLIPS IN REVERSE

1. Throttle valve cable binding or improperly adjusted.
2. Manual linkage improperly adjusted.
3. Throttle valve binding.
4. Reverse boost valve binding in bore.
5. Low overrun clutch valve binding in bore.
6. Reverse clutch piston cracked, broken or has missing seals.
7. Reverse clutch plates burned.
8. Reverse clutch has incorrect selective spacer ring.
9. Porosity in passages to direct clutch.
10. Pump to case gasket improperly installed or missing.
11. Pump passages cross leaking or restricted.
12. Pump cover seals damaged or missing.
13. Direct clutch piston or housing cracked.
14. Direct clutch piston seals cut or missing.
15. Direct clutch housing ball check, stuck, leaking or missing.
16. Direct clutch plates burned.
17. Incorrect direct clutch piston.
18. Direct clutch orifices plugged in spacer plate.
19. Intermediate servo to case seal cut or missing.
20. Shift T.V. valve binding in valve body bore.

SLIPS 1-2 SHIFT

1. Aerated oil due to low level.
2. 2nd speed feed orifice in spacer plate partially blocked.
3. Improperly installed or missing spacer plate gasket.
4. 1-2 accumulator valve stuck, causing low 1-2 accumulator pressure.
5. Weak or missing 1-2 accumulator valve spring.
6. 1-2 accumulator piston seal leaking or spring missing or broken.
7. Leakage between 1-2 accumulator piston and pin.
8. Incorrect intermediate band apply pin.
9. Excessive leakage between intermediate band apply pin and case.
10. Porous intermediate servo piston.
11. Servo cover to servo seal damaged or missing.
12. Incorrect servo and cover.
13. Throttle valve cable improperly adjusted.
14. Shift throttle valve or throttle valve binding.
15. Intermediate band worn or burned.
16. Case porosity in 2nd clutch passages.

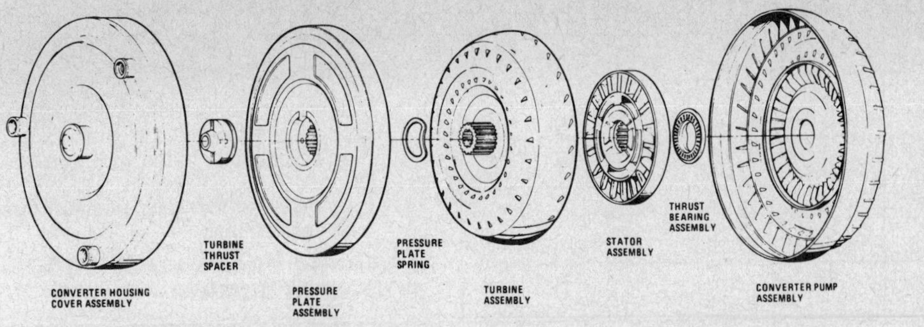

Fig. 2 Torque converter clutch assembly

ROUGH 1-2 SHIFT

1. Throttle valve cable improperly adjusted or binding.
2. Throttle valve or plunger binding.
3. Shift throttle or 1-2 accumulator valve binding.
4. Incorrect intermediate servo pin.
5. Intermediate servo piston to case seal damaged or missing.
6. 1-2 accumulator oil ring damaged, piston stuck, bore damaged or spring broken or missing.

SLIPS 2-3 SHIFT

1. Low oil level.
2. Throttle valve cable improperly adjusted.
3. Throttle valve binding.
4. Direct clutch orifice in spacer plate partially blocked.
5. Spacer plate gaskets improperly installed or missing.
6. Intermediate servo to case seal damaged.
7. Porous direct clutch feed passages in case.
8. Pump to case gasket improperly installed or missing.
9. Pump passages cross feeding, leaking or restricted.
10. Pump cover oil seal rings damaged or missing.
11. Direct clutch piston or housing cracked.
12. Direct clutch piston seals cut or missing.
13. Direct clutch plates burned.

ROUGH 2-3 SHIFT

1. Throttle valve cable improperly installed or missing.
2. Throttle valve or throttle valve plunger binding.
3. Shift throttle valve binding.
4. Intermediate servo exhaust hole undrilled or plugged between intermediate servo piston seals.
5. Direct clutch exhaust valve number 4 check ball missing or improperly installed.

NO ENGINE BRAKING IN 2ND SPEED

1. Intermediate boost valve binding in valve body.
2. Intermediate-Reverse number 3 check ball improperly installed or missing.
3. Shift throttle valve number 3 check ball improperly installed or missing.
4. Intermediate servo to cover seal missing or damaged.
5. Intermediate band off anchor pin, broken or burned.

NO ENGINE BRAKING IN 1ST SPEED

1. Low overrun clutch valve binding in valve body. **The following conditions will also cause no reverse.**
2. Low-reverse clutch piston seals broken or missing.
3. Porosity in low-reverse piston or housing.
4. Low-reverse clutch housing snap ring out of case.
5. Cup plug or rubber seal missing or damaged between case and low-reverse clutch housing.

NO PART THROTTLE DOWNSHIFT

1. Throttle plunger bushing passages obstructed.
2. 2-3 throttle valve bushing passages obstructed.
3. Valve body gaskets improperly installed or damaged.
4. Spacer plate hole obstructed or undrilled.
5. Throttle valve cable improperly adjusted.
6. Throttle valve or shift throttle valve binding.

LOW OR HIGH SHIFT POINTS

1. Throttle valve cable binding or disconnected.
2. Throttle valve or shift throttle valve binding.
3. Number 1 throttle shift check ball improperly installed or missing.
4. Throttle valve plunger, 1-2 or 2-3 throttle valves binding.
5. Valve body gaskets improperly installed or missing.
6. Pressure regulator valve binding.
7. Throttle valve exhaust number 5 check ball and lifter, improperly installed, disconnected or missing.
8. Throttle lever binding, disconnected or loose at valve body mounting bolt or not positioned at the throttle valve plunger bushing pin locator.
9. Governor shaft to cover seal broken or missing.
10. Governor cover O-rings broken or missing. **Outer ring will leak externally and the inner ring will leak internally.**
11. Case porosity.
12. Missing pump body check ball (2-3 only).

WILL NOT HOLD IN PARK

1. Manual linkage improperly adjusted.
2. Parking pawl binding in case.
3. Actuator rod or plunger damaged.
4. Parking pawl damaged.
5. Parking bracket loose or damaged.
6. Detent lever nut loose.
7. Detent lever hole worn or damaged.
8. Detent roller to valve body bolt loose.
9. Detent roller or pin damaged, incorrectly installed or missing.

CONVERTER CLUTCH APPLIED IN ALL RANGES, ENGINE STALLS WHEN TRANSMISSION PUT IN GEAR

1. Converter clutch valve stuck in apply position.

CONVERTER CLUTCH APPLIES ERRATICALLY

1. Vacuum hose leak.
2. Vacuum switch malfunction.
3. Release oil exhaust orifice at pump blocked or restricted.
4. Turbine shaft O-ring damaged.
5. Converter malfunction, clutch pressure plate warped.
6. O-ring damaged at solenoid.
7. Solenoid bolts loose.
8. Governor pressure switch malfunction.

MAINTENANCE

To check fluid, drive vehicle for at least 15 minutes to bring fluid to operating temperature (200° F). With vehicle on a level surface, engine idling in Park and parking brake applied, the level on the dipstick should be at the "F" mark. To bring the fluid level from the ADD mark to the FULL mark requires 1 pint of fluid. If vehicle cannot be driven sufficiently to bring fluid to operating temperature, the level on the dipstick should be between the two dimples on the dipstick with fluid temperature at 70° F.

If additional fluid is required, use only Dexron or Dexron II automatic transmission fluid.

An early change to a darker color from the usual red color and or a strong odor that is usually associated with overheated fluid is normal and should not be considered as a positive sign of required maintenance or unit failure.

Every 100,000 the oil should be drained, the oil pan removed, the screen cleaned and fresh fluid added. For vehicles subjected to more severe use such as heavy city traffic, especially in hot weather, and prolonged periods of idling or towing, this maintenance should be performed every 15,000 miles.

DRAINING BOTTOM PAN

1. Remove front and side oil pan attaching bolts, then loosen the rear oil pan attaching bolts.
2. Carefully pry oil pan loose and allow fluid to drain into a suitable container.
3. Remove the oil pan and gasket, then remove the screen attaching bolts and remove screen.
4. Thoroughly clean oil screen and oil pan with solvent.
5. Install oil screen using a new gasket and torque attaching bolts to 6-10 ft. lbs., then install oil pan using a new gasket and torque attaching bolts to 10-13 ft. lbs.
6. Add 3 quarts of fluid, then with engine idling and parking brake applied, move selector lever through each range and return selector lever to PARK.
7. Check fluid level and add fluid as required to bring level between the two dimples on the dipstick.

ADDING FLUID TO DRY TRANSMISSION & CONVERTER

1. Add 9 1/2 quarts of fluid.
2. With transmission in PARK and parking brake applied, start engine and place carburetor on fast idle cam.
3. Move shifter lever through each range, then with transmission in PARK, add additional fluid as required to bring the level between the two dimples on the dipstick.

IN-VEHICLE ADJUSTMENTS

MANUAL LINKAGE, ADJUST

CONSOLE SHIFT

1982–83 Chevette & 1000

1. Place shift lever (A) in neutral position, **Fig. 3.**
2. Move lever (E) clockwise to maximum detent to PARK, then move lever counterclockwise two detent positions to NEUTRAL.
3. With lever (E) in NEUTRAL, insert pin (F) on fork (G). Adjust rod (H) until hole in rod aligns with shifter assembly pin (B) and install rod on pin.

1984 Chevette & 1000

1. Snap cable (1) into bracket (2), **Fig. 4.**
2. Turn ignition switch to Lock position.
3. Snap end of cable (1) onto sliding pin (3).
4. Place shifter lever (4) in Park position.
5. Install cable (1) onto shifter lever pin (5).
6. Attach cable (1) to shifter mounting bracket (7) by pressing lock assembly against spring (9) and dropping cable through slot in bracket.
7. Depress lock button (10) to complete adjustment.

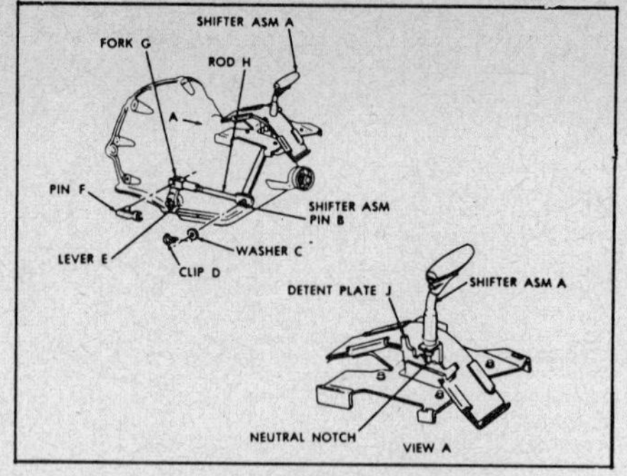

Fig. 3 Console shift manual linkage adjustment. 1982–83 Chevette & 1000

1982–83 Cutlass, Malibu, Monte Carlo & Regal, 1984–85 Cutlass, Grand Prix, Monte Carlo & Regal

1. Loosen shift rod clamp screw, then the pin in transmission manual lever, **Fig. 5.**
2. Place shift lever and manual lever in Park position and ignition key in Lock position.
3. Torque cable pin nut to 20 ft. lbs., then rotate manual lever fully against Park stop and release lever.
4. Pull shift rod downward against lock stop, then torque clamp screw to 20 ft. lbs.

1986–87 Cutlass, Grand Prix, Monte Carlo, Regal

1. Position shift and transmission levers in Park position. **Verify that transmission lever is in Park position by rotating propeller shaft until parking pawl in transmission is fully engaged.**
2. Move pin, **Fig. 5**, until free pin fit is evident in transmission lever, then torque attaching nut to 15 ft. lbs. (20 Nm).

COLUMN SHIFT

Intermediate Models

1. Place shift lever and transmission lever in Neutral position, **Figs. 6.**
2. Assemble clamp, spring washer and screw to equalizer lever and control rod.
3. Hold clamp flush against equalizer lever and lightly tighten clamping screw against rod.
4. Torque clamp screw to 20 ft. lbs. **Do not exert force in either direction on rod or equalizer rod while tightening screw.**

Full Size Models

1. Position shift lever and transmission lever in Neutral position, **Fig. 7.**
2. Hold clamp flush against equalizer lever and lightly tighten.
3. Torque bolt to 20 ft. lbs. **Do not exert force in either direction on rod or equalizer rod while tightening screw.**

T.V./DETENT CABLE, ADJUST

All 1982–87 Models

1. Disengage snap lock. Cable should be free to slide through snap lock.
2. Place carburetor in the wide open position.
3. Engage snap lock and position flush with cable fitting.

1982–84 Chevette & 1000 w/Diesel Engine

1. Remove cruise control rod on vehicles equipped with cruise control.
2. Disconnect throttle valve linkage from throttle assembly.
3. Loosen locknut on pump rod, then shorten rod by rotating several turns.
4. Secure throttle lever assembly in full throttle position.
5. Lengthen pump rod by rotating in opposite direction as described in step 3 until injection pump lever contacts full throttle stop.
6. Release throttle lever assembly and tighten pump rod locknut.
7. Disconnect pump rod from throttle lever.
8. Connect throttle valve linkage to throttle assembly.
9. Depress metal locking tab on upper end of cable and hold in this position.
10. Position slider through fitting and away from lever assembly until slider contacts metal fitting.
11. Release metal tab, then rotate throttle lever assembly to full throttle position and release.
12. Connect pump rod to lever assembly, then connect cruise control throttle rod, if equipped.
13. On models equipped with cruise control, adjust servo throttle rod until minimum amount of slack is present. Install clip into first hole closest to bellcrank that is within servo bail.

All 1982–87 Models w/Gasoline Engine

1. With engine off, depress locking tab and move slider rearward through fitting until slider contacts fitting, **Fig. 8.**
2. Release locking tab, then move carburetor throttle lever to wide open position and release.
3. On Camaro and Firebird with 4-151 engine, rotate idler lever to the maximum travel stop position. The cable will ratchet through its slider and automatically adjust itself. Release throttle idler lever. Do not adjust using the TBI or carburetor lever.
4. On all models, check cable for sticking or binding, then test vehicle for proper operation.
5. If transmission does not shift properly, raise and support vehicle and remove transmission oil pan. Inspect throttle lever and bracket assembly on valve body for damage. Check to ensure that throttle valve exhaust valve rod is not worn or damaged. Check to ensure that lifter spring holds lifter rod against bottom of valve body and that throttle valve plunger is not sticking.

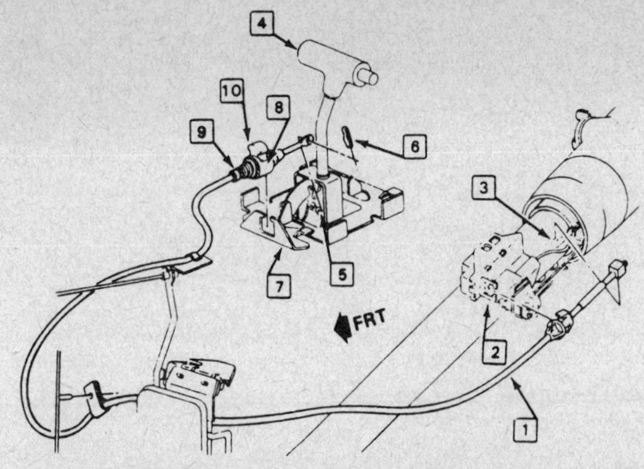

Fig. 4 Console shift manual linkage adjustment. 1984 Chevette & 1000

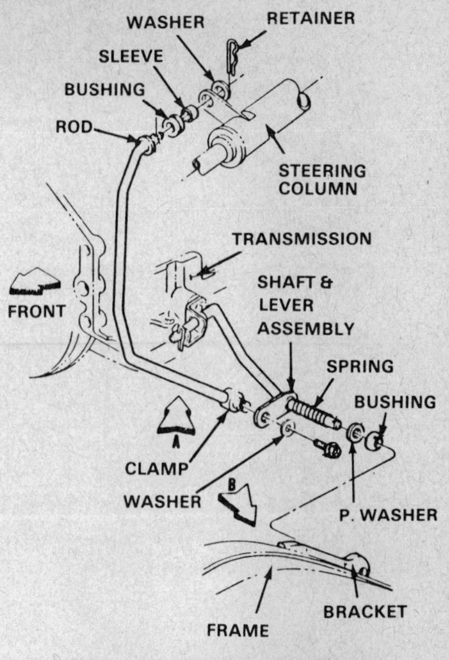

Fig. 6 Column shift manual linkage adjustment. Intermediate models (typical)

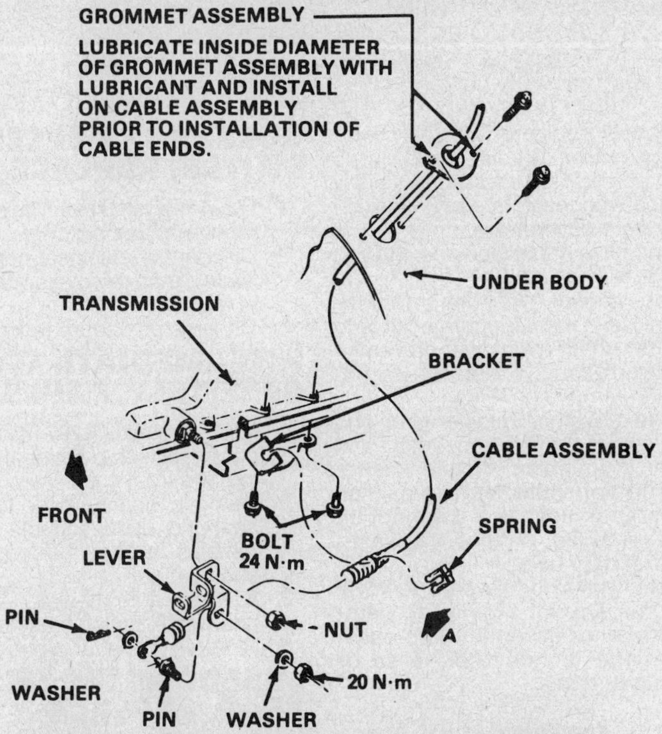

Fig. 5 Console shift manual linkage adjustment. 1982–83 Cutlass, Malibu, Monte Carlo & Regal, 1984–87 Cutlass, Grand Prix, Monte Carlo & Regal

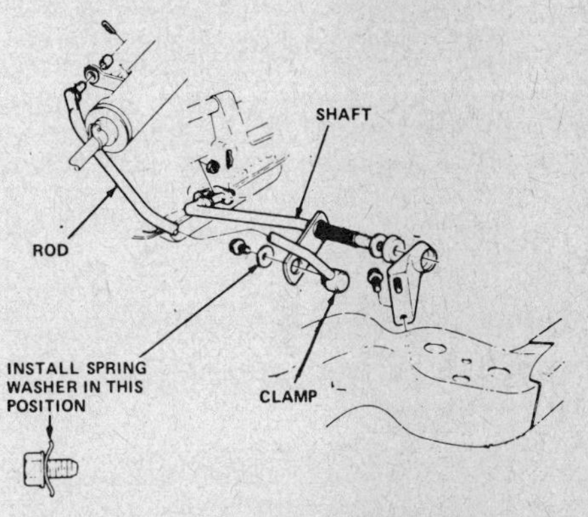

Fig. 7 Column shift linkage adjustment. Full size models

TORQUE CONVERTER CLUTCH SWITCH ADJUSTMENTS

Low Vacuum Switch

1. Disconnect vacuum and electrical connectors from low vacuum switch, **Fig. 11.**
2. Connect a suitable test light to either terminal of vacuum switch. Connect a suitable jumper cable from the other terminal to a good ground.
3. Connect remaining lead of test light to power side of removed vacuum switch connector.
4. Attach suitable vacuum pump to vacuum port of switch.
5. Turn ignition on, then actuate vacuum pump. On V6-231 and 252 engines, test light should remain off until vacuum pump gauge reads 5.5-6.5 in. Hg. On V8-265 and 301 engines the test light should remain off until vacuum gauge reads 6.5-7.5 in. Hg. On V8-307 engines, the test light should remain off until vacuum gauge reads 8 in. Hg. On V8-350 gas engines, light should remain off until vacuum gauge reads 7.5-8.5 in. Hg. On V8-350 diesel engines, test light should remain off until vacuum gauge reads 5-6 in. Hg.
6. Decrease vacuum slowly. Light should remain on until vacuum drops to .3-1.3 in. Hg on V6-231 and 252 engines, 1.2-2.2 in. Hg on V8-265 and 301 engines, 1.5-2.5 in. Hg on V8-307 and 350 gas engines and 3.5-4.5 in. Hg on V8-350 diesel engines. Decreasing vacuum beyond above values should cause light to go out.
7. If above results cannot be obtained, switch is defective.
8. The point at which light comes on and the point at which light goes out must have at least 4 in. of vacuum difference.

High Vacuum Switch

The high vacuum switch must be adjusted anytime the throttle rod, transmission vacuum valve and high idle speed adjustments are changed.

1. Disconnect high vacuum switch electrical connector, **Fig. 9.**
2. Connect suitable test light across the terminals of the high vacuum switch.
3. Energize fast idle solenoid by disconnecting pink and green wire from coolant switch and operate engine at high idle speed, then remove cap from back of high vacuum switch.
4. Before adjustment is performed, the test light must be on, indicating that the switch contacts are closed. If test light is off, close the switch contacts by turning switch adjusting screw clockwise until contacts close.

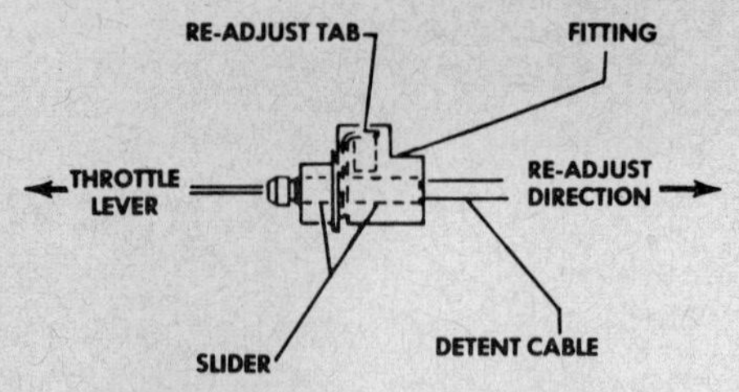

Fig. 8 Self-adjusting throttle valve cable

Fig. 10 Removing or installing pressure regulator

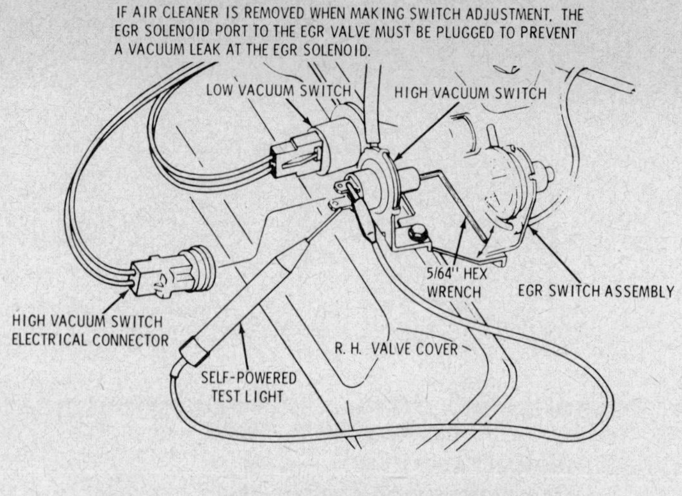

Fig. 9 Vacuum switch location

5. Adjust vacuum switch by turning adjusting screw counterclockwise until switch contact just opens and test light goes off. Turn adjusting screw counterclockwise an additional 1/8-3/16 turn.
6. Reinstall cap on back of vacuum switch and reconnect high vacuum switch and coolant switch electrical connectors.

IN-VEHICLE REPAIRS

VALVE BODY ASSEMBLY, REPLACE

1. Drain transmission fluid, then remove oil pan and screen.
2. Remove detent cable retaining bolt and disconnect cable.
3. Remove throttle lever and bracket assembly. Use care to avoid bending throttle lever link.
4. Remove detent roller and spring.
5. Support valve body and remove retaining bolts, then while holding manual valve, remove valve assembly, spacer plate and gaskets as an assembly to prevent dropping the five check balls. **After removing valve body assembly, the intermediate band anchor band pin, and reverse cup plug may be removed.**
6. To install control valve, reverse removal procedure and torque all valve body bolts to 8 ft. lbs. **Ensure that intermediate band anchor pin is located on intermediate band prior to installation of valve body, as damage will result.**

GOVERNOR, REPLACE

Exc. Camaro & Firebird

1. Disconnect battery ground cable and remove air cleaner.
2. On models equipped with air conditioning, remove the five heater core cover screws, then disconnect the electrical connectors and position heater core cover aside.
3. Disconnect exhaust pipe and allow to hang down.
4. Support transmission, then remove transmission rear support bolts and propeller shaft and lower transmission until enough clearance is obtained to remove governor.
5. Remove governor retainer ring and cover, then remove governor and washer. **If governor to case washer falls into transmission, use a small magnet to remove it. If it cannot be easily removed, replace the washer with a new one.**
6. To install governor, reverse removal procedure. **Do not attempt to hammer governor assembly into case, as damage to governor, case or cover may result.**

Camaro & Firebird

1. Raise and support vehicle.
2. Remove governor retaining ring and cover and the two seal rings.
3. Remove governor from case.
4. Reverse procedure to install.

PRESSURE REGULATOR VALVE, REPLACE

1. Drain transmission fluid, then remove oil pan and screen.
2. Using a small screwdriver or tool J-24684, **Fig. 10**, compress regulator spring.
3. Remove retaining ring and slowly release spring tension.
4. Remove pressure regulator bore plug, valve, spring and guide.
5. To assemble, install pressure regulator spring, guide and valve with stem end first and bore plug with hole side out.
6. Using a small screwdriver or tool J-24684, **Fig. 10,** compress regulator spring and install retaining ring.

GOVERNOR PRESSURE SWITCH, REPLACE

1. Drain transmission fluid from pan, then remove pan.
2. Disconnect electrical connector from switch, then remove switch using suitable socket.
3. Reverse procedure to install.

INTERMEDIATE SERVO ASSEMBLY, REPLACE

1. Using tool No. J-29714 or equivalent, compress servo cover and pry retaining ring from case. Remove tool.
2. Remove servo cover together with seal ring, using suitable pliers. If ring remains in case, pry out gently with suitable tool.
3. Remove intermediate servo piston and band apply pin assembly.
4. Reverse procedure to install.

SPEEDOMETER DRIVEN GEAR, REPLACE

1. Raise and support vehicle.
2. Disconnect speedometer cable.
3. Remove retainer bolt and retainer, then the driven gear and O-ring seal.
4. Reverse procedure to install.

REAR OIL SEAL, REPLACE

1. Raise and support vehicle.
2. Remove propeller shaft, then pry seal out of housing using suitable tool.
3. Coat outer casing of new seal with non-hardening sealer, then tap seal into place with tool No. J-21426 or equivalent.
4. Install propeller shaft, then check and adjust fluid level.

TRANSMISSION REPLACE

BUICK

1. Disconnect battery ground cable.
2. Remove oil lever dipstick and bolt from upper end of oil filler tube.
3. Raise and properly support vehicle.
4. Disconnect T.V. cable at both ends.

5. Disconnect transmission cooler lines, and remove catalytic converter bracket, if necessary.
6. Remove flywheel inspection cover, then the flywheel to converter bolts.
7. If equipped with console shift, disconnect shift control cable from transmission. If equipped with column shift, remove cotter pin and disconnect manual shift linkage.
8. Disconnect speedometer cable and remove propeller shaft.
9. Remove transmission support to mount bolts, and transmission support to frame bolts. Support engine, then raise transmission with a jack and remove support.
10. Lower transmission slightly and remove the engine to transmission bolts.
11. Carefully lower transmission using care to avoid damaging the detent cable and shift linkage.
12. Reverse procedure to install.

CHEVROLET

Exc. Chevette & Camaro

1. Disconnect battery ground cable and the detent cable from carburetor. Remove filler tube and air cleaner.
2. On models with air conditioning, remove five heater core cover screws from heater assembly. Disconnect electrical connector and, with hoses attached, place heater core cover aside.
3. On all models, raise vehicle and remove propeller shaft.
4. Disconnect speedometer cable, electrical lead to case, oil cooler pipes and the shift linkage.
5. Support transmission with a suitable jack and remove the four rear transmission support bolts.
6. Remove nuts securing catalytic converter bracket to support.
7. Disconnect exhaust pipe at rear of catalytic converter, then at the manifold. Remove exhaust pipe catalytic converter and converter bracket as an assembly.
8. On all models, remove torque converter under pan.
9. Remove converter to flywheel bolts.
10. Lower transmission slightly and remove engine to transmission bolts.
11. Raise transmission and move rearward, then lower from vehicle.
12. Reverse procedure to install.

Chevette

1. Disconnect battery ground cable then disconnect detent downshift cable from bracket.
2. Remove air cleaner and dipstick, then on vehicles with air conditioning, remove the 5 heater core cover retaining screws, disconnect connector and place heater core cover assembly aside.
3. Raise and support vehicle and remove propeller shaft.
4. Disconnect speedometer cable, electrical lead, oil cooler lines, and shift control linkage.
5. Support transmission with suitable jack and remove the crossmember retaining bolts.
6. Remove converter to bracket retaining nuts, then disconnect exhaust pipes from rear of catalytic converter and from exhaust manifolds and remove catalytic converter and converter bracket as an assembly.
7. Remove converter dust shield and remove converter to flywheel bolts.
8. Lower transmission slightly and remove transmission to engine bolts.
9. Raise transmission, then support engine with jack and lower and remove transmission from vehicle. **Use converter holding tool J-5384, or keep rear of transmission lower than the front to prevent the converter from sliding out.**
10. Before installing transmission, place two inch blocks between rack and pinion housing assembly and oil pan to align engine and transmission.
11. Reverse removal procedure to install and torque converter to flywheel bolts to 30-40 ft. lbs. (40-54 Nm).

Camaro

1. Disconnect battery ground cable, then remove air cleaner.
2. Disconnect T.V. cable from carburetor, then remove filler tube.
3. Raise and support vehicle.
4. Remove prop. shaft and disconnect catalytic converter to transmission bracket.
5. Disconnect speedometer cable and T.C.C. electrical connector.
6. Remove torque arm to transmission bolts. **When arm is disconnected from transmission, rear spring force will cause torque arm to move toward the floor pan. When disconnecting the arm, carefully place a piece of wood between the floor pan and torque arm to avoid personal injury and damage to the floor pan.**
7. Remove flywheel cover and converter to flywheel attaching bolts. Mark flywheel and converter for reference.
8. Support transmission with a suitable jack, then remove transmission rear mount bolt and crossmember.
9. Lower transmission slightly and remove T.V. cable and oil cooler lines.
10. Support engine using tool BT-6424 or equivalent and remove transmission to engine bolts.
11. Remove transmission from vehicle.
12. Reverse procedure to install.

OLDSMOBILE

1. Disconnect battery ground cable, then remove air cleaner assembly and filler tube.
2. Disconnect T.V. cable at its upper end, then raise vehicle and remove shift linkage and oil cooler pipes.
3. Remove catalytic converter support bracket and flywheel cover pan.
4. Remove flywheel to converter bolts.
5. Disconnect speedometer cable and remove propeller shaft.
6. Remove transmission support to transmission bolts and the transmission support to frame bolts.
7. Support and raise transmission with a suitable jack, then remove support.
8. Lower transmission slightly and remove engine to transmission bolts.
9. Move transmission rearward and lower from vehicle.
10. Reverse procedure to install.

PONTIAC

Exc. Firebird & 1000

1. Disconnect battery ground cable.
2. Disconnect T.V. cable, then remove dipstick and oil filler tube from transmission.
3. Raise and support vehicle.
4. Remove detent cable retaining bolt and cable and plug opening.
5. Disconnect transmission cooler lines and speedometer cable from transmission.
6. Disconnect shift linkage from selector lever. If equipped with console, remove spring clip and T.V. from transmission bracket.
7. Remove catalytic converter support bracket.
8. Remove flywheel cover and then the flywheel to converter bolts.
9. Remove propeller shaft.
10. Remove transmission support to transmission mount bolts and transmission support to mount bolts.
11. Raise transmission with a suitable jack and remove support, then lower transmission and remove transmission to engine bolts.
12. Remove transmission. Do not damage oil cooler lines and detent cable.
13. Reverse procedure to install.

1000

Refer to "Transmission, Replace" under "Chevette" for procedure.

Firebird

Refer to "Transmission Replace" under "Camaro" for procedure.

Turbo Hydra-Matic 200-4R Automatic Transmission

INDEX

IDENTIFICATION

The transmission identification number is stamped on the lefthand side of the transmission.

DESCRIPTION

This transmission is a fully automatic unit consisting primarily of a three-element hydraulic torque converter with a converter clutch, a compound planetary gear set and an overdrive unit, **Fig. 1.** Five multiple-disc clutches and a band provide the friction elements required to obtain the desired function of the compound planetary gear set and the overdrive unit.

The torque converter couples the engine to the overdrive unit and planetary gears through oil and provides torque multiplication. The combination of the compound planetary gear set and the overdrive unit provides four forward ratios and one reverse. Fully automatic changing of the gear ratios is determined by vehicle speed and engine torque.

The hydraulic system in this transmission is pressurized by a variable capacity vane type pump to provide the working pressure required to operate the friction elements and automatic controls.

TROUBLESHOOTING

NO DRIVE

1. Low fluid level.
2. Manual linkage improperly adjusted.
3. Low fluid pressure.
   a. Plugged or restricted oil filter.
   b. Cut or missing oil filter O-ring seals.
   c. Faulty pressure regulator valve.
   d. Damaged pump rotor tangs.
   e. Porosity in oil filter to pump intake bore.
4. Springs missing in overdrive unit roller clutch.
5. Overdrive unit rollers galled or missing.
6. Forward Clutch.
   a. Forward clutch does not apply—piston cracked, seals missing, damaged; clutch plates burned; snap ring out of groove.
   b. Missing or damaged forward clutch oil seal rings; leak in feed circuits; pump to case gasket improperly positioned or damaged.
   c. Stuck or missing clutch housing ball check.
   d. Cup plug leaking or missing in the rear of the forward clutch shaft in the clutch apply passage.
7. Low and reverse roller clutch springs missing.
8. Low and reverse roller clutch rollers galled or missing.

HIGH OR LOW OIL PRESSURE

1. Throttle valve cable improperly adjusted, binding, unhooked, broken, or wrong link.
2. Damaged or leaking throttle valve assembly.
   a. Throttle lever and bracket assembly binding, unhooked or improperly positioned.
   b. Binding throttle valve or plunger valve.
3. Pressure regulator valve binding.
4. Throttle valve boost valve.
   a. Valve binding.
   b. Wrong valve (causing low oil pressure only).
5. Reverse boost valve binding.
6. Manual valve unhooked or improperly positioned.
7. Pressure relief valve ball missing or spring damaged.
8. Pump.
   a. Slide stuck.
   b. Slide seal damaged or missing.
   c. Decrease air bleed orifice missing or damaged causing high oil pressure.
   d. Decrease air bleed orifice plugged causing low oil pressure.
9. Throttle valve limit valve binding.
10. Line bias valve binding in open position causing high oil pressure.
11. Line bias valve binding in closed position causing low oil pressure.
12. Incorrect orifices or passages in control valve assembly spacer plate or case.

1-2 SHIFT ONLY AT FULL THROTTLE

1. Throttle valve cable binding, unhooked, broken, or improperly adjusted.
2. Throttle lever and bracket assembly binding or unhooked.
3. Throttle valve exhaust ball lifter or #5 ball binding, improperly positioned, or unhooked.
4. #5 ball sealed causing full throttle valve pressure regardless of throttle valve position.
5. Throttle valve and plunger binding.
6. Control valve body gaskets leaking, damaged, or incorrectly installed.
7. Porous case assembly.

NO 1-2 SHIFT

1. Governor and governor feed passages.
   a. Plugged governor oil feed orifice in spacer plate.
   b. Check balls missing in governor assembly.
   c. Missing or leaking inner governor cover rubber O-ring seal.
   d. Governor shaft seal missing or damaged.
   e. Stripped governor driven gear.
   f. Governor weights binding on pin.
   g. Governor driven gear not engaged with governor shaft.
2. Control valve assembly.
   a. 1-2 shift, low 1st/Detent, or 1-2 throttle valve stuck in downshift position.
   b. Spacer plate gaskets improperly positioned.

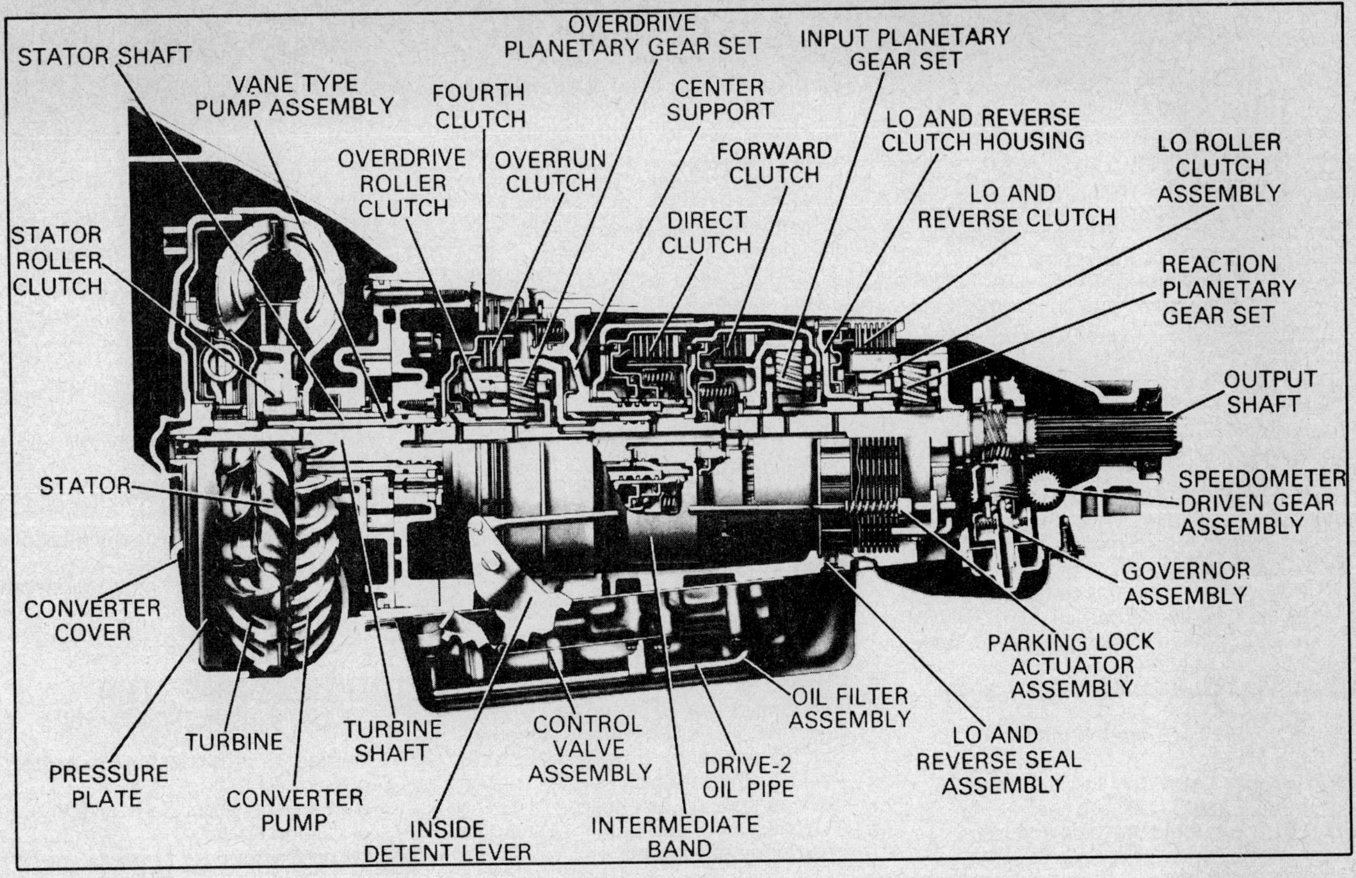

Fig. 1 THM 200-4R cross sectional view

3. Case.
   a. Case channels porous or 2nd oil feed hole undrilled.
   b. Excessive leakage between case bore and intermediate band apply rings.
   c. Intermediate band anchor pin missing or unhooked from band.
   d. Broken or missing band.
4. Intermediate servo assembly.
   a. Missing servo cover oil seal.
   b. Porosity in serve; cover, inner piston, or outer piston.
   c. Incorrect intermediate band apply pin.
   d. Incorrect usage of cover and piston.
5. 1-2 accumulator.
   a. Loose 1-2 accumulator housing bolts.
   b. Damaged 1-2 accumulator housing face.
   c. Missing or damaged accumulator plate.

NO 2-3 SHIFT

1. Control valve assembly and spacer plate.
   a. 2-3 shift valve or 2-3 throttle valve stuck in the downshift position.
   b. Leaking, damaged or incorrectly installed valve body gaskets.
   c. Reverse/3rd check ball not seating, damaged or missing.
2. Case channels porous.
3. Center support.
   a. Plugged or undrilled center support direct clutch feed passage.
   b. Damaged steel oil seal rings on center support.
4. Direct clutch.
   a. Inner oil seal ring on piston damaged or missing.
   b. Center oil seal ring on direct clutch hub damaged or missing.
   c. Check ball and/or retainer damaged or missing from direct clutch piston.
   d. Damaged or missing direct clutch piston or housing.
   e. Damaged or missing direct clutch plates.
   f. Direct clutch backing plate snap ring not in groove.
   g. Release spring guide improperly located, preventing piston check ball from seating in retainer.
5. Intermediate servo assembly (third clutch accumulator oil passages).
   a. Broken or missing servo to case oil seal ring on intermediate servo piston.
   b. Intermediate servo and/or capsule missing or damaged.
   c. Plugged or undrilled exhaust hole in case between servo piston seal rings.
   d. Bleed orifice cup plug missing from intermediate servo pocket in case.

NO DRIVE IN R OR SLIPS IN R

1. Binding or improperly adjusted throttle valve cable.
2. Improperly adjusted manual linkage.
3. Binding throttle valve.
4. Throttle valve limit valve binding.
5. Binding line bias valve.
6. Reverse boost valve binding in pressure regulator bore.
7. Reverse/3rd or Low/Reverse check ball missing or seat in spacer plate damaged.
8. Reverse clutch.
   a. Cracked piston, or missing inner or outer seals.
   b. Clutch plates burned.
   c. Missing or damaged reverse oil seal in case.
   d. Missing clutch plate or wave plate.
9. Center support.
   a. Loose or missing center support attaching bolts.
   b. Blocked or undrilled passages.
   c. Porosity.
10. Direct clutch housing.
    a. Cracked housing or piston.
    b. Missing or damaged inner or outer piston seal.
    c. Missing or damaged check ball in either the direct clutch housing or the piston.
    d. Plates burned.
11. Plugged Low/Reverse overrun clutch orifice in spacer plate.

DRIVE IN NEUTRAL

1. Manual linkage improperly adjusted or disconnected.
2. Forward clutch.
   a. Clutch does not release.
   b. Sticking exhaust check ball.
   c. Plates burned together.

3. Case cross leaking to forward clutch passage (D4).

SLIPPING 1-2 SHIFT

1. Low fluid level.
2. Spacer plate gaskets damaged or incorrectly installed.
3. Accumulator valve.
   a. Valve sticking in valve body causing low 1-2 accumulator pressure.
   b. Weak or missing spring.
4. 1-2 accumulator piston.
   a. Leaking seal, broken or missing spring.
   b. Leak between piston and pin.
   c. Binding 1-2 accumulator piston.
   d. Damaged 1-2 accumulator piston bore.
5. Intermediate band apply pin.
   a. Incorrect selection of apply pin.
   b. Excessive leakage between apply pin and case.
   c. Apply pin feed hole not completely drilled.
6. Intermediate servo assembly.
   a. Porosity in piston.
   b. Damaged or missing cover to servo oil seal ring.
   c. Leak between servo apply pin and case.
7. Improperly adjusted throttle valve cable.
8. Throttle valve binding, causing low throttle valve pressure.
9. Binding throttle valve limit valve.
10. Line bias valve sticking, causing low line pressure.
11. Worn or burned intermediate band.
12. Case porosity in 2nd clutch passage.

ROUGH 1-2 SHIFT

1. Throttle valve cable binding or improperly adjusted.
2. Binding throttle valve to throttle valve plunger.
3. Binding throttle valve limit valve.
4. Binding accumulator valve.
5. Binding line bias valve.
6. Intermediate servo assembly.
   a. Incorrect selection apply pin.
   b. Damaged or missing servo piston to case oil seal ring.
   c. Bleed cup plug missing in case.
7. 1-2 accumulator.
   a. Oil ring damaged.
   b. Piston stuck.
   c. Broken or missing spring.
   d. Damaged bore.
8. 1-2 shift check ball ¯8 missing or sticking.

SLIPPING 2-3 SHIFT

1. Low fluid level.
2. Improperly adjusted throttle valve cable.
3. Binding throttle valve.
4. Spacer plate and gaskets.
   a. Direct clutch orifice partially blocked in spacer plate.
   b. Gaskets out of position or damaged.
5. Intermediate servo assembly.
   a. Damaged or missing servo to case oil seal ring.
   b. Damaged piston or servo bore.
   c. Intermediate servo orifice bleed cup plug in case missing.
   d. Case porous in the servo bore area.
6. Direct clutch feed.
   a. Direct clutch feed channels porous.
   b. Loose case to support bolts causing leakage.
   c. Cracked direct clutch piston or housing.
   d. Cut or missing piston seals.
   e. Burned direct clutch plates.
   f. Check ball in piston and/or housing missing, damaged, or leaking.
   g. Check ball capsule damaged.
   h. Release spring guide improperly located preventing check ball from seating in piston.
7. Center support.
   a. Channels cross feeding, leaking, or restricted.
   b. Damaged or missing oil seal rings.

ROUGH 2-3 SHIFT

1. Missing or improperly positioned throttle valve cable.
2. Throttle valve and plunger.
   a. Throttle valve plunger binding.
   b. Throttle valve binding.
3. Throttle valve limit valve binding.
4. Intermediate servo assembly exhaust hole undrilled or plugged between intermediate servo piston seals, preventing intermediate servo piston from completing its stroke.
5. 3-2 exhaust check ball ¯4 missing or improperly positioned.
6. 3rd accumulator check ball ¯2 missing or improperly positioned.

SLIPPING 3-4 SHIFT

1. Low fluid level.
2. Control valve assembly and spacer plate.
   a. Gaskets of space plate damaged or incorrectly installed.
   b. Accumulator valve sticking causing low 3-4 accumulator pressure.
   c. Weak or missing accumulator valve spring.
3. 3-4 accumulator.
   a. Piston stuck.
   b. Damaged bore or oil ring.
4. Center support porosity.
5. Loose center support attaching bolts.
6. Fourth clutch piston surface or seals damaged.
7. Improper clutch plate usage.
8. Burned fourth clutch plates.
9. Case.
   a. Porosity.
   b. 1-2 accumulator housing bolts loose.
   c. 3-4 accumulator piston seal damaged.
   d. 3-4 accumulator leaking between the piston and pin.
   e. 3-4 accumulator bore damaged.

ROUGH 3-4 SHIFT

1. Throttle valve cable improperly positioned or missing.
2. Throttle valve and plunger.
   a. Throttle valve plunger binding.
   b. Throttle valve binding.
3. Throttle valve limit valve binding.
4. 3-4 accumulator.
   a. Piston stuck.
   b. Bore damaged.
5. Fourth clutch piston binding.

NO CONVERTER CLUTCH APPLICATION

1. Electrical problem.
   a. 12 volts not being supplied to clutch solenoid.
   b. Defective solenoid.
   c. Damaged electrical connector.
   d. Defective pressure switch.
   e. Wire grounded.
2. Converter clutch shift valve or throttle valve stuck.
3. Pump Assembly.
   a. Plugged converter signal oil orifice in pump.
   b. Damaged or missing solenoid O-ring.
   c. Orifice cup plug missing in oil cooler passage in pump.
   d. Damaged or improperly positioned pump to case gasket.
   e. Converter clutch application valve stuck.
   f. Cup plug missing from application passage.

ROUGH CONVERTER CLUTCH APPLICATION

1. Damaged converter clutch pressure plate.
2. Damaged or missing check ball in end of turbine shaft.

CONVERTER CLUTCH DOES NOT RELEASE

1. Converter clutch apply valve stuck.
2. Damaged converter.
3. Missing cup plug in pump release passage.
4. Missing or damaged turbine shaft end seal.
5. Hole not drilled through turbine shaft.

FIRST, SECOND & THIRD SPEED ONLY, NO 3-4 SHIFT

1. Control valve assembly and spacer plate.
   a. 3-4 shift valve or 3-4 throttle valve stuck.
   b. Plugged spacer plate orifice.
2. Center support.
   a. Plugged or undrilled oil passages.
   b. Loose or missing center support attaching bolts.
   c. Cracked or damaged fourth clutch piston.
   d. Damaged, missing or improperly assembled fourth clutch piston seals.
   e. Improper plate usage.
   f. Burned fourth clutch plates.
   g. Binding overrun clutch plates.
3. Case porosity.
4. Orifice cup plug missing in 3-4 accumulator passage in case.
5. Leakage between accumulator piston and pin.
6. 3-4 accumulator bore damaged.

NO ENGINE BRAKING IN L1

1. Improperly adjusted manual linkage.

2. D-3 orifice in spacer plate plugged.
3. Control valve body gaskets leaking, damaged, or incorrectly installed.
4. D-2 oil pipe leaking or out of position.
5. L1 overrun clutch valve binding in valve body.
6. L1/Reverse check ball 10 improperly positioned or missing.
7. L1/Detent check ball 9 improperly positioned or missing.
8. PT/D-3 check ball 3 improperly positioned or missing.
9. Turbine shaft and overrun clutch. No manual 3rd or 2nd should also be a complaint with the following:
   a. Plugged or undrilled D-3 oil passage in turbine shaft.
   b. D-3 oil passage not drilled through in overrun clutch hub.
   c. Missing or damaged oil seals in the overrun clutch piston.
   d. Burned overrun clutches.
   e. Overrun clutch backing plate snap ring out of groove.
10. Case porosity.
11. L1/Reverse clutch assembly. No reverse should also be a complaint with any of the following conditions:
   a. Broken or missing piston seals.
   b. Clutch housing snap ring out of case.
   c. Cracked/porous piston or housing.
   d. Missing or damaged cup plug or rubber seal between case and L1/Reverse clutch housing.

NO ENGINE BRAKING IN L2

1. Manual linkage improperly adjusted.
2. Valve body gaskets leaking, damaged, or improperly installed.
3. Leaking or out of position D-2 oil pipe.
4. Plugged D-3 orifice in spacer plate.
5. PT/D-3 check ball 3 improperly positioned or missing.
6. Porous case.
7. Missing or damaged intermediate servo cover to case oil seal ring.
8. Intermediate band off anchor pin.
9. Broken or burned intermediate band.
10. D-3 oil passage not drilled through in overrun clutch hub.
11. Missing or damaged oil seals in the overrun clutch piston.
12. Undrilled or plugged D-3 oil hole in turbine shaft.
13. Burned overrun clutches.
14. Overrun clutch backing plate snap ring out of groove.

NO ENGINE BRAKING IN 3RD GEAR

1. Control valve assembly and spacer plate.
   a. Manual linkage improperly adjusted.
   b. D-3 orifice in spacer plate clogged.
   c. Valve body gaskets damaged, leaking or improperly installed.
   d. PT/D-3 check ball 3 improperly positioned or missing.
2. Turbine shaft and overrun clutch.
   a. D-3 oil passage clogged or undrilled in turbine shaft.
   b. D-3 oil hole not drilled through in overrun clutch hub.
   c. Overrun clutches burned.
   d. Overrun clutch backing plate snap ring out of groove.
   e. Oil seals damaged or missing in clutch piston.
3. Overrun clutch backing plate snap ring out of groove.

NO ENGINE BRAKING IN D

1. Manual linkage improperly adjusted.
2. Plugged D-3 orifice in spacer plate.
3. Leaking, damaged, or incorrectly installed valve body gaskets.
4. PT/D-3 check ball 3 improperly positioned or missing.
5. Undrilled or plugged D-3 oil passage in turbine shaft.
6. D-3 oil hole not drilled through in overrun clutch hub.
7. Missing or damaged oil seals in the overrun clutch piston.
8. Burned overrun clutches.
9. Overrun clutch backing plate snap ring out of groove.

WILL NOT HOLD IN PARK

1. Manual linkage improperly adjusted.
2. Internal linkage.
   a. Parking pawl binding in case.
   b. Damaged actuator rod, spring, or plunger.
   c. Broken parking pawl.
   d. Loose or damaged parking bracket.
   e. Missing or improperly positioned manual shaft to case pin.
3. Inside detent lever and pin assembly.
   a. Loose nut.
   b. Worn or damaged hole in lever.
4. Manual detent roller and spring assembly.
   a. Roller assembly to valve body bolt loose.
   b. Pin or roller damaged, improperly positioned, or missing.

NO PART THROTTLE DOWNSHIFTS

1. Binding throttle valve.
2. Throttle valve limit valve binding.
3. Plugged or undrilled spacer plate hole.
4. Improperly positioned or damaged valve body gaskets.
5. Throttle valve modulator downshift valve stuck.
6. Improperly set throttle valve cable.

NO PART THROTTLE 4-3 DOWNSHIFTS

On selected models with a part throttle passage in the throttle plunger bushing.

1. Throttle plunger bushing passages not open.
2. 3-4 throttle valve bushing passages not open.
3. PT/D-3 check ball 3 incorrectly positioned or missing.
4. Improperly positioned or damaged valve body gaskets.
5. Improperly set throttle valve cable.
6. Throttle valve limit valve binding.

LOW OR HIGH SHIFT POINT

1. Binding or improperly adjusted throttle valve cable.
2. Throttle valve limit valve binding.
3. Throttle valve binding.
4. Throttle valve modulator upshift valve binding.
5. Throttle valve modulator downshift valve binding.
6. Improperly positioned, leaking, or damaged valve body gaskets.
7. Throttle valve plunger binding.
8. 1-2, 2-3, or 3-4 throttle valves binding in bushings.
9. Pressure regulator valve binding.
10. Throttle valve exhaust ball 5 and lifter improperly positioned, unhooked, or missing.
11. Throttle lever and bracket assembly.
   a. Binding, unhooked, or loose at mounting valve body bolt.
   b. Not positioned at the throttle valve plunger bushing pin locator.
12. Broken or missing governor shaft to cover seal ring.
13. Broken or missing governor cover gasket.
14. Porous case.

MAINTENANCE

To check fluid, drive vehicle for at least 15 minutes to bring fluid to operating temperature (200° F). With vehicle on a level surface and engine idling in Park and parking brake applied, the level on the dipstick should be at the "F" mark. To bring the fluid level from the ADD mark to the FULL mark requires 1 pint of fluid. If vehicle cannot be driven sufficiently to bring fluid to operating temperature, the level on the dipstick should be between the two dimples on the dipstick with fluid temperature at 70° F.

If additional fluid is required, use only Dexron II automatic transmission fluid.

An early change to a darker color from the usual red color and or a strong odor that is usually associated with overheated fluid is normal and should not be considered as a positive sign of required maintenance of unit failure.

When adding fluid, do not overfill, as foaming and loss of fluid through the vent may occur as the fluid heats up. Also, if fluid level is too low, complete loss of drive may occur especially when cold, which can cause transmission failure.

Every 100,000 miles, the oil should be drained, the oil pan removed, the screen cleaned and fresh fluid added. For vehicles subjected to more severe use such as heavy city traffic especially in hot weather, prolonged periods of idling or towing, this maintenance should be performed every 15,000 miles.

DRAINING BOTTOM PAN

1. Remove front and side oil pan attaching bolts, then loosen the rear oil pan attaching bolts.
2. Carefully pry oil pan loose and allow fluid to drain into a suitable container.
3. Remove the oil pan and gasket, then remove the screen attaching bolts and remove screen.
4. Thoroughly clean oil screen and oil pan with solvent.
5. Install oil screen using a new gasket, then install oil pan using a new gasket

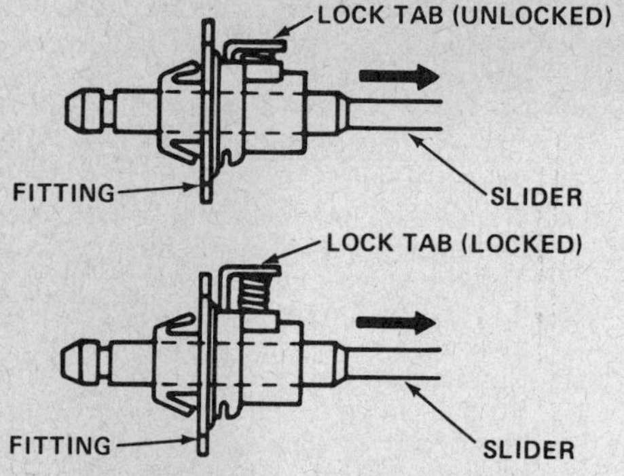

Fig. 2 Self adjusting throttle valve linkage

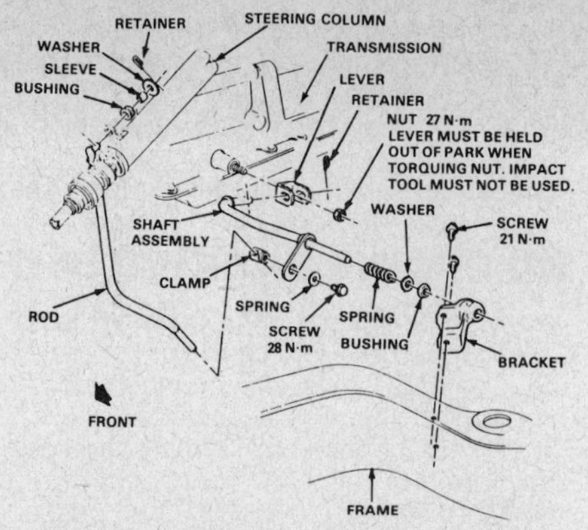

Fig. 3 Column mounted shift linkage adjustment

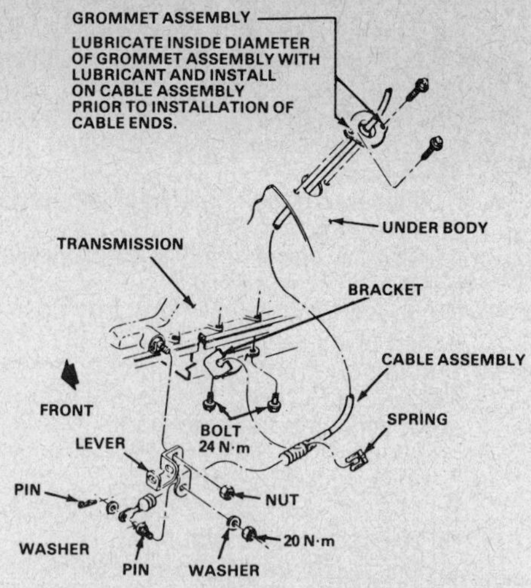

Fig. 4 Console mounted shift linkage adjustment

and torque attaching bolts to 10-13 ft. lbs.

6. Add approximately 3 quarts of fluid, then with engine idling and parking brake applied, move selector lever through each range and return selector lever to PARK.
7. Check fluid level and add fluid as required to bring level between the two dimples on the dipstick.

IN-VEHICLE ADJUSTMENTS

THROTTLE VALVE LINKAGE, ADJUST

Models Equipped With Diesel Engine

1. Remove cruise control rod on vehicles equipped with cruise control.
2. Disconnect throttle valve linkage from throttle assembly.
3. Loosen locknut on pump rod, then shorten rod by rotating several turns.
4. Rotate throttle lever assembly to full throttle position and secure in this position.
5. Lengthen pump rod by rotating in opposite direction as described in step 3 until injection pump lever contacts full throttle stop.
6. Release throttle lever assembly and tighten pump rod locknut.
7. Disconnect pump rod from throttle lever assembly.
8. Connect throttle valve linkage to throttle assembly.
9. Depress metal locking tab on upper end of cable and hold in this position.
10. Position slider through fitting and away from lever assembly until slider contacts metal fitting.
11. Release metal tab, then rotate throttle lever assembly to full throttle position and release.
12. Connect pump rod to lever assembly, then connect cruise control throttle rod, if equipped.
13. On models equipped with cruise control, adjust servo throttle rod until minimum amount of slack is present. Install clip into first hole closest to bellcrank that is within servo bail.

Models Equipped With Gasoline Engine, Manual Type Linkage

1. With engine off, disconnect throttle valve linkage retaining lock.
2. Rotate throttle lever to wide open position and hold in this position.
3. Connect throttle valve linkage retaining lock.

Self Adjusting Linkage, All Models

1. With engine off, depress locking tab and move slider rearward through fitting until slider contacts fitting, **Fig. 2.**
2. Release locking tab, then move carburetor throttle lever to wide open position and release.
3. Check cable for sticking or binding, then test vehicle for proper operation.
4. If transmission does not shift properly, raise and support vehicle and remove transmission oil pan. Inspect throttle lever and bracket assembly on valve body for damage. Check to ensure that throttle valve exhaust valve rod is not worn or damaged. Check to ensure that lifter spring holds lifter rod against bottom of valve body and that throttle valve plunger is not sticking.

MANUAL LINKAGE, ADJUST

Column Mounted

1. Position transmission shift lever in Neutral.
2. Position transmission manual valve lever in Neutral detent.
3. With clamp spring washer and screw assembled onto equalizer lever and control rod, hold clamp against equalizer lever, then snug tighten clamp screw against control rod, **Fig. 3.**

Console Mounted

1. Position console shift lever in Park position.
2. Position transmission manual valve lever in Park detent.
3. Position pin, **Fig. 4,** until pin fits loosely in transmission lever, then tighten attaching nut.

IN-VEHICLE REPAIRS

INTERMEDIATE SERVO, REPLACE

1. Remove intermediate servo cover retaining ring, using a small screwdriver.
2. Remove servo cover and discard seal ring.
3. Remove servo piston and band apply pin assembly.
4. Reverse procedure to install.

SPEEDOMETER DRIVEN GEAR, REPLACE

1. Disconnect speedometer cable.
2. Remove bolt, retainer, speedometer driven gear and the O-ring seal.
3. Reverse procedure to install.

REAR OIL SEAL, REPLACE

1. Remove propeller shaft.
2. Pry seal from extension housing with a suitable tool.
3. Drive new oil seal into extension housing, using a suitable tool.
4. Install propeller shaft.

VALVE BODY, REPLACE

1. Drain transmission oil pan.
2. Remove oil pan and filter.
3. Remove screw and washer securing T.V. cable to transmission and disconnect the cable.
4. Remove throttle lever and bracket assembly. Use caution not to bend throttle lever link.
5. Disconnect electrical connectors at the 4-3 pressure switch and the 4th clutch pressure switch.
6. Remove solenoid attaching bolts, clips and solenoid assembly.
7. Remove manual detent roller and spring assembly.
8. Remove valve body retaining bolts while supporting valve body. Secure manual valve and remove valve body. Use caution not to lose the three check balls.
9. Reverse procedure to install. Torque valve body bolts to 12 ft. lbs.

1-2 & 3-4 ACCUMULATOR, REPLACE

1. Remove valve body.
2. While supporting 1-2 accumulator housing, remove housing retaining bolts. Then, remove housing and gasket.
3. Support valve body spacer plate, gaskets and accumulator plate to prevent loss of the eight check balls and the 3-4 accumulator spring piston and pin located in the case. Remove remaining retaining bolt on accumulator plate. **The intermediate band anchor pin may become dislodged after removing spacer plate and gaskets.**
4. Reverse procedure to install.

GOVERNOR, REPLACE

1. Drain transmission oil pan.
2. Remove oil pan and filter.
3. Remove governor attaching bolts, cover and gasket. The governor may come out with the cover. Also, it may be necessary to rotate output shaft counterclockwise while removing governor.
4. Reverse procedure to install.

TRANSMISSION

REPLACE

1. Disconnect battery ground cable and remove air cleaner.
2. Disconnect throttle valve cable from carburetor.
3. Remove transmission oil level dipstick. Remove upper bolt on dipstick tube.
4. Raise and support vehicle.
5. Mark driveshaft and companion flange for reference during installation, then remove driveshaft.
6. Disconnect speedometer cable and manual shift linkage from transmission.
7. Disconnect torque converter clutch solenoid electrical connector.
8. Remove flywheel under cover. Mark flywheel and converter for reference during installation. Remove three flywheel to converter attaching bolts.
9. Remove catalytic converter support bracket bolts and the tunnel strap.
10. Remove transmission crossmember to transmission mount bolts. Remove transmission crossmember to frame bolts.
11. Support transmission with suitable jack, then move crossmember rearward.
12. Lower transmission slightly and disconnect throttle valve cable and oil cooler lines.
13. Support engine with suitable jack, then remove engine to transmission mounting bolts.
14. Lower jack and remove transmission from vehicle. Use caution not to drop torque converter as transmission is removed. Install suitable converter holding tool to secure converter.
15. Reverse procedure to install noting the following:
    a. Torque converter to flexplate bolts to 46 ft. lbs. (62 Nm).
    b. Adjust T.V. cable and linkage.

Turbo Hydra-Matic 250C, 350C Automatic Transmission

INDEX

IDENTIFICATION

A production day and shift built number, transmission model and model year are stamped on the 1-2 accumulator cover, which is located on the middle lower right side of the transmission case.

DESCRIPTION

The Turbo Hydra-Matic 250C & 350C, **Fig. 1**, are fully automatic three-speed transmissions consisting of a four-element torque converter and two compound planetary gear sets. The Turbo Hydra-Matic 350C transmission has four multiple-disc clutches, two roller clutches and a band to provide the required friction elements to obtain the desired function of the planetary gear set. The Turbo Hydra-Matic 250C transmission uses an adjustable intermediate band in place of the intermediate clutch found in the Turbo Hydra-Matic 350C. Also, the Turbo Hydra-Matic 250C has three multiple-disc clutches and one roller clutch.

The friction elements couple the engine to the planetary gears through oil pressure, providing three forward speeds and one reverse.

The four-element torque converter is of welded construction and is serviced as an assembly. The unit consists of a pump or a turbine, a stator assembly, and converter clutch, **Fig. 2.** When required, the torque converter supplements the gears by multiplying engine torque. The converter clutch

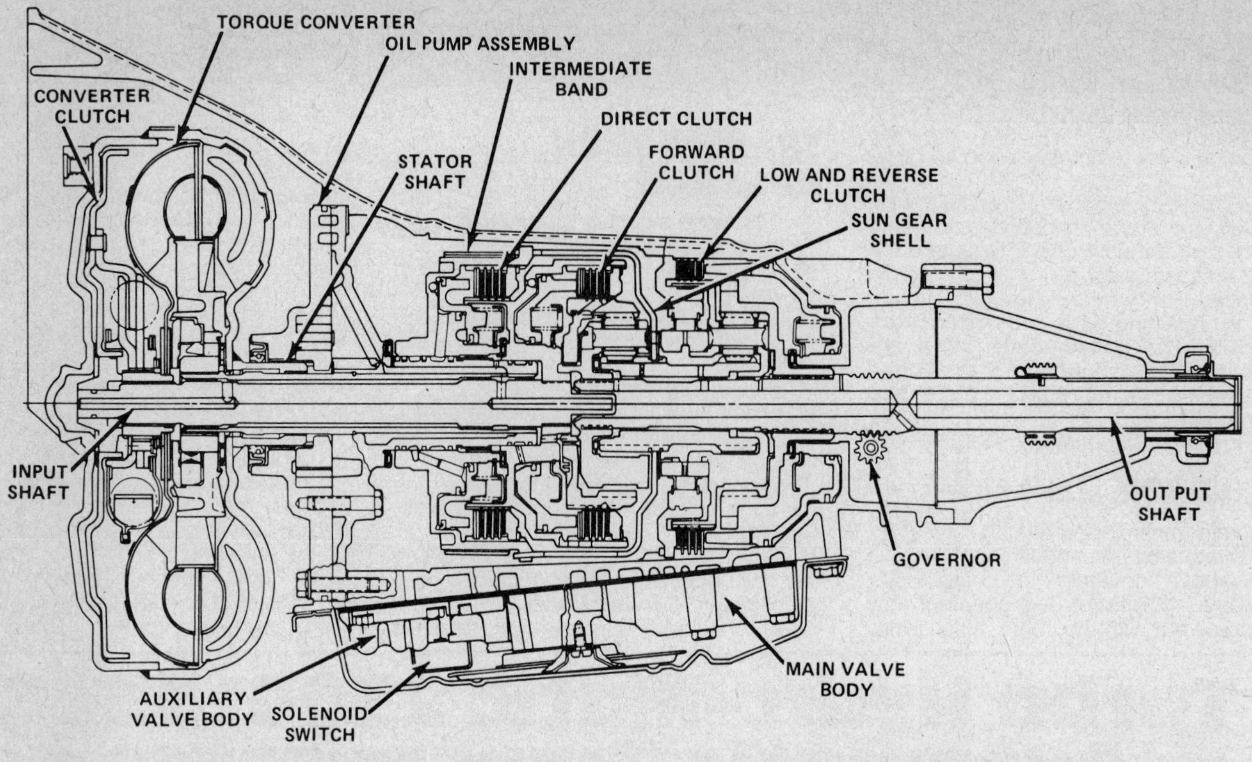

Fig. 1 Typical cross sectional view of Turbo Hydra-Matic transmission. (250C)

assembly consists of a three element torque converter with a converter clutch. The converter clutch is splined to the turbine assembly and, when operated, applies against the converter cover, providing a mechanical direct drive coupling of the engine to the planetary gears. When the converter clutch is released the assembly operates as a normal torque converter.

TROUBLESHOOTING

NO DRIVE IN DRIVE RANGE

1. Low oil level (check for leaks).
2. Manual control linkage improperly adjusted.
3. Low oil pressure due to blocked strainer, defective pressure regulator, pump assembly or pump drive gear. See that tangs have not been damaged by converter. Check case for porosity in intake bore.
4. Check control valve assembly to be sure manual valve has not been disconnected from inner lever.
5. Forward clutch may be stuck or damaged. Check pump feed circuits to forward clutch, including clutch drum ball check.
6. Roller clutch assembly broken or damaged.

OIL PRESSURE HIGH OR LOW

High Pressure

1. Vacuum line or fittings leaking.
2. Vacuum modulator.
3. Modulator valve.
4. Pressure regulator.
5. Oil pump.

Low Pressure

1. Vacuum line or fittings obstructed.
2. Vacuum modulator.
3. Modulator valve.
4. Pressure regulator.
5. Governor.
6. Oil pump.

1-2 SHIFT AT FULL THROTTLE ONLY

1. Detent valve may be sticking or linkage may be improperly adjusted.
2. Vacuum line or fittings leaking.
3. Control valve body gaskets leaking, damaged or incorrectly installed. Detent valve train or 1-2 valve stuck.
4. Check case for porosity.

FIRST SPEED ONLY, NO 1-2 SHIFT

T.H.M. 250C & 350C

1. Governor valve may be sticking.
2. Driven gear in governor assembly loose, worn or damaged. If driven gear shows damage, check output shaft drive gear for nicks or rough finish.
3. Control valve governor feed channel blocked or gaskets leaking. 1-2 shift valve train stuck closed.
4. Check case for blocked governor feed channels or for scored governor bore which will allow cross pressure leak. Check case for porosity.
5. Intermediate clutch or seals damaged.
6. Intermediate roller clutch damaged.

T.H.M. 250C

1. Intermediate servo piston seals damaged, missing or installed improperly.
2. Intermediate band improperly adjusted.
3. Intermediate servo apply rod broken.

1ST & 2ND ONLY, NO 2-3 SHIFT

1. Control valve 2-3 shift train stuck. Valve body gaskets leaking, damaged or improperly installed.
2. Pump hub-to-direct clutch oil seal rings broken or missing.
3. Direct clutch piston seals damaged. Piston ball check stuck or missing.

NO FIRST SPEED

T.H.M. 250C

1. Intermediate band adjusted too tightly.
2. 1-2 shift valve stuck in upshift position.

T.H.M. 350C

1. Excessive number of clutch plates in intermediate clutch pack.
2. Incorrect intermediate clutch piston.

MOVES FORWARD IN NEUTRAL

1. Manual linkage improperly adjusted.
2. Forward clutch not releasing.

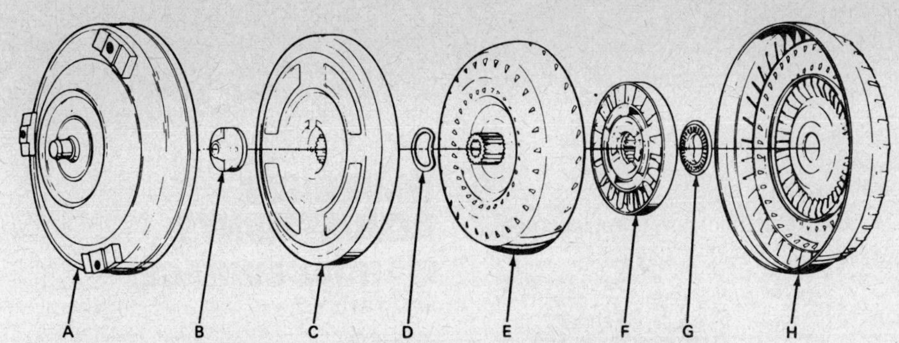

Fig. 2 Torque converter clutch

3. Internal linkage manual valve disconnected or end broken.

NO FORWARD OR REVERSE OPERATION

1. Fatigue failure of forward clutch housing due to excessive pinion pin runout in output carrier.

NO DRIVE IN REVERSE OR SLIPS IN REVERSE

1. Low oil level.
2. Manual linkage improperly adjusted.
3. Modulator valve stuck.
4. Modulator and reverse boost valve stuck.
5. Pump hub-to-direct clutch oil seal rings broken or missing.
6. Direct clutch piston seal cut or missing.
7. Low and reverse clutch piston seal cut or missing.
8. Number 1 check ball missing.
9. Control valve body gaskets leaking or damaged.
10. 2-3 valve train stuck in upshifted position.
11. 1-2 valve train stuck in upshifted position.
12. Intermediate servo piston or pin stuck so intermediate band is applied.
13. Low and reverse clutch piston out or seal damaged.
14. Direct clutch plates burned—may be caused by stuck ball check in piston.
15. Forward clutch not releasing.

SLIPS IN ALL RANGES

1. Low oil level.
2. Vacuum modulator valve defective or sticking.
3. Filter assembly plugged or leaking.
4. Pressure regulator valve stuck.
5. Pump to case gasket damaged.
6. Check case for cross leaks or porosity.
7. Forward clutch slipping.

SLIPS 1-2 SHIFT

T.H.M. 250C & 350C

1. Low oil level.
2. Vacuum modulator assembly defective.
3. Modulator valve sticking.
4. Pump pressure regulator valve defective.
5. 1-2 accumulator oil ring damaged or missing. Case bore damaged.
6. Pump to case gasket mispositioned or damaged.
7. Check for case porosity.
8. Intermediate clutch piston seals damaged. Clutch plates burned.

T.H.M. 250C

1. Intermediate servo piston seals damaged ormissing.
2. Burned intermediate band.

T.H.M. 350C

1. 2-3 accumulator oil ring damaged or missing.

ROUGH 1-2 SHIFT

T.H.M. 250C & 350C

1. Vacuum modulator, check for loose fittings, restrictions in line or defective modulator assembly.
2. Modulator valve stuck.
3. Valve body regulator or boost valve stuck.
4. Pump to case gasket mispositioned or damaged.
5. Check case for porosity.
6. Check 1-2 accumulator assembly for damaged oil rings, stuck piston, broken or missing spring, or damaged case bore.

T.H.M. 250C

1. Intermediate band improperly adjusted.
2. Improper or broken servo spring.

T.H.M. 350C

1. Burned intermediate clutch plates.
2. Improper number of intermediate clutch plates.

SLIPS 2-3 SHIFT

1. Low oil level.
2. Modulator valve or vacuum modulator assembly defective.
3. Pump pressure regulator valve or boost valve; pump to case gasket mispositioned.
4. Check case for porosity.
5. Direct clutch piston seals or ball check leaking.

ROUGH 2-3 SHIFT

1. High oil pressure. Vacuum leak, modulator valve sticking or pressure regulator or boost valve inoperative.
2. 2-3 accumulator piston stuck, spring broken or missing.

NO ENGINE BRAKING IN 2ND SPEED

1. Intermediate servo or 2-3 accumulator oil rings or bores leaking or accumulator piston stuck.
2. Intermediate band burned or broken.
3. Low oil pressure: Pressure regulator and/or boost valve stuck.

NO ENGINE BRAKING IN 1ST SPEED

1. Manual low control valve assembly stuck.
2. Low oil pressure: Pressure regulator and/or boost valve stuck.
3. Low and reverse clutch piston inner seal damaged.

NO PART THROTTLE DOWNSHIFT

1. Oil pressure: Vacuum modulator assembly, modulator valve or pressure regulator valve train malfunctioning.
2. Detent valve and linkage sticking, disconnected or broken.
3. 2-3 shift valve stuck.

NO DETENT DOWNSHIFTS

1. 2-3 valve stuck.
2. Detent valve and linkage sticking, disconnected or broken.

LOW OR HIGH SHIFT POINTS

1. Oil pressure: Check engine vacuum at transmission end of modulator pipe.
2. Vacuum modulator assembly, vacuum line connections at engine and transmission, modulator valve, pressure regulator valve train.
3. Check governor for sticking valve, restricted or leaking feed holes, damaged pipes or plugged feed line.
4. Detent valve stuck open.
5. 1-2 or 2-3 valve train sticking.
6. Check case for porosity.

NO HOLD IN PARK

1. Manual linkage improperly adjusted.
2. Parking brake lever and actuator assembly defective.
3. Parking pawl broken or inoperative.
4. Defective or improperly installed inner lever and actuating rod assembly.
5. Parking lock bracket loose, burred or rough edges, or improperly installed.
6. Parking pawl disengaging spring missing, broken or installed improperly.

BURNED FORWARD CLUTCH PLATES

1. Check ball in clutch drum damaged, stuck or missing.
2. Clutch piston cracked, seals damaged or missing.
3. Low line pressure.
4. Pump cover oil seal rings missing, broken or undersize; ring groove oversize.
5. Transmission case valve body face not flat or porosity between channels.

BURNED INTERMEDIATE CLUTCH PLATES

T.H.M. 350C

1. Intermediate clutch piston seals damaged or missing.
2. Low line pressure.
3. Transmission case valve body face not flat or porosity between channels.

BURNED INTERMEDIATE BAND

T.H.M. 250C

1. Intermediate servo piston seals damaged or missing.
2. Low line pressure.
3. Transmission case valve body face not flat or porosity between channels.

BURNED DIRECT CLUTCH PLATES

1. Restricted orifice in vacuum line to modulator.
2. Check ball in clutch drum damaged, stuck or missing.
3. Defective modulator.
4. Clutch piston cracked, seals damaged or missing.
5. Transmission case valve body face not flat or porosity between channels.

NOISY TRANSMISSION

Before checking transmission for noise, ensure noise is not coming from water pump, alternator or any belt driven accessory.

Park, Neutral & All Driving Ranges

1. Low fluid level.
2. Plugged or restricted screen.
3. Damaged screen to valve body gasket.
4. Porosity in valve body intake area.
5. Transmission fluid contaminated with water.
6. Porosity at transmission case intake port.
7. Improperly installed case to pump gasket.
8. Pump gears damaged.
9. Driving gear assembled backwards.
10. Crescent interference in pump.
11. Damaged or worn pump oil seals.
12. Loose converter to flywheel bolts.
13. Damaged converter.

1st, 2nd And/Or Reverse Gear

1. Planetary gears or thrust bearings damaged.
2. Damaged input or output ring gear.

Acceleration In Any Gear

1. Transmission case or transmission oil cooler lines contacting underbody.
2. Broken or loose engine mounts.

Squeal At Low Vehicle Speed

1. Speedometer driven gear shaft seal requires lubrication or replacement.

CONVERTER CLUTCH APPLIED IN ALL RANGES, ENGINE STALLS WHEN TRANSMISSION PUT IN GEAR

1. Converter clutch apply valve in auxiliary valve body stuck in apply position.

CONVERTER CLUTCH APPLIES ERRATICALLY

1. Vacuum hose leak.
2. Vacuum switch malfunction.
3. Release oil orifice at pump blocked or restricted.
4. Turbine shaft O-ring damaged or missing.
5. Converter malfunction, clutch pressure plate warped, etc.
6. O-ring at solenoid damaged or missing.
7. Solenoid bolts loose.

CONVERTER CLUTCH APPLIES AT VERY LOW OR VERY HIGH 3RD GEAR SPEEDS

1. Governor switch malfunction.
2. Governor malfunction.
3. High line pressures.
4. Converter clutch valve sticking or binding.
5. Solenoid malfunction.

CONVERTER CLUTCH APPLIED AT ALL TIMES IN 3RD GEAR

1. Governor pressure switch shorted to ground.
2. Ground wire from solenoid shorted to case.

MAINTENANCE

Fluid should be checked every 6,000 miles with engine idling, selector lever in neutral position, parking brake set and transmission at operating temperature. Use only General Motors Dexron transmission fluid when adding oil. Do not overfill.

Every 100,000 miles, remove drain plug, then drain transmission oil sump. Add $2^1/_2$ quarts on vehicles equipped with THM 250C units and 3 quarts on vehicles equipped with THM 350C units. After replacing plug, check fluid and add enough fluid to bring level to $^1/_2$ inch below Add mark.

A revised type Dexron fluid is used in these transmissions. An early change to a darker color from the usual red color and or a strong odor that is usually associated with overheated fluid is normal, and should not be treated as a positive sign of needed maintenance or failure.

The normal maintenance schedule for drain and refill of this type fluid is every 15,000 miles under severe operating conditions, such as trailer towing. Under normal operating conditions, drain and refill every 100,000 miles.

IN-VEHICLE ADJUSTMENTS

MANUAL LINKAGE, ADJUST

BUICK

Console Shift

1. Place selector lever in Park position.
2. Place transmission lever in Park position.
3. Position pin to obtain a free pin fit in the transmission lever and torque nut to 15-25 ft. lbs.
4. Check for proper operation.

Column Shift

Refer to **Fig. 3** for procedure.

CADILLAC

Refer to **Fig. 3** for procedure.

CHEVROLET

Console Shift

1. Loosen swivel screw so rod is free to move in swivel, **Fig. 4.**
2. Place transmission control lever in Drive and loosen pin in transmission lever, so it moves in the slot.
3. Move transmission lever counterclockwise to L1 detent and then three detents clockwise to Drive position. Tighten nut on transmission lever to 20 ft. lbs.
4. Place transmission control lever in Park and ignition switch in the Lock position and pull lightly against lock stop, then tighten swivel screw to 20 ft. lbs. Check for proper operation.

Column Shift

Refer to **Fig. 3** for procedure.

OLDSMOBILE

Console Shift

1. Loosen shift rod clamp screw and pin in transmission manual lever. Place shift handle and transmission manual lever in Park position.
2. With rod held lightly against Park stop, tighten screw in clamp at lower end of shift rod.
3. Move pin to give "free pin" fit in manual lever and tighten nut.

Column Shift

Refer to **Fig. 3** for procedure.

PONTIAC

Console Shift

1. Disconnect shift cable at transmission lever.
2. Adjust back drive, as outlined under "Back Drive, Adjust" procedure.
3. Unlock ignition switch, move transmission lever two detents counter-

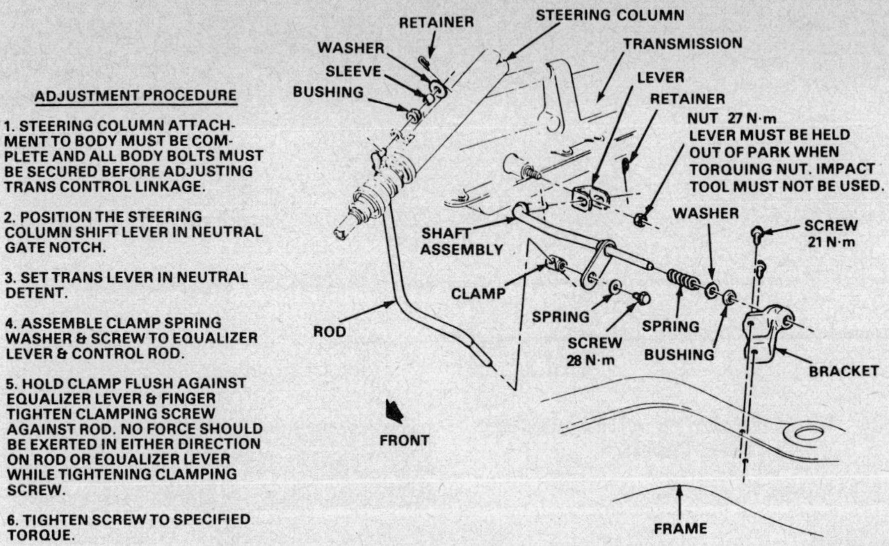
ADJUSTMENT PROCEDURE
1. STEERING COLUMN ATTACHMENT TO BODY MUST BE COMPLETE AND ALL BODY BOLTS MUST BE SECURED BEFORE ADJUSTING TRANS CONTROL LINKAGE.
2. POSITION THE STEERING COLUMN SHIFT LEVER IN NEUTRAL GATE NOTCH.
3. SET TRANS LEVER IN NEUTRAL DETENT.
4. ASSEMBLE CLAMP SPRING WASHER & SCREW TO EQUALIZER LEVER & CONTROL ROD.
5. HOLD CLAMP FLUSH AGAINST EQUALIZER LEVER & FINGER TIGHTEN CLAMPING SCREW AGAINST ROD. NO FORCE SHOULD BE EXERTED IN EITHER DIRECTION ON ROD OR EQUALIZER LEVER WHILE TIGHTENING CLAMPING SCREW.
6. TIGHTEN SCREW TO SPECIFIED TORQUE.
RETAINER
STEERING COLUMN
WASHER
SLEEVE
BUSHING
TRANSMISSION
LEVER
RETAINER
NUT 27 N·m
LEVER MUST BE HELD OUT OF PARK WHEN TORQUING NUT. IMPACT TOOL MUST NOT BE USED.
WASHER
SHAFT ASSEMBLY
SCREW 21 N·m
CLAMP
SPRING
SPRING
SCREW 28 N·m
BUSHING
BRACKET
ROD
FRONT
FRAME

Fig. 3 Column shift linkage

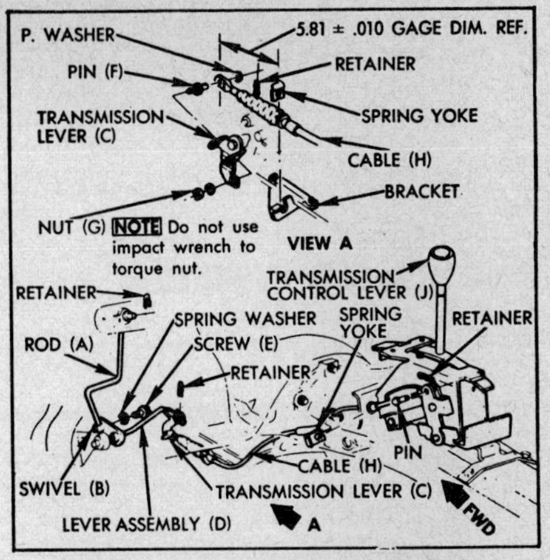
P. WASHER
5.81 ± .010 GAGE DIM. REF.
PIN (F)
RETAINER
TRANSMISSION LEVER (C)
SPRING YOKE
CABLE (H)
BRACKET
NUT (G) NOTE Do not use impact wrench to torque nut.
VIEW A
RETAINER
TRANSMISSION CONTROL LEVER (J)
SPRING WASHER
SPRING YOKE
RETAINER
ROD (A)
SCREW (E)
RETAINER
PIN
CABLE (H)
SWIVEL (B)
TRANSMISSION LEVER (C)
LEVER ASSEMBLY (D)
A
FWD

Fig. 4 Manual linkage adjustment. Camaro, Malibu & Monte Carlo

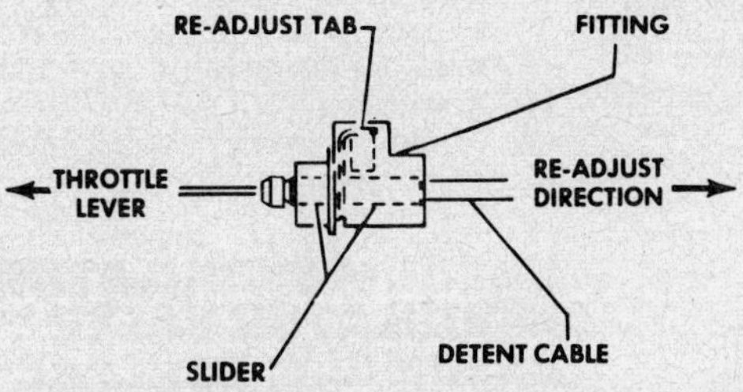
RE-ADJUST TAB
FITTING
THROTTLE LEVER
RE-ADJUST DIRECTION
SLIDER
DETENT CABLE

Fig. 5 Self adjusting throttle valve cable

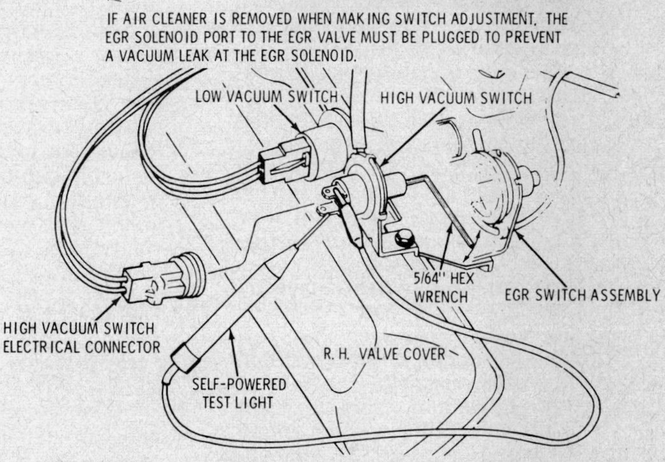
IF AIR CLEANER IS REMOVED WHEN MAKING SWITCH ADJUSTMENT, THE EGR SOLENOID PORT TO THE EGR VALVE MUST BE PLUGGED TO PREVENT A VACUUM LEAK AT THE EGR SOLENOID.
LOW VACUUM SWITCH
HIGH VACUUM SWITCH
5/64" HEX WRENCH
EGR SWITCH ASSEMBLY
HIGH VACUUM SWITCH ELECTRICAL CONNECTOR
R. H. VALVE COVER
SELF-POWERED TEST LIGHT

Fig. 6 Vacuum switch location

clockwise, then place transmission shift lever against Neutral stop.

4. Assemble cable to transmission lever, torque nut to 20 ft. lbs.

Column Shift

Refer to **Fig. 3** for procedure.

STEERING COLUMN LOCK BACK DRIVE, ADJUST

The steering column back drive is used on models equipped with console shift only.

1. Disconnect lower rod at transmission lever.
2. Move transmission lever to Park position.
3. Place transmission selector lever in Park position.
4. Attach lower rod to transmission lever and check for proper operation. **Any inaccuracies in the above adjustments may result in premature failure of the transmission due to operation without the controls in full detent. Such operation results in reduced oil pressure and in turn partial engagement of the affected clutches.**

T.V./DETENT CABLE, ADJUST

Models Equipped With Diesel Engine

1. Remove cruise control rod on vehicles equipped with cruise control.
2. Disconnect throttle valve linkage from throttle assembly.
3. Loosen locknut on pump rod, then shorten rod by rotating several turns.
4. Rotate throttle lever assembly to full throttle position and secure in this position.
5. Lengthen pump rod by rotating in opposite direction as described in step 3 until injection pump lever contacts full throttle stop.
6. Release throttle lever assembly and tighten pump rod locknut.
7. Disconnect pump rod from throttle lever assembly.
8. Connect throttle valve linkage to throttle assembly.
9. Depress metal locking tab on upper end of cable and hold in this position.
10. Position slider through fitting and away from lever assembly until slider contacts metal fitting.
11. Release metal tab, then rotate throttle lever assembly to full throttle position and release.
12. Connect pump rod to lever assembly, then connect cruise control throttle rod, if equipped.
13. On models equipped with cruise control, adjust servo throttle rod until minimum amount of slack is present. Install clip into first hole closest to bellcrank that is within servo bail.

Models Equipped With Gasoline Engine

1. With engine off, depress locking tab and move slider rearward through fitting until slider contacts fitting, **Fig. 5.**
2. Release locking tab, then move carburetor throttle lever to wide open position and release.
3. Check cable for sticking or binding, then test vehicle for proper operation.
4. If transmission does not shift properly, raise and support vehicle and remove transmission oil pan. Inspect throttle lever and bracket assembly on valve body for damage. Check to ensure that throttle valve exhaust valve rod is not worn or damaged. Check to ensure that lifter spring holds lifter rod against bottom of valve body and that throttle valve plunger is not sticking.

INTERMEDIATE BAND, ADJUST

T.H.M. 250C

Since the Turbo Hydra-Matic 250C transmission uses an intermediate band instead of a clutch (used in the Turbo Hydra-Matic 350 transmission) to control the operation of the planetary gear sets, it is necessary to adjust the intermediate band as follows:

1. Loosen adjusting screw locknut, located on case right side, 1/2 turn.
2. Torque adjusting screw to 30 inch pounds, then back off screw 3 turns.
3. Torque adjusting screw locknut to 15 foot pounds while holding adjusting screw in position.

TORQUE CONVERTER CLUTCH SWITCH ADJUSTMENTS

Low Vacuum Switch

1. Disconnect vacuum and electrical connectors from low vacuum switch, **Fig. 6.**
2. Connect a suitable test light to either terminal of vacuum switch. Connect a suitable jumper cable from the other terminal to a good ground.
3. Connect remaining lead of test light to power side of removed vacuum switch connector.
4. Attach suitable vacuum pump to vacuum port of switch.
5. Turn ignition on, then actuate vacuum pump. On V6-231, 252 engines, test light should remain off until vacuum pump gauge reads 5.5-6.5 in. Hg. On V8-265, 301 engines the test light should remain off until vacuum gauge reads 6.5-7.5 in. Hg. On V8-350 gas engines, test light should remain off until vacuum gauge reads 7.5-8.5 in. Hg. On V8-350 diesel engines, test light should remain off until vacuum gauge reads 5-6 in. Hg.
6. Decrease vacuum slowly. Light should remain on until vacuum drops to .3-1.3 in. Hg on V6-231, 252 engines, 1.2-2.2 in. Hg on V8-265, 301 engines, 1.5-2.5 in. Hg on V8-350 gas engines and 3.5-4.5 in. Hg on V8-350 diesel engines. Decreasing vacuum beyond above values should cause light to go out.
7. If above results cannot be obtained, switch is defective and must be replaced.
8. The point at which light comes on and the point at which light goes out must have at least 4 in. of vacuum difference.

High Vacuum Switch

The high vacuum switch must be adjusted anytime the throttle rod, transmission vacuum valve and high idle speed adjustments are changed.

1. Disconnect high vacuum switch electrical connector, **Fig. 6.**
2. Connect the leads of a suitable test light across the terminals of the high vacuum switch.
3. Energize fast idle solenoid by disconnecting pink and green wire from coolant switch and operate engine at high idle speed, then remove cap from back of high vacuum switch.
4. Before adjustment is performed, the test light must be on, indicating that the switch contacts are closed. If test light is off, close the switch contacts by turning switch adjusting screw clockwise until contacts close.

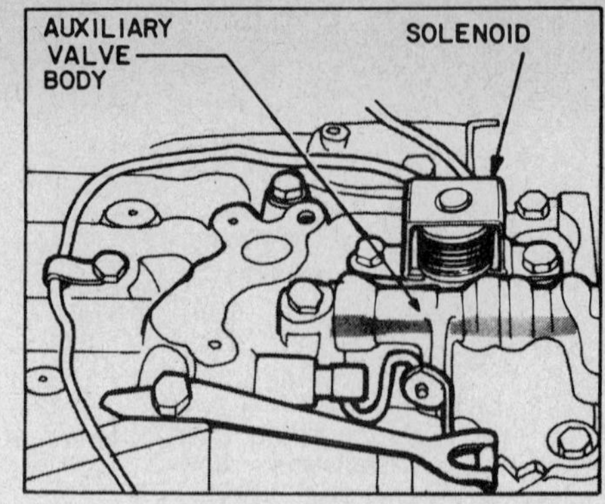

Fig. 7 Auxiliary valve body solenoid

5. Adjust vacuum switch by turning adjusting screw counterclockwise until switch contact just opens and test light goes off. Turn adjusting screw counterclockwise an additional 1/8-3/16 turn.
6. Reinstall cap on back of vacuum switch and reconnect high vacuum switch and coolant switch electrical connectors.

IN-VEHICLE REPAIRS

VALVE BODY ASSEMBLY, REPLACE

1. Remove oil pan and filter.
2. Remove detent roller spring assembly from valve body, then disconnect solenoid wires from governor pressure switch and case electrical connector.
3. Remove solenoid attaching bolts, then the solenoid.
4. Remove manual shaft retaining clip and slide manual shaft outward.
5. Remove valve body attaching bolts, then the valve body.
6. Remove auxiliary valve body attaching bolts, then the auxiliary valve body from the valve body.
7. Reverse procedure to install.

AUXILIARY VALVE BODY & SOLENOID, REPLACE

1. Remove oil pan and filter.
2. Remove solenoid wire clip, then disconnect solenoid electrical connectors.
3. Remove two solenoid attaching bolts, then the solenoid, **Fig. 7.**
4. Reverse procedure to install.

AUXILIARY VALVE BODY & VALVE, REPLACE

1. Remove solenoid as outlined above.
2. Remove retaining bolts, then the auxiliary valve body.
3. Remove apply valve retaining pin, retainer, spring, then the apply valve, **Fig. 8.**
4. Reverse procedure to install.

GOVERNOR PRESSURE SWITCH, REPLACE

1. Drain transmission fluid from pan, then remove pan.
2. Disconnect electrical connector from switch, then remove switch using suitable socket.
3. Reverse procedure to install.

GOVERNOR, REPLACE

1. Remove governor cover retainer and cover.
2. Remove governor.

INTERMEDIATE CLUTCH ACCUMULATOR PISTON ASSEMBLY, REPLACE

1. Remove two oil pan bolts adjacent to accumulator piston cover, install compressor on pan lip and retain with these two bolts, **Fig. 9.**
2. Compress intermediate clutch accumulator piston cover and remove retaining ring piston cover and O-ring from case.
3. Remove spring and intermediate clutch accumulator piston.

VACUUM MODULATOR & MODULATOR VALVE ASSEMBLY, REPLACE

1. Disconnect vacuum hose from modulator stem and remove vacuum modulator screw and retainer.
2. Remove modulator and its O-ring.
3. Remove modulator valve from case.

EXTENSION HOUSING OIL SEAL, REPLACE

1. Remove propeller shaft.
2. Pry out lip seal with screwdriver or small chisel.

MANUAL SHAFT, RANGE SELECTOR INNER LEVER & PARKING LINKAGE ASSEMBLIES, REPLACE

1. Remove oil pan and strainer.
2. Remove manual shaft to case retainer and loosen jam nut holding range selector inner lever to manual shaft.
3. Remove jam nut and remove manual shaft from range selector inner lever and case. Do not remove manual shaft lip seal unless replacement is required.
4. Disconnect parking pawl actuating rod from range selector inner lever and remove bolt from case.
5. Remove bolts and parking lock bracket.
6. Remove pawl disengaging spring.
7. If necessary to replace pawl or shaft, clean up bore in case and remove shaft retaining plug, shaft and pawl.

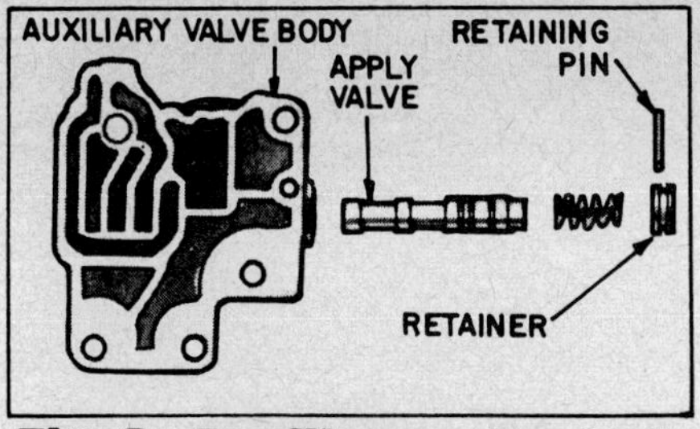

Fig. 8 Auxiliary valve body & valve

TRANSMISSION REPLACE

BUICK

1. Disconnect battery ground cable.
2. Raise car and remove propeller shaft. If necessary, disconnect exhaust crossover pipe. On Turbo 350 units, remove catalytic converter support bracket, if equipped.
3. Place suitable jack under transmission and fasten transmission securely to jack.
4. Remove vacuum line from vacuum modulator.
5. Loosen cooler line nuts and separate cooler lines from transmission.
6. Remove detent cable from accelerator or carburetor lever assembly. Do not bend cable. Remove plastic guide from bracket and slide cable out through slot.
7. Remove detent cable from detent valve link.
8. Remove crossmember.
9. Disconnect speedometer cable, shift linkage and filler pipe. Remove filler pipe.
10. Support engine at oil pan.
11. Remove transmission flywheel cover pan.
12. Mark flywheel and converter for reassembly and remove three flywheel to converter bolts.
13. Be sure transmission is supported by transmission jack and remove transmission case to engine block bolts.
14. Move transmission rearward to provide clearance between converter and crankshaft. Install converter holding tool, lower transmission and remove.

CADILLAC

1. Disconnect negative battery cable and disconnect detent cable at upper end, then remove top two transmission to engine bolts.
2. Raise and support vehicle.
3. Disconnect transmission linkage and remove speedometer drive cable at transmission, then, using suitable tools, disconnect oil cooler lines at transmission and cap lines and plug connector holes. Move oil cooler lines aside.
4. Disconnect vacuum pipe hose from modulator and position out of way, then remove propeller shaft and lower flexplate inspection cover.
5. Remove the three converter to flexplate attaching bolts, rotating converter and flexplate for bolt accessibility. Do not pry on flexplate ring gear or transmission case.
6. Place suitable jack under rear of engine, then remove four bolts from tunnel strap and remove strap.
7. Remove two rear engine mount to extension housing bolts, then position suitable jack under transmission and raise it sufficiently to take load off rear engine support and remove converter bracket.
8. Remove one bolt from strut support to crossmember, then remove two bolts from each side of rear engine support and slide support back out of position. Support will hang from parking brake cable and exhaust pipe.
9. Remove rear engine support crossmember and remove four remaining transmission housing to engine attaching bolts, lowering engine and transmission, if necessary, to gain access.
10. Disengaging transmission case from locating dowels on engine, move transmission toward rear of car.
11. Install converter holding clamp, J-21366, or equivalent, on front of transmission case and lower transmission from car.
12. Reverse procedure to install.

CHEVROLET

1. Disconnect negative battery cable and raise car.
2. Remove propeller shaft, disconnect speedometer cable, detent cable, modulator vacuum line and oil cooler lines. Disconnect catalytic converter support bracket from transmission.
3. Disconnect shift linkage.
4. Support transmission with suitable jack and remove crossmember.
5. Remove converter under pan.
6. Remove converter to flywheel bolts.
7. loosen exhaust pipe to manifold bolts approximately 1/4 inch. Lower transmission until jack is barely supporting transmission. **On V8 engines, care must be taken not to lower the rear of the transmission too far as the distributor housing may be forced against firewall causing damage to the distributor.**
8. Remove transmission to engine mounting bolts and remove oil filler tube at transmission.
9. Raise transmission to its normal position, support engine with jack and slide transmission rearward from engine and lower it away from vehicle.
10. Reverse procedure to install.

OLDSMOBILE

1. Disconnect battery ground cable.
2. Disconnect detent cable from accelerator or carburetor lever assembly.
3. Remove transmission oil level dipstick. Remove catalytic converter support bracket, if equipped.
4. Raise car and remove detent cable from link. Plug hole.
5. Disconnect oil cooler lines at transmission.
6. Remove flywheel cover pan and mark converter and flywheel for reassembly. Remove three flywheel to converter bolts.
7. Disconnect vacuum modulator line. Remove speedometer clip and driven gear. Plug hole.
8. Disconnect shift linkage.
9. Remove propeller shaft.
10. Support transmission with a suitable jack and remove crossmember.
11. Lower transmission slightly and remove transmission to engine bolts.
12. Remove oil level indicator tube and clip holding detent cable to tube.
13. Lower transmission being careful not to damage cooler lines, detent cable, modulator line and shift linkage.
14. Reverse procedure to install.

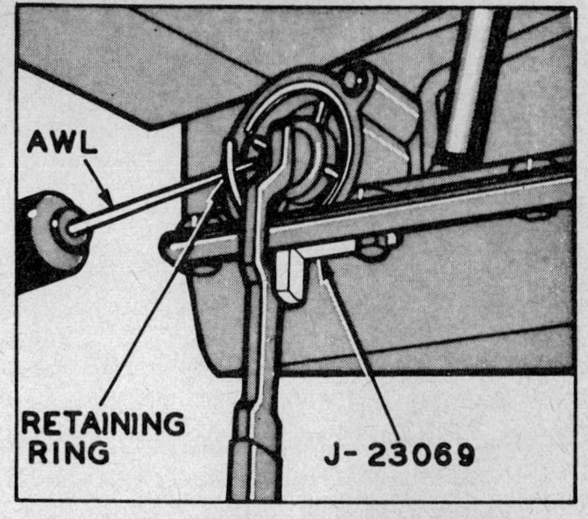

Fig. 9 Intermediate clutch accumulator piston removal

PONTIAC

1. Disconnect battery ground cable and release parking brake.
2. Raise car and remove propeller shaft. Remove catalytic converter support bracket, if equipped.
3. Disconnect speedometer cable, vacuum hose at modulator, detent cable at transmission and shift linkage. **When removing detent cable, be careful not to bend it.**
4. Support transmission with a suitable jack and remove crossmember.
5. Remove converter dust pan, mark flywheel and converter for reassembly and remove flywheel to converter bolts. Make sure converter hub is free of converter.
6. Disconnect transmission filler pipe at engine and remove pipe from transmission.
7. Lower transmission and engine to gain access to cooler line fitting nuts and disconnect cooler lines. On some models it may be necessary to loosen the exhaust system.
8. With transmission in lowered position, remove the transmission to engine bolts.
9. Raise transmission to its normal position, support engine and slide transmission rearward and lower it away from car. **When lowering transmission, keep rear of transmission lower than the front so as not to lose the converter.**
10. Reverse procedure to install.

Turbo Hydra-Matic 325-4L Automatic Transmission

INDEX

IDENTIFICATION

This transmission may be identified by a model tag attached to the transmission on the left side of the converter housing.

DESCRIPTION

The Turbo Hydra-Matic 325-4L transmission, **Fig. 1,** is a fully automatic front wheel drive unit consisting of a four-element torque converter with converter clutch, three compound planetary gear sets and an overdrive unit. Five multiple disc clutches, two roller clutches and a band provide the friction elements required to obtain the desired function of the compound planetary gear sets and the overdrive unit. The combination of the compound planetary gear sets and the overdrive unit provides four forward ratios and one reverse. Changing of the gear ratios is fully automatic in relation to vehicle speed and engine torque.

The torque converter couples the engine to the overdrive unit and planetary gears through oil and hydraulically provides torque multiplication. It consists of a pump or driven member, a turbine or driven member and a stator assembly. With the engine running, the converter pump acts as a centrifugal pump, picking up oil at its center and discharging it at the rim located between the blades. The shape of the converter pump blades causes the oil to leave the pump spinning in a clockwise direction towards the turbine blades. As the oil strikes the turbine blades, it creates a force which enables the turbine to turn. After the oil has imparted its force to the turbine, it follows the contour of the turbine shell and blades and leaves the turbine in a counterclockwise direction, or opposite engine rotation. If this oil is allowed to enter the inner section of the converter pump, it will hinder the ability of the pump to deliver oil with any force due to the opposing rotation of pump blades to oil flow. To prevent this from happening, a stator assembly is added to redirect the oil returning from the

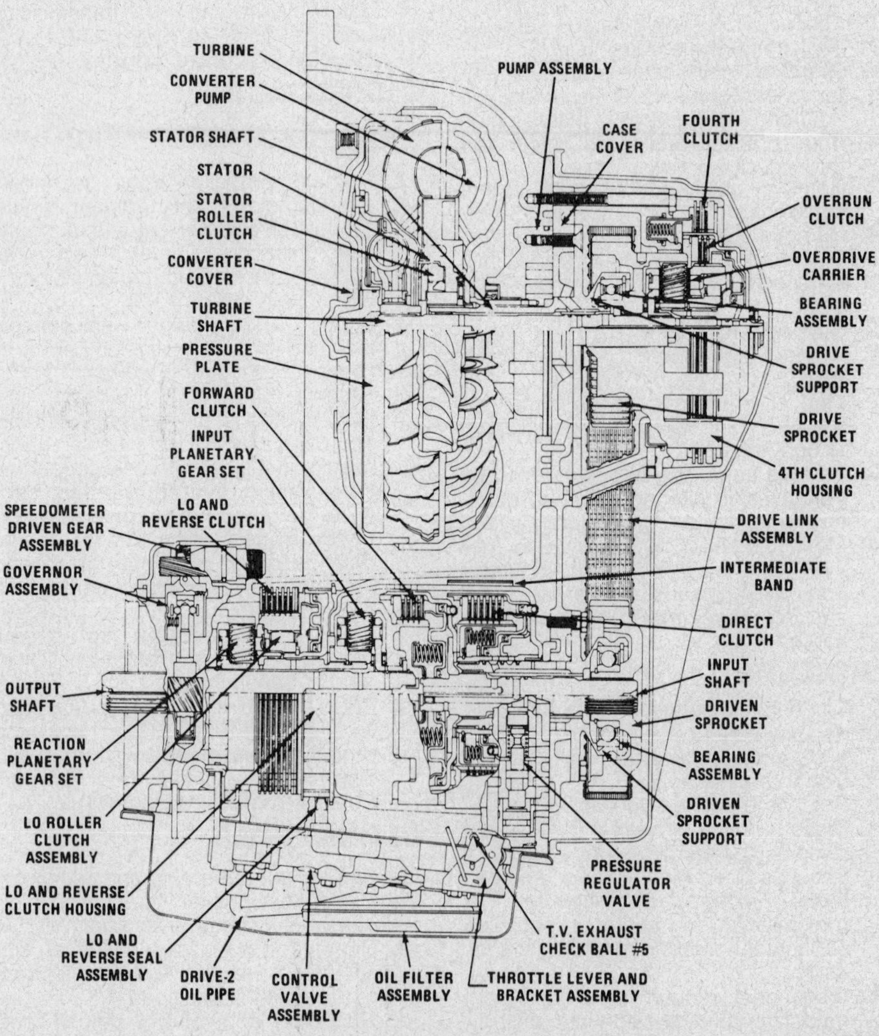

Fig. 1 Cross sectional view of Turbo Hydra-Matic 325-4L transmission

turbine and change its rotation back to that of the converter pump blades. The stator is located between the pump and turbine and is mounted on a one-way roller clutch which allows it to rotate clockwise, but not counterclockwise. The clockwise flow of oil is used to assist the engine in turning the converter pump. This increases the force of the oil driving the turbine and results in the multiplication of torque from the engine. As turbine and vehicle speed increase, the stator becomes inactive and torque multiplication ceases. At this point, the converter is acting as a fluid coupling, since the converter pump and turbine are turning at approximately the same speed.

The converter clutch provides a direct mechanical coupling of the engine to the transmission. This mechanical coupling prevents the slippage that occurs in conventional torque converters and results in improved fuel economy. The application and release of the converter clutch is determined by a series of controls and by drive range selection.

The hydraulic system in this transmission is pressurized by a gear-type pump to provide the working pressures required to operate the friction elements and automatic controls.

TROUBLESHOOTING

FLUID LEAK

1. Broken sealant bead around bottom pan and sprocket cover.
2. Improperly torqued oil pan attaching bolts.
3. Cracked sprocket cover.
4. Distorted sealing surface.
5. Missing or damaged T.V. cable or filler pipe seal.
6. Interference between T.V. cable and engine mount.
7. Damaged manual shaft seal assembly.
8. Damaged governor cover, servo cover and speedometer gear O-ring seal.
9. Incorrectly torqued or cross threaded pressure taps and cooler line fittings.
10. Damaged case gasket or low attaching bolt torque.
11. Leaking converter welded seam.
12. Damaged square cut pump seal or low pump attaching bolt torque.
13. Improperly seated governor oil cup plug.

FLUID LEAKAGE FROM VENT

1. High fluid level.
2. Blocked drive sprocket support drain holes.
3. Contaminated fluid.
4. Overheating engine.

HIGH OR LOW FLUID PRESSURE

1. Improper fluid level.
2. Broken, disconnected, binding or misadjusted T.V. cable.
3. Improperly assembled T.V lever and bracket assembly or binding roll pin.
4. Stuck or binding throttle valve and plunger.
5. Stuck, binding or improperly assembled pressure regulator valve.
6. Stuck, binding or improperly assembled pressure regulator valve.
7. Stuck, binding or improperly assembled reverse boot valve and bushing.
8. Stuck, binding or improperly assembled M.T.V. valve and bushing.
9. Missing pressure relief valve ball or, distorted spring.
10. Stuck or binding T.V. limit or line bias valve.
11. Clogged oil filter, cracked pickup tube or damaged filter O-ring seal.
12. Damaged gears in oil pump assembly.

NO DRIVE IN D

1. Low fluid Level.
2. Low oil pressure.
3. Improperly adjusted manual linkage.
4. Broken torque converter stator roller clutch.
5. Damaged overdrive roller clutch springs or rollers.
6. Damaged overdrive carrier assembly pinions, sun gear or internal gear.
7. Damaged oil pump assembly gears.
8. Broken drive link assembly, sprockets or bearings.
9. Damaged forward clutch assembly piston seals, improperly assembled clutch, cracked piston, damaged input shaft seals, clutch plates, release springs and/or retainer.
10. Damaged input and reaction carrier assembly pinions, sun gear or integral gear.
11. Broken forward clutch input shaft.

1ST SPEED ONLY, NO 1-2 SHIFT

1. Binding governor weights, broken or bent springs, blocked valve body spacer plate/gaskets, worn or damaged drive or driven gear, damaged seals, blocked case passages or damaged governor oil seal.
2. Stuck 1-2 shift, Lo/1st detent or 1-2 throttle valve.
3. Damaged or burned intermediate band, missing anchor band or improperly assembled band.
4. Short intermediate servo assembly pin, wrong piston/cover combination or damaged seal.
5. Loose 1-2, 3-4 accumulator housing attaching bolts, mispositioned or blocked spacer plate, damaged gasket or porous housing.

1-2 SHIFT AT FULL THROTTLE ONLY

1. Disconnected or misadjusted T.V. cable or bent T.V. link.
2. Improperly assembled T.V.lever and bracket assembly.
3. Broken or missing T.V. link.
4. Stuck or binding throttle valve or plunger.
5. Mispositioned or blocked spacer plates and gaskets.
6. Low governor pressure.

1ST & 2ND SPEEDS ONLY, NO 2-3 SHIFT

1. Stuck or binding 2-3 shift valve or throttle valve or mispositioned or blocked spacer plate.
2. Porous case or interconnected passages.
3. Unseated ¯7 pellet and spring in case cover, porosity or interconnected case cover passages, damaged gasket or improperly torqued case cover attaching bolts.
4. Loose driven sprocket support attaching bolts, mispositioned, cut or leaking oil seal rings or damaged sprocket support gasket.
5. Missing or leaking ¯6 check ball.
6. Improperly assembled direct clutch assembly, damaged pistons or seals or damaged ball capsule.
7. Worn governor driven gear, unseated check ball, binding weights or damaged springs.

NO REVERSE OR SLIPS IN REVERSE

1. Improperly adjusted manual link.
2. Damaged Low and reverse clutch pistons and seals or cup plug and seal.
3. Improperly assembled direct clutch, damaged piston seals or ball capsule damaged.
4. Binding or stuck reverse boot valve.
5. Leaking reverse oil pipe.
6. Missing or leaking ¯6 check ball.
7. Missing or leaking ¯10 check ball.
8. Mispositioned or damaged Spacer plate.
9. Leaking case cover reverse passage.

DRIVE IN NEUTRAL

1. Improperly adjusted manual linkage.
2. Leak into D4 oil passage.
3. Fused clutch plates or stuck ball capsule.

SLIPPING 1-2 SHIFT

1. Low fluid level.
2. Mispositioned or blocked spacer plate and gaskets.
3. Loose 1-2 accumulator piston housing bolts, porous housing, damaged stuck or binding 1-2 piston or seal.
4. Damaged or burned intermediate band lining.
5. Incorrect intermediate servo apply pin, porosity, damaged piston or seal.
6. Sticking or binding pressure regulator valve.
7. Binding or stuck line bias, throttle valve or plunger.
8. Improperly adjusted T.V. cable.
9. Leaking case cover 2nd oil passage.

ROUGH 1-2 SHIFT

1. Improperly adjusted or binding T.V. cable.
2. Binding or stuck throttle valve or plunger, or T.V. limit valve, line bias valve or accumulator.
3. Incorrect intermediate servo apply pin or missing piston bleed orifice.
4. Damaged, binding or stuck 1-2 accumulator piston.
5. Missing or leaking ¯8 check ball.
6. Missing or blocked servo bleed orifice.

SLIPPING 2-3 SHIFT

1. Low fluid level.
2. Improperly adjusted T.V. cable.

3. Mispositioned or blocked spacer plate/gaskets.
4. Leaking 7 pellet and spring.
5. Damaged servo piston seal rings.
6. Missing or blocked servo bleed orifice.
7. Leak in 3rd clutch passage.
8. Damaged direct clutch ball capsule, piston, housing and seal, improperly assembled direct clutch or burned clutch plates.

ROUGH 2-3 SHIFT

1. Improperly adjusted T.V. cable.
2. Binding or stuck throttle valve or plunger.
3. Binding or stuck T.V. limit or line bias valve.
4. Binding or stuck M.T.V. up valve.

NO 3-4 SHIFT

1. Stuck or binding shift valve or 3-4 throttle valve.
2. Damaged 4th clutch piston or seals, or 4th feed O-ring seal missing or leaking.
3. Leaking 3-4 accumulator circuit.
4. Mispositioned or blocked spacer plate/gaskets.
5. Binding governor weights, broken or bent springs, blocked valve body spacer plate/gaskets, worn or damaged drive or driven gear, damaged seals, blocked case passages or damaged governor oil seal.

SLIPPING 3-4 SHIFT

1. Damaged accumulator housing piston or seal or loose housing bolts.
2. Binding or stuck accumulator valve.
3. Internal leak, damaged 4th clutch piston seal, damaged O-ring, or loose 4th clutch clutch housing bolts.

ROUGH 3-4 SHIFT

1. Improperly adjusted T.V. cable.
2. Binding or stuck throttle valve or plunger.
3. Damaged or stuck 3-4 accumulator valve or missing or weak spring.

NO CONVERTER CLUTCH APPLY

1. Stuck converter clutch shift valve.
2. Open solenoid.
3. Sticking or binding converter clutch apply valve or spring.
4. Leaking converter clutch signal pipe or plugged screen.
5. Shorted electrical wire or pinched wire.

ROUGH CONVERTER CLUTCH APPLY

1. Plugged converter clutch apply valve bushing orifice.

NO CONVERTER CLUTCH RELEASE

1. Stuck converter clutch apply valve (in apply position).

NO ENGINE BRAKING IN MANUAL RANGES

1. Improperly adjusted manual linkage.
2. Mispositioned, damaged or plugged spacer plate or gaskets.

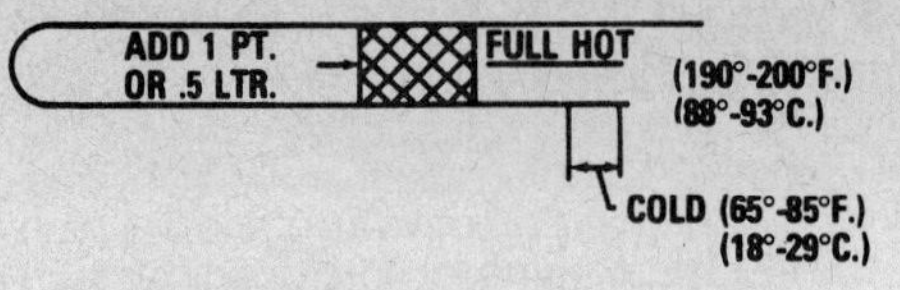

Fig. 2 Transmission oil dipstick level

3. Binding or stuck 4-3 control valve.
4. Leaking D2 signal pipe.
5. Leaking or missing 3 check ball.
6. Binding or stuck Low overrun clutch valve.
7. Missing 10 check ball.
8. Missing or leaking 9 check ball.
9. Damaged overrun clutch pistons, seals or clutch plates.
10. Blocked turbine shaft oil passages.

NO PART THROTTLE DOWNSHIFTS

1. Sticking or binding T.V. valve or plunger.
2. Mispositioned or blocked spacer plates or gaskets.
3. Improperly adjusted T.V. cable.
4. Binding or stuck T.V. modulator downshift valve.

NO HOLD IN PARK

1. Improperly adjusted manual linkage.
2. Damaged, mispositioned or improperly assembled internal linkage.

HIGH OR LOW SHIFT POINTS

1. Improperly adjusted or damaged T.V. cable.
2. Sticking or binding T.V. limit valve.
3. Sticking or binding throttle valve or plunger.
4. Sticking or binding T.V. modulator upshift or downshift valves.
5. Mispositioned or binding spacer plates or gaskets.
6. Unhooked, mispositioned or improperly assembled T.V. lever and bracket assembly.
7. Damaged or leaking governor assembly or cover.

MAINTENANCE

CHECKING FLUID LEVEL

To check fluid level, drive vehicle at least 15 miles to allow fluid to reach normal operating temperature (190°-200° F). With vehicle on level surface, parking brake applied and engine running at slow idle, move selector lever through each range, then into Park position. The level on the dipstick should be at the Full Hot mark. To bring fluid level from the Add to Full mark requires only one pint of fluid. If vehicle cannot be driven sufficiently to bring fluid to normal operating temperature, the level on the dipstick should be approximately 1/2 inch above the Full mark with fluid temperature at 65-85° F, **Fig. 2.**

If additional fluid is required, use Dexron II, or equivalent, automatic transmission fluid.

The transmission fluid now being used may appear to be darker or have a stronger odor. This is normal and not a positive sign of required transmission maintenance or transmission failure.

An overfilled transmission can cause foaming and loss of fluid through the vent, resulting in slippage and/or transmission failure. A low fluid level can also cause slippage, particularly when the transmission is cold or the vehicle is driven on a steep hill.

Every 100,000 miles, the transmission fluid should be drained, the oil pan removed, the screen cleaned and fresh fluid added. For vehicles subjected to more severe use such as heavy city traffic, where temperatures reach 90° F, or prolonged periods of idle or towing, this maintenance should be performed every 15,000 miles.

CHANGING FLUID

1. Raise and support vehicle, then position drain pan under transmission oil pan.
2. Remove front and side oil pan attaching bolts, then loosen rear bolts approximately four turns.
3. Carefully pry transmission oil pan loose with screwdriver and allow fluid to drain.
4. Remove remaining bolts, pan and gasket.
5. Drain remaining fluid from pan, clean with solvent and dry with compressed air.
6. Remove transmission screen, clean thoroughly with solvent and dry with compressed air. **Paper or felt type filters should be replaced.**
7. Install new gasket and O-ring onto screen assembly. Lubricate O-ring with petroleum jelly.
8. Install transmission screen, then position new gasket onto pan and install pan. Torque pan attaching bolts to 12 ft. lbs. **Some THM 325-4L transmissions may be built using R.T.V. (Room Temperature Vulcanizing) silicone sealant in place of standard gaskets. If oil pan or side cover is equipped with flat or depressed rib flanges, Fig. 3,** use, a 1/16 inch bead of R.T.V. sealant to seal surfaces. If pan or side cover is equipped with a raised rib flange, **Fig. 4,** conventional gaskets must be used.
9. Lower vehicle and add approximately 5 qts. of Dexron II type transmission fluid through filler tube.
10. Apply parking brake, start engine and allow to idle. Do not race engine.
11. Move selector lever through each range, then position lever in Park and check fluid level.

IN-VEHICLE ADJUSTMENTS

SHIFT CONTROL CABLE, ADJUST

The following procedure applies to all

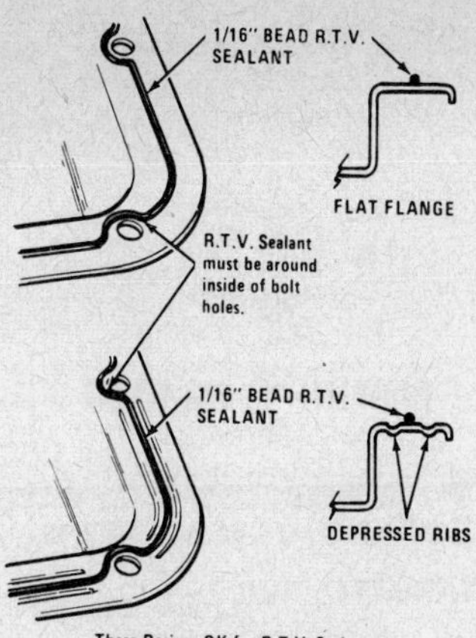

Fig. 3 Flat or depressed rib sealing flange

models except Cadillac. For shift control adjustment on Cadillac models, refer to "Manual Linkage, Adjust."

1. Position steering column shift lever in neutral gate notch, then loosen attaching nut at column lever, **Fig. 5.**
2. Set transmission lever in neutral detent, then move pin to give "free pin" fit in column lever and torque attaching nut two to 20 ft. lbs.
3. Check that starter will not crank in any position except Neutral or Park. Adjust neutral start switch, if necessary.

MANUAL LINKAGE, ADJUST

1. Position steering column shift lever in neutral, then place transmission (A) in neutral, **Fig. 6.**
2. Assemble linkage as shown in figure.
3. Hold clamp (B) flush against transmission control equalizer shaft assembly (C), then finger tighten screw (D) against Rod (E).
4. Torque screw to 20 ft. lbs., noting not to exert force in either direction on shafts (E) or (C).

THROTTLE VALVE (T.V.) CABLE, ADJUST

SELF-ADJUSTING TYPE

Gasoline Engine

1. Depress lock tab, then move slider in direction away from carburetor throttle body, **Fig. 7.**
2. Release lock tab and open carburetor lever to full throttle stop position to automatically adjust T.V. cable.

Diesel Engine

1. Remove cruise control rod from bellcrank, if equipped.
2. Unlock T.V. cable snap-lock button, then disconnect T.V. cable and throttle rod from bellcrank, **Fig. 8.**
3. Rotate bellcrank to full throttle stop and hold in this position.
4. Pull throttle rod and pump lever to full throttle stop position, **Fig. 9,** then adjust throttle rod to meet bellcrank. Do not connect throttle rod to bellcrank at this time.

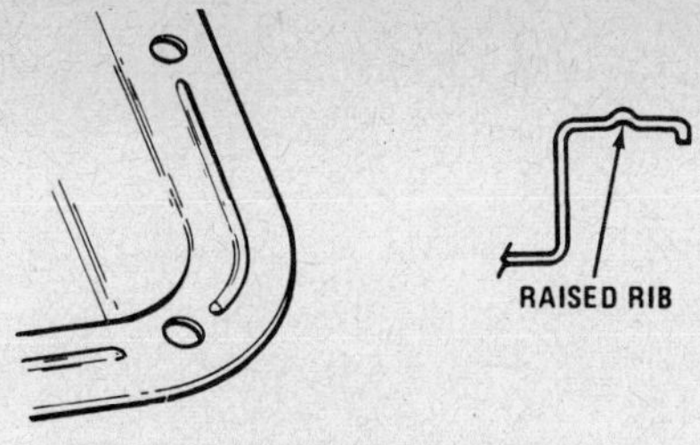

Fig. 4 Raised rib sealing flange

5. Release bellcrank, then reconnect T.V. cable.
6. Rotate and hold bellcrank to full throttle stop, then lock T.V. cable snap-lock button.
7. Reconnect throttle and cruise control rods. **If bellcrank full throttle stop is not obtained when accelerator pedal is completely depressed, all full throttle adjustments must be made by completely depressing the accelerator pedal instead of rotating the bellcrank by hand.**

MANUAL TYPE

1. Pushing upward, unlock T.V. cable snap-lock button, **Fig. 10.**
2. Rotate carburetor lever to wide open throttle position and hold.
3. Pushing downward, lock T.V. cable snap lock-button, then release carburetor throttle lever.

IN-VEHICLE REPAIRS

VALVE BODY, REPLACE

1. Drain transmission fluid and remove oil pan and screen.
2. Remove screw and disconnect T.V. cable from transmission.
3. Remove throttle lever and bracket assembly, then disconnect converter clutch wiring connections.
4. Remove oil transfer pipes and hold-down brackets.
5. Support valve body and remove retaining bolts.
6. Remove valve body, noting location of check ball. **If accumulator housing is removed, support spacer plate during removal and note location of check balls in spacer plate and accumulator housing.**
7. Reverse procedure to install. Torque valve body retaining bolts to 10 ft. lbs. **Intermediate band anchor pin must locate on intermediate band, or damage to transmission may result.**

INTERMEDIATE SERVO, REPLACE

1. Install tool No. J-28493 on transmission case and tighten bolt to depress servo cover.
2. Using a small screwdriver, remove servo cover retaining ring, then remove tool.
3. Remove servo cover, then remove servo piston and band apply pin assembly.
4. Reverse procedure to install.

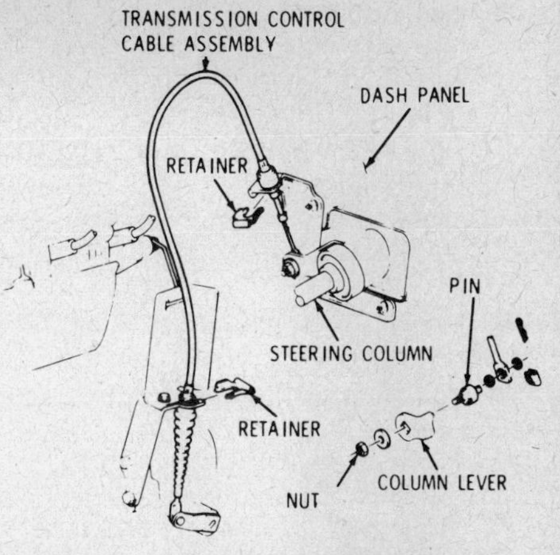

Fig. 5 Shift control cable adjustment

SPEEDOMETER GEARS, REPLACE

1. Disconnect speedometer cable, then remove driven gear attaching bolt, retainer and driven gear.
2. Remove governor cover attaching screws and governor cover.
3. Remove governor and speedometer drive gear assembly.
4. Remove speedometer drive gear from governor assembly.
5. Reverse procedure to install.

PRESSURE REGULATOR VALVE, REPLACE

1. Drain transmission fluid and remove oil pan and screen.
2. Push in on pressure regulator valve, and compress valve spring with a small screwdriver.
3. Remove retaining ring, then slowly release spring tension.
4. Remove Drive 2 or T.V. boost valve and bushing, reverse boost plunger and bushing, spacer, then the pressure regulator spring and valve.

TRANSMISSION REPLACE

EXC. MODELS WITH TURBOCHARGED ENGINE

1. Disconnect battery ground cable, then the speedometer cable.
2. Remove air cleaner assembly, then disconnect T.V. cable from bellcrank (diesel engine) or carburetor throttle lever (gasoline engine).
3. Support engine with suitable engine holding fixture.
4. Remove top and the two left upper final drive-to-transmission attaching bolts.
5. Remove remaining accessible engine-to-transmission bolts.
6. Raise and support vehicle, then remove starter.
7. Disconnect converter clutch electrical connections from transmission.
8. Disconnect and plug transmission cooler lines, then remove flywheel in-

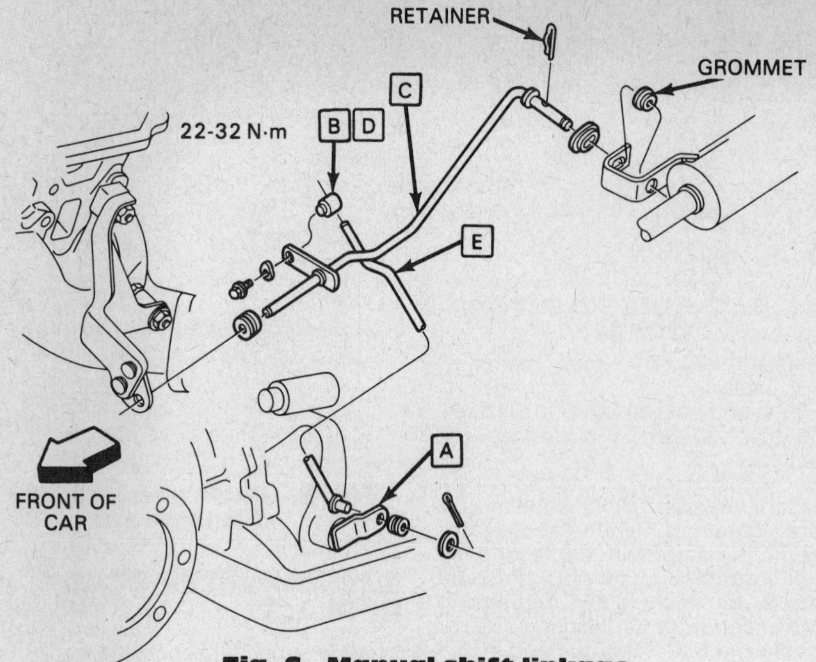

Fig. 6 Manual shift linkage adjustment

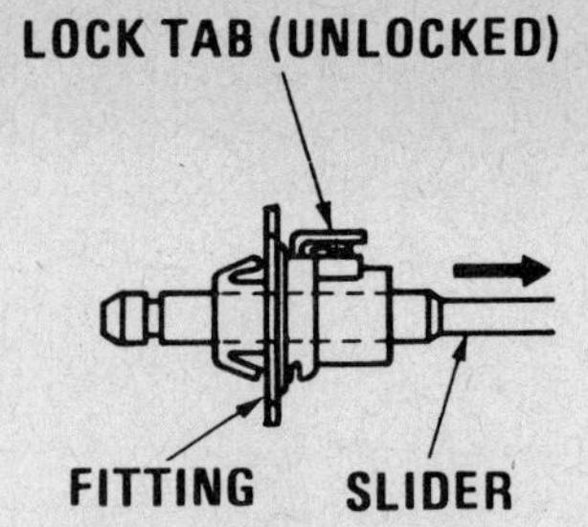

Fig. 7 Adjusting T.V. cable. Self-adjusting type

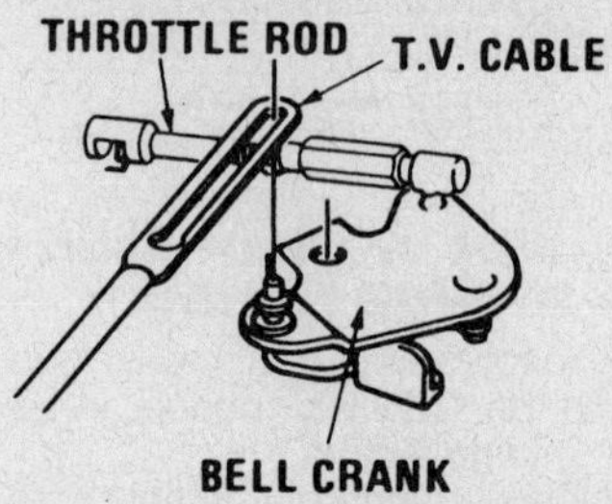

Fig. 8 Disconnecting T.V. cable & throttle rod

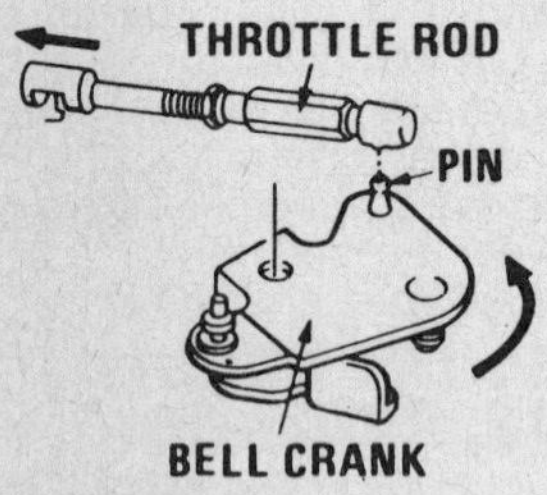

Fig. 9 Adjusting throttle rod

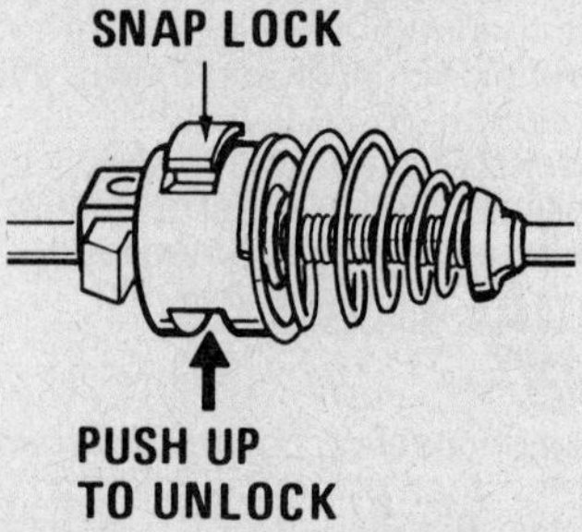

Fig. 10 Adjusting T.V. cable. Manual type (gasoline engine)

spection cover.

9. On vehicles equipped with V-8 engines, disconnect "Y" pipe from left exhaust pipe.
10. Disconnect right exhaust pipe from exhaust manifold.
11. On all gasoline engine equipped vehicles, disconnect catalytic converter hanger bolts.
12. Lower and support exhaust system approximately five inches, then remove crossmember attaching bolts and the crossmember.
13. Position a suitable transmission jack under transmission, then remove the three remaining final drive-to-transmission bolts.
14. Remove torque converter-to-flywheel attaching bolts, then disconnect shift linkage from transmission.
15. Remove final drive-support bracket bolt and the right transmission mount-through, and bracket bolts.
16. Remove left transmission mount-through bolt, then the lower support bracket-to-transmission bolt.
17. Raise transmission about two inches and remove remaining upper bracket-to-transmission bolts and the last engine-to-transmission bolt.
18. Carefully lower transmission while disengaging the final drive.
19. Install torque converter holding fixture and remove transmission from vehicle.
20. Reverse procedure to install. Torque starter mounting bolts to 30 ft. lbs., transmission mount-to-frame nut to 40 ft. lbs., transmission-to-engine attaching bolts to 35 ft. lbs., flywheel-to-converter bolts to 35 ft. lbs., final drive-to-transmission bolts to 30 ft. lbs. and final drive-support bracket bolt to 35 ft. lbs.

MODELS WITH TURBOCHARGED ENGINE

1. Disconnect battery ground cable, then the speedometer cable.
2. Remove heated air pipe.
3. Remove turbocharger assembly, then the four top engine-to-transmission attaching bolts.
4. Remove top final drive-to-transmission bolt and two final drive-to-engine attaching bolts, then loosen retaining bracket at engine.
5. Support engine with a suitable engine holding fixture, then raise and support vehicle.
6. Disconnect shift linkage from transmission.
7. Disconnect and cap transmission cooler lines, then remove remaining final drive-to-transmission bolts.
8. Remove final drive cover, then disconnect right output shaft bearing support from engine.
9. Turn wheels to gain clearance between final drive and steering linkage, then separate final drive from transmission. Support final drive unit.
10. Remove outlet pipe/converter assembly which was disconnected when turbocharger was removed.
11. Remove starter and the two remaining transmission-to-engine attaching bolts.
12. Disconnect converter cover and position aside.
13. Remove flex plate-to-converter attaching bolts, then position transmission jack under transmission.
14. Remove both transmission mount-through bolts, then the right-mount bracket from transmission.
15. Remove left-mount brackets from both frame and transmission by pulling out inner fender liner and removing attaching bolts through access holes in frame.
16. Separate transmission from engine, then carefully lower and remove from vehicle.
17. Reverse procedure to install. Torque starter mounting bolts to 30 ft. lbs., transmission mount-to-frame nut to 40 ft. lbs., transmission-to-engine attaching bolts to 35 ft. lbs., flywheel-to-converter bolts to 35 ft. lbs., final drive-to-transmission bolts to 30 ft. lbs. and final drive-support bracket bolt to 35 ft. lbs.

Turbo Hydra-Matic 400 Automatic Transmission

INDEX

IDENTIFICATION

An identification plate is attached to the transmission. The plate indicates year of production, code letters, and serial number.

DESCRIPTION

This transmission, **Fig. 1**, is a fully automatic unit consisting of a three-element hydraulic torque converter and a compound planetary gear set. Three multiple-disc clutches, two one-way clutches, and two bands provide the friction elements required to obtain the desired functions of the planetary gear set.

The torque converter, the multiple-disc clutches and the one-way clutches couple the engine to the planetary gears through oil pressure, providing three forward speeds and reverse. The torque converter, when required, supplements the gears by multiplying engine torque.

TORQUE CONVERTER

The torque converter is of welded construction and is serviced as an assembly. The unit is made up of two vaned sections, or halves, that face each other in an oil-filled housing. The pump half of the converter is connected to the engine and the turbine half is connected to the transmission.

When the engine makes the converter pump revolve, it sends oil against the turbine, making it revolve also. The oil then returns in a circular flow back to the converter pump, continuing this flow as long as the engine is running.

STATOR

The converter also has a smaller vaned section, called a stator, that funnels the oil back to the converter pump through smaller openings, at increased speed. The speeded up oil directs additional force to the engine-driven converter pump, thereby multiplying engine torque. In other words, without the stator, the unit is nothing more than a fluid coupling.

EXTERNAL CONTROLS

The external control connections to the transmission are:

1. Manual linkage to select the desired operating range.
2. Engine vacuum to operate the vacuum modulator unit.
3. An electrical signal to operate an electric detent solenoid.

VACUUM MODULATOR

A vacuum modulator is used to sense engine torque input to the transmission automatically. The vacuum modulator transmits this signal to the pressure regulator, which controls line pressure, so that all torque requirements of the transmission are met and proper shift spacing is obtained at all throttle openings.

DETENT SOLENOID

The detent solenoid is activated by an electric switch at the carburetor. When the throttle is opened sufficiently to close this switch, the solenoid in the transmission is activated, causing a downshift at speeds below 70 mph. At lower speeds, downshifts will occur at lesser throttle openings without use of the electric switch.

TROUBLESHOOTING

OIL PRESSURE HIGH OR LOW

1. Vacuum line or fittings clogged or leaking.
2. Vacuum modulator.
3. Modulator valve.
4. Pressure regulator.
5. Oil pump.
6. Governor.

NO DRIVE IN DRIVE RANGE

1. Low oil level (check for leaks).
2. Manual control linkage not adjusted properly.
3. Low oil pressure. Check for blocked strainer, defective pressure regulator, pump assembly or pump drive gear. See that tangs have not been damaged by converter.
4. Check control valve assembly to see if manual valve has been disconnected from manual lever pin.
5. Forward clutch may be struck or damaged. Check pump feed circuits to forward clutch including clutch drum ball check.
6. Sprag or roller clutch assembled incorrectly.

1-2 SHIFT AT FULL THROTTLE ONLY

1. Detent switch may be sticking or defective.
2. Detent solenoid may be stuck open, loose or have leaking gasket.
3. Control valve assembly may be leaking, damaged or incorrectly installed.
4. Porous transmission case.

1ST SPEED ONLY—NO 1-2 SHIFT

1. Governor valve may be sticking.
2. Driven gear in governor assembly loose, worn or damaged.
3. The 1-2 shift valve in control valve assembly stuck closed. Check governor feed channels for blocks, leaks, and position. Also check control valve body gaskets for leaks and damage.
4. Intermediate clutch plug in case may be leaking or blown out.
5. Check for porosity between channels

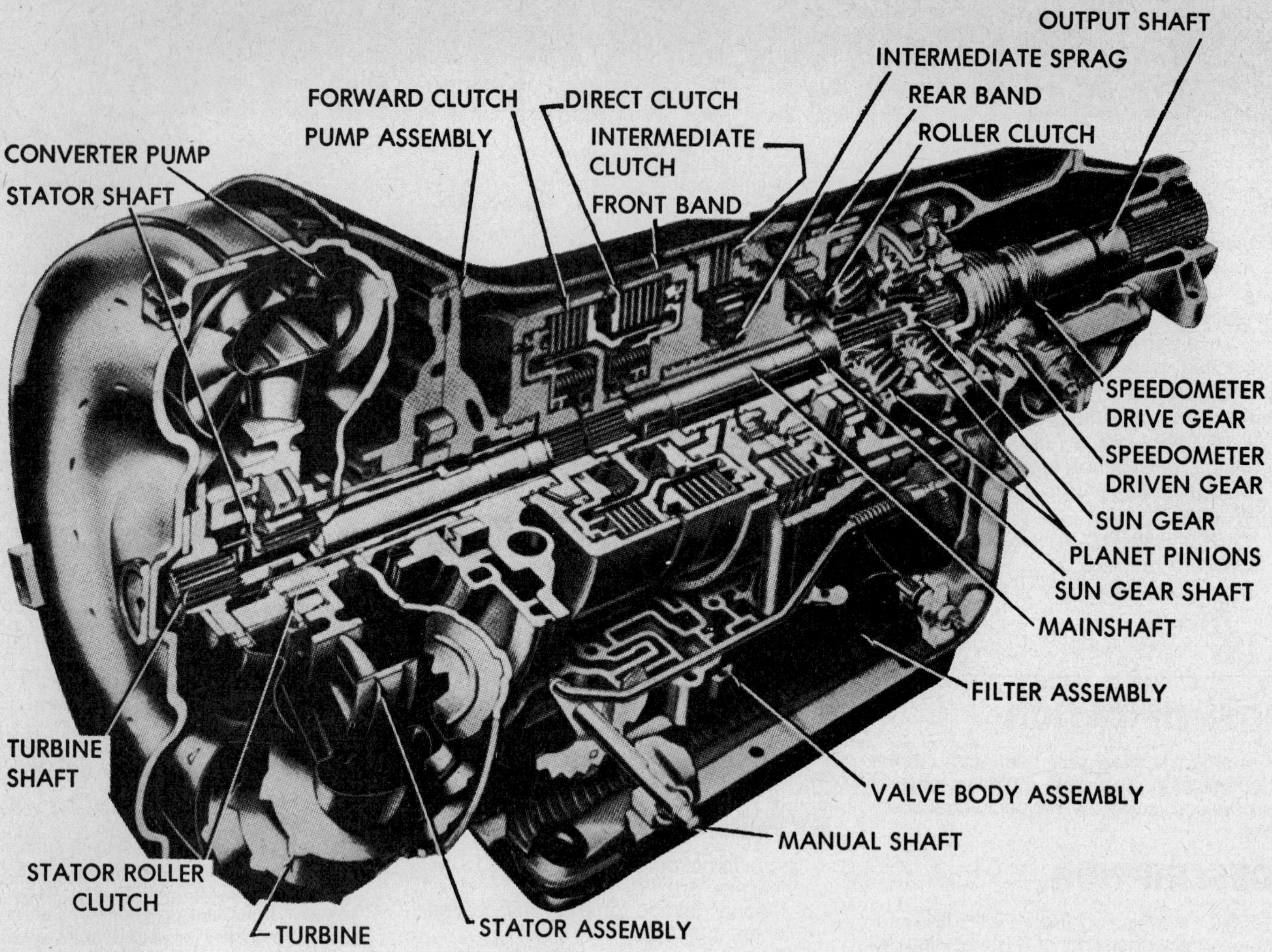

Fig. 1 Cutaway view of transmission assembly

and for blocked governor feed channels in case.
6. Check intermediate clutch for proper operation.

NO 2-3 SHIFT—1ST & 2ND ONLY

1. Detent solenoid may be stuck open.
2. Detent switch may not be properly adjusted.
3. Control valve assembly may be stuck, leaking, damaged, or incorrectly installed.
4. Check direct clutch case center support for broken, leaking or missing oil rings.
5. Check clutch piston seals and piston ball check in clutch assembly.

MOVES FORWARD IN NEUTRAL

1. Manual control linkage improperly adjusted.
2. Forward clutch does not release.
3. Oil pump.
4. Internal linkage.

NO DRIVE IN REVERSE OR SLIPS IN REVERSE

1. Check oil level.
2. Manual control linkage improperly adjusted.
3. Vacuum modulator assembly may be defective.
4. Vacuum modulator valve sticking.
5. Strainer may be restricted or leaking at intake.
6. Regulator or boost valve in pump assembly may be sticking.
7. Control valve assembly may be stuck, leaking or damaged.
8. Rear servo and accumulator may have damaged or missing servo piston seal ring.
9. Reverse band burned out or damaged. Determine that apply pin or anchor pins engage properly.
10. Direct clutch may be damaged or may have stuck ball check in piston.
11. Forward clutch does not release.
12. Low-reverse ball check missing from case.

SLIPS IN ALL RANGES & ON STARTS

1. Check oil level.
2. Vacuum modulator defective.
3. Modulator valve sticking.
4. Strainer assembly plugged or leaking at neck.
5. Pump assembly regulator or boost valve sticking.
6. Leaks from damaged gaskets or cross leaks from porosity of case.
7. Forward and direct clutches burned.

SLIPS 1-2 SHIFT

1. Incorrect oil level.
2. Vacuum modulator valve sticking.
3. Vacuum modulator defective.
4. Pump pressure regulator valve defective.
5. Porosity between channels in case.
6. Control valve assembly.
7. Pump-to-case gasket may be mispositioned.
8. Intermediate clutch plug in case may be missing or leaking excessively.
9. Intermediate clutch piston seal missing or damaged.
10. Intermediate clutch plates burned.
11. Front or rear accumulator oil ring may be damaged.

SLIPS 2-3 SHIFT

1. Items 1 through 6 under Slips 1-2 Shift will also cause 2-3 shift slips.
2. Direct clutch plates burned.
3. Oil seal rings on direct clutch may be damaged permitting excessive leaking between tower and bushing.

ROUGH 1-2 SHIFT

1. Modulator valve sticking.
2. Modulator assembly defective.

3. Pump pressure regulator or boost valve stuck or inoperative.
4. Control valve assembly loosened from case, damaged or mounted with wrong gaskets.
5. Intermediate clutch ball missing or not sealing.
6. Porosity between channels in case.
7. Rear servo accumulator assembly may have oil rings damaged, stuck piston, broken or missing spring or damaged bore.

ROUGH 2-3 SHIFT

1. Items 1, 2 and 3 under Rough 1-2 Shift will also cause rough 2-3 shift.
2. Front servo accumulator spring broken or missing. Accumulator piston may be sticking.

NO ENGINE BRAKING IN 2ND SPEED

1. Front servo or accumulator oil rings may be leaking.
2. Front band may be broken or burned out.
3. Front bank not engaged on anchor pin and/or servo pin.

NO ENGINE BRAKING IN LOW RANGE

1. Low-reverse check ball may be missing from control valve assembly.
2. Rear servo may have damaged oil seal ring, bore or piston.
3. Rear servo apply pressure, leaking.
4. Rear band broken, burned out or not engaged on anchor pins or servo pin.

NO PART THROTTLE DOWNSHIFTS

1. Vacuum modulator assembly.
2. Modulator valve.
3. Regulator valve train.
4. Control valve assembly has stuck 3-2 valve or broken spring.

NO DETENT DOWNSHIFTS

1. Detent switch needs fuse, connections tightened or adjustment.
2. Detent solenoid may be inoperative.
3. Detent valve train in control valve assembly malfunctioning.

LOW OR HIGH SHIFT POINTS

1. Oil pressure. Check vacuum modulator assembly, vacuum line connections, modulator valve, and pressure regulator valve train.
2. Governor may have sticking valve or feed holes that are leaking, plugged or damaged.
3. Detent solenoid may be stuck open or loose.
4. Control valve assembly. Check detent, 3-2, and 1-2 shift valve trains, and check spacer plate gaskets for positioning.
5. Check case for porosity, missing or leaking intermediate plug.

NO HOLD IN PARK

1. Manual control linkage improperly adjusted.
2. Internal linkage defective; check for chamfer on actuator rod sleeve.
3. Parking pawl broken or inoperative.

NOISY TRANSMISSION

1. Pump noises caused by high or low oil level.
2. Cavitation due to plugged strainer, porosity in intake circuit or water in oil.
3. Pump gears may be damaged.
4. Gear noise in low gear of Drive Range.
5. Transmission contacting body.
6. Defective planetary gear set.
7. Clutch noises during application can be worn or burned clutch plates.

FORWARD CLUTCH PLATES BURNED

1. Check ball in clutch housing damaged, stuck or missing.
2. Clutch piston cracked, seals damaged or missing.
3. Low line pressure.
4. Manual valve mispositioned.
5. Restricted oil feed to forward clutch.
6. Pump cover oil seal rings missing, broken or undersize; ring groove oversize.
7. Case valve body face not flat or porosity between channels.
8. Manual valve bent and center land not properly ground.

INTERMEDIATE CLUTCH PLATES BURNED

1. Constant bleed orifice in center support missing.
2. Rear accumulator piston oil ring damaged or missing.
3. 1-2 accumulator valve stuck in control valve assembly.
4. Intermediate clutch piston seal damaged or missing.
5. Center support bolt loose.
6. Low line pressure.
7. Intermediate clutch plug in case missing.
8. Case valve body face not flat or porosity between channels.
9. Manual valve bent and center land not ground properly.

DIRECT CLUTCH PLATES BURNED

1. Restricted orifice in vacuum line to modulator.
2. Check ball in direct clutch piston damaged, stuck or missing.
3. Defective modulator bellows.
4. Center support bolt loose.
5. Center support oil rings or grooves damaged or missing.
6. Clutch piston seals damaged or missing.
7. Front and rear servo pistons and seals damaged.
8. Manual valve bent and center land not cleaned up.
9. Case valve body face not flat or porosity between channels.
10. Intermediate sprag clutch installed backwards.
11. 3-2 valve, 3-2 spring or 3-2 spacer pin installed in wrong location in 3-2 valve bore.

MAINTENANCE

CHECKING & ADDING FLUID

Fluid level should be checked at every engine oil change. The full ("F") and ADD marks on the transmission dipstick are one pint apart and determine the correct fluid level at normal operating temperature (170° F). Careful attention to transmission oil temperature is necessary as proper fluid level at low operating temperatures will be below the ADD mark on the dipstick. Proper fluid level at higher operating temperatures will rise above the "F" mark.

Fluid level must always be checked with the car on a level surface, and with the engine running to make certain the converter is full. To determine proper fluid level, proceed as follows:

1. Operate engine at a fast idle for about 1 1/2 minutes with selector lever in park ("P") position.
2. Reduce engine speed to slow idle and check fluid level.
3. With engine running add Dexron fluid as required. **An extended-life Dexron transmission fluid is used. With this fluid, strainer replacement and fluid change is recommended at 100,000 miles under normal operating conditions and 50,000 miles under severe or abnormal service such as trailer towing.**

This recommendation applies only to the improved fluid and its availability for service. If the new fluid is not available, the former fluid can be used but then the 24,000 mile maintenance rule will apply.

The normal maintenance schedule for drain and refill of this type fluid remains unchanged at 24,000 miles under normal service and 12,000 miles under severe operating conditions, such as trailer towing.

Do not overfill as foaming might occur when the fluid heats up. If fluid level is too low, especially when cold, complete loss of drive may result after quick stops. Extremely low fluid level will result in damage to transmission.

DRAINING BOTTOM PAN ONLY

1. Disconnect filler tube at bottom pan and allow fluid to drain. Remove and discard filler tube O-ring.
2. Use a new O-ring on filler tube and install tube on pan.
3. Lower car and add three quarts of Dexron transmission fluid through filler tube when replacing intake pipe and strainer assembly. When just draining bottom pan, add only two quarts.
4. Operate engine at a fast idle for about 1 1/2 minutes with selector lever in park ("P") position.
5. Reduce engine speed to slow idle and check fluid level. Then add fluid as required to bring it to the proper level.

ADDING FLUID TO FILL DRY TRANSMISSION & CONVERTER

1. Add seven quarts of fluid through filler tube.

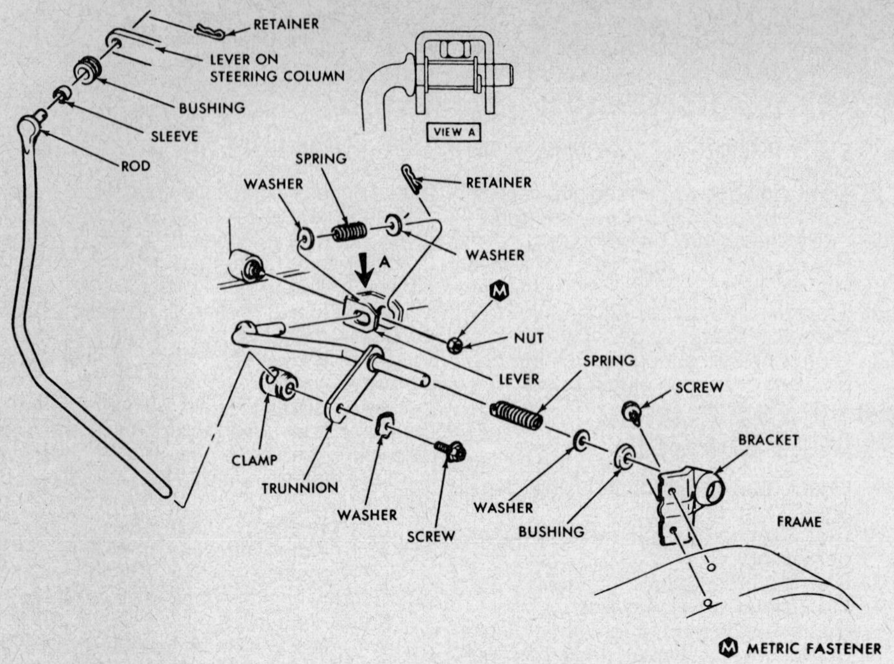

Fig. 2 Manual linkage adjustment

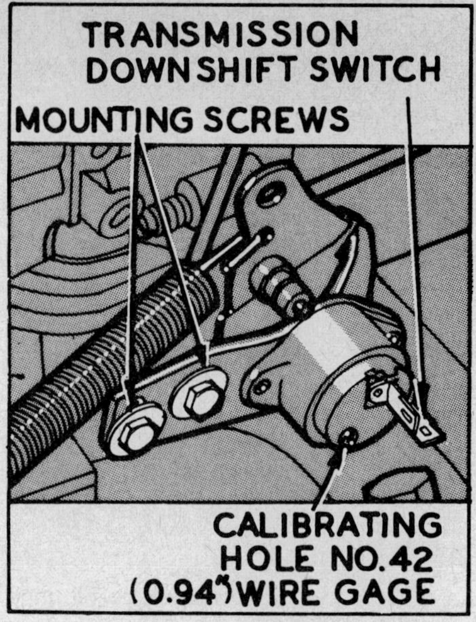

Fig. 3 Detent switch adjustment

2. Operate engine at a fast idle for about 1½ minutes with selector lever in park ("P") position.
3. Reduce engine speed to slow idle and add three more quarts of fluid.
4. Check fluid level and add as required to bring it to the proper level.

IN-VEHICLE ADJUSTMENTS

BACK DRIVE LINKAGE, ADJUST

Adjust back drive at trunnion so that:

1. Transmission is in full detent in each selector position.
2. With key in Run position and transmission in Reverse, key cannot be removed and steering wheel is not locked.
3. With key in Lock position and transmission in Park, key can be removed and steering wheel is locked.

MANUAL LINKAGE, ADJUST

1. Loosen nut or screw on shift rod trunnion, **Fig. 2.**
2. Pull trunnion lever upward to Park position, then downward to the third (Neutral) step.
3. Place steering column selector lever in Neutral position.
4. Tighten the shift rod trunnion nut or screw.
5. Check for proper operation.

DOWNSHIFT SWITCHES, ADJUST

1. Remove air cleaner.
2. Make certain carburetor is adjusted to specification and that linkage is at low speed idle setting.
3. Loosen two mounting screws and insert a 42 drill through calibrating hole below lower wire terminal extending through to carburetor side of switch, **Fig. 3.** Adjust position of switch so that lever just touches the carburetor adapter plate arm.
4. Tighten mounting screws and remove drill.
5. Install air cleaner.

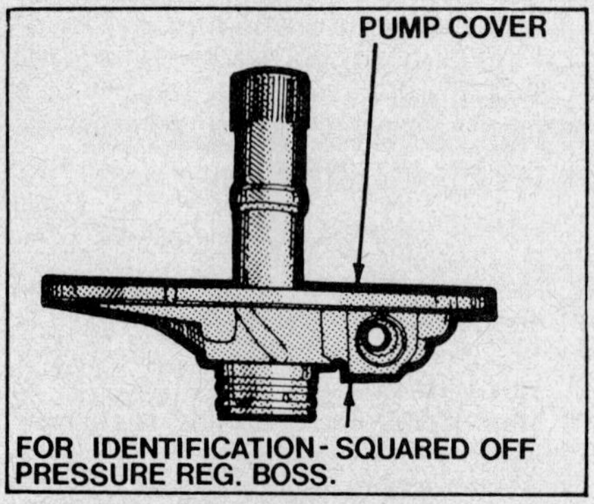

Fig. 4 Pressure regulator identification

IN-VEHICLE REPAIRS

PRESSURE REGULATOR, REPLACE

A solid type pressure regulator valve must be used only in a pump cover with a "Squared Off" (machined) pressure regulator boss, **Fig. 4.** A pressure regulator valve with oil holes and an orifice cup plug may be used with either type pump.

1. Remove bottom pan and strainer.
2. Using a screwdriver or steel rod, compress regulator boost valve bushing against pressure regulator spring, **Fig. 5. Pressure regulator spring is under extreme pressure and will force valve bushing out of bore when snap ring is removed if valve bushing is not held securely.**
3. Continue to exert pressure on valve bushing and remove snap ring. Gradually release pressure on valve bushing until spring force is exhausted.
4. Carefully remove regulator boost valve bushing and valve, and pressure regulator spring. Be careful not to drop parts as they will fall out if they are not held.
5. Remove pressure regulator valve and spring retainer. Remove spacers if present.
6. Reverse procedure to install.

CONTROL VALVE BODY, REPLACE

1. Remove bottom pan and strainer.
2. Disconnect pressure switch lead wire.
3. Remove control valve body attaching screws and detent roller spring assembly. Do not remove solenoid attaching screws.
4. Remove control valve body and governor pipes. If care is used in removing control valve body, the six check balls will stay in place above spacer plate.
5. Remove governor pipes and manual valve from control valve body.
6. Reverse procedure to install.

GOVERNOR, REPLACE

1. Remove governor cover and discard gasket.
2. Withdraw governor from case.
3. Reverse procedure to install, using a new gasket.

MODULATOR & MODULATOR VALVE, REPLACE

1. Remove modulator attaching screw and retainer.
2. Remove modulator assembly from case and discard O-ring seal.

3. Remove modulator valve from case.
4. Reverse procedure to install, using a new O-ring seal.

PARKING LINKAGE, REPLACE

1. Remove bottom pan and oil strainer.
2. Loosen jam nut holding detent lever to manual shaft.
3. Remove manual shaft retaining pin from case.
4. Remove manual shaft and jam nut from case.
5. Remove O-ring seal from manual shaft.
6. Remove parking actuator rod and detent lever assembly.
7. Remove parking pawl bracket, pawl return spring and pawl shaft retainer.
8. Remove parking pawl shaft, O-ring seal and parking pawl.
9. Reverse procedure to install, using new seals and gasket.

REAR SEAL, REPLACE

1. Remove propeller shaft.
2. Pry out seal with screwdriver.
3. Install new seal with a suitable seal driver.
4. Install propeller shaft.

TRANSMISSION REPLACE

1. Disconnect battery ground cable and raise vehicle.

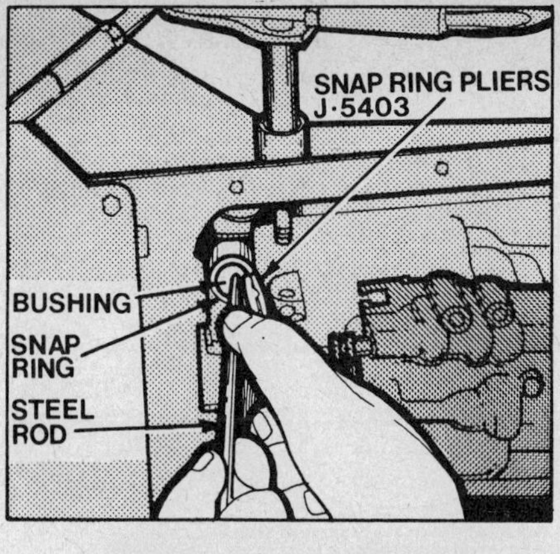

Fig. 5 Removing & installing pressure regulator valve

2. Disconnect transmission shift linkage, speedometer cable, downshift connector, and the Track Master electrical connector, if equipped.
3. Disconnect and plug oil cooler lines from transmission and position aside. Also, plug transmission ports.
4. Disconnect vacuum line from vacuum modulator and position aside.
5. Remove propeller shaft.
6. Remove lower flywheel housing cover and the three converter to flywheel attaching bolts. **This is accomplished by inserting a heavy screwdriver in open slot under one of the converter weld nuts and rotating the converter with a 1¼ inch deep socket until the bolts are accessible. Do not pry on ring gear or transmission case to rotate converter as damage may result.**
7. Support rear of engine with a suitable jack.
8. Remove two nuts from tunnel strap, then the strap.
9. Remove two rear engine mounts to extension housing screws.
10. Support transmission with a suitable jack and raise transmission slightly, releasing load from rear engine support crossmember, and remove shim.
11. Remove rear engine support crossmember bolts, then the space from crossmember right side.
12. Disconnect exhaust pipe from manifold and remove rear engine support crossmember.
13. Remove engine to transmission bolts. **It may be necessary to slightly lower the engine and transmission to gain access to the upper attaching bolts.**
14. Move transmission rearward, disengaging transmission case from engine locating dowels, and install a suitable converter holding tool.
15. Lower transmission from vehicle.
16. Reverse procedure to install. Torque engine to transmission case bolts to 35 ft. lbs. and the converter to flywheel bolts to 30 ft. lbs.

Turbo Hydra-Matic 700-R4 Automatic Transmission

INDEX

IDENTIFICATION

Transmission identification code can be located in one of two positions: right rear pan to case mounting flange or right side transmission to engine mounting flange. The second and third digits of the transmission identification code denotes transmission model.

DESCRIPTION

The model 700-R4, **Fig. 1**, is a fully automatic transmission consisting of a 3-element hydraulic torque converter with the addition of a converter clutch.

Also two planetary gear sets, five multiple-disc type clutches, two roller or one-way clutches and a band are used which provide the friction elements to produce four forward speeds, the last of which is overdrive.

The torque converter, through oil, couples the engine power to the gear sets and hydraulically provides additional torque multiplication when required. Also, through the converter clutch, the converter drive and driven members operate as one unit when applied, providing mechanical drive from the engine through the transmission.

The gear ratio changes are fully automatic in relation to the vehicle speed and engine torque. Vehicle speed and engine torque are directed to the transmission providing the proper gear ratio for maximum efficiency and performance at all throttle openings.

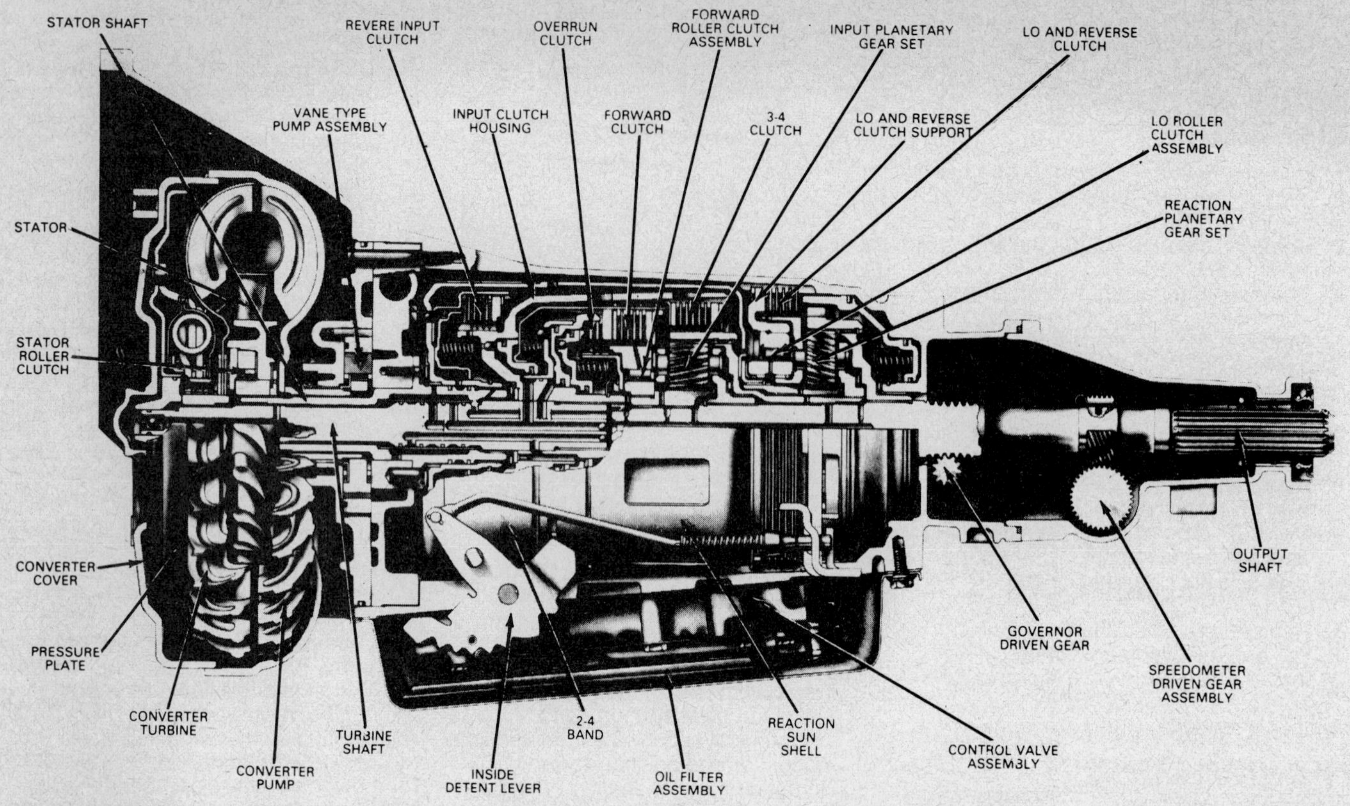

Fig. 1 700-R4 automatic transmission

A hydraulic system pressurized by a variable capacity vane-type pump, provides the operating pressure required for the operation of the friction elements and automatic controls.

TROUBLESHOOTING

OIL PRESSURE HIGH OR LOW

1. Oil pump assembly pressure regulator valve stuck.
2. Oil pump assembly pressure regulator valve spring damaged.
3. Oil pump rotor guide missing or incorrectly installed.
4. Oil pump rotor cracked or damaged.
5. T.V. valve and reverse boost valve or bushing stuck, damaged or incorrectly installed.
6. Orifice hole in pressure regulator valve plugged.
7. Oil pump assembly slide sticking or excessive rotor clearance.
8. Oil pump pressure relief ball not sealed or damaged.
9. Oil pump cover or body porous.
10. Incorrect pump cover or defective pump faces.
11. Oil filter intake pipe and filter body restricted or cracked.
12. Oil filter O-ring seal missing, cut or damaged.
13. T.V. exhaust ball stuck or damaged.
14. Throttle lever and bracket assembly or throttle link binding, damaged or incorrectly installed.
15, Valve body manual valve scored or damaged.
16. Valve body spacer plate or gaskets incorrect, damaged or incorrectly installed.
17. Valve body throttle valve sticking, sleeve rotated in bore or retaining pin not seated.
18. T.V. limit valve, line bias valve, modulated downshift valve or 2-3 shift valve stuck.
19. Valve body check balls missing or incorrectly installed.

HIGH OR LOW SHIFT POINTS

1. T.V. cable binding or incorrectly adjusted.
2. T.V. exhaust ball stuck or damaged.
3. Throttle lever and bracket assembly binding, damaged or incorrectly installed.
4. Sticking oil pump slide, pressure regulator valve or T.V. boost valve.
5. Valve body modulated T.V. up or down valves sticking.
6. T.V. limit valve, throttle valve or plunger sticking.
7. Valve body spacer plate or gaskets damaged or incorrect.

FIRST SPEED ONLY—NO UPSHIFT

1. Governor valve sticking.
2. Governor driven gear loose or damaged.
3. Governor driven gear retaining pin missing.
4. Nicks or burrs on output shaft, governor sleeve or case bore.
5. Governor support pin in case too long or short.
6. Governor weights or springs missing, binding or damaged.
7. 1-2 shift valve sticking.
8. Valve body spacer plate or gaskets damaged or incorrectly installed.
9. Case to valve body face not flat or damaged.
10. Governor screen restricted or damaged.
11. Restricted or blocked 2-4 servo assembly apply passages.
12. Nicks or burrs on 2-4 servo assembly pin or pin bore in case.
13. Missing or damaged 2-4 servo assembly piston or pin seals.
14. Fourth servo piston installed backwards.
15. 2-4 band assembly worn or damaged.
16. 2-4 band assembly anchor pin not engaged.

SLIPS IN FIRST GEAR

1. Forward clutch assembly plates worn.
2. Porosity or damage in forward clutch piston.
3. Forward clutch piston inner and outer seals missing, cut or damaged.
4. Input housing to forward clutch housing O-ring seal missing, cut or damaged.
5. Forward clutch housing damaged.
6. Forward clutch housing retainer and ball assembly not sealing or damaged.
7. Turbine shaft seals missing, cut or damaged.
8. Valve body accumulator valve stuck.
9. Valve body face not flat, damaged lands or interconnected passages.
10. Valve body spacer plate or gaskets incorrect, damaged or incorrectly installed.

11. T.V. cable binding or broken.
12. Damaged ring grooves on 1-2 accumulator piston.
13. 1-2 accumulator piston seal missing, cut or damaged.
14. 1-2 accumulator cover gasket missing or damaged.
15. Leak between 1-2 accumulator piston and pin.
16. Broken 1-2 accumulator spring.
17. Fourth servo piston installed backwards.
18. Incorrect oil pressure. Refer to "High Or Low Oil Pressure."

1-2 SHIFT SPEED HIGH OR LOW

1. T.V. cable binding, broken or incorrectly adjusted.
2. Faulty governor assembly. Refer to "First Speed Only – No Upshift."
3. Throttle lever and bracket assembly damaged, binding or incorrectly installed.
4. T.V. link missing, binding or damaged.
5. T.V. exhaust check ball and T.V. plunger sticking.
6. Valve body or oil pump assembly face not flat.

1-2 SHIFT SLIPPING OR ROUGH

1. Throttle lever and bracket assembly incorrectly installed or damaged.
2. T.V. cable damaged.
3. Throttle valve sticking.
4. T.V. bushing turned in its bore.
5. 1-2 shift valve train stuck.
6. Valve body assembly gaskets or spacer plate incorrect, damaged or incorrectly installed.
7. T.V. limit valve, line bias valve or accumulator valve stuck.
8. Valve body face not flat.
9. 2-4 servo assembly apply pin too long or short.
10. 2-4 servo seals or O-ring seals missing, cut or damaged.
11. 2-4 servo assembly bore damaged.
12. Restricted or missing 2-4 servo assembly oil passages.
13. Porosity in 1-2 accumulator housing or piston.
14. Second accumulator piston seal or groove damaged.
15. Nicks or burrs in 1-2 accumulator housing.
16. 2-4 band worn or incorrectly installed.
17. Oil pump assembly faces not flat.

NO 2-3 SHIFT OR 2-3 SHIFT SLIPPING, ROUGH OR HUNTING

1. Internal converter damage.
2. Governor valve stuck.
3. Governor assembly drive gear retaining pin missing or loose.
4. Governor weights binding.
5. Governor drive gear damaged.
6. Governor support pin in case too long or short.
7. Oil pump stator shaft sleeve scored or improperly installed.
8. Accumulator valve, throttle valve, T.V. limit valve or 2-3 valve train stuck.
9. Valve body spacer plate or gaskets incorrect, damaged or incorrectly installed.
10. Forward or 3-4 clutch plates worn.
11. Excessive clutch plate travel.
12. Cut or damaged piston seals in input housing assembly.
13. Porosity in 3-4 clutch housing or piston.
14. 3-4 piston check ball stuck, damaged or incorrectly sealing.
15. Restricted input housing assembly apply passages.
16. Forward clutch piston retainer and ball assembly not seating.
17. Input housing assembly sealing balls loose or missing.
18. Third accumulator retainer and ball assembly not seating.
19. Second apply piston seals missing, cut or damaged.
20. 2-4 servo pin seals missing, cut or damaged.

NO 3-4 SHIFT OR ROUGH 3-4 SHIFT

1. Governor weights bonding.
2. Governor valve stuck.
3. Governor drive gear retaining pin missing or loose.
4. Governor drive gear damaged.
5. Governor support pin in case too long or short.
6. Oil pump assembly faces not flat.
7. Pump cover retainer and ball assembly missing or damaged.
8. Accumulator valve, throttle valve, T.V. limit valve, 3-2 control valve, 1-2 shift valve train or 2-3 shift valve train stuck.
9. Manual valve link bent or damaged.
10. Valve body assembly spacer plates or gaskets incorrect, damaged or incorrectly installed.
11. Incorrect 2-4 servo assembly band apply pin.
12. Missing or damaged 2-4 servo seals.
13. Porosity in 2-4 servo pistons, cover and case.
14. Damaged 2-4 servo piston seal grooves.
15. Plugged or missing orifice cup plug in 2-4 servo assembly.
16. Third accumulator retainer and ball assembly leaking.
17. Porosity in 3-4 accumulator piston or bore.
18. 3-4 accumulator piston seal or seal grooves damaged.
19. Plugged or missing orifice cup plug.
20. Restricted case oil passage.
21. Faulty input housing assembly. Refer to "No 2-3 Shift Or 2-3 Shift Slipping, Rough Or Hunting."
22. 2-4 band assembly worn or incorrectly installed.

NO REVERSE OR SLIPS IN REVERSE

1. 3-4 apply ring stuck in applied position.
2. Forward clutch not releasing.
3. Turbine shaft seals missing, cut or damaged.
4. Manual linkage incorrectly adjusted.
5. Oil pump retainer and ball assembly missing or damaged.
6. Oil pump stator shaft sleeve scored or damaged.
7. Reverse boost valve stuck, damaged or incorrectly installed.
8. Oil pump cup plug missing.
9. Oil pump converter clutch apply valve stuck.
10. Oil pump face not flat or restricted oil passage.
11. 2-3 shift valve stuck.
12. Valve body spacer plate and gaskets incorrect, damaged or incorrectly installed.
13. Reverse input clutch plate worn.
14. Reverse input housing and drum assembly cracked at weld.
15. Reverse input clutch plate retaining ring out of groove.
16. Reverse input clutch return spring assembly retaining ring out of groove.
17. Reverse input clutch seals cut or damaged.
18. Reverse input clutch retainer and ball assembly not sealing.
19. Restricted oil apply passage in reverse input clutch.
20. Lo and reverse clutch plates worn.
21. Lo and reverse clutch plate retaining ring incorrectly installed.
22. Porosity in low and reverse clutch piston.
23. Low and reverse clutch seals damaged or oil apply passage restricted.
24. Case cover plate gasket missing, damaged or incorrectly torqued.

NO PART THROTTLE OR DELAYED DOWNSHIFTS

1. Throttle linkage incorrectly adjusted.
2. 2-4 servo assembly apply pin cut or damaged.
3. 2-4 servo cover retaining ring missing or incorrectly installed.
4. Fourth apply piston damaged or incorrectly installed.
5. 2-4 servo inner housing damaged or incorrectly installed.
6. Governor weights binding.
7. Governor valve stuck.
8. Throttle valve, 3-2 control valve or T.V. modulated downshift valve stuck.
9. T.V. sleeve turned in bore.
10. 4-3 sequence valve body channel blocked.
11. Number 5 check ball missing from valve body.

NO OVERRUN BRAKING — MANUAL 3-2-1

1. Throttle linkage incorrectly adjusted.
2. Throttle valve or 4-3 sequence valve stuck.
3. Number 3 check ball incorrectly installed.
4. Valve body spacer plate and gaskets incorrect, damaged or incorrectly installed.
5. Turbine shaft oil passages plugged or not drilled.
6. Turbine shaft seal rings damaged.
7. Turbine shaft sealing balls loose or missing.
8. Porosity in forward or overrun clutch piston.
9. Overrun piston seals cut or damaged.
10. Overrun piston check ball not seating.

NO CONVERTER CLUTCH APPLY

1. 12 volts not being applied to the transmission.
2. Defective outside electrical connector.
3. Defective inside electrical connector, wiring harness or solenoid.
4. Solenoid shorted or incorrectly grounded.
5. Incorrect or damaged pressure switches.
6. Internal converter damage.
7. Oil pump converter clutch apply valve stuck or incorrectly installed.
8. Oil pump converter clutch apply valve retaining ring incorrectly installed.
9. Oil pump to case gasket incorrectly installed.
10. Oil pump orifice cup plug clogged.
11. Oil pump solenoid O-ring seal cut or damaged.
12. Oil pump orifice cup plug missing from cooler in passage.
13. High or uneven oil pump body to cover bolt torque.
14. Converter clutch shift valve or throttle valve stuck.
15. Turbine shaft O-ring seal cut or damaged.
16. Turbine shaft retainer and ball assembly plugged.

CONVERTER SHUDDER

1. Internal torque converter damage.
2. Converter clutch shift valve stuck.
3. Oil pump converter clutch apply valve stuck.
4. Restricted oil pump oil passage.
5. Crack in oil filter body or restriction in filter neck.
6. Oil filter O-ring seal cut or damaged.
7. Low oil pressure or engine not properly tuned.
8. Turbine shaft O-ring cut or damaged.
9. Turbine shaft retainer and ball assembly damaged.

NO CONVERTER CLUTCH RELEASE

1. Oil pump converter clutch apply valve stuck.
2. Internal torque converter damage.
3. Solenoid grounded.

DRIVES IN NEUTRAL

1. Forward clutch burned or not releasing.
2. Manual linkage disconnected or incorrectly adjusted.
3. Internal leakage in case or case face not flat.

SECOND GEAR START IN DRIVE RANGE

1. Governor valve stuck.
2. Governor support pin too long or missing.
3. Forward sprag clutch assembly installed backwards.

NO PARK

1. Parking linkage actuator rod assembly bent or damaged.
2. Parking linkage actuator rod spring binding or improperly crimped.
3. Parking linkage actuator rod not attached to inside detent lever.
4. Parking linkage bracket damaged or not torqued properly.
5. Inside detent lever not torqued properly.
6. Detent roller improperly installed.
7. Parking pawl binding or damaged.

RATCHETING NOISE

1. Parking pawl return spring weak, damaged or incorrectly installed.

OIL OUT OF THE VENT

1. Chamfer in oil pump body rotor pocket too large.
2. T.V. limit valve stuck.

VIBRATION IN REVERSE & WHINING NOISE IN PARK

1. Broken vane rings in oil pump.

MAINTENANCE

Fluid level should be checked at every engine oil change. Frequency of change for transmission fluid is dependent on the type of driving conditions in which the vehicle is used. If the transmission is subjected to severe service such as: use in heavy city traffic when the outside temperature regularly reaches 90° F, use in very hilly or mountainous areas, commercial use such as taxi or delivery service, the fluid should be changed every 15,000 miles. Otherwise, change the fluid every 100,000 miles, using Dexron II or equivalent automatic transmission fluid. To check fluid at operating temperature (190°-200° F), which is obtained only after 15 miles of highway-type driving:

1. Apply parking brake and block wheels.
2. Place selector lever in park and start, but do not race, engine. Move selector lever through each range.
3. Check fluid immediately with selector lever in park, engine running at slow idle, and vehicle on level surface. Fluid level should be at full hot mark.

CHANGING FLUID

1. Raise and support vehicle.
2. Place drain pan under transmission oil pan, loosen pan bolts on front of pan, pry carefully with screwdriver to loosen oil pan, and allow fluid to drain.
3. Remove remaining oil pan bolts, oil pan, and gasket.
4. Drain fluid from pan, then clean pan and dry thoroughly with compressed air.
5. Remove oil filter to valve body bolt, then remove filter and gasket, replace with new filter and gasket and install filter attaching bolt. Torque to specification.
6. Install new gasket on oil pan, then install oil pan and torque bolts to 8 ft. lbs.
7. Lower vehicle and add five quarts of automatic transmission fluid through filler tube.
8. With selector lever in park and parking brake applied, start engine and let idle. Do not race engine.
9. Move selector lever through each range, return to park position, check fluid, and add additional fluid to bring level between dimples on dipstick.

ADDING FLUID TO FILL DRY TRANSMISSION & CONVERTER

1. Add 11½ quarts of transmission fluid through filler tube.
2. Place selector lever in park, depress accelerator to place carburetor on fast idle cam, and move selector lever through each range. Do not race engine.
3. With selector lever in park, engine running at idle (1-3 minutes), and vehicle on level surface, check fluid level and add additional fluid to bring level between dimples on dipstick.

IN-VEHICLE ADJUSTMENTS

MANUAL LINKAGE, ADJUST

CAMARO & FIREBIRD

1. Loosen manual lever attaching screw, **Fig. 2.**
2. Place transmission manual shaft in neutral position.
3. Place console shift lever in neutral position.
4. Position shift cable pin so that it is centered in manual lever slot, then torque attaching bolts to 12-18 ft. lbs.

CAPRICE, IMPALA, PARISIENNE, EL CAMINO & MONTE CARLO

1. Loosen swivel clamp screw.
2. Position shift lever in neutral gate.
3. Position transmission lever in neutral detent.
4. While holding swivel clamp flush against equalizer lever, tighten swivel clamp screw, **Fig. 3. Do not exert force in either direction on rod or equalizer lever while tightening swivel clamp screw.**

CORVETTE

1982

1. Place selector lever (A) in PARK position, **Fig. 4.**
2. Place transmission lever (C) in PARK position by rotating lever clockwise to last detent position.
3. Connect cable (B) to levers (A) and (C).

1984

1. Attach cable (1), **Fig. 5,** to top of steering column lock lever by routing cable through retaining bracket and seating cable retaining clip firmly in place.
2. Press cable connector firmly over pin on steering column lock lever.
3. Place lock lever in locked position and move shifter assembly park lever to Park position.
4. Apply rearward tension to shift lever (3) to hold it against park stop.

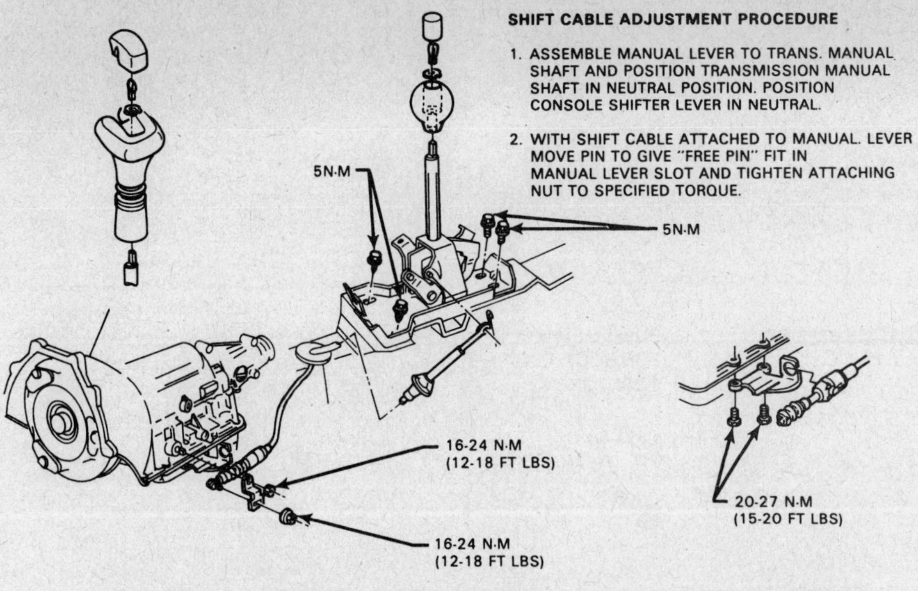
SHIFT CABLE ADJUSTMENT PROCEDURE
1. ASSEMBLE MANUAL LEVER TO TRANS. MANUAL SHAFT AND POSITION TRANSMISSION MANUAL SHAFT IN NEUTRAL POSITION. POSITION CONSOLE SHIFTER LEVER IN NEUTRAL.
2. WITH SHIFT CABLE ATTACHED TO MANUAL. LEVER MOVE PIN TO GIVE "FREE PIN" FIT IN MANUAL LEVER SLOT AND TIGHTEN ATTACHING NUT TO SPECIFIED TORQUE.
5N·M
5N·M
16-24 N·M (12-18 FT LBS)
16-24 N·M (12-18 FT LBS)
20-27 N·M (15-20 FT LBS)

Fig. 2 Shift linkage adjustment. Camaro & Firebird

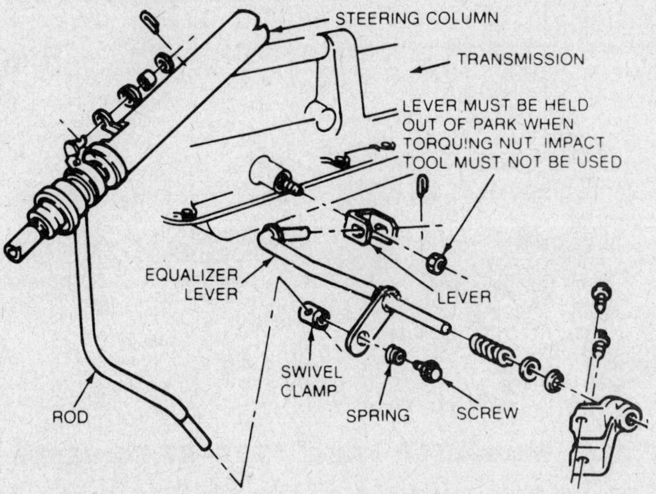
STEERING COLUMN
TRANSMISSION
LEVER MUST BE HELD OUT OF PARK WHEN TORQUING NUT IMPACT TOOL MUST NOT BE USED
EQUALIZER LEVER
LEVER
SWIVEL CLAMP
SPRING
SCREW
ROD

Fig. 3 Column shift manual linkage. Caprice, Impala, Parisienne, El Camino & Monte Carlo

5. Pull adjusting key (5) up on cable and install cable to park lock lever pin on shifter. Secure cable with retainer (2). **Secure retainer in slot in bracket portion of shifter assembly, then push adjusting key down to lock in place.**

1985–87

1. Place shift control lever in park position.
2. Loosen cable pin retaining nut at transmission lever, **Fig. 6.**
3. Place transmission lever in Park position by rotating lever clockwise to last detent position.
4. Torque cable pin attaching nut at transmission lever as shown, **Fig. 6.**

T.V. CABLE, ADJUST

The T.V. cable should not be thought of as an automatic downshift cable. It controls line pressures, shift points, shift feel, part throttle downshifts, and detent downshifts. The function of the cable is similar to the combined functions of a vacuum modulator and detent downshift cable. The T.V. cable operates the throttle lever and bracket assembly, **Figs. 7 and 8.**

1. Stop engine.
2. Depress readjust tab and move slider through fitting, away from lever assembly, until slider stops against fitting. Release readjust tab.
3. Open carburetor lever to full throttle stop position to automatically adjust cable, then release carburetor lever and check cable for sticking or binding.
4. Road test vehicle. If delayed or only full throttle shifts still occur, proceed as follows:
   a. Remove oil pan and inspect throttle lever and bracket assembly, **Fig. 9.**
   b. Check T.V. exhaust valve lifter rod for distortion, or binding in control valve assembly or spacer plate.
   c. Make sure T.V. exhaust check ball moves up and down in conjunction with lifter.
   d. Make sure lifter spring holds lifter rod up against control valve assembly.
   e. Make sure T.V. plunger is not stuck.
   f. Inspect transmission for correct throttle lever to cable link.

IN-VEHICLE REPAIRS

SERVO ASSEMBLY, REPLACE

1. On 1984-87 Corvette models, raise and support vehicle, then disconnect exhaust system and remove propeller shaft and torque arm. **On 1986 Corvette convertible models, the upper and lower underbody braces must be removed prior to disconnecting the exhaust system. Also, on all 1986-87 Corvette models, the driveline support beam must be removed before disconnecting propeller shaft.**
2. On all models, remove two oil pan bolts and install tool No. J-29714 or equivalent on oil pan flange to depress servo cover.
3. Remove servo cover retaining ring, then remove tool.
4. Remove cover and seal ring which may be in case.
5. Remove servo piston and bore-apply pin assembly.
6. Reverse procedure to install.

SPEEDOMETER DRIVEN GEAR, REPLACE

1. Disconnect speedometer cable or P.M. generator electrical connector from transmission.
2. Remove retainer bolt, retainer, P.M. generator (if equipped), speedometer driven gear and O-ring seal.
3. Reverse procedure to install, using new O-ring and adjusting fluid level.

REAR OIL SEAL, REPLACE

1. Remove driveshaft, and tunnel strap, if equipped.
2. Using suitable tool, pry out lip oil seal.
3. Coat outer casting of new oil seal with suitable sealer and drive into place with installer J-21426.
4. Install tunnel strap if used, then install driveshaft.

GOVERNOR, REPLACE

1. Raise and support vehicle, then if necessary, remove exhaust system.
2. Remove governor cover from case using extreme care not to damage cover. If cover is damaged, it must be replaced.
3. Remove governor.
4. Reverse procedure to install and check fluid level.

CONTROL VALVE ASSEMBLY, REPLACE

1. Drain and remove oil pan and remove filter and gasket.
2. Disconnect electrical connectors at valve body.

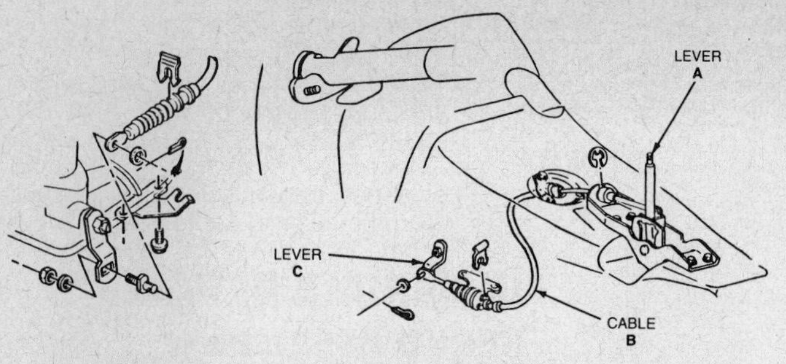

Fig. 4 Manual linkage. 1982 Corvette

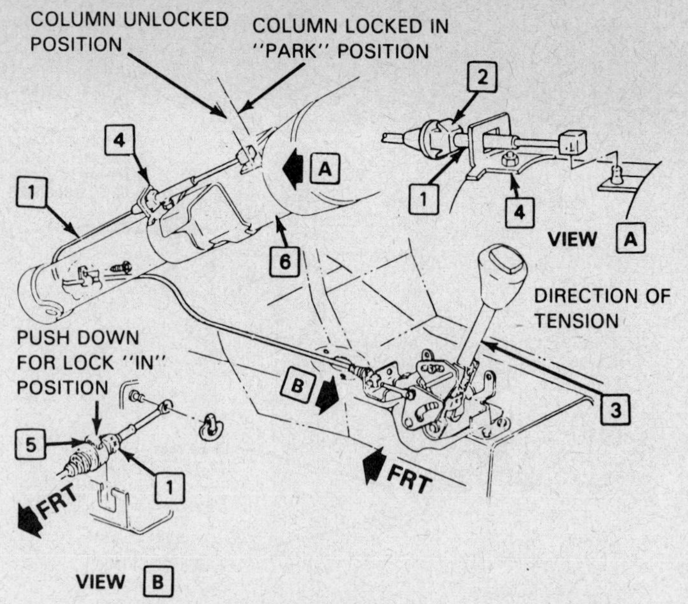

Fig. 5 Manual linkage. 1984 Corvette

3. Remove detent spring and roller assembly from valve body and remove valve body to case bolts.
4. Remove valve body assembly while disconnecting manual control valve link from range selector inner lever and removing throttle lever bracket from T.V. link.
5. Reverse procedure to install. Torque bolts to 8 ft. lbs. and replenish fluid.

TRANSMISSION

REPLACE

CAMARO & FIREBIRD

1. Disconnect battery ground cable.
2. Remove oil dipstick tube, if necessary, then disconnect all transmission electrical connectors.
3. Remove air cleaner assembly and disconnect T.V. cable at upper end.
4. Raise and support vehicle.
5. Remove torque arm clamp from transmission.
6. Place a wooden block between floor pan and torque arm and disconnect torque arm from rear axle.
7. Remove propeller shaft, then disconnect speedometer cable, or P.M. generator, and T.V. cable from transmission.
8. Disconnect transmission cooler lines and shift linkage.
9. Remove exhaust bracket, then the upper-to-lower support bolts.
10. Support transmission with a suitable jack and remove transmission rear lower support.
11. Remove flywheel cover, then mark relationship between flywheel and converter and remove torque converter attaching bolts.
12. Remove transmission-to-engine attaching bolts and carefully lower transmission from vehicle.
13. Reverse procedure to install.

CAPRICE, IMPALA & PARISIENNE

1. Remove air cleaner assembly, then, disconnect T.V. cable at its upper end. Remove transmission oil dipstick and bolt holding dipstick tube, if accessible.
2. Raise and support vehicle and remove driveshaft.
3. Disconnect speedometer cable, shift linkage, and all electrical leads at transmission as well as any clips that retain the leads to the transmission case.
4. Remove flywheel cover, mark flywheel and torque converter to maintain original balance. Remove torque converter to flywheel bolts and/or nuts.
5. On gasoline engine vehicles, disconnect catalytic converter support bracket.
6. On all models equipped, remove floor pan reinforcement if it interferes with removal or installation of driveshaft.
7. Remove transmission support to transmission mount bolt and transmission support to frame bolts and insulators, if used.
8. Position a suitable jack under transmission, raise transmission slightly, and slide transmission support rearward.
9. Lower transmission to gain access to oil cooler lines and T.V. cable attachments, disconnect oil cooler lines and T.V. cable, and cap all openings.
10. Support engine with suitable tool, remove transmission to engine bolts, and disconnect transmission assembly.
11. Install torque converter holding tool J-21366 or equivalent, and remove transmission assembly from vehicle.
12. Reverse procedure to install.

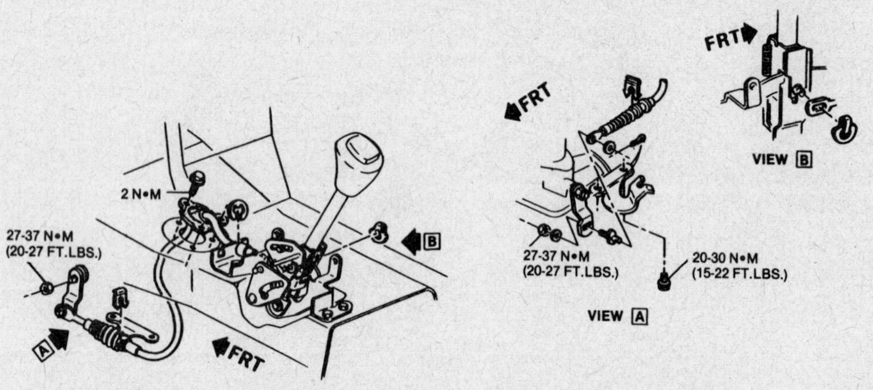

Fig. 6 Manual Linkage. 1985–87 Corvette

CORVETTE

1. Disconnect battery ground cable.
2. Disconnect T.V. cable at upper end, then remove transmission oil dipstick.
3. Raise and support vehicle.
4. On 1986-87 convertible models, remove upper and lower underbody braces.
5. On all models, disconnect speedometer cable or P.M. generator electrical connector, shift linkage and all electrical leads from transmission as well as any clips that retain the leads to transmission case.
6. Remove flywheel cover, then mark flywheel and torque converter to maintain original balance. Remove torque converter to flywheel bolts and/or nuts.
7. Remove exhaust system components as necessary.
8. Install suitable jack under transmission, then raise transmission slightly.

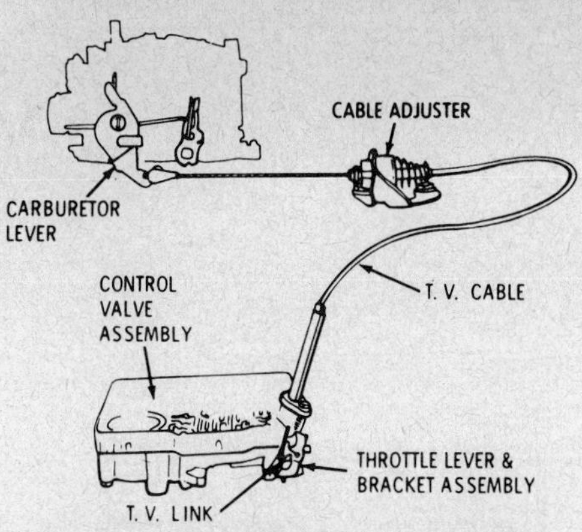

Fig. 7 T.V. cable & linkage

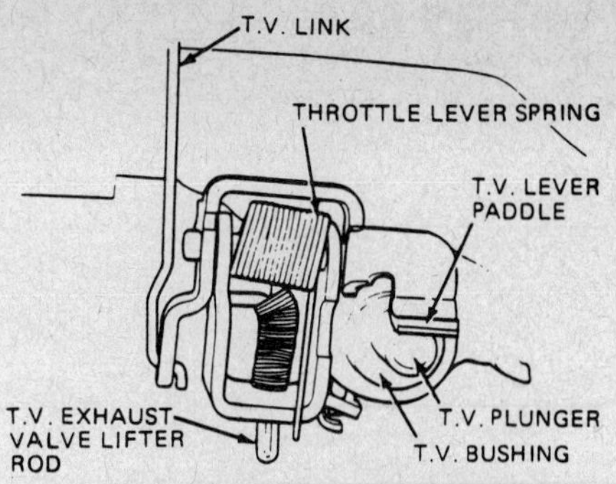

Fig. 8 Throttle lever & bracket assembly

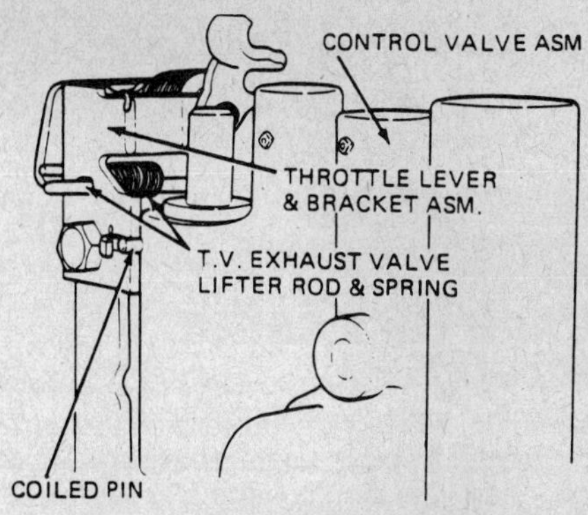

Fig. 9 Throttle lever & bracket assembly alignment

9. Remove driveline beam and propeller shaft.
10. Lower transmission to gain access to oil cooler lines and T.V. cable attachments, then disconnect oil cooler lines and T.V. cable and cap all openings.
11. Support engine using suitable jack, then remove transmission-to-engine attaching bolts.
12. Separate transmission assembly from engine, then install torque converter holding tool No. J-21366 and lower transmission from vehicle.
13. Reverse procedure to install.

EL CAMINO & MONTE CARLO

1. Disconnect battery ground cable.
2. Remove air cleaner assembly and disconnect T.V. cable at upper end.
3. Remove transmission oil dipstick and bolt holding dipstick tube, if necessary.
4. Raise and support vehicle.
5. Remove floor pan reinforcement, if it interferes with removal or installation of driveshaft, then remove driveshaft.
6. Disconnect speedometer cable, shift linkage, and all electrical connectors as well as any clips that retain electrical connectors to the transmission case.
7. Remove flexplate cover, mark flexplate and torque converter to maintain original balance, then remove torque converter to flexplate attaching nuts and/or bolts.
8. Remove catalytic converter support bracket.
9. Remove transmission support to transmission mount bolt, then transmission support to frame bolts and insulator, if used.
10. Position a suitable jack under transmission, raise transmission slightly and slide transmission support rearward.
11. Lower transmission slightly to gain access to oil cooler lines and T.V. cable attachments, then disconnect oil cooler lines and T.V. cable, and cap all openings.
12. Support engine with suitable tool, then remove transmission to engine bolts and disconnect transmission assembly. **Take care not to damage any cables, lines or linkage.**
13. Using tool J-21366 or equivalent, remove transmission assembly from vehicle.
14. Reverse procedure to install noting the following:
    a. Torque converter to flexplate attaching bolts to 46 ft. lbs. (62 Nm).
    b. Adjust T.V. cable and linkage.

Automatic Overdrive Unit (Doug Nash), 1984–87 Corvette

INDEX

DESCRIPTION

The automatic overdrive unit used on the 1984-87 Corvette, **Fig. 1,** and the 4 speed manual transmission is essentially a combination of two separate transmission units. The first unit is a conventional 4 speed (83 mm) manual system with a 1.1 ratio in 4th gear. On 1984 models, the second unit is a two speed overdrive system electronically controlled by the ECM which operates with a 1.1 or .68 to 1 ratio. On 1985-87 models, the second unit is a two speed overdrive system electronically controlled by the ECM which operates with a 1.1 and a .68 to 1 ratio or 1.1 and a .59 to 1 ratio. The two speed or overdrive unit performs its functions using a planetary gear set in combination with two sets of clutch components.

The ECM is programmed to control the shift solenoid and the overdrive unit. The overdrive mode cannot occur when the transmission is in first gear. It can occur when the transmission is in the remaining three gears.

The hydraulic circuit, **Figs. 2 and 3,** consists of a gerotor type pump on the overdrive unit output shaft, a shift valve, solenoid, accumulator valve and a pressure relief valve located in the valve body assembly. In the normal (direct drive) mode, fluid circulates from the pump through a 90-110 psi pressure relief valve on 1984 models and 115-125 psi pressure relief on 1985-87 models, and through the cooler lines then back to the pan or sump. When the overdrive switch is closed by the ECM, the solenoid plunger is activated, opening the shift valve passage for fluid flow into the piston. When the solenoid de-energizes, the shift valve returns to its original position.

TROUBLESHOOTING

Refer to **Fig. 4** for automatic overdrive unit troubleshooting procedure.

IN-VEHICLE ADJUSTMENTS

PARK LOCK CABLE, ADJUST

1. Lift adjusting key upward and release cable, **Fig. 5.**
2. Place steering column lock lever into lock park position.
3. Place transmission shift lever into Reverse.
4. Insert a .060 inch feeler gauge against reverse stop, then pull reverse lever until reverse pawl contacts feeler gauge.
5. Push adjusting key downward to set cable.
6. Remove feeler gauge and pull back on shift lever.
7. Ensure reverse pawl hits reverse stop and locks shifter lever in Reverse.

T.V. CABLE, ADJUST

1. Depress and hold metal lock tab, **Fig. 6.**
2. Move slider back, away from throttle body lever until slider contacts fitting.
3. Release metal lock tab.
4. Rotate throttle lever to the Full throttle stop position to obtain a minimum of one click adjustment.

IN-VEHICLE REPAIRS

SIDE COVER, REPLACE

1. Place transmission shift lever into 2nd gear.
2. Raise and support vehicle.
3. Disconnect electrical connector(s) from side cover switch(s), then remove switch(s) from side cover, if applicable.
4. Remove shift levers from shifter shafts.
5. Remove side cover attaching bolts, then the side cover.
6. Reverse procedure to install.

SHIFTER ASSEMBLY, REPLACE

Removal

1. Disconnect battery ground cable.
2. Disconnect electrical connector from power seat switch(s).
3. Remove left seat from vehicle.
4. Remove knob from shift lever.
5. Remove console cover attaching screws, then the console cover.
6. Remove glove compartment lock and left side panel from console.
7. Remove shifter cover.
8. Disconnect three rods from shifter.
9. Disconnect park lock cable from shifter, then disconnect overdrive switch electrical connector, if applicable.
10. Remove shifter cross bolt and shifter mounting bracket.
11. Remove shifter mounting bolt from body panel, then the shifter assembly from vehicle.

Installation

1. Position shifter into underbody and install mounting bolt. Torque bolt to 40-51 ft. lbs.
2. Position mounting bracket onto shifter and install bracket bolts. Torque cross bolt to 15-22 ft. lbs. Torque mounting bracket to underbody mount bolt to 10-15 ft. lbs.
3. Install three shifter rods onto shifter assembly.
4. Install park lock cable onto shifter. Adjust cable as outlined previously, then reconnect overdrive switch electrical connector, if applicable.
5. Reverse removal steps 1 through 7 for remaining installation procedure.

T.V. CABLE, REPLACE

Refer to **Fig. 7** for T.V. cable routing and attachments. Refer to "T.V. Cable, Adjust" for adjustment procedure.

OVERDRIVE SWITCH, REPLACE

1. Disconnect battery ground cable.
2. Remove instrument cluster trim plate adjusting screws, then the headlight switch knob, tilt column lever and trim plate.

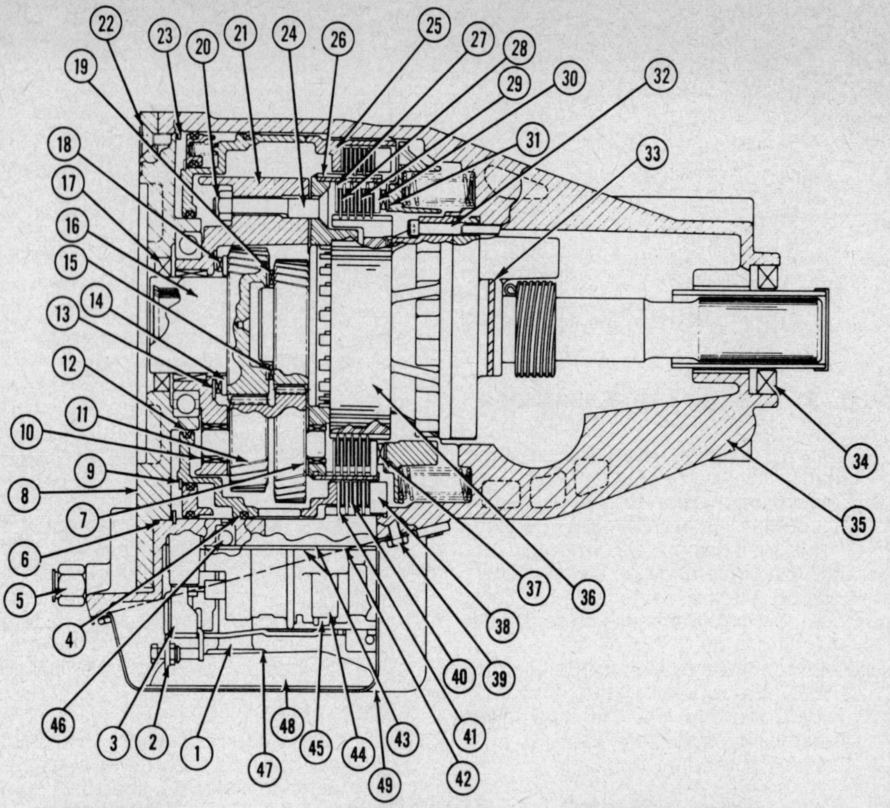

1. PICKUP TUBE
2. LEVER ARM ASSEMBLY
3. LEVER CAM
4. SEAL, "QUAD"
5. FITTING
6. SEAL, 'O' RING
7. PLATE, THRUST
8. PLATE, ADAPTOR
9. PISTON-ACCUM. ASS'Y
10. WASHER, THRUST
11. GEAR, PLANET
12. SEAL, "QUAD"
13. WASHER, THRUST
14. WASHER, THRUST
15. WASHER, THRUST
16. GEAR, SUN
17. SEAL, INPUT
18. BEARING, THRUST
19. BEARING, THRUST
20. NUT, LOCK TORQUE TO 16-18 FT. LBS.
21. CARRIER-BRG. ASS'Y
22. SCREWS, C.S. TORQUE TO 18-20 FT. LBS.
23. RING, RETAINING
24. SCREWS, C.S.
25. PLATE, FINGER PRES.
26. CLUTCH HUB ASS'Y
27. PLATE, SEL. CLUTCH
28. DISC, CLUTCH (5)
29. PLATE, CLUTCH (4)
30. PLATE, BEARING
31. WASHER, THRUST
32. SCREW, ALLEN 6m x 40mm TORQUE TO 6-8 FT. LBS.
33. SEAL, PUMP
34. SEAL, OUTPUT
35. HOUSING ASS'Y
36. SHAFT ASS'Y
37. BEARING, THRUST
38. CLUTCH, STOP
39. SCREW, 6m x 12mm lg. TORQUE TO 6-8 FT. LBS.
40. DISC, CLUTCH (4)
41. PLATE, CLUTCH (4)
42. PLATE, VALVE
43. GASKET, VALVE
44. VALVE BODY ASS'Y
45. SCREW, HEX. 6m x 45mm TORQUE TO 6-8 FT. LBS.
46. BALL, 5/16" STEEL
47. GROMMET
48. OIL FILTER
49. OIL PAN

Fig. 1 Cross sectional view of overdrive unit. Typical

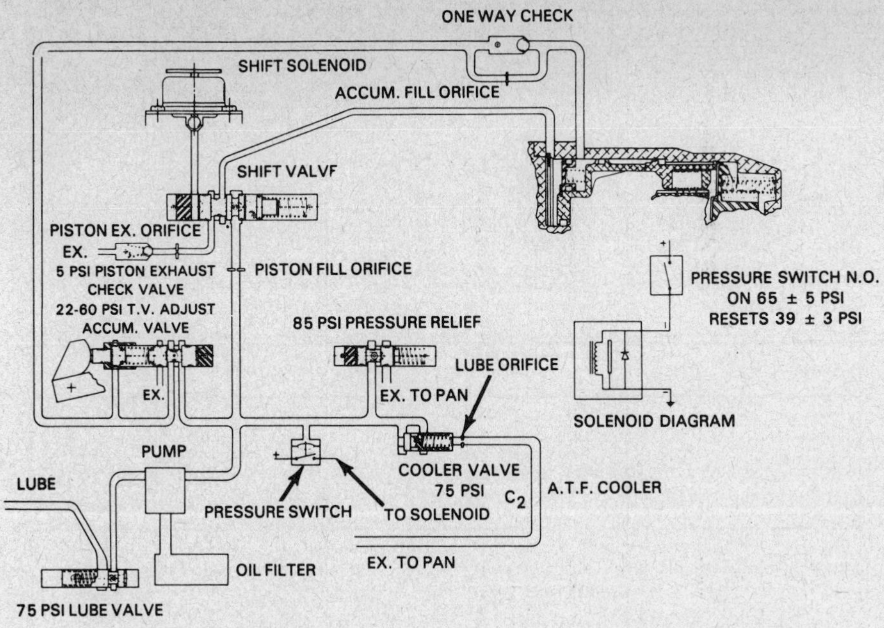

Fig. 2 Overdrive unit hydraulic circuit. 1984–85

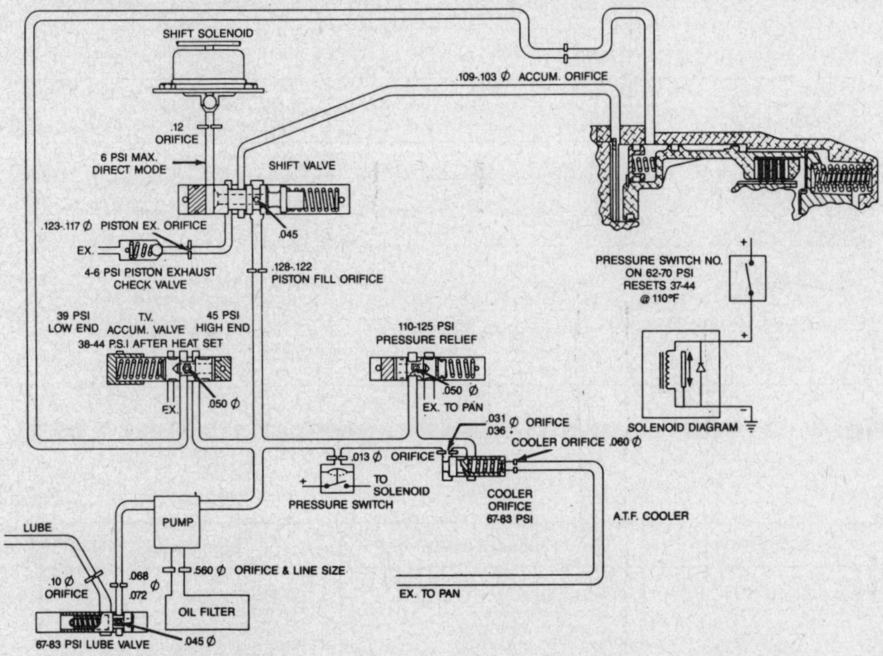

Fig. 3 Overdrive unit hydraulic circuit. 1986–87

3. Remove instrument panel accessory trim plate attaching screws, then the plate.
4. Remove console trim plate attaching screws, pull trim plate rearward, then disconnect cigar lighter electrical connector.
5. Remove shift boot-to-trim plate attaching screws, then the trim plate.
6. Carefully pry overdrive switch button from shifter knob.
7. Disconnect overdrive switch rod from shifter. Count the number of turns required to disconnect rod for installation reference.
8. Loosen overdrive switch-to-shifter retaining nut, then remove switch and slide block. **Use care to prevent losing slide block return spring.**
9. Disconnect switch electrical connector, then remove switch-to-slide block retaining pin.
10. Reverse procedure to install, noting the following:
    a. When installing switch rod, screw rod into switch block the same number of turns noted during removal.
    b. After installing switch button, ensure button is flush with top of shift knob. If not, remove button and turn rod in or out as required.

OIL FILTER, REPLACE

1. Disconnect battery ground cable.
2. Raise and support vehicle.
3. Position a suitable drain pan under overdrive unit oil pan. Remove oil pan attaching bolts from front and side of pan.
4. Loosen rear pan attaching bolts approximately 4 turns.
5. Carefully pry oil pan loose, allowing fluid to drain.
6. Remove remaining pan attaching bolts.
7. Clean oil pan with a suitable solvent and dry thoroughly with compressed air.
8. Remove filter from overdrive unit.
9. Install a new filter.
10. During oil pan installation, note the following:
    a. Apply a bead of RTV sealant number 1052366 or equivalent, onto oil pan flange and install oil pan onto overdrive housing. **The RTV sealant must be wet when installing oil pan onto overdrive housing. RTV sealant should be applied around inside of bolt holes, Fig. 8.**
    b. Install magnet onto oil pan as shown in **Fig. 8.**
    c. Install oil pan attaching bolts. Torque bolts to 6-8 ft. lbs.
11. Fill overdrive unit with Dexron II automatic transmission fluid.

VALVE BODY, REPLACE

1. Disconnect battery ground cable.
2. Disconnect T.V. cable from throttle body lever, if applicable.
3. Remove transmission oil pan and filter assembly as described previously.
4. Disconnect tan colored electrical connector from low pressure cut-off switch.
5. Disconnect T.V. cable from throttle body lever, if applicable, then remove bolt retaining T.V. cable to valve body.
6. Remove remaining valve body to transmission case attaching bolts.
7. Remove valve body and spacer plate assembly from overdrive unit. **Care must be taken when removing valve body to prevent loss of the 2 check balls, Fig. 9. One check ball is spring loaded under the valve body. The other is located under the transmission case above the separator plate.**
8. To install valve body, reverse removal procedure and note the following, if applicable:
    a. Remove T.V. cable attaching bolt from overdrive case. Install tool No. J-34671-1 or equivalent into T.V. cable bore, then hook T.V. cable onto top step, **Fig. 10.**
    b. Unhook T.V. cable from top step, then connect T.V. cable onto lower step.
    c. Position tool No. J-34671-2 or equivalent, between piston and solenoid bracket, **Fig. 11.** Adjust screw/bolt on T.V. lever until bolt contacts cam stop.

OVERDRIVE SOLENOID, REPLACE

1. Disconnect battery ground cable.
2. Remove transmission oil pan and filter assembly as described previously.
3. Disconnect T.V. cable from throttle body lever, if applicable.
4. Remove valve body as described previously.
5. Using tool No. J-34529 or equivalent, compress shift valve spring, then remove retaining pin.
6. Using tool No. J-34529 or equivalent, compress relief valve springs, then remove retaining pin.
7. Remove solenoid valve body attaching bolts.
8. Remove solenoid valve and check ball assembly from valve body.
9. Reverse procedure to install.

PRESSURE SWITCH, REPLACE

1. Disconnect battery ground cable.
2. Remove transmission oil pan and filter assembly as described previously.
3. Disconnect electrical connectors from pressure switch.
4. Remove switch from valve body.
5. Reverse procedure to install.

OVERDRIVE UNIT OUTPUT SEAL, REPLACE

1. Disconnect battery ground cable.
2. Remove propeller shaft as follows:
   a. Raise and support vehicle.
   b. Disconnect AIR pipe from catalytic converter.
   c. Disconnect AIR pipe clamps from exhaust pipe.
   d. Disconnect oxygen sensor lead.
   e. Remove muffler to support hanger attaching bolts.
   f. Disconnect exhaust pipes from exhaust manifolds.
   g. Remove bolts attaching support beam at the axle and transmission.
   h. Mark relationship of propeller shaft to companion flange. Remove trunnion bearing straps, then the rear universal joint. Tape bearings caps to trunnion to prevent bearing loss.
   i. Slide slip yoke from transmission and remove propeller shaft.
3. Using a suitable tool, remove seal from overdrive output shaft.
4. Coat new seal lip with automatic transmission fluid.
5. Using tool No. J-21426 or equivalent, install new seal onto overdrive output shaft seal groove.
6. Reverse removal steps 1 and 2 for remaining installation procedure.

OVERDRIVE UNIT REPLACE

Transmission and overdrive unit are removed as an assembly.

1. Disconnect battery ground cable.
2. Remove air cleaner assembly from engine.
3. Disconnect T.V. cable from left TBI unit, if applicable.

CONDITION	PROBABLE CAUSE	CORRECTION
Overdrive Inop	a. Insufficient Lubricant b. Speedometer Inop c. Blown Fuse d. Temperature Gage Inop e. O/D Switch at Shifter Knob f. Solenoid Inop Check for (12 volts at O/D Connector—Engine at operating temp.—wheels off the ground shift trans from 1st into 2nd gear at 12-15 MPH—solenoid should energize at this point) g. Solenoid Check Ball Missing h. Low Pressure Switch i. Shift Valve Inop j. Pressure Regulator Valve Inop k. Drive Pin Broken or Missing in Pump	a. Fill to correct level b. Replace speedometer sensors. Replace speedometer drive or driven gears. c. Replace fuse d. Replace gage or sending unit e. Replace switch or repair wires f. Replace solenoid or repair wires. g. Install check ball h. Replace switch i. Free up valve or replace valve body j. Free up valve or replace valve body k. Replace pin or pump gears
Overdrive in All Gears	a. Solenoid Plunger Stuck b. Solenoid Exhaust Hole Plugged c. Shift Valve Stuck	a. Replace Solenoid b. Clear exhaust passage c. Free up shift valve or replace valve body
Harsh Up Shifts	a. Stuck T.V. Valve b. Stuck Accumulator Piston c. Accumulator Seal Damaged	a. Free up valve or replace valve body b. Free up or replace c. Replace seal
Harsh Down Shifts	a. Stuck T.V. Valve	a. Free up valve or replace valve body
Soft Up Shift	a. Stuck T.V. Valve b. O/D Clutch Plates Burn't	a. Free up valve or replace valve body b. Replace clutch plates and disc's
Soft Downshift	a. Stuck T.V. Valve	a. Free up valve or replace valve body
No Downshift	a. E.C.M., throttle position switch	a. Repair or replace E.C.M. or throttle position switch
Slips on Upshift	a. Direct Clutch Plates Burn't b. Excessive Clutch Pack Clearance	a. Replace direct clutch plates and disc's b. Adjust clutch pack clearance
Chatters on Upshifts	a. Piston Seals Damaged b. Direct Clutch Plates Burn't c. Low mainline pressure	a. Replace seals b. Replace direct clutch plates and disc's c. Check lines for restrictions. Check pump.

Fig. 4 Overdrive unit troubleshooting chart (Part 1 of 2)

CONDITION	PROBABLE CAUSE	CORRECTION
O/D Overheats	a. Insufficient Lubricant b. Stuck Cooler Valve c. Cooler Line Restriction d. Restriction in Radiator	a. Fill to correct level b. Free up cooler valve or replace valve c. Flush lines or replace d. Flush radiator or replace
No Reverse	a. Direct Clutch Plates Burn't	a. Replace direct clutch plates and disc's
Noisy in Direct Drive	a. Front Carrier Bearing b. Thrust Bearing in Direct Clutch	a. Replace carrier cover b. Replace thrust bearing
Noisy in Overdrive	a. Pinion Roller Bearings b. Pinion Gears (scored, chipped or burn't) c. Input Sun Gear (scored, chipped or burn't) d. Output Sun Gear (scored, chipped or burn't)	a. Replace carrier cover or housing b. Replace pinion gears c. Replace input sun gear d. Replace output sun gear
No Direct Drive	a. Sprag Clutch Damaged	a. Replace Sprag Clutch

Fig. 4 Overdrive unit troubleshooting chart (Part 2 of 2)

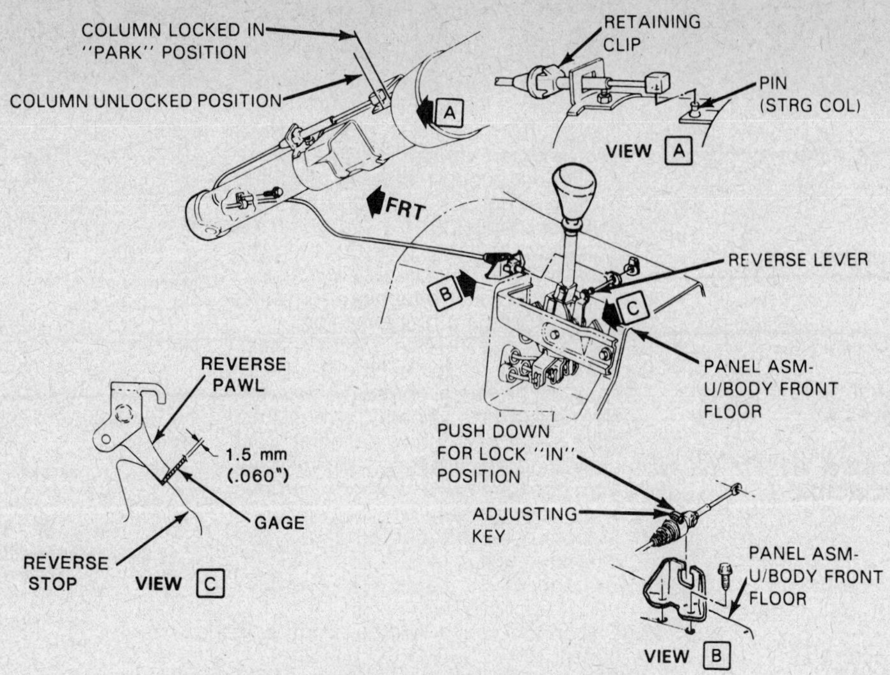

Fig. 5 Park lock cable, adjust

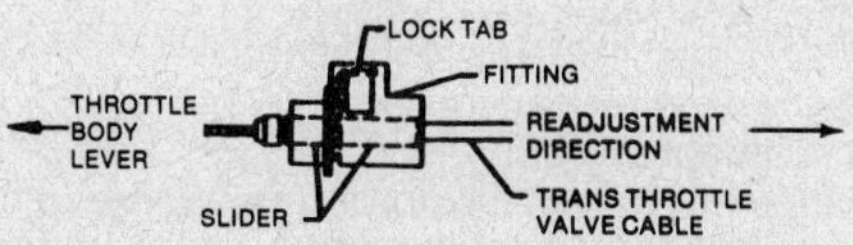

Fig. 6 T.V. cable, adjust

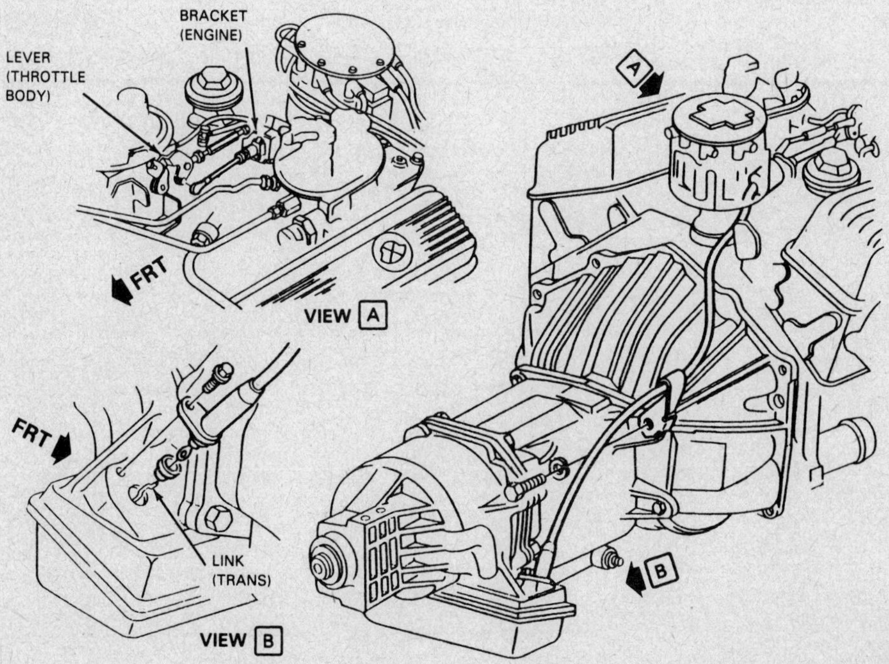

Fig. 7 T.V. cable routing & attachments. Typical

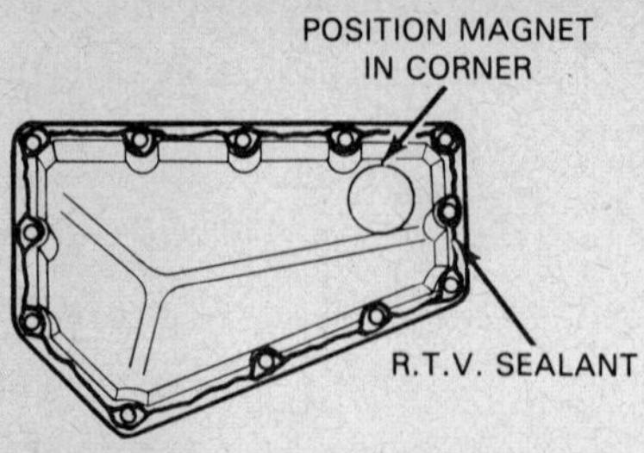

NOTE:

1. INSTALL THE OIL PAN ON HOUSING WHILE R.T.V. SEALANT IS WET.
   PAN AND HOUSING FLANGE SURFACE MUST BE DRY AND FREE OF OIL FILM.

Fig. 8 Magnet & RTV sealant location

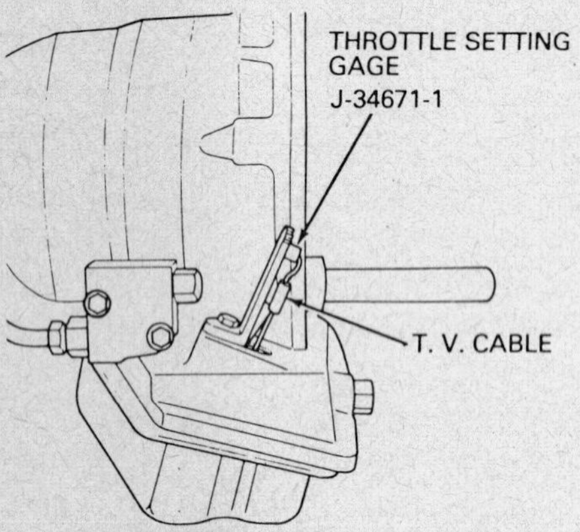

Fig. 10 Hooking T.V. cable onto throttle setting gauge

4. Remove distributor cap and position aside.
5. Raise and support vehicle.
6. Disconnect AIR pipe from catalytic converter. Disconnect AIR pipe clamps from exhaust pipe. Disconnect oxygen sensor lead. Remove muffler to support hanger attaching bolts. Disconnect exhaust pipes from exhaust manifolds.
7. Position a suitable jack under transmission.
8. Remove bolts attaching driveline beam at axle and transmission.
9. Remove driveline beam from vehicle.
10. Mark relationship of the propeller shaft to the axle companion flange. Remove trunnion bearing straps, then disconnect rear universal joint from axle. Slide propeller shaft slip yoke out from the overdrive unit and remove shaft from the vehicle.
11. Disconnect fluid cooler lines from overdrive unit.
12. Disconnect T.V. cable from overdrive unit, if applicable.
13. Disconnect shift linkage from shift cover.
14. Disconnect electrical connector from side cover switches, back-up light switch and overdrive unit. Disconnect speedometer cable.
15. Place a suitable jack under engine oil pan with a block of wood placed between jack and pan.
16. Lower transmission slightly.
17. Remove transmission to bellhousing attaching bolts.
18. Slide transmission and overdrive unit rearward to disengage input shaft from clutch.
19. Lower transmission and overdrive unit from vehicle.
20. Remove (7) transmission to overdrive unit attaching bolts and separate overdrive unit from transmission.
21. Reverse procedure to install.

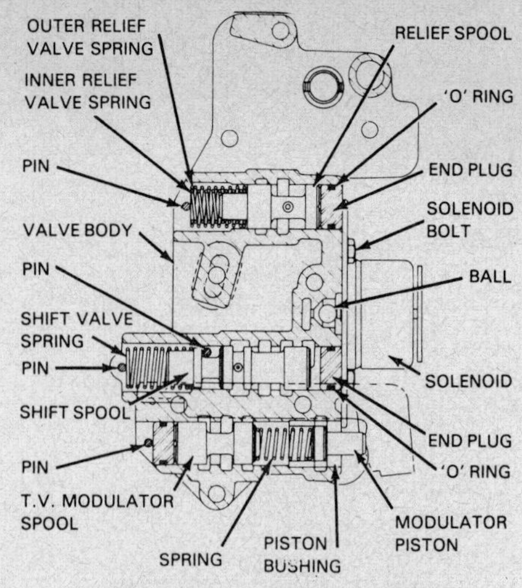

Fig. 9 Valve body components. 1984–85 (1986–87 similar)

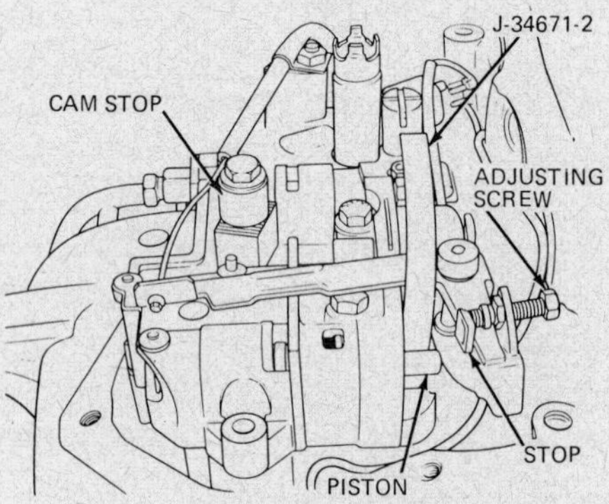

Fig. 11 Positioning tool J-34671-2 between piston & solenoid bracket

FRONT WHEEL DRIVE AXLES

INDEX

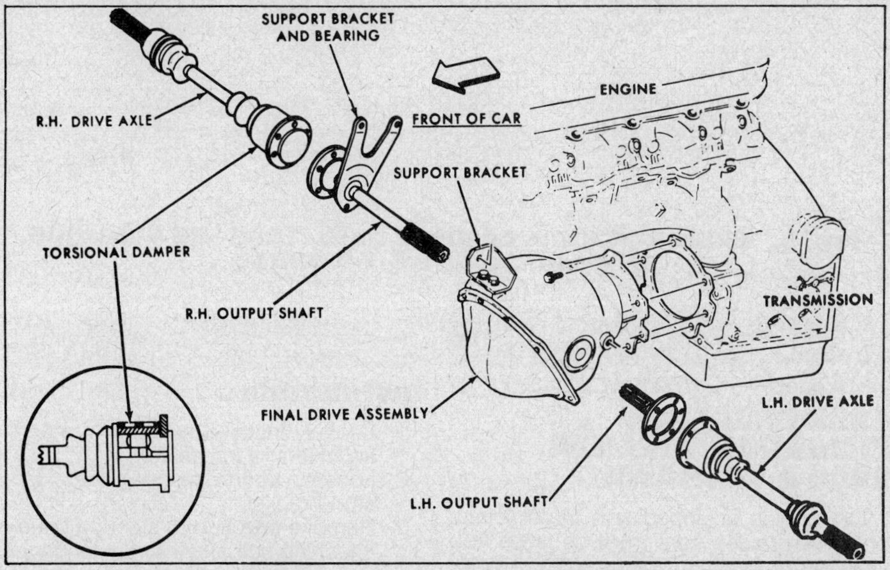

Fig. 1 Front wheel drive components. 1982–85 Eldorado, Riviera, Seville & Toronado

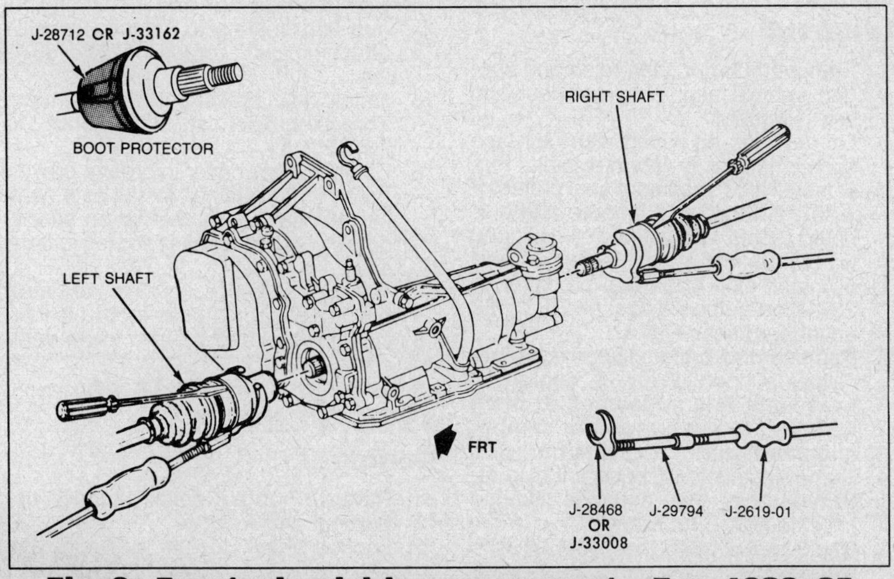

Fig. 2 Front wheel drive components. Exc. 1982–85 Eldorado, Riviera, Seville & Toronado (Typical)

DESCRIPTION

The front wheel drive system, **Figs. 1 and 2,** consists of a final drive unit, left and righthand output shafts and drive axles. On 1982-85 Eldorado, Riviera, Seville and Toronado models, the output shafts are splined to the side gears and are retained by a retaining ring. Each drive axle, **Figs. 3 and 4,** consists of an axle shaft, with a ball type constant velocity joint at the outboard end and a tri-pot joint at the inboard end.

On 1982-84 Citation, Omega, Phoenix, Skylark and 1982-84 Cavalier, Celebrity, Century, Cimarron, Cutlass Ciera, Firenza, 2000, Skyhawk and 6000 models, two different types of drive axle design are used. Both designs use the same ball type constant velocity joint at the outboard end. One design uses a ball type constant velocity joint at the inboard end, **Fig. 5,** the other design uses a tri-pot joint at the inboard end, **Fig. 6.** Both designs incorporate male splines which lock on the transaxle gears with snap rings, except for the left side inboard joint used with the automatic transaxles. The left side inboard joint used on automatic transaxle models utilizes a female spline which installs over a transaxle stub shaft.

On 1985-87 models except Nova and 1985 Eldorado, Riviera, Seville and Toronado, a ball type constant velocity joint is used at the outboard end, while a tri-pot type joint is used at the inboard end, **Fig. 4.** Snap rings are used to lock the male splines of the axle shafts into the transaxle gears, except for the left side inboard joint used with the automatic transaxles. The left side inboard joint used on automatic transaxle models utilizes a female spline which installs over a transaxle stub shaft.

On 1985-87 Nova models, a ball type constant velocity joint is used at the outboard end, while a tri-pot type joint is used at the inboard end. Snap rings are used to lock the male splines of the axle shafts into the transaxle gears, **Fig. 4.**

DRIVE AXLE
REPLACE

EXC. 1982–85 ELDORADO, RIVIERA, SEVILLE, TORONADO; 1982 CAVALIER, CIMARRON, FIRENZA, 2000, SKYHAWK; 1985–87 NOVA

On models equipped with tri-pot joints on inboard axles, care must be taken not to overextend joints. When either or both ends are disconnected, overextending the tri-pot joint could result in internal joint separation.

Removal

1. Remove hub nut, then raise and support vehicle and remove wheel and tire assembly.
2. On vehicles equipped with ball type constant velocity inboard joints, **Fig. 5,** install axle shaft boot seal protector J-28712, **Fig. 2,** on inboard and outboard seals. On vehicles equipped with tri-pot inboard joints, **Figs. 4 and 6,** install axle boot seal protector J-28712 on outboard seal and J-33162 on inboard seal, **Fig. 2.**
3. Disconnect brake line clip at strut.
4. Remove disc brake caliper and caliper support.
5. Mark cam bolt to ensure proper camber alignment during installation.
6. Remove bolts attaching steering knuckle to strut.
7. Using tool J-28468 or J-33008 and J-2619-01, **Fig. 2,** disengage snap rings retaining drive axles.
8. Separate steering knuckle from strut.
9. Carefully pull drive axles from transaxle. On vehicles equipped with tri-pot inboard joints, **Fig. 6,** do not overextend joints.
10. Using tool J-28733, remove axle shaft from hub and bearing assembly.

Installation

1. Loosely install drive axle to steering knuckle and transaxle.
2. Loosely attach steering knuckle to strut bracket.
3. Install disc brake caliper, torque attaching bolts to 30 ft. lbs.
4. Install drive axle to steering knuckle. The drive axle is an interference fit. Install hub nut, when shaft begins to rotate, insert a brass drift in slot on rotor to prevent shaft from turning. It will take approximately 70 ft. lbs. of torque to seat axle shaft.
5. Apply load on hub by lowering vehicle on jack stand. Align cam bolt alignment marks, then torque nut to 140 ft. lbs.
6. Using a screwdriver in groove provided on inner retainer, install axle shaft on transaxle, **Fig. 2.** Tap on screwdriver until axle shaft is seated in transaxle.
7. Connect brake line clip to strut bracket, then install wheel and tire assembly and lower vehicle.
8. Torque hub nut to 225 ft. lbs. on 1982 models and to 185 ft. lbs. on 1983-87 models.

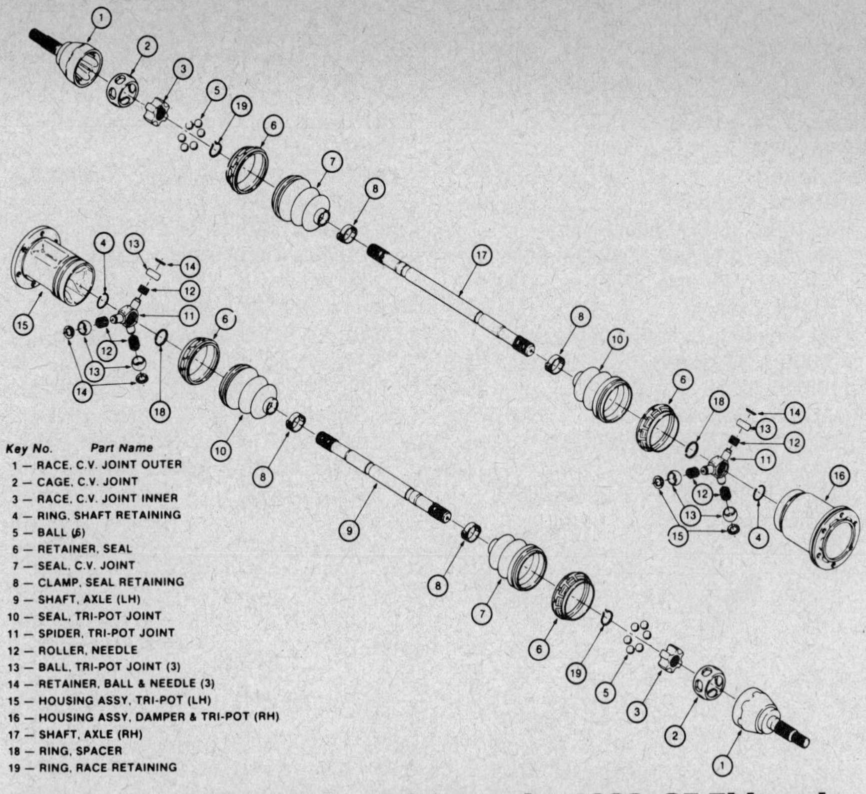

Fig. 3 Exploded view of drive axle. 1982–85 Eldorado, Riviera, Seville & Toronado

1982 CAVALIER, CIMARRON, FIRENZA, 2000 & SKYHAWK

On models equipped with tri-pot joints on inboard axles, care must be taken not to overextend joints. When either or both ends are disconnected, over extending the tri-pot joint could result in internal joint separation.

Removal

1. Remove hub nut, then raise and support vehicle and remove wheel and tire assembly.
2. On vehicles equipped with ball type constant velocity inboard joints, **Fig. 5,** install axle shaft boot seal protector J-28712, **Fig. 2,** on inboard and outboard seals. On vehicles equipped with tri-pot inboard joints, **Figs. 4 and 6,** install axle boot seal protector J-28712 on outboard seal and J-33162 on inboard seal, **Fig. 2.**
3. Remove disc brake caliper, rotor and caliper support. **Prior to beginning next step, it is suggested to mark cam bolt to ensure proper camber alignment during installation.**
4. Remove strut to steering knuckle attaching bolts, then separate steering knuckle from strut bracket.
5. Using tool J-28468 or J-33008 with extension J-29794, remove axle shaft from transaxle, **Fig. 2.**
6. Using tool J-28733, remove axle shaft from hub and bearing assembly.

Installation

1. Loosely install drive axle to steering knuckle and transaxle.
2. Loosely attach steering knuckle to strut bracket.
3. Remove one hub to steering knuckle attaching bolt and install a longer bolt through hub cutout to prevent hub from turning. Install hub nut and washer and torque to 70 ft. lbs.
4. Remove long bolt and install original hub and bearing to steering knuckle attaching bolt. Torque bolts to 63 ft. lbs.
5. Install disc brake caliper and rotor. Torque caliper attaching bolts to 21-35 ft. lbs.
6. Using a screwdriver in groove provided on inner retainer, install axle shaft into transaxle, **Fig. 2.** Tap on screwdriver until axle shaft is seated in transaxle.
7. Torque steering knuckle to strut bracket attaching bolts to 140 ft. lbs.
8. Install wheel and tire and lower vehicle.
9. Torque hub nut to 185 ft. lbs.

1985–87 NOVA

Removal

1. Remove hub nut cotter pin, then the hub nut and washer.
2. Loosen wheel lug nuts, then raise and support vehicle.
3. Remove wheel and tire assembly, then lower control arm to ball joint attaching nuts and bolts.

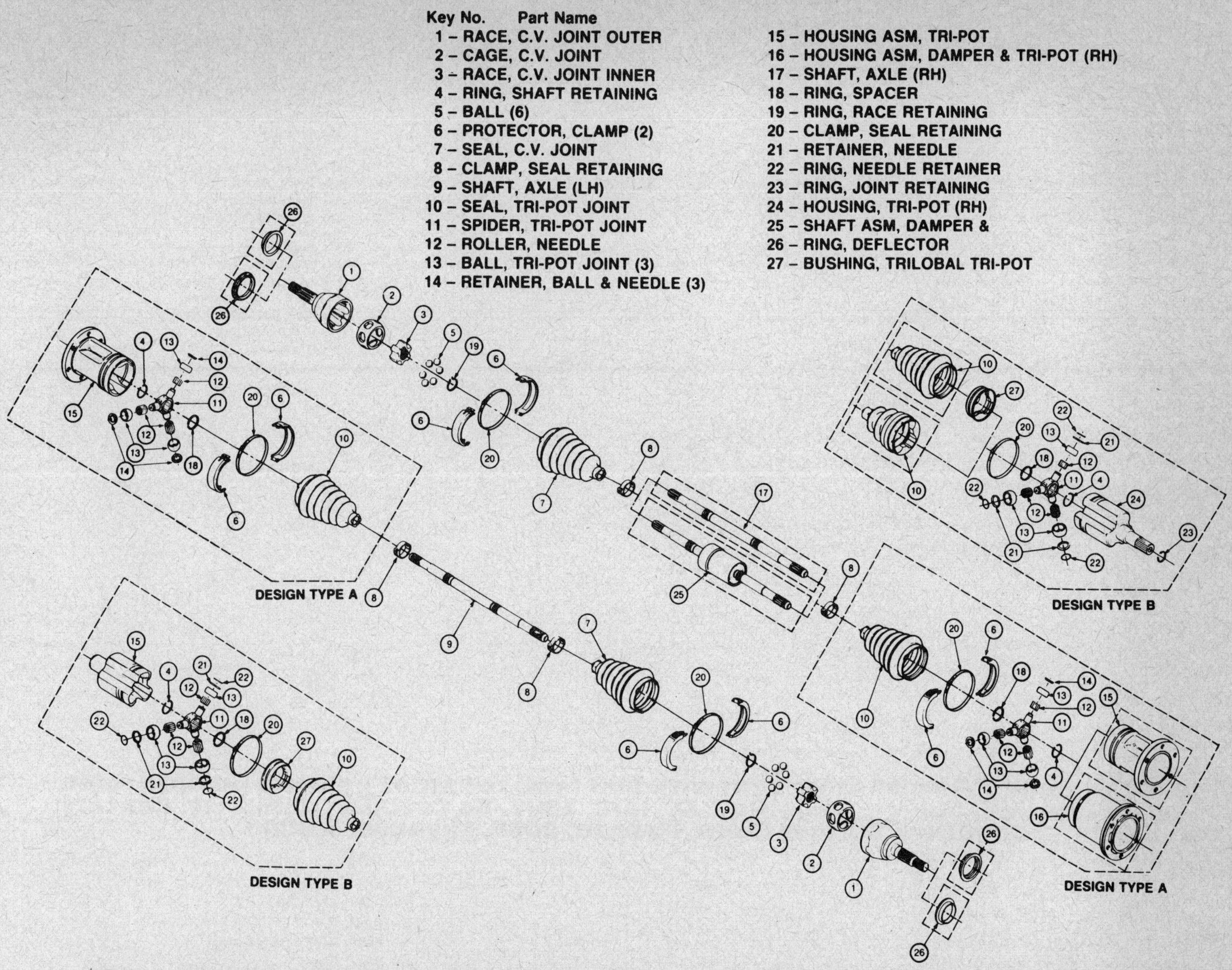

Fig. 4 Exploded view of drive axle with tri-pot inboard joint. 1985–87 models

4. Using tool J-24319-01, remove tie rod end from steering knuckle.
5. Remove brake caliper support-to-steering knuckle attaching bolts, then the caliper. Support caliper to prevent brake hose damage.
6. Remove rotor, then using tool J-25287, push axle assembly from hub, **Fig. 7.**
7. Using tools J-2619-01 and J-35762, pull axle assembly from transaxle. **When removing axle assembly, do not pull on axle shaft. To prevent axle boot damage, do not allow them to contact any parts during removal.**

Installation

Prior to installing axle assembly, inspect knuckle inner grease seal. Replace if distorted or worn. Also check for foreign material at hub bearing area.

1. Install axle assembly into transaxle. Use a long brass drift and hammer positioned on the tri-pot housing ribs to drive in.
2. Install axle into wheel hub, then lower control arm to ball joint. Torque ball joint nuts and bolts to 47 ft. lbs.
3. Install tie rod end. Torque nut to 38 ft. lbs.
4. Install rotor, then the brake caliper. Torque attaching bolts to 65 ft. lbs.
5. Install tire and wheel assembly, then drive axle nut and washer.
6. Lower vehicle to floor, then torque lug nuts to 76 ft. lbs. and drive axle nut to 137 ft. lbs.
7. Install nut cap and cotter pin.

RIGHTHAND DRIVE AXLE, OUTPUT SHAFT & SEAL

REPLACE

1982–85 ELDORADO, RIVIERA, SEVILLE & TORONADO

Removal

1. Disconnect battery ground cable.
2. Raise front of vehicle and place jack stands under front frame horns.
3. Remove wheel and tire assembly.
4. Remove cotter pin, nut and shield from tie rod pivot, then using puller J-24319, detach tie rod end from steering knuckle.
5. Install drive shaft seal protector J-28712, then remove cotter pin, nut and washer from drive axle, then remove six screws attaching drive axle to output shaft. **To prevent axle shaft from rotating when removing nut or attaching screws, insert a drift through opening on top of caliper into corresponding rotor vane.**
6. Remove cotter pin and nut from upper ball joint stud nut, then remove brake hose clip from stud and loosely reinstall nut.
7. Using a hammer and brass drift, rap on steering knuckle to free upper ball joint stud. Use care not to damage brake hose or steering knuckle.
8. Remove nut and separate upper ball joint from steering knuckle.
9. Guide drive axle out of steering knuckle and remove from vehicle.

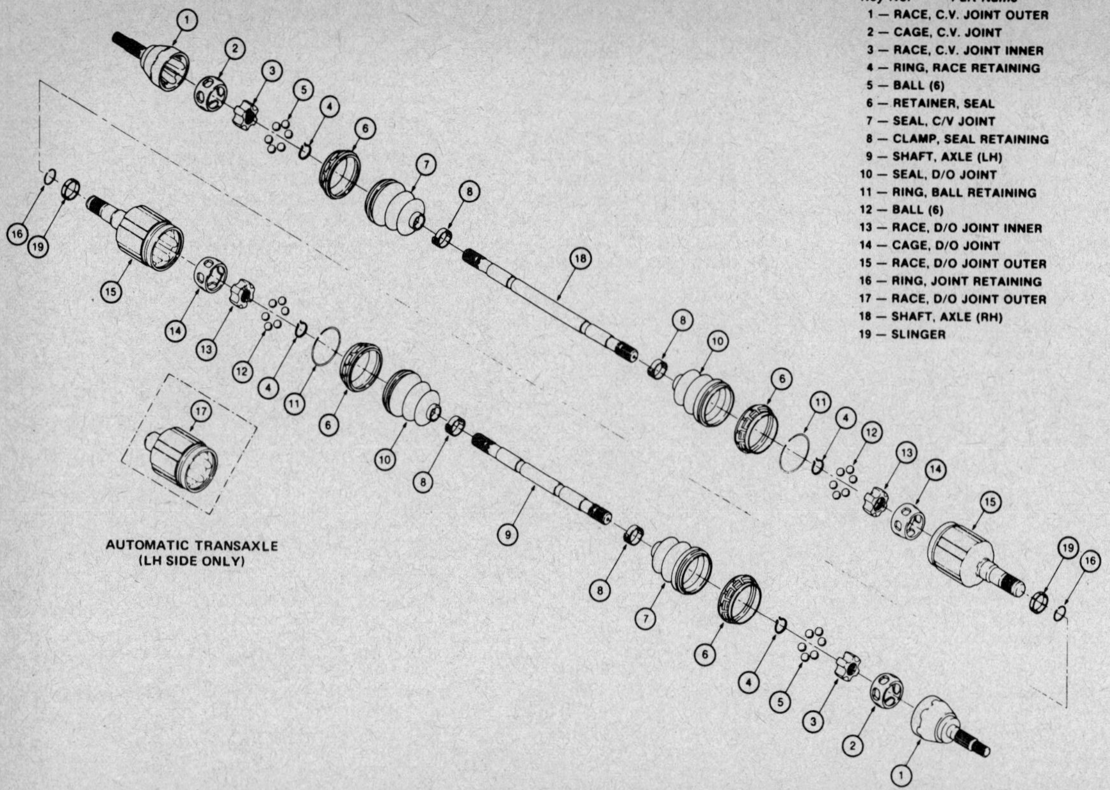

Key No. — Part Name

1 — RACE, C.V. JOINT OUTER
2 — CAGE, C.V. JOINT
3 — RACE, C.V. JOINT INNER
4 — RING, RACE RETAINING
5 — BALL (6)
6 — RETAINER, SEAL
7 — SEAL, C/V JOINT
8 — CLAMP, SEAL RETAINING
9 — SHAFT, AXLE (LH)
10 — SEAL, D/O JOINT
11 — RING, BALL RETAINING
12 — BALL (6)
13 — RACE, D/O JOINT INNER
14 — CAGE, D/O JOINT
15 — RACE, D/O JOINT OUTER
16 — RING, JOINT RETAINING
17 — RACE, D/O JOINT OUTER
18 — SHAFT, AXLE (RH)
19 — SLINGER

Fig. 5 Exploded view of drive axle with ball type constant velocity inboard joint. 1982–84 Citation, Omega, Phoenix & Skylark; 1982–84 Cavalier, Celebrity, Century, Cimarron, Cutlass Ciera, Firenza, 2000, Skyhawk & 6000

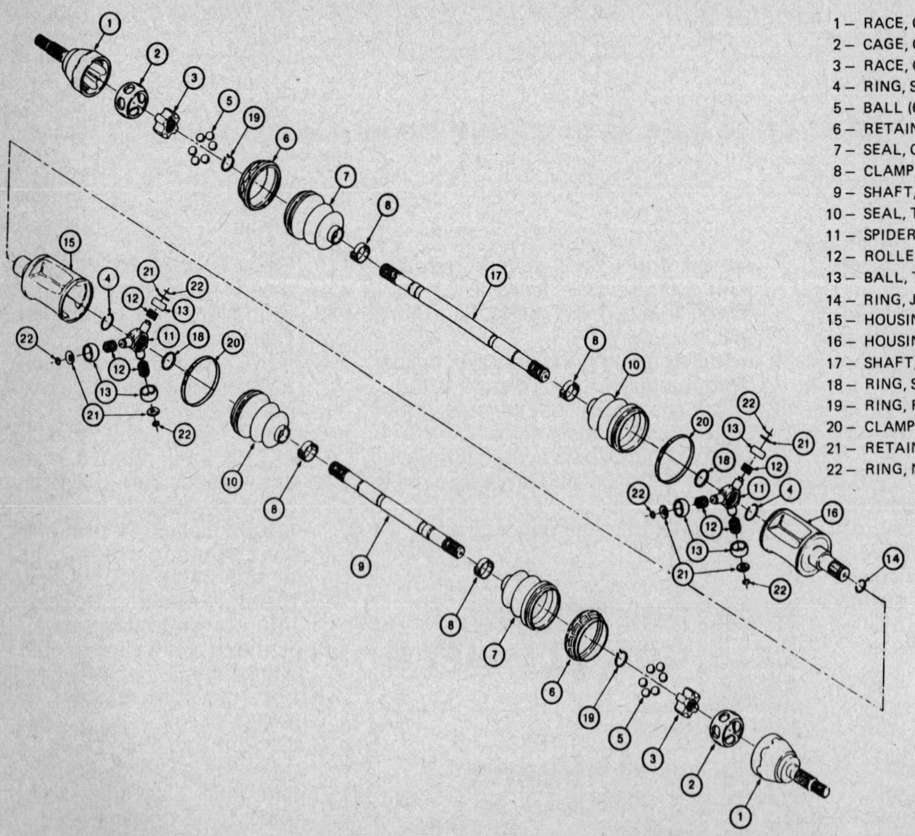

1 – RACE, C.V. JOINT OUTER
2 – CAGE, C.V. JOINT
3 – RACE, C.V. JOINT INNER
4 – RING, SHAFT RETAINING
5 – BALL (6)
6 – RETAINER, SEAL
7 – SEAL, C.V. JOINT
8 – CLAMP, SEAL RETAINING
9 – SHAFT, AXLE (LH)
10 – SEAL, TRI-POT JOINT
11 – SPIDER, TRI-POT JOINT
12 – ROLLER, NEEDLE
13 – BALL, TRI-POT JOINT (3)
14 – RING, JOINT RETAINING
15 – HOUSING ASSY, TRI-POT (LH)
16 – HOUSING ASSY, TRI-POT (RH)
17 – SHAFT, AXLE (RH)
18 – RING, SPACER
19 – RING, RACE RETAINING
20 – CLAMP, SEAL RETAINING
21 – RETAINER, NEEDLE
22 – RING, NEEDLE RETAINER

Fig. 6 Exploded view of drive axle with tri-pot inboard joint. 1982–84 Citation, Omega, Phoenix & Skylark; 1982–84 Cavalier, Celebrity, Century, Cimarron, Cutlass Ciera, Firenza, 2000, Skyhawk & 6000

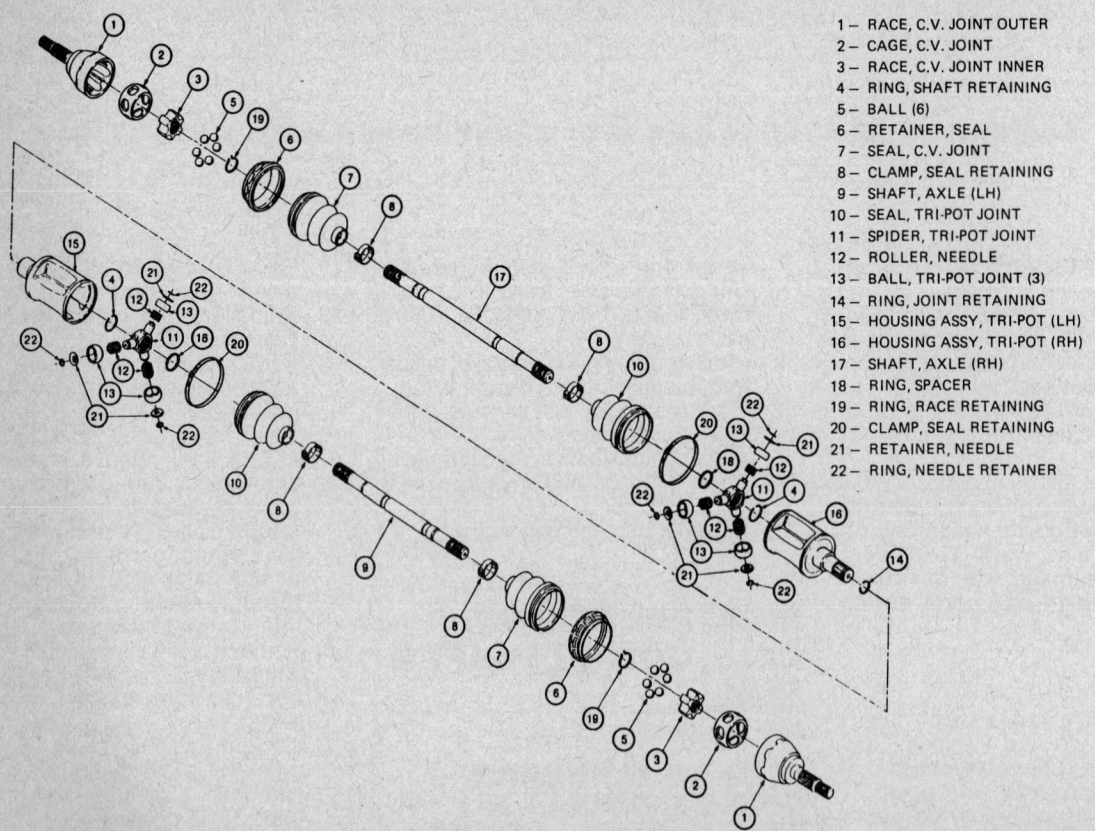

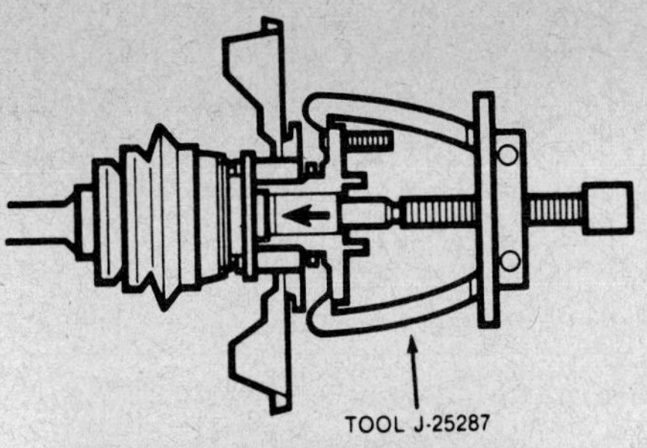

Fig. 7 Pushing axle assembly from hub. 1985–87 Nova

10. Remove two screws attaching battery cable retainer to support and remove two screws attaching output support to engine, then rotate support downward.
11. Remove front nut and bolt from righthand frame brace, then pivot brace outward to provide clearance.
12. Using a plastic mallet, drive on flange end of output shaft until shaft releases from retaining ring, then remove output shaft and support. Use care not to damage output shaft seal surfaces or splines.
13. Using a suitable pry bar, pry output shaft seal out of housing. Pry at two or three different places to avoid cocking seal. Use care not to damage housing.

Installation

1. Using tool No. J-28518, install output shaft seal. Rotate tool to maintain proper alignment when installing seal.
2. Apply wheel bearing grease between lips of seal.
3. Index splines of output shaft with splines of side gear in final drive assembly, then install shaft by tapping on flange end with a soft faced mallet until retaining ring snaps into shaft groove. Ensure shaft is securely locked into position. **When installing output shaft, use care not to damage seal.**
4. Align output shaft support and engine block attaching screw holes, then install two support attaching screws. Torque screws to 50 ft. lbs.
5. Install two screws attaching battery cable retainer to support.
6. Guide drive axle into position and install splined end axle into steering knuckle.
7. Position upper ball joint stud into steering knuckle, then place brake hose clip on stud and install stud nut. Torque stud nut to 60 ft. lbs., then install cotter pin. The nut may be tightened an additional 1/6 turn to align cotter pin slots.
8. Install six screws attaching output shaft to drive axle. Torque screws to 60 ft. lbs.
9. Install drive axle washer, nut, retainer and cotter pin. Torque nut to 175 ft. lbs. Align cotter pin slot by rotating retainer and bend cotter pin so that retainer is held snugly.
10. Install tie rod pivot on steering knuckle. Torque nut to 44 ft. lbs. The nut may be tightened an additional 1/6 turn to align cotter pin slots.

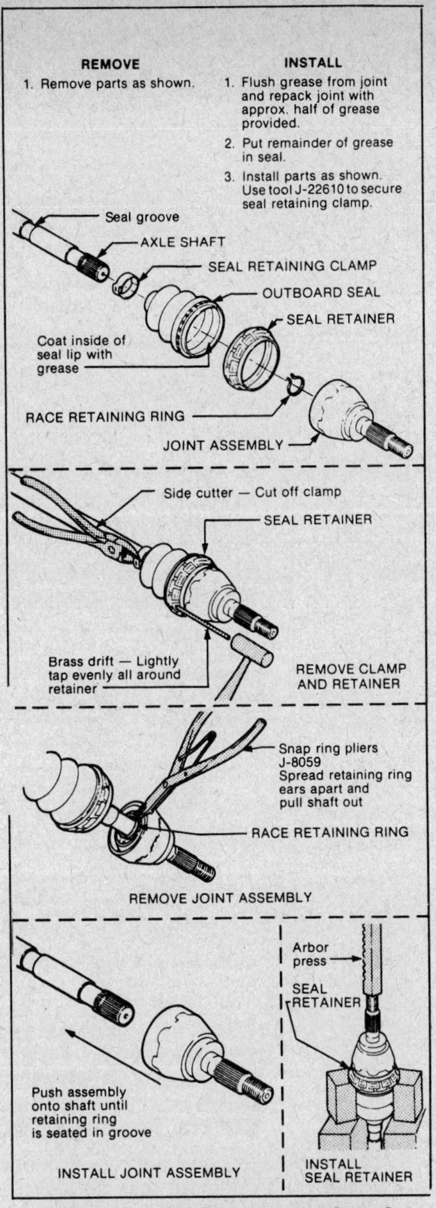

Fig. 8 Outer constant velocity joint seal removal & installation. 1982–84 models

11. Install righthand frame brace bolt and nut. Torque belt to 50 ft. lbs.
12. Install front wheel and tire assembly, then lower vehicle and connect battery ground cable.
13. Check output shaft seal for leakage.

LEFTHAND DRIVE AXLE, OUTPUT SHAFT & SEAL REPLACE

1982–85 ELDORADO, RIVIERA, SEVILLE & TORONADO

Removal

1. Raise front of vehicle and place jack stands under front frame horns.

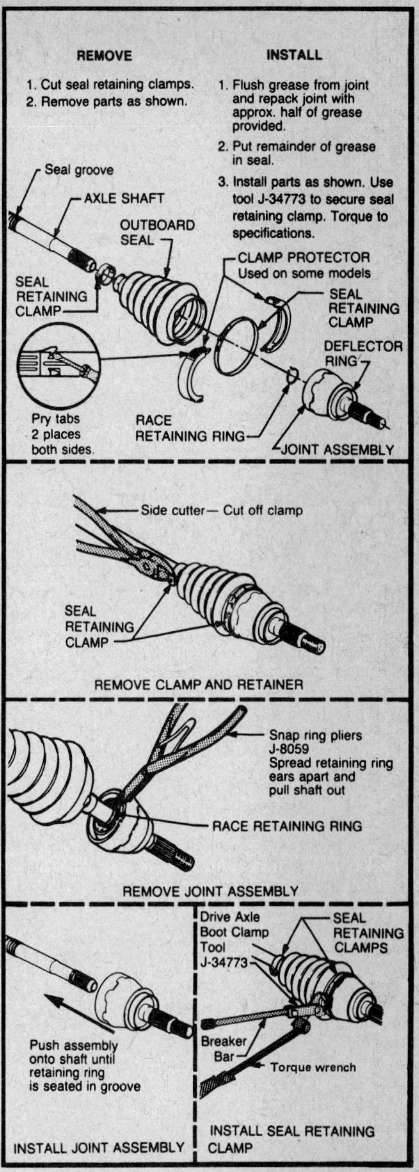

Fig. 9 Outer constant velocity joint seal removal & installation. 1985–87 models

2. Remove wheel and tire assembly.
3. Remove cotter pin, nut and shield from tie rod pivot, then using puller J-24319, detach tie rod end from steering knuckle.
4. Remove cotter pin, nut and washer from drive axle, then remove six screws attaching drive axle to output shaft. **To prevent drive axle from rotating when removing nut or attaching screws, insert a drift through opening on top of caliper into corresponding rotor vane.**
5. Remove cotter pin and nut from upper ball joint stud nut, then remove brake hose clip from stud and loosely reinstall nut.
6. Using a hammer and brass drift, rap on steering knuckle to free upper ball joint stud. Use care not to damage brake hose or steering knuckle.
7. Remove nut and separate upper ball joint from steering knuckle.

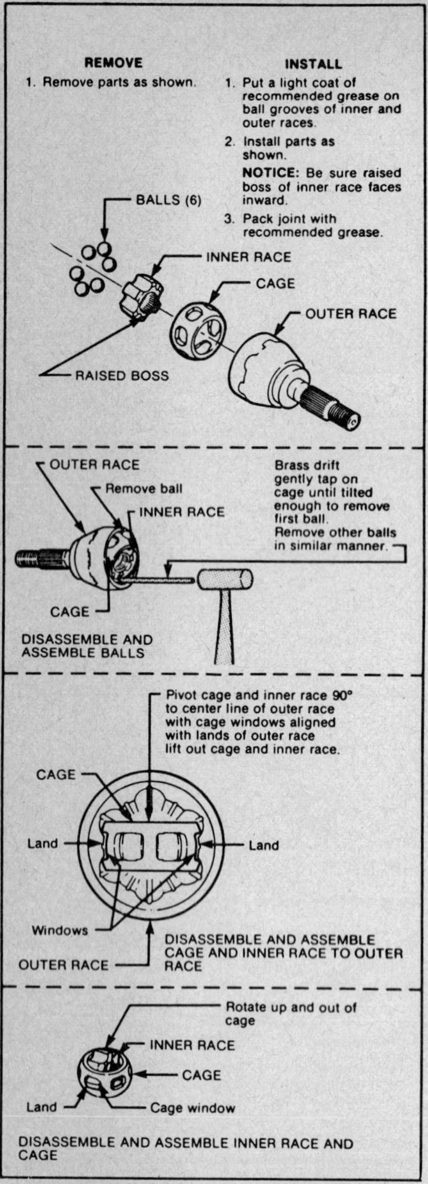

Fig. 10 Outer constant velocity joint disassembly & assembly. 1982–87 models

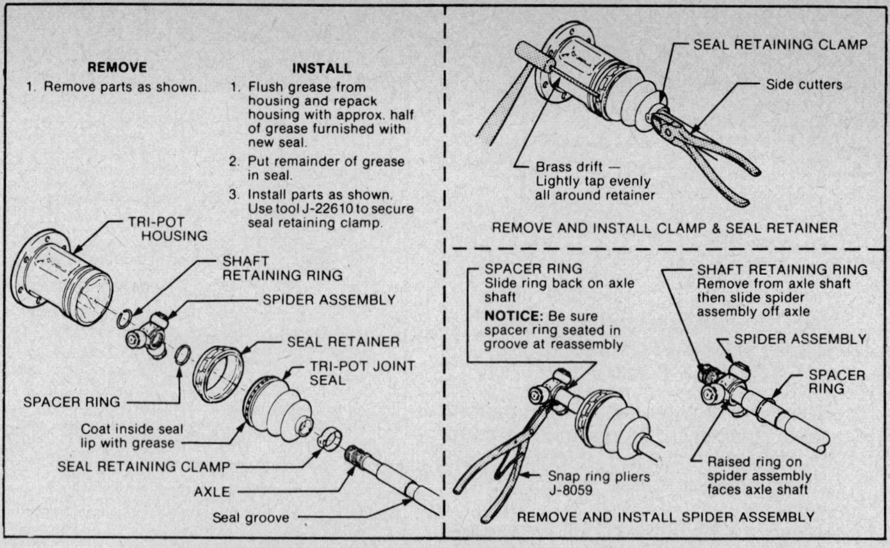

Fig. 11 Inner tri-pot seal removal & installation. 1982–85 Eldorado, Riviera, Seville & Toronado

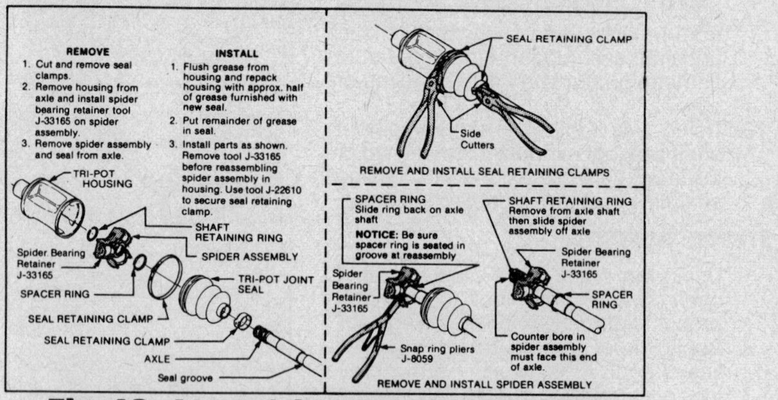

Fig. 12 Inner tri-pot seal removal & installation. 1982–84 Citation, Omega, Phoenix & Skylark; 1982–84 Cavalier, Celebrity, Century, Cimarron, Cutlass Ciera, Firenza, 2000, Skyhawk & 6000

8. Guide drive axle out of steering knuckle and remove from vehicle.
9. Remove front nut and bolt from lefthand frame brace, then pivot brace outward to provide clearance.
10. Using a hammer and brass drift, drive on flange end of output shaft until shaft releases from retaining ring, then remove output shaft.
11. Using a suitable pry bar, pry output shaft seal from housing. Pry at two or three locations to avoid cocking seal. Use care not to damage housing.

Installation

1. Using tool No. J-28518, install output shaft seal. Rotate tool to maintain proper alignment when installing seal.
2. Apply wheel bearing grease between lips of seal.
3. Index splines of output shaft with splines of side gear in final drive assembly then install shaft by tapping center of flange end with a soft faced mallet until retaining ring snaps into shaft groove. Ensure shaft is securely locked into position. **When installing output shaft, use care not to damage seal.**
4. Guide drive axle into position and install splined end into steering knuckle.
5. Position upper ball joint stud into steering knuckle, then place brake hose clip on stud and install nut. Torque nut to 60 ft. lbs., then install cotter pin. The nut may be tightened an additional 1/6 turn to align cotter pin slots.
6. Install six screws attaching output shaft to drive axle. Torque screws to 60 ft. lbs.
7. Install drive axle water nut, retainer and cotter pin. Torque nut to 175 ft. lbs. and bend cotter pin so that retainer is held snugly.
8. Install tie rod pivot on steering knuckle. Torque nut to 44 ft. lbs. The nut may be tightened an additional 1/6 turn to align cotter pin slots.
9. Install lefthand frame brace bolt and nut. Torque bolt to 50 ft. lbs.
10. Install wheel and tire assembly, then lower vehicle and check output shaft seal for leakage.

RIGHTHAND OUTPUT SHAFT SUPPORT BEARING

REPLACE

1982–85 ELDORADO, RIVIERA, SEVILLE & TORONADO

1. Remove righthand output shaft as described under Righthand Drive Axle, Output Shaft and Seal, Replace.
2. Remove three screws securing bearing retainer to support.
3. Install tool No. J-22912 between flange end of output shaft and flat area of shaft support, with flat surface of tool against flat area of shaft support. Position assembly on a suitable press and press shaft support, bearing, retainer and slinger from output shaft.
4. Remove bearing from output shaft support.

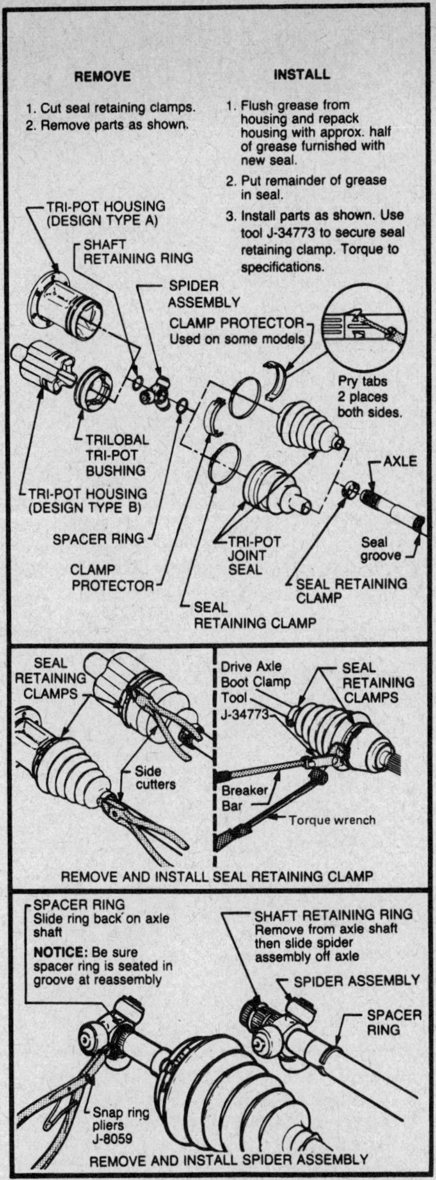

Fig. 13 Inner tri-pot seal removal & installation. 1985–87 models

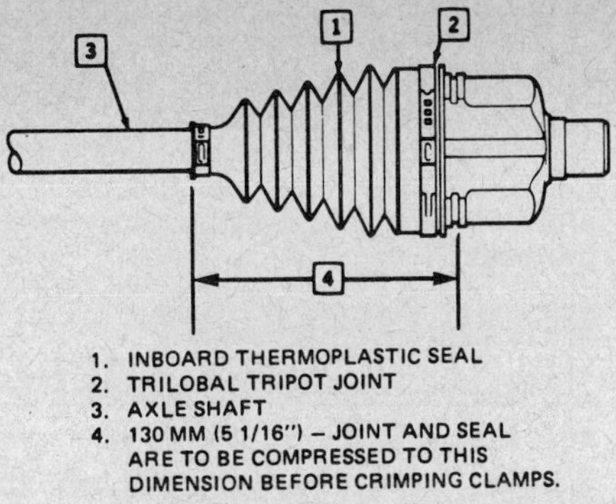

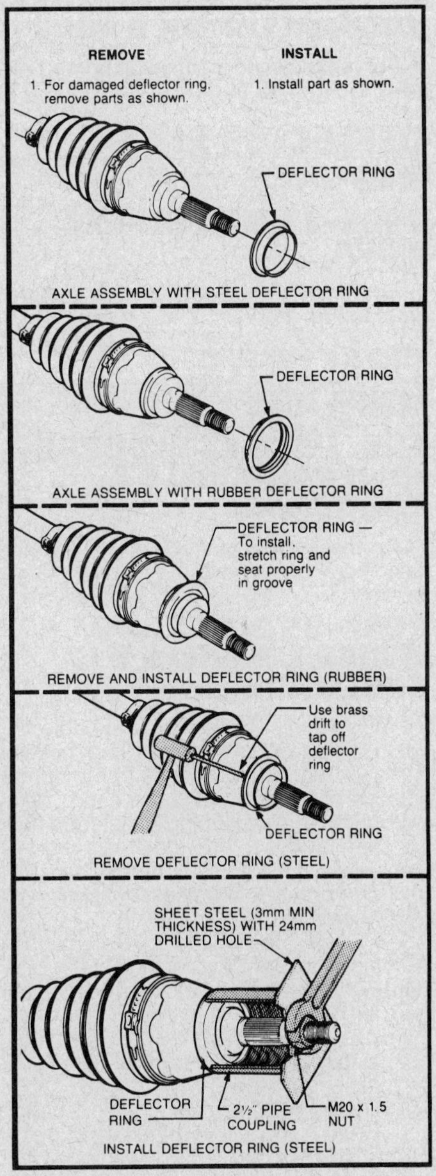

Fig. 14 Inboard thermoplastic seal installation. 1986–87 models

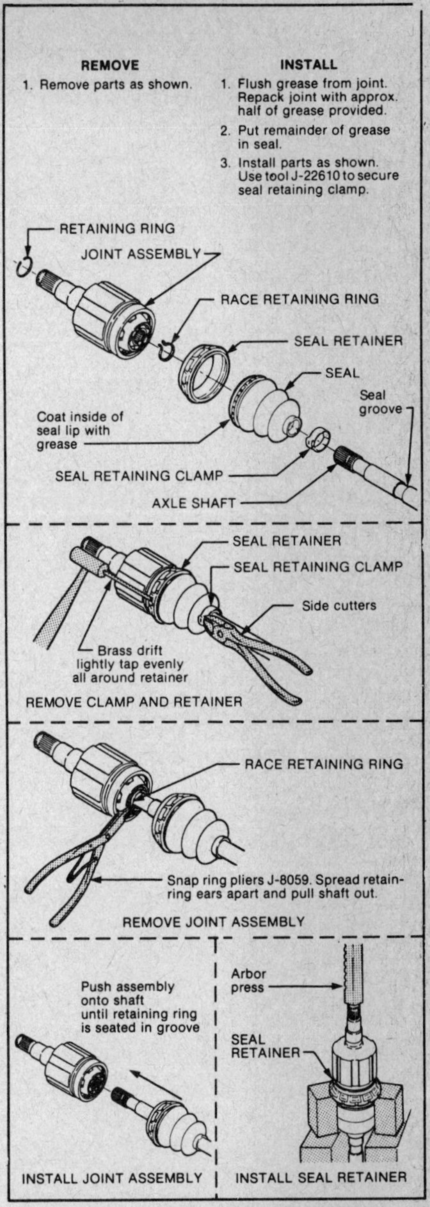

Fig. 15 Inner constant velocity joint seal removal & installation. 1982–84 Citation, Omega, Phoenix & Skylark; 1982–84 Cavalier, Celebrity, Century, Cimarron, Cutlass Ciera, Firenza, 2000, Skyhawk & 6000

5. Lubricate output shaft support and bearing, then position bearing into support.
6. Pack bearing with wheel bearing grease, then install retainer and three attaching screws.
7. Place assembled components and slinger on output shaft, then position components and output shaft on a press. Using a standard 1¼ inch inside diameter pipe, press bearing and assembled components onto shaft.
8. Check to ensure bearing and support rotate smoothly, then install righthand output shaft.

OUTER CONSTANT VELOCITY JOINT & SEAL REPLACE

ALL MODELS

For removal and installation procedures refer to Figs. 8, 9 and 10.

INNER TRI-POT SEAL REPLACE

1982–85 ELDORADO, RIVIERA, SEVILLE & TORONADO

For removal and installation procedures refer to Fig. 11.

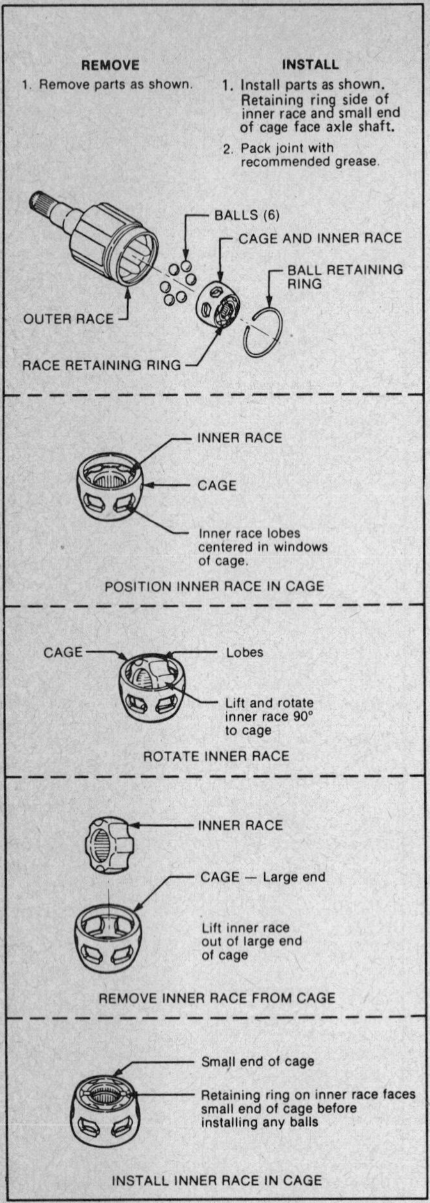

Fig. 16 Inner constant velocity joint removal & installation. 1982–84 Citation, Omega, Phoenix & Skylark; 1982–84 Cavalier, Celebrity, Century, Cimarron, Cutlass Ciera, Firenza, 2000, Skyhawk & 6000

1982–84 CITATION, OMEGA, PHOENIX & SKYLARK; 1982–84 CAVALIER, CELEBRITY, CENTURY, CIMARRON, CUTLASS CIERA, FIRENZA, 2000, SKYHAWK & 6000

For removal and installation procedures, refer to **Fig. 12.**

1985–87 MODELS

For removal and installation procedures, refer to **Fig. 13. On 1986-87 models, when installing the thermo-plastic seal, the drive axle must be collapsed as shown in Fig. 14 to prevent distortion of the seal.**

INNER CONSTANT VELOCITY JOINT & SEAL

REPLACE

1982–84 CITATION, OMEGA, PHOENIX & SKYLARK; 1982–84 CAVALIER, CELEBRITY, CENTURY, CIMARRON, CUTLASS CIERA, FIRENZA, 2000, SKYHAWK & 6000

For removal and installation procedures, refer to **Figs. 15 and 16.**

DEFLECTOR RING

REPLACE

1985–87 MODELS EXC. NOVA

For removal and installation procedures, refer to **Fig. 17.**

FINAL DRIVE

REPLACE

EXC. 1982–85 ELDORADO, RIVIERA, SEVILLE & TORONADO

On these models, the final drive unit is an integral component of the transaxle assembly.

1982–85 ELDORADO, RIVIERA, SEVILLE & TORONADO

1. Disconnect battery ground cable.
2. Raise front of vehicle and position jack stands under front frame horns.
3. Remove right and lefthand frame brace front attaching bolts, then position braces to provide clearance.
4. Position drain pan under final drive cover, then loosen cover and allow lubricant to drain.
5. Remove final drive cover attaching screws, cover and gasket.
6. Remove screws attaching right and left output shafts to drive axles. Separate output shaft flanges from drive axles to permit clearance of final drive assembly with shafts installed.
7. Remove two screws attaching battery cable retainer to righthand output shaft support, then remove two screws securing support to engine. Rotate support downward to provide clearance for removal.

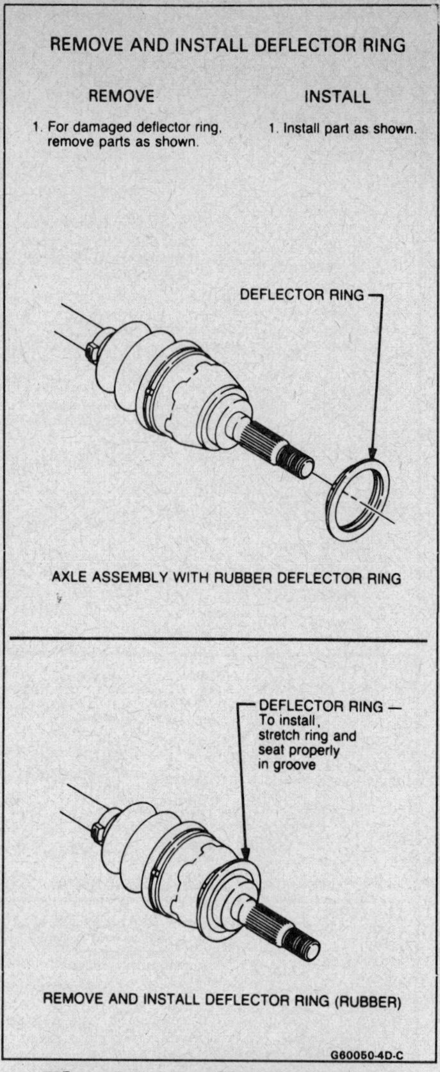

Fig. 17 Deflector ring removal & installation. 1985–87 models exc. Nova

8. Remove final drive to transmission attaching screws that secures rear of final drive shield, then loosen support bracket screws that secure front of shield and remove shield.
9. Remove five remaining final drive to transmission attaching screws.
10. Remove screws attaching final drive support bracket to engine block.
11. Using tool J-24319, disconnect steering linkage intermediate shaft from pitman and idler arms. Push linkage forward to ensure adequate clearance for final drive assembly removal.
12. Slide final drive assembly forward, off transmission splined shaft and remove unit with output shafts attached. Use care not to damage output shaft seal or splines.
13. Reverse procedure to install. Torque final drive to transaxle attaching bolts to 30 ft. lbs., support bracket bolts to 50 ft. lbs. and output shaft to drive shaft attaching bolts to 60 ft. lbs.

UNIVERSAL JOINTS

INDEX

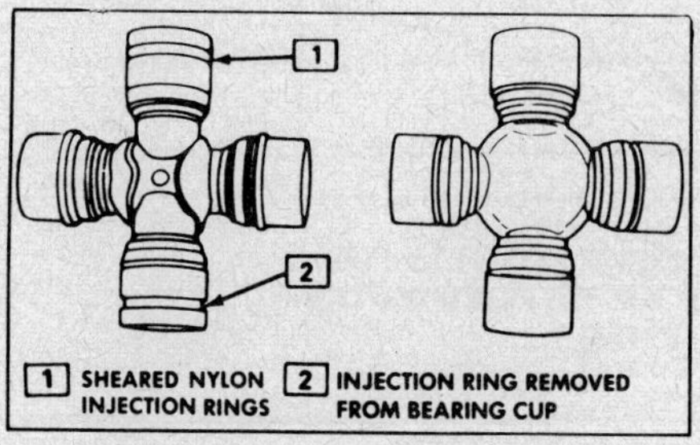

Fig. 1 Production type universal joints

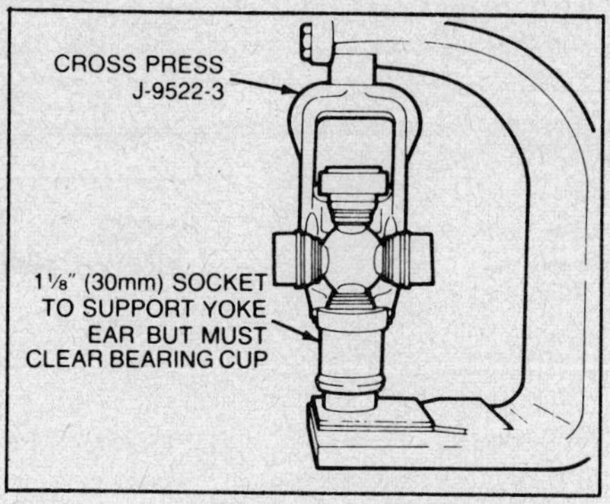

Fig. 2 Removing bearing using cross press

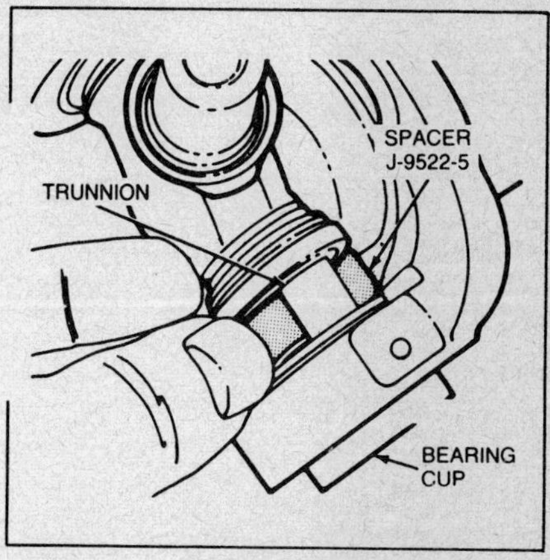

Fig. 3 Installing spacer J-9522-5

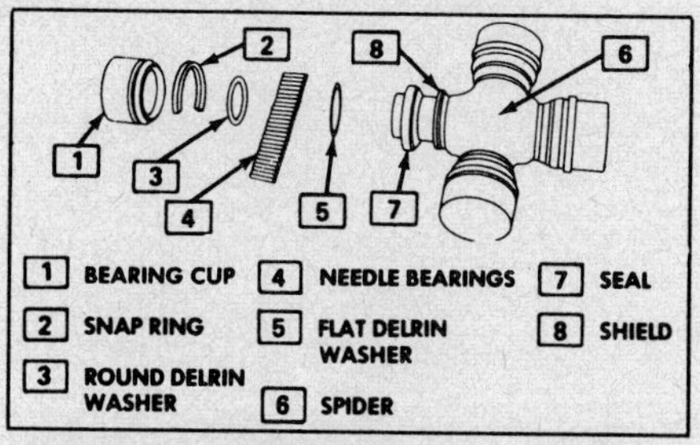

Fig. 4 Service universal joint kit

SERVICE NOTES

Before disassembling any universal joint, examine the assembly carefully and note the position of the grease fitting (if used). Also, be sure to mark the yokes with relation to the propeller shaft so they may be reassembled in the same relative position. Failure to observe these precautions may produce rough car operation which results in rapid wear and failure of parts, and place an unbalanced load on transmission, engine and rear axle.

When universal joints are disassembled for lubrication or inspection, and the old parts are to be reinstalled, special care must be exercised to avoid damage to universal joint spider or cross and bearing cups.

Some late model cars use an injected nylon retainer on the universal joint bearings. When service is necessary, pressing the bearings out will sheer the nylon retainer. Replacement with the conventional steel snap ring type is then necessary.

CROSS & ROLLER TYPE

DISASSEMBLY

During disassembly, two types of universal joints may be found, **Fig. 1.**

1. Support propeller shaft horizontally, in line with base plate of a suitable press.
2. Position universal joint so that lower ear of shaft yoke is supported on a 1⅛ inch socket.
3. Position universal joint bearing separator tool No. J-2522-3 or equivalent, onto open portion of horizontal bearing cups, then press lower bearing cup out of yoke ear, **Fig. 2.** This will shear the plastic retaining ring on the lower bearing cup. If the bearing cup is not completely removed, lift bearing separator and insert spacer remover tool No. J-9522-5 or equivalent, between the seal and bearing cup, **Fig. 3.** Complete removal of bearing cup by pressing out from yoke.
4. Rotate propeller shaft, shear the opposite plastic retainer, and press opposite bearing cup out from yoke. **There are no bearing retainer grooves in production type bearing cups, and they cannot be reused.**
5. If the front universal joint is being replaced, remove bearing cup from the slip yoke in the same manner described in steps 2, 3 and 4.

ASSEMBLY

During assembly of universal joint, always install a complete universal service kit. This kit includes one pre-lubricated cross assembly, four service bearing cup assemblies with seals, needle roller bearings, washers, bearing retainers and grease, **Fig. 4.** Ensure seals are in place on the service bearing cups.

1. Install one bearing cup partially into one side of the yoke, then turn yoke ear toward bottom.
2. Insert universal joint bearing separator tool No. J-9522-3 or equivalent, so that trunnion seats freely into bearing cup, **Fig. 5.**

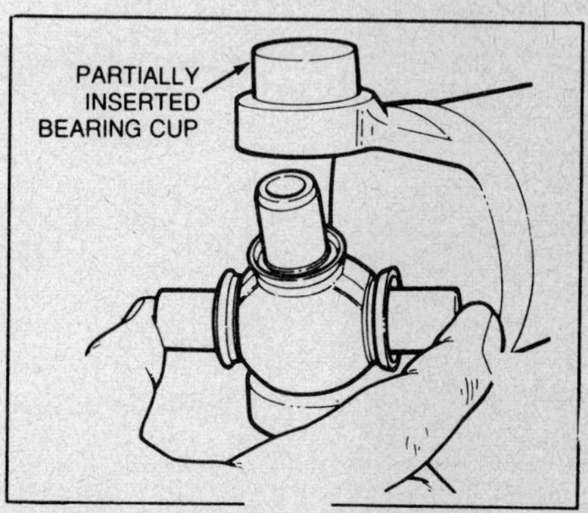

Fig. 5 Partially installed bearing cap

3. Partially install opposite bearing cup. Ensure both trunions are installed straight into both bearing cups.
4. Press against opposite bearing cups, moving the cross to ensure free movement of the trunnions in the bearings. If the bearing cups bind, check needle roller bearings.
5. When one bearing retainer groove clears the inside of the yoke, stop pressing and insert bearing retainer into position, **Fig. 6.**
6. Continue pressing bearing cup until opposite bearing retainer can be installed into position.
7. If opposite bearing retainer cannot be installed, firmly tap yoke and install bearing retainer, **Fig. 7.**
8. Install other half of the universal joint in the same manner.

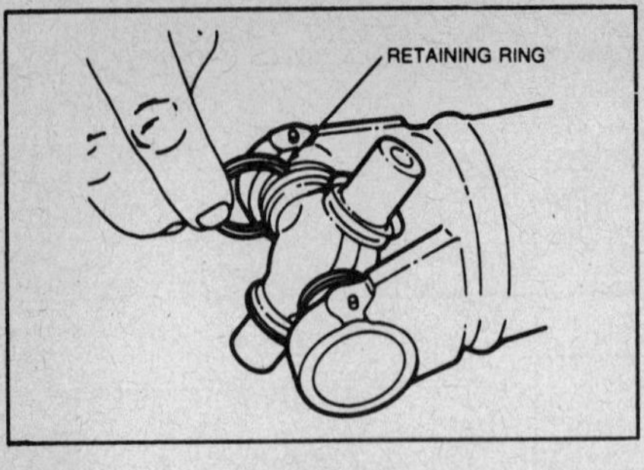

Fig. 6 Installing retaining ring

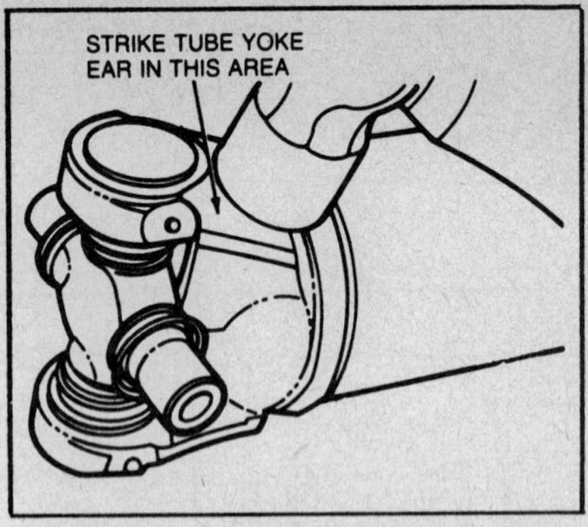

Fig. 7 Taping yoke with hammer to seat retaining ring

ELECTRONIC IGNITION SYSTEMS

TABLE OF CONTENTS

High Energy Ignition (H.E.I.) System

INDEX

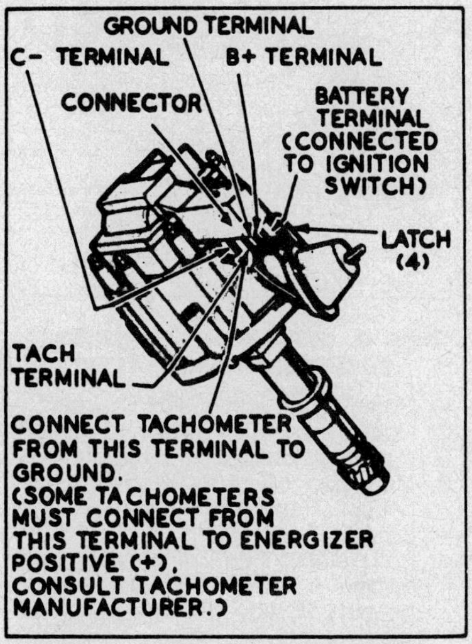

Fig. 1 H.E.I. distributor external components. Except units with external coil

DESCRIPTION

The H.E.I. system, **Figs. 1, 2 and 3,** utilizes an all-electronic module, pickup coil and timer core.

The magnetic pickup consists of a rotating timer core attached to the distributor shaft, a stationary pole piece, permanent magnet and pickup coil.

When the distributor shaft rotates, the teeth of the timer core line up and pass the teeth of the pole piece inducing voltage in the pickup coil which signals the all-electronic module to open the ignition coil primary circuit. Maximum inductance occurs at the moment the timer core teeth are lined up with the teeth on the pole piece. At the instant the timer core teeth start to pass the pole teeth, the primary current decreases and a high voltage is induced in the ignition coil secondary winding and is directed through the rotor and high voltage leads to fire the spark plugs. **Since this is a full 12 volt system it does not require a resistance wire.**

The vacuum diaphragm is connected by linkage to the pole piece. When the diaphragm moves against spring pressure it rotates the pole piece allowing the poles to advance relative to the timer core. The timer core is rotated about the shaft by conventional advance weights, thus providing centrifugal advance. **Never connect a wire directly between the "Tach" terminal, Figs. 1 and 3** of the distributor connector and the ground since this will damage the electronic circuitry of the module.

A convenient tachometer connection is incorporated in the wiring connector on the side of the distributor, **Figs. 1 and 3.** However, due to its transistorized design, the high energy ignition system will not trigger some models of engine tachometers. **When using a timing light to adjust ignition timing, the connection should be made at the No. 1 spark plug. Forcing foreign objects through the boot at the No. 1 terminal of the distributor cap will damage the boot and could cause engine misfiring.**

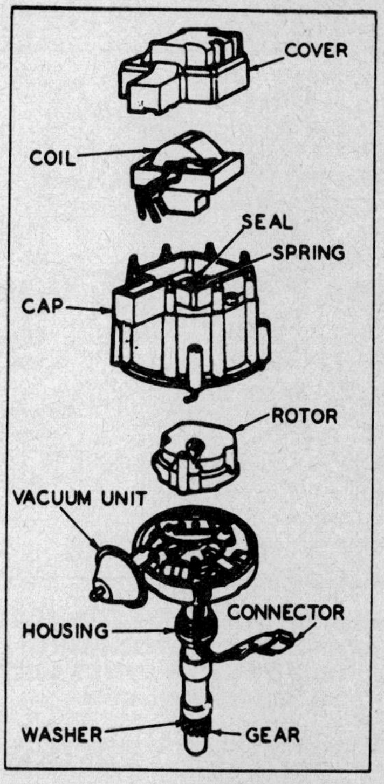

Fig. 2 H.E.I. distributor internal components. Except units with external coil

The spark plug boot has been designed to form a tight seal around the spark plug and should be twisted 1/2 turn before removal.

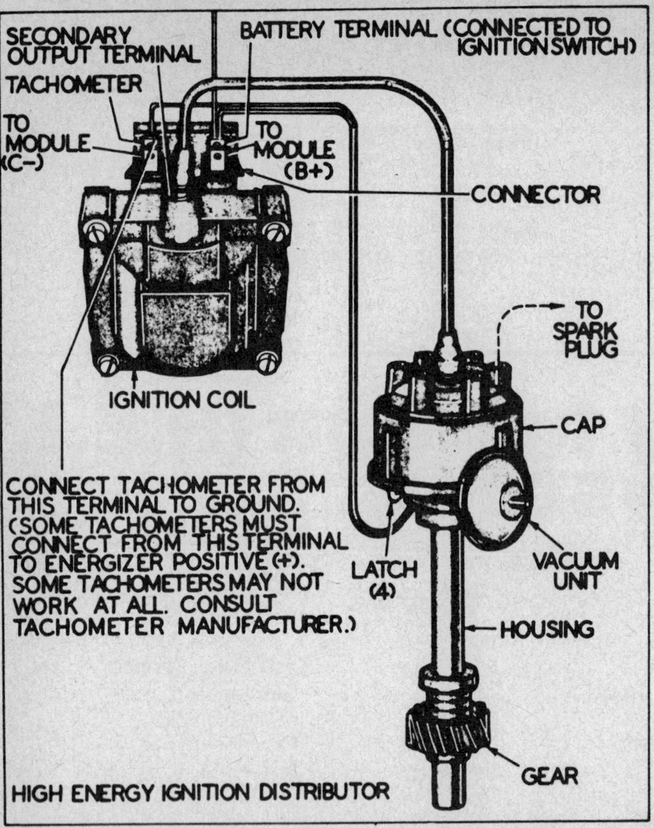

Fig. 3 H.E.I. distributor components. 1982–84 inline 4 cyl. units with external coil. 6 cylinder shown (4 cylinder similar)

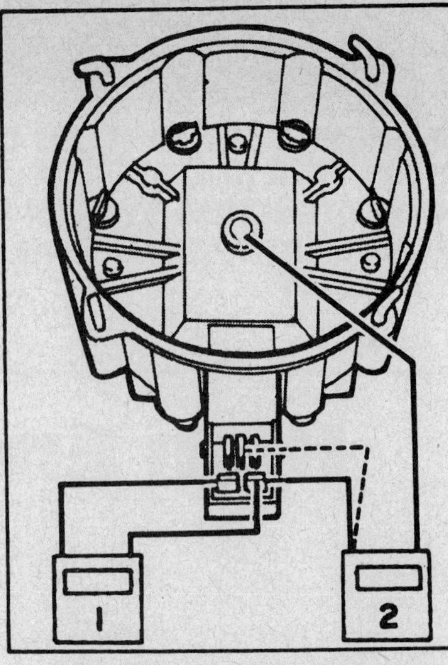

Fig. 4 H.E.I. distributor ignition coil ohmmeter test. Except units with external coil

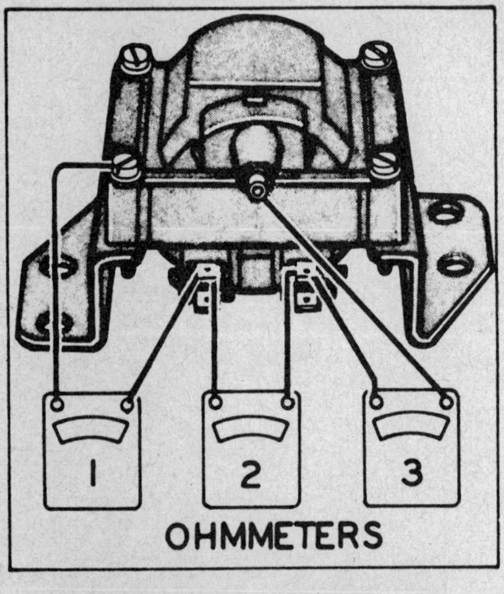

Fig. 5 H.E.I. distributor ignition coil ohmmeter test. 1982–84 units with external coil

COMPONENT TESTING

1. Remove cap and coil assembly.
2. Inspect cap, coil and rotor for spark arc-over.
3. On V6 and V8 engines:
   a. Connect ohmmeter, **Fig. 4,** step 1. If ohmmeter reading is other than zero or very near to zero, the ignition coil must be replaced.
   b. If no ohmmeter reading was observed in step 1, reconnect ohmmeter both ways, **Fig. 4**, step 2. If both ohmmeter readings are infinite on high scale, replace ignition coil.
4. On inline engines:
   a. Connect ohmmeter, **Fig. 5**, step 1. If reading is not infinite, replace coil.
   b. Connect ohmmeter, **Fig. 5**, step 2. If reading is not zero or near zero, replace coil.
   c. Connect ohmmeter, **Fig. 5**, step 3. If reading is infinite, replace coil.
5. Connect an external vacuum source to the vacuum advance unit. Replace vacuum unit if inoperative.
6. If vacuum unit is operating properly, connect ohmmeter, **Fig. 6**, step 1. If ohmmeter reading on middle scale is not infinite at all times, pickup coil must be replaced.
7. With ohmmeter connected, **Fig. 6**, step 2, reading should be within 500 to 1500 ohms. **Tester J-24624 is required to test the module. If this tester is not available, and malfunction still exists after performing the above checks, replace module.**

DISTRIBUTOR REPLACE

EXC. CHEVETTE

Removal

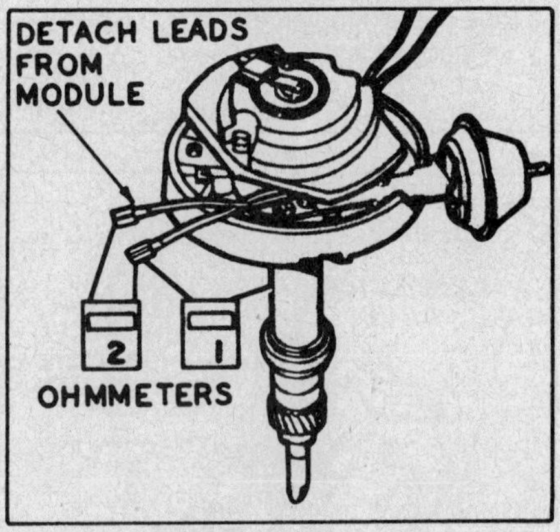

Fig. 6 Distributor pickup coil ohmmeter test

1. Disconnect electrical connectors from distributor cap. On Cadillac models with fuel injection, disconnect speed sensor connector at distributor trigger. Remove cap and position aside.
2. Remove vacuum advance hose and mark position of distributor in engine.
3. Mark position of rotor on distributor housing, then remove distributor hold-down bolt and clamp.
4. Pull distributor up until rotor just stops turning and mark this position on housing. Remove distributor from engine.

Installation

1. If engine was not cranked after distributor was removed from engine, proceed as follows:
   a. Position rotor to align with mark made on housing in step 4 of Removal procedure.
   b. Slide distributor into engine, aligning distributor housing to engine mark made in step 2 of Removal procedure. With distributor fully seated, rotor should align with mark made on housing in step 3 of Removal procedure.

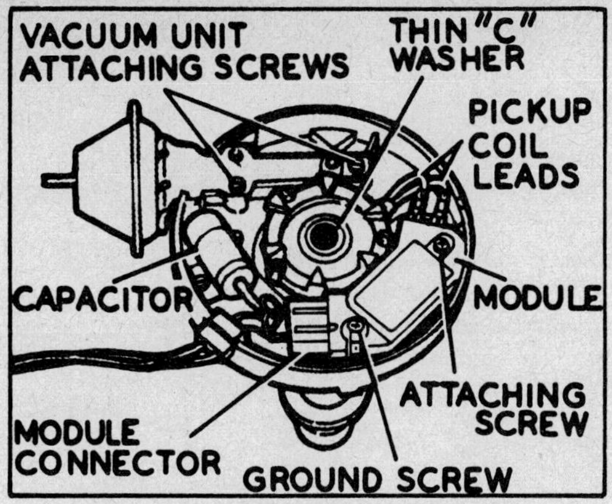

Fig. 7 H.E.I. distributor component replacement

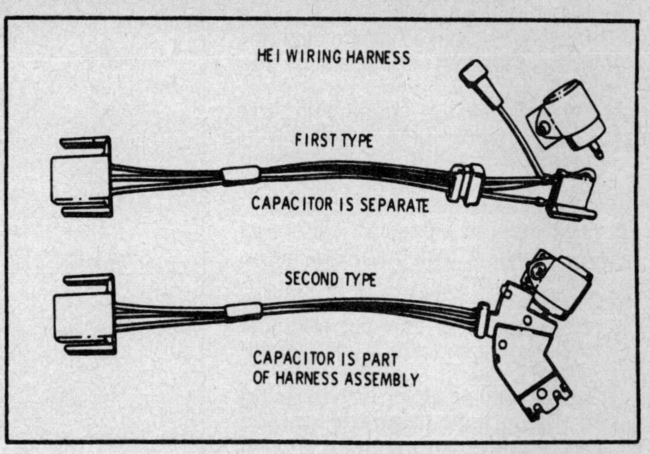

Fig. 8 H.E.I. wiring harness identification

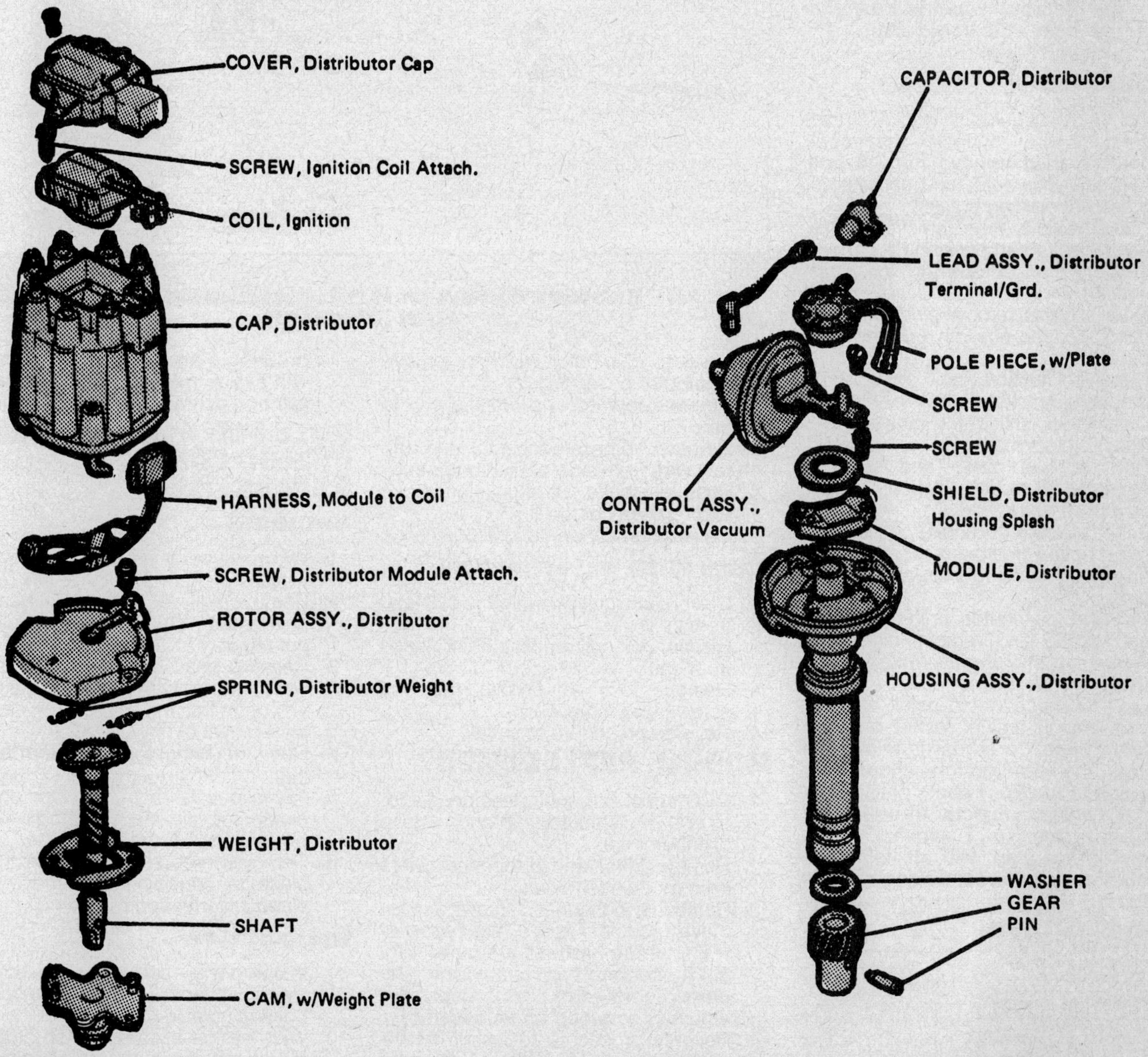

Fig. 9 Exploded view of H.E.I. distributor (Typical). All except Cadillac with fuel injection

c. Install distributor cap, connect electrical connectors and attach vacuum advance hose.
d. Adjust ignition timing.

2. If engine was cranked after distributor was removed from engine, proceed as follows:
   a. Remove No. 1 spark plug and crank engine until compression pressure is felt in No. 1 cylinder. Slowly rotate engine until Top Dead Center (TDC) is indicated.
   b. Turn rotor to a position just ahead of the No. 1 distributor cap terminal.
   c. Slide distributor into engine. Install distributor cap, connect electrical connectors and attach vacuum advance hose.
   d. Adjust ignition timing. **When using a timing light to adjust ignition timing, the connection should be made at the No. 1 spark plug. Forcing foreign objects through the boot at the No. 1 terminal of the distributor cap will damage the boot and could cause engine misfiring.**

CHEVETTE

1. On models equipped with A/C, disconnect wire connector from compressor, then remove through bolt, two adjusting bolts, and upper compressor mounting bracket.
2. Raise vehicle, then remove two retaining bolts and position lower compressor bracket outward for clearance.
3. On all models, remove air cleaner and distributor cap, position distributor cap out of way.
4. Remove ignition coil cover and mounting bracket bolts.
5. Disconnect distributor primary lead from coil terminal.
6. Remove fuel pump and pushrod. **Pushrod must be installed in same direction as removed.**
7. Scribe a mark on engine in line with rotor, noting approximate position of distributor housing in relation to engine.
8. Remove distributor hold-down bolt and clamp and remove distributor. **Avoid rotating engine while distributor is removed.**
9. Reverse procedure to install, then adjust ignition timing. **When using a timing light to adjust ignition timing, the connection should be made at the No. 1 spark plug. Forcing foreign objects through the boot at the No. 1 terminal of the distributor cap will damage the boot and could cause engine misfiring.**

COMPONENTS REPLACE

IGNITION COIL REPLACEMENT

Except Units With External Coil

1. Remove screws holding distributor cover to distributor cap and remove distributor cover, Fig. 2.
2. Remove four screws holding coil to cap.
3. Remove harness connector and battery wire from side of distributor cap.
4. Push coil leads out of position in cap and remove coil.
5. Reverse procedure to install.

Units With External Coil

1. Disconnect ignition switch to coil lead from coil.
2. Disconnect coil to distributor leads from coil.
3. Remove coil to engine retaining screws and remove coil.
4. Reverse procedure to install.

MODULE REPLACEMENT

1. Disconnect wiring harness connector at side of distributor cap and remove distributor cap.
2. Remove rotor and disconnect wires from module terminals.
3. Remove two mounting screws and remove module, **Fig. 7. Two types of H.E.I. wiring harness are used, Fig. 8. The second type is a wiring harness, connector and capacitor which is serviced as an assembly.**
4. Reverse procedure to install. **At installation, coat bottom of new module with dielectric lubricant (furnished with new module) to aid in heat transfer into distributor housing. Failure to apply lubricant will cause excessive heat at module and premature module failure.**

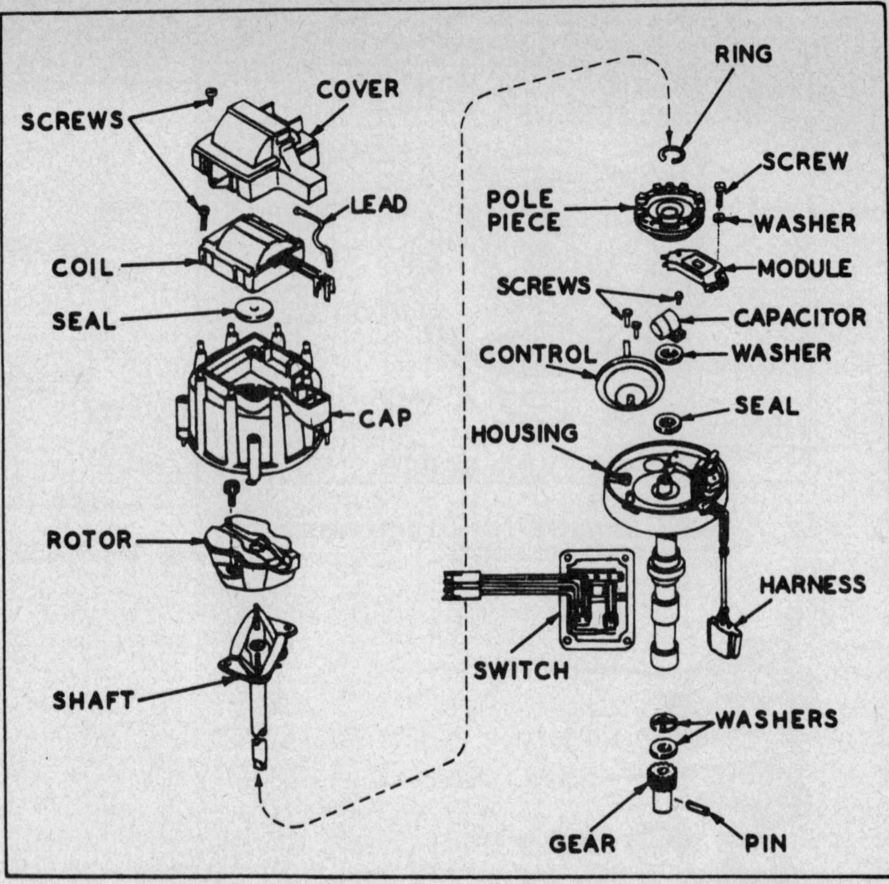

Fig. 10 Exploded view of H.E.I. distributor. Cadillac with fuel injection

POLE PIECE, MAGNET OR PICKUP COIL REPLACEMENT

Removal

1. With distributor removed, disconnect wires at module terminals, **Fig. 7.**
2. Remove roll pin from drive gear by driving out with 1/8 inch diameter drift punch.
3. Remove gear, shim and the tanged washer from distributor shaft. Remove any burrs that may have been caused by removal of pin.
4. Remove distributor shaft from housing.
5. Remove washer from upper end of distributor housing. **Bushings in the housing are not serviceable.**
6. Remove three screws securing pole piece to housing and remove pole piece, magnet and pickup coil.

Installation

1. Install pickup coil, magnet and pole piece and loosely install three screws holding pole piece.
2. With washer installed at top of housing, install distributor shaft and rotate to check for proper clearance between pole piece teeth and timer core teeth.

3. If necessary, realign pole piece to provide adequate clearance and secure properly.
4. Install tanged washer, shim and drive gear (teeth up) to bottom of shaft. Align drive gear and install new roll pin.

DISTRIBUTOR SERVICE

DISASSEMBLY

Some of the following steps do not apply to the Cadillac DEFI or units with EST systems.

1. Remove distributor, **Figs. 9 and 10.**
2. Remove rotor.
3. Remove advance springs and weights (if equipped).
4. Remove module retaining screws and move module to a position where connector may be removed.
5. Remove wires from module terminals.
6. Support distributor gear so that distributor shaft will not be damaged, then remove roll pin by driving it out with a punch.
7. Remove gear, shim and tanged washer from shaft. Remove any burrs that may have been caused by removal of roll pin. **Some distributors do not use a shim or tanged washer.**
8. On Cadillac models with EFI:
   a. Remove the four screws retaining speed sensor, then remove speed sensor and gasket, **Fig. 11.**
   b. Remove plug from opposite side of sensor housing on distributor.
   c. Remove roll pin from magnet assembly.
9. Remove distributor shaft and magnet assembly.
10. Remove pole piece retaining screws, pole piece, magnet and pickup coil.
11. Remove lock ring from top of housing, pickup coil retainer and felt washer.
12. Remove vacuum advance unit (if equipped).

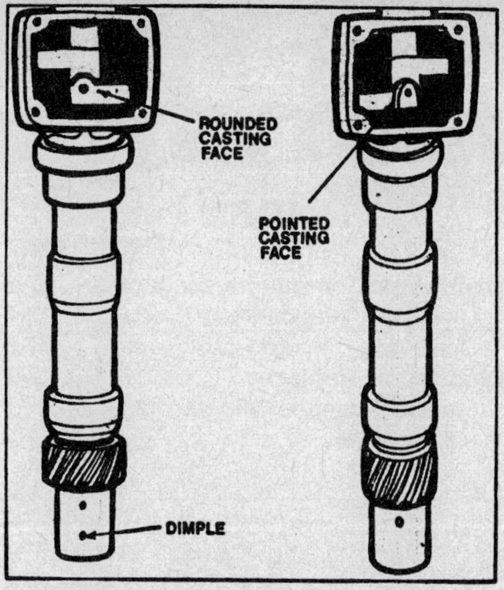

Fig. 11 Speed sensor location

13. Remove capacitor and wiring harness from distributor housing.

ASSEMBLY

1. Install vacuum advance unit (if used) and secure with two screws, **Figs. 9 and 10.**
2. Place felt washer over lubricant reservoir at top of housing.
3. Position pickup coil retainer onto housing with vacuum advance arm over actuating pin of vacuum advance mechanism and secure with lock ring.
4. Install pickup coil magnet and pole piece. Loosely install the three retaining screws.
5. Install distributor shaft and rotate to check for even clearance all around between pole piece and shaft projections.
6. Move pole piece to provide even clearance and secure with three retaining screws.
7. On Cadillac models with EFI:
   a. Position distributor shaft so speed sensor rotating magnet can be installed in distributor housing, **Fig. 11.**
   b. Engage speed sensor rotating magnet on distributor shaft and install shaft into position. Do not install roll pin.
8. Install drive with teeth up onto shaft. **Drive gear has a dimple on one side next to drive pin hole. Align drive gear so that dimple is on same side of shaft as the rotor pointer. Temporarily install rotor to ensure correct alignment.**
9. Install tanged washer, shim and drive gear, then retain with a new roll pin.
10. On Cadillac models with EFI:
    a. Install speed sensor rotating magnet and retain with new roll pin.
    b. Using a new gasket, position speed sensor onto distributor housing with wiring harness coming out of top of sensor (directly below distributor housing) and retain with four screws.
11. Install capacitor and loosely install retaining screw.
12. Install connector on module with tab on top, then liberally apply silicone grease to bottom of module and install screws. **Failure to apply silicone grease to module will cause excessive heat build-up of module and premature failure.**
13. Position wiring harness with grommet in housing notch, then connect pink wire to capacitor stud and black wire to capacitor retaining screw. Tighten screw.
14. Reconnect wires to module, then install centrifugal advance weights and springs.

High Energy Ignition W/Electronic Spark Timing (HEI-EST) System

INDEX

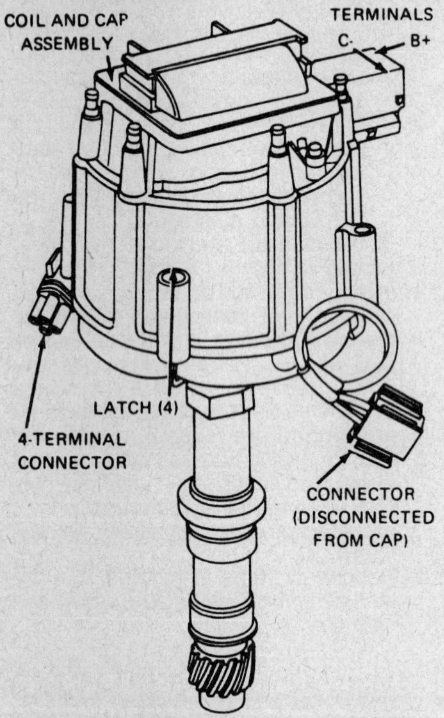

Fig. 1 HEI-EST Distributor with internal coil. Models with 6 & 8 cylinder engine

DESCRIPTION

The High Energy Ignition System with Electronic Spark Timing (HEI-EST) is used on 1982-87 GM models except the following:

a. 1982-84 Chevette and 1000 w/4 terminal ignition module.
b. 1984-87 models w/C³I (Computer-Controlled Coil Ignition).
c. 1985-87 Nova w/Solid State Ignition system.
d. 1987 models with Direct Ignition System (DIS).

All Models equipped with HEI-EST can be identified by the addition of a four-wire distributor connector and the lack of a distributor vacuum advance chamber.

The HEI-EST system consists of an electronic distributor, **Figs. 1 and 2,** with the ignition coil mounted on the distributor cap on 6 and 8 cylinder models, or with an externally mounted coil on 4 cylinder models. All spark timing changes in the HEI-EST system are performed electronically by the Electronic Control Module (ECM). The ECM monitors information from various engine sensors, determines the correct spark timing and signals the distributor to change timing as necessary. A secondary spark advance system is incorporated into the system to signal the ignition module in case of ECM failure. The HEI-EST system does not use vacuum or mechanical advance.

On some HEI-EST systems, Electronic Spark Control (ESC) is used to retard spark advance when detonation occurs. The spark is retarded for 20 seconds, then the spark control returns to EST.

The ESC system consists of three basic components: sensor, distributor and controller. The ESC sensor is an accelerometer or magneto-strictive device, mounted on the engine block. It detects presence, or absence, and intensity of detonation by vibration characteristics of the engine. The sensor's output is an electrical signal which is sent to the controller. A failure of the sensor would allow no retard.

The distributor is an HEI-EST unit with an electronic module modified so that it can respond to ESC controller signal. The command is delayed when detonation is detected, providing the level of retard required. The amount of retard is determined by the severity of detonation.

The ESC controller processes the sensor signal into a command signal to the distributor to adjust spark timing. This is a continuous process monitoring and controlling detonation. The controller is a hard-wired signal processor and amplifier which operates from 6 to 16 volts. Controller failure would be indicated by no ignition, no retard or full retard. **Since this is a full 12 volt system, no resistance wire is used. Also, a diagnostic connector is used on some models. This connector is located in the engine compartment on the left side front fender skirt. On vehicles equipped with this connector, a tachometer may be connected between terminals 6 and G.**

A tachometer connection is incorporated in the wiring connector on the side of the distributor on 6 and 8 cylinder models, or next to the coil battery terminal on 4 cylinder models. **Never connect a wire directly between the Tach terminal of the distributor connector and ground as this will damage the electronic circuitry of the module. When using a timing light to adjust ignition timing, the connection should be made at the No. 1 spark plug. Forcing foreign objects through the boot at the No. 1 spark plug terminal will damage the boot and cause engine misfire.**

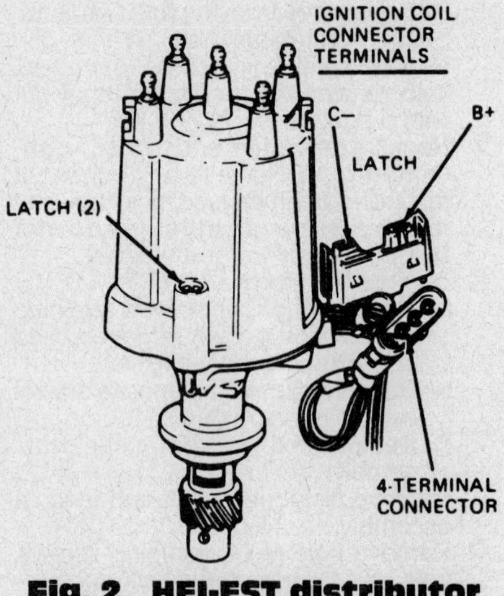

Fig. 2 HEI-EST distributor with external coil. Models with 4 cylinder engine

DISTRIBUTOR COMPONENT DIAGNOSIS

UNITS WITH REMOTE COIL

Testing Ignition Coil

1. Connect a suitable ohmmeter as shown in **Fig. 3**, step 1. Using the high scale, read ohmmeter. Should read very high or infinite. If not, replace coil.
2. Connect ohmmeter as shown in **Fig. 3,** step 2. Using the low scale, read ohmmeter. Should read very low or zero. If not, replace coil.
3. Connect ohmmeter as shown in **Fig. 3,** step 3. Using the high scale, read ohmmeter. Should not read infinite. If it does, replace coil.

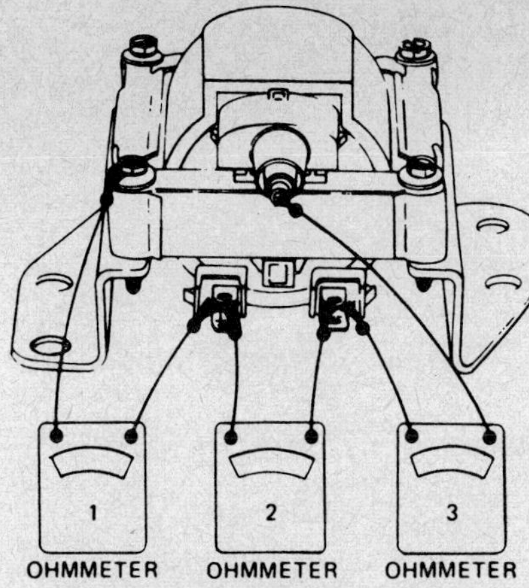

Fig. 3 Testing remote ignition coil

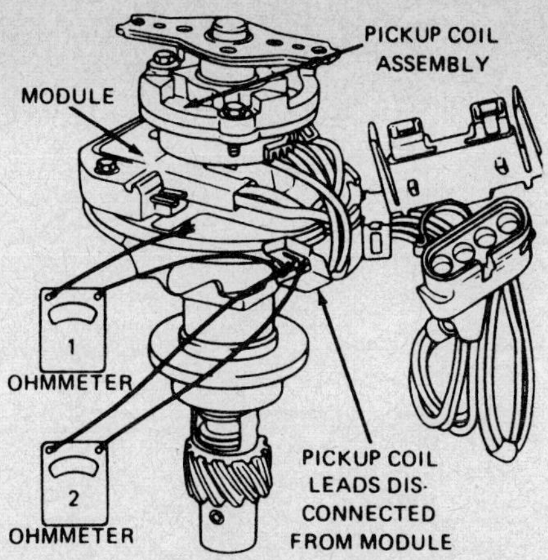

Fig. 4 Testing remote coil distributor pickup coil less Hall Effect switch

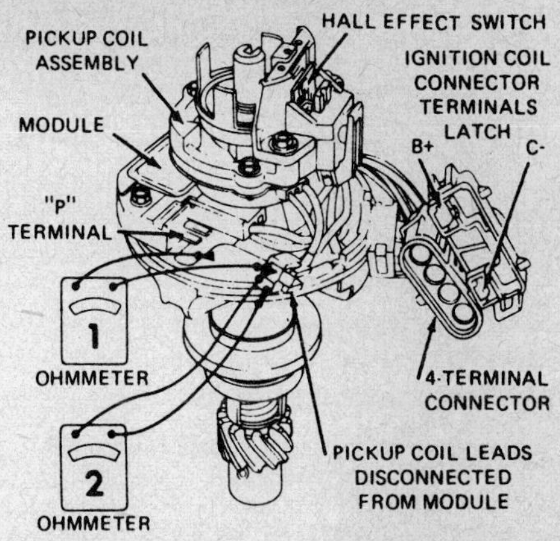

Fig. 5 Testing remote coil distributor pickup coil w/ Hall Effect switch

Testing Pickup Coil

1. Remove distributor rotor, then disconnect pickup coil leads from module.
2. Connect ohmmeter as shown in **Figs. 4 and 5,** step 1. Connect a suitable vacuum source to vacuum advance chamber (if equipped) and note ohmmeter reading throughout entire vacuum advance range. If no vacuum advance is used, flex leads by hand to check for opens. Ohmmeter should read infinite at all times. If not, pickup coil is defective and must be replaced.
3. Connect ohmmeter as shown in **Figs. 4 and 5,** step 2. Repeat step 2. Ohmmeter should read one steady value between 500-1500 ohms. If not, pickup coil is defective and must be replaced. **Ohmmeter may deflect if vacuum advance range causes timing core teeth to align. This is not to be considered a defect.**

Testing Hall Effect Switch (If Equipped)

Refer to Fig. 5 during the following procedures.

1. Carefully noting polarity, connect battery and suitable voltmeter as shown in **Fig. 6.**
2. Voltmeter should read less than 0.5 volts. If not, replace Hall Effect switch.
3. Insert knife blade as shown in **Fig. 6.** Voltmeter should read within 0.5 volts of battery voltage. If not, replace Hall Effect switch.

UNITS WITH INTEGRAL COIL

Testing Ignition Coil

1. Connect a suitable ohmmeter as shown in **Fig. 7,** step 1. Using the low scale, read ohmmeter. Should be near zero or zero. If not, replace coil.
2. Connect ohmmeter both ways as shown in **Fig. 7,** step 2. Using the high scale, read ohmmeter. If both readings are infinite, replace coil.

Testing Pickup Coil

1. Remove distributor rotor, then disconnect pickup coil leads from module.
2. Connect ohmmeter as shown in **Fig. 8,** step 1. Connect a suitable vacuum source to vacuum advance chamber (if equipped) and note ohmmeter reading throughout entire vacuum advance range. If no vacuum advance is used, flex leads by hand to check for opens. Ohmmeter should read infinite at all times. If not, pickup coil is defective and must be replaced.
3. Connect ohmmeter as shown in **Fig. 8,** step 2. Repeat step 2. Ohmmeter should read one steady value between 500-1500 ohms. If not, pickup coil is defective and must be replaced. **Ohmmeter may deflect if vacuum advance range causes timing core teeth to align. This is not to be considered a defect.**

Testing Hall Effect Switch (If Equipped)

Refer to "Units With Remote Coil."

DISTRIBUTOR REPLACE

MODELS EQUIPPED WITH INTEGRAL COIL DISTRIBUTOR

1. Disconnect battery and tachometer lead from distributor cap.
2. Disconnect coil connectors from distributor cap and 4 terminal connector (if equipped). **Do not use a tool of any kind to release coil connectors or damage to lock tabs will result.**
3. Remove distributor cap with ignition high tension wires connected and position aside. Remove vacuum hose (if equipped).
4. Remove distributor clamp screw and hold-down clamp.
5. Mark relationship of rotor to distributor housing, then lift distributor from engine slightly until rotor stops turning. Mark relationship of new rotor position on distributor housing, then remove distributor from engine.
6. If engine was not cranked after distributor was removed from engine, proceed as follows:
   a. Position rotor to align with second mark made on distributor housing prior to removing distributor.
   b. Install distributor into engine and align rotor with first mark made on distributor housing prior to removing distributor.
   c. Install distributor cap and connect all electrical connectors.
   d. Adjust ignition timing.
7. If engine was cranked after distributor was removed from engine, proceed as follows:
   a. Remove No. 1 spark plug and crank engine until compression pressure is felt in No. 1 cylinder. Slowly rotate engine until top dead center is indicated.
   b. Turn rotor to a position just ahead of No. 1 spark plug tower on distributor cap.
   c. Install distributor. Connect 4 terminal connector (if equipped).
   d. Install distributor cap, coil connectors, tachometer lead and battery feed wire.
   e. Adjust ignition timing.

MODELS EQUIPPED WITH REMOTE COIL DISTRIBUTOR

Chevette & 1000

1. Disconnect battery ground cable, then disconnect wiring harness from distributor.
2. Remove distributor cap with ignition cables connected and position aside.
3. Remove ignition coil as described under "Ignition Coil, Replace."
4. Remove air cleaner and disconnect fuel pump hoses at fuel pump.
5. Remove fuel pump and pushrod.
6. Mark relationship of rotor to distributor housing and distributor housing to engine, then remove distributor hold-down clamp and remove distributor from engine.
7. Install distributor checking to ensure that marks made during removal align.
8. Install hold-down clamp and distributor cap.
9. Connect distributor wiring harness electrical connector.

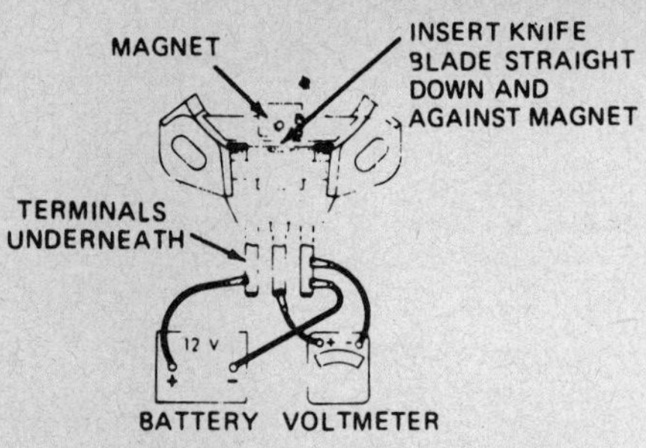

Fig. 6 Testing Hall Effect switch

10. Install fuel pump, air cleaner and ignition coil.
11. Adjust ignition timing.

1982–85 Skylark, 1982–87 Celebrity, Century, Citation, Cutlass Ciera, Omega, 6000 & 1984–87 Cutlass Cruiser w/4 Cylinder Engine

1. Raise and support vehicle.
2. Remove two bolts securing rear engine cradle.
3. Lower cradle enough to allow for access to distributor.
4. Remove five brake line support to floorpan retaining screws.
5. Remove coil wire and distributor cap and position aside.
6. Mark relationship of rotor to distributor housing and distributor housing to engine block, then remove distributor hold-down clamp and remove distributor from engine.
7. Reverse procedure to install. Ensure marks made during disassembly are correctly lined up during distributor installation.
8. Adjust ignition timing.

1982–85 Skylark, 1982–87 Celebrity, Century, Citation, Cutlass Ciera, Omega, 6000 & 1984–87 Cutlass Cruiser w/6 Cylinder Engine

1. Disconnect battery ground cable.
2. Disconnect ignition switch battery feed wire, then if equipped, the tachometer lead from distributor cap. **Do not use a tool of any kind to release locking tabs.**
3. Remove distributor cap by turning four retaining latches counterclockwise, then position cap aside.
4. Remove distributor clamp screw, then the hold-down clamp.
5. Note position of rotor, then pull distributor up until rotor just stops turning counterclockwise and again note position of rotor. **To ensure correct timing of distributor it must be installed with rotor correctly positioned as described.**
6. Reverse procedure to install.
7. Adjust ignition timing.

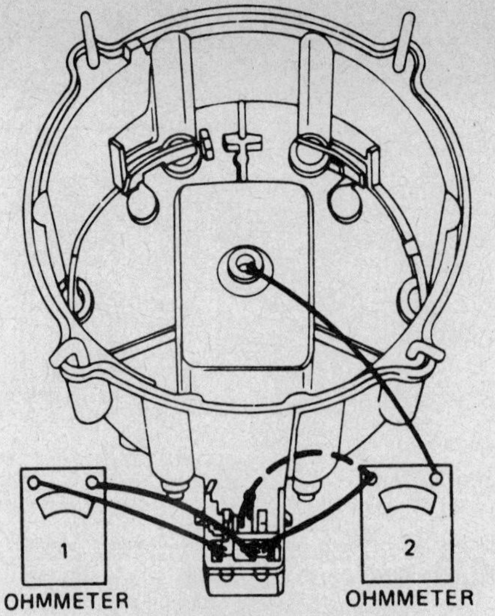

Fig. 7 Testing integral ignition coil

Cavalier, Cimarron, Firenza, 2000, Sunbird & Skyhawk Exc. 1982–86 Firenza, Skyhawk, Sunbird & 2000 with 1.8L OHC Engine

1. Disconnect battery ground cable and remove air cleaner.
2. Release distributor cap latches, then remove distributor cap and position aside.
3. Disconnect AIR pipe to exhaust manifold hose at AIR management valve.
4. Remove rear engine lift bracket bolt and nut from stud, then position assembly aside.
5. Mark relationship of rotor to distributor housing and distributor housing to block.
6. Remove distributor hold-down clamp, then remove distributor from engine.
7. Reverse procedure to install. Check to ensure that marks made during removal align after distributor is installed.

1982–86 Firenza, Skyhawk, Sunbird & 2000 with 1.8L OHC Engine

1. Disconnect battery ground cable.
2. Remove spark plug wires and ignition coil.
3. Disconnect distributor wiring.
4. Remove two nuts securing distributor body to cylinder head and remove distributor.
5. Reverse procedure to install. Adjust ignition timing. Torque nuts 9-15 ft. lbs. **No gear is used to drive the distributor. A lug at the distributor base engages a slot on camshaft end.**

Camaro, Fiero & Firebird

1. Disconnect battery ground cable.
2. Disconnect ignition switch battery feed wire, then if equipped, the tachometer lead from distributor cap. **Do not use a tool of any kind to release locking tabs.**

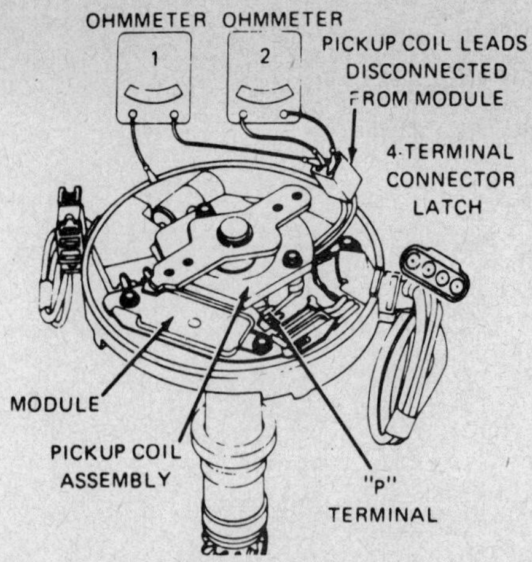

Fig. 8 Testing integral coil distributor pickup coil

3. Remove distributor cap by turning four retaining latches counterclockwise, then position cap aside.
4. Disconnect 4 terminal ECM harness connector from distributor.
5. If necessary, disconnect spark plug cables from cap.
6. Remove distributor clamp screw, then the hold-down clamp.
7. Note position of rotor, then pull distributor up until rotor just stops turning counterclockwise and again note position of rotor. **To ensure correct timing of distributor it must be installed with rotor correctly positioned as described.**
8. Reverse procedure to install.
9. Adjust ignition timing.

COMPONENTS REPLACE

IGNITION COIL REPLACEMENT

Units With Internal Coil

1. Remove electrical connector from distributor cap by lifting retaining tabs.
2. Remove three coil cover attaching screws, then remove cover, **Fig. 9.**
3. Remove coil attaching screws, then remove ignition coil with leads from distributor cap.
4. Remove coil arc seal.
5. Reverse procedure to install.

Units With External Coil

1. On 1982-85 Skylark, 1982-86 Citation, Omega, Phoenix, 1982-86 Celebrity, Century, Cutlass Ciera, 6000 & 1984-86 Cutlass Cruiser, proceed as follows:
   a. Remove bolt securing radio capacitor to coil.
   b. Disconnect coil electrical connector and high tension lead.
   c. Remove three coil mounting bolts, then remove coil.
   d. Reverse procedure to install.
2. On Chevette and 1000 models, proceed as follows:

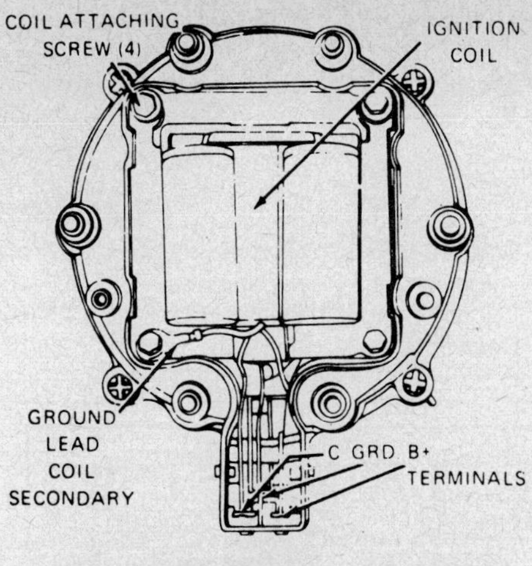

Fig. 9 Removing ignition coil cover. 1982–87 models with internal coil

a. Remove coil cover, then disconnect ignition switch to coil lead at coil.
b. Disconnect coil high tension lead, then remove coil retaining bolts and the coil.
c. Reverse procedure to install.

3. On Cavalier, Cimarron, Firenza, 2000, Sunbird & Skyhawk models, proceed as follows: **On 1982-86 Firenza, Skyhawk, Sunbird & 2000 with 1.8L OHC engine, the coil is located at the rear of the engine near the end of the cam cover.**
   a. Disconnect battery ground cable, then raise and support vehicle.
   b. Disconnect fuel pump lines at fuel pump, then remove vacuum pipe retaining bracket nut at coil and position pipe aside.
   c. Remove fuel pump, then remove coil mounting bolts.

MODULE REPLACEMENT

1. Remove distributor cap and rotor.
2. Remove module retaining screws, then lift module upward.
3. Disconnect module electrical connector. Note position of electrical connector prior to disconnecting. Remove module from distributor.
4. Reverse procedure to install. Check to ensure that module electrical connector is installed in proper position. If module is not being replaced, do not wipe grease from module or distributor base. If new module is to be installed, coat module and distributor base with pack of grease supplied with replacement module.

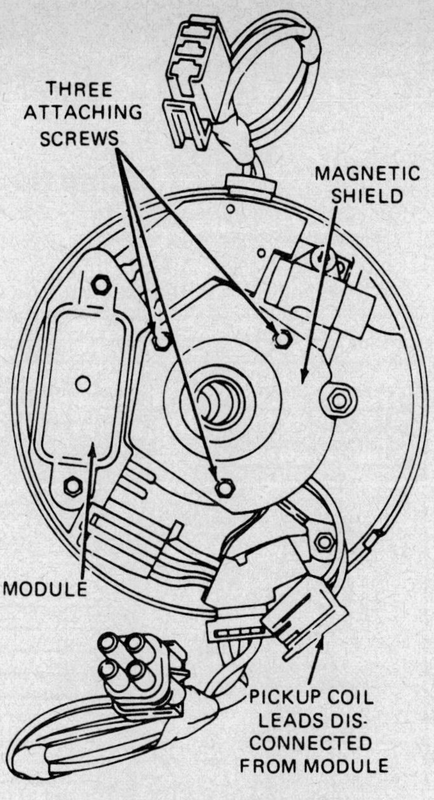

Fig. 10 Removing distributor shield. Models equipped with 6 & 8 cylinder engines

PICKUP COIL, REPLACE

1. Remove distributor from engine.
2. Mark relationship of distributor shaft and driven gear for reference during assembly.
3. Remove roll pin and driven gear from shaft.
4. Remove distributor cap, magnetic shield (if equipped), shaft and rotor.
5. Remove C-washer on top of pickup coil assembly, then disconnect pickup coil leads from module and remove pickup coil assembly.
6. Reverse procedure to install.

HALL EFFECT SWITCH (IF EQUIPPED), REPLACE

1. Remove distributor cap and rotor.
2. Remove switch retaining screws, then while pulling switch away, remove wiring connector. Remove switch.
3. Reverse procedure to install. **After Hall Effect switch is installed, spin distributor shaft to ensure teeth do**

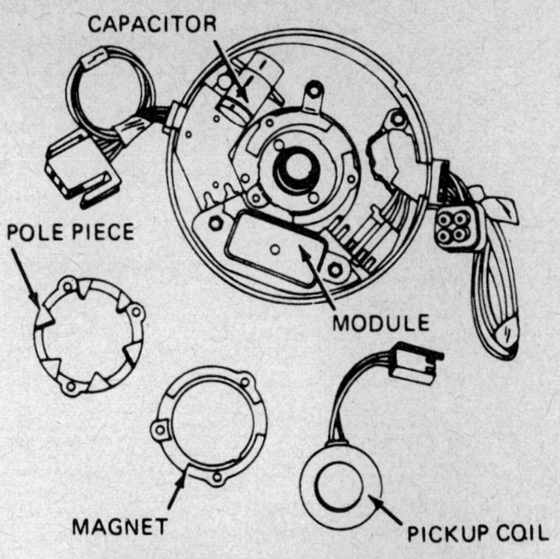

Fig. 11 Pickup coil disassembled. Models equipped with 6 & 8 cylinder engines

not touch. If necessary loosen, then retighten pickup coil teeth and Hall Effect switch to eliminate contact.

DISTRIBUTOR SERVICE

V6 & V8 ENGINES

1. Remove cap and coil as an assembly.
2. Remove rotor and pickup coil leads from module.
3. Mark relationship of distributor shaft and driven gear for reference during assembly.
4. Remove roll pin and driven gear.
5. Remove distributor shaft assembly.
6. Remove shield, **Fig. 10.**
7. Remove retaining ring, pickup coil, magnet and pole piece, **Fig. 11.**
8. Remove module retaining screws and capacitor screw, then remove module, capacitor and harness assembly from distributor.
9. Disconnect wiring harness from module. Reverse procedure to assemble.

4 CYLINDER ENGINE

1. Remove rotor, then disconnect pickup coil leads from module.
2. Mark relationship of distributor shaft and driven gear for reference during assembly.
3. Remove roll pin and driven gear from distributor shaft.
4. Remove C-washer retaining ring, then remove pickup coil assembly.
5. Disconnect module electrical connectors, then remove module retaining screws and the module.
6. Clean distributor base, then apply suitable silicone lubricant between module and base.
7. Reverse procedure to assemble.

Computer Controlled Coil Ignition (C³I) System

INDEX

DESCRIPTION

The Computer-Controlled Coil Ignition (C³I) System is an Electronic Spark Timing (EST) system which consists of an Electronic Control Module (ECM), ignition (coil) module, electro-magnetic camshaft and crankshaft position sensors and necessary wiring, **Figs. 1 through 9.**

The ignition (coil) module replaces the conventional ignition coil and distributor and has an integral microprocessor which receives and buffers information from the crankshaft and camshaft position sensors to determine the proper firing sequence, then selects and triggers each of the three interconnected coils to fire the spark plugs.

The three interconnected coils must fire two spark plugs simultaneously. Therefore, cylinder Nos. one and four, five and two and three and six are selected for each coil. When cylinder No. one is approaching TDC on the compression stroke, cylinder No. 4 is on the exhaust stroke, and so on through the entire spark plug firing sequence. Very little energy is required to fire the spark plug in the cylinder on the exhaust stroke, so the remaining high voltage is used to fire the spark plug in the cylinder on the compression stoke.

Ignition timing is determined by the Electronic Control Module (ECM) which monitors crankshaft position, engine RPM, engine temperature and amount of air the engine is consuming, then signals the ignition (coil) module accordingly. Electronic Spark Control (ESC) is also used to retard timing during times of spark detonation. The ESC system is comprised of a knock sensor and an ESC module, **Figs. 10 and 11.** As the knock sensor detects detonation, the ESC module to ECM voltage is shut off, signalling the ECM to retard the spark. An electronic filter is used to filter out vibrations not related to detonation.

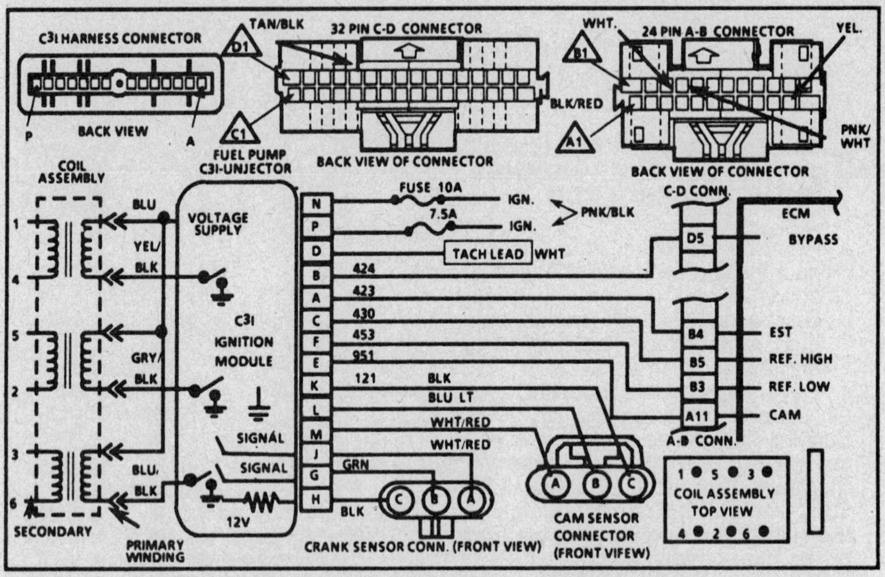

Fig. 1 C³I ignition system wiring schematic. 1984–85 V6-231/3.8L turbocharged engine

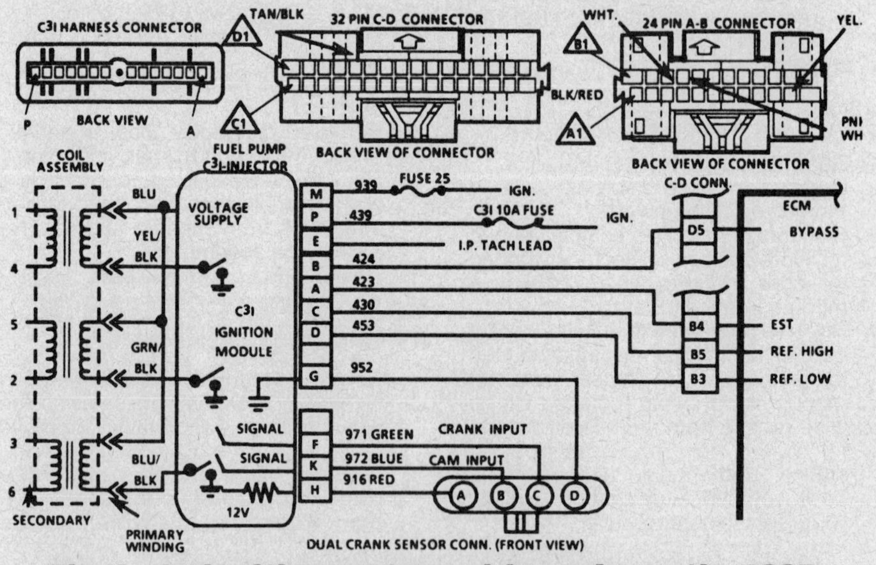

Fig. 2 C³I ignition system wiring schematic. 1985 V6-181/3.0L engine

COMPONENTS REPLACE

IGNITION COIL REPLACEMENT

1. Disconnect battery ground cable.
2. Disconnect spark plug wires from ignition coil.
3. Remove screws securing coil to ignition module, then tilt coil back and disconnect module connectors.
4. Remove coil.
5. Reverse procedure to install.

IGNITION MODULE REPLACEMENT

1. Disconnect battery ground cable, then the ignition module 14-way connector.
2. Disconnect spark plug wires from ignition coil.
3. Remove ignition module-to-bracket attaching nuts and washers.
4. Remove screws securing coil to ignition module, then disconnect coil-to-module wire connectors.
5. Remove ignition module.
6. Reverse procedure to install.

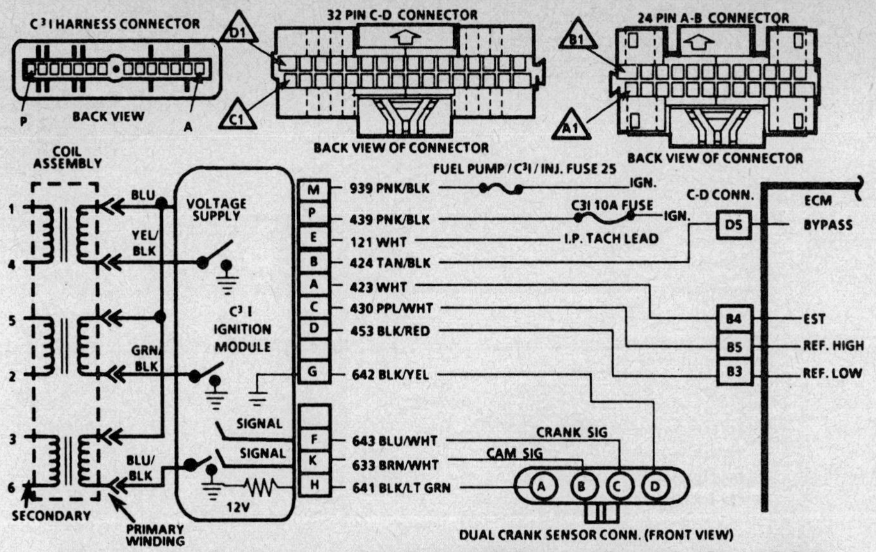

Fig. 3 C³I ignition system wiring schematic. 1986 V6-181/3.0L engine

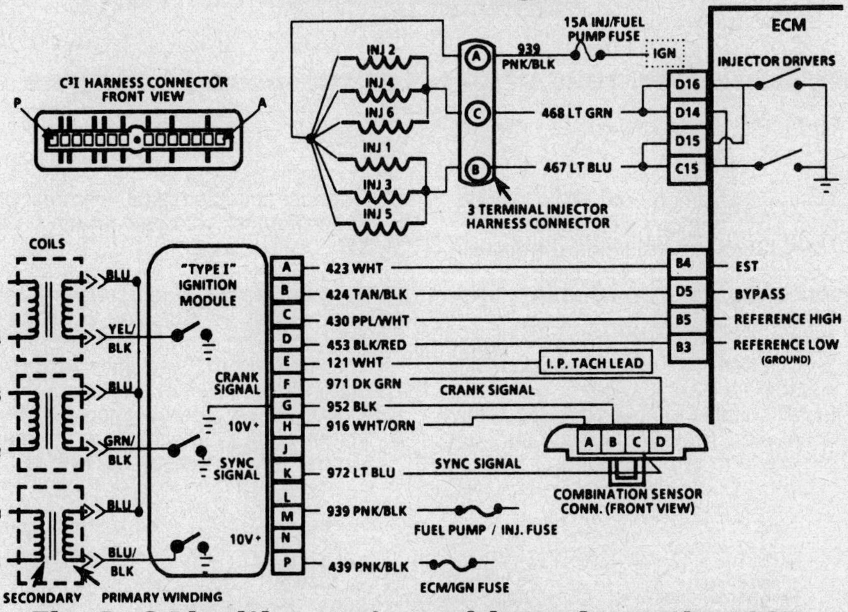

Fig. 4 C³I ignition system wiring schematic. 1987 V6-181/3.0L engine

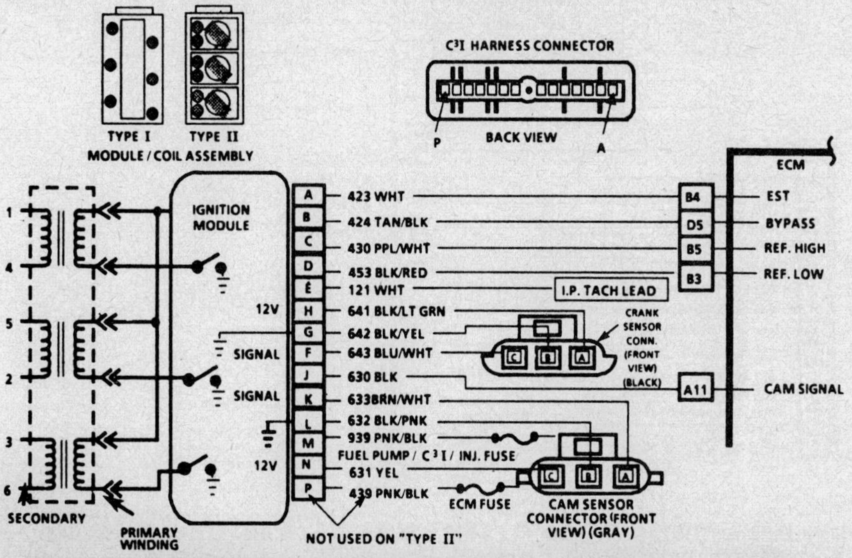

Fig. 5 C³I ignition system wiring schematic. 1986 V6-231/3.8L non-turbocharged engine

CRANKSHAFT SENSOR REPLACEMENT

1. Disconnect battery ground cable, then remove sensor 3-way connector.
2. Raise and support vehicle.
3. Rotate harmonic balancer so slot in disc is aligned with sensor.
4. Loosen sensor attaching bolt, then slide sensor outboard and remove through notch in sensor housing.
5. Reverse procedure to install. Adjust sensor so that an equal clearance exists on both sides of disc (approximately .030 inch), then tighten attaching bolt and check clearance. Readjust as necessary.

CAMSHAFT POSITION SENSOR REPLACEMENT

To replace camshaft position sensor, it is not necessary to remove drive assembly. If drive assembly replacement is required, refer to "Camshaft Position Sensor Drive Assembly Replacement."

1. Disconnect battery ground cable, then remove ignition module 14-way connector.
2. Disconnect spark plug wires from ignition coil.
3. Remove ignition module bracket assembly.
4. Disconnect sensor wiring, then remove sensor securing screws and sensor.
5. Reverse procedure to install.

CAMSHAFT POSITION SENSOR DRIVE ASSEMBLY REPLACEMENT

1. Remove camshaft position sensor as outlined previously.
2. Make note of position of slot in rotating vane in drive assembly.
3. Remove bolt securing drive assembly in engine block, then pull drive assembly to remove.
4. Install drive assembly so dot on drive gear faces the opposite direction of cam sensor disc window. **When installed correctly, the dot on the sensor drive gear will face away from the timing chain when No. 1 cylinder is at TDC. Also, the sensor wiring harness should be facing the timing chain.**
5. Loosely install drive assembly securing bolt.
6. Install camshaft position sensor as outlined previously.
7. Set camshaft sensor timing. Refer to "Camshaft Sensor Timing."

COMBINATION CAMSHAFT & CRANKSHAFT SENSOR REPLACEMENT

V6-181/3.0L Engine

1. Disconnect battery ground cable.
2. Disconnect electrical connector from sensor.
3. Raise and support vehicle.
4. Position harmonic balancer so slot in disc aligns with sensor, then remove sensor retaining bolt and the sensor. **It may be necessary to remove the**

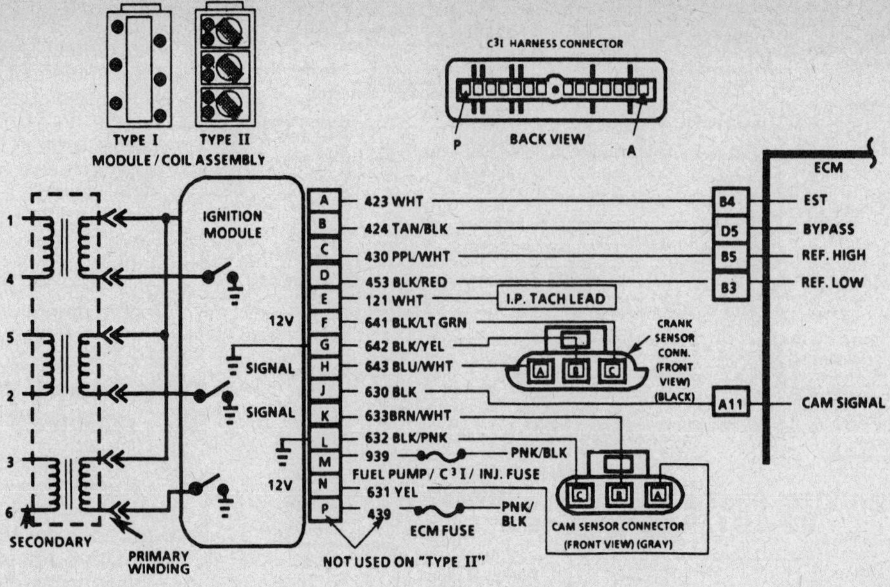

Fig. 6 C³I ignition system wiring schematic. 1986 V6-231/3.8L turbocharged engine

harmonic balancer to gain access to sensor.

5. Reverse procedure to install. Adjust sensor to obtain approximately .030 inch clearance between disc and each side of sensor.

ADJUSTMENTS

CAMSHAFT SENSOR TIMING

The following adjustment does not affect spark timing.

1. Rotate crankshaft until No. 1 cylinder is at TDC, compression stroke.
2. Mark harmonic balancer, then rotate crankshaft to 25° after TDC.
3. Remove spark plug wires from ignition coil.
4. Remove terminal "B" of wire sensor 3-way connector on module side with suitable tool.
5. Install suitable jumper wire into 3-way connector "B" terminal, then connect other end to removed wire.
6. Connect suitable digital voltmeter between jumper wire and ground, **Fig. 12.**
7. Turn ignition On, then rotate sensor counterclockwise until sensor switch closes. This is indicated by voltage reading going from a high of 5 to 12 volts to a low of 0 to 2 volts. Low voltage indicates switch closing.
8. Tighten drive assembly securing bolt.
9. Install spark plug wires, then remove jumper wire and repair connection.

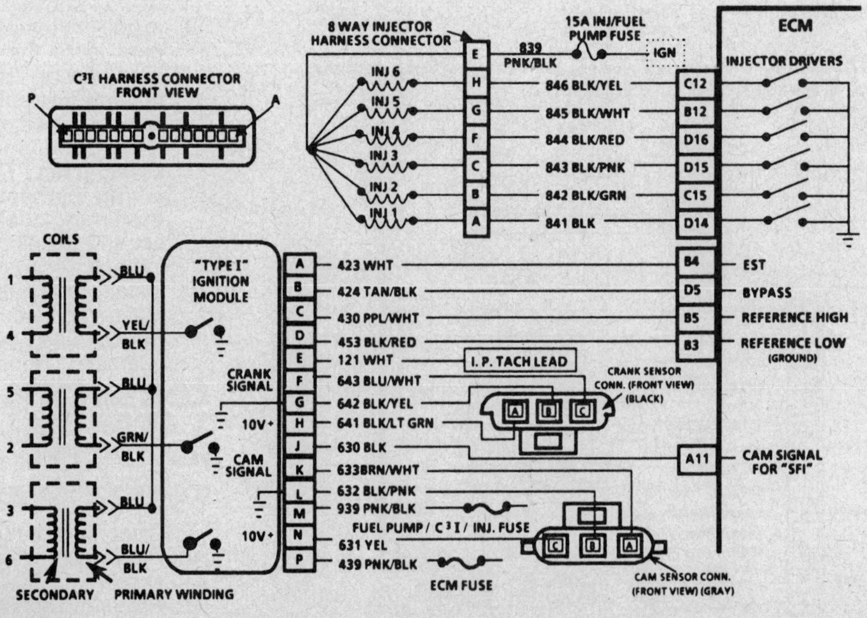

Fig. 7 C³I ignition system wiring schematic (Type I). 1987 V6-231/3.8L exc. Cutlass Supreme, Grand Prix, Monte Carlo & Regal

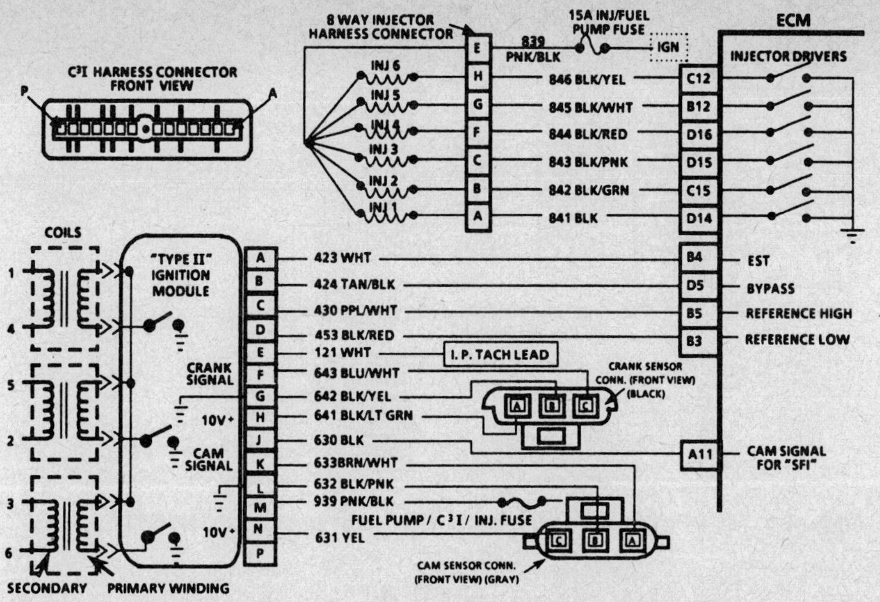

Fig. 8 C³I ignition system wiring schematic (Type II). 1987 V6-231/3.8L exc. Cutlass Supreme, Grand Prix, Monte Carlo & Regal

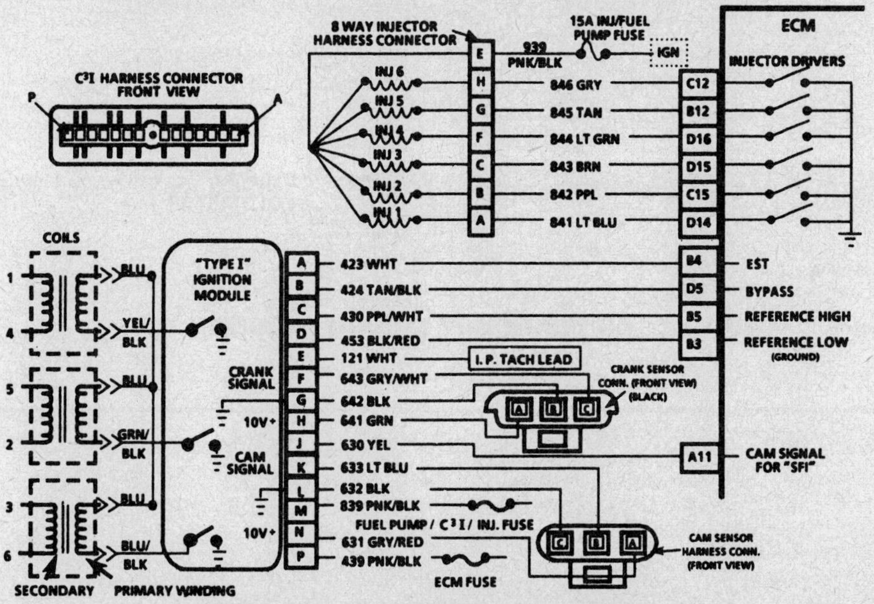

Fig. 9 C³I ignition system wiring schematic (Type I). 1987 V6-231/3.8L Cutlass Supreme, Grand Prix, Monte Carlo & Regal

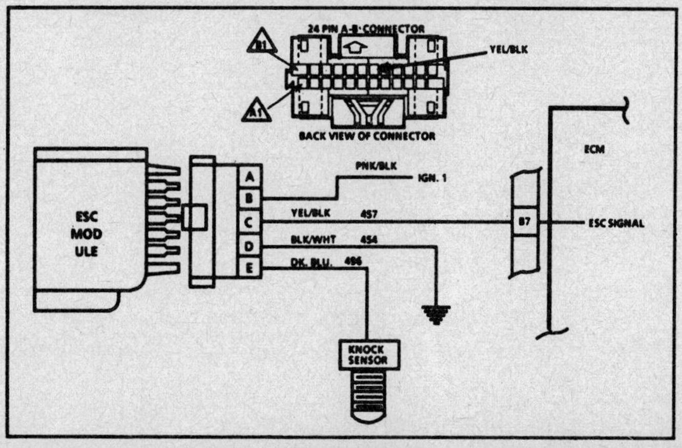

Fig. 10 C³I ignition system ESC wiring schematic. 1984–86

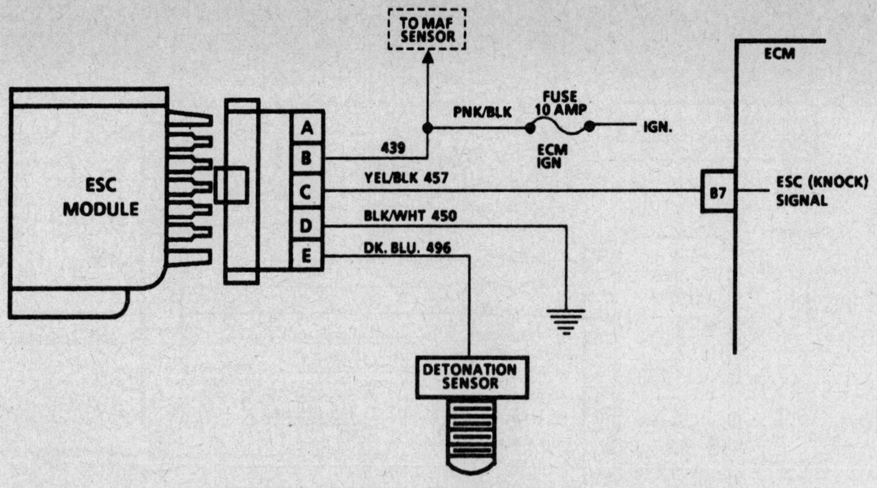

Fig. 11 C³I ignition system ESC wiring schematic. 1987

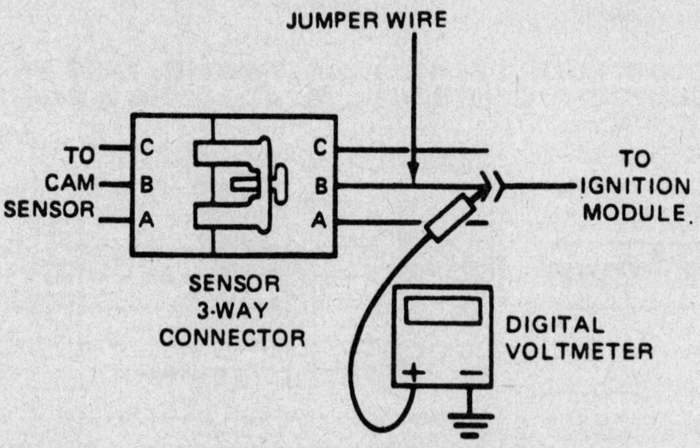

Fig. 12 C³I camshaft sensor adjustment

Solid State Ignition, 1985–87 Nova

INDEX

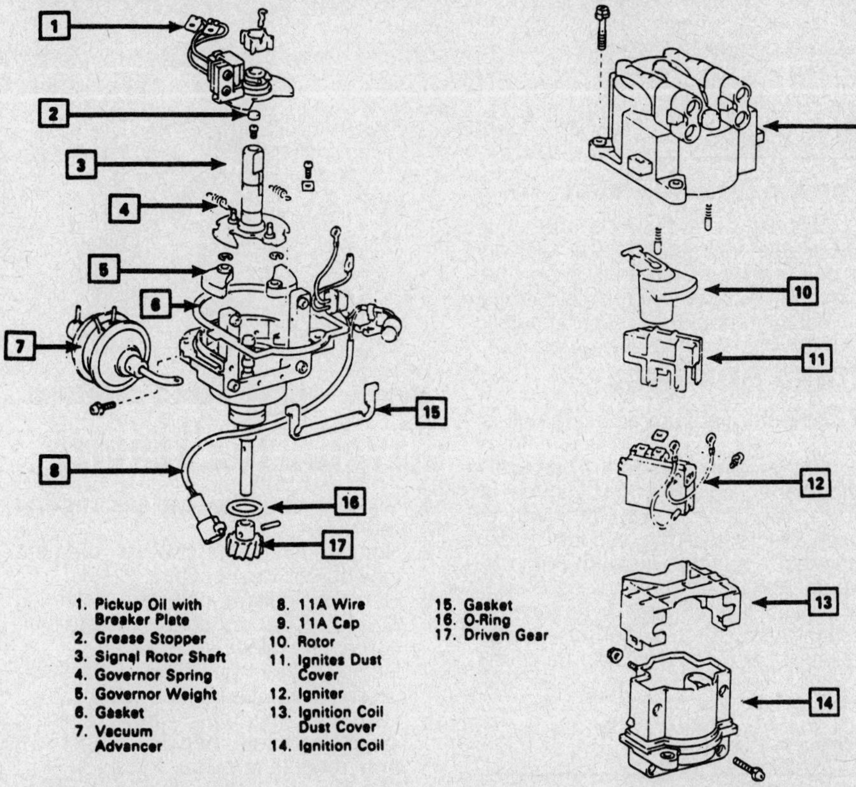

Fig. 1 Exploded view of solid state ignition system

DESCRIPTION

The principle components of a solid state ignition system are the spark plugs, ignition coil and distributor. The distributor, **Fig. 1,** has a rotor, module, pole piece, vacuum advance and a centrifugal advance.

The pickup coil is used to generate the ignition signal and consists of a pole piece, magnet and a pickup coil. The pole piece is attached to the distributor shaft. The magnet along with the pickup coil, is attached to the pickup coil base plate.

When the distributor shaft rotates, the magnetic flux passing through the pickup coil varies due to the change in the air gap between the pickup coil and the pole piece. As a result, the alternating current voltage is induced in the pickup coil. The voltage induced, turns the module off and on which switches off the ignition coil primary current. Thus the high voltage is induced in the secondary winding of the ignition coil and ignition sparks are generated at the plugs, **Fig. 2.**

TROUBLESHOOTING

Ignition related problems such as overheating, backfiring, afterfire and engine run-on can be corrected by adjusting ignition timing.

ENGINE WILL NOT START/HARD START (CRANKS OK)

1. Incorrect ignition timing.
2. Faulty ignition coil.
3. Faulty module.
4. Faulty 11A.
5. Faulty spark plug wiring.
6. Faulty spark plugs.
7. Disconnected or broken 11A wiring.

ENGINE CRANKS SLOWLY

1. Insufficient battery voltage.
2. Loose, corroded or worn battery cables.
3. Faulty starter.

ENGINE WILL NOT CRANK

1. Insufficient battery voltage.
2. Loose, corroded or worn battery cables.
3. Faulty neutral safety switch.
4. Blown fusible link.
5. Faulty starter.
6. Faulty ignition switch.

ROUGH IDLE OR STALLS

1. Faulty spark plugs.
2. Faulty 11A wiring.
3. Incorrect ignition timing.
4. Faulty ignition coil.
5. Faulty module.
6. Faulty 11A.
7. Faulty spark plug wiring.

ENGINE HESITATES OR POOR ACCELERATION

1. Faulty spark plugs.
2. Faulty ignition wiring.
3. Incorrect ignition timing.

POOR GAS MILEAGE

1. Incorrect ignition timing.
2. Faulty spark plugs.

SYSTEM TESTING

PICKUP COIL

1. Place ignition switch in "Off" position.
2. Remove distributor cap, then disconnect pickup coil wire from module.
3. Measure resistance across pickup coil as shown, **Fig. 3.**

IGNITION COIL

1. Disconnect ignition coil wiring at positive andnegative leads, then the high tension coil wire.
2. Measure resistance between positive and negative terminals using a suitable ohmmeter.
3. Resistance should be .3-.5 ohms (cold).
4. Measure resistance between positive terminal and high tension terminal.
5. Secondary coil resistance (coil) should be 7.5-10.5 ohms.
6. If resistance values are not as specified, replace coil.
7. Reconnect terminal leads, then the high tension coil wire.

MODULE

1. Remove distributor cap, then turn ignition switch to "On" position.

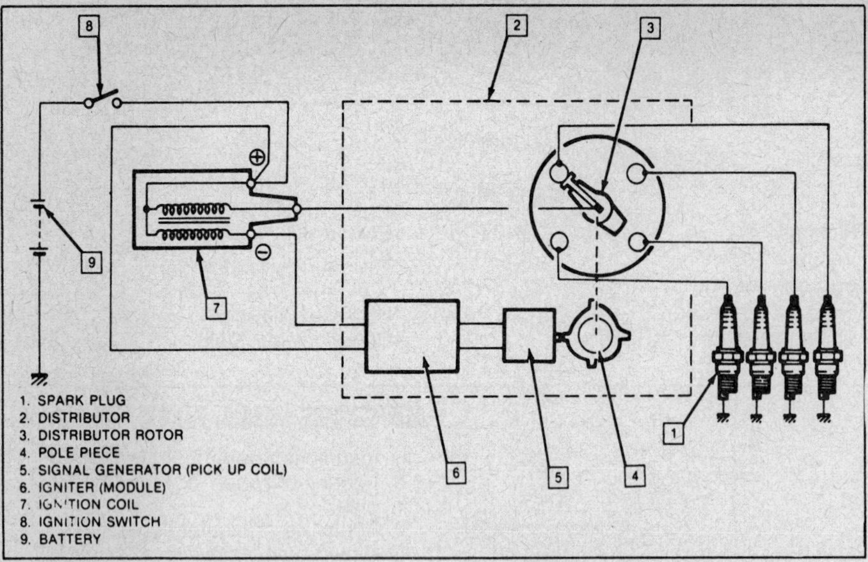

Fig. 2 Schematic view of solid state ignition system

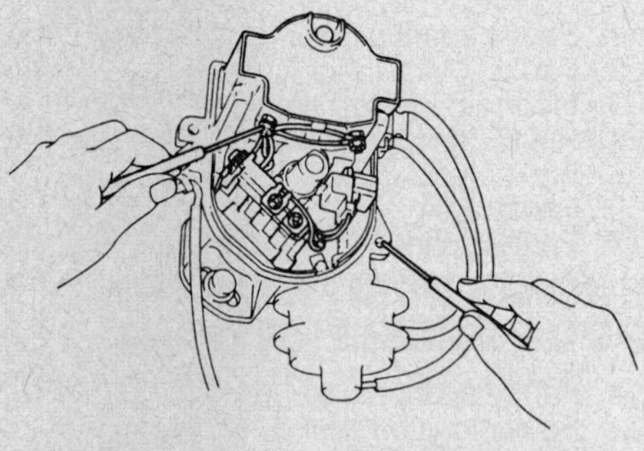

Fig. 4 Testing power transistor

2. Check for line voltage at power source as follows:
   a. Connect the positive probe from a suitable voltmeter to the positive terminal of the ignition coil.
   b. Connect the negative probe of voltmeter to a suitable ground.
   c. Voltage reading should be approximately 12 volts.
3. Inspect power transistor as follows:
   a. Connect positive probe of a suitable ohmmeter to the ignition coil negative terminal, then the negative probe to ground, **Fig. 4.** Voltage reading should be approximately 12 volts.
   b. Connect the positive pole of a 1.5 volt dry cell battery to the pink wire terminal, then the negative pole to the white wire terminal, **Fig. 5. Do not apply voltage for more than 5 seconds or damage to power transistor will occur.**
   c. Connect the positive probe of a suitable voltmeter to the ignition coil negative terminal, then the negative probe to ground. Voltage reading should be approximately 0-3 volts. If not, replace module.

VACUUM ADVANCE

The distributor vacuum advance unit is controlled by negative air pressure from the vacuum advance port on the carburetor. During normal operation, this vacuum is sufficient to regulate the vacuum advance. To check, disconnect the vacuum hose, then connect a suitable vacuum pump to diaphragm. Apply vacuum and ensure advancer moves. If not, repair or replace as necessary. Also, rotate rotor clockwise, then release it and ensure it returns counterclockwise. Ensure rotor is not excessively loose.

DISTRIBUTOR

REPLACE

1. Disconnect battery ground cable.
2. Disconnect distributor wire at electrical connector.
3. Disconnect vacuum hoses, then the vacuum advance unit.
4. Disconnect distributor cap with spark plug cables connected, then position aside.
5. Remove distributor hold-down bolts.
6. Note position of rotor, then pull distributor outward until it stops rotating counterclockwise.
7. Reverse procedure to install. Check to ensure marks made during removal are correctly aligned during installation.
8. Adjust ignition timing.

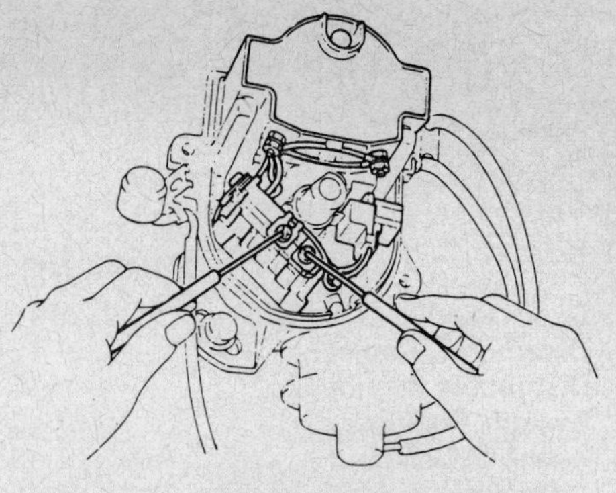

Fig. 3 Measuring pickup coil resistance

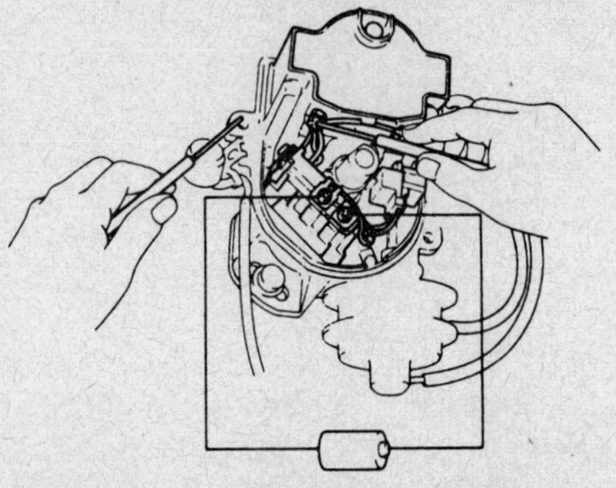

Fig. 5 Inspecting module

DISTRIBUTOR SERVICE

1. Remove distributor cap, packing and rotor.
2. Remove ignition dust cover, then the ignition coil dust cover.
3. Remove ignition coil wire retaining nuts, then disconnect wires from ignition coil terminal.
4. Remove four ignition coil retaining screws, then the ignition coil.
5. Remove module wire retaining screws and nuts, then disconnect wire from module terminal.
6. Remove module retaining screws, then the module.
7. Pry off rotor and spring using suitable tool, then remove vacuum advance retaining screws.
8. Separate advance unit link hole from breaker plate pin, then remove advance unit.
9. Remove breaker plate retaining screws and washers, then the breaker plate and pickup coil.
10. Remove governor springs, then the grease stopper at end of governor shaft.
11. Remove governor shaft end screw, then the signal rotor shaft.
12. Remove C-clip, then the governor weights.
13. Reverse procedure to assemble.

Direct Ignition System (DIS)

INDEX

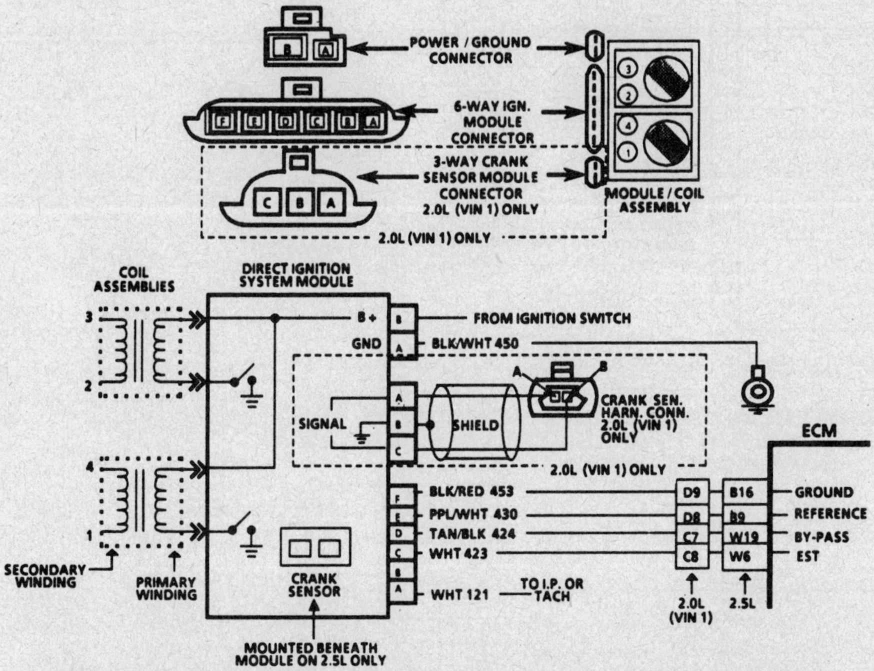

Fig. 1 DIS ignition system wiring schematic. 1987 4-121/2.0L Firenza & 4-151/2.5L Calais & Cutlass Ciera w/TBI

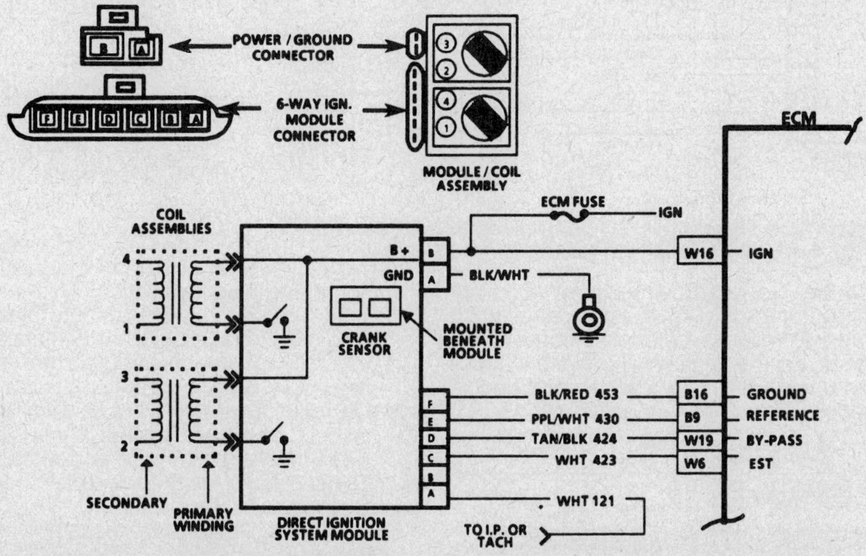

Fig. 2 DIS ignition system wiring schematic. 1987 4-151/2.5L Celebrity, Grand Am, Fiero & 6000 w/TBI

DESCRIPTION

The Direct Ignition System (DIS), **Figs. 1 through 4**, is a distributorless type ignition system which consists of: two separate ignition coils on 4 cylinder models or 3 separate ignition coils on 6 cylinder models; a "DIS" ignition module; a Crankshaft Sensor; and the Electronic Spark Timing (EST) portion of the ECM (Electronic Control Module).

A "Waste Spark" method of distribution is used on this distributorless ignition system. Each cylinder is paired with its opposing cylinder in firing order so that one cylinder on the compression stroke fires simultaneously with its opposing cylinder on the exhaust stroke. Requiring less voltage to fire the plug on the exhaust stroke, most of the available voltage is sent to the compression stroke cylinder. This process is reversed as the cylinders roles are reversed.

In much the same manner as the distributor type ignition system, these systems use the EST signal from the ECM. The DIS module controls spark timing under 400 RPM and the ECM controls spark timing over 400 RPM.

The DIS module monitors the Crankshaft Sensor signals and based on these signals, sends a reference signal to the ECM to allow the correct spark and fuel injector control to be maintained during all driving conditions. At the point of ignition firing, the DIS module monitors the "sync-pulse," and below 400 RPM the module controls spark advance by triggering each of the two coils at a predetermined interval based on engine speed only. The ECM controls the spark above 400 RPM and compensates for all driving conditions. The DIS module must receive a "sync-pulse" followed by a Crank Signal in that order to enable engine start up.

The EST system utilizes the same EST to ECM circuits that distributor type ignition systems use. These system circuits include the DIS reference circuit, reference ground, bypass and the EST circuit.

In the DIS reference circuit, the Crankshaft Sensor generates a signal to the ignition module which results in a reference pulse being sent to the ECM. The ECM uses this pulse to calculate crankshaft position, engine speed and injector pulse width.

In the reference ground circuit, the wire is grounded through the module and insures that the ground circuit has no voltage drop between the ignition module and the ECM, which could affect performance.

In the bypass circuit, the ECM applies approximately 5 volts at about 400 RPM to switch spark timing control from the DIS module to the ECM. An open or grounded

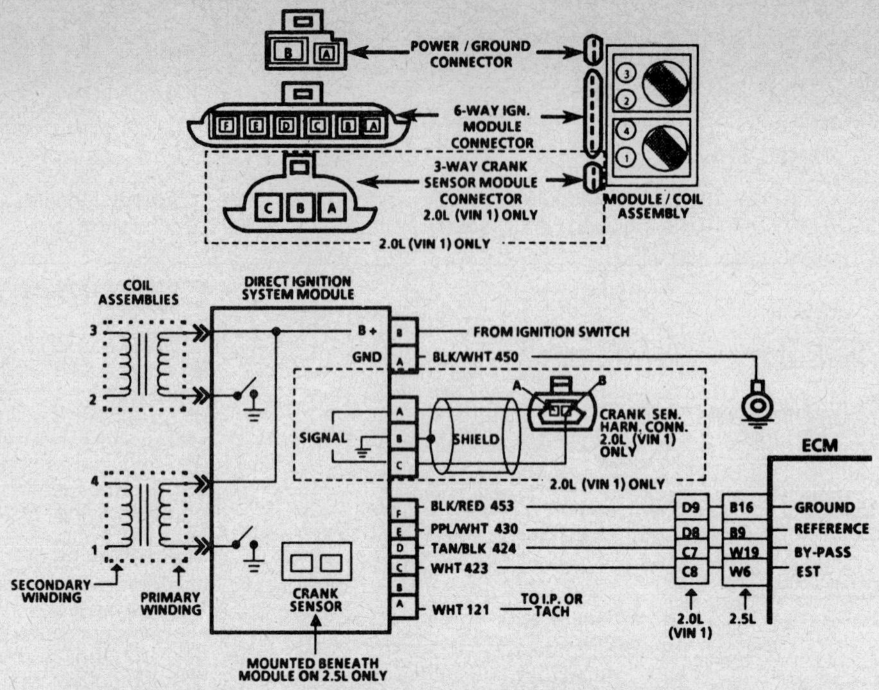

Fig. 3 DIS ignition system wiring schematic. 1987 4-121/2.0L Skyhawk & 4-151/2.5L Century, Skylark & Somerset Regal w/TBI

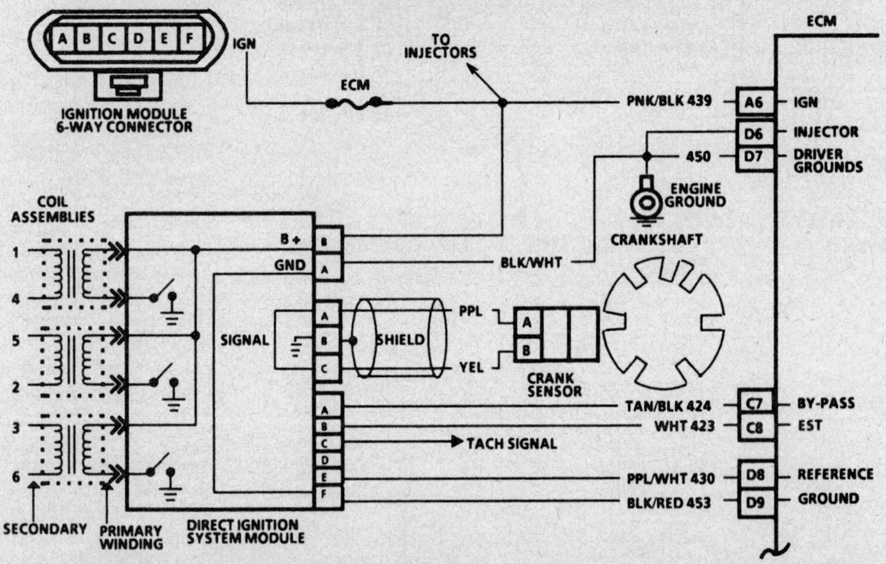

Fig. 4 DIS ignition system wiring schematic. 1987 V6-173/2.8L models w/port injection

bypass circuit will set a code 42 and result in the engine operating in a backup ignition timing mode (module timing) at a calculated timing value. This may cause poor performance and reduce fuel economy.

In the EST circuit, the DIS module sends a reference signal to the ECM when the engine is cranking. While the engine is under 400 RPM, the DIS module controls the ignition timing. When engine speed exceeds 400 RPM, the DIS module controls ignition timing. When engine speed exceeds 400 RPM, the ECM applies 5 volts to the bypass line to switch the timing to the ECM control (EST). An open or ground in the EST circuit will result in the engine continuing to run but in a backup ignition timing mode at a calculated timing value and the "Service Engine Soon" lamp will not light. If the EST fault is present the next time the engine is restarted, a code 42 will be set and the engine will operate in module timing. This may cause poor performance and reduce fuel economy.

COMPONENTS REPLACE

DIS MODULE ASSEMBLY

1. Disconnect battery ground cable.
2. Disconnect DIS module assembly electrical connectors, **Figs. 5 through 7.**
3. Disconnect spark plug wires from module assembly, noting proper location to facilitate installation.
4. Remove DIS module assembly to engine block attaching bolts, then separate DIS module assembly from engine.
5. On models with 4-151/2.5L engines, inspect crankshaft sensor O-ring for wear, cracks, or leakage and replace as necessary. Apply engine oil to new O-ring prior to installation.
6. Assemble DIS module assembly to engine.
7. Insert attaching bolts, then torque to 20 ft. lbs. on 4 cylinder models and 19 ft. lbs. on V6 models.
8. Connect spark plug wires to their respectful coils.
9. Connect DIS module assembly elec-

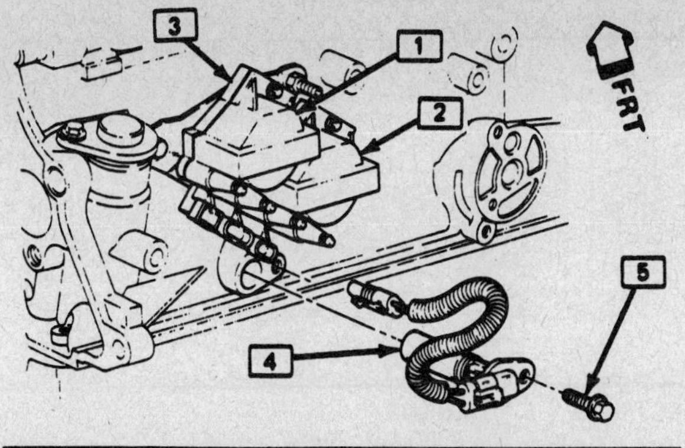

1	2-3 COIL	4	CRANK SENSOR ASM
2	1-4 COIL	5	BOLT 10 N·m (88 LBS. IN.)
3	MODULE		

Fig. 5 Removing DIS module assembly. 4-121/2.0L models

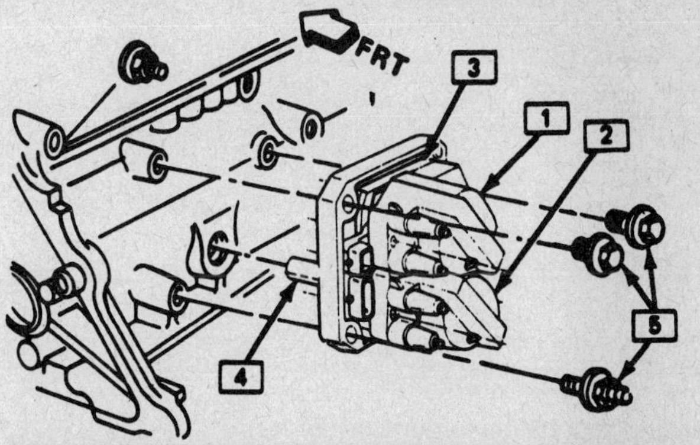

1	#2/3 IGN. COIL	4	CRANKSHAFT SENSOR
2	#1/4 IGN. COIL	5	BOLT (3) 27 N·m (20 LBS. FT.)
3	IGN. MODULE		

Fig. 6 Removing DIS module assembly. 4-151/2.5L models

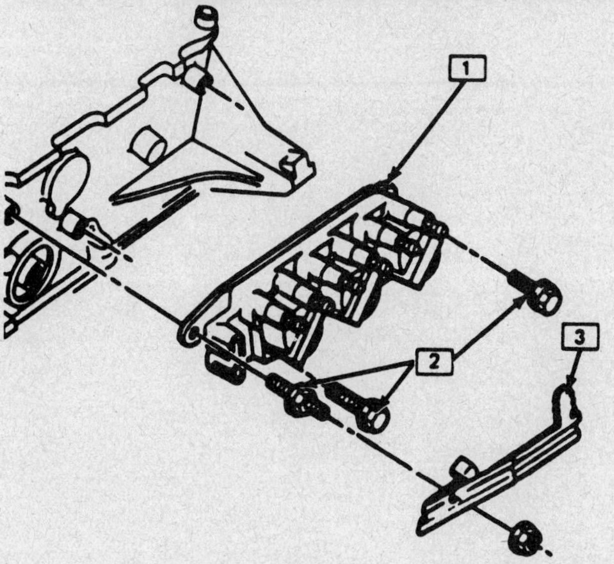

1	DIS ASM
2	BOLTS (3) 25 N·m (19 FT. LBS.)
3	BRACKET

Fig. 7 Removing DIS module assembly. V6-173 2.8L models

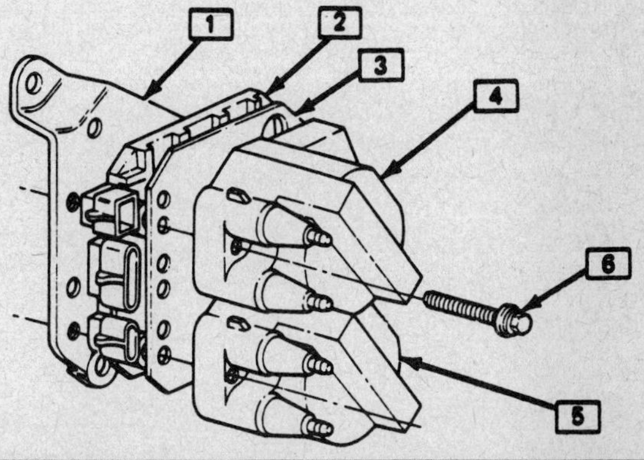

1	BRACKET	4	2-3 COIL	6	SCREWS (4) 4.5 N·m (40 LBS. IN.)
2	MODULE	5	1-4 COIL		
3	SHIELD				

Fig. 8 Exploded view of DIS module assembly. 4-121/2.0L models

trical connectors, then the battery ground cable.

CRANKSHAFT SENSOR

4-121 2.0L Engines

1. Disconnect sensor harness connector at module, then remove sensor to block attaching bolt.
2. Remove sensor from engine.
3. Inspect crankshaft sensor O-ring for wear, cracks, or leakage and replace as necessary. Apply engine oil to new O-ring prior to installation.
4. Insert sensor in block.
5. Insert sensor attaching bolt, then torque to 88 inch lbs.
6. Connect sensor harness connector at module.

4-151/2.5L Engines

1. Disconnect battery ground cable.
2. Remove DIS module assembly as previously described.
3. Remove two Crankshaft sensor attaching screws, then separate Crankshaft sensor from DIS assembly.
4. Inspect crankshaft sensor O-ring for wear, cracks, or leakage and replace as necessary. Apply engine oil to new O-ring prior to installation.
5. Assemble sensor to DIS module assembly.
6. Insert sensor attaching screws, then torque to 20 inch lbs.
7. Install DIS module assembly as previously described.
8. Connect battery ground cable.

V6-173/2.8L Engines

1. Disconnect battery ground cable.
2. Disconnect sensor electrical connector.
3. Remove sensor attaching bolts, then separate sensor from engine.

4. Inspect crankshaft sensor O-ring for wear, cracks, or leakage and replace as necessary. Apply engine oil to new O-ring prior to installation.
5. Reverse procedure to install.
6. Torque sensor attaching bolt to 88 inch lbs.

IGNITION COIL

1. Remove coil retaining screws on 4-121/2.0L and V6-173 models or nuts on 4-151/2.5L models, then separate coils from module, **Figs. 8 and 9.**
2. Connect coil
3. Insert attaching nuts or screws as applicable, then torque to 40 inch lbs.

IGNITION MODULE

1. Disconnect battery ground cable.
2. Remove DIS module assembly from engine as previously described.
3. Remove coils from engine as previously described.
4. Remove module from assembly plate.
5. Reverse procedure to install.

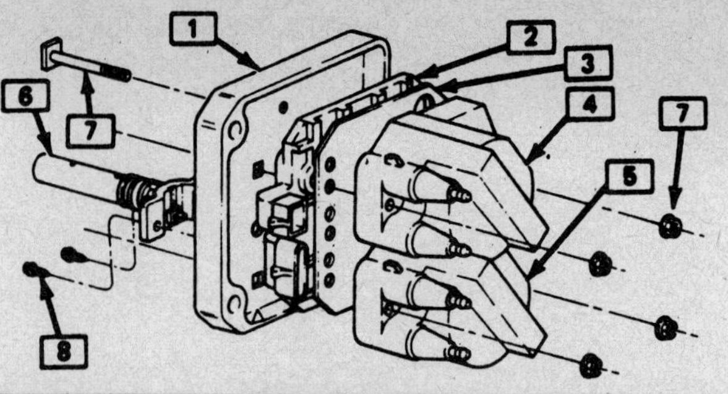

1	BASE PLATE	6	SENSOR
2	MODULE	7	STUDS (4), NUTS 4.5 N·m (40 LBS. IN.)
3	SHIELD	8	SCREWS 2.3 N·m (20 LBS. IN.)
4	2/3 COIL		
5	1/4 COIL		

Fig. 9 Exploded view of DIS module assembly. 4-151/2.5L models

CARBURETOR SECTION

TABLE OF CONTENTS

Holley 6510-C Carburetor

INDEX

ADJUSTMENT SPECIFICATIONS

Year	Carb. Model	Float Level	Fast Idle Cam	Vacuum Break	Unloader	Choke Coil	Secondary Throttle Stop Screw
1982	14032364	.500	.080	.270	.350	②	①
	14032365	.500	.080	.270	.350	②	①
	14032366	.500	.080	.270	.350	②	①
	14032367	.500	.080	.270	.350	②	①
	14032368	.500	.080	.270	.350	②	①
	14032369	.500	.080	.270	.350	②	①
	14032370	.500	.080	.270	.350	②	①
	14032371	.500	.080	.270	.350	②	①
	14033392	.500	.080	.270	.350	②	①
	14033393	.500	.080	.270	.350	②	①
	14047072	.500	.080	.270	.350	②	①
1983	14048827	.500	.080	.270	.350	②	①
	14048828	.500	.080	.300	.350	②	①
	14048829	.500	.080	.270	.350	②	①
1984	14068690	.500	.080	.270	.350	②	①
	14068691	.500	.080	.270	.350	②	①
	14068692	.500	.080	.300	.350	②	①
1985-87	14068690	.500	.080	.270	.350	②	①
	14068691	.500	.080	.270	.350	②	①
	14068692	.500	.080	.300	.350	②	①
	14076363	.500	.080	.300	.350	②	①

①—Refer to text for adjustment.
②—Not adjustable.

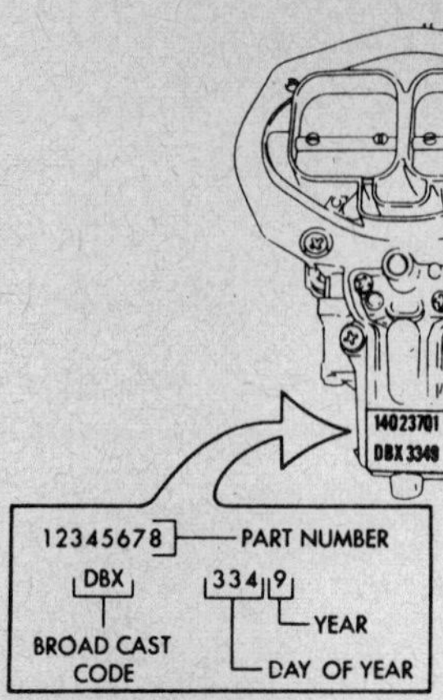

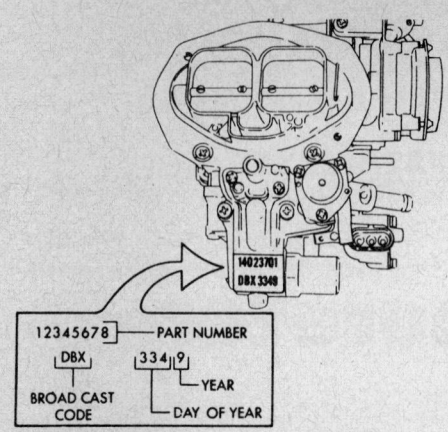

Fig. 1 Carburetor identification location

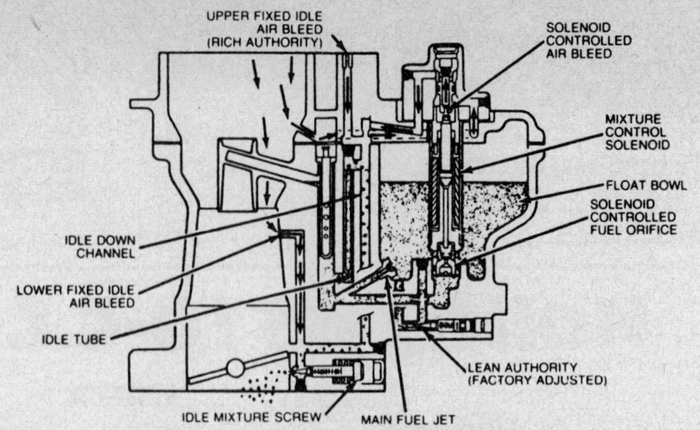

Fig. 2 Idle circuit schematic

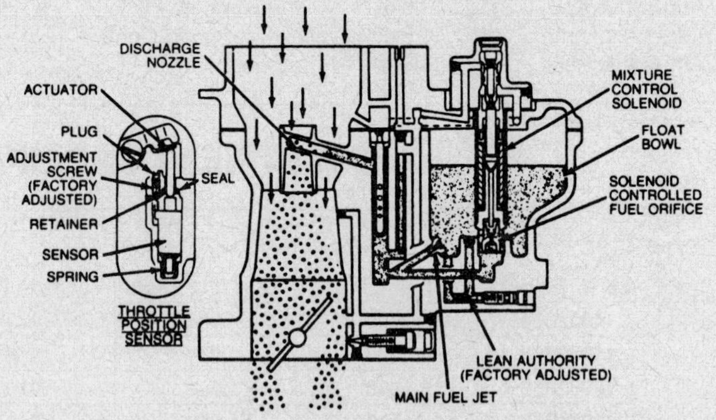

Fig. 3 Primary main metering circuit schematic

IDENTIFICATION LOCATION

The identification number is stamped near the fuel inlet, **Fig. 1,** along with production codes and a matching code for the electronic control module calibration unit.

DESCRIPTION

The 6510-C carburetor used with Computer Command Control (C-3) systems is a staged 2 barrel downdraft carburetor which uses solenoid operated fuel metering and air bleed valves to control air/fuel mixtures in the primary side. The primary side of the carburetor includes 5 systems; conventional float and acceleration enrichment systems, an electrically heated choke, and Mixture Control (MC) solenoid controlled idle and main metering systems. The MC solenoid is an on/off type solenoid, cycled at a fixed rate by the C-3 system computer which monitors various sensors in order to determine proper air fuel mixtures for operating conditions. The computer controls air fuel mixtures by varying the solenoid "on" time (dwell period) during each cycle. The secondary side of the carburetor, which draws fuel from the common float bowl, includes conventional main metering and pull over fuel enrichment systems which supplement primary side systems. The secondary throttle is controlled by interconnecting linkage which prevents it from opening until the primary side throttle is almost fully open.

In the primary idle circuit, **Fig. 2,** fuel flows into the idle fuel well through the main jet, a factory adjusted lean authority orifice and through the solenoid controlled fuel orifice. Fuel is drawn through a calibrated tube into the idle circuit and emulsified by air entering the upper and lower fixed air bleeds and through a cross-channel to the solenoid controlled air bleed. The emulsified fuel is discharged through idle and transition ports, and regulated by a sealed mixture adjusting screw. The MC solenoid controls air/fuel mixtures during idle and transition acceleration by controlling the air bleed and fuel orifice openings.

In the primary main metering circuit, fuel is metered through the main jet, lean authority orifice, and the solenoid controlled fuel orifice, **Fig. 3.** Air is drawn into the main circuit through a main air bleed and used to emulsify fuel which is discharged through a nozzle in the booster venturi. The MC solenoid controls air/fuel mixtures during off-idle through wide open throttle operation by controlling the opening of the fuel orifice located in the float bowl floor.

Additional carburetor or carburetor mounted controls include a solenoid operated bowl vent valve, throttle position sensor, integral automatic choke with a non-adjustable, electrically heated thermostat, and on 1983-87 models a Stepped Speed Control (SSC) system. The SSC system consists of a vacuum operated actuator which opens the primary throttle when vacuum is applied, a solenoid controlled Vacuum Control Valve (VCV), and an engine speed sensor. The VCV is held open when energized, applying vacuum to the actuator which in turn opens the throttle a preset amount to prevent stalling or deceleration backfire. The VCV is energized under the following conditions: excessive coolant temperature, during first 10 seconds of engine operation and with A/C compressor clutch engaged on models with A/C; power steering pump output pressure above calibrated pressure; engine speed above calibrated RPM on models with manual transmission.

ON-VEHICLE ADJUSTMENTS

CURB IDLE SPEED ADJUSTMENT

Make all adjustments with engine at normal operating temperature, choke fully open and air cleaner removed.

1. Disconnect and plug vacuum hoses as directed on vehicle emission control label.
2. Connect tachometer following tool manufacturer's instructions.
3. Check and, if necessary, adjust ignition timing to specifications.
4. Set parking brake and block drive wheels.
5. Adjust curb idle speed by turning idle speed screw in or out as required, **Fig. 4.**
6. If equipped with idle speed solenoid, adjust solenoid as follows:
   a. Set parking brake and block drive wheels.
   b. On vehicles equipped with A/C, disconnect electrical connector from A/C compressor, then turn A/C control On. Ensure actuator is fully extended, then turn actuator adjusting screw to obtain specified RPM, then reconnect electrical connector.

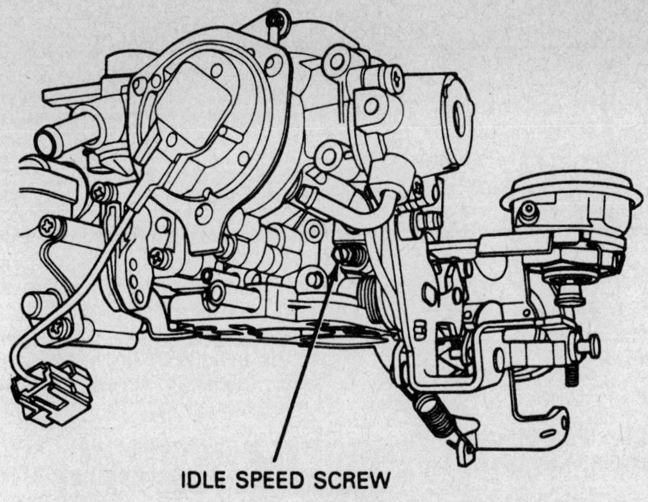

Fig. 4 Idle speed adjusting screw

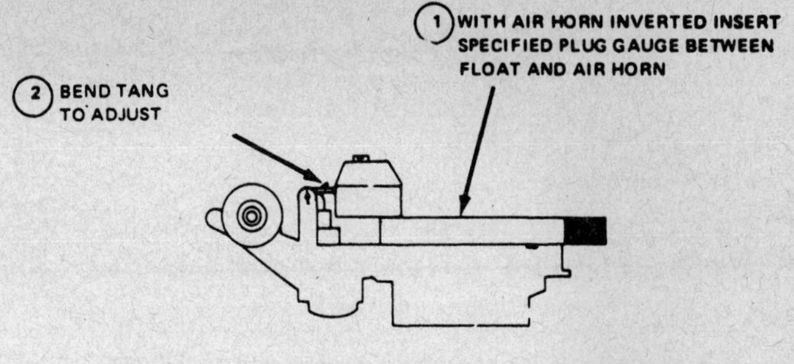

Fig. 5 Float level adjustment

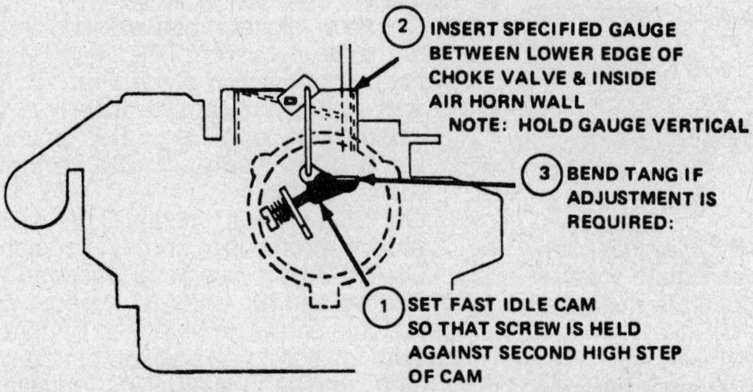

NOTE: HOLD GAUGE VERTICAL

Fig. 6 Fast idle cam index adjustment

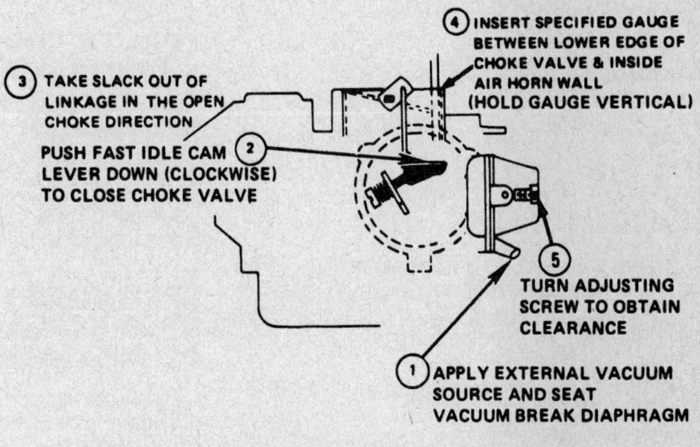

3 TAKE SLACK OUT OF LINKAGE IN THE OPEN CHOKE DIRECTION

Fig. 7 Vacuum break adjustment

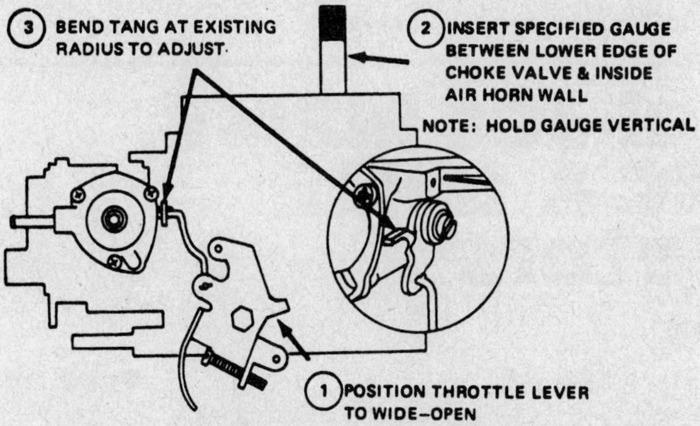

NOTE: HOLD GAUGE VERTICAL

Fig. 8 Choke unloader adjustment

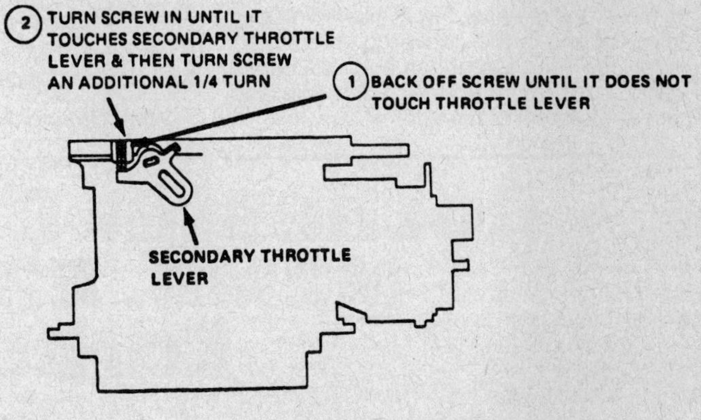

1 BACK OFF SCREW UNTIL IT DOES NOT TOUCH THROTTLE LEVER

Fig. 9 Secondary throttle stop screw adjustment

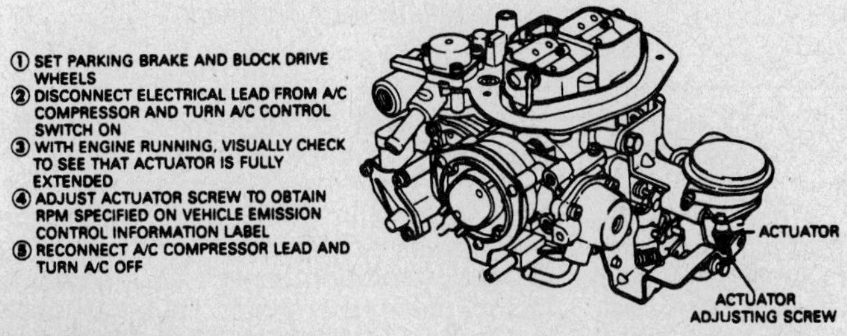

① SET PARKING BRAKE AND BLOCK DRIVE WHEELS
② DISCONNECT ELECTRICAL LEAD FROM A/C COMPRESSOR AND TURN A/C CONTROL SWITCH ON
③ WITH ENGINE RUNNING, VISUALLY CHECK TO SEE THAT ACTUATOR IS FULLY EXTENDED
④ ADJUST ACTUATOR SCREW TO OBTAIN RPM SPECIFIED ON VEHICLE EMISSION CONTROL INFORMATION LABEL
⑤ RECONNECT A/C COMPRESSOR LEAD AND TURN A/C OFF
ACTUATOR
ACTUATOR ADJUSTING SCREW

Fig. 10 Stepped Speed Control (SSC) adjustment. With A/C

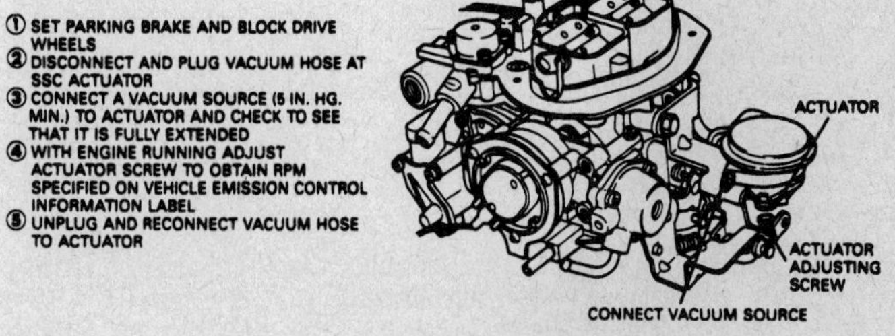

① SET PARKING BRAKE AND BLOCK DRIVE WHEELS
② DISCONNECT AND PLUG VACUUM HOSE AT SSC ACTUATOR
③ CONNECT A VACUUM SOURCE (5 IN. HG. MIN.) TO ACTUATOR AND CHECK TO SEE THAT IT IS FULLY EXTENDED
④ WITH ENGINE RUNNING ADJUST ACTUATOR SCREW TO OBTAIN RPM SPECIFIED ON VEHICLE EMISSION CONTROL INFORMATION LABEL
⑤ UNPLUG AND RECONNECT VACUUM HOSE TO ACTUATOR
ACTUATOR
ACTUATOR ADJUSTING SCREW
CONNECT VACUUM SOURCE

Fig. 11 Stepped Speed Control (SSC) adjustment. Less A/C

c. On vehicles less A/C, disconnect and plug vacuum hose from ISS actuator. Apply minimum 5 inches Hg vacuum to actuator, then turn actuator adjusting screw to obtain specified RPM. Unplug and reconnect actuator vacuum hose.

FAST IDLE SPEED ADJUSTMENT

1. Disconnect and plug vacuum hoses as directed on vehicle emission label.
2. Place fast idle adjusting screw on highest step of fast idle cam.
3. Turn adjusting screw inward or outward as required until specified fast idle speed is obtained.

FLOAT LEVEL ADJUSTMENT

With air horn inverted, **Fig. 5**, insert specified gauge between float and air horn. Bend tang to adjust.

FAST IDLE CAM ADJUSTMENT

Set fast idle cam in position, **Fig. 6**, so the screw contacts second high step. Insert specified gauge between lower edge of choke valve and air horn wall. Bend tang to adjust.

VACUUM BREAK ADJUSTMENT

On 1983-87 units, remove adjusting screw plug. On all units, apply an external vacuum source to vacuum break to seat diaphragm. Rotate fast idle cam clockwise to close choke valve, **Fig. 7.** Remove slack from linkage in the choke open direction. Insert the specified gauge between choke valve and air horn wall. Turn adjusting screw to obtain clearance.

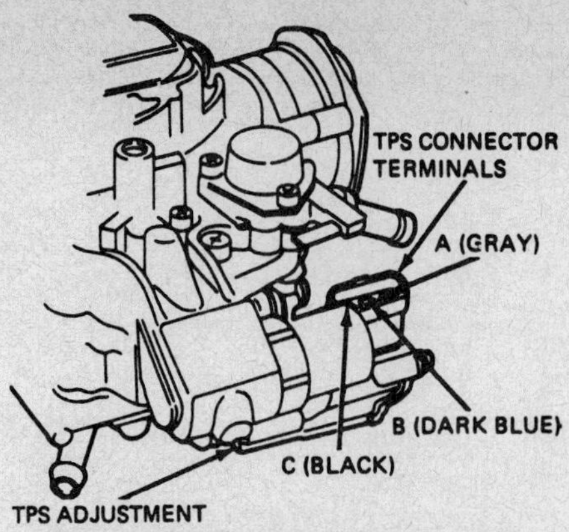

Fig. 12 Throttle Position Sensor (TPS) adjustment

UNLOADER ADJUSTMENT

Place throttle lever in wide open position. Insert specified gauge between lower edge of choke valve and air horn wall. Bend tang at existing radius to adjust, **Fig. 8.**

SECONDARY THROTTLE STOP SCREW ADJUSTMENT

Back off secondary throttle stop screw until clear of throttle lever. Rotate screw inward until the screw contacts secondary throttle lever, then an additional 1/4 turn, **Fig. 9.**

STEPPED SPEED CONTROL ADJUSTMENT

1983–87 Models W/Air Conditioning

With parking brake applied and drive wheels blocked, disconnect electrical lead at A/C compressor and turn A/C system on. With engine running, check that actuator is fully extended. Turn actuator adjusting screw to adjust speed as necessary, **Fig. 10.**

1983–87 Models Less Air Conditioning

With parking brake applied and drive wheels blocked, disconnect and plug vacuum hose at SSC actuator. Using an outside vacuum source, apply a minimum of 5 inches Hg to the actuator and ensure that it extends fully. With engine running, turn actuator adjusting screw to adjust speed as necessary, **Fig. 11.**

THROTTLE POSITION SENSOR ADJUSTMENT

1. Remove TPS adjustment screw and apply thread sealing compound to screw.
2. Connect digital voltmeter between terminals B and C of TPS, leaving harness connector in place, **Fig. 12. Insert voltmeter probes into rear of connector, ensuring that probes make proper contact with connector terminals.**
3. On 1982 with full function C-3 system, ensure throttle is in curb idle position. On 1982 with minimum function C-3 system and all 1983-87 models, set fast idle screw on high step of cam.
4. Turn ignition to on position but do not start engine. Install TPS adjusting screw and adjust quickly to obtain voltmeter reading of 0.42 volts on 1982 with full function C-3 system or 0.92 volts on 1982 with minimum function C-3 system and all 1983-87 models.

Rochester Dual-Jet M2MC, M2ME, E2MC & E2ME Carburetors

INDEX

IDENTIFICATION LOCATION

The carburetor model identification is stamped vertically on the rear left edge of the float bowl, **Fig. 1.**

DESCRIPTION

The Dual Jet carburetor, **Figs. 2 and 3,** is a two barrel, single stage unit, incorporating the design features of the primary side of the Quadrajet (four barrel) carburetor. The E2M model is used with the Computer Controlled Catalytic Converter System (C-4 System) or Computer Control Command System. The triple venturi stack up, plus the smaller 1 3/8 inch bores result in good fuel metering control during all phases of operation.

The main metering system has a separate main well for each main nozzle for good fuel flow through the venturi.

On models except E2M models, an adjustable part throttle screw is used in the float bowl to aid in controlling fuel mixtures for good emission control. This screw is factory preset and should not be adjusted in service. However, if it becomes necessary to replace the float bowl, the new service float bowl will include the adjustable part throttle screw which has been preset.

ADJUSTMENT SPECIFICATIONS

Year	Carb. Production No.	Float Level	Choke Coil Lever	Choke Rod	Vacuum Break		Choke Unloader	Choke Setting
					Front	Rear		
1982	17082130	3/8	.120	20°	27°	—	38°	④
	17082132	3/8	.120	20°	27°	—	38°	④
	17082138	3/8	.120	20°	27°	—	38°	④
	17082140	3/8	.120	20°	27°	—	38°	④
	17082150	13/32	.120	14°	24°	38°	35°	④
	17082150①	13/32	.120	14°	24°	40°	35°	④
	17082182	5/16	.120	18°	28°	24°	32°	④
	17082184	5/16	.120	18°	28°	24°	32°	④
	17082186	5/16	.120	18°	21°	19°	27°	④
	17082192	5/16	.120	18°	28°	24°	32°	④
	17082194	5/16	.120	18°	28°	24°	32°	④
	17082196	5/16	.120	18°	21°	19°	27°	④
	17082497	5/16	.120	24.5°	28°	24°	32°	④
	17082916	5/16	—	25°	21°	19°	27°	④
1983	17082130	3/8	.120	20°	27°	—	38°	④
	17082132	3/8	.120	20°	27°	—	38°	④
	17083130	3/8	.120	20°	27°	—	38°	④
	17083132	3/8	.120	20°	27°	—	38°	④
	17083190	5/16	.120	18°	28°	24°	32°	④
	17083192	5/16	.120	18°	28°	24°	32°	④
	17083193	5/16	.120	②	③	28°	27°	④
	17083194	5/16	.120	17°	27°	25°	35°	④
	17084195	5/16	.120	17°	23°	28°	27°	④
1984	17082130	3/8	.120	20°	27°	—	38°	④
	17084132	3/8	.120	20°	27°	—	38°	④
	17084191	5/16	.120	18°	28°	24°	32°	④
	17084193	5/16	.120	17°	27°	25°	35°	④
	17084194	5/16	.120	17°	27°	25°	35°	④
	17084195	5/16	.120	17°	27°	25°	35°	④
1985	17085190	5/16	.120	18°	28°	24°	32°	④
	17085192	11/32	.120	17°	27°	25°	35°	④
	17085194	11/32	.120	17°	27°	25°	35°	④
1986-87	17086190	5/16	.120	18°	28°	24°	32°	④

①—High Altitude.
②—Chevrolet models and Oldsmobile front wheel drive models, 17°; all others, 18°.
③—Chevrolet models and Oldsmobile front wheel drive models, 23°; all others, 24°.
④—Tamper-resistant.

On E2M models, an electrically operated mixture control solenoid, mounted in the fuel bowl, is used to control the fuel-air mixture metered to the idle and main metering systems. Fuel metering is controlled by two stepped metering rods positioned by a plunger in the mixture control solenoid. The solenoid plunger is controlled or "Pulsed" by an electrical output signal from the Electronic Control Module (ECM). The ECM, responding to a signal from the oxygen sensor, energizes the solenoid, to move the plunger and metering rods to control fuel delivery to the idle and main metering systems. At the same time, air metering to the idle system is controlled by an idle air bleed valve, located in the air horn, which follows movement of the mixture control solenoid plunger to control the amount of air bleed into the idle system to lean or richen the mixture. The movement or "Cycling" of the solenoid plunger occurs approximately 10 times per second, thereby controlling the fuel-air mixture to achieve optimum mixture ratios. The positioning of the mixture control solenoid in the float bowl, rich stop setting and idle air bleed valve in the air horn are factory adjusted and no attempt should be made to alter these settings except during major carburetor overhaul or when air horn or float bowl replacement is necessary.

On some E2M units, an idle speed control mounted on the float bowl is used to control idle speed. On these units, the curb idle speed is programmed into the Electronic Control Module and no attempt should be made to adjust idle speed. On some models with V8 engine, an idle load compensator mounted on the float bowl is used to control idle speed. The compensator uses manifold vacuum to sense changes in engine load and compensates by adjusting curb idle speed. This unit should not be adjusted, unless if during diagnosis, curb idle speed is not within specifications.

The choke cover is retained to the choke housing by three pop rivets. With float bowl and throttle body properly supported, carefully align a No. 21 drill on pop rivet head. Drill only deep enough to remove rivet head, then using a small hammer and drift, drive remainder of rivet from choke housing. A service kit is available for choke cover installation. The choke cover should be removed only during major carburetor overhaul or if the choke coil is damaged.

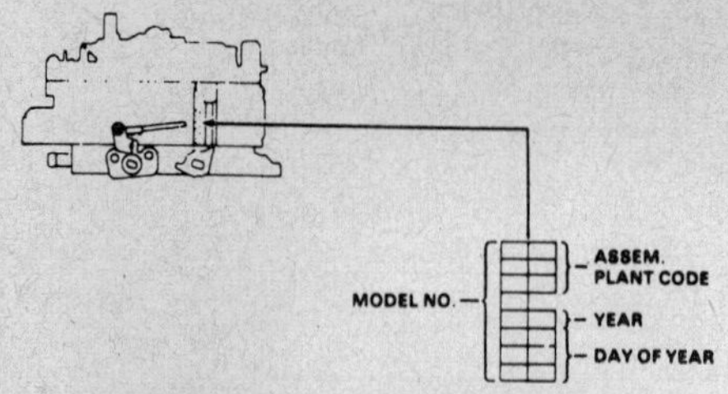
ASSEM. PLANT CODE
MODEL NO.
YEAR
DAY OF YEAR

Fig. 1 Carburetor identification location

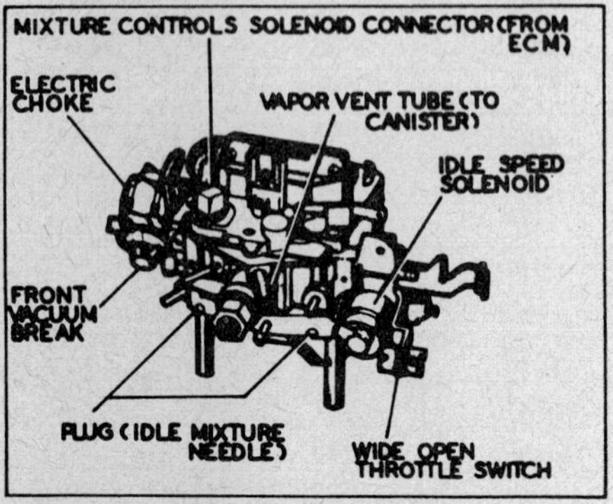
MIXTURE CONTROLS SOLENOID CONNECTOR (FROM ECM)
ELECTRIC CHOKE
VAPOR VENT TUBE (TO CANISTER)
IDLE SPEED SOLENOID
FRONT VACUUM BREAK
PLUG (IDLE MIXTURE NEEDLE)
WIDE OPEN THROTTLE SWITCH

Fig. 3 Rochester Dual-Jet model E2ME

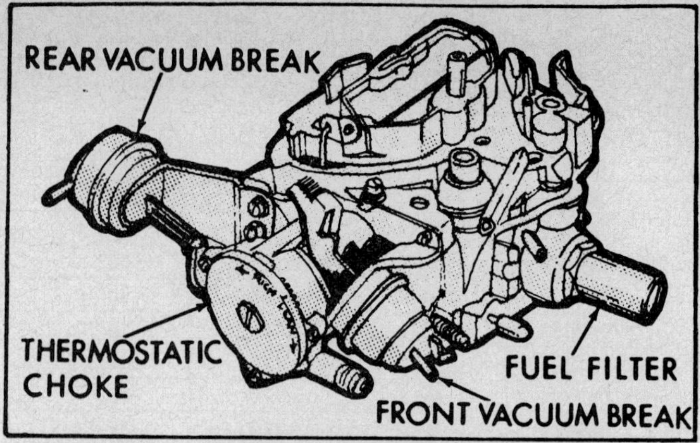
REAR VACUUM BREAK
THERMOSTATIC CHOKE
FUEL FILTER
FRONT VACUUM BREAK

Fig. 2 Rochester Dual-Jet M2MC carburetor

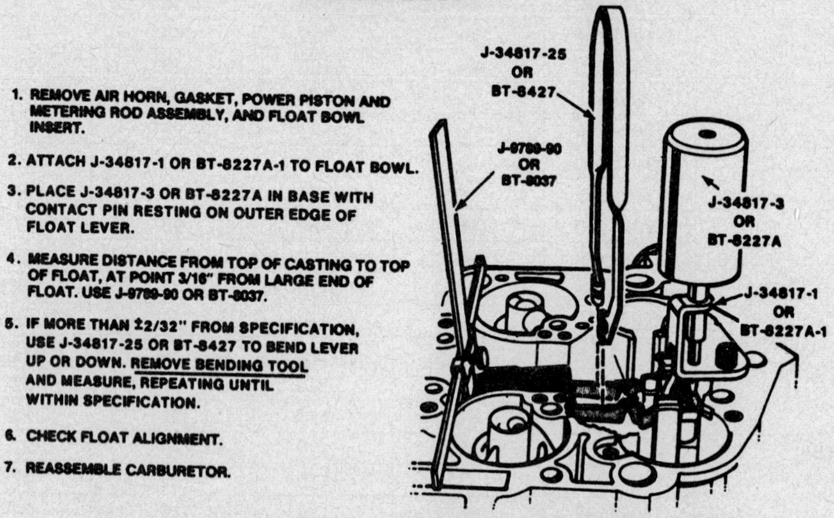
1. REMOVE AIR HORN, GASKET, POWER PISTON AND METERING ROD ASSEMBLY, AND FLOAT BOWL INSERT.
2. ATTACH J-34817-1 OR BT-8227A-1 TO FLOAT BOWL.
3. PLACE J-34817-3 OR BT-8227A IN BASE WITH CONTACT PIN RESTING ON OUTER EDGE OF FLOAT LEVER.
4. MEASURE DISTANCE FROM TOP OF CASTING TO TOP OF FLOAT, AT POINT 3/16" FROM LARGE END OF FLOAT. USE J-9789-90 OR BT-8037.
5. IF MORE THAN ±2/32" FROM SPECIFICATION, USE J-34817-25 OR BT-8427 TO BEND LEVER UP OR DOWN. REMOVE BENDING TOOL AND MEASURE, REPEATING UNTIL WITHIN SPECIFICATION.
6. CHECK FLOAT ALIGNMENT.
7. REASSEMBLE CARBURETOR.
J-34817-25 OR BT-8427
J-9789-90 OR BT-8037
J-34817-3 OR BT-8227A
J-34817-1 OR BT-8227A-1

Fig. 4 Float level adjustment. M2M units

ON-VEHICLE ADJUSTMENTS

CURB IDLE SPEED ADJUSTMENT

E2M Units

On carburetors equipped with an Idle Speed Control (ISC) motor or an Idle Load Compensator (ILC), idle speed is not adjustable. If the ISC or ILC is found defective, a new one can be installed and must be adjusted to specifications. This procedure applies to carburetors without an ISC or ILC.

Make all adjustments with engine at normal operating temperature, choke fully open, air cleaner installed and A/C off, if equipped, except where noted.

1. Disconnect and plug vacuum hoses as directed on vehicle emissions label.
2. Check and, if necessary, adjust ignition timing to specifications.
3. On vehicles less A/C, turn idle speed screw inward or outward until specified idle speed is obtained.
4. On models equipped with A/C, proceed as follows:
   a. Turn idle speed screw inward or outward until specified RPM (base idle) is obtained.
   b. With transmission in Drive (manual transmission in Neutral), disconnect A/C compressor electrical connector and switch A/C control to On position.
   c. Open throttle and allow A/C solenoid plunger to fully extend.
   d. Turn solenoid adjusting screw inward or outward until specified RPM (solenoid energized) is obtained.
   e. Reconnect compressor electrical connector.

M2M Units

Check and, if necessary, adjust ignition timing before adjusting curb idle speed.

Make all adjustments with engine at normal operating temperature, choke fully open, air cleaner installed and A/C system, if equipped, off, except where noted.

1. Disconnect and plug vacuum hoses as directed on vehicle emission control label.
2. On vehicles less idle solenoid, adjust idle speed screw in or out to obtain specified curb idle speed.
3. On vehicles equipped with idle solenoid, open throttle slightly to allow solenoid plunger to extend, then adjust solenoid screw in or out to obtain specified curb idle speed. Disconnect solenoid electrical connector, then adjust idle speed screw in or out to obtain specified base idle speed.
4. On vehicles equipped with A/C, turn idle speed screw in or out to obtain specified curb idle speed with A/C control off. Disconnect electrical connector from A/C compressor, then turn A/C switch on. With transmission in Drive (manual transmission in Neutral), open throttle and allow solenoid plunger to extend fully. Adjust solenoid screw to obtain specified speed. Reconnect compressor electrical connector.

FAST IDLE SPEED ADJUSTMENT

Check and, if necessary, adjust ignition timing before adjusting fast idle speed.

Make all adjustments with engine at normal operating temperature, choke fully open, air cleaner installed and A/C control Off, if equipped.

1. Disconnect and plug vacuum hoses as directed on vehicles emissions label.
2. Position fast idle speed screw on specified step of fast idle cam as directed on emissions label, then start engine.
3. Turn fast idle screw inward or outward and adjust fast idle speed to specifications.

FLOAT LEVEL ADJUSTMENT

M2M Units

Refer to **Fig. 4** for float adjustment procedure. Adjust as directed to dimension listed in Adjustment Specifications.

E2M Units

Refer to **Fig. 5** for float adjustment procedure. Adjust as directed to dimension listed in Adjustment Specifications.

1. REMOVE AIR HORN & GASKET.
2. REMOVE SOLENOID PLUNGER, METERING RODS, FLOAT BOWL INSERT. IF NECESSARY TO REMOVE SOLENOID (LEAN MIXTURE) ADJUSTING SCREW, COUNT AND MAKE RECORD OF NUMBER OF TURNS IT TAKES TO LIGHTLY BOTTOM SCREW, USING J-28696-10 OR BT-7928. (RETURN TO EXACT POSITION WHEN REASSEMBLING.)
3. ATTACH J-34817-1 OR BT-8227A-1 TO FLOAT BOWL.
4. PLACE J-34817-3 OR BT-8227A IN BASE WITH CONTACT PIN RESTING ON OUTER EDGE OF FLOAT LEVER.
5. MEASURE DISTANCE FROM TOP OF CASTING TO TOP OF FLOAT, AT POINT 3/16" FROM LARGE END OF FLOAT. USE J-9789-90 OR BT-8037.
6. IF MORE THAN ±2/32" FROM SPECIFICATION, USE J-34817-15 OR BT-8233 TO BEND LEVER UP OR DOWN. REMOVE BENDING TOOL AND MEASURE, REPEATING UNTIL WITHIN SPECIFICATION.
7. CHECK FLOAT ALIGNMENT.
8. REASSEMBLE CARBURETOR.

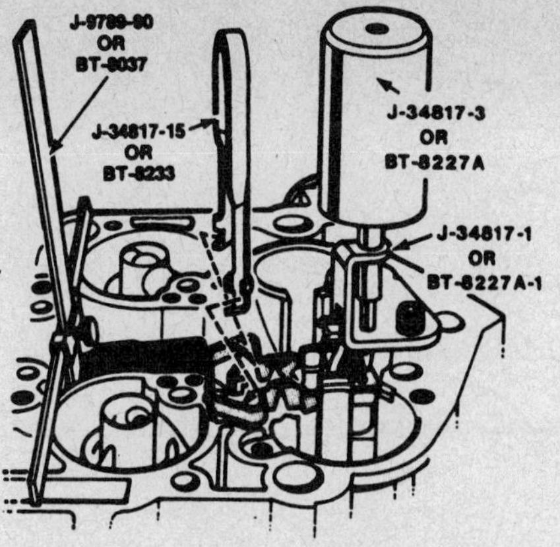
J-9789-90
OR
BT-8037
J-34817-15
OR
BT-8233
J-34817-3
OR
BT-8227A
J-34817-1
OR
BT-8227A-1

Fig. 5 Float level adjustment. E2M units

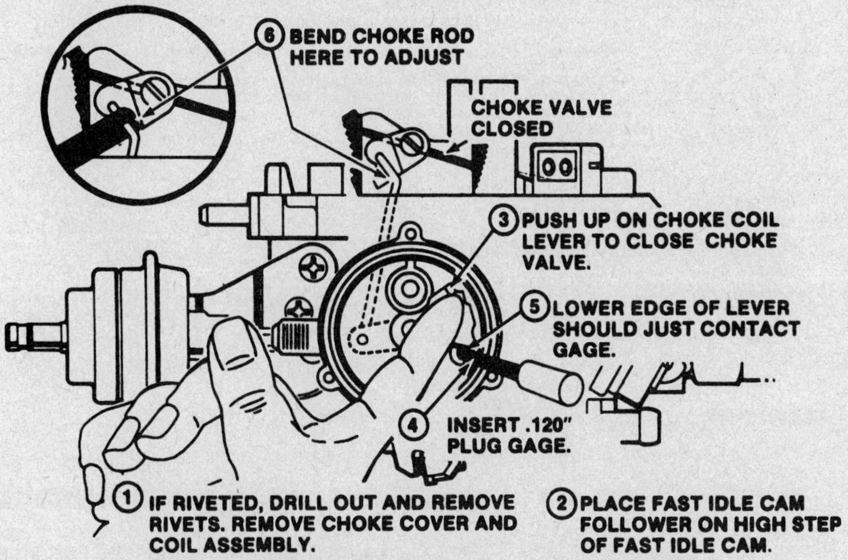
6 BEND CHOKE ROD HERE TO ADJUST
CHOKE VALVE CLOSED
3 PUSH UP ON CHOKE COIL LEVER TO CLOSE CHOKE VALVE.
5 LOWER EDGE OF LEVER SHOULD JUST CONTACT GAGE.
4 INSERT .120" PLUG GAGE.
1 IF RIVETED, DRILL OUT AND REMOVE RIVETS. REMOVE CHOKE COVER AND COIL ASSEMBLY.
2 PLACE FAST IDLE CAM FOLLOWER ON HIGH STEP OF FAST IDLE CAM.

Fig. 6 Choke coil lever adjustment

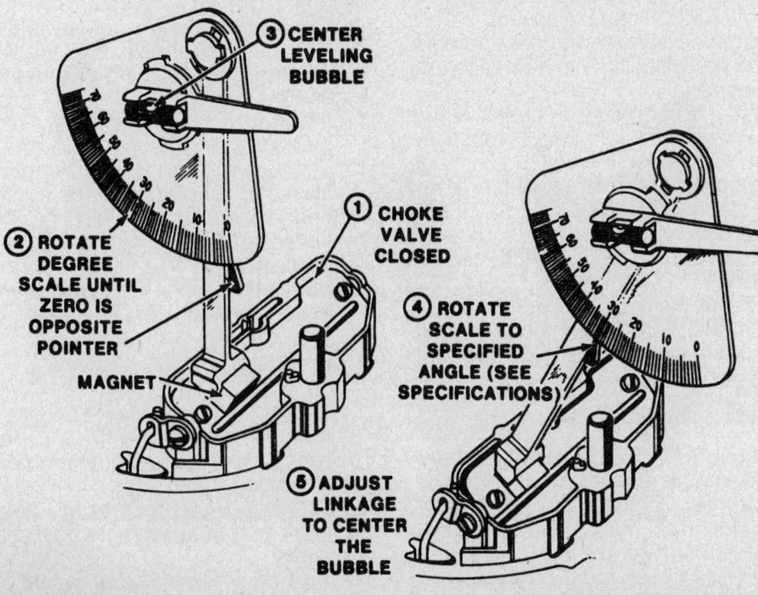
3 CENTER LEVELING BUBBLE
1 CHOKE VALVE CLOSED
2 ROTATE DEGREE SCALE UNTIL ZERO IS OPPOSITE POINTER
MAGNET
4 ROTATE SCALE TO SPECIFIED ANGLE (SEE SPECIFICATIONS)
5 ADJUST LINKAGE TO CENTER THE BUBBLE

Fig. 7 Choke valve angle gauge installation

CHOKE COIL LEVER ADJUSTMENT

Refer to **Fig. 6** for choke lever adjustment procedure. Adjust as directed to dimension listed in Adjustment Specifications.

CHOKE ROD ADJUSTMENT

Install choke valve angle gauge tool No. J-26701 or BT-7704 as shown in **Fig. 7.**

With gauge installed, adjust choke rod as outlined in **Fig. 8.** Adjust as directed to dimension listed in Adjustment Specifications.

VACUUM BREAK ADJUSTMENT

Prior to adjusting vacuum breaks, refer to **Fig. 9** for air bleed hole blocking procedures.

Front Unit

Install choke valve angle gauge tool No. J-26701 or BT-7704 as shown in **Fig. 7.**

With gauge installed, adjust vacuum break as outlined in **Fig. 10.** Adjust as directed to dimension listed in Adjustment Specifications.

Rear Unit

Install choke valve angle gauge tool No. J-26701 or BT-7704 as shown in **Fig. 7.**

With gauge installed, adjust vacuum break as outlined in **Fig. 11.** Adjust as directed to dimension listed in Adjustment Specifications.

CHOKE UNLOADER ADJUSTMENT

1982 Units

Rotate degree scale until the zero is opposite pointer, then with choke valve completely closed, place magnet squarely on top of choke valve and rotate bubble until centered, **Fig. 12.** Refer to the Specification Chart for proper setting for adjustment. Rotate scale until specified degree for adjustment is opposite pointer. Install choke cover and coil assembly and align index mark with specified point on housing. Hold throttle valves wide open. On a warm engine close choke valve by pushing upward on tang on vacuum break lever and hold in position with a rubber band. To adjust, bend fast idle lever tang until the bubble is centered.

1983–87 Units

Attach rubber band to green tang of intermediate choke shaft, then open throttle to allow choke valve to close, **Fig. 13.** Install angle gauge, then rotate scale until degree indicated on Specification Chart is opposite pointer. Hold secondary lockout lever away from pin, if applicable, then place throttle lever in wide open position. To adjust, bend fast idle lever tang until bubble is centered.

IDLE LOAD COMPENSATOR ADJUSTMENT

1982 E2M Units

On some 1982 models with V8 engine, an idle load compensator mounted on the

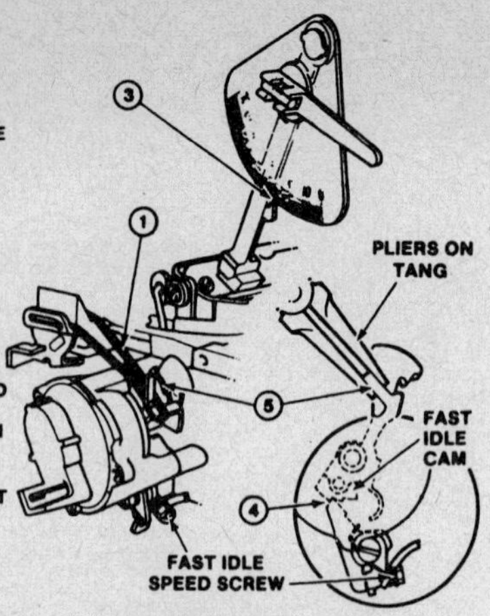

① ATTACH RUBBER BAND TO GREEN TANG OF INTERMEDIATE CHOKE SHAFT
② OPEN THROTTLE TO ALLOW CHOKE VALVE TO CLOSE
③ SET UP ANGLE GAGE AND SET ANGLE TO SPECIFICATIONS
④ PLACE CAM FOLLOWER ON SECOND STEP OF CAM, AGAINST RISE OF HIGH STEP. IF CAM FOLLOWER DOES NOT CONTACT CAM, TURN IN FAST IDLE SPEED SCREW ADDITIONAL TURN(S).
NOTICE: FINAL FAST IDLE SPEED ADJUSTMENT MUST BE PERFORMED ACCORDING TO UNDER-HOOD EMISSION CONTROL INFORMATION LABEL.
⑤ ADJUST BY BENDING TANG OF FAST IDLE CAM UNTIL BUBBLE IS CENTERED.
PLIERS ON TANG
FAST IDLE CAM
FAST IDLE SPEED SCREW

Fig. 8 Choke rod adjustment

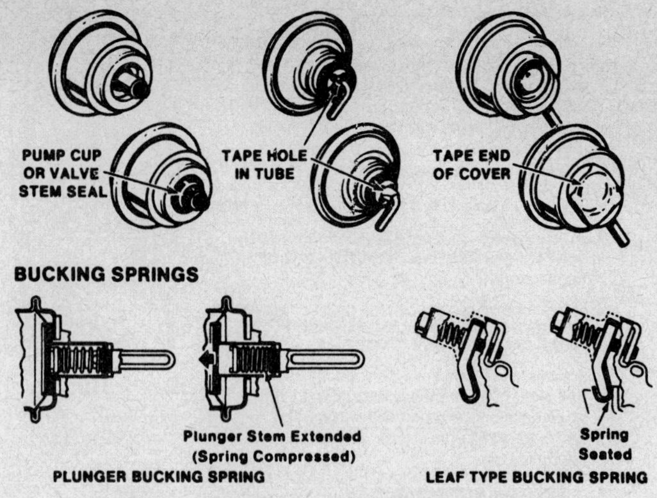

Fig. 9 Blocking air bleed holes

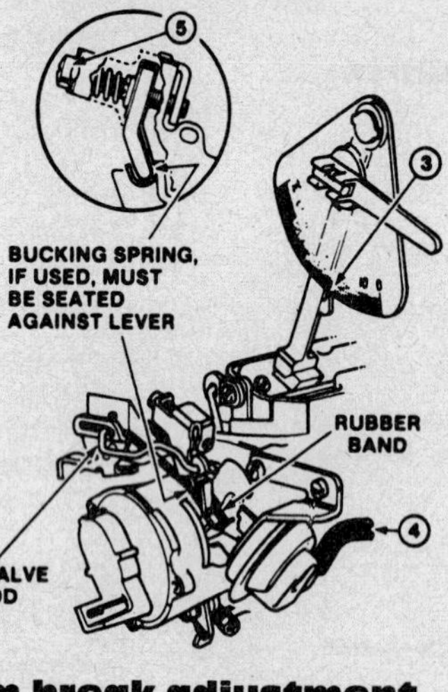

Fig. 10 Front vacuum break adjustment

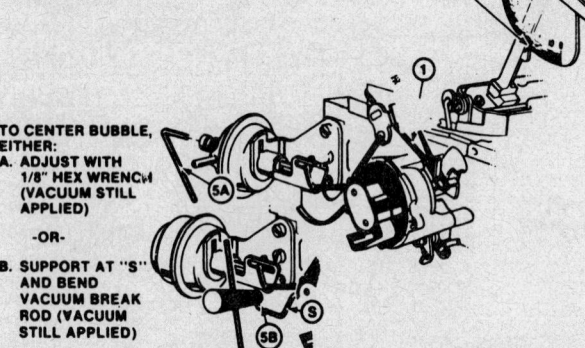

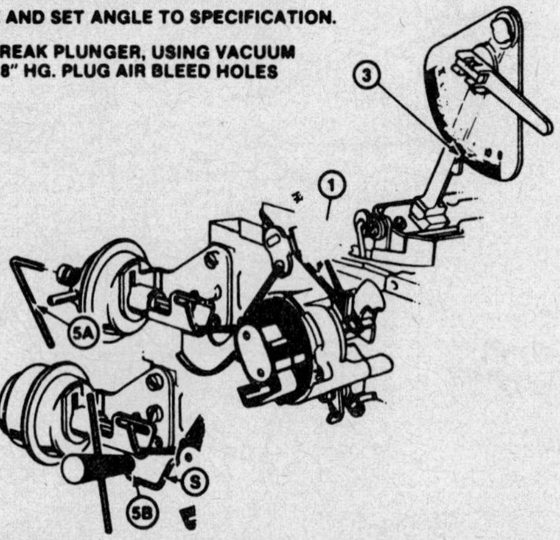

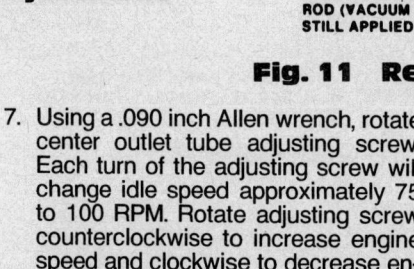

Fig. 11 Rear vacuum break adjustment

float bowl is used to control idle speed. This unit should not be adjusted, unless if during diagnosis, curb idle speed is not within specifications. This adjustment should be performed with engine at operating temperature and choke and A/C off.

1. Remove air cleaner assembly and plug vacuum hose to thermal vacuum valve.
2. Disconnect and plug hoses to EGR valve, canister purge port and idle load compensator.
3. Apply parking brake and block wheels, then back throttle stop screw out 3 turns.
4. With engine operating, place transmission selector lever in drive position, adjust plunger to obtain 750 RPM. The jam nut on the plunger must be held in position to prevent damage to guide tabs. If a replacement idle load compensator is being installed, the plunger should be set to obtain a clearance of 61/64 inch from jam nut to tip of plunger.
5. Connect vacuum hose to idle load compensator and note idle speed. If idle speed requires adjustment, stop engine and remove idle load compensator.
6. With idle load compensator removed, remove rubber and metal plug from center outlet tube.
7. Using a .090 inch Allen wrench, rotate center outlet tube adjusting screw. Each turn of the adjusting screw will change idle speed approximately 75 to 100 RPM. Rotate adjusting screw counterclockwise to increase engine speed and clockwise to decrease engine speed.
8. Reinstall rubber plug on center outlet tube, then install idle load compensator on carburetor. If a final adjustment is necessary, it will be necessary to repeat steps 6, 7 and 8.
9. Apply a suitable vacuum source to idle load compensator to fully retract plunger.
10. Adjust throttle body idle stop screw to obtain 500 RPM, then reconnect all vacuum hoses and install air cleaner.

IDLE SPEED CONTROL (ISC) ADJUSTMENT

Do not use ISC plunger to adjust curb idle speed, as idle speed is controlled by the Electronic Control Module (ECM). When a new ISC is installed, a base (minimum authority) and a high (maximum authority) RPM check must be made and adjustments performed as needed. When making low and high speed adjustments, low speed adjustment must be performed first.

Preliminary Check

1. Check ISC plunger for an identification letter as shown, **Fig. 14.** If letter appears, proceed to "Adjustment Procedure."
2. If letter does not appear, remove plunger using tool No. J-29607 or equivalent, then measure distance from back of plunger head to plunger end (dimension "A"), **Fig. 14.** Record dimension for use during "Adjustment Procedure."
3. Reinstall plunger to a dimension less than dimension "B," **Fig. 14.**

Adjustment Procedure

1. Connect a tachometer to engine. If vehicle is equipped with tachometer, connect remote tachometer to distributor side of tach filter.
2. Connect dwell meter to MC solenoid dwell lead, then set meter to 6 cylinder scale.
3. Start engine and run at fast idle until engine reaches normal operating temperature and dwell readings start

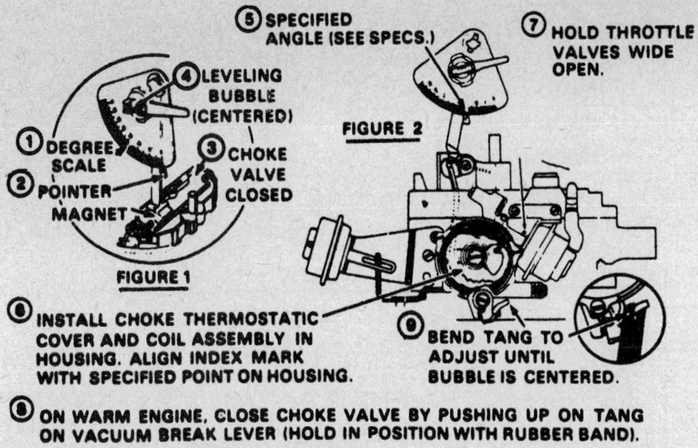

(5) SPECIFIED ANGLE (SEE SPECS.)
(7) HOLD THROTTLE VALVES WIDE OPEN.
(4) LEVELING BUBBLE (CENTERED)
(1) DEGREE SCALE
(3) CHOKE VALVE CLOSED
(2) POINTER
MAGNET
FIGURE 1
FIGURE 2
(6) INSTALL CHOKE THERMOSTATIC COVER AND COIL ASSEMBLY IN HOUSING. ALIGN INDEX MARK WITH SPECIFIED POINT ON HOUSING.
(9) BEND TANG TO ADJUST UNTIL BUBBLE IS CENTERED.
(8) ON WARM ENGINE, CLOSE CHOKE VALVE BY PUSHING UP ON TANG ON VACUUM BREAK LEVER (HOLD IN POSITION WITH RUBBER BAND).

Fig. 12 Choke unloader adjustment. 1982 units

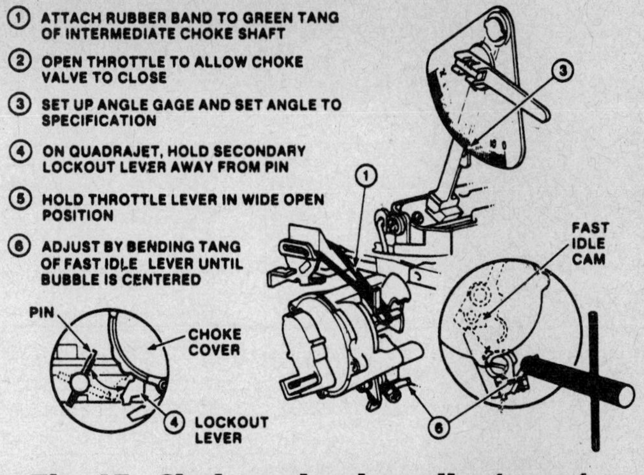

(1) ATTACH RUBBER BAND TO GREEN TANG OF INTERMEDIATE CHOKE SHAFT
(2) OPEN THROTTLE TO ALLOW CHOKE VALVE TO CLOSE
(3) SET UP ANGLE GAGE AND SET ANGLE TO SPECIFICATION
(4) ON QUADRAJET, HOLD SECONDARY LOCKOUT LEVER AWAY FROM PIN
(5) HOLD THROTTLE LEVER IN WIDE OPEN POSITION
(6) ADJUST BY BENDING TANG OF FAST IDLE LEVER UNTIL BUBBLE IS CENTERED
PIN
CHOKE COVER
(4) LOCKOUT LEVER
FAST IDLE CAM

Fig. 13 Choke unloader adjustment. 1983–87 units

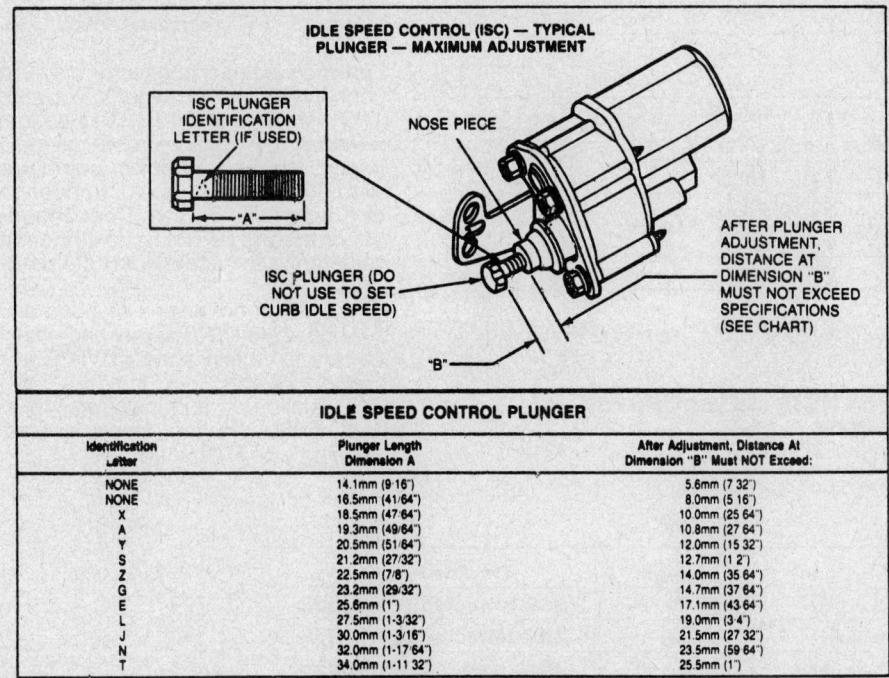

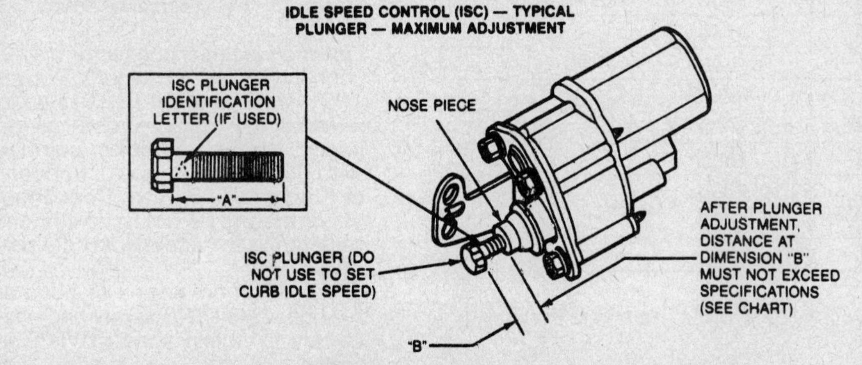

IDLE SPEED CONTROL (ISC) — TYPICAL PLUNGER — MAXIMUM ADJUSTMENT
ISC PLUNGER IDENTIFICATION LETTER (IF USED)
"A"
NOSE PIECE
AFTER PLUNGER ADJUSTMENT, DISTANCE AT DIMENSION "B" MUST NOT EXCEED SPECIFICATIONS (SEE CHART)
ISC PLUNGER (DO NOT USE TO SET CURB IDLE SPEED)
"B"

IDLE SPEED CONTROL PLUNGER

Identification Letter	Plunger Length Dimension A	After Adjustment, Distance At Dimension "B" Must NOT Exceed:
NONE	14.1mm (9/16")	5.6mm (7/32")
NONE	16.5mm (41/64")	8.0mm (5/16")
X	18.5mm (47/64")	10.0mm (25/64")
A	19.3mm (49/64")	10.8mm (27/64")
Y	20.5mm (51/64")	12.0mm (15/32")
S	21.2mm (27/32")	12.7mm (1/2")
Z	22.5mm (7/8")	14.0mm (35/64")
G	23.2mm (29/32")	14.7mm (37/64")
E	25.6mm (1")	17.1mm (43/64")
L	27.5mm (1-3/32")	19.0mm (3/4")
J	30.0mm (1-3/16")	21.5mm (27/32")
N	32.0mm (1-17/64")	23.5mm (59/64")
T	34.0mm (1-11/32")	25.5mm (1")

Fig. 14 Idle Speed Control (ISC) plunger specifications

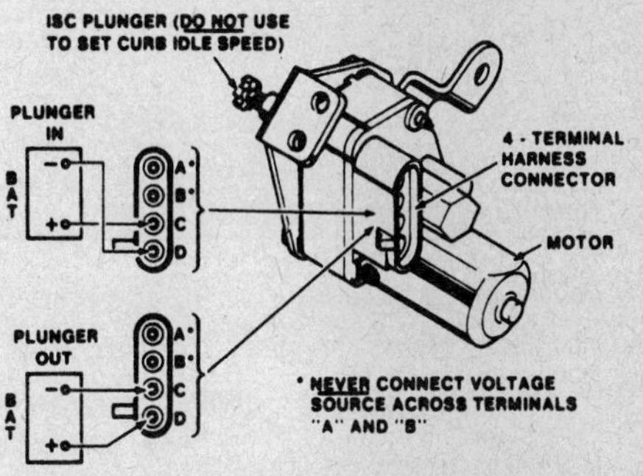

ISC PLUNGER (DO NOT USE TO SET CURB IDLE SPEED)
PLUNGER IN
BAT
PLUNGER OUT
4 - TERMINAL HARNESS CONNECTOR
MOTOR
* NEVER CONNECT VOLTAGE SOURCE ACROSS TERMINALS "A" AND "B"

Fig. 15 Idle Speed Control (ISC) test connections

to fluctuate.

4. Turn ignition to "Off" position, then disconnect ISC motor connector.
5. Apply battery voltage to terminal C of ISC motor connector to retract plunger, **Fig. 15,** then ground terminal D. **Do not leave battery voltage connected to ISC motor longer than necessary to retract plunger. Do not connect battery voltage to terminals A or B on motor. ISC motor will be damaged if connections are improperly made.**
6. Start engine and run until dwell reading begins to fluctuate, then place automatic transmissions in Drive (manual transmission in Neutral).
7. With ISC plunger fully retracted, adjust idle speed to specified minimum authority RPM, **Fig. 16,** using throttle stop screw.
8. Place automatic transmission in Park, manual transmission in Neutral, then reverse jumper wire connections. Apply battery voltage to terminal D, then ground terminal C. **Only leave jumper wires connected long enough to extend ISC plunger.**
9. On vehicles with manual transmission, adjust idle speed to specified maximum authority RPM, **Fig. 16,** by turning ISC plunger using tool No. J-29607 or equivalent.
10. On vehicles with automatic transmission, place selector level in Park, then adjust idle to 1500 RPM by turning ISC plunger using tool mentioned above. Set parking brake, then block drive wheels and place selector lever in Drive. Adjust idle speed to specified maximum authority RPM, **Fig. 16,** by turning ISC plunger using tool No. J-29607 ore equivalent.
11. On all vehicles, recheck ISC maximum authority adjustment RPM with battery voltage applied to motor. Motor will ratchet at full extension with power applied.
12. Measure distance from back of plunger head to ISC nosepiece, dimension "B," **Fig. 14.** Dimension must not exceed specification shown in chart.
13. Fully retract ISC plunger, then place automatic transmission in Park, manual transmission in Neutral and turn ignition "Off." Disconnect 12 volt power source, ground lead, tachometer and dwell meter. Connect four terminal harness to ISC motor. **This procedure will cause the "Check Engine" lamp to light and an ISC motor trouble code to be set. Restoring the system to normal operation will cause the lamp to go out, but the trouble code will continue to be stored as an intermittent problem.**

Year	Engine (VIN Code)	Carburetor Number	Minimum Authority①	Maximum Authority②
1982	V6-181/3.0L(E)	17082183	450D	1050D
		17082186	450D	1050D
		17082196	450D	1050D
	V6-229/3.8L(K)	17082130	475D	800D
		17082132	475D	800D
	V6-231/3.8L(A)	17082182	450D	900D
		17082184	450D	900D
		17082192	450D	900D
		17082194	450D	900D
1983	V6-181/3.0L(E)	All	500D	1300D
	V6-229/3.8L(9)	17082130	475D	750D
		17082132	475D	800D
	V6-231/3.8L(A)	All	450D	900D
1984	V6-181/3.0L(E)	17084193	500D	1350D
		17084194	500D	1350D
		17084195	500D	1350D
	V6-229/3.8L(9)	17082130	475D	③
		17082132	475D	④
	V6-231/3.8L(A)	450D	1000D	
1985	V6-181/3.0L(E)	17083194	500D	1350D
		17084193	500D	1350D
	V6-181/3.0L(E)	All	500D	1300D
	V6-231/3.8L(A)	All	450D	900D
1986	V6-231/3.8L(E)	All	450D	900D

①—Plunger retracted.
②—Plunger extended.
③—750D less A/C; 800D with A/C.

Fig. 16 Idle Speed Control (ISC) adjustment specifications

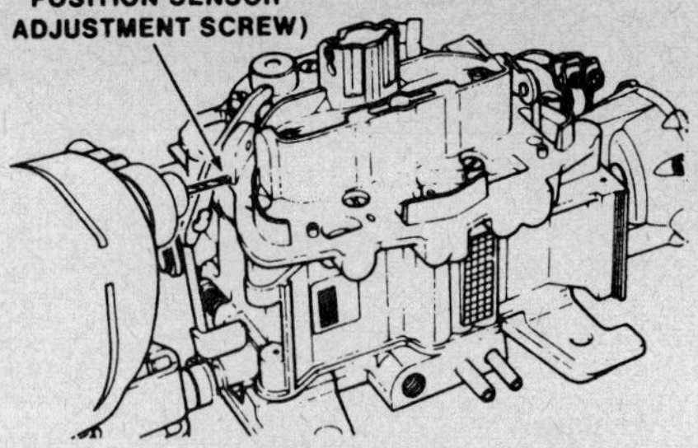

Fig. 17 Throttle Position Sensor (TPS) adjustment screw plug removal

THROTTLE POSITION SENSOR (TPS) ADJUSTMENT

1. Remove TPS adjusting screw, **Fig. 17.**
2. Leaving electrical connector in place, connect a digital voltmeter between TPS center terminal (B) and bottom terminal (C), using jumper wires if necessary. **Only a digital voltmeter with 10 megohm input impedance or higher can be used. Conventional voltmeters do not have sufficient resistance to obtain accurate readings.**
3. With ignition on, engine stopped and A/C off, install TPS screw and adjust quickly to obtain specified TPS idle voltage, **Fig. 18.**
4. Turn ignition off and install new plug over TPS adjusting screw or seal opening with RTV sealer.

Year	Engine (VIN Code)	Voltage	Throttle Position
1982	V6-181/3.0L(E)	.46	ISC retracted at slow idle
	V6-229/3.8L(K)	.51	ISC retracted at slow idle
	V6-231/3.8L(A)	.77	High step of fast idle cam
	V8-260/4.3L(8)	.46	Stopped at curb idle
	V8-267/4.4L(J)	.51	Stopped at curb idle.
1983	V6-181/3.0L(E)	.42	ISC retracted at base idle
	V6-229/3.8L(9)	.51	ISC retracted at base idle
	V6-231/3.8L(A)	.77	High step of fast idle cam
1984	V6-181/3.0L(E)	①	ISC retracted at base idle
	V6-229/3.8L(9)	.28	ISC retracted at base idle
	V6-231/3.8L(A)	②	ISC retracted at base idle
1985	V6-181/3.0L(E)	.31	ISC retracted at base idle
	V6-231/3.8L(A)	.31	ISC retracted at base idle
1986	V6-231/3.8L(A)	.46	ISC retracted at base idle

①—Chevrolet and Oldsmobile models, .42 volts. Buick and Pontiac models: with 3 speed trans., .57 volt; with 4 speed trans, .65 volt.

②—Chevrolet and Oldsmobile models, .39 volt; Buick and Pontiac models, .46 volt.

Fig. 18 Throttle Position Sensor (TPS) adjustment specifications

Rochester Varajet 2SE & E2SE Series Carburetors

INDEX

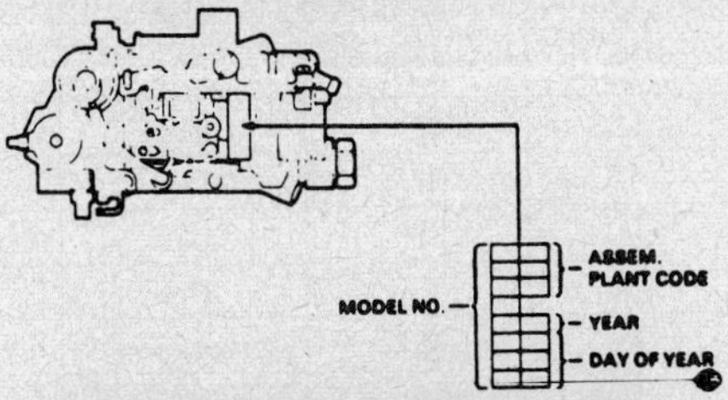

Fig. 1 Carburetor model identification number location

IDENTIFICATION LOCATION

The carburetor model identification is stamped vertically on the float bowl in the flat area adjacent to the vacuum tube, **Fig. 1**.

DESCRIPTION

The Varajet models 2SE and E2SE, **Figs. 2 and 3**, are two barrel, two stage, down draft design carburetors. Aluminum die castings are used for the air horn, float bowl and throttle body. A heat insulator gasket is used between the throttle body and float bowl to reduce heat transfer to the float bowl.

The primary stage has a triple venturi with a small 35 mm bore, resulting in good fuel metering control during idle and part throttle operation. The secondary stage has a 46 mm bore, providing sufficient air capacity for engine power requirements. An air valve is used in the secondary stage with a single tapered metering rod.

The float chamber is internally vented through a vertical vent cavity in the air horn. The float chamber is also externally vented through a tube in the air horn. A hose connects this tube directly to a vacuum operated vapor vent valve located in the vapor canister. When the engine is not running, the canister vapor vent valve is open, allowing fuel vapor from the float chamber to pass into the canister where the vapor is stored until normally purged.

An adjustable part throttle screw is used in the float bowl to aid emission control. This screw is factory pre-set and a plug is installed to prevent further adjustment or fuel leakage. The plug should not be removed or the screw setting disturbed. If float bowl replacement is required, the ser-

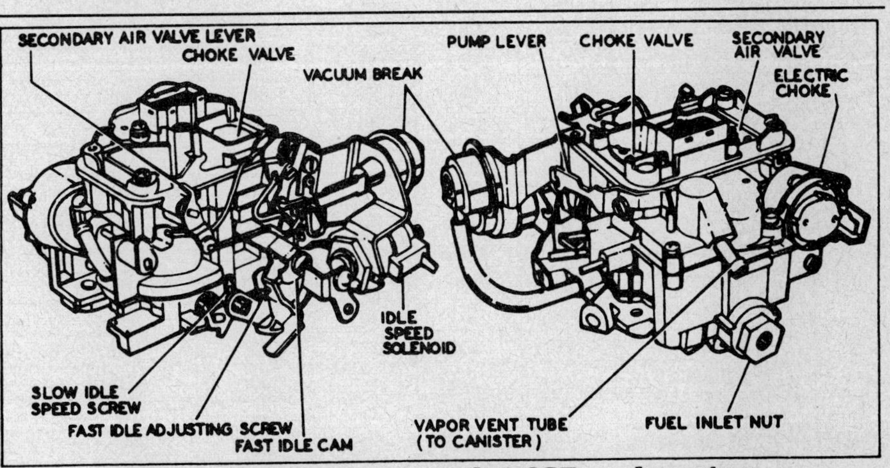

Fig. 2 Rochester Varajet 2SE carburetor

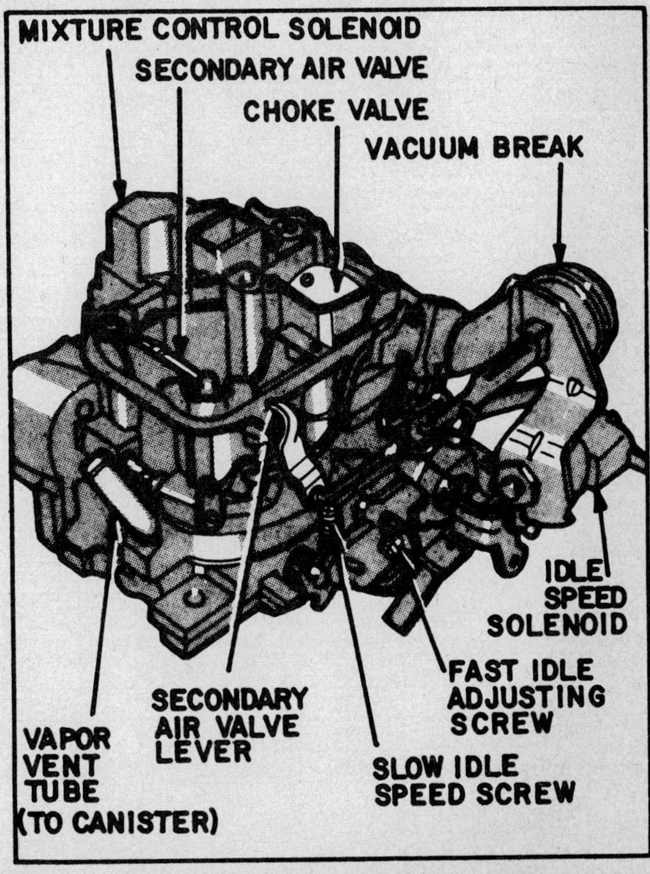

Fig. 3 Rochester Varajet E2SE carburetor

ADJUSTMENT SPECIFICATIONS

Year	Carb. Production No.	Float Level	Choke Coil Lever	Choke Rod	Vacuum Break		Air Valve Rod	Choke Setting	Unloader	Secondary Lockout
					Primary	Secondary				
1982	17081600, 06	5/16	.085	18°	23°	27°	1°	①	35°	.025
	17081601	5/16	.085	18°	21°	27°	1°	①	35°	.025
	17081607, 09	5/16	.085	21°	27°	27°	1°	①	35°	.025
	17082300, 04	5/16	.085	18°	23°	27°	1°	①	35°	.025
	17082301, 03	5/16	.085	18°	21°	27°	1°	①	35°	.025
	17082305	5/16	.085	21°	23°	27°	1°	①	35°	.025
	17082316	1/4	.085	17°	30°	34°	1°	①	45°	.025
	17082317	1/4	.085	17°	30°	35°	1°	①	45°	.025
	17082320, 21	1/4	.085	25°	30°	35°	1°	①	45°	.025
	17082390	13/32	.085	17°	30°	34°	1°	①	45°	.025
	17082391	13/32	.085	25°	30°	35°	1°	①	45°	.025
	17082446, 48	5/16	.085	18°	20°	27°	1°	①	35°	.025
	17082447, 49	5/16	.085	18°	20°	25°	1°	①	35°	.025
	17082490	13/32	.085	17°	30°	34°	1°	①	45°	.025
	17082491	13/32	.085	25°	30°	35°	1°	①	45°	.025
	17082630	5/16	.085	18°	23°	27°	1°	①	35°	.025
	17082631	5/16	.085	18°	23°	25°	1°	①	35°	.025
	17082632	5/16	.085	18°	20°	27°	1°	①	35°	.025
	17082640	1/4	.085	17°	30°	34°	1°	①	45°	.025
	17082641	1/4	.085	17°	30°	35°	1°	①	45°	.025
	17082642	1/4	.085	25°	30°	35°	1°	①	45°	.025
1983	17083356	13/32	.085	22°	25°	35°	1°	①	30°	.025
	17083357	13/32	.085	22°	25°	35°	1°	①	30°	.025
	17083358	13/32	.085	22°	25°	35°	1°	①	30°	.025
	17083359	13/32	.085	22°	25°	35°	1°	①	30°	.025
	17083368	1/8	.085	22°	25°	35°	1°	①	30°	.025
	17083370	1/8	.085	22°	25°	35°	1°	①	30°	.025
	17083430	11/32	.085	15°	26°	38°	1°	①	42°	.025
	17083431	11/32	.085	15°	26°	38°	1°	①	42°	.025
	17083434	11/32	.085	15°	26°	38°	1°	①	42°	.025
	17083435	11/32	.085	15°	26°	38°	1°	①	42°	.025
	17083450	1/8	.085	28°	27°	35°	1°	①	45°	.025
	17083451	1/8	.085	28°	27°	35°	1°	①	45°	.025
	17083452	1/8	.085	28°	27°	35°	1°	①	45°	.025
	17083453	1/8	.085	28°	27°	35°	1°	①	45°	.025
	17083454	1/8	.085	28°	27°	35°	1°	①	45°	.025
	17083455	1/8	.085	28°	27°	35°	1°	①	45°	.025
	17083456	1/8	.085	28°	27°	35°	1°	①	45°	.025
	17083458	1/4	.085	28°	27°	35°	1°	①	45°	.025
	17083459	1/4	.085	28°	27°	35°	1°	①	45°	.025
	17083630	1/4	.085	28°	27°	35°	1°	①	45°	.025
	17083631	1/4	.085	28°	27°	35°	1°	①	45°	.025
	17083632	1/4	.085	28°	27°	35°	1°	①	45°	.025
	17083633	1/4	.085	28°	27°	35°	1°	①	45°	.025
	17083634	1/4	.085	28°	27°	35°	1°	①	45°	.025
	17083635	1/4	.085	28°	27°	35°	1°	①	45°	.025
	17083636	1/4	.085	28°	27°	35°	1°	①	45°	.025
	17083650	1/8	.085	28°	27°	35°	1°	①	45°	.025

Continued

ADJUSTMENT SPECIFICATIONS continued

Year	Carb. Production No.	Float Level	Choke Coil Lever	Choke Rod	Vacuum Break		Air Valve Rod	Choke Setting	Unloader	Secondary Lockout
					Primary	Secondary				
1984	17072683	9/32	.085	28°	25°	35°	1°	①	45°	.025
	17074812	9/32	.085	28°	25°	35°	1°	①	45°	.025
	17084356	9/32	.085	22°	25°	30°	1°	①	30°	.025
	17084357	9/32	.085	22°	25°	30°	1°	①	30°	.025
	17084358	9/32	.085	22°	25°	30°	1°	①	30°	.025
	17084359	9/32	.085	22°	25°	30°	1°	①	30°	.025
	17084368	1/8	.085	22°	25°	30°	1°	①	30°	.025
	17084370	1/8	.085	22°	25°	30°	1°	①	30°	.025
	17084430	11/32	.085	15°	26°	38°	1°	①	42°	.025
	17084431	11/32	.085	15°	26°	38°	1°	①	42°	.025
	17084434	11/32	.085	15°	26°	38°	1°	①	42°	.025
	17084435	11/32	.085	15°	26°	38°	1°	①	42°	.025
	17084452	5/32	.085	28°	25°	35°	1°	①	45°	.025
	17084453	5/32	.085	28°	25°	35°	1°	①	45°	.025
	17084455	5/32	.085	28°	25°	35°	1°	①	45°	.025
	17084456	5/32	.085	28°	25°	35°	1°	①	45°	.025
	17084458	5/32	.085	28°	25°	35°	1°	①	45°	.025
	17084532	5/32	.085	28°	25°	35°	1°	①	45°	.025
	17084534	5/32	.085	28°	25°	35°	1°	①	45°	.025
	17084535	5/32	.085	28°	25°	35°	1°	①	45°	.025
	17084537	5/32	.085	28°	25°	35°	1°	①	45°	.025
	17084538	5/32	.085	28°	25°	35°	1°	①	45°	.025
	17084540	5/32	.085	28°	25°	35°	1°	①	45°	.025
	17084542	1/8	.085	28°	25°	35°	1°	①	45°	.025
	17084632	9/32	.085	28°	25°	35°	1°	①	45°	.025
	17084633	9/32	.085	28°	25°	35°	1°	①	45°	.025
	17084635	9/32	.085	28°	25°	35°	1°	①	45°	.025
	17084636	9/32	.085	28°	25°	35°	1°	①	45°	.025
1985	17084534	5/32	.085	28°	25°	35°	1°	①	35°	.025
	17084535	5/32	.085	28°	25°	35°	1°	①	35°	.025
	17084540	5/32	.085	28°	25°	35°	1°	①	35°	.025
	17084542	1/8	.085	28°	25°	35°	1°	①	35°	.025
	17085006	1/8	.085	22°	21°	—	1°	①	30°	.025
	17085356	1/8	.085	22°	25°	30°	1°	①	30°	.025
	17085357	9/32	.085	22°	25°	30°	1°	①	30°	.025
	17085358	1/8	.085	22°	25°	30°	1°	①	30°	.025
	17085359	9/32	.085	22°	25°	30°	1°	①	30°	.025
	17085368	1/8	.085	22°	25°	30°	1°	①	30°	.025
	17085369	9/32	.085	22°	25°	30°	1°	①	30°	.025
	17085370	1/8	.085	22°	25°	30°	1°	①	30°	.025
	17085371	9/32	.085	22°	25°	30°	1°	①	30°	.025
	17085388	1/8	.085	22°	21°	—	1°	①	30°	.025
	17085452	5/32	.085	28°	25°	35°	1°	①	35°	.025
	17085453	5/32	.085	28°	25°	35°	1°	①	35°	.025
	17085458	5/32	.085	28°	25°	35°	1°	①	35°	.025
1986	17084534	5/32	.085	28°	25°	35°	1°	①	45°	.025
	17084535	5/32	.085	28°	25°	35°	1°	①	45°	.025
	17084540	5/32	.085	28°	25°	35°	1°	①	45°	.025
	17084542	1/8	.085	28°	25°	35°	1°	①	45°	.025

①—Tamper-resistant.

vice float bowl will include a factory pre-set and plugged adjustable part throttle screw.

A hot idle compensator is used on some models and is located in the air horn. The opening and closing of the hot idle compensator valve is controlled by a bi-metal strip that is calibrated to a specific temperature. When the valve opens, additional air is allowed to bypass the throttle valves and enter the intake manifold to prevent rough idle during periods of hot engine operation.

The idle mixture screw is recessed in the throttle body and is sealed with a hardened steel plug to prevent alteration of the factory pre-set mixture setting. The plug should not be removed and the mixture screw readjusted unless required by major carburetor overhaul or throttle body replacement.

The E2SE carburetor includes special design features for use with the Computer Controlled Catalytic Converter (C4) System or the Computer Command Control (C3) System. An electrically operated mixture control solenoid mounted in the air horn, controls air and fuel metering to the idle and main metering systems of the carburetor. The plunger located at the end of the solenoid is submerged in the fuel chamber of the float bowl. This plunger is controlled by an electrical signal from the Electronic Control Module (ECM). The Electronic Control Module responding to signals from the oxygen sensor in the exhaust and other engine operating condition signals, energizes the solenoid to move the plunger down to the lean position or de-energizes the solenoid to move the plunger up to the rich position to control fuel delivery to the idle and main metering systems. When the plunger is in the lean position, fuel metering is controlled by a lean mixture screw located in the float bowl. When the plunger is in the rich position, the additional fuel is metered to the main fuel well through a rich mixture screw located at the end of the fuel supply channel in the float bowl. Air metered to the idle system is controlled by the up and down movement of the mixture control solenoid plunger. The plunger increases or decreases air supplied to the idle system which is further metered by the idle air bleed screw. The plunger cycles up and down approximately 10 times per second, controlling air and fuel mixtures.

On 1982 models with 4-112 (1.8L) and 4-121 (2.0L) engines, an idle speed control motor which is controlled by the Electronic Control Module is used to control idle speed, **Fig. 4.** The curb idle speed is programmed into the Electronic Control Module and no attempt should be made to adjust idle speed using the idle speed control motor.

ON-VEHICLE ADJUSTMENTS

Use care not to remove the special friction reducing coating applied to the primary and secondary throttle shafts, the secondary actuating lever and lockout lever. A special graphite compound is also applied to the secondary throttle bore and valve.

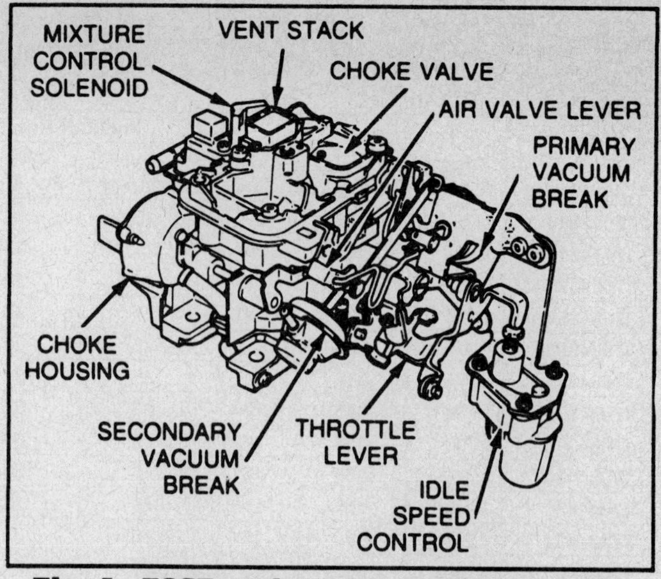

Fig. 4 E2SE carburetor equipped with idle speed control motor

1. REMOVE AIR HORN, AIR HORN GASKET AND UPPER FLOAT BOWL INSERT.
2. ATTACH J-34817-1 OR BT-8227A-1 TO FLOAT BOWL.
3. PLACE J-34817-3 OR BT-8227A IN BASE, WITH CONTACT PIN RESTING ON OUTER EDGE OF FLOAT LEVER.
4. MEASURE DISTANCE FROM TOP OF CASTING TO TOP OF FLOAT, AT POINT FARTHEST FROM FLOAT HINGE. USE J-9789-90 OR BT-8037.
5. IF MORE THAN ±1.59mm (2/32") FROM SPECIFICATION, USE J-34817-20 OR BT-8045A TO BEND LEVER UP OR DOWN. REMOVE BENDING TOOL AND MEASURE, REPEATING UNTIL WITHIN SPECIFICATION.
6. VISUALLY CHECK FLOAT ALIGNMENT.
7. REASSEMBLE CARBURETOR.

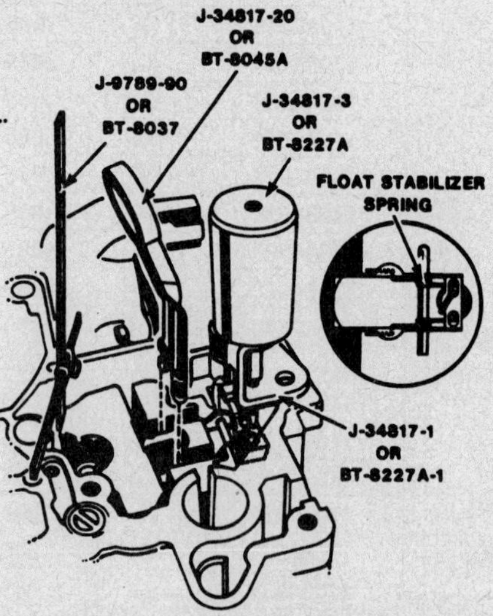

Fig. 5 Float level adjustment. 2SE & E2SE carburetors

(1) IF RIVETED, DRILL OUT AND REMOVE RIVETS. REMOVE CHOKE COVER AND
(2) STAT ASSEMBLY.

PLACE FAST IDLE SCREW ON HIGH STEP OF FAST IDLE CAM.

(5) PUSH ON INTERMEDIATE CHOKE LEVER UNTIL CHOKE VALVE IS CLOSED.

(3) INSERT .085" (2.18mm) PLUG GAGE IN HOLE.

(4) EDGE OF LEVER SHOULD JUST CONTACT SIDE OF GAGE.

(6) SUPPORT AT "S" AND BEND INTERMEDIATE CHOKE LINK TO ADJUST.

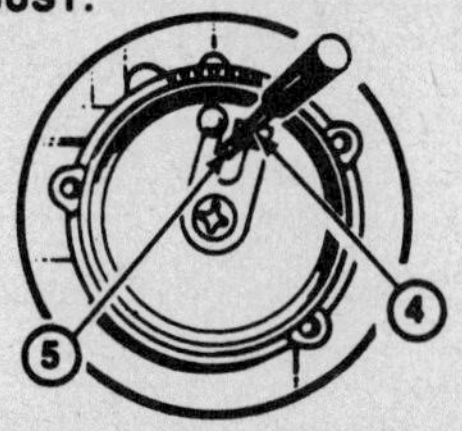

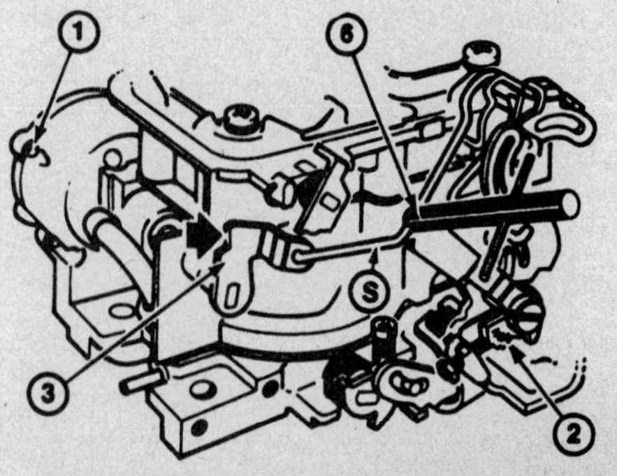

Fig. 6 Choke coil lever adjustment w/single tang lever. 2SE & E2SE carburetors

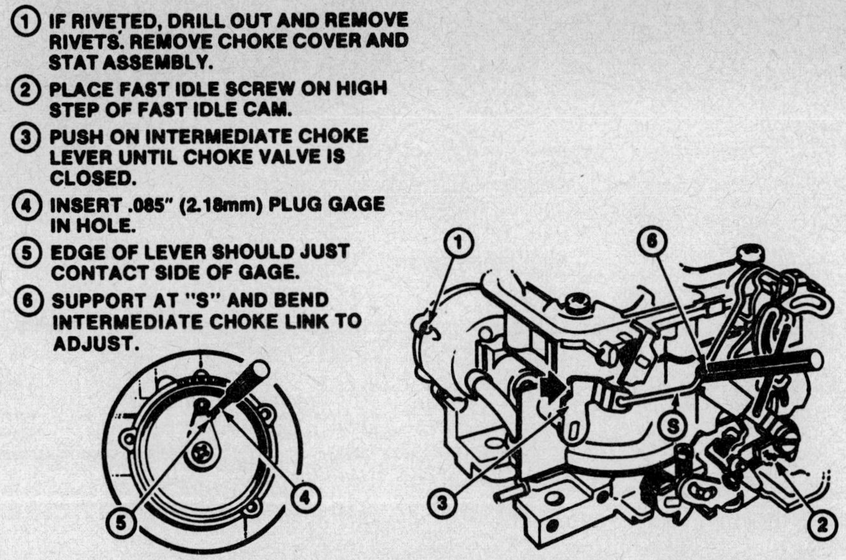

Fig. 7 Choke coil lever adjustment w/dual tang lever. 2SE & E2SE carburetors

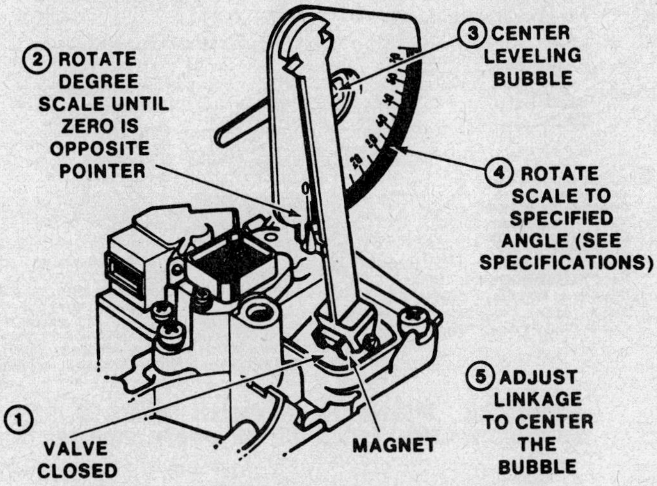

Fig. 8 Carburetor angle gauge installation

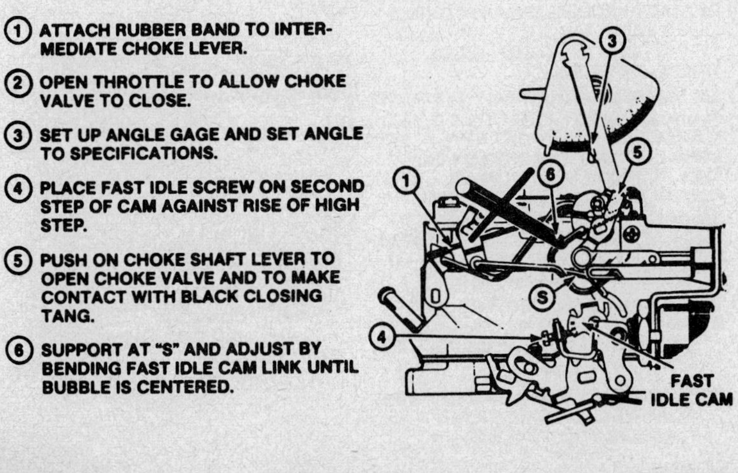
1 ATTACH RUBBER BAND TO INTERMEDIATE CHOKE LEVER.
2 OPEN THROTTLE TO ALLOW CHOKE VALVE TO CLOSE.
3 SET UP ANGLE GAGE AND SET ANGLE TO SPECIFICATIONS.
4 PLACE FAST IDLE SCREW ON SECOND STEP OF CAM AGAINST RISE OF HIGH STEP.
5 PUSH ON CHOKE SHAFT LEVER TO OPEN CHOKE VALVE AND TO MAKE CONTACT WITH BLACK CLOSING TANG.
6 SUPPORT AT "S" AND ADJUST BY BENDING FAST IDLE CAM LINK UNTIL BUBBLE IS CENTERED.
S
FAST IDLE CAM

Fig. 9 Choke rod adjustment (Typical) 2SE & E2SE carburetors

CURB IDLE SPEED ADJUSTMENT

On some vehicles equipped with computerized emission control systems, idle speed is controlled by the Idle Speed Control (ISC) motor and is not adjustable. Refer to vehicle emission label for specific applications. If the ISC is found defective, a new one can be installed and must be adjusted to specifications. The procedure below applies to carburetors without an ISC motor.

Make all adjustments with engine at normal operating temperature, choke fully open, air cleaner installed and A/C off, except where noted.

1. Disconnect and plug vacuum hoses as directed on vehicle emission label.
2. Check and, if necessary, adjust ignition timing to specifications.
3. On vehicles less A/C without idle speed solenoid, turn idle speed screw inward or outward until specified idle speed is obtained.
4. On vehicles less A/C with idle speed solenoid, proceed as follows:
   a. With solenoid energized and transmission in Drive (manual transmission in Neutral), open throttle and allow solenoid plunger to fully extend.
   b. Turn solenoid actuating screw inward or outward until specified RPM (solenoid energized) is obtained.
   c. Disconnect solenoid electrical connector, then turn idle speed adjusting screw inward or outward until specified RPM (base idle) is obtained.
   d. Reconnect solenoid electrical connector.
5. On vehicles equipped with A/C, proceed as follows:
   a. Turn idle speed adjusting screw inward or outward until specified RPM (base idle) is obtained.
   b. With transmission in Drive (manual transmission in Neutral), disconnect A/C compressor electrical connector and switch A/C control to On position.
   c. Open throttle and allow A/C solenoid plunger to fully extend.
   d. Turn solenoid actuating screw inward or outward until specified RPM (solenoid energized) is obtained.
   e. Reconnect compressor electrical lead.

FAST IDLE SPEED ADJUSTMENT

Check and, if necessary, adjust ignition timing before adjusting fast idle speed.

Make all adjustments with engine at normal operating temperature, choke fully open, air cleaner installed and A/C control Off, if equipped.

1. Disconnect and plug vacuum hoses as directed on vehicle emissions label.
2. Position fast idle screw on specified step of fast idle cam as directed on emissions label, then start engine.

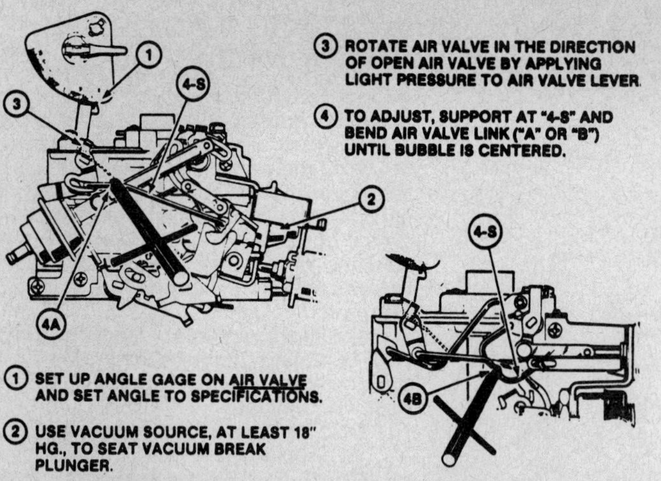

③ ROTATE AIR VALVE IN THE DIRECTION OF OPEN AIR VALVE BY APPLYING LIGHT PRESSURE TO AIR VALVE LEVER.
④ TO ADJUST, SUPPORT AT "4-S" AND BEND AIR VALVE LINK ("A" OR "B") UNTIL BUBBLE IS CENTERED.
① SET UP ANGLE GAGE ON AIR VALVE AND SET ANGLE TO SPECIFICATIONS.
② USE VACUUM SOURCE, AT LEAST 18" HG., TO SEAT VACUUM BREAK PLUNGER.
4-S
4A
4B

Fig. 10 Air valve rod adjustment (Typical). 2SE & E2SE carburetors

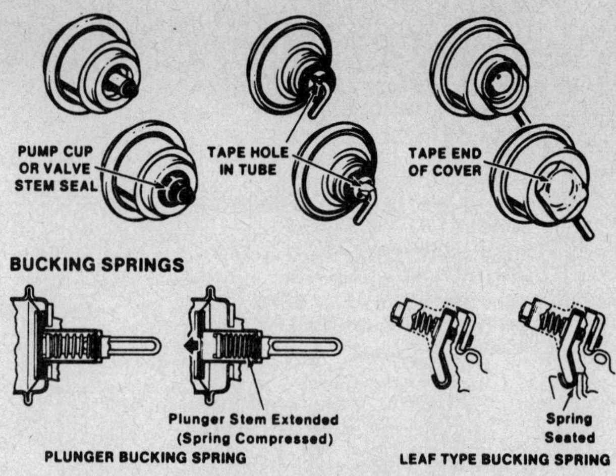

Fig. 11 Blocking air bleed holes

3. Turn fast idle screw inward or outward and adjust fast idle speed to specifications.

FLOAT LEVEL ADJUSTMENT

Refer to **Fig. 5**, for float adjustment procedure. Adjust as directed to dimension listed in Adjustment Specifications.

CHOKE COIL LEVER ADJUSTMENT

Refer to **Figs. 6 and 7** for choke coil lever adjustment.

CHOKE ROD ADJUSTMENT

Install carburetor angle gauge tool No. J-26701 or BT-7704 as shown in **Fig. 8.**

With gauge installed, adjust choke rod as outlined in **Fig. 9.** Adjust as directed to dimension listed in Adjustment Specifications.

AIR VALVE ROD ADJUSTMENT

Install carburetor angle gauge tool No. J-26701 or BT-7704 as shown in **Fig. 8.**

With gauge installed, adjust air valve rod as outlined in **Fig. 10.** Adjust as directed to dimension listed in Adjustment Specifications.

PRIMARY VACUUM BREAK ADJUSTMENT

Prior to adjusting vacuum break, refer to **Fig. 11** for air bleed hole blocking procedures.

1982 E2SE

Before performing adjustment procedure, remove primary vacuum break from carburetor and position bracket in vise, then grind off adjusting screw cap and reinstall vacuum break.

1. Rotate degree scale until zero is opposite pointer, then with choke valve completely closed and fast idle screw on high step of fast idle cam, place magnet squarely on top of choke valve and rotate bubble until it is centered, **Fig. 12.**

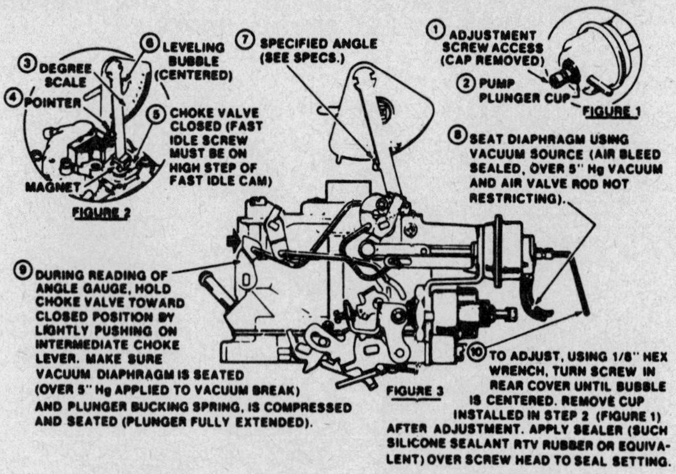

Fig. 12 Primary vacuum break adjustment. 1982 E2SE carburetor

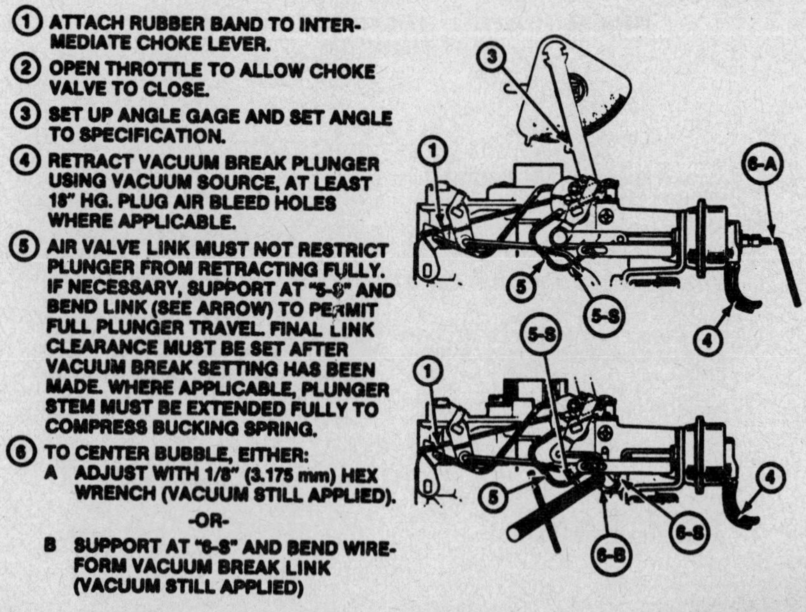

Fig. 13 Primary vacuum break adjustment w/single break unit. 1983–86 E2SE carburetor

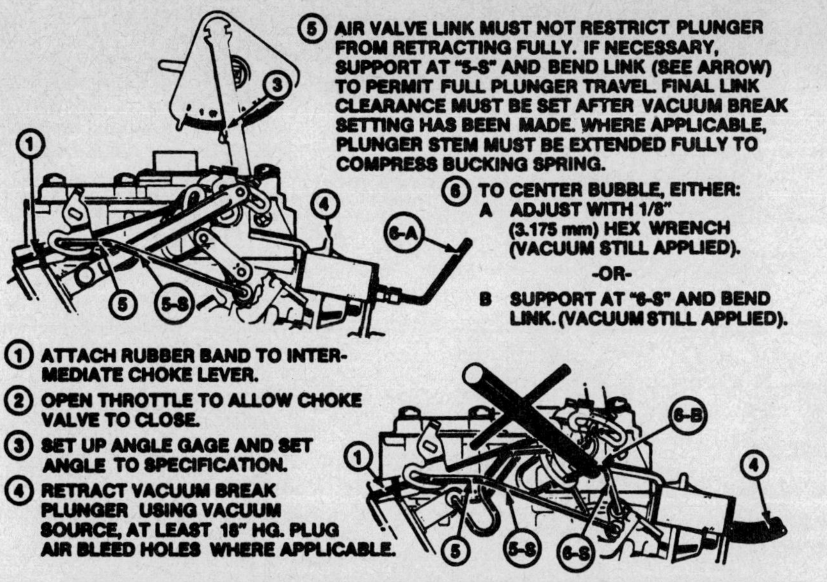

5 AIR VALVE LINK MUST NOT RESTRICT PLUNGER FROM RETRACTING FULLY. IF NECESSARY, SUPPORT AT "5-S" AND BEND LINK (SEE ARROW) TO PERMIT FULL PLUNGER TRAVEL. FINAL LINK CLEARANCE MUST BE SET AFTER VACUUM BREAK SETTING HAS BEEN MADE. WHERE APPLICABLE, PLUNGER STEM MUST BE EXTENDED FULLY TO COMPRESS BUCKING SPRING.
6 TO CENTER BUBBLE, EITHER:
A ADJUST WITH 1/8" (3.175 mm) HEX WRENCH (VACUUM STILL APPLIED).
-OR-
B SUPPORT AT "6-S" AND BEND LINK. (VACUUM STILL APPLIED).
1 ATTACH RUBBER BAND TO INTERMEDIATE CHOKE LEVER.
2 OPEN THROTTLE TO ALLOW CHOKE VALVE TO CLOSE.
3 SET UP ANGLE GAGE AND SET ANGLE TO SPECIFICATION.
4 RETRACT VACUUM BREAK PLUNGER USING VACUUM SOURCE, AT LEAST 18" HG. PLUG AIR BLEED HOLES WHERE APPLICABLE.
6-A
6-B
5-S
6-S

Fig. 14 Primary vacuum break adjustment w/dual break units. 1983–86 E2SE carburetor

2. Rotate scale so that specified degree for adjustment is opposite pointer.
3. Seat choke vacuum diaphragm using a vacuum source with over 5 inches Hg of vacuum. Check to ensure that air valve rod is not restricting the vacuum diaphragm from being seated. It may be necessary to bend air valve rod to obtain a slight clearance between rod and end of slot in air valve lever. If the air valve rod adjustment is disturbed, refer to the Air Valve Rod Adjustment procedure after completing the primary vacuum break adjustment.
4. Hold choke valve toward the closed position by lightly pushing on intermediate lever and note angle gauge reading.
5. If adjustment is necessary, use a 1/8 inch hex wrench to rotate adjusting screw in rear cover until bubble is centered.
6. After completing adjustment, apply a suitable sealer over adjusting screw head.

1983–86 E2SE

Install carburetor angle gauge tool No. J-26701 or BT-7704 as shown in **Fig. 8.**

With gauge installed, adjust primary vacuum break as outlined in **Figs. 13 and 14.** Adjust as directed to dimension listed in Adjustment Specification.

SECONDARY VACUUM BREAK ADJUSTMENT

Prior to adjusting vacuum break, refer to **Fig. 11** for air bleed hole blocking procedures.

1982 E2SE

Before performing adjustment procedure, remove secondary vacuum break from carburetor and position bracket in vise, then grind off adjusting screw cap and reinstall vacuum break. Plug vacuum break end cover using an accelerator pump plunger cup or equivalent. After completing adjusting remove pump plunger cup.

1. Rotate degree scale so that zero is opposite pointer, then with choke valve completely closed and fast idle screw on high step of fast idle cam, place magnet on top of choke valve and rotate until bubble is centered, **Fig. 15.**
2. Rotate scale so that specified degree for adjustment is opposite pointer.
3. Seat choke diaphragm using a vacuum source with over 5 inches Hg of vacuum.
4. Hold choke valve toward the closed position by lightly pushing on intermediate choke lever and note angle gauge reading. When noting reading check to ensure that vacuum diaphragm is seated.
5. Rotate adjusting screw in rear cover until bubble is centered. After completing adjustment, apply a suitable sealer over adjusting screw head. **Remove pump plunger cup from end cover before applying sealer over adjusting screw head.**

1983–86 E2SE

Install carburetor angle gauge tool No. J-26701 or BT-7704 as shown in **Fig. 8.**

With gauge installed, adjust secondary vacuum break as outlined in **Fig. 16.** Adjust as directed to dimension listed in Adjustment Specifications.

UNLOADER ADJUSTMENT

1982 Units

1. Rotate degree scale until zero is opposite pointer, then with choke valve completely closed, place magnet on top of choke valve and rotate bubble until centered, **Fig. 17.**
2. Rotate degree scale so specified degree for adjustment is opposite pointer.
3. With choke setting properly adjusted, hold primary throttle valve wide open.
4. On warm engines and 1983-84 units, close choke valve by pushing on intermediate choke lever and hold in position with a rubber band.
5. To adjust, bend tang on throttle lever until bubble is centered.

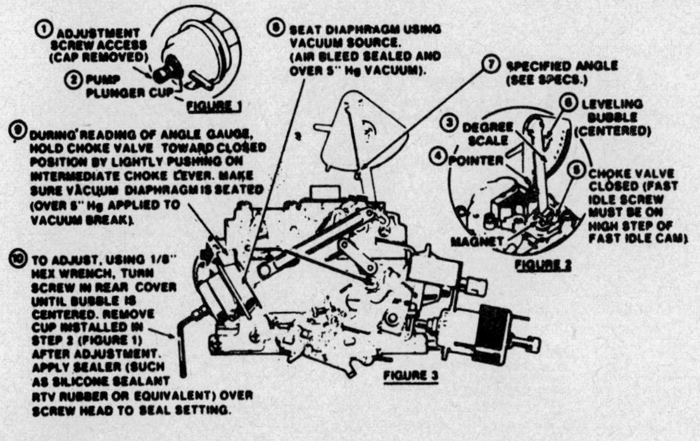

1 ADJUSTMENT SCREW ACCESS (CAP REMOVED)
2 PUMP PLUNGER CUP
FIGURE 1
8 SEAT DIAPHRAGM USING VACUUM SOURCE. (AIR BLEED SEALED AND OVER 5" Hg VACUUM).
7 SPECIFIED ANGLE (SEE SPECS.)
6 LEVELING BUBBLE (CENTERED)
3 DEGREE SCALE
4 POINTER
5 CHOKE VALVE CLOSED (FAST IDLE SCREW MUST BE ON HIGH STEP OF FAST IDLE CAM)
MAGNET
FIGURE 2
9 DURING READING OF ANGLE GAUGE, HOLD CHOKE VALVE TOWARD CLOSED POSITION BY LIGHTLY PUSHING ON INTERMEDIATE CHOKE LEVER. MAKE SURE VACUUM DIAPHRAGM IS SEATED (OVER 5" Hg APPLIED TO VACUUM BREAK).
10 TO ADJUST, USING 1/8" HEX WRENCH, TURN SCREW IN REAR COVER UNTIL BUBBLE IS CENTERED. REMOVE CUP INSTALLED IN STEP 2 (FIGURE 1) AFTER ADJUSTMENT. APPLY SEALER (SUCH AS SILICONE SEALANT RTV RUBBER OR EQUIVALENT) OVER SCREW HEAD TO SEAL SETTING.
FIGURE 3

Fig. 15 Secondary vacuum break adjustment. 1982 E2SE carburetor

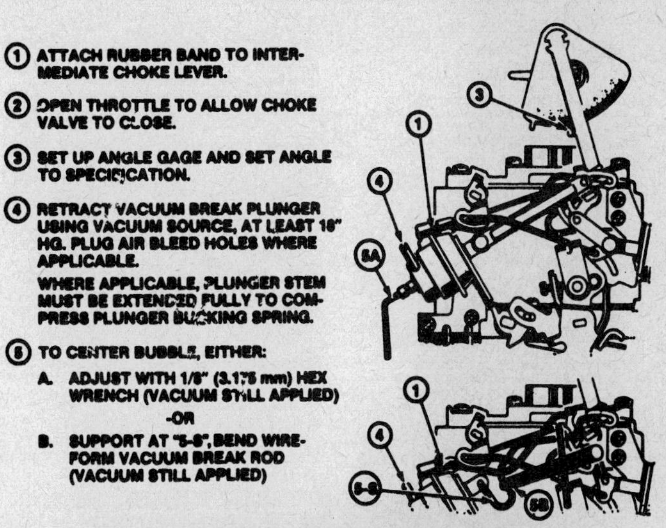

1 ATTACH RUBBER BAND TO INTERMEDIATE CHOKE LEVER.
2 OPEN THROTTLE TO ALLOW CHOKE VALVE TO CLOSE.
3 SET UP ANGLE GAGE AND SET ANGLE TO SPECIFICATION.
4 RETRACT VACUUM BREAK PLUNGER USING VACUUM SOURCE, AT LEAST 18" HG. PLUG AIR BLEED HOLES WHERE APPLICABLE.
WHERE APPLICABLE, PLUNGER STEM MUST BE EXTENDED FULLY TO COMPRESS PLUNGER BUCKING SPRING.
5 TO CENTER BUBBLE, EITHER:
A. ADJUST WITH 1/8" (3.175 mm) HEX WRENCH (VACUUM STILL APPLIED)
-OR
B. SUPPORT AT "5-S", BEND WIRE-FORM VACUUM BREAK ROD (VACUUM STILL APPLIED)
5A
5-S

Fig. 16 Secondary vacuum break adjustment. 1983–86 E2SE carburetor

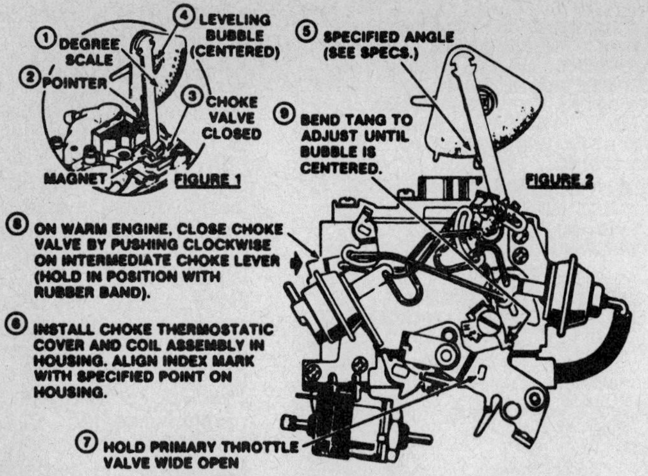

Fig. 17 Unloader adjustment. 1982 2SE & E2SE carburetors

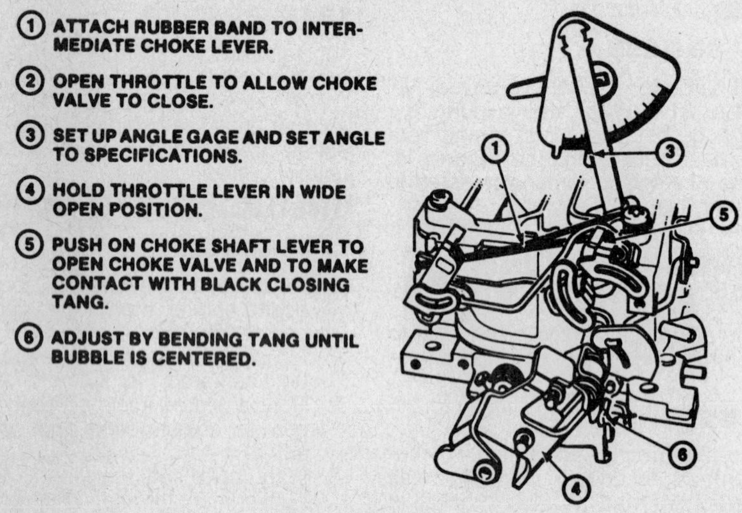
① ATTACH RUBBER BAND TO INTERMEDIATE CHOKE LEVER.
② OPEN THROTTLE TO ALLOW CHOKE VALVE TO CLOSE.
③ SET UP ANGLE GAGE AND SET ANGLE TO SPECIFICATIONS.
④ HOLD THROTTLE LEVER IN WIDE OPEN POSITION.
⑤ PUSH ON CHOKE SHAFT LEVER TO OPEN CHOKE VALVE AND TO MAKE CONTACT WITH BLACK CLOSING TANG.
⑥ ADJUST BY BENDING TANG UNTIL BUBBLE IS CENTERED.

Fig. 18 Unloader adjustment. 1983–86 2SE & E2SE carburetor

1983–86 Units

Install carburetor angle gauge tool No. J-26701 or BT-7704 as shown in **Fig. 8.**

With gauge installed, adjust unloader as outlined in **Fig. 18.** Adjust as directed to dimension listed in Adjustment Specifications.

SECONDARY LOCKOUT ADJUSTMENT

1. Hold choke valve wide open by pulling on intermediate choke lever.
2. Position throttle lever until end of secondary actuating lever is opposite toe of lockout lever, **Fig. 19.**
3. Insert specified gauge between throttle lever and secondary lockout lever toe.
4. To adjust, bend lockout lever tang contacting fast idle cam.

AIR VALVE SPRING ADJUSTMENT

1982–84 E2SE Carburetor

1. Loosen lock screw, then turn adjusting screw clockwise until air valve is partially open, **Fig. 20. On 1983-86 units, it may be necessary to remove the intermediate choke rod to gain access to the lock screw.**
2. Turn adjusting screw counterclockwise until air valve just closes, then turn screw an additional turn counterclockwise and tighten lock screw. **On 1983 units with part No. 17083650, rotate the screw 1/2 turn only.**
3. Lubricate air valve shaft pin and closing spring with lithium base grease.

IDLE SPEED CONTROL (ISC) ADJUSTMENT

Do not use ISC plunger to adjust curb idle speed, as idle speed is controlled by the Electronic Control Module (ECM). When a new ISC is installed, a base (minimum authority) and a high (maximum authority) RPM check must be made, and adjustments performed as needed. When

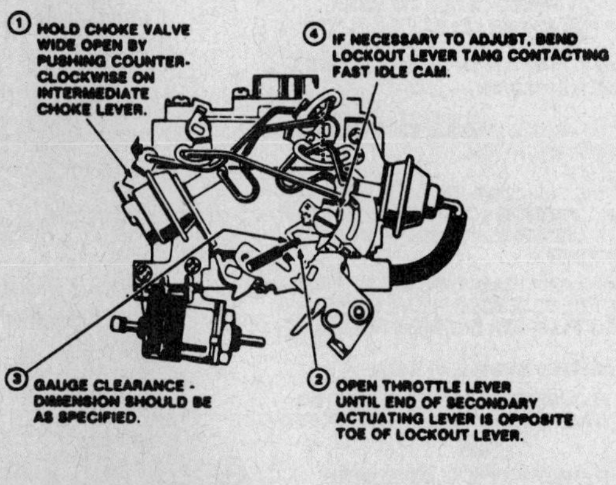

Fig. 19 Secondary lockout adjustment (Typical). 2SE & E2SE carburetor

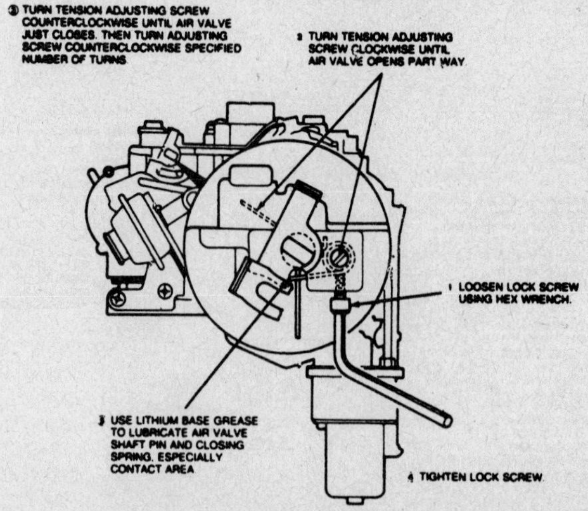

Fig. 20 Air valve spring adjustment. 1982–84 E2SE carburetor

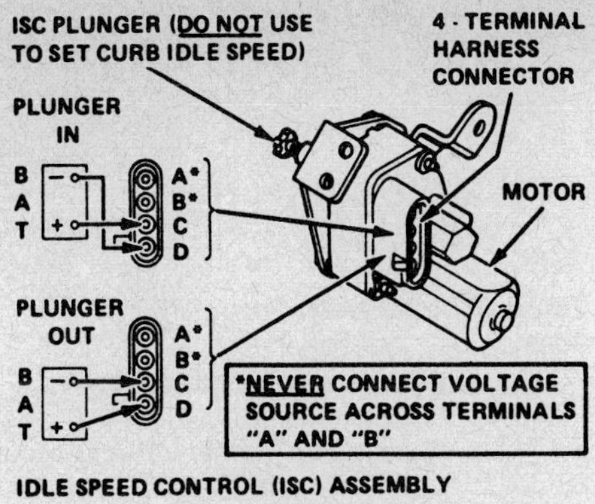

Fig. 21 Idle Speed Control (ISC) motor test connections. E2SE carburetor

Year/Engine (VIN Code)	Carburetor Number	Minimum Authority①	Maximum Authority②
1982 4-112/1.8 (G)	17081600	700D	2300P
	17082300	700D	2300P
	17081601	750N	1700N
	17082301	750N	1700N
	17081606	830D	2300P
	17082304	830D	2300P
	17081607	700N	1200N
	17082303	700N	1200N
	17081609	800N	1700N
	17082305	800N	1700N
	17081700	③	1600P
	17081701	④	1900N
1982 4-121/ 2.0 (B)	17082630	700D	2300P
	17082631	750N	1700N

①—Plunger retracted.
②—Plunger extended.
③—Exc. Chevrolet, 680D RPM; Chevrolet, 725D RPM.
④—Exc. Chevrolet, 680 RPM; Chevrolet, 725 RPM.

Fig. 22 Idle Speed Control (ISC) motor adjustment specifications. E2SE carburetor

Year	Engine (VIN Code)	Volt.	Throttle Position
1982	4-112/1.8 (G)	.26	ISC retracted at slow idle
	V6-173/2.8 (B, X, Z & 1)	.26	Engine stopped, curb idle position
1983	V6-173/2.9 (L, X & Z)	.26	Curb idle, solenoid retracted
1984	V6-173/2.8 (B, Z)	.26	Curb idle, solenoid retracted
	V6-173/2.8 (X)	.31	Curb idle, solenoid retracted
1985-86	V6-173/2.8 (X)	.3	Curb idle, solenoid retracted

Fig. 23 Throttle Position Sensor (TPS) adjustment specifications. E2SE carburetor

making low and high speed adjustments, low speed adjustment must be performed first.

1982 4-112, 121 W/E2SE Carburetor

1. Connect dwell meter to test lead in MC solenoid harness (usually a green wire) and set meter on 6 cylinder scale. Connect tachometer to engine following manufacturer's instructions.
2. Start engine and run at fast idle until it reaches normal operating temperature and dwell reading begins to fluctuate.
3. Stop engine and disconnect wiring harness connector to ISC motor. **Do not connect or disconnect wiring harness connector to ILC motor with ignition in on position, as ECM will be damaged.**
4. Using a jumper wire, connect battery voltage to terminal "C" on ISC motor, **Fig. 21**, then connect a jumper wire between terminal "D" and ground. **Do not leave battery voltage connected to ISC motor longer than necessary to retract solenoid plunger. Do not connect battery voltage to terminals "A" or "B" on motor. ISC motor will be damaged if connections are improperly made.**
5. Start engine and run until dwell reading begins to fluctuate. Place transmission in drive (manual transmission in neutral).
6. With ISC plunger fully retracted, adjust idle speed to specified minimum authority RPM, **Fig. 22**, with throttle stop screw.
7. Place transmission in neutral and reverse jumper wire connections. Connect battery voltage to terminal "D," and connect terminal "C" to ground. **Leave jumper wires connected only long enough to fully extend ISC plunger.**
8. With plunger fully extended, adjust idle speed to specified maximum authority RPM, **Fig. 22**, by turning ISC plunger with tool J-29607 or equivalent. **Adjustments must be made as quickly as possible. If engine RPM increases, adjustment cannot be performed, engine will have to be stopped and the procedure will have to be restarted from step 2.**
9. Stop engine. Reconnect wiring harness connector to ISC motor. **Test connections to ISC motor will cause "Check Engine" light to remain on until wiring harness is reconnected to motor. An intermittent trouble code will then be stored in the ECM memory which must be cleared.**

THROTTLE POSITION SENSOR (TPS) ADJUSTMENT

Do not remove plug sealing TPS adjustment or adjust TPS unless carburetor is overhauled or "Computer Command Control (C3)" system diagnosis indicates a problem with the sensor.

1982–86

1. Using a 5/64 inch drill, make a hole in TPS adjustment screw hole plug. **Use caution to prevent damaging TPS adjustment screw.**
2. Using suitable slide hammer, remove plug from hole.
3. Disconnect TPS connector, then using suitable wires, jumper all three terminals.
4. Connect digital ohmmeter J-29125-A or equivalent to TPS connector center terminal (B) to bottom terminal (C).
5. With ignition On and engine not running, turn TPS screw with suitable screwdriver to obtain specified TPS idle voltage, **Fig. 23.**
6. Turn ignition Off, then install new plug over TPS adjustment hole.

Rochester E4M & M4M Series Carburetors

INDEX

ADJUSTMENT SPECIFICATIONS

Year	Carb. Production No.	Float Level	Choke Coil Lever	Choke Rod	Vacuum Break		Air Valve Dash Pot	Choke Setting	Choke Unloader	Air Valve Valve Spring Wind-Up
					Front	Rear				
1982	17082202	11/32	.120	20°	27°	—	.025	①	38°	7/8
	17082203	11/32	.120	38°	27°	—	.025	①	38°	7/8
	17082204	11/32	.120	20°	27°	—	.025	①	38°	7/8
	17082207	11/32	.120	38°	27°	—	.025	①	38°	7/8
	17082244	7/16	.120	24.5°	21°	16°	.025	①	32°	9/16
	17082245	3/8	.120	24.5°	26°	26°	.025	①	32°	5/8
	17082246	3/8	.120	24.5°	26°	26°	.025	①	32°	5/8
	17082247	3/8	.120	18°	26°	26°	.025	①	32°	5/8
	17082248	13/32	.120	24.5°	28°	24°	.025	①	38°	5/8
	17082251	15/32	.120	14°	25°	45°	.025	①	35°	1/2
	17082253	15/32	.120	14°	25°	36°	.025	①	35°	1/2
	17082264	7/16	.120	24.5°	21°	16°	.025	①	32°	9/16
	17082265	3/8	.120	24.5°	26°	26°	.025	①	32°	5/8
	17082266	3/8	.120	24.5°	26°	26°	.025	①	32°	5/8
	17082267	3/8	.120	24.5°	28°	24°	.025	①	38°	5/8
	17082268	13/32	.120	24.5°	28°	24°	.025	①	38°	5/8
1983	17082265	3/8	.120	24.5°	26°	26°	.025	①	32°	5/8
	17082266	3/8	.120	24.5°	26°	26°	.025	①	32°	5/8
	17082267	11/32	.120	18°	26°	26°	.025	①	32°	5/8
	17082268	3/8	.120	18°	26°	26°	.025	①	32°	5/8
	17083202	11/32	.120	20°	—	27°	.025	①	38°	7/8
	17083203	11/32	.120	38°	—	27°	.025	①	38°	7/8
	17083204	11/32	.120	20°	27°	—	.025	①	38°	7/8
	17083205	11/32	.120	38°	27°	—	.025	①	38°	7/8
	17083206	11/32	.120	20°	27°	—	.025	①	38°	7/8
	17083207	11/32	.120	38°	27°	—	.025	①	38°	7/8
	17083216	11/32	.120	20°	—	27°	.025	①	38°	7/8
	17083218	11/32	.120	20°	27°	—	.025	①	38°	7/8
	17083236	11/32	.120	20°	27°	—	.025	①	38°	7/8
	17083242	9/32	.120	24.5°	20°	—	.025	①	38°	9/16
	17083244	1/4	.120	24.5°	21°	16°	.025	①	32°	9/16
	17083248	3/8	.120	24.5°	26°	26°	.025	①	32°	5/8
	17083250	7/16	.120	14°	27°	42°	.025	①	35°	1/2
	17082253	7/16	.120	14°	27°	41°	.025	①	35°	1/2
	17083506	7/16	.120	20°	27°	36°	.025	①	36°	1
	17083508	7/16	.120	20°	27°	36°	.025	①	36°	1

ADJUSTMENT SPECIFICATIONS Continued

Year	Carb. Production No.	Float Level	Choke Coil Lever	Choke Rod	Vacuum Break Front	Vacuum Break Rear	Air Valve Dash Pot	Choke Setting	Choke Unloader	Air Valve Valve Spring Wind-Up
	17083524	7/16	.120	20°	25°	36°	.025	①	36°	1
	17083526	7/16	.120	20°	25°	36°	.025	①	36°	1
	17083553	7/16	.120	14°	27°	41°	.025	①	35°	1/2
1984	17084201	11/32	.120	20°	27°	—	.025	①	38°	7/8
	17084205	11/32	.120	38°	27°	—	.025	①	38°	7/8
	17084208	11/32	.120	20°	27°	—	.025	①	38°	7/8
	17084209	11/32	.120	38°	27°	—	.025	①	38°	7/8
	17084210	11/32	.120	20°	27°	—	.025	①	38°	7/8
	17084240	5/16	.120	24.5°	24°	—	.025	①	32°	1
	17084244	5/16	.120	24.5°	24°	—	.025	①	32°	1
	17084246	5/16	.120	24.5°	22°	24°	.025	①	32°	1
	17084248	5/16	.120	24.5°	24°	—	.025	①	32°	1
	17084252	7/16	.120	14°	27°	41°	.025	①	35°	1/2
	17084254	7/16	.120	14°	27°	41°	.025	①	35°	1/2
	17084256	11/32	.120	14°	27°	41°	.025	①	35°	1/2
	17084258	11/32	.120	14°	27°	41°	.025	①	35°	1/2
	17084507	7/16	.120	20°	27°	36°	.025	①	36°	1
	17084509	7/16	.120	20°	27°	36°	.025	①	36°	1
	17084525	7/16	.120	20°	25°	36°	.025	①	36°	1
	17084527	7/16	.120	20°	25°	36°	.025	①	36°	1
	17084554	7/16	.120	14°	27°	41°	.025	①	35°	1/2
1985	17085202	11/32	.120	20°	27°	—	.025	①	38°	7/8
	17085203	11/32	.120	20°	27°	—	.025	①	38°	7/8
	17085204	11/32	.120	20°	27°	—	.025	①	38°	7/8
	17085207	11/32	.120	38°	27°	—	.025	①	38°	7/8
	17085218	11/32	.120	20°	27°	—	.025	①	38°	7/8
	17085282	11/32	.120	14°	25°	43°	.025	①	35°	1/2
	17085502	7/16	.120	20°	26°	36°	.025	①	39°	7/8
	17085503	7/16	.120	20°	26°	36°	.025	①	39°	7/8
	17085506	7/16	.120	20°	27°	36°	.025	①	36°	1
	17085508	7/16	.120	20°	27°	36°	.025	①	36°	1
	17085524	7/16	.120	20°	25°	36°	.025	①	36°	1
	17085526	7/16	.120	20°	25°	36°	.025	①	36°	1
	17085554	7/16	.120	14°	27°	41°	.025	①	35°	1/2
1986-87	17085502	7/16	.120	20°	26°	36°	.025	①	39°	7/8
	17085503	7/16	.120	20°	26°	36°	.025	①	39°	7/8
	17085506	7/16	.120	20°	27°	36°	.025	①	36°	1
	17085508	7/16	.120	20°	27°	36°	.025	①	36°	1
	17085524	7/16	.120	20°	25°	36°	.025	①	36°	1
	17085526	7/16	.120	20°	25°	36°	.025	①	36°	1
	17086003	11/32	.120	20°	27°	—	.025	①	38°	7/8
	17086004	11/32	.120	20°	27°	—	.025	①	38°	7/8
	17086005	11/32	.120	38°	27°	—	.025	①	38°	7/8
	17086006	11/32	.120	20°	27°	—	.025	①	38°	7/8
	17086008	11/32	.120	14°	25°	43°	.025	①	38°	7/8
	17086009	7/16	.120	14°	25°	43°	.025	①	35°	1/2
	17086040	11/32	.120	20°	27°	—	.025	①	38°	7/8
	17086077	11/32	.120	14°	25°	43°	.025	①	35°	1/2
	17086190	5/16	.120	18°	28°	24°	—	①	32°	—

①—Tamper-resistant.

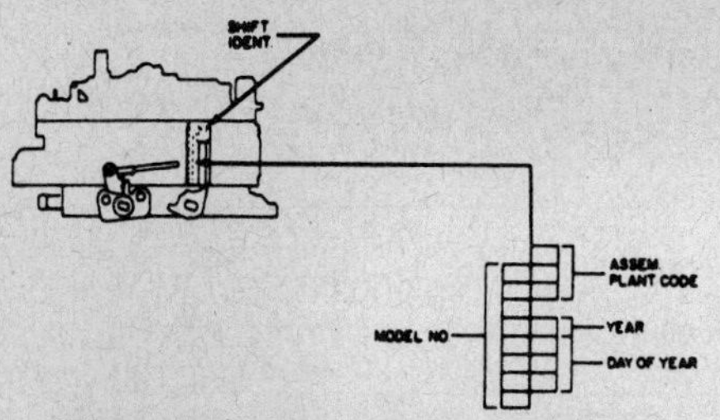

Fig. 1 Rochester E4M & M4M series identification number location

IDENTIFICATION LOCATION

The carburetor identification number is a vertically stamped 8 digit number. The number can be found on the left rear corner of the float bowl casting, adjacent to the secondary pickup lever, **Fig. 1.**

DESCRIPTION

The M4M Series (M4MC and M4ME) Quadrajet carburetor, **Fig. 2**, are two stage, downdraft carburetors.

The primary side of the carburetor has six systems of operation: float, idle, main metering, power, pump and choke. The secondary side has one metering system which supplements the primary main metering system and receives fuel from a common float chamber.

An Adjustable Part Throttle (A.P.T.) feature incorporates an adjustable metering rod assembly operating in a fixed jet. On some models, a barometric pressure-sensitive aneroid (Bellows) is an integral part of the A.P.T. metering rod assembly. This provides a close tolerance control of fuel flow to the main metering system, thereby controlling air/fuel ratios during part throttle operation.

Some units use a multiple stage power enrichment system with two power pistons. One piston is an auxiliary power piston with a single metering rod operating in a fixed jet. The primary power piston with two metering rods operates in replaceable metering jets. This system provides sensitive control of the air/fuel ratio during light engine power requirements while providing richer mixtures during moderate to heavy engine loads.

All units use a bowl mounted choke housing with a thermostatic coil assembly. Also, a dual vacuum break system is used to improve cold engine warm-up and drive-away performance. Cadillac units use a three stage electric choke with a ceramic resistor for precise timing of the choke valve opening to improve engine warm-up performance.

The E4M series (E4MC and E4ME) carburetors are used on vehicles equipped with the C3 (Computer Control Command) System, **Fig. 3.** An electrically operated mixture control solenoid is mounted in the float bowl and is used to control air and fuel metering to idle and main metering systems of the carburetor. Fuel metering is controlled by two special stepped primary metering rods, operating in removable jets and positioned by a plunger in the solenoid which is controlled by an electrical signal from the Electronic Control Module. Air metering to the idle system is controlled by an idle air bleed valve located in the air horn, which follows movement of the mixture control solenoid plunger to control the amount of bleed air into the idle system. A throttle position sensor mounted in the float bowl, is used to electrically signal the Electronic Control module of various throttle position changes.

On some 1982-84 units, an Idle Speed Control (ISC) mounted on the float bowl is used to control idle speed. On these units, the curb idle speed is programmed into the Electronic Control Module and no attempt should be made to adjust idle speed. On some 1982-87 models an Idle Load Compensator (ILC) mounted on the float bowl is used to control idle speed. The compensator uses manifold vacuum to sense changes in engine load and compensates by adjusting curb idle speed. This unit should not be adjusted, unless if during diagnosis, curb idle speed is not within specifications.

On 1982-84 air conditioned models, not equipped with ISC or ILC and all 1985-87 models not equipped with ILC, an Idle Speed Solenoid (ISS), mounted on the float bowl, is used to control engine curb idle speed. On 1982-84 models, the ISS is energized whenever the A/C compressor is engaged. On 1985-87 models, the ISS is actuated by a relay that is controlled by the ECM during two different modes of operation:

a. On models equipped with A/C, the ISS plunger will extend when the A/C switch is On to maintain curb idle speed.
b. On all models, the ISS plunger will extend during certain deceleration modes (above 40 mph) to maintain emissions.

On all models, the ISS is adjustable.

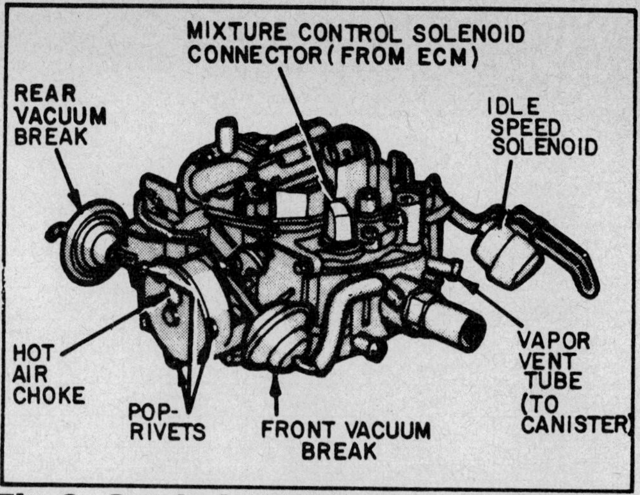

Fig. 2 Quadrajet M4M series carburetor (Typical)

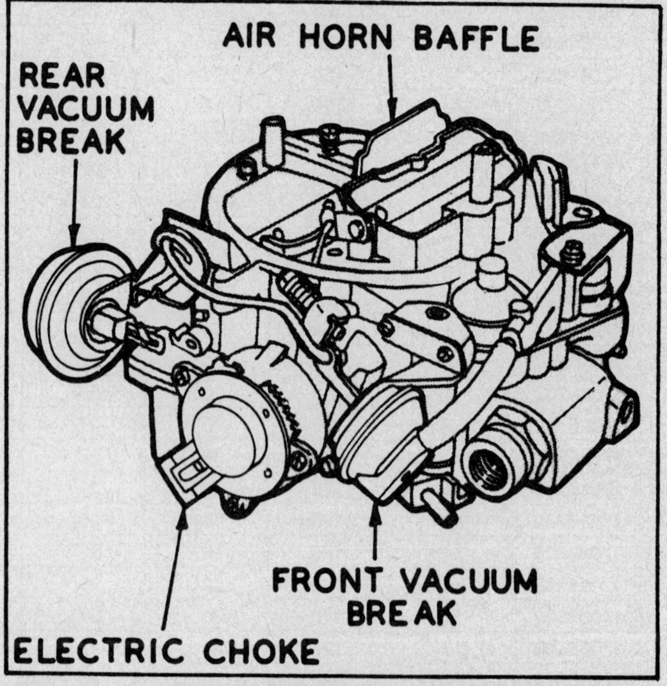

Fig. 3 Quadrajet E4M series carburetor (Typical)

1. REMOVE AIR HORN, GASKET, POWER PISTON AND METERING ROD ASSEMBLY, AND FLOAT BOWL INSERT.
2. ATTACH J-34817-1 OR BT-8227A-1 TO FLOAT BOWL.
3. PLACE J-34817-3 OR BT-8227A IN BASE WITH CONTACT PIN RESTING ON OUTER EDGE OF FLOAT LEVER.
4. MEASURE DISTANCE FROM TOP OF CASTING TO TOP OF FLOAT, AT POINT 3/16" FROM LARGE END OF FLOAT. USE J-9789-90 OR BT-8037.
5. IF MORE THAN ±2/32" FROM SPECIFICATION, USE J-34817-25 OR BT-8427 TO BEND LEVER UP OR DOWN. REMOVE BENDING TOOL AND MEASURE, REPEATING UNTIL WITHIN SPECIFICATION.
6. CHECK FLOAT ALIGNMENT.
7. REASSEMBLE CARBURETOR.

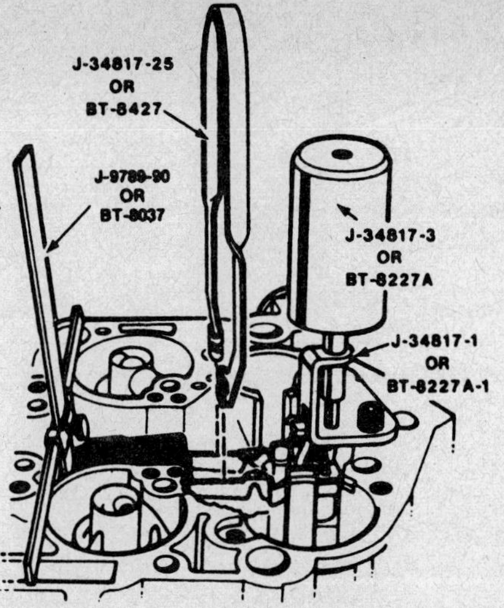
J-34817-25
OR
BT-8427
J-9789-90
OR
BT-8037
J-34817-3
OR
BT-8227A
J-34817-1
OR
BT-8227A-1

Fig. 4 Float level adjustment. MEM series

1. REMOVE AIR HORN & GASKET.
2. REMOVE SOLENOID PLUNGER, METERING RODS, FLOAT BOWL INSERT. IF NECESSARY TO REMOVE SOLENOID (LEAN MIXTURE) ADJUSTING SCREW, COUNT AND MAKE RECORD OF NUMBER OF TURNS IT TAKES TO LIGHTLY BOTTOM SCREW, USING J-28696-10 OR BT-7928. (RETURN TO EXACT POSITION WHEN REASSEMBLING.)
3. ATTACH J-34817-1 OR BT-8227A-1 TO FLOAT BOWL.
4. PLACE J-34817-3 OR BT-8227A IN BASE WITH CONTACT PIN RESTING ON OUTER EDGE OF FLOAT LEVER.
5. MEASURE DISTANCE FROM TOP OF CASTING TO TOP OF FLOAT, AT POINT 3/16" FROM LARGE END OF FLOAT. USE J-9789-90 OR BT-8037.
6. IF MORE THAN ±2/32" FROM SPECIFICATION, USE J-34817-15 OR BT-8233 TO BEND LEVER UP OR DOWN. REMOVE BENDING TOOL AND MEASURE, REPEATING UNTIL WITHIN SPECIFICATION.
7. CHECK FLOAT ALIGNMENT.
8. REASSEMBLE CARBURETOR.

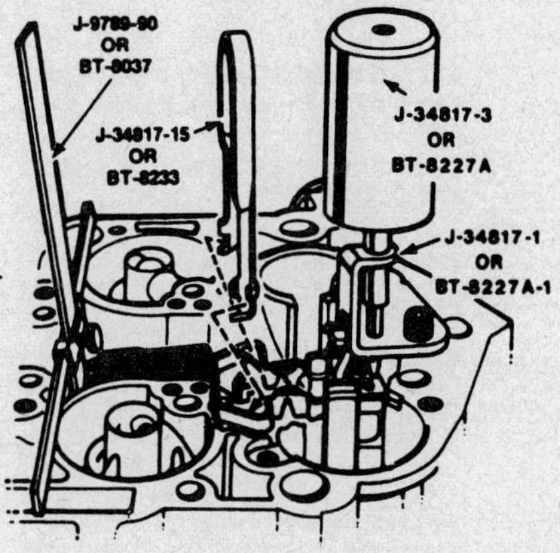
J-9789-90
OR
BT-8037
J-34817-15
OR
BT-8233
J-34817-3
OR
BT-8227A
J-34817-1
OR
BT-8227A-1

Fig. 5 Float level adjustment. E4M

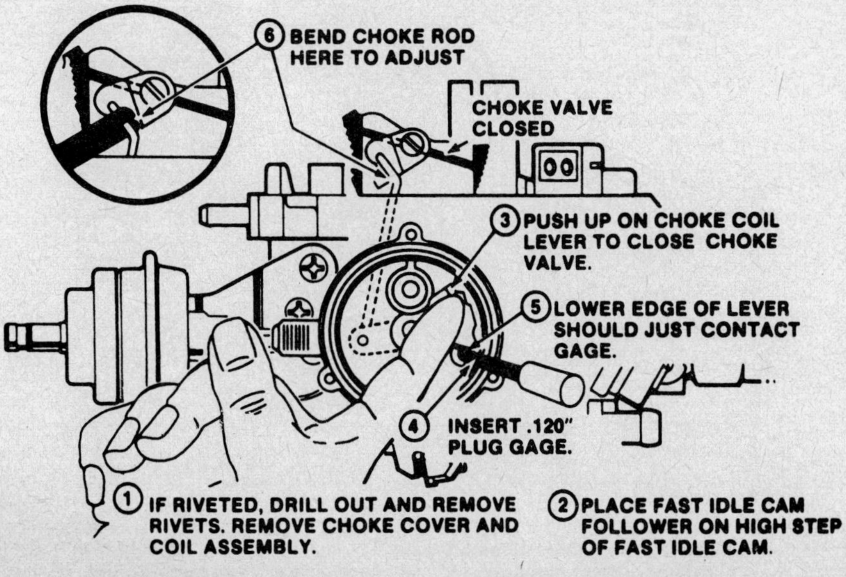
6 BEND CHOKE ROD HERE TO ADJUST
CHOKE VALVE CLOSED
3 PUSH UP ON CHOKE COIL LEVER TO CLOSE CHOKE VALVE.
5 LOWER EDGE OF LEVER SHOULD JUST CONTACT GAGE.
4 INSERT .120" PLUG GAGE.
1 IF RIVETED, DRILL OUT AND REMOVE RIVETS. REMOVE CHOKE COVER AND COIL ASSEMBLY.
2 PLACE FAST IDLE CAM FOLLOWER ON HIGH STEP OF FAST IDLE CAM.

Fig. 6 Choke coil lever adjustment

ON-VEHICLE ADJUSTMENTS

The choke cover is retained to the choke housing by three pop rivets. With float bowl and throttle body properly supported, carefully align a No. 21 drill on pop rivet head. Drill only enough to remove the rivet heads, then using a small hammer and drift, drive remainder of rivet from choke housing. A service kit is available for choke cover installation. The choke cover should be removed only during major carburetor overhaul or if the choke coil is damaged.

CURB IDLE SPEED ADJUSTMENT

E4M UNITS

On carburetors equipped with an Idle Speed Control (ISC) motor or an Idle Load Compensator (ILC), idle speed is not adjustable. If the ISC or ILC is found defective, a new one can be installed and must be adjusted to specifications. This procedure applies to carburetors without an ISC or ILC.

Make all adjustments with engine at normal operating temperature, choke fully open, air cleaner installed and A/C off, if equipped, except where noted.

1. Disconnect and plug vacuum hoses as directed on vehicle emissions label.
2. Check and, if necessary, adjust ignition timing to specifications.
3. On vehicles less A/C, turn idle speed screw inward or outward until specified idle speed is obtained.
4. On models equipped with A/C, proceed as follows:
   a. Turn idle speed screw inward or outward until specified RPM (base idle) is obtained.
   b. With transmission in Drive (manual transmission in Neutral), disconnect A/C compressor electrical connector and switch A/C control to On position.
   c. Open throttle and allow A/C solenoid plunger to fully extend.
   d. Turn solenoid adjusting screw inward or outward until specified RPM (solenoid energized) is obtained.
   e. Reconnect compressor electrical connector.

M4M UNITS

Check and, if necessary, adjust ignition timing before adjusting curb idle speed.

Make all adjustments with engine at normal operating temperature, choke fully open, air cleaner installed and A/C system, if equipped, off, except where noted.

1. Disconnect and plug vacuum hoses as directed on emission control label.
2. On vehicles less idle solenoid, adjust idle speed screw in or out to obtain specified curb idle speed.
3. On vehicles equipped with idle solenoid, open throttle slightly to allow solenoid plunger to extend, then adjust solenoid screw to obtain specified curb idle speed. Disconnect solenoid electrical lead, then adjust idle speed

screw in or out to obtain specified slow idle speed.

4. On vehicles equipped with A/C, turn idle speed screw in or out to obtain specified curb idle speed with A/C control off. Disconnect electrical lead from A/C compressor, then turn A/C switch on. With transmission in Drive (manual transmission in Neutral), open throttle and allow solenoid plunger to fully extend, then adjust solenoid screw to obtain specified speed. Reconnect compressor electrical connector.

FAST IDLE SPEED ADJUSTMENT

Check and, if necessary, adjust ignition timing before adjusting fast idle speed.

Make all adjustments with engine at normal operating temperature, choke fully open, air cleaner installed and A/C control Off, if equipped.

1. Disconnect and plug vacuum hoses as directed on vehicle emissions label.
2. Position fast idle speed screw on specified step of fast idle cam as directed on emissions label, then start engine.
3. Turn fast idle screw inward or outward and adjust fast idle speed to specifications.

FLOAT LEVEL ADJUSTMENT

M4M Units

Refer to **Fig. 4** for float adjustment procedure. Adjust as directed to dimension listed in Adjustment Specifications.

E4M Units

Refer to **Fig. 5** for float adjustment procedure. Adjust as directed to dimension listed in Adjustment Specifications.

CHOKE COIL LEVER ADJUSTMENT

Refer to **Fig. 6** for choke coil lever adjustment procedure. Adjust as directed to dimension listed in Adjustment Specifications.

CHOKE ROD ADJUSTMENT

Install carburetor angle gauge tool No. J-26701 or BT-7704 as shown in **Fig. 7**.

With gauge installed, adjust choke rod as outlined in **Fig. 8.** Adjust as directed to dimension listed in Adjustment Specifications.

VACUUM BREAKS ADJUSTMENT

Prior to adjusting vacuum breaks, refer to **Fig. 9** for air bleed hole blocking procedures.

Front Unit

Install carburetor angle gauge tool No. J-26701 or BT-7704 as shown in **Fig. 7**.

With gauge installed, adjust vacuum break as outlined in **Fig. 10.** Adjust as directed to dimension listed in Adjustment Specifications.

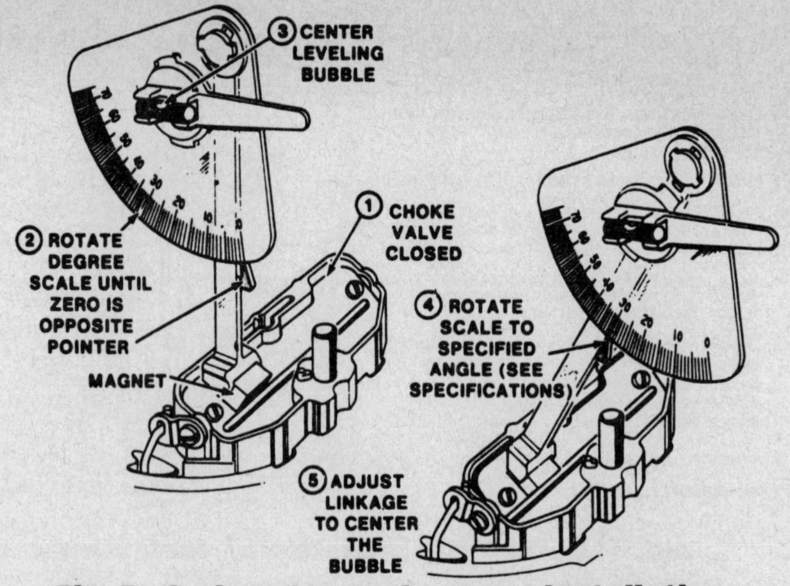

Fig. 7 Carburetor angle gauge installation

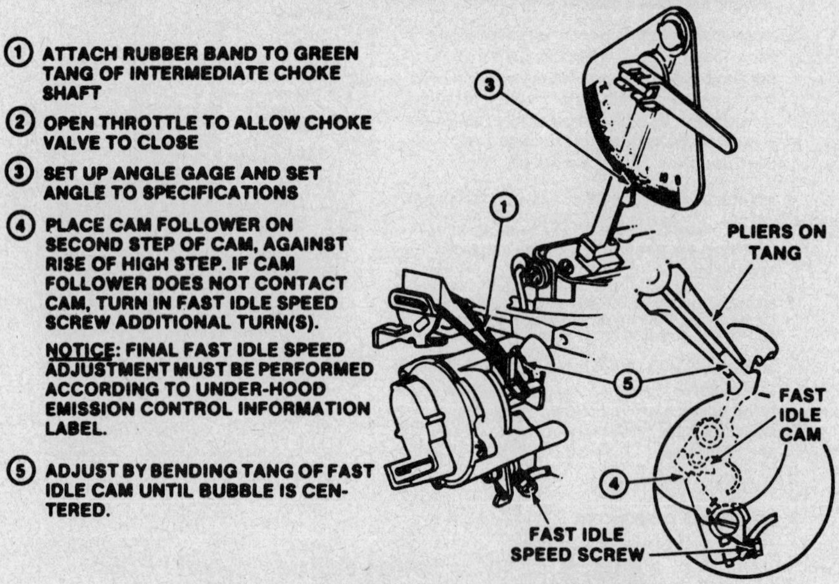
① ATTACH RUBBER BAND TO GREEN TANG OF INTERMEDIATE CHOKE SHAFT
② OPEN THROTTLE TO ALLOW CHOKE VALVE TO CLOSE
③ SET UP ANGLE GAGE AND SET ANGLE TO SPECIFICATIONS
④ PLACE CAM FOLLOWER ON SECOND STEP OF CAM, AGAINST RISE OF HIGH STEP. IF CAM FOLLOWER DOES NOT CONTACT CAM, TURN IN FAST IDLE SPEED SCREW ADDITIONAL TURN(S).
NOTICE: FINAL FAST IDLE SPEED ADJUSTMENT MUST BE PERFORMED ACCORDING TO UNDER-HOOD EMISSION CONTROL INFORMATION LABEL.
⑤ ADJUST BY BENDING TANG OF FAST IDLE CAM UNTIL BUBBLE IS CENTERED.
PLIERS ON TANG
FAST IDLE CAM
FAST IDLE SPEED SCREW

Fig. 8 Choke rod adjustment

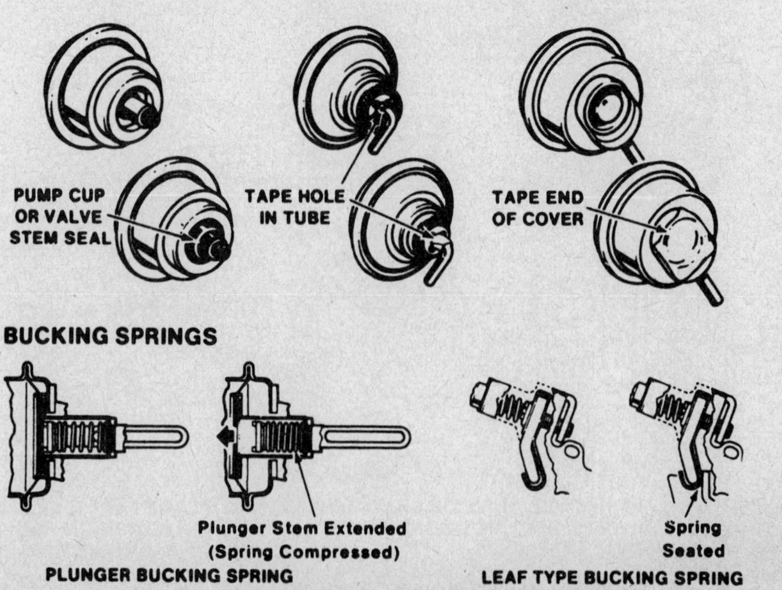
PUMP CUP OR VALVE STEM SEAL
TAPE HOLE IN TUBE
TAPE END OF COVER
BUCKING SPRINGS
Plunger Stem Extended (Spring Compressed)
PLUNGER BUCKING SPRING
Spring Seated
LEAF TYPE BUCKING SPRING

Fig. 9 Blocking air bleed holes

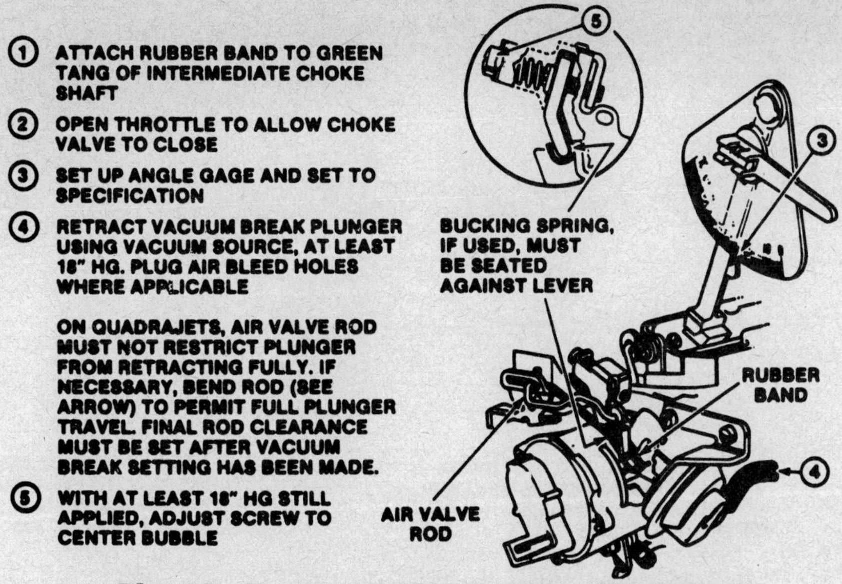

1 ATTACH RUBBER BAND TO GREEN TANG OF INTERMEDIATE CHOKE SHAFT
2 OPEN THROTTLE TO ALLOW CHOKE VALVE TO CLOSE
3 SET UP ANGLE GAGE AND SET TO SPECIFICATION
4 RETRACT VACUUM BREAK PLUNGER USING VACUUM SOURCE, AT LEAST 18" HG. PLUG AIR BLEED HOLES WHERE APPLICABLE
ON QUADRAJETS, AIR VALVE ROD MUST NOT RESTRICT PLUNGER FROM RETRACTING FULLY. IF NECESSARY, BEND ROD (SEE ARROW) TO PERMIT FULL PLUNGER TRAVEL. FINAL ROD CLEARANCE MUST BE SET AFTER VACUUM BREAK SETTING HAS BEEN MADE.
5 WITH AT LEAST 18" HG STILL APPLIED, ADJUST SCREW TO CENTER BUBBLE
BUCKING SPRING, IF USED, MUST BE SEATED AGAINST LEVER
RUBBER BAND
AIR VALVE ROD
5
3
4

Fig. 10 Front vacuum break adjustment

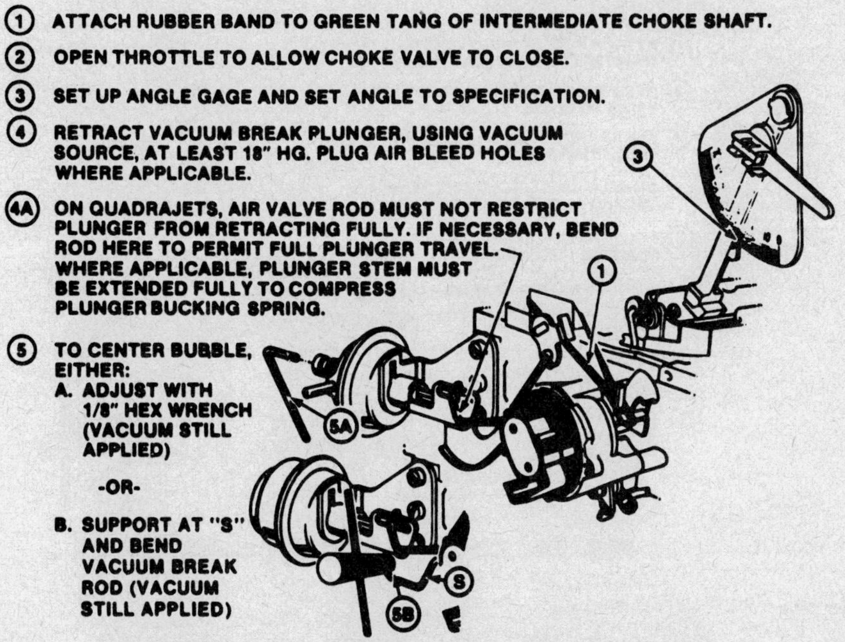

1 ATTACH RUBBER BAND TO GREEN TANG OF INTERMEDIATE CHOKE SHAFT.
2 OPEN THROTTLE TO ALLOW CHOKE VALVE TO CLOSE.
3 SET UP ANGLE GAGE AND SET ANGLE TO SPECIFICATION.
4 RETRACT VACUUM BREAK PLUNGER, USING VACUUM SOURCE, AT LEAST 18" HG. PLUG AIR BLEED HOLES WHERE APPLICABLE.
4A ON QUADRAJETS, AIR VALVE ROD MUST NOT RESTRICT PLUNGER FROM RETRACTING FULLY. IF NECESSARY, BEND ROD HERE TO PERMIT FULL PLUNGER TRAVEL. WHERE APPLICABLE, PLUNGER STEM MUST BE EXTENDED FULLY TO COMPRESS PLUNGER BUCKING SPRING.
5 TO CENTER BUBBLE, EITHER:
A. ADJUST WITH 1/8" HEX WRENCH (VACUUM STILL APPLIED)
-OR-
B. SUPPORT AT "S" AND BEND VACUUM BREAK ROD (VACUUM STILL APPLIED)
3
1
5A
S
5B

Fig. 11 Rear vacuum break adjustment

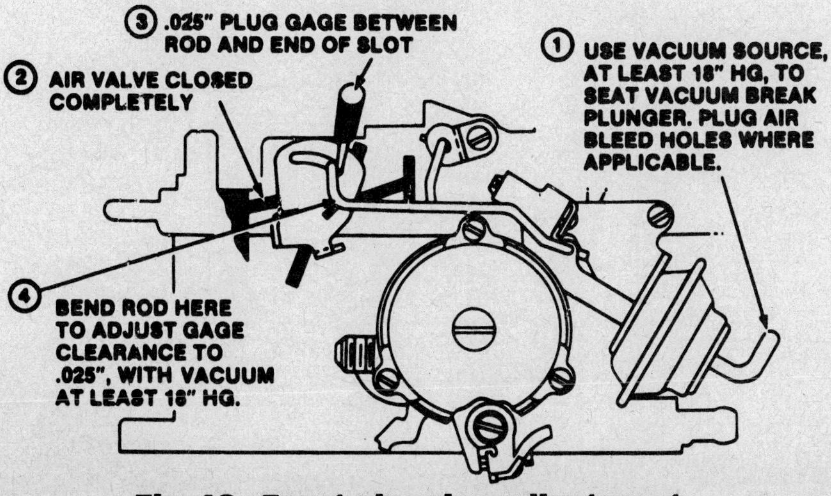

2 AIR VALVE CLOSED COMPLETELY
4 BEND ROD HERE TO ADJUST GAGE CLEARANCE TO .025", WITH VACUUM AT LEAST 18" HG.

Fig. 12 Front air valve adjustment

Rear Unit

Install carburetor angle gauge tool No. J-26701 or BT-7704 as shown in **Fig. 7.**

With gauge installed, adjust vacuum break as outlined in **Fig. 11.** Adjust as directed to dimension listed in Adjustment Specifications.

AIR VALVE DASH POT ADJUSTMENT

Refer to **Figs. 12 and 13** for air valve dash pot adjustments. Adjust as directed to dimension listed in Adjustment Specifications.

CHOKE UNLOADER ADJUSTMENT

Refer to **Fig. 14** for choke unloader adjustments. Adjust as directed to dimension listed in Adjustment Specifications.

SECONDARY THROTTLE VALVE LOCKOUT ADJUSTMENT

Refer to **Fig. 15** for secondary throttle valve adjustment.

SECONDARY THROTTLE VALVES ADJUSTMENT

1982 UNITS

Throttle Closing

With curb idle speed set, hold choke valve open with cam follower lever off fast idle cam steps, **Fig. 16.** Measure clearance between forward edge of slot in the secondary throttle valve pickup lever and the secondary actuating rod. Clearance should be .020 inch. To adjust, bend secondary closing tang on primary throttle lever.

Throttle Opening

Open primary throttle lever until link lightly contacts secondary lever tang, **Fig. 17.** The bottom end of the link should be in the center of the slot in secondary lever. To adjust, bend tang on secondary lever.

AIR VALVE SPRING WIND-UP ADJUSTMENT

Refer to **Fig. 18** for air valve spring wind-up adjustment. Adjust as directed to dimension listed in Adjustment Specifications.

IDLE LOAD COMPENSATOR (ILC) ADJUSTMENT

1. Remove air cleaner and plug related vacuum fittings. Disconnect and plug vacuum hoses at canister purge port, EGR valve and ILC unit.
2. Turn throttle stop screw counterclockwise 3 turns.
3. Start engine and place transmission in drive (manual transmission in neutral).
4. With ILC plunger fully extended (vacuum hose disconnected), adjust plunger with tool J-29607, or equivalent, to obtain 725 RPM. **Jam nut on plunger must be held with a suitable tool to prevent damage to guide tabs.**

5. Reconnect vacuum hose to ILC while observing tachometer. If idle speed is within specifications, proceed to step 12.
6. If idle speed is not within specifications, remove ILC from carburetor.
7. Remove rubber plug from ILC center outlet tube, **Fig. 19**, then remove metal plug from outlet tube.
8. Reinstall ILC unit. Install a spare rubber cap over outlet tube with a hole punched to accept a 3/32 inch Allen wrench.
9. Insert Allen wrench through spare cap, start engine and place transmission in drive.
10. Adjust ILC as needed to obtain 500 RPM, then remove wrench and install a new cap over center outlet tube. **Turning ILC adjusting screw changes engine speed 75-100 RPM for each complete turn. Turning screw clockwise decreases engine speed; turning screw counterclockwise raises engine speed.**
11. If idle speed is not within specifications, repeat steps 8-10.
12. After adjusting ILC plunger, measure distance between jam nut and tip of plunger. Distance must not exceed 1 inch.
13. Disconnect and plug vacuum hose to ILC plunger and connect an external vacuum source to fitting on ILC.
14. Retract ILC plunger with external vacuum source, then adjust idle speed to 500 RPM in Drive with throttle stop screw.
15. Stop engine and remove external vacuum source. Reconnect vacuum hoses to proper fittings and install air cleaner.

IDLE SPEED CONTROL (ISC) ADJUSTMENT

Do not use ISC plunger to adjust curb idle speed, as idle speed is controlled by the Electronic Control Module (ECM).

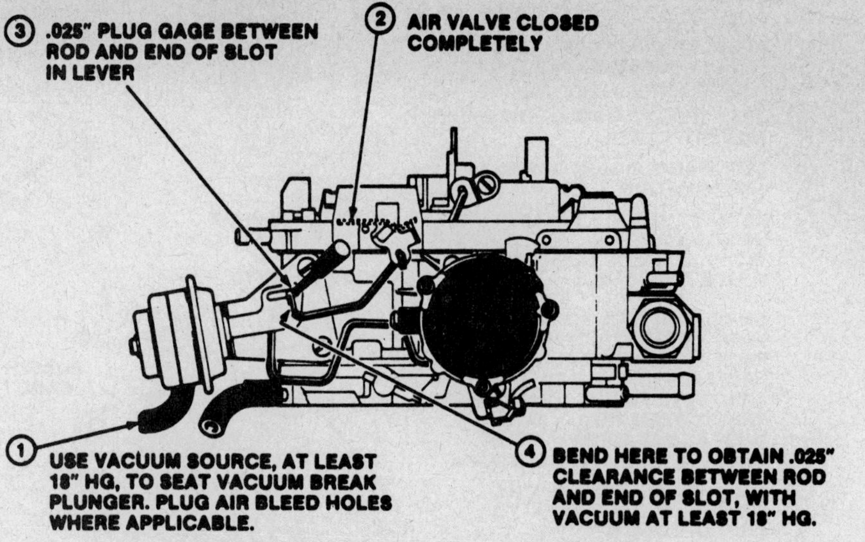

② AIR VALVE CLOSED COMPLETELY

Fig. 13 Rear air valve adjustment

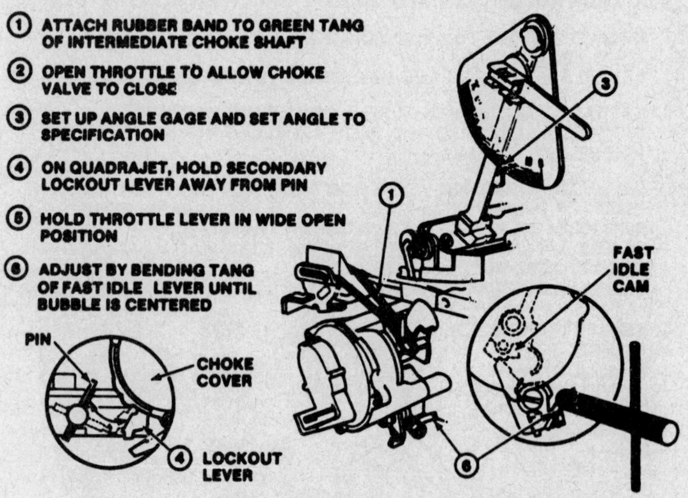

① ATTACH RUBBER BAND TO GREEN TANG OF INTERMEDIATE CHOKE SHAFT
② OPEN THROTTLE TO ALLOW CHOKE VALVE TO CLOSE
③ SET UP ANGLE GAGE AND SET ANGLE TO SPECIFICATION
④ ON QUADRAJET, HOLD SECONDARY LOCKOUT LEVER AWAY FROM PIN
⑤ HOLD THROTTLE LEVER IN WIDE OPEN POSITION
⑥ ADJUST BY BENDING TANG OF FAST IDLE LEVER UNTIL BUBBLE IS CENTERED
PIN
CHOKE COVER
LOCKOUT LEVER
BEND PIN TO ADJUST
.015 MAX. CLEARANCE
FAST IDLE CAM

Fig. 14 Choke unloader adjustment

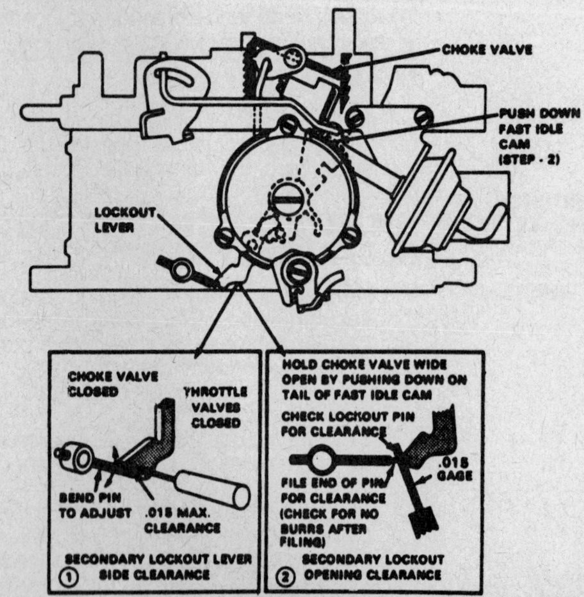

CHECK LOCKOUT PIN FOR CLEARANCE

FILE END OF PIN FOR CLEARANCE (CHECK FOR NO BURRS AFTER FILING)

Fig. 15 Secondary throttle valve lockout adjustment

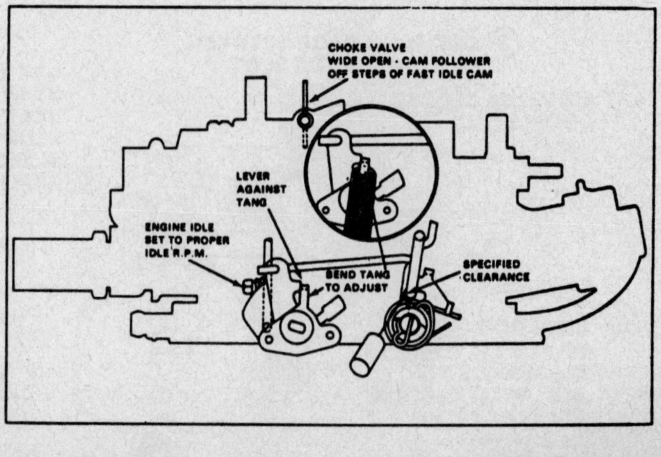

LEVER AGAINST TANG
ENGINE IDLE SET TO PROPER IDLE R.P.M.

Fig. 16 Secondary throttle valve closing adjustment. 1981–82 units

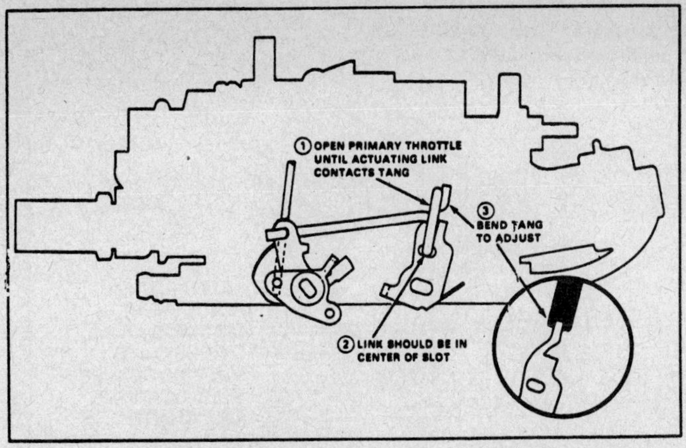
① OPEN PRIMARY THROTTLE UNTIL ACTUATING LINK CONTACTS TANG
③ BEND TANG TO ADJUST
② LINK SHOULD BE IN CENTER OF SLOT

Fig. 17 Secondary throttle valve opening adjustment. 1981–82 units

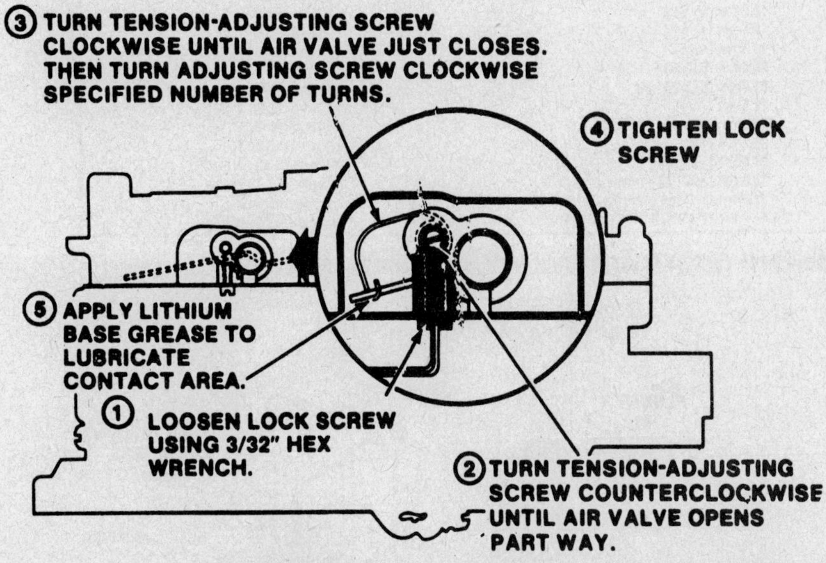
③ TURN TENSION-ADJUSTING SCREW CLOCKWISE UNTIL AIR VALVE JUST CLOSES. THEN TURN ADJUSTING SCREW CLOCKWISE SPECIFIED NUMBER OF TURNS.
④ TIGHTEN LOCK SCREW
⑤ APPLY LITHIUM BASE GREASE TO LUBRICATE CONTACT AREA.
① LOOSEN LOCK SCREW USING 3/32" HEX WRENCH.
② TURN TENSION-ADJUSTING SCREW COUNTERCLOCKWISE UNTIL AIR VALVE OPENS PART WAY.

Fig. 18 Quadrajet E4M & M4M series air-valve spring windup adjustment

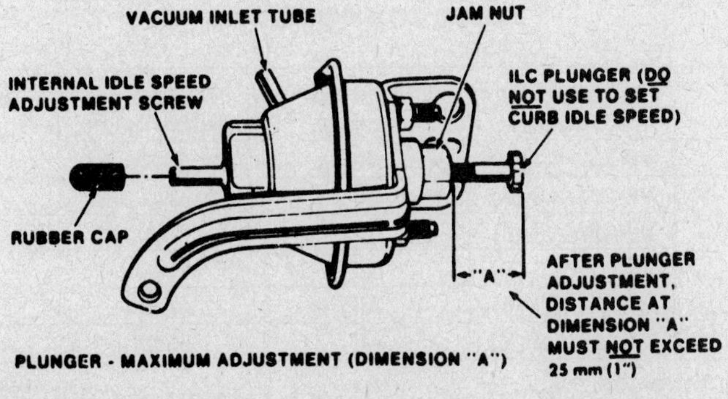
VACUUM INLET TUBE
JAM NUT
INTERNAL IDLE SPEED ADJUSTMENT SCREW
ILC PLUNGER (DO NOT USE TO SET CURB IDLE SPEED)
RUBBER CAP
"A"
AFTER PLUNGER ADJUSTMENT, DISTANCE AT DIMENSION "A" MUST NOT EXCEED 25 mm (1")
PLUNGER - MAXIMUM ADJUSTMENT (DIMENSION "A")

Fig. 19 Idle Load Compensator (ILC) assembly

When a new ISC is installed, a base (minimum authority) and a high (maximum authority) RPM check must be made, and adjustments performed as needed. When making low and high speed adjustments, low speed adjustment must be performed first.

Preliminary Check

1. Check for an identification letter on ISC plunger, **Fig. 20.** If a letter appears, proceed to "Adjustment Procedure."
2. If no letter appears, remove plunger using tool J-29607 or equivalent, and measure distance from back of plunger head to end of plunger (dimension "A"), **Fig. 20.** Record dimension for use in step 11 of "Adjustment Procedure."
3. Reinstall plunger, turning plunger in to a preset dimension that is less than dimension "B," **Fig. 20.**

Adjustment Procedure

1. Connect dwell meter to test lead in MC solenoid harness (usually a green wire) and set meter on 6 cylinder scale. Connect tachometer to engine following manufacturer's instructions.
2. Start engine and run at fast idle until it reaches normal operating temperature and dwell reading begins to fluctuate.
3. Stop engine and disconnect wiring harness connector to ISC motor. **Do not connect or disconnect wiring harness connector to ILC motor with ignition in on position, as ECM will be damaged.**
4. Using a jumper wire, connect battery voltage to terminal "C" on ISC motor, **Fig. 21,** then connect a jumper wire between terminal "D" and ground. **Do not leave battery voltage connected to ISC motor longer than necessary to retract solenoid plunger. Do not connect battery voltage to terminals "A" or "B" on motor. ISC motor will be damaged if connections are improperly made.**
5. Start engine and run until dwell reading begins to fluctuate. Place transmission in drive (manual transmission in neutral).
6. With ISC plunger fully retracted, adjust idle speed to specified minimum authority RPM, **Fig. 22,** with throttle stop screw.
7. Place transmission in neutral and reverse jumper wire connections. Connect battery voltage to terminal "D", and connect terminal "C" to ground. **Leave jumper wires connected only long enough to fully extend ISC plunger.**
8. With plunger fully extended, adjust idle speed to specified maximum authority RPM (manual transmission), **Fig. 22,** or 1500 RPM (automatic transmission), by turning ISC plunger with tool J-29607 or equivalent.
9. Place automatic transmission in drive and adjust idle speed to specified maximum authority RPM with ISC plunger. **Adjustments must be made as quickly as possible. If en-**

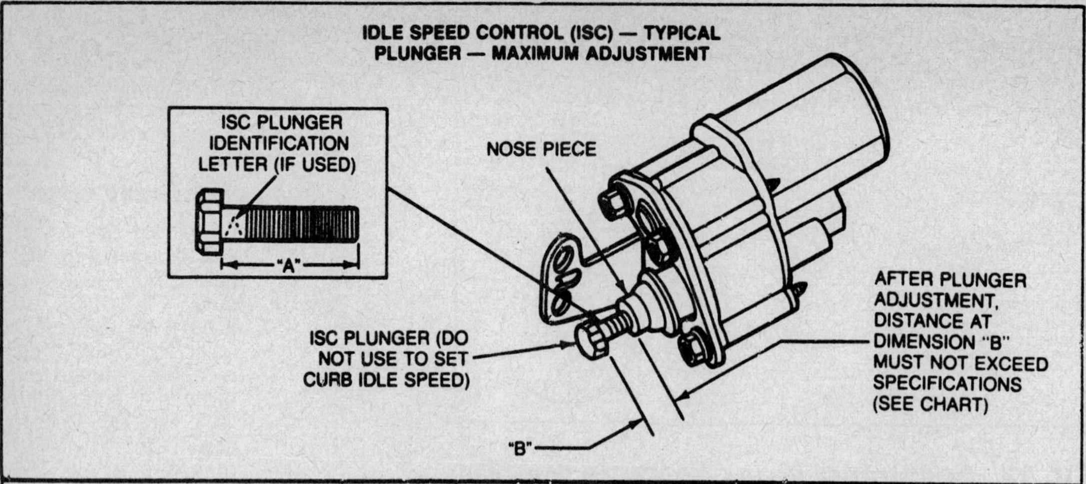

IDLE SPEED CONTROL PLUNGER

Identification Letter	Plunger Length Dimension A	After Adjustment, Distance At Dimension "B" Must NOT Exceed:
NONE	14.1mm (9/16")	5.6mm (7/32")
NONE	16.5mm (41/64")	8.0mm (5/16")
X	18.5mm (47/64")	10.0mm (25/64")
A	19.3mm (49/64")	10.8mm (27/64")
Y	20.5mm (51/64")	12.0mm (15/32")
S	21.2mm (27/32")	12.7mm (1/2")
Z	22.5mm (7/8")	14.0mm (35/64")
G	23.2mm (29/32")	14.7mm (37/64")
E	25.6mm (1")	17.1mm (43/64")
L	27.5mm (1-3/32")	19.0mm (3/4")
J	30.0mm (1-3/16")	21.5mm (27/32")
N	32.0mm (1-17/64")	23.5mm (59/64")
T	34.0mm (1-11/32")	25.5mm (1")

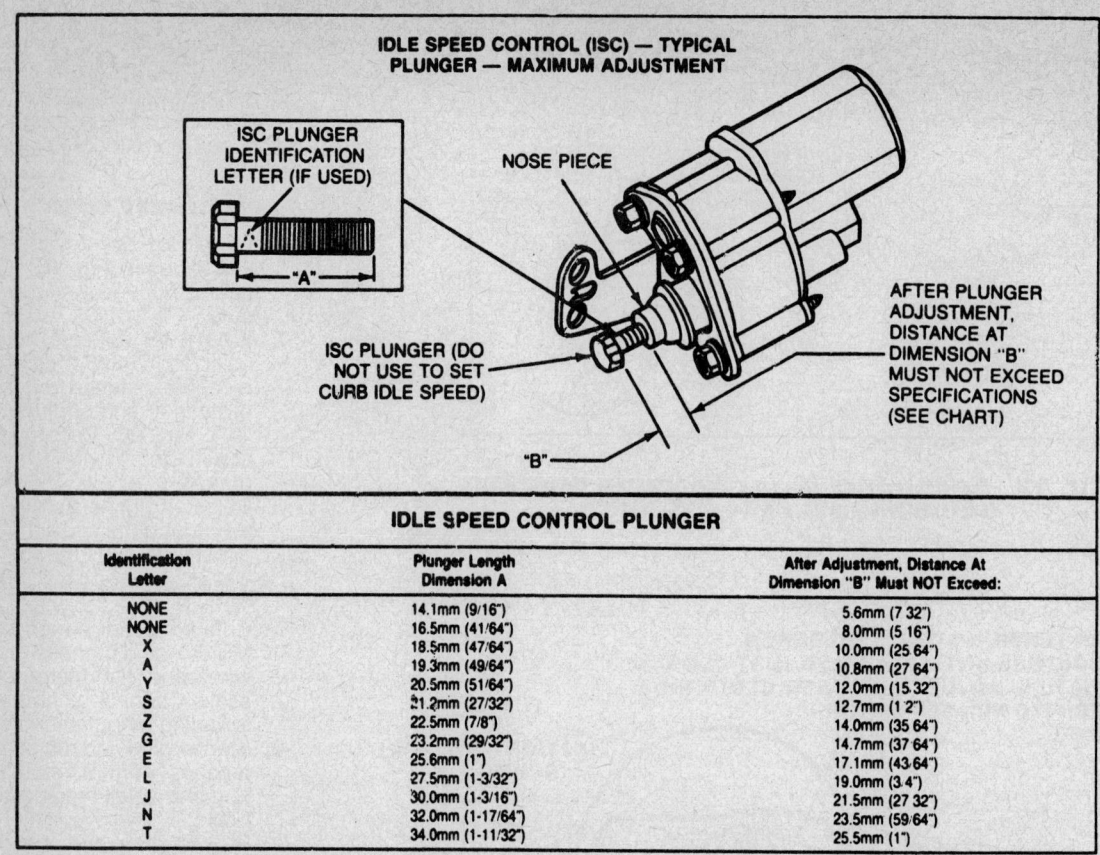

Fig. 20 Idle Speed Control (ISC) plunger adjustment specifications

gine RPM increases, adjustment cannot be performed, engine will have to be stopped and the procedure will have to be restarted from step 2.

10. Reconnect jumper wires as in step 7 and recheck maximum authority RPM. Motor will ratchet at full extension with voltage applied.
11. Remove jumper wires and measure dimension "B", **Fig. 20.** Dimension must not exceed specifications shown in chart.
12. Connect jumper wires to ISC motor, as in step 4, to fully retract ISC plunger, then remove jumper wires.
13. Stop engine. Reconnect wiring harness connector to ISC motor. **Test connections to ISC motor will cause "Check Engine" light to remain on until wiring harness is reconnected to motor. An intermittent trouble code will then be stored in the ECM memory which must be cleared.**

THROTTLE POSITION SENSOR (TPS) ADJUSTMENT

Do not remove plug sealing TPS adjustment or adjust TPS unless carburetor is overhauled or "Computer Command Control (C3)" system diagnosis indicates a problem with the switch.

1. Drill a .078 (5/64) inch hole, 1/16-1/8 inch deep, in plug covering TPS adjustment, **Fig. 23.**

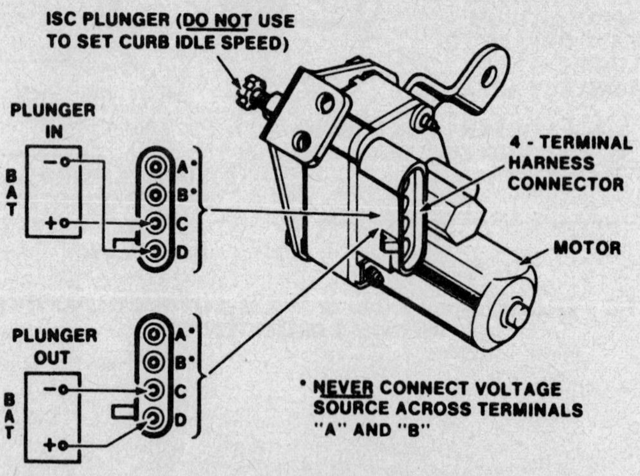

Fig. 21 Idle Speed Control (ISC) motor test connections

Year	Engine (VIN Code)	Carburetor Number	Minimum Authority ①	Maximum Authority ②
1982	V6-252/4.1 (4)	All	470D	900D
1983	V6-231/3.8 (8)	All	450	900
	V6-252/4.1 (4)	All	470	900
	V8-307/5.0 (Y)	All	500D	725
1984	V6-252/4.1 (4)	All	470D	900D
	V6-307/5.0 (Y)	All	500D	725D

①—Plunger retracted.
②—Plunger extended.

Fig. 22 Idle Speed Control (ISC) adjustment specifications

Fig. 23 Throttle Position Sensor (TPS) adjustment screw plug removal

2. Thread a No. 8 sheet metal screw into hole and pry out plug using a suitable lever.
3. Remove TPS adjusting screw using tool J-28696 or equivalent.
4. Leaving electrical connector in place, connect a digital voltmeter between TPS center terminal (B) and bottom terminal (C), using jumper wires if necessary. **Only a digital voltmeter with 10 mega-ohm input impedance or higher can be used. Conventional voltmeters do not have sufficient resistance to obtain accurate readings.**
5. With ignition on, engine stopped and A/C off, install TPS screw and adjust quickly to obtain specified TPS idle voltage, **Fig. 24.**
6. Turn ignition off and install new plug over TPS adjusting screw.

Year	Engine (VIN Code)	Voltage	Throttle Position
1982	V6-231/3.8 (3)	1.28	High step of fast idle cam
	V6-252/4.1 (4)	.97	High step of fast idle cam
	V8-305/5.0 (H)	.51	Stopped at curb idle
	V8-307/5.0 (Y)	.46	Stopped at curb idle
1983	V6-231/3.8 (8) ①	.77	High step of fast idle cam
	V6-252/4.1 (4)	.97	High step of fast idle cam
	V8-305/5.0 (H)	.51	Curb idle
	V8-305/5.0 (G)	.51	Curb idle
	V8-307/5.0 (Y)	.46	ILC retracted
1984	V6-252/4.1 (4)	.57	Minimum authority
	V8-305/5.0 (G)	.48	Curb idle
	V8-305/5.0 (H)	.48	Curb idle
	V8-307/5.0 (Y)	.46	Minimum authority, trans. in drive
1985	V8-305/5.0 (G)	.48	Curb idle
	V8-305/5.0 (H)	.48	Curb idle
	V8-307/5.0 (Y)	.41	ILC retracted, trans. in drive
	V8-307/5.0 (9)	.41	550 RPM (minimum authority) in drive
1986	V8-305/5.0 (G)	.46	Curb idle
	V8-305/5.0 (H)	.46	Curb idle
	V8-307/5.0 (Y)	.41	ILC retracted, trans. in drive
	V8-307/5.0 (9) ②	.46	ILC retracted, trans. in drive
	V8-307/5.0 (9) ③	.41	ILC retracted, trans. in drive

①—Turbocharged.
②—Exc. carb. No. 17086190.
③—Carb. No. 17086190.

Fig. 24 Throttle Position Sensor (TPS) adjustment specifications

Aisin Two Barrel Carburetor

INDEX

ADJUSTMENT SPECIFICATIONS

Year	Float Level	Float Drop	Primary Throttle Valve Opening Angle	Secondary Throttle Valve Opening Inches	Secondary Throttle Valve Kickup Inches	Secondary Touch Inches	Fast Idle Setting Inches	Choke Unloader Inches	Choke Vacuum Break	Pump Stroke Inches
1985-87	③	.0657-.0783	90° ①	.500	.006	.170	.045	.120	②	.151

①—From horizontal plane.
②—With vacuum applied to 1st diaphragm, .095 inch; with vacuum applied to 1st & 2nd diaphragms, .245 inch.
③—1985-86, .283 inch; 1987, .275 inch.

DESCRIPTION

The Aisin two barrel carburetor, used on the Chevrolet Nova is of the downdraft type with a vacuum operated secondary throttle plate.

The carburetor operating circuits consist of the float, primary low speed, secondary low speed, secondary high speed, power enrichment, accelerator and choke.

An Auxiliary Acceleration Pump (AAP) system is used during cold engine operation to supplement the main accelerator pump system. During times of high engine vacuum, the Thermostatic Vacuum Switching Valve (TVSV) is open, allowing intake manifold vacuum to draw the AAP diaphragm inward. As the AAP diaphragm is drawn in, fuel is drawn into the AAP chamber, where it is retained by a check valve. When manifold vacuum drops, the AAP diaphragm is forced inwards, forcing the fuel in the AAP chamber through a check valve and into the accelerator pump nozzle. When the engine warms up, the TVSV is closed, blocking intake manifold vacuum to the AAP.

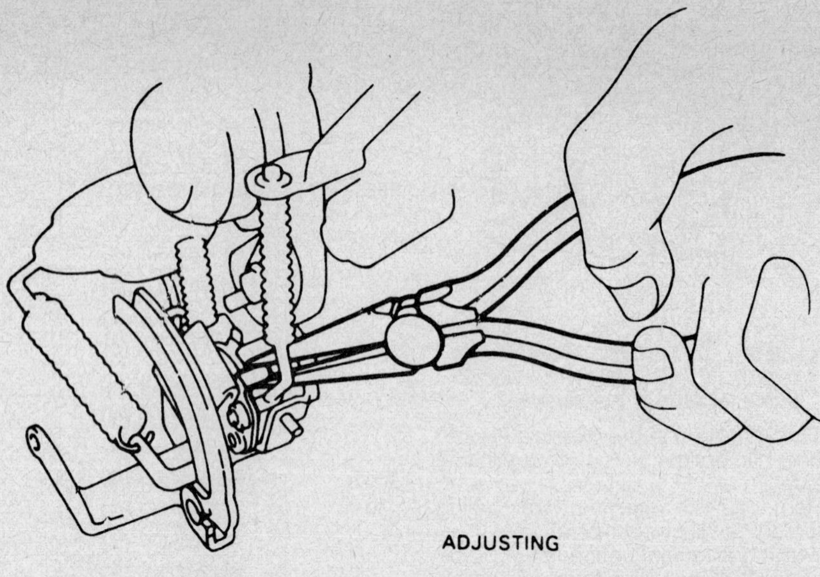

Fig. 1 Adjusting primary throttle valve opening

ON-VEHICLE ADJUSTMENTS

CURB IDLE SPEED ADJUSTMENT

1. Start and idle engine until coolant reaches normal operating temperature.
2. Check and, if necessary, adjust ignition timing.
3. Connect a suitable tachometer to engine according to manufacturer's instructions.
4. Adjust idle speed to specifications by turning idle speed adjusting screw.

FAST IDLE SPEED ADJUSTMENT

1. Remove air cleaner.
2. Plug hot idle compensator hose to prevent rough idling.
3. Disconnect and plug hose from thermal vacuum switch valve M port. This will shut off the choke opener and EGR systems.
4. While holding throttle open slightly, push choke valve closed and hold it closed as you release the throttle.
5. Start engine, but do not depress the accelerator pedal.
6. Set fast idle speed to specifications by fast idle adjusting screw as necessary.

PRIMARY THROTTLE VALVE OPENING ADJUSTMENT

1. While holding throttle fully open, measure primary throttle valve opening angle with suitable carburetor angle gauge.
2. Compare measurement to Adjustment Specifications.
3. If measurement is not within specifications, adjust by bending primary throttle lever stopper, **Fig. 1.**

SECONDARY THROTTLE VALVE OPENING ADJUSTMENT

1. While holding throttle fully open, measure secondary throttle valve-to-bore clearance.
2. Compare measurement to Adjustment Specifications.
3. If measurement is not within specifications, adjust by bending secondary throttle lever stopper, **Fig. 2.**

SECONDARY THROTTLE VALVE KICKUP ADJUSTMENT

1. With primary throttle valve fully open, measure secondary throttle valve-to-bore clearance.
2. Compare measurement to Adjustment Specifications.
3. If measurement is not within specifications, adjust by bending secondary throttle lever, **Fig. 3.**

SECONDARY TOUCH ADJUSTMENT

1. Open throttle to the point where primary kick lever just touches secondary kick lever, then measure primary throttle valve-to-bore clearance.
2. Compare measurement to Adjustment Specifications.
3. If measurement is not within specifications, adjust by bending primary kick lever, **Fig. 4.**

FAST IDLE SETTING

1. Position throttle shaft lever on first step of fast idle cam.
2. With choke valve fully closed, measure primary throttle valve angle-to-bore clearance.
3. Compare measurement to Adjustment Specifications.
4. If measurement is not within specifications, adjust by turning fast idle screw.

CHOKE UNLOADER ADJUSTMENT

1. With primary throttle valve fully open, measure choke valve-to-primary bore clearance.
2. Compare measurement to Adjustment Specifications.
3. If measurement is not within specifications, adjust by bending fast idle lever, **Fig. 5.**

CHOKE VACUUM BREAK ADJUSTMENT

1. Set fast idle cam by applying slight pressure to choke valve while opening throttle. Hold choke plate closed and release throttle.
2. Apply vacuum to 1st vacuum break and measure choke valve-to-primary bore clearance.
3. Compare measurement to Adjustment Specifications.
4. If measurement is not within specifications, adjust by bending relief lever.
5. Apply vacuum to 1st and 2nd vacuum breaks and measure choke valve-to-primary bore clearance.
6. Compare measurements to Adjustment Specifications.
7. If measurement is not within specifications, adjust by turning diaphragm adjusting screw.

PUMP STROKE ADJUSTMENT

1. With choke valve fully open, measure accelerator pump stroke.
2. Compare measurement to Adjustment Specifications.
3. If measurement is outside specifications, adjust by bending pump link.

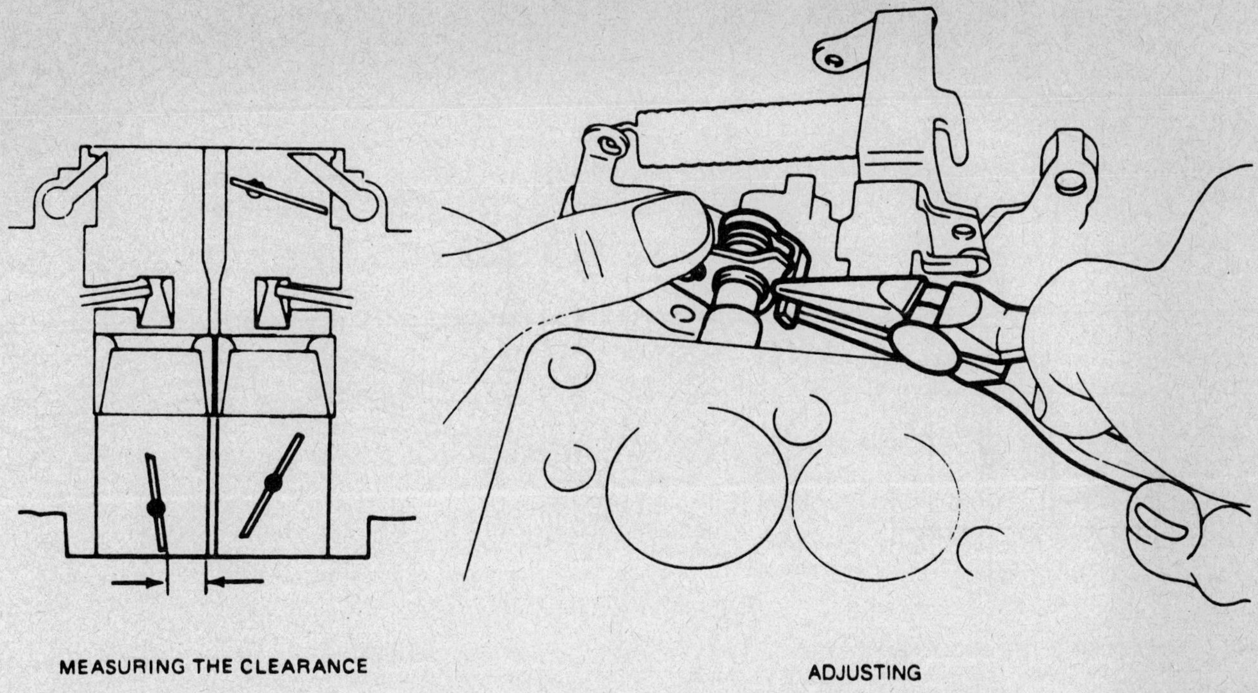

Fig. 2 Adjusting secondary throttle valve opening

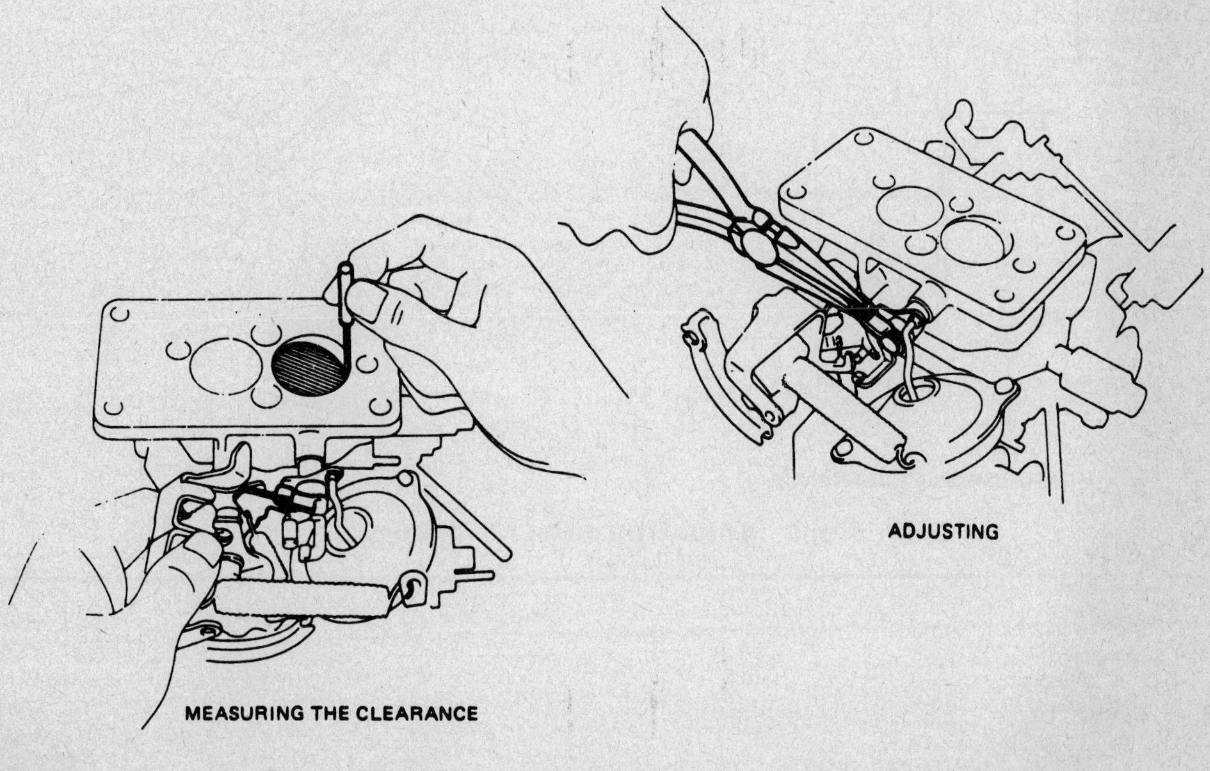

Fig. 3 Adjusting secondary throttle valve kickup

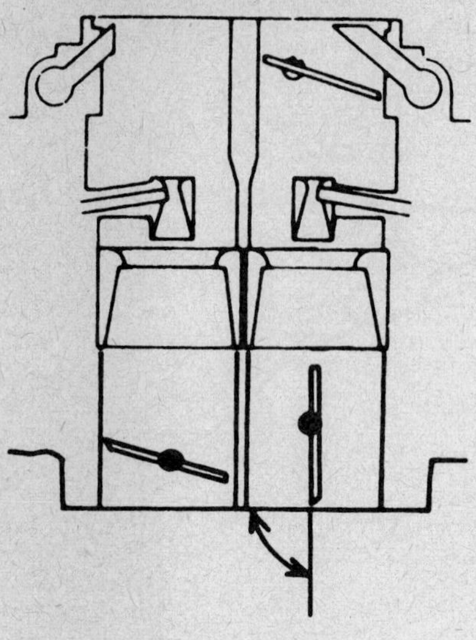

MEASURING THE ANGLE

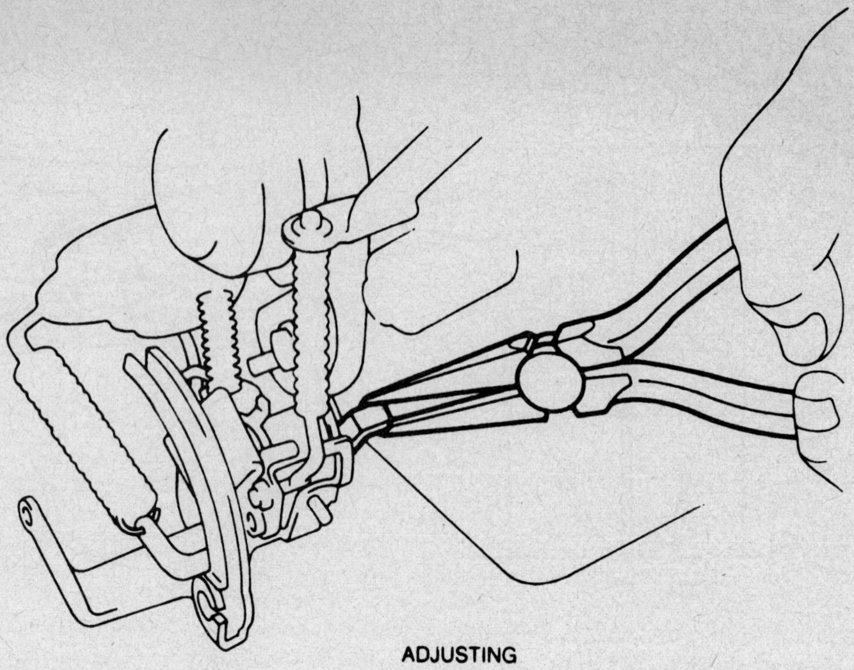

ADJUSTING

Fig. 4 Adjusting secondary touch

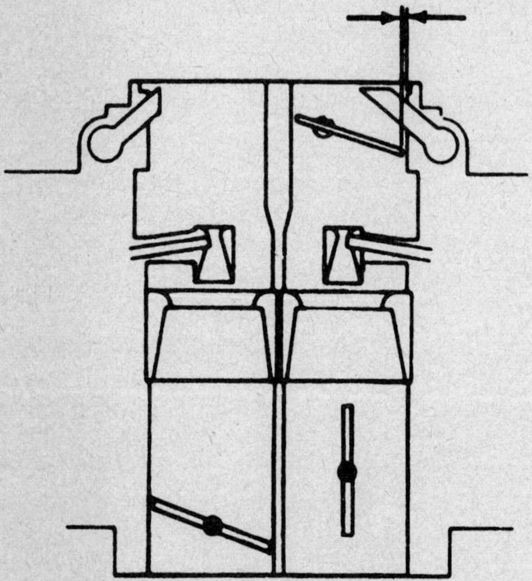

MEASURING THE CLEARANCE

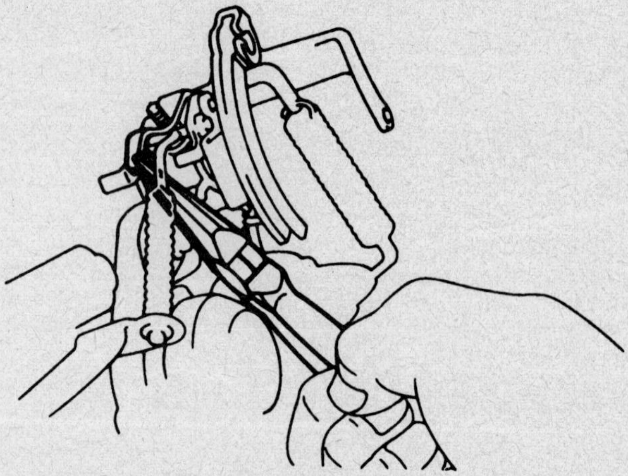

ADJUSTING

Fig. 5 Adjusting choke unloader

FUEL INJECTION SECTION

TABLE OF CONTENTS

Digital Electronic Fuel Injection (DEFI), Cadillac Rear Wheel Drive Models & 1982–85 Eldorado & Seville

INDEX

DESCRIPTION

All 1982-85 Cadillac rear wheel drive models and Eldorado and Sevilles with V8 gasoline engines are equipped with the Digital Electronic Fuel Injection (DEFI) system.

Digital Electronic Fuel Injection, **Fig. 1**, provides a means of fuel distribution for controlling exhaust emissions by precisely controlling the air/fuel mixture under all operating conditions. This is accomplished by establishing a program for the digital Electronic Control Module (ECM), which will provide the correct quantity of fuel for a wide range of operating conditions. Several sensors are used to determine which operating conditions exist and the ECM can then signal the injectors to provide the precise amount of fuel required.

The DEFI consists of a pair of electrically actuated fuel metering valves which, when actuated, spray a calculated quantity of fuel into the engine intake manifold. These valves or injectors are mounted on the throttle body above the throttle blades with the metering tip pointed into the throttle throats. The injectors are normally actuated alternately.

Fuel is supplied to the inlet of the injectors through the fuel lines and is maintained at a constant pressure across the injector inlets. When the solenoid operated valves are energized, the injector call valve moves to the full open position and since the pressure differential across the valve is constant, the fuel quantity is changed by varying the time that the injector is held open.

The amount of air entering the engine is measured by monitoring the intake manifold absolute pressure (MAP), the intake manifold air temperature (MAT) and the engine speed (in RPM). This information allows the ECM to compute the flow rate of air being inducted into the engine and, consequently, the flow rate of fuel required to achieve the desired air/fuel mixture for the particular engine operating condition.

SUBSYSTEMS

The DEFI subsystems are: fuel supply system and injectors, air induction system, sensors, electronic control module (ECM) and wiring harness, electronic spark timing (EST) system, idle speed control (ISC) system, EGR control, system failure operation, system diagnostics, cruise control, closed loop fuel control and torque converter clutch.

FUEL SUPPLY SYSTEM

The fuel supply system components, **Fig. 2**, provide fuel at the correct pressure for metering by the injectors into the throttle bores. The pressure regulator controls fuel pressure to a nominal 10.5 psi across the injectors. The fuel supply system consists of a fuel tank mounted electric pump, a full-flow fuel filter mounted on a vehicle frame, a fuel pressure regulator integral with the throttle body, fuel supply and fuel return lines and two fuel injectors. The timing and amount of fuel supplied is controlled by the ECM.

An electric motor driven twin turbine type pump, integral with the fuel tank float unit, provides fuel at a positive pressure to the throttle body and fuel pressure regulator. The pump is specific for DEFI application and is not serviceable; however, the pump may be serviced separately from the fuel gage unit.

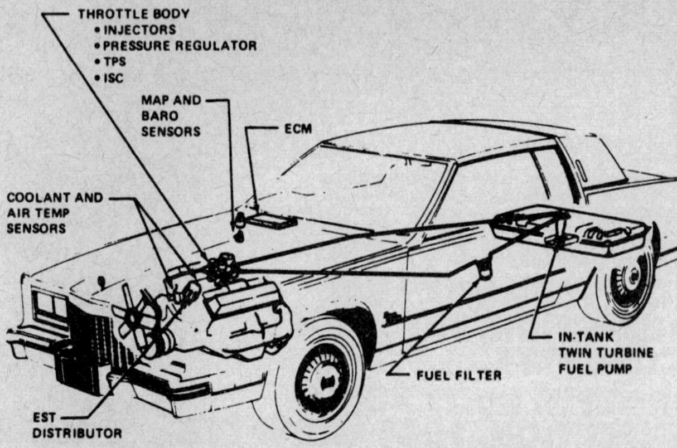

Fig. 1 Digital electronic fuel injection system components (Typical)

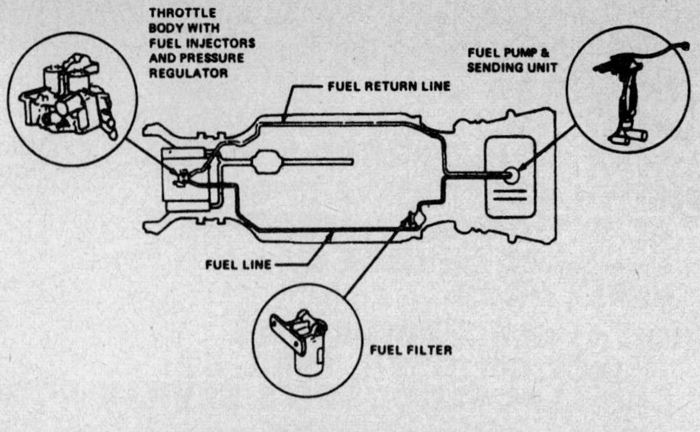

Fig. 2 Digital electronic fuel injection fuel supply system

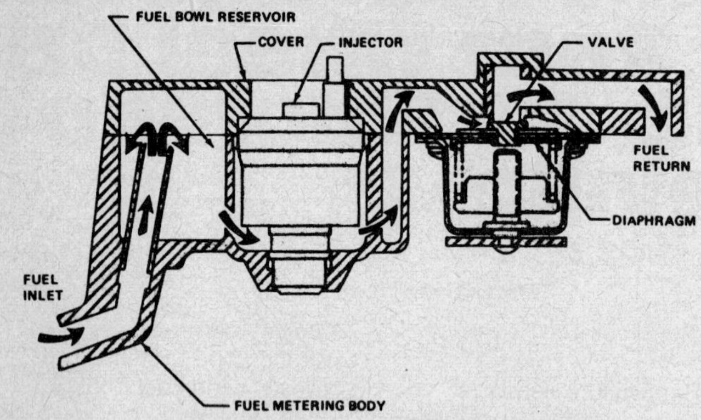

Fig. 3 Digital electronic fuel injection fuel pressure regulator

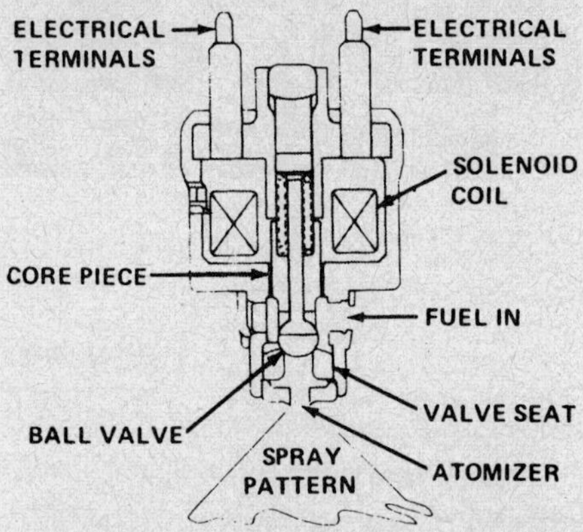

Fig. 4 Digital electronic fuel injection fuel injector

Fuel pump operation is controlled by the fuel pump relay, located in the relay center. Operation of the relay is controlled by a signal from the ECM. The fuel pump circuit is protected by a 10 amp fuse located in the fuse block. The ECM activates the pump with the ignition ON or START. However, if the engine is not cranked within one second after ignition is turned on, the ECM signal is removed and the pump is deactivated.

Fuel is pumped from the fuel tank through the supply line into the filter to the throttle body and pressure regulator. The injections supply fuel to the engine in precisely timed bursts as a result of electrical signals from the ECM. Excess fuel is returned to the fuel tank through the fuel return line.

The fuel tank incorporates a reservoir directly below the sending unit-in-tank pump assembly. The "bath tub" shaped reservoir is used to ensure a constant supply of fuel for the in-tank pump even at low fuel level and severe maneuvering conditions.

The fuel filter consists of a casing with an internal paper filter element capable of filtering foreign particles down to the 10 micron size. The filter element is a throw-away type and should be replaced when recommended. The filter is mounted to the frame near the left rear wheel.

The fuel pressure regulator, **Fig. 3,** is integral with the throttle body. The valve, which regulates pressure, is a diaphragm-operated relief valve in which one side of the valve senses fuel pressure and the other side is exposed to atmospheric pressure. Nominal pressure is established by the pre-load spring. Constant pressure drop across the injectors is maintained by referencing to the ambient pressure at the throttle body. Fuel in excess of that is used to maintain constant pressure by the engine is returned through the fuel return line to the fuel tank. The regulator is not serviced separately from the fuel body assembly.

During normal operation, the two fuel injectors, **Fig. 4,** are actuated alternately by the ECM and are used to meter and direct the atomized fuel into the throttle bores above the throttle blades. During cranking, both injectors are actuated simultaneously to aid starting.

The injector body contains a solenoid. The plunger or core piece is pulled upward by the solenoid allowing the spring loaded ball valve to come off the valve seat, which then allows fuel through to the atomizer/spray nozzle. Injectors may be replaced individually.

A 3/8 inch fuel delivery line is routed along the left frame side rail between the fuel pump/sending unit assembly and the throttle body. A braided stainless steel covered Teflon hose is used to connect the metal fuel line to the fuel line on the engine to provide high system integrity and protection against abrasion.

The fuel return line is 5/16 inch in diameter and is routed along the right frame side rail. Flexible connection in this line is also by braided stainless steel covered Teflon hose at the engine to frame junction.

AIR INDUCTION SYSTEM

The Air Induction System consists of the throttle body assembly, idle speed control and intake manifold.

Air enters the throttle body and is distributed to each cylinder through the intake manifold. The air flow rate is controlled by the throttle valves which are connected to the accelerator pedal linkage. Idle speed is determined by position of the throttle valves and is controlled by the Idle Speed Control (ISC) actuator.

Additional air for cold starts and warm-up is provided by opening the throttle valves further. This is accomplished by the ISC actuator moving out further in response to commands from the ECM.

The throttle body, **Fig. 5,** consists of a housing with two bores and two shaft mounted throttle valves connected to the vehicle accelerator pedal by mechanical linkage. Fittings are incorporated to accommodate vacuum connections. The end of the throttle shaft opposite from the accelerator lever controls the Throttle Position Sensor.

The intake manifold used with the DEFI system is constructed of aluminum and is of the dual plane design and incorporates an exhaust heat crossover passage since DEFI uses the EFE heat riser system.

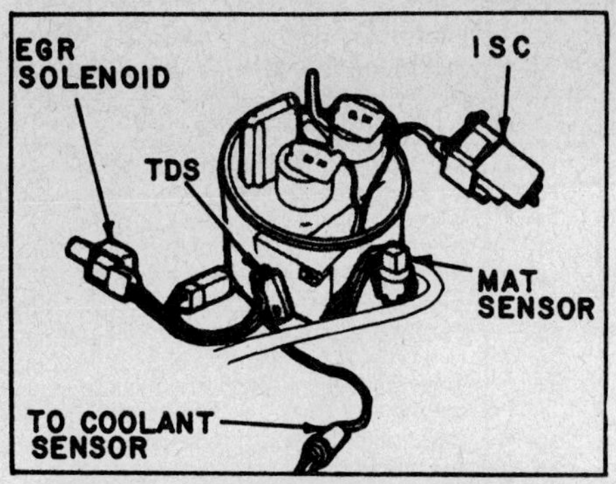

Fig. 5 Digital electronic fuel injection engine controls

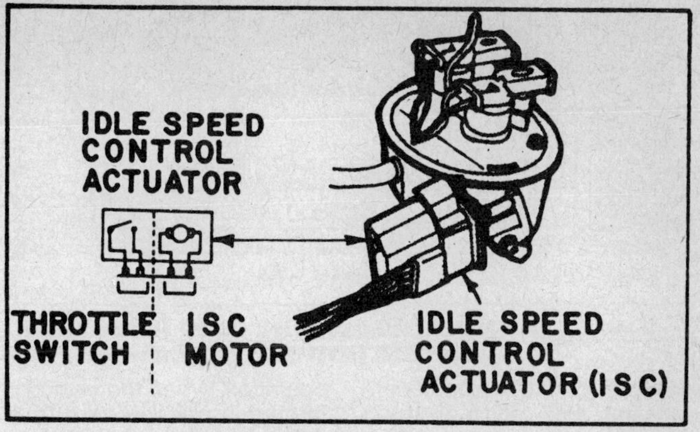

Fig. 6 Digital electronic fuel injection idle speed control

SENSORS

The sensors consist of the manifold air temperature sensor (MAT), engine coolant temperature sensor, barometric pressure sensor (BARO), vehicle speed sensor (VSS), throttle position sensor (TPS) and engine speed sensor, which is provided by pulses from the EST distributor.

The manifold air temperature (MAT) sensor is installed in the intake manifold in front of the throttle body. This sensor measures the temperature of the fuel/air mixture in the intake manifold and provides this information to the ECM. The sensor is a thermistor whose resistance changes as a function of temperature. Low temperature provides high resistance and as temperature increases sensor resistance decreases.

The coolant temperature sensor is similar in function to the MAT sensor and is usually installed in the right front corner of the engine directly below the thermostat. This sensor provides data to the ECM for fuel enrichment during cold operation, for idle speed control, ignition timing and EGR operation.

The manifold absolute pressure (MAP) sensor monitors the changes in intake manifold pressure which result from engine load and speed changes. These pressure changes are supplied to the ECM in the form of electrical signals. As intake manifold pressure increases, additional fuel is required. The MAP sensor sends this information to the ECM so the injector "On" time (or pulse width) will be increased. Conversely as manifold pressure decreases, the pulse width will be shortened. The MAP sensor is mounted under the instrument panel near the righthand A/C outlet and is connected electrically to the ECM. A hose from the throttle body provides a vacuum signal to the sensor.

The barometric pressure sensor (BARO) senses ambient or barometric pressure and provides information to the ECM on ambient pressure changes due to altitude and/or weather. The sensor is mounted under the instrument panel near the righthand A/C outlet and is electrically connected to the ECM.

The vehicle speed sensor (VSS) informs the ECM as to how fast the vehicle is being operated. The ECM uses this information to determine the logic required to operate the fuel economy data panel (if applicable), cruise control and idle speed control system. A speed sensor buffer is positioned between the speed sensor and the ECM to amplify the weak signal generated by the sensor. The speed sensor and buffer are located behind the speedometer cluster.

The Throttle Position Sensor is a variable resistor mounted to the throttle body and is connected to the throttle valve shaft. Movement of the accelerator causes the throttle shaft to rotate (opening or closing the throttle blades). The sensor determines shaft position and transmits an appropriate electrical signal to the ECM. The ECM processes these signals to determine conditions for the idle speed control system.

The engine speed signal is originated from the electronic module in the EST distributor. Pulses from the distributor are sent to the ECM where the time between these pulses is used to calculate engine speed and spark advance.

ELECTRONIC CONTROL MODULE (ECM)

The Electronic Control Module provides all computation and controls for the DEFI system. Sensor inputs are fed into the ECM from the various sensors and processed to produce the appropriate pulse duration for the injectors, the correct idle speed for the particular operating condition and the proper spark advance. Analog inputs from the sensors are converted to digital signals before processing. The ECM is mounted under the instrument panel and consists of various printed circuit boards mounted in a protective metal box.

The ECM receives power from the vehicle battery and when the ignition is set to the "On" or "Crank" position. The following information is received from the sensors:

a. Engine coolant temperature.
b. Intake manifold air temperature.
c. Intake manifold absolute pressure.
d. Barometric pressure.
e. Engine speed.
f. Throttle position.

The following commands are transmitted by the ECM:

a. Electric fuel pump activation.
b. ISC motor control.
c. Spark advance control.
d. Injection valve activation.
e. EGR solenoid activation.

The desired air/fuel mixture for various operating atmospheric conditions are programmed into the ECM. As the above signals are received from the sensors, the ECM processes the signals and computes the engine's fuel requirements. The ECM issues commands to the injection valves to open for a specific time duration. The duration of command pulses varies as the operating conditions change.

The DEFI System is activated when the ignition switch is turned to the "On" position. The following events occur at that moment:

1. The ECM receives ignition "On" signal.
2. The fuel pump is activated by the ECM. (The pump will operate for approximately one second only, unless the engine is cranking or running.)
3. All engine sensors are activated and begin transmitting signals to the ECM.
4. The EGR solenoid is activated to block the vacuum signal to the EGR valve at coolant temperatures below 110° F.
5. The "Check Engine" and "Coolant" lights are illuminated as a functional check of the bulb and circuit. On 1983-85 models, the "Check Engine" light is replaced by "Service Now" and "Service Soon" telltale lights.
6. Operation of the fuel economy lamp begins.

The following events occur when the engine is started:

1. The fuel pump is activated for continuous operation.
2. The ISC motor will begin controlling idle speed (including fast idle speed) if the throttle switch is closed.
3. The spark advance shifts from base (bypass) timing to the ECM programmed spark curve.
4. The fuel pressure regulator maintains the fuel pressure at 10.5 psi by returning excess fuel to the fuel tank.
5. The following sensor signals are continuously received and processed by the ECM:
   a. Engine coolant temperature.
   b. Intake manifold temperature.
   c. Barometric pressure.
   d. Intake manifold absolute air pressure.
   e. Engine speed.
   f. Throttle position changes.
6. The ECM alternately grounds each in-

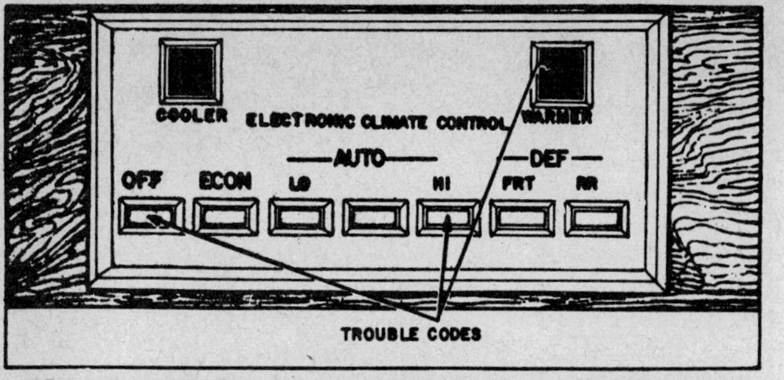

Fig. 7 Digital electronic fuel injection diagnostic panel (Typical)

jector, precisely controlling the opening and closing time (pulse width) to deliver fuel to the engine.

The ECM's control of fuel delivery can be considered in three basic modes: cranking, part throttle and wide open throttle.

If the engine is determined to be in the cranking mode by the presence of a voltage in the cranking signal wire from the ignition switch, the starting fuel delivery consists of one lone "Prime" pulse from both injectors followed by a series of "Starting" pulses until the cranking mode signal is no longer present.

In addition, there is a "clear flood" condition where smaller alternating fuel pulses are delivered if the throttle is held wide open and cranking exceeds five seconds.

Once the engine is running, injector pulse width is then adjusted to account for operating conditions such as idle, part throttle, acceleration, deceleration, and altitude.

For wide open throttle conditions, which are sensed by matching the MAP and BARO sensor inputs, additional enrichment is provided.

Engine ignition timing is controlled by the ECM. The two basic operating modes are "Cranking" (or bypass) and "Normal Engine" operation.

When the engine is in the cranking/bypass mode, ignition timing occurs at a reference setting (distributor timing set point) regardless of other engine operating parameters. Under all other normal operating conditions, basic engine ignition timing is controlled by the ECM and modified, or added to, depending on particular conditions, such as altitude and/or engine loading.

The Idle Speed Control system is controlled by the ECM. The system acts to control engine idle speed in three ways: normal idle (RPM) control, as a fast idle device, and as a "dash pot" on decelerations and throttle closing.

The normal engine idle speed is programmed into the ECM and no adjustments are possible. Under normal engine operating conditions, idle speed is maintained by monitoring idle speed in a "Closed Loop" fashion. To accomplish this loop, the ECM periodically senses the engine idle speed and issues commands to the ISC to move the throttle stop to maintain the designed speed.

For engine starting, the throttle is either held open by the ISC for a longer period (cold) or a shorter time (hot) to provide adequate engine warm-up prior to normal operation. When the engine is shut off, the throttle is opened by fully extending the ISC actuator to get ready for the next start.

Signal inputs for transmission gear, air conditioning compressor clutch (engaged or not engaged) and throttle open or closed are used to either increase or decrease throttle angle in response to these particular engine loadings.

ELECTRONIC SPARK TIMING (EST)

The EST type HEI distributor receives all spark timing information from the ECM when the engine is running. The ECM provides spark plug firing pulses based upon the various engine operating parameters. The electronic components for the EST system are integral with ECM. The Electronic Spark Timing system consists of the ECM and a modified HEI distributor which uses a seven terminal HEI module. The HEI distributor receives input signals from the ECM and delivers output signals to the ECM through four circuits: distributor reference circuit, bypass circuit, EST circuit and ground circuit. When the pickup coil signals the HEI module to open the primary circuit, it also sends the spark timing signals to the ECM through the reference circuit. During engine cranking when HEI bypass line voltage is zero, the HEI module operates in bypass mode. At this point, the HEI module is supplying spark advance according to a fixed value and disregards spark advance signals from the ECM. When the engine is running, voltage on the HEI bypass circuit is increased to five volts and this signals the HEI module to accept spark timing signals from the ECM. The ECM monitors engine speed through the HEI reference circuit and engine operating conditions through various sensors. Using these parameters, the ECM calculates the correct spark advance and sends this signal to the HEI module via the EST circuit.

IDLE SPEED CONTROL SYSTEM (ISC)

Vehicle idle speed is controlled by an electrically driven actuator (ISC), **Fig. 6**, which changes the throttle angle by acting as a moveable idle stop. Inputs to the ISC actuator motor come from the ECM and are determined by the idle speed required for the particular operating condition. The electronic components for the ISC system are integral with the ECM. An integral part of the ISC is the throttle switch. Position of the switch determines whether the ISC should control idle speed or not. When the switch is closed, as determined by the throttle lever resting upon the end of the ISC actuator, the ECM will issue the appropriate commands to move the ISC to provide the programmed idle speed. When the throttle lever moves off the ISC actuator from idle, the throttle switch is opened, the ECM extends the actuator and then stops sending idle speed commands and the driver controls engine speed.

1982 DIAGNOSTIC CODES

CODE	CIRCUIT AFFECTED
12	NO DISTRIBUTOR (TACH) SIGNAL
13	O_2 SENSOR NOT READY
14	SHORTED COOLANT SENSOR CIRCUIT
15	OPEN COOLANT SENSOR CIRCUIT
16	GENERATOR VOLTAGE OUT OF RANGE
18	OPEN CRANK SIGNAL CIRCUIT
19	SHORTED FUEL PUMP CIRCUIT
20	OPEN FUEL PUMP CIRCUIT
21	SHORTED THROTTLE POSITION SENSOR CIRCUIT
22	OPEN THROTTLE POSITION SENSOR CIRCUIT
23	EST CIRCUIT PROBLEM IN RUN MODE
24	SPEED SENSOR CIRCUIT PROBLEM
25	EST CIRCUIT PROBLEM IN BYPASS MODE
26	SHORTED THROTTLE SWITCH CIRCUIT
27	OPEN THROTTLE SWITCH CIRCUIT
28	OPEN FOURTH GEAR CIRCUIT
29	SHORTED FOURTH GEAR CIRCUIT
30	ISC CIRCUIT PROBLEM
31	SHORTED MAP SENSOR CIRCUIT
32	OPEN MAP SENSOR CIRCUIT
33	MAP/BARO SENSOR CORRELATION
34	MAP SIGNAL TOO HIGH
35	SHORTED BARO SENSOR CIRCUIT
36	OPEN BARO SENSOR CIRCUIT
37	SHORTED MAT SENSOR CIRCUIT
38	OPEN MAT SENSOR CIRCUIT
39	TCC ENGAGEMENT PROBLEM
44	LEAN EXHAUST SIGNAL
45	RICH EXHAUST SIGNAL
51	PROM ERROR INDICATOR
52	ECM MEMORY RESET INDICATOR
60	TRANSMISSION NOT IN DRIVE
63	CAR AND SET SPEED TOLERANCE EXCEEDED
64	CAR ACCELERATION EXCEEDS MAX. LIMIT
65	COOLANT TEMPERATURE EXCEEDS MAXIMUM LIMIT
66	ENGINE RPM EXCEEDS MAXIMUM LIMIT
67	SHORTED SET OR RESUME CIRCUIT
.7.0	SYSTEM READY FOR FURTHER TESTS
.7.1	CRUISE CONTROL BRAKE CIRCUIT TEST
.7.2	THROTTLE SWITCH CIRCUIT TEST
.7.3	DRIVE (ADL) CIRCUIT TEST
.7.4	REVERSE CIRCUIT TEST
.7.5	CRUISE ON/OFF CIRCUIT TEST
.7.6	"SET/COAST" CIRCUIT TEST
.7.7	"RESUME/ACCELERATION" CIRCUIT TEST
.7.8	"INSTANT/AVERAGE" CIRCUIT TEST
.7.9	"RESET" CIRCUIT TEST
.8.0	A/C CLUTCH CIRCUIT TEST
-1.8.8	DISPLAY CHECK
.9.0	SYSTEM READY TO DISPLAY ENGINE DATA
.9.5	SYSTEM READY FOR OUTPUT CYCLING OR IN FIXED SPARK MODE
.9.6	OUTPUT CYCLING
.0.0	ALL DIAGNOSTICS COMPLETE

Fig. 8 DEFI diagnostic codes. 1982

SYSTEM DIAGNOSTICS

The dash-mounted light(s) in the right-hand information center is used to inform the driver of certain ECM detected DEFI system malfunctions or abnormalities. These malfunctions may be related to the various sensors or to the ECM itself. The light resets automatically when the fault clears; however, the ECM stores the trouble code associated with the detected fail-

PARAMETER NO.	PARAMETER	RANGE	DISPLAY UNITS
0 1	THROTTLE POSITION	10 to 90	DEGREES
0 2	MAP	14 to 108	kPa
0 3	BARO	14 to 108	kPa
0 4	COOLANT	40 to 151	C
0 5	MAT	40 to 151	C
0 6	INJECTOR PULSE WIDTH	0 to 19 9	MSEC
0 7	O_2 SENSOR	0 to 1 99	VOLTS
0 8	SPARK ADVANCE	0 to 52	DEGREES
0 9	IGNITION CYCLES	0 to 50	KEY CYCLES
1 0	BATTERY VOLTAGE	0 to 19 9	VOLTS
1 1	ENGINE RPM	0 to 1990	RPM 10
1 2	VEHICLE SPEED	0 to 199	MPH
1 3	PROM I D	0 to 199	CODE

Fig. 9 Engine data display chart. 1982–85

ure until the diagnostic system is cleared.

The dash-mounted digital display panel normally used for the Electronic Climate Control (ECC) system, is used to display trouble codes stored in the ECM when desired.

Any codes that may be stored can be called up and/or cleared by properly exercising the ECC controls.

OPERATION WITH SYSTEM FAILURES

In the event the ECM detects a system malfunction, the light will be activated, the corresponding trouble code stored and substitute values to replace missing data may be made available for computations by the ECM. This can be thought of as a "Fail Safe" operation. In this mode, driveability of the car may be poor under certain condition and the diagnostic procedures should be exercised.

EGR CONTROL

A vacuum solenoid is utilized to control the EGR supply vacuum. The solenoid is controlled by the ECM in response to the engine coolant temperatures signal. When the engine coolant temperature signal indicates that coolant temperature is below 110° F, a signal from the ECM energizes the EGR solenoid blocking vacuum to the EGR valve. The solenoid is also activated during cranking and at wide open throttle. Above 160° F the EGR solenoid is deactivated and the EGR valve is actuated according to normal (ported) vacuum and exhaust backpressure signals.

CLOSED LOOP FUEL CONTROL

This system maintains an air/fuel mixture ratio of 14.7/1. At this mixture ratio, the catalytic converter operates at maximum efficiency, resulting in lower emission levels. The ECM receives information from the oxygen sensor, enabling it to correct fuel mixture for maintaining an ideal air/fuel ratio.

TORQUE CONVERTER CLUTCH (TCC) CONTROL

The ECM controls a transmission mounted electrical solenoid. When vehicle reaches a specific speed, the ECM energizes the solenoid, causing the torque converter to mechanically couple the engine to the transmission. When operating conditions indicate transmission should operate as a normal fluid-coupled transmission, solenoid is de-energized, and transmission returns to normal automatic operation when brake pedal is depressed.

Diagnosis of intermittent problems should be a visual and physical inspection of the connectors involved in the affected circuit. Some causes of the problems are: improperly formed terminals or connector bodies, damaged terminals or connector bodies, corrosion, body sealer, or other contaminants on the terminal mating surfaces, incomplete mating of the connector halves, terminals not fully seated in the connector body ("backed-out" terminals) and inadequate terminal crimps to the wire.

DIAGNOSIS

"TROUBLE CODE" DIAGNOSIS

On 1983-85 models, "Service Now" and "Service Soon" lights are used to indicate that a malfunction has been detected in the system.

The dash-mounted light(s) is used to indicate system malfunctions or abnormalities. These malfunctions may be related to the various operating sensors or to the ECM. The light(s) goes out automatically if the fault clears (intermittent). However, the ECM stores the trouble code associated with the detected failure until the diagnostic system is "Cleared" or until 20 ignition switch on-off cycles (50 on 1982-85 models) have occurred without the fault reappearing.

Proper operation of the light(s) is as follows:

a. The light(s) is normally off.
b. A bulb check is performed when the ignition is in the "On" and "Crank" positions (crank position only on 1983-85 models). When the engine starts, the bulb(s) go out.
c. On 1982 models, the light comes on and remains on when a constant malfunction is detected.
d. On 1983-85 models, either the "Service Now" or "Service Soon" light will illuminate and remain lit depending on the malfunction detected.
e. If a malfunction is intermittent, the light will go out when the malfunction is not present. The light will come on or flash on and off each time a malfunction is detected.
f. On 1983-85 models, when "Service Soon" and "Service Now" malfunctions are detected simultaneously, only the "Service Now" light will illuminate.
g. On 1982 models, the light goes out when the system is in diagnostic mode.
h. On 1983-85 models, both lights remain lit when the system is in diagnostic mode.

CODE	CIRCUIT AFFECTED
■■ 12	NO DISTRIBUTOR (TACH) SIGNAL
□ 13	O_2 SENSOR NOT READY
□ 14	SHORTED COOLANT SENSOR CIRCUIT
□ 15	OPEN COOLANT SENSOR CIRCUIT
■■ 16	GENERATOR VOLTAGE OUT OF RANGE
□ 18	OPEN CRANK SIGNAL CIRCUIT
□ 19	SHORTED FUEL PUMP CIRCUIT
■■ 20	OPEN FUEL PUMP CIRCUIT
□ 21	SHORTED THROTTLE POSITION SENSOR CIRCUIT
□ 22	OPEN THROTTLE POSITION SENSOR CIRCUIT
□ 23	EST/BYPASS CIRCUIT PROBLEM
□ 24	SPEED SENSOR CIRCUIT PROBLEM
□ 26	SHORTED THROTTLE SWITCH CIRCUIT
□ 27	OPEN THROTTLE SWITCH CIRCUIT
□ 28	OPEN FOURTH GEAR CIRCUIT
□ 29	SHORTED FOURTH GEAR CIRCUIT
□ 30	ISC CIRCUIT PROBLEM
■■ 31	SHORTED MAP SENSOR CIRCUIT
■■ 32	OPEN MAP SENSOR CIRCUIT
■■ 33	MAP/BARO SENSOR CORRELATION
□ 34	MAP SIGNAL TOO HIGH
□ 35	SHORTED BARO SENSOR CIRCUIT
□ 36	OPEN BARO SENSOR CIRCUIT
□ 37	SHORTED MAT SENSOR CIRCUIT
□ 38	OPEN MAT SENSOR CIRCUIT
□ 39	TCC ENGAGEMENT PROBLEM
■■ 44	LEAN EXHAUST SIGNAL
■■ 45	RICH EXHAUST SIGNAL
■■ 51	PROM ERROR INDICATOR
▼ 52	ECM MEMORY RESET INDICATOR
▼ 53	DISTRIBUTOR SIGNAL INTERRUPT
▼ 60	TRANSMISSION NOT IN DRIVE
▼ 63	CAR AND SET SPEED TOLERANCE EXCEEDED
▼ 64	CAR ACCELERATION EXCEEDS MAX. LIMIT
▼ 65	COOLANT TEMPERATURE EXCEEDS MAX. LIMIT
▼ 66	ENGINE RPM EXCEEDS MAXIMUM LIMIT
▼ 67	SHORTED SET OR RESUME CIRCUIT
.7.0	SYSTEM READY FOR FURTHER TESTS
.7.1	CRUISE CONTROL BRAKE CIRCUIT TEST
.7.2	THROTTLE SWITCH CIRCUIT TEST
.7.3	DRIVE (ADL) CIRCUIT TEST
.7.4	REVERSE CIRCUIT TEST
.7.5	CRUISE ON/OFF CIRCUIT TEST
.7.6	"SET/COAST" CIRCUIT TEST
.7.7	"RESUME/ACCELERATION" CIRCUIT TEST
.7.8	"INSTANT/AVERAGE" CIRCUIT TEST
.7.9	"RESET" CIRCUIT TEST
.8.0	A/C CLUTCH CIRCUIT TEST
-1.8.8	DISPLAY CHECK
.9.0	SYSTEM READY TO DISPLAY ENGINE DATA
.9.5	SYSTEM READY FOR OUTPUT CYCLING OR IN FIXED SPARK MODE
.9.6	OUTPUT CYCLING
.0.0	ALL DIANOSTICS COMPLETE
■■	TURNS ON "SERVICE NOW" LIGHT
□	TURNS ON "SERVICE SOON" LIGHT
▼	DOES NOT TURN ON ANY TELLTALE LIGHT

NOTE: CRUISE IS DISENGAGED WITH ANY "SERVICE NOW" LIGHT OR WITH CODES 60-67.

Fig. 10 DEFI diagnostic codes. 1983–84

The dash-mounted digital display panel, normally used for the ECC system, can be temporarily directed to display trouble codes stored in the ECM, **Fig. 7.**

ENTERING DIAGNOSTIC MODE

1. Turn ignition "On."
2. Depress "Off" and "Warmer" buttons

on the ECC panel simultaneously and hold until ".." appears, **Fig. 7.** "88" ("−1.8.8" on 1982-85 models) will then be displayed which indicates the beginning of the diagnostic readout.

3. Trouble codes will be displayed on the digital ECC panel beginning with the lowest numbered code. Note that the fuel data panel does not display when the system is in the diagnostic mode. Refer to **Figs. 8 through 11** for display information.

Trouble codes stored in the ECM's memory may be cleared (erased) by entering the diagnostic mode and then depressing the "Off" and "Hi" buttons simultaneously, **Fig. 7.** Hold until ".0.0" appears. After ".0.0" is displayed, ".7.0" will appear. With this displayed, turn off ignition for at least 10 seconds before re-entering the diagnostic mode.

EXITING FROM DIAGNOSTIC MODE

To get out of the diagnostic mode, depress any of the ECC "Function" keys (except Outside Temperature) or turn ignition switch "Off" for ten seconds. Trouble codes are not erased when this is done.

ADJUSTMENTS

THROTTLE POSITION SENSOR, ADJUST

The TPS adjustment is preset and then spot welded to prevent tampering and retain the original setting. Do not remove spot welds and loosen screws unless diagnosis indicates that TPS sensor is incorrectly adjusted, or it becomes necessary to replace the TPS sensor or throttle body assembly. Since this is a critical adjustment, it must be performed accurately to ensure proper vehicle performance and exhaust emission control.

1982

1. Check voltage at TPS test leads with a suitable digital voltmeter as follows:
   a. Turn ignition on. Do not start engine.
   b. Connect positive lead of voltmeter to test point corresponding to pin A (blue-dark blue wire) and negative lead to test point corresponding to pin B (black wire).
   c. Retract ICS motor by pressing plunger in while holding throttle open.
   d. Open throttle and let it snap fully shut. If voltmeter reading is not between .45 and .55 volts, proceed with TSP adjustment.
2. Remove throttle body from intake manifold. Invert throttle body assembly and support assembly to prevent damage to injector electrical connections. Using 5/16 inch drill bit, drill through TPS screw access holes in base of throttle body to insure spot weld removal. Install throttle body assembly and loosen screws until sensor can be rotated.
3. With engine idling at 400 RPM, position TPS lever so that the voltmeter reads .50 volts.

1985 DIAGNOSTIC CODES	
CODE	CIRCUIT AFFECTED
■■ 12	NO DISTRIBUTOR (TACH) SIGNAL
□ 13	O_2 SENSOR NOT READY
□ 14	SHORTED COOLANT SENSOR CIRCUIT
□ 15	OPEN COOLANT SENSOR CIRCUIT
■■ 16	GENERATOR VOLTAGE OUT OF RANGE
□ 18	OPEN CRANK SIGNAL CIRCUIT
□ 19	SHORTED FUEL PUMP CIRCUIT
■■ 20	OPEN FUEL PUMP CIRCUIT
□ 21	SHORTED THROTTLE POSITION SENSOR CIRCUIT
□ 22	OPEN THROTTLE POSITION SENSOR CIRCUIT
□ 23	EST/BYPASS CIRCUIT PROBLEM
□ 24	SPEED SENSOR CIRCUIT PROBLEM
□ 26	SHORTED THROTTLE SWITCH CIRCUIT
□ 27	OPEN THROTTLE SWITCH CIRCUIT
□ 28	OPEN FOURTH GEAR CIRCUIT
□ 29	SHORTED FOURTH GEAR CIRCUIT
□ 30	ISC CIRCUIT PROBLEM
■■ 31	SHORTED MAP SENSOR CIRCUIT
■■ 32	OPEN MAP SENSOR CIRCUIT
■■ 33	MAP/BARO SENSOR CORRELATION
■■ 34	MAP SIGNAL TOO HIGH
□ 35	SHORTED BARO SENSOR CIRCUIT
□ 36	OPEN BARO SENSOR CIRCUIT
□ 37	SHORTED MAT SENSOR CIRCUIT
□ 38	OPEN MAT SENSOR CIRCUIT
□ 39	TCC ENGAGEMENT PROBLEM
■■ 44	LEAN EXHAUST SIGNAL
■■ 45	RICH EXHAUST SIGNAL
■■ 51	PROM ERROR INDICATOR
▼ 52	ECM MEMORY RESET INDICATOR
▼ 53	DISTRIBUTOR SIGNAL INTERRUPT
▼ 60	TRANSMISSION NOT IN DRIVE
▼ 63	CAR AND SET SPEED TOLERANCE EXCEEDED
▼ 64	CAR ACCELERATION EXCEEDS MAX. LIMIT
▼ 65	COOLANT TEMPERATURE EXCEEDS MAX. LIMIT
▼ 66	ENGINE RPM EXCEEDS MAXIMUM LIMIT
▼ 67	SHORTED SET OR RESUME CIRCUIT
.7.0	SYSTEM READY FOR FURTHER TESTS
.7.1	CRUISE CONTROL BRAKE CIRCUIT TEST
.7.2	THROTTLE SWITCH CIRCUIT TEST
.7.3	DRIVE (ADL) CIRCUIT TEST
.7.4	REVERSE CIRCUIT TEST
.7.5	CRUISE ON/OFF CIRCUIT TEST
.7.6	"SET/COAST" CIRCUIT TEST
.7.7	"RESUME/ACCELERATION" CIRCUIT TEST
.7.8	"INSTANT/AVERAGE" CIRCUIT TEST
.7.9	"RESET" CIRCUIT TEST
.8.0	A/C CLUTCH CIRCUIT TEST
-1.8.8	DISPLAY CHECK
.9.0	SYSTEM READY TO DISPLAY ENGINE DATA
.9.5	SYSTEM READY FOR OUTPUT CYCLING OR IN FIXED SPARK MODE
.9.6	OUTPUT CYCLING
.0.0	ALL DIANOSTICS COMPLETE
■■	TURNS ON "SERVICE NOW" LIGHT
□	TURNS ON "SERVICE SOON" LIGHT
▼	DOES NOT TURN ON ANY TELLTALE LIGHT
NOTE: CRUISE IS DISENGAGED WITH ANY "SERVICE NOW" LIGHT OR WITH CODES 60-67.	

Fig. 11 DEFI diagnostic codes. 1985

4. Tighten TPS mounting screws and recheck voltmeter reading to make sure adjustment has not changed.
5. If TPS adjustment was necessary, perform ICS motor adjustment.

ISC MOTOR, ADJUST

This adjustment is necessary only to establish the initial position of the motor after replacement.

1982

1. Check adjustment of as described under "Throttle Position Sensor, Adjust."
2. Fully extend ICS actuator nosepiece as follows:
   a. With ignition on, disconnect throttle position sensor.
   b. Disconnect ICS at fullest extension of nosepiece (top of ratcheting cycle). This may require several tries of touching ICS connectors to ICS motor.
   c. Reconnect throttle position sensor.
3. Turn ICS motor nosepiece adjustment screw to obtain a reading of 1.06 ± .01 volts at the TPS test point.
4. Disconnect test equipment and reconnect all electrical connectors.
5. Turn ignition off for 10 seconds and check that ISC motor moves to its extended position.
6. The above procedure may have caused the "Check Engine" lamp to light and trouble codes to set. By restoring system to normal operation, the light will go out, but the trouble codes will be stored as intermittents. With ignition on, enter diagnostics, clear trouble codes, then turn ignition off for 10 seconds.

COMPONENT REPLACEMENT

THROTTLE BODY, REPLACE

Removal

1. Raise hood and remove air cleaner assembly.
2. Disconnect the following electrical connectors: ISC motor, IPS and both injectors.
3. Remove both throttle return springs, cruise control and throttle linkage and downshift cable, **Fig. 12.**
4. Disconnect the following hoses and lines from rear of throttle body: fuel inlet line, fuel return line, brake booster line, MAP hose and AIR hose.
5. Remove PCV, EVAP and EGR hoses from front of throttle body.
6. Remove three throttle body mounting screws, then the throttle body and gasket, **Fig. 12.**

Installation

1. Install new throttle body gasket to intake manifold, then the throttle body. Torque three retaining screws to 15 ft. lbs.
2. Connect vacuum lines and fittings to front and rear of throttle body, **Fig. 13.**
3. Install downshift cable, cruise control, throttle linkages and both throttle return springs.
4. Refer to "Throttle Position Sensor, Adjust" and check adjustment of throttle position sensor.
5. Refer to "ISC Motor, Adjust" and check adjustment of ISC motor.

MANIFOLD ABSOLUTE PRESSURE SENSOR, REPLACE

When replacing a Bendix MAP or BARO sensor with a Delco sensor, both MAP and BARO sensors must be replaced and a sensor mounting kit used to complete the installation.

1. Remove instrument panel lower cover.
2. From under righthand end of instrument panel, disconnect MAP hose from sensor.
3. Disconnect MAP sensor electrical connector using caution not to damage small gauge wires on sensor side.

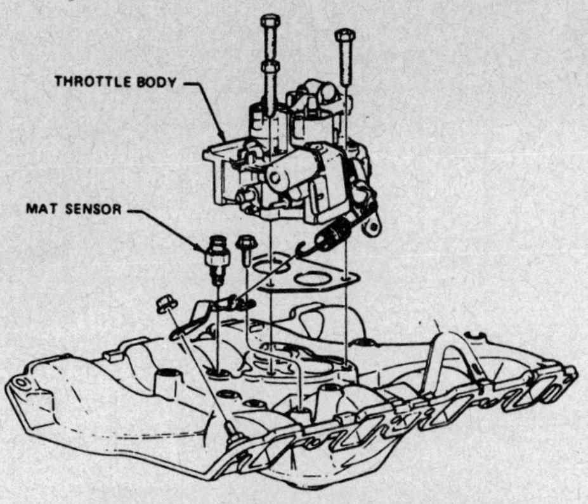

Fig. 12 Throttle body removal

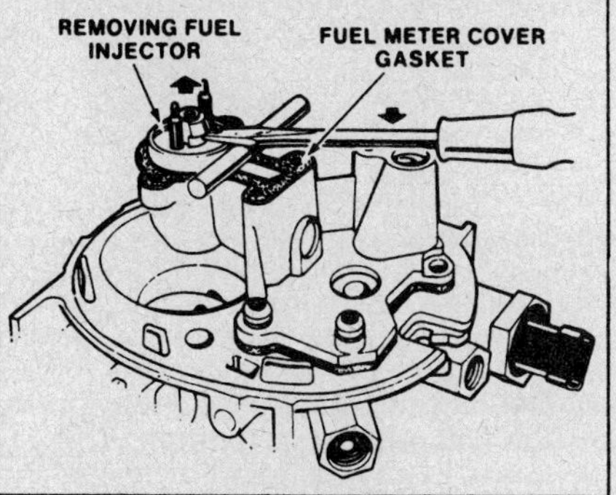

Fig. 14 Fuel injector removal

Note that MAP sensor has female connector on sensor and male connector on harness, while BARO connectors are the reverse.

4. Remove screw securing MAP sensor to MAP/BARO bracket, then the sensor.
5. Reverse procedure to install. Torque bracket retaining screw to 3 ft. lbs.

BAROMETRIC SENSOR, REPLACE

When replacing a Bendix MAP or BARO sensor with a Delco sensor, both MAP and BARO sensors must be replaced and a sensor mounting kit used to complete the installation.

1. Remove instrument panel lower cover.
2. Remove four glove box liner retaining screws, then the glove box liner.
3. Disconnect BARO sensor electrical connector using caution not to damage small gauge wires on sensor side. Note that BARO sensor has male connector on sensor and female connector on harness, while MAP connectors are reverse.
4. Remove screw securing MAP/BARO bracket to instrument panel, then the screw securing BARO sensor and ground strap to bracket. Remove sensor through glove box opening.
5. Reverse procedure to install. Torque sensor and ground strap to bracket screw to 3 ft. lbs.

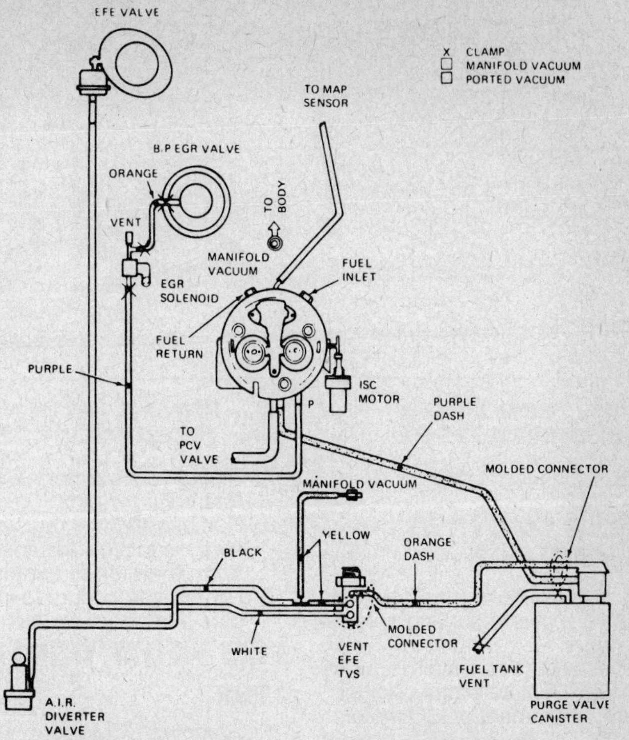

Fig. 13 DEFI vacuum schematic

ELECTRONIC CONTROL MODULE, REPLACE

1. Remove lower instrument panel cover.
2. Remove three nuts securing module to instrument panel mounting brackets, then lower module to gain access to electrical connectors.
3. Remove one nut securing ground strap, then disconnect three module electrical connectors.
4. Reverse procedure to install. Torque ground strap nut to 3 ft. lbs.

MANIFOLD AIR TEMPERATURE SENSOR, REPLACE

The MAT sensor threads should be coated with a suitable sealant whenever sensor is replaced. Torque sensor to 15 ft. lbs.

COOLANT SENSOR, REPLACE

1. Drain radiator until coolant is below level of sensor.
2. Disconnect sensor electrical connector then remove sensor.
3. Reverse procedure to install. Coat threads of sensor with suitable sealant, and torque sensor to 15 ft. lbs.

THROTTLE POSITION SENSOR, REPLACE

1982

Removal

1. Disconnect TPS electrical connector.
2. Remove throttle body assembly from intake manifold as described under "Throttle Body, Replace."
3. Invert and support throttle body assembly to prevent damage to injector electrical connectors.
4. Using 5/16 inch drill bit, drill through TPS screw access holes in base of throttle body.
5. Remove TPS attaching screws, washers and retainers.
6. Remove TPS from throttle body noting location of TPS pickup lever in relation to tang on lever of throttle shaft for reference during installation.

Installation

1. Position TPS over throttle shaft checking to ensure TPS pickup lever locates tang on throttle actuator lever.
2. Install retainers and new attaching screws, then install throttle body onto intake manifold as described under "Throttle Body, Replace."

1983–85

Removal

1. Disconnect electrical connector from sensor pigtail.
2. Remove two mounting screws, then the sensor from throttle body.

Installation

1. Position sensor over throttle shaft on right side of throttle body.
2. Snug tighten mounting screws and connect electrical connector.
3. Refer to "Throttle Position Sensor, Adjust," and check adjustment of sensor.

MILES PER GALLON DISPLAY, REPLACE

1. Remove center instrument panel applique.
2. Remove two display mounting screws and pull display outward away from instrument panel. Disconnect electrical connector.

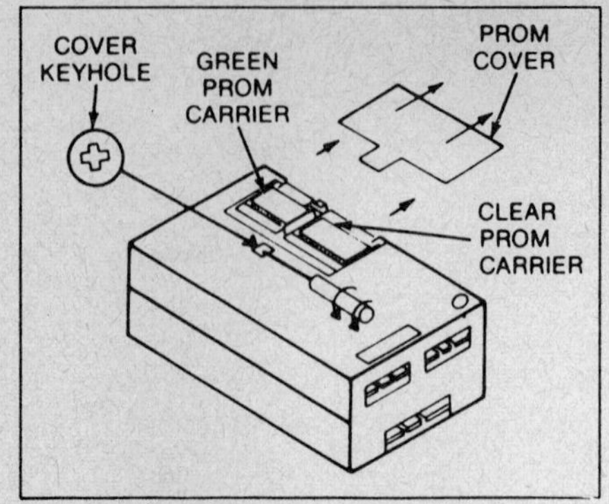

Fig. 15 ECM PROM replacement. 1982

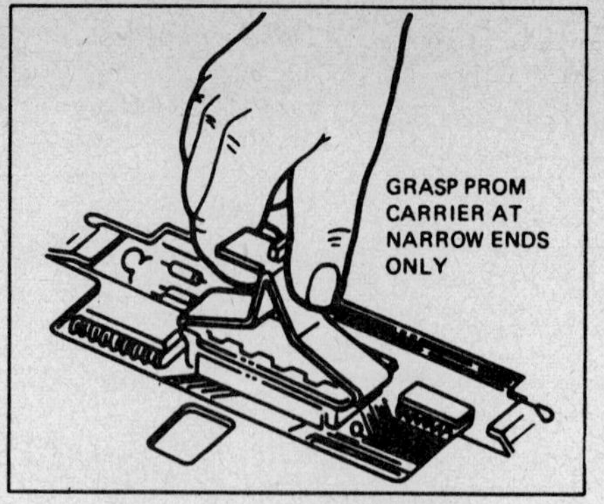

Fig. 16 ECM PROM removal. 1983–85

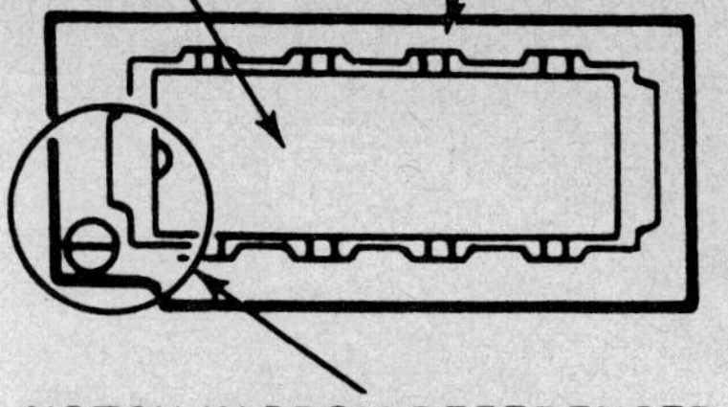

Fig. 17 ECM PROM installation. 1983–85

3. Reverse procedure to install.

IDLE SPEED CONTROL MOTOR, REPLACE

1. Disconnect electrical connector, then remove two motor mounting screws and the motor.
2. Reverse procedure to install. Refer to "Idle Speed Control Motor, Adjust," and check adjustment of ISC motor.

INJECTORS, REPLACE

Removal

1. Raise hood and remove air cleaner housing and extension.
2. Remove injector electrical connectors, then the eight pressure regulator attaching screws and the regulator.
3. Remove injector from fuel meter body by carefully lifting out with a screwdriver, **Fig. 14.** Leave fuel meter cover gasket in place to prevent damage to body casting.
4. Discard upper and lower O-rings.

Installation

1. Lubricate, then install new O-ring over injector nozzle.
2. Position upper O-ring back-up washer and a new lubricated upper O-ring into housing bore.
3. Position injector into throttle body, then center nozzle into bottom housing bore, and install injector. Align electrical terminals so that pin in bottom of injector fits into locating hole in bottom of injector cavity.
4. Install pressure regulator, then start engine and check for leaks and proper injector operation.
5. Connect injector electrical connectors.

PRESSURE REGULATOR, REPLACE

1. Raise hood and remove air cleaner housing and extension.
2. Disconnect injector electrical connectors.
3. Remove eight screws securing pressure regulator assembly to throttle body, then the regulator.
4. Reverse procedure to install. Start engine and check for leaks.

ECM PROM, REPLACE

1982

1. Remove ECM from vehicle as described under "Electronic Control Module, Replace."
2. Remove PROM access cover by inserting tip of small blade screwdriver into keyhole of locking tab. Bend tab slightly to unlock access cover, then remove cover, **Fig. 15. Note position of PROMs in ECM. PROMs are not interchangeable. Replacement PROMs must be installed in same position and direction as defective PROM. The small reference boss, or dimple, on the PROM carrier must align with boss, or dimple in the PROM socket.**
3. Grasp clear PROM carrier and rock carrier from side to side while applying firm upward force, **Fig. 15.**
4. Repeat step 3 for green PROM carrier.
5. Place replacement clear PROM carrier and position upside down on flat surface so pins face upward. Using narrow, blunt instrument press downward on body of PROM on both sides of retainer bar until top of PROM is flush with top of carrier.
6. Repeat step 5 for PROM mounted in green carrier.
7. Position clear PROM carrier over PROM socket and press down firmly on top of carrier. With carrier held in this position, press down on body of PROM with blunt, narrow tool.
8. Repeat step 7 for PROM mounted in green carrier.
9. Replace PROM access cover, then install ECM on vehicle.
10. Start engine, enter diagnostics and check for code 51. If code 51 does not display, PROM is installed correctly. If code 51 is displayed, one or both PROMs are installed incorrectly. If PROM is not fully seated, remove access cover and set PROM fully. If any pins are broken or if either PROM is installed backwards, replace both PROMs.

1983–85

1. Remove ECM from vehicle as described under "Electronic Control Module, Replace."
2. Depress PROM access cover locking tab and remove cover from ECM.
3. Grasp PROM carrier with removal tool and remove PROM from ECM, **Fig. 16.** Rock carrier from end to end while applying a firm upward force. **Before installing replacement PROM, ensure that part number matches that on defective PROM unit. Install PROM so that dimple is properly positioned in carrier, Fig. 17.**
4. Place replacement PROM mounted in carrier upside down on flat surface so pins face upward. Using narrow, blunt instrument, press downward on body of PROM on both sides of retainer bar until top of PROM is flush with top of carrier.
5. Position PROM carrier over PROM socket and press down firmly on top of carrier.
6. Replace PROM access cover, then install ECM on vehicle.
7. Start engine, enter diagnostics and check for Code 51. If Code 51 does not display, PROM is installed correctly. If Code 51 is displayed, the PROM is installed improperly, has bent pins or is defective. If PROM is not fully seated, remove access cover and press firmly on carrier. If pins are bent, remove PROM, straighten pins and reinstall PROM. If pins are broken or cracked while straightening, replace PROM. If PROM is installed backwards, it must be replaced.

Throttle Body Fuel Injection, 1984 Corvette

INDEX

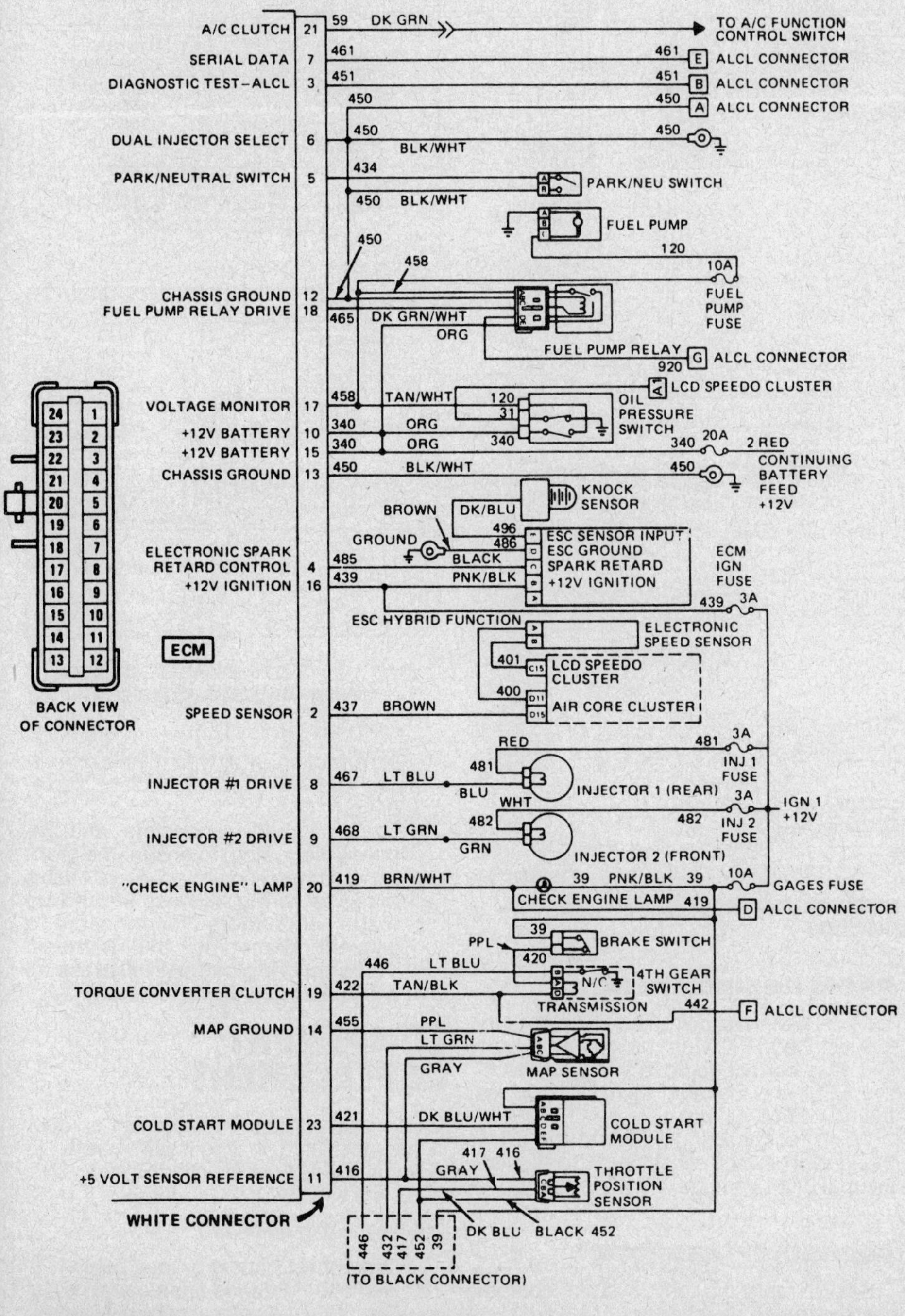

Fig. 1 Throttle body fuel injection wiring circuit. White ECM connector

For system description, refer to "Throttle Body Fuel Injection Systems, Exc. 1984 Corvette."

DIAGNOSIS

Refer to **Figs. 1 and 2** when troubleshooting the system.

SELF DIAGNOSIS SYSTEM

A built-in, self diagnostic system will identify problems most likely to occur in the Throttle Body Fuel Injection System. When a problem is detected, the diagnostic system will illuminate a "Check Engine" light in the instrument panel. The "Check Engine" light will flash a trouble code or codes when a trouble code "Test" terminal under the dash is grounded with ignition on and engine not running.

The "Check Engine" light will illuminate with the ignition switch on and the engine off. If the "Test" terminal is then grounded and the light flashes a Code 12, the self-diagnostic system is functioning properly. A Code 12 consists of one flash, a short pause, then two flashes in rapid succession. After a longer pause, the code will repeat twice.

When the engine is started, the "Check Engine" light should turn off. If the light remains lit, the self-diagnostic system has detected a problem. To determine where the problem exists, ground the "Test" terminal with ignition on and engine off, and observe trouble code display. Each trouble code will flash three times in numerical order. Each trouble code will indicate a fault in a particular circuit.

Trouble Code "Test" Lead

The trouble code "Test" lead is located in a 12 volt terminal connector under the dash. When this terminal is grounded, the ECM will flash any trouble codes stored in the memory. To ground the terminal, connect a jumper wire between the "Test" lead terminal and the adjacent ground terminal.

If the "Test" terminal is grounded with ignition on and engine off, the system will enter the diagnostic mode. In the diagnostic mode, the ECM will flash a code 12 and energize all ECM controlled relays.

If the "Test" terminal is grounded with the engine running, the system will enter the field service mode. In this mode, the "Check Engine" light will indicate whether the system is in open or closed loop operation. If the light flashes approximately twice

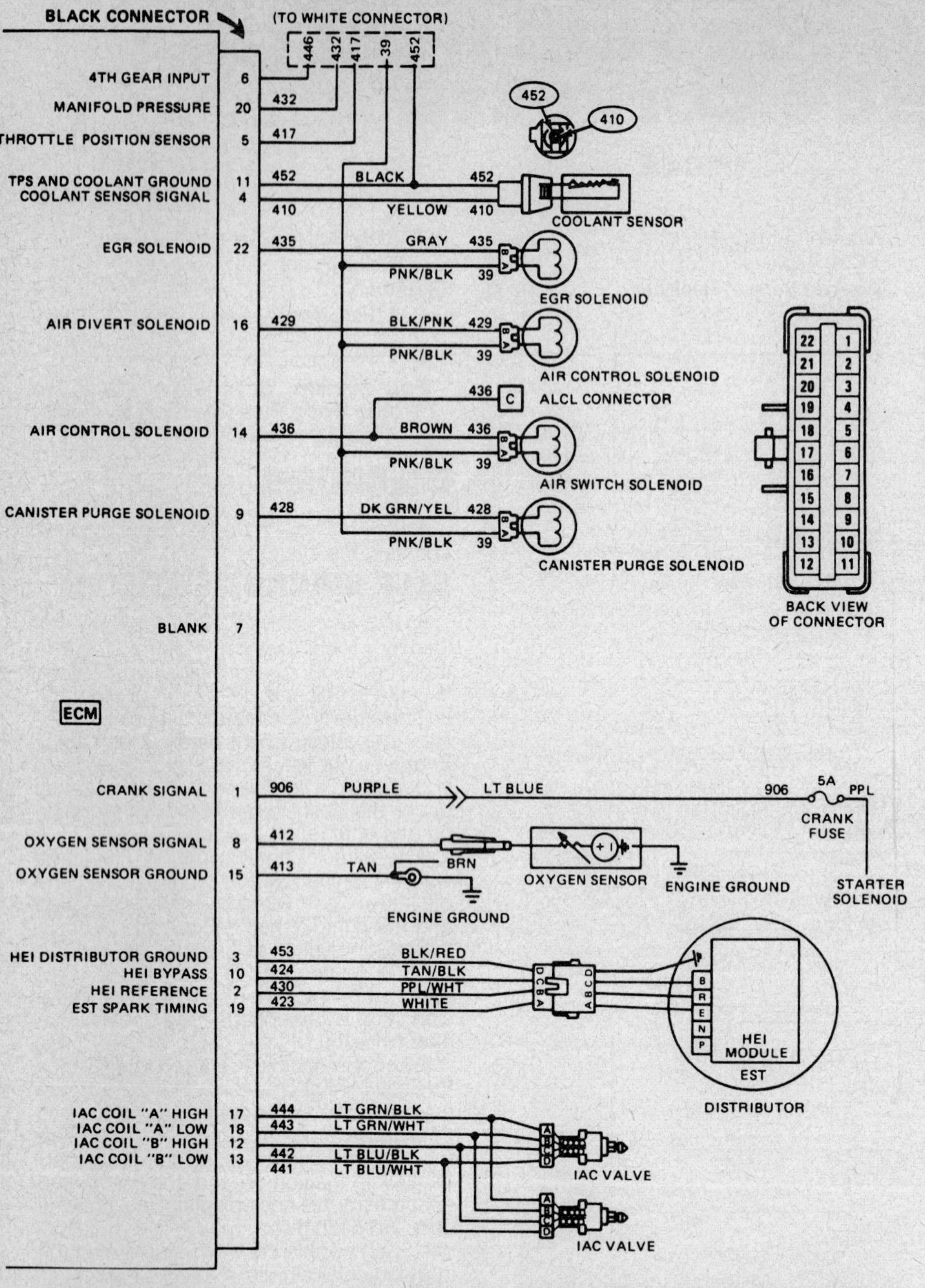

Fig. 2 Throttle body fuel injection wiring circuit. Black ECM connector

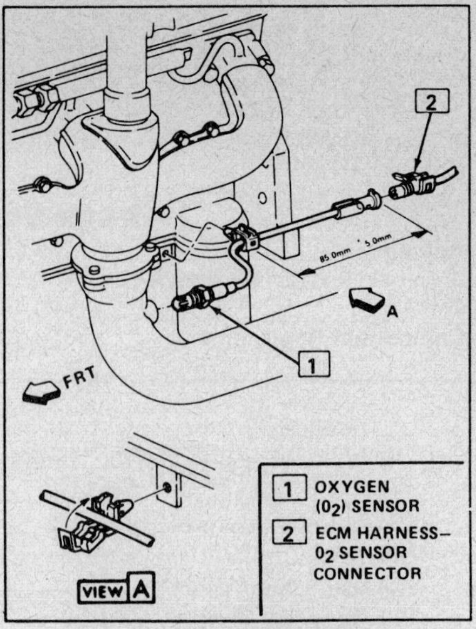

Fig. 3 Oxygen sensor replacement

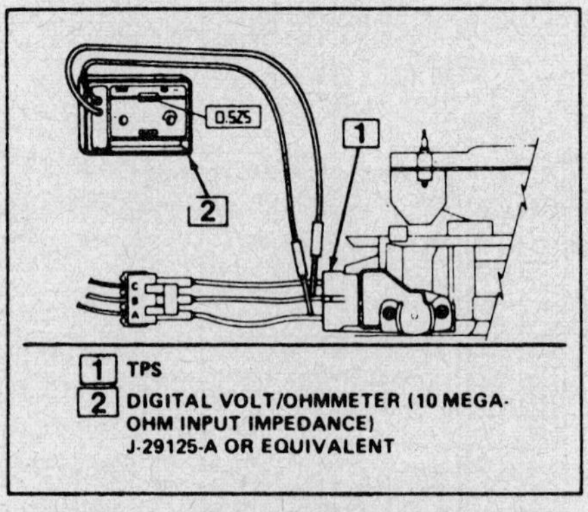

Fig. 4 Throttle position sensor adjustment

per second, the system is in open loop operation. Closed loop operation is indicated by the light flashing approximately once per second.

Trouble Code Memory

When a problem develops in the system, the "Check Engine" light will illuminate and a trouble code will be set in the ECM memory. If the problem is intermittent, the "Check Engine" light will turn off approximately ten seconds after the fault goes away. The trouble code, however, will be retained in the ECM memory until battery voltage to the ECM is removed. To clear all stored trouble codes, disconnect battery positive cable for ten seconds and reconnect.

PROM Replacement

If the ECM must be replaced, first ensure the installed PROM is the correct part. If PROM is correct, remove from the defective ECM and install in the new ECM, as the new ECM will not contain a PROM.

When reconnecting power to the ECM, the ignition switch must be off to prevent internal ECM damage.

Connector Inspection

Before replacing any system components, proceed as follows:

1. Disconnect connector(s) associated with suspected defective component and check for improper installation, bent, broken, or dirty terminals or mating tabs and repair or replace as required.
2. Reconnect all connectors and recheck the system to ensure the problem has been corrected. **Any repairs made to wiring harness should be made with battery disconnected to prevent damaging the harness. Disconnecting battery will erase all trouble codes stored in the ECM.**

COMPONENT REPLACEMENT

For component replacement procedures not listed in this section, refer to "Throttle Body Fuel Injection System, Exc. 1984 Corvette."

ECM, REPLACE

1. Disconnect battery ground cable.
2. Remove righthand hush panel.
3. Disconnect electrical connectors from ECM.
4. Remove ECM attaching screws and the ECM.

5. Reverse procedure to install. **Replacement ECM is supplied without engine calibration unit (PROM). Care should be taken when removing the PROM from a defective unit, as it will be used in the replacement ECM.**

THROTTLE POSITION SENSOR (TPS), REPLACE

1. Disconnect battery ground cable.
2. Remove air cleaner, then disconnect electrical connector from sensor.
3. Remove sensor attaching screws, lockwashers, retainers and the sensor. Discard attaching screws. **It may be necessary to remove TPS actuating lever attaching screw from end of throttle shaft to remove sensor.**
4. Reverse procedure to install, noting the following:
   a. Install TPS on throttle body assembly with throttle valve in the normal closed idle position.
   b. Ensure TPS pickup lever is above tang on throttle actuator lever.
   c. Apply suitable locking compound to screws prior to installation.
   d. Do not tighten screws until TPS has been adjusted. Refer to "Throttle Position Sensor, Adjust."

OXYGEN SENSOR, REPLACE

The oxygen sensor should be removed when engine temperature is above 120° F to prevent damage to threads in exhaust pipe or manifold.

1. Disconnect battery ground cable.
2. Raise and support vehicle.
3. Disconnect inline electrical connector, then remove oxygen sensor using a suitable wrench, **Fig. 3.**
4. Reverse procedure to install. Apply suitable anti-seize compound to sensor threads and torque sensor to 30 ft. lbs.

COOLANT SENSOR, REPLACE

1. Disconnect battery ground cable.
2. Drain cooling system.
3. Remove accessory drive belts, then the belt tensioner.
4. Disconnect electrical connector from coolant sensor.
5. Carefully back out sensor.
6. Reverse procedure to install.

ADJUSTMENTS

THROTTLE POSITION SENSOR (TPS), ADJUST

1. Remove air cleaner, then disconnect electrical connector from TPS.
2. Connect 3 jumper wires between TPS electrical connector and TPS, **Fig. 4.**
3. With ignition on and engine off, measure voltage between sensor terminals A and B, **Fig. 4,** using a digital voltmeter.
4. In the closed throttle position, voltmeter should read .450-.600 volt.
5. Rotate TPS as necessary to bring voltage within specifications. Tighten screws and recheck voltage.
6. Turn ignition off and remove jumper wires.

Digital Electronic Fuel Injection (DEFI), 1985–87 Cadillac DeVille & Fleetwood

INDEX

DESCRIPTION

Digital Electronic Fuel Injection (DEFI) provides a means of fuel distribution for controlling exhaust emissions by precisely controlling the air/fuel mixture under all operating conditions. This is accomplished through the use of an Electronic Control Module (ECM). The ECM receives signals from various sensors and signals the injectors to provide the precise amount of fuel required.

A Body Computer Module (BCM) used in conjunction with the ECM provides for additional control capability. The BCM monitors various body operating parameters and shares this information with the ECM through an electronic communications process.

The ECM and BCM are both capable of diagnosing faults with the various inputs and systems they control. When the ECM detects a malfunction, a Service Now or Service Soon warning lamp on the instrument panel is illuminated.

FUEL CONTROL SYSTEM COMPONENTS

INJECTOR UNIT

The injector unit, **Fig. 1,** is composed of two major assemblies; a throttle body and a fuel body.

The throttle body contains an Idle Speed Control (ISC) control assembly and a Throttle Position Sensor (TPS). The throttle body portion of the injector unit may contain ports located at, above, or below the throttle valve. The ports are used to produce the vacuum signals for the canister purge system and the Manifold Absolute Pressure (MAP) sensor.

The fuel body portion of the injector unit contains a fuel meter cover with integral pressure regulator and a fuel injector to supply fuel to the engine.

FUEL INJECTOR

The fuel injector is solenoid operated and controlled by the ECM. The ECM energizes the solenoid, which lifts a ball valve off its seat. Pressurized fuel is then injected in a conical spray pattern at the walls of the throttle body bore above the throttle valve. Fuel not used by the injector passes through the pressure regulator, then back to the fuel tank.

PRESSURE REGULATOR

The pressure regulator is a diaphragm type relief valve with injector pressure acting on one side and air cleaner pressure acting on the opposite side. The regulator maintains a constant injector pressure at all times by controlling flow in the return line.

IDLE SPEED CONTROL (ISC) ASSEMBLY

The ISC controls idle speed using a plunger to change throttle angle. Idle speed is monitored by the ECM which moves the plunger to maintain idle speed required for the operating condition. The throttle switch, integral with the ISC, determines when the ISC controls idle speed. When throttle lever rests against ISC plunger, the switch contacts are closed and the ECM moves ISC to predetermined idle speed position. When throttle lever breaks contact with ISC plunger, the ECM stops sending idle speed commands and engine speed is controlled by the accelerator pedal.

The following listed sensors and/or switches are parameter information transmitters. The status lights and parameter displays can be utilized to monitor each sensor or input.

ENGINE COOLANT TEMPERATURE SENSOR

The coolant sensor is a thermistor mounted in the engine coolant flow. The ECM supplies a 5 volt signal to the coolant sensor through a resistor in the ECM and measures voltage. Voltage will be high when engine is cold and low when engine is hot. The sensor provides coolant temperature information to the ECM for ignition timing, fuel enrichment, canister purge control, EGR operation, EFE operation, air management, closed loop fuel control and idle speed control.

MANIFOLD ABSOLUTE PRESSURE (MAP) SENSOR

The MAP sensor measures changes in intake manifold pressure resulting from changes in engine load and speed, and converts this to a voltage output. The ECM, by monitoring sensor output voltage, increases or decreases injector "on" time to compensate for the addition or reduction of fuel as required.

The MAP sensor is used by the ECM to control fuel delivery and ignition timing. In addition, the sensor is also used to measure barometric pressure under certain conditions, allowing the ECM to automatically adjust for different altitudes.

MANIFOLD AIR TEMPERATURE (MAT) SENSOR

The MAT sensor, mounted in the intake manifold, in front of throttle body, measures temperature of air/fuel mixture in intake manifold and relays a signal to the ECM. The sensor is a thermistor, whose resistance decreases as temperature increases.

OXYGEN SENSOR

The exhaust oxygen sensor, mounted in the exhaust system, monitors oxygen content of exhaust gas stream and produces a corresponding voltage output which is relayed to the ECM. The ECM, by monitoring this voltage signal, sends a fuel mixture command to the injector.

THROTTLE POSITION SENSOR (TPS)

The TPS, connected to the throttle shaft, is a variable resistor with one end connected to 5 volts from the ECM and the other to ground. A third wire, connected to the ECM, measures TPS voltage. TPS voltage changes with movement of the throttle valve. The ECM modifies fuel delivery according to throttle valve angle, by monitoring TPS voltage.

VEHICLE SPEED SENSOR (VSS)

The VSS, located in the transaxle, provides vehicle speed information to the ECM. The ECM uses this signal to operate fuel economy data panel, integral cruise control, idle speed control system, VCC and to modify fuel delivery under certain conditions. A VSS buffer is installed between speed sensor and ECM to amplify the signal.

ENGINE SPEED SENSOR

The engine speed signal is produced by the seven terminal HEI module in the distributor. The ECM receives pulses from the distributor and the time between these pulses is used to determine engine speed. The ECM adds spark advance modifications to the signal and relays this signal back to the distributor.

PARK/NEUTRAL SWITCH

The park/neutral switch signals the ECM when the transaxle is in Park or Neutral. This information is used for cruise control, ISC operation and the VCC system.

POWER STEERING PRESSURE SWITCH

The power steering pressure switch opens during high pressure power steering situations and signals the ECM to increase idle speed to compensate for the increased engine load.

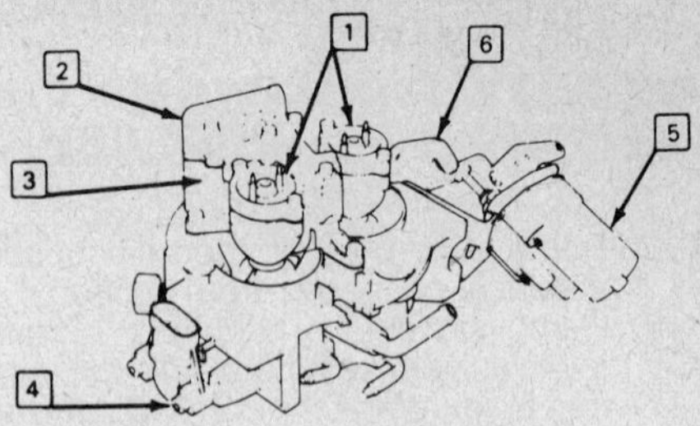

1 FUEL INJECTORS
2 FUEL METER COVER
3 FUEL METER BODY
4 THROTTLE POSITION SENSOR
5 IDLE SPEED CONTROL (ISC)
6 THROTTLE LEVER

Fig. 1 Digital electronic fuel injection unit

DEFI/ECM SYSTEM OPERATION

STARTING MODE

When ignition is first turned On, the ECM energizes the fuel pump for two seconds and pressure is built up at the injector unit. The ECM then checks coolant temperature sensor, TPS and crank signal and determines proper air/fuel mixture for starting.

CLEAR FLOOD MODE

A flooded engine should be cleared by fully depressing the accelerator pedal, which causes the ECM to pulse injectors at a rate of 25.5:1. The ECM will maintain this injector rate as long as throttle is wide open and engine RPM is less than 600. When throttle position becomes less than 80%, the ECM returns to the "starting" mode.

RUN MODE

The "run" mode consists of two separate operating conditions; open loop and closed loop.

The system goes into open loop operation when the engine is first started and RPM is above 400. In open loop operation, the ECM disregards oxygen sensor signal and determines air/fuel mixture primarily on inputs from coolant and MAP sensors. The system will remain in open loop operation until the oxygen sensor has varying voltage output and is hot enough to operate, or the coolant sensor is above 158° F and 60 seconds has elapsed after starting engine. When these conditions are met, the system switches to closed loop operation.

In closed loop operation, the ECM calculates the air/fuel mixture based on signals from the oxygen sensor. This allows the air/fuel mixture to stay close to the optimum 14.7:1 ratio.

ACCELERATION MODE

In the "acceleration" mode, the ECM senses rapid changes in throttle position and manifold pressure and provides a corresponding amount of added fuel.

DECELERATION MODE

During deceleration, fuel remaining in intake manifold can cause excessive emissions and backfiring. To compensate for this, the ECM senses changes in throttle

ECM DIAGNOSTIC CODES	
CODE	MALFUNCTION
■■ E12	NO DISTRIBUTOR SIGNAL
□ E13	OXYGEN SENSOR NOT READY (CANISTER PURGE)
□ E14	SHORTED COOLANT SENSOR CIRCUIT
□ E15	OPEN COOLANT SENSOR CIRCUIT
■■ E16	GENERATOR VOLTAGE OUT OF RANGE (ALL SOLENOIDS)
□ E18	OPEN CRANK SIGNAL CIRCUIT
□ E19	SHORTED FUEL PUMP CIRCUIT
■■ E20	OPEN FUEL PUMP CIRCUIT
□ E21	SHORTED THROTTLE POSITION SENSOR CIRCUIT
□ E22	OPEN THROTTLE POSITION SENSOR CIRCUIT
□ E23	EST/BYPASS CIRCUIT PROBLEM (AIR)
□ E24	SPEED SENSOR CIRCUIT PROBLEM (VCC)
□ E26	SHORTED THROTTLE SWITCH CIRCUIT
□ E27	OPEN THROTTLE SWITCH CIRCUIT
□ E28	OPEN THIRD OR FOURTH GEAR CIRCUIT
□ E30	ISC CIRCUIT PROBLEM
■■ E31	SHORTED MAP SENSOR CIRCUIT (AIR)
■■ E32	OPEN MAP SENSOR CIRCUIT (AIR)
■■ E34	MAP SENSOR SIGNAL TOO HIGH (AIR)
□ E37	SHORTED MAT SENSOR CIRCUIT
□ E38	OPEN MAT SENSOR CIRCUIT
□ E39	VCC ENGAGEMENT PROBLEM
□ E40	OPEN POWER STEERING PRESSURE CIRCUIT
■■ E44	LEAN EXHAUST SIGNAL (AIR & CL & CANISTER PURGE)
■■ E45	RICH EXHAUST SIGNAL (AIR & CL & CANISTER PURGE)
□ E47	BCM - ECM DATA PROBLEM
■■ E51	ECM PROM ERROR
▼ E52	ECM MEMORY RESET INDICATOR
▼ E53	DISTRIBUTOR SIGNAL INTERRUPT
▼ E59	VCC TEMPERATURE SENSOR CIRCUIT
▼ E60	TRANSMISSION NOT IN DRIVE
▼ E63	CAR SPEED AND SET SPEED DIFFERENCE TOO HIGH
▼ E64	CAR ACCELERATION TOO HIGH
▼ E65	COOLANT TEMPERATURE TOO HIGH
▼ E66	ENGINE RPM TOO HIGH
▼ E67	CRUISE SWITCH SHORTED DURING ENABLE

ECM AND CRUISE CONTROL COMMENTS:

■■	TURNS ON "SERVICE NOW" LIGHT
□	TURNS ON "SERVICE SOON" LIGHT
▼	DOES NOT TURN ON ANY TELLTALE LIGHT
( )	FUNCTIONS WITHIN BRACKETS ARE DISENGAGED WHILE SPECIFIED MALFUNCTION REMAINS CURRENT (HARD)

E16 & E24 DISABLE VCC FOR ENTIRE IGNITION CYCLE

E24 & E67 DISABLE CRUISE FOR ENTIRE IGNITION CYCLE

CRUISE IS DISENGAGED WITH CODE(S) E16, E51 OR E60 - E67

Fig. 2 ECM diagnostic codes

position and manifold pressure and reduces fuel delivery. When decelerating very rapidly, the ECM will cut off the fuel supply for short periods.

BATTERY VOLTAGE CORRECTION MODE

When battery is low, the ECM compensates to maintain acceptable system performance by increasing injector "on" time, idle RPM and ignition dwell time.

DEFI/ECM SYSTEM DIAGNOSTIC MODE

TROUBLE CODES

The ECM and BCM continually monitor operating conditions of their controlled systems for possible malfunctions. When a problem is detected, a two-digit numerical "trouble code," **Figs. 2 and 3,** is stored in computer memory. These codes can be displayed as aid in system repair. Any malfunctions which the vehicle operator should be aware of will illuminate Service Now or Service Soon warning lamps on the dashboard.

If a malfunction which would result in unacceptable system operation is encountered, the self-diagnostics will minimize the effect by taking "failsoft" action to compensate for the detected problem. A typical "failsoft" action, for example, would be the substitution of a fixed input value when a sensor is detected to be open or shorted.

ENTERING DIAGNOSTIC MODE

To enter diagnostic mode, turn ignition On, then depress Off and Warmer buttons on the Climate Control Panel (CCP), **Fig. 4.** Hold buttons until all display panel segments illuminate, indicating beginning of diagnostic readout. The two display panels must be illuminated to ensure all segments are operating. Do not attempt diagnosis unless all segments appear, as a incorrect diagnosis could result. If any segments are inoperative, the display panel must be replaced.

TROUBLE CODE DISPLAY

When segment check is completed, any codes stored in computer memory will be displayed on the data display as follows:

1. Trouble code display begins with "8.8.8" for approximately one second, followed by "..E". The first pass of ECM codes includes all detected malfunctions, whether currently present or not. If no ECM codes are stored, the "..E" display is bypassed.
2. Following the "..E" display, all stored ECM codes, beginning with the lowest numbered, will be displayed for approximately two seconds. All ECM codes will be prefixed with an "E".
3. After all ECM codes have been displayed, ".E.E" will illuminate, indicating beginning of the second pass. In the second pass of ECM codes, only "hard" codes are displayed. These are codes which indicate a currently present malfunction. If there are no stored "hard" codes, the ".E.E" display is bypassed.
4. When all ECM codes have been displayed, BCM codes will then be displayed in a similar fashion. BCM codes are prefixed with an "F." Before first pass of BCM codes, "..F" is displayed, and ".F.F" is displayed before second pass of BCM codes.
5. After all ECM and BCM codes have been displayed, or if no codes are present, Code .7.0 will be displayed, indicating that system is ready for next diagnostic feature to be selected.
6. If a Code E51 is currently being detected, it will be continuously displayed until diagnostic mode is exited. When Code E51 is displayed, no other diagnostic features are possible.

ECM DATA DISPLAY

To display ECM data, depress and release Lo button on CCP. ECM data display is initiated as display switches from Code .7.0 to Code E.9.0. To advance display, depress Hi button on CCP. To return to a lower parameter, or go directly from Code E.9.0 to end of parameter list, depress Lo button. When troubleshooting a malfunction, then ECM data display can be used to compare vehicle to a properly functioning vehicle. The various data parameters and their values are described in **Fig. 5.**

BCM DIAGNOSTIC CODES	
CODE	CIRCUIT AFFECTED
▼ F10	OUTSIDE TEMP SENSOR CKT
▼ F11	A/C HIGH SIDE TEMP SENSOR CKT
▼ F12	A/C LOW SIDE TEMP SENSOR CKT
▼ F13	IN-CAR TEMP SENSOR CKT
▼ F14	DIESEL COOLANT SENSOR CKT
▼ F30	CCP TO BCM DATA CKT
▼ F31	FDC/DDC TO BCM DATA CKT
▼ F32	ECM-BCM DATA CKT'S
▼ F40	AIR MIX DOOR PROBLEM
▼ F41	COOLING FANS PROBLEM
☑ F46	LOW REFRIGERANT WARNING
☑ F47	LOW REFRIGERANT CONDITION
☑ F48	LOW REFRIGERANT PRESSURE
▼ F49	HIGH TEMP CLUTCH DISENGAGE
▼ F51	BCM PROM ERROR

☑ TURNS ON "SERVICE AIR COND" LIGHT

▼ DOES NOT TURN ON ANY LIGHT

COMMENTS:

F11 TURNS ON COOLING FANS WHEN A/C CLUTCH IS ENGAGED

F12 DISENGAGES A/C CLUTCH

F14 & F32 TURN ON COOLING FANS

F30 TURNS ON FT. DEFOG AT 75° F

F41 TURNS ON "COOLANT TEMP/FANS" LIGHT WHEN FANS SHOULD BE ON

F47 & F48 SWITCHES FROM "AUTO" TO "ECON"

Fig. 3 BCM diagnostic codes

BCM DATA DISPLAY

To display BCM data, depress and release Outside Temp button on CCP. BCM data display is initiated as display switches from Code .7.0 to Code F.8.0. To advance to a lower number parameter, or go directly from Code F.8.0 to end of parameter list, depress Lo button. When troubleshooting a malfunction, the BCM data display can be used to compare vehicle to a properly functioning vehicle. The various data parameters and their values are described in **Fig. 6.**

CLEARING TROUBLE CODES

Stored ECM codes may be cleared by entering diagnostic mode, then simultaneously depressing Off and Hi buttons on the CCP until "E.0.0" is displayed. Stored BCM codes may be cleared by entering the diagnostic mode and simultaneously depressing Off and Lo buttons until "F.0.0" is displayed. After "E.0.0" or "F.0.0" is displayed, ".7.0" will appear. With ".7.0" displayed, turn ignition Off for at least ten seconds before re-entering diagnostic mode.

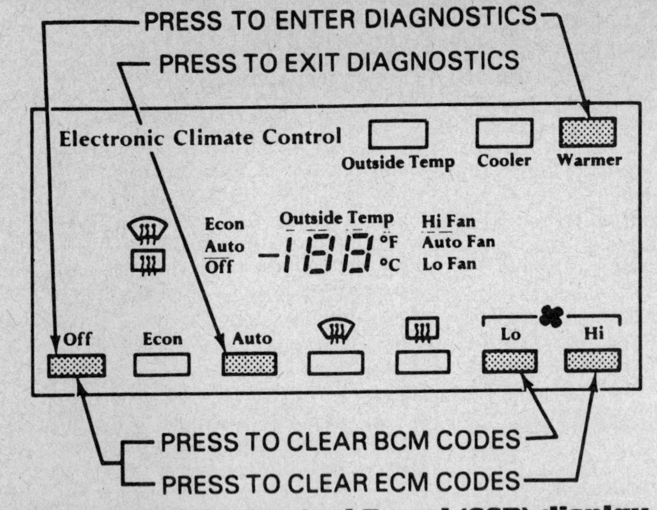

Fig. 4 Climate Control Panel (CCP) display

E.9.0 ENGINE DATA DISPLAY			
PARAMETER NUMBER	PARAMETER	PARAMETER RANGE	DISPLAY UNITS
P.0.1	Throttle Position	-10 - 90	Degrees
P.0.2	MAP	14 - 109	kPa
P.0.3	Computed BARO	61 - 103	kPa
P.0.4	Coolant Temperature	-40 - 151	°C
P.0.5	MAT	-40 - 151	°C
P.0.6	Injector Pulse Width	0 - 99.9	ms
P.0.7	Oxygen Sensor Voltage	0 - 1.14	Volts
P.0.8	Spark Advance	0 - 52	Degrees
P.0.9	Ignition Cycle Counter	0 - 50	Key Cycles
P.1.0	Battery Voltage	0 - 25.5	Volts
P.1.1	Engine RPM	0 - 6370	RPM ÷ 10
P.1.2	Car Speed	0 - 255	MPH
P.1.3	ECM PROM I.D.	0 - 255	Code

Fig. 5 ECM data display chart

F.8.0 BCM DATA DISPLAY			
PARAMETER NUMBER	PARAMETER	PARAMETER RANGE	DISPLAY UNITS
P.2.0	Commanded Blower Voltage	-3.3 - 18.0	Volts
P.2.1	Coolant Temperature	-40 - 215	°C
P.2.2	Commanded Air Mix Door Position	0 - 100	%
P.2.3	Actual Air Mix Door Position	0 - 100	%
P.2.4	Air Delivery Mode 0 = Max A/C 4 = Off 1 = A/C 5 = Normal Purge 2 = Intermediate 6 = Cold Purge 3 = Heater 7 = Front Defog	0 - 7	Code
P.2.5	In-Car Temperature	-40 - 102	°C
P.2.6	Actual Outside Temperature	-40 - 93	°C
P.2.7	High Side Temperature (Condenser Out)	-40 - 215	°C
P.2.8	Low Side Temperature (Evaporator In)	-40 - 93	°C
P.2.9	Actual Fuel Level	0 - 19.0	Gallons
P.3.0	Ignition Cycle Counter	0 - 99	Key Cycles
P.3.1	BCM PROM I.D.	0 - 255	Code

Fig. 6 BCM data display chart

EXITING DIAGNOSTIC MODE

To get out of diagnostic mode, depress Auto button on CCP or turn ignition Off for ten seconds until the temperature setting is displayed. The action does not clear the stored codes.

CLIMATE CONTROL IN DIAGNOSTIC MODE

When the diagnostic mode is entered, the ECC operates in the mode being commanded just before depressing Off and Warmer buttons. If display changes to Off mode as buttons are pushed, the prior operating mode is remembered and will resume after diagnostics are entered.

INTERMITTENT CODES VS. HARD FAILURES

An intermittent "trouble code" can be an ECM code which has occurred within the last 50 ignition cycles, or a BCM code which has occurred within the last 100 ignition cycles. A hard "trouble code" indicates a failure which has been detected the last time the ECM or BCM tested the circuit.

For ECM codes E12 through E51, the Service Soon or Service Now warning lamp will automatically go out if the malfunction clears.

For ECM codes E52 through E67, the warning lamps will never illuminate.

STATUS DISPLAY

When in the diagnostic mode, mode indicators on the CCP indicate the status of certain system operating modes. Different modes of operation are indicated by light being turned On or Off. Operation of the status lights is as follows:

1. The Auto status light is illuminated when ECM is operating in closed loop mode. The light will come on after coolant and oxygen sensors have reached normal operating temperatures.
2. The Econ status light is illuminated when oxygen sensor signal to ECM indicates a rich exhaust condition. The light will flash on and off during warm, steady throttle operation.
3. The Off status light is illuminated when ECM senses that throttle switch is closed. The light will be off whenever throttle is applied.
4. The Front Defog status light is illuminated when ECM commands transaxle VCC to engage. The light only indicates whether or not VCC is enabled by the ECM and does not indicate actual operation of the VCC system.
5. The Rear Defog status light is illuminated when ECM senses that 4th gear pressure switch is open. This light should only be on while in 4th gear operation.
6. The Outside Temp status light is illuminated when BCM commands ECC compressor clutch to engage. The light only indicates whether or not clutch is enabled by BCM and does not indicate actual operation of the compressor clutch system.
7. The Auto Fan status light is illuminated when feedback signal from cooling fan control module to BCM indicates that fans are operating. The light should be off whenever fans are off.
8. The Hi Fan status light is illuminated when BCM is commanding up-down mode door to divert air flow up away from heater outlet. The light will be off whenever ECC system is in "heater" or "normal purge" modes.
9. The Lo Fan status light is illuminated when BCM is commanding A/C-DEF mode door to divert air flow to A/C outlets as in "A/C" or "normal purge" modes. The light will be off whenever ECC system is in "heater," "intermediate," "defrost" and "cold" modes.
10. The °F status light is illuminated when BCM senses refrigerant low pressure switch is open. The light will come on when ambient temperature falls below approximately −5° F because of pressure-temperature relationship of refrigerant. The light will remain off under all other conditions if refrigerant system is fully charged and properly controlled.
11. The °C status light is illuminated when BCM is commanding heater water valve to block coolant flow through heater core. The light will remain off except when air mix door is commanded to "Max A/C" position.

COMPONENT REPLACEMENT

THROTTLE POSITION SENSOR, REPLACE

Removal

1. Remove air cleaner, then disconnect sensor electrical connector.

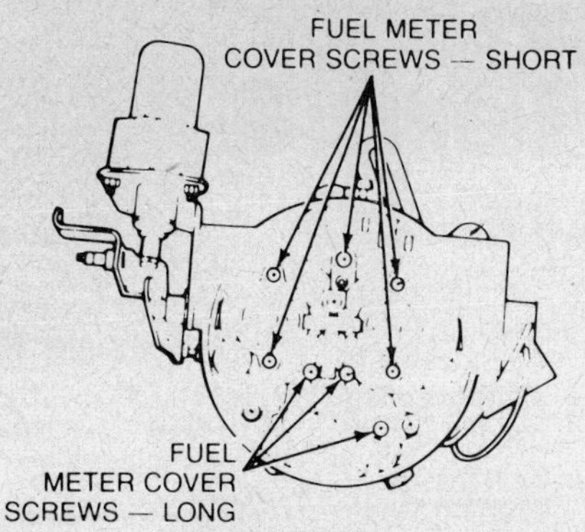

Fig. 7 Fuel meter cover replacement

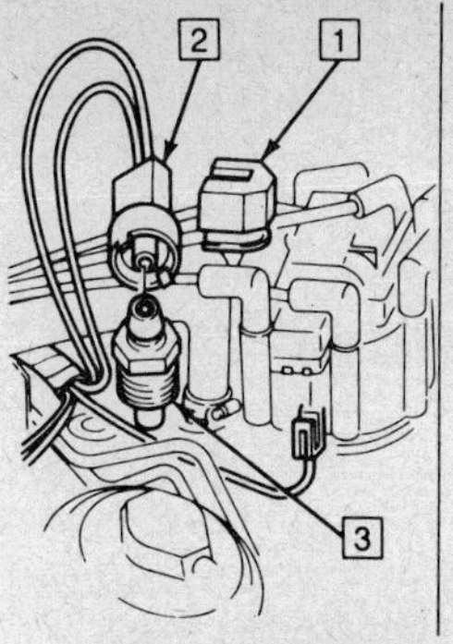

1 COOLANT TEMPERATURE SENSOR RETAINER
2 ECM HARNESS-CONNECTOR TO COOLANT SENSOR
3 COOLANT SENSOR

Fig. 8 Coolant sensor replacement

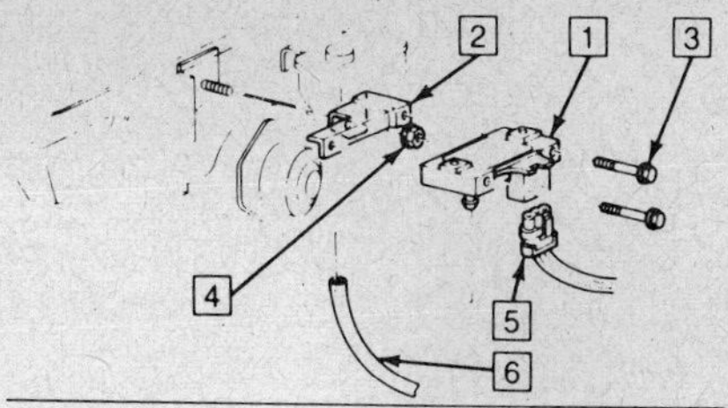

1 MAP SENSOR
2 BRACKET
3 SCREW (1.4 N•m)
4 NUT (8 N•m)
5 ECM HARNESS-CONNECTOR TO MAP SENSOR
6 MAP HOSE TO TBI MANIFOLD VACUUM PORT

Fig. 9 Manifold Absolute Pressure (MAP) sensor replacement

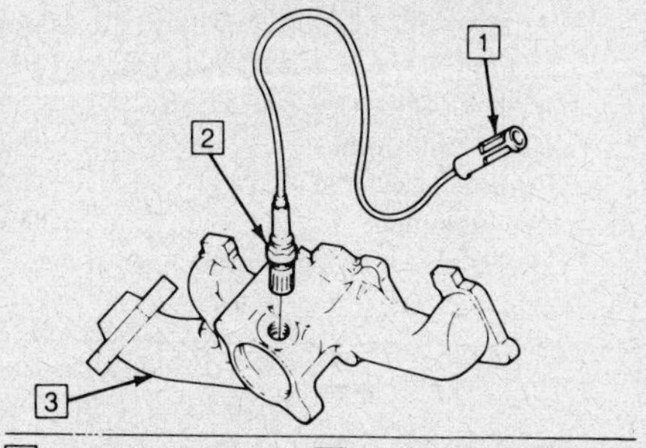

1 ECM HARNESS-CONNECTOR TO OXYGEN SENSOR
2 OXYGEN SENSOR
3 EXHAUST MANIFOLD

Fig. 10 Oxygen sensor replacement

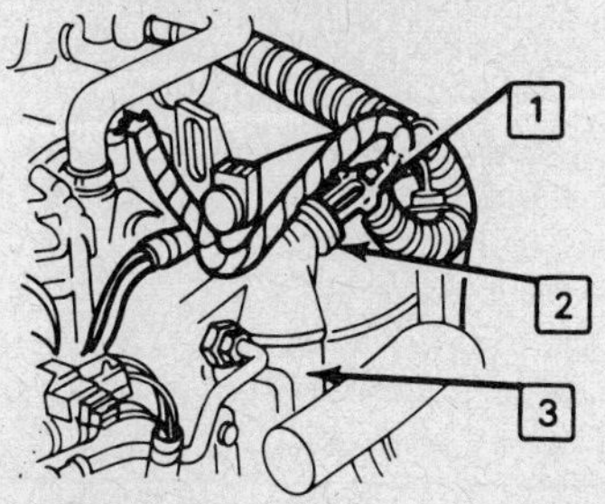

1 ECM HARNESS — CONNECTOR TO OIL PRESSURE SWITCH
2 OIL PRESSURE SWITCH
3 OIL FILTER

Fig. 11 Oil pressure switch replacement

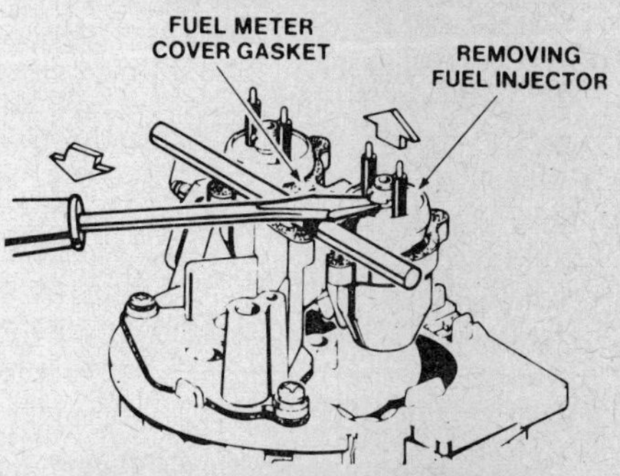

Fig. 12 Fuel injector removal

2. Remove two sensor attaching screws and the sensor. Discard screws. **It may be necessary to remove sensor actuator lever-to-throttle shaft screw.**

Installation

1. Install sensor with throttle valve in normal closed position. Ensure sensor pickup lever is located above tang on throttle actuator lever.
2. Install retainers and two new attaching screws and lockwashers, using a suitable locking compound on screw threads.
3. Adjust sensor, then tighten attaching screws.

FUEL METER COVER, REPLACE

1. Remove air cleaner assembly, then disconnect injector electrical connectors.
2. Remove fuel meter cover attaching screws and the cover. Note location of four short screws, **Fig. 7**, for installation reference.
3. Reverse procedure to install, using new seal and gaskets.

IDLE SPEED CONTROL (ISC) MOTOR, REPLACE

1. Remove air cleaner assembly, then disconnect motor electrical connectors.
2. Remove ISC motor attaching screws and the motor.
3. Reverse procedure to install, then adjust motor.

COOLANT SENSOR, REPLACE

1. Drain radiator until coolant level is below sensor.
2. Disconnect sensor electrical connector and remove sensor, **Fig. 8**.
3. Reverse procedure to install.

MANIFOLD ABSOLUTE PRESSURE (MAP) SENSOR, REPLACE

Removal

1. Disconnect sensor electrical connector.
2. Remove sensor attaching screw and the sensor, **Fig. 9**.
3. Reverse procedure to install.

Installation

1. Lubricate, then install new O-ring over injector nozzle.
2. Position upper O-ring back-up washer and a new lubricated O-ring into housing bore.
3. Position injector into throttle body, then center nozzle into bottom housing bore and install injector. Align electrical terminals so that pin in bottom of injector fits into locating hole in bottom of injector cavity.
4. Install fuel meter cover as previously described, then start engine and check for leaks and proper injector operation.
5. Connect injector electrical connectors, then install air cleaner assembly.

OXYGEN SENSOR, REPLACE

1. Disconnect battery ground cable.
2. Raise and support vehicle.
3. Disconnect sensor electrical connector and remove sensor, **Fig. 10.**
4. Reverse procedure to install. Coat sensor threads with a suitable anti-seize compound and torque sensor to 30 ft. lbs.

OIL PRESSURE SWITCH, REPLACE

1. Remove oil pressure switch lock collar.
2. Disconnect switch electrical connector and remove switch from rear of engine, **Fig. 11.**
3. Reverse procedure to install.

INJECTORS, REPLACE

1. Remove air cleaner assembly, then disconnect injector electrical connectors.
2. Remove fuel meter cover as previously described.
3. Remove injector from fuel meter body by carefully lifting out with a screwdriver, **Fig. 12.** Leave fuel meter cover gasket in place to prevent damage to body casting.
4. Discard upper and lower O-rings.

Port Fuel Injection, Exc. 1986–87 Buick Riviera & Oldsmobile Toronado

INDEX

DESCRIPTION

Multi-port Fuel Injection (MFI) and Sequential Fuel Injection (SFI) provide a means of fuel metering which insures a precise air/fuel mixture and superior fuel distribution, resulting in reduced exhaust emissions and improved driveability under all driving conditions.

The MFI & SFI engines share many similar components. The main operating difference between two types of injection systems is in fuel delivery. The MFI engines inject metered fuel into all cylinder inlet ports at the same time once every engine revolution. Using this method, two injections of fuel are required to produce the charge for each combustion cycle. The SFI engines inject metered fuel sequentially into each cylinder inlet port once per working cycle (every two revolutions) just prior to the opening of each intake valve.

An Electronic Control Module (ECM) is used to determine the amount of fuel delivered to the engine. The ECM receives signals from several sensors and devices to know what mode of operation the engine is being subjected to, then analyzes the information and adjusts the fuel mixture accordingly. Because of this constant measuring and adjusting of the air/fuel ratio, these systems are referred to as a "Closed Loop."

The ECM is capable of diagnosing faults with the various inputs and systems it controls. When the ECM detects a malfunction, a "Check Engine" or "Service Engine Soon" lamp in the instrument panel is illuminated, warning the driver to have the system checked.

Fuel is supplied to the injector fuel rail by a tank mounted high pressure fuel pump. A pressure regulator is integral with the fuel rail to keep fuel available to the injectors at a constant pressure. The fuel pump is operated by the ECM through the fuel pump relay and oil pressure switch.

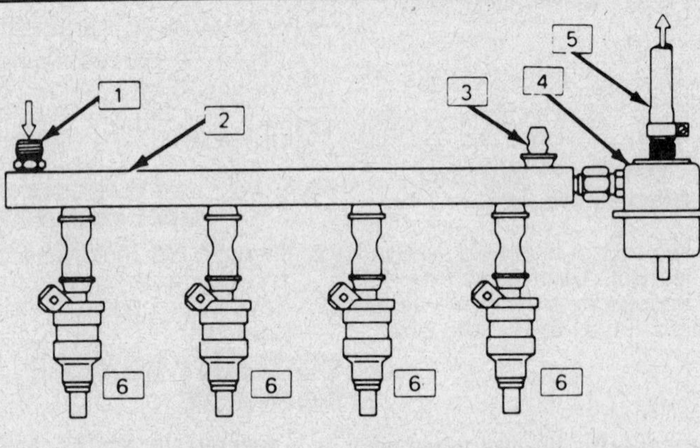

Fig. 1 Fuel rail assembly (Typical)

SYSTEM COMPONENTS

THROTTLE BODY UNIT

The throttle body unit is used to control the amount of air entering the engine. This is accomplished through the use of a throttle valve. The Idle Air Control (IAC) valve and Throttle Position Sensor (TPS) are also mounted on the throttle body unit.

The throttle body unit contains vacuum ports located above or below the throttle valve. These ports provide vacuum signals to operate various components.

FUEL RAIL

The fuel rail is mounted directly above the engine intake manifold runners. At one end, high pressure fuel enters and is made available to the individual injectors. At the other end, a fuel pressure regulator is mounted to keep the fuel pressure at a steady level. Remaining fuel is returned to the fuel tank, **Fig. 1.**

FUEL INJECTOR

The fuel injector is solenoid operated and ECM controlled. The ECM energizes the solenoid, which opens a valve, allowing fuel delivery. The fuel, which is stored under pressure in the fuel rail, is injected in a conical spray pattern into the intake manifold near the intake valve, **Fig. 2.**

PRESSURE REGULATOR

The pressure regulator is a diaphragm type relief valve with injector pressure acting on one side of the diaphragm and manifold and spring pressure acting on the other, **Fig. 3.** The regulator maintains constant pressure in the fuel rail by controlling flow in the return line. The pressure regulator also serves as a load compensator by increasing fuel pressure at times of low manifold vacuum.

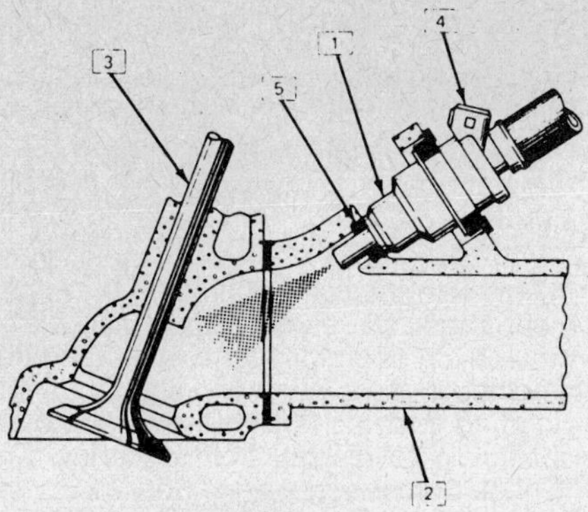

Fig. 2 Fuel injector assembly

IDLE AIR CONTROL (IAC) VALVE

The Idle Air Control (IAC) Valve is located in the throttle body unit and is used to control engine idle speed. The valve operates by allowing air to bypass the throttle valve in the throttle body unit. If engine RPM is too low, the ECM will move the IAC conical valve in to allow more air to bypass the throttle valve. If engine RPM is too high, the ECM will move the IAC conical valve out to allow less air to bypass the throttle valve, **Fig. 4.**

If IAC connector is removed with the engine running, the idle set RPM may be lost. To reset idle set RPM, turn ignition On, then Off.

ELECTRONIC CONTROL MODULE (ECM)

The Electronic Control Module (ECM), located in the passenger compartment, is the control center for the fuel injection system. The ECM continually monitors and processes the input information and generates output commands to the various systems affecting vehicle performance.

A removable calibration unit (PROM) enables the ECM to recognize and adjust for vehicle variations (vehicle weight, axle ratio, etc.). There are specific ECM/PROM combinations for each specific vehicle which are not interchangeable.

A CALPAK is also installed in the ECM. The CALPAK allows fuel delivery if other parts of the ECM are damaged.

The ECM also performs the diagnostic function of the fuel injection system. When the ECM senses an operational problem, it will illuminate the "Check Engine" lamp and store the appropriate code(s) to identify the problem area.

DATA SENSORS

Engine Coolant Temperature Sensor

The engine temperature sensor is located in the flow of the engine coolant and sends information concerning temperature to the ECM.

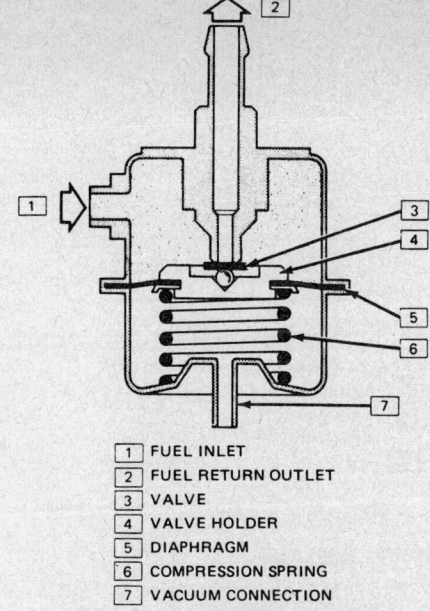

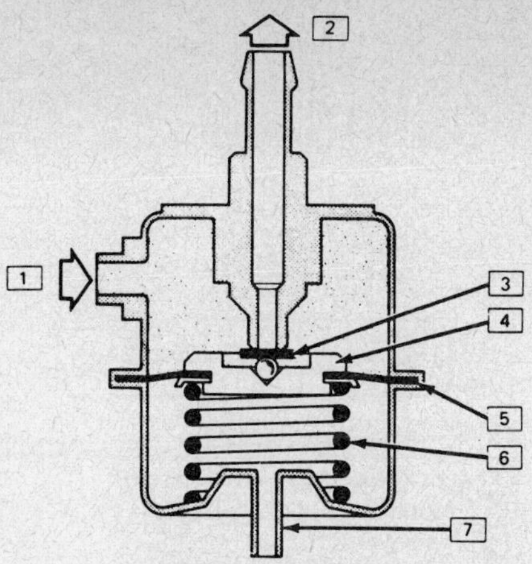

Fig. 3 Fuel pressure regulator

Mass Air Flow (MAF) Sensor (Exc. 4-110/1.8L Turbo)

The mass air flow (MAF) sensor measures the amount of air being consumed by the engine and sends the information to the ECM. The ECM uses this information to determine the operating condition of the engine and to meter the fuel accordingly. If the MAF sensor indicates a large quantity of air is being consumed, the ECM will recognize the engine is accelerating. If the MAF sensor indicates a small quantity of air is being consumed, the ECM will recognize this as deceleration or idle.

V6-173 Engine W/AC Delco MAF Sensor (Exc. Fiero)

The MAF sensor used on this engine produces a frequency output which is directly proportional to the air entering the engine. The output will vary from approximately 32 Hertz at idle to 150 Hertz during wide open throttle applications. If the sensor fails at a low frequency, a code 34 will be set and stored. A code 44 or 45 may also be caused by a faulty MAF sensor.

V8-305 Engine W/Bosch MAF Sensor

The Bosch MAF Sensor is of the hot wire type. Current is supplied to the sensing wire (hot wire) to maintain a calibrated temperature, and as air flow increases or decreases the current will vary. This varying of current causes a voltage drop within the meter circuitry which is directly proportional to the incoming air mass. The ECM supplies a current limiting 5 volt source on the signal line. The MAF sensor draws approximately .4 volts with a low air flow and up to 5 volts with a high air flow (during wide open throttle applications).

Manifold Air Temperature (MAT) Sensor (4-110/1.8L Turbo)

The manifold air temperature (MAT)

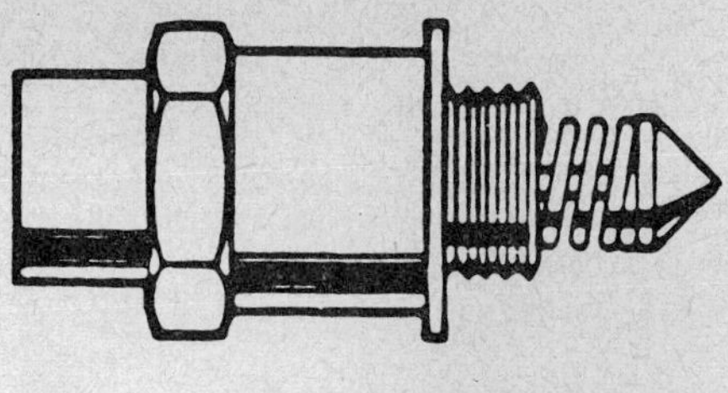

Fig. 4 Idle Air Control (IAC) valve

sensor is a thermistor mounted in the intake manifold. Low intake air temperature produces a high resistance, while high intake air resistance produces low resistance. The ECM supplies a 5 volt signal to the sensor through a resistor and measures the voltage. By measuring the voltage, the ECM can determine MAT.

Manifold Absolute Pressure (MAP) Sensor (4-110/1.8L Turbo)

The manifold absolute pressure (MAP) sensor measures changes in the intake manifold pressure resulting from engine load and speed changes and converts this to a voltage output. By monitoring the sensor output voltage, the ECM can determine the MAP. The higher the MAP, the lower the engine vacuum and the higher the sensor output, which requires more fuel. The lower the MAP, the higher the engine vacuum and the lower the sensor output, which requires less fuel.

Vehicle Speed Sensor (VSS)

The vehicle speed sensor (VSS) sends a pulsating voltage signal to the ECM, which the ECM converts to mph. This sensor mainly controls the operation of the Transmission Controlled Clutch (TCC) system.

Oxygen Sensor

The exhaust oxygen sensor is located in the exhaust system and monitors oxygen content in the exhaust gas stream. The oxygen content of the exhaust gas reacts with the oxygen sensor to produce a voltage output. By monitoring the oxygen sensor output voltage, the ECM can determine the amount of oxygen in the exhaust gas and adjust the air/fuel mixture accordingly.

Throttle Position Sensor (TPS)

The throttle position sensor is connected to the throttle valve shaft in the throttle body unit. The TPS is a potentiometer with one connection to ground and the other to a ECM 5 volt voltage source. A third wire from the ECM is used to measure the voltage from the TPS. As the throttle angle changes, so does the TPS voltage output. By monitoring TPS voltage output, the ECM can determine fuel delivery rate based on throttle valve angle.

DATA SIGNALS

Park/Neutral Switch

The park/neutral switch indicates to the ECM when the transmission is in park or neutral. This information is used by the ECM for ignition timing, IAC operation and Transmission Controlled Clutch (TCC) operation.

Do not drive vehicle with park/neutral switch disconnected, as idle quality may be affected.

Crank Signal (4-110/1.8L Turbo)

This signal is used to inform the ECM that the engine is cranking. The ECM uses this information to tell when the engine is in the starting mode.

Distributor (EST) Reference Signal

This signal is used to inform the ECM of engine RPM and crankshaft position.

Power Steering Pressure Switch

The power steering pressure switch opens during high pressure power steering situations. When the power steering switch is open, power to the air conditioning relay is shut off, resulting in compressor clutch disengagement. A signal is also sent to the ECM. The ECM uses this signal for idle control.

Air Conditioning "On" Signal

The air conditioning "On" signal informs the ECM the A/C selector switch is turned on, and the A/C pressure cycling switch is closed. Using this information, the ECM adjusts the engine idle speed as necessary to ensure a smooth idle.

OPERATION

STARTING MODE

When the ignition is switched On, the ECM energizes the fuel pump for two seconds and pressure is built up in the fuel rail. The ECM then checks the coolant temperature sensor, the TPS and crank signal and determines the proper air/fuel ratio for starting.

The ECM controls the air/fuel ratio by changing how long the injectors are turned on and off. This is accomplished by "Pulsing" the injectors for short periods of time.

The cold start valve, used on V6-173, V8-305 and 350 engines, is not controlled by the ECM. This valve is used to provide additional fuel during the starting mode of operation to improve cold start-ups. The cold start circuit is important when engine coolant temperature is very low because the other eight injectors will not be pulsed ON long enough to provide the needed amount of fuel to start the engine.

CLEAR FLOOD MODE

A flooded engine is cleared by fully depressing the accelerator pedal, which causes the ECM to pulse the injectors at a air/fuel ratio of 20:1. The ECM will maintain this air/fuel ratio as long as the throttle is wide open and engine RPM is less than 600. If throttle position becomes less than 80% of wide open throttle, the ECM returns to "Starting Mode."

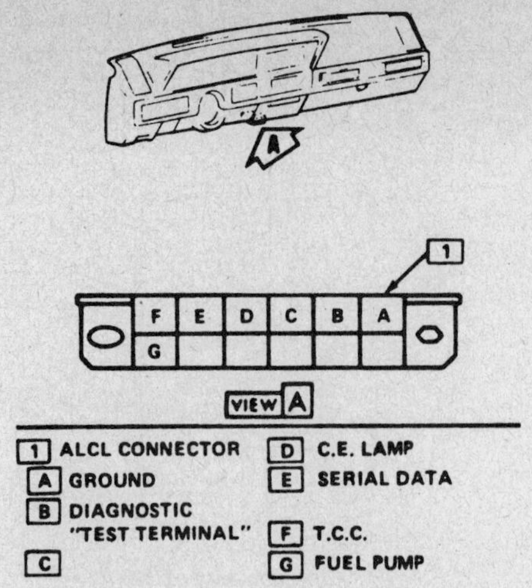

Fig. 5 ALCL connector

RUN MODE

The Run Mode consists of two separate operating conditions; open loop and closed loop. The engine operates in open loop when it is first started and RPM is above 400 RPM. During open loop operation, the ECM disregards the oxygen sensor signal and determines air/fuel mixture primarily from coolant and MAF sensors on V6-173/2.8L (except Fiero), V6-181/3.0L, V6-231/3.8L, V8-305/5.0L and V8-350/5.7L engines or from the coolant and MAP sensors on 4-110/1.8L Turbo and Fiero V6-173/2.8L engines. The engine will continue to operate in open loop until the following conditions are met:

1. The oxygen sensor has varying voltage output, indicating it is hot enough to operate properly.
2. The coolant sensor is above a specified temperature.
3. A specific amount of time has elapsed since the engine was started. **The specified values for conditions mentioned above vary from model to model, and are stored in the ECM PROM.**

When the above conditions are met, the engine goes into closed loop operation. When operating in closed loop, the ECM determines the air/fuel ratio (injector pulse rate) based on signals from the oxygen sensor. This allows the air/fuel mixture to remain close to the optimum 14.7:1 ratio.

ACCELERATION MODE

In the Acceleration Mode, the ECM senses rapid change in throttle position and manifold pressure or air flow and provides a corresponding amount of added fuel.

DECELERATION MODE

In the Deceleration Mode, the ECM senses changes in throttle position and manifold pressure of air flow and reduces fuel delivery. When decelerating very rapidly, the ECM can cut off fuel completely for short periods of time.

BATTERY VOLTAGE CORRECTION MODE

When battery voltage is low, the ECM compensates to maintain acceptable system performance by increasing injector pulses, idle speed and ignition dwell time.

DIAGNOSIS

"CHECK ENGINE" OR "SERVICE ENGINE SOON" LIGHT

This warning light, located on the instrument panel, serves two purposes: to alert the vehicle operator that a fault has been detected in the system and should be serviced as soon as possible and as a diagnostic aid to display trouble codes. The "Check Engine" light and "Service Engine Soon" light perform the same function and which light is used depends on particular vehicle application.

This light will illuminate with the ignition key on and the engine not running. When the engine is started, the light should go out. If the light remains lit, the self-diagnostic system has detected a malfunction. If the malfunction clears, the light will go out after ten seconds and a trouble code will be stored in the ECM.

TROUBLE CODES

The ECM uses sensors to monitor various engine operating conditions and compares present values with preset values stored in its memory. When the ECM detects a malfunction in any of the monitored systems, it will turn on the "Check Engine" or "Service Engine Soon" light and store a corresponding trouble code in the memory. Each trouble code indicates which circuit a particular problem is in.

ALCL CONNECTOR

To extract a trouble code from the ECM for diagnostic purposes, the Assembly Line Communication Link (ALCL) connector, **Fig. 5**, is used.

The ALCL diagnostic connector is located in the passenger compartment. Terminal B of the connector is the test terminal and terminal A is the ground used for diagnostic display.

If the test terminal is grounded with ignition on and engine not running, the system will enter the diagnostic mode. In this mode, the ECM will display a Code 12 three consecutive times by flashing the "Check Engine" or "Service Engine Soon" light. A Code 12 consists of one flash, a short pause, then two flashes in rapid succession. After Code 12 is displayed, any stored trouble codes will be displayed three times each by flashing the "Check Engine" or "Service Engine Soon" light. In the diagnostic mode, the ECM will also energize all ECM controlled relays and solenoids.

If the test terminal is grounded with the engine running, the system will enter the field service mode. In this mode, the "Check Engine" or "Service Engine Soon" light will indicate whether the system is in open or closed loop operation. If the system is in open loop operation, the light will flash approximately two and one-half times per second. Closed loop operation is indicated by the light flashing approximately once per second. In closed loop operation, the light will stay out most of the time if system is too lean and remain on

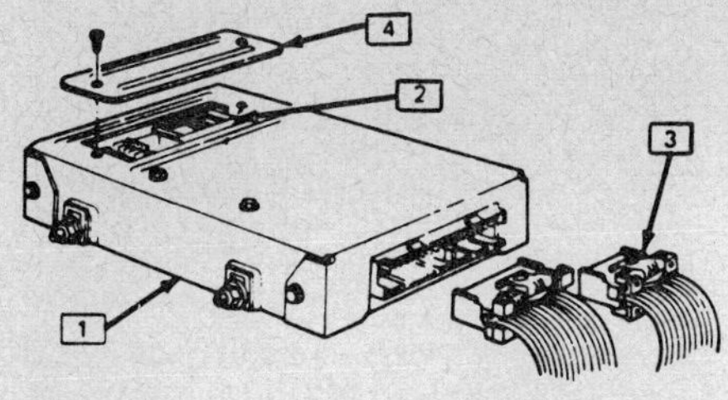

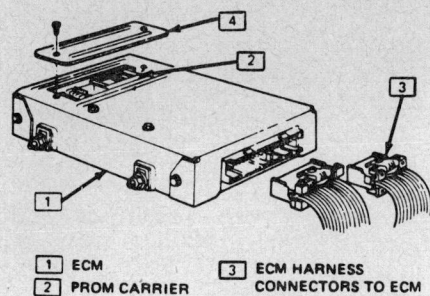

[1] ECM
[2] PROM CARRIER
[3] ECM HARNESS CONNECTORS TO ECM
[4] PROM ACCESS COVER

Fig. 6 PROM access cover removal

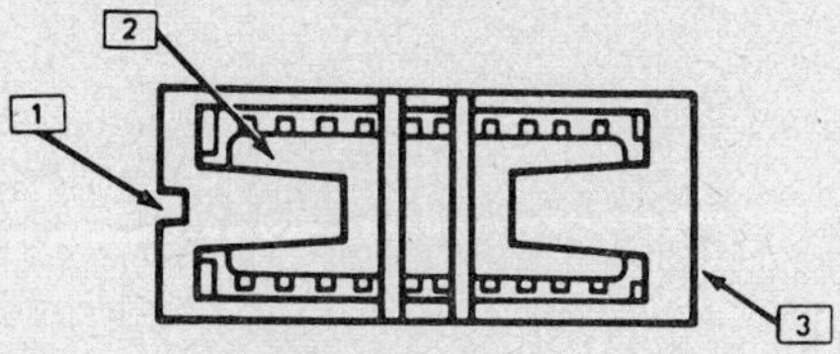

[1] REFERENCE END
[2] PROM
[3] PROM CARRIER

Fig. 8 Installing PROM in carrier

most of the time if system is too rich.

CLEARING TROUBLE CODES

Stored trouble codes in the ECM memory can be cleared by removing battery voltage from the ECM. To do this, disconnect the ECM harness from positive battery pigtail for ten seconds with ignition off. Trouble codes should be cleared after any repairs have been performed.

After the ECM memory has been cleared, a change may be noted in vehicle performance. To restore the vehicle to normal, drive with engine at normal operating temperature at part throttle with moderate acceleration and idle conditions until normal performance is restored.

INTERMITTENT TROUBLE CODES VS. HARD FAILURES

A hard trouble code is one which is present when performing diagnostic procedures on the vehicle. An intermittent code is one which does not reset itself and is not present when performing diagnostic procedures.

Because many intermittent malfunctions are caused at electrical connections, diagnosis of such problems should begin with a visual and physical inspection of connectors involved with the code. Appropriate connectors should be disconnected, examined and reconnected before replacing any components.

ADJUSTMENTS

THROTTLE POSITION SENSOR (TPS), ADJUST

Exc. 4-110/1.8L Turbo

1. Disconnect TPS electrical connector.
2. Remove TPS attaching screws, then apply thread locking compound 1052624 or equivalent to screw threads and reinstall. Do not tighten screws.
3. Install three jumper wires between TPS and TPS wire connector.
4. With ignition On and engine not running, measure voltage between sensor terminals B and C on non-turbocharged models or sensor terminals A and B on turbocharged models with a digital voltmeter.
5. With throttle in closed position, adjust TPS to obtain .55 ± .05 volts on V6-173/2.8L and V6-181/3.0L; .40 ± .05 volts on V6-231/3.8L; .54 ± .075 volts on V8-305/5.0L & V8-350/5.7L.
6. Tighten screws, then recheck adjustment to ensure it did not change.
7. Turn ignition Off, then remove jumper wires and connect TPS wire connector.

4-110/1.8L Turbo

The TPS used on these models is not adjustable. The ECM uses the reading at idle for the zero reading, so adjustment is not necessary.

COLD START VALVE, ADJUST

1. Bend tang backward and turn valve completely into body.
2. Turn valve back one full turn, until electrical connector is facing up.
3. Bend tang back to limit rotation of valve less than a full turn.
4. Reinstall and check for leaks.

COMPONENT REPLACEMENT

Always relieve fuel system pressure prior to disconnecting fuel system components.

ECM, REPLACE

When replacing a production ECM with a service ECM, transfer the broadcast code and production number from the production unit to the service unit. Also, during replacement, the PROM must be removed from the ECM being replaced and transferred to the new unit. Refer to "PROM, Replace" for procedure.

1. Disconnect battery ground cable.
2. Disconnect two ECM electrical connectors.
3. Remove ECM mounting hardware.
4. Remove ECM from passenger compartment.
5. Reverse procedure to install.

PROM, REPLACE

1. Remove ECM from vehicle as described under "ECM, Replace."
2. Remove PROM access cover, **Fig. 6. Note position of PROM unit in ECM. PROMs are not interchangeable. Replacement PROMs must be installed in the same position and direction as defective PROM.**
3. Grasp PROM carrier with PROM removal tool, **Fig. 7.**

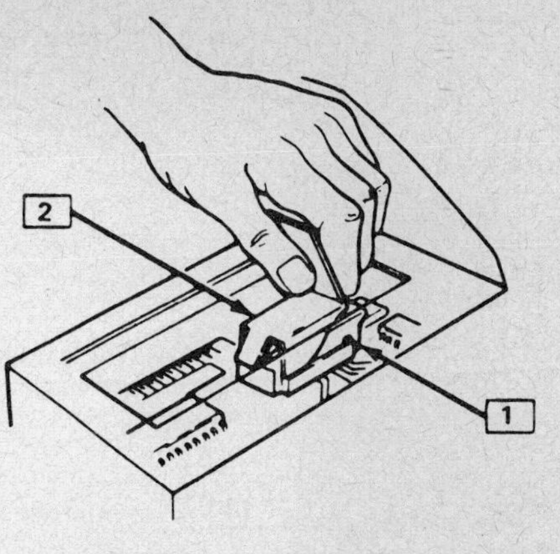

[1] PROM CARRIER
[2] PROM REMOVAL TOOL

Fig. 7 PROM removal

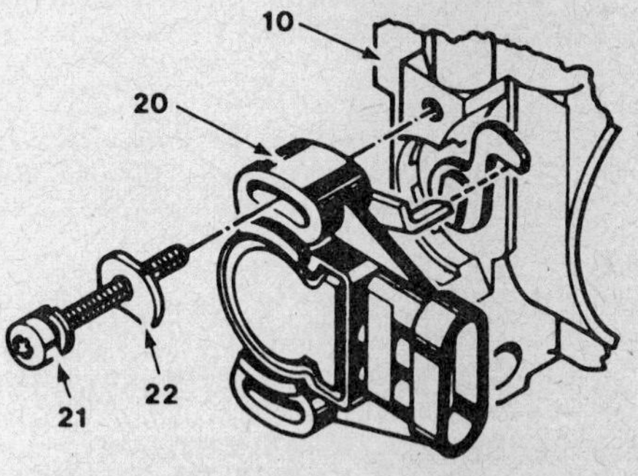

10 THROTTLE BODY ASSEMBLY
20 THROTTLE POSITION SENSOR (TPS)
21 TPS ATTACHING SCREW
22 TPS RETAINER

Fig. 9 Throttle position sensor

4. Rock carrier side-to-side while applying a firm upward force, then remove PROM and carrier. Remove PROM from carrier. **Inspect replacement PROM to ensure the part number is the same as the removed PROM.**
5. Install replacement PROM in carrier, **Fig. 8.**
6. Position PROM and carrier assembly over PROM socket and press down firmly on top of carrier. Press down on carrier and ensure it seats squarely.
7. Replace PROM access cover, then install ECM in vehicle.
8. Start engine, enter diagnosis and check for code 51. If code 51 does not display, PROM is installed correctly. If code 51 is displayed, PROM is installed incorrectly and installation procedure must be repeated. **If PROM is installed backwards, it will be destroyed.**

MEM-CAL, REPLACE

1. Remove ECM from vehicle and access cover from ECM.
2. Push both retaining clips back away from MEM-CAL. At the same time grasp both ends of the MEM-CAL and lift it from socket.

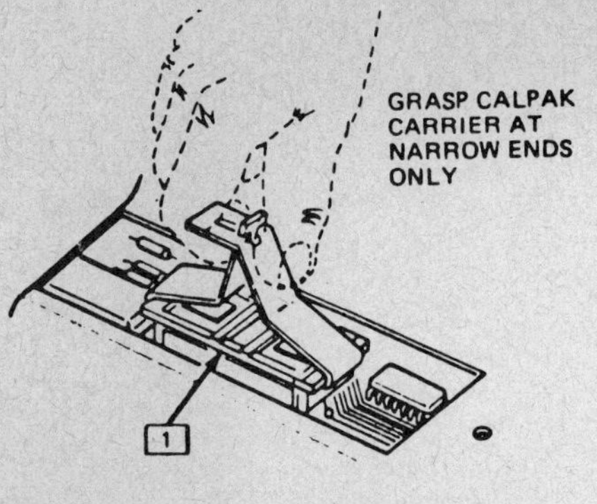

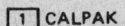

1 CALPAK   2 REMOVAL TOOL

Fig. 10 CALPAK removal

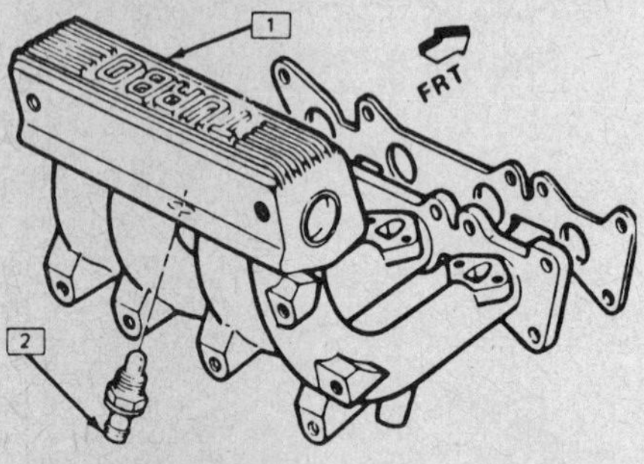

1 INTAKE MANIFOLD
2 SENSOR-MANIFOLD TEMP.

Fig. 13 MAT sensor removal. 4-110/1.8L Turbo

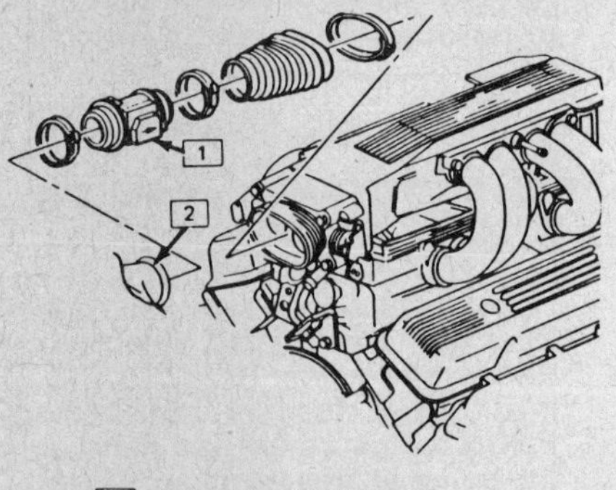

1 MASS AIR FLOW SENSOR
2 AIR CLEANER ASSEMBLY

Fig. 16 MAF sensor removal

3. Align small notches of MEM-CAL with notches in ECM and position MEM-CAL in socket.
4. Evenly press on both ends of MEM-CAL, until retaining clips snap onto ends of MEM-CAL. **Do not press on center of MEM-CAL. Only press on ends or MEM-CAL will be damaged.**
5. Replace access cover, then install ECM in vehicle.

THROTTLE POSITION SENSOR, REPLACE

1. Disconnect TPS electrical connector.
2. Remove two TPS attaching screws, lockwashers and retainers.
3. Remove TPS.

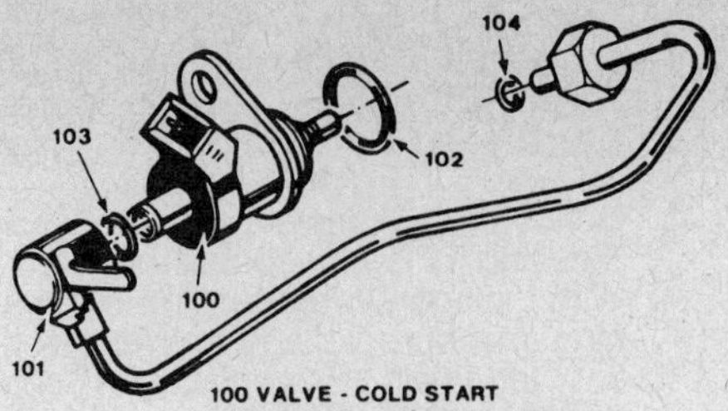

100 VALVE - COLD START
101 TUBE AND BODY ASSEMBLY
102 O-RING SEAL - VALVE
103 O-RING SEAL - BODY
104 O-RING SEAL - TUBE

Fig. 11 MAP sensor removal

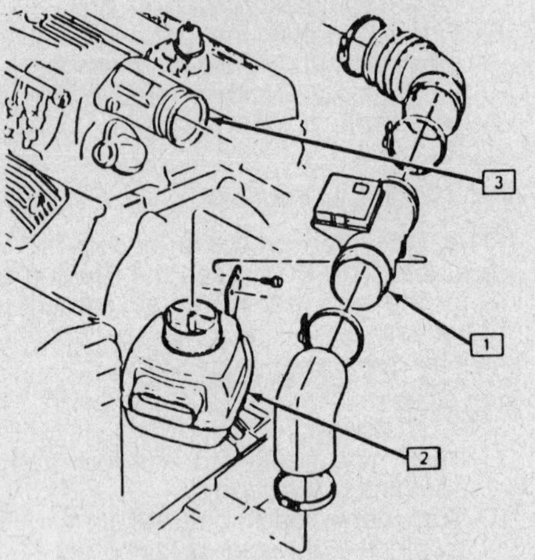

1 MASS AIR FLOW SENSOR
2 AIR CLEANER ASSEMBLY
3 THROTTLE BODY ASSEMBLY

Fig. 14 MAF sensor removal. V6-231/3.8L Non-Turbo

4. With throttle valve in normal closed idle position, install TPS. Ensure TPS pickup lever is located above tang on throttle actuator lever, **Fig. 9.**
5. Apply thread locking compound 1052624 or equivalent to screw threads, then install retainers, lockwashers and screws. On 4-110/1.8L Turbo models, tighten screws. On all other models, adjust TPS. Refer to "Throttle Position Sensor (TPS) Sensor, Adjust" for procedure.

CALPAK, REPLACE

To replace CALPAK, refer to **Fig. 10.**

COLD START VALVE & TUBE ASSEMBLY, REPLACE

V6-173/2.8L 1986 Ciera

1. Disconnect negative ground cable.
2. Remove plenum, IAC tube and engine mount strut brace.
3. Remove fuel line at fuel rail.
4. Remove electrical connector from valve.
5. Remove valve attaching bolt, then valve, **Fig. 11.**
6. Replace O-rings.
7. Reverse procedure to install.

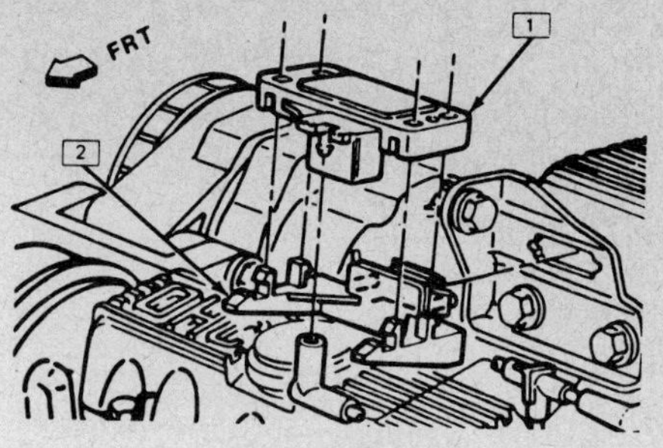

1 M.A.P. SENSOR
2 BRACKET

Fig. 12 MAP sensor removal. 4-110/1.8L Turbo

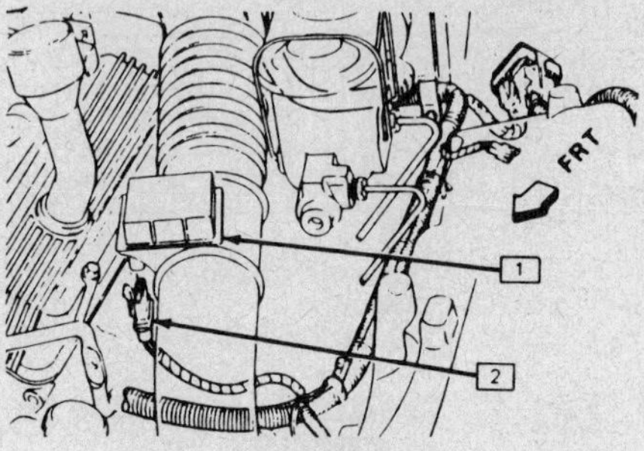

1 M.A.F. SENSOR
2 M.A.F. SENSOR CONNECTOR

Fig. 15 MAF sensor removal. V6-231/3.8L Turbo

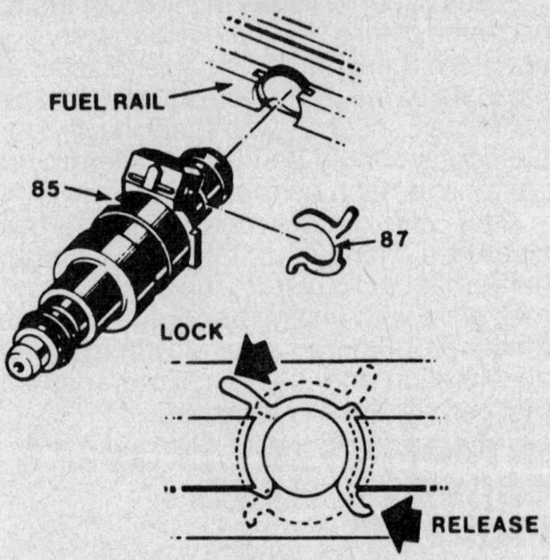

85 INJECTOR - PORT
87 CLIP-INJECTOR RETAINER

Fig. 17 Port injector retainer clip removal

V6-173/2.8L 1986 Firenza

1. Remove negative ground cable.
2. Remove alternator.
3. Remove plenum and IAC tube.
4. Remove electrical connector from valve.
5. Remove valve attaching bolt, then valve, **Fig. 11.**
6. Replace O-rings.
7. Reverse procedure to install.

V8-305/5.0L

1. Remove negative ground cable.
2. Remove plenum.
3. Remove distributor cap.

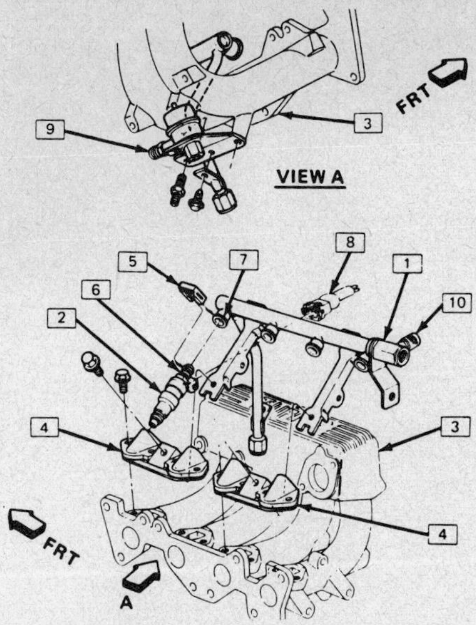

1 FUEL RAIL ASSEMBLY
2 INJECTOR
3 INTAKE MANIFOLD
4 INJECTOR HOUSING ASSEMBLY
5 INJECTOR RETAINING CLIP
6 INJECTOR ASM. RETAINING GROOVE
7 INJECTOR CUP FLANGE
8 INJECTOR CONTROL HARNESS ASM.
9 PRESSURE REGULATOR ASM.
10 FUEL PRESSURE GAGE TEST POINT

Fig. 18 Fuel rail removal. 4-110/1.8L Turbo

4. Remove electrical connector from valve.
5. Remove valve attaching bolt, then valve, **Fig. 11.**
6. Replace O-rings.
7. Reverse procedure to install.

V8-350/5.7L

1. Remove negative ground cable.
2. Remove brake booster line.
3. Remove fuel line at fuel rail.
4. Remove PCV pipe retaining screws.
5. Remove electrical connector from valve.
6. Remove valve attaching bolts, then valve, **Fig. 11.**
7. Replace O-rings.
8. Reverse procedure to install.

MAP & MAT SENSOR, REPLACE

4-110/1.8L Turbo Only

To replace MAP sensor, refer to **Fig. 12.** To replace MAT sensor, refer to **Fig. 13.**

MAF SENSOR, REPLACE

V6-181/3.0 & V6-231/3.8L All

To replace MAF sensor on non-turbocharged models, refer to **Fig. 14.** To replace MAF sensor on turbocharged models, refer to **Fig. 15.**

V6-173/2.8L, V6-181/3.0L & V8-305/5.0L

Refer to **Fig. 16** for removal procedure.

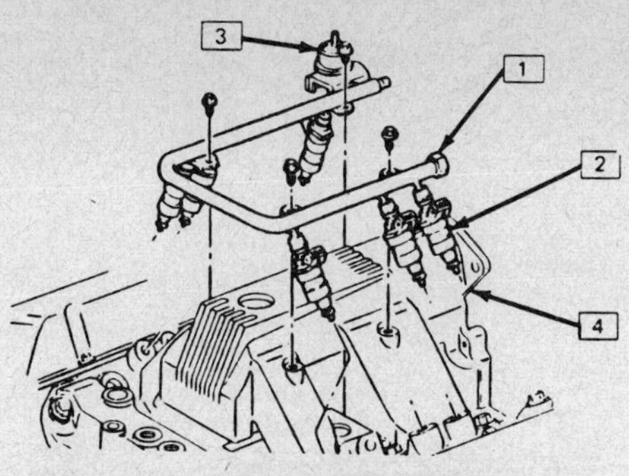

Fig. 19 Fuel rail removal. V6-231/3.8L

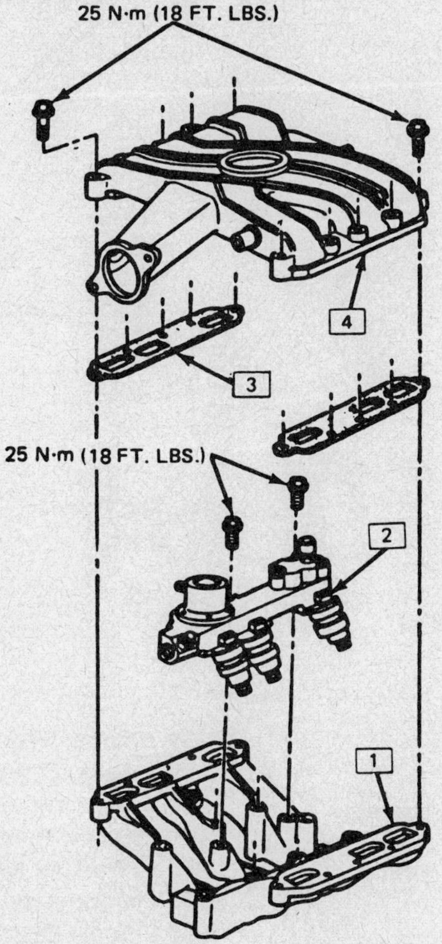

1 INTAKE MANIFOLD
2 FUEL RAIL ASSEMBLY
3 GASKET
4 PLENUM

Fig. 21 Fuel rail removal. V6-173/2.8L

OXYGEN SENSOR, REPLACE

The following procedure should be performed with engine temperature over 120° F, otherwise the oxygen sensor may be difficult to remove.

1. Disconnect battery ground cable.
2. Disconnect oxygen sensor electrical connector, then remove sensor.
3. Reverse procedure to install. Torque sensor to 30 ft. lbs. **Replacement sensors should have a special anti-seize compound applied to threads. If a replacement sensor is lacking anti-seize compound or original sensor is to be reinstalled, coat threads with suitable anti-seize compound.**

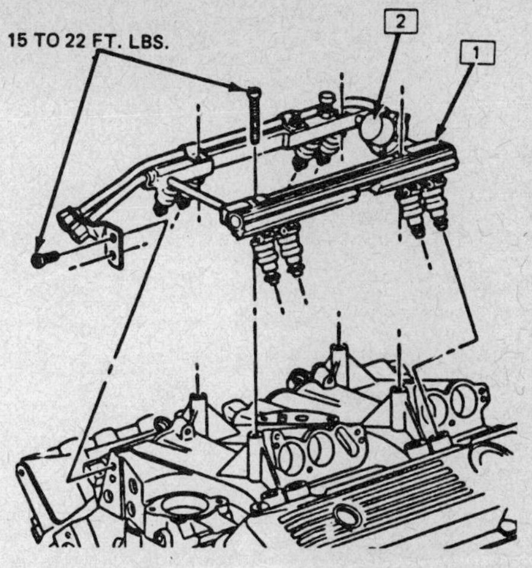

1 FUEL RAIL
2 PRESSURE REGULATOR

Fig. 20 Fuel rail removal. V8-305/5.0L

FUEL INJECTOR, REPLACE

1. With ignition Off, disconnect injector electrical connection(s).
2. Relieve fuel pressure. Refer to "Fuel Pressure Relief" procedure.
3. Remove fuel rail. Refer to "Fuel Rail, Replace."
4. Rotate injector retainer clips to release, **Fig. 17.**
5. Remove injector(s).
6. Reverse procedure to install. If original injector(s) are being reinstalled or replacement injector(s) do not come equipped with new O-rings, install new O-rings.

FUEL RAIL, REPLACE

1. Relieve fuel pressure. Refer to "Fuel Pressure Relief Procedure."
2. Remove fuel rail. Refer to **Figs. 18 through 21** for procedures.
3. Reverse procedure to install.

FUEL PRESSURE REGULATOR, REPLACE

4-110/1.8L Turbo

1. Relieve fuel pressure. Refer to "Fuel Pressure Relief" procedure.
2. Place suitable shop cloths around base of regulator to catch any fuel spills, then remove pressure regulator.
3. Reverse procedure to install.

V6-173/2.8L

The pressure regulator is factory adjusted. Under no circumstances should the regulator be removed from the fuel rail.

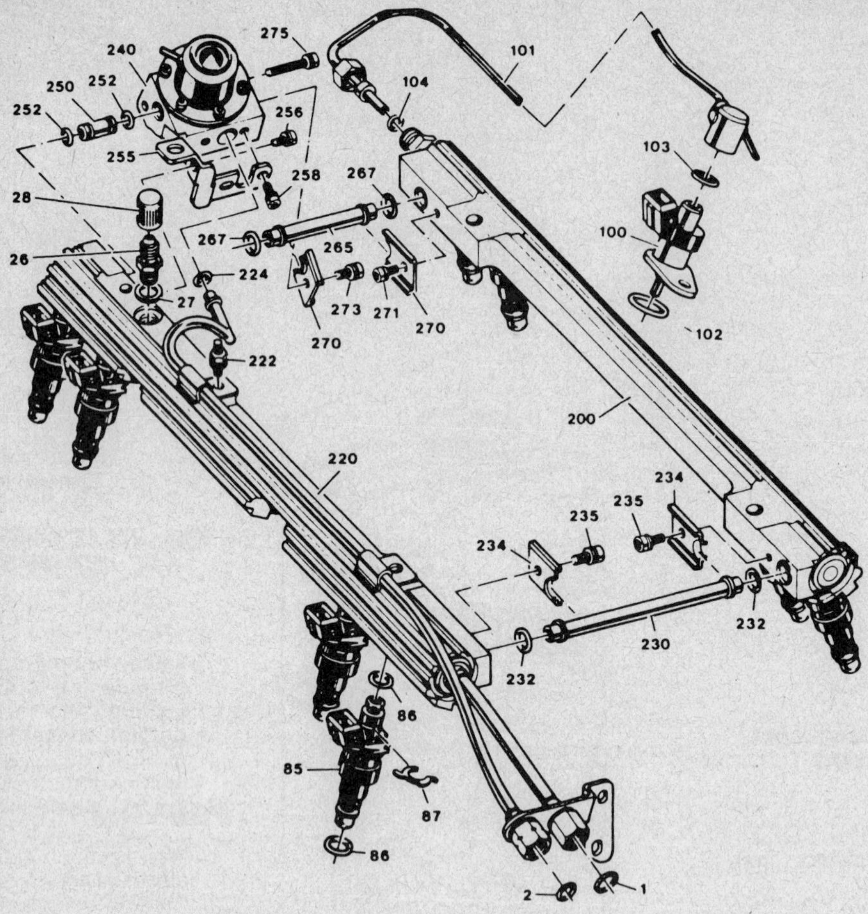

1 O-ring - Fuel Inlet Line
2 - O-ring - Fuel Return line
26 Fuel Pressure Connection Assembly
27 Seal - Fuel Pressure Connection Assembly
28 Cap - Fuel Pressure Connection
85 Injector - Port
86 Seal - O-ring - Injector
87 Clip - Injector Retainer
100 Valve - Cold Start
101 Tube & Body Assembly
102 Seal - O-ring - Valve
103 Seal - O-ring - Body
104 Seal - O-ring - Tube
200 Fuel Rail & Plug Assembly (LH)
220 Fuel Rail & Tube Assembly (RH)
222 Stud Assembly - Rear Bracket Attaching
224 Seal - O-ring - Fuel Outlet Tube
230 Tube - Front Crossover
232 Seal - O-ring - Front Crossover Tube
234 Retainer - Crossover Tube
235 Screw Assembly - Retainer Attaching
240 Pressure Regulator & Base Assembly
250 Connector - Base to Rail
252 Seal - O-ring - Connector
255 Bracket - Pressure Regulator and Base Assembly
256 Screw Assembly - Bracket to Rail Attaching
258 Screw Assembly - Bracket to Base Attaching
265 Tube - Rear Crossover
267 Seal - O-ring - Crossover Tube
270 Retainer - Rear Crossover Tube
271 Screw Assembly - Retainer to LH Rail
273 Screw Assembly - Retainer to Base
275 Screw Assembly - Base to RH Rail

Fig. 22 Pressure regulator removal. V8-305/5.0L & V8-350/5.7L

V8-305/5.0L, V8-350/5.7L

The pressure regulator is factory adjusted and no attempt should be made to remove the cover.

1. Remove crossover tube retainer attaching bolts (235) **Fig. 22,** then retainers (234).
2. Remove rear crossover retainer attaching bolt (273), then retainer (270).
3. Remove left side fuel rail and plug assembly (220) from the right side fuel rail (200).
4. Remove regulator bracket assembly attaching bolts (256 & 258), then bracket.
5. Remove rear stud assembly (222).
6. Remove right side rail attaching bolts (275), then regulator and base assembly (240).
7. Remove regulator from fuel outlet tube.
8. Remove base to rail connector (250).
9. Reverse procedure to install, noting the following:
   a. Replace all O-rings and coat with suitable oil prior to installation.

IDLE AIR CONTROL (IAC) VALVE, REPLACE

Removal

1. Disconnect IAC valve electrical connector.
2. Remove IAC valve using a suitable 1¼ inch wrench and discard gasket.

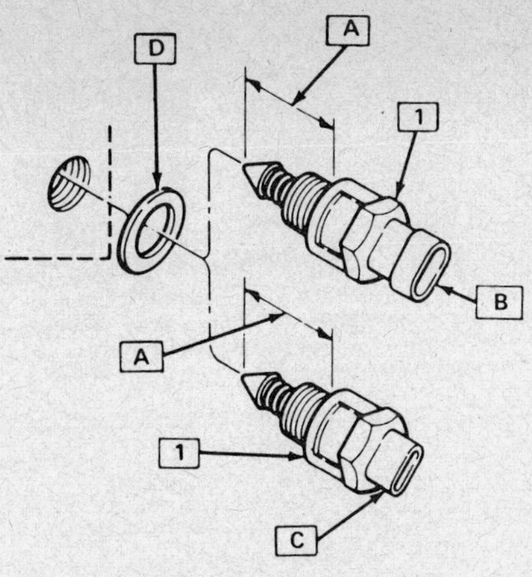

Fig. 23 IAC valve installation (Typical)

Installation

Prior to installation, identify IAC valve as being either Type 1 or Type 2, **Fig. 23.** If dimension "A" is greater than 1⅛ inch, reduce as follows:

On Type 1, exert a firm pressure on conical valve to retract it.

On Type 2, while turning valve in clockwise rotation, compress retaining spring from conical valve. Return spring to original position with straight part of spring end aligned with flat surface of valve.

1. Install IAC valve in throttle body using new gasket. Torque IAC valve to 13 ft. lbs.
2. Connect IAC valve electrical connector.
3. Start engine and allow to reach operating temperature.
4. On 4-110/1.8L Turbo engines, IAC valve will reset idle speed when vehicle is driven at 30 mph. On V6-231/3.8L engines, ECM will reset idle speed when ignition is turned On, then Off.

SYSTEM SERVICE

FUEL PRESSURE RELIEF PROCEDURE

1. Remove fuel pump fuse from fuse block.
2. Start engine and allow to run out of fuel, then crank engine an additional 3 seconds.
3. Service fuel system as necessary.

Throttle Body Fuel Injection System, Exc. 1984 Corvette

INDEX

DESCRIPTION

The Throttle Body Fuel Injection Systems provide a means of fuel distribution for controlling exhaust emissions within the required limits by precisely controlling the air/fuel ratio under all operating conditions. This is accomplished by means of an Electronic Control Module (ECM) which receives electrical signals from various sensors indicating engine operating conditions, and varies the fuel delivery time (pulse width) of the injector(s) accordingly. The ECM may modify the fuel pulse to compensate for special operating conditions such as cranking, cold starting, altitude, acceleration and deceleration. By increasing the injector pulse, more fuel is delivered and the air/fuel mixture is enriched. When the injector pulse is decreased, the air/fuel ratio is decreased.

In the fuel injection system used with the 4 cylinder engines, **Fig. 1,** the throttle body injector (TBI) is located on the intake manifold where fuel and air are distributed through a single bore in the throttle body, **Fig. 2.** Air for combustion is controlled by a single throttle valve which is connected to the accelerator pedal linkage by a throttle shaft and lever assembly. Fuel for combustion is supplied by a single fuel injector mounted on the TBI assembly, **Fig. 2.**

The fuel injection system used on 6 cylinder engines, **Fig. 3,** is similar to the system used on 4 cylinder engines except that the throttle body injection unit on 6 cylinder engines has two fuel injectors.

On fuel injected V8 applications, the "2 x 1" or "Crossfire" fuel injection system is used. This system incorporates a front and rear TBI unit, **Fig. 4,** each controlled by an ECM. Each TBI unit supplies the correct air/fuel mixture through long runners in the intake manifold to the bank of cylinders located on the opposite side of the engine. A fuel pressure compensator is located on the fuel meter cover of the front unit, **Fig. 5.** The compensator will equalize fuel pressure between the two TBI units during the momentary pressure drop which may occur at injector "on" time. The TBI units in both systems utilize a special "swirl" plate located directly beneath the throttle valve

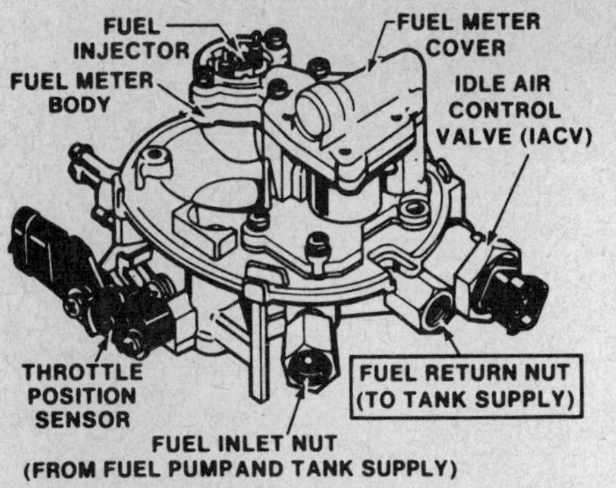

Fig. 1 Throttle body injector unit. Four cylinder engine

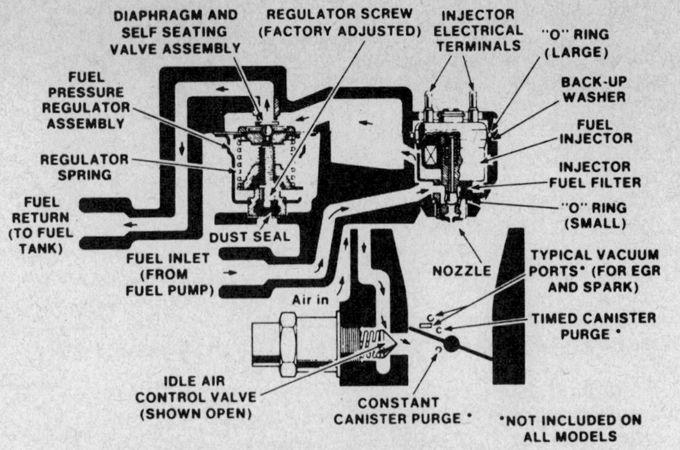

Fig. 2 Fuel metering schematic. Four cylinder engine

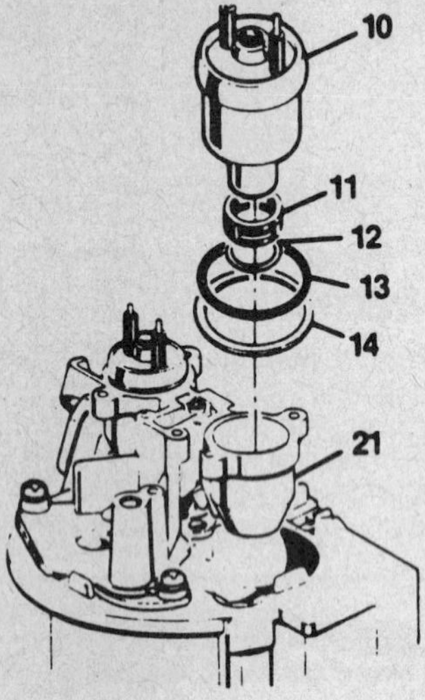

10 - INJECTOR - FUEL
11 - FILTER - FUEL INJECTOR INLET
12 - "O" RING - FUEL INJECTOR - LOWER
13 - "O" RING - FUEL INJECTOR - UPPER
14 - WASHER - FUEL INJECTOR
21 - FUEL METER BODY ASSEMBLY

Fig. 3 Throttle body injector unit. V6 engine

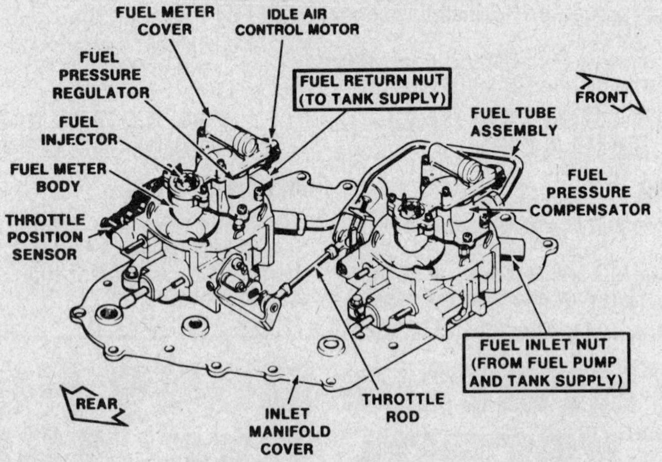

Fig. 4 Throttle body injector units. Crossfire injection system. V8 engine

to aid in mixture distribution.

When the ignition key is turned on, the ECM will energize the fuel pump relay. The fuel pump pressurizes the system to approximately 10 psi. If a distributor reference pulse is not received by the ECM within two seconds, the fuel pump relay will be de-energized, turning off the fuel pump. If a distributor reference pulse is later received by the ECM, the fuel pump relay will be re-energized and the pump will resume operation.

SUBSYSTEMS

The Throttle Body Fuel Injection systems are comprised of the following major sub-systems: Fuel Supply, Throttle Body Injector Assembly (TBI), Idle Air Control (IAC), Data Sensors, Electronic Control Module (ECM), Electronic Spark Timing (EST), and, on 6 and 8 cylinder engines, Electronic Spark Control (ESC).

FUEL SUPPLY

Fuel is supplied by an electric fuel pump located in the fuel tank. The fuel passes through an inline filter before reaching the TBI. Fuel pump operation is controlled by a fuel pump relay.

THROTTLE BODY INJECTOR ASSEMBLY

The TBI unit is made up of two major castings: a throttle body with a valve to control air flow and a fuel body assembly with an integral pressure regulator and fuel injector to supply the necessary fuel. The TBI unit also includes an electronically operated device to control idle speed and a device which provides information regarding throttle valve position.

The throttle body portion of the TBI unit contains several ports which generate vacuum signals for the EGR valve, MAP sensor and canister purge system.

The fuel injector is a solenoid operated device controlled by the ECM. Incoming fuel is directed to the lower end of the injector assembly which has a fine screen surrounding the injector inlet. When the ECM actuates the solenoid, the normally closed ball valve is lifted off its seat and pressurized fuel is injected in a conical spray pattern at the walls of the throttle body bore above the throttle valve. Excess fuel passes through a pressure regulator and returns to the fuel tank.

The fuel pressure regulator on all systems, and the fuel pressure compensator on the front TBI unit of the "Crossfire" injection system are serviced as a unit with the fuel meter cover assembly and must not be interchanged from one unit to another.

ELECTRONIC CONTROL MODULE

The Electronic Control Module (ECM), located in the passenger compartment, is the control center of the fuel injection system. The ECM continually monitors and processes the input information and generates output commands to the various systems affecting vehicle performance.

The throttle body injection system uses three basic types of electronic control modules. Most ECMs have a removable calibration unit (PROM) that enables the ECM to recognize and adjust for vehicle variations (vehicle weight, axle ratio, etc.). There are specific ECM/PROM combinations for each specific vehicle which are not interchangeable. Some PROM equipped ECMs also have a CALPAK unit that allows fuel delivery if other parts of the ECM are damaged. Some vehicles use a MEM-CAL unit that functions as a combined PROM/CALPAK assembly.

The ECM also performs the diagnostic function of the fuel injection system. When the ECM senses an operational problem, it will illuminate the "Check Engine" or "Service Engine Soon" light and store the appropriate code(s) to identify the problem area.

DATA SENSORS

Engine Coolant Temperature Sensor

The engine temperature sensor is located in the flow of the engine coolant and sends information concerning temperature to the ECM.

Oxygen Sensor

The exhaust oxygen sensor is located in the exhaust system and monitors oxygen content in the exhaust gas stream. The ECM receives this information and adjusts the air/fuel ratio as necessary.

Manifold Absolute Pressure Sensor

The manifold absolute pressure (MAP) sensor measures changes in the intake manifold pressure resulting from engine load and speed changes. As the pressure changes, the electrical resistance of the sensor changes. This change in resistance causes a voltage change which is amplified and sent to the ECM.

Vehicle Speed Sensor

The vehicle speed sensor (VSS) is located behind the speedometer in the instrument cluster. The sensor sends a series of pulses to the ECM used to determine road speed. The ECM uses this information to reset the idle air control motor, canister purge and torque converter clutch.

Do not drive vehicle without VSS, as idle quality may be affected.

Throttle Position Sensor

The throttle position sensor (TPS) is connected to the throttle shaft and is controlled by the throttle mechanism. The TPS converts the throttle valve angle to an electrical signal and transmits the signal to the ECM.

Hall Effect Unit

The Hall Effect Unit is located above the pickup coil in the distributor and sends engine RPM information to the ECM. This unit is used in place of the "R" terminal of the conventional HEI module.

Park/Neutral Switch

The park/neutral switch indicates to the ECM when the transmission is in park or neutral.

Do not drive vehicle with park/neutral switch disconnected, as idle quality may be affected in park or neutral.

A/C Compressor Clutch Engagement

The A/C compressor clutch engagement signal tells the ECM that the A/C compressor clutch is engaged.

Manifold Air Temperature (MAT) Sensor, 1987

The manifold air temperature (MAT) sensor is a termistor or resistor that changes its value based on temperature. The MAT sensor is mounted on the engine air cleaner on 4-121 overhead cam engine, on the TBI air bonnet on 4-121 overhead valve engines and on the intake manifold on 4-151 engines. Low air temperatures produce a high resistance while high temperatures produce a low resistance. The ECM supplies a 5 volt signal to the MAT sensor, through a resistor in the ECM and monitors the voltage. The voltage will be high when the air is cold and low when the air is hot. By monitoring the voltage, the ECM calculates the air temperature and adjusts fuel and spark advance.

Ignition Module, 1987

The ignition module, used on 4-121 overhead cam engines, receives a signal from the pickup coil which is sent to the ECM as a reference signal. The ECM uses this reference signal to calculate RPM and crankshaft position.

Crankshaft Sensor, 1987

The crankshaft sensor sends a signal through the "DIS" (Direct Ignition System) module to the ECM. The ECM uses this reference signal to calculate RPM and crankshaft position.

Electronic Spark Timing

The Electronic Spark Timing (EST) distributor contains no vacuum or centrifugal advance and uses a seven-terminal distributor module. In addition to the connectors normally found on HEI distributors, the EST distributor also has four wires going to a four-terminal connector. A reference pulse, indicating engine RPM and crankshaft position is sent to the ECM. The ECM determines the proper spark advance for the engine operating conditions and sends an "EST" pulse to the distributor.

The EST system provides better control of exhaust emissions and improves fuel economy by optimizing spark timing. The ECM monitors information from various engine sensors and computes the spark timing changes accordingly. In case of EST failure, a backup spark advance system is incorporated in the module.

Electronic Spark ControL

In vehicles equipped with 6 or 8 cylinder engines, Electronic Spark Control (ESC) is used in conjunction with EST to reduce spark advance when detonation occurs. A knock sensor signals a separate ESC controller to retard the timing when it senses knock. The ESC controller signals the ECM which will reduce spark advance until no more signals are received from the knock sensor.

Idle Air Control

The idle air control (IAC) system is designed to control engine idle speeds while preventing stalls due to changes in engine load. The IAC assembly, mounted on the throttle body, provides control of bypass air around the throttle plate by extending or retracting a conical valve to divert air around the throttle plate. If RPM is lower than desired, more air is diverted around the throttle plate to increase RPM. If RPM is too high, less air is diverted around the throttle plate to decrease RPM.

At idle speeds, the ECM calculates the desired position depending on battery voltage, coolant temperature, engine load and engine RPM. If RPM drops below a specified RPM and the throttle plate is closed, the ECM will sense a near stall condition and will calculate a position based on barometric pressure to prevent stalls.

DIAGNOSIS

SELF DIAGNOSIS SYSTEM

A built-in, self diagnostic system will identify problems most likely to occur in the Throttle Body Fuel Injection System. When a problem is detected, the diagnostic system will illuminate a "Check Engine" or "Service Engine Soon" light in the instrument panel. The "Check Engine" light will flash a trouble code or codes when a trouble code "Test" terminal under the dash is grounded with ignition on and engine not running.

The "Check Engine" or "Service Engine Soon" light will illuminate with the ignition switch on and the engine not running. If the "Test" terminal is then grounded and the light flashes a Code 12, the self-diagnostic system is functioning properly. A Code 12 consists of one flash, a short pause, then two flashes in rapid succession. After a longer pause, the code will repeat two more times.

When the engine is started, the "Check Engine" or "Service Engine Soon" light should turn off. If the light remains lit, the self-diagnostic system has detected a problem. To determine where the problem exists, ground the "Test" terminal with ignition on and engine not running and observe trouble code display. Each trouble code will flash three times in numeric order. Each trouble code will indicate a fault in a particular circuit.

TROUBLE CODE "TEST" LEAD

On Corvette models, the 12 terminal connector is located behind the ashtray.

The trouble code "Test" lead is located in a 12 volt terminal connector under the dash. When this terminal is grounded, the ECM will flash any trouble codes stored in the memory. To ground the terminal, connect a jumper wire between the "Test" lead terminal and the adjacent ground terminal.

If the "Test" terminal is grounded with ignition on and engine not running, the system will enter the diagnostic mode. In the diagnostic mode, the ECM will flash a code 12 and energize all ECM controlled relays.

If the "Test" terminal is grounded with the engine running, the system will enter the field service mode. In this mode, the "Check Engine" light will indicate whether the system is in open or closed loop operation. If the light flashes approximately twice per second, the system is in open loop operation. Closed loop operation is indicated by the light flashing approximately once per second.

"SCAN" DIAGNOSTICS

Terminal "E" or "M" of the underdash ALDL connector allows access to a variety of system information known as "Serial Data" using SCAN type testers. Terminal "E" is used to transmit data on 1986 models and 1987 models that retain the 160 baud transmission rate ECM. Terminal "M" Is used on 1987 models with the 8192 baud transmission rate ECM.

Serial data access can be useful in obtaining information regarding intermittent malfunctions, as the SCAN tool can be installed and monitored while operating the vehicle under the conditions where the malfunction was reported to occur. If the malfunction seems to be related to specific functions that are monitored by the SCAN tool, the system can be checked in the applicable positions, under actual operating conditions. If the malfunction is not related to any specific area, the system can be monitored in all tester positions for a period of time or under a group of operating conditions. This allows the technician to observe the system and monitor changes in tester readings that may indicate a system malfunction.

The use of the SCAN tool is required to diagnose malfunctions on some 1987 models. The SCAN tool is capable of monitoring sensor inputs to the ECM and ECM commands to the various system operating elements, and provides the means to save time in diagnosis and prevent replacement of satisfactory components. Successful use of the SCAN tool for diagnosis requires an understanding of how the C-3 system functions, a thorough acquaintance with the tool manufacturer's recommendations and knowledge of the SCAN tool's limitations. **Not all SCAN testers are compatible with every system. A SCAN tool that produces faulty readings should not be used, and problems should be reported to the tool manufacturer. Use of a faulty SCAN tool can result in improper diagnosis and unnecessary component replacement.**

The SCAN tool can be used in 3 different modes: the normal or open mode; the 10K, special or ALDL mode; the factory test, backup or 3.9K mode. Most SCAN tools are programmed so that the system will enter the special (ALDL, 10K) mode directly, and the "normal" or "factory test" modes must be selected manually, if available. In the special mode, all information incorporated into an engine/ECM combination is available. However, in the special mode engine operating characteristics are modified as follows: The closed loop timers are bypassed, EST spark is at full advance, the IAC (if equipped) controls idle speed at 1000 RPM, the park/neutral restrict functions are disabled, and on some

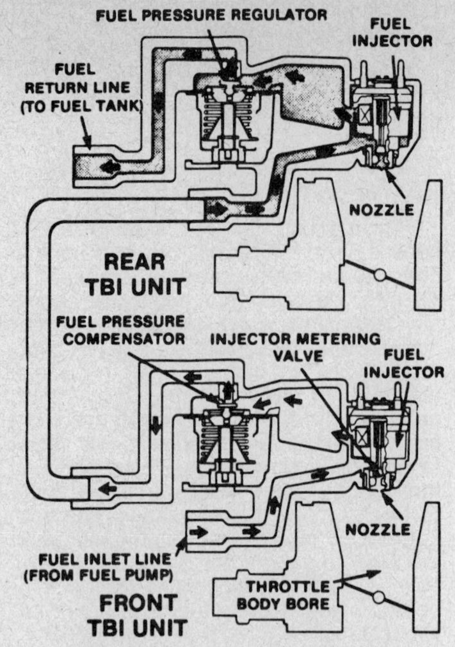

Fig. 5 Fuel metering schematic. Crossfire injection system. V8 engine

engines the canister purge solenoid is activated. Although not all engine/ECM "families" are able to transmit information on the serial data line with the SCAN tool in the normal (open) mode, on engines that can be monitored in the open mode the SCAN tool allows data on certain operating parameters to be obtained without changing engine operating characteristics. Selecting the factory test or back-up mode causes the ECM to operate on the fuel back-up logic programming, designed to allow system operation in the event of an ECM failure. While selection of this mode verifies that the back-up programming is functioning properly, parameters that can be checked with the tool in this mode are of little value in diagnosing system malfunctions.

In the generally used special or normal test modes the SCAN tool allows a quick check of sensors and switches which provide inputs to the ECM, but on models with a 160 baud ECM, the data only updates once every 1.25 seconds making the tool less effective than a voltmeter for locating intermittent conditions which may last for less than 1.25 seconds. However, the SCAN tool does allow the technician to manipulate wiring harnesses or underhood components while observing the SCAN readout. This aids in locating intermittent malfunctions while the engine is not running.

It is also important to note that while the SCAN tool may indicate that a component has been activated by the ECM, this indication only represents the ECM command to the specific circuit. The only way to verify that the command has been transmitted and carried out is to observe operation of the specific component activated by the ECM, or by noting changes in the system that the device controls. However, the SCAN tool allows the technician to compare operating parameters of a poorly operating engine with the parameters of an engine which is operating properly. Therefore, system malfunctions that may not ordinarily set a trouble code in the ECM memory, such as a shift in sensor values or excessive resistance in an operating element, can be uncovered by comparing operation of like systems.

The SCAN tool is capable of testing a variety of electronic engine control systems, and therefore not all tester positions will be applicable for each engine/ECM combination being tested. If a position is selected that is not applicable to the particular combination, this condition will be indicated on the tester. Refer to the manufacturer's instructions and the following descriptions for information regarding the SCAN tester positions and how they can aid diagnosis.

COMPONENT REPLACEMENT

ECM, REPLACE

1. Disconnect battery ground cable.
2. Disconnect two ECM electrical connectors.
3. Remove the ECM mounting hardware.
4. Remove ECM from passenger compartment.
5. Reverse procedure to install. **Replacement ECM is supplied without engine calibration unit (PROM) and, on 1984-85 models equipped with 4-121 engine, 1985-87 models equipped with V6 engine and 1986-87 models equipped with 4-121 and auto. trans., the CALPAK. 1986-87 models equipped with 4-121 engine and man. trans. are equipped with a MEM-CAL in place of the PROM. Care must be taken when removing the PROM, CALPAK or MEM-CAL from a defective ECM as they will be used in the replacement ECM.**

ECM PROM, REPLACE

A PROM (Programmable Read Only Memory) is used in all ECM's except 1986-87 models equipped with 4-121 and manual transmission. 1986-87 models equipped with 4-121 and manual transmission have an ECM utilizing a MEM-CAL in place of the PROM.

1. Remove ECM from vehicle as described under "Electronic Control Module, Replace."
2. Remove PROM access cover. **Note position of PROM in ECM. PROM's are not interchangeable. Replacement PROMs must be installed in some position and direction as defective PROM.**
3. Grasp PROM carrier with the PROM removal tool, **Figs. 6 through 8.**
4. Gently rock the carrier from side to side while applying a firm upward force.
5. Remove PROM and carrier. **Check part number of the new PROM to ensure it is the same as the defective PROM.**

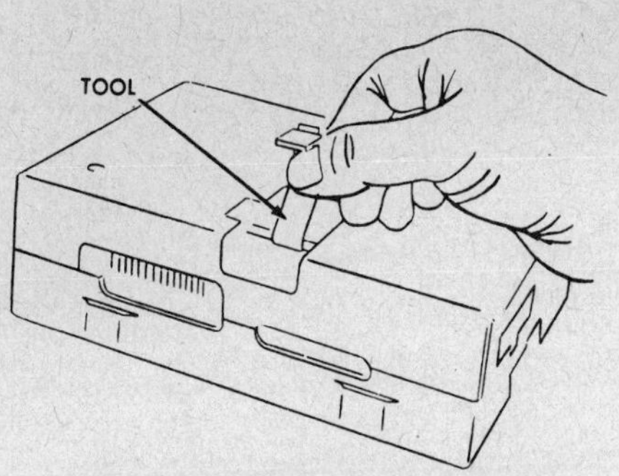

Fig. 6 Removing PROM carrier. 1982 models

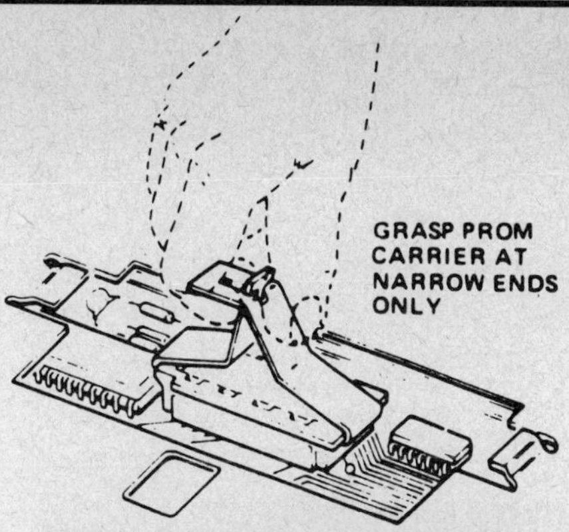

Fig. 7 Removing PROM carrier. 1983 models

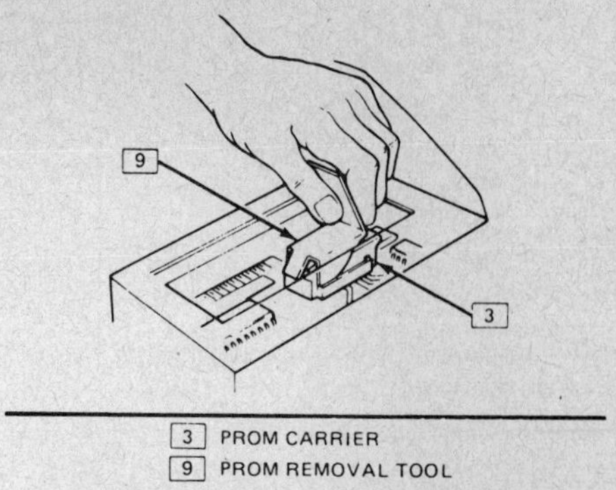

Fig. 8 Removing PROM carrier. 1984–87 models

6. Position replacement PROM and carrier over PROM socket and press down firmly on top of carrier. Press down on carrier and ensure it seats squarely.
7. Replace PROM access cover, then install ECM on vehicle.
8. Start engine, enter diagnosis and check for code 51. If code 51 does not display, PROM is installed correctly. If code 51 is displayed, PROM is installed incorrectly and must repeat procedure. **If PROM is installed backwards, it will be destroyed.**

CALPAK, REPLACE

A CALPAK is used on 1984-85 4-121 engines, 1985-87 V6 Engines and 1986-87 4-121 engines equipped with auto. trans.

1. Remove ECM from vehicle as described under "Electronic Control Module, Replace."
2. Remove PROM access cover.
3. Carefully remove CALPAK.
4. Install replacement CALPAK, then access cover.
5. Install ECM in vehicle.

MEM-CAL, REPLACE

A MEM-CAL is used on 1986-87 4-121 engines equipped with man. trans. in place of the PROM.

1. Remove ECM from vehicle as described under "Electronic Control Module, Replace."
2. Remove access cover from ECM.
3. Using two fingers, push MEM-CAL retaining clips aside, then using other hand, grasp MEM-CAL at both ends and lift up and out.
4. Align replacement MEM-CAL notches with MEM-CAL socket notches, then press MEM-CAL into position by pressing on ends only. MEM-CAL is properly installed when retaining clips snap over ends of MEM-CAL. **Press on ends of MEM-CAL only. Do not press in the middle or damage to MEM-CAL will result.**
5. Install ECM access cover.
6. Install ECM in vehicle.

THROTTLE POSITION SENSOR, REPLACE

Removal

1. On 1982 models, remove TBI unit, if necessary, then position throttle body unit on a clean, flat surface.
2. On 1982 models, using a 5/16 inch drill bit, drill completely through TPS screw access holes in base on throttle body to ensure removing the spot welds holding TPS screws in place. On Corvette models, remove TPS screws by using a suitable screwdriver.
3. On all models, remove TPS screws, lockwashers, and retainers. Remove TPS sensor from the throttle body. Discard and replace screws.

Installation

1. Position sensor over throttle body. Ensure TPS pickup lever is located above tang on actuator lever.
2. Using new screws and lockwashers, apply thread locking compound to screws and install. Adjust TPS as described under "Throttle Position Sensor, Adjust."

MAP SENSOR, REPLACE

MAP sensors are located in the engine compartment. Exact location depends on model application. Besides checking hoses and electrical connections, the only service possible is unit replacement if sensor is diagnosed as being faulty. To prevent sensor damage, exercise care when disconnecting vacuum hose from sensor.

OXYGEN SENSOR, REPLACE

1. Disconnect battery ground cable.
2. With engine temperature above 120° F disconnect electrical connector and remove sensor.
3. Reverse procedure to install. Coat oxygen sensor threads with a suitable anti-seize compound and torque sensor to 30 ft. lbs. **On 1984-87 models equipped with 4-121 engine, remember to install shield when replacing oxygen sensor. If a new shield is not used, an air leak will occur, resulting in a false Code 44 or rich system operation.**

IDLE AIR CONTROL ASSEMBLY, REPLACE

Removal

1. Remove air cleaner, then disconnect electrical connection from Idle Air Control (IAC).
2. Using a suitable wrench, remove IAC assembly from throttle body and discard valve gaskets. **Before installing new IAC assembly, measure extension of conical valve, Fig. 9. Make measurement from motor housing to end of pintle. The extension should be 1 1/8 inch. If cone is extended too far, the motor may be damaged during installation.**

Installation

Identify replacement IAC assembly as being either Type 1 or Type 2, **Fig. 9.** If dimension "A" is greater than 1 1/8 inch, reduce distance as follows:

On Type 1, exert a firm pressure on conical valve to retract it.

On Type 2, while turning valve in clockwise rotation, compress retaining spring from conical valve. Return spring to original position with straight part of spring end aligned with flat surface of valve.

1. Install new IAC assembly to throttle body. Torque motor to 13 ft. lbs.
2. Reconnect IAC electrical connection and install air cleaner.
3. Start engine and run until normal operating temperature is reached. **On 1982-83 vehicles equipped with man. trans., idle speed will be controlled when normal operating temperature is reached. On 1982-83 vehicles equipped with auto. trans., place gear selector in "Drive" when normal operating temperature is reached. This will enable ECM to control idle speed.**

On 1984-87 vehicles, the ECM will reset idle speed when vehicle is driven over 35 mph.

INJECTOR, REPLACE

Removal

1. Raise hood and remove air cleaner.
2. Relieve fuel system pressure as described under "Fuel System Pressure Test."
3. Disconnect injector connector by squeezing two tabs together and pulling straight up.
4. Remove fuel meter cover, **Fig. 10.** Do not remove gasket from fuel meter body.
5. Lift injector out of fuel meter body using a suitable screwdriver, **Fig. 11.**
6. Remove small O-ring from injector nozzle or from bottom of injector cavity.

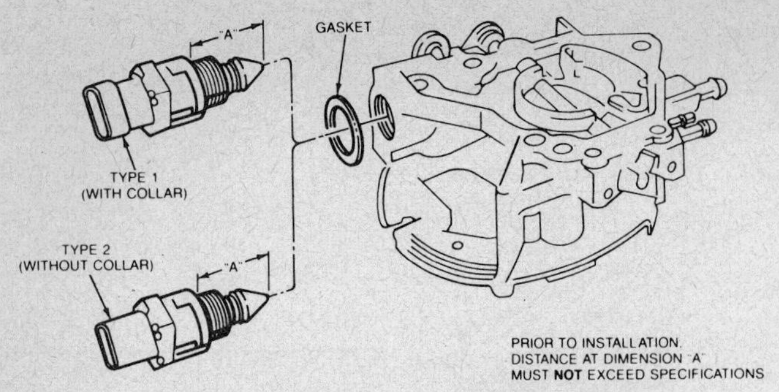

Fig. 9 Idle air control assembly

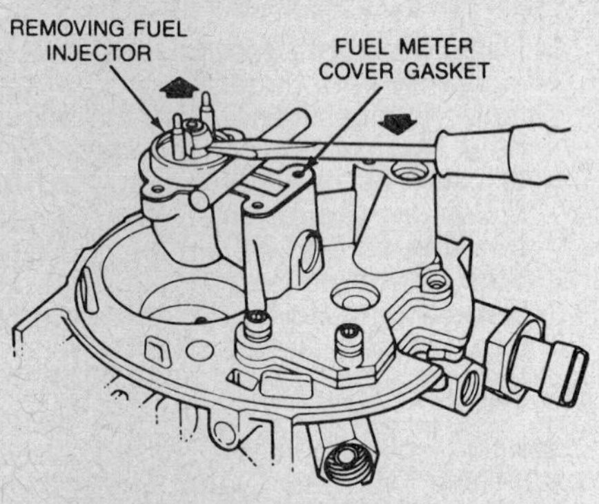

Fig. 11 Removing fuel injector

7. If necessary, remove injector fuel filter by rotating filter back and forth while lightly pulling filter.
8. Remove fuel meter cover gasket.
9. Remove large O-ring and steel back-up washer from top counterbore of fuel meter body injector cavity.

Installation

1. Using a twisting motion, install injector fuel filter (if removed) with larger end of filter facing injector, so that filter covers raised ribs at base of injector.
2. Lubricate new, small O-ring with automatic transmission fluid, then install O-ring. Push O-ring on injector until seated against injector fuel filter.
3. Install back-up washer in fuel meter body injector counterbore.
4. Lubricate new, large O-ring with automatic transmission fluid, then install over back-up washer. Ensure O-ring is seated properly and top of O-ring is flush with top of fuel meter casting surface.
5. Install injector by pushing into position while aligning raised lug on injector body with fuel meter body cover. Push until injector is fully seated in cavity.
6. Install fuel meter cover using new gasket. **Thread locking compound must be used on fuel meter cover attaching screws.**
7. Connect electrical connector, then install air cleaner.

COOLANT SENSOR, REPLACE

1. Disconnect battery ground cable.
2. Disconnect electrical connector, then carefully back out coolant sensor. **Damage to coolant sensor will affect proper operation of the E.F.I. system.**
3. Reverse procedure to install. Ensure electrical connector is fully seated.

VEHICLE SPEED SENSOR, REPLACE

1. Disconnect battery ground cable.
2. Remove instrument cluster assembly.
3. Remove screw attaching V.S.S. pick-up to rear of speedometer head.
4. Remove screw attaching V.S.S. to instrument cluster.
5. Disconnect printed circuit connector from V.S.S.
6. Remove V.S.S.
7. Reverse procedure to install.

THROTTLE BODY INJECTION (TBI) UNIT, REPLACE

4 Cyl. Engines, Removal

1. Raise hood and remove air cleaner assembly.
2. Relieve fuel system pressure as described under "Fuel System Pressure Test."
3. Disconnect electrical connectors to idle air control, throttle position sensor and injector.
4. Disconnect throttle linkage, return spring, and cruise control linkage if so equipped.
5. Disconnect vacuum hoses from TBI unit.
6. Disconnect fuel supply and return lines at TBI unit. This will require use of back-up wrench to hold fuel inlet and outlet nuts on throttle body.
7. On 4-112 and 4-151 engine, remove three TBI unit-to-engine attaching bolts, then the TBI unit.
8. On 4-121 engine, remove the two long air cleaner isolator-to-TBI unit attaching bolts and the isolator. Remove injector harness and grommet from TBI unit, then the remaining attaching bolt and TBI unit.

4 Cyl. Engines, Installation

1. Ensure TBI and intake manifold sealing surfaces are clean.
2. Position replacement TBI-to-intake manifold gasket on manifold.
3. Position TBI unit on intake manifold, then install 3 attaching bolts. Torque bolts to 13 ft. lbs. on 4-112 and 4-151 engine, or 17 ft. lbs. on 4-121 engine.

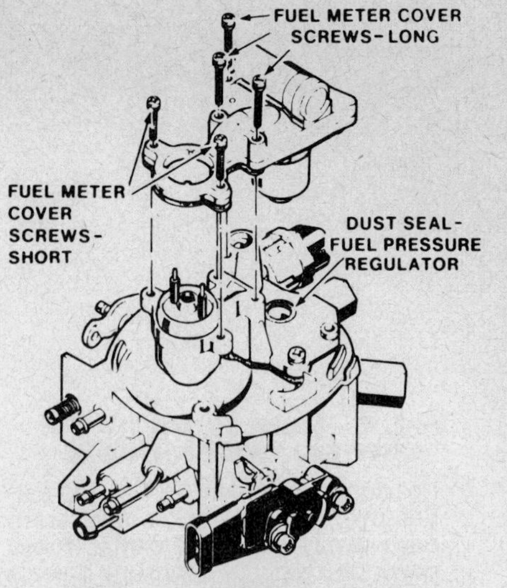

Fig. 10 Removal & installation of fuel meter cover

4. Install fuel return line. Torque to 17 ft. lbs. **Inspect fuel return line O-ring prior to installation. If O-ring shows signs of tears or wear, it must be replaced.**
5. Install fuel pressure line. On models equipped with banjo type connection, torque fitting to 21 ft. lbs. On models equipped with O-ring type fitting, torque fitting to 17 ft. lbs. **Inspect fuel pressure line O-ring or washers prior to installation. If O-ring (if equipped) shows signs of tears or wear, it must be replaced. If washers (if equipped) and sealing surfaces are scratched or damaged in any way, they must be replaced.**
6. Connect electrical connectors to idle air control, throttle position sensor and injector.
7. Connect throttle linkage, return spring and cruise control linkage (if equipped).

V6 Engines, Removal

1. Disconnect battery ground cable.
2. Disconnect THERMAC hose from engine fitting.
3. Disconnect electrical connectors from idle control valve, throttle position sensor and the injectors, then remove injector harness and grommet from TBI unit.
4. Disconnect throttle cable, return spring, transmission control cable and cruise control cable, if equipped.
5. Disconnect vacuum hoses from throttle body, noting positions for proper installation.
6. Disconnect fuel feed and return lines from throttle body unit.
7. Remove three hold-down bolts securing TBI to manifold and remove unit from manifold.

V6 Engines, Installation

1. Ensure throttle body to intake manifold sealing surface is clean.
2. Install new throttle body to manifold gasket.

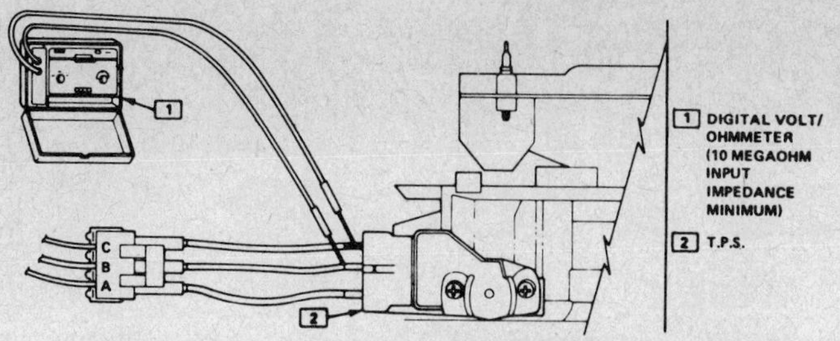

Fig. 12 Adjusting throttle position sensor

3. Install throttle body on intake manifold.
4. Install injector harness and grommet on TBI unit.
5. Install air cleaner gasket on TBI unit.
6. Install throttle body attaching bolts, torquing alternately to 26 ft. lbs.
7. Install fuel feed and return lines to throttle body, torquing to 23 ft. lbs.
8. Connect electrical connectors to idle air control, TPS and injectors.
9. Connect throttle cable, return spring, transmission control cable and cruise control cable.
10. Install air cleaner.
11. Start engine and check for fuel leaks.

V8 Engines With Crossfire Injection

1. Remove air cleaner.
2. Relieve fuel system pressure as described under "Fuel System Pressure Test."
3. Disconnect electrical connectors from injectors, idle air control motors and throttle position sensor.
4. Remove necessary vacuum hoses.
5. If removing rear TBI unit only, proceed as follows:
   a. Remove throttle cable and cruise control cable, if equipped.
   b. Disconnect fuel return line and fuel line to front TBI unit.
   c. Disconnect throttle rod between front and rear TBI units.
   d. Remove attaching bolts and the rear TBI unit.
6. If removing front TBI unit only, proceed as follows:
   a. Disconnect transmission detent cable, then the fuel feed line and fuel line to rear TBI unit.
   b. Disconnect throttle rod between front and rear TBI units.
   c. Remove attaching bolts and the front TBI unit.
7. If removing both TBI units as an assembly, proceed as follows:
   a. Remove throttle cable and transmission detent cable.
   b. Remove cruise control cable, if equipped.
   c. Disconnect fuel feed and return lines.
   d. Remove attaching bolts and the TBI unit.
8. Reverse procedure to install. Torque attaching bolts and nuts to 120-168 inch lbs. **If only one of the TBI units is being removed, check and adjust minimum idle speed.**

ADJUSTMENTS

THROTTLE POSITION SENSOR, ADJUST

1985–87 Exc. 1985 V6 Engine

On 1985-87 4 cylinder engines and 1986 V6 engines, the Throttle Position Sensor (TPS) does not require adjustment. The ECM reads the TPS voltage at idle for the zero reading, therefore, no adjustment is necessary.

1985 V6 Engine

With ignition on, use a digital voltmeter connected to terminals "A" and "B" and rotate TPS to obtain .45-.6 volts.

1982–84 Models

1. On 1982 models, remove TBI unit, then the TPS as previously described. Loosely reinstall sensor and position TBI unit on intake manifold without installing bolts. Remove fuel pump fuse from fuse block.
2. On 1983-84 models, remove air cleaner.
3. On all models, connect three jumper wires between TPS harness and TPS, **Fig. 12.**
4. With ignition on and engine not running, measure voltage between sensor terminals B and C, **Fig. 12,** using a digital voltmeter.
5. In the closed throttle position, voltmeter should read .795-.845 volts on 1982-83 4-112 engine, .450-.600 volts on 1982 4-151 and V8-305 and 1983-84 4-121 engines, or .450-1.250 volts on all other models.
6. Rotate TPS as necessary to bring voltage within specifications. Tighten screws and recheck voltage.
7. Turn ignition off and remove jumper wires.
8. On 1982 models, install TBI unit.

SYSTEM SERVICE

FUEL SYSTEM PRESSURE TEST

4 & 8 Cylinder Engines

1. With engine Off, remove fuel pump fuse from fuse block.
2. Start engine and allow to run until fuel supply is exhausted.
3. Crank engine an additional 3 seconds to ensure fuel supply is exhausted.
4. Install fuel pump fuse.
5. On 4-112 and 4-121 engines, install fuel pressure gauge between throttle body side of fuel filter at the rear of the car. On 4-151 engines, install fuel pressure gauge between TBI unit and steel fuel line. On V8 engines, install fuel gauge between front and rear TBI units steel fuel line.
6. Start engine and observe fuel pressure. It should be 9 to 13 psi.
7. Relieve fuel system pressure. Refer to steps 1 through 3 above.
8. Remove fuel pressure gauge and reinstall fuel lines.
9. Start engine and check for fuel leaks.

1985 V6 Engine

1. Turn engine off and relieve fuel pressure.
2. Remove air cleaner and plug THERMAC vacuum port on TBI.
3. Remove flexible fuel line between fuel tank and filter.
4. Install suitable fuel pressure gauge.
5. Start vehicle and observe fuel pressure reading, which should be 9-13 psi.
6. Relieve fuel pressure.
7. Remove fuel pressure gauge.
8. Reinstall fuel line.
9. Start vehicle and check for fuel leaks.
10. Remove plug covering THERMAC vacuum port on TBI and install air cleaner.

1986–87 V6 Engine

1. Obtain two sections of 3/8 inch steel tubing, each approximately 10 inches long, and double-flare one end of each section.
2. Install flare nut on each section, then connect each of the two sections of tubing into the "flare nut to flare nut adapters" that are included in J-29658-82 Gage Adapters.
3. Attach pipe and adapter assemblies to the J-29658 gage.
4. Raise and support vehicle. **This engine has a bleed in the pressure regulator to relieve pressure any time the engine is turned off, but a small amount of fuel may be released when the fuel line is disconnected. To reduce the risk of personal injury, cover the fuel line with a shop cloth to collect the fuel, then place cloth in suitable container.**
5. Disconnect front fuel feed hose from fuel pipe on body.
6. Install a ten inch length of 3/8 inch fuel hose onto fuel feed pipe on body and attach other end of hose onto one of the sections of pipe obtained in step 1.
7. Attach front fuel feed hose onto other end of tubing.
8. Start engine and check for leaks.
9. Observe fuel gauge reading, which should be 9-13 psi.
10. Depressurize fuel system and remove gage with adapters, then reconnect fuel feed hose to pipe and torque clamp to 15 inch lbs.
11. Lower vehicle, start engine and check for leaks.

Digital Electronic Fuel Injection (DEFI), 1986–87 Cadillac Eldorado & Seville

INDEX

DESCRIPTION

Digital Electronic Fuel Injection (DEFI) provides a means of fuel distribution for controlling exhaust emissions by precisely controlling the air/fuel mixture under all operating conditions. This is accomplished through the use of an Electronic Control Module (ECM). The ECM receives signals from various sensors and signals the injectors to provide the precise amount of fuel required.

A Body Computer Module (BCM) used in conjunction with the ECM provides for additional control capability. The BCM monitors various body operating parameters and shares this information with the ECM through an electronic communications process.

The ECM and BCM are both capable of diagnosing faults with the various inputs and systems they control. When the ECM detects a malfunction, a Service Now or Service Soon warning lamp on the instrument panel is illuminated.

SYSTEM COMPONENTS

Injector Unit

The injector unit, **Fig. 1**, is composed of two major assemblies; a throttle body and a fuel body.

The throttle body contains an Idle Speed Control (ISC) control assembly and a Throttle Position Sensor (TPS). The throttle body portion of the injector unit may contain ports located at, above, or below the throttle valve. The ports are used to produce the vacuum signals for the canister purge system and the Manifold Absolute Pressure (MAP) sensor.

The fuel body portion of the injector unit contains a fuel meter cover with integral pressure regulator and two fuel injectors to supply fuel to the engine.

Fuel Injectors

The fuel injectors are solenoid operated and controlled by the ECM. The ECM energizes the solenoid, which lifts a ball valve off its seat. Pressurized fuel is then injected in a conical spray pattern at the walls of the throttle body bore above the throttle valve. Fuel not used by the injector passes through the pressure regulator, then back to the fuel tank.

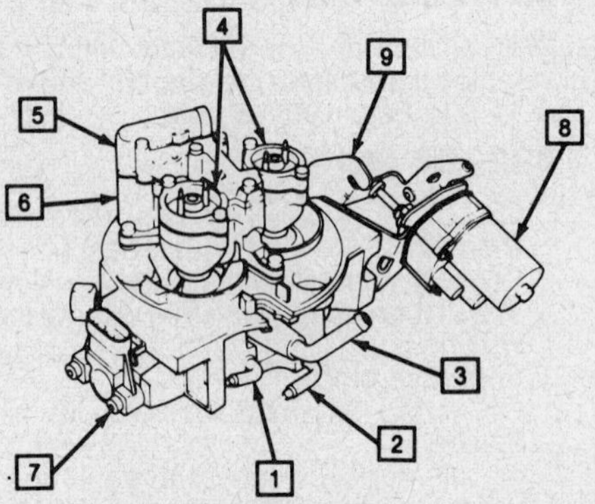

1 MAP SENSOR
2 CANISTER PURGE
3 PCV
4 FUEL INJECTORS
5 FUEL METER COVER
6 FUEL METER BODY
7 THROTTLE POSITION SENSOR
8 IDLE SPEED CONTROL (ISC)
9 THROTTLE LEVER

Fig. 1 Digital electronic fuel injection unit

Pressure Regulator

The pressure regulator is a diaphragm type relief valve with injector pressure acting on one side and air cleaner pressure acting on the opposite side. The regulator maintains a constant injector pressure at all times by controlling flow in the return line.

Idle Speed Control (ISC) Assembly

The ISC controls idle speed using a plunger to change throttle angle. Idle speed is monitored by the ECM which moves the plunger to maintain idle speed required for the operating condition. The throttle switch, integral with the ISC, determines when the ISC controls idle speed. When throttle lever rests against ISC plunger, the switch contacts are closed and the ECM moves ISC to predetermined idle speed position. When throttle lever breaks contact with ISC plunger, the ECM stops sending idle speed commands and engine speed is controlled by the accelerator pedal.

Engine Coolant Temperature Sensor

The coolant sensor is a thermistor mounted in the engine coolant flow. The ECM supplies a 5 volt signal to the coolant sensor through a resistor in the ECM and measures voltage. Voltage will be high when engine is cold and low when engine is hot. The sensor provides coolant temperature information to the ECM for ignition timing, fuel enrichment, canister purge control, EGR operation, EFE operation, air management, closed loop fuel control and idle speed control.

Manifold Absolute Pressure (MAP) Sensor

The MAP sensor measures changes in intake manifold pressure resulting from changes in engine load and speed, and converts this to a voltage output. The ECM, by monitoring sensor output voltage, increases or decreases injector "on" time to compensate for the addition or reduction of fuel as required.

STATUS LIGHTS

ECM STATUS LIGHT DISPLAY							
	LIGHT ON	VCC ENABLED	CLOSED LOOP	RICH	3RD GEAR	4TH & 3RD	4TH W/O 3RD
	LIGHT OFF	VCC DISABLED	OPEN LOOP	LEAN	NOT IN 3RD OR 4TH GEAR		
	INDICATOR	OFF	AUTO	ECON	°C	°F	°E
	FUNCTION	VCC OUTPUT	ECM OPERATING MODE	OXYGEN SENSOR INPUT	4TH & 3RD GEAR INPUT		

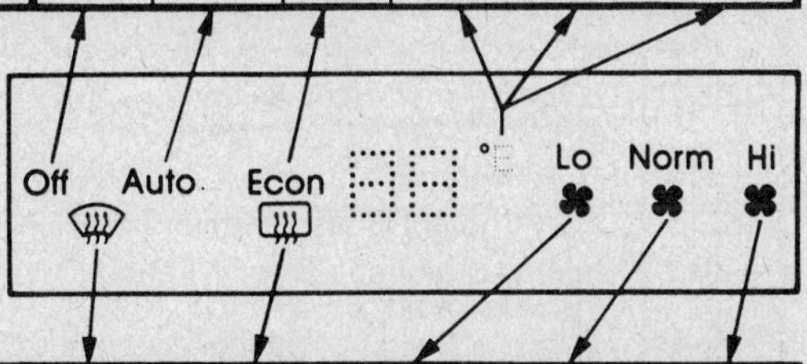

BCM STATUS LIGHT DISPLAY						
	FUNCTION	A/C CLUTCH OUTPUT	COMPRESSOR LOW PRESSURE SWITCH INPUT	A/C-DEF MODE DOOR OUTPUT	HEATER WATER VALVE OUTPUT	UP/DOWN MODE DOOR OUTPUT
	INDICATOR	FRONT DEF	REAR DEF	LO FAN	NORMAL FAN	HI FAN
	LIGHT ON	ENERGIZED	OPEN (LOW PRESSURE)	A/C	CLOSED (NO WATER FLOW)	UP
	LIGHT OFF	DE-ENERGIZED	CLOSED	DEF	OPEN	DOWN

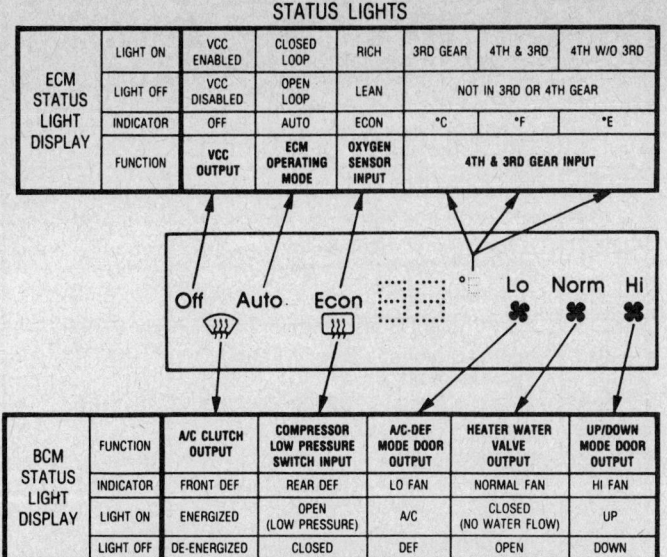

Fig. 2 Climate Control Panel (CCP) display

The MAP sensor is used by the ECM to control fuel delivery and ignition timing. In addition, the sensor is also used to measure barometric pressure under certain conditions, allowing the ECM to automatically adjust for different altitudes.

Manifold Air Temperature (MAT) Sensor

The MAT sensor, mounted in the intake manifold, in front of throttle body, measures temperature of air/fuel mixture in intake manifold and relays a signal to the ECM. The sensor is a thermistor, whose resistance decreases as temperature increases.

Oxygen Sensor

The exhaust oxygen sensor, mounted in the exhaust system, monitors oxygen content of exhaust gas stream and produces a corresponding voltage output which is relayed to the ECM. The ECM, by monitoring this voltage signal, sends a fuel mixture command to the injector.

Throttle Position Sensor (TPS)

The TPS, connected to the throttle shaft, is a variable resistor with one end connected to 5 volts from the ECM and the other to ground. A third wire, connected to the ECM, measures TPS voltage. TPS voltage changes with movement of the throttle valve. The ECM modifies fuel delivery according to throttle valve angle, by monitoring TPS voltage.

Vehicle Speed Sensor (VSS)

The VSS, located in the transaxle, provides vehicle speed information to the ECM. The ECM uses this signal to operate fuel economy data panel, integral cruise control, idle speed control system, VCC and to modify fuel delivery under certain conditions.

Engine Speed Sensor

The engine speed signal is produced by the seven terminal HEI module in the distributor. The ECM receives pulses from the distributor and the time between these pulses is used to determine engine speed. The ECM adds spark advance modifications to the signal and relays this signal back to the distributor.

Park/Neutral Switch

The park/neutral switch signals the ECM when the transaxle is in Park or Neutral. This information is used for cruise control, ISC operation and the VCC system.

Power Steering Pressure Switch

The power steering pressure switch opens during high pressure power steering situations and signals the ECM to increase idle speed to compensate for the increased engine load.

OPERATION

STARTING MODE

When ignition is first turned On, the ECM energizes the fuel pump for two seconds and pressure is built up at the injector unit. The ECM then checks coolant temperature sensor, TPS and crank signal and determines proper air/fuel mixture for starting.

CLEAR FLOOD MODE

A flooded engine should be cleared by fully depressing the accelerator pedal, which causes the ECM to pulse injectors at a rate of 25.5:1. The ECM will maintain this injector rate as long as throttle is wide open and engine RPM is less than 600. When throttle position becomes less than 80%, the ECM returns to the "starting" mode.

RUN MODE

The "run" mode consists of two separate operating conditions; open loop and closed loop.

The system goes into open loop operation when the engine is first started and RPM is above 400. In open loop operation, the ECM disregards oxygen sensor signal and determines air/fuel mixture primarily on inputs from coolant and MAP sensors. The system will remain in open loop operation until the oxygen sensor has varying voltage output and is hot enough to operate, or the coolant sensor is above 158° F and 60 seconds has elapsed after starting engine. When these conditions are met, the system switches to closed loop operation.

In closed loop operation, the ECM calculates the air/fuel mixture based on signals from the oxygen sensor. This allows the air/fuel mixture to stay close to the optimum 14.7:1 ratio.

ACCELERATION MODE

In the "acceleration" mode, the ECM senses rapid changes in throttle position and manifold pressure and provides a corresponding amount of added fuel.

DECELERATION MODE

During deceleration, fuel remaining in intake manifold can cause excessive emissions and backfiring. To compensate for this, the ECM senses changes in throttle position and manifold pressure and reduces fuel delivery. When decelerating very rapidly, the ECM will cut off the fuel supply for short periods.

BATTERY VOLTAGE CORRECTION MODE

When battery is low, the ECM compensates to maintain acceptable system performance by increasing injector "on" time, idle RPM and ignition dwell time.

DIAGNOSIS

The DEFI system is a highly complex computer system which includes the use of both an Electronic Control Module (ECM) and Body Control Module (BCM). The information contained in this section is intended for use as an aid in diagnosing engine fuel and emissions related complaints only.

TROUBLE CODES

The ECM continually monitors operating conditions of the various systems it control. When a problem is detected, a trouble code will be stored in the computer memory. These codes can be displayed as an aid in system repair. Any malfunctions which the vehicle operator should be aware of will illuminate an "Engine Control Systems" warning lamp on the dashboard. If a malfunction which would result in unacceptable system operation is encountered, the self-diagnostics will minimize the effect by taking "failsoft" action to compensate for the detected problem.

Entering Diagnostic Mode

To enter diagnostic mode, turn ignition On, then depress Off and Warmer buttons on the Climate Control Panel (CCP), **Fig. 2.** Hold buttons until all display panel segments illuminate, indicating beginning of diagnostic readout. The two display panels must be illuminated to ensure all segments are operating. Do not attempt diagnosis unless all segments appear, since an improper diagnosis could result. If any segments are inoperative, the display panel must be replaced.

Trouble Code Display

When segment check is completed, any codes stored in computer memory will be displayed on the data display as follows:

1. All ECM codes, **Fig. 3,** will be displayed first. Codes will be displayed with the lowest code first, followed by progressively higher codes present. All ECM codes will be prefixed with an "E" (EO14, EO15, etc.) before the code. If no ECM codes are stored, a "No ECM Codes" message will be displayed.
2. When all ECM codes or a "No ECM Codes" message has been displayed, all BCM codes will be displayed. BCM codes are prefixed with a "B" (BI15, BI19, etc.). If no BCM codes are stored, a "No BCM Codes" message will be displayed.
3. Any ECM or BCM codes displayed will also be accompanied by "Current" or "History". "History" indicates the failure was not present the last time the code was present, while "Current" indicates the fault still exists.
4. At any time during the display of the ECM or BCM codes, if the Lo button on the CCP is depressed, the display of codes will be bypassed. If the "Reset/Recall" button on the Driver Information Center (DIC) is depressed, the system will exit the diagnostic mode and go back to normal vehicle operation.
5. After all ECM and BCM codes have been displayed, or if no codes are present, a decision point is reached. "ECM" is displayed, and the technician may select from ECM, BCM or IPC data. Refer to "Diagnostic Procedures" for complete operations.

Clearing Trouble Codes

After all ECM and BCM codes are displayed and appropriate measures are taken to correct malfunctions, trouble codes may be cleared.

1. To clear ECM codes, proceed as follows:
   a. With ECM displayed on CCP (Climate Control Panel), depress the Hi button on the panel. This will permit access to ECM options (ECM data, inputs, outputs, code clearing, etc.).
   b. With ECM data displayed, continue to depress the Lo button on CCP until "ECM Clear Codes" is displayed.
   c. Depress Hi button on CCP. A "Codes Clear" message will be displayed on panel. This message will appear for approximately 3 seconds to indicate that all trouble codes have been erased from system memory. After clearing codes, turn the ignition off for 10 seconds before re-entering the diagnostic mode.

ECM DIAGNOSTIC CODES

CODE	DESCRIPTION	COMMENTS
E012	No Distributor Signal	Ⓐ
E013	Oxygen Sensor Not Ready [AIR, CL & Canister Purge]	Ⓑ
E014	Shorted Coolant Sensor Circuit [AIR]	Ⓑ Ⓕ
E015	Open Coolant Sensor Circuit [AIR]	Ⓑ Ⓕ
E016	Generator Voltage Out Of Range [All Solenoids]	Ⓐ Ⓔ
E018	Open Crank Signal Circuit	Ⓑ
E019	Shorted Fuel Pump Circuit	Ⓑ
E020	Open Fuel Pump Circuit	Ⓐ
E021	Shorted Throttle Position Sensor Circuit	Ⓑ
E022	Open Throttle Position Sensor Circuit	Ⓑ
E023	EST/Bypass Circuit Problem [AIR]	Ⓑ Ⓓ
E024	Speed Sensor Circuit Problem [VCC]	Ⓑ Ⓔ
E026	Shorted Throttle Switch Circuit	Ⓑ
E027	Open Throttle Switch Circuit	Ⓑ
E028	Open Third or Fourth Gear Circuit	Ⓑ
E030	ISC Circuit Problem	Ⓑ
E031	Shorted MAP Sensor Circuit [AIR]	Ⓐ
E032	Open MAP Sensor Circuit [AIR]	Ⓐ
E034	MAP Sensor Signal Too High [AIR]	Ⓐ
E037	Shorted MAT Sensor Circuit [AIR]	Ⓑ
E038	Open MAT Sensor Circuit [AIR]	Ⓑ
E039	VCC Engagement Problem	Ⓑ
E040	Open Power Steering Pressure Switch Circuit	Ⓑ
E044	Lean Exhaust Signal [AIR, CL & Canister Purge]	Ⓐ
E045	Rich Exhaust Signal [AIR, CL & Canister Purge]	Ⓐ
E047	BCM — ECM Data Problem	Ⓑ
E048	EGR System Fault [EGR]	Ⓑ
E051	ECM PROM Error	Ⓐ Ⓕ
E052	ECM Memory Reset Indicator	Ⓒ
E053	Distributor Signal Interrupt	Ⓒ
E055	TPS Misadjusted	Ⓒ
E059	VCC Temperature Sensor Circuit Problem	Ⓒ

DIAGNOSTIC CODE COMMENTS

Ⓐ	Displays "SERVICE NOW" Message And Turns On "ENGINE CONTROL SYSTEM" Light.
Ⓑ	Displays "SERVICE SOON" Message And Turns On "ENGINE CONTROL SYSTEM" Light.
Ⓒ	Does Not Turn On Any Telltale Light Or Display Any Message.
Ⓓ	Causes System To Operate On Bypass Spark.
Ⓔ	Disengages VCC For Entire Ignition Cycle.
Ⓕ	Forces Cooling Fans On Full Speed.
[ ]	Functions Within Bracket Are Disengaged While Specified Malfunction Remains Current.

Fig. 3 ECM diagnostic codes

ECM DATA			
PARAMETER NUMBER	PARAMETER	DISPLAY	
		RANGE	UNITS
ED01	Throttle Position	– 10.0 - 90.0	Degrees
ED02	MAP	14 - 109	kPa
ED03	Computed BARO	61 - 103	kPa
ED04	Coolant Temperature	– 40 - 151	°C
ED05	MAT	– 40 - 151	°C
ED06	Injector Pulse Width	0 - 99.9	ms
ED07	Oxygen Sensor Voltage	0 - .99	Volts
ED08	Spark Advance	– 30 - 60	Degrees
ED10	Battery Voltage	0 - 25.5	Volts
ED11	Engine RPM	0 - 6370	RPM ÷ 10
ED12	Car Speed	0 - 255	MPH
ED18	Oxygen Sensor Cross	0 - 255	Number
ED19	Fuel Integrator	0 - 255	Counts
ED26	VCC Temp. Sensor Volts	0 - 5.1	Volts
ED98	Ignition Cycle Counter	0 - 50	Key Cycles
ED99	ECM PROM ID	0 - 999	Code •

Fig. 4 ECM data display chart

2. To clear BCM codes:
   a. With ECM displayed on CCP (Climate Control Panel), depress the Lo button on the panel. This will permit bypassing of the ECM options and lead the technician to a BCM message.
   b. With BCM displayed on CCP (Climate Control Panel), depress the Hi button on the panel. This will permit access to BCM options.
   c. Depress the Lo button on CCP until "BCM Clear Codes" is displayed.
   d. Depress Hi button on CCP. A "Codes Clear" message will be displayed on panel. This message will appear for approximately 3 seconds to indicate that all trouble codes have been erased from system memory. After clearing codes, turn the ignition off for 10 seconds before re-entering the diagnostic mode.

Exiting Diagnostic Mode

To get out of diagnostic mode, depress Reset/Recall button on the DIC or turn the ignition switch off for 10 seconds. Temperature setting will reappear in the display panel.

CLIMATE CONTROL IN DIAGNOSTIC MODE

When the diagnostic mode is entered, the ECC operates in the mode being commanded before depressing the Off and Warmer buttons. Even though the display may change as the buttons are depressed, the prior operating mode is remembered and will resume after the diagnostic mode is entered.

SET TIMING MODE

The set timing mode instructs the ECM to control spark timing to the 10° BTDC base timing setting to allow setting and verification of spark timing. To enter the set timing mode, proceed as follows:

1. Start engine and run until coolant temperature reaches 85°C.
2. Ensure transmission is in Park position and engine idle speed is less than 900 RPM.
3. Exit diagnostics by depressing Off button on CCP until display returns to standard climate control mode.
4. Connect suitable jumper wire between ALDL connector pins A and B. "Set Timing" will be displayed and engine will operate at base idle. At this point, timing can be checked with a standard timing light.
5. Exit set timing mode by removing jumper wire from connector.

STATUS DISPLAY

While in the diagnostic mode, the mode indicators on the CCP are used to indicate the status of certain operating modes. The different modes of operation are indicated by the status light either being illuminated or off. A summary of the fuel and emission control systems status indicators is as follows:

1. The "Off" indicator is illuminated whenever the ECM is commanding the VCC to engage. This light only indicates whether the VCC is engaged or disabled by the ECM.
2. The "Auto" indicator shows the open/closed loop status of the DEFI system. The light is illuminated when operating in the closed loop mode.
3. The "Econ" indicator displays the rich/lean status of the oxygen sensor. The light is illuminated when the oxygen sensor is transmitting a "rich" voltage (above approximately .6 volt), or an increasing voltage from rich to lean (from approximately .4 to .6 volt).
4. The "°" indicator illustrates the status of the transmission third and fourth gear switch input to the ECM. The "°C" indicator is illuminated as the transmission shifts from second to third gear. The "°F" indicator is illuminated when the transmission shifts from third to fourth gear. The "°E" indicator is illuminated when a fault in the system results in the fourth gear input to the ECM to be open without the third gear input also being open.

DIAGNOSTIC SYSTEMS

After all trouble codes are displayed, diagnostics may be exited or any of the following diagnostic features may be displayed: Data, Inputs, Outputs, Snapshot and Clear Codes.

ECM Data Display

When troubleshooting a system malfunction, the data display can be used to compare the vehicle being serviced to a vehicle which is operating normally.

Following the trouble code displays, ECM will appear on CCP. With the ECM message displayed on the panel, depress the Hi button to access ECM data. Selection of the "Data" test type will result in the first available test being displayed. Four characters of the display will contain a test code to identify the selection. The first two characters are letters which identify the system and test type. The last two characters are numerals which identify the test itself (Example: ED01). Depressing the Hi button will display the next largest number for the selected test type, while depressing the Lo button will display the next smaller test number for the selected test. Depressing the Off button will stop the test selection process and return the display to the next available test type for the selected system (Example: ECM Inputs). The various data parameters and their values are shown in **Fig. 4.**

ECM Input Display

When troubleshooting a system malfunction, the input display can be used to test the four switch inputs to the ECM.

Following the ECM and BCM trouble code displays, ECM will appear on CCP as outlined previously. With the ECM message displayed on the panel, depress the Hi, then the Lo button. This will allow the technician to bypass ECM data and proceed directly to ECM inputs. Selection of the "Input" test type will result in the first available test being displayed. Input status is displayed as HI or LO and will be shown as "0" until detects that input has cycled from HI to LO or LO to HI. When the cycle is complete, the "0" will be replaced by an "X", indicating that the input being checked has passed the input test. if the inputs will not cycle, or an intermittent input is suspected, refer to "ECM Input Display Diagnosis." Four characters of the display will contain a test code to identify the selection. The first two characters are letters which identify the system and test type. The last two characters are numerals which identify the test itself (Example: EI71). Depressing the Hi button will display the next largest test number for the selected test type, while depressing the Lo button will display the next smaller test number for the selected test. Depressing the Off button will stop the test selection process and return the display to the next available test type for the selected system

ECM INPUTS▼	
INPUT NUMBER	INPUT
EI71	Brake Switch
EI72	Throttle Switch
EI74	Park/Neutral Switch
EI78	Power Steering Pressure Switch (Engine Running)

▼ *"HI" = High Signal Voltage
▼ *"LO" = Low Signal Voltage
▼ "0" = Input Same Since Displayed
▼ "X" = Input Changed Since Displayed

Fig. 5 ECM input display chart

(Example ECM Outputs). Available input displays are shown in **Fig. 5.**

ECM Output Display

If "--" message appears when trying to test device, device must be tested with engine off.

When troubleshooting a system malfunction, the output display can be used to determine if the output tests can be actuated regardless of the inputs and normal program instructions.

With the ECM message displayed on the panel as outlined above, depress the Hi, then the Lo button twice. This will allow the technician to bypass ECM data and inputs and proceed directly to ECM outputs. Selection of the "Output" test type will result in the first available test being displayed. When a test has been selected, HI and LO will be illuminated for three seconds in each state to indicate the command and output terminal voltage. Four characters of the display will contain a test code to identify the selection. The first two characters are letters which identify the system and test type. The last two characters are numerals which identify the test itself (Example: EO01). Depressing the Hi button will display the next largest test number for the selected test type, while depressing the Lo button will display the next smaller test number for the selected test. Depressing the Off button will stop the test selection process and return the display to the next available test type for the selected system (Example: ECM Clear Codes). Available output displayed are shown in **Fig. 6.**

ECM Snapshot

The ECM snapshot feature can be used when troubleshooting intermittent malfunctions in the system. When the snapshot is requested, a set of all ECM data parameter values and output status indications will be stored at that moment.

With the ECM message displayed on the panel as outlined above, depress the Hi button, then depress the Lo button until "Snapshot?" is displayed. Selection of the "Snapshot" test type will result in a "Snapshot Taken" display with selected system name preceding it. This message will remain for three seconds to indicate that all data and inputs have been stored in memory. The system will then automatically

ECM OUTPUTS*■	
OUTPUT NUMBER	OUTPUT
E000	No Outputs
E001	Canister Purge Solenoid
E002	VCC Solenoid
E003	EFE Relay
E004	EGR Solenoid
E005	AIR Switch Solenoid
E006	AIR Divert Solenoid
E007	ISC Motor
E099	Cycle All Outputs

■If " ≡ ≡ ≡ ≡ " Message Appears You Are Trying To Test A Device That Is Not Allowed With Engine Running. Turn Engine Off And Try Again.

Fig. 6 ECM output display chart

proceed to the first available snapshot test. Depressing the Lo button will move display to the next snapshot test. Depressing the Hi button with "Snap Inputs" or "Snapdata" displayed will select that test type. The display will then be controlled as for normal data and input displays, however, all values and status information will represent memorized vehicle conditions. Depressing the Hi button with "Snapshot?" displayed will display "Snapshot Taken," indicating that new information has been stored in the memory.

ECM Clear Codes

Refer to "Clearing Trouble Codes" for procedure.

COMPONENT REPLACEMENT

ELECTRONIC CONTROL MODULE (ECM), REPLACE

When replacing a production ECM with a service ECM, transfer the broadcast code and production number from the production unit to the service unit. Also, during replacement, the PROM and CALPAK must be removed from the ECM being replaced and transferred to the new unit. Refer to applicable heading for replacement procedure.

1. Disconnect battery ground cable.
2. Remove righthand hush panel to gain access to ECM.
3. Disconnect two electrical connectors from ECM.
4. Remove ECM retaining screw, then the ECM and related mounting hardware.
5. Reverse procedure to install.

PROM, REPLACE

1. Remove ECM as previously described.
2. Remove PROM/CALPAK access cover, **Fig. 7.**
3. Grasp PROM carrier with PROM removal tool, **Fig. 8.** Engage one end of carrier with hooked end of tool, then

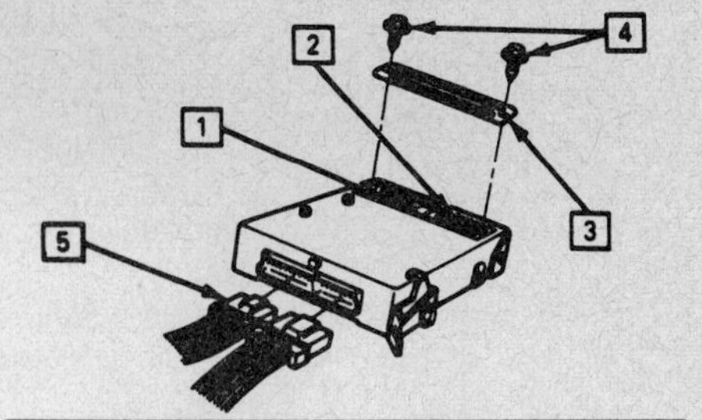

1 CALPAK
2 PROM
3 ACCESS COVER
4 SCREW
5 CONNECTOR

Fig. 7 PROM/CALPAK access cover removal

press on vertical bar of tool and rock engaged end of carrier out as far as possible. Repeat procedure on opposite end of carrier until removed from socket.
4. Inspect replacement PROM to ensure part number matches that of original PROM.
5. Ensure new PROM is properly installed in carrier, **Fig. 9. The PROM must never be removed from the carrier. If a PROM is found to be reversed in the carrier, a new PROM/carrier assembly must be installed.**
6. Position PROM and carrier over socket and press down firmly on top of carrier. Press down on carrier and ensure it seats squarely.
7. Install PROM/CALPAK access cover, then position ECM in vehicle.

CALPAK, REPLACE

1. Remove ECM as previously described.
2. Remove PROM/CALPAK access cover, **Fig. 7.**
3. Grasp narrow end of CALPAK carrier with CALPAK removal tool, **Fig. 10.** Carefully rock carrier from end to end while applying a firm upward force to remove CALPAK and carrier assembly from ECM.
4. Inspect replacement CALPAK to ensure part number matches that of original CALPAK.
5. Ensure new CALPAK is properly installed in carrier, **Fig. 11. The CALPAK must never be removed from the carrier. If a CALPAK is found to be reversed in the carrier, a new CALPAK/carrier assembly must be installed.**
6. Position CALPAK and carrier over socket and press down firmly on top of carrier. Press down on carrier and ensure it seats squarely.
7. Install PROM/CALPAK access cover, then position ECM in vehicle.

THROTTLE BODY INJECTOR UNIT, REPLACE

1. Remove air cleaner assembly and disconnect Thermactor hose from engine fitting.
2. Disconnect electrical connectors from ISC motor, TPS and injectors.

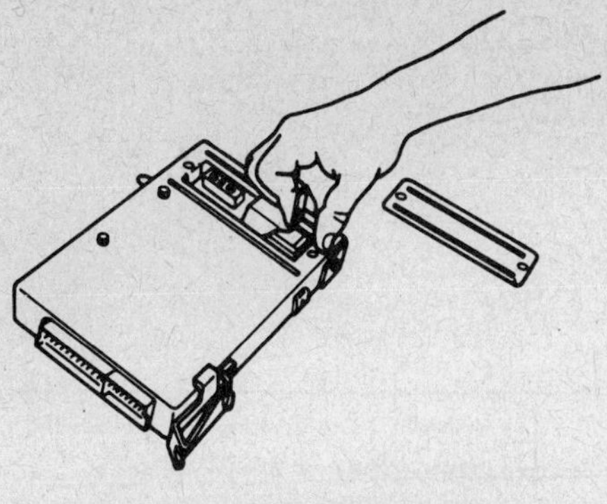

Fig. 8 PROM removal

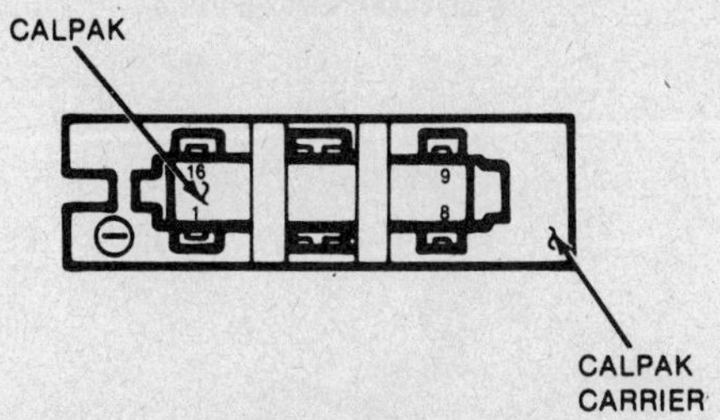

Fig. 11 CALPAK installed in carrier

3. Disconnect throttle cable, transmission control cable and cruise control cable, if equipped.
4. Disconnect vacuum hoses from throttle body, noting positions for installation reference.
5. Disconnect fuel lines from throttle body.
6. Remove throttle body attaching bolts and the throttle body.
7. Reverse procedure to install, noting the following:
   a. Inspect EFE gasket for wear of damage and replace if necessary.
   b. Install new throttle body gasket.
   c. Torque attaching bolts to 11 ft. lbs.
   d. Torque fuel line fittings to 17 ft. lbs.

FUEL METER COVER, REPLACE

The pressure regulator is integral with the fuel meter cover and is serviced as an assembly only. To avoid personal injury, the pressure regulator attaching screws must never be removed from the cover, as the regulator spring is under heavy compression.

1. Remove air cleaner assembly.
2. Disconnect fuel injector electrical connectors.
3. Remove fuel meter cover attaching screws and the cover, **Fig. 12. Do not immerse fuel meter cover in any type of cleaning agent.**
4. Reverse procedure to install, noting the following:
   a. Install new dust seal in fuel meter body recess.
   b. Install new fuel return passage gasket and fuel meter cover gasket.
   c. Torque cover attaching screws to 28 inch lbs., noting locations of long and short screws, **Fig. 12.**

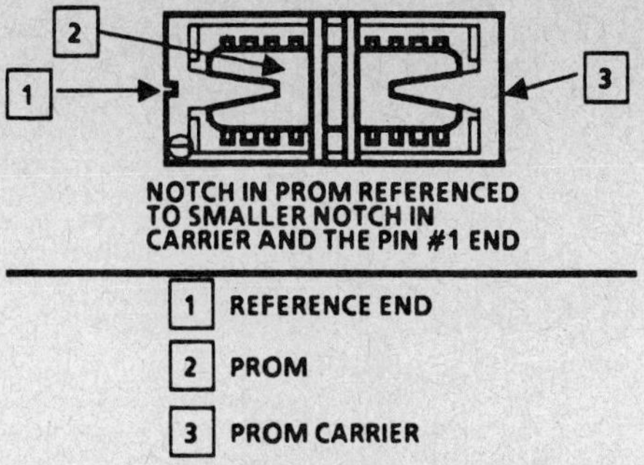

Fig. 9 PROM installed in carrier

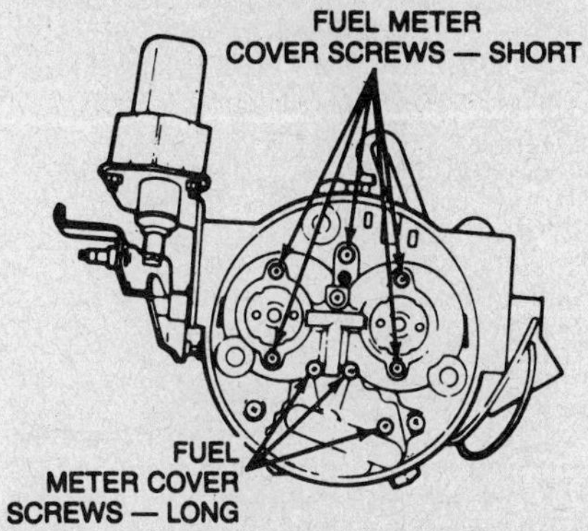

Fig. 12 Fuel meter cover removal

FUEL METER BODY, REPLACE

1. Remove fuel meter cover as previously described.
2. Remove fuel meter cover gasket, fuel meter outlet gasket and pressure regulator seal.
3. Remove fuel injectors as described under "Fuel Injectors, Replace."
4. Remove fuel inlet and outlet nuts and gaskets from fuel meter body.
5. Remove fuel meter body attaching screws, then separate body from throttle body unit. Remove and discard body gasket. **Do not remove center screw and staking at either end securing fuel distribution skirt in throttle body unit.**
6. Reverse procedure to install, noting the following:
   a. Apply suitable locking compound to attaching screws.
   b. Install new gaskets on fuel inlet and outlet fittings and torque inlet nut to 30 ft. lbs. and outlet nut to 21 ft. lbs.

IDLE SPEED CONTROL (ISC) MOTOR, REPLACE

The ISC motor is serviced as an assembly only and should not be immersed in any type of cleaning agent.

1. Remove air cleaner assembly.
2. Disconnect electrical connector from ISC motor.
3. Remove motor attaching screws and the motor.

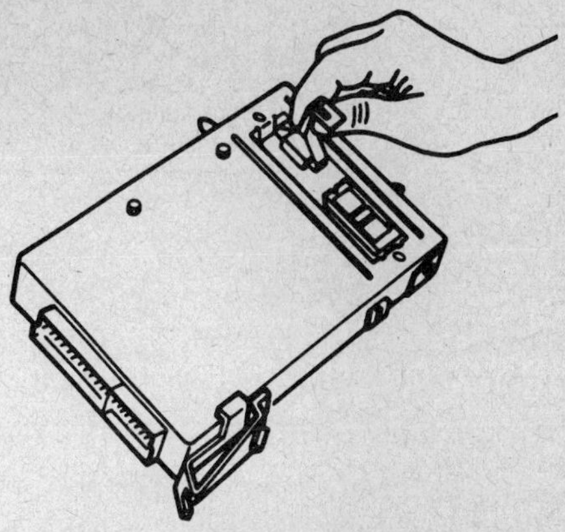

Fig. 10 CALPAK removal

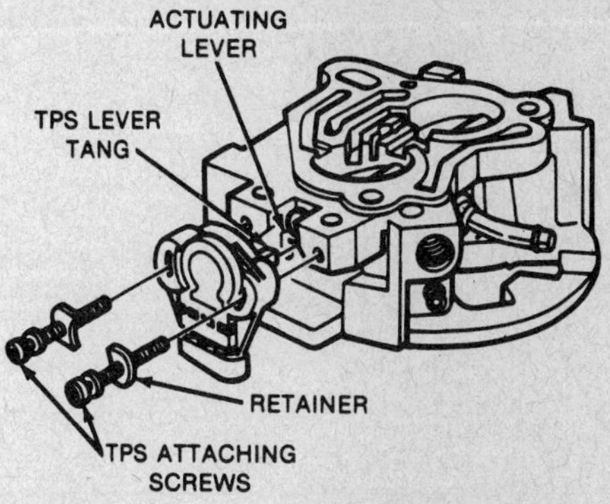

Fig. 13 Throttle Position Sensor (TPS) removal

4. Reverse procedure to install.

THROTTLE POSITION SENSOR (TPS), REPLACE

1. Remove air cleaner assembly.
2. Disconnect electrical connector from TPS.
3. Remove TPS attaching screws and the TPS, **Fig. 13.**
4. Reverse procedure to install, noting the following:
   a. Install TPS with throttle in normal closed idle position.
   b. When installing TPS, ensure pick-up lever on the sensor is located above tang on throttle actuator lever.
   c. Do not apply locking compound to TPS attaching screws.
   d. Do not tighten TPS attaching screws until TPS has been properly adjusted. Refer to "Adjustments."

FUEL INJECTORS, REPLACE

The fuel injectors are serviced as an assembly only and should not be immersed in any type of cleaning agent.

1. Remove air cleaner assembly, then disconnect injector electrical connector.
2. Remove fuel meter cover as previously described.
3. Remove injector from fuel meter body by carefully lifting out with a screwdriver, **Fig. 14. Leave fuel meter cover gasket in position when remov-**

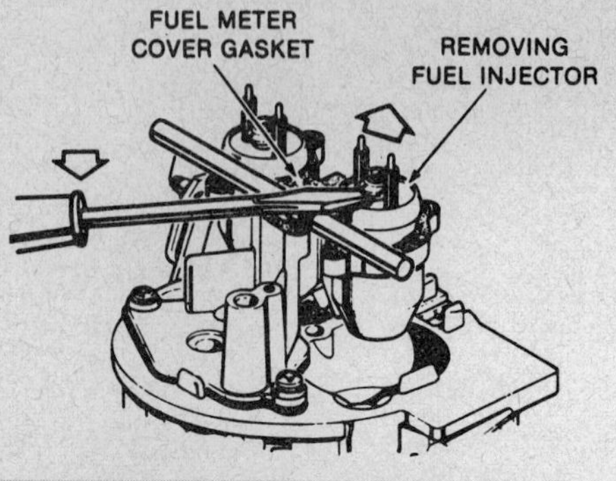

Fig. 14 Fuel injector removal

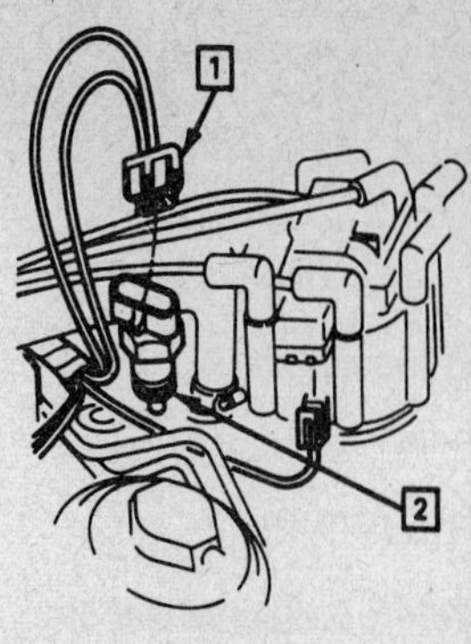

Fig. 15 Coolant sensor replacement

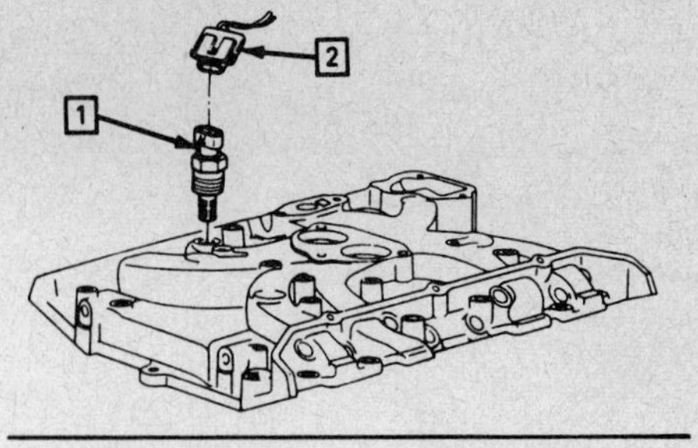

Fig. 16 Manifold Air Temperature (MAT) sensor replacement

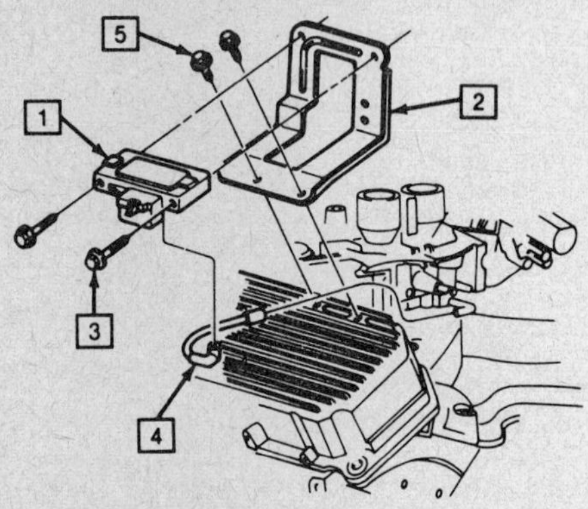

Fig. 17 Manifold Absolute Pressure (MAP) sensor replacement

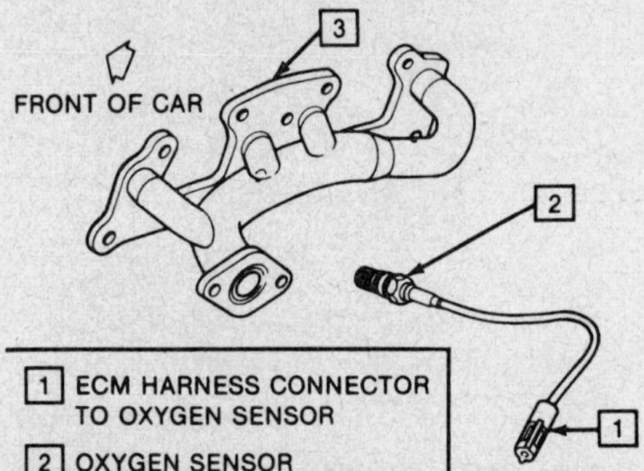

Fig. 18 Oxygen sensor replacement

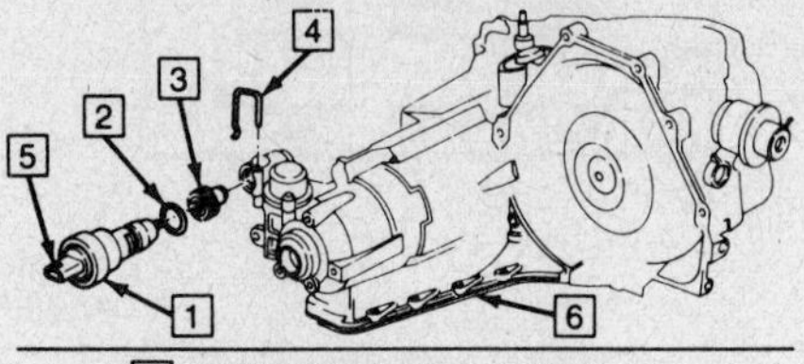

Fig. 19 Vehicle speed sensor (VSS) replacement

ing injector to prevent damage to body casting.

4. Remove large O-ring and back-up washer, then the small O-ring from injector. Discard both O-rings.
5. Carefully remove fuel filter from base of injector.
6. Reverse procedure to install, noting the following:
   a. Install filter on nozzle end of injector with large end of filter toward injector. Ensure filter covers raised rib at bottom of injector, then position filter against base of injector using a twisting motion.
   b. Lubricate new small O-ring with automatic transmission fluid, then press O-ring onto injector until it contacts filter.
   c. Lubricate new large O-ring with automatic transmission fluid, then install O-ring above back-up washer until flush with top of fuel meter body casting surface.
   d. When installing injector, align raised lug on injector base with notch in fuel meter body, then push down on injector until fully seated.

COOLANT SENSOR, REPLACE

1. Partially drain engine coolant from radiator.
2. Disconnect electrical connector from coolant sensor, then carefully back sensor out of engine, **Fig. 15.**
3. Reverse procedure to install.

MANIFOLD AIR TEMPERATURE (MAT) SENSOR, REPLACE

1. Remove air cleaner assembly.
2. Disconnect electrical connector from MAT sensor, then carefully back sensor out of engine, **Fig. 16.**
3. Reverse procedure to install. Apply suitable sealant to sensor threads and torque to 15 ft. lbs.

MANIFOLD ABSOLUTE PRESSURE (MAP) SENSOR, REPLACE

1. Remove air cleaner assembly.
2. Disconnect electrical connector from MAP sensor.
3. Remove two MAP sensor attaching screws and the sensor, **Fig. 17.**
4. Reverse procedure to install. Torque sensor attaching screws to 3 ft. lbs.

OXYGEN SENSOR, REPLACE

The pigtail and connector are permanently attached to the oxygen sensor and must not be disturbed.

1. Run engine until normal operating temperature is reached, then stop engine.
2. Disconnect battery ground cable, then the oxygen sensor electrical connector. **Keep sensor electrical connector free of grease and other contaminants.**
3. Raise and support vehicle.
4. Carefully back out oxygen sensor, **Fig. 18.**
5. Reverse procedure to install. Torque sensor to 30 ft. lbs. **If original oxygen sensor is to be returned to service, a suitable anti-seize compound should be applied to sensor threads. New sensors will already have the compound applied to the threads.**

VEHICLE SPEED SENSOR (VSS), REPLACE

1. Disconnect electrical connector from speed sensor.
2. Remove retainer, then the speed sensor and gear from transmission, **Fig. 19.**
3. Reverse procedure to install.

Port Fuel Injection, 1986–87 Buick Riviera & Oldsmobile Toronado

INDEX

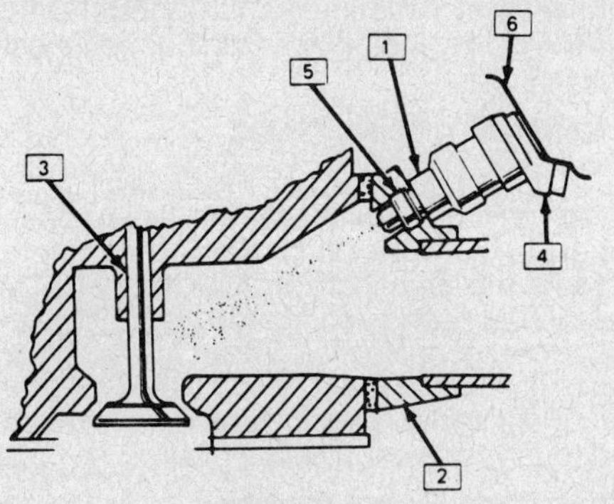

1 FUEL INJECTOR
2 INTAKE MANIFOLD
3 INTAKE VALVE
4 ELECTRICAL TERMINAL
5 "O" RING
6 FUEL RAIL

Fig. 1 Port fuel injection nozzle

DESCRIPTION

Port Fuel Injection provide a means of fuel metering which insures a precise air/fuel mixture and superior fuel distribution resulting in reduced exhaust emissions and improved driveability under all driving conditions.

This Fuel Injection system is of the Sequential Fuel Injection (SFI) type, whereby metered fuel is injected sequentially into each intake port once per working cycle (every two revolutions), just prior to the opening of the intake valve.

An Electronic Control Module (ECM) is used to determine the amount of fuel delivered to the engine. The ECM receives signals from various sensors and devices to know what mode of operation the engine is being subjected to, then analyzes the information and adjusts the air/fuel mixture accordingly.

A Body Computer Module (BCM) used in conjunction with the ECM, provides for additional control capacity. The BCM monitors various body operating functions and shares this information with the ECM through an electronic communications process called the serial data line.

The ECM and BCM are both capable of diagnosing faults within the various inputs and sensors they control. When the ECM detects a malfunction, a dash mounted "Service Engine Soon" lamp is illuminated.

SYSTEM COMPONENTS

Throttle Body

The throttle body regulates the amount of air entering the engine through the use of a throttle plate, which rotates in response to the accelerator pedal. The throttle body also contain vacuum ports, which are located above and below the throttle plate and are used to generate vacuum signals to control various components.

Fuel Rail

The fuel rail is used to distribute fuel to the fuel injectors. One end is connected to the fuel supply line, while the other end is connected to the fuel pressure regulator. The fuel injectors are mounted at various points along the rail so the injector nozzles are positioned above each intake valve.

Fuel Injectors

The fuel injectors, **Fig. 1,** are solenoid operated and controlled by the ECM. The ECM energizes the injector solenoid, which opens a valve that permits fuel delivery. The pressurized fuel is then injected in a conical spray pattern at the intake valve opening.

Fuel Pressure Regulator

The fuel pressure regulator, **Fig. 2,** is a diaphragm operated relief valve with intake manifold vacuum operating on one side and fuel pressure operating on the other. The regulator function is to maintain constant fuel pressure in the fuel rail at all times. The fuel pressure regulator also compensates for engine load by increasing fuel pressure during periods of low manifold vacuum. The pressure regulator is mounted on the fuel rail and is serviced separately as a unit.

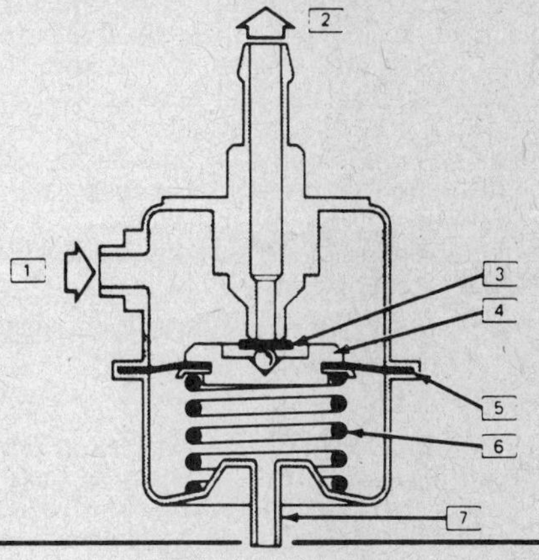

1 FUEL INLET
2 FUEL RETURN OUTLET
3 VALVE
4 VALVE HOLDER
5 DIAPHRAGM
6 COMPRESSION SPRING
7 VACUUM CONNECTION

Fig. 2 Fuel pressure regulator assembly

Idle Air Control Valve (IAC)

The throttle body mounted IAC valve, **Fig. 3,** is used to control engine idle speed by moving a conical valve in or out of the throttle valve air bypass channel. The ECM monitors battery voltage, coolant temperature, engine load and engine RPM and then uses this information to determine IAC valve position. If the IAC valve is dis-

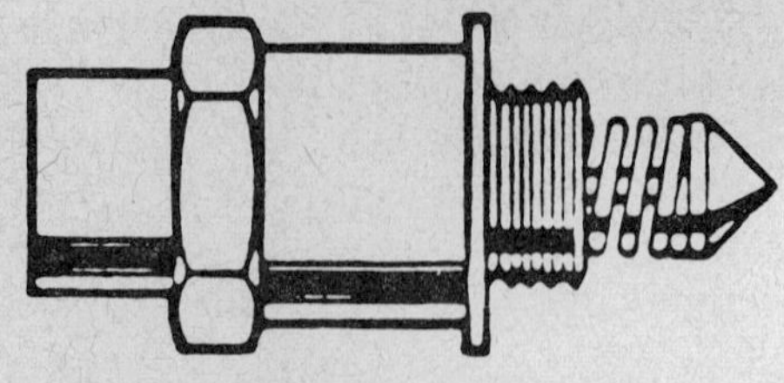

Fig. 3 Idle Air Control (IAC) valve

connected and reconnected while the engine is running, the idle speed may be incorrect. If this occurs, reset the IAC valve. To reset the IAC valve, turn ignition On, then Off.

Electric Fuel Pump

The fuel tank mounted electric fuel pump provides the injection system's fuel quantity and pressure. When the ignition switch is turned On, but the engine is not started, the ECM energizes the fuel pump relay to provide power to the fuel pump for two seconds to build up fuel pressure. If the engine is not started within two seconds, the ECM de-energizes the fuel pump relay. When the engine is cranked, the ECM energizes the fuel pump relay and the fuel pump. As a back-up system, the oil pressure switch can also operate the fuel pump. When oil pressure reaches 28 psi, and the fuel pump relay fails, the oil pressure switch will close and operate the fuel pump.

Mass Air Flow (MAF) & Mass Air Temperature (MAT) Sensors

The MAF & MAT sensors work in conjunction to measure the density of the air entering the intake manifold. This is accomplished by measuring incoming air flow and incoming air temperature. This information is used by the ECM to calculate the proper air/fuel mixture.

Oxygen Sensor

The exhaust oxygen sensor, **Fig. 4**, mounted in the exhaust system, monitors oxygen content in the exhaust gas stream and produces a corresponding voltage output which is monitored by the ECM. If the ECM determines the air/fuel mixture is incorrect, it will change the injector opening duration as necessary to correct the air/fuel mixture.

Electronic Control Module

The ECM, located in the passenger compartment, is the control center for the fuel injection system. The ECM continually monitors and processes the input information and generates output commands to the various systems affecting vehicle performance.

A Programmable Read Only Memory (PROM) removable calibration unit, enables the ECM to recognize and adjust for vehicle variations (vehicle weight, axle ratio, etc.). There are specific ECM/PROM combinations for each specific vehicle which are not interchangeable.

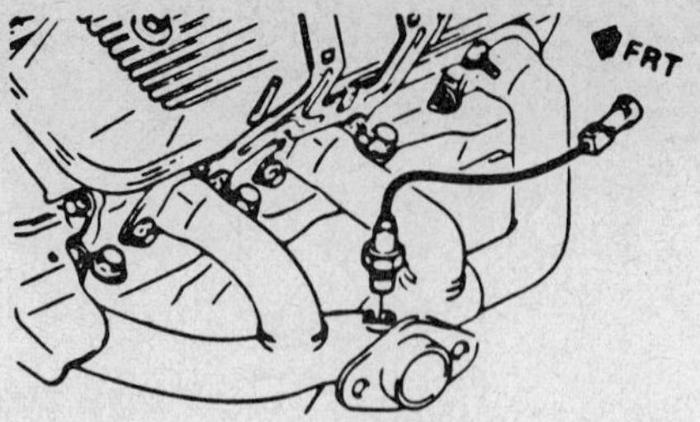

Fig. 4 Oxygen sensor location

A CALPAK is also installed in the ECM. The CALPAK allows fuel delivery if other parts of the ECM are damaged.

The ECM can also perform the diagnostic functions of the fuel injection system. When the ECM detects a system malfunction, it will illuminate the Service Engine Soon lamp and store the appropriate code(s) to identify the problem area(s).

Engine Coolant Temperature Sensor

The engine coolant temperature sensor is a thermistor mounted in the engine coolant stream flow. The ECM supplies a 5 volt signal to the sensor through a resistor in the ECM and measures voltage. Voltage will be high when the engine is cold and low when the engine is hot. The sensor provides coolant temperature information to the ECM for most ECM operated systems.

Throttle Position Sensor (TPS)

The TPS, **Fig. 5**, connected to the throttle shaft, is a potentiometer with one end connected to 5 volts from the ECM and the other to ground. A third wire, connected to the TPS, measures TPS wiper voltage and relays the information to the ECM. TPS voltage changes with each movement of the throttle valve. The ECM calculates fuel delivery and spark advance based on throttle valve angle.

Gear Selector Switch

The gear selector switch indicates to the ECM when the transaxle is in the park or neutral position. This information is used by the ECM for EGR control, IAC valve operation and Transaxle Converter Clutch (TCC) operation.

Air Conditioning ON Signal

When the A/C is switched On, a signal is sent to the BCM. If all systems are satisfactory, the BCM signals the ECM to turn on the A/C. If the Low R-12 and Power Steering Pressure switches are closed, the A/C will operate.

Power Steering Pressure Switch

The power steering pressure switch, **Fig. 6**, opens during high pressure power steering situations and signals the ECM to shut Off the A/C compressor and increase the idle speed to compensate for the increased engine load.

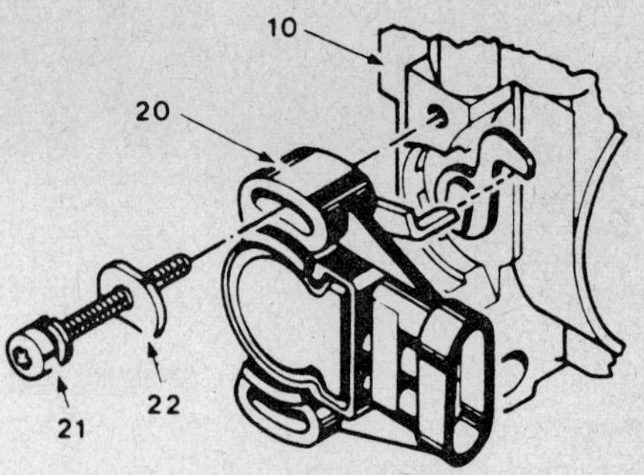

10 THROTTLE BODY ASSEMBLY
20 THROTTLE POSITION SENSOR (TPS)
21 TPS ATTACHING SCREW
22 TPS RETAINER

Fig. 5 TPS switch

Crankshaft Sensor

The crankshaft sensor, **Fig. 7**, is used by the ECM to determine engine RPM and crankshaft position. The sensor is a Hall Effect switch mounted on a pedestal at the front of the engine near the harmonic balancer.

Camshaft Sensor

The camshaft sensor, **Fig. 7**, is a Hall Effect switch mounted on the timing cover behind the water pump. The sensor represents the camshaft position to the ECM, which uses this information to time the sequential port injection. When the camshaft position signal is not seen by the ECM, the fuel injection system operates simultaneously, instead of sequentially.

Fourth Gear Switch

The fourth gear switch, located on the transaxle, signals the ECM when the fourth gear clutch hydraulic circuit has been reached the apply pressure level. The ECM uses this information to engage the Transaxle Converter Clutch (TCC) and to calculate EGR Duty Cycle.

Detonation Sensor

The detonation sensor, **Fig. 8**, is a piezoelectric sensor located near the transmission end of the engine. The sensor generates electrical impulses which are directly proportional to the frequency of the knock being detected. The signal is sent to a buffer, which sorts the signals and eliminates all those that are not within the proper detonation frequency. The modified signal is then sent to the Electronic Spark Control (ESC) module and to the ECM where the timing is retarded until detonation ceases.

OPERATION

STARTING MODE

When ignition is first turned On, the ECM energizes the fuel pump for two seconds and pressure is built up in the fuel rail. The ECM then checks coolant temperature sensor, TPS, MAT sensor and crank signal

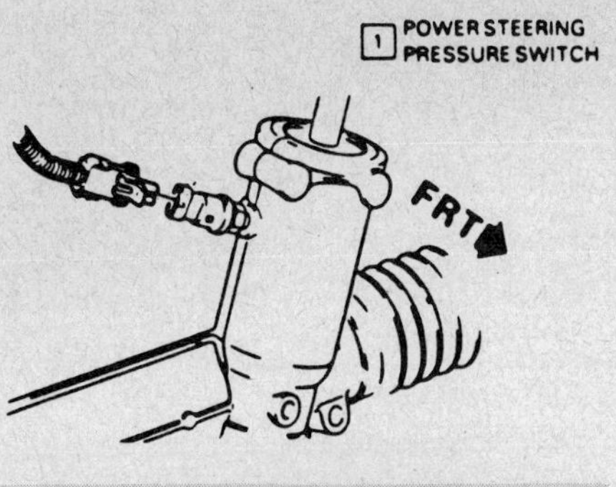

Fig. 6 Power steering pressure switch

and determines proper air/fuel mixture for starting. **While in the starting mode only, the ECM pulses the injectors once for each crankshaft revolution.**

CLEAR FLOOD MODE

A flooded engine can be cleared by fully depressing the accelerator pedal, which causes the ECM to shut off the fuel flow. The ECM will maintain this operational mode as long as throttle is wide open and engine RPM is less than 600. When throttle position becomes less than 62%, the ECM returns to the "starting" mode.

RUN MODE

The "run" mode consists of two separate operating conditions; open loop and closed loop.

The system goes into open loop operation when the engine is first started and RPM is above 400. In open loop operation, the ECM disregards oxygen sensor signal and determines air/fuel mixture primarily on inputs from coolant, MAF, MAT and TPS sensors. The system will remain in open loop operation until the oxygen sensor has varying voltage output and is hot enough to operate, the coolant sensor is above 156° F and 70 seconds has elapsed after starting a cold engine or 30 seconds after starting warm engine. When these conditions are met, the system switches to closed loop operation.

In closed loop operation, the ECM calculates the air/fuel mixture based on signals from the oxygen sensor. This allows the air/fuel mixture to stay close to the optimum 14.7:1 ratio.

ACCELERATION MODE

In the "acceleration" mode, the ECM senses rapid changes in throttle position and air flow and provides a corresponding amount of added fuel.

DECELERATION MODE

In the "deceleration mode" the ECM senses changes in throttle position and manifold vacuum and makes necessary changes in the air/fuel mixture. When decelerating very rapidly, the ECM will cut off the fuel supply completely for short periods of time.

BATTERY VOLTAGE CORRECTION MODE

When battery is low, the ECM compen-

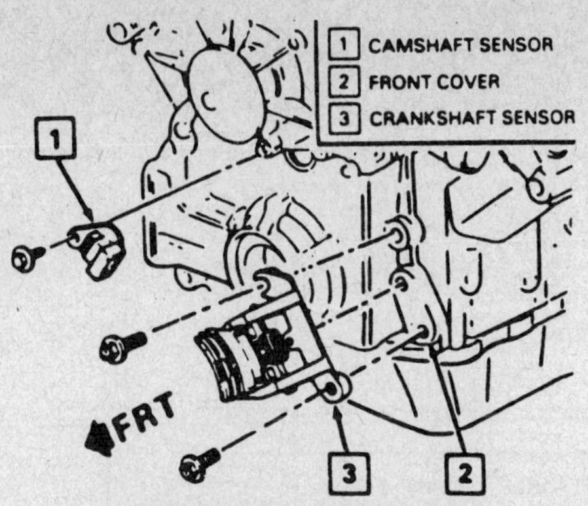

Fig. 7 Camshaft & crankshaft sensors

sates to maintain charging system performance by increasing engine idle speed.

SELF-DIAGNOSIS

This fuel injection system is a highly complex computer system which includes the use of both an Electronic Control Module (ECM) and Body Control Module (BCM). The information contained in this section is intended for use as an aid in diagnosing engine fuel and emissions related complaints only.

TROUBLE CODES

The ECM continually monitors operating conditions of the various systems it control. When a problem is detected, a trouble code will be stored in the computer memory. These codes can be displayed as an aid in system repair. Any malfunctions which the vehicle operator should be aware of will illuminate an "Service Engine Soon" warning lamp on the instrument panel. If a malfunction which would result in unacceptable system operation is encountered, the self-diagnostics will minimize the effect by taking "failsoft" action to compensate for the detected problem.

Entering Service Mode

If the vehicle is to be in the Service Mode for more than a 1/2 hour with the engine Off, hook suitable trickle charger to battery to prevent the possibility of false diagnostic readings or a no start condition.

On Toronado models, turn ignition On, then touch Off and Warm buttons simultaneously on the Electronic Climate Control (ECC) Panel, **Fig. 9.** Hold buttons until a segment check is displayed on the ECC panel and Instrument Panel Cluster (IPC). The segment check usually occurs within three seconds.

On Riviera Models, turn ignition On, then touch Off and Warm buttons on Cathode Ray Tube's (CRT) Climate Control page simultaneously, **Fig. 10.** Hold buttons until a double beep is heard or a page entitled "Service Mode" appears.

Climate Control In Service Mode

When the service mode is entered, the climate control operates in the mode com-

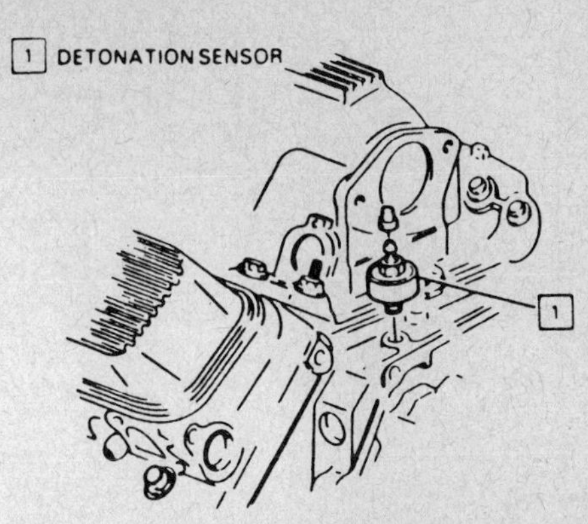

Fig. 8 Detonation sensor

manded just prior to touching the Off and Warm buttons. Even though the display may change as the buttons are touched during diagnosis, the prior operating mode is remembered and will resume after the service mode is entered.

Trouble Code Display

After the Service Mode is entered, any codes stored in computer memory will be displayed as follows:

1. All ECM codes will be displayed first. Codes will be displayed for approximately two seconds with the lowest code first, followed by progressively higher codes present. All ECM codes will be prefixed with an "E" (EO13, EO14, etc.) before the code. If no ECM codes are stored, a "No ECM Codes" message will be displayed .
2. When all ECM codes or a "No ECM Codes" message has been displayed, all BCM codes will be displayed. BCM codes are prefixed with a "B"(B110, B111, etc.). If no BCM codes are stored, a "No BCM Codes" message will be displayed.
3. BCM codes displayed will be accompanied by a "Current" or "History" designation. "History" indicates the failure was not present the last time the code was tested. "Current" indicates the fault still exists.
4. At any time during the display of the ECM or BCM codes, if the Lo button on the IPC is touched on Toronado models, or the NO button is touched on the CRT on Riviera models, the display of codes will be bypassed. If the Bi-Lev button on the ECC panel is touched on Toronado models, or the EXIT button is touched on the CRT on Riviera models, the system will exit the service mode and go back to normal vehicle operation.
5. After all ECM and BCM codes have been displayed, or if no codes are present, a decision point is reached. "ECM" is displayed, and a selection from ECM, BCM or IPC data may be made. Refer to "Service Diagnostics" for complete operations.

Exiting Service Mode

On Toronado models, touch Bi-Lev button on ECC panel. The trouble codes will not be erased and the system will go back to normal vehicle operation.

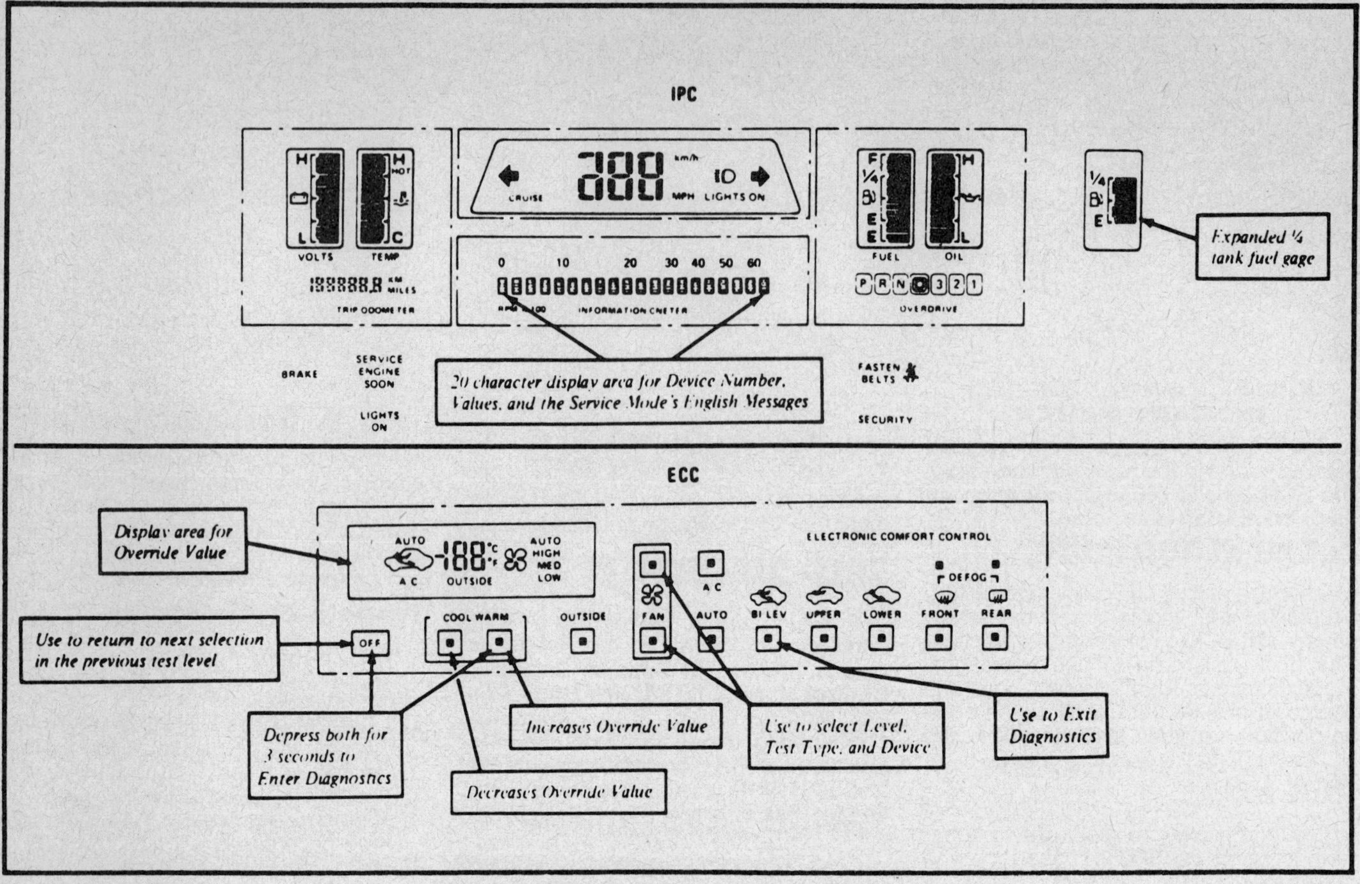

Fig. 9 ECC & IPC Panel. Toronado

On Riviera models, repeatedly touch EXIT button until "Service Mode" page disappears or turn ignition Off. The trouble codes will not be erased and the system will go back to normal vehicle operation.

Clearing Trouble Codes

After all ECM and BCM codes are displayed and appropriate measures are taken to correct malfunctions, trouble codes may be cleared.

1. To clear ECM codes on Toronado models, proceed as follows:
   a. With ECM displayed on ECC panel, touch the Hi button on the panel. This will permit access to ECM options (ECM data, inputs, outputs, code clearing, etc.)
   b. With ECM data displayed, touch the Lo button on ECC panel until "ECM Clear Codes" is displayed.
   c. Touch Hi button on ECC panel. A "Codes Clear" message will be displayed on panel. This message will appear for approximately 3 seconds to indicate that all trouble codes have been erased from system memory. After clearing codes, touch "Bi-Lev" button on ECC panel to exit diagnostics.
2. To clear ECM codes on Riviera models, proceed as follows:
   a. With ECM displayed on CRT, touch the YES button on the panel. This will permit access to ECM options (ECM data, inputs, outputs, code clearing, etc.)

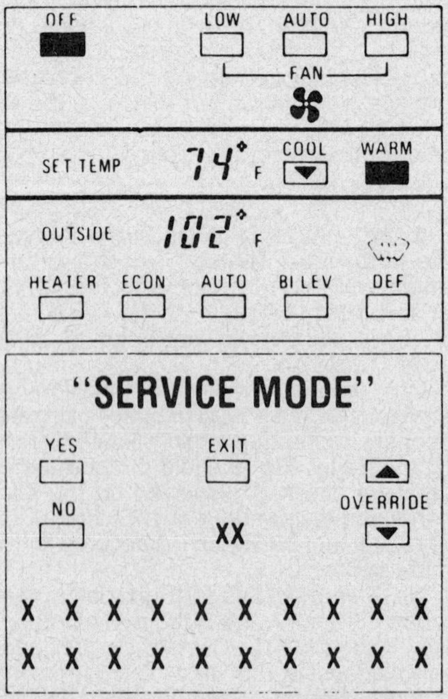

Fig. 10 CRT Climate Control page. Riviera

   b. With ECM data displayed, touch the NO button on CRT until "Code Reset" is displayed.
   c. Touch YES button on CRT. A "Codes Clear" message will be displayed on CRT. This message will appear for approximately 3 seconds to indicate that all trouble codes have been erased from system memory. After clearing codes, touch EXIT button repeatedly until "Service Mode" page disappears to exit diagnostics.
3. To clear BCM codes on Toronado models, proceed as follows:
   a. With ECM displayed on ECC panel, touch the Lo button on the panel. This will permit bypassing of the ECM options and lead to a BCM message.
   b. With BCM displayed on ECC panel, touch the Hi button on the panel. This will permit access to BCM options.
   c. Touch the Lo button on ECC panel until "BCM Clear Codes" is displayed.
   d. Touch Hi button on ECC panel. A "Codes Clear" message will be displayed on panel. This message will appear for approximately 3 seconds to indicate that all trouble codes have been erased from system memory. After clearing codes, touch Bi-Lev button on ECC panel to exit diagnostics.

4. To clear BCM codes on Riviera models, proceed as follows:
   a. With ECM displayed on CRT, touch the NO button on the panel. This will permit bypassing of the ECM options and lead to a BCM message.
   b. With BCM displayed on CRT, touch the YES button on the panel. This will permit access to BCM options.
   c. Touch the NO button on CRT until "Code Reset" is displayed.
   d. Touch YES button on CRT. A "Codes Clear" message will be displayed on CRT. This message will appear for approximately 3 seconds to indicate that all trouble codes have been erased from system memory. After clearing codes, touch EXIT button repeatedly until "Service Mode" page disappears to exit diagnostics.

SERVICE DIAGNOSTICS

TORONADO MODELS

After all trouble codes are displayed, diagnostics may be exited or any of the following diagnostic features may be displayed: Data, Inputs, Outputs, and Clear Codes, **Fig. 11.**

ECM Data Display

When troubleshooting a system malfunction, the data display can be used to compare the vehicle being serviced to a vehicle which is operating normally.

Following the trouble code displays, ECM will appear on ECC panel. With the ECM message displayed on the panel, touch the Hi button to access ECM data. Selection of the "Data" test type will result in the first available test being displayed. Four characters of the display will contain a test code to identify the selection. The first two characters are letters which identify the system and test type. The last two characters are numerals which identify the test itself (Example: ED01). Depressing the Hi button will display the next largest number for the selected test type, while touching the Lo button will display the next smaller test number for the selected test. Depressing the Off button will stop the test selection process and return the display to the next available system selection (Example: ECM Inputs). The various data parameters and their values are shown in **Fig. 12.**

ECM Input Display

When troubleshooting a system malfunction, the input display can be used to test the switch inputs to the ECM.

Following the ECM and BCM trouble code displays, ECM will appear on ECC panel as outlined previously. With the ECM message displayed on the panel, touch the Hi, then the Lo button. This will allow bypassing the ECM data and proceed directly to ECM inputs. Selection of the "Input" test type will result in the first available test being displayed. Input status is displayed as HI or LO and w ill be shown as "0" until it detects that input has cycled from HI to LO or LO to HI. When the cycle is com-

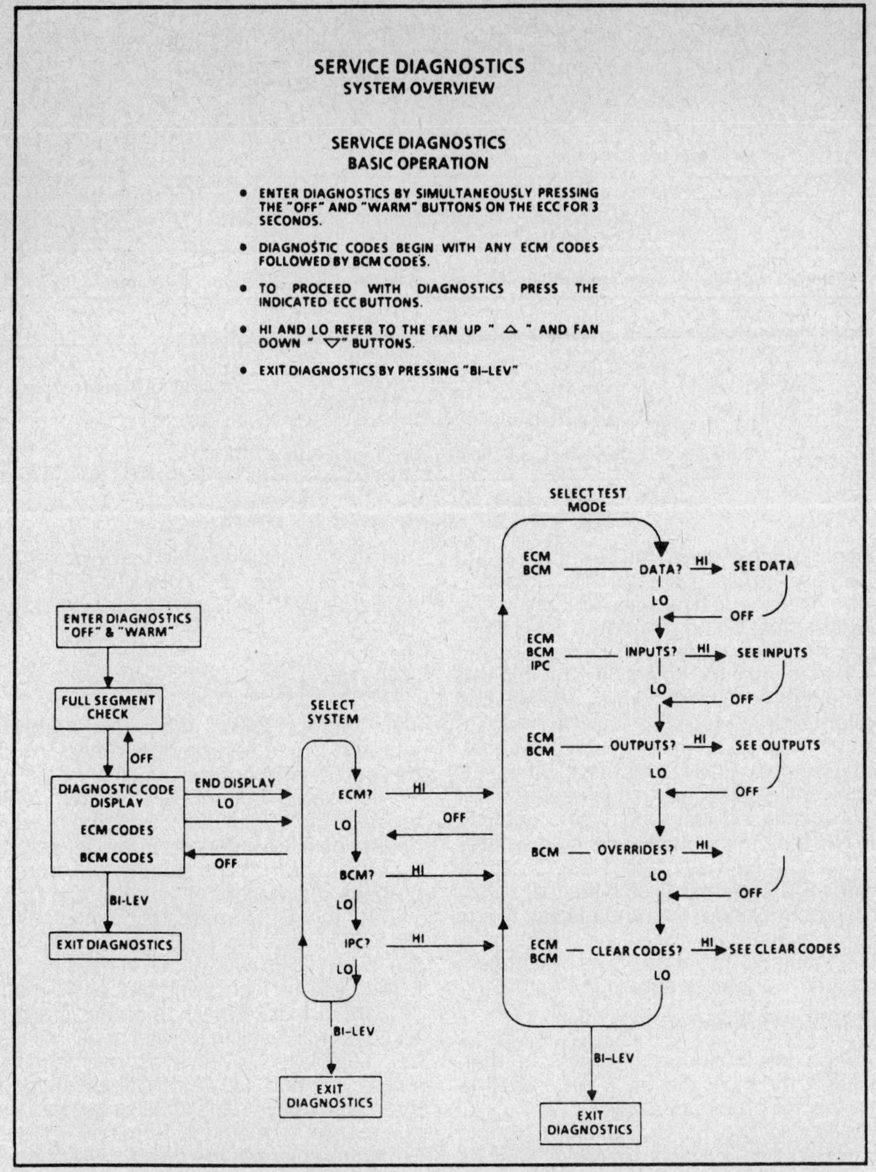

Fig. 11 Self-diagnostic system flow chart. Toronado

Data Number	Description	Message	Display	
			Range	Units
ED01	Throttle Position	TPS	0 - 5100	mv
ED04	Coolant Temperature	COOLANT	-40 - 306/152	°F/°C*
ED05	Air Temperature	MAT	-40 - 306/152	°F/°C*
ED06	Injector Pulse Width	INJ PW	0 - 1002	ms
ED07	Oxygen Sensor Voltage	OXY	0 - 1128	mv
ED08	Spark Avance	SPARK	0 - 70	Degrees
ED09	Transaxle Convertor Clutch	TCC	0 - 1	0 = OFF 1 = ON
ED10	Battery Voltage	VOLTS	0 - 25.5	VOLTS
ED11	Engine RPM	RPM	0 - 6375	RPM
ED12	Vehicle Speed	MPH	0 - 159	MPH
ED15	Closed or Open Loop	MODE	0 - 1	0 = OL 1 = CL
ED16	ESC (Knock Retard)	ESC	0 - 20	Degrees
ED17	OLDPA3 (Knock Signal)	OLDPA3	0 - 255	Counts
ED18	Cross Counts 0^2	X CTS	0 - 255	Counts
ED19	Fuel Integrator	INT	0 - 255	Counts
ED20	Block Learn Memory (Fuel)	BLM	0 - 255	Counts
ED21	Air Flow	AIR FLOW	0 - 255	Grams Per Sec.
ED22	Idle Air Control	IAC	0 - 255	Steps
ED23	LV8 (Engine Load)	LV8	0 - 255	Counts
ED98	Ignition Cycle Counter	IGN C	0 - 50	Key Cycles
ED99	ECM PROM ID	PROM	0 - 9999	CODE **

*°F or °C selectable with the E/M button on the Left Switch Assy.

**PROM ID code number identifies an individual OEM ECM and PROM (last digits).If a service PROM has been installed, the displayed value represents the last digits of the service package # (not stamped on PROM). Refer to the latest Service Publications for the correct ID number.

Fig. 12 ECM data chart

plete, the "0" will be replaced by an "X", indicating that the input being checked has passed the input test. if the inputs will not cycle, or an intermittent input is suspected, refer to "ECM Input Display Diagnosis." Four characters of the display will containa test code to identify the selection. The first two characters are letters which identify the system and test type. The last two characters are numerals which identify the test itself (Example: EI71). Depressing the Hi button will display the next largest test number for the selected test type, while touching the Lo button will display the next smaller test number for the selected test. Depressing the Off button will stop the test selection process and return the display to the next available test type for the selected system (Example: ECM Outputs). Available input displays are shown in **Fig. 13.**

ECM Output Display

If "EEEE" message appears when trying to test device, device must be tested with engine off.

When troubleshooting a system malfunction, the output display can be used to determine if the output tests can be actuated regardless of the inputs and normal program instructions.

With the ECM message displayed on the panel as outlined above, touch the Hi, then the Lo button twice. This will allow bypassing the ECM data and inputs and proceed directly to ECM outputs. Selection of the "Output" test type will result in the first available test being displayed. When a test has been selected, HI and LO will be illuminated for three seconds in each state to indicate the command and output terminal voltage. Four characters of the display will contain a test code to identify the selection. The first two characters are letters which identify the system and test type. The last two characters are numerals which identify the test itself (Example: EO01). Depressing the Hi button will display the next largest test number for the selected test type, while touching the Lo button will display the next smaller test number for the selected test. Depressing the Off button will stop the test selection process and return the display to the next available test type for the selected system (Example: ECM Clear Codes). Available output displays are shown in **Fig. 14.**

ECM Clear Codes

Refer to "Clearing Trouble Codes" for procedure.

RIVIERA MODELS

After all trouble codes are displayed, diagnostics may be exited or any of the following diagnostic features may be displayed: Data, Inputs, Outputs, and Clear Codes.

ECM Data Display

When troubleshooting a system malfunction, the data display can be used to compare the vehicle being serviced to a vehicle which is operating normally.

Following the trouble code displays, ECM will appear on CRT. With the ECM message displayed on the panel, touch the YES button to access ECM data. Selection of the "Data" test type will result in the first available test being displayed. Four characters of the display will contain a test code to identify the selection. The first two characters are letters which identify the system and test type. The last two characters are numerals which identify the test itself (Example: ED01). Depressing the YES button will display the next largest number for the selected test type, while touching the NO button will display the next smaller test number for the selected test. Depressing the EXIT button will stop the test selection process and return the display to the next available system selection (Example: ECM Inputs). The various data parameters and their values are shown in **Fig. 12.**

ECM Input Display

When troubleshooting a system malfunction, the input display can be used to test the switch inputs to the ECM.

Following the ECM and BCM trouble code displays, ECM will appear on CRT as outlined previously. With the ECM message displayed on the panel, touch the YES, then the NO button. This will allow bypassing the ECM data and proceed directly to ECM inputs. Selection of the "Input" test type will result in the first available test being displayed. Input status is displayed as HI or LO and will be shown as "0" until it detects that input has cycled from HI to LO or LO to HI. When the cycle is complete, the "0" will be replaced by an "X", indicating that the input being checked has passed the input test. if the inputs will not cycle, or an intermittent input is suspected, refer to "ECM Input Display Diagnosis." Four characters of the display will contain a test code to identify the selection. The first two characters are letters which identify the system and test type. The last two characters are numerals which identify the test itself (Example: EI71). Depressing the YES button will display the next largest test number for the selected test type, while touching the NO button will display the next smaller test number for the selected test. Depressing the EXIT button will stop the test selection process and return the display to the next available test type for the selected system (Example: ECM Outputs). Available input displays are shown in **Fig. 13.**

Input Number	Description	Message	Status	Ign. "ON" Display
EI60	EVRV EGR Vac. Switch	EVRV	HI/LO	HI
EI74	Park/Neutral Switch	P/N	HI/LO	LO
EI78	Power Steering Press.Switch	PS	HI/LO	HI
EI82	Fourth Gear Switch	4TH	HI/LO	LO

* In park, engine not running.

Fig. 13 ECM inputs chart

Output Number	Description	Message	Status
EO00	No Outputs	None	
EO01	Canister Purge Solenoid	Purge	HI/LO
EO02	TCC Solenoid	TCC	HI/LO
EO04	EGR Solenoid	EGR	HI/LO
EO07	IAC Motor Set	IAC	Pintle Fully Extended*
EO08	A/C Clutch	A/C Clutch	HI/LO
EO09	Coolant Fan Relay	Fan	Hi/LO

*Minimum air adjustment can be made when pintle is fully extended.

Fig. 14 ECM outputs chart

ECM Output Display

If "Select ERR" message appears when trying to test device, device must be tested with engine off.

When troubleshooting a system malfunction, the output display can be used to determine if the output tests can be actuated regardless of the inputs and normal program instructions.

With the ECM message displayed on the CRT, touch the YES, then the NO button twice. This will allow bypassing the ECM data and inputs and proceed directly to ECM outputs. Selection of the "Output" test type will result in the first available test being displayed. When a test has been selected, HI and LO will be illuminated for three seconds in each state to indicate the command and output terminal voltage. Four characters of the display will contain a test code to identify the selection. The first two characters are letters which identify the system and test type. The last two characters are numerals which identify the test itself (Example: EO01). Depressing the YES button will display the next largest test number for the selected test type, while touching the NO button will display the next smaller test number for the selected test. Depressing the EXIT button will stop the test selection process and return the display to the next available test type for the selected system (Example: ECM Clear Codes). Available output displays are shown in **Fig. 14.**

ECM Clear Codes

Refer to "Clearing Trouble Codes" for procedure.

SYSTEM SERVICE

FUEL PRESSURE RELIEF PROCEDURE

1. Connect fuel gauge J-34730 or equiv-

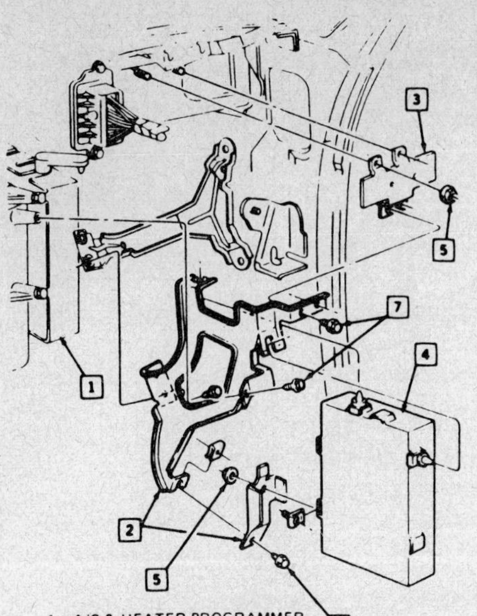

1. A/C & HEATER PROGRAMMER
2. ECM BRACKET
3. MULTIUSE RELAY BRACKET
4. ECM
5. 6 N•m (53 LBS. IN.)
6. 2 N•m (18 LBS. IN.)
7. FULLY DRIVEN, SEATED AND NOT STRIPPED

Fig. 15 ECM mounting

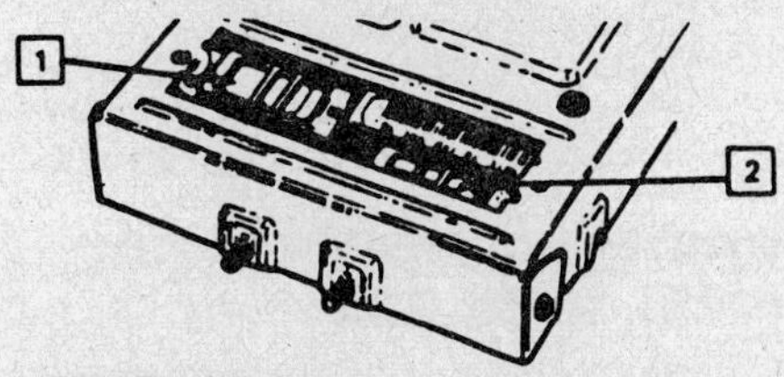

[1] CALIBRATOR (PROM)
[2] CALPAK

Fig. 18 PROM & CALPAK location

alent to fuel pressure valve. **Wrap shop towel around fitting while connecting gauge to prevent fuel spillage.**

2. Install bleed hose into suitable container, then slowly open valve to relieve system fuel pressure.

ECM, REPLACE

If diagnostic procedures indicate ECM replacement, the engine calibrator (PROM) and ECM should be checked first to ensure they are the correct parts. After proper identification, remove the PROM and CALPAK from faulty ECM and install them in new service ECM. The service ECM will not contain a PROM or CALPAK. Trouble code EO51 indicates PROM is installed improperly or has malfunctioned. If code EO51 appears, check PROM installation for bent pins or pins not properly seated in socket. If PROM is installed correctly and code EO51 still appears, replace PROM.

When replacing a production ECM with a service ECM, transfer broadcast code and production ECM number to the service ECM label.

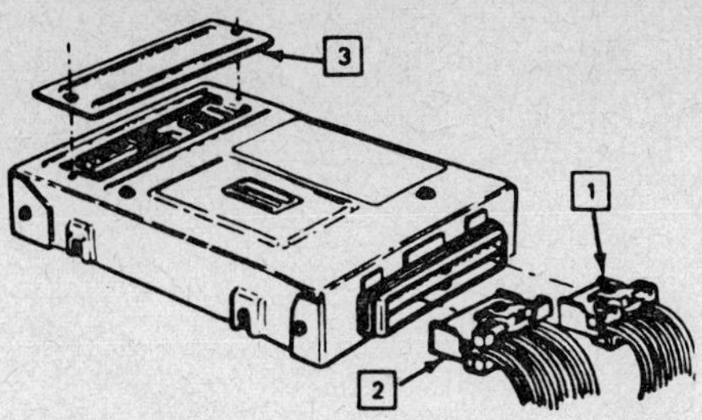

[1] 24 PIN "A"-"B" CONNECTOR
[2] 32 PIN "C"-"D" CONNECTOR
[3] ACCESS COVER

Fig. 16 PROM & CALPAK access cover

To prevent internal ECM damage, ignition switch must be "Off" when disconnecting or reconnecting power to ECM.

1. Disconnect battery ground cable.
2. Remove righthand sound absorber to I.P. and cowl attaching screws.
3. Remove righthand courtesy bulb and socket to panel, then the righthand sound absorber panel.
4. Remove lefthand sound absorber to I.P. and cowl attaching screws.
5. Remove lefthand courtesy bulb and socket to panel, then the lefthand sound absorber panel.
6. Disconnect ECM and A/C programmer electrical connectors.
7. Remove ECM to mounting bracket attaching screws, then the ECM, **Fig. 15.**
8. Reverse procedure to install.

PROM, REPLACE

Use caution not to install PROM backwards. If PROM is installed incorrectly and ignition switch is placed in "On" position, then PROM circuit will be destroyed, requiring PROM replacement.

1. Remove ECM from vehicle, refer to "ECM, Replace" procedure.
2. Remove PROM access cover on ECM, **Fig. 16.**
3. Grasp PROM carrier with suitable PROM removal tool, **Fig. 17.**
4. Rock carrier side-to-side while applying a firm upward force, then remove PROM and carrier. Remove PROM from carrier. **Inspect replacement PROM to ensure the part number is the same the removed PROM.**
5. Install replacement PROM in carrier.
6. Position PROM and carrier assembly over PROM socket, aligning small notch of carrier with small notch in socket. Press on PROM carrier until PROM is fully seated in socket, **Fig. 18.**
7. Replace PROM access cover, then install ECM on vehicle.
8. Start engine, enter diagnostic mode and check for code EO51. If code EO51 does not display, PROM is installed correctly. If code EO51 is displayed, PROM is installed incorrectly and installation procedure must be repeated.

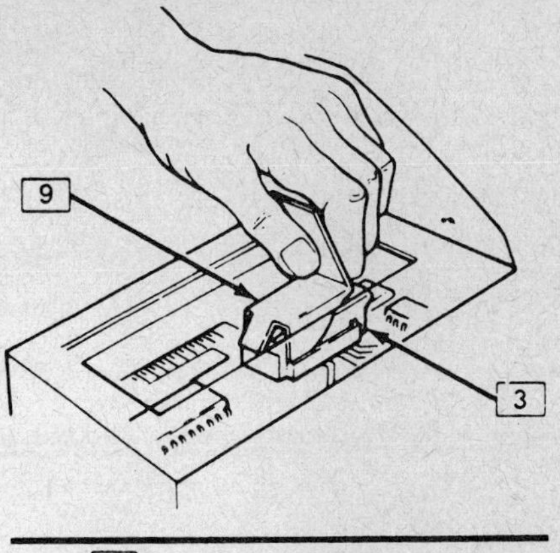

[3] PROM CARRIER
[9] PROM REMOVAL TOOL

Fig. 17 PROM removal

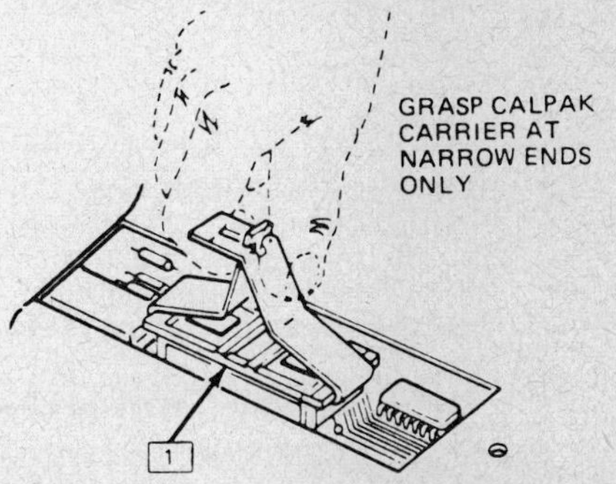

[1] CALPAK [2] REMOVAL TOOL

Fig. 19 CALPAK removal

CALPAK, REPLACE

Replacement of CALPAK is the same procedure used to replace PROM. When removing CALPAK refer "PROM, Replace" procedure and to **Figs. 18 and 19.**

COOLANT SENSOR, REPLACE

1. Disconnect battery ground cable.
2. Partially drain engine coolant from radiator.
3. Disconnect coolant sensor electrical connector, then remove sensor.
4. Reverse procedure to install.

MAT SENSOR, REPLACE

The MAT sensor is located in the air cleaner plenum near left side inner strut tower.

1. Disconnect battery ground cable.
2. Disconnect MAT sensor electrical connector, then remove sensor from air cleaner plenum.
3. Reverse procedure to install.

MAF SENSOR, REPLACE

1. Disconnect battery ground cable.
2. Disconnect MAF sensor electrical connector, then remove sensor from intake runner system, **Fig. 20.**
3. Reverse procedure to install.

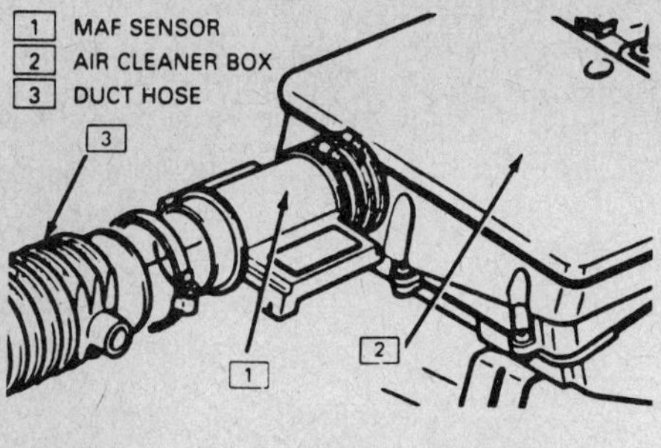

Fig. 20 MAF sensor removal

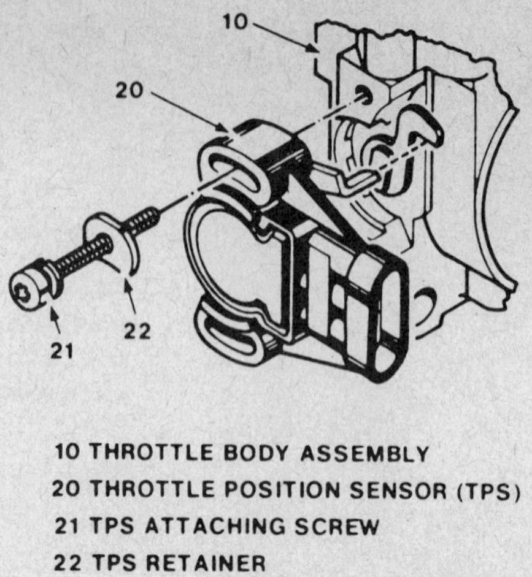

Fig. 21 Throttle position sensor

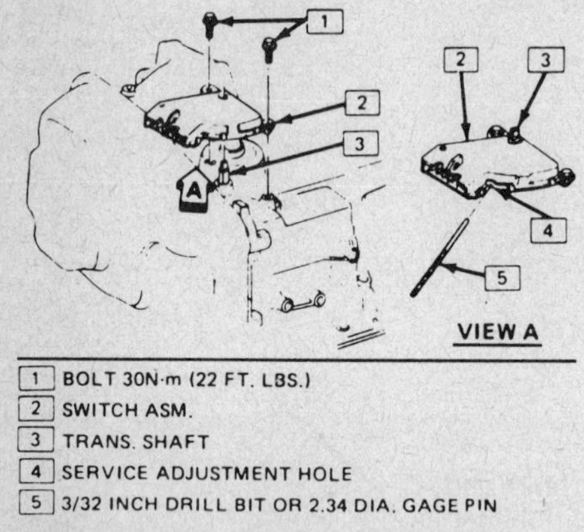

Fig. 22 Adjusting gear selector switch

OXYGEN SENSOR, REPLACE

The following procedure should be performed with engine temperature over 120° F, otherwise the oxygen sensor may be difficult to remove.

1. Disconnect battery ground cable.
2. Disconnect oxygen sensor electrical connector, then remove sensor.
3. Reverse procedure to install. Torque sensor to 30 ft. lbs. **Replacement sensors should have a suitable anti-seize compound applied to threads. If replacement sensor is lacking anti-seize compound or original sensor is to be reinstalled, coat threads with suitable anti-seize compound.**

THROTTLE POSITION SENSOR (TPS), REPLACE

1. Disconnect battery ground cable.
2. Disconnect vacuum port and steel vacuum lines, then TPS electrical connector.
3. Remove two TPS attaching screws, lock washers and retainers, then the sensor.
4. With throttle valve in normal closed idle position, install TPS on throttle body assembly. Ensure TPS pickup lever is located above tang on throttle actuator lever, **Fig. 21.**
5. Apply suitable locking compound to TPS attaching screws, then install retainers, lock washers and TPS attaching screws. **Do not tighten attaching screws until TPS has been adjusted.**
6. Adjust TPS as follows:
   a. Install three jumper wires between TPS and harness connector.
   b. Place ignition switch in "On" position, then connect a suitable digital voltmeter between terminals "B" and "C" and adjust TPS to obtain .35-.45 volts.
   c. Tighten TPS attaching screws.

GEAR SELECTOR SWITCH, REPLACE

1. Disconnect battery ground cable.
2. Disconnect shift linkage, then the switch electrical connector.
3. Remove switch attaching bolts, then the switch.
4. Place selector lever in "Neutral" position, then align flats of shifter lever to flats in switch.
5. Loosely install switch attaching bolts, then insert 3/32 inch maximum diameter gauge pin in service adjustment hole. Rotate switch until pin drops in to a depth of 15/32 inch, **Fig. 22. New switch is pre-pinned in "Neutral" position. No adjustment is necessary unless adjustment pin has been broken.**
6. Tighten switch attaching bolts, then remove gauge pin.
7. After switch installation, ensure engine can only be started in "Neutral" or "Park" position. If engine can be started in any other position, repeat step 5.

POWER STEERING PRESSURE SWITCH, REPLACE

1. Disconnect battery ground cable.
2. Raise and support vehicle.
3. Disconnect power steering pressure switch electrical connector, then remove switch.
4. Reverse procedure to install.

VEHICLE SPEED SENSOR (VSS), REPLACE

1. Disconnect battery ground cable.
2. Raise and support vehicle.
3. Disconnect VSS electrical connector, then remove sensor.
4. Reverse procedure to install.

DETONATION SENSOR, REPLACE

1. Disconnect battery ground cable.
2. Disconnect vacuum port and steel vacuum lines.
3. Disconnect detonation sensor electrical connector, then remove sensor.
4. Reverse procedure to install.

CAMSHAFT SENSOR, REPLACE

1. Disconnect battery ground cable.
2. Disconnect camshaft sensor electrical connector.
3. Remove sensor attaching bolts, then the sensor.
4. Reverse procedure to install.

CRANKSHAFT SENSOR, REPLACE

1. Disconnect battery ground cable.
2. Disconnect crankshaft sensor electrical connector.
3. Rotate harmonic balancer using suitable tool until any window in interrupter is aligned with crank sensor.
4. Loosen pinch bolt on sensor pedestal until sensor is free to slide in the pedestal, then remove pedestal to engine attaching bolts.

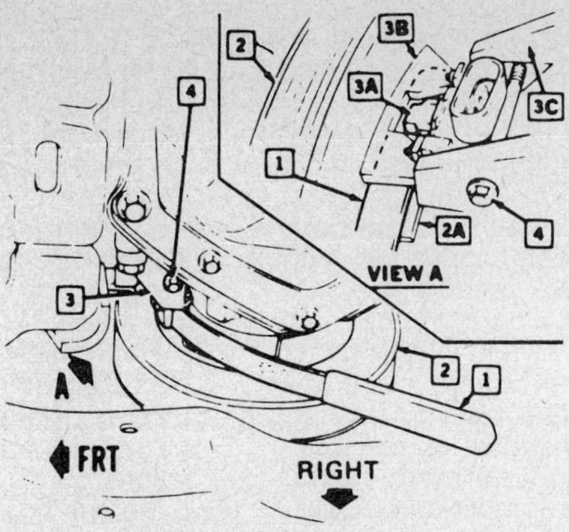

1. TOOL J 36179
2. CRANKSHAFT HARMONIC BALANCER ASSY.
   A. INTERRUPTER RING
3. CRANKSHAFT POSITION SENSOR ASSY.
   A. SENSOR
   B. DEFLECTOR
   C. PEDESTAL
4. PINCH BOLT

Fig. 23 Adjusting crankshaft sensor

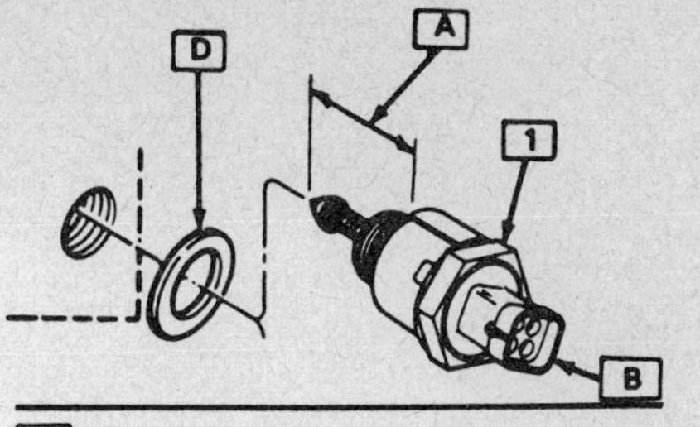

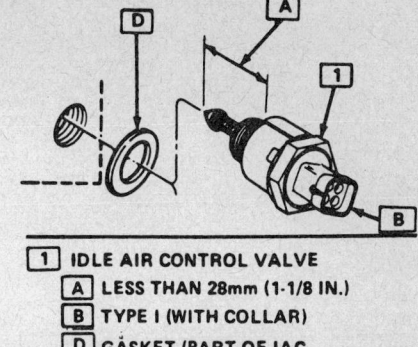

1 IDLE AIR CONTROL VALVE
A LESS THAN 28mm (1-1/8 IN.)
B TYPE I (WITH COLLAR)
D GASKET (PART OF IAC VALVE SERVICE KIT)

Fig. 24 Installing IAC valve

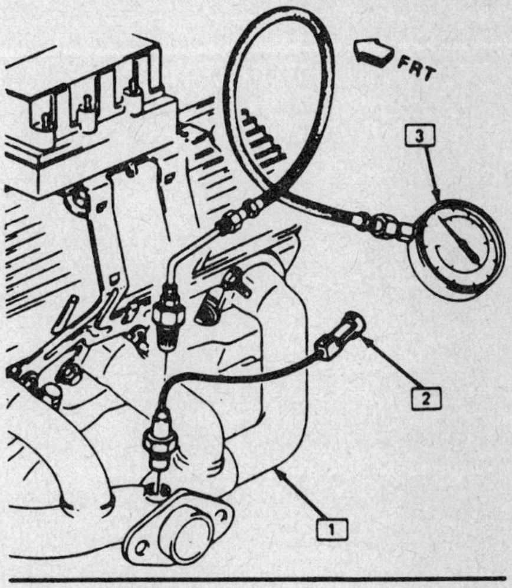

1 EXHAUST MANIFOLD
2 O_2 SENSOR
3 BACK PRESSURE TESTER

Fig. 25 Connecting exhaust back pressure tester

5. Carefully remove sensor and pedestal as a unit.
6. Loosen pinch bolt on new sensor pedestal until sensor is free to slide in pedestal.
7. Ensure window in interrupter is properly positioned, then install sensor and pedestal as a unit. Ensure interrupter ring is aligned within proper slot.
8. Install pedestal to engine attaching bolts. Torque attaching bolts to 22 ft. lbs.
9. Adjust crankshaft sensor as follows:
   a. Rotate harmonic balancer using suitable tool until interrupter ring(s) fills sensor slot(s) and edge of interrupter window is aligned with edge of deflector on pedestal.
   b. Install adjustment tool J36179 or equivalent, **Fig. 23,** into gap between sensor and interrupter on each side of interrupter ring. This clearance should be checked at three positions approximately 120° apart. If gauge will slide past sensor on either side of interrupter ring, adjustment is satisfactory. If gauge will not slide past sensor on either side of interrupter ring, sensor is out of adjustment, proceed to step c. **If found out of adjustment, check interrupter ring and sensor for damage.**
   c. Loosen pinch bolt on sensor pedestal and insert adjustment tool J36179 or equivalent into gap between sensor and interrupter on each side of interrupter ring.
   d. Slide sensor into contact against gauge and interrupter ring.
   e. Torque sensor pinch bolt to 30 inch lbs. while maintaining light pressure on sensor against gauge and interrupter ring. Recheck clearance at three positions around interrupter ring, approximately 120° apart. If interrupter ring contacts sensor at any point during harmonic balancer rotation, the interrupter ring has excessive runout and should be replaced.

FOURTH GEAR SWITCH, REPLACE

1. Disconnect battery ground cable.
2. Remove case side cover pan, then the switch at transaxle valve body.
3. Reverse procedure to install.

FUEL PUMP RELAY, REPLACE

The fuel pump relay is located in the relay center under hood.

FUEL INJECTOR, REPLACE

The fuel injector is an electrical component and should not be immersed in any type of cleaner. The fuel injector is not serviceable and should be replaced as a complete assembly.

1. Disconnect battery ground cable.
2. Remove fuel injector electrical connectors.
3. Remove fuel rail, refer to "Fuel Rail, Replace" procedure.
4. Remove fuel injectors. **Use caution when removing injectors to prevent damage to electrical connector pins on injector and at nozzle.**
5. Reverse procedure to install. If injector is to be reused, original O-ring should be replaced.

FUEL RAIL, REPLACE

1. Relieve fuel pressure, refer to "Fuel Pressure Relief Procedure."
2. Disconnect battery ground cable.
3. Disconnect all electrical connectors to fuel rail.
4. Remove fuel rail assembly attaching screws, then the fuel rail and injectors as an assembly. Cap all fittings and plug holes to prevent dirt from entering fuel passages.
5. Reverse procedure to install. Replace all O-ring seals during installation.

FUEL PRESSURE REGULATOR, REPLACE

1. Relieve fuel pressure, refer to "Fuel Pressure Relief Procedure."
2. Remove pressure regulator from fuel rail. Place shop cloth around base of

regulator to catch any spilled fuel.
3. Reverse procedure to install.

IDLE AIR CONTROL (IAC) VALVE, REPLACE

1. Disconnect battery ground cable.
2. Disconnect IAC valve electrical connector.
3. Remove IAC valve attaching bolts, then the IAC valve.
4. Before installing new idle air control valve, proceed as follows:
   a. Measure distance that valve is extended. This measurement should be made from motor housing to end of cone (A), **Fig. 24.**
   b. Dimension (A) should be no greater than 1 1/8 inch or damage may occur to valve when installed. If dimension (A) is less than 1 1/8 inch, proceed to step 5. If dimension (A) is greater than 1 1/8 inch, proceed to step c.
   c. Compress retaining spring from valve while turning valve in a clockwise motion. Return spring to original position with straight portion of spring end aligned with flat surface of valve, then proceed to step 5.
5. Install air control valve to throttle body using new gasket. Torque valve attaching bolts to 13 ft. lbs.
6. Connect valve electrical connectors, then start engine and allow to reach normal operating temperature. ECM will automatically adjust IAC valve to correct position.

RESTRICTED EXHAUST SYSTEM CHECK

1. Remove oxygen sensor, refer to "Oxygen Sensor, Replace" procedure, then install back pressure tester BT8515 or equivalent in place of sensor, **Fig. 25.**
2. Start engine and allow to reach normal operating temperature, then run engine at 2500 RPM and note exhaust system back pressure reading on gauge.
3. If back pressure exceeds 1 1/4 psi, a restricted exhaust system is indicated. Inspect exhaust system for damaged pipe, heat distress or internal muffler failure.
4. If there is no obvious reasons for excessive back pressure, catalytic converter should be replaced.

EMISSION CONTROL SYSTEMS

INDEX

INDEX—Continued

AIR INJECTION REACTOR (AIR)

Description

In this system, fresh air is pumped into the exhaust system, usually in the area of the exhaust valves, to ignite and burn the unburned portion of exhaust gases in the exhaust system, thus minimizing exhaust contaminants.

Air systems, **Fig. 1,** consist of an air pump, **Figs. 2 and 3,** injection tubes (one for each cylinder), diverter valve, check valves (one for Inline engines, two for V8s), air manifolds and the tubes and hoses necessary to connect the various components.

Carburetors, distributors and control valves are designed for specific engine applications and should not be interchanged with other units.

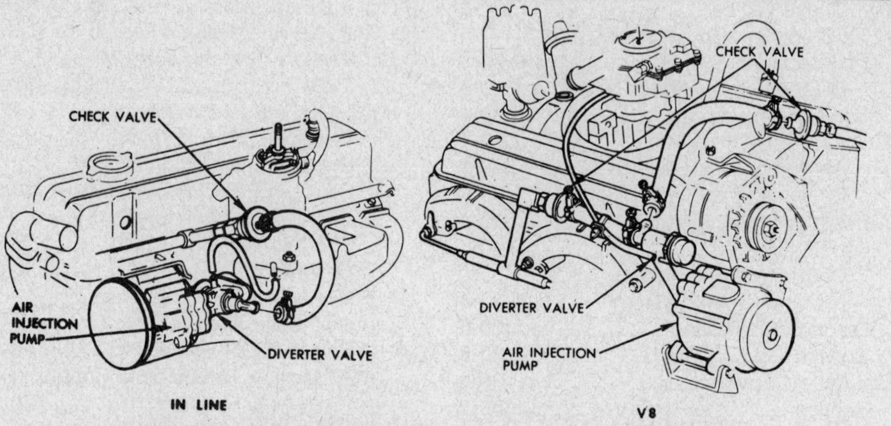

Fig. 1 Typical AIR system installation

DIVERTER VALVE

The diverter or air bypass valve, **Figs. 4 and 5,** when triggered by a sharp increase in manifold vacuum, shuts off the injected air to the exhaust and prevents backfiring during this richer period. On engine overrun the total air supply is dumped through the diverter valve muffler. At high engine speeds the excess air is dumped through the pressure relief valve located either in the pump assembly, **Fig. 3,** or the diverter valve, **Fig. 5.**

The check valves prevent hot gases from backing up into the hoses or pump, yet allow fresh air to circulate from the pump to the exhaust ports.

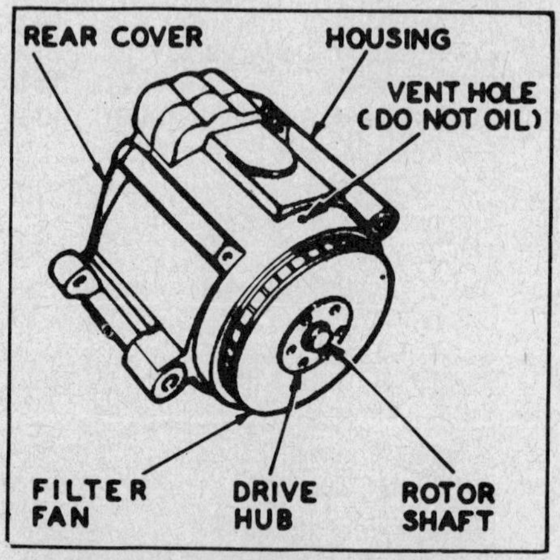

Fig. 2 Air pump without integral pressure relief valve

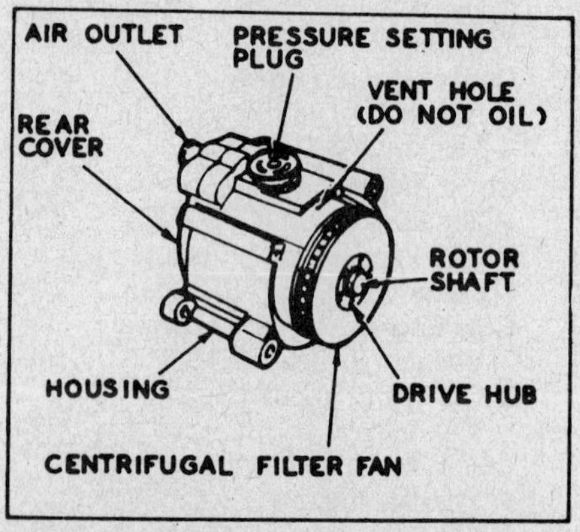

Fig. 3 Air pump w/integral pressure relief valve

DIFFERENTIAL VACUUM DELAY & SEPARATOR VALVE

Used on some engines, the differential vacuum delay and separator valve delays the vacuum signal to the air bypass or air control valve, thereby preventing air from diverting under normal operating conditions except during extended heavy engine loads. Under extended heavy load conditions, the differential vacuum delay and separator valve permits vacuum to flow to the air bypass or air control valve, which then diverts air to atmosphere to prevent exhaust system overheating.

PRESSURE OPERATED ELECTRIC DIVERT/ELECTRIC SWITCHING VALVE (PEDES)

Used on some engines, the divert and switching functions are electronically controlled by the ECM. Pressure from AIR pump is used to operate the valve. Operation is completely independent of manifold vacuum.

As air enters body of valve from pump, air pressure builds up against control valve. During the code mode, port solenoid is energized which in turn opens the port valve and allows flow to the exhaust ports. During the warm mode, port solenoid is deenergized and the converter solenoid energized which closes the port valve and keeps converter valve seated. This forces flow past converter valve and to the converter. During the convert mode, both solenoids are deenergized which opens the converter valve, allowing air to take the path of least resistance. The relieve valve operates to limit overall system pressure.

Diagnosis & Testing

AIR INJECTION PUMP

1. Accelerate engine to approximately

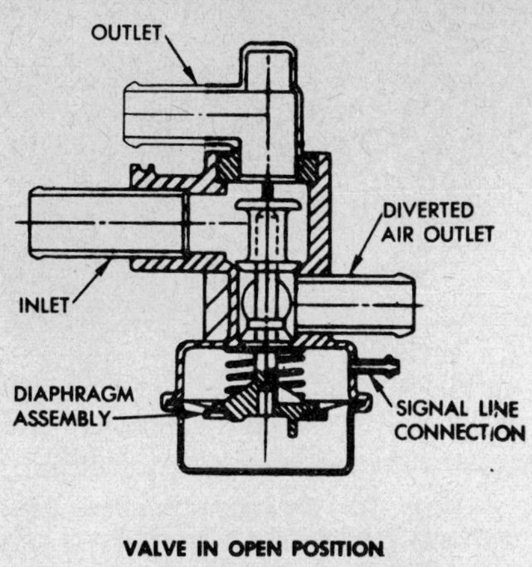

Fig. 4 Typical diverter air bypass valve without pressure relief valve

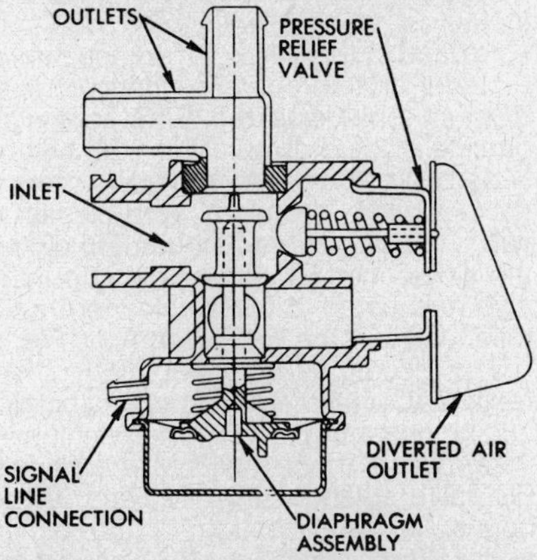

Fig. 5 Typical diverter air bypass valve w/pressure relief valve

1500 RPM and observe air flow from hose. If air flow increases as engine is accelerated, the pump is operating satisfactorily. If not proceed as follows:

2. Check for proper drive belt tension.
3. Check for leaky pressure relief valve. Air may be heard leaking with the pump running. The air pump is not completely noiseless. Under normal operating conditions, the noise from the pump rises in pitch as engine speed is increased. To determine if excessive noise is the fault of the system, operate the engine with the pump drive belt removed.
4. If excessive noise does not exist with pump drive belt removed, proceed as follows:
5. Check for proper installation of the relief valve silencer, if equipped.
6. Check for a seized air injection pump.
7. Check hoses, tubes and all connections for leaks and proper mounting.
8. Check air injection pump for proper mounting.
9. On vehicles equipped with C3 or C4 systems, perform air management systems check as outlined under "Air Management Systems."
10. Replace air injection pump, if defective.

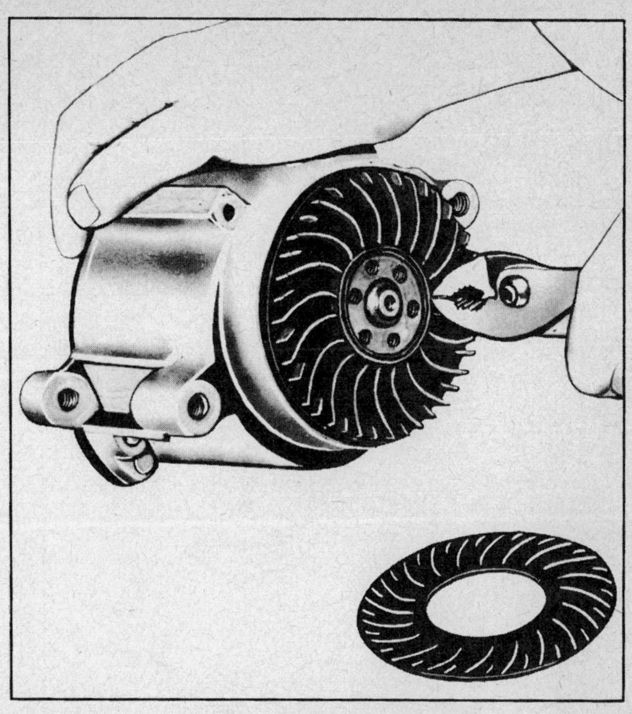

Fig. 6 Removing air pump centrifugal filter

CHECK VALVES

1. Remove check valve(s) from vehicle.
2. Blow through check valve in direction of air manifold or cylinder head, then attempt to suck back in reverse direction. Air flow should only be towards air manifold or cylinder head. If not, replace check valve.

DIFFERENTIAL VACUUM DELAY & SEPARATOR VALVE

1. Start engine and allow to reach normal operating temperature.
2. Disconnect vacuum line from valve.
3. After a delay of 15 to 35 seconds, air should exhaust from diverter valve muffler. If not, check hoses for proper routing and connections.
4. Reconnect vacuum line to valve. The diverter valve should immediately stop diverting air. If not, check other components for proper operation, then replace valve.

DIVERTER OR AIR BYPASS VALVE

1. Check condition and routing of all lines. All lines must be secure without crimps or leaks.
2. Disconnect vacuum signal line at diverter valve, making sure vacuum is present at line opening.
3. With engine warmed to operating temperature and carburetor at curb idle, no air should be escaping through the diverter valve muffler. Manually open and close the throttle; a momentary blast of air should discharge through the diverter valve muffler for at least one second. If not, replace diverter valve.

Service

AIR PUMP DRIVE BELT

Check drive belt for cracks, fraying, wear and proper tension. Adjust or replace belts as necessary. Using a suitable belt tension gauge, adjust belt according to the following specifications: 5/16 inch—80 lbs. Max. (New), 50 lbs. Min. (Used); 3/8 inch—140 lbs. Max. (New), 70 lbs. Min. (Used); 15/32 inch—165 lbs. Max. (New), 90 lbs. Min. (Used).

AIR PUMP FILTER, REPLACE

1. Remove air pump drive belt and pulley.
2. Carefully pry outer disc from filter fan, then remove remaining portion of filter with pliers, **Fig. 6.**
3. Position new filter onto pump, install pulley and pulley retaining bolts and draw filter down evenly by alternately torquing retaining bolts.
4. Install and adjust air pump drive belt. The new filter may squeal upon initial operation until sealing lip outer edge has worn in.

PRESSURE RELIEF VALVE, REPLACE

The relief valve may be serviced separately only if incorporated into the air pump. If the relief valve is incorporated into the diverter valve, the diverter valve must be replaced.

1. Using suitable puller, remove relief valve from pump assembly, **Fig. 7.**
2. Lightly tap new relief valve into pump housing until valve shoulders on housing. Various length pressure setting plugs designed for the particular

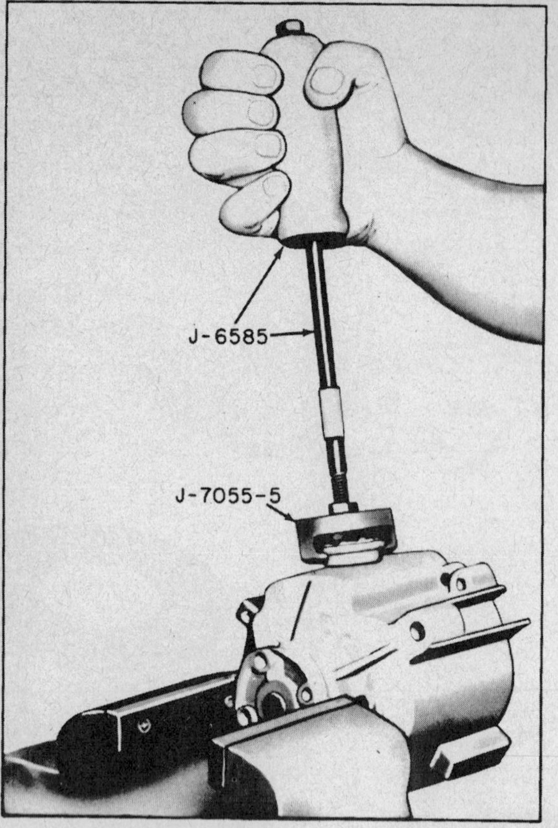

Fig. 7 Removing air pump pressure relief valve

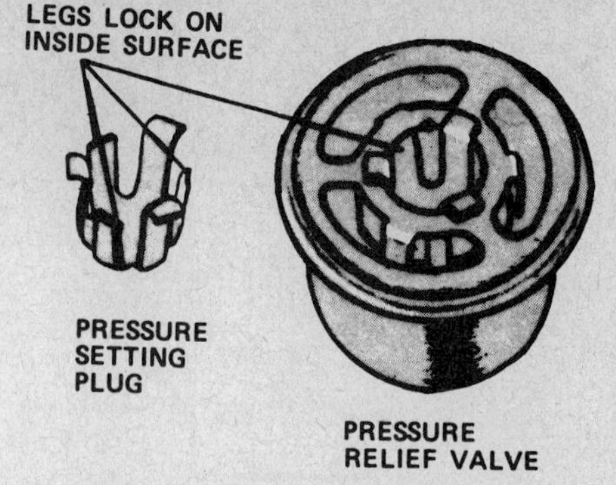

Fig. 8 Pressure relief valve pressure setting plug

requirements of the vehicle being serviced determine the pressure required to open the relief valve. Usually, the pressure setting plugs are color coded. To remove the pressure setting plug, **Fig. 8,** carefully unlock the legs from the inside surface of the relief valve with a small screwdriver. To install the plug, carefully push it into the relief valve until the legs lock into place.

AIR MANAGEMENT SYSTEM

Description

COMPUTER CONTROLLED AIR MANAGEMENT SYSTEM

MANAGED AIR INJECTION REACTOR (MAIR)

This system, **Fig. 9,** consists of a belt driven pump, internal passages in the cylinder heads or manifolds, piping and hoses, air management valves and check valves. The dual bed catalytic converter, if equipped, is also considered part of this system. The air pump operates whenever engine is running, drawing air in through an integral filter, and delivering the air to air management valves for distribution. Excess air is discharged through a pressure relief valve, located either on the pump or in the air management valve assembly.

When engine is cold, air is routed to the exhaust port area of the cylinder head or manifold, **Fig. 9.** Unburned exhaust gases combine with oxygen in the air, reducing HC and CO levels and speeding warm-up of the catalyst and oxygen sensor. During normal operation, air is either routed to the dual bed catalyst to provide additional oxygen for the oxidizing catalyst, or diverted to the air cleaner or atmosphere. During deceleration or wide open throttle on most models, air is diverted from the system to the air cleaner or directly to atmosphere. Check valves prevent exhaust gases from flowing back through the air distribution system.

Electric Air Control & Electric Air Switching (EAC/ES)

Models with this system have 2 valves which provide air control and air switching. The system can be identified by the separate mounting of the 2 valves or by the vacuum divert hose position on the integral type EAC/ES valve, **Fig. 10.** The first valve (EAC) directs air pump output into the system, or diverts it to the air cleaner. The second valve (ES) directs EAC valve output to either the exhaust ports or catalytic converter. Vacuum signals, controlled by an Electronic Control Module (ECM), operate both valves.

During normal operation, the EAC valve solenoid is energized by the ECM, **Fig. 11.** Air pump output is directed to the air switching valve unless there is a sudden rise in intake manifold vacuum, such as during deceleration. A sudden vacuum rise closes the valve, diverting air pump output to the air cleaner until the vacuum has equalized in the decel timing assembly.

Under certain operating conditions, the ECM de-energizes the EAC solenoid to provide electric divert. When the solenoid is de-energized pressurized air enters the decel timing chamber and closes the valve, causing air pump output to divert to the air cleaner. Excess air pump output is also exhausted to the air cleaner through relief valve in the EAC assembly, **Fig. 11.**

The Electric Air Switching (ES) valve directs EAC valve output depending upon engine operating mode. When engine is in "Open Loop" mode the ECM energized the ES valve solenoid, **Fig. 12,** and vacuum opens the air passage to the exhaust ports. When engine is in "Closed Loop" mode the solenoid is de-energized, the vacuum signal is blocked, and spring tension opens the air passage to the catalytic converter.

Electric Divert/Electric Air Switching (ED/ES)

Electric divert air control and electric air switching are combined into one valve assembly, which can be identified by the vacuum signal hose position, **Fig. 13.** The valve is operated by vacuum signals which are solenoid-controlled through an Electronic Control Module (ECM).

During normal operation the ECM energizes the air control (lower) solenoid, **Fig. 14.** Manifold vacuum holds the valve open and air is directed to the air switching valve. If engine is operating in "Open Loop" mode, the ECM energizes the air switching (upper) solenoid, **Fig. 15,** and manifold vacuum opens the air passage to the exhaust ports. If engine is operating in "Closed Loop" mode, the air switching solenoid is de-energized, and spring tension opens the air passage to the catalytic converter.

When the ECM determines that air should be diverted from the system, the solenoids are de-energized, spring tension closes the valves, and air pump output is diverted to the air cleaner, **Fig. 15.** Under low manifold vacuum conditions, as in wide open throttle operation, vacuum in the air control chamber drops, spring tension closes the air control valve, and air is

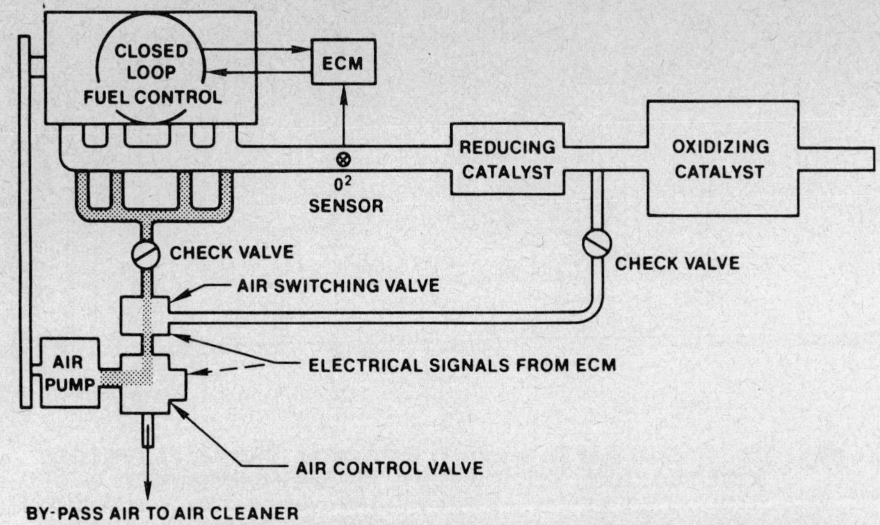

Fig. 9 Computer controlled Managed Air Injection Reactor (MAIR) system. Typical of models w/dual bed catalytic converter

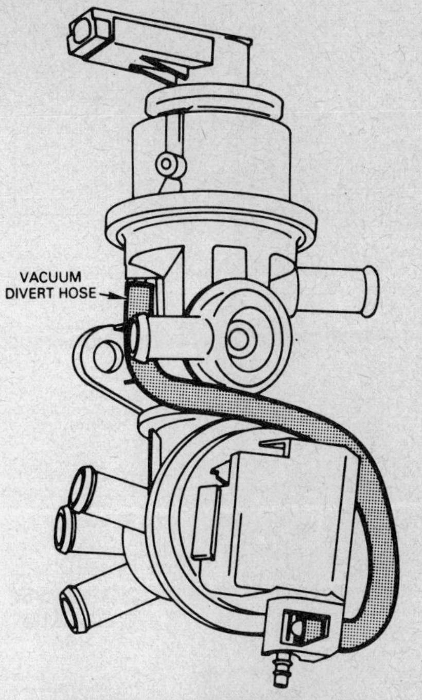

Fig. 10 Electric Air Control/Electric Air Switching (EAC/ES) valve. Integral type

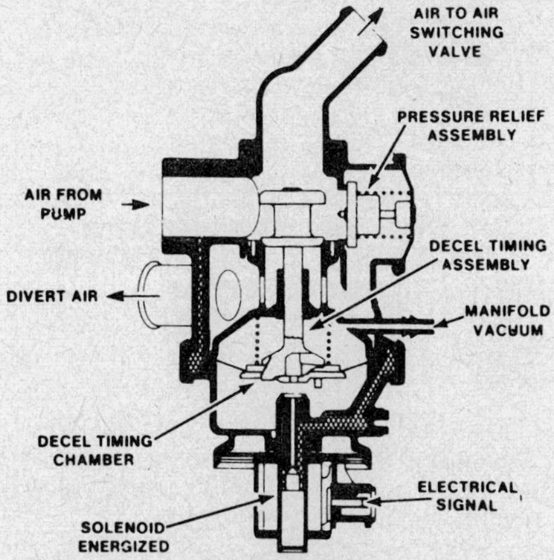

Fig. 11 Electric air control valve operation

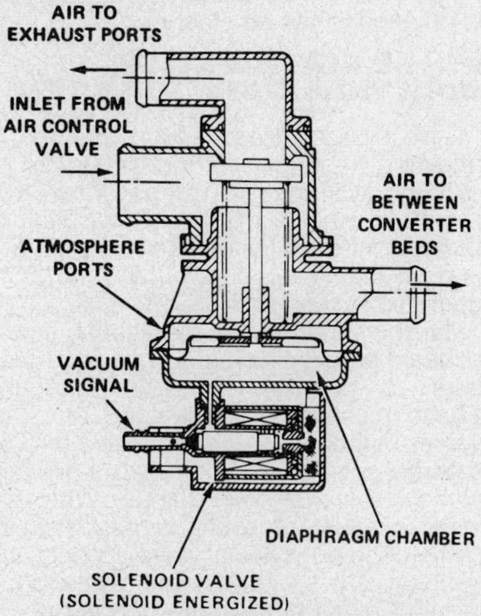

Fig. 12 Electric air switching valve operation

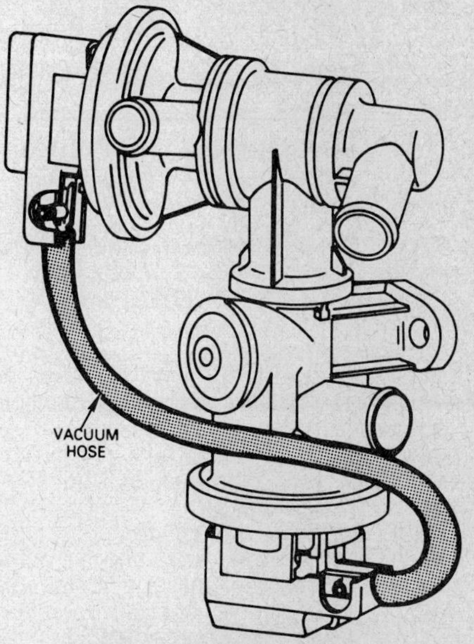

Fig. 13 Electric Divert/Electric Air Switching (ED/ES) valve

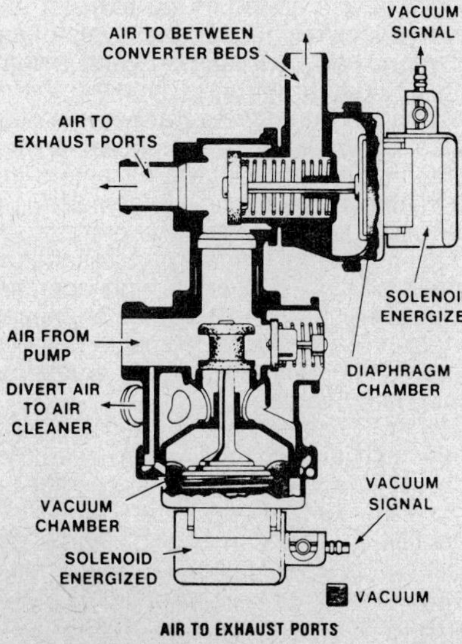

Fig. 14 ED/ES valve normal operation. "Open Loop" mode

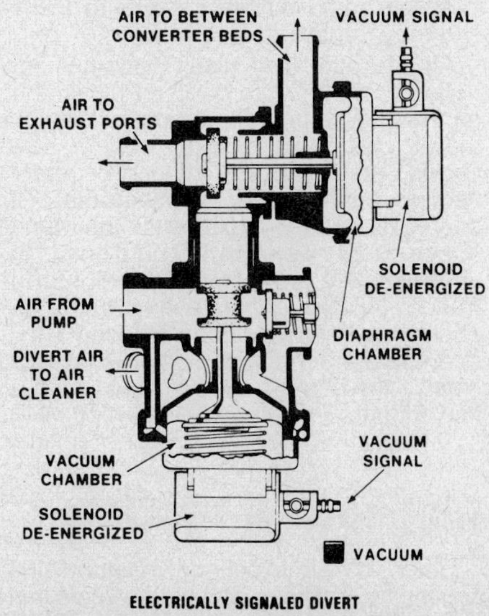

Fig. 15 ED/ES valve electric divert operation

diverted to the air cleaner, **Fig. 16.** Excess air pump output is also exhausted through a pressure relief valve.

On some L-4 and V6 engines a deceleration valve is used with this system. This valve eliminates the need for deceleration divert by providing additional air to the intake manifold, leaning the normally rich mixtures created by high vacuum operation.

Pressure Operated Electric Divert/Electric Switching (PEDES)

This valve, **Fig. 17,** is ECM operated

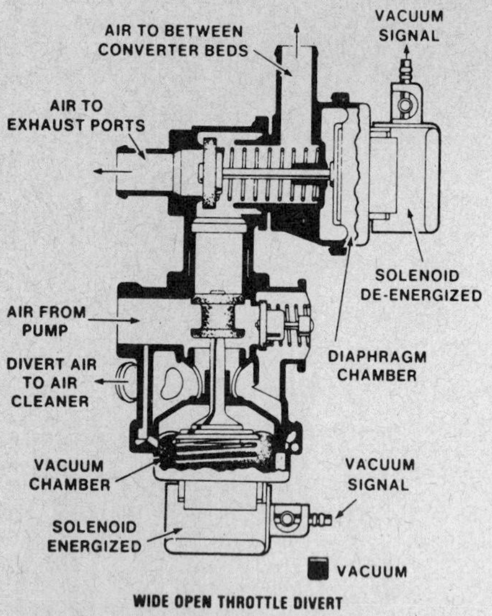

Fig. 16 ED/ES valve low vacuum divert operation

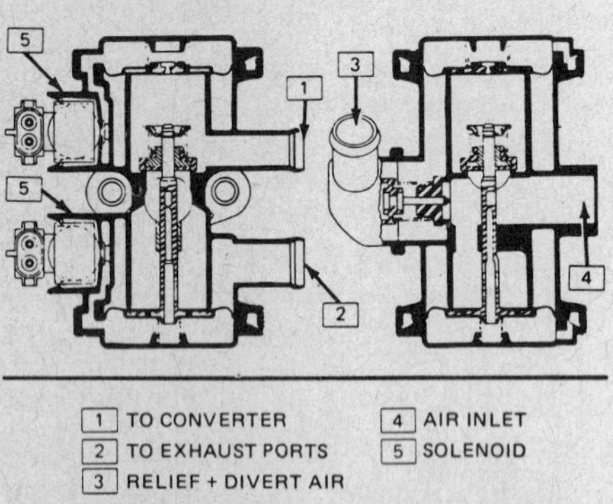

Fig. 17 Pressure Operated Electric Divert/Electric Switching (PEDES) valve

similarly to the ED/ES type, but uses air pump pressure rather than intake manifold vacuum to operate control valves. Air pump pressure builds up against a control valve which is operated by the ECM through 2 solenoids.

When engine is cold ("Open Loop"), the port solenoid is energized and air pump pressure opens the passage to the exhaust ports. During normal operation, ("Closed Loop"), the port solenoid is de-energized, the converter solenoid is energized, and air pump pressure opens the passage to the catalytic converter. When the ECM determines that air divert is necessary, both solenoids are de-energized and air pump output is diverted to the air cleaner through a divert/relief valve. The divert/relief valve limits system pressure.

Electric Divert (EDV)

This system is used on models that do not require air injection into the catalytic converter, and is controlled by an Electronic Control Module (ECM). When engine is operating in "Open Loop" mode, the valve is energized and air pump output is directed to the exhaust ports. However, a sudden rise in manifold vacuum will close the valve, momentarily diverting air to the air cleaner. When engine is operating in "Closed Loop" mode, the valve is not energized and the vacuum signal is blocked. Air pump pressure closes the valve and air is diverted to the air cleaner.

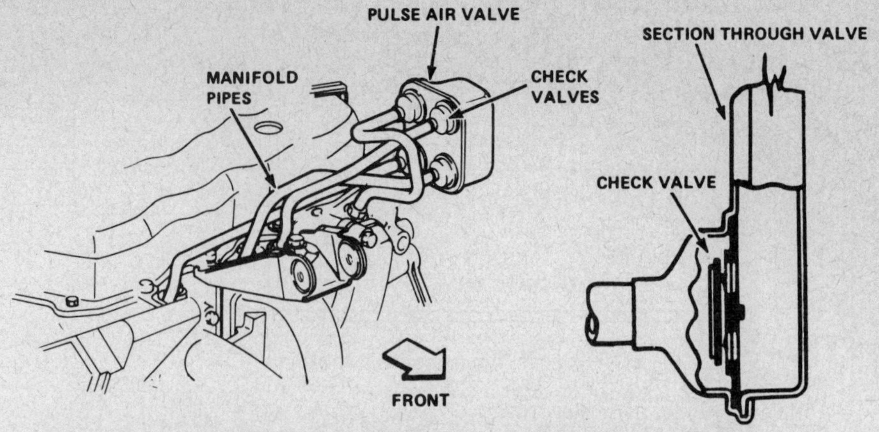

Fig. 18 Pulse Air Injection Reactor (PulsAir) system installation. Typical of 4 cylinder engines.

PULSE AIR INJECTION REACTION (PAIR, PULSAIR)

This system uses vacuum created by engine exhaust pulses to draw air into the exhaust system. Fresh air is drawn from the clean side of the engine air filter. Air flow is controlled by a Pulsair control valve and an Electronic Control Module (ECM) operated Pulsair air shut-off valve.

Engine firing creates a pulsating flow of exhaust gases which are of positive pressure or negative pressure (vacuum). These pulses are transmitted to check valves in the Pulsair control valve through external pipes, **Fig. 18.** There is a pipe and a check valve for each cylinder. When cylinder exhaust pressure is negative, the corresponding check valve opens and fresh air mixes with exhaust gases. When cylinder exhaust pressure is positive, the check valve is forced closed, preventing exhaust gases from flowing back through system. At high RPM the check valves fail to follow rapid pulsations due to inertia, and they remain closed.

Air intake for the Pulsair system is controlled by the ECM through a Pulsair shut-off valve. This valve is mounted between the air cleaner and Pulsair control valve, and is operated by an integral or remote vacuum control solenoid. When the ECM energizes the solenoid, such as during "Open Loop" operation, vacuum opens the shut-off valve and air is allowed into the Pulsair system. When the valve is de-energized, such as during "Closed Loop" operation, the vacuum signal is blocked, closing the shutoff valve and blocking air flow into the Pulsair system.

Diagnosis & Testing

Refer to "Air Injection Reactor (AIR)" section for air pump and check valve testing or "Pulse Air Injection Reactor (PAIR, PulsAir)" section for testing of PulsAir reed valve assemblies.

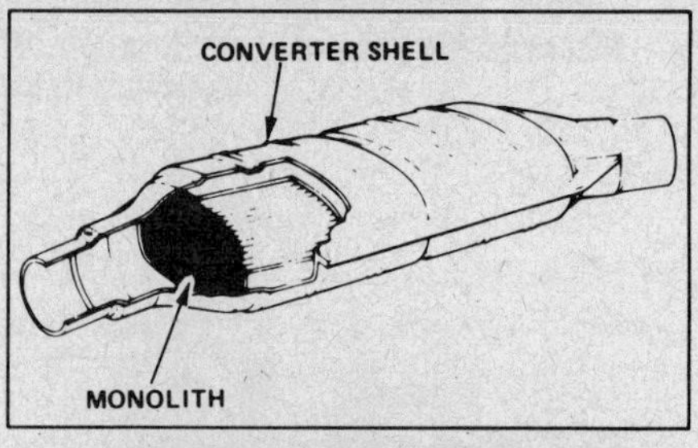

Fig. 19 Single bed monolith type catalytic converter

Service

The air management system control valves and switches are not serviceable. If testing shows a defective control valve or switch, replace as necessary.

CATALYTIC CONVERTERS

The catalytic converter is an emission control device added to the exhaust system to effectively reduce the levels of carbon monoxide, hydrocarbons, and in some cases oxides of nitrogen, entering the atmosphere. The converter serves two purposes: it permits a faster chemical reaction to take place and although it enters into the chemical reaction, it remains unchanged, ready to repeat the process.

This device sometimes requires the use of heat shields, due to its high operating temperatures. The heat shields are necessary to protect chassis components, passenger compartment and other areas from heat related damage.

General Motors uses four different converter designs in conjunction with two types of catalysts. The four converter designs, **Figs. 19 through 22,** are: single bed monolith, dual bed monolith, single bed pellet and dual bed pellet. The two types of catalysts used are an oxidation catalyst and a three-way (reduction) catalyst. The oxidation catalyst is coated with material containing platinum and palladium which lowers levels of carbon monoxide and hydrocarbons. The three-way (reduction)

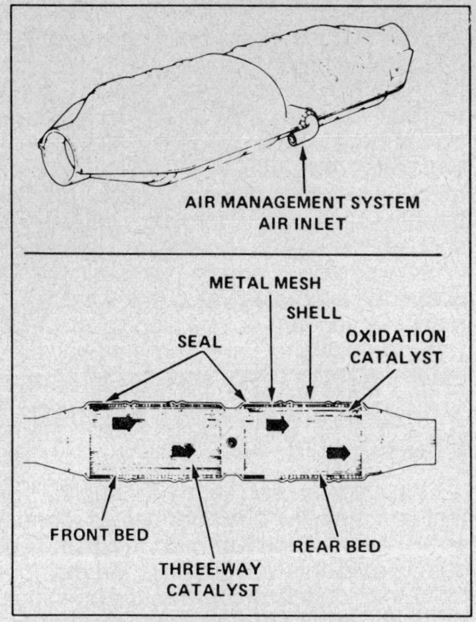

Fig. 20 Dual bed monolith type catalytic converter

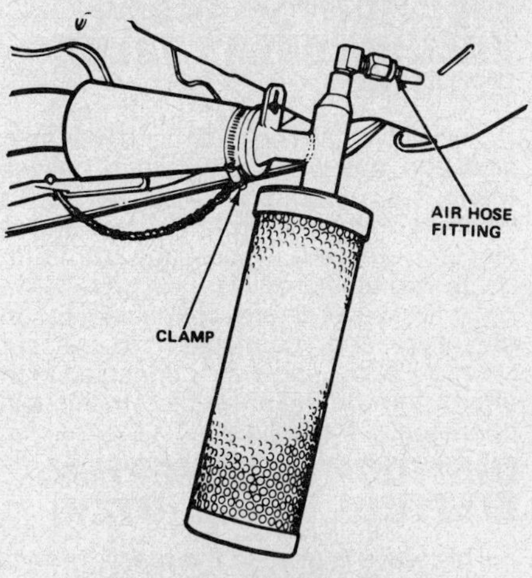

Fig. 23 Aspirator installation

catalyst is coated with platinum and rhodium which lowers levels of oxides of nitrogen (NOx), as well as carbon monoxide and hydrocarbons.

All dual bed converters, whether monolith or pellet type, contain both oxidation and three-way catalysts.

A small diameter fuel tank filler tube is used on catalytic converter equipped vehicles to prevent the larger service station pump nozzle, used for leaded fuels, being inserted into the filler tube. **Since the use of leaded fuels contaminates the catalysts, rendering them ineffective, the use of unleaded fuels is mandatory in catalytic converter equipped vehicles.**

Service

CATALYST REMOVAL

Monolith type converters are not serviceable. The following procedure applies only to pellet type catalytic converters.

1. Raise and support vehicle.
2. Install aspirator, **Fig. 23,** and connect an air line to aspirator, creating a vacuum in the converter, thereby holding pellets in place when fill plug is removed.
3. If converter is equipped with threaded fill plug, use a 3/4 inch Allen wrench and remove fill plug from converter.
4. If converter is equipped with pressed fill plug, lightly drive a small chisel between converter shell and fill plug until fill plug distorts. Remove fill plug with pliers. **Do not pry fill plug from converter, since damage to fill plug sealing surface may result.**
5. Install vibrator and catalyst container, then adapter J-25077-6, if equipped with pressed fill plug, **Fig. 24.**
6. Disconnect air line from aspirator and connect to vibrator. Catalyst will now drain from converter.
7. When all catalyst has been drained from converter, remove container and discard the used catalyst.

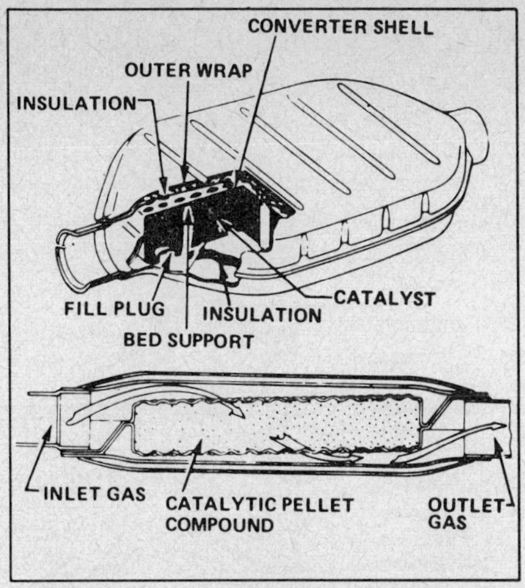

Fig. 21 Single bed pellet type catalytic converter

CATALYST INSTALLATION

1. Fill container with recommended replacement catalyst and install fill tube extension to fixture.
2. Connect air line to aspirator and vibrator, then secure container to fixture.
3. When catalyst stops flowing, disconnect air line from vibrator making sure catalyst has filled converter flush with fill plug. Add catalyst, if necessary.
4. If equipped with threaded fill plug, apply suitable anti-seize compound to threads and install into converter. Torque fill plug to 50-60 ft. lbs.
5. If equipped with pressed fill plug, install service fill plug kit with dished fill plug facing outward, **Fig. 25.**
6. Disconnect air supply from aspirator, then remove aspirator from converter.

CONTROL SWITCHES & VALVES

Description

Refer to the number stamped on the base of the switch or valve for calibrated switching or activation temperatures.

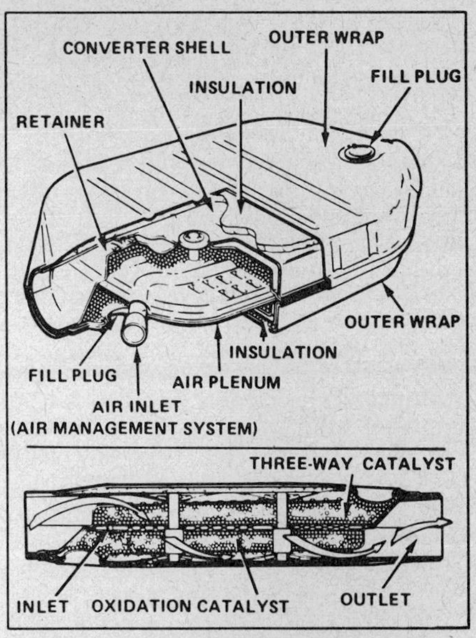

Fig. 22 Dual bed pellet type catalytic converter

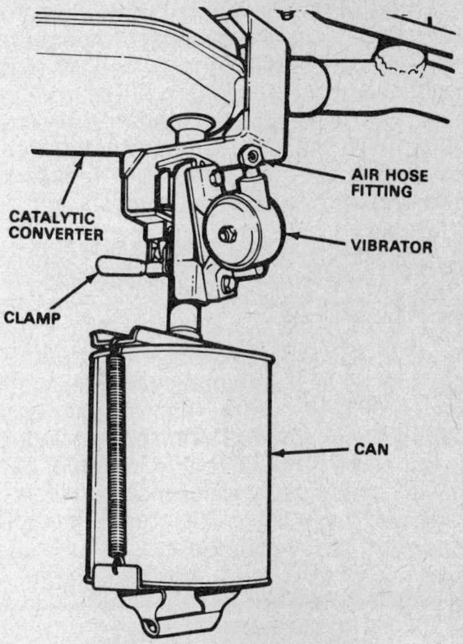

Fig. 24 Vibrator installation

CANISTER PURGE THERMAL VACUUM SWITCH (CP-TVS)

When coolant temperatures are below the switching point, canister purge is controlled by the internal orifice within the switch. However, when coolant temperature is above the switching point, the switch opens and permits canister purge to be controlled by manifold vacuum from the carburetor port.

COLD ENGINE AIR BLEED THERMAL VACUUM SWITCH (CEAB-TVS)

This switch remains open to allow cold air bleed through the switch to the intake manifold when engine coolant temperature is below the switching point. When engine coolant temperature is above the switching point, the switch closes and stops air flow to the manifold.

CHOKE VACUUM BREAK DISTRIBUTOR THERMAL VACUUM SWITCH (CVB-DTVS)

This switch is located in the air cleaner and permits the choke to run richer below the switching point, then to the leanest point above the switching point. The distributor vacuum advance receives full manifold vacuum below the switching point of the CVB-DTVS. When temperatures exceed the calibration value of the switch, manifold vacuum is directed to the thermostatic air cleaner and choke vacuum break ports while the port to the vacuum advance is blocked, preventing distributor advance above the switching point.

CHOKE VACUUM BREAK THERMAL VACUUM SWITCH (CVB-TVS)

The CVB-TVS provides a richer choke operation when the air entering the carburetor is less than the specified temperature. The CVB-TVS controls the vacuum to the secondary vacuum break. When the engine is started and the air temperature is less than specified, the CVB-TVS closes and prevents the vacuum break from pulling, to provide a richer start and improved driveability. If the air temperature is greater than specified, both vacuum breaks pull the choke to its leanest position.

CHOKE VACUUM BREAK-VACUUM DELAY VALVE (CVB-VDV)

When a sudden increase in vacuum occurs, the orifice within the valve delays the vacuum to the carburetor vacuum break. This delay is caused when higher vacuum is sensed by the valve and length of delay is dependent of the difference between the high and low values. The greater the difference the greater the delay.

DELAY VALVE TRAPPED SPARK (DV-TS)

The DV-TS is used to help control exhaust emissions by delaying vacuum advance during some acceleration modes and is located in the vacuum line between the carburetor and the distributor advance unit.

DISTRIBUTOR SPARK CANISTER PURGE THERMAL VACUUM SWITCH (DS-CP-TVS)

The two upper ports and the two lower ports of this valve are sealed when cold and connected to each other when warm. The two upper ports are not connected to the two lower ports.

DISTRIBUTOR SPARK THERMAL VACUUM SWITCH (DS-TVS)

This switch allows no vacuum flow to the distributor when engine coolant temperature is below the calibration temperature. When engine coolant temperature is above the calibration temperature, the DS-TVS allows ported vacuum to the distributor. The ported vacuum signal is controlled by a distributor spark vacuum delay valve (DS-VDV) which maintains vacuum advance during rapid throttle openings, thereby improving engine response during cold engine operation.

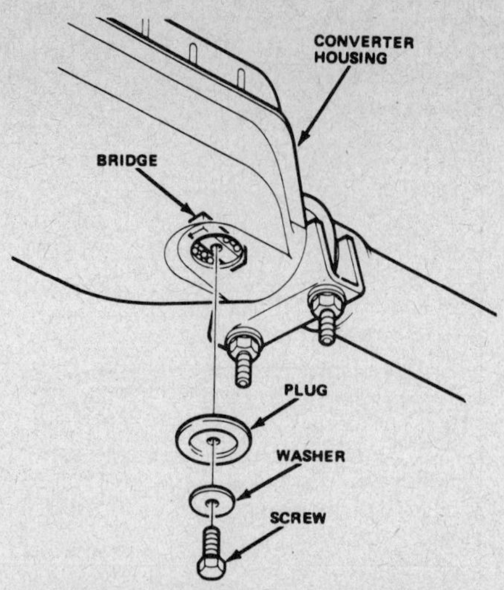

Fig. 25 Catalytic converter service plug installation

DISTRIBUTOR SPARK THERMAL VACUUM VALVE (DS-TVV)

This valve supplies manifold vacuum through a distributor spark vacuum delay valve (DS-VDV) to the distributor when the carburetor air inlet temperature is below the specified temperature. The DS-VDV maintains vacuum advance during rapid throttle opening to improve engine response during cold engine operation. When engine coolant temperature is above the calibration temperature, ported vacuum is supplied to the distributor through a distributor spark thermal vacuum switch (DS-TVS) with no additional vacuum controls.

DISTRIBUTOR SPARK VACUUM MODULATOR VALVE (DS-VMV)

This valve limits distributor spark vacuum to a calibrated value until ported vacuum applied to the control port of the DS-VMV is greater than the calibration value. When ported vacuum is greater than the calibration value, the distributor spark vacuum is equal to the ported vacuum signal.

DISTRIBUTOR SPARK VACUUM REGULATOR VALVE (DS-VRV)

This valve limits the spark vacuum to a calibrated value until ported vacuum applied to the control port of the VRV is greater than the calibration value. When ported vacuum is greater than the calibration value, full manifold vacuum signal is applied to the distributor.

Manifold and ported vacuum is applied to the VRV through two distributor spark thermal vacuum valves (DS-TVV). Ported vacuum is available to the VRV at all times with no vacuum control. When carburetor air inlet temperature is below the specified temperature, manifold vacuum is supplied to the VRV through a distributor spark thermal vacuum valve (DS-TVV) and controlled by an inline distributor spark vacuum delay valve (DS-VDV). DS-VDV maintains vacuum advance during quick throttle openings, improving engine response during cold engine operation. When engine coolant temperature is above the calibrated value of the valve, full manifold vacuum is supplied to the VRV with no additional vacuum controls.

DISTRIBUTOR SPARK VACUUM RETARD DELAY VALVE (DS-VRDV)

This valve is used with a thermal switch that connects the chamber halves (ports 2 and 3) after engine warm-up. When the engine is cold, this valve delays the distributor retard during quick throttle openings. When the engine is warm, the thermal vacuum switch allows the advance unit to respond directly to ported vacuum changes when the TVS bypasses the delay valve.

DISTRIBUTOR SPARK VACUUM DELAY VALVE (DS-VDV)

This valve has two chambers with an orifice and one-way check valve between them. This arrangement allows free air passage toward source vacuum and restricted (delayed) air passage toward the controlled unit or units.

Ports 1 and 2 are connected to one chamber and connected to vacuum source. Ports 3 and 4 are connected to the other chamber and are subject to the delay operation of the valve.

DISTRIBUTOR THERMAL CONTROL VALVE (DTCV)

This valve is used in the manifold vacuum line to the distributor vacuum advance to improve driveability during cold engine operation.

DISTRIBUTOR THERMAL CONTROL SWITCH (DTCS)

This switch has a check valve that holds the highest manifold vacuum reached to the distributor vacuum advance until switching occurs at the specified coolant temperature. After the valve switches, unchecked vacuum is directed to the distributor, to give better engine operation.

DISTRIBUTOR VACUUM MODULATOR VALVE (DVMV)

This valve has a calibration point of 8.7 inches of vacuum. Whenever manifold or ported vacuum is less than the calibration point, the DVMV switches to full manifold vacuum. Whenever the manifold or ported vacuum is greater than the calibration point, the DVMV switches to the highest vacuum, either manifold or ported.

DISTRIBUTOR VACUUM SOLENOID VALVE (DVSV)

This valve isused on some automatic

transmission equipped vehicles with air conditioning. The function of the DVSV is to prevent detonation when the A/C is on and coolant temperature is above 120°F, by supplying ported vacuum rather than manifold vacuum to the distributor vacuum advance unit. The solenoid is energized whenever the air conditioning is in use.

EARLY FUEL EVAPORATION CHECK VALVE (EFE-CV)

This valve is located in the vacuum line from the carburetor to the EFE thermal vacuum switch. The EFE-CV holds the highest vacuum reached, enabling the EFE heat valve to remain closed until the TVS switches modes. It also prevents the heat valve from rattling during severe low vacuum conditions (heavy acceleration).

EARLY FUEL EVAPORATION DELAY VALVE (EFE-DV)

When vacuum at the EGR-EFE-EMR-DTVS port is greater than the vacuum at the EFE valve actuator port, the check valve closes and vacuum from the TVS is metered through the restriction to the EFE valve actuator port within 28-42 seconds. When vacuum at the TVS is less than the vacuum at the EFE port, vacuum from the EFE port flows through the unseated check valve to the TVS port.

EARLY FUEL EVAPORATION DISTRIBUTOR THERMAL VACUUM SWITCH (EFE-DTVS)

The EFE-DTVS is an engine coolant sensitive vacuum switch which controls vacuum to both the distributor and EFE valve. When engine coolant temperatures are below the calibration point of the switch, manifold vacuum is directed to the EFE system and the distributor vacuum advance is vented to atmosphere. When engine coolant temperatures are above the calibration point of the switch, the EFE actuator is vented to atmosphere while the distributor receives ported vacuum for proper spark advance.

EARLY FUEL EVAPORATION THERMAL VACUUM SWITCH (EFE-TVS)

When engine coolant temperature is below the calibration point of the switch, manifold vacuum flows through ports 2 and 3 of this switch to the EFE actuator, closing the EFE actuator. Above the switching point, port 3 of this switch is blocked and the EFE vacuum actuator is vented to atmosphere through port 1.

EGR CANISTER PURGE THERMAL VACUUM SWITCH (EGR-CP-TVS)

When engine coolant temperature is below the calibration point of the switch, ported vacuum is blocked from the canister and the EGR valve. Above the switching point, ported vacuum is directed to both the canister purge port and the EGR valve.

EGR EARLY FUEL EVAPORATION ELECTRONIC MODULE RETARD DISTRIBUTOR THERMAL VACUUM SWITCH (EGR-EFE-EMR-DTVS)

When engine coolant temperature is below the calibration value of the switch, the EFE valve actuator and the EMR vacuum switch receive manifold vacuum from port 2, which is directed through the TVS from port 1. Port 3 is vented through port 6 while ported vacuum at port 4 and the distributor ports are sealed.

When engine coolant temperature is above the switching point, distributor port 5 receives vacuum from port 1; the EFE actuator and the EMR vacuum switch are vented at port 6; while port 3 receives ported vacuum from port 4.

EGR EARLY FUEL EVAPORATION THERMAL VACUUM SWITCH (EGR-EFE-TVS)

This switch controls vacuum to the EGR and EFE valves according to engine coolant temperature. This switch allows the EFE system to operate only during engine warm-up periods, by supplying manifold vacuum to the EFE valve when coolant temperature is below the switching point. Above the switching point, the vacuum is blocked and the EFE actuator is vented to atmosphere.

This switch also permits EGR operation at a reduced rate during warm-up and at full operation after warm-up. When engine coolant temperature is below the switching point, vacuum is directed from the ported vacuum port to the EGR port. Above the switching point, the vent orifice is blocked so full ported vacuum is directed to the EGR port.

EGR ELECTRONIC MODULE RETARD DISTRIBUTOR THERMAL VACUUM SWITCH (EGR-EMR-DTVS)

When engine coolant temperature is below the switching point, this switch receives manifold vacuum from port 2, which is directed through the TVS from port 1. Port 3 is vented through port 6 while ported vacuum at port 4 and distributor ports are sealed.

When engine coolant temperature is above the switching point, the distributor port 5 receives manifold vacuum from port 1. Port 2 is now vented through port 6, while port 3 receives ported vacuum from port 4.

EGR MIXTURE TEMPERATURE CONTROL (EGR-MTC)

On models with this system, EGR valve operating vacuum is controlled by a temperature sensitive vacuum switch mounted in the intake manifold. The valve senses intake mixture temperatures and blocks the EGR valve vacuum signal when temperatures are below 70°F. The valve is a two port type with the bottom port connected to the vacuum source and the top port connected to the EGR valve.

EGR RESPONSE VACUUM REDUCER VALVE (EGR-RVR)

This valve is used on diesel engines. The Response Vacuum Reducer Valve is located in the vacuum line between the torque converter clutch solenoid and the vacuum regulator valve and allows the EGR valve to change position quickly as throttle position is changed.

EGR THERMAL VACUUM SWITCH (EGR-TVS)

This valve is used to allow vacuum to be directed to the EGR valve when engine coolant reaches the calibration value of the switch. This valve is located in the coolant outlet on the engine.

EGR-VACUUM DELAY VALVE (EGR-VDV)

This valve is used on some V8 engines and is located in the vacuum hose to the EGR valve. Its purpose is to delay vacuum from bleeding down at the EGR valve. The vacuum is metered through a .005 inch orifice and requires up to 4 seconds from vacuum to bleed down completely.

EGR VACUUM SWITCH (EGR-VS)

This switch is used on some V8-350 diesel engines. When vacuum at this switch is below 8 inches Hg, the switch's electrical contacts are normally closed. Regulated vacuum from the vacuum regulator valve is directed to the EGR-VS. When vacuum is above 8 inches Hg, the switch's electrical contacts close and complete the circuit to ground. The EGR vacuum solenoid valve is energized allowing unregulated vacuum from the vacuum pump to be directed through the EGR vacuum solenoid valve to the EGR valve.

ELECTRONIC MODULE RETARD-VACUUM SWITCH (EMR-VS)

The electrical contacts of this switch are normally closed. When the TVS directs vacuum to the EMR-VS, the contacts close and complete the circuit to ground. The circuit is energized when 4 or more inches Hg are applied and de-energized when vacuum is reduced to 5.75 inches Hg or less.

ENGINE TEMPERATURE SWITCH (ETS)

This switch is used on some diesel engines to control fast idle speed.

On 1982-86 vehicles, the switch contacts are closed below 125°F, which completes the circuit and activates the solenoids. At the calibration point, the contacts open, creating an open circuit which deac-

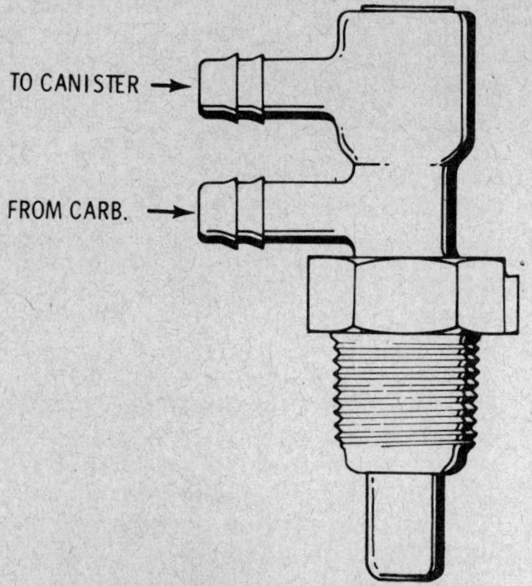

Fig. 26 Typical Canister Purge Thermal Vacuum Switch (CP-TVS)

tivates the fast idle and Housing Pressure Cold Advance solenoids.

QUICK VACUUM RESPONSE VALVE (QVRV)

These valves, used in EGR and TCC systems on diesel engines, function as quick acting vacuum release valves. As long as vacuum input to the valves remains constant or is increasing, vacuum output is equal to vacuum input. However, if the vacuum input signal decreases, the vacuum output signal will be vented until vacuum trapped within the operated device equalizes with input vacuum or input vacuum increases.

SPARK RETARD DELAY VALVE (SRDV)

This valve is used to maintain vacuum advance during quick throttle openings when engine coolant temperature is below the calibration point. Above the calibration point, full manifold vacuum is used for distributor spark on vehicles without A/C or ported spark on vehicles with A/C.

When manifold vacuum suddenly decreases, the orifice within the valve delays dropping vacuum to the distributor vacuum advance. This delay is caused when lower vacuum is sensed by the valve. The length of delay is dependent on the difference between the high and low values. The greater the difference, the longer the delay.

THERMAC SECONDARY VACUUM BREAK THERMAL VACUUM SWITCH (SVB-TVS)

This switch acts as a vacuum connection for the thermac air cleaner control and a thermal control for the secondary vacuum break diaphragm. Ports 1 and 2 of this switch are always connected and port 3 is sealed when cold and connected to the other ports when warm .

THERMOSTATIC AIR CLEANER DISTRIBUTOR THERMAL VACUUM SWITCH (TAC-DTVS)

When TAC inlet air temperature is below the switching point, vacuum from the carburetor port is directed to the distributor vacuum advance and the TAC sensor. Above the switching point, vacuum is directed to the TAC sensor but not to the distributor vacuum advance.

TRAPPED VACUUM SPARK ADVANCE (TVSA)

This system improves engine warm-up during heavy acceleration. A vacuum delay unit is located in the vacuum advance line and connected to the distributor Thermal Vacuum Switch (TVS). When engine coolant temperature is below the switching point, full vacuum signal is supplied through a delay valve to the distributor when manifold vacuum is increasing. A small orifice is provided in the delay valve to allow for leakdown when manifold vacuum is decreasing. When engine coolant temperature is above the switching point, the TVS opens ports 1 and 2 and full vacuum bypasses the delay valve through the TVS to the distributor.

VACUUM ADVANCE DELAY

This valve controls exhaust emissions by delaying vacuum advance under some acceleration conditions. This valve is located inline between the carburetor and distributor vacuum advance.

During light acceleration, the ported spark signal to the vacuum advance diaphragm is delayed by the spark delay valve which causes the vacuum advance to delay during acceleration. During cruising conditions with no change in vacuum, the restrictor does not affect vacuum advance. During closed throttle and heavy acceleration conditions when the ported vacuum decreases, the pressure differential across the restrictor disc reverses and causes the choke valve to open so that transfer of the decreasing vacuum signal is not delayed by the resistor disc.

VACUUM MODULATOR VALVE (VMV)

The vacuum modulator valve is installed between the Transmission Converter Clutch (TCC) solenoid and the EGR/EPR valves on V6 and V8 diesel engines. The VMV limits the vacuum signal to the EGR/EPR valves to 13 inches Hg.

VACUUM MODULATOR CHECK VALVE (VM-CV)

This valve is used on vehicles equipped with Electronic Fuel Control. The VM-CV is located in the line from the fresh air vent port of the vacuum modulator to the fresh air vent at the carburetor. It is used to make sure fresh air is drawn from the fresh air port at the carburetor and not from the fresh air vent of the vacuum modulator when the CEAB-TVS is open.

VACUUM REDUCER VALVE

This valve reduces vacuum by 1 1/2 inches Hg to prevent detonation when engine coolant is above 220°F and the DTVS "MT" is open to the distributor vacuum advance.

The VRV has one port on the manifold side and two ports on the DTVS side of the valve. The center port is open to vent at the

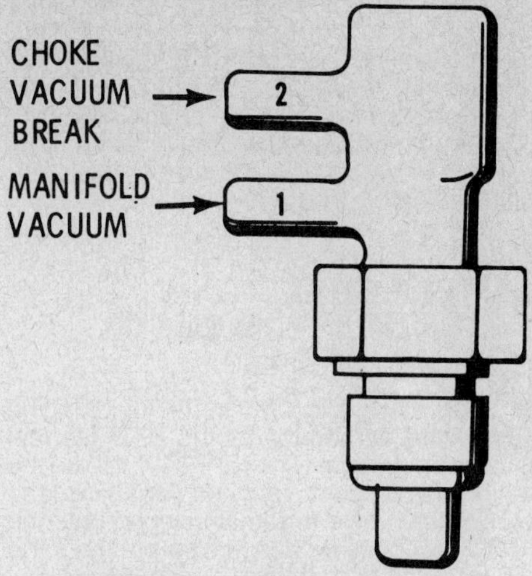

Fig. 27 Choke Break Thermal Vacuum Switch (CB-TVS). 2 port type

carburetor air horn, and the outboard port to the "MT" port of the DTVS.

VACUUM REGULATOR VALVE (VRV)

This valve is used on diesel engines, attached to the side of the injection pump, and regulates vacuum in proportion to throttle angle. Vacuum is supplied to port 1 and vacuum from port 2 is reduced as the throttle is opened. At closed throttle, the vacuum is 15 inches Hg and at wide open throttle the vacuum is zero.

Vacuum from the vacuum regulator valve port 2 is directed to the EGR vacuum switch and the vacuum modulator valve and transmission converter clutch.

Diagnosis & Testing

Refer to "Emission Control Application Charts" to determine application of control switches and valves. Also refer to the number stamped on the base of the switch or valve for calibrated switching or activation temperatures.

CANISTER PURGE THERMAL VACUUM SWITCH (CP-TVS)

With engine coolant temperature below the calibration point, connect a vacuum gauge to upper port and a vacuum pump to lower port, **Fig. 26.** Apply vacuum, then disconnect pump. The gauge should indicate that the vacuum is slowly bleeding off. Replace valve if operation is not as specified.

Make same connections as "Cold Check," then with engine coolant temperature above the calibration point, apply vacuum. Vacuum gauge reading should be the same as that applied with vacuum pump. Disconnect vacuum pump from valve. The vacuum reading on the gauge should drop to zero immediately. Replace valve if operation is not as specified.

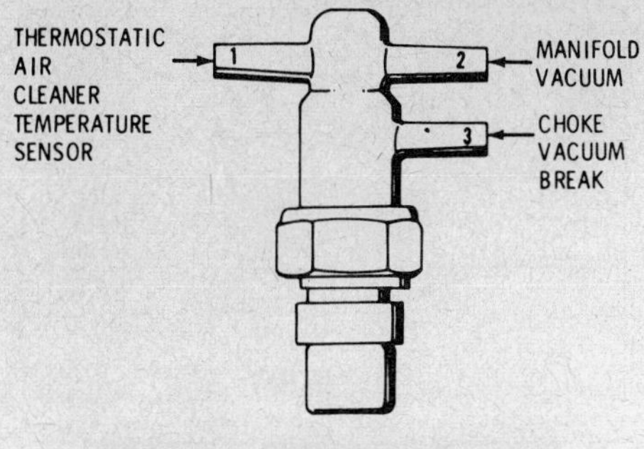

Fig. 28 Choke Break Thermal Vacuum Switch (CB-TVS). 3 port type

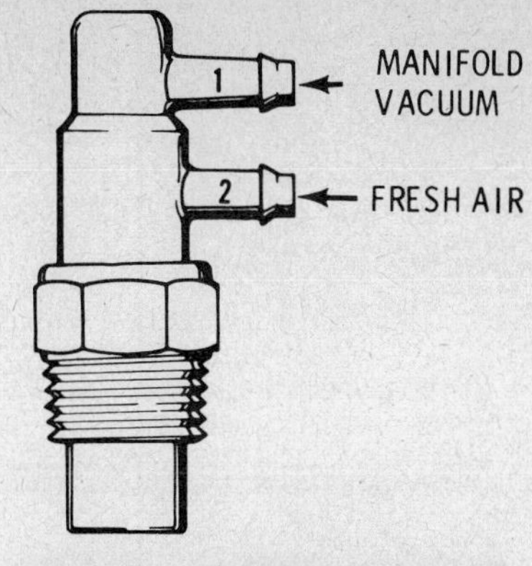

Fig. 29 Cold Engine Air Bleed Thermal Vacuum Switch (CEAB-TVS)

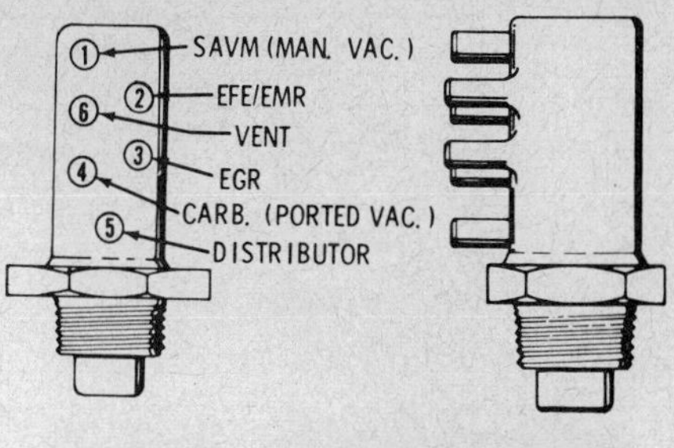

Fig. 30 EGR/EFE/EMR Thermal Vacuum Switch

CHOKE VACUUM BREAK THERMAL VACUUM SWITCH (CVB-TVS)

When cold, the valve should be closed. If necessary, cool the valve below its calibration point. Replace if defective.

At normal operating temperature, the valve should be open. This can be checked by disconnecting the top hose and connecting a vacuum gauge to it. There should be vacuum present with engine running. A valve stuck in the closed position can cause poor start condition and/or stalling after start up.

2 Port Type

With engine coolant temperature below the switching point, passage of vacuum should be restricted between ports 1 and 2, **Fig. 27.**

With engine coolant temperature above the switching point, vacuum should pass freely through ports 1 and 2, **Fig. 27.**

3 Port Type

When engine coolant temperature is below the switching point, vacuum should pass through ports 1 and 2, **Fig. 28.** When engine coolant temperature is above the switching point, vacuum should pass through ports 1 and 3, **Fig. 28.**

COLD ENGINE AIR BLEED TVS (CEAB-TVS)

With engine coolant temperature below 170°F, connect a vacuum gauge to either port and connect a vacuum pump to the remaining port, then apply vacuum, **Fig. 29.** The vacuum reading on the gauge should be the same as that applied by the pump. Replace valve if operation is not as specified.

Make same connections as "Cold Check," then with engine coolant temperature above 170°F and vacuum applied, there should be no reading on vacuum gauge. Replace valve if operation is not as specified.

DISTRIBUTOR VACUUM MODULATOR VALVE (DVMV)

This valve has a calibration point of 8.7 inches Hg. Whenever the manifold or ported vacuum is less than 8.7 inches, the DVMV switches to full manifold vacuum. Whenever manifold or ported vacuum is greater than 8.7 inches Hg, the DVMV switches to the highest vacuum, either ported or manifold.

EFE CHECK VALVE (EFE-CV)

1. Remove check valve from vacuum hoses.
2. Connect a vacuum gauge to EFE side of check valve and connect a vacuum pump to other side of valve, then apply vacuum.
3. The vacuum gauge should show a reading and hold that reading. If not, replace check valve. A slow leak-down indicates the check valve is defective. If leak-down is fast, check to see if valve is backwards.

EFE THERMAL VACUUM SWITCH (EFE-TVS)

Start engine and allow it to reach normal operating temperature. With transmission in Park or Neutral, disconnect vacuum hose from EFE and check for vacuum. No vacuum should be available. If vacuum is present, replace switch.

EGR CANISTER PURGE THERMAL VACUUM SWITCH (EGR-CP-TVS)

Below the switching point, Ports 1 and 2 should be blocked and no ported vacuum should be directed to the canister and EGR valve.

Above the switching point, Ports 1 and 2 should be open, allowing ported vacuum to be directed to the canister and EGR valve. Replace valve, if defective.

EGR EARLY FUEL EVAPORATION ELECTRONIC MODULE RETARD DISTRIBUTOR THERMAL VACUUM SWITCH (EGR-EFE-EMR-DTVS)

Below the switching point, Ports 1 and 2 and 3 and 6 should be connected, while Ports 4 and 5 should be sealed, **Fig. 30.**

Above the switching point, Port 1 should be connected to Port 5, Port 2 should be connected to Port 6, and Port 3 should be connected to Port 4.

EGR EARLY FUEL EVAPORATION THERMAL VACUUM SWITCH (EGR-EFE-TVS)

Below the switching point, the EFE and Manifold Vacuum ports should be open, the EGR and Ported Vacuum ports should be opened and vented through the Vent port, and the Vent port should be blocked to the EFE port.

Above the switching point, the Manifold Vacuum port should be blocked, the EFE port should be vented at the Vent port, and the EGR and Ported Vacuum ports should be open, while the Vent port is blocked at the EGR port.

EGR RESPONSE VACUUM REDUCER VALVE (EGR-RVR)

Connect a vacuum gauge to the "EGR" or "T.C.C." solenoid port, while connecting a suitable vacuum pump to the "Vacuum Regulator Valve" port. Apply 15 inches Hg vacuum draw to "VRV" port, while noting reading of vacuum gauge. Vacuum gauge should read 2.5 inches lower than vacuum pump on all High Altitude V8 engines; and .75 inches lower on V6 and V8 (Exc. High Alt.) engines.

EGR THERMAL VACUUM CONTROL VALVE (EGR-TCV)

This valve is used on some engines in the vacuum line to the EGR valve. The valve is closed below 61°F to block the vacuum to the EGR valve to permit better cold engine operation. The valve is open above 76°F to provide normal EGR operation.

If vacuum is present at the EGR valve when temperature is below 61°F, or there is no vacuum present when temperature is above 76°F, replace the valve.

EGR THERMAL VACUUM SWITCH (EGR-TVS)

Hot Check

The EGR-TVS should be open when coolant temperature is above the calibrated switching point, permitting ported vacuum to reach the EGR valve.

1. Disconnect hose from EGR valve and connect a vacuum gauge to hose.
2. Start engine and partially open throttle. As throttle is opened, the vacuum gauge should respond with an in-

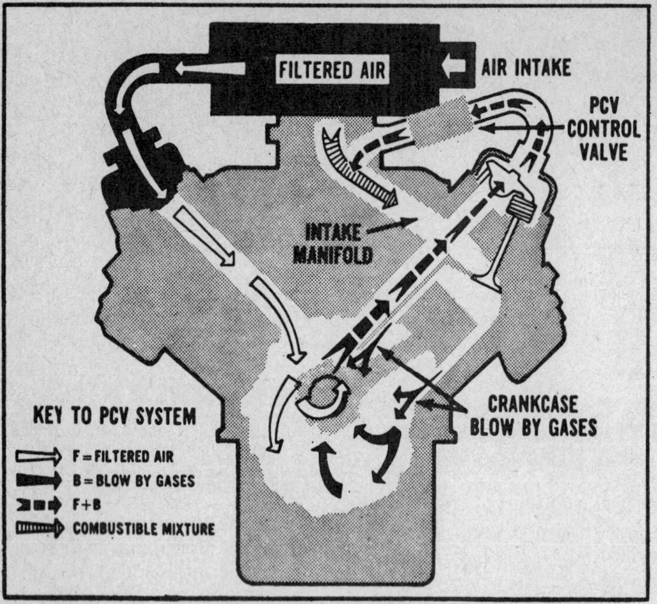

Fig. 31 Typical gasoline engine PCV system

crease in vacuum. Engine coolant temperature must be above the calibration temperature.

3. If operation is as specified, remove gauge and reconnect hose to EGR valve. If operation was not as specified, proceed to step 4.
4. Remove vacuum source hose from switch and connect hose to vacuum gauge, then repeat step 2.
5. If vacuum gauge responds to throttle opening, the EGR-TVS is defective and should be replaced.
6. If gauge does not respond to throttle opening, then check for obstructed hoses, fittings, etc.

Cold Check

1. Drain engine coolant below level of switch.
2. Disconnect vacuum lines and remove switch from thermostat housing.
3. Connect a vacuum gauge to "EGR" port and a hand held vacuum pump to vacuum source port of switch.
4. Place switch in water that is below the calibration temperature of the switch, and submerge for two minutes while agitating water.
5. Apply 12 inches Hg vacuum and observe vacuum gauge. The switch should be closed and hold vacuum.
6. If operation of switch is not as specified, it should be replaced. Leakage of up to 2 inches Hg vacuum in 2 minutes is acceptable.

QUICK VACUUM RESPONSE VALVE (QVRV)

1. Connect vacuum gauge in line between QVRV valve output and operated device and connect suitable vacuum pump to QVRV input port.
2. Apply 22 inches Hg vacuum to valve while observing gauge. Output vacuum should be approximately 20.7 inches Hg within 1.7 seconds.
3. Reduce vacuum at input side of valve to 0.9 inches Hg while observing gauge. Output vacuum should equalize within 0.5 second.
4. If valve fails to perform as outlined, replace valve.

SECONDARY VACUUM BREAK THERMAL VACUUM SWITCH (SVB-TVS)

With engine at normal operating temperature, the SVB-TVS must be open. Check by applying either engine vacuum or auxiliary vacuum to the inlet port on top of the TVS and checking for vacuum at the outlet. If there is no vacuum, replace the TVS.

THERMOSTATIC AIR CLEANER THERMAL CHECK VALVE (TAC-TCV)

This valve is a one-way check valve and closes at 80°F. When the valve's temperature reaches 95°F, it opens and allows vacuum to flow in both directions.

VACUUM REDUCER VALVE (VRV)

1. Connect a vacuum gauge to the outlet port of the valve and a hand operated vacuum pump to the inlet port.
2. Apply 15 inches Hg vacuum. The reading at the outlet port should be 1½ inches lower and should read 13 to 13½ inches Hg.
3. If the valve is not seating and bleeding off to vent, replace valve. If valve is defective, engine idle will be rough and driveability of the vehicle will be affected.

VACUUM MODULATOR VALVE

1. Block drive wheels, apply parking brake and place transmission in park.
2. Start engine and run at slow idle.
3. Connect vacuum gauge to hose leading to VMV port "M." If reading is less than 14 inches Hg, check vacuum pump, VRV, solenoid and connecting hoses.
4. Reconnect hose to VMV port "M" and connect gauge to VMV port "D."
5. Gauge should read 13 inches Hg. If not, VMV is defective.

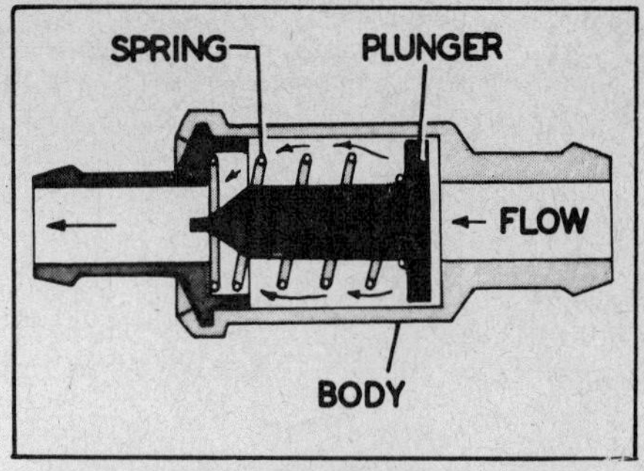

Fig. 32 Gasoline engine PCV valve. Cross sectional view

CRANKCASE VENTILATION (PCV) SYSTEM

Description

All engines produce small amounts of blow-by gases which seep past the piston rings and into the crankcase. These blow-by gases are the result of the high pressures developed within the combustion chamber during the combustion process, and contain undesirable pollutants. To prevent blow-by gases from entering the atmosphere while allowing proper crankcase ventilation, all engines use a PCV system.

GASOLINE ENGINES

The gasoline engine PCV system, **Fig. 31,** prevents blow-by gases from escaping by routing them through a vacuum controlled ventilating valve and a hose into the intake manifold. The blow-by gases mix with the air/fuel mixture and are burned in the combustion chambers. When the engine is running, fresh air is drawn into the crankcase through a tube or hose connected to the air cleaner housing.

The PCV valve, **Fig. 32,** consists of a needle valve, spring and housing. When the engine is off, the spring holds the needle valve closed to stop vapors from entering the intake manifold. When the engine is running, manifold vacuum unseats the valve allowing crankcase vapors to enter the intake manifold. In case of a backfire in the intake manifold, the valve closes, stopping the backflow and preventing ignition of fumes in the crankcase. During certain engine conditions, more blow-by gases are created than the ventilator valve can handle. The excess is returned through the air intake tube to the air cleaner and carburetor where it is burned in the engine.

DIESEL ENGINES

Although the function of the crankcase ventilation system is the same for both gasoline and diesel engines, the systems and control valves are different. Diesel en-

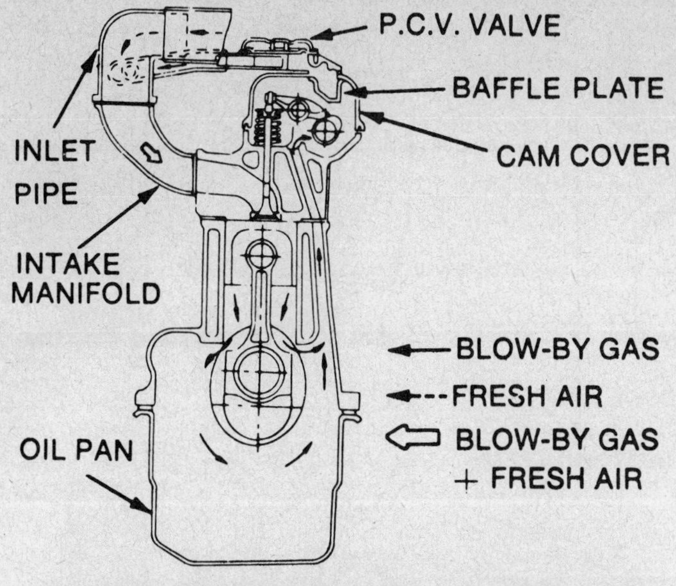

Fig. 33 Closed Crankcase Ventilation (CCV) system. 4-110/1.8L diesel engines

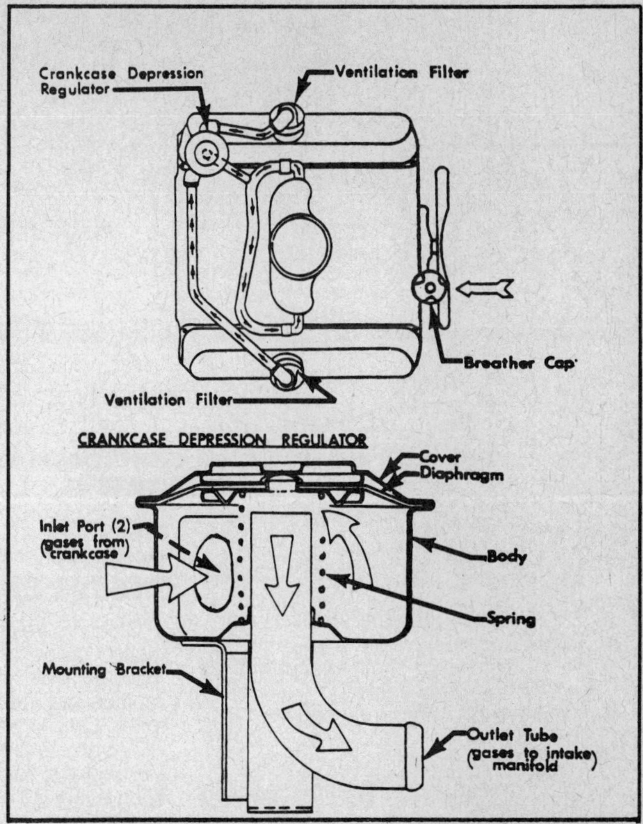

Fig. 34 Crankcase ventilation system w/Constant Depression Regulator (CDR). V6-262/4.3L & V8-350/5.7L diesel engines

gines use either a Closed Crankcase Ventilation system or Crankcase Depression Regulator to regulate flow of blow-by gases back into the engine.

Closed Crankcase Ventilation

This system, used on L-4 diesel engines, consists of a baffle plate oil separator inside the cam cover, PCV valve on the cover, and a hose connecting the valve and intake manifold, **Fig. 33.** The baffle plate separates oil particles from blow-by gases and provides an area in the cam cover for gases to collect. When pressure in the cam cover exceeds intake manifold pressure by a specified amount, the PCV valve opens and blow-by gases are forced into the intake manifold and drawn into the engine.

Crankcase Depression Regulator

This system, **Fig. 34**, is used on V6 and V8 diesel engines to regulate the flow of blow-by gases back into the engine. It is designed to limit vacuum in the crankcase as the gases are drawn from the valve cover(s) through the CDRV and into the intake manifold.

Fresh air enters the engine through the combination check valve, filter and oil fill cap. The fresh air combines with blow-by gases and enters one (V6) or both (V8) valve cover(s). These gases then pass through the valve cover filter into the connecting pipes. Intake manifold vacuum then determines the flow of the gases by acting on the spring loaded diaphragm of the CDRV. During periods of high vacuum, the diaphragm is pulled closer to the top of the outlet tube, reducing the amount of gases being drawn from the crankcase and decreasing the vacuum level in the crankcase. As vacuum decreases, the spring pushes the diaphragm away from the top of the outlet tube, permitting more gases to flow to the intake manifold.

Diagnosis & Testing

GASOLINE ENGINES

SYSTEM AIR INTAKE QUICK CHECK

A quick check of the system can be made by pulling the end of the valve out of the valve cover and, with the engine idling, placing a finger over the end of the valve to block the air flow. A vacuum should be felt and the engine speed should drop approximately 50 RPM if the system is satisfactory. If there is no change in engine speed a clogged system is indicated. To isolate the problem, remove the valve from the hose. If the ventilator hoses and carburetor passages are clear, a strong vacuum will be felt and the engine idle will change drastically or the engine will stall when the end of the hose is uncovered. If this occurs, the trouble is in the valve. If the engine continues to idle approximately as it did before the hose was uncovered, the hoses or carburetor passages are blocked.

PCV VALVE TEST

1. Install a PCV valve known to be good in the crankcase ventilation system.
2. Start engine and compare engine idle condition to the prior idle condition.
3. If the loping or rough idle condition remains when the good PCV valve is installed, the crankcase ventilation system is not at fault. Further engine component diagnosis will have to be made to find the cause of the malfunction.
4. If the idle condition proves satisfactory, replace the PCV valve and clean hoses, fittings, etc.

SYSTEM TESTING WITH TESTER

This test uses the AC positive crankcase ventilation tester, **Fig. 35,** which is operated by the engine vacuum through the oil filler opening.

1. With engine at normal operating temperature, remove oil filler cap and dipstick.
2. Connect one end of the hose to the tester body and connect the other end of the hose to the tester adapter.
3. Use the dipstick hole plug to plug the opening in the dipstick tube.
4. Insert the tester adapter in the filler cap opening and turn the selector knob to No. 2, **Fig. 35.**
5. If the vehicle has a system with the tube from the air cleaner going into the oil filler cap, disconnect the tube at the filler cap and plug the tube.
6. Start engine and let it idle.
7. With plugs secure and tube free of kinks, hold tester body upright and note color in the tester windows. Following lists the various colors and probable cause or related condition of the system.

Green

1. System operating properly.

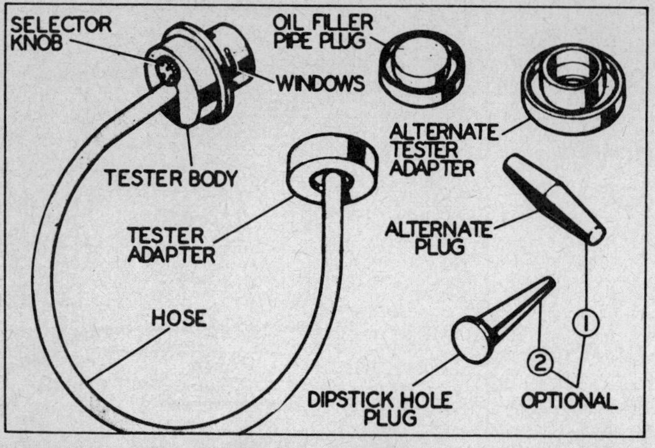

Fig. 35 AC positive crankcase ventilation system tester

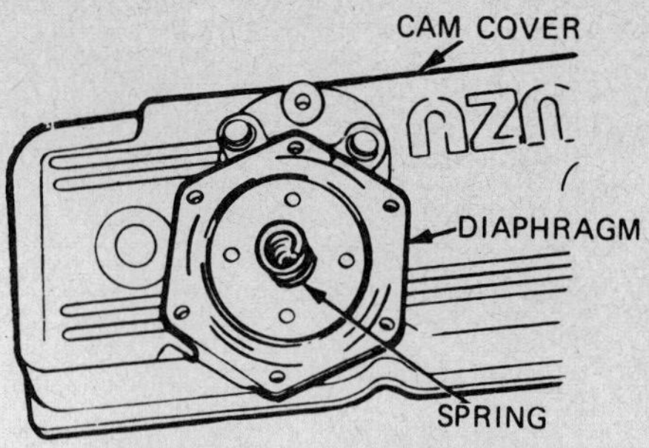

Fig. 36 PCV valve. 4-110/1.8L diesel engine

Green & Yellow

1. PCV valve or system partially plugged.
2. Slight kink in tester hose.
3. Slight engine blow-by.
4. Plugs from kit or engine vacuum lines are not properly sealed.
5. Tester knob improperly set.

Yellow

1. PCV valve or system partially plugged.
2. Tester hose kinked or blocked.
3. Blow-by at maximum capacity of PCV valve.
4. Plugs from kit or engine vacuum lines are not properly sealed.
5. Tester knob improperly set.

Yellow & Red

1. PCV valve or system partially or fully plugged.
2. More engine blow-by than PCV valve can handle.
3. Vent hose plugged or collapsed.

Red

1. PCV valve or system fully plugged or stuck.
2. Vent hose plugged or collapsed.
3. Extreme blow-by.

DIESEL ENGINES

1. Check hoses for deterioration and blockage, and replace as needed.
2. On L-4 engines, remove PCV and cam covers:
   a. Check PCV valve diaphragm, spring and housing for dirt or damage, **Fig. 36,** and repair as needed.
   b. Check baffle in cam cover and clean as needed.
3. On V6 and V8 engines, check for plugged CDR valve or breather, check CDR for binding or sticking, and replace as needed.

Service

GASOLINE ENGINES

Replace PCV valve and filter element every 30,000 miles. If vehicle is driven under dusty conditions, replace filter element as necessary. Inspect and replace any hoses that show signs of damage or plugged condition.

DIESEL ENGINES

Clean valve cover filter assemblies, ventilation pipes and connecting tube every 15,000 miles. Inspect rubber fittings and replace as necessary, or every 15,000 miles. On L-4 engines, inspect and service PCV valve every 15,000 miles. On V6 and V8 engines, replace breather cap assemblies every 30,000 miles.

EARLY FUEL EVAPORATION (EFE)

Description

This system is used to provide a source of rapid heat for quick induction system warm-up during cold engine operation. Rapid heat is more desirable because it provides for better fuel evaporation and a more uniform mixture.

VACUUM OPERATED TYPE

The vacuum operated EFE heat control valve mounted between the exhaust manifold and pipe, **Fig. 37,** directs a portion of the exhaust gases through the intake manifold and to the base of the carburetor during engine warm-up. Some vehicles rely on a thermal vacuum switch (TVS) to control the activation of the EFE valve while others use a solenoid to control the activation function.

Solenoid Controlled Type

This system uses a vacuum actuator controlled by a solenoid. The solenoid controls vacuum to the EFE valve from an electrical signal supplied by the Electronic Control Module (ECM). When engine coolant temperature is below the calibration value programmed into the ECM, the solenoid is energized, increasing the exhaust gas flow under the intake manifold. When engine coolant is above the calibration value, the solenoid is deactivated and vacuum no longer flows to the EFE valve.

Thermal Vacuum Switch Controlled

The thermal vacuum switch is used to regulate the EFE valve at or below a predetermined temperature.

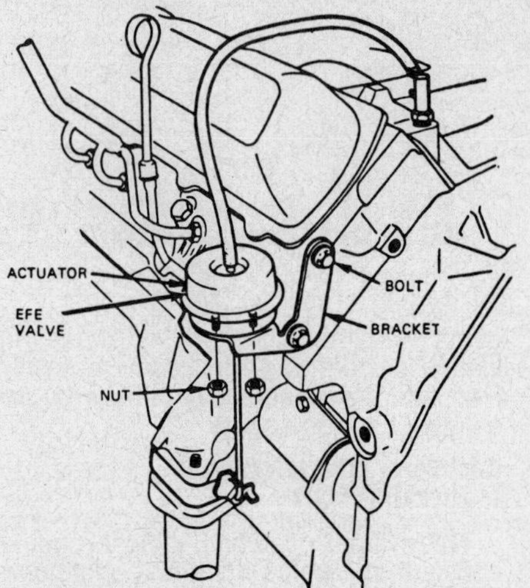

Fig. 37 Typical EFE valve installation. Vacuum operated type

When engine coolant (oil on some engines) is at or below the specified temperature, the TVS will cause vacuum to flow to the EFE control valve, diverting the exhaust gases through the intake manifold to the base of the carburetor. At temperatures above those specified, the TVS closes off vacuum to the EFE control valve, stopping the flow of exhaust gases through the intake manifold. For calibration temperature of thermal vacuum switch, see number stamped at head of switch.

CERAMIC HEATER GRID TYPE

This system, **Fig. 38,** uses a ceramic heater grid located underneath the primary bore of the carburetor. When the ignition is turned on and engine coolant temperature is low, voltage is applied to the EFE relay through the ECM. With the EFE relay energized, voltage is applied to the EFE heater. When coolant temperature increases, the ECM de-energizes the relay which shuts off the EFE heater.

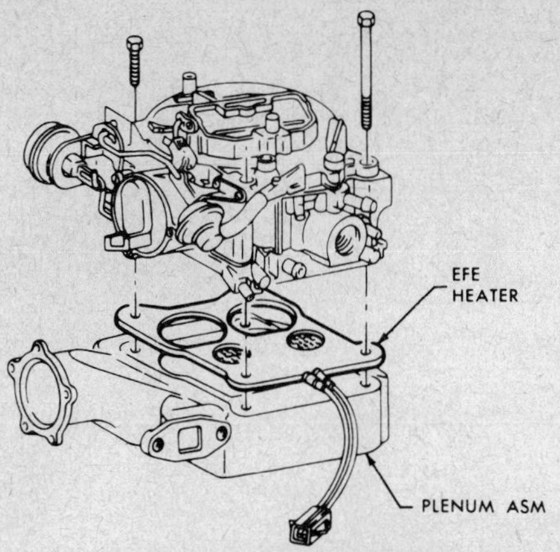

Fig. 38 Typical EFE heater grid installation

Diagnosis & Testing

VACUUM OPERATED EFE VALVE FUNCTIONAL CHECK

1. Note position of actuator arm of EFE valve with engine off, then start engine and observe EFE valve movement.
2. When engine is started cold, the valve should close, pulling the actuator link into the diaphragm housing.
3. If valve does not close, stop engine and disconnect vacuum line from EFE valve.
4. Apply 10 inches Hg vacuum load to EFE valve and note position of valve. Valve should be closed and remain closed for approximately 20 seconds without applying additional vacuum. If leak-down time is less than specified, replace EFE valve.
5. If valve does not close it may be seized. Lubricate valve with heat valve lubricant and recheck. If valve remains open, it is defective and should be replaced.
6. If valve is closed and problem continues, check for pinched, loose, kinked or plugged vacuum hoses. Repair or replace as necessary.
7. Run engine and allow to reach normal operating temperature. Valve should be open.
8. If valve does not open, remove vacuum hose from EFE valve and check if it opens. If valve opens there is no air bleed for the valve diaphragm, the TVS or EFE solenoid plunger is stuck in the cold mode, or the engine is not reaching normal operating temperature. Check and replace thermostat, TVS or EFE solenoid, if defective.

Service

EFE VALVE REPLACEMENT

1. Raise and support vehicle, then disconnect vacuum line from EFE valve.
2. Remove exhaust pipe to manifold nuts, washers and tension springs, if used.
3. Lower exhaust crossover pipe and remove EFE valve.
4. Reverse procedure to install using new seals and gaskets.

EFE THERMAL VACUUM SWITCH REPLACEMENT

1. Drain coolant level below outlet housing, then disconnect vacuum hoses from switch.
2. Noting position of ports, remove switch from outlet housing.
3. Apply soft setting sealant to threads of replacement TVS and install into outlet housing. **No sealant should be applied to sensor end of TVS, since improper operation may result.**
4. Torque switch to 120 inch lbs. and continue turning clockwise until ports align with vacuum hoses.
5. Connect vacuum hoses to switch, then add coolant as necessary.
6. Start engine and check for leaks.

EFE SOLENOID REPLACEMENT

1. Disconnect battery ground cable and remove air cleaner.
2. Disconnect electrical leads and vacuum hoses from solenoid, then remove solenoid to valve cover bracket retaining screw and the solenoid.
3. Reverse procedure to install.

CERAMIC HEATER GRID REPLACEMENT

1. Disconnect battery ground cable and remove air cleaner.
2. Disconnect all electrical, vacuum and fuel connections from carburetor.
3. Disconnect heater electrical connector, then remove carburetor and heater assembly.
4. Reverse procedure to install, then start engine and check for leaks.

HEATER RELAY REPLACEMENT

1. Disconnect battery ground cable and relay electrical connections.
2. Remove relay retaining bolts, then the relay.
3. Reverse procedure to install.

ELECTRIC ASSIST CHOKE

Description

The electric assist choke is designed to give a more rapid choke opening at temperatures above 60° to 65°F and a slower choke opening when temperatures are below 60° to 65°F.

The electric assist choke system does not change any carburetor service procedures and cannot be adjusted. If system is found out of calibration, the choke unit must be replaced.

The main components of the system, **Fig. 39**, consist of the thermostatic coil, ceramic resistor, cover, bi-metal snap disc and contact spring. The ceramic resistor is divided into a small center section for gradual heating and a larger outer section for rapid heating of the thermostatic coil. The electric actuated ceramic resistor

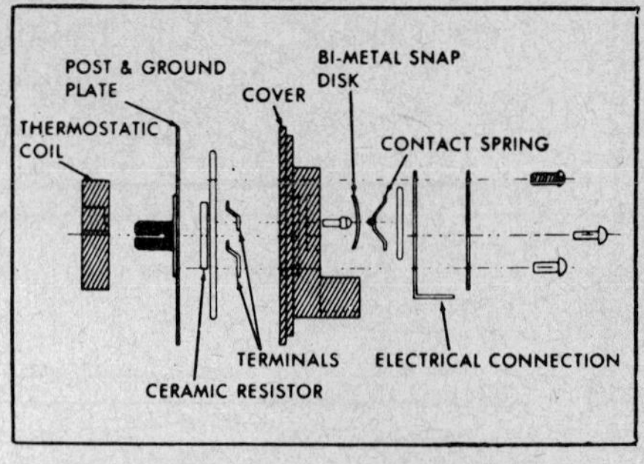

Fig. 39 Electric Choke assembly exploded view

heats the thermostatic coil, gradually relaxing coil tension and allowing the choke valve to open.

At air temperatures below 50°F, electric current applied to the small section of the ceramic resistor, allows slow opening of the choke valve for good engine warm-up. As the small section of the ceramic resistor continues to heat, a bi-metal disc causes the spring loaded contact to close and apply electric current to the large section of the ceramic resistor which increases the heat flow to the thermostatic coil for more rapid opening of the choke valve.

At air temperatures between 50-70°F, electric current applied to the small section, or both the small and large sections of the ceramic resistor, will produce the amount of heat required to control the choke valve position for good engine operation in these temperature ranges.

At air temperatures above 70°F, electric current applied to the small section of the ceramic resistor and through the spring contact to the large section of the ceramic resistor, provides rapid heating of the thermostatic coil for quicker choke valve opening when leaner air/fuel mixtures are required at warmer temperatures.

Diagnosis & Testing

CHOKE FAILS TO OPEN

If choke fails to open, proceed as follows:

1. With engine running, check voltage at choke heater connection.
2. Voltage should be 12 to 15 volts. If within specifications, replace electric choke unit.
3. If voltage is low or zero, check all wires and connections. If any connections in the oil pressure switch circuitry are defective or circuit is open, the oil pressure warning light will be on with engine running. Repair wires or connections as necessary.
4. If, after completing Steps 2 and 3, choke still fails to open, replace oil pressure switch.

EXHAUST GAS RECIRCULATION (EGR)

Description

The Exhaust Gas Recirculation (EGR)

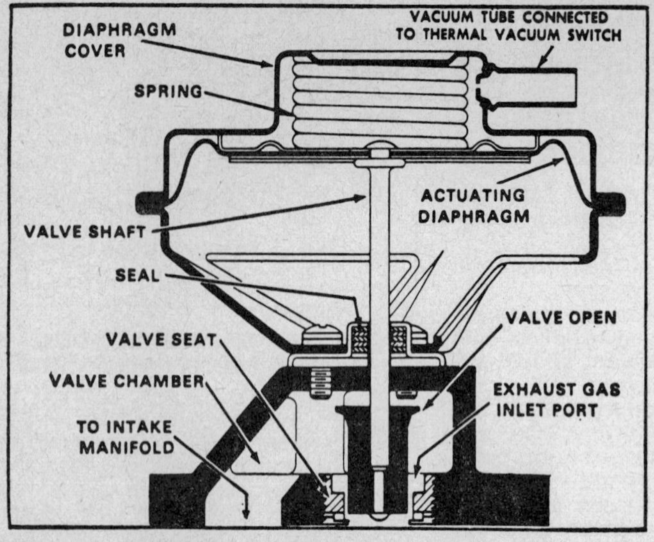

Fig. 40 Single diaphragm EGR valve cross sectional view

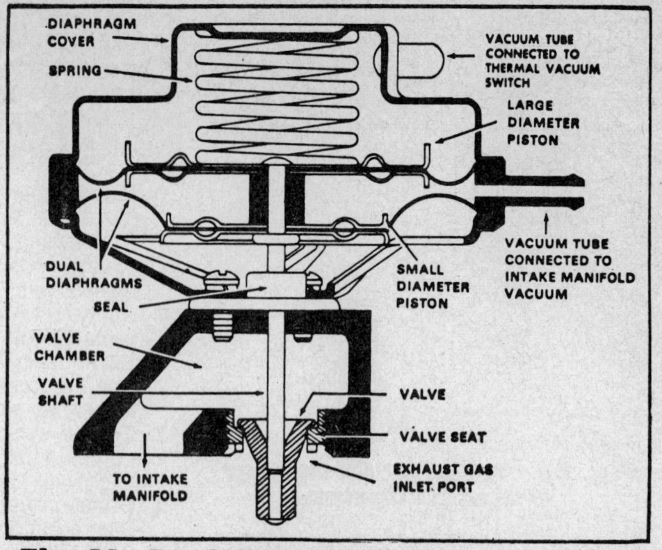

Fig. 41 Dual diaphragm EGR valve cross sectional view

System is used to reduce the levels of oxides of nitrogen (NOx) entering the atmosphere. The tremendous heat encountered during the combustion process enables nitrogen to combine with oxygen to form oxides of nitrogen. In order to reduce levels of NOx, combustion temperatures must be lowered. The EGR system lowers combustion temperatures by introducing small amounts of exhaust gases into the intake manifold, where they are reburned. This recirculation of exhaust can lower combustion temperatures as much as 500°F.

The EGR system consists of an EGR valve mounted on a special intake manifold. The exhaust gas intake port of the EGR valve is connected to the intake manifold exhaust crossover channels where it can pick up exhaust gases.

GASOLINE ENGINE EGR

As the throttle valves are opened and the engine speeds up, ported vacuum is applied to a vacuum diaphragm in the E.G.R. valve through a connecting tube. When the vacuum reaches approximately 3 inch Hg, the diaphragm moves upward against spring tension and is in the full-up position at approximately 7 inch to 8 inch hg. of vacuum. This diaphragm is connected by a shaft to a valve which closes off the exhaust gas port, **Fig. 40.** As the diaphragm moves up, it opens the valve in the exhaust gas port which allows exhaust gas to be pulled into the intake manifold and enter the cylinders. The exhaust gas port must be closed during idle as the mixing of exhaust gases with the fuel air mixture at this point would cause rough running.

The dual diaphragm EGR valve, **Fig. 41,** is designed to provide increased exhaust gas recirculation rates when engine loads increase. Manifold vacuum is used as the signal to indicate the engine load.

The valve is similar to the single diaphragm valve except that a second diaphragm has been added to the valve and is connected to the upper diaphragm with a spacer, thus both diaphragms move together. A manifold vacuum signal is applied to the volume between the two diaphragms. The upper diaphragm has a larger diameter piston than the lower diaphragm, therefore the load caused by the manifold vacuum between the two diaphragms aids the spring load. Thus as the engine load increases and manifold vacuum decreases the combined load of the spring and the vacuum chamber are reduced allowing the valve to open further for a given EGR vacuum signal.

Therefore, for high intake manifold vacuums (such as cruising), the opening is less than for low manifold vacuums obtained during accelerations. The valve now is capable of providing more recirculation on accelerations where loads are higher and the tendency to produce NOx is greater.

Integrated Electronic EGR Valve

This valve functions like a port valve with a remote vacuum regulator, except the regulator and pintle position sensor are sealed in the black plastic cover, **Fig. 42.** The regulator and position sensor are not serviceable. There is a serviceable filter, that provides clean fresh air to the regulator.

The ECM provides variable current to the vacuum regulator. This correct produces desired EGR flow using inputs from mass air flow sensor, coolant temperature sensor and engine RPM.

This valve can be identified by a part number engraved on the non-removable black plastic top.

Back Pressure EGR Valve

This valve is used on some vehicles to regulate the EGR flow according to engine load. The back pressure EGR valve is equipped with a transducer located inside the valve. The transducer uses exhaust gas pressure to control an air bleed within the valve to modify the vacuum signal from the carburetor.

A small diaphragm controlled valve inside the EGR valve assembly acts as a pressure regulator. The control valve receives an exhaust back pressure signal through the hollow shaft which exerts a force on the bottom of the control valve diaphragm, opposed by light spring pressure. A metal deflector plate prevents hot exhaust gases from flowing directly on the diaphragm.

Vacuum is applied to the EGR valve from the carburetor spark port, to ensure no exhaust gas recirculation during idle. During off-idle operation, manifold vacuum is applied to the vacuum chamber through a restriction in the signal tube. When engine load is light, and back pressure is low, the control valve is open, allowing air to flow from the bleeds in the diaphragm plate, through the control valve orifice, and into the vacuum chamber. The air bleeds off vacuum, decreasing the signal trying to open the EGR valve. If back pressure does not close the control valve, sealing off the air flow, there will not be any vacuum buildup to open the EGR valve for exhaust gas recirculation.

When power demands are made on the engine, and exhaust gas recirculation is required, exhaust back pressure increases, closing the control valve, thereby shutting off air flow through the valve. Vacuum builds up in the vacuum chamber until the spring force holding the EGR valve closed is overcome.

When the EGR valve opens, the exhaust pressure decreases because some of the exhaust gas is flowing into the intake manifold through the EGR passage. In actual operation, the system will reach a balanced condition providing maximum EGR operation.

Any increase in engine load will momentarily increase the exhaust signal, causing the control valve to close, allowing a stronger vacuum signal. The system will then stabilize at a greater EGR flow.

At maximum engine load, when manifold vacuum is nearly zero, there will be no EGR flow momentarily. This is due to the insufficient vacuum required to pull the valve open, even though high exhaust back pressure has closed the control valve.

Two types of back pressure EGR valves

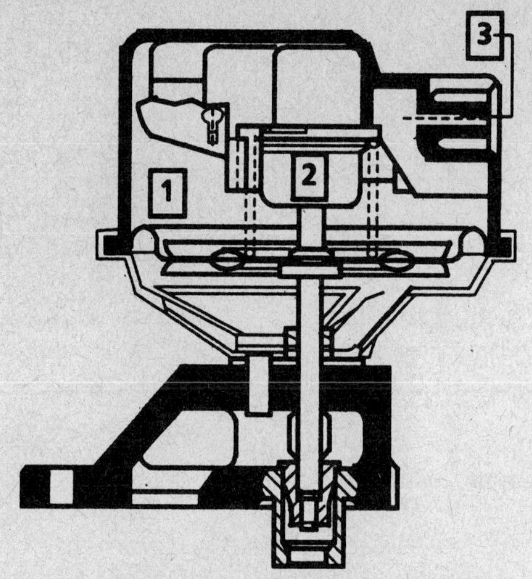

1 Diaphragm

2 Pintle Position Sensor

3 Vacuum Connection

Fig. 42 Integrated electronic EGR valve

are used on General Motors vehicles. A Positive Back Pressure EGR Valve, **Fig. 43,** is used on most engines. A Negative Back Pressure EGR Valve, **Fig. 44,** is used on those engines with relatively low back pressure to provide the desired opening point and flow rate.

Most EGR valves can be identified by the raised pattern on the diaphragm plate. Ported Vacuum valves have a raised circular rib. Positive Back Pressure valves have a slightly raised "X" shaped rib, and Negative Back Pressure valves have a substantially raised "X" shaped rib. However, on some engines it is not possible to determine valve type in this manner. On these models, a letter "N" for negative or "P" for positive is stamped next to the date code below the model number on the top of the valve and no identification letter stamped after model number for ported vacuum valves. Refer to this letter for valve identification.

EGR Control

Vacuum signals to the EGR valve are controlled by either temperature operated valves and switches or by electrically operated solenoids.

On Thermal Vacuum Switch (TVS) controlled models, vacuum signals to the EGR valve are blocked when engine coolant temperature is below switch calibration point. When engine coolant is at or above switch calibration temperature, the switch opens and allows vacuum to reach the EGR valve.

Two types of electrically controlled vacuum solenoids are used to allow Electronic Control Module (ECM) control of the EGR valve operation. A solenoid which operates similar to the TVS and a solenoid that bleeds-off a portion of the EGR valve vacuum signal are used. Depending upon application, either one or both of these solenoids may be used to control EGR.

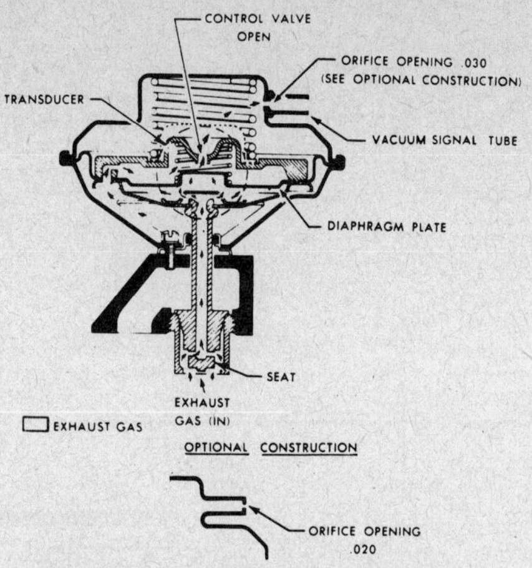

Fig. 43 Positive back pressure EGR valve cross sectional view

The EGR solenoid is energized by the ECM to block vacuum signals to the EGR valve. When engine is cold and operating within specified load and RPM range, the ECM completes the solenoid ground circuit. When engine reaches the temperature programmed into the ECM, the solenoid ground circuit is opened and vacuum signals are allowed to reach the EGR valve.

The EGR bleed solenoid is used to bleed-off a portion of the EGR vacuum signal, limiting the amount of recirculation under certain operating conditions. The bleed solenoid is operated by the ECM when engine is cold and/or when the Transmission Converter Clutch (TCC), if equipped, is engaged. Most models use a Pulse Width Modulated (PWM) type bleed solenoid. The solenoid is turned "on and off" 32 times per second by the ECM, with the amount of vacuum bleed determined by the solenoid "on time" per cycle. This allows the ECM to bleed-off up to one half of the EGR vacuum signal, or allow full vacuum by de-energizing the solenoid.

DIESEL ENGINE EGR

V8-350 ENGINES

1982–83

On this system, **Fig. 45,** vacuum from the vacuum pump is modulated by the Vacuum Regulator Valve (VRV) mounted on the injection pump. Vacuum is highest at idle and decreases to zero at wide open throttle. The EGR valve is therefore fully open at idle and fully closed at wide open throttle. A Response Vacuum Reducer (RVR) valve is used between the VRV and the EGR valve to permit the EGR valve to change position quickly as throttle position is changed. A torque converter clutch solenoid shuts off vacuum to the EGR valve whenever the T.C.C. is engaged.

The torque converter clutch operated solenoid is not used on 1982 Caprice, Custom Cruiser and LeSabre wagons equipped with V8-350 diesel engine.

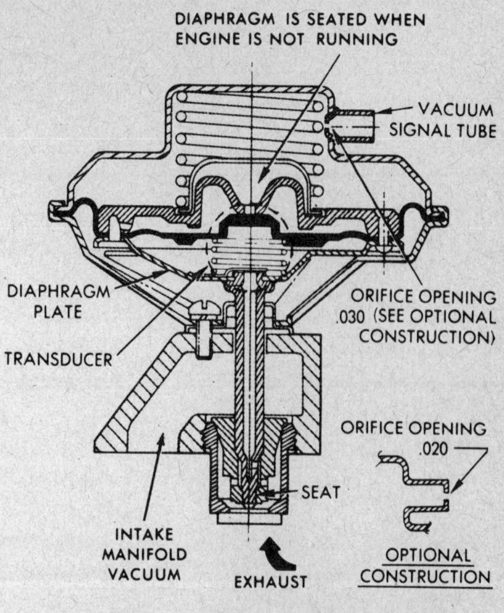

Fig. 44 Negative back pressure EGR valve cross sectional view

1984–85

The EGR vacuum control circuit on these engines includes an injection pump mounted Vacuum Regulator Valve (VRV), TCC vacuum cut solenoid, Quick Response Valve (EGR-QRV), Thermal Vacuum Switch (EGR-TVS), and an altitude compensation circuit, **Figs. 46 and 47.** The VRV and TCC solenoid operate as outlined for 1982-83 models, providing high vacuum at idle and decreasing operating vacuum as throttle lever angles increase, and cutting off vacuum to the EGR valve when the converter clutch is engaged. The QRV allows the EGR valve to respond rapidly to decreasing vacuum by venting vacuum trapped in the EGR valve diaphragm chamber when vacuum input to the QRV decreases. The EGR-TVS operates in a conventional manner, venting EGR valve operating vacuum when coolant temperature is below switch calibration temperature. The altitude compensation circuit uses an altitude sensitive switch to operate an Altitude Trim Solenoid (ATS) and an Altitude Vacuum Reducer Valve (AVRV). The components in the altitude compensation circuit allow vehicles calibrated for low altitude operation to meet emission standards when operated at high altitudes and vehicles calibrated for high altitude operation to meet emission standards when operated at low altitudes.

On vehicles calibrated for low altitude operation, vacuum signals transmitted through the EGR-TVS are applied to port 3 of the ATS and port 3 of the AVRV. During low altitude operation, the ATS is not energized and vacuum is transmitted through the ATS to AVRS port 2. Vacuum at AVRV ports 2 and 3 is equal and full output from the VRV is applied to the EGR valve through the QRV. At altitudes above 4000 feet the ATS is energized and vacuum applied to ATS port 3 is vented to atmosphere. Vacuum applied to AVRV port 3 is greater than vacuum at port 2, causing the vacuum applied to the AVRV to be routed through the valve's reducing circuit,

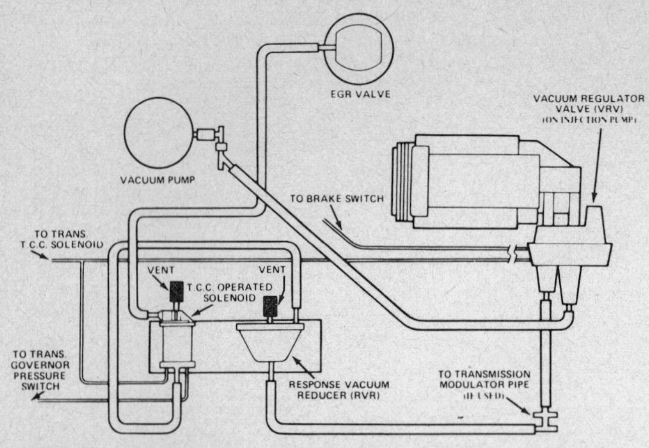

Fig. 45 EGR system schematic. 1982–83 V8-350/5.7L diesel engine

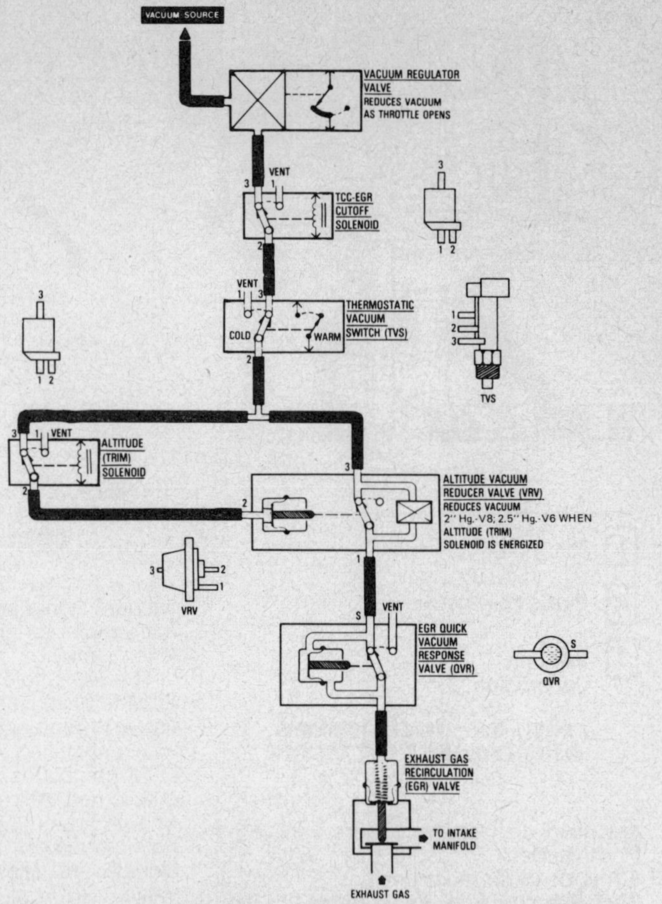

Fig. 46 Low altitude EGR vacuum control system schematic. 1984–85 V6 & V8 diesel engines exc. front wheel drive models & models w/DEC system

and vacuum applied to the EGR valve is reduced by 2-2.5 inches Hg.

On vehicles calibrated for high altitude operation, vacuum signals transmitted through the EGR-TVS are applied to port 1 of the ATS and port 3 of the AVRV. During high altitude operation, the ATS is not energized and vacuum applied to port 1 is vented. Vacuum applied to port 3 of the AVRV is greater than vacuum applied to port 2 and is routed through the valves reducing circuit, reducing vacuum applied to the EGR valve by 2-2.5 inches Hg. At altitudes below 4000 feet, the ATS is energized, the ATS vent is closed and vacuum is transmitted through the ATS to port 2 of the AVRV. Vacuum at ports 2 and 3 of the AVRV is then equal, the reducing circuit is closed and full VRV vacuum is applied to the EGR valve through the QRV.

V6-262 ENGINES

1982–83

On this system, **Figs. 48 and 49** vacuum from the vacuum pump is modulated by a Vacuum Regulator Valve (VRV) mounted on the injection pump. The EGR valve is open to its fullest at idle and decreases to zero at wide open throttle. The amount of EGR valve opening is further determined by a Vacuum Modulator Valve (VMV), which permits an increase in vacuum to the EGR valve when the throttle is closed up to the switching point of the VMV. A Response Vacuum Reducer (RVR) valve is used between the vacuum regulator valve and the torque converter clutch solenoid to allow the EGR valve to change position quickly as throttle position is changed. The solenoid blocks vacuum to the EGR valve whenever the torque converter clutch is applied and is fed 12 volts from the T.C.C. switch portion of the VRV. Grounding is supplied through the transmission governor pressure switch.

An Exhaust Pressure Regulator (EPR) valve is incorporated into the EGR system, **Fig. 49.** This valve is situated between the righthand exhaust manifold and the exhaust pipe and is used to increase backpressure in the exhaust system, resulting in increased exhaust gas flow through the EGR system. The EPR valve operates from the same vacuum source as the EGR valve and is fully closed at idle and fully open at wide open throttle position.

1984–85 Rear Wheel Drive Models Exc. Calif.

The system used on these models operates as outlined for 1984-85 V8-350 Engines.

1984–85 Front Wheel Drive Models Exc. Calif. & High Altitude

The basic EGR vacuum control system on these models operates in a manner similar to the system used on 1984-85 V8-350 engines, but the layout of components is varied, and some components have been added to further control EGR and TCC operation. All models use an injection pump mounted Vacuum Regulator Valve (VRV) to provide high vacuum at idle and progressively lower operating vacuum as throttle lever angle increases, a TCC cut-off solenoid to vent EGR vacuum when the converter clutch is engaged, and an Altitude Trim Solenoid (ATS) and Altitude Vacuum Regulator Valve (AVRV) to reduce EGR valve operating vacuum when the vehicle is operated above 4000 feet.

The system used on models with 3 speed automatic transmissions and 4 speed manual transmissions is the same as the 1984 V8-350 engine system, but the EGR-TVS is located between the AVRV and QRV, and the ATS and AVRV receive vacuum directly from the TCC solenoid, **Fig. 50.**

The system used on models with 4 speed automatic transmissions, except station wagons, includes a Transaxle Modulator Quick Response Valve (TM-QRV), Exhaust Pressure Regulator (EPR) valve, EPR Delay Valve (EPR-DV) and EPR-QVR, as well as all components used on other 1984-85 systems, **Fig. 51.** The EPR valve receives operating vacuum from the outlet port of the ATS, through the delay valve and QRV. At low altitudes, when the ATS is de-energized, the EPR valve receives the same vacuum signal as the EGR valve, after a 20-30 second delay caused by the inline delay valve. However, during high altitude operation when the ATS is energized, the EPR valve receives no vacuum as the signal is vented by the ATS. The EPR valve is fully closed when VRV vacuum exceeds 13 inches Hg, open when VRV vacuum is below 6.9 inches Hg, and serves to increase exhaust back pressure when closed or partially closed. The EPR-QRV and TM-QRV operate the same as the EGR-QRV, venting diaphragm chamber vacuum until it is constant with decreasing signal vacuum.

The system used on station wagon models with 4 speed automatic transmis-

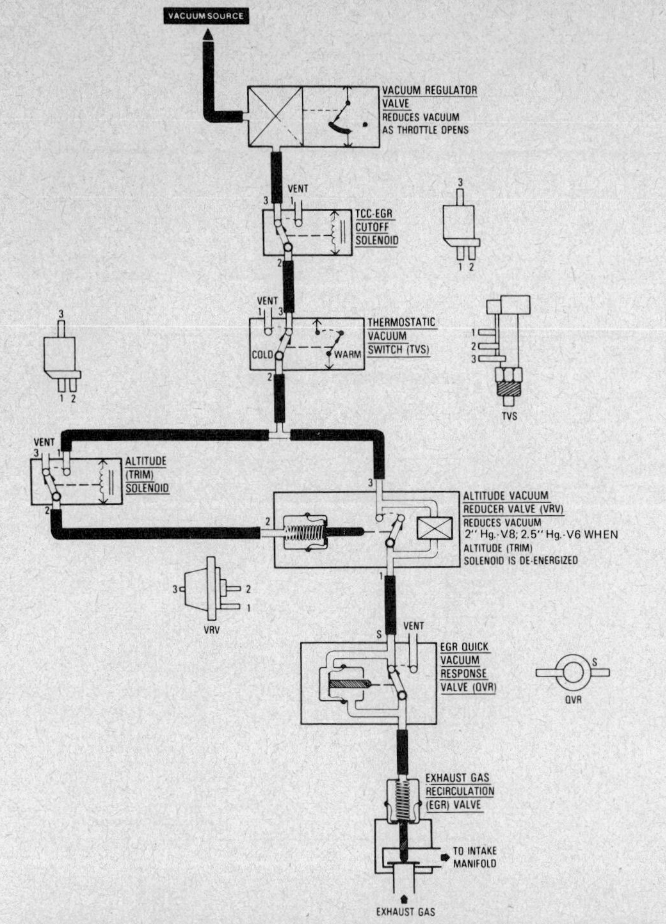

Fig. 47 High altitude EGR vacuum control system schematic. 1984–85 V6 & V8 diesel engines exc. front wheel drive w/V6-262/4.3L & models w/DEC system

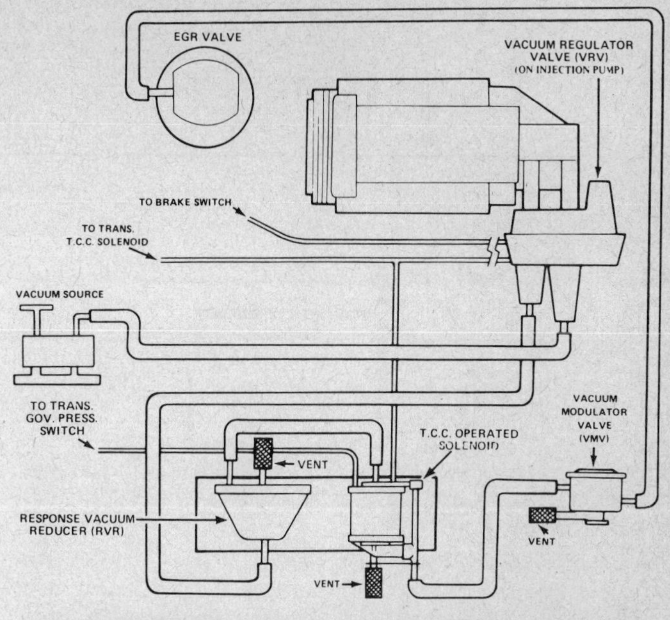

Fig. 48 EGR system schematic. 1982–83 V6-262/4.3L diesel engine less Exhaust Pressure Regulator (EPR) valve

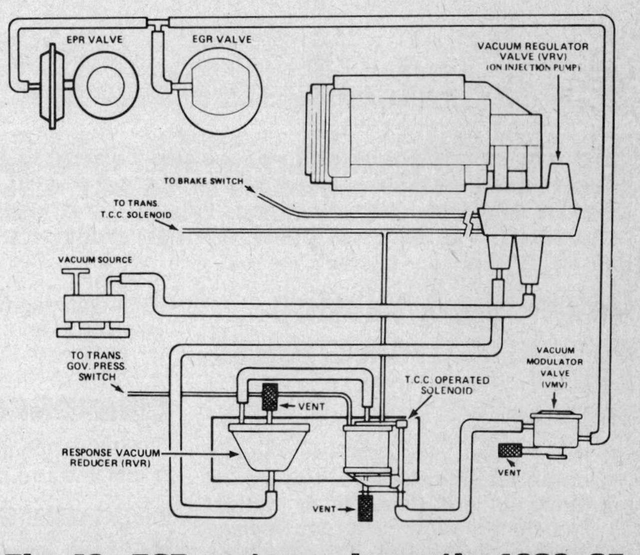

Fig. 49 EGR system schematic. 1982–83 V6-262/4.3L diesel engine w/Exhaust Pressure Regulator (EPR) valve

sions includes a Transaxle Modulator Vacuum Reducer Valve (TM-VRV) and Transaxle Modulator Quick Response Valve (TM-QRV) as well as all components used on 1984-85 V8-350 engines, and the EGR-TVS and TCC cut-off solenoid is located between the AVRV and EGR-QRV, **Fig. 52.** Vacuum is applied to the ATS, AVRV and TM-VRV directly from the injection pump mounted VRV. At low altitudes, when the ATS is not energized, vacuum is transmitted to both the EGR valve and transaxle modulator, and regulated by the VRV. However, at altitudes above 4000 feet when the ATS is energized, VRV vacuum is reduced 2.5 inches Hg to the EGR valve and 1 inch Hg to the modulator by their respective vacuum reducer valves.

1984–85 Front Wheel Drive High Altitude

This system operates as outlined for 1984-85 V8-350 engines. However, on models with 4 speed automatic transaxles, a Quick Response Valve has been added between the VRV and transaxle modulator and the EGR-TVS is located between the AVRS valve and the EGR-QRV, **Fig. 53.**

4-110 ENGINES

1984–86

The EGR system includes an intake manifold mounted EGR valve and stainless steel exhaust pickup tube, vacuum pump, vacuum switching valve, control module, and sensors that monitor engine and vehicle operating conditions. Operating vacuum for the EGR valve is provided by the vacuum pump through the vacuum switching valve which is controlled by the module. The module transmits ON-OFF electrical pulses to the vacuum switching valve according to engine RPM, injection pump lever angle, vehicle speed and coolant temperature. When the switching valve is energized, vacuum is supplied to the EGR valve, opening the valve; when the switching valve is off, the EGR valve closes.

The engine speed sensor, coolant sensor, control lever position sensor and vehicle speed sensor convert measured operating conditions into voltage signals which are transmitted to the control module. The module uses these signals to compute proper amounts of EGR, then controls operation of the vacuum switching valve accordingly. This allows the module to provide EGR only under conditions where it is needed to reduce NOx emissions and prevents recirculation under conditions where it will adversely affect driveability as shown in **Fig. 54.**

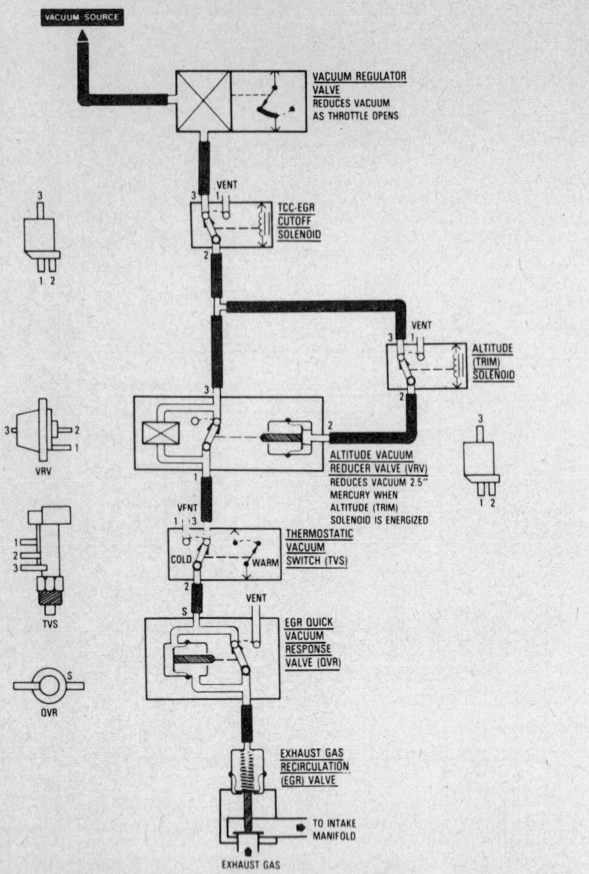

Fig. 50 EGR system schematic. 1984–85 front wheel drive models w/V6-262/4.3L diesel engine, 3 spd. auto. trans. or 4 spd. manual trans. exc. Calif. & high altitude

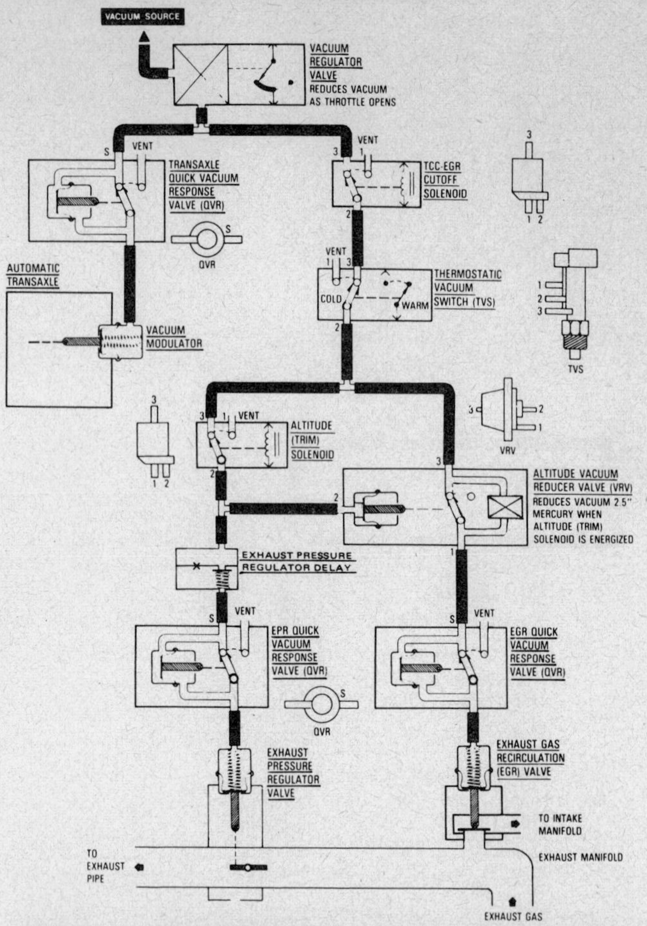

Fig. 51 EGR system schematic. 1984–85 front wheel drive models w/V6-262/4.3L diesel engine & 4 spd. auto. trans. exc. station wagon, Calif. & high altitude

Diagnosis & Testing

EGR SYSTEM FUNCTIONAL CHECK

1982–86

1. Place finger under EGR valve and lift up on diaphragm plate. Plate should move up and down freely without binding or sticking. If not, replace valve. **If valve is hot, it may be necessary to wear gloves to avoid injury.**
2. Connect vacuum gauge to EGR valve vacuum signal line using a T-fitting. Start engine and run at part throttle.
3. Vacuum gauge should indicate at least 5 inches Hg at part throttle once engine reaches normal operating temperature. If not, check control valves, hoses and vacuum source, and repair as needed.
4. With engine running as in step 3, disconnect vacuum hose to EGR valve. Diaphragm plate should move and engine speed should increase.
5. Reconnect vacuum hose to EGR valve. Diaphragm plate should move and engine speed should decrease.
6. If diaphragm moves but there is no change in engine speed, check manifold passages for blockage. If passages are clear, EGR valve is defective.
7. If diaphragm does not move in steps 4 or 5 and vacuum signal is within specifications, EGR valve is defective.

COMPONENT TESTING

Refer to "Control Switches and Valves" to test vacuum circuit controls.

GASOLINE ENGINES

Ported Vacuum & Negative Back Pressure EGR Valves

1. Check vacuum hoses for correct routing and EGR valve signal tube orifice for obstructions.
2. Connect vacuum gauge between EGR valve and carburetor and check that at least 5 inches Hg vacuum is available with engine running at normal operating temperature.
3. Depress valve diaphragm, then position finger over source tube. Release diaphragm.
4. Valve is good if diaphragm takes at least 20 seconds to move to closed position. If diaphragm closes in less than 20 seconds, replace EGR valve.

Positive Back Pressure EGR Valve

1. Check vacuum hoses for correct routing and EGR valve signal tube orifice for obstructions. **On engines equipped with EGR thermal vacuum switch or solenoid, there should be no EGR valve movement below the calibration temperature. If movement occurs, check TVS or solenoid for proper operation.**
2. Remove EGR valve from vehicle, then apply a constant 10 inches Hg vacuum to EGR valve signal tube and observe position of valve. Valve should be closed. If not, replace EGR valve.
3. With vacuum supply still applied, direct a low pressure stream of air into EGR valve exhaust inlet. Valve should open. If not, replace EGR valve.

DIESEL ENGINE

V8-350 EGR Valve

1. Apply vacuum to valve using vacuum pump with integral gauge and observe valve diaphragm.
2. On all except 1983 Bonneville, Cutlass, Malibu, Monte Carlo and Regal, valve should remain closed below 6 inches Hg and should be fully open above 10.5 inches Hg.
3. On 1983 Bonneville, Cutlass, Malibu, Monte Carlo and Regal, valve should remain closed below 5 inches Hg and should be fully open above 9.5 inches Hg.

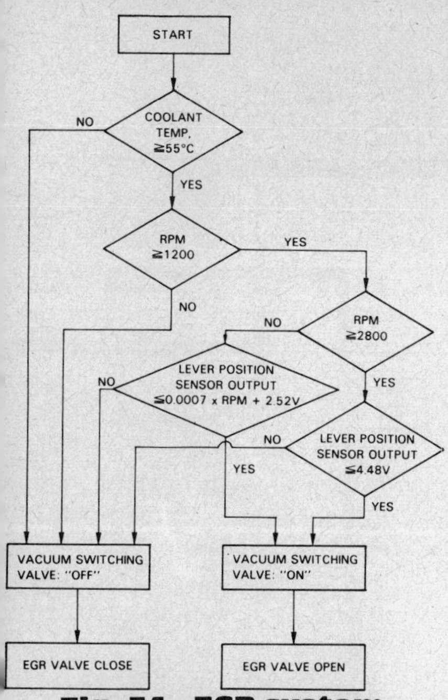

Fig. 54 EGR system operation. 1984–85 4-110/1.8L diesel engine

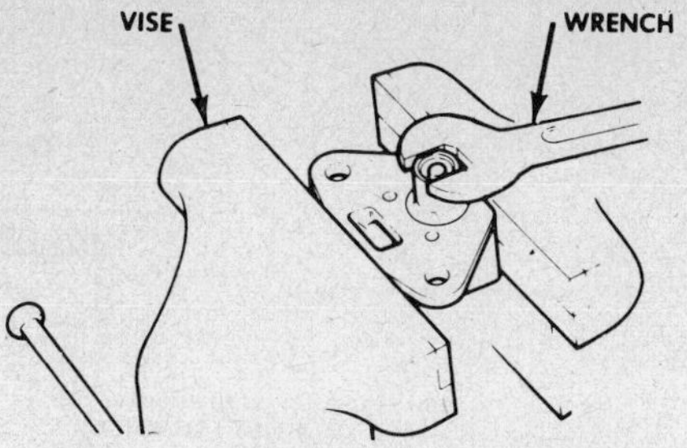

Fig. 55 Removing valve seat on serviceable type EGR valve

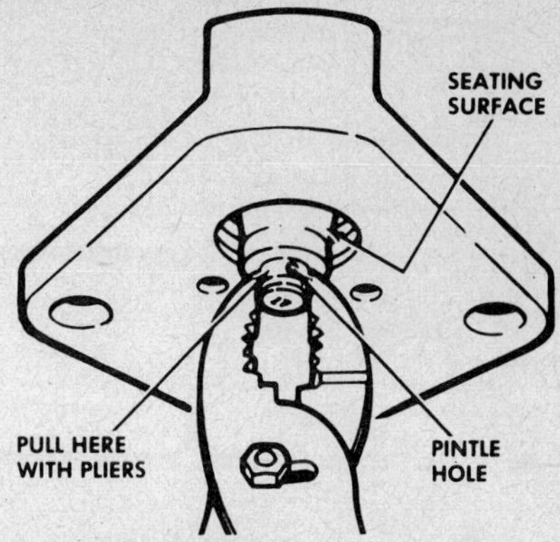

Fig. 56 Removing pintle on serviceable type EGR valve

4. Inspect valve outlet and remove deposits with suitable sharp tool.
5. Clean intake manifold to EGR valve mounting surface with wire brush, then install EGR valve assembly using new gasket.

Serviceable Type

1. Remove EGR valve from vehicle.
2. Clean seat and base, then inspect for alignment marks located on base and seat. These marks must align and alignment be retained during reassembly.
3. Measure distance from base surface to seal shoulder. Record this measurement to aid in reassembly.
4. Secure EGR valve in bench vise, then remove seat from pintle using suitable wrench, Fig. 55. **If pintle seat is difficult to remove, rock fore and aft to overcome tightness due to factory shaking.**
5. Holding valve in upright position:
   a. Remove pintle by pulling downward with pliers, making sure jaws are not located on sealing surface, **Fig. 56.**
   b. Using drill bit slightly smaller than shaft inside diameter, turn bit clockwise up into shaft for approximately one inch, then pull out without turning.
   c. Tap shaft lightly to loosen debris from shaft inner surface.
6. Clean holes in pintle with suitable drill bit, then brush and air blow pintle and shaft to complete cleaning. **Safety glasses should be worn to protect eyes from flying debris.**
7. Position pintle over end of shaft and press down until pintle lock ring feels seated, then proceed as follows:
   a. Screw seat into base until distance between base and seal shoulder is the same as recorded in Step 3.

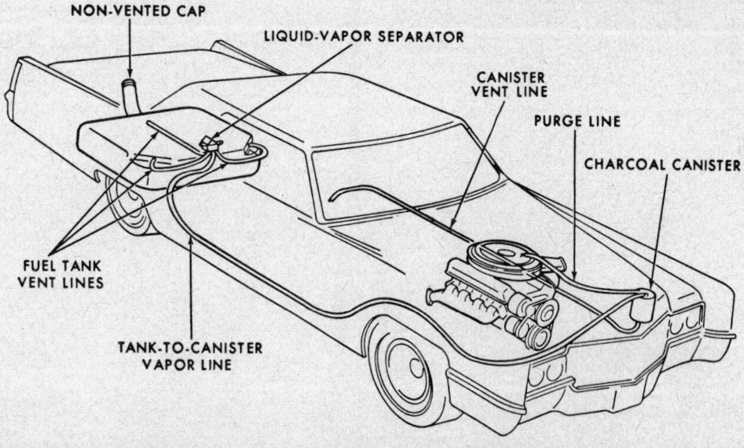

Fig. 57 Evaporative Emission Control (EEC) system. Typical of General Motors vehicles

   b. Position scribe marks on base and seat so that they are in alignment.
8. Supporting valve at base, restake seat at original staking locations.
9. Install EGR valve using new gasket.

EVAPORATIVE EMISSION CONTROL SYSTEM

Description

This system, **Fig. 57,** allows evaporating fuel vapors to be stored for burning during combustion, rather than being vented to atmosphere when the engine is not running. This is accomplished by venting the fuel tank and usually the carburetor float bowl through a canister containing activated charcoal. The canister absorbs fuel vapors and retains them until it is purged or cleared by air drawn through a filter located either at the bottom of the canister or in the air cleaner snorkel. The canister absorbs fuel vapors when the engine is off. When the engine is running, vapors are drawn from the canister into the engine, where they are burned.

FUEL TANK

A specially designed domed fuel tank is used on the EEC system. The dome allows for expansion of fuel and collection of fuel vapors. A fill pipe which prevents complete filling of the tank is used on these special design tanks. A liquid vapor separator is provided to prevent liquid fuel from entering the system. Liquid fuel entering the separator is spilled back into the tank while raw fuel vapors are passed into the lines.

FILLER CAP

The filler cap used on the EEC system is not vented under normal conditions. However, to prevent damage to the tank from excessive internal or external pressure resulting from the closed system, the filler cap contains a two-way relief valve which allows the cap to vent when abnormal pressure or vacuum develops within the tank. **Installation of a fill cap from a non-emission fuel tank will render the system inoperative, since the non-emission fill cap is vented and the system must be sealed to function properly. Also, if a non-vented fill cap is installed on a conventional tank, the result will be a serious deformation or a total collapse of the fuel tank.**

VAPOR STORAGE CANISTER

Several types of vapor storage canisters are used on General Motors Vehicles.

Single Stage Type Vapor Canister

This canister, **Fig. 58,** absorbs fuel vapors from the fuel tank through a tube on

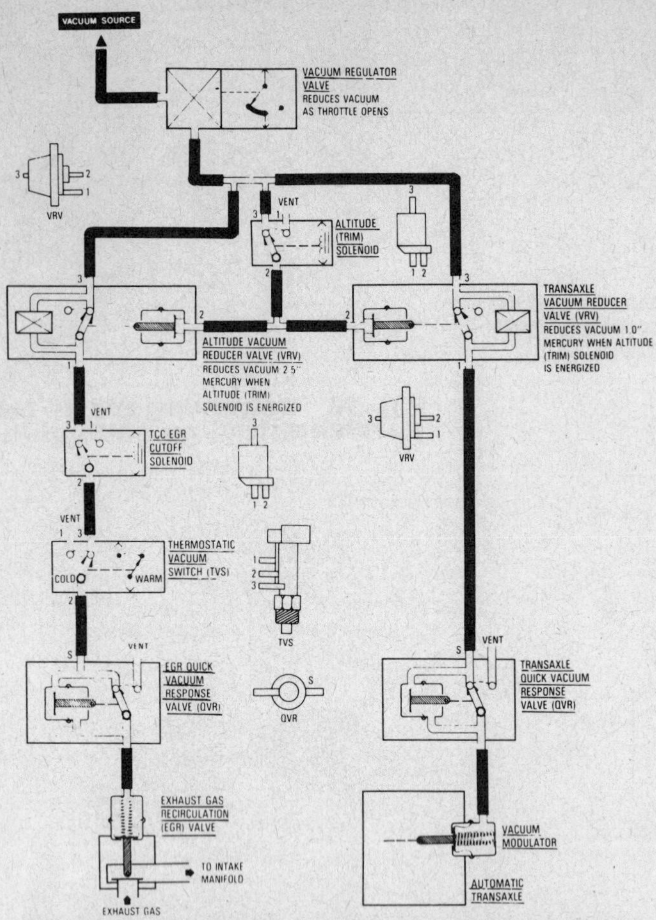

Fig. 52 EGR system schematic. 1984–85 front wheel drive station wagon w/V6-262/4.3L diesel engine & 4 spd. auto. trans. exc. Calif. & high altitude

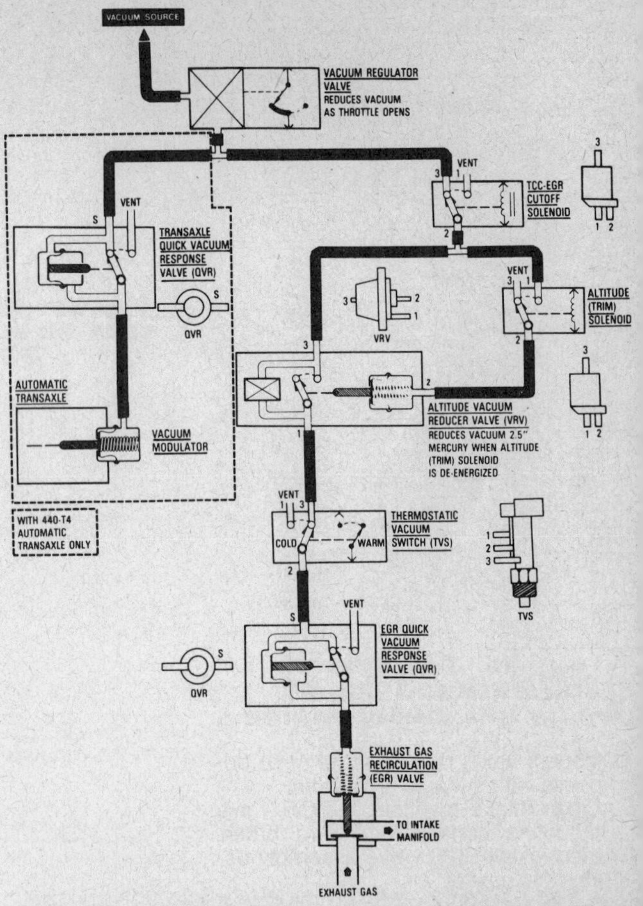

Fig. 53 EGR system schematic. 1984–85 high altitude front wheel drive models w/V6-262/4.3L diesel engine exc. Calif.

4. If valve fails to perform as outlined, valve should be replaced.

V6-262 Engine EGR Valve

1. Apply vacuum to valve using vacuum pump with integral gauge and observe valve diaphragm.
2. On 1982-83 models, valve should be fully open above 12 inches Hg and valve should remain closed below 6 inches Hg on 1982 models or 7.5 inches Hg on 1983 models.
3. On 1984-85 rear wheel drive models, except California models with DEC system, valve should remain closed below 8.5 inches Hg and should be fully open above 13 inches Hg.
4. On 1984 front wheel drive models, except California models with DEC system, valve should remain closed below 7.5 inches Hg and be fully open above 12 inches Hg.
5. On 1984-85 California models with DEC system and 1985 Electra, Fleetwood Brougham and Ninety-Eight, valve should remain closed below 6 inches Hg and should be fully open above 18 inches Hg.
6. If valve fails to perform as outlined, valve should be replaced.

4-110 Engine EGR Valve

1. Apply vacuum to valve using vacuum pump with integral gauge and observe valve diaphragm.
2. Valve should move to fully open position at approximately 13.8 inches Hg, and should not leak down as long as constant vacuum is applied.

4-110 Engine Control Module

1. Connect voltmeter between light green/black and black/yellow wire terminals at vacuum switching valve.
2. Start engine and run until it reaches normal operating temperature.
3. Run engine at speed above 1200 RPM.
4. Module is operating properly if voltmeter indicates 12 volts with engine running above 1200 RPM.

Service

INTAKE MANIFOLD EGR PASSAGES

When cleaning intake manifold EGR passages, care should be taken to ensure that all loose particles are completely removed to prevent them from clogging the EGR valve or from being ingested into the engine.

1. Remove carburetor.
2. Disconnect vacuum hose from EGR valve, then remove EGR valve manifold retaining bolts and valve.
3. Remove deposits from EGR ports b hand using a suitable drill bit an screwdriver.
4. Brush small deposits down EGR po into passages, then using com pressed air, blow ports clean. **So vents should not be used to clea EGR valve or passages, since dam age to system may result.**
5. Install EGR valve, using new gasket
6. Install carburetor.

EGR VALVE CLEANING

Some General Motors EGR valves hav a removable pintle and seat, while other are non-serviceable. Serviceable valve can be identified by punch marks locate on valve seat and base.

Non-Serviceable Type

1. Remove EGR valve from vehicle.
2. Holding valve assembly in hand, ta on round pintle with plastic hammer remove deposits from valve sea Empty loose particles from valve.
3. Clean mounting base and pintle usin a wire brush, then depress valve dia phragm and check seating area fo cleanliness. If pintle or seat are no completely clean, repeat Step 2.

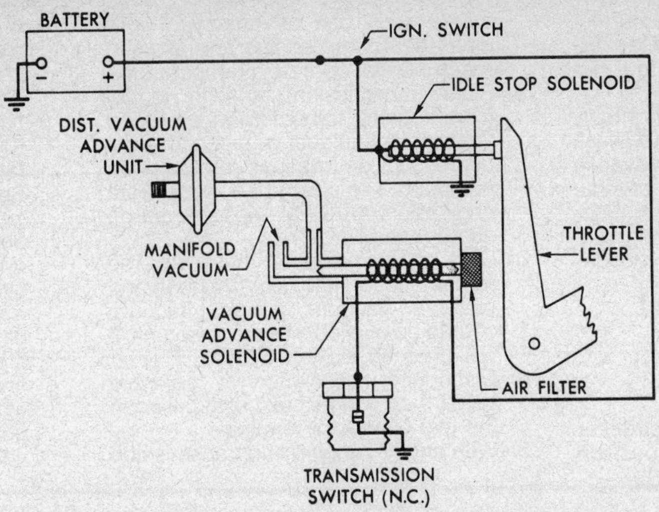

Fig. 68 Basic TCS system wiring circuit

um motor causes the control damper to partially open, allowing outside air to blend with heated air. This regulated air then enters the air cleaner assembly, **Fig. 65.**

During periods of wide open throttle or when ambient temperatures are very high, there is not enough vacuum available to the vacuum motor to overcome diaphragm spring tension. The diaphragm then causes the control damper to move downward, closing the hot air duct and allowing only outside air to enter the air cleaner, **Fig. 66.**

Some vehicles are equipped with a built-in vacuum trap to hold the control damper door in the hot air mode during acceleration, when ambient temperatures are below 70°F. The length of time that the vacuum will be trapped is dependent upon sensor temperature, varying from several minutes at very cold temperatures to a few seconds at approximately 70°F. Once the sensor reaches its calibration temperature, the trapped vacuum feature no longer applies.

Trapped vacuum is accomplished through the use of a check valve located in the small orifice leg of the temperature sensor.

Diagnosis & Testing

SYSTEM CHECK

1. Check system to make sure that all hoses and ducts are connected. Check for kinked, plugged or deteriorated hoses.
2. If engine temperature is above 80°F, remove air cleaner and allow it to cool below 80°F. Place a cool wet cloth over sensor to aid cooling.
3. Install cooled air cleaner with cold air intake disconnected.
4. Start engine. When engine is first started, damper door should be closed. As engine warms up, damper door should open slowly. Some air cleaner sensors have a check valve that delays the opening of the damper door. Length of time depends on temperature, which may vary from a few minutes at 0°F to a few seconds at 70°F.
5. Disconnect vacuum hose from vacuum diaphragm and apply at least 7 inches Hg vacuum. Damper door should completely block off the snorkel passage. If not, check linkage for proper connections.
6. With vacuum still applied, trap vacuum in vacuum motor by bending hose. Damper should remain closed. If not, replace vacuum motor assembly. **Failure of vacuum diaphragm motor is more likely to be caused from that linkage binding or corroded snorkel than a failed diaphragm. Check this first, before replacing the vacuum motor.**
7. Reinstall the air cleaner. As the engine warms up, damper door should start to allow outside air and heated air to enter the carburetor.
8. If air cleaner operation is not as specified previously, or operation is doubtful, check sensor as follows:
   a. Start test with air cleaner temperature below approximately 86°F. If engine was running recently, remove air cleaner cover and place thermometer as close as possible to sensor, **Fig. 67.** Allow air cleaner to cool until thermometer reads below approximately 86°F for about 5 to 10 minutes.
   b. Start engine and allow to idle. Damper door should move to close the snorkel passage immediately if engine is cool enough. When damper door starts to open the snorkel passage (within a few minutes), remove air cleaner cover and read thermometer. Thermometer should read 100-131°F. If not, sensor is malfunctioning and should be replaced.

Service

VACUUM MOTOR, REPLACE

1. Remove air cleaner, then disconnect vacuum hose from motor.
2. Using 1/16 inch drill bit, drill out the two spot welds holding retaining strap to snorkel. Continue to enlarge as required until retaining strap breaks loose from snorkel.
3. Lift motor and twist until linkage unhooks from control damper assembly. Remove vacuum motor from vehicle.
4. Using a 7/64 inch drill bit, drill hole in snorkel tube half way between the two spot welds.
5. Connect linkage to control damper and install vacuum motor into snorkel tube.
6. Using new retaining strap and sheet metal screw provided in service kit, secure vacuum motor to snorkel. **Make certain that screw does not interfere with operation of damper assembly. Shorten screw if necessary.**
7. Connect vacuum hose to motor and install air cleaner.

TEMPERATURE SENSOR, REPLACE

1. Remove air cleaner and disconnect hoses from sensor.
2. Pry upward on retaining clip tabs, then remove retaining clip and sensor from air cleaner.
3. Reverse procedure to install.

TRANSMISSION CONTROLLED SPARK (TCS) SYSTEM

The Transmission Controlled Spark system is designed to provide vacuum spark advance during high gear operation only. The retarded ignition timing in the lower gears results in significantly reduced exhaust emissions.

The basic TCS system, **Fig. 68,** consists of a solenoid operated vacuum control valve and a transmission control switch. The solenoid operated valve, located in the vacuum line between the carburetor and distributor, controls vacuum to the distributor advance unit in response to a signal from the transmission switch.

The transmission switch is normally closed, energizing the solenoid to block vacuum signals to the distributor advance capsule. Selecting high gear or reverse opens the transmission switch, de-energizing the solenoid, and allowing vacuum to be applied to the advance capsule.

Diagnosis & Testing

SYSTEM CHECK

With Normally Closed Transmission Switch

1. Connect vacuum gauge to distributor advance vacuum line, then position gauge so it can be observed from driver seat. Start engine and allow to reach normal operating temperature.
2. Place transmission shifter in neutral for automatic transmission equipped vehicles or first gear with clutch pedal depressed on manual transmission equipped vehicles, then accelerate engine to 1000 RPM. Vacuum gauge should read zero.
3. Shift transmission into reverse (automatic) or high gear (manual) and observe vacuum gauge. Vacuum should be available to advance unit. If not, proceed to Step 4.
4. Disconnect connector at solenoid valve, then connect test light between the two connector terminals.
5. With engine running and transmission in reverse (automatic) or high gear with clutch pedal depressed (manual), observe test light. Test light should be off. If not, check for grounded wire between solenoid connector and transmission. If wire is not grounded, replace transmission switch.
6. Shift transmission into neutral (automatic) or first gear (manual) and observe test light. Test light should be on. If not, check for open circuit between solenoid connector and transmission. If there is no open circuit, replace transmission switch.
7. If the above checks are satisfactory, and still there is no vacuum reading when transmission is shifted into high gear or reverse, replace solenoid valve.

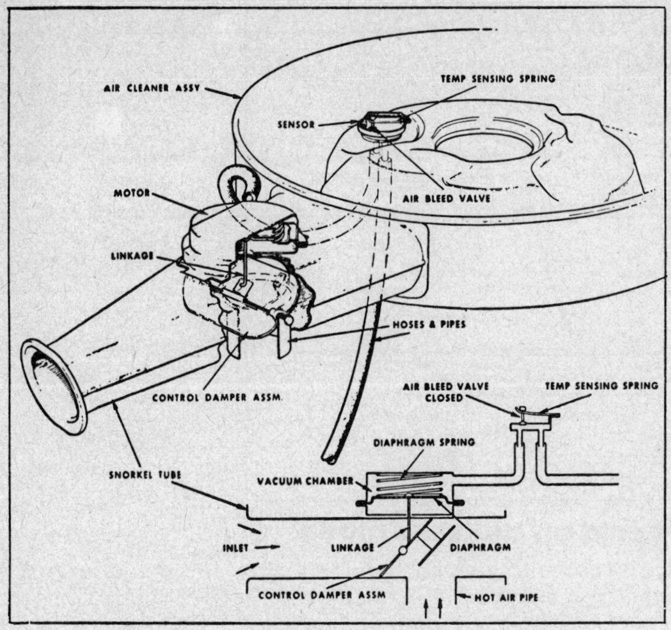

Fig. 64 TAC hot air delivery mode

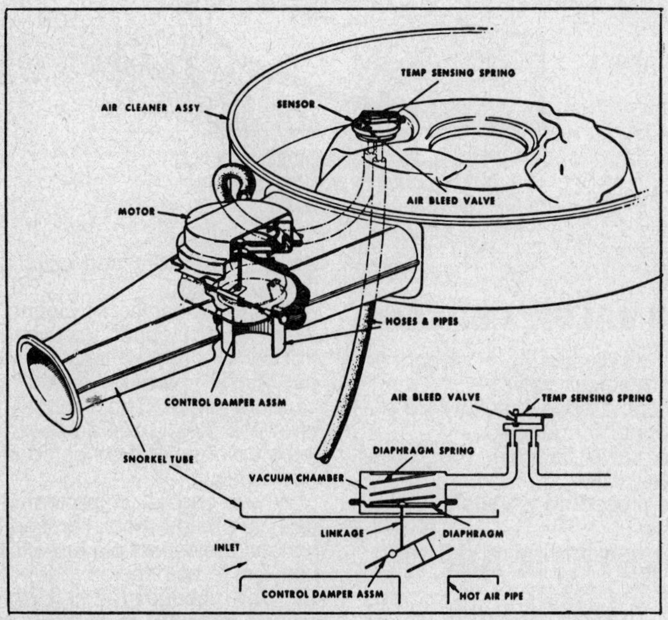

Fig. 65 TAC blend air regulation mode

TANK PRESSURE CONTROL VALVE (TPCV)

This valve is a spring based diaphragm valve which normally closed. When vapor pressure in the fuel tank exceeds a predetermined pressure, the valve will open allowing the vapors to vent to the canister and then be purged. When tank pressure drops sufficiently, the tank pressure control valve will close, keeping vapors in the fuel tank.

CANISTER PURGE VALVE SOLENOID

Most vehicles with Computer Command Control (C3) or Electronic Fuel Injection (DFI, TBI, MFI, etc.) use a solenoid to control vacuum signals transmitted to the canister purge valve. This solenoid allows the system Electronic Control Module (ECM) to control canister purge operation.

Diagnosis & Testing

CANISTER PURGE VALVE

1. Disconnect purge valve vacuum line and check for vacuum with engine operating above 1500 RPM. If no vacuum is present, perform EGR check.
2. Using hand-held vacuum pump, apply vacuum to purge valve control diaphragm and note vacuum reading. Valve should hold vacuum. If purge valve loses vacuum, replace vacuum canister.
3. If purge valve holds vacuum, disconnect purge line and check for presence of vacuum with engine running. If no vacuum is present, check PCV hoses and system. Repair or replace as necessary.

CANISTER VENT VALVE

1. Disconnect carburetor bowl vent vapor hose.
2. Using hand-held vacuum pump, apply vacuum to hose and note gauge reading. Reading should not be more than .5 inches Hg. If vacuum is greater than specified, check for plugged hose or canister filter. If reading remains high, replace vacuum canister.
3. With engine idling at normal operating temperature, again apply vacuum to vapor hose. The line should be blocked and a high vacuum reading obtained. If line is not blocked, remove vacuum line from canister and check for presence of vacuum. If no vacuum is available, repair line. If vacuum is available, replace canister.

Service

The only service required is that the filter mounted at the bottom of the canister or in the air cleaner snorkel be replaced at recommended intervals.

PULSE AIR INJECTION REACTOR (PAIR)

This system, **Fig. 18**, utilizes exhaust

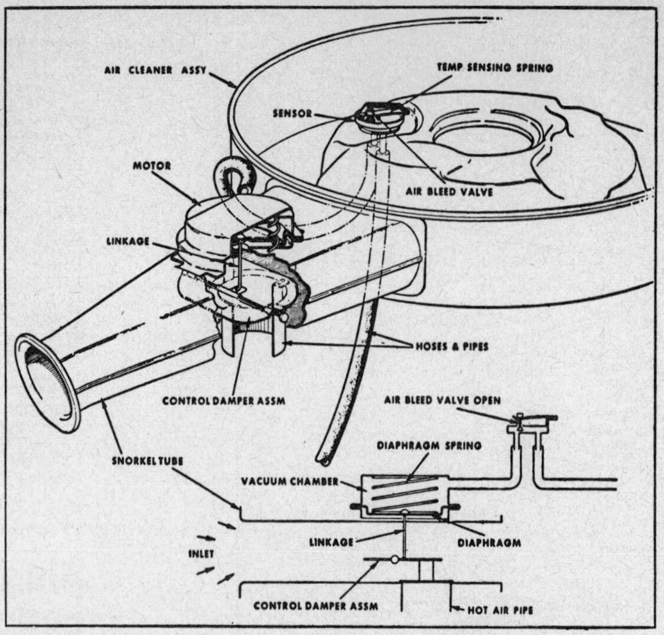

Fig. 66 TAC cold air delivery mode

pressure pulsations to draw fresh air from the air into the exhaust system.

This system uses a series of pipes and check valves in the pulse air valve to route fresh air into the exhaust manifold, **Fig. 18.**

Engine operation causes a pulsating flow of exhaust gases which are of positive or negative pressure depending on whether the exhaust valve is seated or not. If pressure is positive, the disc is forced to the closed position, allowing no air flow into the exhaust system. If pressure is negative, the disc will open allowing fresh air flow into the exhaust system. Due to the inertia at high engine RPM, the disc fails to follow pressure pulsations. Therefore, the disc will remain closed preventing air flow into the exhaust system.

Throttle closure during deceleration momentarily causes air fuel mixtures too rich to burn. These mixtures, when combined with air will become combustible, causing after fire.

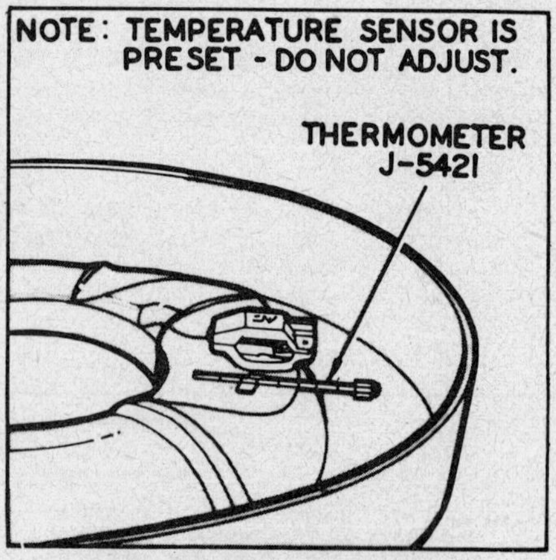

Fig. 67 Checking TAC sensor in air cleaner

Diagnosis & Testing

PULSAIR VALVE

1. Inspect pulsair valve and hoses for leaks and cracks. Replace as necessary.
2. Disconnect pulsair hose from valve fitting. **On V6 engines, both Pulsair valves must be tested individually.**
3. Disconnect pulsair solenoid from valve, if equipped.
4. Connect a suitable hand-held vacuum pump to valve and apply a minimum of 15 inches of vacuum to valve. Time vacuum loss from 15 inches to 5 inches of mercury. If vacuum drops in less than two seconds, replace pulsair valve.

Service

PULSAIR VALVE, REPLACE

1. Remove air cleaner, then disconnect hose from pulsair valve.
2. Disconnect support bracket and pulsair solenoid, if equipped.
3. Remove valve attaching nuts, then the pulsair valve.
4. Reverse procedure to install.

THERMOSTATIC AIR CLEANER (TAC)

The Thermostatic Air Cleaner is designed to keep air entering the engine above 100-120°F, depending on application. Keeping intake air above this temperature reduces exhaust emissions by permitting leaner mixtures and shorter choke on periods. The TAC also improves cold engine driveability and helps prevent carburetor icing.

The thermostatic air cleaner includes a temperature sensor, vacuum motor, control damper and connecting vacuum hoses. The temperature sensor controls the vacuum motor. The vacuum motor then operates the control damper, which regulates the flow of pre-heated and non preheated air.

When engine compartment temperatures are below the calibration value of the sensor, the sensor closes, allowing engine vacuum to be directed to the vacuum motor. The vacuum motor then closes the control damper to outside air, allowing heated air from the exhaust manifold to flow up through the heat tube to the air cleaner, **Fig. 64.**

As the temperature in the air cleaner reaches the calibration value of the sensor, the sensor begins to open, bleeding off vacuum to the vacuum motor. The vacu-

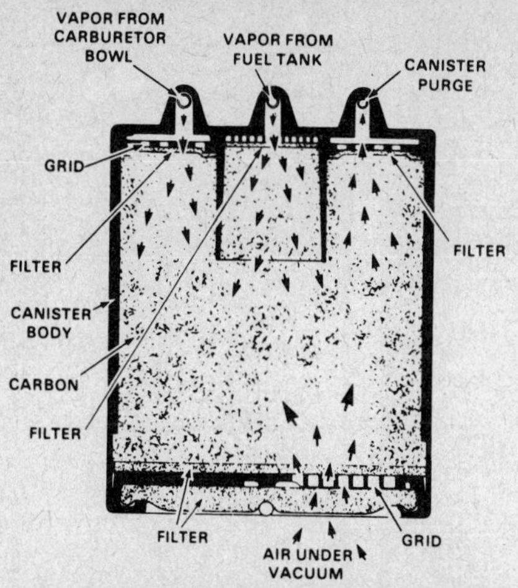

Fig. 58 Single stage type vapor storage canister

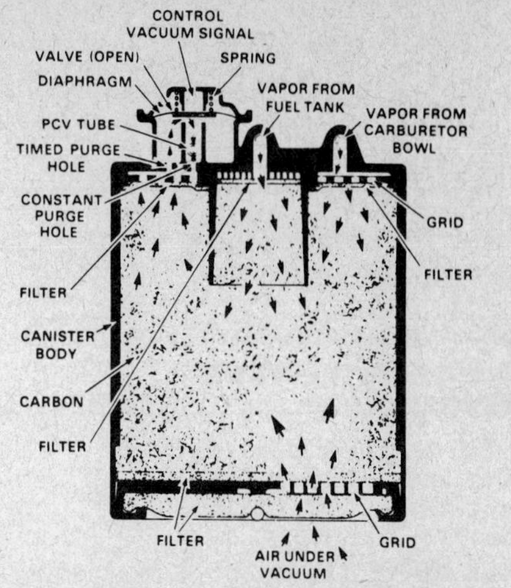

Fig. 59 Purge valve type vapor storage canister

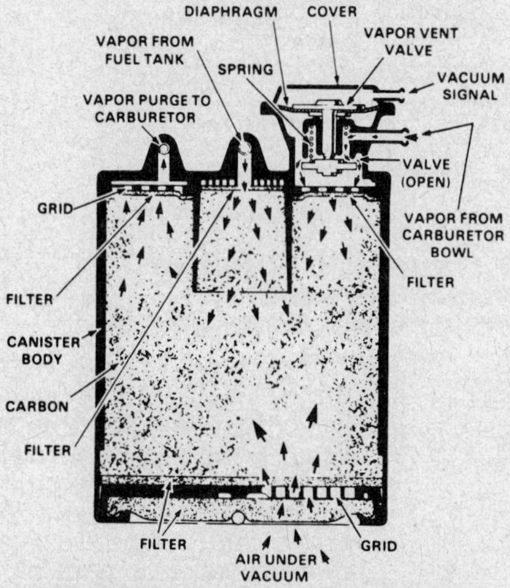

Fig. 60 Vent valve type vapor storage canister

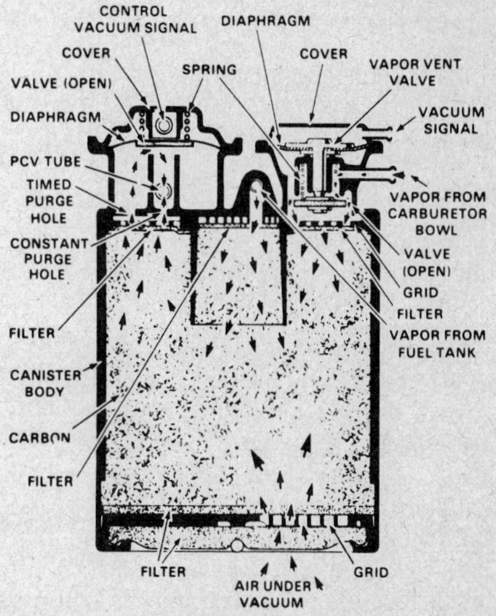

Fig. 61 Vent & purge valve type vapor storage canister

the canister marked "Fuel Tank" and from an area just above the carburetor float bowl through a tube marked "Carb Bowl." The storage of fuel vapors occurs when the engine is not running.

During engine operation, fuel vapors pass through a hose connected to the canister tube marked "Purge" and into a port on the carburetor, where they are mixed with carburetor inlet air and burned during the combustion process. Some single stage type vapor canisters are equipped with two, rather than three tube ports. However, the principles of operation are identical for both models.

Purge Valve Type Vapor Canister

This canister, **Fig. 59,** absorbs fuel vapors from the fuel tank through a tube on the canister marked "Fuel Tank" and from the carburetor through a tube marked "Carb Bowl." The fuel vapors enter the canister and are absorbed by activated charcoal when the engine is not running.

The canister is equipped with a purge valve which is an integral part of the vapor canister. The purge valve consists of a housing and tube molded into the canister cover, and a diaphragm, valve assembly, valve spring and diaphragm cover with an integral control vacuum signal tube.

When the engine is idling, spring tension holds the purge valve closed. A small amount of fuel vapor is then drawn from the canister through a calibrated bleed hole which leads from the charcoal bed to the tube marked "PCV," enabling some purge of the canister through the PCV hose while the engine is at idle.

As engine speed increases, the carburetor throttle valve passes by a timed vacuum port and vacuum is supplied through a tube leading to the top of the purge valve diaphragm marked "Control Vac." This vacuum lifts the purge valve off its seat, opening another channel leading to the charcoal bed. This enables more fuel vapors to be combined with the increased air/fuel ratio of the carburetor.

Both purge channels in the canister lead to a common "PCV" tube, which is directly connected to the PCV hose from the engine.

Vent Valve Type Vapor Canister

This canister, **Fig. 60,** has a vent valve system which is an integral part of the canister assembly. The canister collects fuel vapors from the carburetor float bowl through a hose to the vent valve. The vent valve assembly consists of a housing and tube molded into the canister cover, vent valve, valve spring, diaphragm, and diaphragm cover with integral vacuum signal line.

When the engine is off, no manifold vacuum is available to the vent valve diaphragm, thereby enabling the valve spring to keep the valve open. At this point, fuel vapors in the carburetor float bowl are pressurized and then directed from a tube in the float bowl, through a connecting hose, to the "Carb Bowl" tube in the canister cover. The vapors then flow past the open vent valve through the upper canister filter and into the charcoal bed, where they are stored until normal purging of the canister occurs.

When the engine is running, manifold vacuum is applied to the vent valve diaphragm through the signal tube marked "Man. Vac." At this point, the vent valve closes against spring tension and seals the passage venting fuel vapors from the float bowl to the canister.

When the engine is stopped, the spring opens the valve to again allow venting of the float bowl.

Vent and Purge Valve Type Vapor Canister

This canister, **Fig. 61,** is equipped with both a vent valve and a canister purge valve. The rate at which fuel vapor is drawn into the engine is controlled by a Thermal Vacuum Switch (TVS), which supplies ported vacuum to the purge valve when engine coolant temperature is above a pre-determined value.

With engine idling at normal operating temperature, the purge valve is forced closed by spring tension and no purging of the canister occurs.

On some models, a small amount of fuel vapor is drawn from the canister through a bleed hole, allowing some canister purge through the PCV system at idle.

When the carburetor throttle plates are opened, the signal port located above the throttle plates is uncovered and a ported vacuum signal is applied to the purge valve. Vacuum then overcomes spring tension, opening the valve and allowing vapors to be drawn into the engine for burning.

Inverter Function Vapor Canister

In this canister, **Fig. 62,** gasoline vapors from fuel tank flow into tube labeled "tank" and are absorbed into the carbon. Any liquid fuel goes into a reservoir in bottom of canister to prevent damage of the carbon bed above. The canister is purged when engine is running above idle speed. Ambient air is allowed into canister through an air tube. This air mixes with vapor which is drawn into the intake manifold.

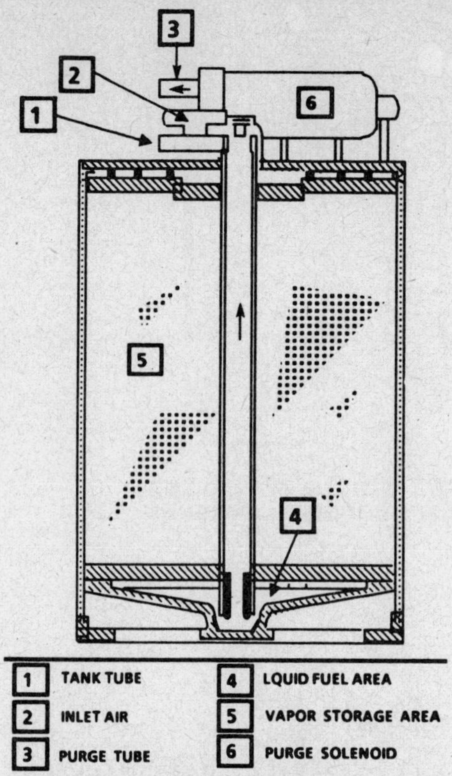

Fig. 62 Inverted function vapor canister w/encapsulated purge solenoid

The ECM operates a solenoid valve which controls vacuum to the purge valve in the charcoal canister.

CANISTER CONTROL VALVE

Some vehicles use a Canister Control Valve (CCV) to control float chamber fuel vapor storage and purging. The system, **Fig. 63,** is comprised of a dual tube vapor canister, a canister control valve mounted near the carburetor, and a thermal vacuum switch located in the intake manifold.

When the engine is shut off, manifold vacuum is lost at the CCV. The CCV then connects the carburetor bowl vent hose to the thermal vacuum switch. If engine coolant temperature is above the calibration point of the TVS, the switch opens and allows fuel vapors to pass into the canister.

When the engine is restarted, manifold vacuum is directed to the CCV. This action closes the bowl vent hose port at the CCV and connects the purge hose to the TVS. When the TVS opens, the canister is purged through the carburetor throttle body which sends ported vacuum through the purge hose.

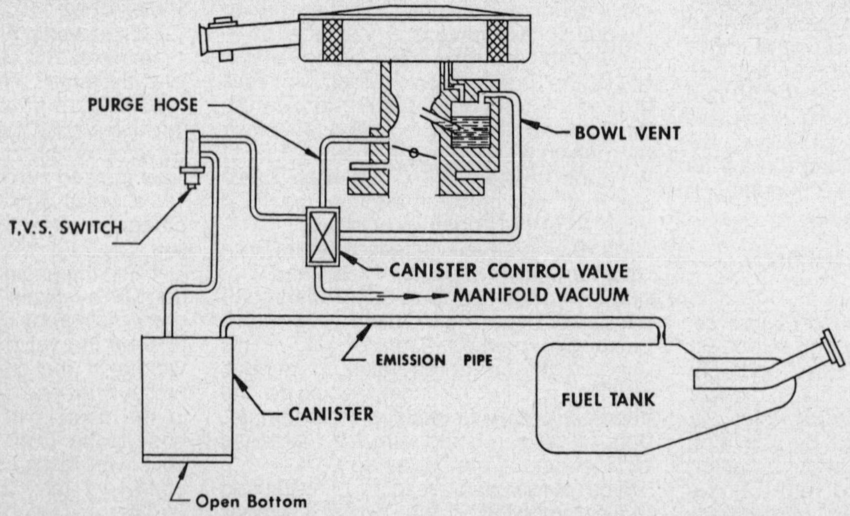

Fig. 63 Typical Canister Control Valve (CCV) installation

DECIMAL & MILLIMETER EQUIVALENTS

INCH	INCH	MM
1/64	.015625	.397
1/32	.03125	.794
3/64	.046875	1.191
1/16	.0625	1.587
5/64	.078125	1.984
3/32	.09375	2.381
7/64	.109375	2.778
1/8	.125	3.175
9/64	.140625	3.572
5/32	.15625	3.969
11/64	.171875	4.366
3/16	.1875	4.762
13/64	.203125	5.159
7/32	.21875	5.556
15/64	.234375	5.953
1/4	.25	6.350
17/64	.265625	6.747
9/32	.28125	7.144
19/64	.296875	7.541
5/16	.3125	7.937
21/64	.328125	8.334
11/32	.34375	8.731
23/64	.359375	9.128
3/8	.375	9.525
25/64	.390625	9.922
13/32	.40625	10.319
27/64	.421875	10.716
7/16	.4375	11.113
29/64	.453125	11.509
15/32	.46875	11.906
31/64	.484375	12.303
1/2	.5	12.700
33/64	.515625	13.097
17/32	.53125	13.494
35/64	.546875	13.890
9/16	.5625	14.287
37/64	.578125	14.684
19/32	.59375	15.081
39/64	.609375	15.478
5/8	.625	15.875
41/64	.640625	16.272
21/32	.65625	16.669
43/64	.671875	17.065
11/16	.6875	17.462
45/64	.703125	17.859
23/32	.71875	18.265
47/64	.734375	18.653
3/4	.75	19.050
49/64	.765625	19.447
25/32	.78125	19.884
51/64	.796875	20.240
13/16	.8125	20.637
53/64	.828125	21.034
27/32	.84375	21.431
55/64	.859375	21.828
7/8	.875	22.225
57/64	.890625	22.622
29/32	.90625	23.019
59/64	.921875	23.415
15/16	.9375	23.812
61/64	.953125	24.209
31/32	.96875	24.606
63/64	.984375	25.003
1		25.400

Special Service Tools

Throughout this manual references are made to and illustrations may depict the use of special tools required to perform certain jobs. These special tools can generally be ordered through the dealers of the make vehicle being serviced. It is also suggested that you check with local automotive supply firms as they also supply tools manufactured by other firms that will assist in the performance of these jobs. The vehicle manufacturers special tools are supplied by:

American Motors & General Motors........... Service Tool Division
Kent-Moore Corporation
29784 Little Mack
Roseville, Michigan 48066

Chrysler Corp.............................. Miller Special Tools
A Division of Utica Tool Co.
32615 Park Lane
Garden City, Michigan 48135

Ford Motor Co. .... Owatonna Tool Company
Owatonna, Minnesota 55060

Flasher Locations

Car	1980		1981		1982		1983		1984		1985–87	
	TSF	HWF	TSF	HWF	TSF	HWF	TSF	HWF	TSF	HWF	TSF	HW
American Motors	12	3	12	3	12	3	12	3	12	3	12	3
Buick—Rear Wheel Drive	3	3	3	3	3	3	3	3	3	3	3	3
1980–85 Buick Skylark & 1982–86 Century	6	15	6	15	6	15	6	15	6	15	6	15
Cadillac—Rear Wheel Drive	6	4	6	4	6	4	6	4	6	4	6	4
Cadillac Seville & Eldorado, 1980–85	6	4	6	4	6	4	6	4	6	4	6	4
Cadillac Fleetwood (1985–86) & DeVille (1985–86); 1986 Eldorado & Seville	—	—	—	—	—	—	—	—	—	—	5	6
Calais, 1985–86 Grand AM & Somerset Regal; 1986 Skylark	—	—	—	—	—	—	—	—	—	—	6	3
Camaro & Firebird	4	3	4	3	6	6	6	6	6	6	6	6
Capri & Mustang	4	14	4	14	4	14	4	14	4	14	4	14
Cavalier, Cimarron, 2000, 1982–86 Skyhawk, Firenza & 1984–86 Sunbird	—	—	—	—	5	3	5	3	5	3	5	3
Chev. Malibu & Monte Carlo	3	3	3	3	3	3	3	3	3	3	3	3
Chevette & 1000	13	3	13	3	13	3	13	3	13	3	13	3
Chevrolet Full Size	3	3	3	3	3	3	3	3	3	3	3	3
Chevrolet Citation & Celebrity	6	15	6	15	6	15	6	15	6	15	6	15
Chevrolet Nova	—	—	—	—	—	—	—	—	—	—	3	3
Chrysler, Imperial & 1980–81 LeBaron	7①	6①	7①	6①	3	3	3	3	3	3	3	3
Chrysler E Class, Executive, 1982–86 LeBaron, 1983–86 New Yorker, Town & Country	—	—	—	—	4	5	4	5	4	5	4	5
Chrysler LeBaron GTS & Dodge Lancer	—	—	—	—	—	—	—	—	—	—	10	10
Chrysler Laser	—	—	—	—	—	—	—	—	3	3	3	3
Cordoba & Mirada	5	5	5	5	3	3	3	3	—	—	—	—
Corvette	3	3	3	3	3	3	—	—	7	7	7	7
Cougar, LTD II & Thunderbird	4	4	4	②	4	②	4	4	4	4	4	4
Dodge & Plymouth Full Size	7	6	7	6	—	—	—	—	—	—	—	—
Dodge & Plymouth Intermed.	3	3	3	3	3	3	3	3	3	3	3	3
Dodge Aries, 400, 600 & Plymouth Reliant, Caravelle	—	—	3	3	4	5	4	5	4	5	4	5
Dodge Daytona	—	—	—	—	—	—	—	—	—	—	3	3
Horizon, Omni & 1983–86 Charger & Turismo	3	3	3	3	3	3	3	3	3	3	3	3
Escort, EXP, LN7 & Lynx	—	—	4	5	4	5	4	5	4	5	4	5
Ford & Mercury Full Size	5	5	5	5	5	5	5	5	5	5	5	5
Fairmont, Zephyr & 1983–86 LTD & Marquis	4	4	4	14	4	14	4	4	4	4	4	4
Ford Pinto & Mercury Bobcat	6	6	—	—	—	—	—	—	—	—	—	—
Ford Tempo & Mercury Topaz	—	—	—	—	—	—	—	—	5	5	5	5
Granada, Monarch & Versailles	10	4	4	14	4	14	—	—	—	—	—	—
Grand Am (Exc. 1985–86), Grand Prix, LeMans & 1982–86 Bonneville	3	3	3	3	3	3	3	3	3	3	3	3
Lincoln	5	5	5	5	5③	5③	5③	5③	5	5	5	5
Oldsmobile (Exc. 1985–86 98 & 1986 88)	3	3	3	3	3	3	3	3	3	3	3	3
Oldsmobile Cutlass (Exc. Ciera, 1984–86 Cruiser)	3	3	3	3	3	3	3	3	3	3	3	3
Olds. Omega, Cutlass Ciera & 1984–86 Cruiser	6	15	6	15	6	15	6	15	6	15	6	15
Oldsmobile Toronado	3	3	3	3	6	4	6	4	6	4	6	4
Pontiac Full Size, 1980–81, 1983–86	3	3	3	3	—	—	3	3	3	3	3	3
Pont. Phoenix & 6000	6	15	6	15	6	15	6	15	6	15	6	15
Pontiac Fiero	—	—	—	—	—	—	—	—	5	16	5	16

TSF: Turn Signal Flasher. HWF: Hazard Warning Flasher.

①—Location 3 on LeBaron. Location 5 on Imperial.

②—Location 14 on Cougar. Location 4 on Cougar XR7 & Thunderbird.

③—Location 4 on Lincoln Continental.

continue